The National Hockey League

Official Guide & Record Book 2001

TOTAL SPORTS PUBLISHING

THE NATIONAL HOCKEY LEAGUE
Official Guide & Record Book/2001

Copyright © 2000 by the National Hockey League.
Compiled by the NHL Public Relations Department and the 30 NHL Club Public Relations Directors.

Printed in Canada. All rights reserved under the Pan-American and International Copyright Conventions.

Published in Canada by:
Dan Diamond and Associates, Inc., 194 Dovercourt Road, Toronto, Ontario M6J 3C8 Canada
  ISBN in Canada 0-920445-70-5

Published in the United States by:
Total Sports Publishing Inc., 100 Enterprise Drive, Kingston, NY 12401
  ISBN in USA 1-892129-46-9

Staff

For the NHL: Brian Jennings; Supervising Editor: Greg Inglis; Statistician: Benny Ercolani;
Editorial Staff: Luc Coulombe, David Keon, Jackie Rinaldi, Kelley Rosset, Chris Tredree.

Managing Editor: Ralph Dinger   **Player Register Editor:** James Duplacey

Photo Editor: Eric Zweig   **Production Editors:** John Pasternak, Alex Dubiel

Assistant Editor: Paul Bontje   **European Statistical Consultant:** Patrick Houda

Senior Contributors: Bob Borgen, Anthony Buccongello, Wil Curry, Bob Duff, Mel Foster, W.D. Lighthall, Ralph Slate.

Contributors: Timo Alenan, Heiko Behrens, Aaron Blackburn, Peter Borkowski, Paul R. Carroll Jr., Steve Cherwonak (WPHL), Matthew Condlin, Bill Crawford, Paul de Montigny, Mark DeWitt, D.A. England, Jeff Fanter (ECAC), Peter Fillman, Ernie Fitzsimmons, Jamey Foster, Brad Freeman, Dan Gognavic, Lloyd Hamshaw (WHL), Gregg Inkpen, Scott Kelly, Jeff Knott, Martin Kogler, Len Kotylo, Eric Lavigne, Eric Leblanc, Roger Leblond, Steve Lederer, Manon Gagnon Leroux (QMJHL); Douglas G. MacEachern, Roy W. Mackie, Al Mason, Pablo Maurelia, Herb Morrell (OHL), Ross Munro, Nicole Norris (IHL), NHL Broadcasters' Association, NHL Central Registry, NHL Players' Association, Michael Olynick, Mark Paddock, John D. Painter (NCAA), Becky Pasternak, Brenda Pasternak, Stephanie Pasternak, John Paton, Gary J. Pearce, Jean Pelland, Curt Phillips, Amy Pickett (CHL), Valentina Riazanova, Jane Rodney, Jason Rothwell (ECHL), Willie Runquist, Ed Saunders (Hockey East), Sherry Skalko (CCHA), Doug Spencer (WCHA), Lane Startin, Bret Stothart (AHL), Tony Techko, Jussi Votila, Drew White, Will Wolper (UHL).

Publisher: Dan Diamond

Data Management and Typesetting: Caledon Data Management, Hillsburgh, Ontario
Digital Image Scanning: Stafford Graphics, Toronto, Ontario
Printing: vistainfo, Scarborough, Ontario
Production Management: Dan Diamond and Associates, Inc., Toronto Ontario

Photo Credits

NHL Images: Anita Cechowski, Jill Oswskey.
Photographers: Graig Abel, Toronto; Marc Archambault, Montreal; Scott Audette, Tampa Bay; Steve Babineau; Greg Bartram/Better Image, Columbus; Bruce Bennett Studios; Andrew D. Bernstein/Andrew Bernstein Associates, Los Angeles; Mark Buckner, St. Louis; Scott Cunningham, Atlanta; Gregg Forwerck, Carolina; Barry Gossage, Phoenix; Jon Hayt, Tampa Bay; Mark A. Hicks/Action Image, Detroit; Hockey Hall of Fame Collections; Glenn James, Dallas; Robert Laberge, Montreal; Mitchell Layton, Washington; Richard C. Lewis, Florida; D. MacMillan, Calgary; Silvia Pecota; Len Redkole, Philadelphia; Debora Robinson, Anaheim; John Russell, Nashville; Slapshot Photo, Chicago; Don Smith, San Jose; Diane Sobolewski; Teckles/McElligott Sports Focus Imaging, Ottawa; Sandra Tenuto, Phoenix; Gerry Thomas, Calgary and Edmonton; Jeff Vinnick, Vancouver; Bill Wippert, Buffalo; Dale Zanine, Atlanta.

Distribution

Trade sales and distribution in Canada by:
North 49 Books, 35 Prince Andrew Drive, Toronto, Ontario M3C 2H2
416/449-4000; FAX 416/449-9924

Dan Diamond and Associates, Inc., 194 Dovercourt Road, Toronto, Ontario M6J 3C8
416/531-6535; FAX 416/531-3939 e-mail: dda.nhl@sympatico.ca

Trade sales and distribution in the United States by:
Publishers Group West, 1700 Fourth Street, Berkeley, CA 94710

International representatives:
Barkers Worldwide Publications, Unit 6/7 The Elms Centre, Glaziers Lane, Normandy, Guildford, Surrey GU3 2DF England
Tel: 011/441/483/811-971 and FAX: 011/441/483/811-972 e-mail: sales@bwpu.demon.co.uk website: www.bwpu.demon.co.uk

Licensed by the National Hockey League.®

The National Hockey League
1251 Avenue of the Americas, 47th Floor, New York, New York 10020-1198
1800 McGill College Ave., Suite 2600, Montreal, Quebec H3A 3J6
50 Bay Street, 11th Floor, Toronto, Ontario M5J 2X8

Table of Contents

13 CLUBS   records, rosters, management

131 FINAL STATISTICS 1999-2000

Table of Contents *continued*

(2000-01 NHL Schedule begins inside front cover)

Introduction

WELCOME TO *THE NHL OFFICIAL GUIDE & RECORD BOOK 2001.* This 69th edition continues the expanded coverage and array of new features that made their debut last season. An expanding National Hockey League combined with upgraded statistical tracking, e-mail and the Internet enable us to provide more information on more players, resulting in the biggest edition of the *Guide & Record Book* ever published. Since 1984, when the book was first produced in today's big-page format, the NHL has grown from 21 teams to 30 and the book has jumped from 352 pages to 624. Extra pages and additions aside, the *Guide's* greatest strength remains unchanged: providing comprehensive statistical coverage of the National Hockey League, its players and top prospects in minor pro, European, junior or college leagues and conferences.

The Player Registers begins on page 265 with a new Prospect Register made up of active forwards and defensemen who have yet to play in the NHL. Players in the Prospect Register either have been recently drafted, signed as free agents or invited to training camp by NHL clubs.

The NHL Player Register begins on page 323. It includes active forwards and defensemen who have appeared in an NHL regular-season or playoff game at any time. Included are the following statistical categories, listed from left to right as they appear in a player's panel: power-play goals (PP), shorthand goals (SH), game-winning goals (GW), shots on goal (S), percentage of shots that score (%), plus-minus rating (+/–), total faceoffs taken (TF*), faceoff winning percentage (F%*), hits (H*), shots blocked (SB*) and average time-on-ice per game played (Min*). Categories marked with an asterisk (*) are NHL Real-Time statistics gathered by teams of trained spotters who, working with laptop computers and custom software, record hits, shots blocked, faceoff wins, etc. "on-the-fly" at each game. These statistics were kept officially for the first time in 1998-99, so no player in this year's *NHL Guide* has more than two year's worth of Real-Time statistics.

Another new feature carried forward from the 2000 edition is the addition of player mug shots. Photos of forwards and defensemen with NHL experience accompany their data panels. Active goaltender photos are found on page 558. In this edition, we've been able to find a photograph of everyone in the NHL Player Register. No one is "camera shy" in the 2001 *NHL Guide & Record Book.*

The order of the Registers is as follows: Prospect, NHL Player, Goaltender, Retired Player and Retired Goaltender.

A key to the abbreviations and symbols used in individual player and goaltender data panels is found on page 322. Late additions to the Registers plus a list of abbreviations for league names used in the Registers are found on page 264. Each NHL club's minor-pro affiliates is found on page 129. NHL and team Websites are listed on page 130.

The *NHL Guide's* Player Register, which includes approximately 1,000 prospects yet to appear in the NHL, enables the book to complement the second edition of the *Total Hockey* encyclopedia published in October 2000. The great success of the first edition of *Total Hockey*—produced by the same editorial team as the *NHL Guide*—has facilitated improvements in the data base that supports both publications. More information on *Total Hockey* is found on page 624.

For 2000-01, the NHL welcomes the Columbus Blue Jackets and Minnesota Wild. Both teams will play in the Western Conference with Columbus in the Central Division and Minnesota in the Northwest. With the addition of these clubs, the NHL will become a 30-team league, organized in two conferences, each of which will be made up of three five-team divisions. Divisional alignment and scheduling for 2000–01 are described on the inside front cover. Columbus coverage begins on page 45; Minnesota on page 67.

As always, our thanks to readers, correspondents and members of the media who take the time to comment on the *Guide & Record Book.* Thanks as well to the people working in the communications departments of the NHL's member clubs and to their counterparts in the AHL, IHL, ECHL, Central, United, West Coast and Western Professional and junior leagues as well as in college athletic conferences and European hockey federations.

Best wishes for an enjoyable 2000-01 NHL season.

ACCURACY REMAINS THE *GUIDE & RECORD BOOK'*S TOP PRIORITY.
We appreciate comments and clarification from our readers. Please direct these to:

- James Duplacey   Player Register Editor, 194 Dovercourt Road, Toronto, Ontario M6J 3C8. e-mail: jj.nhl@sympatico.ca.
- Greg Inglis   47th floor, 1251 Avenue of the Americas, New York, New York 10020-1198 . . . or . . .
- David Keon   50 Bay Street, 11th Floor, Toronto, Ontario, M5J 2X8

Your involvement makes a better book.

NATIONAL HOCKEY LEAGUE

Established November 22, 1917

New York, 1251 Avenue of the Americas, 47th Floor, New York, NY 10020-1198, 212/789-2000, Fax: 212/789-2020, PR Fax: 212/789-2080
Montréal, 1800 McGill College Avenue, Suite 2600, Montréal, Québec, H3A 3J6, 514/841-9220, Fax: 514/284-0300
Toronto, 50 Bay Street, 11th Floor, Toronto, Ontario, M5J 2X8, 416/981-2777, Fax: 416/981-2779
NHL Enterprises, L.P. — 1251 Avenue of the Americas, 47th Floor, New York, NY 10020-1198, (212) 789-2000, Fax: (212) 789-2020
NHL Enterprises Canada, L.P. — 50 Bay Street, 11th Floor, Toronto, Ontario, M5J 2X8, 416/981-2777, Fax: 416/981-2779
NHL Productions — 183 Oak Tree Road, Tappan, NY 10983-2809, 914/365-6701, Fax: 914/365-6010

EXECUTIVE

Commissioner..Gary B. Bettman
Executive Vice President & Chief Legal Officer................................William Daly
Executive Vice President & Director of Hockey Operations................Colin Campbell
Executive Vice President & Chief Operating Officer................................Jon Litner
Executive Vice President & Chief Financial Officer................................Craig Harnett
Director, Administration & Executive Assistant to the Commissioner................Debbie Jordan

ADMINISTRATION

Director of Administration..Debbie Jordan
Director, Human Resources..Janet Meyers

BROADCASTING/SCHEDULING

Vice President, Broadcasting & Programming................................Adam Acone
Manager, Business & Special Events................................Phyllis DeCongilio
Manager, T.V. Production & Operations................................Anthony Triano

Vice President, Scheduling, Operations & Research (Montreal)................Steve Hatze Petros
Manager, Research & Scheduling................................Mark Erlichson
Manager, Scheduling & Operations................................William Bredin

NHL PRODUCTIONS

Executive Producer..Ken Rosen
Vice President..Patti Fallick
Coordinating Producer..Darryl Lepik
Senior Producer..Keith Wetzler
Producer..Gary Waksman
Senior Associate Producers................................Janice Arbour, Michele Giordano
Senior Editor..Chip Swain
Senior Operations Manager..Peg Walsh
Senior Production Manager................................Christine Cortez
Manager, Video Services..Chris Cesa

NHL IMAGES
Director, NHL Images..Anita Cechowski
Manager..Jill Oswskey

COMMUNICATIONS

Group Vice President, Communications................................Bernadette Mansur
Vice President, Media Relations................................Frank Brown
Vice President, Public Relations & Media Services (Toronto)................Gary Meagher
Chief Statistician (Toronto)................................Benny Ercolani
Director, Communications................................Jamey Horan
Director, Corporate Communications................................John Krisiukenas
Director, Media Relations................................Amy Early
Director, News Services................................Greg Inglis
Manager, Community Relations................................Adrienne Brautigan
Manager, Corporate Communications & Player Publicity................Sandra Carreon
Manager, Corporate Communications................................Joy Kalfus
Manager, Diversity Task Force................................Nirva Milord
Manager, News Services................................Adam Schwartz
Managers, Public Relations (Toronto)................David Keon, Chris Tredree

EVENTS & ENTERTAINMENT

Group Vice President..Frank Supovitz
Vice President..Anne I. Grotefeld
Senior Director..Ken Chin
Managers................Susan Aglietti, Sammy Choi, Danny Frank, Kimberly Guarachi, Bill Miller

FINANCE

Executive Vice President & Chief Financial Officer................Craig Harnett
Senior Vice President, Finance................................Joseph DeSousa
Vice President, Finance and Office Manager (Montreal)................Olivia Pietrantonio
Director, Financial Systems................................Belinda Haeberlein
Director, Finance..Lowell Heit

HOCKEY OPERATIONS

Executive Vice President & Director of Hockey Operations................Colin Campbell
Senior Vice President, Hockey Operations (Toronto)................Jim Gregory
Vice President, Hockey Operations (Toronto)................Mike Murphy
Hockey Operations Manager................................Claude Loiselle
Vice President & Managing Director, Central Registry (Montreal)................Stephen Pellegrini
Assistant Director, Central Registry (Montreal)................Madeleine Supino
Director, Central Scouting (Toronto)................................Frank Bonello
Director of Officiating (Toronto)................................Andy VanHellemond
Consultant (Montreal)................................Brian F. O'Neill
Director of Alumni Relations (Toronto)................................Patrick Flatley
Video Director..Damian Echevarrieta
Video Coordinator (Toronto)................................Paul Brighty
Ice Technician..Dan Craig

INFORMATION TECHNOLOGY

Vice President, Information Technology................................Peter DelGiacco
Assistant Director (Montreal)................................Luc Coulombe
Manager, Network Communication................................Patrick Powers
Manager, Technical Systems & Support................................John Ho
Manager, RTSS Support..Dan O'Neill

LEGAL

Executive Vice President & Chief Legal Officer................................William Daly
Senior Vice President, General Counsel................................David Zimmerman
Deputy General Counsel..Julie Grand

NHL INTERACTIVE CYBERENTERPRISES (NHL ICE)

President, NHL ICE..Tom Richardson
Vice President, Editorial & Production................................Richard Libero
Vice President, Sales & Marketing................................Kenneth Nova
Director, Web Operations................................Grant Nodine

PENSION

Director, Pension (Montreal)................................Yvon Chamberland
Controller, Pension (Montreal)................................Mary Skiadopoulos
Manager, Pension (Montreal)................................Lise de Jocas

SECURITY

Vice President, Security................................Dennis Cunningham
Director, Security..Joseph Caporicci

TELEVISION AND BUSINESS AFFAIRS

Group Vice President, Media Ventures & Strategic Development................Douglas L. Perlman
Vice President, Television & Business Affairs................................Leslie Gittess
Director, NHL Center Ice & Program Development................Ken Gelman
Director, Team Television & Business Affairs................................John Tortora

NHL ENTERPRISES

President, NHL Enterprises..Ed Horne

CONSUMER PRODUCTS MARKETING

Group Vice President, Consumer Products Marketing................Brian Jennings
Vice President, Consumer Products Marketing (Toronto)................Glenn Wakefield
Senior Director, Consumer Products Marketing................James Haskins
Director, Retail Sales, Canada (Toronto)................Barry Monahan
Director, Center Ice Program and Sporting Goods................Lloyd Haymes
Director, Consumer Products Marketing, Canada (Toronto)................Karen Hanson
Director, Non-Apparel................................Judith Salsberg
Sales Director, Eastern Region................................Adam Blinderman
Sales Director, Midwest Region................................Cathy Groves
Manager, Youth Licensing................................Nelly Campana

CLUB MARKETING

Vice President, Club Marketing................................Scott Carmichael
Senior Director..Susan Cohig
Manager..Maryann Thorgrimson

CORPORATE MARKETING

Vice President, Corporate Marketing................................Andrew Judelson
Director, Canada (Toronto)................................Laurie Kepron
Managers................................Eustace King, Ian Lasher, Pam Perlman
Manager, Canada (Toronto)................................Mark Leno

CREATIVE SERVICES

Associate Director, Creative Services................................Kathy Drew

FAN DEVELOPMENT

Vice President, Fan Development................................Alysse Soll
Director, Off-Ice Programs................................Brian Mullen
Manager, Fan Development................................Roy Edmondson
Account Executives................................Rachel Podradchik, Suzanne Sherman

FINANCE

Vice President, Finance, NHL Enterprises................................Mary McCarthy
Director, Finance..Scott Weinfeld
Director, Accounting Operations................................Deborah Corletta

INTERNATIONAL

Group Vice President & Managing Director, NHL International................Ken Yaffe
Senior Director, International Business Operations................Frank Nakano
Director, International Marketing................................Kamini Sharma
Director, International Broadcasting................................Susanna Mandel-Mantello
Manager, International Licensing & Special Projects................Lynn White

NHLE LEGAL

Senior Vice President & General Counsel................................Richard Zahnd
Vice President & Associate General Counsel................................Mary Sotis
Associate Counsel and Secretary................................Robert Hawkins
Associate Counsel, Intellectual Property................................Tom Prochnow
Associate Counsel..Yvette Quinson
Staff Attorney..Matthew Kline
Vice President, Licensing and Trademark Compliance................Ruth Gruhin
Director, Contract Administration................................Heather Bell
Director, Intellectual Property................................Maria Liuzzo
Intellectual Property Administrator................................Alison Nunez

BOARD OF GOVERNORS
Chairman of the Board – Harley N. Hotchkiss

Mighty Ducks of Anaheim
Tony Tavares ....Governor
Michael D. Eisner ....Alternate Governor
Pierre Gauthier................................Alternate Governor
Rick Schlesinger ....Alternate Governor

Atlanta Thrashers
Stan Kasten ....Governor
Don Waddell ....Alternate Governor

Boston Bruins
Jeremy M. Jacobs ....Governor
Louis Jacobs ....Alternate Governor
Harry J. Sinden ....Alternate Governor
Mike O'Connell ....Alternate Governor

Buffalo Sabres
John Rigas.. Governor
Timothy J. Rigas ....Alternate Governor
Michael J. Rigas ....Alternate Governor
James Rigas......................................Alternate Governor
Ed Hartman......................................Alternate Governor
Darcy Regier ....Alternate Governor
Kevin Billet ....Alternate Governor

Calgary Flames
Harley N. Hotchkiss..Governor
Byron J. Seaman...............................Alternate Governor
Ron Bremner ....Alternate Governor
N. Murray Edwards ....Alternate Governor
Grant Bartlett...................................Alternate Governor

Carolina Hurricanes
Peter Karmanos, Jr..Governor
Jim Rutherford ....Alternate Governor
Jason Karmanos ....Alternate Governor
Jim Cain...Alternate Governor

Chicago Blackhawks
William W. Wirtz ....Governor
John A. Ziegler, Jr. ....Alternate Governor
Robert J. Pulford ....Alternate Governor
Peter Wirtz.......................................Alternate Governor

Colorado Avalanche
Stan Kroenke..Governor
Don Elliman ....Alternate Governor
Pierre Lacroix...................................Alternate Governor

Columbus Blue Jackets
John H. McConnell...Governor
John P. McConnell.............................Alternate Governor
John S. Christie ....Alternate Governor
Doug MacLean..................................Alternate Governor

Dallas Stars
Tom Hicks...Governor
James R. Lites ....Alternate Governor
Robert Gainey ....Alternate Governor

Detroit Red Wings
Michael Ilitch..Governor
Jay A. Bielfield ....Alternate Governor
Jim Devellano...................................Alternate Governor
Atanas Ilitch ....Alternate Governor
Christopher Ilitch.............................Alternate Governor
Denise Ilitch ....Alternate Governor
Ken Holland ....Alternate Governor

Edmonton Oilers
Cal Nichols ....Governor
Kevin Lowe ....Alternate Governor
Gordon Buchanan ....Alternate Governor
Patrick LaForge................................Alternate Governor

Florida Panthers
William A. Torrey ....Governor
H. Wayne Huizenga.........................Alternate Governor
Bryan Murray ....Alternate Governor

Los Angeles Kings
Timothy J. Leiweke ....Governor
Philip F. Anschutz ....Alternate Governor
David Taylor ....Alternate Governor

Minnesota Wild
Robert O. Naegele, Jr......................................Governor
Jac Sperling......................................Alternate Governor

Montréal Canadiens
Pierre Boivin..Governor
Fred Steer...Alternate Governor
Rejean Houle....................................Alternate Governor

Nashville Predators
Craig Leipold ....Governor
David Poile ....Alternate Governor
Jack Diller...Alternate Governor
Terry London ....Alternate Governor

New Jersey Devils
Louis A. Lamoriello ....Governor
Harvey Schiller.................................Alternate Governor
Michael Gilfillan ....Alternate Governor

New York Islanders
Charles B. Wang...Governor
Sanjay Kumar ....Alternate Governor
Mike Picker ....Alternate Governor
Roy Reichbach...................................Alternate Governor
William Skehan ....Alternate Governor

New York Rangers
David W. Checketts ....Governor
Kenneth W. Munoz......................Alternate Governor
James L. Dolan ....Alternate Governor
Glen Sather.......................................Alternate Governor

Ottawa Senators
Roderick M. Bryden ....Governor
Roy Mlakar.......................................Alternate Governor

Philadelphia Flyers
Edward M. Snider..Governor
Bob Clarke ....Alternate Governor
Ronald K. Ryan ....Alternate Governor
Philip I. Weinberg ....Alternate Governor

Phoenix Coyotes
Richard T. Burke...Governor
Shawn Hunter...................................Alternate Governor
Robert D. Smith ....Alternate Governor

Pittsburgh Penguins
Mario Lemieux..Governor
Craig Patrick ....Alternate Governor
Kenneth Sawyer................................Alternate Governor
Ronald Burkle....................................Alternate Governor
Anthony Liberati ....Alternate Governor

St. Louis Blues
William J. Laurie ....Governor
Richard C. Thomas ....Alternate Governor
Mark Sauer ....Alternate Governor
Larry Pleau ....Alternate Governor
Brent P. Karasiuk ....Alternate Governor

San Jose Sharks
George Gund III..Governor
Gordon Gund....................................Alternate Governor
Irvin A. Leonard ....Alternate Governor
Greg Jamison ....Alternate Governor
Dean Lombardi.................................Alternate Governor

Tampa Bay Lightning
Thomas S. Wilson...Governor
Ronald J. Campbell ....Alternate Governor
Jay H. Feaster ....Alternate Governor

Toronto Maple Leafs
Steve A. Stavro ....Governor
Brian P. Bellmore ....Alternate Governor
Ken Dryden.......................................Alternate Governor
Richard A. Peddie.............................Alternate Governor

Vancouver Canucks
John E. McCaw, Jr. ....Governor
Stanley McCammon ....Alternate Governor
Brian Burke ....Alternate Governor
David Nonis.......................................Alternate Governor
David Cobb.......................................Alternate Governor

Washington Capitals
Richard M. Patrick ....Governor
Ted Leonsis......................................Alternate Governor
Jon Ledecky ....Alternate Governor
George McPhee ....Alternate Governor

Commissioner and League Presidents

Gary B. Bettman

Gary B. Bettman took office as the NHL's first Commissioner on February 1, 1993. Since the League was formed in 1917, there have been five League Presidents.

NHL President	Years in Office
Frank Calder	1917-1943
Mervyn "Red" Dutton	1943-1946
Clarence Campbell	1946-1977
John A. Ziegler, Jr.	1977-1992
Gil Stein	1992-1993

Hockey Hall of Fame

BCE Place
30 Yonge Street
Toronto, Ontario M5E 1X8
Phone: 416/360-7735
Executive Fax: 416/360-1501
Resource Center/Retail Fax: 416/360-1316
www.hhof.com

William C. Hay – Chairman
Jeff Denomme – President
Craig Baines – Director, Marketing and Facilities Services
Ron Ellis – Director, Public Affairs and Ass't to the President
Ray Paquet – Creative Director, Exhibit Development
Phil Pritchard – Director, Hockey Operations and Curator
Craig Campbell – Manager, Resource Center and Archives
Jan Barrina – Manager, Special Events and Hospitality
Kelly Massé – Manager, Corportae and Media Relations
Tim McWilliams – Manager, Attractions and Retail Services
Craig Beckim – Associate Manager, Merchandising
Anthony Fusco – Manager, Information Systems
Sandra Walters – Controller and Office Manager
Pearl Rajwanth – Executive Assistant to the President

National Hockey League Players' Association

777 Bay Street, Suite 2400
Toronto, Ontario M5G 2C8
Phone: 416/313-2300
Fax: 416/313-2301
E-mail: www.nhlpa.com

Robert W. Goodenow – Executive Director and General Counsel
Ian Pulver, Ian Penny, Roland Lee – Associate Counsels
Ted Saskin – Senior Director, Business Affairs and Licensing
Mike Ouellet, Jordan Banks– Associate Counsels, Licensing
Mike Gartner – Director, Business Relations
Kenneth Kim – Director, Marketing
Barbara Larcina – Director, Business Operations
Kim Murdoch – Manager, Pensions and Benefits
Devin Smith – Manager, Goals and Dreams Fund
Dave Tredgett – Manager, Television and Media Projects
Tim Wharnsby – Manager, Media Relations ext. 2390
e-mail: twharnsby@nhlpa.com
Michael Fox – Assistant, Media Relations ext. 2316

NHL On-Ice Officials

Total NHL Games and 1999-2000 Games columns count regular-season games only.

Referees

#	Name	Birthplace	Birthdate	First NHL Game	Total NHL Games	99-2000 Games
9	Blaine Angus	Shawville, Que	9/25/1961	10/17/1992	174	63
41	Stephane Auger	Montreal, Que.	12/9/1970	4/1/2000	1	1
30	Bernard DeGrace	Lameque, N.B.	5/1/1967	10/15/1991	245	66
10	Paul Devorski	Guelph, Ont.	8/18/1958	10/14/1989	603	74
44	Harry Dumas	Mount Laurel, N.J.	7/7/1973			
11	Mark Faucette	Springfield, MA	6/9/1958	12/23/1987	702	78
2	Kerry Fraser	Sarnia, Ont.	5/30/1952	4/6/1975	1263	78
39	Eric Furlatt	Cap de la Madelaine, QC	12/2/1971			
4	Terry Gregson	Erin, Ont.	11/7/1953	12/19/1981	1147	69
34	Conrad Haché	Sudbury, Ont.	5/15/1972	2/27/1995	37	8
58	Dave Hansen	New Haven, CT	12/1/1972			
36	Mike Hasenfratz	Regina, Sask.	7/19/1966			
64	Shane Heyer	Summerland, B.C.	2/7/1964	**10/1/99	*814	29
8	Dave Jackson	Montreal, Que.	11/28/1964	12/23/1990	466	79
33	Marc Joannette	Verdun, Que.	11/3/1968	10/27/1999	3	3
18	Greg Kimmerly	Toronto, Ont.	12/8/1964	11/30/1996	89	62
12	Don Koharski	Halifax, N.S.	12/2/1955	10/14/1977	*1293	80
32	Tom Kowal	Vernon, B.C.	11/2/1967	10/29/1999	5	5
76	Bob Langdon	Woodstock, Ont	3/11/1971			
14	Dennis LaRue	Savannah, GA	7/14/1959	3/26/1991	289	72
49	Chris Lee	Saint John, N.B.	7/7/1970	4/2/2000	1	1
28	Mike Leggo	North Bay, Ont.	10/7/1964	3/3/1998	81	67
27	Kevin Maguire	Toronto, Ont.	5/1/1963	1/22/1998	87	61
6	Dan Marouelli	Edmonton, Alta.	7/16/1955	11/2/1984	991	82
26	Rob Martell	Winnipeg, Man.	10/21/1963	3/14/1984	*34	14
7	Bill McCreary	Guelph, Ont.	11/17/1955	11/3/1984	1016	80
19	Mick McGeough	Regina, Sask.	6/20/1957	1/19/1989	592	78
40	Brad Meier	Dayton, OH	4/11/1967	10/23/1999	9	9
85	Dean Morton	Peterborough, Ont.	2/27/1968			
93	Brian Murphy	Dover, NH	12/13/1964	**10/18/99	*743	29
15	Dan O'Halloran	Essex, Ont.	3/25/1964	10/14/1995	156	71
37	Tim Peel	Toronto, Ont.	4/27/1966	10/21/1999	10	10
52	Kevin Pollock	Kincardine, Ont.	2/7/1970	3/28/2000	1	1
20	Lance Roberts	Edmonton, Alta.	5/28/1957	11/3/1989	483	74
43	Chris Rooney	Boston, MA	5/26/1974			
57	Jay Sharrers	Jamaica, West Indies	7/3/1967	10/6/1990	642	63
16	Rob Shick	Port Alberni, B.C.	12/4/1957	4/6/1986	785	75
60	Kelly Sutherland	Victoria, B.C.	4/18/1971			
22	Paul Stewart	Boston, MA	3/21/1955	3/27/1987	804	68
17	Richard Trottier	Laval, Que.	2/28/1957	12/13/1989	477	71
21	Don Van Massenhoven	London, Ont.	7/17/1960	11/11/1993	402	74
24	Stephen Walkom	North Bay, Ont.	8/8/1963	10/18/1992	403	76
53	Ian Walsh	Philadelphia, PA	5/9/1972			
35	Dean Warren	Toronto, Ont.	7/22/1963	10/8/1999	6	6
23	Brad Watson	Regina, Sask.	10/4/1961	2/5/1994	111	68
29	Scott Zelkin	Wilmette, IL	9/12/1968	4/13/1997	90	65

* Includes some games worked as a linesman.   ** First game as an NHL referee. Previousl worked as a linesman.

Linesmen

#	Name	Birthplace	Birthdate	First NHL Game	Total NHL Games	99-2000 Games
75	Derek Amell	Port Colborne, Ont.	9/16/1968	10/13/1997	145	62
59	Steve Barton	Ottawa, Ont.	12/27/1971			
94	Wayne Bonney	Ottawa, Ont.	5/27/1953	10/10/1979	1456	71
96	David Brisebois	Sudbury, Ont.	4/14/1976	10/11/1999	45	45
55	Gord Broseker	Baltimore, MD	7/8/1950	1/14/1975	1791	69
74	Lonnie Cameron	Victoria, B.C.	7/15/1964	10/5/1996	259	60
67	Pierre Champoux	Ville St-Pierre, Que.	4/18/1963	10/8/1988	770	64
50	Kevin Collins	Springfield, MA	12/15/1950	10/13/1977	1758	73
88	Mike Cvik	Calgary, Alta.	7/6/1962	10/8/1987	851	71
38	Angelo D'Amico	Etobicoke, Ont.	5/29/1974			
45	Pat Dapuzzo	Hoboken, NJ	12/29/1958	12/5/1984	1142	70
54	Greg Devorski	Guelph, Ont.	8/3/1969	10/9/1993	431	63
68	Scott Driscoll	Seaforth, Ont.	5/2/1968	10/10/1992	493	59
63	Gerard Gauthier	Montreal, Que.	9/5/1948	10/16/1971	2138	63
66	Darren Gibbs	Edmonton, Alta.	9/30/1966	10/1/1997	162	66
91	Don Henderson	Calgary, Alta.	9/23/1968	3/10/1995	248	58
71	Brad Kovachik	Woodstock, Ont.	3/7/1971	10/10/1996	231	70
86	Brad Lazarowich	Vancouver, B.C.	8/4/1962	10/9/1986	953	62
78	Brian Mach	Little Falls, MN	4/15/1974			
46	Dan McCourt	Falconbridge, Ont.	8/14/1954	12/27/1980	1341	63
90	Andy McElman	Chicago Heights, IL	8/4/1961	10/7/1993	435	70
89	Steve Miller	Stratford, Ont.	6/22/1972			
98	Randy Mitton	Fredericton, N.B.	9/22/1950	2/2/1974	1832	66
97	Jean Morin	Sorel, Que.	8/10/1963	10/5/1991	561	66
95	Jonny Murray	Beauport, Quebec	8/10/1974			
80	Thor Nelson	Westminister, CA	1/6/1968	2/16/1995	174	22
77	Tim Nowak	Buffalo, NY	9/6/1967	10/8/1993	444	71
92	Dan O'Rourke	Calgary, Alta.	8/31/1972	10/2/1999	54	54
79	Mark Paré	Windsor, Ont.	7/26/1957	10/11/1979	1538	70
72	Stephane Provost	Montreal, Que.	5/5/1967	1/25/1995	407	78
65	Pierre Racicot	Verdun, Que.	2/15/1967	10/12/1993	466	75
73	Vaughan Roddy	Winnipeg, MB	12/13/1968			
81	Troy Sartison	Swift Current, Sask.	2/25/1970	10/6/1999	59	59
42	Ray Scapinello	Guelph, Ont.	11/5/1946	10/17/1971	2224	65
47	Dan Schachte	Madison, WI	7/13/1958	10/6/1982	1253	69
31	Lyle Seitz	Brooks, Alta.	1/22/1969	10/6/1992	*179	67
84	Anthony Sericolo	Troy, NY	7/17/1968	10/21/1998	91	62
56	Mark Wheler	North Battleford, Sask.	9/20/1965	10/10/1992	515	65

* Includes some games worked as a referee.

NHL History

1917 — National Hockey League organized November 22 in Montreal following suspension of operations by the National Hockey Association of Canada Limited (NHA). Montreal Canadiens, Montreal Wanderers, Ottawa Senators and Quebec Bulldogs attended founding meeting. Delegates decided to use NHA rules.

Toronto Arenas were later admitted as fifth team; Quebec decided not to operate during the first season. Quebec players allocated to remaining four teams.

Frank Calder elected president and secretary-treasurer.

First NHL games played December 19, with Toronto only arena with artificial ice. Clubs played 22-game split schedule.

1918 — Emergency meeting held January 3 due to destruction by fire of Montreal Arena which was home ice for both Canadiens and Wanderers.

Wanderers withdrew, reducing the NHL to three teams; Canadiens played remaining home games at 3,250-seat Jubilee rink.

Quebec franchise sold to P.J. Quinn of Toronto on October 18 on the condition that the team operate in Quebec City for 1918-19 season. Quinn did not attend the November League meeting and Quebec did not play in 1918-19.

1919-20 — NHL reactivated Quebec Bulldogs franchise. Former Quebec players returned to the club. New Mount Royal Arena became home of Canadiens. Toronto Arenas changed name to St. Patricks. Clubs played 24-game split schedule.

1920-21 — H.P. Thompson of Hamilton, Ontario made application for the purchase of an NHL franchise. Quebec franchise shifted to Hamilton with other NHL teams providing players to strengthen the club.

1921-22 — Split schedule abandoned. First and second place teams at the end of full schedule to play for championship.

1922-23 — Clubs agreed that players could not be sold or traded to clubs in any other league without first being offered to all other clubs in the NHL. In March, Foster Hewitt broadcasts radio's first hockey game.

1923-24 — Ottawa's new 10,000-seat arena opened. First U.S. franchise granted to Boston for following season.

Dr. Cecil Hart Trophy donated to NHL to be awarded to the player judged most useful to his team.

1924-25 — Canadian Arena Company of Montreal granted a franchise to operate Montreal Maroons. NHL now six team league with two clubs in Montreal. Inaugural game in new Montreal Forum played November 29, 1924 as Canadiens defeated Toronto 7-1. Forum was home rink for the Maroons, but no ice was available in the Canadiens arena November 29, resulting in shift to Forum.

Hamilton finished first in the standings, receiving a bye into the finals. But Hamilton players, demanding $200 each for additional games in the playoffs, went on strike. Stanley Cup finalist to be the winner of NHL semi-final between Toronto and Canadiens.

Prince of Wales and Lady Byng trophies donated to NHL.

Clubs played 30-game schedule.

1925-26 — Hamilton club dropped from NHL. Players signed by new New York Americans franchise. Franchise granted to Pittsburgh.

Clubs played 36-game schedule.

1926-27 — New York Rangers granted franchise May 15, 1926. Chicago Black Hawks and Detroit Cougars granted franchises September 25, 1926. NHL now ten-team league with an American and a Canadian Division.

Stanley Cup came under the control of NHL. In previous seasons, winners of the now-defunct Western or Pacific Coast leagues would play NHL champion in Cup finals.

Toronto franchise sold to a new company controlled by Hugh Aird and Conn Smythe. Name changed from St. Patricks to Maple Leafs.

Clubs played 44-game schedule.

The Montreal Canadiens donated the Vezina Trophy to be awarded to the team allowing the fewest goals-against in regular season play. The winning team would, in turn, present the trophy to the goaltender playing in the greatest number of games during the season.

1930-31 — Detroit franchise changed name from Cougars to Falcons. Pittsburgh transferred to Philadelphia for one season. Pirates changed name to Philadelphia Quakers. Trading deadline for teams set at February 15 of each year. NHL approved operation of farm teams by Rangers, Americans, Falcons and Bruins. Four-sided electric arena clock first demonstrated.

1931-32 — Philadelphia dropped out. Ottawa withdrew for one season. New Maple Leaf Gardens completed.

Clubs played 48-game schedule.

1932-33 — Detroit franchise changed name from Falcons to Red Wings. Franchise application received from St. Louis but refused because of additional travel costs. Ottawa team resumed play.

1933-34 — First All-Star Game played as a benefit for injured player Ace Bailey. Leafs defeated All-Stars 7-3 in Toronto.

1934-35 — Ottawa franchise transferred to St. Louis. Team called St. Louis Eagles and consisted largely of Ottawa's players.

1935-36 — Ottawa-St. Louis franchise terminated. Montreal Canadiens finished season with very poor record. To strengthen the club, NHL gave Canadiens first call on the services of all French-Canadian players for three seasons.

1937-38 — Second benefit all-star game staged November 2 in Montreal in aid of the family of the late Canadiens star Howie Morenz.

Montreal Maroons withdrew from the NHL on June 22, 1938, leaving seven clubs in the League.

1938-39 — Expenses for each club regulated at $5 per man per day for meals and $2.50 per man per day for accommodation.

1939-40 — Benefit All-Star Game played October 29, 1939 in Montreal for the children of the late Albert (Babe) Siebert.

1940-41 — Ross-Tyer puck adopted as the official puck of the NHL. Early in the season it was apparent that this puck was too soft. The Spalding puck was adopted in its place.

After the playoffs, Arthur Ross, NHL governor from Boston, donated a perpetual trophy to be awarded annually to the player voted outstanding in the league.

1941-42 — New York Americans changed name to Brooklyn Americans.

1942-43 — Brooklyn Americans withdrew from NHL, leaving six teams: Boston, Chicago, Detroit, Montreal, New York and Toronto. Playoff format saw first-place team play third-place team and second play fourth.

Clubs played 50-game schedule.

Frank Calder, president of the NHL since its inception, died in Montreal. Meryn "Red" Dutton, former manager of the New York Americans, became president. The NHL commissioned the Calder Memorial Trophy to be awarded to the League's outstanding rookie each year.

1945-46 — Philadelphia, Los Angeles and San Francisco applied for NHL franchises.

The Philadelphia Arena Company of the American Hockey League applied for an injunction to prevent the possible operation of an NHL franchise in that city.

1946-47 — Mervyn Dutton retired as president of the NHL prior to the start of the season. He was succeeded by Clarence S. Campbell.

Individual trophy winners and all-star team members to receive $1,000 awards.

Playoff guarantees for players introduced.

Clubs played 60-game schedule.

1947-48 — The first annual All-Star Game for the benefit of the players' pension fund was played when the All-Stars defeated the Stanley Cup Champion Toronto Maple Leafs 4-3 in Toronto on October 13, 1947.

Ross Trophy, awarded to the NHL's outstanding player since 1941, to be awarded annually to the League's scoring leader.

Philadelphia and Los Angeles franchise applications refused.

National Hockey League Pension Society formed.

1949-50 — Clubs played 70-game schedule.

First intra-league draft held April 30, 1950. Clubs allowed to protect 30 players. Remaining players available for $25,000 each.

1951-52 — Referees included in the League's pension plan.

1952-53 — In May of 1952, City of Cleveland applied for NHL franchise. Application denied. In March of 1953, the Cleveland Barons of the AHL challenged the NHL champions for the Stanley Cup. The NHL governors did not accept this challenge.

1953-54 — The James Norris Memorial Trophy presented to the NHL for annual presentation to the League's best defenseman.

Intra-league draft rules amended to allow teams to protect 18 skaters and two goaltenders, claiming price reduced to $15,000.

1954-55 — Each arena to operate an "out-of-town" scoreboard. Referees and linesmen to wear shirts of black and white vertical stripes.

1956-57 — Standardized signals for referees and linesmen introduced.

1960-61 — Canadian National Exhibition, City of Toronto and NHL reach agreement for the construction of a Hockey Hall of Fame on the CNE grounds. Hall opens on August 26, 1961.

1963-64 — Player development league established with clubs operated by NHL franchises located in Minneapolis, St. Paul, Indianapolis, Omaha and, beginning in 1964-65, Tulsa. First universal amateur draft took place. All players of qualifying age (17) unaffected by sponsorship of junior teams available to be drafted.

1964-65 — Conn Smythe Trophy presented to the NHL to be awarded annually to the outstanding player in the Stanley Cup playoffs.

Minimum age of players subject to amateur draft changed to 18.

1965-66 — NHL announced expansion plans for a second six-team division to begin play in 1967-68.

1966-67 — Fourteen applications for NHL franchises received.

Lester Patrick Trophy presented to the NHL to be awarded annually for outstanding service to hockey in the United States.

NHL sponsorship of junior teams ceased, making all players of qualifying age not already on NHL-sponsored lists eligible for the amateur draft.

1967-68 — Six new teams added: California Seals, Los Angeles Kings, Minnesota North Stars, Philadelphia Flyers, Pittsburgh Penguins, St. Louis Blues. New teams to play in West Division. Remaining six teams to play in East Division.

Minimum age of players subject to amateur draft changed to 20.

Clubs played 74-game schedule.

Clarence S. Campbell Trophy awarded to team finishing the regular season in first place in West Division.

California Seals changed name to Oakland Seals on December 8, 1967.

1968-69 — Clubs played 76-game schedule.

Amateur draft expanded to cover any amateur player of qualifying age throughout the world.

1970-71 — Two new teams added: Buffalo Sabres and Vancouver Canucks. These teams joined East Division: Chicago switched to West Division.

Clubs played 78-game schedule.

1971-72 — Playoff format amended. In each division, first to play fourth; second to play third.

1972-73 — Soviet Nationals and Canadian NHL stars play eight-game pre-season series. Canadians win 4-3-1.

Two new teams added. Atlanta Flames join West Division; New York Islanders join East Division.

1974-75 — Two new teams added: Kansas City Scouts and Washington Capitals. Teams realigned into two nine-team conferences, the Prince of Wales made up of the Norris and Adams Divisions, and the Clarence Campbell made up of the Smythe and Patrick Divisions.

Clubs played 80-game schedule.

1976-77 — California franchise transferred to Cleveland. Team named Cleveland Barons. Kansas City franchise transferred to Denver. Team named Colorado Rockies.

1977-78 — Clarence S. Campbell retires as NHL president. Succeeded by John A. Ziegler, Jr.

1978-79 — Cleveland and Minnesota franchises merge, leaving NHL with 17 teams. Merged team placed in Adams Division, playing home games in Minnesota.

Minimum age of players subject to amateur draft changed to 19.

1979-80 — Four new teams added: Edmonton Oilers, Hartford Whalers, Quebec Nordiques and Winnipeg Jets.

Minimum age of players subject to entry draft changed to 18.

1980-81 — Atlanta franchise shifted to Calgary, retaining "Flames" name.

1981-82 — Teams realigned within existing divisions. New groupings based on geographical areas. Unbalanced schedule adopted.

1982-83 — Colorado Rockies franchise shifted to East Rutherford, New Jersey. Team named New Jersey Devils. Franchise moved to Patrick Division from Smythe; Winnipeg moved to Smythe Division from Norris.

NHL History — *continued*

1991-92 — San Jose Sharks added, making the NHL a 22-team league. NHL celebrates 75th Anniversary Season. The 1991-92 regular season suspended due to a strike by members of the NHL Players' Association on April 1, 1992. Play resumed April 12, 1992.

1992-93 — Gil Stein named NHL president (October, 1992). Gary Bettman named first NHL Commissioner (February, 1993). Ottawa Senators and Tampa Bay Lightning added, making the NHL a 24-team league. NHL celebrates Stanley Cup Centennial. Clubs played 84-game schedule.

1993-94 — Mighty Ducks of Anaheim and Florida Panthers added, making the NHL a 26-team league. Minnesota franchise shifted to Dallas, team named Dallas Stars. Prince of Wales and Clarence Campbell Conferences renamed Eastern and Western. Adams, Patrick, Norris and Smythe Divisions renamed Northeast, Atlantic, Central and Pacific. Winnipeg moved to Central Division from Pacific; Tampa Bay moved to Atlantic Division from Central; Pittsburgh moved to Northeast Division from Atlantic.

1994-95 — A labor disruption forced the cancellation of 468 games from October 1, 1994 to January 19, 1995. Clubs played a 48-game schedule that began January 20, 1995 and ended May 3, 1995. No inter-conference games were played.

1995-96 — Quebec franchise transferred to Denver. Team named Colorado Avalanche and placed in Pacific Division of Western Conference. Clubs to play 82-game schedule.

1996-97 — Winnipeg franchise transferred to Phoenix. Team named Phoenix Coyotes and placed in Central Division of Western Conference.

1997-98 — Hartford franchise transferred to Raleigh. Team named Carolina Hurricanes and remains in Northeast Division of Eastern Conference.

1998-99 — The addition of the Nashville Predators made the NHL a 27-team league and brought about the creation of two new divisions and a League-wide realignment in preparation for further expansion to 30 teams by 2000-2001. Nashville was added to the Central Division of the Western Conference, while Toronto moved into the Northeast Division of the Eastern Conference. Pittsburgh was shifted from the Northeast to the Atlantic, while Carolina left the Northeast for the newly created Southeast Division of the Eastern Conference. Florida, Tampa Bay and Washington also joined the Southeast. In the Western Conference, Calgary, Colorado, Edmonton and Vancouver make up the new Northwest Division. Dallas and Phoenix moved from the Central to the Pacific Division.

The NHL retired uniform number 99 in honor of all-time scoring leader Wayne Gretzky who retired at the end of the season.

1999-2000 — Atlanta Thrashers added, making the NHL a 28-team league.

2000-01 — Columbus Blue Jackets and Minnesota Wild added, making the NHL a 30-team league.

Major Rule Changes

1910-11 — Game changed from two 30-minute periods to three 20-minute periods.

1911-12 — National Hockey Association (forerunner of the NHL) originated six-man hockey, replacing seven-man game.

1917-18 — Goalies permitted to fall to the ice to make saves. Previously a goaltender was penalized for dropping to the ice.

1918-19 — Penalty rules amended. For minor fouls, substitutes not allowed until penalized player had served three minutes. For major fouls, no substitutes for five minutes. For match fouls, no substitutes allowed for the remainder of the game.

  With the addition of two lines painted on the ice twenty feet from center, three playing zones were created, producing a forty-foot neutral center ice area in which forward passing was permitted. Kicking the puck was permitted in this neutral zone.

  Tabulation of assists began.

1921-22 — Goaltenders allowed to pass the puck forward up to their own blue line.

  Overtime limited to twenty minutes.

  Minor penalties changed from three minutes to two minutes.

1923-24 — Match foul defined as actions deliberately injuring or disabling an opponent. For such actions, a player was fined not less than $50 and ruled off the ice for the balance of the game. A player assessed a match penalty may be replaced by a substitute at the end of 20 minutes. Match penalty recipients must meet with the League president who can assess additional punishment.

1925-26 — Delayed penalty rules introduced. Each team must have a minimum of four players on the ice at all times.

  Two rules were amended to encourage offense: No more than two defensemen permitted to remain inside a team's own blue line when the puck has left the defensive zone. A faceoff to be called for ragging the puck unless short-handed.

  Team captains only players allowed to talk to referees.

  Goaltender's leg pads limited to 12-inch width.

  Timekeeper's gong to mark end of periods rather than referee's whistle. Teams to dress a maximum of 12 players for each game from a roster of no more than 14 players.

1926-27 — Blue lines repositioned to sixty feet from each goal-line, thereby enlarging the neutral zone and standardizing distance from blueline to goal.

  Uniform goal nets adopted throughout NHL with goal posts securely fastened to the ice.

1927-28 — To further encourage offense, forward passes allowed in defending and neutral zones and goaltender's pads reduced in width from 12 to 10 inches.

  Game standardized at three twenty-minute periods of stop-time separated by ten-minute intermissions. Teams to change ends after each period.

  Ten minutes of sudden-death overtime to be played if the score is tied after regulation time.

  Minor penalty to be assessed to any player other than a goaltender for deliberately picking up the puck while it is in play. Minor penalty to be assessed for deliberately shooting the puck out of play.

  The Art Ross goal net adopted as the official net of the NHL.

  Maximum length of hockey sticks limited to 53 inches measured from heel of blade to end of handle. No minimum length stipulated.

  Home teams given choice of goals to defend at start of game.

1928-29 — Forward passing permitted in defensive and neutral zones and into attacking zone if pass receiver is in neutral zone when pass is made. No forward passing allowed inside attacking zone.

  Minor penalty to be assessed to any player who delays the game by passing the puck back into his defensive zone.

  Ten-minute overtime without sudden-death provision to be played in games tied after regulation time. Games tied after this overtime period declared a draw.

  Exclusive of goaltenders, team to dress at least 8 and no more than 12 skaters.

NHL Attendance

Season	Regular Season Games	Regular Season Attendance	Playoffs Games	Playoffs Attendance	Total Attendance
1960-61	210	2,317,142	17	242,000	2,559,142
1961-62	210	2,435,424	18	277,000	2,712,424
1962-63	210	2,590,574	16	220,906	2,811,480
1963-64	210	2,732,642	21	309,149	3,041,791
1964-65	210	2,822,635	20	303,859	3,126,494
1965-66	210	2,941,164	16	249,000	3,190,184
1966-67	210	3,084,759	16	248,336	3,333,095
1967-68[1]	444	4,938,043	40	495,089	5,433,132
1968-69	456	5,550,613	33	431,739	5,982,352
1969-70	456	5,992,065	34	461,694	6,453,759
1970-71[2]	546	7,257,677	43	707,633	7,965,310
1971-72	546	7,609,368	36	582,666	8,192,034
1972-73[3]	624	8,575,651	38	624,637	9,200,288
1973-74	624	8,640,978	38	600,442	9,241,420
1974-75[4]	720	9,521,536	51	784,181	10,305,717
1975-76	720	9,103,761	48	726,279	9,830,040
1976-77	720	8,563,890	44	646,279	9,210,169
1977-78	720	8,526,564	45	686,634	9,213,198
1978-79	680	7,758,053	45	694,521	8,452,574
1979-80[5]	840	10,533,623	63	976,699	11,510,322
1980-81	840	10,726,198	68	966,390	11,692,588
1981-82	840	10,710,894	71	1,058,948	11,769,842
1982-83	840	11,020,610	66	1,088,222	12,028,832
1983-84	840	11,359,386	70	1,107,400	12,466,786
1984-85	840	11,633,730	70	1,107,500	12,741,230
1985-86	840	11,621,000	72	1,152,503	12,773,503
1986-87	840	11,855,880	87	1,383,967	13,239,847
1987-88	840	12,117,512	83	1,336,901	13,454,413
1988-89	840	12,417,969	83	1,327,214	13,745,183
1989-90	840	12,579,651	85	1,355,593	13,935,244
1990-91	840	12,343,897	92	1,442,203	13,786,100
1991-92[6]	880	12,769,676	86	1,327,920	14,097,596
1992-93[7]	1,008	14,158,177[8]	83	1,346,034	15,504,211
1993-94[9]	1,092	16,105,604[10]	90	1,440,095	17,545,699
1994-95	624[11]	9,233,884	81	1,329,130	10,563,014
1995-96	1,066	17,041,614	86	1,540,140	18,581,754
1996-97	1,066	17,640,529	82	1,494,878	19,135,407
1997-98	1,066	17,264,678	82	1,507,416	18,772,094
1998-99[12]	1,107	18,001,741	86	1,509,411	19,511,152
1999-2000[13]	1,148	18,800,139	83	1,524,629	20,324,768

[1] First expansion: Los Angeles, Pittsburgh, California (Cleveland),Philadelphia, St. Louis and Minnesota (Dallas)
[2] Second expansion: Buffalo and Vancouver
[3] Third expansion: Atlanta (Calgary) and New York Islanders
[4] Fourth expansion: Kansas City (Colorado, New Jersey) and Washington
[5] Fifth expansion: Edmonton, Hartford, Quebec (Colorado) and Winnipeg
[6] Sixth expansion: San Jose
[7] Seventh expansion: Ottawa and Tampa Bay
[8] Includes 24 neutral site games
[9] Eighth expansion: Anaheim and Florida
[10] Includes 26 neutral site games
[11] Lockout resulted in the cancellation of 468 regular-season games.
[12] Ninth expansion: Nashville
[13] Tenth expansion: Atlanta

Major Rule Changes — *continued*

1929-30 — Forward passing permitted inside all three zones but not permitted across either blue line.

Kicking the puck allowed, but a goal cannot be scored by kicking the puck in.

No more than three players including the goaltender may remain in their defensive zone when the puck has gone up ice. Minor penalties to be assessed for the first two violations of this rule in a game; major penalties thereafter.

Goaltenders forbidden to hold the puck. Pucks caught must be cleared immediately. For infringement of this rule, a faceoff to be taken ten feet in front of the goal with no player except the goaltender standing between the faceoff spot and the goal-line.

Highsticking penalties introduced.

Maximum number of players in uniform increased from 12 to 15.

December 21, 1929 — Forward passing rules instituted at the beginning of the 1929-30 season more than doubled number of goals scored. Partway through the season, these rules were further amended to read, "No attacking player allowed to precede the play when entering the opposing defensive zone." This is similar to modern offside rule.

1930-31 — A player without a complete stick ruled out of play and forbidden from taking part in further action until a new stick is obtained. A player who has broken his stick must obtain a replacement at his bench.

A further refinement of the offside rule stated that the puck must first be propelled into the attacking zone before any player of the attacking side can enter that zone; for infringement of this rule a faceoff to take place at the spot where the infraction took place.

1931-32 — Though there is no record of a team attempting to play with two goaltenders on the ice, a rule was instituted which stated that each team was allowed only one goaltender on the ice at one time.

Attacking players forbidden to impede the movement or obstruct the vision of opposing goaltenders.

Defending players with the exception of the goaltender forbidden from falling on the puck within 10 feet of the net.

1932-33 — Each team to have captain on the ice at all times.

If the goaltender is removed from the ice to serve a penalty, the manager of the club to appoint a substitute.

Match penalty with substitution after five minutes instituted for kicking another player.

1933-34 — Number of players permitted to stand in defensive zone restricted to three including goaltender.

Visible time clocks required in each rink.

Two referees replace one referee and one linesman.

1934-35 — Penalty shot awarded when a player is tripped and thus prevented from having a clear shot on goal, having no player to pass to other than the offending player. Shot taken from inside a 10-foot circle located 38 feet from the goal. The goaltender must not advance more than one foot from his goal-line when the shot is taken.

1937-38 — Rules introduced governing icing the puck.

Penalty shot awarded when a player other than a goaltender falls on the puck within 10 feet of the goal.

1938-39 — Penalty shot modified to allow puck carrier to skate in before shooting.

One referee and one linesman replace two referee system.

Blue line widened to 12 inches.

Maximum number of players in uniform increased from 14 to 15.

1939-40 — A substitute replacing a goaltender removed from ice to serve a penalty may use a goaltender's stick and gloves but no other goaltending equipment.

1940-41 — Flooding ice surface between periods made obligatory.

1941-42 — Penalty shots classified as minor and major. Minor shot to be taken from a line 28 feet from the goal. Major shot, awarded when a player is tripped with only the goaltender to beat, permits the player taking the penalty shot to skate right into the goalkeeper and shoot from point-blank range.

One referee and two linesmen employed to officiate games.

For playoffs, standby minor league goaltenders employed by NHL as emergency substitutes.

1942-43 — Because of wartime restrictions on train scheduling, regular-season overtime was discontinued on November 21, 1942.

Player limit reduced from 15 to 14. Minimum of 12 men in uniform abolished.

1943-44 — Red line at center ice introduced to speed up the game and reduce offside calls. This rule is considered to mark the beginning of the modern era in the NHL.

Delayed penalty rules introduced.

1945-46 — Goal indicator lights synchronized with official time clock required at all rinks.

1946-47 — System of signals by officials to indicate infractions introduced.

Linesmen from neutral cities employed for all games.

1947-48 — Goal awarded when a player with the puck has an open net to shoot at and a thrown stick prevents the shot on goal. Major penalty to any player who throws his stick in any zone other than defending zone. If a stick is thrown by a player in his defending zone but the thrown stick is not considered to have prevented a goal, a penalty shot is awarded.

All playoff games played until a winner determined, with 20-minute sudden-death overtime periods separated by 10-minute intermissions.

1949-50 — Ice surface painted white.

Clubs allowed to dress 17 players exclusive of goaltenders.

Major penalties incurred by goaltenders served by a member of the goaltender's team instead of resulting in a penalty shot.

1950-51 — Each team required to provide an emergency goaltender in attendance with full equipment at each game for use by either team in the event of illness or injury to a regular goaltender.

1951-52 — Home teams to wear basic white uniforms; visiting teams basic colored uniforms.

Goal crease enlarged from 3 × 7 feet to 4 × 8 feet.

Number of players in uniform reduced to 15 plus goaltenders.

Faceoff circles enlarged from 10-foot to 15-foot radius.

1952-53 — Teams permitted to dress 15 skaters on the road and 16 at home.

1953-54 — Number of players in uniform set at 16 plus goaltenders.

1954-55 — Number of players in uniform set at 18 plus goaltenders up to December 1 and 16 plus goaltenders thereafter. Teams agree to wear colored uniforms at home and white uniforms on the road.

1956-57 — Player serving a minor penalty allowed to return to ice when a goal is scored by opposing team.

1959-60 — Players prevented from leaving their benches to enter into an altercation. Substitutions permitted providing substitutes do not enter into altercation.

1960-61 — Number of players in uniform set at 16 plus goaltenders.

1961-62 — Penalty shots to be taken by the player against whom the foul was committed. In the event of a penalty shot called in a situation where a particular player hasn't been fouled, the penalty shot to be taken by any player on the ice when the foul was committed.

1964-65 — No bodily contact on faceoffs.

In playoff games, each team to have its substitute goaltender dressed in his regular uniform except for leg pads and body protector. All previous rules governing standby goaltenders terminated.

1965-66 — Teams required to dress two goaltenders for each regular-season game. Maximum stick length increased to 55 inches.

1966-67 — Substitution allowed on coincidental major penalties.

Between-periods intermissions fixed at 15 minutes.

1967-68 — If a penalty incurred by a goaltender is a co-incident major, the penalty to be served by a player of the goaltender's team on the ice at the time the penalty was called. Limit of curvature of hockey stick blade set at 1-½ inches.

1969-70 — Limit of curvature of hockey stick blade set at 1 inch.

1970-71 — Home teams to wear basic white uniforms; visiting teams basic colored uniforms.

Limit of curvature of hockey stick blade set at ½ inch.

Minor penalty for deliberately shooting the puck out of the playing area.

1971-72 — Number of players in uniform set at 17 plus 2 goaltenders.

Third man to enter an altercation assessed an automatic game misconduct penalty.

1972-73 — Minimum width of stick blade reduced to 2 inches from 2-½ inches.

1974-75 — Bench minor penalty imposed if a penalized player does not proceed directly and immediately to the penalty box.

1976-77 — Rule dealing with fighting amended to provide a major and game misconduct penalty for any player who is clearly the instigator of a fight.

1977-78 — Teams requesting a stick measurement to be assessed a minor penalty in the event that the measured stick does not violate the rules.

1979-80 — Wearing of helmets made mandatory for players entering the NHL.

1980-81 — Maximum stick length increased to 58 inches.

1981-82 — If both of a team's listed goaltenders are incapacitated, the team can dress and play any eligible goaltender who is available.

1982-83 — Number of players in uniform set at 18 plus 2 goaltenders.

1983-84 — Five-minute sudden-death overtime to be played in regular-season games that are tied at the end of regulation time.

1985-86 — Substitutions allowed in the event of co-incidental minor penalties. Maximum stick length increased to 60 inches.

1986-87 — Delayed off-side is no longer in effect once the players of the offending team have cleared the opponents' defensive zone.

1990-91 — The goal lines, blue lines, defensive zone face-off circles and markings all moved one foot out from the end boards, creating 11 feet of room behind the nets and shrinking the neutral zone from 60 to 58 feet.

1991-92 — Video replays employed to assist referees in goal/no goal situations. Size of goal crease increased. Crease changed to semi-circular configuration. Time clock to record tenths of a second in last minute of each period and overtime. Major and game misconduct penalty for checking from behind into boards. Penalties added for crease infringement and unnecessary contact with goaltender. Goal disallowed if puck enters net while a player of the attacking team is standing on the goal crease line, is in the goal crease or places his stick in the goal crease.

1992-93 — No substitutions allowed in the event of coincidental minor penalties called when both teams are at full strength. Wearing of helmets made optional for forwards and defensemen. Minor penalty for attempting to draw a penalty ("diving"). Major and game misconduct penalty for checking from behind into goal frame. Game misconduct penalty for instigating a fight. Highsticking redefined to include any use of the stick above waist-height. Previous rule stipulated shoulder-height.

1993-94 — High sticking redefined to allow goals scored with a high stick below the height of the crossbar of the goal frame.

1996-97 — Maximum stick length increased to 63 inches.

1998-99 — The league instituted a two-referee system with each team to play 20 regular-season games with two referees and a pair of linesmen. Also, the goal lines, blue lines, defensive zone face-off circles and markings all moved two feet closer to center, creating 13 feet of room behind the nets and cutting the neutral zone from 58 to 54 feet. The goal crease was altered so that it extends only one foot beyond each goal post (eight feet across in total) and has square sides for the first 4'6". Only the top of the crease remains rounded.

1999-2000 — Each team to play 25 home and 25 road games using the two-referee system. Crease rule revised to implement a "no harm, no foul, no video review" standard. An attacking player's position, whether inside or outside the crease, does not, in itself, determine whether a goal should be allowed or disallowed. The on-ice judgement of the referee(s) — instead of video review — will determine if a goal is "good" or not. Also, regular-season games tied at the end of three periods will result in each team being awarded one point in the standings. As before, there will be a five-minute sudden death overtime when the score is tied after three periods, but each team will play "four on four," with four skaters and a goalkeeper. In the event that penalties dictate that one team has a two-man advantage, the penalized team plays with three skaters while the team with the two-man advantage adds a fifth skater. A team scoring in overtime will receive one additional point in the standings.

2000-01 — All games to be played using the two-referee system.

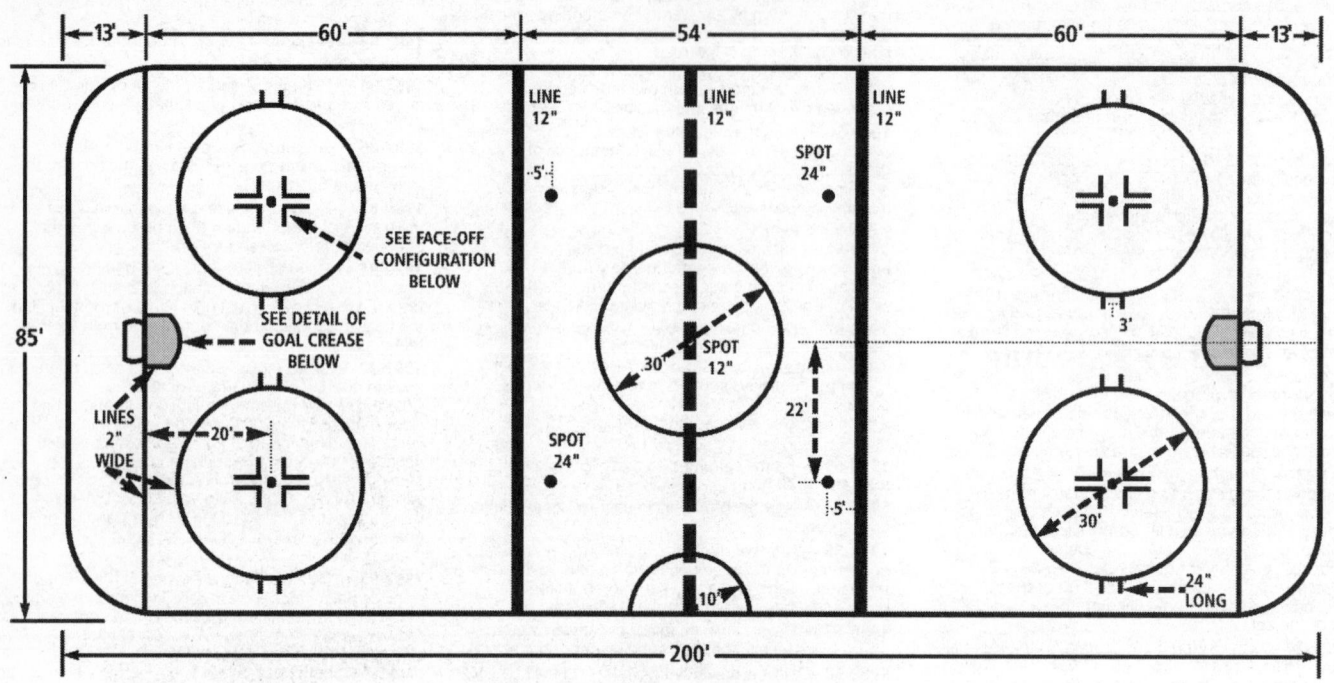

NHL RINK DIMENSIONS

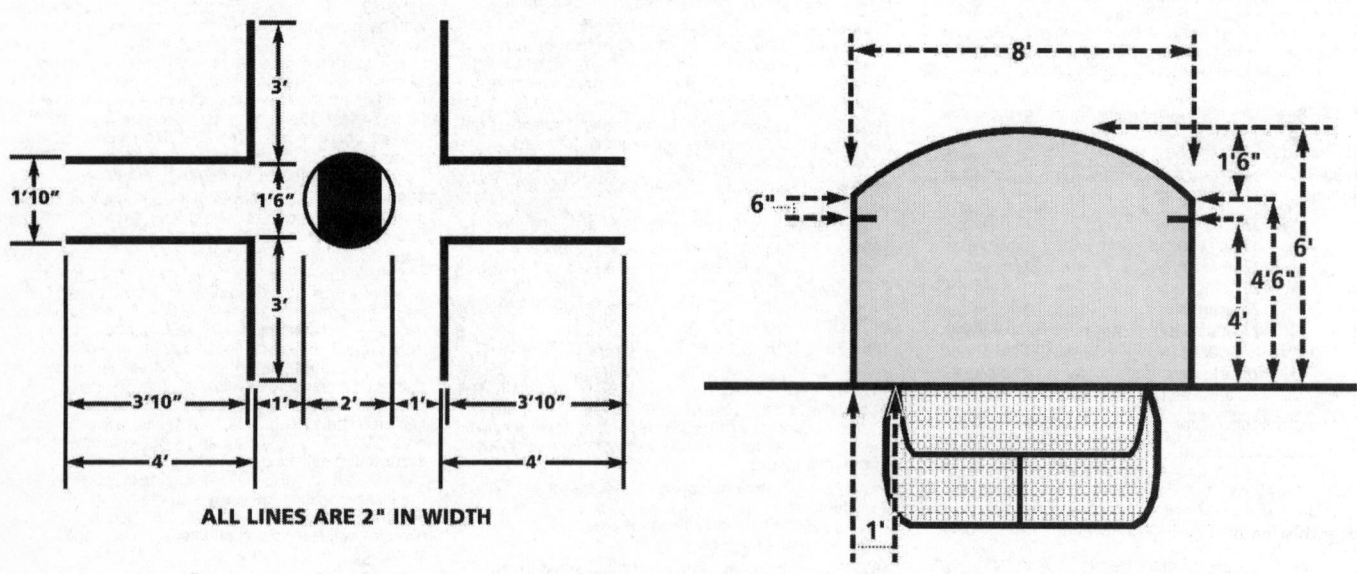

FACEOFF CONFIGURATION

CREASE DIMENSIONS

Mighty Ducks of Anaheim

1999-2000 Results: 34w-36L-12T 83PTS. Fifth, Pacific Division

Year-by-Year Record

Season	GP	Home W	L	T	Road W	L	T	Overall W	L	T	GF	GA	Pts.	Finished		Playoff Result
1999-2000	82	19	15	7	15	21	5	34	36	12	217	227	83	5th,	Pacific Div.	Out of Playoffs
1998-99	82	21	14	6	14	20	7	35	34	13	215	206	83	3rd,	Pacific Div.	Lost Conf. Quarter-Final
1997-98	82	12	23	6	14	20	7	26	43	13	205	261	65	6th,	Pacific Div.	Out of Playoffs
1996-97	82	23	12	6	13	21	7	36	33	13	245	233	85	2nd,	Pacific Div.	Lost Conf. Semi-Final
1995-96	82	22	15	4	13	24	4	35	39	8	234	247	78	4th,	Pacific Div.	Out of Playoffs
1994-95	48	11	9	4	5	18	1	16	27	5	125	164	37	6th,	Pacific Div.	Out of Playoffs
1993-94	84	14	26	2	19	20	3	33	46	5	229	251	71	4th,	Pacific Div.	Out of Playoffs

2000-01 Schedule

Oct.	Fri.	6	Minnesota
	Sun.	8	St. Louis*
	Wed.	11	Boston
	Sat.	14	at New Jersey
	Mon.	16	at NY Rangers
	Tue.	17	at NY Islanders
	Fri.	20	at Buffalo
	Sat.	21	at Philadelphia
	Mon.	23	Los Angeles
	Wed.	25	at Los Angeles
	Fri.	27	Edmonton
	Sun.	29	at Calgary
	Mon.	30	at Edmonton
Nov.	Wed.	1	Phoenix
	Sat.	4	at Nashville
	Sun.	5	at Chicago
	Wed.	8	Vancouver
	Sat.	11	at Colorado
	Sun.	12	Detroit*
	Wed.	15	Colorado
	Sat.	18	at Phoenix
	Sun.	19	NY Islanders*
	Wed.	22	New Jersey
	Fri.	24	at Calgary
	Sat.	25	at Edmonton
	Tue.	28	at Vancouver
	Thu.	30	at San Jose
Dec.	Sun.	3	Los Angeles*
	Tue.	5	at St. Louis
	Wed.	6	at Columbus
	Fri.	8	at Minnesota
	Sun.	10	Dallas*
	Wed.	13	Columbus
	Fri.	15	NY Rangers
	Sun.	17	Tampa Bay*
	Wed.	20	Atlanta
	Fri.	22	at Detroit
	Sat.	23	at St. Louis
	Wed.	27	at Dallas
	Thu.	28	at Nashville
	Sun.	31	at Minnesota*
Jan.	Wed.	3	Florida
	Fri.	5	Calgary
	Wed.	10	St. Louis
	Fri.	12	Buffalo
	Sun.	14	at Carolina*
	Mon.	15	at Pittsburgh*
	Wed.	17	at Atlanta
	Fri.	19	Phoenix
	Sun.	21	Colorado*
	Wed.	24	Minnesota
	Fri.	26	at Detroit
	Sat.	27	at Columbus
	Wed.	31	Nashville
Feb.	Thu.	1	at Phoenix
	Wed.	7	Chicago
	Fri.	9	Washington
	Sun.	11	Carolina*
	Wed.	14	Edmonton
	Fri.	16	at Dallas
	Mon.	19	Calgary
	Wed.	21	San Jose
	Fri.	23	at San Jose
	Sun.	25	Columbus*
	Wed.	28	Detroit
Mar.	Fri.	2	Dallas
	Sun.	4	Los Angeles*
	Wed.	7	Montreal
	Fri.	9	Chicago
	Sun.	11	Nashville*
	Tue.	13	at Washington
	Wed.	14	at Toronto
	Fri.	16	at Ottawa
	Sun.	18	at Chicago*
	Wed.	21	at Dallas
	Sat.	24	at Los Angeles*
	Thu.	29	at San Jose
	Fri.	30	at Vancouver
Apr.	Sun.	1	Vancouver*
	Wed.	4	at Colorado
	Fri.	6	Phoenix
	Sun.	8	San Jose*

* Denotes afternoon game.

Franchise date: June 15, 1993

WESTERN CONFERENCE

PACIFIC DIVISION

8th NHL Season

With 42 goals and 44 assists in 1999-2000, Paul Kariya continues to be one of the game's elite players. Kariya ranked fourth in the NHL in scoring and led the Mighty Ducks in most offensive categories.

Note: In each club's Year-by-Year Record, 1999-2000 point totals include regulation ties.

2000-01 Player Personnel

FORWARDS	HT	WT	S	Place of Birth	Date	1999-00 Club
AALTO, Antti	6-2	210	L	Lappeenranta, Finland	3/4/75	Anaheim
BALMOCHNYKH, Maxim	6-1	180	L	Lipetsk, USSR	3/7/79	Anaheim-Cincinnati Ducks
BYLSMA, Dan	6-2	209	L	Grand Haven, MI	9/19/70	Los Angeles-Long Beach-Lowell
CHOUINARD, Marc	6-5	204	R	Charlesbourg, Que.	5/6/77	Cincinnati Ducks
CULLEN, Matt	6-1	197	L	Virginia, MN	11/2/76	Anaheim
CUMMINS, Jim	6-2	219	R	Dearborn, MI	5/17/70	Montreal
DIROBERTO, Torrey	5-11	186	L	Utica, NY	4/17/78	Cincinnati Ducks-Huntington-Dayton Bombers
HRKAC, Tony	5-11	170	L	Thunder Bay, Ont.	7/7/66	NY Islanders-Anaheim
KARIYA, Paul	5-10	173	L	Vancouver, B.C.	10/16/74	Anaheim
KOHN, Ladislav	5-11	194	L	Uherske Hradiste, Czech.	3/4/75	Anaheim
LECLERC, Mike	6-1	206	L	Winnipeg, Man.	11/10/76	Anaheim
LEGAULT, Jay	6-4	205	L	Peterborough, Ont.	5/15/79	Cincinnati Ducks-Dayton Bombers
McDONALD, Andy	5-10	185	L	Strathroy, Ont.	8/25/77	Colgate
McINNIS, Marty	6-0	192	R	Weymouth, MA	6/2/70	Anaheim
RONNQVIST, Jonas	6-1	200	R	Kalix, Sweden	8/22/73	Lulea HF
RUCCHIN, Steve	6-3	212	L	Thunder Bay, Ont.	7/4/71	Anaheim
SAWYER, Kevin	6-2	205	L	Christina Lake, B.C.	2/21/74	Phoenix-Springfield
SELANNE, Teemu	6-0	204	R	Helsinki, Finland	7/3/70	Anaheim
SMITH, Jarrett	6-1	190	L	Edmonton, Alta.	6/15/79	Prince Albert
TENKRAT, Petr	6-1	185	R	Kladno, Czech.	5/31/77	HPK Hameenlinna-Ilves Tampere
TITOV, German	6-1	201	L	Moscow, USSR	10/16/65	Pittsburgh-Edmonton
WREN, Bob	5-10	185	L	Preston, Ont.	9/16/74	Cincinnati Ducks

DEFENSEMEN						
HAVELID, Niclas	6-0	192	L	Stockholm, Sweden	4/12/73	Anaheim-Cincinnati Ducks
MALKOC, Dean	6-3	215	L	Vancouver, B.C.	1/26/70	Chicago Wolves
MARSHALL, Jason	6-2	200	R	Cranbrook, B.C.	2/22/71	Anaheim
NIEMI, Antti-Jussi	6-1	183	L	Vantaa, Finland	9/22/77	Jokerit Helsinki
O'SULLIVAN, Chris	6-2	205	L	Dorchester, MA	5/15/74	Vancouver-Syracuse Crunch
PODHRADSKY, Peter	6-2	194	R	Bratislava, Czech.	12/10/79	HK Trnava-2-HC Bratislava
SALEI, Ruslan	6-1	212	L	Minsk, USSR	11/2/74	Anaheim
TRAVERSE, Patrick	6-3	190	L	Montreal, Que.	3/14/74	Ottawa
TREPANIER, Pascal	6-0	210	R	Gaspe, Que.	9/4/73	Anaheim
TRNKA, Pavel	6-3	200	L	Plzen, Czech.	7/27/76	Anaheim
TVERDOVSKY, Oleg	6-0	200	L	Donetsk, USSR	5/18/76	Anaheim
VISHNEVSKI, Vitaly	6-2	200	L	Kharkov, USSR	3/18/80	Anaheim-Cincinnati Ducks

GOALTENDERS	HT	WT	C	Place of Birth	Date	1999-00 Club
GIGUERE, Jean-Sebastien	6-1	175	L	Montreal, Que.	5/16/77	Calgary-Saint John Flames
HEBERT, Guy	5-11	186	L	Troy, NY	1/7/67	Anaheim
NAUMENKO, Gregg	6-1	201	L	Chicago, IL	3/30/77	Cincinnati Ducks
ROUSSEL, Dominic	6-2	200	L	Hull, Que.	2/22/70	Anaheim

1999-2000 Scoring
* – rookie

Regular Season

Pos	#	Player	Team	GP	G	A	Pts	+/–	PIM	PP	SH	GW	GT	S	%
L	9	Paul Kariya	ANA	74	42	44	86	22	24	11	3	3	0	324	13.0
R	8	Teemu Selanne	ANA	79	33	52	85	6	12	8	0	6	2	236	14.0
C	20	Steve Rucchin	ANA	71	19	38	57	9	16	10	0	2	2	131	14.5
D	10	Oleg Tverdovsky	ANA	82	15	36	51	5	30	5	0	5	0	153	9.8
C	11	Kip Miller	PIT	44	4	15	19	–1	10	0	0	1	0	50	8.0
			ANA	30	6	17	23	1	4	2	0	1	0	32	18.8
			TOTAL	74	10	32	42	0	14	2	0	2	0	82	12.2
C	17	Matt Cullen	ANA	80	13	26	39	5	24	1	0	1	0	137	9.5
D	2	Fredrik Olausson	ANA	70	15	19	34	–13	28	8	0	1	1	120	12.5
C	22	Jorgen Jonsson	NYI	68	11	17	28	–6	16	1	2	0	0	95	11.6
			ANA	13	1	2	3	–2	0	0	0	1	0	21	4.8
			TOTAL	81	12	19	31	–8	16	1	2	1	0	116	10.3
L	21	Ted Donato	ANA	81	11	19	30	–3	26	2	0	3	0	138	8.0
L	16	Marty McInnis	ANA	62	10	18	28	–4	26	2	1	2	0	129	7.8
R	29 *	Ladislav Kohn	ANA	77	5	16	21	–17	27	1	0	1	1	123	4.1
L	12	Mike Leclerc	ANA	69	8	11	19	–15	70	0	0	2	0	105	7.6
R	19	Jeff Nielsen	ANA	79	8	10	18	4	14	1	0	0	0	113	7.1
C	14	Antti Aalto	ANA	63	7	11	18	–13	26	1	0	1	0	102	6.9
D	7	Pavel Trnka	ANA	57	2	15	17	12	34	0	0	1	0	54	3.7
C	15	Tony Hrkac	NYI	7	0	2	2	–1	0	0	0	0	0	2	0.0
			ANA	60	4	7	11	–2	8	1	0	0	0	37	10.8
			TOTAL	67	4	9	13	–3	8	1	0	0	0	39	10.3
D	24	Ruslan Salei	ANA	71	5	5	10	3	94	1	0	0	0	116	4.3
D	28	Niclas Havelid	ANA	50	2	7	9	0	20	0	0	2	0	70	2.9
D	5	Kevin Haller	ANA	67	3	5	8	–8	61	0	0	2	0	50	6.0
R	33	Ed Ward	ATL	44	5	1	6	–5	44	0	2	0	0	51	9.8
			ANA	8	1	0	1	–2	15	0	0	0	0	5	20.0
			TOTAL	52	6	1	7	–7	59	0	2	0	0	56	10.7
D	27	Pascal Trepanier	ANA	37	0	4	4	2	54	0	0	0	0	33	0.0
L	32	Stu Grimson	ANA	50	1	2	3	0	116	0	0	0	0	14	7.1
D	23	Jason Marshall	ANA	55	0	3	3	–10	88	0	0	0	0	41	0.0
D	6 *	Vitaly Vishnevski	ANA	31	1	1	2	0	26	1	0	0	0	17	5.9
G	31	Guy Hebert	ANA	68	0	2	2	0	2	0	0	0	0	0	0.0
L	18 *	Maxim Balmochnykh	ANA	6	0	1	1	2	2	0	0	0	0	6	0.0
L	26	Jeremy Stevenson	ANA	3	0	0	0	–1	7	0	0	0	0	2	0.0
R	25 *	Frank Banham	ANA	3	0	0	0	0	2	0	0	0	0	4	0.0
G	30	Dominic Roussel	ANA	20	0	0	0	0	6	0	0	0	0	0	0.0

Goaltending

No.	Goaltender	GPI	Mins	Avg	W	L	T	EN	SO	GA	SA	S%
31	Guy Hebert	68	3976	2.51	28	31	9	8	4	166	1805	.908
30	Dominic Roussel	20	988	3.16	6	5	3	1	1	52	445	.883
	Totals	**82**	**4992**	**2.73**	**34**	**36**	**12**	**9**	**5**	**227**	**2259**	**.900**

President and General Manager

GAUTHIER, PIERRE
President and General Manager, Mighty Ducks of Anaheim.
Born in Montreal, Que., May 28, 1953.

Pierre Gauthier enters his third season as president and general manager of the Mighty Ducks. He is responsible for the overall hockey and front office operations of the club. Gauthier rejoined the Mighty Ducks on July 16, 1998. Under Gauthier, the Mighty Ducks returned to the playoffs in 1999 and just missed a playoff spot in 2000.

An original member of Anaheim's management team in 1993, Gauthier spent two-and-a-half seasons as general manager of the Ottawa Senators from 1995 to 1998. He has earned a reputation as one of the most astute judges of hockey talent in the NHL during his 19 years in the league. Gauthier joined Ottawa as the team's general manager in December of 1995. Just 17 months later, the club had earned its first-ever playoff berth.

Gauthier served as assistant general manager of the Mighty Ducks from 1993 to 1995 before joining the Senators. He was a key part of management in starting up the Anaheim franchise in 1993.

Prior to his first stint with the Mighty Ducks, Gauthier had spent 12 seasons in the scouting department with the Quebec Nordiques. He had joined the club as a scout in 1983 and worked in that capacity for three seasons before being named assistant director of scouting in 1986. Gauthier was promoted to chief scout in 1988, serving at that capacity until he joined Anaheim in 1993.

Gauthier received a master's degree in sports administration in 1983 from the University of Minnesota, where he also served as a teaching associate in physical education. He is also a graduate of Syracuse University, where he earned a bachelor of science degree in physical education.

A native of Montreal, Gauthier and his wife, Manon Roberge, have a daughter, Catherine, and a son Vincent. The family resides in Irvine, California.

Steve Rucchin usually centers Paul Kariya and Teemu Selanne on the Ducks' top line.

Club Records

Team

(Figures in brackets for season records are games played; records for fewest points, wins, ties, losses, goals, goals against are for 70 or more games)

Most Points	85	1996-97 (82)
Most Wins	36	1996-97 (82)
Most Ties	13	1996-97 (82); 1997-98 (82); 1998-99 (82)
Most Losses	46	1993-94 (84)
Most Goals	245	1996-97 (82)
Most Goals Against	261	1998-99 (82)
Fewest Points	65	1997-98 (82)
Fewest Wins	26	1997-98 (82)
Fewest Ties	5	1993-94 (84)
Fewest Losses	33	1996-97 (82)
Fewest Goals	205	1997-98 (82)
Fewest Goals Against	206	1998-99 (82)

Longest Winning Streak
Overall	7	Feb. 20-Mar. 7/99
Home	5	Twice
Away	5	Nov. 26-Dec. 26/99

Longest Undefeated Streak
Overall	12	Feb. 22-Mar. 19/97 (7 wins, 5 ties)
Home	14	Feb. 12-Apr. 9/97 (10 wins, 4 ties)
Away	5	Three times

Longest Losing Streak
Overall	8	Oct. 12-30/96
Home	6	Feb. 7-Mar. 11/98
Away	6	Three times

Longest Winless Streak
Overall	9	Twice
Home	6	Twice
Away	10	Mar. 26-Oct. 11/95 (9 losses, 1 tie)

Most Shutouts, Season	7	1998-99 (82)
Most PIM, Season	1,843	1997-98 (82)
Most Goals, Game	8	Jan. 21/98 (Ana. 8, Fla. 3)

Individual

Most Seasons	7	Guy Hebert
Most Games	400	Guy Hebert
Most Goals, Career	210	Paul Kariya
Most Assists, Career	254	Paul Kariya
Most Points, Career	464	Paul Kariya (210G, 254A)
Most PIM, Career	788	Dave Karpa
Most Shutouts, Career	25	Guy Hebert
Longest Consecutive Games Streak	159	Bobby Dollas (Oct. 9/95-Mar. 30/97)
Most Goals, Season	52	Teemu Selanne (1997-98)
Most Assists, Season	62	Paul Kariya (1998-99)
Most Points, Season	109	Teemu Selanne (1996-97; 51G, 58A)

Most PIM, Season	285	Todd Ewen (1995-96)
Most Points, Defenseman, Season	56	Fredrik Olausson (1998-99; 16G, 40A)
Most Points, Center, Season	67	Steve Rucchin (1996-97; 19G, 48A)
Most Points, Right Wing, Season	109	Teemu Selanne (1996-97; 51G, 58A)
Most Points, Left Wing, Season	108	Paul Kariya (1995-96; 50G, 58A)
Most Points, Rookie, Season	39	Paul Kariya (1994-95; 18G, 21A)
Most Shutouts, Season	6	Guy Hebert (1998-99)
Most Goals, Game	3	Thirteen times
Most Assists, Game	5	Dmitri Mironov (Dec. 12/97)
Most Points, Game	5	Six times

General Managers' History

Jack Ferreira, 1993-94 to 1997-98; Pierre Gauthier, 1998-99 to date.

Coaching History

Ron Wilson, 1993-94 to 1996-97; Pierre Page, 1997-98; Craig Hartsburg, 1998-99 to date.

Captains' History

Troy Loney, 1993-94; Randy Ladouceur, 1994-95, 1995-96; Paul Kariya, 1996-97; Paul Kariya and Teemu Selanne, 1997-98; Paul Kariya, 1998-99 to date.

All-time Record vs. Other Clubs

Regular Season

		At Home						On Road							Total					
	GP	W	L	T	GF	GA	PTS	GP	W	L	T	GF	GA	PTS	GP	W	L	T	GF	GA	PTS
Atlanta	1	1	0	0	4	1	2	0	0	0	0	0	0	0	1	1	0	0	4	1	2
Boston	6	2	3	1	11	15	5	6	3	3	0	18	18	6	12	5	6	1	29	33	11
Buffalo	6	2	4	0	12	18	4	6	2	2	2	16	14	6	12	4	6	2	28	32	10
Calgary	18	8	7	3	55	47	19	17	6	11	0	38	51	12	35	14	18	3	93	98	31
Carolina	5	3	2	0	21	17	6	6	1	4	1	12	18	3	11	4	6	1	33	35	9
Chicago	14	7	6	1	34	32	15	16	6	8	2	36	47	14	30	13	14	3	70	79	29
Colorado	13	4	6	3	32	31	11	13	4	7	2	39	48	10	26	8	13	5	71	79	21
Dallas	17	8	9	0	42	44	16	16	2	13	1	30	66	5	33	10	22	1	72	110	21
Detroit	14	5	7	2	32	44	12	14	1	10	3	36	58	5	28	6	17	5	68	102	17
Edmonton	18	12	5	1	56	47	25	17	8	9	0	37	34	16	35	20	14	1	93	81	41
Florida	6	2	4	0	19	22	4	5	1	2	2	13	13	5	11	3	6	2	32	35	9
Los Angeles	19	9	5	5	61	46	24	20	8	10	2	54	56	18	39	17	15	7	115	102	42
Montreal	5	1	4	0	16	19	2	6	2	3	1	16	19	5	11	3	7	1	32	38	7
Nashville	4	4	0	0	13	4	8	4	2	2	0	11	9	4	8	6	2	0	24	13	12
New Jersey	6	3	3	0	18	14	6	6	1	5	0	10	24	2	12	4	8	0	28	38	8
NY Islanders	6	1	3	2	13	18	4	5	2	2	1	15	12	5	11	3	5	3	28	30	9
NY Rangers	6	5	1	0	24	15	11	5	2	2	1	14	14	5	11	7	3	1	38	29	16
Ottawa	6	3	1	2	16	9	8	6	3	2	1	17	17	7	12	6	3	3	33	26	15
Philadelphia	6	2	2	2	21	20	6	6	1	2	3	12	17	5	12	3	4	5	33	37	11
Phoenix	16	10	5	1	48	42	21	16	7	8	1	48	54	15	32	17	13	2	96	96	36
Pittsburgh	6	3	3	0	20	22	6	6	1	3	2	20	22	4	12	4	6	2	40	44	10
St. Louis	14	4	9	1	35	43	9	14	5	6	3	42	47	13	28	9	15	4	77	90	22
San Jose	20	8	10	2	58	68	18	19	10	7	2	59	54	22	39	18	17	4	117	122	40
Tampa Bay	6	3	2	1	19	16	7	6	4	2	0	19	12	8	12	7	4	1	38	28	15
Toronto	10	4	5	1	29	27	9	12	2	6	4	25	36	8	22	6	11	5	54	63	17
Vancouver	17	4	7	6	44	54	14	18	6	12	0	44	67	12	35	10	19	6	88	121	26
Washington	6	4	1	1	21	17	9	6	3	3	0	15	10	6	12	7	4	1	36	27	15
Totals	**271**	**122**	**114**	**35**	**774**	**752**	**281**	**271**	**93**	**144**	**34**	**696**	**837**	**221**	**542**	**215**	**258**	**69**	**1470**	**1589**	**502**

Playoffs

	Series	W	L	GP	W	L	T	GF	GA
Detroit	2	0	2	8	0	8	0	14	30
Phoenix	1	1	0	7	4	3	0	17	17
Totals	**3**	**1**	**2**	**15**	**4**	**11**	**0**	**31**	**47**

Playoff Results 2000-1996

Year	Round	Opponent	Result	GF	GA	Last Mtg. Round	Result
1999	CQF	Detroit	L 0-4	6	17	1999 CQF	L 0-4
1997	CSF	Detroit	L 0-4	8	13	1997 CQF	W 4-3
	CQF	Phoenix	W 4-3	17	17		

Abbreviations: Round: CSF – conference semi-final; **CQF** – conference quarter-final

Carolina totals include Hartford, 1993-94 to 1996-97.
Colorado totals include Quebec, 1993-94 to 1994-95.
Phoenix totals include Winnipeg, 1993-94 to 1995-96.

1999-2000 Results

Oct.	2	at Dallas	0-2	8	at Detroit	3-5
	5	at Phoenix	0-4	12	Ottawa	0-2
	8	Dallas	3-0	14	St. Louis	3-1
	11	San Jose	5-3	15	at Phoenix	2-4
	13	at New Jersey	2-3	17	Buffalo	0-5
	15	at Tampa Bay	3-2	19	Dallas	3-1
	16	at Florida	2-3 *	21	Colorado	3-3
	19	at Washington	7-1	22	at San Jose	3-4
	21	at Chicago	5-5	26	NY Islanders	2-4
	24	Boston	2-3	29	at Pittsburgh	7-1
	27	Pittsburgh	2-1 *	31	at Boston	4-2
	29	Washington	5-2	Feb. 1	at Buffalo	2-2
	31	Phoenix	0-3	3	at Philadelphia	3-3
Nov.	3	Philadelphia	3-3	8	at Los Angeles	5-3
	7	Edmonton	3-1	9	Dallas	3-5
	9	at Toronto	2-0	12	at St. Louis	3-6
	11	at Montreal	1-2	14	at Chicago	4-3
	13	at Ottawa	2-4	16	Calgary	6-5 *
	15	at Detroit	3-6	18	San Jose	4-4
	17	Calgary	2-1	21	St. Louis	2-4
	19	Chicago	4-2	23	Vancouver	4-4
	22	Montreal	1-2	27	Edmonton	3-2
	24	New Jersey	1-2	29	at San Jose	4-2
	26	at Dallas	4-2	Mar. 2	at Vancouver	1-3
Dec.	1	Tampa Bay	2-4	3	at Calgary	1-4
	3	Los Angeles	1-1	5	Nashville	1-0
	4	at Phoenix	2-1	8	NY Rangers	3-4 *
	8	Vancouver	2-2	11	at St. Louis	1-1
	10	Colorado	1-2	14	at Colorado	2-2
	12	Atlanta	4-1	15	Los Angeles	2-2
	15	at Colorado	4-2	19	Detroit	3-1
	17	Chicago	2-0	21	at Los Angeles	5-2
	19	Detroit	3-1	22	at Edmonton	1-2
	22	Phoenix	2-8	24	at Vancouver	1-8
	26	at San Jose	1-0	26	Phoenix	4-3 *
	27	at Edmonton	1-4	Apr. 1	at Los Angeles	1-2
	29	at Calgary	1-3	3	Nashville	3-1
	31	at Dallas	4-5	5	at Chicago	2-5
Jan.	5	Florida	1-5	7	at Nashville	5-1
	7	at Carolina	4-4	9	Los Angeles	3-4 *

* – Overtime

Entry Draft
Selections 2000-1993

2000
Pick
12	Alexei Smirnov
44	Ilja Bryzgalov
98	Jonas Ronnqvist
134	Peter Podhradsky
153	Bill Cass

1999
Pick
44	Jordan Leopold
83	Niclas Havelid
105	Alexander Chagodayev
141	Maxim Rybin
173	Jan Sandstrom
230	Petr Tenkrat
258	Brian Gornick

1998
Pick
5	Vitaly Vishnevski
32	Stephen Peat
112	Viktor Wallin
150	Trent Hunter
178	Jesse Fibiger
205	David Bernier
233	Pelle Prestberg
245	Andreas Andersson

1997
Pick
18	Mikael Holmqvist
45	Maxim Balmochnykh
72	Jay Legault
125	Luc Vaillancourt
178	Tony Mohagen
181	Mat Snesrud
209	Rene Stussi
235	Tommi Degerman

1996
Pick
9	Ruslan Salei
35	Matt Cullen
117	Brendan Buckley
149	Blaine Russell
172	Timo Ahmaoja
198	Kevin Kellett
224	Tobias Johansson

1995
Pick
4	Chad Kilger
29	Brian Wesenberg
55	Mike Leclerc
107	Igor Nikulin
133	Peter LeBoutillier
159	Mike LaPlante
185	Igor Karpenko

1994
Pick
2	Oleg Tverdovsky
28	Johan Davidsson
67	Craig Reichert
80	Byron Briske
106	Pavel Trnka
132	Bates Battaglia
158	Rocky Welsing
184	Brad Englehart
236	Tommi Miettinen
262	Jeremy Stevenson

1993
Pick
4	Paul Kariya
30	Nikolai Tsulygin
56	Valeri Karpov
82	Joel Gagnon
108	Mikhail Shtalenkov
134	Antti Aalto
160	Matt Peterson
186	Tom Askey
212	Vitali Kozel
238	Anatoli Fedotov
264	David Penney

Coach

HARTSBURG, CRAIG
Coach, Mighty Ducks of Anaheim. Born in Stratford, Ont., June 29, 1959.

Craig Hartsburg became the third head coach in the history of the Mighty Ducks of Anaheim on July 21, 1998. He guided the Ducks to their second appearance in the postseason in 1999 and just missed a playoff spot in 2000. Hartsburg came to the Mighty Ducks after serving three seasons as head coach of the Chicago Blackhawks. During his tenure with Chicago, Hartsburg compiled a 104-102-40 record. He was the 30th head coach in Chicago Blackhawks history.

The Blackhawks posted a 40-28-14 record in Hartsburg's first season behind the bench in Chicago (1995-96), finishing second in the Central Division and third overall in the Western Conference. After a sweep of the Calgary Flames in the opening round of the playoffs, the Blackhawks fell to the eventual Stanley Cup champion Colorado Avalanche. Hartsburg led Chicago back to the Stanley Cup Playoffs in 1997, pushing the top-seeded Avalanche to six games in the first round before falling, four games to two. In 1997-98, Chicago stayed in contention for postseason play until the last week of the season, finishing just five points out of a playoff spot. Hartsburg's Blackhawks had the seventh-most rookie man-games played in the league (230) that year.

Before joining the Blackhawks, Hartsburg received his first head coaching job in 1994 with the Guelph Storm of the Ontario Hockey League. He was named OHL coach of the year after leading the Storm to a 47-14-5 record for a .750 winning percentage in 1994-95. Hartsburg also spent four years as an assistant coach with the Philadelphia Flyers from 1990 to 1994 and one season as an assistant coach with the Minnesota North Stars in 1989-90.

Hartsburg played his entire 10-year NHL career with Minnesota from 1979 to 1989. Known as an offensive defenseman, he was the North Stars' captain for six seasons until injuries forced him to retire from active play on January 13, 1989. Hartsburg was Minnesota's first round selection (sixth overall) in the 1979 NHL Entry Draft and immediately made an impact on the North Stars' blueline, scoring 44 points in 79 games during his rookie season. Hartsburg led all Minnesota defensemen in scoring each of his first four seasons. During the 1981 playoffs, he was a key player for the North Stars, scoring three goals and 12 assists to help lead the club to its first appearance in the Stanley Cup finals. Hartsburg also became the first North Stars defenseman to record a hat trick, netting three goals on November 1, 1986 vs. Chicago.

Hartsburg played in 570 games during his NHL career, scoring 98 goals and 315 assists for 413 points with 818 penalty minutes. He also appeared in 61 playoff games during his career, posting 15 goals and 27 assists for 42 points. Hartsburg holds or shares seven Stars' team records, including most assists (60) and most points (77) by a defenseman in one season. In February of 1992, he was voted to the North Stars' 25th Anniversary Dream Team by Minnesota fans.

A participant in three NHL All-Star Games (1980, 1982 and 1983), Hartsburg also competed in three World championship tournaments for Team Canada, including being chosen as best defenseman of the 1987 World Championships. He lists winning the Canada Cup championship in 1987 as his most memorable moment in hockey.

Hartsburg and his wife Peggy have two children, Christopher and Katie.

Coaching Record

Season	Team	Regular Season					Playoffs			
		Games	W	L	T	%	Games	W	L	%
1994-95	Guelph (OHL)	66	47	14	5	.750	14	10	4	.714
1995-96	Chicago (NHL)	82	40	28	14	.573	10	6	4	.600
1996-97	Chicago (NHL)	82	34	35	13	.494	6	2	4	.333
1997-98	Chicago (NHL)	82	30	39	13	.455	....	....	....	....
1998-99	Anaheim (NHL)	82	35	34	13	.506	4	0	4	.000
1999-2000	Anaheim (NHL)	82	34	36	12	.506•	....	....	....	....
	NHL Totals	410	173	172	65	.505•	20	8	12	.400

• Includes points from regulation ties

Club Directory

Arrowhead Pond of Anaheim

Mighty Ducks of Anaheim
Arrowhead Pond of Anaheim
2695 Katella Ave.
Anaheim, CA 92806
Phone **714/940-2900**
FAX 714/940-2953
Ticket Information 714/704-2701
Website: www.mightyducks.com
Capacity: 17,174

Executive Management
Chairman and Governor	Tony Tavares
President and General Manager	Pierre Gauthier
Assistant General Manager	David McNab
Vice President, Finance and Administration	Andy Roundtree
Vice President, Advertising Sales and Broadcasting	John Covarrubias
Vice President, Communications	Tim Mead
Vice President, Business and Legal Affairs	Rick Schlesinger
Vice President, Sales and Marketing	Kevin Uhlich
Admin. Assistant, Chairman	Meta Maynard
Admin. Assistant, President and General Manager	Maureen Nyeholt
Admin. Assistant, Finance/Administration	Monica Campanis
Admin. Assistant, Advertising Sales and Broadcasting	Sonia Salem
Sr. Paralegal	Tia Wood
Admin. Assistant, Communications	Lisa Parris
Admin. Assistant. Sales and Marketing	Leslie Flammini

Coaching Staff
Head Coach	Craig Hartsburg
Assistant Coaches	Guy Charron, Terry Simpson
Goaltending Consultant	Francois Allaire

Hockey Club Operations
Chief Amateur Scout	Alain Chainey
Pro Scout	Lucien DeBlois
Scouts	Jan-Åke Danielson, Richard Green, Mark Odnokon
Scouting Staff	Ross Ainsworth, Donald Marier, Konstantin Krylov, Al MacPherson, Mike McGraw
Scouting Coordinator	Greg Carvel
Head Athletic Trainer	Chris Phillips
Assistant Athletic Trainer	Greg Thayer
Equipment Manager	Mark O'Neill
Assistant Equipment Manager	John Allaway
Cincinnati Mighty Ducks (AHL) Head Coach	Mike Babcock
Team Physicians	Dr. Ronald Glousman, Dr. Craig Milhouse
Oral Surgeon	Dr. Jeff Pulver
Visiting Team Equipment Attendant	Chris Kincaid

Communications Department
Manager, Communications and Team Services	Alex Gilchrist
Manager, Publications	Doug Ward
Media Relations Representative	Merit Tully
Community Development Representative	Renee Zidan
Team Photographer	V.J. Lovero (Lovero Group)

Finance and Administration Department
Director, Finance	TBA
Sr. Financial Analyst	Amy Langdale
Manager, Business Development	Marc Kolin
Manager, Human Resources	Jenny Price
Manager, Information Services	Al Castro
Sr. Network Engineer	Neil Fariss
Sr. End User Analyst	Phil Alger
Assistant Controller	Melody Martin
Accountants	Jean Ouyang, Rosanna Sitzman
Accounting Assistants	Rob Dumlao, Trang Nguyen
Administrative Assistant, Human Resources	Cindy Williams
Human Resources Assistant	Alex Oftelie
Manager, Ballpark Operations	John Drum
Assistant Operations Manager	Sam Maida
Administrative Assistant, Operations	Debbie Tierney
Sr. Travel Consultant	Chantelle Ball
General Manager, Disney ICE	Art Trottier

Sales and Marketing Department
Director, Ticket Sales and Customer Service	Bill Chapin
Manager, Premium Ticket Services	Anne McNiff-Gaeta
Manager, Marketing and Promotions	Robert Alvarado
Promotions Representatives	Joel Hobson, Jared Rice, Cindy Ryan, Colby Sato
Ticketing Operations Manager	Christa Richards
Telemarketing Supervisor	Ari Rubinstein
Group Sales Manager	Brian Clark
Account Executives	Ron Campbell, Bob Ruiz
Group Ticket Sales Executives	Kristen Atkinson, Ken Bamberg, Joe Furmanski, Angel Rodriguez
Outside Sales Account Executives	John Slebel, Brian Stracke
Ticketing Supervisor	Jonas Calicdan
Ticketing Representative	Lisa Yamamoto
Director, Entertainment	Rod Murray
Manager, Entertainment	Tim Beach
Producer, Video & Scoreboard Operations	Robert Castillo
Assistant Producer, Video & Scoreboard Operations	David Tsuruda
Marketing/Database Coordinator	Angela Carbaugh
Administrative Assistant, Sales	Pat Navarro
Administrative Assistant, Group Sales	Alison Honeyman

Advertising Sales and Broadcasting Department
Director, Advertising Sales & Broadcasting	Richard McClemmy
Director, Broadcasting	Mark Vittorio
Television, KCAL (Ch. 9) & Fox Sports West 2 (Cable)	Chris Madsen, Brian Hayward
Radio, XTRA Sports (690 AM) & Mighty Ducks Radio Network	Steve Carroll, Mike Greenlay
Practice Facilities	Disney ICE (300 W. Lincoln Ave.) and the Arrowhead Pond (2695 Katella Ave.)

Atlanta Thrashers

1999-2000 Results: 14w-61L-7t 39pts. Fifth, Southeast Division

Year-by-Year Record

Season	GP	Home W	L	T	Road W	L	T	Overall W	L	T	GF	GA	Pts.	Finished		Playoff Result
1999-2000	82	9	29	3	5	32	4	14	61	7	170	313	39	5th,	Southeast Div.	Out of Playoffs

2000-01 Schedule

Oct.	Sat.	7	NY Rangers		Wed.	10	Dallas
	Wed.	11	Washington		Fri.	12	Montreal
	Sun.	15	at Tampa Bay		Sat.	13	at Washington
	Tue.	17	New Jersey		Wed.	17	Anaheim
	Fri.	20	NY Islanders		Sat.	20	at New Jersey*
	Sat.	21	at Ottawa		Sun.	21	NY Islanders*
	Wed.	25	at Edmonton		Tue.	23	at Nashville
	Fri.	27	at Vancouver		Thu.	25	Toronto
	Sat.	28	at San Jose		Sat.	27	at Pittsburgh
Nov.	Thu.	2	Los Angeles		Mon.	29	at NY Rangers
	Sat.	4	at Boston		Tue.	30	Pittsburgh
	Mon.	6	Ottawa	Feb.	Thu.	1	Carolina
	Sun.	12	at Washington*		Wed.	7	at Toronto
	Mon.	13	at Florida		Fri.	9	Boston
	Wed.	15	Nashville		Sat.	10	Florida
	Fri.	17	Philadelphia		Tue.	13	Buffalo
	Sat.	18	at Pittsburgh		Thu.	15	at Buffalo
	Wed.	22	at Tampa Bay		Sat.	17	at Philadelphia
	Thu.	23	Montreal		Wed.	21	at Carolina
	Sat.	25	Washington		Fri.	23	at Chicago
	Mon.	27	at Montreal		Sun.	25	at Colorado*
	Wed.	29	Detroit		Tue.	27	Carolina
Dec.	Fri.	1	Tampa Bay	Mar.	Fri.	2	at Florida
	Sat.	2	at Columbus		Sat.	3	Florida
	Mon.	4	Boston		Tue.	6	Colorado
	Wed.	6	Carolina		Thu.	8	Pittsburgh
	Fri.	8	Florida		Sat.	10	at Boston*
	Sat.	9	at NY Islanders		Sun.	11	Calgary
	Mon.	11	at New Jersey		Wed.	14	at Ottawa
	Wed.	13	Chicago		Fri.	16	Columbus
	Fri.	15	St. Louis		Sun.	18	Vancouver*
	Tue.	19	at Los Angeles		Wed.	21	Tampa Bay
	Wed.	20	at Anaheim		Thu.	22	at Tampa Bay
	Fri.	22	at Phoenix		Sat.	24	at Montreal
	Tue.	26	Toronto		Mon.	26	Buffalo
	Thu.	28	at NY Rangers		Wed.	28	New Jersey
	Fri.	29	at NY Islanders		Fri.	30	at Buffalo
Jan.	Mon.	1	at Washington*	Apr.	Sun.	1	NY Rangers*
	Wed.	3	at Minnesota		Tue.	3	Ottawa
	Fri.	5	Philadelphia		Thu.	5	at Detroit
	Sat.	6	at Philadelphia		Fri.	6	at Carolina

* Denotes afternoon game.

Ray Ferraro provided a veteran presence in Atlanta in 1999-2000. Both he and Andrew Brunette took part in 81 of 82 games last season and proved to be the team's offensive leaders.

Franchise date: June 25, 1997

SOUTHEAST DIVISION

2nd NHL Season

2000-01 Player Personnel

FORWARDS	HT	WT	S	Place of Birth	Date	1999-00 Club
ADAMS, Bryan	6-0	185	L	Fort St. James, B.C.	3/20/77	Atlanta-Orlando
AUDETTE, Donald	5-8	190	R	Laval, Que.	9/23/69	Los Angeles-Atlanta
BOISVERT, Hugo	6-0	200	L	St-Eustache, Que.	2/11/76	Canada
BRUNETTE, Andrew	6-1	210	L	Sudbury, Ont.	8/24/73	Atlanta
DOMENICHELLI, Hnat	6-0	194	L	Edmonton, Alta.	2/17/76	Calgary-Saint John-Atlanta
DONOVAN, Shean	6-3	210	R	Timmins, Ont.	1/22/75	Colorado-Atlanta
FERRARO, Ray	5-9	200	L	Trail, B.C.	8/23/64	Atlanta
GUOLLA, Stephen	6-0	190	L	Scarborough, Ont.	3/15/73	Tampa Bay-Atlanta
JOHNSON, Matt	6-5	232	L	Welland, Ont.	11/23/75	Atlanta
KALLIO, Tomi	6-1	180	L	Turku, Finland	1/27/77	TPS Turku
KARLSSON, Andreas	6-3	195	L	Luvicka, Sweden	8/19/75	Atlanta-Orlando
LAMBERT, Denny	5-10	215	L	Wawa, Ont.	1/7/70	Atlanta
SARAULT, Yves	6-0	200	L	Valleyfield, Que.	12/23/72	Ottawa-Grand Rapids
SKALDE, Jarrod	6-0	185	L	Niagara Falls, Ont.	2/26/71	Utah Grizzlies
STEFAN, Patrik	6-3	205	L	Pribram, Czech.	9/16/80	Atlanta
SVARTVADET, Per	6-1	190	L	Solleftea, Sweden	5/17/75	Atlanta-Orlando
SYLVESTER, Dean	6-2	210	R	Hanson, MA	12/30/72	Atlanta-Orlando
VASILJEVS, Herbert	5-11	180	R	Riga, Latvia	5/27/76	Atlanta-Orlando
VLASENKOV, Dmitri	5-11	183	L	Safonovo, USSR	1/1/78	Torpedo Yaroslavl
WESENBERG, Brian	6-3	187	R	Peterborough, Ont.	5/9/77	Philadelphia (AHL)-Orlando

DEFENSEMEN						
BURT, Adam	6-2	205	L	Detroit, MI	1/15/69	Philadelphia
BUZEK, Petr	6-0	205	L	Jihlava, Czech.	4/26/77	Atlanta
CLARK, Brett	6-1	185	L	Wapella, Sask.	12/23/76	Atlanta-Orlando
HARLOCK, David	6-2	220	L	Toronto, Ont.	3/16/71	Atlanta
KABERLE, Frantisek	6-0	185	L	Kladno, Czech.	11/8/73	L.A.-Long Beach-Atl.-Lowell (AHL)
KINNEAR, Geordie	6-1	195	L	Simcoe, Ont.	7/9/73	Atlanta-Orlando
MURPHY, Gord	6-2	195	R	Willowdale, Ont.	3/23/67	Atlanta
NDUR, Rumun	6-2	222	L	Zaria, Nigeria	7/7/75	Hartford-Atlanta
STAIOS, Steve	6-1	200	R	Hamilton, Ont.	7/28/73	Atlanta
TAMER, Chris	6-2	215	L	Dearborn, MI	11/17/70	Atlanta
TREMBLAY, Yannick	6-2	185	R	Pointe-aux-Trembles, Que.	11/15/75	Atlanta
VYSHEDKEVICH, Sergei	6-0	195	L	Dedovsk, USSR	1/3/75	Atlanta-Orlando

GOALTENDERS	HT	WT	C	Place of Birth	Date	1999-00 Club
FANKHOUSER, Scott	6-2	195	L	Bismark, ND	7/1/75	Atlanta-Greenville-Orlando-Louisville
HNILICKA, Milan	6-0	180	L	Litomerice, Czech.	6/25/73	NY Rangers-Hartford
LANGKOW, Scott	5-11	190	L	Sherwood Park, Alta.	4/21/75	Atlanta-Orlando
MARACLE, Norm	5-8	195	L	Belleville, Ont.	10/2/74	Atlanta
RHODES, Damian	6-0	190	L	St. Paul, MN	5/28/69	Atlanta

General Managers' History

Don Waddell, 1999-2000 to date.

General Manager

WADDELL, DON
General Manager, Atlanta Thrashers. Born in Detroit, MI, August 19, 1958.

Don Waddell serves as vice president and general manager of the Atlanta Thrashers. He came to the Thrashers on June 23, 1998, - almost a year to the day after the NHL granted Atlanta a franchise - bringing with him more than 20 years in professional hockey as a player, coach and general manager. He brings extensive organizational experience to the Thrashers having previously built two professional hockey franchises, the San Diego Gulls and the Orlando Solar Bears of the International Hockey League. He's also no stranger to winning through his role as assistant general manager for the NHL's two-time Stanley Cup champion Detroit Red Wings during the 1997-98 season.

Prior to Detroit, he was vice president of RDV Sports, where he served on the Executive Committee which oversaw operations of the National Basketball Association's Orlando Magic, the International Hockey League's Orlando Solar Bears, Magic Fanattics (retail) and Magic Carpet Aviation. While at RDV Sports, Waddell was vice president and general manager of the IHL's Orlando Solar Bears from 1995 to 1997. Prior to the Solar Bears, he held the same role with the IHL's San Diego Gulls from 1990 to 1995. He also served as the club's head coach for the 1991-92 season, guiding the team to the franchise's first playoff berth. He spent two seasons with the IHL's Flint Spirits where he served as head coach and general manager in 1988-89, and general manager in 1989-90.

Waddell's playing experience includes being player/coach for the Flint Spirits from 1986 to 1988, and the Goaldiggers Hockey Club in Toledo, Ohio for the 1985-86 season. He was drafted by the NHL's Los Angeles Kings back in 1978, and spent three years with the organization from 1980 to 1983. He was a member of the 1983 U.S. National Team and had been a member of the 1980 gold medal Olympic hockey team, but was injured prior to play.

Waddell played Division I hockey at Northern Michigan University from 1976 to 1980, where he majored in business management. He was inducted into the Northern Michigan University Sports Hall of Fame in 1992.

He and his wife, Cheryl, have a daughter named Chelsea.

1999-2000 Scoring

* – rookie

Regular Season

Pos	#	Player	Team	GP	G	A	Pts	+/–	PIM	PP	SH	GW	GT	S	%
L	15	Andrew Brunette	ATL	81	23	27	50	-32	30	9	0	2	1	107	21.5
C	21	Ray Ferraro	ATL	81	19	25	44	-33	88	10	0	3	0	170	11.2
R	28	Donald Audette	L.A.	49	12	20	32	6	45	1	0	3	0	112	10.7
			ATL	14	7	4	11	-4	12	0	1	1	0	50	14.0
			TOTAL	63	19	24	43	2	57	1	1	4	0	162	11.7
D	38	Yannick Tremblay	ATL	75	10	21	31	-42	22	4	1	2	1	139	7.2
C	9	Hnat Domenichelli	CGY	32	5	9	14	0	12	1	0	1	0	57	8.8
			ATL	27	6	9	15	-21	4	0	0	0	0	68	8.8
			TOTAL	59	11	18	29	-21	16	1	0	1	0	125	8.8
L	12	Stephen Guolla	T.B	46	6	10	16	2	11	2	0	1	0	52	11.5
			ATL	20	4	9	13	-13	4	2	0	0	0	34	11.8
			TOTAL	66	10	19	29	-11	15	4	0	1	0	86	11.6
R	11	Dean Sylvester	ATL	52	16	10	26	-14	24	1	0	2	0	98	16.3
C	13 *	Patrik Stefan	ATL	72	5	20	25	-20	30	1	0	0	0	117	4.3
C	14	Mike Stapleton	ATL	62	10	12	22	-29	30	4	0	1	0	146	6.8
D	2 *	Petr Buzek	ATL	63	5	14	19	-22	41	3	0	0	0	90	5.6
L	29	Johan Garpenlov	ATL	73	2	14	16	-30	31	0	0	0	0	79	2.5
D	8 *	Frantisek Kaberle	L.A	37	0	9	9	3	4	0	0	0	0	41	0.0
			ATL	14	1	6	7	-13	6	0	1	0	0	35	2.9
			TOTAL	51	1	15	16	-10	10	0	1	0	0	76	1.3
C	24 *	Andreas Karlsson	ATL	51	5	9	14	-17	14	1	0	0	0	74	6.8
R	22	Shean Donovan	COL	18	1	0	1	-4	8	0	0	0	0	13	7.7
			ATL	33	4	7	11	-13	18	1	0	1	0	53	7.5
			TOTAL	51	5	7	12	-17	26	1	0	1	0	66	7.6
L	27	Denny Lambert	ATL	73	5	6	11	-17	219	2	0	0	0	83	6.0
D	5	Gord Murphy	ATL	58	1	10	11	-26	38	0	0	0	0	74	1.4
D	4	Chris Tamer	ATL	69	2	8	10	-32	91	0	0	0	0	61	3.3
D	33	Maxim Galanov	ATL	40	4	3	7	-12	20	0	0	0	0	47	8.5
L	39 *	Per Svartvadet	ATL	38	3	4	7	-8	6	0	0	0	0	36	8.3
L	17	Matt Johnson	ATL	64	2	5	7	-11	144	0	0	0	0	54	3.7
D	6	David Harlock	ATL	44	0	6	6	-8	36	0	0	0	0	29	0.0
R	25	Steve Staios	ATL	27	2	3	5	-5	66	0	0	0	0	38	5.3
D	7	Chris McAlpine	STL	21	1	1	2	1	14	0	0	0	1	25	4.0
			T.B	10	1	1	2	-5	10	0	0	0	0	5	20.0
			ATL	3	0	0	0	-4	2	0	0	0	0	4	0.0
			TOTAL	34	2	2	4	-8	26	0	0	0	1	34	5.9
D	3 *	Sergei Vyshedkevich	ATL	7	1	3	4	-3	2	1	0	0	0	5	20.0
R	37 *	Herbert Vasiljevs	ATL	7	1	0	1	-3	4	0	0	0	0	2	50.0
D	36	Rumun Ndur	ATL	27	1	0	1	-17	71	0	0	0	0	6	16.7
L	23	Martin Prochazka	ATL	3	0	1	1	-1	0	0	0	0	0	5	0.0
D	23	Brett Clark	ATL	14	0	1	1	-12	4	0	0	0	0	13	0.0
L	26 *	Bryan Adams	ATL	2	0	0	0	-1	0	0	0	0	0	1	0.0
C	9	Vladimir Vujtek	ATL	3	0	0	0	0	0	0	0	0	0	0	0.0
D	28 *	Geordie Kinnear	ATL	4	0	0	0	-1	13	0	0	0	0	2	0.0
L	22 *	Eric Bertrand	N.J	4	0	0	0	-1	0	0	0	0	0	1	0.0
			ATL	8	0	0	0	-5	4	0	0	0	0	11	0.0
			TOTAL	12	0	0	0	-6	4	0	0	0	0	12	0.0
G	35 *	Scott Langkow	ATL	15	0	0	0	0	0	0	0	0	0	0	0.0
G	30 *	Scott Fankhouser	ATL	16	0	0	0	0	4	0	0	0	0	0	0.0
G	1	Damian Rhodes	ATL	28	0	0	0	0	0	0	0	0	0	0	0.0
G	34 *	Norm Maracle	ATL	32	0	0	0	0	0	0	0	0	0	0	0.0

Goaltending

No.	Goaltender	GPI	Mins	Avg	W	L	T	EN	SO	GA	SA	S%
30	* Scott Fankhouser	16	920	3.20	2	11	2	1	0	49	451	.891
34	* Norm Maracle	32	1618	3.49	4	19	2	5	1	94	852	.890
1	Damian Rhodes	28	1561	3.88	5	19	3	3	1	101	803	.874
35	Rick Tabaracci	1	59	4.07	0	1	0	0	0	4	32	.875
35	* Scott Langkow	15	765	4.31	3	11	0	1	0	55	395	.861
	Totals	**82**	**4966**	**3.78**	**14**	**61**	**7**	**10**	**2**	**313**	**2543**	**.877**

Captains' History

Kelly Buchberger, 1999-2000.

Coaching History

Curt Fraser, 1999-2000 to date.

Club Records

Team

(Figures in brackets for season records are games played.)

Most Points	39	1999-2000 (82)
Most Wins	14	1999-2000 (82)
Most Ties	7	1999-2000 (82)
Most Losses	61	1999-2000 (82)
Most Goals	170	1999-2000 (82)
Most Goals Against	313	1999-2000 (82)
Fewest Points	39	1999-2000 (82)
Fewest Wins	14	1999-2000 (82)
Fewest Ties	7	1999-2000 (82)
Fewest Losses	61	1999-2000 (82)
Fewest Goals	170	1999-2000 (82)
Fewest Goals Against	313	1999-2000 (82)

Longest Winning Streak
Overall .... 2 Dec. 3-4/99, Jan. 4-6/00
Home .... 2 Nov. 3-17/99
Away .... 1 Five times

Longest Undefeated Streak
Overall .... 3 Oct. 9-16/99 (1 win, 2 ties), Dec. 22-26/99 (1 win, 2 ties)
Home .... 2 Nov. 3-17/99 (2 wins)
Away .... 2 Dec. 22-23/99 (2 ties)

Longest Losing Streak
Overall .... 12 Jan. 24-Feb. 20/00
Home .... 11 Jan. 24-Mar. 16/00
Away .... 8 Oct. 17-Nov. 27/99

Longest Winless Streak
Overall .... 16 Jan. 16-Feb. 20/00 (2 ties, 14 losses)
Home .... 17 Jan. 19-Mar. 29/00 (2 ties, 15 losses)
Away .... 9 Oct. 16-Nov. 27/99 (1 tie, 8 losses), Jan. 8-Feb. 20/00 (1 tie, 8 losses)

Most Shutouts, Season 2 1999-2000 (82)
Most PIM, Season 1,422 1999-2000 (82)
Most Goals, Game .... 6 Nov. 22/99 (Van. 3 at Atl. 6), Dec. 26/99 (T.B. 3 at Atl. 6)

Individual

Most Seasons .... 1 Many players
Most Games .... 81 Andrew Brunette, Ray Ferrarro
Most Goals, Career .... 23 Andrew Brunette
Most Assists, Career .... 27 Andrew Brunette
Most Points, Career .... 50 Andrew Brunette (23G, 27A)
Most PIM, Career .... 219 Denny Lambert
Most Shutouts, Career .... 1 Norm Maracle, Damian Rhodes
Most Goals, Season .... 23 Andrew Brunette (1999-2000)
Most Assists, Season .... 27 Andrew Brunette (1999-2000)

Most Points, Season .... 50 Andrew Brunette (1999-2000; 23G, 27A)
Most PIM, Season .... 219 Denny Lambert (1999-2000)
Most Points, Defenseman, Season .... 31 Yannick Tremblay (1999-2000; 10G, 21A)
Most Points, Center, Season .... 44 Ray Ferraro (1999-2000; 19G, 25A)
Most Points, Right Wing, Season .... 33 Nelson Emmerson (1999-2000; 14G, 19A)
Most Points, Left Wing, Season .... 50 Andrew Brunette (1999-2000; 23G, 27A)
Most Points, Rookie, Season .... 25 Patrick Stefan (1999-2000; 5G, 20A)
Most Shutouts, Season .... 1 Norm Maracle (1999-2000), Damian Rhodes (1999-2000)
Most Goals, Game .... 3 Dean Sylvester (Nov. 22/99)
Most Assists, Game .... 3 Andrew Brunette (Nov. 22/99)
Most Points, Game .... 4 Dean Sylvester (Nov. 22/99; 3G, 1A)

All-time Record vs. Other Clubs

Regular Season

		At Home						On Road							Total					
	GP	W	L	T	GF	GA	PTS	GP	W	L	T	GF	GA	PTS	GP	W	L	T	GF	GA	PTS
Anaheim	0	0	0	0	0	0	0	1	0	1	0	1	4	0	1	0	1	0	1	4	0
Boston	2	0	2	0	4	7	0	1	0	1	0	5	7	1	3	0	3	1	9	14	1
Buffalo	2	0	1	1	5	9	1	2	1	1	0	8	8	2	4	1	2	1	13	17	3
Calgary	1	1	0	0	2	1	2	1	0	1	0	2	5	0	2	1	1	0	4	6	2
Carolina	2	0	2	0	5	8	0	3	0	3	0	4	11	0	5	0	5	0	9	19	0
Chicago	1	0	1	0	3	4	0	0	0	0	0	0	0	0	1	0	1	0	3	4	0
Colorado	1	0	1	0	2	3	1	1	0	1	0	4	3	2	2	1	0	6	6	3
Dallas	1	0	1	0	2	4	0	1	0	1	0	2	2	0	2	0	2	0	3	6	0
Detroit	1	0	1	0	1	7	0	1	0	1	0	2	3	1	2	0	2	0	3	10	1
Edmonton	1	0	1	0	0	3	0	1	0	1	0	4	5	0	2	0	2	0	4	8	0
Florida	2	1	0	1	5	4	3	3	0	2	1	4	10	1	5	1	2	2	9	14	4
Los Angeles	1	0	1	0	1	4	0	1	0	1	0	4	4	0	2	0	2	0	1	8	0
Montreal	2	0	1	1	2	6	1	2	0	2	0	4	7	0	4	0	3	1	6	13	1
Nashville	1	0	0	1	3	4	1	1	0	1	0	0	6	0	2	0	1	1	3	10	1
New Jersey	2	0	2	0	1	13	0	2	0	2	0	1	11	0	4	0	4	0	2	24	0
NY Islanders	2	1	1	0	7	8	2	2	2	0	0	6	3	4	4	3	1	0	13	11	6
NY Rangers	2	0	2	0	6	12	0	2	0	2	0	4	10	0	4	0	4	0	10	22	0
Ottawa	2	0	2	0	7	12	0	2	0	2	0	3	10	0	4	0	4	0	10	22	0
Philadelphia	2	1	1	0	4	5	2	2	1	1	0	5	7	1	4	2	1	1	9	12	3
Phoenix	1	0	1	0	2	3	0	1	0	1	0	2	4	0	2	0	2	0	4	7	0
Pittsburgh	2	0	2	0	4	7	1	2	0	2	0	3	9	0	4	0	4	0	7	16	1
St. Louis	1	0	1	0	2	5	0	1	0	1	0	1	4	0	2	0	3	0	3	9	0
San Jose	1	0	1	0	3	0	1	0	1	0	1	4	0	2	0	2	0	1	8	0
Tampa Bay	3	3	0	0	15	8	6	2	0	1	1	5	6	1	5	3	1	1	20	14	7
Toronto	1	0	1	0	0	4	0	2	0	2	0	4	5	3	1	0	2	0	4	9	2
Vancouver	1	1	0	0	6	3	2	0	0	0	0	0	0	1	1	1	0	0	6	3	2
Washington	3	1	2	0	5	10	2	4	0	4	0	8	5	1	4	0	7	0	18	2
Totals	**41**	**9**	**29**	**3**	**94**	**157**	**24**	**41**	**5**	**32**	**4**	**76**	**156**	**15**	**82**	**14**	**61**	**7**	**170**	**313**	**39**

1999-2000 Results

Oct.	2	New Jersey	1-4		14	Philadelphia	1-0
	7	Detroit	1-7		16	at NY Rangers	3-6
	9	Buffalo	5-5		17	at Boston	3-3
	14	at NY Islanders	2-0		19	Boston	3-4
	16	at Tampa Bay	4-4		21	Florida	3-3
	17	at NY Rangers	1-4		24	NY Rangers	3-6
	23	Colorado	2-3*		27	at Pittsburgh	1-4
	26	Calgary	2-1		29	at Tampa Bay	1-2
	27	at Toronto	0-4		31	Pittsburgh	1-2*
	31	Ottawa	4-6	Feb.	2	at Dallas	1-2
Nov.	3	Tampa Bay	4-1		3	NY Rangers	3-6
	6	at Boston	2-4		9	at Pittsburgh	2-5
	10	at Florida	1-4		11	San Jose	0-3
	12	at New Jersey	1-5		12	Chicago	3-4
	13	at Montreal	2-4		15	at St. Louis	1-4
	17	Tampa Bay	5-4		16	Montreal	1-5
	19	Buffalo	0-4		20	at Phoenix	2-4
	20	at Buffalo	3-4		22	at Colorado	4-3
	22	Vancouver	6-3		25	at Edmonton	4-5
	25	Ottawa	3-6		26	at Calgary	2-5
	27	at Florida	0-3		29	Toronto	0-4
	28	Dallas	2-4	Mar.	2	St. Louis	2-5
Dec.	3	Florida	2-1		4	at Ottawa	2-3
	4	at NY Islanders	4-3		6	at Montreal	2-3
	6	Nashville	3-4*		10	New Jersey	0-9
	8	at Los Angeles	0-4		12	at Carolina	1-5
	10	at San Jose	1-4		13	Edmonton	0-3
	12	at Anaheim	1-4		16	NY Islanders	2-4
	15	Washington	0-4		18	at Toronto	4-1
	17	Boston	1-3		21	at Ottawa	1-7
	18	at Carolina	2-4		22	Montreal	1-1
	22	at Florida	3-3		24	Pittsburgh	3-5
	23	at Philadelphia	4-4		26	Los Angeles	1-4
	26	Tampa Bay	6-3		28	at Washington	2-5
	27	at Detroit	2-3*		29	Phoenix	2-3
	30	at Nashville	0-6		31	at New Jersey	0-6
Jan.	1	Carolina	2-4	Apr.	2	NY Islanders	5-4
	4	at Buffalo	5-4		4	Philadelphia	2-5
	6	Washington	3-1		6	at Philadelphia	1-3
	8	at Washington	0-3		8	Carolina	3-4
	12	Washington	2-5		9	at Carolina	1-2

* – Overtime

Entry Draft
Selections 2000-1999

2000 Pick		1999 Pick	
2	Dany Heatley	1	Patrik Stefan
31	Ilja Nikulin	30	Luke Sellars
42	Libor Ustrnul	68	Zdenek Blatny
107	Carl Mallette	98	David Kaczowka
108	Blake Robson	99	Rob Zepp
147	Matt McRae	128	Derek MacKenzie
168	Zdenek Smid	159	Yuri Dobryshkin
178	Jeff Dwyer	188	Stephan Baby
180	Darcy Hordichuk	217	Garnet Exelby
230	Samu Isosalo	245	Tommi Santala
242	Evan Nielsen	246	Raymond DiLauro
244	Eric Bowen		
288	Mark McRae		
290	Simon Gamache		

Club Directory

Philips Arena

Atlanta Thrashers
One CNN Center, Box 105583
Atlanta, GA 30348-5583
Phone **404/827-5300**
FAX 404/827-5909
www.atlantathrashers.com
Capacity: 18,575

Club Officers and Officials
President and Governor......................... Stan Kasten
Vice President and General Manager
  (Alternate Governor)........................ Don Waddell
Vice President of Sales and Marketing........... Derek Schiller
Vice President of Public Relations .... Greg Hughes
Director of Player Evaluation and Development.... Bob Owen
Chief Scout .... Dan Marr
Director of Ticket Sales .... Dan Froehlich
Director of Marketing .... Jim Pfeifer
Director of Team Services .... Michele Zarzaca

Coaching Staff
Head Coach................................. Curt Fraser
Assistant Coaches .... George Kingston, Jay Leach
Strength and Conditioning Coach.............. Chris Reichart

Media Relations Information
Director of Media Relations.................. Tom Hughes   tom.hughes@turner.com
  (404) 827-5232
Manager of Media Relations .... Rob Koch   rob.koch@turner.com
  (404) 827-5467
Manager of Publications .... Matt Musgrove   matt.musgrove@turner.com
  (404) 827-4516
Multimedia Specialist....................... John Heid   john.heid@turner.com
  (404) 827-5717
Junior Publicist............................ Susan Sanderman
  susan.sanderman@turner.com
  (404) 827-2346
Main Media Relations Phone: .... (404) 827-2828
Media Relations Fax: .... (404) 827-5769

General Information
Practice Facility .... The IceForum, 2500 Satellite Bvld.,
  Duluth, Ga., 30097
Affiliates .... Orlando Solar Bears (IHL) and
  Greenville Grrrowl (ECHL)
Television................................. Turner South, WUPA/UPN69
Flagship Radio Stations .... WQXI AM 790 "The Zone,"
  WLKQ Lake 102.3 and WZGC, Z93 FM

Coach

FRASER, CURT
Coach, Atlanta Thrashers. Born in Cincinnati, OH, January 12, 1958.

Curt Fraser became the first head coach in the history of the Atlanta Thrashers on July 14, 1999. Fraser had spent the previous four seasons as the head coach of the IHL's Orlando Solar Bears, where he worked with Thrashers G.M. Don Waddell from 1995 to 1997.

During Fraser's four years with Orlando, the Solar Bears posted a 192-111-25 record for a .624 winning percentage along with four consecutive playoff appearances, including reaching the Eastern Conference Finals on three occasions and two Turner Cup Finals (1995-96 and 1998-99). He won eight of 12 playoff rounds and posted a 17-4 record in playoff elimination games during that span.

In 1996-97, Fraser led the club to its second consecutive 50-plus win season and eclipsed the 100-point plateau for the second time with Orlando and the third time in his IHL career. He led the club to a 16-game winning streak, the third longest in professional hockey history. He was also named as co-coach for the Eastern Conference at the 1997 IHL All-Star Game for the second consecutive season (with Orlando) and for the third time in his IHL career. He also represented Milwaukee in 1993.

During their 1995-96 inaugural season, the Solar Bears clinched the Central Division championship and became the first Eastern Conference expansion team to reach the Turner Cup Finals in the history of the IHL.

Fraser came to Orlando in 1995 after 12 years as a player in the NHL and five years as a coach in the professional ranks. He spent the 1994-95 season as an associate coach with the AHL's Syracuse Crunch, the top affiliate for the Vancouver Canucks. Before joining Syracuse, Fraser served as an assistant coach and later head coach of the IHL's Milwaukee Admirals.

Prior to reaching the coaching ranks, Fraser was a highly respected left winger in the NHL with Vancouver, Chicago and Minnesota. In 704 career games, he scored 193 goals, notched 433 points and amassed 1,306 penalty minutes. Originally a second round pick of Vancouver in 1978, Fraser established himself as a hard working and fearless player, who combined toughness with the ability to score.

Fraser and his wife, Rhonda, have three sons, Casey, Jesse and Luke.

Coaching Record

| Season | Team | Regular Season | | | | | Playoffs | | | |
		Games	W	L	T	%	Games	W	L	%
1992-93	Milwaukee (IHL)	82	49	23	10	.659	6	2	4	.333
1993-94	Milwaukee (IHL)	81	40	24	17	.599	4	0	4	.000
1995-96	Orlando (IHL)	82	52	24	6	.671	23	11	12	.478
1996-97	Orlando (IHL)	82	53	24	5	.677	10	4	6	.400
1997-98	Orlando (IHL)	82	42	30	10	.573	17	9	8	.529
1998-99	Orlando (IHL)	82	45	33	4	.573	17	10	7	.588
1999-2000	**Atlanta (NHL)**	82	14	61	7	.238•	....	....	....	....
	NHL Totals	82	14	61	7	.238•	....	....	....	....

• Includes points from regulation ties

Injuries limited Damian Rhodes to just 28 games last year. Still, he recorded the club's first victory — and its first shutout — on October 14, 1999.

Boston Bruins

1999-2000 Results: 24w-39l-19t 73pts. Fifth, Northeast Division

Kyle McLaren had a career-high eight goals last season. Three of them were game winners.

2000-01 Schedule

Oct.	Thu.	5	Ottawa
	Sat.	7	at Philadelphia
	Mon.	9	Florida*
	Wed.	11	at Anaheim
	Fri.	13	at Los Angeles
	Sat.	14	at San Jose
	Tue.	17	at Edmonton
	Fri.	20	at Calgary
	Thu.	26	Washington
	Sat.	28	Toronto
	Sun.	29	at NY Rangers
	Tue.	31	at NY Islanders
Nov.	Thu.	2	Chicago
	Sat.	4	Atlanta
	Sun.	5	at Toronto
	Thu.	9	Ottawa
	Sat.	11	Nashville
	Thu.	16	New Jersey
	Sat.	18	Minnesota
	Tue.	21	at Ottawa
	Wed.	22	at Detroit
	Fri.	24	Carolina*
	Sun.	26	Los Angeles
	Tue.	28	Pittsburgh
Dec.	Fri.	1	at Washington
	Sat.	2	Washington
	Mon.	4	at Atlanta
	Wed.	6	at Pittsburgh
	Fri.	8	at Columbus
	Sat.	9	NY Rangers
	Tue.	12	Buffalo
	Sat.	16	Carolina
	Tue.	19	Philadelphia
	Thu.	21	Toronto
	Sat.	23	Detroit
	Wed.	27	at NY Islanders
	Fri.	29	at Florida
	Sat.	30	at Tampa Bay
Jan.	Mon.	1	at Buffalo*
	Fri.	5	at Washington
	Sat.	6	Dallas

	Tue.	9	Pittsburgh
	Wed.	10	at Montreal
	Sat.	13	NY Rangers*
	Tue.	16	at New Jersey
	Thu.	18	at Carolina
	Fri.	19	at Nashville
	Mon.	22	Florida
	Wed.	24	at Toronto
	Fri.	26	at Buffalo
	Sat.	27	New Jersey
	Tue.	30	St. Louis
Feb.	Thu.	1	Montreal
	Tue.	6	Philadelphia
	Fri.	9	at Atlanta
	Sat.	10	Tampa Bay
	Thu.	15	at Tampa Bay
	Fri.	16	at Florida
	Sun.	18	at Carolina*
	Wed.	21	at Colorado
	Fri.	23	at Dallas
	Sat.	24	at St. Louis
	Tue.	27	Phoenix
Mar.	Thu.	1	Tampa Bay
	Sat.	3	San Jose*
	Mon.	5	at Philadelphia
	Tue.	6	Buffalo
	Thu.	8	Ottawa
	Sat.	10	Atlanta*
	Thu.	15	Vancouver
	Sat.	17	at Montreal
	Tue.	20	at Pittsburgh
	Thu.	22	Montreal
	Sat.	24	Colorado*
	Sun.	25	at NY Rangers
	Wed.	28	at Toronto
	Fri.	30	at Ottawa
	Sat.	31	NY Islanders
Apr.	Mon.	2	Montreal
	Wed.	4	at Buffalo
	Fri.	6	at New Jersey
	Sat.	7	NY Islanders

* Denotes afternoon game.

Franchise date: November 1, 1924

NORTHEAST DIVISION

77th NHL Season

Year-by-Year Record

Season	GP	Home W	L	T	Road W	L	T	Overall W	L	T	GF	GA	Pts.	Finished		Playoff Result
1999-2000	82	12	18	11	12	21	8	24	39	19	210	248	73	5th,	Northeast Div.	Out of Playoffs
1998-99	82	22	10	9	17	20	4	39	30	13	214	181	91	3rd,	Northeast Div.	Lost Conf. Semi-Final
1997-98	82	19	16	6	20	14	7	39	30	13	221	194	91	2nd,	Northeast Div.	Lost Conf. Quarter-Final
1996-97	82	14	20	7	12	27	2	26	47	9	234	300	61	6th,	Northeast Div.	Out of Playoffs
1995-96	82	22	14	5	18	17	6	40	31	11	282	269	91	2nd,	Northeast Div.	Lost Conf. Quarter-Final
1994-95	48	15	7	2	12	11	1	27	18	3	150	127	57	3rd,	Northeast Div.	Lost Conf. Quarter-Final
1993-94	84	20	14	8	22	15	5	42	29	13	289	252	97	2nd,	Northeast Div.	Lost Conf. Semi-Final
1992-93	84	29	10	3	22	16	4	51	26	7	332	268	109	1st,	Adams Div.	Lost Div. Semi-Final
1991-92	80	23	11	6	13	21	6	36	32	12	270	275	84	2nd,	Adams Div.	Lost Conf. Championship
1990-91	80	26	9	5	18	15	7	44	24	12	299	264	100	1st,	Adams Div.	Lost Conf. Championship
1989-90	80	23	13	4	23	12	5	46	25	9	289	232	101	1st,	Adams Div.	Lost Final
1988-89	80	17	15	8	20	14	6	37	29	14	289	256	88	2nd,	Adams Div.	Lost Div. Final
1987-88	80	24	13	3	20	17	3	44	30	6	300	251	94	2nd,	Adams Div.	Lost Final
1986-87	80	25	11	4	14	23	3	39	34	7	301	276	85	3rd,	Adams Div.	Lost Div. Semi-Final
1985-86	80	24	9	7	13	22	5	37	31	12	311	288	86	3rd,	Adams Div.	Lost Div. Semi-Final
1984-85	80	21	15	4	15	19	6	36	34	10	303	287	82	4th,	Adams Div.	Lost Div. Semi-Final
1983-84	80	25	12	3	24	13	3	49	25	6	336	261	104	1st,	Adams Div.	Lost Div. Semi-Final
1982-83	80	28	6	6	22	14	4	50	20	10	327	228	110	1st,	Adams Div.	Lost Conf. Championship
1981-82	80	24	12	4	19	15	6	43	27	10	323	285	96	2nd,	Adams Div.	Lost Div. Final
1980-81	80	26	10	4	11	20	9	37	30	13	316	272	87	2nd,	Adams Div.	Lost Prelim. Round
1979-80	80	27	9	4	19	12	9	46	21	13	310	234	105	2nd,	Adams Div.	Lost Quarter-Final
1978-79	80	25	10	5	18	13	9	43	23	14	316	270	100	1st,	Adams Div.	Lost Semi-Final
1977-78	80	29	6	5	22	12	6	51	18	11	333	218	113	1st,	Adams Div.	Lost Final
1976-77	80	27	7	6	22	16	2	49	23	8	312	240	106	1st,	Adams Div.	Lost Final
1975-76	80	27	5	8	21	10	9	48	15	17	313	237	113	1st,	Adams Div.	Lost Semi-Final
1974-75	80	29	5	6	11	21	8	40	26	14	345	245	94	2nd,	Adams Div.	Lost Prelim. Round
1973-74	78	33	4	2	19	13	7	52	17	9	349	221	113	1st,	East Div.	Lost Final
1972-73	78	27	10	2	24	12	3	51	22	5	330	235	107	2nd,	East Div.	Lost Quarter-Final
1971-72	**78**	**28**	**4**	**7**	**26**	**9**	**4**	**54**	**13**	**11**	**330**	**204**	**119**	**1st,**	**East Div.**	**Won Stanley Cup**
1970-71	78	33	4	2	24	10	5	57	14	7	399	207	121	1st,	East Div.	Lost Quarter-Final
1969-70	**76**	**27**	**3**	**8**	**13**	**14**	**11**	**40**	**17**	**19**	**277**	**216**	**99**	**2nd,**	**East Div.**	**Won Stanley Cup**
1968-69	76	29	3	6	13	15	10	42	18	16	303	221	100	2nd,	East Div.	Lost Semi-Final
1967-68	74	22	9	6	15	18	4	37	27	10	259	216	84	3rd,	East Div.	Lost Quarter-Final
1966-67	70	10	21	4	7	22	6	17	43	10	182	253	44	6th,		Out of Playoffs
1965-66	70	15	17	3	6	26	3	21	43	6	174	275	48	5th,		Out of Playoffs
1964-65	70	12	17	6	9	26	0	21	43	6	166	253	48	6th,		Out of Playoffs
1963-64	70	13	15	7	5	25	5	18	40	12	170	212	48	6th,		Out of Playoffs
1962-63	70	7	18	10	7	21	7	14	39	17	198	281	45	6th,		Out of Playoffs
1961-62	70	9	22	4	6	25	4	15	47	8	177	306	38	6th,		Out of Playoffs
1960-61	70	13	17	5	2	25	8	15	42	13	176	254	43	6th,		Out of Playoffs
1959-60	70	21	11	3	7	23	5	28	34	8	220	241	64	5th,		Out of Playoffs
1958-59	70	21	11	3	11	18	6	32	29	9	205	215	73	2nd,		Lost Semi-Final
1957-58	70	15	14	6	12	14	9	27	28	15	199	194	69	4th,		Lost Final
1956-57	70	20	9	6	14	15	6	34	24	12	195	174	80	3rd,		Lost Final
1955-56	70	14	14	7	9	20	6	23	34	13	147	185	59	5th,		Out of Playoffs
1954-55	70	16	10	9	7	16	12	23	26	21	169	188	67	4th,		Lost Semi-Final
1953-54	70	22	8	5	10	20	5	32	28	10	177	181	74	4th,		Lost Semi-Final
1952-53	70	19	10	6	9	19	7	28	29	13	152	172	69	3rd,		Lost Final
1951-52	70	15	12	8	10	17	8	25	29	16	162	176	66	4th,		Lost Semi-Final
1950-51	70	13	12	10	9	18	8	22	30	18	178	197	62	4th,		Lost Semi-Final
1949-50	70	15	12	8	7	20	8	22	32	16	198	228	60	5th,		Out of Playoffs
1948-49	60	18	10	2	11	13	6	29	23	8	178	163	66	2nd,		Lost Semi-Final
1947-48	60	12	8	10	11	16	3	23	24	13	167	168	59	3rd,		Lost Semi-Final
1946-47	60	18	7	5	8	16	6	26	23	11	190	175	63	3rd,		Lost Semi-Final
1945-46	50	11	5	4	13	13	4	24	18	8	167	156	56	2nd,		Lost Final
1944-45	50	11	12	2	5	18	2	16	30	4	179	219	36	4th,		Lost Semi-Final
1943-44	50	15	8	2	4	18	3	19	26	5	223	268	43	5th,		Out of Playoffs
1942-43	50	13	3	5	11	14	0	24	17	9	195	176	57	2nd,		Lost Final
1941-42	48	17	4	3	8	13	3	25	17	6	160	118	56	3rd,		Lost Semi-Final
1940-41	**48**	**15**	**4**	**5**	**12**	**4**	**8**	**27**	**8**	**13**	**168**	**102**	**67**	**1st,**		**Won Stanley Cup**
1939-40	48	20	3	1	11	9	4	31	12	5	170	98	67	1st,		Lost Semi-Final
1938-39	**48**	**20**	**2**	**2**	**16**	**8**	**0**	**36**	**10**	**2**	**156**	**76**	**74**	**1st,**		**Won Stanley Cup**
1937-38	48	18	3	3	12	8	4	30	11	7	142	89	67	1st,	Amn. Div.	Lost Semi-Final
1936-37	48	9	11	4	14	7	3	23	18	7	120	110	53	2nd,	Amn. Div.	Lost Quarter-Final
1935-36	48	15	8	1	7	12	5	22	20	6	92	83	50	2nd,	Amn. Div.	Lost Quarter-Final
1934-35	48	17	7	0	9	9	6	26	16	6	129	112	58	1st,	Amn. Div.	Lost Semi-Final
1933-34	48	11	11	2	7	14	3	18	25	5	111	130	41	4th,	Amn. Div.	Out of Playoffs
1932-33	48	15	4	5	10	11	3	25	15	8	124	88	58	1st,	Amn. Div.	Lost Semi-Final
1931-32	48	11	10	3	4	11	9	15	21	12	122	117	42	4th,	Amn. Div.	Out of Playoffs
1930-31	44	16	1	5	12	9	1	28	10	6	143	90	62	1st,	Amn. Div.	Lost Semi-Final
1929-30	44	21	1	0	17	4	1	38	5	1	179	98	77	1st,	Amn. Div.	Lost Final
1928-29	**44**	**15**	**6**	**1**	**11**	**7**	**4**	**26**	**13**	**5**	**89**	**52**	**57**	**1st,**	**Amn. Div.**	**Won Stanley Cup**
1927-28	44	13	4	5	7	9	6	20	13	11	77	70	51	1st,	Amn. Div.	Lost Semi-Final
1926-27	44	15	7	0	6	13	3	21	20	3	97	89	45	2nd,	Amn. Div.	Lost Final
1925-26	36	10	7	1	7	13	0	17	15	4	92	85	38	4th,		Out of Playoffs
1924-25	30	3	12	0	3	12	0	6	24	0	49	119	12	6th,		Out of Playoffs

2000-01 Player Personnel

FORWARDS	HT	WT	S	Place of Birth	Date	1999-00 Club
ALLISON, Jason	6-3	218	R	North York, Ont.	5/29/75	Boston
AXELSSON, P.J.	6-1	176	L	Kungalv, Sweden	2/26/75	Boston
BATES, Shawn	5-11	212	R	Melrose, MA	4/3/75	Boston
BELANGER, Ken	6-4	225	L	Sault Ste. Marie, Ont.	5/14/74	Boston
CARTER, Anson	6-1	200	R	Toronto, Ont.	6/6/74	Boston
ELORANTA, Mikko	6-0	190	L	Turku, Finland	8/24/72	Boston
FERRARO, Peter	5-10	180	R	Port Jefferson, NY	1/24/73	Boston-Providence Bruins
GOREN, Lee	6-3	200	R	Winnipeg, Man.	12/26/77	North Dakota
HENDERSON, Jay	5-11	190	L	Edmonton, Alta.	9/17/78	Boston-Providence Bruins
HULBIG, Joe	6-3	215	L	Norwood, MA	9/29/73	Boston-Providence Bruins
KARLIN, Mattias	5-11	183	L	Ornskoldsvik, Sweden	7/4/79	MoDo Hockey
KNUBLE, Mike	6-3	208	R	Toronto, Ont.	7/4/72	NY Rangers-Boston
KOVALENKO, Andrei	5-10	200	L	Balakovo, USSR	6/7/70	Carolina
MANLOW, Eric	6-0	190	L	Belleville, Ont.	4/7/75	Florida (ECHL)-Providence
MANN, Cameron	6-0	195	R	Thompson, Man.	4/20/77	Boston-Providence Bruins
NICKULAS, Eric	5-11	200	R	Hyannis, MA	3/25/75	Boston-Providence Bruins
PAHLSSON, Samuel	5-11	190	L	Ornskoldsvik, Sweden	12/17/77	MoDo Hockey
PRONGER, Sean	6-2	205	L	Dryden, Ont.	11/30/72	Boston-Providence Bruins-Manitoba Moose
ROLSTON, Brian	6-2	205	L	Flint, MI	2/21/73	New Jersey-Colorado-Boston
SAMSONOV, Sergei	5-8	180	R	Moscow, USSR	10/27/78	Boston
SAVAGE, Andre	6-0	195	R	Ottawa, Ont.	5/27/75	Boston-Providence Bruins
THORNTON, Joe	6-4	215	L	London, Ont.	7/2/79	Boston
TROTTIER, Joel	6-0	200	R	Alexandria, Ont.	2/11/77	Greenville-Providence (AHL)
ZEHR, Jeff	6-3	195	L	Woodstock, Ont.	12/10/78	Boston-Providence Bruins
ZULTEK, Matt	6-4	222	L	Windsor, Ont.	3/12/79	Ottawa 67's
DEFENSEMEN						
ABRAHAMSSON, Elias	6-3	240	L	Uppsala, Sweden	6/15/77	Providence (AHL)-Hamilton
AITKEN, Johnathan	6-4	215	L	Edmonton, Alta.	5/24/78	Boston-Providence Bruins
BELTER, Shane	6-1	205	R	Swift Current, Sask.	10/5/77	Providence Bruins
BOYNTON, Nick	6-2	202	R	Nobleton, Ont.	1/14/79	Boston-Providence Bruins
CECH, Vratislav	6-3	196	L	Tabor, Czech.	1/28/79	Providence (AHL)-Greenville
COFFEY, Paul	6-0	205	L	Weston, Ont.	6/1/61	Carolina
GILL, Hal	6-7	235	L	Concord, MA	4/6/75	Boston
GIRARD, Jonathan	5-11	196	R	Joliette, Que.	5/27/80	Moncton Wildcats-Boston-Providence Bruins
GRENIER, Martin	6-5	231	L	Laval, Que.	11/2/80	Quebec Remparts
KOLARIK, Pavel	6-1	207	L	Vyskov, Czech.	10/24/72	Slavia Praha
KULTANEN, Jarno	6-2	198	L	Luumaki, Finland	1/8/73	HIFK Helsinki
KUTLAK, Zdenek	6-3	207	L	Budejovice, Czech.	2/13/80	HC Budejovice-Jr.-SHC Hradec-IHC Pisek-HC Budejovice
McCAMBRIDGE, Keith	6-2	205	L	Thompson, Man.	2/1/74	Providence (AHL)-Manitoba
McLAREN, Kyle	6-4	230	L	Humboldt, Sask.	6/18/77	Boston
POPOVIC, Peter	6-6	243	L	Koping, Sweden	2/10/68	Pittsburgh
SMITH, Brandon	6-1	198	L	Hazelton, B.C.	2/25/73	Boston-Providence Bruins
SWEENEY, Don	5-10	186	L	St. Stephen, N.B.	8/17/66	Boston
VAN ACKER, Eric	6-5	246	L	St-Jean, Que.	3/1/79	Greenville-Providence (AHL)
VAN IMPE, Darren	6-1	205	L	Saskatoon, Sask.	5/18/73	Boston

GOALTENDERS	HT	WT	C	Place of Birth	Date	1999-00 Club
DAFOE, Byron	5-11	200	L	Sussex, England	2/25/71	Boston
GRAHAME, John	6-2	214	L	Denver, CO	8/31/75	Boston-Providence Bruins
RAYCROFT, Andrew	6-0	150	L	Belleville, Ont.	5/4/80	Kingston
WHITMORE, Kay	5-11	175	L	Sudbury, Ont.	4/10/67	Providence Bruins

Coaching History

Art Ross, 1924-25 to 1927-28; Cy Denneny, 1928-29; Art Ross, 1929-30 to 1933-34; Frank Patrick, 1934-35, 1935-36; Art Ross, 1936-37 to 1938-39; Cooney Weiland, 1939-40, 1940-41; Art Ross, 1941-42 to 1944-45; Dit Clapper, 1945-46 to 1948-49; George Boucher, 1949-50; Lynn Patrick, 1950-51 to 1953-54; Lynn Patrick and Milt Schmidt, 1954-55; Milt Schmidt, 1955-56 to 1960-61; Phil Watson, 1961-62; Phil Watson and Milt Schmidt, 1962-63; Milt Schmidt, 1963-64 to 1965-66; Harry Sinden, 1966-67 to 1969-70; Tom Johnson, 1970-71, 1971-72; Tom Johnson and Bep Guidolin, 1972-73; Bep Guidolin, 1973-74; Don Cherry, 1974-75 to 1978-79; Fred Creighton and Harry Sinden, 1979-80; Gerry Cheevers, 1980-81 to 1983-84; Gerry Cheevers and Harry Sinden, 1984-85; Butch Goring, 1985-86; Butch Goring and Terry O'Reilly, 1986-87; Terry O'Reilly, 1987-88, 1988-89; Mike Milbury, 1989-90, 1990-91; Rick Bowness, 1991-92; Brian Sutter, 1992-93 to 1994-95; Steve Kasper, 1995-96, 1996-97; Pat Burns, 1997-98 to date.

1999-2000 Scoring

* – rookie

Regular Season

Pos	#	Player	Team	GP	G	A	Pts	+/–	PIM	PP	SH	GW	GT	S	%
C	6	Joe Thornton	BOS	81	23	37	60	–5	82	5	0	3	0	171	13.5
L	33	Anson Carter	BOS	59	22	25	47	8	14	4	0	1	1	144	15.3
L	14	Sergei Samsonov	BOS	77	19	26	45	–6	4	6	0	3	0	145	13.1
L	12	Brian Rolston	N.J	11	3	1	4	–2	0	1	0	2	0	33	9.1
			COL	50	8	10	18	–6	12	1	0	3	0	107	7.5
			BOS	16	5	4	9	–4	6	3	0	1	0	66	7.6
			TOTAL	77	16	15	31	–12	18	5	0	6	0	206	7.8
C	41	Jason Allison	BOS	37	10	18	28	5	20	3	0	1	1	66	15.2
D	20	Darren Van Impe	BOS	79	5	23	28	–19	73	4	0	0	0	97	5.2
R	11	P.J. Axelsson	BOS	81	10	16	26	1	24	0	0	4	0	186	5.4
R	23	Steve Heinze	BOS	75	12	13	25	–8	36	2	0	2	2	145	8.3
R	26	Mike Knuble	NYR	59	9	5	14	–5	18	1	0	1	0	50	18.0
			BOS	14	3	3	6	–2	8	1	0	1	0	28	10.7
			TOTAL	73	12	8	20	–7	26	2	0	2	0	78	15.4
C	28	* Andre Savage	BOS	43	7	13	20	–8	10	2	0	1	1	70	10.0
D	18	Kyle McLaren	BOS	71	8	11	19	–4	67	2	0	3	0	142	5.6
C	22	Mikko Eloranta	BOS	50	6	12	18	–10	36	1	0	0	0	59	10.2
D	32	Don Sweeney	BOS	81	1	13	14	–14	48	0	0	0	0	82	1.2
R	10	Cameron Mann	BOS	32	8	4	12	–6	13	1	0	0	1	48	16.7
C	17	Shawn Bates	BOS	44	5	7	12	–17	14	0	0	1	0	65	7.7
D	25	Hal Gill	BOS	81	3	9	12	0	51	0	0	0	0	120	2.5
R	21	* Eric Nickulas	BOS	20	5	6	11	–1	12	1	0	0	0	28	17.9
L	57	* Antti Laaksonen	BOS	27	6	3	9	3	2	0	0	1	0	23	26.1
D	37	Mattias Timander	BOS	60	0	8	8	–11	22	0	0	0	0	39	0.0
D	53	Brandon Smith	BOS	22	2	4	6	–4	10	0	0	0	0	24	8.3
D	29	Marty McSorley	BOS	27	2	3	5	2	62	0	0	0	0	24	8.3
L	48	Joe Hulbig	BOS	24	2	2	4	–8	8	0	0	0	0	15	13.3
L	16	Ken Belanger	BOS	37	2	2	4	–4	44	0	0	0	0	20	10.0
L	51	* Jay Henderson	BOS	16	1	3	4	1	9	0	0	0	0	18	5.6
R	27	Landon Wilson	BOS	40	1	3	4	–6	18	0	0	0	0	67	1.5
D	55	* Jonathan Girard	BOS	23	1	2	3	–1	2	0	0	0	0	17	5.9
C	39	* Joel Prpic	BOS	14	0	3	3	–6	0	0	0	0	0	13	0.0
C	61	Marquis Mathieu	BOS	6	0	2	2	–2	4	0	0	0	0	3	0.0
R	42	Peter Ferraro	BOS	5	0	1	1	–1	0	0	0	0	0	3	0.0
C	46	Sean Pronger	BOS	11	0	1	1	–4	13	0	0	0	0	7	0.0
G	47	* John Grahame	BOS	24	0	1	1	0	8	0	0	0	0	0	0.0
R	45	Aaron Downey	BOS	1	0	0	0	0	0	0	0	0	0	0	0.0
D	49	* Johnathan Aitken	BOS	3	0	0	0	–3	0	0	0	0	0	2	0.0
L	54	* Jeff Zehr	BOS	4	0	0	0	–1	2	0	0	0	0	3	0.0
D	44	* Nicholas Boynton	BOS	5	0	0	0	–5	0	0	0	0	0	6	0.0
G	35	Robbie Tallas	BOS	27	0	0	0	0	6	0	0	0	0	0	0.0
G	34	Byron Dafoe	BOS	41	0	0	0	0	0	0	0	0	0	0	0.0

Goaltending

No.	Goaltender	GPI	Mins	Avg	W	L	T	EN	SO	GA	SA	S%
47	* John Grahame	24	1344	2.46	7	10	5	1	2	55	609	.910
34	Byron Dafoe	41	2307	2.96	13	16	10	2	3	114	1030	.889
35	Robbie Tallas	27	1363	3.17	4	13	4	4	0	72	628	.885
	Totals	**82**	**5028**	**2.96**	**24**	**39**	**19**	**7**	**6**	**248**	**2274**	**.891**

Coach

BURNS, PAT
Coach, Boston Bruins. Born in St-Henri, Que., April 4, 1952.

Pat Burns has led the Bruins into the playoffs two of his three seasons behind the Bruins bench. The club's 30-point improvement in 1997-98 saw Burns honored with the Jack Adams Award, making him the first man to be named coach of the year on three occasions. The three victories have come with three different clubs.

Burns began his coaching career with the Hull Olympiques of the QMJHL. During his four seasons behind the Hull bench, he compiled a 138-136-6 record and a berth in the 1986 Memorial Cup finals. In 1987-88, he moved to the professional ranks, assuming the head coaching position with Montreal's AHL affiliate in Sherbrooke. After leading that team to a 42-34-4 record, he was named as the head coach in Montreal.

He was the NHL's winningest coach over his four-year tenure in Montreal, with a 174-104-42 record and .609 winning percentage from 1988-89 through 1991-92.

On May 29, 1992, Burns was named as the head coach for the Toronto Maple Leafs. In his first season with Toronto, he led the team to the highest single-season turnaround in club history with club records in regular season wins, points, home wins, playoff games and victories. Their 44-29-11 record in 1992-93 was a 32-point improvement from their 1991-92 campaign. His second season behind the Toronto bench earned the team consecutive 40-win seasons for the first time in club history.

Coaching Record

		Regular Season					Playoffs			
Season	Team	Games	W	L	T	%	Games	W	L	%
1983-84	Hull (QMJHL)	70	25	45	0	.357	....	....	....	....
1984-85	Hull (QMJHL)	68	33	34	1	.493	5	1	4	.200
1985-86	Hull (QMJHL)	72	54	18	0	.750	15	15	0	1.000
1986-87	Hull (QMJHL)	70	26	39	5	.407	8	4	4	.500
1987-88	Sherbrooke (AHL)	80	42	34	4	.550	6	2	4	.333
1988-89	**Montreal (NHL)**	**80**	**53**	**18**	**9**	**.719**	**21**	**14**	**7**	**.667**
1989-90	**Montreal (NHL)**	**80**	**41**	**28**	**11**	**.581**	**11**	**5**	**6**	**.455**
1990-91	**Montreal (NHL)**	**80**	**39**	**30**	**11**	**.556**	**13**	**7**	**6**	**.538**
1991-92	**Montreal (NHL)**	**80**	**41**	**28**	**11**	**.581**	**11**	**4**	**7**	**.364**
1992-93	**Toronto (NHL)**	**84**	**44**	**29**	**11**	**.589**	**21**	**11**	**10**	**.524**
1993-94	**Toronto (NHL)**	**84**	**43**	**29**	**12**	**.583**	**18**	**9**	**9**	**.500**
1994-95	**Toronto (NHL)**	**48**	**21**	**19**	**8**	**.521**	**7**	**3**	**4**	**.429**
1995-96	**Toronto (NHL)**	**65**	**25**	**30**	**10**	**.462**	....	....	....	....
1997-98	**Boston (NHL)**	**82**	**39**	**30**	**13**	**.555**	**6**	**2**	**4**	**.333**
1998-99	**Boston (NHL)**	**82**	**39**	**30**	**13**	**.555**	**12**	**6**	**6**	**.500**
1999-2000	**Boston (NHL)**	**82**	**24**	**39**	**19**	**.445•**	....	....	....	....
	NHL Totals	**847**	**409**	**310**	**128**	**.562•**	**120**	**61**	**59**	**.508**

• Includes points from regulation ties

Club Records

Team

(Figures in brackets for season records are games played; records for fewest points, wins, ties, losses, goals, goals against are for 70 or more games)

Most Points	121	1970-71 (78)
Most Wins	57	1970-71 (78)
Most Ties	21	1954-55 (70)
Most Losses	47	1961-62 (70), 1996-97 (82)
Most Goals	399	1970-71 (78)
Most Goals Against	306	1961-62 (70)
Fewest Points	38	1961-62 (70)
Fewest Wins	14	1962-63 (70)
Fewest Ties	5	1972-73 (78)
Fewest Losses	13	1971-72 (78)
Fewest Goals	147	1955-56 (70)
Fewest Goals Against	172	1952-53 (70)
Longest Winning Streak		
Overall	14	Dec. 3/29-Jan. 9/30
Home	*20	Dec. 3/29-Mar. 18/30
Away	8	Feb. 17-Mar. 8/72, Mar. 15-Apr. 14/93
Longest Undefeated Streak		
Overall	23	Dec. 22/40-Feb. 23/41 (15 wins, 8 ties)
Home	27	Nov. 22/70-Mar. 20/71 (26 wins, 1 tie)
Away	15	Dec. 22/40-Mar. 16/41 (9 wins, 6 ties)
Longest Losing Streak		
Overall	11	Dec. 3/24-Jan. 5/25
Home	*11	Dec. 8/24-Feb. 17/25
Away	14	Dec. 27/64-Feb. 21/65
Longest Winless Streak		
Overall	20	Jan. 28-Mar. 11/62 (16 losses, 4 ties)
Home	11	Dec. 8/24-Feb. 17/25 (11 losses)
Away	14	Three times
Most Shutouts, Season	15	1927-28 (44)
Most PIM, Season	2,443	1987-88 (80)
Most Goals, Game	14	Jan. 21/45 (NYR 3 at Bos. 14)

Individual

Most Seasons	21	John Bucyk, Ray Bourque
Most Games	1,518	Ray Bourque
Most Goals, Career	545	John Bucyk
Most Assists, Career	1,111	Ray Bourque
Most Points, Career	1,506	Ray Bourque (395G, 1,111A)
Most PIM, Career	2,095	Terry O'Reilly
Most Shutouts, Career	74	Tiny Thompson
Longest Consecutive Games Streak	418	John Bucyk (Jan. 23/69-Mar. 2/75)
Most Goals, Season	76	Phil Esposito (1970-71)
Most Assists, Season	102	Bobby Orr (1970-71)
Most Points, Season	152	Phil Esposito (1970-71; 76G, 76A)
Most PIM, Season	302	Jay Miller (1987-88)
Most Points, Defenseman, Season	*139	Bobby Orr (1970-71; 37G, 102A)
Most Points, Center, Season	152	Phil Esposito (1970-71; 76G, 76A)
Most Points, Right Wing, Season	105	Ken Hodge (1970-71; 43G, 62A), (1973-74; 50G, 55A), Rick Middleton (1983-84; 47G, 58A)
Most Points, Left Wing, Season	116	John Bucyk (1970-71; 51G, 65A)
Most Points, Rookie, Season	102	Joe Juneau (1992-93; 32G, 70A)
Most Shutouts, Season	15	Hal Winkler (1927-28)
Most Goals, Game	4	Twenty times
Most Assists, Game	6	Ken Hodge (Feb. 9/71), Bobby Orr (Jan. 1/73)
Most Points, Game	7	Bobby Orr (Nov. 15/73; 3G, 4A), Phil Esposito (Dec. 19/74; 3G, 4A), Barry Pederson (Apr. 4/82; 3G, 4A), Cam Neely (Oct. 16/88; 3G, 4A)

* NHL Record.

Retired Numbers

2	Eddie Shore	1926-1940
3	Lionel Hitchman	1925-1934
4	Bobby Orr	1966-1976
5	Dit Clapper	1927-1947
7	Phil Esposito	1967-1975
9	John Bucyk	1957-1978
15	Milt Schmidt	1936-1955

All-time Record vs. Other Clubs

Regular Season

	At Home							On Road							Total						
	GP	W	L	T	GF	GA	PTS	GP	W	L	T	GF	GA	PTS	GP	W	L	T	GF	GA	PTS
Anaheim	6	3	3	0	18	18	6	6	3	2	1	15	11	7	12	6	5	1	33	29	13
Atlanta	2	1	0	1	7	5	3	2	2	0	0	7	4	4	4	3	0	1	14	9	7
Buffalo	97	55	29	13	369	286	123	97	32	50	15	290	360	80	194	87	79	28	659	646	203
Calgary	44	26	12	6	155	121	59	42	22	17	3	149	154	47	86	48	29	9	304	275	106
Carolina	70	44	19	7	261	186	95	68	32	29	7	237	230	71	138	76	48	14	498	416	166
Chicago	281	159	88	34	1015	800	352	283	94	145	44	758	913	233	564	253	233	78	1773	1713	585
Colorado	60	31	20	9	236	185	71	62	34	22	6	261	219	74	122	65	42	15	497	404	145
Dallas	57	40	8	9	249	136	89	58	29	16	13	213	168	71	115	69	24	22	462	304	160
Detroit	284	152	89	43	1002	757	347	282	77	153	52	711	946	206	566	229	242	95	1713	1703	553
Edmonton	27	18	6	3	115	76	39	27	14	10	3	92	89	31	54	32	16	6	207	165	70
Florida	14	4	7	3	34	41	11	13	7	6	0	39	40	15	27	11	13	3	73	81	26
Los Angeles	59	43	11	5	278	165	91	58	31	20	7	216	199	69	117	74	31	12	494	364	160
Montreal	324	148	120	56	957	879	352	324	93	185	46	769	1098	232	648	241	305	102	1726	1977	584
Nashville	2	1	1	0	9	4	2	2	2	0	0	10	4	4	4	3	1	0	19	8	6
New Jersey	48	28	13	7	195	145	63	45	23	12	10	150	119	57	93	51	25	17	345	264	120
NY Islanders	51	27	14	10	194	147	64	53	25	22	6	175	177	56	104	52	36	16	369	324	120
NY Rangers	290	155	93	42	1049	813	352	294	112	127	55	831	895	279	584	267	220	97	1880	1708	631
Ottawa	22	14	6	2	89	63	30	21	14	4	3	74	45	32	43	28	10	5	163	108	62
Philadelphia	68	43	16	9	265	189	95	65	27	30	8	185	220	62	133	70	46	17	450	409	157
Phoenix	27	20	4	3	122	83	43	28	14	12	2	100	98	30	55	34	16	5	222	181	73
Pittsburgh	70	51	13	6	317	201	108	72	27	31	14	259	256	68	142	78	44	20	576	457	176
St. Louis	56	34	13	9	239	152	77	56	23	24	9	192	179	55	112	57	37	18	431	331	132
San Jose	7	5	0	2	26	17	12	8	5	1	2	32	19	12	15	10	1	4	58	36	24
Tampa Bay	15	11	1	3	56	32	25	15	7	6	2	43	40	16	30	18	7	5	99	72	41
Toronto	288	156	85	47	946	764	359	288	87	150	51	748	979	225	576	243	235	98	1694	1743	584
Vancouver	48	36	6	6	206	113	78	49	25	16	8	201	162	58	97	61	22	14	407	275	136
Washington	48	27	14	7	180	132	61	47	24	12	11	169	134	59	95	51	26	18	349	266	120
Defunct Clubs	164	112	39	13	525	306	237	164	79	67	18	496	440	176	328	191	106	31	1021	746	413
Totals	**2529**	**1444**	**730**	**355**	**9114**	**6816**	**3244**	**2529**	**964**	**1169**	**396**	**7422**	**8198**	**2329**	**5058**	**2408**	**1899**	**751**	**16536**	**15014**	**5573**

Playoffs

	Series	W	L	GP	W	L	T	GF	GA	Last Mtg.	Round	Result
Buffalo	7	5	2	39	21	18	0	146	130	1999	CSF	L 2-4
Carolina	3	3	0	19	12	7	0	63	48	1999	CQF	W 4-2
Chicago	6	5	1	22	16	5	1	97	63	1978	QF	W 4-0
Colorado	2	1	1	11	6	5	0	37	36	1983	DSF	W 3-1
Dallas	1	0	1	3	0	3	0	13	20	1981	PR	L 0-3
Detroit	7	4	3	33	19	14	0	96	98	1957	SF	W 4-1
Edmonton	2	0	2	9	1	8	0	20	41	1990	F	L 1-4
Florida	1	0	1	5	1	4	0	16	22	1996	CQF	L 1-4
Los Angeles	2	2	0	13	8	5	0	56	38	1977	QF	W 4-2
Montreal	28	7	21	139	52	87	0	339	430	1994	CQF	W 4-3
New Jersey	3	1	2	18	7	11	0	52	55	1995	CQF	L 1-4
NY Islanders	2	0	2	11	3	8	0	35	49	1983	CF	L 2-4
NY Rangers	9	6	3	42	22	18	2	114	104	1973	QF	L 1-4
Philadelphia	4	2	2	20	11	9	0	60	57	1978	SF	W 4-1
Pittsburgh	4	2	2	19	9	10	0	62	67	1992	CF	L 0-4
St. Louis	2	2	0	8	8	0	0	48	15	1972	SF	W 4-0
Toronto	13	5	8	62	30	31	1	153	150	1974	QF	W 4-0
Washington	2	1	1	10	6	4	0	28	21	1998	CQF	L 2-4
Defunct Clubs	3	1	2	11	4	5	2	20	20			
Totals	**101**	**47**	**54**	**494**	**236**	**252**	**6**	**1448**	**1464**			

Calgary totals include Atlanta Flames, 1972-73 to 1979-80.
Carolina totals include Hartford, 1979-80 to 1996-97.
Colorado totals include Quebec, 1979-80 to 1994-95.
Dallas totals include Minnesota North Stars, 1967-68 to 1992-93.
New Jersey totals include Kansas City, 1974-75 to 1975-76, and Colorado Rockies, 1976-77 to 1981-82.
Phoenix totals include Winnipeg, 1979-80 to 1995-96.

Playoff Results 2000-1996

Year	Round	Opponent	Result	GF	GA
1999	CSF	Buffalo	L 2-4	14	17
	CQF	Carolina	W 4-2	16	10
1998	CQF	Washington	L 2-4	13	15
1996	CQF	Florida	L 1-4	16	22

Abbreviations: Round: F – Final; **CF** – conference final; **CSF** – conference semi-final; **CQF** – conference quarter-final; **DSF** – division semi-final; **SF** – semi-final; **QF** – quarter-final; **PR** – preliminary round.

1999-2000 Results

Month	Day		Opponent	Score
Oct.	2		Carolina	1-3
	4	at	Toronto	0-4
	7	at	Ottawa	3-4
	9		Philadelphia	1-1
	11		Colorado	3-3
	13	at	Colorado	1-2
	15	at	Dallas	2-2
	16	at	Phoenix	1-2
	20	at	Los Angeles	2-2
	23	at	San Jose	3-1
	24	at	Anaheim	3-2
	28		Tampa Bay	7-3
	30		Buffalo	3-0
Nov.	4		New Jersey	3-1
	6		Atlanta	4-2
	10	at	Buffalo	2-6
	11		Toronto	4-3 *
	13	at	NY Rangers	5-2
	17	at	New Jersey	2-2
	18		NY Rangers	5-3
	20		Washington	0-3
	22	at	Carolina	2-1
	24	at	Nashville	5-2
	26		Vancouver	2-2
	28		NY Islanders	1-2
Dec.	2	at	Washington	2-2
	4		Chicago	3-9
	9		Edmonton	2-2
	11		Detroit	4-5
	13		Phoenix	2-0
	14	at	Pittsburgh	2-4
	17	at	Atlanta	3-1
	18	at	St. Louis	0-4
	21		Nashville	1-3
	23		Montreal	3-3
	27	at	NY Islanders	0-3
	29	at	New Jersey	4-5 *
	30	at	Ottawa	4-5 *
Jan.	1		New Jersey	2-2
	4	at	NY Islanders	7-3
	6		Carolina	3-7
	8		NY Islanders	2-5
	11		Toronto	2-3
	13		Buffalo	0-0
	15	at	Montreal	2-2
	17		Atlanta	3-3
	19	at	Atlanta	4-3
	20	at	Tampa Bay	4-2
	22	at	Florida	3-4 *
	24		Calgary	3-4 *
	29		Buffalo	1-0
	31		Anaheim	2-4
Feb.	1	at	Ottawa	4-4
	3		Toronto	4-2
	8		Washington	2-2
	11	at	NY Rangers	2-5
	12		Florida	1-5
	16	at	Toronto	3-3
	21	at	Vancouver	2-5
	23	at	Edmonton	2-4
	25	at	Washington	3-0
	26	at	Pittsburgh	2-2
	29		Ottawa	3-5
Mar.	2		Montreal	2-5
	4		Philadelphia	0-3
	6		Ottawa	1-5
	8	at	Buffalo	1-2 *
	10	at	Carolina	5-3
	11	at	Montreal	5-3
	16	at	Chicago	4-5 *
	18		Pittsburgh	3-2
	19	at	Philadelphia	2-6
	21		Tampa Bay	4-0
	23		Florida	1-3
	25		Los Angeles	4-4
	29	at	Montreal	3-4
	30		St. Louis	2-3
Apr.	1		NY Rangers	2-2
	4	at	Tampa Bay	4-5
	5	at	Florida	3-6
	8	at	Philadelphia	0-3
	9		Pittsburgh	3-1

* – Overtime

Entry Draft
Selections 2000-1986

2000
Pick
7	Lars Jonsson
27	Martin Samuelsson
37	Andy Hilbert
59	Ivan Huml
66	Tuukka Makela
73	Sergei Zinovjev
102	Brett Nowak
174	Jarno Kultanen
204	Chris Berti
237	Zdenek Kutlak
268	Pavel Kolarik
279	Andreas Lindstrom

1999
Pick
21	Nick Boynton
56	Matt Zultek
89	Kyle Wanvig
118	Jaakko Harikkala
147	Seamus Kotyk
179	Donald Choukalos
207	Greg Barber
236	John Cronin
247	Mikko Eloranta
264	Georgy Pujacs

1998
Pick
48	Jonathan Girard
52	Bobby Allen
78	Peter Nordstrom
135	Andrew Raycroft
165	Ryan Milanovic

1997
Pick
1	Joe Thornton
8	Sergei Samsonov
27	Ben Clymer
54	Mattias Karlin
63	Lee Goren
81	Karol Bartanus
135	Denis Timofeev
162	Joel Trottier
180	Jim Baxter
191	Antti Laaksonen
218	Eric Van Acker
246	Jay Henderson

1996
Pick
8	Johnathan Aitken
45	Henry Kuster
53	Eric Naud
80	Jason Doyle
100	Trent Whitfield
132	Elias Abrahamsson
155	Chris Lane
182	Thomas Brown
208	Bob Prier
234	Anders Soderberg

1995
Pick
9	Kyle McLaren
21	Sean Brown
47	Paxton Schafer
73	Bill McCauley
99	Cameron Mann
151	Yevgeny Shaldybin
177	P.J. Axelsson
203	Sergei Zhukov
229	Jonathon Murphy

1994
Pick
21	Evgeni Ryabchikov
47	Daniel Goneau
99	Eric Nickulas
125	Darren Wright
151	Andre Roy
177	Jeremy Schaefer
229	John Grahame
255	Neil Savary
281	Andrei Yakhanov

1993
Pick
25	Kevyn Adams
51	Matt Alvey
88	Charles Paquette
103	Shawn Bates
129	Andrei Sapozhnikov
155	Milt Mastad
181	Ryan Golden
207	Hal Gill
233	Joel Prpic
259	Joakim Persson

1992
Pick
16	Dmitri Kvartalnov
55	Sergei Zholtok
112	Scott Bailey
133	Jiri Dopita
136	Grigori Panteleev
184	Kurt Seher
208	Mattias Timander
232	Chris Crombie
256	Denis Chervyakov

1991
Pick
18	Glen Murray
40	Jozef Stumpel
62	Marcel Cousineau
84	Brad Tiley
106	Mariusz Czerkawski
150	Gary Golczewski
172	Jay Moser
194	Daniel Hodge
216	Steve Norton
238	Stephen Lombardi
260	Torsten Kienass

1990
Pick
21	Bryan Smolinski
63	Cam Stewart
84	Jerome Buckley
105	Mike Bales
126	Mark Woolf
147	Jim Mackey
168	John Gruden
189	Darren Wetherill
210	Dean Capuano
231	Andy Bezeau
252	Ted Miskolczi

1989
Pick
17	Shayne Stevenson
38	Mike Parson
57	Wes Walz
80	Jackson Penney
101	Mark Montanari
122	Stephen Foster
143	Otto Hascak
164	Rick Allain
185	James Lavish
206	Geoff Simpson
227	David Franzosa

1988
Pick
18	Robert Cimetta
60	Steve Heinze
81	Joe Juneau
102	Daniel Murphy
123	Derek Geary
165	Mark Krys
186	Jon Rohloff
228	Eric Reisman
249	Doug Jones

1987
Pick
3	Glen Wesley
14	Stephane Quintal
56	Todd Lalonde
67	Darwin McPherson
77	Matt DelGuidice
98	Ted Donato
119	Matt Glennon
140	Rob Cheevers
161	Chris Winnes
182	Paul Ohman
203	Casey Jones
224	Eric Lemarque
245	Sean Gorman

1986
Pick
13	Craig Janney
34	Pekka Tirkkonen
76	Dean Hall
97	Matt Pesklewis
118	Garth Premak
139	Paul Beraldo
160	Brian Ferreira
181	Jeff Flaherty
202	Greg Hawgood
223	Steffan Malmqvist
244	Joel Gardner

President and General Manager

SINDEN, HARRY
President and General Manager, Boston Bruins.
Born in Collins Bay, Ont., September 14, 1932.

Harry Sinden enters his 12th season as the Bruins' president and his 29th season as the club's general manager.

Sinden's name has been synonymous with the Bruins organization for over 38 years. He has been instrumental in bringing a Stanley Cup, six Conference titles and 10 Division championships to Boston. On October 17, 1995 with a 7-4 Boston win at St. Louis, he became the first general manager in the history of the NHL to record 1,000 victories as a g.m.

His many accomplishments, in addition to his knowledge and experience, led to his 1983 induction into the Hockey Hall of Fame in the Builder's category as he became the 23rd Bruin enshrined.

Sinden was a top amateur player in Canada as a defenseman who captained his Whitby Dunlops team to both the 1957 Allan Cup as Canada's Senior Amateur Champions and the 1958 World Championship title. He also competed in the 1960 Olympics in Squaw Valley, bringing a silver medal home to Canada.

He came to the Bruins organization in 1961 when he assumed the position of player-coach in Kingston, Ontario. After coaching Boston's minor league affiliate in Minneapolis, he became a player-coach in Oklahoma City and led that team to the 1966 CHL championship with eight consecutive playoff victories. He moved to Boston to assume the Bruins head coaching reins in 1966-67.

In 1972 he served as coach of Team Canada in the classic series between NHL players and the Soviet Union.

Sinden and his wife, Eleanor, reside in Winchester, MA. They have four daughters.

NHL Coaching Record

		Regular Season					Playoffs			
Season	Team	Games	W	L	T	%	Games	W	L	%
1966-67	Boston	70	17	43	10	.314	....	....	....	....
1967-68	Boston	74	37	27	10	.608	4	0	4	.000
1968-69	Boston	76	42	18	16	.658	10	6	4	.600
1969-70	Boston	76	40	17	19	.651	14	12	2	.857*
1979-80	Boston	7	6	1	0	.857	10	4	6	.400
1984-85	Boston	24	11	10	3	.521	5	2	3	.400
	NHL Totals	**327**	**153**	**116**	**58**	**.557**	**43**	**24**	**19**	**.558**

* Stanley Cup win.

Club Directory

FleetCenter

Boston Bruins
FleetCenter
One FleetCenter, Suite 250
Boston, Massachusetts 02114
Phone **617/624-1900**
FAX 617/523-7184
www.bostonbruins.com
Capacity: 17,565

Executive
Owner and Governor	Jeremy M. Jacobs
Alternate Governor	Louis Jacobs
President, General Manager and Alternate Governor	Harry Sinden
Vice President of Hockey Operations and Assistant General Manager	Mike O'Connell
Executive Vice President	Richard Krezwick
Senior Assistant to the President	Nate Greenberg
Assistant to the Vice President of Hockey Operations	Jeff Gorton
General Counsel	Michael Wall
Director of Administration	Dale Hamilton
Assistant to the President	Joe Curnane
Team Travel Coordinator/Administrative Assistant	Carol Gould
Receptionist	Karen Ondo

Coaching Staff
Coach	Pat Burns
Assistant Coaches	Jacques Laperriere, Peter Laviolette
Goaltending Consultant	Brian Daccord
Coach, Providence Bruins	Bill Armstrong
Coach, Greenville Grrrowl	John Marks

Scouting Staff
Director of Scouting	Scott Bradley
Director of Development	Bob Tindall
Scouting Information/Video Coordinator	Nickolai Bobrov
Scouting Staff	Don Saatzer, Jean Ratelle, Daniel Dore, Don Matheson, David McNamara, Svenake Svensson, Yuri Karmanov, Gerry Cheevers, Jim Morrison, Tom McVie, Tom Songin

Communications & Marketing Staff
Director of Media Relations	Heidi Holland
Media Relations Assistant	Mark Awdycki
Director of Marketing and Community Relations	Sue Byrne
Promotions Manager	Dave Murray
Community Relations Coordinator	Heather Wright
Game Presentation and Marketing Coordinator	Mike Burns
Director of Alumni Community Relations	John Bucyk
Administrative Assistant, Alumni Office	Mal Viola

Medical and Training Staff
Athletic Trainer	Don Del Negro
Physical Therapist	Scott Waugh
Equipment Manager	Peter Henderson
Assistant Equipment Managers	Chris "Muggsy" Aldrich, Keith Robinson
Team Physicians	Dr. Bertram Zarins, Dr. Ashby Moncure, Dr. James Dineen, Dr. Tom Gill, Dr. Arthur Boland
Team Dentists	Dr. Edwin Riley, DMD; Dr. Bruce Donoff, DMD, MD; Dr. Robert Amato, DMD
Team Opthalmic Consultant	Dr. Bradford Shingleton
Team Psychologist	Dr. Fred Neff

Ticketing and Finance Staff
Director of Ticket Operations	Matt Brennan
Assistant Director of Ticket Operations	Jim Foley
Ticket Office Receptionist	Jo-Ann Connolly-White
Controller	Richard McGlinchey
Payroll Manager	Barbara Johnson
Accounts Payable	Linda Bartlett

Television and Radio
Broadcasters	(Television) Dale Arnold & Dave Shea (play-by-play), Gord Kluzak, Andy Brickley & Gerry Cheevers (color) (Radio) Dave Goucher and Bob Beers
TV Channels	New England Sports Network (NESN) and UPN38 WSBK-TV
Radio Station	WBZ (1030 AM) and Bruins Radio Network

General Managers' History

Art Ross, 1924-25 to 1953-54; Lynn Patrick, 1954-55 to 1964-65; Hap Emms, 1965-66, 1966-67; Milt Schmidt, 1967-68 to 1971-72; Harry Sinden, 1972-73 to date.

Captains' History

No captain, 1924-25 to 1926-27; Lionel Hitchman, 1927-28 to 1930-31; George Owen, 1931-32; Dit Clapper, 1932-33 to 1937-38; Cooney Weiland, 1938-39; Dit Clapper, 1939-40 to 1945-46; Dit Clapper and John Crawford, 1946-47; John Crawford 1947-48 to 1949-50; Milt Schmidt, 1950-51 to 1953-54; Milt Schmidt, Ed Sanford, 1954-55; Fern Flaman, 1955-56 to 1960-61; Don McKenney, 1961-62, 1962-63; Leo Boivin, 1963-64 to 1965-66; John Bucyk, 1966-67; no captain, 1967-68 to 1972-73; John Bucyk, 1973-74 to 1976-77; Wayne Cashman, 1977-78 to 1982-83; Terry O'Reilly, 1983-84, 1984-85; Ray Bourque, Rick Middleton (co-captains) 1985-86 to 1987-88; Ray Bourque, 1988-89 to 1999-2000.

Buffalo Sabres

1999-2000 Results: 35w-36L-11T 85PTS. Third, Northeast Division

A gritty two-way player, Michael Peca rebounded from a slow start in 1999-2000 to reach the 20-goal plateau for the third time in his five years in Buffalo. Peca has been captain of the Sabres since 1998.

2000-01 Schedule

Oct.	Thu.	5	Chicago
	Sat.	7	Los Angeles
	Fri.	13	at Edmonton
	Sat.	14	at Vancouver
	Tue.	17	at Montreal
	Fri.	20	Anaheim
	Sat.	21	at Detroit
	Wed.	25	Carolina
	Fri.	27	Toronto
	Sat.	28	at Chicago
Nov.	Fri.	3	Montreal
	Sat.	4	at Philadelphia
	Thu.	9	NY Islanders
	Sat.	11	at New Jersey
	Mon.	13	Calgary
	Wed.	15	Dallas
	Fri.	17	Minnesota
	Sat.	18	at St. Louis
	Wed.	22	Philadelphia
	Fri.	24	NY Rangers
	Sat.	25	at Montreal
	Tue.	28	at Ottawa
Dec.	Fri.	1	Pittsburgh
	Sat.	2	at Pittsburgh
	Tue.	5	at Montreal
	Wed.	6	New Jersey
	Fri.	8	at NY Rangers
	Tue.	12	at Boston
	Fri.	15	at Carolina
	Sat.	16	Florida
	Wed.	20	at Washington
	Thu.	21	Washington
	Sat.	23	San Jose*
	Tue.	26	Pittsburgh
	Fri.	29	Ottawa
	Sat.	30	at NY Islanders
Jan.	Mon.	1	Boston*
	Wed.	3	at Toronto
	Fri.	5	Toronto
	Sat.	6	at Nashville
	Tue.	9	at San Jose

	Thu.	11	at Los Angeles
	Fri.	12	at Anaheim
	Tue.	16	Tampa Bay
	Fri.	19	Florida
	Sat.	20	at Toronto
	Tue.	23	Columbus
	Fri.	26	Boston
	Sat.	27	at NY Islanders
	Wed.	31	at Florida
Feb.	Thu.	1	at Tampa Bay
	Tue.	6	at NY Rangers
	Wed.	7	NY Islanders
	Sat.	10	at Ottawa
	Sun.	11	Montreal
	Tue.	13	at Atlanta
	Thu.	15	Atlanta
	Sat.	17	New Jersey
	Mon.	19	Ottawa
	Thu.	22	at New Jersey
	Fri.	23	Phoenix
	Sun.	25	Tampa Bay*
	Tue.	27	at Ottawa
Mar.	Thu.	1	at Philadelphia
	Sat.	3	at Colorado*
	Sun.	4	at Dallas*
	Tue.	6	at Boston
	Fri.	9	Edmonton
	Wed.	14	NY Rangers
	Fri.	16	Vancouver
	Sat.	17	at Washington
	Tue.	20	Toronto
	Wed.	21	at Carolina
	Sat.	24	Carolina
	Mon.	26	at Atlanta
	Tue.	27	at Pittsburgh
	Fri.	30	Atlanta
Apr.	Sun.	1	at Tampa Bay
	Mon.	2	at Florida
	Wed.	4	Boston
	Fri.	6	Washington
	Sun.	8	Philadelphia*

* Denotes afternoon game.

Franchise date: May 22, 1970

EASTERN NHL CONFERENCE

NORTHEAST DIVISION

31st NHL Season

Year-by-Year Record

Season	GP	Home W	L	T	Road W	L	T	Overall W	L	T	GF	GA	Pts.	Finished		Playoff Result
1999-2000	82	21	15	5	14	21	6	35	36	11	213	204	85	3rd,	Northeast Div.	Lost Conf. Quarter-Final
1998-99	82	23	12	6	14	16	11	37	28	17	207	175	91	4th,	Northeast Div.	Lost Final
1997-98	82	20	13	8	16	16	9	36	29	17	211	187	89	3rd,	Northeast Div.	Lost Conf. Final
1996-97	82	24	11	6	16	19	6	40	30	12	237	208	92	1st,	Northeast Div.	Lost Conf. Semi-Final
1995-96	82	19	17	5	14	25	2	33	42	7	247	262	73	5th,	Northeast Div.	Out of Playoffs
1994-95	48	15	8	1	7	11	6	22	19	7	130	119	51	4th,	Northeast Div.	Lost Conf. Quarter-Final
1993-94	84	22	17	3	21	15	6	43	32	9	282	218	95	4th,	Northeast Div.	Lost Conf. Quarter-Final
1992-93	84	25	15	2	13	21	8	38	36	10	335	297	86	4th,	Adams Div.	Lost Div. Final
1991-92	80	22	13	5	9	24	7	31	37	12	289	299	74	3rd,	Adams Div.	Lost Div. Semi-Final
1990-91	80	15	13	12	16	17	7	31	30	19	292	278	81	3rd,	Adams Div.	Lost Div. Semi-Final
1989-90	80	27	11	2	18	16	6	45	27	8	286	248	98	2nd,	Adams Div.	Lost Div. Semi-Final
1988-89	80	25	12	3	13	23	4	38	35	7	291	299	83	3rd,	Adams Div.	Lost Div. Semi-Final
1987-88	80	19	14	7	18	18	4	37	32	11	283	305	85	3rd,	Adams Div.	Lost Div. Semi-Final
1986-87	80	18	18	4	10	26	4	28	44	8	280	308	64	5th,	Adams Div.	Out of Playoffs
1985-86	80	23	16	1	14	21	5	37	37	6	296	291	80	5th,	Adams Div.	Out of Playoffs
1984-85	80	23	10	4	15	18	7	38	28	14	290	237	90	3rd,	Adams Div.	Lost Div. Semi-Final
1983-84	80	25	9	6	23	16	1	48	25	7	315	257	103	2nd,	Adams Div.	Lost Div. Semi-Final
1982-83	80	25	7	8	13	22	5	38	29	13	318	285	89	3rd,	Adams Div.	Lost Div. Final
1981-82	80	23	8	9	16	18	6	39	26	15	307	273	93	3rd,	Adams Div.	Lost Div. Semi-Final
1980-81	80	21	7	12	18	13	9	39	20	21	327	250	99	1st,	Adams Div.	Lost Quarter-Final
1979-80	80	27	5	8	20	12	8	47	17	16	318	201	110	1st,	Adams Div.	Lost Semi-Final
1978-79	80	19	13	8	17	15	8	36	28	16	280	263	88	2nd,	Adams Div.	Lost Prelim. Round
1977-78	80	25	7	8	19	12	9	44	19	17	288	215	105	2nd,	Adams Div.	Lost Quarter-Final
1976-77	80	27	8	5	21	16	3	48	24	8	301	220	104	2nd,	Adams Div.	Lost Quarter-Final
1975-76	80	28	7	5	18	14	8	46	21	13	339	240	105	2nd,	Adams Div.	Lost Quarter-Final
1974-75	80	28	6	6	21	10	9	49	16	15	354	240	113	1st,	Adams Div.	Lost Final
1973-74	78	23	10	6	9	24	6	32	34	12	242	250	76	5th,	East Div.	Out of Playoffs
1972-73	78	30	6	3	7	21	11	37	27	14	257	219	88	4th,	East Div.	Lost Quarter-Final
1971-72	78	11	19	9	5	24	10	16	43	19	203	289	51	6th,	East Div.	Out of Playoffs
1970-71	78	16	13	10	8	26	5	24	39	15	217	291	63	5th,	East Div.	Out of Playoffs

2000-01 Player Personnel

FORWARDS	HT	WT	S	Place of Birth	Date	1999-00 Club
ADDUONO, Jeremy	6-0	183	R	Thunder Bay, Ont.	8/4/78	Rochester
AFINOGENOV, Maxim	6-0	195	L	Moscow, USSR	9/4/79	Buffalo-Rochester
ANDREYCHUK, Dave	6-4	220	R	Hamilton, Ont.	9/29/63	Boston-Colorado
BARNES, Stu	5-11	180	R	Spruce Grove, Alta.	12/25/70	Buffalo
BARTOVIC, Milan	6-0	194	L	Trencin, Czech.	4/9/81	Tri-City-Brandon
BOULTON, Eric	6-1	215	L	Halifax, N.S.	8/17/76	Rochester
BROWN, Curtis	6-0	196	L	Unity, Sask.	2/12/76	Buffalo
BRUNEL, Craig	6-0	200	R	Winnipeg, Man.	11/12/79	Prince Albert-Red Deer Rebels
DUMONT, Jean-Pierre	6-2	202	L	Montreal, Que.	4/1/78	Chicago-Cleveland-Rochester
GILMOUR, Doug	5-11	180	L	Kingston, Ont.	6/25/63	Chicago-Buffalo
GRATTON, Chris	6-4	226	L	Brantford, Ont.	7/5/75	Tampa Bay-Buffalo
HAMEL, Denis	6-2	200	L	Lachute, Que.	5/10/77	Buffalo-Rochester
HEISTEN, Barrett	6-1	189	L	Anchorage, AK	3/19/80	University of Maine
METHOT, Francois	6-0	184	R	Montreal, Que.	4/26/78	Rochester
MILLEY, Norman	6-0	200	R	Toronto, Ont.	2/14/80	Sudbury Wolves
PECA, Michael	5-11	190	R	Toronto, Ont.	3/26/74	Buffalo
PETERS, Andrew	6-4	213	L	St. Catharines, Ont.	5/5/80	Kitchener
PRESTON, Tim	6-1	190	L	Vancouver, B.C.	6/30/81	Seattle T-Birds
RASMUSSEN, Erik	6-3	208	L	Minneapolis, MN	3/28/77	Buffalo
RAY, Rob	6-0	216	L	Stirling, Ont.	6/8/68	Buffalo
SATAN, Miroslav	6-3	192	L	Topolcany, Czech.	10/22/74	Dukla Trencin-Buffalo
TAYLOR, Chris	6-2	195	L	Stratford, Ont.	3/6/72	Buffalo-Rochester
VAN OENE, Darren	6-4	216	L	Edmonton, Alta.	1/18/78	Rochester
VARADA, Vaclav	6-0	214	L	Vsetin, Czech.	4/26/76	HC Vitkovice-Buffalo
ZIGOMANIS, Michael	6-1	189	R	North York, Ont.	1/17/81	Kingston
DEFENSEMEN						
CAMPBELL, Brian	6-0	190	L	Strathroy, Ont.	5/23/79	Buffalo-Rochester
HOLLAND, Jason	6-3	209	R	Morinville, Alta.	4/30/76	Buffalo-Rochester
HOUDA, Doug	6-2	209	R	Blairmore, Alta.	6/3/66	Buffalo-Rochester
HURLBUT, Mike	6-2	206	L	Massena, NY	10/7/66	Buffalo-Rochester
KALININ, Dmitri	6-2	206	L	Chelyabinsk, USSR	7/22/80	Buffalo-Rochester
KINCH, Matthew	6-0	195	L	Red Deer, Alta.	2/17/80	Calgary Hitmen
McKEE, Jay	6-4	201	L	Kingston, Ont.	9/8/77	Buffalo
PATRICK, James	6-3	201	R	Winnipeg, Man.	6/14/63	Buffalo
SMEHLIK, Richard	6-4	222	L	Ostrava, Czech.	1/23/70	Buffalo
WARRENER, Rhett	6-1	206	R	Shaunavon, Sask.	1/27/76	Buffalo
WOOLLEY, Jason	6-0	200	L	Toronto, Ont.	7/27/69	Buffalo
ZHITNIK, Alexei	5-11	215	L	Kiev, USSR	10/10/72	Buffalo
GOALTENDERS	**HT**	**WT**	**C**	**Place of Birth**	**Date**	**1999-00 Club**
BIRON, Martin	6-2	163	L	Lac St-Charles, Que.	8/15/77	Buffalo-Rochester
HASEK, Dominik	5-11	180	L	Pardubice, Czech.	1/29/65	Buffalo
NORONEN, Mika	6-1	206	L	Tampere, Finland	6/17/79	Rochester

Coaching History

Punch Imlach, 1970-71; Punch Imlach, Floyd Smith and Joe Crozier, 1971-72; Joe Crozier, 1972-73, 1973-74; Floyd Smith, 1974-75 to 1976-77; Marcel Pronovost, 1977-78; Marcel Pronovost and Billy Inglis, 1978-79; Scotty Bowman, 1979-80; Roger Neilson, 1980-81; Jim Roberts and Scotty Bowman, 1981-82; Scotty Bowman 1982-83 to 1984-85; Jim Schoenfeld and Scotty Bowman, 1985-86; Scotty Bowman, Craig Ramsay and Ted Sator, 1986-87; Ted Sator, 1987-88, 1988-89; Rick Dudley, 1989-90, 1990-91; Rick Dudley and John Muckler, 1991-92; John Muckler, 1992-93 to 1994-95; Ted Nolan, 1995-96, 1996-97; Lindy Ruff, 1997-98 to date.

Head Coach

RUFF, LINDY

Head Coach, Buffalo Sabres. Born in Warburg, Alta., February, 17, 1960.

A former captain of the Sabres, Lindy Ruff was appointed as the club's 15th head coach on July 21, 1997. In 1999, he led the Sabres to the Stanley Cup Finals for just the second time in club history. As a player, Ruff was drafted 32nd overall by the Sabres in the 1979 Entry Draft. He played both defense and left wing in an NHL career that spanned 12 seasons including 608 regular-season games with Buffalo. He became a playing assistant coach with Rochester of the AHL in 1991-92 and San Diego of the IHL in 1992-93. Ruff's San Diego club set a pro hockey record with 62 wins. In 1993-94 he became an NHL assistant coach with the Florida Panthers.

Ruff and his wife Gaye have four children.

Coaching Record

		Regular Season					Playoffs			
Season	Team	Games	W	L	T	%	Games	W	L	%
1997-98	Buffalo (NHL)	82	36	29	17	.543	15	10	5	.667
1998-99	Buffalo (NHL)	82	37	28	17	.555	21	14	7	.667
1999-2000	Buffalo (NHL)	82	35	36	11	.518•	5	1	4	.200
	NHL Totals	246	108	93	45	.539•	41	25	16	.610

• Includes points from regulation ties

1999-2000 Scoring

* – rookie

Regular Season

Pos	#	Player	Team	GP	G	A	Pts	+/–	PIM	PP	SH	GW	GT	S	%
C	93	Doug Gilmour	CHI	63	22	34	56	–12	51	8	0	3	1	100	22.0
			BUF	11	3	14	17	3	12	2	0	0	0	13	23.1
			TOTAL	74	25	48	73	–9	63	10	0	3	1	113	22.1
L	81	Miroslav Satan	BUF	81	33	34	67	16	32	5	3	5	1	265	12.5
C	37	Curtis Brown	BUF	74	22	29	51	19	42	5	0	4	1	149	14.8
C	77	Chris Gratton	T.B	58	14	27	41	–24	121	4	0	1	1	168	8.3
			BUF	14	1	7	8	1	15	0	0	0	0	34	2.9
			TOTAL	72	15	34	49	–23	136	4	0	1	1	202	7.4
C	41	Stu Barnes	BUF	82	20	25	45	–3	16	8	2	2	0	137	14.6
C	27	Michael Peca	BUF	73	20	21	41	6	67	2	0	3	0	144	13.9
R	25	Vaclav Varada	BUF	76	10	27	37	12	62	0	0	0	0	140	7.1
R	61	* Maxim Afinogenov	BUF	65	16	18	34	–4	41	2	0	2	0	128	12.5
D	5	Jason Woolley	BUF	74	8	25	33	14	52	2	0	2	0	113	7.1
L	29	Vladimir Tsyplakov	L.A	29	6	7	13	6	4	1	0	1	0	30	20.0
			BUF	34	6	13	19	17	10	0	0	1	0	46	13.0
			TOTAL	63	12	20	32	23	14	1	0	2	0	76	15.8
L	8	Geoff Sanderson	BUF	67	13	13	26	4	22	4	0	3	0	136	9.6
R	15	Dixon Ward	BUF	71	11	9	20	1	41	1	2	2	0	101	10.9
D	74	Jay McKee	BUF	78	5	12	17	5	50	1	0	1	0	84	6.0
C	9	Erik Rasmussen	BUF	67	8	6	14	1	43	0	0	2	0	76	10.5
D	3	James Patrick	BUF	66	5	8	13	8	22	0	0	3	0	40	12.5
D	44	Alexei Zhitnik	BUF	74	2	11	13	–6	95	1	0	0	0	139	1.4
D	42	Richard Smehlik	BUF	64	2	9	11	13	50	0	0	0	0	67	3.0
D	51	* Brian Campbell	BUF	12	1	4	5	–2	4	0	0	0	0	10	10.0
R	32	Rob Ray	BUF	69	1	3	4	0	158	0	0	0	0	17	5.9
D	4	Rhett Warrener	BUF	61	0	3	3	18	89	0	0	0	0	68	0.0
C	16	Chris Taylor	BUF	11	1	1	2	–2	2	0	0	0	0	15	6.7
L	55	* Denis Hamel	BUF	3	1	0	1	–1	0	0	0	0	0	3	33.3
C	12	* Domenic Pittis	BUF	7	1	0	1	1	6	0	0	0	0	6	16.7
D	20	* Jason Holland	BUF	9	0	1	1	0	0	0	0	0	0	8	0.0
G	39	Dominik Hasek	BUF	35	0	1	1	0	12	0	0	0	0	0	0.0
D	20	Doug Houda	BUF	1	0	0	0	0	12	0	0	0	0	0	0.0
D	21	Mike Hurlbut	BUF	1	0	0	0	1	2	0	0	0	0	1	0.0
L	64	David Moravec	BUF	1	0	0	0	–1	0	0	0	0	0	2	0.0
D	45	* Dimitri Kalinin	BUF	4	0	0	0	0	4	0	0	0	0	3	0.0
L	24	Paul Kruse	BUF	11	0	0	0	–2	43	0	0	0	0	7	0.0
D	34	* Jean-Luc Grand-Pierre	BUF	11	0	0	0	–1	15	0	0	0	0	10	0.0
G	30	Dwayne Roloson	BUF	14	0	0	0	0	0	0	0	0	0	0	0.0
G	43	* Martin Biron	BUF	41	0	0	0	0	6	0	0	0	0	0	0.0

Goaltending

No.	Goaltender	GPI	Mins	Avg	W	L	T	EN	SO	GA	SA	S%
39	Dominik Hasek	35	2066	2.21	15	11	6	2	3	76	937	.919
43	* Martin Biron	41	2229	2.42	19	18	2	2	5	90	988	.909
30	Dwayne Roloson	14	677	2.84	1	7	3	2	0	32	277	.884
	Totals	**82**	**4996**	**2.45**	**35**	**36**	**11**	**6**	**8**	**204**	**2208**	**.908**

Playoffs

Pos	#	Player	Team	GP	G	A	Pts	+/–	PIM	PP	SH	GW	OT	S	%
L	81	Miroslav Satan	BUF	5	3	2	5	2	0	0	0	0	0	11	27.3
C	37	Curtis Brown	BUF	5	1	3	4	1	6	1	0	0	0	10	10.0
C	41	Stu Barnes	BUF	5	3	0	3	–1	2	2	0	1	1	11	27.3
L	8	Geoff Sanderson	BUF	5	0	2	2	0	8	0	0	0	0	9	0.0
D	5	Jason Woolley	BUF	5	0	2	2	1	2	0	0	0	0	10	0.0
D	42	Richard Smehlik	BUF	5	1	0	1	0	0	0	0	0	0	6	16.7
C	93	Doug Gilmour	BUF	5	0	1	1	–1	0	0	0	0	0	3	0.0
D	3	James Patrick	BUF	5	0	1	1	1	2	0	0	0	0	3	0.0
R	15	Dixon Ward	BUF	5	0	1	1	1	2	0	0	0	0	4	0.0
C	27	Michael Peca	BUF	5	0	1	1	–1	4	0	0	0	0	7	0.0
C	77	Chris Gratton	BUF	5	0	1	1	–1	4	0	0	0	0	4	0.0
L	29	Vladimir Tsyplakov	BUF	5	0	1	1	1	4	0	0	0	0	4	0.0
R	61	* Maxim Afinogenov	BUF	5	0	1	1	–2	2	0	0	0	0	9	0.0
D	20	* Jason Holland	BUF	1	0	0	0	0	0	0	0	0	0	1	0.0
D	74	Jay Mckee	BUF	1	0	0	0	0	0	0	0	0	0	0	0.0
C	16	Chris Taylor	BUF	2	0	0	0	–1	2	0	0	0	0	2	0.0
C	9	Erik Rasmussen	BUF	3	0	0	0	0	4	0	0	0	0	5	0.0
D	44	Alexei Zhitnik	BUF	4	0	0	0	–1	8	0	0	0	0	4	0.0
D	34	* Jean-Luc Grand-Pierre	BUF	4	0	0	0	0	4	0	0	0	0	5	0.0
G	39	Dominik Hasek	BUF	5	0	0	0	0	2	0	0	0	0	0	0.0
D	4	Rhett Warrener	BUF	5	0	0	0	–1	2	0	0	0	0	8	0.0
R	25	Vaclav Varada	BUF	5	0	0	0	1	8	0	0	0	0	8	0.0

Goaltending

No.	Goaltender	GPI	Mins	Avg	W	L	EN	SO	GA	SA	S%
39	Dominik Hasek	5	301	2.39	1	4	2	0	12	147	.918
	Totals	**5**	**305**	**2.75**	**1**	**4**	**2**	**0**	**14**	**149**	**.906**

Captains' History

Floyd Smith, 1970-71; Gerry Meehan, 1971-72 to 1973-74; Gerry Meehan and Jim Schoenfeld, 1974-75; Jim Schoenfeld, 1975-76, 1976-77; Danny Gare, 1977-78 to 1980-81; Danny Gare and Gilbert Perreault, 1981-82; Gilbert Perreault, 1982-83 to 1985-86; Gilbert Perreault and Lindy Ruff, 1986-87; Lindy Ruff, 1987-88; Lindy Ruff and Mike Foligno, 1988-89; Mike Foligno, 1989-90; Mike Foligno and Mike Ramsey, 1990-91; Mike Ramsey, 1991-92; Mike Ramsey and Pat LaFontaine, 1992-93; Pat LaFontaine and Alexander Mogilny, 1993-94; Pat LaFontaine, 1994-95 to 1996-97; Donald Audette and Michael Peca, 1997-98; Michael Peca, 1998-99 to date.

Club Records

Team

(Figures in brackets for season records are games played; records for fewest points, wins, ties, losses, goals, goals against are for 70 or more games)

Most Points	113	1974-75 (80)
Most Wins	49	1974-75 (80)
Most Ties	21	1980-81 (80)
Most Losses	44	1986-87 (80)
Most Goals	354	1974-75 (80)
Most Goals Against	308	1986-87 (80)
Fewest Points	51	1971-72 (78)
Fewest Wins	16	1971-72 (78)
Fewest Ties	6	1985-86 (80)
Fewest Losses	16	1974-75 (80)
Fewest Goals	203	1971-72 (78)
Fewest Goals Against	175	1998-99 (82)

Longest Winning Streak

Overall	10	Jan. 4-23/84
Home	12	Nov. 12/72-Jan. 7/73, Oct. 13-Dec. 10/89
Away	10	Dec. 10/83-Jan. 23/84

Longest Undefeated Streak

Overall	14	Mar. 6-Apr. 6/80 (8 wins, 6 ties)
Home	21	Oct. 8/72-Jan. 7/73 (18 wins, 3 ties)
Away	10	Dec. 10/83-Jan. 23/84 (10 wins)

Longest Losing Streak

Overall	7	Oct. 25-Nov. 8/70, Apr. 3-15/93, Oct. 9-22/93
Home	6	Oct. 10-Nov. 10/93, Mar. 3-Apr. 3/96
Away	7	Oct. 14-Nov. 7/70, Feb. 6-27/71, Jan. 10-Feb. 3/96

Longest Winless Streak

Overall	12	Nov. 23-Dec. 20/91 (8 losses, 4 ties)
Home	12	Jan. 27-Mar. 10/91 (7 losses, 5 ties)
Away	23	Oct. 30/71-Feb. 19/72 (15 losses, 8 ties)

Most Shutouts, Season	13	1997-98 (82)
Most PIM, Season	2,713	1991-92 (80)
Most Goals, Game	14	Jan. 21/75 (Wsh. 2 at Buf. 14), Mar. 19/81 (Tor. 4 at Buf. 14)

Individual

Most Seasons	17	Gilbert Perreault
Most Games	1,191	Gilbert Perreault
Most Goals, Career	512	Gilbert Perreault
Most Assists, Career	814	Gilbert Perreault
Most Points, Career	1,326	Gilbert Perreault (512G, 814A)
Most PIM, Career	2,687	Rob Ray
Most Shutouts, Career	44	Dominik Hasek

Longest Consecutive Games Streak	776	Craig Ramsay (Mar. 27/73-Feb. 10/83)
Most Goals, Season	76	Alexander Mogilny (1992-93)
Most Assists, Season	95	Pat LaFontaine (1992-93)
Most Points, Season	148	Pat LaFontaine (1992-93; 53G, 95A)
Most PIM, Season	354	Rob Ray (1991-92)
Most Points, Defenseman, Season	81	Phil Housley (1989-90; 21G, 60A)
Most Points, Center, Season	148	Pat LaFontaine (1992-93; 53G, 95A)

Most Points, Right Wing, Season	127	Alexander Mogilny (1992-93; 76G, 51A)
Most Points, Left Wing, Season	95	Rick Martin (1974-75; 52G, 43A)
Most Points, Rookie, Season	74	Rick Martin (1971-72; 44G, 30A)
Most Shutouts, Season	13	Dominik Hasek (1997-98)
Most Goals, Game	5	Dave Andreychuk (Feb. 6/86)
Most Assists, Game	5	Gilbert Perreault (Feb. 1/76, Mar. 9/80, Jan. 4/84), Dale Hawerchuk (Jan. 15/92), Pat LaFontaine (Dec. 31/92, Feb. 10/93)
Most Points, Game	7	Gilbert Perreault (Feb. 1/76; 2G, 5A)

Retired Numbers

2	Tim Horton	1972-1974
7	Rick Martin	1971-1981
11	Gilbert Perreault	1970-1987
14	Rene Robert	1971-1979

All-time Record vs. Other Clubs

Regular Season

			At Home							On Road							Total				
	GP	W	L	T	GF	GA	PTS	GP	W	L	T	GF	GA	PTS	GP	W	L	T	GF	GA	PTS
Anaheim	6	2	2		14	16	6	6	4	2	0	18	12	8	12	6	4	2	32	28	14
Atlanta	2	1	1	0	8	8	2	2	1	0	1	9	5	3	4	2	1	1	17	13	5
Boston	97	50	32	15	360	290	115	97	29	55	13	286	369	71	194	79	87	28	646	659	186
Calgary	43	25	13	5	181	127	55	43	17	15	11	143	146	45	86	42	28	16	324	273	100
Carolina	69	40	22	7	279	210	87	70	32	28	10	213	210	74	139	72	50	17	492	420	161
Chicago	50	31	13	6	189	129	68	48	16	26	6	133	158	38	98	47	39	12	322	287	106
Colorado	61	35	17	9	242	197	79	61	20	30	11	189	221	51	122	55	47	20	431	418	130
Dallas	49	26	13	10	177	131	62	51	21	24	6	152	162	48	100	47	37	16	329	293	110
Detroit	50	32	10	8	219	145	72	52	18	29	5	151	190	41	102	50	39	13	370	335	113
Edmonton	28	10	11	7	109	105	27	26	5	19	2	70	112	12	54	15	30	9	179	217	39
Florida	15	10	4	1	50	24	22	13	6	7	0	40	38	12	28	16	10	2	90	62	34
Los Angeles	50	26	15	9	203	147	61	51	22	20	9	178	177	53	101	48	35	18	381	324	114
Montreal	92	46	27	19	287	249	111	92	28	52	12	274	361	68	184	74	79	31	561	610	179
Nashville	2	0	2	0	5	8	0	2	2	0	0	5	2	4	4	2	2	0	10	10	4
New Jersey	46	28	13	5	192	148	61	46	24	13	9	163	135	57	92	52	26	14	355	283	118
NY Islanders	53	29	16	8	184	147	66	53	21	23	9	148	156	51	106	50	39	17	332	303	117
NY Rangers	60	35	17	8	253	189	78	58	19	24	15	155	189	53	118	54	41	23	408	378	131
Ottawa	21	14	5	2	71	29	30	22	11	5	6	66	48	28	43	25	10	8	137	77	58
Philadelphia	55	27	21	7	188	163	61	59	13	34	12	153	212	39	114	40	55	19	341	375	100
Phoenix	27	20	2	5	118	64	45	27	12	13	2	88	86	26	54	32	15	7	206	150	71
Pittsburgh	63	32	15	16	256	169	81	63	16	31	16	201	239	48	126	48	46	32	457	408	129
St. Louis	49	29	14	6	195	151	64	47	14	26	7	122	170	35	96	43	40	13	317	321	99
San Jose	8	8	0	0	41	23	16	8	1	4	3	30	32	6	16	9	4	3	71	55	22
Tampa Bay	15	8	6	1	39	45	17	15	11	3	1	50	31	23	30	19	9	2	89	76	40
Toronto	58	37	17	4	244	159	78	57	25	23	9	205	178	60	115	62	40	13	449	337	138
Vancouver	49	24	17	8	177	144	56	49	16	23	10	160	182	42	98	40	40	18	337	326	98
Washington	48	31	11	6	192	127	68	48	27	13	8	169	124	62	96	58	24	14	361	251	130
Defunct Clubs	23	13	5	5	94	63	31	23	12	8	3	97	76	27	46	25	13	8	191	139	58
Totals	**1189**	**669**	**340**	**180**	**4567**	**3407**	**1519**	**1189**	**443**	**550**	**196**	**3668**	**4021**	**1085**	**2378**	**1112**	**890**	**376**	**8235**	**7428**	**2604**

Playoffs

	Series	W	L	GP	W	L	T	GF	GA	Last Mtg.	Round	Result
Boston	7	2	5	39	18	21	0	130	146	1999	CSF	W 4-2
Chicago	2	2	0	9	8	1	0	36	17	1980	QF	W 4-0
Colorado	2	0	2	8	2	6	0	27	35	1985	DSF	L 2-3
Dallas	3	1	2	13	5	8	0	37	39	1999	F	L 2-4
Montreal	7	3	4	35	17	18	0	111	124	1998	CSF	W 4-0
New Jersey	1	0	1	7	3	4	0	14	14	1994	CQF	L 3-4
NY Islanders	3	0	3	16	4	12	0	45	59	1980	SF	L 2-4
NY Rangers	1	1	0	3	2	1	0	6	9	1978	PR	W 2-1
Ottawa	2	2	0	11	8	3	0	26	19	1999	CQF	W 4-0
Philadelphia	6	1	5	31	10	21	0	75	97	2000	CQF	L 1-4
Pittsburgh	1	0	1	2	0	2	0	9	9	1979	PR	L 1-2
St. Louis	1	1	0	3	2	1	0	7	8	1976	PR	W 2-1
Toronto	1	1	0	5	4	1	0	21	16	1999	CF	W 4-1
Vancouver	2	2	0	7	6	1	0	28	14	1981	PR	W 3-0
Washington	1	0	1	6	2	4	0	11	13	1998	CF	L 2-4
Totals	**40**	**16**	**24**	**196**	**92**	**104**	**0**	**588**	**609**			

Playoff Results 2000-1996

Year	Round	Opponent	Result	GF	GA
2000	CQF	Philadelphia	L 1-4	8	14
1999	F	Dallas	L 2-4	9	13
	CF	Toronto	W 4-1	21	16
	CSF	Boston	W 4-2	17	14
	CQF	Ottawa	W 4-0	12	6
1998	CF	Washington	L 2-4	11	13
	CSF	Montreal	W 4-0	17	10
	CQF	Philadelphia	W 4-1	18	9
1997	CSF	Philadelphia	L 1-4	13	21
	CQF	Ottawa	W 4-3	14	13

Abbreviations: Round: F – final; **CF** – conference final; **CSF** – conference semi-final; **CQF** – conference quarter-final; **DSF** – division semi-final; **SF** – semi-final; **QF** – quarter-final; **PR** – preliminary round.

Calgary totals include Atlanta Flames, 1972-73 to 1979-80.
Colorado totals include Quebec, 1979-80 to 1994-95.
New Jersey totals include Kansas City, 1974-75 to 1975-76, and Colorado Rockies, 1976-77 to 1981-82.
Phoenix totals include Winnipeg, 1979-80 to 1995-96.
Carolina totals include Hartford, 1979-80 to 1996-97.
Dallas totals include Minnesota North Stars, 1970-71 to 1992-93.

1999-2000 Results

Oct.	2	at Detroit	0-2		8	at Ottawa	7-4
	8	Washington	2-3		13	at Boston	0-0
	9	at Atlanta	5-5		14	Montreal	1-2
	11	Phoenix	2-2		17	at Anaheim	5-0
	16	at Montreal	1-2		18	at Los Angeles	3-5
	17	at Philadelphia	2-5		20	at Phoenix	1-2
	20	Nashville	3-4		22	at Carolina	1-4
	22	Carolina	7-3		25	Tampa Bay	2-1
	23	at Ottawa	0-4		28	Ottawa	1-0
	27	Tampa Bay	4-3		29	at Boston	0-1
	29	Florida	3-2 *	Feb.	1	Anaheim	2-2
	30	at Boston	0-3		3	Ottawa	4-2
Nov.	3	at Dallas	3-1		8	at Colorado	2-0
	4	Chicago	5-4 *		10	at Nashville	2-1 *
	6	NY Islanders	2-1		12	at Philadelphia	2-3 *
	10	Boston	6-2		13	Edmonton	3-2
	12	at Tampa Bay	2-4		16	at Pittsburgh	1-1
	13	at Florida	1-3		17	Vancouver	1-2
	16	at Pittsburgh	2-4		19	Los Angeles	4-1
	19	at Atlanta	4-0		21	New Jersey	3-2
	20	Atlanta	4-3		25	NY Rangers	3-6
	24	Washington	5-2		26	at Toronto	2-5
	26	St. Louis	0-2		28	at Florida	5-2
	28	at Tampa Bay	3-2 *	Mar.	1	at NY Rangers	3-3
	30	Pittsburgh	1-4		4	at NY Islanders	2-4
Dec.	2	Philadelphia	2-4		5	at Washington	1-2
	4	NY Rangers	1-1		8	Boston	2-1 *
	6	at Toronto	2-3 *		9	Montreal	2-3
	8	Ottawa	0-0		12	NY Islanders	4-2
	10	Chicago	2-1		15	at San Jose	5-6 *
	14	Philadelphia	3-1		16	at Vancouver	3-6
	17	Florida	2-4		18	at Calgary	5-1
	18	at NY Islanders	2-2		20	Montreal	4-1
	21	at NY Rangers	3-1		23	Calgary	4-2
	23	Colorado	2-1		27	at Carolina	5-1
	27	at New Jersey	3-2		31	Carolina	1-3
	28	Detroit	2-7	Apr.	1	at Montreal	2-0
Jan.	1	Toronto	8-1		3	Toronto	3-2
	3	at Toronto	2-6		6	at New Jersey	5-0
	4	Atlanta	4-5		7	Pittsburgh	1-2 *
	6	New Jersey	3-6		9	at Washington	1-1

* – Overtime

Entry Draft Selections 2000-1986

2000

Pick	
15	Artem Kryukov
48	Gerard Dicaire
111	Ghyslain Rousseau
149	Denis Denisov
213	Vasili Bizyayev
220	Paul Gaustad
258	Sean McMorrow
277	Ryan Courtney

1999

Pick	
20	Barrett Heisten
35	Milan Bartovic
55	Doug Janik
64	Michael Zigomanis
73	Tim Preston
117	Karel Mosovsky
138	Ryan Miller
146	Matthew Kinch
178	Seneque Hyacinthe
206	Bret Dececco
235	Brad Self
263	Craig Brunel

1998

Pick	
18	Dmitri Kalinin
34	Andrew Peters
47	Norman Milley
50	Jaroslav Kristek
77	Mike Pandolfo
137	Aaron Goldade
164	Ales Kotalik
191	Brad Moran
218	David Moravec
249	Edo Terglav

1997

Pick	
21	Mika Noronen
48	Henrik Tallinder
69	Maxim Afinogenov
75	Jeff Martin
101	Luc Theoret
128	Torrey DiRoberto
156	Brian Campbell
184	Jeremy Adduono
212	Kamil Piros
238	Dylan Kemp

1996

Pick	
7	Erik Rasmussen
27	Cory Sarich
33	Darren Van Oene
54	Francois Methot
87	Kurt Walsh
106	Mike Martone
115	Alexei Tezikov
142	Ryan Davis
161	Darren Mortier
222	Scott Buhler

1995

Pick	
14	Jay McKee
16	Martin Biron
42	Mark Dutiaume
68	Mathieu Sunderland
94	Matt Davidson
111	Marian Menhart
119	Kevin Popp
123	Daniel Bienvenue
172	Brian Scott
198	Mike Zanutto
224	Rob Skrlac

1994

Pick	
17	Wayne Primeau
43	Curtis Brown
69	Rumun Ndur
121	Sergei Klimentiev
147	Cal Benazic
168	Steve Plouffe
173	Shane Hnidy
176	Steve Webb
199	Bob Westerby
225	Craig Millar
251	Mark Polak
277	Shayne Wright

1993

Pick	
38	Denis Tsygurov
64	Ethan Philpott
116	Richard Safarik
142	Kevin Pozzo
168	Sergei Petrenko
194	Mike Barrie
220	Barrie Moore
246	Chris Davis
272	Scott Nichol

1992

Pick	
11	David Cooper
35	Jozef Cierny
59	Ondrej Steiner
80	Dean Melanson
83	Matthew Barnaby
107	Markus Ketterer
108	Yuri Khmylev
131	Paul Rushforth
179	Dean Tiltgen
203	Todd Simon
227	Rick Kowalsky
251	Chris Clancy

1991

Pick	
13	Philippe Boucher
35	Jason Dawe
57	Jason Young
72	Peter Ambroziak
101	Steve Shields
123	Sean O'Donnell
124	Brian Holzinger
145	Chris Snell
162	Jiri Kuntos
189	Tony Iob
211	Spencer Meany
233	Mikhail Volkov
255	Michael Smith

1990

Pick	
14	Brad May
82	Brian McCarthy
97	Richard Smehlik
100	Todd Bojcun
103	Brad Pascall
142	Viktor Gordiouk
166	Milan Nedoma
187	Jason Winch
208	Sylvain Naud
229	Kenneth Martin
250	Brad Rubachuk

1989

Pick	
14	Kevin Haller
56	Scott Thomas
77	Doug MacDonald
98	Ken Sutton
107	Bill Pye
119	Mike Barkley
161	Derek Plante
183	Donald Audette
194	Mark Astley
203	John Nelson
224	Todd Henderson
245	Michael Bavis

1988

Pick	
13	Joel Savage
55	Darcy Loewen
76	Keith Carney
89	Alexander Mogilny
97	Rob Ray
106	David Di Vita
118	Mike McLaughlin
139	Mike Griffith
160	Daniel Ruoho
181	Wade Flaherty
223	Thomas Nieman
243	Michael Pohl

1987

Pick	
1	Pierre Turgeon
22	Brad Miller
53	Andrew MacVicar
84	John Bradley
85	David Pergola
106	Chris Marshall
127	Paul Flanagan
148	Sean Dooley
153	Tim Roberts
169	Grant Tkachuk
190	Ian Herbers
211	David Littman
232	Allan MacIsaac

1986

Pick	
5	Shawn Anderson
26	Greg Brown
47	Bob Corkum
56	Kevin Kerr
68	David Baseggio
89	Larry Rooney
110	Miguel Baldris
131	Mike Hartman
152	Francois Guay
173	Shawn Whitham
194	Kenton Rein
215	Tony Arndt

General Managers' History

Punch Imlach, 1970-71 to 1977-78; John Anderson, 1978-79; Scotty Bowman, 1979-80 to 1985-86; Scotty Bowman and Gerry Meehan, 1986-87; Gerry Meehan, 1987-88 to 1992-93; John Muckler, 1993-94 to 1996-97; Darcy Regier, 1997-98 to date.

General Manager

REGIER, DARCY
General Manager, Buffalo Sabres. Born in Swift Current, Sask., Nov. 27, 1957.

Darcy Regier became the sixth general manager of the Buffalo Sabres on June 11, 1997 after a lengthy management apprenticeship in the New York Islanders organization. As a player, Regier played eight pro seasons, including part of the 1977-78 season with the Cleveland Barons and parts of the 1982-83 and 1983-84 campaigns with the New York Islanders.

He began his career as an administrator with the Islanders in 1984-85 and went on to serve in a variety of capacities including director of administration, assistant director of hockey operations, assistant coach and assistant general manager. He also served as an assistant coach with Hartford in 1991-92.

While with the Islanders, Regier benefitted from working with talented managers and coaches including Bill Torrey and Al Arbour. As a minor pro player with Indianapolis of the CHL he became associated with another important influence on his hockey career, current Detroit Red Wing executive Jim Devellano.

Regier and his wife Kathy have three sons, Jonathan, Justin and Jarrett.

Club Directory

HSBC Arena

Buffalo Sabres
HSBC Arena
One Seymour H. Knox III Plaza
Buffalo, NY 14203
Phone **716/855-4100**
Fax 716/855-4110
Ticket Office: 716/888-4000
Capacity: 18,690

Board of Patmos Inc.

Chairman of the Board	John J. Rigas
Chief Executive Officer	Timothy J. Rigas
Directors	Michael J. Rigas, James P. Rigas

Executive Department

Executive Vice President/Administration	Ron Bertovich
Executive Vice President/Finance & Business Development	Ed Hartman
Executive Vice President/Integrated Marketing	John Cimperman
Senior Vice President/ Sales	Kerry Atkinson
Senior Vice President/Legal & Business Affairs	Kevin Billet
Senior Vice President/Marketing	Christye Peterson
Vice President/Communications	Michael Gilbert
Vice President/Corporate Relations	Seymour H. Knox, IV
Vice President/Ticket Sales & Operations	John Sinclair
Senior Director of Sports & Arena Planning	Chris Schoepflin
Special Consultant	Joe Crozier
Executive Assistants	Eleanore MacKenzie, Carol Smith

Hockey Department

General Manager	Darcy Regier
Assistant to the General Manager	Larry Carriere
Director of Player Personnel	Don Luce
Executive Assistant	Elaine Burzynski
On-Site Travel Coordinator	Kim Christiano
Professional Scouts	Kevin Devine, Terry Martin
Scouting Staff	Don Barrie, Jim Benning, Bo Berglund, Paul Merritt, Darryl Plandowski, Mike Racicot, Rudy Migay, David Volek
Head Coach	Lindy Ruff
Associate Coach	Don Lever
Assistant Coach	Brian McCutcheon
Strength & Conditioning Coach	Doug McKenney
Assistant Strength Coach	Dennis Cole
Goaltender Coach	Jim Corsi
Administrative Assistant Coach	Jeff Holbrook
Head Trainer/Massage Therapist	Jim Pizzutelli
Head Equipment Manager	Rip Simonick
Assistant Equipment Manager	George Babcock
Equipment Assistant	Encil "Porky" Palmer

Medical

Club Doctors	Les Bisson, M.D., John Marzo, M.D.
Doctors	Nicholas Aquino, M.D., William Hartrich, M.D.
Oral Surgeon	Steven Jensen, DDS
Club Dentist	Daniel Yustin, DDS, M.S.
Physical Therapist	Joe Acquino
Club Doctor Emeritus	John L. Butsch, M.D.

Broadcast Production

Director of Broadcast & Production Services	Joe Guarnieri
Broadcast Team	Rick Jeanneret (play-by-play) Jim Lorentz (color commentary) Danny Gare (reporter)
Radio Producer/Host	Mark Jeanneret

Merchandise

Director of Merchandise	Mike Kaminska
Store Manager	Tammy Preteroti

Communications

Director of Communications	Gregg Huller
Director of Alumni Relations	Larry Playfair
Corporate & Community Relations Liaison	Gilbert Perreault

Empire Sports Sales

General Sales Manager	Dan Rozanski
National Account Manager	Mark Kennedy
Radio General Sales Manager	Steve Cuccia
Local Radio Sales Manager	Paul Cooper

Finance

Controller	John Marsh
Financial Analyst	Mark Raymond

Marketing

Director of Advertising & Promotions	Amy Reese
Director of Game Presentation & Special Events	Kathy Manley
Director of Community Relations	Ken Martin, Jr.

Canadian Sales & Marketing

Director of Canadian Sales & Marketing	Steve Katzman
Canadian Sales & Marketing Manager	Dorian Anderson

Ticket Sales & Operations

Ticket Sales Manager	Dan Carroll
Box Office Manager	Michael Tout

HSBC Arena

Senior Director of Facilities Management	Stan Makowski
Director of Event Booking	Jennifer Stich
Director of Event Services	John Faso
Chief Engineer	Barry Becker
Director of Premium Sales	Nick Turano
Director of Suite Services	Natalie DeSilva
Director of Lacrosse & Amateur Athletics	Kurt Silcott
Team Photographer	Bill Wippert

General Information

Location of Press Box	South side (S. Park Street) of building (above sections 318-322).
Practice Site	Pepsi Center; Amherst, NY
TV Station	Empire Sports Network
Radio Flagship Station	WNUC FM 107.7

Calgary Flames

1999-2000 Results: 31W-41L-10T 77PTS. Fourth, Northwest Division

2000-01 Schedule

Oct.	Thu.	5	Detroit	Sat.	6	at Los Angeles
	Tue.	10	Colorado	Thu.	11	Nashville
	Thu.	12	Columbus	Sat.	13	Ottawa
	Sat.	14	at NY Islanders	Sun.	14	at Vancouver
	Sun.	15	at Detroit	Wed.	17	at San Jose
	Wed.	18	at Vancouver	Sun.	21	Detroit
	Fri.	20	Boston	Tue.	23	Phoenix
	Sat.	21	Toronto*	Thu.	25	at Los Angeles
	Tue.	24	Phoenix	Sat.	27	Vancouver
	Thu.	26	at St. Louis	Tue.	30	Edmonton
	Fri.	27	at Minnesota	**Feb.** Thu.	1	Chicago
	Sun.	29	Anaheim	Tue.	6	San Jose
Nov.	Wed.	1	at Edmonton	Fri.	9	at Colorado
	Sat.	4	Pittsburgh	Sat.	10	at Vancouver
	Sun.	5	Minnesota	Tue.	13	Washington
	Wed.	8	at Minnesota	Thu.	15	at St. Louis
	Fri.	10	at Florida	Sun.	18	at Phoenix
	Sat.	11	at Tampa Bay	Mon.	19	at Anaheim
	Mon.	13	at Buffalo	Thu.	22	Los Angeles
	Thu.	16	Chicago	Sat.	24	Edmonton
	Sat.	18	NY Rangers	Mon.	26	Dallas
	Sun.	19	at Edmonton	**Mar.** Thu.	1	Minnesota
	Wed.	22	at Minnesota	Sat.	3	St. Louis
	Fri.	24	Anaheim	Tue.	6	Toronto
	Sat.	25	at Colorado	Thu.	8	at Philadelphia
	Tue.	28	at Nashville	Sat.	10	at Pittsburgh
	Wed.	29	at Dallas	Sun.	11	at Atlanta
Dec.	Sat.	2	Montreal*	Wed.	14	at Columbus
	Mon.	4	San Jose	Thu.	15	at Detroit
	Thu.	7	Nashville	Sat.	17	St. Louis
	Sat.	9	Carolina	Mon.	19	New Jersey
	Wed.	13	at Montreal	Thu.	22	Philadelphia
	Thu.	14	at Ottawa	Sat.	24	at Columbus*
	Sat.	16	at Toronto	Sun.	25	at Chicago*
	Tue.	19	at Colorado	Tue.	27	Columbus
	Wed.	20	at Phoenix	Thu.	29	Colorado
	Fri.	22	Edmonton	Sat.	31	Dallas
	Fri.	29	Vancouver	**Apr.** Mon.	2	at Dallas
	Sun.	31	Montreal	Wed.	4	at Chicago
Jan.	Wed.	3	at San Jose	Thu.	5	at Nashville
	Fri.	5	at Anaheim	Sat.	7	Los Angeles

Denotes afternoon game.

Franchise date: June 6, 1972
Transferred from Atlanta to Calgary, June 24, 1980.

WESTERN CONFERENCE

NORTHWEST DIVISION

29th NHL Season

Marc Savard had 22 goals in his first season with Calgary in 1999-2000, more than double the total he had scored over two seasons with the Rangers. Savard added 31 assists to rank as one of Calgary's top offensive threats.

Year-by-Year Record

		Home			Road			Overall							
Season	GP	W	L	T	W	L	T	W	L	T	GF	GA	Pts.	Finished		Playoff Result
1999-2000	82	20	15	6	11	26	4	31	41	10	211	256	77	4th,	Northwest Div.	Out of Playoffs
1998-99	82	15	20	6	15	20	6	30	40	12	211	234	72	3rd,	Northwest Div.	Out of Playoffs
1997-98	82	18	17	6	8	24	9	26	41	15	217	252	67	5th,	Pacific Div.	Out of Playoffs
1996-97	82	21	18	2	11	23	7	32	41	9	214	239	73	5th,	Pacific Div.	Out of Playoffs
1995-96	82	18	18	5	16	19	6	34	37	11	241	240	79	2nd,	Pacific Div.	Lost Conf. Quarter-Final
1994-95	48	15	7	2	9	10	5	24	17	7	163	135	55	1st,	Pacific Div.	Lost Conf. Quarter-Final
1993-94	84	25	12	5	17	17	8	42	29	13	302	256	97	1st,	Pacific Div.	Lost Conf. Quarter-Final
1992-93	84	23	14	5	20	16	6	43	30	11	322	282	97	2nd,	Smythe Div.	Lost Div. Semi-Final
1991-92	80	19	14	7	12	23	5	31	37	12	296	305	74	5th,	Smythe Div.	Out of Playoffs
1990-91	80	29	8	3	17	18	5	46	26	8	344	263	100	2nd,	Smythe Div.	Lost Div. Semi-Final
1989-90	80	28	7	5	14	16	10	42	23	15	348	265	99	1st,	Smythe Div.	Lost Div. Semi-Final
1988-89	**80**	**32**	**4**	**4**	**22**	**13**	**5**	**54**	**17**	**9**	**354**	**226**	**117**	**1st,**	**Smythe Div.**	**Won Stanley Cup**
1987-88	80	26	11	3	22	12	6	48	23	9	397	305	105	1st,	Smythe Div.	Lost Div. Final
1986-87	80	25	13	2	21	18	1	46	31	3	318	289	95	2nd,	Smythe Div.	Lost Div. Semi-Final
1985-86	80	23	11	6	17	20	3	40	31	9	354	315	89	2nd,	Smythe Div.	Lost Final
1984-85	80	23	11	6	18	16	6	41	27	12	363	302	94	3rd,	Smythe Div.	Lost Div. Semi-Final
1983-84	80	22	11	7	12	21	7	34	32	14	311	314	82	3rd,	Smythe Div.	Lost Div. Final
1982-83	80	21	11	8	11	22	7	32	34	14	321	317	78	2nd,	Smythe Div.	Lost Div. Final
1981-82	80	20	11	9	9	23	8	29	34	17	334	345	75	3rd,	Smythe Div.	Lost Div. Semi-Final
1980-81	80	25	5	10	14	22	4	39	27	14	329	298	92	3rd,	Patrick Div.	Lost Semi-Final
1979-80*	80	18	15	7	17	17	6	35	32	13	282	269	83	4th,	Patrick Div.	Lost Prelim. Round
1978-79*	80	25	11	4	16	20	4	41	31	8	327	280	90	4th,	Patrick Div.	Lost Prelim. Round
1977-78*	80	20	13	7	14	14	12	34	27	19	274	252	87	3rd,	Patrick Div.	Lost Prelim. Round
1976-77*	80	22	11	7	12	23	5	34	34	12	264	265	80	3rd,	Patrick Div.	Lost Prelim. Round
1975-76*	80	19	14	7	16	19	5	35	33	12	262	237	82	3rd,	Patrick Div.	Lost Prelim. Round
1974-75*	80	24	9	7	10	22	8	34	31	15	243	233	83	4th,	Patrick Div.	Out of Playoffs
1973-74*	78	17	15	7	13	19	7	30	34	14	214	238	74	4th,	West Div.	Lost Quarter-Final
1972-73*	78	16	16	7	9	22	8	25	38	15	191	239	65	7th,	West Div.	Out of Playoffs

Atlanta Flames

2000-01 Player Personnel

FORWARDS	HT	WT	S	Place of Birth	Date	1999-00 Club
ANDERSSON, Niklas	5-9	180	L	Kungalv, Sweden	5/20/71	NYI-Chicago Wolves-Nsh
BEGIN, Steve	5-11	190	L	Trois-Rivières, Que.	6/14/78	Calgary-Saint John Flames
BETTS, Blair	6-1	204	L	Edmonton, Alta.	2/16/80	Prince George
BOTTERILL, Jason	6-4	220	L	Edmonton, Alta.	5/19/76	Atl.-Orlando-Cgy-St. Jn.
BURE, Valeri	5-10	185	R	Moscow, USSR	6/13/74	Calgary
BUREAU, Marc	6-1	203	R	Trois-Rivières, Que.	5/19/66	Philadelphia-Calgary
CLARK, Chris	6-0	202	R	Manchester, CT	3/8/76	Calgary-Saint John Flames
COWAN, Jeff	6-2	192	L	Scarborough, Ont.	9/27/76	Calgary-Saint John Flames
ELOMO, Miika	6-0	200	L	Turku, Finland	4/21/77	Washington-Portland (AHL)
FATA, Rico	5-11	197	L	Sault Ste. Marie, Ont.	2/12/80	Calgary-Saint John Flames
GRATTON, Benoit	5-11	194	L	Montreal, Que.	12/28/76	Calgary-Saint John Flames
HENTUNEN, Jukka	5-10	187	R	Joroinen, Finland	5/3/74	HPK Hameenlinna
IGINLA, Jarome	6-1	202	R	Edmonton, Alta.	7/1/77	Calgary
LINDSAY, Bill	6-0	195	L	Big Fork, MT	5/17/71	Calgary
LOWRY, Dave	6-1	200	L	Sudbury, Ont.	2/14/65	San Jose
MURRAY, Marty	5-9	178	L	Deloraine, Man.	2/16/75	Kolner Haie
NAZAROV, Andrei	6-5	234	R	Chelyabinsk, USSR	5/22/74	Calgary
PETROVICKY, Ronald	5-11	188	R	Zilina, Czech.	2/15/77	Saint John Flames
ROCHE, Dave	6-4	230	L	Lindsay, Ont.	6/13/75	Calgary-Saint John Flames
SAPRYKIN, Oleg	6-0	195	L	Moscow, USSR	2/12/81	Seattle T-Birds-Calgary
SAVARD, Marc	5-10	184	L	Ottawa, Ont.	7/17/77	Calgary
SHANTZ, Jeff	6-0	195	R	Duchess, Alta.	10/10/73	Calgary
STILLMAN, Cory	6-0	194	L	Peterborough, Ont.	12/20/73	Calgary
SUTTER, Shaun	6-1	175	R	Red Deer, Alta.	6/2/80	Medicine Hat-Calgary Hitmen
TKACZUK, Daniel	6-1	197	L	Toronto, Ont.	6/10/79	Saint John Flames
VARLAMOV, Sergei	5-11	195	L	Kiev, USSR	7/21/78	Calgary-Saint John Flames
WIEMER, Jason	6-1	220	L	Kimberley, B.C.	4/14/76	Calgary
WILM, Clarke	6-0	202	L	Central Butte, Sask.	10/24/76	Calgary

DEFENSEMEN						
ALBELIN, Tommy	6-1	194	L	Stockholm, Sweden	5/21/64	Calgary
BELAK, Wade	6-5	222	R	Saskatoon, Sask.	7/3/76	Calgary
EAKINS, Dallas	6-2	200	L	Dade City, FL	2/27/67	NY Islanders-Chicago Wolves
FOSTER, Kurtis	6-5	205	R	Carp, Ont.	11/24/81	Peterborough
GAUTHIER, Denis	6-2	210	L	Montreal, Que.	10/1/76	Calgary
HOUSLEY, Phil	5-10	185	L	St. Paul, MN	3/9/64	Calgary
LYDMAN, Toni	6-1	200	L	Lahti, Finland	9/25/77	HIFK Helsinki
MARTIN, Mike	6-2	205	R	Stratford, Ont.	10/27/76	Michigan
MORRIS, Derek	5-11	200	R	Edmonton, Alta.	8/24/78	Calgary
REGEHR, Robyn	6-2	225	L	Recife, Brazil	4/19/80	Calgary-Saint John Flames
ST. CROIX, Chris	6-1	199	R	Voorhees, NJ	5/2/79	Saint John Flames
SCOVILLE, Darryl	6-3	214	L	Swift Current, SK	10/13/75	Calgary-Saint John Flames
SMITH, Steve	6-4	215	L	Glasgow, Scotland	4/30/63	Calgary
VELLINGA, Mike	6-2	212	L	Chatham, Ont.	8/19/78	Saint John Flames-Johnstown
WALSER, Derrick	5-10	190	L	New Glasgow, N.S.	5/12/78	Saint John Flames-Johnstown
WERENKA, Brad	6-1	218	L	Two Hills, Alta.	2/12/69	Pittsburgh-Calgary

GOALTENDERS	HT	WT	C	Place of Birth	Date	1999-00 Club
BRATHWAITE, Fred	5-7	175	L	Ottawa, Ont.	11/24/72	Calgary-Saint John Flames
BROCHU, Martin	6-0	199	L	Anjou, Que.	3/10/73	Portland Pirates
FUHR, Grant	5-10	201	R	Spruce Grove, Alta.	9/28/62	Calgary-Saint John Flames
GARNER, Tyrone	6-1	200	L	Stoney Creek, Ont.	7/27/78	Saint John-Dayton-Johnstown
SABOURIN, Dany	6-2	182	L	Val d'Or, Que.	9/2/80	Sherbrooke
SZUPER, Levente	5-10	178	L	Budapest, Hungary	6/11/80	Ottawa 67's
VERNON, Mike	5-9	180	L	Calgary, Alta.	2/24/63	San Jose-Florida

1999-2000 Scoring

* – rookie

Regular Season

Pos	#	Player	Team	GP	G	A	Pts	+/–	PIM	PP	SH	GW	GT	S	%
R	8	Valeri Bure	CGY	82	35	40	75	–7	50	13	0	6	1	308	11.4
C	12	Jarome Iginla	CGY	77	29	34	63	0	26	12	0	4	0	256	11.3
D	6	Phil Housley	CGY	78	11	44	55	–12	24	5	0	2	1	176	6.3
C	27	Marc Savard	CGY	78	22	31	53	–2	56	4	0	3	1	184	12.0
D	53	Derek Morris	CGY	78	9	29	38	2	80	3	0	2	0	193	4.7
R	25	Sergei Krivokrasov	NSH	63	9	17	26	–7	40	3	0	2	1	132	6.8
			CGY	12	1	10	11	2	4	0	0	0	0	27	3.7
			TOTAL	75	10	27	37	–5	44	3	0	2	1	159	6.3
R	62	Andrei Nazarov	CGY	76	10	22	32	3	78	1	0	1	0	110	9.1
C	11	Jeff Shantz	CGY	74	13	18	31	–13	30	6	0	1	0	112	11.6
D	2	Darryl Shannon	ATL	49	5	13	18	–14	65	1	0	1	0	66	7.6
			CGY	27	1	8	9	–13	22	0	0	0	0	46	2.2
			TOTAL	76	6	21	27	–27	87	1	0	1	0	112	5.4
C	24	Jason Wiemer	CGY	64	11	11	22	–10	120	2	0	3	0	104	10.6
C	23	Clarke Wilm	CGY	78	10	12	22	–6	67	1	3	0	0	81	12.3
L	16	Cory Stillman	CGY	37	12	9	21	–9	12	6	0	3	1	59	20.3
L	22	Bill Lindsay	CGY	80	8	12	20	–7	86	0	0	2	0	147	5.4
L	15	* Martin St. Louis	CGY	56	3	15	18	–5	22	0	0	1	0	73	4.1
L	21	Andreas Johansson	T.B	12	2	3	5	1	8	0	0	0	0	11	18.2
			CGY	28	3	7	10	–3	14	1	0	0	0	47	6.4
			TOTAL	40	5	10	15	–2	22	1	0	0	0	58	8.6
D	33	Brad Werenka	PIT	61	3	8	11	15	69	0	0	1	0	42	7.1
			CGY	12	1	1	2	–2	21	0	0	0	0	20	5.0
			TOTAL	73	4	9	13	13	90	0	0	1	0	62	6.5
D	28	* Robyn Regehr	CGY	57	5	7	12	–2	46	2	0	0	0	64	7.8
D	5	Tommy Albelin	CGY	41	4	6	10	–3	12	1	1	1	0	37	10.8
D	4	Bobby Dollas	OTT	1	0	0	0	0	0	0	0	0	0	0	0.0
			CGY	49	3	7	10	4	28	1	0	0	0	36	8.3
			TOTAL	50	3	7	10	6	28	1	0	0	0	36	8.3
C	7	Marc Bureau	PHI	54	2	2	4	–1	10	0	1	0	0	46	4.3
			CGY	9	1	3	4	–3	2	0	0	0	0	5	20.0
			TOTAL	63	3	5	8	–4	12	0	1	0	0	51	5.9
D	32	Cale Hulse	CGY	47	1	6	7	–11	47	0	0	1	0	43	2.4
L	38	* Jeff Cowan	CGY	13	4	1	5	2	16	0	0	0	0	26	15.4
L	17	* Jason Botterill	ATL	25	1	4	5	–7	17	0	0	1	0	17	5.9
			CGY	2	0	0	0	–4	0	0	0	0	0	2	0.0
			TOTAL	27	1	4	5	–11	17	0	0	1	0	19	5.3
D	55	Steve Smith	CGY	20	0	4	4	–13	42	0	0	0	0	10	0.0
L	37	* Sergei Varlamov	CGY	7	3	0	3	0	0	0	0	1	0	11	27.3
C	26	* Steve Begin	CGY	13	1	1	2	–3	18	0	0	0	0	3	33.3
D	3	Denis Gauthier	CGY	39	1	1	2	–4	50	0	0	0	0	29	3.4
L	39	Benoit Gratton	CGY	10	0	2	2	1	10	0	0	0	0	4	0.0
L	26	* Travis Brigley	CGY	17	0	2	2	–6	4	0	0	0	0	0	0.0
D	29	Wade Belak	CGY	40	0	2	2	–4	122	0	0	0	0	11	0.0
D	34	Stewart Malgunas	CGY	4	0	1	1	1	2	0	0	0	0	0	0.0
C	19	* Oleg Saprykin	CGY	4	0	1	1	–4	2	0	0	0	0	2	0.0
R	17	Chris Clark	CGY	22	0	1	1	–3	14	0	0	0	0	17	0.0
C	18	Steve Dubinsky	CGY	23	0	1	1	–12	4	0	0	0	0	29	0.0
D	32	* Lee Sorochan	CGY	1	0	0	0	0	0	0	0	0	0	0	0.0
L	25	Dave Roche	CGY	2	0	0	0	–1	5	0	0	0	0	3	0.0
R	15	Rico Fata	CGY	2	0	0	0	–1	0	0	0	0	0	4	0.0
D	45	* Darrel Scoville	CGY	6	0	0	0	1	2	0	0	0	0	1	0.0
G	47	J-S Giguere	CGY	7	0	0	0	0	2	0	0	0	0	0	0.0
D	36	Eric Charron	CGY	21	0	0	0	–3	37	0	0	0	0	8	0.0
G	31	Grant Fuhr	CGY	23	0	0	0	0	0	0	0	0	0	0	0.0
G	40	Fred Brathwaite	CGY	61	0	0	0	0	0	0	0	0	0	0	0.0

Goaltending

No.	Goaltender	GPI	Mins	Avg	W	L	T	EN	SO	GA	SA	S%
47	J-S Giguere	7	330	2.73	1	3	1	1	0	15	175	.914
40	Fred Brathwaite	61	3448	2.75	25	25	7	3	5	158	1664	.905
31	Grant Fuhr	23	1205	3.83	5	13	2	2	0	77	536	.856
	Totals	**82**	**5007**	**3.07**	**31**	**41**	**10**	**6**	**5**	**256**	**2381**	**.892**

General Manager

BUTTON, CRAIG
Vice President/General Manager, Calgary Flames.
Born in Montreal, Que., January 3, 1963.

Craig Button is entering his first season with the Calgary Flames having been named vice-president and general manager of the team on June 6, 2000. Button spent the previous 12 seasons with the Dallas Stars organization, serving as the director of player personnel for the last two seasons after spending six years as the director of scouting. Button oversaw the Stars' top minor league team in Kalamazoo, aiding in the evaluation and development of the Stars' minor league prospects. His other responsibilities included the management and development of the Stars' amateur and professional scouting program, the evaluation of players as it relates to movement within the organization, including the Entry Draft, trades and free agent signings, and the player development program for their amateur prospects.

A native of Montreal, Button graduated from Concordia University in Montreal in 1987 with a BA in Economics with an emphasis in international finance.

Button's family has a long history in hockey. His late father, Jack, was a former NHL general manager and a highly respected 34-year veteran of NHL management. His mother, Bridget, worked for Punch Imlach and the Toronto Maple Leafs, and his brother Tod is a pro scout with the Flames. Craig and his wife, Cara, have two daughters, Chandler and Quinn.

General Managers' History

Cliff Fletcher, 1972-73 to 1990-91; Doug Risebrough, 1991-92 to 1994-95; Doug Risebrough and Al Coates, 1995-96; Al Coates, 1996-97 to 1999-2000; Craig Button, 2000-01.

Coaching History

Bernie Geoffrion, 1972-73, 1973-74; Bernie Geoffrion and Fred Creighton, 1974-75; Fred Creighton, 1975-76 to 1978-79; Al MacNeil, 1979-80 to 1981-82; Bob Johnson, 1982-83 to 1986-87; Terry Crisp, 1987-88 to 1989-90; Doug Risebrough, 1990-91; Doug Risebrough and Guy Charron, 1991-92; Dave King, 1992-93 to 1994-95; Pierre Page, 1995-96, 1996-97; Brian Sutter, 1997-98 to 1999-2000; Don Hay, 2000-01.

Club Records

Team

(Figures in brackets for season records are games played; records for fewest points, wins, ties, losses, goals, goals against are for 70 or more games)

Most Points **117** 1988-89 (80)
Most Wins **54** 1988-89 (80)
Most Ties **19** 1977-78 (80)
Most Losses **41** 1996-97 (82), 1997-98 (82), 1999-2000 (82)
Most Goals **397** 1987-88 (80)
Most Goals Against **345** 1981-82 (80)
Fewest Points **65** 1972-73 (78)
Fewest Wins **25** 1972-73 (78)
Fewest Ties **3** 1986-87 (80)
Fewest Losses **17** 1988-89 (80)
Fewest Goals **191** 1972-73 (78)
Fewest Goals Against **226** 1988-89 (80)
Longest Winning Streak
Overall .... **10** Oct. 14-Nov. 3/78
Home .... **9** Oct. 17-Nov. 15/78, Jan. 3-Feb. 5/89, Mar. 3-Apr. 1/90, Feb. 21-Mar. 14/91
Away .... **7** Nov. 10-Dec. 4/88
Longest Undefeated Streak
Overall .... **13** Nov. 10-Dec. 8/88 (12 wins, 1 tie)
Home .... **18** Dec. 29/90-Mar. 14/91 (17 wins, 1 tie)
Away .... **9** Feb. 20-Mar. 21/88 (6 wins, 3 ties), Nov. 11-Dec. 16/90 (6 wins, 3 ties)
Longest Losing Streak
Overall .... **11** Dec. 14/85-Jan. 7/86
Home .... **6** Dec. 5-31/98
Away .... **9** Dec. 1/85-Jan. 12/86
Longest Winless Streak
Overall .... **11** Dec. 14/85-Jan. 7/86 (11 losses), Jan. 5-26/93 (9 losses, 2 ties)
Home .... **6** Four times
Away .... **13** Feb. 3-Mar. 29/73 (10 losses, 3 ties)
Most Shutouts, Season **8** 1974-75 (80)
Most PIM, Season **2,655** 1991-92 (80)
Most Goals, Game .... **13** Feb. 10/93 (S.J. 1 at Cgy. 13)

Individual

Most Seasons .... **13** Al MacInnis
Most Games .... **803** Al MacInnis
Most Goals, Career .... **364** Theoren Fleury
Most Assists, Career ..... **609** Al MacInnis
Most Points, Career ...... **830** Theoren Fleury (364G, 466A)
Most PIM, Career .... **2,405** Tim Hunter
Most Shutouts, Career .... **20** Dan Bouchard
Longest Consecutive Games Streak .... **257** Brad Marsh (Oct. 11/78-Nov. 10/81)
Most Goals, Season .... **66** Lanny McDonald (1982-83)
Most Assists, Season ..... **82** Kent Nilsson (1980-81)
Most Points, Season ...... **131** Kent Nilsson (1980-81) (49G, 82A)
Most PIM, Season .... **375** Tim Hunter (1988-89)
Most Points, Defenseman, Season .... **103** Al MacInnis (1990-91; 28G, 75A)
Most Points, Center, Season .... **131** Kent Nilsson (1980-81; 49G, 82A)
Most Points, Right Wing, Season .... **110** Joe Mullen (1988-89; 51G, 59A)
Most Points, Left Wing, Season .... **90** Gary Roberts (1991-92; 53G, 37A)
Most Points, Rookie, Season .... **92** Joe Nieuwendyk (1987-88; 51G, 41A)
Most Shutouts, Season .... **5** Dan Bouchard (1973-74), Phil Myre (1974-75), Fred Brathwaite (1999-2000)
Most Goals, Game .... **5** Joe Nieuwendyk (Jan. 11/89)
Most Assists, Game .... **6** Guy Chouinard (Feb. 25/81), Gary Suter (Apr. 4/86)
Most Points, Game .... **7** Sergei Makarov (Feb. 25/90; 2G, 5A)

Records include Atlanta Flames, 1972-73 through 1979-80.

Retired Numbers

9	Lanny McDonald	1981-1989

Captains' History

Keith McCreary, 1972-73 to 1974-75; Pat Quinn, 1975-76, 1976-77; Tom Lysiak, 1977-78, 1978-79; Jean Pronovost, 1979-80; Brad Marsh, 1980-81; Phil Russell, 1981-82, 1982-83; Lanny McDonald, Doug Risebrough (co-captains), 1983-84; Lanny McDonald, Doug Risebrough, Jim Peplinski (tri-captains), 1984-85 to 1986-87; Lanny McDonald, Jim Peplinski (co-captains), 1987-88; Lanny McDonald, Jim Peplinski, Tim Hunter (tri-captains), 1988-89; Brad McCrimmon, 1989-90; alternating captains, 1990-91; Joe Nieuwendyk, 1991-92 to 1994-95; Theoren Fleury, 1995-96, 1996-97; Todd Simpson, 1997-98, 1998-99; Steve Smith, 1999-2000 to date.

All-time Record vs. Other Clubs

Regular Season

	At Home							On Road							Total						
	GP	W	L	T	GF	GA	PTS	GP	W	L	T	GF	GA	PTS	GP	W	L	T	GF	GA	PTS
Anaheim	17	11	6	0	51	38	22	18	7	8	3	47	55	18	35	18	14	3	98	93	40
Atlanta	1	1	0	0	5	2	2	1	0	1	0	1	2	0	2	1	1	0	6	4	2
Boston	42	17	22	3	154	149	37	44	12	26	6	121	155	30	86	29	48	9	275	304	67
Buffalo	43	15	17	11	146	143	41	43	13	25	5	127	181	31	86	28	42	16	273	324	72
Carolina	26	19	5	2	129	86	40	27	13	10	4	100	88	30	53	32	15	6	229	174	70
Chicago	55	25	19	11	178	169	61	53	17	23	13	152	177	47	108	42	42	24	330	346	108
Colorado	37	19	12	6	143	117	44	36	12	15	9	121	143	33	73	31	27	15	264	260	77
Dallas	54	31	11	12	196	135	74	54	18	27	9	174	201	45	108	49	38	21	370	336	119
Detroit	52	30	16	6	210	159	66	51	15	26	10	155	191	40	103	45	42	16	365	350	106
Edmonton	70	39	25	6	305	251	84	71	24	37	10	243	286	58	141	63	62	16	548	537	142
Florida	6	2	3	1	14	17	5	6	4	2	0	16	12	8	12	6	5	1	30	29	13
Los Angeles	86	51	25	10	390	289	112	83	31	43	9	298	320	72	169	82	68	19	688	609	184
Montreal	43	13	25	5	129	151	31	43	11	24	8	106	154	30	86	24	49	13	235	305	61
Nashville	4	2	1	1	13	12	5	5	3	2	0	14	13	6	9	5	3	1	27	25	11
New Jersey	40	27	5	8	177	103	62	42	26	13	3	157	118	55	82	53	18	11	334	221	117
NY Islanders	48	24	13	11	171	142	59	47	13	25	9	129	185	35	95	37	38	20	300	327	94
NY Rangers	47	27	10	10	211	141	64	49	21	23	5	174	174	48	96	48	33	15	385	315	112
Ottawa	8	5	2	1	32	17	11	7	2	3	2	17	17	6	15	7	5	3	49	34	17
Philadelphia	50	24	17	9	201	166	57	48	13	32	3	128	190	29	98	37	49	12	329	356	86
Phoenix	63	36	19	8	280	206	80	62	21	30	11	213	242	53	125	57	49	19	493	448	133
Pittsburgh	43	26	10	7	193	132	59	42	10	22	10	130	159	30	85	36	32	17	323	291	89
St. Louis	54	26	24	4	186	165	57	56	21	26	9	176	201	51	110	47	50	13	362	366	108
San Jose	24	15	7	2	101	63	32	26	16	8	2	88	77	34	50	31	15	4	189	140	66
Tampa Bay	7	5	2	0	25	14	10	8	3	4	1	26	25	7	15	8	6	1	51	39	17
Toronto	54	31	18	5	222	174	67	50	17	26	7	180	190	41	104	48	44	12	402	364	108
Vancouver	88	56	19	13	375	254	125	88	39	32	17	299	305	96	176	95	51	30	674	559	221
Washington	36	24	6	6	152	85	54	38	14	19	5	132	143	33	74	38	25	11	284	228	87
Defunct Clubs	13	8	4	1	51	34	17	13	7	3	3	43	33	17	26	15	7	4	94	67	34
Totals	**1111**	**609**	**343**	**159**	**4440**	**3414**	**1378**	**1111**	**403**	**535**	**173**	**3567**	**4037**	**983**	**2222**	**1012**	**878**	**332**	**8007**	**7451**	**2361**

Playoffs

	Series	W	L	GP	W	L	T	GF	GA	Last Mtg.	Round	Result
Chicago	3	2	1	12	7	5	0	37	33	1996	CQF	L 0-4
Dallas	1	0	1	6	2	4	0	18	25	1981	SF	L 2-4
Detroit	1	0	1	2	0	2	0	5	8	1978	PR	L 0-2
Edmonton	5	1	4	30	11	19	0	96	132	1991	DSF	L 3-4
Los Angeles	6	2	4	26	13	13	0	102	105	1993	DSF	L 2-4
Montreal	2	1	1	11	5	6	0	32	31	1989	F	W 4-2
NY Rangers	1	0	1	4	1	3	0	8	14	1980	PR	L 1-3
Philadelphia	2	1	1	11	4	7	0	28	43	1981	QF	W 4-3
St. Louis	1	1	0	7	4	3	0	28	22	1986	CF	W 4-3
San Jose	1	0	1	7	3	4	0	35	26	1995	CQF	L 3-4
Toronto	1	0	1	2	0	2	0	5	9	1979	PR	L 0-2
Vancouver	5	3	2	25	13	12	0	82	80	1994	CQF	L 3-4
Winnipeg	3	1	2	13	6	7	0	43	45	1987	DSF	L 2-4
Totals	**32**	**12**	**20**	**156**	**69**	**87**	**0**	**529**	**590**			

Playoff Results 2000-1996

Year	Round	Opponent	Result	GF	GA
1996	CQF	Chicago	L 0-4	7	16

Abbreviations: Round: F – Final; **CF** – conference final; **CQF** – conference quarter-final; **DSF** – division semi-final; **SF** – semi-final; **QF** – quarter-final; **PR** – preliminary round.

Carolina totals include Hartford, 1979-80 to 1996-97.
Colorado totals include Quebec, 1979-80 to 1994-95.
Dallas totals include Minnesota North Stars, 1972-73 to 1992-93.
New Jersey totals include Kansas City, 1974-75 to 1975-76, and Colorado Rockies, 1976-77 to 1981-82.
Phoenix totals include Winnipeg, 1979-80 to 1995-96.

1999-2000 Results

Oct.	2	at	San Jose	3-5		8		Tampa Bay	3-2 *
	6		St. Louis	1-4		12		Dallas	2-1 *
	8		Montreal	1-4		15		Toronto	4-0
	11		Carolina	3-3		18		Detroit	6-1
	13	at	Vancouver	4-3 *		19	at	Edmonton	0-7
	15		Los Angeles	1-4		21		Nashville	5-4 *
	16		Vancouver	4-4		24	at	Boston	4-3 *
	19	at	St. Louis	1-7		26	at	Washington	1-2
	22	at	Florida	3-2 *		28	at	Detroit	1-4
	23	at	Tampa Bay	1-2		29	at	Nashville	1-3
	26	at	Atlanta	1-2	**Feb.**	1		St. Louis	4-5 *
	28	at	Ottawa	4-3 *		3		Chicago	5-5
	30	at	Toronto	1-2		9	at	Vancouver	3-4 *
Nov.	3		Nashville	5-4 *		10	at	Colorado	2-3
	6		Florida	3-6		12	at	Phoenix	3-4
	10		San Jose	4-3 *		14	at	Los Angeles	3-4 *
	13		Colorado	2-5		16	at	Anaheim	5-6 *
	16	at	Phoenix	1-2		18		Edmonton	4-2
	17	at	Anaheim	1-2		19	at	Edmonton	3-2 *
	19		Detroit	3-1		23		Los Angeles	2-7
	23		NY Islanders	3-2		25		Phoenix	3-3
	25		Chicago	2-1 *		26		Atlanta	5-2
	27	at	Colorado	1-7	**Mar.**	1		Pittsburgh	8-2
	30	at	Carolina	3-4		3		Anaheim	4-1
Dec.	2	at	NY Islanders	5-0		5		New Jersey	2-2
	4	at	New Jersey	4-2		7		Colorado	3-8
	6	at	NY Rangers	2-3 *		9		Toronto	2-6
	7	at	Montreal	3-3		11	at	Los Angeles	1-3
	10		Vancouver	3-2		13	at	San Jose	3-5
	12	at	Chicago	2-1		15		Ottawa	1-3
	14	at	St. Louis	1-1		18		Buffalo	1-5
	15	at	Dallas	1-5		19	at	Edmonton	3-2
	18		Ottawa	2-1		22	at	Detroit	2-2
	21		Dallas	0-0		23	at	Buffalo	2-4
	23		Edmonton	2-1		25	at	Nashville	2-1
	26	at	Vancouver	2-0		31		Phoenix	1-3
	27		Philadelphia	1-5	**Apr.**	1		San Jose	3-0
	29		Anaheim	3-1		3	at	Dallas	2-2
Jan.	2		Vancouver	4-2		5	at	St. Louis	5-6
	5	at	Colorado	0-4		7		Colorado	1-3
	6	at	Chicago	2-5		8		Edmonton	3-6

* – Overtime

Entry Draft
Selections 2000-1986

2000
Pick
9   Brent Krahn
40 Kurtis Foster
46 Jarret Stoll
116 Levente Szuper
141 Wade Davis
155 Travis Moen
176 Jukka Hentunen
239 David Hajek
270 Micki Dupont

1999
Pick
11 Oleg Saprykin
38 Dan Cavanaugh
77 Craig Andersson
106 Rail Rozakov
135 Matt Doman
153 Jesse Cook
166 Cory Pecker
170 Matt Underhill
190 Blair Stayzer
252 Dmitri Kirilenko

1998
Pick
6   Rico Fata
33 Blair Betts
62 Paul Manning
102 Shaun Sutter
108 Dany Sabourin
120 Brent Gauvreau
192 Radek Duda
206 Jonas Frogren
234 Kevin Mitchell

1997
Pick
6   Daniel Tkaczuk
32 Evan Lindsay
42 John Tripp
51 Dmitri Kokorev
60 Derek Schutz
70 Erik Andersson
92 Chris St. Croix
100 Ryan Ready
113 Martin Moise
140 Ilja Demidov
167 Jeremy Rondeau
223 Dustin Paul

1996
Pick
13 Derek Morris
39 Travis Brigley
40 Steve Begin
73 Dmitri Vlasenkov
89 Toni Lydman
94 Christian Lefebvre
122 Josef Straka
202 Ryan Wade
228 Ronald Petrovicky

1995
Pick
20 Denis Gauthier
46 Pavel Smirnov
72 Rocky Thompson
98 Jan Labraaten
150 Clarke Wilm
176 Ryan Gillis
233 Steve Shirreffs

1994
Pick
19 Chris Dingman
45 Dmitri Ryabykin
77 Chris Clark
91 Ryan Duthie
97 Johan Finnstrom
107 Nils Ekman
123 Frank Appel
149 Patrick Haltia
175 Ladislav Kohn
201 Keith McCambridge
227 Jorgen Jonsson
253 Mike Peluso
279 Pavel Torgaev

1993
Pick
18 Jesper Mattsson
44 Jamie Allison
70 Dan Tompkins
95 Jason Smith
96 Marty Murray
121 Darryl Lafrance
122 John Emmons
148 Andreas Karlsson
200 Derek Sylvester
252 German Titov
278 Burke Murphy

1992
Pick
6   Cory Stillman
30 Chris O'Sullivan
54 Mathias Johansson
78 Robert Svehla
102 Sami Helenius
126 Ravil Yakubov
129 Joel Bouchard
150 Pavel Rajnoha
174 Ryan Mulhern
198 Brandon Carper
222 Jonas Hoglund
246 Andrei Potaichuk

1991
Pick
19 Niklas Sundblad
41 Francois Groleau
52 Sandy McCarthy
63 Brian Caruso
85 Steven Magnusson
107 Jerome Butler
129 Bobby Marshall
140 Matt Hoffman
151 Kelly Harper
173 David St. Pierre
195 David Struch
217 Sergei Zolotov
239 Marko Jantunen
261 Andrei Trefilov

1990
Pick
11 Trevor Kidd
26 Nicolas Perreault
32 Vesa Viitakoski
41 Etienne Belzile
62 Glen Mears
83 Paul Kruse
125 Chris Tschupp
146 Dimitri Frolov
167 Shawn Murray
188 Mike Murray
209 Rob Sumner
230 invalid claim
251 Leo Gudas

1989
Pick
24 Kent Manderville
42 Ted Drury
50 Veli-Pekka Kautonen
63 Corey Lyons
70 Robert Reichel
84 Ryan O'Leary
105 Toby Kearney
147 Alex Nikolic
168 Kevin Wortman
189 Sergei Gomolyako
210 Dan Sawyer
231 Alexander Yudin
252 Kenneth Kennholt

1988
Pick
21 Jason Muzzatti
42 Todd Harkins
84 Gary Socha
85 Tomas Forslund
90 Scott Matusovich
126 Jonas Bergqvist
168 Troy Kennedy
189 Brett Peterson
210 Guy Darveau
231 Dave Tretowicz
252 Sergei Priakin

1987
Pick
19 Bryan Deasley
25 Stephane Matteau
40 Kevin Grant
61 Scott Mahoney
70 Tim Harris
103 Tim Corkery
124 Joe Aloi
145 Peter Ciavaglia
166 Theoren Fleury
187 Mark Osiecki
208 William Sedergren
229 Peter Hasselblad
250 Magnus Svensson

1986
Pick
16 George Pelawa
37 Brian Glynn
79 Tom Quinlan
100 Scott Bloom
121 John Parker
142 Rick Lessard
163 Mark Olsen
184 Scott Sharples
205 Doug Pickell
226 Anders Lindstrom
247 Antonin Stavjana

Coach

HAY, DON
Coach, Calgary Flames. Born in Kamloops, B.C., February 13, 1954.

The Calgary Flames announced the appointment of Don Hay as head coach on August 1, 2000. Hay had spent the two previous seasons as head coach and general manager of the Tri-City Americans of the Western Hockey League. He was named the 1998-99 WHL Coach of the Year and Executive of the Year after leading the Americans to a 43-23-6 record. This is Hay's second coaching position in Calgary, as he served as an assistant coach under Pierre Page in the 1995-96 season. The Flames finished second in the Pacific Division that season with a 34-37-11 record.

Hay served as an assistant coach to Pierre Page in Anaheim during the 1996-97 season when the Mighty Ducks finished second in the Pacific Division. Prior to joining the Mighty Ducks, Hay was the first head coach of the Phoenix Coyotes in 1996-97.

Prior to Hay's first tenure with the Flames, he spent three seasons as head coach of the Kamloops Blazers of the WHL from 1992 to 1995 and led the team to two-straight Memorial Cup championships in 1994 and 1995. Hay was named by the Canadian Hockey League as the Western Hockey League's Best All-Time Coach at the 1999 Memorial Cup in Ottawa.

Serving as head coach of the Canadian national junior team at the 1995 World Junior Championships, Hay led the team to the gold medal. Canada's 7-0 record in the 1995 World Junior Competition marked the first time any team had gone undefeated in the tournament.

Coaching Record

Season	Team	Games	Regular Season W	L	T	%	Playoffs Games	W	L	%
1992-93	Kamloops (WHL)	72	42	28	2	.597	13	8	5	.615
1993-94	Kamloops (WHL)	72	50	16	6	.736	19	12	7	.632
1994-95	Kamloops (WHL)	72	52	14	6	.764	21	15	6	.714
1996-97	**Phoenix (NHL)**	**82**	**38**	**37**	**7**	**.506**	**7**	**3**	**4**	**.429**
1998-99	Tri-City (WHL)	72	43	23	6	.639	12	7	5	.583
1999-2000	Tri-City (WHL)	72	24	41	7	.396•	4	0	4	.000
	NHL Totals	**82**	**38**	**37**	**7**	**.506**	**7**	**3**	**4**	**.429**

• Includes points from regulation ties

Club Directory

Pengrowth Saddledome

Calgary Flames
Pengrowth Saddledome
P.O. Box 1540 Station M
Calgary, Alberta T2P 3B9
Phone **403/777-2177**
FAX 403/777-2199
Website: www.calgaryflames.com
Capacity: 17,139

Owners: Grant A. Bartlett (Alt. Governor), N. Murray Edwards (Alt. Governor), Harley N. Hotchkiss (Governor), Ronald V. Joyce, Alvin G. Libin, Allan P. Markin, J.R. (Bud) McCaig, Byron J. Seaman, Daryl K. Seaman

Management
President & Chief Executive Officer - Alt. Governor . Ron Bremner
Vice President, Finance & Administration . . . . Michael Holditch
Vice President, Marketing & Sales . . . . Garry McKenzie

Hockey Club Personnel
Vice-President/General Manager . . . . Craig Button
Assistant to the General Manager . . . . Dan Stuchal
Head Coach. . . . . Don Hay
Assistant Coaches . . . . Brad McCrimmon, Greg Gilbert, Rob Cookson
Development Coach . . . . Jamie Hislop
Director, Hockey Administration . . . . Mike Burke
Pro Scout. . . . . Tod Button
Scouts. . . . . Ian McKenzie, Bob Atrill, Mike Sands, Bob Richardson, Lars Norrman, Nikolai Ladigan, Tomas Jelinek, Dave Polano
Video Coordinator. . . . . Gary Taylor
Saint John Flames Head Coach . . . . Jim Playfair
Saint John Flames Asst. Coach. . . . . Ron Wilson
Exec. Asst. to President/CEO . . . . Yvette Mutcheson
Exec. Asst. to GM and Hockey Operations. . . . . . . Brenda Koyich
Exec. Asst. to VP, Finance & Corporate Development . Gita Nayak

Medical/Training Staff
Physical Therapist . . . . Terry Kane
Athletic Therapist . . . . Morris Boyer
Equipment Manager . . . . Gus Thorson
Strength & Conditioning . . . . Rich Hesketh
Assistant Equipment Manager. . . . . Les Jarvis
Head Physician - Sport Medicine . . . . Dr. Willem Meeuwisse
Orthopedic Surgeon . . . . Dr. Nicholas Mohtadi
Internal Medicine. . . . . Dr. Terry Groves
Team Dentist . . . . Dr. Bill Blair
Dressing Room Attendant . . . . Jules Carriere

Communications
Director, Communications. Peter Hanlon
Manager, Media Relations . . . . Sean O'Brien
Administrative Assistant, Communications . . . . Bernie Hargrave

Community Relations
Director, Community Relations . . . . TBA
Community Relations Ambassador . . . . Jim "Bearcat" Murray
Community Relations Coordinator . . . . Allanah Mooney

Administration/Human Resources
Controller . . . . TBA
Assistant Controller . . . . Karen Kingham
Director, Human Resources . . . . Eleanor Culver

Marketing
Director of Marketing . . . . John Vidalin
Director, Retail Operations . . . . Dean Borle
Director, Advertising and Publishing . . . . Pat Halls
Director, Executive Suites . . . . Bob White
Business Development Manager . . . . Al Molnar
Director, Game Presentation . . . . Dave Imbach

Sales/Customer Relations
Director, Ticket Operations . . . . Jack Maloney
Director, Ticket Sales . . . . Dave Sclanders

Pengrowth Saddledome
GM, Building Operations . . . . Libby Raines
Operations Manager . . . . George Greenwood
Food Services Manager . . . . Art Hernandez
Concessions Manager . . . . Sheila Parisien
Security/Parking Superintendent . . . . Bob Godun
Mascot . . . . Harvey the Hound

Calgary Hitmen
General Manager . . . . Kelly Kisio
Asst. General Manager . . . . Blaine Forsythe
Head Coach. . . . . Dean Clark
Asst. Coach. . . . . Jeff Maher

Miscellaneous Data
Radio Affiliation. . . . . 66 CFR (660 AM)
TV Affiliation . . . . CTV Sportsnet, CBC-TV

Carolina Hurricanes

1999-2000 Results: 37W-35L-10T 84PTS. Third, Southeast Division

Year-by-Year Record

Season	GP	Home W	L	T	Road W	L	T	Overall W	L	T	GF	GA	Pts.	Finished		Playoff Result
1999-2000	82	20	16	5	17	19	5	37	35	10	217	216	84	3rd,	Southeast Div.	Out of Playoffs
1998-99	82	20	12	9	14	18	9	34	30	18	210	202	86	1st,	Southeast Div.	Lost Conf. Quarter-Final
1997-98	82	16	18	7	17	23	1	33	41	8	200	219	74	6th,	Northeast Div.	Out of Playoffs
1996-97*	82	23	15	3	9	24	8	32	39	11	226	256	75	5th,	Northeast Div.	Out of Playoffs
1995-96*	82	22	15	4	12	24	5	34	39	9	237	259	77	4th,	Northeast Div.	Out of Playoffs
1994-95*	48	12	10	2	7	14	3	19	24	5	127	141	43	5th,	Northeast Div.	Out of Playoffs
1993-94*	84	14	22	6	13	26	3	27	48	9	227	288	63	6th,	Northeast Div.	Out of Playoffs
1992-93*	84	12	25	5	14	27	1	26	52	6	284	369	58	5th,	Adams Div.	Out of Playoffs
1991-92*	80	13	17	10	13	24	3	26	41	13	247	283	65	4th,	Adams Div.	Lost Div. Semi-Final
1990-91*	80	18	16	6	13	22	5	31	38	11	238	276	73	4th,	Adams Div.	Lost Div. Semi-Final
1989-90*	80	17	18	5	21	15	4	38	33	9	275	268	85	4th,	Adams Div.	Lost Div. Semi-Final
1988-89*	80	21	17	2	16	21	3	37	38	5	299	290	79	4th,	Adams Div.	Lost Div. Semi-Final
1987-88*	80	21	14	5	14	24	2	35	38	7	249	267	77	4th,	Adams Div.	Lost Div. Semi-Final
1986-87*	80	26	9	5	17	21	2	43	30	7	287	270	93	1st,	Adams Div.	Lost Div. Semi-Final
1985-86*	80	21	17	2	19	19	2	40	36	4	332	302	84	4th,	Adams Div.	Lost Div. Final
1984-85*	80	17	18	5	13	23	4	30	41	9	268	318	69	5th,	Adams Div.	Out of Playoffs
1983-84*	80	19	16	5	9	26	5	28	42	10	288	320	66	5th,	Adams Div.	Out of Playoffs
1982-83*	80	13	22	5	6	32	2	19	54	7	261	403	45	5th,	Adams Div.	Out of Playoffs
1981-82*	80	13	17	10	8	24	8	21	41	18	264	351	60	5th,	Adams Div.	Out of Playoffs
1980-81*	80	14	17	9	7	24	9	21	41	18	292	372	60	4th,	Norris Div.	Out of Playoffs
1979-80*	80	22	12	6	5	22	13	27	34	19	303	312	73	4th,	Norris Div.	Lost Prelim. Round

* Hartford Whalers

2000-01 Schedule

Oct.	Sat.	7	Washington	Sun.	14	Anaheim*
	Tue.	10	Dallas	Tue.	16	at Montreal
	Fri.	13	at Florida	Thu.	18	Boston
	Sat.	14	at Nashville	Sat.	20	Los Angeles*
	Wed.	18	at Pittsburgh	Mon.	22	NY Rangers
	Sat.	21	at Montreal	Wed.	24	at NY Rangers
	Tue.	24	San Jose	Sat.	27	Philadelphia*
	Wed.	25	at Buffalo	Mon.	29	Tampa Bay
	Fri.	27	New Jersey	Wed.	31	Toronto
	Sun.	29	St. Louis	**Feb.** Thu.	1	at Atlanta
	Tue.	31	Tampa Bay	Wed.	7	at Phoenix
Nov.	Fri.	3	at Colorado	Thu.	8	at Los Angeles
	Sat.	4	at San Jose	Sun.	11	at Anaheim*
	Wed.	8	at Toronto	Wed.	14	at Detroit
	Fri.	10	Toronto	Fri.	16	Phoenix
	Sun.	12	Ottawa*	Sun.	18	Boston*
	Wed.	15	Florida	Mon.	19	at Philadelphia
	Thu.	16	at Ottawa	Wed.	21	Atlanta
	Sat.	18	at New Jersey*	Fri.	23	New Jersey
	Wed.	22	at Pittsburgh	Sat.	24	Washington
	Fri.	24	at Boston*	Tue.	27	at Atlanta
	Sun.	26	Nashville*	**Mar.** Thu.	1	at NY Islanders
	Wed.	29	at Florida	Fri.	2	at New Jersey
	Thu.	30	Philadelphia	Sun.	4	at Chicago*
Dec.	Sun.	3	Ottawa*	Wed.	7	Columbus
	Wed.	6	at Atlanta	Thu.	8	at Tampa Bay
	Sat.	9	at Calgary	Sun.	11	Edmonton*
	Wed.	13	at Minnesota	Wed.	14	Montreal
	Fri.	15	Buffalo	Thu.	15	at Washington
	Sat.	16	at Boston	Sun.	18	NY Islanders*
	Tue.	19	at NY Islanders	Wed.	21	Buffalo
	Sat.	23	at Philadelphia*	Fri.	23	Pittsburgh
	Tue.	26	at Tampa Bay	Sat.	24	at Buffalo
	Wed.	27	NY Rangers	Mon.	26	Montreal
	Fri.	29	at Columbus	Wed.	28	at Washington
	Sun.	31	Chicago	Fri.	30	Washington
Jan.	Wed.	3	Tampa Bay	**Apr.** Sun.	1	at Ottawa*
	Sat.	6	Colorado	Tue.	3	at St. Louis
	Sun.	7	NY Islanders*	Wed.	4	at NY Rangers
	Tue.	9	Florida	Fri.	6	Atlanta
	Fri.	12	at Florida	Sun.	8	Pittsburgh*

* Denotes afternoon game.

Franchise date: June 22, 1979
Transferred from Hartford to Carolina,
June 25, 1997.

**SOUTHEAST
DIVISION**

**22nd
NHL
Season**

*Injuries limited Rod Brind'Amour to just four goals in 33 games for Carolina last season. A return to the form that
has seen him score at least 24 goals eight times in his career would make Brind'Amour a key contributor in 2000-01.*

2000-01 Player Personnel

FORWARDS

	HT	WT	S	Place of Birth	Date	1999-00 Club
ADAMS, Craig	6-0	200	R	Calgary, Alta.	4/26/77	Cincinnati (IHL)
BATTAGLIA, Bates	6-2	205	L	Chicago, IL	12/13/75	Carolina
BRIND'AMOUR, Rod	6-1	202	L	Ottawa, Ont.	8/9/70	Philadelphia-Carolina
COLE, Erik	6-1	200	L	Oswego, NY	11/6/78	Clarkson-Cincinnati (IHL)
DANIELS, Jeff	6-1	200	L	Oshawa, Ont.	6/24/68	Carolina
DiMAIO, Rob	5-10	190	R	Calgary, Alta.	2/19/68	Boston-NY Rangers
FRANCIS, Ron	6-3	200	L	Sault Ste. Marie, Ont.	3/1/63	Carolina
GELINAS, Martin	5-11	195	L	Shawinigan, Que.	6/5/70	Carolina
KAPANEN, Sami	5-10	195	L	Vantaa, Finland	6/14/73	Carolina
KOEHLER, Greg	6-2	195	L	Scarborough, Ont.	2/27/75	Cincinnati (IHL)
LANGDON, Darren	6-1	205	L	Deer Lake, Nfld.	1/8/71	NY Rangers
MacDONALD, Craig	6-2	195	L	Antigonish, N.S.	4/7/77	Cincinnati (IHL)
MacNEIL, Ian	6-2	190	L	Halifax, N.S.	4/27/77	Cincinnati (IHL)
O'NEILL, Jeff	6-1	190	R	Richmond Hill, Ont.	2/23/76	Carolina
RITCHIE, Byron	5-10	185	L	Burnaby, B.C.	4/24/77	Carolina-Cincinnati (IHL)
SVOBODA, Jaroslav	6-2	190	L	Cervenka, Czech.	6/1/80	Kootenay Ice
VASICEK, Josef	6-4	200	L	Havlickuv Brod, Czech.	9/12/80	Sault Ste. Marie
WESTLUND, Tommy	6-0	210	R	Fors, Sweden	12/29/74	Carolina
WILLIS, Shane	6-0	185	R	Edmonton, Alta.	6/13/77	Carolina-Cincinnati (IHL)

DEFENSEMEN

	HT	WT	S	Place of Birth	Date	1999-00 Club
HALKO, Steven	6-1	200	R	Etobicoke, Ont.	3/8/74	Carolina
HATCHER, Kevin	6-3	230	R	Detroit, MI	9/9/66	NY Rangers
KARPA, Dave	6-1	210	R	Regina, Sask.	5/7/71	Carolina-Cincinnati (IHL)
MALIK, Marek	6-5	215	L	Ostrava, Czech.	6/24/75	Carolina
OZOLINSH, Sandis	6-3	205	L	Riga, Latvia	8/3/72	Colorado
ROHLOFF, Jon	5-11	220	R	Mankato, MN	10/3/69	Kansas City
RUCINSKI, Mike	5-11	179	L	Trenton, MI	3/30/75	Cincinnati (IHL)
TANABE, David	6-1	190	R	Minneapolis, MN	7/19/80	Carolina-Cincinnati (IHL)
TSELIOS, Nikos	6-5	210	L	Oak Park, IL	1/20/79	Cincinnati (IHL)
WALLIN, Niclas	6-3	220	L	Boden, Sweden	2/20/75	Brynas IF
WESLEY, Glen	6-1	205	L	Red Deer, Alta.	10/2/68	Carolina

GOALTENDERS

	HT	WT	C	Place of Birth	Date	1999-00 Club
AMIDOVSKI, Bujar	5-11	180	L	Toronto, Ont.	2/19/77	Trenton Titans-Phi (AHL)
IRBE, Arturs	5-8	190	L	Riga, Latvia	2/2/67	Carolina
MAGLIARDITI, Marc	6-0	180	L	Niagara Falls, NY	7/9/76	Cin (IHL)-Florida Everblades
MOSS, Tyler	6-0	185	R	Ottawa, Ont.	6/29/75	Wilkes-Barre-Kansas City
PELLETIER, Jean-Marc	6-3	200	L	Atlanta, GA	3/4/78	Phi (AHL)-Cin (IHL)
PETRUK, Randy	5-9	180	R	Cranbrook, B.C.	4/23/78	Florida Everblades-Cin (IHL)

1999-2000 Scoring

*– rookie

Regular Season

Pos	#	Player	Team	GP	G	A	Pts	+/–	PIM	PP	SH	GW	GT	S	%
C	21	Ron Francis	CAR	78	23	50	73	10	18	7	0	4	0	150	15.3
C	92	Jeff O'Neill	CAR	80	25	38	63	–9	72	4	0	7	0	189	13.2
L	10	Gary Roberts	CAR	69	23	30	53	–10	62	12	0	1	0	150	15.3
R	24	Sami Kapanen	CAR	76	24	24	48	10	12	7	0	5	2	229	10.5
D	22	Sean Hill	CAR	62	13	31	44	3	59	8	0	2	0	150	8.7
R	18	Robert Kron	CAR	81	13	27	40	–4	8	2	1	3	1	134	9.7
D	77	Paul Coffey	CAR	69	11	29	40	–6	40	6	0	3	1	155	7.1
L	51	Andrei Kovalenko	CAR	76	15	24	39	–13	38	2	0	3	0	114	13.2
L	13	Bates Battaglia	CAR	77	16	18	34	20	39	3	0	3	0	86	18.6
L	23	Martin Gelinas	CAR	81	14	16	30	–10	40	3	0	0	0	139	10.1
C	27	Rod Brind'Amour	PHI	33	5	3	8	–1	4	0	0	0	0	26	19.2
			CAR	33	4	10	14	–12	22	0	1	1	0	61	6.6
			TOTAL	45	9	13	22	–13	26	4	1	1	0	87	10.3
L	28	Paul Ranheim	CAR	79	9	13	22	–14	6	0	0	2	0	98	9.2
D	2	Glen Wesley	CAR	78	7	15	22	–4	38	1	0	0	0	99	7.1
D	5	Marek Malik	CAR	57	4	10	14	13	63	0	0	1	0	57	7.0
R	16	* Tommy Westlund	CAR	81	4	8	12	–10	19	1	0	0	0	67	6.0
L	20	Sandy McCarthy	PHI	58	6	5	11	–5	111	1	0	0	0	68	8.8
			CAR	13	0	0	0	2	9	0	0	0	0	12	0.0
			TOTAL	71	6	5	11	–3	120	1	0	0	0	80	7.5
D	14	Steven Halko	CAR	58	0	8	8	0	25	0	0	0	0	54	0.0
L	17	* Jeff Daniels	CAR	69	3	4	7	–8	10	0	0	0	1	28	10.7
D	33	Dave Karpa	CAR	27	1	4	5	9	52	0	0	0	0	24	4.2
D	45	* David Tanabe	CAR	31	4	0	4	–4	14	3	0	0	0	28	14.3
D	4	Nolan Pratt	CAR	64	3	1	4	–22	90	0	0	1	0	47	6.4
C	15	* Byron Ritchie	CAR	26	0	2	2	–10	17	0	0	0	0	13	0.0
D	7	Curtis Leschyshyn	CAR	53	0	2	2	–19	14	0	0	0	0	31	0.0
G	1	Arturs Irbe	CAR	75	0	1	1	0	14	0	0	0	0	0	0.0
R	25	* Shane Willis	CAR	2	0	0	0	–1	0	0	0	0	1	0	0.0
G	30	Mark Fitzpatrick	CAR	3	0	0	0	0	0	0	0	0	0	0	0.0

Goaltending

No.	Goaltender	GPI	Mins	Avg	W	L	T	EN	SO	GA	SA	S%
1	Arturs Irbe	75	4345	2.42	34	28	9	8	5	175	1858	.906
41	Eric Fichaud	9	490	2.94	3	5	1	0	1	24	206	.883
30	Mark Fitzpatrick	3	107	4.49	0	2	0	1	0	8	68	.882
	Totals	**82**	**4974**	**2.61**	**37**	**35**	**10**	**9**	**6**	**216**	**2141**	**.899**

Arturs Irbe led all NHL netminders with 75 games played last season. His 34 wins broke Mike Liut's franchise record of 31.

Coach

MAURICE, PAUL
Coach, Carolina Hurricanes. Born in Sault Ste. Marie, Ont., January 30, 1967.

Paul Maurice is entering his sixth year as the franchise's head coach and is the first head coach of the Carolina Hurricanes. Maurice became the tenth coach in the history of the franchise on November 6, 1995, just 12 games into the 1995-96 season. Maurice stepped in as the youngest coach in the National Hockey League and remains the youngest head coach in the NHL despite ranking in the top five in tenure among NHL head coaches. In franchise history, Maurice ranks first in all-time wins (165) and games coached (398). In the 1996-97 season, Maurice was chosen to coach in the 1997 NHL All-Star Game.

Maurice joined the Whalers in June of 1995 as an assistant coach after serving as the head coach of the Detroit Junior Red Wings for two seasons. The Junior Wings won the OHL Western Division regular season title and played for the 1995 Memorial Cup by winning the OHL playoffs. The Wings lost in the Cup finals to Kamloops. For his efforts, Maurice was the runner-up for OHL coach of the year honors in 1995. In the 1993-94 season, Maurice's squad won the OHL Hap Emms Division title and advanced to the finals of the OHL playoffs before losing in seven games to North Bay.

Maurice began his coaching career in 1986 as an assistant coach for the Detroit Junior Red Wings after an eye injury ended his junior playing career. He served six seasons in that capacity before taking over the head coaching responsibilities in the 1993-94 season.

Coaching Record

Season	Team	Games	W	L	T	%	Games	W	L	%
			Regular Season					Playoffs		
1993-94	Detroit (OHL)	66	42	20	4	.697	17	11	6	.647
1994-95	Detroit (OHL)	66	44	18	4	.727	21	16	5	.762
1995-96	Hartford (NHL)	70	29	33	8	.471	....	....	....	....
1996-97	Hartford (NHL)	82	32	39	11	.457	....	....	....	....
1997-98	Carolina (NHL)	82	33	41	8	.451	....	....	....	....
1998-99	Carolina (NHL)	82	34	30	18	.524	6	2	4	.333
1999-2000	Carolina (NHL)	82	37	35	10	.512	....	....	....	....
	NHL Totals	**398**	**165**	**178**	**55**	**.484**	**6**	**2**	**4**	**.333**

General Managers' History

Jack Kelly, 1979-80, 1980-81; Larry Pleau, 1981-82, 1982-83; Emile Francis, 1983-84 to 1988-89; Ed Johnston, 1989-90 to 1991-92; Brian Burke, 1992-93; Paul Holmgren, 1993-94; Jim Rutherford, 1994-95 to date.

Coaching History

Don Blackburn, 1979-80; Don Blackburn and Larry Pleau, 1980-81; Larry Pleau, 1981-82; Larry Kish, Larry Pleau and John Cuniff, 1982- 83; Jack Evans, 1983-84 to 1986-87; Jack Evans and Larry Pleau, 1987-88; Larry Pleau, 1988-89; Rick Ley, 1989-90, 1990-91; Jim Roberts, 1991-92; Paul Holmgren, 1992-93; Paul Holmgren and Pierre Maguire, 1993-94; Paul Holmgren, 1994-95; Paul Holmgren and Paul Maurice, 1995-96; Paul Maurice, 1996-97 to date.

Captains' History

Rick Ley, 1979-80; Rick Ley and Mike Rogers, 1980-81; Dave Keon, 1981-82; Russ Anderson, 1982-83; Mark Johnson, 1983-84; Mark Johnson and Ron Francis, 1984-85; Ron Francis, 1985-86 to 1990-91; Randy Ladouceur, 1991-92; Pat Verbeek, 1992-93 to 1994-95; Brendan Shanahan, 1995-96; Kevin Dineen, 1996-97, 1997-98; Keith Primeau, 1998-99; Keith Primeau and Ron Francis, 1999-2000; Ron Francis, 2000-01.

Club Records

Team

(Figures in brackets for season records are games played; records for fewest points, wins, ties, losses, goals, goals against are for 70 or more games)

Most Points	93	1986-87 (80)
Most Wins	43	1986-87 (80)
Most Ties	19	1979-80 (80)
Most Losses	54	1982-83 (80)
Most Goals	332	1985-86 (80)
Most Goals Against	403	1982-83 (80)
Fewest Points	45	1982-83 (80)
Fewest Wins	19	1982-83 (80)
Fewest Ties	4	1985-86 (80)
Fewest Losses	30	1986-87 (80); 1998-99 (82)
Fewest Goals	200	1997-98 (82)
Fewest Goals Against	202	1998-99 (82)

Longest Winning Streak
Overall	7	Mar. 16-29/85
Home	5	Mar. 17-29/85
Away	6	Nov. 10-Dec. 7/90

Longest Undefeated Streak
Overall	10	Jan. 20-Feb. 10/82 (6 wins, 4 ties)
Home	7	Mar. 15-Apr. 5/86 (5 wins, 2 ties)
Away	8	Nov. 11-Dec. 5/96 (4 wins, 4 ties)

Longest Losing Streak
Overall	9	Feb. 19-Mar. 8/83
Home	6	Feb. 19-Mar. 12/83, Feb. 10-Mar. 3/85
Away	13	Dec. 18/82-Feb. 5/83

Longest Winless Streak
Overall	14	Jan. 4-Feb. 9/92 (8 losses, 6 ties)
Home	13	Jan. 15-Mar. 10/85 (11 losses, 2 ties)
Away	15	Nov. 11/79-Jan. 9/80 (11 losses, 4 ties)

Most Shutouts, Season	8	1998-99 (82)
Most PIM, Season	2,354	1992-93 (84)
Most Goals, Game	11	Feb. 12/84 (Edm. 0 at Hfd. 11), Oct. 19/85 (Mtl. 6 at Hfd. 11), Jan. 17/86 (Que. 6 at Hfd. 11), Mar. 15/86 (Chi. 4 at Hfd. 11)

Individual

Most Seasons	12	Kevin Dineen, Ron Francis
Most Games	874	Ron Francis
Most Goals, Career	308	Ron Francis
Most Assists, Career	638	Ron Francis
Most Points, Career	946	Ron Francis (308g, 638a)
Most PIM, Career	1,439	Kevin Dineen
Most Shutouts, Career	13	Mike Liut
Longest Consecutive Games Streak	419	Dave Tippett (Mar. 3/84-Oct. 7/89)
Most Goals, Season	56	Blaine Stoughton (1979-80)
Most Assists, Season	69	Ron Francis (1989-90)
Most Points, Season	105	Mike Rogers (1979-80; 44g, 61a), (1980-81; 40g, 65a)
Most PIM, Season	358	Torrie Robertson (1985-86)

Most Points, Defenseman, Season	69	Dave Babych (1985-86; 14g, 55a)
Most Points, Center, Season	105	Mike Rogers (1979-80; 44g, 61a), (1980-81; 40g, 65a)
Most Points, Right Wing, Season	100	Blaine Stoughton (1979-80; 56g, 44a)
Most Points, Left Wing, Season	89	Geoff Sanderson (1992-93; 46g, 43a)
Most Points, Rookie, Season	72	Sylvain Turgeon (1983-84; 40g, 32a)
Most Shutouts, Season	6	Arturs Irbe (1998-99)
Most Goals, Game	4	Jordy Douglas (Feb. 3/80), Ron Francis (Feb. 12/84)
Most Assists, Game	6	Ron Francis (Mar. 5/87)
Most Points, Game	6	Paul Lawless (Jan. 4/87; 2g, 4a), Ron Francis (Mar. 5/87; 6a) (Oct. 8/89; 3g, 3a)

Records include Hartford Whalers, 1979-80 through 1996-97.

All-time Record vs. Other Clubs

Regular Season

		At Home							On Road							Total					
	GP	W	L	T	GF	GA	PTS	GP	W	L	T	GF	GA	PTS	GP	W	L	T	GF	GA	PTS
Anaheim	6	4	1	1	18	12	9	5	2	3	0	17	21	4	11	6	4	1	35	33	13
Atlanta	3	3	0	0	11	4	6	2	2	0	0	8	5	4	5	5	0	0	19	9	10
Boston	68	29	32	7	230	237	65	70	19	44	7	186	261	45	138	48	76	14	416	498	110
Buffalo	70	28	32	10	210	213	66	69	22	40	7	210	279	51	139	50	72	17	420	492	117
Calgary	27	10	13	4	88	100	24	26	5	19	2	86	129	12	53	15	32	6	174	229	36
Chicago	28	13	12	3	92	89	29	26	7	16	3	72	111	17	54	20	28	6	164	200	46
Colorado	60	24	25	11	199	209	59	62	17	36	9	186	261	43	122	41	61	20	385	470	102
Dallas	28	10	14	4	91	105	24	27	10	16	1	81	109	21	55	20	30	5	172	214	45
Detroit	27	16	10	1	95	73	33	28	7	15	6	76	107	20	55	23	25	7	171	180	53
Edmonton	27	11	10	6	109	94	28	28	5	18	5	84	114	15	55	16	28	11	193	208	43
Florida	15	7	7	1	46	44	15	15	4	6	5	30	43	13	30	11	13	6	76	87	28
Los Angeles	27	13	10	4	105	105	30	27	10	14	3	108	115	23	54	23	24	7	213	220	53
Montreal	70	28	33	9	212	248	65	67	15	45	7	191	284	37	137	43	78	16	403	532	102
Nashville	2	2	0	0	7	2	4	2	0	2	0	4	6	0	4	2	2	0	11	8	4
New Jersey	36	16	13	7	122	113	39	37	13	21	3	121	132	29	73	29	34	10	243	245	68
NY Islanders	37	18	14	5	132	125	41	36	15	17	4	105	120	34	73	33	31	9	237	245	75
NY Rangers	35	19	13	3	123	115	41	37	11	23	3	100	147	25	72	30	36	6	223	262	66
Ottawa	19	15	2	2	62	37	32	21	10	8	3	63	57	23	40	25	10	5	125	94	55
Philadelphia	36	11	18	7	122	140	29	35	9	23	3	90	133	21	71	20	41	10	212	273	50
Phoenix	26	12	8	6	99	82	30	29	14	13	2	108	105	30	55	26	21	8	207	187	60
Pittsburgh	40	18	19	3	155	155	39	38	12	21	5	144	173	29	78	30	40	8	299	328	68
St. Louis	28	11	15	2	86	88	24	28	9	17	2	88	111	20	56	20	32	4	174	199	44
San Jose	8	4	4	0	26	18	8	8	4	4	0	28	36	8	16	8	8	0	54	54	16
Tampa Bay	16	11	2	3	56	40	25	16	6	7	3	45	46	15	32	17	9	6	101	86	40
Toronto	29	16	8	5	125	98	37	29	15	9	5	112	100	35	58	31	17	10	237	198	72
Vancouver	27	12	10	5	87	90	29	28	10	12	6	79	96	26	55	22	22	11	166	186	55
Washington	38	13	19	7	103	121	33	37	11	23	3	98	124	25	75	24	41	10	201	245	58
Totals	**833**	**374**	**343**	**116**	**2811**	**2757**	**864**	**833**	**264**	**472**	**97**	**2520**	**3225**	**625**	**1666**	**638**	**815**	**213**	**5331**	**5982**	**1489**

Playoffs

	Series	W	L	GP	W	L	T	GF	GA	Last Mtg.	Round	Result
Boston	3	0	3	19	7	12	0	48	63	1999	CQF	L 2-4
Colorado	2	1	1	9	5	4	0	35	34	1987	DSF	L 2-4
Montreal	5	0	5	27	8	19	0	70	96	1992	DSF	L 3-4
Totals	**10**	**1**	**9**	**55**	**20**	**35**	**0**	**153**	**193**			

Calgary totals include Atlanta Flames, 1979-80.
Dallas totals include Minnesota North Stars, 1979-80 to 1992-93.
Phoenix totals include Winnipeg, 1979-80 to 1995-96.

Colorado totals include Quebec, 1979-80 to 1994-95.
New Jersey totals include Colorado Rockies, 1979-80 to 1981-82.

Playoff Results 2000-1996

Year	Round	Opponent	Result	GF	GA
1999	CQF	Boston	L 2-4	10	16

Abbreviations: Round: CQF – conference quarter-final; **DSF** – division semi-final.

1999-2000 Results

Oct.	2	at Boston	3-1		9	NY Rangers	1-0
	7	at Philadelphia	2-0		11	Philadelphia	3-4
	8	at NY Rangers	1-3		14	at Florida	1-5
	11	at Calgary	3-3		17	at New Jersey	2-5
	13	at Edmonton	3-3		18	at NY Rangers	2-3
	15	at Vancouver	4-1		20	NY Rangers	1-4
	20	at Toronto	3-3		22	Buffalo	4-1
	22	at Buffalo	3-7		24	Montreal	3-2 *
	23	at Pittsburgh	3-2		27	Phoenix	2-4
	29	New Jersey	2-4		28	New Jersey	4-3 *
	30	at NY Islanders	4-0		30	at Montreal	0-3
Nov.	3	Toronto	0-6	**Feb.**	1	Florida	4-2
	5	at Detroit	2-3		3	at Washington	1-2
	7	Washington	3-2		8	at NY Islanders	4-3
	10	NY Islanders	0-2		12	at Tampa Bay	5-2
	11	at Philadelphia	1-4		14	at Toronto	5-2
	13	Tampa Bay	4-2		15	at Ottawa	1-5
	17	Ottawa	2-1		17	Montreal	0-3
	19	at Washington	3-3		19	Tampa Bay	4-2
	20	Dallas	1-0		21	Washington	1-1
	22	Boston	2-2		24	Florida	2-4
	24	Vancouver	1-1		26	at Florida	2-1 *
	26	at Tampa Bay	3-3	**Mar.**	1	at Phoenix	5-7
	27	Pittsburgh	5-3		2	at Los Angeles	5-2
	30	Calgary	4-3		4	at San Jose	5-2
Dec.	2	Toronto	2-2		8	Chicago	4-1
	4	at Colorado	1-3		10	Boston	3-5
	7	at St. Louis	4-2		12	Atlanta	5-1
	8	at Dallas	1-2		15	Edmonton	2-2
	10	at Tampa Bay	2-3		17	at Washington	2-4
	15	Pittsburgh	3-6		18	at Montreal	2-3
	18	Atlanta	4-2		21	at New Jersey	5-0
	20	Colorado	2-4		22	St. Louis	1-2
	22	Detroit	1-4		26	NY Islanders	4-1
	23	at Ottawa	3-4		27	Buffalo	1-5
	26	Florida	4-3 *		29	Nashville	3-1
	28	at Nashville	2-3		31	at Buffalo	3-1
Jan.	1	at Atlanta	4-2	**Apr.**	2	Philadelphia	1-0
	4	Ottawa	1-2		3	at Pittsburgh	2-3
	6	at Boston	7-3		8	at Atlanta	4-3
	7	Anaheim	4-4		9	Atlanta	2-1

* – Overtime

Entry Draft
Selections 2000-1986

2000
Pick
- 32 Tomas Kurka
- 80 Ryan Bayda
- 97 Niclas Wallin
- 110 Jared Newman
- 181 Justin Forrest
- 212 Magnus Kahnberg
- 235 Craig Kowalski
- 276 Troy Ferguson

1999
Pick
- 16 David Tanabe
- 49 Brett Lysak
- 84 Brad Fast
- 113 Ryan Murphy
- 174 Damian Surma
- 231 David Evans
- 237 Antti Jokela
- 259 Yevgeny Kurilin

1998
Pick
- 11 Jeff Heerema
- 70 Kevin Holdridge
- 71 Erik Cole
- 91 Josef Vasicek
- 93 Tommy Westlund
- 97 Chris Madden
- 184 Donald Smith
- 208 Jaroslav Svoboda
- 211 Mark Kosick
- 239 Brent McDonald

1997
Pick
- 22 Nikos Tselios
- 28 Brad DeFauw
- 80 Francis Lessard
- 142 Kyle Dafoe
- 169 Andrew Merrick
- 195 Niklas Nordgren
- 199 Randy Fitzgerald
- 225 Kent McDonell

1996
Pick
- 34 Trevor Wasyluk
- 61 Andrei Petrunin
- 88 Craig MacDonald
- 104 Steve Wasylko
- 116 Mark McMahon
- 143 Aaron Baker
- 171 Greg Kuznik
- 197 Kevin Marsh
- 223 Craig Adams
- 231 Askhat Rakhmatullin

1995
Pick
- 13 Jean-Sebastien Giguere
- 35 Sergei Fedotov
- 85 Ian MacNeil
- 87 Sami Kapanen
- 113 Hugh Hamilton
- 165 Byron Ritchie
- 191 Milan Kostolny
- 217 Mike Rucinski

1994
Pick
- 5 Jeff O'Neill
- 83 Hnat Domenichelli
- 109 Ryan Risidore
- 187 Tom Buckley
- 213 Ashlin Halfnight
- 230 Matt Ball
- 239 Brian Regan
- 265 Steve Nimigon

1993
Pick
- 2 Chris Pronger
- 72 Marek Malik
- 84 Trevor Roenick
- 115 Nolan Pratt
- 188 Manny Legace
- 214 Dmitri Gorenko
- 240 Wes Swinson
- 266 Igor Chibirev

1992
Pick
- 9 Robert Petrovicky
- 47 Andrei Nikolishin
- 57 Jan Vopat
- 79 Kevin Smyth
- 81 Jason McBain
- 143 Jarrett Reid
- 153 Ken Belanger
- 177 Konstantin Korotkov
- 201 Greg Zwakman
- 225 Steven Halko
- 249 Joacim Esbjors

1991
Pick
- 9 Patrick Poulin
- 31 Martin Hamrlik
- 53 Todd Hall
- 59 Michael Nylander
- 75 Jim Storm
- 119 Mike Harding
- 141 Brian Mueller
- 163 Steve Yule
- 185 Chris Belanger
- 207 Jason Currie
- 229 Mike Santonelli
- 251 Rob Peters

1990
Pick
- 15 Mark Greig
- 36 Geoff Sanderson
- 57 Mike Lenarduzzi
- 78 Chris Bright
- 120 Cory Keenan
- 141 Jergus Baca
- 162 Martin D'Orsonnens
- 183 Corey Osmak
- 204 Espen Knutsen
- 225 Tommie Eriksen
- 246 Denis Chalifoux

1989
Pick
- 10 Bobby Holik
- 52 Blair Atcheynum
- 73 Jim McKenzie
- 94 James Black
- 115 Jerome Bechard
- 136 Scott Daniels
- 157 Raymond Saumier
- 178 Michel Picard
- 199 Trevor Buchanan
- 220 John Battice
- 241 Peter Kasowski

1988
Pick
- 11 Chris Govedaris
- 32 Barry Richter
- 74 Dean Dyer
- 95 Scott Morrow
- 116 Corey Beaulieu
- 137 Kerry Russell
- 158 Jim Burke
- 179 Mark Hirth
- 200 Wayde Bucsis
- 221 Rob White
- 242 Dan Slatalla

1987
Pick
- 18 Jody Hull
- 39 Adam Burt
- 81 Terry Yake
- 102 Marc Rousseau
- 123 Jeff St. Cyr
- 144 Greg Wolf
- 165 John Moore
- 186 Joe Day
- 228 Kevin Sullivan
- 249 Steve Laurin

1986
Pick
- 11 Scott Young
- 32 Marc Laforge
- 74 Brian Chapman
- 95 Bill Horn
- 116 Joe Quinn
- 137 Steve Torrel
- 158 Ron Hoover
- 179 Robert Glasgow
- 200 Sean Evoy
- 221 Cal Brown
- 242 Brian Verbeek

President and General Manager

RUTHERFORD, JIM
President and General Manager, Carolina Hurricanes.
Born in Beeton, Ont., February 17, 1949.

Jim Rutherford, a former NHL goaltender, is the franchise's seventh general manager and the first general manager of the Carolina Hurricanes. Entering his seventh season, Rutherford has taken an aggressive approach towards improving the fortunes of the franchise through trades and the NHL draft.

A veteran of 13 NHL seasons, Rutherford began his professional goaltending career in 1969 as a first-round selection of the Detroit Red Wings. While playing for Detroit, Pittsburgh, Toronto and Los Angeles, Rutherford collected 14 career shutouts. For five seasons he also served as the Red Wings' player representative. Rutherford also played for Team Canada in the IIHF World Championships in Vienna in 1977 and Moscow in 1979.

After his playing days with the Red Wings, Rutherford joined Compuware to serve as the director of hockey operations for Compuware Sports Corporation. Rutherford gained a wealth of experience in youth hockey and junior programs. As a former player, coach, and general manager, his ability to develop players and produce winning programs is widely respected throughout the hockey community.

He started his management career by guiding Compuware Sports Corporation's purchase of the Windsor Spitfires of the Ontario Hockey League in April of 1984. During the next four years, Rutherford acted as general manager of the Spitfires. After the Spitfires advanced to the 1988 Memorial Cup finals, Rutherford led Compuware's efforts to bring the first American-based OHL franchise to Detroit on December 11, 1989. Rutherford was voted the 1987 executive of the year in both the OHL and the Canadian Hockey League and won the OHL executive of the year award again in 1988.

Club Directory

Entertainment and Sports Arena

Carolina Hurricanes
1400 Edwards Mill Rd.
Raleigh, NC 27607-3624
Phone **919/467-7825**
FAX 919/462-0123
Capacity: 18,730

Executive Management
Owner/Governor	Peter Karmanos, Jr.
General Partner	Thomas Thewes
Chief Executive Officer/General Manager	Jim Rutherford
President/Chief Operating Officer	Jim Cain
Vice President/Assistant General Manager	Jason Karmanos
Chief Financial Officer	Mike Amendola
Executive Vice President, Hockey Operations	Doug Piper

Hockey Operations
Head Coach	Paul Maurice
Assistant Coaches	Randy Ladouceur, Kevin McCarthy
Director of Amateur Scouting	Sheldon Ferguson
Amateur Scouts	Laurence Ferguson, Willy Langer, Willy Lindstrom, Tony MacDonald, Bert Marshall, Terry E. McDonnell
Pro Scout	Claude Larose
Goaltender Coach/Pro Scout	Steve Weeks
Video Coordinator	Chris Huffine
Head Athletic Therapist/Strength and Conditioning Coach	Peter Friesen
Assistant Athletic Therapist	Stu Lempke
Massage Therapist	Dave Duffy
Equipment Managers	Wally Tatomir, Skip Cunningham, Bob Gorman
Team Services Manager	Brian Tatum
Executive Assistant for Hockey Operations	Debbie Shannon

Administration
Receptionists	Mary Lou Ruetz, Rachel Cortez
General Office Assistant	Norris Bridges
Executive Assistant to Jim Cain	Lynn Reese

Arena Operations
Vice President and General Manager, ESA	Davin Olsen
Assistant General Manager, ESA	Larry Perkins
Booking Manager	Emma Bennett
Executive Assistant to Dave Olsen	Terri Cohen
Executive Assistant to Larry Perkins	Karla Timpani
Event Services Manager	Rhonda Watlington
Security Coordinator	Clinton Peterson
Parking Manager	Terry Putman
Director of Premium Services	Bene Wills
Premium Services Coordinator	Matt Shaw
Premium Services Assistant	Katie Schmitt
Event Coordinators	Stephanie Clark, Rob Douglas
Special Events Coordinator	Amie Becton
Facility Systems Manager	Ron Roach
Production Manager	Niles Ray
Event Production Technician	Joel Becker
Operations Supervisors	Adam Forchelli, Tom Lee, Dan McGowan, Timm Miller
Box Office Manager	Bill Nowicki
Box Office Supervisors	Eric Della Rocco, Joe Sousa, Kathy Voss
Arena Office Manager	Hillman Huskey
Group Sales Manager	Brian Slais
Guest Services Representatives	Nancy Hodge, Chris Jovino, Kelly Kirwin, Airen Murray

Broadcasters
Television Play-by-Play/Radio Analyst	John Forslund
Television Analyst	Tripp Tracy
Radio Play-by-Play	Chuck Kaiton

Communications
Director of Media Relations	Jerry Peters
Media Relations Assistant	Mike Sundheim
Director of Corporate Communications	Mary-Ann Baldwin
Motivational Consultant and Community Relations Development Manager	Doris E. Barksdale

Finance/Information Technology
Director of Arena Finance	Billy Traurig
Senior Accountant	Kevin Atamian
Accounting Manager	Melissa Anderson
Accounts Payable	Michael Arrington, Karen Kirby
Accounts Receivable	Patty Hilliard, Temika Smith
Payroll/Human Resources Manager	Sharon Khachadourian
Assistant to the Chief Financial Officer	Regina Bennett
Director of Information Technology	Glenn Johnson
Client/Server Technologist	Andrew Pollara
Programmer/Analyst	Kevin Slinkman

Marketing
Senior Director of Marketing	Ken Lehner
Director of Website/Creative Design	Howard Sadel
Marketing Manager	Sheila Carter
Manager of New Media & Graphics	Ami Herrman
Fan Development Manager	Brian Mehm
Director of In Game Entertainment	Bob Becker
Manager of In Game Entertainment	Pete Soto
Promotions Manager	Mike Bosasia
Community Relations Coordinator	Heather Wyson

Merchandise
Director of Merchandise	Kevin Murphy
Assistant Director of Merchandise	John Weinum

Sales
Vice President of Sales and Marketing	Rick Francis
New Business Development	Tony Gilliam
Account Executives	George Bliss, Susan Rotman, Bruce Weber
Corporate Sales and Client Services Manager	Kim Moore
Director of Ticket Operations	Scott Tippins
Hurricanes Box Office Manager	Mike Gilsenan
Ticket Sales Manager	Brian Tatum

Chicago Blackhawks

1999-2000 Results: 33W-39L-10T 78PTS. Third, Central Division

Alexei Zhamnov's 23 goals last season marked the most he has scored in four seasons with the Blackhawks. His seven game-winning goals led the team.

2000-01 Schedule

Oct.	Thu.	5	at Buffalo
	Sat.	7	at Columbus
	Thu.	12	Detroit
	Sat.	14	at Montreal
	Sun.	15	Columbus
	Wed.	18	NY Rangers
	Fri.	20	Dallas
	Sat.	21	at St. Louis
	Thu.	26	Colorado
	Sat.	28	Buffalo
	Sun.	29	at Minnesota
Nov.	Thu.	2	at Boston
	Fri.	3	at Detroit
	Sun.	5	Anaheim
	Wed.	8	San Jose
	Fri.	10	Minnesota
	Sat.	11	at Toronto
	Tue.	14	at Vancouver
	Thu.	16	at Calgary
	Fri.	17	at Edmonton
	Tue.	21	at Phoenix
	Wed.	22	at San Jose
	Fri.	24	at Minnesota*
	Mon.	27	at Detroit
	Thu.	30	Nashville
Dec.	Fri.	1	at Nashville
	Sun.	3	Columbus
	Thu.	7	Minnesota
	Sat.	9	at St. Louis
	Sun.	10	St. Louis
	Wed.	13	at Atlanta
	Fri.	15	at Dallas
	Sat.	16	at Nashville
	Thu.	21	Vancouver
	Sat.	23	at Ottawa*
	Wed.	27	Phoenix
	Fri.	29	Detroit
	Sun.	31	at Carolina
Jan.	Wed.	3	Vancouver
	Fri.	5	Edmonton
	Sun.	7	Tampa Bay

	Tue.	9	at NY Islanders
	Wed.	10	at New Jersey
	Fri.	12	at Columbus
	Sun.	14	Colorado
	Wed.	17	Florida
	Fri.	19	Washington
	Sun.	21	Pittsburgh
	Thu.	25	Philadelphia
	Fri.	26	at Colorado
	Sun.	28	at Vancouver
	Wed.	31	at Edmonton
Feb.	Thu.	1	at Calgary
	Tue.	6	at Los Angeles
	Wed.	7	at Anaheim
	Sat.	10	at San Jose
	Sun.	11	at Phoenix
	Wed.	14	San Jose
	Fri.	16	St. Louis
	Sun.	18	Los Angeles*
	Mon.	19	at NY Rangers*
	Wed.	21	Detroit
	Fri.	23	Atlanta
	Sun.	25	Toronto
	Tue.	27	at Washington
Mar.	Thu.	1	Los Angeles
	Sun.	4	Carolina*
	Wed.	7	at Dallas
	Fri.	9	at Anaheim
	Sat.	10	at Los Angeles
	Tue.	13	Dallas
	Thu.	15	Nashville
	Sun.	18	Anaheim*
	Thu.	22	Nashville
	Sat.	24	at St. Louis*
	Sun.	25	Calgary*
	Wed.	28	Ottawa
	Thu.	29	at Pittsburgh
Apr.	Sun.	1	Edmonton*
	Wed.	4	Calgary
	Fri.	6	Toronto
	Sun.	8	at Columbus

* Denotes afternoon game.

Franchise date: September 25, 1926

CENTRAL DIVISION

75th NHL Season

Year-by-Year Record

Season	GP	Home W	Home L	Home T	Road W	Road L	Road T	Overall W	Overall L	Overall T	GF	GA	Pts.	Finished		Playoff Result
1999-2000	82	16	20	5	17	19	5	33	39	10	242	245	78	3rd,	Central Div.	Out of Playoffs
1998-99	82	20	17	4	9	24	8	29	41	12	202	248	70	3rd,	Central Div.	Out of Playoffs
1997-98	82	14	19	8	16	20	5	30	39	13	192	199	73	5th,	Central Div.	Out of Playoffs
1996-97	82	16	21	4	18	14	9	34	35	13	223	210	81	5th,	Central Div.	Lost Conf. Quarter-Final
1995-96	82	22	13	6	18	15	8	40	28	14	273	220	94	2nd,	Central Div.	Lost Conf. Semi-Final
1994-95	48	11	10	3	13	9	2	24	19	5	156	115	53	3rd,	Central Div.	Lost Conf. Championship
1993-94	84	21	16	5	18	20	4	39	36	9	254	240	87	5th,	Central Div.	Lost Conf. Quarter-Final
1992-93	84	25	11	6	22	14	6	47	25	12	279	230	106	1st,	Norris Div.	Lost Div. Semi-Final
1991-92	80	23	9	8	13	20	7	36	29	15	257	236	87	2nd,	Norris Div.	Lost Final
1990-91	80	28	8	4	21	15	4	49	23	8	284	211	106	1st,	Norris Div.	Lost Div. Semi-Final
1989-90	80	25	13	2	16	20	4	41	33	6	316	294	88	1st,	Norris Div.	Lost Conf. Championship
1988-89	80	16	14	10	11	27	2	27	41	12	297	335	66	4th,	Norris Div.	Lost Conf. Championship
1987-88	80	21	17	2	9	24	7	30	41	9	284	328	69	3rd,	Norris Div.	Lost Div. Semi-Final
1986-87	80	18	13	9	11	24	5	29	37	14	290	310	72	3rd,	Norris Div.	Lost Div. Semi-Final
1985-86	80	23	12	5	16	21	3	39	33	8	351	349	86	1st,	Norris Div.	Lost Div. Semi-Final
1984-85	80	22	16	2	16	19	5	38	35	7	309	299	83	2nd,	Norris Div.	Lost Conf. Championship
1983-84	80	25	13	2	5	29	6	30	42	8	277	311	68	4th,	Norris Div.	Lost Div. Semi-Final
1982-83	80	29	8	3	18	15	7	47	23	10	338	268	104	1st,	Norris Div.	Lost Conf. Championship
1981-82	80	20	13	7	10	25	5	30	38	12	332	363	72	4th,	Norris Div.	Lost Conf. Championship
1980-81	80	21	11	8	10	22	8	31	33	16	304	315	78	2nd,	Smythe Div.	Lost Prelim. Round
1979-80	80	21	12	7	13	15	12	34	27	19	241	250	87	1st,	Smythe Div.	Lost Quarter-Final
1978-79	80	18	12	10	11	24	5	29	36	15	244	277	73	1st,	Smythe Div.	Lost Quarter-Final
1977-78	80	20	9	11	12	20	8	32	29	19	230	220	83	1st,	Smythe Div.	Lost Quarter-Final
1976-77	80	19	16	5	7	27	6	26	43	11	240	298	63	3rd,	Smythe Div.	Lost Prelim. Round
1975-76	80	17	15	8	15	15	10	32	30	18	254	261	82	1st,	Smythe Div.	Lost Quarter-Final
1974-75	80	24	12	4	13	23	4	37	35	8	268	241	82	3rd,	Smythe Div.	Lost Quarter-Final
1973-74	78	26	6	13	21	8	10	41	14	23	272	164	105	2nd,	West Div.	Lost Semi-Final
1972-73	78	26	9	4	16	18	5	42	27	9	284	225	93	1st,	West Div.	Lost Final
1971-72	78	28	3	8	18	14	7	46	17	15	256	166	107	1st,	West Div.	Lost Semi-Final
1970-71	78	30	6	3	19	14	6	49	20	9	277	184	107	1st,	West Div.	Lost Final
1969-70	76	26	7	5	19	15	4	45	22	9	250	170	99	1st,	East Div.	Lost Semi-Final
1968-69	76	20	14	4	14	19	5	34	33	9	280	246	77	6th,	East Div.	Out of Playoffs
1967-68	74	20	13	4	12	13	12	32	26	16	212	222	80	4th,	East Div.	Lost Semi-Final
1966-67	70	24	5	6	17	12	6	41	17	12	264	170	94	1st,		Lost Semi-Final
1965-66	70	21	8	6	16	17	2	37	25	8	240	187	82	2nd,		Lost Semi-Final
1964-65	70	20	13	2	14	15	6	34	28	8	224	176	76	3rd,		Lost Final
1963-64	70	26	4	5	10	18	7	36	22	12	218	169	84	2nd,		Lost Semi-Final
1962-63	70	17	9	9	15	12	8	32	21	17	194	178	81	2nd,		Lost Semi-Final
1961-62	70	20	10	5	11	16	8	31	26	13	217	186	75	3rd,		Lost Final
1960-61	**70**	**20**	**6**	**9**	**9**	**18**	**8**	**29**	**24**	**17**	**198**	**180**	**75**	**3rd,**		**Won Stanley Cup**
1959-60	70	18	11	6	10	18	7	28	29	13	191	180	69	3rd,		Lost Semi-Final
1958-59	70	14	12	9	14	17	4	28	29	13	197	208	69	3rd,		Lost Semi-Final
1957-58	70	15	17	3	9	22	4	24	39	7	163	202	55	5th,		Out of Playoffs
1956-57	70	12	15	8	4	24	7	16	39	15	169	225	47	6th,		Out of Playoffs
1955-56	70	9	19	7	10	20	5	19	39	12	155	216	50	6th,		Out of Playoffs
1954-55	70	6	21	8	7	19	9	13	40	17	161	235	43	6th,		Out of Playoffs
1953-54	70	8	21	6	4	30	1	12	51	7	133	242	31	6th,		Out of Playoffs
1952-53	70	14	11	10	13	17	5	27	28	15	169	175	69	4th,		Lost Semi-Final
1951-52	70	9	19	7	8	25	2	17	44	9	158	241	43	6th,		Out of Playoffs
1950-51	70	8	22	5	5	25	5	13	47	10	171	280	36	6th,		Out of Playoffs
1949-50	70	13	18	4	9	20	6	22	38	10	203	244	54	6th,		Out of Playoffs
1948-49	60	13	12	5	8	19	3	21	31	8	173	211	50	5th,		Out of Playoffs
1947-48	60	10	17	3	10	17	3	20	34	6	195	225	46	6th,		Out of Playoffs
1946-47	60	10	17	3	9	20	1	19	37	4	193	274	42	6th,		Out of Playoffs
1945-46	50	15	5	5	8	15	2	23	20	7	200	178	53	3rd,		Lost Semi-Final
1944-45	50	9	14	2	4	16	5	13	30	7	141	194	33	5th,		Out of Playoffs
1943-44	50	15	6	4	7	16	2	22	23	5	178	187	49	4th,		Lost Final
1942-43	50	14	3	8	3	15	7	17	18	15	179	180	49	5th,		Out of Playoffs
1941-42	48	15	8	1	7	15	2	22	23	3	145	155	47	4th,		Lost Quarter-Final
1940-41	48	11	10	3	5	15	4	16	25	7	112	139	39	5th,		Lost Semi-Final
1939-40	48	15	7	2	8	12	4	23	19	6	112	120	52	4th,		Lost Quarter-Final
1938-39	48	5	13	6	7	15	2	12	28	8	91	132	32	7th,		Out of Playoffs
1937-38	**48**	**10**	**10**	**4**	**4**	**15**	**5**	**14**	**25**	**9**	**97**	**139**	**37**	**3rd,**	**Amn. Div.**	**Won Stanley Cup**
1936-37	48	8	13	3	6	14	4	14	27	7	99	131	35	4th,	Amn. Div.	Out of Playoffs
1935-36	48	15	7	2	6	12	6	21	19	8	93	92	50	3rd,	Amn. Div.	Lost Quarter-Final
1934-35	48	19	3	2	14	8	2	26	17	5	118	88	57	2nd,	Amn. Div.	Lost Quarter-Final
1933-34	**48**	**13**	**4**	**7**	**7**	**13**	**4**	**20**	**17**	**11**	**88**	**83**	**51**	**2nd,**	**Amn. Div.**	**Won Stanley Cup**
1932-33	48	12	7	5	4	13	7	16	20	12	88	101	44	4th,	Amn. Div.	Out of Playoffs
1931-32	48	13	5	6	5	14	5	18	19	11	86	101	47	2nd,	Amn. Div.	Lost Quarter-Final
1930-31	44	13	8	1	11	9	2	24	17	3	108	78	51	2nd,	Amn. Div.	Lost Final
1929-30	44	12	9	1	9	9	4	21	18	5	117	111	47	2nd,	Amn. Div.	Lost Quarter-Final
1928-29	44	3	13	6	4	16	2	7	29	8	33	85	22	5th,	Amn. Div.	Out of Playoffs
1927-28	44	4	18	2	3	16	1	7	34	3	68	134	17	5th,	Amn. Div.	Out of Playoffs
1926-27	44	12	8	2	7	14	1	19	22	3	115	116	41	3rd,	Amn. Div.	Lost Quarter-Final

2000-01 Player Personnel

FORWARDS	HT	WT	S	Place of Birth	Date	1999-00 Club
AMONTE, Tony	6-0	200	L	Hingham, MA	8/2/70	Chicago
ATCHEYNUM, Blair	6-2	198	R	Estevan, Sask.	4/20/69	Chicago
BELL, Mark	6-3	198	L	St. Paul's, Ont.	8/5/80	Ottawa 67's
CALDER, Kyle	5-11	180	L	Mannville, Alta.	1/5/79	Chicago-Cleveland
DAZE, Eric	6-6	234	L	Montreal, Que.	7/2/75	Chicago
DOWNEY, Aaron	6-0	210	R	Shelburne, Ont.	8/27/74	Boston-Providence Bruins
DUBINSKY, Steve	6-0	190	L	Montreal, Que.	7/9/70	Calgary
GROSEK, Michal	6-2	207	R	Vyskov, Czech.	6/1/75	Buffalo-Chicago
HANKINSON, Casey	6-1	187	L	Edina, MN	5/8/76	Cleveland
HERPERGER, Chris	6-0	190	L	Esterhazy, Sask.	2/24/74	Cleveland-Chicago
JANSSENS, Mark	6-3	212	L	Surrey, B.C.	5/19/68	Chicago
JONES, Ty	6-3	218	R	Richland, WA	2/22/79	Cleveland-Florida Everblades
LEROUX, Jean-Yves	6-2	211	L	Montreal, Que.	6/24/76	Chicago
MARHA, Josef	6-0	176	L	Havlickuv, Czech.	6/2/76	Chicago
McAMMOND, Dean	5-11	200	L	Grand Cache, Alta.	6/15/73	Chicago
NYLANDER, Michael	5-11	195	L	Stockholm, Sweden	10/3/72	Tampa Bay-Chicago
PROBERT, Bob	6-3	225	L	Windsor, Ont.	6/5/65	Chicago
SULLIVAN, Steve	5-9	160	R	Timmins, Ont.	7/6/74	Toronto-Chicago
VANDENBUSSCHE, Ryan	6-0	200	R	Simcoe, Ont.	2/28/73	Chicago
ZELEPUKIN, Valeri	6-1	200	L	Voskresensk, USSR	9/17/68	Philadelphia
ZHAMNOV, Alexei	6-1	200	L	Moscow, USSR	10/1/70	Chicago

DEFENSEMEN						
ALLISON, Jamie	6-1	200	L	Lindsay, Ont.	5/13/75	Chicago
BAUMGARTNER, Nolan	6-2	205	R	Calgary, Alta.	3/23/76	Washington-Portland Pirates
BROWN, Brad	6-4	218	R	Baie Verte, Nfld.	12/27/75	Chicago
DEAN, Kevin	6-3	210	L	Madison, WI	4/1/69	Atlanta-Dallas-Chicago
ERIKSSON, Anders	6-2	220	L	Bollnas, Sweden	1/9/75	Chicago
McALPINE, Chris	6-0	210	R	Roseville, MN	12/1/71	StL-Worcester-T.B.-Atl.-Detroit Vipers
McCABE, Bryan	6-1	210	L	St. Catharines, Ont.	6/8/75	Chicago
McCARTHY, Steve	6-0	197	L	Trail, B.C.	2/3/81	Chicago-Kootenay Ice
MIRONOV, Boris	6-3	223	R	Moscow, USSR	3/21/72	Chicago
POAPST, Steve	6-0	200	L	Cornwall, Ont.	1/3/69	Portland Pirates
TOLKUNOV, Dmitri	6-2	190	R	Kiev, USSR	5/5/79	Cleveland
WILFORD, Marty	6-0	216	L	Cobourg, Ont.	4/17/77	Cleveland-Houston Aeros
ZMOLEK, Doug	6-2	222	L	Rochester, MN	11/3/70	Chicago

GOALTENDERS	HT	WT	C	Place of Birth	Date	1999-00 Club
LAROCQUE, Michel	5-11	200	L	Lahr, West Germany	10/3/76	Cleveland-Wilkes-Barre-Saint John-Greensboro
MAUND, Jeff	6-2	195	L	Mississauga, Ont.	4/8/76	Florida Everblades
SALTARELLI, Erasmo	5-11	190	L	Montreal, Que.	2/20/74	B.C. Icemen-Springfield
TALLAS, Robbie	6-0	170	L	Edmonton, Alta.	3/20/73	Boston
THIBAULT, Jocelyn	5-11	170	L	Montreal, Que.	1/12/75	Chicago

1999-2000 Scoring
* – rookie

Regular Season

Pos	#	Player	Team	GP	G	A	Pts	+/–	PIM	PP	SH	GW	GT	S	%
R	10	Tony Amonte	CHI	82	43	41	84	10	48	11	5	2	1	260	16.5
C	26	Steve Sullivan	TOR	7	0	1	1	–1	4	0	0	0	0	11	0.0
			CHI	73	22	42	64	20	52	2	1	6	0	169	13.0
			TOTAL	80	22	43	65	19	56	2	1	6	0	180	12.2
C	13	Alexei Zhamnov	CHI	71	23	37	60	7	61	5	0	7	0	175	13.1
C	92	Michael Nylander	T.B	11	1	2	3	–3	4	1	0	0	0	10	10.0
			CHI	66	23	28	51	9	26	4	0	2	0	112	20.5
			TOTAL	77	24	30	54	6	30	5	0	2	0	122	19.7
L	17	Michal Grosek	BUF	61	11	23	34	12	35	2	0	2	0	96	11.5
			CHI	14	2	4	6	–1	12	1	0	0	0	18	11.1
			TOTAL	75	13	27	40	11	47	3	0	2	0	114	11.4
D	2	Boris Mironov	CHI	58	9	28	37	–3	72	4	2	1	1	144	6.3
L	55	Eric Daze	CHI	59	23	13	36	–16	28	6	0	1	1	143	16.1
L	19	Dean McAmmond	CHI	76	14	18	32	11	72	1	0	1	0	118	11.9
D	8	Anders Eriksson	CHI	73	3	25	28	4	20	0	0	1	0	86	3.5
D	44	Bryan McCabe	CHI	79	6	19	25	–8	139	2	0	2	0	119	5.0
C	11	Josef Marha	CHI	81	10	12	22	–10	18	2	1	3	0	91	11.0
R	17 *	Jean-Pierre Dumont	CHI	47	10	8	18	–6	18	0	0	1	0	86	11.6
L	24	Bob Probert	CHI	69	4	11	15	10	114	0	0	0	0	38	10.5
R	34	Blair Atcheynum	CHI	47	5	7	12	–8	4	0	0	0	0	48	10.4
D	6	Kevin Dean	ATL	23	1	0	1	–5	14	0	1	0	0	9	11.1
			DAL	14	0	0	0	–1	10	0	0	0	0	6	0.0
			CHI	27	2	8	10	9	12	0	0	0	0	32	6.3
			TOTAL	64	3	8	11	3	36	0	1	0	0	47	6.4
D	4	Doug Zmolek	CHI	43	2	7	9	6	60	0	0	0	0	24	8.3
D	3	Brad Brown	CHI	57	0	9	9	–1	134	0	0	0	0	15	0.0
L	23	Jean-Yves Leroux	CHI	54	3	5	8	–10	43	0	0	1	0	36	8.3
C	20	Mark Janssens	CHI	36	0	6	6	–2	73	0	0	0	0	14	0.0
R	16	Ed Olczyk	CHI	33	2	2	4	–8	12	0	0	0	0	33	6.1
C	12	Derek Plante	DAL	16	1	1	2	–4	2	0	0	0	0	17	5.9
			CHI	17	1	1	2	–1	2	0	0	0	0	14	7.1
			TOTAL	33	2	2	4	–5	4	1	0	0	0	31	6.5
D	33	Jamie Allison	CHI	59	1	3	4	–5	102	0	0	0	0	24	4.2
D	32	Radim Bicanek	CHI	11	0	3	3	7	4	0	0	0	0	8	0.0
D	5 *	Steve McCarthy	CHI	5	1	1	2	4	0	0	0	0	0	4	25.0
L	25 *	Kyle Calder	CHI	8	1	1	2	–3	2	0	0	0	0	5	20.0
R	14	Ryan Vandenbussche	CHI	52	0	1	1	–3	143	0	0	0	0	19	0.0
G	31 *	Marc Lamothe	CHI	2	0	0	0	0	0	0	0	0	0	0	0.0
C	36 *	Chris Herperger	CHI	9	0	0	0	–2	5	0	0	0	0	2	0.0
G	29	Steve Passmore	CHI	24	0	0	0	0	0	0	0	0	0	0	0.0
G	41	Jocelyn Thibault	CHI	60	0	0	0	0	2	0	0	0	0	0	0.0

Goaltending

No.	Goaltender	GPI	Mins	Avg	W	L	T	EN	SO	GA	SA	S%
29	Steve Passmore	24	1388	2.72	7	12	3	4	1	63	654	.904
41	Jocelyn Thibault	60	3438	2.76	25	26	7	10	3	158	1679	.906
31	* Marc Lamothe	2	116	5.17	1	1	0	0	0	10	50	.800
	Totals	82	4984	2.95	33	39	10	14	4	245	2397	.898

Steve Sullivan registered career highs with 22 goals and 43 assists to trail only Tony Amonte among Blackhawks scorers in 1999-2000.

Coach

SUHONEN, ALPO
Coach, Chicago Blackhawks. Born in Valkeakoski, Finland, June 17, 1948.

Alpo Suhonen brings more than 34 years of hockey experience to the Blackhawks. As a coach, he is known for a free-flowing, creative and offensively imaginative team philosophy while not overlooking the importance of defense.

Suhonen played most of his career in the Finnish Elite League before taking over that country's national team programs in 1977, a post he held to 1986. Under his guidance, the Finnish Under-18 Team won the 1978 European Junior Championship on an overtime goal by Jari Kurri. That victory marked the first time any Finnish team had won an International tournament. Suhonen took over the reigns as head coach of the Finnish national team from 1982 to 1986 before coaching two years in the Swiss Elite League. He accepted his first North American coaching position as head coach of the Winnipeg Jets' American Hockey League affiliate in Moncton in February 1989.

Suhonen joined the Winnipeg Jets as an assistant coach for the 1989-90 season. Then, he returned to Finland to pursue the other passion in his life, the theater, for more than two years. Suhonen returned to the ice in 1995 as head coach of Kloten of the Swiss Elite League. Alpo guided his team to back-to-back league championships in 1995 and 1996.

In the spring of 1997, Suhonen returned to North America to be head coach of the Chicago Wolves of the International Hockey League. He then returned to Finland for a season before joining the Toronto Maple Leafs as an assistant coach on August 26, 1998. Suhonen's extensive coaching experience includes more than 1,500 games in Europe as a head coach and over 300 games as an assistant coach in the NHL.

Coaching Record

		Regular Season					Playoffs			
Season	Team	Games	W	L	T	%	Games	W	L	%
1986-87	Zurcher SC (Swiss-2)	36	26	8	2	.750	....	....	....	....
1987-88	Zurcher SC (Swiss-2)	36	22	8	6	.694	....	....	....	....
1988-89	Moncton (AHL)	23	7	13	3	.370	10	6	4	.600
1994-95	Kloten (Swiss)	36	15	13	8	.528	....	....	....	....
1995-96	Kloten (Swiss)	36	20	10	6	.639	....	....	....	....
1996-97	Chicago (IHL)	15	9	5	1	.633	4	1	3	.250
1997-98	HPK Hameenlinna (Finn)	35	14	16	5	.471	....	....	....	....

Captains' History

Dick Irvin, 1926-27 to 1928-29; Duke Dukowski, 1929-30; Ty Arbour, 1930-31; Cy Wentworth, 1931-32; Helge Bostrom, 1932-33; Chuck Gardiner, 1933-34; no captain, 1934-35; Johnny Gottselig, 1935-36 to 1939-40; Earl Seibert, 1940-41, 1941-42; Doug Bentley, 1942-43, 1943-44; Clint Smith 1944-45; John Mariucci, 1945-46; Red Hamill, 1946-47; John Mariucci, 1947-48; Gaye Stewart, 1948-49; Doug Bentley, 1949-50; Jack Stewart, 1950-51, 1951-52; Bill Gadsby, 1952-53, 1953-54; Gus Mortson, 1954-55 to 1956-57; no captain, 1957-58; Ed Litzenberger, 1958-59 to 1960-61; Pierre Pilote, 1961-62 to 1967-68, no captain, 1968-69; Pat Stapleton, 1969-70; no captain, 1970-71 to 1974-75; Stan Mikita and Pit Martin, 1975-76; Stan Mikita, Pit Martin and Keith Magnuson, 1976-77; Keith Magnuson, 1977-78, 1978-79; Keith Magnuson and Terry Ruskowski, 1979-80; Terry Ruskowski, 1980-81, 1981-82; Darryl Sutter, 1982-83 to 1984-85; Darryl Sutter and Bob Murray, 1985-86; Darryl Sutter, 1986-87; no captain, 1987-88; Denis Savard and Dirk Graham, 1988-89; Dirk Graham, 1989-90 to 1994-95; Chris Chelios, 1995-96 to 1998-99; Doug Gilmour, 1999-2000.

Club Records

Team

(Figures in brackets for season records are games played; records for fewest points, wins, ties, losses, goals, goals against are for 70 or more games)

Most Points	107	1970-71 (78), 1971-72 (78)
Most Wins	49	1970-71 (78), 1990-91 (80)
Most Ties	23	1973-74 (78)
Most Losses	51	1953-54 (70)
Most Goals	351	1985-86 (80)
Most Goals Against	363	1981-82 (80)
Fewest Points	31	1953-54 (70)
Fewest Wins	12	1953-54 (70)
Fewest Ties	6	1989-90 (80)
Fewest Losses	14	1973-74 (78)
Fewest Goals	*133	1953-54 (70)
Fewest Goals Against	164	1973-74 (78)

Longest Winning Streak

Overall	8	Dec. 9-26/71, Jan. 4-21/81
Home	13	Nov. 11-Dec. 20/70
Away	7	Dec. 9-29/64

Longest Undefeated Streak

Overall	15	Jan. 14-Feb. 16/67 (12 wins, 3 ties)
Home	18	Oct. 11-Dec. 20/70 (16 wins, 2 ties)
Away	12	Nov. 2-Dec. 16/67 (6 wins, 6 ties)

Longest Losing Streak

Overall	13	Feb. 25-Oct. 11/51
Home	11	Feb. 8-Nov. 22/28
Away	17	Jan. 2-Oct. 7/54

Longest Winless Streak

Overall	21	Dec. 17/50-Jan. 28/51 (18 losses, 3 ties)
Home	15	Dec. 16/28-Feb. 28/29 (11 losses, 4 ties)
Away	23	Dec. 19/50-Oct. 11/51 (21 losses, 2 ties)

Most Shutouts, Season	15	1969-70 (76)
Most PIM, Season	2,663	1991-92 (80)
Most Goals, Game	12	Jan. 30/69 (Chi. 12 at Phi. 0)

Individual

Most Seasons	22	Stan Mikita
Most Games	1,394	Stan Mikita
Most Goals, Career	604	Bobby Hull
Most Assists, Career	926	Stan Mikita
Most Points, Career	1,467	Stan Mikita (541G, 926A)
Most PIM, Career	1,495	Chris Chelios
Most Shutouts, Career	74	Tony Esposito

Longest Consecutive Games Streak	884	Steve Larmer (Oct. 6/82-Apr. 15/93)
Most Goals, Season	58	Bobby Hull (1968-69)
Most Assists, Season	87	Denis Savard (1981-82, 1987-88)
Most Points, Season	131	Denis Savard (1987-88; 44G, 87A)
Most PIM, Season	408	Mike Peluso (1991-92)

Most Points, Defenseman, Season	85	Doug Wilson (1981-82; 39G, 46A)
Most Points, Center, Season	131	Denis Savard (1987-88; 44G, 87A)
Most Points, Right Wing, Season	101	Steve Larmer (1990-91; 44G, 57A)
Most Points, Left Wing, Season	107	Bobby Hull (1968-69; 58G, 49A)
Most Points, Rookie, Season	90	Steve Larmer (1982-83; 43G, 47A)
Most Shutouts, Season	15	Tony Esposito (1969-70)
Most Goals, Game	5	Grant Mulvey (Feb. 3/82)
Most Assists, Game	6	Pat Stapleton (Mar. 30/69)
Most Points, Game	7	Max Bentley (Jan. 28/43; 4G, 3A), Grant Mulvey (Feb. 3/82; 5G, 2A)

* NHL Record.

Retired Numbers

1	Glenn Hall	1957-1967
9	Bobby Hull	1957-1972
18	Denis Savard	1980-1990, 1995-1997
21	Stan Mikita	1958-1980
35	Tony Esposito	1969-1984

All-time Record vs. Other Clubs

Regular Season

	At Home GP	W	L	T	GF	GA	PTS	On Road GP	W	L	T	GF	GA	PTS	Total GP	W	L	T	GF	GA	PTS
Anaheim	16	8	6	2	47	36	18	14	6	7	1	32	34	13	30	14	13	3	79	70	31
Atlanta	0	0	0	0	0	0	0	1	1	0	0	4	3	2	1	1	0	0	4	3	2
Boston	283	145	94	44	913	758	334	281	88	159	34	800	1015	210	564	233	253	78	1713	1773	544
Buffalo	48	26	16	6	158	133	59	50	13	31	6	129	189	32	98	39	47	12	287	322	91
Calgary	53	23	17	13	177	152	59	55	19	25	11	169	178	50	108	42	42	24	346	330	109
Carolina	26	16	7	3	111	72	35	28	12	13	3	89	92	27	54	28	20	6	200	164	62
Colorado	33	19	12	2	122	106	40	32	11	16	5	113	128	27	65	30	28	7	235	234	67
Dallas	102	63	26	13	405	264	139	104	43	46	15	323	350	101	206	106	72	28	728	614	240
Detroit	327	149	127	51	983	914	349	325	95	199	31	802	1116	221	652	244	326	82	1785	2030	570
Edmonton	36	19	12	5	145	129	43	37	17	16	4	133	138	38	73	36	28	9	278	267	81
Florida	6	2	3	1	18	23	5	6	4	2	0	25	16	8	12	6	5	1	43	39	13
Los Angeles	67	31	28	8	241	205	70	66	30	30	6	230	227	66	133	61	58	14	471	432	136
Montreal	272	93	124	55	729	758	241	272	53	171	48	639	1050	154	544	146	295	103	1368	1808	395
Nashville	6	3	2	1	21	19	7	6	2	3	1	15	19	5	12	5	5	2	36	38	12
New Jersey	44	24	11	9	173	122	57	43	16	16	11	133	129	43	87	40	27	20	306	251	100
NY Islanders	46	25	16	5	156	150	55	44	12	17	15	130	153	39	90	37	33	20	286	303	94
NY Rangers	283	127	114	42	861	785	296	283	112	116	55	801	834	279	566	239	230	97	1662	1619	575
Ottawa	6	3	1	2	15	13	8	7	4	3	0	21	19	8	13	7	4	2	36	32	16
Philadelphia	57	25	13	19	202	162	69	59	16	32	11	155	191	43	116	41	45	30	357	353	112
Phoenix	41	25	10	6	174	117	56	42	14	24	4	131	149	32	83	39	34	10	305	266	88
Pittsburgh	56	38	9	9	233	151	85	56	23	26	7	185	199	53	112	61	35	16	418	350	138
St. Louis	108	60	33	15	406	324	135	104	37	50	17	325	348	91	212	97	83	32	731	672	226
San Jose	17	9	6	2	57	50	20	18	9	9	0	52	48	18	35	18	15	2	109	98	38
Tampa Bay	10	5	3	2	30	25	12	9	3	4	2	23	22	8	19	8	7	4	53	47	20
Toronto	314	155	117	42	960	821	352	312	96	163	53	813	1063	245	626	251	280	95	1773	1884	597
Vancouver	63	42	15	6	237	143	90	64	20	29	15	187	192	55	127	62	44	21	424	335	145
Washington	37	21	11	5	146	113	47	38	13	20	5	119	137	31	75	34	31	10	265	250	78
Defunct Clubs	139	79	40	20	408	268	178	140	52	67	21	316	346	125	279	131	107	41	724	614	303
Totals	2496	1235	873	388	8128	6813	2859	2496	821	1294	381	6894	8385	2024	4992	2056	2167	769	15022	15198	4883

Playoffs

	Series	W	L	GP	W	L	T	GF	GA	Last Mtg.	Round	Result
Boston	6	1	5	22	5	16	1	63	97	1978	QF	L 0-4
Buffalo	2	0	2	9	1	8	0	17	36	1980	QF	L 0-4
Calgary	3	1	2	12	5	7	0	33	37	1996	CQF	W 4-0
Colorado	2	0	2	12	4	8	0	28	49	1997	CQF	L 2-4
Dallas	6	4	2	33	19	14	0	120	118	1991	DSF	L 2-4
Detroit	14	8	6	69	38	31	0	210	190	1995	CF	L 1-4
Edmonton	4	1	3	20	8	12	0	77	102	1992	CF	W 4-0
Los Angeles	1	1	0	5	4	1	0	10	7	1974	QF	W 4-1
Montreal	17	5	12	81	29	50	2	185	261	1976	QF	L 0-4
NY Islanders	2	0	2	6	0	6	0	6	21	1979	QF	L 0-4
NY Rangers	5	4	1	24	14	10	0	66	54	1973	SF	W 4-1
Philadelphia	1	1	0	4	4	0	0	20	8	1971	QF	W 4-0
Pittsburgh	2	1	1	8	4	4	0	24	23	1992	F	L 0-4
St. Louis	9	7	2	45	27	18	0	166	129	1993	DSF	L 2-4
Toronto	9	3	6	38	15	22	1	89	111	1995	CQF	W 4-3
Vancouver	2	1	1	9	5	4	0	24	24	1995	CSF	W 4-0
Defunct Clubs	4	2	2	9	5	3	1	16	15			
Totals	89	40	49	406	187	214	5	1154	1282			

Calgary totals include Atlanta Flames, 1972-73 to 1979-80.
Colorado totals include Quebec, 1979-80 to 1994-95.
New Jersey totals include Kansas City, 1974-75 to 1975-76, and Colorado Rockies, 1976-77 to 1981-82.
Phoenix totals include Winnipeg, 1979-80 to 1995-96.
Carolina totals include Hartford, 1979-80 to 1996-97.
Dallas totals include Minnesota North Stars, 1967-68 to 1992-93.

Playoff Results 2000-1996

Year	Round	Opponent	Result	GF	GA
1997	CQF	Colorado	L 2-4	14	28
1996	CSF	Colorado	L 2-4	14	21
	CQF	Calgary	W 4-0	16	7

Abbreviations: Round: F – Final; **CF** – conference final; **CSF** – conference semi-final; **CQF** – conference quarter-final; **DSF** – division semi-final; **SF** – semi-final; **QF** – quarter-final.

1999-2000 Results

Oct.	4	at San Jose	1-7		9	Colorado	5-3
	6	at Vancouver	4-5		12	Vancouver	3-2 *
	8	Phoenix	3-3		13	at Detroit	5-3
	10	Nashville	3-3		15	at Colorado	1-3
	15	Toronto	1-2		17	San Jose	5-4 *
	16	at Pittsburgh	3-3		19	at New Jersey	1-4
	21	Anaheim	5-5		21	St. Louis	0-3
	23	Detroit	0-1		23	Dallas	2-3
	27	at Montreal	1-0		27	Colorado	6-4
	29	at Detroit	4-2		30	at Vancouver	3-1
	30	Los Angeles	1-3	Feb.	2	at Edmonton	1-4
Nov.	4	Buffalo	4-5 *		3	at Calgary	5-5
	5	at Nashville	3-1		12	at Atlanta	4-3
	7	NY Rangers	1-3		14	Anaheim	3-4
	10	Nashville	2-4		16	Los Angeles	1-4
	12	NY Islanders	5-0		18	Washington	4-5
	14	Edmonton	3-6		20	Detroit	6-4
	16	at Los Angeles	2-3		22	at Philadelphia	1-3
	19	at Anaheim	2-4		23	Nashville	2-4
	20	at Phoenix	1-3		25	at Dallas	4-3 *
	24	at Edmonton	3-2		27	at St. Louis	4-1
	25	at Calgary	1-2 *	Mar.	1	Montreal	1-4
	27	at St. Louis	3-8		3	Tampa Bay	5-1
	30	at Ottawa	1-2		5	Phoenix	7-3
Dec.	3	Detroit	4-7		7	at Nashville	1-3
	4	at Boston	9-3		8	at Carolina	1-4
	6	Edmonton	5-1		11	at Florida	5-2
	9	New Jersey	0-4		12	at Tampa Bay	4-1
	10	at Buffalo	1-2		15	at Toronto	5-2
	12	Calgary	1-2		16	Boston	5-4 *
	14	at San Jose	5-2		18	Dallas	2-2
	17	at Anaheim	0-2		21	at Phoenix	3-0
	18	at Los Angeles	8-4		24	at Dallas	1-5
	23	Dallas	5-2		26	St. Louis	1-1
	26	Pittsburgh	2-4		27	at Colorado	1-3
	27	at Washington	2-2		30	Toronto	4-0
	30	Florida	2-1	Apr.	1	at NY Islanders	2-2
	31	at Detroit	4-4		2	Vancouver	2-2
Jan.	2	San Jose	1-4		5	Anaheim	5-2
	6	Calgary	5-2		7	at St. Louis	4-3 *
	8	at Nashville	3-6		9	St. Louis	3-1

* – Overtime

Entry Draft
Selections 2000-1986

2000
Pick

10	Mikhail Yakubov
11	Pavel Vorobjev
49	Jonas Nordqvist
74	Igor Radulov
106	Scott Balan
117	Olli Malmivaara
151	Alexander Barkunov
177	Michael Ayers
193	Joey Martin
207	Cliff Loya
225	Vladislav Luchkin
240	Adam Berkhoel
262	Peter Flache
271	Reto Von Arx
291	Arne Ramholt

1999
Pick

23	Steve McCarthy
46	Dimitri Levinski
63	Stepan Mokhov
134	Michael Jacobsen
165	Michael Leighton
194	Mattias Wennerberg
195	Yorick Treille
223	Andrew Carver

1998
Pick

8	Mark Bell
94	Matthias Trattnig
156	Kent Huskins
158	Jari Viuhkola
166	Jonathan Pelletier
183	Tyler Arnason
210	Sean Griffin
238	Alexandre Couture
240	Andrei Yershov

1997
Pick

13	Daniel Cleary
16	Ty Jones
39	Jeremy Reich
67	Mike Souza
110	Benjamin Simon
120	Peter Gardiner
130	Kyle Calder
147	Heath Gordon
174	Jerad Smith
204	Sergei Shikhanov
230	Chris Feil

1996
Pick

31	Remi Royer
42	Jeff Paul
46	Geoff Peters
130	Andy Johnson
184	Mike Vellinga
210	Chris Twerdun
236	Andrei Kozyrev

1995
Pick

19	Dmitri Nabokov
45	Christian Laflamme
71	Kevin McKay
82	Chris Van Dyk
97	Pavel Kriz
146	Marc Magliarditi
149	Marty Wilford
175	Steve Tardif
201	Casey Hankinson
227	Mike Pittman

1994
Pick

14	Ethan Moreau
40	Jean-Yves Leroux
85	Steve McLaren
118	Marc Dupuis
144	Jim Enson
170	Tyler Prosofsky
196	Mike Josephson
222	Lubomir Jandera
248	Lars Weibel
263	Rob Mara

1993
Pick

24	Eric Lecompte
50	Eric Manlow
54	Bogdan Savenko
76	Ryan Huska
90	Eric Daze
102	Patrik Pysz
128	Jonni Vauhkonen
180	Tom White
206	Sergei Petrov
232	Mike Rusk
258	Mike McGhan
284	Tom Noble

1992
Pick

12	Sergei Krivokrasov
36	Jeff Shantz
41	Sergei Klimovich
89	Andy MacIntyre
113	Tim Hogan
137	Gerry Skrypec
161	Mike Prokopec
185	Layne Roland
209	David Hymovitz
233	Richard Raymond

1991
Pick

22	Dean McAmmond
39	Mike Pomichter
44	Jamie Matthews
66	Bobby House
71	Igor Kravchuk
88	Zac Boyer
110	Maco Balkovec
112	Kevin St. Jacques
132	Jacques Auger
154	Scott Kirton
176	Roch Belley
198	Scott MacDonald
220	Alexander Andrievski
242	Mike Larkin
264	Scott Dean

1990
Pick

16	Karl Dykhuis
37	Ivan Droppa
79	Chris Tucker
121	Brett Stickney
124	Derek Edgerly
163	Hugo Belanger
184	Owen Lessard
205	Erik Peterson
226	Steve Dubinsky
247	Dino Grossi

1989
Pick

6	Adam Bennett
27	Michael Speer
48	Bob Kellogg
111	Tommi Pullola
132	Tracy Egeland
153	Milan Tichy
174	Jason Greyerbiehl
195	Matt Saunders
216	Mike Kozak
237	Michael Doneghey

1988
Pick

8	Jeremy Roenick
50	Trevor Dam
71	Stefan Elvenas
92	Joe Cleary
113	Justin Lafayette
134	Craig Woodcroft
155	Jon Pojar
176	Mathew Hentges
197	Daniel Maurice
218	Dirk Tenzer
239	Andreas Lupzig

1987
Pick

8	Jimmy Waite
29	Ryan McGill
50	Cam Russell
60	Mike Dagenais
92	Ulf Sandstrom
113	Mike McCormick
134	Stephen Tepper
155	John Reilly
176	Lance Werness
197	Dale Marquette
218	Bill Lacouture
239	Mike Lappin

1986
Pick

14	Everett Sanipass
35	Mark Kurzawski
77	Frantisek Kucera
98	Lonnie Loach
119	Mario Doyon
140	Mike Hudson
161	Marty Nanne
182	Geoff Benic
203	Glen Lowes
224	Chris Thayer
245	Sean Williams

Coaching History

Pete Muldoon, 1926-27; Barney Stanley and Hugh Lehman, 1927-28; Herb Gardiner and Dick Irvin, 1928-29; Tom Shaughnessy and Bill Tobin, 1929-30; Dick Irvin, 1930-31; Bill Tobin, 1931-32; Emil Iverson, Godfrey Matheson and Tommy Gorman, 1932-33; Tommy Gorman, 1933-34; Clem Loughlin, 1934-35 to 1936-37; Bill Stewart, 1937-38; Bill Stewart and Paul Thompson, 1938-39; Paul Thompson, 1939-40 to 1943-44; Paul Thompson and Johnny Gottselig, 1944-45; Johnny Gottselig, 1945-46, 1946-47; Johnny Gottselig and Charlie Conacher, 1947-48; Charlie Conacher, 1948-49, 1949-50; Ebbie Goodfellow, 1950-51, 1951-52; Sid Abel, 1952-53, 1953-54; Frank Eddolls, 1954-55; Dick Irvin, 1955-56; Tommy Ivan, 1956-57; Tommy Ivan and Rudy Pilous, 1957-58; Rudy Pilous, 1958-59 to 1962-63; Billy Reay, 1963-64 to 1975-76; Billy Reay and Bill White, 1976-77; Bob Pulford, 1977-78, 1978-79; Eddie Johnston, 1979-80; Keith Magnuson, 1980-81; Keith Magnuson and Bob Pulford, 1981-82; Orval Tessier, 1982-83, 1983-84; Orval Tessier and Bob Pulford, 1984-85; Bob Pulford, 1985-86, 1986-87; Bob Murdoch, 1987-88; Mike Keenan, 1988-89 to 1991-92; Darryl Sutter, 1992-93 to 1994-95; Craig Hartsburg, 1995-96 to 1997-98; Dirk Graham and Lorne Molleken, 1998-99; Lorne Molleken and Bob Pulford, 1999-2000; Alpo Suhonen, 2000-01.

Manager of Hockey Operations

SMITH, MIKE
Manager of Hockey Operations, Chicago Blackhawks.
Born in Potsdam, New York, August 31, 1945.

Mike Smith joined the Chicago Blackhawks as Manager of Hockey Operations on December 12, 1999. Smith served as Associate General Manager of the Toronto Maple Leafs for two seasons (1997-98 to 1998-99) before joining the Blackhawks. Previously, he had served as a consultant under Bob Pulford with Chicago from 1995 to 1997. Smith held a variety of positions with the Winnipeg Jets from 1979 to 1994, including general manager. Under Smith, the Jets entered into a formal agreement with Sokol Kiev in 1989, the first of its kind for any NHL team.

Smith has a doctorate in Political Science and Russian Studies from Syracuse University. He has authored 10 books, mostly on coaching hockey. Mike and his wife Judy have a son, Jason.

NHL Coaching Record

		Regular Season					Playoffs			
Season	Team	Games	W	L	T	%	Games	W	L	%
1980-81	Winnipeg	23	2	17	4	.174	....	....	....	....
	NHL Totals	**23**	**2**	**17**	**4**	**.174**	....	....	....	....

Club Directory

United Center

Chicago Blackhawks
United Center
1901 W. Madison Street
Chicago, IL 60612
Phone 312/455-7000
FAX 312/455-7041
www.chicagoblackhawks.com
Capacity: 20,500

President	William W. Wirtz
Senior Vice President	Robert J. Pulford
Vice President	Jack Davison
Vice President	Peter R. Wirtz
Manager of Hockey Operations	Mike Smith
Assistant General Manager	Nick Beverley
Director of Pro Scouting	Joe Yannetti
Director of Player Personnel	Dale Tallon
Head Coach	Alpo Suhonen
Assistant Coach	Denis Savard
Assistant Coach	Don Jackson
Asst Coach, Strength & Conditioning	Phil Walker
Goaltending Consultant	Vladislav Tretiak
Chief Amateur Scout	Michel Dumas
Amateur Scout	Bruce Franklin
Amateur Scout	Tim Higgins
Amateur Scout	Ron Anderson
European Scout	Sakari Pietela
Executive Assistant	Cindy Brueck
Manager of Team Services	David Stensby

Medical Staff

Club Doctors	Mark Bowen, Gordon Nuber, Greg Ewert
Team Dentist	Dr. Daniel Mackey, Dr. Dean Sana
Oral Surgeon	Dr. Eric Pulver
Eye Doctor	Dr. Robert Stein
Head Trainer	Michael Gapski
Equipment Manager	Troy Parchman
Asst. Equipment Mgr.	Lou Varga
Asst. Equipment Mgr.	Bill Stehle
Massage Therapist	Pawel Prylinski
Equipment Assistant	Jim Terracino

Public Relations/Marketing

Executive Director of Communications	Jim De Maria
Director of Communiation Relations/PR Assistant	Barbara Davidson
Manager of Public Relations	Tony Ommen
Exec. Director of Marketing and New Business Development	Jim Sofranko
Director of Corporate Sponsorships	Steve Waight
Account Executive, Corporate Sponsorship	Matt Colleran
Manager, Client Services	Kelly Bodnarchuk
Executive Director of Fan Development, Oper., Charities	Carol Czaplicki
Manager, Youth and Fan Development	Drew Stevenson
Manager, Game Operations	Mike Sullivan
Web Producer	Kellett McConville
Marketing Coordinator	Maxine Ohlava
Marketing Associate	Alison Tragesser
Administrative Assistant	Angela Armbruster

Finance

Treasurer	Robert Rinkus
Controller	Tracy Hernandez
Accounting Manager	Deb Kulir
Accounting Clerk	Rita Loretto

Ticketing

Director, Ticket Operations	James K. Bare
Director, Ticket Sales	Doug Ryan
Account Executive	Jamie Arbuckle
Account Executive	Andy Blackburn
Account Executive	Brad Bober
Account Executive	Ryan Francescatti
Account Executive	Katie Golem
Account Executive	Steve Rigney
Ticket Operations Manager	Kathie Raimondi
Administrative Assistant	Martha Webster

Miscellaneous Information

Team Photographer	Bill Smith
Organist	Frank Pellico
Public Address Announcer	Harvey Wittenberg
Executive Offices/Home Ice	United Center
Location of Press Box	South Side of United Center
Radio Station	WSCR (AM 670)
Television Station	Fox Sports Chicago
Broadcasters	Pat Foley, Bill Gardner

General Managers' History

Major Frederic McLaughlin, 1926-27 to 1941-42; Bill Tobin, 1942-43 to 1953-54; Tommy Ivan, 1954-55 to 1976-77; Bob Pulford, 1977-78 to 1989-90; Mike Keenan, 1990-91, 1991-92; Mike Keenan and Bob Pulford, 1992-93; Bob Pulford, 1993-94 to 1996-97; Bob Murray, 1997-98 to 1998-99; Bob Murray and Bob Pulford, 1999-2000; Bob Pulford, 2000-01.

Colorado Avalanche

1999-2000 Results: 42W-29L-11T 96PTS. First, Northwest Division

2000-01 Schedule

Oct.	Wed.	4	at Dallas		Sun.	7	at Detroit
	Sat.	7	at Edmonton		Wed.	10	at Columbus
	Tue.	10	at Calgary		Fri.	12	at Minnesota
	Thu.	12	at Vancouver		Sun.	14	at Chicago
	Sat.	14	Columbus		Tue.	16	NY Islanders
	Tue.	17	at Washington		Thu.	18	Vancouver
	Wed.	18	at Columbus		Sat.	20	at San Jose*
	Fri.	20	Florida		Sun.	21	at Anaheim*
	Wed.	25	Nashville		Fri.	26	Chicago
	Thu.	26	at Chicago		Sat.	27	at Nashville
	Sat.	28	Edmonton		Tue.	30	at San Jose
	Mon.	30	Phoenix	Feb.	Thu.	1	at Vancouver
Nov.	Wed.	1	at Vancouver		Wed.	7	Washington
	Fri.	3	Carolina		Fri.	9	Calgary
	Tue.	7	Minnesota		Sat.	10	St. Louis
	Thu.	9	St. Louis		Tue.	13	at Montreal
	Sat.	11	Anaheim		Thu.	15	at Ottawa
	Mon.	13	Pittsburgh		Sat.	17	at Toronto
	Wed.	15	at Anaheim		Mon.	19	at Pittsburgh*
	Thu.	16	at Phoenix		Wed.	21	Boston
	Sat.	18	at Los Angeles*		Fri.	23	Minnesota
	Wed.	22	Columbus		Sun.	25	Atlanta*
	Sat.	25	Calgary	Mar.	Sat.	3	Buffalo*
	Wed.	29	Phoenix		Sun.	4	at Phoenix
Dec.	Fri.	1	Dallas		Tue.	6	at Atlanta
	Sun.	3	at NY Rangers		Thu.	8	at St. Louis
	Tue.	5	at New Jersey		Sat.	10	at Dallas*
	Fri.	8	at Tampa Bay		Sun.	11	Dallas
	Sat.	9	at Florida		Tue.	13	New Jersey
	Mon.	11	Tampa Bay		Sat.	17	Detroit*
	Wed.	13	Philadelphia		Sun.	18	Minnesota*
	Fri.	15	Detroit		Tue.	20	San Jose
	Tue.	19	Calgary		Thu.	22	at St. Louis
	Thu.	21	Los Angeles		Sat.	24	at Boston*
	Sat.	23	Vancouver		Wed.	28	at Edmonton
	Tue.	26	at Nashville		Thu.	29	at Calgary
	Wed.	27	Edmonton		Sat.	31	at Los Angeles*
	Fri.	29	Nashville	Apr.	Mon.	2	Edmonton
Jan.	Tue.	2	Los Angeles		Wed.	4	Anaheim
	Thu.	4	San Jose		Sat.	7	at Detroit*
	Sat.	6	at Carolina		Sun.	8	at Minnesota*

* Denotes afternoon game.

Franchise date: June 22, 1979
Transferred from Quebec to Denver,
June 21, 1995

22nd NHL Season

NORTHWEST DIVISION

Patrick Roy enters the 2000-01 campaign with 444 career victories. His fourth win this season will move him past Terry Sawchuk into first place on the NHL's all-time win list.

Year-by-Year Record

Season	GP	Home W	L	T	Road W	L	T	Overall W	L	T	GF	GA	Pts.	Finished		Playoff Result
1999-2000	82	25	12	4	17	17	7	42	29	11	233	201	96	1st,	Northwest Div.	Lost Conf. Championship
1998-99	82	21	14	6	23	14	4	44	28	10	239	205	98	1st,	Northwest Div.	Lost Conf. Championship
1997-98	82	21	10	10	18	16	7	39	26	17	231	205	95	1st,	Pacific Div.	Lost Conf. Quarter-Final
1996-97	82	26	10	5	23	14	4	49	24	9	277	205	107	1st,	Pacific Div.	Lost Conf. Championship
1995-96	**82**	**24**	**10**	**7**	**23**	**15**	**3**	**47**	**25**	**10**	**326**	**240**	**104**	**1st,**	**Pacific Div.**	**Won Stanley Cup**
1994-95*	48	19	1	4	11	12	1	30	13	5	185	134	65	1st,	Northeast Div.	Lost Conf. Quarter-Final
1993-94*	84	19	17	6	15	25	2	34	42	8	277	292	76	5th,	Northeast Div.	Out of Playoffs
1992-93*	84	23	17	2	24	10	8	47	27	10	351	300	104	2nd,	Adams Div.	Lost Div. Semi-Final
1991-92*	80	18	19	3	2	29	9	20	48	12	255	318	52	5th,	Adams Div.	Out of Playoffs
1990-91*	80	9	23	8	7	27	6	16	50	14	236	354	46	5th,	Adams Div.	Out of Playoffs
1989-90*	80	8	26	6	4	35	1	12	61	7	240	407	31	5th,	Adams Div.	Out of Playoffs
1988-89*	80	16	20	4	11	26	3	27	46	7	269	342	61	5th,	Adams Div.	Out of Playoffs
1987-88*	80	15	23	2	17	20	3	32	43	5	271	306	69	5th,	Adams Div.	Out of Playoffs
1986-87*	80	20	13	7	11	26	3	31	39	10	267	276	72	4th,	Adams Div.	Lost Div. Final
1985-86*	80	23	13	4	20	18	2	43	31	6	330	289	92	1st,	Adams Div.	Lost Div. Semi-Final
1984-85*	80	24	12	4	17	18	5	41	30	9	323	275	91	2nd,	Adams Div.	Lost Conf. Championship
1983-84*	80	24	11	5	18	17	5	42	28	10	360	278	94	3th,	Adams Div.	Lost Div. Final
1982-83*	80	23	10	7	11	24	5	34	34	12	343	336	80	4th,	Adams Div.	Lost Div. Semi-Final
1981-82*	80	24	13	3	9	18	13	33	31	16	356	345	82	4th,	Adams Div.	Lost Conf. Championship
1980-81*	80	18	11	11	12	21	7	30	32	18	314	318	78	4th,	Adams Div.	Lost Prelim. Round
1979-80*	80	17	16	7	8	28	4	25	44	11	248	313	61	5th,	Adams Div.	Out of Playoffs

* Quebec Nordiques

2000-01 Player Personnel

FORWARDS	HT	WT	S	Place of Birth	Date	1999-00 Club
AULIN, Jared	6-0	180	R	Calgary, Alta.	3/15/82	Kamloops Blazers
BABENKO, Yuri	6-1	200	L	Penza, USSR	1/2/78	Hershey Bears
BOOTLAND, Nick	6-3	215	L	Shelbourne, Ont.	7/31/78	Hershey Bears
CRAIG, Mike	6-1	180	R	St. Mary's, Ont.	6/6/71	Kentucky
DEADMARSH, Adam	6-0	195	R	Trail, B.C.	5/10/75	Colorado
DINGMAN, Chris	6-4	245	L	Edmonton, Alta.	7/6/76	Colorado
DRURY, Chris	5-10	180	R	Trumbull, CT	8/20/76	Colorado
FAIRCHILD, Kelly	5-11	180	L	Hibbing, MN	4/9/73	Michigan K-Wings
FORSBERG, Peter	6-0	190	L	Ornskoldsvik, Sweden	7/20/73	Colorado
HEJDUK, Milan	5-11	185	R	Usti-nad-Labem, Czech.	2/14/76	Colorado
HINOTE, Dan	6-0	190	R	Leesburg, FL	1/30/77	Colorado-Hershey Bears
KLIAZMINE, Sergei	6-3	190	L	Mozhajsk, USSR	1/3/82	Dynamo Moscow-2
KOVAC, Kristian	6-2	205	R	Kosice, Czech.	1/1/81	Victoriaville Tigres
KRESTANOVICH, Jordan	6-0	168	L	Surrey, B.C.	6/14/81	Calgary Hitmen-Hershey Bears
LARSEN, Brad	5-11	212	L	Nakusp, B.C.	1/28/77	Hershey Bears
LAZAREV, Yevgeny	6-2	205	L	Kharkov, USSR	4/25/80	Hershey Bears
LOVDAHL, Anders	6-4	189	L	Borlange, Sweden	2/4/81	Calgary Hitmen-Moose Jaw
NIEMINEN, Ville	6-0	200	L	Tampere, Finland	4/6/77	Colorado-Hershey Bears
PARKER, Scott	6-5	230	R	Hanford, CA	1/29/78	Hershey Bears
PODEIN, Shjon	6-2	200	L	Rochester, MN	3/5/68	Colorado
PRPIC, Joel	6-7	225	L	Sudbury, Ont.	9/25/74	Boston-Providence Bruins
RADIVOJEVIC, Branko	6-1	200	R	Piestany, Czech.	11/24/80	Belleville Bulls
REID, Dave	6-1	217	L	Toronto, Ont.	5/15/64	Colorado
SAKIC, Joe	5-11	185	L	Burnaby, B.C.	7/7/69	Colorado
SHEARER, Rob	5-10	190	L	Kitchener, Ont.	10/19/76	Hershey Bears
TANGUAY, Alex	6-0	180	L	Ste-Justine, Que.	11/21/79	Colorado
TIMMONS, K.C.	6-4	215	L	Victoria, B.C.	4/6/80	Tri-City Americans-Hershey
VRBATA, Radim	6-1	185	R	Mlada Boleslav, Czech.	6/13/81	Hull Olympiques
WILLSIE, Brian	6-1	195	R	London, Ont.	3/16/78	Colorado-Hershey Bears
YELLE, Stephane	6-1	190	L	Ottawa, Ont.	5/9/74	Colorado

DEFENSEMEN	HT	WT	S	Place of Birth	Date	1999-00 Club
BERRY, Rick	6-2	210	L	Brandon, Man.	11/4/78	Hershey Bears
BOURQUE, Ray	5-11	219	L	Montreal, Que.	12/28/60	Boston-Colorado
de VRIES, Greg	6-3	215	L	Sundridge, Ont.	1/4/73	Colorado
FOOTE, Adam	6-1	205	R	Toronto, Ont.	7/10/71	Colorado
GUSAROV, Alexei	6-3	185	L	Leningrad, USSR	7/8/64	Colorado
KLEMM, Jon	6-3	200	R	Cranbrook, B.C.	1/8/70	Colorado
LINDSTROM, Sanny	6-2	205	L	Huddinge, Sweden	12/24/79	Hershey Bears-Baton Rouge
MALGUNAS, Stewart	6-0	200	L	Prince George, B.C.	4/21/70	Utah Grizzlies-Calgary
MESSIER, Eric	6-2	200	L	Drummondville, Que.	10/29/73	Colorado
MILLER, Aaron	6-3	200	R	Buffalo, NY	8/11/71	Colorado
PRATT, Nolan	6-2	210	L	Fort McMurray, Alta.	8/14/75	Carolina
RIAZANTSEV, Alexander	6-0	210	R	Moscow, USSR	3/15/80	Victoriaville Tigres-Hershey
SAUER, Kurt	6-4	220	L	St. Cloud, MN	1/16/81	Spokane Chiefs
SAVIELS, Agris	6-2	200	L	Riga, Latvia	1/15/82	Owen Sound
SCORSUNE, Matthew	6-2	210	L	Morristown, NJ	6/27/77	Harvard University
SKOULA, Martin	6-2	195	L	Litomerice, Czech.	10/28/79	Colorado
SMITH, Dan	6-2	200	L	Fernie, B.C.	10/19/76	Colorado-Hershey Bears
STOREY, Ben	6-2	200	L	Ottawa, Ont.	6/22/77	Hershey Bears
WHITE, Brian	6-1	195	R	Winchester, MA	2/7/76	Hershey Bears

GOALTENDERS	HT	WT	C	Place of Birth	Date	1999-00 Club
AEBISCHER, David	6-1	190	L	Fribourg, Switz.	2/7/78	Hershey Bears
CASSIVI, Frederic	6-4	205	L	Sorel, Que.	6/12/75	Hershey Bears
ROY, Patrick	6-2	192	L	Quebec City, Que.	10/5/65	Colorado
SAUVE, Phillipe	6-0	180	L	Buffalo, NY	2/27/80	Drummondville-Hull Olympiques

General Managers' History

Maurice Filion, 1979-80 to 1987-88; Martin Madden, 1988-89; Martin Madden and Maurice Filion, 1989-90; Pierre Page, 1990-91 to 1993-94; Pierre Lacroix, 1994-95 to date.

President and General Manager

LACROIX, PIERRE
President and General Manager, Colorado Avalanche.
Born in Montreal, Que., August 3, 1948.

Pierre Lacroix was appointed to the general manager's post on May 24, 1994 after 21 years as a respected player agent. In his first season as general manager, his leadership was instrumental in moving the team from 11th to second place in the NHL. Lacroix's second season began with the club's move to Denver. He set out to improve the team and did so through acquisitions that brought Claude Lemieux, Sandis Ozolinsh, Patrick Roy and Mike Keane to Colorado. The revamped Avs finished atop the Pacific Division and went on to win the Stanley Cup. He was named NHL executive of the year by *The Hockey News* and became president of the club's hockey operations in August, 1995.

Lacroix and his wife Colombe have two children. Martin is a player agent, Eric plays in the NHL.

1999-2000 Scoring

* – rookie

Regular Season

Pos	#	Player	Team	GP	G	A	Pts	+/–	PIM	PP	SH	GW	GT	S	%
C	19	Joe Sakic	COL	60	28	53	81	30	28	5	1	5	0	242	11.6
R	23	Milan Hejduk	COL	82	36	36	72	14	16	13	0	9	2	228	15.8
C	37	Chris Drury	COL	82	20	47	67	8	42	7	0	2	0	213	9.4
D	77	Ray Bourque	BOS	65	10	28	38	–11	20	6	0	0	0	217	4.6
			COL	14	8	6	14	9	6	7	0	0	0	43	18.6
			TOTAL	79	18	34	52	–2	26	13	0	0	0	260	6.9
D	8	Sandis Ozolinsh	COL	82	16	36	52	17	46	6	0	1	0	210	7.6
L	40	Alex Tanguay	COL	76	17	34	51	6	22	5	0	3	1	74	23.0
C	21	Peter Forsberg	COL	49	14	37	51	9	52	3	0	2	0	105	13.3
R	18	Adam Deadmarsh	COL	71	18	27	45	–10	106	5	0	4	0	153	11.8
L	38	Dave Andreychuk	BOS	63	19	14	33	–11	28	7	0	2	1	192	9.9
			COL	14	1	2	3	–9	2	1	0	1	0	41	2.4
			TOTAL	77	20	16	36	–20	30	8	0	3	1	233	8.6
C	26	Stephane Yelle	COL	79	8	14	22	9	28	0	1	1	0	90	8.9
L	25	Shjon Podein	COL	75	11	8	19	12	29	0	1	3	0	104	10.6
L	14	Dave Reid	COL	65	11	7	18	12	28	0	0	2	0	86	12.8
D	52	Adam Foote	COL	59	5	13	18	5	98	1	0	2	0	63	7.9
D	55	* Martin Skoula	COL	80	3	13	16	5	20	2	0	0	0	66	4.5
D	24	Jon Klemm	COL	73	5	7	12	26	34	0	0	0	0	64	7.8
L	11	Chris Dingman	COL	68	8	3	11	–2	132	2	0	1	0	54	14.8
D	29	Eric Messier	COL	61	3	6	9	0	24	1	0	0	0	28	10.7
D	7	Greg De Vries	COL	69	2	7	9	–7	73	0	0	0	0	40	5.0
D	3	Aaron Miller	COL	53	1	7	8	3	36	0	0	0	0	44	2.3
D	5	Alexei Gusarov	COL	34	2	2	4	–8	10	0	0	0	0	16	12.5
R	38	* Dan Hinote	COL	27	1	3	4	0	10	0	0	0	0	14	7.1
C	49	* Serge Aubin	COL	15	2	1	3	1	6	0	0	0	0	14	14.3
R	36	Jeff Odgers	COL	62	1	2	3	–7	162	0	0	1	0	29	3.4
G	33	Patrick Roy	COL	63	0	3	3	0	10	0	0	0	0	0	0.0
G	30	* Marc Denis	COL	23	0	2	2	0	0	0	0	0	0	0	0.0
R	17	* Christian Matte	COL	5	0	1	1	–2	4	0	0	0	0	1	0.0
R	50	* Brian Willsie	COL	1	0	0	0	0	0	0	0	0	0	0	0.0
L	39	* Ville Nieminen	COL	1	0	0	0	0	0	0	0	0	0	1	0.0
G	35	Rick Tabaracci	ATL	1	0	0	0	0	0	0	0	0	0	0	0.0
			COL	2	0	0	0	0	0	0	0	0	0	0	0.0
			TOTAL	3	0	0	0	0	0	0	0	0	0	0	0.0
D	43	* Dan Smith	COL	3	0	0	0	2	0	0	0	0	0	0	0.0
D	44	* Sami Helenius	COL	33	0	0	0	–5	46	0	0	0	0	6	0.0

Goaltending

No.	Goaltender	GPI	Mins	Avg	W	L	T	EN	SO	GA	SA	S%
35	Rick Tabaracci	2	60	2.00	1	0	0	0	0	2	18	.889
33	Patrick Roy	63	3704	2.28	32	21	8	5	2	141	1640	.914
30	* Marc Denis	23	1203	2.54	9	8	3	2	3	51	618	.917
	Totals	82	4990	2.42	42	29	11	7	5	201	2283	.912

Playoffs

Pos	#	Player	Team	GP	G	A	Pts	+/–	PIM	PP	SH	GW	OT	S	%
C	21	Peter Forsberg	COL	16	7	8	15	9	12	2	1	4	0	54	13.0
R	18	Adam Deadmarsh	COL	17	4	11	15	7	21	1	0	1	0	41	9.8
C	37	Chris Drury	COL	17	4	10	14	7	4	1	0	2	0	44	9.1
D	8	Sandis Ozolinsh	COL	17	5	5	10	1	20	3	0	1	0	42	11.9
R	23	Milan Hejduk	COL	17	5	4	9	–7	6	3	0	1	0	50	10.0
C	19	Joe Sakic	COL	17	2	7	9	–5	8	2	0	0	0	48	4.2
D	77	Ray Bourque	COL	13	1	8	9	4	8	0	0	0	0	28	3.6
D	52	Adam Foote	COL	16	0	7	7	6	28	0	0	0	0	15	0.0
L	25	Shjon Podein	COL	17	5	0	5	4	8	0	0	1	0	26	19.2
L	38	Dave Andreychuk	COL	17	3	2	5	–3	18	2	0	1	0	38	7.9
L	14	Dave Reid	COL	17	1	3	4	4	0	0	0	0	0	24	4.2
D	24	Jon Klemm	COL	17	2	1	3	4	9	0	0	0	0	16	12.5
L	40	* Alex Tanguay	COL	17	2	1	3	–2	2	1	0	1	0	13	15.4
C	26	Stephane Yelle	COL	17	1	2	3	3	4	0	0	0	0	25	4.0
D	3	Aaron Miller	COL	17	1	1	2	4	6	0	0	0	0	10	10.0
D	55	* Martin Skoula	COL	17	0	2	2	–3	4	0	0	0	0	14	0.0
D	29	Eric Messier	COL	14	0	1	1	1	4	0	0	0	0	3	0.0
G	33	Patrick Roy	COL	17	0	1	1	0	4	0	0	0	0	0	0.0
C	49	* Serge Aubin	COL	17	0	1	1	1	6	0	0	0	0	8	0.0
R	36	Jeff Odgers	COL	4	0	0	0	0	4	0	0	0	0	1	0.0
D	7	Greg De Vries	COL	5	0	0	0	2	4	0	0	0	0	1	0.0

Goaltending

No.	Goaltender	GPI	Mins	Avg	W	L	EN	SO	GA	SA	S%
33	Patrick Roy	17	1039	1.79	11	6	1	3	31	431	.928
	Totals	17	1043	1.84	11	6	1	3	32	432	.926

Club Records

Team

(Figures in brackets for season records are games played; records for fewest points, wins, ties, losses, goals, goals against are for 70 or more games)

Most Points	107	1996-97 (82)
Most Wins	49	1996-97 (82)
Most Ties	18	1980-81 (80)
Most Losses	61	1989-90 (80)
Most Goals	360	1983-84 (80)
Most Goals Against	407	1989-90 (80)
Fewest Points	31	1989-90 (80)
Fewest Wins	12	1989-90 (80)
Fewest Ties	5	1987-88 (80)
Fewest Losses	24	1996-97 (82)
Fewest Goals	231	1997-98 (82)
Fewest Goals Against	201	1999-2000 (82)

Longest Winning Streak
Overall	12	Jan. 10-Feb. 7/99
Home	10	Nov. 26/83-Jan. 10/84, Mar. 6-Apr. 16/95
Away	7	Jan. 10-Feb. 7/99

Longest Undefeated Streak
Overall	12	Dec. 23/96-Jan. 20/97 (9 wins, 3 ties), Jan. 10-Feb. 7/99 (12 wins)
Home	14	Nov. 19/83-Jan. 21/84 (11 wins, 3 ties)
Away	10	Jan. 10-Mar. 3/99 (8 wins, 2 ties)

Longest Losing Streak
Overall	14	Oct. 21-Nov. 19/90
Home	8	Oct. 21-Nov. 24/90
Away	18	Jan. 18-Apr. 1/90

Longest Winless Streak
Overall	17	Oct. 21-Nov. 25/90 (15 losses, 2 ties)
Home	11	Nov. 14-Dec. 26/89 (7 losses, 4 ties)
Away	33	Oct. 8/91-Feb. 27/92 (25 losses, 8 ties)

Most Shutouts, Season	8	1996-97 (82)
Most PIM, Season	2,104	1989-90 (80)
Most Goals, Game	12	Three times

Individual

Most Seasons	12	Joe Sakic
Most Games	852	Joe Sakic
Most Goals, Career	456	Michel Goulet
Most Assists, Career	668	Peter Stastny
Most Points, Career	1,060	Joe Sakic (403G, 657A)
Most PIM, Career	1,562	Dale Hunter
Most Shutouts, Career	19	Patrick Roy
Longest Consecutive Games Streak	312	Dale Hunter (Oct. 9/80-Mar. 13/84)
Most Goals, Season	57	Michel Goulet (1982-83)
Most Assists, Season	93	Peter Stastny (1981-82)
Most Points, Season	139	Peter Stastny (1981-82; 46G, 93A)
Most PIM, Season	301	Gord Donnelly (1987-88)
Most Points, Defenseman, Season	82	Steve Duchesne (1992-93; 20G, 62A)
Most Points, Center, Season	139	Peter Stastny (1981-82; 46G, 93A)
Most Points, Right Wing, Season	103	Jacques Richard (1980-81; 52G, 51A)
Most Points, Left Wing, Season	121	Michel Goulet (1983-84; 56G, 65A)
Most Points, Rookie, Season	109	Peter Stastny (1980-81; 39G, 70A)
Most Shutouts, Season	7	Patrick Roy (1996-97)
Most Goals, Game	5	Mats Sundin (Mar. 5/92), Mike Ricci (Feb. 17/94)
Most Assists, Game	5	Six times
Most Points, Game	8	Peter Stastny (Feb. 22/81; 4G, 4A), Anton Stastny (Feb. 22/81; 3G, 5A)

Records include Quebec Nordiques, 1979-80 through 1994-95.

Quebec Nordiques Retired Numbers

3	J.C. Tremblay	1972-1979
8	Marc Tardif	1979-1983
16	Michel Goulet	1979-1990

Captains' History

Marc Tardif, 1979-80, 1980-81; Robbie Ftorek and Andre Dupont, 1981-82; Mario Marois, 1982-83 to 1984-85; Mario Marois and Peter Stastny, 1985-86; Peter Stastny, 1986-87 to 1989-90; Joe Sakic and Steven Finn, 1990-91; Mike Hough, 1991-92; Joe Sakic, 1992-93 to date.

All-time Record vs. Other Clubs

Regular Season

	At Home GP	W	L	T	GF	GA	PTS	On Road GP	W	L	T	GF	GA	PTS	Total GP	W	L	T	GF	GA	PTS
Anaheim	13	7	4	2	48	39	16	13	6	4	3	31	32	15	26	13	8	5	79	71	31
Atlanta	1	0	1	0	3	4	0	1	1	0	0	3	2	2	2	1	1	0	6	6	2
Boston	62	22	34	6	219	261	50	60	20	31	9	185	236	49	122	42	65	15	404	497	99
Buffalo	61	30	20	11	221	189	71	61	17	35	9	197	242	43	122	47	55	20	418	431	114
Calgary	36	15	12	9	143	121	39	37	12	19	6	117	143	30	73	27	31	15	260	264	69
Carolina	62	36	17	9	261	186	81	60	25	24	11	209	199	61	122	61	41	20	470	385	142
Chicago	32	16	11	5	128	113	37	33	12	19	2	106	122	26	65	28	30	7	234	235	63
Dallas	33	19	10	4	131	92	42	33	13	16	4	98	106	30	66	32	26	8	229	198	72
Detroit	34	18	12	4	129	116	40	32	12	19	1	100	121	25	66	30	31	5	229	237	65
Edmonton	36	16	17	3	145	145	35	36	14	20	2	113	158	30	72	30	37	5	258	303	65
Florida	8	2	3	3	20	21	7	8	7	1	0	35	22	14	16	9	4	3	55	43	21
Los Angeles	34	17	14	3	139	123	37	35	11	21	3	115	149	25	69	28	35	6	254	272	62
Montreal	62	31	26	5	209	216	67	61	15	37	9	192	254	39	123	46	63	14	401	470	106
Nashville	4	3	0	1	13	6	7	4	1	2	1	11	11	4	8	4	2	2	24	17	11
New Jersey	31	16	12	3	115	90	35	33	12	17	4	115	137	28	64	28	29	7	230	227	63
NY Islanders	31	18	11	2	117	95	38	30	13	16	1	104	120	27	61	31	27	3	221	215	65
NY Rangers	32	16	13	3	132	124	35	30	8	18	4	83	121	20	62	24	31	7	215	245	55
Ottawa	13	11	1	1	64	34	23	14	7	5	2	61	44	16	27	18	6	3	125	78	39
Philadelphia	31	11	9	11	115	110	33	32	8	22	2	87	120	19	63	19	31	13	202	230	52
Phoenix	33	15	14	4	121	120	34	32	14	12	6	119	121	34	65	29	26	10	240	241	68
Pittsburgh	30	15	13	2	135	119	32	33	13	15	5	134	138	31	63	28	28	7	269	257	63
St. Louis	33	18	11	4	117	92	40	32	8	21	3	97	134	19	65	26	32	7	214	226	59
San Jose	15	10	2	3	65	31	23	16	9	7	0	63	53	18	31	19	9	3	128	84	41
Tampa Bay	10	7	2	1	46	22	15	9	1	7	1	22	31	3	19	8	9	2	68	53	18
Toronto	29	17	7	5	111	87	39	31	14	14	3	122	104	31	60	31	21	8	233	191	70
Vancouver	37	17	13	7	123	105	41	36	18	12	6	144	125	42	73	35	25	13	267	230	83
Washington	30	14	12	4	98	107	32	31	10	17	4	100	126	24	61	24	29	8	198	233	56
Totals	**833**	**417**	**301**	**115**	**3168**	**2768**	**949**	**833**	**301**	**430**	**102**	**2763**	**3171**	**705**	**1666**	**718**	**731**	**217**	**5931**	**5939**	**1654**

Playoffs

	Series	W	L	GP	W	L	T	GF	GA	Last Mtg.	Round	Result
Boston	2	1	1	11	5	6	0	36	37	1983	DSF	L 1-3
Buffalo	2	2	0	8	6	2	0	35	27	1985	DSF	W 3-2
Chicago	2	2	0	12	8	4	0	49	28	1997	CQF	W 4-2
Dallas	2	0	2	14	6	8	0	29	37	2000	CF	L 3-4
Detroit	4	3	1	23	14	9	0	66	54	2000	CSF	W 4-1
Edmonton	2	1	1	12	7	5	0	35	30	1998	CQF	W 3-4
Florida	1	1	0	4	4	0	0	15	4	1996	F	W 4-0
Hartford	2	1	1	9	4	5	0	34	35	1987	DSF	W 4-2
Montreal	5	2	3	31	14	17	0	85	105	1993	DSF	L 2-4
NY Islanders	1	0	1	4	0	4	0	9	18	1982	CF	L 0-4
NY Rangers	1	0	1	6	2	4	0	19	25	1995	CQF	L 2-4
Philadelphia	2	0	2	11	4	7	0	29	39	1985	CF	L 2-4
Phoenix	1	1	0	5	4	1	0	17	10	2000	CQF	W 4-1
San Jose	1	1	0	6	4	2	0	19	17	1999	CQF	W 4-2
Vancouver	1	1	0	6	4	2	0	24	17	1996	CQF	W 4-2
Totals	**29**	**16**	**13**	**162**	**86**	**76**	**0**	**501**	**483**			

Playoff Results 2000-1996

Year	Round	Opponent	Result	GF	GA
2000	CF	Dallas	L 3-4	13	14
	CSF	Detroit	W 4-1	13	8
	CQF	Phoenix	W 4-1	17	10
1999	CF	Dallas	L 3-4	16	23
	CSF	Detroit	W 4-2	21	14
	CQF	San Jose	W 4-2	19	17
1998	CQF	Edmonton	L 3-4	16	19
1997	CF	Detroit	L 2-4	12	16
	CSF	Edmonton	W 4-1	19	11
	CQF	Chicago	W 4-2	28	14
1996	**F**	**Florida**	**W 4-0**	**15**	**4**
	CF	Detroit	W 4-2	20	16
	CSF	Chicago	W 4-2	21	14
	CQF	Vancouver	W 4-2	24	17

Abbreviations: Round: F – Final; **CF** – conference final; **CSF** – conference semi-final; **CQF** – conference quarter-final; **DSF** – division semi-final.

Calgary totals include Atlanta Flames, 1979-80.
Dallas totals include Minnesota North Stars, 1979-80 to 1992-93.
Phoenix totals include Winnipeg, 1979-80 to 1995-96.

Carolina totals include Hartford, 1979-80 to 1996-97.
New Jersey totals include Colorado Rockies, 1979-80 to 1981-82.

1999-2000 Results

Oct.	5	at Nashville	3-2		9	at Chicago	3-5
	6	at Toronto	1-2		11	Nashville	4-2
	8	at Pittsburgh	3-3		13	Pittsburgh	4-3
	10	at NY Islanders	2-4		15	Chicago	3-1
	11	at Boston	3-3		17	Phoenix	2-0
	13	Boston	2-1		19	San Jose	0-0
	16	Ottawa	3-1		21	at Anaheim	3-3
	20	at Montreal	2-1		23	at Los Angeles	2-3
	21	at Ottawa	1-4		25	at San Jose	4-3
	23	at Atlanta	3-2 *		27	at Chicago	4-6
	27	at Detroit	3-5		29	at St. Louis	0-4
	28	at Philadelphia	4-5 *	Feb.	1	Vancouver	2-1
Nov.	3	Phoenix	3-5		3	San Jose	3-3
	3	St. Louis	5-0		8	Buffalo	0-2
	5	NY Rangers	4-1		10	Calgary	3-2
	11	at Los Angeles	2-5		13	Detroit	3-4
	13	at Calgary	5-2		15	at Washington	1-2
	15	at Vancouver	2-2		17	at New Jersey	5-5
	17	Florida	1-2		18	at NY Rangers	4-2
	19	NY Islanders	2-3		20	Dallas	1-2
	22	at Dallas	3-2 *		22	Atlanta	3-4
	23	Los Angeles	2-6		25	at St. Louis	2-3
	26	at Phoenix	0-7		27	at Dallas	1-1
	27	Calgary	7-1		29	Edmonton	1-3
	30	at Vancouver	4-2	Mar.	2	New Jersey	5-0
Dec.	1	at Edmonton	1-3		4	Tampa Bay	4-1
	4	Carolina	3-1		7	at Calgary	8-3
	6	Vancouver	5-2		10	at Edmonton	4-2
	8	at San Jose	2-4		12	Philadelphia	3-1
	10	at Anaheim	2-1		14	Anaheim	4-2
	12	at Vancouver	3-2 *		16	Nashville	2-2
	15	Anaheim	2-4		18	Detroit	3-4
	17	at Detroit	2-5		20	Vancouver	2-3
	18	at Nashville	2-2		23	at Phoenix	2-2
	20	at Carolina	4-2		26	at Dallas	2-1 *
	23	at Buffalo	1-2		27	Chicago	3-1
	27	St. Louis	5-1		29	Edmonton	3-2
	29	Los Angeles	4-2	Apr.	2	Dallas	3-2 *
Jan.	3	Edmonton	2-2		5	at Edmonton	3-2
	5	Calgary	4-0		7	at Calgary	3-1
	7	Montreal	4-1		9	Detroit	3-2

* – Overtime

Entry Draft
Selections 2000-1986

2000 Pick		1996 Pick		1992 Pick		1988 Pick	
14	Vaclav Nedorost	25	Peter Ratchuk	4	Todd Warriner	3	Curtis Leschyshyn
47	Jared Aulin	51	Yuri Babenko	28	Paul Brousseau	5	Daniel Dore
50	Sergei Soin	79	Mark Parrish	29	Tuomas Gronman	24	Stephane Fiset
63	Agris Saviels	98	Ben Storey	52	Manny Fernandez	45	Petri Aaltonen
88	Kurt Sauer	107	Randy Petruk	76	Ian McIntyre	66	Darin Kimble
92	Sergei Kliazmine	134	Luke Curtin	100	Charlie Wasley	87	Stephane Venne
119	Brian Fahey	146	Brian Willsie	124	Paxton Schulte	108	Ed Ward
159	John-Michael Liles	160	Kai Fischer	148	Martin Lepage	129	Valeri Kamensky
189	Chris Bahen	167	Dan Hinote	172	Mike Jickling	150	Sakari Lindfors
221	Aaron Molnar	176	Samuel Pahlsson	196	Steve Passmore	171	Dan Wiebe
252	Darryl Bootland	188	Roman Pylner	220	Anson Carter	213	Alexei Gusarov
266	Sean Kotary	214	Matthew Scorsune	244	Aaron Ellis	234	Claude Lapointe
285	Blake Ward	240	Justin Clark				

1999 Pick		1995 Pick		1991 Pick		1987 Pick	
25	Mikhail Kuleshov	25	Marc Denis	1	Eric Lindros	9	Bryan Fogarty
45	Martin Grenier	51	Nic Beaudoin	24	Rene Corbet	15	Joe Sakic
93	Branko Radivojevic	77	John Tripp	46	Rich Brennan	51	Jim Sprott
112	Sanny Lindstrom	81	Tomi Kallio	68	Dave Karpa	72	Kip Miller
122	Kristian Kovac	129	Brent Johnson	90	Patrick Labrecque	93	Rob Mendel
142	William Magnuson	155	John Cirjak	103	Bill Lindsay	114	Garth Snow
152	Jordan Krestanovich	181	Dan Smith	134	Mikael Johansson	135	Tim Hanus
158	Anders Lovdahl	207	Tomi Hirvonen	156	Janne Laukkanen	156	Jake Enebak
183	Riku Hahl	228	Chris George	157	Aaron Asp	177	Jaroslav Sevcik
212	Radim Vrbata			178	Adam Bartell	183	Ladislav Tresl
240	Jeff Finger			188	Brent Brekke	198	Darren Nauss
				200	Paul Koch	219	Mike Williams
				222	Doug Friedman		
				244	Eric Meloche		

1998 Pick		1994 Pick		1990 Pick		1986 Pick	
12	Alex Tanguay	12	Wade Belak	1	Owen Nolan	18	Ken McRae
17	Martin Skoula	22	Jeff Kealty	22	Ryan Hughes	39	Jean-Marc Routhier
19	Robyn Regehr	35	Josef Marha	43	Brad Zavisha	41	Stephane Guerard
20	Scott Parker	61	Sebastien Bety	106	Jeff Parrott	81	Ron Tugnutt
28	Ramzi Abid	72	Chris Drury	127	Dwayne Norris	102	Gerald Bzdel
38	Phillipe Sauve	87	Milan Hejduk	148	Andrei Kovalenko	117	Scott White
53	Steve Moore	113	Tony Tuzzolino	158	Alexander Karpovtsev	123	Morgan Samuelsson
79	Yevgeny Lazarev	139	Nicholas Windsor	169	Pat Mazzoli	134	Mark Vermette
141	K.C. Timmons	165	Calvin Elfring	190	Scott Davis	144	Jean F. Nault
167	Alexander Riazantsev	191	Jay Bertsch	211	Mika Stromberg	165	Keith Miller
		217	Tim Thomas	232	Wade Klippenstein	186	Pierre Millier
		243	Chris Pittman			207	Chris Lappin
		285	Steven Low			228	Martin Latreille
						249	Sean Boudreault

1997 Pick		1993 Pick		1989 Pick	
26	Kevin Grimes	10	Jocelyn Thibault	1	Mats Sundin
53	Graham Belak	14	Adam Deadmarsh	22	Adam Foote
55	Rick Berry	49	Ashley Buckberger	43	Stephane Morin
78	Ville Nieminen	75	Bill Pierce	54	John Tanner
87	Brad Larsen	101	Ryan Tocher	68	Niklas Andersson
133	Aaron Miskovich	127	Anders Myrvold	85	Kevin Kaiser
161	David Aebischer	137	Nicholas Checco	106	Dan Lambert
217	Doug Schmidt	153	Christian Matte	127	Sergei Mylnikov
243	Kyle Kidney	179	David Ling	148	Paul Krake
245	Stephen Lafleur	205	Petr Franek	169	Vyacheslav Bykov
		231	Vincent Auger	190	Andrei Khomutov
		257	Mark Pivetz	211	Byron Witkowski
		283	John Hillman	232	Noel Rahn

Club Directory

Pepsi Center

Colorado Avalanche
Pepsi Center
1000 Chopper Place
Denver, CO 80204
Phone **303/405-1100**
FAX 303/893-0614
Press Box 303/575-1926
www.coloradoavalanche.com
Capacity: 18,007

Owner & Governor	E. Stanley Kroenke
Alternate Governor, President & General Manager	Pierre Lacroix
Vice President, Hockey Operations	Francois Giguere
Assistant General Manager	Brian MacDonald
Head Coach	Bob Hartley
Assistant Coach	Jacques Cloutier
Assistant Coach	Bryan Trottier
Video Coach	Paul Fixter
Vice President, Player Personnel	Michel Goulet
Director of Hockey Administration	Charlotte Grahame
Team Services Assistant	Ronnie Jameson
Consultant to the President	Dave Draper
Chief Scout	TBA
Pro Scout	Brad Smith
Scout	Yvon Gendron
Scout	Jim Hammett
Scout	Garth Joy
Scout	Steve Lyons
Scout	Don Paarup
Scout	Orval Tessier
European Scout	Joni Lehto
Computer Research Consultant	John Donohue
Strength & Conditioning Coach	Paul Goldberg
Head Athletic Trainer	Pat Karns
Kinesiologist	Matt Sokolowski
Massage Therapist	Gregorio Pradera
Equipment Manager	Wayne Flemming
Equipment Manager	Mark Miller
Assistant Equipment Manager	Dave Randolph

Communications Department

Vice President, Communications & Team Services	Jean Martineau
Director of Special Projects/New Media	Hayne Ellis
Assistant Director of Communications	Damen Zier
Team Founded	1979 Quebec Nordiques - Relocated to Colorado 1995
Press Box Location	West Side - Level 6
Practice Facility	Family Sports Center
Minor League Affiliate	Hershey Bears (AHL)
Television Outlets	FOX Sports Net Rocky Mountain, KTVD UPN-20
Radio Flagship	KKFN AM-950

Coach

HARTLEY, BOB
Coach, Colorado Avalanche. Born in Hawkesbury, Ont., September 7, 1960.

Bob Hartley became the second coach of the Colorado Avalanche and the 11th coach in franchise history when he was named to the position on June 30, 1998. Hartley spent four years as a head coach with the organization's American Hockey League affiliates in Cornwall and Hershey compiling a record of 151-136-33 for a .523 winning percentage.

Hartley began his coaching career with the Hawksbury Hawks, where he won two Central Ontario Junior A championships in four seasons. In 1991 he became head coach of the Laval Titans of the Quebec Major Junior Hockey League, where he won another championship prior to becoming an assistant coach with the Cornwall Aces in 1993. He became head coach in Cornwall the following year and remained with the Avalanche affiliate after it relocated to Hershey for the 1996-97 season. Hartley coached Hershey to the Calder Cup championship that year. In addition to his on-ice success in Hershey, Hartley was known for his summer hockey camps and volunteer work within the community.

Hartley and his wife Micheline have two children, Kristin and Steve.

Coaching Record

		Regular Season					Playoffs			
Season	Team	Games	W	L	T	%	Games	W	L	%
1991-92	Laval (QMJHL)	70	38	27	5	.579	10	4	6	.400
1992-93	Laval (QMJHL)	70	43	25	2	.629	13	12	1	.923
1994-95	Cornwall (AHL)	80	38	33	9	.531	15	8	7	.533
1995-96	Cornwall (AHL)	80	34	39	7	.469	8	3	5	.375
1996-97	Hershey (AHL)	80	43	27	10	.600	23	15	8	.652
1997-98	Hershey (AHL)	80	36	37	7	.494	7	3	4	.429
1998-99	**Colorado (NHL)**	82	44	28	10	.598	19	11	8	.579
1999-2000	**Colorado (NHL)**	82	42	29	11	.585•	17	11	6	.647
	NHL Totals	164	86	57	21	.591•	36	22	14	.611

• Includes points from regulation ties

Traded to Colorado after 20+ years in Boston, Ray Bourque's brilliance down the stretch helped propel the Avalanche to their sixth straight divisional title in 1999-2000.

Coaching History

Jacques Demers, 1979-80; Maurice Filion and Michel Bergeron, 1980-81; Michel Bergeron, 1981-82 to 1986-87; Andre Savard and Ron Lapointe, 1987-88; Ron Lapointe and Jean Perron, 1988-89; Michel Bergeron, 1989-90; Dave Chambers, 1990-91; Dave Chambers and Pierre Page, 1991-92; Pierre Page, 1992-93, 1993-94; Marc Crawford, 1994-95 to 1997-98; Bob Hartley, 1998-99 to date.

Columbus Blue Jackets

General manager Doug MacLean welcomes Lyle Odelein to Columbus following the 2000 Expansion Draft. Odelein will be counted on to anchor the defense in front of goaltender Ron Tugnutt.

2000-01 Schedule

Oct.	Sat.	7	Chicago		Sat.	6	at Vancouver
	Mon.	9	Los Angeles		Sun.	7	at Edmonton
	Thu.	12	at Calgary		Wed.	10	Colorado
	Sat.	14	at Colorado		Fri.	12	Chicago
	Sun.	15	at Chicago		Mon.	15	Minnesota
	Wed.	18	Colorado		Wed.	17	at Minnesota
	Sat.	21	at Pittsburgh		Sun.	21	Tampa Bay
	Sun.	22	Detroit		Tue.	23	at Buffalo
	Wed.	25	San Jose		Sat.	27	Anaheim
	Fri.	27	Washington		Wed.	31	Detroit
	Sat.	28	at Detroit	Feb.	Thu.	1	at St. Louis
	Tue.	31	Los Angeles		Tue.	6	St. Louis
Nov.	Wed.	1	at Dallas		Thu.	8	at Nashville
	Sat.	4	at Ottawa		Sat.	10	Nashville
	Sun.	5	Edmonton		Mon.	12	NY Rangers
	Thu.	9	San Jose		Wed.	14	at Toronto
	Sat.	11	Phoenix		Fri.	16	at Detroit
	Tue.	14	Dallas		Sat.	17	Pittsburgh
	Thu.	16	at Nashville		Tue.	20	at San Jose
	Fri.	17	Florida		Wed.	21	at Phoenix
	Sun.	19	Vancouver		Sat.	24	at Los Angeles*
	Wed.	22	at Colorado		Sun.	25	at Anaheim*
	Fri.	24	at Dallas		Wed.	28	Phoenix
	Sat.	25	Dallas	Mar.	Thu.	1	at Nashville
	Wed.	29	Philadelphia		Wed.	7	at Carolina
Dec.	Sat.	2	Atlanta		Fri.	9	at Florida
	Sun.	3	at Chicago		Sat.	10	at Tampa Bay
	Wed.	6	Anaheim		Wed.	14	Calgary
	Fri.	8	Boston		Fri.	16	at Atlanta
	Sun.	10	at Phoenix		Sat.	17	NY Islanders
	Wed.	13	at Anaheim		Mon.	19	Nashville
	Thu.	14	at San Jose		Wed.	21	Vancouver
	Sat.	16	at Vancouver		Sat.	24	Calgary*
	Mon.	18	at Montreal		Mon.	26	at Edmonton
	Thu.	21	Ottawa		Tue.	27	at Calgary
	Sat.	23	at NY Islanders		Thu.	29	at Los Angeles
	Tue.	26	at St. Louis	Apr.	Sun.	1	St. Louis
	Wed.	27	at New Jersey		Tue.	3	Detroit
	Fri.	29	Carolina		Thu.	5	at St. Louis
	Sun.	31	New Jersey		Fri.	6	at Minnesota
Jan.	Wed.	3	Edmonton		Sun.	8	Chicago

* Denotes afternoon game.

Franchise date: June 25, 1997

CENTRAL DIVISION

1st NHL Season

2000-01 Player Personnel

FORWARDS	HT	WT	S	Place of Birth	Date	1999-00 Club
ADAMS, Kevyn	6-1	195	R	Washington, D.C.	10/8/74	Toronto-St. John's Leafs
AUBIN, Serge	6-1	194	L	Val d'Or, Que.	2/15/75	Colorado-Hershey Bears
BELLEFEUILLE, Blake	5-10	208	R	Framingham, MA	12/27/77	Boston College
BOWLER, Bill	5-9	180	L	Toronto, Ont.	9/25/74	Manitoba Moose
CALOUN, Jan	5-10	190	R	Usti-Nad-Labem, Czech.	12/20/72	HIFK Helsinki
DARCHE, Mathieu	6-1	225	L	St-Laurent, Que.	11/26/76	McGill University
DAVIDSON, Matt	6-2	190	R	Flin Flon, Man.	8/9/77	Rochester
DINEEN, Kevin	5-11	190	R	Quebec City, Que.	10/28/63	Ottawa
DRURY, Ted	6-0	208	L	Boston, MA	9/13/71	Anaheim-NY Islanders
GARDINER, Bruce	6-1	193	R	Barrie, Ont.	2/11/72	Ottawa-Tampa Bay
HEINZE, Steve	5-11	202	R	Lawrence, MA	1/30/70	Boston
HOLLIS, Scott	6-0	185	R	Kingston, Ont.	9/18/72	SB Rosenheim
KNUTSEN, Espen	5-11	180	L	Oslo, Norway	1/12/72	Djurgardens IF
KRON, Robert	5-11	185	L	Brno, Czech.	2/27/67	Carolina
MANELUK, Mike	5-11	190	R	Winnipeg, Man.	10/1/73	Phi-Phi (AHL)
McDONELL, Kent	6-0	200	R	Williamstown, Ont.	3/1/79	Guelph Storm
MORAN, Brad	5-11	180	L	Abbotsford, B.C.	3/20/79	Calgary Hitmen
NIELSEN, Chris	6-1	190	R	Moshi, Tanzania	2/16/80	Calgary Hitmen
OLIWA, Krzysztof	6-5	235	L	Tychy, Poland	4/12/73	New Jersey
REICH, Jeremy	6-1	190	L	Craik, Sask.	2/11/79	Swift Current
SANDERSON, Geoff	6-0	190	L	Hay River, N.W.T.	2/1/72	Buffalo
SAVAGE, Reggie	5-10	197	L	Montreal, Que.	5/1/70	Syracuse Crunch
SCHILL, Jonathan	6-1	201	R	Kitchener, Ont.	6/28/79	Kingston
SELMSER, Sean	6-1	195	L	Calgary, Alta.	11/10/74	Hamilton Bulldogs
SPANHEL, Martin	6-2	202	L	Zlin, Czech.	7/1/77	HCK Plzen
VYBORNY, David	5-10	183	R	Jihlava, Czech.	6/2/75	Sparta Praha
WILLIAMS, Jeff	6-1	200	L	Pointe-Claire, Que.	2/11/76	Orlando-Albany River Rats
WRIGHT, Tyler	6-0	185	R	Canora, Sask.	4/6/73	Pittsburgh-Wilkes-Barre

DEFENSEMEN	HT	WT	S	Place of Birth	Date	1999-00 Club
ANDERSSON-JUNKKA, Jonas	6-2	170	R	Kiruna, Sweden	5/4/75	HPK Hameenlinna
BICANEK, Radim	6-1	195	L	Uherske Hradiste, Czech.	1/18/75	Chicago-Cleveland
DAHL, Kevin	5-11	190	R	Regina, Sask.	12/30/68	Chicago Wolves
GAUL, Michael	6-1	200	L	Lachine, Que.	4/22/73	Hershey Bears
GRAND-PIERRE, Jean-Luc	6-3	207	R	Montreal, Que.	2/2/77	Buffalo-Rochester
HEWARD, Jamie	6-2	207	R	Regina, Sask.	3/30/71	NY Islanders
KLESLA, Rostislav	6-2	198	L	Novy Jicin, Czech.	3/21/82	Brampton
KLIMENTIEV, Sergei	5-11	200	L	Kiev, USSR	4/5/75	Ak Bars Kazan
KUCERA, Frantisek	6-2	205	L	Prague, Czech.	2/3/68	Sparta Praha
NUMMELIN, Petteri	5-10	196	L	Turku, Finland	11/25/72	HC Davos
ODELEIN, Lyle	5-11	210	R	Quill Lake, Sask.	7/21/68	New Jersey-Phoenix
PUSHOR, Jamie	6-3	218	R	Lethbridge, Alta.	2/11/73	Dallas
QUINT, Deron	6-2	219	L	Durham, NH	3/12/76	Phoenix-New Jersey
ROBERTSSON, Bert	6-3	205	L	Sodertalje, Sweden	6/30/74	Edmonton-Hamilton Bulldogs
SRYUBKO, Andrei	6-3	205	L	Kiev, USSR	10/21/75	P. Huron-Utah-Grand Rapids
TIMANDER, Mattias	6-2	210	L	Solleftea, Sweden	4/16/74	Boston-Hershey Bears
WATSON, Dan	6-2	221	R	Glencoe, Ont.	10/5/79	Sarnia Sting

GOALTENDERS	HT	WT	C	Place of Birth	Date	1999-00 Club
CHABOT, Frederic	5-11	187	L	Hebertville Station, Que.	2/12/68	Houston Aeros
DENIS, Marc	6-0	190	L	Montreal, Que.	8/1/77	Colorado
GARDNER, Greg	6-0	190	L	Mississauga, Ont.	11/21/75	Niagara University
TUGNUTT, Ron	5-11	160	L	Scarborough, Ont.	10/22/67	Ottawa-Pittsburgh

Entry Draft Selections 2000

General Managers' History
Doug MacLean, 2000-01.

Coaching History
Dave King, 2000-01.

Captains' History
TBD, 2000-01.

2000
Pick

Pick	Player
4	Rostislav Klesla
69	Ben Knopp
133	Petteri Nummelin
138	Scott Heffernan
150	Tyler Kolarik
169	Shane Bendera
200	Janne Jokila
231	Peter Zingoni
278	Martin Paroulek
286	Andrej Nedorost
292	Louis Mandeville

General Manager

MacLEAN, DOUG
General Manager, Columbus Blue Jackets.
Born in Summerside, P.E.I., April 12, 1954.

Doug MacLean joined the Columbus Blue Jackets in February, 1998, after a successful stint with the Florida Panthers that saw him lead the team to the Stanley Cup Finals in 1996 during his first season as head coach. He was selected as coach of the year by *The Hockey News* and was runner-up for the Jack Adams Award that same season.

MacLean began his NHL coaching career in 1986 as an assistant to Jacques Martin in St. Louis. He spent two seasons with the Blues before joining the Washington Capitals in 1988, assisting Bryan Murray behind the bench. He was named coach of the Capitals' American Hockey League affiliate in Baltimore for the final 35 games of the 1989-90 season.

The following season, MacLean joined Murray on the Detroit Red Wings, serving as an assistant coach for two years. In 1992, MacLean was named assistant general manager of the Red Wings and also served as general manager of the team's AHL affiliate in Adirondack for two years. MacLean followed Murray to the Panthers in 1994, becoming the expansion club's director of player development. He was named head coach on July 24, 1995.

A collegiate hockey player at the University of Prince Edward Island, MacLean graduated with a bachelor's degree in education. He also played for the Montreal Jr. Canadiens and was invited to training camp with the St. Louis Blues in 1974. Following his playing career, MacLean enrolled at the University of Western Ontario, where he received a master's degree in educational psychology. While attending Western, MacLean began his coaching career as an assistant with London of the Ontario Hockey League.

NHL Coaching Record

Season	Team	Games	W	L	T	%	Games	W	L	%
1995-96	Florida (NHL)	82	41	31	10	.561	22	12	10	.545
1996-97	Florida (NHL)	82	35	28	19	.543	5	1	4	.200
1997-98	Florida (NHL)	23	7	12	4	.391	....	....	....	....
	NHL Totals	**187**	**83**	**71**	**33**	**.532**	**27**	**13**	**14**	**.481**

Coach

KING, DAVE
Coach, Columbus Blue Jackets. Born in Saskatoon, Sask., December 22, 1947.

Former Canadian national team coach Dave King was named the first head coach of the Columbus Blue Jackets on July 5, 2000. King joined the Blue Jackets after spending three seasons with the Montreal Canadiens organization.

King enjoyed a successful three-year stint as the head coach of the NHL's Calgary Flames from 1992 to 1995, guiding the club to consecutive Pacific Division titles in 1994 and 1995. He joined the Flames after spending nine seasons with the Canadian national hockey program. King coached Canada to the gold medal at the 1982 World Junior Championships and served as an assistant coach with the bronze medal-winning Team Canada at the 1982 World Championships. He later coached Canada at the Olympics in 1984, 1988 and 1992 and at the World Championships from 1989 to 1992.

King began his coaching career at the University of Saskatchewan in 1972-73. He then coached the Saskatoon Junior B Quakers to a pair of provincial and divisional championships from 1974 to 1976. After splitting the 1976-77 season between the Tier II Saskatoon Olympiques and Saskatoon Blades of the Western Hockey League, he joined the Billings Bighorns in 1977 and captured WHL Coach of the Year honors after leading the club to the 1978 WHL Finals. He then returned to the University of Saskatchewan, where he led the Huskies to three conference championships and the 1983 CIAU national title.

King and his wife Linda have two sons, Andrew and Scott, and a daughter, Jennifer.

Coaching Record

Year	Team	Games	W	L	T	%	Games	W	L	T	%
1984	Canadian National	....	....	....	....	....	7	4	3	0	.571
1987	Canadian National	10	3	5	2	.400	....	....	....	....	....
1988	Canadian National	....	....	....	....	....	8	5	2	1	.688
1989	Canadian National	10	7	3	0	.700	....	....	....	....	....
1990	Canadian National	10	6	3	1	.650	....	....	....	....	....
1991	Canadian National	10	5	2	3	.650	....	....	....	....	....
1992	Canadian National	6	2	3	1	.417	8	6	2	0	.750
1992-93	**Calgary (NHL)**	84	43	30	11	.577	6	2	4		.333
1993-94	**Calgary (NHL)**	84	42	29	13	.577	7	3	4		.429
1994-95	**Calgary (NHL)**	48	24	17	7	.573	7	3	4		.429
	NHL Totals	216	109	76	31	.576	20	8	12	....	.400

Club Directory

Nationwide Arena

Columbus Blue Jackets
Nationwide Arena
200 W. Nationwide Blvd.
Columbus, Ohio 43215
Phone **614/246-4625**
FAX 614/246-4007
Website: www.BlueJackets.com

Ownership
Majority Owner/Governor . . . . John H. McConnell
Alternate Governor . . . . John P. McConnell
Ownership Group . . . . John F. Wolfe, Ron Pizzuti, The Crane Family

Hockey Operations
President/General Manager/Alternate Governor . . . Doug MacLean
Assistant General Manager . . . . Jim Clark
Head Coach. . . . . Dave King
Associate Coach . . . . Newell Brown
Assistant Coach . . . . Gerard Gallant
Goaltending Coach, Pro Scout. . . . . Rick Wamsley
Director of Amateur Scouting . . . . Don Boyd
Hockey Operations Coordinator . . . . Chris MacFarland
Amateur Scouts. . . . . Paul Castron, Sam McMaster
Pro Scouts . . . . Bill Davidge, Peter Dineen, Bob Strumm
European Scout . . . . Kjell Larsson
Regional Scouts . . . . Brian Bates, Scott Fitzgerald, Erin Ginnell,
Denis LeBlanc, Artem Telepin Nicholaevich,
Bryan Raymond, Wayne Smith, Milan Tichy
Head Athletic Trainer. Chris Mizer
Equipment Manager. . . . . Tim LeRoy
Assistant Equipment Manager. . . . . Jamie Healy
Strength and Conditioning Coach. . . . . Mark Casterline
Team Services Coordinator . . . . Jim Rankin
Executive Assistant . . . . Kari Pitzer

Business and Corporate Development
Vice-President of Business Development and
Broadcasting. . . . . Mike Humes
Executive Director of Sales. . . . . Paul D'Aiuto
Senior Account Executive . . . . Andy Loughnane
Account Executive . . . . Scott Klein
Director of Client Services . . . . Terri Murphy
Client Services Manager . . . . Chris Rooks

Communications and Media Relations
Director of Communications . . . . Todd Sharrock
Assistant Director of Communications. . . . . Dan Jones
Manager of Multimedia and Publications . . . . Gary Kohn

Marketing and Community Development
Vice-President of Marketing . . . . David Paitson
Director of Advertising and Promotions. . . . . Marc Gregory
Director of Game Operations. . . . . Kimberly Kershaw
Director of Fan Development. . . . . J.D. Kershaw
Fan Development Coordinator . . . . Joel Siegman
Director of Community Development . . . . Wendy Peterson
Manager of Community Development . . . . Stacey Segal

Broadcasting
Director of Broadcasting . . . . Russ Mollohan
Television Play-By-Play Announcer. . . . . Dan Kelly
Television Color Commentator . . . . Steve Konroyd
Radio Play-By-Play Announcer . . . . George Matthews
Radio Color Commentator . . . . Bill Davidge

Business Operations
Director of Finance . . . . T.J. LaMendola
General Counsel . . . . Greg Kirstein
Controller . . . . Rich Gross
Financial Analyst . . . . Dana Fletcher
MIS Manager. . . . . Jim Connolly
Human Resources Manager . . . . Harry Coder
Project Construction Manager. . . . . Don McCarthy
Merchandise Manager (FMI) . . . . Jennfier Emerich
Merchandise/Retail Consultant . . . . Carl Bassewitz
Office Coordinator . . . . Rachel Durham

Ticket Operations
Vice-President of Ticket Sales . . . . Andy Silverman
Director of Ticket Operations and Customer Service . . Mark Morris
Director of Group Sales . . . . Brooks Jordan
Manager of Premium and Suite Services . . . . Derrill Smith
Premium and Suite Services Coordinator . . . . Brian Lane
Manager of Ticket Operations and Customer Service . Karen Bierley
Assistant Manager of Ticket Operations and
Customer Service . . . . Mark Metz
Senior Account Executives . . . . Paul Howard, Todd Taylor
Account Executives . . . . Belinda Slay, Carson Woods
Group Sales Account Executive . . . . John Davis

Nationwide Arena
Regional General Manager . . . . Bob Newman
General Manager . . . . Jay Cooper
Assistant Director of Operations . . . . Andy Gorchov
Director of Marketing . . . . Cliff Clinger
Marketing Manager. . . . . Tricia Smith
Marketing Coordinator . . . . Marie Hagen
Public Relations Manager . . . . Karen Davis
Event Manager . . . . Eric Granger
Event Coordinator . . . . Gwen Leidy
Engineering Supervisor . . . . Chris Beatty
Facility Engineer. . . . . Rob Myers
Lead Maintenance Technician . . . . Mark Grainer
Changeover Manager . . . . Dave Seal
Assistant Box Office Manager . . . . Marilyn Gates
Executive Assistant . . . . Kim Faught

Dallas Stars

1999-2000 Results: 43W-29L-10T 102PTS. First, Pacific Division

Though he's always been known for his offense, Mike Modano finished among the NHL's top-10 scorers for the first time in his career in 1999-2000. His shooting percentage of 20.2 ranked fifth in the NHL.

2000-01 Schedule

Oct.	Wed.	4	Colorado	Fri.	12	Detroit
	Sat.	7	at Ottawa	Sun.	14	at Tampa Bay
	Mon.	9	at Toronto	Mon.	15	at Florida
	Tue.	10	at Carolina	Wed.	17	Nashville
	Thu.	12	Philadelphia	Fri.	19	Pittsburgh
	Sat.	14	Washington	Sun.	21	at Phoenix
	Wed.	18	San Jose	Mon.	22	Vancouver
	Fri.	20	at Chicago	Wed.	24	New Jersey
	Sat.	21	Los Angeles	Fri.	26	San Jose
	Wed.	25	Vancouver	Tue.	30	at Los Angeles
	Fri.	27	Phoenix	**Feb.** Thu.	1	at San Jose
	Sat.	28	at St. Louis	Wed.	7	Edmonton
Nov.	Wed.	1	Columbus	Fri.	9	Minnesota
	Fri.	3	at Phoenix	Sun.	11	St. Louis
	Sat.	11	Montreal	Tue.	13	at Nashville
	Tue.	14	at Columbus	Wed.	14	Los Angeles
	Wed.	15	at Buffalo	Fri.	16	Anaheim
	Fri.	17	at Detroit	Sun.	18	Detroit
	Mon.	20	Tampa Bay	Wed.	21	Minnesota
	Wed.	22	at Nashville	Fri.	23	Boston
	Fri.	24	Columbus	Sun.	25	at Edmonton
	Sat.	25	at Columbus	Mon.	26	at Calgary
	Wed.	29	Calgary	Wed.	28	at Vancouver
Dec.	Fri.	1	at Colorado	**Mar.** Fri.	2	at Anaheim
	Sat.	2	at Phoenix	Sun.	4	Buffalo*
	Wed.	6	at San Jose	Wed.	7	Chicago
	Thu.	7	at Los Angeles	Sat.	10	Colorado*
	Sun.	10	at Anaheim*	Sun.	11	at Colorado
	Wed.	13	Edmonton	Tue.	13	at Chicago
	Fri.	15	Chicago	Fri.	16	Phoenix
	Sun.	17	at Minnesota*	Sun.	18	Ottawa*
	Wed.	20	at New Jersey	Mon.	19	at Minnesota
	Thu.	21	at NY Islanders	Wed.	21	Anaheim
	Sat.	23	at Pittsburgh	Fri.	23	NY Islanders
	Wed.	27	Anaheim	Sun.	25	St. Louis
	Fri.	29	Los Angeles	Wed.	28	at Vancouver
	Sun.	31	NY Rangers	Fri.	30	at Edmonton
Jan.	Thu.	4	at Detroit	Sat.	31	at Calgary
	Sat.	6	at Boston	**Apr.** Mon.	2	Calgary
	Mon.	8	at NY Rangers	Wed.	4	Nashville
	Wed.	10	at Atlanta	Sat.	7	at San Jose*

* Denotes afternoon game.

Franchise date: June 5, 1967
Transferred from Minnesota to Dallas,
June 9, 1993.

**34th
NHL
Season**

**PACIFIC
DIVISION**

Year-by-Year Record

Season	GP	Home W	Home L	Home T	Road W	Road L	Road T	Overall W	Overall L	Overall T	GF	GA	Pts.	Finished		Playoff Result
1999-2000	82	21	15	5	22	14	5	43	29	10	211	184	102	1st,	Pacific Div.	Lost Final
1998-99	**82**	**29**	**8**	**4**	**22**	**11**	**8**	**51**	**19**	**12**	**236**	**168**	**114**	**1st,**	**Pacific Div.**	**Won Stanley Cup**
1997-98	82	26	8	7	23	14	4	49	22	11	242	167	109	1st,	Central Div.	Lost Conf. Final
1996-97	82	25	13	3	23	13	5	48	26	8	252	198	104	1st,	Central Div.	Lost Conf. Quarter-Final
1995-96	82	14	18	9	12	24	5	26	42	14	227	280	66	6th,	Central Div.	Out of Playoffs
1994-95	48	9	10	5	8	13	3	17	23	8	136	135	42	5th,	Central Div.	Lost Conf. Quarter-Final
1993-94	84	23	12	7	19	17	6	42	29	13	286	265	97	3rd,	Central Div.	Lost Conf. Semi-Final
1992-93*	84	18	17	7	18	21	3	36	38	10	272	293	82	5th,	Norris Div.	Out of Playoffs
1991-92*	80	20	16	4	12	26	2	32	42	6	246	278	70	4th,	Norris Div.	Lost Div. Semi-Final
1990-91*	80	19	15	6	8	24	8	27	39	14	256	266	68	4th,	Norris Div.	Lost Final
1989-90*	80	26	12	2	10	28	2	36	40	4	284	291	76	4th,	Norris Div.	Lost Div. Semi-Final
1988-89*	80	17	15	8	10	22	8	27	37	16	258	278	70	3rd,	Norris Div.	Lost Div. Semi-Final
1987-88*	80	10	24	6	9	24	7	19	48	13	242	349	51	5th,	Norris Div.	Out of Playoffs
1986-87*	80	17	20	3	13	20	7	30	40	10	296	314	70	5th,	Norris Div.	Out of Playoffs
1985-86*	80	21	15	4	17	18	5	38	33	9	327	305	85	2nd,	Norris Div.	Lost Div. Semi-Final
1984-85*	80	14	19	7	11	24	5	25	43	12	268	321	62	4th,	Norris Div.	Lost Div. Final
1983-84*	80	22	14	4	17	17	6	39	31	10	345	344	88	1st,	Norris Div.	Lost Conf. Championship
1982-83*	80	23	6	11	17	18	5	40	24	16	321	290	96	2nd,	Norris Div.	Lost Div. Final
1981-82*	80	21	7	12	16	16	8	37	23	20	346	288	94	1st,	Norris Div.	Lost Div. Semi-Final
1980-81*	80	23	10	7	12	18	10	35	28	17	291	263	87	3rd,	Adams Div.	Lost Final
1979-80*	80	25	8	7	11	20	9	36	28	16	311	253	88	3rd,	Adams Div.	Lost Semi-Final
1978-79*	80	19	15	6	9	25	6	28	40	12	257	289	68	4th,	Adams Div.	Out Of Playoffs
1977-78*	80	12	24	4	6	29	5	18	53	9	218	325	45	5th,	Smythe Div.	Out of Playoffs
1976-77*	80	17	14	9	6	25	9	23	39	18	240	310	64	2nd,	Smythe Div.	Lost Prelim. Round
1975-76*	80	15	22	3	5	31	4	20	53	7	195	303	47	4th,	Smythe Div.	Out of Playoffs
1974-75*	80	17	20	3	6	30	4	23	50	7	221	341	53	4th,	Smythe Div.	Out of Playoffs
1973-74*	78	18	15	6	5	23	11	23	38	17	235	275	63	7th,	West Div.	Out of Playoffs
1972-73*	78	26	8	5	11	22	6	37	30	11	254	230	85	3rd,	West Div.	Lost Quarter-Final
1971-72*	78	22	11	6	15	18	6	37	29	12	212	191	86	2nd,	West Div.	Lost Quarter-Final
1970-71*	78	16	15	8	12	19	8	28	34	16	191	223	72	4th,	West Div.	Lost Semi-Final
1969-70*	76	11	16	11	8	19	11	19	35	22	224	257	60	3rd,	West Div.	Lost Quarter-Final
1968-69*	76	11	21	6	7	22	9	18	43	15	189	270	51	6th,	West Div.	Out of Playoffs
1967-68*	74	17	12	8	10	20	7	27	32	15	191	226	69	4th,	West Div.	Lost Semi-Final

* Minnesota North Stars

2000-01 Player Personnel

FORWARDS	HT	WT	S	Place of Birth	Date	1999-00 Club
DONATO, Ted	5-10	178	L	Boston, MA	4/28/69	Anaheim
HOUDE, Eric	5-11	191	L	Montreal, Que.	12/19/76	Hamilton Bulldogs-Springfield
HULL, Brett	5-11	203	R	Belleville, Ont.	8/9/64	Dallas
KEANE, Mike	6-0	185	R	Winnipeg, Man.	5/29/67	Dallas
LANGENBRUNNER, Jamie	6-1	200	R	Duluth, MN	7/24/75	Dallas
LEHTINEN, Jere	6-0	200	R	Espoo, Finland	6/24/73	Dallas
LING, David	5-9	185	R	Halifax, N.S.	1/9/75	Kansas City
LYASHENKO, Roman	6-0	189	R	Murmansk, Russia	5/2/79	Dallas-Michigan K-Wings
MARSHALL, Grant	6-1	200	R	Mississauga, Ont.	6/9/73	Dallas
MODANO, Mike	6-3	205	L	Livonia, MI	6/7/70	Dallas
MORROW, Brenden	5-11	200	L	Carlyle, Sask.	1/16/79	Dallas-Michigan K-Wings
MULLER, Kirk	6-0	205	L	Kingston, Ont.	2/8/66	Dallas
NIEUWENDYK, Joe	6-1	205	L	Oshawa, Ont.	9/10/66	Dallas
SIM, Jonathan	5-10	184	L	New Glasgow, N.S.	9/29/77	Michigan K-Wings-Dallas
SLOAN, Blake	5-10	196	R	Park Ridge, IL	7/27/75	Dallas
VAN ALLEN, Shaun	6-1	204	L	Calgary, Alta.	8/29/67	Ottawa
WELLS, Chris	6-6	223	L	Calgary, Alta.	11/12/75	Florida-Louisville-Hartford
WRIGHT, Jamie	6-0	195	L	Kitchener, Ont.	5/13/76	Dallas-Michigan K-Wings
DEFENSEMEN						
HATCHER, Derian	6-5	230	L	Sterling Heights, MI	6/4/72	Dallas
HELENIUS, Sami	6-5	225	L	Helsinki, Finland	1/22/74	Colorado-Hershey Bears
JACKMAN, Richard	6-2	192	R	Toronto, Ont.	6/28/78	Dallas-Michigan K-Wings
LETANG, Alan	6-0	205	L	Renfrew, Ont.	9/4/75	Dallas-Michigan K-Wings
LUKOWICH, Brad	6-1	200	L	Cranbrook, B.C.	8/12/76	Dallas
MATVICHUK, Richard	6-2	215	L	Edmonton, Alta.	2/5/73	Dallas
SYDOR, Darryl	6-1	205	L	Edmonton, Alta.	5/13/72	Dallas
TORY, Jeff	5-11	190	R	Burnaby, B.C.	5/9/73	Philadelphia (AHL)
WOTTON, Mark	6-1	195	L	Foxwarren, Man.	11/16/73	Michigan K-Wings
ZUBOV, Sergei	6-1	200	R	Moscow, USSR	7/22/70	Dallas

GOALTENDERS	HT	WT	C	Place of Birth	Date	1999-00 Club
BALES, Mike	6-1	200	L	Prince Albert, Sask.	8/6/71	Michigan K-Wings
BELFOUR, Ed	5-11	192	L	Carman, Man.	4/21/65	Dallas
TABARACCI, Rick	6-1	190	L	Toronto, Ont.	1/2/69	Canada-Atl.-Clev-Orlando-Col-Utah Grizzlies
TURCO, Marty	5-11	183	L	Sault Ste. Marie, Ont.	8/13/75	Michigan K-Wings

Coach

HITCHCOCK, KEN

Coach, Dallas Stars. Born in Edmonton, Alberta, December 17, 1951.

Ken Hitchcock coached the Dallas Stars to the first Stanley Cup championship in franchise history in 1999. That success culminated a season in which the Stars set franchise records with 51 victories (51-19-12) and 114 points, marking the third straight season in which Hitchcock's club established new highs in those categories. Hitchcock led Dallas back to the Stanley Cup finals in 2000.

Named to his current position on January 8, 1996, Hitchcock had previously enjoyed winning seasons in every year at every level at which he had coached. He posted an incredible 575-69 mark in 10 seasons of Canadian Triple A midget hockey with Sherwood Park in suburban Edmonton, and then went on to record-breaking success with a .693 winning percentage in six seasons with Kamloops of the Western Hockey League. Hitchcock was the WHL coach of the year in 1986-87 and again in 1989-90, when he also added honors as Canadian Major Junior coach of the year.

After a three-year stint (1990-93) as an assistant coach for the Philadelphia Flyers, Hitchcock returned to head coaching duties in the International Hockey League before earning his promotion to Dallas.

Coaching Record

		Regular Season					Playoffs			
Season	Team	Games	W	L	T	%	Games	W	L	%
1984-85	Kamloops (WHL)	71	52	17	2	.746	15	10	5	.667
1985-86	Kamloops (WHL)	72	49	19	4	.708	16	14	2	.875
1986-87	Kamloops (WHL)	72	55	14	3	.785	13	8	5	.615
1987-88	Kamloops (WHL)	72	45	26	1	.632	18	12	6	.667
1988-89	Kamloops (WHL)	72	34	33	5	.507	16	8	8	.500
1989-90	Kamloops (WHL)	72	56	16	0	.778	17	14	3	.824
1993-94	Kalamazoo (IHL)	81	48	26	7	.636	5	1	4	.200
1994-95	Kalamazoo (IHL)	81	43	24	14	.617	16	10	6	.625
1995-96	Michigan (IHL)	40	19	10	11	.613	....	....	....	....
	Dallas (NHL)	**43**	**15**	**23**	**5**	**.407**	....	....	....	....
1996-97	**Dallas (NHL)**	**82**	**48**	**26**	**8**	**.634**	**7**	**3**	**4**	**.429**
1997-98	**Dallas (NHL)**	**82**	**49**	**22**	**11**	**.665**	**17**	**10**	**7**	**.588**
1998-99	**Dallas (NHL)**	**82**	**51**	**19**	**12**	**.695**	**23**	**16**	**7**	**.696***
1999-2000	**Dallas (NHL)**	**82**	**43**	**29**	**10**	**.622•**	**23**	**14**	**9**	**.609**
	NHL Totals	**371**	**206**	**119**	**46**	**.625•**	**70**	**43**	**27**	**.614**

* Stanley Cup win.
• Includes points from regulation ties

1999-2000 Scoring

* – rookie

Regular Season

Pos	#	Player	Team	GP	G	A	Pts	+/–	PIM	PP	SH	GW	GT	S	%
C	9	Mike Modano	DAL	77	38	43	81	0	48	11	1	8	3	188	20.2
L	16	Brett Hull	DAL	79	24	35	59	–21	43	11	0	3	0	223	10.8
D	56	Sergei Zubov	DAL	77	9	33	42	–2	18	3	1	3	0	179	5.0
L	15	Jamie Langenbrunner	DAL	65	18	21	39	16	68	4	2	6	0	153	11.8
D	3	Sylvain Cote	TOR	3	0	1	1	1	0	0	0	0	0	3	0.0
			CHI	45	6	18	24	–4	14	5	0	2	0	78	7.7
			DAL	28	2	8	10	6	14	0	0	0	0	47	4.3
			TOTAL	76	8	27	35	3	28	5	0	2	0	128	6.3
C	25	Joe Nieuwendyk	DAL	48	15	19	34	–1	26	7	0	2	0	110	13.6
R	12	Mike Keane	DAL	81	13	21	34	9	41	0	4	3	0	85	15.3
D	5	Darryl Sydor	DAL	74	8	26	34	6	32	5	0	1	0	132	6.1
L	45	* Brenden Morrow	DAL	64	14	19	33	8	81	3	0	3	0	113	12.4
D	24	Richard Matvichuk	DAL	70	4	21	25	7	42	0	0	1	0	73	5.5
D	2	Derian Hatcher	DAL	57	2	22	24	6	68	0	0	0	0	90	2.2
C	22	Kirk Muller	DAL	47	7	15	22	–3	24	3	0	2	0	57	12.3
R	11	* Blake Sloan	DAL	67	4	13	17	11	50	0	0	1	0	78	5.1
C	21	Guy Carbonneau	DAL	69	10	6	16	10	36	0	1	4	0	70	14.3
C	17	Scott Thornton	MTL	35	2	3	5	–7	70	0	0	1	0	36	5.6
			DAL	30	6	3	9	–5	38	1	0	0	0	47	12.8
			TOTAL	65	8	6	14	–12	108	1	0	1	0	83	9.6
C	44	Aaron Gavey	DAL	41	7	6	13	0	44	1	0	2	0	39	17.9
C	36	* Roman Lyashenko	DAL	58	6	6	12	–2	10	0	0	1	0	51	11.8
D	6	Dave Manson	CHI	37	0	7	7	2	40	0	0	0	0	45	0.0
			DAL	26	1	2	3	10	22	0	0	0	0	21	4.8
			TOTAL	63	1	9	10	12	62	0	0	0	0	66	1.5
C	49	* Jonathan Sim	DAL	25	5	3	8	4	10	2	0	1	0	44	11.4
R	26	Jere Lehtinen	DAL	17	3	5	8	1	0	0	0	1	0	29	10.3
R	29	Grant Marshall	DAL	45	2	6	8	–5	38	1	0	0	0	43	4.7
D	4	Jamie Pushor	DAL	62	0	8	8	0	53	0	0	0	0	27	0.0
L	22	Pavel Patera	DAL	12	1	4	5	–1	4	0	0	0	0	18	5.6
L	46	Jamie Wright	DAL	23	1	4	5	4	16	0	0	0	0	15	6.7
D	18	Joel Bouchard	NSH	52	1	4	5	–11	23	0	0	0	0	60	1.7
			DAL	2	0	0	0	1	2	0	0	0	0	1	0.0
			TOTAL	54	1	4	5	–10	25	0	0	0	0	61	1.6
D	37	* Brad Lukowich	DAL	60	3	1	4	–14	50	0	0	1	0	33	9.1
R	23	Chris Murray	DAL	32	2	1	3	–7	62	0	0	0	1	25	8.0
C	10	Brian Skrudland	DAL	22	1	2	3	0	22	0	0	0	0	16	6.3
D	28	* Richard Jackman	DAL	22	1	2	3	–1	6	1	0	0	0	16	6.3
G	20	Ed Belfour	DAL	62	0	3	3	0	10	0	0	0	0	0	0.0
G	30	* Manny Fernandez	DAL	24	0	2	2	0	2	0	0	0	0	0	0.0
R	17	Warren Luhning	DAL	10	0	1	1	–2	13	0	0	0	0	7	0.0
D	27	Shawn Chambers	DAL	4	0	0	0	–2	4	0	0	0	0	2	0.0
R	41	Keith Aldridge	DAL	4	0	0	0	1	0	0	0	0	0	6	0.0
L	50	* Ryan Christie	DAL	5	0	0	0	–1	0	0	0	0	0	1	0.0
D	38	* Alan Letang	DAL	8	0	0	0	–5	2	0	0	0	0	1	0.0

Goaltending

No.	Goaltender	GPI	Mins	Avg	W	L	T	EN	SO	GA	SA	S%
20	Ed Belfour	62	3620	2.10	32	21	7	6	4	127	1571	.919
30	* Manny Fernandez	24	1353	2.13	11	8	3	3	1	48	603	.920
	Totals	**82**	**4992**	**2.21**	**43**	**29**	**10**	**9**	**5**	**184**	**2183**	**.916**

Playoffs

Pos	#	Player	Team	GP	G	A	Pts	+/–	PIM	PP	SH	GW	OT	S	%
L	16	Brett Hull	DAL	23	11	13	24	3	4	3	0	4	0	79	13.9
C	9	Mike Modano	DAL	23	10	13	23	3	10	4	0	2	1	67	14.9
C	25	Joe Nieuwendyk	DAL	23	7	3	10	–2	18	3	0	2	1	45	15.6
D	56	Sergei Zubov	DAL	18	2	7	9	1	6	1	1	0	0	34	5.9
C	17	Scott Thornton	DAL	23	2	7	9	1	28	0	0	1	0	33	6.1
L	15	Jamie Langenbrunner	DAL	15	1	7	8	–1	18	1	0	0	0	27	3.7
D	24	Richard Matvichuk	DAL	23	2	5	7	7	14	0	0	0	0	19	10.5
D	5	Darryl Sydor	DAL	23	1	6	7	1	6	0	0	0	0	39	2.6
L	45	* Brenden Morrow	DAL	21	2	4	6	2	22	1	0	0	0	30	6.7
C	21	Guy Carbonneau	DAL	23	2	4	6	2	12	0	1	1	0	12	16.7
R	12	Mike Keane	DAL	23	2	4	6	1	14	0	0	0	0	27	7.4
R	26	Jere Lehtinen	DAL	13	1	5	6	1	2	0	0	0	0	23	4.3
C	22	Kirk Muller	DAL	23	2	3	5	–2	18	0	0	1	0	20	10.0
D	2	Derian Hatcher	DAL	23	1	3	4	–4	29	0	0	0	0	34	2.9
C	36	* Roman Lyashenko	DAL	16	2	1	3	–1	0	0	0	2	0	15	13.3
D	3	Sylvain Cote	DAL	23	2	1	3	0	8	2	0	0	0	24	8.3
C	44	Aaron Gavey	DAL	13	1	2	3	1	10	0	0	1	0	6	16.7
C	49	* Jonathan Sim	DAL	7	1	0	1	0	6	0	0	0	0	9	11.1
R	29	Grant Marshall	DAL	14	0	1	1	0	4	0	0	0	0	15	0.0
G	30	* Manny Fernandez	DAL	1	0	0	0	0	0	0	0	0	0	0	0.0
D	4	Jamie Pushor	DAL	5	0	0	0	–1	5	0	0	0	0	2	0.0
R	11	* Blake Sloan	DAL	16	0	0	0	2	12	0	0	0	0	10	0.0
G	20	Ed Belfour	DAL	23	0	0	0	0	8	0	0	0	0	0	0.0
D	6	Dave Manson	DAL	23	0	0	0	2	33	0	0	0	0	19	0.0

Goaltending

No.	Goaltender	GPI	Mins	Avg	W	L	EN	SO	GA	SA	S%
20	Ed Belfour	23	1443	1.87	14	9	0	4	45	651	.931
30	* Manny Fernandez	1	17	3.53	0	0	0	0	1	8	.875
	Totals	**23**	**1467**	**1.88**	**14**	**9**	**0**	**4**	**46**	**659**	**.930**

Club Records

Team

(Figures in brackets for season records are games played; records for fewest points, wins, ties, losses, goals, goals against are for 70 or more games)

Most Points **114** 1998-99 (82)
Most Wins **51** 1998-99 (82)
Most Ties **22** 1969-70 (76)
Most Losses **53** 1975-76, 1977-78 (80)
Most Goals **346** 1981-82 (80)
Most Goals Against **349** 1987-88 (80)
Fewest Points **45** 1977-78 (80)
Fewest Wins **18** 1968-69 (76), 1977-78 (80)
Fewest Ties **4** 1989-90 (80)
Fewest Losses **19** 1998-99 (82)
Fewest Goals **189** 1968-69 (76)
Fewest Goals Against **167** 1997-98 (82)
Longest Winning Streak
Overall .... **7** Mar. 16-28/80, Mar. 16-Apr. 2/97, Nov. 22-Dec. 5/97
Home .... **11** Nov. 4-Dec. 27/72
Away .... **7** Three times
Longest Undefeated Streak
Overall .... **15** Dec. 6/98-Jan. 6/99 (12 wins, 3 ties)
Home .... **13** Oct. 28-Dec. 27/72 (12 wins, 1 tie), Nov. 21/79-Jan. 9/80 (10 wins, 3 ties), Jan. 17-Mar. 17/91 (11 wins, 2 ties)
Away .... **10** Jan. 12-Mar. 4/99 (8 wins, 2 ties)
Longest Losing Streak
Overall .... **10** Feb. 1-20/76
Home .... **6** Jan. 17-Feb. 4/70
Away .... **8** Oct. 19-Nov. 13/75, Jan. 28-Mar. 3/88
Longest Winless Streak
Overall .... **20** Jan. 15-Feb. 28/70 (15 losses, 5 ties)
Home .... **12** Jan. 17-Feb. 25/70 (8 losses, 4 ties)
Away .... **23** Oct. 25/74-Jan. 28/75 (19 losses, 4 ties)
Most Shutouts, Season **10** 1997-98 (82)
Most PIM, Season **2,313** 1987-88 (80)
Most Goals, Game .... **15** Nov. 11/81 (Wpg. 2 at Min. 15)

Individual

Most Seasons .... **16** Neal Broten
Most Games .... **992** Neal Broten
Most Goals, Career .... **349** Mike Modano
Most Assists, Career .... **593** Neal Broten
Most Points, Career .... **867** Neal Broten (274G, 593A)
Most PIM, Career .... **1,883** Shane Churla
Most Shutouts, Career .... **26** Cesare Maniago
Longest Consecutive Games Streak .... **442** Danny Grant (Dec. 4/68-Apr. 7/74)
Most Goals, Season .... **55** Dino Ciccarelli (1981-82), Brian Bellows (1989-90)
Most Assists, Season .... **76** Neal Broten (1985-86)
Most Points, Season .... **114** Bobby Smith (1981-82; 43G, 71A)
Most PIM, Season .... **382** Basil McRae (1987-88)
Most Points, Defenseman, Season .... **77** Craig Hartsburg (1981-82; 17G, 60A)
Most Points, Center, Season .... **114** Bobby Smith (1981-82; 43G, 71A)
Most Points, Right Wing, Season .... **107** Dino Ciccarelli (1981-82; 55G, 52A)
Most Points, Left Wing, Season .... **99** Brian Bellows (1989-90; 55G, 44A)
Most Points, Rookie, Season .... **98** Neal Broten (1981-82; 38G, 60A)
Most Shutouts, Season .... **9** Ed Belfour (1997-98)
Most Goals, Game .... **5** Tim Young (Jan. 15/79)
Most Assists, Game .... **5** Murray Oliver (Oct. 24/71), Larry Murphy (Oct. 17/89)
Most Points, Game .... **7** Bobby Smith (Nov. 11/81; 4G, 3A)

Records include Minnesota North Stars, 1967-68 through 1992-93.

Dallas Stars Retired Numbers

7	Neal Broten	1980-1995, 1996-1997

Minnesota North Stars Retired Numbers

8	Bill Goldsworthy	1967-1976
19	Bill Masterton	1967-1968

All-time Record vs. Other Clubs

Regular Season

	At Home							On Road							Total						
	GP	W	L	T	GF	GA	PTS	GP	W	L	T	GF	GA	PTS	GP	W	L	T	GF	GA	PTS
Anaheim	16	13	2	1	66	30	27	17	9	8	0	44	42	18	33	22	10	1	110	72	45
Atlanta	1	1	0	0	2	1	2	1	1	0	0	4	2	2	2	2	0	0	6	3	4
Boston	58	16	29	13	168	213	45	57	8	40	9	136	249	25	115	24	69	22	304	462	70
Buffalo	51	24	21	6	162	152	54	49	13	26	10	131	177	36	100	37	47	16	293	329	90
Calgary	54	27	18	9	201	174	63	54	11	31	12	135	196	35	108	38	49	21	336	370	98
Carolina	27	16	10	1	109	81	33	28	14	10	4	105	91	32	55	30	20	5	214	172	65
Chicago	104	46	43	15	350	323	108	102	26	63	13	264	405	65	206	72	106	28	614	728	173
Colorado	33	16	13	4	106	98	38	33	10	19	4	92	131	25	66	26	32	8	198	229	63
Detroit	98	50	33	15	352	295	115	98	35	49	14	322	383	84	196	85	82	29	674	678	199
Edmonton	37	18	13	6	136	113	42	36	11	17	8	120	149	30	73	29	30	14	256	262	72
Florida	6	3	1	2	21	16	8	6	3	2	1	21	17	7	12	6	3	3	42	33	15
Los Angeles	73	45	16	12	294	194	102	72	25	29	18	218	244	68	145	70	45	30	512	438	170
Montreal	56	15	30	11	145	201	41	56	11	37	8	137	245	30	112	26	67	19	282	446	71
Nashville	4	3	1	0	8	3	6	4	2	2	0	11	11	4	8	5	3	0	19	14	10
New Jersey	42	25	11	6	161	110	56	41	19	19	3	128	137	41	83	44	30	9	289	247	97
NY Islanders	44	17	20	7	131	162	42	44	13	23	8	126	165	34	88	30	43	15	257	327	76
NY Rangers	58	18	30	10	174	215	46	59	14	34	11	161	205	39	117	32	64	21	335	420	85
Ottawa	7	4	3	0	26	15	8	7	5	2	0	21	16	10	14	9	5	0	47	31	18
Philadelphia	63	26	23	14	207	206	66	64	9	41	14	145	249	32	127	35	64	28	352	455	98
Phoenix	45	23	16	6	173	138	52	43	22	19	2	148	140	46	88	45	35	8	321	278	98
Pittsburgh	62	35	21	6	237	207	76	60	18	36	6	168	227	42	122	53	57	12	405	434	118
St. Louis	107	49	39	19	365	322	117	110	30	60	20	312	402	80	217	79	99	39	677	724	197
San Jose	19	9	8	2	55	49	20	19	11	8	0	54	46	22	38	20	16	2	109	95	42
Tampa Bay	9	6	2	1	32	21	13	10	7	1	2	30	16	16	19	13	3	3	62	37	29
Toronto	95	49	35	11	362	302	109	99	34	49	16	311	350	84	194	83	84	27	673	652	193
Vancouver	63	33	18	12	240	191	78	63	24	29	10	190	232	58	126	57	47	22	430	423	136
Washington	37	18	11	8	138	103	44	38	15	15	8	118	117	38	75	33	26	16	256	220	82
Defunct Clubs	33	19	8	6	123	86	44	32	10	16	6	84	105	26	65	29	24	12	207	191	70
Totals	**1302**	**624**	**475**	**203**	**4544**	**4021**	**1455**	**1302**	**410**	**685**	**207**	**3736**	**4749**	**1029**	**2604**	**1034**	**1160**	**410**	**8280**	**8770**	**2484**

Playoffs

	Series	W	L	GP	W	L	T	GF	GA	Last Mtg.	Round	Result
Boston	1	1	0	3	3	0	0	20	13	1981	PR	W 3-0
Buffalo	3	2	1	13	8	5	0	39	37	1999	F	W 4-2
Calgary	1	1	0	6	4	2	0	25	18	1981	SF	W 4-2
Chicago	6	2	4	33	14	19	0	118	120	1991	DSF	W 4-2
Colorado	2	2	0	14	8	6	0	37	29	2000	CF	W 4-3
Detroit	3	0	3	18	6	12	0	40	55	1998	CF	L 2-4
Edmonton	6	4	2	30	19	11	0	82	80	2000	CQF	W 4-1
Los Angeles	1	1	0	7	4	3	0	26	21	1968	QF	W 4-3
Montreal	2	1	1	13	6	7	0	37	48	1980	QF	W 4-3
New Jersey	1	0	1	6	2	4	0	9	15	2000	F	L 2-4
NY Islanders	1	0	1	5	1	4	0	16	26	1981	F	L 1-4
Philadelphia	2	0	2	11	3	8	0	26	41	1980	SF	L 1-4
Pittsburgh	1	0	1	6	2	4	0	16	28	1991	F	L 2-4
St. Louis	11	6	5	62	34	28	0	191	174	1999	CSF	W 4-2
San Jose	2	2	0	11	8	3	0	31	19	2000	CSF	W 4-1
Toronto	2	2	0	7	6	1	0	35	26	1983	DSF	W 3-1
Vancouver	1	0	1	5	1	4	0	11	18	1994	CSF	L 1-4
Totals	**46**	**24**	**22**	**250**	**129**	**121**	**0**	**760**	**767**			

Calgary totals include Atlanta Flames, 1972-73 to 1979-80.
Carolina totals include Hartford, 1979-80 to 1996-97.
Colorado totals include Quebec, 1979-80 to 1994-95.
New Jersey totals include Kansas City, 1974-75 to 1975-76, and Colorado Rockies, 1976-77 to 1981-82.
Phoenix totals include Winnipeg, 1979-80 to 1995-96.

Playoff Results 2000-1996

Year	Round	Opponent	Result	GF	GA
2000	F	New Jersey	L 2-4	9	15
	CF	Colorado	W 4-3	14	13
	CSF	San Jose	W 4-1	15	7
	CQF	Edmonton	W 4-1	14	11
1999	**F**	**Buffalo**	**W 4-2**	**13**	**9**
	CF	Colorado	W 4-3	23	16
	CSF	St. Louis	W 4-2	17	12
	CQF	Edmonton	W 4-0	11	7
1998	CF	Detroit	L 2-4	11	15
	CSF	Edmonton	W 4-1	9	5
	CQF	San Jose	W 4-2	16	12
1997	CQF	Edmonton	L 3-4	18	21

Abbreviations: Round: F – Final; **CF** – conference final; **CSF** – conference semi-final; **CQF** – conference quarter-final; **DSF** – division semi-final; **SF** – semi-final; **QF** – quarter-final; **PR** – preliminary round.

1999-00 Results

Oct.	1		Pittsburgh	6-4		7		Vancouver	1-3
	2		Anaheim	2-0		11	at	Edmonton	3-2
	5	at	Detroit	3-2		12	at	Calgary	1-2 *
	8	at	Anaheim	0-3		15	at	Vancouver	2-1
	9	at	San Jose	3-2		19	at	Anaheim	1-3
	13		San Jose	0-2		20	at	Los Angeles	5-2
	15		Boston	2-2		23	at	Chicago	3-2
	16	at	Nashville	2-3		26		Los Angeles	3-1
	20		Edmonton	2-1		28		St. Louis	1-3
	22		New Jersey	2-1 *		31		Edmonton	2-1
	25	at	Toronto	0-4	**Feb.**	2		Atlanta	2-1
	30		Tampa Bay	1-2		3	at	Phoenix	2-0
Nov.	3		Buffalo	1-3		9	at	Anaheim	5-3
	5	at	Phoenix	6-4		11	at	Los Angeles	2-3
	6	at	San Jose	1-2		13		Washington	2-1
	9	at	St. Louis	5-2		16		Nashville	3-0
	10		Detroit	2-4		18		Phoenix	3-4
	17	at	Washington	2-2		20	at	Colorado	2-1
	18	at	Philadelphia	1-1		21	at	Nashville	2-5
	20	at	Carolina	0-1		23	at	Detroit	5-2
	22		Colorado	2-3 *		25		Chicago	3-4 *
	24		Los Angeles	3-2 *		27		Colorado	1-1
	26		Anaheim	2-4	**Mar.**	1		Philadelphia	2-0
	28	at	Atlanta	4-2		3	at	Phoenix	4-1
	30	at	NY Islanders	2-1		5		Detroit	3-5
Dec.	1	at	Montreal	3-2		8		Vancouver	3-3
	4	at	Ottawa	3-1		10		NY Islanders	3-4 *
	6		Phoenix	2-3		12		St. Louis	4-2
	8		Carolina	2-1		13	at	NY Rangers	4-3
	10		Florida	4-3		15	at	New Jersey	3-2
	11	at	St. Louis	2-4		18	at	Chicago	2-2
	15		Calgary	5-1		19		San Jose	5-3
	17	at	Edmonton	2-2		24		Chicago	5-1
	18	at	Vancouver	4-2		26		Colorado	1-2 *
	21	at	Calgary	0-0		28	at	Tampa Bay	4-2
	23	at	Chicago	2-5		29	at	Florida	4-1
	27		San Jose	1-3	**Apr.**	2	at	Colorado	2-3 *
	29		NY Rangers	4-3 *		3		Calgary	2-2
	31		Anaheim	5-4		5	at	San Jose	2-5
Jan.	3		Los Angeles	4-1		7	at	Los Angeles	2-3
	5		Nashville	3-1		9		Phoenix	2-2

* – Overtime

Entry Draft
Selections 2000-1986

2000
Pick

25	Steve Ott
60	Dan Ellis
68	Joel Lundqvist
91	Alexei Tereschenko
123	Vadim Khomitsky
139	Ruslan Bernikov
162	Artem Chernov
192	Ladislav Vlcek
219	Marco Tuokko
224	Antti Miettinen

1999
Pick

32	Michael Ryan
66	Dan Jancevski
96	Mathias Tjarnqvist
126	Jeff Bateman
156	Gregor Baumgartner
184	Justin Cox
186	Brett Draney
215	Jeff MacMillan
243	Brian Sullivan
265	Jamie Chamberlain
272	Mikhail Donika

1998
Pick

39	John Erskine
57	Tyler Bouck
86	Gabriel Karlsson
153	Pavel Patera
173	Niko Kapanen
200	Scott Perry

1997
Pick

25	Brenden Morrow
52	Roman Lyashenko
77	Steve Gainey
105	Marc Kristofferson
132	Teemu Elomo
160	Alexei Timkin
189	Jeff McKercher
216	Alexei Komarov
242	Brett McLean

1996
Pick

5	Richard Jackman
70	Jonathan Sim
90	Mike Hurley
112	Ryan Christie
113	Yevgeny Tsybuk
166	Eoin McInerney
194	Joel Kwiatkowski
220	Nick Bootland

1995
Pick

11	Jarome Iginla
37	Patrick Cote
63	Petr Buzek
69	Sergey Gusev
115	Wade Strand
141	Dominic Marleau
173	Jeff Dewar
193	Anatoli Koveshnikov
202	Sergei Luchinkin
219	Stephen Lowe

1994
Pick

20	Jason Botterill
46	Lee Jinman
98	Jamie Wright
124	Marty Turco
150	Evgeny Petrochinin
228	Marty Flichel
254	Jimmy Roy
280	Chris Szysky

1993
Pick

9	Todd Harvey
35	Jamie Langenbrunner
87	Chad Lang
136	Rick Mrozik
139	Per Svartvadet
165	Jeremy Stasiuk
191	Rob Lurtsema
243	Jordan Willis
249	Bill Lang
269	Cory Peterson

1992
Pick

34	Jarkko Varvio
58	Jeff Bes
88	Jere Lehtinen
130	Michael Johnson
154	Kyle Peterson
178	Juha Lind
202	Lars Edstrom
226	Jeff Romfo
250	Jeffrey Moen

1991
Pick

8	Richard Matvichuk
74	Mike Torchia
97	Mike Kennedy
118	Mark Lawrence
137	Geoff Finch
174	Michael Burkett
184	Derek Herlofsky
206	Tom Nemeth
228	Shayne Green
250	Jukka Suomalainen

1990
Pick

8	Derian Hatcher
50	Laurie Billeck
70	Cal McGowan
71	Frank Kovacs
92	Enrico Ciccone
113	Roman Turek
134	Jeff Levy
155	Doug Barrault
176	Joe Biondi
197	Troy Binnie
218	Ole-Eskild Dahlstrom
239	John McKersie

1989
Pick

7	Doug Zmolek
28	Mike Craig
60	Murray Garbutt
75	Jean-Francois Quintin
87	Pat MacLeod
91	Bryan Schoen
97	Rhys Hollyman
112	Scott Cashman
154	Jonathon Pratt
175	Kenneth Blum
196	Arturs Irbe
217	Tom Pederson
238	Helmut Balderis

1988
Pick

1	Mike Modano
40	Link Gaetz
43	Shaun Kane
64	Jeffrey Stolp
148	Ken MacArthur
169	Travis Richards
190	Ari Matilainen
211	Grant Bischoff
232	Trent Andison

1987
Pick

6	Dave Archibald
35	Scott McCrady
48	Kevin Kaminski
73	John Weisbrod
88	Teppo Kivela
109	D'arcy Norton
130	Timo Kulonen
151	Don Schmidt
172	Jarmo Myllys
193	Larry Olimb
214	Mark Felicio
235	Dave Shields

1986
Pick

12	Warren Babe
30	Neil Wilkinson
33	Dean Kolstad
54	Rick Bennett
55	Rob Zettler
58	Brad Turner
75	Kirk Tomlinson
96	Jari Gronstrand
159	Scott Mathias
180	Lance Pitlick
201	Dan Keczmer
222	Garth Joy
243	Kurt Stahura

Club Directory

Reunion Arena

Dallas Stars
Dr Pepper StarCenter
211 Cowboys Parkway
Irving, TX 75063
Phone **972/831-2401**
FAX 972/868-2860
Ticket Information 214/GO STARS
Capacity: 17,001

Chairman of the Board & Owner	Thomas O. Hicks
President/Alternate Governor	James R. Lites
V.P. of Hockey Operations/General Manager	Bob Gainey
V.P. of Marketing and Broadcasting	Bill Strong
V.P. of Marketing and Promotion	Jeff Cogen
V.P. of Communications	John Blake
Assistant General Manager	Doug Armstrong
Director of Player Personnel	Les Jackson
Director of Hockey Administration	Brian Poile
Head Coach	Ken Hitchcock
Assistant Coaches	Doug Jarvis, Rick Wilson
Head Athletic Trainer	Dave Surprenant
Equipment Managers	Dave Smith, Steve Sumner
Strength and Conditioning Coach	J.J. McQueen
Director of Media Relations	Larry Kelly (972) 868-2807
Media Relations Assistant	Mark Janko (972) 868-2818
P.R. Fax	(972) 868-2860
Radio Station	WBAP, 820 AM
TV Stations	KDFI, Ch. 27; Fox Sports Southwest
Web site	www.dallasstars.com

The solid work of rookies like Brenden Morrow (left) and Roman Lyashenko helped Dallas return to the Stanley Cup finals in 2000. This time, however, they were beaten by Scott Gomez and the New Jersey Devils.

General Managers' History

Wren Blair, 1967-68 to 1973-74; Jack Gordon, 1974-75 to 1976-77; Lou Nanne, 1977-78 to 1987-88; Jack Ferreira, 1988-89, 1989-90; Bob Clarke 1990-91, 1991-92; Bob Gainey, 1992-93 to date.

Coaching History

Wren Blair, 1967-68; Wren Blair and John Muckler, 1968-69; Wren Blair and Charlie Burns, 1969-70; Jackie Gordon, 1970-71 to 1972-73; Jackie Gordon and Parker MacDonald, 1973-74; Jackie Gordon and Charlie Burns, 1974-75; Ted Harris, 1975-76, 1976-77; Ted Harris, André Beaulieu and Lou Nanne, 1977-78; Harry Howell and Glen Sonmor, 1978-79; Glen Sonmor, 1979-80 to 1981-82; Glen Sonmor and Murray Oliver, 1982-83; Bill Mahoney, 1983-84, 1984-85; Lorne Henning, 1985-86; Lorne Henning and Glen Sonmor, 1986-87; Herb Brooks, 1987-88; Pierre Page, 1988-89, 1989-90; Bob Gainey, 1990-91 to 1994-95; Bob Gainey and Ken Hitchcock, 1995-96; Ken Hitchcock, 1996-97 to date.

Captains' History

Bob Woytowich, 1967-68; Elmer Vasko, 1968-69; Claude Larose, 1969-70; Ted Harris, 1970-71 to 1973-74; Bill Goldsworthy, 1974-75, 1975-76; Bill Hogaboam, 1976-77; Nick Beverley, 1977-78; J.P. Parise, 1978-79; Paul Shmyr, 1979-80, 1980-81; Tim Young, 1981-82; Craig Hartsburg, 1982-83; Craig Hartsburg and Brian Bellows, 1983-84; Craig Hartsburg, 1984-85 to 1987-88; Curt Fraser, Bob Rouse and Curt Giles, 1988-89; Curt Giles, 1989-90, 1990-91; Mark Tinordi, 1991-92 to 1993-94; Neal Broten and Derian Hatcher, 1994-95; Derian Hatcher, 1995-96 to date.

General Manager

GAINEY, BOB
Vice President of Hockey Operations/General Manager, Dallas Stars.
Born in Peterborough, Ont., December 13, 1953.

Bob Gainey enters his fifth season as the full-time general manager for the Dallas Stars after building the team into a Stanley Cup champion in 1999 and a finalist in 2000. Named general manager of the team on June 8, 1992, he held the dual role of coach and g.m. for over three seasons before relinquishing his head coaching duties on January 8, 1996. He is the Stars' sixth general manager and was the team's 16th head coach.

Under Gainey's tutelage, the Stars improved their regular-season record in each of his first four seasons as coach, going from 27 wins and 68 points in his first year to 42 wins and 97 points in 1993-94. In his first season, 1990-91, Gainey led the Stars through to the Stanley Cup finals, surprising Chicago and St. Louis and eliminating defending champion Edmonton before bowing in six games to Pittsburgh. He finished his reign behind the Stars bench with a 165-190-60 regular season record.

Elected to the Hockey Hall of Fame in 1992, Gainey was Montreal's first choice (eighth overall) in the 1973 Amateur Draft. During his 16-year career with the Canadiens, Gainey was a member of five Stanley Cup-winning teams and was named the Conn Smythe Trophy winner in 1979. He was a four-time recipient of the Frank Selke Trophy (1978-81), awarded to the League's top defensive forward, and participated in four NHL All-Star Games (1977, 1978, 1980 and 1981). He served as team captain for eight seasons (1981-89). During his career, he played in 1,160 regular-season games, registering 239 goals and 262 assists for 501 points. In addition, he tallied 73 points (25-48-73) in 182 post-season games.

NHL Coaching Record

		Regular Season					Playoffs			
Season	Team	Games	W	L	T	%	Games	W	L	%
1990-91	Minnesota	80	27	39	14	.425	23	14	9	.643
1991-92	Minnesota	80	32	42	6	.438	7	3	4	.429
1992-93	Minnesota	84	36	38	10	.488	....	....	....	....
1993-94	Dallas	84	42	29	13	.577	9	5	4	.556
1994-95	Dallas	48	17	23	8	.438	5	1	4	.200
1995-96	Dallas	39	11	19	9	.397	....	....	....	....
	NHL Totals	**415**	**165**	**190**	**60**	**.470**	**44**	**23**	**21**	**.523**

Detroit Red Wings

1999-2000 Results: 48W-24L-10T 108PTS. Second, Central Division

Brendan Shanahan continues to rank as one of hockey's top power forwards. His 78 points last season (including 41 goals) trailed only Steve Yzerman among Red Wings scorers, while his 105 penalty minutes rated second to Martin Lapointe.

2000-01 Schedule

Oct.	Thu.	5	at Calgary	**Jan.**	Thu.	4	Dallas
	Fri.	6	at Edmonton		Fri.	5	at Minnesota
	Wed.	11	Edmonton		Sun.	7	Colorado
	Thu.	12	at Chicago		Tue.	9	Phoenix
	Sun.	15	Calgary		Fri.	12	at Dallas
	Tue.	17	St. Louis		Mon.	15	at San Jose*
	Thu.	19	Nashville		Tue.	16	at Vancouver
	Sat.	21	Buffalo		Sat.	20	at Edmonton
	Sun.	22	at Columbus		Sun.	21	at Calgary
	Wed.	25	Tampa Bay		Wed.	24	Nashville
	Sat.	28	Columbus		Fri.	26	Anaheim
	Tue.	31	at Washington		Tue.	30	at New Jersey
Nov.	Wed.	1	at Montreal		Wed.	31	at Columbus
	Fri.	3	Chicago	**Feb.**	Tue.	6	Ottawa
	Wed.	8	at Phoenix		Thu.	8	Toronto
	Sat.	11	at Los Angeles		Sat.	10	at Toronto
	Sun.	12	at Anaheim*		Wed.	14	Carolina
	Wed.	15	San Jose		Fri.	16	Columbus
	Fri.	17	Dallas		Sun.	18	at Dallas
	Sat.	18	at Nashville		Tue.	20	at Nashville
	Mon.	20	Nashville		Wed.	21	at Chicago
	Wed.	22	Boston		Fri.	23	St. Louis
	Fri.	24	Vancouver		Sun.	25	Phoenix*
	Sat.	25	at NY Islanders		Wed.	28	at Anaheim
	Mon.	27	Chicago	**Mar.**	Fri.	2	at Phoenix
	Wed.	29	at Atlanta		Sat.	3	at Los Angeles
Dec.	Fri.	1	at Florida		Tue.	6	at Vancouver
	Sat.	2	at Tampa Bay		Sat.	10	at St. Louis*
	Wed.	6	Toronto		Sun.	11	at Minnesota*
	Fri.	8	Philadelphia		Tue.	13	Vancouver
	Sun.	10	Pittsburgh		Thu.	15	Calgary
	Wed.	13	Florida		Sat.	17	at Colorado*
	Fri.	15	at Colorado		Sun.	18	at San Jose*
	Sat.	16	at St. Louis		Thu.	22	Minnesota
	Mon.	18	Edmonton		Sat.	24	at NY Rangers*
	Wed.	20	San Jose		Wed.	28	St. Louis
	Fri.	22	Anaheim		Sat.	31	at Philadelphia*
	Sat.	23	at Boston	**Apr.**	Sun.	1	Washington
	Wed.	27	Minnesota		Tue.	3	at Columbus
	Fri.	29	at Chicago		Thu.	5	Atlanta
	Sun.	31	Los Angeles		Sat.	7	Colorado*

* Denotes afternoon game.

Franchise date: September 25, 1926

CENTRAL DIVISION

75th NHL Season

Year-by-Year Record

		Home			Road			Overall							
Season	**GP**	**W**	**L**	**T**	**W**	**L**	**T**	**W**	**L**	**T**	**GF**	**GA**	**Pts.**	**Finished**	**Playoff Result**
1999-2000	82	28	10	3	20	14	7	48	24	10	278	210	108	2nd, Central Div.	Lost Conf. Semi-Final
1998-99	82	27	12	2	16	20	5	43	32	7	245	202	93	1st, Central Div.	Lost Conf. Semi-Final
1997-98	**82**	**25**	**8**	**8**	**19**	**15**	**7**	**44**	**23**	**15**	**250**	**196**	**103**	**2nd, Central Div.**	**Won Stanley Cup**
1996-97	**82**	**20**	**12**	**9**	**18**	**14**	**9**	**38**	**26**	**18**	**253**	**197**	**94**	**2nd, Central Div.**	**Won Stanley Cup**
1995-96	82	36	3	2	26	10	5	62	13	7	325	181	131	1st, Central Div.	Lost Conf. Championship
1994-95	48	17	4	3	16	7	1	33	11	4	180	117	70	1st, Central Div.	Lost Final
1993-94	84	23	13	6	23	17	2	46	30	8	356	275	100	1st, Central Div.	Lost Conf. Quarter-Final
1992-93	84	25	14	3	22	14	6	47	28	9	369	280	103	2nd, Norris Div.	Lost Div. Semi-Final
1991-92	80	24	12	4	19	13	8	43	25	12	320	256	98	1st, Norris Div.	Lost Div. Final
1990-91	80	26	14	0	8	24	8	34	38	8	273	298	76	3rd, Norris Div.	Lost Div. Semi-Final
1989-90	80	20	14	6	8	24	8	28	38	14	288	323	70	5th, Norris Div.	Out of Playoffs
1988-89	80	20	14	6	14	20	6	34	34	12	313	316	80	1st, Norris Div.	Lost Div. Semi-Final
1987-88	80	24	10	6	17	18	5	41	28	11	322	269	93	1st, Norris Div.	Lost Conf. Championship
1986-87	80	20	14	6	14	22	4	34	36	10	260	274	78	2nd, Norris Div.	Lost Conf. Championship
1985-86	80	10	26	4	7	31	2	17	57	6	266	415	40	5th, Norris Div.	Out of Playoffs
1984-85	80	19	14	7	8	27	5	27	41	12	313	357	66	3rd, Norris Div.	Lost Div. Semi-Final
1983-84	80	18	20	2	13	22	5	31	42	7	298	323	69	3rd, Norris Div.	Lost Div. Semi-Final
1982-83	80	14	19	7	7	25	8	21	44	15	263	344	57	5th, Norris Div.	Out of Playoffs
1981-82	80	15	19	6	6	28	6	21	47	12	270	351	54	6th, Norris Div.	Out of Playoffs
1980-81	80	16	15	9	3	28	9	19	43	18	252	339	56	5th, Norris Div.	Out of Playoffs
1979-80	80	14	21	5	12	22	6	26	43	11	268	306	63	5th, Norris Div.	Out of Playoffs
1978-79	80	15	17	8	8	24	8	23	41	16	252	295	62	5th, Norris Div.	Out of Playoffs
1977-78	80	22	11	7	10	23	7	32	34	14	252	266	78	2nd, Norris Div.	Lost Quarter-Final
1976-77	80	12	22	6	4	33	3	16	55	9	183	309	41	5th, Norris Div.	Out of Playoffs
1975-76	80	17	15	8	9	29	2	26	44	10	226	300	62	4th, Norris Div.	Out of Playoffs
1974-75	80	17	17	6	6	28	6	23	45	12	259	335	58	4th, Norris Div.	Out of Playoffs
1973-74	78	21	12	6	8	27	4	29	39	10	255	319	68	6th, East Div.	Out of Playoffs
1972-73	78	22	12	5	15	17	7	37	29	12	265	243	86	5th, East Div.	Out of Playoffs
1971-72	78	25	11	3	8	24	7	33	35	10	261	262	76	5th, East Div.	Out of Playoffs
1970-71	78	17	15	7	5	30	4	22	45	11	209	308	55	7th, East Div.	Out of Playoffs
1969-70	76	20	11	7	20	10	8	40	21	15	246	199	95	3rd, East Div.	Lost Quarter-Final
1968-69	76	23	8	7	10	23	5	33	31	12	239	221	78	5th, East Div.	Out of Playoffs
1967-68	74	18	15	4	9	20	8	27	35	12	245	257	66	6th, East Div.	Out of Playoffs
1966-67	70	21	11	3	6	28	1	27	39	4	212	241	58	5th,	Out of Playoffs
1965-66	70	20	8	7	11	19	5	31	27	12	221	194	74	4th,	Lost Final
1964-65	70	25	7	3	15	16	4	40	23	7	224	175	87	1st,	Lost Semi-Final
1963-64	70	23	9	3	7	20	8	30	29	11	191	204	71	4th,	Lost Final
1962-63	70	19	10	6	13	15	7	32	25	13	200	194	77	4th,	Lost Final
1961-62	70	17	11	7	6	22	7	23	33	14	184	219	60	5th,	Out of Playoffs
1960-61	70	15	13	7	10	16	9	25	29	16	195	215	66	4th,	Lost Final
1959-60	70	18	14	3	8	15	12	26	29	15	186	197	67	4th,	Lost Semi-Final
1958-59	70	13	17	5	12	20	3	25	37	8	167	218	58	6th,	Out of Playoffs
1957-58	70	16	11	8	13	18	4	29	29	12	176	207	70	3rd,	Lost Semi-Final
1956-57	70	23	7	5	15	13	7	38	20	12	198	157	88	1st,	Lost Semi-Final
1955-56	70	21	6	8	9	18	8	30	24	16	183	148	76	2nd,	Lost Final
1954-55	**70**	**25**	**5**	**5**	**17**	**12**	**6**	**42**	**17**	**11**	**204**	**134**	**95**	**1st,**	**Won Stanley Cup**
1953-54	**70**	**24**	**4**	**7**	**13**	**15**	**7**	**37**	**19**	**14**	**191**	**132**	**88**	**1st,**	**Won Stanley Cup**
1952-53	70	20	5	10	16	11	8	36	16	18	222	133	90	1st,	Lost Semi-Final
1951-52	**70**	**24**	**7**	**4**	**20**	**7**	**8**	**44**	**14**	**12**	**215**	**133**	**100**	**1st,**	**Won Stanley Cup**
1950-51	70	25	3	7	19	10	6	44	13	13	236	139	101	1st,	Lost Semi-Final
1949-50	**70**	**19**	**9**	**7**	**18**	**10**	**7**	**37**	**19**	**14**	**229**	**164**	**88**	**1st,**	**Won Stanley Cup**
1948-49	60	21	6	3	13	13	4	34	19	7	195	145	75	1st,	Lost Final
1947-48	60	16	9	5	14	9	7	30	18	12	187	148	72	2nd,	Lost Final
1946-47	60	14	10	6	8	17	5	22	27	11	190	193	55	4th,	Lost Semi-Final
1945-46	50	16	5	4	4	15	6	20	20	10	146	159	50	4th,	Lost Semi-Final
1944-45	50	19	5	1	12	9	4	31	14	5	218	161	67	2nd,	Lost Final
1943-44	50	18	5	2	8	13	4	26	18	6	214	177	58	2nd,	Lost Semi-Final
1942-43	**50**	**16**	**4**	**5**	**9**	**10**	**6**	**25**	**14**	**11**	**169**	**124**	**61**	**1st,**	**Won Stanley Cup**
1941-42	48	14	7	3	5	18	1	19	25	4	140	147	42	5th,	Lost Final
1940-41	48	14	5	5	7	11	6	21	16	11	112	102	53	3rd,	Lost Final
1939-40	48	11	10	3	5	16	3	16	26	6	90	126	38	5th,	Lost Semi-Final
1938-39	48	14	8	2	4	16	4	18	24	6	107	128	42	5th,	Lost Semi-Final
1937-38	48	8	10	6	4	15	5	12	25	11	99	133	35	4th, Amn. Div.	Out of Playoffs
1936-37	**48**	**14**	**5**	**5**	**11**	**9**	**4**	**25**	**14**	**9**	**128**	**102**	**59**	**1st, Amn. Div.**	**Won Stanley Cup**
1935-36	**48**	**14**	**5**	**5**	**10**	**11**	**3**	**24**	**16**	**8**	**124**	**103**	**56**	**1st, Amn. Div.**	**Won Stanley Cup**
1934-35	48	11	8	5	8	14	2	19	22	7	127	114	45	4th, Amn. Div.	Out of Playoffs
1933-34	48	15	5	4	9	9	6	24	14	10	113	98	58	1st, Amn. Div.	Lost Final
1932-33*	48	17	3	4	8	12	4	25	15	8	111	93	58	2nd, Amn. Div.	Lost Semi-Final
1931-32	48	15	3	6	3	17	4	18	20	10	95	108	46	3rd, Amn. Div.	Lost Quarter-Final
1930-31**	44	10	7	5	6	14	2	16	21	7	102	105	39	4th, Amn. Div.	Out of Playoffs
1929-30	44	9	10	3	5	14	3	14	24	6	117	133	34	4th, Amn. Div.	Out of Playoffs
1928-29	44	11	6	5	8	10	4	19	16	9	72	63	47	3rd, Amn. Div.	Lost Quarter-Final
1927-28	44	9	10	3	10	9	3	19	19	6	88	79	44	4th, Amn. Div.	Out of Playoffs
1926-27***	44	5	16	0	7	12	4	12	28	4	76	105	28	5th, Amn. Div.	Out of Playoffs

* Team name changed to Red Wings. ** Team name changed to Falcons. *** Team named Cougars.

2000-01 Player Personnel

FORWARDS	HT	WT	S	Place of Birth	Date	1999-00 Club
BROWN, Doug	5-10	185	R	Southborough, MA	6/12/64	Detroit
BUTSAYEV, Yuri	6-1	183	L	Togliatti, USSR	10/11/78	Detroit-Cincinnati Ducks
DANDENAULT, Mathieu	6-0	200	R	Sherbrooke, Que.	2/3/76	Detroit
DEVEREAUX, Boyd	6-2	195	L	Seaforth, Ont.	4/16/78	Edmonton
DRAPER, Kris	5-11	190	L	Toronto, Ont.	5/24/71	Detroit
FEDOROV, Sergei	6-1	200	L	Pskov, USSR	12/13/69	Detroit
GILCHRIST, Brent	5-11	180	L	Moose Jaw, Sask.	4/3/67	Detroit
HOLMSTROM, Tomas	6-0	200	L	Pitea, Sweden	1/23/73	Detroit
KOZLOV, Vyacheslav	5-10	180	L	Voskresensk, USSR	5/3/72	Detroit
LAPOINTE, Martin	5-11	200	R	Ville Ste. Pierre, Que.	9/12/73	Detroit
MALTBY, Kirk	6-0	180	R	Guelph, Ont.	12/22/72	Detroit
McCARTY, Darren	6-1	210	R	Burnaby, B.C.	4/1/72	Detroit
RODGERS, Marc	5-9	185	R	Shawville, Que.	3/16/72	Detroit-Manitoba Moose
SHANAHAN, Brendan	6-3	218	R	Mimico, Ont.	1/23/69	Detroit
VERBEEK, Pat	5-9	192	R	Sarnia, Ont.	5/24/64	Detroit
YZERMAN, Steve	5-11	185	R	Cranbrook, B.C.	5/9/65	Detroit
DEFENSEMEN						
CHELIOS, Chris	6-1	190	R	Chicago, IL	1/25/62	Detroit
DUCHESNE, Steve	5-11	195	L	Sept-Iles, Que.	6/30/65	Detroit
FISCHER, Jiri	6-5	225	L	Horovice, Czech.	7/31/80	Detroit-Cincinnati Ducks
GILL, Todd	6-0	185	L	Cardinal, Ont.	11/9/65	Phoenix-Detroit
GOLUBOVSKY, Yan	6-3	183	R	Novosibirsk, USSR	3/9/76	Detroit
KUZNETSOV, Maxim	6-5	198	L	Pavlodar, USSR	3/24/77	Cincinnati Ducks
LIDSTROM, Nicklas	6-2	185	L	Vasteras, Sweden	4/28/70	Detroit
MURPHY, Larry	6-2	210	R	Scarborough, Ont.	3/8/61	Detroit
WALLIN, Jesse	6-2	190	L	Saskatoon, Sask.	3/10/78	Detroit-Cincinnati Ducks
WARD, Aaron	6-2	200	R	Windsor, Ont.	1/17/73	Detroit

GOALTENDERS	HT	WT	C	Place of Birth	Date	1999-00 Club
LEGACE, Manny	5-9	162	L	Toronto, Ont.	2/4/73	Detroit-Manitoba Moose
OSGOOD, Chris	5-10	175	L	Peace River, Alta.	11/26/72	Detroit
WREGGET, Ken	6-1	201	L	Brandon, Man.	3/25/64	Detroit

Coach

BOWMAN, WILLIAM SCOTT (SCOTTY)
Coach, Detroit Red Wings. Born in Montreal, Que. September 18, 1933.

Scotty Bowman is entering his eighth season as coach of the Red Wings and his 29th as a coach in the NHL. Bowman equalled Toe Blake's record for coaches in 1998 when he guided the Detroit Red Wings to a second consecutive Stanley Cup championship. The victory gave Bowman his eighth title as a coach and the ninth of his career including his victory as director of player development with the Pittsburgh Penguins in 1991. Bowman, who is also the all-time coaching leader in both regular-season and playoff victories, is the first coach to win the Stanley Cup with three different teams.

Bowman began his NHL coaching career with the St. Louis Blues and led the team to the Stanley Cup finals three years in a row from 1968 to 1970. He was then appointed head coach of the Montreal Canadiens and led the team to five Stanley Cup titles in eight years.

Following an eight-season term as the general manager of the Buffalo Sabres, and a brief stint as a commentator for CBC Television, Bowman joined the Pittsburgh Penguins as director of player development, but returned to coaching when head coach Bob Johnson became ill in September, 1991. Bowman was elected to the Hockey Hall of Fame as a builder in 1991.

NHL Coaching Record

		Regular Season					Playoffs			
Season	Team	Games	W	L	T	%	Games	W	L	%
1967-68	St. Louis	58	23	21	14	.517	18	8	10	.444
1968-69	St. Louis	76	37	25	14	.579	12	8	4	.667
1969-70	St. Louis	76	37	27	12	.566	16	8	8	.500
1970-71	St. Louis	28	13	10	5	.554	6	2	4	.333
1971-72	Montreal	78	46	16	16	.692	6	2	4	.333
1972-73	Montreal	78	52	10	16	.769	17	12	5	.706*
1973-74	Montreal	78	45	24	9	.635	6	2	4	.333
1974-75	Montreal	80	47	14	19	.706	11	6	5	.545
1975-76	Montreal	80	58	11	11	.794	13	12	1	.923*
1976-77	Montreal	80	60	8	12	.825	14	12	2	.857*
1977-78	Montreal	80	59	10	11	.806	15	12	3	.800*
1978-79	Montreal	80	52	17	11	.719	16	12	4	.750*
1979-80	Buffalo	80	47	17	16	.688	14	9	5	.643
1981-82	Buffalo	35	18	10	7	.614	4	1	3	.250
1982-83	Buffalo	80	38	29	13	.556	10	6	4	.600
1983-84	Buffalo	80	48	25	7	.644	3	0	3	.000
1984-85	Buffalo	80	38	28	14	.563	5	2	3	.400
1985-86	Buffalo	37	18	18	1	.500	....	....	....	....
1986-87	Buffalo	12	3	7	2	.333	....	....	....	....
1991-92	Pittsburgh	80	39	32	9	.544	21	16	5	.762*
1992-93	Pittsburgh	84	56	21	7	.708	12	7	5	.583
1993-94	Detroit	84	46	30	8	.595	7	3	4	.429
1994-95	Detroit	48	33	11	4	.729	18	12	6	.667
1995-96	Detroit	82	62	13	7	.799	19	10	9	.526
1996-97	Detroit	82	38	26	18	.573	20	16	4	.800*
1997-98	Detroit	82	44	23	15	.628	22	16	6	.727*
1998-99	Detroit	77	39	32	6	.545	10	6	4	.600
1999-2000	Detroit	82	48	24	10	.659•	9	5	4	.556
	NHL Totals	**1977**	**1144**	**539**	**294**	**.654•**	**324**	**205**	**119**	**.633**

* Stanley Cup win.
• Includes points from regulation ties

1999-2000 Scoring

* – rookie

Regular Season

Pos	#	Player	Team	GP	G	A	Pts	+/–	PIM	PP	SH	GW	GT	S	%
C	19	Steve Yzerman	DET	78	35	44	79	28	34	15	2	6	1	234	15.0
L	14	Brendan Shanahan	DET	78	41	37	78	24	105	13	1	9	1	283	14.5
D	5	Nicklas Lidstrom	DET	81	20	53	73	19	18	9	4	3	0	218	9.2
C	91	Sergei Fedorov	DET	68	27	35	62	8	22	4	4	7	0	263	10.3
R	15	Pat Verbeek	DET	68	22	26	48	22	95	7	0	5	1	138	15.9
C	8	Igor Larionov	DET	79	9	38	47	13	28	3	0	4	0	69	13.0
R	20	Martin Lapointe	DET	82	16	25	41	17	121	1	1	2	1	127	12.6
D	28	Steve Duchesne	DET	79	10	31	41	12	42	1	0	1	0	154	6.5
D	55	Larry Murphy	DET	81	10	30	40	4	45	7	0	0	0	146	6.8
L	13	Vyacheslav Kozlov	DET	72	18	18	36	11	28	4	0	3	0	165	10.9
L	96	Tomas Holmstrom	DET	72	13	22	35	4	43	4	0	1	0	71	18.3
D	24	Chris Chelios	DET	81	3	31	34	48	103	0	0	0	0	135	2.2
R	17	Doug Brown	DET	51	10	8	18	8	12	0	1	0	0	67	14.9
R	11	Mathieu Dandenault	DET	81	6	12	18	–12	20	0	0	0	0	98	6.1
C	39	Stacy Roest	DET	49	7	9	16	–1	12	1	0	1	0	56	12.5
L	18	Kirk Maltby	DET	41	6	8	14	1	24	0	2	1	0	71	8.5
R	25	Darren McCarty	DET	24	6	6	12	1	48	0	0	1	0	40	15.0
C	33	Kris Draper	DET	51	5	7	12	3	28	0	0	3	0	76	6.6
D	23	Todd Gill	PHX	41	1	6	7	–10	30	0	0	1	0	41	2.4
			DET	13	2	0	2	2	15	0	0	1	0	20	10.0
			TOTAL	54	3	6	9	–8	45	0	0	2	0	61	4.9
C	22	* Yuri Butsayev	DET	57	5	3	8	–6	12	0	0	0	0	46	10.9
D	2	* Jiri Fischer	DET	52	0	8	8	1	45	0	0	0	0	41	0.0
C	41	Brent Gilchrist	DET	24	4	2	6	1	24	0	0	0	0	33	12.1
C	21	* Darryl Laplante	DET	30	0	6	6	–2	10	0	0	0	0	19	0.0
D	27	Aaron Ward	DET	36	1	3	4	–4	24	0	0	0	0	25	4.0
D	44	Yan Golubovsky	DET	21	1	2	3	3	8	0	0	0	0	7	14.3
R	37	Marc Rodgers	DET	21	1	1	2	–3	10	0	0	0	0	17	5.9
G	31	Ken Wregget	DET	29	0	1	1	0	0	0	0	0	0	0	0.0
G	30	Chris Osgood	DET	53	0	1	1	0	18	0	0	0	0	0	0.0
D	3	* Jesse Wallin	DET	1	0	0	0	–2	0	0	0	0	0	0	0.0
R	36	* B.J. Young	DET	1	0	0	0	0	0	0	0	0	0	1	0.0
G	34	Manny Legace	VAN	0	0	0	0	0	0	0	0	0	0	0	0.0
			DET	4	0	0	0	0	0	0	0	0	0	0	0.0
			TOTAL	4	0	0	0	0	0	0	0	0	0	0	0.0

Goaltending

No.	Goaltender	GPI	Mins	Avg	W	L	T	EN	SO	GA	SA	S%
30	Chris Osgood	53	3148	2.40	30	14	8	2	6	126	1349	.907
31	Ken Wregget	29	1579	2.66	14	10	2	1	0	70	700	.900
34	Manny Legace	4	240	2.75	4	0	0	0	0	11	117	.906
	Totals	**82**	**4985**	**2.53**	**48**	**24**	**10**	**3**	**6**	**210**	**2169**	**.903**

Playoffs

Pos	#	Player	Team	GP	G	A	Pts	+/–	PIM	PP	SH	GW	OT	S	%
C	91	Sergei Fedorov	DET	9	4	4	8	2	4	2	0	1	0	34	11.8
D	5	Nicklas Lidstrom	DET	9	2	4	6	–6	4	1	0	0	0	21	9.5
L	14	Brendan Shanahan	DET	9	3	2	5	0	10	0	0	0	0	41	7.3
D	55	Larry Murphy	DET	9	2	3	5	1	2	1	1	0	0	16	12.5
R	20	Martin Lapointe	DET	9	3	1	4	–1	20	2	0	1	0	12	25.0
L	96	Tomas Holmstrom	DET	9	3	1	4	3	16	1	0	1	0	14	21.4
C	19	Steve Yzerman	DET	8	0	4	4	–4	0	0	0	0	0	20	0.0
D	28	Steve Duchesne	DET	9	0	4	4	2	10	0	0	0	0	14	0.0
L	13	Vyacheslav Kozlov	DET	8	2	1	3	–3	12	1	0	1	0	18	11.1
C	8	Igor Larionov	DET	9	1	2	3	–2	6	1	0	0	0	5	20.0
C	33	Kris Draper	DET	9	2	0	2	4	6	0	0	0	0	16	12.5
R	15	Pat Verbeek	DET	9	1	1	2	–4	2	1	0	1	0	12	8.3
R	17	Doug Brown	DET	3	0	1	1	0	0	0	0	0	0	4	0.0
L	18	Kirk Maltby	DET	8	0	1	1	0	4	0	0	0	0	8	0.0
D	24	Chris Chelios	DET	9	0	1	1	–3	8	0	0	0	0	11	0.0
D	23	Todd Gill	DET	9	0	1	1	2	4	0	0	0	0	7	0.0
G	30	Chris Osgood	DET	9	0	1	1	0	4	0	0	0	0	0	0.0
R	25	Darren Mccarty	DET	9	0	1	1	3	12	0	0	0	0	7	0.0
D	27	Aaron Ward	DET	3	0	0	0	0	0	0	0	0	0	1	0.0
C	39	Stacy Roest	DET	3	0	0	0	0	0	0	0	0	0	2	0.0
C	41	Brent Gilchrist	DET	6	0	0	0	–3	6	0	0	0	0	7	0.0
R	11	Mathieu Dandenault	DET	6	0	0	0	2	2	0	0	0	0	1	0.0

Goaltending

No.	Goaltender	GPI	Mins	Avg	W	L	EN	SO	GA	SA	S%
30	Chris Osgood	9	547	1.97	5	4	1	2	18	237	.924
	Totals	**9**	**550**	**2.07**	**5**	**4**	**1**	**2**	**19**	**238**	**.920**

Coaching History

Art Duncan, 1926-27; Jack Adams, 1927-28 to 1946-47; Tommy Ivan, 1947-48 to 1953-54; Jimmy Skinner, 1954-55 to 1956-57; Jimmy Skinner and Sid Abel, 1957-58; Sid Abel, 1958-59 to 1967-68; Bill Gadsby, 1968-69; Bill Gadsby and Sid Abel, 1969-70; Ned Harkness and Doug Barkley, 1970-71; Doug Barkley and John Wilson, 1971-72; John Wilson, 1972-73; Ted Garvin and Alex Delvecchio, 1973-74; Alex Delvecchio, 1974-75; Doug Barkley and Alex Delvecchio, 1975-76; Alex Delvecchio and Larry Wilson, 1976-77; Bobby Kromm, 1977-78, 1978-79; Bobby Kromm and Ted Lindsay, 1979-80; Ted Lindsay and Wayne Maxner, 1980-81; Wayne Maxner and Billy Dea, 1981-82; Nick Polano, 1982-83 to 1984-85; Harry Neale and Brad Park, 1985-86; Jacques Demers, 1986-87 to 1989-90; Bryan Murray, 1990-91 to 1992-93; Scotty Bowman, 1993-94 to 1997-98; Dave Lewis, Barry Smith (co-coaches) and Scotty Bowman, 1998-99; Scotty Bowman, 1999-2000 to date.

Club Records

Team

(Figures in brackets for season records are games played; records for fewest points, wins, ties, losses, goals, goals against are for 70 or more games)

Most Points	131	1995-96 (82)
Most Wins	*62	1995-96 (82)
Most Ties	18	1952-53 (70), 1980-81 (80), 1996-97 (82)
Most Losses	57	1985-86 (80)
Most Goals	369	1992-93 (84)
Most Goals Against	415	1985-86 (80)
Fewest Points	40	1985-86 (80)
Fewest Wins	16	1976-77 (80)
Fewest Ties	4	1966-67 (70)
Fewest Losses	13	1950-51 (70), 1995-96 (82)
Fewest Goals	167	1958-59 (70)
Fewest Goals Against	132	1953-54 (70)
Longest Winning Streak		
Overall	9	Mar. 3-21/51, Feb. 27-Mar. 20/55, Dec. 12-31/95, Mar. 3-22/96
Home	14	Jan. 21-Mar. 25/65
Away	7	Mar. 25-Apr. 14/95, Feb. 18-Mar. 20/96
Longest Undefeated Streak		
Overall	15	Nov. 27-Dec. 28/52 (8 wins, 7 ties)
Home	18	Nov. 19/31-Feb.28/32 (13 wins, 5 ties), Dec. 26/54-Mar. 20/55 (13 wins, 5 ties)
Away	15	Oct. 18-Dec. 20/51 (10 wins, 5 ties)
Longest Losing Streak		
Overall	14	Feb. 24-Mar. 25/82
Home	7	Feb. 20-Mar. 25/82
Away	14	Oct. 19-Dec. 21/66
Longest Winless Streak		
Overall	19	Feb. 26-Apr. 3/77 (18 losses, 1 tie)
Home	10	Dec. 11/85-Jan. 18/86 (9 losses, 1 tie)
Away	26	Dec. 15/76-Apr. 3/77 (23 losses, 3 ties)
Most Shutouts, Season	13	1953-54 (70)
Most. PIM, Season	2,393	1985-86 (80)
Most Goals, Game	15	Jan. 23/44 (NYR 0 at Det. 15)

Individual

Most Seasons	25	Gordie Howe
Most Games	1,687	Gordie Howe
Most Goals, Career	786	Gordie Howe
Most Assists, Career	1,023	Gordie Howe
Most Points, Career	1,809	Gordie Howe (786G, 1,023A)
Most PIM, Career	2,090	Bob Probert
Most Shutouts, Career	85	Terry Sawchuk
Longest Consecutive Games Streak	548	Alex Delvecchio (Dec. 13/56-Nov. 11/64)
Most Goals, Season	65	Steve Yzerman (1988-89)
Most Assists, Season	90	Steve Yzerman (1988-89)
Most Points, Season	155	Steve Yzerman (1988-89; 65G, 90A)
Most PIM, Season	398	Bob Probert (1987-88)
Most Points, Defenseman, Season	77	Paul Coffey (1993-94; 14G, 63A)
Most Points, Center, Season	155	Steve Yzerman (1988-89; 65G, 90A)
Most Points, Right Wing, Season	103	Gordie Howe (1968-69; 44G, 59A)
Most Points, Left Wing, Season	105	John Ogrodnick (1984-85; 55G, 50A)
Most Points, Rookie, Season	87	Steve Yzerman (1983-84; 39G, 48A)
Most Shutouts, Season	12	Terry Sawchuk (1951-52, 1953-54, 1954-55), Glenn Hall (1955-56)
Most Goals, Game	6	Syd Howe (Feb. 3/44)
Most Assists, Game	*7	Billy Taylor (Mar. 16/47)
Most Points, Game	7	Carl Liscombe (Nov. 5/42; 3G, 4A), Don Grosso (Feb. 3/44; 1G, 6A), Billy Taylor (Mar. 16/47; 7A)

* NHL Record.

Retired Numbers

1	Terry Sawchuk	1949-55, 57-64, 68-69
7	Ted Lindsay	1944-57, 64-65
9	Gordie Howe	1946-1971
10	Alex Delvecchio	1951-1973
12	Sid Abel	1938-43, 45-52

All-time Record vs. Other Clubs

Regular Season

	At Home							On Road							Total						
	GP	W	L	T	GF	GA	PTS	GP	W	L	T	GF	GA	PTS	GP	W	L	T	GF	GA	PTS
Anaheim	14	10	1	3	58	36	23	14	7	5	2	44	32	16	28	17	6	5	102	68	39
Atlanta	1	1	0	0	3	2	2	1	1	0	0	7	1	2	2	2	0	0	10	3	4
Boston	282	153	77	52	946	711	358	284	89	152	43	757	1002	221	566	242	229	95	1703	1713	579
Buffalo	52	29	18	5	190	151	63	50	10	32	8	145	219	28	102	39	50	13	335	370	91
Calgary	51	26	15	10	191	155	62	52	16	30	6	159	210	38	103	42	45	16	350	365	100
Carolina	28	15	7	6	107	76	36	27	10	16	1	73	95	21	55	25	23	7	180	171	57
Chicago	325	199	95	31	1116	802	429	327	127	149	51	914	983	305	652	326	244	82	2030	1785	734
Colorado	32	19	12	1	121	100	39	34	12	18	4	116	129	28	66	31	30	5	237	229	67
Dallas	98	49	35	14	383	322	112	98	33	50	15	295	352	81	196	82	85	29	678	674	193
Edmonton	36	19	14	3	138	126	41	36	13	17	6	141	152	32	72	32	31	9	279	278	73
Florida	5	3	1	1	21	15	7	6	3	1	2	19	13	8	11	6	2	3	40	28	15
Los Angeles	72	30	30	12	277	255	72	72	21	38	13	225	296	55	144	51	68	25	502	551	127
Montreal	279	130	96	53	803	714	313	279	65	171	43	628	988	173	558	195	267	96	1431	1702	486
Nashville	6	6	0	0	25	12	12	6	4	2	0	22	16	8	12	10	2	0	47	28	20
New Jersey	37	22	13	2	152	123	46	37	10	18	9	101	130	29	74	32	31	11	253	253	75
NY Islanders	42	23	17	2	152	132	48	43	17	23	3	126	155	37	85	40	40	5	278	287	85
NY Rangers	283	162	76	45	998	696	369	281	90	133	58	726	862	238	564	252	209	103	1724	1558	607
Ottawa	6	3	3	0	20	13	6	7	4	2	1	21	19	9	13	7	5	1	41	32	15
Philadelphia	56	28	18	10	198	177	66	56	13	32	11	166	226	37	112	41	50	21	364	403	103
Phoenix	43	21	17	5	173	152	47	41	14	16	11	131	131	39	84	35	33	16	304	283	86
Pittsburgh	63	39	12	12	243	171	90	62	15	43	4	183	274	34	125	54	55	16	426	445	124
St. Louis	99	43	39	17	359	311	103	100	28	55	17	273	353	74	199	71	94	34	632	664	177
San Jose	17	16	1	0	80	30	32	18	10	5	3	75	55	23	35	26	6	3	155	85	55
Tampa Bay	9	8	1	0	38	17	16	11	8	2	1	57	36	17	20	16	3	1	95	53	33
Toronto	317	165	106	46	949	779	377	313	104	163	46	839	1036	254	630	269	269	92	1788	1815	631
Vancouver	58	36	15	7	251	168	79	57	22	25	10	189	211	54	115	58	40	17	440	379	133
Washington	44	19	14	11	155	129	49	43	18	20	5	135	160	41	87	37	34	16	290	289	90
Defunct Clubs	141	76	40	25	430	307	177	141	49	63	29	364	375	127	282	125	103	54	794	682	304
Totals	**2496**	**1350**	**773**	**373**	**8577**	**6682**	**3074**	**2496**	**813**	**1281**	**402**	**6931**	**8511**	**2029**	**4992**	**2163**	**2054**	**775**	**15508**	**15193**	**5103**

Playoffs

	Series	W	L	GP	W	L	T	GF	GA	Last Mtg.	Round	Result
Anaheim	2	2	0	8	8	0	0	30	14	1999	CQF	W 4-0
Boston	7	3	4	33	14	19	0	98	96	1957	SF	L 1-4
Calgary	1	1	0	2	2	0	0	8	5	1978	PR	W 2-0
Chicago	14	6	8	69	31	38	0	190	210	1995	CF	W 4-1
Colorado	4	1	3	23	9	14	0	54	66	2000	CSF	L 1-4
Dallas	3	3	0	18	12	6	0	55	40	1998	CF	W 4-2
Edmonton	2	0	2	10	2	8	0	26	39	1988	CF	L 1-4
Los Angeles	1	1	0	4	4	0	0	15	6	2000	CQF	W 4-0
Montreal	12	7	5	62	29	33	0	149	161	1978	QF	L 1-4
New Jersey	1	0	1	4	0	4	0	7	16	1995	F	L 0-4
NY Rangers	5	4	1	23	13	10	0	57	49	1950	F	W 4-3
Philadelphia	1	1	0	4	4	0	0	16	6	1997	F	W 4-0
Phoenix	2	2	0	12	8	4	0	44	28	1998	CQF	W 4-2
St. Louis	6	4	2	35	20	15	0	111	92	1998	CSF	W 4-2
San Jose	2	1	1	11	7	4	0	51	27	1995	CSF	W 4-0
Toronto	23	11	12	117	59	58	0	321	311	1993	DSF	L 3-4
Washington	1	1	0	4	4	0	0	13	7	1998	F	W 4-0
Defunct Clubs	4	3	1	10	7	2	1	21	13			
Totals	**91**	**51**	**40**	**449**	**233**	**215**	**1**	**1266**	**1186**			

Playoff Results 2000-1996

Year	Round	Opponent	Result	GF	GA
2000	CSF	Colorado	L 1-4	8	13
	CQF	Los Angeles	W 4-0	15	6
1999	CSF	Colorado	L 2-4	14	21
	CQF	Anaheim	W 4-0	17	6
1998	**F**	**Washington**	**W 4-0**	**13**	**7**
	CF	Dallas	W 4-2	15	11
	CSF	St. Louis	W 4-2	23	13
	CQF	Phoenix	W 4-2	24	18
1997	**F**	**Philadelphia**	**W 4-0**	**16**	**6**
	CF	Colorado	W 4-2	16	12
	CSF	Anaheim	W 4-0	13	8
	CQF	St. Louis	W 4-2	13	12
1996	CF	Colorado	L 2-4	16	20
	CSF	St. Louis	W 4-3	22	16
	CQF	Winnipeg	W 4-2	20	10

Abbreviations: Round: F – Final; **CF** – conference final; **CSF** – conference semi-final; **CQF** – conference quarter-final; **DSF** – division semi-final; **SF** – semi-final; **QF** – quarter-final; **PR** – preliminary round.

Calgary totals include Atlanta Flames, 1972-73 to 1979-80.
Colorado totals include Quebec, 1979-80 to 1994-95.
New Jersey totals include Kansas City, 1974-75 to 1975-76, and Colorado Rockies, 1976-77 to 1981-82.
Phoenix totals include Winnipeg, 1979-80 to 1995-96.
Carolina totals include Hartford, 1979-80 to 1996-97.
Dallas totals include Minnesota North Stars, 1967-68 to 1992-93.

1999-2000 Results

Oct.	2		Buffalo	2-0		8		Anaheim	5-3
	5		Dallas	2-3		11	at	Montreal	0-3
	7	at	Atlanta	7-1		13		Chicago	3-5
	9	at	Florida	2-2		16	at	Edmonton	3-3
	13		St. Louis	4-2		18	at	Calgary	1-6
	16		Philadelphia	3-2		19	at	Vancouver	3-3
	20		San Jose	6-3		22	at	Ottawa	3-2
	23	at	Chicago	1-0		26		Toronto	4-2
	27		Colorado	5-3		28		Calgary	4-1
	29		Chicago	2-4		29		New Jersey	3-1
	30	at	St. Louis	4-5 *		31	at	Phoenix	3-5
Nov.	3		Los Angeles	1-1	**Feb.**	3	at	Los Angeles	3-6
	5		Carolina	3-2		8		St. Louis	1-4
	7	at	Tampa Bay	2-3		10	at	St. Louis	2-0
	10	at	Dallas	4-2		13	at	Colorado	4-3
	12		Pittsburgh	3-2 *		14	at	Phoenix	3-1
	13	at	Toronto	1-1		16		Vancouver	5-2
	15		Anaheim	6-3		18		Los Angeles	2-3
	17	at	Vancouver	7-2		20	at	Chicago	4-6
	19	at	Calgary	1-3		21	at	NY Islanders	2-0
	20	at	Edmonton	1-2		23		Dallas	2-5
	24		St. Louis	4-2		25		NY Islanders	5-2
	26		Edmonton	4-2		27		Tampa Bay	3-1
	28		Phoenix	3-4	**Mar.**	3	at	Washington	2-2
Dec.	1		San Jose	4-2		5	at	Dallas	5-3
	3	at	Chicago	7-4		7	at	Los Angeles	3-1
	4	at	Nashville	1-4		8	at	San Jose	1-1
	8		Nashville	6-3		10	at	Nashville	3-1
	10		Los Angeles	3-1		14		Nashville	3-2 *
	11	at	Boston	5-4		16		Toronto	3-4 *
	15		Edmonton	5-1		18	at	Colorado	4-3
	17		Colorado	5-2		19	at	Anaheim	1-3
	19	at	Anaheim	1-3		22		Calgary	2-2
	20	at	San Jose	4-3		23	at	Nashville	6-3
	22	at	Carolina	4-1		26		NY Rangers	8-2
	27		Atlanta	3-2 *		27	at	NY Rangers	6-0
	28	at	Buffalo	7-2		29		Vancouver	6-3
	31		Chicago	4-4	**Apr.**	1	at	St. Louis	0-0
Jan.	2	at	Pittsburgh	3-4		2		Montreal	6-5 *
	4		Phoenix	2-5		7		Washington	2-4
	6		Nashville	5-2		9	at	Colorado	2-3

* – Overtime

Entry Draft
Selections 2000-1986

2000
Pick
29	Niklas Kronwall
38	Tomas Kopecky
102	Stefan Liv
127	Dmitri Semenov
128	Alexander Seluyanov
130	Aaron Van Leusen
187	Par Backer
196	Paul Ballantyne
228	Jimmie Svensson
251	Todd Jackson
260	Yevgeny Bumagin

1999
Pick
120	Jari Tolsa
149	Andrei Maximenko
181	Kent McDonell
210	Henrik Zetterberg
238	Anton Borodkin
266	Ken Davis

1998
Pick
25	Jiri Fischer
55	Ryan Barnes
76	Tomek Valtonen
84	Jake McCracken
111	Brent Hobday
142	Calle Steen
151	Adam DeLeeuw
171	Pavel Datsyuk
198	Jeremy Goetzinger
226	David Petrasek
256	Petja Pietilainen

1997
Pick
49	Yuri Butsayev
76	Petr Sykora
102	Quintin Laing
129	John Wikstrom
157	B.J. Young
186	Mike Laceby
213	Steve Willejto
239	Greg Willers

1996
Pick
26	Jesse Wallin
52	Aren Miller
108	Johan Forsander
135	Michal Podolka
144	Magnus Nilsson
162	Alexandre Jacques
189	Colin Beardsmore
215	Craig Stahl
241	Eugeny Afanasiev

1995
Pick
26	Maxim Kuznetsov
52	Philippe Audet
58	Darryl Laplante
104	Anatoli Ustyugov
125	Chad Wilchynski
126	David Arsenault
156	Tyler Perry
182	Per Eklund
208	Andrei Samokhvalov
234	David Engblom

1994
Pick
23	Yan Golubovsky
49	Mathieu Dandenault
75	Sean Gillam
114	Frederic Deschenes
127	Doug Battaglia
153	Pavel Agarkov
205	Jason Elliot
231	Jeff Mikesch
257	Tomas Holmstrom
283	Toivo Suursoo

1993
Pick
5	Benoit Larose
22	Anders Eriksson
48	Jon Coleman
74	Kevin Hilton
97	John Jakopin
126	Norm Maracle
152	Tim Spitzig
178	Yuri Yeresko
204	Vitezslav Skuta
230	Ryan Shanahan
256	James Kosecki
282	Gordon Hunt

1992
Pick
22	Curtis Bowen
46	Darren McCarty
70	Sylvain Cloutier
118	Mike Sullivan
142	Jason MacDonald
166	Greg Scott
183	Justin Krall
189	C. J. Denomme
214	Jeff Walker
238	Dan McGillis
262	Ryan Bach

1991
Pick
10	Martin Lapointe
32	Jamie Pushor
54	Chris Osgood
76	Mike Knuble
98	Dimitri Motkov
142	Igor Malykhin
186	Jim Bermingham
208	Jason Firth
230	Bart Turner
252	Andrew Miller

1990
Pick
3	Keith Primeau
45	Vyacheslav Kozlov
66	Stewart Malgunas
87	Tony Burns
108	Claude Barthe
129	Jason York
150	Wes McCauley
171	Anthony Gruba
192	Travis Tucker
213	Brett Larson
234	John Hendry

1989
Pick
11	Mike Sillinger
32	Bob Boughner
53	Nicklas Lidstrom
74	Sergei Fedorov
95	Shawn McCosh
116	Dallas Drake
137	Scott Zygulski
158	Andy Suhy
179	Bob Jones
200	Greg Bignell
204	Rick Judson
221	Vladimir Konstantinov
242	Joseph Frederick
246	Jason Glickman

1988
Pick
17	Kory Kocur
38	Serge Anglehart
47	Guy Dupuis
59	Petr Hrbek
80	Sheldon Kennedy
143	Kelly Hurd
164	Brian McCormack
185	Jody Praznik
206	Glen Goodall
227	Darren Colbourne
248	Donald Stone

1987
Pick
11	Yves Racine
32	Gord Kruppke
41	Bob Wilkie
52	Dennis Holland
74	Mark Reimer
95	Radomir Brazda
116	Sean Clifford
137	Mike Gober
158	Kevin Scott
179	Mikko Haapakoski
200	Darin Bannister
221	Craig Quinlan
242	Tomas Jansson

1986
Pick
1	Joe Murphy
22	Adam Graves
43	Derek Mayer
64	Tim Cheveldae
85	Johan Garpenlov
106	Jay Stark
127	Per Djoos
148	Dean Morton
169	Marc Potvin
190	Scott King
211	Tom Bissett
232	Peter Ekroth

Club Directory

Joe Louis Arena

Detroit Red Wings
Joe Louis Arena
600 Civic Center Drive
Detroit, Michigan 48226
Phone **313/396-7544**
FAX PR: 313/567-0296
www.detroitredwings.com
Capacity: 19,983

Owner/Governor	Mike Ilitch
Owner/Secretary-Treasurer	Marian Ilitch
Senior Vice-President/Alternate Governor	Jim Devellano
Vice-President, Red Wings/President, Ilitch Holdings, Inc./Alternate Governor	Christopher Ilitch
President, Ilitch Holdings, Inc./Alternate Governor	Denise Ilitch
General Counsel	Rob Carr
General Manager/Alternate Governor	Ken Holland
Assistant General Manager	Jim Nill
Head Coach	Scotty Bowman
Associate Coaches	Barry Smith, Dave Lewis
Goaltending Consultant	Jim Bedard
NHL Scout	Dan Belisle
Pro Scouts	Mark Howe, Glenn Merkosky
Eastern Scout	Joe McDonnell
Western Scout	Bruce Haralson
Eastern USA, High School and College Scout	Mark Leach
Director of European Scouting	Hakan Andersson
European Scout	Vladimir Havluj
Part-Time European Scouts	Jan Blomgren, Evgeni Jerfilov, Igor Parashkin
Scouts	Marty Stein, Bruce Southern
Executive Assistant	Nancy Beard
Office Assistant	David Kolb
Senior Director of Finance	Paul MacDonald
Accounting Assistant	Bridget Merritt
Athletic Therapist	John Wharton
Assistant Athletic Therapist	Piet Van Zant
Equipment Manager	Paul Boyer
Assistant Equipment Managers	Tim Abbott, Rob Gagne
Director of Public Relations	John Hahn
Community Relations Manager	Anne Marie Krappmann
Public Relations Coordinator	Michael Kuta
Public Relations Assistant	Jennie Hagler
General Manager - Joe Louis Arena	Randy Lippe
Director of Operations	Tim Padgett
Senior Director of Merchandise	Jim Urban
Senior Director of Box Office Operations	Bob Kerlin
Senior Director of Advertising Sales/ General Sales Manager	Bill Ley
Senior Account Executives	Scott Miller, Kurt Buehler
Account Executive	Mary Greener
Sales Coordinator	Mark Kelly
Broadcast Coordinator	Lori Mariles
Administrative Assistant	Jennifer Jones
Senior Director of Marketing and Communications	Ted Speers
Marketing Manager	Kevin Vaughn
Marketing Manager	Lori Shiels
Marketing Coordinator	Keri McCartney
Season Ticket Sales Manager	Chuck Smith
Group Sales Coordinator	Lisa Maselli
Director of Publishing & New Media	Mike Bayoff
Director of Information Services	Bob Dinges
Team Physicians	John Finley, D.O.; David Collon, M.D.
Team Dentist	C.J. Regula, D.M.D.
Aviation Department Manager/Chief Pilot	Dennis Gease
Senior Captain	Robert Mintari
Pilots	Larry Henry, Al Long
Chief of Maintenance/Flight Engineer	George Zuchelkowski
Mechanic/Flight Engineer	Greg Vinyard
Radio Announce Team, TBA	Ken Kal, Paul Woods
TV Announce Team, WKBD UPN-50 & FOX Sports Net Detroit	Ken Daniels, Mickey Redmond

General Manager

HOLLAND, KEN
General Manager, Detroit Red Wings. Born in Vernon, B.C., Nov. 10, 1955.
Ken Holland is entering his fourth season as a general manager and his 18th year with the Red Wings organization. In his three seasons as Detroit's general manager, Holland has established himself as one of the most innovative and aggressive GMs in the National Hockey League. Holland began his tenure as the club's general manager after serving as assistant general manager for the previous three seasons. Holland was elevated to his present position July 18, 1997.

In his new and expanded role, he oversees all aspects of hockey operations including all matters relating to player personnel, development, contract negotiations and player movements. Holland also continues to be Detroit's point person at the NHL Entry Draft, as he has for the past eight years. In that capacity, he was instrumental in selecting some of Detroit's best young talent, including Vyacheslav Kozlov, Darren McCarty, Chris Osgood and Martin Lapointe, along with several other top prospects.

Holland has deftly handled several different front-office duties for the club over the past 18 years. At the conclusion of his playing days as a goaltender, spending most of his pro career at the American Hockey League level, Holland began his off-ice career in 1985 as a western Canada scout followed by five years as amateur scouting director before promotions leading to his current position as general manager.

A native of Vernon, BC, Holland played in the junior ranks for Medicine Hat (WHL) in 1974-75. He was Toronto's 13th pick (188th overall) in the 1975 draft but never saw action with the Maple Leafs. Holland twice signed with NHL teams as a free agent — in 1980 with Hartford and 1983 with Detroit. He spent most of his pro career with AHL clubs in Binghamton and Springfield, along with Adirondack, but did appear in four NHL games, making his debut with Hartford in 1980-81 and playing three contests for Detroit in 1983-84.

Ken and wife Cindy have four children, Brad, Julie, Rachel and Greg, and reside in suburban Detroit.

General Managers' History

Art Duncan and Duke Keats, 1926-27; Jack Adams, 1927-28 to 1961-62; Sid Abel, 1962-63 to 1969-70; Sid Abel and Ned Harkness, 1970-71; Ned Harkness, 1971-72 to 1973-74; Alex Delvecchio, 1974-75, 1975-76; Alex Delvecchio and Ted Lindsay, 1976-77; Ted Lindsay, 1977-78 to 1979-80; Jimmy Skinner, 1980-81, 1981-82; Jim Devellano, 1982-83 to 1989-90; Bryan Murray, 1990-91 to 1993-94; Jim Devellano (Senior Vice President), 1994-95 to 1996-97; Ken Holland, 1997-98 to date.

Captains' History

Art Duncan, 1926-27; Reg Noble, 1927-28 to 1929-30; George Hay, 1930-31; Carson Cooper, 1931-32; Larry Aurie, 1932-33; Herbie Lewis, 1933-34; Ebbie Goodfellow, 1934-35; Doug Young, 1935-36 to 1937-38; Ebbie Goodfellow, 1938-39 to 1940-41; Ebbie Goodfellow and Syd Howe, 1941-42; Sid Abel, 1942-43; Mud Bruneteau, Bill Hollett (co-captains), 1943-44; Bill Hollett, 1944-45; Bill Hollett and Sid Abel, 1945-46; Sid Abel, 1946-47 to 1951-52; Ted Lindsay, 1952-53 to 1955-56; Red Kelly, 1956-57, 1957-58; Gordie Howe, 1958-59 to 1961-62; Alex Delvecchio, 1962-63 to 1972-73; Alex Delvecchio, Nick Libett, Red Berenson, Gary Bergman, Ted Harris, Mickey Redmond and Larry Johnston, 1973-74; Marcel Dionne, 1974-75; Danny Grant and Terry Harper, 1975-76; Danny Grant and Dennis Polonich, 1976-77; Dan Maloney and Dennis Hextall, 1977-78; Dennis Hextall, Nick Libett and Paul Woods, 1978-79; Dale McCourt, 1979-80; Errol Thompson and Reed Larson, 1980-81; Reed Larson, 1981-82; Danny Gare, 1982-83 to 1985-86; Steve Yzerman, 1986-87 to date.

Edmonton Oilers

1999-2000 Results: 32w-34L-16T 88PTS. Second, Northwest Division

Year-by-Year Record

		Home			Road			Overall						
Season	GP	W	L	T	W	L	T	W	L	T	GF	GA	Pts.	Finished	Playoff Result
1999-2000	82	18	14	9	14	20	7	32	34	16	226	212	88	2nd, Northwest Div.	Lost Conf. Quarter-Final
1998-99	82	17	19	5	16	18	7	33	37	12	230	226	78	2nd, Northwest Div.	Lost Conf. Quarter-Final
1997-98	82	20	16	5	15	21	5	35	37	10	215	224	80	3rd, Pacific Div.	Lost Conf. Semi-Final
1996-97	82	21	16	4	15	21	5	36	37	9	252	247	81	3rd, Pacific Div.	Lost Conf. Semi-Final
1995-96	82	15	21	5	15	23	3	30	44	8	240	304	68	5th, Pacific Div.	Out of Playoffs
1994-95	48	11	12	1	6	15	3	17	27	4	136	183	38	5th, Pacific Div.	Out of Playoffs
1993-94	84	17	22	3	8	23	11	25	45	14	261	305	64	6th, Pacific Div.	Out of Playoffs
1992-93	84	16	21	5	10	29	3	26	50	8	242	337	60	5th, Smythe Div.	Out of Playoffs
1991-92	80	22	13	5	14	21	5	36	34	10	295	297	82	3rd, Smythe Div.	Lost Conf. Championship
1990-91	80	22	15	3	15	22	3	37	37	6	272	272	80	3rd, Smythe Div.	Lost Conf. Championship
1989-90	**80**	**23**	**11**	**6**	**15**	**17**	**8**	**38**	**28**	**14**	**315**	**283**	**90**	**2nd, Smythe Div.**	**Won Stanley Cup**
1988-89	80	21	16	3	17	18	5	38	34	8	325	306	84	3rd, Smythe Div.	Lost Div. Semi-Final
1987-88	**80**	**28**	**8**	**4**	**16**	**17**	**7**	**44**	**25**	**11**	**363**	**288**	**99**	**2nd, Smythe Div.**	**Won Stanley Cup**
1986-87	**80**	**29**	**6**	**5**	**21**	**18**	**1**	**50**	**24**	**6**	**372**	**284**	**106**	**1st, Smythe Div.**	**Won Stanley Cup**
1985-86	80	32	6	2	24	11	5	56	17	7	426	310	119	1st, Smythe Div.	Lost Div. Final
1984-85	**80**	**26**	**7**	**7**	**23**	**13**	**4**	**49**	**20**	**11**	**401**	**298**	**109**	**1st, Smythe Div.**	**Won Stanley Cup**
1983-84	**80**	**31**	**5**	**4**	**26**	**13**	**1**	**57**	**18**	**5**	**446**	**314**	**119**	**1st, Smythe Div.**	**Won Stanley Cup**
1982-83	80	25	9	6	22	12	6	47	21	12	424	315	106	1st, Smythe Div.	Lost Final
1981-82	80	31	5	4	17	12	11	48	17	15	417	295	111	1st, Smythe Div.	Lost Div. Semi-Final
1980-81	80	17	13	10	12	22	6	29	35	16	328	327	74	4th, Smythe Div.	Lost Quarter-Final
1979-80	80	17	14	9	11	25	4	28	39	13	301	322	69	4th, Smythe Div.	Lost Prelim. Round

2000-01 Schedule

Oct.	Fri.	6	Detroit
	Sat.	7	Colorado
	Tue.	10	at Montreal
	Wed.	11	at Detroit
	Fri.	13	Buffalo
	Sun.	15	at Minnesota*
	Tue.	17	Boston
	Thu.	19	Toronto
	Sun.	22	Phoenix
	Wed.	25	Atlanta
	Fri.	27	at Anaheim
	Sat.	28	at Colorado
	Mon.	30	Anaheim
Nov.	Wed.	1	Calgary
	Fri.	3	Minnesota
	Sun.	5	at Columbus
	Tue.	7	at NY Rangers
	Thu.	9	at Philadelphia
	Sat.	11	at Pittsburgh
	Sun.	12	at Minnesota
	Tue.	14	St. Louis
	Fri.	17	Chicago
	Sun.	19	Calgary
	Wed.	22	at Toronto
	Thu.	23	at Ottawa
	Sat.	25	Anaheim
	Wed.	29	Montreal
Dec.	Sat.	2	at Vancouver
	Sun.	3	San Jose
	Wed.	6	Nashville
	Sat.	9	Los Angeles
	Wed.	13	at Dallas
	Thu.	14	at Nashville
	Sat.	16	at Washington
	Mon.	18	at Detroit
	Wed.	20	Vancouver
	Fri.	22	at Calgary
	Wed.	27	at Colorado
	Thu.	28	at San Jose
	Sat.	30	Montreal*
Jan.	Mon.	1	at St. Louis*
	Wed.	3	at Columbus
	Fri.	5	at Chicago
	Sun.	7	Columbus
	Wed.	10	Nashville
	Fri.	12	Vancouver
	Sun.	14	Ottawa
	Tue.	16	at Nashville
	Thu.	18	at St. Louis
	Sat.	20	Detroit
	Mon.	22	San Jose
	Wed.	24	at San Jose
	Fri.	26	Phoenix
	Tue.	30	at Calgary
	Wed.	31	Chicago
Feb.	Wed.	7	at Dallas
	Fri.	9	at Phoenix
	Mon.	12	at Los Angeles
	Wed.	14	at Anaheim
	Fri.	16	NY Islanders
	Sat.	17	Vancouver
	Tue.	20	Los Angeles
	Sat.	24	at Calgary
	Sun.	25	Dallas
	Wed.	28	St. Louis
Mar.	Fri.	2	Minnesota
	Wed.	7	Toronto
	Fri.	9	at Buffalo
	Sun.	11	at Carolina*
	Tue.	13	at Tampa Bay
	Wed.	14	at Florida
	Sat.	17	New Jersey
	Mon.	19	Philadelphia
	Wed.	21	at Los Angeles
	Sat.	24	at Phoenix
	Mon.	26	Columbus
	Wed.	28	Colorado
	Fri.	30	Dallas
Apr.	Sun.	1	at Chicago*
	Mon.	2	at Colorado
	Wed.	4	Minnesota
	Sat.	7	at Vancouver

* Denotes afternoon game.

Franchise date: June 22, 1979

NORTHWEST DIVISION

22nd NHL Season

Only Olaf Kolzig faced more flying rubber (1957 shots against) than Tommy Salo (1875) in 1999-2000. Salo made his first appearance in the All-Star Game last season and picked up the win as the World beat North America 9-4.

2000-01 Player Personnel

FORWARDS	HT	WT	S	Place of Birth	Date	1999-00 Club
CHIMERA, Jason	6-0	180	L	Edmonton, Alta.	5/2/79	Hamilton Bulldogs
CLEARY, Daniel	6-0	203	L	Carbonear, Nfld.	12/18/78	Edmonton-Hamilton Bulldogs
COMRIE, Mike	5-9	172	L	Edmonton, Alta.	9/11/80	U. of Michigan
COMRIE, Paul	5-11	192	L	Edmonton, Alta.	2/7/77	Edmonton-Hamilton Bulldogs
COTE, Patrick	6-3	220	L	Lasalle, Que.	1/24/75	Nashville
DICKENSON, Lou	6-1	192	L	Ottawa, Ont.	8/15/82	Mississauga
GREEN, Josh	6-4	212	L	Camrose, Alta.	11/16/77	NY Islanders-Lowell
GRIER, Mike	6-1	227	R	Detroit, MI	1/5/75	Edmonton
GUERIN, Bill	6-2	210	R	Wilbraham, MA	11/9/70	Edmonton
HEALEY, Paul	6-2	185	R	Edmonton, Alta.	3/20/75	Milwaukee
HENRICH, Michael	6-2	206	R	Thornhill, Ont.	3/3/80	Barrie Colts
HINZ, Chad	5-10	190	R	Saskatoon, Sask.	3/21/79	Hamilton Bulldogs-Tallahasee
HORCOFF, Shawn	6-1	202	L	Trail, B.C.	9/17/78	Michigan State
KILGER, Chad	6-3	215	L	Cornwall, Ont.	11/27/76	Edmonton-Hamilton Bulldogs
LaCOUTURE, Dan	6-3	210	L	Hyannis, MA	4/18/77	Edmonton-Hamilton Bulldogs
LARAQUE, Georges	6-3	240	R	Montreal, Que.	12/7/76	Edmonton
MARCHANT, Todd	5-10	178	L	Buffalo, NY	8/12/73	Edmonton
MOREAU, Ethan	6-2	211	L	Huntsville, Ont.	9/22/75	Edmonton
MURRAY, Rem	6-2	195	L	Stratford, Ont.	10/9/72	Edmonton
NORRIE, Shaun	6-2	190	R	Calgary, Alta.	9/15/82	Calgary Hitman
PISANI, Fernando	6-1	185	L	Edmonton, Alta.	12/27/76	Providence
PITTIS, Domenic	5-11	190	L	Calgary, Alta.	10/1/74	Buffalo-Rochester
RIESEN, Michel	6-2	190	R	Oberbalm, Switzerland	4/11/79	Hamilton Bulldogs
RITA, Jani	6-1	206	R	Helsinki, Finland	7/25/81	Jokerit Helsinki
SARNO, Peter	5-11	185	L	Toronto, Ont.	7/26/79	Hamilton Bulldogs
SMYTH, Ryan	6-1	195	L	Banff, Alta.	2/21/76	Edmonton
SPIRIDONOV, Maxim	5-10	185	L	Moscow, USSR	4/7/78	Tallahasee-Hamilton Bulldogs
URICK, Brian	6-1	195	R	Minneapolis, MN	1/25/77	Hamilton-Tallahasee
VOLCHKOV, Alexandre	6-2	204	R	Moscow, USSR	9/25/77	Wsh-Portland-Hamilton
WEIGHT, Doug	5-11	200	L	Warren, MI	1/21/71	Edmonton

DEFENSEMEN						
BREWER, Eric	6-3	220	L	Vernon, B.C.	4/17/79	NY Islanders-Lowell
BROWN, Sean	6-3	205	L	Oshawa, Ont.	11/5/76	Edmonton
FAUTEUX, Jonathan	6-2	232	R	Terrebone, Que.	12/3/80	Val-d'Or-Victoriaville
FERGUSON, Scott	6-1	202	L	Camrose, Alta.	1/6/73	Cincinnati Ducks
FLACHE, Paul	6-5	195	R	Toronto, Ont.	3/4/82	Brampton
HAJT, Chris	6-3	206	L	Saskatoon, Sask.	7/5/78	Hamilton Bulldogs
HAUER, Brett	6-2	210	R	Richfield, MN	7/11/71	Edmonton-Manitoba Moose
HENRY, Alex	6-5	220	L	Elliot Lake, Ont.	10/18/79	Hamilton Bulldogs
MUSIL, Frantisek	6-3	215	L	Pardubice, Czech.	12/17/64	Edmonton
NASREDDINE, Alain	6-1	201	L	Montreal, Que.	7/10/75	Quebec (AHL)-Hamilton
NIINIMAA, Janne	6-1	220	L	Raahe, Finland	5/22/75	Edmonton
NORTON, Brad	6-4	225	L	Cambridge, MA	2/13/75	Hamilton Bulldogs
POTI, Tom	6-3	215	L	Worcester, MA	3/22/77	Edmonton
SANDWITH, Terran	6-4	210	L	Edmonton, Alta.	4/17/72	St. John's Leafs
SEMENOV, Alexei	6-6	210	L	Murmansk, USSR	4/10/81	Sudbury-Hamilton
SMITH, Jason	6-3	210	R	Calgary, Alta.	11/2/73	Edmonton
ULANOV, Igor	6-3	211	L	Krasnokamsk, USSR	10/1/69	Montreal-Edmonton

GOALTENDERS	HT	WT	C	Place of Birth	Date	1999-00 Club
ANTILA, Kristian	6-3	207	L	Vammala, Finland	1/10/80	Ilves Tampere
GAGE, Joaquin	6-0	200	L	Vancouver, B.C.	10/19/73	Canada-Hamilton Bulldogs
HAUSER, Adam	6-2	192	L	Bovey, MN	5/27/80	U. of Minnesota
HEFFLER, Eric	6-3	190	L	Williamsville, NY	2/29/76	Hamilton Bulldogs
RANFORD, Bill	5-11	185	L	Brandon, Man.	12/14/66	Edmonton
SALO, Tommy	5-11	173	L	Surahammar, Sweden	2/1/71	Edmonton

Coaching History

Glen Sather, 1979-80; Bryan Watson and Glen Sather, 1980-81; Glen Sather, 1981-82 to 1988-89; John Muckler, 1989-90, 1990-91; Ted Green, 1991-92, 1992-93; Ted Green and Glen Sather, 1993-94; George Burnett and Ron Low, 1994-95; Ron Low, 1995-96 to 1998-99; Kevin Lowe, 1999-2000; Craig MacTavish, 2000-01.

Coach

MacTAVISH, CRAIG
Coach, Edmonton Oilers. Born in London, Ont., August 15, 1958.

The Edmonton Oilers named Craig MacTavish as their head coach on June 22, 2000. He becomes the eighth person in the club's NHL history to hold the position. MacTavish joins Kevin Lowe and Glen Sather as head coaches who were former captains of the Oilers.

MacTavish played for 17 seasons in the NHL, including eight-and-a-half campaigns with the Oilers. He was instrumental in helping his teams win four Stanley Cup titles; three with Edmonton and one with the New York Rangers. Although he was the last player in the NHL to play without a helmet, MacTavish was known for his aggressive style, combined with above average skills.

MacTavish retired as a player in 1997 and was immediately named an assistant coach with the New York Rangers. He was with the Rangers for two seasons, prior to joining the Oilers' coaching staff as an assistant under Kevin Lowe in 1999-2000. Craig, his wife, Debbie, and their three children make their home in Edmonton.

1999-2000 Scoring
* – rookie

Regular Season

Pos	#	Player	Team	GP	G	A	Pts	+/–	PIM	PP	SH	GW	GT	S	%
C	39	Doug Weight	EDM	77	21	51	72	6	54	3	1	4	0	167	12.6
L	94	Ryan Smyth	EDM	82	28	26	54	–2	58	11	0	4	1	238	11.8
R	29	Alex Selivanov	EDM	67	27	20	47	2	46	10	0	5	0	122	22.1
R	9	Bill Guerin	EDM	70	24	22	46	4	123	11	0	2	0	188	12.8
L	13	German Titov	PIT	63	17	25	42	–3	34	4	2	3	0	111	15.3
			EDM	7	0	4	4	2	4	0	0	0	0	11	0.0
			TOTAL	70	17	29	46	–1	38	4	2	3	0	122	13.9
D	22	Roman Hamrlik	EDM	80	8	37	45	1	68	5	0	1	0	180	4.4
L	26	Todd Marchant	EDM	82	17	23	40	7	70	0	1	0	2	170	10.0
D	5	Tom Poti	EDM	76	9	26	35	8	65	2	1	1	0	125	7.2
D	44	Janne Niinimaa	EDM	81	8	25	33	14	89	2	2	0	0	133	6.0
R	25	Mike Grier	EDM	65	9	22	31	9	68	0	3	2	0	115	7.8
L	18	Ethan Moreau	EDM	73	17	10	27	8	62	1	0	3	0	106	16.0
C	19	Boyd Devereaux	EDM	76	8	19	27	7	20	0	1	2	1	108	7.4
C	34	Jim Dowd	EDM	69	5	18	23	10	45	0	0	1	1	103	4.9
R	27	Georges Laraque	EDM	76	8	8	16	5	123	0	0	0	0	56	14.3
L	17	Rem Murray	EDM	44	9	5	14	–2	8	2	0	3	0	65	13.8
D	21	Jason Smith	EDM	80	3	11	14	16	60	0	0	1	0	96	3.1
D	23	Sean Brown	EDM	72	4	8	12	1	192	0	0	2	0	36	11.1
D	55	Igor Ulanov	MTL	43	1	5	6	–11	76	0	0	0	0	33	3.0
			EDM	14	0	3	3	–3	10	0	0	0	0	6	0.0
			TOTAL	57	1	8	9	–14	86	0	0	0	0	39	2.6
L	37	Daniel Cleary	EDM	17	3	2	5	–1	8	0	0	1	0	18	16.7
C	15	Chad Kilger	EDM	40	3	2	5	–6	18	0	0	0	0	32	9.4
D	14	Bert Robertsson	EDM	52	0	4	4	–3	34	0	0	0	0	31	0.0
C	47 *	Paul Comrie	EDM	15	1	2	3	–2	4	0	0	0	0	11	9.1
D	2	Brett Hauer	EDM	5	0	2	2	–2	2	0	0	0	0	8	0.0
G	35	Tommy Salo	EDM	70	0	1	1	0	8	0	0	0	0	0	0.0
G	1 *	Mike Minard	EDM	1	0	0	0	0	0	0	0	0	0	0	0.0
L	12	Michel Picard	EDM	2	0	0	0	0	2	0	0	0	0	2	0.0
L	33 *	Dan LaCouture	EDM	5	0	0	0	0	10	0	0	0	0	5	0.0
R	10	Kevin Brown	EDM	7	0	0	0	0	0	0	0	0	0	5	0.0
G	30	Bill Ranford	EDM	16	0	0	0	0	2	0	0	0	0	0	0.0

Goaltending

No.	Goaltender	GPI	Mins	Avg	W	L	T	EN	SO	GA	SA	S%
35	Tommy Salo	70	4164	2.33	27	28	13	0	2	162	1875	.914
1 *	Mike Minard	1	60	3.00	1	0	0	0	0	3	36	.917
30	Bill Ranford	16	785	3.59	4	6	3	0	0	47	407	.885
	Totals	82	5030	2.53	32	34	16	0	2	212	2318	.909

Playoffs

Pos	#	Player	Team	GP	G	A	Pts	+/–	PIM	PP	SH	GW	OT	S	%
R	9	Bill Guerin	EDM	5	3	2	5	–1	9	1	0	0	0	12	25.0
C	39	Doug Weight	EDM	5	3	2	5	–3	4	2	0	1	0	8	37.5
C	34	Jim Dowd	EDM	5	2	1	3	–2	4	0	0	0	0	6	33.3
L	13	German Titov	EDM	5	1	1	2	–2	0	0	0	0	0	3	33.3
D	44	Janne Niinimaa	EDM	5	0	2	2	1	2	0	0	0	0	8	0.0
L	26	Todd Marchant	EDM	3	1	0	1	–1	2	0	0	0	0	6	16.7
L	94	Ryan Smyth	EDM	5	1	0	1	–2	6	0	0	1	0	13	7.7
L	37	Daniel Cleary	EDM	4	0	1	1	1	2	0	0	0	0	3	0.0
D	22	Roman Hamrlik	EDM	5	0	1	1	–4	4	0	0	0	0	10	0.0
D	21	Jason Smith	EDM	5	0	1	1	–1	2	0	0	0	0	5	0.0
L	17	Rem Murray	EDM	5	0	1	1	–1	2	0	0	0	0	9	0.0
L	18	Ethan Moreau	EDM	5	0	1	1	0	0	0	0	0	0	6	0.0
R	27	Georges Laraque	EDM	5	0	1	1	–1	6	0	0	0	0	5	0.0
D	5	Tom Poti	EDM	5	0	1	1	–3	0	0	0	0	0	7	0.0
R	10	Kevin Brown	EDM	1	0	0	0	0	0	0	0	0	0	0	0.0
L	33 *	Dan Lacouture	EDM	3	0	0	0	0	0	0	0	0	0	1	0.0
C	15	Chad Kilger	EDM	3	0	0	0	0	0	0	0	0	0	4	0.0
D	23	Sean Brown	EDM	3	0	0	0	–1	23	0	0	0	0	4	0.0
D	55	Igor Ulanov	EDM	5	0	0	0	1	6	0	0	0	0	4	0.0
G	35	Tommy Salo	EDM	5	0	0	0	0	2	0	0	0	0	0	0.0
D	14	Bert Robertsson	EDM	5	0	0	0	–1	0	0	0	0	0	2	0.0
R	29	Alex Selivanov	EDM	5	0	0	0	0	8	0	0	0	0	6	0.0

Goaltending

No.	Goaltender	GPI	Mins	Avg	W	L	EN	SO	GA	SA	S%
35	Tommy Salo	5	297	2.83	1	4	0	0	14	133	.895
	Totals	5	300	2.80	1	4	0	0	14	133	.895

General Managers' History

Larry Gordon, 1979-80; Glen Sather, 1980-81 to 1999-2000; Kevin Lowe, 2000-01.

Club Records

Team

(Figures in brackets for season records are games played; records for fewest points, wins, ties, losses, goals, goals against are for 70 or more games)

Most Points	119	1983-84 (80), 1985-86 (80)
Most Wins	57	1983-84 (80)
Most Ties	16	1980-81 (80), 1999-2000 (82)
Most Losses	50	1992-93 (84)
Most Goals	*446	1983-84 (80)
Most Goals Against	327	1980-81 (80)
Fewest Points	60	1992-93 (84)
Fewest Wins	25	1993-94 (84)
Fewest Ties	5	1983-84 (80)
Fewest Losses	17	1981-82 (80), 1985-86 (80)
Fewest Goals	215	1997-98 (82)
Fewest Goals Against	212	1999-2000 (82)

Longest Winning Streak

Overall	8	Five times
Home	8	Jan. 19-Feb. 22/85, Feb. 24-Apr. 2/86
Away	8	Dec. 9/86-Jan. 17/87

Longest Undefeated Streak

Overall	15	Oct. 11-Nov. 9/84 (12 wins, 3 ties)
Home	14	Nov. 15/89-Jan. 6/90 (11 wins, 3 ties)
Away	9	Jan. 17-Mar. 2/82 (6 wins, 3 ties), Nov. 23/82-Jan. 18/83 (7 wins, 2 ties)

Longest Losing Streak

Overall	11	Oct. 16-Nov. 7/93
Home	9	Oct. 16-Nov. 24/93
Away	9	Nov. 25-Dec. 30/80

Longest Winless Streak

Overall	14	Oct. 11-Nov. 7/93 (13 losses, 1 tie)
Home	9	Oct. 16-Nov. 24/93 (9 losses)
Away	9	Three times
Most Shutouts, Season	8	1997-98 (82)
Most PIM, Season	2,173	1987-88 (80)
Most Goals, Game	13	Nov. 19/83 (N.J. 4 at Edm. 13), Nov. 8/85 (Van. 0 at Edm. 13)

Individual

Most Seasons	15	Kevin Lowe
Most Games	1,037	Kevin Lowe
Most Goals, Career	583	Wayne Gretzky
Most Assists, Career	1,086	Wayne Gretzky
Most Points, Career	1,669	Wayne Gretzky (583G, 1,086A)
Most PIM, Career	1,747	Kelly Buchberger
Most Shutouts, Career	14	Curtis Joseph
Longest Consecutive Games Streak	521	Craig MacTavish (Oct. 11/86-Jan. 2/93)
Most Goals, Season	*92	Wayne Gretzky (1981-82)
Most Assists, Season	*163	Wayne Gretzky (1985-86)
Most Points, Season	*215	Wayne Gretzky (1985-86; 52G, 163A)
Most PIM, Season	286	Steve Smith (1987-88)

Most Points, Defenseman, Season	138	Paul Coffey (1985-86; 48G, 90A)
Most Points, Center, Season	*215	Wayne Gretzky (1985-86; 52G, 163A)
Most Points, Right Wing, Season	135	Jari Kurri (1984-85; 71G, 64A)
Most Points, Left Wing, Season	106	Mark Messier (1982-83; 48G, 58A)
Most Points, Rookie, Season	75	Jari Kurri (1980-81; 32G, 43A)
Most Shutouts, Season	8	Curtis Joseph (1997-98)
Most Goals, Game	5	Wayne Gretzky (Feb. 18/81, Dec. 30/81, Dec. 15/84, Dec. 6/87), Jari Kurri (Nov. 19/83), Pat Hughes (Feb. 3/84)
Most Assists, Game	*7	Wayne Gretzky (Feb. 15/80, Dec. 11/85, Feb. 14/86)
Most Points, Game	8	Wayne Gretzky (Nov. 19/83; 3G, 5A), (Jan. 4/84; 4G, 4A), Paul Coffey (Mar. 14/86; 2G, 6A)

* NHL Record.

Retired Numbers

3	Al Hamilton	1972-1980
99	Wayne Gretzky	1979-1988

Captains' History

Ron Chipperfield, 1979-80; Blair MacDonald and Lee Fogolin, 1980-81; Lee Fogolin, 1981-82, 1982-83; Wayne Gretzky, 1983-84 to 1987-88; Mark Messier, 1988-89 to 1990-91; Kevin Lowe, 1991-92; Craig MacTavish, 1992-93, 1993-94; Shayne Corson, 1994-95; Kelly Buchberger, 1995-96 to 1998-99; Doug Weight, 1999-2000 to date.

All-time Record vs. Other Clubs

Regular Season

		At Home							On Road							Total					
	GP	W	L	T	GF	GA	PTS	GP	W	L	T	GF	GA	PTS	GP	W	L	T	GF	GA	PTS
Anaheim	17	9	8	0	34	37	18	18	5	12	1	47	56	11	35	14	20	1	81	93	29
Atlanta	1	1	0	0	5	4	2	1	1	0	0	3	0	2	2	2	0	0	8	4	4
Boston	27	10	14	3	89	92	23	27	6	18	3	76	115	15	54	16	32	6	165	207	38
Buffalo	26	19	5	2	112	70	40	28	11	10	7	105	109	29	54	30	15	9	217	179	69
Calgary	71	37	24	10	286	243	85	70	25	39	6	251	305	56	141	62	63	16	537	548	141
Carolina	28	18	5	5	114	84	41	27	10	11	6	94	109	26	55	28	16	11	208	193	67
Chicago	37	16	17	4	138	133	36	36	12	19	5	129	145	29	73	28	36	9	267	278	65
Colorado	36	20	14	2	158	113	42	36	17	16	3	145	145	37	72	37	30	5	303	258	79
Dallas	36	17	11	8	149	120	42	37	13	18	6	113	136	32	73	30	29	14	262	256	74
Detroit	36	17	13	6	152	141	40	36	14	19	3	126	138	31	72	31	32	9	278	279	71
Florida	5	2	2	1	14	12	5	6	1	4	1	14	17	3	11	3	6	2	28	29	8
Los Angeles	69	36	19	14	327	256	86	69	28	26	15	288	280	71	138	64	45	29	615	536	157
Montreal	29	14	15	0	94	93	28	27	9	14	4	87	95	22	56	23	29	4	181	188	50
Nashville	4	3	1	0	13	9	7	5	1	3	1	12	15	3	9	4	4	1	25	24	10
New Jersey	29	14	9	6	130	106	34	30	15	13	2	101	102	32	59	29	22	8	231	208	66
NY Islanders	27	16	6	5	103	78	37	28	7	12	9	105	117	23	55	23	18	14	208	195	60
NY Rangers	27	11	13	3	97	93	25	27	13	8	6	103	99	33	54	24	21	9	200	192	58
Ottawa	8	5	1	2	32	21	12	6	3	2	1	14	10	7	14	8	3	3	46	31	19
Philadelphia	26	14	7	5	94	77	33	28	7	19	2	79	124	16	54	21	26	7	173	201	49
Phoenix	64	41	19	4	286	214	86	63	34	25	4	286	256	73	127	75	44	8	572	470	159
Pittsburgh	28	21	6	1	144	94	43	28	12	13	3	122	108	27	56	33	19	4	266	202	70
St. Louis	36	18	15	3	135	129	39	36	16	15	5	140	131	37	72	34	30	8	275	260	77
San Jose	25	16	5	4	92	54	36	24	10	12	2	75	82	23	49	26	17	6	167	136	59
Tampa Bay	8	6	2	0	22	17	12	8	4	2	2	25	22	10	16	10	4	2	47	39	22
Toronto	36	19	11	6	160	122	45	34	14	18	2	145	142	30	70	33	29	8	305	264	75
Vancouver	70	46	17	7	326	216	99	72	35	28	9	294	267	80	142	81	45	16	620	483	179
Washington	27	13	10	4	111	87	30	26	9	15	2	91	109	20	53	22	25	6	202	196	50
Totals	**833**	**459**	**269**	**105**	**3417**	**2715**	**1026**	**833**	**332**	**391**	**110**	**3070**	**3234**	**779**	**1666**	**791**	**660**	**215**	**6487**	**5949**	**1805**

Playoffs

	Series	W	L	GP	W	L	T	GF	GA	Last Mtg.	Round	Result
Boston	2	2	0	9	8	1	0	41	20	1990	F	W 4-1
Calgary	5	4	1	30	19	11	0	132	96	1991	DSF	W 4-3
Chicago	4	3	1	20	12	8	0	102	77	1992	CF	L 0-4
Colorado	2	1	1	12	5	7	0	30	35	1998	CQF	W 4-3
Dallas	6	2	4	30	11	19	0	80	82	2000	CQF	L 1-4
Detroit	2	2	0	10	8	2	0	39	26	1988	CF	W 4-1
Los Angeles	7	5	2	36	24	12	0	154	127	1992	DSF	W 4-2
Montreal	1	1	0	3	3	0	0	15	6	1981	PR	W 3-0
NY Islanders	3	1	2	15	6	9	0	47	58	1984	F	W 4-1
Philadelphia	3	2	1	15	8	7	0	49	44	1987	F	W 4-3
Vancouver	2	2	0	9	7	2	0	35	20	1992	DF	W 4-2
Winnipeg	6	6	0	26	22	4	0	120	75	1990	DSF	W 4-3
Totals	**43**	**31**	**12**	**215**	**133**	**82**	**0**	**844**	**666**			

Playoff Results 2000-1996

Year	Round	Opponent	Result	GF	GA
2000	CQF	Dallas	L 1-4	14	14
1999	CQF	Dallas	L 0-4	7	11
1998	CSF	Dallas	L 1-4	5	9
	CQF	Colorado	W 4-3	19	16
1997	CSF	Colorado	L 1-4	11	19
	CQF	Dallas	W 4-3	21	18

Abbreviations: Round: F – Final; **CF** – conference final; **CSF** – conference semi-final; **CQF** – conference quarter-final; **DF** – division final; **DSF** – division semi-final; **PR** – preliminary round.

Calgary totals include Atlanta Flames, 1979-80.
Colorado totals include Quebec, 1979-80 to 1994-95.
New Jersey totals include Colorado Rockies, 1979-80 to 1981-82.

Carolina totals include Hartford, 1979-80 to 1996-97.
Dallas totals include Minnesota North Stars, 1979-80 to 1992-93.
Phoenix totals include Winnipeg, 1979-80 to 1995-96.

1999-2000 Results

Oct.	1	NY Rangers	1-1		7	Tampa Bay	5-1
	6	Montreal	2-1		11	Dallas	2-3
	7	at San Jose	2-3 *		14	Toronto	2-3 *
	9	St. Louis	2-4		16	Detroit	3-3
	13	Carolina	3-3		19	Calgary	7-0
	16	Los Angeles	5-4		22	Vancouver	3-3
	20	at Dallas	1-2		24	Nashville	2-3 *
	21	at St. Louis	2-3 *		25	at Vancouver	5-4 *
	23	Nashville	3-4		28	at Tampa Bay	7-3
	26	Phoenix	3-1		29	at Florida	1-2
	31	Nashville	4-2		31	at Dallas	1-2
Nov.	3	Florida	2-2	Feb.	2	Chicago	4-1
	5	St. Louis	1-2		8	at Montreal	5-4 *
	7	at Anaheim	1-3		10	at Philadelphia	3-2
	9	at Los Angeles	1-1		11	at Pittsburgh	2-2
	10	at Phoenix	4-5 *		13	at Buffalo	2-2
	12	at St. Louis	2-2		15	at Nashville	2-1
	14	at Chicago	6-3		18	at Calgary	2-4
	20	Detroit	2-1		19	Calgary	2-3 *
	21	NY Islanders	4-4		21	Los Angeles	6-3
	24	Chicago	2-3		23	Boston	4-2
	26	at Detroit	2-4		25	Atlanta	5-4
	27	at Toronto	2-5		27	at Anaheim	2-3
Dec.	1	Colorado	3-1		29	at Colorado	3-1
	2	at Vancouver	2-3 *	Mar.	4	Pittsburgh	2-3
	4	Vancouver	3-2		7	Toronto	0-2
	6	at Chicago	1-5		10	Colorado	2-4
	8	NY Rangers	1-2 *		12	at Nashville	3-4
	9	at Boston	2-3		13	at Atlanta	3-0
	11	at New Jersey	3-1		15	at Carolina	2-2
	14	at NY Islanders	4-2		17	Ottawa	4-2
	15	at Detroit	1-5		19	Calgary	2-3
	17	Dallas	2-2		22	Anaheim	2-1
	19	Ottawa	3-3		25	Vancouver	2-3
	21	Washington	6-2		27	at San Jose	2-1
	23	at Calgary	1-2		29	at Colorado	2-3
	27	Anaheim	4-1	Apr.	1	Phoenix	4-3 *
	30	at Los Angeles	2-8		3	San Jose	0-1
Jan.	1	at Phoenix	5-4		5	Colorado	2-2
	3	Colorado	2-2		7	at Vancouver	5-4
	5	San Jose	1-1		8	at Calgary	6-3
				* – Overtime			

Entry Draft
Selections 2000-1986

2000		1996		1992		1988	
Pick		**Pick**		**Pick**		**Pick**	
17	Alexei Mikhnov	6	Boyd Devereaux	13	Joe Hulbig	19	Francois Leroux
35	Brad Winchester	19	Matthieu Descoteaux	37	Martin Reichel	39	Petro Koivunen
83	Alexander Lyubimov	32	Chris Hajt	61	Simon Roy	53	Trevor Sim
113	Lou Dickenson	59	Tom Poti	65	Kirk Maltby	61	Collin Bauer
152	Paul Flache	114	Brian Urick	96	Ralph Intranuovo	82	Cam Brauer
184	Shaun Norrie	141	Bryan Randall	109	Joaquin Gage	103	Don Martin
211	Joe Cullen	168	David Bernier	157	Steve Gibson	124	Len Barrie
215	Matthew Lombardi	170	Brandon Lafrance	181	Kyuin Shim	145	Mike Glover
247	Jason Platt	195	Fernando Pisani	190	Colin Schmidt	166	Shjon Podein
274	Yevgeny Muratov	221	John Hultberg	205	Marko Tuomainen	187	Tim Cole
				253	Bryan Rasmussen	208	Vladimir Zubkov
1999		**1995**				229	Darin MacDonald
Pick		**Pick**		**1991**		250	Tim Tisdale
13	Jani Rita	6	Steve Kelly	**Pick**			
36	Alexei Semenov	31	Georges Laraque	12	Tyler Wright	**1987**	
41	Tony Salmelainen	57	Lukas Zib	20	Martin Rucinsky	**Pick**	
81	Adam Hauser	83	Mike Minard	34	Andrew Verner	21	Peter Soberlak
91	Mike Comrie	109	Jan Snopek	56	George Breen	42	Brad Werenka
139	Jonathan Fauteux	161	Martin Cerven	78	Mario Nobili	63	Geoff Smith
171	Chris Legg	187	Stephen Douglas	93	Ryan Haggerty	64	Peter Eriksson
199	Christian Chartier	213	Jiri Antonin	144	David Oliver	105	Shaun Van Allen
256	Tamas Groschl			166	Gary Kitching	126	Radek Toupal
		1994		210	Vegar Barlie	147	Tomas Srsen
1998		**Pick**		232	Yevgeny Belosheiken	168	Age Ellingsen
Pick		4	Jason Bonsignore	254	Juha Riihijarvi	189	Gavin Armstrong
13	Michael Henrich	6	Ryan Smyth			210	Mike Tinkham
67	Alex Henry	32	Mike Watt	**1990**		231	Jeff Pauletti
99	Shawn Horcoff	53	Corey Neilson	**Pick**		241	Jesper Duus
113	Kristian Antila	60	Brad Symes	17	Scott Allison	252	Igor Vyazmikin
128	Paul Elliott	79	Adam Copeland	38	Alexandre Legault		
144	Oleg Smirnov	95	Jussi Tarvainen	59	Joe Crowley	**1986**	
159	Trevor Ettinger	110	Jon Gaskins	67	Joel Blain	**Pick**	
186	Michael Morrison	136	Terry Marchant	101	Greg Louder	21	Kim Issel
213	Christian Lefebvre	160	Chris Sheptak	122	Keijo Sailynoja	42	Jamie Nichols
241	Maxim Spiridonov	162	Dmitri Shulga	143	Mike Power	63	Ron Shudra
		179	Chris Wickenheiser	164	Roman Mejzlik	84	Dan Currie
1997		185	Rob Guinn	185	Richard Zemlicka	105	David Haas
Pick		188	Jason Reid	206	Petr Korinek	126	Jim Ennis
14	Michel Riesen	214	Jeremy Jablonski	227	invalid claim	147	Ivan Matulik
41	Patrick Dovigi	266	Ladislav Benysek	248	Sami Nuutinen	168	Nicolas Beaulieu
68	Sergei Yerkovich					189	Mike Greenlay
94	Jonas Elofsson	**1993**		**1989**		210	Matt Lanza
121	Jason Chimera	**Pick**		**Pick**		231	Mojmir Bozik
141	Peter Sarno	7	Jason Arnott	15	Jason Soules	252	Tony Hand
176	Kevin Bolibruck	16	Nick Stajduhar	36	Richard Borgo		
187	Chad Hinz	33	David Vyborny	78	Josef Beranek		
205	Chris Kerr	59	Kevin Paden	92	Peter White		
231	Alexander Fomitchev	60	Alexander Kerch	120	Anatoli Semenov		
		111	Miroslav Satan	140	Davis Payne		
		163	Alexander Zhurik	141	Sergei Yashin		
		189	Martin Bakula	162	Darcy Martini		
		215	Brad Norton	225	Roman Bozek		
		241	Oleg Maltsev				
		267	Ilja Byakin				

General Manager

LOWE, KEVIN
General Manager, Edmonton Oilers. Born in Lachute, Que., April 15, 1959.

The Edmonton Oilers named Kevin Lowe as their new general manager on June 9, 2000, filling the position left vacant when Glen Sather resigned on May 19th. Lowe moves into the front office after spending the 1999-2000 season as coach of the Oilers.

After a brilliant 19-year playing career with the Edmonton Oilers and New York Rangers, Kevin Lowe announced his retirement on July 30, 1998 and joined the Edmonton Oilers coaching staff. He replaced Ron Low as head coach on June 18, 1999.

Lowe was the Oilers' first-ever draft pick when he was selected 21st overall in the 1979 NHL Amateur Draft. He went on to play in 1,254 regular season games and 214 playoff games, winning six Stanley Cup championships; the first five with Edmonton (1984, 1985, 1987, 1988, 1990) followed by a sixth title with the Rangers in 1994.

Besides being the first draft choice in Oilers history, Lowe also scored the first goal in team history on October 10, 1979. He holds the Oilers' record for most games played in both the regular season (1,037) and playoffs (172), and became the sixth captain in team history in 1990-91. He was no less a leader off the ice, becoming the only player to win the King Clancy Memorial Trophy and the Budweiser/NHL Man of the Year Award in the same season (1989-90). Both awards are presented for leadership qualities and humanitarian contributions. His work with the Edmonton Christmas Bureau has set the standard for the Oilers' commitment to community involvement.

Lowe and his wife Karen, a two-time Olympic bronze medalist for Canada at the 1988 Winter Olympics in Calgary, have four children.

NHL Coaching Record

		Regular Season					Playoffs			
Season	Team	Games	W	L	T	%	Games	W	L	%
1999-2000	Edmonton	82	32	43	16	.537•	5	1	4	.200
	NHL Totals	**82**	**32**	**43**	**16**	**.537•**	**5**	**1**	**4**	**.200**

• Includes points from regulation ties

Club Directory

Skyreach Centre

Edmonton Oilers
11230 – 110 Street
Edmonton, Alberta T5G 3H7
Phone **780/414-4000**
· Ticketing 780/414-4400
FAX 780/414-4659
Website: www.edmontonoilers.com
Capacity: 17,100

Owner	Edmonton Investors Group Ltd.
Governor	Cal Nichols
Alternate Governors	Patrick R. LaForge, Kevin Lowe & Gordon Buchanan
President & Chief Executive Officer	Patrick R. LaForge
Executive Vice-President & General Manager	Kevin Lowe
Vice-President, Hockey Operations	Kevin Prendergast
Assistant to the General Manager	Scott Howson
Head Coach	Craig MacTavish
Assistant Coaches	Charlie Huddy, Bill Moores
Assistant Coach, Development	Mark Lamb
Vice President, Public Relations, Hockey	Bill Tuele
Public Relations Coordinator	Warren Suitor
Information Coordinator	Steve Knowles
Director of Research, Analysis and Software Development	Sean Draper
Video Coordinator	Brian Ross
Scouting Staff	Ed Chadwick, Brad Davis, Lorne Davis, Stu MacGregor, Bob Mancini, Chris McCarthy, Kent Nilsson, Gord Pell, Dave Semenko,
Executive Assistant to the President	Trena Jackson
Executive Assistant to the General Manager	Yvonne Ewaskow
Administrative Assistant	Cheryl Zaruk

Medical and Training Staff

Head Medical Trainer	Ken Lowe
Head Equipment Manager	Barrie Stafford
Equipment Manager	Lyle Kulchisky
Assistant Equipment Manager	Chris Delaney
Massage Therapist	Stewart Poirier
Team Medical Chief of Staff/ Director of Glen Sather Sports Medicine Clinic	Dr. David C. Reid
Team Physician	Dr. Boris Boyko
Team Dermatologist	Dr. Don Groot
Team Dentists	Dr. Tony Sneazwell, Dr. Ben Eastwood
Fitness Consultants	Dr. Art Quinney, Dr. Gordon Bell
Physical Therapy Consultant	Dr. Dave Magee
Team Optometrist	Dr. Brent Saik
Strength & Conditioning Consultant	Daryl Duke

Finance

Vice-President, Finance and Administration	Doug Thomson
Director of Finance	Darryl Boessenkool
Manager Payroll & Benefits	Pat Stanic
Financial Analyst	Colleen Stewart
Systems Administrators	Terry Rhoades, Rod Pruden
Finance Staff	Donna Chizen, Lynn Schmidl, Michelle Schwendeman

Marketing & Communications

Vice-President, Marketing & Communications	Allan Watt
Director of Community Relations Development	Bryn Griffiths
Community Relations Coordinator	Fiona Liew
Managers, Corporate Sponsorships	Brad MacGregor, Greg McDannold, Darren Simmons
Coordinator, Sponsorships, Sales & Services	Nicole Wiens
Director of Corporate Communications & Marketing	Natalie Minckler
Marketing & Promotions Manager	Melanie Harysh
Director of Broadcast	Don Metz
Game Night Director	Glenn Wiun
Game Night Supervisor	Marilyn Riddell
Publications Coordinator	Steve Sandor
New Media Production Manager	Andreas Schwabe

Properties

Vice President, Properties	Darrell Holowaychuk
Product Manager	Brent Gibbs
Properties Manager	Linda Malito
Administrative Asst. to VP, Properties	Heather Allen
Operations Manager	Doug Wadlow
Administration	Nycole Kindree

Ticket Operations

Director of Ticket Operations	John Yeomans
Box Office Manager	Bob Haromy
Ticket Client Services	Sheila McCaskill, Sandy Langley, Sherry Smith
Call Centre Supervisor	Cathy Cookson
Suite Manager	Lori-Ann Rothfos

Ticket Sales

Director of Ticket Sales	Michael Lake
Coordinator, Ticket Sales and Service	Heather Willson
Account Executives, Corporate Ticket Sales	Damon Bunting, Scott Jacques, Bruce Rakoczy, Teresa Powanda, Kristie Brown
Account Executives, Group Ticket Sales	Emiliano Diaz-Page, Marran Vogelesang
Account Services Representative	Lisa Saskiw
Location of Press Box	East Side at top (Radio/TV) West Side at top (Media)
Training Camp Site	Strathcona County Millennium Arena; Sherwood Park, Alberta
Television Outlets	A-Channel (Local) CBXT TV & CTV SportsNet (Regional & National)
Radio Flagship Station	630 CHED (AM); Rod Phillips (Play-by-play) & Morley Scott (colour)

Florida Panthers

1999-2000 Results: 43W-33L-6T 98PTS. Second, Southeast Division

Year-by-Year Record

		Home			Road			Overall							
Season	GP	W	L	T	W	L	T	W	L	T	GF	GA	Pts.	Finished	Playoff Result
1999-2000	82	26	11	4	17	22	2	43	33	6	244	209	98	2nd, Southeast Div.	Lost Conf. Quarter-Final
1998-99	82	17	17	7	13	17	11	30	34	18	210	228	78	2nd, Southeast Div.	Out of Playoffs
1997-98	82	11	24	6	13	19	9	24	43	15	203	256	63	6th, Atlantic Div.	Out of Playoffs
1996-97	82	21	12	8	14	16	11	35	28	19	221	201	89	3rd, Atlantic Div.	Lost Conf. Quarter-Final
1995-96	82	25	12	4	16	19	6	41	31	10	254	234	92	3rd, Atlantic Div.	Lost Final
1994-95	48	9	12	3	11	10	3	20	22	6	115	127	46	5th, Atlantic Div.	Out of Playoffs
1993-94	84	15	18	9	18	16	8	33	34	17	233	233	83	5th, Atlantic Div.	Out of Playoffs

2000-01 Schedule

Oct.	Fri.	6	Vancouver
	Mon.	9	at Boston*
	Fri.	13	Carolina
	Wed.	18	at Phoenix
	Fri.	20	at Colorado
	Sun.	22	at Minnesota*
	Wed.	25	New Jersey
	Fri.	27	at Nashville
	Sat.	28	Ottawa
	Mon.	30	at New Jersey
Nov.	Wed.	1	NY Islanders
	Sat.	4	Washington
	Wed.	8	Montreal
	Fri.	10	Calgary
	Mon.	13	Atlanta
	Wed.	15	at Carolina
	Fri.	17	at Columbus
	Sat.	18	at Ottawa
	Tue.	21	at Montreal
	Fri.	24	at Tampa Bay
	Sat.	25	Tampa Bay
	Wed.	29	Carolina
Dec.	Fri.	1	Detroit
	Sat.	2	at St. Louis
	Mon.	4	at Toronto
	Wed.	6	NY Islanders
	Fri.	8	at Atlanta
	Sat.	9	Colorado
	Wed.	13	at Detroit
	Fri.	15	at Pittsburgh
	Sat.	16	at Buffalo
	Mon.	18	at NY Rangers
	Wed.	20	Pittsburgh
	Fri.	22	New Jersey
	Sat.	23	at Washington
	Wed.	27	Philadelphia
	Fri.	29	Boston
	Sat.	30	Toronto
Jan.	Wed.	3	at Anaheim
	Thu.	4	at Los Angeles
	Sat.	6	at San Jose

	Tue.	9	at Carolina
	Fri.	12	Carolina
	Sat.	13	Philadelphia
	Mon.	15	Dallas
	Wed.	17	at Chicago
	Fri.	19	at Buffalo
	Sat.	20	at Philadelphia
	Mon.	22	at Boston
	Wed.	24	at Washington
	Fri.	26	Ottawa
	Sat.	27	Tampa Bay
	Tue.	30	at Tampa Bay
	Wed.	31	Buffalo
Feb.	Wed.	7	Minnesota
	Fri.	9	NY Rangers
	Sat.	10	at Atlanta
	Wed.	14	Phoenix
	Fri.	16	Boston
	Mon.	19	St. Louis
	Wed.	21	at Pittsburgh
	Thu.	22	at Ottawa
	Sat.	24	at NY Islanders*
	Mon.	26	at New Jersey
	Wed.	28	at NY Rangers
Mar.	Fri.	2	Atlanta
	Sat.	3	at Atlanta
	Wed.	7	San Jose
	Fri.	9	Columbus
	Sun.	11	at NY Islanders*
	Wed.	14	Edmonton
	Fri.	16	Pittsburgh
	Sat.	17	Toronto
	Tue.	20	at Montreal
	Wed.	21	at Toronto
	Fri.	23	Washington
	Wed.	28	Montreal
	Fri.	30	Tampa Bay
Apr.	Mon.	2	Buffalo
	Tue.	3	at Philadelphia
	Thu.	5	at Washington
	Sat.	7	NY Rangers*

* Denotes afternoon game.

Franchise date: June 14, 1993

SOUTHEAST
DIVISION

8th
NHL
Season

Viktor Kozlov had a breakthrough season in 1999-2000, tallying a career-high 70 points. Centering a line with Pavel Bure on his right wing helped Kozlov finish tied for fourth in the NHL with 53 assists.

2000-01 Player Personnel

FORWARDS	HT	WT	S	Place of Birth	Date	1999-00 Club
BARRIE, Len	6-0	200	L	Kimberley, B.C.	6/4/69	L.A.-Long Beach-Fla.
BOGUNIECKI, Eric	5-8	192	R	New Haven, CT	5/6/75	Florida-Louisville
BROUSSEAU, Paul	6-2	203	R	Pierrefonds, Que.	9/18/73	Louisville
BURE, Pavel	5-10	189	L	Moscow, USSR	3/31/71	Florida
DUERDEN, Dave	6-2	201	L	Oshawa, Ont.	4/11/77	Florida-Louisville
EMMA, David	5-10	185	L	Cranston, RI	1/14/69	KAC Klagenfurt
JOKINEN, Olli	6-3	208	L	Kuopio, Finland	12/5/78	NY Islanders
KOZLOV, Viktor	6-5	232	R	Togliatti, USSR	2/14/75	Florida
LARIONOV, Igor	5-9	170	L	Voskresensk, USSR	12/3/60	Detroit
LAUS, Paul	6-1	212	R	Beamsville, Ont.	9/26/70	Florida
MELLANBY, Scott	6-1	205	R	Montreal, Que.	6/11/66	Florida
NIEDERMAYER, Rob	6-2	204	L	Cassiar, B.C.	12/28/74	Florida
NILSON, Marcus	6-2	193	R	Balsta, Sweden	3/1/78	Florida-Louisville
NOVOSELTSEV, Ivan	6-1	183	L	Golitsino, USSR	1/23/79	Florida-Louisville
SHVIDKI, Denis	6-0	195	L	Kharkov, USSR	11/21/80	Barrie Colts
SILLINGER, Mike	5-10	190	R	Regina, Sask.	6/29/71	Tampa Bay-Florida
THOMPSON, Rocky	6-2	205	R	Calgary, Alta.	8/8/77	Saint John Flames-Louisville
WHITNEY, Ray	5-10	175	R	Fort Saskatchewan, Alta.	5/8/72	Florida
WORRELL, Peter	6-6	235	L	Pierrefonds, Que.	8/18/77	Florida
DEFENSEMEN						
BOYLE, Dan	5-11	190	R	Ottawa, Ont.	7/12/76	Florida-Louisville
DOELL, Curtis	5-11	209	R	Saskatoon, Sask.	10/3/76	Louisville
FERENCE, Brad	6-3	196	R	Calgary, Alta.	4/2/79	Florida-Louisville
HEDICAN, Bret	6-2	205	L	St. Paul, MN	8/10/70	Florida
JAKOPIN, John	6-5	239	R	Toronto, Ont.	5/16/75	Florida-Louisville
PITLICK, Lance	6-0	205	R	Minneapolis, MN	11/5/67	Florida
RATCHUK, Peter	6-1	185	L	Buffalo, NY	9/10/77	Louisville
SIMPSON, Todd	6-3	215	L	North Vancouver, B.C.	5/28/73	Florida
SPACEK, Jaroslav	5-11	198	L	Rokycany, Czech.	2/11/74	Florida
SVEHLA, Robert	6-1	210	R	Martin, Czech.	1/2/69	Florida
TETARENKO, Joey	6-2	212	R	Prince Albert, Sask.	3/3/78	Louisville
THOMPSON, Brent	6-2	205	L	Calgary, Alta.	1/9/71	Louisville
WARD, Lance	6-3	215	L	Lloydminster, Alta.	6/2/78	Louisville
WILSON, Mike	6-6	212	L	Brampton, Ont.	2/26/75	Florida

GOALTENDERS	HT	WT	C	Place of Birth	Date	1999-00 Club
GAUTHIER, Sean	5-11	200	L	Sudbury, Ont.	3/28/71	Louisiana-Louisville
KIDD, Trevor	6-2	190	L	Dugald, Man.	3/29/72	Florida-Louisville
LUONGO, Roberto	6-3	175	L	Montreal, Que.	4/4/79	NY Islanders-Lowell
SHULMISTRA, Richard	6-2	185	R	Sudbury, Ont.	4/1/71	Florida-Louisville-Orlando

General Managers' History

Bob Clarke, 1993-94; Bryan Murray, 1994-95 to date.

General Manager

MURRAY, BRYAN CLARENCE
Vice President and General Manager, Florida Panthers.
Born in Shawville, Que., December 5, 1942.

Bryan Murray is entering his seventh season as vice president and general manager of the Panthers. Bryan hired his brother, Terry, as head coach prior to the 1998-99 season and, on January 17, 1999, orchestrated the biggest trade in franchise history when he acquired All-Star wing Pavel Bure from the Vancouver Canucks in a multiplayer deal.

Before joining the Panthers, he served as coach and general manager of the Detroit Red Wings from 1990-93 and as general manager during the 1993-94 campaign. In 328 games under Murray's control, the Wings won a total of 170 games, while losing 121 and tying 37, an average of 43 wins and 94 points a season. Bryan left his mark in the NHL record book as a coach with a career record of 484-368-123 (.559 winning pct.) in 975 regular-season games, placing him seventh on the all-time victory list.

Murray broke into the NHL coaching ranks with the Washington Capitals on November 11, 1981. He spent the next 8½ seasons with the Caps and earned the Jack Adams Award as the NHL's coach of the year in 1983-84. In 1988-89, he led the Capitals to the Patrick Division title, but on January 15, 1990, Bryan was replaced by his brother, Terry.

Born in Shawville, Quebec on Dec. 5, 1942, Bryan is a graduate of McGill University in Montreal. He spent four years as athletic director and hockey coach at the school before leaving to coach the Regina Pats to a WHL title in 1979-80. Bryan moved up to the Hershey Bears (AHL) the following season and was named *The Hockey News'* minor league coach of the year after guiding that team to its best record in 40 years.

Bryan and his wife, Geri, have two daughters, Heide and Brittany.

1999-2000 Scoring

* – rookie

Regular Season

Pos	#	Player	Team	GP	G	A	Pts	+/–	PIM	PP	SH	GW	GT	S	%
R	10	Pavel Bure	FLA	74	58	36	94	25	16	11	2	14	0	360	16.1
C	14	Ray Whitney	FLA	81	29	42	71	16	35	5	0	3	2	198	14.6
C	25	Viktor Kozlov	FLA	80	17	53	70	24	16	6	0	2	0	223	7.6
C	16	Mike Sillinger	T.B	67	19	25	44	–29	86	6	3	1	0	126	15.1
			FLA	13	4	4	8	–1	16	2	0	1	0	20	20.0
			TOTAL	80	23	29	52	–30	102	8	3	2	0	146	15.8
D	24	Robert Svehla	FLA	82	9	40	49	23	64	3	0	1	0	143	6.3
R	27	Scott Mellanby	FLA	77	18	28	46	14	126	6	0	2	1	134	13.4
R	21	Mark Parrish	FLA	81	26	18	44	1	39	6	0	3	0	152	17.1
D	28	Jaroslav Spacek	FLA	82	10	26	36	7	53	4	0	1	0	111	9.0
C	44	Rob Niedermayer	FLA	81	10	23	33	–5	46	1	0	4	0	135	7.4
D	4	Bret Hedican	FLA	76	6	19	25	4	68	2	0	1	0	58	10.3
L	13	Oleg Kvasha	FLA	78	5	20	25	3	34	2	0	0	0	110	4.5
C	9	Len Barrie	L.A	46	5	8	13	5	56	0	0	0	0	46	10.9
			FLA	14	4	6	10	4	6	0	0	0	0	15	26.7
			TOTAL	60	9	14	23	9	62	0	0	0	0	61	14.8
R	26	Ray Sheppard	FLA	47	10	10	20	–4	4	5	0	2	0	74	13.5
D	7	Mike Wilson	FLA	60	4	16	20	10	35	0	0	2	0	65	6.2
L	18	Cameron Stewart	FLA	65	9	7	16	–2	30	0	0	3	0	52	17.3
D	3	Paul Laus	FLA	77	3	8	11	–1	172	0	0	0	0	44	6.8
L	8	Peter Worrell	FLA	48	3	6	9	–7	169	2	0	1	0	45	6.7
D	2	Lance Pitlick	FLA	62	3	5	8	7	44	0	0	1	0	26	11.5
D	22	Todd Simpson	FLA	82	1	6	7	5	202	0	0	0	0	50	2.0
D	5 *	Filip Kuba	FLA	13	1	5	6	–3	2	1	0	1	0	16	6.3
R	16 *	Ivan Novoseltsev	FLA	14	2	1	3	–3	8	2	0	0	0	8	25.0
L	12	Alex Hicks	FLA	8	1	2	3	3	4	0	0	0	0	6	16.7
D	6 *	Dan Boyle	FLA	13	0	3	3	–2	4	0	0	0	0	9	0.0
G	30	Mikhail Shtalenkov	PHX	15	0	3	3	0	2	0	0	0	0	0	0.0
			FLA	15	0	0	0	0	2	0	0	0	0	0	0.0
			TOTAL	30	0	3	3	0	4	0	0	0	0	0	0.0
G	29	Mike Vernon	S.J	15	0	0	0	0	0	0	0	0	0	0	0.0
			FLA	34	0	3	3	0	2	0	0	0	0	0	0.0
			TOTAL	49	0	3	3	0	2	0	0	0	0	0	0.0
L	48 *	Marcus Nilson	FLA	9	0	2	2	2	2	0	0	0	0	6	0.0
D	45 *	Brad Ference	FLA	13	0	2	2	2	46	0	0	0	0	10	0.0
G	32	Rich Shulmistra	FLA	1	0	0	0	0	0	0	0	0	0	0	0.0
L	48 *	Dave Duerden	FLA	2	0	0	0	0	0	0	0	0	0	1	0.0
C	47	Craig Ferguson	FLA	3	0	0	0	–2	0	0	0	0	0	2	0.0
C	40 *	Eric Boguniecki	FLA	4	0	0	0	–1	2	0	0	0	0	5	0.0
C	23	Chris Wells	FLA	13	0	0	0	–5	14	0	0	0	0	5	0.0
D	15 *	John Jakopin	FLA	17	0	0	0	–2	26	0	0	0	0	1	0.0
G	37	Trevor Kidd	FLA	28	0	0	0	0	0	0	0	0	0	0	0.0

Goaltending

No.	Goaltender	GPI	Mins	Avg	W	L	T	EN	SO	GA	SA	S%
32	Rich Shulmistra	1	60	1.00	1	0	0	0	0	1	21	.952
30	Mikhail Shtalenkov	15	882	2.31	8	4	2	0	0	34	369	.908
29	Mike Vernon	34	2019	2.47	18	13	2	2	1	83	1020	.919
1	Sean Burke	7	418	2.58	2	5	0	2	0	18	208	.913
37	Trevor Kidd	28	1574	2.63	14	11	2	0	1	69	809	.915
	Totals	**82**	**4966**	**2.53**	**43**	**33**	**6**	**4**	**2**	**209**	**2431**	**.914**

Playoffs

Pos	#	Player	Team	GP	G	A	Pts	+/–	PIM	PP	SH	GW	OT	S	%
R	10	Pavel Bure	FLA	4	1	3	4	–3	2	1	0	0	0	15	6.7
C	16	Mike Sillinger	FLA	4	2	1	3	–1	2	0	0	0	0	7	28.6
C	14	Ray Whitney	FLA	4	1	0	1	–2	4	0	0	0	0	17	5.9
C	44	Rob Niedermayer	FLA	4	1	0	1	–1	6	0	0	0	0	5	20.0
L	8	Peter Worrell	FLA	4	1	0	1	–2	8	0	0	0	0	6	16.7
R	27	Scott Mellanby	FLA	4	0	1	1	0	2	0	0	0	0	4	0.0
D	2	Lance Pitlick	FLA	4	0	1	1	0	0	0	0	0	0	2	0.0
D	24	Robert Svehla	FLA	4	0	1	1	0	4	0	0	0	0	4	0.0
L	12	Alex Hicks	FLA	4	0	1	1	–1	4	0	0	0	0	4	0.0
C	25	Viktor Kozlov	FLA	4	0	1	1	–3	0	0	0	0	0	6	0.0
R	21	Mark Parrish	FLA	4	0	1	1	–2	0	0	0	0	0	5	0.0
C	9	Len Barrie	FLA	4	0	0	0	–1	0	0	0	0	0	3	0.0
G	29	Mike Vernon	FLA	4	0	0	0	0	10	0	0	0	0	0	0.0
D	4	Bret Hedican	FLA	4	0	0	0	1	0	0	0	0	0	5	0.0
D	3	Paul Laus	FLA	4	0	0	0	0	8	0	0	0	0	5	0.0
D	7	Mike Wilson	FLA	4	0	0	0	–5	0	0	0	0	0	1	0.0
D	22	Todd Simpson	FLA	4	0	0	0	–4	4	0	0	0	0	2	0.0
L	13	Oleg Kvasha	FLA	4	0	0	0	0	0	0	0	0	0	6	0.0
D	28	Jaroslav Spacek	FLA	4	0	0	0	–1	0	0	0	0	0	7	0.0

Goaltending

No.	Goaltender	GPI	Mins	Avg	W	L	EN	SO	GA	SA	S%
29	Mike Vernon	4	237	3.04	0	4	0	0	12	136	.912
	Totals	**4**	**240**	**3.00**	**0**	**4**	**0**	**0**	**12**	**136**	**.912**

NHL Coaching Record

		Regular Season					Playoffs			
Season	Team	Games	W	L	T	%	Games	W	L	%
1981-82	Washington	76	25	28	13	.477	....	....	....	....
1982-83	Washington	80	39	25	16	.588	4	1	3	.250
1983-84	Washington	80	48	27	5	.631	8	4	4	.500
1984-85	Washington	80	46	25	9	.631	5	2	3	.400
1985-86	Washington	80	50	23	7	.669	9	5	4	.556
1986-87	Washington	80	38	32	10	.538	7	3	4	.429
1987-88	Washington	80	38	33	9	.531	14	7	7	.500
1988-89	Washington	80	41	29	10	.575	6	2	4	.333
1989-90	Washington	46	18	24	4	.435	....	....	....	....
1990-91	Detroit	80	34	38	8	.475	7	3	4	.429
1991-92	Detroit	80	43	25	12	.613	11	4	7	.364
1992-93	Detroit	84	47	28	9	.613	7	3	4	.429
1997-98	Florida	59	17	31	11	.381	....	....	....	....
	NHL Totals	**975**	**484**	**368**	**123**	**.559**	**78**	**34**	**44**	**.436**

Club Records

Team

(Figures in brackets for season records are games played; records for fewest points, wins, ties, losses, goals, goals against are for 70 or more games)

Most Points 98 1999-2000 (82)
Most Wins 43 1999-2000 (82)
Most Ties 19 1996-97 (82)
Most Losses 43 1997-98 (82)
Most Goals 254 1995-96 (82)
Most Goals Against 256 1997-98 (82)
Fewest Points 63 1997-98 (82)
Fewest Wins 24 1997-98 (82)
Fewest Ties 6 1999-2000 (82)
Fewest Losses 28 1996-97 (82)
Fewest Goals 203 1997-98 (82)
Fewest Goals Against 201 1996-97 (82)

Longest Winning Streak
Overall .... 7 Nov. 2-14/95
Home .... 5 Nov. 5-14/95
Away .... 4 Dec. 2-12/95, Nov. 13-Dec 1/96, Oct. 25-Nov. 22/97

Longest Undefeated Streak
Overall .... 12 Oct. 5-30/96 (8 wins, 4 ties)
Home .... 8 Nov. 5-26/95 (7 wins, 1 tie)
Away .... 7 Twice

Longest Losing Streak
Overall .... 13 Feb. 7-Mar. 23/98
Home .... 6 Feb. 25-Mar. 23/98
Away .... 7 Feb. 7-Mar. 21/98

Longest Winless Streak
Overall .... 15 Feb. 1-Mar. 23/98 (14 losses, 1 tie)
Home .... 8 Feb. 1-Mar. 23/98 (7 losses, 1 tie)
Away .... 16 Jan. 2-Mar. 21/98 (12 losses, 4 ties)

Most Shutouts, Season 6 1994-95 (48)
Most PIM, Season 1,676 1997-98 (82)
Most Goals, Game .... 10 Nov. 26/97 (Bos. 5 at Fla. 10)

Individual

Most Seasons .... 7 Scott Mellanby, Paul Laus, Rob Niedermayer
Most Games .... 512 Scott Mellanby
Most Goals, Career .... 153 Scott Mellanby
Most Assists, Career ..... 188 Scott Mellanby
Most Points, Career ...... 341 Scott Mellanby (153g, 188a)
Most PIM, Career .... 1,479 Paul Laus
Most Shutouts, Career .... 13 John Vanbiesbrouck

Longest Consecutive
Games Streak .... 221 Robert Svehla (Oct. 13/95-Mar. 4/98)

Most Goals, Season .... 58 Pavel Bure (1999-2000)
Most Assists, Season ..... 53 Viktor Kozlov (1999-2000)
Most Points, Season ...... 94 Pavel Bure (1999-2000; 58g, 36a)
Most PIM, Season .... 313 Paul Laus (1996-97)
Most Shutouts, Season .... 4 John Vanbiesbrouck (1994-95, 1997-98)

Most Points, Defenseman,
Season .... 57 Robert Svehla (1995-96; 8g, 49a)

Most Points, Center,
Season .... 70 Viktor Kozlov (1999-2000; 17g, 53a)

Most Points, Right Wing,
Season .... 94 Pavel Bure (1999-2000; 58g, 36a)

Most Points, Left Wing,
Season .... 71 Ray Whitney (1999-2000; 29g, 42a)

Most Points, Rookie,
Season .... 50 Jesse Belanger (1993-94; 17g, 33a)

Most Goals, Game .... 4 Mark Parrish (Oct. 30/98); Pavel Bure (Jan. 1/00)

Most Assists, Game .... 4 Scott Mellanby (Nov. 26/97)

Most Points, Game .... 4 Eight times

Coaching History

Roger Neilson, 1993-94, 1994-95; Doug MacLean, 1995-96, 1996-97; Doug MacLean and Bryan Murray, 1997-98; Terry Murray, 1998-99 to date.

Captains' History

Brian Skrudland, 1993-94 to 1996-97; Scott Mellanby, 1997-98 to date.

All-time Record vs. Other Clubs

Regular Season

	At Home							On Road							Total						
	GP	W	L	T	GF	GA	PTS	GP	W	L	T	GF	GA	PTS	GP	W	L	T	GF	GA	PTS
Anaheim	5	2	1	2	13	13	6	6	4	2	0	22	19	8	11	6	3	2	35	32	14
Atlanta	3	2	0	1	10	4	5	2	0	1	1	4	5	1	5	2	1	2	14	9	6
Boston	13	6	7	0	40	39	12	14	7	4	3	41	34	17	27	13	11	3	81	73	29
Buffalo	13	7	6	0	38	40	14	15	3	10	2	24	50	9	28	10	16	2	62	90	23
Calgary	6	2	4	0	12	16	5	6	3	2	1	17	14	7	12	5	6	1	29	30	12
Carolina	15	6	4	5	43	30	18	15	7	7	1	44	46	16	30	13	11	6	87	76	34
Chicago	6	2	4	0	16	25	4	6	3	2	1	23	18	7	12	5	6	1	39	43	11
Colorado	8	1	7	0	22	35	2	8	3	2	3	21	20	9	16	4	9	3	43	55	11
Dallas	6	2	3	1	17	21	5	6	1	3	2	16	21	4	12	3	6	3	33	42	9
Detroit	6	1	3	2	13	19	4	5	1	3	1	15	21	3	11	2	6	3	28	40	7
Edmonton	6	4	1	1	17	14	9	5	5	2	1	12	14	5	11	6	3	2	29	28	14
Los Angeles	6	3	0	3	18	9	9	6	2	4	0 .	19	19	4	12	5	4	3	37	28	13
Montreal	14	8	4	2	48	36	18	13	6	6	1	30	39	13	27	14	10	3	78	75	31
Nashville	2	2	0	0	7	3	4	2	2	0	0	5	2	4	4	4	0	0	12	5	8
New Jersey	17	7	6	4	43	39	18	16	4	9	3	30	45	11	15	7	15	7	73	84	30
NY Islanders	17	10	4	3	56	44	23	17	9	6	2	45	41	20	34	19	10	5	101	85	43
NY Rangers	17	8	8	1	46	46	17	16	6	6	4	42	45	16	33	14	14	5	88	91	33
Ottawa	14	8	5	1	49	41	17	14	7	5	2	41	36	16	28	15	10	3	90	77	33
Philadelphia	16	5	11	0	42	55	10	17	6	7	4	39	39	16	33	11	18	4	81	94	26
Phoenix	5	2	3	0	17	13	4	7	3	2	2	22	16	8	12	5	5	2	39	29	12
Pittsburgh	14	7	7	0	36	33	14	15	3	10	2	40	56	8	29	10	17	2	76	89	22
St. Louis	6	1	3	2	13	16	4	6	1	4	1	9	16	3	12	2	7	3	22	32	7
San Jose	6	2	0	4	17	11	8	6	2	2	2	16	14	6	12	4	2	6	33	25	14
Tampa Bay	17	12	2	3	53	29	27	18	10	4	4	54	37	24	35	22	6	7	107	66	51
Toronto	9	3	3	3	28	25	9	7	1	6	0	16	29	2	16	4	9	3	44	54	11
Vancouver	6	3	2	1	16	18	7	6	2	3	1	13	18	5	12	5	5	2	29	36	12
Washington	18	8	8	2	47	50	18	17	5	8	4	43	50	11	35	13	16	6	90	100	33
Totals	271	124	106	41	777	724	291	271	102	119	50	703	764	258	542	226	225	91	1480	1488	549

Playoffs

	Series	W	L	GP	W	L	T	GF	GA
Boston	1	1	0	5	4	1	0	22	16
Colorado	1	0	1	4	0	4	0	4	15
New Jersey	1	0	1	4	0	4	0	6	12
NY Rangers	1	0	1	5	1	4	0	10	13
Philadelphia	1	1	0	6	4	2	0	15	11
Pittsburgh	1	1	0	7	4	3	0	20	15
Totals	6	3	3	31	13	18	0	77	82

Playoff Results 2000-1996

Year	Round	Opponent	Result	GF	GA
2000	CQF	New Jersey	L 0-4	6	12
1997	CQF	NY Rangers	L 1-4	10	13
1996	F	Colorado	L 0-4	4	15
	CF	Pittsburgh	W 4-3	20	15
	CSF	Philadelphia	W 4-2	15	11
	CQF	Boston	W 4-1	22	16

Abbreviations: Round: F – Final;
CF – conference final; CSF – conference semi-final;
CQF – conference quarter-final.

Colorado totals include Quebec, 1993-94 to 1994-95.
Phoenix totals include Winnipeg, 1993-94 to 1995-96.

Carolina totals include Hartford, 1993-94 to 1996-97.

Last Mtg. / Round / Result column (Playoffs)

Last Mtg.	Round	Result
1996	CQF	W 4-1
1996	F	L 0-4
2000	CQF	L 0-4
1997	CQF	L 1-4
1996	CSF	W 4-2
1996	CF	W 4-3

1999-2000 Results

Oct.	2	Washington	4-3		14		Carolina	5-1
	6	Los Angeles	4-2		15	at	Tampa Bay	5-2
	9	Detroit	2-2		17		Philadelphia	3-1
	12	at Montreal	2-1		19		Washington	1-3
	13	at Toronto	2-3		21	at	Atlanta	3-3
	16	Anaheim	3-2 *		22		Boston	4-3 *
	20	Vancouver	5-2		26		New Jersey	2-3
	22	Calgary	2-3 *		27	at	Philadelphia	2-4
	24	at Philadelphia	0-2		29		Edmonton	2-1
	27	NY Islanders	6-3	Feb.	1	at	Carolina	2-4
	29	at Buffalo	2-3 *		2		Montreal	3-1
	30	at Ottawa	0-5		9		San Jose	4-1
Nov.	3	at Edmonton	2-2		11	at	Ottawa	3-5
	5	at Vancouver	2-3		12	at	Boston	5-1
	6	at Calgary	6-3		14	at	Montreal	1-4
	10	Atlanta	4-1		16		NY Rangers	3-0
	13	Buffalo	3-1		19		Pittsburgh	1-2
	17	at Colorado	2-1		21		Ottawa	2-4
	18	at St. Louis	0-3		23	at	Washington	2-3 *
	20	Pittsburgh	2-1 *		24	at	Carolina	2-4
	24	Philadelphia	1-6		26		Carolina	1-2 *
	26	NY Rangers	6-2		28		Buffalo	2-5
	27	Atlanta	3-0	Mar.	1		Toronto	3-1
Dec.	3	at Atlanta	1-2		3	at	NY Rangers	2-4
	4	Washington	2-1		4		St. Louis	1-1
	8	at Phoenix	6-1		7	at	Washington	2-4
	10	at Dallas	3-4		10	at	Tampa Bay	4-3
	11	at Nashville	4-2		11		Chicago	2-5
	15	Nashville	3-2		16	at	Pittsburgh	2-4
	17	at Buffalo	4-2		18	at	NY Islanders	4-2
	18	at Pittsburgh	5-2		19	at	New Jersey	2-5
	20	Toronto	4-6		21	at	NY Rangers	4-3
	22	Atlanta	3-3		23	at	Boston	3-1
	26	at Carolina	3-4 *		25		Montreal	4-2
	27	at Tampa Bay	6-1		29		Dallas	1-4
	30	at Chicago	1-2		31		Ottawa	3-1
Jan.	1	Tampa Bay	7-5	Apr.	1		Tampa Bay	1-3
	5	at Anaheim	5-1		3		New Jersey	5-2
	6	at Los Angeles	2-4		5		Boston	6-3
	8	at San Jose	4-2		8	at	New Jersey	1-2 *
	12	NY Islanders	4-3		9	at	NY Islanders	2-3

* – Overtime

Entry Draft
Selections 2000-1993

2000
Pick
- 58 Vladimir Sapozhnikov
- 77 Robert Fried
- 82 Sean O'Connor
- 115 Chris Eade
- 120 Davis Parley
- 190 Josh Olson
- 234 Janis Sprukts
- 253 Mathew Sommerfeld

1999
Pick
- 12 Denis Shvidki
- 40 Alexander Auld
- 70 Niklas Hagman
- 80 Jean-Francois Laniel
- 103 Morgan McCormick
- 109 Rod Sarich
- 169 Brad Woods
- 198 Travis Eagles
- 227 Jonathon Charron

1998
Pick
- 30 Kyle Rossiter
- 61 Joe DiPenta
- 63 Lance Ward
- 89 Ryan Jardine
- 117 Jaroslav Spacek
- 148 Chris Ovington
- 176 B.J. Ketcheson
- 203 Ian Jacobs
- 231 Adrian Wichser

1997
Pick
- 20 Mike Brown
- 47 Kristian Huselius
- 56 Vratislav Cech
- 74 Nick Smith
- 95 Ivan Novoseltsev
- 127 Pat Parthenais
- 155 Keith Delaney
- 183 Tyler Palmer
- 211 Doug Schueller
- 237 Benoit Cote

1996
Pick
- 20 Marcus Nilson
- 60 Chris Allen
- 65 Oleg Kvasha
- 82 Joey Tetarenko
- 129 Andrew Long
- 156 Gaetan Poirier
- 183 Alexandre Couture
- 209 Denis Khloptonov
- 235 Russell Smith

1995
Pick
- 10 Radek Dvorak
- 36 Aaron MacDonald
- 62 Mike O'Grady
- 80 Dave Duerden
- 88 Daniel Tjarnqvist
- 114 Francois Cloutier
- 166 Peter Worrell
- 192 Filip Kuba
- 218 David Lemanowicz

1994
Pick
- 1 Ed Jovanovski
- 27 Rhett Warrener
- 31 Jason Podollan
- 36 Ryan Johnson
- 84 David Nemirovsky
- 105 Dave Geris
- 157 Matt O'Dette
- 183 Jason Boudrias
- 235 Tero Lehtera
- 261 Per Gustafsson

1993
Pick
- 5 Rob Niedermayer
- 41 Kevin Weekes
- 57 Chris Armstrong
- 67 Mikael Tjallden
- 78 Steve Washburn
- 83 Bill McCauley
- 109 Todd MacDonald
- 135 Alain Nasreddine
- 161 Trevor Doyle
- 187 Briane Thompson
- 213 Chad Cabana
- 239 John Demarco
- 265 Eric Montreuil

Coach

MURRAY, TERRY RODNEY
Coach, Florida Panthers. Born in Shawville, Que., July 20, 1950.

Florida vice president and general manager Bryan Murray appointed his brother Terry Murray to the Panthers coaching position on June 21, 1998. Terry is the fourth coach in franchise history, taking over from his brother who served on an interim basis after taking over from Doug MacLean during the 1997-98 season. Terry previously took over the coaching reigns from Bryan when he replaced him as bench boss with the Washington Capitals during the 1989-90 campaign.

Terry Murray coached the Panthers to a franchise-best 43 wins and 98 points in 1999-2000. The club finished second in the Southeast Conference standings and returned to the playoffs for the first time since 1997.

Murray was named head coach of the Philadelphia Flyers on June 23, 1994 and coached the team for three seasons. He compiled a record of 118-64-30 and won two Atlantic Division titles. Murray was a finalist for the Jack Adams Award as coach of the year following the 1994-95 season and guided the Flyers to the Stanley Cup finals in 1997. His playoff winning percentage of .609 in Philadelphia is better than Fred Shero (.578), Pat Quinn (.564) or Mike Keenan (.561).

Terry replaced Bryan as coach of the Capitals back on January 15, 1990. In his first full season behind the bench in 1990-91, he led Washington to the Wales Conference finals for the first time in club history. During his tenure with the Capitals, Murray had a record of 163-134-28. In between his coaching stints in Washington and Philadelphia, he served briefly as coach of the Panthers' International Hockey League affiliate in Cincinnati. Murray had a record of 17-7-4 in 28 games with the Cyclones to close out the 1993-94 season and guide them to a second-place finish in the IHL's Central Division.

Over a 12-year professional playing career, Terry Murray appeared in 302 NHL regular-season games with the California Golden Seals, Philadelphia Flyers, Detroit Red Wings and Washington Capitals. He had four goals and 76 assists for 80 points and had 199 penalty minutes. Terry and his wife Linda have two daughters, Megan and Lindsey.

Coaching Record

Season	Team	Regular Season					Playoffs			
		Games	W	L	T	%	Games	W	L	%
1988-89	Baltimore (AHL)	80	30	46	4	.400	....	....	....	....
1989-90	Baltimore (AHL)	44	26	17	1	.603	....	....	....	....
1989-90	**Washington (NHL)**	34	18	14	2	.559	15	8	7	.533
1990-91	**Washington (NHL)**	80	37	36	7	.506	11	5	6	.455
1991-92	**Washington (NHL)**	80	45	27	8	.613	7	3	4	.429
1992-93	**Washington (NHL)**	84	43	34	7	.554	6	2	4	.333
1993-94	**Washington (NHL)**	47	20	23	4	.468	....	....	....	....
	Cincinnati (IHL)	28	17	7	4	.679	11	6	5	.545
1994-95	**Philadelphia (NHL)**	48	28	16	4	.625	15	10	5	.667
1995-96	**Philadelphia (NHL)**	82	45	24	13	.628	12	6	6	.500
1996-97	**Philadelphia (NHL)**	82	45	24	13	.628	19	12	7	.632
1998-99	**Florida (NHL)**	82	30	34	18	.476	....	....	....	....
1999-2000	**Florida (NHL)**	82	43	33	6	.598•	4	0	4	.000
	NHL Totals	701	354	265	82	.568•	89	46	43	.517

• Includes points from regulation ties

Club Directory

National Car Rental Center

Florida Panthers
National Car Rental Center
One Panthers Parkway
Sunrise, FL 33323
Phone **954/835-7000**
FAX 954/835-7600
Website: www.flpanthers.com
Capacity: 19,200

Chairman and Chief Executive Officer . . . . H. Wayne Huizenga
Vice Chairman & President . . . . Richard C. Rochon
Senior Vice President . . . . Alex Muxo

Executive
President and Governor . . . . William A. Torrey
Senior Vice President . . . . Steve Dangerfield
Vice President and General Manager . . . . Bryan Murray
Vice President of Corporate Sales and Client Services . Kimberly Terranova Sciarretta
Executive Assistants to President . . . . Deanna Cocozzelli, Cathy Stevenson
Executive Assistant to Senior Vice President . . . . . . Janine Shea
Executive Assistant to Vice President and
   General Manager . . . . Vanessa Rey
Executive Assistant to Vice President of
   Corporate Sales . . . . Susan Ferro

Hockey Operations
Assistant General Manager . . . . Chuck Fletcher
Head Coach . . . . Terry Murray
Assistant Coaches . . . . Slavomir Lener, Bill Smith
Director of Professional Player Evaluation . . . . Michael Abbamont
Pro Scout . . . . Duane Sutter
Director of Amateur Player Relations . . . . Tim Murray
Amateur Scouts . . . . Billy Dea, Ron Harris, Todd Hearty, Wayne
   Meier, Marty Nanne, Sean O'Brien
Chief European Scout . . . . Pavel Routa
Scouting and Video Coordinator . . . . Brent Flahr
Head Medical Trainer . . . . Stan Wong
Strength and Conditioning Coach . . . . Ian Pyka
Head Equipment Manager . . . . Mark Brennan
Associate Equipment Manager . . . . Scott Tinkler
Equipment Staff . . . . Jon Korman
Team Services Coordinator . . . . Marni Share
Internist . . . . Charles Posternack, M.D.
Orthopedic Surgeon . . . . Jeffrey Minkoff, M.D.
Assistant Orthopedist . . . . Steve Stecker, M.D.
Massage Therapist . . . . Mikhail Manchik
Team Cardiologist . . . . Howard Bush, M.D.
Plastic Surgeon . . . . Harry K. Moon, M.D.
Team Dentist . . . . Martin Robins, D.D.S.

Communications Department
Director of Broadcasting and Communications . . . . Mike Hanson
Media Relations Manager . . . . Randy Sieminski
Community Development Manager . . . . Hillary Reynolds
Communications/Publications Coordinator . . . . Michael Citro
Communications Coordinator . . . . Mary Lou Veroline
Administrative Assistant,
   Communications Department . . . . Giselle Seoane

Corporate Sales and Client Services Department
Director of Client Services . . . . Brette Sadler
Director of Corporate Sales . . . . Chris Trinceri
Retail Sales Manager . . . . Scott Baynes
Corporate Account Manager . . . . Jason Camp

Finance and Administration
Director of Information Technology . . . . Kelly Connor
Director of Finance/Controller . . . . Evelyn Lopez
Office Manager . . . . Laura Barrera
Accounting Manager . . . . Michele Gilbert
Manager of Human Resources/Payroll . . . . Mary Santimaw

Game Presentation/Promotions Department
Director of Game Presentation . . . . Scott Cunningham
Director of Promotions . . . . Ed Krajewski
Game Presentation Producer . . . . Marc Bick
Youth and Amateur Hockey Coordinator . . . . Keith Martin
Promotions Coordinator . . . . Garrison Grund
Special Projects Coordinator . . . . Anthony Van Daley

Merchandise Department
Director of Merchandising . . . . Ron Dennis
Retail Manager . . . . Maria Cocozzelli

Ticket Operations and Sales Department
Director of Group and Season Ticket Sales . . . . Chris Gallagher
Director of Ticket and Game-day Operations . . . . . . Scott Wampold
Director of Suite and Club Level Services . . . . Steve Woznick
Manager of Ticket Operations . . . . Matt Coyne
Managers of Suite and Club Level Services . . . . Kathy Stock, Peter Cameron

General Information
Press Box Phone . . . . (954) 835-7753 fax (954) 835-7750
Television . . . . Fox Sports Net
Television Announcers . . . . Jeff Rimer, Denis Potvin
Radio Flagship . . . . WQAM (560 AM)
Radio Announcers . . . . Jiggs McDonald, Randy Moller, Steve Goldstein

Los Angeles Kings

1999-2000 Results: 39w-31l-12t 94pts. Second, Pacific Division

2000-01 Schedule

Oct.	Fri.	6	at Washington	Sat.	6	Calgary
	Sat.	7	at Buffalo	Thu.	11	Buffalo
	Mon.	9	at Columbus	Sat.	13	St. Louis
	Wed.	11	St. Louis	Tue.	16	at Ottawa
	Fri.	13	Boston	Wed.	17	at Toronto
	Sun.	15	Phoenix*	Sat.	20	at Carolina*
	Tue.	17	at Nashville	Mon.	22	at Philadelphia
	Thu.	19	at St. Louis	Thu.	25	Calgary
	Sat.	21	at Dallas	Sat.	27	Minnesota*
	Mon.	23	at Anaheim	Tue.	30	Dallas
	Wed.	25	Anaheim	**Feb.** Thu.	1	Nashville
	Sat.	28	at Phoenix	Tue.	6	Chicago
	Tue.	31	at Columbus	Thu.	8	Carolina
Nov.	Thu.	2	at Atlanta	Sat.	10	Washington
	Sat.	4	at New Jersey*	Mon.	12	Edmonton
	Sun.	5	at NY Islanders*	Wed.	14	at Dallas
	Tue.	7	Phoenix	Fri.	16	at Minnesota
	Thu.	9	Vancouver	Sun.	18	at Chicago*
	Sat.	11	Detroit	Tue.	20	at Edmonton
	Thu.	16	NY Islanders	Thu.	22	at Calgary
	Sat.	18	Colorado*	Sat.	24	Columbus*
	Thu.	23	New Jersey*	Tue.	27	at Nashville
	Sat.	25	at Pittsburgh	**Mar.** Thu.	1	at Chicago
	Sun.	26	at Boston	Sat.	3	Detroit
	Tue.	28	at NY Rangers	Sun.	4	at Anaheim*
Dec.	Sat.	2	Minnesota	Tue.	6	Montreal
	Sun.	3	at Anaheim*	Thu.	8	Nashville
	Thu.	7	Dallas	Sat.	10	Chicago
	Sat.	9	at Edmonton	Wed.	14	at San Jose
	Sun.	10	at Vancouver	Sat.	17	San Jose*
	Thu.	14	NY Rangers	Mon.	19	Phoenix
	Sat.	16	Tampa Bay	Wed.	21	Edmonton
	Tue.	19	Atlanta	Sat.	24	Anaheim*
	Thu.	21	at Colorado	Mon.	26	San Jose
	Fri.	22	at Minnesota	Tue.	27	at San Jose
	Tue.	26	San Jose	Thu.	29	Columbus
	Thu.	28	at St. Louis	Sat.	31	Colorado*
	Fri.	29	at Dallas	**Apr.** Mon.	2	Vancouver
	Sun.	31	at Detroit	Tue.	3	at Phoenix
Jan.	Tue.	2	at Colorado	Thu.	5	at Vancouver
	Thu.	4	Florida	Sat.	7	at Calgary

* Denotes afternoon game.

Franchise date: June 5, 1967

**PACIFIC
DIVISION**

**34th
NHL
Season**

Originally drafted 171st overall by Los Angeles in 1984, and later re-acquired in 1997, Luc Robitaille's 483 goals in a Kings uniform trail only Marcel Dionne's total of 550. His 991 points are 78 behind Dave Taylor for third spot in team history.

Year-by-Year Record

		Home			Road			Overall							
Season	GP	W	L	T	W	L	T	W	L	T	GF	GA	Pts.	Finished	Playoff Result
1999-2000	82	21	15	5	18	16	7	39	31	12	245	228	94	2nd, Pacific Div.	Lost Conf. Quater-Final
1998-99	82	18	20	3	14	25	2	32	45	5	189	222	69	5th, Pacific Div.	Out of Playoffs
1997-98	82	22	16	3	16	17	8	38	33	11	227	225	87	2nd, Pacific Div.	Lost Conf. Quater-Final
1996-97	82	18	16	7	10	27	4	28	43	11	214	268	67	6th, Pacific Div.	Out of Playoffs
1995-96	82	16	16	9	8	24	9	24	40	18	256	302	66	6th, Pacific Div.	Out of Playoffs
1994-95	48	7	11	6	9	12	3	16	23	9	142	174	41	4th, Pacific Div.	Out of Playoffs
1993-94	84	18	19	5	9	26	7	27	45	12	294	322	66	5th, Pacific Div.	Out of Playoffs
1992-93	84	22	15	5	17	20	5	39	35	10	338	340	88	3rd, Smythe Div.	Lost Final
1991-92	80	20	11	9	15	20	5	35	31	14	287	296	84	2nd, Smythe Div.	Lost Div. Semi-Final
1990-91	80	26	9	5	20	15	5	46	24	10	340	254	102	1st, Smythe Div.	Lost Div. Final
1989-90	80	21	16	3	13	23	4	34	39	7	338	337	75	4th, Smythe Div.	Lost Div. Final
1988-89	80	25	12	3	17	19	4	42	31	7	376	335	91	2nd, Smythe Div.	Lost Div. Final
1987-88	80	19	18	3	11	24	5	30	42	8	318	359	68	4th, Smythe Div.	Lost Div. Semi-Final
1986-87	80	20	17	3	11	24	5	31	41	8	318	341	70	4th, Smythe Div.	Lost Div. Semi-Final
1985-86	80	9	27	4	14	22	4	23	49	8	284	389	54	5th, Smythe Div.	Out of Playoffs
1984-85	80	20	14	6	14	18	8	34	32	14	339	326	82	4th, Smythe Div.	Lost Div. Semi-Final
1983-84	80	13	19	8	10	25	5	23	44	13	309	376	59	5th, Smythe Div.	Out of Playoffs
1982-83	80	20	13	7	7	28	5	27	41	12	308	365	66	5th, Smythe Div.	Out of Playoffs
1981-82	80	19	15	6	5	26	9	24	41	15	314	369	63	4th, Smythe Div.	Lost Div. Final
1980-81	80	22	11	7	21	13	6	43	24	13	337	290	99	2nd, Norris Div.	Lost Prelim. Round
1979-80	80	18	13	9	12	23	5	30	36	14	290	313	74	2nd, Norris Div.	Lost Prelim. Round
1978-79	80	20	13	7	14	21	5	34	34	12	292	286	80	3rd, Norris Div.	Lost Prelim. Round
1977-78	80	18	16	6	13	18	9	31	34	15	243	245	77	3rd, Norris Div.	Lost Prelim. Round
1976-77	80	20	13	7	14	18	8	34	31	15	271	241	83	2nd, Norris Div.	Lost Quarter-Final
1975-76	80	22	13	5	16	20	4	38	33	9	263	265	85	2nd, Norris Div.	Lost Quarter-Final
1974-75	80	22	7	11	20	10	10	42	17	21	269	185	105	2nd, Norris Div.	Lost Prelim. Round
1973-74	78	22	13	4	11	20	8	33	33	12	233	231	78	3rd, West Div.	Lost Quarter-Final
1972-73	78	21	11	7	10	25	4	31	36	11	232	245	73	6th, West Div.	Out of Playoffs
1971-72	78	14	23	2	6	26	7	20	49	9	206	305	49	7th, West Div.	Out of Playoffs
1970-71	78	17	14	8	8	26	5	25	40	13	239	303	63	5th, West Div.	Out of Playoffs
1969-70	76	12	22	4	2	30	6	14	52	10	168	290	38	6th, West Div.	Out of Playoffs
1968-69	76	19	14	5	5	28	5	24	42	10	185	260	58	4th, West Div.	Lost Semi-Final
1967-68	74	20	13	4	11	20	6	31	33	10	200	224	72	2nd, West Div.	Lost Quarter-Final

2000-01 Player Personnel

FORWARDS	HT	WT	S	Place of Birth	Date	1999-00 Club
BELANGER, Eric	6-0	177	L	Sherbrooke, Que.	12/16/77	Lowell
BLAKE, Jason	5-10	185	L	Moorhead, MN	9/2/73	Los Angeles-Long Beach
BRENNAN, Kip	6-4	210	L	Kingston, Ont.	8/27/80	Sudbury Wolves
BUCHBERGER, Kelly	6-2	210	L	Langenburg, Sask.	12/2/66	Atlanta-Los Angeles
CHARTRAND, Brad	5-11	191	L	Winnipeg, Man.	12/14/74	Los Angeles-Lowell-Long Beach
CORKUM, Bob	6-0	222	R	Salisbury, MA	12/18/67	Los Angeles
EMERSON, Nelson	5-11	180	R	Hamilton, Ont.	8/17/67	Atlanta-Los Angeles
GRIMSON, Stu	6-5	227	L	Kamloops, B.C.	5/20/65	Anaheim
HYMOVITZ, David	5-11	191	L	Boston, MA	5/30/73	Lowell-Houston Aeros
JOHNSON, Craig	6-2	200	L	St. Paul, MN	3/8/72	Los Angeles
LAPERRIERE, Ian	6-1	201	R	Montreal, Que.	1/19/74	Los Angeles
LeBOUTILLIER, Peter	6-1	190	R	Minnedosa, Man.	1/11/75	Cincinnati Ducks
MILLER, Nate	6-3	192	L	Anoka, MN	6/3/76	U. of Minnesota
MURRAY, Glen	6-3	225	R	Halifax, N.S.	11/1/72	Los Angeles
PALFFY, Ziggy	5-10	183	L	Skalica, Czech.	5/5/72	Los Angeles
PHILLIPS, Greg	6-2	205	R	Winnipeg, Man.	3/27/78	Lowell
PODOLLAN, Jason	6-1	198	R	Vernon, B.C.	2/18/76	Los Angeles-Lowell
REINPRECHT, Steve	6-0	190	L	Edmonton, AB	5/7/76	U. of Wisconsin-Los Angeles
ROBITAILLE, Luc	6-1	215	L	Montreal, Que.	2/17/66	Los Angeles
SMITHSON, Jerred	6-2	190	R	Vernon, B.C.	2/4/79	Calgary Hitmen
SMOLINSKI, Bryan	6-1	208	R	Toledo, OH	12/27/71	Los Angeles
STUMPEL, Jozef	6-3	225	R	Nitra, Czech.	7/20/72	Los Angeles
VLASAK, Tomas	5-10	175	R	Prague, Czech.	2/1/75	HPK Hameenlinna
DEFENSEMEN						
BERG, Aki	6-3	215	L	Turku, Finland	7/28/77	Los Angeles
BLAKE, Rob	6-4	227	R	Simcoe, Ont.	12/10/69	Los Angeles
BOUCHER, Philippe	6-2	221	R	St. Apollinaire, Que.	3/24/73	Los Angeles-Long Beach
BRENNAN, Rich	6-2	200	R	Schenectady, NY	11/26/72	Lowell
CORVO, Joseph	6-0	205	R	Oak Park, IL	6/20/77	Los Angeles
KARALAHTI, Jere	6-2	210	R	Helsinki, Finland	3/25/75	HIFK Helsinki-L.A.-Long Beach
LILJA, Andreas	6-3	222	L	Landskrona, Sweden	7/13/75	Malmo IF
MODRY, Jaroslav	6-2	215	L	Ceske-Budejovice, Czech.	2/27/71	Los Angeles-Long Beach
NORSTROM, Mattias	6-2	201	L	Stockholm, Sweden	1/2/72	Los Angeles
PUDLICK, Michael	6-3	190	L	Blaine, MN	2/24/78	St. Cloud State
RULLIER, Joe	6-3	200	R	Montreal, Que.	1/28/80	Rimouski Oceanic
SCHNEIDER, Mathieu	5-10	192	L	New York, NY	6/12/69	NY Rangers
SEELEY, Richard	6-2	205	L	Powell River, B.C.	4/30/79	Lowell
VISNOVSKY, Lubomir	5-10	183	L	Topolcany, Czech.	8/11/76	Slovan Bratislava

GOALTENDERS	HT	WT	C	Place of Birth	Date	1999-00 Club
COUSINEAU, Marcel	5-9	183	L	Delson, Que.	4/30/73	Los Angeles-Long Beach
FISET, Stephane	6-1	215	L	Montreal, Que.	6/17/70	Los Angeles
PASSMORE, Steve	5-9	165	L	Thunder Bay, Ont.	1/29/73	Chicago-Cleveland
SCOTT, Travis	6-2	185	L	Kanata, Ont.	9/14/75	Lowell
STORR, Jamie	6-2	195	L	Brampton, Ont.	12/28/75	Los Angeles
VOLKOV, Alexei	6-1	195	L	Yekaterinburg, USSR	3/15/80	Halifax

General Managers' History

Larry Regan, 1967-68 to 1972-73; Larry Regan and Jake Milford, 1973-74; Jake Milford, 1974-75 to 1976-77; George Maguire, 1977-78 to 1982-83; George Maguire and Rogie Vachon, 1983-84; Rogie Vachon, 1984-85 to 1991-92; Nick Beverley, 1992-93, 1993-94; Sam McMaster, 1994-95 to 1996-97; Dave Taylor, 1997-98 to date.

General Manager

TAYLOR, DAVE
General Manager, Los Angeles Kings. Born in Levack, Ont., December 4, 1955.

No player in the history of the Kings ever wore the uniform with more distinction and class than Dave Taylor. For 17 seasons, Taylor gave his all, both on and off the ice, receiving All-Star status for his outstanding play.

Fittingly, after finishing his illustrious career during the 1993-94 season, Taylor remains a key part of the Kings organization, now serving as vice president and general manager for the NHL club. Taylor assumed his current responsibilities on April 22, 1997, becoming the seventh GM in team history. He joined the Kings front office four years earlier as an assistant to his predecessor, Sam McMaster.

An All-American hockey player while at Clarkson College, Taylor was relatively unknown when the Kings picked him in the 15th round of the 1975 draft. His grit and work ethic kept him around long enough to hook up with a center named Marcel Dionne, who virtually ignited Taylor's career. As a member of the renowned Triple Crown line with Dionne and left winger Charlie Simmer, Taylor became a prolific scorer and a fearsome checker. Taylor's NHL career stats include a Kings-record 1,111 games, 431 goals, 638 assists and 1,069 points.

A five-time NHL All-Star Game selection, Taylor served as the Kings captain for four seasons (1985-89). After posting career highs in goals (47) and points (112) during the 1980-81 season, Taylor earned a spot on the NHL Second All-Star Team. On April 3, 1995, Taylor's jersey No. 18 was retired, joining Rogie Vachon (No. 30) and Marcel Dionne (No. 16). For all his individual accomplishments in hockey, his crowning glory was reaching the Stanley Cup Finals with the 1992-93 Kings.

Away from the ice, Taylor has worked tirelessly for numerous charities throughout the years. Each year he hosts the Dave Taylor Golf Classic benefiting the Cystic Fibrosis Foundation, which annually raises more than $125,000. In 1991, the NHL honored Taylor's contributions to hockey and the community by awarding him both the Bill Masterton and King Clancy trophies.

Dave and his wife, Beth, live in Tarzana, CA with their daughters Jamie and Katie.

1999-2000 Scoring

* – rookie

Regular Season

Pos	#	Player	Team	GP	G	A	Pts	+/–	PIM	PP	SH	GW	GT	S	%
L	20	Luc Robitaille	L.A.	71	36	38	74	11	68	13	0	7	0	221	16.3
R	33	Zigmund Palffy	L.A.	64	27	39	66	18	32	4	0	3	1	186	14.5
R	27	Glen Murray	L.A.	78	29	33	62	13	60	10	1	2	1	202	14.4
C	15	Jozef Stumpel	L.A.	57	17	41	58	23	10	3	0	7	1	126	13.5
D	4	Rob Blake	L.A.	77	18	39	57	10	112	12	0	5	0	327	5.5
C	21	Bryan Smolinski	L.A.	79	20	36	56	2	48	2	0	0	2	160	12.5
R	17	Nelson Emerson	ATL	58	14	19	33	–24	47	4	0	0	1	183	7.7
			L.A	5	1	1	2	1	0	0	0	0	0	13	7.7
			TOTAL	63	15	20	35	–23	47	4	0	0	1	196	7.7
D	3	Garry Galley	L.A.	70	9	21	30	9	52	2	0	1	0	96	9.4
L	23	Craig Johnson	L.A.	76	9	14	23	–10	28	1	0	1	0	106	8.5
C	11	Jason Blake	L.A.	64	5	18	23	4	26	0	0	1	0	131	3.8
C	22	Ian Laperriere	L.A.	79	9	13	22	–14	185	0	0	1	0	87	10.3
R	9	Kelly Buchberger	ATL	68	5	12	17	–34	139	0	0	0	0	56	8.9
			L.A	13	2	1	3	–2	13	0	0	0	0	20	10.0
			TOTAL	81	7	13	20	–36	152	0	0	0	0	76	9.2
R	12	Marko Tuomainen	L.A.	63	9	8	17	–12	80	2	1	1	0	74	12.2
D	8	* Jere Karalahti	L.A.	48	6	10	16	3	18	4	0	1	0	69	8.7
D	5	Aki Berg	L.A.	70	3	13	16	–1	45	0	0	0	0	70	4.3
D	6	Sean O'Donnell	L.A.	80	2	12	14	4	114	0	0	1	0	51	3.9
D	14	Mattias Norstrom	L.A.	82	1	13	14	22	66	0	0	0	0	62	1.6
R	29	* Brad Chartrand	L.A.	50	6	6	12	4	17	0	1	3	0	51	11.8
C	19	Bob Corkum	L.A.	45	5	6	11	0	14	0	0	0	0	45	11.1
D	44	Jaroslav Modry	L.A.	26	5	4	9	–2	18	5	0	1	1	32	15.6
L	42	Dan Bylsma	L.A.	64	3	6	9	–2	55	0	1	0	0	43	7.0
L	7	Steve McKenna	L.A.	46	0	5	5	3	125	0	0	0	0	14	0.0
G	35	Stephane Fiset	L.A.	47	0	2	2	0	4	0	0	0	0	0	0.0
C	37	Jason Podollan	L.A.	1	0	1	1	0	2	0	0	0	0	2	0.0
G	1	Jamie Storr	L.A.	42	0	1	1	0	4	0	0	0	0	0	0.0
L	28	Bill Huard	L.A.	1	0	0	0	0	2	0	0	0	0	0	0.0
D	43	Philippe Boucher	L.A.	1	0	0	0	0	0	0	0	0	0	3	0.0
D	54	* Jan Nemecek	L.A.	1	0	0	0	0	0	0	0	0	0	0	0.0
C	28	* Steven Reinprecht	L.A.	1	0	0	0	0	2	0	0	0	0	0	0.0
R	55	Pavel Rosa	L.A.	3	0	0	0	–1	0	0	0	0	0	1	0.0
G	34	Marcel Cousineau	L.A.	5	0	0	0	0	0	0	0	0	0	0	0.0

Goaltending

No.	Goaltender	GPI	Mins	Avg	W	L	T	EN	SO	GA	SA	S%
34	Marcel Cousineau	5	171	2.11	1	1	0	0	0	6	64	.906
1	Jamie Storr	42	2206	2.53	18	15	5	5	1	93	1008	.908
35	Stephane Fiset	47	2592	2.75	20	15	7	5	1	119	1208	.901
	Totals	**82**	**4997**	**2.74**	**39**	**31**	**12**	**10**	**2**	**228**	**2290**	**.900**

Playoffs

Pos	#	Player	Team	GP	G	A	Pts	+/–	PIM	PP	SH	GW	GT	S	%
L	20	Luc Robitaille	L.A.	4	2	2	4	–1	6	0	0	0	0	8	25.0
C	15	Jozef Stumpel	L.A.	4	0	4	4	0	8	0	0	0	0	5	0.0
R	33	Zigmund Palffy	L.A.	4	2	0	2	0	0	0	0	0	0	8	25.0
D	4	Rob Blake	L.A.	4	0	2	2	1	4	0	0	0	0	19	0.0
L	23	Craig Johnson	L.A.	4	1	0	1	0	2	0	0	0	0	6	16.7
D	6	Sean O'Donnell	L.A.	4	1	0	1	0	4	0	0	0	0	4	25.0
D	8	* Jere Karalahti	L.A.	4	0	1	1	–3	2	0	0	0	0	5	0.0
R	17	Nelson Emerson	L.A.	1	0	0	0	0	0	0	0	0	0	2	0.0
R	12	Marko Tuomainen	L.A.	1	0	0	0	0	0	0	0	0	0	0	0.0
G	1	Jamie Storr	L.A.	1	0	0	0	0	0	0	0	0	0	0	0.0
D	44	Jaroslav Modry	L.A.	2	0	0	0	0	2	0	0	0	0	2	0.0
D	5	Aki Berg	L.A.	2	0	0	0	0	2	0	0	0	0	5	0.0
L	42	Dan Bylsma	L.A.	3	0	0	0	–1	0	0	0	0	0	2	0.0
C	11	Jason Blake	L.A.	3	0	0	0	0	0	0	0	0	0	9	0.0
R	9	Kelly Buchberger	L.A.	4	0	0	0	–1	4	0	0	0	0	1	0.0
C	19	Bob Corkum	L.A.	4	0	0	0	–1	0	0	0	0	0	2	0.0
G	35	Stephane Fiset	L.A.	4	0	0	0	0	0	0	0	0	0	0	0.0
D	3	Garry Galley	L.A.	4	0	0	0	–2	0	0	0	0	0	9	0.0
C	21	Bryan Smolinski	L.A.	4	0	0	0	–1	2	0	0	0	0	7	0.0
R	27	Glen Murray	L.A.	4	0	0	0	–3	2	0	0	0	0	3	0.0
D	14	Mattias Norstrom	L.A.	4	0	0	0	1	6	0	0	0	0	3	0.0
C	22	Ian Laperriere	L.A.	4	0	0	0	0	2	0	0	0	0	5	0.0
R	29	* Brad Chartrand	L.A.	4	0	0	0	–1	6	0	0	0	0	5	0.0

Goaltending

No.	Goaltender	GPI	Mins	Avg	W	L	EN	SO	GA	SA	S%
35	Stephane Fiset	4	200	3.00	0	3	2	0	10	98	.898
1	Jamie Storr	1	36	3.33	0	1	1	0	2	25	.920
	Totals	**4**	**240**	**3.75**	**0**	**4**	**3**	**0**	**15**	**126**	**.881**

Captains' History

Bob Wall, 1967-68, 1968-69; Larry Cahan, 1969-70, 1970-71; Bob Pulford, 1971-72, 1972-73; Terry Harper, 1973-74, 1974-75; Mike Murphy, 1975-76 to 1980-81; Dave Lewis, 1981-82, 1982-83; Terry Ruskowski, 1983-84, 1984-85; Dave Taylor, 1985-86 to 1988-89; Wayne Gretzky, 1989-90 to 1991-92; Wayne Gretzky and Luc Robitaille, 1992-93; Wayne Gretzky, 1993-94, 1994-95; Wayne Gretzky and Rob Blake, 1995-96; Rob Blake, 1996-97 to date.

Club Records

Team

(Figures in brackets for season records are games played; records for fewest points, wins, ties, losses, goals, goals against are for 70 or more games)

Most Points	**105**	1974-75 (80)
Most Wins	**46**	1990-91 (80)
Most Ties	**21**	1974-75 (80)
Most Losses	**52**	1969-70 (76)
Most Goals	**376**	1988-89 (80)
Most Goals Against	**389**	1985-86 (80)
Fewest Points	**38**	1969-70 (76)
Fewest Wins	**14**	1969-70 (76)
Fewest Ties	**5**	1998-99 (82)
Fewest Losses	**17**	1974-75 (80)
Fewest Goals	**168**	1969-70 (76)
Fewest Goals Against	**185**	1974-75 (80)
Longest Winning Streak		
Overall	8	Oct. 21-Nov. 7/72
Home	12	Oct. 10-Dec. 5/92
Away	8	Dec. 18/74-Jan. 16/75
Longest Undefeated Streak		
Overall	11	Feb. 28-Mar. 24/74 (9 wins, 2 ties)
Home	13	Oct. 10-Dec. 8/92 (12 wins, 1 tie)
Away	11	Oct. 10-Dec. 11/74 (6 wins, 5 ties)
Longest Losing Streak		
Overall	10	Feb. 22-Mar. 9/84
Home	9	Feb. 8-Mar. 12/86
Away	12	Jan. 11-Feb. 15/70
Longest Winless Streak		
Overall	17	Jan. 29-Mar. 5/70 (13 losses, 4 ties)
Home	9	Jan. 29-Mar. 5/70 (8 losses, 1 tie), Feb. 8-Mar. 12/86 (9 losses)
Away	21	Jan. 11-Apr. 3/70 (17 losses, 4 ties)
Most Shutouts, Season	**9**	1974-75 (80)
Most PIM, Season	**2,228**	1990-91 (80)
Most Goals, Game	**12**	Nov. 28/84 (Van. 1 at L.A. 12)

Individual

Most Seasons	**17**	Dave Taylor
Most Games	**1,111**	Dave Taylor
Most Goals, Career	**550**	Marcel Dionne
Most Assists, Career	**757**	Marcel Dionne
Most Points Career	**1,307**	Marcel Dionne (550G, 757A)
Most PIM, Career	**1,846**	Marty McSorley
Most Shutouts, Career	**32**	Rogie Vachon
Longest Consecutive Games Streak	**324**	Marcel Dionne (Jan. 7/78-Jan. 9/82)
Most Goals, Season	**70**	Bernie Nicholls (1988-89)
Most Assists, Season	**122**	Wayne Gretzky (1990-91)
Most Points, Season	**168**	Wayne Gretzky (1988-89; 54G, 114A)
Most PIM, Season	**399**	Marty McSorley (1992-93)
Most Points, Defenseman, Season	**76**	Larry Murphy (1980-81; 16G, 60A)
Most Points, Center, Season	**168**	Wayne Gretzky (1988-89; 54G, 114A)
Most Points, Right Wing, Season	**112**	Dave Taylor (1980-81; 47G, 65A)
Most Points, Left Wing, Season	***125**	Luc Robitaille (1992-93; 63G, 62A)
Most Points, Rookie, Season	**84**	Luc Robitaille (1986-87; 45G, 39A)
Most Shutouts, Season	**8**	Rogie Vachon (1976-77)
Most Goals, Game	**4**	Sixteen times
Most Assists, Game	**6**	Bernie Nicholls (Dec. 1/88), Tomas Sandstrom (Oct. 9/93)
Most Points, Game	**8**	Bernie Nicholls (Dec. 1/88; 2G, 6A)

* NHL Record.

Coaching History

Red Kelly, 1967-68, 1968-69; Hal Laycoe and John Wilson, 1969-70; Larry Regan, 1970-71; Larry Regan and Fred Glover, 1971-72; Bob Pulford, 1972-73 to 1976-77; Ron Stewart, 1977-78; Bob Berry, 1978-79 to 1980-81; Parker MacDonald and Don Perry, 1981-82; Don Perry, 1982-83; Don Perry, Rogie Vachon and Roger Neilson, 1983-84; Pat Quinn, 1984-85, 1985-86; Pat Quinn and Mike Murphy 1986-87; Mike Murphy, Rogie Vachon and Robbie Ftorek, 1987-88; Robbie Ftorek, 1988-89; Tom Webster, 1989-90 to 1991-92; Barry Melrose, 1992-93, 1993-94; Barry Melrose and Rogie Vachon, 1994-95; Larry Robinson, 1995-96 to 1998-99; Andy Murray, 1999-2000 to date.

Retired Numbers

16	Marcel Dionne	1975-1987
18	Dave Taylor	1977-1994
30	Rogie Vachon	1971-1978

All-time Record vs. Other Clubs

Regular Season

	At Home							On Road							Total						
	GP	W	L	T	GF	GA	PTS	GP	W	L	T	GF	GA	PTS	GP	W	L	T	GF	GA	PTS
Anaheim	20	10	8	2	56	54	22	19	5	9	5	46	61	15	39	15	17	7	102	115	37
Atlanta	1	1	0	0	4	0	2	1	1	0	0	4	1	2	2	2	0	0	8	1	4
Boston	58	20	31	7	199	216	47	59	11	43	5	165	278	27	117	31	74	12	364	494	74
Buffalo	51	20	22	9	177	178	49	50	15	26	9	147	203	39	101	35	48	18	324	381	88
Calgary	83	43	31	9	320	298	95	86	25	51	10	289	390	60	169	68	82	19	609	688	155
Carolina	27	14	10	3	115	108	31	27	10	13	4	105	105	24	54	24	23	7	220	213	55
Chicago	66	30	30	6	227	230	66	67	28	31	8	205	241	64	133	58	61	14	432	471	130
Colorado	35	21	11	3	149	115	45	34	14	17	3	123	139	31	69	35	28	6	272	254	76
Dallas	72	29	25	18	244	218	76	73	16	45	12	194	294	45	145	45	70	30	438	512	121
Detroit	72	38	21	13	296	225	89	72	30	30	12	255	277	72	144	68	51	25	551	502	161
Edmonton	69	26	28	15	280	288	67	69	19	36	14	256	327	52	138	45	64	29	536	615	119
Florida	6	4	2	0	19	19	8	6	0	3	3	9	18	3	12	4	5	3	28	37	11
Montreal	62	17	36	9	191	248	43	62	8	43	11	158	284	27	124	25	79	20	349	532	70
Nashville	4	1	3	0	8	11	3	4	3	1	0	14	8	6	8	4	4	0	22	19	9
New Jersey	39	27	6	6	198	119	60	40	17	18	5	141	136	39	79	44	24	11	339	255	99
NY Islanders	42	20	15	7	154	136	47	41	13	24	4	115	154	30	83	33	39	11	269	290	77
NY Rangers	57	23	25	9	188	203	55	55	15	34	6	156	224	36	112	38	59	15	344	427	91
Ottawa	7	6	1	0	38	17	12	6	1	4	1	14	20	3	13	7	5	1	52	37	15
Philadelphia	63	20	35	8	187	216	48	61	16	38	7	156	236	39	124	36	73	15	343	452	87
Phoenix	63	22	31	10	250	257	55	66	25	32	9	228	268	59	129	47	63	19	478	525	114
Pittsburgh	67	42	17	8	258	178	92	69	22	38	9	218	256	53	136	64	55	17	476	434	145
St. Louis	70	33	27	10	242	206	76	70	16	44	10	179	263	42	140	49	71	20	421	469	118
San Jose	26	18	6	2	95	66	38	27	9	15	3	82	97	22	53	27	21	5	177	163	60
Tampa Bay	8	1	6	1	19	29	3	7	4	3	0	19	16	8	15	5	9	1	38	45	11
Toronto	64	34	21	9	230	187	77	65	20	34	11	215	260	51	129	54	55	20	445	447	128
Vancouver	91	48	29	14	373	289	110	89	29	45	15	286	344	73	180	77	74	29	659	633	183
Washington	44	26	12	6	175	134	58	43	18	18	7	161	181	43	87	44	30	13	336	315	101
Defunct Clubs	35	27	6	2	141	76	56	34	11	14	9	91	109	31	69	38	20	11	232	185	87
Totals	**1302**	**621**	**495**	**186**	**4833**	**4321**	**1430**	**1302**	**401**	**709**	**192**	**4031**	**5190**	**996**	**2604**	**1022**	**1204**	**378**	**8864**	**9511**	**2426**

Playoffs .

	Series	W	L	GP	W	L	T	GF	GA	Last Mtg.	Round	Result
Boston	2	0	2	13	5	8	0	38	56	1977	QF	L 2-4
Calgary	6	4	2	26	13	13	0	105	112	1993	DSF	W 4-2
Chicago	1	0	1	5	1	4	0	7	10	1974	QF	L 1-4
Dallas	1	0	1	7	3	4	0	21	26	1968	QF	L 3-4
Detroit	1	0	1	4	0	4	0	6	15	2000	CQF	L 0-4
Edmonton	7	2	5	36	12	24	0	127	154	1992	DSF	L 2-4
Montreal	1	0	1	5	1	4	0	12	15	1993	F	L 1-4
NY Islanders	1	0	1	4	1	3	0	10	21	1980	PR	L 1-3
NY Rangers	2	0	2	6	1	5	0	14	32	1981	PR	L 1-3
St. Louis	2	0	2	8	0	8	0	13	32	1998	CQF	L 0-4
Toronto	3	1	2	12	5	7	0	31	41	1993	CF	W 4-3
Vancouver	3	2	1	17	9	8	0	66	60	1993	DF	W 4-2
Defunct Clubs	1	1	0	7	4	3	0	23	25			
Totals	**31**	**10**	**21**	**150**	**55**	**95**	**0**	**473**	**599**			

Playoff Results 2000-1996

Year	Round	Opponent	Result	GF	GA
2000	CQF	Detroit	L 0-4	6	15
1998	CQF	St. Louis	L 0-4	8	16

Abbreviations: Round: F – Final; **CF** – conference final; **CQF** – conference quarter-final; **DF** – division final; **DSF** – division semi-final; **QF** – quarter-final; **PR** – preliminary round.

Calgary totals include Atlanta Flames, 1972-73 to 1979-80.
Carolina totals include Hartford, 1979-80 to 1996-97.
Colorado totals include Quebec, 1979-80 to 1994-95.
Dallas totals include Minnesota North Stars, 1967-68 to 1992-93.
New Jersey totals include Kansas City, 1974-75 to 1975-76, and Colorado Rockies, 1976-77 to 1981-82.
Phoenix totals include Winnipeg, 1979-80 to 1995-96.

1999-2000 Results

Oct.	2	at	Nashville	2-0		13		St. Louis	2-3
	4	at	St. Louis	3-2		15	at	San Jose	2-3 *
	6	at	Florida	2-4		18		Buffalo	5-3
	7	at	Tampa Bay	5-2		20		Dallas	2-5
	9	at	Washington	2-2		23		Colorado	3-2
	15	at	Calgary	4-1		26	at	Dallas	1-3
	16	at	Edmonton	4-5		27	at	Nashville	6-2
	20		Boston	2-2		29	at	Toronto	2-3
	22		Phoenix	3-6		31		NY Islanders	5-2
	24		San Jose	4-3	**Feb.**	3		Detroit	6-3
	26		Washington	5-2		8		Anaheim	3-5
	28		Pittsburgh	5-3		9	at	Phoenix	5-2
	30	at	Chicago	3-1		11		Dallas	3-2
Nov.	2	at	Pittsburgh	5-4		14		Calgary	4-3 *
	3	at	Detroit	1-1		16	at	Chicago	4-1
	6		Philadelphia	3-5		18	at	Detroit	3-2
	9		Edmonton	1-1		19	at	Buffalo	1-4
	11		Colorado	5-2		21	at	Edmonton	3-6
	14	at	Phoenix	3-2		23	at	Calgary	7-2
	16		Chicago	3-2		25	at	Vancouver	5-2
	18		Phoenix	2-3		26	at	San Jose	3-6
	20		Montreal	3-5		29		Vancouver	1-1
	23	at	Colorado	6-2	**Mar.**	2		Carolina	2-5
	24	at	Dallas	2-3 *		4		Nashville	3-2 *
	27		San Jose	4-1		7		Detroit	1-3
Dec.	3	at	Anaheim	1-1		9		NY Rangers	3-1
	4		Tampa Bay	3-3		11		Calgary	3-1
	8		Atlanta	4-0		13		Vancouver	3-2 *
	10	at	Detroit	1-3		15	at	Anaheim	2-2
	11	at	Montreal	4-2		17		St. Louis	0-4
	14	at	New Jersey	1-7		19		Nashville	1-2 *
	15	at	NY Rangers	3-8		21		Anaheim	2-5
	18		Chicago	4-8		23	at	Philadelphia	3-2 *
	22	at	San Jose	1-2		25	at	Boston	4-4
	26		Phoenix	2-3 *		26	at	Atlanta	4-1
	29	at	Colorado	2-4		29		San Jose	1-1
	30		Edmonton	8-2	**Apr.**	1		Anaheim	2-1
Jan.	3	at	Dallas	1-4		3	at	Phoenix	1-2
	4	at	St. Louis	2-2		5	at	Vancouver	1-1
	6		Florida	4-2		7		Dallas	3-2
	11		Ottawa	3-4		9	at	Anaheim	4-3 *

* – Overtime

Entry Draft Selections 2000-1986

2000

Pick	
20	Alexander Frolov
54	Andreas Lilja
86	Yanick Lehoux
118	Lubomir Visnovsky
165	Nathan Marsters
201	Yevgeny Fedorov
206	Tim Eriksson
218	Craig Olynick
245	Dan Welch
250	Flavien Conne
282	Carl Grahn

1999

Pick	
43	Andrei Shefer
74	Jason Crain
76	Frantisek Kaberle
92	Cory Campbell
104	Brian McGrattan
125	Daniel Johansson
133	Jean-Francois Nogues
193	Kevin Baker
222	George Parros
250	Noah Clarke

1998

Pick	
21	Mathieu Biron
46	Justin Papineau
76	Alexei Volkov
103	Kip Brennan
133	Joe Rullier
163	Tomas Zizka
190	Tommi Hannus
217	Jim Henkel
248	Matthew Yeats

1997

Pick	
3	Olli Jokinen
15	Matt Zultek
29	Scott Barney
83	Joseph Corvo
99	Sean Blanchard
137	Richard Seeley
150	Jeff Katcher
193	Jay Kopischke
220	Konrad Brand

1996

Pick	
30	Josh Green
37	Marian Cisar
57	Greg Phillips
84	Mikael Simons
96	Eric Belanger
120	Jesse Black
123	Peter Hogan
190	Stephen Valiquette
193	Kai Nurminen
219	Sebastien Simard

1995

Pick	
3	Aki Berg
33	Don MacLean
50	Pavel Rosa
59	Vladimir Tsyplakov
118	Jason Morgan
137	Igor Melyakov
157	Benoit Larose
163	Juha Vuorivirta
215	Brian Stewart

1994

Pick	
7	Jamie Storr
33	Matt Johnson
59	Vitali Yachmenev
111	Chris Schmidt
163	Luc Gagne
189	Andrew Dale
215	Jan Nemecek
241	Sergei Shalomai

1993

Pick	
42	Shayne Toporowski
68	Jeff Mitchell
94	Bob Wren
105	Frederick Beaubien
117	Jason Saal
120	Tomas Vlasak
146	Jere Karalahti
172	Justin Martin
198	John-Tra Dillabough
224	Martin Strbak
250	Kimmo Timonen
276	Patrick Howald

1992

Pick	
39	Justin Hocking
63	Sandy Allan
87	Kevin Brown
111	Jeff Shevalier
135	Rem Murray
207	Magnus Wernblom
231	Ryan Pisiak
255	Jukka Tiilikainen

1991

Pick	
42	Guy Leveque
79	Keith Redmond
81	Alexei Zhitnik
108	Pauli Jaks
130	Brett Seguin
152	Kelly Fairchild
196	Craig Brown
218	Mattias Olsson
240	Andre Bouliane
262	Michael Gaul

1990

Pick	
7	Darryl Sydor
28	Brandy Semchuk
49	Bill Berg
91	David Goverde
112	Erik Andersson
133	Robert Lang
154	Dean Hulett
175	Denis Leblanc
196	Patrik Ross
217	K.J.(Kevin) White
238	Troy Mohns

1989

Pick	
39	Brent Thompson
81	Jim Maher
102	Eric Ricard
103	Thomas Newman
123	Daniel Rydmark
144	Ted Kramer
165	Sean Whyte
182	Jim Giacin
186	Martin Maskarinec
207	Jim Hiller
228	Steve Jaques
249	Kevin Sneddon

1988

Pick	
7	Martin Gelinas
28	Paul Holden
49	John Van Kessel
70	Rob Blake
91	Jeff Robison
109	Micah Aivazoff
112	Robert Larsson
133	Jeff Kruesel
154	Timo Peltomaa
175	Jim Larkin
196	Brad Hyatt
217	Doug Laprade
238	Joe Flanagan

1987

Pick	
4	Wayne McBean
27	Mark Fitzpatrick
43	Ross Wilson
90	Mike Vukonich
111	Greg Batters
132	Kyosti Karjalainen
174	Jeff Gawlicki
195	John Preston
216	Rostislav Vlach
237	Mikael Lindholm

1986

Pick	
2	Jimmy Carson
44	Denis Larocque
65	Sylvain Couturier
86	Dave Guden
107	Robb Stauber
128	Sean Krakiwsky
149	Rene Chapdelaine
170	Trevor Pochipinski
191	Paul Kelly
212	Russ Mann
233	Brian Hayton

Coach

MURRAY, ANDY

Coach, Los Angeles Kings. Born in Gladstone, Man., March 3, 1951.

Andy Murray became the 19th head coach in Kings history on June 14, 1999 and led the team to a playoff spot in 1999-2000. His coaching experience dates back to 1974 and includes seven seasons as an NHL assistant or associate coach with the Winnipeg Jets (1993 to 1995), Minnesota North Stars (1990 to 1992) and Philadelphia Flyers (1988 to 1990). As an assistant coach in Minnesota, Murray reached the Stanley Cup Finals in 1991.

In addition to his NHL service, Murray brings to the Kings a tremendous amount of international coaching experience. As head coach of the Canadian national team, he guided his team to a 77-29-14 record and the gold medal in the 1997 World Hockey Championships with a team that featured Kings captain Rob Blake.

From 1976 to 1978, Murray served his first head coaching position with the Brandon Travelers of the Manitoba Junior Hockey League. He moved on to become head coach for Brandon University from 1978 to 1981, leading the Bobcats to the #1 ranking in Canadian University hockey during his final year. In 1981-82, Murray moved to Switzerland, where for the next seven years he coached several Swiss-A Division teams.

Murray returned to North America as an assistant coach for the Hershey Bears of the American Hockey League in 1987 and helped guide the Bears to the 1988 Calder Cup Championship. In 1992, Murray returned to Europe to coach Lugano in Switzerland and then Eisbaren Berlin in Germany a year later. Most recently, Murray served as the head coach for Shattuck-St. Mary's in Faribault, Minnesota, where he led the prep school to a 70-9-2 record and the Midget Triple A USA Hockey national championship in 1998-99.

Murray and his wife, Ruth, have three children, sons Braden and Jordan, and daughter, Sarah.

Coaching Record

		Regular Season					Playoffs			
Season	Team	Games	W	L	T	%	Games	W	L	%
1999-2000	Los Angeles (NHL)	82	39	31	12	.573•	4	0	4	.000
	NHL Totals	82	39	31	12	.573•	4	0	4	.000

• Includes points from regulation ties

Club Directory

STAPLES Center

Los Angeles Kings
STAPLES Center
1111 South Figueroa Street
Los Angeles, CA 90015
Phone **213/742-7100**
GM FAX 310/535-4504
PR FAX 310/535-4507
Website: www.lakings.com
Capacity: 18,118

Executive

Owner	Philip F. Anschutz
Owner	Edward P. Roski
President/Governor	Timothy J. Leiweke
Executive Vice President/General Counsel	Ted Fikre
Special Assistant to the President	Rogie Vachon
Manager of Special Services/Office of the President	Lisa Tran
Executive Assistant to the President	Ruth Resendiz
Executive Assistant To Executive Vice President, General Counsel	Francis Inomata

Hockey Operations

Senior Vice President/General Manager	Dave Taylor
Assistant General Manager	Kevin Gilmore
Director, Player Personnel	Bill O'Flaherty
Assistant to the General Manager	John Wolf
Executive Assistant to the General Manager	Marcia Galloway
Head Coach	Andy Murray
Assistant Coaches	Dave Tippett, Mark Hardy, Ray Bennett
Director, Amateur Scouting	Al Murray
Director, Pro Scouting	Ace Bailey
Scouting Staff	Mark Bavis, Greg Dreschel, Rob Laird, Vaclav Nedomansky, Parry Shockey, John Stanton, Ari Vuori, Michel Boucher, Gary Harker, Victor Tjumenev
Video Coordinator	Bill Gurney

Medical

Trainer	Peter Demers, ATC
Assistant Athletic Trainer	Rick Burrill, ATC
Rehabilitation Trainer	Robert Zolg, MPT, ATC
Head Speed-Strength and Conditioning Coach	Joseph Horrigan, DC, CSCS
Assistant Speed-Strength and Conditioning Coach	Dave Good, CSCS, SSC
Assistant Strength and Conditioning Coach	Ken Vick, CSCS
Nutrition Consultant	Doug Andersen, DC, CCN
Team Physician	Dr. Ronald Kvitne
Jobe Orthopaedic Clinic	
Internist	Dr. Michael Mellman
Dentist	Dr. Jeffrey Hoy
Opthamologist	Dr. Howard Lazerson

Equipment Staff

Equipment Manager	Peter Millar
Assistant Equipment Manager	Rick Garcia
Equipment Coordinator	Grady Clark

Media Relations/Team Services

Director, Media Relations/Team Services	Mike Altieri
Manager, Media Relations/Team Services	Jeff Moeller
Media Relations Assistant	Lee Callans
Team Photography	Andrew D. Bernstein, Robert Mora, Juan Ocampo, Catherine Steenkeste

Finance/Accounting/Ticket Operations

Executive Vice President, Chief Financial Officer	Dan Beckerman
Director, Finance	Peter Mazur
Payroll Manager	Elcee Prendergast
Ticket Operations	Bobby Anderson, Nell Nicolas
Assistant to Executive Vice President, Chief Financial Officer	Kely Lyon

Sales & Marketing

Vice President, Sales & Marketing	Kurt Schwartzkopf
Director, Sales	Chris McGowan
Marketing Coordinator	Shelby Russell
Graphic Designer	Brooke Lingle, Lynette Fowler
Corporate Account Executives	Shawn Jeffers, Justin Apmadoc, Randy Bechtold, April Aryuyo, Geno Zicarelli
Group Sales Account Managers	Charisse Gopez, Stephanie Henderson, Tony Barnachea, Matt Rosenfeld, Glenn Kamimura
Inside Sales Account Executives	Marc Entin, Patricia Peterson, Mark La Ferr, Peter Kwon, Jampier Arias
Sales Coordinator	Lara Frandzel

Human Resources

Vice President, Human Resources	Kevin McDowell
Manager, Human Resources	Margaret Castaneda, Ed Perne

Corporate Partnerships

Director, Corporate Partnerships	Susan Long
Manager, Corporate Partnerships	Kevin Donovan

Community/Fan Development

Fan Development Manager	Annie Camins
Community Relations Manager	Kris Nakamura
Fan Development Coordinator	Stacy Schwartz
Community Relations Coordinator	Noy Louer
Public Address Announcer	David Courtney
Supervisor, Off-Ice Officials	Bill Meuris

Broadcasting/Press Info

TV Play-by-Play Announcer-FOX Sports Net	Bob Miller
Radio Play-by-Play Announcer-KRLA 1110 AM	Nick Nickson
TV Color Commentator-FOX Sports Net	Jim Fox
Radio Color Commentator- KRLA 1110 AM	Daryl Evans
Training Center	HealthSouth Training Center
Location of Bob Miller Press Box	Upper concourse, west side

Minnesota Wild

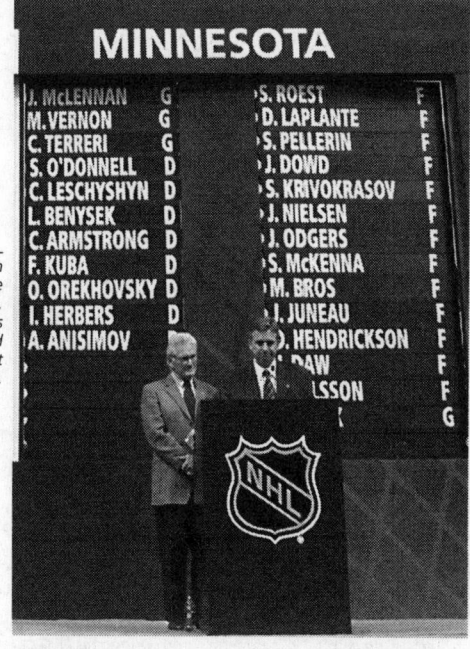

General manager Doug Risebrough (right) began to put the Wild on ice at the Expansion Draft on June 23, 2000. Among the team's 26 picks was Sergei Krivokrasov, who led Nashville with 25 goals during that club's inaugural season of 1998-99.

2000-01 Schedule

Oct.	Fri.	6	at Anaheim		Wed.	10	Washington
	Sat.	7	at Phoenix		Fri.	12	Colorado
	Wed.	11	Philadelphia		Sun.	14	at NY Rangers
	Fri.	13	at St. Louis		Mon.	15	at Columbus
	Sun.	15	Edmonton*		Wed.	17	Columbus
	Wed.	18	Tampa Bay		Fri.	19	NY Islanders
	Fri.	20	San Jose		Sun.	21	New Jersey*
	Sun.	22	Florida*		Wed.	24	at Anaheim
	Tue.	24	at Montreal		Sat.	27	at Los Angeles*
	Wed.	25	at Toronto		Tue.	30	at Vancouver
	Fri.	27	Calgary	Feb.	Tue.	6	at Tampa Bay
	Sun.	29	Chicago		Wed.	7	at Florida
Nov.	Fri.	3	at Edmonton		Fri.	9	at Dallas
	Sun.	5	at Calgary		Sun.	11	Pittsburgh*
	Tue.	7	at Colorado		Wed.	14	at Pittsburgh
	Wed.	8	Calgary		Fri.	16	Los Angeles
	Fri.	10	at Chicago		Sun.	18	San Jose*
	Sun.	12	Edmonton		Wed.	21	at Dallas
	Wed.	15	NY Rangers		Fri.	23	at Colorado
	Fri.	17	at Buffalo		Sat.	24	at Nashville
	Sat.	18	at Boston		Mon.	26	Vancouver
	Wed.	22	Calgary	Mar.	Thu.	1	at Calgary
	Fri.	24	Chicago*		Fri.	2	at Edmonton
	Sun.	26	Vancouver*		Sun.	4	at Vancouver
	Tue.	28	at San Jose		Tue.	6	St. Louis
	Thu.	30	at Phoenix		Thu.	8	at New Jersey
Dec.	Sat.	2	at Los Angeles		Fri.	9	at NY Islanders
	Thu.	7	at Chicago		Sun.	11	Detroit*
	Fri.	8	Anaheim		Wed.	14	St. Louis
	Sun.	10	Nashville*		Thu.	15	at Philadelphia
	Wed.	13	Carolina		Sun.	18	at Colorado*
	Thu.	14	at Washington		Mon.	19	Dallas
	Sun.	17	Dallas*		Wed.	21	Nashville
	Wed.	20	Ottawa		Thu.	22	at Detroit
	Fri.	22	Los Angeles		Sun.	25	Vancouver*
	Wed.	27	at Detroit		Wed.	28	Phoenix
	Fri.	29	Phoenix		Sat.	31	at Nashville
	Sun.	31	Anaheim*	Apr.	Mon.	2	at San Jose
Jan.	Wed.	3	Atlanta		Wed.	4	at Edmonton
	Fri.	5	Detroit		Fri.	6	Columbus
	Sat.	6	at St. Louis		Sun.	8	Colorado*

* Denotes afternoon game.

Franchise date: June 25, 1997

NORTHWEST
DIVISION

**1st
NHL
Season**

2000-01 Player Personnel

FORWARDS	HT	WT	S	Place of Birth	Date	1999-00 Club
ARONSON, Steve	6-1	205	R	Minnetonka, MN	7/15/78	U. of St. Thomas
BARTOS, Peter	6-0	185	R	Martin, Czech.	9/5/73	HC Budejovice
BONIN, Brian	5-10	186	L	St. Paul, MN	11/28/73	Syracuse Crunch
DAW, Jeff	6-3	190	R	Carlyle, Ont.	2/28/72	Houston-Lowell (AHL)
DOWD, Jim	6-1	190	R	Brick, NJ	12/25/68	Edmonton
FITZGERALD, Randy	5-11	174	L	Toronto, Ont.	9/5/79	Plymouth Whalers
GABORIK, Marian	6-1	183	L	Trencin, Czech.	2/14/82	Dukla Trencin
GARDINER, Peter	6-5	220	R	Toronto, Ont.	9/29/77	RPI Engineers
GAVEY, Aaron	6-2	200	L	Sudbury, Ont.	2/22/74	Dallas-Michigan K-Wings
HENDRICKSON, Darby	6-1	195	L	Richfield, MN	8/28/72	Vancouver-Syracuse Crunch
KRIVOKRASOV, Sergei	5-11	185	L	Angarsk, USSR	4/15/74	Nashville-Calgary
LAAKSONEN, Antti	6-0	180	L	Tammela, Finland	10/3/73	Boston-Providence Bruins
LAPLANTE, Darryl	6-0	198	L	Calgary, Alta.	3/28/77	Detroit-Cincinnati Ducks
LAROSE, Cory	6-0	188	L	Campbellton, N.B.	5/14/75	U. of Maine
MATTE, Christian	6-0	190	R	Hull, Que.	1/20/75	Colorado-Hershey Bears
McKENNA, Steve	6-8	255	L	Toronto, Ont.	8/21/73	Los Angeles
McLEAN, Brett	5-11	194	L	Comox, B.C.	8/14/78	Johnstown Chiefs-Saint John Flames
NIELSEN, Jeff	6-0	200	L	Grand Rapids, MN	9/20/71	Anaheim
NURMINEN, Kai	6-1	198	L	Turku, Finland	3/29/69	TPS Turku
ODGERS, Jeff	6-0	200	R	Spy Hill, Sask.	5/31/69	Colorado
PARK, Richard	5-11	190	R	Seoul, South Korea	5/27/76	Utah Grizzlies
PATERA, Pavel	6-1	181	L	Kladno, Czech.	9/6/71	Dallas-Slovnaft Vsetin
PELLERIN, Scott	5-11	172	L	Shediac, N.B.	1/9/70	St. Louis
ROEST, Stacy	5-9	185	R	Lethbridge, Alta.	3/15/74	Detroit
STEWART, Cam	5-11	196	L	Kitchener, Ont.	9/18/71	Florida
SUSHINSKY, Maxim	5-8	165	L	Leningrad, USSR	6/1/74	Avangard Omsk
WALSH, Brendan	5-9	181	R	Dorchester, MA	10/22/74	U. of Maine
WALZ, Wes	5-10	180	R	Calgary, Alta.	5/15/70	Long Beach-HC Lugano

DEFENSEMEN						
ARMSTRONG, Chris	6-0	205	L	Regina, Sask.	6/26/75	Kentucky
BENYSEK, Ladislav	6-2	190	L	Olomouc, Czech.	3/24/75	Sparta Praha
BOMBARDIR, Brad	6-1	205	L	Powell River, B.C.	5/5/72	New Jersey
CHARRON, Eric	6-3	195	L	Verdun, Que.	1/14/70	Calgary-Saint John Flames
DAIGNEAULT, J.J.	5-10	192	L	Montreal, Que.	10/12/65	Phoenix
HERBERS, Ian	6-4	225	L	Jasper, Alta.	7/18/67	T.B.-Detroit Vipers-NYI
KUBA, Filip	6-3	205	L	Ostrava, Czech.	12/29/76	Florida-Houston Aeros
LESCHYSHYN, Curtis	6-1	205	L	Thompson, Man.	9/21/69	Carolina
MATTEUCCI, Mike	6-2	210	L	Trail, B.C.	12/27/71	Long Beach
NAUMENKO, Nick	5-11	185	R	Chicago, IL	7/7/74	Kansas City
NYCHOLAT, Lawrence	6-0	192	L	Calgary, Alta.	5/7/79	Swift Current
O'DONNELL, Sean	6-3	230	L	Ottawa, Ont.	10/13/71	Los Angeles
REITZ, Erik	6-0	192	R	Detroit, MI	7/29/82	Barrie Colts
SCHULTZ, Nick	6-0	187	L	Regina, Sask.	8/25/82	Prince Albert
SEKERAS, Lubomir	6-0	183	L	Trencin, Czech.	11/18/68	HC Trinec
SUTTON, Andy	6-6	245	L	Edmonton, Alta.	3/10/75	San Jose-Kentucky

GOALTENDERS	HT	WT	C	Place of Birth	Date	1999-00 Club
BIERK, Zac	6-4	205	L	Peterborough, Ont.	9/17/76	Tampa Bay-Detroit Vipers
BRUMBY, David	6-1	190	L	Victoria, B.C.	5/21/75	Jackson Bandits-Providence Bruins
FERNANDEZ, Manny	6-0	180	L	Etobicoke, Ont.	8/27/74	Dallas
GUSTAFSON, Derek	5-11	210	L	Gresham, OR	6/21/79	St. Lawrence
McLENNAN, Jamie	6-0	190	L	Edmonton, Alta.	6/30/71	St. Louis

Entry Draft Selections 2000

2000
Pick

3	Marian Gaborik
33	Nick Schultz
99	Marc Cavosie
132	Maxim Sushinsky
199	Brian Passmore
214	Peter Bartos
232	Lubomir Sekeras
255	Eric Johansson

General Managers' History

Doug Risebrough, 2000-01.

Coaching History

Jacques Lemaire, 2000-01.

Captains' History

TBD, 2000-01.

General Manager

RISEBROUGH, DOUG
Executive Vice President and General Manager, Minnesota Wild.
Born in Guelph, Ont., January 29, 1954.

Doug Risebrough was hired as the first Executive Vice President and General Manager of the Minnesota Wild on September 2, 1999. He is responsible for the club's overall hockey operations. After ending his 14-year NHL playing career with the Flames in 1987, Risebrough was named as assistant coach with Calgary and joined Terry Crisp behind the bench. Risebrough was appointed head coach of the Flames on May 18, 1990 and on May 16, 1991, he also assumed the role of general manager. Late in the 1991-92 campaign he directed his energies full-time to general manager, handing the coaching responsibilities over to Guy Charron for the balance of the season. Risebrough served as G.M. in Calgary through the 1995-96 season.

Risebrough was Montreal's first selection, seventh overall, in the 1974 Amateur Draft. During his nine years with the Canadiens, he helped his club to four consecutive Stanley Cup championships between 1976 and 1979. He joined the Flames prior to the start of the club's 1982 training camp. During his NHL career, his clubs have won five Stanley Cup titles (1976-1979 and 1989 with Calgary) and two Presidents' Trophies (1987-88 and 1988-89).

NHL Coaching Record

Season	Team	Regular Season					Playoffs			
		Games	W	L	T	%	Games	W	L	%
1990-91	Calgary	80	46	26	8	.625	7	3	4	.429
1991-92	Calgary	64	25	30	9	.461	....	....	....	....
	NHL Totals	**144**	**71**	**56**	**17**	**.522**	**7**	**3**	**4**	**.429**

Coach

LEMAIRE, JACQUES GERARD
Coach, Minnesota Wild. Born in LaSalle, Quebec, September 7, 1945.

The Minnesota Wild announced the signing of Jacques Lemaire as the club's first head coach on June 19, 2000. Lemaire had spent parts of the previous two seasons as a senior consultant to the general manager for the Montreal Canadiens, the franchise with which he captured eight Stanley Cup championships as a player.

Lemaire spent five seasons behind the New Jersey Devils bench and compiled a 199-122-57 mark. In 1994-95, he coached the Devils to their first Stanley Cup Championship. In his first season with the team (1993-94), he was awarded the Jack Adams Trophy as the NHL's outstanding coach.

Lemaire began his NHL coaching career with the Montreal Canadiens in 1983-84. The next year, he coached Montreal to the Adams Division Championship. He stepped aside as head coach following the 1984-85 campaign and moved to the front office where he held the position of assistant to the managing director for seven of his last eight years with the Canadiens. During that time, Lemaire played a role in Montreal's Stanley Cup Championships of 1986 and 1993.

Lemaire spent his entire NHL playing career with Montreal from 1967 to 1979. He then began his coaching career in Switzerland where he served as player/coach of the Sierre club. He returned to North America in 1981 and was named the first head coach of the Quebec Major Junior Hockey League's expansion Longueuil Chevaliers. In his first season at the helm (1982-83), Lemaire guided the team to the QMJHL finals.

He and his wife, Mychele, have three children, sons Patrice and Danyk, and daughter Magalie.

Coaching Record

Season	Team	Regular Season					Playoffs			
		Games	W	L	T	%	Games	W	L	%
1979-80	Sierre (Switzerland)					UNAVAILABLE				
1980-81	Sierre (Switzerland)					UNAVAILABLE				
1982-83	Longueuil (QMJHL)	70	37	29	4	.557	15	9	6	.600
1983-84	Montreal (NHL)	17	7	10	0	.412	15	9	6	.600
1984-85	Montreal (NHL)	80	41	27	12	.588	12	6	6	.500
1993-94	New Jersey (NHL)	84	47	25	12	.631	20	11	9	.550
1994-95	New Jersey (NHL)	48	22	18	8	.542	20	16	4	.800*
1995-96	New Jersey (NHL)	82	37	33	12	.524	....	....	....	....
1996-97	New Jersey (NHL)	82	45	23	14	.634	10	5	5	.500
1997-98	New Jersey (NHL)	82	48	23	11	.652	6	2	4	.333
	NHL Totals	**475**	**247**	**159**	**69**	**.593**	**83**	**49**	**34**	**.590**

* Stanley Cup win.

Club Directory

Xcel Energy Center

Minnesota Wild
317 Washington Street
St. Paul, MN 55102
Phone **651/602-6000**
FAX 651/222-1055
Tickets 651/222-9453
Website: http://www.wild.com/
Capacity: 18,600

Executive Management
Chairman	Bob Naegele, Jr.
Chief Executive Officer	Jac K. Sperling
President	Tod Leiweke
President of Saint Paul Arena Company	Chris Hansen
Executive Vice President/General Manager	Doug Risebrough
Chief Financial Officer	Martha Fuller
Vice President of Corporate Partnerships	Laura Day
Vice President of Customer Sales and Service	Steve Griggs
Vice President of Marketing	Matt Majka
Vice President of Communications & Broadcasting	Bill Robertson
Vice President of Saint Paul Arena Company	Jim Ibister
Xcel Energy Center Project Director	Ray Chandler
Assistant Xcel Energy Center Project Director	Mark Anger
Executive Assistant	Kris Brown
Executive Assistant	Stephane Huseby
Executive Assistant	Maggie Stiffler
Executive Assistant	Cindy Sweiger
Executive Assistant	C.J. Neale

Coaching Staff
Head Coach	Jacques Lemaire
Assistant Coaches	Mike Ramsey, Mario Tremblay
Strength and Conditioning Coach	George Kinnear

Hockey Operations
Director of Hockey Administration & Legal Affairs	Thomas Lynn
Chief Amateur Scout	Tom Thompson
Coordinator of Amateur Scouting	Guy Lapointe
Scouts	Marc Chamard, Paul Charles, Frank Effinger, Glen Giovanucci, Doug Mosher, Jeff Perry, Noel Rahn, Glen Sonmor, Rich Sutter, Matti Vaisanen
Head Athletic Therapist	Don Fuller
Assistant Athletic Therapist	Michael Vogt
Head Equipment Manager	Tony DaCosta
Assistant Equipment Managers	Rick Szuber, Brent Proulx
Medical Director	Dr. Sheldon Burns
Orthopedic Surgeon	Dr. Joel Boyd
Team Dentists	Dr. Dennis Killian, Dr. Frank Milnar, Dr. Michael Nanne

Corporate Partnerships
Director of Corporate Services	Carin Anderson
Manager of Suite Service and Operations	Rachael Johnson
Corporate Partnerships Account Executives	Greg Gerlach, Greg Nelson, Mike Snee
Corporate Account Coordinators	Cory Effertz, Marnie Moore, Joel Stenman

Customer Sales and Service
Manager of Ticket Operations/Customer Service	Holly Cedarblade
Manager of Group Sales	Kelly Harens
Manager of Sales	Jamie Spencer
New Business Development	Matt Cords
New Business Development	Bryan Dan
Club/Premier Account Coordinator	Mike Kimbell
Hockey Association Account Executive	Shawn Reid
Account Services	Jeff Bednar, Dana Dummer, John Swing
Administrative Assistant	Kelly Novara

Marketing Department
Director of Production Services	John Maher
Director of Marketing	Heather McGinty
Director of Retail Operations	Chris Poitras
Retail Manager	Dave Krolow
Production Services Manager	Wayne Peterson
10,000 Rinks Manager	Pat Sullivan
Community Relations Manager	Marlene Wall
Marketing Event Coordinator	Annie Gleason
Museum Curator	Roger Godin
Administrative Assistant	Melisa Hubbard
Game Presentation Intern	Bill Freeman

Communications and Broadcasting
Manager of Internet Services	Brian Hutchinson
Publications Manager	Brian Israel
Manager of Media Relations/Team Services	Chris Kelleher
Broadcast Manager	Pat O'Connor
Associate Producer	Kevin Falness
Corporate Communications Coordinator	Aaron Sickman
Media Relations Coordinator	Brad Smith
Administrative Assistant	Kathy Ross
Communications Intern	Jason Ball

Finance and Administration
Director of Information Technologies	Brian Jore
Financial Analyst	Brian Gramm
Human Resources Manager	Ellen Hughes
Manager of Network Communication	Chris Monicatti
Travel Coordinator	Mary Kenna
Receptionist	Gillian Mitchell

Miscellaneous
Training Site	Parade Ice Garden, Minneapolis
Radio Network flagship	WCCO (830 AM)
Radio Play-By-Play Broadcaster	Bob Kurtz
Radio Analyst	Barry Buetel
Television Station	Fox Sports Net (cable), KMSP 9 (over-the-air)
Television Play-By-Play Broadcaster	Mike Goldberg
Television Analyst	Tom Reid
Team Photographer	Bruce Kluckhohn
PA Announcer	Jim Carroll
Press Box PA Announcer	Dave Lee
Head Off-Ice Official	Barry Fritz

Montreal Canadiens

1999-2000 Results: 35W-38L-9T 83PTS. Fourth, Northeast Division

Jose Theodore's goals-against average of 2.10 was fourth best in the NHL last season, while his save percentage of .91911 was second to Ed Belfour's mark of .91916.

2000-01 Schedule

Month	Day	Date	Opponent
Oct.	Fri.	6	at New Jersey
	Sat.	7	at Toronto
	Tue.	10	Edmonton
	Wed.	11	at NY Rangers
	Sat.	14	Chicago
	Tue.	17	Buffalo
	Thu.	19	at Philadelphia
	Sat.	21	Carolina
	Tue.	24	Minnesota
	Fri.	27	at NY Islanders
	Sat.	28	NY Islanders
Nov.	Wed.	1	Detroit
	Fri.	3	at Buffalo
	Sat.	4	NY Rangers
	Wed.	8	at Florida
	Fri.	10	at Tampa Bay
	Sat.	11	at Dallas
	Tue.	14	Tampa Bay
	Fri.	17	at Washington
	Sat.	18	Toronto
	Tue.	21	Florida
	Thu.	23	at Atlanta
	Sat.	25	Buffalo
	Mon.	27	Atlanta
	Wed.	29	at Edmonton
	Thu.	30	at Vancouver
Dec.	Sat.	2	at Calgary*
	Tue.	5	Buffalo
	Fri.	8	at Ottawa
	Sat.	9	Ottawa
	Wed.	13	Calgary
	Fri.	15	at New Jersey
	Sat.	16	Pittsburgh
	Mon.	18	Columbus
	Thu.	21	Nashville
	Sat.	23	Toronto
	Wed.	27	at Vancouver
	Sat.	30	at Edmonton*
	Sun.	31	at Calgary
Jan.	Tue.	2	at NY Islanders
	Fri.	5	at Pittsburgh
	Sat.	6	at Ottawa
	Wed.	10	Boston
	Fri.	12	at Atlanta
	Sat.	13	Phoenix
	Tue.	16	Carolina
	Thu.	18	Tampa Bay
	Sat.	20	NY Rangers
	Tue.	23	St. Louis
	Wed.	24	at Pittsburgh
	Sat.	27	Washington*
	Sun.	28	Ottawa*
	Wed.	31	at NY Rangers
Feb.	Thu.	1	at Boston
	Tue.	6	New Jersey
	Sat.	10	NY Islanders
	Sun.	11	at Buffalo
	Tue.	13	Colorado
	Sat.	17	Washington
	Sun.	18	at Ottawa
	Wed.	21	Vancouver
	Fri.	23	at Washington
	Sat.	24	at Toronto
	Tue.	27	at Philadelphia
	Wed.	28	Pittsburgh
Mar.	Sat.	3	Philadelphia
	Tue.	6	at Los Angeles
	Wed.	7	at Anaheim
	Sat.	10	at Phoenix*
	Mon.	12	at San Jose
	Wed.	14	at Carolina
	Sat.	17	Boston
	Tue.	20	Florida
	Thu.	22	at Boston
	Sat.	24	Atlanta
	Mon.	26	at Carolina
	Wed.	28	at Florida
	Thu.	29	at Tampa Bay
	Sat.	31	Toronto
Apr.	Mon.	2	at Boston
	Thu.	5	Philadelphia
	Sat.	7	New Jersey

* Denotes afternoon game.

Franchise date: November 22, 1917

NORTHEAST DIVISION

84th NHL Season

Year-by-Year Record

Season	GP	Home W	Home L	Home T	Road W	Road L	Road T	Overall W	Overall L	Overall T	GF	GA	Pts.	Finished		Playoff Result
1999-2000	82	18	18	5	17	20	4	35	38	9	196	194	83	4th,	Northeast Div.	Out of Playoffs
1998-99	82	21	15	5	11	24	6	32	39	11	184	209	75	5th,	Northeast Div.	Out of Playoffs
1997-98	82	15	17	9	22	15	4	37	32	13	235	208	87	4th,	Northeast Div.	Lost Conf. Semi-Final
1996-97	82	17	17	7	14	19	8	31	36	15	249	276	77	4th,	Northeast Div.	Lost Conf. Quarter-Final
1995-96	82	23	12	6	17	20	4	40	32	10	265	248	90	3rd,	Northeast Div.	Lost Conf. Quarter-Final
1994-95	48	15	5	4	3	18	3	18	23	7	125	148	43	6th,	Northeast Div.	Out of Playoffs
1993-94	84	26	12	4	15	17	10	41	29	14	283	248	96	3rd,	Northeast Div.	Lost Conf. Quarter-Final
1992-93	**84**	**27**	**13**	**2**	**21**	**17**	**4**	**48**	**30**	**6**	**326**	**280**	**102**	**3rd,**	**Adams Div.**	**Won Stanley Cup**
1991-92	80	27	8	5	14	20	6	41	28	11	267	207	93	1st,	Adams Div.	Lost Div. Final
1990-91	80	23	12	5	16	18	6	39	30	11	273	249	89	2nd,	Adams Div.	Lost Div. Final
1989-90	80	26	8	6	15	20	5	41	28	11	288	234	93	3rd,	Adams Div.	Lost Div. Final
1988-89	80	30	6	4	23	12	5	53	18	9	315	218	115	1st,	Adams Div.	Lost Final
1987-88	80	26	8	6	19	14	7	45	22	13	298	238	103	1st,	Adams Div.	Lost Div. Final
1986-87	80	27	9	4	14	20	6	41	29	10	277	241	92	2nd,	Adams Div.	Lost Conf. Championship
1985-86	**80**	**25**	**11**	**4**	**15**	**22**	**3**	**40**	**33**	**7**	**330**	**280**	**87**	**2nd,**	**Adams Div.**	**Won Stanley Cup**
1984-85	80	24	10	6	17	17	6	41	27	12	309	262	94	1st,	Adams Div.	Lost Div. Final
1983-84	80	19	19	2	16	21	3	35	40	5	286	295	75	4th,	Adams Div.	Lost Conf. Championship
1982-83	80	25	6	9	17	18	5	42	24	14	350	286	98	2nd,	Adams Div.	Lost Div. Semi-Final
1981-82	80	25	6	9	21	11	8	46	17	17	360	223	109	1st,	Adams Div.	Lost Div. Semi-Final
1980-81	80	31	7	2	14	15	11	45	22	13	332	232	103	1st,	Norris Div.	Lost Prelim. Round
1979-80	80	30	7	3	17	13	10	47	20	13	328	240	107	1st,	Norris Div.	Lost Quarter-Final
1978-79	**80**	**29**	**6**	**5**	**23**	**11**	**6**	**52**	**17**	**11**	**337**	**204**	**115**	**1st,**	**Norris Div.**	**Won Stanley Cup**
1977-78	**80**	**32**	**4**	**4**	**27**	**6**	**7**	**59**	**10**	**11**	**359**	**183**	**129**	**1st,**	**Norris Div.**	**Won Stanley Cup**
1976-77	**80**	**33**	**1**	**6**	**27**	**7**	**6**	**60**	**8**	**12**	**387**	**171**	**132**	**1st,**	**Norris Div.**	**Won Stanley Cup**
1975-76	**80**	**32**	**3**	**5**	**26**	**8**	**6**	**58**	**11**	**11**	**337**	**174**	**127**	**1st,**	**Norris Div.**	**Won Stanley Cup**
1974-75	80	27	8	5	20	6	14	47	14	19	374	225	113	1st,	Norris Div.	Lost Semi-Final
1973-74	78	24	12	3	21	12	6	45	24	9	293	240	99	2nd,	East Div.	Lost Quarter-inal
1972-73	**78**	**29**	**4**	**6**	**23**	**6**	**10**	**52**	**10**	**16**	**329**	**184**	**120**	**1st,**	**East Div.**	**Won Stanley Cup**
1971-72	78	29	3	7	17	13	9	46	16	16	307	205	108	3rd,	East Div.	Lost Quarter-Final
1970-71	**78**	**29**	**7**	**3**	**13**	**16**	**10**	**42**	**23**	**13**	**291**	**216**	**97**	**3rd,**	**East Div.**	**Won Stanley Cup**
1969-70	76	21	9	8	17	13	8	38	22	16	244	201	92	5th,	East Div.	Out of Playoffs
1968-69	**76**	**26**	**7**	**5**	**20**	**12**	**6**	**46**	**19**	**11**	**271**	**202**	**103**	**1st,**	**East Div.**	**Won Stanley Cup**
1967-68	**74**	**26**	**5**	**6**	**16**	**17**	**4**	**42**	**22**	**10**	**236**	**167**	**94**	**1st,**	**East Div.**	**Won Stanley Cup**
1966-67	70	19	9	7	13	16	6	32	25	13	202	188	77	2nd,		Lost Final
1965-66	**70**	**23**	**11**	**1**	**18**	**10**	**7**	**41**	**21**	**8**	**239**	**173**	**90**	**1st,**		**Won Stanley Cup**
1964-65	**70**	**20**	**8**	**7**	**16**	**15**	**4**	**36**	**23**	**11**	**211**	**185**	**83**	**2nd,**		**Won Stanley Cup**
1963-64	70	22	7	6	14	14	7	36	21	13	209	167	85	1st,		Lost Semi-Final
1962-63	70	15	10	10	13	9	13	28	19	23	225	183	79	3rd,		Lost Semi-Final
1961-62	70	26	2	7	16	12	7	42	14	14	259	166	98	1st,		Lost Semi-Final
1960-61	70	24	6	5	17	13	5	41	19	10	254	188	92	1st,		Lost Semi-Final
1959-60	**70**	**23**	**4**	**8**	**17**	**14**	**4**	**40**	**18**	**12**	**255**	**178**	**92**	**1st,**		**Won Stanley Cup**
1958-59	**70**	**21**	**8**	**6**	**18**	**10**	**7**	**39**	**18**	**13**	**258**	**158**	**91**	**1st,**		**Won Stanley Cup**
1957-58	**70**	**23**	**8**	**4**	**20**	**9**	**6**	**43**	**17**	**10**	**250**	**158**	**96**	**1st,**		**Won Stanley Cup**
1956-57	**70**	**23**	**6**	**6**	**12**	**17**	**6**	**35**	**23**	**12**	**210**	**155**	**82**	**2nd,**		**Won Stanley Cup**
1955-56	**70**	**29**	**5**	**1**	**16**	**10**	**9**	**45**	**15**	**10**	**222**	**131**	**100**	**1st,**		**Won Stanley Cup**
1954-55	70	26	5	4	15	13	7	41	18	11	228	157	93	2nd,		Lost Final
1953-54	70	27	5	3	8	19	8	35	24	11	195	141	81	2nd,		Lost Final
1952-53	**70**	**18**	**12**	**5**	**10**	**11**	**14**	**28**	**23**	**19**	**155**	**148**	**75**	**2nd,**		**Won Stanley Cup**
1951-52	70	22	8	5	12	18	5	34	26	10	195	164	78	2nd,		Lost Final
1950-51	70	17	10	8	8	20	7	25	30	15	173	184	65	3rd,		Lost Final
1949-50	70	17	8	10	12	14	9	29	22	19	172	150	77	2nd,		Lost Semi-Final
1948-49	60	19	8	3	9	15	6	28	23	9	152	126	65	3rd,		Lost Semi-Final
1947-48	60	13	13	4	7	16	7	20	29	11	147	169	51	5th,		Out of Playoffs
1946-47	60	19	6	5	15	10	5	34	16	10	189	138	78	1st,		Lost Final
1945-46	**50**	**16**	**6**	**3**	**12**	**11**	**2**	**28**	**17**	**5**	**172**	**134**	**61**	**1st,**		**Won Stanley Cup**
1944-45	50	21	2	2	17	6	2	38	8	4	228	121	80	1st,		Lost Semi-Final
1943-44	**50**	**22**	**0**	**3**	**16**	**5**	**4**	**38**	**5**	**7**	**234**	**109**	**83**	**1st,**		**Won Stanley Cup**
1942-43	50	14	4	7	5	15	5	19	19	12	181	191	50	4th,		Lost Semi-Final
1941-42	48	12	10	2	6	17	1	18	27	3	134	173	39	6th,		Lost Quarter-Final
1940-41	48	11	9	4	5	17	2	16	26	6	121	147	38	6th,		Lost Quarter-Final
1939-40	48	5	14	5	5	19	0	10	33	5	90	167	25	7th,		Out of Playoffs
1938-39	48	8	11	5	7	13	4	15	24	9	115	146	39	6th,		Lost Quarter-Final
1937-38	48	13	4	7	5	13	6	18	17	13	123	128	49	3rd,	Cdn. Div.	Lost Quarter-Final
1936-37	48	16	8	0	8	10	6	24	18	6	115	111	54	1st,	Cdn. Div.	Lost Semi-Final
1935-36	48	5	11	8	6	15	3	11	26	11	82	123	33	4th,	Cdn. Div.	Out of Playoffs
1934-35	48	11	11	2	8	12	4	19	23	6	110	145	44	3rd,	Cdn. Div.	Lost Quarter-Final
1933-34	48	16	6	2	6	14	4	22	20	6	99	101	50	2nd,	Cdn. Div.	Lost Quarter-Final
1932-33	48	15	5	4	3	20	1	18	25	5	92	115	41	3rd,	Cdn. Div.	Lost Quarter-Final
1931-32	48	18	3	3	7	13	4	25	16	7	128	111	57	1st,	Cdn. Div.	Lost Semi-Final
1930-31	**44**	**15**	**3**	**4**	**11**	**7**	**4**	**26**	**10**	**8**	**129**	**89**	**60**	**1st,**	**Cdn. Div.**	**Won Stanley Cup**
1929-30	**44**	**13**	**5**	**4**	**8**	**9**	**5**	**21**	**14**	**9**	**142**	**114**	**51**	**2nd,**	**Cdn. Div.**	**Won Stanley Cup**
1928-29	44	12	4	6	10	3	9	22	7	15	71	43	59	1st,	Cdn. Div.	Lost Semi-Final
1927-28	44	12	7	3	14	4	4	26	11	7	116	48	59	1st,	Cdn. Div.	Lost Semi-Final
1926-27	44	15	5	2	13	9	0	28	14	2	99	67	58	2nd,	Cdn. Div.	Lost Semi-Final
1925-26	36	5	12	1	6	12	0	11	24	1	79	108	23	7th,		Out of Playoffs
1924-25	30	10	5	0	7	6	2	17	11	2	93	56	36	3rd,		Lost Final
1923-24	**24**	**10**	**2**	**0**	**3**	**9**	**0**	**13**	**11**	**0**	**59**	**48**	**26**	**2nd,**		**Won Stanley Cup**
1922-23	24	10	2	0	3	7	2	13	9	2	73	61	28	2nd,		Lost NHL Final
1921-22	24	8	3	1	4	8	0	12	11	1	88	94	25	3rd,		Out of Playoffs
1920-21	24	9	3	0	4	8	0	13	11	0	112	99	26	3rd and 2nd*		Out of Playoffs
1919-20	24	8	4	0	5	7	0	13	11	0	129	113	26	2nd and 3rd*		Out of Playoffs
1918-19	18	7	2	0	3	6	0	10	8	0	88	78	20	1st and 2nd*		Cup Final but no Decision
1917-18	22	8	3	0	5	6	0	13	9	0	115	84	26	1st and 3rd*		Lost NHL Final

* Season played in two halves with no combined standing at end.
From 1917-18 through 1925-26, NHL champions played against PCHA/WCHL champions for Stanley Cup.

2000-01 Player Personnel

FORWARDS	HT	WT	S	Place of Birth	Date	1999-00 Club
ASHAM, Arron	5-11	191	R	Portage La Prairie, Man.	4/13/78	Montreal-Quebec Citadelles
BASHKIROV, Andrei	6-0	215	L	Shelehov, USSR	6/22/70	Montreal-Quebec Citadelles
BERTRAND, Eric	6-1	205	L	St-Ephrem, Que.	4/16/75	N.J.-Atl.-Phi (AHL)-Milw
BLOUIN, Sylvain	6-2	207	L	Montreal, Que.	5/21/74	Worcester
BRUNET, Benoit	5-11	198	L	Ste-Anne-de-Bellevue, Que.	8/24/68	Montreal
CAMPBELL, Jim	6-2	205	R	Worcester, MA	4/3/73	Manitoba-StL-Worcester
CHOUINARD, Eric	6-3	202	L	Atlanta, GA	7/8/80	Quebec Remparts
DARBY, Craig	6-3	200	R	Oneida, NY	9/26/72	Montreal
DELISLE, Xavier	5-11	182	R	Quebec City, Que.	5/24/77	Detroit (IHL)-Toledo-Quebec (AHL)
HARRIS, Darcy	6-2	196	R	O'Leary, P.E.I.	12/22/78	Quebec Citadelles
HIGGINS, Matt	6-2	190	L	Calgary, Alta.	10/29/77	Montreal-Quebec Citadelles
KOIVU, Saku	5-10	181	L	Turku, Finland	11/23/74	Montreal
LANDRY, Eric	5-11	190	L	Gatineau, Que.	1/20/75	Kentucky
LIND, Juha	5-11	185	L	Helsinki, Finland	1/2/74	Dallas-Montreal
LINDEN, Trevor	6-5	211	R	Medicine Hat, Alta.	4/11/70	Montreal
McCLEARY, Trent	6-0	182	R	Swift Current, Sask.	9/8/72	Montreal
MORIN, Olivier	6-0	184	R	Montreal, Que.	4/2/78	Tallahasee-Quebec Citadelles
PETROV, Oleg	5-9	175	L	Moscow, USSR	4/18/71	Montreal-Quebec Citadelles
POULIN, Patrick	6-1	216	L	Vanier, Que.	4/23/73	Montreal
RIBEIRO, Mike	5-11	164	L	Montreal, Que.	2/10/80	Mtl-Quebec (AHL)-Rouyn-Noranda-Quebec (QMJHL)
RUCINSKY, Martin	6-1	205	L	Most, Czech.	3/11/71	Montreal
RYDER, Michael	6-0	187	R	St. John's, Nfld.	3/31/80	Hull Olympiques
SAVAGE, Brian	6-2	193	L	Sudbury, Ont.	2/24/71	Montreal
STOCK, P.J.	5-10	190	L	Victoriaville, Que.	5/26/75	NY Rangers-Hartford
WARD, Jason	6-3	193	R	Chapleau, Ont.	1/16/79	Montreal-Quebec Citadelles
ZHOLTOK, Sergei	6-2	191	R	Riga, Latvia	2/12/72	Montreal-Quebec Citadelles
ZUBRUS, Dainius	6-4	227	L	Elektrenai, USSR	6/16/78	Montreal
DEFENSEMEN						
BOUILLON, Francis	5-9	189	L	New York, NY	10/17/75	Montreal
BRISEBOIS, Patrice	6-1	203	R	Montreal, Que.	1/27/71	Montreal
CICCONE, Enrico	6-5	220	L	Montreal, Que.	4/10/70	Moskitos Essen
DESCOTEAUX, Matthieu	6-3	220	L	Pierreville, Que.	9/23/77	Hamilton-Quebec Citadelles
DeWOLF, Josh	6-2	200	L	Bloomington, MN	7/25/77	Albany-Quebec Citadelles
DYKHUIS, Karl	6-3	214	L	Sept-Iles, Que.	7/8/72	Philadelphia-Montreal
GUREN, Miloslav	6-2	213	L	Uherske Hradiste, Czech.	9/24/76	Montreal-Quebec Citadelles
LAFLAMME, Christian	6-1	210	R	St-Charles, Que.	11/24/76	Edmonton-Montreal
MARKOV, Andrei	6-0	185	L	Voskresensk, USSR	12/20/78	Dynamo Moscow
McBAIN, Mike	6-2	195	L	Kimberley, B.C.	1/12/77	Detroit (IHL)-Quebec (AHL)
RAZIN, Gennady	6-4	200	L	Kharkov, USSR	2/3/78	Quebec Citadelles
RICHTER, Barry	6-2	200	L	Madison, WI	9/11/70	Mtl-Quebec (AHL)-Manitoba
RIVET, Craig	6-2	197	R	North Bay, Ont.	9/13/74	Montreal
ROBIDAS, Stephane	5-11	180	R	Sherbrooke, Que.	3/3/77	Montreal-Quebec Citadelles
SOURAY, Sheldon	6-4	230	L	Elk Point, Alta.	7/13/76	New Jersey-Montreal
WEINRICH, Eric	6-1	213	L	Roanoke, VA	12/19/66	Montreal

GOALTENDERS	HT	WT	C	Place of Birth	Date	1999-00 Club
FICHAUD, Eric	5-11	171	L	Anjou, Que.	11/4/75	Carolina-Quebec Citadelles
GARON, Mathieu	6-3	182	R	Chandler, Que.	1/9/78	Quebec Citadelles
HACKETT, Jeff	6-1	198	L	London, Ont.	6/1/68	Montreal
THEODORE, Jose	5-11	189	R	Laval, Que.	9/13/76	Montreal

1999-2000 Scoring

* – rookie

Regular Season

Pos	#	Player	Team	GP	G	A	Pts	+/–	PIM	PP	SH	GW	GT	S	%
L	26	Martin Rucinsky	MTL	80	25	24	49	1	70	7	1	4	1	242	10.3
R	15	Dainius Zubrus	MTL	73	14	28	42	–1	54	3	0	1	0	139	10.1
C	34	Sergei Zholtok	MTL	68	26	12	38	2	28	9	0	7	1	163	16.0
D	43	Patrice Brisebois	MTL	54	10	25	35	–1	18	5	0	2	2	88	11.4
C	14	Trevor Linden	MTL	50	13	17	30	–3	34	4	0	3	0	87	14.9
L	49	Brian Savage	MTL	38	17	12	29	–4	19	6	1	5	0	107	15.9
L	17	Benoit Brunet	MTL	50	14	15	29	3	13	6	1	2	0	103	13.6
D	22	Eric Weinrich	MTL	77	4	25	29	4	39	2	0	0	0	120	3.3
L	27	Shayne Corson	MTL	70	8	20	28	–2	115	2	0	1	0	121	6.6
R	32	Oleg Petrov	MTL	44	2	24	26	10	8	1	0	0	1	96	2.1
R	23	Turner Stevenson	MTL	64	8	13	21	–1	61	0	0	2	0	94	8.5
C	11	Saku Koivu	MTL	24	3	18	21	7	14	1	0	0	1	53	5.7
D	28	Karl Dykhuis	PHI	5	0	1	1	–2	6	0	0	0	0	5	0.0
			MTL	67	7	12	19	–3	40	3	1	0	0	64	10.9
			TOTAL	72	7	13	20	–5	46	3	1	0	0	69	10.1
C	63	Craig Darby	MTL	76	7	10	17	–14	14	0	1	2	0	90	7.8
D	52	Craig Rivet	MTL	61	3	14	17	11	76	0	0	1	1	71	4.2
D	51	* Francis Bouillon	MTL	74	3	13	16	–7	38	2	0	1	0	76	3.9
C	37	Patrick Poulin	MTL	82	10	5	15	–15	17	0	1	2	0	82	12.2
D	44	Sheldon Souray	N.J	52	0	8	8	–6	70	0	0	0	0	74	0.0
			MTL	19	3	0	3	7	44	0	0	0	0	39	7.7
			TOTAL	71	3	8	11	1	114	0	0	0	0	113	2.7
L	47	Juha Lind	DAL	34	3	4	7	–1	6	0	0	0	0	36	8.3
			MTL	13	1	2	3	–2	4	0	0	0	0	6	16.7
			TOTAL	47	4	6	10	–3	10	0	0	0	0	42	9.5
C	40	Jesse Belanger	MTL	16	3	6	9	2	2	0	0	0	0	21	14.3
R	29	Jim Cummins	MTL	47	3	5	8	–5	92	0	0	0	0	33	9.1
D	24	Christian Laflamme	EDM	50	0	5	5	–4	32	0	0	0	0	18	0.0
			MTL	15	0	2	2	–5	8	0	0	0	0	6	0.0
			TOTAL	65	0	7	7	–9	40	0	0	0	0	24	0.0
C	45	* Arron Asham	MTL	33	4	2	6	–7	24	0	1	1	0	29	13.8
D	20	Scott Lachance	MTL	57	0	6	6	–4	22	0	0	0	0	41	0.0
R	61	* Jason Ward	MTL	32	2	1	3	–1	10	1	0	0	0	24	8.3
D	48	* Miloslav Guren	MTL	24	1	2	3	–5	12	1	0	0	0	20	5.0
C	71	* Mike Ribeiro	MTL	19	1	1	2	–6	2	1	0	0	0	18	5.6
D	21	Barry Richter	MTL	23	0	2	2	–5	8	0	0	0	0	13	0.0
C	46	* Matt Higgins	MTL	25	0	2	2	–6	4	0	0	0	0	9	0.0
C	6	Trent McCleary	MTL	12	1	0	1	2	4	0	0	0	0	4	25.0
L	36	Dave Morissette	MTL	1	0	0	0	0	5	0	0	0	0	0	0.0
D	44	* Stephane Robidas	MTL	1	0	0	0	0	0	0	0	0	0	0	0.0
L	35	Andrei Bashkirov	MTL	2	0	0	0	0	0	0	0	0	0	0	0.0
G	41	Eric Fichaud	CAR	9	0	0	0	0	2	0	0	0	0	0	0.0
			MTL	0	0	0	0	0	0	0	0	0	0	0	0.0
			TOTAL	9	0	0	0	0	2	0	0	0	0	0	0.0
G	60	Jose Theodore	MTL	30	0	0	0	0	0	0	0	0	0	0	0.0
G	31	Jeff Hackett	MTL	56	0	0	0	0	4	0	0	0	0	0	0.0

Goaltending

No.	Goaltender	GPI	Mins	Avg	W	L	T	EN	SO	GA	SA	S%
60	Jose Theodore	30	1655	2.10	12	13	2	2	5	58	717	.919
31	Jeff Hackett	56	3301	2.40	23	25	7	2	3	132	1543	.914
	Totals	**82**	**4983**	**2.34**	**35**	**38**	**9**	**4**	**8**	**194**	**2264**	**.914**

Coach

VIGNEAULT, ALAIN
Coach, Montreal Canadiens. Born in Quebec, Que., May 14, 1961.

Alain Vigneault was named the 24th head coach in the history of the Montreal Canadiens on May 26, 1997, becoming the second youngest coach in team history.

Vigneault, who guided the Canadiens to the Eastern Conference semi-finals during his first season, possesses more than 11 years of coaching experience. He coached the QMJHL Beauport Harfangs for two seasons (1995-96 and 1996-97), following more than three years as an assistant coach with the NHL Ottawa Senators.

Vigneault was the head coach of the Hull Olympiques for five seasons (1987 to 1992), leading his team to the Memorial Cup Tournament in his first season. His coaching career began in 1986-87 with the Trois-Rivières Draveurs of the QMJHL. As head coach at the junior hockey level, Vigneault had a record of 257 victories, 213 losses and 35 ties. In 580 games (season and playoffs), he posted a .541 winning percentage.

Vigneault was assistant coach on Canada's national junior team in 1989 and 1991, winning the gold medal at the 1991 World Junior Championships in Saskatoon. He was honored once as CHL coach of the year (1987-88), and twice as head coach of the QMJHL Second All-Star Team.

Alain Vigneault played a total of 42 games in the NHL from 1981 to 1983 with the St. Louis Blues. He resides in Montreal with his spouse, Josée Doucet, and their two daughters, Andréanne and Janie.

Coaching Record

		Regular Season					Playoffs			
Season	Team	Games	W	L	T	%	Games	W	L	%
1986-87	Trois-Rivières (QMJHL)	65	26	37	2	.415	....	....	....	....
1987-88	Hull (QMJHL)	70	43	23	4	.643	19	12	7	.632
1988-89	Hull (QMJHL)	66	36	25	5	.583	9	5	4	.556
1989-90	Hull (QMJHL)	70	36	29	5	.550	11	4	7	.364
1990-91	Hull (QMJHL)	65	33	25	7	.562	6	2	4	.333
1991-92	Hull (QMJHL)	68	40	23	5	.625	6	2	4	.333
1995-96	Beauport (QMJHL)	31	19	7	5	.694	20	13	7	.650
1996-97	Beauport (QMJHL)	70	24	44	2	.357	4	1	3	.250
1997-98	**Montreal (NHL)**	**82**	**37**	**32**	**13**	**.530**	**10**	**4**	**6**	**.400**
1998-99	**Montreal (NHL)**	**82**	**32**	**39**	**11**	**.457**	....	....	....	....
1999-2000	**Montreal (NHL)**	**82**	**35**	**38**	**9**	**.506•**	....	....	....	....
	NHL Totals	**246**	**104**	**109**	**33**	**.498•**	**10**	**4**	**6**	**.400**

• Includes points from regulation ties

Coaching History

Jack Laviolette, 1909-10; Adolphe Lecours, 1910-11; Napoleon Dorval, 1911-12, 1912-13; Jimmy Gardner, 1913-14, 1914-15; Newsy Lalonde, 1915-16 to 1920-21; Newsy Lalonde and Léo Dandurand, 1921-22; Léo Dandurand, 1922-23 to 1925-26; Cecil Hart, 1926-27 to 1931-32; Newsy Lalonde, 1932-33, 1933-34; Newsy Lalonde and Léo Dandurand, 1934-35; Sylvio Mantha, 1935-36; Cecil Hart, 1936-37, 1937-38; Cecil Hart and Jules Dugal, 1938-39; Babe Siebert, 1939*; Pit Lepine, 1939-40; Dick Irvin 1940-41 to 1954-55; Toe Blake, 1955-56 to 1967-68; Claude Ruel, 1968-69, 1969-70; Claude Ruel and Al MacNeil, 1970-71; Scotty Bowman, 1971-72 to 1978-79; Bernie Geoffrion and Claude Ruel, 1979-80; Claude Ruel, 1980-81; Bob Berry, 1981-82, 1982-83; Bob Berry and Jacques Lemaire, 1983-84; Jacques Lemaire, 1984-85; Jean Perron, 1985-86 to 1987-88; Pat Burns, 1988-89 to 1991-92; Jacques Demers, 1992-93 to 1994-95; Jacques Demers and Mario Tremblay, 1995-96; Mario Tremblay, 1996-97; Alain Vigneault, 1997-98 to date.

* Named coach in summer but died before 1939-40 season began.

Captains' History

Jack Laviolette, 1909-10; Newsy Lalonde, 1910-11; Jack Laviolette, 1911-12; Newsy Lalonde, 1912-13; Jimmy Gardner, 1913-14, 1914-15; Howard McNamara, 1915-16; Newsy Lalonde, 1916-17 to 1921-22; Sprague Cleghorn, 1922-23 to 1924-25; Bill Coutu, 1925-26; Sylvio Mantha, 1926-27 to 1931-32; George Hainsworth, 1932-33; Sylvio Mantha, 1933-34 to 1935-36; Babe Siebert, 1936-37 to 1938-39; Walter Buswell, 1939-40; Toe Blake, 1940-41 to 1946-47; Toe Blake and Bill Durnan, 1947-48; Emile Bouchard, 1948-49 to 1955-56; Maurice Richard, 1956-57 to 1959-60; Doug Harvey, 1960-61; Jean Béliveau, 1961-62 to 1970-71; Henri Richard, 1971-72 to 1974-75; Yvan Cournoyer, 1975-76 to 1978-79; Serge Savard, 1979-80, 1980-81; Bob Gainey, 1981-82 to 1988-89; Guy Carbonneau and Chris Chelios (co-captains), 1989-90; Guy Carbonneau, 1990-91 to 1993-94; Kirk Muller and Mike Keane, 1994-95; Mike Keane and Pierre Turgeon, 1995-96; Pierre Turgeon and Vincent Damphousse, 1996-97; Vincent Damphousse, 1997-98, 1998-99; Saku Koivu, 1999-2000 to date.

Club Records

Team

(Figures in brackets for season records are games played; records for fewest points, wins, ties, losses, goals, goals against are for 70 or more games)

Most Points	*132	1976-77 (80)
Most Wins	60	1976-77 (80)
Most Ties	23	1962-63 (70)
Most Losses	40	1983-84 (80)
Most Goals	387	1976-77 (80)
Most Goals Against	295	1983-84 (80)
Fewest Points	65	1950-51 (70)
Fewest Wins	25	1950-51 (70)
Fewest Ties	5	1983-84 (80)
Fewest Losses	*8	1976-77 (80)
Fewest Goals	155	1952-53 (70)
Fewest Goals Against	*131	1955-56 (70)
Longest Winning Streak		
Overall	12	Jan. 6-Feb. 3/68
Home	13	Nov. 2/43-Jan. 8/44, Jan. 30-Mar. 26/77
Away	8	Dec. 18/77-Jan. 18/78, Jan. 21-Feb. 21/82
Longest Undefeated Streak		
Overall	28	Dec. 18/77-Feb. 23/78 (23 wins, 5 ties)
Home	*34	Nov. 1/76-Apr. 2/77 (28 wins, 6 ties)
Away	*23	Nov. 27/74-Mar. 12/75 (14 wins, 9 ties)
Longest Losing Streak		
Overall	12	Feb. 13-Mar. 13/26
Home	7	Dec. 16/39-Jan. 18/40
Away	10	Jan. 16-Mar. 13/26
Longest Winless Streak		
Overall	12	Feb. 13-Mar. 13/26 (12 losses), Nov. 28-Dec. 29/35 (8 losses, 4 ties)
Home	15	Dec. 16/39-Mar. 7/40 (12 losses, 3 ties)
Away	12	Nov. 26/33-Jan. 28/34 (8 losses, 4 ties), Oct. 20/50-Dec. 13/51 (8 losses, 4 ties)
Most Shutouts, Season	*22	1928-29 (44)
Most PIM, Season	1,847	1995-96 (82)
Most Goals, Game	*16	Mar. 3/20 (Mtl. 16 at Que. 3)

Individual

Most Seasons	20	Henri Richard, Jean Béliveau
Most Games	1,256	Henri Richard
Most Goals, Career	544	Maurice Richard
Most Assists, Career	728	Guy Lafleur
Most Points, Career	1,246	Guy Lafleur (518G, 728A)
Most PIM, Career	2,248	Chris Nilan
Most Shutouts, Career	75	George Hainsworth
Longest Consecutive Games Streak	560	Doug Jarvis (Oct. 8/75-Apr. 4/82)
Most Goals, Season	60	Steve Shutt (1976-77), Guy Lafleur (1977-78)
Most Assists, Season	82	Peter Mahovlich (1974-75)
Most Points, Season	136	Guy Lafleur (1976-77; 56G, 80A)
Most PIM, Season	358	Chris Nilan (1984-85)
Most Points, Defenseman, Season	85	Larry Robinson (1976-77; 19G, 66A)
Most Points, Center, Season	117	Peter Mahovlich (1974-75; 35G, 82A)
Most Points, Right Wing, Season	136	Guy Lafleur (1976-77; 56G, 80A)
Most Points, Left Wing, Season	110	Mats Naslund (1985-86; 43G, 67A)
Most Points, Rookie, Season	71	Mats Naslund (1982-83; 26G, 45A), Kjell Dahlin (1985-86; 32G, 39A)
Most Shutouts, Season	*22	George Hainsworth (1928-29)
Most Goals, Game	6	Newsy Lalonde (Jan. 10/20)
Most Assists, Game	6	Elmer Lach (Feb. 6/43)
Most Points, Game	8	Maurice Richard (Dec. 28/44; 5G, 3A), Bert Olmstead (Jan. 9/54; 4G, 4A)

* NHL Record.

Retired Numbers

1	Jacques Plante	1952-1963
2	Doug Harvey	1947-1961
4	Jean Béliveau	1950-1971
7	Howie Morenz	1923-1937
9	Maurice Richard	1942-1960
10	Guy Lafleur	1971-1984
16	Henri Richard	1955-1975

All-time Record vs. Other Clubs

Regular Season

	At Home							On Road							Total						
	GP	W	L	T	GF	GA	PTS	GP	W	L	T	GF	GA	PTS	GP	W	L	T	GF	GA	PTS
Anaheim	6	3	2	1	19	16	7	5	4	1	0	19	16	8	11	7	3	1	38	32	15
Atlanta	2	2	0	0	7	4	4	2	1	0	1	6	2	3	4	3	0	1	13	6	7
Boston	324	185	93	46	1098	769	416	324	120	148	56	879	957	296	648	305	241	102	1977	1726	712
Buffalo	92	52	28	12	361	274	116	92	27	46	19	249	287	73	184	79	74	31	610	561	189
Calgary	43	24	11	8	154	106	56	43	25	13	5	151	129	55	86	49	24	13	305	235	111
Carolina	67	45	15	7	284	191	97	70	33	28	9	248	212	76	137	78	43	16	532	403	173
Chicago	272	171	53	48	1050	639	390	272	124	93	55	758	729	303	544	295	146	103	1808	1368	693
Colorado	61	37	15	9	254	192	83	62	26	31	5	216	209	57	123	63	46	14	470	401	140
Dallas	56	37	11	8	245	137	82	56	30	15	11	201	145	71	112	67	26	19	446	282	153
Detroit	279	171	65	43	988	628	385	279	96	130	53	714	803	246	558	267	195	96	1702	1431	631
Edmonton	27	14	9	4	95	87	33	29	15	14	0	93	94	30	56	29	23	4	188	181	63
Florida	13	6	6	1	39	30	13	14	4	8	2	36	48	10	27	10	14	3	75	78	23
Los Angeles	62	43	8	11	284	158	97	62	36	17	9	248	191	81	124	79	25	20	532	349	178
Nashville	1	1	0	0	3	2	2	2	0	1	1	3	8	1	3	1	1	1	6	10	3
New Jersey	46	29	11	6	170	120	64	46	24	19	3	178	134	51	92	53	30	9	348	254	115
NY Islanders	52	30	13	9	193	154	69	52	23	24	5	153	164	52	104	53	37	14	346	318	121
NY Rangers	282	188	56	38	1108	644	414	282	114	114	54	825	819	282	564	302	170	92	1933	1463	696
Ottawa	23	13	7	3	72	63	29	20	11	8	1	61	56	23	43	24	15	4	133	119	52
Philadelphia	66	32	20	14	239	203	78	65	24	26	15	196	199	63	131	56	46	29	435	402	141
Phoenix	27	23	3	1	134	61	47	26	11	9	6	101	86	28	53	34	12	7	235	147	75
Pittsburgh	74	56	10	8	356	187	120	74	35	26	13	262	223	83	148	91	36	21	618	410	203
St. Louis	56	40	9	7	246	149	87	56	28	13	15	195	144	71	112	68	22	22	441	293	158
San Jose	9	6	1	2	32	16	14	8	4	2	2	22	22	10	17	10	3	4	54	38	24
Tampa Bay	14	8	5	1	44	35	17	15	6	6	3	35	35	15	29	14	11	4	79	70	32
Toronto	322	196	86	40	1140	794	432	323	114	165	44	842	975	272	645	310	251	84	1982	1769	704
Vancouver	50	38	8	4	240	127	80	49	32	9	8	188	123	72	99	70	17	12	428	250	152
Washington	52	30	15	7	202	109	67	51	21	21	9	157	139	51	103	51	36	16	359	248	118
Defunct Clubs	231	148	58	25	779	469	321	230	98	97	35	586	606	231	461	246	155	60	1365	1075	552
Totals	**2609**	**1628**	**618**	**363**	**9836**	**6364**	**3620**	**2609**	**1086**	**1084**	**439**	**7622**	**7555**	**2614**	**5218**	**2714**	**1702**	**802**	**17458**	**13919**	**6234**

Playoffs

	Series	W	L	GP	W	L	T	GF	GA	Last Mtg.	Round	Result
Boston	28	21	7	139	87	52	0	430	339	1994	CQF	L 3-4
Buffalo	7	4	3	35	18	17	0	124	111	1998	CSF	L 0-4
Calgary	2	1	1	11	6	5	0	31	32	1989	F	L 2-4
Chicago	17	12	5	81	50	29	2	261	185	1976	QF	W 4-0
Colorado	5	3	2	31	17	14	0	105	85	1993	DSF	W 4-2
Dallas	2	1	1	13	7	6	0	48	37	1980	QF	L 3-4
Detroit	12	5	7	62	33	29	0	161	149	1978	QF	W 4-1
Edmonton	1	0	1	3	0	3	0	6	15	1981	PR	L 0-3
Hartford	5	5	0	27	19	8	0	96	70	1992	DSF	W 4-3
Los Angeles	1	1	0	5	4	1	0	15	12	1993	F	W 4-1
NY Islanders	4	3	1	22	14	8	0	64	55	1993	CF	W 4-1
NY Rangers	14	7	7	61	34	25	2	188	158	1996	CQF	L 2-4
New Jersey	1	0	1	5	1	4	0	11	22	1997	CQF	L 1-4
Philadelphia	4	3	1	21	14	7	0	72	52	1989	CF	W 4-2
Pittsburgh	1	1	0	6	4	2	0	18	15	1998	CQF	W 4-2
St. Louis	3	3	0	12	12	0	0	42	14	1977	QF	W 4-0
Toronto	15	8	7	71	42	29	0	215	160	1979	QF	W 4-0
Vancouver	1	1	0	5	4	1	0	20	9	1975	QF	W 4-1
Defunct Clubs	11*	6	4	28	15	9	4	70	71			
Totals	**134***	**85**	**48**	**638**	**381**	**249**	**8**	**1977**	**1591**			

* 1919 Final incomplete due to influenza epidemic.

Playoff Results 2000-1996

Year	Round	Opponent	Result	GF	GA
1998	CSF	Buffalo	L 0-4	10	17
	CQF	Pittsburgh	W 4-2	18	15
1997	CQF	New Jersey	L 1-4	11	22
1996	CQF	NY Rangers	L 2-4	17	19

Abbreviations: Round: F – Final; **CF** – conference final; **CSF** – conference semi-final; **CQF** – conference quarter-final; **DSF** – division semi-final; **QF** – quarter-final; **PR** – preliminary round.

Calgary totals include Atlanta Flames, 1972-73 to 1979-80.
Colorado totals include Quebec, 1979-80 to 1994-95.
New Jersey totals include Kansas City, 1974-75 to 1975-76, and Colorado Rockies, 1976-77 to 1981-82.
Phoenix totals include Winnipeg, 1979-80 to 1995-96.
Carolina totals include Hartford, 1979-80 to 1996-97.
Dallas totals include Minnesota North Stars, 1967-68 to 1992-93.

1999-2000 Results

Oct.	2		Toronto	1-4		11		Detroit	3-0
	6	at	Edmonton	1-2		14	at	Buffalo	2-1
	8	at	Calgary	4-1		15		Boston	2-2
	9	at	Vancouver	1-4		19		NY Islanders	3-0
	12		Florida	1-2		22		Pittsburgh	4-2
	14	at	Philadelphia	5-4 *		24	at	Carolina	2-3 *
	16		Buffalo	2-1		29		Philadelphia	2-2
	18		NY Islanders	2-4		30		Carolina	3-0
	20		Colorado	1-2	Feb.	2	at	Florida	1-3
	23	at	Toronto	2-3		3	at	Tampa Bay	2-1 *
	27		Chicago	0-1		8		Edmonton	4-5 *
	30		NY Rangers	2-2		10		Washington	0-1
Nov.	3	at	New Jersey	2-3		12		Ottawa	5-4
	4	at	NY Islanders	1-2 *		14		Florida	4-1
	6	at	Ottawa	1-2		16	at	Atlanta	5-1
	10	at	Pittsburgh	4-5		17	at	Carolina	3-0
	11		Anaheim	2-1		19		Toronto	2-1
	13		Atlanta	4-2		22		Phoenix	1-0
	16		San Jose	1-4		24		New Jersey	3-2 *
	18	at	Nashville	1-6		26		Washington	0-3
	20	at	Los Angeles	5-3		27	at	New Jersey	0-3
	22	at	Anaheim	2-1	Mar.	1	at	Chicago	4-1
	23	at	San Jose	3-2 *		2	at	Boston	5-2
	27		Vancouver	2-1		4	at	Toronto	3-4
Dec.	1		Dallas	2-3		6		Atlanta	3-2
	3	at	NY Rangers	2-3		8	at	Pittsburgh	3-0
	4		Philadelphia	2-3		10	at	Buffalo	3-2
	7		Calgary	3-3		11		Boston	3-5
	9	at	NY Islanders	4-2		14		Tampa Bay	3-4
	11		Los Angeles	2-4		16	at	Philadelphia	1-1
	13	at	Washington	1-0		18		Carolina	3-2
	16		New Jersey	1-2		20	at	Buffalo	1-4
	18	at	Toronto	1-2		22	at	Atlanta	1-1
	20		Pittsburgh	5-1		25	at	Florida	2-4
	23	at	Boston	3-3		26	at	Tampa Bay	3-1
	27	at	Ottawa	4-4		29		Boston	4-3
	29		Ottawa	2-3	Apr.	1		Buffalo	0-2
Jan.	2		NY Rangers	2-2		2	at	Detroit	5-6 *
	4	at	Washington	1-6		5	at	NY Rangers	3-0
	6	at	St. Louis	3-4		6		Tampa Bay	5-1
	7	at	Colorado	1-4		8		Ottawa	1-3

* – Overtime

Entry Draft
Selections 2000-1986

2000	**1996**	**1992**	**1988**
Pick	**Pick**	**Pick**	**Pick**
13 Ron Hainsey	18 Matt Higgins	20 David Wilkie	20 Eric Charron
16 Marcel Hossa	44 Mathieu Garon	33 Valeri Bure	34 Martin St. Amour
78 Jozef Balej	71 Arron Asham	44 Keli Corpse	46 Neil Carnes
79 Tyler Hanchuck	92 Kim Staal	68 Craig Rivet	83 Patric Kjellberg
109 Johan Eneqvist	99 Etienne Drapeau	82 Louis Bernard	93 Peter Popovic
114 Christian Larrivee	127 Daniel Archambault	92 Marc Lamothe	104 Jean-Claude Bergeron
145 Ryan Glenn	154 Brett Clark	116 Don Chase	125 Patrik Carnback
172 Scott Selig	181 Timo Vertala	140 Martin Sychra	146 Tim Chase
182 Petr Chvojka	207 Mattia Baldi	164 Christian Proulx	167 Sean Hill
243 Joni Puurula	233 Michel Tremblay	188 Michael Burman	188 Harijs Vitolinsh
275 Jonathan Gauthier		212 Earl Cronan	209 Yuri Krivokhizha
	1995	236 Trent Cavicchi	230 Kevin Dahl
1999	**Pick**	260 Hiroyuki Miura	251 Dave Kunda
Pick	8 Terry Ryan		
39 Alexander Buturlin	60 Miloslav Guren	**1991**	**1987**
58 Matt Carkner	74 Martin Hohenberger	**Pick**	**Pick**
97 Chris Dyment	86 Jonathan Delisle	17 Brent Bilodeau	17 Andrew Cassels
107 Evan Lindsay	112 Niklas Anger	28 Jim Campbell	33 John LeClair
136 Dusty Jamieson	138 Boyd Olson	43 Craig Darby	38 Eric Desjardins
145 Marc-Andre Thinel	164 Stephane Robidas	61 Yves Sarault	44 Mathieu Schneider
150 Matt Shasby	190 Greg Hart	73 Vladimir Vujtek	58 Francois Gravel
167 Sean Dixon	216 Eric Houde	83 Sylvain Lapointe	80 Kris Miller
196 Vadim Tarasov		100 Brad Layzell	101 Steve McCool
225 Mikko Hyytia	**1994**	105 Tony Prpic	122 Les Kuntar
253 Jerome Marois	**Pick**	127 Oleg Petrov	143 Rob Kelley
	18 Brad Brown	149 Brady Kramer	164 Will Geist
1998	44 Jose Theodore	171 Brian Savage	185 Eric Tremblay
Pick	54 Chris Murray	193 Scott Fraser	206 Barry McKinlay
16 Eric Chouinard	70 Marko Kiprusoff	215 Greg MacEachern	227 Ed Ronan
45 Mike Ribeiro	74 Martin Belanger	237 Paul Lepler	248 Bryan Herring
75 Francois Beauchemin	96 Arto Kuki	259 Dale Hooper	
132 Andrei Bashkirov	122 Jimmy Drolet		**1986**
152 Gordie Dwyer	148 Joel Irving	**1990**	**Pick**
162 Andrei Markov	174 Jessie Rezansoff	**Pick**	15 Mark Pederson
189 Andrei Kruchinin	200 Peter Strom	12 Turner Stevenson	27 Benoit Brunet
201 Craig Murray	226 Tomas Vokoun	39 Ryan Kuwabara	57 Jyrki Lumme
216 Michael Ryder	252 Chris Aldous	58 Charles Poulin	78 Brent Bobyck
247 Darcy Harris	278 Ross Parsons	60 Robert Guillet	94 Eric Aubertin
		81 Gilbert Dionne	99 Mario Milani
1997	**1993**	102 Paul Di Pietro	120 Steve Bisson
Pick	**Pick**	123 Craig Conroy	141 Lyle Odelein
11 Jason Ward	21 Saku Koivu	144 Stephen Rohr	162 Rick Hayward
37 Gregor Baumgartner	47 Rory Fitzpatrick	165 Brent Fleetwood	183 Antonin Routa
65 Ilkka Mikkola	73 Sebastien Bordeleau	186 Derek Maguire	204 Eric Bohemier
91 Daniel Tetrault	85 Adam Wiesel	207 Mark Kettelhut	225 Charlie Moore
118 Konstantin Sidulov	99 Jean-Francois Houle	228 John Uniac	246 Karel Svoboda
122 Gennady Razin	113 Jeff Lank	249 Sergei Martynyuk	
145 Jonathan Desroches	125 Dion Darling		
172 Ben Guite	151 Darcy Tucker	**1989**	
197 Petr Kubos	177 David Ruhly	**Pick**	
202 Andrei Sidyakin	203 Alan Letang	13 Lindsay Vallis	
228 Jarl Espen Ygranes	229 Alexandre Duchesne	30 Patrice Brisebois	
	255 Brian Larochelle	41 Steve Larouche	
	281 Russell Guzior	51 Pierre Sevigny	
		76 Eric Dubois	
		83 Andre Racicot	
		104 Marc Deschamps	
		146 Craig Ferguson	
		167 Patrick Lebeau	
		188 Roy Mitchell	
		209 Ed Henrich	
		230 Justin Duberman	
		251 Steve Cadieux	

General Managers' History

Jack Laviolette and Joseph Cattarinich, 1909-1910; George Kennedy, 1910-11 to 1920-21; Leo Dandurand, 1921-22 to 1934-35; Ernest Savard, 1935-36; Cecil Hart, 1936-37 to 1938-39; Jules Dugal, 1939-40; Tom P. Gorman, 1940-41 to 1945-46; Frank J. Selke, 1946-47 to 1963-64; Sam Pollock, 1964-65 to 1977-78; Irving Grundman, 1978-79 to 1982-83; Serge Savard, 1983-84 to 1994-95; Serge Savard and Réjean Houle, 1995-96; Réjean Houle, 1996-97 to date.

General Manager

HOULE, RÉJEAN
Vice President, Hockey and General Manager, Montreal Canadiens.
Born in Rouyn-Noranda, Que., October 25, 1949.

Réjean Houle was appointed general manager of the Montreal Canadiens on October 21, 1995. His appointment represents the high point of a career that began at age 16 with the Montreal Junior Canadiens.

Houle was a member of five Stanley Cup Championship teams during his playing career with the Canadiens. From 1969 to 1983, he played for 11 seasons with the Canadiens, with the exception of a three-year stint with the Quebec Nordiques of the World Hockey Association (1973 to 1976). Houle played in 635 NHL regular season games, posting totals of 161 goals and 247 assists (408 points). He also participated in the NHL playoffs on 10 occasions (90 games).

Prior to becoming general manager of the Canadiens, and following his playing career, Houle was an executive with Molson Breweries.

Club Directory

Centre Molson

Centre Molson
1260 de La Gauchetière St. W.
Montréal, QC H3B 5E8
Phone **514/932-2582**
FAX (Hockey) 514/932-8736
Team Services 514/989-2717
P.R. 514/932-9296
Media 514/932-8285
www.canadiens.com
Capacity: 21,273

President of Club de Hockey Canadien and the Molson Centre	Pierre Boivin
Executive Assistant to the President	Lise Beaudry
Vice-President, Finance and Administration and Alternate Governor	Fred Steer
Executive Vice-President and General Manager Entertainment	Aldo Giampaolo
Vice-President, Marketing, Communications and Sales	Pierre Ladouceur
Vice-President, Operations, Molson Centre	Alain Gauthier
Vice-President Hockey, General Manager and Alternate Governor	Réjean Houle
Director of Hockey Personnel	André Savard
Director of Team Services	Michèle Lapointe
Supervisor of Prospect Development	Guy Carbonneau
Chief Scout	Pierre Dorion
Professional Scouts	Pierre Mondou, Doug Robinson
Amateur and Professional Scout	Martin Madden
Amateur Scouts	Fred E. Bandel, Elmer Benning, Hannu Laine, Mats Naslund, Gerry O'Flaherty, Antonin Routa, Claude Ruel, Richard Scammell, Nikolai Vakourov
Executive Assistant to the V.P. & General Manager	Donna Stuart
Administrative Assistant, Team Services	Claudine Crépin
Head Coach	Alain Vigneault
Assistant Coaches	Clément Jodoin, Roland Melanson

Medical and Training Staff

Club Physician and Chief Surgeon	Dr. David Mulder
Senior Medical Consultant	Dr. D.G. Kinnear
Orthopaedist	Dr. Eric Lenczner
Ophthalmologist	Dr. John Little
Dentist	Dr. Pierre Desautels
General Physician	Dr. Vincent Lacroix
Athletic Therapist	Gaétan Lefebvre
Athletic Therapist	Graham Rynbend
Strength & Conditioning Coach	Stéphane Dubé
Equipment Manager	Pierre Gervais
Assistants to the Equipment Manager	Robert Boulanger, Pierre Ouellette
Video Supervisor	Mario Leblanc

AHL Affiliation
Les Citadelles de Québec
Colisée de Québec – 250, Wilfrid Laurier Blvd. – Québec, QC G1L 5A7 – Tel.: (418) 525-5333

President	Maurice Tanguay
General Manager	Raymond Bolduc
Head Coach	Michel Therrien
Assistant Coach	Éric Lavigne
Managing Assistant - Communications and Hockey Operations	Nicole Bouchard

Communications

Director, Communications	Donald Beauchamp
Assistant, Director Communications	Dominick Saillant
Administrative-Assistant, Communications	Sylvie Lambert

Marketing/Community Relations/Game Presentation/Web Site

Director of Marketing	Patrice St-Amour
Marketing Manager	Frédérique Cardinal
Marketing Coordinator	Geneviève Paquette
Executive Assistant to the V.P. Marketing, Communications and Sales	Normande Herget
Supervisor-Production Room (Jumbotron)	Paul Shubin
Executive Director, Sales	Richard Primeau
Assistant Director, Souvenir Boutiques	Gilles Trudeau
Coordinator - Photos and Archives	Claude Rompré

Advertising and Sponsorship

EFFIX Inc.	Franois-Xavier Seigneur

Finance

Executive Director of Finance	Jacques Aubé
Controller Budgeting & Analysis	Dennis McKinley
Administrative Supervisor CHC/Molson Centre	Dave Poulton
Controller - Financial Reporting	Franoise Brault
Accounting Supervisor, Molson Centre	Paule Jolicoeur
Accounting Supervisor CHC	Marleine Bédard
Director of Information Technology	Pierre-Éric Belzile
Executive Assistant to the V.P. Finance	Susan Cryans

Centre Molson

Director, Ticket Office	Cathy D'Ascoli
Executive Assistant to the V.P. Operations	Maryse Carthwright

Entertainment

Executive Director, Events	Louise Laliberté
Executive Assistant to the V.P. & General Manager Entertainment	Vicki Mercuri
Location of Press Box	Suspended above ice - East Side
Location of Radio and TV booth	Suspended above ice - West side
Club trains at	Centre Molson
Play-by-play - Radio/TV	Claude Quenneville, Pierre Houde, André Côté, Pierre Rinfret (French)
	Dino Sisto (English), Paul Romanuk (English)
TV Channels	CBFT (2), TQS (35) (French)
Cable TV	RDS (33) (French), TSN (28) (English)
Radio Stations	CKAC (730) (French), CJAD (800) (English)

Nashville Predators

1999-2000 Results: 28W-47L-7T 70PTS. Fourth, Central Division

Year-by-Year Record

Season	GP	Home W	L	T	Road W	L	T	Overall W	L	T	GF	GA	Pts.	Finished		Playoff Result
1999-2000	82	15	23	3	13	24	4	28	47	7	199	240	70	4th,	Central Div.	Out of Playoffs
1998-99	82	15	22	4	13	25	3	28	47	7	190	261	63	4th,	Central Div.	Out of Playoffs

2000-01 Schedule

Oct.	Sat.	7	at Pittsburgh (in Japan)
	Sun.	8	Pittsburgh (in Japan)
	Fri.	13	Washington
	Sat.	14	Carolina
	Tue.	17	Los Angeles
	Thu.	19	at Detroit
	Sat.	21	San Jose
	Tue.	24	Vancouver
	Wed.	25	at Colorado
	Fri.	27	Florida
	Tue.	31	St. Louis
Nov.	Thu.	2	at Philadelphia
	Sat.	4	Anaheim
	Tue.	7	at NY Islanders
	Wed.	8	at New Jersey
	Sat.	11	at Boston
	Wed.	15	at Atlanta
	Thu.	16	Columbus
	Sat.	18	Detroit
	Mon.	20	at Detroit
	Wed.	22	Dallas
	Fri.	24	St. Louis
	Sun.	26	at Carolina*
	Tue.	28	Calgary
	Thu.	30	at Chicago
Dec.	Fri.	1	Chicago
	Mon.	4	at Vancouver
	Wed.	6	at Edmonton
	Thu.	7	at Calgary
	Sun.	10	at Minnesota*
	Tue.	12	Philadelphia
	Thu.	14	Edmonton
	Sat.	16	Chicago
	Wed.	20	at Toronto
	Thu.	21	at Montreal
	Sat.	23	at NY Rangers*
	Tue.	26	Colorado
	Thu.	28	Anaheim
	Fri.	29	at Colorado
Jan.	Mon.	1	Vancouver*

	Thu.	4	at St. Louis
	Sat.	6	Buffalo
	Mon.	8	at Vancouver
	Wed.	10	at Edmonton
	Thu.	11	at Calgary
	Sat.	13	at San Jose
	Tue.	16	Edmonton
	Wed.	17	at Dallas
	Fri.	19	Boston
	Sun.	21	St. Louis*
	Tue.	23	Atlanta
	Wed.	24	at Detroit
	Sat.	27	Colorado
	Mon.	29	at Phoenix
	Wed.	31	at Anaheim
Feb.	Thu.	1	at Los Angeles
	Thu.	8	Columbus
	Sat.	10	at Columbus
	Tue.	13	Dallas
	Fri.	16	San Jose
	Sun.	18	Tampa Bay*
	Tue.	20	Detroit
	Wed.	21	at Washington
	Sat.	24	Minnesota
	Tue.	27	Los Angeles
Mar.	Thu.	1	Columbus
	Sun.	4	NY Rangers*
	Tue.	6	at Phoenix
	Thu.	8	at Los Angeles
	Sat.	10	at San Jose
	Sun.	11	at Anaheim*
	Thu.	15	at Chicago
	Sat.	17	Phoenix
	Mon.	19	at Columbus
	Wed.	21	at Minnesota
	Thu.	22	at Chicago
	Sat.	24	Ottawa
	Thu.	29	Phoenix
	Sat.	31	Minnesota
Apr.	Wed.	4	at Dallas
	Thu.	5	Calgary
	Sat.	7	at St. Louis

* Denotes afternoon game.

Franchise date: June 25, 1997

CENTRAL DIVISION

3rd NHL Season

A veteran of seven seasons in the Finnish Elite League, defenseman Kimmo Timonen entered the NHL with Nashville during the 1998-99 season. In 1999-2000, he was the club's top-scoring blueliner with 33 points on eight goals and 25 assists.

2000-01 Player Personnel

FORWARDS	HT	WT	S	Place of Birth	Date	1999-00 Club
ANDERSSON, Jonas	6-3	200	L	Stockholm, Sweden	2/24/81	North Bay-Milwaukee
ARKHIPOV, Denis	6-3	210	L	Kazan, USSR	5/19/79	Ak Bars Kazan
BARTEK, Martin	6-1	200	R	Kindgssed Jill, Czech.	7/17/80	Moncton Wildcats
BORDELEAU, Sebastien	5-11	185	L	Vancouver, B.C.	2/15/75	Nashville
CISAR, Marian	6-0	197	R	Bratislava, Czech.	2/25/78	Nashville-Milwaukee
CLASSEN, Greg	6-1	194	L	Aylsham, Sask.	8/24/77	Merrimack College-Milwaukee
FITZGERALD, Tom	6-0	195	R	Billerica, MA	8/28/68	Nashville
GOSSELIN, David	6-1	200	R	Levis, Que.	6/22/77	Nashville-Milwaukee
HAGGERTY, Sean	6-1	186	L	Rye, NY	2/11/76	NY Islanders-Kansas City
HARTNELL, Scott	6-3	198	L	Regina, Sask.	4/18/82	Prince Albert
JOHNSON, Greg	5-11	202	L	Thunder Bay, Ont.	3/16/71	Nashville
KJELLBERG, Patric	6-3	210	L	Trelleborg, Sweden	6/7/69	Nashville
KREVSUN, Alexander	6-1	210	L	Togliatti, USSR	6/2/80	Krylja Sovetov-CSK Samara-2
LEGWAND, David	6-2	190	L	Detroit, MI	8/17/80	Nashville
MOWERS, Mark	5-11	187	R	Whitesboro, NY	2/16/74	Nashville-Milwaukee
MYHRES, Brantt	6-3	220	R	Edmonton, Alta.	3/18/74	San Jose-Kentucky
PELTONEN, Ville	5-11	188	L	Vantaa, Finland	5/24/73	Nashville
RIVA, Danny	6-0	190	R	Framingham, MA	9/17/75	Milwaukee
ROBITAILLE, Randy	5-11	196	L	Ottawa, Ont.	10/12/75	Nashville
RONNING, Cliff	5-8	165	L	Burnaby, B.C.	10/1/65	Nashville
SACHL, Peter	6-2	205	L	Jindrichuv Hradec, Czech.	12/2/77	Tacoma-Asheville-Fort Wayne
TOBLER, Ryan	6-3	222	L	Calgary, Alta.	5/13/76	Milwaukee
VALICEVIC, Robert	6-1	198	L	Detroit, MI	1/6/71	Nashville
WALKER, Scott	5-10	195	R	Cambridge, Ont.	7/19/73	Nashville
WATT, Mike	6-2	212	L	Seaforth, Ont.	3/31/76	NY Islanders-Lowell
YACHMENEV, Vitali	5-11	195	L	Chelyabinsk, USSR	1/8/75	Nashville

DEFENSEMEN						
BEREHOWSKY, Drake	6-2	225	R	Toronto, Ont.	1/3/72	Nashville
BERENZWEIG, Bubba	6-1	215	L	Arlington Heights, IL	8/8/77	Nashville-Milwaukee
BOIKOV, Alexandre	6-0	198	L	Chelyabinsk, USSR	2/7/75	Nashville-Milwaukee
FILIPOWICZ, Jayme	6-2	215	L	Arlington Heights, IL	6/15/76	Milwaukee
FITZPATRICK, Rory	6-2	208	R	Rochester, NY	1/11/75	Worcester-Milwaukee
HOULDER, Bill	6-2	215	L	Thunder Bay, Ont.	3/11/67	Tampa Bay-Nashville
HULSE, Cale	6-3	220	R	Edmonton, Alta.	11/10/73	Calgary
LINTNER, Richard	6-3	214	L	Trencin, Czech.	11/15/77	Milwaukee-Nashville
MILLAR, Craig	6-2	212	L	Winnipeg, Man.	7/12/76	Nashville-Milwaukee
MORO, Marc	6-1	220	L	Toronto, Ont.	7/17/77	Nashville-Milwaukee
NAMESTNIKOV, John	5-11	190	R	Arzamis-Ig, USSR	10/9/71	Hartford-Nashville-Milwaukee
SAUER, Kent	6-2	230	L	St. Cloud, MN	5/10/79	Portland (WHL)-Milwaukee
SKRASTINS, Karlis	6-1	208	L	Riga, USSR	7/9/74	Nashville-Milwaukee
SKRBEK, Pavel	6-3	215	L	Kladno, Czech.	8/9/78	Wilkes-Barre-Milwaukee
TIMONEN, Kimmo	5-10	196	L	Kuopio, Finland	3/18/75	Nashville

GOALTENDERS	HT	WT	C	Place of Birth	Date	1999-00 Club
DUNHAM, Mike	6-3	200	L	Johnson City, NY	6/1/72	Nashville-Milwaukee
FINLEY, Brian	6-4	183	R	Sault Ste. Marie, Ont.	7/3/81	Barrie Colts
MASON, Chris	6-0	198	L	Red Deer, Alta.	4/20/76	Milwaukee
LASAK, Jan	6-1	205	L	Zvolen, Czech.	10/4/79	Hampton Roads
VOKOUN, Tomas	6-0	197	R	Karlovy Vary, Czech.	7/2/76	Nashville-Milwaukee

1999-2000 Scoring

* – rookie

Regular Season

Pos	#	Player	Team	GP	G	A	Pts	+/-	PIM	PP	SH	GW	GT	S	%
C	7	Cliff Ronning	NSH	82	26	36	62	–13	34	7	0	2	0	248	10.5
R	10	Patric Kjellberg	NSH	82	23	23	46	–11	14	9	0	3	0	129	17.8
C	22	Greg Johnson	NSH	82	11	33	44	–15	40	2	0	1	0	133	8.3
D	44	Kimmo Timonen	NSH	51	8	25	33	–5	26	2	1	2	0	97	8.2
R	43	Vitali Yachmenev	NSH	68	16	16	32	5	12	1	1	3	0	120	13.3
D	15	Drake Berehowsky	NSH	79	12	20	32	–4	87	5	0	1	0	102	11.8
C	11	* David Legwand	NSH	71	13	15	28	–6	30	4	0	2	0	111	11.7
R	24	Scott Walker	NSH	69	7	21	28	–16	90	0	1	0	1	98	7.1
L	16	Ville Peltonen	NSH	79	6	22	28	–1	22	2	0	2	0	125	4.8
C	12	Robert Valicevic	NSH	80	14	11	25	–11	21	2	1	3	0	113	12.4
C	27	* Randy Robitaille	NSH	69	11	14	25	–13	10	2	0	1	0	113	9.7
C	71	Sebastien Bordeleau	NSH	60	10	13	23	–12	30	0	2	1	1	127	7.9
R	21	Tom Fitzgerald	NSH	82	13	9	22	–18	66	0	3	1	0	119	10.9
D	23	Bill Houlder	T.B	14	1	2	3	–3	2	1	0	0	0	21	4.8
			NSH	57	2	12	14	–6	24	1	0	1	0	68	2.9
			TOTAL	71	3	14	17	–9	26	2	0	1	0	89	3.4
D	8	Craig Millar	NSH	57	3	11	14	–6	28	0	0	1	0	50	6.0
D	3	* Karlis Skrastins	NSH	59	5	6	11	–7	20	1	0	2	0	51	9.8
L	36	Niklas Andersson	NYI	17	3	7	10	–3	8	1	0	0	0	24	12.5
			NSH	7	0	1	1	0	0	0	0	0	0	7	0.0
			TOTAL	24	3	8	11	–3	8	1	0	0	0	31	9.7
R	18	Mark Mowers	NSH	41	4	5	9	0	10	0	0	0	0	50	8.0
R	41	* Richard Lintner	NSH	33	1	5	6	–6	22	0	0	0	0	58	1.7
D	2	Dan Keczmer	NSH	24	0	5	5	–2	28	0	0	0	0	21	0.0
R	40	* David Gosselin	NSH	10	2	1	3	–4	6	0	0	0	0	14	14.3
C	9	Darren Turcotte	NSH	9	0	1	1	0	4	0	0	0	0	13	0.0
G	29	Tomas Vokoun	NSH	33	0	1	1	0	8	0	0	0	0	0	0.0
D	20	Yevgeny Namestnikov	NSH	2	0	0	0	2	0	0	0	0	0	3	0.0
D	38	* Alexandre Boikov	NSH	2	0	0	0	0	2	0	0	0	0	1	0.0
D	26	* Andy Berenzweig	NSH	2	0	0	0	–1	0	0	0	0	0	3	0.0
L	39	* Marian Cisar	NSH	3	0	0	0	–2	4	0	0	0	0	2	0.0
R	26	Philip Crowe	NSH	6	0	0	0	0	6	0	0	0	0	1	0.0
D	5	Jan Vopat	NSH	6	0	0	0	0	1	0	0	0	0	3	0.0
D	33	* Marc Moro	NSH	8	0	0	0	–3	40	0	0	0	0	1	0.0
L	17	Patrick Cote	NSH	21	0	0	0	–7	70	0	0	0	0	8	0.0
G	1	Mike Dunham	NSH	52	0	0	0	0	0	0	0	0	0	0	0.0

Goaltending

No.	Goaltender	GPI	Mins	Avg	W	L	T	EN	SO	GA	SA	S%
29	Tomas Vokoun	33	1879	2.78	9	20	1	4	1	87	908	.904
1	Mike Dunham	52	3077	2.85	19	27	6	3	0	146	1584	.908
	Totals	82	4986	2.89	28	47	7	7	1	240	2499	.904

General Manager

POILE, DAVID
General Manager, Nashville Predators.
Born in Toronto, Ont., February 14, 1949.

Known for his patience, loyalty, determination and thoroughness, David Poile exhausted every conceivable option to launch and build the Nashville Predators.

Since joining the Predators on July 9, 1997, Poile made a commitment to building for the future, surrounding himself with one of the youngest and most talented staffs in the National Hockey League.

Prior to joining Nashville, Poile spent 15 seasons as vice president/general manager of the Washington Capitals. During his tenure in Washington, the Capitals made 14 post-season appearances, winning their first Patrick Division title in 1989 and advancing to the Conference Finals in 1990. During Poile's 15 years in Washington, the Capitals compiled a record of 594-454-132, finished first or second in the Atlantic Division eight seasons and recorded 90-or-more points seven different seasons. Poile's Capitals were ranked in the NHL's top five in winning percentage during his fifteen years with a .559 mark.

Poile started his professional hockey career as an administrative assistant for the Atlanta Flames in 1972, shortly after graduating from Northeastern University in Boston. At Northeastern, he was hockey team captain, leading scorer and most valuable player for two years.

In 1977, he was named assistant general manager of the Atlanta Flames (moved to Calgary in 1980), serving as the manager and coordinator of the Calgary farm club.

Poile is a member of the NHL's general managers committee and was instrumental in the NHL's adoption of the instant replay rule in 1991. He was awarded *Inside Hockey*'s Man of the Year for his leadership on the issue. He was also twice honored as *The Sporting News* NHL Executive of the Year following the 1982-83 and 1983-84 seasons. Poile served as general manager of the 1998 and 1999 U.S. National Team for the International Ice Hockey Federation World Championships.

Poile was introduced to hockey by watching his father, Norman "Bud" Poile, play seven seasons in the NHL. Bud later became general manager for the Vancouver Canucks and the Philadelphia Flyers, both NHL expansion franchises at the time. In 1989, Bud was a co-winner of the Lester Patrick Award (an annual award for outstanding service to hockey in the United States), and was inducted into the Hockey Hall of Fame a year later.

David and his wife, Elizabeth, reside in Nashville and have two children, Brian and Lauren.

David Legwand was the first draft choice in the history of the Nashville Predators, selected second overall behind Vincent Lecavalier in 1998. He collected his first NHL goal and assist on October 11, 1999.

Club Records

Team

(Figures in brackets for season records are games played; records for fewest points, wins, ties, losses, goals, goals against are for 70 or more games)

Most Points	70	1999-2000 (82)
Most Wins	28	1998-99 (82)
		1999-2000 (82)
Most Ties	7	1998-99 (82)
		1999-2000 (82)
Most Losses	47	1998-99 (82)
		1999-2000 (82)
Most Goals	199	1999-2000 (82)
Most Goals Against	261	1998-99 (82)
Fewest Points	63	1998-99 (82)
Fewest Wins	28	1998-99 (82)
Fewest Ties	7	1998-99 (82)
		1999-2000 (82)
Fewest Losses	47	1998-99 (82)
		1999-2000 (82)
Fewest Goals	190	1998-99 (82)
Fewest Goals Against	240	1999-2000 (82)

Longest Winning Streak
Overall	4	Dec. 26/99-Jan. 1/00
Home	4	Dec. 28/99-Jan. 8/00
Away	3	Feb. 12-24/99

Longest Undefeated Streak
Overall	8	Dec. 18/99-Jan. 1/00
Home	6	Dec. 18/99-Jan. 1/00
Away	3	Five times

Longest Losing Streak
Overall	7	Nov. 20-Dec. 2/99
Home	6	Jan. 21-Feb. 15/99
Away	5	Twice

Longest Winless Streak
Overall	7	Twice
Home	9	Jan. 21-Mar. 2/99
Away	5	Five times
Most Shutouts, Season	2	1998-99 (82)
Most PIM, Season	1,420	1998-99 (82)
Most Goals, Game	6	Five times

Individual

Most Seasons	2	Many players
Most Games	162	Tom Fitzgerald
Most Goals, Career	44	Cliff Ronning
Most Assists, Career	71	Cliff Ronning
Most Points, Career	115	Cliff Ronning (44G, 71A)
Most PIM, Career	312	Patrick Cote
Most Shutouts, Career	2	Tomas Vokoun
Longest Consecutive Games Streak	131	Tom Fitzgerald (Dec. 30/98-date)
Most Goals, Season	26	Cliff Ronning (1999-2000)
Most Assists, Season	36	Cliff Ronning (1999-2000)
Most Points, Season	62	Cliff Ronning (1999-2000; 26G, 36A)
Most PIM, Season	242	Patrick Cote (1999-2000)
Most Points, Defenseman, Season	33	Kimmo Timonen (1999-2000; 8G, 25A)
Most Points, Center, Season	62	Cliff Ronning (1999-2000; 26G, 36A)
Most Points, Right Wing, Season	48	Sergei Krivokrasov (1998-99; 25G, 23A)
Most Points, Left Wing, Season	46	Patrick Kjellberg (1999-2000; 23G, 23A)
Most Points, Rookie, Season	28	David Legwand (1999-2000; 13G, 15A)
Most Shutouts, Season	1	Mike Dunham (1998-99), Tomas Vokoun (1998-99, 1999-2000)
Most Goals, Game	3	Rob Valicevic (Nov. 10/99)
Most Assists, Game	3	Sebastien Bordeleau (Mar. 7/99), Drake Berehowsky (Feb. 2/00)
Most Points, Game	4	Sebastien Bordeleau (Dec. 19/98; 2G, 2A), Sergei Krivokrasov (Dec. 19/98; 2G, 2A)

General Managers' History

David Poile, 1998-99 to date.

Coaching History

Barry Trotz, 1998-99 to date.

Captains' History

Tom Fitzgerald, 1998-99 to date.

A fine defensive forward and a top penalty killer, Nashville captain Tom Fitzgerald led the Predators with three shorthand goals in 1999-2000. He has missed only 25 games over the last nine seasons.

1999-2000 Results

Date	Opponent	Result	Date	Opponent	Result
Oct. 2	Los Angeles	0-2	8	Chicago	6-3
5	Colorado	2-3	11	at Colorado	2-4
10	at Chicago	3-3	13	Vancouver	3-4*
11	at Toronto	4-2	15	Pittsburgh	4-2
14	San Jose	1-5	18	Phoenix	4-4
16	Dallas	3-2	21	at Calgary	4-5*
20	at Buffalo	4-3	23	at Vancouver	2-1
23	Edmonton	4-3	24	at Edmonton	3-2*
28	at San Jose	2-3	27	Los Angeles	2-6
30	at Vancouver	1-4	29	Calgary	3-1
31	at Edmonton	2-4	31	at NY Rangers	1-5
Nov. 3	at Calgary	4-5*	Feb. 2	at NY Islanders	6-4
5	Chicago	1-3	3	at New Jersey	1-4
10	at Chicago	4-2	10	Buffalo	1-2*
11	at Ottawa	2-1	12	Washington	2-4
13	at Pittsburgh	2-6	15	Edmonton	1-2
18	Montreal	6-1	16	at Dallas	0-3
20	Vancouver	1-3	18	St. Louis	1-2
22	at St. Louis	2-3*	21	Dallas	5-2
24	Boston	2-5	23	at Chicago	4-2
26	at Washington	0-1	26	Tampa Bay	2-3
27	Anaheim	3-4	29	New Jersey	1-2
30	Phoenix	3-6	Mar. 2	at San Jose	3-4
Dec. 2	at St. Louis	1-3	4	at Los Angeles	2-3*
4	Detroit	4-1	5	at Anaheim	0-1
6	at Atlanta	4-3*	7	Chicago	3-1
8	at Detroit	3-6	10	Detroit	1-3
10	St. Louis	2-4	12	Edmonton	4-3
11	Florida	2-4	14	at Detroit	2-3*
14	at Tampa Bay	4-4	16	at Colorado	2-2
15	at Florida	2-3	17	at Phoenix	4-3*
18	Colorado	2-2	19	at Los Angeles	2-1*
19	at Philadelphia	1-1	21	Philadelphia	0-2
21	at Boston	3-1	23	Detroit	3-6
23	St. Louis	2-2	25	Calgary	1-2
26	at St. Louis	3-2	28	NY Islanders	3-2
28	Carolina	3-2	29	at Carolina	1-3
30	Atlanta	3-2	29	at Vancouver	2-1
Jan. 1	San Jose	3-2	Apr. 3	at Anaheim	1-3
5	at Dallas	1-3	5	at Phoenix	2-3
6	at Detroit	2-5	7	Anaheim	1-5

* – Overtime

All-time Record vs. Other Clubs

Regular Season

	At Home							On Road							Total						
	GP	W	L	T	GF	GA	PTS	GP	W	L	T	GF	GA	PTS	GP	W	L	T	GF	GA	PTS
Anaheim	4	2	2	0	9	11	4	4	0	4	0	4	13	0	8	2	6	0	13	24	4
Atlanta	1	1	0	0	6	0	2	1	1	0	0	4	3	2	2	2	0	0	10	3	4
Boston	2	0	2	0	4	10	0	2	1	1	0	4	9	2	4	1	3	0	8	19	2
Buffalo	2	0	2	0	2	5	0	1	1	0	0	8	4	2	3	1	2	0	10	10	2
Calgary	5	2	3	0	13	14	4	4	2	1	1	12	13	5	9	4	4	1	25	27	9
Carolina	2	2	0	0	6	4	4	2	0	2	0	5	7	0	4	2	2	0	11	11	4
Chicago	6	3	2	1	19	15	7	6	2	3	1	19	21	5	12	5	5	2	38	36	12
Colorado	4	1	1	2	11	11	4	4	0	3	1	6	13	1	8	1	4	3	17	24	5
Dallas	4	2	2	0	11	11	4	3	0	3	0	3	8	0	7	2	5	0	14	19	4
Detroit	6	2	4	0	16	22	4	6	0	6	0	12	25	0	12	2	10	0	28	47	4
Edmonton	5	3	1	1	15	12	7	4	0	4	0	9	13	0	9	3	5	1	24	25	7
Florida	2	0	2	0	2	5	0	2	0	2	0	3	7	0	4	0	4	0	5	12	0
Los Angeles	4	1	3	0	8	14	2	4	3	1	0	11	8	6	8	4	4	0	19	22	8
Montreal	2	1	0	1	8	3	3	1	0	1	0	2	3	0	3	1	1	1	10	6	3
New Jersey	2	0	2	0	2	6	0	2	1	1	0	1	4	2	4	1	3	0	3	10	2
NY Islanders	2	1	1	0	6	8	2	2	2	0	0	8	5	4	4	3	1	0	14	13	6
NY Rangers	1	0	1	0	4	7	0	2	0	2	0	2	10	0	3	0	3	0	6	17	0
Ottawa	1	0	1	0	1	3	0	1	1	0	0	2	1	2	2	1	1	0	3	4	2
Philadelphia	2	0	2	0	2	4	0	2	0	1	1	1	9	1	3	1	2	1	4	13	2
Phoenix	4	1	1	2	10	15	3	4	2	2	0	13	13	4	8	3	3	2	23	28	7
Pittsburgh	2	1	1	0	6	5	2	2	0	2	0	3	7	0	4	1	3	0	9	12	2
St. Louis	6	1	4	1	14	21	3	6	2	4	0	11	20	5	12	3	8	1	25	41	8
San Jose	4	2	2	0	9	12	4	4	1	3	0	10	12	2	8	3	5	0	19	24	6
Tampa Bay	2	0	2	0	4	6	0	2	1	0	1	7	4	3	4	1	2	1	11	10	3
Toronto	0	0	0	0	0	0	0	1	1	0	0	4	2	2	1	1	0	0	4	2	2
Vancouver	5	3	2	0	15	13	7	4	2	2	0	12	14	4	9	5	4	0	27	27	11
Washington	2	1	1	0	5	5	2	1	0	1	0	2	4	0	3	1	2	0	7	9	2
Totals	**82**	**30**	**45**	**7**	**207**	**242**	**69**	**82**	**26**	**49**	**7**	**182**	**259**	**64**	**164**	**56**	**94**	**14**	**389**	**501**	**133**

Entry Draft
Selections 2000-1998

2000 Pick		1999 Pick		1998 Pick	
6	Scott Hartnell	6	Brian Finley	2	David Legwand
36	Daniel Widing	33	Jonas Andersson	60	Denis Arkhipov
72	Mattias Nilsson	52	Adam Hall	85	Geoff Koch
89	Libor Pivko	54	Andrew Hutchinson	88	Kent Sauer
131	Matt Hendricks	61	Ed Hill	138	Martin Beauchesne
137	Mike Stuart	65	Jan Lasak	147	Craig Brunel
154	Matt Koalska	72	Brett Angel	202	Martin Bartek
173	Tomas Harant	121	Yevgeny Pavlov	230	Karlis Skrastins
197	Zybynek Irgl	124	Alexander Krevsun		
203	Jure Penko	131	Konstantin Panov		
236	Mats Christeen	162	Timo Helbling		
284	Martin Hohener	191	Martin Erat		
		205	Kyle Kettles		
		220	Miroslav Durak		
		248	Darren Haydar		

Coach

TROTZ, BARRY
Coach, Nashville Predators. Born in Winnipeg, Man., July 15, 1962.

Barry Trotz realized his dream of becoming an NHL Head Coach on August 6, 1997, after serving four seasons as head coach and director of hockey operations for the American Hockey League's Portland Pirates. He and assistant Paul Gardner spent the 1997-98 season scouting in preparation for the inaugural season of the Nashville Predators.

Trotz began his coaching career in 1984 as assistant coach with the University of Manitoba for one season, before serving two seasons as the head coach and general manager of the Dauphin Kings Junior Hockey Club from 1985-87. He became head coach of the University of Manitoba during the 1987 season and also served as a scout for the Spokane Chiefs of the Western Hockey League that season. Trotz joined the Washington Capitals organization as their chief western scout during the 1988 season. The Winnipeg, Manitoba native was appointed an assistant coach of the Capitals' American Hockey League affiliate in Baltimore prior to the 1991 season before being named head coach prior to the 1992 season. When the franchise relocated to Portland, he guided the Pirates to two AHL Calder Cup Final appearances in the club's first four seasons. He led the Pirates to a league-best 43-27-10 record, captured the Calder Cup Championship and was named the American Hockey League Coach of the Year following the 1994-95 season.

In 1995, Trotz guided Portland to a new North American professional hockey league record 17-game unbeaten streak (14-0-3) to start the season. He was named head coach for the U.S. Team at the American Hockey League All-Star Game in 1996.

Prior to his coaching career, Trotz played junior hockey for the Western Hockey League's Regina Pats from 1979-83. During that time, he recorded 39 goals, 121 assists for 160 points, along with 490 penalty minutes in 204 games.

Barry and his wife, Kim reside in Brentwood along with their three children Shalan, Tyson and Tiana.

Coaching Record

			Regular Season				Playoffs			
Season	Team	Games	W	L	T	%	Games	W	L	%
1992-93	Baltimore (AHL)	80	28	40	12	.425	7	3	4	.429
1993-94	Portland (AHL)	80	43	27	10	.600	8	6	2	.750
1994-95	Portland (AHL)	80	46	22	12	.650	7	3	4	.429
1995-96	Portland (AHL)	80	32	38	10	.463	24	14	10	.583
1996-97	Portland (AHL)	80	37	33	10	.525	5	2	3	.400
1998-99	**Nashville (NHL)**	**82**	**28**	**47**	**7**	**.384**	....	....	....	....
1999-2000	**Nashville (NHL)**	**82**	**28**	**47**	**7**	**.427•**	....	....	....	....
	NHL Totals	**164**	**56**	**94**	**14**	**.405•**	....	....	....	....

• Includes points from regulation ties

Club Directory

Gaylord Entertainment Center

Nashville Predators
Gaylord Entertainment Center
501 Broadway
Nashville, TN 37203
Phone 615/770-2300
FAX 615/770-2309
Ticket Information 615/770-PUCK
www.nashvillepredators.com
Capacity: 17,113

Owner, Chairman and Governor	Craig Leipold
General Partner	Nashville Predators, LLC
Limited Partner	Gaylord Entertainment Company
President, COO and Alternate Governor	Jack Diller
Executive Vice President/General Manager and Alternate Governor	David Poile
Executive Vice President/Business Operations	Tom Ward
Vice President/Chief Financial Officer	Ed Lang
Vice President/Communications & Development	Gerry Helper

Hockey Operations

Assistant General Manager	Ray Shero
Head Coach	Barry Trotz
Assistant Coaches	Paul Gardner, Brent Peterson
Strength and Conditioning Coach	Mark Nemish
Goaltending Coach	Mitch Korn
Video Coach	Robert Bouchard
Director of Player Personnel	Paul Fenton
Chief Amateur Scout	Craig Channell
Scouting Coordinator	Dan MacKinnon
Professional Scout	Fred Devereaux
Amateur Scouts - Europe	Lucas Bergman, Alexei Dementiev, Janne Kekalainen
Amateur Scouts - North America	Luc Gauthier, Alan Hepple, Rick Knickle, Greg Royce, Mike Rooney, Dennis Schueller
Head Athletic Trainer	Dan Redmond
Equipment Manager	Pete Rogers
Assistant Equipment Manager	Chris Scoppetto
Equipment Assistant	Chris Moody
Massage Therapist	Anthony Garrett
Nutritionist	Donna Gurchiek
Director of Team Services/Media Relations	Frank Buonomo
Executive Assistant	Kalli Quinn
Hockey Operations Assistant	Mike Corbett

Team Doctors

Team Physician	Dr. Michael J. Pagnani, MD
Team Dentist	Dr. James W. McPherson Jr., DDS
Team Ophthalmologist	Dr. Daniel Weikert, MD
Team Plastic Surgeons	Dr. Bryan D. Oslin, MD
	Dr. Donald Griffin, MD
Team Neuropsychologist	Dr. Gary S. Solomon, Ph. D.
Team Neurosurgeon	Dr. Carl Hampf, MD
Team Internist	Dr. Richard W. Garman, MD

Communications/Development

Communications Manager	Ken Anderson
Communications Coordinator	Gregory Harvey
Corporate Communications Coordinator	Cathy Lewandowski
Director of Community Relations/ Executive Director of Predators Foundation	Jenny Hannon
Community Relations Manager	Alexis Herbster
Community Relations Assistant	Angel Winter
Manager, Amateur Hockey	Marc Spigel
Graphic Artist, Communications & Development	Maggie Bizwell
Team Photographer	John Russell

Business/Marketing/Corporate Sales

Vice President, Corporate Services	Susie Masotti
Executive Director of Business Development	Mark Perrone
National Sales Manager	Bill McKay
Local Sales Manager, Corporate Sponsorship	David Nivison
Account Executives	Allison Gay, Tommy Lynch
Sponsor Services, Account Managers	Evelyn Finch, Lisa Hays, Kristin Snyder
Premium Seating Manager	Britt Kincheloe
Account Manager, Premium Seating	Myron Murray
Director of Marketing	Randy Campbell
Marketing Manager/Special Events	Polly Pearce
Advertising Manager	Julia Robinson
Marketing Assistant	Carrie Poss
Promotions Manager	Mark Iralson
Entertainment Coordinator	Brett Rhinehardt
Graphic Artist, Marketing	Mike Towsen
Executive Assistant	Linda Adams
Sponsor Sales Administrative Assistant	Kelly Preuett

Finance/Human Resources

Director of Finance	Beth Snider
Director of Human Resources	Stephanie Ditenhafer
Administrator Payroll & Accounting	Susan Charnley
Accountant, Gaylord Entertainment Center	Tracy Hardes
Accountant, Team	Sjar Toney
Accounts Payable Clerk	Carter Lynch
Project Coordinator	Scott Pilkinton
Financial Project Coordinator	Denton McClane
Benefits and Office Administrator	Robin Krokker
Administrative Assistant	Elaine Lewis

Broadcast and Game Presentation Department

Vice President, Broadcasting	John Guagliano
Director of Operations	Jimmy Corn
Producer	Erik Barnhart
Game Presentations Manager	Bryan Shaffer
Broadcast and Entertainment Manager	Susan Morgan
Game Presentation/Promotions Coordinator	Christel Foley
Game Video Producer	Blake Grant
Broadcast Assistant Producer	Robert Hill
Broadcasters	Pete Weber, Terry Crisp

Ticket Operations

Vice President, Ticket Sales	Scott Loft
Ticket Operations Manager	Jamie Hall
Computer Operator	Cordell Johnson
Business Development Manager	Geoff Dunnuck
Club/Suite Sales Executive	Tom Phillips
Account Executives	Tony Hall, Nat Harden, Jonathan Tuschl, Bill Walker
Ticket Sales Administrative Assistant	Annie Snelgrove
Fan Relations Manager	Gene Connelly
Fan Relations Account Service Representatives	Bob Milhizer, Tiffany Williams
Radio Flagship	WTN-FM (99.7 FM)
TV Flagship	FOX Sports Net

New Jersey Devils

1999-2000 Results: 45w-29l-8t 103pts. Second, Atlantic Division

Year-by-Year Record

Season	GP	Home W	L	T	Road W	L	T	Overall W	L	T	GF	GA	Pts.	Finished		Playoff Result
1999-2000	**82**	**28**	**10**	**3**	**17**	**19**	**5**	**45**	**29**	**8**	**251**	**203**	**103**	**2nd,**	**Atlantic Div.**	**Won Stanley Cup**
1998-99	82	19	14	8	28	10	3	47	24	11	248	196	105	1st,	Atlantic Div.	Lost Conf. Quarter-Final
1997-98	82	29	10	2	19	13	9	48	23	11	225	166	107	1st,	Atlantic Div.	Lost Conf. Quarter-Final
1996-97	82	23	9	9	22	14	5	45	23	14	231	182	104	1st,	Atlantic Div.	Lost Conf. Semi-Final
1995-96	82	22	17	2	15	16	10	37	33	12	215	202	86	6th,	Atlantic Div.	Out of Playoffs
1994-95	**48**	**14**	**4**	**6**	**8**	**14**	**2**	**22**	**18**	**8**	**136**	**121**	**52**	**2nd,**	**Atlantic Div.**	**Won Stanley Cup**
1993-94	84	29	11	2	18	14	10	47	25	12	306	220	106	2nd,	Atlantic Div.	Lost Conf. Championship
1992-93	84	24	14	4	16	23	3	40	37	7	308	299	87	4th,	Patrick Div.	Lost Div. Semi-Final
1991-92	80	24	12	4	14	19	3	38	31	11	289	259	87	4th,	Patrick Div.	Lost Div. Semi-Final
1990-91	80	23	10	7	9	23	8	32	33	15	272	264	79	4th,	Patrick Div.	Lost Div. Semi-Final
1989-90	80	22	15	3	15	19	6	37	34	9	295	288	83	2nd,	Patrick Div.	Lost Div. Semi-Final
1988-89	80	17	18	5	10	23	7	27	41	12	281	325	66	5th,	Patrick Div.	Out of Playoffs
1987-88	80	23	16	1	15	20	5	38	36	6	295	296	82	4th,	Patrick Div.	Lost Conf. Championship
1986-87	80	20	17	3	9	28	3	29	45	6	293	368	64	6th,	Patrick Div.	Out of Playoffs
1985-86	80	17	21	2	11	28	1	28	49	3	300	374	59	6th,	Patrick Div.	Out of Playoffs
1984-85	80	13	21	6	9	27	4	22	48	10	264	346	54	5th,	Patrick Div.	Out of Playoffs
1983-84	80	10	28	2	7	28	5	17	56	7	231	350	41	5th,	Patrick Div.	Out of Playoffs
1982-83	80	11	20	9	6	29	5	17	49	14	230	338	48	5th,	Patrick Div.	Out of Playoffs
1981-82**	80	14	21	5	4	28	8	18	49	13	241	362	49	5th,	Smythe Div.	Out of Playoffs
1980-81**	80	15	16	9	7	29	4	22	45	13	258	344	57	5th,	Smythe Div.	Out of Playoffs
1979-80**	80	12	20	8	7	28	5	19	48	13	234	308	51	6th,	Smythe Div.	Out of Playoffs
1978-79**	80	8	24	8	7	29	4	15	53	12	210	331	42	4th,	Smythe Div.	Out of Playoffs
1977-78**	80	17	14	9	2	26	12	19	40	21	257	305	59	2nd,	Smythe Div.	Lost Prelim. Round
1976-77*	80	12	20	8	8	26	6	20	46	14	226	307	54	5th,	Smythe Div.	Out of Playoffs
1975-76*	80	8	24	8	4	32	4	12	56	12	190	351	36	5th,	Smythe Div.	Out of Playoffs
1974-75*	80	12	20	8	3	34	3	15	54	11	184	328	41	5th,	Smythe Div.	Out of Playoffs

* Kansas City Scouts.   ** Colorado Rockies.

2000-01 Schedule

Oct.	Fri.	6	Montreal
	Fri.	13	at Ottawa
	Sat.	14	Anaheim
	Tue.	17	at Atlanta
	Thu.	19	at Washington
	Sat.	21	Tampa Bay
	Wed.	25	at Florida
	Fri.	27	at Carolina
	Sat.	28	at Pittsburgh
	Mon.	30	Florida
Nov.	Wed.	1	Philadelphia
	Thu.	2	at Toronto
	Sat.	4	Los Angeles*
	Wed.	8	Nashville
	Fri.	10	Pittsburgh
	Sat.	11	Buffalo
	Tue.	14	San Jose
	Thu.	16	at Boston
	Sat.	18	Carolina*
	Wed.	22	at Anaheim
	Thu.	23	at Los Angeles*
	Sat.	25	at San Jose
	Wed.	29	NY Rangers
Dec.	Fri.	1	NY Islanders
	Sun.	3	at NY Islanders*
	Tue.	5	Colorado
	Wed.	6	at Buffalo
	Sat.	9	Washington*
	Mon.	11	Atlanta
	Fri.	15	Montreal
	Sat.	16	at Philadelphia
	Wed.	20	Dallas
	Fri.	22	at Florida
	Sat.	23	at Tampa Bay
	Wed.	27	Columbus
	Fri.	29	Washington
	Sun.	31	at Columbus
Jan.	Tue.	2	Philadelphia
	Thu.	4	NY Islanders
	Sat.	6	at NY Rangers*
	Sun.	7	Phoenix

	Wed.	10	Chicago
	Sat.	13	Toronto
	Tue.	16	Boston
	Thu.	18	at Philadelphia
	Sat.	20	Atlanta*
	Sun.	21	at Minnesota
	Wed.	24	at Dallas
	Thu.	25	at St. Louis
	Sat.	27	at Boston
	Tue.	30	Detroit
	Wed.	31	at NY Islanders
Feb.	Tue.	6	at Montreal
	Thu.	8	at Ottawa
	Sat.	10	at Pittsburgh*
	Sun.	11	at NY Rangers*
	Wed.	14	Ottawa
	Fri.	16	Pittsburgh
	Sat.	17	at Buffalo
	Mon.	19	at Toronto
	Thu.	22	Buffalo
	Fri.	23	at Carolina
	Mon.	26	Florida
	Tue.	27	at NY Islanders
Mar.	Fri.	2	Carolina
	Sun.	4	Tampa Bay*
	Tue.	6	Ottawa
	Thu.	8	Minnesota
	Sat.	10	at Philadelphia*
	Tue.	13	at Colorado
	Wed.	14	at Phoenix
	Sat.	17	at Edmonton
	Mon.	19	at Calgary
	Wed.	21	NY Rangers
	Fri.	23	Vancouver
	Sun.	25	Pittsburgh*
	Tue.	27	at Tampa Bay
	Wed.	28	at Atlanta
	Sat.	31	NY Rangers*
Apr.	Tue.	3	at Washington
	Fri.	6	Boston
	Sat.	7	at Montreal

* Denotes afternoon game.

Franchise date: June 11, 1974
Transferred from Denver to New Jersey,
June 30, 1982.
Previously transferred from Kansas City
to Denver.

EASTERN CONFERENCE

ATLANTIC DIVISION

27th NHL Season

A member of the New Jersey Devils during his entire NHL career, Ken Daneyko played his 1,000th game last season and was awarded the Masterton Trophy for perseverance, sportsmanship and dedication to hockey.

2000-01 Player Personnel

FORWARDS	HT	WT	S	Place of Birth	Date	1999-00 Club
ARNOTT, Jason	6-4	225	R	Collingwood, Ont.	10/11/74	New Jersey
BICEK, Jiri	5-10	195	L	Kosice, Czech.	12/3/78	Albany River Rats
BIRBRAER, Maxim	6-2	185	L	Ust-Kamenogorsk, USSR	12/15/80	Newmarket
BRYLIN, Sergei	5-10	190	L	Moscow, USSR	1/13/74	New Jersey
CAMERON, Scott	6-0	180	L	Sudbury, Ont.	4/11/81	Barrie Colts-North Bay-Albany River Rats
CLOUTHIER, Brett	6-4	220	L	Ottawa, Ont.	6/9/81	Kingston
CLOUTIER, Sylvain	6-0	195	L	Mont-Laurier, Que.	2/13/74	Albany River Rats-Orlando
DAGENAIS, Pierre	6-4	210	L	Blainville, Que.	3/4/78	Albany River Rats
DUCE, Bryan	6-0	200	R	Thunder Bay, Ont.	1/15/78	Augusta Lynx
ELIAS, Patrik	6-1	200	L	Trebic, Czech.	4/13/76	SK Trebic-2-HC Pardubice-N.J.
FERRARO, Chris	5-10	180	R	Port Jefferson, NY	1/24/73	NYI-Prov (AHL)-Chi (IHL)
GOMEZ, Scott	5-11	200	L	Anchorage, AK	12/23/79	New Jersey
GRON, Stanislav	6-2	210	L	Bratislava, Czech.	10/28/78	Albany River Rats
HOLIK, Bobby	6-4	230	R	Jihlava, Czech.	1/1/71	New Jersey
JEFFERSON, Mike	5-9	190	R	Brampton, Ont.	10/21/80	Barrie Colts
KELLY, Steve	6-2	210	L	Vancouver, B.C.	10/26/76	Detroit Vipers-N.J.-Albany
LEHOUX, Jason	6-2	227	L	Ste-Marie-Beauce, Que.	7/21/79	Rouyn-Noranda-Hull
LEWIS, Carlyle	6-3	230	R	Middleton, N.S.	3/1/78	Albany River Rats
MADDEN, John	5-11	195	L	Barrie, Ont.	5/4/75	New Jersey
McKAY, Randy	6-2	210	R	Montreal, Que.	1/25/67	New Jersey
McKENZIE, Jim	6-4	220	L	Gull Lake, Sask.	11/3/69	Anaheim-Washington
MOGILNY, Alexander	5-11	200	L	Khabarovsk, USSR	2/18/69	Vancouver-New Jersey
NEMCHINOV, Sergei	6-0	205	L	Moscow, USSR	1/14/64	New Jersey
PANDOLFO, Jay	6-1	190	L	Winchester, MA	12/27/74	New Jersey
ROCHEFORT, Richard	5-10	195	R	North Bay, Ont.	1/7/77	Albany River Rats
RUPP, Michael	6-5	230	L	Cleveland, OH	1/13/80	Erie Otters
SKRLAC, Rob	6-5	240	L	Campbell, B.C.	6/10/76	Albany River Rats
STEVENSON, Turner	6-3	225	R	Prince George, B.C.	5/18/72	Montreal
STIENSTRA, Doug	6-1	210	L	Kelowna, B.C.	6/18/76	Cornell Big Red
SYKORA, Petr	6-0	190	L	Plzen, Czech.	11/19/76	New Jersey
THOMPSON, Chris	6-1	200	L	Prince Albert, Sask.	4/10/78	Augusta Lynx
WARD, Ed	6-3	220	R	Edmonton, Alta.	11/10/69	Atlanta-Anaheim
DEFENSEMEN						
ANDREWS, Daryl	6-2	205	L	Campbell River, B.C.	4/27/77	Western Michigan-Albany
BOUMEDIENNE, Josef	6-1	190	L	Stockholm, Sweden	1/12/78	Tappara Tampere
COLE, Phil	6-4	190	L	Winnipeg, Man.	9/6/82	Lethbridge
COMMODORE, Mike	6-4	225	R	Fort Saskatchewan, Alta.	11/7/79	North Dakota
DANEYKO, Ken	6-1	215	L	Windsor, Ont.	4/17/64	New Jersey
ENGELLAND, Deryk	6-2	200	R	Edmonton, Alta.	4/5/82	Moose Jaw
GOC, Sascha	6-2	220	R	Calw, West Germany	4/17/79	Albany River Rats
JOHNSTONE, Alex	6-1	200	L	Halifax, N.S.	12/28/79	Albany River Rats-Augusta Lynx
JOKELA, Mikko	6-1	215	R	Lappeenranta, Finland	3/4/80	SaiPa
LAKOS, Andre	6-6	230	R	Vienna, Austria	7/29/79	Albany River Rats
MITCHELL, Willie	6-3	205	L	Port McNeill, B.C.	4/23/77	New Jersey-Albany River Rats
NEHRLING, Lucas	6-5	225	R	Peterborough, Ont.	8/14/79	Augusta Lynx-Arkansas-Muskegon Fury-Albany
NIEDERMAYER, Scott	6-1	200	L	Edmonton, Alta.	8/31/73	New Jersey
RAFALSKI, Brian	5-9	200	R	Dearborn, MI	9/28/73	New Jersey
REHNBERG, Henrik	6-2	195	L	Grava, Sweden	7/20/77	Farjestads BK
STEVENS, Scott	6-1	215	L	Kitchener, Ont.	4/1/64	New Jersey
SUTTON, Ken	6-1	205	L	Edmonton, Alta.	11/5/69	New Jersey-Albany River Rats
WHITE, Colin	6-4	210	L	New Glasgow, N.S.	12/12/77	New Jersey-Albany River Rats

GOALTENDERS	HT	WT	C	Place of Birth	Date	1999-00 Club
AHONEN, Ari	6-2	170	L	Jyvaskyla, Finland	2/6/81	HIFK Helsinki-HIFK Helsinki Jr.
BRODEUR, Martin	6-2	205	L	Montreal, Que.	5/6/72	New Jersey
DAMPHOUSSE, J-F	6-0	175	L	St-Alexis-des-Monts, Que.	7/21/79	Augusta Lynx-Albany River Rats
HENRY, Frederic	5-11	180	L	Cap-Rouge, Que.	8/9/77	Albany River Rats
KOSTUR, Matus	6-2	185	L	Banska Bystrica, Czech.	3/28/80	HKm Zvolen
TERRERI, Chris	5-9	170	L	Providence, RI	11/15/64	New Jersey

General Managers' History

Sid Abel, 1974-75, 1975-76; Ray Miron, 1976-77 to 1980-81; Billy MacMillan, 1981-82, 1982-83; Billy MacMillan and Max McNab, 1983-84; Max McNab 1984-85 to 1986-87; Lou Lamoriello, 1987-88 to date.

General Manager

LAMORIELLO, LOU
CEO/President/General Manager, New Jersey Devils.
Born in Providence, RI, October 21, 1942.

Lou Lamoriello's life-long dedication to the game of hockey was rewarded in 1992 when he was named a recipient of the Lester Patrick Trophy for outstanding service to hockey in the United States. Lamoriello is entering his 14th season as president and general manager of the Devils following more than 20 years with Providence College as a player, coach and administrator. His trades, signings and draft choices helped lead the Devils to their first Stanley Cup championship in 1995 and another in 2000. A member of the varsity hockey Friars during his undergraduate days, he became an assistant coach with the college club after graduating in 1963. Lamoriello was later named head coach and in the ensuing 15 years, led his teams to a 248-179-13 record, a .578 winning percentage and appearances in 10 post-season tournaments, including the 1983 NCAA Final Four. Lamoriello also served a five-year term as athletic director at Providence and was a co-founder of Hockey East, one of the strongest collegiate hockey conferences in the U.S. He remained as athletic director until he was hired as president of the Devils on April 30, 1987. He assumed the dual responsibility of general manager on September 10, 1987. He was g.m. of Team USA for the first World Cup of Hockey in 1996 as the U.S. captured the championship. He was also the g.m. for the 1998 U.S. Olympic Team.

1999-2000 Scoring

* – rookie

Regular Season

Pos	#	Player	Team	GP	G	A	Pts	+/–	PIM	PP	SH	GW	GT	S	%
L	26	Patrik Elias	N.J.	72	35	37	72	16	58	9	0	9	1	183	19.1
C	23	* Scott Gomez	N.J.	82	19	51	70	14	78	7	0	1	2	204	9.3
C	17	Petr Sykora	N.J.	79	25	43	68	24	26	5	1	4	0	222	11.3
R	25	Jason Arnott	N.J.	76	22	34	56	22	51	7	0	4	0	244	9.0
R	22	Claude Lemieux	COL	13	3	6	9	0	4	0	0	0	0	36	8.3
			N.J	70	17	21	38	–3	86	7	0	3	0	221	7.7
			TOTAL	83	20	27	47	–3	90	7	0	3	0	257	7.8
C	16	Bobby Holik	N.J.	79	23	23	46	7	106	7	0	4	1	257	8.9
R	89	Alexander Mogilny	VAN	47	21	17	38	7	16	3	1	1	2	126	16.7
			N.J	12	3	3	6	–4	4	2	0	0	0	35	8.6
			TOTAL	59	24	20	44	3	20	5	1	1	2	161	14.9
R	21	Randy McKay	N.J.	67	16	23	39	8	80	3	0	4	0	116	13.8
D	27	Scott Niedermayer	N.J.	71	7	31	38	19	48	1	0	0	0	109	6.4
D	28	* Brian Rafalski	N.J.	75	5	27	32	21	28	1	0	1	0	128	3.9
D	4	Scott Stevens	N.J.	78	8	21	29	30	103	0	1	1	0	133	6.0
C	12	Sergei Nemchinov	N.J.	53	10	16	26	1	18	0	1	1	0	55	18.2
L	11	* John Madden	N.J.	74	16	9	25	7	6	0	6	3	0	115	13.9
C	18	Sergei Brylin	N.J.	64	9	11	20	0	20	1	0	1	0	84	10.7
L	29	Krzysztof Oliwa	N.J.	69	6	10	16	–2	184	1	0	2	0	61	9.8
L	20	Jay Pandolfo	N.J.	71	7	8	15	0	4	0	0	0	0	86	8.1
D	2	Deron Quint	PHX	50	3	7	10	0	22	0	0	1	0	88	3.4
			N.J	4	1	0	1	–2	2	0	0	0	0	6	16.7
			TOTAL	54	4	7	11	–2	24	0	0	1	0	94	4.3
D	3	Ken Daneyko	N.J.	78	0	6	6	13	98	0	0	0	0	74	0.0
D	7	Vladimir Malakhov	MTL	7	0	0	0	0	4	0	0	0	0	7	0.0
			N.J	17	1	4	5	1	19	1	0	1	0	11	9.1
			TOTAL	24	1	4	5	1	23	1	0	1	0	18	5.6
G	30	Martin Brodeur	N.J.	72	1	4	5	0	16	0	0	1	0	1	100.0
D	6	Brad Bombardir	N.J.	32	3	1	4	–6	6	0	0	0	0	24	12.5
D	5	* Colin White	N.J.	21	2	1	3	3	40	0	0	1	0	29	6.9
D	2	Ken Sutton	N.J.	6	0	2	2	2	2	0	0	0	0	10	0.0
C	15	Steve Kelly	N.J.	1	0	0	0	0	0	0	0	0	0	0	0.0
D	24	* Willie Mitchell	N.J.	2	0	0	0	1	0	0	0	0	0	2	0.0
G	31	Chris Terreri	N.J.	12	0	0	0	0	2	0	0	0	0	0	0.0

Goaltending

No.	Goaltender	GPI	Mins	Avg	W	L	T	EN	SO	GA	SA	S%
30	Martin Brodeur	72	4312	2.24	43	20	8	3	6	161	1797	.910
31	Chris Terreri	12	649	3.42	2	9	0	2	0	37	299	.876
	Totals	**82**	**4975**	**2.45**	**45**	**29**	**8**	**5**	**6**	**203**	**2101**	**.903**

Playoffs

Pos	#	Player	Team	GP	G	A	Pts	+/–	PIM	PP	SH	GW	OT	S	%
R	25	Jason Arnott	N.J.	23	8	12	20	7	18	3	0	1	1	56	14.3
L	26	Patrik Elias	N.J.	23	7	13	20	9	9	2	1	1	0	60	11.7
C	17	Petr Sykora	N.J.	23	9	8	17	8	10	1	0	3	0	45	20.0
D	4	Scott Stevens	N.J.	23	3	8	11	9	6	0	0	2	0	29	10.3
R	22	Claude Lemieux	N.J.	23	4	6	10	7	28	1	0	0	0	78	5.1
C	23	* Scott Gomez	N.J.	23	4	6	10	1	4	1	0	2	0	53	7.5
C	16	Bobby Holik	N.J.	23	3	7	10	–1	14	0	0	1	0	73	4.1
C	18	Sergei Brylin	N.J.	17	3	5	8	2	0	0	0	0	0	24	12.5
D	28	* Brian Rafalski	N.J.	23	2	6	8	5	8	0	0	1	0	31	6.5
D	27	Scott Niedermayer	N.J.	22	5	2	7	5	10	0	2	1	0	40	12.5
R	89	Alexander Mogilny	N.J.	23	4	3	7	1	4	2	0	1	0	55	7.3
L	11	* John Madden	N.J.	20	3	4	7	4	0	0	1	2	0	38	7.9
D	5	* Colin White	N.J.	23	1	5	6	9	18	0	0	1	0	23	4.3
R	21	Randy Mckay	N.J.	23	0	6	6	–1	9	0	0	0	0	31	0.0
C	12	Sergei Nemchinov	N.J.	21	3	2	5	1	2	1	0	0	0	20	15.0
D	7	Vladimir Malakhov	N.J.	23	1	4	5	3	18	1	0	0	0	29	3.4
L	20	Jay Pandolfo	N.J.	23	0	5	5	3	0	0	0	0	0	28	0.0
D	3	Ken Daneyko	N.J.	23	1	2	3	–2	14	0	0	0	0	9	11.1
D	6	Brad Bombardir	N.J.	1	0	0	0	0	0	0	0	0	0	0	0.0
C	10	* Steve Brule	N.J.	1	0	0	0	0	0	0	0	0	0	0	0.0
C	15	Steve Kelly	N.J.	10	0	0	0	–1	4	0	0	0	0	5	0.0
G	30	Martin Brodeur	N.J.	23	0	0	0	0	10	0	0	0	0	0	0.0

Goaltending

No.	Goaltender	GPI	Mins	Avg	W	L	EN	SO	GA	SA	S%
30	Martin Brodeur	23	1450	1.61	16	7	0	2	39	537	.927
	Totals	**23**	**1455**	**1.61**	**16**	**7**	**0**	**2**	**39**	**537**	**.927**

Coaching History

Bep Guidolin, 1974-75; Bep Guidolin, Sid Abel and Eddie Bush, 1975-76; John Wilson, 1976-77; Pat Kelly, 1977-78; Pat Kelly and Aldo Guidolin, 1978-79; Don Cherry, 1979-80; Bill MacMillan, 1980-81; Bert Marshall and Marshall Johnston, 1981-82; Bill MacMillan, 1982-83; Bill MacMillan and Tom McVie, 1983-84; Doug Carpenter, 1984-85 to 1986-87; Doug Carpenter and Jim Schoenfeld, 1987-88; Jim Schoenfeld, 1988-89; Jim Schoenfeld and John Cunniff, 1989-90; John Cunniff and Tom McVie, 1990-91; Tom McVie, 1991-92; Herb Brooks, 1992-93; Jacques Lemaire, 1993-94 to 1997-98; Robbie Ftorek, 1998-99; Robbie Ftorek and Larry Robinson, 1999-2000; Larry Robinson, 2000-01.

Captains' History

Simon Nolet, 1974-75 to 1976-77; Wilf Paiement, 1977-78; Gary Croteau, 1978-79; Mike Christie, Rene Robert and Lanny McDonald, 1979-80; Lanny McDonald, 1980-81; Lanny McDonald and Rob Ramage, 1981-82; Don Lever, 1982-83; Don Lever and Mel Bridgman, 1983-84; Mel Bridgman, 1984-85 to 1986-87; Kirk Muller, 1987-88 to 1990-91; Bruce Driver, 1991-92; Scott Stevens, 1992-93 to date.

Club Records

Team

(Figures in brackets for season records are games played; records for fewest points, wins, ties, losses, goals, goals against are for 70 or more games)

Most Points	107	1997-98 (82)
Most Wins	48	1997-98 (82)
Most Ties	21	1977-78 (80)
Most Losses	56	1983-84 (80),
		1975-76 (80)
Most Goals	308	1992-93 (84)
Most Goals Against	374	1985-86 (80)
Fewest Points	*36	1975-76 (80)
	41	1983-84 (80)
Fewest Wins	*12	1975-76 (80)
	17	1982-83 (80),
		1983-84 (80)
Fewest Ties	3	1985-86 (80)
Fewest Losses	23	1996-97 (82);
		1997-98 (82)
Fewest Goals	*184	1974-75 (80)
	225	1997-98 (82)
Fewest Goals Against	166	1997-98 (82)

Longest Winning Streak

Overall	8	Oct. 27-Nov. 15/97
Home	8	Oct. 9-Nov. 7/87
Away	6	Jan. 3-26/00

Longest Undefeated Streak

Overall	13	Jan. 24-Feb. 20/97
		(6 wins, 7 ties),
		Jan. 31-Mar. 12/98
		(9 wins, 4 ties)
Home	15	Jan. 8-Mar. 15/97
		(9 wins, 6 tie)
Away	8	Nov. 5-Dec. 2/93
		(5 wins, 3 ties),
		Jan. 31-Mar. 12/98
		(5 wins, 3 ties),
		Dec. 26/99-Jan. 26/00
		(6 wins, 2 ties)

Longest Losing Streak

Overall	*14	Dec. 30/75-Jan. 29/76
	10	Oct. 14-Nov. 4/83
Home	9	Dec. 22/85-Feb. 6/86
Away	12	Oct. 19-Dec. 1/83

Longest Winless Streak

Overall	*27	Feb. 12-Apr. 4/76
		(21 losses, 6 ties)
	18	Oct. 20-Nov. 26/82
		(14 losses 4 ties)
Home	*14	Feb. 12-Mar. 30/76
		(10 losses, 4 ties),
		Feb. 4-Mar. 31/79
		(12 losses, 2 ties)
	9	Dec. 22/85-Feb. 6/86
		(9 losses)
Away	*32	Nov. 12/77-Mar. 15/78
		(22 losses, 10 ties)
	14	Dec. 26/82-Mar. 5/83
		(13 losses, 1 tie)

Most Shutouts, Season	13	1996-97 (82)
Most PIM, Season	2,494	1988-89 (80)
Most Goals, Game	9	Eight times

Individual

Most Seasons	17	Ken Daneyko
Most Games	1,070	Ken Daneyko
Most Goals, Career	347	John MacLean
Most Assists, Career	354	John MacLean
Most Points, Career	701	John MacLean
		(347G, 354A)
Most PIM, Career	2,339	Ken Daneyko
Most Shutouts, Career	42	Martin Brodeur

Longest Consecutive

Games Streak	388	Ken Daneyko
		(Nov. 4/89-Mar. 29/94)

Most Goals, Season	46	Pat Verbeek
		(1987-88)
Most Assists, Season	60	Scott Stevens
		(1993-94)
Most Points, Season	94	Kirk Muller
		(1987-88; 37G, 57A)
Most PIM, Season	295	Krzysztof Oliwa
		(1997-98)
Most Points, Defenseman, Season	78	Scott Stevens
		(1993-94; 18G, 60A)
Most Points, Center, Season	94	Kirk Muller
		(1987-88; 37G, 57A)
Most Points, Right Wing, Season	*87	Wilf Paiement
		(1977-78; 31G, 56A)
	87	John MacLean
		(1988-89; 42G, 45A)
Most Points, Left Wing, Season	86	Kirk Muller
		(1989-90; 30G, 56A)
Most Points, Rookie, Season	70	Scott Gomez
		(1999-2000; 19G, 51A)
Most Shutouts, Season	10	Martin Brodeur
		(1996-97, 1997-98)
Most Goals, Game	4	Bob MacMillan
		(Jan. 8/82),
		Pat Verbeek
		(Feb. 28/88)
Most Assists, Game	5	Greg Adams
		(Oct. 10/85),
		Kirk Muller
		(Mar. 25/87),
		Tom Kurvers
		(Feb. 13/89)
Most Points, Game	6	Kirk Muller
		(Nov. 29/86; 3G, 3A)

* Records include Kansas City Scouts and Colorado Rockies, 1974-75 through 1981-82.

All-time Record vs. Other Clubs

Regular Season

	GP	W	L	T	At Home GF	GA	PTS	GP	W	L	T	On Road GF	GA	PTS	GP	W	L	T	Total GF	GA	PTS
Anaheim	6	5	1	0	24	10	10	6	3	3	0	14	18	6	12	8	4	0	38	28	16
Atlanta	2	2	0	0	11	1	4	2	2	0	0	13	1	4	4	4	0	0	24	2	8
Boston	45	12	23	10	119	150	34	48	13	28	7	145	195	33	93	25	51	17	264	345	67
Buffalo	46	13	24	9	135	163	35	46	13	28	5	148	192	31	92	26	52	14	283	355	66
Calgary	42	13	26	3	118	157	29	40	5	27	8	103	177	18	82	18	53	11	221	334	47
Carolina	37	21	13	3	132	121	45	36	13	16	7	113	122	34	73	34	29	10	245	243	79
Chicago	43	16	16	11	129	133	43	44	11	24	9	122	173	31	87	27	40	20	251	306	74
Colorado	33	17	12	4	137	115	38	31	12	16	3	90	115	27	64	29	28	7	227	230	65
Dallas	41	19	19	3	137	128	41	42	11	25	6	110	161	29	83	30	44	9	247	289	70
Detroit	37	18	10	9	130	101	45	37	13	22	2	123	152	28	74	31	32	11	253	253	73
Edmonton	30	13	15	2	102	101	28	29	9	14	6	106	130	24	59	22	29	8	208	231	52
Florida	16	9	4	3	45	30	21	17	6	7	4	39	43	16	33	15	11	7	84	73	37
Los Angeles	40	18	17	5	136	141	41	39	6	27	6	119	198	18	79	24	44	11	255	339	59
Montreal	46	19	24	3	134	178	41	46	11	29	6	120	170	29	92	30	53	9	254	348	70
Nashville	2	1	1	0	6	4	2	2	0	0	2	4	4	3	1	0	6	12	6	6
NY Islanders	74	29	35	10	249	271	68	74	14	51	9	215	330	37	148	43	86	19	464	601	105
NY Rangers	75	38	32	5	259	258	81	74	20	39	15	223	298	55	149	58	71	20	482	556	136
Ottawa	15	10	3	2	53	33	22	16	10	4	2	43	33	22	31	20	7	4	96	66	44
Philadelphia	73	39	29	5	265	266	83	74	19	47	8	188	299	46	147	58	76	13	453	565	129
Phoenix	26	10	10	6	84	81	26	28	5	20	3	74	108	13	54	15	30	9	158	189	39
Pittsburgh	70	34	24	12	265	240	80	69	27	38	4	236	269	58	139	61	62	16	501	509	138
St. Louis	44	20	17	7	142	127	47	43	10	26	7	131	183	27	87	30	43	14	273	310	74
San Jose	9	5	3	1	33	18	11	8	4	3	1	24	18	10	17	9	6	2	57	36	21
Tampa Bay	18	15	2	1	66	25	31	17	10	4	3	53	42	23	35	25	6	4	119	67	54
Toronto	39	14	13	12	137	122	40	40	9	27	4	127	169	22	79	23	40	16	264	291	62
Vancouver	45	19	20	6	143	149	44	46	9	26	11	128	171	29	91	28	46	17	271	320	73
Washington	71	33	31	7	221	214	74	71	21	45	5	201	281	47	142	54	76	12	422	495	121
Defunct Clubs	8	4	2	2	25	19	10	8	2	3	3	19	27	7	16	6	5	5	44	46	17
Totals	1033	466	426	141	3437	3356	1074	1033	290	599	144	3033	4077	728	2066	756	1025	285	6470	7433	1802

Playoffs

	Series	W	L	GP	W	L	T	GF	GA	Last Mtg.	Round	Result
Boston	3	2	1	18	11	7	0	55	52	1995	CQF	W 4-1
Buffalo	1	1	0	7	4	3	0	14	14	1994	CQF	W 4-3
Dallas	1	1	0	6	4	2	0	15	9	2000	F	W 4-2
Detroit	1	1	0	4	4	0	0	16	7	1995	F	W 4-0
Florida	1	1	0	4	4	0	0	12	6	2000	CQF	W 4-0
Montreal	1	1	0	5	4	1	0	22	11	1997	CQF	W 4-1
NY Islanders	1	1	0	6	4	2	0	23	18	1988	DSF	W 4-2
NY Rangers	3	0	3	19	7	12	0	46	56	1997	CSF	L 1-4
Ottawa	1	0	1	6	2	4	0	13	19	1998	CQF	L 2-4
Philadelphia	3	2	1	15	8	7	0	41	35	2000	CF	W 4-3
Pittsburgh	4	1	3	24	11	13	0	69	73	1999	CQF	L 3-4
Toronto	1	1	0	6	4	2	0	16	9	2000	CSF	W 4-2
Washington	2	1	1	13	6	7	0	43	44	1990	DSF	L 2-4
Totals	23	13	10	133	73	50	0	380	351			

Calgary totals include Atlanta Flames, 1974-75 to 1979-80.
Colorado totals include Quebec, 1979-80 to 1994-95.
Phoenix totals include Winnipeg, 1979-80 to 1995-96.

Carolina totals include Hartford, 1979-80 to 1996-97.
Dallas totals include Minnesota North Stars, 1974-75 to 1992-93.

Playoff Results 2000-1996

Year	Round	Opponent	Result	GF	GA
2000	F	Dallas	W 4-2	15	9
	CF	Philadelphia	W 4-3	18	15
	CSF	Toronto	W 4-2	16	9
	CQF	Florida	W 4-0	12	6
1999	CQF	Pittsburgh	L 3-4	18	21
1998	CQF	Ottawa	L 2-4	12	13
1997	CSF	NY Rangers	L 1-4	5	10
	CQF	Montreal	W 4-1	22	11

Abbreviations: Round: F – Final;
CF – conference final; **CSF** – conference semi-final;
CQF – conference quarter-final; **DSF** – division semi-final.

1999-2000 Results

Oct.	2	at Atlanta	4-1		8		Phoenix	4-3
	7	Pittsburgh	5-7		11	at	Tampa Bay	6-5
	9	Tampa Bay	1-0		14		Washington	2-3 *
	11	at Ottawa	2-2		15	at	Philadelphia	4-1
	13	Anaheim	3-2		17		Carolina	5-2
	16	NY Islanders	4-1		19		Chicago	4-1
	22	at Dallas	1-2 *		21		NY Islanders	4-0
	23	at St. Louis	1-3		26	at	Florida	3-2
	27	St. Louis	2-1		28	at	Carolina	3-4 *
	29	at Carolina	4-2		29	at	Detroit	1-3
	30	at Philadelphia	3-5	Feb.	2	at	NY Rangers	3-1
Nov.	3	Montreal	3-2		3		Nashville	4-1
	4	at Boston	1-3		8	at	NY Rangers	2-2
	6	Toronto	3-3		9		NY Rangers	4-1
	9	Philadelphia	2-1		13		San Jose	3-1
	12	Atlanta	5-1		15		Philadelphia	4-2
	13	at Washington	2-4		17		Colorado	5-5
	17	Boston	2-2		19		NY Islanders	2-4
	20	Ottawa	3-1		21	at	Buffalo	2-3
	24	at Anaheim	2-1		24	at	Montreal	2-3 *
	25	at Phoenix	2-4		25		Toronto	1-3
	28	at San Jose	3-4 *		27		Montreal	3-0
Dec.	1	NY Rangers	3-2		29	at	Nashville	2-1
	3	Ottawa	7-4	Mar.	2	at	Colorado	0-5
	4	Calgary	2-4		4	at	Vancouver	2-4
	7	Pittsburgh	2-4		5	at	Calgary	2-2
	9	at Chicago	4-0		10	at	Atlanta	9-0
	11	Edmonton	1-3		11	at	Washington	2-4
	14	Los Angeles	7-1		13	at	Pittsburgh	3-2
	16	at Montreal	2-1		15		Dallas	2-3
	18	Washington	5-4		17		Tampa Bay	1-3
	19	at NY Islanders	3-5		19		Florida	5-2
	22	Philadelphia	3-2		21		Carolina	0-5
	23	at Toronto	1-4		24	at	NY Islanders	8-2
	26	at NY Rangers	3-2		25	at	Toronto	3-5
	27	Buffalo	4-1		28	at	Pittsburgh	2-3
	29	Boston	5-4 *		31		Atlanta	6-0
Jan.	1	at Boston	2-2	Apr.	2	at	Tampa Bay	4-1
	3	at Ottawa	4-3 *		3	at	Florida	2-5
	5	at Pittsburgh	3-1		6		Buffalo	0-5
	6	at Buffalo	6-3		8		Florida	2-1 *

* – Overtime

Entry Draft
Selections 2000-1986

2000
Pick
22	David Hale
39	Teemu Laine
56	Alexander Suglobov
57	Matt DeMarchi
62	Paul Martin
67	Maxim Birbraer
76	Michael Rupp
125	Phil Cole
135	Mike Jefferson
164	Matus Kostur
194	Deryk Engelland
198	Ken Magowan
257	Warren McCutcheon

1999
Pick
27	Ari Ahonen
42	Mike Commodore
50	Brett Clouthier
95	Andre Lakos
100	Teemu Kesa
185	Scott Cameron
214	Chris Hartsburg
242	Justin Dziama

1998
Pick
26	Mike Van Ryn
27	Scott Gomez
37	Christian Berglund
82	Brian Gionta
96	Mikko Jokela
105	Pierre Dagenais
119	Anton But
143	Ryan Flinn
172	Jacques Lariviere
199	Erik Jensen
227	Marko Ahosilta
257	Ryan Held

1997
Pick
24	J-F Damphousse
38	Stanislav Gron
104	Lucas Nehrling
131	Jiri Bicek
159	Sascha Goc
188	Mathieu Benoit
215	Scott Clemmensen
241	Jan Srdinko

1996
Pick
10	Lance Ward
38	Wes Mason
41	Josh DeWolf
47	Pierre Dagenais
49	Colin White
63	Scott Parker
91	Josef Boumedienne
101	Josh MacNevin
118	Glenn Crawford
145	Sean Ritchlin
173	Daryl Andrews
199	Willie Mitchell
205	Jay Bertsch
225	Pasi Petrilainen

1995
Pick
18	Petr Sykora
44	Nathan Perrott
70	Sergei Vyshedkevich
78	David Gosselin
79	Alyn McCauley
96	Henrik Rehnberg
122	Chris Mason
148	Adam Young
174	Richard Rochefort
200	Frederic Henry
226	Colin O'Hara

1994
Pick
25	Vadim Sharifijanov
51	Patrik Elias
71	Sheldon Souray
103	Zdenek Skorepa
129	Christian Gosselin
134	Ryan Smart
155	Luciano Caravaggio
181	Jeff Williams
207	Eric Bertrand
233	Steve Sullivan
259	Scott Swanjord
269	Mike Hanson

1993
Pick
13	Denis Pederson
32	Jay Pandolfo
39	Brendan Morrison
65	Krzysztof Oliwa
110	John Guirestante
143	Steve Brule
169	Nikolai Zavarukhin
195	Thomas Cullen
221	Judd Lambert
247	Jimmy Provencher
273	Mike Legg

1992
Pick
18	Jason Smith
42	Sergei Brylin
66	Cale Hulse
90	Vitali Tomilin
94	Scott McCabe
114	Ryan Black
138	Daniel Trebil
162	Geordie Kinnear
186	Stephane Yelle
210	Jeff Toms
234	Heath Weenk
258	Vladislav Yakovenko

1991
Pick
3	Scott Niedermayer
11	Brian Rolston
33	Donevan Hextall
55	Fredrik Lindquist
77	Bradley Willner
121	Curt Regnier
143	David Craievich
165	Paul Wolanski
187	Daniel Reimann
231	Kevin Riehl
253	Jason Hehr

1990
Pick
20	Martin Brodeur
24	David Harlock
29	Chris Gotziaman
53	Mike Dunham
56	Brad Bombardir
64	Mike Bodnarchuk
95	Dean Malkoc
106	Petr Kuchyna
116	Lubomir Kolnik
137	Chris McAlpine
179	Jaroslav Modry
200	Corey Schwab
221	Valeri Zelepukin
242	Todd Reirden

1989
Pick
5	Bill Guerin
18	Jason Miller
26	Jarrod Skalde
47	Scott Pellerin
89	Mike Heinke
110	David Emma
152	Sergei Starikov
173	Andre Faust
215	Jason Simon
236	Peter Larsson

1988
Pick
12	Corey Foster
23	Jeff Christian
54	Zdeno Ciger
65	Matt Ruchty
75	Scott Luik
96	Chris Nelson
117	Chad Johnson
138	Chad Erickson
159	Bryan Lafort
180	Sergei Svetlov
201	Bob Woods
207	Alexander Semak
222	Charles Hughes
244	Robert Wallwork

1987
Pick
2	Brendan Shanahan
23	Ricard Persson
65	Brian Sullivan
86	Kevin Dean
107	Ben Hankinson
128	Tom Neziol
149	Jim Dowd
170	John Blessman
191	Peter Fry
212	Alain Charland

1986
Pick
3	Neil Brady
24	Todd Copeland
45	Janne Ojanen
66	Marc Laniel
108	Troy Crowder
129	Kevin Todd
150	Ryan Pardoski
171	Scott McCormack
192	Frederic Chabot
213	John Andersen
236	Doug Kirton

Coach

ROBINSON, LARRY
Coach, New Jersey Devils. Born in Winchester, Ont., June 2, 1951.

On March 23, 2000, Larry Robinson was moved up from assistant coach to replace Robbie Ftorek as head coach in New Jersey. He went on to lead the Devils to the second Stanley Cup championship in franchise history. Previously, Robinson had been an assistant coach with the Devils when they won their first Stanley Cup title in 1995. He had first joined the Devils in 1993 following a one-year absence from hockey after concluding a 20-year NHL career that included six Stanley Cup championships and two Norris Trophy titles with the Montreal Canadiens.

Robinson returned to New Jersey for his second stint with the Devils when he was named to an assistant coaching position on May 26, 1999. He had spent the previous four seasons as the head coach of the Los Angeles Kings. Robinson spent the first 17 seasons of his Hall of Fame playing career with Montreal, before signing as a free agent with the Kings on July 25, 1989. He spent the final three years of his playing career with Los Angeles before retiring after the 1991-92 season.

Larry and his wife Jeannette have one son, Jeffrey, and one daughter, Rachelle.

Coaching Record

Season	Team	Games	Regular Season W	L	T	%	Games	Playoffs W	L	%
1995-96	Los Angeles (NHL)	82	24	40	18	.402	....	....	....	....
1996-97	Los Angeles (NHL)	82	28	43	11	.409	....	....	....	....
1997-98	Los Angeles (NHL)	82	38	33	11	.530	4	0	4	.000
1998-99	Los Angeles (NHL)	82	32	45	5	.421	....	....	....	....
1999-2000	New Jersey (NHL)	8	4	4	0	.500	23	16	7	.696*
	NHL Totals	336	126	165	45	.422	27	16	11	.593

* Stanley Cup win.

Club Directory

Continental Airlines Arena

New Jersey Devils
Continental Airlines Arena
50 Route 120 North
P.O. Box 504
East Rutherford, NJ 07073
Phone **201/935-6050**
FAX 201/935-2127
www.newjerseydevils.com
Capacity: 19,040

CEO/President/General Manager	Louis A. Lamoriello
Executive Vice President	Peter S. McMullen
Executive Vice President	Chris Modrzynski
Vice President, General Counsel	Joseph C. Benedetti
Vice President, Ticket Operations	Terry Farmer
Vice President, Corporate Partnerships	Kenneth F. Ferriter
Vice President, Sales/Marketing	Jason Siegel
Vice President, Finance	Scott Struble

Hockey Club Personnel
Head Coach	Larry Robinson
Assistant Coaches	Viacheslav Fetisov, Kurt Kleinendorst
Goaltending Coach	Jacques Caron
Director of Scouting	David Conte
Assistant Director of Scouting	Claude Carrier
Scouting Staff	Glen Dirk, Milt Fisher, Ferny Flaman, Dan Labraaten, Chris Lamoriello, Joe Mahoney, Larry Perris, Marcel Pronovost, Lou Reycroft, Vaclav Slansky, Jr., Geoff Stevens, Ed Thomlinson, Les Widdifield
Pro Scouting Staff	Andre Boudrias, Bob Hoffmeyer, Jan Ludvig
Special Assignment Scouts	Robbie Ftorek, Dennis Gendron
Hockey Operations Video Coordinator	Taran Singleton
Scouting Staff Assistant	Callie A. Smith
Medical Trainer	Bill Murray
Strength/Conditioning Coordinator	Michael Vasalani
Equipment Manager	Rich Matthews
Assistant Equipment Managers	Alex Abasto, Lou Centanni
Massage Therapist	Juergen Merz
Team Cardiologist	Dr. Joseph Niznik
Team Dentist	Dr. H. Hugh Gardy
Team Optometrist	Dr. Paul Berman
Team Orthopedists	Dr. Barry Fisher, Dr. Len Jaffe
Exercise Physiologist	Dr. Garret Caffrey
Head Coach, Albany	John Cunniff
Associate Coach, Albany	Bob Carpenter
Athletic Trainer, Albany	Curtis Bell
Equipment Manager, Albany	Jason McGrath

Administration Department
Hockey Operations Executive Assistant to the President/General Manager	Marie Carnevale
Corporate Executive Assistant to the President/General Manager	Mary K. Morrison
Staff Attorney	John Ruzich
Receptionists	Jelsa Belotta, Pat Maione
Corporate Staff Assistant	Christie Zdanowicz
Operations Staff Assistant	Adam Manger

Ticket Department
Director, Ticket Operations	Tom Bates
Director, Customer Service/ Season Ticket Accounts	Dave Beck
Customer Service Representative	Andrea Marchesani
Director, Group Sales	Neil Desormeaux
Group Account Manager	Rich Davis

Marketing Department
Director, Season Ticket Sales	Mike Yencik
Account Managers	Chris Brehm, Carmine D'Urso, Todd Hyland, Justin Keshish, Joe Lawrence, Nick Mike-Mayer, Vincent Occhipinti, Mauricio Ramirez, D.J. Semenza
Account Managers, Corporate Partnerships	Michael DeMartino, Mike Kozak
Coordinator, Corporate Partner Services	Kelly A. Klunk
Staff Assistant, Corporate Partner Services	Matt Dugan
Assistant Director, Community Development	Paul Viola
Community Development Assistant	Brad Preston
Coordinator, Game Entertainment	Bruce Cohn
Sales Receptionist	Elizabeth Grace

Communications Department
Director, Public Relations	Kevin Dessart
Director, Information/Publications	Mike Levine
Coordinator, Communications	Jana Spaulding

Finance Department
Assistant Controller	Craig Wolman
Staff Accountants	Suzanne McDowell, Patrick Kennedy, Michael Merolla
Administrative Assistant	Eileen Musikant

Merchandise Department
Merchandise Manager	David Perricone
Assistant Merchandise Manager	TBA

Computer Operations
Director, Programming/Computer Operations	Jack Skelley
Systems Administrator	Mike Tukes
Director, Website Operations	Antonio Barrera
Assistant Director, Computer Operations	Anthony Danzi

Television/Radio
Television Outlet	FOX Sports Net New York
Broadcasters	Mike Emrick, Play-by-Play Glenn Resch, Color
Radio Outlet	WABC 77AM
Broadcasters	Mike Miller, Play-by-Play Randy Velischek, Color

New York Islanders

1999-2000 Results: 24w-49L-9T 58PTS. Fifth, Atlantic Division

2000-01 Schedule

Oct.	Fri.	6	at Tampa Bay		Tue.	9	Chicago
	Wed.	11	at Toronto		Fri.	12	at Pittsburgh
	Sat.	14	Calgary		Sat.	13	Pittsburgh
	Tue.	17	Anaheim		Tue.	16	at Colorado
	Fri.	20	at Atlanta		Fri.	19	at Minnesota
	Sat.	21	at Washington		Sun.	21	at Atlanta*
	Fri.	27	Montreal		Tue.	23	Ottawa
	Sat.	28	at Montreal		Fri.	26	at NY Rangers
	Tue.	31	Boston		Sat.	27	Buffalo
Nov.	Wed.	1	at Florida		Wed.	31	New Jersey
	Fri.	3	at Tampa Bay	Feb.	Thu.	1	at Philadelphia
	Sun.	5	Los Angeles*		Wed.	7	at Buffalo
	Tue.	7	Nashville		Fri.	9	Philadelphia
	Thu.	9	at Buffalo		Sat.	10	at Montreal
	Sat.	11	San Jose		Mon.	12	at Ottawa
	Thu.	16	at Los Angeles		Wed.	14	Philadelphia
	Sat.	18	at San Jose		Fri.	16	at Edmonton
	Sun.	19	at Anaheim*		Sun.	18	at Vancouver
	Wed.	22	NY Rangers		Thu.	22	Philadelphia
	Fri.	24	at Washington		Sat.	24	Florida*
	Sat.	25	Detroit		Sun.	25	at Pittsburgh*
	Mon.	27	Tampa Bay		Tue.	27	New Jersey
	Thu.	30	Toronto	Mar.	Thu.	1	Carolina
Dec.	Fri.	1	at New Jersey		Sat.	3	Tampa Bay
	Sun.	3	New Jersey*		Mon.	5	at NY Rangers
	Wed.	6	at Florida		Tue.	6	Washington
	Sat.	9	Atlanta		Fri.	9	Minnesota
	Sun.	10	at Philadelphia		Sun.	11	Florida*
	Tue.	12	Washington		Wed.	14	at Pittsburgh
	Fri.	15	Toronto		Sat.	17	at Columbus
	Sat.	16	at Ottawa		Sun.	18	at Carolina*
	Tue.	19	Carolina		Tue.	20	at St. Louis
	Thu.	21	Dallas		Fri.	23	at Dallas
	Sat.	23	Columbus		Sun.	25	at Phoenix
	Wed.	27	Boston		Wed.	28	at NY Rangers
	Fri.	29	Atlanta		Thu.	29	NY Rangers
	Sat.	30	Buffalo		Sat.	31	at Boston
Jan.	Tue.	2	Montreal	Apr.	Mon.	2	at Pittsburgh
	Thu.	4	at New Jersey		Wed.	4	at Toronto
	Sat.	6	Phoenix		Fri.	6	Ottawa
	Sun.	7	at Carolina*		Sat.	7	at Boston

* Denotes afternoon game.

Franchise date: June 6, 1972

ATLANTIC DIVISION

29th NHL Season

Tim Connolly's strength as a one-on-one player was the reason that the Islanders made him their first of three top-10 picks in the 1999 NHL Entry Draft. He made the club last season as a 19-year-old and finished third on the team in scoring.

Year-by-Year Record

Season	GP	Home W	L	T	Road W	L	T	Overall W	L	T	GF	GA	Pts.	Finished		Playoff Result
1999-2000	82	10	26	5	14	23	4	24	49	9	194	275	58	5th,	Atlantic Div.	Out of Playoffs
1998-99	82	11	23	7	13	25	3	24	48	10	194	244	58	5th,	Atlantic Div.	Out of Playoffs
1997-98	82	17	20	4	13	21	7	30	41	11	212	225	71	4th,	Atlantic Div.	Out of Playoffs
1996-97	82	19	18	4	10	23	8	29	41	12	240	250	70	7th,	Atlantic Div.	Out of Playoffs
1995-96	82	14	21	6	8	29	4	22	50	10	229	315	54	7th,	Atlantic Div.	Out of Playoffs
1994-95	48	10	11	3	5	17	2	15	28	5	126	158	35	7th,	Atlantic Div.	Out of Playoffs
1993-94	84	23	15	4	13	21	8	36	36	12	282	264	84	4th,	Atlantic Div.	Lost Conf. Quarter-Final
1992-93	84	20	19	3	20	18	4	40	37	7	335	297	87	3rd,	Patrick Div.	Lost Conf. Championship
1991-92	80	20	15	5	14	20	6	34	35	11	291	299	79	5th,	Patrick Div.	Out of Playoffs
1990-91	80	15	19	6	10	26	4	25	45	10	223	290	60	6th,	Patrick Div.	Out of Playoffs
1989-90	80	15	17	8	16	21	3	31	38	11	281	288	73	4th,	Patrick Div.	Lost Div. Semi-Final
1988-89	80	19	18	3	9	29	2	28	47	5	265	325	61	6th,	Patrick Div.	Out of Playoffs
1987-88	80	24	10	6	15	21	4	39	31	10	308	267	88	1st,	Patrick Div.	Lost Div. Semi-Final
1986-87	80	20	15	5	15	18	7	35	33	12	279	281	82	3rd,	Patrick Div.	Lost Div. Final
1985-86	80	22	11	7	17	18	5	39	29	12	327	284	90	3rd,	Patrick Div.	Lost Div. Semi-Final
1984-85	80	26	11	3	14	23	3	40	34	6	345	312	86	3rd,	Patrick Div.	Lost Div. Final
1983-84	80	28	11	1	22	15	3	50	26	4	357	269	104	1st,	Patrick Div.	Lost Final
1982-83	**80**	**26**	**11**	**3**	**16**	**15**	**9**	**42**	**26**	**12**	**302**	**226**	**96**	**2nd,**	**Patrick Div.**	**Won Stanley Cup**
1981-82	**80**	**33**	**3**	**4**	**21**	**13**	**6**	**54**	**16**	**10**	**385**	**250**	**118**	**1st,**	**Patrick Div.**	**Won Stanley Cup**
1980-81	**80**	**23**	**6**	**11**	**25**	**12**	**3**	**48**	**18**	**14**	**355**	**260**	**110**	**1st,**	**Patrick Div.**	**Won Stanley Cup**
1979-80	**80**	**26**	**9**	**5**	**13**	**19**	**8**	**39**	**28**	**13**	**281**	**247**	**91**	**2nd,**	**Patrick Div.**	**Won Stanley Cup**
1978-79	80	31	3	6	20	12	8	51	15	14	358	214	116	1st,	Patrick Div.	Lost Semi-Final
1977-78	80	29	3	8	19	14	7	48	17	15	334	210	111	1st,	Patrick Div.	Lost Quarter-Final
1976-77	80	24	11	5	23	10	7	47	21	12	288	193	106	2nd,	Patrick Div.	Lost Semi-Final
1975-76	80	24	8	8	18	13	9	42	21	17	297	190	101	2nd,	Patrick Div.	Lost Semi-Final
1974-75	80	22	6	12	11	19	10	33	25	22	264	221	88	3rd,	Patrick Div.	Lost Semi-Final
1973-74	78	13	17	9	6	24	9	19	41	18	182	247	56	8th,	East Div.	Out of Playoffs
1972-73	78	10	25	4	2	35	2	12	60	6	170	347	30	8th,	East Div.	Out of Playoffs

2000-01 Player Personnel

FORWARDS	HT	WT	S	Place of Birth	Date	1999-00 Club
BELANGER, Jesse	6-1	190	R	St. Georges de Beauce, Que.	6/15/69	Montreal-Quebec Citadelles
CONNOLLY, Tim	6-0	186	R	Syracuse, NY	5/7/81	NY Islanders
CZERKAWSKI, Mariusz	6-0	195	L	Radomsko, Poland	4/13/72	NY Islanders
ISBISTER, Brad	6-4	227	R	Edmonton, Alta.	5/7/77	NY Islanders
KROG, Jason	5-11	191	R	Fernie, B.C.	10/9/75	NYI-Lowell (AHL)-Prov (AHL)
KVASHA, Oleg	6-5	215	R	Moscow, USSR	7/26/78	Florida
LAPOINTE, Claude	5-9	181	L	Lachine, Que.	10/11/68	NY Islanders
LAWRENCE, Mark	6-4	215	R	Burlington, Ont.	1/27/72	NY Islanders-Chicago Wolves-Lowell (AHL)
LINDGREN, Mats	6-2	202	L	Skelleftea, Sweden	10/1/74	NY Islanders
MUCKALT, Bill	6-1	200	R	Surrey, B.C.	7/15/74	Vancouver-NY Islanders
NABOKOV, Dmitri	6-2	209	R	Novosibirsk, USSR	1/4/77	NY Islanders-Lowell (AHL)
PARRISH, Mark	5-11	191	R	Edina, MN	2/2/77	Florida
PETROVICKY, Robert	5-11	172	L	Kosice, Czech.	10/26/73	Tampa Bay-Grand Rapids
PYATT, Taylor	6-4	220	L	Thunder Bay, Ont.	8/19/81	Sudbury Wolves
SCATCHARD, Dave	6-2	220	R	Hinton, Alta.	2/20/76	Vancouver-NY Islanders
STAPLETON, Mike	5-10	183	R	Sarnia, Ont.	5/5/66	Atlanta
TOMS, Jeff	6-5	200	L	Swift Current, Sask.	6/4/74	Washington-Portland Pirates
TORRES, Raffi	5-11	207	L	Toronto, Ont.	10/8/81	Brampton
WEBB, Steve	6-0	195	R	Peterborough, Ont.	4/30/75	NY Islanders
DEFENSEMEN						
BIRON, Mathieu	6-6	212	R	Lac St. Charles, Que.	4/29/80	NY Islanders
BRIMANIS, Aris	6-3	210	R	Cleveland, OH	3/14/72	NYI-K.C.-Providence Bruins
CAIRNS, Eric	6-6	230	L	Oakville, Ont.	6/27/74	NY Islanders-Providence Bruins
CHARA, Zdeno	6-9	255	L	Trencin, Czech.	3/18/77	NY Islanders
GIROUX, Ray	6-0	180	L	North Bay, Ont.	7/20/76	NY Islanders-Lowell (AHL)
HALLER, Kevin	6-2	199	L	Trochu, Alta.	12/5/70	Anaheim
HAMRLIK, Roman	6-2	215	L	Gottwaldov, Czech.	4/12/74	Barum Zlin-Edmonton
JONSSON, Kenny	6-3	195	L	Angelholm, Sweden	10/6/74	NY Islanders
KOROLEV, Evgeny	6-1	186	L	Moscow, USSR	7/24/78	NY Islanders-Lowell (AHL)
MEZEI, Branislav	6-4	221	L	Nitra, Czech.	10/8/80	Belleville Bulls
MYRVOLD, Anders	6-2	200	L	Lorenskog, Norway	8/12/75	AIK Solna
SCHULTZ, Ray	6-2	200	L	Red Deer, Alta.	11/14/76	NY Islanders-Kansas City
TREBIL, Daniel	6-3	210	R	Bloomington, MN	4/10/74	Cincinnati Ducks-Pittsburgh

GOALTENDERS	HT	WT	C	Place of Birth	Date	1999-00 Club
DiPIETRO, Rick	5-11	185	R	Winthrop, MA	9/19/81	Boston University
FLAHERTY, Wade	6-0	170	L	Terrace, B.C.	1/11/68	NY Islanders
VANBIESBROUCK, John	5-8	176	L	Detroit, MI	9/4/63	Philadelphia

1999-2000 Scoring

* – rookie

Regular Season

Pos	#	Player	Team	GP	G	A	Pts	+/–	PIM	PP	SH	GW	GT	S	%
R	21	Mariusz Czerkawski	NYI	79	35	35	70	–16	34	16	0	4	1	276	12.7
R	15	Brad Isbister	NYI	64	22	20	42	–18	100	9	0	1	1	135	16.3
C	18	* Tim Connolly	NYI	81	14	20	34	–25	44	2	1	1	1	114	12.3
C	13	Claude Lapointe	NYI	76	15	16	31	–22	60	2	1	3	0	129	11.6
C	38	Dave Scatchard	VAN	21	0	4	4	–3	24	0	0	0	0	25	0.0
			NYI	44	12	14	26	0	93	0	1	1	0	103	11.7
			TOTAL	65	12	18	30	–3	117	0	1	1	0	128	9.4
L	25	Josh Green	NYI	49	12	14	26	–7	41	2	0	3	0	109	11.0
D	29	Kenny Jonsson	NYI	65	1	24	25	–15	32	1	0	0	0	84	1.2
C	62	Olli Jokinen	NYI	82	11	10	21	0	80	1	2	3	0	138	8.0
R	11	Bill Muckalt	VAN	33	4	8	12	6	17	1	0	1	0	53	7.5
			NYI	12	4	3	7	5	4	0	0	0	1	26	15.4
			TOTAL	45	8	11	19	11	21	1	0	1	1	79	10.1
R	6	Jamie Heward	NYI	54	6	11	17	–9	26	2	0	1	0	92	6.5
D	20	Jamie Rivers	NYI	75	1	16	17	–4	84	1	0	0	0	95	1.1
C	10	Mats Lindgren	NYI	43	9	7	16	0	24	1	0	1	0	68	13.2
L	12	Mike Watt	NYI	45	5	6	11	–8	17	0	1	0	0	49	10.2
C	37	* Dmitri Nabokov	NYI	26	4	7	11	–8	16	0	0	0	0	40	10.0
D	3	Zdeno Chara	NYI	65	2	9	11	–27	57	0	0	1	1	47	4.3
D	33	Eric Cairns	NYI	67	2	7	9	–5	196	0	0	0	0	55	3.6
D	41	* Raymond Giroux	NYI	14	0	9	9	0	10	0	0	0	0	24	0.0
D	34	* Mathieu Biron	NYI	60	4	4	8	–13	38	2	0	2	0	70	5.7
L	43	Mikael Andersson	PHI	36	2	3	5	–2	0	0	1	0	0	38	5.3
			NYI	19	0	3	3	–1	4	0	0	0	0	19	0.0
			TOTAL	55	2	6	8	–3	4	0	1	0	0	57	3.5
C	24	Johan Davidsson	ANA	5	1	0	1	0	2	0	0	1	0	8	12.5
			NYI	14	2	4	6	0	0	0	0	0	0	21	9.5
			TOTAL	19	3	4	7	0	2	0	0	1	0	29	10.3
C	28	* Jason Krog	NYI	17	2	4	6	–1	6	1	0	0	0	22	9.1
R	44	Mark Lawrence	NYI	29	1	5	6	–13	26	0	0	0	1	33	3.0
C	17	Ted Drury	ANA	11	1	1	2	–1	6	0	0	0	0	9	11.1
			NYI	55	2	1	3	–8	31	1	0	0	0	48	4.2
			TOTAL	66	3	2	5	–9	37	1	0	0	0	57	5.3
R	14	Chris Ferraro	NYI	11	1	3	4	1	8	0	0	0	0	15	6.7
R	8	Steve Webb	NYI	65	1	3	4	–4	103	0	0	0	0	27	3.7
R	16	Vladimir Orszagh	NYI	11	2	1	3	1	4	0	0	0	0	16	12.5
D	58	Aris Brimanis	NYI	18	2	1	3	–5	6	2	0	0	0	16	12.5
D	36	* Evgeny Korolev	NYI	17	1	2	3	–10	8	0	0	0	0	7	14.3
D	56	Ian Herbers	T.B	37	0	0	0	–12	45	0	0	0	0	11	0.0
			NYI	6	0	3	3	6	2	0	0	0	0	3	0.0
			TOTAL	43	0	3	3	–6	47	0	0	0	0	14	0.0
L	39	* Sean Haggerty	NYI	5	1	1	2	3	4	0	0	0	0	2	50.0
D	55	* Vlad Chebaturkin	NYI	17	1	1	2	–3	8	0	0	0	0	9	11.1
D	4	Eric Brewer	NYI	26	0	2	2	–11	20	0	0	0	0	30	0.0
L	39	Scott Pearson	NYI	2	0	1	1	1	0	0	0	0	0	5	0.0
D	7	Dallas Eakins	NYI	2	0	1	1	3	2	0	0	0	0	4	0.0
D	7	* Ray Schultz	NYI	9	0	1	1	1	30	0	0	0	0	2	0.0
G	80	Kevin Weekes	VAN	20	0	0	0	0	0	0	0	0	0	0	0.0
			NYI	36	0	1	1	0	0	0	0	0	0	1	0.0
			TOTAL	56	0	1	1	0	0	0	0	0	0	1	0.0
C	16	Daniel Lacroix	NYI	1	0	0	0	–1	0	0	0	0	0	0	0.0
R	32	* Petr Mika	NYI	3	0	0	0	–1	0	0	0	0	0	1	0.0
G	30	Wade Flaherty	NYI	4	0	0	0	0	0	0	0	0	0	0	0.0
G	35	* Stephen Valiquette	NYI	6	0	0	0	0	0	0	0	0	0	0	0.0
G	1	* Roberto Luongo	NYI	24	0	0	0	0	0	0	0	0	0	0	0.0

Goaltending

No.	Goaltender	GPI	Mins	Avg	W	L	T	EN	SO	GA	SA	S%
35	* Stephen Valiquette	6	193	1.87	2	0	0	0	0	6	117	.949
30	Wade Flaherty	4	182	2.31	0	1	1	1	0	7	81	.914
29	Felix Potvin	22	1273	3.21	5	14	3	3	1	68	632	.892
1	* Roberto Luongo	24	1292	3.25	7	14	1	2	1	70	730	.904
80	Kevin Weekes	36	2026	3.41	10	20	4	3	1	115	1173	.902
	Totals	**82**	**4981**	**3.31**	**24**	**49**	**9**	**9**	**3**	**275**	**2742**	**.900**

Coaching History

Phil Goyette and Earl Ingarfield, 1972-73; Al Arbour, 1973-74 to 1985-86; Terry Simpson, 1986-87, 1987-88; Terry Simpson and Al Arbour, 1988-89; Al Arbour, 1989-90 to 1993-94; Lorne Henning, 1994-95; Mike Milbury, 1995-96; Mike Milbury and Rick Bowness, 1996-97; Rick Bowness and Mike Milbury, 1997-98; Mike Milbury and Bill Stewart, 1998-99; Butch Goring, 1999-2000 to date.

General Managers' History

Bill Torrey, 1972-73 to 1991-92; Don Maloney, 1992-93 to 1994-95; Don Maloney and Mike Milbury, 1995-96; Mike Milbury, 1996-97 to date.

Coach

GORING, BUTCH
Coach, New York Islanders. Born in St. Boniface, Man., October 22, 1949.

Former New York Islanders star Butch Goring re-joined the team as its head coach on April 30, 1999 and has been entrusted with the task of trying to restore a little bit of the Islanders tradition to a franchise that last made the playoffs during the 1993-1994 season. He spent his first season behind the bench with the club in 1999-2000.

Goring played 16 seasons in the NHL with three different teams - the Los Angeles Kings, New York Islanders, and Boston Bruins - but it was his stay on Long Island that defined his career. Goring was the last piece of the puzzle that included the likes of Mike Bossy, Billy Smith, Denis Potvin, Bryan Trottier, and Bob Nystrom, and he helped the Isles win four consecutive Stanley Cup titles from 1980 to 1983. Perhaps Goring's greatest individual accomplishment as a player came in the 1981 playoffs when he had 10 goals and 10 assists in 18 games to earn the Conn Smythe Trophy as the most valuable player of the post-season.

Along with an impressive resume as a player, Goring's coaching background also has plenty of peaks, including back-to-back Turner Cup titles with the International Hockey League's Denver/Utah Grizzlies in 1995 and 1996. Goring began his head coaching career with the Boston Bruins in 1985-86. In a little over a season in Boston, Goring had a winning 42-38-13 record. Goring was an Islanders assistant under Al Arbour in 1989-90. He has also had head coaching stints in the Western Hockey League (WHL) and the American Hockey League (AHL).

Goring and his wife, Cathy, have two daughters, Shannon and Kellie.

Coaching Record

		Regular Season					Playoffs			
Season	Team	Games	W	L	T	%	Games	W	L	%
1985-86	**Boston (NHL)**	**80**	**37**	**31**	**12**	**.538**	**3**	**0**	**3**	**.000**
1986-87	**Boston (NHL)**	**13**	**5**	**7**	**1**	**.423**	....	....	....	....
1987-88	Spokane (WHL)	72	37	32	3	.535	15	7	8	.467
1988-89	Spokane (WHL)	11	2	9	0	.182	....	....	....	....
1990-91	Capital Dist. (AHL)	80	28	43	9	.406	....	....	....	....
1991-92	Capital Dist. (AHL)	80	32	37	11	.469	7	3	4	.429
1992-93	Capital Dist. (AHL)	80	34	34	12	.500	4	0	4	.000
1993-94	Las Vegas (IHL)	81	52	18	11	.710	5	1	4	.200
1994-95	Denver (IHL)	81	57	18	6	.741	17	15	2	.882
1995-96	Utah (IHL)	82	49	29	4	.622	22	15	7	.682
1996-97	Utah (IHL)	82	43	33	6	.561	7	3	4	.429
1997-98	Utah (IHL)	82	47	27	8	.622	4	1	3	.250
1998-99	Utah (IHL)	82	39	34	9	.530	....	....	....	....
1999-2000	**NY Islanders (NHL)**	**82**	**24**	**49**	**9**	**.354•**	....	....	....	....
	NHL Totals	**175**	**66**	**87**	**22**	**.443•**	**3**	**0**	**3**	**.000**

• Includes points from regulation ties

Club Records

Team

(Figures in brackets for season records are games played; records for fewest points, wins, ties, losses, goals, goals against are for 70 or more games)

Most Points	118	1981-82 (80)
Most Wins	54	1981-82 (80)
Most Ties	22	1974-75 (80)
Most Losses	60	1972-73 (78)
Most Goals	385	1981-82 (80)
Most Goals Against	347	1972-73 (78)
Fewest Points	30	1972-73 (78)
Fewest Wins	12	1972-73 (78)
Fewest Ties	4	1983-84 (80)
Fewest Losses	15	1978-79 (80)
Fewest Goals	170	1972-73 (78)
Fewest Goals Against	190	1975-76 (80)

Longest Winning Streak

Overall	15	Jan. 21-Feb. 20/82
Home	14	Jan. 2-Feb. 27/82
Away	8	Feb. 27-Mar. 31/81

Longest Undefeated Streak

Overall	15	Jan. 21-Feb. 20/82 (15 wins), Nov. 4-Dec. 4/80 (13 wins, 2 ties)
Home	23	Oct. 17/78-Jan. 27/79 (19 wins, 4 ties), Jan. 2-Apr. 3/82 (21 wins, 2 ties)
Away	8	Four times

Longest Losing Streak

Overall	12	Dec. 27/72-Jan. 16/73, Nov. 22-Dec. 15/88
Home	7	Nov. 13-Dec. 14/99
Away	15	Jan. 20-Mar. 31/73

Longest Winless Streak

Overall	15	Nov. 22-Dec. 21/72 (12 losses, 3 ties)
Home	9	Mar. 2-Apr. 6/99 (7 losses, 2 ties)
Away	20	Nov. 3/72-Jan. 13/73 (19 losses, 1 tie)
Most Shutouts, Season	10	1975-76 (80)
Most PIM, Season	1,857	1986-87 (80)
Most Goals, Game	11	Dec. 20/83 (Pit. 3 at NYI 11), Mar. 3/84 (NYI 11 at Tor. 6)

Individual

Most Seasons	17	Billy Smith
Most Games	1,123	Bryan Trottier
Most Goals, Career	573	Mike Bossy
Most Assists, Career	853	Bryan Trottier
Most Points, Career	1,353	Bryan Trottier (500G, 853A)
Most PIM, Career	1,879	Mick Vukota
Most Shutouts, Career	25	Glenn Resch
Longest Consecutive Games Streak	576	Bill Harris (Oct. 7/72-Nov. 30/79)

Most Goals, Season	69	Mike Bossy (1978-79)
Most Assists, Season	87	Bryan Trottier (1978-79)
Most Points, Season	147	Mike Bossy (1981-82; 64G, 83A)
Most PIM, Season	356	Brian Curran (1986-87)
Most Points, Defenseman, Season	101	Denis Potvin (1978-79; 31G, 70A)
Most Points, Center, Season	134	Bryan Trottier (1978-79; 47G, 87A)
Most Points, Right Wing, Season	147	Mike Bossy (1981-82; 64G, 83A)
Most Points, Left Wing, Season	100	John Tonelli (1984-85; 42G, 58A)
Most Points, Rookie, Season	95	Bryan Trottier (1975-76; 32G, 63A)
Most Shutouts, Season	7	Glenn Resch (1975-76)
Most Goals, Game	5	Bryan Trottier (Dec. 23/78, Feb. 13/82), John Tonelli (Jan. 6/81)
Most Assists, Game	6	Mike Bossy (Jan. 6/81)
Most Points, Game	8	Bryan Trottier (Dec. 23/78; 5G, 3A)

Captains' History

Ed Westfall, 1972-73 to 1975-76; Ed Westfall and Clark Gillies, 1976-77; Clark Gillies, 1977-78, 1978-79; Denis Potvin, 1979-80 to 1986-87; Brent Sutter, 1987-88 to 1990-91; Brent Sutter and Pat Flatley, 1991-92; Pat Flatley, 1992-93 to 1995-96; no captain, 1996-97; Bryan McCabe and Trevor Linden, 1997-98; Trevor Linden, 1998-99; Kenny Jonsson, 1999-2000 to date.

Retired Numbers

5	Denis Potvin	1973-1988
9	Clark Gillies	1974-1986
22	Mike Bossy	1977-1987
23	Bob Nystrom	1972-1986
31	Billy Smith	1972-1989

All-time Record vs. Other Clubs

Regular Season

		At Home							On Road							Total					
	GP	W	L	T	GF	GA	PTS	GP	W	L	T	GF	GA	PTS	GP	W	L	T	GF	GA	PTS
Anaheim	5	2	2	1	12	15	5	6	3	1	2	18	13	8	11	5	3	3	30	28	13
Atlanta	2	0	2	0	3	6	0	2	1	1	0	8	7	2	4	1	3	0	11	13	2
Boston	53	22	25	6	177	175	50	51	14	27	10	147	194	38	104	36	52	16	324	369	88
Buffalo	53	23	21	9	156	148	55	53	16	29	8	147	184	40	106	39	50	17	303	332	95
Calgary	47	25	13	9	185	129	59	48	13	24	11	142	171	37	95	38	37	20	327	300	96
Carolina	36	17	15	4	120	105	38	37	14	18	5	125	132	33	73	31	33	9	245	237	71
Chicago	44	17	12	15	153	130	49	46	16	25	5	150	156	37	90	33	37	20	303	286	86
Colorado	30	16	13	1	120	104	33	31	11	18	2	95	117	24	61	27	31	3	215	221	57
Dallas	44	23	13	8	165	126	54	44	20	17	7	162	131	47	88	43	30	15	327	257	101
Detroit	43	23	17	3	155	126	49	42	17	23	2	132	152	36	85	40	40	5	287	278	85
Edmonton	28	12	7	9	117	105	33	27	6	16	5	78	103	17	55	18	23	14	195	208	50
Florida	17	6	9	2	41	45	14	17	4	10	3	44	56	11	34	10	19	5	85	101	25
Los Angeles	41	24	13	4	154	115	52	42	15	20	7	136	154	37	83	39	33	11	290	269	89
Montreal	52	24	23	5	164	153	53	52	13	30	9	154	193	35	104	37	53	14	318	346	88
Nashville	2	0	2	0	5	8	0	2	1	1	0	8	6	2	4	1	3	0	13	14	2
New Jersey	74	51	14	9	330	215	111	74	35	29	10	271	249	80	148	86	43	19	601	464	191
NY Rangers	86	53	26	7	345	263	114	85	25	50	10	256	329	60	171	78	76	17	601	592	173
Ottawa	16	3	9	4	54	64	11	15	4	7	4	45	49	12	31	7	16	8	99	113	23
Philadelphia	87	47	26	14	333	252	108	85	24	51	10	249	321	58	172	71	77	24	582	573	166
Phoenix	28	13	7	8	110	86	34	27	14	10	3	97	86	31	55	27	17	11	207	172	65
Pittsburgh	76	39	29	8	304	255	86	79	29	37	11	270	296	69	153	68	66	19	574	551	155
St. Louis	46	24	11	11	176	118	59	44	18	17	9	144	158	45	90	42	28	20	320	276	104
San Jose	9	5	3	1	38	29	11	8	5	2	1	28	17	11	17	10	5	2	66	46	22
Tampa Bay	17	7	9	1	47	50	15	18	8	9	1	53	47	17	35	15	18	2	100	97	32
Toronto	45	24	18	3	180	135	51	47	22	22	3	166	159	47	92	46	40	6	346	294	98
Vancouver	44	23	11	10	164	122	56	45	21	21	3	148	148	45	89	44	32	13	312	270	101
Washington	73	40	32	1	279	229	81	73	29	34	10	234	238	68	146	69	66	11	513	467	149
Defunct Clubs	13	11	0	2	75	33	24	13	4	5	4	35	41	12	26	15	5	6	110	74	36
Totals	**1111**	**574**	**382**	**155**	**4162**	**3341**	**1304**	**1111**	**402**	**554**	**155**	**3542**	**3907**	**959**	**2222**	**976**	**936**	**310**	**7704**	**7248**	**2263**

Playoffs

	Series	W	L	GP	W	L	T	GF	GA	Last Mtg.	Round	Result
Boston	2	2	0	11	8	3	0	49	35	1983	CF	W 4-2
Buffalo	3	3	0	16	12	4	0	59	45	1980	SF	W 4-2
Chicago	2	2	0	6	6	0	0	21	6	1979	QF	W 4-0
Colorado	1	1	0	4	4	0	0	18	9	1982	CF	W 4-0
Dallas	1	1	0	5	4	1	0	26	16	1981	F	W 4-1
Edmonton	3	2	1	15	9	6	0	58	47	1984	F	L 1-4
Los Angeles	1	1	0	4	3	1	0	21	10	1980	PR	W 3-1
Montreal	4	1	3	22	8	14	0	55	64	1993	CF	L 1-4
New Jersey	1	0	1	6	2	4	0	18	23	1988	DSF	L 2-4
NY Rangers	8	5	3	39	20	19	0	129	132	1994	CQF	L 0-4
Philadelphia	4	1	3	25	11	14	0	69	83	1987	DF	L 3-4
Pittsburgh	3	3	0	19	11	8	0	67	58	1993	DF	W 4-3
Toronto	2	1	1	10	6	4	0	33	20	1981	PR	W 3-0
Vancouver	2	2	0	6	6	0	0	26	14	1982	F	W 4-0
Washington	6	5	1	30	18	12	0	99	88	1993	DSF	W 4-2
Totals	**43**	**30**	**13**	**218**	**128**	**90**	**0**	**748**	**650**			

Calgary totals include Atlanta Flames, 1972-73 to 1979-80.
Colorado totals include Quebec, 1979-80 to 1994-95.
New Jersey totals include Kansas City, 1974-75 to 1975-76, and Colorado Rockies, 1976-77 to 1981-82.
Phoenix totals include Winnipeg, 1979-80 to 1995-96.

Carolina totals include Hartford, 1979-80 to 1996-97.
Dallas totals include Minnesota North Stars, 1972-73 to 1992-93.

Playoff Results 2000-1996

Year	Round	Opponent	Result	GF	GA

(Last playoff appearance: 1994)

Abbreviations: Round: F – Final;
CF – conference final; **CQF** – conference quarter-final;
DF – division final; **DSF** – division semi-final;
SF – semi-final; **QF** – quarter-final;
PR – preliminary round.

1999-2000 Results

Oct.	2	at Tampa Bay	2-4		13	at Tampa Bay	2-4
	10	Colorado	4-2		15	NY Rangers	2-5
	11	NY Rangers	2-4		17	Ottawa	3-4 *
	14	Atlanta	2-4		19	at Montreal	0-3
	16	at New Jersey	1-4		21	at New Jersey	0-4
	18	at Montreal	4-2		22	Tampa Bay	2-0
	23	Vancouver	2-2		26	at Anaheim	4-2
	27	at Florida	3-6		29	at San Jose	3-2 *
	30	Carolina	0-4		31	at Los Angeles	2-4
Nov.	3	at NY Rangers	3-3	Feb.	2	Nashville	4-6
	4	Montreal	2-1 *		3	at Pittsburgh	2-4
	6	at Buffalo	1-2		8	Carolina	3-4
	10	at Carolina	2-0		10	Tampa Bay	5-4 *
	12	at Chicago	0-5		12	Pittsburgh	5-1
	13	St. Louis	3-5		13	at NY Rangers	4-2
	19	at Colorado	3-2		15	San Jose	1-4
	21	at Edmonton	4-4		17	at Philadelphia	2-2
	23	at Calgary	2-3		19	at New Jersey	4-2
	27	Washington	3-4		21	Detroit	0-2
	28	at Boston	2-1		25	at Detroit	2-5
	30	Dallas	1-2		26	Philadelphia	1-5
Dec.	2	Calgary	0-5		28	at Washington	2-3
	4	Atlanta	3-4	Mar.	2	Ottawa	5-5
	7	at Washington	2-4		4	Buffalo	4-2
	9	Montreal	2-4		5	at Philadelphia	4-3 *
	11	at Ottawa	1-1		9	at Phoenix	0-5
	14	Edmonton	2-4		10	at Dallas	4-3 *
	15	at Toronto	1-5		12	at Buffalo	2-4
	18	Buffalo	2-3		15	at Washington	3-4
	19	New Jersey	5-3		16	at Atlanta	4-2
	21	Pittsburgh	0-4		18	Florida	2-4
	23	NY Rangers	4-2		21	Pittsburgh	2-8
	27	Boston	3-0		22	at Toronto	5-2
	29	Toronto	1-2		24	New Jersey	2-8
	30	at Pittsburgh	3-9		26	at Carolina	1-4
Jan.	2	Philadelphia	1-4		28	at Nashville	2-3
	6	Boston	3-7	Apr.	1	Chicago	2-2
	6	at Philadelphia	2-3		2	at Atlanta	4-5
	8	at Boston	5-2		6	at Ottawa	2-1
	10	Phoenix	2-2		7	Toronto	1-2
	12	at Florida	3-4		9	Florida	3-2

* – Overtime

Entry Draft
Selections 2000-1986

2000
Pick
1 Rick DiPietro
5 Raffi Torres
101 Arto Tukio
105 Vladimir Gorbunov
136 Dmitri Upper
148 Kristofer Ottosson
202 Ryan Caldwell
264 Dmitri Altarev
267 Tomi Pettinen

1999
Pick
5 Tim Connolly
8 Taylor Pyatt
10 Branislav Mezei
28 Kristian Kudroc
78 Mattias Weinhandl
87 Brian Collins
101 Juraj Kolnik
102 Johan Halvardsson
130 Justin Mapletoft
140 Adam Johnson
163 Bjorn Melin
228 Radek Martinek
255 Brett Henning
268 Tyler Scott

1998
Pick
9 Michael Rupp
36 Chris Nielsen
95 Andy Burnham
123 Jiri Dopita
155 Kevin Clauson
182 Evgeny Korolev
209 Frederik Brindamour
237 Ben Blais
242 Jason Doyle
250 Radek Matejovsky

1997
Pick
4 Roberto Luongo
6 Eric Brewer
31 Jeff Zehr
59 Jarrett Smith
79 Robert Schnabel
85 Petr Mika
115 Adam Edinger
139 Bobby Leavins
166 Kris Knoblauch
196 Jeremy Symington
222 Ryan Clark

1996
Pick
3 Jean-Pierre Dumont
29 Dan Lacouture
56 Zdeno Chara
83 Tyrone Garner
109 Bubba Berenzweig
128 Peter Sachl
138 Todd Miller
165 J.R. Prestifilippo
192 Evgeny Korolev
218 Mike Muzechka

1995
Pick
2 Wade Redden
28 Jan Hlavac
41 D.J. Smith
106 Vladimir Orszagh
158 Andrew Taylor
210 David MacDonald
211 Mike Broda

1994
Pick
9 Brett Lindros
38 Jason Holland
63 Jason Strudwick
90 Brad Lukowich
112 Mark McArthur
116 Albert O'Connell
142 Jason Stewart
194 Mike Loach
203 Peter Hogardh
220 Gord Walsh
246 Kirk Dewaele
272 Dick Tarnstrom

1993
Pick
23 Todd Bertuzzi
40 Bryan McCabe
66 Vladimir Chebaturkin
92 Warren Luhning
118 Tommy Salo
144 Peter LeBoutillier
170 Darren Van Impe
196 Rod Hinks
222 Daniel Johansson
248 Stephane Larocque
274 Carl Charland

1992
Pick
5 Darius Kasparaitis
56 Jarrett Deuling
104 Thomas Klimt
105 Ryan Duthie
128 Derek Armstrong
152 Vladimir Grachev
159 Steve O'Rourke
176 Jason Widmer
200 Daniel Paradis
224 David Wainwright
248 Andrei Vasilyev

1991
Pick
4 Scott Lachance
26 Ziggy Palffy
48 Jamie McLennan
70 Milan Hnilicka
92 Steve Junker
114 Robert Valicevic
136 Andreas Johansson
158 Todd Sparks
180 John Johnson
202 Robert Canavan
224 Marcus Thuresson
246 Marty Schriner

1990
Pick
6 Scott Scissons
27 Chris Taylor
48 Dan Plante
90 Chris Marinucci
111 Joni Lehto
132 Michael Guilbert
153 Sylvain Fleury
174 John Joyce
195 Richard Enga
216 Martin Lacroix
237 Andy Shier

1989
Pick
2 Dave Chyzowski
23 Travis Green
44 Jason Zent
65 Brent Grieve
86 Jace Reed
90 Steve Young
99 Kevin O'Sullivan
128 Jon Larson
133 Brett Harkins
149 Phil Huber
170 Matthew Robbins
191 Vladimir Malakhov
212 Kelly Ens
233 Iain Fraser

1988
Pick
16 Kevin Cheveldayoff
29 Wayne Doucet
37 Sean Lebrun
58 Danny Lorenz
79 Andre Brassard
100 Paul Rutherford
111 Pavel Gross
121 Jason Rathbone
142 Yves Gaucher
163 Marty McInnis
173 Shorty Forrest
184 Jeff Blumer
205 Jeff Kampersal
226 Phillip Neururer
247 Joe Caprinni

1987
Pick
13 Dean Chynoweth
34 Jeff Hackett
55 Dean Ewen
76 George Maneluk
97 Petr Vlk
118 Rob DiMaio
139 Knut Walbye
160 Jeff Saterdalen
181 Shawn Howard
202 John Herlihy
223 Michael Erickson
244 Will Averill

1986
Pick
17 Tom Fitzgerald
38 Dennis Vaske
59 Bill Berg
80 Shawn Byram
101 Dean Sexsmith
104 Todd McLellan
122 Tony Schmalzbauer
138 Will Anderson
143 Richard Pilon
164 Peter Harris
185 Jeff Jablonski
206 Kerry Clark
227 Dan Beaudette
248 Paul Thompson

General Manager

MILBURY, MIKE
General Manager, New York Islanders. Born in Walpole, MA, June 17, 1952.

Milbury came to the Islanders with 20 years of professional hockey experience with the Boston Bruins — as a player, assistant coach, assistant general manager, general manager and coach on both the NHL and AHL levels. Milbury took over as general manager from Don Maloney on December 12, 1995.

His recent trades have brought the Islanders John Vanbiesbrouck, Roman Hamrlik, Mark Parrish, Oleg Kvasha, Bill Muckalt, Dave Scatchard and draft picks used to select Taylor Pyatt, Raffi Torres and Branislav Mezei. In addition, his staff has used first round picks to take Tim Connolly (fifth overall, 1999) and Rick DiPietro (first overall, 2000). Milbury has also added two top-line forwards in a pair of excellent deals — Brad Isbister from Phoenix for Robert Reichel, and Mariusz Czerkawski from Edmonton for Dan Lacouture.

Milbury joined the Boston organization after graduating from Colgate University with a degree in urban sociology and enjoyed a 10-year playing career with the team. He retired May 6, 1985 and took over as assistant coach. He returned to the ice late in the 1985-86 season when injuries decimated the Bruins defense.

Milbury's playing career concluded after the 1986-87 season and on July 16, 1987 he took over as coach of the Maine Mariners, Boston's top AHL affiliate. In his first year with the team he guided the Mariners to the AHL's Northern Division title and was named both AHL coach of the year and *The Hockey News* minor league coach of the year.

Mike and his wife, Ginger, live in Garden City. He has four sons, Owen, Luke, Jake and Jack, and two daughters, Alison and Caitlin.

NHL Coaching Record

		Regular Season					Playoffs			
Season	Team	Games	W	L	T	%	Games	W	L	%
1989-90	Boston	80	46	25	9	.631	21	13	8	.619
1990-91	Boston	80	44	24	12	.606	19	10	9	.526
1995-96	NY Islanders	82	22	50	10	.329	....	....	....	....
1996-97	NY Islanders	45	13	23	9	.389	....	....	....	....
1997-98	NY Islanders	19	8	9	2	.474	....	....	....	....
	NHL Totals	**306**	**133**	**131**	**42**	**.503**	**40**	**23**	**17**	**.575**

Club Directory

Nassau Veterans' Memorial Coliseum

New York Islanders
Nassau Veterans'
Memorial Coliseum
Uniondale, NY 11553
Phone **516/832-4200**
FAX 516/542-9348
www.newyorkislanders.com
Capacity: 16,297

New York Islanders Executive Office
Owner and Governor . . . . Charles B. Wang
Owner and Alternate Governor . . . . Sanjay Kumar
Alternate Governor . . . . Michael J. Picker
Alternate Governor and General Counsel . . . . Roy E. Reichbach
Alternate Governor . . . . William M. Skehan
Executive Assistant . . . . Alice Vanderveldt

Hockey Operations
General Manager . . . . Mike Milbury
Asst. General Manager and Director of
  Player Personnel . . . . Gordie Clark
Head Coach . . . . Butch Goring
Assistant General Manager/Director of
  Hockey Operations . . . . Mike Santos
Manager, Hockey Administration . . . . Joanne Holewa
Assistant Manager of Player Contracts . . . . Pam Genzardi
Associate Coach . . . . Lorne Henning
Assistant Coach . . . . Greg Cronin
Scout and Organizational Coach . . . . Gilles Gilbert
Organizational Coach . . . . Steve Stirling
Head Amateur Scout . . . . Tony Feltrin
Western Scout . . . . Earl Ingarfield
Director of European Scouting . . . . Anders Kallur
Director of Pro Scouting . . . . Ken Morrow
Assistant Director of Pro Scouting . . . . Kevin Maxwell
Scouting Staff . . . . Jim Madigan, Mario Saraceno, Karel Pavlik,
  Doug Gibson, Brian Hunter, Harri Rindell
Video Coordinator . . . . Bob Smith

Medical Staff
Director of Medical Services . . . . Dr. Elliot Pellman
Internist . . . . Dr. Clifford Cooper
Team Orthopedists . . . . Dr. Elliott Hershman, Dr. Kenneth Montgomery,
  Dr. Stephen Nicholas
Team Dentists . . . . Dr. Bruce Michnick, Dr. Jan Sherman

Training/Equipment Staff
Head Trainer . . . . Rich Campbell
Strength & Conditioning Coach . . . . Sean Donellan
Head Equipment Manager . . . . Joe McMahon
Assistant Equipment Managers . . . . Rick Harper, Eric Miklich
Lockerroom Attendants . . . . Charles E. Nass, Matt Brager, Robert
  Dobrzeniecki, Arthur Verdi

Administration and Sales
Senior Vice President/CFO . . . . Arthur McCarthy
Senior Vice President of Operations . . . . Bob Brennfleck
Vice President of Administration . . . . Janet L. Kask
Vice President of Communications . . . . Chris Botta
Vice President of Corporate Sales . . . . Bill Kain
Director of Corporate Relations . . . . Bob Nystrom
Director of Merchandise . . . . Chris DiPierri
Director of Ticket Sales and Operations . . . . Kyle Draper
Controller . . . . Ralph Selitti
Assistant Controller . . . . Ginna Cotton
Ticket Sales Manager . . . . Larry Fitzpatrick
Manager of Media Relations . . . . Jason Lagnese
Event Operations Manager . . . . Ryan Halkett
Customer Service Manager . . . . Kerry Cornils
Payroll Manager . . . . Christine Bowler
Corporate Marketing Managers . . . . Erik Scheibe, Ted Van Zelst, Jamie Fabos
Creative Services Manager . . . . Mauricio Acosta
Team Store Managers . . . . Danny DiPierri, Maryanne Steves
Group Sales Manager . . . . Cliff Gault
Corporate Ticket Sales . . . . Anthony Mercogliano, Brian Reynolds
Customer Service Representative . . . . Heather Cozzens
Group Sales Representative . . . . Adam Ortiz
Sales Representatives . . . . Mike Clough, Patrick Duffy
Staff Accountant . . . . Heather Jabick
Accounts Payable Bookkeeper . . . . Maria Corvino
Premium Seating Coordinator . . . . Linda Statkevicus
Publications Coordinator . . . . Kerry Gwydir
Special Events Coordinator . . . . Kevin Schwab
Promotional Coordinator . . . . Randy Risorto
Community Relations Coordinator . . . . Melissa Harding
Sponsor Services Coordinator . . . . Erica Blauberg
Communications Assistant . . . . Rocky Bonanno
Receptionist . . . . Chere O'Neill
Office Attendant . . . . Todd Aronovitch

Team Information
Television Coverage . . . . FOX Sports New York
Announcers . . . . Howie Rose, Joe Micheletti
Radio . . . . ONE-ON-ONE SPORTS AM 620
Radio Announcers . . . . Jim Cerny, Chris King

New York Rangers

1999-2000 Results: 29w-41L-12T 73PTS. Fourth, Atlantic Division

Petr Nedved led the Rangers with 68 points last season. Once traded to the Rangers for ex-Oiler Esa Tikanen, Nedved will be joined in New York this season by a trio of prominent former Oilers — Glen Sather, Ron Low and Mark Messier.

2000-01 Schedule

Oct.	Sat.	7	at Atlanta		Mon.	8	Dallas
	Wed.	11	Montreal		Sat.	13	at Boston*
	Sat.	14	at Pittsburgh		Sun.	14	Minnesota
	Mon.	16	Anaheim		Tue.	16	Philadelphia
	Wed.	18	at Chicago		Thu.	18	Toronto
	Sun.	22	Tampa Bay		Sat.	20	at Montreal
	Tue.	24	Philadelphia		Mon.	22	at Carolina
	Thu.	26	at Philadelphia		Wed.	24	Carolina
	Fri.	27	Pittsburgh		Fri.	26	NY Islanders
	Sun.	29	Boston		Sat.	27	at Toronto
Nov.	Wed.	1	Tampa Bay		Mon.	29	Atlanta
	Thu.	2	at Ottawa		Wed.	31	Montreal
	Sat.	4	at Montreal	Feb.	Tue.	6	Buffalo
	Tue.	7	Edmonton		Fri.	9	at Florida
	Thu.	9	at Washington		Sun.	11	New Jersey
	Sun.	12	Phoenix		Mon.	12	at Columbus
	Wed.	15	at Minnesota		Sat.	17	at Tampa Bay
	Fri.	17	at Vancouver		Mon.	19	Chicago*
	Sat.	18	at Calgary		Fri.	23	at Pittsburgh
	Tue.	21	Toronto		Sun.	25	at Philadelphia
	Wed.	22	at NY Islanders		Mon.	26	Ottawa
	Fri.	24	at Buffalo		Wed.	28	Florida
	Sun.	26	Ottawa	Mar.	Fri.	2	Pittsburgh
	Tue.	28	Los Angeles		Sun.	4	at Nashville*
	Wed.	29	at New Jersey		Mon.	5	NY Islanders
Dec.	Sat.	2	at Toronto		Fri.	9	at Washington
	Sun.	3	Colorado		Sat.	10	at Ottawa
	Wed.	6	Washington		Mon.	12	Pittsburgh
	Fri.	8	Buffalo		Wed.	14	at Buffalo
	Sat.	9	at Boston		Sat.	17	at Philadelphia*
	Tue.	12	at San Jose		Mon.	19	Washington
	Thu.	14	at Los Angeles		Wed.	21	at New Jersey
	Fri.	15	at Anaheim		Sat.	24	Detroit*
	Mon.	18	Florida		Sun.	25	Boston
	Wed.	20	St. Louis		Wed.	28	NY Islanders
	Sat.	23	Nashville*		Thu.	29	at NY Islanders
	Wed.	27	at Carolina		Sat.	31	at New Jersey*
	Thu.	28	Atlanta	Apr.	Sun.	1	at Atlanta*
	Sun.	31	at Dallas		Wed.	4	Carolina
Jan.	Thu.	4	at Phoenix		Thu.	5	at Tampa Bay
	Sat.	6	New Jersey*		Sat.	7	at Florida*

* Denotes afternoon game.

Franchise date: May 15, 1926

EASTERN NHL CONFERENCE

75th NHL Season

ATLANTIC DIVISION

Year-by-Year Record

Season	GP	Home W	L	T	Road W	L	T	Overall W	L	T	GF	GA	Pts.	Finished	Playoff Result
1999-2000	82	15	21	5	14	20	7	29	41	12	218	246	73	4th, Atlantic Div.	Out of Playoffs
1998-99	82	17	19	5	16	19	6	33	38	11	217	227	77	4th, Atlantic Div.	Out of Playoffs
1997-98	82	14	18	9	11	21	9	25	39	18	197	231	68	5th, Atlantic Div.	Out of Playoffs
1996-97	82	21	14	6	17	20	4	38	34	10	258	231	86	4th, Atlantic Div.	Lost Conf. Final
1995-96	82	22	10	9	19	17	5	41	27	14	272	237	96	2nd, Atlantic Div.	Lost Conf. Semi-Final
1994-95	48	11	10	3	11	13	0	22	23	3	139	134	47	4th, Atlantic Div.	Lost Conf. Semi-Final
1993-94	**84**	**28**	**8**	**6**	**24**	**16**	**2**	**52**	**24**	**8**	**299**	**231**	**112**	**1st, Atlantic Div.**	**Won Stanley Cup**
1992-93	84	20	17	5	14	22	6	34	39	11	304	308	79	6th, Patrick Div.	Out of Playoffs
1991-92	80	28	8	4	22	17	1	50	25	5	321	246	105	1st, Patrick Div.	Lost Div. Final
1990-91	80	22	11	7	14	20	6	36	31	13	297	265	85	2nd, Patrick Div.	Lost Div. Semi-Final
1989-90	80	20	11	9	16	20	4	36	31	13	279	267	85	1st, Patrick Div.	Lost Div. Final
1988-89	80	21	17	2	16	18	6	37	35	8	310	307	82	3rd, Patrick Div.	Lost Div. Semi-Final
1987-88	80	22	13	5	14	21	5	36	34	10	300	283	82	5th, Patrick Div.	Out of Playoffs
1986-87	80	18	18	4	16	20	4	34	38	8	307	323	76	4th, Patrick Div.	Lost Div. Semi-Final
1985-86	80	20	18	2	16	20	4	36	38	6	280	276	78	4th, Patick Div.	Lost Conf. Championship
1984-85	80	16	18	6	10	26	4	26	44	10	295	345	62	4th, Patrick Div.	Lost Div. Semi-Final
1983-84	80	27	12	1	15	17	8	42	29	9	314	304	93	4th, Patrick Div.	Lost Div. Semi-Final
1982-83	80	24	13	3	11	22	7	35	35	10	306	287	80	4th, Patrick Div.	Lost Div. Final
1981-82	80	19	15	6	20	12	8	39	27	14	316	306	92	2nd, Patrick Div.	Lost Div. Final
1980-81	80	17	13	10	13	23	4	30	36	14	312	317	74	4th, Patrick Div.	Lost Semi-Final
1979-80	80	22	10	8	16	22	2	38	32	10	308	284	86	3rd, Patrick Div.	Lost Quarter-Final
1978-79	80	19	13	8	21	16	3	40	29	11	316	292	91	3rd, Patrick Div.	Lost Final
1977-78	80	18	15	7	12	22	6	30	37	13	279	280	73	4th, Patrick Div.	Lost Prelim. Round
1976-77	80	17	18	5	12	19	9	29	37	14	272	310	72	4th, Patrick Div.	Out of Playoffs
1975-76	80	16	16	8	13	26	1	29	42	9	262	333	67	4th, Patrick Div.	Out of Playoffs
1974-75	80	21	11	8	16	18	6	37	29	14	319	276	88	2nd, Patrick Div.	Lost Prelim. Round
1973-74	78	26	7	6	14	17	8	40	24	14	300	251	94	3rd, East Div.	Lost Semi-Final
1972-73	78	26	8	5	21	15	3	47	23	8	297	208	102	3rd, East Div.	Lost Semi-Final
1971-72	78	26	6	7	22	11	6	48	17	13	317	192	109	2nd, East Div.	Lost Final
1970-71	78	30	7	2	19	16	4	49	18	11	259	177	109	2nd, East Div.	Lost Semi-Final
1969-70	76	22	8	8	16	14	8	38	22	16	246	189	92	4th, East Div.	Lost Quarter-Final
1968-69	76	27	7	4	14	19	5	41	26	9	231	196	91	3rd, East Div.	Lost Quarter-Final
1967-68	74	22	8	7	17	15	5	39	23	12	226	183	90	4th, East Div.	Lost Quarter-Final
1966-67	70	18	12	5	12	16	7	30	28	12	188	189	72	4th,	Lost Semi-Final
1965-66	70	12	16	7	6	25	4	18	41	11	195	261	47	6th,	Out of Playoffs
1964-65	70	18	19	8	12	19	4	20	38	12	179	246	52	5th,	Out of Playoffs
1963-64	70	14	13	8	8	25	2	22	38	10	186	242	54	5th,	Out of Playoffs
1962-63	70	12	17	6	10	19	6	22	36	12	211	233	56	5th,	Out of Playoffs
1961-62	70	16	11	8	10	21	4	26	32	12	195	207	64	4th,	Lost Semi-Final
1960-61	70	15	15	5	7	23	5	22	38	10	204	248	54	5th,	Out of Playoffs
1959-60	70	10	15	10	7	23	5	17	38	15	187	247	49	6th,	Out of Playoffs
1958-59	70	14	16	5	12	16	7	26	32	12	201	217	64	5th,	Out of Playoffs
1957-58	70	14	15	6	18	10	7	32	25	13	195	188	77	2nd,	Lost Semi-Final
1956-57	70	15	12	8	11	18	6	26	30	14	184	227	66	4th,	Lost Semi-Final
1955-56	70	20	7	8	12	21	2	32	28	10	204	203	74	3rd,	Lost Semi-Final
1954-55	70	10	12	13	7	23	5	17	35	18	150	210	52	5th,	Out of Playoffs
1953-54	70	18	12	5	11	19	5	29	31	10	161	182	68	5th,	Out of Playoffs
1952-53	70	11	14	10	6	23	6	17	37	16	152	211	50	6th,	Out of Playoffs
1951-52	70	16	13	6	7	21	7	23	34	13	192	219	59	5th,	Out of Playoffs
1950-51	70	14	11	10	6	18	11	20	29	21	169	201	61	5th,	Out of Playoffs
1949-50	70	19	12	4	9	19	7	28	31	11	170	189	67	4th,	Lost Final
1948-49	60	13	12	5	5	19	6	18	31	11	133	172	47	6th,	Out of Playoffs
1947-48	60	11	12	7	10	14	6	21	26	13	176	201	55	4th,	Lost Semi-Final
1946-47	60	11	14	5	11	18	1	22	32	6	167	186	50	5th,	Out of Playoffs
1945-46	50	8	12	5	5	16	4	13	28	9	144	191	35	6th,	Out of Playoffs
1944-45	50	7	11	7	4	18	3	11	29	10	154	247	32	6th,	Out of Playoffs
1943-44	50	4	17	4	2	22	1	6	39	5	162	310	17	6th,	Out of Playoffs
1942-43	50	7	13	5	4	18	3	11	31	8	161	253	30	6th,	Out of Playoffs
1941-42	48	15	8	1	14	9	1	29	17	2	177	143	60	1st,	Lost Semi-Final
1940-41	48	13	7	4	8	12	4	21	19	8	143	125	50	4th,	Lost Quarter-Final
1939-40	**48**	**17**	**4**	**3**	**10**	**7**	**7**	**27**	**11**	**10**	**136**	**77**	**64**	**2nd,**	**Won Stanley Cup**
1938-39	48	13	8	3	13	8	3	26	16	6	149	105	58	2nd,	Lost Semi-Final
1937-38	48	15	5	4	12	10	2	27	15	6	149	96	60	2nd,	Lost Quarter-Final
1936-37	48	9	7	8	10	13	1	19	20	9	117	106	47	3rd, Amn. Div.	Lost Final
1935-36	48	11	6	7	8	11	5	19	17	12	91	96	50	4th, Amn. Div.	Out of Playoffs
1934-35	48	11	6	5	11	12	1	22	20	6	137	139	50	4th, Amn. Div.	Lost Semi-Final
1933-34	48	11	8	5	10	12	2	21	19	8	120	113	50	3rd, Amn. Div.	Lost Semi-Final
1932-33	**48**	**12**	**7**	**5**	**11**	**10**	**3**	**23**	**17**	**8**	**135**	**107**	**54**	**3rd, Amn. Div.**	**Won Stanley Cup**
1931-32	48	13	11	4	10	10	4	23	17	8	134	112	54	1st,	Lost Final
1930-31	44	10	9	3	9	7	6	19	16	9	106	87	47	3rd,	Lost Semi-Final
1929-30	44	11	5	6	6	12	4	17	17	10	136	143	44	3rd, Amn. Div.	Lost Semi-Final
1928-29	44	12	6	4	9	7	6	21	13	10	72	65	52	2nd,	Lost Final
1927-28	**44**	**10**	**8**	**4**	**9**	**8**	**5**	**19**	**16**	**9**	**94**	**79**	**47**	**2nd, Amn. Div.**	**Won Stanley Cup**
1926-27	44	13	5	4	12	8	2	25	13	6	95	72	56	1st, Amn. Div.	Lost Quarter-Final

2000-01 Player Personnel

FORWARDS	HT	WT	S	Place of Birth	Date	1999-00 Club
ARMSTRONG, Derek	5-11	188	R	Ottawa, Ont.	4/23/73	NY Rangers-Hartford
BRENDL, Pavel	6-1	204	R	Opocno, Czech.	3/23/81	Calgary Hitmen
CHERNESKI, Stefan	6-0	195	L	Winnipeg, Man.	9/19/78	Hartford
DAWE, Jason	5-10	189	L	North York, Ont.	5/29/73	Milwaukee-NYR-Hartford
DIETRICH, Brandon	6-0	190	R	Waterloo, Ont.	3/22/78	St. Lawrence
DVORAK, Radek	6-1	194	R	Tabor, Czech.	3/9/77	Florida-NY Rangers
FLEURY, Theoren	5-6	180	R	Oxbow, Sask.	6/29/68	NY Rangers
FORTIER, Francois	5-11	194	L	Beauport, Que.	6/13/79	Hartford
GERNANDER, Ken	5-10	175	L	Coleraine, MN	6/30/69	Hartford
GONEAU, Daniel	6-0	195	L	Montreal, Que.	1/16/76	NY Rangers-Hartford
GRAVES, Adam	6-0	205	L	Toronto, Ont.	4/12/68	NY Rangers
GUSAKOV, Yevgeny	6-6	225	L	Togliatti, USSR	3/6/81	Baie-Comeau
HALL, Todd	6-1	200	L	Hamden, CT	1/22/73	Hartford
HARDER, Mike	6-0	185	R	Winnipeg, Man.	2/8/73	Hartford
HELFENSTEIN, Sven	5-10	176	R	Winterthur, Switz.	7/30/82	EHC Kloten
HLAVAC, Jan	6-0	185	L	Prague, Czech.	9/20/76	NY Rangers-Hartford
KANE, Boyd	6-2	218	L	Swift Current, Sask.	4/18/78	Charlotte-Hartford-B.C. Icemen
LACROIX, Eric	6-1	210	L	Montreal, Que.	7/15/71	NY Rangers
LUNDMARK, Jamie	6-0	174	R	Edmonton, Alta.	1/16/81	Moose Jaw
MacLEAN, John	6-0	200	R	Oshawa, Ont.	11/20/64	NY Rangers
MALHOTRA, Manny	6-2	210	L	Mississauga, Ont.	5/18/80	NYR-Guelph Storm-Hart
McCARTHY, Sandy	6-3	225	R	Toronto, Ont.	6/15/72	Philadelphia-Carolina
MESSIER, Mark	6-1	210	L	Edmonton, Alta.	1/18/61	Vancouver
NEDVED, Petr	6-3	195	L	Liberec, Czech.	12/9/71	NY Rangers
SMYTH, Brad	6-0	195	R	Ottawa, Ont.	3/13/73	Hartford
TAYLOR, Tim	6-1	185	L	Stratford, Ont.	2/6/69	NY Rangers
ULMER, Jeff	5-11	190	R	Wilcox, Sask.	4/27/77	Team Canada-Houston Aeros
WITEHALL, Johan	6-1	198	L	Goteborg, Sweden	1/7/72	NY Rangers-Hartford
YORK, Mike	5-10	185	R	Waterford, MI	1/3/78	NY Rangers
DEFENSEMEN						
BANNISTER, Drew	6-2	200	R	Belleville, Ont.	9/4/74	Hartford
BROWN, Jeff	6-2	218	R	Mississauga, Ont.	4/24/78	Hartford-Charlotte
CARPENTIER, Benjamin	6-2	195	L	Grand-Mere, Que.	6/13/78	Hartford
DOIG, Jason	6-3	228	R	Montreal, Que.	1/29/77	NY Rangers-Hartford
DUBEN, Premysl	6-3	220	L	Jihlava, Czech.	10/5/81	Dukla Jihlava-Jr.-Dukla Jihlava-2
HENRY, Burke	6-3	190	L	Ste. Rose, Man.	1/21/79	Hartford
JARVIS, Wes	6-5	215	L	Toronto, Ont.	4/16/79	Canada
JOHNSSON, Kim	6-1	178	L	Malmo, Sweden	3/16/76	NY Rangers
KLOUCEK, Tomas	6-3	203	L	Prague, Czech.	3/7/80	Hartford
LEETCH, Brian	6-1	190	L	Corpus Christi, TX	3/3/68	NY Rangers
LEFEBVRE, Sylvain	6-2	205	L	Richmond, Que.	10/14/67	NY Rangers
MALAKHOV, Vladimir	6-4	230	L	Ekaterinburg, USSR	8/30/68	Montreal-New Jersey
PILON, Richard	6-2	220	L	Saskatoon, Sask.	4/30/68	NY Islanders-NY Rangers
PURINTON, Dale	6-3	214	L	Fort Wayne, IN	10/11/76	NY Rangers-Hartford
QUINTAL, Stephane	6-3	228	R	Boucherville, Que.	10/22/68	NY Rangers
RICHTER, Martin	6-1	196	R	Prostejov, Czech.	12/6/77	SaiPa
VASILIEV, Alexei	6-1	192	L	Yaroslavl, USSR	9/1/77	NY Rangers-Hartford
VIRTUE, Terry	6-0	207	R	Scarborough, Ont.	8/12/70	NY Rangers-Hartford
WILKIE, David	6-3	215	R	Ellensburgh, WA	5/30/74	Houston-Hartford-Chicago Wolves

GOALTENDERS	HT	WT	C	Place of Birth	Date	1999-00 Club
HOLMQVIST, Johan	6-3	190	L	Tolfta, Sweden	5/24/78	Brynas IF
LABARBERA, Jason	6-2	205	L	Prince George, B.C.	1/18/80	Portland (WHL)-Spokane
LABBE, Jean-Francois	5-10	172	L	Sherbrooke, Que.	6/15/72	NY Rangers-Hartford
McLEAN, Kirk	6-0	180	L	Willowdale, Ont.	6/26/66	NY Rangers
RICHTER, Mike	5-11	185	L	Abington, PA	9/22/66	NY Rangers
WANDLER, Bryce	6-0	180	L	Lacombe, Alta.	2/25/79	Swift Current
YEREMEYEV, Vitali	5-10	167	L	Ust-Kamenogorsk, USSR	9/23/75	Dynamo Moscow

Captains' History

Bill Cook, 1926-27 to 1936-37; Art Coulter, 1937-38 to 1941-42; Ott Heller, 1942-43 to 1944-45; Neil Colville 1945-46 to 1948-49; Buddy O'Connor, 1949-50; Frank Eddolls, 1950-51; Frank Eddolls and Allan Stanley, 1951-52; Allan Stanley, 1952-53; Allan Stanley and Don Raleigh, 1953-54; Don Raleigh, 1954-55; Harry Howell, 1955-56, 1956-57; Red Sullivan, 1957-58 to 1960-61; Andy Bathgate, 1961-62, 1962-63; Andy Bathgate and Camille Henry, 1963-64; Camille Henry and Bob Nevin, 1964-65; Bob Nevin 1965-66 to 1970-71; Vic Hadfield, 1971-72 to 1973-74; Brad Park, 1974-75; Brad Park and Phil Esposito, 1975-76; Phil Esposito, 1976-77, 1977-78; Dave Maloney, 1978-79, 1979-80; Dave Maloney, Walt Tkaczuk and Barry Beck, 1980-81; Barry Beck, 1981-82 to 1985-86; Ron Greschner, 1986-87; Ron Greschner and Kelly Kisio, 1987-88; Kelly Kisio, 1988-89 to 1990-91; Mark Messier, 1991-92 to 1996-97; Brian Leetch, 1997-98 to 1999-2000; Mark Messier, 2000-01.

General Managers' History

Lester Patrick, 1927-28 to 1945-46; Frank Boucher, 1946-47 to 1954-55; Muzz Patrick, 1955-56 to 1963-64; Emile Francis, 1964-65 to 1974-75; Emile Francis and John Ferguson, 1975-76; John Ferguson, 1976-77, 1977-78; John Ferguson and Fred Shero, 1978-79; Fred Shero, 1979-80; Fred Shero and Craig Patrick, 1980-81; Craig Patrick, 1981-82 to 1985-86; Phil Esposito, 1986-87 to 1988-89; Neil Smith, 1989-90 to 1999-2000; Glen Sather, 2000-01.

1999-2000 Scoring

* – rookie

Regular Season

Pos	#	Player	Team	GP	G	A	Pts	+/–	PIM	PP	SH	GW	GT	S	%
C	93	Petr Nedved	NYR	76	24	44	68	2	40	6	2	4	0	201	11.9
R	14	Theoren Fleury	NYR	80	15	49	64	–4	68	1	0	1	0	246	6.1
C	18 *	Michael York	NYR	82	26	24	50	–17	18	8	0	4	2	177	14.7
R	20	Radek Dvorak	FLA	35	7	10	17	5	6	0	0	1	0	67	10.4
			NYR	46	11	22	33	0	10	2	1	0	0	90	12.2
			TOTAL	81	18	32	50	5	16	2	1	1	0	157	11.5
L	27 *	Jan Hlavac	NYR	67	19	23	42	3	16	6	0	2	0	134	14.2
R	15	John MacLean	NYR	77	18	24	42	–2	52	6	2	3	0	158	11.4
L	9	Adam Graves	NYR	77	23	17	40	–15	14	11	0	4	0	194	11.9
L	13	Valeri Kamensky	NYR	58	13	19	32	–13	24	3	0	1	0	88	14.8
D	21	Mathieu Schneider	NYR	80	10	20	30	–6	78	3	0	1	1	228	4.4
R	12	Alexandre Daigle	NYR	58	8	18	26	–5	23	1	0	1	1	52	15.4
D	2	Brian Leetch	NYR	50	7	19	26	–16	20	3	0	2	1	124	5.6
R	16	Rob Dimaio	BOS	50	5	16	21	–1	42	0	0	0	0	93	5.4
			NYR	12	1	3	4	–8	8	0	0	0	0	18	5.6
			TOTAL	62	6	19	25	–9	50	0	0	0	0	111	5.4
D	4	Kevin Hatcher	NYR	74	4	19	23	–10	38	2	0	0	1	112	3.6
D	3 *	Kim Johnsson	NYR	76	6	15	21	–13	46	1	0	1	0	101	5.9
C	26	Tim Taylor	NYR	76	9	11	20	–4	72	0	0	2	1	79	11.4
D	5	Stephane Quintal	NYR	75	2	14	16	–10	77	0	0	1	0	102	2.0
L	28	Eric Lacroix	NYR	70	4	8	12	–12	24	0	0	1	0	46	8.7
D	24	Sylvain Lefebvre	NYR	82	2	10	12	–13	43	0	0	0	1	67	3.0
L	17	Kevin Stevens	NYR	38	3	5	8	–7	43	1	0	0	0	44	6.8
D	47	Richard Pilon	NYI	9	0	2	2	–2	34	0	0	0	0	0	0.0
			NYR	45	0	4	4	0	36	0	0	0	0	16	0.0
			TOTAL	54	0	6	6	–2	70	0	0	0	0	16	0.0
L	29	Johan Witehall	NYR	9	1	1	2	0	2	0	0	0	0	6	16.7
R	22	Jason Dawe	NYR	3	0	1	1	0	2	0	0	0	0	8	0.0
D	25	Jason Doig	NYR	7	0	1	1	–2	22	0	0	0	0	3	0.0
C	32	P.J. Stock	NYR	11	0	1	1	1	11	0	0	0	0	2	0.0
L	19	Darren Langdon	NYR	21	0	1	1	–2	26	0	0	0	0	13	0.0
G	30	Kirk McLean	NYR	22	0	1	1	0	2	0	0	0	0	0	0.0
C	37	Derek Armstrong	NYR	1	0	0	0	0	0	0	0	0	0	1	0.0
G	31	Jean Labbe	NYR	1	0	0	0	0	0	0	0	0	0	0	0.0
D	32	Terry Virtue	NYR	1	0	0	0	–2	0	0	0	0	0	2	0.0
L	39	Daniel Goneau	NYR	1	0	0	0	–1	0	0	0	0	0	3	0.0
D	36 *	Alexei Vasiljev	NYR	1	0	0	0	–1	2	0	0	0	0	0	0.0
D	45 *	Dale Purinton	NYR	1	0	0	0	–1	7	0	0	0	0	1	0.0
G	32	Milan Hnilicka	NYR	2	0	0	0	0	0	0	0	0	0	0	0.0
R	29	Christopher Kenady	NYR	2	0	0	0	–1	0	0	0	0	0	1	0.0
C	6	Manny Malhotra	NYR	27	0	0	0	–6	4	0	0	0	0	18	0.0
G	35	Mike Richter	NYR	61	0	0	0	0	4	0	0	0	0	0	0.0

Goaltending

No.	Goaltender	GPI	Mins	Avg	W	L	T	EN	SO	GA	SA	S%
35	Mike Richter	61	3622	2.87	22	31	8	4	0	173	1815	.905
30	Kirk McLean	22	1206	2.89	7	8	4	2	0	58	558	.896
31	Jean Labbe	1	60	3.00	0	1	0	0	0	3	22	.864
32	Milan Hnilicka	2	86	3.49	0	1	0	1	0	5	44	.886
	Totals	**82**	**4996**	**2.95**	**29**	**41**	**12**	**7**	**0**	**246**	**2446**	**.899**

President and General Manager

SATHER, GLEN CAMERON
President and General Manager, New York Rangers
Born in High River, Alta., Sept. 2, 1943.

Glen Sather, who spent parts of four seasons with the New York Rangers as a player from 1970 to 1974, became the franchise's 12th President and 10th General Manager on June 1, 2000. He joined the club following a 24-year career with the Edmonton Oilers, where he was the architect of five Stanley Cup Championships between 1984 and 1990. One of the most respected executives in the National Hockey League, Sather was honored for his tremendous achievements by becoming the first member of the Oilers organization to be selected to the Hockey Hall of Fame.

Named coach and vice president of hockey operation for the Oilers when the franchise joined the NHL in June of 1979, Sather became coach, general manager and club president in May of 1980. He coached through the 1988-89 season and also returned for 60 games behind the bench in 1993-94. His .616 winning percentage in 842 regular-season games ranks seventh on the NHL's all-time coaching list. His playoff winning percentage of .706 ranks first.

Sather-coached teams won the Stanley Cup four times in the 1980s. As general manager, Sather was instrumental in the Oilers' fifth Cup triumph in 1990.

He played for six different teams during a 10-year NHL career. He scored 80 goals in 658 games.

NHL Coaching Record

		Regular Season					Playoffs			
Season	Team	Games	W	L	T	%	Games	W	L	%
1979-80	Edmonton	80	28	39	13	.431	3	0	3	.000
1980-81	Edmonton	62	25	26	11	.492	9	5	4	.555
1981-82	Edmonton	80	48	17	15	.694	5	2	3	.400
1982-83	Edmonton	80	47	21	12	.663	16	11	5	.687
1983-84	Edmonton	80	57	18	5	.744	19	15	4	.789*
1984-85	Edmonton	80	49	20	11	.681	18	15	3	.833*
1985-86	Edmonton	80	56	17	7	.744	10	6	4	.600
1986-87	Edmonton	80	50	24	6	.663	21	16	5	.762*
1987-88	Edmonton	80	44	25	11	.619	18	16	2	.889*
1988-89	Edmonton	80	38	34	8	.538	7	3	4	.429
1993-94	Edmonton	60	22	27	11	.458	....	....	....	....
	NHL Totals	**842**	**464**	**268**	**110**	**.616**	**126**	**89**	**37**	**.706**

* Stanley Cup win.

Club Records

Team

(Figures in brackets for season records are games played; records for fewest points, wins, ties, losses, goals, goals against are for 70 or more games)

Most Points **112** 1993-94 (84)
Most Wins **52** 1993-94 (84)
Most Ties **21** 1950-51 (70)
Most Losses **44** 1984-85 (80)
Most Goals **371** 1991-92 (80)
Most Goals Against **345** 1984-85 (80)
Fewest Points **47** 1965-66 (70)
Fewest Wins **17** 1952-53 (70), 1954-55 (70), 1959-60 (70)
Fewest Ties **5** 1991-92 (80)
Fewest Losses **17** 1971-72 (78)
Fewest Goals **150** 1954-55 (70)
Fewest Goals Against **177** 1970-71 (78)
Longest Winning Streak
Overall .... **10** Dec. 19/39-Jan. 13/40, Jan. 19-Feb. 10/73
Home .... **14** Dec. 19/39-Feb. 25/40
Away .... **7** Jan. 12-Feb. 12/35, Oct. 28-Nov. 29/78
Longest Undefeated Streak
Overall .... **19** Nov. 23/39-Jan. 13/40 (14 wins, 5 ties)
Home .... **26** Mar. 29/70-Jan. 31/71 (19 wins, 7 ties)
Away .... **11** Nov. 5/39-Jan. 13/40 (6 wins, 5 ties)
Longest Losing Streak
Overall .... **11** Oct. 30-Nov. 27/43
Home .... **7** Oct. 20-Nov. 14/76, Mar. 24-Apr. 14/93
Away .... **10** Oct. 30-Dec. 23/43
Longest Winless Streak
Overall .... **21** Jan. 23-Mar. 19/44 (17 losses, 4 ties)
Home .... **10** Jan. 30-Mar. 19/44 (7 losses, 3 ties)
Away .... **16** Oct. 9-Dec. 20/52 (12 losses, 4 ties)
Most Shutouts, Season **13** 1928-29 (44)
Most PIM, Season **2,018** 1989-90 (80)
Most Goals, Game .... **12** Nov. 21/71 (Cal. 1 at NYR 12)

Individual

Most Seasons .... **17** Harry Howell
Most Games .... **1,160** Harry Howell
Most Goals, Career .... **406** Rod Gilbert
Most Assists, Career .... **615** Rod Gilbert
Most Points, Career .... **1,021** Rod Gilbert (406G, 615A)
Most PIM, Career .... **1,226** Ron Greschner
Most Shutouts, Career ...... **49** Ed Giacomin
Longest Consecutive Games Streak .... **560** Andy Hebenton (Oct. 7/55-Mar. 24/63)
Most Goals, Season .... **52** Adam Graves (1993-94)
Most Assists, Season .... **80** Brian Leetch (1991-92)
Most Points, Season .... **109** Jean Ratelle (1971-72; 46G, 63A)
Most PIM, Season .... **305** Troy Mallette (1989-90)
Most Points, Defenseman, Season .... **102** Brian Leetch (1991-92; 22G, 80A)
Most Points, Center, Season .... **109** Jean Ratelle (1971-72; 46G, 63A)
Most Points, Right Wing, Season .... **97** Rod Gilbert (1971-72; 43G, 54A), (1974-75; 36G, 61A)
Most Points, Left Wing, Season .... **106** Vic Hadfield (1971-72; 50G, 56A)
Most Points, Rookie, Season .... **76** Mark Pavelich (1981-82; 33G, 43A)
Most Shutouts, Season ...... **13** John Ross Roach (1928-29)
Most Goals, Game .... **5** Don Murdoch (Oct. 12/76), Mark Pavelich (Feb. 23/83)
Most Assists, Game .... **5** Walt Tkaczuk (Feb. 12/72), Rod Gilbert (Mar. 2/75, Mar. 30/75, Oct. 8/76), Don Maloney (Jan. 3/87), Brian Leetch (Apr. 18/95), Wayne Gretzky (Feb. 15/99)
Most Points, Game .... **7** Steve Vickers (Feb. 18/76; 3G, 4A)

Retired Numbers

1	Ed Giacomin	1965-1976
7	Rod Gilbert	1960-1978

All-time Record vs. Other Clubs

Regular Season

	At Home							On Road							Total						
	GP	W	L	T	GF	GA	PTS	GP	W	L	T	GF	GA	PTS	GP	W	L	T	GF	GA	PTS
Anaheim	5	2	2	1	14	14	5	6	1	5	0	15	24	2	11	3	7	1	29	38	7
Atlanta	2	2	0	0	10	4	4	2	2	0	0	12	6	4	4	4	0	0	22	10	8
Boston	294	127	112	55	895	831	309	290	93	155	42	813	1049	228	584	220	267	97	1708	1880	537
Buffalo	58	24	19	15	189	155	63	60	17	35	8	189	253	42	118	41	54	23	378	408	105
Calgary	49	23	21	5	174	174	51	47	10	27	10	141	211	30	96	33	48	15	315	385	81
Carolina	37	23	11	3	147	100	49	35	13	19	3	115	123	29	72	36	30	6	262	223	78
Chicago	283	116	112	55	834	801	287	283	114	127	42	785	861	270	566	230	239	97	1619	1662	557
Colorado	30	18	8	4	121	83	40	32	13	16	3	124	132	29	62	31	24	7	245	215	69
Dallas	59	34	14	11	205	161	79	58	30	18	10	215	174	71	117	64	32	21	420	335	150
Detroit	281	133	90	58	862	726	324	283	76	162	45	696	998	197	564	209	252	103	1558	1724	521
Edmonton	27	8	13	6	99	103	22	27	13	11	3	93	97	29	54	21	24	9	192	200	51
Florida	16	6	6	4	45	42	16	17	8	8	1	46	46	17	33	14	14	5	91	88	33
Los Angeles	55	34	15	6	224	156	74	57	25	23	9	203	188	59	112	59	38	15	427	344	133
Montreal	282	114	114	54	819	825	282	282	56	188	38	644	1108	150	564	170	302	92	1463	1933	432
Nashville	2	2	0	0	10	2	4	1	1	0	0	7	4	2	3	3	0	0	17	6	6
New Jersey	74	39	20	15	298	223	93	75	32	38	5	258	259	69	149	71	58	20	556	482	162
NY Islanders	85	50	25	10	329	256	110	86	26	53	7	263	345	59	171	76	78	17	592	601	169
Ottawa	15	8	7	0	54	44	16	15	9	4	2	44	39	20	30	17	11	2	98	83	36
Philadelphia	100	43	34	23	322	289	109	98	37	47	14	282	326	88	198	80	81	37	604	615	197
Phoenix	27	17	8	2	125	98	36	28	13	11	4	97	97	30	55	30	19	6	222	195	66
Pittsburgh	90	47	35	8	362	304	102	90	40	36	14	338	324	94	180	87	71	22	700	628	196
St. Louis	58	44	8	6	240	134	94	60	28	23	9	193	174	65	118	72	31	15	433	308	159
San Jose	8	6	1	1	37	23	13	9	7	1	1	35	19	15	17	13	2	2	72	42	28
Tampa Bay	19	10	7	2	69	67	22	17	7	7	3	59	57	17	36	17	14	5	128	124	39
Toronto	275	117	102	56	848	804	290	274	82	153	39	721	942	204	549	199	255	95	1569	1746	494
Vancouver	52	37	10	5	232	133	79	49	33	13	3	200	156	69	101	70	23	8	432	289	148
Washington	74	34	32	8	280	260	77	76	30	37	9	251	282	69	150	64	69	17	531	542	146
Defunct Clubs	139	87	30	22	460	290	196	139	82	34	23	441	291	187	278	169	64	45	901	581	383
Totals	**2496**	**1205**	**856**	**435**	**8304**	**7102**	**2846**	**2496**	**898**	**1251**	**347**	**7280**	**8585**	**2145**	**4992**	**2103**	**2107**	**782**	**15584**	**15687**	**4991**

Playoffs

	Series	W	L	GP	W	L	T	GF	GA	Last Mtg.	Round	Result
Boston	9	3	6	42	18	22	2	104	114	1973	QF	W 4-1
Buffalo	1	0	1	3	1	2	0	6	11	1978	PR	L 1-2
Calgary	1	1	0	4	3	1	0	14	8	1980	PR	W 3-1
Chicago	5	1	4	24	10	14	0	54	66	1973	SF	L 1-4
Colorado	1	1	0	6	4	2	0	25	19	1995	CQF	W 4-2
Detroit	5	1	4	23	10	13	0	49	57	1950	F	L 3-4
Florida	1	1	0	5	4	1	0	13	10	1997	CQF	W 4-1
Los Angeles	2	2	0	6	5	1	0	32	14	1981	PR	W 3-1
Montreal	14	7	7	61	25	34	2	158	188	1996	CQF	W 4-2
New Jersey	3	3	0	19	12	7	0	56	46	1997	CSF	W 4-1
NY Islanders	8	3	5	39	19	20	0	132	129	1994	CQF	W 4-0
Philadelphia	10	4	6	47	20	27	0	153	158	1997	CF	L 1-4
Pittsburgh	3	0	3	15	3	12	0	45	64	1996	CSF	L 1-4
St. Louis	1	1	0	6	4	2	0	29	22	1981	QF	W 4-2
Toronto	8	5	3	35	19	16	0	86	86	1971	QF	W 4-2
Vancouver	1	1	0	7	4	3	0	21	19	1994	F	W 4-3
Washington	4	2	2	22	11	11	0	71	75	1994	CSF	W 4-1
Defunct	9	6	3	22	11	7	4	43	29			
Totals	**86**	**42**	**44**	**386**	**183**	**195**	**8**	**1091**	**1115**			

Calgary totals include Atlanta Flames, 1972-73 to 1979-80.
Colorado totals include Quebec, 1979-80 to 1994-95.
New Jersey totals include Kansas City, 1974-75 to 1975-76, and Colorado Rockies, 1976-77 to 1981-82.
Phoenix totals include Winnipeg, 1979-80 to 1995-96.
Carolina totals include Hartford, 1979-80 to 1996-97.
Dallas totals include Minnesota North Stars, 1967-68 to 1992-93.

Playoff Results 2000-1996

Year	Round	Opponent	Result	GF	GA
1997	CF	Philadelphia	L 1-4	13	20
	CSF	New Jersey	W 4-1	10	5
	CQF	Florida	W 4-1	13	10
1996	CSF	Pittsburgh	L 1-4	15	21
	CQF	Montreal	W 4-2	19	17

Abbreviations: Round: F – Final; **CF** – conference final; **CSF** – conference semi-final; **CQF** – conference quarter-final; **SF** – semi-final; **QF** – quarter-final; **PR** – preliminary round.

1999-2000 Results

Oct.	1	at	Edmonton	1-1		15	at	NY Islanders	5-2
	2	at	Vancouver	1-2		16		Atlanta	6-3
	5		Ottawa	1-2		18		Carolina	3-2
	8		Carolina	3-1		20	at	Carolina	4-1
	10		Phoenix	4-2		22	at	St. Louis	4-1
	11	at	NY Islanders	4-2		24	at	Atlanta	6-3
	14		Pittsburgh	2-5		25	at	Pittsburgh	4-3
	17		Atlanta	4-1		27		Toronto	3-4
	19		San Jose	1-2		29	at	Ottawa	2-3
	20	at	Philadelphia	0-5		31		Nashville	5-1
	22		Philadelphia	0-2	**Feb.**	2		New Jersey	1-3
	24		Vancouver	0-3		3	at	Atlanta	6-3
	30	at	Montreal	2-2		8		New Jersey	2-2
Nov.	3		NY Islanders	3-3		9	at	New Jersey	1-4
	5	at	Colorado	1-4		11		Boston	5-2
	7	at	Chicago	3-1		13		NY Islanders	2-4
	10		Ottawa	3-4		15	at	Tampa Bay	2-2
	11	at	Washington	5-4*		16	at	Florida	0-3
	13		Boston	2-5		18		Colorado	2-4
	18	at	Boston	3-5		20		Philadelphia	2-3
	20	at	Toronto	3-4*		22		Pittsburgh	4-3
	24	at	Tampa Bay	6-3		25	at	Buffalo	6-3
	26	at	Florida	2-6		26	at	Ottawa	2-4
Dec.	1	at	New Jersey	2-3	**Mar.**	1		Buffalo	3-3
	3		Montreal	3-2		3		Florida	4-2
	4	at	Buffalo	1-1		6	at	San Jose	1-2
	6		Calgary	3-2*		8	at	Anaheim	4-3*
	8		Edmonton	2-1*		9	at	Los Angeles	1-3
	15		Los Angeles	8-3		11	at	Pittsburgh	1-3
	17		Washington	2-3*		13		Dallas	3-4
	19		Tampa Bay	5-4*		15		Tampa Bay	4-4
	21		Buffalo	1-3		18	at	Philadelphia	3-2
	23	at	NY Islanders	2-4		19	at	Pittsburgh	4-5
	26		New Jersey	3-3		21		Florida	3-4
	28	at	Phoenix	2-2		23		Washington	1-4
	29	at	Dallas	3-4*		26	at	Detroit	2-8
Jan.	2	at	Montreal	2-2		27		Detroit	0-6
	3		St. Louis	2-5	**Apr.**	1	at	Boston	2-2
	5		Toronto	3-2*		3	at	Washington	1-4
	8	at	Toronto	5-3		5		Montreal	0-3
	9	at	Carolina	0-1		9		Philadelphia	1-4

* – Overtime

Entry Draft
Selections 2000-1986

2000	**1996**	**1992**	**1988**
Pick	Pick	Pick	Pick
64 Filip Novak	22 Jeff Brown	24 Peter Ferraro	22 Troy Mallette
95 Dominic Moore	48 Daniel Goneau	48 Mattias Norstrom	26 Murray Duval
112 Premysl Duben	76 Dmitri Subbotin	72 Eric Cairns	68 Tony Amonte
140 Nathan Martz	131 Colin Pepperall	85 Chris Ferraro	99 Martin Bergeron
143 Brandon Snee	158 Ola Sandberg	120 Dmitri Starostenko	110 Dennis Vial
175 Sven Helfenstein	185 Jeff Dessner	144 David Dal Grande	131 Mike Rosati
205 Henrik Lundqvist	211 Ryan McKie	168 Matt Oates	152 Eric Couvrette
238 Dan Eberly	237 Ronnie Sundin	192 Mickey Elick	194 Paul Cain
269 Martin Richter		216 Daniel Brierley	202 Eric Fenton
	1995	240 Vladimir Vorobiev	215 Peter Fiorentino
1999	Pick		236 Keith Slifstein
Pick	39 Christian Dube	**1991**	
4 Pavel Brendl	65 Mike Martin	Pick	**1987**
9 Jamie Lundmark	91 Marc Savard	15 Alexei Kovalev	Pick
59 David Inman	110 Alexei Vasiliev	37 Darcy Werenka	10 Jay More
79 Johan Asplund	117 Dale Purinton	96 Corey Machanic	31 Daniel Lacroix
90 Patrick Aufiero	143 Peter Slamiar	125 Fredrik Jax	46 Simon Gagne
137 Garrett Bembridge	169 Jeff Heil	128 Barry Young	69 Mike Sullivan
177 Jay Dardis	195 Ilja Gorokhov	147 John Rushin	94 Eric O'Borsky
197 Arto Laatikainen	221 Bob Maudie	169 Corey Hirsch	115 Ludek Cajka
226 Yevgeny Gusakov		191 Vyachesl Uvayev	136 Clint Thomas
251 Petter Henning	**1994**	213 Jamie Ram	157 Charles Wiegand
254 Alexei Bulatov	Pick	235 Vitali Chinakhov	178 Eric Burrill
	26 Dan Cloutier	257 Brian Wiseman	199 David Porter
1998	52 Rudolf Vercik		205 Brett Barnett
Pick	78 Adam Smith	**1990**	220 Lance Marciano
7 Manny Malhotra	100 Alexander Korobolin	Pick	
40 Randy Copley	104 Sylvain Blouin	13 Michael Stewart	**1986**
66 Jason Labarbera	130 Martin Ethier	34 Doug Weight	Pick
114 Boyd Kane	135 Yuri Litvinov	55 John Vary	9 Brian Leetch
122 Patrick Leahy	156 David Brosseau	69 Jeff Nielsen	51 Bret Walter
131 Tomas Kloucek	182 Alexei Lazarenko	76 Rick Willis	53 Shawn Clouston
180 Stefan Lundqvist	208 Craig Anderson	85 Sergei Zubov	72 Mark Janssens
207 Johan Witehall	209 Vitali Yeremeyev	99 Lubos Rob	93 Jeff Bloemberg
235 Jan Mertzig	234 Eric Boulton	118 Jason Weinrich	114 Darren Turcotte
	260 Radoslav Kropac	139 Brian Lonsinger	135 Robb Graham
1997	267 Jamie Butt	160 Todd Hedlund	156 Barry Chyzowski
Pick	286 Kim Johnsson	181 Andrew Silverman	177 Pat Scanlon
19 Stefan Cherneski		202 Jon Hillebrandt	198 Joe Ranger
46 Wes Jarvis	**1993**	223 Brett Lievers	219 Russell Parent
73 Burke Henry	Pick	244 Sergei Nemchinov	240 Soren True
93 Tomi Kallarsson	8 Niklas Sundstrom		
126 Jason McLean	34 Lee Sorochan	**1989**	
134 Johan Lindbom	61 Maxim Galanov	Pick	
136 Mike York	86 Sergei Olimpiyev	20 Steven Rice	
154 Shawn Degagne	112 Gary Roach	40 Jason Prosofsky	
175 Johan Holmqvist	138 Dave Trofimenkoff	45 Rob Zamuner	
182 Mike Mottau	162 Sergei Kondrashkin	49 Louie DeBrusk	
210 Andrew Proskurnicki	164 Todd Marchant	67 Jim Cummins	
236 Richard Miller	190 Ed Campbell	88 Aaron Miller	
	216 Ken Shepard	118 Joby Messier	
	242 Andrei Kudinov	139 Greg Leahy	
	261 Pavel Komarov	160 Greg Spenrath	
	268 Maxim Smelnitsky	181 Mark Bavis	
		202 Roman Oksiuta	
		223 Steve Locke	
		244 Ken MacDermid	

Coach

LOW, RON
Coach, New York Rangers. Born in Birtie, Man., June 21, 1950.

Ron Low was hired as head coach of the New York Rangers on July 12, 2000, after spending the 1999-2000 season with the Houston Aeros of the International Hockey League. He guided the club to the IHL Western Conference Finals.

Prior to his stint in Houston, Low served as head coach of the Edmonton Oilers, where he compiled a 139-162-40 mark in four-plus years behind the bench. As one of the NHL's youngest coaches, Low earned a reputation for successfully developing talented young prospects into solid NHL performers.

Low's history with Glen Sather and the Edmonton franchise dates back to the 1979-80 season, when the Oilers obtained his playing rights from the Quebec Nordiques. An NHL veteran of 11 years, Low's career in the crease saw him tend goal for Toronto, Washington, Detroit, Quebec, Edmonton and New Jersey from 1972 to 1985.

In 1985-86, Low was named player/assistant coach for the Nova Scotia Oilers, Edmonton's American Hockey League affiliate. Following two years as an assistant coach, he was named Nova Scotia's head coach in 1987-88 and kept that position when the team became the Cape Breton Oilers in 1988-89. He joined the NHL coaching ranks in August 1989 as an assistant coach for the Oilers, and was a member of the 1990 Stanley Cup championship team.

Ron and his wife, Linda, have two daughters, Alexandra Juliana and Taylor.

Coaching Record

Season	Team	Regular Season					Playoffs			
		Games	W	L	T	%	Games	W	L	%
1987-88	Nova Scotia (AHL)	80	35	36	9	.506	5	1	4	.200
1988-89	Cape Breton (AHL)	80	27	47	6	.375	....	....	....	....
1994-95	Edmonton (NHL)	13	5	7	1	.423	....	....	....	....
1995-96	Edmonton (NHL)	82	30	44	8	.415	....	....	....	....
1996-97	Edmonton (NHL)	82	36	37	9	.494	12	5	7	.417
1997-98	Edmonton (NHL)	82	35	37	10	.488	12	5	7	.417
1998-99	Edmonton (NHL)	82	33	37	12	.476	4	0	4	.000
1999-2000	Houston (IHL)	82	44	29	9	.591	11	6	5	.545
	NHL Totals	341	139	162	40	.466	28	10	18	.357

Club Directory

Madison Square Garden

New York Rangers
14th Floor
2 Pennsylvania Plaza
New York, New York 10121
Phone **212/465-6000**
PR FAX 212/465-6494
www.newyorkrangers.com
Capacity: 18,200

Team Executive Management
President and Chief Executive Officer/Governor,
   Madison Square Garden . . . . David W. Checketts
President and General Manager/Alternate Governor . . Glen Sather
Executive Vice President and General Counsel/
   Alternate Governor. . . . . Kenneth W. Munoz
Senior Vice President, MSG Sports. . . . . Francis P. Murphy
Vice President, Controller . . . . John Cudmore
Vice President, Legal and Business Affairs . . . . Marc Schoenfeld

Madsion Square Garden Executive Management
President, MSG Facilities . . . . Robert Russo
Executive Vice President, Finance. . . . . Robert Pollichino
Senior Vice President, Sports & Facility Event Sales . . . Joel Fisher
Senior Vice President, Advertising Sales. . . . . Joe Gangone
Senior Vice President, Human Resources . . . . Aimee Kaye
Senior Vice President, Communications . . . . Barry Watkins

Hockey Club Personnel
Vice President, Player Development and
   Assistant General Manager. . . . . Don Maloney
Director, Player Personnel . . . . Tom Renney
Head Coach. . . . . Ron Low
Assistant Coaches . . . . Ted Green and Walt Kyle
Goaltending Analyst . . . . Sam St. Laurent
Amateur Scouting Staff. . . . . Darwin Bennett, Ray Clearwater, Andre
   Beaulieu, Jan Gajdosik, Ernie Gare, Martin
   Madden Jr., Christer Rockstom, Bob Crocker,
   Dick Todd
Professional Scouting Staff . . . . Dave Brown, Harry Howell and Kevin McDonald
Scouting Manager . . . . Bill Short
Video Analyst . . . . Jerry Dineen

Operations Department
Vice President, Operations. . . . . Mark Piazza
Director, Business Operations . . . . Barbara Dand
Director, Team Operations . . . . Darren Blake
Executive Assistant to the President and
   General Manager . . . . Sara Adamson
Operations Assistant . . . . Victor Saljanin
Operations Assistant . . . . Chris Smith

Public Relations Department
Vice President, Public Relations . . . . John Rosasco
Manager, Public Relations . . . . Jason Vogel
Public Relations Coordinator . . . . Keith Soutar
Public Relations Assistant. . . . . Jennifer Schoenfeld

Marketing Department
Vice President, Marketing . . . . Jeanie Baumgartner
Director, Marketing Partnerships . . . . Rob Scolaro
Game Presentation Coordinator . . . . TBD
Marketing Coordinator . . . . Janet Duch
Marketing Assistant. . . . . Adam Evert
Marketing Partnerships Assistant. . . . . Alessandra Savarese

Business and Community Development Department
Vice President, Business and
   Community Development . . . . Patricia Kerr
Director, Business Development. . . . . Rob Capilli
Community Relations Representative and
   Director of Special Projects . . . . Rod Gilbert
Manager, Community Development . . . . TBD
Business and Community Development Assistant . . TBD

Medical/Training Staff
Team Physician and Orthopedic Surgeon. . . . . Dr. Barton Nisonson
Assistant Team Physician . . . . Dr. Anthony Maddalo
Medical Consultants . . . . Drs. Howard Chester and Ronald Weissman
Team Dentists . . . . Drs. Irwin Miller and Don Soloman
Medical Trainer . . . . Jim Ramsay
Equipment Manager . . . . Acacio Marques
Assistant Equipment Manager . . . . James Johnson
Massage Therapist. . . . . Bruce Lifrieri
Strength and Conditioning Coordinator . . . . Scott Livingston
Coaching Staff Assistant . . . . Pat Boller

Additional Information
Media Entrance . . . . 8 Penn Plaza (8th Avenue and 33rd Street)
Press Room . . . . 6th Floor, Madison Square Garden
Television Network . . . . MSG Network
Radio Network . . . . MSG Radio
Uniforms . . . . Home- Base color white, trimmed with blue
   and red
   Road- Base color blue, trimmed with red and
   white
   Third- Base color navy blue, trimmed with
   silver, red and white
Practice Facility . . . . Rye, New York (212.465.5850)

Ottawa Senators

1999-2000 Results: 41W-30L-11T 95PTS. Second, Northeast Division

Year-by-Year Record

		Home			Road			Overall						
Season	GP	W	L	T	W	L	T	W	L	T	GF	GA	Pts.	Finished	Playoff Result
1999-2000	82	24	12	5	17	18	6	41	30	11	244	210	95	2nd, Northeast Div.	Lost Conf. Quarter-Final
1998-99	82	22	11	8	22	12	7	44	23	15	239	179	103	1st, Northeast Div.	Lost Conf. Quarter-Final
1997-98	82	18	16	7	16	17	8	34	33	15	193	200	83	5th, Northeast Div.	Lost Conf. Semi-Final
1996-97	82	16	17	8	15	19	7	31	36	15	226	234	77	3rd, Northeast Div.	Lost Conf. Quarter-Final
1995-96	82	8	28	5	10	31	0	18	59	5	191	291	41	6th, Northeast Div.	Out of Playoffs
1994-95	48	5	16	3	4	18	2	9	34	5	117	174	23	7th, Northeast Div.	Out of Playoffs
1993-94	84	8	30	4	6	31	5	14	61	9	201	397	37	7th, Northeast Div.	Out of Playoffs
1992-93	84	9	29	4	1	41	0	10	70	4	202	395	24	6th, Adams Div.	Out of Playoffs

2000-01 Schedule

Oct. Thu. 5 at Boston
Sat. 7 Dallas
Fri. 13 New Jersey
Sat. 14 at Toronto
Tue. 17 at Philadelphia
Thu. 19 Pittsburgh
Sat. 21 Atlanta
Wed. 25 at Pittsburgh
Fri. 27 at Tampa Bay
Sat. 28 at Florida
Tue. 31 Toronto
Nov. Thu. 2 NY Rangers
Sat. 4 Columbus
Mon. 6 at Atlanta
Thu. 9 at Boston
Sat. 11 at Philadelphia*
Sun. 12 at Carolina*
Thu. 16 Carolina
Sat. 18 Florida
Tue. 21 Boston
Thu. 23 Edmonton
Sat. 25 at Toronto
Sun. 26 at NY Rangers
Tue. 28 Buffalo
Dec. Sat. 2 Philadelphia
Sun. 3 at Carolina*
Tue. 5 Pittsburgh
Fri. 8 Montreal
Sat. 9 at Montreal
Thu. 14 Calgary
Sat. 16 NY Islanders
Wed. 20 at Minnesota
Thu. 21 at Columbus
Sat. 23 Chicago*
Wed. 27 Washington
Fri. 29 at Buffalo
Sat. 30 at Pittsburgh
Jan. Tue. 2 St. Louis
Thu. 4 Tampa Bay
Sat. 6 Montreal
Wed. 10 at Vancouver

Sat. 13 at Calgary
Sun. 14 at Edmonton
Tue. 16 Los Angeles
Thu. 18 Washington
Sat. 20 Tampa Bay
Tue. 23 at NY Islanders
Thu. 25 at Tampa Bay
Fri. 26 at Florida
Sun. 28 at Montreal*
Tue. 30 at Washington
Feb. Tue. 6 at Detroit
Thu. 8 New Jersey
Sat. 10 Buffalo
Mon. 12 NY Islanders
Wed. 14 at New Jersey
Thu. 15 Colorado
Sun. 18 Montreal
Mon. 19 at Buffalo
Thu. 22 Florida
Sat. 24 Vancouver*
Mon. 26 at NY Rangers
Tue. 27 Buffalo
Mar. Thu. 1 San Jose
Sat. 3 at Toronto
Tue. 6 at New Jersey
Thu. 8 at Boston
Sat. 10 NY Rangers
Sun. 11 at Washington*
Wed. 14 Atlanta
Fri. 16 Anaheim
Sun. 18 at Dallas*
Wed. 21 at Phoenix
Thu. 22 at San Jose
Sat. 24 at Nashville
Mon. 26 Philadelphia
Wed. 28 at Chicago
Fri. 30 Boston
Apr. Sun. 1 Carolina*
Tue. 3 at Atlanta
Fri. 6 at NY Islanders
Sat. 7 Toronto

* Denotes afternoon game.

Franchise date: December 16, 1991

9th NHL Season

NORTHEAST DIVISION

Runner-up for the Calder Trophy in 1998-99, Marian Hossa nearly doubled his scoring output as a second-year player and led the Senators with 29 goals. His brother Marcel was selected 16th by the Montreal Canadiens in the 2000 Entry Draft.

2000-01 Player Personnel

FORWARDS	HT	WT	S	Place of Birth	Date	1999-00 Club
ALFREDSSON, Daniel	5-11	195	R	Gothenburg, Sweden	12/11/72	Ottawa
ARVEDSON, Magnus	6-2	198	L	Karlstad, Swe.	11/25/71	Ottawa
BONK, Radek	6-3	210	L	Krnov, Czech.	1/9/76	HC Pardubice-Ottawa
BUTSAYEV, Viacheslav	6-2	228	L	Togliatti, USSR	6/13/70	T.B.-Ott-Grand Rapids
CIERNIK, Ivan	6-1	234	L	Levice, Czech.	10/30/77	Grand Rapids
DACKELL, Andreas	5-11	195	R	Gavle, Sweden	12/29/72	Ottawa
EMMONS, John	6-1	203	L	San Jose, CA	8/17/74	Ottawa-Grand Rapids
FISHER, Mike	6-1	193	R	Peterborough, Ont.	6/5/80	Ottawa
FORBES, Colin	6-3	205	L	New Westminster, B.C.	2/16/76	Tampa Bay-Ottawa
GOROVIKOV, Konstantin	5-11	172	L	Novosibirsk, USSR	8/31/77	Grand Rapids
HAVLAT, Martin	6-1	178	L	Mlada Boleslav, Czech.	4/19/81	HC Trinec
HOSSA, Marian	6-1	199	L	Stara Lubovna, Czech.	1/12/79	Ottawa
KING, Derek	6-1	203	L	Hamilton, Ont.	2/11/67	Tor-St.L-Grand Rapids
McEACHERN, Shawn	5-11	193	L	Waltham, MA	2/28/69	Ottawa
NEIL, Christopher	6-1	213	R	Markdale, Ont.	6/18/79	Mobile-Grand Rapids
OLIVER, David	6-0	190	R	Sechelt, B.C.	4/17/71	Phoenix-Houston Aeros
PAVLIKOVSKY, Rastislav	5-11	193	L	Dubnica, Czech.	9/8/79	Grand Rapids-Phi (AHL)-Cincinnati Ducks
PROSPAL, Vaclav	6-2	195	L	Ceske-Budejovice, Czech.	2/17/75	Ottawa
ROY, Andre	6-4	213	L	Port Chester, NY	2/8/75	Ottawa
SCHASTLIVY, Petr	6-1	204	L	Angarsk, USSR	4/18/79	Ottawa-Grand Rapids
SZYSKY, Chris	6-0	208	R	White City, Sask.	6/8/76	Grand Rapids
WHITE, Todd	5-10	180	L	Kanata, Ont.	5/21/75	Chi-Clev-Phi-Phi (AHL)
YASHIN, Alexei	6-3	225	R	Sverdlovsk, USSR	11/5/73	Ottawa
ZAMUNER, Rob	6-3	203	L	Oakville, Ont.	9/17/69	Ottawa
DEFENSEMEN						
DEMIDOV, Ilja	6-3	185	L	Moscow, USSR	4/14/79	Oshawa Generals
GAGNON, Sean	6-2	219	L	Sault Ste. Marie, Ont.	9/11/73	Jokerit Helsinki
GRIMES, Kevin	6-3	218	L	Ottawa, Ont.	8/19/79	Pee Dee Pride-Grand Rapids
GRUDEN, John	6-0	203	L	Virginia, MN	6/4/70	Ottawa-Grand Rapids
HNIDY, Shane	6-2	210	R	Neepawa, Man.	11/8/75	Cincinnati Ducks
KRAVCHUK, Igor	6-1	218	L	Ufa, USSR	9/13/66	Ottawa
KWIATKOWSKI, Joel	6-2	206	L	Kindersley, Sask.	3/22/77	Cincinnati Ducks
PERSSON, Ricard	6-1	201	L	Ostersund, Sweden	8/24/69	St. Louis-Worcester
PHILLIPS, Chris	6-3	215	L	Fort McMurray, Alta.	3/9/78	Ottawa
RACHUNEK, Karel	6-2	202	R	Gottwaldov, Czech.	8/27/79	Ottawa-Grand Rapids
REDDEN, Wade	6-2	205	L	Lloydminster, Sask.	6/12/77	Ottawa
SALO, Sami	6-3	192	R	Turku, Finland	9/2/74	Ottawa
YORK, Jason	6-1	200	R	Nepean, Ont.	5/20/70	Ottawa

GOALTENDERS	HT	WT	C	Place of Birth	Date	1999-00 Club
CHOUINARD, Mathieu	6-1	211	L	Laval, Que.	4/11/80	Shawinigan
FOUNTAIN, Mike	6-1	180	L	North York, Ont.	1/26/72	Ottawa-Grand Rapids
HURME, Jani	6-0	187	L	Turku, Finland	1/7/75	Ottawa-Grand Rapids
LALIME, Patrick	6-3	185	L	St-Bonaventure, Que.	7/7/74	Ottawa

General Managers' History

Mel Bridgman, 1992-93; Randy Sexton, 1993-94, 1994-95; Randy Sexton and Pierre Gauthier, 1995-96; Pierre Gauthier, 1996-97, 1997-98; Rick Dudley, 1998-99; Marshall Johnston, 1999-2000 to date.

General Manager

JOHNSTON, MARSHALL

General Manager, Ottawa Senators. Born in Birch Hills, Sask., June 6, 1941.

Marshall Johnston was named general manager of the Ottawa Senators on June 8, 1999, replacing Rick Dudley. Johnston joined the Senators in July 1996 as director of player personnel. He worked through his first season in 1996-97 with the Senators' pro and amateur scouts and guided the staff during the 1997 NHL Entry Draft that saw the club pick Marian Hossa of Slovakia as its first selection, 12th overall.

After a successful seven-year NHL career on the ice (1967 to 1974), Johnston coached the California Golden Seals during parts of the 1973-74 and 1974-75 seasons. He then became head coach of Denver University, his alma mater, for four seasons, leading the Pioneers to the WCHA title and being named the Conference Coach of the Year in 1976-77.

Johnston joined the Colorado Rockies as assistant general manager and assistant coach on May 4, 1981 and served as head coach for the final 56 games of the 1981-82 season. Following the season, Johnston was named head coach of Canada's entry at the World Championships. After the Colorado franchise moved to New Jersey, he remained with the club as an assistant coach until being promoted to director of player personnel. He spent 10 years in New Jersey (1983 to 1993) as director of player personnel for the Devils, the 1995 Stanley Cup champions. While heading New Jersey's scouting department, the Devils drafted, among others, Scott Niedermayer, Brian Rolston, Martin Brodeur, Bill Guerin, Zdeno Ciger, Brendan Shanahan, Craig Wolanin, Sean Burke, Kirk Muller and Kirk McLean.

Johnston spent two years as executive director of CIPRO, a hockey scouting group jointly owned and operated by the Dallas Stars, Hartford Whalers, Philadelphia Flyers and Winnipeg Jets, prior to joining the New York Islanders' scouting staff in 1995-96.

Marshall and his wife Barbara have two daughters, Jill and Amy.

1999-2000 Scoring

* – rookie

Regular Season

Pos	#	Player	Team	GP	G	A	Pts	+/–	PIM	PP	SH	GW	GT	S	%
C	14	Radek Bonk	OTT	80	23	37	60	–2	53	10	0	5	1	167	13.8
R	11	Daniel Alfredsson	OTT	57	21	38	59	11	28	4	2	0	0	164	12.8
R	18	Marian Hossa	OTT	78	29	27	56	5	32	5	0	4	0	240	12.1
C	13	Vaclav Prospal	OTT	79	22	33	55	–2	40	5	0	4	0	204	10.8
L	15	Shawn McEachern	OTT	69	29	22	51	2	24	10	0	4	1	219	13.2
C	39	Joe Juneau	OTT	65	13	24	37	3	22	2	0	2	0	126	10.3
D	6	Wade Redden	OTT	81	10	26	36	–1	49	3	0	2	1	163	6.1
R	10	Andreas Dackell	OTT	82	10	25	35	5	18	0	0	1	1	99	10.1
D	33	Jason York	OTT	79	8	22	30	–3	60	1	0	1	0	159	5.0
L	20	Magnus Arvedson	OTT	47	15	13	28	4	36	1	1	4	1	91	16.5
C	22	Shaun Van Allen	OTT	75	9	19	28	20	37	0	2	4	0	75	12.0
D	3	Patrick Traverse	OTT	66	6	17	23	17	21	1	0	0	0	73	8.2
L	7	Rob Zamuner	OTT	57	9	12	21	–6	32	0	1	0	0	103	8.7
D	4	Chris Phillips	OTT	65	5	14	19	12	39	0	0	1	0	96	5.2
D	29	Igor Kravchuk	OTT	64	6	12	18	–5	20	5	0	1	0	126	4.8
D	5	Sami Salo	OTT	37	6	8	14	6	2	3	0	1	0	85	7.1
R	9	Kevin Dineen	OTT	67	4	8	12	2	57	0	0	1	0	71	5.6
C	12 *	Mike Fisher	OTT	32	4	5	9	–6	15	0	0	1	0	49	8.2
R	26 *	Andre Roy	OTT	73	4	3	7	3	145	0	0	1	0	39	10.3
L	56 *	Petr Schastlivy	OTT	13	2	5	7	4	2	1	0	1	0	22	9.1
L	17	Colin Forbes	T.B	8	0	0	0	–4	18	0	0	0	0	3	0.0
			OTT	45	2	5	7	–1	12	0	0	0	0	54	3.7
			TOTAL	53	2	5	7	–5	30	0	0	0	0	57	3.5
D	2	Grant Ledyard	OTT	40	2	4	6	–3	8	0	0	1	0	42	4.8
C	21	Kevin Miller	OTT	9	3	2	5	1	2	1	0	2	0	11	27.3
L	23	Yves Sarault	OTT	11	0	2	2	–3	7	0	0	0	0	13	0.0
G	30	Michael Fountain	OTT	1	0	0	0	0	0	0	0	0	0	0	0.0
D	52 *	David Van Drunen	OTT	1	0	0	0	0	0	0	0	0	0	0	0.0
D	59 *	Erich Goldmann	OTT	1	0	0	0	0	0	0	0	0	0	0	0.0
G	1 *	Jani Hurme	OTT	1	0	0	0	0	0	0	0	0	0	0	0.0
C	25	Viacheslav Butsayev	T.B	2	0	0	0	–2	0	0	0	0	0	1	0.0
			OTT	3	0	0	0	–2	0	0	0	0	0	1	0.0
			TOTAL	5	0	0	0	–4	0	0	0	0	0	2	0.0
D	44 *	Karel Rachunek	OTT	6	0	0	0	0	2	0	0	0	0	3	0.0
D	24	John Gruden	OTT	9	0	0	0	0	4	0	0	0	0	3	0.0
C	38 *	John Emmons	OTT	10	0	0	0	–2	6	0	0	0	0	3	0.0
G	35	Tom Barrasso	PIT	18	0	0	0	0	6	0	0	0	0	0	0.0
			OTT	7	0	0	0	0	0	0	0	0	0	0	0.0
			TOTAL	25	0	0	0	0	6	0	0	0	0	0	0.0
G	40	Patrick Lalime	OTT	38	0	0	0	0	4	0	0	0	0	0	0.0

Goaltending

No.	Goaltender	GPI	Mins	Avg	W	L	T	EN	SO	GA	SA	S%
1	* Jani Hurme	1	60	2.00	1	0	0	0	0	2	19	.895
40	Patrick Lalime	38	2038	2.33	19	14	3	1	3	79	834	.905
31	Ron Tugnutt	44	2435	2.54	18	12	8	2	4	103	1020	.899
35	Tom Barrasso	7	418	3.16	3	4	0	0	0	22	182	.879
30	Michael Fountain	1	16	3.75	0	0	0	0	0	1	6	.833
	Totals	**82**	**4986**	**2.53**	**41**	**30**	**11**	**3**	**7**	**210**	**2064**	**.898**

Playoffs

Pos	#	Player	Team	GP	G	A	Pts	+/–	PIM	PP	SH	GW	OT	S	%
R	11	Daniel Alfredsson	OTT	6	1	3	4	0	2	1	0	0	0	11	9.1
C	13	Vaclav Prospal	OTT	6	0	4	4	–1	4	0	0	0	0	8	0.0
C	39	Joe Juneau	OTT	6	2	1	3	–1	0	0	0	0	0	13	15.4
R	10	Andreas Dackell	OTT	6	2	1	3	0	2	0	0	1	0	13	15.4
L	15	Shawn Mceachern	OTT	6	0	3	3	0	4	0	0	0	0	14	0.0
L	7	Rob Zamuner	OTT	6	2	0	2	1	2	0	0	1	0	7	28.6
D	29	Igor Kravchuk	OTT	6	1	1	2	–5	0	0	0	0	0	19	5.3
D	5	Sami Salo	OTT	6	1	1	2	–8	0	1	0	0	0	19	5.3
D	33	Jason York	OTT	6	0	2	2	1	2	0	0	0	0	8	0.0
L	17	Colin Forbes	OTT	5	1	0	1	0	14	0	0	0	0	7	14.3
C	22	Shaun Van Allen	OTT	6	0	1	1	0	9	0	0	0	0	5	0.0
D	4	Chris Phillips	OTT	6	0	1	1	0	4	0	0	0	0	9	0.0
C	21	Kevin Miller	OTT	1	0	0	0	0	0	0	0	0	0	0	0.0
L	56 *	Petr Schastlivy	OTT	1	0	0	0	0	0	0	0	0	0	0	0.0
R	26 *	Andre Roy	OTT	5	0	0	0	0	2	0	0	0	0	4	0.0
G	35	Tom Barrasso	OTT	6	0	0	0	0	2	0	0	0	0	0	0.0
D	2	Grant Ledyard	OTT	6	0	0	0	0	16	0	0	0	0	3	0.0
D	3	Patrick Traverse	OTT	6	0	0	0	–2	2	0	0	0	0	4	0.0
C	14	Radek Bonk	OTT	6	0	0	0	–6	8	0	0	0	0	8	0.0
R	18	Marian Hossa	OTT	6	0	0	0	–8	2	0	0	0	0	14	0.0
L	20	Magnus Arvedson	OTT	6	0	0	0	–6	6	0	0	0	0	7	0.0

Goaltending

No.	Goaltender	GPI	Mins	Avg	W	L	EN	SO	GA	SA	S%
35	Tom Barrasso	6	372	2.58	2	4	1	0	16	168	.905
	Totals	**6**	**375**	**2.72**	**2**	**4**	**1**	**0**	**17**	**169**	**.899**

NHL Coaching Record

		Regular Season					Playoffs			
Season	Team	Games	W	L	T	%	Games	W	L	%
1973-74	California	21	2	17	2	.143	....	....	....	....
1974-75	California	48	11	28	9	.323	....	....	....	....
1981-82	Colorado	56	15	32	9	.348	....	....	....	....
	NHL Totals	**125**	**28**	**77**	**20**	**.304**	....	....	....	....

Club Records

Team

(Figures in brackets for season records are games played; records for fewest points, wins, ties, losses, goals, goals against are for 70 or more games)

Most Points	103	1998-99 (82)
Most Wins	44	1998-99 (82)
Most Ties	15	1996-97 (82), 1997-98 (82), 1998-99 (82)
Most Losses	70	1992-93 (84)
Most Goals	244	1999-2000 (82)
Most Goals Against	397	1993-94 (84)
Fewest Points	24	1992-93 (84)
Fewest Wins	10	1992-93 (84)
Fewest Ties	4	1992-93 (84)
Fewest Losses	36	1996-97 (82)
Fewest Goals	191	1995-96 (82)
Fewest Goals Against	179	1998-99 (82)

Longest Winning Streak

Overall	5	Twice
Home	7	Feb. 13-Mar. 8/99
Away	5	Apr. 3-19/98

Longest Undefeated Streak

Overall	11	Dec. 28/98-Jan. 16/99 (8 wins, 3 ties)
Home	8	Feb. 5-Mar. 20/98 (5 wins, 3 ties)
Away	7	Twice

** NHL records do not include neutral site games

Longest Losing Streak

Overall	14	Mar. 2-Apr. 7/93
Home	*11	Oct. 27-Dec. 8/93
Away	*38	Oct. 10/92-Apr. 3/93**

Longest Winless Streak

Overall	21	Oct. 10-Nov. 23/92 (20 losses, 1 tie)
Home	*17	Oct. 28/95-Jan. 27/96 (15 losses, 2 ties)
Away	*38	Oct. 10/92-Apr. 3/93 (38 losses)

Most Shutouts, Season	8	1997-98 (82)
Most PIM, Season	1,716	1992-93 (84)
Most Goals, Game	9	Twice

Individual

Most Seasons	6	Alexei Yashin, Radek Bonk
Most Games, Career	422	Alexei Yashin
Most Goals, Career	178	Alexei Yashin
Most Assists, Career	225	Alexei Yashin
Most Points, Career	403	Alexei Yashin (178G, 225A)
Most PIM, Career	625	Dennis Vial
Most Shutouts, Career	13	Ron Tugnutt

Longest Consecutive

Games Streak	210	Alexei Yashin (Feb. 23/95-Apr. 17/99)

Most Goals, Season	44	Alexei Yashin (1998-99)
Most Assists, Season	50	Alexei Yashin (1998-99)
Most Points, Season	94	Alexei Yashin (1998-99; 44G, 50A)
Most PIM, Season	318	Mike Peluso (1992-93)
Most Points, Defenseman, Season	63	Norm Maciver (1992-93; 17G, 46A)
Most Points, Center, Season	94	Alexei Yashin (1998-99; 44G, 50A)
Most Points, Right Wing, Season	71	Daniel Alfredsson (1996-97; 24G, 47A)
Most Points, Left Wing, Season	56	Shawn McEachern (1998-99; 31G, 25A), Marian Hossa (1999-2000; 29G, 27A)
Most Points, Rookie, Season	79	Alexei Yashin (1993-94; 30G, 49A)
Most Shutouts, Season	5	Damian Rhodes (1997-98)
Most Goals, Game	3	Thirteen times
Most Assists, Game	4	Alexei Yashin (Nov. 5/93), Vaclav Prospal (Mar. 21/00)
Most Points, Game	6	Dan Quinn (Oct. 15/95; 3G, 3A)

* NHL Record.

Coaching History

Rick Bowness, 1992-93 to 1994-95; Rick Bowness, Dave Allison and Jacques Martin, 1995-96; Jacques Martin, 1996-97 to date.

Captains' History

Laurie Boschman, 1992-93; Brad Shaw, Mark Lamb and Gord Dineen, 1993-94; Randy Cunneyworth, 1994-95 to 1997-98; Alexei Yashin, 1998-99; Daniel Alfredsson, 1999-2000 to date.

Retired Numbers

8	Frank Finnigan	1924-1934

All-time Record vs. Other Clubs

Regular Season

	GP	W	L	T	GF	GA	PTS	GP	W	L	T	GF	GA	PTS	GP	W	L	T	GF	GA	PTS
				At Home							**On Road**							**Total**			
Anaheim	6	2	3	1	17	17	5	6	1	3	2	9	16	4	12	3	6	3	26	33	9
Atlanta	2	2	0	0	10	3	4	2	2	0	0	12	7	4	4	4	0	0	22	10	8
Boston	21	4	14	3	45	74	11	22	6	14	2	63	89	14	43	10	28	5	108	163	25
Buffalo	22	5	11	6	48	66	16	21	5	14	2	29	71	12	43	10	25	8	77	137	28
Calgary	7	3	2	2	17	17	9	8	2	5	1	17	32	5	15	5	7	3	34	49	14
Carolina	21	8	10	3	57	63	19	19	2	15	2	37	62	6	40	10	25	5	94	125	25
Chicago	7	3	4	0	19	21	6	6	1	3	2	13	15	4	13	4	7	2	32	36	10
Colorado	14	5	7	2	44	61	12	13	1	11	1	34	64	3	27	6	18	3	78	125	15
Dallas	7	2	5	0	16	21	4	7	3	4	0	15	26	6	14	5	9	0	31	47	10
Detroit	7	2	4	1	19	21	5	6	3	3	0	13	20	6	13	5	7	1	32	41	11
Edmonton	6	2	3	1	10	14	5	8	1	5	2	21	32	4	14	3	8	3	31	46	9
Florida	14	5	7	2	36	41	12	14	5	8	1	41	49	11	28	10	15	3	77	90	23
Los Angeles	6	4	1	1	20	14	9	7	1	6	0	17	38	2	13	5	7	1	37	52	11
Montreal	20	8	11	1	56	61	17	23	7	13	3	63	72	17	43	15	24	4	119	133	34
Nashville	2	1	1	0	4	3	2	1	1	0	0	3	1	2	3	2	1	0	7	4	4
New Jersey	16	4	10	2	33	43	11	15	3	10	2	33	53	8	31	7	20	4	66	96	19
NY Islanders	15	7	4	4	49	45	18	16	9	3	4	64	54	22	31	16	7	8	113	99	40
NY Rangers	15	4	9	2	39	44	10	15	7	8	0	44	54	14	30	11	17	2	83	98	24
Philadelphia	16	5	9	2	44	55	12	15	4	10	1	36	56	9	31	9	19	3	80	111	21
Phoenix	9	2	6	1	21	33	5	7	3	3	1	27	28	7	16	5	9	2	48	61	12
Pittsburgh	19	5	11	3	46	62	13	19	1	14	4	36	77	6	38	6	25	7	82	139	19
St. Louis	7	1	6	0	13	33	2	7	3	3	1	21	21	7	14	4	9	1	34	54	9
San Jose	7	2	1	4	19	19	8	6	2	4	0	8	11	4	13	4	5	4	27	30	12
Tampa Bay	15	8	7	0	53	38	16	15	7	1	7	46	49	15	30	15	8	7	99	87	31
Toronto	10	6	3	1	28	24	13	11	3	7	1	27	36	7	21	9	10	2	55	60	20
Vancouver	7	3	3	1	16	21	7	7	3	4	1	15	25	7	15	6	7	2	31	46	14
Washington	15	7	7	1	55	49	15	16	5	10	1	35	59	11	31	12	17	2	90	108	26
Totals	**313**	**110**	**159**	**44**	**834**	**963**	**266**	**313**	**91**	**187**	**35**	**779**	**1117**	**217**	**626**	**201**	**346**	**79**	**1613**	**2080**	**483**

Playoffs

	Series	W	L	GP	W	L	T	GF	GA	Last Mtg.	Round	Result
Buffalo	2	0	2	8	1	0	19	26	1999	CQF	L 0-4
New Jersey	1	1	0	6	4	2	0	13	12	1998	CQF	W 4-2
Toronto	1	0	1	6	2	4	0	10	17	2000	CQF	L 2-4
Washington	1	0	1	5	1	4	0	7	18	1998	CSF	L 1-4
Totals	**5**	**1**	**4**	**28**	**10**	**18**	**0**	**49**	**73**			

Playoff Results 2000-1996

Year	Round	Opponent	Result	GF	GA
2000	CQF	Toronto	L 2-4	10	17
1999	CQF	Buffalo	L 0-4	6	12
1998	CSF	Washington	L 1-4	7	18
	CQF	New Jersey	W 4-2	13	12
1997	CQF	Buffalo	L 3-4	13	14

Abbreviations: Round: CSF – conference semi-final; **CQF** – conference quarter-final.

Colorado totals include Quebec, 1992-93 to 1994-95.
Dallas totals include Minnesota North Stars, 1992-93.
Carolina totals include Hartford, 1992-93 to 1996-97.
Phoenix totals include Winnipeg, 1992-93 to 1995-96.

1999-2000 Results

Oct.	2	at	Philadelphia	3-0		11	at	Los Angeles	4-3
	5	at	NY Rangers	2-1		12	at	Anaheim	2-0
	7		Boston	4-3		16	at	Washington	1-2
	9		Toronto	4-3		17	at	NY Islanders	4-3 *
	11		New Jersey	2-2		20	at	Philadelphia	1-1
	14	at	Phoenix	3-4		22		Detroit	2-3
	16	at	Colorado	1-3		24	at	Toronto	3-3
	21		Colorado	4-1		26		St. Louis	1-4
	23		Buffalo	4-0		28	at	Buffalo	0-1
	28		Calgary	3-4 *		29		NY Rangers	3-2
	30		Florida	5-0	Feb.	1		Boston	4-4
	31	at	Atlanta	6-4		3	at	Buffalo	2-4
Nov.	3	at	Washington	1-3		11		Florida	5-3
	4		Pittsburgh	2-1		12	at	Montreal	4-5
	6		Montreal	2-1		15		Carolina	5-1
	10	at	NY Rangers	4-3		17	at	Tampa Bay	6-2
	11		Nashville	1-2		19		Vancouver	1-3
	13		Anaheim	4-2		21	at	Florida	4-2
	17	at	Carolina	1-2		24	at	Tampa Bay	4-5
	18		San Jose	1-4		26		NY Rangers	4-3
	20	at	New Jersey	1-3		28	at	Pittsburgh	1-1
	25	at	Atlanta	6-3		29	at	Boston	5-3
	26	at	Pittsburgh	0-5	Mar.	2	at	NY Islanders	5-5
	28		Philadelphia	3-3		4		Atlanta	3-2
	30		Chicago	2-1		6	at	Boston	5-1
Dec.	3	at	New Jersey	4-7		9		Pittsburgh	7-0
	4		Dallas	1-3		11		Toronto	2-4
	8	at	Buffalo	0-0		15	at	Calgary	3-1
	11		NY Islanders	1-1		17	at	Edmonton	2-4
	13	at	Toronto	3-1		18	at	Vancouver	1-6
	16	at	Vancouver	2-1		21		Atlanta	7-1
	18	at	Calgary	1-2		23		Toronto	3-2
	19	at	Edmonton	3-3		25		Washington	2-2
	23		Carolina	4-3		28		Philadelphia	5-2
	27		Montreal	4-4		30	at	Tampa Bay	3-6
	29	at	Montreal	3-2		31	at	Florida	1-3
	30		Boston	5-4 *	Apr.	2	at	St. Louis	1-4
Jan.	3		New Jersey	3-4 *		4		Washington	4-0
	4	at	Carolina	2-1		6		NY Islanders	1-2
	6		Phoenix	5-2		8	at	Montreal	3-1
	8		Buffalo	4-7		9		Tampa Bay	5-2

* – Overtime

Entry Draft
Selections 2000-1992

2000
Pick
21	Anton Volchenkov
45	Mathieu Chouinard
55	Antoine Vermette
87	Jan Bohac
122	Derrick Byfuglien
156	Greg Zanon
157	Grant Potulny
158	Sean Connolly
188	Jason Maleyko
283	James Demone

1999
Pick
26	Martin Havlat
48	Simon Lajeunesse
62	Teemu Sainomaa
94	Chris Kelly
154	Andrew Ianiero
164	Martin Prusek
201	Mikko Ruutu
209	Layne Ulmer
213	Alexandre Giroux
269	Konstantin Gorovikov

1998
Pick
15	Mathieu Chouinard
44	Mike Fisher
58	Chris Bala
74	Julien Vauclair
101	Petr Schastlivy
130	Gavin McLeod
161	Christopher Neil
188	Michel Periard
223	Sergei Verenikin
246	Rastislav Pavlikovsky

1997
Pick
12	Marian Hossa
58	Jani Hurme
66	Josh Langfeld
119	Magnus Arvedson
146	Jeff Sullivan
173	Robin Bacul
203	Nick Gillis
229	Karel Rachunek

1996
Pick
1	Chris Phillips
81	Antti-Jussi Niemi
136	Andreas Dackell
163	Francois Hardy
212	Erich Goldmann
216	Ivan Ciernik
239	Sami Salo

1995
Pick
1	Bryan Berard
27	Marc Moro
53	Brad Larsen
89	Kevin Bolibruck
103	Kevin Boyd
131	David Hruska
183	Kaj Linna
184	Ray Schultz
231	Erik Kaminski

1994
Pick
3	Radek Bonk
29	Stanislav Neckar
81	Bryan Masotta
131	Mike Gaffney
133	Daniel Alfredsson
159	Doug Sproule
210	Frederic Cassivi
211	Danny Dupont
237	Stephen MacKinnon
274	Antti Tormanen

1993
Pick
1	Alexandre Daigle
27	Radim Bicanek
53	Patrick Charbonneau
91	Cosmo Dupaul
131	Rick Bodkin
157	Sergei Poleschuk
183	Jason Disher
209	Toby Kvalevog
227	Pavol Demitra
235	Rick Schuwerk

1992
Pick
2	Alexei Yashin
25	Chad Penney
50	Patrick Traverse
73	Radek Hamr
98	Daniel Guerard
121	Al Sinclair
146	Jaroslav Miklenda
169	Jay Kenney
194	Claude Savoie
217	Jake Grimes
242	Tomas Jelinek
264	Petter Ronnqvist

Club Directory

Corel Centre

Ottawa Senators
Corel Centre
1000 Palladium Drive
Kanata, Ontario
K2V 1A5
Phone **613/599-0250**
FAX 613/599-5562
Website:
www.ottawasenators.com
Capacity: 18,500

Chairman and Governor	Rod Bryden
President and CEO	Roy Mlakar
General Manager	Marshall Johnston
Director of Hockey Operations	Trevor Timmins
Director of Player Personnel	Jarmo Kekalainen
Chief Amateur Scout	Frank Jay
Head Coach	Jacques Martin
Assistant Coaches	Perry Pearn, Roger Neilson
Strength & Conditioning & Video Coach	Randy Lee
Pro Scout/Goaltending Coach	Phil Myre
VP, Communications	Phil Legault
Director, Communications	Steve Keogh
Manager, Communications	Ian Mendes
Communications/Hockey Operations Assistant	Jennifer Eves
Head Athletic Trainer	Kevin Wagner
Head Equipment Manager	Ed Georgica
Assistant Equipment Manager	John Gervais
Massage Therapist	Brad Joyal
Radio	The Team 1200 Radio (English), Radio 1150 CJRC (French)
Commercial TV	NEW RO TV
Cable TV	CTV Sportsnet
Internet	www.ottawasenators.com

Wade Redden has emerged as one of the top young defensemen in the NHL. Solid in his own zone, he also led all Ottawa blueliners with 36 points and ranked among the top-25 scoring defensemen in the NHL.

Coach

MARTIN, JACQUES
Coach, Ottawa Senators. Born in St. Pascal, Ont., October 1, 1952.

Jacques Martin led the Ottawa Senators to their best season in team history in 1998-99, breaking team records for wins (44) and points (103) the club had established the year before. He was rewarded with the Jack Adams Award as coach of the year. Ottawa approached both of these team records again in 1999-2000.

When appointed the Senators' third head coach on January 24, 1996, Martin brought 10 years of NHL coaching experience, including five with the Quebec Nordiques, an organization often compared with the Senators, in that both teams were built around young, talented players requiring patience and teaching.

Martin's coaching career began at the collegiate level in 1976. He was appointed head coach of the Guelph Platers (now Storm) in 1985, winning the OHL title, the Memorial Cup and being named the OHL coach of the year. That summer, Martin became head coach of the St. Louis Blues. In his NHL rookie year, he lead the Blues to the Norris Division championship and, in two seasons with the Blues, posted a 66-71-23 record. He then spent two seasons as an assistant to Chicago's head coach Mike Keenan, before joining the Nordiques in 1990. With Quebec, he worked four years as assistant coach and one year (1993-94) as both head coach and general manager of the AHL Cornwall Aces.

Coaching Record

Season	Team	Regular Season					Playoffs			
		Games	W	L	T	%	Games	W	L	%
1983-84	Peterborough (OHL)	70	43	23	4	.643	....	....	....	....
1984-85	Peterborough (OHL)	66	42	20	4	.667	....	....	....	....
1985-86	Guelph (OHL)	66	41	23	2	.636	....	....	....	....
1986-87	**St. Louis (NHL)**	80	32	33	15	.494	6	2	4	.333
1987-88	**St. Louis (NHL)**	80	34	38	8	.475	10	5	5	.500
1993-94	Cornwall (AHL)	80	33	36	11	.481	13	8	5	.615
1995-96	**Ottawa (NHL)**	38	10	24	4	.316	....	....	....	....
1996-97	**Ottawa (NHL)**	82	31	36	15	.470	7	3	4	.429
1997-98	**Ottawa (NHL)**	82	34	33	15	.506	11	5	6	.455
1998-99	**Ottawa (NHL)**	82	44	23	15	.628	4	0	4	.000
1999-2000	**Ottawa (NHL)**	82	41	30	11	.579•	6	2	4	.333
	NHL Totals	526	226	217	83	.510•	44	17	27	.386

• Includes points from regulation ties

Philadelphia Flyers

1999-2000 Results: 45w-25l-12t 105pts. First, Atlantic Division

2000-01 Schedule

Oct.	Thu.	5	Vancouver	Mon.	8	at St. Louis
	Sat.	7	Boston	Fri.	12	at Tampa Bay
	Wed.	11	at Minnesota	Sat.	13	at Florida
	Thu.	12	at Dallas	Tue.	16	at NY Rangers
	Sat.	14	at Phoenix	Thu.	18	New Jersey
	Tue.	17	Ottawa	Sat.	20	Florida
	Thu.	19	Montreal	Mon.	22	Los Angeles
	Sat.	21	Anaheim	Thu.	25	at Chicago
	Tue.	24	at NY Rangers	Sat.	27	at Carolina*
	Thu.	26	NY Rangers	Sun.	28	at Washington*
	Sun.	29	Washington	Wed.	31	at Pittsburgh
Nov.	Wed.	1	at New Jersey	Feb. Thu.	1	NY Islanders
	Thu.	2	Nashville	Tue.	6	at Boston
	Sat.	4	Buffalo	Wed.	7	at Pittsburgh
	Wed.	8	at Pittsburgh	Fri.	9	at NY Islanders
	Thu.	9	Edmonton	Wed.	14	at NY Islanders
	Sat.	11	Ottawa*	Thu.	15	Toronto
	Wed.	15	at Toronto	Sat.	17	Atlanta
	Fri.	17	at Atlanta	Mon.	19	Carolina
	Sat.	18	Washington	Thu.	22	at NY Islanders
	Wed.	22	at Buffalo	Sat.	24	Tampa Bay*
	Fri.	24	Pittsburgh*	Sun.	25	NY Rangers
	Sun.	26	Phoenix	Tue.	27	Montreal
	Wed.	29	at Columbus	Mar. Thu.	1	Buffalo
	Thu.	30	at Carolina	Sat.	3	at Montreal
Dec.	Sat.	2	at Ottawa	Mon.	5	Boston
	Wed.	6	Tampa Bay	Thu.	8	Calgary
	Fri.	8	at Detroit	Sat.	10	New Jersey*
	Sun.	10	NY Islanders	Tue.	13	St. Louis
	Tue.	12	at Nashville	Thu.	15	Minnesota
	Wed.	13	at Colorado	Sat.	17	NY Rangers*
	Sat.	16	New Jersey	Mon.	19	at Edmonton
	Tue.	19	at Boston	Thu.	22	at Calgary
	Thu.	21	San Jose	Sat.	24	at Toronto
	Sat.	23	Carolina*	Mon.	26	at Ottawa
	Wed.	27	at Florida	Thu.	29	Toronto
	Thu.	28	at Tampa Bay	Sat.	31	Detroit*
	Sat.	30	at Washington	Apr. Tue.	3	Florida
Jan.	Tue.	2	at New Jersey	Thu.	5	at Montreal
	Fri.	5	at Atlanta	Sat.	7	Pittsburgh*
	Sat.	6	Atlanta	Sun.	8	at Buffalo*

* Denotes afternoon game.

Franchise date: June 5, 1967

ATLANTIC DIVISION

34th NHL Season

Mark Recchi established himself among the NHL's scoring elite once again in his first full season back in a Flyers uniform. His 63 assists led the NHL in 1999-2000, while his 91 points trailed only Jaromir Jagr and Pavel Bure.

Year-by-Year Record

Season	GP	Home W	L	T	Road W	L	T	Overall W	L	T	GF	GA	Pts.	Finished		Playoff Result
1999-2000	82	25	9	7	20	16	5	45	25	12	237	179	105	1st,	Atlantic Div.	Lost Conf. Championship
1998-99	82	21	9	11	16	17	8	37	26	19	231	196	93	2nd,	Atlantic Div.	Lost Conf. Quarter-Final
1997-98	82	24	11	6	18	18	5	42	29	11	242	193	95	2nd,	Atlantic Div.	Lost Conf. Quarter-Final
1996-97	82	23	12	6	22	12	7	45	24	13	274	217	103	2nd,	Atlantic Div.	Lost Final
1995-96	82	27	9	5	18	15	8	45	24	13	282	208	103	1st,	Atlantic Div.	Lost Conf. Semi-Final
1994-95	48	16	7	1	12	9	3	28	16	4	150	132	60	1st,	Atlantic Div.	Lost Conf. Championship
1993-94	84	19	20	3	16	19	7	35	39	10	294	314	80	6th,	Atlantic Div.	Out of Playoffs
1992-93	84	23	14	5	13	23	6	36	37	11	319	319	83	5th,	Patrick Div.	Out of Playoffs
1991-92	80	22	11	7	10	26	4	32	37	11	252	273	75	6th,	Patrick Div.	Out of Playoffs
1990-91	80	18	16	6	15	21	4	33	37	10	252	267	76	5th,	Patrick Div.	Out of Playoffs
1989-90	80	17	19	4	13	20	7	30	39	11	290	297	71	6th,	Patrick Div.	Out of Playoffs
1988-89	80	22	15	3	14	21	5	36	36	8	307	285	80	4th,	Patrick Div.	Lost Conf. Championship
1987-88	80	20	14	6	18	19	3	38	33	9	292	292	85	3rd,	Patrick Div.	Lost Div. Semi-Final
1986-87	80	29	9	2	17	17	6	46	26	8	310	245	100	1st,	Patrick Div.	Lost Final
1985-86	80	33	6	1	20	17	3	53	23	4	335	241	110	1st,	Patrick Div.	Lost Div. Semi-Final
1984-85	80	32	4	4	21	16	3	53	20	7	348	241	113	1st,	Patrick Div.	Lost Final
1983-84	80	25	10	5	19	16	5	44	26	10	350	290	98	3rd,	Patrick Div.	Lost Div. Semi-Final
1982-83	80	29	8	3	20	15	5	49	23	8	326	240	106	1st,	Patrick Div.	Lost Div. Semi-Final
1981-82	80	25	10	5	13	21	6	38	31	11	325	313	87	3rd,	Patrick Div.	Lost Div. Semi-Final
1980-81	80	23	9	8	18	15	7	41	24	15	313	249	97	2nd,	Patrick Div.	Lost Quarter-Final
1979-80	80	27	5	8	21	7	12	48	12	20	327	254	116	1st,	Patrick Div.	Lost Final
1978-79	80	26	10	4	14	15	11	40	25	15	281	248	95	2nd,	Patrick Div.	Lost Quarter-Final
1977-78	80	29	6	5	16	14	10	45	20	15	296	200	105	2nd,	Patrick Div.	Lost Semi-Final
1976-77	80	33	6	1	15	10	15	48	16	16	323	213	112	1st,	Patrick Div.	Lost Semi-Final
1975-76	80	36	2	2	15	11	14	51	13	16	348	209	118	1st,	Patrick Div.	Lost Final
1974-75	**80**	**32**	**6**	**2**	**19**	**12**	**9**	**51**	**18**	**11**	**293**	**181**	**113**	**1st,**	**Patrick Div.**	**Won Stanley Cup**
1973-74	**78**	**28**	**6**	**5**	**22**	**10**	**7**	**50**	**16**	**12**	**273**	**164**	**112**	**1st,**	**West Div.**	**Won Stanley Cup**
1972-73	78	27	8	4	10	22	7	37	30	11	296	256	85	2nd,	West Div.	Lost Semi-Final
1971-72	78	19	13	7	7	25	7	26	38	14	200	236	66	5th,	West Div.	Out of Playoffs
1970-71	78	20	10	9	8	23	8	28	33	17	207	225	73	3rd,	West Div.	Lost Quarter-Final
1969-70	76	11	14	13	6	21	11	17	35	24	197	225	58	5th,	West Div.	Out of Playoffs
1968-69	76	14	16	8	6	19	13	20	35	21	174	225	61	3rd,	West Div.	Lost Quarter-Final
1967-68	74	17	13	7	14	19	4	31	32	11	173	179	73	1st,	West Div.	Lost Quarter-Final

2000-01 Player Personnel

FORWARDS	HT	WT	S	Place of Birth	Date	1999-00 Club
DIVISEK, Tomas	6-2	194	L	Most, Czech.	7/19/79	Philadelphia (AHL)
GAGNE, Simon	6-0	185	L	Ste-Foy, Que.	2/29/80	Philadelphia
GREIG, Mark	5-11	190	R	High River, Alta.	1/25/70	Phi-Phi (AHL)
HULL, Jody	6-2	200	R	Petrolia, Ont.	2/2/69	Orlando-Philadelphia
JONES, Keith	6-2	200	L	Brantford, Ont.	11/8/68	Philadelphia
LANGKOW, Daymond	5-11	175	L	Edmonton, Alta	9/27/76	Philadelphia
LeCLAIR, John	6-3	226	L	St. Albans, VT	7/5/69	Philadelphia
MANDERVILLE, Kent	6-3	210	L	Edmonton, Alta.	4/12/71	Carolina-Philadelphia
ODJICK, Gino	6-3	210	L	Maniwaki, Que.	9/7/70	NY Islanders-Philadelphia
PICARD, Michel	5-11	190	L	Beauport, Que.	11/7/69	Grand Rapids-Edmonton
PLANTE, Derek	5-11	181	L	Cloquet, MN	1/17/71	Dallas-Michigan K-Wings-Chicago-Chicago Wolves
PRIMEAU, Keith	6-4	210	L	Toronto, Ont.	11/24/71	Philadelphia
RANHEIM, Paul	6-1	210	R	St. Louis, MO	1/25/66	Carolina
RECCHI, Mark	5-10	185	L	Kamloops, B.C.	2/1/68	Philadelphia
STEVENS, Kevin	6-3	230	L	Brockton, MA	4/15/65	NY Rangers
TOCCHET, Rick	6-0	210	R	Scarborough, Ont.	4/9/64	Phoenix-Philadelphia
WHITE, Peter	5-11	200	L	Montreal, Que.	3/15/69	Phi-Phi (AHL)

DEFENSEMEN						
DELMORE, Andy	6-1	192	R	LaSalle, Ont.	12/26/76	Phi-Phi (AHL)
DESJARDINS, Eric	6-1	200	R	Rouyn, Que.	6/14/69	Philadelphia
EATON, Mark	6-2	205	L	Wilmington, DE	5/6/77	Phi-Phi (AHL)
McGILLIS, Dan	6-2	225	L	Hawkesbury, Ont.	7/1/72	Philadelphia
RICHARDSON, Luke	6-3	210	L	Ottawa, Ont.	3/26/69	Philadelphia
SYKORA, Michal	6-5	225	L	Pardubice, Czech.	7/5/73	Sparta Praha
THERIEN, Chris	6-4	230	L	Ottawa, Ont.	12/14/71	Philadelphia

GOALTENDERS	HT	WT	C	Place of Birth	Date	1999-00 Club
BOUCHER, Brian	6-1	190	L	Woonsocket, RI	1/2/77	Phi-Phi (AHL)
CECHMANEK, Roman	6-3	176	L	Gottwaldov, Czech.	3/2/71	HC Vsetin

Captains' History

Lou Angotti, 1967-68; Ed Van Impe, 1968-69 to 1971-72; Ed Van Impe and Bobby Clarke, 1972-73; Bobby Clarke, 1973-74 to 1978-79; Mel Bridgman, 1979-80, 1980-81; Bill Barber, 1981-82; Bill Barber and Bobby Clarke, 1982-83; Bobby Clarke, 1983-84; Dave Poulin, 1984-85 to 1988-89; Dave Poulin and Ron Sutter, 1989-90; Ron Sutter, 1990-91; Rick Tocchet, 1991-92; no captain, 1992-93; Kevin Dineen, 1993-94; Eric Lindros, 1994-95 to 1998-99; Eric Lindros and Eric Desjardins, 1999-2000; Eric Desjardins, 2000-01.

Coaching History

Keith Allen, 1967-68, 1968-69; Vic Stasiuk, 1969-70, 1970-71; Fred Shero, 1971-72 to 1977-78; Bob McCammon and Pat Quinn, 1978-79; Pat Quinn, 1979-80, 1980-81; Pat Quinn and Bob McCammon, 1981-82; Bob McCammon, 1982-83, 1983-84; Mike Keenan, 1984-85 to 1987-88; Paul Holmgren, 1988-89 to 1990-91; Paul Holmgren and Bill Dineen, 1991-92; Bill Dineen, 1992-93; Terry Simpson, 1993-94; Terry Murray, 1994-95 to 1996-97; Wayne Cashman and Roger Neilson, 1997-98; Roger Neilson, 1998-99, 1999-2000; Craig Ramsay, 2000-01.

General Managers' History

Bud Poile, 1967-68, 1968-69; Bud Poile and Keith Allen, 1969-70; Keith Allen, 1970-71 to 1982-83; Bob McCammon, 1983-84; Bob Clarke, 1984-85 to 1989-90; Russ Farwell, 1990-91 to 1993-94; Bob Clarke, 1994-95 to date.

President and General Manager

CLARKE, ROBERT EARLE (BOB)
President/General Manager, Philadelphia Flyers.
Born in Flin Flon, Man., August 13, 1949.

Bob Clarke was named president and general manager of the Philadelphia Flyers on June 15, 1994. Clarke's appointment marks the second time he has served as the Flyers' general manager. The Flin Flon native was the Flyers' vice president and general manager from 1984-90. During his 12 years as the team's general manager, the Flyers have won six divisional titles, three conference championships, reached the Stanley Cup semifinals six times and the Finals three times.

Prior to re-joining the Flyers' family in 1994, Clarke served as vice president and general manager of the Florida Panthers. In 1993-94, their first season in the NHL, the Panthers established NHL records for wins (33) and points (83) by an expansion franchise. Clarke also served as the vice president and general manager of the Minnesota North Stars from 1990-92, guiding the team to the Stanley Cup Finals in 1991.

As a player, the former Philadelphia captain led his club to Stanley Cup championships in 1974 and 1975 and captured numerous individual awards, including the Hart Trophy as the League's most valuable player in 1973, 1975 and 1976. The four-time All-Star also received the Bill Masterton Memorial Trophy (perseverance and dedication) in 1972 and the Frank J. Selke Trophy (top defensive forward) in 1983. He appeared in eight All-Star Games and was elected to the Hockey Hall of Fame in 1987. He was awarded the Lester Patrick Trophy in 1979-80 in recognition of his contribution to hockey in the United States. Clarke appeared in 1,144 regular season games, recording 358 goals and 852 assists for 1,210 points. He also added 119 points in 136 playoff games.

1999-2000 Scoring

* – rookie

Regular Season

Pos	#	Player	Team	GP	G	A	Pts	+/−	PIM	PP	SH	GW	GT	S	%
R	8	Mark Recchi	PHI	82	28	63	91	20	50	7	1	5	1	223	12.6
L	10	John LeClair	PHI	82	40	37	77	8	36	13	0	7	2	249	16.1
C	88	Eric Lindros	PHI	55	27	32	59	11	83	10	1	2	1	187	14.4
D	37	Eric Desjardins	PHI	81	14	41	55	20	32	8	0	4	1	207	6.8
C	18	Daymond Langkow	PHI	82	18	32	50	1	56	5	0	7	0	222	8.1
C	12	* Simon Gagne	PHI	80	20	28	48	11	22	8	1	4	0	159	12.6
R	92	Rick Tocchet	PHX	64	12	17	29	−5	67	2	0	1	0	107	11.2
			PHI	16	3	3	6	4	23	2	0	0	0	23	13.0
			TOTAL	80	15	20	35	−1	90	4	0	1	1	130	11.5
R	26	Valeri Zelepukin	PHI	77	11	21	32	−3	55	2	0	3	1	125	8.8
R	20	Keith Jones	PHI	57	9	16	25	8	82	1	0	0	0	92	9.8
L	29	Gino Odjick	NYI	46	5	10	15	−7	90	0	0	3	0	91	5.5
			PHI	13	3	1	4	2	10	0	0	0	0	24	12.5
			TOTAL	59	8	11	19	−5	100	0	0	3	0	115	7.0
D	3	Daniel McGillis	PHI	68	4	14	18	16	55	3	0	1	0	128	3.1
C	25	Keith Primeau	PHI	23	7	10	17	10	31	1	0	1	0	51	13.7
R	11	Jody Hull	PHI	67	10	3	13	8	4	0	2	2	0	63	15.9
D	6	Chris Therien	PHI	80	4	9	13	11	66	1	0	1	0	126	3.2
L	32	Craig Berube	PHI	77	4	8	12	3	162	0	0	0	0	63	6.3
C	28	Kent Manderville	CAR	56	1	4	5	−8	12	0	0	1	0	45	2.2
			PHI	13	0	3	3	2	4	0	0	0	0	17	0.0
			TOTAL	69	1	7	8	−6	16	0	0	1	0	62	1.6
D	43	* Andy Delmore	PHI	27	2	5	7	−1	8	0	0	1	0	55	3.6
D	22	Luke Richardson	PHI	74	2	5	7	14	140	0	0	1	0	50	4.0
D	2	Adam Burt	PHI	67	1	6	7	−2	45	0	0	1	0	49	2.0
C	15	Peter White	PHI	21	1	5	6	1	6	0	0	0	0	24	4.2
R	9	Mark Greig	PHI	11	3	2	5	0	6	0	0	0	0	14	21.4
D	55	Ulf Samuelsson	PHI	49	1	2	3	8	58	0	0	1	0	17	5.9
D	44	* Mark Eaton	PHI	27	1	1	2	1	8	0	0	0	0	25	4.0
D	24	Zarley Zalapski	PHI	12	0	2	2	0	6	0	0	0	0	6	0.0
C	23	Todd White	CHI	1	0	0	0	0	0	0	0	0	0	0	0.0
			PHI	3	1	0	1	−1	0	0	0	0	0	4	25.0
			TOTAL	4	1	0	1	−1	0	0	0	0	0	4	25.0
G	33	* Brian Boucher	PHI	35	0	1	1	0	0	0	0	0	0	0	0.0
G	34	John Vanbiesbrouck	PHI	50	0	1	1	0	6	0	0	0	0	0	0.0
C	38	Steve Washburn	PHI	1	0	0	0	0	0	0	0	0	0	0	0.0
R	14	Mike Maneluk	PHI	1	0	0	0	4	0	0	0	0	0	2	0.0
D	39	* Jeff Lank	PHI	2	0	0	0	0	0	0	0	0	0	0	0.0

Goaltending

No.	Goaltender	GPI	Mins	Avg	W	L	T	EN	SO	GA	SA	S%
33	* Brian Boucher	35	2038	1.91	20	10	3	3	4	65	790	.918
34	John Vanbiesbrouck	50	2950	2.20	25	15	9	3	3	108	1143	.906
	Totals	**82**	**5008**	**2.14**	**45**	**25**	**12**	**6**	**7**	**179**	**1939**	**.908**

Playoffs

Pos	#	Player	Team	GP	G	A	Pts	+/−	PIM	PP	SH	GW	OT	S	%
R	8	Mark Recchi	PHI	18	6	12	18	3	6	2	0	1	0	53	11.3
L	10	John Leclair	PHI	18	6	7	13	3	6	4	0	2	0	64	9.4
C	25	Keith Primeau	PHI	18	2	11	13	−4	13	0	0	1	1	37	5.4
D	37	Eric Desjardins	PHI	18	2	10	12	1	2	1	0	1	0	31	6.5
R	92	Rick Tocchet	PHI	18	5	6	11	−2	49	2	0	1	0	46	10.9
C	18	Daymond Langkow	PHI	16	5	5	10	2	23	1	1	2	0	47	10.6
C	12	* Simon Gagne	PHI	17	5	5	10	0	2	2	0	1	0	34	14.7
D	3	Daniel Mcgillis	PHI	18	2	6	8	−1	12	0	0	0	0	51	3.9
D	43	* Andy Delmore	PHI	18	5	2	7	0	14	1	0	1	1	31	16.1
R	20	Keith Jones	PHI	18	3	3	6	−1	14	1	0	0	0	18	16.7
R	26	Valeri Zelepukin	PHI	18	1	2	3	3	12	1	0	0	0	23	4.3
C	15	Peter White	PHI	16	0	2	2	−1	0	0	0	0	0	17	0.0
C	88	Eric Lindros	PHI	2	1	0	1	0	0	0	0	0	0	3	33.3
L	32	Craig Berube	PHI	18	1	0	1	−4	23	0	0	1	0	13	7.7
D	2	Adam Burt	PHI	11	0	1	1	4	4	0	0	0	0	3	0.0
R	11	Jody Hull	PHI	18	0	1	1	−4	0	0	0	0	0	29	0.0
D	22	Luke Richardson	PHI	18	0	1	1	−5	41	0	0	0	0	10	0.0
C	28	Kent Manderville	PHI	18	0	1	1	−3	22	0	0	0	0	4	0.0
D	6	Chris Therien	PHI	18	0	1	1	−1	12	0	0	0	0	25	0.0
R	9	Mark Greig	PHI	3	0	0	0	−1	0	0	0	0	0	2	0.0
D	44	* Mark Eaton	PHI	7	0	0	0	−2	0	0	0	0	0	2	0.0
G	33	* Brian Boucher	PHI	18	0	0	0	0	0	0	0	0	0	0	0.0

Goaltending

No.	Goaltender	GPI	Mins	Avg	W	L	EN	SO	GA	SA	S%
33	* Brian Boucher	18	1183	2.03	11	7	0	1	40	484	.917
	Totals	**18**	**1188**	**2.02**	**11**	**7**	**0**	**1**	**40**	**484**	**.917**

Club Records

Team

(Figures in brackets for season records are games played; records for fewest points, wins, ties, losses, goals, goals against are for 70 or more games)

Most Points	118	1975-76 (80)
Most Wins	53	1984-85 (80), 1985-86 (80)
Most Ties	*24	1969-70 (76)
Most Losses	39	1993-94 (84)
Most Goals	350	1983-84 (80)
Most Goals Against	319	1992-93 (84)
Fewest Points	58	1969-70 (76)
Fewest Wins	17	1969-70 (76)
Fewest Ties	4	1985-86 (80)
Fewest Losses	12	1979-80 (80)
Fewest Goals	173	1967-68 (74)
Fewest Goals Against	164	1973-74 (78)
Longest Winning Streak		
Overall	13	Oct. 19-Nov. 17/85
Home	*20	Jan. 4-Apr. 3/76
Away	8	Dec. 22/82-Jan. 16/83
Longest Undefeated Streak		
Overall	*35	Oct. 14/79-Jan. 6/80 (25 wins, 10 ties)
Home	26	Oct. 11/79-Feb. 3/80 (19 wins, 7 ties)
Away	16	Oct. 20/79-Jan. 6/80 (11 wins, 5 ties)
Longest Losing Streak		
Overall	6	Mar. 25-Apr. 4/70, Dec. 5-Dec. 17/92, Jan. 25-Feb. 5/94
Home	5	Jan. 30-Feb. 15/69
Away	8	Oct. 25-Nov. 26/72
Longest Winless Streak		
Overall	12	Feb. 24-Mar. 16/99 (8 losses, 4 ties)
Home	8	Dec. 19/68-Jan. 18/69 (4 losses, 4 ties)
Away	19	Oct. 23/71-Jan. 27/72 (15 losses, 4 ties)
Most Shutouts, Season	13	1974-75 (80)
Most PIM, Season	2,621	1980-81 (80)
Most Goals, Game	13	Mar. 22/84 (Pit. 4 at Phi. 13), Oct. 18/84 (Van. 2 at Phi. 13)

Individual

Most Seasons	15	Bobby Clarke
Most Games	1,144	Bobby Clarke
Most Goals, Career	420	Bill Barber
Most Assists, Career	852	Bobby Clarke
Most Points, Career	1,210	Bobby Clarke (358G, 852A)
Most PIM, Career	1,706	Rick Tocchet
Most Shutouts, Career	50	Bernie Parent
Longest Consecutive Game Streak	484	Rod Brind'Amour (Feb. 24/93-Apr. 18/99)
Most Goals, Season	61	Reggie Leach (1975-76)
Most Assists, Season	89	Bobby Clarke (1974-75, 1975-76)
Most Points, Season	123	Mark Recchi (1992-93; 53G, 70A)
Most PIM, Season	*472	Dave Schultz (1974-75)
Most Points, Defenseman, Season	82	Mark Howe (1985-86; 24G, 58A)
Most Points, Center, Season	119	Bobby Clarke (1975-76; 30G, 89A)
Most Points, Right Wing, Season	123	Mark Recchi (1992-93; 53G, 70A)
Most Points, Left Wing, Season	112	Bill Barber (1975-76; 50G, 62A)
Most Points, Rookie, Season	82	Mikael Renberg (1993-94; 38G, 44A)
Most Shutouts, Season	12	Bernie Parent (1973-74, 1974-75)
Most Goals, Game	4	Fourteen times
Most Assists, Game	6	Eric Lindros (Feb. 26/97)
Most Points, Game	8	Tom Bladon (Dec. 11/77; 4G, 4A)

* NHL Record.

Retired Numbers

1	Bernie Parent	1967-1971, 1973-1979
4	Barry Ashbee	1970-1974
7	Bill Barber	1972-1985
16	Bobby Clarke	1969-1984

All-time Record vs. Other Clubs

Regular Season

	At Home							On Road							Total						
	GP	W	L	T	GF	GA	PTS	GP	W	L	T	GF	GA	PTS	GP	W	L	T	GF	GA	PTS
Anaheim	6	2	1	3	17	12	7	6	2	2	2	20	21	6	12	4	3	5	37	33	13
Atlanta	2	1	0	1	7	5	3	2	1	1	0	5	4	2	4	2	1	1	12	9	5
Boston	65	30	27	8	220	185	68	68	16	43	9	189	265	41	133	46	70	17	409	450	109
Buffalo	59	34	13	12	212	153	80	55	21	27	7	163	188	49	114	55	40	19	375	341	129
Calgary	48	32	13	3	190	128	67	50	17	24	9	166	201	43	98	49	37	12	356	329	110
Carolina	35	23	9	3	133	90	49	36	18	11	7	140	122	43	71	41	20	10	273	212	92
Chicago	59	32	16	11	191	155	75	57	13	25	19	162	202	45	116	45	41	30	353	357	120
Colorado	32	22	8	2	120	87	46	31	9	11	11	110	115	29	63	31	19	13	230	202	75
Dallas	64	41	9	14	249	145	96	63	23	26	14	206	207	60	127	64	35	28	455	352	156
Detroit	56	32	13	11	226	166	75	56	18	28	10	177	198	46	112	50	41	21	403	364	121
Edmonton	28	19	7	2	124	79	40	26	7	14	5	77	94	19	54	26	21	7	201	173	59
Florida	17	7	6	4	39	39	18	16	11	5	0	55	42	22	33	18	11	4	94	81	40
Los Angeles	61	38	16	7	236	156	84	63	35	20	8	216	187	78	124	73	36	15	452	343	162
Montreal	65	26	24	15	199	196	68	66	20	32	14	203	239	54	131	46	56	29	402	435	122
Nashville	2	1	0	1	9	1	3	2	2	0	0	4	1	4	4	3	0	1	13	2	7
New Jersey	74	47	19	8	299	188	102	73	29	39	5	266	265	63	147	76	58	13	565	453	165
NY Islanders	85	51	24	10	321	249	113	87	26	47	14	252	333	66	172	77	71	24	573	582	179
NY Rangers	98	47	37	14	326	282	108	100	34	43	23	289	322	91	198	81	80	37	615	604	199
Ottawa	15	10	4	1	56	36	21	16	9	5	2	55	44	20	31	19	9	3	111	80	41
Phoenix	28	21	7	0	124	77	42	27	15	10	2	96	81	32	55	36	17	2	220	158	74
Pittsburgh	96	74	15	7	417	241	155	95	34	42	19	308	333	87	191	108	57	26	725	574	242
St. Louis	64	43	11	10	252	145	96	64	31	26	7	201	188	69	128	74	37	17	453	333	165
San Jose	8	5	2	1	28	17	11	9	7	1	1	28	15	15	17	12	3	2	56	32	26
Tampa Bay	17	11	1	5	60	28	27	18	11	6	1	56	50	23	35	22	7	6	116	78	50
Toronto	59	39	12	8	235	138	86	59	25	21	13	202	195	63	118	64	33	21	437	333	149
Vancouver	50	34	15	1	220	149	69	50	28	10	12	201	143	68	100	62	25	13	421	292	137
Washington	75	46	24	5	281	207	97	72	31	28	13	240	241	75	147	77	52	18	521	448	172
Defunct Clubs	34	24	4	6	137	67	54	35	13	14	8	102	89	34	69	37	18	14	239	156	88
Totals	**1302**	**792**	**337**	**173**	**4928**	**3421**	**1760**	**1302**	**506**	**561**	**235**	**4189**	**4385**	**1247**	**2604**	**1298**	**898**	**408**	**9117**	**7806**	**3007**

Playoffs

	Series	W	L	GP	W	L	T	GF	GA	Last Mtg.	Round	Result
Boston	4	2	2	20	9	11	0	57	60	1978	QF	L 1-4
Buffalo	6	5	1	31	21	10	0	97	75	2000	CQF	W 4-1
Calgary	2	1	1	11	7	4	0	43	28	1981	QF	L 3-4
Chicago	1	0	1	4	0	4	0	8	20	1971	QF	L 0-4
Colorado	2	2	0	11	7	4	0	39	29	1985	CF	W 4-2
Dallas	2	2	0	11	8	3	0	41	26	1980	SF	W 4-1
Detroit	1	0	1	4	0	4	0	6	16	1997	F	L 0-4
Edmonton	3	1	2	15	7	8	0	44	49	1987	F	L 3-4
Florida	1	0	1	6	2	4	0	11	15	1996	CSF	L 2-4
Montreal	4	1	3	21	6	15	0	52	72	1989	CF	L 2-4
New Jersey	3	1	2	15	7	8	0	35	41	2000	CF	L 3-4
NY Islanders	4	3	1	25	14	11	0	83	69	1987	DF	W 4-3
NY Rangers	10	6	4	47	27	20	0	158	153	1997	CF	W 4-1
Pittsburgh	3	3	0	18	12	6	0	66	51	2000	CSF	W 4-2
St. Louis	2	0	2	11	3	8	0	20	34	1969	QF	L 0-4
Tampa Bay	1	1	0	6	4	2	0	26	13	1996	CQF	W 4-2
Toronto	4	3	1	23	14	9	0	78	56	1999	CQF	L 2-4
Vancouver	1	1	0	3	2	1	0	15	9	1979	PR	W 2-1
Washington	3	1	2	16	7	9	0	55	65	1989	DSF	W 4-2
Totals	**57**	**33**	**24**	**298**	**158**	**140**	**0**	**933**	**881**			

Calgary totals include Atlanta Flames, 1972-73 to 1979-80.
Carolina totals include Hartford, 1979-80 to 1996-97.
Colorado totals include Quebec, 1979-80 to 1994-95.
Dallas totals include Minnesota North Stars, 1967-68 to 1992-93.
New Jersey totals include Kansas City, 1974-75 to 1975-76, and Colorado Rockies, 1976-77 to 1981-82.
Phoenix totals include Winnipeg, 1979-80 to 1995-96.

Playoff Results 2000-1996

Year	Round	Opponent	Result	GF	GA
2000	CF	New Jersey	L 3-4	15	18
	CSF	Pittsburgh	W 4-2	15	14
	CQF	Buffalo	W 4-1	14	8
1999	CQF	Toronto	L 2-4	11	9
1998	CQF	Buffalo	L 1-4	9	18
1997	F	Detroit	L 0-4	6	16
	CF	NY Rangers	W 4-1	20	13
	CSF	Buffalo	W 4-1	21	13
	CQF	Pittsburgh	W 4-1	20	13
1996	CSF	Florida	L 2-4	11	15
	CQF	Tampa Bay	W 4-2	26	13

Abbreviations: Round: F – Final;
CF – conference final; **CSF** – conference semi-final;
CQF – conference quarter-final; **DF** – division final;
DSF – division semi-final; **SF** – semi-final;
QF – quarter-final; **PR** – preliminary round.

1999-2000 Results

Oct.	2		Ottawa	0-3		11	at	Carolina	4-3
	7		Carolina	0-2		14	at	Atlanta	0-1
	9	at	Boston	1-1		15		New Jersey	1-4
	12	at	Washington	4-5		17	at	Florida	1-3
	14		Montreal	4-5 *		20		Ottawa	1-1
	16	at	Detroit	2-3		23	at	Pittsburgh	4-4
	17		Buffalo	5-2		27		Florida	4-2
	20		NY Rangers	5-0		29	at	Montreal	2-2
	22	at	NY Rangers	2-0		30	at	Washington	0-2
	24		Florida	2-0	**Feb.**	3		Anaheim	3-3
	26		Vancouver	2-5		9	at	Toronto	4-2
	28		Colorado	5-4 *		10		Edmonton	2-3
	30		New Jersey	5-3		12		Buffalo	3-2 *
Nov.	3	at	Anaheim	3-3		15	at	New Jersey	2-4
	5	at	San Jose	3-1		17		NY Islanders	2-2
	6	at	Los Angeles	5-3		19		Washington	4-2
	9	at	New Jersey	1-2		20	at	NY Rangers	3-2
	11		Carolina	4-1		22		Chicago	3-1
	13		San Jose	3-2		24		Pittsburgh	4-3 *
	18		Dallas	1-1		26	at	NY Islanders	5-1
	20		Tampa Bay	4-1		29	at	St. Louis	2-3
	22	at	Tampa Bay	1-4	**Mar.**	1	at	Dallas	0-2
	24	at	Florida	6-1		4	at	Boston	3-0
	26		Toronto	3-2 *		5		NY Islanders	3-4 *
	28	at	Ottawa	3-3		8	at	Tampa Bay	3-2 *
Dec.	2	at	Buffalo	4-2		9		Washington	3-1
	4	at	Montreal	3-2		12	at	Colorado	1-3
	5		St. Louis	3-2		13	at	Phoenix	4-1
	9		Toronto	4-2		16		Montreal	1-1
	11	at	Toronto	4-6		18		NY Rangers	2-3
	14	at	Buffalo	1-3		19		Boston	6-2
	16		Phoenix	5-3		21	at	Nashville	2-0
	18		Tampa Bay	4-0		23		Los Angeles	2-3 *
	19		Nashville	1-1		26		Pittsburgh	3-1
	22	at	New Jersey	2-3		28	at	Ottawa	2-5
	23		Atlanta	4-4	**Apr.**	1	at	Pittsburgh	3-2
	27	at	Calgary	5-1		2	at	Carolina	0-1
	29	at	Vancouver	3-2 *		4	at	Atlanta	5-3
Jan.	2	at	NY Islanders	4-1		6		Atlanta	3-1
	6		NY Islanders	3-2		8		Boston	3-0
	8		Pittsburgh	6-2		9	at	NY Rangers	4-1

* – Overtime

Entry Draft
Selections 2000-1986

2000 Pick		1995 Pick		1991 Pick		1988 Pick	
28	Justin Williams	22	Brian Boucher	6	Peter Forsberg	14	Claude Boivin
94	Alexander Drozdetsky	48	Shane Kenny	50	Yanick Dupre	35	Pat Murray
171	Roman Cechmanek	100	Radovan Somik	86	Aris Brimanis	56	Craig Fisher
195	Colin Shields	132	Dimitri Tertyshny	94	Yanick Degrace	63	Dominic Roussel
210	John Eichelberger	135	Jamie Sokolsky	116	Clayton Norris	77	Scott Lagrand
227	Guillaume Lefebvre	152	Martin Spanhel	122	Dimitry Yushkevich	98	Edward O'Brien
259	Regan Kelly	178	Martin Streit	138	Andrei Lomakin	119	Gordie Frantti
287	Milan Kopecky	204	Ruslan Shafikov	182	James Bode	140	Jamie Cooke
		230	Jeff Lank	204	Josh Bartell	161	Johan Salle
1999				226	Neil Little	182	Brian Arthur
Pick		**1994**		248	John Porco	203	Jeff Dandretta
22	Maxime Ouellet	**Pick**				224	Scott Billey
119	Jeff Feniak	62	Artem Anisimov	**1990**		245	Drahomir Kadlec
160	Konstantin Rudenko	88	Adam Magarrell	**Pick**			
200	Pavel Kasparik	101	Sebastien Vallee	4	Mike Ricci	**1987**	
208	Vaclav Pletka	140	Alex Selivanov	25	Chris Simon	**Pick**	
224	David Nystrom	166	Colin Forbes	40	Mikael Renberg	20	Darren Rumble
		192	Derek Diener	44	Kimbi Daniels	30	Jeff Harding
1998		202	Ray Giroux	46	Bill Armstrong	62	Martin Hostak
Pick		218	Johan Hedberg	47	Chris Therien	83	Tomaz Eriksson
22	Simon Gagne	244	Andre Payette	52	Al Kinisky	104	Bill Gall
42	Jason Beckett	270	Jan Lipiansky	88	Dan Kordic	125	Tony Link
51	Ian Forbes			109	Viacheslav Butsayev	146	Mark Strapon
109	Jean-Philippe Morin	**1993**		151	Patrik Englund	167	Darryl Ingham
124	Francis Belanger	**Pick**		172	Toni Porkka	188	Bruce McDonald
139	Garrett Prosofsky	36	Janne Niinimaa	193	Greg Hanson	209	Steve Morrow
168	Antero Niittymaki	71	Vaclav Prospal	214	Tommy Soderstrom	230	Darius Rusnak
175	Cam Ondrik	77	Milos Holan	235	William Lund	251	Dale Roehl
195	Tomas Divisek	114	Vladimir Krechin				
222	Lubomir Pistek	140	Mike Crowley	**1989**		**1986**	
243	Petr Hubacek	166	Aaron Israel	**Pick**		**Pick**	
253	Bruno St. Jacques	192	Paul Healey	33	Greg Johnson	20	Kerry Huffman
258	Sergei Skrobot	218	Tripp Tracy	34	Patrik Juhlin	23	Jukka Seppo
		226	E.J. Bradley	72	Reid Simpson	28	Kent Hawley
1997		244	Jeff Staples	117	Niklas Eriksson	83	Mark Bar
Pick		270	Ken Hemenway	138	John Callahan Jr.	125	Steve Scheifele
30	Jean-Marc Pelletier			159	Sverre Sears	146	Sami Wahlsten
50	Pat Kavanagh	**1992**		180	Glen Wisser	167	Murray Baron
62	Kris Mallette	**Pick**		201	Al Kummu	188	Blaine Rude
103	Mikhail Chernov	7	Ryan Sittler	222	Matt Brait	209	Shaun Sabol
158	Jordon Flodell	15	Jason Bowen	243	James Pollio	230	Brett Lawrence
164	Todd Fedoruk	31	Denis Metlyuk			251	Daniel Stephano
214	Marko Kauppinen	103	Vladislav Buljin				
240	Par Styf	127	Roman Zolotov				
		151	Kirk Daubenspeck				
1996		175	Claude Jutras				
Pick		199	Jonas Hakansson				
15	Dainius Zubrus	223	Chris Herperger				
64	Chester Gallant	247	Patrice Paquin				
124	Per-Ragnar Bergqvist						
133	Jesse Boulerice						
187	Roman Malov						
213	Jeff Milleker						

Coach

RAMSAY, CRAIG
Coach, Philadelphia Flyers. Born in Weston, Ont., March 17, 1951.

On June 8, 2000, the Philadelphia Flyers named Craig Ramsay head coach. He is the 13th head coach in Flyers' history. Ramsay had taken over the club on February 20, 2000, when he replaced Roger Neilson, who left the team to seek treatment for multiple myeloma. Over the last 25 games of the 1999-2000 season, Ramsay guided the Flyers to a 16-8-1 record as the team finished first in the Eastern Conference. He previously served as interim head coach for the Flyers for two games (March 21 and 22, 1999) when Neilson served a league-imposed suspension. (The Flyers won both games.)

Ramsay originally joined the Flyers as an assistant coach under Roger Neilson on July 7, 1998. He has been a hockey disciple of Neilson since his playing days with the Peterborough Petes (1967-68 through 1970-71) of the Ontario Hockey Association. Ramsay spent two seasons (1993-94 and 1994-95) with the Florida Panthers as an associate coach under Neilson.

A 14-year NHL veteran (1971-72 through 1984-85, all with the Buffalo Sabres), Ramsay spent eight seasons (1985-86 through 1992-93) in the Sabres organization after his playing days. He also served as an assistant coach for the Ottawa Senators for two seasons (1996-97 and 1997-98) and as a scout for the Dallas Stars during the 1995-96 season.

Craig and his wife, Susan, have three sons, Travis, Jad and Brendon, and a daughter, Summer.

Coaching Record

Season	Team	Regular Season Games	W	L	T	%	Playoffs Games	W	L	%
1986-87	Buffalo (NHL)	21	4	15	2	.238	....	....	....	....
	NHL Totals	21	4	15	2	.238	....	....	....	....

Posted a 16-8-1 regular-season record and an 11-7 playoff record as interim coach after Roger Neilson was sidelined for treatment of bone-marrow cancer on February 20, 2000. All games are credited to Neilson's coaching record.

Club Directory

First Union Center

Philadelphia Flyers
First Union Center
3601 South Broad Street
Philadelphia, PA 19148
Phone **215/465-4500**
PR FAX 215/389-9403
www.philadelphiaflyers.com
Capacity: 19,519

Executive Management
Chairman	Ed Snider
Limited Partners	Pat Croce, Jay Snider, Sylvan and Fran Tobin
President and General Manager	Bob Clarke
Chairman of the Board, Emeritus	Joe Scott
Executive Vice President and Chief Operating Officer	Ron Ryan
Executive Vice President	Keith Allen
Governor	Ed Snider
Alternate Governors	Bob Clarke, Ron Ryan, Phil Weinberg
Executive Assistant	Kathy Nasevich
Receptionist	Maureen McGuckin

Hockey Club Personnel
Assistant General Manager	Paul Holmgren
Head Coach	Craig Ramsay
Assistant Coach	Bill Barber
Assistant Coach	Mike Stothers
Goaltending Coach	Rejean Lemelin
Skating Coach	David Roy
Chief Scout	Dennis Patterson
Scouting Staff	Serge Boudreault, John Chapman, Inge Hammarstrom, Simon Nolet, Chris Pryor, Vaclav Slansky, Evgeny Zimin
Pro Scouts	Ron Hextall, Al Hill
Assistant to the President	Barry Hanrahan
Video Coordinator	Steve Romanowski
Scouting Information Coordinator	Bryan Hardenbergh
Massage Therapist	Tom D'Ancona
Executive Assistant	Dianna Taylor
Receptionist	Judy DiCinti

Medical/Training Staff
Team Physicians	Arthur Bartolozzi, M.D.; Jeff Hartzell, M.D.; Gary Dorshimer, M.D.; Michael Weinik, D.O.; Guy Lanzi, D.M.D.
Athletic Trainer	John Worley
Strength and Conditioning Instructor	Jim McCrossin
Head Equipment Manager	Jim Evers
Equipment Managers	Anthony Oratorio, Harry Bricker, Luke Clarke
Training Center Maintenance	Tim Tocci

Public Relations Department
Director of Public Relations	Zack Hill
Director of Publications	Steve Majewski
Director of Fan Services	Joe Kadlec
Director of Community Relations	Linda Panasci
Director of Youth Hockey and Fan Development	Eric Turner
Manager of Game Operations and Special Events	Linda Held
Assistant Director of Public Relations	Jill Lipson
Asst. Dir. of Youth Hockey and Fan Development	Melissa Wilson
Archivist	Kerrianne Farrelly
Public Relations Assistant	Kristin Lewandowski

Sales/Marketing Department
Vice President, Sales	Jack Betson
Vice President, Sales and Marketing	Kathi Gillin
Ticket Manager	Cecilia Baker
Ticket Office Administration	Joan Kadlec
Manager, Sales and Services	Nicole Allison
Marketing Assistant	Kevin Morley
Assistant Manager, Sales and Services	Diane Smith
Ticket Office Assistants	Pat Piazza, Lisa Albertson, Linda DiTommaso
Receptionist	Debbie Brown

Finance Department
Director of Finance	Dave Jablonski
Controller	Lisa Cataldo
Payroll Accountant	Susan Schaffer
Accounts Payable Manager	Marilyn Trout

Advertising Sales Department
Vice President, Sales	Joe Croce
Administrative Assistant	Donna Schroeder
Director, Advertising Sales	Jeffrey Kirk
General Sales Manager	Brian Monihan
National Sales Manager	Bill Drolet
Senior Account Executive	Joe Watson
Account Executives	Sean Baedke, Nick Battista, Mike Garrity, Robert Kasilowski, Bo Koelle, Ray Lyons, Tanya Orliw, Chris Pezzello, Steve Rex, Vince Santroni
Sponsorship Manager	Maura Hood
Manager of Client Services	Thea Vogel
Senior Account Coordinator	Colleen Molloy
Account Coordinators	Shannan Reed, Kimberly Windt
Advertising Services Coordinator	Jimmy Dunk
Director of Premium Seating	Rick Campbell
Financial Project Manager	Randy Mintz
Sales Executives	Chris Genther, Colleen Kearns, Pete Seelaus

Broadcast Department
TV Play-by-Play, Analyst, Color Commentary	Jim Jackson, Gary Dornhoefer, Steve Coates
Radio Play-by-Play, Color Commentary	Tim Saunders, Brian Propp
Executive Producer/Director of Broadcasting	Bryan Cooper
Associate Producer	Jennifer Roman
Director, Flyers Game Operations	Brian Mantai
Public Address Announcer	Lou Nolan
TV Rightsholders	Comcast SportsNet, UPN-57 WPSG-TV
Radio Rightsholder	SportsRadio 610 WIP (610 AM)

Flyers Wives Charities
Executive Director	Fran Tobin
Director	Rita Johanson
Event Coordinators	Laurie Mellon, Susan Wechsler

Phoenix Coyotes

1999-2000 Results: 39w-35L-8T 90PTS. Third, Pacific Division

2000-01 Schedule

Oct.	Thu.	5	St. Louis	Fri.	12	at Toronto
	Sat.	7	Minnesota	Sat.	13	at Montreal
	Thu.	12	at San Jose	Mon.	15	St. Louis
	Sat.	14	Philadelphia	Wed.	17	Pittsburgh
	Sun.	15	at Los Angeles*	Fri.	19	at Anaheim
	Wed.	18	Florida	Sun.	21	Dallas
	Sat.	21	at Vancouver	Tue.	23	at Calgary
	Sun.	22	at Edmonton	Wed.	24	at Vancouver
	Tue.	24	at Calgary	Fri.	26	at Edmonton
	Fri.	27	at Dallas	Mon.	29	Nashville
	Sat.	28	Los Angeles	**Feb.** Thu.	1	Anaheim
	Mon.	30	at Colorado	Wed.	7	Carolina
Nov.	Wed.	1	at Anaheim	Fri.	9	Edmonton
	Fri.	3	Dallas	Sun.	11	Chicago
	Tue.	7	at Los Angeles	Tue.	13	at Tampa Bay
	Wed.	8	Detroit	Wed.	14	at Florida
	Sat.	11	at Columbus	Fri.	16	at Carolina
	Sun.	12	at NY Rangers	Sun.	18	Calgary
	Tue.	14	at Washington	Wed.	21	Columbus
	Thu.	16	Colorado	Fri.	23	at Buffalo
	Sat.	18	Anaheim	Sun.	25	at Detroit*
	Tue.	21	Chicago	Tue.	27	at Boston
	Sat.	25	at St. Louis	Wed.	28	at Columbus
	Sun.	26	at Philadelphia	**Mar.** Fri.	2	Detroit
	Wed.	29	at Colorado	Sun.	4	Colorado
	Thu.	30	Minnesota	Tue.	6	Nashville
Dec.	Sat.	2	Dallas	Thu.	8	Vancouver
	Wed.	6	Vancouver	Sat.	10	Montreal*
	Sun.	10	Columbus	Wed.	14	New Jersey
	Thu.	14	Tampa Bay	Fri.	16	at Dallas
	Sat.	16	San Jose	Sat.	17	at Nashville
	Wed.	20	Calgary	Mon.	19	at Los Angeles
	Fri.	22	Atlanta	Wed.	21	Ottawa
	Wed.	27	at Chicago	Sat.	24	Edmonton
	Fri.	29	at Minnesota	Sun.	25	NY Islanders
	Sat.	30	at St. Louis	Wed.	28	at Minnesota
Jan.	Mon.	1	San Jose	Thu.	29	at Nashville
	Thu.	4	NY Rangers	Sat.	31	San Jose
	Sat.	6	at NY Islanders	**Apr.** Tue.	3	Los Angeles
	Sun.	7	at New Jersey	Thu.	5	at San Jose
	Tue.	9	at Detroit	Fri.	6	at Anaheim

* Denotes afternoon game.

Franchise date: June 22, 1979
Transferred from Winnipeg to Phoenix,
July 1, 1996

**PACIFIC
DIVISION**

**22nd
NHL
Season**

Only Thomas Steen has played more games for the Phoenix Coyotes/Winnipeg Jets than Teppo Numminen. Numminen, who has spent his entire 11-year career with the club, holds the franchise record for points and assists by a defenseman.

Year-by-Year Record

Season	GP	Home			Road			Overall					Pts.	Finished		Playoff Result
		W	L	T	W	L	T	W	L	T	GF	GA				
1999-2000	82	22	17	2	17	18	6	39	35	8	232	228	90	3rd,	Pacific Div.	Lost Conf. Quarter-Final
1998-99	82	23	13	5	16	18	7	39	31	12	205	197	90	2nd,	Pacific Div.	Lost Conf. Quarter-Final
1997-98	82	19	16	6	16	19	6	35	35	12	224	227	82	4th,	Central Div.	Lost Conf. Quarter-Final
1996-97	82	15	19	7	23	18	0	38	37	7	240	243	83	3rd,	Central Div.	Lost Conf. Quarter-Final
1995-96*	82	22	16	3	14	24	3	36	40	6	275	291	78	5th,	Central Div.	Lost Conf. Quarter-Final
1994-95*	48	10	10	4	6	15	3	16	25	7	157	177	39	6th,	Central Div.	Out of Playoffs
1993-94*	84	15	23	4	9	28	5	24	51	9	245	344	57	6th,	Central Div.	Out of Playoffs
1992-93*	84	23	16	3	17	21	4	40	37	7	322	320	87	4th,	Smythe Div.	Lost Div. Semi-Final
1991-92*	80	20	14	6	13	18	9	33	32	15	251	244	81	4th,	Smythe Div.	Lost Div. Semi-Final
1990-91*	80	17	18	5	9	25	6	26	43	11	260	288	63	5th,	Smythe Div.	Out of Playoffs
1989-90*	80	22	13	5	15	19	6	37	32	11	298	290	85	3rd,	Smythe Div.	Lost Div. Semi-Final
1988-89*	80	17	18	5	9	24	7	26	42	12	300	355	64	5th,	Smythe Div.	Out of Playoffs
1987-88*	80	20	14	6	13	22	5	33	36	11	292	310	77	3rd,	Smythe Div.	Lost Div. Semi-Final
1986-87*	80	25	12	3	15	20	5	40	32	8	279	271	88	3rd,	Smythe Div.	Lost Div. Final
1985-86*	80	18	19	3	8	28	4	26	47	7	295	372	59	4th,	Smythe Div.	Lost Div. Semi-Final
1984-85*	80	21	13	6	22	14	4	43	27	10	358	332	96	2nd,	Smythe Div.	Lost Div. Final
1983-84*	80	17	15	8	14	23	3	31	38	11	340	374	73	4th,	Smythe Div.	Lost Div. Semi-Final
1982-83*	80	22	16	2	11	23	6	33	39	8	311	333	74	4th,	Smythe Div.	Lost Div. Semi-Final
1981-82*	80	18	13	9	15	20	5	33	33	14	319	332	80	2nd,	Norris Div.	Lost Div. Semi-Final
1980-81*	80	7	25	8	2	32	6	9	57	14	246	400	32	6th,	Smythe Div.	Out of Playoffs
1979-80*	80	13	19	8	7	30	3	20	49	11	214	314	51	5th,	Smythe Div.	Out of Playoffs

* Winnipeg Jets

2000-01 Player Personnel

FORWARDS	HT	WT	S	Place of Birth	Date	1999-00 Club
ABID, Ramzi	6-2	210	L	Montreal, Que.	3/24/80	Acadie-Bathurst-Halifax
ALATALO, Mika	6-0	202	L	Oulu, Finland	6/11/71	Phoenix
AUDET, Philippe	6-2	202	L	Ottawa, Ont.	6/4/77	Cincinnati Ducks-Springfield
BRIERE, Daniel	5-10	181	R	Gatineau, Que.	10/6/77	Phoenix-Springfield
DeBRUSK, Louie	6-2	238	L	Cambridge, Ont.	3/19/71	Phoenix
DOAN, Shane	6-2	218	R	Halkirk, Alta.	10/10/76	Phoenix
GREEN, Travis	6-2	200	R	Castlegar, B.C.	12/20/70	Phoenix
HANSEN, Tavis	6-1	205	R	Prince Albert, Sask.	6/17/75	Phoenix-Springfield
HEALEY, Eric	5-11	196	L	Hull, MA	1/20/75	Springfield
JUNEAU, Joe	6-0	195	L	Pont-Rouge, Que.	1/5/68	Ottawa
LETOWSKI, Trevor	5-10	176	R	Thunder Bay, Ont.	4/5/77	Phoenix
MAY, Brad	6-1	210	L	Toronto, Ont.	11/29/71	Vancouver
MILLS, Craig	6-0	190	R	Toronto, Ont.	8/27/76	Springfield
ROENICK, Jeremy	6-0	207	R	Boston, MA	1/17/70	Phoenix
SMITH, Wyatt	5-11	208	L	Thief River Falls, MN	2/13/77	Phoenix-Springfield
SULLIVAN, Mike	6-2	201	L	Marshfield, MA	2/27/68	Phoenix
TKACHUK, Keith	6-2	225	L	Melrose, MA	3/28/72	Phoenix
TRUDEL, Jean-Guy	5-11	202	L	Sudbury, Ont.	10/18/75	Phoenix-Springfield
WILSON, Landon	6-2	216	R	St. Louis, MO	3/13/75	Boston-Providence Bruins
YLONEN, Juha	6-1	189	L	Helsinki, Finland	2/13/72	Phoenix

DEFENSEMEN	HT	WT	S	Place of Birth	Date	1999-00 Club
BOUCHARD, Joel	6-0	202	L	Montreal, Que.	1/23/74	Nashville-Dallas
CARNEY, Keith	6-2	211	L	Providence, RI	2/3/70	Phoenix
CULLEN, David	6-2	209	R	St. Catharines, Ont.	12/30/76	Springfield
HOCKING, Justin	6-4	215	R	Stettler, Alta.	1/9/74	St. John's Leafs
JOSEPH, Chris	6-3	212	R	Burnaby, B.C.	9/10/69	Vancouver-Phoenix
LEROUX, Francois	6-6	247	L	Ste-Adele, Que.	4/18/70	Springfield
LUMME, Jyrki	6-1	209	L	Tampere, Finland	7/16/66	Phoenix
MacINTYRE, Dave	5-11	190	L	New Glascow, N.S.	10/20/68	JyP Jyvaskyla
NECKAR, Stanislav	6-1	207	L	Ceske Budejovice, Czech.	12/22/75	Phoenix
NUMMINEN, Teppo	6-2	199	R	Tampere, Finland	7/3/68	Phoenix
SAFRONOV, Kirill	6-2	209	L	Leningrad, USSR	2/26/81	Quebec Remparts
SCHNABEL, Robert	6-6	234	L	Prague, Czech.	11/10/78	Springfield
SUCHY, Radoslav	6-1	185	L	Kezmarok, Czech.	4/7/76	Phoenix-Springfield
VAANANEN, Ossi	6-4	205	L	Vantaa, Finland	8/18/80	Jokerit Helsinki

GOALTENDERS	HT	WT	C	Place of Birth	Date	1999-00 Club
DESROCHERS, Patrick	6-4	207	L	Penetanguishene, Ont.	10/27/79	Springfield
ESCHE, Robert	6-1	200	L	Utica, NY	1/22/78	Phx-Houston-Springfield
KHABIBULIN, Nikolai	6-1	195	L	Sverdlovsk, USSR	1/13/73	Long Beach

Coach

FRANCIS, BOB

Coach, Phoenix Coyotes. Born in North Battleford, Sask., December 5, 1958.

The Phoenix Coyotes named Bob Francis as the team's new head coach on June 16, 1999. Francis became the 14th Head Coach in franchise history and the third since moving to Phoenix in 1996.

Francis joined the Coyotes after two successful seasons as an assistant coach with the Boston Bruins. The son of former NHL great Emile Francis joined the Bruins as an assistant on June 27, 1997. He had previously spent two seasons in the Boston organization as head coach of the Bruins' AHL affiliate in Providence.

Francis began his coaching career with the Calgary Flames organization in the 1986-87 season, first as a player/assistant coach with Calgary's IHL affiliate in Salt Lake City. Francis helped guide the Golden Eagles to the IHL championship, winning the Turner Cup that season and successfully defending its title the following year with Francis serving as a full-time assistant coach. In 1989-90, Francis became the Golden Eagles' head coach and held that position for four seasons. The highlight of his coaching career at Salt Lake City was a 50-win season during the 1990-91 campaign. When Calgary moved their development team to Saint John (AHL) in 1993-94, Francis moved as well and served as their head coach before joining Providence.

Before his move to the coaching ranks, Francis played four years of college hockey at the University of New Hampshire (ECAC). Francis spent most of his professional career at the minor-league level though he did play 14 NHL games with Detroit during the 1982-83 season.

Coaching Record

		Regular Season					Playoffs			
Season	Team	Games	W	L	T	%	Games	W	L	%
1989-90	Salt Lake (IHL)	82	37	36	9	.506	10	5	5	.500
1990-91	Salt Lake (IHL)	83	50	28	5	.633	4	0	4	.000
1991-92	Salt Lake (IHL)	82	33	40	9	.457	5	1	4	.200
1992-93	Salt Lake (IHL)	82	38	39	5	.494	....	....	....	....
1993-94	Saint John (AHL)	80	37	33	10	.512	7	3	4	.429
1994-95	Saint John (AHL)	80	27	40	13	.419	5	1	4	.200
1995-96	Providence (AHL)	80	30	40	10	.438	4	1	3	.250
1996-97	Providence (AHL)	80	35	40	5	.469	10	4	6	.400
1999-2000	**Phoenix (NHL)**	**82**	**39**	**35**	**8**	**.549•**	**5**	**1**	**4**	**.200**
	NHL Totals	**82**	**39**	**35**	**8**	**.549•**	**5**	**1**	**4**	**.200**

• Includes points from regulation ties

1999-2000 Scoring

* – rookie

Regular Season

Pos	#	Player	Team	GP	G	A	Pts	+/–	PIM	PP	SH	GW	GT	S	%
C	97	Jeremy Roenick	PHX	75	34	44	78	11	102	6	3	12	1	192	17.7
R	19	Shane Doan	PHX	81	26	25	51	6	66	1	1	4	0	221	11.8
C	39	Travis Green	PHX	78	25	21	46	–4	45	6	0	2	1	157	15.9
L	17	Greg Adams	PHX	69	19	27	46	–1	14	5	0	0	0	129	14.7
R	11	Dallas Drake	PHX	79	15	30	45	11	62	0	2	5	0	127	11.8
L	7	Keith Tkachuk	PHX	50	22	21	43	7	82	5	1	1	0	183	12.0
D	27	Teppo Numminen	PHX	79	8	34	42	21	16	2	0	2	0	126	6.3
D	21	Jyrki Lumme	PHX	74	8	32	40	9	44	4	0	3	0	142	5.6
C	10	* Trevor Letowski	PHX	82	19	20	39	2	20	3	4	3	0	125	15.2
R	20	Mikael Renberg	PHI	62	8	21	29	–1	30	3	0	1	0	106	7.5
			PHX	10	2	4	6	0	2	0	0	0	0	16	12.5
			TOTAL	72	10	25	35	–1	32	3	0	1	0	122	8.2
C	36	Juha Ylonen	PHX	76	6	23	29	–6	12	0	1	1	0	82	7.3
L	18	Mika Alatalo	PHX	82	10	17	27	–3	36	1	0	1	0	107	9.3
D	3	Keith Carney	PHX	82	4	20	24	11	87	0	0	1	0	73	5.5
D	4	Lyle Odelein	N.J	57	1	15	16	–10	104	0	0	1	0	59	1.7
			PHX	16	1	7	8	1	19	1	0	0	0	30	3.3
			TOTAL	73	2	22	24	–9	123	1	0	1	0	89	2.2
L	26	Mike Sullivan	PHX	79	5	10	15	–4	10	0	2	1	0	59	8.5
C	12	Benoit Hogue	PHX	27	3	10	13	–1	10	0	0	0	0	39	7.7
D	23	Chris Joseph	VAN	38	2	9	11	–4	6	1	0	0	0	73	2.7
			PHX	9	0	0	0	–5	0	0	0	0	0	13	0.0
			TOTAL	47	2	9	11	–9	6	1	0	0	0	86	2.3
D	24	Stan Neckar	PHX	66	2	8	10	1	36	0	0	0	0	34	5.9
L	29	Louie Debrusk	PHX	61	4	3	7	1	78	0	0	0	0	24	16.7
D	33	J.J. Daigneault	PHX	53	1	6	7	–16	22	0	0	0	0	44	2.3
D	15	* Radoslav Suchy	PHX	60	0	6	6	2	16	0	0	0	0	36	0.0
C	8	Daniel Briere	PHX	13	1	1	2	0	0	0	0	0	1	9	11.1
R	20	David Oliver	PHX	9	1	0	1	0	2	1	0	0	0	6	16.7
L	62	* Jean-Guy Trudel	PHX	1	0	0	0	–1	0	0	0	0	0	0	0.0
C	64	* Wyatt Smith	PHX	2	0	0	0	–2	0	0	0	0	0	0	0.0
L	70	* Kevin Sawyer	PHX	3	0	0	0	1	12	0	0	0	0	0	0.0
C	14	* Tavis Hansen	PHX	5	0	0	0	0	0	0	0	0	0	2	0.0
G	42	* Robert Esche	PHX	8	0	0	0	0	4	0	0	0	0	1	0.0
G	31	Bob Essensa	PHX	30	0	0	0	0	0	0	0	0	0	0	0.0
G	1	Sean Burke	FLA	7	0	0	0	0	2	0	0	0	0	0	0.0
			PHX	35	0	0	0	0	10	0	0	0	0	0	0.0
			TOTAL	42	0	0	0	0	12	0	0	0	0	0	0.0

Goaltending

No.	Goaltender	GPI	Mins	Avg	W	L	T	EN	SO	GA	SA	S%
30	Mikhail Shtalenkov	15	904	2.39	7	6	2	3	2	36	370	.903
1	Sean Burke	35	2074	2.55	17	14	3	1	3	88	1022	.914
31	Bob Essensa	30	1573	2.78	13	10	3	3	1	73	719	.898
42	* Robert Esche	8	408	3.38	2	5	0	1	0	23	215	.893
	Totals	**82**	**4987**	**2.74**	**39**	**35**	**8**	**8**	**6**	**228**	**2334**	**.902**

Playoffs

Pos	#	Player	Team	GP	G	A	Pts	+/–	PIM	PP	SH	GW	OT	S	%
C	97	Jeremy Roenick	PHX	5	2	2	4	–4	10	1	0	0	0	14	14.3
C	39	Travis Green	PHX	5	2	1	3	0	2	0	0	0	0	8	25.0
R	19	Shane Doan	PHX	4	1	2	3	–2	8	1	0	0	0	7	14.3
C	12	Benoit Hogue	PHX	5	1	2	3	2	2	0	0	0	0	4	25.0
R	20	Mikael Renberg	PHX	5	1	2	3	–2	4	0	0	1	0	7	14.3
D	27	Teppo Numminen	PHX	5	1	1	2	1	0	0	0	0	0	12	8.3
L	7	Keith Tkachuk	PHX	5	1	1	2	–4	4	1	0	0	0	11	9.1
C	10	* Trevor Letowski	PHX	5	1	1	2	1	4	0	0	0	0	7	14.3
D	21	Jyrki Lumme	PHX	5	0	1	1	–2	2	0	0	0	0	9	0.0
R	11	Dallas Drake	PHX	5	0	1	1	1	4	0	0	0	0	8	0.0
L	26	Mike Sullivan	PHX	5	0	1	1	–1	0	0	0	0	0	4	0.0
D	15	* Radoslav Suchy	PHX	5	0	1	1	3	0	0	0	0	0	2	0.0
D	33	J.J. Daigneault	PHX	1	0	0	0	–1	0	0	0	0	0	2	0.0
C	36	Juha Ylonen	PHX	1	0	0	0	–1	0	0	0	0	0	1	0.0
C	8	Daniel Briere	PHX	1	0	0	0	0	0	0	0	0	0	1	0.0
L	29	Louie Debrusk	PHX	3	0	0	0	0	0	0	0	0	0	0	0.0
L	17	Greg Adams	PHX	5	0	0	0	–1	0	0	0	0	0	3	0.0
G	1	Sean Burke	PHX	5	0	0	0	0	0	0	0	0	0	0	0.0
D	4	Lyle Odelein	PHX	5	0	0	0	–3	16	0	0	0	0	9	0.0
L	18	Mika Alatalo	PHX	5	0	0	0	1	2	0	0	0	0	2	0.0
D	3	Keith Carney	PHX	5	0	0	0	–4	17	0	0	0	0	5	0.0
D	24	Stan Neckar	PHX	5	0	0	0	0	0	0	0	0	0	1	0.0

Goaltending

No.	Goaltender	GPI	Mins	Avg	W	L	EN	SO	GA	SA	S%
1	Sean Burke	5	296	3.24	1	4	1	0	16	167	.904
	Totals	**5**	**300**	**3.40**	**1**	**4**	**1**	**0**	**17**	**168**	**.899**

Coaching History

Tom McVie and Bill Sutherland, 1979-80; Tom McVie, Bill Sutherland and Mike Smith, 1980-81; Tom Watt, 1981-82, 1982-83; Tom Watt and Barry Long, 1983-84; Barry Long, 1984-85; Barry Long and John Ferguson, 1985-86; Dan Maloney, 1986-87, 1987-88; Dan Maloney and Rick Bowness, 1988-89; Bob Murdoch, 1989-90, 1990-91; John Paddock, 1991-92 to 1993-94; John Paddock and Terry Simpson, 1994-95; Terry Simpson, 1995-96; Don Hay, 1996-97; Jim Schoenfeld, 1997-98, 1998-99; Bob Francis, 1999-2000 to date.

Club Records

Team

(Figures in brackets for season records are games played; records for fewest points, wins, ties, losses, goals, goals against are for 70 or more games)

Most Points	96	1984-85 (80)
Most Wins	43	1984-85 (80)
Most Ties	15	1991-92 (80)
Most Losses	57	1980-81 (80)
Most Goals	358	1984-85 (80)
Most Goals Against	400	1980-81 (80)
Fewest Points	32	1980-81 (80)
Fewest Wins	9	1980-81 (80)
Fewest Ties	6	1995-96 (82)
Fewest Losses	27	1984-85 (80)
Fewest Goals	205	1998-99 (82)
Fewest Goals Against	197	1998-99 (82)

Longest Winning Streak

Overall	9	Mar. 8-27/85
Home	9	Dec. 27/92-Jan. 23/93
Away	8	Feb. 25-Apr. 6/85

Longest Undefeated Streak

Overall	14	Oct. 25-Nov. 28/98 (12 wins, 2 ties)
Home	11	Dec. 23/83-Feb. 5/84 (6 wins, 5 ties), Oct. 15-Dec. 20/98 (10 wins, 1 tie)
Away	9	Feb. 25-Apr. 7/85 (8 wins, 1 tie)

Longest Losing Streak

Overall	10	Nov. 30-Dec. 20/80, Feb. 6-25/94
Home	5	Twice
Away	13	Jan. 26-Apr. 14/94

Longest Winless Streak

Overall	*30	Oct. 19-Dec. 20/80 (23 losses, 7 ties)
Home	14	Oct. 19-Dec. 14/80 (9 losses, 5 ties)
Away	18	Oct. 10-Dec. 20/80 (16 losses, 2 ties)

Most Shutouts, Season	9	1998-99 (82)
Most PIM, Season	2,278	1987-88 (80)
Most Goals, Game	12	Feb. 25/85 (Wpg. 12 at NYR 5)

Individual

Most Seasons	14	Thomas Steen
Most Games	950	Thomas Steen
Most Goals, Career	379	Dale Hawerchuk
Most Assists, Career	553	Thomas Steen
Most Points, Career	929	Dale Hawerchuk (379G, 550A)
Most PIM, Career	1,400	Keith Tkachuk
Most Shutouts, Career	21	Nikolai Khabibulin
Longest Consecutive Games Streak	475	Dale Hawerchuk (Dec. 19/82-Dec. 10/88)
Most Goals, Season	76	Teemu Selanne (1992-93)
Most Assists, Season	79	Phil Housley (1992-93)
Most Points, Season	132	Teemu Selanne (1992-93; 76G, 56A)
Most PIM, Season	347	Tie Domi (1993-94)

Most Points, Defenseman, Season	97	Phil Housley (1992-93; 18G, 79A)
Most Points, Center, Season	130	Dale Hawerchuk (1984-85; 53G, 77A)
Most Points, Right Wing, Season	132	Teemu Selanne (1992-93; 76G, 56A)
Most Points, Left Wing, Season	98	Keith Tkachuk (1995-96; 50G, 48A)
Most Points, Rookie, Season	*132	Teemu Selanne (1992-93; 76G, 56A)
Most Shutouts, Season	8	Nikolai Khabibulin (1998-99)
Most Goals, Game	5	Willy Lindstrom (Mar. 2/82), Alexei Zhamnov (Apr. 1/95)
Most Assists, Game	5	Dale Hawerchuk (Mar. 6/84, Mar. 18/89, Mar. 4/90), Phil Housley (Jan. 18/93)
Most Points, Game	6	Willy Lindstrom (Mar. 2/82; 5G, 1A), Dale Hawerchuk (Dec. 14/83; 3G, 3A, Mar. 5/88; 2G, 4A, Mar. 18/89; 1G, 5A), Thomas Steen (Oct. 24/84; 2G, 4A), Ed Olczyk (Dec. 21/91; 2G, 4A)

* NHL Record.

Records include Winnipeg Jets, 1979-80 through 1995-96.

General Managers' History

John Ferguson, 1979-80 to 1987-88; John Ferguson and Mike Smith, 1988-89; Mike Smith, 1989-90 to 1992-93; Mike Smith and John Paddock, 1993-94; John Paddock, 1994-95, 1995-96; John Paddock and Bobby Smith, 1996-97; Bobby Smith, 1997-98 to date.

Captains' History

Lars-Erik Sjoberg, 1979-80; Morris Lukowich, 1980-81; Dave Christian, 1981-82; Dave Christian and Lucien DeBlois, 1982-83; Lucien DeBlois, 1983-84; Dale Hawerchuk, 1984-85 to 1988-89; Randy Carlyle, Dale Hawerchuk and Thomas Steen (tri-captains), 1989-90; Randy Carlyle and Thomas Steen (co-captains), 1990-91; Troy Murray, 1991-92; Troy Murray and Dean Kennedy, 1992-93; Dean Kennedy and Keith Tkachuk, 1993-94; Keith Tkachuk, 1994-95; Kris King, 1995-96; Keith Tkachuk, 1996-97 to date.

Winnipeg Jets Retired Numbers

9	Bobby Hull	1972-1980
25	Thomas Steen	1981-1995

All-time Record vs. Other Clubs

Regular Season

	At Home							On Road							Total						
	GP	W	L	T	GF	GA	PTS	GP	W	L	T	GF	GA	PTS	GP	W	L	T	GF	GA	PTS
Anaheim	16	8	7	1	54	48	17	16	5	10	1	42	48	12	32	13	17	2	96	96	29
Atlanta	1	1	0	0	4	2	2	1	1	0	0	3	2	2	2	2	0	0	7	4	4
Boston	28	12	14	2	98	100	26	27	4	20	3	83	122	11	55	16	34	5	181	222	37
Buffalo	27	13	12	2	86	88	28	27	2	20	5	64	118	9	54	15	32	7	150	206	37
Calgary	62	30	21	11	242	213	71	63	19	36	8	206	280	46	125	49	57	19	448	493	117
Carolina	29	13	14	2	105	108	28	26	8	12	6	82	99	22	55	21	26	8	187	207	50
Chicago	42	24	14	4	149	131	52	41	10	25	6	117	174	26	83	34	39	10	266	305	78
Colorado	32	12	14	6	121	119	30	33	14	15	4	120	121	32	65	26	29	10	241	240	62
Dallas	43	19	22	2	140	148	40	45	16	23	6	138	173	38	88	35	45	8	278	321	78
Detroit	41	16	14	11	131	131	43	43	17	21	5	152	173	39	84	33	35	16	283	304	82
Edmonton	63	25	34	4	256	286	54	64	19	41	4	214	286	43	127	44	75	8	470	572	97
Florida	7	2	3	2	16	22	6	5	3	2	0	13	17	6	12	5	5	2	29	39	12
Los Angeles	66	32	25	9	268	228	73	63	31	22	10	257	250	72	129	63	47	19	525	478	145
Montreal	26	9	11	6	86	101	24	27	3	23	1	61	134	7	53	12	34	7	147	235	31
Nashville	4	2	2	0	13	13	5	4	2	1	1	15	10	5	8	4	3	1	28	23	10
New Jersey	28	20	5	3	108	74	43	26	10	10	6	81	84	26	54	30	15	9	189	158	69
NY Islanders	27	10	14	3	86	97	23	28	7	13	8	86	110	22	55	17	27	11	172	207	45
NY Rangers	28	11	13	4	97	97	26	27	8	17	2	98	125	18	55	19	30	6	195	222	44
Ottawa	7	3	3	1	28	27	7	9	6	2	1	33	21	13	16	9	5	2	61	48	20
Philadelphia	27	10	15	2	81	96	22	28	7	21	0	77	124	14	55	17	36	2	158	220	36
Pittsburgh	27	11	13	3	98	95	25	28	8	20	0	79	118	16	55	19	33	3	177	213	41
St. Louis	43	20	17	6	140	139	46	42	12	20	10	119	152	34	85	32	37	16	259	291	80
San Jose	24	14	7	3	79	64	31	22	10	10	2	77	78	22	46	24	17	5	156	142	53
Tampa Bay	8	5	3	0	25	17	10	7	4	2	1	14	22	8	15	9	6	0	39	18	18
Toronto	38	20	12	6	157	137	46	40	21	17	2	153	143	44	78	41	29	8	310	280	90
Vancouver	61	30	23	8	234	223	68	64	18	37	9	186	241	45	125	48	60	17	420	464	113
Washington	28	14	7	7	104	99	35	27	6	18	3	76	114	16	55	20	25	10	180	213	51
Totals	**833**	**386**	**339**	**108**	**3006**	**2903**	**881**	**833**	**271**	**459**	**103**	**2657**	**3339**	**648**	**1666**	**657**	**798**	**211**	**5663**	**6242**	**1529**

Playoffs

	Series	W	L	GP	W	L	T	GF	GA	Last Mtg.	Round	Result
Anaheim	1	0	1	7	3	4	0	17	17	1997	CQF	L 3-4
Calgary	3	2	1	13	7	6	0	45	43	1987	DSF	W 4-2
Colorado	1	0	1	5	1	4	0	10	17	2000	CQF	L 1-4
Detroit	2	0	2	12	4	8	0	28	44	1998	CQF	L 2-4
Edmonton	6	0	6	26	4	22	0	75	120	1990	DSF	L 3-4
St. Louis	2	0	2	11	4	7	0	29	39	1999	CQF	L 3-4
Vancouver	2	0	2	13	5	8	0	34	50	1993	DSF	L 2-4
Totals	**17**	**2**	**15**	**87**	**28**	**59**	**0**	**238**	**330**			

Playoff Results 2000-1996

Year	Round	Opponent	Result	GF	GA
2000	CQF	Colorado	L 1-4	10	17
1999	CQF	St. Louis	L 3-4	16	19
1998	CQF	Detroit	L 2-4	18	24
1997	CQF	Anaheim	L 3-4	17	17
1996	CQF	Detroit	L 2-4	10	20

Abbreviations: Round: CQF – conference quarter-final; **DSF** – division semi-final.

Calgary totals include Atlanta Flames, 1979-80.
Colorado totals include Quebec, 1979-80 to 1994-95.
New Jersey totals include Colorado Rockies, 1979-80 to 1981-82.
Carolina totals include Hartford, 1979-80 to 1996-97.
Dallas totals include Minnesota North Stars, 1979-80 to 1992-93.

1999-2000 Results

Oct.	2	at St. Louis	2-1		10	at NY Islanders	2-2
	5	Anaheim	4-0		12	Pittsburgh	3-1
	8	at Chicago	3-3		15	Anaheim	4-2
	10	at NY Rangers	2-4		17	at Colorado	0-2
	11	at Buffalo	2-2		18	at Nashville	4-4
	14	Ottawa	4-3		20	Buffalo	2-1
	16	Boston	2-1		23	San Jose	3-2 *
	22	at Los Angeles	6-3		27	at Carolina	4-2
	23	Washington	2-2		28	at Washington	2-3 *
	26	at Edmonton	1-1		31	at Detroit	5-3
	28	at Vancouver	4-1	**Feb.**	1	at San Jose	1-0 *
	30	at Colorado	5-3		3	Dallas	0-2
	31	at Anaheim	3-0		9	Los Angeles	2-5
Nov.	3	at San Jose	3-6		12	Calgary	4-3
	5	Dallas	4-6		14	Detroit	1-3
	10	Edmonton	5-4 *		18	at Dallas	4-3
	12	Vancouver	2-3		20	Atlanta	4-2
	14	Los Angeles	2-3		22	at Montreal	0-1
	16	Calgary	2-1		23	at Toronto	3-5
	18	at Los Angeles	3-2		25	at Calgary	3-3
	20	Chicago	3-1		27	at Vancouver	1-2
	25	New Jersey	4-2	**Mar.**	1	Carolina	7-5
	26	Colorado	7-0		3	Dallas	1-4
	28	at Detroit	4-3		5	at Chicago	3-7
	30	at Nashville	6-3		7	at St. Louis	0-4
Dec.	2	Tampa Bay	3-1		9	NY Islanders	5-0
	4	Anaheim	2-3		11	Vancouver	5-0
	6	at Dallas	3-2		13	Philadelphia	1-4
	8	Florida	1-6		15	St. Louis	3-5
	11	at Pittsburgh	2-4		17	Nashville	3-4 *
	13	at Boston	3-2		21	Chicago	0-3
	16	at Philadelphia	3-5		23	Colorado	2-4
	19	San Jose	4-3		24	at San Jose	1-5
	21	St. Louis	0-6		26	at Anaheim	3-4 *
	22	at Anaheim	3-3		29	at Atlanta	3-2
	26	at Los Angeles	3-2 *		31	at Calgary	3-1
	28	NY Rangers	2-2	**Apr.**	1	at Edmonton	3-4 *
Jan.	1	Edmonton	4-5		3	Los Angeles	2-1
	4	at Detroit	5-2		5	Nashville	3-2
	6	at Ottawa	2-5		7	San Jose	1-3
	8	at New Jersey	3-4		9	at Dallas	2-2

* -- Overtime

Entry Draft
Selections 2000-1986

2000 Pick	1995 Pick	1991 Pick	1988 Pick
19 Krys Kolanos	7 Shane Doan	5 Aaron Ward	10 Teemu Selanne
53 Alexander Tatarinov	32 Marc Chouinard	49 Dmitri Filimonov	31 Russell Romaniuk
85 Ramzi Abid	34 Jason Doig	91 Juha Ylonen	52 Stephane Beauregard
160 Nate Kiser	67 Brad Isbister	99 Yan Kaminsky	73 Brian Hunt
186 Brent Gauvreau	84 Justin Kurtz	115 Jeff Sebastian	94 Tony Joseph
217 Igor Samoilov	121 Brian Elder	159 Jeff Ricciardi	101 Benoit Lebeau
249 Sami Venalainen	136 Sylvain Daigle	181 Sean Gauthier	115 Ronald Jones
281 Peter Fabus	162 Paul Traynor	203 Igor Ulanov	127 Markus Akerblom
	188 Jaroslav Obsut	225 Jason Jennings	136 Jukka Marttila
1999 **Pick**	189 Fredrik Loven	247 Sergei Sorokin	157 Mark Smith
15 Scott Kelman	214 Rob Deciantis		178 Mike Helber
19 Kirill Safronov		**1990** **Pick**	199 Pavel Kostichkin
53 Brad Ralph	**1994** **Pick**	19 Keith Tkachuk	220 Kevin Heise
71 Jason Jaspers	30 Deron Quint	35 Mike Muller	241 Kyle Galloway
116 Ryan Lauzon	56 Dorian Anneck	74 Roman Meluzin	
123 Preston Mizzi	58 Tavis Hansen	75 Scott Levins	**1987** **Pick**
168 Erik Lewerstrom	82 Steve Cheredaryk	77 Alexei Zhamnov	16 Bryan Marchment
234 Goran Bezina	108 Craig Mills	98 Craig Martin	37 Patrik Ericksson
262 Alexei Litvinenko	143 Steve Vezina	119 Daniel Jardemyr	79 Don McLennan
	146 Chris Kibermanis	140 John Lilley	96 Ken Gernander
1998 **Pick**	186 Ramil Saifullin	161 Henrik Andersson	100 Darrin Amundson
14 Patrick Desrochers	212 Henrik Smangs	182 Rauli Raitanen	121 Joe Harwell
43 Ossi Vaananen	238 Mike Mader	203 Mika Alatalo	142 Todd Hartje
73 Pat O'Leary	264 Jason Issel	224 Sergei Selyanin	163 Markku Kyllonen
100 Ryan VanBuskirk		245 Keith Morris	184 Jim Fernholz
115 Jay Leach	**1993** **Pick**		226 Roger Rougelot
116 Josh Blackburn	15 Mats Lindgren	**1989** **Pick**	247 Hans Goran Elo
129 Robert Schnabel	31 Scott Langkow	4 Stu Barnes	
160 Rickard Wallin	43 Alexei Budayev	25 Dan Ratushny	**1986** **Pick**
187 Erik Westrum	79 Ruslan Batyrshin	46 Jason Cirone	8 Pat Elynuik
214 Justin Hansen	93 Ravil Gusmanov	62 Kris Draper	29 Teppo Numminen
	119 Larry Courville	64 Mark Brownschidle	50 Esa Palosaari
1997 **Pick**	145 Michal Grosek	69 Allain Roy	71 Hannu Jarvenpaa
43 Juha Gustafsson	171 Martin Woods	109 Dan Bylsma	92 Craig Endean
96 Scott McCallum	197 Adrian Murray	130 Pekka Peltola	113 Robertson Bateman
123 Curtis Suter	217 Vladimir Potapov	131 Doug Evans	155 Frank Furlan
151 Robert Francz	223 Ilja Stashenkov	151 Jim Solly	176 Mark Green
207 Alexander Andreyev	228 Harijs Vitolinsh	172 Stephane Gauvin	197 John Blue
233 Wyatt Smith	285 Russell Hewson	193 Joe Larson	218 Matt Cote
		214 Bradley Podiak	239 Arto Blomsten
1996 **Pick**	**1992** **Pick**	235 Evgeny Davydov	
11 Dan Focht	17 Sergei Bautin	240 Sergei Kharin	
24 Daniel Briere	27 Boris Mironov		
62 Per-Anton Lundstrom	60 Jeremy Stevenson		
119 Richard Lintner	84 Mark Visheau		
139 Robert Esche	132 Alexander Alexeyev		
174 Trevor Letowski	155 Artur Oktyabrev		
200 Nicholas Lent	156 Andrei Raisky		
226 Marc-Etienne Hubert	204 Nikolai Khabibulin		
	228 Yevgeny Garanin		
	229 Teemu Numminen		
	252 Andrei Karpovstev		
	254 Ivan Vologzhaninov		

General Manager

SMITH, BOBBY
General Manager, Phoenix Coyotes.
Born in North Sydney, N.S., February 12, 1958.

After 15 outstanding seasons as a National Hockey League player, including eight years as the vice president of the NHL Players' Association, Bobby Smith became the Phoenix Coyotes' first executive vice president of hockey operations on May 21, 1996.

A product of Ottawa's minor hockey system, in 1978 Smith was named Canadian Major Junior player of the year and was drafted by the Minnesota North Stars first overall in the NHL Entry Draft. A year later, he was named the Calder Trophy winner as the NHL's top rookie after scoring 30 goals and 74 points in his first season. Smith went on to have a remarkable NHL career with Minnesota and Montreal. Smith played in 1,077 games with the North Stars and Canadiens recording (357-679) 1,036 points. He led the North Stars in scoring three of his first four years with the club. His finest season with Minnesota came during the 1981-82 campaign when Smith achieved career highs in games played (80), goals (43), assists (71) and points (114). He was one of three players who played on both of Minnesota's Stanley Cup Finalist teams in 1981 and 1991. Following a trade to Montreal in 1983, Smith played seven seasons with the Canadiens, recording 70-plus points in five of those years. In 1986, he helped guide the Canadiens to a Stanley Cup victory over the Calgary Flames. Smith scored the Stanley Cup game-winning goal in a 4-3 win over Calgary. After 13 playoff seasons and 184 games with Minnesota and Montreal, Smith retired with 64 goals and 96 assists for 160 points, ranking him 12th on the NHL all-time playoff point leaders list. Smith also played in four NHL All-Star Games (1981, 1982, 1989, 1991) during his career.

After retiring from hockey, Smith focused his energy on education and completed two degrees at the Curt Carlson School of Management at the University of Minnesota; a Bachelor of Science (in business) and a Masters of Business Administration.

Bobby and his wife Elizabeth along with their three children Ryan, Megan and Daniel reside in Scottsdale, AZ.

Club Directory

America West Arena

Phoenix Coyotes
ALLTEL Ice Den
9375 E. Bell Road
Scottsdale, AZ 85260
Phone **480/473-5600**
FAX 480/473-5699
Website: www.PhoenixCoyotes.com
Capacity: 16,210

CEO & Governor	Richard Burke
President & Alternate Governor	Shawn Hunter
General Manager & Alternate Governor	Bobby Smith
Senior Vice President/Chief Financial Officer	Mark Peterson
Executive Assistant to the President	Lisa Mardeusz
Executive Assistant, Hockey Operations	Lesa Guth

Hockey Operations

Assistant General Manager	Taylor Burke
Director of Hockey Operations	Laurence Gilman
Director of Player Personnel	Sean Coady
Director of Player Development	Gordie Roberts
Director of Amateur Scouting	Vaughn Karpan
Professional Scout	Tom Kurvers
Director of Hockey Information	Igor Kuperman
Head Coach	Bob Francis
Assistant Coach	Rick Bowness
Assistant Coach	TBA
Goaltending Coach	Benoit Allaire
Strength & Conditioning Coach	Stieg Theander
Amateur Scouts	Connie Broden, Blair Mackasey, Paul Coady, Evzen Slansky, Pelle Eklund, Boris Yemeljanov, Blair Reid, Paul Henry
Athletic Therapist	Gord Hart
Equipment Manager	Stan Wilson
Massage Therapist	Jukka Nieminen
Assistant Equipment Managers	Tony Silva, Kevin Smith
Video Coordinator	Steve Peters
Team Physician	Matt Maddox, D.O.
Team Dentists	Dr. Rick Lawson, Dr. Lawrence Emmott
Springfield Falcons (AHL) Head Coach	Marc Potvin
Springfield Falcons (AHL) Assistant Coach	Norm Maciver

Communications

Vice President of Media & Player Relations	Richard Nairn
Manager of Media Relations	Rick Braunstein
Publications & Media Relations Coordinator	Jeff Altstadter
Media Relations Interns	Tom Enders, Eric McGraw

Broadcasting

TV Play-by-Play	Doug McLeod
TV Color Commentator	Charlie Simmer
Radio Play-by-Play	Curt Keilback
Radio Color Commentator	Jim Johnson
Broadcast Coordinator	Graham Taylor

Business Development

Vice President of Business Operations	Joe Levy
Director of Suite Sales	Renee Tauer
Suite Sales Coordinator	Lisa Gonzalez
Website Coordinator	John Mellor

Community Relations

Manager of Community Relations/ Phoenix Coyotes Goals For Kids Foundation	Marcy Fileccia

Corporate Sales & Service

Director of Corporate Sales	Matt Stys
Manager of Corporate Sales	Kelly Staley
Senior Corporate Account Executive	Tara Pisciotta
Corporate Account Executives	Jason Levy, Amy Robertson
Corporate Account Coordinator	Justin Kemp

Fan Development

Director of Fan Development	Bruce Bielenberg

Finance & Administration

Controller	Joe Leibfried
Assistant Controller	Larry Silver
Payroll Administrator	Cheri Sedor

Marketing

Director of Marketing	Dave Groff
Game Operations Coordinator	Jen Town
Marketing Coordinator	Jason Shughart

Ticket Sales & Service

Director of Ticket Operations	Lori Blanche
Box Office Manager	Kevin Prebil
Box Office Assistant	Karen Sabo
Director of Ticket Sales	Jim Willits
Ticket Sales Manager	Brian Tollefson
Senior Account Executive	Scott Newhouse
Account Executives	John Allen, Randy Just , E.A. McDonough, Tiffany Rojas, Tom Schimpf
Senior Customer Service Representative	Brian Wilkinson
Customer Service Representatives	Cortney Guinn, Tudor Waddell

ALLTEL Ice Den

President, Coyotes Ice, LLC	Mike O'Hearn
Executive Director	Justin Maloof
Director of Administration	Mica Berroteran
Director of Facility Operations	Don Moffatt
Coordinator of Facility Operations	Scott Gruber
Director of Amateur Hockey	Keith Blase
Director of Programming/Skating	Julie Patterson
Manager, Coyotes Ice Sports	Kristen DeBenny

Team Information

Training Camp	Scottsdale, Arizona
Press Box Location	East Side of Arena
Cable Television Station	FOX SPORTS NET Arizona
Broadcast Television Stations	KTVK (Ch. 3), KASW (WB-61)
Radio Stations	KDKB 93.3 FM, KDUS 1060 AM

Pittsburgh Penguins

1999-2000 Results: 37w-37L-8T 88PTS. Third, Atlantic Division

Year-by-Year Record

Season	GP	Home W	L	T	Road W	L	T	Overall W	L	T	GF	GA	Pts.	Finished		Playoff Result
1999-2000	82	23	11	7	14	26	1	37	37	8	241	236	88	3rd,	Atlantic Div.	Lost Conf. Semi-Final
1998-99	82	21	10	10	17	20	4	38	30	14	242	225	90	3rd,	Atlantic Div.	Lost Conf. Semi-Final
1997-98	82	21	10	10	19	14	8	40	24	18	228	188	98	1st,	Northeast Div.	Lost Conf. Quarter-Final
1996-97	82	25	11	5	13	25	3	38	36	8	285	280	84	2nd,	Northeast Div.	Lost Conf. Quarter-Final
1995-96	82	32	9	0	17	20	4	49	29	4	362	284	102	1st,	Northeast Div.	Lost Conf. Championship
1994-95	48	18	5	1	11	11	2	29	16	3	181	158	61	2nd,	Northeast Div.	Lost Conf. Semi-Final
1993-94	84	25	9	8	19	18	5	44	27	13	299	285	101	1st,	Northeast Div.	Lost Conf. Quarter-Final
1992-93	84	32	6	4	24	15	3	56	21	7	367	268	119	1st,	Patrick Div.	Lost Div. Final
1991-92	**80**	**21**	**13**	**6**	**18**	**19**	**3**	**39**	**32**	**9**	**343**	**308**	**87**	**3rd,**	**Patrick Div.**	**Won Stanley Cup**
1990-91	**80**	**25**	**12**	**3**	**16**	**21**	**3**	**41**	**33**	**6**	**342**	**305**	**88**	**1st,**	**Patrick Div.**	**Won Stanley Cup**
1989-90	80	22	15	3	10	25	5	32	40	8	318	359	72	5th,	Patrick Div.	Out of Playoffs
1988-89	80	24	13	3	16	20	4	40	33	7	347	349	87	2nd,	Patrick Div.	Lost Div. Final
1987-88	80	22	12	6	14	23	3	36	35	9	319	316	81	6th,	Patrick Div.	Out of Playoffs
1986-87	80	19	15	6	11	23	6	30	38	12	297	290	72	5th,	Patrick Div.	Out of Playoffs
1985-86	80	20	15	5	14	23	3	34	38	8	313	305	76	5th,	Patrick Div.	Out of Playoffs
1984-85	80	17	20	3	7	31	2	24	51	5	276	385	53	6th,	Patrick Div.	Out of Playoffs
1983-84	80	7	29	4	9	29	2	16	58	6	254	390	38	6th,	Patrick Div.	Out of Playoffs
1982-83	80	14	22	4	4	31	5	18	53	9	257	394	45	6th,	Patrick Div.	Out of Playoffs
1981-82	80	21	11	8	10	25	5	31	36	13	310	337	75	4th,	Patrick Div.	Lost Div. Semi-Final
1980-81	80	21	16	3	9	21	10	30	37	13	302	345	73	3rd,	Norris Div.	Lost Prelim. Round
1979-80	80	20	13	7	10	24	6	30	37	13	251	303	73	3rd,	Norris Div.	Lost Prelim. Round
1978-79	80	23	12	5	13	19	8	36	31	13	281	279	85	2nd,	Norris Div.	Lost Quarter-Final
1977-78	80	16	15	9	9	22	9	25	37	18	254	321	68	4th,	Norris Div.	Out of Playoffs
1976-77	80	22	12	6	12	21	7	34	33	13	240	252	81	3rd,	Norris Div.	Lost Prelim. Round
1975-76	80	23	11	6	12	22	6	35	33	12	339	303	82	3rd,	Norris Div.	Lost Prelim. Round
1974-75	80	25	5	10	12	23	5	37	28	15	326	289	89	3rd,	Norris Div.	Lost Quarter-Final
1973-74	78	15	18	6	13	23	3	28	41	9	242	273	65	5th,	West Div.	Out of Playoffs
1972-73	78	24	11	4	8	26	5	32	37	9	257	265	73	5th,	West Div.	Out of Playoffs
1971-72	78	18	15	6	8	23	8	26	38	14	220	258	66	4th,	West Div.	Lost Quarter-Final
1970-71	78	18	12	9	3	25	11	21	37	20	221	240	62	6th,	West Div.	Out of Playoffs
1969-70	76	17	13	8	9	25	4	26	38	12	182	238	64	2nd,	West Div.	Lost Semi-Final
1968-69	76	12	20	6	8	25	5	20	45	11	189	252	51	5th,	West Div.	Out of Playoffs
1967-68	74	15	12	10	12	22	3	27	34	13	195	216	67	5th,	West Div.	Out of Playoffs

2000-01 Schedule

Oct. Sat. 7 Nashville (in Japan)
Sun. 8 at Nashville (in Japan)
Fri. 13 Tampa Bay
Sat. 14 NY Rangers
Wed. 18 Carolina
Thu. 19 at Ottawa
Sat. 21 Columbus
Wed. 25 Ottawa
Fri. 27 at NY Rangers
Sat. 28 New Jersey

Nov. Wed. 1 at San Jose
Fri. 3 at Vancouver
Sat. 4 at Calgary
Wed. 8 Philadelphia
Fri. 10 at New Jersey
Sat. 11 Edmonton
Mon. 13 at Colorado
Thu. 16 at St. Louis
Sat. 18 Atlanta
Wed. 22 Carolina
Fri. 24 at Philadelphia*
Sat. 25 Los Angeles
Tue. 28 at Boston

Dec. Fri. 1 at Buffalo
Sat. 2 Buffalo
Tue. 5 at Ottawa
Wed. 6 Boston
Sat. 9 at Toronto
Sun. 10 at Detroit
Wed. 13 Toronto
Fri. 15 Florida
Sat. 16 at Montreal
Wed. 20 at Florida
Thu. 21 at Tampa Bay
Sat. 23 Dallas
Tue. 26 at Buffalo
Wed. 27 Toronto
Sat. 30 Ottawa

Jan. Wed. 3 Washington
Fri. 5 Montreal

Mon. 8 at Washington
Tue. 9 at Boston
Fri. 12 NY Islanders
Sat. 13 at NY Islanders
Mon. 15 Anaheim*
Wed. 17 at Phoenix
Fri. 19 at Dallas
Sun. 21 at Chicago
Wed. 24 Montreal
Sat. 27 Atlanta
Tue. 30 at Atlanta
Wed. 31 Philadelphia

Feb. Wed. 7 Philadelphia
Sat. 10 New Jersey*
Sun. 11 at Minnesota*
Wed. 14 Minnesota
Fri. 16 at New Jersey
Sat. 17 at Columbus
Mon. 19 Colorado*
Wed. 21 Florida
Fri. 23 NY Rangers
Sun. 25 NY Islanders*
Wed. 28 at Montreal

Mar. Fri. 2 at NY Rangers
Sat. 3 at Washington
Wed. 7 Washington
Thu. 8 at Atlanta
Sat. 10 Calgary
Mon. 12 at NY Rangers
Wed. 14 NY Islanders
Fri. 16 at Florida
Sat. 17 at Tampa Bay
Tue. 20 Boston
Fri. 23 at Carolina
Sun. 25 at New Jersey*
Tue. 27 Buffalo
Thu. 29 Chicago
Sat. 31 St. Louis*

Apr. Mon. 2 at NY Islanders
Wed. 4 Tampa Bay
Sat. 7 at Philadelphia*
Sun. 8 at Carolina*

* Denotes afternoon game.

Franchise date: June 5, 1967

EASTERN
NHL CONFERENCE

34th
NHL
Season

ATLANTIC
DIVISION

Jean-Sebastein Aubin played 51 games in goal for the Penguins last season, the most by any rookie netminder in 1999-2000. His .914 save percentage ranked among the best in the NHL.

2000-01 Player Personnel

FORWARDS	HT	WT	S	Place of Birth	Date	1999-00 Club
BARNABY, Matthew	6-0	189	L	Ottawa, Ont.	5/4/73	Pittsburgh
BERANEK, Josef	6-2	195	L	Litvinov, Czech.	10/25/69	Edmonton-Pittsburgh
BONVIE, Dennis	5-11	205	R	Antigonish, N.S.	7/23/73	Pittsburgh-Wilkes-Barre
CORBET, Rene	6-0	195	L	Victoriaville, Que.	6/25/73	Calgary-Pittsburgh
CROZIER, Greg	6-3	200	L	Calgary, Alta.	7/6/76	Wilkes-Barre
DOME, Robert	6-0	210	L	Skalica, Czech.	1/29/79	Pittsburgh-Wilkes-Barre
FADRNY, Jan	6-0	182	R	Brno, Czech.	6/14/80	Brandon
GYORI, Dylan	5-11	190	L	Rimbey, Alta.	2/20/79	Wilkes-Barre-Richmond
HRDINA, Jan	6-0	200	R	Hradec Kralove, Czech.	2/5/76	Pittsburgh
JAGR, Jaromir	6-2	234	L	Kladno, Czech.	2/15/72	Pittsburgh
KOLKUNOV, Alexei	6-0	201	L	Belgorod, USSR	2/3/77	Wilkes-Barre
KOSTOPOULOS, Tom	6-0	205	R	Mississauga, Ont.	1/24/79	Wilkes-Barre
KOVALEV, Alexei	6-1	215	L	Togliatti, USSR	2/24/73	Pittsburgh
KRAFT, Milan	6-3	195	R	Plzen, Czech.	1/17/80	Prince Albert
LANG, Robert	6-2	216	R	Teplice, Czech.	12/19/70	Pittsburgh
MATHIEU, Alexandre	6-2	177	L	Repentigny, Que.	2/12/79	Wilkes-Barre
MELOCHE, Eric	5-11	195	R	Montreal, Que.	5/1/76	Ohio State
MORAN, Ian	6-0	206	R	Cleveland, OH	8/24/72	Pittsburgh
MOROZOV, Aleksey	6-1	196	L	Moscow, USSR	2/16/77	Pittsburgh
PETERSEN, Toby	5-10	196	L	Minneapolis, MN	10/27/78	Colorado College
PROTSENKO, Boris	5-11	192	R	Kiev, USSR	8/21/78	Wilkes-Barre
SIMICEK, Roman	6-3	210	L	Ostrava, Czech.	11/4/71	HPK Hameenlinna
SONNENBERG, Martin	6-0	184	L	Wetaskiwin, Alta.	1/23/78	Pittsburgh-Wilkes-Barre
STRAKA, Martin	5-9	176	L	Plzen, Czech.	9/3/72	Pittsburgh
TIBBETTS, Billy	6-2	215	R	Boston, MA	10/14/74	DID NOT PLAY
VEROT, Darcy	6-0	190	L	Radville, Sask.	7/13/76	Wheeling-Wilkes-Barre
ZEVAKHIN, Alexander	6-0	187	L	Perm, USSR	12/30/78	CSKA Moscow
DEFENSEMEN						
BOUGHNER, Bob	6-0	203	R	Windsor, Ont.	3/8/71	Nashville-Pittsburgh
BUTENSCHON, Sven	6-4	215	L	Itzehoe, West Germany	3/22/76	Pittsburgh-Wilkes-Barre
CULL, Trent	6-2	215	L	Brampton, Ont.	9/27/73	Springfield-Houston Aeros
FERENCE, Andrew	5-10	190	L	Edmonton, Alta.	3/17/79	Pittsburgh-Wilkes-Barre
JONSSON, Hans	6-1	202	L	Jarved, Sweden	8/2/73	Pittsburgh
KASPARAITIS, Darius	5-11	212	L	Elektrenai, USSR	10/16/72	Pittsburgh
KELLEHER, Chris	6-1	210	L	Cambridge, MA	3/23/75	Wilkes-Barre
LAUKKANEN, Janne	6-1	194	L	Lahti, Finland	3/19/70	Ottawa-Pittsburgh
MELICHAR, Josef	6-2	214	L	Ceske Budejovice, Czech.	1/20/79	Wilkes-Barre
MOORE, Mark	6-3	185	R	Windsor, Ont.	2/18/77	Harvard University
ROZSIVAL, Michal	6-1	208	R	Vlasim, Czech.	9/3/78	Pittsburgh
SLANEY, John	6-0	189	L	St. John's, Nfld.	2/2/72	Pittsburgh-Wilkes-Barre
SLEGR, Jiri	6-0	216	L	Jihlava, Czech.	5/30/71	Pittsburgh

GOALTENDERS	HT	WT	C	Place of Birth	Date	1999-00 Club
AUBIN, Jean-Sebastien	5-11	176	R	Montreal, Que.	7/17/77	Pittsburgh-Wilkes-Barre
CARON, Sebastian	6-1	160	L	Amqui, Que.	6/25/80	Rimouski Oceanic
HILLIER, Craig	6-1	183	L	Cole Harbour, N.S.	2/28/78	Wilkes-Barre-Johnstown-Toledo-Charlotte

Coach

HLINKA, IVAN

Coach, Pittsburgh Penguins. Born in Most, Czechoslovakia, January 26, 1950.

The Pittsburgh Penguins named Ivan Hlinka as the 19th head coach in team history on June 21, 2000. He becomes the 16th different person to hold the head coaching title. Hlinka first joined the Penguins coaching staff as an associate coach on February 20, 2000, and takes over the head coaching duties from Herb Brooks, who replaced Kevin Constantine behind the bench during the 1999-2000 season.

Before joining the Penguins, Hlinka served as head coach of the Czech Republic national team, and is generally credited with building the country's ice hockey program into one of the finest in the world today. While serving as head coach, Hlinka led the team to two world championships and three Olympic medals in the 1990s. The high point of Hlinka's international coaching career came when he led the 1998 Czech Olympic Team — featuring Penguins Jaromir Jagr, Robert Lang, Jiri Slegr, Martin Straka and Josef Beranek — to the country's first gold medal in hockey at the Winter Olympics in Nagano, Japan.

Hlinka began his professional playing career in 1969 with CHZ Litvinov in the Czech League, and quickly established himself as one of his country's top players. He also distinguished himself as a member of Czechoslovakia's national team during the 1970s and 1980s, playing in 11 World Championship tournaments and bringing home gold medals in 1972, 1976 and 1977. He also participated in the 1972 and 1976 Olympic Games, and was named the top forward at the 1976 Canada Cup tournament.

In 1981, Hlinka and fellow Czech Jiri Bubla made the transition to the NHL by joining the Vancouver Canucks. Hlinka returned to Europe in 1983 and finished out his playing career with EV Zug in the Swiss League from 1983 to 1985 before turning to coaching.

Coaching Record

		Regular Season					Playoffs			
Season	Team	Games	W	L	T	%	Games	W	L	%
1985-86	CHZ Litvinov (Czech)	34	20	10	4	.647	....	....	....	....
1987-88	CHZ Litvinov (Czech)	34	18	13	3	.632	....	....	....	....
1988-89	CHZ Litvinov (Czech)	34	13	15	6	.471	....	....	....	....
1989-90	EHC Frieburg (Germany)	28	2	23	3	.125	....	....	....	....

1999-2000 Scoring

* – rookie

Regular Season

Pos	#	Player	Team	GP	G	A	Pts	+/–	PIM	PP	SH	GW	GT	S	%
R	68	Jaromir Jagr	PIT	63	42	54	96	25	50	10	0	5	1	290	14.5
C	27	Alexei Kovalev	PIT	82	26	40	66	–3	94	9	2	4	1	254	10.2
C	20	Robert Lang	PIT	78	23	42	65	–9	14	13	0	5	1	142	16.2
C	82	Martin Straka	PIT	71	20	39	59	24	26	3	1	2	0	146	13.7
C	38	Jan Hrdina	PIT	70	13	33	46	13	43	3	0	1	0	84	15.5
R	95	Alexei Morozov	PIT	68	12	19	31	12	14	0	1	0	0	101	11.9
D	71	Jiri Slegr	PIT	74	11	20	31	20	82	0	0	2	1	144	7.6
R	14	Pat Falloon	EDM	33	5	13	18	6	4	1	0	0	0	51	9.8
			PIT	30	4	9	13	–2	10	0	0	0	0	41	9.8
			TOTAL	63	9	22	31	4	14	1	0	0	0	92	9.8
L	18	Josef Beranek	EDM	58	9	8	17	–6	39	3	0	1	0	107	8.4
			PIT	13	4	4	8	–6	18	1	0	0	0	32	12.5
			TOTAL	71	13	12	25	–12	57	4	0	1	0	139	9.4
R	36	Matthew Barnaby	PIT	64	12	12	24	3	197	0	0	3	0	80	15.0
R	44	Rob Brown	PIT	50	10	13	23	–13	10	4	0	3	0	73	13.7
C	29	Tyler Wright	PIT	50	12	10	22	4	45	0	0	1	0	68	17.6
D	28 *	Michal Rozsival	PIT	75	4	17	21	11	48	1	0	1	0	73	5.5
D	5	Janne Laukkanen	OTT	60	1	11	12	14	55	0	0	0	0	62	1.6
			PIT	11	1	7	8	3	12	1	0	0	0	19	5.3
			TOTAL	71	2	18	20	17	67	1	0	0	0	81	2.5
L	9	Rene Corbet	CGY	48	4	10	14	–7	60	0	0	0	0	100	4.0
			PIT	4	1	0	1	–4	0	1	0	0	0	9	11.1
			TOTAL	52	5	10	15	–11	60	1	0	0	0	109	4.6
D	11	Darius Kasparaitis	PIT	73	3	12	15	–12	146	1	0	1	0	76	3.9
D	8	Hans Jonsson	PIT	68	3	11	14	–5	12	0	1	1	0	49	6.1
D	24	Ian Moran	PIT	73	4	8	12	–10	28	0	0	0	0	58	6.9
D	6	Bob Boughner	NSH	62	2	4	6	–13	97	0	0	0	0	32	6.3
			PIT	11	1	0	1	2	69	1	0	1	0	8	12.5
			TOTAL	73	3	4	7	–11	166	1	0	1	0	40	7.5
C	59	Robert Dome	PIT	22	2	5	7	1	0	0	0	0	0	27	7.4
D	7 *	Andrew Ference	PIT	30	2	4	6	3	20	0	0	1	0	26	7.7
R	17	Tom Chorske	PIT	33	1	5	6	–2	2	0	0	0	0	14	7.1
D	34	Peter Popovic	PIT	54	1	5	6	–8	30	0	0	0	0	23	4.3
R	23	Stephen Leach	PIT	56	2	3	5	–11	24	0	0	1	0	41	4.9
D	32	John Slaney	PIT	29	1	4	5	–10	10	1	0	0	0	27	3.7
L	12	Martin Sonnenberg	PIT	14	1	2	3	0	0	1	0	0	0	19	5.3
D	3	Daniel Trebil	PIT	3	1	0	1	2	0	0	0	0	0	2	50.0
G	30 *	J-Sebastien Aubin	PIT	51	0	1	1	0	2	0	0	0	0	0	0.0
D	22	Sven Butenschon	PIT	3	0	0	0	3	0	0	0	0	0	2	0.0
G	1	Peter Skudra	PIT	20	0	0	0	0	0	0	0	0	0	0	0.0
R	16	Dennis Bonvie	PIT	28	0	0	0	–2	80	0	0	0	0	6	0.0
G	31	Ron Tugnutt	OTT	44	0	0	0	0	0	0	0	0	0	0	0.0
			PIT	7	0	0	0	0	0	0	0	0	0	0	0.0
			TOTAL	51	0	0	0	0	0	0	0	0	0	0	0.0

Goaltending

No.	Goaltender	GPI	Mins	Avg	W	L	T	EN	SO	GA	SA	S%
31	Ron Tugnutt	7	374	2.41	4	2	0	0	0	15	197	.924
30	* J-Sebastien Aubin	51	2789	2.58	23	21	3	3	2	120	1392	.914
1	Peter Skudra	20	922	3.12	5	7	3	2	1	48	374	.872
35	Tom Barrasso	18	870	3.17	5	7	2	2	1	46	386	.881
	Totals	**82**	**4984**	**2.84**	**37**	**37**	**8**	**7**	**4**	**236**	**2356**	**.900**

Playoffs

Pos	#	Player	Team	GP	G	A	Pts	+/–	PIM	PP	SH	GW	OT	S	%
R	68	Jaromir Jagr	PIT	11	8	8	16	5	6	2	0	4	1	42	19.0
C	38	Jan Hrdina	PIT	9	4	8	12	9	2	1	0	0	0	9	44.4
C	82	Martin Straka	PIT	11	3	9	12	5	10	1	0	0	0	23	13.0
C	20	Robert Lang	PIT	11	3	3	6	–1	0	2	0	0	0	18	16.7
D	5	Janne Laukkanen	PIT	11	2	4	6	6	10	1	0	1	0	16	12.5
C	27	Alexei Kovalev	PIT	11	1	5	6	–1	10	0	0	0	0	37	2.7
D	71	Jiri Slegr	PIT	10	2	3	5	5	19	0	0	1	0	17	11.8
C	29	Tyler Wright	PIT	11	3	1	4	0	17	0	0	0	0	13	23.1
R	44	Rob Brown	PIT	11	1	2	3	1	0	0	0	0	0	17	5.9
L	18	Josef Beranek	PIT	11	0	3	3	2	4	0	0	0	0	16	0.0
L	9	Rene Corbet	PIT	7	1	1	2	–2	9	0	0	0	0	13	7.7
D	11	Darius Kasparaitis	PIT	11	1	1	2	–3	10	0	0	0	0	6	16.7
D	6	Bob Boughner	PIT	11	0	2	2	6	15	0	0	0	0	6	0.0
R	36	Matthew Barnaby	PIT	11	0	2	2	–1	29	0	0	0	0	11	0.0
D	32	John Slaney	PIT	2	1	0	1	0	2	1	0	0	0	1	100.0
R	14	Pat Falloon	PIT	10	1	0	1	0	2	0	0	0	0	12	8.3
D	24	Ian Moran	PIT	11	0	1	1	0	2	0	0	0	0	9	0.0
D	8	Hans Jonsson	PIT	11	0	1	1	2	6	0	0	0	0	2	0.0
G	1	Peter Skudra	PIT	1	0	0	0	0	0	0	0	0	0	0	0.0
D	28 *	Michal Rozsival	PIT	2	0	0	0	0	4	0	0	0	0	5	0.0
R	95	Alexei Morozov	PIT	5	0	0	0	–1	0	0	0	0	0	5	0.0
D	34	Peter Popovic	PIT	10	0	0	0	–2	10	0	0	0	0	6	0.0
G	31	Ron Tugnutt	PIT	11	0	0	0	0	2	0	0	0	0	0	0.0

Goaltending

No.	Goaltender	GPI	Mins	Avg	W	L	EN	SO	GA	SA	S%
31	Ron Tugnutt	11	746	1.77	6	5	0	2	22	398	.945
1	Peter Skudra	1	20	3.00	0	0	0	0	1	11	.909
	Totals	**11**	**769**	**1.79**	**6**	**5**	**0**	**2**	**23**	**409**	**.944**

General Managers' History

Jack Riley, 1967-68 to 1969-70; Red Kelly, 1970-71; Red Kelly and Jack Riley, 1971-72; Jack Riley, 1972-73; Jack Riley and Jack Button, 1973-74; Jack Button, 1974-75; Wren Blair, 1975-76; Wren Blair and Baz Bastien, 1976-77; Baz Bastien, 1977-78 to 1982-83; Ed Johnston, 1983-84 to 1987-88; Tony Esposito, 1988-89; Tony Esposito and Craig Patrick, 1989-90; Craig Patrick, 1990-91 to date.

Club Records

Team

(Figures in brackets for season records are games played; records for fewest points, wins, ties, losses, goals, goals against are for 70 or more games)

Most Points	119	1992-93 (84)
Most Wins	56	1992-93 (84)
Most Ties	20	1970-71 (78)
Most Losses	58	1983-84 (80)
Most Goals	367	1992-93 (84)
Most Goals Against	394	1982-83 (80)
Fewest Points	38	1983-84 (80)
Fewest Wins	16	1983-84 (80)
Fewest Ties	4	1995-96 (82)
Fewest Losses	21	1992-93 (84)
Fewest Goals	182	1969-70 (76)
Fewest Goals Against	188	1997-98 (82)

Longest Winning Streak
Overall ... *17 Mar. 9-Apr. 10/93
Home ... 11 Jan. 5-Mar. 7/91
Away ... 7 Mar. 14-Apr. 9/93

Longest Undefeated Streak
Overall ... 18 Mar. 9-Apr. 14/93 (17 wins, 1 tie)
Home ... 20 Nov. 30/74-Feb. 22/75 (12 wins, 8 ties)
Away ... 8 Mar. 14-Apr. 14/93 (7 wins, 1 tie)

Longest Losing Streak
Overall ... 11 Jan. 22-Feb. 10/83
Home ... 7 Oct. 8-29/83
Away ... 18 Dec. 23/82-Mar. 4/83

Longest Winless Streak
Overall ... 18 Jan. 2-Feb. 10/83 (17 losses, 1 tie)
Home ... 11 Oct. 8-Nov. 19/83 (9 losses, 2 ties)
Away ... 18 Oct. 25/70-Jan. 14/71 (11 losses, 7 ties), Dec. 23/82-Mar. 4/83 (18 losses)

Most Shutouts, Season ... 9 1998-99 (82)
Most PIM, Season ... 2,670 1988-89 (80)
Most Goals, Game ... 12 Mar. 15/75 (Wsh. 1 at Pit. 12), Dec. 26/91 (Tor. 1 at Pit. 12)

Individual

Most Seasons	12	Mario Lemieux
Most Games	753	Jean Pronovost
Most Goals, Career	613	Mario Lemieux
Most Assists, Career	881	Mario Lemieux
Most Points, Career	1,494	Mario Lemieux (613G, 881A)
Most PIM, Career	980	Troy Loney
Most Shutouts, Career	22	Tom Barrasso

Longest Consecutive Games Streak ... 320 Ron Schock (Oct. 24/73-Apr. 3/77)
Most Goals, Season ... 85 Mario Lemieux (1988-89)
Most Assists, Season ... 114 Mario Lemieux (1988-89)
Most Points, Season ... 199 Mario Lemieux (1988-89; 85G, 114A)
Most PIM, Season ... 409 Paul Baxter (1981-82)

Most Points, Defenseman, Season ... 113 Paul Coffey (1988-89; 30G, 83A)
Most Points, Center, Season ... 199 Mario Lemieux (1988-89; 85G, 114A)
Most Points, Right Wing, Season ... *149 Jaromir Jagr (1995-96; 62G, 87A)
Most Points, Left Wing, Season ... 123 Kevin Stevens (1991-92; 54G, 69A)
Most Points, Rookie, Season ... 100 Mario Lemieux (1984-85; 43G, 57A)
Most Shutouts, Season ... 7 Tom Barrasso (1997-98)
Most Goals, Game ... 5 Mario Lemieux (Three times)
Most Assists, Game ... 6 Ron Stackhouse (Mar. 8/75), Greg Malone (Nov. 28/79), Mario Lemieux (Three times)
Most Points, Game ... 8 Mario Lemieux (Oct. 15/88; 3G, 5A, Dec. 31/88; 5G, 3A)

* NHL Record.

Captains' History

Ab McDonald, 1967-68; no captain, 1968-69 to 1972-73; Ron Schock, 1973-74 to 1976-77; Jean Pronovost, 1977-78; Orest Kindrachuk, 1978-79 to 1980-81; Randy Carlyle, 1981-82 to 1983-84; Mike Bullard, 1984-85; Mike Bullard and Terry Ruskowski, 1986-87; Dan Frawley and Mario Lemieux, 1987-88; Mario Lemieux, 1988-89 to 1993-94; Ron Francis, 1994-95; Mario Lemieux, 1995-96, 1996-97; Ron Francis, 1997-98; Jaromir Jagr, 1998-99 to date.

Retired Numbers

21	Michel Brière	1969-1970
66	Mario Lemieux	1984-1997

All-time Record vs. Other Clubs

Regular Season

	At Home							On Road							Total						
	GP	W	L	T	GF	GA	PTS	GP	W	L	T	GF	GA	PTS	GP	W	L	T	GF	GA	PTS
Anaheim	6	3	1	2	22	20	8	6	3	3	0	22	20	7	12	6	4	2	44	40	15
Atlanta	2	2	0	0	9	3	4	2	0	2	0	7	4	4	4	0	0	16	7	8
Boston	72	31	27	14	256	259	76	70	13	51	6	201	317	32	142	44	78	20	457	576	108
Buffalo	63	31	16	16	239	201	78	63	16	32	15	169	256	46	126	46	48	32	408	457	124
Calgary	42	22	10	10	159	130	54	43	10	26	7	132	193	27	85	32	36	17	291	323	81
Carolina	38	21	12	5	173	144	47	40	19	18	3	155	155	41	78	40	30	8	328	299	88
Chicago	56	26	23	7	199	185	59	56	9	38	9	151	233	27	112	35	61	16	350	418	86
Colorado	33	15	13	5	138	134	35	30	13	15	2	119	135	28	63	28	28	7	257	269	63
Dallas	60	36	18	6	227	168	78	62	21	35	6	207	237	48	122	57	53	12	434	405	126
Detroit	62	43	15	4	274	183	90	63	12	39	12	171	243	37	125	55	54	16	445	426	127
Edmonton	28	13	12	3	108	122	29	28	6	21	1	94	144	13	56	19	33	4	202	266	42
Florida	15	10	3	2	56	40	22	14	7	7	0	33	36	15	29	17	10	2	89	76	37
Los Angeles	69	38	22	9	256	218	85	67	17	42	8	178	258	42	136	55	64	17	434	476	127
Montreal	74	26	35	13	223	262	65	74	10	56	8	187	356	28	148	36	91	21	410	618	93
Nashville	2	1	0	1	7	3	3	2	1	1	0	5	6	2	4	2	1	1	12	9	5
New Jersey	69	38	27	4	269	236	80	70	24	34	12	240	265	60	139	62	61	16	509	501	140
NY Islanders	77	37	29	11	296	270	85	76	29	39	8	255	304	46	153	66	68	19	551	574	151
NY Rangers	90	36	40	14	324	338	86	90	35	47	8	304	362	78	180	71	87	22	628	700	164
Ottawa	19	14	1	4	77	36	32	19	11	5	3	62	46	25	38	25	6	7	139	82	57
Philadelphia	95	42	34	19	333	308	103	96	15	74	7	241	417	38	191	57	108	26	574	725	141
Phoenix	28	20	8	0	118	79	40	27	13	11	3	95	98	29	55	33	19	3	213	177	69
St. Louis	61	30	19	12	230	182	72	61	15	40	6	165	238	36	122	45	59	18	395	420	108
San Jose	7	3	3	1	34	25	7	9	6	1	2	48	17	14	16	9	4	3	82	42	21
Tampa Bay	15	10	3	2	65	38	22	15	8	6	1	49	42	17	30	18	9	3	114	80	39
Toronto	61	34	21	6	258	192	74	60	21	28	11	199	241	54	121	55	49	17	457	433	128
Vancouver	48	33	8	7	224	164	73	47	22	21	4	178	169	48	95	55	29	11	402	333	121
Washington	75	41	27	7	294	240	89	77	18	31	6	289	330	70	153	72	67	14	583	570	159
Defunct Clubs	35	22	6	7	148	93	51	34	13	10	11	108	101	37	69	35	16	18	256	194	88
Totals	**1302**	**678**	**433**	**191**	**5016**	**4273**	**1547**	**1302**	**401**	**740**	**161**	**4064**	**5223**	**969**	**2604**	**1079**	**1173**	**352**	**9080**	**9496**	**2516**

Playoffs

	Series	W	L	GP	W	L	T	GF	GA	Last Mtg.	Round	Result
Boston	4	2	2	19	10	9	0	67	62	1992	CF	W 4-0
Buffalo	1	1	0	3	2	1	0	9	9	1979	PR	W 2-1
Chicago	2	1	1	8	4	4	0	23	24	1992	F	W 4-0
Dallas	1	1	0	6	4	2	0	28	16	1991	F	W 4-2
Florida	1	0	1	7	3	4	0	15	20	1996	CF	L 3-4
Montreal	1	0	1	6	2	4	0	15	18	1998	CQF	L 2-4
New Jersey	4	3	1	24	13	11	0	73	69	1999	CQF	W 4-3
NY Islanders	3	0	3	19	8	11	0	58	67	1993	DF	L 3-4
NY Rangers	3	3	0	15	12	3	0	64	45	1996	CSF	W 4-1
Philadelphia	3	0	3	18	6	12	0	51	66	2000	CSF	L 2-4
St. Louis	3	1	2	13	6	7	0	40	45	1981	PR	L 2-3
Toronto	3	0	3	12	4	8	0	27	39	1999	CSF	L 2-4
Washington	6	5	1	36	22	14	0	123	111	2000	CQF	W 4-1
Defunct Clubs	1	1	0	4	4	0	0	13	6			
Totals	**36**	**18**	**18**	**190**	**100**	**90**	**0**	**606**	**597**			

Playoff Results 2000-1996

Year	Round	Opponent	Result	GF	GA
2000	CSF	Philadelphia	L 2-4	14	15
	CQF	Washington	W 4-1	17	8
1999	CSF	Toronto	L 2-4	14	18
	CQF	New Jersey	W 4-3	21	18
1998	CQF	Montreal	L 2-4	15	18
1997	CQF	Philadelphia	L 1-4	13	20
1996	CF	Florida	L 3-4	15	20
	CSF	NY Rangers	W 4-1	21	15
	CQF	Washington	W 4-2	21	17

Abbreviations: Round: F – Final;
CF – conference final; **CSF** – conference semi-final;
CQF – conference quarter-final; **DF** – division final;
PR – preliminary round.

Calgary totals include Atlanta Flames, 1972-73 to 1979-80.
Colorado totals include Quebec, 1979-80 to 1994-95.
New Jersey totals include Kansas City, 1974-75 to 1975-76, and Colorado Rockies, 1976-77 to 1981-82.
Phoenix totals include Winnipeg, 1979-80 to 1995-96.
Carolina totals include Hartford, 1979-80 to 1996-97.
Dallas totals include Minnesota North Stars, 1967-68 to 1992-93.

1999-2000 Results

Oct.	1	at Dallas	4-6
	7	at New Jersey	7-5
	8	Colorado	3-3
	14	at NY Rangers	5-2
	16	Chicago	3-3
	23	Carolina	2-3
	27	at Anaheim	1-2 *
	28	at Los Angeles	3-5
	30	at San Jose	1-1
Nov.	2	Los Angeles	4-5
	4	at Ottawa	1-2
	6	Tampa Bay	4-7
	10	Montreal	5-4
	12	at Detroit	2-3 *
	13	Nashville	6-2
	16	Buffalo	3-2
	18	at Tampa Bay	1-2
	20	at Florida	1-2 *
	23	Toronto	3-1
	26	Ottawa	5-0
	27	at Carolina	3-5
	30	at Buffalo	4-1
Dec.	2	San Jose	2-5
	4	at Toronto	2-3 *
	7	at New Jersey	1-2
	9	Washington	3-0
	11	Phoenix	4-2
	14	Boston	4-2
	15	at Carolina	6-3
	18	Florida	2-5
	20	at Montreal	1-5
	21	at NY Islanders	4-0
	23	Tampa Bay	4-3
	26	at Chicago	4-2
	29	at Washington	2-3 *
	30	NY Islanders	9-3
Jan.	2	Detroit	4-3
	5	New Jersey	1-3
	7	Toronto	5-2
	8	at Philadelphia	2-6
	12	at Phoenix	1-3

	13	at Colorado	3-4
	15	at Nashville	2-4
	19	St. Louis	3-1
	22	at Montreal	2-4
	23	Philadelphia	4-4
	25	NY Rangers	3-4
	27	Atlanta	4-1
	29	Anaheim	1-7
	31	at Atlanta	2-1 *
Feb.	1	Washington	3-2
	3	NY Islanders	4-2
	5	Atlanta	5-2
	11	Edmonton	2-2
	12	at NY Islanders	1-5
	14	Vancouver	3-0
	16	Buffalo	1-1
	19	at Florida	2-1
	21	at Tampa Bay	1-2
	22	at NY Rangers	3-4
	24	at Philadelphia	3-4 *
	26	Boston	2-2
	28	Ottawa	1-1
Mar.	1	at Calgary	2-8
	4	at Edmonton	3-2
	8	Montreal	0-3
	9	at Ottawa	0-7
	11	NY Rangers	3-1
	13	New Jersey	2-3
	16	Florida	4-2
	18	at Boston	2-3
	19	NY Rangers	5-4
	21	at NY Islanders	8-2
	24	at Atlanta	5-3
	26	at Philadelphia	1-3
	28	New Jersey	3-2
	30	at Washington	4-3 *
Apr.	1	Philadelphia	2-3
	3	Carolina	3-2
	5	at Toronto	4-2
	7	at Buffalo	2-1 *
	9	at Boston	1-3

* – Overtime

Entry Draft
Selections 2000-1986

2000
Pick
18	Brooks Orpik
52	Shane Endicott
84	Peter Hamerlik
124	Michel Ouellet
146	David Koci
185	Patrick Foley
216	Jim Abbott
248	Steven Crampton
273	Roman Simicek
280	Nick Boucher

1999
Pick
18	Konstantin Koltsov
51	Matt Murley
57	Jeremy Van Hoof
86	Sebastian Caron
115	Ryan Malone
144	Tomas Skvaridlo
157	Vladimir Malenkykh
176	Doug Meyer
204	Tom Kostopoulos
233	Darcy Robinson
261	Andrew McPherson

1998
Pick
23	Milan Kraft
54	Alexander Zevakhin
80	David Cameron
110	Scott Myers
134	Robert Scuderi
169	Jan Fadrny
196	Joel Scherban
224	Mika Lehto
244	Toby Petersen
254	Matt Hussey

1997
Pick
17	Robert Dome
44	Brian Gaffaney
71	Josef Melichar
97	Alexandre Mathieu
124	Harlan Pratt
152	Petr Havelka
179	Mark Moore
208	Andrew Ference
234	Eric Lind

1996
Pick
23	Craig Hillier
28	Pavel Skrbek
72	Boyd Kane
77	Boris Protsenko
105	Michal Rozsival
150	Peter Bergman
186	Eric Meloche
238	Timo Seikkula

1995
Pick
24	Aleksey Morozov
76	Jean-Sebastien Aubin
102	Oleg Belov
128	Jan Hrdina
154	Alexei Kolkunov
180	Derrick Pyke
206	Sergei Voronov
232	Frank Ivankovic

1994
Pick
24	Chris Wells
50	Richard Park
57	Sven Butenschon
73	Greg Crozier
76	Alexei Krivchenkov
102	Tom O'Connor
128	Clint Johnson
154	Valentin Morozov
161	Serge Aubin
180	Drew Palmer
206	Boris Zelenko
232	Jason Godbout
258	Mikhail Kazakevich
284	Brian Leitza

1993
Pick
26	Stefan Bergkvist
52	Domenic Pittis
62	Dave Roche
104	Jonas Andersson-Junkka
130	Chris Kelleher
156	Patrick Lalime
182	Sean Selmser
208	Larry McMorran
234	Timothy Harberts
260	Leonid Toropchenko
286	Hans Jonsson

1992
Pick
19	Martin Straka
43	Marc Hussey
67	Travis Thiessen
91	Todd Klassen
115	Philippe DeRouville
139	Artem Kopot
163	Jan Alinc
187	Fran Bussey
211	Brian Bonin
235	Brian Callahan

1991
Pick
16	Markus Naslund
38	Rusty Fitzgerald
60	Shane Peacock
82	Joe Tamminen
104	Robert Melanson
126	Brian Clifford
148	Ed Patterson
170	Peter McLaughlin
192	Jeff Lembke
214	Chris Tok
236	Paul Dyck
258	Pasi Huura

1990
Pick
5	Jaromir Jagr
61	Joe Dziedzic
68	Chris Tamer
89	Brian Farrell
107	Ian Moran
110	Denis Casey
130	Mika Valila
131	Ken Plaquin
145	Pat Neaton
152	Petteri Koskimaki
173	Ladislav Karabin
194	Timothy Fingerhut
215	Michael Thompson
236	Brian Bruininks

1989
Pick
16	Jamie Heward
37	Paul Laus
58	John Brill
79	Todd Nelson
100	Tom Nevers
121	Mike Markovich
126	Mike Needham
142	Patrick Schafhauser
163	Dave Shute
184	Andrew Wolf
205	Greg Hagen
226	Scott Farrell
247	Jason Smart

1988
Pick
4	Darrin Shannon
25	Mark Major
62	Daniel Gauthier
67	Mark Recchi
88	Greg Andrusak
130	Troy Mick
151	Jeff Blaeser
172	Rob Gaudreau
193	David Pancoe
214	Cory Laylin
235	Darren Stolk

1987
Pick
5	Chris Joseph
26	Rick Tabaracci
47	Jamie Leach
68	Risto Kurkinen
89	Jeff Waver
110	Shawn McEachern
131	Jim Bodden
152	Jiri Kucera
173	Jack MacDougall
194	Daryn McBride
215	Mark Carlson
236	Ake Lilljebjorn

1986
Pick
4	Zarley Zalapski
25	Dave Capuano
46	Brad Aitken
67	Rob Brown
88	Sandy Smith
109	Jeff Daniels
130	Doug Hobson
151	Steve Rohlik
172	Dave McLlwain
193	Kelly Cain
214	Stan Drulia
235	Rob Wilson

General Manager

PATRICK, CRAIG
General Manager, Pittsburgh Penguins. Born in Detroit, MI, May 20, 1946.

Known for his calm and patient management style, Craig Patrick has led the Penguins to two Stanley Cup championships, one Presidents' Trophy title and five division championships since taking over as g.m. on Dec. 5, 1989. In 2000, he and Mario Lemieux were recipients of the Lester Patrick Trophy for their contributions to hockey in the United States.

A member of one of hockey's most famous families — including grandfather Lester, father Lynn and uncle Muzz — Patrick played collegiate hockey at the University of Denver and captained the Pioneers to the NCAA championship in 1969. He played eight NHL seasons with four different teams, registering 72 goals and 163 points in 401 games before retiring in 1979. He made the transition to management and coaching when he landed the dual role of assistant coach and assistant g.m. of the 1980 U.S. Olympic Team that won the gold medal at Lake Placid.

Patrick joined the New York Rangers organization as director of operations in 1980 and became the youngest general manager in club history one year later. He served in that capacity through the 1985-86 season, leading his team to the playoffs every year.

Prior to joining the Penguins, Patrick spent two years as director of athletics and recreation at the University of Denver.

NHL Coaching Record

Season	Team	Games	Regular Season W	L	T	%	Playoffs Games	W	L	%
1980-81	NY Rangers	60	26	23	11	.525	14	7	7	.500
1984-85	NY Rangers	35	11	22	2	.343	3	0	3	.000
1989-90	Pittsburgh	54	22	26	6	.463	....	....	....	....
1996-97	Pittsburgh	20	7	10	3	.425	5	1	4	.200
	NHL Totals	**169**	**66**	**81**	**22**	**.456**	**22**	**8**	**14**	**.364**

Club Directory

Mellon Arena

Pittsburgh Penguins
Mellon Arena
66 Mario Lemieux Place
Pittsburgh, PA 15219
Phone **412/642-1300**
FAX 412/642-1859
Media Relations FAX 412/642-1322
Capacity: 16,958

Ownership
Mario Lemieux and The Lemieux Group

Administration
Chairman/CEO	Mario Lemieux
Executive Vice President/COO	Tom Rooney
Executive Vice President/CFO	Ken Sawyer
Vice President & General Counsel	Ted Black
Executive Assistant	Elaine Heufelder
Executive Assistant	Fay McNamara
Receptionist	Kelly Hart

Hockey Operations
Executive Vice President/General Manager	Craig Patrick
Assistant General Manager	Ed Johnston
Head Coach	Ivan Hlinka
Assistant Coaches	Rick Kehoe, Joe Mullen, Randy Hillier
Goaltending Coach and Scout	Gilles Meloche
Head Scout	Greg Malone
Scouts	Herb Brooks, Wayne Daniels, Charlie Hodge, Mark Kelley, Neil Shea
Strength and Conditioning Coach	John Welday
Equipment Manager	Steve Latin
Trainers	Mark Mortland, Scott Johnson
Team Physician	Dr. Charles Burke
Executive Assistant	Tracey Botsford
Assistant Equipment Manager	Paul Flati
Team Equipment Staff	Paul DeFazio
Head Coach, Wilkes-Barre/Scranton Penguins	Glenn Patrick

Communications and Marketing
Vice President, Communications/Marketing	Tom McMillan
Director of Media Relations	Steve Bovino
Manager, Media Relations	Keith Wehner
Director of Public & Alumni Relations	Cindy Himes
Director, Community Relations	Renee Petrichevich
Director of Entertainment	Paul Barto
Assistant Director, Entertainment	Mike Wurman
Youth Hockey Coordinator	Mark Shuttleworth

Finance
Executive Vice President/CFO	Ken Sawyer
Vice President/Controller	Kevin Hart
Accounting Staff	Tawni Love, Mark Oresic, Troy Ussack, Andrea Winschel

Properties
Vice President of Properties	Mike Lee
Director of Publications	Brian Coe
Creative Director	Barb Pilarski

Ticketing
Vice President, Ticketing	Mark Anderson
Director, Premium Seating	Terri Smith
Manager, Premium Services	Michelle Follen
Assistant Manager, Premium Services	Sherry Huggins
Director, Ticket Sales	James Santilli
Manager, Group Sales	Mike Guiffre
Director, Ticket Operations	Laura Bryer
Manager, Inside Ticket Sales	Chad Slencak
Box Office Manager	Carol Coulson
Box Office Staff	Kelly Gabany, Jason Onufer
Group Sales	Ted Miller, Chuck Pukansky
Ticket Sales Representatives	Peter Bakarat, George Birman, Bonnie Golinski, Mike McLaughlin, Joe Traynor, Craig Wheeler, Jason Florian, George Murphy
Customer Service Representatives	Kristen Abbott, Lynda Gladding, Jill Weisbrod

Corporate Sales
Vice President, Corporate Sales	David Soltesz
Managers, Corporate Sponsorships	Kimberly Bogesdorfer, Carl D'Alicandro, Mark DeAndrea
Manager, Sales Service	Marie Mays
Assistant Managers, Sales Service	Amy Gillespie, Beth McQuiston

General Information
TV Station	Fox Sports Net Pittsburgh
TV Announcers	Mike Lange, TBA
Flagship Radio Station	3WS (94.5 FM, 970 AM)
Radio Announcers	Paul Steigerwald, Bob Errey
Minor League Affiliates	Wilkes-Barre/Scranton (AHL), Wheeling (ECHL)

Coaching History

Red Sullivan, 1967-68, 1968-69; Red Kelly, 1969-70 to 1971-72; Red Kelly and Ken Schinkel, 1972-73; Ken Schinkel and Marc Boileau, 1973-74; Marc Boileau, 1974-75; Marc Boileau and Ken Schinkel, 1975-76; Ken Schinkel, 1976-77; John Wilson, 1977-78 to 1979-80; Eddie Johnston, 1980-81 to 1982-83; Lou Angotti, 1983-84; Bob Berry, 1984-85 to 1986-87; Pierre Creamer, 1987-88; Gene Ubriaco, 1988-89; Gene Ubriaco and Craig Patrick, 1989-90; Bob Johnson, 1990-91, 1991-92; Scotty Bowman, 1991-92, 1992-93; Eddie Johnston, 1993-94 to 1995-96; Eddie Johnston and Craig Patrick, 1996-97; Kevin Constantine, 1997-98, 1998-99; Kevin Constantine and Herb Brooks, 1999-2000; Ivan Hlinka, 2000-01.

St. Louis Blues

1999-2000 Results: 51w-20L-11T 114PTS. First, Central Division

Year-by-Year Record

Season	GP	Home W	L	T	Road W	L	T	Overall W	L	T	GF	GA	Pts.	Finished		Playoff Result
1999-2000	82	24	10	7	27	10	4	51	20	11	248	165	114	1st,	Central Div.	Lost Conf. Quarter-Final
1998-99	82	18	17	6	19	15	7	37	32	13	237	209	87	2nd,	Central Div.	Lost Conf. Semi-Final
1997-98	82	26	10	5	19	19	3	45	29	8	256	204	98	3rd,	Central Div.	Lost Conf. Semi-Final
1996-97	82	17	20	4	19	15	7	36	35	11	236	239	83	4th,	Central Div.	Lost Conf. Quarter-Final
1995-96	82	15	17	9	17	17	7	32	34	16	219	248	80	4th,	Central Div.	Lost Conf. Semi-Final
1994-95	48	16	6	2	12	9	3	28	15	5	178	135	61	2nd,	Central Div.	Lost Conf. Quarter-Final
1993-94	84	23	11	8	17	22	3	40	33	11	270	283	91	4th,	Central Div.	Lost Conf. Quarter-Final
1992-93	84	22	13	7	15	23	4	37	36	11	282	278	85	4th,	Norris Div.	Lost Div. Final
1991-92	80	25	12	3	11	21	8	36	33	11	279	266	83	3rd,	Norris Div.	Lost Div. Semi-Final
1990-91	80	24	9	7	23	13	4	47	22	11	310	250	105	2nd,	Norris Div.	Lost Div. Final
1989-90	80	20	15	5	17	19	4	37	34	9	295	279	83	2nd,	Norris Div.	Lost Div. Final
1988-89	80	22	11	7	11	24	5	33	35	12	275	285	78	2nd,	Norris Div.	Lost Div. Final
1987-88	80	18	17	5	16	21	3	34	38	8	278	294	76	2nd,	Norris Div.	Lost Div. Final
1986-87	80	21	12	7	11	21	8	32	33	15	281	293	79	1st,	Norris Div.	Lost Div. Semi-Final
1985-86	80	23	11	6	14	23	3	37	34	9	302	291	83	3rd,	Norris Div.	Lost Conf. Championship
1984-85	80	21	12	7	16	19	5	37	31	12	299	288	86	1st,	Norris Div.	Lost Div. Semi-Final
1983-84	80	23	14	3	9	27	4	32	41	7	293	316	71	2nd,	Norris Div.	Lost Div. Final
1982-83	80	16	16	8	9	24	7	25	40	15	285	316	65	4th,	Norris Div.	Lost Div. Semi-Final
1981-82	80	22	14	4	10	26	4	32	40	8	315	349	72	3rd	Norris Div.	Lost Div. Final
1980-81	80	29	7	4	16	11	13	45	18	17	352	281	107	1st,	Smythe Div.	Lost Quarter-Final
1979-80	80	20	13	7	14	21	5	34	34	12	266	278	80	2nd,	Smythe Div.	Lost Prelim. Round
1978-79	80	14	20	6	4	30	6	18	50	12	249	348	48	3rd,	Smythe Div.	Out of Playoffs
1977-78	80	12	20	8	8	27	5	20	47	13	195	304	53	4th,	Smythe Div.	Out of Playoffs
1976-77	80	22	13	5	10	26	4	32	39	9	239	276	73	1st,	Smythe Div.	Lost Quarter-Final
1975-76	80	20	12	8	9	25	6	29	37	14	249	290	72	3rd,	Smythe Div.	Lost Prelim. Round
1974-75	80	23	13	4	12	18	10	35	31	14	269	267	84	2nd,	Smythe Div.	Lost Prelim. Round
1973-74	78	16	16	7	10	24	5	26	40	12	206	248	64	6th,	West Div.	Out of Playoffs
1972-73	78	21	11	7	11	23	5	32	34	12	233	251	76	4th,	West Div.	Lost Quarter-Final
1971-72	78	17	17	5	11	22	6	28	39	11	208	247	67	3rd,	West Div.	Lost Semi-Final
1970-71	78	23	7	9	11	18	10	34	25	19	223	208	87	2nd,	West Div.	Lost Quarter-Final
1969-70	76	24	9	5	13	18	7	37	27	12	224	179	86	1st,	West Div.	Lost Final
1968-69	76	21	8	9	16	17	5	37	25	14	204	157	88	1st,	West Div.	Lost Final
1967-68	74	18	12	7	9	19	9	27	31	16	177	191	70	3rd,	West Div.	Lost Final

2000-01 Schedule

Oct.	Thu.	5	at Phoenix		Thu.	11	at San Jose
	Fri.	6	at San Jose		Sat.	13	at Los Angeles
	Sun.	8	at Anaheim*		Mon.	15	at Phoenix
	Wed.	11	at Los Angeles		Thu.	18	Edmonton
	Fri.	13	Minnesota		Sat.	20	Vancouver
	Tue.	17	at Detroit		Sun.	21	at Nashville*
	Thu.	19	Los Angeles		Tue.	23	at Montreal
	Sat.	21	Chicago		Thu.	25	New Jersey
	Thu.	26	Calgary		Sat.	27	San Jose
	Sat.	28	Dallas		Tue.	30	at Boston
	Sun.	29	at Carolina	Feb.	Thu.	1	Columbus
	Tue.	31	at Nashville		Tue.	6	at Columbus
Nov.	Thu.	2	Washington		Thu.	8	Tampa Bay
	Sat.	4	Toronto		Sat.	10	at Colorado
	Thu.	9	at Colorado		Sun.	11	at Dallas
	Sat.	11	at Vancouver		Thu.	15	Calgary
	Tue.	14	at Edmonton		Fri.	16	at Chicago
	Thu.	16	Pittsburgh		Mon.	19	at Florida
	Sat.	18	Buffalo		Tue.	20	at Tampa Bay
	Tue.	21	Vancouver		Fri.	23	at Detroit
	Fri.	24	at Nashville		Sat.	24	Boston
	Sat.	25	Phoenix		Mon.	26	San Jose
	Wed.	29	at Toronto		Wed.	28	at Edmonton
Dec.	Sat.	2	Florida	Mar.	Fri.	2	at Vancouver
	Tue.	5	Anaheim		Sat.	3	at Calgary
	Thu.	7	Toronto		Tue.	6	at Minnesota
	Sat.	9	Chicago		Thu.	8	Colorado
	Sun.	10	at Chicago		Sat.	10	Detroit*
	Fri.	15	at Atlanta		Tue.	13	at Philadelphia
	Sat.	16	Detroit		Wed.	14	at Minnesota
	Wed.	20	at NY Rangers		Sat.	17	at Calgary
	Sat.	23	Anaheim		Tue.	20	NY Islanders
	Tue.	26	Columbus		Thu.	22	Colorado
	Thu.	28	Los Angeles		Sat.	24	Chicago*
	Sat.	30	Phoenix		Sun.	25	at Dallas
Jan.	Mon.	1	Edmonton*		Wed.	28	at Detroit
	Tue.	2	at Ottawa		Sat.	31	at Pittsburgh*
	Thu.	4	Nashville	Apr.	Sun.	1	at Columbus
	Sat.	6	Minnesota		Tue.	3	Carolina
	Mon.	8	Philadelphia		Thu.	5	Columbus
	Wed.	10	at Anaheim		Sat.	7	Nashville

* Denotes afternoon game.

Franchise date: June 5, 1967

CENTRAL DIVISION

34th NHL Season

Chris Pronger led a parade of Blues to the podium at the NHL Awards following the club's stellar 1999-2000 season. Pronger became the first defenseman to win the Hart Trophy as the NHL's most valuable player since Bobby Orr in 1972.

2000-01 Player Personnel

FORWARDS

	HT	WT	S	Place of Birth	Date	1999-00 Club
BARTECKO, Lubos	6-1	200	L	Kezmarok, Czech.	7/14/76	St. Louis-Worcester
CONROY, Craig	6-2	198	R	Potsdam, NY	9/4/71	St. Louis
DEMITRA, Pavol	6-0	196	L	Dubnica, Czech.	11/29/74	St. Louis
DRAKE, Dallas	6-1	190	L	Trail, B.C.	2/4/69	Phoenix
EASTWOOD, Mike	6-3	209	R	Ottawa, Ont.	7/1/67	St. Louis
HANDZUS, Michal	6-5	210	L	Banska Bystrica, Czech.	3/11/77	St. Louis
HECHT, Jochen	6-3	196	L	Mannheim, West Germany	6/21/77	St. Louis
LOW, Reed	6-3	220	R	Moose Jaw, Sask.	6/21/76	Worcester
MAYERS, Jamal	6-1	212	R	Toronto, Ont.	10/24/74	St. Louis
MURRAY, Chris	6-2	209	R	Port Hardy, B.C.	10/25/74	Dallas-Michigan K-Wings
NAGY, Ladislav	5-11	183	L	Saca, Czech.	6/1/79	St. Louis-Worcester
NASH, Tyson	6-0	185	L	Edmonton, Alta.	3/11/75	St. Louis
REASONER, Marty	6-1	203	L	Rochester, NY	2/26/77	St. Louis-Worcester
RHEAUME, Pascal	6-1	209	L	Quebec, Que.	6/21/73	St. Louis-Worcester
SIMPSON, Reid	6-2	220	L	Flin Flon, Man.	5/21/69	Cleveland-Tampa Bay
TURGEON, Pierre	6-1	199	L	Rouyn, Que.	8/28/69	St. Louis
YOUNG, Scott	6-1	200	R	Clinton, MA	10/1/67	St. Louis

DEFENSEMEN

	HT	WT	S	Place of Birth	Date	1999-00 Club
BERGEVIN, Marc	6-1	214	L	Montreal, Que.	8/11/65	St. Louis
CHEBATURKIN, Vladimir	6-2	226	L	Tyumen, USSR	4/23/75	NY Islanders-Lowell
FINLEY, Jeff	6-2	205	L	Edmonton, Alta.	4/14/67	St. Louis
HILL, Sean	6-0	205	R	Duluth, MN	2/14/70	Carolina
MacINNIS, Al	6-2	209	R	Inverness, N.S.	7/11/63	St. Louis
OBSUT, Jaroslav	6-1	200	L	Presov, Czech.	9/3/76	Worcester
PRONGER, Chris	6-6	220	L	Dryden, Ont.	10/10/74	St. Louis
REIRDEN, Todd	6-5	220	L	Deerfield, IL	6/25/71	St. Louis
RUMBLE, Darren	6-1	200	L	Barrie, Ont.	1/23/69	Grand Rapids-Worcester
SALVADOR, Bryce	6-2	215	L	Brandon, Man.	2/11/76	Worcester
VAN RYN, Mike	6-1	190	R	London, Ont.	5/14/79	Sarnia Sting

GOALTENDERS

	HT	WT	C	Place of Birth	Date	1999-00 Club
JOHNSON, Brent	6-2	200	L	Farmington, MI	3/12/77	Worcester
ROLOSON, Dwayne	6-1	190	L	Simcoe, Ont.	10/12/69	Buffalo
RUDKOWSKY, Cody	6-1	200	L	Willingdon, Alta.	7/21/78	Worcester-Peoria Rivermen
TUREK, Roman	6-3	190	R	Pisek, Czech.	5/21/70	St. Louis

Coaching History

Lynn Patrick and Scotty Bowman, 1967-68; Scotty Bowman, 1968-69, 1969-70; Al Arbour and Scotty Bowman, 1970-71; Sid Abel, Bill McCreary and Al Arbour, 1971-72; Al Arbour and Jean-Guy Talbot, 1972-73; Jean-Guy Talbot and Lou Angotti, 1973-74; Lou Angotti, Lynn Patrick and Garry Young, 1974-75; Garry Young, Lynn Patrick and Leo Boivin, 1975-76; Emile Francis, 1976-77; Leo Boivin and Barclay Plager, 1977-78; Barclay Plager, 1978-79; Barclay Plager and Red Berenson, 1979-80; Red Berenson, 1980-81; Red Berenson and Emile Francis, 1981-82; Emile Francis and Barclay Plager, 1982-83; Jacques Demers, 1983-84 to 1985-86; Jacques Martin, 1986-87, 1987-88; Brian Sutter, 1988-89 to 1991-92; Bob Plager and Bob Berry, 1992-93; Bob Berry, 1993-94; Mike Keenan, 1994-95, 1995-96; Mike Keenan, Jim Roberts and Joel Quenneville, 1996-97; Joel Quenneville, 1997-98 to date.

Coach

QUENNEVILLE, JOEL
Head Coach, St. Louis Blues.
Born in Windsor, Ont., September 15, 1958.

Joel Quenneville was named head coach on January 6, 1997, becoming the 20th head coach in Blues history. His first game in St. Louis was on January 7, 1997. He won the Jack Adams Award as coach of the year in 1999-2000 after leading the Blues to the Presidents' Trophy with a club record 51 wins and 114 points.

Prior to joining the Blues the former NHL defenseman spent three seasons with the Colorado Avalanche organization as an assistant coach. He was instrumental in the Avalanche's drive for their first Stanley Cup championship during the 1995-96 season.

Prior to joining the Avalanche he was head coach for the Springfield Indians of the American Hockey League during the 1993-94 season. He retired from hockey after the 1991-92 season after serving the St. John's Maple Leafs (AHL) as a player/coach. Quenneville played 13 NHL seasons and finished with 803 career games played, 54 goals, 136 assists and 705 penalty minutes. His best years on the ice were spent with Hartford where he earned most valuable defenseman honors in 1985 and 1986. He played an integral part in helping Hartford win a divisional championship in 1986-87.

Quenneville and his wife Elizabeth have three children: Dylan, Lily and Anna.

1999-2000 Scoring

* – rookie

Regular Season

Pos	#	Player	Team	GP	G	A	Pts	+/-	PIM	PP	SH	GW	GT	S	%
R	38	Pavol Demitra	STL	71	28	47	75	34	8	8	0	4	0	241	11.6
C	77	Pierre Turgeon	STL	52	26	40	66	30	8	8	0	3	0	139	18.7
D	44	Chris Pronger	STL	79	14	48	62	52	92	8	0	3	2	192	7.3
C	26	Michal Handzus	STL	81	25	28	53	19	44	3	4	5	1	166	15.1
R	48	Scott Young	STL	75	24	15	39	12	18	6	1	7	1	244	9.8
R	23	Lubos Bartecko	STL	67	16	23	39	24	51	3	0	3	0	75	21.3
D	2	Al MacInnis	STL	61	11	28	39	20	34	6	0	7	0	245	4.5
R	19	Stephane Richer	T.B	20	7	5	12	2	4	1	0	0	0	47	14.9
			STL	36	8	17	25	7	14	4	0	1	0	63	12.7
			TOTAL	56	15	22	37	9	18	5	0	1	0	110	13.6
C	32	Mike Eastwood	STL	79	19	15	34	5	32	1	3	3	1	83	22.9
C	17	* Jochen Hecht	STL	63	13	21	34	20	28	5	.0	1	0	140	9.3
C	22	Craig Conroy	STL	79	12	15	27	5	36	1	2	3	0	98	12.2
D	28	Todd Reirden	STL	56	4	21	25	18	32	0	0	1	0	77	5.2
C	15	* Marty Reasoner	STL	32	10	14	24	9	20	3	0	2	0	51	19.6
L	33	Scott Pellerin	STL	80	8	15	23	9	48	0	2	2	0	120	6.7
C	21	Jamal Mayers	STL	79	7	10	17	0	90	0	0	1	0	99	7.1
C	9	* Tyson Nash	STL	66	4	9	13	6	150	0	1	1	0	68	5.9
D	6	Dave Ellett	STL	52	2	8	10	-4	12	0	0	1	0	41	4.9
D	37	Jeff Finley	STL	74	2	8	10	26	38	0	0	2	0	31	6.5
L	12	Derek King	TOR	3	0	0	0	-2	2	0	0	0	0	4	0.0
			STL	19	2	7	9	0	6	1	0	0	0	29	6.9
			TOTAL	22	2	7	9	-2	8	1	0	0	0	33	6.1
D	4	Marc Bergevin	STL	81	1	8	9	27	75	0	0	0	0	54	1.9
D	7	Ricard Persson	STL	41	0	8	8	-2	38	0	0	0	0	30	0.0
C	47	* Ladislav Nagy	STL	11	2	4	6	2	2	1	0	0	0	15	13.3
L	14	Geoff Courtnall	STL	6	2	2	4	3	6	0	0	1	0	15	13.3
L	41	Bob Bassen	STL	27	1	3	4	-3	26	0	0	0	0	26	3.8
C	25	Pascal Rheaume	STL	7	1	1	2	-2	6	0	0	0	0	5	20.0
D	36	Bryan Helmer	STL	15	1	1	2	-3	10	1	0	1	0	19	5.3
R	39	Kelly Chase	STL	25	0	1	1	-5	118	0	0	0	0	14	0.0
G	1	Roman Turek	STL	67	0	1	1	0	4	0	0	0	0	0	0.0
C	46	* Derek Bekar	STL	1	0	0	0	0	0	0	0	0	0	6	0.0
R	10	Jim Campbell	STL	2	0	0	0	0	9	0	0	0	0	6	0.0
D	20	Rudy Poeschek	STL	12	0	0	0	-3	24	0	0	0	0	8	0.0
G	29	Jamie McLennan	STL	19	0	0	0	0	0	0	0	0	0	0	0.0

Goaltending

No.	Goaltender	GPI	Mins	Avg	W	L	T	EN	SO	GA	SA	S%
1	Roman Turek	67	3960	1.95	42	15	9	3	7	129	1470	.912
29	Jamie McLennan	19	1009	1.96	9	5	2	0	2	33	341	.903
	Totals	**82**	**4988**	**1.98**	**51**	**20**	**11**	**3**	**9**	**165**	**1814**	**.909**

Playoffs

Pos	#	Player	Team	GP	G	A	Pts	+/-	PIM	PP	SH	GW	OT	S	%
C	17	* Jochen Hecht	STL	7	4	6	10	1	2	1	0	1	0	13	30.8
R	48	Scott Young	STL	6	6	2	8	1	8	3	0	0	0	15	40.0
D	44	Chris Pronger	STL	7	3	4	7	0	32	2	0	2	0	22	13.6
C	77	Pierre Turgeon	STL	7	0	7	7	-2	0	0	0	0	0	11	0.0
D	2	Al MacInnis	STL	7	1	3	4	-1	14	1	0	0	0	40	2.5
C	21	Jamal Mayers	STL	7	0	4	4	1	2	0	0	0	0	7	0.0
C	15	* Marty Reasoner	STL	7	2	1	3	3	4	1	0	0	0	9	22.2
C	26	Michal Handzus	STL	7	0	3	3	-2	6	0	0	0	0	16	0.0
C	47	* Ladislav Nagy	STL	6	1	1	2	-1	0	0	0	0	0	8	12.5
C	32	Mike Eastwood	STL	7	1	1	2	-2	6	0	0	0	0	6	16.7
R	23	Lubos Bartecko	STL	7	1	1	2	1	4	0	0	0	0	8	12.5
D	37	Jeff Finley	STL	7	0	2	2	2	4	0	0	0	0	4	0.0
C	22	Craig Conroy	STL	7	0	2	2	1	2	0	0	0	0	8	0.0
R	19	Stephane Richer	STL	3	1	0	1	0	0	0	0	0	0	3	33.3
D	7	Ricard Persson	STL	3	1	0	1	0	0	0	0	0	0	1	100.0
L	9	* Tyson Nash	STL	6	1	0	1	-1	24	0	0	0	0	7	14.3
D	28	Todd Reirden	STL	4	0	1	1	1	0	0	0	0	0	7	0.0
D	4	Marc Bergevin	STL	7	0	1	1	2	6	0	0	0	0	2	0.0
D	6	Dave Ellett	STL	7	0	1	1	1	2	0	0	0	0	2	0.0
L	33	Scott Pellerin	STL	7	0	0	0	2	4	0	0	0	0	8	0.0
G	1	Roman Turek	STL	7	0	0	0	0	0	0	0	0	0	0	0.0

Goaltending

No.	Goaltender	GPI	Mins	Avg	W	L	EN	SO	GA	SA	S%
1	Roman Turek	7	415	2.75	3	4	1	0	19	161	.882
	Totals	**7**	**420**	**2.86**	**3**	**4**	**1**	**0**	**20**	**162**	**.877**

Coaching Record

Season	Team	Regular Season					Playoffs			
		Games	W	L	T	%	Games	W	L	%
1993-94	Springfield (AHL)	80	29	38	13	.443	6	2	4	.333
1996-97	St. Louis (NHL)	40	18	15	7	.538	6	2	4	.333
1997-98	St. Louis (NHL)	82	45	29	8	.598	10	6	4	.600
1998-99	St. Louis (NHL)	82	37	32	13	.530	13	6	7	.462
1999-2000	St. Louis (NHL)	82	51	20	11	.695•	7	3	4	.429
	NHL Totals	**286**	**151**	**96**	**39**	**.598•**	**36**	**17**	**19**	**.472**

• Includes points from regulation ties

Club Records

Team

(Figures in brackets for season records are games played; records for fewest points, wins, ties, losses, goals, goals against are for 70 or more games)

Most Points	114	1999-2000 (82)
Most Wins	51	1999-2000 (82)
Most Ties	19	1970-71 (78)
Most Losses	50	1978-79 (80)
Most Goals	352	1980-81 (80)
Most Goals Against	349	1981-82 (80)
Fewest Points	48	1978-79 (80)
Fewest Wins	18	1978-79 (80)
Fewest Ties	7	1983-84 (80)
Fewest Losses	18	1980-81 (80)
Fewest Goals	177	1967-68 (74)
Fewest Goals Against	157	1968-69 (76)

Longest Winning Streak
Overall .... 7 Jan. 21-Feb. 3/88, Mar. 19-31/91, Oct. 3-18/97
Home .... 9 Jan. 26-Feb. 26/91
Away .... *10 Jan. 21-Mar. 2/00

Longest Undefeated Streak
Overall .... 12 Nov. 10-Dec. 8/68 (5 wins, 7 ties)
Home .... 11 Three times
Away .... 11 Jan. 21-Mar. 4/00 (10 wins, 1 tie)

Longest Losing Streak
Overall .... 7 Nov. 12-26/67, Feb. 12-25/89
Home .... 6 Nov. 23-Dec. 19/96
Away .... 10 Jan. 20-Mar. 8/82

Longest Winless Streak
Overall .... 12 Jan. 17-Feb. 15/78 (10 losses, 2 ties)
Home .... 7 Dec. 28/82-Jan. 25/83 (5 losses, 2 ties)
Away .... 17 Jan. 23-Oct. 9/74 (13 losses, 4 ties)

Most Shutouts, Season 13 1968-69 (76)
Most PIM, Season 2,041 1990-91 (80)
Most Goals, Game .... 11 Feb. 26/94 (St.L. 11 at Ott. 1)

Individual

Most Seasons	13	Bernie Federko
Most Games	927	Bernie Federko
Most Goals, Career	527	Brett Hull
Most Assists, Career	721	Bernie Federko
Most Points, Career	1,073	Bernie Federko (352G, 721A)
Most PIM, Career	1,786	Brian Sutter
Most Shutouts, Career	16	Glenn Hall

Longest Consecutive
Games Streak .... 662 Garry Unger (Feb. 7/71-Apr. 8/79)
Most Goals, Season .... 86 Brett Hull (1990-91)
Most Assists, Season .... 90 Adam Oates (1990-91)
Most Points, Season .... 131 Brett Hull (1990-91) (86G, 45A)
Most PIM, Season .... 306 Bob Gassoff (1975-76)

Most Points, Defenseman,
Season .... 78 Jeff Brown (1992-93; 25G, 53A)
Most Points, Center,
Season .... 115 Adam Oates (1990-91; 25G, 90A)
Most Points, Right Wing,
Season .... 131 Brett Hull (1990-91; 86G, 45A)
Most Points, Left Wing,
Season .... 102 Brendan Shanahan (1993-94; 52G, 50A)
Most Points, Rookie,
Season .... 73 Jorgen Pettersson (1980-81; 37G, 36A)
Most Shutouts, Season .... 8 Glenn Hall (1968-69)
Most Goals, Game .... 6 Red Berenson (Nov. 7/68)
Most Assists, Game .... 5 Brian Sutter (Nov. 22/83), Bernie Federko (Feb. 27/88), Adam Oates (Jan. 26/91)
Most Points, Game .... 7 Red Berenson (Nov. 7/68; 6G, 1A), Garry Unger (Mar. 13/71; 3G, 4A)

* NHL Record.

Retired Numbers

3	Bob Gassoff	1973-1977
8	Barclay Plager	1967-1977
11	Brian Sutter	1976-1988
24	Bernie Federko	1976-1989

All-time Record vs. Other Clubs

Regular Season

			At Home							On Road							Total			
	GP	W	L	T	GF	GA	PTS	GP	W	L	T	GF	GA	PTS	GP	W	L	T	GF	GA	PTS
Anaheim	14	6	5	3	47	42	15	14	9	4	1	43	35	19	28	15	9	4	90	77	34
Atlanta	1	1	0	0	4	1	2	1	1	0	0	5	2	2	2	2	0	0	9	3	4
Boston	56	24	23	9	179	192	57	56	13	34	9	152	239	35	112	37	57	18	331	431	92
Buffalo	47	26	14	7	170	122	59	49	14	29	6	151	195	34	96	40	43	13	321	317	93
Calgary	56	26	21	9	201	176	61	54	24	26	4	165	186	52	110	50	47	13	366	362	113
Carolina	28	17	9	2	111	88	36	28	15	11	2	88	86	32	56	32	20	4	199	174	68
Chicago	104	50	37	17	348	325	118	108	33	60	15	324	406	81	212	83	97	32	672	731	199
Colorado	32	21	8	3	134	97	45	33	11	18	4	92	117	26	65	32	26	7	226	214	71
Dallas	110	60	30	20	402	312	140	107	39	49	19	322	365	97	217	99	79	39	724	677	237
Detroit	100	55	28	17	353	273	127	99	39	43	17	311	359	95	199	94	71	34	664	632	222
Edmonton	36	15	16	5	131	140	35	36	15	18	3	129	135	33	72	30	34	8	260	275	68
Florida	6	4	1	1	16	9	9	6	3	1	2	16	13	8	12	7	2	3	32	22	17
Los Angeles	70	44	16	10	263	179	98	70	27	33	10	206	242	64	140	71	49	20	469	421	162
Montreal	56	13	28	15	144	195	41	56	9	40	7	149	246	25	112	22	68	22	293	441	66
Nashville	6	4	2	0	20	11	8	6	4	1	1	21	14	9	12	8	3	1	41	25	17
New Jersey	43	26	10	7	183	131	59	44	17	20	7	127	142	41	87	43	30	14	310	273	100
NY Islanders	44	17	18	9	158	144	43	46	11	24	11	118	176	33	90	28	42	20	276	320	76
NY Rangers	60	23	28	9	174	193	55	58	8	44	6	134	240	22	118	31	72	15	308	433	77
Ottawa	7	3	3	1	21	21	7	7	6	1	0	33	13	12	14	9	4	1	54	34	19
Philadelphia	64	26	31	7	188	201	59	64	11	43	10	145	252	32	128	37	74	17	333	453	91
Phoenix	42	20	12	10	152	119	50	43	17	20	6	139	140	40	85	37	32	16	291	259	90
Pittsburgh	61	40	15	6	238	165	86	61	19	30	12	182	230	50	122	59	45	18	420	395	136
San Jose	20	14	5	1	68	44	29	16	13	2	1	58	35	27	36	27	7	2	126	79	56
Tampa Bay	8	7	1	0	31	19	14	10	5	3	2	35	29	12	18	12	4	2	66	48	26
Toronto	98	56	29	13	337	275	125	96	27	58	11	278	360	65	194	83	87	24	615	635	190
Vancouver	63	36	18	9	238	182	81	64	32	25	7	209	188	71	127	68	43	16	447	370	152
Washington	38	17	13	8	155	125	42	37	13	20	4	108	132	30	75	30	33	12	263	257	72
Defunct Clubs	32	25	4	3	131	55	53	33	11	10	12	95	100	34	65	36	14	15	226	155	87
Totals	1302	676	425	201	4597	3836	1554	1302	446	667	189	3835	4677	1081	2604	1122	1092	390	8432	8513	2635

Playoffs

	Series	W	L	GP	W	L	T	GF	GA	Last Mtg.	Round	Result
Boston	2	0	2	8	0	8	0	15	48	1972	SF	L 0-4
Buffalo	1	0	1	3	1	2	0	8	7	1976	PR	L 1-2
Calgary	1	0	1	7	3	4	0	22	28	1986	CF	L 3-4
Chicago	9	2	7	45	18	27	0	129	166	1993	DSF	W 4-0
Dallas	11	5	6	62	28	34	0	174	191	1999	CQF	L 2-4
Detroit	6	2	4	35	15	20	0	92	111	1998	CQF	L 2-4
Los Angeles	2	2	0	8	8	0	0	32	13	1998	CSF	W 4-0
Montreal	3	0	3	12	0	12	0	14	42	1977	QF	L 0-4
NY Rangers	1	0	1	6	2	4	0	22	29	1981	QF	L 2-4
Philadelphia	2	2	0	11	8	3	0	34	20	1969	QF	W 4-0
Phoenix	2	2	0	11	7	4	0	39	29	1999	CQF	W 4-3
Pittsburgh	3	2	1	13	7	6	0	45	40	1981	PR	W 3-2
San Jose	1	0	1	7	3	4	0	22	20	2000	CQF	L 3-4
Toronto	5	3	2	31	17	14	0	88	90	1996	CQF	W 4-2
Vancouver	1	0	1	7	3	4	0	27	27	1995	CQF	L 3-4
Totals	50	20	30	266	120	146	0	763	861			

Playoff Results 2000-1996

Year	Round	Opponent	Result	GF	GA
2000	CQF	San Jose	L 3-4	22	20
1999	CSF	Dallas	L 2-4	12	17
	CQF	Phoenix	W 4-3	19	16
1998	CSF	Detroit	L 2-4	13	23
	CQF	Los Angeles	W 4-0	16	8
1997	CQF	Detroit	L 2-4	12	13
1996	CSF	Detroit	L 3-4	16	22
	CQF	Toronto	W 4-2	21	15

Abbreviations: Round: CF – conference final; CSF – conference semi-final; CQF – conference quarter-final; DSF – division semi-final; SF – semi-final; QF – quarter-final; PR – preliminary round.

Calgary totals include Atlanta Flames, 1972-73 to 1979-80.
Colorado totals include Quebec, 1979-80 to 1994-95.
New Jersey totals include Kansas City, 1974-75 to 1975-76, and Colorado Rockies, 1976-77 to 1981-82.
Phoenix totals include Winnipeg, 1979-80 to 1995-96.
Carolina totals include Hartford, 1979-80 to 1996-97.
Dallas totals include Minnesota North Stars, 1967-68 to 1992-93.

1999-2000 Results

Oct. 2	Phoenix	1-2		8	Vancouver	4-2
4	Los Angeles	2-3		11 at	San Jose	5-2
6 at	Calgary	4-1		13 at	Los Angeles	3-2
9 at	Edmonton	4-2		14 at	Anaheim	1-3
13 at	Detroit	2-4		19 at	Pittsburgh	1-3
16	Toronto	4-2		21 at	Chicago	3-0
19	Calgary	7-1		22	NY Rangers	1-4
21	Edmonton	3-2 *		26 at	Ottawa	4-1
23	New Jersey	3-1		28 at	Dallas	3-1
27 at	New Jersey	1-2		29	Colorado	4-0
30	Detroit	5-4 *	Feb. 1 at	Calgary	5-4 *
Nov. 3 at	Colorado	0-5		3 at	Vancouver	5-2
5 at	Edmonton	2-1		8 at	Detroit	4-1
7 at	Vancouver	6-1		10	Detroit	0-2
9	Dallas	2-5		12	Anaheim	6-3
12	Edmonton	2-3		15	Atlanta	4-1
13 at	NY Islanders	5-3		18 at	Nashville	2-1
17 at	Toronto	3-2		21 at	Anaheim	4-2
18	Florida	3-0		23 at	San Jose	4-1
20	San Jose	1-1		25	Colorado	4-2
22	Nashville	3-2 *		27	Chicago	1-4
24 at	Detroit	2-4		29	Philadelphia	3-2
26 at	Buffalo	2-0	Mar. 2 at	Atlanta	5-2
27	Chicago	8-3		4 at	Florida	1-1
Dec. 2	Nashville	3-1		7	Phoenix	4-0
4	San Jose	4-2		9	Vancouver	2-2
5 at	Philadelphia	2-3		11	Anaheim	1-1
7	Carolina	2-4		12 at	Dallas	2-4
10 at	Nashville	4-2		15 at	Phoenix	5-3
11	Dallas	4-2		17 at	Los Angeles	4-0
14	Calgary	1-1		20	Washington	2-1
18	Boston	4-0		22 at	Carolina	2-1
21 at	Phoenix	6-0		24 at	Tampa Bay	5-1
23 at	Nashville	2-2		26 at	Chicago	1-1
26	Nashville	2-3		29	Toronto	2-3
27 at	Colorado	1-5		30 at	Boston	3-2
30	San Jose	2-1 *	Apr. 1	Detroit	0-0
Jan. 1 at	Washington	1-1		2	Ottawa	4-1
3 at	NY Rangers	5-2		5	Calgary	6-5
4	Los Angeles	2-2		7	Chicago	3-4 *
6	Montreal	4-3		9 at	Chicago	1-3

* – Overtime

Entry Draft
Selections 2000-1986

2000
Pick
30	Jeff Taffe
65	David Morisset
75	Justin Papineau
96	Antoine Bergeron
129	Troy Riddle
167	Craig Weller
229	Brett Lutes
261	Reinhard Divis
293	Lauri Kinos

1999
Pick
17	Barret Jackman
85	Peter Smrek
114	Chad Starling
143	Trevor Byrne
180	Tore Vikingstad
203	Phil Osaer
221	Colin Hemingway
232	Alexander Khavanov
260	Brian McMeekin
270	James Desmarais

1998
Pick
24	Christian Backman
41	Maxim Linnik
83	Matt Walker
157	Brad Voth
170	Andrei Trochinsky
197	Brad Twordik
225	Yevgeny Pastukh
255	John Pohl

1997
Pick
40	Tyler Rennette
86	Didier Tremblay
98	Jan Horacek
106	Jame Pollock
149	Nicholas Bilotto
177	Ladislav Nagy
206	Bobby Haglund
232	Dmitri Plekhanov
244	Marek Ivan

1996
Pick
14	Marty Reasoner
67	Gordie Dwyer
95	Jonathan Zukiwsky
97	Andrei Petrakov
159	Stephen Wagner
169	Daniel Corso
177	Reed Low
196	Andrei Podkonicky
203	Tony Hutchins
229	Konstantin Shafranov

1995
Pick
49	Jochen Hecht
75	Scott Roche
101	Michal Handzus
127	Jeff Ambrosio
153	Denis Hamel
179	Jean-Luc Grand-Pierre
205	Derek Bekar
209	Libor Zabransky

1994
Pick
68	Stephane Roy
94	Tyler Harlton
120	Edvin Frylen
172	Roman Vopat
198	Steve Noble
224	Marc Stephan
250	Kevin Harper
276	Scott Fankhouser

1993
Pick
37	Maxim Bets
63	Jamie Rivers
89	Jamal Mayers
141	Todd Kelman
167	Mike Buzak
193	Eric Boguniecki
219	Mike Grier
245	Libor Prochazka
271	Alexander Vasilevski
275	Christer Olsson

1992
Pick
38	Igor Korolev
62	Vitali Karamnov
64	Vitali Prokhorov
86	Lee Leslie
134	Bob Lachance
158	Ian Laperriere
160	Lance Burns
180	Igor Boldin
182	Nick Naumenko
206	Todd Harris
230	Yuri Gunko
259	Wade Salzman

1991
Pick
27	Steve Staios
64	Kyle Reeves
65	Nathan LaFayette
87	Grayden Reid
109	Jeff Callinan
131	Bruce Gardiner
153	Terry Hollinger
175	Chris Kenady
197	Jed Fiebelkorn
219	Chris MacKenzie
241	Kevin Rappana
263	Mike Veisor

1990
Pick
33	Craig Johnson
54	Patrice Tardif
96	Jason Ruff
117	Kurtis Miller
138	Wayne Conlan
180	Parris Duffus
201	Steve Widmeyer
222	Joe Hawley
243	Joe Fleming

1989
Pick
9	Jason Marshall
31	Rick Corriveau
55	Denny Felsner
93	Daniel Laperriere
114	David Roberts
124	Derek Frenette
135	Jeff Batters
156	Kevin Plager
177	John Roderick
198	John Valo
219	Brian Lukowski

1988
Pick
9	Rod Brind'Amour
30	Adrien Plavsic
51	Rob Fournier
72	Jaan Luik
105	Dave Lacouture
114	Dan Fowler
135	Matt Hayes
156	John McCoy
177	Tony Twist
198	Bret Hedican
219	Heath DeBoer
240	Michael Francis

1987
Pick
12	Keith Osborne
54	Kevin Miehm
59	Robert Nordmark
75	Darren Smith
82	Andy Rymsha
117	Rob Robinson
138	Todd Crabtree
159	Guy Hebert
180	Robert Dumas
201	David Marvin
207	Andy Cesarski
222	Dan Rolfe
243	Ray Savard

1986
Pick
10	Jocelyn Lemieux
31	Mike Posma
52	Tony Hejna
73	Glen Featherstone
87	Michael Wolak
115	Mike O' Toole
136	Andy May
157	Randy Skarda
178	Martyn Ball
199	Rod Thacker
220	Terry MacLean
234	Bill Butler
241	David O'Brien

General Manager

PLEAU, LARRY
General Manager, St. Louis Blues. Born in Lynn, MA, June 29, 1947.

Larry Pleau was named general manager on June 9, 1997, becoming the tenth person to hold that position in team history.

Pleau joined the Blues after spending eight seasons with the New York Rangers organization, most recently as vice president of player personnel. He joined the Rangers in 1989 as assistant general manager of player development. During Pleau's tenure in New York, the Rangers drafted NHL stars Sergei Zubov, Doug Weight, Alexei Kovalev, Niklas Sundstrom, Todd Marchant and Sergei Nemchinov, along with Corey Hirsch, Daniel Goneau and Mattias Norstrom. Prior to joining the Rangers, Pleau spent 17 seasons with the Hartford Whalers organization as a player, assistant coach, head coach, general manager and minor league general manager and head coach. He was also instrumental in drafting Ray Ferraro, Ron Francis, Kevin Dineen and Ulf Samuelsson while a member of the Whalers organization.

Pleau played three seasons with the Montreal Canadiens (1969-1972) in the National Hockey League before being the first player signed by the Hartford Whalers of the World Hockey Association. He was a center/left wing for the Whalers from 1972 until his retirement in 1979. He played in 468 regular season games for Hartford, accumulating 157 goals and 215 assists for 372 points. He also played for the 1968 United States Olympic Team, the 1969 U.S. National Team and for Team USA in the 1976 Canada Cup tournament.

Pleau and his wife, Wendy, have a son, Steve, and a daughter, Shannon.

NHL Coaching Record

		Regular Season					Playoffs			
Season	Team	Games	W	L	T	%	Games	W	L	%
1980-81	Hartford	20	6	12	2	.350	....	....	....	....
1981-82	Hartford	80	21	41	18	.375	....	....	....	....
1982-83	Hartford	18	4	13	1	.250	....	....	....	....
1987-88	Hartford	26	13	13	0	.500	6	2	4	.333
1988-89	Hartford	80	37	38	5	.494	4	0	4	.000
	NHL Totals	**224**	**81**	**117**	**26**	**.420**	**10**	**2**	**8**	**.200**

Club Directory

Savvis Center

St. Louis Blues
Savvis Center
1401 Clark Avenue
St. Louis, MO 63103
Phone **314/622-2500**
FAX 314/622-2533
Website: www.stlouisblues.com
Capacity: TBA

Owner and Chairman	Bill Laurie
President & CEO	Mark Sauer
Senior Vice President, Marketing & Communications	Jim Woodcock
Senior Vice President, Finance and Hockey Administration	Jerry Jasiek
Senior Vice President, Sales	Bruce Affleck
Vice President, Marketing	JoAnn Miles
Senior Vice President, Savvis Center	Dennis Petrullo
Vice President, Human Resources	David Coverstone
Executive to the President	Lisa Cwiklowski
Executive to the General Manager	Donna Lembke

Executive, Paige Sports Entertainment
President	Richard Thomas
Executive Vice President	Brent Karasiuk
Executive Assistant	Deborah Belsheim
Assistant	Cynthia Morrison
Receptionist	Sharon Odom

Hockey Operations
Senior Vice President & General Manager	Larry Pleau
Assistant General Manager	John Ferguson Jr.
Head Coach	Joel Quenneville
Assistant Coaches	Mike Kitchen, Jim Roberts
Golatending Coach	Keith Allain
Director of Pro Scouting	Bob Plager
Pro Scouts	Bill Dineen
Special Assignment	Ralph Backstrom, Jack Evans, Rick Meagher, Peter Stastny
Director of Amateur Scouting	Teddy Hampson
Amateur Scouts	Mike Antonovich, Pat Ginnell, Anders Steen, Bill Terry
Part-time Scouts	Jim Bzdel, Paul Guay, Wayne Mundey, Miroslav Termer, Georgi Zhuravlev, Jack Gardiner
Director of Team Services	Michael Caruso
Video Coach	Jamie Kompon
Head Coach, Worcester IceCats	Don Granato
Associate Coach, Worcester IceCats	Steve Pleau

Medical Staff
Athletic Trainer	Ray Barile
Equipment Manager	Bert Godin
Assistant Equipment Manager	Eric Bechtol
Equipment Assistant	Greg Cable
Massage Therapist	Jeffrey Wright
Strength & Conditioning Coordinator	Aaron Komarek
Orthopedic Surgeons	Dr. Jerome Gilden, Dr. Rick Wright, Dr. Matt Matava
Internists	Dr. Aaron Birenbaum, Dr. William Birenbaum
Neurosurgeon	Dr. Ralph Dacey
General Surgery	Dr. Michael Brunt
Dentist	Dr. Glenn Edwards
Optometrist	Dr. N. Rex Ghormley

Communications/Marketing
Director of Communications	Jeff Trammel
Assistant Director of Communications	Greg Franklin
Communications Manager	Stanley Richardson
Manager of Publications	Renee St. John
Marketing/Public Relations Assistant	Donna Quirk

Marketing
Director of Corporate Sponsorships	Chris Arger
Director of Marketing Programs	Lou Siville
Manager of Corporate Sales and Promotions	Rob Rixford
Sponsorship Service Coordinator	Jeff Floerke
Community Relations/Youth Marketing Manager	Maureen Cierpiot

Finance
Director of Finance	Jeff Horstman
Accounting Staff	Jim Bergman, Craig Bryant, Phil Siddle, Pam Pflasterer, Crystal Strasburg, Michelle Daily, Traci Hinterser, Mindy Wallace, Sirena Moore

Sales
Director of Sales	Jennifer Gruner
Season Ticket Manager	Jill Hahn
Season Ticket Account Executive	Paula Barnes
Group Sales Account Executives	Kari Palmer, Jill Serve
Sales Executives	Kourtney Hacker, Katie Kelley, Ashley Zurawski
Sales Coordinator	Kris Francis
Retail Director	George Pavlik
Radio Stations	KTRS 550 am
TV Stations	Fox Sports Net, KPLR-TV, WBII

General Managers' History

Lynn Patrick, 1967-68; Scotty Bowman, 1968-69 to 1970-71; Lynn Patrick, 1971-72; Sid Abel, 1972-73; Charles Catto, 1973-74; Gerry Ehman, 1974-75; Dennis Ball, 1975-76; Emile Francis, 1976-77 to 1982-83; Ron Caron, 1983-84 to 1993-94; Mike Keenan, 1994-95, 1995-96; Mike Keenan and Ron Caron, 1996-97; Larry Pleau, 1997-98 to date.

Captains' History

Al Arbour, 1967-68 to 1969-70; Red Berenson and Barclay Plager, 1970-71; Barclay Plager, 1971-72 to 1975-76; no captain, 1976-77; Red Berenson, 1977-78; Barry Gibbs, 1978-79; Brian Sutter, 1979-80 to 1987-88; Bernie Federko, 1988-89; Rick Meagher, 1989-90; Scott Stevens, 1990-91; Garth Butcher, 1991-92; Brett Hull, 1992-93 to 1994-95; Brett Hull, Shayne Corson and Wayne Gretzky, 1995-96; no captain, 1996-97; Chris Pronger, 1997-98 to date.

San Jose Sharks

1999-2000 Results: 35W-37L-10T 87PTS. Fourth, Pacific Division

Year-by-Year Record

		Home			Road			Overall					
Season	GP	W	L	T	W	L	T	W	L	T	GF	GA	Pts.	Finished	Playoff Result
1999-2000	82	21	17	3	14	20	7	35	37	10	225	214	87	4th, Pacific Div.	Lost Conf. Semi-Final
1998-99	82	17	15	9	14	18	9	31	33	18	196	191	80	4th, Pacific Div.	Lost Conf. Quarter-Final
1997-98	82	17	19	5	17	19	5	34	38	10	210	216	78	4th, Pacific Div.	Lost Conf. Quarter-Final
1996-97	82	14	23	4	13	24	4	27	47	8	211	278	62	7th, Pacific Div.	Out of Playoffs
1995-96	82	12	26	3	8	29	4	20	55	7	252	357	47	7th, Pacific Div.	Out of Playoffs
1994-95	48	10	13	1	9	12	3	19	25	4	129	161	42	3rd, Pacific Div.	Lost Conf. Semi-Final
1993-94	84	19	13	10	14	22	6	33	35	16	252	265	82	3rd, Pacific Div.	Lost Conf. Semi-Final
1992-93	84	8	33	1	3	38	1	11	71	2	218	414	24	6th, Smythe Div.	Out of Playoffs
1991-92	80	14	23	3	3	35	2	17	58	5	219	359	39	6th, Smythe Div.	Out of Playoffs

2000-01 Schedule

Oct.	Fri.	6	St. Louis		Thu.	11	St. Louis
	Thu.	12	Phoenix		Sat.	13	Nashville
	Sat.	14	Boston		Mon.	15	Detroit*
	Wed.	18	at Dallas		Wed.	17	Calgary
	Fri.	20	at Minnesota		Sat.	20	Colorado*
	Sat.	21	at Nashville		Mon.	22	at Edmonton
	Tue.	24	at Carolina		Wed.	24	Edmonton
	Wed.	25	at Columbus		Fri.	26	at Dallas
	Sat.	28	Atlanta		Sat.	27	at St. Louis
Nov.	Wed.	1	Pittsburgh		Tue.	30	Colorado
	Sat.	4	Carolina	Feb.	Thu.	1	Dallas
	Sun.	5	at Vancouver		Tue.	6	at Calgary
	Wed.	8	at Chicago		Thu.	8	at Vancouver
	Thu.	9	at Columbus		Sat.	10	Chicago
	Sat.	11	at NY Islanders		Wed.	14	at Chicago
	Tue.	14	at New Jersey		Fri.	16	at Nashville
	Wed.	15	at Detroit		Sun.	18	at Minnesota*
	Sat.	18	NY Islanders		Tue.	20	Columbus
	Wed.	22	Chicago		Wed.	21	at Anaheim
	Sat.	25	New Jersey		Fri.	23	Anaheim
	Tue.	28	Minnesota		Mon.	26	at St. Louis
	Thu.	30	Anaheim		Wed.	28	at Toronto
Dec.	Sun.	3	at Edmonton	Mar.	Thu.	1	at Ottawa
	Mon.	4	at Calgary		Sat.	3	at Boston*
	Wed.	6	Dallas		Tue.	6	at Tampa Bay
	Fri.	8	Vancouver		Wed.	7	at Florida
	Tue.	12	NY Rangers		Sat.	10	Nashville
	Thu.	14	Columbus		Mon.	12	Montreal
	Sat.	16	at Phoenix		Wed.	14	Los Angeles
	Mon.	18	at Washington		Sat.	17	at Los Angeles*
	Wed.	20	at Detroit		Sun.	18	Detroit*
	Thu.	21	at Philadelphia		Tue.	20	at Colorado
	Sat.	23	at Buffalo*		Thu.	22	Ottawa
	Tue.	26	at Los Angeles		Mon.	26	at Los Angeles
	Thu.	28	Edmonton		Tue.	27	Los Angeles
	Sat.	30	Vancouver		Thu.	29	Anaheim
Jan.	Mon.	1	at Phoenix		Sat.	31	at Phoenix
	Wed.	3	Calgary	Apr.	Mon.	2	Minnesota
	Thu.	4	at Colorado		Thu.	5	Phoenix
	Sat.	6	Florida		Sat.	7	Dallas*
	Tue.	9	Buffalo		Sun.	8	at Anaheim*

* Denotes afternoon game.

Franchise date: May 9, 1990

WESTERN CONFERENCE

PACIFIC DIVISION

10th NHL Season

Jeff Friesen is the Sharks' all-time leader in games played, goals (tied with Owen Nolan), assists and points. He was the 11th player taken in the 1994 NHL Entry Draft, and has been the top scorer to emerge from among that season's selections.

2000-01 Player Personnel

FORWARDS	HT	WT	S	Place of Birth	Date	1999-00 Club
BATOVSKY, Zoltan	5-11	186	L	Slovad, Czech.	3/27/79	Drummondville
BRADLEY, Matt	6-2	195	R	Stittsville, Ont.	6/13/78	Kentucky
CHEECHOO, Jonathan	6-0	200	R	Moose Factory, Ont.	7/15/80	Belleville Bulls
COLAGIACOMO, Adam	6-2	200	R	Toronto, Ont.	3/17/79	Kentucky-New Orleans
COURVILLE, Larry	6-1	180	L	Timmins, Ont.	4/2/75	Kentucky
DAMPHOUSSE, Vincent	6-1	200	L	Montreal, Que.	12/17/67	San Jose
DEULING, Jarrett	6-0	205	L	Vernon, B.C.	3/4/74	Kentucky
FRIEDMAN, Doug	6-1	205	L	Cape Elizabeth, ME	9/1/71	Kentucky
FRIESEN, Jeff	6-0	205	L	Meadow Lake, Sask.	8/5/76	San Jose
GRANATO, Tony	5-10	185	R	Downers Grove, IL	7/25/64	San Jose
HARVEY, Todd	6-0	205	R	Hamilton, Ont.	2/17/75	NY Rangers-San Jose
KOROLYUK, Alexander	5-9	195	L	Moscow, USSR	1/15/76	San Jose
KRAFT, Ryan	5-9	181	L	Bottineau, ND	11/7/75	Richmond-Cleveland-Kentucky
LAPLANTE, Eric	6-0	195	L	St-Maurice, Que.	12/1/79	Quebec Remparts
LUNDBOHM, Andy	6-3	225	L	Roseau, MN	3/24/77	New Orleans-Kentucky
MARLEAU, Patrick	6-2	210	L	Aneroid, Sask.	9/15/79	San Jose
MATTEAU, Stephane	6-4	220	L	Rouyn-Noranda, Que.	9/2/69	San Jose
MONTGOMERY, Jim	5-10	180	R	Montreal, Que.	6/30/69	Phi (AHL)-Manitoba Moose
NITTEL, Adam	6-2	225	R	Kitchener, Ont.	7/17/78	Kentucky-New Orleans
NOLAN, Owen	6-1	210	R	Belfast, Ireland	2/12/72	San Jose
RICCI, Mike	6-0	190	L	Scarborough, Ont.	10/27/71	San Jose
SAMUELSSON, Mikael	6-1	195	L	Mariefred, Sweden	12/23/76	Brynas IF
SMITH, Mark	5-10	200	L	Eyebrow, Sask.	10/24/77	Kentucky
STRINGER, Rejean	5-11	205	L	Gravelbourg, Sask.	8/21/74	New Orleans Brass-Kentucky
STURM, Marco	6-0	195	L	Dingolfing, Germany	9/8/78	San Jose
SUNDSTROM, Niklas	6-0	200	L	Ornskoldsvik, Sweden	6/6/75	San Jose
THORNTON, Scott	6-3	216	L	London, Ont.	1/9/71	Montreal-Dallas
ZALESAK, Miroslav	6-0	185	L	Skalica, Czech.	1/2/80	Drummondville
DEFENSEMEN						
ANDRUSAK, Greg	6-1	195	R	Cranbrook, B.C.	11/14/69	Toronto-Chicago Wolves
BANCROFT, Steve	6-1	214	L	Toronto, Ont.	10/6/70	Cincinnati (IHL)-Houston Aeros
DAVISON, Rob	6-2	220	L	St. Catharines, Ont.	5/1/80	North Bay
GOSSELIN, Christian	6-5	235	R	Laval, Que.	8/21/76	Kentucky
HANNAN, Scott	6-2	220	L	Richmond, B.C.	1/23/79	San Jose-Kentucky
HEINS, Shawn	6-4	210	L	Eganville, Ont.	12/24/73	San Jose-Kentucky
JILLSON, Jeff	6-3	220	R	Providence, RI	7/24/80	U. of Michigan
JINDRICH, Robert	5-11	190	L	Plzen, Czech.	10/14/76	Kentucky
MacISAAC, Dave	6-2	225	L	Cambridge, MA	4/23/72	Lowell
MARCHMENT, Bryan	6-1	195	L	Scarborough, Ont.	5/1/69	San Jose
MULICK, Robert	6-2	205	R	Toronto, Ont.	10/23/79	Kentucky
RAGNARSSON, Marcus	6-1	215	L	Ostervala, Sweden	8/13/71	San Jose
RATHJE, Mike	6-5	235	L	Mannville, Alta.	5/11/74	San Jose
STUART, Brad	6-2	210	L	Rocky Mountain House, Alta.	11/6/79	San Jose
SUTER, Gary	6-0	215	L	Madison, WI	6/24/64	San Jose

GOALTENDERS	HT	WT	C	Place of Birth	Date	1999-00 Club
FRIESEN, Terry	5-11	195	L	Winkler, Man.	10/29/77	New Orleans Brass
HEDBERG, Johan	5-11	185	L	Leksand, Sweden	5/5/73	Kentucky
KIPRUSOFF, Miikka	6-2	190	L	Turku, Finland	10/26/76	Kentucky
NABOKOV, Evgeni	6-0	200	L	Ust-Kamenogorsk, USSR	7/25/75	San Jose-Cleveland-Kentucky
SHIELDS, Steve	6-3	215	L	Toronto, Ont.	7/19/72	San Jose
TOSKALA, Vesa	5-9	175	L	Tampere, Finland	5/20/77	Farjestads BK

Coach

SUTTER, DARRYL JOHN
Coach, San Jose Sharks. Born in Viking, Alta., August 19, 1958.

Darryl Sutter became the Sharks' fifth head coach on June 9, 1997. He led the club to a team record 87 points in 1999-2000. Sutter played eight NHL seasons, all with the Chicago Blackhawks (1979-87). He began his coaching career as an assistant in Chicago in 1987-88 before taking over as head coach of the Blackhawks' IHL affiliate that played in Saginaw (1988-89) and in Indianapolis (1989-90). His club won an IHL Turner Cup championship in 1990 and Sutter was named coach of the year.

He later served as an associate coach under Mike Keenan in Chicago in 1990-91 and 1991-92 and began a three-year tenure as head coach of the Blackhawks in 1992-93. As coach of Chicago, Sutter's teams reached the playoffs in all three seasons. His career winning percentage of .569 ranks second among Chicago coaches. He resigned as head coach following the 1994-95 season to spend more time with his family and worked as a consultant to the Blackhawks for special assignments in 1995-96 and 1996-97.

In 18 years of hockey as a player and coach, Sutter has never failed to qualify for post-season play. During his eight-year playing career, he scored 161 goals and added 118 assists in 406 regular-season games. He added 24 goals and 19 assists in 51 playoff games. Drafted 179th overall by Chicago in the 1978 NHL Entry Draft, he scored a remarkable 40 goals during his rookie season. The left winger served as team captain from 1982-83 until injuries forced his retirement after the 1986-87 season.

He is one of six brothers to play in the NHL. The others are Brian, Brent, Duane, Rich and Ron. All are involved in the Sutter Foundation which raises raises money for non-profit organizations in their home province of Alberta.

Coaching Record

		Regular Season					Playoffs			
Season	Team	Games	W	L	T	%	Games	W	L	%
1988-89	Saginaw (IHL)	82	46	26	10	.560	6	2	4	.333
1989-90	Indianapolis (IHL)	82	53	21	8	.646	14	12	2	.857
1992-93	**Chicago (NHL)**	**84**	**47**	**25**	**12**	**.631**	**4**	**0**	**4**	**.000**
1993-94	**Chicago (NHL)**	**84**	**39**	**36**	**9**	**.518**	**6**	**2**	**4**	**.333**
1994-95	**Chicago (NHL)**	**48**	**24**	**19**	**5**	**.552**	**16**	**9**	**7**	**.563**
1997-98	**San Jose (NHL)**	**82**	**34**	**38**	**10**	**.476**	**6**	**2**	**4**	**.333**
1998-99	**San Jose (NHL)**	**82**	**31**	**33**	**18**	**.488**	**6**	**2**	**4**	**.333**
1999-2000	**San Jose (NHL)**	**82**	**35**	**37**	**10**	**.530•**	**12**	**5**	**7**	**.417**
	NHL Totals	**462**	**210**	**188**	**64**	**.531•**	**50**	**20**	**30**	**.400**

• Includes points from regulation ties

1999-2000 Scoring

* – rookie

Regular Season

Pos	#	Player	Team	GP	G	A	Pts	+/–	PIM	PP	SH	GW	GT	S	%
R	11	Owen Nolan	S.J.	78	44	40	84	–1	110	18	4	6	2	261	16.9
C	25	Vincent Damphousse	S.J.	82	21	49	70	4	58	3	1	1	1	204	10.3
L	39	Jeff Friesen	S.J.	82	26	35	61	–2	47	11	3	7	0	191	13.6
C	18	Mike Ricci	S.J.	82	20	24	44	14	60	10	0	5	0	134	14.9
C	14	Patrick Marleau	S.J.	81	17	23	40	–9	36	3	0	3	0	161	10.6
R	24	Niklas Sundstrom	S.J.	79	12	25	37	9	22	2	1	2	3	90	13.3
D	7 *	Brad Stuart	S.J.	82	10	26	36	3	32	5	1	3	0	133	7.5
R	15	Alexander Korolyuk	S.J.	57	14	21	35	4	35	3	0	1	1	124	11.3
D	20	Gary Suter	S.J.	76	6	28	34	7	52	2	1	0	0	175	3.4
C	19	Marco Sturm	S.J.	74	12	15	27	4	22	2	4	3	0	120	10.0
L	32	Stephane Matteau	S.J.	69	12	12	24	–3	61	0	0	3	0	73	16.4
D	5	Jeff Norton	S.J.	62	0	20	20	–2	49	0	0	0	0	45	0.0
R	9	Todd Harvey	NYR	31	3	3	6	–9	62	0	0	0	0	31	9.7
			S.J	40	8	4	12	–2	78	2	0	0	0	59	13.6
			TOTAL	71	11	7	18	–11	140	2	0	0	0	90	12.2
D	10	Marcus Ragnarsson	S.J.	63	3	13	16	13	38	0	0	0	0	60	5.0
D	40	Mike Rathje	S.J.	66	2	14	16	–2	31	0	0	0	0	46	4.3
L	21	Tony Granato	S.J.	48	6	7	13	2	39	1	0	0	0	67	9.0
C	12	Ron Sutter	S.J.	78	5	6	11	–3	34	0	1	1	0	68	7.4
R	22	Ronnie Stern	S.J.	67	4	5	9	–9	151	0	0	0	0	63	6.3
L	26	Dave Lowry	S.J.	32	1	4	5	1	18	0	0	0	0	25	4.0
D	27	Bryan Marchment	S.J.	49	0	4	4	3	72	0	0	0	0	51	0.0
D	43 *	Scott Hannan	S.J.	30	1	2	3	7	10	0	0	0	0	28	3.6
D	42	Andy Sutton	S.J.	40	1	1	2	–5	80	0	0	0	0	29	3.4
L	32	Murray Craven	S.J.	19	0	2	2	–2	4	0	0	0	0	18	0.0
R	33	Brantt Myhres	S.J.	13	0	1	1	0	97	0	0	0	0	2	0.0
D	3	Bob Rouse	S.J.	26	0	1	1	–3	19	0	0	0	0	20	0.0
G	31	Steve Shields	S.J.	67	0	1	1	0	29	0	0	0	0	0	0.0
D	23 *	Shawn Heins	S.J.	1	0	0	0	–1	2	0	0	0	0	1	0.0
G	35 *	Evgeni Nabokov	S.J.	11	0	0	0	0	0	0	0	0	0	0	0.0

Goaltending

No.	Goaltender	GPI	Mins	Avg	W	L	T	EN	SO	GA	SA	S%
35	* Evgeni Nabokov	11	414	2.17	2	2	1	2	1	15	166	.910
29	Mike Vernon	15	772	2.49	6	5	1	0	0	32	360	.911
31	Steve Shields	67	3797	2.56	27	30	8	3	4	162	1826	.911
	Totals	**82**	**5004**	**2.57**	**35**	**37**	**10**	**5**	**5**	**214**	**2357**	**.909**

Playoffs

Pos	#	Player	Team	GP	G	A	Pts	+/–	PIM	PP	SH	GW	OT	S	%
R	11	Owen Nolan	S.J.	10	8	2	10	–2	6	2	2	3	0	32	25.0
C	25	Vincent Damphousse	S.J.	12	1	7	8	–5	16	1	0	0	0	28	3.6
D	20	Gary Suter	S.J.	12	2	5	7	–6	12	1	0	1	0	33	6.1
C	18	Mike Ricci	S.J.	12	5	1	6	–3	2	3	0	1	0	20	25.0
L	39	Jeff Friesen	S.J.	11	2	2	4	–4	10	0	0	0	0	22	9.1
D	40	Mike Rathje	S.J.	12	1	3	4	1	8	0	0	0	0	8	12.5
C	19	Marco Sturm	S.J.	12	1	3	4	0	6	0	0	0	0	16	6.3
D	27	Bryan Marchment	S.J.	11	2	1	3	2	12	0	0	0	0	16	12.5
L	26	Dave Lowry	S.J.	12	1	2	3	0	6	0	0	0	0	7	14.3
R	15	Alexander Korolyuk	S.J.	9	0	3	3	1	6	0	0	0	0	13	0.0
D	10	Marcus Ragnarsson	S.J.	12	0	3	3	3	10	0	0	0	0	7	0.0
C	14	Patrick Marleau	S.J.	5	1	1	2	–3	2	1	0	0	0	4	25.0
L	32	Stephane Matteau	S.J.	10	0	2	2	–2	8	0	0	0	0	16	0.0
C	12	Ron Sutter	S.J.	12	0	2	2	0	10	0	0	0	0	11	0.0
R	24	Niklas Sundstrom	S.J.	12	0	2	2	–3	2	0	0	0	0	9	0.0
R	22	Ronnie Stern	S.J.	3	1	0	1	–2	11	0	0	0	0	4	25.0
R	9	Todd Harvey	S.J.	12	1	0	1	–2	8	1	0	0	0	9	11.1
D	7 *	Brad Stuart	S.J.	12	1	0	1	–11	6	1	0	0	0	12	8.3
D	43 *	Scott Hannan	S.J.	1	0	1	1	0	0	0	0	0	0	2	0.0
L	21	Tony Granato	S.J.	12	0	1	1	1	14	0	0	0	0	15	0.0
D	5	Jeff Norton	S.J.	12	0	1	1	–3	7	0	0	0	0	11	0.0
G	35 *	Evgeni Nabokov	S.J.	1	0	0	0	0	0	0	0	0	0	0	0.0
G	31	Steve Shields	S.J.	12	0	0	0	0	0	0	0	0	0	0	0.0

Goaltending

No.	Goaltender	GPI	Mins	Avg	W	L	EN	SO	GA	SA	S%
35	* Evgeni Nabokov	1	20	.00	0	0	0	0	0	10	1.000
31	Steve Shields	12	696	3.10	5	7	1	0	36	323	.889
	Totals	**12**	**720**	**3.08**	**5**	**7**	**1**	**0**	**37**	**334**	**.889**

Captains' History

Doug Wilson, 1991-92, 1992-93; Bob Errey, 1993-94; Bob Errey and Jeff Odgers, 1994-95; Jeff Odgers, 1995-96; Todd Gill, 1996-97, 1997-98; Owen Nolan, 1998-99 to date.

Coaching History

George Kingston, 1991-92, 1992-93; Kevin Constantine, 1993-94, 1994-95; Kevin Constantine and Jim Wiley, 1995-96; Al Sims, 1996-97; Darryl Sutter, 1997-98 to date.

Club Records

Team

(Figures in brackets for season records are games played; records for fewest points, wins, ties, losses, goals, goals against are for 70 or more games)

Most Points	87	1999-2000 (82)
Most Wins	35	1999-2000 (82)
Most Ties	18	1998-99 (82)
Most Losses	*71	1992-93 (84)
Most Goals	252	1993-94 (84), 1995-96 (82)
Most Goals Against	414	1992-93 (84)
Fewest Points	24	1992-93 (84)
Fewest Wins	11	1992-93 (84)
Fewest Ties	*2	1992-93 (84)
Fewest Losses	33	1998-99 (82)
Fewest Goals	196	1998-99 (82)
Fewest Goals Against	191	1998-99 (82)

Longest Winning Streak

Overall	7	Mar. 24-Apr. 5/94
Home	5	Jan. 21-Feb. 15/95
Away	4	Four times

Longest Undefeated Streak

Overall	9	Mar. 20-Apr. 5/94 (7 wins, 2 ties)
Home	6	Three times
Away	6	Twice

Longest Losing Streak

Overall	*17	Jan. 4-Feb. 12/93
Home	9	Nov. 19-Dec. 19/92
Away	19	Nov. 27/92-Feb. 12/93

Longest Winless Streak

Overall	20	Dec. 29/92-Feb. 12/93 (19 losses, 1 tie)
Home	9	Nov. 19-Dec. 19/92 (9 losses)
Away	19	Nov. 27/92-Feb. 12/93 (19 losses)
Most Shutouts, Season	8	1998-99 (82)
Most PIM, Season	2134	1992-93 (84)
Most Goals, Game	10	Jan. 13/96 (S.J. 10 at Pit. 8)

Individual

Most Seasons	7	Mike Rathje
Most Games, Career	448	Jeff Friesen
Most Goals, Career	137	Jeff Friesen, Owen Nolan
Most Assists, Career	177	Jeff Friesen
Most Points, Career	314	Jeff Friesen (137G, 177A)
Most PIM, Career	1,001	Jeff Odgers
Most Shutouts, Career	9	Mike Vernon
Longest Consecutive Games Streak	141	Mike Ricci (Nov. 22/97-date)
Most Goals, Season	44	Owen Nolan (1999-2000)
Most Assists, Season	52	Kelly Kisio (1992-93)
Most Points, Season	84	Owen Nolan (1999-2000; 44G, 40A)
Most PIM, Season	326	Link Gaetz (1991-92)
Most Shutouts, Season	5	Mike Vernon (1997-98)
Most Points, Defenseman, Season	64	Sandis Ozolnish (1993-94; 26G, 38A)
Most Points, Center, Season	78	Kelly Kisio (1992-93; 26G, 52A)
Most Points, Right Wing, Season	84	Owen Nolan (1999-2000; 44G, 40A)
Most Points, Left Wing, Season	66	Johan Garpenlov (1992-93; 22G, 44A)
Most Points, Rookie, Season	59	Pat Falloon (1991-92; 25G, 34A)
Most Goals, Game	4	Owen Nolan (Dec. 19/95)
Most Assists, Game	4	Three times
Most Points, Game	5	Owen Nolan (Dec. 19/95; 4G, 1A), Marco Sturm (Dec. 23/98; 3G, 2A)

* NHL Record.

General Manager

LOMBARDI, DEAN
Executive Vice President and General Manager, San Jose Sharks.
Born in Holyoke, MA, March 5, 1958.

Dean Lombardi is the architect who built the San Jose hockey club. A charter member of the Sharks management team, Lombardi joined the club in 1990 as assistant general manager after having served in a similar capacity with the Minnesota North Stars. He was named San Jose's director of hockey operations on June 26, 1992 and became the club's general manager on March 6, 1996. As the team's top hockey executive, he oversees player personnel decisions, negotiates player contracts and coordinates the efforts of the Sharks' scouting and player evaluation departments.

Lombardi has spent considerable effort in building a professional scouting staff, reorganizing the amateur scouting department, and establishing a system to evaluate pro players at all levels. He has stood firm in building the Sharks through the draft. San Jose draft picks making important contributions to the club include forwards Jeff Friesen, Patrick Marleau and Marco Sturm. Trades have brought players like Owen Nolan and Vincent Damphousse.

After the 1993-94 season that saw the Sharks post an NHL record single-season improvement of 58 points, Lombardi finished third in *The Hockey News* award voting for executive of the year.

General Managers' History

Jack Ferreira, 1991-92; Chuck Grillo (V.P. Director of Player Personnel), 1992-93 to 1995-96; Dean Lombardi, 1996-97 to date.

All-time Record vs. Other Clubs

Regular Season

	At Home						On Road						Total					
	GP	W	L	T	GF	GA	PTS	GP	W	L	T	GF	GA	PTS	GP	W	L	T	GF	GA	PTS
Anaheim	19	7	10	2	54	59	16	20	10	8	2	68	58	22	39	17	18	4	122	117	38
Atlanta	1	1	0	0	4	1	2	1	1	0	0	3	0	2	2	2	0	0	7	1	4
Boston	8	1	5	2	19	32	4	7	0	5	2	17	26	2	15	1	10	4	36	58	6
Buffalo	8	4	1	3	32	30	11	8	0	8	0	23	41	0	16	4	9	3	55	71	11
Calgary	26	8	16	2	77	88	18	24	7	15	2	63	101	17	50	15	31	4	140	189	35
Carolina	8	4	4	0	36	28	8	8	4	4	0	18	26	8	16	8	8	0	54	54	16
Chicago	18	9	9	0	48	52	18	17	6	9	2	50	57	15	35	15	18	2	98	109	33
Colorado	16	7	9	0	53	63	14	15	2	10	3	31	65	7	31	9	19	3	84	128	21
Dallas	19	8	11	0	46	54	16	19	8	9	2	49	55	18	38	16	20	2	95	109	34
Detroit	18	5	10	3	55	75	13	17	1	16	0	30	80	2	35	6	26	3	85	155	15
Edmonton	24	12	10	2	82	75	26	25	5	16	4	54	92	14	49	17	26	6	136	167	40
Florida	6	2	2	2	14	16	6	6	0	2	4	11	17	4	12	2	4	6	25	33	10
Los Angeles	27	15	9	3	97	82	33	26	6	18	2	66	95	14	53	21	27	5	163	177	47
Montreal	8	2	4	2	22	22	7	9	1	6	2	16	32	4	17	3	10	4	38	54	11
Nashville	4	3	1	0	12	10	6	4	2	2	0	12	9	4	8	5	3	0	24	19	10
New Jersey	8	3	4	1	18	24	7	9	3	5	1	18	33	7	17	6	9	2	36	57	14
NY Islanders	8	2	5	1	17	28	6	9	3	5	1	29	38	7	17	5	10	2	46	66	13
NY Rangers	9	1	7	1	19	35	3	8	1	6	1	23	37	3	17	2	13	2	42	72	6
Ottawa	6	4	2	0	11	8	8	7	1	2	4	19	19	6	13	5	4	4	30	27	14
Philadelphia	9	1	7	1	15	28	3	8	2	5	1	17	28	5	17	3	12	2	32	56	8
Phoenix	22	10	10	2	78	77	23	24	7	14	3	64	79	18	46	17	24	5	142	156	41
Pittsburgh	9	1	6	2	17	48	4	7	3	3	1	25	34	7	16	4	9	3	42	82	11
St. Louis	16	2	13	1	35	58	5	20	5	14	1	44	68	12	36	7	27	2	79	126	17
Tampa Bay	8	5	2	1	27	29	5	8	4	4	0	24	20	8	16	9	6	1	51	49	13
Toronto	14	5	7	2	30	38	12	15	4	10	1	40	60	9	29	9	17	3	70	98	21
Vancouver	26	9	12	5	78	83	23	24	6	16	2	60	95	14	50	15	28	7	138	178	37
Washington	8	4	3	1	22	22	9	8	3	5	0	20	25	6	16	7	8	1	42	47	15
Totals	**353**	**132**	**182**	**39**	**1018**	**1165**	**306**	**353**	**95**	**217**	**41**	**894**	**1290**	**235**	**706**	**227**	**399**	**80**	**1912**	**2455**	**541**

Playoffs

	Series	W	L	GP	W	L	T	GF	GA	Last Mtg.	Round	Result
Calgary	1	1	0	7	4	3	0	26	35	1995	CQF	W 4-3
Colorado	1	0	1	6	2	4	0	17	19	1999	CQF	L 2-4
Dallas	2	0	2	11	3	8	0	19	31	2000	CSF	L 1-4
Detroit	2	1	1	11	4	7	0	27	51	1995	CSF	L 0-4
St. Louis	1	1	0	7	4	3	0	20	22	2000	CQF	W 4-3
Toronto	1	0	1	7	3	4	0	21	26	1994	CSF	L 3-4
Totals	**8**	**3**	**5**	**49**	**20**	**29**	**0**	**130**	**184**			

Carolina totals include Hartford, 1991-92 to 1996-97.
Dallas totals include Minnesota North Stars, 1991-92 to 1992-93.

Colorado totals include Quebec, 1991-92 to 1994-95.
Phoenix totals include Winnipeg, 1991-92 to 1995-96.

Playoff Results 2000-1996

Year	Round	Opponent	Result	GF	GA
2000	CSF	Dallas	L 1-4	7	15
	CQF	St. Louis	W 4-3	20	22
1999	CQF	Colorado	L 2-4	17	19
1998	CQF	Dallas	L 2-4	12	16

Abbreviations: Round: CSF – conference semi-final;
CQF – conference quarter-final.

1999-2000 Results

Oct.	2	Calgary	5-3	Jan.	1	at Nashville	2-3
	4	Chicago	7-1		2	at Chicago	4-1
	7	Edmonton	3-2 *		5	at Edmonton	1-1
	9	Dallas	2-3		8	Florida	2-4
	11	at Anaheim	3-5		11	St. Louis	2-5
	13	at Dallas	2-0		15	Los Angeles	3-2 *
	14	at Nashville	5-1		17	at Chicago	4-5 *
	16	at Washington	3-2		19	at Colorado	0-0
	19	at NY Rangers	2-1		22	Anaheim	4-3
	20	at Detroit	3-6		23	at Phoenix	2-3 *
	23	Boston	1-3		25	Colorado	3-4
	24	at Los Angeles	3-4		28	at Vancouver	1-4
	28	Nashville	3-2		29	NY Islanders	2-3 *
	30	Pittsburgh	1-1	Feb.	1	Phoenix	0-1 *
	31	Washington	2-1		3	at Colorado	3-3
Nov.	3	Phoenix	6-3		8	at Tampa Bay	8-0
	5	Philadelphia	1-5		9	at Florida	1-4
	6	Dallas	2-1		11	at Atlanta	3-0
	9	at Vancouver	4-4		13	at New Jersey	1-3
	10	at Calgary	3-4 *		15	at NY Islanders	4-1
	13	at Philadelphia	2-3		18	at Anaheim	4-4
	15	at Toronto	2-4		23	St. Louis	1-4
	16	at Montreal	4-1		26	Los Angeles	6-3
	18	at Ottawa	4-1		29	Anaheim	2-4
	20	at St. Louis	1-1	Mar.	2	Nashville	4-3
	23	Montreal	2-3 *		4	Carolina	2-4
	27	at Los Angeles	1-4		6	NY Rangers	2-1
	28	New Jersey	4-3 *		8	Detroit	1-1
Dec.	1	at Detroit	2-4		13	Calgary	5-3
	2	at Pittsburgh	5-2		15	Buffalo	6-5 *
	4	St. Louis	2-4		17	at Anaheim	2-4
	6	Tampa Bay	3-3		19	at Dallas	3-5
	8	Colorado	4-2		22	Vancouver	4-3
	10	Atlanta	4-1		24	Phoenix	5-1
	14	Chicago	2-5		27	Edmonton	1-2
	19	at Phoenix	3-4		29	at Los Angeles	1-1
	20	Detroit	3-4	Apr.	1	at Calgary	0-3
	22	Los Angeles	2-3		3	at Edmonton	1-0
	26	Anaheim	0-1		5	Dallas	2-2
	27	at Dallas	3-1		7	at Phoenix	3-1
	30	at St. Louis	1-2 *		9	Vancouver	2-5

* – Overtime

Entry Draft
Selections 2000-1991

2000 Pick	1998 Pick	1997 Pick	1995 Pick	1994 Pick	1993 Pick	1992 Pick	1991 Pick
41 Tero Maatta	3 Brad Stuart	2 Patrick Marleau	12 Teemu Riihijarvi	11 Jeff Friesen	6 Viktor Kozlov	3 Mike Rathje	2 Pat Falloon
104 Jon Disalvatore	29 Jonathan Cheechoo	23 Scott Hannan	38 Peter Roed	37 Angel Nikolov	28 Shean Donovan	10 Andrei Nazarov	23 Ray Whitney
142 Michal Pinc	65 Eric Laplante	82 Adam Colagiacomo	64 Marko Makinen	66 Alexei Yegorov	45 Vlastimil Kroupa	51 Alexander Cherbayev	30 Sandis Ozolinsh
166 Nolan Schaefer	98 Rob Davison	107 Adam Nittel	90 Vesa Toskala	89 Vaclav Varada	58 Ville Peltonen	75 Jan Caloun	45 Dody Wood
183 Michal Macho	104 Miroslav Zalesak	163 Joe Dusbabek	116 Miikka Kiprusoff	115 Brian Swanson	80 Alexander Osadchy	99 Marcus Ragnarsson	67 Kerry Toporowski
246 Chad Wiseman	127 Brandon Coalter	192 Cam Severson	130 Michal Bros	141 Alexander Korolyuk	106 Andrei Buschan	123 Michal Sykora	89 Dan Ryder
256 Pasi Saarinen	145 Mikael Samuelsson	219 Mark Smith	140 Timo Hakanen	167 Sergei Gorbachev	132 Petri Varis	147 Eric Bellerose	111 Frank Nilsson
	185 Robert Mulick		142 Jaroslav Kudrna	193 Eric Landry	154 Fredrik Oduya	171 Ryan Smith	133 Jaroslav Otevrel
1999 Pick	212 Jim Fahey	**1996** Pick	167 Brad Mehalko	219 Evgeni Nabokov	158 Anatoli Filatov	195 Chris Burns	155 Dean Grillo
14 Jeff Jillson		2 Andrei Zyuzin	168 Robert Jindrich	240 Tomas Pisa	184 Todd Holt	219 Alexander Kholomeyev	177 Corwin Saurdiff
82 Mark Concannon		21 Marco Sturm	194 Ryan Kraft	245 Aniket Dhadphale	210 Jonas Forsberg	243 Victor Ignatjev	199 Dale Craigwell
111 Willie Levesque		55 Terry Friesen	220 Mikko Markkanen	271 David Beauregard	236 Jeff Salajko		221 Aaron Kriss
155 Nicholas Dimitrakos		102 Matt Bradley			262 Jamie Matthews		243 Mikhail Kravets
229 Eric Betournay		137 Michel Larocque					
241 Doug Murray		164 Jake Deadmarsh					
257 Hannes Hyvonen		191 Cory Cyrenne					
		217 David Thibeault					

Club Directory

San Jose Arena

San Jose Sharks
San Jose Arena
525 West Santa Clara Street
San Jose, CA 95113
Phone **408/287-7070**
FAX 408/999-5797
Internet http://www.sjsharks.com
Capacity: 17,496

Executive Staff
Owner & Chairman	George Gund III
Co-Owner	Gordon Gund
President & Chief Executive Officer	Greg Jamison
Executive Vice President of Business Operations	Malcolm Bordelon
Executive Vice President & General Manager (San Jose Arena)	Jim Goddard
Executive Vice President & General Counsel	Don Gralnek
Executive Vice President & General Manager (Sharks)	Dean Lombardi
Executive Vice President & Chief Financial Officer	Gregg Olson
Vice President of Corporate Partnerships	Greg Elliott
Vice President of Building Operations	Rich Sotelo
Vice President of Sales & Marketing	Kent Russell
Executive Assistant	Tricia Nordquist, Michelle Simmons, Kristen Fuce

Hockey
Vice President and Assistant General Manager	Wayne Thomas
Head Coach	Darryl Sutter
Assistant Coach	Rich Preston
Assistant Coach	Cap Raeder
Goaltender Coach	Warren Strelow
Director of Pro Development	Doug Wilson
Senior Professional Scout	John Ferguson
Professional Scout	Barry Long
Director of Amateur Scouting	Tim Burke
Special Assistant to the General Manager	Bob Berry
Chief Scout	Ray Payne
Assistant to the General Manager	Joe Will
Scouts	Pat Funk, Rob Grillo, Brian Gross, Karel Masopust
Executive Assistant	Brenda Will
Video Scouting Coordinator	Bob Friedlander
Head Athletic Trainer	Ray Tufts, ATC
Athletic Trainer	Tom Woodcock ATC, L
Strength & Conditioning Coordinator	Mac Read
Massage Therapist	Jeffrey Sjoblom-Powell
Equipment Manager	Mike Aldrich
Assistant Equipment Manager	Kurt Harvey
Equipment Assistant & Equipment Transportation	Jason Rudee
Team Services Coordinator	Aaron Abrams
Director of Hockey Operations, Kentucky Thoroughblades	Jim Wiley
Head Coach, Kentucky Thoroughblades	Roy Sommer
Assistant Coach, Kentucky Thoroughblades	Nick Fotiu
Head Trainer, Kentucky Thoroughblades	Jerry Iannarelli
Team Physician	Arthur J. Ting, M.D.
Team Dentist	Robert Bonahoom, D.D.S.
Team Vision Specialist	Vincent S. Zuccaro, O.D., F.A.A.O.
Medical Staff	Warren King, M.D., Mark Sontag, M.D., Will Straw, M.D.

Business Operations
Director of Broadcasting	Frank Albin
Director of Media Relations	Ken Arnold
Director of Advertising & Publicity	Beth Brigino
Director of Ticket Operations	Mary Enriquez
Director of Ticket Sales	Andy Fiske
Director of Sponsorship Sales	Mark Foxton
Director of Event Presentation	Jason Minsky
Director of Suite Hospitality	Jay O'Sullivan
Director of Internet Services	Roger Ross
Director of Community Development	TBA
Sponsorship Sales Manager	Jennifer Birmingham, Bryan Deierling, Chris Parker
Account Sales Manager	Jeff Goda, Mike Hollywood, Andy Fiske
Account Service Manager	Sharon Holman, Kristin Lyon, Kathy Payne
Internet Services Manager	Kimberly Brown
Advertising Sales Representative	Jon Chin
The Sharks Foundation Manager	Jackie Fuce
Media Relations Manager	Scott Emmert
Marketing Manager	Jim Sparaco
Sponsorship Services Manager	Anna Traggio
Community Development Manager	Julie Vennewitz-Pierce
Suite Hospitality Manager	Bruce Ross
Event Sponsorship Sales Manager	Rip Reynolds
Ticket Operations Coordinator	John Castro
Marketing Coordinator	TBA
Media Relations Coordinator	Ben Stephenson
Sponsorship Services Coordinator	Christine Guerrero
Community Development Coordinator	Kimberly McIntyre
Event Presentation Coordinator	Joi Smith
Mascot Operations Coordinator	Tim Patnode
Sponsorship Sales Representative	Michele Tabarez
Community Development Assistant	Mike Bruins
Executive Assistant	Mary Grace Miller

Finance
Director of Finance	Ken Caveney
Director of Information Technology	James Struckle
Human Resources Manager	TBA
Senior Staff Accountant	Tina Park
Payroll Accounting Associate	Sue Feachen
Accounts Payable Accounting Associate	Tammy Link
Accounts Receivable Accounting Associate	Diane Rubino
Senior Systems Administrator	Joseph Lee
Systems Administrator	Frank Frasula
Executive Assistant	Pat Gonzales

Building Operations
Director of Ticket Operations	Daniel DeBoer
Director of Booking & Events	Steve Kirsner
Director of Guest Services	Ken Sweezey
Facilities Technical Director	Greg Carrolan
Director of Building Services	Monte Chavez
Chief Engineer	Jay Farr
Telephone Systems Manager	Bob Davis
Building Services Manager	Bruce Tharaldson
Assistant Building Services Manager	Frank Peinado
Security Manager	Geoff Pepe
Ticket Operations Manager	Judy Jones
Ushering & Emergency Medical Manager	James Hamnett
Parking and Carousel Manager	Kimberley Gutierrez
Recruiting and Training Manager	Jason Parker
Building Services Coordinator	George Gund IV, Greg Gund, Peggy Roland, Elida Chavez
Mailroom Coordinator	Richard Perez
Guest Services Coordinator	Vikki Klass
Executive Assistant	Rebecca Gomez
Administrative Assistant	Maureen Miller
Engineers	Michael Garcia, Jeff Cassidy, Rob Dean, Robert Dougherty, Eric Gold, Mike Murphy
Administrative Assistant	Melanie Mathis
Cleaning Supervisor	Ray Romero
Conversion Supervisor	Carlos Munoz
Parking Coordinator	Patrick Doherty
Receptionist	Keri Lucero, Tricia Holman

Ice Centre of San Jose
Jon Gustafson	General Manager

Miscellaneous
Television Station	Fox Sports Net
Radio Network Flagship	KFOX 98.5 FM
Television Play-By-Play Broadcaster	Randy Hahn
Television Color Analyst	Drew Remenda
Radio Play-By-Play Broadcaster	Dan Rusanowsky
Radio Color Analyst	TBA
Team Photographers	Don Smith, Rocky Widner
P.A. Announcer	Joe Ike
Organist	Jim Sealy
Primary Anthem Singers	Dennis Leach, Kristin Rapinchuk
In Game Host	Danny Miller
Mascot	S.J. Sharkie

Tampa Bay Lightning

1999-2000 Results: 19w-54l-9t 54pts. Fourth, Southeast Division

Year-by-Year Record

Season	GP	Home			Road			Overall			GF	GA	Pts.	Finished		Playoff Result
		W	L	T	W	L	T	W	L	T						
1999-2000	82	13	24	4	6	30	5	19	54	9	204	310	54	4th,	Southeast Div.	Out of Playoffs
1998-99	82	12	25	4	7	29	5	19	54	9	179	292	47	4th,	Southeast Div.	Out of Playoffs
1997-98	82	11	23	7	6	32	3	17	55	10	151	269	44	7th,	Atlantic Div.	Out of Playoffs
1996-97	82	15	18	8	17	22	2	32	40	10	217	247	74	6th,	Atlantic Div.	Out of Playoffs
1995-96	82	22	14	5	16	18	7	38	32	12	238	248	88	5th,	Atlantic Div.	Lost Conf. Quarter-Final
1994-95	48	10	14	0	7	14	3	17	28	3	120	144	37	6th,	Atlantic Div.	Out of Playoffs
1993-94	84	14	22	6	16	21	5	30	43	11	224	251	71	7th,	Atlantic Div.	Out of Playoffs
1992-93	84	12	27	3	11	27	4	23	54	7	245	332	53	6th,	Norris Div.	Out of Playoffs

2000-01 Schedule

Oct.	Fri.	6	NY Islanders		Fri.	12	Philadelphia
	Sun.	8	Vancouver		Sun.	14	Dallas
	Fri.	13	at Pittsburgh		Tue.	16	at Buffalo
	Sun.	15	Atlanta		Thu.	18	at Montreal
	Wed.	18	at Minnesota		Sat.	20	at Ottawa
	Sat.	21	at New Jersey		Sun.	21	at Columbus
	Sun.	22	at NY Rangers		Tue.	23	Washington
	Wed.	25	at Detroit		Thu.	25	Ottawa
	Fri.	27	Ottawa		Sat.	27	at Florida
	Tue.	31	at Carolina		Mon.	29	at Carolina
Nov.	Wed.	1	at NY Rangers		Tue.	30	Florida
	Fri.	3	NY Islanders	**Feb.**	Thu.	1	Buffalo
	Sun.	5	Washington		Tue.	6	Minnesota
	Fri.	10	Montreal		Thu.	8	at St. Louis
	Sat.	11	Calgary		Sat.	10	at Boston
	Tue.	14	at Montreal		Tue.	13	Phoenix
	Fri.	17	at Toronto		Thu.	15	Boston
	Mon.	20	at Dallas		Sat.	17	NY Rangers
	Wed.	22	Atlanta		Sun.	18	at Nashville*
	Fri.	24	Florida		Tue.	20	St. Louis
	Sat.	25	at Florida		Sat.	24	at Philadelphia*
	Mon.	27	at NY Islanders		Sun.	25	at Buffalo*
	Wed.	29	at Washington	**Mar.**	Thu.	1	at Boston
Dec.	Fri.	1	at Atlanta		Sat.	3	at NY Islanders
	Sat.	2	Detroit		Sun.	4	at New Jersey*
	Wed.	6	at Philadelphia		Tue.	6	San Jose
	Fri.	8	Colorado		Thu.	8	Carolina
	Mon.	11	at Colorado		Sat.	10	Columbus
	Thu.	14	at Phoenix		Tue.	13	Edmonton
	Sat.	16	at Los Angeles		Thu.	15	Toronto
	Sun.	17	at Anaheim*		Sat.	17	Pittsburgh
	Thu.	21	Pittsburgh		Wed.	21	at Atlanta
	Sat.	23	New Jersey		Thu.	22	Atlanta
	Tue.	26	Carolina		Sat.	24	Washington
	Thu.	28	Philadelphia		Tue.	27	New Jersey
	Sat.	30	Boston		Thu.	29	Montreal
	Sun.	31	Toronto		Fri.	30	at Florida
Jan.	Wed.	3	at Carolina	**Apr.**	Sun.	1	Buffalo
	Thu.	4	at Ottawa		Wed.	4	at Pittsburgh
	Sun.	7	at Chicago		Thu.	5	NY Rangers
	Wed.	10	at Toronto		Sun.	8	at Washington*

* Denotes afternoon game.

Franchise date: December 16, 1991

9th NHL Season

SOUTHEAST DIVISION

Mike Johnson was acquired from the Toronto Maple Leafs in February and combined with Vincent Lecavalier and fellow former Leaf Fredrik Modin to give the Lightning three 20-goal scorers last season.

2000-01 Player Personnel

FORWARDS	HT	WT	S	Place of Birth	Date	1999-00 Club
AFANASENKOV, Dmitry	6-2	200	R	Arkhangelsk, USSR	5/12/80	Sherbrooke
ALEXEEV, Nikita	6-5	215	L	Murmansk, USSR	12/27/81	Erie Otters
DRULIA, Stan	5-11	190	R	Elmira, NY	1/5/68	Tampa Bay
DWYER, Gordie	6-2	216	L	Dalhousie, NB	1/25/78	Que (AHL)-T.B.-Det (IHL)
EKMAN, Nils	5-11	175	L	Stockholm, Sweden	3/11/76	Detroit Vipers-T.B.-Long Beach
ELICH, Matt	6-3	196	R	Detroit, MI	9/22/79	Tampa Bay-Detroit Vipers
FREADRICH, Kyle	6-7	260	L	Edmonton, Alta.	12/28/78	T.B.-Louisiana-Detroit Vipers
HAY, Dwayne	6-0	219	L	London, Ont.	2/11/77	Florida-Louisville-Tampa Bay
HOLZINGER, Brian	5-11	190	R	Parma, OH	10/10/72	Buffalo-Tampa Bay
JOHNSON, Mike	6-2	197	R	Scarborough, Ont.	10/3/74	Toronto-Tampa Bay
JOHNSON, Ryan	6-1	200	L	Thunder Bay, Ont.	6/14/76	Florida-Tampa Bay
KEEFE, Sheldon	5-11	185	R	Brampton, Ont.	9/17/80	Barrie Colts
KESA, Dan	6-0	198	R	Vancouver, B.C.	11/23/71	Tampa Bay-Manitoba-Detroit (IHL)
KHARITONOV, Alexander	5-9	169	R	Moscow, USSR	3/30/76	Dynamo Moscow
LECAVALIER, Vincent	6-4	180	L	Ile Bizard, Que.	4/21/80	Tampa Bay
MARTINS, Steve	5-9	175	L	Gatineau, Que.	4/13/72	Ottawa-Tampa Bay
MODIN, Fredrik	6-4	220	L	Sundsvall, Sweden	10/8/74	Tampa Bay
PRIMEAU, Wayne	6-3	220	L	Scarborough, Ont.	6/4/76	Buffalo-Tampa Bay
RICHARDS, Brad	6-1	187	L	Montague, P.E.I.	5/2/80	Rimouski Oceanic
ROMINSKI, Dale	6-2	200	R	Farmington Hills, MI	10/1/75	Tampa Bay-Detroit Vipers
ST. PIERRE, Samuel	6-2	201	R	Laurierville, Que.	6/28/79	Detroit Vipers
ST-LOUIS, Martin	5-9	185	L	Laval, Que.	6/18/75	Calgary-Saint John Flames
SVEJKOVSKY, Jaroslav	6-1	193	R	Plzen, Czech.	10/1/76	Washington-Tampa Bay
WARRINER, Todd	6-1	200	L	Blenheim, Ont.	1/3/74	Toronto-Tampa Bay
ZIEGLER, Thomas	5-11	174	L	Zurich, Switz.	6/9/78	Ambri-Piotta
DEFENSEMEN						
ASTASHENKO, Kaspars	6-2	183	L	Riga, Latvia	2/17/75	T.B.-Detroit Vipers-Long Beach
CLYMER, Ben	6-1	195	L	Edina, MN	4/11/78	Tampa Bay-Detroit Vipers
CULLIMORE, Jassen	6-5	225	L	Simcoe, Ont.	12/4/72	Tampa Bay-Providence Bruins
GUSEV, Sergey	6-1	205	L	Nizhny Tagil, USSR	7/31/75	Tampa Bay
KOS, Kyle	6-3	184	L	Hope, B.C.	5/25/79	Detroit Vipers-Utah Grizzlies
KUBINA, Pavel	6-3	213	R	Celadna, Czech.	4/15/77	Tampa Bay
KUDROC, Kristian	6-6	229	R	Michalovce, Czech.	5/21/81	Quebec Remparts
KUPARINEN, Mikko	6-3	213	L	Kerava, Finland	3/29/77	HIFK Helsinki-Detroit Vipers-Long Beach
LAROCQUE, Mario	6-2	182	L	Montreal, Que.	4/24/78	Detroit Vipers
MARA, Paul	6-4	202	L	Ridgewood, NJ	9/7/79	Tampa Bay-Detroit Vipers
MUIR, Bryan	6-4	220	L	Winnipeg, Man.	6/8/73	Chicago-Tampa Bay
POSMYK, Marek	6-5	228	R	Jihlava, Czech.	9/15/78	Tampa Bay-Detroit Vipers
SARICH, Cory	6-3	193	R	Saskatoon, Sask.	8/16/78	Buffalo-Rochester-Tampa Bay
SVOBODA, Petr	6-1	198	L	Most, Czech.	2/14/66	Tampa Bay
ZYUZIN, Andrei	6-1	210	R	Ufa, USSR	1/21/78	Tampa Bay
GOALTENDERS	**HT**	**WT**	**C**	**Place of Birth**	**Date**	**1999-00 Club**
CLOUTIER, Dan	6-1	182	L	Mont-Laurier, Que.	4/22/76	Tampa Bay
KOCHAN, Dieter	6-1	180	L	Saskatoon, SK	5/11/74	Bing-Orlando-Sprfld-T.B.-Grand Rapids
WEEKES, Kevin	6-0	195	L	Toronto, Ont.	4/4/75	Vancouver-NY Islanders

Coaching History

Terry Crisp, 1992-93 to 1996-97; Terry Crisp, Rick Paterson and Jacques Demers, 1997-98; Jacques Demers, 1998-99; Steve Ludzik, 1999-2000 to date.

Coach

LUDZIK, STEVE
Coach, Tampa Bay Lightning. Born in Toronto, Ont., April 3, 1962.

Steve Ludzik was named as the Lightning head coach on July 14, 1999, rejoining friend, and once-again boss, Rick Dudley. Ludzik became the fourth head coach in franchise history, and the first under the new ownership of Palace Sports and Entertainment, following a successful three-year run with the Detroit Vipers in which he racked up a regular-season record of 154-58-34 behind the bench. Also during his time in Detroit, Ludzik took the IHL franchise to the Turner Cup Finals two years in a row, winning it on the first trip in 1997. The Vipers' 122 points in 1996-97 marked the third-highest point total in IHL history. His .695 winning percentage is tops all-time in the IHL.

The position in Tampa Bay marks Ludzik's first as a head coach in the NHL. In addition to his coaching time in Detroit, Ludzik also had a successful tenure as bench boss for the Muskegon Fury then of the Colonial Hockey League (now UHL). With Ludzik behind the bench the Fury posted a 77-51-10 record in his two seasons and reached the League finals in 1994-95. Ludzik became an associate coach under Rick Dudley in Detroit the following season.

During his playing career, Ludzik spent nine seasons in the NHL with the Chicago Blackhawks and Buffalo Sabres, playing 424 games, scoring 46 goals with 93 assists.

1999-2000 Scoring

* – rookie

Regular Season

Pos	#	Player	Team	GP	G	A	Pts	+/–	PIM	PP	SH	GW	GT	S	%
C	4	Vincent Lecavalier	T.B.	80	25	42	67	–25	43	6	0	3	1	166	15.1
L	33	Fredrik Modin	T.B.	80	22	26	48	–26	18	3	0	5	0	167	13.2
R	10	Mike Johnson	TOR	52	11	14	25	8	23	2	1	3	0	89	12.4
			T.B	28	10	12	22	–2	4	4	0	0	0	43	23.3
			TOTAL	80	21	26	47	6	27	6	1	3	0	132	15.9
R	20	Stan Drulia	T.B.	68	11	22	33	–18	24	1	2	1	1	94	11.7
C	9	Brian Holzinger	BUF	59	7	17	24	4	30	0	1	2	0	81	8.6
			T.B	14	3	3	6	–7	21	1	1	0	0	23	13.0
			TOTAL	73	10	20	30	–3	51	1	2	2	0	104	9.6
L	8	Todd Warriner	TOR	18	3	1	4	6	2	0	0	0	0	33	9.1
			T.B	55	11	13	24	–14	34	3	1	0	0	100	11.0
			TOTAL	73	14	14	28	–8	36	3	1	0	0	133	10.5
D	13	Pavel Kubina	T.B.	69	8	18	26	–19	93	6	0	3	0	128	6.3
D	23	Petr Svoboda	T.B.	70	2	23	25	–11	170	2	0	0	0	93	2.2
D	2	* Paul Mara	T.B.	54	7	11	18	–27	73	4	0	1	0	78	9.0
C	17	* Ryan Johnson	FLA	66	4	12	16	1	14	0	0	0	0	44	9.1
			T.B	14	0	2	2	–9	2	0	0	0	0	5	0.0
			TOTAL	80	4	14	18	–8	16	0	0	0	0	49	8.2
C	14	Robert Petrovicky	T.B.	43	7	10	17	2	14	1	0	0	0	50	14.0
C	22	Wayne Primeau	BUF	41	5	7	12	–8	38	2	0	1	0	40	12.5
			T.B	17	2	3	5	–4	25	0	0	0	0	35	5.7
			TOTAL	58	7	10	17	–12	63	2	0	1	0	75	9.3
R	25	Dan Kesa	T.B.	50	4	10	14	–11	21	0	1	1	0	55	7.3
L	15	Jaroslav Svejkovsky	WSH	23	1	2	3	–7	2	1	0	0	0	18	5.6
			T.B	29	5	5	10	–7	28	0	0	0	0	42	11.9
			TOTAL	52	6	7	13	–14	30	1	0	0	0	60	10.0
C	19	Steve Martins	OTT	2	1	0	1	–1	0	0	0	0	0	3	33.3
			T.B	57	5	7	12	–11	37	0	1	1	0	62	8.1
			TOTAL	59	6	7	13	–12	37	0	1	1	0	65	9.2
C	5	Bruce Gardiner	OTT	10	0	3	3	1	4	0	0	0	0	18	0.0
			T.B	41	3	6	9	–21	37	0	0	0	0	30	10.0
			TOTAL	51	3	9	12	–20	41	0	0	0	0	48	6.3
D	30	Andrei Zyuzin	T.B.	34	2	9	11	–11	33	0	0	0	0	47	4.3
D	7	* Ben Clymer	T.B.	60	2	6	8	–26	87	2	0	0	0	98	2.0
D	6	Bryan Muir	CHI	11	2	3	5	–1	13	0	1	0	0	19	10.5
			T.B	30	1	1	2	–8	32	0	0	0	0	32	3.1
			TOTAL	41	3	4	7	–9	45	0	1	0	0	51	5.9
D	21	* Cory Sarich	BUF	42	0	4	4	2	35	0	0	0	0	49	0.0
			T.B	17	0	2	2	–8	42	0	0	0	0	20	0.0
			TOTAL	59	0	6	6	–6	77	0	0	0	0	69	0.0
D	3	Sergey Gusev	T.B.	28	2	3	5	–9	6	1	0	0	0	23	8.7
L	28	* Nils Ekman	T.B.	28	2	2	4	–8	36	1	0	0	0	42	4.8
L	29	Pavel Torgaev	CGY	9	0	2	2	0	4	0	0	0	0	12	0.0
			T.B	5	0	2	2	1	2	0	0	0	0	6	0.0
			TOTAL	14	0	4	4	1	6	0	0	0	0	18	0.0
D	18	* Marek Posmyk	T.B.	18	1	2	3	1	20	0	0	0	0	22	4.5
R	42	* Matt Elich	T.B.	8	1	1	2	–1	0	0	0	0	0	5	20.0
L	25	* Dwayne Hay	FLA	6	0	0	0	–2	2	0	0	0	0	3	0.0
			T.B	13	1	1	2	0	2	0	0	0	0	11	9.1
			TOTAL	19	1	1	2	–2	4	0	0	0	0	14	7.1
D	27	Jassen Cullimore	T.B.	46	1	1	2	–12	66	0	0	0	0	23	4.3
L	11	Shawn Burr	T.B.	4	0	2	2	2	0	0	0	0	0	6	0.0
L	24	Reid Simpson	T.B.	26	1	0	1	–3	103	0	0	0	0	13	7.7
R	51	* Dale Rominski	T.B.	3	0	1	1	1	2	0	0	0	0	0	0.0
D	49	* Kaspars Astashenko	T.B.	8	0	1	1	–2	4	0	0	0	0	3	0.0
G	1	* Zac Bierk	T.B.	12	0	1	1	0	0	0	0	0	0	0	0.0
L	34	* Gordie Dwyer	T.B.	24	0	1	1	–6	135	0	0	0	0	7	0.0
D	46	Andrei Skopintsev	T.B.	4	0	0	0	–4	6	0	0	0	0	0	0.0
G	93	Daren Puppa	T.B.	5	0	0	0	0	2	0	0	0	0	0	0.0
L	9	Jeff Shevalier	T.B.	5	0	0	0	–1	2	0	0	0	0	2	0.0
G	35	* Dieter Kochan	T.B.	5	0	0	0	0	0	0	0	0	0	0	0.0
L	43	* Kyle Freadrich	T.B.	10	0	0	0	–1	39	0	0	0	0	0	0.0
G	31	Rich Parent	T.B.	14	0	0	0	0	2	0	0	0	0	0	0.0
G	35	Kevin Hodson	T.B.	24	0	0	0	0	2	0	0	0	0	0	0.0
G	39	Dan Cloutier	T.B.	52	0	0	0	0	29	0	0	0	0	0	0.0

Goaltending

No.	Goaltender	GPI	Mins	Avg	W	L	T	EN	SO	GA	SA	S%
39	Dan Cloutier	52	2492	3.49	9	30	3	3	0	145	1258	.885
1	* Zac Bierk	12	509	3.65	4	4	1	0	0	31	308	.899
35	Kevin Hodson	24	769	3.67	2	7	4	3	0	47	327	.856
31	Rich Parent	14	698	3.70	2	7	1	1	0	43	353	.878
35	* Dieter Kochan	5	238	4.29	1	4	0	1	0	17	111	.847
93	Daren Puppa	5	249	4.58	1	2	0	0	0	19	129	.853
	Totals	**82**	**4982**	**3.73**	**19**	**54**	**9**	**8**	**0**	**310**	**2494**	**.876**

Coaching Record

		Regular Season					Playoffs			
Season	Team	Games	W	L	T	%	Games	W	L	%
1993-94	Muskegon (ColHL)	64	35	24	5	.586	3	0	3	.000
1994-95	Muskegon (ColHL)	74	42	27	5	.601	17	10	7	.588
1996-97	Detroit (IHL)	82	57	17	8	.744	17	12	5	.706
1997-98	Detroit (IHL)	82	47	20	15	.665	23	14	9	.609
1998-99	Detroit (IHL)	82	50	21	11	.677	11	6	5	.545
1999-2000	**Tampa Bay (NHL)**	**82**	**19**	**54**	**9**	**.329•**	....	....	....	....
	NHL Totals	**82**	**19**	**54**	**9**	**.329•**	**....**	**....**	**....**	**....**

• Includes points from regulation ties

Club Records

Team

(Figures in brackets for season records are games played; records for fewest points, wins, ties, losses, goals, goals against are for 70 or more games)

Most Points	88	1995-96 (82)
Most Wins	38	1995-96 (82)
Most Ties	12	1995-96 (82)
Most Losses	55	1997-98 (82)
Most Goals	245	1992-93 (84)
Most Goals Against	332	1992-93 (84)
Fewest Points	44	1997-98 (82)
Fewest Wins	17	1997-98 (82)
Fewest Ties	7	1992-93 (84)
Fewest Losses	32	1995-96 (82)
Fewest Goals	151	1997-98 (82)
Fewest Goals Against	247	1996-97 (82)

Longest Winning Streak

Overall	5	Twice
Home	6	Feb. 15-Mar. 10/96
Away	4	Jan. 6-13/97

Longest Undefeated Streak

Overall	7	Feb. 28-Mar. 13/96 (5 wins, 2 ties)
Home	8	Twice
Away	6	Dec. 28/93-Jan. 12/94 (5 wins, 1 tie)

Longest Losing Streak

Overall	13	Jan. 3-Feb. 2/98
Home	10	Jan. 3-Feb. 26/98
Away	11	Oct. 24-Dec. 10/98

Longest Winless Streak

Overall	16	Twice
Home	11	Jan. 2-Feb. 26/98 (10 losses, 1 tie)
Away	16	Oct. 10-Dec. 10/97 (15 losses, 1 ties)
Most Shutouts, Season	6	1996-97 (82)
Most PIM, Season	1,823	1997-98 (82)
Most Goals, Game	7	Five times

Individual

Most Seasons	7	Mikael Andersson, Rob Zamuner
Most Games, Career	475	Rob Zamuner
Most Goals, Career	111	Brian Bradley
Most Assists, Career	189	Brian Bradley
Most Points, Career	300	Brian Bradley (111G, 189A)
Most PIM, Career	782	Chris Gratton
Most Shutouts, Career	12	Daren Puppa
Longest Consecutive Games Streak	226	Rob Zamuner (Nov. 1/95-Mar. 30/98)
Most Goals, Season	42	Brian Bradley (1992-93)
Most Assists, Season	56	Brian Bradley (1995-96)
Most Points, Season	86	Brian Bradley (1992-93; 42G, 44A)
Most PIM, Season	258	Enrico Ciccone (1995-96)
Most Shutouts, Season	5	Daren Puppa (1995-96)
Most Points, Defenseman, Season	65	Roman Hamrlik (1995-96; 16G, 49A)
Most Points, Center, Season	86	Brian Bradley (1992-93; 42G, 44A)
Most Points, Right Wing, Season	60	Dino Ciccarelli (1996-97; 35G, 25A)
Most Points, Left Wing, Season	51	Chris Kontos (1992-93; 27G, 24A)
Most Points, Rookie, Season	43	Rob Zamuner (1992-93; 15G, 28A)
Most Goals, Game	4	Chris Kontos (Oct. 7/92)
Most Assists, Game	4	Joe Reekie (Oct. 7/92), Marc Bureau (Feb. 1/93)
Most Points, Game	6	Doug Crossman (Nov. 7/92; 3G, 3A)

Captains' History

No captain, 1992-93 to 1994-95; Paul Ysebaert, 1995-96, 1996-97; Paul Ysebaert and Mikael Renberg, 1997-98; Rob Zamuner, 1998-99; Bill Houlder, Chris Gratton and Vincent Lecavalier, 1999-2000.

All-time Record vs. Other Clubs

Regular Season

	GP	W	L	T	GF	GA	PTS	GP	W	L	T	GF	GA	PTS	GP	W	L	T	GF	GA	PTS
				At Home							**On Road**							**Total**			
Anaheim	6	2	4	0	12	19	4	6	2	3	1	16	19	5	12	4	7	1	28	38	9
Atlanta	2	1	0	1	6	5	3	3	0	8		15	0	5	1	3	1		14	20	3
Boston	15	6	7	2	40	43	14	15	1	11	3	32	56	5	30	7	18	5	72	99	19
Buffalo	15	3	11	1	31	50	8	15	6	8	1	45	39	13	30	9	19	2	76	89	21
Calgary	8	4	3	1	25	26	9	7	2	5	0	14	25	5	15	6	8	1	39	51	14
Carolina	16	7	6	3	46	45	17	16	2	11	3	40	56	7	32	9	17	6	86	101	24
Chicago	9	4	3	2	22	23	10	10	3	5	2	25	30	8	19	7	8	4	47	53	18
Colorado	9	7	1	1	31	22	15	10	2	7	1	22	46	5	19	9	8	2	53	68	20
Dallas	10	1	7	2	16	30	4	9	2	6	1	21	32	5	19	3	13	3	37	62	9
Detroit	11	2	8	1	36	57	5	9	1	8	0	17	38	2	20	3	16	1	53	95	7
Edmonton	8	2	4	2	22	25	6	8	2	6	0	17	22	4	16	4	10	2	39	47	10
Florida	18	4	10	4	37	54	12	17	2	12	3	29	53	7	35	6	22	7	66	107	19
Los Angeles	7	3	4	0	16	19	6	8	1	1	1	29	19	13	15	9	5	1	45	38	19
Montreal	15	6	6	3	35	35	16	14	5	8	1	35	44	11	29	11	14	4	70	79	27
Nashville	2	0	1	1	4	7	1	2	2	0	0	6	4	4	4	2	1	1	10	11	5
New Jersey	17	4	10	3	42	53	11	18	2	15	1	25	66	5	35	6	25	4	67	119	16
NY Islanders	18	9	8	1	47	53	19	17	9	7	1	50	47	20	35	18	15	2	97	100	39
NY Rangers	17	7	7	3	57	59	17	19	7	10	2	67	69	17	36	14	17	5	124	128	34
Ottawa	15	7	7	1	49	46	15	15	7	8	0	38	53	14	30	14	15	1	87	99	29
Philadelphia	18	6	11	1	50	56	14	17	1	11	5	28	60	7	35	7	22	6	78	116	21
Phoenix	7	3	4	0	22	25	6	8	3	5	0	17	25	6	15	6	9	0	39	50	12
Pittsburgh	15	6	8	1	42	49	13	15	3	10	2	38	65	8	30	9	18	3	80	114	21
St. Louis	10	3	5	2	29	35	8	8	1	7	0	19	31	2	18	4	12	2	48	66	10
San Jose	8	4	4	0	20	24	8	8	5	2	1	29	27	11	16	9	6	1	49	51	19
Toronto	12	1	11	0	23	47	2	13	5	6	0	33	50	10	25	6	19	0	56	97	12
Vancouver	7	3	4	0	24	27	7	7	0	6	1	12	34	1	14	3	10	1	36	61	8
Washington	18	4	13	1	37	62	9	19	5	10	4	45	72	14	37	9	23	5	82	134	23
Totals	**313**	**109**	**167**	**37**	**821**	**996**	**259**	**313**	**86**	**193**	**34**	**757**	**1097**	**209**	**626**	**195**	**360**	**71**	**1578**	**2093**	**468**

Playoffs

	Series	W	L	GP	W	L	T	GF	GA	Last Mtg.	Round	Result
Philadelphia	1	0	1	6	2	4	0	13	26	1996	CQF	L 2-4
Totals	**1**	**0**	**1**	**6**	**2**	**4**	**0**	**13**	**26**			

Playoff Results 2000-1996

Year	Round	Opponent	Result	GF	GA
1996	CQF	Philadelphia	L 2-4	13	26

Abbreviations: Round: CQF – conference quarter-final.

Carolina totals include Hartford, 1992-93 to 1996-97.
Dallas totals include Minnesota North Stars, 1992-93.

Colorado totals include Quebec, 1992-93 to 1994-95.
Phoenix totals include Winnipeg, 1992-93 to 1995-96.

1999-2000 Results

Oct.	2	NY Islanders	4-2		15		Florida	2-5
	7	Los Angeles	2-5		17		Washington	3-6
	9	at New Jersey	0-1		20		Boston	2-4
	15	Anaheim	2-3		22	at	NY Islanders	0-2
	16	Atlanta	4-4		24	at	Washington	2-8
	19	Vancouver	5-6 *		25	at	Buffalo	1-2
	23	Calgary	2-1		28		Edmonton	3-7
	27	at Buffalo	3-4		29		Atlanta	2-1
	28	at Boston	3-7	Feb.	1		Toronto	3-5
	30	at Dallas	2-1		3		Montreal	1-2 *
Nov.	3	at Atlanta	1-4		8		San Jose	0-8
	6	at Pittsburgh	7-4		10	at	NY Islanders	4-5 *
	7	Detroit	3-2		12		Carolina	2-5
	9	at Washington	1-2		15		NY Rangers	2-2
	12	Buffalo	4-2		17	at	Ottawa	2-6
	13	at Carolina	2-4		19	at	Carolina	2-4
	17	at Atlanta	4-5		21		Pittsburgh	2-1
	18	Pittsburgh	2-1		24		Ottawa	5-4
	20	at Philadelphia	1-4		26	at	Nashville	3-2
	22	Philadelphia	4-1		27	at	Detroit	1-3
	24	NY Rangers	3-6	Mar.	1		Washington	2-4
	26	Carolina	3-3		3	at	Chicago	1-5
	28	Buffalo	2-3 *		4	at	Colorado	1-4
Dec.	1	at Anaheim	4-2		8		Philadelphia	2-3 *
	2	at Phoenix	1-3		10		Florida	3-4
	4	at Los Angeles	3-3		12		Chicago	1-4
	6	at San Jose	3-3		14	at	Montreal	4-3
	10	Carolina	3-2		15	at	NY Rangers	4-4
	14	Nashville	4-4		17	at	New Jersey	3-1
	18	at Philadelphia	0-4		19	at	Washington	2-5
	19	at NY Rangers	4-5 *		21	at	Boston	0-4
	21	Toronto	2-4		24		St. Louis	1-5
	23	at Pittsburgh	3-4		26		Montreal	1-3
	26	at Atlanta	3-6		28		Dallas	2-3
	27	Florida	1-6		30		Ottawa	6-3
Jan.	1	at Florida	5-7	Apr.	1	at	Florida	3-3
	5	at Vancouver	3-3		2		New Jersey	1-4
	7	at Edmonton	1-5		4		Boston	5-4
	8	at Calgary	2-3 *		6	at	Montreal	1-5
	11	New Jersey	5-6		8	at	Toronto	2-4
	13	NY Islanders	4-2		9	at	Ottawa	2-5

* – Overtime

Entry Draft
Selections 2000-1992

2000 Pick	1998 Pick	1996 Pick	1993 Pick
8 Nikita Alexeev	1 Vincent Lecavalier	16 Mario Larocque	3 Chris Gratton
34 Ruslan Zainullin	64 Brad Richards	69 Curtis Tipler	29 Tyler Moss
81 Alexander Kharitonov	72 Dmitry Afanasenkov	125 Jason Robinson	55 Allan Egeland
126 Johan Hagglund	92 Eric Beaudoin	152 Nikolai Ignatov	81 Marian Kacir
161 Pavel Sedov	121 Curtis Rich	157 Xavier Delisle	107 Ryan Brown
191 Aaron Gionet	146 Sergei Kuznetsov	179 Pavel Kubina	133 Kiley Hill
222 Marek Priechodsky	174 Brett Allan		159 Matthieu Raby
226 Brian Eklund	194 Oak Hewer	1995 Pick	185 Ryan Nauss
233 Alexander Polukeyev	221 Daniel Hulak	5 Daymond Langkow	211 Alexandre Laporte
263 Thomas Ziegler	229 Chris Lyness	30 Mike McBain	237 Brett Duncan
	252 Martin Cibak	56 Shane Willis	263 Mark Szoke

1999 Pick	1997 Pick	1996 Pick (cont.)	1992 Pick
47 Sheldon Keefe	7 Paul Mara	108 Konstantin Golokhvastov	1 Roman Hamrlik
67 Evgeny Konstantinov	33 Kyle Kos	134 Eduard Pershin	26 Drew Bannister
75 Brett Scheffelmaier	61 Matt Elich	160 Cory Murphy	49 Brent Gretzky
88 Jimmie Olvestad	108 Mark Thompson	186 Joe Cardarelli	74 Aaron Gavey
127 Kaspars Astashenko	109 Jan Sulc	212 Zac Bierk	97 Brantt Myhres
148 Michal Lanicek	112 Karel Betik		122 Martin Tanguay
182 Fedor Fedorov	153 Andrei Skopintsev	1994 Pick	145 Derek Wilkinson
187 Ivan Rachunek	168 Justin Jack	8 Jason Wiemer	170 Dennis Maxwell
216 Erkki Rajamaki	170 Eero Somervuori	34 Colin Cloutier	193 Andrew Kemper
244 Mikko Kuparinen	185 Samuel St. Pierre	55 Vadim Epanchintsev	218 Marc Tardif
	198 Shawn Skolney	86 Dmitri Klevakin	241 Tom MacDonald
	224 Paul Comrie	137 Daniel Juden	
		138 Bryce Salvador	
		164 Chris Maillet	
		190 Alexei Baranov	
		216 Yuri Smirnov	
		242 Shawn Gervais	
		268 Brian White	

General Managers' History

Phil Esposito, 1992-93 to 1997-98; Jacques Demers, 1998-99; Rick Dudley, 1999-2000 to date.

General Manager

DUDLEY, RICK
General Manager, Tampa Bay Lightning.
Born in Toronto, Ont., January 31, 1949.

Rick Dudley was named Vice President of Hockey Operations for Palace Sports and Entertainment (PS&E) on June 8, 1999 and took on the job of overseeing all aspects of Tampa Bay Lightning hockey operations when PS&E consummated its acquisition of the hockey club. On July 14, 1999, Dudley was officially named the club's General Manager.

The hiring of Dudley in Tampa Bay was made possible after the Ottawa Senators reached a compensation agreement with Palace Sports and Entertainment. The move returned Dudley to his former employer (PS&E) after one season as the General Manager in Ottawa. In his one season there, the Senators finished with 103 points, an increase of 20 points from the previous campaign. Ottawa finished with the third best overall record in the NHL during the 1998-99 season.

Before joining Ottawa, Dudley was the General Manager of PS&E's Detroit Vipers in the International Hockey League. In Detroit, he served as general manager and head coach during the team's first two years of existence before handing over the coaching duties to Steve Ludzik and concentrating solely on his front office work for the next two seasons.

Dudley is credited with finding the likes of Detroit's first two players in Petr Sykora and Miroslav Satan as well as bringing over 17-year-old phenom Sergei Samsonov. Samsonov helped lead the Vipers to the 1996 Turner Cup Championship and became the NHL's Rookie of the Year the following season.

A lifetime hockey man, Dudley was the head coach of the IHL's Phoenix Roadrunners in 1993-94. He took over the reigns of a last-place club and led them to the league's best record over the rest of the season. His other head coaching jobs came with the IHL's San Diego Gulls (1992-93), NHL's Buffalo Sabres (1989 to 1992), AHL's New Haven Nighthawks (1988-89), IHL's Flint Spirits (1986 to 1988), and ECHL's Carolina Thunderbirds (1981 to 1986). Dudley amassed a 476-196-51 lifetime record as a head coach.

His professional playing career spanned 13 seasons where he spent time in the AHL (Cleveland, Cincinnati, Fredericton), IHL (Flint), WHA (Cincinnati) and National Hockey League (Buffalo and Winnipeg).

NHL Coaching Record

		Regular Season					Playoffs			
Season	Team	Games	W	L	T	%	Games	W	L	%
1989-90	Buffalo	80	45	27	8	.613	6	2	4	.333
1990-91	Buffalo	80	31	30	9	.506	6	2	4	.333
1991-92	Buffalo	28	9	15	4	.393	....	....	....	....
	NHL Totals	**188**	**85**	**72**	**31**	**.535**	**12**	**4**	**8**	**.333**

Club Directory

Ice Palace

Tampa Bay Lightning
Ice Palace
401 Channelside Drive
Tampa, FL 33602
Phone **813/301-6500**
FAX 813/301-1480
Ticket Info. 813/301-6600
www.icepalace.com
Capacity: 19,758

Executive Staff
Owners . . . . Palace Sports & Entertainment, Bill Davidson, David Hermelin
President of Palace Sports & Entertainment/Governor . . . . Tom Wilson
President of Tampa Bay Lightning/ Alternate Governor. . . . . Ron Campbell
Senior Vice President of Arena Management . . . . Hugh Lombardi
Senior Vice President of Sales and Marketing . . . Michael Yormark

Hockey Operations
Vice President of Hockey Operations/ General Manager. Rick Dudley
Assistant General Manager/Alternate Governor . . . Jay H. Feaster
Head Coach. . . . . Steve Ludzik
Associate Coach . . . . John Tortorella
Associate Coach . . . . John Torchetti
Special Skills Coach . . . . Paul Vincent
Goaltending Consultant . . . . Jeff Reese
Scouting Coordinator . . . . Jake Goertzen
Scouting Staff . . . . Stephen Baker, Randy Hansch, Dave Heitz, Karri Kettunen, Scott Luce, Dennis McIvor, Craig Muni, Rick Paterson, Miroslav Prihoda, Richard Rose, Buck Steele, Luke Williams, Niklas Blomgren, Lou Claire, Sergei Grigorkin, Mike Guest, Martin Loucher, John McLean, Jr., Sergei Tizhnich, Glen Zacharias, Yuri Yanchenkov
Player Relations Coordinator . . . . Ryan Belec
Director or Team Services . . . . Phil Thibodeau
Head Medical Trainer. . . . . Dave Boyer
Strength & Conditioning Trainer . . . . Brian Peterson
Equipment Manager . . . . Ray Thill
Assistant Equipment Manager. . . . . Jim Pickard
Skate Sharpening Technician/ Assistant Equipment Mgr. . . . . Ken Fleger
Message Therapist. . . . . Mike Griebel
Hockey Operations Assistant . . . . Kathy Skelton
Video Coordinator . . . . Nigel Kirwan
Medical Director . . . . Dr. Richard Lehman
Minor League Affiliate. . . . . Detroit Vipers (IHL)
Minor League Affiliate. . . . . Johnstown Chiefs (ECHL)
General Manager Detroit Vipers . . . . Grant Sonier
Head Coach Detroit Vipers . . . . Brad Shaw

Community Relations
Director of Community Development . . . . Donna Ferris
Community Youth Development Manager . . . . . . David Walkowiak
Community Development Manager . . . . Stephanie Hanchey
Community Business Development Manager . . . . . Martin Quessenberry
Mascot Coordinator . . . . Jason Franke

Executive Suites & Premium Seating
Director of Suite Sales . . . . Don Rossman
Director of Suite Services. . . . . Marie Wenger
Suite Services Coordinators . . . . Lisa Klassen
Premium Seating Manager . . . . Missy Davis
Premium Seating Coordinator . . . . Ken Kacsur
Suite Ticket Supervisor. . . . . Lakeisha Sharpe

Finance
Director of Finance . . . . Brad Whalen
Senior Accountant. . . . . Doug Riefler
Senior Accountant. . . . . David Weber
Accounting Manager. Foster Atteberry
Accounts Payable . . . . Tim Winans
Accounts Receivable . . . . Alina Simonds
Staff Accountant . . . . Kelly Papas
Administrative Assistant. . . . . Evie Williams

Internal Support Staff
Support Services . . . . ManagerNikki Mays
Support Services . . . . CoordinatorIrving Belsky
Information Services Manager . . . . Dave Everett
Assistant Information Services Manager . . . . Roberto Camejo
Receptionists . . . . Mary Sharpe, Gina Maqueira, Aria Robinson, Stephanie Skubina

Box Office
Box Office Manager. Mary Ruth Hughey
Assistant Box Office Managers . . . . Marilyn Brace, Aaron Corso, Jim Mannino
Box Office Supervisors . . . . Adam Burr, Andy Myers

Sales
Vice President of Sales . . . . Chad Estis
Director of Group Events . . . . Lynn Wittenburg
Sales Manager . . . . Doug Dawson, Chris Gargani
Database Marketing Manager . . . . Damion Chatmon
Corporate Account Managers . . . . Chris Hibbs, Heather Johnson, Mike Ondrejko, Chad Johnson, Alex Ramati
Group Event Coordinators . . . . Kristy Bauer, Brent Stehlik, Rebecca Rogers, Jon Duff, Adam Gesacion, Matt Martin, Marcia Steinberg
Account Executives . . . . Eric Campailla, Chris Kremer, Eric Toledo, Peter Kramer, Sonny Wasko, Michael Ryan, Evan Sitar, Scott Shepherd
Sales Coordinator . . . . Ashlie Rolley

Marketing
Vice President of Integrated Sales . . . . Pedro Goncalves
Senior Director of Corporate Marketing/

Toronto Maple Leafs

1999-2000 Results: 45W-30L-7T 100PTS. First, Northeast Division

A star both on the ice and off, Curtis Joseph (left) received the King Clancy Trophy for his humanitarian efforts. The award was presented by teammates Steve Thomas and Bryan Berard. Berard hopes to come back from a serious eye injury.

2000-01 Schedule

Month	Day	Date	Opponent
Oct.	Sat.	7	Montreal
	Mon.	9	Dallas
	Wed.	11	NY Islanders
	Sat.	14	Ottawa
	Mon.	16	at Vancouver
	Thu.	19	at Edmonton
	Sat.	21	at Calgary*
	Wed.	25	Minnesota
	Fri.	27	at Buffalo
	Sat.	28	at Boston
	Tue.	31	at Ottawa
Nov.	Thu.	2	New Jersey
	Sat.	4	at St. Louis
	Sun.	5	Boston
	Wed.	8	Carolina
	Fri.	10	at Carolina
	Sat.	11	Chicago
	Wed.	15	Philadelphia
	Fri.	17	Tampa Bay
	Sat.	18	at Montreal
	Tue.	21	at NY Rangers
	Wed.	22	Edmonton
	Sat.	25	Ottawa
	Wed.	29	St. Louis
	Thu.	30	at NY Islanders
Dec.	Sat.	2	NY Rangers
	Mon.	4	Florida
	Wed.	6	at Detroit
	Thu.	7	at St. Louis
	Sat.	9	Pittsburgh
	Wed.	13	at Pittsburgh
	Fri.	15	at NY Islanders
	Sat.	16	Calgary
	Wed.	20	Nashville
	Thu.	21	at Boston
	Sat.	23	at Montreal
	Tue.	26	at Atlanta
	Wed.	27	at Pittsburgh
	Sat.	30	at Florida
	Sun.	31	at Tampa Bay
Jan.	Wed.	3	Buffalo
	Fri.	5	at Buffalo
	Sat.	6	Washington
	Wed.	10	Tampa Bay
	Fri.	12	Phoenix
	Sat.	13	at New Jersey
	Wed.	17	Los Angeles
	Thu.	18	at NY Rangers
	Sat.	20	Buffalo
	Wed.	24	Boston
	Thu.	25	at Atlanta
	Sat.	27	NY Rangers
	Wed.	31	at Carolina
Feb.	Thu.	1	at Washington
	Wed.	7	Atlanta
	Thu.	8	at Detroit
	Sat.	10	Detroit
	Wed.	14	Columbus
	Thu.	15	at Philadelphia
	Sat.	17	Colorado
	Mon.	19	New Jersey
	Thu.	22	Vancouver
	Sat.	24	Montreal
	Sun.	25	at Chicago
	Wed.	28	San Jose
Mar.	Thu.	1	at Washington
	Sat.	3	Ottawa
	Tue.	6	at Calgary
	Wed.	7	at Edmonton
	Sat.	10	at Vancouver
	Wed.	14	Anaheim
	Thu.	15	at Tampa Bay
	Sat.	17	at Florida
	Tue.	20	at Buffalo
	Wed.	21	Florida
	Sat.	24	Philadelphia
	Wed.	28	Boston
	Thu.	29	at Philadelphia
	Sat.	31	at Montreal
Apr.	Wed.	4	NY Islanders
	Fri.	6	at Chicago
	Sat.	7	at Ottawa

* Denotes afternoon game.

Franchise date: November 22, 1917

84th NHL Season

NORTHEAST DIVISION

Year-by-Year Record

		Home			Road			Overall							
Season	**GP**	**W**	**L**	**T**	**W**	**L**	**T**	**W**	**L**	**T**	**GF**	**GA**	**Pts.**	**Finished**	**Playoff Result**
1999-2000	82	24	12	5	21	18	2	45	30	7	246	222	100	1st, Northeast Div.	Lost Conf. Semi-Final
1998-99	82	23	13	5	22	17	2	45	30	7	268	231	97	2nd, Northeast Div.	Lost Conf. Championship
1997-98	82	16	20	5	14	23	4	30	43	9	194	237	69	6th, Central Div.	Out of Playoffs
1996-97	82	18	20	3	12	24	5	30	44	8	230	273	68	6th, Central Div.	Out of Playoffs
1995-96	82	19	15	7	15	21	5	34	36	12	247	252	80	3rd, Central Div.	Lost Conf. Quarter-Final
1994-95	48	15	7	2	6	12	6	21	19	8	135	146	50	4th, Central Div.	Lost Conf. Quarter-Final
1993-94	84	23	15	4	20	14	8	43	29	12	280	243	98	2nd, Central Div.	Lost Conf. Championship
1992-93	84	25	11	6	19	18	5	44	29	11	288	241	99	3rd, Norris Div.	Lost Conf. Championship
1991-92	80	21	16	3	9	27	4	30	43	7	234	294	67	5th, Norris Div.	Out of Playoffs
1990-91	80	15	21	4	8	25	7	23	46	11	241	318	57	5th, Norris Div.	Out of Playoffs
1989-90	80	24	14	2	14	24	2	38	38	4	337	358	80	3rd, Norris Div.	Lost Div. Semi-Final
1988-89	80	15	20	5	13	26	1	28	46	6	259	342	62	5th, Norris Div.	Out of Playoffs
1987-88	80	14	20	6	7	29	4	21	49	10	273	345	52	4th, Norris Div.	Lost Div. Semi-Final
1986-87	80	22	14	4	10	28	2	32	42	6	286	319	70	4th, Norris Div.	Lost Div. Final
1985-86	80	16	21	3	9	27	4	25	48	7	311	386	57	4th, Norris Div.	Lost Div. Final
1984-85	80	10	28	2	10	24	6	20	52	8	253	358	48	5th, Norris Div.	Out of Playoffs
1983-84	80	17	16	7	9	29	2	26	45	9	303	387	61	5th, Norris Div.	Out of Playoffs
1982-83	80	20	15	5	8	25	7	28	40	12	293	330	68	3rd, Norris Div.	Lost Div. Semi-Final
1981-82	80	12	20	8	8	24	8	20	44	16	298	380	56	5th, Norris Div.	Out of Playoffs
1980-81	80	14	21	5	14	16	10	28	37	15	322	367	71	5th, Adams Div.	Lost Prelim. Round
1979-80	80	17	19	4	18	21	1	35	40	5	304	327	75	4th, Adams Div.	Lost Prelim. Round
1978-79	80	20	12	8	14	21	5	34	33	13	267	252	81	3rd, Adams Div.	Lost Quarter-Final
1977-78	80	21	13	6	20	16	4	41	29	10	271	237	92	3rd, Adams Div.	Lost Semi-Final
1976-77	80	18	13	9	15	19	6	33	32	15	301	285	81	3rd, Adams Div.	Lost Quarter-Final
1975-76	80	23	12	5	11	19	10	34	31	15	294	276	83	3rd, Adams Div.	Lost Quarter-Final
1974-75	80	19	12	9	12	21	7	31	33	16	280	309	78	3rd, Adams Div.	Lost Quarter-Final
1973-74	78	21	11	7	14	16	9	35	27	16	274	230	86	4th, East Div.	Lost Quarter-Final
1972-73	78	20	12	7	7	29	3	27	41	10	247	279	64	6th, East Div.	Out of Playoffs
1971-72	78	21	11	7	12	20	7	33	31	14	209	208	80	4th, East Div.	Lost Quarter-Final
1970-71	78	24	9	6	13	24	2	37	33	8	248	211	82	4th, East Div.	Lost Quarter-Final
1969-70	76	18	13	7	11	21	6	29	34	13	222	242	71	6th, East Div.	Out of Playoffs
1968-69	76	20	8	10	15	18	5	35	26	15	234	217	85	4th, East Div.	Lost Quarter-Final
1967-68	74	24	9	4	9	22	6	33	31	10	209	176	76	5th, East Div.	Out of Playoffs
1966-67	**70**	**21**	**8**	**6**	**11**	**19**	**5**	**32**	**27**	**11**	**204**	**211**	**75**	**3rd,**	**Won Stanley Cup**
1965-66	70	22	9	4	12	16	7	34	25	11	208	187	79	3rd,	Lost Semi-Final
1964-65	70	17	15	3	13	11	11	30	26	14	204	173	74	4th,	Lost Semi-Final
1963-64	**70**	**22**	**7**	**6**	**11**	**18**	**6**	**33**	**25**	**12**	**192**	**172**	**78**	**3rd,**	**Won Stanley Cup**
1962-63	**70**	**21**	**8**	**6**	**14**	**15**	**6**	**35**	**23**	**12**	**221**	**180**	**82**	**1st,**	**Won Stanley Cup**
1961-62	**70**	**25**	**5**	**5**	**12**	**17**	**6**	**37**	**22**	**11**	**232**	**180**	**85**	**2nd,**	**Won Stanley Cup**
1960-61	70	21	6	8	18	13	4	39	19	12	234	176	90	2nd,	Lost Semi-Final
1959-60	70	20	9	6	15	17	3	35	26	9	199	195	79	2nd,	Lost Final
1958-59	70	17	13	5	10	19	6	27	32	11	189	201	65	4th,	Lost Final
1957-58	70	12	16	7	9	22	4	21	38	11	192	226	53	6th,	Out of Playoffs
1956-57	70	12	16	7	9	18	8	21	34	15	174	192	57	5th,	Out of Playoffs
1955-56	70	19	10	6	5	23	7	24	33	13	153	181	61	4th,	Lost Semi-Final
1954-55	70	14	10	11	10	14	11	24	24	22	147	135	70	3rd,	Lost Semi-Final
1953-54	70	22	6	7	10	18	7	32	24	14	152	131	78	3rd,	Lost Semi-Final
1952-53	70	17	12	6	10	18	7	27	30	13	156	167	67	5th,	Out of Playoffs
1951-52	70	17	10	8	12	15	8	29	25	16	168	157	74	3rd,	Lost Semi-Final
1950-51	**70**	**22**	**8**	**5**	**19**	**8**	**8**	**41**	**16**	**13**	**212**	**138**	**95**	**2nd,**	**Won Stanley Cup**
1949-50	70	18	9	8	13	18	4	31	27	12	176	173	74	3rd,	Lost Semi-Final
1948-49	**60**	**12**	**8**	**10**	**10**	**17**	**3**	**22**	**25**	**13**	**147**	**161**	**57**	**4th,**	**Won Stanley Cup**
1947-48	**60**	**22**	**3**	**5**	**10**	**12**	**8**	**32**	**15**	**13**	**182**	**143**	**77**	**1st,**	**Won Stanley Cup**
1946-47	**60**	**20**	**8**	**2**	**11**	**11**	**8**	**31**	**19**	**10**	**209**	**172**	**72**	**2nd,**	**Won Stanley Cup**
1945-46	50	10	13	2	9	11	5	19	24	7	174	185	45	5th,	Out of Playoffs
1944-45	**50**	**13**	**9**	**3**	**11**	**13**	**1**	**24**	**22**	**4**	**183**	**161**	**52**	**3rd,**	**Won Stanley Cup**
1943-44	50	13	11	1	10	12	3	23	23	4	214	174	50	3rd,	Lost Semi-Final
1942-43	50	17	6	2	5	13	7	22	19	9	198	159	53	3rd,	Lost Semi-Final
1941-42	**48**	**18**	**6**	**0**	**9**	**12**	**3**	**27**	**18**	**3**	**158**	**136**	**57**	**2nd,**	**Won Stanley Cup**
1940-41	48	16	5	3	12	9	3	28	14	6	145	99	62	2nd,	Lost Semi-Final
1939-40	48	15	3	6	10	14	0	25	17	6	134	110	56	3rd,	Lost Final
1938-39	48	13	8	3	6	12	6	19	20	9	114	107	47	3rd,	Lost Final
1937-38	48	13	6	5	11	9	4	24	15	9	151	127	57	1st, Cdn. Div.	Lost Final
1936-37	48	14	9	1	8	12	4	22	21	5	119	115	49	3rd, Cdn. Div.	Lost Quarter-Final
1935-36	48	15	4	5	8	15	1	23	19	6	126	106	52	2nd, Cdn. Div.	Lost Final
1934-35	48	16	6	2	14	8	2	30	14	4	157	111	64	1st, Cdn. Div.	Lost Final
1933-34	48	19	2	3	7	11	6	26	13	9	174	119	61	1st, Cdn. Div.	Lost Semi-Final
1932-33	48	16	4	4	8	14	2	24	18	6	119	111	54	1st, Cdn. Div.	Lost Final
1931-32	**48**	**17**	**4**	**3**	**6**	**14**	**4**	**23**	**18**	**7**	**155**	**127**	**53**	**2nd, Cdn. Div.**	**Won Stanley Cup**
1930-31	44	15	4	3	7	9	6	22	13	9	118	99	53	2nd, Cdn. Div.	Lost Quarter-Final
1929-30	44	10	8	4	7	13	2	17	21	6	116	124	40	4th, Cdn. Div.	Out of Playoffs
1928-29	44	15	5	2	6	13	3	21	18	5	85	69	47	3rd, Cdn. Div.	Lost Semi-Final
1927-28	44	9	8	5	9	10	3	18	18	8	89	88	44	4th, Cdn. Div.	Out of Playoffs
1926-27*	44	10	10	2	5	14	3	15	24	5	79	94	35	5th, Cdn. Div.	Out of Playoffs
1925-26	36	11	5	2	1	16	1	12	21	3	92	114	27	6th,	Out of Playoffs
1924-25	30	10	5	0	9	6	0	19	11	0	90	84	38	2nd,	Lost NHL S-Final
1923-24	24	7	5	0	3	9	0	10	14	0	59	85	20	3rd,	Out of Playoffs
1922-23	24	10	1	1	3	9	0	13	10	1	82	88	27	3rd,	Out of Playoffs
1921-22	**24**	**8**	**4**	**0**	**5**	**6**	**1**	**13**	**10**	**1**	**98**	**97**	**27**	**2nd,**	**Won Stanley Cup**
1920-21	24	9	3	0	6	6	0	15	9	0	105	100	30	2nd and 1st***	Lost NHL Final
1919-20**	24	8	4	0	4	8	0	12	12	0	119	106	24	3rd and 2nd***	Out of Playoffs
1918-19	18	5	4	0	0	9	0	5	13	0	64	92	10	3rd and 3rd***	Out of Playoffs
1917-18	**22**	**10**	**1**	**0**	**3**	**8**	**0**	**13**	**9**	**0**	**108**	**109**	**26**	**2nd and 1st*** **	**Won Stanley Cup**

* Name changed from St. Patricks to Maple Leafs. ** Name changed from Arenas to St. Patricks.
*** Season played in two halves with no combined standing at end.
From 1917-18 through 1925-26, NHL champions played against PCHA/WCHL champions for Stanley Cup.

2000-01 Player Personnel

FORWARDS	HT	WT	S	Place of Birth	Date	1999-00 Club
ANTROPOV, Nik	6-5	203	L	Vost, USSR	2/18/80	Toronto-St. John's Leafs
BEREZIN, Sergei	5-10	200	R	Voskresensk, USSR	11/5/71	Toronto
BOYES, Brad	6-0	181	R	Mississauga, Ont.	4/17/82	Erie Otters
CORSON, Shayne	6-1	202	L	Barrie, Ont.	8/13/66	Montreal
DOMI, Tie	5-10	200	R	Windsor, Ont.	11/1/69	Toronto
FARKAS, Jeff	6-0	185	L	Amherst, MA	1/24/78	Boston College-Toronto
HAKANSSON, Mikael	6-2	204	L	Stockholm, Sweden	5/31/74	Djurgardens IF
HOGLUND, Jonas	6-3	215	R	Hammaro, Swe.	8/29/72	Toronto
KHRISTICH, Dmitri	6-2	195	R	Kiev, USSR	7/23/69	Toronto
KOROLEV, Igor	6-1	190	L	Moscow, USSR	9/6/70	Toronto
MacLEAN, Don	6-2	199	L	Sydney, N.S.	1/14/77	Lowell-St. John's Leafs
MAIR, Adam	6-2	195	R	Hamilton, Ont.	2/15/79	Toronto-St. John's Leafs
McCAULEY, Alyn	5-11	190	L	Brockville, Ont.	5/29/77	Toronto-St. John's Leafs
PERREAULT, Yanic	5-10	185	L	Sherbrooke, Que.	4/4/71	Toronto
ROBERTS, Gary	6-1	190	L	North York, Ont.	5/23/66	Carolina
SUNDIN, Mats	6-4	220	R	Bromma, Sweden	2/13/71	Toronto
THOMAS, Steve	5-10	185	L	Stockport, England	7/15/63	Toronto
TUCKER, Darcy	5-11	185	L	Castor, Alta.	3/15/75	Tampa Bay-Toronto
VALK, Garry	6-1	200	L	Edmonton, Alta.	11/27/67	Toronto
DEFENSEMEN						
BERARD, Bryan	6-1	195	L	Woonsocket, RI	3/5/77	Toronto
CROSS, Cory	6-5	220	L	Lloydminster, Alta.	1/3/71	Toronto
DEMPSEY, Nathan	6-0	190	R	Spruce Grove, Alta.	7/14/74	Toronto-St. John's Leafs
DIDUCK, Gerald	6-1	216	R	Edmonton, Alta.	4/6/65	Canada-Toronto
KABERLE, Tomas	6-2	200	L	Rakovnik, Czech.	3/2/78	Toronto
KARPOVTSEV, Alexander	6-3	215	R	Moscow, USSR	4/7/70	Toronto
MANSON, Dave	6-2	200	L	Prince Albert, Sask.	1/27/67	Chicago-Dallas
MARKOV, Danny	6-1	190	L	Moscow, USSR	7/11/76	Toronto
McALLISTER, Chris	6-8	225	L	Saskatoon, Sask.	6/16/75	Toronto
SMITH, D.J.	6-2	205	L	Windsor, Ont.	5/13/77	Toronto-St. John's Leafs
SVOBODA, Petr	6-3	200	R	Jihlava, Czech.	6/20/80	HC Ocelari Trinec
YAKUSHIN, Dmitri	6-0	200	L	Kharkov, USSR	1/21/78	Toronto-St. John's Leafs
YUSHKEVICH, Dimitry	5-11	208	R	Yaroslavl, USSR	11/19/71	Toronto

GOALTENDERS	HT	WT	C	Place of Birth	Date	1999-00 Club
HEALY, Glenn	5-9	190	L	Pickering, Ont.	8/23/62	Toronto
JOSEPH, Curtis	5-11	190	L	Keswick, Ont.	4/29/67	Toronto
WAITE, Jimmy	6-1	180	L	Sherbrooke, Que.	4/15/69	St. John's Leafs

1999-2000 Scoring

* – rookie

Regular Season

Pos	#	Player	Team	GP	G	A	Pts	+/–	PIM	PP	SH	GW	GT	S	%
C	13	Mats Sundin	TOR	73	32	41	73	16	46	10	2	7	0	184	17.4
L	32	Steve Thomas	TOR	81	26	37	63	1	68	9	0	9	0	151	17.2
R	14	Jonas Hoglund	TOR	82	29	27	56	–2	10	9	1	3	0	215	13.5
C	16	Darcy Tucker	T.B	50	14	20	34	–15	108	1	0	2	0	98	14.3
			TOR	27	7	10	17	3	55	0	2	3	0	40	17.5
			TOTAL	77	21	30	51	–12	163	1	2	5	0	138	15.2
C	22	Igor Korolev	TOR	80	20	26	46	12	22	5	3	4	1	101	19.8
C	44	Yanic Perreault	TOR	58	18	27	45	3	22	5	0	4	0	114	15.8
D	15	Tomas Kaberle	TOR	82	7	33	40	3	24	2	0	0	0	82	8.5
L	94	Sergei Berezin	TOR	61	26	13	39	8	2	5	0	4	0	241	10.8
R	8	Dmitri Khristich	TOR	53	12	18	30	8	24	3	0	0	1	79	15.2
C	9	* Nik Antropov	TOR	66	12	18	30	14	41	0	0	2	0	89	13.5
D	34	Bryan Berard	TOR	64	3	27	30	11	42	1	0	0	0	98	3.1
D	36	Dimitri Yushkevich	TOR	77	3	24	27	2	55	2	1	1	0	103	2.9
R	10	Garry Valk	TOR	73	10	14	24	–2	44	0	1	1	1	91	11.0
D	52	Alexander Karpovtsev	TOR	69	3	14	17	9	54	3	0	0	0	51	5.9
D	4	Cory Cross	TOR	71	4	11	15	13	64	0	0	1	0	60	6.7
R	28	Tie Domi	TOR	70	5	9	14	–5	198	0	0	2	0	64	7.8
C	42	* Kevyn Adams	TOR	52	5	8	13	–7	39	0	0	0	0	70	7.1
C	18	Alyn McCauley	TOR	45	5	5	10	–6	10	1	0	0	0	41	12.2
D	55	Danny Markov	TOR	59	0	10	10	13	28	0	0	0	0	38	0.0
L	17	Wendel Clark	CHI	13	2	0	2	–2	13	0	0	0	0	27	7.4
			TOR	20	2	2	4	–3	21	0	0	1	0	36	5.6
			TOTAL	33	4	2	6	–5	34	0	0	1	0	63	6.3
L	12	Kris King	TOR	39	2	4	6	4	55	0	0	0	0	24	8.3
D	2	Gerald Diduck	TOR	26	0	3	3	2	33	0	0	0	0	18	0.0
D	33	Chris McAllister	TOR	36	0	3	3	–4	68	0	0	0	0	12	0.0
L	43	* Nathan Dempsey	TOR	6	0	2	2	2	2	0	0	0	0	3	0.0
C	21	* Adam Mair	TOR	8	1	0	1	–1	6	0	0	0	0	7	14.3
D	25	Greg Andrusak	TOR	9	0	1	1	1	4	0	0	0	0	5	0.0
G	30	Glenn Healy	TOR	20	0	1	1	0	2	0	0	0	0	0	0.0
G	31	Curtis Joseph	TOR	63	0	1	1	0	14	0	0	0	0	1	0.0
D	49	* Dmitriy Yakushin	TOR	2	0	0	0	0	2	0	0	0	0	1	0.0
D	24	* D.J. Smith	TOR	3	0	0	0	–1	5	0	0	0	0	2	0.0

Goaltending

No.	Goaltender	GPI	Mins	Avg	W	L	T	EN	SO	GA	SA	S%
31	Curtis Joseph	63	3801	2.49	36	20	7	4	4	158	1854	.915
30	Glenn Healy	20	1164	3.04	9	10	0	1	2	59	527	.888
	Totals	**82**	**4983**	**2.67**	**45**	**30**	**7**	**5**	**6**	**222**	**2386**	**.907**

Playoffs

Pos	#	Player	Team	GP	G	A	Pts	+/–	PIM	PP	SH	GW	OT	S	%
L	32	Steve Thomas	TOR	12	6	3	9	8	10	0	0	1	1	32	18.8
L	94	Sergei Berezin	TOR	12	4	4	8	2	0	0	0	1	0	37	10.8
C	13	Mats Sundin	TOR	12	3	5	8	8	10	0	0	1	0	20	15.0
C	16	Darcy Tucker	TOR	12	4	2	6	0	15	1	0	2	0	27	14.8
R	14	Jonas Hoglund	TOR	12	2	4	6	4	2	0	0	0	0	21	9.5
D	15	Tomas Kaberle	TOR	12	1	4	5	2	0	0	0	1	0	11	9.1
C	22	Igor Korolev	TOR	12	0	4	4	–1	6	0	0	0	0	13	0.0
R	8	Dmitri Khristich	TOR	12	1	2	3	–3	0	1	0	0	0	13	7.7
R	10	Garry Valk	TOR	12	1	2	3	2	14	0	0	0	0	18	5.6
D	52	Alexander Karpovtsev	TOR	11	0	3	3	4	4	0	0	0	0	7	0.0
D	55	Danny Markov	TOR	12	0	3	3	3	10	0	0	0	0	7	0.0
L	17	Wendel Clark	TOR	6	1	1	2	2	4	0	0	0	0	15	6.7
D	36	Dimitri Yushkevich	TOR	12	1	1	2	4	4	0	0	0	0	19	5.3
D	4	Cory Cross	TOR	12	0	2	2	1	2	0	0	0	0	7	0.0
C	39	* Jeff Farkas	TOR	3	1	0	1	2	0	0	0	0	0	3	33.3
C	42	* Kevyn Adams	TOR	12	1	0	1	–2	7	0	1	0	0	13	7.7
C	44	Yanic Perreault	TOR	1	0	1	1	0	0	0	0	0	0	2	0.0
D	2	Gerald Diduck	TOR	10	0	1	1	–1	14	0	0	0	0	4	0.0
R	28	Tie Domi	TOR	12	0	1	1	–5	20	0	0	0	0	3	0.0
L	12	Kris King	TOR	1	0	0	0	0	2	0	0	0	0	0	0.0
D	25	Greg Andrusak	TOR	3	0	0	0	–1	2	0	0	0	0	2	0.0
C	9	* Nik Antropov	TOR	3	0	0	0	1	4	0	0	0	0	2	0.0
C	18	Alyn Mccauley	TOR	5	0	0	0	–4	6	0	0	0	0	3	0.0
C	21	* Adam Mair	TOR	5	0	0	0	–3	8	0	0	0	0	7	0.0
G	31	Curtis Joseph	TOR	12	0	0	0	0	10	0	0	0	0	0	0.0

Goaltending

No.	Goaltender	GPI	Mins	Avg	W	L	EN	SO	GA	SA	S%
31	Curtis Joseph	12	729	2.06	6	6	1	1	25	369	.932
	Totals	**12**	**735**	**2.12**	**6**	**6**	**1**	**1**	**26**	**370**	**.930**

Coach and General Manager

QUINN, PAT
Coach and General Manager, Toronto Maple Leafs.
Born in Hamilton, Ont., January 29, 1943.

Pat Quinn became the 25th head coach of the Toronto Maple Leafs on June 26, 1998 and quickly turned the club's fortunes around. He earned a nomination for the Jack Adams Award as coach of the year in his first year behind the bench in Toronto after guiding the Leafs to a club record 45 victories. After the season, Quinn was named General Manager on July 14, 1999. He becomes the first man since Punch Imlach in the 1960s to serve the dual role in Toronto. Quinn served as both coach and general manager during much of his time with the Vancouver Canucks. He led the Leafs to their first 100-point season in 1999-2000.

Quinn joined the Canucks as president and general manager in 1987 and took over the coaching reigns on January 31, 1991. He guided the Canucks to single-season records for wins (46) and points (101) in 1992-93, and led the team to the Stanley Cup Finals in 1994. Quinn had previously guided Philadelphia to the Stanley Cup Finals in 1980. He won the Jack Adams Award with the Flyers in 1979-80 and in Vancouver in 1992-93. He also coached in Los Angeles from 1984 to 1987.

Quinn spent the 1968-69 and 1969-70 seasons in a Maple Leafs uniform. He played 99 games for Toronto and later played for Vancouver and the Atlanta Flames. He holds a law degree from Widener University, Delaware School of Law.

NHL Coaching Record

		Regular Season					Playoffs			
Season	Team	Games	W	L	T	%	Games	W	L	%
1978-79	Philadelphia	30	18	8	4	.667	8	3	5	.375
1979-80	Philadelphia	80	48	12	20	.725	19	13	6	.684
1980-81	Philadelphia	80	41	24	15	.606	12	6	6	.500
1981-82	Philadelphia	72	34	29	9	.535	....	....	....	....
1984-85	Los Angeles	80	34	32	14	.513	3	0	3	.000
1985-86	Los Angeles	80	23	49	8	.338	....	....	....	....
1986-87	Los Angeles	42	18	20	4	.476	....	....	....	....
1990-91	Vancouver	26	9	13	4	.423	6	2	4	.333
1991-92	Vancouver	80	42	26	12	.600	13	6	7	.462
1992-93	Vancouver	84	46	29	9	.601	12	6	6	.500
1993-94	Vancouver	84	41	40	3	.506	24	15	9	.625
1995-96	Vancouver	6	3	3	0	.500	6	2	4	.333
1998-99	Toronto	82	45	30	7	.591	17	9	8	.529
1999-2000	Toronto	82	45	30	7	.610•	12	6	6	.500
	NHL Totals	**908**	**447**	**345**	**116**	**.558•**	**132**	**68**	**64**	**.515**

• Includes points from regulation ties

Coaching History

Conn Smythe, 1927-28 to 1929-30; Conn Smythe and Art Duncan, 1930-31; Art Duncan and Dick Irvin, 1931-32; Dick Irvin, 1932-33 to 1939-40; Hap Day, 1940-41 to 1949-50; Joe Primeau, 1950-51 to 1952-53; King Clancy, 1953-54 to 1955-56; Howie Meeker, 1956-57; Billy Reay, 1957-58; Billy Reay and Punch Imlach, 1958-59; Punch Imlach, 1959-60 to 1968-69; John McLellan, 1969-70 to 1972-73; Red Kelly, 1973-74 to 1976-77; Roger Neilson, 1977-78, 1978-79; Floyd Smith, Dick Duff and Punch Imlach, 1979-80; Punch Imlach, Joe Crozier and Mike Nykoluk, 1980-81; Mike Nykoluk, 1981-82 to 1983-84; Dan Maloney, 1984-85, 1985-86; John Brophy, 1986-87, 1987-88; John Brophy and George Armstrong, 1988-89; Doug Carpenter, 1989-90; Doug Carpenter and Tom Watt, 1990-91; Tom Watt, 1991-92; Pat Burns, 1992-93 to 1994-95; Pat Burns and Nick Beverley, 1995-96; Mike Murphy, 1996-97, 1997-98; Pat Quinn, 1998-99 to date.

Club Records

Team

(Figures in brackets for season records are games played; records for fewest points, wins, ties, losses, goals, goals against are for 70 or more games)

Most Points	**100**	1999-2000 (82)
Most Wins	**45**	1998-99 (82), 1999-2000 (82)
Most Ties	**22**	1954-55 (70)
Most Losses	**52**	1984-85 (80)
Most Goals	**337**	1989-90 (80)
Most Goals Against	**387**	1983-84 (80)
Fewest Points	**48**	1984-85 (80)
Fewest Wins	**20**	1981-82 (80), 1984-85 (80)
Fewest Ties	**4**	1989-90 (80)
Fewest Losses	**16**	1950-51 (70)
Fewest Goals	**147**	1954-55 (70)
Fewest Goals Against	***131**	1953-54 (70)
Longest Winning Streak		
Overall	**10**	Oct. 7-28/93
Home	**9**	Nov. 11-Dec. 26/53
Away	**7**	Nov. 14-Dec. 15/40, Dec. 4/60-Jan. 5/61
Longest Undefeated Streak		
Overall	**11**	Oct. 15-Nov. 8/50 (8 wins, 3 ties), Jan. 6-Feb. 1/94 (7 wins, 4 ties)
Home	**18**	Nov. 28/33-Mar. 10/34 (15 wins, 3 ties), Oct. 31/53-Jan. 23/54 (16 wins, 2 ties)
Away	**9**	Nov. 30/47-Jan. 11/48 (4 wins, 5 ties)
Longest Losing Streak		
Overall	**10**	Jan. 15-Feb. 8/67
Home	**7**	Nov. 11-Dec. 5/84
Away	**11**	Feb. 20-Apr. 1/88
Longest Winless Streak		
Overall	**15**	Dec. 26/87-Jan. 25/88 (11 losses, 4 ties)
Home	**11**	Dec. 19/87-Jan. 25/88 (7 losses, 4 ties)
Away	**18**	Oct. 6/82-Jan. 5/83 (13 losses, 5 ties)
Most Shutouts, Season	**13**	1953-54 (70)
Most PIM, Season	**2,419**	1989-90 (80)
Most Goals, Game	**14**	Mar. 16/57 (NYR 1 at Tor. 14)

Individual

Most Seasons	**21**	George Armstrong
Most Games	**1,187**	George Armstrong
Most Goals, Career	**389**	Darryl Sittler
Most Assists, Career	**620**	Borje Salming
Most Points, Career	**916**	Darryl Sittler (389G, 527A)
Most PIM, Career	**1,670**	Dave Williams
Most Shutouts, Career	**62**	Turk Broda
Longest Consecutive Games Streak	**486**	Tim Horton (Feb. 11/61-Feb. 4/68)
Most Goals, Season	**54**	Rick Vaive (1981-82)
Most Assists, Season	**95**	Doug Gilmour (1992-93)
Most Points, Season	**127**	Doug Gilmour (1992-93; 32G, 95A)
Most PIM, Season	**365**	Tie Domi (1997-98)
Most Points, Defenseman, Season	**79**	Ian Turnbull (1976-77; 22G, 57A)
Most Points, Center, Season	**127**	Doug Gilmour (1992-93; 32G, 95A)
Most Points, Right Wing, Season	**97**	Wilf Paiement (1980-81; 40G, 57A)
Most Points, Left Wing, Season	**99**	Dave Andreychuk (1993-94; 53G, 46A)
Most Points, Rookie, Season	**66**	Peter Ihnacak (1982-83; 28G, 38A)
Most Shutouts, Season	**13**	Harry Lumley (1953-54)
Most Goals, Game	**6**	Corb Denneny (Jan. 26/21), Darryl Sittler (Feb. 7/76)
Most Assists, Game	**6**	Babe Pratt (Jan. 8/44), Doug Gilmour (Feb. 13/93)
Most Points, Game	***10**	Darryl Sittler (Feb. 7/76; 6G, 4A)

* NHL Record.

Retired Numbers

5	Bill Barilko	1946-1951
6	Ace Bailey	1926-1934

Honored Numbers

1	Turk Broda	1936-43, 45-52
	Johnny Bower	1958-1970
7	King Clancy	1930-1937
	Tim Horton	1949-50, 51-70
9	Charlie Conacher	1929-1938
	Ted Kennedy	1942-55, 56-57
10	Syl Apps	1936-43, 45-48
	George Armstrong	1949-50, 51-71

All-time Record vs. Other Clubs

Regular Season

	At Home							On Road							Total						
	GP	W	L	T	GF	GA	PTS	GP	W	L	T	GF	GA	PTS	GP	W	L	T	GF	GA	PTS
Anaheim	12	6	2	4	36	25	16	10	5	4	1	27	29	11	22	11	6	5	63	54	27
Atlanta	2	1	1	0	5	4	2	1	1	0	0	4	0	2	3	2	1	0	9	4	4
Boston	288	150	87	51	979	748	351	288	85	156	47	764	946	218	576	235	243	98	1743	1694	569
Buffalo	57	23	25	9	178	205	55	58	17	37	4	159	244	38	115	40	62	13	337	449	93
Calgary	50	26	17	7	190	180	59	54	18	31	5	174	222	41	104	44	48	12	364	402	100
Carolina	29	9	15	5	100	112	23	29	8	16	5	98	125	21	58	17	31	10	198	237	44
Chicago	312	163	96	53	1063	813	379	314	117	155	42	821	960	276	626	280	251	95	1884	1773	655
Colorado	31	14	14	3	104	122	31	29	7	17	5	87	111	19	60	21	31	8	191	233	50
Dallas	99	49	34	16	350	311	114	95	35	49	11	302	362	81	194	84	83	27	652	673	195
Detroit	313	163	104	46	1036	839	372	317	106	165	46	779	949	258	630	269	269	92	1815	1788	630
Edmonton	34	18	14	2	142	145	38	36	11	19	6	122	160	28	70	29	33	8	264	305	66
Florida	7	6	1	0	29	16	12	9	3	3	3	25	28	9	16	9	4	3	54	44	21
Los Angeles	65	34	20	11	260	215	79	64	21	34	9	187	230	51	129	55	54	20	447	445	130
Montreal	323	165	114	44	975	842	374	322	86	196	40	794	1140	212	645	251	310	84	1769	1982	586
Nashville	2	0	1	1	4	6	1	0	0	0	0	0	0	0	2	0	1	1	4	6	1
New Jersey	40	27	9	4	169	127	58	39	13	14	12	122	137	38	79	40	23	16	291	264	96
NY Islanders	47	22	22	3	159	166	47	45	18	24	3	135	180	39	92	40	46	6	294	346	86
NY Rangers	274	153	82	39	942	721	345	275	102	117	56	804	848	261	549	255	199	95	1746	1569	606
Ottawa	11	7	3	1	36	27	15	10	3	6	1	24	28	7	21	10	9	2	60	55	22
Philadelphia	59	21	25	13	195	202	55	59	12	39	8	138	235	33	118	33	64	21	333	437	88
Phoenix	40	17	21	2	143	153	36	38	12	20	6	137	157	30	78	29	41	8	280	310	66
Pittsburgh	60	28	21	11	241	199	67	61	21	34	6	192	258	48	121	49	55	17	433	457	115
St. Louis	96	58	27	11	360	278	127	98	29	56	13	275	337	71	194	87	83	24	635	615	198
San Jose	15	10	4	1	60	40	21	14	7	5	2	38	30	16	29	17	9	3	98	70	37
Tampa Bay	13	8	5	0	50	33	16	12	11	1	0	47	23	22	25	19	6	0	97	56	38
Vancouver	57	26	21	10	210	190	62	57	20	27	10	193	200	50	114	46	48	20	403	390	112
Washington	41	22	14	5	187	144	49	42	13	27	2	116	163	28	83	35	41	7	303	307	77
Defunct Clubs	232	158	53	21	860	515	337	233	84	120	29	607	745	197	465	242	173	50	1467	1260	534
Totals	**2609**	**1384**	**852**	**373**	**9063**	**7378**	**3141**	**2609**	**865**	**1372**	**372**	**7171**	**8847**	**2105**	**5218**	**2249**	**2224**	**745**	**16234**	**16225**	**5246**

Playoffs

	Series	W	L	GP	W	L	T	GF	GA	Last Mtg.	Round	Result
Boston	13	8	5	62	31	30	1	150	153	1974	QF	L 0-4
Buffalo	1	0	1	5	1	4	0	16	21	1999	CF	L 1-4
Calgary	1	1	0	2	2	0	0	9	5	1979	PR	W 2-0
Chicago	9	6	3	38	22	15	1	111	89	1995	CQF	L 3-4
Dallas	2	0	2	7	1	6	0	26	35	1983	DSF	L 1-3
Detroit	23	12	11	117	58	59	0	311	321	1993	DSF	W 4-3
Los Angeles	3	2	1	12	7	5	0	41	31	1993	CF	L 3-4
Montreal	15	7	8	71	29	42	0	160	215	1979	QF	L 0-4
New Jersey	1	0	1	6	2	4	0	9	16	2000	CSF	L 2-4
NY Islanders	2	1	1	10	4	6	0	20	33	1981	PR	L 0-3
NY Rangers	8	3	5	35	16	19	0	86	86	1971	QF	L 2-4
Ottawa	1	1	0	6	4	2	0	17	10	2000	CQF	W 4-2
Philadelphia	4	1	3	23	9	14	0	56	78	1999	CQF	W 4-2
Pittsburgh	3	3	0	12	8	4	0	39	27	1999	CSF	W 4-2
St. Louis	5	2	3	31	14	17	0	90	88	1996	CQF	L 2-4
San Jose	1	1	0	7	4	3	0	26	21	1994	CSF	W 4-3
Vancouver	1	0	1	5	1	4	0	9	16	1994	CF	L 1-4
Defunct	8	6	2	24	12	10	2	59	57			
Totals	**101**	**54**	**47**	**473**	**225**	**244**	**4**	**1235**	**1302**			

Playoff Results 2000-1996

Year	Round	Opponent	Result	GF	GA
2000	CSF	New Jersey	L 2-4	9	16
	CQF	Ottawa	W 4-2	17	10
1999	CF	Buffalo	L 1-4	16	21
	CSF	Pittsburgh	W 4-2	18	14
	CQF	Philadelphia	W 4-2	9	11
1996	CQF	St. Louis	L 2-4	15	21

Abbreviations: Round: CF – conference final; **CSF** – conference semi-final; **CQF** – conference quarter-final; **DSF** – division semi-final; **QF** – quarter-final; **PR** – preliminary round.

Calgary totals include Atlanta Flames, 1972-73 to 1979-80.
Carolina totals include Hartford, 1979-80 to 1996-97.
Colorado totals include Quebec, 1979-80 to 1994-95.
Dallas totals include Minnesota North Stars, 1967-68 to 1992-93.
New Jersey totals include Kansas City, 1974-75 to 1975-76, and Colorado Rockies, 1976-77 to 1981-82.
Phoenix totals include Winnipeg, 1979-80 to 1995-96.

1999-2000 Results

Oct.	2	at	Montreal	4-1		7	at	Pittsburgh	2-5
	4		Boston	4-0		8		NY Rangers	3-5
	6		Colorado	2-1		11	at	Boston	3-2
	9	at	Ottawa	3-4		14	at	Edmonton	3-2 *
	11		Nashville	2-4		15	at	Calgary	0-4
	13		Florida	3-2		17	at	Vancouver	5-4 *
	15	at	Chicago	2-1		22		Washington	5-5
	16	at	St. Louis	2-4		24		Ottawa	3-3
	20		Carolina	3-3		26	at	Detroit	2-4
	23		Montreal	3-2		27	at	NY Rangers	4-3
	25		Dallas	4-0		29		Los Angeles	3-2
	27		Atlanta	4-0	**Feb.**	1	at	Tampa Bay	5-3
	30		Calgary	2-1		3	at	Boston	2-4
Nov.	3	at	Carolina	6-0		9		Philadelphia	2-4
	5	at	Washington	3-5		12		Vancouver	1-4
	6	at	New Jersey	3-3		14		Carolina	2-5
	9		Anaheim	0-2		16		Boston	3-3
	11	at	Boston	3-4 *		19	at	Montreal	1-2
	13		Detroit	1-1		23		Phoenix	5-3
	15		San Jose	4-2		25	at	New Jersey	3-1
	17		St. Louis	2-3		26		Buffalo	5-2
	20		NY Rangers	4-3 *		29	at	Atlanta	4-0
	23	at	Pittsburgh	1-3	**Mar.**	1	at	Florida	1-3
	26	at	Philadelphia	2-3 *		4		Montreal	4-3
	27		Edmonton	5-2		6	at	Vancouver	6-5 *
	29		Washington	3-1		7	at	Edmonton	2-0
Dec.	2	at	Carolina	2-2		9	at	Calgary	6-2
	4		Pittsburgh	3-2 *		11	at	Ottawa	4-2
	6		Buffalo	3-2 *		15		Chicago	2-5
	9	at	Philadelphia	2-4		16	at	Detroit	4-3 *
	11		Philadelphia	6-4		18		Atlanta	1-4
	13		Ottawa	1-3		22		NY Islanders	2-5
	15		NY Islanders	5-1		23	at	Ottawa	2-3
	18		Montreal	2-1		25		New Jersey	5-3
	20	at	Florida	6-4		29	at	St. Louis	3-2
	21	at	Tampa Bay	4-2		30	at	Chicago	0-4
	23		New Jersey	4-1	**Apr.**	1	at	Washington	4-3
	29	at	NY Islanders	2-1		3	at	Buffalo	2-3
Jan.	1	at	Buffalo	1-8		5		Pittsburgh	2-4
	3		Buffalo	6-2		7	at	NY Islanders	2-1
	5	at	NY Rangers	2-3 *		8		Tampa Bay	4-2

* – Overtime

Entry Draft
Selections 2000-1986

2000
Pick
24 Brad Boyes
51 Kris Vernarsky
70 Mikael Tellqvist
90 Jean-Francois Racine
100 Miguel Delisle
179 Vadim Sozinov
209 Markus Seikola
223 Lubos Velebny
254 Alexander Shinkar
265 Jean-Philippe Cote

1999
Pick
24 Luca Cereda
60 Peter Reynolds
108 Mirko Murovic
110 Jonathon Zion
151 Vaclav Zavoral
161 Jan Sochor
211 Vladimir Kulikov
239 Pierre Hedin
267 Peter Metcalf

1998
Pick
10 Nik Antropov
35 Petr Svoboda
69 Jamie Hodson
87 Alexei Ponikarovsky
126 Morgan Warren
154 Allan Rourke
181 Jonathan Gagnon
215 Dwight Wolfe
228 Michal Travnicek
236 Sergei Rostov

1997
Pick
57 Jeff Farkas
84 Adam Mair
111 Frantisek Mrazek
138 Eric Gooldy
165 Hugo Marchand
190 Shawn Thornton
194 Russ Bartlett
221 Jonathan Hedstrom

1996
Pick
36 Marek Posmyk
50 Francis Larivee
66 Mike Lankshear
68 Konstantin Kalmikov
86 Jason Sessa
103 Vladimir Antipov
110 Peter Cava
111 Brandon Sugden
140 Dmitri Yakushin
148 Chris Bogas
151 Lucio DeMartinis
178 Reggie Berg
204 Tomas Kaberle
230 Jared Hope

1995
Pick
15 Jeff Ware
54 Ryan Pepperall
139 Doug Bonner
145 Yannick Tremblay
171 Marek Melenovsky
197 Mark Murphy
223 Danny Markov

1994
Pick
16 Eric Fichaud
48 Sean Haggerty
64 Fredrik Modin
126 Mark Deyell
152 Karri White
178 Tommi Rajamaki
204 Rob Butler
256 Sergei Berezin
282 Doug Nolan

1993
Pick
12 Kenny Jonsson
19 Landon Wilson
123 Zdenek Nedved
149 Paul Vincent
175 Jeff Andrews
201 David Brumby
253 Kyle Ferguson
279 Mikhail Lapin

1992
Pick
8 Brandon Convery
23 Grant Marshall
77 Nikolai Borschevsky
95 Mark Raiter
101 Janne Gronvall
106 Chris Deruiter
125 Mikael Hakansson
149 Patrik Augusta
173 Ryan Vandenbussche
197 Wayne Clarke
221 Sergei Simonov
245 Nathan Dempsey

1991
Pick
47 Yanic Perreault
69 Terry Chitaroni
102 Alexei Kudashov
113 Jeff Perry
120 Alexander Kuzminsky
135 Martin Prochazka
160 Dmitri Mironov
164 Robb McIntyre
167 Tomas Kucharcik
179 Guy Lehoux
201 Gary Miller
223 Johnathon Kelley
245 Chris O'Rourke

1990
Pick
10 Drake Berehowsky
31 Felix Potvin
73 Darby Hendrickson
80 Greg Walters
115 Alexander Godynyuk
136 Eric Lacroix
157 Dan Stiver
178 Robert Horyna
199 Rob Chebator
220 Scott Malone
241 Nick Vachon

1989
Pick
3 Scott Thornton
12 Rob Pearson
21 Steve Bancroft
66 Matt Martin
96 Keith Carney
108 David Burke
125 Michael Doers
129 Keith Merkler
150 Derek Langille
171 Jeffrey St. Laurent
192 Justin Tomberlin
213 Mike Jackson
234 Steve Chartrand

1988
Pick
6 Scott Pearson
27 Tie Domi
48 Peter Ing
69 Ted Crowley
86 Len Esau
132 Matt Mallgrave
153 Peter Elvenas
174 Mike Delay
195 David Sacco
216 Mike Gregorio
237 Peter DeBoer

1987
Pick
7 Luke Richardson
28 Daniel Marois
49 John McIntyre
71 Joe Sacco
91 Mike Eastwood
112 Damian Rhodes
133 Trevor Jobe
175 Brian Blad
196 Ron Bernacci
217 Ken Alexander
238 Alex Weinrich

1986
Pick
6 Vincent Damphousse
36 Darryl Shannon
48 Sean Boland
69 Kent Hulst
90 Scott Taylor
111 Stephane Giguere
132 Danny Hie
153 Stephen Brennan
174 Brian Bellefeuille
195 Sean Davidson
216 Mark Holick
237 Brian Hoard

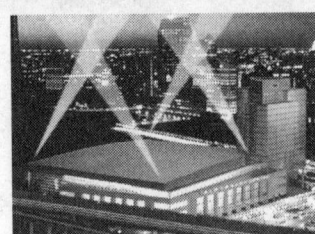
Air Canada Centre

Club Directory

Toronto Maple Leafs
Air Canada Centre
40 Bay St., Suite 400
Toronto, Ontario M5J 2X2
Phone **416/815-5700**
FAX 416/359-9331
Website:
www.torontomapleleafs.com
Capacity: 18,819

Board of Directors
Steve A. Stavro (Chairman of the Board and NHL Governor), Brian P. Bellmore (Alternate NHL Governor), Robert G. Bertram, Dale Lastman, John MacIntyre, Dean Metcalf

Maple Leaf Sports & Entertainment Ltd.
Chairman of the Board and NHL Governor . . . . Steve A. Stavro
Alternate NHL Governor . . . . Brian P. Bellmore
President and Chief Executive Officer . . . . Richard Peddie
Executive Vice-President . . . . Ken Dryden
Sr. Vice-President and General Manager,
Air Canada Centre . . . . Bob Hunter
Sr. Vice-President, Business . . . . Tom Anselmi
Sr. Vice-President, Chief Financial Officer . . . . Ian Clarke
Vice-President, Sports Communications and
Community Development . . . . John Lashway
Vice-President, People . . . . Mardi Walker
Vice-President, General Counsel . . . . Robin Brudner
Vice-President, Marketing . . . . Derek Chalmers
Vice-President, Sales and Service . . . . Chris Overholt
Corporate Secretary. . . . . Paul Perantinos

Maple Leafs Management
President and Alternate NHL Governor . . . . Ken Dryden
General Manager and Head Coach . . . . Pat Quinn
Assistant to the President . . . . Bill Watters
Director, Player Personnel . . . . Mike Penny
Assistant Coaches . . . . Keith Acton, Rick Ley
Development Coach . . . . Paul Dennis
Community Representative . . . . Darryl Sittler
Chief European Scout . . . . Thommie Bergman
Director, Amateur Scouting . . . . Mark Hillier
Scouts . . . . George Armstrong, Larry Hornung, Bob Johnson, Garth Malarchuk, Murray Oliver, Floyd Smith, Mark Yannetti
European Scouts . . . . Leonid Vaysfeld, Jan Kovac
Director, Hockey Operations . . . . Casey Vanden Heuvel
Travel Coordinator . . . . Mary Speck
Scout Coordinator . . . . Christine Buchanan
Executive Assistant to President. . . . . Ann Clark
Executive Assistant to General Manager . . . . Maria Tomasevic

Maple Leafs Communications and Community Development
Vice-President, Sports Communications and
Community Development. . . . . John Lashway
Director, Media Relations . . . . Pat Park
Coordinators, Media Relations. . . . . Dave Griffiths, Reid Mitchell
Director, Community Relations . . . . Kristy Fletcher
Director, Leaf Community Fund. . . . . Angela McManus
Coordinator, Leaf Community Fund . . . . Cora Mattholie
Assistant, Leaf Community Fund . . . . Joanna Korach
Coordinators, Community Relations . . . . Sefu Bernard, Paulette Minard
Coordinator, Game Presentation. . . . . Mike Ferriman
Manager, Game Operations . . . . Nancy Gilks
Assistant, Game Operations . . . . Shannon Nolan
Manager, Community Youth Outreach . . . . Al Quance
Coordinator, Youth Hockey Development. . . . . Greg Schell
Alumni Relations . . . . Jennifer Woods
Executive Assistant, Communications . . . . Laura Leite

Maple Leafs Medical and Training Staff
Head Athletic Therapist . . . . Chris Broadhurst
Athletic Therapist . . . . Brent Smith
Equipment Manager . . . . Brian Papineau
Assistant Equipment Manager. . . . . Dave Aleo
Trainer. . . . . Scott McKay
Team Doctors . . . . Dr. Michael Clarfield, Dr. Darrell,Ogilvie-Harris, Dr. Leith Douglas, Dr. Rob Devenyi, Dr. Simon McGrail
Team Dentist . . . . Dr. Ernie Lewis
Team Psychologist . . . . Robert Offenberger, Ph. D.

Broadcast Information
Radio Play-By-Play . . . . Joe Bowen, Dennis Beyak
Radio Analyst. . . . . Jim Ralph
Television Play-By-Play . . . . Bob Cole, Joe Bowen
Television Analyst . . . . Harry Neale

St. John's Maple Leafs (American Hockey League Affiliate)
Head Coach. . . . . Lou Crawford
Assistant Coach. . . . . Kevin McClelland
Vice President, Hockey Operations . . . . Glenn Stanford
Communications Manager . . . . Chris Schwartz
Athletic Therapist . . . . Nick Addey-Jibb
Equipment Manager . . . . Don Alcock
Assistant Equipment Manager. . . . . Shannon Coady
Executive Assistant to the GM . . . . Carolyn Dooling
Marketing Manager. . . . . Michelle Collins
Financial and Administration Manager . . . . Lisa Neville

Air Canada Centre
Director, Building Operations. . . . . Diego Roccasalva
Director, Event Operations and Production . . . . Jim Roe
Director, Event Personnel and Guest Services . . . . . Kim Bedier
Director, Programming and Event Marketing . . . . . Patti-Anne Tarlton
Sr. Manager, Ticket Operations . . . . Donna Henderson
Manager, Video and Scoreboard Production . . . . . . Curtis Emerson
Director, Marketing Services . . . . Joyce Van Zeumeren
Director, Executive Suites Services . . . . Nancy Read
Director, Food and Beverage Operations . . . . Garth Essery
Director, Consumer Products. . . . . Jeff Newman

Though ticketed to spend the season in the minors, the fine play of Nik Antropov earned him a spot in the Leafs lineup in 1999-2000. The 6'5" native of Kazakhstan is a big part of Toronto's future.

Captains' History
Hap Day, 1927-28 to 1936-37; Charlie Conacher, 1937-38; Red Horner, 1938-39, 1939-40; Syl Apps, 1940-41 to 1942-43; Bob Davidson, 1943-44, 1944-45; Syl Apps, 1945-46 to 1947-48; Ted Kennedy, 1948-49 to 1954-55; Sid Smith, 1955-56; Jim Thomson, Ted Kennedy, 1956-57; George Armstrong, 1957-58 to 1968-69; Dave Keon, 1969-70 to 1974-75; Darryl Sittler, 1975-76 to 1980-81; Rick Vaive, 1981-82 to 1985-86; no captain, 1986-87 to 1988-89; Rob Ramage, 1989-90, 1990-91; Wendel Clark, 1991-92 to 1993-94; Doug Gilmour, 1994-95 to 1996-97; Mats Sundin, 1997-98 to date.

General Managers' History
Conn Smythe, 1927-28 to 1956-57; Hap Day, 1957-58; Punch Imlach, 1958-59 to 1968-69; Jim Gregory, 1969-70 to 1978-79; Punch Imlach, 1979-80, 1980-81; Punch Imlach and Gerry McNamara, 1981-82; Gerry McNamara, 1982-83 to 1987-88; Gord Stellick, 1988-89; Floyd Smith, 1989-90, 1990-91; Cliff Fletcher, 1991-92 to 1996-97; Ken Dryden, 1997-98, 1998-99; Pat Quinn, 1999-2000 to date.

Vancouver Canucks

1999-2000 Results: 30w-37l-15t 83pts. Third, Northwest Division

Year-by-Year Record

Season	GP	Home W	L	T	Road W	L	T	Overall W	L	T	GF	GA	Pts.	Finished		Playoff Result
1999-2000	82	16	20	5	14	17	10	30	37	15	227	237	83	3rd,	Northwest Div.	Out of Playoffs
1998-99	82	14	21	6	9	26	6	23	47	12	192	258	58	4th,	Northwest Div.	Out of Playoffs
1997-98	82	15	22	4	10	21	10	25	43	14	224	273	64	7th,	Pacific Div.	Out of Playoffs
1996-97	82	20	17	4	15	23	3	35	40	7	257	273	77	4th,	Pacific Div.	Out of Playoffs
1995-96	82	15	19	7	17	16	8	32	35	15	278	278	79	3rd,	Pacific Div.	Lost Conf. Quarter-Final
1994-95	48	10	8	6	8	10	6	18	18	12	153	148	48	2nd,	Pacific Div.	Lost Conf. Semi-Final
1993-94	84	20	19	3	21	21	0	41	40	3	279	276	85	2nd,	Pacific Div.	Lost Final
1992-93	84	27	11	4	19	18	5	46	29	9	346	278	101	1st,	Smythe Div.	Lost Div. Final
1991-92	80	23	10	7	19	16	5	42	26	12	285	250	96	1st,	Smythe Div.	Lost Div. Final
1990-91	80	18	17	5	10	26	4	28	43	9	243	315	65	4th,	Smythe Div.	Lost Div. Semi-Final
1989-90	80	13	16	11	12	25	3	25	41	14	245	306	64	5th,	Smythe Div.	Out of Playoffs
1988-89	80	19	15	6	14	24	2	33	39	8	251	253	74	4th,	Smythe Div.	Lost Div. Semi-Final
1987-88	80	15	20	5	10	26	4	25	46	9	272	320	59	5th,	Smythe Div.	Out of Playoffs
1986-87	80	17	19	4	12	24	4	29	43	8	282	314	66	5th,	Smythe Div.	Out of Playoffs
1985-86	80	17	18	5	6	26	8	23	44	13	282	333	59	4th,	Smythe Div.	Lost Div. Semi-Final
1984-85	80	15	21	4	10	25	5	25	46	9	284	401	59	5th,	Smythe Div.	Out of Playoffs
1983-84	80	20	16	4	12	23	5	32	39	9	306	328	73	3rd,	Smythe Div.	Lost Div. Semi-Final
1982-83	80	20	12	8	10	23	7	30	35	15	303	309	75	3rd,	Smythe Div.	Lost Div. Semi-Final
1981-82	80	20	8	12	10	25	5	30	33	17	290	286	77	2nd,	Smythe Div.	Lost Final
1980-81	80	17	12	11	11	20	9	28	32	20	289	301	76	3rd,	Smythe Div.	Lost Prelim. Round
1979-80	80	14	17	9	13	20	7	27	37	16	256	281	70	3rd,	Smythe Div.	Lost Prelim. Round
1978-79	80	15	18	7	10	24	6	25	42	13	217	291	63	2nd,	Smythe Div.	Lost Prelim. Round
1977-78	80	13	15	12	7	28	5	20	43	17	239	320	57	3rd,	Smythe Div.	Out of Playoffs
1976-77	80	13	21	6	12	21	7	25	42	13	235	294	63	4th,	Smythe Div.	Out of Playoffs
1975-76	80	22	11	7	11	21	8	33	32	15	271	272	81	2nd,	Smythe Div.	Lost Prelim. Round
1974-75	80	23	12	5	15	20	5	38	32	10	271	254	86	1st,	Smythe Div.	Lost Quarter-Final
1973-74	78	14	18	7	10	25	4	24	43	11	224	296	59	7th,	East Div.	Out of Playoffs
1972-73	78	17	18	4	5	29	5	22	47	9	233	339	53	7th,	East Div.	Out of Playoffs
1971-72	78	14	20	5	6	30	3	20	50	8	203	297	48	7th,	East Div.	Out of Playoffs
1970-71	78	17	18	4	7	28	4	24	46	8	229	296	56	6th,	East Div.	Out of Playoffs

2000-01 Schedule

Oct.	Thu.	5	at Philadelphia
	Fri.	6	at Florida
	Sun.	8	at Tampa Bay
	Thu.	12	Colorado
	Sat.	14	Buffalo
	Mon.	16	Toronto
	Wed.	18	Calgary
	Sat.	21	Phoenix
	Tue.	24	at Nashville
	Wed.	25	at Dallas
	Fri.	27	Atlanta
Nov.	Wed.	1	Colorado
	Fri.	3	Pittsburgh
	Sun.	5	San Jose
	Wed.	8	at Anaheim
	Thu.	9	at Los Angeles
	Sat.	11	St. Louis
	Tue.	14	Chicago
	Fri.	17	NY Rangers
	Sun.	19	at Columbus
	Tue.	21	at St. Louis
	Wed.	22	at Washington
	Fri.	24	at Detroit
	Sun.	26	at Minnesota*
	Tue.	28	Anaheim
	Thu.	30	Montreal
Dec.	Sat.	2	Edmonton
	Mon.	4	Nashville
	Wed.	6	at Phoenix
	Fri.	8	at San Jose
	Sun.	10	Los Angeles
	Sat.	16	Columbus
	Wed.	20	at Edmonton
	Thu.	21	at Chicago
	Sat.	23	at Colorado
	Wed.	27	Montreal
	Fri.	29	at Calgary
	Sat.	30	at San Jose
Jan.	Mon.	1	at Nashville*
	Wed.	3	at Chicago
	Sat.	6	Columbus
	Mon.	8	Nashville
	Wed.	10	Ottawa
	Fri.	12	at Edmonton
	Sun.	14	Calgary
	Tue.	16	Detroit
	Thu.	18	at Colorado
	Sat.	20	at St. Louis
	Mon.	22	at Dallas
	Wed.	24	Phoenix
	Sat.	27	at Calgary
	Sun.	28	Chicago
	Tue.	30	Minnesota
Feb.	Thu.	1	Colorado
	Thu.	8	San Jose
	Sat.	10	Calgary
	Wed.	14	Washington
	Sat.	17	at Edmonton
	Sun.	18	NY Islanders
	Wed.	21	at Montreal
	Thu.	22	at Toronto
	Sat.	24	at Ottawa*
	Mon.	26	at Minnesota
	Wed.	28	Dallas
Mar.	Fri.	2	St. Louis
	Sun.	4	Minnesota
	Tue.	6	Detroit
	Thu.	8	at Phoenix
	Sat.	10	Toronto
	Tue.	13	at Detroit
	Thu.	15	at Boston
	Fri.	16	at Buffalo
	Sun.	18	at Atlanta*
	Wed.	21	at Columbus
	Fri.	23	at New Jersey
	Sun.	25	at Minnesota*
	Wed.	28	Dallas
	Fri.	30	Anaheim
Apr.	Sun.	1	at Anaheim*
	Mon.	2	at Los Angeles
	Thu.	5	Los Angeles
	Sat.	7	Edmonton

* Denotes afternoon game.

Franchise date: May 22, 1970

NORTHWEST DIVISION

31st NHL Season

After reaching a career high with 36 goals in 1998-99, Markus Naslund established a career high in assists with 38 last season. Vancouver's scoring leader should get offensive support from fellow Swedes Daniel and Henrik Sedin this season.

2000-01 Player Personnel

FORWARDS	HT	WT	S	Place of Birth	Date	1999-00 Club
BERTUZZI, Todd	6-3	235	L	Sudbury, Ont.	2/2/75	Vancouver
BRASHEAR, Donald	6-2	225	L	Bedford, IN	1/7/72	Vancouver
BROWN, Mike	6-5	185	L	Surrey, B.C.	4/27/79	Syracuse Crunch
CASSELS, Andrew	6-1	185	L	Bramalea, Ont.	7/23/69	Vancouver
CHUBAROV, Artem	6-1	189	L	Gorky, USSR	12/12/79	Vancouver-Syracuse Crunch
COOKE, Matt	5-11	205	L	Belleville, Ont.	9/7/78	Vancouver-Syracuse Crunch
DAVIDSSON, Johan	6-1	185	R	Jonkoping, Swe.	1/6/76	Ana-Cincinnati Ducks-NYI
DRUKEN, Harold	6-0	205	L	St. John's, Nfld.	1/26/79	Vancouver-Syracuse Crunch
HOLDEN, Josh	6-0	190	L	Calgary, Alta.	1/18/78	Vancouver-Syracuse Crunch
KARIYA, Steve	5-8	170	R	North Vancouver, B.C.	12/22/77	Vancouver-Syracuse Crunch
KLATT, Trent	6-1	210	R	Robbinsdale, MN	1/30/71	Vancouver-Syracuse Crunch
LEEB, Brad	5-11	180	R	Red Deer, Alta.	8/27/79	Vancouver-Syracuse Crunch
MORRISON, Brendan	5-11	190	L	Pitt Meadows, B.C.	8/15/75	SK Trebic-2-HC Pardubice-New Jersey-Vancouver
NASLUND, Markus	5-11	195	L	Ornskoldsvik, Sweden	7/30/73	Vancouver
PEDERSON, Denis	6-2	205	R	Prince Albert, Sask.	9/10/75	New Jersey-Vancouver
RUUTU, Jarkko	6-2	194	L	Vantaa, Finland	8/23/75	Vancouver-Syracuse Crunch
SCHAEFER, Peter	5-11	195	L	Yellow Grass, Sask.	7/12/77	Vancouver-Syracuse Crunch
SEDIN, Daniel	6-1	200	L	Ornskoldsvik, Sweden	9/26/80	MoDo Hockey
SEDIN, Henrik	6-2	200	L	Ornskoldsvik, Sweden	9/26/80	MoDo Hockey
SHARIFIJANOV, Vadim	6-0	205	L	Ufa, USSR	12/23/75	New Jersey-Vancouver
WOOD, Dody	6-0	200	L	Chelwynd, B.C.	3/18/72	Kansas City

DEFENSEMEN	HT	WT	S	Place of Birth	Date	1999-00 Club
ALLEN, Bryan	6-4	215	L	Kingston, Ont.	8/21/80	Oshawa Generals-Syracuse
AUCOIN, Adrian	6-2	210	R	Ottawa, Ont.	7/3/73	Canada-Vancouver
BARON, Murray	6-3	220	L	Prince George, B.C.	6/1/67	Vancouver
BONNI, Ryan	6-4	190	L	Winnipeg, Man.	2/18/79	Vancouver-Syracuse Crunch
HAWGOOD, Greg	5-10	190	L	Edmonton, Alta.	8/10/68	Vancouver
HELMER, Bryan	6-1	200	R	Sault Ste. Marie, Ont.	7/15/72	St. Louis-Worcester
JOVANOVSKI, Ed	6-2	210	L	Windsor, Ont.	6/26/76	Vancouver
KOMARNISKI, Zenith	6-0	200	L	Edmonton, Alta.	8/13/78	Vancouver-Syracuse Crunch
LACHANCE, Scott	6-1	215	L	Charlottesville, VA	10/22/72	Montreal
OHLUND, Mattias	6-2	220	L	Pitea, Sweden	9/9/76	Vancouver
SOPEL, Brent	6-1	205	R	Calgary, Alta.	1/7/77	Vancouver-Syracuse Crunch
STRUDWICK, Jason	6-3	225	L	Edmonton, Alta.	7/17/75	Vancouver

GOALTENDERS	HT	WT	C	Place of Birth	Date	1999-00 Club
ESSENSA, Bob	6-0	188	L	Toronto, Ont.	1/14/65	Phoenix
POTVIN, Felix	6-1	190	L	Anjou, Que.	6/23/71	NY Islanders-Vancouver
SCHWAB, Corey	6-0	180	L	North Battleford, Sask.	11/4/70	Orlando-Van-Syracuse Crunch

1999-2000 Scoring

* – rookie

Regular Season

Pos	#	Player	Team	GP	G	A	Pts	+/–	PIM	PP	SH	GW	GT	S	%
L	19	Markus Naslund	VAN	82	27	38	65	-5	64	6	2	3	1	271	10.0
C	25	Andrew Cassels	VAN	79	17	45	62	8	16	6	0	1	0	109	15.6
C	11	Mark Messier	VAN	66	17	37	54	-15	30	6	0	4	0	131	13.0
L	44	Todd Bertuzzi	VAN	80	25	25	50	-2	126	4	0	2	0	173	14.5
C	7	Brendan Morrison	N.J	44	5	21	26	8	8	2	0	1	0	79	6.3
			VAN	12	2	7	9	4	10	0	0	0	0	17	11.8
			TOTAL	56	7	28	35	12	18	2	0	1	0	96	7.3
L	72	* Peter Schaefer	VAN	71	16	15	31	0	20	2	2	4	0	101	15.8
D	55	Ed Jovanovski	VAN	75	5	21	26	-3	54	1	0	1	0	109	4.6
D	6	Adrian Aucoin	VAN	57	10	14	24	7	30	4	0	1	0	126	7.9
D	4	Greg Hawgood	VAN	79	5	17	22	5	26	2	0	0	0	70	7.1
R	26	Trent Klatt	VAN	47	10	10	20	-8	26	8	0	0	0	100	10.0
D	2	Mattias Ohlund	VAN	42	4	16	20	6	24	2	1	1	0	63	6.3
L	18	* Steve Kariya	VAN	45	8	11	19	9	22	0	0	0	0	41	19.5
C	27	Harry York	VAN	54	4	13	17	-4	20	1	1	0	1	50	8.0
L	9	Brad May	VAN	59	9	7	16	-2	90	0	0	3	0	66	13.6
C	15	* Harold Druken	VAN	33	7	9	16	14	10	2	0	0	0	69	10.1
L	8	Donald Brashear	VAN	60	11	2	13	-9	136	1	0	3	0	83	13.3
C	24	Matt Cooke	VAN	51	5	7	12	3	39	0	1	1	0	58	8.6
D	23	Murray Baron	VAN	81	2	10	12	8	67	0	0	0	0	48	4.2
C	20	Denis Pederson	N.J	35	3	3	6	-7	16	0	0	0	0	41	7.3
			VAN	12	3	2	5	1	2	0	0	0	0	15	20.0
			TOTAL	47	6	5	11	-6	18	0	0	0	0	56	10.7
R	17	Vadim Sharifijanov	N.J	20	3	4	7	-6	8	0	0	0	0	20	15.0
			VAN	17	2	1	3	-7	14	1	0	0	0	26	7.7
			TOTAL	37	5	5	10	-13	22	1	0	0	0	46	10.9
C	14	Darby Hendrickson	VAN	40	5	4	9	-3	14	0	1	0	0	39	12.8
C	13	* Artem Chubarov	VAN	49	1	8	9	-4	10	0	0	0	0	53	1.9
D	3	* Brent Sopel	VAN	18	2	4	6	9	12	0	0	0	0	11	18.2
C	21	Josh Holden	VAN	6	1	5	6	2	2	0	0	0	0	5	20.0
D	39	Chris O'Sullivan	VAN	11	0	5	5	2	2	0	0	0	0	16	0.0
D	34	Jason Strudwick	VAN	63	1	3	4	-13	64	0	0	0	0	18	5.6
D	5	* Zenith Komarniski	VAN	18	1	1	2	-1	8	0	0	0	0	21	4.8
G	30	Garth Snow	VAN	32	0	2	2	0	8	0	0	0	0	0	0.0
G	29	Felix Potvin	NYI	22	0	0	0	0	2	0	0	0	0	0	0.0
			VAN	34	0	2	2	0	0	0	0	0	0	0	0.0
			TOTAL	56	0	2	2	0	2	0	0	0	0	0	0.0
L	37	* Jarkko Ruutu	VAN	8	0	1	1	-1	6	0	0	0	0	4	0.0
D	3	Doug Bodger	VAN	13	0	1	1	-6	4	0	0	0	0	11	0.0
R	38	* Brad Leeb	VAN	2	0	0	0	-2	2	0	0	0	0	3	0.0
G	33	* Alfie Michaud	VAN	2	0	0	0	0	0	0	0	0	0	0	0.0
D	36	* Ryan Bonni	VAN	3	0	0	0	-1	0	0	0	0	0	1	0.0
C	31	* Lubomir Vaic	VAN	4	0	0	0	0	0	0	0	0	0	2	0.0
G	32	Corey Schwab	VAN	6	0	0	0	0	0	0	0	0	0	0	0.0

Goaltending

No.	Goaltender	GPI	Mins	Avg	W	L	T	EN	SO	GA	SA	S%
29	Felix Potvin	34	1966	2.59	12	13	7	4	0	85	906	.906
30	Garth Snow	32	1712	2.66	10	15	3	1	0	76	775	.902
80	Kevin Weekes	20	987	2.86	6	7	4	3	1	47	461	.898
32	Corey Schwab	6	269	3.57	2	1	1	0	0	16	115	.861
33	* Alfie Michaud	2	69	4.35	1	1	0	0	0	5	27	.815
	Totals	82	5033	2.83	30	37	15	8	1	237	2292	.897

Coach

CRAWFORD, MARC
Coach, Vancouver Canucks. Born in Belleville, Ont., February 13, 1961.

Marc Crawford became the 15th Head Coach in Canucks history on January 24, 1999. Crawford began his NHL coaching career with the Quebec Nordiques in 1994 and won a Stanley Cup in 1996 when the team moved to Denver to become the Colorado Avalanche. With the win, Crawford became the third-youngest coach in NHL history to win a Stanley Cup. Crawford coached the Avalanche for two seasons after winning the Cup before leaving following the 1997-98 season. He began the 1998-99 season as a colour commentator for CBC's Hockey Night in Canada before joining the Canucks. He led the team to 83 points in his first full season behind the bench in 1999-2000.

Crawford was the Head Coach for Team Canada at the 1998 Olympic Winter Games in Nagano, Japan and he was an assistant coach with Canada's silver medal-winning team in the 1996 World Cup of Hockey. He began his coaching career when he was hired by Brian Burke as a playing assistant with Fredericton (AHL) for the 1987-88 season. At the end of the year he moved to Milwaukee where he served as an assistant coach for the Canucks' IHL minor league affiliate for the 1988-89 campaign. He then moved to Cornwall where he served as the Royals' General Manager and Head Coach in 1989-90.

After two seasons with Cornwall, Crawford went on to coach the St. John's Maple Leafs of the AHL before joining the Nordiques in 1994. He received the 1995 Jack Adams Award as the NHL Coach of the Year, becoming the first rookie coach to win the award since it was inaugurated in 1974.

Crawford played every game of his six-year NHL career with the Vancouver Canucks, recording 19 goals and 31 assists in 176 games. He was a rookie on the Canucks team that made a run to the Stanley Cup finals to face the NY Islanders in 1982.

Coaching History

Hal Laycoe, 1970-71, 1971-72; Vic Stasiuk, 1972-73; Bill McCreary and Phil Maloney, 1973-74; Phil Maloney, 1974-75, 1975-76; Phil Maloney and Orland Kurtenbach, 1976-77; Orland Kurtenbach, 1977-78; Harry Neale, 1978-79 to 1980-81; Harry Neale and Roger Neilson, 1981-82; Roger Neilson, 1982-83; Roger Neilson and Harry Neale, 1983-84; Harry Neale and Bill Laforge, 1984-85; Tom Watt, 1985-86, 1986-87; Bob McCammon, 1987-88 to 1989-90; Bob McCammon and Pat Quinn, 1990-91; Pat Quinn, 1991-92 to 1993-94; Rick Ley, 1994-95; Rick Ley and Pat Quinn, 1995-96; Tom Renney, 1996-97; Tom Renney and Mike Keenan, 1997-98; Mike Keenan and Marc Crawford, 1998-99; Marc Crawford, 1999-2000 to date.

Coaching Record

Season	Team	Regular Season					Playoffs			
		Games	W	L	T	%	Games	W	L	%
1989-90	Cornwall (OHL)	66	24	38	4	.394	6	2	4	.333
1990-91	Cornwall (OHL)	66	23	42	1	.356	....			
1991-92	St. John's (AHL)	80	39	29	12	.562	16	11	5	.688
1992-93	St. John's (AHL)	80	41	26	13	.594	9	4	5	.444
1993-94	St. John's (AHL)	80	45	23	12	.638	11	6	5	.545
1994-95	Quebec (NHL)	48	30	13	5	.677	6	2	4	.333
1995-96	Colorado (NHL)	82	47	25	10	.634	22	16	6	.727*
1996-97	Colorado (NHL)	82	49	24	9	.652	17	10	7	.588
1997-98	Colorado (NHL)	82	39	26	17	.579	7	3	4	.429
1998-99	Vancouver (NHL)	37	8	23	6	.297				
1999-2000	Vancouver (NHL)	82	30	37	15	.506•				
	NHL Totals	413	203	148	62	.576•	52	31	21	.596

* Stanley Cup win.
• Includes points from regulation ties

Club Records

Team

(Figures in brackets for season records are games played; records for fewest points, wins, ties, losses, goals, goals against are for 70 or more games)

Most Points	101	1992-93 (84)
Most Wins	46	1992-93 (84)
Most Ties	20	1980-81 (80)
Most Losses	50	1971-72 (78)
Most Goals	346	1992-93 (84)
Most Goals Against	401	1984-85 (80)
Fewest Points	48	1971-72 (78)
Fewest Wins	20	1971-72 (78), 1977-78 (80)
Fewest Ties	3	1993-94 (84)
Fewest Losses	26	1991-92 (80)
Fewest Goals	192	1998-99 (82)
Fewest Goals Against	237	1999-2000 (82)

Longest Winning Streak

Overall	7	Feb. 10-23/89
Home	9	Nov. 6-Dec. 9/92
Away	5	Jan. 14-25/92, Oct. 6-Nov. 2/93

Longest Undefeated Streak

Overall	10	Mar. 5-25/77 (5 wins, 5 ties)
Home	18	Nov. 4/92-Jan. 16/93 (16 wins, 2 ties)
Away	5	Six times

Longest Losing Streak

Overall	10	Oct. 23-Nov. 11/97
Home	6	Dec. 18/70-Jan. 20/71
Away	12	Nov. 28/81-Feb. 6/82

Longest Winless Streak

Overall	13	Nov. 9-Dec. 7/73 (10 losses, 3 ties)
Home	11	Dec. 18/70-Feb. 6/71 (10 losses, 1 tie)
Away	20	Jan. 2-Apr. 2/86 (14 losses, 6 ties)

Most Shutouts, Season	8	1974-75 (80)
Most PIM, Season	2,326	1992-93 (84)
Most Goals, Game	11	Mar. 28/71 (Cal. 5 at Van. 11), Nov. 25/86 (L.A. 5 at Van. 11), Mar. 1/92 (Cgy. 0 at Van. 11)

Individual

Most Seasons	13	Stan Smyl
Most Games	896	Stan Smyl
Most Goals, Career	262	Stan Smyl
Most Assists, Career	411	Stan Smyl
Most Points, Career	673	Stan Smyl (262G, 411A)
Most PIM, Career	2,127	Gino Odjick
Most Shutouts, Career	20	Kirk McLean
Longest Consecutive Games Streak	482	Trevor Linden (Oct. 4/90-Dec. 1/96)
Most Goals, Season	60	Pavel Bure (1992-93, 1993-94)
Most Assists, Season	62	André Boudrias (1974-75)
Most Points, Season	110	Pavel Bure (1992-93; 60G, 50A)
Most PIM, Season	372	Donald Brashear (1997-98)

Most Points, Defenseman, Season	63	Doug Lidster (1986-87; 12G, 51A)
Most Points, Center, Season	91	Patrik Sundstrom (1983-84; 38G, 53A)
Most Points, Right Wing, Season	110	Pavel Bure (1992-93; 60G, 50A)
Most Points, Left Wing, Season	81	Darcy Rota (1982-83; 42G, 39A)
Most Points, Rookie, Season	60	Ivan Hlinka (1981-82; 23G, 37A), Pavel Bure (1991-92; 34G, 26A)
Most Shutouts, Season	6	Gary Smith (1974-75), Garth Snow (1998-99)
Most Goals, Game	4	Several times
Most Assists, Game	6	Patrik Sundstrom (Feb. 29/84)
Most Points, Game	7	Patrik Sundstrom (Feb. 29/84; 1G, 6A)

Retired Numbers

12	Stan Smyl	1978-1991

Captains' History

Orland Kurtenbach, 1970-71 to 1973-74; no captain, 1974-75; Andre Boudrias, 1975-76; Chris Oddleifson, 1976-77; Don Lever, 1977-78; Don Lever and Kevin McCarthy, 1978-79; Kevin McCarthy, 1979-80 to 1981-82; Stan Smyl, 1982-83 to 1989-90; Dan Quinn, Doug Lidster and Trevor Linden, 1990-91; Trevor Linden, 1991-92 to 1996-97; Mark Messier, 1997-98 to 1999-2000.

General Managers' History

Bud Poile, 1970-71 to 1972-73; Hal Laycoe, 1973-74; Phil Maloney, 1974-75 to 1976-77; Jake Milford, 1977-78 to 1981-82; Harry Neale, 1982-83 to 1984-85; Jack Gordon, 1985-86, 1986-87; Pat Quinn, 1987-88 to 1997-98; Brian Burke, 1998-99 to date.

All-time Record vs. Other Clubs

Regular Season

	GP	W	L	T	GF	GA	PTS	GP	W	L	T	GF	GA	PTS	GP	W	L	T	GF	GA	PTS
	\	At Home							On Road							Total					
Anaheim	18	12	6	0	67	44	24	17	7	4	6	54	44	20	35	19	10	6	121	88	44
Atlanta	0	0	0	0	0	0	0	1	0	1	0	3	6	0	1	0	1	0	3	6	0
Boston	49	16	25	8	162	201	40	48	6	36	6	113	206	18	97	22	61	14	275	407	58
Buffalo	49	23	16	10	182	160	56	49	17	24	8	144	177	42	98	40	40	18	326	337	98
Calgary	88	32	39	17	305	299	82	88	19	56	13	254	375	51	176	51	95	30	559	674	133
Carolina	28	12	10	6	96	79	30	27	10	12	5	90	87	25	55	22	22	11	186	166	55
Chicago	64	29	20	15	192	187	73	63	15	42	6	143	237	37	127	44	62	21	335	424	110
Colorado	36	12	18	6	125	144	31	37	13	17	7	105	123	33	73	25	35	13	230	267	64
Dallas	63	29	24	10	232	190	68	63	18	33	12	191	240	48	126	47	57	22	423	430	116
Detroit	57	25	22	10	211	189	60	58	15	36	7	168	251	37	115	40	58	17	379	440	97
Edmonton	72	28	35	9	267	294	66	70	17	46	7	216	326	41	142	45	81	16	483	620	107
Florida	6	2	1	3	18	13	7	6	2	3	1	18	16	5	12	4	4	4	36	29	12
Los Angeles	89	45	29	15	344	286	105	91	29	48	14	289	373	73	180	74	77	29	633	659	178
Montreal	49	9	32	8	123	188	26	50	8	38	4	127	240	20	99	17	70	12	250	428	46
Nashville	4	2	2	0	14	12	4	5	2	3	0	15	15	4	9	4	5	0	27	27	8
New Jersey	46	26	9	11	171	128	63	45	20	19	6	149	143	46	91	46	28	17	320	271	109
NY Islanders	45	21	21	3	148	148	45	44	11	23	10	122	164	32	89	32	44	13	270	312	77
NY Rangers	49	13	33	3	156	200	29	52	10	37	5	133	232	25	101	23	70	8	289	432	54
Ottawa	8	4	3	1	25	15	9	7	3	3	1	21	16	7	15	7	6	2	46	31	16
Philadelphia	50	10	28	12	143	201	33	50	15	34	1	149	220	31	100	25	62	13	292	421	64
Phoenix	64	37	18	9	241	186	83	61	23	30	8	223	234	54	125	60	48	17	464	420	137
Pittsburgh	47	21	22	4	169	178	46	48	8	33	7	164	224	23	95	29	55	11	333	402	69
St. Louis	64	25	32	7	188	209	57	63	18	36	9	182	238	45	127	43	68	16	370	447	102
San Jose	24	16	6	2	95	60	34	26	12	9	5	83	78	29	50	28	15	7	178	138	63
Tampa Bay	7	6	0	1	34	12	13	7	4	3	0	27	24	8	14	10	3	1	61	36	21
Toronto	57	27	20	10	200	193	66	57	21	26	10	190	210	52	114	48	46	20	390	403	118
Washington	37	17	15	5	127	119	39	37	12	21	4	107	127	28	74	29	36	9	234	246	67
Defunct Clubs	19	14	3	2	82	48	30	19	10	8	1	71	68	21	38	24	11	3	153	116	51
Totals	**1189**	**513**	**489**	**187**	**4117**	**3983**	**1219**	**1189**	**345**	**681**	**163**	**3549**	**4694**	**855**	**2378**	**858**	**1170**	**350**	**7666**	**8677**	**2074**

Playoffs

	Series	W	L	GP	W	L	T	GF	GA	Last Mtg.	Round	Result
Buffalo	2	0	2	7	1	6	0	14	28	1981	PR	L 0-3
Calgary	5	2	3	25	12	13	0	80	82	1994	CQF	W 4-3
Chicago	2	1	1	9	4	5	0	24	24	1995	CSF	L 0-4
Colorado	1	0	1	6	2	4	0	17	24	1996	CQF	L 2-4
Dallas	1	1	0	5	4	1	0	18	11	1994	CSF	W 4-1
Edmonton	2	0	2	9	2	7	0	20	35	1992	DF	L 2-4
Los Angeles	3	1	2	17	8	9	0	60	66	1993	DF	L 2-4
Montreal	1	0	1	5	1	4	0	9	20	1975	QF	L 1-4
NY Islanders	2	0	2	6	0	6	0	14	26	1982	F	L 0-4
NY Rangers	1	0	1	7	3	4	0	19	21	1994	F	L 3-4
Philadelphia	1	0	1	3	1	2	0	9	15	1979	PR	L 1-2
St. Louis	1	1	0	7	4	3	0	27	27	1995	CQF	W 4-3
Toronto	1	1	0	5	4	1	0	16	9	1994	CF	W 4-1
Winnipeg	2	2	0	13	8	5	0	50	34	1993	DSF	W 4-2
Totals	**25**	**9**	**16**	**124**	**54**	**70**	**0**	**377**	**422**			

Calgary totals include Atlanta Flames, 1972-73 to 1979-80.
Colorado totals include Quebec, 1979-80 to 1994-95.
New Jersey totals include Kansas City, 1974-75 to 1975-76, and Colorado Rockies, 1976-77 to 1981-82.
Phoenix totals include Winnipeg, 1979-80 to 1995-96.
Carolina totals include Hartford, 1979-80 to 1996-97.
Dallas totals include Minnesota North Stars, 1970-71 to 1992-93.

Playoff Results 2000-1996

Year	Round	Opponent	Result	GF	GA
1996	CQF	Colorado	L 2-4	17	24

Abbreviations: Round: F – Final;
CF – conference final; **CSF** – conference semi-final;
CQF – conference quarter-final; **DF** – division final;
DSF – division semi-final; **QF** – quarter-final;
PR – preliminary round.

1999-2000 Results

Oct. 2	NY Rangers	2-1		13	at Nashville	4-3*
6	Chicago	5-4		15	Dallas	1-2
9	Montreal	4-1		17	Toronto	4-5*
13	Calgary	3-4*		19	Detroit	3-3
15	Carolina	1-4		22	at Edmonton	3-3
16	at Calgary	4-4		23	Nashville	1-2
19	at Tampa Bay	6-5*		25	Edmonton	4-5*
20	at Florida	2-5		28	San Jose	4-1
23	at NY Islanders	2-2		30	Chicago	1-3
24	NY Rangers	3-0	Feb. 1	at Colorado	1-2
26	at Philadelphia	5-2		3	St. Louis	2-5
28	Phoenix	1-4		9	Calgary	4-3*
30	Nashville	4-1		12	at Toronto	4-1
Nov. 5	Florida	3-2		14	at Pittsburgh	0-3
7	St. Louis	1-6		16	at Detroit	2-5
9	San Jose	4-4		17	at Buffalo	2-1
12	at Phoenix	3-2		19	at Ottawa	3-1
15	Colorado	2-2		21	Boston	5-2
17	Detroit	2-7		23	at Anaheim	4-4
20	at Nashville	3-1		25	Los Angeles	2-5
22	at Atlanta	3-6		27	Phoenix	2-1
24	at Carolina	1-1		29	at Los Angeles	1-1
26	at Boston	2-2	Mar. 2	Anaheim	3-1
27	at Montreal	1-2		4	New Jersey	1-2
30	Colorado	2-4		6	Toronto	5-6*
Dec. 2	Edmonton	3-2*		8	at Dallas	3-3
4	at Edmonton	2-3		9	at St. Louis	2-2
6	at Colorado	2-3		11	at Phoenix	0-5
8	at Anaheim	2-2		13	at Los Angeles	2-3*
10	at Calgary	2-3		16	Buffalo	6-3
12	Colorado	2-3*		18	Ottawa	6-1
16	Ottawa	1-2		20	at Colorado	3-2
18	Dallas	2-4		22	at San Jose	3-4
22	Washington	6-3		24	Anaheim	8-1
26	Calgary	0-2		25	at Edmonton	3-2
29	Philadelphia	2-3*		29	at Detroit	3-6
Jan. 2	at Calgary	2-4		31	at Nashville	1-2
5	Tampa Bay	3-3	Apr. 2	at Chicago	3-2
7	at Dallas	3-1		5	Los Angeles	1-1
8	at St. Louis	2-4		7	Edmonton	4-5
12	at Chicago	2-3*		9	at San Jose	5-2

* – Overtime

Entry Draft
Selections 2000-1986

2000 Pick	1996 Pick	1992 Pick	1988 Pick
23 Nathan Smith	12 Josh Holden	21 Libor Polasek	2 Trevor Linden
71 Thatcher Bell	75 Zenith Komarniski	40 Michael Peca	33 Leif Rohlin
93 Tim Branham	93 Jonas Soling	45 Mike Fountain	44 Dane Jackson
144 Pavel Duma	121 Tyler Prosofsky	69 Jeff Connolly	107 Corrie D'Alessio
208 Brandon Reid	147 Nolan McDonald	93 Brent Tully	122 Phil Von Stefenelli
241 Nathan Barrett	175 Clint Cabana	110 Brian Loney	128 Dixon Ward
272 Tim Smith	201 Jeff Scissons	117 Adrian Aucoin	149 Greg Geldart
	227 Lubomir Vaic	141 Jason Clark	170 Roger Akerstrom
1999 Pick		165 Scott Hollis	191 Paul Constantin
2 Daniel Sedin	**1995 Pick**	213 Sonny Mignacca	212 Chris Wolanin
3 Henrik Sedin	40 Chris McAllister	237 Mark Wotton	233 Steffan Nilsson
69 Rene Vydareny	61 Larry Courville	261 Aaron Boh	
129 Ryan Thorpe	66 Peter Schaefer		**1987 Pick**
172 Josh Reed	92 Lloyd Shaw	**1991 Pick**	24 Rob Murphy
189 Kevin Swanson	120 Todd Norman	7 Alek Stojanov	45 Steve Veilleux
218 Markus Kankaanpera	144 Brent Sopel	29 Jassen Cullimore	66 Doug Torrel
271 Darrell Hay	170 Stewart Bodtker	51 Sean Pronger	87 Sean Fabian
	196 Tyler Willis	95 Dan Kesa	108 Garry Valk
1998 Pick	222 Jason Cugnet	117 John Namestnikov	129 Todd Fanning
4 Bryan Allen		139 Brent Thurston	150 Viktor Tyumenev
31 Artem Chubarov	**1994 Pick**	161 Eric Johnson	171 Greg Daly
68 Jarkko Ruutu	13 Mattias Ohlund	183 David Neilson	192 John Fletcher
81 Justin Morrison	39 Robb Gordon	205 Brad Barton	213 Roger Hansson
90 Regan Darby	42 Dave Scatchard	227 Jason Fitzsimmons	233 Neil Eisenhut
136 David Ytfeldt	65 Chad Allan	249 Xavier Majic	234 Matt Evo
140 Rick Bertran	92 Mike Dubinsky		
149 Paul Cabana	117 Yanick Dube	**1990 Pick**	**1986 Pick**
177 Vincent Malts	169 Yuri Kuznetsov	2 Petr Nedved	7 Dan Woodley
204 Graig Mischler	195 Rob Trumbley	18 Shawn Antoski	49 Don Gibson
219 Curtis Valentine	221 Bill Muckalt	23 Jiri Slegr	70 Ron Stern
232 Jason Metcalfe	247 Tyson Nash	65 Darin Bader	91 Eric Murano
	273 Robert Longpre	86 Gino Odjick	112 Steve Herniman
1997 Pick		128 Daryl Filipek	133 Jon Helgeson
10 Brad Ference	**1993 Pick**	149 Paul O'Hagan	154 Jeff Noble
34 Ryan Bonni	20 Mike Wilson	170 Mark Cipriano	175 Matt Merton
36 Harold Druken	46 Rick Girard	191 Troy Neumier	196 Marc Lyons
64 Kyle Freadrich	98 Dieter Kochan	212 Tyler Ertel	217 Todd Hawkins
90 Chris Stanley	124 Scott Walker	233 Karri Kivi	238 Vladimir Krutov
114 David Darguzas	150 Troy Creurer		
117 Matt Cockell	176 Yevgeni Babariko	**1989 Pick**	
144 Matt Cooke	202 Sean Tallaire	8 Jason Herter	
148 Larry Shapley	254 Bert Robertsson	29 Robert Woodward	
171 Rod Leroux	280 Sergei Tkachenko	71 Brett Hauer	
201 Denis Martynyuk		113 Pavel Bure	
227 Peter Brady		134 James Revenberg	
		155 Rob Sangster	
		176 Sandy Moger	
		197 Gus Morschauser	
		218 Hayden O'Rear	
		239 Darcy Cahill	
		248 Jan Bergman	

President and General Manager

BURKE, BRIAN
President and General Manager, Vancouver Canucks.
Born in Providence, RI, June 30, 1955.

The Vancouver Canucks announced the appointment of Brian Burke to the position of president and general manager on June 22, 1998. Burke became the eighth general manager in Canucks history after serving as the National Hockey League's senior vice president and director of hockey operations for the past five years.

Burke's prior experience with the Canucks began when he was named vice president and director of hockey operations on June 2, 1987. Burke worked with former Canucks president and general manager Pat Quinn for five seasons and assisted in rebuilding Vancouver's team through his contract negotiation skills and his overseeing of the club's scouting systems and its minor league affiliates. Burke helped reshape the Canucks from a 59 point team in 1987-88, to a 96 point team in his final season of 1991-92. It was the first time since the 1974-75 regular season that the Canucks finished first in the Smythe Division.

Brian Burke was appointed general manager of the Hartford Whalers on May 26, 1992. In his only season in Hartford, Brian made a number of player moves, changed the team's uniform and completed a major draft-day trade in 1993. After acquiring a second overall selection from San Jose, Burke selected Chris Pronger who has developed into one of the NHL's premier defencemen.

Burke joined the NHL front office in September of 1993. In five years as NHL senior vice president, Burke was most visible in his role as the league's chief disciplinarian. He spent much of his time overseeing the league's on-ice officials and was responsible for many disciplinary decisions handed down by the NHL based on his interpretation of league rules. Brian worked closely with NHL commissioner Gary Bettman on the direction of the league and was a key member of the group that introduced NHL excitement to Japan when the Vancouver Canucks and Mighty Ducks of Anaheim opened the 1997-98 regular season in Tokyo.

Brian has four children who reside in the Boston area.

Club Directory

Vancouver Canucks
General Motors Place
800 Griffiths Way
Vancouver, B.C. V6B 6G1
Phone **604/899-4600**
FAX 604/899-4640
Website: www.canucks.com
Capacity: 18,422

General Motors Place

Executive
Chairman, OBSE; Governor, NHL . . . . John E. McCaw Jr.
President, Chief Executive Officer, OBSE . . . . Stanley B. McCammon
President & General Manager, Vancouver Canucks,
   Alternate Governor, NHL . . . . Brian P. Burke
Chief Operating Officer, Alternate Governor, NHL . . . David Cobb
Senior Vice-President, Sales and Marketing . . . . John Rizzardini
Vice President & General Manager,
   Arena Operations . . . . Harvey Jones
Vice President, Finance & Chief Financial Officer . . . Victor de Bonis
Vice President, Broadcast and New Media . . . . Chris Hebb

Hockey Operations
President & General Manager . . . . Brian P. Burke
Senior Vice-President, Director Hockey Operations . . . David M. Nonis
Vice President, Player Personnel . . . . Steve Tambellini
Head Coach . . . . Marc Crawford
Assistant Coaches . . . . Jack McIlhargey, Mike Johnston
Head Coach, Kansas City Blades . . . . Stan Smyl
Assistant Coach, Kansas City Blades . . . . Barry Smith
Strength & Conditioning Coach . . . . Peter Twist
Goaltending Consultant . . . . Andy Moog
Assistant Coach, Video . . . . Eric Crawford
Senior Editor, Alumni Liaison . . . . Norm Jewison
Manager, Media Relations . . . . Chris Brumwell
Coordinator, Media Relations . . . . T.C. Carling
Assistant, Media Relations . . . . Rob Viccars
Manager, Community Relations . . . . Veronica Varhaug
Coordinator, Community Relations . . . . Lisa Denton
Executive Assistant to Mr. Burke . . . . Patti Timms
Executive Assistant to Mr. Nonis . . . . Chris Stephens
Coordinator, Team Services . . . . Lisa McFadden

Scoutig Staff
Professional Scouts . . . . Bob Murray, Shawn Dineen
European Scout . . . . Thomas Gradin
Russian Scout . . . . Sergei Chibisov
Amateur Scouts . . . . Ron Delorme, Ken Slater, Jack McCartan, Barry
   Dean, Dave Morrison, Daryl Stanley, Jim Eagle,
   Mike McHugh, Tim Lenardon, Mario Marois
Scouting Information Coordinator . . . . Jonathan Wall

Medical and Training Staff
Medical Trainer . . . . Mike Burnstein
Massage Therapist . . . . Dave Schima
Assistant Medical Trainer . . . . Jon Sanderson
Equipment Manager . . . . Pat ONeill
Assistant Equipment Manager . . . . Darren Granger
Assistant Equipment Trainer . . . . Tim Gross
Game Dressing Room Attendants . . . . Ron Shute, Jamie Henricks, John Jukitch
Team Doctors . . . . Dr. Rui Avelar, Dr. Bill Regan
Team Dentist . . . . Dr. David Lawson
Team Chiropractor . . . . Dr. Sid Sheard
Team Optometrist . . . . Dr. Alan R. Boyco

Corporate Communications
Director, Corporate Communications . . . . Nancy McHarg
Manager, Creative Services . . . . Anna-Lea Dahl
Design & Production, Creative Services . . . . Jessica Fish, Kiley Redhead, Jackie Boucher
Photo Librarian . . . . Kathy McAdam

Broadcasting
Vice President, Broadcasting and New Media . . . . . Chris Hebb
Broadcast Coordinator . . . . Shannon Baker
Director, Facilities and In-house Productions . . . . . Paul Brettell
Director, Production Services . . . . Mike Hall

Business and Legal
Corporate Counsel . . . . James Conrad
Vice President, Business Development . . . . Ric Thomsen
Director, Business Development . . . . David Altman
Director, Business Development . . . . Dave Cannon

Executive Suites
Director, Executive Suite Sales & Marketing . . . . . . Chris Bradley
Director, Executive Suite Service & Operations . . . . . Valerie Lewis

Customer Sales and Service
Vice President, Customer Sales and Service . . . . John Rocha
Executive Assistant . . . . Annabelle Kroes
Director, Customer Sales and Service . . . . Caley Denton
Director, Customer Sales . . . . Jordan Thorstenstein
Senior Managers, Customer Sales . . . . Sharon Butler, Graham Wall

Marketing and Game Operations
Director, Marketing . . . . Paul Dal Monte
Manager, Game Presentation & Events . . . . Karen Brydon
Coordinator, Game Presentation & Events . . . . Jamie Levchuk

Finance, Administration and People Development
Vice President, Finance . . . . Victor de Bonis
Director of Finance . . . . Chris Samis
Vice President, People Development & Admin. . . . . Susanne Haine
People Development Coach . . . . Catherine Anderson

Authentix Fan Apparel and Collectibles
Director of Retail Operations . . . . Alan Fey

Washington Capitals

1999-2000 Results: 44w-26L-12T 102PTS. First, Southeast Division

2000-01 Schedule

Oct. Fri.	6	Los Angeles	
Sat.	7	at Carolina	
Wed.	11	at Atlanta	
Fri.	13	at Nashville	
Sat.	14	at Dallas	
Tue.	17	Colorado	
Thu.	19	New Jersey	
Sat.	21	NY Islanders	
Thu.	26	at Boston	
Fri.	27	at Columbus	
Sun.	29	at Philadelphia	
Tue.	31	Detroit	
Nov. Thu.	2	at St. Louis	
Sat.	4	at Florida	
Sun.	5	at Tampa Bay	
Thu.	9	NY Rangers	
Sun.	12	Atlanta*	
Tue.	14	Phoenix	
Fri.	17	Montreal	
Sat.	18	at Philadelphia	
Wed.	22	Vancouver	
Fri.	24	NY Islanders	
Sat.	25	at Atlanta	
Wed.	29	Tampa Bay	
Dec. Fri.	1	Boston	
Sat.	2	at Boston	
Wed.	6	at NY Rangers	
Sat.	9	at New Jersey*	
Tue.	12	at NY Islanders	
Thu.	14	Minnesota	
Sat.	16	Edmonton	
Mon.	18	San Jose	
Wed.	20	Buffalo	
Thu.	21	at Buffalo	
Sat.	23	Florida	
Wed.	27	at Ottawa	
Fri.	29	at New Jersey	
Sat.	30	Philadelphia	
Jan. Mon.	1	Atlanta*	
Wed.	3	at Pittsburgh	
Fri.	5	Boston	

Sat.	6	at Toronto	
Mon.	8	Pittsburgh	
Wed.	10	at Minnesota	
Sat.	13	Atlanta	
Thu.	18	at Ottawa	
Fri.	19	at Chicago	
Tue.	23	at Tampa Bay	
Wed.	24	Florida	
Sat.	27	at Montreal*	
Sun.	28	Philadelphia*	
Tue.	30	Ottawa	
Feb. Thu.	1	Toronto	
Wed.	7	at Colorado	
Fri.	9	at Anaheim	
Sat.	10	at Los Angeles	
Tue.	13	at Calgary	
Wed.	14	at Vancouver	
Sat.	17	at Montreal	
Wed.	21	Nashville	
Fri.	23	Montreal	
Sat.	24	at Carolina	
Tue.	27	Chicago	
Mar. Thu.	1	Toronto	
Sat.	3	Pittsburgh	
Tue.	6	at NY Islanders	
Wed.	7	at Pittsburgh	
Fri.	9	NY Rangers	
Sun.	11	Ottawa*	
Tue.	13	Anaheim	
Thu.	15	Carolina	
Sat.	17	Buffalo	
Mon.	19	at NY Rangers	
Fri.	23	at Florida	
Sat.	24	at Tampa Bay	
Wed.	28	Carolina	
Fri.	30	at Carolina	
Apr. Sun.	1	at Detroit	
Tue.	3	New Jersey	
Thu.	5	Florida	
Fri.	6	at Buffalo	
Sun.	8	Tampa Bay*	

* Denotes afternoon game.

Franchise date: June 11, 1974

EASTERN CONFERENCE

SOUTHEAST DIVISION

27th NHL Season

Not exactly known for his soft hands before, Chris Simon emerged as Washington's leading goal scorer with 29 last season — a total that nearly doubled his previous career best of 16. Simon also led the Capitals with 146 penalty minutes.

Year-by-Year Record

		Home			Road			Overall							
Season	GP	W	L	T	W	L	T	W	L	T	GF	GA	Pts.	Finished	Playoff Result
1999-2000	82	26	7	8	18	19	4	44	26	12	227	194	102	1st, Southeast Div.	Lost Conf. Quarter-Final
1998-99	82	16	23	2	15	22	4	31	45	6	200	218	68	3rd, Southeast Div.	Out of Playoffs
1997-98	82	23	12	6	17	18	6	40	30	12	219	202	92	3rd, Atlantic Div.	Lost Final
1996-97	82	19	17	5	14	23	4	33	40	9	214	231	75	5th, Atlantic Div.	Out of Playoffs
1995-96	82	21	15	5	18	17	6	39	32	11	234	204	89	4th, Atlantic Div.	Lost Conf. Quarter-Final
1994-95	48	15	6	3	7	12	5	22	18	8	136	120	52	3rd, Atlantic Div.	Lost Conf. Quarter-Final
1993-94	84	17	16	9	22	19	1	39	35	10	277	263	88	3rd, Atlantic Div.	Lost Conf. Semi-Final
1992-93	84	21	15	6	22	19	1	43	34	7	325	286	93	2nd, Patrick Div.	Lost Div. Semi-Final
1991-92	80	25	12	3	20	15	5	45	27	8	330	275	98	2nd, Patrick Div.	Lost Div. Semi-Final
1990-91	80	21	14	5	16	22	2	37	36	7	258	258	81	3rd, Patrick Div.	Lost Div. Final
1989-90	80	19	18	3	17	20	3	36	38	6	284	275	78	3rd, Patrick Div.	Lost Conf. Championship
1988-89	80	25	12	3	16	17	7	41	29	10	305	259	92	1st, Patrick Div.	Lost Div. Semi-Final
1987-88	80	22	14	4	16	19	5	38	33	9	281	249	85	2nd, Patrick Div.	Lost Div. Final
1986-87	80	22	15	3	16	17	7	38	32	10	285	278	86	2nd, Patrick Div.	Lost Div. Semi-Final
1985-86	80	30	8	2	20	15	5	50	23	7	315	272	107	2nd, Patrick Div.	Lost Div. Final
1984-85	80	27	11	2	19	14	7	46	25	9	322	240	101	2nd, Patrick Div.	Lost Div. Semi-Final
1983-84	80	26	11	3	22	16	2	48	27	5	308	226	101	2nd, Patrick Div.	Lost Div. Semi-Final
1982-83	80	22	12	6	17	13	10	39	25	16	306	283	94	3rd, Patrick Div.	Lost Div. Semi-Final
1981-82	80	16	16	8	10	25	5	26	41	13	319	338	65	5th, Patrick Div.	Out of Playoffs
1980-81	80	16	17	7	10	19	11	26	36	18	286	317	70	5th, Patrick Div.	Out of Playoffs
1979-80	80	20	14	6	7	26	7	27	40	13	261	293	67	5th, Patrick Div.	Out of Playoffs
1978-79	80	15	19	6	9	22	9	24	41	15	273	338	63	4th, Norris Div.	Out of Playoffs
1977-78	80	10	23	7	7	26	7	17	49	14	195	321	48	5th, Norris Div.	Out of Playoffs
1976-77	80	17	15	8	7	27	6	24	42	14	221	307	62	4th, Norris Div.	Out of Playoffs
1975-76	80	6	26	8	5	33	2	11	59	10	224	394	32	5th, Norris Div.	Out of Playoffs
1974-75	80	7	28	5	1	39	0	8	67	5	181	446	21	5th, Norris Div.	Out of Playoffs

2000-01 Player Personnel

FORWARDS	HT	WT	S	Place of Birth	Date	1999-00 Club
BEECH, Kris	6-2	178	L	Salmon Arm, B.C.	2/5/81	Calgary Hitmen
BERUBE, Craig	6-1	205	L	Calahoo, Alta.	12/17/65	Philadelphia
BLACK, James	6-0	202	L	Regina, Sask.	8/15/69	Washington
BONDRA, Peter	6-1	205	L	Luck, USSR	2/7/68	Washington
BULIS, Jan	6-1	208	L	Pardubice, Czech.	3/18/78	Washington
DAHLEN, Ulf	6-3	195	L	Ostersund, Sweden	1/12/67	Washington
EAGLES, Mike	5-10	195	L	Sussex, N.B.	3/7/63	Washington
HALPERN, Jeff	6-0	195	R	Potomac, MD	5/3/76	Washington
HALVERSON, Trevor	6-0	200	L	White River, Ont.	4/6/71	Washington
HERR, Matt	6-2	204	L	Hackensack, NJ	5/26/76	Portland (AHL)
KONOWALCHUK, Steve	6-2	207	L	Salt Lake City, UT	11/11/72	Washington
METROPOLIT, Glen	5-11	185	R	Toronto, Ont.	6/25/74	Washington-Portland Pirates
MULHERN, Ryan	6-1	202	R	Philadelphia, PA	1/11/73	Portland Pirates
MURPHY, Joe	6-0	190	L	London, Ont.	10/16/67	Boston-Washington
MURPHY, Mark	5-11	200	L	Stoughton, MA	8/6/76	Wilkes-Barre-Trenton-Phi (AHL)
NELSON, Jeff	5-11	190	L	Prince Albert, Sask.	12/18/72	Portland Pirates
NIKOLISHIN, Andrei	5-11	214	L	Vorkuta, USSR	3/25/73	Washington
OATES, Adam	5-11	180	R	Weston, Ont.	8/27/62	Washington
PELUSO, Mike	6-1	208	R	Bismark, ND	9/2/74	Portland Pirates
RICHER, Stephane	6-2	215	R	Ripon, Que.	6/7/66	T.B.-Detroit Vipers-St. Louis
SACCO, Joe	6-1	190	L	Medford, MA	2/4/69	Washington
SIMON, Chris	6-4	235	L	Wawa, Ont.	1/30/72	Washington
SIVEK, Michal	6-3	209	L	Nachod, Czech.	1/21/81	Prince Albert
USTORF, Stefan	6-0	195	L	Kaufbeuren, Germany	1/3/74	Cincinnati (IHL)
WHITFIELD, Trent	5-11	200	L	Estevan, Sask.	6/17/77	Portland Pirates-Washington
YAKE, Terry	5-11	190	R	New Westminster, B.C.	10/22/68	St. Louis-Washington
ZEDNIK, Richard	6-0	199	L	Bystrica, Czech.	1/6/76	Washington
DEFENSEMEN						
BOILEAU, Patrick	6-0	202	R	Montreal, Que.	2/22/75	Portland Pirates
COTE, Sylvain	6-0	190	R	Quebec City, Que.	1/19/66	Toronto-Chicago-Dallas
FARRELL, Michael	6-1	205	R	Edina, MN	10/20/78	Providence-Portland Pirates
FORTIN, Jean-Francois	6-2	200	R	Laval, Que.	3/15/79	Portland (AHL)-Hampton Roads
GONCHAR, Sergei	6-2	212	L	Chelyabinsk, USSR	4/13/74	Washington
HUSCROFT, Jamie	6-3	210	R	Creston, B.C.	1/9/67	Washington-Portland Pirates
JOHANSSON, Calle	5-11	200	L	Goteborg, Sweden	2/14/67	Washington
KLEE, Ken	6-1	212	R	Indianapolis, IN	4/24/71	Washington
MIRONOV, Dmitri	6-4	224	R	Moscow, USSR	12/25/65	Washington
NORD, Bjorn	6-0	196	R	Huddinge, Sweden	4/5/72	Djurgardens IF
REEKIE, Joe	6-3	220	L	Victoria, B.C.	2/22/65	Washington
ROHLOFF, Todd	6-3	213	L	Grand Rapids, IL	1/16/74	Cleveland
ROYER, Remi	6-2	200	R	Donnacona, Que.	2/12/78	Cleveland
SHIRREFFS, Steve	6-3	220	R	Norwich, VT	2/18/76	Portland (AHL)-Hampton Roads
STORK, Dean	6-3	223	L	Edmonton, Alta.	10/2/75	Portland (AHL)-Hampton Roads
TEZIKOV, Alexei	6-1	208	L	Togliatti, USSR	6/22/78	Washington-Portland Pirates
VanBUSKIRK, Ryan	6-1	190	L	Sault Ste. Marie, MI	1/12/80	Sarnia Sting
WITT, Brendan	6-2	226	L	Humbolt, Sask.	2/20/75	Washington
ZETTLER, Rob	6-3	200	L	Sept Iles, Que.	3/8/68	Washington-Portland Pirates

GOALTENDERS	HT	WT	C	Place of Birth	Date	1999-00 Club
BILLINGTON, Craig	5-10	170	L	London, Ont.	9/11/66	Washington
KOLZIG, Olaf	6-3	225	L	Johannesburg, South Africa	4/9/70	Washington

Coach

WILSON, RON
Coach, Washington Capitals. Born in Windsor, Ont., May 28, 1955.

In his first season as head coach of the Washington Capitals, Wilson's team came within reach of the Cup when, after posting a 40-30-12 regular season record, the Caps advanced to the Stanley Cup finals for the first time in the franchise's 24-year history. He led the team to first place in the Southeast Division with 102 points in 1999-2000.

Prior to joining the Capitals, Wilson served as head coach of the Mighty Ducks of Anaheim for four years. In his last season with the Ducks (1996-97) he led the team to its first playoff appearance. Wilson posted a 120-145-31 (.458) overall record in Anaheim. He also spent three years in Vancouver as an assistant coach to Pat Quinn from 1990-93.

Wilson, 44, also served as the head coach for Team USA at the 1996 World Cup of Hockey. Team USA won the championship series, two games to one, over Canada.

Wilson has significant playing experience in professional, amateur and international hockey. He played four years at Providence College where he was a two-time All-American and two-time ECAC First Team All-Star. Wilson was ECAC player of the year in 1975 when he led the nation in scoring with 26-61-87 points in 27 games. He remains Providence's all-time leading scorer and ranks as the NCAA all-time leading scorer among defensemen with 250 points. Wilson received a Bachelor of Arts degree in economics from Providence College.

Drafted by the Toronto Maple Leafs (132nd overall) in 1975, Wilson began his professional hockey career in 1976-77 with the Dallas Blackhawks in the Central Hockey League. He joined the Toronto Maple Leafs in 1977-78, playing in 64 NHL contests over three seasons. Wilson then moved to Switzerland in 1980 and competed for the Swiss teams Kloten and Davos for six seasons. The former defenseman/winger signed with the Minnesota North Stars as a free agent in 1985 where he played through 1988. Ron enjoyed his finest offensive season in 1986-87 when he recorded 12 goals and 29 assists in 65 games with the North Stars.

Although born in Canada, Wilson was raised in the United States and remains a U.S. citizen. He was a four-time player for U.S. National Teams (1975, 1981, 1983, 1987) and coached the 1994 squad at the World Championships in Italy, leading Team USA to a 4-4-0 record with a fourth-place finish. Wilson also coached the 1996 squad, earning a bronze medal for Team USA.

1999-2000 Scoring

* – rookie

Regular Season

Pos	#	Player	Team	GP	G	A	Pts	+/–	PIM	PP	SH	GW	GT	S	%
C	77	Adam Oates	WSH	82	15	56	71	13	14	5	0	6	0	93	16.1
D	55	Sergei Gonchar	WSH	73	18	36	54	26	52	5	0	3	0	181	9.9
L	17	Chris Simon	WSH	75	29	20	49	11	146	7	0	5	1	201	14.4
L	22	Steve Konowalchuk	WSH	82	16	27	43	19	80	3	0	1	0	146	11.0
R	12	Peter Bondra	WSH	62	21	17	38	5	30	5	3	5	0	187	11.2
R	10	Ulf Dahlen	WSH	75	15	23	38	11	8	5	0	4	1	106	14.2
L	44	Richard Zednik	WSH	69	19	16	35	6	54	1	0	2	3	179	10.6
D	6	Calle Johansson	WSH	82	7	25	32	13	24	1	0	3	0	138	5.1
C	8	Jan Bulis	WSH	56	9	22	31	7	30	0	0	1	0	92	9.8
C	11 *	Jeff Halpern	WSH	79	18	11	29	21	39	4	4	1	0	108	16.7
R	9	Joe Murphy	BOS	26	7	7	14	–7	41	3	0	0	1	68	10.3
			WSH	29	5	8	13	8	53	1	0	2	0	50	10.0
			TOTAL	55	12	15	27	1	94	4	0	2	1	118	10.2
C	13	Andrei Nikolishin	WSH	76	11	14	25	6	28	0	2	2	0	98	11.2
R	27	Terry Yake	STL	26	4	9	13	2	22	2	0	2	0	26	15.4
			WSH	35	6	5	11	2	12	1	0	1	0	29	20.7
			TOTAL	61	10	14	24	4	34	3	0	3	0	55	18.2
L	14	Joe Sacco	WSH	79	7	16	23	7	50	0	0	1	0	117	6.0
D	15	Dmitri Mironov	WSH	73	3	19	22	7	28	1	0	0	0	99	3.0
D	2	Ken Klee	WSH	80	7	13	20	8	79	0	0	2	2	113	6.2
C	20 *	Glen Metropolit	WSH	30	6	13	19	5	4	1	0	1	0	57	10.5
C	28	James Black	WSH	49	8	9	17	–1	6	1	0	1	0	71	11.3
L	33	Jim McKenzie	ANA	31	3	3	6	–5	48	0	0	0	0	22	13.6
			WSH	30	1	2	3	0	16	0	0	0	0	10	10.0
			TOTAL	61	4	5	9	–5	64	0	0	0	0	32	12.5
D	19	Brendan Witt	WSH	77	1	7	8	5	114	0	0	0	0	64	1.6
D	29	Joe Reekie	WSH	59	0	7	7	21	50	0	0	0	0	32	0.0
L	21	Jeff Toms	WSH	20	1	2	3	–1	4	0	0	1	0	18	5.6
L	36	Mike Eagles	WSH	25	2	0	2	–7	15	0	0	1	0	13	15.4
D	4 *	Alexei Tezikov	WSH	23	1	1	2	–2	2	1	0	1	0	18	5.6
D	24	Rob Zettler	WSH	12	0	2	2	–1	19	0	0	0	0	15	0.0
G	37	Olaf Kolzig	WSH	73	0	2	2	0	6	0	0	0	0	0	0.0
C	23 *	Miika Elomo	WSH	2	0	1	1	1	2	0	0	0	0	3	0.0
D	38 *	Nolan Baumgartner	WSH	8	0	1	1	1	2	0	0	0	0	6	0.0
L	25	Barrie Moore	WSH	1	0	0	0	0	0	0	0	0	0	2	0.0
L	39 *	Alexander Volchkov	WSH	3	0	0	0	–2	0	0	0	0	0	1	0.0
D	3	Jamie Huscroft	WSH	7	0	0	0	–5	11	0	0	0	0	4	0.0
G	1	Craig Billington	WSH	13	0	0	0	0	0	0	0	0	0	0	0.0

Goaltending

No.	Goaltender	GPI	Mins	Avg	W	L	T	EN	SO	GA	SA	S%
37	Olaf Kolzig	73	4371	2.24	41	20	11	1	5	163	1957	.917
1	Craig Billington	13	611	2.75	3	6	1	2	2	28	310	.910
	Totals	**82**	**4999**	**2.33**	**44**	**26**	**12**	**3**	**7**	**194**	**2270**	**.915**

Playoffs

Pos	#	Player	Team	GP	G	A	Pts	+/–	PIM	PP	SH	GW	OT	S	%
C	11 *	Jeff Halpern	WSH	5	2	1	3	–1	0	1	0	1	0	11	18.2
D	6	Calle Johansson	WSH	5	1	2	3	–4	0	1	0	0	0	13	7.7
C	77	Adam Oates	WSH	5	0	3	3	0	4	0	0	0	0	3	0.0
L	17	Chris Simon	WSH	4	2	0	2	1	24	0	0	0	0	13	15.4
R	12	Peter Bondra	WSH	5	1	1	2	–4	4	1	0	0	0	13	7.7
C	13	Andrei Nikolishin	WSH	5	0	2	2	–3	4	0	0	0	0	7	0.0
L	22	Steve Konowalchuk	WSH	5	1	0	1	0	2	0	1	0	0	13	7.7
D	55	Sergei Gonchar	WSH	5	1	0	1	–3	6	0	0	0	0	16	6.3
R	10	Ulf Dahlen	WSH	5	0	1	1	–1	2	0	0	0	0	11	0.0
D	29	Joe Reekie	WSH	5	0	1	1	–1	2	0	0	0	0	0	0.0
D	2	Ken Klee	WSH	5	0	1	1	–1	10	0	0	0	0	16	0.0
G	1	Craig Billington	WSH	1	0	0	0	0	0	0	0	0	0	0	0.0
L	33	Jim Mckenzie	WSH	1	0	0	0	0	0	0	0	0	0	0	0.0
C	20 *	Glen Metropolit	WSH	2	0	0	0	–1	2	0	0	0	0	5	0.0
R	27	Terry Yake	WSH	3	0	0	0	–2	0	0	0	0	0	2	0.0
D	19	Brendan Witt	WSH	3	0	0	0	–3	0	0	0	0	0	4	0.0
C	23 *	Trent Whitfield	WSH	3	0	0	0	0	0	0	0	0	0	0	0.0
D	15	Dmitri Mironov	WSH	4	0	0	0	2	4	0	0	0	0	6	0.0
G	37	Olaf Kolzig	WSH	5	0	0	0	0	0	0	0	0	0	0	0.0
R	9	Joe Murphy	WSH	5	0	0	0	–2	8	0	0	0	0	8	0.0
L	14	Joe Sacco	WSH	5	0	0	0	–2	4	0	0	0	0	6	0.0
D	24	Rob Zettler	WSH	5	0	0	0	–2	2	0	0	0	0	4	0.0
L	44	Richard Zednik	WSH	5	0	0	0	–1	5	0	0	0	0	9	0.0

Goaltending

No.	Goaltender	GPI	Mins	Avg	W	L	EN	SO	GA	SA	S%
1	Craig Billington	1	20	3.00	0	0	0	0	1	6	.833
37	Olaf Kolzig	5	284	3.38	1	4	0	0	16	103	.845
	Totals	**5**	**306**	**3.33**	**1**	**4**	**0**	**0**	**17**	**109**	**.844**

Coaching Record

		Regular Season					Playoffs			
Season	**Team**	**Games**	**W**	**L**	**T**	**%**	**Games**	**W**	**L**	**%**
1993-94	**Anaheim (NHL)**	**84**	**33**	**46**	**5**	**.423**	....	....	....	....
1994-95	**Anaheim (NHL)**	**48**	**16**	**27**	**5**	**.385**	....	....	....	....
1995-96	**Anaheim (NHL)**	**82**	**35**	**39**	**8**	**.476**	....	....	....	....
1996-97	**Anaheim (NHL)**	**82**	**36**	**33**	**13**	**.518**	**11**	**4**	**7**	**.364**
1997-98	**Washington (NHL)**	**82**	**40**	**30**	**12**	**.561**	**21**	**12**	**9**	**.571**
1998-99	**Washington (NHL)**	**82**	**31**	**45**	**6**	**.415**	....	....	....	....
1999-2000	**Washington (NHL)**	**82**	**44**	**26**	**12**	**.622•**	**5**	**1**	**4**	**.200**
	NHL Totals	**542**	**235**	**246**	**61**	**.492•**	**37**	**17**	**20**	**.459**

• Includes points from regulation ties

Club Records

Team

(Figures in brackets for season records are games played; records for fewest points, wins, ties, losses, goals, goals against are for 70 or more games)

Most Points	107	1985-86 (80)
Most Wins	50	1985-86 (80)
Most Ties	18	1980-81 (80)
Most Losses	67	1974-75 (80)
Most Goals	330	1991-92 (80)
Most Goals Against	*446	1974-75 (80)
Fewest Points	*21	1974-75 (80)
Fewest Wins	*8	1974-75 (80)
Fewest Ties	5	1974-75 (80), 1983-84 (80)
Fewest Losses	23	1985-86 (80)
Fewest Goals	181	1974-75 (80)
Fewest Goals Against	202	1997-98 (82)

Longest Winning Streak

Overall	10	Jan. 27-Feb. 18/84
Home	9	Mar. 3-Oct. 6/89
Away	6	Feb. 26-Apr. 1/84

Longest Undefeated Streak

Overall	14	Nov. 24-Dec. 23/82 (9 wins, 5 ties), Jan. 17-Feb. 18/84 (13 wins, 1 tie)
Home	13	Nov. 25/92-Jan. 31/93 (9 wins, 4 ties)
Away	10	Nov. 24/82-Jan. 8/83 (6 wins, 4 ties)

Longest Losing Streak

Overall	*17	Feb. 18-Mar. 26/75
Home	*11	Feb. 18-Mar. 30/75
Away	37	Oct. 9/74-Mar. 26/75

Longest Winless Streak

Overall	25	Nov. 29/75-Jan. 21/76 (22 losses, 3 ties)
Home	14	Dec. 3/75-Jan. 21/76 (11 losses, 3 ties)
Away	37	Oct. 9/74-Mar. 26/75 (37 losses)

Most Shutouts, Season	9	1995-96 (82)
Most PIM, Season	2,204	1989-90 (80)
Most Goals, Game	12	Feb. 6/90 (Que. 2 at Wsh. 12)

Individual

Most Seasons	13	Michal Pivonka, Kelly Miller
Most Games	940	Kelly Miller
Most Goals, Career	397	Mike Gartner
Most Assists, Career	418	Michal Pivonka
Most Points, Career	789	Mike Gartner (397G, 392A)
Most PIM, Career	2,003	Dale Hunter
Most Shutouts, Career	14	Jim Carey
Longest Consecutive Games Streak	422	Bob Carpenter (Oct. 7/81-Nov. 22/86)
Most Goals, Season	60	Dennis Maruk (1981-82)
Most Assists, Season	76	Dennis Maruk (1981-82)
Most Points, Season	136	Dennis Maruk (1981-82; 60G, 76A)
Most PIM, Season	339	Alan May (1989-90)

Most Points, Defenseman, Season	81	Larry Murphy (1986-87; 23G, 58A)
Most Points, Center, Season	136	Dennis Maruk (1981-82; 60G, 76A)
Most Points, Right Wing, Season	102	Mike Gartner (1984-85; 50G, 52A)
Most Points, Left Wing, Season	87	Ryan Walter (1981-82; 38G, 49A)
Most Points, Rookie, Season	67	Bobby Carpenter (1981-82; 32G, 35A), Chris Valentine (1981-82; 30G, 37A)
Most Shutouts, Season	9	Jim Carey (1995-96)
Most Goals, Game	5	Bengt Gustafsson (Jan. 8/84), Peter Bondra (Feb. 5/94)
Most Assists, Game	6	Mike Ridley (Jan. 7/89)
Most Points, Game	7	Dino Ciccarelli (Mar. 18/89; 4G, 3A)

* NHL Record.

Retired Numbers

5	Rod Langway	1982-1993
7	Yvon Labre	1974-1981

Coaching History

Jim Anderson, Red Sullivan and Milt Schmidt, 1974-75; Milt Schmidt and Tom McVie, 1975-76; Tom McVie, 1976-77, 1977-78; Danny Belisle, 1978-79; Danny Belisle and Gary Green, 1979-80; Gary Green, 1980-81; Gary Green, Roger Crozier and Bryan Murray, 1981-82; Bryan Murray, 1982-83 to 1988-89; Bryan Murray and Terry Murray, 1989-90; Terry Murray, 1990-91 to 1992-93; Terry Murray and Jim Schoenfeld, 1993-94; Jim Schoenfeld, 1994-95 to 1996-97; Ron Wilson, 1997-98 to date.

Captains' History

Doug Mohns, 1974-75; Bill Clement and Yvon Labre, 1975-76; Yvon Labre, 1976-77, 1977-78; Guy Charron, 1978-79; Ryan Walter, 1979-80 to 1981-82; Rod Langway, 1982-83 to 1991-92; Rod Langway and Kevin Hatcher, 1992-93; Kevin Hatcher, 1993-94; Dale Hunter, 1994-95 to 1998-99; Adam Oates, 1999-2000 to date.

All-time Record vs. Other Clubs

Regular Season

	At Home							On Road							Total					
	GP	W	L	T	GF	GA	PTS	GP	W	L	T	GF	GA	PTS	GP	W	L	T	GF	GA	PTS
Anaheim	6	3	3	0	10	15	6	6	1	4	1	17	21	3	12	4	7	1	27	36	9
Atlanta	2	2	0	0	8	2	4	3	2	1	0	5	4	4	5	4	1	0	13	6	8
Boston	47	12	24	11	134	169	35	48	14	27	7	132	180	35	95	26	51	18	266	349	70
Buffalo	48	13	27	8	124	169	34	48	11	31	6	127	192	28	96	24	58	14	251	361	62
Calgary	38	19	14	5	143	132	43	36	6	24	6	85	152	18	74	25	38	11	228	284	61
Carolina	37	23	11	3	124	98	49	38	18	13	7	121	103	43	75	41	24	10	245	201	92
Chicago	38	20	13	5	137	119	45	37	11	21	5	113	146	27	75	31	34	10	250	265	72
Colorado	31	17	10	4	126	100	38	30	12	14	4	107	98	28	61	29	24	8	233	198	66
Dallas	38	15	15	8	117	118	38	37	11	18	8	103	138	30	75	26	33	16	220	256	68
Detroit	43	20	18	5	160	135	45	44	14	19	11	129	155	39	87	34	37	16	289	290	84
Edmonton	26	15	9	2	109	91	32	27	10	13	4	87	111	24	53	25	22	6	196	202	56
Florida	17	8	5	4	50	43	20	18	8	8	2	50	47	18	35	16	13	6	100	90	38
Los Angeles	43	18	18	7	181	161	43	44	12	26	6	134	175	30	87	30	44	13	315	336	73
Montreal	51	21	21	9	139	157	51	52	15	30	7	109	202	37	103	36	51	16	248	359	88
Nashville	2	1	1	0	3	3	2	2	1	1	0	5	5	2	4	2	2	0	8	8	4
New Jersey	71	45	21	5	281	201	95	71	31	33	7	214	221	69	142	76	54	12	495	422	164
NY Islanders	73	34	29	10	238	234	78	73	32	40	1	229	279	65	146	66	69	11	467	513	143
NY Rangers	76	37	30	9	282	251	84	74	32	34	8	260	280	72	150	69	64	17	542	531	156
Ottawa	16	10	5	1	59	35	21	15	7	7	1	49	55	15	31	17	12	2	108	90	36
Philadelphia	72	28	31	13	241	240	69	75	24	46	5	207	281	53	147	52	77	18	448	521	122
Phoenix	27	18	6	3	114	76	39	28	7	14	7	99	104	21	55	25	20	10	213	180	60
Pittsburgh	78	40	31	7	330	289	88	75	27	41	7	240	294	61	153	67	72	14	570	583	149
St. Louis	37	20	13	4	132	108	44	38	13	17	8	125	155	34	75	33	30	12	257	263	78
San Jose	8	5	3	0	25	20	10	8	3	4	1	22	22	7	16	8	7	1	47	42	17
Tampa Bay	19	10	5	4	72	45	24	18	13	4	1	62	37	27	37	23	9	5	134	82	51
Toronto	42	27	13	2	163	116	56	41	14	22	5	144	187	33	83	41	35	7	307	303	89
Vancouver	37	21	12	4	127	107	46	37	15	17	5	119	127	35	74	36	29	9	246	234	81
Defunct Clubs	10	2	8	0	28	42	4	10	4	5	1	30	39	9	20	6	13	1	58	81	13
Totals	1033	504	396	133	3657	3276	1143	1033	368	534	131	3129	3811	867	2066	872	930	264	6786	7087	2010

Playoffs

	Series	W	L	GP	W	L	T	GF	GA	Last Mtg.	Round	Result
Boston	2	1	1	10	4	6	0	15	13	1998	CQF	W 4-2
Buffalo	1	1	0	6	4	2	0	13	11	1998	CF	W 4-2
Detroit	1	0	1	4	0	4	0	7	13	1998	F	L 0-4
New Jersey	2	1	1	13	7	6	0	44	43	1990	DSF	W 4-2
NY Islanders	6	1	5	30	12	18	0	88	89	1993	DSF	L 2-4
NY Rangers	4	2	2	22	11	11	0	75	71	1994	CSF	L 1-4
Ottawa	1	1	0	5	4	1	0	18	7	1998	CSF	W 4-1
Philadelphia	3	2	1	16	9	7	0	65	55	1989	DSF	L 2-4
Pittsburgh	6	1	5	36	14	22	0	111	123	2000	CQF	L 1-4
Totals	26	10	16	142	65	77	0	442	450			

Playoff Results 2000-1996

Year	Round	Opponent	Result	GF	GA
2000	CQF	Pittsburgh	L 1-4	8	17
1998	F	Detroit	L 0-4	7	13
	CF	Buffalo	W 4-2	13	11
	CSF	Ottawa	W 4-1	18	7
	CQF	Boston	W 4-2	15	13
1996	CQF	Pittsburgh	L 2-4	17	21

Abbreviations: Round: F – Final; **CF** – conference final; **CSF** – conference semi-final; **CQF** – conference quarter-final; **DSF** – division semi-final.

Calgary totals include Atlanta Flames, 1974-75 to 1979-80. Colorado totals include Quebec, 1979-80 to 1994-95. New Jersey totals include Kansas City, 1974-75 to 1975-76, and Colorado Rockies, 1976-77 to 1981-82. Phoenix totals include Winnipeg, 1979-80, 1995-96.

Carolina totals include Hartford, 1979-80 to 1996-97. Dallas totals include Minnesota North Stars, 1974-75 to 1992-93.

1999-2000 Results

Oct.	2	at	Florida	3-4		16		Ottawa	2-1
	8	at	Buffalo	3-2		17	at	Tampa Bay	6-3
	9		Los Angeles	2-2		19	at	Florida	3-1
	12		Philadelphia	5-4		22	at	Toronto	5-5
	16		San Jose	2-3		24		Tampa Bay	8-2
	19		Anaheim	1-7		26		Calgary	2-3
	23	at	Phoenix	2-2		28		Phoenix	3-2 *
	26	at	Los Angeles	2-5		30		Philadelphia	2-0
	29	at	Anaheim	2-5	**Feb.**	1	at	Pittsburgh	2-3
	31	at	San Jose	1-2		3		Carolina	2-1
Nov.	3		Ottawa	3-1		5	at	Boston	2-2
	5		Toronto	5-3		10	at	Montreal	1-0
	7	at	Carolina	2-3		12	at	Nashville	4-2
	9		Tampa Bay	2-1		13	at	Dallas	1-2
	11		NY Rangers	4-5 *		15		Colorado	2-1
	13		New Jersey	4-2		18	at	Chicago	5-4
	17		Dallas	2-2		19	at	Philadelphia	2-4
	19		Carolina	3-3		21	at	Carolina	1-1
	20	at	Boston	3-0		23		Florida	3-2 *
	24	at	Buffalo	2-5		25		Boston	0-3
	26		Nashville	1-0		26	at	Montreal	3-0
	27	at	NY Islanders	4-3		28	at	NY Islanders	3-2
	29	at	Toronto	1-3	**Mar.**	1	at	Tampa Bay	4-2
Dec.	2		Boston	2-2		3		Detroit	2-2
	4	at	Florida	1-2		5		Buffalo	2-1
	7		NY Islanders	4-2		7		Florida	4-2
	9	at	Pittsburgh	0-3		9	at	Philadelphia	1-3
	13		Montreal	0-1		11		New Jersey	4-2
	15	at	Atlanta	4-0		15		NY Islanders	4-3
	17	at	NY Rangers	3-2 *		17		Carolina	4-2
	18	at	New Jersey	4-5		19		Tampa Bay	5-2
	21	at	Edmonton	2-6		20	at	St. Louis	1-2
	22	at	Vancouver	3-6		23	at	NY Rangers	4-1
	27		Chicago	2-2		25	at	Ottawa	4-3
	29		Pittsburgh	3-2 *		28		Atlanta	5-2
Jan.	1		St. Louis	1-1		30		Pittsburgh	3-4 *
	4		Montreal	6-1	**Apr.**	1		Toronto	3-4
	6	at	Atlanta	1-3		3		NY Rangers	4-1
	8		Atlanta	3-0		4	at	Ottawa	0-4
	12	at	Atlanta	5-2		7	at	Detroit	4-2
	14	at	New Jersey	3-2 *		9		Buffalo	1-1

* – Overtime

Entry Draft
Selections 2000-1986

2000
Pick
26 Brian Sutherby
43 Matt Pettinger
61 Jakub Cutta
121 Ryan VanBuskirk
163 Ivan Nepryayev
289 Bjorn Nord

1999
Pick
7 Kris Beech
29 Michal Sivek
31 Charlie Stephens
34 Ross Lupaschuk
37 Nolan Yonkman
132 Roman Tvrdon
175 Kyle Clark
192 David Johansson
219 Maxim Orlov
249 Igor Schadilov

1998
Pick
49 Jomar Cruz
59 Todd Hornung
106 Krys Barch
107 Chris Corrinet
118 Mike Siklenka
125 Erik Wendell
179 Nathan Forster
193 Ratislav Stana
220 Michael Farrell
251 Blake Evans

1997
Pick
9 Nick Boynton
35 Jean-Francois Fortin
89 Curtis Cruickshank
116 Kevin Caulfield
143 Henrik Petre
200 Pierre-Luc Therrien
226 Matt Oikawa

1996
Pick
4 Alexandre Volchkov
17 Jaroslav Svejkovsky
43 Jan Bulis
58 Sergei Zimakov
74 Dave Weninger
78 Shawn McNeil
85 Justin Davis
126 Matthew Lahey
153 Andrew Van Bruggen
180 Michael Anderson
206 Oleg Orekhovsky
232 Chad Cavanagh

1995
Pick
17 Brad Church
23 Miika Elomo
43 Dwayne Hay
93 Sebastien Charpentier
95 Joel Theriault
105 Benoit Gratton
124 Joel Cort
147 Frederick Jobin
199 Vasili Turkovsky
225 Scott Swanson

1994
Pick
10 Nolan Baumgartner
15 Alexander Kharlamov
41 Scott Cherrey
93 Matt Herr
119 Yanick Jean
145 Dmitri Mekeshkin
171 Daniel Reja
197 Chris Patrick
223 John Tuohy
249 Richard Zednik
275 Sergei Tertyshny

1993
Pick
11 Brendan Witt
17 Jason Allison
69 Patrick Boileau
147 Frank Banham
173 Daniel Hendrickson
174 Andrew Brunette
199 Joel Poirier
225 Jason Gladney
251 Mark Seliger
277 Dany Bousquet

1992
Pick
14 Sergei Gonchar
32 Jim Carey
53 Stefan Ustorf
71 Martin Gendron
119 John Varga
167 Mark Matier
191 Mike Mathers
215 Brian Stagg
239 Gregory Callahan
263 Billy Jo MacPherson

1991
Pick
14 Pat Peake
21 Trevor Halverson
25 Eric Lavigne
36 Jeff Nelson
58 Steve Konowalchuk
80 Justin Morrison
146 Dave Morissette
168 Rick Corriveau
190 Trevor Duhaime
209 Rob Leask
212 Carl Leblanc
234 Rob Puchniak
256 Bill Kovacs

1990
Pick
9 John Slaney
30 Rod Pasma
51 Chris Longo
72 Randy Pearce
93 Brian Sakic
94 Mark Ouimet
114 Andrei Kovalev
135 Roman Kontsek
156 Peter Bondra
159 Steve Martell
177 Ken Klee
198 Michael Boback
219 Alan Brown
240 Todd Hlushko

1989
Pick
19 Olaf Kolzig
35 Byron Dafoe
59 Jim Mathieson
61 Jason Woolley
82 Trent Klatt
145 Dave Lorentz
166 Dean Holoien
187 Victor Gervais
208 Jiri Vykoukal
229 Sidorov Sidorov
250 Ken House

1988
Pick
15 Reggie Savage
36 Tim Taylor
41 Todd Bartley
57 Duane Derksen
78 Bob Krauss
120 Dmitri Khristich
141 Keith Jones
144 Brad Schlegel
162 Todd Hilditch
183 Petr Pavlas
192 Mark Sorensen
204 Claudio Scremin
225 Chris Venkus
246 Ron Pascucci

1987
Pick
36 Jeff Ballantyne
57 Steve Maltais
78 Tyler Larter
99 Pat Beauchesne
120 Rich Defreitas
141 Devon Oleniuk
162 Thomas Sjogren
204 Chris Clarke
225 Milos Vanik
240 Dan Brettschneider
246 Ryan Kummo

1986
Pick
19 Jeff Greenlaw
40 Steve Seftel
60 Shawn Simpson
61 Jim Hrivnak
82 Erin Ginnell
103 John Purves
124 Stefan Nilsson
145 Peter Choma
166 Lee Davidson
187 Tero Toivola
208 Bobby Babcock
229 John Schratz
250 Scott McCrory

General Managers' History

Milt Schmidt, 1974-75; Milt Schmidt and Max McNab, 1975-76; Max McNab, 1976-77 to 1980-81; Max McNab and Roger Crozier, 1981-82; David Poile, 1982-83 to 1996-97; George McPhee, 1997-98 to date.

General Manager

McPHEE, GEORGE
General Manager, Washington Capitals. Born in Guelph, Ont., July 2, 1958.
On June 9, 1997, George McPhee became the fifth General Manager of the Washington Capitals. In his first year on the job, McPhee led the Caps to the Stanley Cup Finals for the first time in franchise history. He provides the Capitals with the leadership and knowledge to bring the Stanley Cup Finals back to Washington in the years to come.

A back injury forced McPhee to retire as an active player at the conclusion of the 1988-89 season, after a seven year playing career with the New York Rangers and New Jersey Devils. McPhee originally signed as a free agent with the Rangers in July, 1982, after graduating from Bowling Green State University with a business degree. McPhee did not waste any time in college, tallying 40 goals and 48 assists in his freshman season and easily winning CCHA rookie of the year honors. His outstanding collegiate hockey career was capped off when he was named the recipient of the Hobey Baker Award as the top U.S. collegiate player in his senior season. McPhee also earned All-America honors as a senior and finished his career at Bowling Green as the CCHA's all-time leading scorer with 114-153-267. He was the first player in CCHA history to make the Conference's all-academic team three straight seasons.

Club Directory

MCI Center

Washington Capitals
MCI Center
401 9th Street, NW
Washington, DC 20004
Phone **202/226-2200**
PR FAX 202/661-5113
www.washingtoncaps.com
Capacity: 18,678

Executive Management
Majority Owner/Chairman . . . . Ted Leonsis
Owner and President . . . . Richard M. Patrick
Executive Assistant . . . . Michelle Trostle
Owners . . . . Jonathan Ledecky, Raul Fernandez, Michael Jordan

Business Operations
Sr. Vice President of Business Operations . . . . Declan J. Bolger
Executive Assistant . . . . Gemma Nocon
Special Advisor - Finance . . . . Tom Stout
Special Advisor - Strategy &
President, Washingtoncaps.com . . . . Dean Silverman
Gen.Council and Corp.Secretary . . . . George Stamas

Communications
Vice President of Communications . . . . Andrew J. McGowan
Executive Assistant . . . . Stefanie Minor
Manager of Media Relations . . . . Brian Potter
Manager of Community Development . . . . Stephanie Boyer
Interactive Marketing Manager . . . . Josh Cole
Ignite Sr. Sports Media Producer . . . . Mike Vogel
Ignite Sports Media Producer . . . . Julie Anastos
Communications Assistant . . . . Carly Minner
Communications Intern . . . . David Stern

Finance
Controller . . . . Keith Burrows
Senior Accountant . . . . Michael Mercer
Accounts Payable . . . . Amber Harris
Accounts Receivable . . . . Shirley Bumpers

Marketing and Advertising
Vice President of Marketing . . . . TBA
Sr. Administrative Assistant . . . . Kirsten Bergman
Director of Game Presentation . . . . Mark Tamar
Fan Development Coordinator . . . . Chris Lewis
Promotions Manager . . . . Missy Rentz
Promotions Coordinator . . . . Ryan Ahern
Marketing Coordinator . . . . Shari Gulley
Mascot Coordinator . . . . Desi Deceder

Sales
Vice President of Sales . . . . Kevin Morgan
Executive Assistant . . . . Ingrid Harrell-Lee
Senior Regional Sales Managers . . . . Darren Bruening, Tim Munchmeyer, Tim Bronaugh
Regional Sales Managers . . . . Ron Bates, Mike Ragan, Darren Montgomery, Letitia Petrillo, Paul Shapiro, Victoria Walker, Greg Voss, Jyermal Jones, David Dzwonkowski

Ticket Operations & Guest Services
Director, Ticket Operations & Guest Services . . . . . . Laini Samuels
Assistant Director of Guest Services . . . . Greg Monares
Manager of Ticket Operations . . . . Chris Turns
Assistant Managers of Guest Services . . . . Stacie Sandridge, Jason Kmet
Coordinators of Ticket Operations . . . . Duane Harris, Kristen Bargmeyer

Hockey Operations
Vice President and General Manager . . . . George McPhee
Executive Assistant . . . . Maria Montilla
Director of Hockey Operations . . . . Shawn Simpson
Assistant to the General Manager . . . . Frank Provenzano
Head Coach . . . . Ron Wilson
Assistant Coaches . . . . Tim Army, Tim Hunter
Goaltending Coach . . . . Dave Prior
Strength/Conditioning Coach . . . . Frank Costello
Director of Team Services . . . . Todd Warren
Scouting Coordinator . . . . Kris Wagner
Piney Orchard Staff . . . . Alex Walker

Scouting Staff
Director of Amateur Scouting . . . . Ross Mahoney
Pro Scouts . . . . Archie Henderson, Mike Backman
Ontario Scout . . . . Steve Bowman
Western Scout . . . . Dale Derkatch
Quebec Scout . . . . Martin Pouliot
European Scout . . . . Ville Siren
European Scout . . . . Gleb Tchistyakov
Western U.S. Scout . . . . Ernie Vargas
Eastern U.S. Scout . . . . Ed McColgan

Medical Staff
Head Athletic Trainer . . . . Greg Smith
Assistant Athletic Trainer . . . . Tim Clark
Massage Therapist . . . . Curt Millar
Team Physician . . . . Ben Shaffer, MD
Internal Medicine . . . . Peter Basch, MD
Team Ophthalmologist . . . . Michael Herr, MD
Team Dentist . . . . Howard Salob, DDS
Team Nutritionist . . . . Tom Fox

Training Staff
Head Equipment Manager . . . . Doug Shearer
Assistant Equipment Manager . . . . Craig Leydig
Equipment Assistant . . . . Brian Metzger

Miscellaneous
Radio Flagship . . . . SportsTalk 980 AM
Radio Play-by-Play . . . . Steve Kolbe
Television Rightsholder . . . . Home Team Sports (HTS)
Television Play-by-Play . . . . Joe Beninati
HTS Color Analyst . . . . Craig Laughlin
HTS Producer . . . . Bill Bell
Team Photographer . . . . Mitchell Layton

NHL Clubs' Minor-League Affiliations, 2000-01

NHL CLUB	MINOR-LEAGUE AFFILIATE
Atlanta	Orlando Solar Bears (IHL) Greenville Grrrowl (ECHL)
Anaheim	Cincinnati Mighty Ducks (AHL)
Boston	Providence Bruins (AHL) Greenville Grrrowl (ECHL)
Buffalo	Rochester Americans (AHL) South Carolina Stingrays (ECHL) B.C. Iceman (UHL)
Calgary	Saint John Flames (AHL) Johnstown Chiefs (ECHL)
Carolina	Cincinnati Cyclones (IHL) Florida Everblades (ECHL)
Chicago	Norfolk Admirals (AHL)
Colorado	Hershey Bears (AHL)
Columbus	Syracuse Crunch (AHL) Dayton Bombers (ECHL) Elmira Jackals (UHL)
Dallas	Utah Grizzlies (IHL)
Detroit	Cincinnati Mighty Ducks (AHL) Toledo Storm (ECHL)
Edmonton	Hamilton Bulldogs (AHL) Tallahassee Tiger Sharks (ECHL)
Florida	Louisville Panthers (AHL) Port Huron Border Cats (UHL)
Los Angeles	Lowell Lock Monsters (AHL) Long Beach Ice Dogs (WCHL)
Minnesota	Cleveland Lumberjacks (IHL) Jackson Bandits (ECHL)

NHL CLUB	MINOR-LEAGUE AFFILIATE
Montreal	Citadelles de Québec (AHL) Tallahassee Tiger Sharks (ECHL)
Nashville	Milwaukee Admirals (IHL) New Orleans Brass (ECHL)
New Jersey	Albany River Rats (AHL)
NY Islanders	Lowell Lock Monsters (AHL) Chicago Wolves (IHL) Trenton Titans (ECHL)
NY Rangers	Hartford Wolf Pack (AHL)
Ottawa	Grand Rapids Griffins (IHL)
Philadelphia	Philadelphia Phantoms (AHL) Trenton Titans (ECHL)
Phoenix	Springfield Falcons (AHL) Las Vegas Thunder (IHL) Mississippi Sea Wolves (ECHL) Binghamton Icemen (UHL)
Pittsburgh	Wilkes-Barre/Scranton Penguins (AHL) Wheeling Nailers (ECHL)
St. Louis	Worcester IceCats (AHL) Peoria Rivermen (ECHL)
San Jose	Kentucky Thoroughblades (AHL) Richmond Renegades (ECHL) New Orleans Brass (ECHL)
Tampa Bay	Detroit Vipers (IHL) Johnstown Chiefs (ECHL)
Toronto	St. John's Maple Leafs (AHL)
Vancouver	Kansas City Blades (IHL)
Washington	Portland Pirates (AHL) Hampton Roads Admirals (ECHL) Quad City Mallards (UHL)

NHL League and Team Websites

National Hockey League ....**www.nhl.com**

NHL Games on Radio ....www.broadcast.com

NHL Site for Kids ....www.nhl.com/kids

Hockey Fights Cancer ....www.hockeyfightscancer.com

Official NHL Team Websites:

Anaheim	www.mightyducks.com
Atlanta	www.atlantathrashers.com
Boston	www.bostonbruins.com
Buffalo	www.sabres.com
Calgary	www.calgaryflames.com
Carolina	www.caneshockey.com
Chicago	www.chicagoblackhawks.com
Colorado	www.coloradoavalanche.com
Columbus	www.columbusbluejackets.com
Dallas	www.dallasstars.com
Detroit	www.detroitredwings.com
Edmonton	www.edmontonoilers.com
Florida	www.flpanthers.com
Los Angeles	www.lakings.com
Minnesota	www.wild.com
Montreal	www.canadiens.com
Nashville	www.nashvillepredators.com
New Jersey	www.newjerseydevils.com
NY Islanders	www.newyorkislanders.com
NY Rangers	www.newyorkrangers.com
Ottawa	www.ottawasenators.com
Philadelphia	www.philadelphiaflyers.com
Phoenix	www.phoenixcoyotes.com
Pittsburgh	www.nhlpenguins.com
St. Louis	www.stlouisblues.com
San Jose	www.sj-sharks.com
Tampa Bay	www.tampabaylightning.com
Toronto	www.torontomapleleafs.com
Vancouver	www.vancouvercanucks.com
Washington	www.washingtoncaps.com

1999-2000 Final Statistics

Standings

Abbreviations: GA – goals against; **GF** – goals for; **GP** – games played; **L** – losses;
PTS – points; **RT** – regulation ties; **T** – ties; **W** – wins; * – rookie eligible for Calder Trophy.

EASTERN CONFERENCE

Northeast Division

	GP	W	L	T	RT	GF	GA	PTS
Toronto	82	45	30	7	3	246	222	100
Ottawa	82	41	30	11	2	244	210	95
Buffalo	82	35	36	11	4	213	204	85
Montreal	82	35	38	9	4	196	194	83
Boston	82	24	39	19	6	210	248	73

Atlantic Division

	GP	W	L	T	RT	GF	GA	PTS
Philadelphia	82	45	25	12	3	237	179	105
New Jersey	82	45	29	8	5	251	203	103
Pittsburgh	82	37	37	8	6	241	236	88
NY Rangers	82	29	41	12	3	218	246	73
NY Islanders	82	24	49	9	1	194	275	58

Southeast Division

	GP	W	L	T	RT	GF	GA	PTS
Washington	82	44	26	12	2	227	194	102
Florida	82	43	33	6	6	244	209	98
Carolina	82	37	35	10	0	217	216	84
Tampa Bay	82	19	54	9	7	204	310	54
Atlanta	82	14	61	7	4	170	313	39

WESTERN CONFERENCE

Central Division

	GP	W	L	T	RT	GF	GA	PTS
St Louis	82	51	20	11	1	248	165	114
Detroit	82	48	24	10	2	278	210	108
Chicago	82	33	39	10	2	242	245	78
Nashville	82	28	47	7	7	199	240	70

Pacific Division

	GP	W	L	T	RT	GF	GA	PTS
Dallas	82	43	29	10	6	211	184	102
Los Angeles	82	39	31	12	4	245	228	94
Phoenix	82	39	35	8	4	232	228	90
San Jose	82	35	37	10	7	225	214	87
Anaheim	82	34	36	12	3	217	227	83

Northwest Division

	GP	W	L	T	RT	GF	GA	PTS
Colorado	82	42	29	11	1	233	201	96
Edmonton	82	32	34	16	8	226	212	88
Vancouver	82	30	37	15	8	227	237	83
Calgary	82	31	41	10	5	211	256	77

With 43 goals in 1999-2000, Tony Amonte has outscored every player in the NHL over the past two seasons. His total of 87 goals surpasses that of Jaromir Jagr (86), John LeClair (83), Paul Kariya (81) and Teemu Selanne (80).

INDIVIDUAL LEADERS

Goal Scoring

Player	Team	GP	G
Pavel Bure	Florida	74	58
Owen Nolan	San Jose	78	44
Tony Amonte	Chicago	82	43
Jaromir Jagr	Pittsburgh	63	42
Paul Kariya	Anaheim	74	42
Brendan Shanahan	Detroit	78	41
John LeClair	Philadelphia	82	40
Mike Modano	Dallas	77	38
Luc Robitaille	Los Angeles	71	36
Milan Hejduk	Colorado	82	36

Assists

Player	Team	GP	A
Mark Recchi	Philadelphia	82	63
Adam Oates	Washington	82	56
Jaromir Jagr	Pittsburgh	63	54
Joe Sakic	Colorado	60	53
Viktor Kozlov	Florida	80	53
Nicklas Lidstrom	Detroit	81	53
Teemu Selanne	Anaheim	79	52
Doug Weight	Edmonton	77	51
*Scott Gomez	New Jersey	82	51
Ron Francis	Carolina	78	50

Power-play Goals

Player	Team	GP	PP
Owen Nolan	San Jose	78	18
Mariusz Czerkawski	NY Islanders	79	16
Steve Yzerman	Detroit	78	15

Short-handed Goals

Player	Team	GP	SH
*John Madden	New Jersey	74	6
Tony Amonte	Chicago	82	5

Game-winning Goals

Player	Team	GP	GW
Pavel Bure	Florida	74	14
Jeremy Roenick	Phoenix	75	12
Patrik Elias	New Jersey	72	9
Brendan Shanahan	Detroit	78	9
Steve Thomas	Toronto	81	9
Milan Hejduk	Colorado	82	9
Mike Modano	Dallas	77	8

Game-tying Goals

Player	Team	GP	GT
Richard Zednik	Washington	69	3
Mike Modano	Dallas	77	3
Niklas Sundstrom	San Jose	79	3
Patrice Brisebois	Montreal	54	2
Alexander Mogilny	Van., N.J	59	2
Steve Rucchin	Anaheim	71	2
Steve Heinze	Boston	75	2
Sergei Krivokrasov	Nsh., Cgy	75	2
Sami Kapanen	Carolina	76	2
Owen Nolan	San Jose	78	2

Shots

Player	Team	GP	S
Pavel Bure	Florida	74	360
Rob Blake	Los Angeles	77	327
Paul Kariya	Anaheim	74	324
Valeri Bure	Calgary	82	308
Jaromir Jagr	Pittsburgh	63	290

Shooting Percentage
(minimum 82 shots)

Player	Team	GP	G	S	%
Mike Eastwood	St Louis	79	19	83	22.9
Alex Selivanov	Edmonton	67	27	122	22.1
Doug Gilmour	Chi., Buf	74	25	113	22.1
Andrew Brunette	Atlanta	81	23	107	21.5
Mike Modano	Dallas	77	38	188	20.2

Penalty Minutes

Player	Team	GP	PIM
Denny Lambert	Atlanta	73	219
Todd Simpson	Florida	82	202
Tie Domi	Toronto	70	198
Matthew Barnaby	Pittsburgh	64	197
Eric Cairns	NY Islanders	67	196

Plus/Minus

Player	Team	GP	+/–
Chris Pronger	St Louis	79	52
Chris Chelios	Detroit	81	48
Pavol Demitra	St Louis	71	34
Pierre Turgeon	St Louis	52	30
Joe Sakic	Colorado	60	30
Scott Stevens	New Jersey	78	30

Individual Leaders

Abbreviations: * – rookie eligible for Calder Trophy; **A** – assists; **G** – goals; **GP** – games played; **GT** – game-tying goals;
GW – game-winning goals; **PIM** – penalties in minutes; **PP** – power play goals; **Pts** – points; **S** – shots on goal; **SH** – short-handed goals;
% – percentage of shots on goal resulting in goals; **+/–** – difference between Goals For (**GF**) scored when a player is on the ice with his
team at even strength or short-handed and Goals Against (**GA**) scored when the same player is on the ice with his team at even
strength or on a power play.

Individual Scoring Leaders for Art Ross Trophy

Player	Team	GP	G	A	Pts	+/–	PIM	PP	SH	GW	GT	S	%
Jaromir Jagr	Pittsburgh	63	42	54	96	25	50	10	0	5	1	290	14.5
Pavel Bure	Florida	74	58	36	94	25	16	11	2	14	0	360	16.1
Mark Recchi	Philadelphia	82	28	63	91	20	50	7	1	5	1	223	12.6
Paul Kariya	Anaheim	74	42	44	86	22	24	11	3	3	0	324	13.0
Teemu Selanne	Anaheim	79	33	52	85	6	12	8	0	6	2	236	14.0
Owen Nolan	San Jose	78	44	40	84	1-	110	18	4	6	2	261	16.9
Tony Amonte	Chicago	82	43	41	84	10	48	11	5	2	1	260	16.5
Mike Modano	Dallas	77	38	43	81	0	48	11	1	8	3	188	20.2
Joe Sakic	Colorado	60	28	53	81	30	28	5	1	5	0	242	11.6
Steve Yzerman	Detroit	78	35	44	79	28	34	15	2	6	1	234	15.0
Brendan Shanahan	Detroit	78	41	37	78	24	105	13	1	9	1	283	14.5
Jeremy Roenick	Phoenix	75	34	44	78	11	102	6	3	12	1	192	17.7
John LeClair	Philadelphia	82	40	37	77	8	36	13	0	7	2	249	16.1
Valeri Bure	Calgary	82	35	40	75	7-	50	13	0	6	1	308	11.4
Pavol Demitra	St. Louis	71	28	47	75	34	8	8	0	4	0	241	11.6
Luc Robitaille	Los Angeles	71	36	38	74	11	68	13	0	7	0	221	16.3
Mats Sundin	Toronto	73	32	41	73	16	46	10	2	7	0	184	17.4
Doug Gilmour	Chi., Buf.	74	25	48	73	9-	63	10	0	3	1	113	22.1
Ron Francis	Carolina	78	23	50	73	10	18	7	0	4	0	150	15.3
Nicklas Lidstrom	Detroit	81	20	53	73	19	18	9	4	3	0	218	9.2
Milan Hejduk	Colorado	82	36	36	72	14	16	13	0	9	2	228	15.8
Patrik Elias	New Jersey	72	35	37	72	16	58	9	0	9	1	183	19.1
Doug Weight	Edmonton	77	21	51	72	6	54	3	1	4	0	167	12.6
Ray Whitney	Florida	81	29	42	71	16	35	5	0	3	2	198	14.6
Adam Oates	Washington	82	15	56	71	13	14	5	0	6	0	93	16.1

Defensemen Scoring Leaders

Player	Team	GP	G	A	Pts	+/–	PIM	PP	SH	GW	GT	S	%
Nicklas Lidstrom	Detroit	81	20	53	73	19	18	9	4	3	0	218	9.2
Chris Pronger	St. Louis	79	14	48	62	52	92	8	0	3	2	192	7.3
Rob Blake	Los Angeles	77	18	39	57	10	112	12	0	5	0	327	5.5
Eric Desjardins	Philadelphia	81	14	41	55	20	32	8	0	4	1	207	6.8
Phil Housley	Calgary	78	11	44	55	12-	24	5	0	2	1	176	6.3
Sergei Gonchar	Washington	73	18	36	54	26	52	5	0	3	0	181	9.9
Ray Bourque	Bos., Col.	79	18	34	52	2-	26	13	0	0	0	260	6.9
Sandis Ozolinsh	Colorado	82	16	36	52	17	46	6	0	1	0	210	7.6
Oleg Tverdovsky	Anaheim	82	15	36	51	5	30	5	0	5	0	153	9.8
Robert Svehla	Florida	82	9	40	49	23	64	3	0	1	0	143	6.3

*Jarome Iginla of the Calgary Flames had last season's longest scoring streak
when he collected points in 16 straight games from January 29 to March 5.
Iginla finished the 1999-2000 season with a career-best 29 goals and 34 assists.*

CONSECUTIVE SCORING STREAKS

Goals

Games	Player	Team	G
7	Joe Sakic	Colorado	11
7	Jaromir Jagr	Pittsburgh	8
6	Paul Kariya	Anaheim	10
6	Owen Nolan	San Jose	8
6	Tony Amonte	Chicago	7
6	Tony Amonte	Chicago	7
5	Pavel Bure	Florida	8
5	Luc Robitaille	Los Angeles	7
5	Brendan Shanahan	Detroit	7
5	Brian Savage	Montreal	7
5	Patrik Elias	New Jersey	7
5	Jarome Iginla	Calgary	7
5	John LeClair	Philadelphia	6
5	Steve Yzerman	Detroit	6
5	Teemu Selanne	Anaheim	6
5	Alexander Mogilny	Vancouver	5
5	Travis Green	Phoenix	5
5	Jozef Stumpel	Los Angeles	5
5	Cory Stillman	Calgary	5
5	Jonas Hoglund	Toronto	5
5	Vincent Lecavalier	Tampa Bay	5

Assists

Games	Player	Team	A
12	Pierre Turgeon	St. Louis	16
10	Joe Sakic	Colorado	15
8	Jeremy Roenick	Phoenix	11
8	Theoren Fleury	NY Rangers	10
7	Doug Gilmour	Chi., Buf.	10
7	Cliff Ronning	Nashville	10
7	Pavel Bure	Florida	9
7	Pavol Demitra	St. Louis	9
6	Daniel Alfredsson	Ottawa	11
6	Adam Oates	Washington	10
6	Peter Forsberg	Colorado	10
6	Jason Allison	Boston	10
6	Mike Modano	Dallas	9
6	Oleg Tverdovsky	Anaheim	9
6	Daymond Langkow	Philadelphia	9
6	Jaromir Jagr	Pittsburgh	8
6	Joe Sakic	Colorado	8
6	Nicklas Lidstrom	Detroit	8
6	Vincent Damphousse	San Jose	7
6	Doug Gilmour	Chicago	7
6	Jaromir Jagr	Pittsburgh	7
6	Al Macinnis	St. Louis	7
6	Luc Robitaille	Los Angeles	7
6	Bryan Smolinski	Los Angeles	7
6	Owen Nolan	San Jose	6
6	Keith Jones	Philadelphia	6

Points

Games	Player	Team	G	A	PTS
16	Jarome Iginla	Calgary	12	14	26
15	Jaromir Jagr	Pittsburgh	14	19	33
15	Luc Robitaille	Los Angeles	11	13	24
15	Pierre Turgeon	St. Louis	7	17	24
15	Patrik Elias	New Jersey	15	9	24
14	Joe Sakic	Colorado	16	11	27
13	Teemu Selanne	Anaheim	8	14	22
13	Pavel Bure	Florida	12	9	21
13	M. Czerkawski	NY Islanders	7	13	20
12	Peter Forsberg	Colorado	5	17	22
11	Pavel Bure	Florida	12	10	22
11	Jeremy Roenick	Phoenix	9	12	21
11	Mike Modano	Dallas	7	11	18
11	Mark Recchi	Philadelphia	7	11	18
10	Owen Nolan	San Jose	8	9	17
10	Joe Sakic	Colorado	2	15	17
10	Mats Sundin	Toronto	6	11	17
10	Nicklas Lidstrom	Detroit	2	15	17
10	Steve Yzerman	Detroit	6	8	14
10	Marc Savard	Calgary	6	8	14
10	Theoren Fleury	NY Rangers	1	12	13

The NHL gained a new star and an engaging new personality when Scott Gomez burst upon the scene last season. An Alaskan-born Hispanic-American, Gomez won the Calder Trophy after leading all rookies in scoring with 70 points.

Individual Rookie Scoring Leaders

Rookie	Team	GP	G	A	Pts	+/–	PIM	PP	SH	GW	GT	S	%
Scott Gomez	New Jersey	82	19	51	70	14	78	7	0	1	2	204	9.3
Alex Tanguay	Colorado	76	17	34	51	6	22	5	0	3	1	74	23.0
Michael York	NY Rangers	82	26	24	50	17-	18	8	0	4	2	177	14.7
Simon Gagne	Philadelphia	80	20	28	48	11	22	8	1	4	0	159	12.6
Jan Hlavac	NY Rangers	67	19	23	42	3	16	6	0	2	0	134	14.2
Trevor Letowski	Phoenix	82	19	20	39	2	20	3	4	3	0	125	15.2
Brad Stuart	San Jose	82	10	26	36	3	32	5	1	3	0	133	7.5
Maxim Afinogenov	Buffalo	65	16	18	34	4-	41	2	0	2	0	128	12.5
Tim Connolly	NY Islanders	81	14	20	34	25-	44	2	1	1	1	114	12.3
Jochen Hecht	St. Louis	63	13	21	34	20	28	5	0	1	0	140	9.3
Brenden Morrow	Dallas	64	14	19	33	8	81	3	0	3	0	113	12.4
Brian Rafalski	New Jersey	75	5	27	32	21	28	1	0	1	0	128	3.9
Peter Schaefer	Vancouver	71	16	15	31	0	20	2	2	4	0	101	15.8
Nik Antropov	Toronto	66	12	18	30	14	41	0	0	2	0	89	13.5

Goal Scoring

Name	Team	GP	G
Michael York	NY Rangers	82	26
Simon Gagne	Philadelphia	80	20
Jan Hlavac	NY Rangers	67	19
Trevor Letowski	Phoenix	82	19
Scott Gomez	New Jersey	82	19
Jeff Halpern	Washington	79	18
Alex Tanguay	Colorado	76	17
Maxim Afinogenov	Buffalo	65	16
Peter Schaefer	Vancouver	71	16
John Madden	New Jersey	74	16
Brenden Morrow	Dallas	64	14
Tim Connolly	NY Islanders	81	14
Jochen Hecht	St. Louis	63	13
David Legwand	Nashville	71	13
Nik Antropov	Toronto	66	12

Assists

Name	Team	GP	A
Scott Gomez	New Jersey	82	51
Alex Tanguay	Colorado	76	34
Simon Gagne	Philadelphia	80	28
Brian Rafalski	New Jersey	75	27
Brad Stuart	San Jose	82	26
Michael York	NY Rangers	82	24
Jan Hlavac	NY Rangers	67	23
Jochen Hecht	St. Louis	63	21
Patrik Stefan	Atlanta	72	20
Tim Connolly	NY Islanders	81	20
Trevor Letowski	Phoenix	82	20
Brenden Morrow	Dallas	64	19
Maxim Afinogenov	Buffalo	65	18
Nik Antropov	Toronto	66	18
Michal Rozsival	Pittsburgh	75	17

Power-play Goals

Name	Team	GP	PP
Simon Gagne	Philadelphia	80	8
Michael York	NY Rangers	82	8
Scott Gomez	New Jersey	82	7
Jan Hlavac	NY Rangers	67	6
Jochen Hecht	St. Louis	63	5
Alex Tanguay	Colorado	76	5
Brad Stuart	San Jose	82	5
Jere Karalahti	Los Angeles	48	4
Paul Mara	Tampa Bay	54	4
David Legwand	Nashville	71	4
Jeff Halpern	Washington	79	4

Short-handed Goals

Name	Team	GP	SH
John Madden	New Jersey	74	6
Jeff Halpern	Washington	79	4
Trevor Letowski	Phoenix	82	4
Peter Schaefer	Vancouver	71	2

Game-winning Goals

Name	Team	GP	GW
Peter Schaefer	Vancouver	71	4
Simon Gagne	Philadelphia	80	4
Michael York	NY Rangers	82	4
Brad Chartrand	Los Angeles	50	3
Brenden Morrow	Dallas	64	3
John Madden	New Jersey	74	3
Alex Tanguay	Colorado	76	3
Trevor Letowski	Phoenix	82	3
Brad Stuart	San Jose	82	3

Game-tying Goals

Name	Team	GP	GT
Michael York	NY Rangers	82	2
Scott Gomez	New Jersey	82	2
Andre Savage	Boston	43	1
Alex Tanguay	Colorado	76	1
Ladislav Kohn	Anaheim	77	1
Tim Connolly	NY Islanders	81	1

Shots

Name	Team	GP	S
Scott Gomez	New Jersey	82	204
Michael York	NY Rangers	82	177
Simon Gagne	Philadelphia	80	159
Jochen Hecht	St. Louis	63	140
Jan Hlavac	NY Rangers	67	134
Brad Stuart	San Jose	82	133
Maxim Afinogenov	Buffalo	65	128
Brian Rafalski	New Jersey	75	128
Trevor Letowski	Phoenix	82	125
Ladislav Kohn	Anaheim	77	123

Shooting Percentage
(minimum 82 shots)

Name	Team	GP	G	S	%
Jeff Halpern	Washington	79	18	108	16.7
Peter Schaefer	Vancouver	71	16	101	15.8
Trevor Letowski	Phoenix	82	19	125	15.2
Michael York	NY Rangers	82	26	177	14.7
Jan Hlavac	NY Rangers	67	19	134	14.2
John Madden	New Jersey	74	16	115	13.9
Nik Antropov	Toronto	66	12	89	13.5
Simon Gagne	Philadelphia	80	20	159	12.6
Maxim Afinogenov	Buffalo	65	16	128	12.5
Brenden Morrow	Dallas	64	14	113	12.4

Penalty Minutes

Name	Team	GP	PIM
Tyson Nash	St. Louis	66	150
Andre Roy	Ottawa	73	145
Gordie Dwyer	Tampa Bay	24	135
Ben Clymer	Tampa Bay	60	87
Brenden Morrow	Dallas	64	81

Plus/Minus

Name	Team	GP	+/–
Brian Rafalski	New Jersey	75	21
Jeff Halpern	Washington	79	21
Jochen Hecht	St. Louis	63	20
Harold Druken	Vancouver	33	14
Nik Antropov	Toronto	66	14
Scott Gomez	New Jersey	82	14

Three-or-More-Goal Games

Player	Team	Date	Final Score		G	Player	Team	Date	Final Score		G
Tony Amonte	Chicago	Mar. 12	Chi. 4	T.B. 1	3	Petr Nedved	NY Rangers	Feb. 25	NYR 6	Buf. 3	3
Dave Andreychuk	Boston	Oct. 28	T.B. 3	Bos. 7	4	Owen Nolan	San Jose	Oct. 04	Chi. 1	S.J. 7	3
*Nik Antropov	Toronto	Dec. 20	Tor. 6	Fla. 4	3	Michael Nylander	Chicago	Dec. 04	Chi. 9	Bos. 3	4
Bates Battaglia	Carolina	Mar. 08	Chi. 1	Car. 4	3	Sandis Ozolinsh	Colorado	Dec. 06	Van. 2	Col. 5	3
Peter Bondra	Washington	Oct. 12	Phi. 4	Wsh 5	3	Michael Peca	Buffalo	Feb. 25	NYR 6	Buf. 3	3
Pavel Bure	Florida	Dec. 08	Fla. 6	Phx. 1	3	Shjon Podein	Colorado	Feb. 18	Col. 4	NYR 2	3
Pavel Bure	Florida	Dec. 17	Fla. 4	Buf. 2	3	Stephane Richer	St. Louis	Feb. 25	Col. 2	St.L. 4	3
Pavel Bure	Florida	Jan. 01	T.B. 3	Fla. 7	4	Luc Robitaille	Los Angeles	Oct. 07	L.A. 5	T.B. 2	3
Pavel Bure	Florida	Mar. 18	Fla. 4	NYI 2	3	Jeremy Roenick	Phoenix	Nov. 25	N.J. 2	Phx. 4	3
Mariusz Czerkawski	NY Islanders	Apr. 09	Fla. 2	NYI 3	3	Jeremy Roenick	Phoenix	Nov. 26	Col. 0	Phx. 7	3
Adam Deadmarsh	Colorado	Jan. 05	Cgy. 0	Col. 4	3	Joe Sakic	Colorado	Mar. 07	Col. 8	Cgy. 3	3
Pavol Demitra	St. Louis	Feb. 12	Ana. 3	St.L. 6	3	Joe Sakic	Colorado	Mar. 23	Col. 4	Phx. 2	3
Boyd Devereaux	Edmonton	Mar. 17	Ott. 2	Edm. 4	3	Miroslav Satan	Buffalo	Jan. 08	Buf. 7	Ott. 2	3
Radek Dvorak	NY Rangers	Jan. 31	Nsh. 1	NYR 5	3	Brian Savage	Montreal	Oct. 08	Mtl. 4	Cgy. 1	3
Mike Eastwood	St. Louis	Dec. 21	St.L. 6	Phx. 0	3	Brian Savage	Montreal	Oct. 14	Mtl. 5	Phi. 4	3
Jeff Friesen	San Jose	Oct. 04	Chi. 1	S.J. 7	3	Marc Savard	Calgary	Apr. 05	Cgy. 5	St.L. 6	4
*Scott Gomez	New Jersey	Dec. 26	N.J. 3	NYR 3	3	Teemu Selanne	Anaheim	Nov. 26	Ana. 4	Dal. 2	3
Sergei Gonchar	Washington	Jan. 04	Mtl. 1	Wsh 6	3	Alex Selivanov	Edmonton	Nov. 14	Edm. 6	Chi. 3	4
*Jan Hlavac	NY Rangers	Feb. 11	Bos. 2	NYR 5	3	Alex Selivanov	Edmonton	Apr. 08	Edm. 6	Cgy. 3	3
Jaromir Jagr	Pittsburgh	Nov. 26	Ott. 0	Pit. 5	3	Ryan Smyth	Edmonton	Mar. 13	Edm. 3	Atl. 0	3
Jaromir Jagr	Pittsburgh	Dec. 30	NYI 3	Pit. 9	3	Dean Sylvester	Atlanta	Nov. 22	Van. 3	Atl. 6	3
Viktor Kozlov	Florida	Jan. 05	Fla. 5	Ana. 1	3	Pierre Turgeon	St. Louis	Dec. 02	Nsh. 1	St.L. 3	3
Martin Lapointe	Detroit	Mar. 26	NYR 2	Det. 8	3	Robert Valicevic	Nashville	Nov. 10	Nsh. 4	Chi. 2	3
Georges Laraque	Edmonton	Feb. 21	L.A. 3	Edm. 6	3						
Trevor Linden	Montreal	Feb. 08	Edm. 5	Mtl. 4	3						
Eric Lindros	Philadelphia	Dec. 09	Tor. 2	Phi. 4	3						
Alexei Morozov	Pittsburgh	Oct. 07	Pit. 7	N.J. 5	3						
Glen Murray	Los Angeles	Oct. 16	L.A. 4	Edm. 5	3						
Petr Nedved	NY Rangers	Jan. 08	NYR 5	Tor. 3	3						
Petr Nedved	NY Rangers	Jan. 24	NYR 6	Atl. 3	3						

Pavel Bure (above) had a trio of three-goal games and one four-goal effort en route to scoring 58 goals last season. Roman Turek (right) finished second in voting for the Vezina Trophy after recording 42 wins, nine shutouts and a 1.95 GAA.

Goaltending Leaders

Minimum 26 games

Goals Against Average

Goaltender	Team	GPI	Mins	GA	Avg
*Brian Boucher	Philadelphia	35	2038	65	1.91
Roman Turek	St. Louis	67	3960	129	1.95
Ed Belfour	Dallas	62	3620	127	2.10
Jose Theodore	Montreal	30	1655	58	2.10
John Vanbiesbrouck	Philadelphia	50	2950	108	2.20

Wins

Goaltender	Team	GPI	MINS	W	L	T
Martin Brodeur	New Jersey	72	4312	43	20	8
Roman Turek	St. Louis	67	3960	42	15	9
Olaf Kolzig	Washington	73	4371	41	20	11
Curtis Joseph	Toronto	63	3801	36	20	7
Arturs Irbe	Carolina	75	4345	34	28	9
Ed Belfour	Dallas	62	3620	32	21	7
Patrick Roy	Colorado	63	3704	32	21	8
Chris Osgood	Detroit	53	3148	30	14	8

Save Percentage

Goaltender	Team	GPI	MINS	GA	SA	S%	W	L	T
Ed Belfour	Dallas	62	3620	127	1571	.919	32	21	7
Jose Theodore	Montreal	30	1655	58	717	.919	12	13	2
Dominik Hasek	Buffalo	35	2066	76	937	.919	15	11	6
*Brian Boucher	Philadelphia	35	2038	65	790	.918	20	10	3
Olaf Kolzig	Washington	73	4371	163	1957	.917	41	20	11
Mike Vernon	S.J., Fla.	49	2791	115	1380	.917	24	18	3

Shutouts

Goaltender	Team	GPI	MINS	SO	W	L	T
Roman Turek	St. Louis	67	3960	7	42	15	9
Chris Osgood	Detroit	53	3148	6	30	14	8
Martin Brodeur	New Jersey	72	4312	6	43	20	8
Jose Theodore	Montreal	30	1655	5	12	13	2
*Martin Biron	Buffalo	41	2229	5	19	18	2
Fred Brathwaite	Calgary	61	3448	5	25	25	7
Arturs Irbe	Carolina	75	4345	5	34	28	9
Olaf Kolzig	Washington	73	4371	5	41	20	11

Team-by-Team Point Totals

1995-96 to 1999-2000
(Ranked by five-year point %)

	99-00	98-99	97-98	96-97	95-96	Pts%
Detroit	108	93	103	94	131	.645
New Jersey	103	105	107	104	86	.616
Colorado	96	98	95	107	104	.610
Philadelphia	105	93	95	103	103	.609
Dallas	102	114	109	104	66	.604
St. Louis	114	87	98	83	80	.563
Pittsburgh	88	90	98	84	102	.563
Buffalo	85	91	89	92	73	.524
Washington	102	68	92	75	89	.520
Phx./Wpg.	90	90	82	83	78	.516
Florida	98	78	63	89	92	.512
Toronto	100	97	69	68	80	.505
Montreal	83	75	87	77	90	.502
Boston	73	91	91	61	91	.496
NY Rangers	73	77	68	86	96	.488
Ottawa	95	103	83	77	41	.487
Chicago	78	70	73	81	94	.483
Car./Hfd.	84	86	74	75	77	.483
Edmonton	88	78	80	81	68	.482
Anaheim	83	83	65	85	78	.480
Los Angeles	94	69	87	67	66	.467
Calgary	77	72	67	73	79	.449
Vancouver	83	58	64	77	79	.440
San Jose	87	80	78	62	47	.432
Nashville	70	63	---	---	---	.405
NY Islanders	58	58	71	70	54	.379
Tampa Bay	54	47	44	74	88	.374
Atlanta	39	---	---	---	---	.238

Team Record When Scoring First Goal of a Game

Team	GP	FG	W	L	T
Detroit	82	49	33	10	6
Dallas	82	49	30	13	6
Chicago	82	48	27	15	6
Philadelphia	82	46	32	8	6
Colorado	82	46	31	11	4
Buffalo	82	46	28	11	11
New Jersey	82	45	28	11	6
Florida	82	45	26	15	4
Montreal	82	44	26	14	4
Pittsburgh	82	44	26	15	3
Washington	82	43	31	6	6
Toronto	82	42	32	9	1
Calgary	82	42	24	14	4
Carolina	82	41	27	11	3
St. Louis	82	40	30	4	6
Phoenix	82	40	27	11	2
Edmonton	82	40	22	9	9
Nashville	82	39	20	15	4
Vancouver	82	39	20	10	9
Ottawa	82	38	30	5	3
Los Angeles	82	38	24	8	6
San Jose	82	38	24	12	2
Anaheim	82	38	23	9	6
Boston	82	38	17	13	8
NY Rangers	82	36	19	13	4
NY Islanders	82	33	16	10	7
Tampa Bay	82	31	12	13	6
Atlanta	82	25	7	15	3

Team Plus/Minus Differential

Team	GF	PPGF	Net GF	GA	PPGA	Net GA	Goal Differential
St. Louis	248	61	**187**	165	42	**123**	+ 64
Detroit	278	69	**209**	210	44	**166**	+ 43
Washington	227	43	**184**	194	47	**147**	+ 37
New Jersey	251	55	**196**	203	39	**164**	+ 32
Philadelphia	237	69	**168**	179	42	**137**	+ 31
Buffalo	213	37	**176**	204	54	**150**	+ 26
Toronto	246	57	**189**	222	58	**164**	+ 25
Colorado	233	59	**174**	201	52	**149**	+ 25
Florida	244	58	**186**	209	47	**162**	+ 24
Los Angeles	245	60	**185**	228	66	**162**	+ 23
Ottawa	244	52	**192**	210	34	**176**	+ 16
Edmonton	226	53	**173**	212	54	**158**	+ 15
Phoenix	232	37	**195**	228	43	**185**	+ 10
San Jose	225	62	**163**	214	61	**153**	+ 10
Pittsburgh	241	54	**187**	236	56	**180**	+ 7
Dallas	211	54	**157**	184	33	**151**	+ 6
Chicago	242	52	**190**	245	58	**187**	+ 3
Vancouver	227	51	**176**	237	63	**174**	+ 2
Anaheim	217	55	**162**	227	62	**165**	– 3
Montreal	196	54	**142**	194	40	**154**	– 12
Carolina	217	58	**159**	216	40	**176**	– 17
Calgary	211	59	**152**	256	74	**182**	– 30
NY Rangers	218	55	**163**	246	49	**197**	– 34
Boston	210	51	**159**	248	55	**193**	– 34
Nashville	199	41	**158**	240	46	**194**	– 36
NY Islanders	194	45	**149**	275	84	**191**	– 42
Tampa Bay	204	51	**153**	310	77	**233**	– 80
Atlanta	170	44	**126**	313	76	**237**	–111

Team Record When Leading, Trailing, Tied

Team	Leading after 1 period W	L	T	2 periods W	L	T	Trailing after 1 period W	L	T	2 periods W	L	T	Tied after 1 period W	L	T	2 periods W	L	T
Anaheim	18	8	3	27	4	2	3	16	2	3	23	4	13	12	7	4	9	6
Atlanta	5	9	1	8	5	3	3	36	2	2	49	2	6	16	3	4	7	2
Boston	17	7	6	18	3	5	4	17	5	2	24	7	3	15	8	4	12	7
Buffalo	20	3	5	28	1	4	1	20	0	1	25	2	14	13	6	6	10	5
Calgary	17	5	2	20	5	2	2	18	5	3	32	5	12	18	3	8	4	3
Carolina	18	6	2	30	3	2	4	18	5	2	23	5	15	11	3	5	9	3
Chicago	22	7	4	26	3	6	4	21	2	4	28	3	7	11	4	3	8	1
Colorado	21	4	3	30	2	3	8	13	4	5	20	1	13	12	4	7	7	7
Dallas	21	6	6	22	7	4	13	14	3	8	18	2	9	9	1	13	4	4
Detroit	28	7	5	41	4	2	8	11	3	1	16	2	12	6	2	6	4	6
Edmonton	14	5	2	20	1	6	4	17	6	4	24	3	10	12	8	8	9	7
Florida	27	6	1	31	2	2	4	15	3	2	22	2	12	12	2	10	9	2
Los Angeles	22	4	2	29	2	2	8	15	4	3	23	1	9	12	6	7	6	9
Montreal	17	7	0	22	4	2	4	20	3	1	29	3	14	11	6	12	5	4
Nashville	14	7	2	21	3	2	4	27	2	3	34	2	10	13	3	4	10	3
New Jersey	21	4	5	30	1	3	11	15	1	4	18	3	13	11	2	11	10	2
NY Islanders	11	6	4	17	2	2	3	33	1	3	41	2	10	10	4	4	6	4
NY Rangers	15	7	0	22	5	2	3	17	4	3	30	6	11	17	8	4	6	4
Ottawa	21	4	3	27	1	4	5	17	4	6	22	3	15	9	7	8	7	4
Philadelphia	27	1	4	34	5	6	7	13	3	3	17	0	11	11	5	8	5	3
Phoenix	17	7	1	24	6	3	6	15	4	3	22	2	16	13	3	12	7	3
Pittsburgh	20	6	3	28	3	2	8	17	3	4	26	2	9	14	2	5	8	4
San Jose	19	5	2	27	3	3	4	25	4	2	24	2	12	7	4	5	10	7
St. Louis	25	4	2	35	1	2	9	11	1	5	15	5	17	5	8	11	4	4
Tampa Bay	6	6	4	12	4	3	8	35	2	1	42	3	5	13	3	6	8	3
Toronto	26	3	1	34	2	2	3	18	5	3	23	2	16	9	1	8	5	3
Vancouver	20	8	8	23	4	2	2	21	3	3	25	3	8	8	4	8	10	10
Washington	20	3	5	26	1	3	8	14	1	3	18	5	16	9	6	15	7	4

Team Statistics

TEAMS' HOME-AND-ROAD RECORD

Eastern Conference

			Home								Road				
	GP	W	L	T	RT	GF	GA	PTS	GP	W	L	T	RT	GF	GA	PTS
PHI	41	25	9	7	3	126	86	60	41	20	16	5	0	111	93	45
N.J.	41	28	10	3	1	133	92	60	41	17	19	5	4	118	111	43
WSH	41	26	7	8	2	120	83	62	41	18	19	4	0	107	111	40
TOR	41	24	12	5	0	128	105	53	41	21	18	2	3	118	117	47
FLA	41	26	11	4	2	129	97	58	41	17	22	2	4	115	112	40
OTT	41	24	12	5	2	139	98	55	41	17	18	6	0	105	112	40
PIT	41	23	11	7	0	134	107	53	41	14	26	1	6	107	129	35
BUF	41	21	15	5	1	112	98	48	41	14	21	6	3	101	106	37
CAR	41	20	16	5	0	99	102	45	41	17	19	5	0	118	114	39
MTL	41	18	18	5	1	95	90	42	41	17	20	4	3	101	104	41
NYR	41	15	21	5	1	109	123	36	41	14	20	7	2	109	123	37
BOS	41	12	18	11	1	99	118	36	41	12	21	8	5	111	130	37
NYI	41	10	26	5	1	94	140	26	41	14	23	4	0	100	135	32
T.B.	41	13	24	4	4	110	151	34	41	6	30	5	3	94	159	20
ATL	41	9	29	3	3	94	157	24	41	5	32	4	1	76	156	15
Total	**615**	**294**	**239**	**82**	**0**	**1721**	**1647**	**692**	**615**	**223**	**324**	**68**	**0**	**1591**	**1812**	**548**

Western Conference

	GP	W	L	T	RT	GF	GA	PTS	GP	W	L	T	RT	GF	GA	PTS
ST.L.	41	24	10	7	1	123	84	56	41	27	10	4	0	125	81	58
DET	41	28	10	3	1	152	106	60	41	20	14	7	1	126	104	48
DAL	41	21	15	5	4	106	91	51	41	22	14	5	2	105	93	51
COL	41	25	12	4	0	122	80	54	41	17	17	7	1	111	121	42
L.A.	41	21	15	5	2	126	115	49	41	18	16	7	2	119	113	45
PHX	41	22	17	2	1	117	110	47	41	17	18	6	3	115	118	43
EDM	41	18	14	9	3	118	94	48	41	14	20	7	5	108	118	40
S.J.	41	21	17	3	2	119	110	48	41	14	20	7	4	106	104	39
ANA	41	19	15	7	2	105	104	47	41	15	21	5	1	112	123	36
VAN	41	16	20	5	6	123	123	43	41	14	17	10	2	104	114	40
CHI	41	16	20	5	1	125	123	38	41	17	19	5	1	117	122	40
CGY	41	20	15	6	1	119	124	47	41	11	26	4	4	92	132	30
NSH	41	15	23	3	2	103	116	35	41	13	24	4	5	96	124	35
Total	**533**	**266**	**203**	**64**	**0**	**1558**	**1380**	**623**	**533**	**219**	**236**	**78**	**0**	**1436**	**1467**	**547**
	1148	**560**	**442**	**146**	**0**	**3279**	**3027**	**1315**	**1148**	**442**	**560**	**146**	**0**	**3027**	**3279**	**1095**

TEAMS' DIVISIONAL RECORD

Northeast Division

			Against Own Division								Against Other Division				
	GP	W	L	T	RT	GF	GA	PTS	GP	W	L	T	RT	GF	GA	PTS
TOR	20	10	8	2	1	59	54	23	62	35	22	5	2	187	168	77
OTT	20	11	5	4	0	64	53	26	62	30	25	7	2	180	157	69
BUF	20	9	9	2	1	47	42	21	62	26	27	9	3	166	162	64
MTL	20	7	10	3	0	47	55	17	62	28	28	6	4	149	139	66
BOS	20	5	10	5	2	50	63	17	62	19	29	14	4	160	185	56
Total	**100**	**42**	**42**	**16**	**0**	**267**	**267**	**104**	**310**	**138**	**131**	**41**	**0**	**842**	**811**	**332**

Atlantic Division

PHI	20	12	6	2	1	64	44	27	62	33	19	10	2	173	135	78
N.J.	20	13	5	2	0	67	46	28	62	32	24	6	5	184	157	75
PIT	20	9	10	1	1	71	62	20	62	28	27	7	5	170	174	68
NYR	20	5	12	3	0	46	65	13	62	24	29	9	3	172	181	60
NYI	20	6	12	2	0	49	80	14	62	18	37	7	1	145	195	44
Total	**100**	**45**	**45**	**10**	**0**	**297**	**297**	**102**	**310**	**135**	**136**	**39**	**0**	**844**	**842**	**325**

Southeast Division

WSH	20	14	4	2	0	69	38	30	62	30	22	10	2	158	156	72
FLA	20	10	7	3	3	65	50	26	62	33	26	3	3	179	159	72
CAR	20	12	5	3	0	60	48	27	62	25	30	7	0	157	168	57
T.B.	20	2	15	3	0	50	88	7	62	17	39	6	7	154	222	47
ATL	20	5	12	3	0	45	65	13	62	9	49	4	4	125	248	26
Total	**100**	**43**	**43**	**14**	**0**	**289**	**289**	**103**	**310**	**114**	**166**	**30**	**0**	**773**	**953**	**274**

Central Division

ST.L.	18	8	7	3	1	46	41	20	64	43	13	8	0	202	124	94
DET	18	10	6	2	1	60	51	23	64	38	18	8	1	218	159	85
CHI	18	7	8	3	0	52	59	17	64	26	31	7	2	190	186	61
NSH	18	6	10	2	2	47	54	16	64	22	37	5	5	152	186	54
Total	**72**	**31**	**31**	**10**	**0**	**205**	**205**	**76**	**256**	**129**	**99**	**28**	**0**	**762**	**655**	**294**

Pacific Division

DAL	24	12	11	1	0	65	60	25	58	31	18	9	6	146	124	77
L.A.	24	8	13	3	3	57	70	22	58	31	18	9	1	188	158	72
PHX	24	13	10	1	1	68	64	28	58	26	25	7	3	164	164	62
S.J.	24	11	11	2	2	67	61	26	58	24	26	8	5	158	153	61
ANA	24	11	10	3	1	65	67	26	58	23	26	9	2	152	160	57
Total	**120**	**55**	**55**	**10**	**0**	**322**	**322**	**127**	**290**	**135**	**113**	**42**	**0**	**808**	**759**	**329**

Northwest Division

COL	18	13	3	2	0	62	35	28	64	29	26	9	1	171	166	68
EDM	18	7	9	2	2	54	48	18	64	25	25	14	6	172	164	70
VAN	18	4	11	3	3	46	58	14	64	26	26	12	5	181	179	69
CGY	18	8	9	1	1	44	65	18	64	23	32	9	4	167	191	59
Total	**72**	**32**	**32**	**8**	**0**	**206**	**206**	**78**	**256**	**103**	**109**	**44**	**0**	**691**	**700**	**266**

TEAM STREAKS

Consecutive Wins

Games	Team	From	To
8	Phoenix	Nov. 16	Dec. 2
8	Colorado	Mar. 23	Apr. 9
7	NY Rangers	Jan. 15	Jan. 25
7	Montreal	Feb. 12	Feb. 24
6	Boston	Oct. 23	Nov. 6
6	Toronto	Dec. 15	Dec. 29
6	Philadelphia	Dec. 27	Jan. 11
6	Washington	Jan. 8	Jan. 19
6	St. Louis	Jan. 26	Feb. 8
6	St. Louis	Feb. 12	Feb. 25
6	Colorado	Mar. 2	Mar. 14

Consecutive Home Wins

Games	Team	From	To
10	Washington	Jan. 4	Feb. 23
7	Buffalo	Oct. 22	Nov. 24
7	Calgary	Dec. 29	Jan. 21
7	New Jersey	Jan. 17	Feb. 15
7	Washington	Mar. 5	Mar. 28
6	Boston	Oct. 28	Nov. 18
6	Philadelphia	Nov. 20	Dec. 18
6	Toronto	Nov. 20	Dec. 11
6	Detroit	Dec. 1	Dec. 27
6	New Jersey	Dec. 14	Jan. 8
6	Colorado	Jan. 5	Jan. 17

Consecutive Road Wins

Games	Team	From	To
10	St. Louis	Jan. 21	Mar. 2
6	New Jersey	Jan. 3	Jan. 26
6	Colorado	Mar. 7	Apr. 7
5	Anaheim	Nov. 26	Dec. 26
5	NY Rangers	Jan. 15	Jan. 25
5	Toronto	Mar. 6	Mar. 16
4	San Jose	Oct. 13	Oct. 19
4	Vancouver	Oct. 24	Nov. 20
4	St. Louis	Nov. 5	Nov. 17
4	Phoenix	Nov. 18	Dec. 6
4	Dallas	Nov. 28	Dec. 4
4	Philadelphia	Dec. 27	Jan. 11
4	Ottawa	Dec. 29	Jan. 12
4	Washington	Jan. 12	Jan. 19
4	Dallas	Jan. 20	Feb. 9
4	Dallas	Feb. 23	Mar. 15
4	Chicago	Mar. 11	Mar. 21
4	St. Louis	Mar. 15	Mar. 24
4	Buffalo	Mar. 18	Apr. 6

Consecutive Undefeated

Games	Team	W	T	From	To
11	Washington	10	1	Jan. 8	Jan. 30
9	New Jersey	7	2	Dec. 26	Jan. 11
8	Phoenix	8	0	Nov. 16	Dec. 2
8	Nashville	5	3	Dec. 18	Jan. 1
8	St. Louis	6	2	Dec. 30	Jan. 13
8	Detroit	6	2	Feb. 25	Mar. 14
8	Colorado	8	0	Mar. 23	Apr. 9
7	Detroit	6	1	Oct. 7	Oct. 27
7	Boston	6	1	Oct. 20	Nov. 6
7	Philadelphia	6	1	Nov. 24	Dec. 9
7	Philadelphia	6	1	Dec. 23	Jan. 11
7	NY Rangers	7	0	Jan. 15	Jan. 25
7	New Jersey	5	2	Feb. 2	Feb. 17
7	Montreal	7	0	Feb. 12	Feb. 24
7	Ottawa	5	2	Feb. 26	Mar. 9
7	Colorado	6	1	Mar. 2	Mar. 16
7	Detroit	5	2	Mar. 22	Apr. 2

Consecutive Home Undefeated

Games	Team	W	T	From	To
15	Philadelphia	12	3	Oct. 28	Jan. 8
13	Washington	11	2	Dec. 27	Feb. 23
12	New Jersey	10	2	Oct. 9	Dec. 3
12	Colorado	9	3	Dec. 27	Feb. 3
8	Boston	6	2	Oct. 9	Nov. 18
8	Edmonton	5	3	Dec. 1	Jan. 7
8	New Jersey	7	1	Jan. 17	Feb. 17
8	Pittsburgh	4	4	Feb. 1	Feb. 28
8	Washington	7	1	Mar. 3	Mar. 28
7	Buffalo	7	0	Oct. 22	Nov. 24
7	St. Louis	5	2	Nov. 12	Dec. 4
7	Calgary	6	1	Nov. 19	Dec. 23
7	Detroit	6	1	Dec. 1	Dec. 31
7	Calgary	7	0	Dec. 29	Jan. 21
7	Montreal	4	3	Jan. 2	Jan. 30

Consecutive Road Undefeated

Games	Team	W	T	From	To
11	St. Louis	10	1	Jan. 21	Mar. 4
8	New Jersey	6	2	Dec. 26	Jan. 26
7	Detroit	5	2	Feb. 21	Mar. 18
7	Dallas	6	1	Feb. 23	Mar. 29
7	Colorado	6	1	Feb. 27	Apr. 7
6	Vancouver	2	4	Feb. 17	Mar. 9
6	St. Louis	5	1	Mar. 15	Mar. 30
5	Vancouver	4	1	Oct. 23	Nov. 20
5	Los Angeles	4	1	Oct. 30	Nov. 23
5	Boston	3	2	Nov. 13	Dec. 2
5	Anaheim	5	0	Nov. 26	Dec. 26
5	Ottawa	4	1	Dec. 19	Jan. 12
5	Washington	4	1	Jan. 12	Jan. 22
5	NY Rangers	5	0	Jan. 15	Jan. 25
5	Anaheim	3	2	Jan. 29	Feb. 8
5	Edmonton	3	2	Feb. 8	Feb. 15
5	Ottawa	3	2	Feb. 28	Mar. 15
5	Toronto	5	0	Mar. 6	Mar. 16
5	Buffalo	4	1	Mar. 18	Apr. 9

TEAM PENALTIES

Abbreviations: GP – games played; **PEN** – total penalty minutes including bench minutes; **BMI** – total bench minor minutes; **AVG** – average penalty minutes/game calculated by dividing total penalty minutes by games played

Team	GP	PEN	BMI	AVG
CAR	82	799	4	9.7
OTT	82	850	14	10.4
BOS	82	865	6	10.5
NYR	82	916	4	11.2
ANA	82	926	8	11.3
NSH	82	946	14	11.5
PHX	82	940	12	11.5
WSH	82	994	14	12.1
DET	82	1014	20	12.4
DAL	82	1029	12	12.5
VAN	82	1047	22	12.8
MTL	82	1067	14	13.0
TOR	82	1103	12	13.5
COL	82	1118	18	13.6
St.L.	82	1139	22	13.9
BUF	82	1173	10	14.3
PIT	82	1221	16	14.9
PHI	82	1233	16	15.0
CGY	82	1267	8	15.5
S.J.	82	1292	6	15.8
L.A.	82	1313	4	16.0
N.J.	82	1313	22	16.0
FLA	82	1329	18	16.2
EDM	82	1344	16	16.4
NYI	82	1376	8	16.8
ATL	82	1422	16	17.3
CHI	82	1444	20	17.6
T.B.	82	1733	20	21.1
Total	**1148**	**32213**	**368**	**28.1**

After a poor first half last season, the Washington Capitals came alive after Christmas. Olaf Kolzig led the team to 10 wins during an 11-game undefeated streak in January. He went on to win the Vezina Trophy.

TEAMS' POWER-PLAY RECORD

Abbreviations: ADV – total advantages; **PPGF** – power-play goals for; **%** – calculated by dividing number of power-play goals by total advantages.

		Home				Home					Overall		
	Team	GP	ADV	PPGF	%	Team	GP	ADV	PPGF	%	Team	GP	ADV	PPGF	%
1	N.J.	41	143	34	23.8	PHI	41	163	34	20.9	DET	82	338	69	20.4
2	DET	41	185	39	21.1	COL	41	141	28	19.9	PHI	82	340	69	20.3
3	TOR	41	171	35	20.5	DET	41	153	30	19.6	N.J.	82	274	55	20.1
4	PHI	41	177	35	19.8	L.A.	41	170	32	18.8	COL	82	302	59	19.5
5	COL	41	161	31	19.3	MTL	41	165	31	18.8	CGY	82	330	59	17.9
6	OTT	41	176	33	18.8	CGY	41	170	31	18.2	TOR	82	321	57	17.8
7	ANA	41	175	32	18.3	CAR	41	171	31	18.1	St.L.	82	342	61	17.8
8	CHI	41	167	30	18.0	FLA	41	166	30	18.1	FLA	82	338	58	17.2
9	St.L.	41	164	29	17.7	St.L.	41	178	32	18.0	CAR	82	342	58	17.0
10	VAN	41	170	30	17.6	NYR	41	165	28	17.0	NYR	82	325	55	16.9
11	PIT	41	170	30	17.6	S.J.	41	173	28	16.2	L.A.	82	356	60	16.9
12	DAL	41	189	33	17.5	N.J.	41	131	21	16.0	OTT	82	310	52	16.8
13	CGY	41	160	28	17.5	EDM	41	172	27	15.7	MTL	82	323	54	16.7
14	NYR	41	160	27	16.9	NSH	41	140	21	15.0	ANA	82	332	55	16.6
15	S.J.	41	204	34	16.7	TOR	41	150	22	14.7	S.J.	82	377	62	16.4
16	FLA	41	172	28	16.3	WSH	41	158	23	14.6	CHI	82	325	52	16.0
17	EDM	41	164	26	15.9	ANA	41	157	23	14.6	EDM	82	336	53	15.8
18	BOS	41	182	29	15.9	OTT	41	134	19	14.2	VAN	82	323	51	15.8
19	T.B.	41	189	30	15.9	CHI	41	158	22	13.9	DAL	82	343	54	15.7
20	CAR	41	171	27	15.8	VAN	41	153	21	13.7	PIT	82	346	54	15.6
21	WSH	41	129	20	15.5	PIT	41	176	24	13.6	WSH	82	287	43	15.0
22	L.A.	41	186	28	15.1	DAL	41	154	21	13.6	BOS	82	355	51	14.4
23	NYI	41	156	23	14.7	NYI	41	164	22	13.4	NYI	82	320	45	14.1
24	MTL	41	158	23	14.6	PHX	41	134	17	12.7	T.B.	82	365	51	14.0
25	ATL	41	175	24	13.7	BOS	41	173	22	12.7	NSH	82	304	41	13.5
26	NSH	41	164	20	12.2	T.B.	41	176	21	11.9	ATL	82	348	44	12.6
27	PHX	41	176	20	11.4	ATL	41	173	20	11.6	PHX	82	310	37	11.9
28	BUF	41	169	19	11.2	BUF	41	182	18	9.9	BUF	82	351	37	10.5
	TOTAL	**1148**	**4763**	**797**	**16.7**		**1148**	**4500**	**699**	**15.5**		**1148**	**9263**	**1496**	**16.2**

TEAMS' PENALTY KILLING RECORD

Abbreviations: TSH – total times short-handed; **PPGA** – power-play goals against; **%** – calculated by dividing times short minus power-play goals against by times short.

		Home				Road					Overall		
	Team	GP	TSH	PPGA	%	Team	GP	TSH	PPGA	%	Team	GP	TSH	PPGA	%
1	CAR	41	127	12	90.6	OTT	41	134	14	89.6	DAL	82	307	33	89.3
2	DAL	41	148	14	90.5	St.L.	41	188	20	89.4	St.L.	82	345	42	87.8
3	N.J.	41	155	17	89.0	DAL	41	159	19	88.1	OTT	82	273	34	87.5
4	COL	41	160	18	88.8	BUF	41	201	25	87.6	N.J.	82	313	39	87.5
5	DET	41	157	18	88.5	PHI	41	164	21	87.2	MTL	82	302	40	86.8
6	MTL	41	142	18	87.3	EDM	41	192	25	87.0	PHI	82	316	42	86.7
7	FLA	41	147	19	87.1	MTL	41	160	22	86.3	WSH	82	341	47	86.2
8	WSH	41	162	21	87.0	N.J.	41	158	22	86.1	DET	82	311	44	85.9
9	NSH	41	152	20	86.8	PHX	41	155	22	85.8	PHX	82	306	43	85.9
10	PHI	41	152	21	86.2	WSH	41	179	26	85.5	EDM	82	369	54	85.4
11	PHX	41	151	21	86.1	L.A.	41	178	27	84.8	FLA	82	323	47	85.4
12	St.L.	41	157	22	86.0	CHI	41	192	30	84.4	NSH	82	309	46	85.1
13	OTT	41	139	20	85.6	FLA	41	176	28	84.1	BUF	82	361	54	85.0
14	NYR	41	138	20	85.5	S.J.	41	184	30	83.7	COL	82	335	52	84.5
15	PIT	41	156	23	85.3	T.B.	41	195	32	83.6	CAR	82	253	40	84.2
16	EDM	41	177	29	83.6	NSH	41	157	26	83.4	CHI	82	355	58	83.7
17	S.J.	41	188	31	83.5	DET	41	154	26	83.1	S.J.	82	372	61	83.6
18	ATL	41	195	33	83.1	TOR	41	164	28	82.9	NYR	82	292	49	83.2
19	BOS	41	122	21	82.8	VAN	41	156	29	81.4	PIT	82	321	56	82.6
20	CHI	41	163	28	82.8	NYR	41	154	29	81.2	TOR	82	330	58	82.4
21	ANA	41	151	26	82.8	COL	41	175	34	80.6	L.A.	82	373	66	82.3
22	CGY	41	161	29	82.0	PIT	41	165	33	80.0	T.B.	82	399	77	80.7
23	TOR	41	166	30	81.9	NYI	41	211	43	79.6	VAN	82	322	63	80.4
24	BUF	41	160	29	81.9	CGY	41	204	45	77.9	ATL	82	386	76	80.3
25	NYI	41	209	41	80.4	CAR	41	126	28	77.8	NYI	82	420	84	80.0
26	L.A.	41	195	39	80.0	ATL	41	191	43	77.5	CGY	82	365	74	79.7
27	VAN	41	166	34	79.5	BOS	41	146	34	76.7	BOS	82	268	55	79.5
28	T.B.	41	204	45	77.9	ANA	41	145	36	75.2	ANA	82	296	62	79.1
	TOTAL	**1148**	**4500**	**699**	**84.5**		**1148**	**4763**	**797**	**83.3**		**1148**	**9263**	**1496**	**83.8**

SHORT-HANDED GOALS FOR

		Home			Road			Overall	
	Team	GP	SHGF	Team	GP	SHGF	Team	GP	SHGF
1	PHX	41	9	S.J.	41	10	S.J.	82	16
2	NYI	41	8	WSH	41	9	DET	82	15
3	DAL	41	7	DET	41	9	PHX	82	14
4	St.L.	41	7	BUF	41	7	St.L.	82	13
5	EDM	41	6	TOR	41	6	TOR	82	11
6	T.B.	41	6	CHI	41	6	CHI	82	10
7	DET	41	6	St.L.	41	6	DAL	82	9
8	NSH	41	6	PHX	41	5	EDM	82	9
9	S.J.	41	6	OTT	41	4	N.J.	82	9
10	VAN	41	5	N.J.	41	4	T.B.	82	9
11	TOR	41	5	ANA	41	4	WSH	82	9
12	N.J.	41	5	PHI	41	4	NSH	82	9
13	PIT	41	5	VAN	41	4	VAN	82	9
14	ATL	41	4	MTL	41	4	NYI	82	8
15	CHI	41	4	EDM	41	3	BUF	82	8
16	PHI	41	3	T.B.	41	3	PIT	82	8
17	NYR	41	3	NSH	41	3	MTL	82	7
18	CGY	41	3	PIT	41	2	PHI	82	7
19	OTT	41	2	NYR	41	2	OTT	82	6
20	COL	41	2	L.A.	41	2	ATL	82	6
21	L.A.	41	2	DAL	41	2	NYR	82	5
22	CAR	41	2	ATL	41	2	L.A.	82	4
23	FLA	41	1	CAR	41	1	ANA	82	4
24	BOS	41	0	CGY	41	1	CGY	82	4
25	BUF	41	1	COL	41	1	CAR	82	3
26	ANA	41	0	FLA	41	1	COL	82	3
27	WSH	41	0	NYI	41	0	FLA	82	2
28				BOS	41	0	BOS	82	0
	TOTAL	**1148**	**112**		**1148**	**104**		**1148**	**216**

SHORT-HANDED GOALS AGAINST

		Home			Road			Overall	
	Team	GP	SHGA	Team	GP	SHGA	Team	GP	SHGA
1	WSH	41	0	St.L.	41	0	WSH	82	3
2	S.J.	41	1	DET	41	0	St.L.	82	3
3	CGY	41	2	BOS	41	1	EDM	82	4
4	BUF	41	2	EDM	41	1	BOS	82	4
5	COL	41	2	TOR	41	2	S.J.	82	4
6	EDM	41	3	PHX	41	2	TOR	82	4
7	FLA	41	3	VAN	41	2	DET	82	6
8	MTL	41	3	CAR	41	3	CAR	82	6
9	FLA	41	3	WSH	41	3	PHI	82	7
10	St.L.	41	3	DAL	41	3	T.B.	82	7
11	TOR	41	3	PHI	41	3	PHX	82	7
12	OTT	41	3	T.B.	41	3	VAN	82	7
13	ANA	41	3	S.J.	41	3	COL	82	7
14	PHI	41	4	NYR	41	4	MTL	82	7
15	ATL	41	4	N.J.	41	4	OTT	82	7
16	T.B.	41	4	NYI	41	4	NYI	82	7
17	CHI	41	4	OTT	41	5	FLA	82	7
18	NYI	41	3	ANA	41	4	ANA	82	7
19	CAR	41	4	COL	41	5	CGY	82	8
20	VAN	41	5	MTL	41	5	DAL	82	8
21	PHX	41	5	NSH	41	5	NYR	82	9
22	N.J.	41	5	FLA	41	5	N.J.	82	9
23	PIT	41	5	PIT	41	5	BUF	82	10
24	DAL	41	5	L.A.	41	5	PIT	82	11
25	NSH	41	6	CGY	41	6	NSH	82	11
26	NSH	41	6	BUF	41	8	L.A.	82	13
27	L.A.	41	6	CHI	41	9	ATL	82	13
28							CHI	82	13
	TOTAL	**1148**	**104**		**1148**	**112**		**1148**	**216**

Overtime Results

1990-91 to 1999-2000

Team	1999-2000 GP	W	L	T	1998-99 GP	W	L	T	1997-98 GP	W	L	T	1996-97 GP	W	L	T	1995-96 GP	W	L	T	1994-95 GP	W	L	T	1993-94 GP	W	L	T	1992-93 GP	W	L	T	1991-92 GP	W	L	T	1990-91 GP	W	L	T
ANA	18	3	3	12	17	1	3	13	20	3	4	13	16	3	0	13	16	6	2	8	7	2	0	5	12	2	5	5												
ATL	11	0	4	7																																				
BOS	26	1	6	19	17	2	2	13	17	3	1	13	15	3	3	9	19	2	6	11	8	2	3	3	17	2	2	13	15	5	3	7	20	6	2	12	17	5	0	12
BUF	20	5	4	11	23	3	3	17	21	3	1	17	21	5	4	12	15	2	6	7	9	1	1	7	13	0	4	9	18	4	4	10	16	2	2	12	24	3	2	19
CGY	26	11	5	10	16	3	1	12	22	4	3	15	16	3	4	9	16	2	3	11	9	1	1	7	18	3	2	13	19	4	4	11	19	2	5	12	15	3	4	8
HFD/CAR	14	4	0	10	24	1	5	18	12	2	2	8	18	3	4	11	14	2	3	9	9	1	1	7	14	4	1	9	18	3	9	6	18	2	3	13	9	1	1	7
CHI	17	5	2	10	15	1	2	12	18	1	4	13	19	1	5	13	19	1	4	14	7	2	0	5	16	2	5	9	16	1	3	12	19	2	2	15	12	3	1	8
QUE/COL	17	5	1	11	12	2	0	10	22	2	3	17	15	2	3	10	6	1	0	5	8	0	0	8	15	3	3	9	15	4	1	10	17	0	5	12	18	1	3	14
MIN/DAL	19	3	6	10	16	3	1	12	17	5	1	11	15	4	3	8	15	1	0	14	9	0	1	8	22	6	3	13	10	0	0	10	8	0	2	6	17	0	3	14
DET	16	4	2	10	10	2	1	7	15	0	0	15	27	7	2	18	11	3	1	7	4	0	0	4	15	5	2	8	11	2	0	9	16	3	1	12	14	2	4	8
EDM	27	3	8	16	20	3	5	12	15	3	2	10	16	1	6	9	14	4	2	8	7	1	2	4	21	1	6	14	17	5	4	8	12	0	2	10	15	4	5	6
FLA	15	3	6	6	21	1	2	18	20	3	2	15	26	3	4	19	13	0	3	10	9	0	3	6	24	2	5	17												
L.A.	21	5	4	12	12	5	2	5	16	3	2	11	14	0	3	11	23	3	2	18	9	0	0	9	18	3	3	12	13	2	1	10	16	1	1	14	16	4	2	10
MTL	17	4	4	9	15	0	4	11	20	3	4	13	21	4	2	15	15	2	3	10	10	1	2	7	19	3	2	14	14	5	3	6	20	6	3	11	17	3	3	11
N.J.	16	3	5	8	15	3	1	11	16	2	3	11	17	1	2	14	19	7	0	12	11	1	2	8	14	1	1	12	11	4	0	7	17	2	4	11	17	1	1	15
NSH	18	4	7	7	10	1	2	7																																
NYI	15	5	1	9	17	1	6	10	13	0	2	11					17	2	5	10	7	1	1	5	19	5	2	12	13	3	3	7	16	3	2	11	15	2	3	10
NYR	21	6	3	12	19	5	3	11	24	2	4	18	13	3	0	10	17	2	1	14	3	0	0	3	12	3	1	8	17	2	4	11	11	5	1	5	16	1	2	13
OTT	15	2	2	11	18	1	2	15	17	2	0	15	17	0	2	15	8	0	3	5	7	1	1	5	17	4	4	9	10	0	6	4								
PHI	21	6	3	12	24	2	3	19	15	3	1	11	18	3	2	13	20	4	3	13	8	3	1	4	18	3	5	10	17	4	2	11	17	2	4	11	11	1	0	10
WPG/PHX	16	4	4	8	15	2	1	12	14	0	2	12	16	5	4	7	8	2	0	6	9	0	2	7	15	1	5	9	11	2	2	7	20	1	4	15	14	1	2	11
PIT	17	3	6	8	22	7	1	14	23	3	2	18	13	1	4	8	9	3	2	4	5	1	1	3	19	4	2	13	10	3	0	7	12	2	1	9	12	4	2	6
ST.L.	17	5	1	11	15	1	1	13	12	2	2	8	13	1	1	11	18	1	1	16	7	1	1	5	17	4	2	11	17	2	4	11	15	2	2	11	18	3	4	11
S.J.	21	4	7	10	21	1	2	18	12	0	2	10	12	3	1	8	9	1	1	7	5	1	0	4	19	2	1	16	10	3	5	2	9	1	3	5				
T.B.	16	0	7	9	12	1	2	9	13	0	3	10	16	4	2	10	16	2	3	12	7	2	2	3	18	3	4	11	14	3	4	7								
TOR	17	7	3	7	14	6	1	7	10	1	0	9	10	1	1	8	18	4	2	12	8	0	0	8	17	4	1	12	13	1	1	11	11	4	0	7	17	4	2	11
VAN	27	4	8	15	13	0	1	12	17	0	3	14	14	5	2	7	20	1	4	15	13	0	1	12	12	5	4	3	10	1	0	9	17	4	1	12	15	3	3	9
WSH	19	5	2	12	11	2	3	6	17	4	1	12	13	2	3	9	16	4	1	11	9	0	1	8	14	2	2	10	11	2	2	7	12	2	2	8	14	4	3	7
Totals	**260**	**114**	**146**		**222**	**60**	**162**		**219**	**54**	**165**		**214**	**70**	**144**		**201**	**64**	**137**		**101**	**26**	**75**		**214**	**74**	**140**		**165**	**65**	**100**		**169**	**52**	**117**		**166**	**54**	**112**	

1999-2000

Home Team Wins: 65
Visiting Team Wins: 49

1999-2000 Penalty Shots

Scored

Miroslav Satan (Buffalo) scored against Damian Rhodes (Atlanta), October 9. Final score: Buffalo 5 at Atlanta 5.

Kimmo Timonen (Nashville) scored against Jeff Hackett (Montreal), November 18. Final score: Montreal 1 at Nashville 6.

Fredrik Olausson (Anaheim) scored against Martin Brodeur (New Jersey), November 24. Final score: New Jersey 2 at Anaheim 1.

Jeremy Roenick (Phoenix) scored against Dan Cloutier (Tampa Bay), December 2. Final score: Tampa Bay 1 at Phoenix 4.

Petr Sykora (New Jersey) scored against Dwayne Roloson (Buffalo), January 6. Final score: New Jersey 6 at Buffalo 3.

Brad Isbister (NY Islanders) scored against Sean Burke (Phoenix), January 10. Final score: Phoenix 2 at NY Islanders 2.

Alexander Korolyuk (San Jose) scored against Roman Turek (St. Louis), January 11. Final score: St. Louis 5 at San Jose 2.

Keith Tkachuk (Phoenix) scored against Jean-Sebastien Aubin (Pittsburgh), January 12. Final score: Pittsburgh 1 at Phoenix 4.

Martin Straka (Pittsburgh) scored against Roman Turek (St. Louis), January 19. Final score: St. Louis 1 at Pittsburgh 3.

Viktor Kozlov (Florida) scored against Olaf Kolzig (Washington), February 23. Final score: Florida 2 at Washington 3.

Daniel Alfredsson (Ottawa) scored against Scott Langkow (Atlanta), March 4. Final score: Atlanta 2 at Ottawa 3.

Olli Jokinen (NY Islanders) scored against Dominik Hasek (Buffalo), March 4. Final score: Buffalo 2 at NY Islanders 4.

Patrik Elias (New Jersey) scored against Damian Rhodes (Atlanta), March 10. Final score: New Jersey 9 at Atlanta 0.

Jeremy Roenick (Phoenix) scored against Tomas Vokoun (Nashville), March 17. Final score: Nashville 4 at Phoenix 3.

Chris Drury (Colorado) scored against Ken Wregget (Detroit), March 18. Final score: Detroit 4 at Colorado 3.

Tim Connolly (NY Islanders) scored against J-Sebastien Aubin (Pittsburgh), March 21. Final score: Pittsburgh 8 at NY Islanders 2.

Stopped

Dominic Roussel (Anaheim) stopped Stan Drulia (Tampa Bay), October 15. Final score: Anaheim 3 at Tampa Bay 2.

Peter Skudra (Pittsburgh) stopped Doug Gilmour (Chicago), October 16. Final score: Chicago 3 at Pittsburgh 3.

Stephane Fiset (Los Angeles) stopped Mike Ricci (San Jose), October 24. Final score: San Jose 3 at Los Angeles 4.

Jean-Sebastien Aubin (Pittsburgh) stopped Teemu Selanne (Anaheim), October 27. Final score: Pittsburgh 1 at Anaheim 2.

Martin Brodeur (New Jersey) stopped Valeri Zelepukin (Philadelphia), October 30. Final score: New Jersey 3 at Philadelphia 5.

Mike Richter (NY Rangers) stopped Richard Zednik (Washington), November 11. Final score: NY Rangers 5 at Washington 4.

Sean Burke (Florida) stopped Terry Yake (St. Louis), November 18. Final score: Florida 0 at St. Louis 3.

Patrick Roy (Colorado) stopped Andrew Cassels (Vancouver), November 30. Final score: Colorado 4 at Vancouver 2.

Jamie Storr (Los Angeles) stopped Martin Rucinsky (Montreal), December 11. Final score: Los Angeles 4 at Montreal 2.

Ken Wregget (Detroit) stopped Miroslav Satan (Buffalo), December 28. Final score: Detroit 7 at Buffalo 2.

Roman Turek (St. Louis) stopped Jeff Friesen (San Jose), December 30. Final score: San Jose 1 at St. Louis 2.

Steve Shields (San Jose) stopped Pierre Turgeon (St. Louis), December 30. Final score: San Jose 1 at St. Louis 2.

Tommy Salo (Edmonton) stopped Mike Sillinger (Tampa Bay), January 7. Final score: Tampa Bay 1 at Edmonton 5.

Martin Biron (Buffalo) stopped Daniel Alfredsson (Ottawa), January 8. Final score: Buffalo 7 at Ottawa 4.

Mike Vernon (Florida) stopped Claude Lapointe (NY Islanders), January 12. Final score: NY Islanders 3 at Florida 4.

Roberto Luongo (NY Islanders) stopped Dan Kesa (Tampa Bay), January 13. Final score: NY Islanders 2 at Tampa Bay 4.

Mike Richter (NY Rangers) stopped Randy Robitaille (Nashville), January 31. Final score: Nashville 1 at NY Rangers 5.

Arturs Irbe (Carolina) stopped Kevyn Adams (Toronto), February 14. Final score: Carolina 5 at Toronto 2.

Mike Dunham (Nashville) stopped John Madden (New Jersey), February 29. Final score: New Jersey 2 at Nashville 1.

Kevin Weekes (NY Islanders) stopped Miroslav Satan (Buffalo), March 4. Final score: Buffalo 2 at NY Islanders 4.

Olaf Kolzig (Washington) stopped Sergei Nemchinov (New Jersey), March 11. Final score: New Jersey 2 at Washington 4.

Emmanuel Fernandez (Dallas) stopped Radek Dvorak (NY Rangers), March 13. Final score: Dallas 4 at NY Rangers 3.

Damian Rhodes (Atlanta) stopped Brad Isbister (NY Islanders), March 16. Final score: NY Islanders 4 at Atlanta 2.

Curtis Joseph (Toronto) stopped Ulf Dahlen (Washington), April 1. Final score: Toronto 4 at Washington 3.

Summary

40 penalty shots resulted in 16 goals

NHL Record Book

Year-By-Year Final Standings & Leading Scorers

*Stanley Cup winner

1917-18

First Half

Team	GP	W	L	T	GF	GA	PTS
Montreal	14	10	4	0	81	47	20
Toronto	14	8	6	0	71	75	16
Ottawa	14	5	9	0	67	79	10
**Mtl. Wanderers	6	1	5	0	17	35	2

**Montreal Arena burned down and Wanderers forced to withdraw from League. Montreal Canadiens and Toronto each counted a win for defaulted games with Wanderers.

Second Half

Team	GP	W	L	T	GF	GA	PTS
*Toronto	8	5	3	0	37	34	10
Ottawa	8	4	4	0	35	35	8
Montreal	8	3	5	0	34	37	6

Leading Scorers

Player	Club	GP	G	A	PTS	PIM
Malone, Joe	Montreal	20	44	4	48	30
Denneny, Cy	Ottawa	20	36	10	46	80
Noble, Reg	Toronto	20	30	10	40	35
Lalonde, Newsy	Montreal	14	23	7	30	51
Denneny, Corb	Toronto	21	20	9	29	14
Cameron, Harry	Toronto	21	17	10	27	28
Pitre, Didier	Montreal	20	17	6	23	29
Gerard, Eddie	Ottawa	20	13	7	20	26
Darragh, Jack	Ottawa	18	14	5	19	26
Nighbor, Frank	Ottawa	10	11	8	19	6
Meeking, Harry	Toronto	21	10	9	19	28

1918-19

First Half

Team	GP	W	L	T	GF	GA	PTS
• Montreal	10	7	3	0	57	50	14
Ottawa	10	5	5	0	39	39	10
Toronto	10	3	7	0	42	49	6

Second Half

Team	GP	W	L	T	GF	GA	PTS
Ottawa	8	7	1	0	32	14	14
Montreal	8	3	5	0	31	28	6
Toronto	8	2	6	0	22	43	4

• NHL Champion. Stanley Cup not awarded due to influenza epidemic.

Leading Scorers

Player	Club	GP	G	A	PTS	PIM
Lalonde, Newsy	Montreal	17	22	10	32	40
Cleghorn, Odie	Montreal	17	22	6	28	22
Nighbor, Frank	Ottawa	18	19	9	28	27
Denneny, Cy	Ottawa	18	18	4	22	58
Pitre, Didier	Montreal	17	14	5	19	12
Skinner, Alf	Toronto	17	12	4	16	26
Cameron, Harry	Tor., Ott.	14	11	3	14	35
Darragh, Jack	Ottawa	14	11	3	14	33
Randall, Ken	Toronto	15	8	6	14	27
Cleghorn, Sprague	Ottawa	18	7	6	13	27

1919-20

First Half

Team	GP	W	L	T	GF	GA	PTS
Ottawa	12	9	3	0	59	23	18
Montreal	12	8	4	0	62	51	16
Toronto	12	5	7	0	52	62	10
Quebec	12	2	10	0	44	81	4

Second Half

Team	GP	W	L	T	GF	GA	PTS
*Ottawa	12	10	2	0	62	41	20
Montreal	12	5	7	0	67	62	10
Toronto	12	7	5	0	67	44	14
Quebec	12	2	10	0	47	96	4

Leading Scorers

Player	Club	GP	G	A	PTS	PIM
Malone, Joe	Quebec	24	39	10	49	12
Lalonde, Newsy	Montreal	23	37	9	46	34
Nighbor, Frank	Ottawa	23	26	15	41	18
Denneny, Corb	Toronto	24	24	12	36	20
Darragh, Jack	Ottawa	23	22	14	36	22
Noble, Reg	Toronto	24	24	9	33	52
Arbour, Amos	Montreal	22	21	5	26	13
Wilson, Cully	Toronto	23	20	6	26	86
Pitre, Didier	Montreal	22	14	12	26	6
Broadbent, Punch	Ottawa	21	19	6	25	40

1920-21

First Half

Team	GP	W	L	T	GF	GA	PTS
*Ottawa	10	8	2	0	49	23	16
Toronto	10	5	5	0	39	47	10
Montreal	10	4	6	0	37	51	8
Hamilton	10	3	7	0	34	38	6

Second Half

Team	GP	W	L	T	GF	GA	PTS
Toronto	14	10	4	0	66	53	20
Montreal	14	9	5	0	75	48	18
Ottawa	14	6	8	0	48	52	12
Hamilton	14	3	11	0	58	94	6

Leading Scorers

Player	Club	GP	G	A	PTS	PIM
Lalonde, Newsy	Montreal	24	33	10	43	36
Dye, Babe	Ham., Tor.	24	35	5	40	32
Denneny, Cy	Ottawa	24	34	5	39	10
Malone, Joe	Hamilton	20	28	9	37	6
Nighbor, Frank	Ottawa	24	19	10	29	10
Noble, Reg	Toronto	24	19	8	27	54
Cameron, Harry	Toronto	24	18	9	27	35
Prodgers, Goldie	Hamilton	24	18	9	27	8
Denneny, Corb	Toronto	20	19	7	26	29
Darragh, Jack	Ottawa	24	11	15	26	20

All-Time Standings of NHL Teams

(ranked by percentage)

Active Clubs

Team	Games	Wins	Losses	Ties	Goals For	Goals Against	Points*	Pts %	First Season
Montreal	5218	2714	1702	802	17458	13919	6234	.597	1917-18
Philadelphia	2604	1298	898	408	9117	7806	3007	.576	1967-68
Boston	5058	2408	1899	751	16536	15014	5573	.551	1924-25
Buffalo	2378	1112	890	376	8235	7428	2604	.547	1970-71
Edmonton	1666	791	660	215	6487	5949	1805	.540	1979-80
Calgary	2222	1012	878	332	8007	7451	2361	.529	1972-73
Detroit	4992	2163	2054	775	15509	15193	5103	.511	1926-27
NY Islanders	2222	976	936	310	7704	7248	2263	.508	1972-73
St. Louis	2604	1122	1092	390	8432	8513	2635	.505	1967-68
Florida	542	226	225	91	1480	1488	549	.503	1993-94
Toronto	5218	2249	2224	745	16234	16225	5246	.502	1917-18
NY Rangers	4992	2103	2107	782	15584	15687	4991	.499	1926-27
Colorado	1666	718	731	217	5931	5939	1654	.495	1979-80
Chicago	4992	2056	2167	769	15022	15197	4883	.489	1926-27
Washington	2066	872	930	264	6786	7087	2010	.485	1974-75
Pittsburgh	2604	1079	1173	352	9080	9496	2516	.482	1967-68
Dallas	2604	1034	1160	410	8280	8770	2484	.476	1967-68
Los Angeles	2604	1022	1204	378	8864	9511	2426	.465	1967-68
Anaheim	542	215	258	69	1470	1589	502	.460	1993-94
Phoenix	1666	657	798	211	5663	6242	1529	.458	1979-80
Carolina	1666	638	815	213	5331	5982	1489	.446	1979-80
New Jersey	2066	756	1025	285	6470	7435	1802	.435	1974-75
Vancouver	2378	858	1170	350	7666	8677	2074	.435	1970-71
Nashville	164	56	94	14	389	501	133	.390	1998-99
Ottawa	626	201	346	79	1613	2080	483	.384	1992-93
San Jose	706	227	399	80	1912	2455	541	.380	1991-92
Tampa Bay	626	195	360	71	1578	2093	468	.372	1992-93
Atlanta	82	14	61	7	170	313	39	.230	1999-2000

Defunct Clubs

Team	Games	Wins	Losses	Ties	Goals For	Goals Against	Points*	Pts %	First Season	Last Season
Ottawa Senators	542	258	221	63	1458	1333	579	.534	1917-18	1933-34
Montreal Maroons	622	271	260	91	1474	1405	633	.509	1924-25	1937-38
NY/Brooklyn Americans	784	255	402	127	1643	2182	637	.406	1925-26	1941-42
Hamilton Tigers	126	47	78	1	414	475	95	.377	1920-21	1924-25
Cleveland Barons	160	47	87	26	470	617	120	.375	1976-77	1977-78
Pittsburgh Pirates	212	67	122	23	376	519	157	.370	1925-26	1929-30
Calif./Oakland Seals	698	182	401	115	1826	2580	479	.343	1967-68	1975-76
St. Louis Eagles	48	11	31	6	86	144	28	.292	1934-35	1934-35
Quebec Bulldogs	24	4	20	0	91	177	8	.167	1919-20	1919-20
Montreal Wanderers	6	1	5	0	17	35	2	.167	1917-18	1917-18
Philadelphia Quakers	44	4	36	4	76	184	12	.136	1930-31	1930-31

Calgary totals include Atlanta Flames, 1972-73 to 1979-80.
Carolina totals include Hartford, 1979-80 to 1996-97.
Colorado totals include Quebec, 1979-80 to 1994-95.
Dallas totals include Minnesota North Stars, 1967-68 to 1992-93.
Detroit totals include Cougars, 1926-27 to 1929-30, and Falcons, 1930-31 to 1931-32.
New Jersey totals include Kansas City, 1974-75 to 1975-76, and Colorado Rockies, 1976-77 to 1981-82.
Phoenix totals include Winnipeg, 1979-80 to 1995-96.
Toronto totals include Arenas, 1917-18 to 1918-19, and St. Patricks, 1919-20 to 1925-56.

* includes regulation ties in 1999-2000.

1921-22

Team	GP	W	L	T	GF	GA	PTS
Ottawa	24	14	8	2	106	84	30
*Toronto	24	13	10	1	98	97	27
Montreal	24	12	11	1	88	94	25
Hamilton	24	7	17	0	88	105	14

Leading Scorers

Player	Club	GP	G	A	PTS	PIM
Broadbent, Punch	Ottawa	24	32	14	46	28
Denneny, Cy	Ottawa	22	27	12	39	20
Dye, Babe	Toronto	24	31	7	38	39
Cameron, Harry	Toronto	24	18	17	35	22
Malone, Joe	Hamilton	24	24	7	31	4
Denneny, Corb	Toronto	24	19	9	28	28
Noble, Reg	Toronto	24	17	11	28	19
Cleghorn, Sprague	Montreal	24	17	9	26	80
Cleghorn, Odie	Montreal	23	21	3	24	26
Reise Sr., Leo	Hamilton	24	9	14	23	11

1922-23

Team	GP	W	L	T	GF	GA	PTS
*Ottawa	24	14	9	1	77	54	29
Montreal	24	13	9	2	73	61	28
Toronto	24	13	10	1	82	88	27
Hamilton	24	6	18	0	81	110	12

Leading Scorers

Player	Club	GP	G	A	PTS	PIM
Dye, Babe	Toronto	22	26	11	37	19
Denneny, Cy	Ottawa	24	21	10	31	20
Adams, Jack	Toronto	23	19	9	28	42
Boucher, Billy	Montreal	24	23	4	27	52
Cleghorn, Odie	Montreal	24	19	7	26	14
Roach, Mickey	Hamilton	23	17	8	25	8
Boucher, George	Ottawa	23	15	9	24	44
Joliat, Aurel	Montreal	24	13	9	22	31
Noble, Reg	Toronto	24	12	10	22	41
Wilson, Cully	Hamilton	23	16	3	19	46

1923-24

Team	GP	W	L	T	GF	GA	PTS
Ottawa	24	16	8	0	74	54	32
*Montreal	24	13	11	0	59	48	26
Toronto	24	10	14	0	59	85	20
Hamilton	24	9	15	0	63	68	18

Leading Scorers

Player	Club	GP	G	A	PTS	PIM
Denneny, Cy	Ottawa	22	22	2	24	10
Boucher, George	Ottawa	21	13	10	23	38
Boucher, Billy	Montreal	23	16	6	22	48
Burch, Billy	Hamilton	24	16	6	22	6
Joliat, Aurel	Montreal	24	15	5	20	27
Dye, Babe	Toronto	19	16	3	19	23
Adams, Jack	Toronto	22	14	4	18	51
Noble, Reg	Toronto	23	12	5	17	79
Morenz, Howie	Montreal	24	13	3	16	20
Clancy, King	Ottawa	24	8	8	16	26

1924-25

Team	GP	W	L	T	GF	GA	PTS
Hamilton	30	19	10	1	90	60	39
Toronto	30	19	11	0	90	84	38
**Montreal	30	17	11	2	93	56	36
Ottawa	30	17	12	1	83	66	35
Mtl. Maroons	30	9	19	2	45	65	20
Boston	30	6	24	0	49	119	12

**NHL Champion (Stanley Cup won by Victoria Cougars, WCHL)

Leading Scorers

Player	Club	GP	G	A	PTS	PIM
Dye, Babe	Toronto	29	38	8	46	41
Denneny, Cy	Ottawa	29	27	15	42	16
Joliat, Aurel	Montreal	25	30	11	41	85
Morenz, Howie	Montreal	30	28	11	39	46
Green, Red	Hamilton	30	19	15	34	81
Adams, Jack	Toronto	27	21	10	31	67
Boucher, Billy	Montreal	30	17	13	30	92
Burch, Billy	Hamilton	27	20	7	27	10
Herbert, Jimmy	Boston	30	17	7	24	55
Smith, Hooley	Ottawa	30	10	13	23	81

1925-26

Team	GP	W	L	T	GF	GA	PTS
Ottawa	36	24	8	4	77	42	52
*Mtl. Maroons	36	20	11	5	91	73	45
Pittsburgh	36	19	16	1	82	70	39
Boston	36	17	15	4	92	85	38
NY Americans	36	12	20	4	68	89	28
Toronto	36	12	21	3	92	114	27
Montreal	36	11	24	1	79	108	23

Leading Scorers

Player	Club	GP	G	A	PTS	PIM
Stewart, Nels	Mtl. Maroons	36	34	8	42	119
Denneny, Cy	Ottawa	36	24	12	36	18
Cooper, Carson	Boston	36	28	3	31	10
Herbert, Jimmy	Boston	36	26	5	31	47
Morenz, Howie	Montreal	31	23	3	26	39
Adams, Jack	Toronto	36	21	5	26	52
Joliat, Aurel	Montreal	35	17	9	26	52
Burch, Billy	NY Americans	36	22	3	25	33
Smith, Hooley	Ottawa	28	16	9	25	53
Nighbor, Frank	Ottawa	35	12	13	25	40

1926-27

Canadian Division

Team	GP	W	L	T	GF	GA	PTS
*Ottawa	44	30	10	4	86	69	64
Montreal	44	28	14	2	99	67	58
Mtl. Maroons	44	20	20	4	71	68	44
NY Americans	44	17	25	2	82	91	36
Toronto	44	15	24	5	79	94	35

American Division

Team	GP	W	L	T	GF	GA	PTS
New York	44	25	13	6	95	72	56
Boston	44	21	20	3	97	89	45
Chicago	44	19	22	3	115	116	41
Pittsburgh	44	15	26	3	79	108	33
Detroit	44	12	28	4	76	105	28

Leading Scorers

Player	Club	GP	G	A	PTS	PIM
Cook, Bill	New York	44	33	4	37	58
Irvin, Dick	Chicago	43	18	18	36	34
Morenz, Howie	Montreal	44	25	7	32	49
Fredrickson, Frank	Det., Bos.	41	18	13	31	46
Dye, Babe	Chicago	41	25	5	30	14
Bailey, Ace	Toronto	42	15	13	28	82
Boucher, Frank	New York	44	13	15	28	17
Burch, Billy	NY Americans	43	19	8	27	40
Oliver, Harry	Boston	42	18	6	24	17
Keats, Duke	Bos., Det.	42	16	8	24	52

1927-28

Canadian Division

Team	GP	W	L	T	GF	GA	PTS
Montreal	44	26	11	7	116	48	59
Mtl. Maroons	44	24	14	6	96	77	54
Ottawa	44	20	14	10	78	57	50
Toronto	44	18	18	8	89	88	44
NY Americans	44	11	27	6	63	128	28

American Division

Team	GP	W	L	T	GF	GA	PTS
Boston	44	20	13	11	77	70	51
*New York	44	19	16	9	94	79	47
Pittsburgh	44	19	17	8	67	76	46
Detroit	44	19	19	6	88	79	44
Chicago	44	7	34	3	68	134	17

Leading Scorers

Player	Club	GP	G	A	PTS	PIM
Morenz, Howie	Montreal	43	33	18	51	66
Joliat, Aurel	Montreal	44	28	11	39	105
Boucher, Frank	New York	44	23	12	35	15
Hay, George	Detroit	42	22	13	35	20
Stewart, Nels	Mtl. Maroons	41	27	7	34	104
Gagne, Art	Montreal	44	20	10	30	75
Cook, Bun	New York	44	14	14	28	45
Carson, Bill	Toronto	32	20	6	26	36
Finnigan, Frank	Ottawa	38	20	5	25	34
Cook, Bill	New York	43	18	6	24	42
Keats, Duke	Det., Chi.	38	14	10	24	60

1928-29

Canadian Division

Team	GP	W	L	T	GF	GA	PTS
Montreal	44	22	7	15	71	43	59
NY Americans	44	19	13	12	53	53	50
Toronto	44	21	18	5	85	69	47
Ottawa	44	14	17	13	54	67	41
Mtl. Maroons	44	15	20	9	67	65	39

American Division

Team	GP	W	L	T	GF	GA	PTS
*Boston	44	26	13	5	89	52	57
New York	44	21	13	10	72	65	52
Detroit	44	19	16	9	72	63	47
Pittsburgh	44	9	27	8	46	80	26
Chicago	44	7	29	8	33	85	22

Leading Scorers

Player	Club	GP	G	A	PTS	PIM
Bailey, Ace	Toronto	44	22	10	32	78
Stewart, Nels	Mtl. Maroons	44	21	8	29	74
Cooper, Carson	Detroit	43	18	9	27	14
Morenz, Howie	Montreal	42	17	10	27	47
Blair, Andy	Toronto	44	12	15	27	41
Boucher, Frank	New York	44	10	16	26	8
Oliver, Harry	Boston	43	17	6	23	24
Cook, Bill	New York	43	15	8	23	41
Ward, Jimmy	Mtl. Maroons	43	14	8	22	46
Seven players tied with 19 points

1929-30

Canadian Division

Team	GP	W	L	T	GF	GA	PTS
Mtl. Maroons	44	23	16	5	141	114	51
*Montreal	44	21	14	9	142	114	51
Ottawa	44	21	15	8	138	118	50
Toronto	44	17	21	6	116	124	40
NY Americans	44	14	25	5	113	161	33

American Division

Team	GP	W	L	T	GF	GA	PTS
Boston	44	38	5	1	179	98	77
Chicago	44	21	18	5	117	111	47
New York	44	17	17	10	136	143	44
Detroit	44	14	24	6	117	133	34
Pittsburgh	44	5	36	3	102	185	13

Leading Scorers

Player	Club	GP	G	A	PTS	PIM
Weiland, Cooney	Boston	44	43	30	73	27
Boucher, Frank	New York	42	26	36	62	16
Clapper, Dit	Boston	44	41	20	61	48
Cook, Bill	New York	44	29	30	59	56
Kilrea, Hec	Ottawa	44	36	22	58	72
Stewart, Nels	Mtl. Maroons	44	39	16	55	81
Morenz, Howie	Montreal	44	40	10	50	72
Himes, Normie	NY Americans	44	28	22	50	15
Lamb, Joe	Ottawa	44	29	20	49	119
Gainor, Norm	Boston	42	18	31	49	39

1930-31

Canadian Division

Team	GP	W	L	T	GF	GA	PTS
*Montreal	44	26	10	8	129	89	60
Toronto	44	22	13	9	118	99	53
Mtl. Maroons	44	20	18	6	105	106	46
NY Americans	44	18	16	10	76	74	46
Ottawa	44	10	30	4	91	142	24

American Division

Team	GP	W	L	T	GF	GA	PTS
Boston	44	28	10	6	143	90	62
Chicago	44	24	17	3	108	78	51
New York	44	19	16	9	106	87	47
Detroit	44	16	21	7	102	105	39
Philadelphia	44	4	36	4	76	184	12

Leading Scorers

Player	Club	GP	G	A	PTS	PIM
Morenz, Howie	Montreal	39	28	23	51	49
Goodfellow, Ebbie	Detroit	44	25	23	48	32
Conacher, Charlie	Toronto	37	31	12	43	78
Cook, Bill	New York	43	30	12	42	39
Bailey, Ace	Toronto	40	23	19	42	46
Primeau, Joe	Toronto	38	9	32	41	18
Stewart, Nels	Mtl. Maroons	42	25	14	39	75
Boucher, Frank	New York	44	12	27	39	20
Weiland, Cooney	Boston	44	25	13	38	14
Cook, Bun	New York	44	18	17	35	72
Joliat, Aurel	Montreal	43	13	22	35	73

1931-32
Canadian Division

Team	GP	W	L	T	GF	GA	PTS
Montreal	48	25	16	7	128	111	57
*Toronto	48	23	18	7	155	127	53
Mtl. Maroons	48	19	22	7	142	139	45
NY Americans	48	16	24	8	95	142	40

American Division

Team	GP	W	L	T	GF	GA	PTS
New York	48	23	17	8	134	112	54
Chicago	48	18	19	11	86	101	47
Detroit	48	18	20	10	95	108	46
Boston	48	15	21	12	122	117	42

Leading Scorers

Player	Club	GP	G	A	PTS	PIM
Jackson, Harvey	Toronto	48	28	25	53	63
Primeau, Joe	Toronto	46	13	37	50	25
Morenz, Howie	Montreal	48	24	25	49	46
Conacher, Charlie	Toronto	44	34	14	48	66
Cook, Bill	New York	48	34	14	48	33
Trottier, Dave	Mtl. Maroons	48	26	18	44	94
Smith, Reg	Mtl. Maroons	43	11	33	44	49
Siebert, Babe	Mtl. Maroons	48	21	18	39	64
Clapper, Dit	Boston	48	17	22	39	21
Joliat, Aurel	Montreal	48	15	24	39	46

1932-33
Canadian Division

Team	GP	W	L	T	GF	GA	PTS
Toronto	48	24	18	6	119	111	54
Mtl. Maroons	48	22	20	6	135	119	50
Montreal	48	18	25	5	92	115	41
NY Americans	48	15	22	11	91	118	41
Ottawa	48	11	27	10	88	131	32

American Division

Team	GP	W	L	T	GF	GA	PTS
Boston	48	25	15	8	124	88	58
Detroit	48	25	15	8	111	93	58
*New York	48	23	17	8	135	107	54
Chicago	48	16	20	12	88	101	44

Leading Scorers

Player	Club	GP	G	A	PTS	PIM
Cook, Bill	New York	48	28	22	50	51
Jackson, Harvey	Toronto	48	27	17	44	43
Northcott, Baldy	Mtl. Maroons	48	22	21	43	30
Smith, Reg	Mtl. Maroons	48	20	21	41	66
Haynes, Paul	Mtl. Maroons	48	16	25	41	18
Joliat, Aurel	Montreal	48	18	21	39	53
Barry, Marty	Boston	48	24	13	37	40
Cook, Bun	New York	48	22	15	37	35
Stewart, Nels	Boston	47	18	18	36	62
Morenz, Howie	Montreal	46	14	21	35	32
Gagnon, Johnny	Montreal	48	12	23	35	64
Shore, Eddie	Boston	48	8	27	35	102
Boucher, Frank	New York	47	7	28	35	4

1933-34
Canadian Division

Team	GP	W	L	T	GF	GA	PTS
Toronto	48	26	13	9	174	119	61
Montreal	48	22	20	6	99	101	50
Mtl. Maroons	48	19	18	11	117	122	49
NY Americans	48	15	23	10	104	132	40
Ottawa	48	13	29	6	115	143	32

American Division

Team	GP	W	L	T	GF	GA	PTS
Detroit	48	24	14	10	113	98	58
*Chicago	48	20	17	11	88	83	51
New York	48	21	19	8	120	113	50
Boston	48	18	25	5	111	130	41

Leading Scorers

Player	Club	GP	G	A	PTS	PIM
Conacher, Charlie	Toronto	42	32	20	52	38
Primeau, Joe	Toronto	45	14	32	46	8
Boucher, Frank	New York	48	14	30	44	4
Barry, Marty	Boston	48	27	12	39	12
Dillon, Cecil	New York	48	13	26	39	10
Stewart, Nels	Boston	48	21	17	38	68
Jackson, Harvey	Toronto	38	20	18	38	38
Joliat, Aurel	Montreal	48	22	15	37	27
Smith, Reg	Mtl. Maroons	47	18	19	37	58
Thompson, Paul	Chicago	48	20	16	36	17

1934-35
Canadian Division

Team	GP	W	L	T	GF	GA	PTS
Toronto	48	30	14	4	157	111	64
*Mtl. Maroons	48	24	19	5	123	92	53
Montreal	48	19	23	6	110	145	44
NY Americans	48	12	27	9	100	142	33
St. Louis	48	11	31	6	86	144	28

American Division

Team	GP	W	L	T	GF	GA	PTS
Boston	48	26	16	6	129	112	58
Chicago	48	26	17	5	118	88	57
New York	48	22	20	6	137	139	50
Detroit	48	19	22	7	127	114	45

Leading Scorers

Player	Club	GP	G	A	PTS	PIM
Conacher, Charlie	Toronto	47	36	21	57	24
Howe, Syd	St.L., Det.	50	22	25	47	34
Aurie, Larry	Detroit	48	17	29	46	24
Boucher, Frank	New York	48	13	32	45	2
Jackson, Harvey	Toronto	42	22	22	44	27
Lewis, Herb	Detroit	47	16	27	43	26
Chapman, Art	NY Americans	47	9	34	43	4
Barry, Marty	Boston	48	20	20	40	33
Schriner, Sweeney	NY Americans	48	18	22	40	6
Stewart, Nels	Boston	47	21	18	39	45
Thompson, Paul	Chicago	48	16	23	39	20

1935-36
Canadian Division

Team	GP	W	L	T	GF	GA	PTS
Mtl. Maroons	48	22	16	10	114	106	54
Toronto	48	23	19	6	126	106	52
NY Americans	48	16	25	7	109	122	39
Montreal	48	11	26	11	82	123	33

American Division

Team	GP	W	L	T	GF	GA	PTS
*Detroit	48	24	16	8	124	103	56
Boston	48	22	20	6	92	83	50
Chicago	48	21	19	8	93	92	50
New York	48	19	17	12	91	96	50

Leading Scorers

Player	Club	GP	G	A	PTS	PIM
Schriner, Sweeney	NY Americans	48	19	26	45	8
Barry, Marty	Detroit	48	21	19	40	16
Thompson, Paul	Chicago	45	17	23	40	19
Thoms, Bill	Toronto	48	23	15	38	29
Conacher, Charlie	Toronto	44	23	15	38	74
Smith, Reg	Mtl. Maroons	47	19	19	38	75
Romnes, Doc	Chicago	48	13	25	38	6
Chapman, Art	NY Americans	47	10	28	38	14
Lewis, Herb	Detroit	45	14	23	37	25
Northcott, Baldy	Mtl. Maroons	48	15	21	36	41

1936-37
Canadian Division

Team	GP	W	L	T	GF	GA	PTS
Montreal	48	24	18	6	115	111	54
Mtl. Maroons	48	22	17	9	126	110	53
Toronto	48	22	21	5	119	115	49
NY Americans	48	15	29	4	122	161	34

American Division

Team	GP	W	L	T	GF	GA	PTS
*Detroit	48	25	14	9	128	102	59
Boston	48	23	18	7	120	110	53
New York	48	19	20	9	117	106	47
Chicago	48	14	27	7	99	131	35

Leading Scorers

Player	Club	GP	G	A	PTS	PIM
Schriner, Sweeney	NY Americans	48	21	25	46	17
Apps Sr., Syl	Toronto	48	16	29	45	10
Barry, Marty	Detroit	48	17	27	44	6
Aurie, Larry	Detroit	45	23	20	43	20
Jackson, Harvey	Toronto	46	21	19	40	12
Gagnon, Johnny	Montreal	48	20	16	36	38
Gracie, Bob	Mtl. Maroons	47	11	25	36	18
Stewart, Nels	Bos., NYA	43	23	12	35	37
Thompson, Paul	Chicago	47	17	18	35	28
Cowley, Bill	Boston	46	13	22	35	4

1937-38
Canadian Division

Team	GP	W	L	T	GF	GA	PTS
Toronto	48	24	15	9	151	127	57
NY Americans	48	19	18	11	110	111	49
Montreal	48	18	17	13	123	128	49
Mtl. Maroons	48	12	30	6	101	149	30

American Division

Team	GP	W	L	T	GF	GA	PTS
Boston	48	30	11	7	142	89	67
New York	48	27	15	6	149	96	60
*Chicago	48	14	25	9	97	139	37
Detroit	48	12	25	11	99	133	35

Leading Scorers

Player	Club	GP	G	A	PTS	PIM
Drillon, Gordie	Toronto	48	26	26	52	4
Apps Sr., Syl	Toronto	47	21	29	50	9
Thompson, Paul	Chicago	48	22	22	44	14
Mantha, Georges	Montreal	47	23	19	42	12
Dillon, Cecil	New York	48	21	18	39	6
Cowley, Bill	Boston	48	17	22	39	8
Schriner, Sweeney	NY Americans	49	21	17	38	22
Thoms, Bill	Toronto	48	14	24	38	14
Smith, Clint	New York	48	14	23	37	0
Stewart, Nels	NY Americans	48	19	17	36	29
Colville, Neil	New York	45	17	19	36	11

1938-39

Team	GP	W	L	T	GF	GA	PTS
*Boston	48	36	10	2	156	76	74
New York	48	26	16	6	149	105	58
Toronto	48	19	20	9	114	107	47
NY Americans	48	17	21	10	119	157	44
Detroit	48	18	24	6	107	128	42
Montreal	48	15	24	9	115	146	39
Chicago	48	12	28	8	91	132	32

Leading Scorers

Player	Club	GP	G	A	PTS	PIM
Blake, Toe	Montreal	48	24	23	47	10
Schriner, Sweeney	NY Americans	48	13	31	44	20
Cowley, Bill	Boston	34	8	34	42	2
Smith, Clint	New York	48	21	20	41	2
Barry, Marty	Detroit	48	13	28	41	4
Apps Sr., Syl	Toronto	44	15	25	40	4
Anderson, Tom	NY Americans	48	13	27	40	14
Gottselig, Johnny	Chicago	48	16	23	39	15
Haynes, Paul	Montreal	47	5	33	38	2
Conacher, Roy	Boston	47	26	11	37	12
Carr, Lorne	NY Americans	46	19	18	37	16
Colville, Neil	New York	48	18	19	37	12
Watson, Phil	New York	48	15	22	37	42

1939-40

Team	GP	W	L	T	GF	GA	PTS
Boston	48	31	12	5	170	98	67
*New York	48	27	11	10	136	77	64
Toronto	48	25	17	6	134	110	56
Chicago	48	23	19	6	112	120	52
Detroit	48	16	26	6	90	126	38
NY Americans	48	15	29	4	106	140	34
Montreal	48	10	33	5	90	168	25

Leading Scorers

Player	Club	GP	G	A	PTS	PIM
Schmidt, Milt	Boston	48	22	30	52	37
Dumart, Woody	Boston	48	22	21	43	16
Bauer, Bobby	Boston	48	17	26	43	2
Drillon, Gordie	Toronto	43	21	19	40	13
Cowley, Bill	Boston	48	13	27	40	24
Hextall Sr., Bryan	New York	48	24	15	39	52
Colville, Neil	New York	48	19	19	38	22
Howe, Syd	Detroit	46	14	23	37	17
Blake, Toe	Montreal	48	17	19	36	48
Armstrong, Murray	NY Americans	48	16	20	36	12

Toe Blake won the NHL scoring title in 1938-39 and ranked among the league's top scorers five more times in the next seven years.

Herb Cain (with coach Art Ross) set a new NHL scoring record of 82 points in 1943-44. Cain is the only retired NHL scoring champion not enshrined in the Hockey Hall of Fame.

1940-41

Team	GP	W	L	T	GF	GA	PTS
*Boston	48	27	8	13	168	102	67
Toronto	48	28	14	6	145	99	62
Detroit	48	21	16	11	112	102	53
New York	48	21	19	8	143	125	50
Chicago	48	16	25	7	112	139	39
Montreal	48	16	26	6	121	147	38
NY Americans	48	8	29	11	99	186	27

Leading Scorers

Player	Club	GP	G	A	PTS	PIM
Cowley, Bill	Boston	46	17	45	62	16
Hextall Sr., Bryan	New York	48	26	18	44	16
Drillon, Gordie	Toronto	42	23	21	44	2
Apps Sr., Syl	Toronto	41	20	24	44	6
Patrick, Lynn	New York	48	20	24	44	12
Howe, Syd	Detroit	48	20	24	44	8
Colville, Neil	New York	48	14	28	42	28
Wiseman, Eddie	Boston	48	16	24	40	10
Bauer, Bobby	Boston	48	17	22	39	2
Schriner, Sweeney	Toronto	48	24	14	38	6
Conacher, Roy	Boston	40	24	14	38	7
Schmidt, Milt	Boston	44	13	25	38	23

1941-42

Team	GP	W	L	T	GF	GA	PTS
New York	48	29	17	2	177	143	60
*Toronto	48	27	18	3	158	136	57
Boston	48	25	17	6	160	118	56
Chicago	48	22	23	3	145	155	47
Detroit	48	19	25	4	140	147	42
Montreal	48	18	27	3	134	173	39
Brooklyn	48	16	29	3	133	175	35

Leading Scorers

Player	Club	GP	G	A	PTS	PIM
Hextall Sr., Bryan	New York	48	24	32	56	30
Patrick, Lynn	New York	47	32	22	54	18
Grosso, Don	Detroit	48	23	30	53	13
Watson, Phil	New York	48	15	37	52	48
Abel, Sid	Detroit	48	18	31	49	45
Blake, Toe	Montreal	47	17	28	45	19
Thoms, Bill	Chicago	47	15	30	45	8
Drillon, Gordie	Toronto	48	23	18	41	6
Apps Sr., Syl	Toronto	38	18	23	41	0
Anderson, Tom	Brooklyn	48	12	29	41	54

1942-43

Team	GP	W	L	T	GF	GA	PTS
*Detroit	50	25	14	11	169	124	61
Boston	50	24	17	9	195	176	57
Toronto	50	22	19	9	198	159	53
Montreal	50	19	19	12	181	191	50
Chicago	50	17	18	15	179	180	49
New York	50	11	31	8	161	253	30

Leading Scorers

Player	Club	GP	G	A	PTS	PIM
Bentley, Doug	Chicago	50	33	40	73	18
Cowley, Bill	Boston	48	27	45	72	10
Bentley, Max	Chicago	47	26	44	70	2
Patrick, Lynn	New York	50	22	39	61	28
Carr, Lorne	Toronto	50	27	33	60	15
Taylor, Billy	Toronto	50	18	42	60	2
Hextall Sr., Bryan	New York	50	27	32	59	28
Blake, Toe	Montreal	48	23	36	59	28
Lach, Elmer	Montreal	45	18	40	58	14
O'Connor, Buddy	Montreal	50	15	43	58	2

1943-44

Team	GP	W	L	T	GF	GA	PTS
*Montreal	50	38	5	7	234	109	83
Detroit	50	26	18	6	214	177	58
Toronto	50	23	23	4	214	174	50
Chicago	50	22	23	5	178	187	49
Boston	50	19	26	5	223	268	43
New York	50	6	39	5	162	310	17

Leading Scorers

Player	Club	GP	G	A	PTS	PIM
Cain, Herb	Boston	48	36	46	82	4
Bentley, Doug	Chicago	50	38	39	77	22
Carr, Lorne	Toronto	50	36	38	74	9
Liscombe, Carl	Detroit	50	36	37	73	17
Lach, Elmer	Montreal	48	24	48	72	23
Smith, Clint	Chicago	50	23	49	72	4
Cowley, Bill	Boston	36	30	41	71	12
Mosienko, Bill	Chicago	50	32	38	70	10
Jackson, Art	Boston	49	28	41	69	8
Bodnar, Gus	Toronto	50	22	40	62	18

1944-45

Team	GP	W	L	T	GF	GA	PTS
Montreal	50	38	8	4	228	121	80
Detroit	50	31	14	5	218	161	67
*Toronto	50	24	22	4	183	161	52
Boston	50	16	30	4	179	219	36
Chicago	50	13	30	7	141	194	33
New York	50	11	29	10	154	247	32

Leading Scorers

Player	Club	GP	G	A	PTS	PIM
Lach, Elmer	Montreal	50	26	54	80	37
Richard, Maurice	Montreal	50	50	23	73	36
Blake, Toe	Montreal	49	29	38	67	15
Cowley, Bill	Boston	49	25	40	65	2
Kennedy, Ted	Toronto	49	29	25	54	14
Mosienko, Bill	Chicago	50	28	26	54	0
Carveth, Joe	Detroit	50	26	28	54	6
DeMarco Sr., Ab	New York	50	24	30	54	10
Smith, Clint	Chicago	50	23	31	54	0
Howe, Syd	Detroit	46	17	36	53	6

1945-46

Team	GP	W	L	T	GF	GA	PTS
*Montreal	50	28	17	5	172	134	61
Boston	50	24	18	8	167	156	56
Chicago	50	23	20	7	200	178	53
Detroit	50	20	20	10	146	159	50
Toronto	50	19	24	7	174	185	45
New York	50	13	28	9	144	191	35

Leading Scorers

Player	Club	GP	G	A	PTS	PIM
Bentley, Max	Chicago	47	31	30	61	6
Stewart, Gaye	Toronto	50	37	15	52	8
Blake, Toe	Montreal	50	29	21	50	2
Smith, Clint	Chicago	50	26	24	50	2
Richard, Maurice	Montreal	50	27	21	48	50
Mosienko, Bill	Chicago	40	18	30	48	12
DeMarco Sr., Ab	New York	50	20	27	47	20
Lach, Elmer	Montreal	50	13	34	47	34
Kaleta, Alex	Chicago	49	19	27	46	17
Taylor, Billy	Toronto	48	23	18	41	14
Horeck, Pete	Chicago	50	20	21	41	34

1946-47

Team	GP	W	L	T	GF	GA	PTS
Montreal	60	34	16	10	189	138	78
*Toronto	60	31	19	10	209	172	72
Boston	60	26	23	11	190	175	63
Detroit	60	22	27	11	190	193	55
New York	60	22	32	6	167	186	50
Chicago	60	19	37	4	193	274	42

Leading Scorers

Player	Club	GP	G	A	PTS	PIM
Bentley, Max	Chicago	60	29	43	72	12
Richard, Maurice	Montreal	60	45	26	71	69
Taylor, Billy	Detroit	60	17	46	63	35
Schmidt, Milt	Boston	59	27	35	62	40
Kennedy, Ted	Toronto	60	28	32	60	27
Bentley, Doug	Chicago	52	21	34	55	18
Bauer, Bobby	Boston	58	30	24	54	4
Conacher, Roy	Detroit	60	30	24	54	6
Mosienko, Bill	Chicago	59	25	27	52	2
Dumart, Woody	Boston	60	24	28	52	12

1947-48

Team	GP	W	L	T	GF	GA	PTS
*Toronto	60	32	15	13	182	143	77
Detroit	60	30	18	12	187	148	72
Boston	60	23	24	13	167	168	59
New York	60	21	26	13	176	201	55
Montreal	60	20	29	11	147	169	51
Chicago	60	20	34	6	195	225	46

Leading Scorers

Player	Club	GP	G	A	PTS	PIM
Lach, Elmer	Montreal	60	30	31	61	72
O'Connor, Buddy	New York	60	24	36	60	8
Bentley, Doug	Chicago	60	20	37	57	16
Stewart, Gaye	Tor., Chi.	61	27	29	56	83
Bentley, Max	Chi., Tor.	59	26	28	54	14
Poile, Bud	Tor., Chi.	58	25	29	54	17
Richard, Maurice	Montreal	53	28	25	53	89
Apps Sr., Syl	Toronto	55	26	27	53	12
Lindsay, Ted	Detroit	60	33	19	52	95
Conacher, Roy	Chicago	52	22	27	49	4

1948-49

Team	GP	W	L	T	GF	GA	PTS
Detroit	60	34	19	7	195	145	75
Boston	60	29	23	8	178	163	66
Montreal	60	28	23	9	152	126	65
*Toronto	60	22	25	13	147	161	57
Chicago	60	21	31	8	173	211	50
New York	60	18	31	11	133	172	47

Leading Scorers

Player	Club	GP	G	A	PTS	PIM
Conacher, Roy	Chicago	60	26	42	68	8
Bentley, Doug	Chicago	58	23	43	66	38
Abel, Sid	Detroit	60	28	26	54	49
Lindsay, Ted	Detroit	50	26	28	54	97
Conacher, Jim	Det., Chi.	59	26	23	49	43
Ronty, Paul	Boston	60	20	29	49	11
Watson, Harry	Toronto	60	26	19	45	0
Reay, Billy	Montreal	60	22	23	45	33
Bodnar, Gus	Chicago	59	19	26	45	14
Peirson, Johnny	Boston	59	22	21	43	45

1949-50

Team	GP	W	L	T	GF	GA	PTS
*Detroit	70	37	19	14	229	164	88
Montreal	70	29	22	19	172	150	77
Toronto	70	31	27	12	176	173	74
New York	70	28	31	11	170	189	67
Boston	70	22	32	16	198	228	60
Chicago	70	22	38	10	203	244	54

Leading Scorers

Player	Club	GP	G	A	PTS	PIM
Lindsay, Ted	Detroit	69	23	55	78	141
Abel, Sid	Detroit	69	34	35	69	46
Howe, Gordie	Detroit	70	35	33	68	69
Richard, Maurice	Montreal	70	43	22	65	114
Ronty, Paul	Boston	70	23	36	59	8
Conacher, Roy	Chicago	70	25	31	56	16
Bentley, Doug	Chicago	64	20	33	53	28
Peirson, Johnny	Boston	57	27	25	52	49
Prystai, Metro	Chicago	65	29	22	51	31
Guidolin, Bep	Chicago	70	17	34	51	42

Teeder Kennedy's hustle made him a fan favorite in Toronto. The future Leafs captain made his first appearance among the NHL's scoring leaders in 1944-45. Ten years later, he became the last Toronto player to date to win the Hart Trophy as MVP.

1950-51

Team	GP	W	L	T	GF	GA	PTS
Detroit	70	44	13	13	236	139	101
*Toronto	70	41	16	13	212	138	95
Montreal	70	25	30	15	173	184	65
Boston	70	22	30	18	178	197	62
New York	70	20	29	21	169	201	61
Chicago	70	13	47	10	171	280	36

Leading Scorers

Player	Club	GP	G	A	PTS	PIM
Howe, Gordie	Detroit	70	43	43	86	74
Richard, Maurice	Montreal	65	42	24	66	97
Bentley, Max	Toronto	67	21	41	62	34
Abel, Sid	Detroit	69	23	38	61	30
Schmidt, Milt	Boston	62	22	39	61	33
Kennedy, Ted	Toronto	63	18	43	61	32
Lindsay, Ted	Detroit	67	24	35	59	110
Sloan, Tod	Toronto	70	31	25	56	105
Kelly, Red	Detroit	70	17	37	54	24
Smith, Sid	Toronto	70	30	21	51	10
Gardner, Cal	Toronto	66	23	28	51	42

1951-52

Team	GP	W	L	T	GF	GA	PTS
*Detroit	70	44	14	12	215	133	100
Montreal	70	34	26	10	195	164	78
Toronto	70	29	25	16	168	157	74
Boston	70	25	29	16	162	176	66
New York	70	23	34	13	192	219	59
Chicago	70	17	44	9	158	241	43

Leading Scorers

Player	Club	GP	G	A	PTS	PIM
Howe, Gordie	Detroit	70	47	39	86	78
Lindsay, Ted	Detroit	70	30	39	69	123
Lach, Elmer	Montreal	70	15	50	65	36
Raleigh, Don	New York	70	19	42	61	14
Smith, Sid	Toronto	70	27	30	57	6
Geoffrion, Bernie	Montreal	67	30	24	54	66
Mosienko, Bill	Chicago	70	31	22	53	10
Abel, Sid	Detroit	62	17	36	53	32
Kennedy, Ted	Toronto	70	19	33	52	33
Schmidt, Milt	Boston	69	21	29	50	57
Peirson, Johnny	Boston	68	20	30	50	30

1952-53

Team	GP	W	L	T	GF	GA	PTS
Detroit	70	36	16	18	222	133	90
*Montreal	70	28	23	19	155	148	75
Boston	70	28	29	13	152	172	69
Chicago	70	27	28	15	169	175	69
Toronto	70	27	30	13	156	167	67
New York	70	17	37	16	152	211	50

Leading Scorers

Player	Club	GP	G	A	PTS	PIM
Howe, Gordie	Detroit	70	49	46	95	57
Lindsay, Ted	Detroit	70	32	39	71	111
Richard, Maurice	Montreal	70	28	33	61	112
Hergesheimer, Wally	New York	70	30	29	59	10
Delvecchio, Alex	Detroit	70	16	43	59	28
Ronty, Paul	New York	70	16	38	54	20
Prystai, Metro	Detroit	70	16	34	50	12
Kelly, Red	Detroit	70	19	27	46	8
Olmstead, Bert	Montreal	69	17	28	45	83
Mackell, Fleming	Boston	65	27	17	44	63
McFadden, Jim	Chicago	70	23	21	44	29

1953-54

Team	GP	W	L	T	GF	GA	PTS
*Detroit	70	37	19	14	191	132	88
Montreal	70	35	24	11	195	141	81
Toronto	70	32	24	14	152	131	78
Boston	70	32	28	10	177	181	74
New York	70	29	31	10	161	182	68
Chicago	70	12	51	7	133	242	31

Leading Scorers

Player	Club	GP	G	A	PTS	PIM
Howe, Gordie	Detroit	70	33	48	81	109
Richard, Maurice	Montreal	70	37	30	67	112
Lindsay, Ted	Detroit	70	26	36	62	110
Geoffrion, Bernie	Montreal	54	29	25	54	87
Olmstead, Bert	Montreal	70	15	37	52	85
Kelly, Red	Detroit	62	16	33	49	18
Reibel, Earl	Detroit	69	15	33	48	18
Sandford, Ed	Boston	70	16	31	47	42
Mackell, Fleming	Boston	67	15	32	47	60
Mosdell, Kenny	Montreal	67	22	24	46	64
Ronty, Paul	New York	70	13	33	46	18

1954-55

Team	GP	W	L	T	GF	GA	PTS
*Detroit	70	42	17	11	204	134	95
Montreal	70	41	18	11	228	157	93
Toronto	70	24	24	22	147	135	70
Boston	70	23	26	21	169	188	67
New York	70	17	35	18	150	210	52
Chicago	70	13	40	17	161	235	43

Leading Scorers

Player	Club	GP	G	A	PTS	PIM
Geoffrion, Bernie	Montreal	70	38	37	75	57
Richard, Maurice	Montreal	67	38	36	74	125
Béliveau, Jean	Montreal	70	37	36	73	58
Reibel, Earl	Detroit	70	25	41	66	15
Howe, Gordie	Detroit	64	29	33	62	68
Sullivan, Red	Chicago	69	19	42	61	51
Olmstead, Bert	Montreal	70	10	48	58	103
Smith, Sid	Toronto	70	33	21	54	14
Mosdell, Kenny	Montreal	70	22	32	54	82
Lewicki, Danny	New York	70	29	24	53	8

1955-56

Team	GP	W	L	T	GF	GA	PTS
*Montreal	70	45	15	10	222	131	100
Detroit	70	30	24	16	183	148	76
New York	70	32	28	10	204	203	74
Toronto	70	24	33	13	153	181	61
Boston	70	23	34	13	147	185	59
Chicago	70	19	39	12	155	216	50

Leading Scorers

Player	Club	GP	G	A	PTS	PIM
Béliveau, Jean	Montreal	70	47	41	88	143
Howe, Gordie	Detroit	70	38	41	79	100
Richard, Maurice	Montreal	70	38	33	71	89
Olmstead, Bert	Montreal	70	14	56	70	94
Sloan, Tod	Toronto	70	37	29	66	100
Bathgate, Andy	New York	70	19	47	66	59
Geoffrion, Bernie	Montreal	59	29	33	62	66
Reibel, Earl	Detroit	68	17	39	56	10
Delvecchio, Alex	Detroit	70	25	26	51	24
Creighton, Dave	New York	70	20	31	51	43
Gadsby, Bill	New York	70	9	42	51	84

1956-57

Team	GP	W	L	T	GF	GA	PTS
Detroit	70	38	20	12	198	157	88
*Montreal	70	35	23	12	210	155	82
Boston	70	34	24	12	195	174	80
New York	70	26	30	14	184	227	66
Toronto	70	21	34	15	174	192	57
Chicago	70	16	39	15	169	225	47

Leading Scorers

Player	Club	GP	G	A	PTS	PIM
Howe, Gordie	Detroit	70	44	45	89	72
Lindsay, Ted	Detroit	70	30	55	85	103
Béliveau, Jean	Montreal	69	33	51	84	105
Bathgate, Andy	New York	70	27	50	77	60
Litzenberger, Ed	Chicago	70	32	32	64	48
Richard, Maurice	Montreal	63	33	29	62	74
McKenney, Don	Boston	69	21	39	60	31
Moore, Dickie	Montreal	70	29	29	58	56
Richard, Henri	Montreal	63	18	36	54	71
Ullman, Norm	Detroit	64	16	36	52	47

1957-58

Team	GP	W	L	T	GF	GA	PTS
*Montreal	70	43	17	10	250	158	96
New York	70	32	25	13	195	188	77
Detroit	70	29	29	12	176	207	70
Boston	70	27	28	15	199	194	69
Chicago	70	24	39	7	163	202	55
Toronto	70	21	38	11	192	226	53

Leading Scorers

Player	Club	GP	G	A	PTS	PIM
Moore, Dickie	Montreal	70	36	48	84	65
Richard, Henri	Montreal	67	28	52	80	56
Bathgate, Andy	New York	65	30	48	78	42
Howe, Gordie	Detroit	64	33	44	77	40
Horvath, Bronco	Boston	67	30	36	66	71
Litzenberger, Ed	Chicago	70	32	30	62	63
Mackell, Fleming	Boston	70	20	40	60	72
Béliveau, Jean	Montreal	55	27	32	59	93
Delvecchio, Alex	Detroit	70	21	38	59	22
McKenney, Don	Boston	70	28	30	58	22

1958-59

Team	GP	W	L	T	GF	GA	PTS
*Montreal	70	39	18	13	258	158	91
Boston	70	32	29	9	205	215	73
Chicago	70	28	29	13	197	208	69
Toronto	70	27	32	11	189	201	65
New York	70	26	32	12	201	217	64
Detroit	70	25	37	8	167	218	58

Leading Scorers

Player	Club	GP	G	A	PTS	PIM
Moore, Dickie	Montreal	70	41	55	96	61
Béliveau, Jean	Montreal	64	45	46	91	67
Bathgate, Andy	New York	70	40	48	88	48
Howe, Gordie	Detroit	70	32	46	78	57
Litzenberger, Ed	Chicago	70	33	44	77	37
Geoffrion, Bernie	Montreal	59	22	44	66	30
Sullivan, Red	New York	70	21	42	63	56
Hebenton, Andy	New York	70	33	29	62	8
McKenney, Don	Boston	70	32	30	62	20
Sloan, Tod	Chicago	59	27	35	62	79

1959-60

Team	GP	W	L	T	GF	GA	PTS
*Montreal	70	40	18	12	255	178	92
Toronto	70	35	26	9	199	195	79
Chicago	70	28	29	13	191	180	69
Detroit	70	26	29	15	186	197	67
Boston	70	28	34	8	220	241	64
New York	70	17	38	15	187	247	49

Leading Scorers

Player	Club	GP	G	A	PTS	PIM
Hull, Bobby	Chicago	70	39	42	81	68
Horvath, Bronco	Boston	68	39	41	80	60
Béliveau, Jean	Montreal	60	34	40	74	57
Bathgate, Andy	New York	70	26	48	74	28
Richard, Henri	Montreal	70	30	43	73	66
Howe, Gordie	Detroit	70	28	45	73	46
Geoffrion, Bernie	Montreal	59	30	41	71	36
McKenney, Don	Boston	70	20	49	69	28
Stasiuk, Vic	Boston	69	29	39	68	121
Prentice, Dean	New York	70	32	34	66	43

1960-61

Team	GP	W	L	T	GF	GA	PTS
Montreal	70	41	19	10	254	188	92
Toronto	70	39	19	12	234	176	90
*Chicago	70	29	24	17	198	180	75
Detroit	70	25	29	16	195	215	66
New York	70	22	38	10	204	248	54
Boston	70	15	42	13	176	254	43

Leading Scorers

Player	Club	GP	G	A	PTS	PIM
Geoffrion, Bernie	Montreal	64	50	45	95	29
Béliveau, Jean	Montreal	69	32	58	90	57
Mahovlich, Frank	Toronto	70	48	36	84	131
Bathgate, Andy	New York	70	29	48	77	22
Howe, Gordie	Detroit	64	23	49	72	30
Ullman, Norm	Detroit	70	28	42	70	34
Kelly, Red	Toronto	64	20	50	70	12
Moore, Dickie	Montreal	57	35	34	69	62
Richard, Henri	Montreal	70	24	44	68	91
Delvecchio, Alex	Detroit	70	27	35	62	26

1961-62

Team	GP	W	L	T	GF	GA	PTS
Montreal	70	42	14	14	259	166	98
*Toronto	70	37	22	11	232	180	85
Chicago	70	31	26	13	217	186	75
New York	70	26	32	12	195	207	64
Detroit	70	23	33	14	184	219	60
Boston	70	15	47	8	177	306	38

Leading Scorers

Player	Club	GP	G	A	PTS	PIM
Hull, Bobby	Chicago	70	50	34	84	35
Bathgate, Andy	New York	70	28	56	84	44
Howe, Gordie	Detroit	70	33	44	77	54
Mikita, Stan	Chicago	70	25	52	77	97
Mahovlich, Frank	Toronto	70	33	38	71	87
Delvecchio, Alex	Detroit	70	26	43	69	18
Backstrom, Ralph	Montreal	66	27	38	65	29
Ullman, Norm	Detroit	70	26	38	64	54
Hay, Bill	Chicago	60	11	52	63	34
Provost, Claude	Montreal	70	33	29	62	22

The NHL's first 50-goal scorer poses with the next two. Maurice Richard had 50 goals in 50 games in 1944-45. Bernie Geoffrion scored 50 during a 70-game season in 1960-61, as did Bobby Hull in 1961-62.

1962-63

Team	GP	W	L	T	GF	GA	PTS
*Toronto	70	35	23	12	221	180	82
Chicago	70	32	21	17	194	178	81
Montreal	70	28	19	23	225	183	79
Detroit	70	32	25	13	200	194	77
New York	70	22	36	12	211	233	56
Boston	70	14	39	17	198	281	45

Leading Scorers

Player	Club	GP	G	A	PTS	PIM
Howe, Gordie	Detroit	70	38	48	86	100
Bathgate, Andy	New York	70	35	46	81	54
Mikita, Stan	Chicago	65	31	45	76	69
Mahovlich, Frank	Toronto	67	36	37	73	56
Richard, Henri	Montreal	67	23	50	73	57
Béliveau, Jean	Montreal	69	18	49	67	68
Bucyk, John	Boston	69	27	39	66	36
Delvecchio, Alex	Detroit	70	20	44	64	8
Hull, Bobby	Chicago	65	31	31	62	27
Oliver, Murray	Boston	65	22	40	62	38

1963-64

Team	GP	W	L	T	GF	GA	PTS
Montreal	70	36	21	13	209	167	85
Chicago	70	36	22	12	218	169	84
*Toronto	70	33	25	12	192	172	78
Detroit	70	30	29	11	191	204	71
New York	70	22	38	10	186	242	54
Boston	70	18	40	12	170	212	48

Leading Scorers

Player	Club	GP	G	A	PTS	PIM
Mikita, Stan	Chicago	70	39	50	89	146
Hull, Bobby	Chicago	70	43	44	87	50
Béliveau, Jean	Montreal	68	28	50	78	42
Bathgate, Andy	NYR, Tor.	71	19	58	77	34
Howe, Gordie	Detroit	69	26	47	73	70
Wharram, Kenny	Chicago	70	39	32	71	18
Oliver, Murray	Boston	70	24	44	68	41
Goyette, Phil	New York	67	24	41	65	15
Gilbert, Rod	New York	70	24	40	64	62
Keon, Dave	Toronto	70	23	37	60	6

1964-65

Team	GP	W	L	T	GF	GA	PTS
Detroit	70	40	23	7	224	175	87
*Montreal	70	36	23	11	211	185	83
Chicago	70	34	28	8	224	176	76
Toronto	70	30	26	14	204	173	74
New York	70	20	38	12	179	246	52
Boston	70	21	43	6	166	253	48

Leading Scorers

Player	Club	GP	G	A	PTS	PIM
Mikita, Stan	Chicago	70	28	59	87	154
Ullman, Norm	Detroit	70	42	41	83	70
Howe, Gordie	Detroit	70	29	47	76	104
Hull, Bobby	Chicago	61	39	32	71	32
Delvecchio, Alex	Detroit	68	25	42	67	16
Provost, Claude	Montreal	70	27	37	64	28
Gilbert, Rod	New York	70	25	36	61	52
Pilote, Pierre	Chicago	68	14	45	59	162
Bucyk, John	Boston	68	26	29	55	24
Backstrom, Ralph	Montreal	70	25	30	55	41
Esposito, Phil	Chicago	70	23	32	55	44

1965-66

Team	GP	W	L	T	GF	GA	PTS
*Montreal	70	41	21	8	239	173	90
Chicago	70	37	25	8	240	187	82
Toronto	70	34	25	11	208	187	79
Detroit	70	31	27	12	221	194	74
Boston	70	21	43	6	174	275	48
New York	70	18	41	11	195	261	47

Leading Scorers

Player	Club	GP	G	A	PTS	PIM
Hull, Bobby	Chicago	65	54	43	97	70
Mikita, Stan	Chicago	68	30	48	78	58
Rousseau, Bobby	Montreal	70	30	48	78	20
Béliveau, Jean	Montreal	67	29	48	77	50
Howe, Gordie	Detroit	70	29	46	75	83
Ullman, Norm	Detroit	70	31	41	72	35
Delvecchio, Alex	Detroit	70	31	38	69	16
Nevin, Bob	New York	69	29	33	62	10
Richard, Henri	Montreal	62	22	39	61	47
Oliver, Murray	Boston	70	18	42	60	30

1966-67

Team	GP	W	L	T	GF	GA	PTS
Chicago	70	41	17	12	264	170	94
Montreal	70	32	25	13	202	188	77
*Toronto	70	32	27	11	204	211	75
New York	70	30	28	12	188	189	72
Detroit	70	27	39	4	212	241	58
Boston	70	17	43	10	182	253	44

Leading Scorers

Player	Club	GP	G	A	PTS	PIM
Mikita, Stan	Chicago	70	35	62	97	12
Hull, Bobby	Chicago	66	52	28	80	52
Ullman, Norm	Detroit	68	26	44	70	26
Wharram, Kenny	Chicago	70	31	34	65	21
Howe, Gordie	Detroit	69	25	40	65	53
Rousseau, Bobby	Montreal	68	19	44	63	58
Esposito, Phil	Chicago	69	21	40	61	40
Goyette, Phil	New York	70	12	49	61	6
Mohns, Doug	Chicago	61	25	35	60	58
Richard, Henri	Montreal	65	21	34	55	28
Delvecchio, Alex	Detroit	70	17	38	55	10

1967-68

East Division

Team	GP	W	L	T	GF	GA	PTS
*Montreal	74	42	22	10	236	167	94
New York	74	39	23	12	226	183	90
Boston	74	37	27	10	259	216	84
Chicago	74	32	26	16	212	222	80
Toronto	74	33	31	10	209	176	76
Detroit	74	27	35	12	245	257	66

West Division

Team	GP	W	L	T	GF	GA	PTS
Philadelphia	74	31	32	11	173	179	73
Los Angeles	74	31	33	10	200	224	72
St. Louis	74	27	31	16	177	191	70
Minnesota	74	27	32	15	191	226	69
Pittsburgh	74	27	34	13	195	216	67
Oakland	74	15	42	17	153	219	47

Leading Scorers

Player	Club	GP	G	A	PTS	PIM
Mikita, Stan	Chicago	72	40	47	87	14
Esposito, Phil	Boston	74	35	49	84	21
Howe, Gordie	Detroit	74	39	43	82	53
Ratelle, Jean	New York	74	32	46	78	18
Gilbert, Rod	New York	73	29	48	77	12
Hull, Bobby	Chicago	71	44	31	75	39
Ullman, Norm	Det., Tor.	71	35	37	72	28
Delvecchio, Alex	Detroit	74	22	48	70	14
Bucyk, John	Boston	72	30	39	69	8
Wharram, Kenny	Chicago	74	27	42	69	18

1968-69

East Division

Team	GP	W	L	T	GF	GA	PTS
*Montreal	76	46	19	11	271	202	103
Boston	76	42	18	16	303	221	100
New York	76	41	26	9	231	196	91
Toronto	76	35	26	15	234	217	85
Detroit	76	33	31	12	239	221	78
Chicago	76	34	33	9	280	246	77

West Division

Team	GP	W	L	T	GF	GA	PTS
St. Louis	76	37	25	14	204	157	88
Oakland	76	29	36	11	219	251	69
Philadelphia	76	20	35	21	174	225	61
Los Angeles	76	24	42	10	185	260	58
Pittsburgh	76	20	45	11	189	252	51
Minnesota	76	18	43	5	189	270	51

Leading Scorers

Player	Club	GP	G	A	PTS	PIM
Esposito, Phil	Boston	74	49	77	126	79
Hull, Bobby	Chicago	74	58	49	107	48
Howe, Gordie	Detroit	76	44	59	103	58
Mikita, Stan	Chicago	74	30	67	97	52
Hodge, Ken	Boston	75	45	45	90	75
Cournoyer, Yvan	Montreal	76	43	44	87	31
Delvecchio, Alex	Detroit	72	25	58	83	8
Berenson, Red	St. Louis	76	35	47	82	43
Béliveau, Jean	Montreal	69	33	49	82	55
Mahovlich, Frank	Detroit	76	49	29	78	38
Ratelle, Jean	New York	75	32	46	78	26

1969-70

East Division

Team	GP	W	L	T	GF	GA	PTS
Chicago	76	45	22	9	250	170	99
*Boston	76	40	17	19	277	216	99
Detroit	76	40	21	15	246	199	95
New York	76	38	22	16	246	189	92
Montreal	76	38	22	16	244	201	92
Toronto	76	29	34	13	222	242	71

West Division

Team	GP	W	L	T	GF	GA	PTS
St. Louis	76	37	27	12	224	179	86
Pittsburgh	76	26	38	12	182	238	64
Minnesota	76	19	35	22	224	257	60
Oakland	76	22	40	14	169	243	58
Philadelphia	76	17	35	24	197	225	58
Los Angeles	76	14	52	10	168	290	38

Leading Scorers

Player	Club	GP	G	A	PTS	PIM
Orr, Bobby	Boston	76	33	87	120	125
Esposito, Phil	Boston	76	43	56	99	50
Mikita, Stan	Chicago	76	39	47	86	50
Goyette, Phil	St. Louis	72	29	49	78	16
Tkaczuk, Walt	New York	76	27	50	77	38
Ratelle, Jean	New York	75	32	42	74	28
Berenson, Red	St. Louis	67	33	39	72	38
Parise, Jean-Paul	Minnesota	74	24	48	72	72
Howe, Gordie	Detroit	76	31	40	71	58
Mahovlich, Frank	Detroit	74	38	32	70	59
Balon, Dave	New York	76	33	37	70	100
McKenzie, John	Boston	72	29	41	70	114

1970-71

East Division

Team	GP	W	L	T	GF	GA	PTS
Boston	78	57	14	7	399	207	121
New York	78	49	18	11	259	177	109
*Montreal	78	42	23	13	291	216	97
Toronto	78	37	33	8	248	211	82
Buffalo	78	24	39	15	217	291	63
Vancouver	78	24	46	8	229	296	56
Detroit	78	22	45	11	209	308	55

West Division

Team	GP	W	L	T	GF	GA	PTS
Chicago	78	49	20	9	277	184	107
St. Louis	78	34	25	19	223	208	87
Philadelphia	78	28	33	17	207	225	73
Minnesota	78	28	34	16	191	223	72
Los Angeles	78	25	40	13	239	303	63
Pittsburgh	78	21	37	20	221	240	62
California	78	20	53	5	199	320	45

Leading Scorers

Player	Club	GP	G	A	PTS	PIM
Esposito, Phil	Boston	78	76	76	152	71
Orr, Bobby	Boston	78	37	102	139	91
Bucyk, John	Boston	78	51	65	116	8
Hodge, Ken	Boston	78	43	62	105	113
Hull, Bobby	Chicago	78	44	52	96	32
Ullman, Norm	Toronto	73	34	51	85	24
Cashman, Wayne	Boston	77	21	58	79	100
McKenzie, John	Boston	65	31	46	77	120
Keon, Dave	Toronto	76	38	38	76	4
Béliveau, Jean	Montreal	70	25	51	76	40
Stanfield, Fred	Boston	75	24	52	76	12

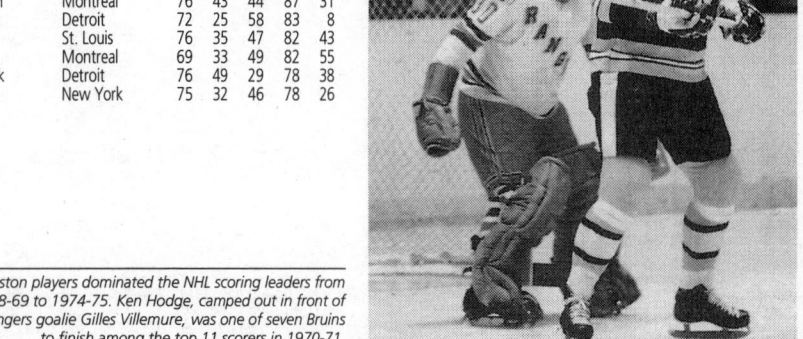

Boston players dominated the NHL scoring leaders from 1968-69 to 1974-75. Ken Hodge, camped out in front of Rangers goalie Gilles Villemure, was one of seven Bruins to finish among the top 11 scorers in 1970-71.

1971-72
East Division

Team	GP	W	L	T	GF	GA	PTS
*Boston	78	54	13	11	330	204	119
New York	78	48	17	13	317	192	109
Montreal	78	46	16	16	307	205	108
Toronto	78	33	31	14	209	208	80
Detroit	78	33	35	10	261	262	76
Buffalo	78	16	43	19	203	289	51
Vancouver	78	20	50	8	203	297	48

West Division

Team	GP	W	L	T	GF	GA	PTS
Chicago	78	46	17	15	256	166	107
Minnesota	78	37	29	12	212	191	86
St. Louis	78	28	39	11	208	247	67
Pittsburgh	78	26	38	14	220	258	66
Philadelphia	78	26	38	14	200	236	66
California	78	21	39	18	216	288	60
Los Angeles	78	20	49	9	206	305	49

Leading Scorers

Player	Club	GP	G	A	PTS	PIM
Esposito, Phil	Boston	76	66	67	133	76
Orr, Bobby	Boston	76	37	80	117	106
Ratelle, Jean	New York	63	46	63	109	4
Hadfield, Vic	New York	78	50	56	106	142
Gilbert, Rod	New York	73	43	54	97	64
Mahovlich, Frank	Montreal	76	43	53	96	36
Hull, Bobby	Chicago	78	50	43	93	24
Cournoyer, Yvan	Montreal	73	47	36	83	15
Bucyk, John	Boston	78	32	51	83	4
Clarke, Bobby	Philadelphia	78	35	46	81	87
Lemaire, Jacques	Montreal	77	32	49	81	26

1972-73
East Division

Team	GP	W	L	T	GF	GA	PTS
*Montreal	78	52	10	16	329	184	120
Boston	78	51	22	5	330	235	107
NY Rangers	78	47	23	8	297	208	102
Buffalo	78	37	27	14	257	219	88
Detroit	78	37	29	12	265	243	86
Toronto	78	27	41	10	247	279	64
Vancouver	78	22	47	9	233	339	53
NY Islanders	78	12	60	6	170	347	30

West Division

Team	GP	W	L	T	GF	GA	PTS
Chicago	78	42	27	9	284	225	93
Philadelphia	78	37	30	11	296	256	85
Minnesota	78	37	30	11	254	230	85
St. Louis	78	32	34	12	233	251	76
Pittsburgh	78	32	37	9	257	265	73
Los Angeles	78	31	36	11	232	245	73
Atlanta	78	25	38	15	191	239	65
California	78	16	46	16	213	323	48

Leading Scorers

Player	Club	GP	G	A	PTS	PIM
Esposito, Phil	Boston	78	55	75	130	87
Clarke, Bobby	Philadelphia	78	37	67	104	80
Orr, Bobby	Boston	63	29	72	101	99
MacLeish, Rick	Philadelphia	78	50	50	100	69
Lemaire, Jacques	Montreal	77	44	51	95	16
Ratelle, Jean	NY Rangers	78	41	53	94	12
Redmond, Mickey	Detroit	76	52	41	93	24
Bucyk, John	Boston	78	40	53	93	12
Mahovlich, Frank	Montreal	78	38	55	93	51
Pappin, Jim	Chicago	76	41	51	92	82

1973-74
East Division

Team	GP	W	L	T	GF	GA	PTS
Boston	78	52	17	9	349	221	113
Montreal	78	45	24	9	293	240	99
NY Rangers	78	40	24	14	300	251	94
Toronto	78	35	27	16	274	230	86
Buffalo	78	32	34	12	242	250	76
Detroit	78	29	39	10	255	319	68
Vancouver	78	24	43	11	224	296	59
NY Islanders	78	19	41	18	182	247	56

West Division

Team	GP	W	L	T	GF	GA	PTS
*Philadelphia	78	50	16	12	273	164	112
Chicago	78	41	14	23	272	164	105
Los Angeles	78	33	33	12	233	231	78
Atlanta	78	30	34	14	214	238	74
Pittsburgh	78	28	41	9	242	273	65
St. Louis	78	26	40	12	206	248	64
Minnesota	78	23	38	17	235	275	63
California	78	13	55	10	195	342	36

Leading Scorers

Player	Club	GP	G	A	PTS	PIM
Esposito, Phil	Boston	78	68	77	145	58
Orr, Bobby	Boston	74	32	90	122	82
Hodge, Ken	Boston	76	50	55	105	43
Cashman, Wayne	Boston	78	30	59	89	111
Clarke, Bobby	Philadelphia	77	35	52	87	113
Martin, Rick	Buffalo	78	52	34	86	38
Apps Jr., Syl	Pittsburgh	75	24	61	85	37
Sittler, Darryl	Toronto	78	38	46	84	55
MacDonald, Lowell	Pittsburgh	78	43	39	82	14
Park, Brad	NY Rangers	78	25	57	82	148
Hextall, Dennis	Minnesota	78	20	62	82	138

1974-75
PRINCE OF WALES CONFERENCE
Norris Division

Team	GP	W	L	T	GF	GA	PTS
Montreal	80	47	14	19	374	225	113
Los Angeles	80	42	17	21	269	185	105
Pittsburgh	80	37	28	15	326	289	89
Detroit	80	23	45	12	259	335	58
Washington	80	8	67	5	181	446	21

Adams Division

Team	GP	W	L	T	GF	GA	PTS
Buffalo	80	49	16	15	354	240	113
Boston	80	40	26	14	345	245	94
Toronto	80	31	33	16	280	309	78
California	80	19	48	13	212	316	51

CLARENCE CAMPBELL CONFERENCE
Patrick Division

Team	GP	W	L	T	GF	GA	PTS
*Philadelphia	80	51	18	11	293	181	113
NY Rangers	80	37	29	14	319	276	88
NY Islanders	80	33	25	22	264	221	88
Atlanta	80	34	31	15	243	233	83

Smythe Division

Team	GP	W	L	T	GF	GA	PTS
Vancouver	80	38	32	10	271	254	86
St. Louis	80	35	31	14	269	267	84
Chicago	80	37	35	8	268	241	82
Minnesota	80	23	50	7	221	341	53
Kansas City	80	15	54	11	184	328	41

Leading Scorers

Player	Club	GP	G	A	PTS	PIM
Orr, Bobby	Boston	80	46	89	135	101
Esposito, Phil	Boston	79	61	66	127	62
Dionne, Marcel	Detroit	80	47	74	121	14
Lafleur, Guy	Montreal	70	53	66	119	37
Mahovlich, Pete	Montreal	80	35	82	117	64
Clarke, Bobby	Philadelphia	80	27	89	116	125
Robert, Rene	Buffalo	74	40	60	100	75
Gilbert, Rod	NY Rangers	76	36	61	97	22
Perreault, Gilbert	Buffalo	68	39	57	96	36
Martin, Rick	Buffalo	68	52	43	95	72

1975-76
PRINCE OF WALES CONFERENCE
Norris Division

Team	GP	W	L	T	GF	GA	PTS
*Montreal	80	58	11	11	337	174	127
Los Angeles	80	38	33	9	263	265	85
Pittsburgh	80	35	33	12	339	303	82
Detroit	80	26	44	10	226	300	62
Washington	80	11	59	10	224	394	32

Adams Division

Team	GP	W	L	T	GF	GA	PTS
Boston	80	48	15	17	313	237	113
Buffalo	80	46	21	13	339	240	105
Toronto	80	34	31	15	294	276	83
California	80	27	42	11	250	278	65

CLARENCE CAMPBELL CONFERENCE
Patrick Division

Team	GP	W	L	T	GF	GA	PTS
Philadelphia	80	51	13	16	348	209	118
NY Islanders	80	42	21	17	297	190	101
Atlanta	80	35	33	12	262	237	82
NY Rangers	80	29	42	9	262	333	67

Smythe Division

Team	GP	W	L	T	GF	GA	PTS
Chicago	80	32	30	18	254	261	82
Vancouver	80	33	32	15	271	272	81
St. Louis	80	29	37	14	249	290	72
Minnesota	80	20	53	7	195	303	47
Kansas City	80	12	56	12	190	351	36

Leading Scorers

Player	Club	GP	G	A	PTS	PIM
Lafleur, Guy	Montreal	80	56	69	125	36
Clarke, Bobby	Philadelphia	76	30	89	119	13
Perreault, Gilbert	Buffalo	80	44	69	113	36
Barber, Bill	Philadelphia	80	50	62	112	104
Larouche, Pierre	Pittsburgh	76	53	58	111	33
Ratelle, Jean	Bos., NYR	80	36	69	105	18
Mahovlich, Pete	Montreal	80	34	71	105	76
Pronovost, Jean	Pittsburgh	80	52	52	104	24
Sittler, Darryl	Toronto	79	41	59	100	90
Apps Jr., Syl	Pittsburgh	80	32	67	99	24

1976-77
PRINCE OF WALES CONFERENCE
Norris Division

Team	GP	W	L	T	GF	GA	PTS
*Montreal	80	60	8	12	387	171	132
Los Angeles	80	34	31	15	271	241	83
Pittsburgh	80	34	33	13	240	252	81
Washington	80	24	42	14	221	307	62
Detroit	80	16	55	9	183	309	41

Adams Division

Team	GP	W	L	T	GF	GA	PTS
Boston	80	49	23	8	312	240	106
Buffalo	80	48	24	8	301	220	104
Toronto	80	33	32	15	301	285	81
Cleveland	80	25	42	13	240	292	63

CLARENCE CAMPBELL CONFERENCE
Patrick Division

Team	GP	W	L	T	GF	GA	PTS
Philadelphia	80	48	16	16	323	213	112
NY Islanders	80	47	21	12	288	193	106
Atlanta	80	34	34	12	264	265	80
NY Rangers	80	29	37	14	272	310	72

Smythe Division

Team	GP	W	L	T	GF	GA	PTS
St. Louis	80	32	39	9	239	276	73
Minnesota	80	23	39	18	240	310	64
Chicago	80	26	43	11	240	298	63
Vancouver	80	25	42	13	235	294	63
Colorado	80	20	46	14	226	307	54

Leading Scorers

Player	Club	GP	G	A	PTS	PIM
Lafleur, Guy	Montreal	80	56	80	136	20
Dionne, Marcel	Los Angeles	80	53	69	122	12
Shutt, Steve	Montreal	80	60	45	105	28
MacLeish, Rick	Philadelphia	79	49	48	97	42
Perreault, Gilbert	Buffalo	80	39	56	95	30
Young, Tim	Minnesota	80	29	66	95	58
Ratelle, Jean	Boston	78	33	61	94	22
McDonald, Lanny	Toronto	80	46	44	90	77
Sittler, Darryl	Toronto	73	38	52	90	89
Clarke, Bobby	Philadelphia	80	27	63	90	71

The son of a Hockey Hall of Famer, Syl Apps Jr. was a star in his own right. A top-10 scorer twice in the mid-1970s, Apps had a career-high 99 points in 1975-76. His son, Syl Apps III, is a Toronto Maple Leafs prospect.

1977-78
PRINCE OF WALES CONFERENCE
Norris Division

Team	GP	W	L	T	GF	GA	PTS
*Montreal	80	59	10	11	359	183	129
Detroit	80	32	34	14	252	266	78
Los Angeles	80	31	34	15	243	245	77
Pittsburgh	80	25	37	18	254	321	68
Washington	80	17	49	14	195	321	48

Adams Division

Team	GP	W	L	T	GF	GA	PTS
Boston	80	51	18	11	333	218	113
Buffalo	80	44	19	17	288	215	105
Toronto	80	41	29	10	271	237	92
Cleveland	80	22	45	13	230	325	57

CLARENCE CAMPBELL CONFERENCE
Patrick Division

Team	GP	W	L	T	GF	GA	PTS
NY Islanders	80	48	17	15	334	210	111
Philadelphia	80	45	20	15	296	200	105
Atlanta	80	34	27	19	274	252	87
NY Rangers	80	30	37	13	279	280	73

Smythe Division

Team	GP	W	L	T	GF	GA	PTS
Chicago	80	32	29	19	230	220	83
Colorado	80	19	40	21	257	305	59
Vancouver	80	20	43	17	239	320	57
St. Louis	80	20	47	13	195	304	53
Minnesota	80	18	53	9	218	325	45

Leading Scorers

Player	Club	GP	G	A	PTS	PIM
Lafleur, Guy	Montreal	79	60	72	132	26
Trottier, Bryan	NY Islanders	77	46	77	123	46
Sittler, Darryl	Toronto	80	45	72	117	100
Lemaire, Jacques	Montreal	76	36	61	97	14
Potvin, Denis	NY Islanders	80	30	64	94	81
Bossy, Mike	NY Islanders	73	53	38	91	6
O'Reilly, Terry	Boston	77	29	61	90	211
Perreault, Gilbert	Buffalo	79	41	48	89	20
Clarke, Bobby	Philadelphia	71	21	68	89	83
McDonald, Lanny	Toronto	74	47	40	87	54
Paiement, Wilf	Colorado	80	31	56	87	114

1978-79
PRINCE OF WALES CONFERENCE
Norris Division

Team	GP	W	L	T	GF	GA	PTS
*Montreal	80	52	17	11	337	204	115
Pittsburgh	80	36	31	13	281	279	85
Los Angeles	80	34	34	12	292	286	80
Washington	80	24	41	15	273	338	63
Detroit	80	23	41	16	252	295	62

Adams Division

Team	GP	W	L	T	GF	GA	PTS
Boston	80	43	23	14	316	270	100
Buffalo	80	36	28	16	280	263	88
Toronto	80	34	33	13	267	252	81
Minnesota	80	28	40	12	257	289	68

CLARENCE CAMPBELL CONFERENCE
Patrick Division

Team	GP	W	L	T	GF	GA	PTS
NY Islanders	80	51	15	14	358	214	116
Philadelphia	80	40	25	15	281	248	95
NY Rangers	80	40	29	11	316	292	91
Atlanta	80	41	31	8	327	280	90

Smythe Division

Team	GP	W	L	T	GF	GA	PTS
Chicago	80	29	36	15	244	277	73
Vancouver	80	25	42	13	217	291	63
St. Louis	80	18	50	12	249	348	48
Colorado	80	15	53	12	210	331	42

Leading Scorers

Player	Club	GP	G	A	PTS	PIM
Trottier, Bryan	NY Islanders	76	47	87	134	50
Dionne, Marcel	Los Angeles	80	59	71	130	30
Lafleur, Guy	Montreal	80	52	77	129	28
Bossy, Mike	NY Islanders	80	69	57	126	25
MacMillan, Bob	Atlanta	79	37	71	108	14
Chouinard, Guy	Atlanta	80	50	57	107	14
Potvin, Denis	NY Islanders	73	31	70	101	58
Federko, Bernie	St. Louis	74	31	64	95	14
Taylor, Dave	Los Angeles	78	43	48	91	124
Gillies, Clark	NY Islanders	75	35	56	91	68

1979-80
PRINCE OF WALES CONFERENCE
Norris Division

Team	GP	W	L	T	GF	GA	PTS
Montreal	80	47	20	13	328	240	107
Los Angeles	80	30	36	14	290	313	74
Pittsburgh	80	30	37	13	251	303	73
Hartford	80	27	34	19	303	312	73
Detroit	80	26	43	11	268	306	63

Adams Division

Team	GP	W	L	T	GF	GA	PTS
Buffalo	80	47	17	16	318	201	110
Boston	80	46	21	13	310	234	105
Minnesota	80	36	28	16	311	253	88
Toronto	80	35	40	5	304	327	75
Quebec	80	25	44	11	248	313	61

CLARENCE CAMPBELL CONFERENCE
Patrick Division

Team	GP	W	L	T	GF	GA	PTS
Philadelphia	80	48	12	20	327	254	116
*NY Islanders	80	39	28	13	281	247	91
NY Rangers	80	38	32	10	308	284	86
Atlanta	80	35	32	13	282	269	83
Washington	80	27	40	13	261	293	67

Smythe Division

Team	GP	W	L	T	GF	GA	PTS
Chicago	80	34	27	19	241	250	87
St. Louis	80	34	34	12	266	278	80
Vancouver	80	27	37	16	256	281	70
Edmonton	80	28	39	13	301	322	69
Winnipeg	80	20	49	11	214	314	51
Colorado	80	19	48	13	234	308	51

Leading Scorers

Player	Club	GP	G	A	PTS	PIM
Dionne, Marcel	Los Angeles	80	53	84	137	32
Gretzky, Wayne	Edmonton	79	51	86	137	21
Lafleur, Guy	Montreal	74	50	75	125	12
Perreault, Gilbert	Buffalo	80	40	66	106	57
Rogers, Mike	Hartford	80	44	61	105	10
Trottier, Bryan	NY Islanders	78	42	62	104	68
Simmer, Charlie	Los Angeles	64	56	45	101	65
Stoughton, Blaine	Hartford	80	56	44	100	16
Sittler, Darryl	Toronto	73	40	57	97	62
MacDonald, Blair	Edmonton	80	46	48	94	6
Federko, Bernie	St. Louis	79	38	56	94	24

1980-81
PRINCE OF WALES CONFERENCE
Norris Division

Team	GP	W	L	T	GF	GA	PTS
Montreal	80	45	22	13	332	232	103
Los Angeles	80	43	24	13	337	290	99
Pittsburgh	80	30	37	13	302	345	73
Hartford	80	21	41	18	292	372	60
Detroit	80	19	43	18	252	339	56

Adams Division

Team	GP	W	L	T	GF	GA	PTS
Buffalo	80	39	20	21	327	250	99
Boston	80	37	30	13	316	272	87
Minnesota	80	35	28	17	291	263	87
Quebec	80	30	32	18	314	318	78
Toronto	80	28	37	15	322	367	71

CLARENCE CAMPBELL CONFERENCE
Patrick Division

Team	GP	W	L	T	GF	GA	PTS
*NY Islanders	80	48	18	14	355	260	110
Philadelphia	80	41	24	15	313	249	97
Calgary	80	39	27	14	329	298	92
NY Rangers	80	30	36	14	312	317	74
Washington	80	26	36	18	286	317	70

Smythe Division

Team	GP	W	L	T	GF	GA	PTS
St. Louis	80	45	18	17	352	281	107
Chicago	80	31	33	16	304	315	78
Vancouver	80	28	32	20	289	301	76
Edmonton	80	29	35	16	328	327	74
Colorado	80	22	45	13	258	344	57
Winnipeg	80	9	57	14	246	400	32

Leading Scorers

Player	Club	GP	G	A	PTS	PIM
Gretzky, Wayne	Edmonton	80	55	109	164	28
Dionne, Marcel	Los Angeles	80	58	77	135	70
Nilsson, Kent	Calgary	80	49	82	131	26
Bossy, Mike	NY Islanders	79	68	51	119	32
Taylor, Dave	Los Angeles	72	47	65	112	130
Stastny, Peter	Quebec	77	39	70	109	37
Simmer, Charlie	Los Angeles	65	56	49	105	62
Rogers, Mike	Hartford	80	40	65	105	32
Federko, Bernie	St. Louis	78	31	73	104	47
Richard, Jacques	Quebec	78	52	51	103	39
Middleton, Rick	Boston	80	44	59	103	16
Trottier, Bryan	NY Islanders	73	31	72	103	74

1981-82
CLARENCE CAMPBELL CONFERENCE
Norris Division

Team	GP	W	L	T	GF	GA	PTS
Minnesota	80	37	23	20	346	288	94
Winnipeg	80	33	33	14	319	332	80
St. Louis	80	32	40	8	315	349	72
Chicago	80	30	38	12	332	363	72
Toronto	80	20	44	16	298	380	56
Detroit	80	21	47	12	270	351	54

Smythe Division

Team	GP	W	L	T	GF	GA	PTS
Edmonton	80	48	17	15	417	295	111
Vancouver	80	30	33	17	290	286	77
Calgary	80	29	34	17	334	345	75
Los Angeles	80	24	41	15	314	369	63
Colorado	80	18	49	13	241	362	49

PRINCE OF WALES CONFERENCE
Adams Division

Team	GP	W	L	T	GF	GA	PTS
Montreal	80	46	17	17	360	223	109
Boston	80	43	27	10	323	285	96
Buffalo	80	39	26	15	307	273	93
Quebec	80	33	31	16	356	345	82
Hartford	80	21	41	18	264	351	60

Patrick Division

Team	GP	W	L	T	GF	GA	PTS
*NY Islanders	80	54	16	10	385	250	118
NY Rangers	80	39	27	14	316	306	92
Philadelphia	80	38	31	11	325	313	87
Pittsburgh	80	31	36	13	310	337	75
Washington	80	26	41	13	319	338	65

Leading Scorers

Player	Club	GP	G	A	PTS	PIM
Gretzky, Wayne	Edmonton	80	92	120	212	26
Bossy, Mike	NY Islanders	80	64	83	147	22
Stastny, Peter	Quebec	80	46	93	139	91
Maruk, Dennis	Washington	80	60	76	136	128
Trottier, Bryan	NY Islanders	80	50	79	129	88
Savard, Denis	Chicago	80	32	87	119	82
Dionne, Marcel	Los Angeles	78	50	67	117	50
Smith, Bobby	Minnesota	80	43	71	114	82
Ciccarelli, Dino	Minnesota	76	55	51	106	138
Taylor, Dave	Los Angeles	78	39	67	106	130

1982-83
CLARENCE CAMPBELL CONFERENCE
Norris Division

Team	GP	W	L	T	GF	GA	PTS
Chicago	80	47	23	10	338	268	104
Minnesota	80	40	24	16	321	290	96
Toronto	80	28	40	12	293	330	68
St. Louis	80	25	40	15	285	316	65
Detroit	80	21	44	15	263	344	57

Smythe Division

Team	GP	W	L	T	GF	GA	PTS
Edmonton	80	47	21	12	424	315	106
Calgary	80	32	34	14	321	317	78
Vancouver	80	30	35	15	303	309	75
Winnipeg	80	33	39	8	311	333	74
Los Angeles	80	27	41	12	308	365	66

PRINCE OF WALES CONFERENCE
Adams Division

Team	GP	W	L	T	GF	GA	PTS
Boston	80	50	20	10	327	228	110
Montreal	80	42	24	14	350	286	98
Buffalo	80	38	29	13	318	285	89
Quebec	80	34	34	12	343	336	80
Hartford	80	19	54	7	261	403	45

Patrick Division

Team	GP	W	L	T	GF	GA	PTS
Philadelphia	80	49	23	8	326	240	106
*NY Islanders	80	42	26	12	302	226	96
Washington	80	39	25	16	306	283	94
NY Rangers	80	35	35	10	306	287	80
New Jersey	80	17	49	14	230	338	48
Pittsburgh	80	18	53	9	257	394	45

Leading Scorers

Player	Club	GP	G	A	PTS	PIM
Gretzky, Wayne	Edmonton	80	71	125	196	59
Stastny, Peter	Quebec	75	47	77	124	78
Savard, Denis	Chicago	78	35	86	121	99
Bossy, Mike	NY Islanders	79	60	58	118	20
Dionne, Marcel	Los Angeles	80	56	51	107	22
Pederson, Barry	Boston	77	46	61	107	47
Messier, Mark	Edmonton	77	48	58	106	72
Goulet, Michel	Quebec	80	57	48	105	51
Anderson, Glenn	Edmonton	72	48	56	104	70
Nilsson, Kent	Calgary	80	46	58	104	10
Kurri, Jari	Edmonton	80	45	59	104	22

1983-84
CLARENCE CAMPBELL CONFERENCE
Norris Division

Team	GP	W	L	T	GF	GA	PTS
Minnesota	80	39	31	10	345	344	88
St. Louis	80	32	41	7	293	316	71
Detroit	80	31	42	7	298	323	69
Chicago	80	30	42	8	277	311	68
Toronto	80	26	45	9	303	387	61

Smythe Division

Team	GP	W	L	T	GF	GA	PTS
*Edmonton	80	57	18	5	446	314	119
Calgary	80	34	32	14	311	314	82
Vancouver	80	32	39	9	306	328	73
Winnipeg	80	31	38	11	340	374	73
Los Angeles	80	23	44	13	309	376	59

PRINCE OF WALES CONFERENCE
Adams Division

Team	GP	W	L	T	GF	GA	PTS
Boston	80	49	25	6	336	261	104
Buffalo	80	48	25	7	315	257	103
Quebec	80	42	28	10	360	278	94
Montreal	80	35	40	5	286	295	75
Hartford	80	28	42	10	288	320	66

Patrick Division

Team	GP	W	L	T	GF	GA	PTS
NY Islanders	80	50	26	4	357	269	104
Washington	80	48	27	5	308	226	101
Philadelphia	80	44	26	10	350	290	98
NY Rangers	80	42	29	9	314	304	93
New Jersey	80	17	56	7	231	350	41
Pittsburgh	80	16	58	6	254	390	38

Leading Scorers

Player	Club	GP	G	A	PTS	PIM
Gretzky, Wayne	Edmonton	74	87	118	205	39
Coffey, Paul	Edmonton	80	40	86	126	104
Goulet, Michel	Quebec	75	56	65	121	76
Stastny, Peter	Quebec	80	46	73	119	73
Bossy, Mike	NY Islanders	67	51	67	118	8
Pederson, Barry	Boston	80	39	77	116	64
Kurri, Jari	Edmonton	64	52	61	113	14
Trottier, Bryan	NY Islanders	68	40	71	111	59
Federko, Bernie	St. Louis	79	41	66	107	43
Middleton, Rick	Boston	80	47	58	105	14

1984-85
CLARENCE CAMPBELL CONFERENCE
Norris Division

Team	GP	W	L	T	GF	GA	PTS
St. Louis	80	37	31	12	299	288	86
Chicago	80	38	35	7	309	299	83
Detroit	80	27	41	12	313	357	66
Minnesota	80	25	43	12	268	321	62
Toronto	80	20	52	8	253	358	48

Smythe Division

Team	GP	W	L	T	GF	GA	PTS
*Edmonton	80	49	20	11	401	298	109
Winnipeg	80	43	27	10	358	332	96
Calgary	80	41	27	12	363	302	94
Los Angeles	80	34	32	14	339	326	82
Vancouver	80	25	46	9	284	401	59

PRINCE OF WALES CONFERENCE
Adams Division

Team	GP	W	L	T	GF	GA	PTS
Montreal	80	41	27	12	309	262	94
Quebec	80	41	30	9	323	275	91
Buffalo	80	38	28	14	290	237	90
Boston	80	36	34	10	303	287	82
Hartford	80	30	41	9	268	318	69

Patrick Division

Team	GP	W	L	T	GF	GA	PTS
Philadelphia	80	53	20	7	348	241	113
Washington	80	46	25	9	322	240	101
NY Islanders	80	40	34	6	345	312	86
NY Rangers	80	26	44	10	295	345	62
New Jersey	80	22	48	10	264	346	54
Pittsburgh	80	24	51	5	276	385	53

Leading Scorers

Player	Club	GP	G	A	PTS	PIM
Gretzky, Wayne	Edmonton	80	73	135	208	52
Kurri, Jari	Edmonton	73	71	64	135	30
Hawerchuk, Dale	Winnipeg	80	53	77	130	74
Dionne, Marcel	Los Angeles	80	46	80	126	46
Coffey, Paul	Edmonton	80	37	84	121	97
Bossy, Mike	NY Islanders	76	58	59	117	38
Ogrodnick, John	Detroit	79	55	50	105	30
Savard, Denis	Chicago	79	38	67	105	56
Federko, Bernie	St. Louis	76	30	73	103	27
Gartner, Mike	Washington	80	50	52	102	71

1985-86
CLARENCE CAMPBELL CONFERENCE
Norris Division

Team	GP	W	L	T	GF	GA	PTS
Chicago	80	39	33	8	351	349	86
Minnesota	80	38	33	9	327	305	85
St. Louis	80	37	34	9	302	291	83
Toronto	80	25	48	7	311	386	57
Detroit	80	17	57	6	266	415	40

Smythe Division

Team	GP	W	L	T	GF	GA	PTS
Edmonton	80	56	17	7	426	310	119
Calgary	80	40	31	9	354	315	89
Winnipeg	80	26	47	7	295	372	59
Vancouver	80	23	44	13	282	333	59
Los Angeles	80	23	49	8	284	389	54

PRINCE OF WALES CONFERENCE
Adams Division

Team	GP	W	L	T	GF	GA	PTS
Quebec	80	43	31	6	330	289	92
*Montreal	80	40	33	7	330	280	87
Boston	80	37	31	12	311	288	86
Hartford	80	40	36	4	332	302	84
Buffalo	80	37	37	6	296	291	80

Patrick Division

Team	GP	W	L	T	GF	GA	PTS
Philadelphia	80	53	23	4	335	241	110
Washington	80	50	23	7	315	272	107
NY Islanders	80	39	29	12	327	284	90
NY Rangers	80	36	38	6	280	276	78
Pittsburgh	80	34	38	8	313	305	76
New Jersey	80	28	49	3	300	374	59

Leading Scorers

Player	Club	GP	G	A	PTS	PIM
Gretzky, Wayne	Edmonton	80	52	163	215	52
Lemieux, Mario	Pittsburgh	79	48	93	141	43
Coffey, Paul	Edmonton	79	48	90	138	120
Kurri, Jari	Edmonton	78	68	63	131	22
Bossy, Mike	NY Islanders	80	61	62	123	14
Stastny, Peter	Quebec	76	41	81	122	60
Savard, Denis	Chicago	80	47	69	116	111
Naslund, Mats	Montreal	80	43	67	110	16
Hawerchuk, Dale	Winnipeg	80	46	59	105	44
Broten, Neal	Minnesota	80	29	76	105	47

1986-87
CLARENCE CAMPBELL CONFERENCE
Norris Division

Team	GP	W	L	T	GF	GA	PTS
St. Louis	80	32	33	15	281	293	79
Detroit	80	34	36	10	260	274	78
Chicago	80	29	37	14	290	310	72
Toronto	80	32	42	6	286	319	70
Minnesota	80	30	40	10	296	314	70

Smythe Division

Team	GP	W	L	T	GF	GA	PTS
*Edmonton	80	50	24	6	372	284	106
Calgary	80	46	31	3	318	289	95
Winnipeg	80	40	32	8	279	271	88
Los Angeles	80	31	41	8	318	341	70
Vancouver	80	29	43	8	282	314	66

PRINCE OF WALES CONFERENCE
Adams Division

Team	GP	W	L	T	GF	GA	PTS
Hartford	80	43	30	7	287	270	93
Montreal	80	41	29	10	277	241	92
Boston	80	39	34	7	301	276	85
Quebec	80	31	39	10	267	276	72
Buffalo	80	28	44	8	280	308	64

Patrick Division

Team	GP	W	L	T	GF	GA	PTS
Philadelphia	80	46	26	8	310	245	100
Washington	80	38	32	10	285	278	86
NY Islanders	80	35	33	12	279	281	82
NY Rangers	80	34	38	8	307	323	76
Pittsburgh	80	30	38	12	297	290	72
New Jersey	80	29	45	6	293	368	64

Leading Scorers

Player	Club	GP	G	A	PTS	PIM
Gretzky, Wayne	Edmonton	79	62	121	183	28
Kurri, Jari	Edmonton	79	54	54	108	41
Lemieux, Mario	Pittsburgh	63	54	53	107	57
Messier, Mark	Edmonton	77	37	70	107	73
Gilmour, Doug	St. Louis	80	42	63	105	58
Ciccarelli, Dino	Minnesota	80	52	51	103	92
Hawerchuk, Dale	Winnipeg	80	47	53	100	54
Goulet, Michel	Quebec	75	49	47	96	61
Kerr, Tim	Philadelphia	75	58	37	95	57
Bourque, Ray	Boston	78	23	72	95	36

1987-88
CLARENCE CAMPBELL CONFERENCE
Norris Division

Team	GP	W	L	T	GF	GA	PTS
Detroit	80	41	28	11	322	269	93
St. Louis	80	34	38	8	278	294	76
Chicago	80	30	41	9	284	328	69
Toronto	80	21	49	10	273	345	52
Minnesota	80	19	48	13	242	349	51

Smythe Division

Team	GP	W	L	T	GF	GA	PTS
Calgary	80	48	23	9	397	305	105
*Edmonton	80	44	25	11	363	288	99
Winnipeg	80	33	36	11	292	310	77
Los Angeles	80	30	42	8	318	359	68
Vancouver	80	25	46	9	272	320	59

PRINCE OF WALES CONFERENCE
Adams Division

Team	GP	W	L	T	GF	GA	PTS
Montreal	80	45	22	13	298	238	103
Boston	80	44	30	6	300	251	94
Buffalo	80	37	32	11	283	305	85
Hartford	80	35	38	7	249	267	77
Quebec	80	32	43	5	271	306	69

Patrick Division

Team	GP	W	L	T	GF	GA	PTS
NY Islanders	80	39	31	10	308	267	88
Washington	80	38	33	9	281	249	85
Philadelphia	80	38	33	9	292	292	85
New Jersey	80	38	36	6	295	296	82
NY Rangers	80	36	34	10	300	283	82
Pittsburgh	80	36	35	9	319	316	81

Leading Scorers

Player	Club	GP	G	A	PTS	PIM
Lemieux, Mario	Pittsburgh	76	70	98	168	92
Gretzky, Wayne	Edmonton	64	40	109	149	24
Savard, Denis	Chicago	80	44	87	131	95
Hawerchuk, Dale	Winnipeg	80	44	77	121	59
Robitaille, Luc	Los Angeles	80	53	58	111	82
Stastny, Peter	Quebec	76	46	65	111	69
Messier, Mark	Edmonton	77	37	74	111	103
Carson, Jimmy	Los Angeles	80	55	52	107	45
Loob, Hakan	Calgary	80	50	56	106	47
Goulet, Michel	Quebec	80	48	58	106	56

1988-89
CLARENCE CAMPBELL CONFERENCE
Norris Division

Team	GP	W	L	T	GF	GA	PTS
Detroit	80	34	34	12	313	316	80
St. Louis	80	33	35	12	275	285	78
Minnesota	80	27	37	16	258	278	70
Chicago	80	27	41	12	297	335	66
Toronto	80	28	46	6	259	342	62

Smythe Division

Team	GP	W	L	T	GF	GA	PTS
*Calgary	80	54	17	9	354	226	117
Los Angeles	80	42	31	7	376	335	91
Edmonton	80	38	34	8	325	306	84
Vancouver	80	33	39	8	251	253	74
Winnipeg	80	26	42	12	300	355	64

PRINCE OF WALES CONFERENCE
Adams Division

Team	GP	W	L	T	GF	GA	PTS
Montreal	80	53	18	9	315	218	115
Boston	80	37	29	14	289	256	88
Buffalo	80	38	35	7	291	299	83
Hartford	80	37	38	5	299	290	79
Quebec	80	27	46	7	269	342	61

Patrick Division

Team	GP	W	L	T	GF	GA	PTS
Washington	80	41	29	10	305	259	92
Pittsburgh	80	40	33	7	347	349	87
NY Rangers	80	37	35	8	310	307	82
Philadelphia	80	36	36	8	307	285	80
New Jersey	80	27	41	12	281	325	66
NY Islanders	80	28	47	5	265	325	61

Leading Scorers

Player	Club	GP	G	A	PTS	PIM
Lemieux, Mario	Pittsburgh	76	85	114	199	100
Gretzky, Wayne	Los Angeles	78	54	114	168	26
Yzerman, Steve	Detroit	80	65	90	155	61
Nicholls, Bernie	Los Angeles	79	70	80	150	96
Brown, Rob	Pittsburgh	68	49	66	115	118
Coffey, Paul	Pittsburgh	75	30	83	113	193
Mullen, Joe	Calgary	79	51	59	110	16
Kurri, Jari	Edmonton	76	44	58	102	69
Carson, Jimmy	Edmonton	80	49	51	100	36
Robitaille, Luc	Los Angeles	78	46	52	98	65

1989-90
CLARENCE CAMPBELL CONFERENCE
Norris Division

Team	GP	W	L	T	GF	GA	PTS
Chicago	80	41	33	6	316	294	88
St. Louis	80	37	34	9	295	279	83
Toronto	80	38	38	4	337	358	80
Minnesota	80	36	40	4	284	291	76
Detroit	80	28	38	14	288	323	70

Smythe Division

Calgary	80	42	23	15	348	265	99
*Edmonton	80	38	28	14	315	283	90
Winnipeg	80	37	32	11	298	290	85
Los Angeles	80	34	39	7	338	337	75
Vancouver	80	25	41	14	245	306	64

PRINCE OF WALES CONFERENCE
Adams Division

Boston	80	46	25	9	289	232	101
Buffalo	80	45	27	8	286	248	98
Montreal	80	41	28	11	288	234	93
Hartford	80	38	33	9	275	268	85
Quebec	80	12	61	7	240	407	31

Patrick Division

NY Rangers	80	36	31	13	279	267	85
New Jersey	80	37	34	9	295	288	83
Washington	80	36	38	6	284	275	78
NY Islanders	80	31	38	11	281	288	73
Pittsburgh	80	32	40	8	318	359	72
Philadelphia	80	30	39	11	290	297	71

Leading Scorers

Player	Club	GP	G	A	PTS	PIM
Gretzky, Wayne	Los Angeles	73	40	102	142	42
Messier, Mark	Edmonton	79	45	84	129	79
Yzerman, Steve	Detroit	79	62	65	127	79
Lemieux, Mario	Pittsburgh	59	45	78	123	78
Hull, Brett	St. Louis	80	72	41	113	24
Nicholls, Bernie	L.A., NYR	79	39	73	112	86
Turgeon, Pierre	Buffalo	80	40	66	106	29
LaFontaine, Pat	NY Islanders	74	54	51	105	38
Coffey, Paul	Pittsburgh	80	29	74	103	95
Sakic, Joe	Quebec	80	39	63	102	27
Oates, Adam	St. Louis	80	23	79	102	30

1990-91
CLARENCE CAMPBELL CONFERENCE
Norris Division

Team	GP	W	L	T	GF	GA	PTS
Chicago	80	49	23	8	284	211	106
St. Louis	80	47	22	11	310	250	105
Detroit	80	34	38	8	273	298	76
Minnesota	80	27	39	14	256	266	68
Toronto	80	23	46	11	241	318	57

Smythe Division

Los Angeles	80	46	24	10	340	254	102
Calgary	80	46	26	8	344	263	100
Edmonton	80	37	37	6	272	272	80
Vancouver	80	28	43	9	243	315	65
Winnipeg	80	26	43	11	260	288	63

PRINCE OF WALES CONFERENCE
Adams Division

Boston	80	44	24	12	299	264	100
Montreal	80	39	30	11	273	249	89
Buffalo	80	31	30	19	292	278	81
Hartford	80	31	38	11	238	276	73
Quebec	80	16	50	14	236	354	46

Patrick Division

*Pittsburgh	80	41	33	6	342	305	88
NY Rangers	80	36	31	13	297	265	85
Washington	80	37	36	7	258	258	81
New Jersey	80	32	33	15	272	264	79
Philadelphia	80	33	37	10	252	267	76
NY Islanders	80	25	45	10	223	290	60

Leading Scorers

Player	Club	GP	G	A	PTS	PIM
Gretzky, Wayne	Los Angeles	78	41	122	163	16
Hull, Brett	St. Louis	78	86	45	131	22
Oates, Adam	St. Louis	61	25	90	115	29
Recchi, Mark	Pittsburgh	78	40	73	113	48
Cullen, John	Pit., Hfd.	78	39	71	110	101
Sakic, Joe	Quebec	80	48	61	109	24
Yzerman, Steve	Detroit	80	51	57	108	34
Fleury, Theoren	Calgary	79	51	53	104	136
MacInnis, Al	Calgary	78	28	75	103	90
Larmer, Steve	Chicago	80	44	57	101	79

1991-92
CLARENCE CAMPBELL CONFERENCE
Norris Division

Team	GP	W	L	T	GF	GA	PTS
Detroit	80	43	25	12	320	256	98
Chicago	80	36	29	15	257	236	87
St. Louis	80	36	33	11	279	266	83
Minnesota	80	32	42	6	246	278	70
Toronto	80	30	43	7	234	294	67

Smythe Division

Vancouver	80	42	26	12	285	250	96
Los Angeles	80	35	31	14	287	296	84
Edmonton	80	36	34	10	295	297	82
Winnipeg	80	33	32	15	251	244	81
Calgary	80	31	37	12	296	305	74
San Jose	80	17	58	5	219	359	39

PRINCE OF WALES CONFERENCE
Adams Division

Montreal	80	41	28	11	267	207	93
Boston	80	36	32	12	270	275	84
Buffalo	80	31	37	12	289	299	74
Hartford	80	26	41	13	247	283	65
Quebec	80	20	48	12	255	318	52

Patrick Division

NY Rangers	80	50	25	5	321	246	105
Washington	80	45	27	8	330	275	98
*Pittsburgh	80	39	32	9	343	308	87
New Jersey	80	38	31	11	289	259	87
NY Islanders	80	34	35	11	291	299	79
Philadelphia	80	32	37	11	252	273	75

Leading Scorers

Player	Club	GP	G	A	PTS	PIM
Lemieux, Mario	Pittsburgh	64	44	87	131	94
Stevens, Kevin	Pittsburgh	80	54	69	123	254
Gretzky, Wayne	Los Angeles	74	31	90	121	34
Hull, Brett	St. Louis	73	70	39	109	48
Robitaille, Luc	Los Angeles	80	44	63	107	95
Messier, Mark	NY Rangers	79	35	72	107	76
Roenick, Jeremy	Chicago	80	53	50	103	98
Yzerman, Steve	Detroit	79	45	58	103	64
Leetch, Brian	NY Rangers	80	22	80	102	26
Oates, Adam	St. L., Bos.	80	20	79	99	22

1992-93
CLARENCE CAMPBELL CONFERENCE
Norris Division

Team	GP	W	L	T	GF	GA	PTS
Chicago	84	47	25	12	279	230	106
Detroit	84	47	28	9	369	280	103
Toronto	84	44	29	11	288	241	99
St. Louis	84	37	36	11	282	278	85
Minnesota	84	36	38	10	272	293	82
Tampa Bay	84	23	54	7	245	332	53

Smythe Division

Vancouver	84	46	29	9	346	278	101
Calgary	84	43	30	11	322	282	97
Los Angeles	84	39	35	10	338	340	88
Winnipeg	84	40	37	7	322	320	87
Edmonton	84	26	50	8	242	337	60
San Jose	84	11	71	2	218	414	24

PRINCE OF WALES CONFERENCE
Adams Division

Boston	84	51	26	7	332	268	109
Quebec	84	47	27	10	351	300	104
*Montreal	84	48	30	6	326	280	102
Buffalo	84	38	36	10	335	297	86
Hartford	84	26	52	6	284	369	58
Ottawa	84	10	70	4	202	395	24

Patrick Division

Pittsburgh	84	56	21	7	367	268	119
Washington	84	43	34	7	325	286	93
NY Islanders	84	40	37	7	335	297	87
New Jersey	84	40	37	7	308	299	87
Philadelphia	84	36	37	11	319	319	83
NY Rangers	84	34	39	11	304	308	79

Leading Scorers

Player	Club	GP	G	A	PTS	PIM
Lemieux, Mario	Pittsburgh	60	69	91	160	38
LaFontaine, Pat	Buffalo	84	53	95	148	63
Oates, Adam	Boston	84	45	97	142	32
Yzerman, Steve	Detroit	84	58	79	137	44
Selanne, Teemu	Winnipeg	84	76	56	132	45
Turgeon, Pierre	NY Islanders	83	58	74	132	26
Mogilny, Alexander	Buffalo	77	76	51	127	40
Gilmour, Doug	Toronto	83	32	95	127	100
Robitaille, Luc	Los Angeles	84	63	62	125	100
Recchi, Mark	Philadelphia	84	53	70	123	95

1993-94
EASTERN CONFERENCE
Northeast Division

Team	GP	W	L	T	GF	GA	PTS
Pittsburgh	84	44	27	13	299	285	101
Boston	84	42	29	13	289	252	97
Montreal	84	41	29	14	283	248	96
Buffalo	84	43	32	9	282	218	95
Quebec	84	34	42	8	277	292	76
Hartford	84	27	48	9	227	288	63
Ottawa	84	14	61	9	201	397	37

Atlantic Division

*NY Rangers	84	52	24	8	299	231	112
New Jersey	84	47	25	12	306	220	106
Washington	84	39	35	10	277	263	88
NY Islanders	84	36	36	12	282	264	84
Florida	84	33	34	17	233	233	83
Philadelphia	84	35	39	10	294	314	80
Tampa Bay	84	30	43	11	224	251	71

WESTERN CONFERENCE
Central Division

Detroit	84	46	30	8	356	275	100
Toronto	84	43	29	12	280	243	98
Dallas	84	42	29	13	286	265	97
St. Louis	84	40	33	11	270	283	91
Chicago	84	39	36	9	254	240	87
Winnipeg	84	24	51	9	245	344	57

Pacific Division

Calgary	84	42	29	13	302	256	97
Vancouver	84	41	40	3	279	276	85
San Jose	84	33	35	16	252	265	82
Anaheim	84	33	46	5	229	251	71
Los Angeles	84	27	45	12	294	322	66
Edmonton	84	25	45	14	261	305	64

Leading Scorers

Player	Club	GP	G	A	PTS	PIM
Gretzky, Wayne	Los Angeles	81	38	92	130	20
Fedorov, Sergei	Detroit	82	56	64	120	34
Oates, Adam	Boston	77	32	80	112	45
Gilmour, Doug	Toronto	83	27	84	111	105
Bure, Pavel	Vancouver	76	60	47	107	86
Roenick, Jeremy	Chicago	84	46	61	107	125
Recchi, Mark	Philadelphia	84	40	67	107	46
Shanahan, Brendan	St. Louis	81	52	50	102	211
Andreychuk, Dave	Toronto	83	53	46	99	98
Jagr, Jaromir	Pittsburgh	80	32	67	99	61

Pat LaFontaine first cracked the top-10 in scoring with the New York Islanders in 1989-90. He finished second in scoring behind Mario Lemieux with 148 points for the Buffalo Sabres in 1992-93.

1994-95
EASTERN CONFERENCE
Northeast Division

Team	GP	W	L	T	GF	GA	PTS
Quebec	48	30	13	5	185	134	65
Pittsburgh	48	29	16	3	181	158	61
Boston	48	27	18	3	150	127	57
Buffalo	48	22	19	7	130	119	51
Hartford	48	19	24	5	127	141	43
Montreal	48	18	23	7	125	148	43
Ottawa	48	9	34	5	117	174	23

Atlantic Division

Team	GP	W	L	T	GF	GA	PTS
Philadelphia	48	28	16	4	150	132	60
*New Jersey	48	22	18	8	136	121	52
Washington	48	22	18	8	136	120	52
NY Rangers	48	22	23	3	139	134	47
Florida	48	20	22	6	115	127	46
Tampa Bay	48	17	28	3	120	144	37
NY Islanders	48	15	28	5	126	158	35

WESTERN CONFERENCE
Central Division

Team	GP	W	L	T	GF	GA	PTS
Detroit	48	33	11	4	180	117	70
St. Louis	48	28	15	5	178	135	61
Chicago	48	24	19	5	156	115	53
Toronto	48	21	19	8	135	146	50
Dallas	48	17	23	8	136	135	42
Winnipeg	48	16	25	7	157	177	39

Pacific Division

Team	GP	W	L	T	GF	GA	PTS
Calgary	48	24	17	7	163	135	55
Vancouver	48	18	18	12	153	148	48
San Jose	48	19	25	4	129	161	42
Los Angeles	48	16	23	9	142	174	41
Edmonton	48	17	27	4	136	183	38
Anaheim	48	16	27	5	125	164	37

Leading Scorers

Player	Club	GP	G	A	PTS	PIM
Jagr, Jaromir	Pittsburgh	48	32	38	70	37
Lindros, Eric	Philadelphia	46	29	41	70	60
Zhamnov, Alexei	Winnipeg	48	30	35	65	20
Sakic, Joe	Quebec	47	19	43	62	30
Francis, Ron	Pittsburgh	44	11	48	59	18
Fleury, Theoren	Calgary	47	29	29	58	112
Coffey, Paul	Detroit	45	14	44	58	72
Renberg, Mikael	Philadelphia	47	26	31	57	20
LeClair, John	Mtl., Phi.	46	26	28	54	30
Messier, Mark	NY Rangers	46	14	39	53	40
Oates, Adam	Boston	48	12	41	53	8

1995-96
EASTERN CONFERENCE
Northeast Division

Team	GP	W	L	T	GF	GA	PTS
Pittsburgh	82	49	29	4	362	284	102
Boston	82	40	31	11	282	269	91
Montreal	82	40	32	10	265	248	90
Hartford	82	34	39	9	237	259	77
Buffalo	82	33	42	7	247	262	73
Ottawa	82	18	59	5	191	291	41

Atlantic Division

Team	GP	W	L	T	GF	GA	PTS
Philadelphia	82	45	24	13	282	208	103
NY Rangers	82	41	27	14	272	237	96
Florida	82	41	31	10	254	234	92
Washington	82	39	32	11	234	204	89
Tampa Bay	82	38	32	12	238	248	88
New Jersey	82	37	33	12	215	202	86
NY Islanders	82	22	50	10	229	315	54

WESTERN CONFERENCE
Central Division

Team	GP	W	L	T	GF	GA	PTS
Detroit	82	62	13	7	325	181	131
Chicago	82	40	28	14	273	220	94
Toronto	82	34	36	12	247	252	80
St. Louis	82	32	34	16	219	248	80
Winnipeg	82	36	40	6	275	291	78
Dallas	82	26	42	14	227	280	66

Pacific Division

Team	GP	W	L	T	GF	GA	PTS
*Colorado	82	47	25	10	326	240	104
Calgary	82	34	37	11	241	240	79
Vancouver	82	32	35	15	278	278	79
Anaheim	82	35	39	8	234	247	78
Edmonton	82	30	44	8	240	304	68
Los Angeles	82	24	40	18	256	302	66
San Jose	82	20	55	7	252	357	47

Leading Scorers

Player	Club	GP	G	A	PTS	PIM
Lemieux, Mario	Pittsburgh	70	69	92	161	54
Jagr, Jaromir	Pittsburgh	82	62	87	149	96
Sakic, Joe	Colorado	82	51	69	120	44
Francis, Ron	Pittsburgh	77	27	92	119	56
Forsberg, Peter	Colorado	82	30	86	116	47
Lindros, Eric	Philadelphia	73	47	68	115	163
Kariya, Paul	Anaheim	82	50	58	108	20
Selanne, Teemu	Wpg., Ana.	79	40	68	108	22
Mogilny, Alexander	Vancouver	79	55	52	107	16
Fedorov, Sergei	Detroit	78	39	68	107	48

1996-97
EASTERN CONFERENCE
Northeast Division

Team	GP	W	L	T	GF	GA	PTS
Buffalo	82	40	30	12	237	208	92
Pittsburgh	82	38	36	8	285	280	84
Ottawa	82	31	36	15	226	234	77
Montreal	82	31	36	15	249	276	77
Hartford	82	32	39	11	226	256	75
Boston	82	26	47	9	234	300	61

Atlantic Division

Team	GP	W	L	T	GF	GA	PTS
New Jersey	82	45	23	14	231	182	104
Philadelphia	82	45	24	13	274	217	103
Florida	82	35	28	19	221	201	89
NY Rangers	82	38	34	10	258	231	86
Washington	82	33	40	9	214	231	75
Tampa Bay	82	32	40	10	217	247	74
NY Islanders	82	29	41	12	240	250	70

WESTERN CONFERENCE
Central Division

Team	GP	W	L	T	GF	GA	PTS
Dallas	82	48	26	8	252	198	104
*Detroit	82	38	26	18	253	197	94
Phoenix	82	38	37	7	240	243	83
St. Louis	82	36	35	11	236	239	83
Chicago	82	34	35	13	223	210	81
Toronto	82	30	44	8	230	273	68

Pacific Division

Team	GP	W	L	T	GF	GA	PTS
Colorado	82	49	24	9	277	205	107
Anaheim	82	36	33	13	245	233	85
Edmonton	82	36	37	9	252	247	81
Vancouver	82	35	40	7	257	273	77
Calgary	82	32	41	9	214	239	73
Los Angeles	82	28	43	11	214	268	67
San Jose	82	27	47	8	211	278	62

Leading Scorers

Player	Club	GP	G	A	PTS	PIM
Lemieux, Mario	Pittsburgh	76	50	72	122	65
Selanne, Teemu	Anaheim	78	51	58	109	34
Kariya, Paul	Anaheim	69	44	55	99	6
LeClair, John	Philadelphia	82	50	47	97	58
Gretzky, Wayne	NY Rangers	82	25	72	97	28
Jagr, Jaromir	Pittsburgh	63	47	48	95	40
Sundin, Mats	Toronto	82	41	53	94	59
Palffy, Ziggy	NY Islanders	80	48	42	90	43
Francis, Ron	Pittsburgh	81	27	63	90	20
Shanahan, Brendan	Hfd., Det.	81	47	41	88	131

Seventh among the NHL's all-time scoring leaders, Ron Francis (left) had his most productive season with the Pittsburgh Penguins in 1995-96. Peter Forsberg (right) made his first appearance among the NHL scoring leaders that season.

1997-98
EASTERN CONFERENCE
Northeast Division

Team	GP	W	L	T	GF	GA	PTS
Pittsburgh	82	40	24	18	228	188	98
Boston	82	39	30	13	221	194	91
Buffalo	82	36	29	17	211	187	89
Montreal	82	37	32	13	235	208	87
Ottawa	82	34	33	15	193	200	83
Carolina	82	33	41	8	200	219	74

Atlantic Division

Team	GP	W	L	T	GF	GA	PTS
New Jersey	82	48	23	11	225	166	107
Philadelphia	82	42	29	11	242	193	95
Washington	82	40	30	12	219	202	92
NY Islanders	82	30	41	11	212	225	71
NY Rangers	82	25	39	18	197	231	68
Florida	82	24	43	15	203	256	63
Tampa Bay	82	17	55	10	151	269	44

WESTERN CONFERENCE
Central Division

Team	GP	W	L	T	GF	GA	PTS
Dallas	82	49	22	11	242	167	109
*Detroit	82	44	23	15	250	196	103
St. Louis	82	45	29	8	256	204	98
Phoenix	82	35	35	12	224	227	82
Chicago	82	30	39	13	192	199	73
Toronto	82	30	43	9	194	237	69

Pacific Division

Team	GP	W	L	T	GF	GA	PTS
Colorado	82	39	26	17	231	205	95
Los Angeles	82	38	33	11	227	225	87
Edmonton	82	35	37	10	215	224	80
San Jose	82	34	38	10	210	216	78
Calgary	82	26	41	15	217	252	67
Anaheim	82	26	43	13	205	261	65
Vancouver	82	25	43	14	224	273	64

Leading Scorers

Player	Club	GP	G	A	PTS	PIM
Jagr, Jaromir	Pittsburgh	77	35	67	102	64
Forsberg, Peter	Colorado	72	25	66	91	94
Bure, Pavel	Vancouver	82	51	39	90	48
Gretzky, Wayne	NY Rangers	82	23	67	90	28
LeClair, John	Philadelphia	82	51	36	87	32
Palffy, Ziggy	NY Islanders	82	45	42	87	34
Francis, Ron	Pittsburgh	81	25	62	87	20
Selanne, Teemu	Anaheim	73	52	34	86	30
Allison, Jason	Boston	81	33	50	83	60
Stumpel, Jozef	Los Angeles	77	21	58	79	53

1998-99
EASTERN CONFERENCE
Northeast Division

Team	GP	W	L	T	GF	GA	PTS
Ottawa	82	44	23	15	239	179	103
Toronto	82	45	30	7	268	231	97
Boston	82	39	30	13	214	181	91
Buffalo	82	37	28	17	207	175	91
Montreal	82	32	39	11	184	209	75

Atlantic Division

Team	GP	W	L	T	GF	GA	PTS
New Jersey	82	47	24	11	248	196	105
Philadelphia	82	37	26	19	231	196	93
Pittsburgh	82	38	30	14	242	225	90
Ny Rangers	82	33	38	11	217	227	77
Ny Islanders	82	24	48	10	194	244	58

Southeast Division

Team	GP	W	L	T	GF	GA	PTS
Carolina	82	34	30	18	210	202	86
Florida	82	30	34	18	210	228	78
Washington	82	31	45	6	200	218	68
Tampa Bay	82	19	54	9	179	292	47

WESTERN CONFERENCE
Central Division

Team	GP	W	L	T	GF	GA	PTS
Detroit	82	43	32	7	245	202	93
St Louis	82	37	32	13	237	209	87
Chicago	82	29	41	12	202	248	70
Nashville	82	28	47	7	190	261	63

Pacific Division

Team	GP	W	L	T	GF	GA	PTS
*Dallas	82	51	19	12	236	168	114
Phoenix	82	39	31	12	205	197	90
Anaheim	82	35	34	13	215	206	83
San Jose	82	31	33	18	196	191	80
Los Angeles	82	32	45	5	189	222	69

Northwest Division

Team	GP	W	L	T	GF	GA	PTS
Colorado	82	44	28	10	239	205	98
Edmonton	82	33	37	12	230	226	78
Calgary	82	30	40	12	211	234	72
Vancouver	82	23	47	12	192	258	58

Leading Scorers

Player	Club	GP	G	A	PTS	PIM
Jagr, Jaromir	Pittsburgh	81	44	83	127	66
Selanne, Teemu	Anaheim	75	47	60	107	30
Kariya, Paul	Anaheim	82	39	62	101	40
Forsberg, Peter	Colorado	78	30	67	97	108
Sakic, Joe	Colorado	73	41	55	96	29
Yashin, Alexei	Ottawa	82	44	50	94	54
Lindros, Eric	Philadelphia	71	40	53	93	120
Fleury, Theoren	Cgy., Col.	75	40	53	93	86
Leclair, John	Philadelphia	76	43	47	90	30
Demitra, Pavol	St Louis	82	37	52	89	16

1999-2000
EASTERN CONFERENCE
Northeast Division

Team	GP	W	L	T	RT	GF	GA	PTS
Toronto	82	45	30	7	3	246	222	100
Ottawa	82	41	30	11	2	244	210	95
Buffalo	82	35	36	11	4	213	204	85
Montreal	82	35	38	9	4	196	194	83
Boston	82	24	39	19	6	210	248	73

Atlantic Division

Team	GP	W	L	T	RT	GF	GA	PTS
Philadelphia	82	45	25	12	3	237	179	105
*New Jersey	82	45	29	8	5	251	203	103
Pittsburgh	82	37	37	8	6	241	236	88
NY Rangers	82	29	41	12	3	218	246	73
NY Islanders	82	24	49	9	1	194	275	58

Southeast Division

Team	GP	W	L	T	RT	GF	GA	PTS
Washington	82	44	26	12	2	227	194	102
Florida	82	43	33	6	6	244	209	98
Carolina	82	37	35	10	0	217	216	84
Tampa Bay	82	19	54	9	7	204	310	54
Atlanta	82	14	61	7	4	170	313	39

WESTERN CONFERENCE
Central Division

Team	GP	W	L	T	RT	GF	GA	PTS
St. Louis	82	51	20	11	1	248	165	114
Detroit	82	48	24	10	2	278	210	108
Chicago	82	33	39	10	2	242	245	78
Nashville	82	28	47	7	7	199	240	70

Pacific Division

Team	GP	W	L	T	RT	GF	GA	PTS
Dallas	82	43	29	10	6	211	184	102
Los Angeles	82	39	31	12	4	245	228	94
Phoenix	82	39	35	8	4	232	228	90
San Jose	82	35	37	10	7	225	214	87
Anaheim	82	34	36	12	3	217	227	83

Northwest Division

Team	GP	W	L	T	RT	GF	GA	PTS
Colorado	82	42	29	11	1	233	201	96
Edmonton	82	32	34	16	8	226	212	88
Vancouver	82	30	37	15	8	227	237	83
Calgary	82	31	41	10	5	211	256	77

Leading Scorers

Player	Club	GP	G	A	PTS	PIM
Jagr, Jaromir	Pittsburgh	63	42	54	96	50
Bure, Pavel	Florida	74	58	36	94	16
Recchi, Mark	Philadelphia	82	28	63	91	50
Kariya, Paul	Anaheim	74	42	44	86	24
Selanne, Teemu	Anaheim	79	33	52	85	12
Nolan, Owen	San Jose	78	44	40	84	110
Amonte, Tony	Chicago	82	43	41	84	48
Modano, Mike	Dallas	77	38	43	81	48
Sakic, Joe	Colorado	60	28	53	81	28
Yzerman, Steve	Detroit	78	35	44	79	34

Note: Detailed statistics for 1999-2000 are listed in the Final Statistics, 1999-2000 section of the *NHL Guide & Record Book*. **See page 131.**

Teemu Selanne has ranked among the NHL's top-10 scorers for five straight seasons since joining the Mighty Ducks of Anaheim during the 1995-96 season. Twice he has finished as the runner-up for the Art Ross Trophy.

Team Records
Regular Season

FINAL STANDINGS

MOST POINTS, ONE SEASON:
132 — Montreal Canadiens, 1976-77. 60w-8L-12T. 80GP
131 — Detroit Red Wings, 1995-96. 62w-13L-7T. 82GP
129 — Montreal Canadiens, 1977-78. 59w-10L-11T. 80GP

BEST WINNING PERCENTAGE, ONE SEASON:
.875 — Boston Bruins, 1929-30. 38w-5L-1T. 77PTS in 44GP
.830 — Montreal Canadiens, 1943-44. 38w-5L-7T. 83PTS in 50GP
.825 — Montreal Canadiens, 1976-77. 60w-8L-12T. 132PTS in 80GP
.806 — Montreal Canadiens, 1977-78. 59w-10L-11T. 129PTS in 80GP
.800 — Montreal Canadiens, 1944-45. 38w-8L-4T. 80PTS in 50GP

FEWEST POINTS, ONE SEASON:
8 — Quebec Bulldogs, 1919-20. 4w-20L-0T. 24GP
10 — Toronto Arenas, 1918-19. 5w-13L-0T. 18GP
12 — Hamilton Tigers, 1920-21. 6w-18L-0T. 24GP
— Hamilton Tigers, 1922-23. 6w-18L-0T. 24GP
— Boston Bruins, 1924-25. 6w-24L-0T. 30GP
— Philadelphia Quakers, 1930-31. 4w-36L-4T. 44GP

FEWEST POINTS, ONE SEASON (MINIMUM 70-GAME SCHEDULE):
21 — Washington Capitals, 1974-75. 8w-67L-5T. 80GP
24 — Ottawa Senators, 1992-93. 10w-70L-4T. 84GP
— San Jose Sharks, 1992-93. 11w-71L-2T. 84GP
30 — NY Islanders, 1972-73. 12w-60L-6T. 78GP

WORST WINNING PERCENTAGE, ONE SEASON:
.131 — Washington Capitals, 1974-75. 8w-67L-5T. 21PTS in 80GP
.136 — Philadelphia Quakers, 1930-31. 4w-36L-4T. 12PTS in 44GP
.143 — Ottawa Senators, 1992-93. 10w-70L-4T. 24PTS in 84GP
.143 — San Jose Sharks, 1992-93. 11w-71L-2T. 24PTS in 84GP
.148 — Pittsburgh Pirates, 1929-30. 5w-36L-3T. 13PTS in 44GP

TEAM WINS

Most Wins

MOST WINS, ONE SEASON:
62 — Detroit Red Wings, 1995-96. 82GP
60 — Montreal Canadiens, 1976-77. 80GP
59 — Montreal Canadiens, 1977-78. 80GP

MOST HOME WINS, ONE SEASON:
36 — Philadelphia Flyers, 1975-76. 40GP
— Detroit Red Wings, 1995-96. 41GP
33 — Boston Bruins, 1970-71. 39GP
— Boston Bruins, 1973-74. 39GP
— Montreal Canadiens, 1976-77. 40GP
— Philadelphia Flyers, 1976-77. 40GP
— NY Islanders, 1981-82. 40GP
— Philadelphia Flyers, 1985-86. 40GP

MOST ROAD WINS, ONE SEASON:
28 — New Jersey Devils, 1998-99. 41**GP**
27 — Montreal Canadiens, 1976-77. 40GP
— Montreal Canadiens, 1977-78. 40GP
— St. Louis Blues, 1999-2000. 41GP
26 — Boston Bruins, 1971-72. 39GP
— Montreal Canadiens, 1975-76. 40GP
— Edmonton Oilers, 1983-84. 40GP
— Detroit Red Wings, 1995-96. 41GP

Fewest Wins

FEWEST WINS, ONE SEASON:
4 — Quebec Bulldogs, 1919-20. 24GP
— Philadelphia Quakers, 1930-31. 44GP
5 — Toronto Arenas, 1918-19. 18GP
— Pittsburgh Pirates, 1929-30. 44GP

FEWEST WINS, ONE SEASON (MINIMUM 70-GAME SCHEDULE):
8 — Washington Capitals, 1974-75. 80GP
9 — Winnipeg Jets, 1980-81. 80GP
10 — Ottawa Senators, 1992-93. 84GP

FEWEST HOME WINS, ONE SEASON:
2 — Chicago Blackhawks, 1927-28. 22GP
3 — Boston Bruins, 1924-25. 15GP
— Chicago Blackhawks, 1928-29. 22GP
— Philadelphia Quakers, 1930-31. 22GP

FEWEST HOME WINS, ONE SEASON (MINIMUM 70-GAME SCHEDULE):
6 — Chicago Blackhawks, 1954-55. 35GP
— Washington Capitals, 1975-76. 40GP
7 — Boston Bruins, 1962-63. 35GP
— Washington Capitals, 1974-75. 40GP
— Winnipeg Jets, 1980-81. 40GP
— Pittsburgh Penguins, 1983-84. 40GP

FEWEST ROAD WINS, ONE SEASON:
0 — Toronto Arenas, 1918-19. 9GP
— Quebec Bulldogs, 1919-20. 12GP
— Pittsburgh Pirates, 1929-30. 22GP
1 — Hamilton Tigers, 1921-22. 12GP
— Toronto St. Patricks, 1925-26. 18GP
— Philadelphia Quakers, 1930-31. 22GP
— NY Americans, 1940-41. 24GP
— Washington Capitals, 1974-75. 40GP
* — Ottawa Senators, 1992-93. 41GP

FEWEST ROAD WINS, ONE SEASON (MINIMUM 70-GAME SCHEDULE):
1 — Washington Capitals, 1974-75. 40GP
* **— Ottawa Senators,** 1992-93. 41GP
2 — Boston Bruins, 1960-61. 35GP
— Los Angeles Kings, 1969-70. 38GP
— NY Islanders, 1972-73. 39GP
— California Seals, 1973-74. 39GP
— Colorado Rockies, 1977-78. 40GP
— Winnipeg Jets, 1980-81. 40GP
— Quebec Nordiques, 1991-92. 40GP

TEAM LOSSES

Fewest Losses

FEWEST LOSSES, ONE SEASON:
5 — Ottawa Senators, 1919-20. 24GP
— Boston Bruins, 1929-30. 44GP
— Montreal Canadiens, 1943-44. 50GP

FEWEST HOME LOSSES, ONE SEASON:
0 — Ottawa Senators, 1922-23. 12GP
— Montreal Canadiens, 1943-44. 25GP
1 — Toronto Arenas, 1917-18. 11GP
— Ottawa Senators, 1918-19. 9GP
— Ottawa Senators, 1919-20. 12GP
— Toronto St. Patricks, 1922-23. 12GP
— Boston Bruins, 1929-30. 22GP
— Boston Bruins, 1930-31. 22GP
— Montreal Canadiens, 1976-77. 40GP
— Quebec Nordiques, 1994-95. 24GP

FEWEST ROAD LOSSES, ONE SEASON:
3 — Montreal Canadiens, 1928-29. 22GP
4 — Ottawa Senators, 1919-20. 12GP
— Montreal Canadiens, 1927-28. 22GP
— Boston Bruins, 1929-30. 20GP
— Boston Bruins, 1940-41. 24GP

FEWEST LOSSES, ONE SEASON (MINIMUM 70-GAME SCHEDULE):
8 — Montreal Canadiens, 1976-77. 80GP
10 — Montreal Canadiens, 1972-73. 78GP
— Montreal Canadiens, 1977-78. 80GP
11 — Montreal Canadiens, 1975-76. 80GP

FEWEST HOME LOSSES, ONE SEASON (MINIMUM 70-GAME SCHEDULE):
1 — Montreal Canadiens, 1976-77. 40GP
2 — Montreal Canadiens, 1961-62. 35GP
— NY Rangers, 1970-71. 39GP
— Philadelphia Flyers, 1975-76. 40GP

FEWEST ROAD LOSSES, ONE SEASON (MINIMUM 70-GAME SCHEDULE):
6 — Montreal Canadiens, 1972-73. 39GP
— Montreal Canadiens, 1974-75. 40GP
— Montreal Canadiens, 1977-78. 40GP
7 — Detroit Red Wings, 1951-52. 35GP
— Montreal Canadiens, 1976-77. 40GP
— Philadelphia Flyers, 1979-80. 40GP

Most Losses

MOST LOSSES, ONE SEASON:
71 — San Jose Sharks, 1992-93. 84GP
70 — Ottawa Senators, 1992-93. 84GP
67 — Washington Capitals, 1974-75. 80GP
61 — Quebec Nordiques, 1989-90. 80GP
—Ottawa Senators, 1993-94. 84GP
—Atlanta Thrashers, 1999-2000. 82GP

MOST HOME LOSSES, ONE SEASON:
***32 — San Jose Sharks,** 1992-93. 41GP
29 — Pittsburgh Penguins, 1983-84. 40GP
* — Ottawa Senators, 1993-94. 41GP
— Atlanta Thrashers, 1999-2000. 41GP

MOST ROAD LOSSES, ONE SEASON:
***40 — Ottawa Senators,** 1992-93. 41GP
39 — Washington Capitals, 1974-75. 40GP
37 — California Seals, 1973-74. 39GP
* — San Jose Sharks, 1992-93. 41GP

* — Does not include neutral site games

TEAM TIES

Most Ties

MOST TIES, ONE SEASON:
   24 — Philadelphia Flyers, 1969-70. 76GP
   23 — Montreal Canadiens, 1962-63. 70GP
      — Chicago Blackhawks, 1973-74. 78GP

MOST HOME TIES, ONE SEASON:
   13 — NY Rangers, 1954-55. 35GP
      — **Philadelphia Flyers,** 1969-70. 38GP
      — **California Seals,** 1971-72. 39GP
      — **California Seals,** 1972-73. 39GP
      — **Chicago Blackhawks,** 1973-74. 39GP

MOST ROAD TIES, ONE SEASON:
   15 — Philadelphia Flyers, 1976-77. 40GP
   14 — Montreal Canadiens, 1952-53. 35GP
      — Montreal Canadiens, 1974-75. 40GP
      — Philadelphia Flyers, 1975-76. 40GP

Fewest Ties

FEWEST TIES, ONE SEASON (Since 1926-27):
   1 — Boston Bruins, 1929-30. 44GP
   2 — Montreal Canadiens, 1926-27. 44GP
      — NY Americans, 1926-27. 44GP
      — Boston Bruins, 1938-39. 48GP
      — NY Rangers, 1941-42. 48GP
      — San Jose Sharks, 1992-93. 84GP

FEWEST TIES, ONE SEASON (MINIMUM 70-GAME SCHEDULE):
   2 — San Jose Sharks, 1992-93. 84GP
   3 — New Jersey Devils, 1985-86. 80GP
      — Calgary Flames, 1986-87. 80GP
      — Vancouver Canucks, 1993-94. 84GP

WINNING STREAKS

LONGEST WINNING STREAK, ONE SEASON:
   17 Games — Pittsburgh Penguins, Mar. 9 - Apr. 10, 1993.
   15 Games — NY Islanders, Jan. 21 - Feb. 20, 1982.
   14 Games — Boston Bruins, Dec. 3, 1929 - Jan. 9, 1930.

LONGEST HOME WINNING STREAK, ONE SEASON:
   20 Games — Boston Bruins, Dec. 3, 1929 - Mar. 18, 1930.
      — **Philadelphia Flyers,** Jan. 4 - Apr. 3, 1976.

LONGEST ROAD WINNING STREAK, ONE SEASON:
   10 Games — Buffalo Sabres, Dec. 10, 1983 - Jan. 23, 1984.
      — **St. Louis Blues,** Jan. 21 - Mar. 2, 2000.
   8 Games — Boston Bruins, Feb. 17 - Mar. 8, 1972.
      — Los Angeles Kings, Dec. 18, 1974 - Jan. 16, 1975.
      — Montreal Canadiens, Dec. 18, 1977 - Jan. 18, 1978.
      — NY Islanders, Feb. 27 - Mar. 29, 1981.
      — Montreal Canadiens, Jan. 21 - Feb. 21, 1982.
      — Philadelphia Flyers, Dec. 22, 1982 - Jan. 16, 1983.
      — Winnipeg Jets, Feb. 25 - Apr. 6, 1985.
      — Edmonton Oilers, Dec. 9, 1986 - Jan. 17, 1987.
      — Boston Bruins, Mar. 15 - Apr. 14, 1993.

LONGEST WINNING STREAK FROM START OF SEASON:
   10 Games — Toronto Maple Leafs, 1993-94.
   8 Games — Toronto Maple Leafs, 1934-35.
      — Buffalo Sabres, 1975-76.
   7 Games — Edmonton Oilers, 1983-84.
      — Quebec Nordiques, 1985-86.
      — Pittsburgh Penguins, 1986-87.
      — Pittsburgh Penguins, 1994-95.

LONGEST HOME WINNING STREAK FROM START OF SEASON:
   11 Games — Chicago Blackhawks, 1963-64.
   10 Games — Ottawa Senators, 1925-26.
   9 Games — Montreal Canadiens, 1953-54.
      — Chicago Blackhawks, 1971-72.

LONGEST ROAD WINNING STREAK FROM START OF SEASON:
   7 Games — Toronto Maple Leafs, Nov. 14 - Dec. 15, 1940.

LONGEST WINNING STREAK, INCLUDING PLAYOFFS:
   15 Games — Detroit Red Wings, Feb. 27 - Apr. 5, 1955. Nine regular-season games, six playoff games.

LONGEST HOME WINNING STREAK, INCLUDING PLAYOFFS:
   24 Games — Philadelphia Flyers, Jan. 4 - Apr. 25, 1976. Twenty regular-season games, four playoff games.

LONGEST ROAD WINNING STREAK, INCLUDING PLAYOFFS:
   8 Games — NY Islanders, Apr. 4 - May 1, 1980. One regular season game, seven playoff games.

UNDEFEATED STREAKS

LONGEST UNDEFEATED STREAK, ONE SEASON:
   35 Games — Philadelphia Flyers, Oct. 14, 1979 - Jan. 6, 1980. 25w-10T.
   28 Games — Montreal Canadiens, Dec. 18, 1977 - Feb. 23, 1978. 23w-5T.
   23 Games — Boston Bruins, Dec. 22, 1940 - Feb. 23, 1941. 15w-8T.
      — Philadelphia Flyers, Jan. 29 - Mar. 18, 1976. 17w-6T.

LONGEST HOME UNDEFEATED STREAK, ONE SEASON:
   34 Games — Montreal Canadiens, Nov. 1, 1976 - Apr. 2, 1977. 28w-6T.
   27 Games — Boston Bruins, Nov. 22, 1970 - Mar. 20, 1971. 26w-1T.

LONGEST ROAD UNDEFEATED STREAK, ONE SEASON:
   23 Games — Montreal Canadiens, Nov. 27, 1974 - Mar. 12, 1975. 14w-9T.
   17 Games — Montreal Canadiens, Dec. 18, 1977 - Mar. 1, 1978. 14w-3T.
   16 Games — Philadelphia Flyers, Oct. 20, 1979 - Jan. 6, 1980. 11w-5T.

LONGEST UNDEFEATED STREAK FROM START OF SEASON:
   15 Games — Edmonton Oilers, 1984-85. 12w-3T.
   14 Games — Montreal Canadiens, 1943-44. 11w-3T.
   13 Games — Montreal Canadiens, 1972-73. 9w-4T.
      — Pittsburgh Penguins, 1994-95. 12w-1T.

LONGEST HOME UNDEFEATED STREAK FROM START OF SEASON:
   25 Games — Montreal Canadiens, Oct. 30, 1943 - Mar. 18, 1944. 22w-3T.

LONGEST ROAD UNDEFEATED STREAK FROM START OF SEASON:
   15 Games — Detroit Red Wings, Oct. 18 - Dec. 20, 1951. 10w-5T.

LONGEST UNDEFEATED STREAK, INCLUDING PLAYOFFS:
   21 Games — Pittsburgh Penguins, Mar. 9 - Apr. 22, 1993. 17w-1T in regular season and 3w in playoffs.

LONGEST HOME UNDEFEATED STREAK, INCLUDING PLAYOFFS:
   38 Games — Montreal Canadiens, Nov. 1, 1976 - Apr. 26, 1977. 28w-6T in regular season and 4w in playoff.

LONGEST ROAD UNDEFEATED STREAK, INCLUDING PLAYOFFS:
   13 Games — Montreal Canadiens, Feb. 26 - Apr. 20, 1980. 6w-4T in regular season and 3w in playoffs.
      — **NY Islanders,** Mar. 16 - May 1, 1980. 3w-3T in regular season and 7w in playoffs.

LOSING STREAKS

LONGEST LOSING STREAK, ONE SEASON:
   17 Games — Washington Capitals, Feb. 18 - Mar. 26, 1975.
      — **San Jose Sharks,** Jan. 4 - Feb. 12, 1993.
   15 Games — Philadelphia Quakers, Nov. 29, 1930 - Jan. 8, 1931.

LONGEST HOME LOSING STREAK, ONE SEASON:
   11 Games — Boston Bruins, Dec. 8, 1924 - Feb. 17, 1925.
      — **Washington Capitals,** Feb. 18 - Mar. 30, 1975.
      — **Ottawa Senators,** Oct. 27 - Dec. 8, 1993.
      — **Atlanta Thrashers,** Jan. 24-Mar. 16, 2000.

LONGEST ROAD LOSING STREAK, ONE SEASON:
   ***38 Games — Ottawa Senators,** Oct. 10, 1992 - Apr. 3, 1993.
   37 Games — Washington Capitals, Oct. 9, 1974 - Mar. 26, 1975.

LONGEST LOSING STREAK FROM START OF SEASON:
   11 Games — NY Rangers, 1943-44.
   7 Games — Montreal Canadiens, 1938-39.
      — Chicago Blackhawks, 1947-48.
      — Washington Capitals, 1983-84.
      — Chicago Blackhawks, 1997-98.

LONGEST HOME LOSING STREAK FROM START OF SEASON:
   8 Games — Los Angeles Kings, Oct. 13 - Nov. 6, 1971.

LONGEST ROAD LOSING STREAK FROM START OF SEASON:
   ***38 Games — Ottawa Senators,** Oct. 10, 1992 - Apr. 3, 1993.

WINLESS STREAKS

LONGEST WINLESS STREAK, ONE SEASON:
   30 Games — Winnipeg Jets, Oct. 19 - Dec. 20, 1980. 23L-7T.
   27 Games — Kansas City Scouts, Feb. 12 - Apr. 4, 1976. 21L-6T.
   25 Games — Washington Capitals, Nov. 29, 1975 - Jan. 21, 1976. 22L-3T.

LONGEST HOME WINLESS STREAK, ONE SEASON:
   17 Games — Ottawa Senators, Oct. 28, 1995 - Jan. 27, 1996. 15L-2T.
      — **Atlanta Thrashers,** Jan. 19-Mar. 29, 2000. 15L-2T.
   15 Games — Chicago Blackhawks, Dec. 16, 1928 - Feb. 28, 1929. 11L-4T.
      — Montreal Canadiens, Dec. 16, 1939 - Mar. 7, 1940. 12L-3T.

LONGEST ROAD WINLESS STREAK, ONE SEASON:
   ***38 Games — Ottawa Senators,** Oct. 10, 1992 - Apr. 3, 1993. 38L-0T.
   37 Games — Washington Capitals, Oct. 9, 1974 - Mar. 26, 1975. 37L-0T.

LONGEST WINLESS STREAK FROM START OF SEASON:
   15 Games — NY Rangers, 1943-44. 14L-1T.
   11 Games — Pittsburgh Pirates, 1927-28. 8L-3T.
      — Minnesota North Stars, 1973-74. 5L-6T.
      — San Jose Sharks, 1995-96. 7L-4T.

LONGEST HOME WINLESS STREAK FROM START OF SEASON:
   11 Games — Pittsburgh Penguins, Oct. 8 - Nov. 19, 1983. 9L-2T.

LONGEST ROAD WINLESS STREAK FROM START OF SEASON:
*38 Games — Ottawa Senators, Oct. 10, 1992 - Apr. 3, 1993. 38L-0T.

NON-SHUTOUT STREAKS

LONGEST NON-SHUTOUT STREAK:
264 Games — Calgary Flames, Nov. 12, 1981 - Jan. 9, 1985.
262 Games — Los Angeles Kings, Mar. 15, 1986 - Oct. 25, 1989.
244 Games — Washington Capitals, Oct. 31, 1989 - Nov. 11, 1993.
230 Games — Quebec Nordiques, Feb. 10, 1980 - Jan. 13, 1983.
229 Games — Edmonton Oilers, Mar. 15, 1981 - Feb. 11, 1984.

LONGEST NON-SHUTOUT STREAK INCLUDING PLAYOFFS:
264 Games — Los Angeles Kings, Mar. 15, 1986 - Apr. 6, 1989.
    (5 playoff games in 1987; 5 in 1988; 2 in 1989).
262 Games — Chicago Blackhawks, Mar. 14, 1970 - Feb. 21, 1973. (8 playoff games in 1970; 18 in 1971; 8 in 1972).
251 Games — Quebec Nordiques, Feb. 10, 1980 - Jan. 13, 1983. (5 playoff games in 1981; 16 in 1982).
245 Games — Pittsburgh Penguins, Jan. 7, 1989 - Oct. 26, 1991. (11 playoff games in 1989; 23 in 1991).

TEAM GOALS

Most Goals

MOST GOALS, ONE SEASON:
446 — Edmonton Oilers, 1983-84. 80GP
426 — Edmonton Oilers, 1985-86. 80GP
424 — Edmonton Oilers, 1982-83. 80GP
417 — Edmonton Oilers, 1981-82. 80GP
401 — Edmonton Oilers, 1984-85. 80GP

MOST GOALS, ONE TEAM, ONE GAME:
16 — Montreal Canadiens, Mar. 3, 1920, at Quebec. Defeated Que. Bulldogs 16-3.

MOST GOALS, BOTH TEAMS, ONE GAME:
21 — Montreal Canadiens, Toronto St. Patricks, at Montreal, Jan. 10, 1920. Montreal won 14-7.
    — Edmonton Oilers, Chicago Blackhawks, at Chicago, Dec. 11, 1985. Edmonton won 12-9.
20 — Edmonton Oilers, Minnesota North Stars, at Edmonton, Jan. 4, 1984. Edmonton won 12-8.
    — Toronto Maple Leafs, Edmonton Oilers, at Toronto, Jan. 8, 1986. Toronto won 11-9.
19 — Montreal Wanderers, Toronto Arenas, at Montreal, Dec. 19, 1917. Montreal won 10-9.
    — Montreal Canadiens, Quebec Bulldogs, at Quebec, Mar. 3, 1920. Montreal won 16-3.
    — Montreal Canadiens, Hamilton Tigers, at Montreal, Feb. 26, 1921. Montreal won 13-6.
    — Boston Bruins, NY Rangers, at Boston, Mar. 4, 1944. Boston won 10-9.
    — Boston Bruins, Detroit Red Wings, at Detroit, Mar. 16, 1944. Detroit won 10-9.
    — Vancouver Canucks, Minnesota North Stars, at Vancouver, Oct. 7, 1983. Vancouver won 10-9.

MOST GOALS, ONE TEAM, ONE PERIOD:
9 — Buffalo Sabres, Mar. 19, 1981, at Buffalo, second period during 14-4 win over Toronto.
8 — Detroit Red Wings, Jan. 23, 1944, at Detroit, third period during 15-0 win over NY Rangers.
    — Boston Bruins, Mar. 16, 1969, at Boston, second period during 11-3 win over Toronto.
    — NY Rangers, Nov. 21, 1971, at New York, third period during 12-1 win over California.
    — Philadelphia Flyers, Mar. 31, 1973, at Philadelphia, second period during 10-2 win over NY Islanders.
    — Buffalo Sabres, Dec. 21, 1975, at Buffalo, third period during 14-2 win over Washington.
    — Minnesota North Stars, Nov. 11, 1981, at Minnesota, second period during 15-2 win over Winnipeg.
    — Pittsburgh Penguins, Dec. 17, 1991, at Pittsburgh, second period during 10-2 win over San Jose.
    — Washington Capitals, Feb. 3, 1999, at Washington, second period during 10-1 win over Tampa Bay.

MOST GOALS, BOTH TEAMS, ONE PERIOD:
12 — Buffalo Sabres, Toronto Maple Leafs, at Buffalo, March 19, 1981, second period. Buffalo scored 9 goals, Toronto 3. Buffalo won 14-4.
    — Edmonton Oilers, Chicago Blackhawks, at Chicago, Dec. 11, 1985, second period. Edmonton scored 6 goals, Chicago 6. Edmonton won 12-9.
10 — NY Rangers, NY Americans, at NY Americans, March 16, 1939, third period. NY Rangers scored 7 goals, NY Americans 3. NY Rangers won 11-5.
    — Toronto Maple Leafs, Detroit Red Wings, at Detroit, March 17, 1946, third period. Toronto scored 6 goals, Detroit 4. Toronto won 11-7.
    — Vancouver Canucks, Buffalo Sabres, at Buffalo, Jan. 8, 1976, third period. Buffalo scored 6 goals, Vancouver 4. Buffalo won 8-5.
    — Buffalo Sabres, Montreal Canadiens, at Montreal, Oct. 26, 1982, first period. Montreal scored 5 goals, Buffalo 5. 7-7 tie.
    — Boston Bruins, Quebec Nordiques, at Quebec, Dec. 7, 1982, second period. Quebec scored 6 goals, Boston 4. Quebec won 10-5.
    — Calgary Flames, Vancouver Canucks, at Vancouver, Jan. 16, 1987, first period. Vancouver scored 6 goals, Calgary 4. Vancouver won 9-5.
    — Winnipeg Jets, Detroit Red Wings, at Detroit, Nov. 25, 1987, third period. Detroit scored 7 goals, Winnipeg 3. Detroit won 10-8.
    — Chicago Blackhawks, St. Louis Blues, at St. Louis, March 15, 1988, third period. Chicago scored 5 goals, St. Louis 5. 7-7 tie.

MOST CONSECUTIVE GOALS, ONE TEAM, ONE GAME:
15 — Detroit Red Wings, Jan. 23, 1944, at Detroit. Defeated NY Rangers 15-0.

Fewest Goals

FEWEST GOALS, ONE SEASON:
33 — Chicago Blackhawks, 1928-29. 44GP
45 — Montreal Maroons, 1924-25. 30GP
46 — Pittsburgh Pirates, 1928-29. 44GP

FEWEST GOALS, ONE SEASON (MINIMUM 70-GAME SCHEDULE):
133 — Chicago Blackhawks, 1953-54. 70GP
147 — Toronto Maple Leafs, 1954-55. 70GP
    — Boston Bruins, 1955-56. 70GP
150 — NY Rangers, 1954-55. 70GP

TEAM POWER-PLAY GOALS

MOST POWER-PLAY GOALS, ONE SEASON:
119 — Pittsburgh Penguins, 1988-89. 80GP
113 — Detroit Red Wings, 1992-93. 84GP
111 — NY Rangers, 1987-88. 80GP
110 — Pittsburgh Penguins, 1987-88. 80GP
    — Winnipeg Jets, 1987-88, 80GP

TEAM SHORTHAND GOALS

MOST SHORTHAND GOALS, ONE SEASON:
36 — Edmonton Oilers, 1983-84. 80GP
28 — Edmonton Oilers, 1986-87. 80GP
27 — Edmonton Oilers, 1985-86. 80GP
    — Edmonton Oilers, 1988-89. 80GP

TEAM GOALS-PER-GAME

HIGHEST GOALS-PER-GAME AVERAGE, ONE SEASON:
5.58 — Edmonton Oilers, 1983-84. 446G in 80GP
5.38 — Montreal Canadiens, 1919-20. 129G in 24GP
5.33 — Edmonton Oilers, 1985-86. 426G in 80GP
5.30 — Edmonton Oilers, 1982-83. 424G in 80GP
5.23 — Montreal Canadiens, 1917-18. 115G in 22GP

LOWEST GOALS-PER-GAME AVERAGE, ONE SEASON:
.75 — Chicago Blackhawks, 1928-29. 33G in 44GP
1.05 — Pittsburgh Pirates, 1928-29. 46G in 44GP
1.20 — NY Americans, 1928-29. 53G in 44GP

TEAM ASSISTS

MOST ASSISTS, ONE SEASON:
737 — Edmonton Oilers, 1985-86. 80GP
736 — Edmonton Oilers, 1983-84. 80GP
706 — Edmonton Oilers, 1981-82. 80GP

FEWEST ASSISTS, ONE SEASON (Since 1926-27):
45 — NY Rangers, 1926-27. 44GP

FEWEST ASSISTS, ONE SEASON (MINIMUM 70-GAME SCHEDULE):
206 — Chicago Blackhawks, 1953-54. 70GP

TEAM TOTAL POINTS

MOST SCORING POINTS, ONE SEASON:
1,182 — Edmonton Oilers, 1983-84. 80GP
1,163 — Edmonton Oilers, 1985-86. 80GP
1,123 — Edmonton Oilers, 1981-82. 80GP

MOST SCORING POINTS, ONE TEAM, ONE GAME:
40 — Buffalo Sabres, Dec. 21, 1975, at Buffalo. Buffalo defeated Washington 14-2, receiving 26A.
39 — Minnesota North Stars, Nov. 11, 1981, at Minnesota. Minnesota defeated Winnipeg 15-2, receiving 24A.
37 — Detroit Red Wings, Jan. 23, 1944, at Detroit. Detroit defeated NY Rangers 15-0, receiving 27A.
    — Toronto Maple Leafs, Mar. 16, 1957, at Toronto. Toronto defeated NY Rangers 14-1, receiving 23A.
    — Buffalo Sabres, Feb. 25, 1978, at Cleveland. Buffalo defeated Cleveland 13-3, receiving 24A.
    — Calgary Flames, Feb. 10, 1993, at Calgary. Calgary defeated San Jose 13-1, receiving 24A.

MOST SCORING POINTS, BOTH TEAMS, ONE GAME:
62 — Edmonton Oilers, Chicago Blackhawks, at Chicago, Dec. 11, 1985. Edmonton won 12-9. Edmonton had 24A, Chicago, 17.
53 — Quebec Nordiques, Washington Capitals, at Washington, Feb. 22, 1981. Quebec won 11-7. Quebec had 22A, Washington, 13.
    — Edmonton Oilers, Minnesota North Stars, at Edmonton, Jan. 4, 1984. Edmonton won 12-8. Edmonton had 20A, Minnesota 13.
    — Minnesota North Stars, St. Louis Blues, at St. Louis, Jan. 27, 1984. Minnesota won 10-8. Minnesota had 19A, St. Louis 16.
    — Toronto Maple Leafs, Edmonton Oilers, at Toronto, Jan. 8, 1986. Toronto won 11-9. Toronto had 17A, Edmonton 16.
52 — Mtl. Maroons, NY Americans, at New York, Feb. 18, 1936. 8-8 tie. New York had 20A, Montreal 16. (3A allowed for each goal.)
    — Vancouver Canucks, Minnesota North Stars, at Vancouver, Oct. 7, 1983. Vancouver won 10-9. Vancouver had 16A, Minnesota 17.

MOST SCORING POINTS, ONE TEAM, ONE PERIOD:
23 — NY Rangers, Nov. 21, 1971, at New York, third period during 12-1 win over California. NY Rangers scored 8G and 15A.
— **Buffalo Sabres,** Dec. 21, 1975, at Buffalo, third period during 14-2 win over Washington. Buffalo scored 8G and 15A.
— **Buffalo Sabres,** March 19, 1981, at Buffalo, second period during 14-4 win over Toronto. Buffalo scored 9G and 14A.
22 — Detroit Red Wings, Jan. 23, 1944, at Detroit, third period during 15-0 win over NY Rangers. Detroit scored 8G and 14A.
— Boston Bruins, March 16, 1969, at Boston, second period during 11-3 win over Toronto Maple Leafs. Boston scored 8G and 14A.
— Minnesota North Stars, Nov. 11, 1981, at Minnesota, second period during 15-2 win over Winnipeg. Minnesota scored 8G and 14A.
— Pittsburgh Penguins, Dec. 17, 1991, at Pittsburgh, second period during 10-2 win over San Jose. Pittsburgh scored 8G and 14A.
— Washington Capitals, Feb. 3, 1999, at Washington, second period during 10-1 win over Tampa Bay. Washington scored 8G and 14A.

MOST SCORING POINTS, BOTH TEAMS, ONE PERIOD:
35 — Edmonton, Oilers, Chicago Blackhawks, at Chicago, Dec. 11, 1985, second period. Edmonton had 6G, 12A; Chicago, 6G, 11A. Edmonton won 12-9.
31 — Buffalo Sabres, Toronto Maple Leafs, at Buffalo, March 19, 1981, second period. Buffalo had 9G, 14A; Toronto, 3G, 5A. Buffalo won 14-4.
29 — Winnipeg Jets, Detroit Red Wings, at Detroit, Nov. 25, 1987, third period. Detroit had 7G, 13A; Winnipeg had 3G, 6A. Detroit won 10-8.
— Chicago Blackhawks, St. Louis Blues, at St. Louis, March 15, 1988, third period. St. Louis had 5G, 10A; Chicago had 5G, 9A. 7-7 tie.

FASTEST GOALS

FASTEST SIX GOALS, BOTH TEAMS
3 Minutes — Quebec Nordiques, Washington Capitals, at Washington, Feb. 22, 1981, second and third periods. Quebec scored 5G, Washington 1. Quebec won 11-7.
3 Minutes, 15 Seconds — Montreal Canadiens, Toronto Maple Leafs, at Montreal, Jan. 4, 1944, first period. Montreal scored 4G, Toronto 2. Montreal won 6-3.

FASTEST FIVE GOALS, BOTH TEAMS:
1 Minute, 24 Seconds — Chicago Blackhawks, Toronto Maple Leafs, at Toronto, Oct. 15, 1983, second period. Scorers: Gaston Gingras, Toronto, 16:49; Denis Savard, Chicago, 17:12; Steve Larmer, Chicago, 17:27; Savard, 17:42; John Anderson, Toronto, 18:13. Toronto won 10-8.
1 Minute, 39 Seconds — Detroit Red Wings, Toronto Maple Leafs, at Toronto, Nov. 15, 1944, third period. Scorers: Ted Kennedy, Toronto, 10:36 and 10:55; Hal Jackson, Detroit, 11:48; Steve Wochy, Detroit, 12:02; Don Grosso, Detroit, 12:15. Detroit won 8-4.

FASTEST FIVE GOALS, ONE TEAM:
2 Minutes, 7 Seconds — Pittsburgh Penguins, at Pittsburgh, Nov. 22, 1972, third period. Scorers: Bryan Hextall, 12:00; Jean Pronovost, 12:18; Al McDonough, 13:40; Ken Schinkel, 13:49; Ron Schock, 14:07. Pittsburgh defeated St. Louis 10-4.
2 Minutes, 37 Seconds — NY Islanders, at New York, Jan. 26, 1982, first period. Scorers: Duane Sutter, 1:31; John Tonelli, 2:30; Bryan Trottier, 2:46; Bryan Trottier, 3:31; Duane Sutter, 4:08. NY Islanders defeated Pittsburgh 9-2.
2 Minutes, 55 Seconds — Boston Bruins, at Boston, Dec. 19, 1974. Scorers: Bobby Schmautz, 19:13 (first period); Ken Hodge, 0:18; Phil Esposito, 0:43; Don Marcotte, 0:58; John Bucyk, 2:08 (second period). Boston defeated NY Rangers 11-3.

FASTEST FOUR GOALS, BOTH TEAMS:
53 Seconds — Chicago Blackhawks, Toronto Maple Leafs, at Toronto, Oct. 15, 1983, second period. Scorers: Gaston Gingras, Toronto, 16:49; Denis Savard, Chicago, 17:12; Steve Larmer, Chicago, 17:27; and Savard, 17:42. Toronto won 10-8.
57 Seconds — Quebec Nordiques, Detroit Red Wings, at Quebec, Jan. 27, 1990, first period. Scorers: Paul Gillis, Quebec, 18:01; Claude Loiselle, Quebec, 18:12; Joe Sakic, Quebec, 18:27; and Jimmy Carson, Detroit, 18:58. Detroit won 8-6.
1 Minute, 1 Second — Colorado Rockies, NY Rangers, at New York, Jan. 15, 1980, first period. Scorers: Doug Sulliman, NY Rangers, 7:52; Ed Johnstone, NY Rangers, 7:57; Warren Miller, NY Rangers, 8:20; Rob Ramage, Colorado, 8:53. 6-6 tie.
— Chicago Blackhawks, Toronto Maple Leafs, at Toronto, Oct. 15, 1983, second period. Scorers: Denis Savard, Chicago, 17:12; Steve Larmer, Chicago, 17:27; Savard, 17:42; John Anderson, Toronto, 18:13. Toronto won 10-8.

FASTEST FOUR GOALS, ONE TEAM:
1 Minute, 20 Seconds — Boston Bruins, at Boston, Jan. 21, 1945, second period. Scorers: Bill Thoms, 6:34; Frank Mario, 7:08 and 7:27; and Ken Smith, 7:54. Boston defeated NY Rangers 14-3.

FASTEST THREE GOALS, BOTH TEAMS:
15 Seconds — Minnesota North Stars, NY Rangers, at Minnesota, Feb. 10, 1983, second period. Scorers: Mark Pavelich, NY Rangers, 19:18; Ron Greschner, NY Rangers, 19:27; Willi Plett, Minnesota, 19:33. Minnesota won 7-5.
18 Seconds — Montreal Canadiens, NY Rangers, at Montreal, Dec. 12, 1963, first period. Scorers: Dave Balon, Montreal, 0:58; Gilles Tremblay, Montreal, 1:04; Camille Henry, NY Rangers, 1:16. Montreal won 6-4.
— California Golden Seals, Buffalo Sabres, at California, Feb. 1, 1976, third period. Scorers: Jim Moxey, California, 19:38; Wayne Merrick, California, 19:45; Danny Gare, Buffalo, 19:56. Buffalo won 9-5.

FASTEST THREE GOALS, ONE TEAM:
20 Seconds — Boston Bruins, at Boston, Feb. 25, 1971, third period. Scorers: John Bucyk, 4:50; Ed Westfall, 5:02; Ted Green, 5:10. Boston defeated Vancouver 8-3.
21 Seconds — Chicago Blackhawks, at New York, Mar. 23, 1952, third period. Bill Mosienko scored all three goals, at 6:09, 6:20 and 6:30. Chicago defeated NY Rangers 7-6.
— Washington Capitals, at Washington, Nov. 23, 1990, first period. Scorers: Michal Pivonka, 16:18; Stephen Leach, 16:29 and 16:39. Washington defeated Pittsburgh 7-3.

FASTEST THREE GOALS FROM START OF PERIOD, BOTH TEAMS:
1 Minute, 5 Seconds — Hartford Whalers, Montreal Canadiens, at Montreal, March 11, 1989, second period. Scorers: Kevin Dineen, Hartford, 0:11; Guy Carbonneau, Montreal, 0:36; Petr Svoboda, Montreal, 1:05. Montreal won 5-3.

FASTEST THREE GOALS FROM START OF PERIOD, ONE TEAM:
53 Seconds — Calgary Flames, at Calgary, Feb. 10, 1993, third period. Scorers: Gary Suter, 0:17; Chris Lindbergh, 0:40; Ron Stern, 0:53. Calgary defeated San Jose 13-1.

FASTEST TWO GOALS, BOTH TEAMS:
2 Seconds — St. Louis Blues, Boston Bruins, at Boston, Dec. 19, 1987, third period. Scorers: Ken Linseman, Boston, 19:50; Doug Gilmour, St. Louis, 19:52. St. Louis won 7-5.
3 Seconds — Chicago Blackhawks, Minnesota North Stars, at Minnesota, Nov. 5, 1988, third period. Scorers: Steve Thomas, Chicago, 6:03; Dave Gagner, Minnesota, 6:06. 5-5 tie.

FASTEST TWO GOALS, ONE TEAM:
4 Seconds — Montreal Maroons, at Montreal, Jan. 3, 1931, third period. Nels Stewart scored both goals, at 8:24 and 8:28. Mtl. Maroons defeated Boston 5-3.
— **Buffalo Sabres,** at Buffalo, Oct. 17, 1974, third period. Scorers: Lee Fogolin, 14:55; Don Luce, 14:59. Buffalo defeated California 6-1.
— **Toronto Maple Leafs,** at Quebec, Dec. 29, 1988, third period. Scorers: Ed Olczyk, 5:24; Gary Leeman, 5:28. Toronto defeated Quebec 6-5.
— **Calgary Flames,** at Quebec, Oct. 17, 1989, third period. Scorers: Doug Gilmour, 19:45; Paul Ranheim, 19:49. Calgary and Quebec tied 8-8.
— **Winnipeg Jets,** at Winnipeg, Dec. 15, 1995, second period. Deron Quint scored both goals, at 7:51 and 7:55. Winnipeg defeated Edmonton 9-4.

FASTEST TWO GOALS FROM START OF GAME, ONE TEAM:
24 Seconds — Edmonton Oilers, Mar. 28, 1982, at Los Angeles. Scorers: Mark Messier, 0:14; Dave Lumley, 0:24. Edmonton defeated Los Angeles 6-2.
29 Seconds — Pittsburgh Penguins, Dec. 6, 1980, at Pittsburgh. Scorers: George Ferguson, 0:17; Greg Malone, 0:29. Pittsburgh defeated Chicago 6-2.
32 Seconds — Calgary Flames, Mar. 11, 1987, at Hartford. Scorers: Doug Risebrough, 0:09; Colin Patterson, 0:32. Calgary defeated Hartford 6-1.

FASTEST TWO GOALS FROM START OF PERIOD, BOTH TEAMS:
14 Seconds — NY Rangers, Quebec Nordiques, at Quebec, Nov. 5, 1983, third period. Scorers: Andre Savard, Quebec, 0:08; Pierre Larouche, NY Rangers, 0:14. 4-4 tie.
26 Seconds — Buffalo Sabres, St. Louis Blues, at Buffalo, Jan. 3, 1993, third period. Scorers: Alexander Mogilny, Buffalo, 0:08; Phillippe Bozon, St. Louis, 0:26. Buffalo won 6-5.
28 Seconds — Boston Bruins, Montreal Canadiens, at Montreal, Oct. 11, 1989, third period. Scorers: Jim Wiemer, Boston 0:10; Tom Chorske, Montreal 0:28. Montreal won 4-2.

FASTEST TWO GOALS FROM START OF PERIOD, ONE TEAM:
21 Seconds — Chicago Blackhawks, Nov. 5, 1983, at Minnesota, second period. Scorers: Ken Yaremchuk, 0:12; Darryl Sutter, 0:21. Minnesota defeated Chicago 10-5.
30 Seconds — Washington Capitals, Jan. 27, 1980, at Washington, second period. Scorers: Mike Gartner, 0:08; Bengt Gustafsson, 0:30. Washington defeated NY Islanders 7-1.
31 Seconds — Buffalo Sabres, Jan. 10, 1974, at Buffalo, third period. Scorers: Rene Robert, 0:21; Rick Martin, 0:31. Buffalo defeated NY Rangers 7-2.
— NY Islanders, Feb. 22, 1986, at New York, third period. Scorers: Roger Kortko, 0:10; Bob Bourne, 0:31. NY Islanders defeated Detroit 5-2.

The Chicago Blackhawks and Toronto Maple Leafs combined to score four goals in 53 seconds and five goals in 1:24 on October 15, 1983. Denis Savard got the Blackhawks going just 23 seconds after Gaston Gingras had scored for Toronto.

50, 40, 30, 20-GOAL SCORERS

MOST 50-OR-MORE-GOAL SCORERS, ONE SEASON:
3 — Edmonton Oilers, 1983-84. Wayne Gretzky, 87; Glenn Anderson, 54; Jari Kurri, 52. 80GP
— **Edmonton Oilers,** 1985-86. Jari Kurri, 68; Glenn Anderson, 54; Wayne Gretzky, 52. 80GP
2 — Boston Bruins, 1970-71. Phil Esposito, 76; John Bucyk, 51. 78GP
— Boston Bruins, 1973-74. Phil Esposito, 68; Ken Hodge, 50. 78GP
— Philadelphia Flyers, 1975-76. Reggie Leach, 61; Bill Barber, 50. 80GP
— Pittsburgh Penguins, 1975-76. Pierre Larouche, 53; Jean Pronovost, 52. 80GP
— Montreal Canadiens, 1976-77. Steve Shutt, 60; Guy Lafleur, 56. 80GP
— Los Angeles Kings, 1979-80. Charlie Simmer, 56; Marcel Dionne, 53. 80GP
— Montreal Canadiens, 1979-80. Pierre Larouche, 50; Guy Lafleur, 50. 80GP
— Los Angeles Kings, 1980-81. Marcel Dionne, 58; Charlie Simmer, 56. 80GP
— Edmonton Oilers, 1981-82. Wayne Gretzky, 92; Mark Messier, 50. 80GP
— NY Islanders, 1981-82. Mike Bossy, 64; Bryan Trottier, 50. 80GP
— Edmonton Oilers, 1984-85. Wayne Gretzky, 73; Jari Kurri, 71. 80GP
— Washington Capitals, 1984-85. Bob Carpenter, 53; Mike Gartner, 50. 80GP
— Edmonton Oilers, 1986-87. Wayne Gretzky, 62; Jari Kurri, 54. 80GP
— Calgary Flames, 1987-88. Joe Nieuwendyk, 51; Hakan Loob, 50. 80GP
— Los Angeles Kings, 1987-88. Jimmy Carson, 55; Luc Robitaille, 53. 80GP
— Los Angeles Kings, 1988-89. Bernie Nicholls, 70; Wayne Gretzky, 54. 80GP
— Calgary Flames, 1988-89. Joe Nieuwendyk, 51; Joe Mullen, 51. 80GP
— Buffalo Sabres, 1992-93. Alexander Mogilny, 76; Pat LaFontaine, 53. 84GP
— Pittsburgh Penguins, 1992-93. Mario Lemieux, 69; Kevin Stevens, 55. 84GP
— St. Louis Blues, 1992-93. Brett Hull, 54; Brendan Shanahan, 51. 84GP
— St. Louis Blues, 1993-94. Brett Hull, 57; Brendan Shanahan, 52. 84GP
— Detroit Red Wings, 1993-94. Sergei Fedorov, 56; Ray Sheppard, 52. 84GP
— Pittsburgh Penguins, 1995-96. Mario Lemieux, 69; Jaromir Jagr, 62. 82GP

MOST 40-OR-MORE-GOAL SCORERS, ONE SEASON:
4 — Edmonton Oilers, 1982-83. Wayne Gretzky, 71; Glenn Anderson, 48; Mark Messier, 48; Jari Kurri, 45. 80GP
— **Edmonton Oilers,** 1983-84. Wayne Gretzky, 87; Glenn Anderson, 54; Jari Kurri, 52; Paul Coffey, 40. 80GP
— **Edmonton Oilers,** 1984-85. Wayne Gretzky, 73; Jari Kurri, 71; Mike Krushelnyski, 43; Glenn Anderson, 42. 80GP
— **Edmonton Oilers,** 1985-86. Jari Kurri, 68; Glenn Anderson, 54; Wayne Gretzky, 52; Paul Coffey, 48. 80GP
— **Calgary Flames,** 1987-88. Joe Nieuwendyk, 51; Hakan Loob, 50; Mike Bullard, 48; Joe Mullen, 40. 80GP
3 — Boston Bruins, 1970-71. Phil Esposito, 76; John Bucyk, 51; Ken Hodge, 43. 78GP
— NY Rangers, 1971-72. Vic Hadfield, 50; Jean Ratelle, 46; Rod Gilbert, 43. 78GP
— Buffalo Sabres, 1975-76. Danny Gare, 50; Rick Martin, 49; Gilbert Perreault, 44. 80GP
— Montreal Canadiens, 1979-80. Guy Lafleur, 50; Pierre Larouche, 50; Steve Shutt, 47. 80GP
— Buffalo Sabres, 1979-80. Danny Gare, 56; Rick Martin, 45; Gilbert Perreault, 40. 80GP
— Los Angeles Kings, 1980-81. Marcel Dionne, 58; Charlie Simmer, 56; Dave Taylor, 47. 80GP
— Los Angeles Kings, 1984-85. Marcel Dionne, 46; Bernie Nicholls, 46; Dave Taylor, 41. 80GP
— NY Islanders, 1984-85. Mike Bossy, 58; Brent Sutter, 42; John Tonelli; 42. 80GP
— Chicago Blackhawks, 1985-86. Denis Savard, 47; Troy Murray, 45; Al Secord, 40. 80GP
— Chicago Blackhawks, 1987-88. Denis Savard, 44; Rick Vaive, 43; Steve Larmer, 41. 80GP
— Edmonton Oilers, 1987-88. Craig Simpson, 43; Jari Kurri, 43; Wayne Gretzky, 40. 80GP
— Los Angeles Kings, 1988-89. Bernie Nicholls, 70; Wayne Gretzky, 54; Luc Robitaille, 46. 80GP
— Los Angeles Kings, 1990-91. Luc Robitaille, 45; Tomas Sandstrom, 45; Wayne Gretzky 41. 80GP
— Pittsburgh Penguins, 1991-92. Kevin Stevens, 54; Mario Lemieux, 44; Joe Mullen, 42. 80GP
— Pittsburgh Penguins, 1992-93. Mario Lemieux, 69; Kevin Stevens, 55; Rick Tocchet, 48. 84GP
— Calgary Flames, 1993-94. Gary Roberts, 41; Robert Reichel, 40; Theoren Fleury, 40. 84GP
— Pittsburgh Penguins, 1995-96. Mario Lemieux, 69; Jaromir Jagr, 62; Petr Nedved, 45. 82GP

MOST 30-OR-MORE GOAL SCORERS, ONE SEASON:
6 — Buffalo Sabres, 1974-75. Rick Martin, 52; Rene Robert, 40; Gilbert Perreault, 39; Don Luce, 33; Rick Dudley, Danny Gare, 31 each. 80GP
— **NY Islanders,** 1977-78. Mike Bossy, 53; Bryan Trottier, 46; Clark Gillies, 35; Denis Potvin, Bob Nystrom, Bob Bourne, 30 each. 80GP
— **Winnipeg Jets,** 1984-85. Dale Hawerchuk, 53; Paul MacLean, 41; Laurie Boschman, Brian Mullen, 32 each; Doug Smail, 31; Thomas Steen, 30. 80GP
5 — Chicago Blackhawks, 1968-69. 76GP
— Boston Bruins, 1970-71. 78GP
— Montreal Canadiens, 1971-72. 78GP
— Philadelphia Flyers, 1972-73. 78GP
— Boston Bruins, 1973-74. 78GP
— Montreal Canadiens, 1974-75. 80GP
— Montreal Canadiens, 1975-76. 80GP
— Pittsburgh Penguins, 1975-76. 80GP
— NY Islanders, 1978-79. 80GP
— Detroit Red Wings, 1979-80. 80GP
— Philadelphia Flyers, 1979-80. 80GP
— NY Islanders, 1980-81. 80GP
— St. Louis Blues, 1980-81. 80GP
— Chicago Blackhawks, 1981-82. 80GP
— Edmonton Oilers, 1981-82. 80GP
— Montreal Canadiens, 1981-82. 80GP
— Quebec Nordiques, 1981-82. 80GP
— Washington Capitals, 1981-82. 80GP
— Edmonton Oilers, 1982-83. 80GP
— Edmonton Oilers, 1983-84. 80GP
— Edmonton Oilers, 1984-85. 80GP
— Los Angeles Kings, 1984-85. 80GP
— Edmonton Oilers, 1985-86. 80GP
— Edmonton Oilers, 1986-87. 80GP
— Edmonton Oilers, 1987-88. 80GP
— Edmonton Oilers, 1988-89. 80GP
— Detroit Red Wings, 1991-92. 80GP
— NY Rangers, 1991-92. 80GP
— Pittsburgh Penguins, 1991-92. 80GP
— Detroit Red Wings, 1992-93. 84GP
— Pittsburgh Penguins, 1992-93. 84GP

MOST 20-OR-MORE GOAL SCORERS, ONE SEASON:
11 — Boston Bruins, 1977-78; Peter McNab, 41; Terry O'Reilly, 29; Bobby Schmautz, Stan Jonathan, 27 each; Jean Ratelle, Rick Middleton, 25 each; Wayne Cashman, 24; Gregg Sheppard, 23; Brad Park, 22; Don Marcotte, Bob Miller, 20 each. 80GP
10 — Boston Bruins, 1970-71. 78GP
— Montreal Canadiens, 1974-75. 80GP
— St. Louis Blues, 1980-81. 80GP

Jacques Plante played 64 of 70 games for Montreal in 1955-56 when the Canadiens allowed just 131 goals in 70 games. (Bob Perreault played the other six games.) Plante led the league with 42 wins and a 1.86 goals-against average that season.

100-POINT SCORERS

MOST 100 OR-MORE-POINT SCORERS, ONE SEASON:
4 — **Boston Bruins,** 1970-71, Phil Esposito, 76G-76A-152PTS; Bobby Orr, 37G-102A-139PTS; John Bucyk, 51G-65A-116PTS; Ken Hodge, 43G-62A-105PTS. 78GP
— **Edmonton Oilers,** 1982-83, Wayne Gretzky, 71G-125A-196PTS; Mark Messier, 48G-58A-106PTS; Glenn Anderson, 48G-56A-104PTS; Jari Kurri, 45G-59A-104PTS. 80GP
— **Edmonton Oilers,** 1983-84, Wayne Gretzky, 87G-118A-205PTS; Paul Coffey, 40G-86A-126PTS; Jari Kurri, 52G-61A-113PTS; Mark Messier, 37G-64A-101PTS. 80GP
— **Edmonton Oilers,**1985-86, Wayne Gretzky, 52G-163A-215PTS; Paul Coffey, 48G-90A-138PTS; Jari Kurri, 68G-63A-131PTS; Glenn Anderson, 54G-48A-102PTS. 80GP
— **Pittsburgh Penguins,**1992-93, Mario Lemieux, 69G-91A-160PTS; Kevin Stevens, 55G-56A-111PTS; Rick Tocchet, 48G-61A-109PTS; Ron Francis, 24G-76A-100PTS. 84GP
3 — Boston Bruins, 1973-74, Phil Esposito, 68G-77A-145PTS; Bobby Orr, 32G-90A-122PTS; Ken Hodge, 50G-55A-105PTS. 78GP
— NY Islanders, 1978-79, Bryan Trottier, 47G-87A-134PTS; Mike Bossy, 69G-57A-126PTS; Denis Potvin, 31G-70A-101PTS. 80GP
— Los Angeles Kings, 1980-81, Marcel Dionne, 58G-77A-135PTS; Dave Taylor, 47 G-65A-112PTS; Charlie Simmer, 56G-49A-105PTS. 80GP
— Edmonton Oilers, 1984-85, Wayne Gretzky, 73G-135A-208PTS; Jari Kurri, 71G-64A-135PTS; Paul Coffey, 37G-84A-121PTS. 80GP
— NY Islanders, 1984-85. Mike Bossy, 58G-59A-117PTS; Brent Sutter, 42G-60A-102PTS; John Tonelli, 42G-58A-100PTS. 80GP
— Edmonton Oilers, 1986-87, Wayne Gretzky, 62G-121A-183PTS; Jari Kurri, 54G-54A-108PTS; Mark Messier, 37G-70A-107PTS. 80GP
— Pittsburgh Penguins, 1988-89, Mario Lemieux, 85G-114A-199PTS; Rob Brown, 49G-66A-115PTS; Paul Coffey, 30G-83A-113PTS. 80GP
— Pittsburgh Penguins, 1995-96, Mario Lemieux, 69G-92A-161PTS; Jaromir Jagr, 62G-87A-149PTS; Ron Francis, 27G-92A-119PTS. 82GP

SHOTS ON GOAL

MOST SHOTS, BOTH TEAMS, ONE GAME:
141 — **NY Americans, Pittsburgh Pirates,** Dec. 26, 1925, at New York. NY Americans, who won game 3-1, had 73 shots; Pit. Pirates, 68 shots.

MOST SHOTS, ONE TEAM, ONE GAME:
83 — **Boston Bruins,** March 4, 1941, at Boston. Boston defeated Chicago 3-2.
73 — NY Americans, Dec. 26, 1925, at New York. NY Americans defeated Pit. Pirates 3-1.
— Boston Bruins, March 21, 1991, at Boston. Boston tied Quebec 3-3.
72 — Boston Bruins, Dec. 10, 1970, at Boston. Boston defeated Buffalo 8-2.

MOST SHOTS, ONE TEAM, ONE PERIOD:
33 — **Boston Bruins,** March 4, 1941, at Boston, second period. Boston defeated Chicago 3-2.

TEAM GOALS-AGAINST

Fewest Goals-Against

FEWEST GOALS AGAINST, ONE SEASON:
42 — **Ottawa Senators,** 1925-26. 36GP
43 — Montreal Canadiens, 1928-29. 44GP
48 — Montreal Canadiens, 1923-24. 24GP
— Montreal Canadiens, 1927-28. 44GP

FEWEST GOALS AGAINST, ONE SEASON (MINIMUM 70-GAME SCHEDULE):
131 — **Toronto Maple Leafs,** 1953-54. 70GP
— **Montreal Canadiens,** 1955-56. 70GP
132 — Detroit Red Wings, 1953-54. 70GP
133 — Detroit Red Wings, 1951-52. 70GP
— Detroit Red Wings, 1952-53. 70GP

LOWEST GOALS-AGAINST-PER-GAME AVERAGE, ONE SEASON:
.98 — **Montreal Canadiens,** 1928-29. 43GA in 44GP.
1.09 — Montreal Canadiens, 1927-28. 48GA in 44GP.
1.17 — Ottawa Senators, 1925-26. 42GA in 36GP.

Most Goals-Against

MOST GOALS AGAINST, ONE SEASON:
446 — **Washington Capitals,** 1974-75. 80GP
415 — Detroit Red Wings, 1985-86. 80GP
414 — San Jose Sharks, 1992-93. 84GP
407 — Quebec Nordiques, 1989-90. 80GP
403 — Hartford Whalers, 1982-83. 80GP

HIGHEST GOALS-AGAINST-PER-GAME AVERAGE, ONE SEASON:
7.38 — **Quebec Bulldogs,** 1919-20, 177GA in 24GP.
6.20 — NY Rangers, 1943-44, 310GA in 50GP.
5.58 — Washington Capitals, 1974-75, 446GA in 80GP.

MOST POWER-PLAY GOALS AGAINST, ONE SEASON:
122 — **Chicago Blackhawks,** 1988-89. 80GP
120 — Pittsburgh Penguins, 1987-88. 80GP
115 — New Jersey Devils, 1988-89. 80GP
— Ottawa Senators, 1992-93. 84GP
114 — Los Angeles Kings, 1992-93. 84GP

MOST SHORTHAND GOALS AGAINST, ONE SEASON:
22 — **Pittsburgh Penguins,** 1984-85. 80GP
— **Minnesota North Stars,** 1991-92. 80GP
— **Colorado Avalanche,** 1995-96. 82GP
21 — Calgary Flames, 1984-85. 80GP
— Pittsburgh Penguins, 1989-90. 80GP

SHUTOUTS

MOST SHUTOUTS, ONE SEASON:
22 — **Montreal Canadiens,** 1928-29. All by George Hainsworth. 44GP
16 — NY Americans, 1928-29. Roy Worters had 13; Flat Walsh 3. 44GP
15 — Ottawa Senators, 1925-26. All by Alex Connell. 36GP
— Ottawa Senators, 1927-28. All by Alex Connell. 44GP
— Boston Bruins, 1927-28. All by Hal Winkler. 44GP
— Chicago Blackhawks, 1969-70. All by Tony Esposito. 76GP

MOST CONSECUTIVE SHUTOUTS, ONE SEASON:
6 — **Ottawa Senators,** Jan. 31 - Feb. 18, 1928.

MOST CONSECUTIVE SHUTOUTS TO START SEASON:
5 — **Toronto Maple Leafs,** Nov. 13 - 22, 1930.

MOST GAMES SHUTOUT, ONE SEASON:
20 — **Chicago Blackhawks,** 1928-29. 44GP

MOST CONSECUTIVE GAMES SHUTOUT:
8 — **Chicago Blackhawks,** Feb. 7 - 28, 1929.

MOST CONSECUTIVE GAMES SHUTOUT TO START SEASON:
3 — **Montreal Maroons,** Nov. 11 - 18, 1930.

TEAM PENALTIES

MOST PENALTY MINUTES, ONE SEASON:
2,713 — **Buffalo Sabres,** 1991-92. 80GP
2,670 — Pittsburgh Penguins, 1988-89. 80GP
2,663 — Chicago Blackhawks, 1991-92. 80GP
2,643 — Calgary Flames, 1991-92. 80GP
2,621 — Philadelphia Flyers, 1980-81. 80GP

MOST PENALTIES, BOTH TEAMS, ONE GAME:
85 Penalties — **Edmonton Oilers (44), Los Angeles Kings (41)** at Los Angeles, Feb. 28, 1990. Edmonton received 26 minors, 7 majors, 6 10-minute misconducts, 4 game misconducts and 1 match penalty; Los Angeles received 26 minors, 9 majors, 3 10-minute misconducts and 3 game misconducts.

MOST PENALTY MINUTES, BOTH TEAMS, ONE GAME:
406 Minutes — **Minnesota North Stars, Boston Bruins** at Boston, Feb. 26, 1981. Minnesota received 18 minors, 13 majors, 4 10-minute misconducts and 7 game misconducts; a total of 211PIM. Boston received 20 minors, 13 majors, 3 10-minute misconducts and six game misconducts; a total of 195PIM.

MOST PENALTIES, ONE TEAM, ONE GAME:
44 — **Edmonton Oilers,** Feb. 28, 1990, at Los Angeles. Edmonton received 26 minors, 7 majors, 6 10-minute misconducts, 4 game misconducts and 1 match penalty.
42 — Minnesota North Stars, Feb. 26, 1981, at Boston. Minnesota received 18 minors, 13 majors, 4 10-minute misconducts and 7 game misconducts.
— Boston Bruins, Feb. 26, 1981, at Boston vs. Minnesota. Boston received 20 minors, 13 majors, 3 10-minute misconducts and 6 game misconducts.

MOST PENALTY MINUTES, ONE TEAM, ONE GAME:
211 — **Minnesota North Stars,** Feb. 26, 1981, at Boston. Minnesota received 18 minors, 13 majors, 4 10-minute misconducts and 7 game misconducts.

MOST PENALTIES, BOTH TEAMS, ONE PERIOD:
67 — **Minnesota North Stars, Boston Bruins,** at Boston, Feb. 26, 1981, first period. Minnesota received 15 minors, 8 majors, 4 10-minute misconducts and 7 game misconducts, a total of 34 penalties. Boston had 16 minors, 8 majors, 3 10-minute misconducts and 6 game misconducts, a total of 33 penalties.

MOST PENALTY MINUTES, BOTH TEAMS, ONE PERIOD:
372 — **Los Angeles Kings, Philadelphia Flyers,** at Philadelphia, March 11, 1979, first period. Philadelphia received 4 minors, 8 majors, 6 10-minute misconducts and 8 game misconducts for 188 minutes. Los Angeles received 2 minors, 8 majors, 6 10-minute misconducts and 8 game misconducts for 184 minutes.

MOST PENALTIES, ONE TEAM, ONE PERIOD:
34 — **Minnesota North Stars,** Feb. 26, 1981, at Boston, first period. 15 minors, 8 majors, 4 10-minute misconducts, 7 game misconducts.

MOST PENALTY MINUTES, ONE TEAM, ONE PERIOD:
188 — **Philadelphia Flyers,** March 11, 1979, at Philadelphia vs. Los Angeles, first period. Flyers received 4 minors, 8 majors, 6 10-minute misconducts and 8 game misconducts.

NHL Individual Scoring Records - History

SIX INDIVIDUAL SCORING RECORDS stand as benchmarks in the history of the game: most goals, single-season and career; most assists, single-season and career; and most points, single-season and career. The evolution of these six records is traced here, beginning with 1917-18, the NHL's first season. New research has resulted in changes to scoring records in the NHL's first four seasons.

MOST GOALS, ONE SEASON

44 —Joe Malone, Montreal, 1917-18.
Scored goal #44 against Toronto's Harry Holmes on March 2, 1918 and finished season with 44 goals.

50 —Maurice Richard, Montreal, 1944-45.
Scored goal #45 against Toronto's Frank McCool on February 25, 1945 and finished the season with 50 goals.

50 —Bernie Geoffrion, Montreal, 1960-61.
Scored goal #50 against Toronto's Cesare Maniago on March 16, 1961 and finished the season with 50 goals.

50 —Bobby Hull, Chicago, 1961-62.
Scored goal #50 against NY Rangers' Gump Worsley on March 25, 1962 and finished the season with 50 goals.

54 —Bobby Hull, Chicago, 1965-66.
Scored goal #51 against NY Rangers' Cesare Maniago on March 12, 1966 and finished the season with 54 goals.

58 —Bobby Hull, Chicago, 1968-69.
Scored goal #55 against Boston's Gerry Cheevers on March 20, 1969 and finished the season with 58 goals.

76 —Phil Esposito, Boston, 1970-71.
Scored goal #59 against Los Angeles' Denis DeJordy on March 11, 1971 and finished the season with 76 goals.

92 —Wayne Gretzky, Edmonton, 1981-82.
Scored goal #77 against Buffalo's Don Edwards on February 24, 1982 and finished the season with 92 goals.

MOST ASSISTS, ONE SEASON

10 —Cy Denneny, Ottawa, 1917-18.
—Reg Noble, Toronto, 1917-18.
—Harry Cameron, Toronto, 1917-18.
15 —Frank Nighbor, Ottawa, 1919-20.
18 —Dick Irvin, Chicago, 1926-27.
18 —Howie Morenz, Montreal, 1927-28.
36 —Frank Boucher, NY Rangers, 1929-30.
37 —Joe Primeau, Toronto, 1931-32.
45 —Bill Cowley, Boston, 1940-41.
45 —Bill Cowley, Boston, 1942-43.
49 —Clint Smith, Chicago, 1943-44.
54 —Elmer Lach, Montreal, 1944-45.
55 —Ted Lindsay, Detroit, 1949-50.
56 —Bert Olmstead, Montreal, 1955-56.
58 —Jean Beliveau, Montreal, 1960-61.
58 —Andy Bathgate, NY Rangers/Toronto, 1963-64.
59 —Stan Mikita, Chicago, 1964-65.
62 —Stan Mikita, Chicago, 1966-67.
77 —Phil Esposito, Boston, 1968-69.
87 —Bobby Orr, Boston, 1969-70.
102 —Bobby Orr, Boston, 1970-71.
109 —Wayne Gretzky, Edmonton, 1980-81.
120 —Wayne Gretzky, Edmonton, 1981-82.
125 —Wayne Gretzky, Edmonton, 1982-83.
135 —Wayne Gretzky, Edmonton, 1984-85.
163 —Wayne Gretzky, Edmonton, 1985-86.

MOST POINTS, ONE SEASON

48 —Joe Malone, Montreal, 1917-18.
49 —Joe Malone, Montreal, 1919-20.
51 —Howie Morenz, Montreal, 1927-28.
73 —Cooney Weiland, Boston, 1929-30.
73 —Doug Bentley, Chicago, 1942-43.
82 —Herb Cain, Boston, 1943-44.
86 —Gordie Howe, Detroit, 1950-51.
95 —Gordie Howe, Detroit, 1952-53.
96 —Dickie Moore, Montreal, 1958-59.
97 —Bobby Hull, Chicago, 1965-66.
97 —Stan Mikita, Chicago, 1966-67.
126 —Phil Esposito, Boston, 1968-69.
152 —Phil Esposito, Boston, 1970-71.
164 —Wayne Gretzky, Edmonton, 1980-81.
212 —Wayne Gretzky, Edmonton, 1981-82.
215 —Wayne Gretzky, Edmonton, 1985-86.

MOST REGULAR-SEASON GOALS, CAREER

44 —Joe Malone, 1917-18, Montreal.
Malone led the NHL in goals in the league's first season and finished with 44 goals in 22 games in 1917-18.

54 —Cy Denneny, 1918-19, Ottawa.
Denneny passed Malone during the 1918-19 season, finishing the year with a two-year total of 54 goals. He held the career goal-scoring mark until 1919-20.

143 —Joe Malone, Montreal, Quebec Bulldogs, Hamilton.
Malone passed Denneny in 1919-20 and remained the NHL's career goal-scoring leader until his retirement. He finished with a career total of 143 goals.

246 —Cy Denneny, Ottawa, Boston.
Denneny passed Malone with goal #144 in 1922-23 and remained the NHL's career goal-scoring leader until his retirement. He finished with a career total of 246 goals.

270 —Howie Morenz, Montreal, NY Rangers, Chicago.
Morenz passed Denneny with goal #247 in 1933-34 and finished his career with 270 goals.

324 —Nels Stewart, Montreal Maroons, Boston, NY Americans.
Stewart passed Morenz with goal #271 in 1936-37 and remained the NHL's career goal-scoring leader until his retirement. He finished his career with 324 goals.

544 —Maurice Richard, Montreal.
Richard passed Nels Stewart with goal #325 on Nov. 8, 1952 and remained the NHL's career goal-scoring leader until his retirement. He finished his career with 544 goals.

801 —Gordie Howe, Detroit, Hartford.
Howe passed Richard with goal #545 on Nov. 10, 1963 and remained the NHL's career goal-scoring leader until his retirement. He finished his career with 801 goals.

894 —Wayne Gretzky, Edmonton, Los Angeles, St. Louis, NYRangers.
Gretzky passed Gordie Howe with goal #802 on March 23, 1994. He retired as the NHL's current goal-scoring leader with 894.

MOST REGULAR-SEASON POINTS, CAREER (minimum 100 points)

100 —Joe Malone, Montreal, Quebec Bulldogs, Hamilton.
In 1919-20, Malone became the first player in NHL history to record 100 points.

200 —Cy Denneny, Ottawa.
In 1923-24, Denneny became the first player in NHL history to record 200 points.

300 —Cy Denneny, Ottawa.
In 1926-27, Denneny became the first player in NHL history to record 300 points.

315 —Cy Denneny, Ottawa, Boston.
Denneny retired as the NHL's career point-scoring leader in 1929 with 315 points.

467 —Howie Morenz, Montreal, Chicago, NY Rangers.
Morenz passed Cy Denneny with point #316 in 1931-32. At the time his career ended in 1937, he was the NHL's career point- scoring leader with 467 points.

515 —Nels Stewart, Montreal Maroons, Boston, NY Americans.
Stewart passed Morenz with point #468 in 1938-39. He retired as the NHL's career point-scoring leader in 1940 with 515 points.

528 —Syd Howe, Ottawa, Philadelphia Quakers, Toronto, St. Louis Eagles, Detroit.
Howe passed Nels Stewart with point #516 on March 8, 1945. He retired as the NHL's career point-scoring leader in 1946 with 528 points.

548 —Bill Cowley, St. Louis Eagles, Boston.
Cowley passed Syd Howe with point #529 on Feb. 12, 1947. He retired as the NHL's career point-scoring leader in 1947 with 548 points.

610 —Elmer Lach, Montreal.
Lach passed Bill Cowley with point #549 on Feb. 23, 1952. He remained the NHL's career point-scoring leader until he was overtaken by Maurice Richard in 1953-54. He finished his career with 623 points.

946 —Maurice Richard, Montreal.
Richard passed teammate Elmer Lach with point #611 on Dec. 12, 1953. He remained the NHL's career point-scoring leader until he was overtaken by Gordie Howe in 1959-60. He finished his career with 965 points.

1,850 —Gordie Howe, Detroit, Hartford.
Howe passed Richard with point #947 on Jan. 16, 1960. He retired as the NHL's career point-scoring leader in 1980 with 1,850 points.

2,857 —Wayne Gretzky, Edmonton, Los Angeles, St. Louis, NY Rangers.
Gretzky passed Howe with point #1,851 on Oct. 15, 1989. He retired as the NHL's current career points leader with 2,857 points.

MOST REGULAR-SEASON ASSISTS, CAREER

(minimum 100 assists)

100 —Frank Boucher, Ottawa, NY Rangers.
In 1930-31, Boucher became the first NHLplayer to reach the 100-assist milestone.

262 —Frank Boucher, Ottawa, NY Rangers.
Boucher retired as the NHL's career assist leader in 1938 with 252. He returned to the NHL in 1943-44 and remained the NHL's career assist leader until he was overtaken by Bill Cowley in 1943-44. He finished his career with 262 assists.

353 —Bill Cowley, St. Louis Eagles, Boston.
Cowley passed Boucher with assist #263 in 1943-44. He retired as the NHL's career assist leader in 1947 with 353.

408 —Elmer Lach, Montreal.
Lach passed Cowley with assist #354 in 1951-52. He retired as the NHL's career assist leader in 1954 with 408.

1,049 —Gordie Howe, Detroit, Hartford.
Howe passed Lach with assist #409 in 1957-58. He retired as the NHL's career assist leader in 1980 with 1,049.

1,963 —Wayne Gretzky, Edmonton, Los Angeles, St. Louis, NY Rangers. Gretzky passed Howe with assist #1,050 in 1988-89. He retired as the NHL's current career assist leader with 1,963.

Individual Records
Regular Season

SEASONS

MOST SEASONS:
26 — Gordie Howe, Detroit, 1946-47 – 1970-71; Hartford, 1979-80.
24 — Alex Delvecchio, Detroit, 1950-51 – 1973-74.
— Tim Horton, Toronto, NY Rangers, Pittsburgh, Buffalo, 1949-50, 1951-52 – 1973-74.
23 — John Bucyk, Detroit, Boston, 1955-56 – 1977-78.
22 — Dean Prentice, NY Rangers, Boston, Detroit, Pittsburgh, Minnesota, 1952-53 – 1973-74.
— Doug Mohns, Boston, Chicago, Minnesota, Atlanta, Washington, 1953-54 – 1974-75.
— Stan Mikita, Chicago, 1958-59 – 1979-80.

GAMES

MOST GAMES:
1,767 — Gordie Howe, Detroit, 1946-47 – 1970-71; Hartford, 1979-80.
1,558 — Larry Murphy, Los Angeles, Washington, Minnesota, Pittsburgh, Toronto, Detroit, 1980-81 – 1999-2000.
1,549 — Alex Delvecchio, Detroit, 1950-51 – 1973-74.

MOST GAMES, INCLUDING PLAYOFFS:
1,924 — Gordie Howe, Detroit, Hartford, 1,767 regular-season and 157 playoff games.
1,767 — Larry Murphy, Los Angeles, Washington, Minnesota, Pittsburgh, Toronto, Detroit, 1,558 regular-season and 209 playoff games.
1,725 — Ray Bourque, Boston, Colorado, 1,532 regular-season and 193 playoff games.

MOST CONSECUTIVE GAMES:
964 — Doug Jarvis, Montreal, Washington, Hartford, from Oct. 8, 1975 – Oct. 10, 1987.
914 — Garry Unger, Toronto, Detroit, St. Louis, Atlanta, from Feb. 24, 1968 – Dec. 21, 1979.
884 — Steve Larmer, Chicago, from Oct. 6, 1982 – Apr. 15, 1993.
776 — Craig Ramsay, Buffalo, from Mar. 27, 1973 – Feb. 10, 1983.
630 — Andy Hebenton, NY Rangers, Boston, from Oct. 7, 1955 – Mar. 22, 1964.

GOALS

MOST GOALS:
894 — Wayne Gretzky, Edmonton, Los Angeles, St. Louis, NY Rangers, in 20 seasons, 1,487GP.
801 — Gordie Howe, Detroit, Hartford, in 26 seasons, 1,767GP.
731 — Marcel Dionne, Detroit, Los Angeles, NY Rangers, in 18 seasons, 1,348GP.
717 — Phil Esposito, Chicago, Boston, NY Rangers, in 18 seasons, 1,282GP.
708 — Mike Gartner, Washington, Minnesota, NY Rangers, Toronto, Phoenix, in 19 seasons, 1,432GP.

MOST GOALS, INCLUDING PLAYOFFS:
1,016 — Wayne Gretzky, Edmonton, Los Angeles, St. Louis, NY Rangers, 894 regular-season and 122 playoff goals.
869 — Gordie Howe, Detroit, Hartford, 801 regular-season and 68 playoff goals.
778 — Phil Esposito, Chicago, Boston, NY Rangers, 717 regular-season and 61 playoff goals.
752 — Marcel Dionne, Detroit, Los Angeles, NY Rangers, 731 regular-season and 21 playoff goals.

MOST GOALS, ONE SEASON:
92 — Wayne Gretzky, Edmonton, 1981-82. 80 game schedule.
87 — Wayne Gretzky, Edmonton, 1983-84. 80 game schedule.
86 — Brett Hull, St. Louis, 1990-91. 80 game schedule.
85 — Mario Lemieux, Pittsburgh, 1988-89. 80 game schedule.
76 — Phil Esposito, Boston, 1970-71. 78 game schedule.
— Alexander Mogilny, Buffalo, 1992-93. 84 game schedule.
— Teemu Selanne, Winnipeg, 1992-93. 84 game schedule.
73 — Wayne Gretzky, Edmonton, 1984-85. 80 game schedule.
72 — Brett Hull, St. Louis, 1989-90. 80 game schedule.
71 — Wayne Gretzky, Edmonton, 1982-83. 80 game schedule.
— Jari Kurri, Edmonton, 1984-85. 80 game schedule.
70 — Mario Lemieux, Pittsburgh, 1987-1988. 80 game schedule.
— Bernie Nicholls, Los Angeles, 1988-89. 80 game schedule.
— Brett Hull, St. Louis, 1991-92. 80 game schedule.

MOST GOALS, ONE SEASON, INCLUDING PLAYOFFS:
100 — Wayne Gretzky, Edmonton, 1983-84, 87G in 74 regular-season games and 13G in 19 playoff games.
97 — Wayne Gretzky, Edmonton, 1981-82, 92G in 80 regular-season games and 5G in 5 playoff games.
— Mario Lemieux, Pittsburgh, 1988-89, 85G in 76 regular-season games and 12G in 11 playoff games.
— Brett Hull, St. Louis, 1990-91, 86G in 78 regular-season games and 11G in 13 playoff games.
90 — Wayne Gretzky, Edmonton, 1984-85, 73G in 80 regular-season games and 17G in 18 playoff games.
— Jari Kurri, Edmonton, 1984-85, 71G in 80 regular-season games and 19G in 18 playoff games.
85 — Mike Bossy, NY Islanders, 1980-81, 68G in 79 regular-season games and 17G in 18 playoff games.
— Brett Hull, St. Louis, 1989-90, 72G in 80 regular-season games and 13G in 12 playoff games.
83 — Wayne Gretzky, Edmonton, 1982-83, 71G in 73 regular-season games and 12G in 16 playoff games.
— Alexander Mogilny, Buffalo, 1992-93, 76G in 77 regular-season games and 7G in 7 playoff games.

MOST GOALS, 50 GAMES FROM START OF SEASON:
61 — Wayne Gretzky, Edmonton, 1981-82. Oct. 7, 1981 - Jan. 22, 1982. (80-game schedule)
— Wayne Gretzky, Edmonton, 1983-84. Oct. 5, 1983 - Jan. 25, 1984. (80-game schedule)
54 — Mario Lemieux, Pittsburgh, 1988-89. Oct. 7, 1988 - Jan. 31, 1989. (80-game schedule)
53 — Wayne Gretzky, Edmonton, 1984-85. Oct. 11, 1984 - Jan. 28, 1985. (80-game schedule)
52 — Brett Hull, St. Louis, 1990-91. Oct. 4, 1990 - Jan. 26, 1991. (80-game schedule).
50 — Maurice Richard, Montreal, 1944-45. Oct. 28, 1944 - March 18, 1945. (50-game schedule)
— Mike Bossy, NY Islanders, 1980-81. Oct. 11, 1980 - Jan. 24, 1981. (80-game schedule)
— Brett Hull, St. Louis, 1991-92. Oct. 5, 1991 – Jan 28, 1992. (80 game schedule)

MOST GOALS, ONE GAME:
7 — Joe Malone, Que. Bulldogs, Jan. 31, 1920, at Quebec. Quebec 10, Toronto 6.
6 — Newsy Lalonde, Montreal, Jan. 10, 1920, at Montreal. Montreal 14, Toronto 7.
— Joe Malone, Que. Bulldogs, March 10, 1920, at Quebec. Quebec 10, Ottawa 4.
— Corb Denneny, Toronto, Jan. 26, 1921, at Toronto. Toronto 10, Hamilton 3.
— Cy Denneny, Ottawa, Mar. 7, 1921, at Ottawa. Ottawa 12, Hamilton 5.
— Syd Howe, Detroit, Feb. 3, 1944, at Detroit. Detroit 12, NY Rangers 2.
— Red Berenson, St. Louis, Nov. 7, 1968, at Philadelphia. St. Louis 8, Philadelphia 0.
— Darryl Sittler, Toronto, Feb. 7, 1976, at Toronto. Toronto 11, Boston 4.

Larry Murphy (right) has now played more NHL games than anyone other than Gordie Howe. He played 336 of his 1,558 games with the Pittsburgh Penguins and 453 of them with the Washington Capitals.

Reg Bentley (left) played briefly with his Hall of Fame brothers Max (center) and Doug (right) in 1942-43. It was during this time that Max collected four goals and three assists in a 10-1 Chicago victory over the New York Rangers.

MOST GOALS, ONE ROAD GAME:

6 — Red Berenson, St. Louis, Nov. 7, 1968, at Philadelphia. St. Louis 8, Philadelphia 0.

5 — Joe Malone, Montreal, Dec. 19, 1917, at Ottawa. Montreal 9, Ottawa 4.
— Red Green, Hamilton, Dec. 5, 1924, at Toronto. Hamilton 10, Toronto 3.
— Babe Dye, Toronto, Dec. 22, 1924, at Boston. Toronto 10, Boston 2.
— Harry Broadbent, Mtl. Maroons, Jan. 7, 1925, at Hamilton. Mtl. Maroons 6, Hamilton 2.
— Don Murdoch, NY Rangers, Oct. 12, 1976, at Minnesota. NY Rangers 10, Minnesota 4.
— Tim Young, Minnesota, Jan. 15, 1979, at NY Rangers. Minnesota 8, NY Rangers 1.
— Willy Lindstrom, Winnipeg, Mar. 2, 1982, at Philadelphia. Winnipeg 7, Philadelphia 6.
— Bengt Gustafsson, Washington, Jan. 8, 1984, at Philadelphia. Washington 7, Philadelphia 1.
— Wayne Gretzky, Edmonton, Dec. 15, 1984, at St. Louis. Edmonton 8, St. Louis 2.
— Dave Andreychuk, Buffalo, Feb. 6, 1986, at Boston. Buffalo 8, Boston 6.
— Mats Sundin, Quebec, Mar. 5, 1992, at Hartford. Quebec 10, Hartford 4.
— Mario Lemieux, Pittsburgh, Apr. 9, 1993, at New York. Pittsburgh 10, NY Rangers 4.
— Mike Ricci, Quebec, Feb. 17, 1994, at San Jose. Quebec 8, San Jose 2.
— Alexei Zhamnov, Winnipeg, Apr. 1, 1995, at Los Angeles. Winnipeg 7, Los Angeles 7.

MOST GOALS, ONE PERIOD:

4 — Harvey Jackson, Toronto, Nov. 20, 1934, at St. Louis, third period. Toronto 5, St. Louis Eagles 2.
— **Max Bentley,** Chicago, Jan. 28, 1943, at Chicago, third period. Chicago 10, NY Rangers 1.
— **Clint Smith,** Chicago, Mar. 4, 1945, at Chicago, third period. Chicago 6, Montreal 4.
— **Red Berenson,** St. Louis, Nov. 7, 1968, at Philadelphia, second period. St. Louis 8, Philadelphia 0.
— **Wayne Gretzky,** Edmonton, Feb. 18, 1981, at Edmonton, third period. Edmonton 9, St. Louis 2.
— **Grant Mulvey,** Chicago, Feb. 3, 1982, at Chicago, first period. Chicago 9, St. Louis 5.
— **Bryan Trottier,** NY Islanders, Feb. 13, 1982, at New York, second period. NY Islanders 8, Philadelphia 2.
— **Al Secord,** Chicago, Jan. 7, 1987, at Chicago, second period. Chicago 6, Toronto 4.
— **Joe Nieuwendyk,** Calgary, Jan. 11, 1989, at Calgary, second period. Calgary 8, Winnipeg 3.
— **Peter Bondra,** Washington, Feb. 5, 1994, at Washington, first period. Washington 6, Tampa Bay 3.
— **Mario Lemieux,** Pittsburgh, Jan. 26, 1997, at Montreal, third period. Pittsburgh 5, Montreal 2.

ASSISTS

MOST ASSISTS:

1,963 — Wayne Gretzky, Edmonton, Los Angeles, St. Louis, NY Rangers, in 20 seasons, 1,487GP.
1,131 — Paul Coffey, Edmonton, Pittsburgh, Los Angeles, Detroit, Hartford, Philadelphia, Chicago, Carolina, in 20 seasons, 1,391GP.
1,117 — Ray Bourque, Boston, Colorado, in 21 seasons, 1,532GP.
1,087 — Mark Messier, Edmonton, NY Rangers, Vancouver, in 21 seasons, 1,479GP.
— Ron Francis, Hartford, Pittsburgh, Carolina, in 19 seasons, 1,407GP.

MOST ASSISTS, INCLUDING PLAYOFFS:

2,223 — Wayne Gretzky, Edmonton, Los Angeles, St. Louis, NY Rangers, 1,963 regular-season and 260 playoff assists.
1,273 — Mark Messier, Edmonton, NY Rangers, Vancouver, 1,087 regular-season and 186 playoff assists.
1,268 — Paul Coffey, Edmonton, Pittsburgh, Los Angeles, Detroit, Hartford, Philadelphia, Chicago, Carolina, 1,131 regular-season and 137 playoff assists.
1,250 — Ray Bourque, Boston, Colorado, 1,117 regular season and 133 playoff assists.
1,170 — Ron Francis, Hartford, Pittsburgh, Carolina, 1,087 regular-season and 83 playoff assists.

MOST ASSISTS, ONE SEASON:

163 — Wayne Gretzky, Edmonton, 1985-86. 80 game schedule.
135 — Wayne Gretzky, Edmonton, 1984-85. 80 game schedule.
125 — Wayne Gretzky, Edmonton, 1982-83. 80 game schedule.
122 — Wayne Gretzky, Los Angeles, 1990-91. 80 game schedule.
121 — Wayne Gretzky, Edmonton, 1986-87. 80 game schedule.
120 — Wayne Gretzky, Edmonton, 1981-82. 80 game schedule.
118 — Wayne Gretzky, Edmonton, 1983-84. 80 game schedule.
114 — Wayne Gretzky, Los Angeles, 1988-89. 80 game schedule.
— Mario Lemieux, Pittsburgh, 1988-89. 80 game schedule.
109 — Wayne Gretzky, Edmonton, 1980-81. 80 game schedule.
— Wayne Gretzky, Edmonton, 1987-88. 80 game schedule.
102 — Bobby Orr, Boston, 1970-71. 78 game schedule.
— Wayne Gretzky, Los Angeles, 1989-90. 80 game schedule.

MOST ASSISTS, ONE SEASON, INCLUDING PLAYOFFS:
174 — **Wayne Gretzky,** Edmonton, 1985-86, 163A in 80 regular-season games and 11A in 10 playoff games.
165 — Wayne Gretzky, Edmonton, 1984-85, 135A in 80 regular-season games and 30A in 18 playoff games.
151 — Wayne Gretzky, Edmonton, 1982-83, 125A in 80 regular-season games and 26A in 16 playoff games.
150 — Wayne Gretzky, Edmonton, 1986-87, 121A in 79 regular-season games and 29A in 21 playoff games.
140 — Wayne Gretzky, Edmonton, 1983-84, 118A in 74 regular-season games and 22A in 19 playoff games.
— Wayne Gretzky, Edmonton, 1987-88, 109A in 64 regular-season games and 31A in 19 playoff games.
133 — Wayne Gretzky, Los Angeles, 1990-91, 122A in 78 regular-season games and 11A in 12 playoff games.
131 — Wayne Gretzky, Los Angeles, 1988-89, 114A in 78 regular-season games and 17A in 11 playoff games.
127 — Wayne Gretzky, Edmonton, 1981-82, 120A in 80 regular-season games and 7A in 5 playoff games.
123 — Wayne Gretzky, Edmonton, 1980-81, 109A in 80 regular-season games and 14A in 9 playoff games.
121 — Mario Lemieux, Pittsburgh, 1988-89, 114A in 76 regular-season games and 7A in 11 playoff games.

MOST ASSISTS, ONE GAME:
7 — **Billy Taylor,** Detroit, Mar. 16, 1947, at Chicago. Detroit 10, Chicago 6.
— **Wayne Gretzky,** Edmonton, Feb. 15, 1980, at Edmonton. Edmonton 8, Washington 2.
— **Wayne Gretzky,** Edmonton, Dec. 11, 1985, at Chicago. Edmonton 12, Chicago 9.
— **Wayne Gretzky,** Edmonton, Feb. 14, 1986, at Edmonton. Edmonton 8, Quebec 2.
6 — Six assists have been recorded in one game on 24 occasions since Elmer Lach of Montreal first accomplished the feat vs. Boston on Feb. 6, 1943. The most recent player is Eric Lindros of Philadelphia (Feb. 26, 1997 at Ottawa)

MOST ASSISTS, ONE ROAD GAME:
7 — **Billy Taylor,** Detroit, Mar. 16, 1947, at Chicago. Detroit 10, Chicago 6.
— **Wayne Gretzky,** Edmonton, Dec. 11, 1985, at Chicago. Edmonton 12, Chicago 9.
6 — Bobby Orr, Boston, Jan. 1, 1973, at Vancouver. Boston 8, Vancouver 2.
— Patrik Sundstrom, Vancouver, Feb. 29, 1984, at Pittsburgh. Vancouver 9, Pittsburgh 5.
— Mario Lemieux, Pittsburgh, Dec. 5, 1992, at San Jose. Pittsburgh 9, San Jose 4.
— Eric Lindros, Philadelphia, Feb. 26, 1997, at Ottawa. Philadelphia 8, Ottawa 5.

MOST ASSISTS, ONE PERIOD:
5 — **Dale Hawerchuk,** Winnipeg, Mar. 6, 1984, at Los Angeles, second period. Winnipeg 7, Los Angeles 3.
4 — Four assists have been recorded in one period on 63 occasions since Mickey Roach of Hamilton first accomplished the feat vs. Toronto St. Pats on Feb. 23, 1921. Most recent player, Paul Kariya of Anaheim, (Dec. 16, 1998 vs Nashville).

POINTS

MOST POINTS:
2,857 — **Wayne Gretzky,** Edmonton, Los Angeles, St. Louis, NY Rangers, in 20 seasons, 1,487GP (894G-1963A).
1,850 — Gordie Howe, Detroit, Hartford, in 26 seasons, 1,767GP (801G-1049A).
1,771 — Marcel Dionne, Detroit, Los Angeles, NY Rangers, in 18 seasons, 1,348GP (731G-1,040A).
1,714 — Mark Messier, Edmonton, NY Rangers, Vancouver, in 21 seasons, 1,479GP (627G-1,087A).
1,590 — Phil Esposito, Chicago, Boston, NY Rangers in 18 seasons, 1,282GP (717G-873A).

MOST POINTS, INCLUDING PLAYOFFS:
3,239 — **Wayne Gretzky,** Edmonton, Los Angeles, St. Louis, NY Rangers, 2,857 regular-season and 382 playoff points.
2,010 — Gordie Howe, Detroit, Hartford, 1,850 regular-season and 160 playoff points.
2,009 — Mark Messier, Edmonton, NY Rangers, Vancouver, 1,714 regular-season and 295 playoff points.
1,816 — Marcel Dionne, Detroit, Los Angeles, NY Rangers, 1,771 regular-season and 45 playoff points.
1,727 — Phil Esposito, Chicago, Boston, NY Rangers, 1,590 regular-season and 137 playoff points.

MOST POINTS, ONE SEASON:
215 — **Wayne Gretzky,** Edmonton, 1985-86. 80 game schedule.
212 — Wayne Gretzky, Edmonton, 1981-82. 80 game schedule.
208 — Wayne Gretzky, Edmonton, 1984-85. 80 game schedule.
205 — Wayne Gretzky, Edmonton, 1983-84. 80 game schedule.
199 — Mario Lemieux, Pittsburgh, 1988-89. 80 game schedule.
196 — Wayne Gretzky, Edmonton, 1982-83. 80 game schedule.
183 — Wayne Gretzky, Edmonton, 1986-87. 80 game schedule.
168 — Mario Lemieux, Pittsburgh, 1987-88, 80 game schedule.
— Wayne Gretzky, Los Angeles, 1988-89. 80 game schedule.
164 — Wayne Gretzky, Edmonton, 1980-81. 80 game schedule.
163 — Wayne Gretzky, Los Angeles, 1990-91. 80 game schedule.
161 — Mario Lemieux, Pittsburgh, 1995-96. 82 game schedule.
160 — Mario Lemieux, Pittsburgh, 1992-93. 84 game schedule.

MOST POINTS, ONE SEASON, INCLUDING PLAYOFFS:
255 — **Wayne Gretzky,** Edmonton, 1984-85, 208PTS in 80 regular-season games and 47PTS in 18 playoff games.
240 — Wayne Gretzky, Edmonton, 1983-84, 205PTS in 74 regular-season games and 35PTS in 19 playoff games.
234 — Wayne Gretzky, Edmonton, 1982-83, 196PTS in 80 regular-season games and 38PTS in 16 playoff games.
— Wayne Gretzky, Edmonton, 1985-86, 215PTS in 80 regular-season games and 19PTS in 10 playoff games.
224 — Wayne Gretzky, Edmonton, 1981-82, 212PTS in 80 regular-season games and 12PTS in 5 playoff games.
218 — Mario Lemieux, Pittsburgh, 1988-89, 199PTS in 76 regular-season games and 19PTS in 11 playoff games.
217 — Wayne Gretzky, Edmonton, 1986-87, 183PTS in 79 regular-season games and 34PTS in 21 playoff games.
192 — Wayne Gretzky, Edmonton, 1987-88, 149PTS in 64 regular-season games and 43PTS in 19 playoff games.
190 — Wayne Gretzky, Los Angeles, 1988-89, 168PTS in 78 regular-season games and 22PTS in 11 playoff games.
188 — Mario Lemieux, Pittsburgh, 1995-96, 161PTS in 70 regular-season games and 27PTS in 18 playoff games.
185 — Wayne Gretzky, Edmonton, 1980-81, 164PTS in 80 regular-season games and 21PTS in 9 playoff games.

Dale Hawerchuk set a record when he set up five goals in the second period of Winnipeg's 7-3 win over Los Angeles on March 6, 1984.

MOST POINTS, ONE GAME:
10 — Darryl Sittler, Toronto, Feb. 7, 1976, at Toronto, 6G-4A. Toronto 11, Boston 4.
 8 — Maurice Richard, Montreal, Dec. 28, 1944, at Montreal, 5G-3A. Montreal 9, Detroit 1.
 — Bert Olmstead, Montreal, Jan. 9, 1954, at Montreal, 4G-4A. Montreal 12, Chicago 1.
 — Tom Bladon, Philadelphia, Dec. 11, 1977, at Philadelphia, 4G-4A. Philadelphia 11, Cleveland 1.
 — Bryan Trottier, NY Islanders, Dec. 23, 1978, at NY Islanders, 5G-3A. NY Islanders 9, NY Rangers 4.
 — Peter Stastny, Quebec, Feb. 22, 1981, at Washington, 4G-4A. Quebec 11, Washington 7.
 — Anton Stastny, Quebec, Feb. 22, 1981, at Washington, 3G-5A. Quebec 11, Washington 7.
 — Wayne Gretzky, Edmonton, Nov. 19, 1983, at Edmonton, 3G-5A. Edmonton 13, New Jersey 4.
 — Wayne Gretzky, Edmonton, Jan. 4, 1984, at Edmonton, 4G-4A. Edmonton 12, Minnesota 8.
 — Paul Coffey, Edmonton, Mar. 14, 1986, at Edmonton, 2G-6A. Edmonton 12, Detroit 3.
 — Mario Lemieux, Pittsburgh, Oct. 15, 1988, at Pittsburgh, 2G-6A. Pittsburgh 9, St. Louis 2.
 — Bernie Nicholls, Los Angeles, Dec. 1, 1988, at Los Angeles, 2G-6A. Los Angeles 9, Toronto 3.
 — Mario Lemieux, Pittsburgh, Dec. 31, 1988, at Pittsburgh, 5G-3A. Pittsburgh 8, New Jersey 6.

MOST POINTS, ONE ROAD GAME:
8 — Peter Stastny, Quebec, Feb. 22, 1981, at Washington, 4G-4A. Quebec 11, Washington 7.
 — **Anton Stastny,** Quebec, Feb. 22, 1981, at Washington, 3G-5A. Quebec 11, Washington 7.
 7 — Red Green, Hamilton, Dec. 5, 1924, at Toronto, 5G-2A. Hamilton 10, Toronto 3.
 — Billy Taylor, Detroit, Mar. 16, 1947, at Chicago, 7A. Detroit 10, Chicago 6.
 — Red Berenson, St. Louis, Nov. 7, 1968, at Philadelphia, 6G-1A. St. Louis 8, Philadelphia 0.
 — Gilbert Perreault, Buffalo, Feb. 1, 1976, at California, 2G-5A. Buffalo 9, California 5.
 — Peter Stastny, Quebec, Apr. 1, 1982, at Boston, 3G-4A. Quebec 8, Boston 5.
 — Wayne Gretzky, Edmonton, Nov. 6, 1983, at Winnipeg, 4G-3A. Edmonton 8, Winnipeg 5.
 — Patrik Sundstrom, Vancouver, Feb. 29, 1984, at Pittsburgh, 1G-6A. Vancouver 9, Pittsburgh 5.
 — Wayne Gretzky, Edmonton, Dec. 11, 1985, at Chicago, 7A, Edmonton 12, Chicago 9.
 — Cam Neely, Boston, Oct. 16, 1988, at Chicago, 3G-4A. Boston 10, Chicago 3.
 — Mario Lemieux, Pittsburgh, Jan. 21, 1989, at Edmonton, 2G-5A. Pittsburgh 7, Edmonton 4.
 — Dino Ciccarelli, Washington, Mar. 18, 1989, at Hartford, 4G-3A. Washington 8, Hartford 2.
 — Mats Sundin, Quebec, Mar. 5, 1992, at Hartford, 5G-2A. Quebec 10, Hartford 4.
 — Mario Lemieux, Pittsburgh, Dec. 5, 1992, at San Jose, 1G-6A. Pittsburgh 9, San Jose 4.
 — Eric Lindros, Philadelphia, Feb. 26, 1997, at Ottawa, 1G-6A. Philadelphia 8, Ottawa 5.

MOST POINTS, ONE PERIOD:
6 — Bryan Trottier, NY Islanders, Dec. 23, 1978, at NY Islanders, second period. 3G-3A. NY Islanders 9, NY Rangers 4.
 5 — Les Cunningham, Chicago, Jan. 28, 1940, at Chicago, third period. 2G- 3A. Chicago 8, Montreal 1.
 — Max Bentley, Chicago, Jan. 28, 1943, at Chicago, third period. 4G-1A, Chicago 10, NY Rangers 1.
 — Leo Labine, Boston, Nov. 28, 1954, at Boston, second period, 3G-2A. Boston 6, Detroit 2.
 — Darryl Sittler, Toronto, Feb. 7, 1976, at Toronto, second period. 3G-2A. Toronto 11, Boston 4.
 — Grant Mulvey, Chicago, Feb. 3, 1982, at Chicago, first period. 4G-1A. Chicago 9, St. Louis 5.
 — Dale Hawerchuk, Winnipeg, Mar. 6, 1984, at Los Angeles, second period. 5A. Winnipeg 7, Los Angeles 3.
 — Jari Kurri, Edmonton, Oct. 26, 1984, at Edmonton, second period. 2G-3A. Edmonton 8, Los Angeles 2.
 — Pat Elynuik, Winnipeg, Jan. 20, 1989, at Winnipeg, second period. 2G- 3A. Winnipeg 7, Pittsburgh 3.
 — Ray Ferraro, Hartford, Dec. 9, 1989, at Hartford, first period. 3G-2A. Hartford 7, New Jersey 3.
 — Stephane Richer, Montreal, Feb. 14, 1990, at Montreal, first period. 2G- 3A. Montreal 10, Vancouver 1.
 — Cliff Ronning, Vancouver, Apr. 15, 1993, at Los Angeles, third period. 3G- 2A. Vancouver 8, Los Angeles 6.
 — Peter Forsberg, Colorado, Mar. 3, 1999, at Florida, third period. 2G- 3A. Colorado 7, Florida 5.

POWER-PLAY and SHORTHAND GOALS

MOST POWER-PLAY GOALS, ONE SEASON:
34 — Tim Kerr, Philadelphia, 1985-86. 80 game schedule.
 32 — Dave Andreychuk, Buffalo, Toronto, 1992-93. 84 game schedule.
 31 — Joe Nieuwendyk, Calgary, 1987-88. 80 game schedule.
 — Mario Lemieux, Pittsburgh, 1988-89. 80 game schedule.
 — Mario Lemieux, Pittsburgh, 1995-96. 82 game schedule.
 29 — Michel Goulet, Quebec, 1987-88. 80 game schedule.
 — Brett Hull, St. Louis, 1990-91. 80 game schedule.
 — Brett Hull, St. Louis, 1992-93. 84 game schedule.

MOST SHORTHAND GOALS, ONE SEASON:
13 — Mario Lemieux, Pittsburgh, 1988-89. 80 game schedule.
 12 — Wayne Gretzky, Edmonton, 1983-84. 80 game schedule.
 11 — Wayne Gretzky, Edmonton, 1984-85. 80 game schedule.
 10 — Marcel Dionne, Detroit, 1974-75. 80 game schedule.
 — Mario Lemieux, Pittsburgh, 1987-88. 80 game schedule.
 — Dirk Graham, Chicago, 1988-89. 80 game schedule.

MOST SHORTHAND GOALS, ONE GAME:
3 —Theoren Fleury, Calgary, Mar. 9, 1991, at St. Louis. Calgary 8, St. Louis 4.

OVERTIME SCORING

MOST OVERTIME GOALS, CAREER:
11 — Steve Thomas, Toronto, Chicago, NY Islanders, New Jersey.
 9 — Mario Lemieux, Pittsburgh.
 — Jaromir Jagr, Pittsburgh.
 8 — Bob Sweeney, Boston, Buffalo, Calgary.
 — Mark Messier, Edmonton, NY Rangers, Vancouver.
 — Tomas Sandstrom, NY Rangers, Los Angeles, Pittsburgh, Detroit, Anaheim.

MOST OVERTIME ASSISTS, CAREER:
15 — Wayne Gretzky, Edmonton, Los Angeles, St. Louis, NY Rangers.
 14 — Adam Oates, Detroit, St. Louis, Boston, Washington.
 13 — Doug Gilmour, St. Louis, Calgary, Toronto, New Jersey, Chicago, Buffalo.
 12 — Mark Messier, Edmonton, NY Rangers, Vancouver.
 — Scott Stevens, Washington, St. Louis, New Jersey.

MOST OVERTIME POINTS, CAREER:
21 — Steve Thomas, Toronto, Chicago, NY Islanders, New Jersey. 11G-10A
 20 — Mark Messier, Edmonton, NY Rangers, Vancouver. 8G-12A
 19 — Mario Lemieux, Pittsburgh. 9G-10A
 18 — Adam Oates, Detroit, St. Louis, Boston, Washington. 4G-14A.
 17 — Wayne Gretzky, Edmonton, Los Angeles, St. Louis, NY Rangers. 2G-15A.
 16 — Doug Gilmour, St. Louis, Calgary, Toronto, New Jersey, Chicago, Buffalo. 3G-13A.
 15 — Pierre Turgeon, Buffalo, NY Islanders, Montreal, St. Louis.. 7G-8A

SCORING BY A CENTER

MOST GOALS BY A CENTER, CAREER
894 — Wayne Gretzky, Edmonton, Los Angeles, St. Louis, NY Rangers, in 20 seasons.
 731 — Marcel Dionne, Detroit, Los Angeles, NY Rangers, in 18 seasons.
 717 — Phil Esposito, Chicago, Boston, NY Rangers, in 18 seasons.
 627 — Mark Messier, Edmonton, NY Rangers, Vancouver, in 21 seasons.
 — Steve Yzerman, Detroit, Detroit, in 17 seasons.

MOST GOALS BY A CENTER, ONE SEASON:
92 — Wayne Gretzky, Edmonton, 1981-82. 80 game schedule.
 87 — Wayne Gretzky, Edmonton, 1983-84. 80 game schedule.
 85 — Mario Lemieux, Pittsburgh, 1988-89. 80 game schedule.
 76 — Phil Esposito, Boston, 1970-71. 78 game schedule.
 73 — Wayne Gretzky, Edmonton, 1984-85. 80 game schedule.

Boston goalie Dave Reece was the unfortunate victim of Darryl Sittler's record 10-point night. The game on February 7, 1976, marked Reece's final appearance in the NHL.

MOST ASSISTS BY A CENTER, CAREER:
1,963 — **Wayne Gretzky,** Edmonton, Los Angeles, St. Louis, NY Rangers, in 20 seasons.
1,087 — Mark Messier, Edmonton, NY Rangers, Vancouver, in 21 seasons.
— Ron Francis, Hartford, Pittsburgh, Carolina, in 19 seasons.
1,040 — Marcel Dionne, Detroit, Los Angeles, NY Rangers, in 18 seasons.
935 — Steve Yzerman, Detroit, in 17 seasons.

MOST ASSISTS BY A CENTER, ONE SEASON:
163 — **Wayne Gretzky,** Edmonton, 1985-86. 80 game schedule.
135 — Wayne Gretzky, Edmonton, 1984-85. 80 game schedule.
125 — Wayne Gretzky, Edmonton, 1982-83. 80 game schedule.
122 — Wayne Gretzky, Los Angeles, 1990-91. 80 game schedule.
121 — Wayne Gretzky, Edmonton, 1986-87. 80 game schedule.

MOST POINTS BY A CENTER, CAREER:
2,857 — **Wayne Gretzky,** Edmonton, Los Angeles, St. Louis, NY Rangers, in 20 seasons.
1,771 — Marcel Dionne, Detroit, Los Angeles, NY Rangers, in 18 seasons.
1,714 — Mark Messier, Edmonton, NY Rangers, Vancouver, in 21 seasons.
1,590 — Phil Esposito, Chicago, Boston, NY Rangers, in 18 seasons.
1,562 — Steve Yzerman, Detroit, in 17 seasons.

MOST POINTS BY A CENTER, ONE SEASON:
215 — **Wayne Gretzky,** Edmonton, 1985-86. 80 game schedule.
212 — Wayne Gretzky, Edmonton, 1981-82. 80 game schedule.
208 — Wayne Gretzky, Edmonton, 1984-85. 80 game schedule.
205 — Wayne Gretzky, Edmonton, 1983-84. 80 game schedule.
199 — Mario Lemieux, Pittsburgh, 1988-89. 80 game schedule.

SCORING BY A LEFT WING

MOST GOALS BY A LEFT WING, CAREER:
610 — **Bobby Hull,** Chicago, Winnipeg, Hartford, in 16 seasons.
556 — John Bucyk, Detroit, Boston, in 23 seasons.
553 — Luc Robitaille, Los Angeles, Pittsburgh, NY Rangers, in 14 seasons.
552 — Dave Andreychuk, Buffalo, Toronto, New Jersey, Boston, Colorado, in 18 seasons.
548 — Michel Goulet, Quebec, Chicago, in 15 seasons.

MOST GOALS BY A LEFT WING, ONE SEASON:
63 — **Luc Robitaille,** Los Angeles, 1992-93. 84 game schedule.
60 — Steve Shutt, Montreal, 1976-77. 80 game schedule.
58 — Bobby Hull, Chicago, 1968-69. 76 game schedule.
57 — Michel Goulet, Quebec, 1982-83. 80 game schedule.
56 — Charlie Simmer, Los Angeles, 1979-80. 80 game schedule.
— Charlie Simmer, Los Angeles, 1980-81. 80 game schedule.
— Michel Goulet, Quebec, 1983-84. 80 game schedule.

MOST ASSISTS BY A LEFT WING, CAREER:
813 — **John Bucyk,** Detroit, Boston, in 23 seasons.
624 — Dave Andreychuk, Buffalo, Toronto, New Jersey, Boston, Colorado, in 18 seasons.
604 — Michel Goulet, Quebec, Chicago, in 15 seasons.
597 — Luc Robitaille, Los Angeles, Pittsburgh, NY Rangers, in 14 seasons.
579 — Brian Propp, Philadelphia, Boston, Minnesota, Hartford, in 15 seasons.

MOST ASSISTS BY A LEFT WING, ONE SEASON:
70 — **Joe Juneau,** Boston, 1992-93. 84 game schedule.
69 — Kevin Stevens, Pittsburgh, 1991-92. 80 game schedule.
67 — Mats Naslund, Montreal, 1985-86. 80 game schedule.
65 — John Bucyk, Boston, 1970-71. 78 game schedule.
— Michel Goulet, Quebec, 1983-84. 80 game schedule.
64 — Mark Messier, Edmonton, 1983-84. 80 game schedule.

MOST POINTS BY A LEFT WING, CAREER:
1,369 — **John Bucyk,** Detroit, Boston, in 23 seasons.
1,176 — Dave Andreychuk, Buffalo, Toronto, New Jersey, Boston, Colorado, in 18 seasons.
1,170 — Bobby Hull, Chicago, Winnipeg, Hartford, in 16 seasons.
1,152 — Michel Goulet, Quebec, Chicago, in 15 seasons.
1,150 — Luc Robitaille, Los Angeles, Pittsburgh, NY Rangers, in 14 seasons.

MOST POINTS BY A LEFT WING, ONE SEASON:
125 — **Luc Robitaille,** Los Angeles, 1992-93. 84 game schedule.
123 — Kevin Stevens, Pittsburgh, 1991-92. 80 game schedule.
121 — Michel Goulet, Quebec, 1983-84. 80 game schedule.
116 — John Bucyk, Boston, 1970-71. 78 game schedule.
112 — Bill Barber, Philadelphia, 1975-76. 80 game schedule.

SCORING BY A RIGHT WING

MOST GOALS BY A RIGHT WING, CAREER:
801 — **Gordie Howe,** Detroit, Hartford, in 26 seasons.
708 — Mike Gartner, Washington, Minnesota, NY Rangers, Toronto, Phoenix, in 19 seasons.
610 — Brett Hull, Calgary, St. Louis, Dallas, in 14 seasons.
608 — Dino Ciccarelli, Minnesota, Washington, Detroit, Tampa Bay, Florida, in 19 seasons.
601 — Jari Kurri, Edmonton, Los Angeles, NY Rangers, Anaheim, Colorado, in 17 seasons.

MOST GOALS BY A RIGHT WING, ONE SEASON:
86 — **Brett Hull,** St. Louis, 1990-91. 80 game schedule.
76 — Alexander Mogilny, Buffalo, 1992-93. 84 game schedule.
— Teemu Selanne, Winnipeg, 1992-93. 84 game schedule.
72 — Brett Hull, St. Louis, 1989-90. 80 game schedule.
71 — Jari Kurri, Edmonton, 1984-85. 80 game schedule.
70 — Brett Hull, St. Louis, 1991-92. 80 game schedule.

MOST ASSISTS BY A RIGHT WING, CAREER:
1,049 — **Gordie Howe,** Detroit, Hartford, in 26 seasons.
797 — Jari Kurri, Edmonton, Los Angeles, NY Rangers, Anaheim, Colorado, in 17 seasons.
793 — Guy Lafleur, Montreal, NY Rangers, Quebec, in 17 seasons.
638 — Dave Taylor, Los Angeles, in 17 seasons.
627 — Mike Gartner, Washington, Minnesota, NY Rangers, Toronto, Phoenix, in 19 seasons.

MOST ASSISTS BY A RIGHT WING, ONE SEASON:
87 — **Jaromir Jagr,** Pittsburgh, 1995-96. 82 game schedule.
83 — Mike Bossy, NY Islanders, 1981-82. 80 game schedule.
— Jaromir Jagr, Pittsburgh, 1998-99. 82 game schedule.
80 — Guy Lafleur, Montreal, 1976-77. 80 game schedule.
77 — Guy Lafleur, Montreal, 1978-79. 80 game schedule.

Dave Andreychuk has quietly become one of the top goal scorers in NHL history. After his fifth goal in 2000-01, Andreychuk will trail only Bobby Hull among left wingers.

MOST POINTS BY A RIGHT WING, CAREER:
1,850 — **Gordie Howe,** Detroit, Hartford, in 26 seasons.
1,398 — Jari Kurri, Edmonton, Los Angeles, NY Rangers, Anaheim, Colorado, in 17 seasons.
1,353 — Guy Lafleur, Montreal, NY Rangers, Quebec, in 17 seasons.
1,335 — Mike Gartner, Washington, Minnesota, NY Rangers, Toronto, Phoenix, in 19 seasons.
1,200 — Dino Ciccarelli, Minnesota, Washington, Detroit, Tampa Bay, Florida, in 19 seasons.

MOST POINTS BY A RIGHT WING, ONE SEASON:
149 — **Jaromir Jagr,** Pittsburgh, 1995-96. 82 game schedule.
147 — Mike Bossy, NY Islanders, 1981-82. 80 game schedule.
136 — Guy Lafleur, Montreal, 1976-77. 80 game schedule.
135 — Jari Kurri, Edmonton, 1984-85. 80 game schedule.
132 — Guy Lafleur, Montreal, 1977-78. 80 game schedule.
— Teemu Selanne, Winnipeg, 1992-93. 84 game schedule.

SCORING BY A DEFENSEMAN

MOST GOALS BY A DEFENSEMAN, CAREER:
403 — **Ray Bourque,** Boston, Colorado, in 21 seasons.
396 — Paul Coffey, Edmonton, Pittsburgh, Los Angeles, Detroit, Hartford, Philadelphia, Chicago, Carolina, in 20 seasons.
313 — Phil Housley, Buffalo, Winnipeg, St. Louis, Calgary, New Jersey, Washington, in 18 seasons.
310 — Denis Potvin, NY Islanders, in 15 seasons.
301 — Al MacInnis, Calgary, St. Louis, in 19 seasons.

MOST GOALS BY A DEFENSEMAN, ONE SEASON:
48 — **Paul Coffey,** Edmonton, 1985-86. 80 game schedule.
46 — Bobby Orr, Boston, 1974-75. 80 game schedule.
40 — Paul Coffey, Edmonton, 1983-84. 80 game schedule.
39 — Doug Wilson, Chicago, 1981-82. 80 game schedule.
37 — Bobby Orr, Boston, 1970-71. 78 game schedule.
— Bobby Orr, Boston, 1971-72. 78 game schedule.
— Paul Coffey, Edmonton, 1984-85. 80 game schedule.

Since entering the NHL directly out of high school with the Buffalo Sabres in 1982, Phil Housley has gone on to become one of the top-scoring defensemen in NHL history.

MOST GOALS BY A DEFENSEMAN, ONE GAME:
5 — **Ian Turnbull,** Toronto, Feb. 2, 1977, at Toronto. Toronto 9, Detroit 1.
4 — Harry Cameron, Toronto, Dec. 26, 1917, at Toronto. Toronto 7, Montreal 5.
— Harry Cameron, Montreal, Mar. 3, 1920, at Quebec City. Montreal 16, Que. Bulldogs 3.
— Sprague Cleghorn, Montreal, Jan. 14, 1922, at Montreal. Montreal 10, Hamilton 6.
— Johnny McKinnon, Pit. Pirates, Nov. 19, 1929, at Pittsburgh. Pit. Pirates 10, Toronto 5.
— Hap Day, Toronto, Nov. 19, 1929, at Pittsburgh. Pit. Pirates 10, Toronto 5.
— Tom Bladon, Philadelphia, Dec. 11, 1977, at Philadelphia. Philadelphia 11, Cleveland 1.
— Ian Turnbull, Los Angeles, Dec. 12, 1981, at Los Angeles. Los Angeles 7, Vancouver 5.
— Paul Coffey, Edmonton, Oct. 26, 1984, at Calgary. Edmonton 6, Calgary 5.

MOST ASSISTS BY A DEFENSEMAN, CAREER:
1,131 — **Paul Coffey,** Edmonton, Pittsburgh, Los Angeles, Detroit, Hartford, Philadelphia, Chicago, Carolina, in 20 seasons.
1,117 — Ray Bourque, Boston, Colorado, in 21 seasons.
910 — Larry Murphy, Los Angeles, Washington, Pittsburgh, Toronto, Detroit, in 20 seasons.
817 — Phil Housley, Buffalo, Winnipeg, St. Louis, Calgary, New Jersey, Washington, in 18 seasons.
803 — Al MacInnis, Calgary, St. Louis, in 19 seasons.

MOST ASSISTS BY A DEFENSEMAN, ONE SEASON:
102 — **Bobby Orr, Boston,** 1970-71. 78 game schedule.
90 — Paul Coffey, Edmonton, 1985-86. 80 game schedule.
90 — Bobby Orr, Boston, 1973-74. 78 game schedule.
89 — Bobby Orr, Boston, 1974-75. 80 game schedule.

MOST ASSISTS BY A DEFENSEMAN, ONE GAME:
6 — **Babe Pratt,** Toronto, Jan. 8, 1944, at Toronto. Toronto 12, Boston 3.
— **Pat Stapleton,** Chicago, Mar. 30, 1969, at Chicago. Chicago 9, Detroit 5.
— **Bobby Orr,** Boston, Jan. 1, 1973, at Vancouver. Boston 8, Vancouver 2.
— **Ron Stackhouse,** Pittsburgh, Mar. 8, 1975, at Pittsburgh. Pittsburgh 8, Philadelphia 2.
— **Paul Coffey,** Edmonton, Mar. 14, 1986, at Edmonton. Edmonton 12, Detroit 3.
— **Gary Suter,** Calgary, Apr. 4, 1986, at Calgary. Calgary 9, Edmonton 3.

MOST POINTS BY A DEFENSEMAN, CAREER:
1,527 — **Paul Coffey,** Edmonton, Pittsburgh, Los Angeles, Detroit, Hartford, Philadelphia, Chicago, Carolina, in 20 seasons.
1,520 — Ray Bourque, Boston, Colorado, in 21 seasons.
1,195 — Larry Murphy, Los Angeles, Washington, Pittsburgh, Toronto, Detroit, in 20 seasons.
1,130 — Phil Housley, Buffalo, Winnipeg, St. Louis, Calgary, New Jersey, Washington, in 18 seasons.
1,104 — Al MacInnis, Calgary, St. Louis, in 19 seasons.

MOST POINTS BY A DEFENSEMAN, ONE SEASON:
139 — **Bobby Orr,** Boston, 1970-71. 78 game schedule.
138 — Paul Coffey, Edmonton, 1985-86. 80 game schedule.
135 — Bobby Orr, Boston, 1974-75. 80 game schedule.
126 — Paul Coffey, Edmonton, 1983-84. 80 game schedule.
122 — Bobby Orr, Boston, 1973-74. 78 game schedule.

MOST POINTS BY A DEFENSEMAN, ONE GAME:
8 — **Tom Bladon,** Philadelphia, Dec. 11, 1977, at Philadelphia. 4G-4A. Philadelphia 11, Cleveland 1.
— **Paul Coffey,** Edmonton, Mar. 14, 1986, at Edmonton. 2G-6A. Edmonton 12, Detroit 3.
7 — Bobby Orr, Boston, Nov. 15, 1973, at Boston. 3G-4A. Boston 10, NY Rangers 2.

SCORING BY A GOALTENDER

MOST POINTS BY A GOALTENDER, CAREER:
48 — **Tom Barrasso,** Buffalo, Pittsburgh, in 17 seasons. (48A)
46 — Grant Fuhr, Edmonton, Toronto, Buffalo, Los Angeles, St. Louis, in 19 seasons. (46A)

MOST POINTS BY A GOALTENDER, ONE SEASON:
14 — **Grant Fuhr,** Edmonton, 1983-84. (14A)
9 — Curtis Joseph, St. Louis, 1991-92. (9A)
8 — Mike Palmateer, Washington, 1980-81. (8A)
— Grant Fuhr, Edmonton, 1987-88. (8A)
— Ron Hextall, Philadelphia, 1988-89. (8A)
— Tom Barrasso, Pittsburgh, 1992-93. (8A)
7 — Ron Hextall, Philadelphia, 1987-88. (1G-6A)
— Mike Vernon, Calgary, 1987-88. (7A)

MOST POINTS BY A GOALTENDER, ONE GAME:
3 — **Jeff Reese,** Calgary, Feb. 10, 1993, at Calgary. Calgary 13, San Jose 1. (3A)

SCORING BY A ROOKIE

MOST GOALS BY A ROOKIE, ONE SEASON:
76 — Teemu Selanne, Winnipeg, 1992-93. 84 game schedule.
53 — Mike Bossy, NY Islanders, 1977-78. 80 game schedule.
51 — Joe Nieuwendyk, Calgary, 1987-88. 80 game schedule.
45 — Dale Hawerchuk, Winnipeg, 1981-82. 80 game schedule.
    — Luc Robitaille, Los Angeles, 1986-87. 80 game schedule.

MOST GOALS BY A PLAYER IN HIS FIRST NHL SEASON, ONE GAME:
5 — Howie Meeker, Toronto, Jan. 8, 1947, at Toronto. Toronto 10, Chicago 4.
    — **Don Murdoch,** NY Rangers, Oct. 12, 1976, at Minnesota. NY Rangers 10, Minnesota 4.

MOST GOALS BY A PLAYER IN HIS FIRST NHL GAME:
3 — Alex Smart, Montreal, Jan. 14, 1943, at Montreal. Montreal 5, Chicago 1.
    — **Real Cloutier,** Quebec, Oct. 10, 1979, at Quebec. Atlanta 5, Quebec 3.

MOST ASSISTS BY A ROOKIE, ONE SEASON:
70 — Peter Stastny, Quebec, 1980-81. 80 game schedule.
    — **Joe Juneau,** Boston, 1992-93. 84 game schedule.
63 — Bryan Trottier, NY Islanders, 1975-76. 80 game schedule.
62 — Sergei Makarov, Calgary, 1989-90. 80 game schedule.
60 — Larry Murphy, Los Angeles, 1980-81. 80 game schedule.

MOST ASSISTS BY A PLAYER IN HIS FIRST NHL SEASON, ONE GAME:
7 — Wayne Gretzky, Edmonton, Feb. 15, 1980, at Edmonton. Edmonton 8, Washington 2.
6 — Gary Suter, Calgary, Apr. 4, 1986, at Calgary. Calgary 9, Edmonton 3.

MOST ASSISTS BY A PLAYER IN HIS FIRST NHL GAME:
4 — Earl Reibel, Detroit, Oct. 8, 1953, at Detroit. Detroit 4, NY Rangers 1.
    — **Roland Eriksson,** Minnesota, Oct. 6, 1976, at New York. NY Rangers 6, Minnesota 5.
3 — Al Hill, Philadelphia, Feb. 14, 1977, at Philadelphia. Philadelphia 6, St. Louis 4.

MOST POINTS BY A ROOKIE, ONE SEASON:
132 — Teemu Selanne, Winnipeg, 1992-93, 84 game schedule.
109 — Peter Stastny, Quebec, 1980-81. 80 game schedule.
103 — Dale Hawerchuk, Winnipeg, 1981-82. 80 game schedule.
102 — Joe Juneau, Boston, 1992-93. 84 game schedule.
100 — Mario Lemieux, Pittsburgh, 1984-85. 80 game schedule.

MOST POINTS BY A PLAYER IN HIS FIRST NHL SEASON, ONE GAME:
8 — Peter Stastny, Quebec, Feb. 22, 1981, at Washington. 4G-4A. Quebec 11, Washington 7.
    — **Anton Stastny,** Quebec, Feb. 22, 1981, at Washington. 3G-5A. Quebec 11, Washington 7.
7 — Wayne Gretzky, Edmonton, Feb. 15, 1980, at Edmonton. 7A. Edmonton 8, Washington 2.
    — Sergei Makarov, Calgary, Feb. 25, 1990, at Calgary. 2G-5A. Calgary 10, Edmonton 4.
6 — Wayne Gretzky, Edmonton, Mar. 29, 1980, at Toronto. 2G-4A. Edmonton 8, Toronto 5.
    — Gary Suter, Calgary, Apr. 4, 1986, at Calgary. 6A. Calgary 9, Edmonton 3.

MOST POINTS BY A PLAYER IN HIS FIRST NHL GAME:
5 — Al Hill, Philadelphia, Feb. 14, 1977, at Philadelphia. 2G-3A. Philadelphia 6, St. Louis 4.
4 — Alex Smart, Montreal, Jan. 14, 1943, at Montreal. 3G-1A. Montreal 5, Chicago 1.
    — Earl Reibel, Detroit, Oct. 8, 1953, at Detroit. 4A. Detroit 4, NY Rangers 1.
    — Roland Eriksson, Minnesota, Oct. 6, 1976 at New York. 4A. NY Rangers 6, Minnesota 5.

SCORING BY A ROOKIE DEFENSEMAN

MOST GOALS BY A ROOKIE DEFENSEMAN, ONE SEASON:
23 — Brian Leetch, NY Rangers, 1988-89. 80 game schedule.
22 — Barry Beck, Col. Rockies, 1977-78. 80 game schedule.
19 — Reed Larson, Detroit, 1977-78. 80 game schedule.
    — Phil Housley, Buffalo, 1982-83. 80 game schedule.

MOST ASSISTS BY A ROOKIE DEFENSEMAN, ONE SEASON:
60 — Larry Murphy, Los Angeles, 1980-81. 80 game schedule.
55 — Chris Chelios, Montreal, 1984-85. 80 game schedule.
50 — Stefan Persson, NY Islanders, 1977-78. 80 game schedule.
    — Gary Suter, Calgary, 1985-86. 80 game schedule.
49 — Nicklas Lidstrom, Detroit, 1991-92. 80 game schedule.

MOST POINTS BY A ROOKIE DEFENSEMAN, ONE SEASON:
76 — Larry Murphy, Los Angeles, 1980-81. 80 game schedule.
71 — Brian Leetch, NY Rangers, 1988-89. 80 game schedule.
68 — Gary Suter, Calgary, 1985-86. 80 game schedule.
66 — Phil Housley, Buffalo, 1982-83. 80 game schedule.
65 — Ray Bourque, Boston, 1979-80. 80 game schedule.

Though he was later dealt to the Washington Capitals for Al Iafrate, Joe Juneau first made his mark in the NHL as a rookie sensation with the Boston Bruins in 1992-93.

PER-GAME SCORING AVERAGES

HIGHEST GOALS-PER-GAME AVERAGE, CAREER
(AMONG PLAYERS WITH 200 OR MORE GOALS):
.823 — **Mario Lemieux,** Pittsburgh, 613G, 745GP, from 1984-85 – 1996-97.
.762 — Mike Bossy, NY Islanders, 573G, 752GP, from 1977-78 – 1986-87.
.756 — Cy Denneny, Ottawa, Boston, 248G, 328GP, from 1917-18 – 1928-29.
.742 — Babe Dye, Toronto, Hamilton, Chicago, NY Americans, 201G, 271GP, from 1919-20 – 1930-31.
.649 — Brett Hull, Calgary, St. Louis, Dallas, 610G, 940GP, from 1986-87 – 1999-2000.
.634 — Pavel Bure, Vancouver, Florida, 325G, 513GP, from 1991-92 – 1999-2000.

HIGHEST GOALS-PER-GAME AVERAGE, ONE SEASON
(AMONG PLAYERS WITH 20-OR-MORE GOALS):
2.20 — **Joe Malone,** Montreal, 1917-18, with 44G in 20GP.
1.80 — Cy Denneny, Ottawa, 1917-18, with 36G in 20GP.
1.64 — Newsy Lalonde, Montreal, 1917-18, with 23G in 14GP.
1.63 — Joe Malone, Quebec, 1919-20, with 39G in 24GP.
1.61 — Newsy Lalonde, Montreal, 1919-20, with 37G in 23GP.

HIGHEST GOALS-PER-GAME AVERAGE, ONE SEASON
(AMONG PLAYERS WITH 50-OR-MORE GOALS):
1.18 — **Wayne Gretzky,** Edmonton, 1983-84, with 87G in 74GP.
1.15 — Wayne Gretzky, Edmonton, 1981-82, with 92G in 80GP.
— Mario Lemieux, Pittsburgh, 1992-93, with 69G in 60GP.
1.12 — Mario Lemieux, Pittsburgh, 1988-89, with 85G in 76GP.
1.10 — Brett Hull, St. Louis, 1990-91, with 86G in 78GP.
1.02 — Cam Neely, Boston, 1993-94, with 50G in 49GP.
1.00 — Maurice Richard, Montreal, 1944-45, with 50G in 50GP.

HIGHEST ASSISTS-PER-GAME AVERAGE, CAREER
(AMONG PLAYERS WITH 300 OR MORE ASSISTS):
1.320 — **Wayne Gretzky,** Edmonton, Los Angeles, St. Louis, NY Rangers, 1,963A, 1,487GP from 1979-80 – 1998-99.
1.183 — Mario Lemieux, Pittsburgh, 881A, 745GP from 1984-85 – 1996-97.
.982 — Bobby Orr, Boston, Chicago, 645A, 657GP from 1966-67 – 1978-79.
.889 — Peter Forsberg, Quebec, Colorado, 349A, 393GP from 1994-95 – 1999-2000.
.852 — Adam Oates, Detroit, St. Louis, Boston, Washington, 894A, 1049GP from 1985-86 – 1999-2000.
.813 — Paul Coffey, Edmonton, Pittsburgh, Los Angeles, Detroit, Hartford, Philadelphia, Chicago, Carolina, 1131A, 1391GP from 1980-81 – 1999-2000.

HIGHEST ASSISTS-PER-GAME AVERAGE, ONE SEASON
(AMONG PLAYERS WITH 35-OR-MORE ASSISTS):
2.04 — **Wayne Gretzky,** Edmonton, 1985-86, with 163A in 80GP.
1.70 — Wayne Gretzky, Edmonton, 1987-88, with 109A in 64GP.
1.69 — Wayne Gretzky, Edmonton, 1984-85, with 135A in 80GP.
1.59 — Wayne Gretzky, Edmonton, 1983-84, with 118A in 74GP.
1.56 — Wayne Gretzky, Edmonton, 1982-83, with 125A in 80GP.
1.56 — Wayne Gretzky, Los Angeles, 1990-91, with 122A in 78GP.
1.53 — Wayne Gretzky, Edmonton, 1986-87, with 121A in 79GP.
1.52 — Mario Lemieux, Pittsburgh, 1992-93, with 91A in 60GP.
1.50 — Wayne Gretzky, Edmonton, 1981-82, with 120A in 80GP.
1.50 — Mario Lemieux, Pittsburgh, 1988-89, with 114A in 76GP.

HIGHEST POINTS-PER-GAME AVERAGE, CAREER:
(AMONG PLAYERS WITH 500 OR MORE POINTS):
2.005 — **Mario Lemieux,** Pittsburgh, 1,494PTS (613G-881A), 745GP from 1984-85 – 1996-97.
1.921 — Wayne Gretzky, Edmonton, Los Angeles, St. Louis, NY Rangers, 2,857PTS (894G-1,963A), 1,487GP from 1979-80 – 1998-99.
1.497 — Mike Bossy, NY Islanders, 1,126PTS (573G-553A), 752GP from 1977-78 – 1986-87.
1.393 — Bobby Orr, Boston, Chicago, 915PTS (270G-645A), 657GP from 1966-67 – 1978-79.
1.356 — Eric Lindros, Philadelphia, 659PTS (290G-369A), 486GP from 1992-93 – 1999-2000.

HIGHEST POINTS-PER-GAME AVERAGE, ONE SEASON
(AMONG PLAYERS WITH 50-OR-MORE POINTS):
2.77 — **Wayne Gretzky,** Edmonton, 1983-84, with 205PTS in 74GP.
2.69 — Wayne Gretzky, Edmonton, 1985-86, with 215PTS in 80GP.
2.67 — Mario Lemieux, Pittsburgh, 1992-93, with 160PTS in 60GP.
2.65 — Wayne Gretzky, Edmonton, 1981-82, with 212PTS in 80GP.
2.62 — Mario Lemieux, Pittsburgh, 1988-89, with 199PTS in 78GP.
2.60 — Wayne Gretzky, Edmonton, 1984-85, with 208PTS in 80GP.
2.45 — Wayne Gretzky, Edmonton, 1982-83, with 196PTS in 80GP.
2.33 — Wayne Gretzky, Edmonton, 1987-88, with 149PTS in 64GP.
2.32 — Wayne Gretzky, Edmonton, 1986-87, with 183PTS in 79GP.
2.30 — Mario Lemieux, Pittsburgh, 1995-96 with 161PTS in 70GP.
2.18 — Mario Lemieux, Pittsburgh, 1987-88 with 168PTS in 77GP.
2.15 — Wayne Gretzky, Los Angeles, 1988-89, with 168PTS in 78GP.
2.09 — Wayne Gretzky, Los Angeles, 1990-91, with 163 PTS in 78GP.
2.08 — Mario Lemieux, Pittsburgh, 1989-90, with 123 PTS in 59GP.
2.05 — Wayne Gretzky, Edmonton, 1980-81, with 164PTS in 80GP.

SCORING PLATEAUS

MOST 20-OR-MORE GOAL SEASONS:
22 — **Gordie Howe,** Detroit, Hartford, in 26 seasons.
18 — Ron Francis, Hartford, Pittsburgh, Carolina, in 19 seasons.
17 — Marcel Dionne, Detroit, Los Angeles, NY Rangers, in 18 seasons.
— Mike Gartner, Washington, Minnesota, NY Rangers, Toronto, Phoenix, in 19 seasons.
— Wayne Gretzky, Edmonton, Los Angeles, St. Louis, NY Rangers, in 20 seasons.
16 — Phil Esposito, Chicago, Boston, NY Rangers, in 18 seasons.
— Norm Ullman, Detroit, Toronto, in 20 seasons.
— John Bucyk, Detroit, Boston, in 23 seasons.
— Mark Messier, Edmonton, NY Rangers, Vancouver, in 21 seasons.

MOST CONSECUTIVE 20-OR-MORE GOAL SEASONS:
22 — **Gordie Howe,** Detroit, 1949-50 – 1970-71.
17 — Marcel Dionne, Detroit, Los Angeles, NY Rangers, 1971-72 – 1987-88.
16 — Phil Esposito, Chicago, Boston, NY Rangers, 1964-65 – 1979-80.
15 — Mike Gartner, Washington, Minnesota, NY Rangers, Toronto, 1979-80 – 1993-94.
14 — Maurice Richard, Montreal, 1943-44 – 1956-57.
— Stan Mikita, Chicago, 1961-62 – 1974-75.
— Michel Goulet, Quebec, Chicago, 1979-80 – 1992-93.

MOST 30-OR-MORE GOAL SEASONS:
17 — **Mike Gartner,** Washington, Minnesota, NY Rangers, Toronto, Phoenix, in 19 seasons.
14 — Gordie Howe, Detroit, Hartford, in 26 seasons.
— Marcel Dionne, Detroit, Los Angeles, NY Rangers, in 18 seasons.
— Wayne Gretzky, Edmonton, Los Angeles, St. Louis, NY Rangers, in 20 seasons.
13 — Bobby Hull, Chicago, Winnipeg, Hartford, in 16 seasons.
— Phil Esposito, Chicago, Boston, NY Rangers, in 18 seasons.

Mike Bossy was one of the most prolific scorers in NHL history. His goals-per-game average of .762 trails only Mario Lemieux, while his average of 1.497 points per game is topped only by Lemieux and Wayne Gretzky.

MOST CONSECUTIVE 30-OR-MORE GOAL SEASONS:
- 15 — **Mike Gartner,** Washington, Minnesota, NY Rangers, Toronto, 1979-80 – 1993-94.
- 13 — Bobby Hull, Chicago, 1959-60 – 1971-72.
  - — Phil Esposito, Boston, NY Rangers, 1967-68 – 1979-80.
  - — Wayne Gretzky, Edmonton, Los Angeles, 1979-80 – 1991-92.
- 12 — Marcel Dionne, Detroit, Los Angeles,1974-75 – 1985-86.
- 10 — Darryl Sittler, Toronto, Philadelphia, 1973-74 – 1982-83.
  - — Mike Bossy, NY Islanders, 1977-78 – 1986-87.
  - — Jari Kurri, Edmonton, 1980-81 – 1989-90.

MOST 40-OR-MORE GOAL SEASONS:
- 12 — **Wayne Gretzky,** Edmonton, Los Angeles, St. Louis, NY Rangers, in 20 seasons.
- 10 — Marcel Dionne, Detroit, Los Angeles, NY Rangers, in 18 seasons.
  - — Mario Lemieux, Pittsburgh, in 12 seasons.
- 9 — Mike Bossy, NY Islanders, in 10 seasons.
  - — Mike Gartner, Washington, Minnesota, NY Rangers, Toronto, Phoenix, in 19 seasons.

MOST CONSECUTIVE 40-OR-MORE GOAL SEASONS:
- 12 — **Wayne Gretzky,** Edmonton, Los Angeles, 1979-80 – 1990-91.
- 9 — Mike Bossy, NY Islanders, 1977-78 – 1985-86.
- 8 — Luc Robitaille, Los Angeles, 1986-87 – 1993-94.
- 7 — Phil Esposito, Boston, 1968-69 – 1974-75.
  - — Michel Goulet, Quebec, 1981-82 – 1987-88.
  - — Jari Kurri, Edmonton, 1982-83 – 1988-89.

MOST 50-OR-MORE GOAL SEASONS:
- 9 — **Mike Bossy,** NY Islanders, in 10 seasons.
  - — **Wayne Gretzky,** Edmonton, Los Angeles, St. Louis, NY Rangers, in 20 seasons.
- 6 — Guy Lafleur, Montreal, NY Rangers, Quebec, in 17 seasons.
  - — Marcel Dionne, Detroit, Los Angeles, NY Rangers, in 18 seasons.
  - — Mario Lemieux, Pittsburgh, in 12 seasons.
- 5 — Bobby Hull, Chicago, Winnipeg, Hartford, in 16 seasons.
  - — Phil Esposito, Chicago, Boston, NY Rangers, in 18 seasons.
  - — Brett Hull, Calgary, St. Louis, Dallas, in 13 seasons.
  - — Steve Yzerman, Detroit, in 16 seasons.

MOST CONSECUTIVE 50-OR-MORE GOAL SEASONS:
- 9 — **Mike Bossy,** NY Islanders, 1977-78 – 1985-86.
- 8 — Wayne Gretzky, Edmonton, 1979-80 – 1986-87.
- 6 — Guy Lafleur, Montreal, 1974-75 – 1979-80.
- 5 — Phil Esposito, Boston, 1970-71 – 1974-75.
  - — Marcel Dionne, Los Angeles, 1978-79 – 1982-83.
  - — Brett Hull, St. Louis, 1989-90 – 1993-94.

MOST 60-OR-MORE GOAL SEASONS:
- 5 — **Mike Bossy,** NY Islanders, in 10 seasons.
  - — **Wayne Gretzky,** Edmonton, Los Angeles, St. Louis, NY Rangers, in 20 seasons.
- 4 — Phil Esposito, Chicago, Boston, NY Rangers, in 18 seasons.
  - — Mario Lemieux, Pittsburgh, in 12 seasons.

MOST CONSECUTIVE 60-OR-MORE GOAL SEASONS:
- 4 — **Wayne Gretzky,** Edmonton, 1981-82 – 1984-85.
- 3 — Mike Bossy, NY Islanders, 1980-81 – 1982-83.
  - — Brett Hull, St. Louis, 1989-90 – 1991-92.
- 2 — Phil Esposito, Boston, 1970-71 – 1971-72, 1973-74 – 1974-75.
  - — Jari Kurri, Edmonton, 1984-85 – 1985-86.
  - — Mario Lemieux, Pittsburgh, 1987-88 – 1988-89.
  - — Steve Yzerman, Detroit, 1988-89 – 1989-90.
  - — Pavel Bure, Vancouver, 1992-93 – 1993-94.

MOST 100-OR-MORE POINT SEASONS:
- 15 — **Wayne Gretzky,** Edmonton, Los Angeles, St. Louis, NY Rangers, in 20 seasons.
- 10 — Mario Lemieux, Pittsburgh, in 12 seasons.
- 8 — Marcel Dionne, Detroit, Los Angeles, NY Rangers, in 18 seasons.
- 7 — Mike Bossy, NY Islanders, in 10 seasons.
  - — Peter Stastny, Quebec, New Jersey, St. Louis, in 15 seasons.

MOST CONSECUTIVE 100-OR-MORE POINT SEASONS:
- 13 — **Wayne Gretzky,** Edmonton, Los Angeles, 1979-80 – 1991-92.
- 6 — Bobby Orr, Boston, 1969-70 – 1974-75.
  - — Guy Lafleur, Montreal, 1974-75 – 1979-80.
  - — Mike Bossy, NY Islanders, 1980-81 – 1985-86.
  - — Peter Stastny, Quebec, 1980-81 – 1985-86.
  - — Mario Lemieux, Pittsburgh, 1984-85 – 1989-90.
  - — Steve Yzerman, Detroit, 1987-88 – 1992-93.

THREE-OR-MORE-GOAL GAMES

MOST THREE-OR-MORE GOAL GAMES, CAREER:
- 50 — **Wayne Gretzky,** Edmonton, Los Angeles, St. Louis, NY Rangers, in 20 seasons, 37 three-goal games, 9 four-goal games, 4 five-goal games.
- 39 — Mike Bossy, NY Islanders, in 10 seasons, 30 three-goal games, 9 four-goal games.
  - — Mario Lemieux, Pittsburgh, in 12 seasons, 26 three-goal games, 10 four-goal games and 3 five-goal games.
- 32 — Phil Esposito, Chicago, Boston, NY Rangers, in 18 seasons, 27 three-goal games, 5 four-goal games.
- 28 — Bobby Hull, Chicago, Winnipeg, Hartford, in 16 seasons, 24 three-goal games, 4 four-goal games.
  - — Marcel Dionne, Detroit, Los Angeles, NY Rangers, in 18 seasons, 25 three-goal games, 3 four-goal games.
  - — Brett Hull, Calgary, St. Louis, Dallas, in 13 seasons, 26 three-goal games, 2 four-goal games.
- 26 — Cy Denneny, Ottawa in 12 seasons. 20 three-goal games, 5 four-goal games, 1 six-goal game.
  - — Maurice Richard, Montreal, in 18 seasons, 23 three-goal games, 2 four-goal games, 1 five-goal game.

MOST THREE-OR-MORE GOAL GAMES, ONE SEASON:
- 10 — **Wayne Gretzky,** Edmonton, 1981-82. 6 three-goal games, 3 four-goal games, 1 five-goal game.
  - — **Wayne Gretzky,** Edmonton, 1983-84. 6 three-goal games, 4 four-goal games.
- 9 — Mike Bossy, NY Islanders, 1980-81. 6 three-goal games, 3 four-goal games.
  - — Mario Lemieux, Pittsburgh, 1988-89. 7 three-goal games, 1 four-goal game, 1 five-goal game.
- 8 — Brett Hull, St. Louis, 1991-92. 8 three-goal games.
- 7 — Joe Malone, Montreal, 1917-18. 2 three-goal games, 2 four-goal games, 3 five-goal games.
  - — Phil Esposito, Boston, 1970-71. 7 three-goal games.
  - — Rick Martin, Buffalo, 1975-76. 6 three-goal games, 1 four-goal game.
  - — Alexander Mogilny, Buffalo, 1992-93. 5 three-goal games, 2 four-goal games.

Mats Sundin collected at least one point in 30 straight games for the Quebec Nordiques in 1992-93. It's the longest scoring steak in NHL history for anyone not named Gretzky or Lemieux. Sundin had a career-high 114 points that season.

SCORING STREAKS

LONGEST CONSECUTIVE GOAL-SCORING STREAK:
16 Games — Harry Broadbent, Ottawa, 1921-22. 27 goals during streak.
14 Games — Joe Malone, Montreal, 1917-18. 35 goals during streak.
13 Games — Newsy Lalonde, Montreal, 1920-21. 24 goals during streak.
— Charlie Simmer, Los Angeles, 1979-80. 17 goals during streak.
12 Games — Cy Denneny, Ottawa, 1917-18. 23 goals during streak.
— Dave Lumley, Edmonton, 1981-82. 15 goals during streak.
— Mario Lemieux, Pittsburgh, 1992-93. 18 goals during streak.

LONGEST CONSECUTIVE ASSIST-SCORING STREAK:
23 Games — Wayne Gretzky, Los Angeles, 1990-91. 48A during streak.
18 Games — Adam Oates, Boston, 1992-93. 28A during streak.
17 Games — Wayne Gretzky, Edmonton, 1983-84. 38A during streak.
— Paul Coffey, Edmonton, 1985-86. 27A during streak.
— Wayne Gretzky, Los Angeles, 1989-90. 35A during streak.
15 Games — Jari Kurri, Edmonton, 1983-84. 21A during streak.
— Brian Leetch, NY Rangers, 1991-92. 23A during streak.

LONGEST CONSECUTIVE POINT SCORING STREAK:
51 Games — Wayne Gretzky, Edmonton, 1983-84. 61G-92A-153PTS during streak.
46 Games — Mario Lemieux, Pittsburgh, 1989-90. 39G-64A-103PTS during streak.
39 Games — Wayne Gretzky, Edmonton, 1985-86. 33G-75A-108PTS during streak.
30 Games — Wayne Gretzky, Edmonton, 1982-83. 24G-52A-76PTS during streak.
— Mats Sundin, Quebec, 1992-93. 21G-25A-46PTS during streak.
28 Games — Guy Lafleur, Montreal, 1976-77. 19G-42A-61PTS during streak.
— Wayne Gretzky, Edmonton, 1984-85. 20G-43A-63PTS during streak.
— Mario Lemieux, Pittsburgh, 1985-86. 21G-38A-59PTS during streak.
— Paul Coffey, Edmonton, 1985-86. 16G-39A-55PTS during streak.
— Steve Yzerman, Detroit, 1988-89. 29G-36A-65PTS during streak.

LONGEST CONSECUTIVE POINT-SCORING STREAK FROM START OF SEASON:
51 Games — Wayne Gretzky, Edmonton, 1983-84. 61G-92A-153PTS during streak which was stopped by goaltender Markus Mattsson and Los Angeles on Jan. 28, 1984.

LONGEST CONSECUTIVE POINT-SCORING STREAK BY A DEFENSEMAN:
28 Games — Paul Coffey, Edmonton, 1985-86. 16G-39A-55PTS during streak.
19 Games — Ray Bourque, Boston, 1987-88. 6G-21A-27PTS during streak.
17 Games — Ray Bourque, Boston, 1984-85. 4G-24A-28PTS during streak.
— Brian Leetch, NY Rangers, 1991-92. 5G-24A-29PTS during streak.
16 Games — Gary Suter, Calgary, 1987-88. 8G-17A-25PTS during streak.
15 Games — Bobby Orr, Boston, 1970-71. 10G-23A-33PTS during streak.
— Bobby Orr, Boston, 1973-74. 8G-15A-23PTS during streak.
— Steve Duchesne, Quebec, 1992-93. 4G-17A-21PTS during streak.
— Chris Chelios, Chicago, 1995-96. 4G-16A-20PTS during streak.

FASTEST GOALS AND ASSISTS

FASTEST GOAL FROM START OF A GAME:
5 Seconds — Doug Smail, Winnipeg, Dec. 20, 1981, at Winnipeg. Winnipeg 5, St. Louis 4.
— **Bryan Trottier,** NY Islanders, Mar. 22, 1984, at Boston. NY Islanders 3, Boston 3.
— **Alexander Mogilny,** Buffalo, Dec. 21, 1991, at Toronto. Buffalo 4, Toronto 1.
6 Seconds — Henry Boucha, Detroit, Jan. 28, 1973, at Montreal. Detroit 4, Montreal 2.
— Jean Pronovost, Pittsburgh, Mar. 25, 1976, at St. Louis. St. Louis 5, Pittsburgh 2.
7 Seconds — Charlie Conacher, Toronto, Feb. 6, 1932, at Toronto. Toronto 6, Boston 0.
— Danny Gare, Buffalo, Dec. 17, 1978, at Buffalo. Buffalo 6, Vancouver 3.
— Dave Williams, Los Angeles, Feb. 14, 1987 at Los Angeles. Los Angeles 5, Harford 2.
8 Seconds — Ron Martin, NY Americans, Dec. 4, 1932, at New York. NY Americans 4, Montreal 2.
— Chuck Arnason, Col. Rockies, Jan. 28, 1977, at Atlanta. Col. Rockies 3, Atlanta 3.
— Wayne Gretzky, Edmonton, Dec. 14, 1983, at New York. Edmonton 9, NY Rangers 4.
— Gaetan Duchesne, Washington, Mar. 14, 1987, at St. Louis. Washington 3, St. Louis 3.
— Tim Kerr, Philadelphia, Mar. 7, 1989, at Philadelphia. Philadelphia 4, Edmonton 3.
— Grant Ledyard, Buffalo, Dec. 4, 1991, at Winnipeg. Buffalo 4, Winnipeg 4.
— Brent Sutter, Chicago, Feb. 5, 1995, at Vancouver. Chicago 9, Vancouver 4.
— Paul Kariya, Anaheim, Mar. 9, 1997, at Colorado. Anaheim 2, Colorado 3.
— Tony Hrkac, Dallas, Nov. 7, 1998, at Los Angeles. Dallas 4, Los Angeles 3.
— Sergei Fedorov, Detroit, Nov. 21, 1998, at Vancouver. Detroit 4, Vancouver 2.

FASTEST GOAL FROM START OF A PERIOD:
4 Seconds — Claude Provost, Montreal, Nov. 9, 1957, at Montreal, second period. Montreal 4, Boston 2.
— **Denis Savard,** Chicago, Jan. 12, 1986, at Chicago, third period. Chicago 4, Hartford 2.

FASTEST GOAL BY A PLAYER IN HIS FIRST NHL GAME:
15 Seconds — Gus Bodnar, Toronto, Oct. 30, 1943. Toronto 5, NY Rangers 2.
18 Seconds — Danny Gare, Buffalo, Oct. 10, 1974. Buffalo 9, Boston 5.
20 Seconds — Alexander Mogilny, Buffalo, Oct. 5, 1989. Buffalo 4, Quebec 3.

FASTEST TWO GOALS:
4 Seconds — Nels Stewart, Mtl. Maroons, Jan. 3, 1931, at Montreal at 8:24 and 8:28, third period. Mtl. Maroons 5, Boston 3.
— **Deron Quint,** Winnipeg, Dec. 15, 1995, at Winnipeg at 7:51 and 7:55, second period. Winnipeg 9, Edmonton 4.
5 Seconds — Pete Mahovlich, Montreal, Feb. 20, 1971, at Montreal at 12:16 and 12:21, third period. Montreal 7, Chicago 1.
6 Seconds — Jim Pappin, Chicago, Feb. 16, 1972, at Chicago at 2:57 and 3:03, third period. Chicago 3, Philadelphia 3.
— Ralph Backstrom, Los Angeles, Nov. 2, 1972, at Los Angeles at 8:30 and 8:36, third period. Los Angeles 5, Boston 2.
— Lanny McDonald, Calgary, Mar. 22, 1984, at Calgary at 16:23 and 16:29, first period. Detroit 6, Calgary 4.
— Sylvain Turgeon, Hartford, Mar. 28, 1987, at Hartford at 13:59 and 14:05, second period. Hartford 5, Pittsburgh 4.

FASTEST THREE GOALS:
21 Seconds — Bill Mosienko, Chicago, Mar. 23, 1952, at New York, against goaltender Lorne Anderson. Mosienko scored at 6:09, 6:20 and 6:30 of third period, all with both teams at full strength. Chicago 7, NY Rangers 6.
44 Seconds — Jean Béliveau, Montreal, Nov. 5, 1955, at Montreal, against goaltender Terry Sawchuk. Béliveau scored at :42, 1:08 and 1:26 of second period, all with Montreal holding a 6-4 man advantage. Montreal 4, Boston 2.

FASTEST THREE ASSISTS:
21 Seconds — Gus Bodnar, Chicago, Mar. 23, 1952, at New York, Bodnar assisted on Bill Mosienko's three goals at 6:09, 6:20 and 6:30 of third period. Chicago 7, NY Rangers 6.
44 Seconds — Bert Olmstead, Montreal, Nov. 5, 1955, at Montreal, Olmstead assisted on Jean Béliveau's three goals at :42, 1:08 and 1:26 of second period. Montreal 4, Boston 2.

SHOTS ON GOAL

MOST SHOTS ON GOAL, ONE SEASON:
550 — Phil Esposito, Boston, 1970-71. 78 game schedule.
429 — Paul Kariya, Anaheim, 1998-99. 82 game schedule.
426 — Phil Esposito, Boston, 1971-72. 78 game schedule.
414 — Bobby Hull, Chicago, 1968-69. 76 game schedule.

PENALTIES

MOST PENALTY MINUTES, CAREER:
3,966 — Dave Williams, Toronto, Vancouver, Detroit, Los Angeles, Hartford, in 14 seasons, 962GP.
3,565 — Dale Hunter, Quebec, Washington, Colorado, in 19 seasons, 1,407GP.
3,381 — Marty McSorley, Pittsburgh, Edmonton, Los Angeles, NY Rangers, San Jose, Boston, in 17 seasons, 961GP.
3,146 — Tim Hunter, Calgary, Quebec, Vancouver, San Jose, in 16 seasons, 815GP.
3,043 — Chris Nilan, Montreal, NY Rangers, Boston, in 13 seasons, 688GP.

MOST PENALTY MINUTES, CAREER, INCLUDING PLAYOFFS:
4,421 — Dave Williams, Toronto, Vancouver, Detroit, Los Angeles, Hartford, 3,966 in regular-season; 455 in playoffs.
4,294 — Dale Hunter, Quebec, Washington, Colorado, 3,565 in regular-season; 729 in playoffs.
3,755 — Marty McSorley, Pittsburgh, Edmonton, Los Angeles, NY Rangers, San Jose, Boston, 3,381 in regular-season; 374 in playoffs.
3,584 — Chris Nilan, Montreal, NY Rangers, Boston, 3,043 in regular-season; 541 in playoffs.
3,572 — Tim Hunter, Calgary, Quebec, Vancouver, San Jose, 3,146 in regular-season; 426 in playoffs.

MOST PENALTY MINUTES, ONE SEASON:
472 — Dave Schultz, Philadelphia, 1974-75.
409 — Paul Baxter, Pittsburgh, 1981-82.
408 — Mike Peluso, Chicago, 1991-92.
405 — Dave Schultz, Los Angeles, Pittsburgh, 1977-78.

MOST PENALTIES, ONE GAME:
  10 — Chris Nilan, Boston, Mar. 31, 1991, at Boston against Hartford.
       6 minors, 2 majors, 1 10-minute misconduct, 1 game misconduct.
   9 — Jim Dorey, Toronto, Oct. 16, 1968, at Toronto against Pittsburgh. 4 minors,
       2 majors, 2 10-minute misconducts, 1 game misconduct.
     — Dave Schultz, Pittsburgh, Apr. 6, 1978, at Detroit. 5 minors,
       2 majors, 2 10-minute misconducts.
     — Randy Holt, Los Angeles, Mar. 11, 1979, at Philadelphia. 1 minor,
       3 majors, 2 10-minute misconducts, 3 game misconducts.
     — Russ Anderson, Pittsburgh, Jan. 19, 1980, at Pittsburgh.
       3 minors, 3 majors, 3 game misconducts.
     — Kim Clackson, Quebec, Mar. 8, 1981, at Quebec. 4 minors, 3 majors,
       2 game misconducts.
     — Terry O'Reilly, Boston, Dec. 19, 1984 at Hartford. 5 minors,
       3 majors, 1 game misconduct.
     — Larry Playfair, Los Angeles, Dec. 9, 1986, at NY Islanders. 6 minors,
       2 majors, 1 10-minute misconduct.
     — Marty McSorley, Los Angeles, Apr. 14, 1992, at Vancouver. 5 minors,
       2 majors, 1 10-minute misconduct, 1 game misconduct.

MOST PENALTY MINUTES, ONE GAME:
  67 — Randy Holt, Los Angeles, Mar. 11, 1979, at Philadelphia. 1 minor,
       3 majors, 2 10-minute misconducts, 3 game misconducts.
   55 — Frank Bathe, Philadelphia, Mar. 11, 1979, at Philadelphia.
       3 majors, 2 10-minute misconducts, 2 game misconducts.
   51 — Russ Anderson, Pittsburgh, Jan. 19, 1980, at Pittsburgh.
       3 minors, 3 majors, 3 game misconducts.

MOST PENALTIES, ONE PERIOD:
   9 — Randy Holt, Los Angeles, Mar. 11, 1979, at Philadelphia, first period.
       1 minor, 3 majors, 2 10-minute misconducts, 3 game misconducts.

MOST PENALTY MINUTES, ONE PERIOD:
  67 — Randy Holt, Los Angeles, Mar. 11, 1979, at Philadelphia, first period.
       1 minor, 3 majors, 2 10-minute misconducts, 3 game misconducts.

GOALTENDING

MOST GAMES APPEARED IN BY A GOALTENDER, CAREER:
  971 — Terry Sawchuk, Detroit, Boston, Toronto, Los Angeles, NY Rangers
       from 1949-50 – 1969-70.
   906 — Glenn Hall, Detroit, Chicago, St. Louis from 1952-53 – 1970-71.
   886 — Tony Esposito, Montreal, Chicago from 1968-69 – 1983-84.
   868 — Grant Fuhr, Edmonton, Toronto, Buffalo, Los Angeles, St. Louis, Calgary
       from 1981-82 – 1999-2000.

MOST CONSECUTIVE COMPLETE GAMES BY A GOALTENDER:
  502 — Glenn Hall, Detroit, Chicago. Played 502 games from beginning of
       1955-56 season - first 12 games of 1962-63. In his 503rd straight game,
       Nov. 7, 1962, at Chicago, Hall was removed from the game against Boston
       with a back injury in the first period.

MOST GAMES APPEARED IN BY A GOALTENDER, ONE SEASON:
  79 — Grant Fuhr, St. Louis, 1995-96.
   77 — Martin Brodeur, New Jersey, 1995-96.
   75 — Grant Fuhr, Edmonton, 1987-88.
     — Arturs Irbe, Carolina, 1999-2000.
   74 — Ed Belfour, Chicago, 1990-91.
     — Arturs Irbe, San Jose, 1993-94.
     — Felix Potvin, Toronto, 1996-97.

MOST MINUTES PLAYED BY A GOALTENDER, CAREER:
  57,194 — Terry Sawchuk, Detroit, Boston, Toronto, Los Angeles, NY Rangers, from
       1949-50 – 1969-70.

MOST MINUTES PLAYED BY A GOALTENDER, ONE SEASON:
  4,433 — Martin Brodeur, New Jersey, 1995-96.

MOST SHUTOUTS, CAREER:
  103 — Terry Sawchuk, Detroit, Boston, Toronto, Los Angeles, NY Rangers
       in 21 seasons.
   94 — George Hainsworth, Montreal, Toronto in 10 seasons.
   84 — Glenn Hall, Detroit, Chicago, St. Louis in 16 seasons.

MOST SHUTOUTS, ONE SEASON:
  22 — George Hainsworth, Montreal, 1928-29. 44GP
   15 — Alex Connell, Ottawa, 1925-26. 36GP
     — Alex Connell, Ottawa, 1927-28. 44GP
     — Hal Winkler, Boston, 1927-28. 44GP
     — Tony Esposito, Chicago, 1969-70. 63GP
   14 — George Hainsworth, Montreal, 1926-27. 44GP

LONGEST SHUTOUT SEQUENCE BY A GOALTENDER:
  461 Minutes, 29 Seconds — Alex Connell, Ottawa, 1927-28, six consecutive
       shutouts. (Forward passing not permitted in attacking zones in 1927-1928.)
   343 Minutes, 5 Seconds — George Hainsworth, Montreal, 1928-29, four consecutive
       shutouts.
   324 Minutes, 40 Seconds — Roy Worters, NY Americans, 1930-31, four consecutive
       shutouts.
   309 Minutes, 21 Seconds — Bill Durnan, Montreal, 1948-49, four consecutive
       shutouts.

MOST WINS BY A GOALTENDER, CAREER:
  447 — Terry Sawchuk, Detroit, Boston, Toronto, Los Angeles, NY Rangers,
       in 21 seasons. 972GP
   444 — Patrick Roy, Montreal, Colorado, in 16 seasons. 841GP
   435 — Jacques Plante, Montreal, NY Rangers, St. Louis, Toronto, Boston,
       in 18 seasons. 837GP
   423 — Tony Esposito, Montreal, Chicago, in 16 seasons. 886GP

MOST WINS BY A GOALTENDER, ONE SEASON:
  47 — Bernie Parent, Philadelphia, 1973-74. 73GP
   44 — Bernie Parent, Philadelphia, 1974-75. 68GP
     — Terry Sawchuk, Detroit, 1950-51. 70GP
     — Terry Sawchuk, Detroit, 1951-52. 70GP

LONGEST WINNING STREAK BY A GOALTENDER, ONE SEASON:
  17 — Gilles Gilbert, Boston, 1975-76.
   14 — Tiny Thompson, Boston, 1929-30.
     — Ross Brooks, Boston, 1973-74.
     — Don Beaupre, Minnesota, 1985-86.
     — Tom Barrasso, Pittsburgh, 1992-93.

LONGEST UNDEFEATED STREAK BY A GOALTENDER, ONE SEASON:
  32 Games — Gerry Cheevers, Boston, 1971-72. 24w-8T
   31 Games — Pete Peeters, Boston, 1982-83. 26w-5T
   27 Games — Pete Peeters, Philadelphia, 1979-80. 22w-5T
   23 Games — Frank Brimsek, Boston, 1940-41. 15w-8T
     — Glenn Resch, NY Islanders, 1978-79. 15w-8T
     — Grant Fuhr, Edmonton, 1981-82. 15w-8T

LONGEST UNDEFEATED STREAK BY A GOALTENDER IN HIS FIRST NHL SEASON:
  23 Games — Grant Fuhr, 1981-82. 15w-8T.

LONGEST UNDEFEATED STREAK BY A GOALTENDER FROM START OF CAREER:
  16 Games — Patrick Lalime, Pittsburgh, 1996-97. 14w-2T.

MOST 40-OR-MORE WIN SEASONS BY A GOALTENDER:
   3 — Terry Sawchuk, Detroit, Boston, Toronto, Los Angeles, NY Rangers,
       in 21 seasons.
     — Jacques Plante, Montreal, NY Rangers, St. Louis, Toronto, Boston,
       in 18 seasons.
   2 — Bernie Parent, Boston, Philadelphia, Toronto, in 13 seasons.
     — Ken Dryden, Montreal, in 8 seasons.
     — Ed Belfour, Chicago, San Jose, Dallas, in 12 seasons.
     — Martin Brodeur, New Jersey, in 8 seasons.

MOST CONSECUTIVE 40-OR-MORE WIN SEASONS BY A GOALTENDER:
   2 — Terry Sawchuk, Detroit, 1950-51 – 1951-52.
     — Bernie Parent, Philadelphia, 1973-74 – 1974-75.
     — Ken Dryden, Montreal, 1975-76 – 1976-77.

MOST 30-OR-MORE WIN SEASONS BY A GOALTENDER:
  10 — Patrick Roy, Montreal, Colorado in 16 seasons.
   8 — Tony Esposito, Montreal, Chicago in 16 seasons.
   7 — Jacques Plante, Montreal, NY Rangers, St. Louis, Toronto, Boston
       in 18 seasons.
     — Ken Dryden, Montreal, in 8 seasons.
   6 — Glenn Hall, Detroit, Chicago, St. Louis in 18 seasons.
     — Ed Belfour, Chicago, San Jose, Dallas, in 12 seasons.

MOST CONSECUTIVE 30-OR-MORE WIN SEASONS BY A GOALTENDER:
   7 — Tony Esposito, Chicago, 1969-70 – 1975-76.
   6 — Jacques Plante, Montreal, 1954-55 – 1959-60.
   5 — Terry Sawchuk, Detroit, 1950-51 – 1954-55.
     — Ken Dryden, Montreal, 1974-75 – 1978-79.
     — Patrick Roy, Montreal, Colorado, 1995-96 – 1999-2000.
     — Martin Brodeur, New Jersey, 1995-96 – 1999-2000.

MOST LOSSES BY A GOALTENDER, CAREER:
  352 — Gump Worsley, NY Rangers, Montreal, Minnesota, in 21 seasons. 861GP
   351 — Gilles Meloche, Chicago, California, Cleveland, Minnesota, Pittsburgh,
       in 18 seasons. 788GP
   332 — Terry Sawchuk, Detroit, Boston, Toronto, Los Angeles, NY Rangers,
       in 21 seasons. 972GP

MOST LOSSES BY A GOALTENDER, ONE SEASON:
  48 — Gary Smith, California, 1970-71.
   47 — Al Rollins, Chicago, 1953-54.

*Patrick Roy first topped 30 wins with the Montreal Canadiens
in 1988-89 and extended his own record when he reached that mark
for the tenth time in 1999-2000.*

Active NHL Players' Three-or-More-Goal Games

Regular Season

Teams named are the ones the players were with at the time of their multiple-scoring games. Players listed alphabetically.

With a pair of hat tricks in 1999-2000, Jaromir Jagr upped his career total to six three-goal games. Jagr scored a hat trick of a different sort last season when he won the Art Ross Trophy for the third year in a row.

Player	Team	3-Goals	4-Goals	5-Goals
Adams, Greg	Vancouver	1	1	—
Alfredsson, Daniel	Ottawa	1	—	—
Allison, Jason	Boston	3	—	—
Amonte, Tony	NYR, Chi	7	—	—
Andersson, Mikael	Tampa Bay	1	—	—
Andersson, Niklas	NY Islanders	1	—	—
Andreychuk, Dave	Buf., Tor., Bos.	7	3	1
Antropov, Nik	Toronto	2	—	—
Arnott, Jason	Edmonton	2	—	—
Arvedson, Magnus	Ottawa	1	—	—
Audette, Donald	Buffalo	2	—	—
Barnes, Stu	Wpg., Pit.	3	—	—
Battaglia, Bates	Carolina	1	—	—
Beranek, Josef	Philadelphia	1	—	—
Berezin, Sergei	Toronto	2	—	—
Bondra, Peter	Washington	9	4	1
Bourque, Ray	Boston	1	—	—
Brind'Amour, Rod	Philadelphia	1	—	—
Brown, Doug	Detroit	1	—	—
Brown, Rob	Pittsburgh	7	—	—
Buchberger, Kelly	Edmonton	1	—	—
Bure, Pavel	Van., Fla.	13	2	—
Bure, Valeri	Calgary	1	—	—
Butsayev, Viacheslav	Philadelphia	1	—	—
Carter, Anson	Boston	1	—	—
Coffey, Paul	Edmonton	4	1	—
Conroy, Craig	St. Louis	1	—	—
Corson, Shayne	Mtl., Edm.	3	—	—
Craven, Murray	Philadelphia	3	—	—
Cunneyworth, Randy	Pittsburgh	1	1	—
Czerkawski, Mariusz	Edm., NYI	3	—	—
Dahlen, Ulf	NYR, Min., S.J.	4	—	—
Daigle, Alexandre	Ott., Phi.	2	—	—
Damphousse, Vincent	Tor., Edm., Mtl., S.J.	11	1	—
Dawe, Jason	Buffalo	2	—	—
Daze, Eric	Chicago	1	1	—
Deadmarsh, Adam	Colorado	1	—	—
Demitra, Pavol	St. Louis	1	—	—
Devereaux, Boyd	Edmonton	1	—	—
Dineen, Kevin	Hfd., Phi.	9	1	—
Dionne, Gilbert	Montreal	1	—	—
Duchesne, Steve	L.A., Phi., St.L.	3	—	—
Dumont, Jean-Pierre	Chicago	1	—	—
Dvorak, Radek	NY Rangers	1	—	—
Eastwood, Mike	St. Louis	1	—	—
Emerson, Nelson	Winnipeg	1	—	—
Fedorov, Sergei	Detroit	1	1	1
Ferraro, Ray	Hfd., NYI, NYR	7	1	—
Fleury, Theoren	Cgy., Col.	14	—	—
Forsberg, Peter	Colorado	4	—	—
Francis, Ron	Hfd., Pit.	10	1	—
Friesen, Jeff	San Jose	2	—	—
Garpenlov, Johan	Det., S.J., Fla.	2	1	—
Gelinas, Martin	Edm., Van.	2	1	—
Gilchrist, Brent	Montreal	1	—	—
Gilmour, Doug	St.L., Tor.	3	—	—
Gomez, Scott	New Jersey	1	—	—
Gonchar, Sergei	Washington	1	—	—
Granato, Tony	NYR, L.A., S.J.	6	1	—
Gratton, Chris	Tampa Bay	1	—	—
Graves, Adam	Edm., NYR	6	—	—
Green, Travis	NY Islanders	1	—	—
Grier, Mike	Edmonton	1	—	—
Grosek, Michal	Buffalo	1	—	—
Guerin, Bill	New Jersey	1	—	—
Harvey, Todd	Dallas	1	—	—
Hatcher, Kevin	Wsh., Dal.	2	—	—
Heinze, Steve	Boston	4	—	—
Hlavac, Jan	NY Rangers	1	—	—
Hogue, Benoit	NY Islanders	1	—	—
Holik, Bobby	New Jersey	3	—	—
Housley, Phil	Buffalo	2	—	—
Hull, Brett	Cgy., St.L.	26	2	—
Hull, Jody	Hartford	1	—	—
Jagr, Jaromir	Pittsburgh	6	—	—
Juneau, Joe	Bos., Wsh.	2	—	—
Kamensky, Valeri	Colorado	5	—	—
Kapanen, Sami	Carolina	2	—	—
Kariya, Paul	Anaheim	3	—	—
Khristich, Dimitri	Was., Bos.	3	—	—
King, Derek	NYI, Tor.	6	1	—
Klatt, Trent	Philadelphia	1	—	—
Konowalchuk, Steve	Washington	2	—	—
Korolev, Igor	Winnipeg	1	—	—
Kovalenko, Andrei	Quebec	1	—	—
Kovalev, Alexei	NY Rangers	2	—	—
Kozlov, Viktor	Florida	1	—	—
Kozlov, Vyacheslav	Detroit	2	1	—
Krupp, Uwe	Quebec	1	—	—
Krygier, Todd	Washington	1	—	—
Lacroix, Eric	Colorado	1	—	—
Lapointe, Martin	Detroit	1	—	—
Laraque, Georges	Edmonton	1	—	—
Larionov, Igor	Van., S.J.	4	—	—
Larouche, Steve	Ottawa	1	—	—
LeClair, John	Philadelphia	7	2	—
Lemieux, Claude	Mtl., N.J., Col.	7	—	—
Linden, Trevor	Van., Mtl.	5	—	—
Lindros, Eric	Philadelphia	10	1	—
MacInnis, Al	Cgy., St.L.	3	—	—
MacLean, John	New Jersey	6	—	—
Malakhov, Vladimir	Montreal	1	—	—
Maltby, Kirk	Detroit	1	—	—
Manderville, Kent	Hartford	1	—	—
McEachern, Shawn	Ottawa	1	—	—
McInnis, Marty	Calgary	1	—	—
McKay, Randy	New Jersey	1	—	—
McKenzie, Jim	Phoenix	1	—	—
Messier, Mark	Edm., NYR	15	4	—
Miller, Kevin	Det., St.L., S.J.	4	—	—
Modano, Mike	Min., Dal.	6	1	—
Mogilny, Alexander	Buf., Van.	12	2	—
Morozov, Alexei	Pittsburgh	1	—	—
Muller, Kirk	N.J., Mtl., Tor.	7	—	—
Murray, Glen	Los Angeles	2	—	—
Murray, Rem	Edmonton	1	—	—
Naslund, Markus	Pit., Van.	3	—	—
Nedved, Petr	Pit., NYR	4	1	—
Nemchinov, Sergei	NY Rangers	1	—	—
Nieuwendyk, Joe	Cgy., Dal.	8	3	1
Nolan, Owen	Que., S.J.	9	1	—
Noonan, Brian	Chi., NYR	3	1	—
Nylander, Michael	Hfd., Chi.	1	1	—
Oates, Adam	Bos., Wsh.	6	1	—
Odelein, Lyle	Montreal	1	—	—
Olczyk, Ed	Tor., NYR, Wpg., L.A.	5	—	—
Oliver, David	Edmonton	1	—	—
O'Neill, Jeff	Hartford	1	—	—
Ozolinsh, Sandis	Colorado	1	—	—
Palffy, Zigmund	NY Islanders	6	—	—
Parrish, Mark	Florida	—	1	—
Peca, Michael	Buffalo	1	—	—
Perreault, Yanic	L.A., Tor.	2	1	—
Pivonka, Michal	Washington	1	—	—
Plante, Derek	Buffalo	1	—	—
Podein, Shjon	Colorado	1	—	—
Probert, Bob	Detroit	1	—	—
Ranheim, Paul	Calgary	1	—	—
Recchi, Mark	Pit., Mtl.	3	—	—
Reichel, Robert	Cgy., NYI	5	—	—
Reid, Dave	Bos., Dal.	2	—	—
Renberg, Mikael	Phi., T.B.	2	—	—
Ricci, Mike	Quebec	—	—	1
Rice, Steven	Hartford	1	—	—
Richer, Stephane	Mtl., N.J., St.L.	9	1	—
Roberts, Gary	Cgy., Car.	10	1	—
Robitaille, Luc	L.A., Pit.	11	3	—
Roenick, Jeremy	Chi., Phx.	6	2	—
Rolston, Brian	New Jersey	1	—	—
Ronning, Cliff	St.L., Van.	3	—	—
Rucinsky, Martin	Montreal	2	—	—
Sakic, Joe	Que., Col.	8	1	—
Salo, Sami	Ottawa	1	—	—
Samsonov, Sergei	Boston	1	—	—
Sanderson, Geoff	Har., Buf.	6	—	—
Sandstrom, Tomas	NYR, L.A.	7	1	—
Satan, Miroslav	Buffalo	3	—	—
Savage, Brian	Montreal	4	1	—
Savard, Marc	Calgary	—	1	—
Selanne, Teemu	Wpg., Ana.	14	2	—
Selivanov, Alexander	Edmonton	2	1	—
Shanahan, Brendan	N.J., St.L., Hfd., Det.	12	—	—
Sheppard, Ray	Buf., Det., S.J., Fla.	12	—	—
Smolinski, Bryan	Boston	1	—	—
Smyth, Ryan	Edmonton	2	—	—
Stevens, Kevin	Pit., NYR	9	2	—
Stillman, Cory	Calgary	1	—	—
Straka, Martin	Pittsburgh	3	—	—
Stumpel, Jozef	Bos., L.A.	2	—	—
Sturm, Marco	San Jose	1	—	—
Sullivan, Steve	Toronto	—	1	—
Sundin, Mats	Que., Tor.	5	—	1
Svejkovsky, Jaroslav	Washington	—	1	—
Sydor, Darryl	Dallas	1	—	—
Sylvester, Dean	Atlanta	1	—	—
Thomas, Steve	Chi., NYI	4	2	—
Titov, German	Calgary	2	—	—
Tkachuk, Keith	Phoenix	6	2	—
Tocchet, Rick	Phi., Pit., L.A., Bos.	12	2	—
Turcotte, Darren	NY Rangers	4	—	—
Turgeon, Pierre	Buf., NYI, Mtl., St.L.	14	—	—
Valicevic, Robert	Nashville	1	—	—
Valk, Garry	Anaheim	1	—	—
Verbeek, Pat	N.J., Hfd., NYR, Dal.	11	1	—
Vukota, Mick	NY Islanders	1	—	—
Ward, Dixon	Buffalo	1	—	—
Weight, Doug	Edmonton	1	—	—
Wesley, Glen	Boston	1	—	—
Wiemer, Jason	Tampa Bay	1	—	—
Yachmenev, Vitali	Los Angeles	1	—	—
Yake, Terry	Anaheim	1	—	—
Yashin, Alexei	Ottawa	5	—	—
Yegorov, Alexei	San Jose	1	—	—
Young, Scott	Que., Col.	4	—	—
Yzerman, Steve	Detroit	17	1	—
Ysebaert, Paul	Detroit	1	—	—
Zamuner, Rob	Tampa Bay	1	—	—
Zhamnov, Alexei	Wpg., Chi.	5	—	1

Top 100 All-Time Goal-Scoring Leaders

* active player

Lanny McDonald is the only player in NHL history to retire with exactly 500 goals in his career. He reached the milestone on March 21, 1989, just two weeks after collecting his 1,000th point.

	Player	Seasons	Games	Goals	Goals per game
1.	Wayne Gretzky, Edm., L.A., St.L., NYR	20	1487	894	.601
2.	Gordie Howe, Det., Hfd.	26	1767	801	.453
3.	Marcel Dionne, Det., L.A., NYR	18	1348	731	.542
4.	Phil Esposito, Chi., Bos., NYR	18	1282	717	.559
5.	Mike Gartner, Wsh., Min., NYR, Tor., Phx.	19	1432	708	.494
* 6.	Mark Messier, Edm., NYR, Van.	21	1479	627	.424
* 7.	Steve Yzerman, Det.	17	1256	627	.499
8.	Mario Lemieux, Pit.	13	745	613	.823
9.	Bobby Hull, Chi., Wpg., Hfd.	16	1063	610	.574
* 10.	Brett Hull, Cgy., St.L., Dal.	15	940	610	.649
11.	Dino Ciccarelli, Min., Wsh., Det., T.B., Fla.	19	1232	608	.494
12.	Jari Kurri, Edm., L.A., NYR, Ana., Col.	17	1251	601	.480
13.	Mike Bossy, NYI	10	752	573	.762
14.	Guy Lafleur, Mtl., NYR, Que.	17	1126	560	.497
15.	John Bucyk, Det., Bos.	23	1540	556	.361
16.	Luc Robitaille, L.A., Pit., NYR	14	1042	553	.531
* 17.	Dave Andreychuk, Buf., Tor., N.J., Bos., Col.	18	1287	552	.429
18.	Michel Goulet, Que., Chi.	15	1089	548	.503
19.	Maurice Richard, Mtl.	18	978	544	.556
20.	Stan Mikita, Chi.	22	1394	541	.388
21.	Frank Mahovlich, Tor., Det., Mtl.	18	1181	533	.451
22.	Bryan Trottier, NYI, Pit.	21	1279	524	.410
23.	Dale Hawerchuk, Wpg., Buf., St.L., Phi.	16	1188	518	.436
24.	Gilbert Perreault, Buf.	17	1191	512	.430
25.	Jean Beliveau, Mtl.	20	1125	507	.451
26.	Joe Mullen, St.L., Cgy., Pit., Bos.	17	1062	502	.473
27.	Lanny McDonald, Tor., Col., Cgy.	16	1111	500	.450
* 28.	Pat Verbeek, N.J., Hfd., NYR, Dal., Det.	18	1293	500	.387
29.	Glenn Anderson, Edm., Tor., NYR, St.L.	16	1129	498	.441
30.	Jean Ratelle, NYR, Bos.	21	1281	491	.383
31.	Norm Ullman, Det., Tor.	20	1410	490	.348
32.	Brian Bellows, Min., Mtl., T.B., Ana., Wsh.	17	1188	485	.408
33.	Darryl Sittler, Tor., Phi., Det.	15	1096	484	.442
34.	Bernie Nicholls, L.A., NYR, Edm., N.J., Chi., S.J.	18	1127	475	.421
35.	Denis Savard, Chi., Mtl., T.B.	18	1196	473	.395
* 36.	Ron Francis, Hfd., Pit., Car.	19	1407	472	.335
37.	Pat LaFontaine, NYI, Buf., NYR	15	865	468	.541
38.	Alex Delvecchio, Det.	25	1549	456	.294
39.	Peter Stastny, Que., N.J., St.L.	15	977	450	.461
40.	Rick Middleton, NYR, Bos.	14	1005	448	.446
41.	Steve Larmer, Chi., NYR	15	1006	441	.438
42.	Rick Vaive, Van., Tor., Chi., Buf.	13	876	441	.503
* 43.	Joe Nieuwendyk, Cgy., Dal.	14	883	440	.498
* 44.	Brendan Shanahan, N.J., St.L., Hfd., Det.	13	947	435	.459
45.	Dave Taylor, L.A.	17	1111	431	.388
46.	Yvan Cournoyer, Mtl.	16	968	428	.442
* 47.	Rick Tocchet, Phi., Pit., L.A., Bos., Wsh., Phx.	16	1070	426	.398
48.	Brian Propp, Phi., Bos., Min., Hfd.	15	1016	425	.418
49.	Steve Shutt, Mtl., L.A.	13	930	424	.456
* 50.	Pierre Turgeon, Buf., NYI, Mtl., St.L.	13	929	423	.455
* 51.	Doug Gilmour, St.L., Cgy., Tor., N.J., Chi., Buf.	17	1271	422	.332
52.	Bill Barber, Phi.	14	903	420	.465
53.	Garry Unger, Tor., Det., St.L., Atl., L.A., Edm.	16	1105	413	.374
* 54.	Stephane Richer, Mtl., N.J., T.B., St.L.	16	986	407	.413
55.	Rod Gilbert, NYR.	18	1065	406	.381
* 56.	John MacLean, N.J., S.J., NYR	17	1144	406	.355
* 57.	Ray Bourque, Bos., Col.	21	1532	403	.263
* 58.	Joe Sakic, Que., Col.	12	852	403	.473
59.	John Ogrodnick, Det., Que., NYR	14	928	402	.433
60.	Dave Keon, Tor., Hfd.	18	1296	396	.306
* 61.	Paul Coffey, Edm., Pit., L.A., Det., Hfd., Phi., Chi., Car.	20	1391	396	.285
62.	Cam Neely, Van., Bos.	13	726	395	.544
63.	Pierre Larouche, Pit., Mtl., Hfd., NYR	14	812	395	.486
* 64.	Tomas Sandstrom, NYR, L.A., Pit., Det., Ana.	15	983	394	.401
65.	Bernie Geoffrion, Mtl., NYR	16	883	393	.445
66.	Jean Pronovost, Pit., Atl., Wsh.	14	998	391	.392
67.	Dean Prentice, NYR, Bos., Det., Pit., Min.	22	1378	391	.284
* 68.	Theoren Fleury, Cgy., Col., NYR	12	886	389	.439
* 69.	Jaromir Jagr, Pit.	10	725	387	.534
70.	Rick Martin, Buf., L.A.	11	685	384	.561
71.	Reggie Leach, Bos., Cal., Phi., Det.	13	934	381	.408
72.	Ted Lindsay, Det., Chi.	17	1068	379	.355
* 73.	Jeremy Roenick, Chi., Phx.	12	828	378	.457
* 74.	Steve Thomas, Tor., Chi., NYI, N.J.	16	1019	378	.371
75.	Butch Goring, L.A., NYI, Bos.	19	1107	375	.339
76.	Rick Kehoe, Tor., Pit.	18	906	371	.409
77.	Tim Kerr, Phi., NYR, Hfd.	13	655	370	.565
78.	Bernie Federko, St.L., Det.	14	1000	369	.369
* 79.	Vincent Damphousse, Tor., Edm., Mtl., S.J.	14	1087	368	.339
80.	Geoff Courtnall, Bos., Edm., Wsh., St.L., Van.	17	1048	367	.350
81.	Jacques Lemaire, Mtl.	16	853	366	.429
* 82.	Ray Ferraro, Hfd., NYI, NYR, L.A., Atl.	16	1101	365	.332
83.	Peter McNab, Buf., Bos., Van., N.J.	14	954	363	.381
84.	Brent Sutter, NYI, Chi.	18	1111	363	.327
* 85.	Mark Recchi, Pit., Phi., Mtl.	12	863	361	.418
86.	Ivan Boldirev, Bos., Cal., Chi., Atl., Van., Det.	15	1052	361	.343
87.	Henri Richard, Mtl.	20	1256	358	.285
88.	Bobby Clarke, Phi.	20	1144	358	.313
* 89.	Ray Sheppard, Buf., NYR, Det., S.J., Fla., Car.	13	817	357	.437
90.	Bobby Smith, Min., Mtl.	15	1077	357	.331
91.	Dennis Maruk, Cal., Cle., Min., Wsh.	14	888	356	.401
92.	Wilf Paiement, K.C., Col., Tor., Que., NYR, Buf., Pit.	14	946	356	.376
93.	Mike Foligno, Det., Buf., Tor., Fla.	16	1018	355	.349
94.	Danny Gare, Buf., Det., Edm.	13	827	354	.428
* 95.	Alexander Mogilny, Buf., Van., N.J.	11	705	353	.501
96.	Andy Bathgate, NYR, Tor., Det., Pit.	17	1069	349	.326
* 97.	Mike Modano, Min., Dal.	12	787	349	.443
98.	Rick MacLeish, Phi., Hfd., Pit., Det.	14	846	349	.413
* 99.	Teemu Selanne, Wpg., Ana.	8	564	346	.613
* 100.	Claude Lemieux, Mtl., N.J., Col.	17	1001	345	.345

Top 100 Active Goal-Scoring Leaders

* active player

	Player	Seasons	Games	Goals	Goals per game
1.	**Mark Messier**, Edm., NYR, Van.	21	1479	**627**	.424
2.	**Steve Yzerman**, Det.	17	1256	**627**	.499
3.	**Brett Hull**, Cgy., St.L., Dal.	15	940	**610**	.649
4.	**Luc Robitaille**, L.A., Pit., NYR	14	1042	**553**	.531
5.	**Dave Andreychuk**, Buf., Tor., N.J., Bos., Col.	18	1287	**552**	.429
6.	**Pat Verbeek**, N.J., Hfd., NYR, Dal., Det.	18	1293	**500**	.387
7.	**Ron Francis**, Hfd., Pit., Car.	19	1407	**472**	.335
8.	**Joe Nieuwendyk**, Cgy., Dal.	14	883	**440**	.498
9.	**Brendan Shanahan**, N.J., St.L., Hfd., Det.	13	947	**435**	.459
10.	**Rick Tocchet**, Phi., Pit., L.A., Bos., Wsh., Phx.	16	1070	**426**	.398
11.	**Pierre Turgeon**, Buf., NYI, Mtl., St.L. . . .	13	929	**423**	.455
12.	**Doug Gilmour**, St.L., Cgy., Tor., N.J., Chi., Buf.	17	1271	**422**	.332
13.	**Stephane Richer**, Mtl., N.J., T.B., St.L. . .	16	986	**407**	.413
14.	**John MacLean**, N.J., S.J., NYR	17	1144	**406**	.355
15.	**Joe Sakic**, Que., Col.	12	852	**403**	.473
16.	**Ray Bourque**, Bos., Col.	21	1532	**403**	.263
17.	**Paul Coffey**, Edm., Pit., L.A., Det., Hfd., Phi., Chi., Car.	20	1391	**396**	.285
18.	**Tomas Sandstrom**, NYR, L.A., Pit., Det., Ana.	15	983	**394**	.401
19.	**Theoren Fleury**, Cgy., Col., NYR	12	886	**389**	.439
20.	**Jaromir Jagr**, Pit.	10	725	**387**	.534
21.	**Jeremy Roenick**, Chi., Phx.	12	828	**378**	.457
22.	**Steve Thomas**, Tor., Chi., NYI, N.J.	16	1019	**378**	.371
23.	**Vincent Damphousse**, Tor., Edm., Mtl., S.J.	14	1087	**368**	.339
24.	**Ray Ferraro**, Hfd., NYI, NYR, L.A., Atl. . .	16	1101	**365**	.332
25.	**Mark Recchi**, Pit., Phi., Mtl.	12	863	**361**	.418
26.	**Ray Sheppard**, Buf., NYR, Det., S.J., Fla., Car.	13	817	**357**	.437
27.	**Alexander Mogilny**, Buf., Van., N.J. . . .	11	705	**353**	.501
28.	**Mike Modano**, Min., Dal.	12	787	**349**	.443
29.	**Teemu Selanne**, Wpg., Ana.	8	564	**346**	.613
30.	**Kirk Muller**, N.J., Mtl., NYI, Tor., Fla., Dal.	16	1161	**345**	.297
31.	**Claude Lemieux**, Mtl., N.J., Col.	17	1001	**345**	.345
32.	**Greg Adams**, N.J., Van., Dal., Phx.	16	996	**344**	.345
33.	**Ed Olczyk**, Chi., Tor., Wpg., NYR, L.A., Pit.	16	1031	**342**	.332
34.	**Kevin Dineen**, Hfd., Phi., Car., Ott.	16	1059	**342**	.323
35.	**Peter Bondra**, Wsh.	10	672	**337**	.501
36.	**Mats Sundin**, Que., Tor.	10	766	**328**	.428
37.	**Pavel Bure**, Van., Fla.	9	513	**325**	.634
38.	**Kevin Stevens**, Pit., Bos., L.A., NYR	13	787	**318**	.404
39.	**Gary Roberts**, Cgy., Car.	14	792	**314**	.396
40.	**Phil Housley**, Buf., Wpg., St.L., Cgy., N.J., Wsh.	18	1288	**313**	.243
41.	**John LeClair**, Mtl., Phi.	10	665	**309**	.465
42.	**Adam Oates**, Det., St.L., Bos., Wsh.	15	1049	**303**	.289
43.	**Al MacInnis**, Cgy., St.L.	19	1203	**301**	.250
44.	**Sergei Fedorov**, Det.	10	672	**301**	.448
45.	**Keith Tkachuk**, Wpg., Phx.	9	576	**294**	.510
46.	**Adam Graves**, Det., Edm., NYR	13	907	**293**	.323
47.	**Tony Amonte**, NYR, Chi.	10	697	**290**	.416
48.	**Eric Lindros**, Phi.	8	486	**290**	.597
49.	**Trevor Linden**, Van., NYI, Mtl.	12	859	**288**	.335
50.	**Larry Murphy**, L.A., Wsh., Min., Pit., Tor., Det.	20	1558	**285**	.183
51.	**Rod Brind'Amour**, St.L., Phi., Car.	12	823	**282**	.343
52.	**Scott Mellanby**, Phi., Edm., Fla.	15	1016	**274**	.270
53.	**Murray Craven**, Det., Phi., Hfd., Van., Chi., S.J.	18	1071	**266**	.248
54.	**Derek King**, NYI, Hfd., Tor., St.L.	14	830	**261**	.314
55.	**Owen Nolan**, Que., Col., S.J.	10	643	**254**	.395
56.	**Ulf Dahlen**, NYR, Min., Dal., S.J., Chi., Wsh.	11	761	**246**	.323
57.	**Tony Granato**, NYR, L.A., S.J.	12	713	**244**	.342
58.	**Cliff Ronning**, St.L., Van., Phx., Nsh.	14	856	**242**	.283
59.	**Shayne Corson**, Mtl., Edm., St.L.	15	942	**241**	.256
60.	**Dmitri Khristich**, Wsh., L.A., Bos., Tor. . .	10	680	**237**	.349
61.	**Scott Young**, Hfd., Pit., Que., Col., Ana., St.L.	12	822	**234**	.285
62.	**Joe Murphy**, Det., Edm., Chi., St.L., S.J., Bos., Wsh.	14	765	**232**	.303
63.	**Geoff Sanderson**, Hfd., Car., Van., Buf.	10	656	**225**	.343
64.	**Kevin Hatcher**, Wsh., Dal., Pit., NYR . . .	16	1100	**223**	.203
65.	**Steve Duchesne**, L.A., Phi., Que., St.L., Ott., Det.	14	995	**218**	.219
66.	**Benoit Hogue**, Buf., NYI, Tor., Dal., T.B., Phx.	13	771	**212**	.275
67.	**Paul Kariya**, Ana.	6	376	**210**	.559
68.	**Robert Reichel**, Cgy., NYI, Phx.	8	602	**209**	.347

Keith Tkachuk was the first American-born player to lead the NHL in goals when he scored 52 times in 1996-97. He enters the 2000-01 season needing to score just six times to reach the 300-goal plateau.

	Player	Seasons	Games	Goals	Goals per game
69.	**Ron Sutter**, Phi., St.L., Que., NYI, Bos., S.J.	18	1072	**204**	.190
70.	**Petr Nedved**, Van., St.L., NYR, Pit.	9	573	**202**	.353
71.	**Donald Audette**, Buf., L.A., Atl.	11	521	**201**	.386
72.	**Bobby Holik**, Hfd., N.J.	10	717	**200**	.279
73.	**Darren Turcotte**, NYR, Hfd., Wpg., S.J., St.L., Nsh.	12	635	**195**	.307
74.	**Martin Gelinas**, Edm., Que., Van., Car.	12	744	**195**	.262
75.	**Ziggy Palffy**, NYI, L.A.	7	395	**195**	.494
76.	**Rob Brown**, Pit., Hfd., Chi., Dal., L.A. . .	11	543	**190**	.350
77.	**Randy Cunneyworth**, Buf., Pit., Wpg., Hfd., Chi., Ott.	16	866	**189**	.218
78.	**Gary Suter**, Cgy., Chi., S.J.	15	995	**187**	.188
79.	**Alexei Zhamnov**, Wpg., Chi.	8	526	**187**	.356
80.	**Keith Primeau**, Det., Hfd., Car., Phi. . . .	10	620	**186**	.300
81.	**Brian Leetch**, NYR	13	857	**184**	.215
82.	**Vyacheslav Kozlov**, Det.	9	535	**182**	.340
83.	**Michal Pivonka**, Wsh.	13	825	**181**	.219
84.	**Kelly Miller**, NYR, Wsh.	15	1057	**181**	.171
85.	**Shawn McEachern**, Pit., L.A., Bos., Ott.	9	593	**180**	.304
86.	**Scott Stevens**, Wsh., St.L., N.J.	18	1353	**179**	.132
87.	**Nelson Emerson**, St.L., Wpg., Hfd., Car., Chi., Ott., Atl., L.A.	10	652	**179**	.275
88.	**Alexei Yashin**, Ott.	7	422	**178**	.422
89.	**Bill Guerin**, N.J., Edm.	9	570	**175**	.307
90.	**Mike Ricci**, Phi., Que., Col., S.J.	10	708	**174**	.246
91.	**Chris Chelios**, Mtl., Chi., Det.	17	1157	**168**	.145
92.	**Alexei Kovalev**, NYR, Pit.	8	547	**165**	.302
93.	**Dave Reid**, Bos., Tor., Dal., Col.	17	888	**164**	.185
94.	**Stu Barnes**, Wpg., Fla., Pit., Buf.	9	596	**161**	.270
95.	**Andrei Kovalenko**, Que., Col., Mtl., Edm., Phi., Car.	8	544	**157**	.289
96.	**Bob Probert**, Det., Chi.	15	795	**155**	.195
97.	**Doug Weight**, NYR, Edm.	10	624	**155**	.248
98.	**Jason Arnott**, Edm., N.J.	7	471	**154**	.327
99.	**Dave Ellett**, Wpg., Tor., N.J., Bos., St.L.	16	1129	**153**	.136
100.	**Doug Brown**, N.J., Pit., Det.	14	794	**151**	.190

Top 100 All-Time Assist Leaders

* active player

Player	Seasons	Games	Assists	Assists per game
1. **Wayne Gretzky**, Edm., L.A., St.L., NYR .	20	1487	**1963**	1.320
* 2. **Paul Coffey**, Edm., Pit., L.A., Det., Hfd., Phi., Chi., Car.	20	1391	**1131**	.813
* 3. **Ray Bourque**, Bos., Col.	21	1532	**1117**	.729
* 4. **Mark Messier**, Edm., NYR, Van.	21	1479	**1087**	.735
* 5. **Ron Francis**, Hfd., Pit., Car.	19	1407	**1087**	.773
6. **Gordie Howe**, Det., Hfd.	26	1767	**1049**	.594
7. **Marcel Dionne**, Det., L.A., NYR.	18	1348	**1040**	.772
* 8. **Steve Yzerman**, Det.	17	1256	**935**	.744
9. **Stan Mikita**, Chi.	22	1394	**926**	.664
* 10. **Larry Murphy**, L.A., Wsh., Min., Pit., Tor., Det.	20	1558	**910**	.584
11. **Bryan Trottier**, NYI, Pit.	21	1279	**901**	.704
* 12. **Adam Oates**, Det., St.L., Bos., Wsh.	15	1049	**894**	.852
13. **Dale Hawerchuk**, Wpg., Buf., St.L., Phi.	16	1188	**891**	.750
* 14. **Doug Gilmour**, St.L., Cgy., Tor., N.J., Chi., Buf.	17	1271	**883**	.695
15. **Mario Lemieux**, Pit.	13	745	**881**	1.183
16. **Phil Esposito**, Chi., Bos., NYR	18	1282	**873**	.681
17. **Denis Savard**, Chi., Mtl., T.B.	18	1196	**865**	.723
18. **Bobby Clarke**, Phi.	20	1144	**852**	.745
19. **Alex Delvecchio**, Det.	25	1549	**825**	.533
* 20. **Phil Housley**, Buf., Wpg., St.L., Cgy., N.J., Wsh.	18	1288	**817**	.634
21. **Gilbert Perreault**, Buf.	17	1191	**814**	.683
22. **John Bucyk**, Det., Bos.	23	1540	**813**	.528
* 23. **Al MacInnis**, Cgy., St.L.	19	1203	**803**	.667
24. **Jari Kurri**, Edm., L.A., NYR, Ana., Col.	17	1251	**797**	.637
25. **Guy Lafleur**, Mtl., NYR, Que.	17	1126	**793**	.704
26. **Peter Stastny**, Que., N.J., St.L.	15	977	**789**	.808
27. **Jean Ratelle**, NYR, Bos.	21	1281	**776**	.606
28. **Bernie Federko**, St.L., Det.	14	1000	**761**	.761
29. **Larry Robinson**, Mtl., L.A.	23	1384	**750**	.542
30. **Denis Potvin**, NYI	15	1060	**742**	.700
31. **Norm Ullman**, Det., Tor.	20	1410	**739**	.524
32. **Bernie Nicholls**, L.A., NYR, Edm., N.J., Chi., S.J.	18	1127	**734**	.651
33. **Jean Beliveau**, Mtl.	20	1125	**712**	.633
34. **Dale Hunter**, Que., Wsh., Col.	20	1407	**697**	.495
35. **Henri Richard**, Mtl.	20	1256	**688**	.548
36. **Brad Park**, NYR, Bos., Det.	17	1113	**683**	.614
37. **Bobby Smith**, Min., Mtl.	15	1077	**679**	.630
* 38. **Chris Chelios**, Mtl., Chi., Det.	17	1157	**664**	.574
* 39. **Joe Sakic**, Que., Col.	12	852	**657**	.771
* 40. **Scott Stevens**, Wsh., St.L., N.J.	18	1353	**649**	.480
41. **Bobby Orr**, Bos., Chi.	12	657	**645**	.982
* 42. **Pierre Turgeon**, Buf., NYI, Mtl., St.L. . .	13	929	**640**	.689
43. **Dave Taylor**, L.A.	17	1111	**638**	.574
44. **Borje Salming**, Tor., Det.	17	1148	**637**	.555
45. **Darryl Sittler**, Tor., Phi., Det.	15	1096	**637**	.581
46. **Neal Broten**, Min., Dal., N.J., L.A.	17	1099	**634**	.577
* 47. **Vincent Damphousse**, Tor., Edm., Mtl., S.J.	14	1087	**631**	.580
48. **Mike Gartner**, Wsh., Min., NYR, Tor., Phx.	19	1432	**627**	.438
49. **Andy Bathgate**, NYR, Tor., Det., Pit. . . .	17	1069	**624**	.584
* 50. **Dave Andreychuk**, Buf., Tor., N.J., Bos., Col.	18	1287	**624**	.485
51. **Rod Gilbert**, NYR.	18	1065	**615**	.577
52. **Michel Goulet**, Que., Chi.	15	1089	**604**	.555
53. **Glenn Anderson**, Edm., Tor., NYR, St.L.	16	1129	**601**	.532
* 54. **Brian Leetch**, NYR.	13	857	**597**	.697
* 55. **Luc Robitaille**, L.A., Pit., NYR	14	1042	**597**	.573
56. **Dino Ciccarelli**, Min., Wsh., Det., T.B., Fla.	19	1232	**592**	.481
* 57. **Gary Suter**, Cgy., Chi., S.J.	15	995	**591**	.594
58. **Doug Wilson**, Chi., S.J.	16	1024	**590**	.576
59. **Dave Keon**, Tor., Hfd.	18	1296	**590**	.455
60. **Dave Babych**, Wpg., Hfd., Van., Phi., L.A.	19	1195	**581**	.486
61. **Brian Propp**, Phi., Bos., Min., Hfd.	15	1016	**579**	.570
* 62. **Mark Recchi**, Pit., Phi., Mtl.	12	863	**572**	.663
63. **Steve Larmer**, Chi., NYR	15	1006	**571**	.568
* 64. **Jaromir Jagr**, Pit.	10	725	**571**	.788
65. **Frank Mahovlich**, Tor., Det., Mtl.	18	1181	**570**	.483
* 66. **Kirk Muller**, N.J., Mtl., NYI, Tor., Fla., Dal.	16	1161	**568**	.489
67. **Craig Janney**, Bos., St.L., S.J., Wpg., Phx., T.B., NYI.	12	760	**563**	.741
68. **Joe Mullen**, St.L., Cgy., Pit., Bos.	17	1062	**561**	.528
69. **Bobby Hull**, Chi., Wpg., Hfd.	16	1063	**560**	.527
70. **Mike Bossy**, NYI	10	752	**553**	.735
71. **Thomas Steen**, Wpg.	14	950	**553**	.582
72. **Ken Linseman**, Phi., Edm., Bos., Tor. . . .	14	860	**551**	.641
73. **Tom Lysiak**, Atl., Chi.	13	919	**551**	.600

Andy Bathgate had 624 assists during his Hall of Fame career. He had 28 goals and a league-high 56 assists to tie Bobby Hull for the scoring title in 1961-62, but was denied the Art Ross Trophy because Hull scored 50 goals that season.

Player	Seasons	Games	Assists	Assist per game
74. **Pat LaFontaine**, NYI, Buf., NYR	15	865	**545**	.630
75. **Mark Howe**, Hfd., Phi., Det.	16	929	**545**	.587
76. **Red Kelly**, Det., Tor., L.A.	21	1316	**542**	.412
77. **Rick Middleton**, NYR, Bos.	14	1005	**540**	.537
78. **Brian Bellows**, Min., Mtl., T.B., Ana., Wsh.	17	1188	**537**	.452
* 79. **Theoren Fleury**, Cgy., Col., NYR	12	886	**529**	.597
80. **Dennis Maruk**, Cal., Cle., Min., Wsh. . .	14	888	**522**	.588
81. **Wayne Cashman**, Bos.	23	1027	**516**	.502
82. **Butch Goring**, L.A., NYI, Bos.	19	1107	**513**	.463
* 83. **Pat Verbeek**, N.J., Hfd., NYR, Dal., Det.	18	1293	**513**	.397
84. **John Tonelli**, NYI, Cgy., L.A., Chi., Que.	14	1028	**511**	.497
85. **Lanny McDonald**, Tor., Col., Cgy.	16	1111	**506**	.455
86. **Ivan Boldirev**, Bos., Cal., Chi., Atl., Van., Det.	15	1052	**505**	.480
87. **Randy Carlyle**, Tor., Pit., Wpg.	19	1055	**499**	.473
* 88. **Brett Hull**, Cgy., St.L., Dal.	15	940	**494**	.526
* 89. **Jeremy Roenick**, Chi., Phx.	12	828	**493**	.595
* 90. **Murray Craven**, Det., Phi., Hfd., Van., Chi., S.J.	18	1071	**493**	.460
* 91. **Steve Duchesne**, L.A., Phi., Que., St.L., Ott., L.A.	14	995	**491**	.493
* 92. **Rick Tocchet**, Phi., Pit., L.A., Bos., Wsh., Phx.	16	1070	**488**	.456
93. **Pit Martin**, Det., Bos., Chi., Van.	17	1101	**485**	.441
94. **Pete Mahovlich**, Det., Mtl., Pit.	16	884	**485**	.549
95. **Ken Hodge**, Chi., Bos., NYR	14	881	**472**	.536
96. **Ted Lindsay**, Det., Chi.	17	1068	**472**	.442
97. **Dean Prentice**, NYR, Bos., Det., Pit., Min.	22	1378	**469**	.340
98. **Jacques Lemaire**, Mtl.	16	853	**469**	.550
* 99. **Mike Modano**, Min., Dal.	12	787	**467**	.593
100. **Phil Goyette**, Mtl., NYR, St.L., Buf.	16	941	**467**	.496

Top 100 Active Assist Leaders

* active player

Player	Seasons	Games	Assists	Assists per game
1. **Paul Coffey**, Edm., Pit., L.A., Det., Hfd., Phi., Chi., Car.	20	1391	**1131**	.813
2. **Ray Bourque**, Bos., Col.	21	1532	**1117**	.729
3. **Mark Messier**, Edm., NYR, Van.	21	1479	**1087**	.735
4. **Ron Francis**, Hfd., Pit., Car.	19	1407	**1087**	.773
5. **Steve Yzerman**, Det.	17	1256	**935**	.744
6. **Larry Murphy**, L.A., Wsh., Min., Pit., Tor., Det.	20	1558	**910**	.584
7. **Adam Oates**, Det., St.L., Bos., Wsh.	15	1049	**894**	.852
8. **Doug Gilmour**, St.L., Cgy., Tor., N.J., Chi., Buf.	17	1271	**883**	.695
9. **Phil Housley**, Buf., Wpg., St.L., Cgy., N.J., Wsh.	18	1288	**817**	.634
10. **Al MacInnis**, Cgy., St.L.	19	1203	**803**	.667
11. **Chris Chelios**, Mtl., Chi., Det.	17	1157	**664**	.574
12. **Joe Sakic**, Que., Col.	12	852	**657**	.771
13. **Scott Stevens**, Wsh., St.L., N.J.	18	1353	**649**	.480
14. **Pierre Turgeon**, Buf., NYI, Mtl., St.L.	13	929	**640**	.689
15. **Vincent Damphousse**, Tor., Edm., Mtl., S.J.	14	1087	**631**	.580
16. **Dave Andreychuk**, Buf., Tor., N.J., Bos., Col.	18	1287	**624**	.485
17. **Luc Robitaille**, L.A., Pit., NYR.	14	1042	**597**	.573
18. **Brian Leetch**, NYR.	13	857	**597**	.697
19. **Gary Suter**, Cgy., Chi., S.J.	15	995	**591**	.594
20. **Mark Recchi**, Pit., Phi., Mtl.	12	863	**572**	.663
21. **Jaromir Jagr**, Pit.	10	725	**571**	.788
22. **Kirk Muller**, N.J., Mtl., NYI, Tor., Fla., Dal.	16	1161	**568**	.489
23. **Theoren Fleury**, Cgy., Col., NYR	12	886	**529**	.597
24. **Pat Verbeek**, N.J., Hfd., NYR, Dal., Det.	18	1293	**513**	.397
25. **Brett Hull**, Cgy., St.L., Dal.	15	940	**494**	.526
26. **Murray Craven**, Det., Phi., Hfd., Van., Chi., S.J.	18	1071	**493**	.460
27. **Jeremy Roenick**, Chi., Phx.	12	828	**493**	.595
28. **Steve Duchesne**, L.A., Phi., Que., St.L., Ott., Det.	14	995	**491**	.493
29. **Rick Tocchet**, Phi., Pit., L.A., Bos., Wsh., Phx.	16	1070	**488**	.456
30. **Mike Modano**, Min., Dal.	12	787	**467**	.593
31. **Tomas Sandstrom**, NYR, L.A., Pit., Det., Ana.	15	983	**462**	.470
32. **Garry Galley**, L.A., Wsh., Bos., Phi., Buf.	16	1093	**461**	.422
33. **Mats Sundin**, Que., Tor.	10	766	**460**	.601
34. **James Patrick**, NYR, Hfd., Cgy., Buf.	17	1046	**454**	.434
35. **Steve Thomas**, Tor., Chi., NYI, N.J.	16	1019	**454**	.446
36. **Ed Olczyk**, Chi., Tor., Wpg., NYR, L.A., Pit.	16	1031	**452**	.438
37. **Brendan Shanahan**, N.J., St.L., Hfd., Det.	13	947	**444**	.469
38. **Rod Brind'Amour**, St.L., Phi., Car.	12	823	**443**	.538
39. **Cliff Ronning**, St.L., Van., Phx., Nsh.	14	856	**439**	.513
40. **Kevin Hatcher**, Wsh., Dal., Pit., NYR	16	1100	**436**	.396
41. **Sergei Fedorov**, Det.	10	672	**433**	.644
42. **Geoff Courtnall**, Bos., Edm., Wsh., St.L., Van.	17	1048	**432**	.412
43. **John MacLean**, N.J., S.J., NYR	17	1144	**424**	.371
44. **Doug Bodger**, Pit., Buf., S.J., N.J., L.A., Van.	16	1071	**422**	.394
45. **Ray Ferraro**, Hfd., NYI, NYR, L.A., Atl.	16	1101	**420**	.381
46. **Michal Pivonka**, Wsh.	13	825	**418**	.507
47. **Joe Nieuwendyk**, Cgy., Dal.	14	883	**417**	.472
48. **Fredrik Olausson**, Wpg., Edm., Ana., Pit.	14	931	**415**	.446
49. **Dave Ellett**, Wpg., Tor., N.J., Bos., St.L.	16	1129	**415**	.368
50. **Alexander Mogilny**, Buf., Van., N.J.	11	705	**405**	.574
51. **Doug Weight**, NYR, Edm.	10	624	**402**	.644
52. **Kevin Dineen**, Hfd., Phi., Car., Ott.	16	1059	**390**	.368
53. **Stephane Richer**, Mtl., N.J., T.B., St.L.	16	986	**384**	.389
54. **Teemu Selanne**, Wpg., Ana.	8	564	**383**	.679
55. **Greg Adams**, N.J., Van., Dal., Phx.	16	996	**376**	.378
56. **Nicklas Lidstrom**, Det.	9	693	**375**	.541
57. **Trevor Linden**, Van., NYI, Mtl.	12	859	**375**	.437
58. **Kevin Stevens**, Pit., Bos., L.A., NYR	13	787	**371**	.471
59. **Eric Lindros**, Phi.	8	486	**369**	.759
60. **Igor Larionov**, Van., S.J., Det.	10	663	**369**	.557
61. **Calle Johansson**, Buf., Wsh.	13	932	**369**	.396
62. **Andrew Cassels**, Mtl., Hfd., Cgy., Van.	11	728	**369**	.507
63. **Shayne Corson**, Mtl., Edm., St.L.	15	942	**368**	.391
64. **Claude Lemieux**, Mtl., N.J., Col.	17	1001	**353**	.353
65. **Derek King**, NYI, Hfd., Tor., St.L.	14	830	**351**	.423
66. **Peter Forsberg**, Que., Col.	6	393	**349**	.888
67. **Scott Mellanby**, Phi., Edm., Fla.	15	1016	**346**	.341
68. **Teppo Numminen**, Wpg., Phx.	12	872	**341**	.391
69. **Joe Juneau**, Bos., Wsh., Buf., Ott.	9	547	**339**	.620

Though best known these days for his crunching body checks, Scott Stevens is a former 20-goal scorer. He also ranks 13th in assists among active NHL players. Six of the 12 players ahead of Stevens are also defensemen.

Player	Games	Assists	Assists per game
70. **Petr Svoboda**, Mtl., Buf., Phi., T.B.	1009	**338**	.335
71. **Glen Wesley**, Bos., Hfd., Car.	955	**337**	.353
72. **Gary Roberts**, Cgy., Car.	792	**335**	.423
73. **Eric Desjardins**, Mtl., Phi.	827	**332**	.401
74. **Sergei Zubov**, NYR, Pit., Dal.	538	**332**	.617
75. **Ron Sutter**, Phi., St.L., Que., NYI, Bos., S.J.	1072	**326**	.304
76. **Jeff Norton**, NYI, S.J., St.L., Edm., T.B., Fla.	725	**316**	.436
77. **Jyrki Lumme**, Mtl., Van., Phx.	788	**313**	.397
78. **Alexei Zhamnov**, Wpg., Chi.	526	**312**	.593
79. **Benoit Hogue**, Buf., NYI, Tor., Dal., T.B., Phx.	771	**306**	.397
80. **John LeClair**, Mtl., Phi.	665	**306**	.460
81. **Tony Amonte**, NYR, Chi.	697	**304**	.436
82. **Scott Young**, Hfd., Pit., Que., Col., Ana., St.L.	822	**302**	.367
83. **Steve Smith**, Edm., Chi., Cgy.	791	**301**	.381
84. **Dmitri Khristich**, Wsh., L.A., Bos., Tor.	680	**300**	.441
85. **Ray Sheppard**, Buf., NYR, Det., S.J., Fla., Car.	817	**300**	.367
86. **Robert Reichel**, Cgy., NYI, Phx.	602	**298**	.495
87. **Sylvain Cote**, Hfd., Wsh., Tor., Chi., Dal.	1032	**291**	.282
88. **Joe Murphy**, Det., Edm., Chi., St.L., S.J., Bos., Wsh.	765	**290**	.379
89. **Zarley Zalapski**, Pit., Hfd., Cgy., Mtl., Phi.	637	**285**	.447
90. **Kelly Miller**, NYR, Wsh.	1057	**282**	.267
91. **Nelson Emerson**, St.L., Wpg., Hfd., Car., Chi., Ott., Atl., L.A.	652	**280**	.429
92. **Dave Manson**, Chi., Edm., Wpg., Phx., Mtl., Dal.	982	**279**	.284
93. **Ulf Samuelsson**, Hfd., Pit., NYR, Det., Phi.	1080	**275**	.255
94. **Ulf Dahlen**, NYR, Min., Dal., S.J., Chi., Wsh.	761	**272**	.357
95. **Grant Ledyard**, NYR, L.A., Wsh., Buf., Dal., Van., Bos., Ott.	953	**270**	.283
96. **Owen Nolan**, Que., Col., S.J.	643	**264**	.411
97. **Pavel Bure**, Van., Fla.	513	**263**	.513
98. **Mike Keane**, Mtl., Col., NYR, Dal.	887	**263**	.297
99. **Mathieu Schneider**, Mtl., NYI, Tor., NYR	708	**260**	.367
100. **Rob Blake**, L.A.	608	**259**	.426

Top 100 All-Time Point Leaders

* active player

Player	Seasons	Games	Goals	Assists	Points	Points per game
1. **Wayne Gretzky**, Edm., L.A., St.L., NYR	20	1487	894	1963	**2857**	1.921
2. **Gordie Howe**, Det., Hfd.	26	1767	801	1049	**1850**	1.047
3. **Marcel Dionne**, Det., L.A., NYR	18	1348	731	1040	**1771**	1.314
* 4. **Mark Messier**, Edm., NYR, Van.	21	1479	627	1087	**1714**	1.159
5. **Phil Esposito**, Chi., Bos., NYR	18	1282	717	873	**1590**	1.240
* 6. **Steve Yzerman**, Det.	17	1256	627	935	**1562**	1.244
* 7. **Ron Francis**, Hfd., Pit., Car.	19	1407	472	1087	**1559**	1.108
* 8. **Paul Coffey**, Edm., Pit., L.A., Det., Hfd., Phi., Chi., Car.	20	1391	396	1131	**1527**	1.098
* 9. **Ray Bourque**, Bos., Col.	21	1532	403	1117	**1520**	.992
10. **Mario Lemieux**, Pit.	13	745	613	881	**1494**	2.005
11. **Stan Mikita**, Chi.	22	1394	541	926	**1467**	1.052
12. **Bryan Trottier**, NYI, Pit.	21	1279	524	901	**1425**	1.114
13. **Dale Hawerchuk**, Wpg., Buf., St.L., Phi.	16	1188	518	891	**1409**	1.186
14. **Jari Kurri**, Edm., L.A., NYR, Ana., Col.	17	1251	601	797	**1398**	1.118
15. **John Bucyk**, Det., Bos.	23	1540	556	813	**1369**	.889
16. **Guy Lafleur**, Mtl., NYR, Que.	17	1126	560	793	**1353**	1.202
17. **Denis Savard**, Chi., Mtl., T.B.	18	1196	473	865	**1338**	1.119
18. **Mike Gartner**, Wsh., Min., NYR, Tor., Phx.	19	1432	708	627	**1335**	.932
19. **Gilbert Perreault**, Buf.	17	1191	512	814	**1326**	1.113
* 20. **Doug Gilmour**, St.L., Cgy., Tor., N.J., Chi., Buf.	17	1271	422	883	**1305**	1.027
21. **Alex Delvecchio**, Det.	25	1549	456	825	**1281**	.827
22. **Jean Ratelle**, NYR, Bos.	21	1281	491	776	**1267**	.989
23. **Peter Stastny**, Que., N.J., St.L.	15	977	450	789	**1239**	1.268
24. **Norm Ullman**, Det., Tor.	20	1410	490	739	**1229**	.872
25. **Jean Beliveau**, Mtl.	20	1125	507	712	**1219**	1.084
26. **Bobby Clarke**, Phi.	20	1144	358	852	**1210**	1.058
27. **Bernie Nicholls**, L.A., NYR, Edm., N.J., Chi., S.J.	18	1127	475	734	**1209**	1.073
28. **Dino Ciccarelli**, Min., Wsh., Det., T.B., Fla.	19	1232	608	592	**1200**	.974
* 29. **Adam Oates**, Det., St.L., Bos., Wsh.	15	1049	303	894	**1197**	1.141
* 30. **Larry Murphy**, L.A., Wsh., Min., Pit., Tor., Det.	20	1558	285	910	**1195**	.767
* 31. **Dave Andreychuk**, Buf., Tor., N.J., Bos., Col.	18	1287	552	624	**1176**	.914
32. **Bobby Hull**, Chi., Wpg., Hfd.	16	1063	610	560	**1170**	1.101
33. **Michel Goulet**, Que., Chi.	15	1089	548	604	**1152**	1.058
* 34. **Luc Robitaille**, L.A., Pit., NYR	14	1042	553	597	**1150**	1.104
35. **Bernie Federko**, St.L., Det.	14	1000	369	761	**1130**	1.130
* 36. **Phil Housley**, Buf., Wpg., St.L., Cgy., N.J., Wsh.	18	1288	313	817	**1130**	.877
37. **Mike Bossy**, NYI	10	752	573	553	**1126**	1.497
38. **Darryl Sittler**, Tor., Phi., Det.	15	1096	484	637	**1121**	1.023
* 39. **Brett Hull**, Cgy., St.L., Dal.	15	940	610	494	**1104**	1.174
* 40. **Al MacInnis**, Cgy., St.L.	19	1203	301	803	**1104**	.918
41. **Frank Mahovlich**, Tor., Det., NYR, St.L., Mtl.	18	1181	533	570	**1103**	.934
42. **Glenn Anderson**, Edm., Tor., NYR, St.L.	16	1129	498	601	**1099**	.973
43. **Dave Taylor**, L.A.	17	1111	431	638	**1069**	.962
* 44. **Pierre Turgeon**, Buf., NYI, Mtl., St.L.	13	929	423	640	**1063**	1.144
45. **Joe Mullen**, St.L., Cgy., Pit., Bos.	17	1062	502	561	**1063**	1.001
* 46. **Joe Sakic**, Que., Col.	12	852	403	657	**1060**	1.244
47. **Denis Potvin**, NYI	15	1060	310	742	**1052**	.992
48. **Henri Richard**, Mtl.	20	1256	358	688	**1046**	.833
49. **Bobby Smith**, Min., Mtl.	15	1077	357	679	**1036**	.962
50. **Brian Bellows**, Min., Mtl., T.B., Ana., Wsh.	17	1188	485	537	**1022**	.860
51. **Rod Gilbert**, NYR.	18	1065	406	615	**1021**	.959
52. **Dale Hunter**, Que., Wsh., Col.	20	1407	323	697	**1020**	.725
* 53. **Pat Verbeek**, N.J., Hfd., NYR, Dal., Det.	18	1293	500	513	**1013**	.783
54. **Pat LaFontaine**, NYI, Buf., NYR	15	865	468	545	**1013**	1.171
55. **Steve Larmer**, Chi., NYR	15	1006	441	571	**1012**	1.006
56. **Lanny McDonald**, Tor., Col., Cgy.	16	1111	500	506	**1006**	.905
57. **Brian Propp**, Phi., Bos., Min., Hfd.	15	1016	425	579	**1004**	.988
* 58. **Vincent Damphousse**, Tor., Edm., Mtl., S.J.	14	1087	368	631	**999**	.919
59. **Rick Middleton**, NYR, Bos.	14	1005	448	540	**988**	.983
60. **Dave Keon**, Tor., Hfd.	18	1296	396	590	**986**	.761
61. **Andy Bathgate**, NYR, Tor., Det., Pit.	17	1069	349	624	**973**	.910
62. **Maurice Richard**, Mtl.	18	978	544	421	**965**	.987

Frank Mahovlich, battling with Barry Ashbee, was the main goal-scorer for the Toronto Maple Leafs in the 1960s, but became a top playmaker with Montreal during the early 1970s. He had 533 goals and 570 assists in his career.

Player	Seasons	Games	Goals	Assists	Points	Points per game
63. **Larry Robinson**, Mtl., L.A.	23	1384	208	750	**958**	.692
* 64. **Jaromir Jagr**, Pit.	10	725	387	571	**958**	1.321
* 65. **Mark Recchi**, Pit., Phi., Mtl.	12	863	361	572	**933**	1.081
66. **Neal Broten**, Min., Dal., N.J., L.A.	17	1099	289	634	**923**	.840
* 67. **Theoren Fleury**, Cgy., Col., NYR	12	886	389	529	**918**	1.036
68. **Bobby Orr**, Bos., Chi.	12	657	270	645	**915**	1.393
* 69. **Rick Tocchet**, Phi., Pit., L.A., Bos., Wsh., Phx.	16	1070	426	488	**914**	.854
* 70. **Kirk Muller**, N.J., Mtl., NYI, Tor., Fla., Dal.	16	1161	345	568	**913**	.786
71. **Brad Park**, NYR, Bos., Det.	17	1113	213	683	**896**	.805
72. **Butch Goring**, L.A., NYI, Bos.	19	1107	375	513	**888**	.802
73. **Bill Barber**, Phi.	14	903	420	463	**883**	.978
* 74. **Brendan Shanahan**, N.J., St.L., Hfd., Det.	13	947	435	444	**879**	.928
75. **Dennis Maruk**, Cal., Cle., Min., Wsh.	14	888	356	522	**878**	.989
* 76. **Jeremy Roenick**, Chi., Phx.	12	828	378	493	**871**	1.052
77. **Ivan Boldirev**, Bos., Cal., Chi., Atl., Van., Det.	15	1052	361	505	**866**	.823
78. **Yvan Cournoyer**, Mtl.	16	968	428	435	**863**	.892
79. **Dean Prentice**, NYR, Bos., Det., Pit., Min.	22	1378	391	469	**860**	.624
* 80. **Joe Nieuwendyk**, Cgy., Dal.	14	883	440	417	**857**	.971
* 81. **Tomas Sandstrom**, NYR, L.A., Pit., Det., Ana.	15	983	394	462	**856**	.871
82. **Ted Lindsay**, Det., Chi.	17	1068	379	472	**851**	.797
83. **Tom Lysiak**, Atl., Chi.	13	919	292	551	**843**	.917
84. **John Tonelli**, NYI, Cgy., L.A., Chi., Que.	14	1028	325	511	**836**	.813
85. **Jacques Lemaire**, Mtl.	16	853	366	469	**835**	.979
* 86. **Steve Thomas**, Tor., Chi., NYI, N.J.	16	1019	378	454	**832**	.816
* 87. **Chris Chelios**, Mtl., Chi., Det.	17	1157	168	664	**832**	.719
* 88. **John MacLean**, N.J., S.J., NYR	17	1144	406	424	**830**	.726
89. **Brent Sutter**, NYI, Chi.	18	1111	363	466	**829**	.746
* 90. **Scott Stevens**, Wsh., St.L., N.J.	18	1353	179	649	**828**	.612
91. **John Ogrodnick**, Det., Que., NYR	14	928	402	425	**827**	.891
92. **Doug Wilson**, Chi., S.J.	16	1024	237	590	**827**	.808
93. **Red Kelly**, Det., Tor., L.A.	21	1316	281	542	**823**	.625
94. **Bernie Geoffrion**, Mtl., NYR.	16	883	393	429	**822**	.931
95. **Pierre Larouche**, Pit., Mtl., Hfd., NYR.	14	812	395	427	**822**	1.012
96. **Thomas Steen**, Wpg.	14	950	264	553	**817**	.860
97. **Steve Shutt**, Mtl., L.A.	13	930	424	393	**817**	.878
* 98. **Mike Modano**, Min., Dal.	12	787	349	467	**816**	1.037
99. **Wilf Paiement**, K.C., Col., Tor., Que., NYR, Buf., Pit.	14	946	356	458	**814**	.860
100. **Peter McNab**, Buf., Bos., Van., N.J.	14	954	363	450	**813**	.852

Top 100 Active Points Leaders

* active player

With a career-high 84 points last season, including 44 goals, Owen Nolan jumped from 96th to 77th among the NHL's top 100 active scoring leaders. Another year like 1999-2000 could see him top 600 career points this season.

#	Player	Seasons	Games	Goals	Assists	Points	Points per game
1.	**Mark Messier**, Edm., NYR, Van.	21	1479	627	1087	**1714**	1.159
2.	**Steve Yzerman**, Det.	17	1256	627	935	**1562**	1.244
3.	**Ron Francis**, Hfd., Pit., Car.	19	1407	472	1087	**1559**	1.108
4.	**Paul Coffey**, Edm., Pit., L.A., Det., Hfd., Phi., Chi., Car.	20	1391	396	1131	**1527**	1.098
5.	**Ray Bourque**, Bos., Col.	21	1532	403	1117	**1520**	.992
6.	**Doug Gilmour**, St.L., Cgy., Tor., N.J., Chi., Buf.	17	1271	422	883	**1305**	1.027
7.	**Adam Oates**, Det., St.L., Bos., Wsh.	15	1049	303	894	**1197**	1.141
8.	**Larry Murphy**, L.A., Wsh., Min., Pit., Tor., Det.	20	1558	285	910	**1195**	.767
9.	**Dave Andreychuk**, Buf., Tor., N.J., Bos., Col.	18	1287	552	624	**1176**	.914
10.	**Luc Robitaille**, L.A., Pit., NYR.	14	1042	553	597	**1150**	1.104
11.	**Phil Housley**, Buf., Wpg., St.L., Cgy., N.J., Wsh.	18	1288	313	817	**1130**	.877
12.	**Brett Hull**, Cgy., St.L., Dal.	15	940	610	494	**1104**	1.174
13.	**Al MacInnis**, Cgy., St.L.	19	1203	301	803	**1104**	.918
14.	**Pierre Turgeon**, Buf., NYI, Mtl., St.L.	13	929	423	640	**1063**	1.144
15.	**Joe Sakic**, Que., Col.	12	852	403	657	**1060**	1.244
16.	**Pat Verbeek**, N.J., Hfd., NYR, Dal., Det.	18	1293	500	513	**1013**	.783
17.	**Vincent Damphousse**, Tor., Edm., Mtl., S.J.	14	1087	368	631	**999**	.919
18.	**Jaromir Jagr**, Pit.	10	725	387	571	**958**	1.321
19.	**Mark Recchi**, Pit., Phi., Mtl.	12	863	361	572	**933**	1.081
20.	**Theoren Fleury**, Cgy., Col., NYR	12	886	389	529	**918**	1.036
21.	**Rick Tocchet**, Phi., Pit., L.A., Bos., Wsh., Phx.	16	1070	426	488	**914**	.854
22.	**Kirk Muller**, N.J., Mtl., NYI, Tor., Fla., Dal.	16	1161	345	568	**913**	.786
23.	**Brendan Shanahan**, N.J., St.L., Hfd., Det.	13	947	435	444	**879**	.928
24.	**Jeremy Roenick**, Chi., Phx.	12	828	378	493	**871**	1.052
25.	**Joe Nieuwendyk**, Cgy., Dal.	14	883	440	417	**857**	.971
26.	**Tomas Sandstrom**, NYR, L.A., Pit., Det., Ana.	15	983	394	462	**856**	.871
27.	**Chris Chelios**, Mtl., Chi., Det.	17	1157	168	664	**832**	.719
28.	**Steve Thomas**, Tor., Chi., NYI, N.J.	16	1019	378	454	**832**	.816
29.	**John MacLean**, N.J., S.J., NYR	17	1144	406	424	**830**	.726
30.	**Scott Stevens**, Wsh., St.L., N.J.	18	1353	179	649	**828**	.612
31.	**Mike Modano**, Min., Dal.	12	787	349	467	**816**	1.037
32.	**Ed Olczyk**, Chi., Tor., Wpg., NYR, L.A., Pit.	16	1031	342	452	**794**	.770
33.	**Stephane Richer**, Mtl., N.J., T.B., St.L.	16	986	407	384	**791**	.802
34.	**Mats Sundin**, Que., Tor.	10	766	328	460	**788**	1.029
35.	**Ray Ferraro**, Hfd., NYI, NYR, L.A., Atl.	16	1101	365	420	**785**	.713
36.	**Brian Leetch**, NYR.	13	857	184	597	**781**	.911
37.	**Gary Suter**, Cgy., Chi., S.J.	15	995	187	591	**778**	.782
38.	**Murray Craven**, Det., Phi., Hfd., Van., Chi., S.J.	18	1071	266	493	**759**	.709
39.	**Alexander Mogilny**, Buf., Van., N.J.	11	705	353	405	**758**	1.075
40.	**Sergei Fedorov**, Det.	10	672	301	433	**734**	1.092
41.	**Kevin Dineen**, Hfd., Phi., Car., Ott.	16	1059	342	390	**732**	.691
42.	**Teemu Selanne**, Wpg., Ana.	8	564	346	383	**729**	1.293
43.	**Rod Brind'Amour**, St.L., Phi., Car.	12	823	282	443	**725**	.881
44.	**Greg Adams**, N.J., Van., Dal., Phx.	16	996	344	376	**720**	.723
45.	**Steve Duchesne**, L.A., Phi., Que., St.L., Ott., Det.	14	995	218	491	**709**	.713
46.	**Claude Lemieux**, Mtl., N.J., Col.	14	1001	345	353	**698**	.697
47.	**Kevin Stevens**, Pit., Bos., L.A., NYR	13	787	318	371	**689**	.875
48.	**Cliff Ronning**, St.L., Van., Phx., Nsh.	14	856	242	439	**681**	.796
49.	**Trevor Linden**, Van., NYI, Mtl.	12	859	288	375	**663**	.772
50.	**Eric Lindros**, Phi.	8	486	290	369	**659**	1.356
51.	**Kevin Hatcher**, Wsh., Dal., Pit., NYR	16	1100	223	436	**659**	.599
52.	**Ray Sheppard**, Buf., NYR, Det., S.J., Fla., Car.	13	817	357	300	**657**	.804
53.	**Gary Roberts**, Cgy., Car.	14	792	314	335	**649**	.819
54.	**Scott Mellanby**, Phi., Edm., Fla.	15	1016	274	346	**620**	.610
55.	**John LeClair**, Mtl., Phi.	10	665	309	306	**615**	.925
56.	**Derek King**, NYI, Hfd., Tor., St.L.	14	830	261	351	**612**	.737
57.	**Shayne Corson**, Mtl., Edm., St.L.	15	942	241	368	**609**	.646
58.	**Michal Pivonka**, Wsh.	13	825	181	418	**599**	.726
59.	**Tony Amonte**, NYR, Chi.	10	697	290	304	**594**	.852
60.	**Pavel Bure**, Van., Fla.	9	513	325	263	**588**	1.146
61.	**James Patrick**, NYR, Hfd., Cgy., Buf.	17	1046	132	454	**586**	.560
62.	**Peter Bondra**, Wsh.	10	672	337	246	**583**	.868
63.	**Garry Galley**, L.A., Wsh., Bos., Phi., Buf.	16	1093	119	461	**580**	.531
64.	**Dave Ellett**, Wpg., Tor., N.J., Bos., St.L.	16	1129	153	415	**568**	.503
65.	**Fredrik Olausson**, Wpg., Edm., Ana., Pit.	14	931	143	415	**558**	.599
66.	**Doug Weight**, NYR, Edm.	10	624	155	402	**557**	.893
67.	**Keith Tkachuk**, Wpg., Phx.	9	576	294	258	**552**	.958
68.	**Adam Graves**, Det., Edm., NYR	13	907	293	248	**541**	.596
69.	**Dmitri Khristich**, Wsh., L.A., Bos., Tor.	10	680	237	300	**537**	.790
70.	**Scott Young**, Hfd., Pit., Que., Col., Ana., St.L.	12	822	234	302	**536**	.652
71.	**Ron Sutter**, Phi., St.L., Que., NYI, Bos., S.J.	18	1072	204	326	**530**	.494
72.	**Doug Bodger**, Pit., Buf., S.J., N.J., L.A., Van.	16	1071	106	422	**528**	.493
73.	**Joe Murphy**, Det., Edm., Chi., St.L., S.J., Bos., Wsh.	14	765	232	290	**522**	.682
74.	**Andrew Cassels**, Mtl., Hfd., Cgy., Van.	11	728	151	369	**520**	.714
75.	**Benoit Hogue**, Buf., NYI, Tor., Dal., T.B., Phx.	13	771	212	306	**518**	.672
76.	**Ulf Dahlen**, NYR, Min., Dal., S.J., Chi., Wsh.	11	761	246	272	**518**	.681
77.	**Owen Nolan**, Que., Col., S.J.	10	643	254	264	**518**	.806
78.	**Igor Larionov**, Van., S.J., Det.	10	663	138	369	**507**	.765
79.	**Robert Reichel**, Cgy., NYI, Phx.	8	602	209	298	**507**	.842
80.	**Alexei Zhamnov**, Wpg., Chi.	8	526	187	312	**499**	.949
81.	**Nicklas Lidstrom**, Det.	9	693	121	375	**496**	.716
82.	**Peter Forsberg**, Que., Col.	6	393	142	349	**491**	1.249
83.	**Tony Granato**, NYR, L.A., S.J.	12	713	244	239	**483**	.677
84.	**Calle Johansson**, Buf., Wsh.	13	932	107	369	**476**	.511
85.	**Joe Juneau**, Bos., Wsh., Buf., Ott.	9	547	127	339	**466**	.852
86.	**Paul Kariya**, Ana.	6	376	210	254	**464**	1.234
87.	**Kelly Miller**, NYR, Wsh.	15	1057	181	282	**463**	.438
88.	**Nelson Emerson**, St.L., Wpg., Hfd., Car., Chi., Ott., Atl., L.A.	10	652	179	280	**459**	.704
89.	**Petr Nedved**, Van., St.L., NYR, Pit.	9	573	202	250	**452**	.789
90.	**Glen Wesley**, Bos., Hfd., Car.	13	955	113	337	**450**	.471
91.	**Bobby Holik**, Hfd., N.J.	10	717	200	247	**447**	.623
92.	**Rob Brown**, Pit., Hfd., Chi., Dal., L.A.	11	543	190	248	**438**	.807
93.	**Geoff Sanderson**, Hfd., Car., Van., Buf.	10	656	225	212	**437**	.666
94.	**Eric Desjardins**, Mtl., Phi.	12	827	102	332	**434**	.525
95.	**Mike Ricci**, Phi., Que., Col., S.J.	10	708	174	257	**431**	.609
96.	**Teppo Numminen**, Wpg., Phx.	12	872	84	341	**425**	.487
97.	**Keith Primeau**, Det., Hfd., Car., Phi.	10	620	186	237	**423**	.682
98.	**Sergei Zubov**, NYR, Pit., Dal.	8	538	83	332	**415**	.771
99.	**Randy Cunneyworth**, Buf., Pit., Wpg., Hfd., Chi., Ott.	16	866	189	225	**414**	.478
100.	**Jyrki Lumme**, Mtl., Van., Phx.	12	788	100	313	**413**	.524

All-Time Games Played Leaders

Regular Season

* active player

	Player	Team	Seasons	GP
1.	Gordie Howe	Detroit	25	1,687
		Hartford	1	80
		Total	**26**	**1,767**
* 2.	Larry Murphy	Los Angeles	3¼	242
		Washington	5½	453
		Minnesota	1¾	121
		Pittsburgh	4½	336
		Toronto	1¾	151
		Detroit	3¼	255
		Total	**20**	**1,558**
3.	Alex Delvecchio	**Detroit**	**24**	**1,549**
4.	John Bucyk	Detroit	2	104
		Boston	21	1,436
		Total	**23**	**1,540**
* 5.	Ray Bourque	Boston	20¾	1,518
		St. Louis	¼	14
		Total	**21**	**1,532**
6.	Wayne Gretzky	Edmonton	9	696
		Los Angeles	7¾	539
		St. Louis	¼	18
		NY Rangers	3	234
		Total	**20**	**1,487**
* 7.	Mark Messier	Edmonton	12	851
		NY Rangers	6	421
		Vancouver	3	207
		Total	**21**	**1,479**
8.	Tim Horton	Toronto	19¾	1,185
		NY Rangers	1¼	93
		Pittsburgh	1	44
		Buffalo	2	124
		Total	**24**	**1,446**
9.	Mike Gartner	Washington	9¾	758
		Minnesota	1	80
		NY Rangers	4	322
		Toronto	2¼	130
		Phoenix	2	142
		Total	**19**	**1,432**
10.	Harry Howell	NY Rangers	17	1,160
		California	1½	83
		Los Angeles	2½	168
		Total	**21**	**1,411**
11.	Norm Ullman	Detroit	12½	875
		Toronto	7½	535
		Total	**20**	**1,410**
12.	Dale Hunter	Quebec	7	523
		Washington	11¾	872
		Colorado	¼	12
		Total	**19**	**1,407**
* 13.	Ron Francis	Hartford	9¾	714
		Pittsburgh	7¼	533
		Carolina	2	160
		Total	**19**	**1,407**
14.	Stan Mikita	**Chicago**	**22**	**1,394**
* 15.	Paul Coffey	Edmonton	7	532
		Pittsburgh	4¾	331
		Los Angeles	¾	60
		Detroit	3½	231
		Hartford	¼	20
		Philadelphia	1¾	94
		Chicago	¼	10
		Carolina	1¾	113
		Total	**20**	**1,391**
16.	Doug Mohns	Boston	11	710
		Chicago	6½	415
		Minnesota	2½	162
		Atlanta	1	28
		Washington	1	75
		Total	**22**	**1,390**
17.	Larry Robinson	Montreal	17	1,202
		Los Angeles	3	182
		Total	**20**	**1,384**
18.	Dean Prentice	NY Rangers	10½	666
		Boston	3	170
		Detroit	3½	230
		Pittsburgh	2	144
		Minnesota	3	168
		Total	**22**	**1,378**
19.	Ron Stewart	Toronto	13	838
		Boston	2	126
		St. Louis	½	19
		NY Rangers	4	306
		Vancouver	1	42
		NY Islanders	½	22
		Total	**21**	**1,353**
* 20.	Scott Stevens	Washington	8	601
		St. Louis	1	78
		New Jersey	9	674
		Total	**18**	**1,353**
21.	Marcel Dionne	Detroit	4	309
		Los Angeles	11¾	921
		NY Rangers	2¼	118
		Total	**18**	**1,348**
22.	Guy Carbonneau	Montreal	13	912
		St. Louis	1	42
		Dallas	5	364
		Total	**19**	**1,318**
23.	Red Kelly	Detroit	12½	846
		Toronto	7½	470
		Total	**20**	**1,316**
24.	Dave Keon	Toronto	15	1,062
		Hartford	3	234
		Total	**18**	**1,296**
* 25.	Pat Verbeek	New Jersey	7	463
		Hartford	5¾	433
		NY Rangers	1¼	88
		Dallas	3	241
		Detroit	1	68
		Total	**18**	**1,293**
* 26.	Phil Housley	Buffalo	8	608
		Winnipeg	3	232
		St. Louis	1	26
		Calgary	3¾	259
		New Jersey	¼	22
		Washington	2	141
		Total	**18**	**1,288**
* 27.	Dave Andreychuk	Buffalo	10½	763
		Toronto	3¼	223
		New Jersey	3¼	224
		Boston	¾	63
		Colorado	¼	14
		Total	**18**	**1,287**
28.	Phil Esposito	Chicago	4	235
		Boston	8¼	625
		NY Rangers	5¾	422
		Total	**18**	**1,282**
29.	Jean Ratelle	NY Rangers	15¼	862
		Boston	5¾	419
		Total	**21**	**1,281**
30.	Bryan Trottier	NY Islanders	15	1,123
		Pittsburgh	3	156
		Total	**18**	**1,279**
* 31.	Doug Gilmour	St. Louis	5	384
		Calgary	3½	266
		Toronto	5¼	392
		New Jersey	1¼	83
		Chicago	1¾	135
		Buffalo	¼	11
		Total	**17**	**1,271**
32.	Craig Ludwig	Montreal	8	597
		NY Islanders	1	75
		Minnesota	2	151
		Dallas	6	433
		Total	**17**	**1,256**
* 33.	Steve Yzerman	**Detroit**	**17**	**1,256**
34.	Henri Richard	**Montreal**	**20**	**1,256**
35.	Kevin Lowe	Edmonton	15	1,037
		NY Rangers	4	217
		Total	**19**	**1,254**
36.	Jari Kurri	Edmonton	10	754
		Los Angeles	4¾	331
		NY Rangers	¼	14
		Anaheim	1	82
		Colorado	1	70
		Total	**17**	**1,251**
37.	Bill Gadsby	Chicago	8½	468
		NY Rangers	6½	457
		Detroit	5	323
		Total	**20**	**1,248**
38.	Allan Stanley	NY Rangers	6¼	307
		Chicago	1¾	111
		Boston	2	129
		Toronto	10	633
		Philadelphia	1	64
		Total	**21**	**1,244**
39.	Dino Ciccarelli	Minnesota	8¾	602
		Washington	3¼	223
		Detroit	4	254
		Tampa Bay	1½	111
		Florida	1½	42
		Total	**19**	**1,232**
40.	Eddie Westfall	Boston	11	734
		NY Islanders	7	493
		Total	**18**	**1,227**
41.	Brad McCrimmon	Boston	3	228
		Philadelphia	5	367
		Calgary	3	231
		Detroit	3	203
		Hartford	3	156
		Phoenix	1	37
		Total	**18**	**1,222**
42.	Eric Nesterenko	Toronto	5	206
		Chicago	16	1,013
		Total	**21**	**1,219**
43.	Marcel Pronovost	Detroit	16	983
		Toronto	5	223
		Total	**21**	**1,206**
* 44.	Al MacInnis	Calgary	13	803
		St. Louis	6	400
		Total	**19**	**1,203**
45.	Denis Savard	Chicago	12¼	881
		Montreal	3	210
		Tampa Bay	1¾	105
		Total	**17**	**1,196**
46.	Dave Babych	Winnipeg	5¼	390
		Hartford	5¾	349
		Vancouver	6¾	409
		Philadelphia	1	39
		Los Angeles	¼	8
		Total	**19**	**1,195**
47.	Gilbert Perreault	**Buffalo**	**17**	**1,191**
48.	Dale Hawerchuk	Winnipeg	9	713
		Buffalo	5	342
		St. Louis	¾	66
		Philadelphia	1¼	67
		Total	**16**	**1,188**
49.	Brian Bellows	Minnesota	10	753
		Montreal	3	200
		Tampa Bay	1¼	86
		Anaheim	¾	62
		Washington	2	87
		Total	**17**	**1,188**
50.	George Armstrong	**Toronto**	**21**	**1,187**
51.	Frank Mahovlich	Toronto	11¾	720
		Detroit	2¾	198
		Montreal	3½	263
		Total	**18**	**1,181**
52.	Bob Carpenter	Washington	6¼	490
		NY Rangers	½	28
		Los Angeles	1¾	120
		Boston	3½	187
		New Jersey	6	353
		Total	**18**	**1,178**
53.	Don Marshall	Montreal	10	585
		NY Rangers	7	479
		Buffalo	1	62
		Toronto	1	50
		Total	**19**	**1,176**
* 54.	Kirk Muller	New Jersey	7	556
		Montreal	3¾	267
		NY Islanders	¾	27
		Toronto	1¼	102
		Florida	2¼	162
		Dallas	1	47
		Total	**16**	**1,161**
55.	Bob Gainey	**Montreal**	**16**	**1,160**
* 56.	Chris Chelios	Montreal	7	402
		Chicago	8¼	65
		Detroit	1¼	91
		Total	**17**	**1,157**
57.	Leo Boivin	Toronto	3¼	137
		Boston	11½	717
		Detroit	1¼	85
		Pittsburgh	1½	114
		Minnesota	1½	97
		Total	**19**	**1,150**
58.	Borje Salming	Toronto	16	1,099
		Detroit	1	49
		Total	**17**	**1,148**
59.	Bobby Clarke	**Philadelphia**	**15**	**1,144**
* 60.	John MacLean	New Jersey	13¼	934
		San Jose	¾	51
		NY Rangers	2	159
		Total	**16**	**1,144**
61.	Glenn Anderson	Edmonton	11½	845
		Toronto	2¾	221
		NY Rangers	¼	12
		St. Louis	1½	51
		Total	**16**	**1,129**

	Player	Team	Seasons	GP
* 62.	**Dave Ellett**	Winnipeg	6¼	475
		Toronto	6½	446
		New Jersey	¼	20
		Boston	2	136
		St. Louis	1	52
		Total	**16**	**1,129**
63.	**Jamie Macoun**	Calgary	8½	586
		Toronto	6¼	466
		Detroit	1¼	76
		Total	**16**	**1,128**
64.	**Bob Nevin**	Toronto	5¾	250
		NY Rangers	7¼	505
		Minnesota	2	138
		Los Angeles	3	235
		Total	**18**	**1,128**
65.	**Murray Oliver**	Detroit	2½	101
		Boston	6½	429
		Toronto	3	226
		Minnesota	5	371
		Total	**17**	**1,127**
66.	**Bernie Nicholls**	Los Angeles	8½	602
		NY Rangers	1¾	104
		Edmonton	1¼	95
		New Jersey	1½	84
		Chicago	2	107
		San Jose	3	135
		Total	**18**	**1,127**
67.	**Guy Lafleur**	Montreal	14	961
		NY Rangers	1	67
		Quebec	2	98
		Total	**17**	**1,126**
68.	**Jean Beliveau**	**Montreal**	**20**	**1,125**
69.	**Brad Park**	NY Rangers	7½	465
		Boston	7½	501
		Detroit	2	147
		Total	**17**	**1,113**
70.	**Doug Harvey**	Montreal	14	890
		NY Rangers	3	151
		Detroit	1	2
		St. Louis	1	70
		Total	**19**	**1,113**
71.	**Lanny McDonald**	Toronto	6½	477
		Colorado	1¾	142
		Calgary	7¾	441
		Total	**16**	**1,111**
72.	**Dave Taylor**	**Los Angeles**	**17**	**1,111**
73.	**Brent Sutter**	NY Islanders	11¼	694
		Chicago	6¾	417
		Total	**18**	**1,111**
74.	**Butch Goring**	Los Angeles	10¾	736
		NY Islanders	4¾	332
		Boston	½	39
		Total	**16**	**1,107**
75.	**Garry Unger**	Toronto	½	15
		Detroit	3	216
		St. Louis	8½	662
		Atlanta	1	79
		Los Angeles	¾	58
		Edmonton	2¼	75
		Total	**16**	**1,105**
76.	**Pit Martin**	Detroit	3¼	119
		Boston	1¾	111
		Chicago	10¼	740
		Vancouver	1¾	131
		Total	**17**	**1,101**
* 77.	**Ray Ferraro**	Hartford	6¼	442
		NY Islanders	4¾	316
		NY Rangers	¾	65
		Los Angeles	3¼	197
		Atlanta	1	81
		Total	**16**	**1,101**
* 78.	**Kevin Hatcher**	Washington	10	685
		Dallas	2	121
		Pittsburgh	3	220
		NY Rangers	1	74
		Total	**16**	**1,100**
79.	**Neal Broten**	Minnesota	13	876
		Dallas	2	116
		New Jersey	1¾	88
		Los Angeles	¼	19
		Total	**17**	**1,099**
80.	**Jay Wells**	Los Angeles	9	604
		Philadelphia	1¾	126
		Buffalo	2	85
		NY Rangers	3¼	186
		St. Louis	1	76
		Tampa Bay	1	21
		Total	**18**	**1,098**
81.	**Gordie Roberts**	Hartford	1½	107
		Minnesota	7	555
		Philadelphia	¼	11
		St. Louis	2½	166
		Pittsburgh	1¾	134
		Boston	2	124
		Total	**15**	**1,097**
82.	**Darryl Sittler**	Toronto	11½	844
		Philadelphia	2½	191
		Detroit	1	61
		Total	**15**	**1,096**
83.	**Craig MacTavish**	Boston	5	217
		Edmonton	8¾	701
		NY Rangers	¼	12
		Philadelphia	1¾	100
		St. Louis	1¼	63
		Total	**17**	**1,093**
* 84.	**Gary Galley**	Los Angeles	5½	361
		Washington	1½	76
		Boston	3½	257
		Philadelphia	3¼	236
		Buffalo	2¼	163
		Total	**16**	**1,093**
85.	**Michel Goulet**	Quebec	10¾	813
		Chicago	4¼	276
		Total	**15**	**1,089**
86.	**Carol Vadnais**	Montreal	2	42
		Oakland	2	152
		California	1¾	94
		Boston	3½	263
		NY Rangers	6¾	485
		New Jersey	1	51
		Total	**17**	**1,087**
* 87.	**Vincent Damphousse**	Toronto	5	394
		Edmonton	1	80
		Montreal	6¾	519
		San Jose	1¼	94
		Total	**14**	**1,087**
88.	**Brad Marsh**	Atlanta	2	160
		Calgary	1¼	97
		Philadelphia	6¾	514
		Toronto	2¾	181
		Detroit	1¼	75
		Ottawa	1	59
		Total	**15**	**1,086**
* 89.	**Ulf Samuelsson**	Hartford	6¾	463
		Pittsburgh	4¼	277
		NY Rangers	3¾	287
		Detroit	¼	4
		Philadelphia	1	49
		Total	**16**	**1,080**
90.	**Bob Pulford**	Toronto	14	947
		Los Angeles	2	132
		Total	**16**	**1,079**
91.	**Bobby Smith**	Minnesota	8¼	572
		Montreal	6¾	505
		Total	**15**	**1,077**
* 92.	**Ron Sutter**	Philadelphia	9	555
		St. Louis	2½	163
		Quebec	½	82
		NY Islanders	1	27
		Boston	1	18
		San Jose	4	272
		Total	**18**	**1,072**
* 93.	**Doug Bodger**	Pittsburgh	4¼	299
		Buffalo	7	479
		San Jose	2¼	166
		New Jersey	½	49
		Los Angeles	1	65
		Vancouver	1	13
		Total	**16**	**1,071**
* 94.	**Murray Craven**	Detroit	2	46
		Philadelphia	7¼	523
		Hartford	1½	128
		Vancouver	1¼	88
		Chicago	3	157
		San Jose	3	129
		Total	**18**	**1,071**
95.	**Craig Ramsay**	**Buffalo**	**14**	**1,070**
* 96.	**Ken Daneyko**	**New Jersey**	**16**	**1,070**
* 97.	**Rick Tocchet**	Philadelphia	8	547
		Pittsburgh	2¼	150
		Los Angelas	1¾	80
		Boston	1	67
		Washington	¼	13
		Phoenix	2¾	213
		Total	**16**	**1,070**
98.	**Mike Ramsey**	Buffalo	13¾	911
		Pittsburgh	1¼	77
		Detroit	3	82
		Total	**18**	**1,070**
99.	**Andy Bathgate**	NY Rangers	11¾	719
		Toronto	1¼	70
		Detroit	2	130
		Pittsburgh	2	150
		Total	**17**	**1,069**
100.	**Ted Lindsay**	Detroit	14	862
		Chicago	3	206
		Total	**17**	**1,068**
101.	**Terry Harper**	Montreal	10	554
		Los Angeles	3	234
		Detroit	4	252
		St. Louis	1	11
		Colorado	1	15
		Total	**19**	**1,066**
102.	**Rod Gilbert**	**NY Rangers**	**18**	**1,065**
103.	**Bobby Hull**	Chicago	15	1,036
		Winnipeg	⅔	18
		Hartford	⅓	9
		Total	**16**	**1,063**
104.	**Joe Mullen**	St. Louis	4½	301
		Calgary	4½	345
		Pittsburgh	6	379
		Boston	1	37
		Total	**16**	**1,062**
* 105.	**Bob Rouse**	Minnesota	5¾	351
		Washington	2	130
		Toronto	3¼	237
		Detroit	4	247
		San Jose	2	96
		Total	**17**	**1,061**
106.	**Denis Potvin**	**NY Islanders**	**15**	**1,060**
* 107.	**Kevin Dineen**	Hartford	8¾	587
		Philadelphia	4¼	284
		Carolina	2	121
		Ottawa	1	67
		Total	**16**	**1,059**
* 108.	**Kelly Miller**	NY Rangers	2½	117
		Washington	12½	940
		Total	**15**	**1,057**
109.	**Jean Guy Talbot**	Montreal	13	791
		Minnesota	¼	4
		Detroit	½	32
		St. Louis	2½	172
		Buffalo	¾	57
		Total	**17**	**1,056**
110.	**Randy Carlyle**	Toronto	2	94
		Pittsburgh	5¾	397
		Winnipeg	9¼	564
		Total	**17**	**1,055**
111.	**Ivan Boldirev**	Boston	1¼	13
		California	2¾	191
		Chicago	4¾	384
		Atlanta	1	65
		Vancouver	2¾	216
		Detroit	2½	183
		Total	**15**	**1,052**
* 112.	**Adam Oates**	Detroit	4	246
		St. Louis	2¾	195
		Boston	5	368
		Washington	3¼	240
		Total	**15**	**1,049**
113.	**Geoff Courtnall**	Boston	4¾	259
		Edmonton	¼	12
		Washington	2	159
		St. Louis	5¾	326
		Vancouver	4¼	292
		Total	**17**	**1,048**
114.	**Eddie Shack**	NY Rangers	2¼	141
		Toronto	8¾	504
		Boston	2	120
		Los Angeles	1¼	84
		Buffalo	1½	111
		Pittsburgh	1¼	87
		Total	**17**	**1,047**
* 115.	**James Patrick**	NY Rangers	10¼	671
		Hartford	½	47
		Calgary	4¼	217
		Buffalo	2	111
		Total	**17**	**1,046**
116.	**Rob Ramage**	Colorado	3	234
		St. Louis	5¾	441
		Calgary	1¼	80
		Toronto	2	160
		Minnesota	1	34
		Tampa Bay	¾	66
		Montreal	½	14
		Philadelphia	¾	15
		Total	**15**	**1,044**
* 117.	**Luc Robitaille**	Los Angeles	11	850
		Pittsburgh	1	46
		NY Rangers	2	146
		Total	**14**	**1,042**
118.	**Serge Savard**	Montreal	15	917
		Winnipeg	2	123
		Total	**17**	**1,040**
119.	**Ron Ellis**	**Toronto**	**16**	**1,034**
120.	**Harold Snepsts**	Vancouver	11¾	781
		Minnesota	1	71
		Detroit	3	120
		St. Louis	1¼	61
		Total	**17**	**1,033**
121.	**Ralph Backstrom**	Montreal	14½	844
		Los Angeles	2¼	172
		Chicago	¼	16
		Total	**17**	**1,032**
* 122.	**Sylvain Cote**	Hartford	7	382
		Washington	6¾	483
		Toronto	1½	94
		Chicago	½	45
		Dallas	¼	28
		Total	**16**	**1,032**
* 123.	**Ed Olczyk**	Chicago	5	322
		Toronto	3¼	257
		Winnipeg	3½	214
		NY Rangers	2¼	103
		Los Angeles	¾	67
		Pittsburgh	1¼	68
		Total	**16**	**1,031**

	Player	Team	Seasons	GP
124.	Dick Duff	Toronto	9¾	582
		NY Rangers	¾	43
		Montreal	5	305
		Los Angeles	¾	39
		Buffalo	1¾	61
		Total	**18**	**1,030**
125.	Russ Courtnall	Toronto	5¼	309
		Montreal	3¾	250
		Minnesota	1	84
		Dallas	1½	116
		Vancouver	2¼	141
		NY Rangers	¼	14
		Los Angeles	2	115
		Total	**16**	**1,029**
126.	John Tonelli	NY Islanders	7¾	584
		Calgary	2¼	161
		Los Angeles	3	231
		Chicago	¾	33
		Quebec	¼	19
		Total	**14**	**1,028**
127.	Gaetan Duchesne	Washington	6	451
		Quebec	2	150
		Minnesota	4	297
		San Jose	1¾	117
		Florida	¼	13
		Total	**14**	**1,028**
128.	Wayne Cashman	Boston	17	1,027
129.	Doug Wilson	Chicago	14	938
		San Jose	2	86
		Total	**16**	**1,024**
130.	Keith Acton	Montreal	4¼	228
		Minnesota	4¼	343
		Edmonton	1	72
		Philadelphia	4½	303
		Washington	¼	6
		NY Islanders	¾	71
		Total	**15**	**1,023**
131.	Jim Neilson	NY Rangers	12	810
		California	2	98
		Cleveland	2	115
		Total	**16**	**1,023**

	Player	Team	Seasons	GP
132.	Don Lever	Vancouver	7⅔	593
		Atlanta	⅓	28
		Calgary	1¼	85
		Colorado	¾	59
		New Jersey	3	216
		Buffalo	2	39
		Total	**15**	**1,020**
* 133.	Steve Thomas	Toronto	5	320
		Chicago	4¼	231
		NY Islanders	3¾	275
		New Jersey	3	193
		Total	**16**	**1,019**
134.	Mike Foligno	Detroit	2½	186
		Buffalo	9	664
		Toronto	2¾	129
		Florida	¾	39
		Total	**15**	**1,018**
135.	Charlie Huddy	Edmonton	11	694
		Los Angeles	3¼	226
		Buffalo	2½	85
		St. Louis	¼	12
		Total	**17**	**1,017**
136.	Phil Russell	Chicago	6¾	504
		Atlanta	1¼	93
		Calgary	3	229
		New Jersey	2¾	172
		Buffalo	1¼	18
		Total	**15**	**1,016**
137.	Brian Propp	Philadelphia	10¾	790
		Boston	¼	14
		Minnesota	3	147
		Hartford	1	65
		Total	**15**	**1,016**
* 138.	Scott Mellanby	Philadelphia	6	355
		Edmonton	2	149
		Florida	7	512
		Total	**15**	**1,016**
139.	Laurie Boschman	Toronto	2¾	187
		Edmonton	1	73
		Winnipeg	7¼	526
		New Jersey	2	153
		Ottawa	1	70
		Total	**14**	**1,009**

	Player	Team	Seasons	GP
140.	Dave Christian	Winnipeg	4	230
		Washington	6½	504
		Boston	1½	128
		St. Louis	1	78
		Chicago	¾	69
		Total	**15**	**1,009**
* 141.	Petr Svoboda	Montreal	7¾	534
		Buffalo	3	139
		Philadelphia	3¾	232
		Tampa Bay	1½	104
		Total	**16**	**1,009**
142.	Dave Lewis	NY Islanders	6¾	514
		Los Angeles	3¼	221
		New Jersey	3	209
		Detroit	2	64
		Total	**15**	**1,008**
143.	Bob Murray	Chicago	15	1,008
144.	Jim Roberts	Montreal	9⅔	611
		St. Louis	5⅓	395
		Total	**15**	**1,006**
145.	Steve Larmer	Chicago	13	891
		NY Rangers	2	115
		Total	**15**	**1,006**
146.	Rick Middleton	NY Rangers	2	124
		Boston	12	881
		Total	**14**	**1,005**
147.	Claude Provost	Montreal	15	1,005
148.	Ryan Walter	Washington	4	307
		Montreal	9	604
		Vancouver	2	92
		Total	**15**	**1,003**
149.	Vic Hadfield	NY Rangers	13	839
		Pittsburgh	3	163
		Total	**16**	**1,002**
* 150.	Claude Lemieux	Montreal	7	281
		New Jersey	5¾	423
		Colorado	4¼	297
		Total	**17**	**1,001**
151.	Bernie Federko	St. Louis	14	927
		Detroit	1	73
		Total	**15**	**1,000**

All-Time Penalty-Minute Leaders

* active player

(Regular season. Minimum 2,000 minutes)

	Player	Seasons	Games	Penalty Minutes	Mins. per game
1.	Tiger Williams, Tor., Van., Det., L.A., Hfd.	14	962	3966	4.12
2.	Dale Hunter, Que., Wsh., Col.	20	1407	3565	2.53
* 3.	Marty McSorley, Pit., Edm., L.A., NYR, S.J., Bos.	17	961	3381	3.52
4.	Tim Hunter, Cgy., Que., Van., S.J.	17	815	3146	3.86
5.	Chris Nilan, Mtl., NYR, Bos.	13	688	3043	4.42
* 6.	Bob Probert, Det., Chi.	15	795	3021	3.80
*7.	Rick Tocchet, Phi., Pit., L.A., Bos., Wsh., Phx.	16	1070	2863	2.68
* 8.	Craig Berube, Phi., Tor., Cgy., Wsh.	14	873	2813	3.22
* 9.	Pat Verbeek, N.J., Hfd., NYR, Dal., Det.	18	1293	2760	2.13
* 10.	Rob Ray, Buf.	11	714	2687	3.76
* 11.	Dave Manson, Chi., Edm., Wpg., Phx., Mtl., Dal.	14	982	2666	2.71
* 12.	Tie Domi, Tor., NYR, Wpg.	11	628	2656	4.23
* 13.	Scott Stevens, Wsh., St.L., N.J.	18	1353	2607	1.93
14.	Willi Plett, Atl., Cgy., Min., Bos.	13	834	2572	3.08
* 15.	Joe Kocur, Det., NYR, Van.	16	820	2519	3.07
16.	Basil McRae, Que., Tor., Det., Min., T.B., St.L., Chi.	16	576	2457	4.27
* 17.	Ulf Samuelsson, Hfd., Pit., NYR, Det., Phi.	16	1080	2453	2.27
* 18.	Gino Odjick, Van., NYI, Phi.	10	539	2391	4.44
* 19.	Chris Chelios, Mtl., Chi., Det.	17	1157	2385	2.06
20.	Jay Wells, L.A., Phi., Buf., NYR, St.L., T.B.	18	1098	2359	2.15
* 21.	Ken Daneyko, N.J.	17	1070	2339	2.19
22.	Garth Butcher, Van., St.L., Que., Tor.	14	897	2302	2.57
23.	Shane Churla, Hfd., Cgy., Min., Dal., L.A., NYR, New York Rangers	12	488	2301	4.72
24.	Dave Schultz, Phi., L.A., Pit., Buf.	9	535	2294	4.29
25.	Laurie Boschman, Tor., Edm., Wpg., N.J., Ott.	14	1009	2265	2.24
26.	Ken Baumgartner, L.A., NYI, Tor., Ana., Bos.	13	696	2244	3.22
27.	Rob Ramage, Col., St.L., Cgy., Tor., Min., T.B., Mtl., Phi.	15	1044	2226	2.13
28.	Bryan Watson, Mtl., Det., Oak., Pit., St.L., Wsh.	16	878	2212	2.52
* 29.	Steve Smith, Edm., Chi., Cgy.	16	791	2122	2.68
30.	Terry O'Reilly, Bos.	14	891	2095	2.35
31.	Al Secord, Bos., Chi., Tor., Phi.	12	766	2093	2.73
* 32.	Gary Roberts, Cgy., Car.	14	792	2079	2.63
33.	Ron Stern, Van., Cgy., S.J.	13	638	2077	3.26
* 34.	Mick Vukota, NYI, T.B., Mtl.	11	574	2071	3.61
35.	Gord Donnelly, Que., Wpg., Buf., Dal.	12	554	2069	3.73
36.	Mike Foligno, Det., Buf., Tor., Fla.	16	1018	2049	2.01
37.	Phil Russell, Chi., Atl., Cgy., N.J., Buf.	15	1016	2038	2.01
* 38.	Kevin Dineen, Hfd., Phi., Car., Ott.	16	1059	2029	1.92
* 39.	Kris King, Det., NYR, Wpg., Phx., Tor.	13	836	2022	2.42
40.	Kelly Chase, St.L., Hfd., Tor.	11	458	2017	4.40
41.	Harold Snepsts, Van., Min., Det., St.L.	17	1033	2009	1.94

Goaltending Records

All-Time Shutout Leaders

Goaltender	Team	Seasons	Games	Shutouts
Terry Sawchuk	Detroit	14	734	85
(1949-1970)	Boston	2	102	11
	Toronto	3	91	4
	Los Angeles	1	36	2
	NY Rangers	1	8	1
	Total	21	971	**103**
George Hainsworth	Montreal	$7\frac{1}{2}$	318	75
(1926-1937)	Toronto	$3\frac{1}{2}$	147	19
	Total	11	465	**94**
Glenn Hall	Detroit	4	148	17
(1952-1971)	Chicago	10	618	51
	St. Louis	4	140	16
	Total	18	906	**84**
Jacques Plante	Montreal	11	556	58
(1952-1973)	NY Rangers	2	98	5
	St. Louis	2	69	10
	Toronto	$2\frac{3}{4}$	106	7
	Boston	$\frac{1}{4}$	8	2
	Total	18	837	**82**
Tiny Thompson	Boston	$10\frac{1}{4}$	468	74
(1928-1940)	Detroit	$1\frac{3}{4}$	85	7
	Total	12	553	**81**
Alex Connell	Ottawa	8	293	64
(1924-1937)	Detroit	1	48	6
	NY Americans	1	1	0
	Mtl. Maroons	2	75	11
	Total	12	417	**81**
Tony Esposito	Montreal	1	13	2
(1968-1984)	Chicago	15	873	74
	Total	16	886	**76**
Lorne Chabot	NY Rangers	2	80	21
(1926-1937)	Toronto	5	214	33
	Montreal	1	47	8
	Chicago	1	48	8
	Mtl. Maroons	1	16	2
	NY Americans	1	6	1
	Total	11	411	**73**
Harry Lumley	Detroit	$6\frac{1}{2}$	324	26
(1943-1960)	NY Rangers	$\frac{1}{2}$	1	0
	Chicago	2	134	5
	Toronto	4	267	34
	Boston	3	78	6
	Total	16	804	**71**
Roy Worters	Pittsburgh Pirates	3	123	22
(1925-1937)	NY Americans	9	360	45
*	Montreal		1	0
	Total	12	484	**67**
Turk Broda	Toronto	14	629	**62**
(1936-1952)				
John Ross Roach	Toronto	7	222	13
(1921-1935)	NY Rangers	4	89	30
	Detroit	3	180	15
	Total	14	491	**58**
Clint Benedict	Ottawa	7	158	19
(1917-1930)	Mtl. Maroons	6	204	38
	Total	13	362	**57**
Bernie Parent	Boston	2	57	1
(1965-1979)	Philadelphia	$9\frac{1}{2}$	486	50
	Toronto	$1\frac{1}{2}$	65	3
	Total	13	608	**54**
Ed Giacomin	NY Rangers	$10\frac{1}{4}$	539	49
(1965-1978)	Detroit	$2\frac{3}{4}$	71	5
	Total	13	610	**54**
David Kerr	Mtl. Maroons	3	101	11
(1930-1941)	NY Americans	1	1	0
	NY Rangers	7	324	40
	Total	11	426	**51**
Rogie Vachon	Montreal	$5\frac{1}{4}$	206	13
(1966-1982)	Los Angeles	$6\frac{3}{4}$	389	32
	Detroit	2	109	4
	Boston	2	91	2
	Total	16	795	**51**
Ed Belfour	Chicago	$7\frac{2}{3}$	415	30
(1988-2000)	San Jose	$\frac{1}{3}$	13	1
	Dallas	3	184	18
	Total	11	612	**49**
Patrick Roy	Montreal	$11\frac{1}{2}$	551	29
(1984-2000)	Colorado	$4\frac{1}{2}$	290	19
	Total	16	841	**48**
Ken Dryden	Montreal	8	397	**46**
(1970-1979)				
Dominik Hasek	Chicago	2	25	1
(1990-2000)	Buffalo	8	424	44
	Total	10	449	**45**
Gump Worsley	NY Rangers	10	582	24
(1952-1974)	Montreal	$6\frac{1}{2}$	172	16
	Minnesota	$4\frac{1}{2}$	107	3
	Total	21	861	**43**
Chuck Gardiner	Chicago	7	316	**42**
(1927-1934)				
Martin Brodeur	New Jersey	8	447	**42**
(1991-2000)				
Frank Brimsek	Boston	9	444	35
(1938-1950)	Chicago	1	70	5
	Total	10	514	**40**
John Vanbiesbrouck	NY Rangers	11	449	16
(1981-2000)	Florida	5	268	13
	Philadelphia	2	112	9
	Total	18	829	**38**
Johnny Bower	NY Rangers	3	77	5
(1953-1970)	Toronto	12	475	32
	Total	15	552	**37**
Tom Barrasso	Buffalo	$5\frac{1}{4}$	226	13
(1983-2000)	Pittsburgh	$11\frac{1}{2}$	460	22
	Ottawa	$\frac{1}{4}$	7	0
	Total	17	733	**35**

*Played 1 game for Canadiens in 1929-30.

Ten or More Shutouts, One Season

Number of Shutouts	Goaltender	Team	Season	Length of Schedule
22	George Hainsworth	Montreal	1928-29	44
15	Alex Connell	Ottawa	1925-26	36
	Alex Connell	Ottawa	1927-28	44
	Hal Winkler	Boston	1927-28	44
	Tony Esposito	Chicago	1969-70	76
14	George Hainsworth	Montreal	1926-27	44
13	Clint Benedict	Mtl. Maroons	1926-27	44
	Alex Connell	Ottawa	1926-27	44
	George Hainsworth	Montreal	1927-28	44
	John Ross Roach	NY Rangers	1928-29	44
	Roy Worters	NY Americans	1928-29	44
	Harry Lumley	Toronto	1953-54	70
	Dominik Hasek	Buffalo	1997-98	82
12	Tiny Thompson	Boston	1928-29	44
	Lorne Chabot	Toronto	1928-29	44
	Chuck Gardiner	Chicago	1930-31	44
	Terry Sawchuk	Detroit	1951-52	70
	Terry Sawchuk	Detroit	1953-54	70
	Terry Sawchuk	Detroit	1954-55	70
	Glenn Hall	Detroit	1955-56	70
	Bernie Parent	Philadelphia	1973-74	78
	Bernie Parent	Philadelphia	1974-75	80
11	Lorne Chabot	NY Rangers	1927-28	44
	Harry Holmes	Detroit	1927-28	44
	Clint Benedict	Mtl. Maroons	1928-29	44
	Joe Miller	Pittsburgh Pirates	1928-29	44
	Tiny Thompson	Boston	1932-33	48
	Terry Sawchuk	Detroit	1950-51	70
10	Lorne Chabot	NY Rangers	1926-27	44
	Roy Worters	Pittsburgh Pirates	1927-28	44
	Clarence Dolson	Detroit	1928-29	44
	John Ross Roach	Detroit	1932-33	48
	Chuck Gardiner	Chicago	1933-34	48
	Tiny Thompson	Boston	1935-36	48
	Frank Brimsek	Boston	1938-39	48
	Bill Durnan	Montreal	1948-49	60
	Gerry McNeil	Montreal	1952-53	70
	Harry Lumley	Toronto	1952-53	70
	Tony Esposito	Chicago	1973-74	78
	Ken Dryden	Montreal	1976-77	80
	Martin Brodeur	New Jersey	1996-97	82
	Martin Brodeur	New Jersey	1997-98	82
	Byron Dafoe	Boston	1998-99	82

All-Time Win Leaders

(Minimum 210 Wins)

Wins	Goaltender	GP	Dec.	Losses	Ties	%
447	Terry Sawchuk	971	949	330	172	.562
444	* Patrick Roy	841	811	264	103	.611
435	Jacques Plante	837	827	247	145	.614
423	Tony Esposito	886	880	306	151	.566
407	Glenn Hall	906	896	326	163	.545
403	* Grant Fuhr	868	812	295	114	.567
372	Andy Moog	713	669	209	88	.622
371	* Mike Vernon	722	698	241	86	.593
358	* John Vanbiesbrouck	829	790	318	114	.525
355	Rogie Vachon	795	773	291	127	.541
353	* Tom Barrasso	733	693	259	81	.568
335	Gump Worsley	861	837	352	150	.490
330	Harry Lumley	803	801	329	142	.501
308	* Ed Belfour	612	585	195	82	.597
305	Billy Smith	680	643	233	105	.556
302	Turk Broda	629	627	224	101	.562
296	Ron Hextall	608	579	214	69	.571
294	Mike Liut	663	639	271	74	.518
289	Ed Giacomin	610	594	208	97	.568
286	Dan Bouchard	655	631	232	113	.543
284	Tiny Thompson	553	553	194	75	.581
284	* Curtis Joseph	587	568	216	68	.560
271	Bernie Parent	608	590	198	121	.562
271	Kelly Hrudey	677	624	265	88	.505
270	Gilles Meloche	788	752	351	131	.446
268	Don Beaupre	667	620	277	75	.493
258	Ken Dryden	397	389	57	74	.758
252	Frank Brimsek	514	514	182	80	.568
252	* Mike Richter	553	522	205	65	.545
250	Johnny Bower	552	535	195	90	.551
246	George Hainsworth	465	465	145	74	.609
246	Pete Peeters	489	452	155	51	.601
244	* Martin Brodeur	447	434	125	65	.637
240	Bill Ranford	647	595	279	76	.467
237	* Kirk McLean	589	560	252	71	.487
236	Reggie Lemelin	507	461	162	63	.580
234	Eddie Johnston	592	571	257	80	.480
231	Glenn Resch	571	537	224	82	.507
230	Gerry Cheevers	418	406	102	74	.658
225	* Ken Wregget	575	526	248	53	.478
219	John Ross Roach	492	491	204	68	.515
218	* Sean Burke	571	543	252	73	.469
215	Greg Millen	604	588	284	89	.441
210	* Dominik Hasek	449	428	150	68	.570

* active player

Active Shutout Leaders

(Minimum 20 Shutouts)

Goaltender	Teams	Seasons	Games	Shutouts
Ed Belfour	Chi., S.J., Dal.	10	612	49
Patrick Roy	Montreal, Colorado	16	841	48
Dominik Hasek	Chicago, Buffalo	10	449	45
Martin Brodeur	New Jersey	8	447	42
John Vanbiesbrouck	NYR, Fla., Phi.	18	829	38
Tom Barrasso	Buf., Pit., Ott.	17	733	35
Chris Osgood	Detroit	7	337	29
Guy Hebert	St. Louis, Anaheim	9	437	26
Curtis Joseph	St.L., Edm., Tor.	11	587	26
Arturs Irbe	S.J., Dal., Van., Car.	9	396	24
Mike Vernon	Cgy., Det., S.J., Fla.	17	722	23
Jeff Hackett	NYI, S.J., Chi., Mtl.	11	403	22
Mike Richter	NY Rangers	11	553	22
Sean Burke	N.J., Hfd., Car., Van., Phi., Fla., Phx.	12	571	22
Kirk McLean	N.J, Van., Car., Fla., NYR	15	589	22
Nikolai Khabibulin	Winnipeg, Phoenix	5	284	21

Active Goaltending Leaders

(Ranked by winning percentage; minimum 250 games played)

Goaltender	Teams	Seasons	GP	Decisions	W	L	T	Winning %
Chris Osgood	Detroit	7	337	329	196	91	42	.660
Martin Brodeur	New Jersey	8	447	434	244	125	65	.637
Patrick Roy	Montreal, Colorado	16	841	811	444	264	103	.611
Ed Belfour	Chi., S.J., Dal.	11	612	585	308	195	82	.597
Mike Vernon	Cgy., Det., S.J., Fla.	17	722	698	371	241	86	.593
Dominik Hasek	Chicago, Buffalo	10	449	428	210	150	68	.570
Tom Barrasso	Buf., Pit., Ott.	17	733	693	353	259	81	.568
Grant Fuhr	Edm., Tor., Buf., L.A., St.L., Cgy.	19	868	812	403	295	114	.567
Curtis Joseph	St. L., Edm., Tor.	11	587	568	284	216	68	.560
Mike Richter	NY Rangers	11	553	522	252	205	65	.545
John Vanbiesbrouck	NYR, Fla., Phi.	18	829	790	358	318	114	.525
Nikolai Khabibulin	Winnipeg, Phoenix	6	284	269	126	113	30	.524
Olaf Kolzig	Washington	9	272	251	114	105	32	.518
Jocelyn Thibault	Que., Col., Mtl., Chi.	7	327	306	136	127	43	.515
Stephane Fiset	Que., Col., L.A.	11	381	356	161	152	43	.513
Trevor Kidd	Cgy., Car., Fla.	8	278	259	114	108	37	.512

Goals Against Average Leaders

(Minimum 13 games played, 1994-95; minimum 27 games played, 1992-93 to 1993-94, 1995-96 to 1997-98; 25 games played, 1926-27 to 1991-92; 15 games played, 1917-18 to 1925-26.)

Season	Goaltender and Club	GP	Mins.	GA	SO	AVG.	Season	Goaltender and Club	GP	Mins.	GA	SO	AVG.
1999-2000	Brian Boucher, Philadelphia	35	2,038	65	4	1.91	1957-58	Jacques Plante, Montreal	57	3,386	119	9	2.11
1998-99	Ron Tugnutt, Ottawa	43	2,508	75	3	1.79	1956-57	Jacques Plante, Montreal	61	3,660	122	9	2.00
1997-98	Ed Belfour, Dallas	61	3,581	112	9	1.88	1955-56	Jacques Plante, Montreal	64	3,840	119	7	1.86
1996-97	Martin Brodeur, New Jersey	67	3,838	120	10	1.88	1954-55	Harry Lumley, Toronto	69	4,140	134	8	1.94
1995-96	Ron Hextall, Philadelphia	53	3,102	112	4	2.17	1953-54	Harry Lumley, Toronto	69	4,140	128	13	1.86
1994-95	Dominik Hasek, Buffalo	41	2,416	85	5	2.11	1952-53	Terry Sawchuk, Detroit	63	3,780	120	9	1.90
1993-94	Dominik Hasek, Buffalo	58	3,358	109	7	1.95	1951-52	Terry Sawchuk, Detroit	70	4,200	133	12	1.90
1992-93	Felix Potvin, Toronto	48	2,781	116	2	2.50	1950-51	Al Rollins, Toronto	40	2,367	70	5	1.77
1991-92	Patrick Roy, Montreal	67	3,935	155	5	2.36	1949-50	Bill Durnan, Montreal	64	3,840	141	8	2.20
1990-91	Ed Belfour, Chicago	74	4,127	170	4	2.47	1948-49	Bill Durnan, Montreal	60	3,600	126	10	2.10
1989-90	Mike Liut, Hartford, Washington	37	2,161	91	4	2.53	1947-48	Turk Broda, Toronto	60	3,600	143	5	2.38
1988-89	Patrick Roy, Montreal	48	2,744	113	4	2.47	1946-47	Bill Durnan, Montreal	60	3,600	138	4	2.30
1987-88	Pete Peeters, Washington	35	1,896	88	2	2.78	1945-46	Bill Durnan, Montreal	40	2,400	104	4	2.60
1986-87	Brian Hayward, Montreal	37	2,178	102	1	2.81	1944-45	Bill Durnan, Montreal	50	3,000	121	1	2.42
1985-86	Bob Froese, Philadelphia	51	2,728	116	5	2.55	1943-44	Bill Durnan, Montreal	50	3,000	109	2	2.18
1984-85	Tom Barrasso, Buffalo	54	3,248	144	5	2.66	1942-43	Johnny Mowers, Detroit	50	3,010	124	6	2.47
1983-84	Pat Riggin, Washington	41	2,299	102	4	2.66	1941-42	Frank Brimsek, Boston	47	2,930	115	3	2.35
1982-83	Pete Peeters, Boston	62	3,611	142	8	2.36	1940-41	Turk Broda, Toronto	48	2,970	99	5	2.00
1981-82	Denis Herron, Montreal	27	1,547	68	3	2.64	1939-40	Dave Kerr, NY Rangers	48	3,000	77	8	1.54
1980-81	Richard Sevigny, Montreal	33	1,777	71	2	2.40	1938-39	Frank Brimsek, Boston	43	2,610	68	10	1.56
1979-80	Bob Sauve, Buffalo	32	1,880	74	4	2.36	1937-38	Tiny Thompson, Boston	48	2,970	89	7	1.80
1978-79	Ken Dryden, Montreal	47	2,814	108	5	2.30	1936-37	Norman Smith, Detroit	48	2,980	102	6	2.05
1977-78	Ken Dryden, Montreal	52	3,071	105	5	2.05	1935-36	Tiny Thompson, Boston	48	2,930	82	10	1.68
1976-77	Michel Larocque, Montreal	26	1,525	53	4	2.09	1934-35	Lorne Chabot, Chicago	48	2,940	88	8	1.80
1975-76	Ken Dryden, Montreal	62	3,580	121	8	2.03	1933-34	Wilf Cude, Detroit, Montreal	30	1,920	47	5	1.47
1974-75	Bernie Parent, Philadelphia	68	4,041	137	12	2.03	1932-33	Tiny Thompson, Boston	48	3,000	88	11	1.76
1973-74	Bernie Parent, Philadelphia	73	4,314	136	12	1.89	1931-32	Chuck Gardiner, Chicago	48	2,989	92	4	1.85
1972-73	Ken Dryden, Montreal	54	3,165	119	6	2.26	1930-31	Roy Worters, NY Americans	44	2,760	74	8	1.61
1971-72	Tony Esposito, Chicago	48	2,780	82	9	1.77	1929-30	Tiny Thompson, Boston	44	2,680	98	3	2.19
1970-71	Jacques Plante, Toronto	40	2,329	73	4	1.88	1928-29	George Hainsworth, Montreal	44	2,800	43	22	0.92
1969-70	Ernie Wakely, St. Louis	30	1,651	58	4	2.11	1927-28	George Hainsworth, Montreal	44	2,730	48	13	1.05
1968-69	Jacques Plante, St. Louis	37	2,139	70	5	1.96	1926-27	Clint Benedict, Mtl. Maroons	43	2,748	65	13	1.42
1967-68	Gump Worsley, Montreal	40	2,213	73	6	1.98	1925-26	Alex Connell, Ottawa	36	2,251	42	15	1.12
1966-67	Glenn Hall, Chicago	32	1,664	66	2	2.38	1924-25	Georges Vezina, Montreal	30	1,860	56	5	1.81
1965-66	Johnny Bower, Toronto	35	1,998	75	3	2.25	1923-24	Georges Vezina, Montreal	24	1,459	48	3	1.97
1964-65	Johnny Bower, Toronto	34	2,040	81	3	2.38	1922-23	Clint Benedict, Ottawa	24	1,478	54	4	2.18
1963-64	Johnny Bower, Toronto	51	3,009	106	5	2.11	1921-22	Clint Benedict, Ottawa	24	1,508	84	2	3.34
1962-63	Don Simmons, Toronto	28	1,680	69	1	2.46	1920-21	Clint Benedict, Ottawa	24	1,457	75	2	3.09
1961-62	Jacques Plante, Montreal	70	4,200	166	4	2.37	1919-20	Clint Benedict, Ottawa	24	1,444	64	5	2.66
1960-61	Charlie Hodge, Montreal	30	1,800	74	4	2.47	1918-19	Clint Benedict, Ottawa	18	1,113	53	2	2.86
1959-60	Jacques Plante, Montreal	69	4,140	175	3	2.54	1917-18	Georges Vezina, Montreal	21	1,282	84	1	3.93
1958-59	Jacques Plante, Montreal	67	4,000	144	9	2.16							

All-Time Regular Season NHL Coaching Register

Regular Season, 1917-99

1999-2000 winning percentage includes regulation ties.

Coach	Team	Games Coached	Wins	Losses	Ties	%Wins	Years	Cup Wins	Career
Abel, Sid	Chicago	140	39	79	22	.357	2		
	Detroit	811	340	339	132	.501	12		
	St. Louis	10	3	6	1	.350	1		
	Kansas City	3	0	3	0	.000	1		
	Total	**964**	**382**	**427**	**155**	**.477**	**16**		1952-76
Adams, Jack	**Detroit**	**964**	**413**	**390**	**161**	**.512**	**20**	**3**	1927-47
Allen, Keith	**Philadelphia**	**150**	**51**	**67**	**32**	**.447**	**2**		1967-69
Allison, Dave	**Ottawa**	**25**	**2**	**22**	**1**	**.100**	**1**		1995-96
Anderson, Jim	**Washington**	**54**	**4**	**45**	**5**	**.120**	**1**		1974-75
Angotti, Lou	St. Louis	32	6	20	6	.281	2		
	Pittsburgh	80	16	58	6	.238	1		
	Total	**112**	**22**	**78**	**12**	**.250**	**3**		1973-84
Arbour, Al	St. Louis	107	42	40	25	.509	3		
	NY Islanders	1499	739	537	223	.567	19	4	
	Total	**1606**	**781**	**577**	**248**	**.564**	**22**	**4**	1970-94
Armstrong, George	**Toronto**	**47**	**17**	**26**	**4**	**.404**	**1**		1988-89
Barkley, Doug	**Detroit**	**77**	**20**	**46**	**11**	**.331**	**3**		1970-76
Beaulieu, Andre	**Minnesota**	**32**	**6**	**23**	**3**	**.234**	**1**		1977-78
Belisle, Danny	**Washington**	**96**	**28**	**51**	**17**	**.380**	**2**		1978-80
Berenson, Red	**St. Louis**	**204**	**100**	**72**	**32**	**.569**	**3**		1979-82
Bergeron, Michel	Quebec	634	265	283	86	.486	8		
	NY Rangers	158	73	67	18	.519	2		
	Total	**792**	**338**	**350**	**104**	**.492**	**10**		1980-90
Berry, Bob	Los Angeles	240	107	94	39	.527	3		
	Montreal	223	116	71	36	.601	3		
	Pittsburgh	240	88	127	25	.419	3		
	St. Louis	157	73	63	21	.532	2		
	Total	**860**	**384**	**355**	**121**	**.517**	**11**		1978-94
Beverley, Nick	**Toronto**	**17**	**9**	**6**	**2**	**.588**	**1**		1995-96
Blackburn, Don	**Hartford**	**140**	**42**	**63**	**35**	**.425**	**2**		1979-81
Blair, Wren	**Minnesota**	**147**	**48**	**65**	**34**	**.442**	**3**		1967-70
Blake, Toe	**Montreal**	**914**	**500**	**255**	**159**	**.634**	**13**	**8**	1955-68
Boileau, Marc	**Pittsburgh**	**151**	**66**	**61**	**24**	**.517**	**3**		1973-76
Boivin, Leo	**St. Louis**	**97**	**28**	**53**	**16**	**.371**	**2**		1975-78
Boucher, Frank	**NY Rangers**	**527**	**181**	**263**	**83**	**.422**	**11**	**1**	1939-54
Boucher, George	Mtl. Maroons	12	6	5	1	.542	1		
	Ottawa	48	13	29	6	.333	1		
	St. Louis	35	9	20	6	.343	1		
	Boston	70	22	32	16	.429	1		
	Total	**165**	**50**	**86**	**29**	**.391**	**4**		1930-50
Bowman, Scotty	St. Louis	238	110	83	45	.557	4		
	Montreal	634	419	110	105	.744	8	5	
	Buffalo	404	210	134	60	.594	7		
	Pittsburgh	164	95	53	16	.628	2	1	
	Detroit	537	310	159	68	.642	7	2	
	Total	**1977**	**1144**	**539**	**294**	**.654**	**28**	**8**	1967-00
Bowness, Rick	Winnipeg	28	8	17	3	.339	1		
	Boston	80	36	32	12	.525	1		
	Ottawa	235	39	178	18	.204	4		
	NY Islanders	100	38	50	12	.440	2		
	Total	**443**	**121**	**277**	**45**	**.324**	**8**		1988-98
Brooks, Herb	NY Rangers	285	131	113	41	.532	4		
	Minnesota	80	19	48	13	.319	1		
	New Jersey	84	40	37	7	.518	1		
	Pittsburgh	58	29	24	5	.560	1		
	Total	**507**	**219**	**222**	**66**	**.499**	**7**		1981-00
Brophy, John	**Toronto**	**193**	**64**	**111**	**18**	**.378**	**3**		1986-89
Burnett, George	**Edmonton**	**35**	**12**	**20**	**3**	**.386**	**1**		1994-95
Burns, Charlie	**Minnesota**	**86**	**22**	**50**	**14**	**.337**	**2**		1969-75
Burns, Pat	Montreal	320	174	104	42	.609	4		
	Toronto	281	133	107	41	.546	4		
	Boston	246	102	99	45	.518	3		
	Total	**847**	**409**	**310**	**128**	**.562**	**11**		1988-00
Bush, Eddie	**Kansas City**	**32**	**1**	**23**	**8**	**.156**	**1**		1975-76
Campbell, Colin	**NY Rangers**	**269**	**118**	**108**	**43**	**.519**	**4**		1994-98
Carpenter, Doug	New Jersey	290	100	166	24	.386	4		
	Toronto	91	39	47	5	.456	2		
	Total	**381**	**139**	**213**	**29**	**.403**	**6**		1984-91
Carroll, Dick	**Toronto**	**40**	**18**	**22**	**0**	**.450**	**2**	**1**	1917-19
Carroll, Frank	**Toronto**	**24**	**15**	**9**	**0**	**.625**	**1**		1920-21
Cashman, Wayne	**Philadelphia**	**61**	**32**	**20**	**9**	**.598**	**1**		1997-98
Chambers, Dave	**Quebec**	**98**	**19**	**64**	**15**	**.270**	**2**		1990-92
Charron, Guy	**Calgary**	**16**	**6**	**7**	**3**	**.469**	**1**		1991-92
Cheevers, Gerry	**Boston**	**376**	**204**	**126**	**46**	**.604**	**5**		1980-85
Cherry, Don	Boston	400	231	105	64	.658	5		
	Colorado	80	19	48	13	.319	1		
	Total	**480**	**250**	**153**	**77**	**.601**	**6**		1974-80
Clancy, King	Mtl. Maroons	18	6	11	1	.361	1		
	Toronto	210	80	81	49	.498	3		
	Total	**228**	**86**	**92**	**50**	**.487**	**4**		1937-56
Clapper, Dit	**Boston**	**230**	**102**	**88**	**40**	**.530**	**4**		1945-49
Cleghorn, Odie	**Pittsburgh**	**168**	**62**	**86**	**20**	**.429**	**4**		1925-29
Cleghorn, Sprague	**Mtl. Maroons**	**48**	**19**	**22**	**7**	**.469**	**1**		1931-32
Colville, Neil	**NY Rangers**	**93**	**26**	**41**	**26**	**.419**	**2**		1950-52
Conacher, Charlie	**Chicago**	**162**	**56**	**84**	**22**	**.414**	**3**		1947-50
Conacher, Lionel	**NY Americans**	**44**	**14**	**25**	**5**	**.375**	**1**		1929-30

Coach	Team	Games Coached	Wins	Losses	Ties	%Wins	Years	Cup Wins	Career
Constantine, Kevin	San Jose	157	55	78	24	.427	3		
	Pittsburgh	188	86	67	35	.550	3		
	Total	**345**	**141**	**145**	**59**	**.500**	**6**		1993-00
Cook, Bill	**NY Rangers**	**117**	**34**	**59**	**24**	**.393**	**2**		1951-53
Crawford, Marc	Quebec	48	30	13	5	.677	1		
	Colorado	246	135	75	36	.622	3	1	
	Vancouver	119	38	60	21	.407	2		
	Total	**413**	**203**	**148**	**62**	**.576**	**6**	**1**	1994-00
Creamer, Pierre	**Pittsburgh**	**80**	**36**	**35**	**9**	**.506**	**1**		1987-88
Creighton, Fred	Atlanta	348	156	136	56	.529	5		
	Boston	73	40	20	13	.637	1		
	Total	**421**	**196**	**156**	**69**	**.548**	**6**		1974-80
Crisp, Terry	Calgary	240	144	63	33	.669	3	1	
	Tampa Bay	391	142	204	45	.421	6		
	Total	**631**	**286**	**267**	**78**	**.515**	**9**	**1**	1987-98
Crozier, Joe	Buffalo	192	77	80	35	.492	3		
	Toronto	40	13	22	5	.388	1		
	Total	**232**	**90**	**102**	**40**	**.474**	**4**		1971-81
Crozier, Roger	**Washington**	**1**	**0**	**1**	**0**	**.000**	**1**		1981-82
Cunniff, John	Hartford	13	3	9	1	.269	1		
	New Jersey	133	59	56	18	.511	2		
	Total	**146**	**62**	**65**	**19**	**.490**	**3**		1982-91
Curry, Alex	**Ottawa**	**36**	**24**	**8**	**4**	**.722**	**1**		1925-26
Dandurand, Leo	**Montreal**	**163**	**78**	**76**	**9**	**.506**	**6**	**1**	1921-35
Day, Hap	**Toronto**	**546**	**259**	**206**	**81**	**.549**	**10**	**5**	1940-50
Dea, Billy	**Detroit**	**11**	**3**	**8**	**0**	**.273**	**1**		1981-82
Delvecchio, Alex	**Detroit**	**245**	**82**	**131**	**32**	**.400**	**4**		1973-77
Demers, Jacques	Quebec	80	25	44	11	.381	1		
	St. Louis	240	106	106	28	.500	3		
	Detroit	320	137	136	47	.502	4		
	Montreal	221	107	87	27	.545	4	1	
	Tampa Bay	145	34	94	17	.293	2		
	Total	**1006**	**409**	**467**	**130**	**.471**	**14**	**1**	1979-99
Denneny, Cy	Boston	44	26	13	5	.648	1	1	
	Ottawa	48	11	27	10	.333	1		
	Total	**92**	**37**	**40**	**15**	**.484**	**2**	**1**	1928-33
Dineen, Bill	**Philadelphia**	**140**	**60**	**60**	**20**	**.500**	**2**		1991-93
Dudley, Rick	**Buffalo**	**188**	**85**	**72**	**31**	**.535**	**3**		1989-92
Duff, Dick	**Toronto**	**2**	**0**	**2**	**0**	**.000**	**1**		1979-80
Dugal, Jules	**Montreal**	**18**	**9**	**6**	**3**	**.583**	**1**		1938-39
Duncan, Art	Detroit	33	10	21	2	.333	1		
	Toronto	47	21	16	10	.553	2	1	
	Total	**80**	**31**	**37**	**12**	**.463**	**3**	**1**	1926-32
Dutton, Red	NY Americans	288	90	151	47	.394	6		
	Brooklyn	48	16	29	3	.365	1		
	Total	**336**	**106**	**180**	**50**	**.390**	**7**		1935-42
Eddolls, Frank	**Chicago**	**70**	**13**	**40**	**17**	**.307**	**1**		1954-55
Esposito, Phil	**NY Rangers**	**45**	**24**	**21**	**0**	**.533**	**2**		1986-89
Evans, Jack	California	80	27	42	11	.406	1		
	Cleveland	160	47	87	26	.375	2		
	Hartford	374	163	174	37	.485	5		
	Total	**614**	**237**	**303**	**74**	**.446**	**8**		1975-88
Fashoway, Gordie	**Oakland**	**10**	**4**	**5**	**1**	**.450**	**1**		1967-68
Ferguson, John	NY Rangers	121	43	59	19	.434	2		
	Winnipeg	14	7	6	1	.536	1		
	Total	**135**	**50**	**65**	**20**	**.444**	**3**		1975-86
Filion, Maurice	**Quebec**	**6**	**1**	**3**	**2**	**.333**	**1**		1980-81
Francis, Bob	**Phoenix**	**82**	**39**	**35**	**8**	**.549**	**1**		1999-00
Francis, Emile	NY Rangers	654	342	209	103	.602	10		
	St. Louis	124	46	64	14	.427	3		
	Total	**778**	**388**	**273**	**117**	**.574**	**13**		1965-83
Fraser, Curt	**Atlanta**	**82**	**14**	**61**	**7**	**.238**	**1**		1999-00

Milt Schmidt retired as a player on Christmas Day 1954, and immediately took over as coach of the Boston Bruins. With the exception of the 1961-62 season, Schmidt remained behind the bench until 1966. He later served as Boston's general manager.

Coach	Team	Games Coached	Wins	Losses	Ties	%Wins	Years	Cup Wins	Career
Fredrickson, Frank	Pittsburgh	44	5	36	3	.148	1		1929-30
Ftorek, Robbie	Los Angeles	132	65	56	11	.534	2		
	New Jersey	156	88	49	19	.641	2		
	Total	288	153	105	30	.592	4		1987-00
Gadsby, Bill	Detroit	78	35	31	12	.526	2		1968-70
Gainey, Bob	Minnesota	244	95	119	30	.451	3		
	Dallas	171	70	71	30	.497	3		
	Total	415	165	190	60	.470	6		1990-96
Gardiner, Herb	Chicago	32	5	23	4	.219	1		1929-30
Gardner, Jimmy	Hamilton	30	19	10	1	.650	1		1924-25
Garvin, Ted	Detroit	11	2	8	1	.227	1		1973-74
Geoffrion, Bernie	NY Rangers	43	22	18	3	.547	1		
	Atlanta	208	77	92	39	.464	3		
	Montreal	30	15	9	6	.600	1		
	Total	281	114	119	48	.491	5		1968-80
Gerard, Eddie	Ottawa	22	9	13	0	.409	1		
	Mtl. Maroons	294	129	122	43	.512	7	1	
	NY Americans	92	34	40	18	.467	2		
	St. Louis	13	2	11	0	.154	1		
	Total	421	174	186	61	.486	11	1	1917-35
Gill, David	Ottawa	132	64	41	27	.587	3	1	1926-29
Glover, Fred	Oakland	152	51	76	25	.418	2		
	California	204	45	131	28	.289	4		
	Los Angeles	68	18	42	8	.324	1		
	Total	424	114	249	61	.341	7		1968-74
Goodfellow, Ebbie	Chicago	140	30	91	19	.282	2		1950-52
Gordon, Jackie	Minnesota	289	116	123	50	.488	5		1970-75
Goring, Butch	Boston	93	42	38	13	.522	2		
	NY Islanders	82	24	49	9	.354	1		
	Total	175	66	87	22	.443	3		1985-00
Gorman, Tommy	NY Americans	80	31	33	16	.488	2		
	Chicago	73	28	28	17	.500	2	1	
	Mtl. Maroons	174	74	71	29	.509	4	1	
	Total	327	133	132	62	.502	8	2	1925-38
Gottselig, Johnny	Chicago	187	62	105	20	.385	4		1944-48
Goyette, Phil	NY Islanders	48	6	38	4	.167	1		1972-73
Graham, Dirk	Chicago	59	16	35	8	.339	1		1998-99
Green, Gary	Washington	157	50	78	29	.411	3		1979-82
Green, Pete	Ottawa	150	94	52	4	.640	6	3	1919-25
Green, Shorty	NY Americans	44	11	27	6	.318	1		1927-28
Green, Ted	Edmonton	188	65	102	21	.402	3		1991-94
Guidolin, Aldo	Colorado	59	12	39	8	.271	1		1978-79
Guidolin, Bep	Boston	104	72	23	9	.736	2		
	Kansas City	125	26	84	15	.268	2		
	Total	229	98	107	24	.480	4		1972-76
Harkness, Ned	Detroit	38	12	22	4	.368	1		1970-71
Harris, Ted	Minnesota	179	48	104	27	.344	3		1975-78
Hart, Cecil	Montreal	394	196	125	73	.590	9	2	1926-39
Hartley, Bob	Colorado	164	86	57	21	.591	2		1998-00
Hartsburg, Craig	Chicago	246	104	102	40	.504	3		
	Anaheim	164	69	70	25	.506	2		
	Total	410	173	172	65	.505	5		1995-00
Harvey, Doug	NY Rangers	70	26	32	12	.457	1		1961-62
Hay, Don	Phoenix	82	38	37	7	.506	1		1996-97
Heffernan, Frank	Toronto	12	5	7	0	.417	1		1919-20
Henning, Lorne	Minnesota	158	68	72	18	.487	2		
	NY Islanders	48	15	28	5	.365	1		
	Total	206	83	100	23	.459	3		1985-95
Hitchcock, Ken	Dallas	371	206	119	46	.626	5	1	1995-00
Holmgren, Paul	Philadelphia	264	107	126	31	.464	4		
	Hartford	161	54	93	14	.379	4		
	Total	425	161	219	45	.432	8		1988-96
Howell, Harry	Minnesota	11	3	6	2	.364	1		1978-79
Imlach, Punch	Toronto	770	370	275	125	.562	12	4	
	Buffalo	119	32	62	25	.374	2		
	Total	889	402	337	150	.537	14	4	1958-80
Ingarfield, Earl	NY Islanders	30	6	22	2	.233	1		1972-73
Inglis, Bill	Buffalo	56	28	18	10	.589	1		1978-79
Irvin, Dick	Chicago	126	45	62	19	.433	3		
	Toronto	427	216	152	59	.575	9	1	
	Montreal	896	431	313	152	.566	15	3	
	Total	1449	692	527	230	.557	27	4	1928-56
Ivan, Tommy	Detroit	470	262	118	90	.653	7	3	
	Chicago	103	26	56	21	.354	2		
	Total	573	288	174	111	.599	9	3	1947-58
Iverson, Emil	Chicago	21	8	7	6	.524	1		1932-33
Johnson, Bob	Calgary	400	193	155	52	.548	5		
	Pittsburgh	80	41	33	6	.550	1	1	
	Total	480	234	188	58	.548	6	1	1982-91
Johnson, Tom	Boston	208	142	43	23	.738	3	1	1970-73
Johnston, Eddie	Chicago	80	34	27	19	.544	1		
	Pittsburgh	516	232	224	60	.508	7		
	Total	596	266	251	79	.513	8		1979-97
Johnston, Marshall	California	69	13	45	11	.268	2		
	Colorado	56	15	32	9	.348	1		
	Total	125	28	77	20	.304	3		1973-82
Kasper, Steve	Boston	164	66	78	20	.463	2		1995-97
Keats, Duke	Detroit	11	2	7	2	.273	1		1926-27
Keenan, Mike	Philadelphia	320	190	102	28	.638	4		
	Chicago	320	153	126	41	.542	4		
	NY Rangers	84	52	24	8	.667	1	1	
	St. Louis	163	75	66	22	.528	3		
	Vancouver	108	36	54	18	.417	2		
	Total	995	506	372	117	.567	14	1	1984-99
Kelly, Pat	Colorado	101	22	54	25	.342	2		1977-79
Kelly, Red	Los Angeles	150	55	75	20	.433	2		
	Pittsburgh	274	90	132	52	.423	4		
	Toronto	318	133	123	62	.516	4		
	Total	742	278	330	134	.465	10		1967-77
King, Dave	Calgary	216	109	76	31	.576	3		1992-95
Kingston, George	San Jose	164	28	129	7	.192	2		1991-93
Kish, Larry	Hartford	49	12	32	5	.296	1		1982-83
Kromm, Bobby	Detroit	231	79	111	41	.431	3		1977-80
Kurtenbach, Orland	Vancouver	125	36	62	27	.396	2		1976-78
LaForge, Bill	Vancouver	20	4	14	2	.250	1		1984-85
Lalonde, Newsy	Montreal	207	96	97	14	.498	8		
	NY Americans	44	17	25	2	.409	1		
	Ottawa	88	31	45	12	.420	2		
	Total	339	144	167	28	.466	11		1917-35
Lapointe, Ron	Quebec	89	33	50	6	.404	2		1987-89
Laycoe, Hal	Los Angeles	24	5	18	1	.229	1		
	Vancouver	156	44	96	16	.333	2		
	Total	180	49	114	17	.319	3		1969-72
Lehman, Hugh	Chicago	21	3	17	1	.167	1		1927-28
Lemaire, Jacques	Montreal	97	48	37	12	.557	2		
	New Jersey	378	199	122	57	.602	5	1	
	Total	475	247	159	69	.593	7	1	1983-98
Lepine, Pit	Montreal	48	10	33	5	.260	1		1939-40
LeSueur, Percy	Hamilton	10	3	7	0	.300	1		1923-24
Lewis, Dave*	Detroit	5	4	1	0	.800	1		1998-99
	*Results shared with co-coach Barry Smith								
Ley, Rick	Hartford	160	69	71	20	.494	2		
	Vancouver	124	47	50	27	.488	2		
	Total	284	116	121	47	.491	4		1989-96
Lindsay, Ted	Detroit	29	5	21	3	.224	2		1979-81
Long, Barry	Winnipeg	205	87	93	25	.485	3		1983-86
Loughlin, Clem	Chicago	144	61	63	20	.493	3		1934-37
Low, Ron	Edmonton	341	139	162	40	.466	5		1994-99
Lowe, Kevin	Edmonton	82	32	34	16	.537	1		1999-00
Ludzik, Steve	Tampa Bay	82	19	54	9	.329	1		1999-00
MacDonald, Parker	Minnesota	61	20	30	11	.418	1		
	Los Angeles	42	13	24	5	.369	1		
	Total	103	33	54	16	.398	2		1973-82
MacLean, Doug	Florida	187	83	71	33	.532	3		1995-98
MacMillan, Bill	Colorado	80	22	45	13	.356	1		
	New Jersey	100	19	67	14	.260	2		
	Total	180	41	112	27	.303	3		1980-84
MacNeil, Al	Montreal	55	31	15	9	.645	1	1	
	Atlanta	80	35	32	13	.519	1		
	Calgary	160	68	61	31	.522	2		
	Total	295	134	108	53	.544	4	1	1970-82
Magnuson, Keith	Chicago	132	49	57	26	.470	2		1980-82
Mahoney, Bill	Minnesota	93	42	39	12	.516	2		1983-85
Maloney, Dan	Toronto	160	45	100	15	.328	2		
	Winnipeg	212	91	93	28	.495	3		
	Total	372	136	193	43	.423	5		1984-89
Maloney, Phil	Vancouver	232	95	105	32	.478	4		1973-77
Mantha, Sylvio	Montreal	48	11	26	11	.344	1		1935-36
Marshall, Bert	Colorado	24	3	17	4	.208	1		1981-82
Martin, Jacques	St. Louis	160	66	71	23	.484	2		
	Ottawa	366	160	146	60	.522	5		
	Total	526	226	217	83	.510	7		1986-00
Matheson, Godfrey	Chicago	2	0	2	0	.000	1		1932-33
Maurice, Paul	Hartford	152	61	72	19	.464	2		
	Carolina	246	104	106	36	.496	3		
	Total	398	165	178	55	.484	5		1995-00
Maxner, Wayne	Detroit	129	34	68	27	.368	2		1980-82
McCammon, Bob	Philadelphia	218	119	68	31	.617	4		
	Vancouver	294	102	156	36	.408	4		
	Total	512	221	224	67	.497	8		1978-91
McCreary, Bill	St. Louis	24	6	14	4	.333	1		
	Vancouver	41	9	25	7	.305	1		
	California	32	8	20	4	.313	1		
	Total	97	23	59	15	.314	3		1971-75
McGuire, Pierre	Hartford	67	23	37	7	.396	1		1993-94
McLellan, John	Toronto	310	126	139	45	.479	4		1969-73
McVie, Tom	Washington	204	49	122	33	.321	3		
	Winnipeg	105	20	67	18	.276	2		
	New Jersey	153	57	74	22	.444	3		
	Total	462	126	263	73	.352	8		1975-92
Meeker, Howie	Toronto	70	21	34	15	.407	1		1956-57
Melrose, Barry	Los Angeles	209	79	101	29	.447	3		1992-95
Milbury, Mike	Boston	160	90	49	21	.628	2		
	NY Islanders	191	56	111	24	.356	4		
	Total	351	146	160	45	.480	6		1989-99
Molleken, Lorne	Chicago	47	18	21	8	.489	2		1998-00
Muckler, John	Minnesota	35	6	23	6	.257	1		
	Edmonton	160	75	65	20	.531	2	1	
	Buffalo	268	125	109	34	.530	4		
	NY Rangers	185	70	91	24	.451	3		
	Total	648	276	288	84	.493	10	1	1968-00
Muldoon, Pete	Chicago	44	19	22	3	.466	1		1926-27
Munro, Dunc	Mtl. Maroons	76	37	29	10	.553	2		1929-31
Murdoch, Bob	Chicago	80	30	41	9	.431	1		
	Winnipeg	160	63	75	22	.463	2		
	Total	240	93	116	31	.452	3		1987-91
Murphy, Mike	Los Angeles	65	20	37	8	.369	2		
	Toronto	164	60	87	17	.418	2		
	Total	229	80	124	25	.404	4		1986-98
Murray, Andy	Los Angeles	82	39	31	12	.573	1		99-2000

Coach	Team	Games Coached	Wins	Losses	Ties	%Wins	Years	Cup Wins	Career
Murray, Bryan	Washington	672	343	246	83	.572	9		
	Detroit	244	124	91	29	.568	3		
	Florida	59	17	31	11	.381	1		
	Total	975	484	368	123	.559	13		1981-98
Murray, Terry	Washington	325	163	134	28	.545	5		
	Philadelphia	212	118	64	30	.627	3		
	Florida	164	73	67	24	.537	2		
	Total	701	354	265	82	.568	10		1989-00
Nanne, Lou	Minnesota	29	7	18	4	.310	1		1977-78
Neale, Harry	Vancouver	407	142	189	76	.442	6		
	Detroit	35	8	23	4	.286	1		
	Total	442	150	212	80	.430	7		1978-86
Neilson, Roger	Toronto	160	75	62	23	.541	2		
	Buffalo	80	39	20	21	.619	1		
	Vancouver	133	51	61	21	.462	3		
	Los Angeles	28	8	17	3	.339	1		
	NY Rangers	280	141	104	35	.566	4		
	Florida	132	53	56	23	.489	2		
	Philadelphia	185	92	60	33	.595	3		
	Total	998	459	380	159	.541	16		1977-00
Nolan, Ted	Buffalo	164	73	72	19	.503	2		1995-97
Nykoluk, Mike	Toronto	280	89	144	47	.402	4		1980-84
O'Donohue, George	Toronto	29	15	13	1	.534	2	1	1921-23
O'Reilly, Terry	Boston	227	115	86	26	.564	3		1986-89
Oliver, Murray	Minnesota	41	21	12	8	.610	2		1981-83
Olmstead, Bert	Oakland	64	11	37	16	.297	1		1967-68
Paddock, John	Winnipeg	281	106	138	37	.443	4		1991-95
Page, Pierre	Minnesota	160	63	77	20	.456	2		
	Quebec	230	98	103	29	.489	3		
	Calgary	164	66	78	20	.463	2		
	Anaheim	82	26	43	13	.396	1		
	Total	636	253	301	82	.462	8		1988-98
Park, Brad	Detroit	45	9	34	2	.222	1		1985-86
Paterson, Rick	Tampa Bay	8	0	8	0	.000	1		1997-98
Patrick, Craig	NY Rangers	95	37	45	13	.458	2		
	Pittsburgh	74	29	36	9	.453	2		
	Total	169	66	81	22	.456	4		1980-97
Patrick, Frank	Boston	96	48	36	12	.563	2		1934-36
Patrick, Lester	NY Rangers	604	281	216	107	.554	13	2	1926-39
Patrick, Lynn	NY Rangers	107	40	51	16	.449	2		
	Boston	310	117	130	63	.479	5		
	St. Louis	26	8	15	3	.365	3		
	Total	443	165	196	82	.465	10		1948-76
Patrick, Muzz	NY Rangers	136	43	66	27	.415	4		1953-63
Perron, Jean	Montreal	240	126	84	30	.588	3	1	
	Quebec	47	16	26	5	.394	1		
	Total	287	142	110	35	.556	4	1	1985-89
Perry, Don	Los Angeles	168	52	85	31	.402	3		1981-84
Pike, Alf	NY Rangers	123	36	66	21	.378	2		1959-61
Pilous, Rudy	Chicago	387	162	151	74	.514	6	1	1957-63
Plager, Barclay	St. Louis	178	49	96	33	.368	4		1977-83
Plager, Bob	St. Louis	11	4	6	1	.409	1		1992-93
Pleau, Larry	Hartford	224	81	117	26	.420	5		1980-89
Polano, Nick	Detroit	240	79	127	34	.400	3		1982-85
Popein, Larry	NY Rangers	41	18	14	9	.549	1		1973-74
Powers, Eddie	Toronto	66	31	32	3	.492	2		1924-26
Primeau, Joe	Toronto	210	97	71	42	.562	3	1	1950-53
Pronovost, Marcel	Buffalo	104	52	29	23	.611	2		1977-79
Pulford, Bob	Los Angeles	396	178	150	68	.535	5		
	Chicago	433	185	180	68	.508	7		
	Total	829	363	330	136	.520	12		1972-00
Quenneville, Joel	St. Louis	286	151	96	39	.598	4		1996-00
Querrie, Charles	Toronto	72	29	38	5	.438	3		1922-27
Quinn, Mike	Quebec	24	4	20	0	.167	1		1919-20
Quinn, Pat	Philadelphia	262	141	73	48	.630	4		
	Los Angeles	202	75	101	26	.436	3		
	Vancouver	280	141	111	28	.554	5		
	Toronto	164	90	60	14	.600	2		
	Total	908	447	345	116	.558	14		1978-00
Ramsay, Craig	Buffalo	21	4	15	2	.238	1		1986-87
Randall, Ken	Hamilton	14	6	8	0	.429	1		1923-24
Reay, Billy	Toronto	90	26	50	14	.367	2		
	Chicago	1012	516	335	161	.589	14		
	Total	1102	542	385	175	.571	16		1957-77
Regan, Larry	Los Angeles	88	27	47	14	.386	2		1970-72
Renney, Tom	Vancouver	101	39	53	9	.431	2		1996-98
Risebrough, Doug	Calgary	144	71	56	17	.552	2		1990-92
Roberts, Jim	Buffalo	45	21	16	8	.556	1		
	Hartford	80	26	41	13	.406	1		
	St. Louis	9	3	3	3	.500	1		
	Total	134	50	60	24	.463	3		1981-97
Robinson, Larry	Los Angeles	328	122	161	45	.441	4		
	New Jersey	8	4	4	0	.500	1		
	Total	336	126	165	45	.442	5		1995-00
Rodden, Mike	Toronto	2	0	2	0	.000	1		1926-27
Romeril, Alex	Toronto	13	7	5	1	.577	1		1926-27
Ross, Art	Mtl. Wanderers	6	1	5	0	.167	1		
	Hamilton	24	6	18	0	.250	1		
	Boston	728	361	277	90	.558	16	1	
	Total	758	368	300	90	.545	18	1	1917-45
Ruel, Claude	Montreal	305	172	82	51	.648	5	2	1968-81
Ruff, Lindy	Buffalo	246	108	93	45	.539	3		1997-00
Sather, Glen	Edmonton	842	464	268	110	.616	11	4	1979-94
Sator, Ted	NY Rangers	99	41	48	10	.465	2		
	Buffalo	207	96	89	22	.517	3		
	Total	306	137	137	32	.500	5		1985-89
Savard, Andre	Quebec	24	10	13	1	.438	1		1987-88
Schinkel, Ken	Pittsburgh	203	83	92	28	.478	4		1972-77
Schmidt, Milt	Boston	726	245	360	121	.421	11		
	Washington	44	5	34	5	.170	2		
	Total	770	250	394	126	.406	13		1954-76
Schoenfeld, Jim	Buffalo	43	19	19	5	.500	1		
	New Jersey	124	50	59	15	.464	3		
	Washington	249	113	102	34	.522	4		
	Phoenix	164	74	66	24	.524	2		
	Total	580	256	248	78	.509	10		1985-99
Shaughnessy, Tom	Chicago	21	10	8	3	.548	1		1929-30
Shero, Fred	Philadelphia	554	308	151	95	.642	7	2	
	NY Rangers	180	82	74	24	.522	3		
	Total	734	390	225	119	.612	10	2	1971-81
Simpson, Joe	NY Americans	144	42	72	30	.396	3		1932-35
Simpson, Terry	NY Islanders	187	81	82	24	.497	3		
	Philadelphia	84	35	39	10	.476	1		
	Winnipeg	97	43	47	7	.479	2		
	Total	368	159	168	41	.488	6		1986-96
Sims, Al	San Jose	82	27	47	8	.378	1		1996-97
Sinden, Harry	Boston	327	153	116	58	.557	6	1	1966-85
Skinner, Jimmy	Detroit	247	123	78	46	.591	4	1	1954-58
Smeaton, Cooper	Philadelphia	44	4	36	4	.136	1		1930-31
Smith, Alf	Ottawa	18	12	6	0	.667	1		1918-19
Smith, Barry*	Detroit	5	4	1	0	.800	1		1998-99
*Results shared with co-coach Dave Lewis									
Smith, Floyd	Buffalo	241	143	62	36	.668	4		
	Toronto	68	30	33	5	.478	1		
	Total	309	173	95	41	.626	5		1971-80
Smith, Mike	Winnipeg	23	2	17	4	.174	1		1980-81
Smith, Ron	NY Rangers	44	15	22	7	.420	1		1992-93
Smythe, Conn	Toronto	134	57	57	20	.500	4		1927-31
Sonmor, Glen	Minnesota	417	174	161	82	.516	7		1978-87
Sproule, Harry	Toronto	12	7	5	0	.583	1		1919-20
Stanley, Barney	Chicago	23	4	17	2	.217	1		1927-28
Stasiuk, Vic	Philadelphia	154	45	68	41	.425	2		
	California	75	21	38	16	.387	1		
	Vancouver	78	22	47	9	.340	1		
	Total	307	88	153	66	.394	4		1969-73
Stewart, Bill	Chicago	69	22	35	12	.406	2	1	1937-39
Stewart, Bill	NY Islanders	37	11	19	7	.329	1		1998-99
Stewart, Ron	NY Rangers	39	15	20	4	.436	1		
	Los Angeles	80	31	34	15	.481	1		
	Total	119	46	54	19	.466	2		1975-78
Sullivan, Red	NY Rangers	196	58	103	35	.385	4		
	Pittsburgh	150	47	79	24	.393	2		
	Washington	18	2	16	0	.111	1		
	Total	364	107	198	59	.375	7		1962-75
Sutherland, Bill	Winnipeg	32	7	22	3	.266	2		1979-81
Sutter, Brian	St. Louis	320	153	124	43	.545	4		
	Boston	216	120	73	23	.609	3		
	Calgary	246	87	122	37	.439	3		
	Total	782	360	319	103	.529	10		1988-00
Sutter, Darryl	Chicago	216	110	80	26	.569	3		
	San Jose	246	100	108	38	.498	3		
	Total	462	210	188	64	.531	6		1992-00
Talbot, Jean-Guy	St. Louis	120	52	53	15	.496	2		
	NY Rangers	80	30	37	13	.456	1		
	Total	200	82	90	28	.480	3		1972-78
Tessier, Orval	Chicago	213	99	93	21	.514	3		1982-85
Thompson, Paul	Chicago	272	104	127	41	.458	7		1938-45
Thompson, Percy	Hamilton	48	13	35	0	.271	2		1920-22
Tobin, Bill	Chicago	71	29	29	13	.500	2		1929-32
Tortorella, John	NY Rangers	4	0	3	1	.125	1		1999-00
Tremblay, Mario	Montreal	159	71	63	25	.525	2		1995-97
Trotz, Barry	Nashville	162	56	94	14	.405	2		1998-00
Ubriaco, Gene	Pittsburgh	106	50	47	9	.514	2		1988-90
Vachon, Rogie	Los Angeles	10	4	3	3	.550	3		1983-95
Vigneault, Alain	Montreal	246	104	109	33	.498	3		1997-00
Watson, Bryan	Edmonton	18	4	9	5	.361	1		1980-81
Watson, Phil	NY Rangers	295	119	124	52	.492	5		
	Boston	84	16	55	13	.268	2		
	Total	379	135	179	65	.442	7		1955-63
Watt, Tom	Winnipeg	181	72	85	24	.464	3		
	Vancouver	160	52	87	21	.391	2		
	Toronto	149	52	80	17	.406	2		
	Total	490	176	252	62	.422	7		1981-92
Webster, Tom	NY Rangers	18	5	9	4	.389	1		
	Los Angeles	240	115	94	31	.544	3		
	Total	258	120	103	35	.533	4		1986-92
Weiland, Cooney	Boston	96	58	20	18	.698	2	1	1939-41
White, Bill	Chicago	46	16	24	6	.413	1		1976-77
Wiley, Jim	San Jose	57	17	37	3	.325	1		1995-96
Wilson, Johnny	Los Angeles	52	9	34	9	.260	1		
	Detroit	145	67	56	22	.538	2		
	Colorado	80	20	46	14	.338	1		
	Pittsburgh	240	91	105	44	.471	3		
	Total	517	187	241	89	.448	7		1969-80
Wilson, Larry	Detroit	36	3	29	4	.139	1		1976-77
Wilson, Ron	Anaheim	296	120	145	31	.458	4		
	Washington	246	115	101	30	.533	3		
	Total	542	235	246	61	.492	7		1993-00
Young, Garry	California	12	2	7	3	.292	1		
	St. Louis	98	41	41	16	.500	2		
	Total	110	43	48	19	.477	3		1972-76

Year-by-Year Individual Regular-Season Leaders

Season	Goals	G	Assists	A	Points	Pts.	Penalty Minutes	PIM
1917-18	Joe Malone	44	Cy Denneny	10	Joe Malone	48	Joe Hall	100
			Reg Noble	10				
			Harry Cameron	10				
1918-19	Newsy Lalonde	23	Newsy Lalonde	10	Newsy Lalonde	33	Joe Hall	135
			Eddie Gerard	10				
1919-20	Joe Malone	39	Frank Nighbor	15	Joe Malone	49	Cully Wilson	86
1920-21	Babe Dye	35	Jack Darragh	15	Newsy Lalonde	43	Bert Corbeau	86
1921-22	Punch Broadbent	32	Punch Broadbent	14	Punch Broadbent	46	Sprague Cleghorn	63
			Leo Reise	14				
1922-23	Babe Dye	26	Edmond Bouchard	12	Babe Dye	37	Billy Boucher	52
1923-24	Cy Denneny	22	King Clancy	8	Cy Denneny	23	Bert Corbeau	55
1924-25	Babe Dye	38	Cy Denneny	15	Babe Dye	44	Billy Boucher	92
1925-26	Nels Stewart	34	Frank Nighbor	13	Nels Stewart	42	Bert Corbeau	121
1926-27	Bill Cook	33	Dick Irvin	18	Bill Cook	37	Nels Stewart	133
1927-28	Howie Morenz	33	Howie Morenz	18	Howie Morenz	51	Eddie Shore	165
1928-29	Ace Bailey	22	Frank Boucher	16	Ace Bailey	32	Red Dutton	139
1929-30	Cooney Weiland	43	Frank Boucher	36	Cooney Weiland	73	Joe Lamb	119
1930-31	Charlie Conacher	31	Joe Primeau	32	Howie Morenz	51	Harvey Rockburn	118
1931-32	Charlie Conacher	34	Joe Primeau	37	Harvey Jackson	53	Red Dutton	107
	Bill Cook	34						
1932-33	Bill Cook	28	Frank Boucher	28	Bill Cook	50	Red Horner	144
1933-34	Charlie Conacher	32	Joe Primeau	32	Charlie Conacher	52	Red Horner	126 *
1934-35	Charlie Conacher	36	Art Chapman	34	Charlie Conacher	57	Red Horner	125
1935-36	Charlie Conacher	23	Art Chapman	28	Sweeney Schriner	45	Red Horner	167
	Bill Thoms	23						
1936-37	Larry Aurie	23	Syl Apps Sr.	29	Sweeney Schriner	46	Red Horner	124
	Nels Stewart	23						
1937-38	Gordie Drillon	26	Syl Apps Sr.	29	Gordie Drillon	52	Red Horner	82 *
1938-39	Roy Conacher	26	Bill Cowley	34	Toe Blake	47	Red Horner	85
1939-40	Bryan Hextall Sr.	24	Milt Schmidt	30	Milt Schmidt	52	Red Horner	87
1940-41	Bryan Hextall Sr.	26	Bill Cowley	45	Bill Cowley	62	Jimmy Orlando	99
1941-42	Lynn Patrick	32	Phil Watson	37	Bryan Hextall Sr.	56	Jimmy Orlando	81 **
1942-43	Doug Bentley	33	Bill Cowley	45	Doug Bentley	73	Jimmy Orlando	89 *
1943-44	Doug Bentley	38	Clint Smith	49	Herb Cain	82	Mike McMahon Sr.	98
1944-45	Maurice Richard	50	Elmer Lach	54	Elmer Lach	80	Pat Egan	86
1945-46	Gaye Stewart	37	Elmer Lach	34	Max Bentley	61	Jack Stewart	73
1946-47	Maurice Richard	45	Billy Taylor	46	Max Bentley	72	Gus Mortson	133
1947-48	Ted Lindsay	33	Doug Bentley	37	Elmer Lach	61	Bill Barilko	147
1948-49	Sid Abel	28	Doug Bentley	43	Roy Conacher	68	Bill Ezinicki	145
1949-50	Maurice Richard	43	Ted Lindsay	55	Ted Lindsay	78	Bill Ezinicki	144
1950-51	Gordie Howe	43	Gordie Howe	43	Gordie Howe	86	Gus Mortson	142
1951-52	Gordie Howe	47	Elmer Lach	50	Gordie Howe	86	Gus Kyle	127
1952-53	Gordie Howe	49	Gordie Howe	46	Gordie Howe	95	Maurice Richard	112
1953-54	Maurice Richard	37	Gordie Howe	48	Gordie Howe	81	Gus Mortson	132
1954-55	Maurice Richard	38	Bert Olmstead	48	Bernie Geoffrion	75	Fernie Flaman	150
	Bernie Geoffrion	38						
1955-56	Jean Beliveau	47	Bert Olmstead	56	Jean Beliveau	88	Lou Fontinato	202
1956-57	Gordie Howe	44	Ted Lindsay	55	Gordie Howe	89	Gus Mortson	147
1957-58	Dickie Moore	36	Henri Richard	52	Dickie Moore	84	Lou Fontinato	152
1958-59	Jean Beliveau	45	Dickie Moore	55	Dickie Moore	96	Ted Lindsay	184
1959-60	Bobby Hull	39	Don McKenney	49	Bobby Hull	81	Carl Brewer	150
1960-61	Bernie Geoffrion	50	Jean Beliveau	58	Bernie Geoffrion	95	Pierre Pilote	165
1961-62	Bobby Hull	50	Andy Bathgate	56	Bobby Hull	84	Lou Fontinato	167
					Andy Bathgate	84		
1962-63	Gordie Howe	38	Henri Richard	50	Gordie Howe	86	Howie Young	273
1963-64	Bobby Hull	43	Andy Bathgate	58	Stan Mikita	89	Vic Hadfield	151
1964-65	Norm Ullman	42	Stan Mikita	59	Stan Mikita	87	Carl Brewer	177
1965-66	Bobby Hull	54	Stan Mikita	48	Bobby Hull	97	Reggie Fleming	166
			Bobby Rousseau	48				
			Jean Beliveau	48				
1966-67	Bobby Hull	52	Stan Mikita	62	Stan Mikita	97	John Ferguson	177
1967-68	Bobby Hull	44	Phil Esposito	49	Stan Mikita	87	Barclay Plager	153
1968-69	Bobby Hull	58	Phil Esposito	77	Phil Esposito	126	Forbes Kennedy	219
1969-70	Phil Esposito	43	Bobby Orr	87	Bobby Orr	120	Keith Magnuson	213
1970-71	Phil Esposito	76	Bobby Orr	102	Phil Esposito	152	Keith Magnuson	291
1971-72	Phil Esposito	66	Bobby Orr	80	Phil Esposito	133	Bryan Watson	212
1972-73	Phil Esposito	55	Phil Esposito	75	Phil Esposito	130	Dave Schultz	259
1973-74	Phil Esposito	68	Bobby Orr	90	Phil Esposito	145	Dave Schultz	348
1974-75	Phil Esposito	61	Bobby Orr	89	Bobby Orr	135	Dave Schultz	472
			Bobby Clarke	89				
1975-76	Reggie Leach	61	Bobby Clarke	89	Guy Lafleur	125	Steve Durbano	370
1976-77	Steve Shutt	60	Guy Lafleur	80	Guy Lafleur	136	Dave Williams	338
1977-78	Guy Lafleur	60	Bryan Trottier	77	Guy Lafleur	132	Dave Schultz	405
1978-79	Mike Bossy	69	Bryan Trottier	87	Bryan Trottier	134	Dave Williams	298
1979-80	Charlie Simmer	56	Wayne Gretzky	86	Marcel Dionne	137	Jimmy Mann	287
	Danny Gare	56			Wayne Gretzky	137		
	Blaine Stoughton	56						
1980-81	Mike Bossy	68	Wayne Gretzky	109	Wayne Gretzky	164	Dave Williams	343
1981-82	Wayne Gretzky	92	Wayne Gretzky	120	Wayne Gretzky	212	Paul Baxter	409
1982-83	Wayne Gretzky	71	Wayne Gretzky	125	Wayne Gretzky	196	Randy Holt	275
1983-84	Wayne Gretzky	87	Wayne Gretzky	118	Wayne Gretzky	205	Chris Nilan	338
1984-85	Wayne Gretzky	73	Wayne Gretzky	135	Wayne Gretzky	208	Chris Nilan	358
1985-86	Jari Kurri	68	Wayne Gretzky	163	Wayne Gretzky	215	Joey Kocur	377
1986-87	Wayne Gretzky	62	Wayne Gretzky	121	Wayne Gretzky	183	Tim Hunter	361
1987-88	Mario Lemieux	70	Wayne Gretzky	109	Mario Lemieux	168	Bob Probert	398
1988-89	Mario Lemieux	85	Mario Lemieux	114	Mario Lemieux	199	Tim Hunter	375
			Wayne Gretzky	114				
1989-90	Brett Hull	72	Wayne Gretzky	102	Wayne Gretzky	142	Basil McRae	351
1990-91	Brett Hull	86	Wayne Gretzky	122	Wayne Gretzky	163	Rob Ray	350
1991-92	Brett Hull	70	Wayne Gretzky	90	Mario Lemieux	131	Mike Peluso	408
1992-93	Teemu Selanne	76	Adam Oates	97	Mario Lemieux	160	Marty McSorley	399
	Alexander Mogilny	76						
1993-94	Pavel Bure	60	Wayne Gretzky	92	Wayne Gretzky	130	Tie Domi	347
1994-95	Peter Bondra	34	Ron Francis	48	Jaromir Jagr	70	Enrico Ciccone	225
					Eric Lindros	70		
1995-96	Mario Lemieux	69	Mario Lemieux	92	Mario Lemieux	161	Matthew Barnaby	335
			Ron Francis	92				
1996-97	Keith Tkachuk	52	Mario Lemieux	72	Mario Lemieux	122	Gino Odjick	371
			Wayne Gretzky	72				
1997-98	Teemu Selanne	52	Jaromir Jagr	67	Jaromir Jagr	102	Donald Brashear	372
	Peter Bondra	52	Wayne Gretzky	67				
1998-99	Teemu Selanne	47	Jaromir Jagr	83	Jaromir Jagr	127	Rob Ray	261
99-2000	Pavel Bure	58	Mark Recchi	63	Jaromir Jagr	96	Denny Lambert	219

* Match Misconduct penalty not included in total penalty minutes. ** Three Match Misconduct penalties not included in total penalty minutes.
1946-47 was the first season that a Match penalty was automatically written into the player's total penalty minutes as 20 minutes.
Beginning in 1947-48 all penalties, Match, Game Misconduct, and Misconduct, are written as 10 minutes.

One Season Scoring Records

Goals-Per-Game Leaders, One Season

(Among players with 20 goals or more in one season)

Player	Team	Season	Games	Goals	Average
Joe Malone	Montreal	1917-18	20	44	2.20
Cy Denneny	Ottawa	1917-18	20	36	1.80
Newsy Lalonde	Montreal	1917-18	14	23	1.64
Joe Malone	Quebec	1919-20	24	39	1.63
Newsy Lalonde	Montreal	1919-20	23	37	1.61
Reg Noble	Toronto	1917-18	20	30	1.50
Babe Dye	Ham., Tor.	1920-21	24	35	1.46
Cy Denneny	Ottawa	1920-21	24	34	1.42
Joe Malone	Hamilton	1920-21	20	28	1.40
Newsy Lalonde	Montreal	1920-21	24	33	1.38
Punch Broadbent	Ottawa	1921-22	24	32	1.33
Babe Dye	Toronto	1924-25	29	38	1.31
Newsy Lalonde	Montreal	1918-19	17	22	1.29
Odie Cleghorn	Montreal	1918-19	17	22	1.29
Babe Dye	Toronto	1921-22	24	31	1.29
Cy Denneny	Ottawa	1921-22	22	27	1.23
Aurel Joliat	Montreal	1924-25	25	30	1.20
Babe Dye	Toronto	1922-23	22	26	1.18
Wayne Gretzky	Edmonton	1983-84	74	87	1.18
Wayne Gretzky	Edmonton	1981-82	80	92	1.15
Mario Lemieux	Pittsburgh	1992-93	60	69	1.15
Frank Nighbor	Ottawa	1919-20	23	26	1.13
Mario Lemieux	Pittsburgh	1988-89	76	85	1.12
Brett Hull	St. Louis	1990-91	78	86	1.10
Frank Nighbor	Ottawa	1918-19	18	19	1.06
Cam Neely	Boston	1993-94	49	50	1.02
Reg Noble	Toronto	1919-20	24	24	1.00
Corb Denneny	Toronto	1919-20	24	24	1.00
Joe Malone	Hamilton	1921-22	24	24	1.00
Billy Boucher	Montreal	1922-23	24	24	1.00
Cy Denneny	Ottawa	1923-24	22	22	1.00
Maurice Richard	Montreal	1944-45	50	50	1.00
Alexander Mogilny	Buffalo	1992-93	77	76	0.99
Mario Lemieux	Pittsburgh	1995-96	70	69	0.99
Cooney Weiland	Boston	1929-30	44	43	0.98
Phil Esposito	Boston	1970-71	78	76	0.97
Jari Kurri	Edmonton	1984-85	73	71	0.97

Though he holds the regular-season and career records for goals, Wayne Gretzky will always been known as hockey's premier playmaker. Gretzky is the only player in NHL history to average better than two assists per game over a full season.

Assists-Per-Game Leaders, One Season

(Among players with 35 assists or more in one season)

Player	Team	Season	Games	Assists	Average
Wayne Gretzky	Edmonton	1985-86	80	163	2.04
Wayne Gretzky	Edmonton	1987-88	64	109	1.70
Wayne Gretzky	Edmonton	1984-85	80	135	1.69
Wayne Gretzky	Edmonton	1983-84	74	118	1.59
Wayne Gretzky	Edmonton	1982-83	80	125	1.56
Wayne Gretzky	Los Angeles	1990-91	78	122	1.56
Wayne Gretzky	Edmonton	1986-87	79	121	1.53
Mario Lemieux	Pittsburgh	1992-93	60	91	1.52
Wayne Gretzky	Edmonton	1981-82	80	120	1.50
Mario Lemieux	Pittsburgh	1988-89	76	114	1.50
Adam Oates	St. Louis	1990-91	61	90	1.48
Wayne Gretzky	Los Angeles	1988-89	78	114	1.46
Wayne Gretzky	Los Angeles	1989-90	73	102	1.40
Wayne Gretzky	Edmonton	1980-81	80	109	1.36
Mario Lemieux	Pittsburgh	1991-92	64	87	1.36
Mario Lemieux	Pittsburgh	1989-90	59	78	1.32
Bobby Orr	Boston	1970-71	78	102	1.31
Mario Lemieux	Pittsburgh	1995-96	70	92	1.31
Mario Lemieux	Pittsburgh	1987-88	77	98	1.27
Bobby Orr	Boston	1973-74	74	90	1.22
Wayne Gretzky	Los Angeles	1991-92	74	90	1.22
Ron Francis	Pittsburgh	1995-96	77	92	1.19
Mario Lemieux	Pittsburgh	1985-86	79	93	1.18
Bobby Clarke	Philadelphia	1975-76	76	89	1.17
Peter Stastny	Quebec	1981-82	80	93	1.16
Adam Oates	Boston	1992-93	84	97	1.15
Doug Gilmour	Toronto	1992-93	83	95	1.14
Wayne Gretzky	Los Angeles	1993-94	81	92	1.14
Paul Coffey	Edmonton	1985-86	79	90	1.14
Bobby Orr	Boston	1969-70	76	87	1.14
Bryan Trottier	NY Islanders	1978-79	76	87	1.14
Bobby Orr	Boston	1972-73	63	72	1.14
Bill Cowley	Boston	1943-44	36	41	1.14
Pat LaFontaine	Buffalo	1992-93	84	95	1.13
Steve Yzerman	Detroit	1988-89	80	90	1.13
Paul Coffey	Pittsburgh	1987-88	46	52	1.13
Bobby Orr	Boston	1974-75	80	89	1.11
Bobby Clarke	Philadelphia	1974-75	80	89	1.11
Paul Coffey	Pittsburgh	1988-89	75	83	1.11
Wayne Gretzky	Los Angeles	1992-93	45	49	1.11
Denis Savard	Chicago	1982-83	78	86	1.10
Denis Savard	Chicago	1981-82	80	87	1.09
Denis Savard	Chicago	1987-88	80	87	1.09
Wayne Gretzky	Edmonton	1979-80	79	86	1.09
Ron Francis	Pittsburgh	1994-95	44	48	1.09
Paul Coffey	Edmonton	1983-84	80	86	1.08
Elmer Lach	Montreal	1944-45	50	54	1.08
Peter Stastny	Quebec	1985-86	76	81	1.07
Jaromir Jagr	Pittsburgh	1995-96	82	87	1.06
Mark Messier	Edmonton	1989-90	79	84	1.06
Peter Forsberg	Colorado	1995-96	82	86	1.05
Paul Coffey	Edmonton	1984-85	80	84	1.05
Marcel Dionne	Los Angeles	1979-80	80	84	1.05
Bobby Orr	Boston	1971-72	76	80	1.05
Mike Bossy	NY Islanders	1981-82	80	83	1.04
Adam Oates	Boston	1993-94	77	80	1.04
Phil Esposito	Boston	1968-69	74	77	1.04
Bryan Trottier	NY Islanders	1983-84	68	71	1.04
Pete Mahovlich	Montreal	1974-75	80	82	1.03
Kent Nilsson	Calgary	1980-81	80	82	1.03
Peter Stastny	Quebec	1982-83	75	77	1.03
Jaromir Jagr	Pittsburgh	1998-99	81	83	1.02
Doug Gilmour	Toronto	1993-94	83	84	1.01
Bernie Nicholls	Los Angeles	1988-89	79	80	1.01
Guy Lafleur	Montreal	1979-80	74	75	1.01
Guy Lafleur	Montreal	1976-77	80	80	1.00
Marcel Dionne	Los Angeles	1984-85	80	80	1.00
Brian Leetch	NY Rangers	1991-92	80	80	1.00
Bryan Trottier	NY Islanders	1977-78	77	77	1.00
Mike Bossy	NY Islanders	1983-84	67	67	1.00
Jean Ratelle	NY Rangers	1971-72	63	63	1.00
Steve Yzerman	Detroit	1993-94	58	58	1.00
Ron Francis	Hartford	1985-86	53	53	1.00
Guy Chouinard	Calgary	1980-81	52	52	1.00
Elmer Lach	Montreal	1943-44	48	48	1.00

Points-Per-Game Leaders, One Season

(Among players with 50 points or more in one season)

Player	Team	Season	Games	Points	Average	Player	Team	Season	Games	Points	Average
Wayne Gretzky	Edmonton	1983-84	74	205	2.77	Peter Stastny	Quebec	1982-83	75	124	1.65
Wayne Gretzky	Edmonton	1985-86	80	215	2.69	Bobby Orr	Boston	1973-74	74	122	1.65
Mario Lemieux	Pittsburgh	1992-93	60	160	2.67	Kent Nilsson	Calgary	1980-81	80	131	1.64
Wayne Gretzky	Edmonton	1981-82	80	212	2.65	Wayne Gretzky	Los Angeles	1991-92	74	121	1.64
Mario Lemieux	Pittsburgh	1988-89	76	199	2.62	Denis Savard	Chicago	1987-88	80	131	1.64
Wayne Gretzky	Edmonton	1984-85	80	208	2.60	Steve Yzerman	Detroit	1992-93	84	137	1.63
Wayne Gretzky	Edmonton	1982-83	80	196	2.45	Marcel Dionne	Los Angeles	1978-79	80	130	1.63
Wayne Gretzky	Edmonton	1987-88	64	149	2.33	Dale Hawerchuk	Winnipeg	1984-85	80	130	1.63
Wayne Gretzky	Edmonton	1986-87	79	183	2.32	Mark Messier	Edmonton	1989-90	79	129	1.63
Mario Lemieux	Pittsburgh	1995-96	70	161	2.30	Bryan Trottier	NY Islanders	1983-84	68	111	1.63
Mario Lemieux	Pittsburgh	1987-88	77	168	2.18	Pat LaFontaine	Buffalo	1991-92	57	93	1.63
Wayne Gretzky	Los Angeles	1988-89	78	168	2.15	Charlie Simmer	Los Angeles	1980-81	65	105	1.62
Wayne Gretzky	Los Angeles	1990-91	78	163	2.09	Guy Lafleur	Montreal	1978-79	80	129	1.61
Mario Lemieux	Pittsburgh	1989-90	59	123	2.08	Bryan Trottier	NY Islanders	1981-82	80	129	1.61
Wayne Gretzky	Edmonton	1980-81	80	164	2.05	Phil Esposito	Boston	1974-75	79	127	1.61
Mario Lemieux	Pittsburgh	1991-92	64	131	2.05	Steve Yzerman	Detroit	1989-90	79	127	1.61
Bill Cowley	Boston	1943-44	36	71	1.97	Peter Stastny	Quebec	1985-86	76	122	1.61
Phil Esposito	Boston	1970-71	78	152	1.95	Mario Lemieux	Pittsburgh	1996-97	76	122	1.61
Wayne Gretzky	Los Angeles	1989-90	73	142	1.95	Michel Goulet	Quebec	1983-84	75	121	1.61
Steve Yzerman	Detroit	1988-89	80	155	1.94	Wayne Gretzky	Los Angeles	1993-94	81	130	1.60
Bernie Nicholls	Los Angeles	1988-89	79	150	1.90	Bryan Trottier	NY Islanders	1977-78	77	123	1.60
Adam Oates	St. Louis	1990-91	61	115	1.89	Bobby Orr	Boston	1972-73	63	101	1.60
Phil Esposito	Boston	1973-74	78	145	1.86	Guy Chouinard	Calgary	1980-81	52	83	1.60
Jari Kurri	Edmonton	1984-85	73	135	1.85	Elmer Lach	Montreal	1944-45	50	80	1.60
Mike Bossy	NY Islanders	1981-82	80	147	1.84	Pierre Turgeon	NY Islanders	1992-93	83	132	1.59
Jaromir Jagr	Pittsburgh	1995-96	82	149	1.82	Steve Yzerman	Detroit	1987-88	64	102	1.59
Mario Lemieux	Pittsburgh	1985-86	79	141	1.78	Mike Bossy	NY Islanders	1978-79	80	126	1.58
Bobby Orr	Boston	1970-71	78	139	1.78	Paul Coffey	Edmonton	1983-84	80	126	1.58
Jari Kurri	Edmonton	1983-84	64	113	1.77	Marcel Dionne	Los Angeles	1984-85	80	126	1.58
Pat LaFontaine	Buffalo	1992-93	84	148	1.76	Bobby Orr	Boston	1969-70	76	120	1.58
Bryan Trottier	NY Islanders	1978-79	76	134	1.76	Eric Lindros	Philadelphia	1995-96	73	115	1.58
Mike Bossy	NY Islanders	1983-84	67	118	1.76	Charlie Simmer	Los Angeles	1979-80	64	101	1.58
Paul Coffey	Edmonton	1985-86	79	138	1.75	Teemu Selanne	Winnipeg	1992-93	84	132	1.57
Phil Esposito	Boston	1971-72	76	133	1.75	Jaromir Jagr	Pittsburgh	1998-99	81	127	1.57
Peter Stastny	Quebec	1981-82	80	139	1.74	Bobby Clarke	Philadelphia	1975-76	76	119	1.57
Wayne Gretzky	Edmonton	1979-80	79	137	1.73	Guy Lafleur	Montreal	1975-76	80	125	1.56
Jean Ratelle	NY Rangers	1971-72	63	109	1.73	Dave Taylor	Los Angeles	1980-81	72	112	1.56
Marcel Dionne	Los Angeles	1979-80	80	137	1.71	Denis Savard	Chicago	1982-83	78	121	1.55
Herb Cain	Boston	1943-44	48	82	1.71	Ron Francis	Pittsburgh	1995-96	77	119	1.55
Guy Lafleur	Montreal	1976-77	80	136	1.70	Mike Bossy	NY Islanders	1985-86	80	123	1.54
Dennis Maruk	Washington	1981-82	80	136	1.70	Kevin Stevens	Pittsburgh	1991-92	80	123	1.54
Phil Esposito	Boston	1968-69	74	126	1.70	Bobby Orr	Boston	1971-72	76	117	1.54
Guy Lafleur	Montreal	1974-75	70	119	1.70	Mike Bossy	NY Islanders	1984-85	76	117	1.54
Mario Lemieux	Pittsburgh	1986-87	63	107	1.70	Kevin Stevens	Pittsburgh	1992-93	72	111	1.54
Adam Oates	Boston	1992-93	84	142	1.69	Doug Bentley	Chicago	1943-44	50	77	1.54
Bobby Orr	Boston	1974-75	80	135	1.69	Doug Gilmour	Toronto	1992-93	83	127	1.53
Marcel Dionne	Los Angeles	1980-81	80	135	1.69	Marcel Dionne	Los Angeles	1976-77	80	122	1.53
Guy Lafleur	Montreal	1977-78	78	132	1.69	**Jaromir Jagr**	**Pittsburgh**	**99-2000**	**63**	**96**	**1.52**
Guy Lafleur	Montreal	1979-80	74	125	1.69	Eric Lindros	Philadelphia	1996-97	52	79	1.52
Rob Brown	Pittsburgh	1988-89	68	115	1.69	Eric Lindros	Philadelphia	1994-95	46	70	1.52
Jari Kurri	Edmonton	1985-86	78	131	1.68	Marcel Dionne	Detroit	1974-75	80	121	1.51
Brett Hull	St. Louis	1990-91	78	131	1.68	Dale Hawerchuk	Winnipeg	1987-88	80	121	1.51
Phil Esposito	Boston	1972-73	78	130	1.67	Paul Coffey	Pittsburgh	1988-89	75	113	1.51
Cooney Weiland	Boston	1929-30	44	73	1.66	Jaromir Jagr	Pittsburgh	1996-97	63	95	1.51
Alexander Mogilny	Buffalo	1992-93	77	127	1.65	Cam Neely	Boston	1993-94	49	74	1.51

Star scorer Cooney Weiland and coach Art Ross helped the Boston Bruins take full advantage of the new rules when the NHL first allowed forward passing in the offensive zone in 1929-30. Weiland set a new NHL record with 73 points that year.

Mario Lemieux (right) and Warren Young (below) were both named to the All-Rookie Team as members of the Pittsburgh Penguins in 1984-85. Lemieux had 43 goals and 57 assists, while Young had 40 goals and 32 assists.

Rookie Scoring Records

All-Time Top 50 Goal-Scoring Rookies

	Rookie	Team	Position	Season	GP	G	A	PTS
1.	* Teemu Selanne	Winnipeg	Right wing	1992-93	84	**76**	56	132
2.	* Mike Bossy	NY Islanders	Right wing	1977-78	73	**53**	38	91
3.	* Joe Nieuwendyk	Calgary	Center	1987-88	75	**51**	41	92
4.	* Dale Hawerchuk	Winnipeg	Center	1981-82	80	**45**	58	103
	* Luc Robitaille	Los Angeles	Left wing	1986-87	79	**45**	39	84
6.	Rick Martin	Buffalo	Left wing	1971-72	73	**44**	30	74
	Barry Pederson	Boston	Center	1981-82	80	**44**	48	92
8.	* Steve Larmer	Chicago	Right wing	1982-83	80	**43**	47	90
	* Mario Lemieux	Pittsburgh	Center	1984-85	73	**43**	57	100
10.	Eric Lindros	Philadelphia	Center	1992-93	61	**41**	34	75
11.	Darryl Sutter	Chicago	Left wing	1980-81	76	**40**	22	62
	Sylvain Turgeon	Hartford	Left wing	1983-84	76	**40**	32	72
	Warren Young	Pittsburgh	Left wing	1984-85	80	**40**	32	72
14.	* Eric Vail	Atlanta	Left wing	1974-75	72	**39**	21	60
	Anton Stastny	Quebec	Left wing	1980-81	80	**39**	46	85
	* Peter Stastny	Quebec	Center	1980-81	77	**39**	70	109
	Steve Yzerman	Detroit	Center	1983-84	80	**39**	48	87
18.	* Gilbert Perreault	Buffalo	Center	1970-71	78	**38**	34	72
	Neal Broten	Minnesota	Center	1981-82	73	**38**	60	98
	Ray Sheppard	Buffalo	Right wing	1987-88	74	**38**	27	65
	Mikael Renberg	Philadelphia	Left wing	1993-94	83	**38**	44	82
22.	Jorgen Pettersson	St. Louis	Left wing	1980-81	62	**37**	36	73
	Jimmy Carson	Los Angeles	Centre	1986-87	80	**37**	42	79
24.	Mike Foligno	Detroit	Right wing	1979-80	80	**36**	35	71
	Mike Bullard	Pittsburgh	Center	1981-82	75	**36**	27	63
	Paul MacLean	Winnipeg	Right wing	1981-82	74	**36**	25	61
	Tony Granato	NY Rangers	Right wing	1988-89	78	**36**	27	63
28.	Marian Stastny	Quebec	Right wing	1981-82	74	**35**	54	89
	Brian Bellows	Minnesota	Right wing	1982-83	78	**35**	30	65
	Tony Amonte	NY Rangers	Right wing	1991-92	79	**35**	34	69
31.	Nels Stewart	Mtl. Maroons	Center	1925-26	36	**34**	8	42
	* Danny Grant	Minnesota	Left wing	1968-69	75	**34**	31	65
	Norm Ferguson	Oakland	Right wing	1968-69	76	**34**	20	54
	Brian Propp	Philadelphia	Left wing	1979-80	80	**34**	41	75
	Wendel Clark	Toronto	Left wing	1985-86	66	**34**	11	45
	* Pavel Bure	Vancouver	Right wing	1991-92	65	**34**	26	60
37.	* Willi Plett	Atlanta	Right wing	1976-77	64	**33**	23	56
	Dale McCourt	Detroit	Center	1977-78	76	**33**	39	72
	Mark Pavelich	NY Rangers	Center	1981-82	79	**33**	43	76
	Ron Flockhart	Philadelphia	Center	1981-82	72	**33**	39	72
	Steve Bozek	Los Angeles	Center	1981-82	71	**33**	23	56
	Jason Arnott	Edmonton	Center	1993-94	78	**33**	35	68
43.	Bill Mosienko	Chicago	Right wing	1943-44	50	**32**	38	70
	Michel Bergeron	Detroit	Right wing	1975-76	72	**32**	27	59
	* Bryan Trottier	NY Islanders	Center	1975-76	80	**32**	63	95
	Don Murdoch	NY Rangers	Right wing	1976-77	59	**32**	24	56
	Jari Kurri	Edmonton	Left wing	1980-81	75	**32**	43	75
	Bobby Carpenter	Washington	Center	1981-82	80	**32**	35	67
	Kjell Dahlin	Montreal	Right wing	1985-86	77	**32**	39	71
	Petr Klima	Detroit	Left wing	1985-86	74	**32**	24	56
	Darren Turcotte	NY Rangers	Right wing	1989-90	76	**32**	34	66
	Joe Juneau	Boston	Center	1992-93	84	**32**	70	102

* Calder Trophy Winner

All-Time Top 50 Point-Scoring Rookies

	Rookie	Team	Position	Season	GP	G	A	PTS
1.	* Teemu Selanne	Winnipeg	Right wing	1992-93	84	76	56	**132**
2.	* Peter Stastny	Quebec	Center	1980-81	77	39	70	**109**
3.	* Dale Hawerchuk	Winnipeg	Center	1981-82	80	45	58	**103**
	Joe Juneau	Boston	Center	1992-93	84	32	70	**102**
5.	* Mario Lemieux	Pittsburgh	Center	1984-85	73	43	57	**100**
6.	Neal Broten	Minnesota	Center	1981-82	73	38	60	**98**
7.	* Bryan Trottier	NY Islanders	Center	1975-76	80	32	63	**95**
8.	Barry Pederson	Boston	Center	1981-82	80	44	48	**92**
	* Joe Nieuwendyk	Calgary	Center	1987-88	75	51	41	**92**
10.	* Mike Bossy	NY Islanders	Right wing	1977-78	73	53	38	**91**
11.	* Steve Larmer	Chicago	Right wing	1982-83	80	43	47	**90**
12.	Marian Stastny	Quebec	Right wing	1981-82	74	35	54	**89**
13.	Steve Yzerman	Detroit	Center	1983-84	80	39	48	**87**
14.	* Sergei Makarov	Calgary	Right wing	1989-90	80	24	62	**86**
15.	Anton Stastny	Quebec	Left wing	1980-81	80	39	46	**85**
16.	* Luc Robitaille	Los Angeles	Left wing	1986-87	79	45	39	**84**
17.	Mikael Renberg	Philadelphia	Left wing	1993-94	83	38	44	**82**
18.	Jimmy Carson	Los Angeles	Center	1986-87	80	37	42	**79**
	Sergei Fedorov	Detroit	Center	1990-91	77	31	48	**79**
	Alexei Yashin	Ottawa	Center	1993-94	83	30	49	**79**
21.	Marcel Dionne	Detroit	Center	1971-72	78	28	49	**77**
22.	Larry Murphy	Los Angeles	Defense	1980-81	80	16	60	**76**
	Mark Pavelich	NY Rangers	Center	1981-82	79	33	43	**76**
	Dave Poulin	Philadelphia	Center	1983-84	73	31	45	**76**
25.	Brian Propp	Philadelphia	Left wing	1979-80	80	34	41	**75**
	Jari Kurri	Edmonton	Left wing	1980-81	75	32	43	**75**
	Denis Savard	Chicago	Center	1980-81	76	28	47	**75**
	Mike Modano	Minnesota	Center	1989-90	80	29	46	**75**
	Eric Lindros	Philadelphia	Center	1992-93	61	41	34	**75**
30.	Rick Martin	Buffalo	Left wing	1971-72	73	44	30	**74**
	* Bobby Smith	Minnesota	Center	1978-79	80	30	44	**74**
32.	Jorgen Pettersson	St. Louis	Left wing	1980-81	62	37	36	**73**
33.	* Gilbert Perreault	Buffalo	Center	1970-71	78	38	34	**72**
	Dale McCourt	Detroit	Center	1977-78	76	33	39	**72**
	Ron Flockhart	Philadelphia	Center	1981-82	72	33	39	**72**
	Sylvain Turgeon	Hartford	Left wing	1983-84	76	40	32	**72**
	Warren Young	Pittsburgh	Left wing	1984-85	80	40	32	**72**
	Carey Wilson	Calgary	Center	1984-85	74	24	48	**72**
	Alexei Zhamnov	Winnipeg	Center	1992-93	68	25	47	**72**
40.	Mike Foligno	Detroit	Right wing	1979-80	80	36	35	**71**
	Dave Christian	Winnipeg	Center	1980-81	80	28	43	**71**
	Mats Naslund	Montreal	Left wing	1982-83	74	26	45	**71**
	Kjell Dahlin	Montreal	Right wing	1985-86	77	32	39	**71**
	* Brian Leetch	NY Rangers	Defense	1988-89	68	23	48	**71**
45.	Bill Mosienko	Chicago	Right wing	1943-44	50	32	38	**70**
	* Scott Gomez	New Jersey	Center	99-2000	82	19	51	**70**
47.	Roland Eriksson	Minnesota	Center	1976-77	80	25	44	**69**
	Tony Amonte	NY Rangers	Right wing	1991-92	79	35	34	**69**
49.	Jude Drouin	Minnesota	Center	1970-71	75	16	52	**68**
	Pierre Larouche	Pittsburgh	Center	1974-75	79	31	37	**68**
	Ron Francis	Hartford	Center	1981-82	59	25	43	**68**
	* Gary Suter	Calgary	Defense	1985-86	80	18	50	**68**
	Jason Arnott	Edmonton	Center	1993-94	84	33	35	**68**

* Calder Trophy Winner

Maurice Richard

Bill Barber

Mike Bullard

50-Goal Seasons

Player	Team	Date of 50th Goal	Score		Goaltender	Player's Game No.	Team Game No.	Total Goals	Total Games	Age When First 50th Scored (Yrs. & Mos.)
Maurice Richard	Mtl.	18-3-45	Mtl. 4	at Bos. 2	Harvey Bennett	50	50	50	50	23.7
Bernie Geoffrion	Mtl.	16-3-61	Tor. 2	at Mtl. 5	Cesare Maniago	62	68	50	64	30.1
Bobby Hull	Chi.	25-3-62	Chi. 1	at NYR 4	Gump Worsley	70	70	50	70	23.2
Bobby Hull	Chi.	2-3-66	Det. 4	at Chi. 5	Hank Bassen	52	57	54	65	
Bobby Hull	Chi.	18-3-67	Chi. 5	at Tor. 9	Bruce Gamble	63	66	52	66	
Bobby Hull	Chi.	5-3-69	NYR 4	at Chi. 4	Ed Giacomin	64	66	58	74	
Phil Esposito	Bos.	20-2-71	Bos. 4	at L.A. 5	Denis DeJordy	58	58	76	78	29.0
John Bucyk	Bos.	16-3-71	Bos. 11	at Det. 4	Roy Edwards	69	69	51	78	35.10
Phil Esposito	Bos.	20-2-72	Bos. 3	at Chi. 1	Tony Esposito	60	60	66	76	
Bobby Hull	Chi.	2-4-72	Det. 1	at Chi. 6	Andy Brown	78	78	50	78	
Vic Hadfield	NYR	2-4-72	Mtl. 6	at NYR 5	Denis DeJordy	78	78	50	78	31.6
Phil Esposito	Bos.	25-3-73	Buf. 1	at Bos. 6	Roger Crozier	75	75	55	78	
Mickey Redmond	Det.	27-3-73	Det. 8	at Tor. 1	Ron Low	73	75	52	76	25.3
Rick MacLeish	Phi.	1-4-73	Phi. 4	at Pit. 5	Cam Newton	78	78	50	78	23.2
Phil Esposito	Bos.	20-2-74	Bos. 5	at Min. 5	Cesare Maniago	56	56	68	78	
Mickey Redmond	Det.	23-3-74	NYR 3	at Det 5	Ed Giacomin	69	71	51	76	
Ken Hodge	Bos.	6-4-74	Bos. 2	at Mtl. 6	Michel Larocque	75	77	50	76	29.10
Rick Martin	Buf.	7-4-74	St. L. 2	at Buf. 5	Wayne Stephenson	78	78	52	78	22.9
Phil Esposito	Bos.	8-2-75	Bos. 8	at Det. 5	Jim Rutherford	54	54	61	79	
Guy Lafleur	Mtl.	29-3-75	K.C. 1	at Mtl. 4	Denis Herron	66	76	53	70	23.6
Danny Grant	Det.	2-4-75	Wsh. 3	at Det. 8	John Adams	78	78	50	80	29.2
Rick Martin	Buf.	3-4-75	Bos. 2	at Buf. 4	Ken Broderick	67	79	52	68	
Reggie Leach	Phi.	14-3-76	Atl. 1	at Phi. 6	Dan Bouchard	69	69	61	80	25.11
Jean Pronovost	Pit.	24-3-76	Bos. 5	at Pit. 5	Gilles Gilbert	74	74	52	80	30.3
Guy Lafleur	Mtl.	27-3-76	K.C. 2	at Mtl. 8	Denis Herron	76	76	56	80	
Bill Barber	Phi.	3-4-76	Buf. 2	at Phi. 5	Al Smith	79	79	50	80	23.9
Pierre Larouche	Pit.	3-4-76	Wsh. 5	at Pit. 4	Ron Low	75	79	53	76	20.5
Danny Gare	Buf.	4-4-76	Tor. 2	at Buf. 5	Gord McRae	79	80	50	79	21.11
Steve Shutt	Mtl.	1-3-77	Mtl. 5	at NYI 4	Glenn Resch	65	65	60	80	24.8
Guy Lafleur	Mtl.	6-3-77	Mtl. 1	at Buf. 4	Don Edwards	68	68	56	80	
Marcel Dionne	L.A.	2-4-77	Min. 2	at L.A. 7	Pete LoPresti	79	79	53	80	25.8
Guy Lafleur	Mtl.	8-3-78	Wsh. 3	at Mtl. 4	Jim Bedard	63	65	60	78	
Mike Bossy	NYI	1-4-78	Wsh. 2	at NYI 3	Bernie Wolfe	69	76	53	73	21.2
Mike Bossy	NYI	24-2-79	Det. 1	at NYI 3	Rogie Vachon	58	58	69	80	
Marcel Dionne	L.A.	11-3-79	L.A. 3	at Phi. 6	Wayne Stephenson	68	68	59	80	
Guy Lafleur	Mtl.	31-3-79	Pit. 3	at Mtl. 5	Denis Herron	76	76	52	80	
Guy Chouinard	Atl.	6-4-79	NYR 2	at Atl. 9	John Davidson	79	79	50	80	22.5
Marcel Dionne	L.A.	12-3-80	L.A. 2	at Pit. 4	Nick Ricci	70	70	53	80	
Mike Bossy	NYI	16-3-80	NYI 6	at Chi. 1	Tony Esposito	68	71	51	75	
Charlie Simmer	L.A.	19-3-80	Det. 3	at L.A. 4	Jim Rutherford	57	73	56	64	26.0
Pierre Larouche	Mtl.	25-3-80	Chi. 4	at Mtl. 8	Tony Esposito	72	75	50	73	
Danny Gare	Buf.	27-3-80	Det. 1	at Buf. 10	Jim Rutherford	71	75	56	76	
Blaine Stoughton	Hfd.	28-3-80	Hfd. 4	at Van. 4	Glen Hanlon	75	75	56	80	27.0
Guy Lafleur	Mtl.	2-4-80	Mtl. 7	at Det. 2	Rogie Vachon	72	78	50	74	
Wayne Gretzky	Edm.	2-4-80	Min. 1	at Edm. 1	Gary Edwards	78	79	51	79	19.2
Reggie Leach	Phi.	3-4-80	Wsh. 2	at Phi. 4	empty net	75	79	50	76	
Mike Bossy	NYI	24-1-81	Que. 3	at NYI 7	Ron Grahame	50	50	68	79	
Charlie Simmer	L.A.	26-1-81	L.A. 7	at Que. 5	Michel Dion	51	51	56	65	
Marcel Dionne	L.A.	8-3-81	L.A. 4	at Wpg. 1	Markus Mattsson	68	68	58	80	
Wayne Babych	St. L.	12-3-81	St. L. 3	at Mtl. 4	Richard Sevigny	70	68	54	78	22.9
Wayne Gretzky	Edm.	15-3-81	Edm. 3	at Cgy. 3	Pat Riggin	69	69	55	80	
Rick Kehoe	Pit.	16-3-81	Pit. 7	at Edm. 6	Eddie Mio	70	70	55	80	29.7
Jacques Richard	Que.	29-3-81	Mtl. 0	at Que. 4	Richard Sevigny	76	75	52	78	28.6
Dennis Maruk	Wsh.	5-4-81	Det. 2	at Wsh. 7	Larry Lozinski	80	80	50	80	25.3
Wayne Gretzky	Edm.	30-12-81	Phi. 5	at Edm. 7	empty net	39	39	92	80	
Dennis Maruk	Wsh.	21-2-82	Wpg. 3	at Wsh. 6	Doug Soetaert	61	61	60	80	
Mike Bossy	NYI	4-3-82	Tor. 1	at NYI 10	Michel Larocque	66	66	64	80	
Dino Ciccarelli	Min.	8-3-82	St. L. 1	at Min. 8	Mike Liut	67	68	55	76	22.1
Rick Vaive	Tor.	24-3-82	St. L. 3	at Tor. 4	Mike Liut	72	75	54	77	22.10
Blaine Stoughton	Hfd.	28-3-82	Min. 5	at Hfd. 2	Gilles Meloche	76	76	52	80	
Rick Middleton	Bos.	28-3-82	Bos. 5	at Buf. 9	Paul Harrison	72	77	51	75	28.11
Marcel Dionne	L.A.	30-3-82	Cgy. 7	at L.A. 5	Pat Riggin	75	77	50	78	
Mark Messier	Edm.	31-3-82	L.A. 3	at Edm. 7	Mario Lessard	78	79	50	78	21.3
Bryan Trottier	NYI	3-4-82	Phi. 3	at NYI 6	Pete Peeters	79	79	50	80	25.9
Lanny McDonald	Cgy.	18-2-83	Cgy. 1	at Buf. 5	Bob Sauve	60	60	66	80	30.0
Wayne Gretzky	Edm.	19-2-83	Edm. 10	at Pit. 7	Nick Ricci	60	60	71	80	
Michel Goulet	Que.	5-3-83	Hfd. 3	at Que. 10	Mike Veisor	67	67	57	80	22.11
Mike Bossy	NYI	12-3-83	Wsh. 2	at NYI 6	Al Jensen	70	71	60	79	
Marcel Dionne	L.A.	17-3-83	Que. 3	at L.A. 4	Dan Bouchard	71	71	56	80	
Al Secord	Chi.	20-3-83	Tor. 3	at Chi. 7	Mike Palmateer	73	73	54	80	25.0
Rick Vaive	Tor.	30-3-83	Tor. 4	at Det. 2	Gilles Gilbert	76	78	51	78	
Wayne Gretzky	Edm.	7-1-84	Hfd. 3	at Edm. 5	Greg Millen	42	42	87	74	
Michel Goulet	Que.	8-3-84	Que. 8	at Pit. 6	Denis Herron	63	69	56	75	
Rick Vaive	Tor.	14-3-84	Min. 3	at Tor. 3	Gilles Meloche	69	72	52	76	
Mike Bullard	Pit.	14-3-84	Pit. 6	at L.A. 7	Markus Mattsson	71	72	51	76	23.0
Jari Kurri	Edm.	15-3-84	Edm. 2	at Mtl. 3	Rick Wamsley	57	73	52	64	23.10
Glenn Anderson	Edm.	21-3-84	Hfd. 3	at Edm. 5	Greg Millen	76	76	54	80	23.6
Tim Kerr	Phi.	22-3-84	Pit. 4	at Phi. 13	Denis Herron	74	75	54	79	24.3
Mike Bossy	NYI	31-3-84	NYI 3	at Wsh. 1	Pat Riggin	67	79	51	67	

Player	Team	Date of 50th Goal	Score	Goaltender	Player's Game No.	Team Game No.	Total Goals	Total Games	Age When First 50th Scored (Yrs. & Mos.)
Wayne Gretzky	Edm.	26-1-85	Pit. 3 at Edm. 6	Denis Herron	49	49	73	80	
Jari Kurri	Edm.	3-2-85	Hfd. 3 at Edm. 6	Greg Millen	50	53	71	73	
Mike Bossy	NYI	5-3-85	Phi. 5 at NYI 4	Bob Froese	61	65	58	76	
Michel Goulet	Que.	6-3-85	Buf. 3 at Que. 4	Tom Barrasso	62	73	55	69	
Tim Kerr	Phi.	7-3-85	Wsh. 6 at Phi. 9	Pat Riggin	63	65	54	74	
John Ogrodnick	Det.	13-3-85	Det. 6 at Edm. 7	Grant Fuhr	69	69	55	79	25.9
Bob Carpenter	Wsh.	21-3-85	Wsh. 2 at Mtl. 3	Steve Penney	72	72	53	80	21.9
Dale Hawerchuk	Wpg.	29-3-85	Chi. 5 at Wpg. 5	W. Skorodenski	77	77	53	80	21.11
Mike Gartner	Wsh.	7-4-85	Pit. 3 at Wsh. 7	Brian Ford	80	80	50	80	25.5
Jari Kurri	Edm.	4-3-86	Edm. 6 at Van. 2	Richard Brodeur	63	65	68	78	
Mike Bossy	NYI	11-3-86	Cgy. 4 at NYI 8	Rejean Lemelin	67	67	61	80	
Glenn Anderson	Edm.	14-3-86	Det. 3 at Edm. 12	Greg Stefan	63	71	54	72	
Michel Goulet	Que.	17-3-86	Que. 8 at Mtl. 6	Patrick Roy	67	72	53	75	
Wayne Gretzky	Edm.	18-3-86	Wpg. 2 at Edm. 4	Brian Hayward	72	72	52	80	
Tim Kerr	Phi.	20-3-86	Pit. 1 at Phi. 5	Roberto Romano	68	72	58	76	
Wayne Gretzky	Edm.	4-2-87	Edm. 6 at Min. 5	Don Beaupre	55	55	62	79	
Dino Ciccarelli	Min.	7-3-87	Pit. 7 at Min. 3	Gilles Meloche	66	66	52	80	
Mario Lemieux	Pit.	12-3-87	Que. 3 at Pit. 6	Mario Gosselin	53	70	54	63	21.5
Tim Kerr	Phi.	17-3-87	NYR 1 at Phi. 4	J. Vanbiesbrouck	67	71	58	75	
Jari Kurri	Edm.	17-3-87	N.J. 4 at Edm. 7	Craig Billington	69	70	54	79	
Mario Lemieux	Pit.	2-2-88	Wsh. 2 at Pit. 3	Pete Peeters	51	54	70	77	
Steve Yzerman	Det.	1-3-88	Buf. 0 at Det. 4	Tom Barrasso	64	64	50	64	22.10
Joe Nieuwendyk	Cgy.	12-3-88	Buf. 4 at Cgy. 10	Tom Barrasso	66	70	51	75	21.5
Craig Simpson	Edm.	15-3-88	Buf. 4 at Edm. 6	Jacques Cloutier	71	71	56	80	21.1
Jimmy Carson	L.A.	26-3-88	Chi. 5 at L.A. 9	Darren Pang	77	77	55	88	19.8
Luc Robitaille	L.A.	1-4-88	L.A. 6 at Cgy. 3	Mike Vernon	79	79	53	80	21.10
Hakan Loob	Cgy.	3-4-88	Min. 1 at Cgy. 4	Don Beaupre	80	80	50	80	27.9
Stephane Richer	Mtl.	3-4-88	Mtl. 4 at Buf. 4	Tom Barrasso	72	80	50	72	21.10
Mario Lemieux	Pit.	20-1-89	Pit. 3 at Wpg. 7	Pokey Reddick	44	46	85	76	
Bernie Nicholls	L.A.	28-1-89	Edm. 7 at L.A. 6	Grant Fuhr	51	51	70	79	27.7
Steve Yzerman	Det.	5-2-89	Det. 6 at Wpg. 2	Pokey Reddick	55	55	65	80	
Wayne Gretzky	L.A.	4-3-89	Phi. 2 at L.A. 6	Ron Hextall	66	67	54	78	
Joe Nieuwendyk	Cgy.	21-3-89	NYI 1 at Cgy. 4	Mark Fitzpatrick	72	74	51	77	
Joe Mullen	Cgy.	31-3-89	Wpg. 1 at Cgy. 4	Bob Essensa	78	79	51	79	32.1
Brett Hull	St. L.	6-2-90	Tor. 4 at St. L. 6	Jeff Reese	54	54	72	80	25.6
Steve Yzerman	Det.	24-2-90	Det. 3 at NYI 3	Glenn Healy	63	63	62	79	
Cam Neely	Bos.	10-3-90	Bos. 3 at NYI 3	Mark Fitzpatrick	69	71	55	76	24.9
Luc Robitaille	L.A.	31-3-90	L.A. 3 at Van. 6	Kirk McLean	79	79	52	80	
Brian Bellows	Min.	22-3-90	Min. 5 at Det. 1	Tim Cheveldae	75	75	55	80	25.6
Pat LaFontaine	NYI	24-3-90	NYI 5 at Edm. 5	Bill Ranford	71	77	54	74	25.1
Stephane Richer	Mtl.	24-3-90	Mtl. 4 at Hfd. 7	Peter Sidorkiewicz	75	77	51	75	
Gary Leeman	Tor.	28-3-90	NYI 6 at Tor. 3	Mark Fitzpatrick	78	78	51	80	26.1
Brett Hull	St. L.	25-1-91	St. L. 9 at Det. 4	David Gagnon	49	49	86	78	
Cam Neely	Bos.	26-3-91	Bos. 7 at Que. 4	empty net	67	78	51	69	
Theoren Fleury	Cgy.	26-3-91	Van. 2 at Cgy. 7	Bob Mason	77	77	51	79	22.9
Steve Yzerman	Det.	30-3-91	NYR 5 at Det. 6	Mike Richter	79	79	51	80	
Brett Hull	St. L.	28-1-92	St. L. 3 at L.A. 3	Kelly Hrudey	50	50	70	73	
Jeremy Roenick	Chi.	7-3-92	Chi. 2 at Bos. 1	Daniel Berthiaume	67	67	53	80	22.2
Kevin Stevens	Pit.	24-3-92	Pit. 3 at Det. 4	Tim Cheveldae	74	74	54	80	26.11
Gary Roberts	Cgy.	31-3-92	Edm. 2 at Cgy. 5	Bill Ranford	73	77	53	76	25.10
Alexander Mogilny	Buf.	3-2-93	Hfd. 2 at Buf. 3	Sean Burke	46	53	76	77	23.11
Teemu Selanne	Wpg.	28-2-93	Min. 6 at Wpg. 7	Darcy Wakaluk	63	63	76	84	22.6
Pavel Bure	Van.	1-3-93	Van. 5 at Buf. 2*	Grant Fuhr	63	63	60	83	21.11
Steve Yzerman	Det.	10-3-93	Det. 6 at Edm. 3	Bill Ranford	70	70	58	84	
Luc Robitaille	L.A.	15-3-93	L.A. 4 at Buf. 2	Grant Fuhr	69	69	63	84	
Brett Hull	St. L.	20-3-93	St. L. 2 at L.A. 3	Robb Stauber	73	73	54	80	
Mario Lemieux	Pit.	21-3-93	Pit. 6 at Edm. 4**	Ron Tugnutt	48	72	69	60	
Kevin Stevens	Pit.	21-3-93	Pit. 6 at Edm. 4**	Ron Tugnutt	62	72	55	72	
Dave Andreychuk	Tor.	22-3-93	Tor. 5 at Wpg. 4	Bob Essensa	72	73	54	83	29.6
Pat LaFontaine	Buf.	28-3-93	Ott. 1 at Buf. 3	Peter Sidorkiewicz	75	75	53	84	
Pierre Turgeon	NYI	2-4-93	NYI 3 at NYR 2	Mike Richter	75	76	58	83	23.8
Mark Recchi	Phi.	3-4-93	T.B. 2 at Phi. 6	J-C Bergeron	77	77	53	84	25.2
Jeremy Roenick	Chi.	15-4-93	Tor. 2 at Chi. 3	Felix Potvin	84	84	50	84	
Brendan Shanahan	St. L.	15-4-93	T.B. 5 at St. L. 6	Pat Jablonski	71	84	51	71	24.3
Cam Neely	Bos.	7-3-94	Wsh. 3 at Bos. 6	Don Beaupre	44	66	50	49	
Sergei Fedorov	Det.	15-3-94	Van. 2 at Det. 5	Kirk McLean	67	69	56	82	24.3
Pavel Bure	Van.	23-3-94	Van. 6 at L.A. 3	empty net	65	73	60	76	
Adam Graves	NYR	23-3-94	NYR 5 at Edm. 3	Bill Ranford	74	74	51	84	25.11
Dave Andreychuk	Tor	24-3-94	S.J. 2 at Tor. 1	Arturs Irbe	73	74	53	83	
Brett Hull	St. L.	25-3-94	Dal. 3 at St. L. 5	Andy Moog	71	74	52	81	
Ray Sheppard	Det.	29-3-94	Hfd. 2 at Det. 6	Sean Burke	74	76	52	82	27.10
Brendan Shanahan	St. L.	12-4-94	St. L. 5 at Dal. 9	Andy Moog	80	83	52	81	
Mike Modano	Dal.	12-4-94	St. L. 5 at Dal. 9	Curtis Joseph	75	83	50	76	23.11
Mario Lemieux	Pit.	23-2-96	Hfd. 4 at Pit. 5	Sean Burke	50	59	69	70	
Jaromir Jagr	Pit.	23-2-96	Hfd. 4 at Pit. 5	Sean Burke	59	59	62	82	24.0
Alexander Mogilny	Van.	29-2-96	St. L. 2 at Van. 2	Grant Fuhr	60	63	55	79	
Peter Bondra	Wsh.	3-4-96	Wsh. 5 at Buf. 1	Andrei Trefilov	62	77	52	67	28.1
Joe Sakic	Col.	7-4-96	Col. 4 at Dal. 1	empty net	79	79	51	82	26.7
John LeClair	Phi.	10-4-96	Phi. 5 at N.J. 1	Corey Schwab	80	80	51	82	26.7
Keith Tkachuk	Wpg.	12-4-96	L.A. 3 at Wpg. 5	empty net	75	81	50	76	24.0
Paul Kariya	Ana.	14-4-96	Wpg. 2 at Ana. 5	N. Khabibulin	82	82	50	82	21.5
Keith Tkachuk	Phx.	6-4-97	Phx. 1 at Col. 2	Patrick Roy	78	79	52	81	
Teemu Selanne	Ana.	9-4-97	L.A. 1 at Ana. 4	empty net	77	81	51	78	
Mario Lemieux	Pit.	11-4-97	Pit. 2 at Fla. 4	J. Vanbiesbrouck	75	81	50	76	
John LeClair	Phi.	13-4-97	N.J. 1 at Phi. 5	Mike Dunham	82	82	50	82	
Teemu Selanne	Ana.	25-3-98	Ana. 3 at Chi. 2	Jeff Hackett	66	71	52	73	
John LeClair	Phi.	13-4-98	Phi. 1 at Buf. 2	Dominik Hasek	79	79	51	82	
Pavel Bure	Van.	17-4-98	Cgy. 4 at Van. 2	Dwayne Roloson	81	81	51	82	
Peter Bondra	Wsh.	18-4-98	Wsh. 4 at Car. 3	Mike Fountain	75	80	52	76	
Pavel Bure	Fla.	18-3-00	Fla. 4 at NYI 2	empty net	63	71	58	74	

* neutral site game played at Hamilton; ** neutral site game played at Cleveland

Luc Robitaille

Pierre Turgeon

Paul Kariya

Phil Esposito

Vic Hadfield

Glenn Anderson

100-Point Seasons

Player	Team	Date of 100th Point	G or A	Score		Player's Game No.	Team Game No.	Points G - A PTS	Total Games	Age when first 100th point scored (Yrs. & Mos.)
Phil Esposito	Bos.	2-3-69	(G)	Pit. 0	at Bos. 4	60	62	49-77 — 126	74	27.1
Bobby Hull	Chi.	20-3-69	(G)	Chi. 5	at Bos. 5	71	71	58-49 — 107	76	30.2
Gordie Howe	Det.	30-3-69	(G)	Det. 5	at Chi. 9	76	76	44-59 — 103	76	41.0
Bobby Orr	Bos.	15-3-70	(G)	Det. 5	at Bos. 5	67	67	33-87 — 120	76	22.11
Phil Esposito	Bos.	6-2-71	(A)	Buf. 3	at Bos. 4	51	51	76-76 — 152	78	
Bobby Orr	Bos.	22-2-71	(A)	Bos. 4	at L.A. 5	58	58	37-102 — 139	78	
John Bucyk	Bos.	13-3-71	(G)	Bos. 6	at Van. 3	68	68	51-65 — 116	78	35.10
Ken Hodge	Bos.	21-3-71	(A)	Buf. 7	at Bos. 5	72	72	43-62 — 105	78	26.9
Jean Ratelle	NYR	18-2-72	(A)	NYR 2	at Cal. 2	58	58	46-63 — 109	63	31.4
Phil Esposito	Bos.	19-2-72	(A)	Bos. 6	at Min. 4	59	59	66-67 — 133	76	
Bobby Orr	Bos.	2-3-72	(A)	Van. 3	at Bos. 7	64	64	37-80 — 117	76	
Vic Hadfield	NYR	25-3-72	(A)	NYR 3	at Mtl. 3	74	74	50-56 — 106	78	31.5
Phil Esposito	Bos.	3-3-73	(A)	Bos. 1	at Mtl. 5	64	64	55-75 — 130	78	
Bobby Clarke	Phi.	29-3-73	(G)	Atl. 2	at Phi. 4	76	76	37-67 — 104	78	23.7
Bobby Orr	Bos.	31-3-73	(G)	Bos. 3	at Tor. 7	62	77	29-72 — 101	63	
Rick MacLeish	Phi.	1-4-73	(G)	Phi. 4	at Pit. 5	78	78	50-50 — 100	78	23.3
Phil Esposito	Bos.	13-2-74	(A)	Bos. 9	at Cal. 6	53	53	68-77 — 145	78	
Bobby Orr	Bos.	12-3-74	(A)	Buf. 0	at Bos. 4	62	66	32-90 — 122	74	
Ken Hodge	Bos.	24-3-74	(G)	Mtl. 3	at Bos. 6	72	72	50-55 — 105	76	
Phil Esposito	Bos.	8-2-75	(A)	Bos. 8	at Det. 5	54	54	61-66 — 127	79	
Bobby Orr	Bos.	13-2-75	(A)	Bos. 1	at Buf. 3	57	57	46-89 — 135	80	
Guy Lafleur	Mtl.	7-3-75	(G)	Wsh. 4	at Mtl. 8	56	66	53-66 — 119	70	24.6
Pete Mahovlich	Mtl.	9-3-75	(G)	Mtl. 5	at NYR 3	67	67	35-82 — 117	80	29.5
Marcel Dionne	Det.	9-3-75	(A)	Det. 5	at Phi. 8	67	67	47-74 — 121	80	23.7
Bobby Clarke	Phi.	22-3-75	(A)	Min. 0	at Phi. 4	72	72	27-89 — 116	80	
Rene Robert	Buf.	5-4-75	(A)	Buf. 4	at Tor. 2	74	80	40-60 — 100	74	26.4
Guy Lafleur	Mtl.	10-3-76	(G)	Mtl. 5	at Chi. 1	69	69	56-69 — 125	80	
Bobby Clarke	Phi.	11-3-76	(A)	Buf. 1	at Phi. 6	64	68	30-89 — 119	76	
Bill Barber	Phi.	18-3-76	(G)	Van. 2	at Phi. 3	71	71	50-62 — 112	80	23.8
Gilbert Perreault	Buf.	21-3-76	(G)	K.C. 1	at Buf. 3	73	73	44-69 — 113	80	25.4
Pierre Larouche	Pit.	24-3-76	(G)	Bos. 5	at Pit. 5	70	74	53-58 — 111	76	20.4
Pete Mahovlich	Mtl.	28-3-76	(A)	Mtl. 2	at Bos. 2	77	77	34-71 — 105	80	
Jean Ratelle	Bos.	30-3-76	(G)	Buf. 4	at Bos. 4	77	77	36-69 — 105	80	
Jean Pronovost	Pit.	3-4-76	(A)	Wsh. 5	at Pit. 4	79	79	52-52 — 104	80	30.4
Darryl Sittler	Tor.	3-4-76	(G)	Bos. 4	at Tor. 2	78	79	41-59 — 100	79	25.7
Guy Lafleur	Mtl.	26-2-77	(A)	Clev. 3	at Mtl. 5	63	63	56-80 — 136	80	
Marcel Dionne	L.A.	5-3-77	(G)	Pit. 3	at L.A. 3	67	67	53-69 — 122	80	
Steve Shutt	Mtl.	27-3-77	(A)	Mtl. 6	at Det. 0	77	77	60-45 — 105	80	24.9
Bryan Trottier	NYI	25-2-78	(A)	Chi. 1	at NYI 7	59	60	46-77 — 123	77	21.7
Guy Lafleur	Mtl.	28-2-78	(G)	Det. 3	at Mtl. 9	69	61	60-72 — 132	78	
Darryl Sittler	Tor.	12-3-78	(A)	Tor. 7	at Pit. 1	67	67	45-72 — 117	80	
Guy Lafleur	Mtl.	27-2-79	(A)	Mtl. 3	at NYI 7	61	61	52-77 — 129	80	
Bryan Trottier	NYI	6-3-79	(A)	Buf. 3	at NYI 2	59	63	47-87 — 134	76	
Marcel Dionne	L.A.	8-3-79	(A)	L.A. 4	at Buf. 6	66	66	59-71 — 130	80	
Mike Bossy	NYI	11-3-79	(G)	NYI 4	at Bos. 4	66	66	69-57 — 126	80	22.2
Bob MacMillan	Atl.	15-3-79	(A)	Atl. 4	at Phi. 5	68	69	37-71 — 108	79	26.6
Guy Chouinard	Atl.	30-3-79	(A)	L.A. 3	at Atl. 5	75	75	50-57 — 107	80	22.5
Denis Potvin	NYI	8-4-79	(A)	NYI 5	at NYR 2	73	80	31-70 — 101	73	25.5
Marcel Dionne	L.A.	6-2-80	(A)	L.A. 3	at Hfd. 7	53	53	53-84 — 137	80	
Guy Lafleur	Mtl.	10-2-80	(A)	Mtl. 3	at Bos. 2	55	55	50-75 — 125	74	
Wayne Gretzky	Edm.	24-2-80	(A)	Bos. 4	at Edm. 2	61	62	51-86 — 137	79	19.2
Bryan Trottier	NYI	30-3-80	(A)	NYI 9	at Que. 6	75	77	42-62 — 104	78	
Gilbert Perreault	Buf.	1-4-80	(A)	Buf. 5	at Atl. 2	77	77	40-66 — 106	80	
Mike Rogers	Hfd.	4-4-80	(A)	Que. 2	at Hfd. 9	79	79	44-61 — 105	80	25.5
Charlie Simmer	L.A.	5-4-80	(A)	Van. 5	at L.A. 3	64	80	56-45 — 101	64	26.0
Blaine Stoughton	Hfd.	6-4-80	(A)	Det. 3	at Hfd. 5	80	80	56-44 — 100	80	27.0
Wayne Gretzky	Edm.	6-2-81	(G)	Wpg. 4	at Edm. 10	53	53	55-109 — 164	80	
Marcel Dionne	L.A.	12-2-81	(A)	L.A. 5	at Chi. 5	58	58	58-77 — 135	80	
Charlie Simmer	L.A.	14-2-81	(A)	Bos. 5	at L.A. 4	59	59	56-49 — 105	65	
Kent Nilsson	Cgy.	27-2-81	(A)	Hfd. 1	at Cgy. 5	64	64	49-82 — 131	80	24.6
Mike Bossy	NYI	3-3-81	(G)	Edm. 8	at NYI 8	65	66	68-51 — 119	79	
Dave Taylor	L.A.	14-3-81	(G)	Min. 4	at L.A. 10	63	70	47-65 — 112	72	25.3
Mike Rogers	Hfd.	22-3-81	(A)	Tor. 3	at Hfd. 3	74	74	40-65 — 105	80	
Bernie Federko	St. L.	28-3-81	(A)	Buf. 4	at St. L. 7	74	76	31-73 — 104	78	24.10
Rick Middleton	Bos.	28-3-81	(A)	Chi. 2	at Bos. 5	74	76	44-59 — 103	80	27.4
Jacques Richard	Que.	29-3-81	(A)	Mtl. 0	at Que. 4	75	76	52-51 — 103	78	28.6
Bryan Trottier	NYI	29-3-81	(G)	NYI 5	at Wsh. 4	69	76	31-72 — 103	73	
Peter Stastny	Que.	29-3-81	(A)	Mtl. 0	at Que. 4	73	76	39-70 — 109	77	24.6
Wayne Gretzky	Edm.	27-12-81	(G)	L.A. 3	at Edm. 10	38	38	92-120 — 212	80	
Mike Bossy	NYI	13-2-82	(A)	Phi. 2	at NYI 8	55	55	64-83 — 147	80	
Peter Stastny	Que.	16-2-82	(A)	Wpg. 3	at Que. 7	60	60	46-93 — 139	80	
Dennis Maruk	Wsh.	20-2-82	(A)	Wsh. 3	at Min. 7	60	60	60-76 — 136	80	26.3
Bryan Trottier	NYI	23-2-82	(G)	Chi. 1	at NYI 5	61	61	50-79 — 129	80	
Denis Savard	Chi.	27-2-82	(A)	Chi. 5	at L.A. 3	64	64	32-87 — 119	80	21.1
Bobby Smith	Min.	3-3-82	(A)	Det. 4	at Min. 6	66	66	43-71 — 114	80	24.1
Marcel Dionne	L.A.	6-3-82	(G)	L.A. 6	at Chi. 5	64	66	50-67 — 117	78	
Dave Taylor	L.A.	20-3-82	(A)	Pit. 5	at L.A. 7	71	72	39-67 — 106	78	
Dale Hawerchuk	Wpg.	24-3-82	(G)	L.A. 3	at Wpg.	74	74	45-58 — 103	80	18.11
Dino Ciccarelli	Min.	27-3-82	(A)	Min. 6	at Bos. 5	72	76	55-52 — 107	76	21.8
Glenn Anderson	Edm.	28-3-82	(G)	Edm. 6	at L.A. 2	78	78	38-67 — 105	80	21.7
Mike Rogers	NYR	2-4-82	(G)	Pit. 7	at NYR 5	79	79	38-65 — 103	80	

Player	Team	Date of 100th Point	G or A	Score		Player's Game No.	Team Game No.	Points G - A PTS	Total Games	Age when first 100th point scored (Yrs. & Mos.)
Wayne Gretzky	Edm.	5-1-83	(A)	Edm. 8	at Wpg. 3	42	42	71-125 — 196	80	
Mike Bossy	NYI	3-3-83	(A)	Tor. 1	at NYI. 5	66	67	60-58 — 118	79	
Peter Stastny	Que.	5-3-83	(A)	Hfd. 3	at Que. 10	62	67	47-77 — 124	75	
Denis Savard	Chi.	6-3-83	(G)	Mtl. 4	at Chi. 5	65	67	35-86 — 121	78	
Mark Messier	Edm.	23-3-83	(A)	Edm. 4	at Wpg. 7	73	76	48-58 — 106	77	22.2
Barry Pederson	Bos.	26-3-83	(A)	Hfd. 4	at Bos. 7	73	76	46-61 — 107	77	22.0
Marcel Dionne	L.A.	26-3-83	(A)	Edm. 9	at L.A. 3	75	75	56-51 — 107	80	
Michel Goulet	Que.	27-3-83	(A)	Que. 6	at Buf. 6	77	77	57-48 — 105	80	22.11
Glenn Anderson	Edm.	29-3-83	(A)	Edm. 7	at Van. 4	70	78	48-56 — 104	72	
Jari Kurri	Edm.	29-3-83	(A)	Edm. 7	at Van. 4	78	78	45-59 — 104	80	22.10
Kent Nilsson	Cgy.	29-3-83	(G)	L.A. 3	at Cgy. 5	78	78	46-58 — 104	80	
Wayne Gretzky	Edm.	18-12-83	(A)	Edm. 7	at Wpg. 5	34	34	87-118 — 205	74	
Paul Coffey	Edm.	4-3-84	(A)	Mtl. 1	at Edm. 6	68	68	40-86 — 126	80	22.9
Michel Goulet	Que.	4-3-84	(A)	Que. 1	at Buf. 1	62	67	56-65 — 121	75	
Jari Kurri	Edm.	7-3-84	(G)	Chi. 4	at Edm. 7	53	69	52-61 — 113	64	
Peter Stastny	Que.	8-3-84	(A)	Que. 8	at Pit. 6	69	69	46-73 — 119	80	
Mike Bossy	NYI	8-3-84	(G)	Tor. 5	at NYI 9	56	68	51-67 — 118	67	
Barry Pederson	Bos.	14-3-84	(A)	Bos. 4	at Det. 2	71	71	39-77 — 116	80	
Bryan Trottier	NYI	18-3-84	(G)	NYI 4	at Hfd. 5	62	73	40-71 — 111	68	
Bernie Federko	St. L.	20-3-84	(A)	Wpg. 3	at St. L. 9	75	76	41-66 — 107	79	
Rick Middleton	Bos.	27-3-84	(G)	Bos. 6	at Que. 4	77	77	47-58 — 105	80	
Dale Hawerchuk	Wpg.	27-3-84	(A)	Wpg. 3	at L.A. 3	77	77	37-65 — 102	80	
Mark Messier	Edm.	27-3-84	(G)	Edm. 9	at Cgy. 2	72	79	37-64 — 101	73	
Wayne Gretzky	Edm.	29-12-84	(A)	Det. 3	at Edm. 6	35	35	73-135 — 208	80	
Jari Kurri	Edm.	29-1-85	(G)	Edm. 4	at Cgy. 2	48	51	71-64 — 135	73	
Mike Bossy	NYI	23-2-85	(A)	Bos. 1	at NYI 7	56	60	58-59 — 117	76	
Dale Hawerchuk	Wpg.	25-2-85	(A)	Wpg. 12	at NYR 5	64	64	53-77 — 130	80	
Marcel Dionne	L.A.	5-3-85	(A)	Pit. 0	at L.A. 6	66	66	46-80 — 126	80	
Brent Sutter	NYI	12-3-85	(A)	NYI 6	at St. L. 5	68	68	42-60 — 102	72	22.10
John Ogrodnick	Det.	22-3-85	(A)	NYR 3	at Det. 5	73	73	55-50 — 105	79	25.9
Paul Coffey	Edm.	26-3-85	(G)	Edm. 7	at NYI 5	74	74	37-84 — 121	80	
Denis Savard	Chi.	29-3-85	(A)	Chi. 5	at Wpg. 5	75	76	38-67 — 105	79	
Peter Stastny	Que.	2-4-85	(A)	Bos. 4	at Que. 6	74	77	32-68 — 100	75	
Bernie Federko	St. L.	4-4-85	(A)	NYR 5	at St. L. 4	74	78	30-73 — 103	76	
John Tonelli	NYI	6-4-85	(G)	N.J. 5	at NYI 5	80	80	42-58 — 100	80	28.1
Paul MacLean	Wpg.	6-4-85	(A)	Wpg. 6	at Edm. 5	78	79	41-60 — 101	79	27.1
Bernie Nicholls	L.A.	6-4-85	(A)	Van. 4	at L.A. 4	80	80	46-54 — 100	80	22.9
Mike Gartner	Wsh.	7-4-85	(G)	Pit. 3	at Wsh. 7	80	80	50-52 — 102	80	25.6
Mario Lemieux	Pit.	7-4-85	(A)	Pit. 3	at Wsh. 7	73	80	43-57 — 100	73	19.6
Wayne Gretzky	Edm.	4-1-86	(A)	Hfd. 3	at Edm. 4	39	39	52-163 — 215	80	
Mario Lemieux	Pit.	15-2-86	(G)	Van. 4	at Pit. 9	55	56	48-93 — 141	79	
Paul Coffey	Edm.	19-2-86	(A)	Tor. 5	at Edm. 9	59	60	48-90 — 138	79	
Peter Stastny	Que.	1-3-86	(A)	Buf. 8	at Que. 4	66	68	41-81 — 122	76	
Jari Kurri	Edm.	2-3-86	(G)	Phi. 1	at Edm. 2	62	64	68-63 — 131	78	
Mike Bossy	NYI	8-3-86	(G)	Wsh. 6	at NYI 2	65	65	61-62 — 123	80	
Denis Savard	Chi.	12-3-86	(A)	Buf. 7	at Chi. 6	69	69	47-69 — 116	80	
Mats Naslund	Mtl.	13-3-86	(A)	Mtl. 2	at Bos. 3	70	70	43-67 — 110	80	26.4
Michel Goulet	Que.	24-3-86	(A)	Que. 1	at Min. 0	70	75	53-50 — 103	75	
Glenn Anderson	Edm.	25-3-86	(G)	Edm. 7	at Det. 2	66	74	54-48 — 102	72	
Neal Broten	Min.	26-3-86	(A)	Min. 6	at Tor. 1	76	76	29-76 — 105	80	26.4
Dale Hawerchuk	Wpg.	31-3-86	(A)	Wpg. 5	at L.A. 2	78	78	46-59 — 105	80	
Bernie Federko	St. L.	5-4-86	(G)	Chi. 5	at St. L. 7	79	79	34-68 — 102	80	
Wayne Gretzky	Edm.	11-1-87	(A)	Cgy. 3	at Edm. 5	42	42	62-121 — 183	79	
Jari Kurri	Edm.	14-3-87	(A)	Buf. 3	at Edm. 5	67	68	54-54 — 108	79	
Mario Lemieux	Pit.	18-3-87	(A)	St. L. 4	at Pit. 5	55	72	54-53 — 107	63	
Mark Messier	Edm.	19-3-87	(A)	Edm. 4	at Cgy. 5	71	71	37-70 — 107	77	
Dino Ciccarelli	Min.	30-3-87	(A)	NYR 6	at Min. 5	78	78	52-51 — 103	80	
Doug Gilmour	St. L.	2-4-87	(A)	Buf. 3	at St. L. 5	78	78	42-63 — 105	80	23.10
Dale Hawerchuk	Wpg.	5-4-87	(A)	Wpg. 3	at Cgy. 1	80	80	47-53 — 100	80	
Mario Lemieux	Pit.	20-1-88	(G)	Pit. 8	at Chi. 3	45	48	70-98 — 168	77	
Wayne Gretzky	Edm.	11-2-88	(A)	Edm. 7	at Van. 2	43	56	40-109 — 149	64	
Denis Savard	Chi.	12-2-88	(A)	St. L. 3	at Chi. 4	57	57	44-87 — 131	80	
Dale Hawerchuk	Wpg.	23-2-88	(G)	Wpg. 4	at Pit. 3	61	61	44-77 — 121	80	
Steve Yzerman	Det.	27-2-88	(A)	Det. 4	at Que. 5	63	63	50-52 — 102	64	22.10
Peter Stastny	Que.	8-3-88	(A)	Hfd. 4	at Que. 6	63	67	46-65 — 111	76	
Mark Messier	Edm.	15-3-88	(A)	Buf. 4	at Edm. 6	68	71	37-74 — 111	77	
Jimmy Carson	L.A.	26-3-88	(A)	Chi. 5	at L.A. 9	77	77	55-52 — 107	80	19.8
Hakan Loob	Cgy.	26-3-88	(A)	Van. 1	at Cgy. 6	76	76	50-56 — 106	80	27.9
Mike Bullard	Cgy.	26-3-88	(A)	Van. 1	at Cgy. 6	76	76	48-55 — 103	79	27.1
Michel Goulet	Que.	27-3-88	(A)	Pit. 6	at Que. 3	76	76	48-58 — 106	80	
Luc Robitaille	L.A.	30-3-88	(G)	Cgy. 7	at L.A. 9	78	78	53-58 — 111	80	22.1
Mario Lemieux	Pit.	31-12-88	(A)	N.J. 6	at Pit. 8	36	38	85-114 — 199	76	
Wayne Gretzky	L.A.	21-1-89	(A)	L.A. 4	at Hfd. 5	47	48	54-114 — 168	78	
Bernie Nicholls	L.A.	21-1-89	(A)	L.A. 4	at Hfd. 5	48	48	70-80 — 150	79	
Steve Yzerman	Det.	27-1-89	(G)	Tor. 1	at Det. 8	50	50	65-90 — 155	80	
Rob Brown	Pit.	16-3-89	(A)	Pit. 2	at N.J. 1	60	72	49-66 — 115	68	20.11
Paul Coffey	Pit.	20-3-89	(A)	Pit. 2	at Min. 7	69	74	30-83 — 113	75	
Joe Mullen	Cgy.	23-3-89	(A)	L.A. 2	at Cgy. 4	74	75	51-59 — 110	79	32.1
Jari Kurri	Edm.	29-3-89	(A)	Edm. 5	at Van. 4	75	79	44-58 — 102	76	
Jimmy Carson	Edm.	2-4-89	(A)	Edm. 2	at Cgy. 4	80	80	49-51 — 100	80	
Mario Lemieux	Pit.	28-1-90	(G)	Pit. 2	at Buf. 7	50	50	45-78 — 123	59	
Wayne Gretzky	L.A.	30-1-90	(A)	N.J. 2	at L.A. 5	51	51	40-102 — 142	73	
Steve Yzerman	Det.	19-2-90	(A)	Mtl. 5	at Det. 5	61	61	62-65 — 127	79	
Mark Messier	Edm.	20-2-90	(A)	Edm. 4	at Van. 2	62	62	45-84 — 129	79	
Brett Hull	St. L.	3-3-90	(A)	NYI 4	at St. L. 5	67	67	72-41 — 113	80	25.7
Bernie Nicholls	NYR	12-3-90	(A)	L.A. 6	at NYR 2	70	71	39-73 — 112	79	
Pierre Turgeon	Buf.	25-3-90	(G)	N.J. 4	at Buf. 3	76	76	40-66 — 106	80	20.7
Paul Coffey	Pit.	25-3-90	(A)	Pit. 2	at Hfd. 4	77	77	29-74 — 103	80	
Pat LaFontaine	NYI	27-3-90	(G)	Cgy. 4	at NYI 2	72	78	54-51 — 105	74	25.1

Bryan Trottier

Rick Middleton

Joe Mullen

Joe Sakic

Peter Forsberg

Jaromir Jagr

Player	Team	Date of 100th Point	G or A	Score		Player's Game No.	Team Game No.	Points G - A PTS	Total Games	Age when first 100th point scored (Yrs. & Mos.)
Adam Oates	St. L.	29-3-90	(G)	Pit 4	at St. L. 5	79	79	23-79 — 102	80	27.7
Joe Sakic	Que.	31-3-90	(G)	Hfd. 3	at Que. 2	79	79	39-63 — 102	80	20.8
Ron Francis	Hfd.	31-3-90	(G)	Hfd. 3	at Que. 2	79	79	32-69 — 101	80	27.0
Luc Robitaille	L.A.	1-4-90	(A)	L.A. 4	at Cgy. 8	80	80	52-49 — 101	80	
Wayne Gretzky	L.A.	30-1-91	(A)	N.J. 4	at L.A. 2	50	51	41-122 — 163	78	
Brett Hull	St. L.	23-2-91	(G)	Bos. 2	at St. L. 9	60	62	86-45 — 131	78	
Mark Recchi	Pit.	5-3-91	(G)	Van. 1	at Pit. 4	66	67	40-73 — 113	78	23.1
Steve Yzerman	Det.	10-3-91	(A)	Det. 4	at St. L. 1	72	72	51-57 — 108	80	
John Cullen	Hfd.	16-3-91	(G)	N.J. 2	at Hfd. 6	71	71	39-71 — 110	78	26.7
Adam Oates	St. L.	17-3-91	(G)	St. L. 4	at Chi. 6	54	73	25-90 — 115	61	
Joe Sakic	Que.	19-3-91	(G)	Edm. 7	at Que. 6	74	74	48-61 — 109	80	
Steve Larmer	Chi.	24-3-91	(A)	Min. 4	at Chi. 5	76	76	44-57 — 101	80	29.9
Theoren Fleury	Cgy.	26-3-91	(G)	Van. 2	at Cgy. 7	77	77	51-53 — 104	79	22.9
Al MacInnis	Cgy.	28-3-91	(G)	Edm. 4	at Cgy. 4	78	78	28-75 — 103	78	27.8
Brett Hull	St. L.	2-3-92	(G)	St. L. 5	at Van. 3	66	66	70-39 — 109	73	
Wayne Gretzky	L.A.	3-3-92	(A)	Phi. 1	at L.A. 4	60	66	31-90 — 121	74	
Kevin Stevens	Pit.	7-3-92	(G)	Pit. 3	at L.A. 5	66	66	54-69 — 123	80	26.11
Mario Lemieux	Pit.	10-3-92	(A)	Cgy. 2	at Pit. 5	53	67	44-87 — 131	64	
Luc Robitaille	L.A.	17-3-92	(G)	Wpg. 4	at L.A. 5	73	73	44-63 — 107	80	
Mark Messier	NYR	22-3-92	(G)	N.J. 3	at NYR 6	74	75	35-72 — 107	79	
Jeremy Roenick	Chi.	29-3-92	(G)	Tor. 1	at Chi. 5	77	77	53-50 — 103	80	22.2
Steve Yzerman	Det.	14-4-92	(G)	Det. 7	at Min. 4	79	80	45-58 — 103	79	
Brian Leetch	NYR	16-4-92	(A)	Pit. 1	at NYR 7	80	80	22-80 — 102	80	24.1
Mario Lemieux	Pit.	31-12-92	(G)	Tor. 3	at Pit. 3	38	39	69-91 — 160	60	
Pat LaFontaine	Buf.	10-2-93	(A)	Buf. 6	at Wpg. 2	55	55	53-95 — 148	84	
Adam Oates	Bos.	14-2-93	(A)	Bos. 3	at T.B. 3	58	58	45-97 — 142	84	
Steve Yzerman	Det.	24-2-93	(A)	Det. 7	at Buf. 10	64	64	58-79 — 137	84	
Pierre Turgeon	NYI	28-2-93	(A)	NYI 7	at Hfd. 6	62	63	58-74 — 132	83	
Doug Gilmour	Tor.	3-3-93	(G)	Min. 1	at Tor. 3	64	64	32-95 — 127	83	
Alexander Mogilny	Buf.	5-3-93	(A)	Hfd. 4	at Buf. 2	58	65	76-51 — 127	77	24.1
Mark Recchi	Phi.	7-3-93	(G)	Phi. 3	at N.J. 7	66	66	53-70 — 123	84	
Teemu Selanne	Wpg.	9-3-93	(A)	Wpg. 4	at T.B. 2	68	68	76-56 — 132	84	22.7
Luc Robitaille	L.A.	15-3-93	(A)	L.A. 4	at Buf. 2	69	69	63-62 — 125	84	
Kevin Stevens	Pit.	23-3-93	(G)	S.J. 2	at Pit. 7	63	73	55-56 — 111	72	
Mats Sundin	Que.	27-3-93	(G)	Phi. 3	at Que. 8	71	75	47-67 — 114	80	22.1
Pavel Bure	Van.	1-4-93	(G)	Van. 5	at T.B. 3	77	77	60-50 — 110	83	22.0
Jeremy Roenick	Chi.	4-4-93	(G)	St. L. 4	at Chi. 5	79	79	50-57 — 107	84	
Craig Janney	St. L.	4-4-93	(A)	St. L. 4	at Chi. 5	79	79	24-82 — 106	84	25.7
Rick Tocchet	Pit.	7-4-93	(G)	Mtl. 3	at Pit. 4	77	81	48-61 — 109	80	28.11
Joe Sakic	Que.	8-4-93	(A)	Que. 2	at Bos. 6	75	81	48-57 — 105	78	
Ron Francis	Pit.	9-4-93	(A)	Pit. 10	at NYR 4	82	82	24-76 — 100	84	
Brett Hull	St. L.	11-4-93	(G)	Min. 1	at St. L. 5	78	82	54-47 — 101	80	
Theoren Fleury	Cgy.	11-4-93	(A)	Cgy. 3	at Van. 6	82	82	34-66 — 100	83	
Joe Juneau	Bos.	14-4-93	(A)	Bos. 4	at Ott. 2	84	84	32-70 — 102	84	25.3
Wayne Gretzky	L.A.	14-2-94	(A)	Bos. 3	at L.A. 2	56	56	38-92 — 130	81	
Sergei Fedorov	Det.	1-3-94	(A)	Cgy. 2	at Det. 5	63	63	56-64 — 120	82	24.2
Doug Gilmour	Tor.	23-3-94	(G)	Tor. 1	at Fla. 1	74	74	27-84 — 111	83	
Adam Oates	Bos.	26-3-94	(A)	Mtl. 3	at Bos. 6	68	75	32-80 — 112	77	
Mark Recchi	Phi.	27-3-94	(A)	Ana. 3	at Phi. 2	76	76	40-67 — 107	84	
Pavel Bure	Van.	28-3-94	(A)	Tor. 2	at Van. 3	68	76	60-47 — 107	76	
Jeremy Roenick	Chi.	31-3-94	(G)	Chi. 3	at Wsh. 6	78	78	46-61 — 107	84	
Brendan Shanahan	St. L.	12-4-94	(G)	St. L. 5	at Dal. 9	80	83	52-50 — 102	81	25.2
Mario Lemieux	Pit.	16-1-96	(G)	Col. 5	at Pit. 2	38	44	69-92 — 161	70	
Jaromir Jagr	Pit.	6-2-96	(G)	Bos. 5	at Pit. 6	52	52	62-87 — 149	82	23.12
Ron Francis	Pit.	9-3-96	(A)	N.J. 4	at Pit. 3	61	66	27-92 — 119	77	
Peter Forsberg	Col.	9-3-96	(A)	Col. 7	at Van. 5	68	68	30-86 — 116	82	22.7
Joe Sakic	Col.	17-3-96	(A)	Edm. 1	at Col. 8	70	70	51-69 — 120	82	
Teemu Selanne	Ana.	25-3-96	(A)	Ana. 1	at Det. 5	70	73	40-68 — 108	79	
Alexander Mogilny	Van.	25-3-96	(A)	L.A. 1	at Van. 4	72	75	55-52 — 107	79	
Eric Lindros	Phi.	25-3-96	(A)	Hfd. 0	at Phi. 3	65	73	47-68 — 115	73	23.0
Wayne Gretzky	St. L.	28-3-96	(G)	N.J. 4	at St. L. 4	76	75	23-79 — 102	80	
Doug Weight	Edm.	30-3-96	(G)	Tor. 4	at Edm. 3	76	76	25-79 — 104	82	25.3
Sergei Fedorov	Det.	2-4-96	(G)	Det. 3	at S.J. 6	72	76	39-68 — 107	78	
Paul Kariya	Ana.	7-4-96	(G)	Ana. 5	at S.J. 3	78	78	50-58 — 108	82	21.5
Mario Lemieux	Pit.	8-3-97	(A)	Phi. 2	at Pit. 3	61	65	50-72 — 122	76	
Teemu Selanne	Ana.	1-4-97	(A)	Chi. 3	at Ana. 3	74	78	51-58 — 109	78	
Jaromir Jagr	Pit.	15-4-98	(G)	T.B. 1	at Pit. 5	76	80	35-67 — 102	77	
Jaromir Jagr	Pit.	13-3-99	(G)	Phi. 0	at Pit. 4	65	65	44-83 — 127	81	
Teemu Selanne	Ana.	5-4-99	(A)	Ana. 2	at Det. 3	69	76	47-60 — 107	75	
Paul Kariya	Ana.	17-4-99	(G)	Ana. 3	at S.J. 3	82	82	39-62 — 101	82	

Five-or-more-Goal Games

Player	Team	Date	Score		Opposing Goaltender
SEVEN GOALS					
Joe Malone	Quebec Bulldogs	Jan. 31/20	Tor. 6	at Que. 10	Ivan Mitchell
SIX GOALS					
Newsy Lalonde	Montreal	Jan. 10/20	Tor. 7	at Mtl. 14	Ivan Mitchell
Joe Malone	Quebec Bulldogs	Mar. 10/20	Ott. 4	at Que. 10	Ivan Mitchell
Corb Denneny	Toronto St. Pats	Jan. 26/21	Ham. 3	at Tor. 10	Howard Lockhart
Cy Denneny	Ottawa Senators	Mar. 7/21	Ham. 5	at Ott. 12	Howard Lockhart
Syd Howe	Detroit	Feb. 3/44	NYR 2	at Det. 12	Ken McAuley
Red Berenson	St. Louis	Nov. 7/68	St. L. 8	at Phil 0	Doug Favell
Darryl Sittler	Toronto	Feb. 7/76	Bos. 4	at Tor. 11	Dave Reece
FIVE GOALS					
Joe Malone	Montreal	Dec. 19/17	Mtl. 7	at Ott. 4	Clint Benedict
Harry Hyland	Mtl. Wanderers	Dec. 19/17	Tor. 9	at Mtl. W. 10	Arthur Brooks
Joe Malone	Montreal	Jan. 12/18	Ott. 4	at Mtl. 9	Clint Benedict
Joe Malone	Montreal	Feb. 2/18	Tor. 2	at Mtl. 11	Harry Holmes
Mickey Roach	Toronto St. Pats	Mar. 6/20	Que. 2	at Tor. 11	Frank Brophy
Newsy Lalonde	Montreal	Feb. 16/21	Ham. 5	at Mtl. 10	Howard Lockhart
Babe Dye	Toronto St. Pats	Dec. 16/22	Mtl. 2	at Tor. 7	Georges Vezina
Red Green	Hamilton Tigers	Dec. 5/24	Ham. 10	at Tor. 3	John Ross Roach
Babe Dye	Toronto St. Pats	Dec. 22/24	Tor. 10	at Bos. 1	Charles Stewart
Harry Broadbent	Mtl. Maroons	Jan. 7/25	Mtl. 6	at Ham. 2	Jake Forbes
Pit Lepine	Montreal	Dec. 14/29	Ott. 4	at Mtl. 6	Alex Connell
Howie Morenz	Montreal	Mar. 18/30	NYA 3	at Mtl. 8	Roy Worters
Charlie Conacher	Toronto	Jan. 19/32	NYA 3	at Tor. 11	Roy Worters
Ray Getliffe	Montreal	Feb. 6/43	Bos. 3	at Mtl. 8	Frank Brimsek
Maurice Richard	Montreal	Dec. 28/44	Det. 1	at Mtl. 9	Harry Lumley
Howie Meeker	Toronto	Jan. 8/47	Chi. 4	at Tor. 10	Paul Bibeault
Bernie Geoffrion	Montreal	Feb. 19/55	NYR 2	at Mtl. 10	Gump Worsley
Bobby Rousseau	Montreal	Feb. 1/64	Det. 3	at Mtl. 9	Roger Crozier
Yvan Cournoyer	Montreal	Feb. 15/75	Chi. 3	at Mtl. 12	Mike Veisor
Don Murdoch	NY Rangers	Oct. 12/76	NYR 10	at Min. 4	Gary Smith
Ian Turnbull	Toronto	Feb. 2/77	Det. 1	at Tor. 9	Ed Giacomin (2) Jim Rutherford (3)
Bryan Trottier	NY Islanders	Dec. 23/78	NYR 4	at NYI 9	Wayne Thomas (4) John Davidson (1)
Tim Young	Minnesota	Jan. 15/79	Min. 8	at NYR 1	Doug Soetaert (3) Wayne Thomas (2)
John Tonelli	NY Islanders	Jan. 6/81	Tor. 3	at NYI 6	Jiri Crha (4) empty net (1)
Wayne Gretzky	Edmonton	Feb. 18/81	St. L. 2	at Edm. 9	Mike Liut (3) Ed Staniowski (2)
Wayne Gretzky	Edmonton	Dec. 30/81	Phi. 5	at Edm. 7	Pete Peeters (4) empty net (1)
Grant Mulvey	Chicago	Feb. 3/82	St. L. 5	at Chi. 9	Mike Liut (4) Gary Edwards (1)
Bryan Trottier	NY Islanders	Feb. 13/82	Phi. 2	at NYI 8	Pete Peeters
Willy Lindstrom	Winnipeg	Mar. 2/82	Wpg. 7	at Phi. 6	Pete Peeters
Mark Pavelich	NY Rangers	Feb. 23/83	Hfd. 3	at NYR 11	Greg Millen
Jari Kurri	Edmonton	Nov. 19/83	N.J. 4	at Edm. 13	Glenn Resch (3) Ron Low (2)
Bengt Gustafsson	Washington	Jan. 8/84	Wsh. 7	at Phi. 1	Pelle Lindbergh
Pat Hughes	Edmonton	Feb. 3/84	Cgy. 5	at Edm. 10	Don Edwards (3) Rejean Lemelin (2)
Wayne Gretzky	Edmonton	Dec. 15/84	Edm. 8	at St. L. 2	Rick Wamsley (4) Mike Liut (1)
Dave Andreychuk	Buffalo	Feb. 6/86	Buf. 8	at Bos. 6	Pat Riggin (1) Doug Keans (4)
Wayne Gretzky	Edmonton	Dec. 6/87	Min. 4	at Edm. 10	Don Beaupre (4) Kari Takko (1)
Mario Lemieux	Pittsburgh	Dec. 31/88	N.J. 6	at Pit. 8	Bob Sauve (3) Chris Terreri (2)
Joe Nieuwendyk	Calgary	Jan. 11/89	Wpg. 3	at Cgy. 8	Daniel Berthiaume
Mats Sundin	Quebec	Mar. 5/92	Que. 10	at Hfd. 4	Peter Sidorkiewicz (3) Kay Whitmore (2)
Mario Lemieux	Pittsburgh	Apr. 9/93	Pit. 10	at NYR 4	Corey Hirsch (3) Mike Richter (2)
Peter Bondra	Washington	Feb. 5/94	T.B. 3	at Wsh. 6	Darren Puppa (4) Pat Jablonski (1)
Mike Ricci	Quebec	Feb. 17/94	Que. 8	at S.J. 2	Arturs Irbe (3) Jimmy Waite (2)
Alexei Zhamnov	Winnipeg	Apr. 1/95	Wpg. 7	at L.A. 7	Kelly Hrudey (3) Grant Fuhr (2)
Mario Lemieux	Pittsburgh	Mar. 26/96	St. L. 4	at Pit. 8	Grant Fuhr (1) Jon Casey (4)
Sergei Fedorov	Detroit	Dec. 26/96	Wsh. 4	at Det. 5	Jim Carey

Players' 500th Goals

Regular Season

Player	Team	Date	Game No.	Score		Opposing Goaltender	Total Goals	Total Games
Maurice Richard	Montreal	Oct. 19/57	863	Chi. 1	at Mtl. 3	Glenn Hall	544	978
Gordie Howe	Detroit	Mar. 14/62	1,045	Det. 2	at NYR 3	Gump Worsley	801	1,767
Bobby Hull	Chicago	Feb. 21/70	861	NYR. 2	at Chi. 4	Ed Giacomin	610	1,063
Jean Béliveau	Montreal	Feb. 11/71	1,101	Min. 2	at Mtl. 6	Gilles Gilbert	507	1,125
Frank Mahovlich	Montreal	Mar. 21/73	1,105	Van. 2	at Mtl. 3	Dunc Wilson	533	1,181
Phil Esposito	Boston	Dec. 22/74	803	Det. 4	at Bos. 5	Jim Rutherford	717	1,282
John Bucyk	Boston	Oct. 30/75	1,370	St. L. 2	at Bos. 3	Yves Bélanger	556	1,540
Stan Mikita	Chicago	Feb. 27/77	1,221	Van. 4	at Chi. 3	Cesare Maniago	541	1,394
Marcel Dionne	Los Angeles	Dec. 14/82	887	L.A. 2	at Wsh. 7	Al Jensen	731	1,348
Guy Lafleur	Montreal	Dec. 20/83	918	Mtl. 6	at N.J. 0	Glenn Resch	560	1,126
Mike Bossy	NY Islanders	Jan. 2/86	647	Bos. 1	at NYI 7	empty net	573	752
Gilbert Perreault	Buffalo	Mar. 9/86	1,159	N.J. 3	at Buf. 4	Alain Chevrier	512	1,191
Wayne Gretzky	Edmonton	Nov. 22/86	575	Van. 2	at Edm. 5	empty net	894	1,487
Lanny McDonald	Calgary	Mar. 21/89	1,107	NYI 1	at Cgy. 4	Mark Fitzpatrick	500	1,111
Bryan Trottier	NY Islanders	Feb. 13/90	1,104	Cgy. 4	at NYI 2	Rick Wamsley	524	1,279
Mike Gartner	NY Rangers	Oct. 14/91	936	Wsh. 5	at NYR 3	Mike Liut	708	1,432
Michel Goulet	Chicago	Feb. 16/92	951	Cgy. 5	at Chi. 5	Jeff Reese	548	1,089
Jari Kurri	Los Angeles	Oct. 17/92	833	Bos. 6	at L.A. 8	empty net	601	1,251
Dino Ciccarelli	Detroit	Jan. 8/94	946	Det. 6	at L.A. 3	Kelly Hrudey	608	1,232
Mario Lemieux	Pittsburgh	Oct. 26/95	605	Pit. 7	at NYI 5	Tommy Soderstrom	613	745
*Mark Messier	NY Rangers	Nov. 6/95	1,141	Cgy. 2	at NYR 4	Rick Tabaracci	627	1,479
*Steve Yzerman	Detroit	Jan. 17/96	906	Col. 2	at Det. 3	Patrick Roy	627	1,256
Dale Hawerchuk	St. Louis	Jan. 31/96	1,103	St. L. 4	at Tor. 0	Felix Potvin	518	1,188
*Brett Hull	St. Louis	Dec. 22/96	693	L.A. 4	at St. L. 7	Stephane Fiset	610	940
Joe Mullen	Pittsburgh	Mar. 14/97	1,052	Pit. 3	at Col. 6	Patrick Roy	502	1,062
*Dave Andreychuk	New Jersey	Mar. 15/97	1,070	Wsh. 2	at N.J. 3	Bill Ranford	552	1,287
*Luc Robitaille	Los Angeles	Jan. 7/99	928	Buf. 4	at L.A. 4	Dwayne Roloson	553	1,042
*Pat Verbeek	Detroit	Mar. 22/00	1,285	Cgy. 2	at Det. 2	Fred Brathwaite	500	1,293

*Active

Joe Malone scored five goals on the very first night in NHL history, leading the Montreal Canadiens to a 7-4 victory over the Ottawa Senators. He set an NHL record that still stands when he scored seven goals on January 31, 1920.

Steve Yzerman (above) and Brett Hull (below) scored their 600th career goals in 1999-2000. Yzerman enters the 2000-01 season with 627 career goals, while Hull has 610. Brett's next goal will move him past his father Bobby on the all-time list.

Players' 1,000th Points

Regular Season

Player	Team	Date	Game No.	G or A		Score	Total Points G A PTS	Total Games
Gordie Howe	Detroit	Nov. 27/60	938	(A)	Tor. 0	at Det. 2	801-1,049–1,850	1,767
Jean Béliveau	Montreal	Mar. 3/68	911	(A)	Mtl. 2	at Det. 5	507-712–1,219	1,125
Alex Delvecchio	Detroit	Feb. 16/69	1,143	(A)	LA 3	at Det. 6	456-825–1,281	1,549
Bobby Hull	Chicago	Dec. 12/70	909	(A)	Minn. 3	at Chi. 5	610-560–1,170	1,063
Norm Ullman	Toronto	Oct. 16/71	1,113	(A)	NYR 5	at Tor. 3	490-739–1,229	1,410
Stan Mikita	Chicago	Oct. 15/72	924	(A)	St. L. 3	at Chi. 1	541-926–1,467	1,394
John Bucyk	Boston	Nov. 9/72	1,144	(G)	Det. 3	at Bos. 8	556-813–1,369	1,540
Frank Mahovlich	Montreal	Feb. 17/73	1,090	(A)	Phi. 7	at Mtl. 6	533-570–1,103	1,181
Henri Richard	Montreal	Dec. 20/73	1,194	(A)	Mtl. 2	at Buf. 2	358-688–1,046	1,256
Phil Esposito	Boston	Feb. 15/74	745	(A)	Bos. 4	at Van. 2	717-873–1,590	1,282
Rod Gilbert	NY Rangers	Feb. 19/77	1,027	(A)	NYR 2	at NYI 5	406-615–1,021	1,065
Jean Ratelle	Boston	Apr. 3/77	1,007	(A)	Tor. 4	at Bos. 7	491-776–1,267	1,281
Marcel Dionne	Los Angeles	Jan. 7/81	740	(G)	L.A. 5	at Hfd. 3	731-1,040–1,771	1,348
Guy Lafleur	Montreal	Mar. 4/81	720	(G)	Mtl. 9	at Wpg. 3	560-793–1,353	1,126
Bobby Clarke	Philadelphia	Mar. 19/81	922	(A)	Bos. 3	at Phi. 5	358-852–1,210	1,144
Gilbert Perreault	Buffalo	Apr. 3/82	871	(A)	Buf. 5	at Mtl.4	512-814–1,326	1,191
Darryl Sittler	Philadelphia	Jan. 20/83	927	(A)	Cgy 2	at Phi. 5	484-637–1,121	1,096
Wayne Gretzky	Edmonton	Dec. 19/84	424	(A)	L.A. 3	at Edm. 7	894-1,963–2,875	1,487
Bryan Trottier	NY Islanders	Jan. 29/85	726	(G)	Min. 4	at NYI 4	524-901–1,425	1,279
Mike Bossy	NY Islanders	Jan. 24/86	656	(A)	NYI 7	at Wsh. 5	573-553–1,126	752
Denis Potvin	NY Islanders	Apr. 4/87	987	(A)	Buf. 6	at NYI 6	310-742–1,052	1,060
Bernie Federko	St. Louis	Mar. 19/88	855	(A)	Hfd. 5	at St. L. 3	369-761–1,130	1,000
Lanny McDonald	Calgary	Mar. 7/89	1,101	(A)	Wpg. 5	at Cgy. 9	500-506–1,006	1,111
Peter Stastny	Quebec	Oct. 19/89	682	(G)	Que. 5	at Chi. 3	450-789–1,239	977
Jari Kurri	Edmonton	Jan. 2/90	716	(A)	Edm. 6	at St. L. 4	601-797–1,398	1,251
Denis Savard	Chicago	Mar. 11/90	727	(A)	St. L. 6	at Chi. 4	473-865–1,338	1,196
*Paul Coffey	Pittsburgh	Dec. 22/90	770	(A)	Pit. 4	at NYI 3	396-1,131–1,527	1,391
*Mark Messier	Edmonton	Jan. 13/91	822	(A)	Edm. 5	at Phi. 3	627-1,087–1,714	1,479
Dave Taylor	Los Angeles	Feb. 5/91	930	(A)	L.A. 3	at Phi. 2	431-638–1,069	1,111
Michel Goulet	Chicago	Feb. 23/91	878	(A)	Chi. 3	at Min. 3	548-604–1,152	1,089
Dale Hawerchuk	Buffalo	Mar. 8/91	781	(G)	Chi. 5	at Buf. 3	518-891–1,409	1,188
Bobby Smith	Minnesota	Nov. 30/91	986	(A)	Min. 4	at Tor. 3	357-679–1,036	1,077
Mike Gartner	NY Rangers	Jan. 4/92	971	(A)	NYR 4	at N.J. 6	708-627–1,335	1,432
*Ray Bourque	Boston	Feb. 29/92	933	(A)	Wsh. 5	at Bos. 5	403-1,117–1,520	1,532
Mario Lemieux	Pittsburgh	Mar. 24/92	513	(A)	Pit. 3	at Det. 4	613-881–1,494	745
Glenn Anderson	Toronto	Feb. 22/93	954	(G)	Tor. 8	at Van. 1	498-601–1,099	1,129
*Steve Yzerman	Detroit	Feb. 24/93	737	(A)	Det. 7	at Buf. 10	627-935–1,562	1,256
*Ron Francis	Pittsburgh	Oct. 28/93	893	(A)	Que. 7	at Pit. 3	472-1,087–1,559	1,407
Bernie Nicholls	New Jersey	Feb. 13/94	858	(A)	N.J. 3	at T.B. 3	475-734–1,209	1,127
Dino Ciccarelli	Detroit	Mar. 9/94	957	(G)	Det. 5	at Cgy. 1	608-592–1,200	1,232
Brian Propp	Hartford	Mar. 19/94	1,008	(G)	Hfd. 5	at Phi. 3	425-579–1,004	1,016
Joe Mullen	Pittsburgh	Feb. 7/95	935	(A)	Fla. 3	at Pit. 7	502-561–1,063	1,062
Steve Larmer	NY Rangers	Mar. 8/95	983	(A)	N.J. 4	at NYR 6	441-571–1,012	1,006
*Doug Gilmour	Toronto	Dec. 23/95	935	(A)	Edm. 1	at Tor. 6	422-883–1,305	1,271
*Larry Murphy	Toronto	Mar. 27/96	1,228	(G)	Tor. 6	at Van. 2	285-910–1,195	1,558
*Dave Andreychuk	New Jersey	Apr. 7/96	998	(G)	NYR 2	at N.J. 4	552-624–1,176	1,287
*Adam Oates	Washington	Oct. 8/97	830	(A)	Wsh. 6	at NYI 3	303-894–1,197	1,049
*Phil Housley	Washington	Nov. 8/97	1,081	(A)	Edm. 1	at Wsh. 2	313-817–1,130	1,288
Dale Hunter	Washington	Jan. 9/98	1,308	(A)	Phi. 1	at Wsh. 4	323-697–1,020	1,407
Pat Lafontaine	NY Rangers	Jan. 22/98	847	(A)	Phi. 4	at NYR 3	468-545–1,013	865
*Luc Robitaille	Los Angeles	Jan. 29/98	882	(A)	Cgy. 3	at L.A. 5	553-597–1,130	1,042
*Al MacInnis	St. Louis	Apr. 7/98	1,056	(A)	St. L. 3	at Det. 5	301-803–1,104	1,203
*Brett Hull	Dallas	Nov. 14/98	815	(A)	Dal. 3	at Bos. 1	610-494–1,104	940
Brian Bellows	Washington	Jan. 2/99	1,147	(A)	Tor. 2	at Wsh. 5	485-537–1,022	1,188
*Pierre Turgeon	St. Louis	Oct. 9/99	881	(G)	St. L. 4	at Edm. 3	423-640–1,063	929
*Joe Sakic	Colorado	Dec. 27/99	810	(A)	St. L. 1	at Col. 5	403-657–1,060	852
*Pat Verbeek	Detroit	Feb. 27/00	1,275	(A)	T.B. 1	at Det. 3	500-513–1,013	1,293

*Active

Individual Awards

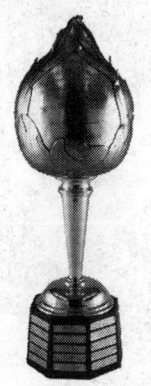

Hart Memorial Trophy

Art Ross Trophy

Calder Memorial Trophy

James Norris Memorial Trophy

HART MEMORIAL TROPHY

An annual award "to the player adjudged to be the most valuable to his team." Winner selected in a poll by the Professional Hockey Writers' Association in the 28 NHL cities (30 in 2000-2001) at the end of the regular schedule. The winner receives $10,000 and the runners-up $6,000 and $4,000.

History: The Hart Memorial Trophy was presented by the National Hockey League in 1960 after the original Hart Trophy was retired to the Hockey Hall of Fame. The original Hart Trophy was donated to the NHL in 1923 by Dr. David A. Hart, father of Cecil Hart, former manager-coach of the Montreal Canadiens.

**1999-2000 Winner:	Chris Pronger, St. Louis Blues**
**	Runners-up:	Jaromir Jagr, Pittsburgh Penguins**
**		Pavel Bure, Florida Panthers**

Defenseman Chris Pronger of the St. Louis Blues captured the Hart Memorial Trophy in the closest vote ever, becoming the first defenseman to win the award since Bobby Orr in 1972. Previously, the closest voting for the Hart Trophy occurred in 1990 when Mark Messier edged Ray Bourque 227-225. This year, Pronger received 25 first-place votes and a total of 396 points. Jaromir Jagr of Pittsburgh had 18 first-place votes and 395 points. Pavel Bure of Florida finished third with 346 points.

Pronger led all NHL players in plus-minus (+52) and ice time per game (30:14), and finished second in scoring among defensemen with a career-high 62 points (14 goals, 48 assists). He helped the Blues establish club records with 51 wins and 114 points while allowing a league-low 165 goals.

CALDER MEMORIAL TROPHY

An annual award "to the player selected as the most proficient in his first year of competition in the National Hockey League." Winner selected in a poll by the Professional Hockey Writers' Association at the end of the regular schedule. The winner receives $10,000 and the runners-up $6,000 and $4,000.

History: From 1936-37 until his death in 1943, Frank Calder, NHL President, bought a trophy each year to be given permanently to the outstanding rookie. After Calder's death, the NHL presented the Calder Memorial Trophy in his memory and the trophy is to be kept in perpetuity. To be eligible for the award, a player cannot have played more than 25 games in any single preceding season nor in six or more games in each of any two preceding seasons in any major professional league. Beginning in 1990-91, to be eligible for this award a player must not have attained his twenty-sixth birthday by September 15th of the season in which he is eligible.

**1999-2000 Winner:	Scott Gomez, New Jersey Devils**
**	Runners-up:	Brad Stuart, San Jose Sharks**
**		Mike York, New York Rangers**

Center Scott Gomez of the New Jersey Devils was selected as the winner of the Calder Memorial Trophy. Gomez received 49 of 58 first-place votes and was the second choice on the other nine ballots for 553 points. Brad Stuart of San Jose had six first-place votes and 250 points, while Mike York of the Rangers earned 209 points.

Gomez led all NHL rookies in points (70), assists (51), power-play points (27) and shots (204), establishing Devils records for assists and points by a rookie. He tied a Devils rookie record with an eight-game point streak (11 points in games from Nov. 12 through Dec. 1) and also recorded streaks of six and seven games. A native of Anchorage, Alaska, Gomez is the third U.S.-born player in four years to earn Calder honors, joining Bryan Berard (1997) and Chris Drury (1999).

ART ROSS TROPHY

An annual award "to the player who leads the league in scoring points at the end of the regular season." The winner receives $10,000 and the runners-up $6,000 and $4,000.

History: Arthur Howie Ross, former manager-coach of the Boston Bruins, presented the trophy to the National Hockey League in 1947. If two players finish the schedule with the same number of points, the trophy is awarded in the following manner: 1. Player with most goals. 2. Player with fewer games played. 3. Player scoring first goal of the season.

**1999-2000 Winner:	Jaromir Jagr, Pittsburgh Penguins**
**	Runners-up:	Pavel Bure, Florida Panthers**
**		Mark Recchi, Philadelphia Flyers**

Right winger Jaromir Jagr of the Pittsburgh Penguins captured the Art Ross Trophy for the third consecutive season and the fourth time in his career by completing the 1999-2000 regular season with 42 goals and 54 assists for 96 points in only 63 games. Pavel Bure, the Maurice Richard Trophy winner, finished second with 94 points in the closest finish since Jagr and Eric Lindros finished tied for the league lead with 70 points in 1994-95. Jagr became the first European-trained player to win the Art Ross Trophy that year because he had scored three more goals than Lindros.

Jagr joins a group of five scoring greats to have won four or more Art Ross Trophy titles: Wayne Gretzky (ten), Gordie Howe (six), Mario Lemieux (six), Phil Esposito (five) and Stan Mikita (four).

JAMES NORRIS MEMORIAL TROPHY

An annual award "to the defense player who demonstrates throughout the season the greatest all-round ability in the position." Winner selected in a poll by the Professional Hockey Writers' Association at the end of the regular schedule. The winner receives $10,000 and the runners-up $6,000 and $4,000.

History: The James Norris Memorial Trophy was presented in 1953 by the four children of the late James Norris in memory of the former owner-president of the Detroit Red Wings.

**1999-2000 Winner:	Chris Pronger, St. Louis Blues**
**	Runners-up:	Nicklas Lidstrom, Detroit Red Wings**
**		Rob Blake, Los Angeles Kings**

Chris Pronger of the St. Louis Blues was awarded the Norris Trophy for the first time in his career. He was a near-unanimous selection, receiving 53 first-place votes and five-second place votes for 565 points. Detroit's Nicklas Lidstrom finished in second place for the third straight year, earning five first-place votes and 400 points. Rob Blake, winner of the Norris Trophy in 1998, was third in balloting with 196 points.

Pronger's defensive play helped St. Louis win the Presidents' Trophy for the first time in franchise history. Coupled with the Norris Trophy win by Al MacInnis in 1999, the Blues become just the second team in NHL history to have two different players win the award in consecutive seasons, joining the Montreal Canadiens who saw Doug Harvey win the Norris in 1958 followed by Tom Johnson in 1959.

Vezina Trophy

Lady Byng Memorial Trophy

Frank J. Selke Trophy

Conn Smythe Trophy

VEZINA TROPHY

An annual award "to the goalkeeper adjudged to be the best at his position" as voted by the general managers of each of the 28 clubs (30 in 2000-01). Over-all winner receives $10,000, runners-up $6,000 and $4,000.

History: Leo Dandurand, Louis Letourneau and Joe Cattarinich, former owners of the Montreal Canadiens, presented the trophy to the National Hockey League in 1926-27 in memory of Georges Vezina, outstanding goalkeeper of the Canadiens who collapsed during an NHL game on November 28, 1925, and died of tuberculosis a few months later. Until the 1981-82 season, the goalkeeper(s) of the team allowing the fewest number of goals during the regular season were awarded the Vezina Trophy.

1999-2000 Winner: Olaf Kolzig, Washington Capitals
Runners-up: Roman Turek, St. Louis Blues
Curtis Joseph, Toronto Maple Leafs

Olaf Kolzig of the Washington Capitals was the winner of the Vezina Trophy for the first time in his career. Kolzig was named on all 28 ballots, receiving 14 first-place votes and 13 second-place votes for 110 points. Roman Turek of St. Louis earned first-place honors on nine ballots and a total of 79 points. Curtis Joseph of Toronto finished third with 23 points.

Kolzig led NHL goaltenders in minutes played (4,371) and shots faced (1,957). He posted a 33-7-5 in his last 45 starts, including a 1.92 goals-against average (his average on the season was 2.24 in 73 games) and a .931 save percentage, as the Capitals rallied to win the Southeast Division. Kolzig finished the season third among goaltenders in wins (41), fourth in shutouts (five) and fifth in save percentage (.917).

CONN SMYTHE TROPHY

An annual award "to the most valuable player for his team in the playoffs." Winner selected by the Professional Hockey Writers' Association at the conclusion of the final game in the Stanley Cup Finals. The winner receives $10,000.

History: Presented by Maple Leaf Gardens Limited in 1964 to honor Conn Smythe, the former coach, manager, president and owner-governor of the Toronto Maple Leafs.

1999-2000 Winner: Scott Stevens, New Jersey Devils

Captain Scott Stevens led the New Jersey Devils to the Stanley Cup in 2000 and was rewarded with the Conn Smythe Trophy. His hard hits and gritty team leadership made Stevens the first defenseman to be named the most valuable player in the playoffs since Brian Leetch in 1994. Stevens is just the sixth blueliner to win the Conn Smythe Award and the first defensive defenseman to be so honored.

LADY BYNG MEMORIAL TROPHY

An annual award "to the player adjudged to have exhibited the best type of sportsmanship and gentlemanly conduct combined with a high standard of playing ability." Winner selected in a poll by the Professional Hockey Writers' Association at the end of the regular schedule. The winner receives $10,000 and the runners-up $6,000 and $4,000.

History: Lady Byng, wife of Canada's Governor-General at the time, presented the Lady Byng Trophy in 1925. After Frank Boucher of the New York Rangers won the award seven times in eight seasons, he was given the trophy to keep and Lady Byng donated another trophy in 1936. After Lady Byng's death in 1949, the National Hockey League presented a new trophy, changing the name to Lady Byng Memorial Trophy.

1999-2000 Winner: Pavol Demitra, St. Louis Blues
Runners-up: Nicklas Lidstrom, Detroit Red Wings
Teemu Selanne, Mighty Ducks of Anaheim

Right Winger Pavol Demitra of the St. Louis Blues won the Lady Byng Trophy for the first time in his career. Demitra received 18 first-place votes and earned 302 points to finish ahead of Detroit's Nicklas Lidstrom. Lidstrom had 263 points, including 17 first-place selections, to finish as the runner-up for the second straight season. Demitra led the Blues in scoring with 75 points (28 goals, 47 assists), as the club captured the Presidents' Trophy for the first time in franchise history. He also posted the NHL's third-best plus-minus rating (+34) and received just eight minutes in penalties.

FRANK J. SELKE TROPHY

An annual award "to the forward who best excels in the defensive aspects of the game." Winner selected in a poll by the Professional Hockey Writers' Association at the end of the regular schedule. The winner receives $10,000 and the runners-up $6,000 and $4,000.

History: Presented to the National Hockey League in 1977 by the Board of Governors of the NHL in honor of Frank J. Selke, one of the great architects of NHL championship teams.

1999-2000 Winner: Steve Yzerman, Detroit Red Wings
Runners-up: Michal Handzus, St. Louis Blues
Mike Ricci, San Jose Sharks

Detroit Red Wings center Steve Yzerman captured the Frank J. Selke Trophy, winning his first major regular-season honor since earning the Pearson Award in 1989. Yzerman was a runaway winner, receiving 32 first-place votes and 431 points. Michal Handzus of St. Louis polled six first-place votes and 188 points, while Mike Ricci of the Sharks received 125 points.

Yzerman was among the NHL's face-off leaders, posting a winning percentage of 56.8 for sixth place overall. He finished second on his team in plus-minus (+28) and led the Red Wings in scoring with 79 points (35 goals, 44 assists).

WILLIAM M. JENNINGS TROPHY

An annual award "to the goalkeeper(s) having played a minimum of 25 games for the team with the fewest goals scored against it." Winners selected on regular-season play. Overall winner receives $10,000, runners-up $6,000 and $4,000.

History: The Jennings Trophy was presented in 1981-82 by the National Hockey League's Board of Governors to honor the late William M. Jennings, longtime governor and president of the New York Rangers and one of the great builders of hockey in the United States.

1999-2000 Winner: Roman Turek, St. Louis Blues
Runners-up: John Vanbiesbrouck and Brian Boucher,
Philadelphia Flyers
Ed Belfour, Dallas Stars

After winning a share of the trophy with the Dallas Stars in 1998-99, Roman Turek of the St. Louis Blues won the William M. Jennings Trophy for the second consecutive season. Turek appeared in 67 of the Blues' 82 games and helped St. Louis post the NHL's best defensive record with just 165 goals against. Turek and Jamie McLennan, who played in 19 games, finished the regular season with a combined goals-against average of 1.97. Turek's win marked just the third time that a goalie or goalies earned the Jennings Trophy in consecutive seasons. It is the first time a goalie has done so with different teams.

LESTER B. PEARSON AWARD

An annual award presented to the NHL's outstanding player as selected by the members of the National Hockey League Players' Association. The winner receives $20,000.

History: The award was presented in 1970-71 by the NHLPA in honor of the late Lester B. Pearson, former Prime Minister of Canada.

1999-2000 Winner: Jaromir Jagr, Pittsburgh Penguins
Runners-up: Pavel Bure, Florida Panthers
Chris Pronger, St. Louis Blues

Jaromir Jagr of the Pittsburgh Penguins won the Lester B. Pearson Award for the second year in a row. His total of 192 votes was 33 more than Pavel Bure of the Florida Panthers and 63 more than Chris Pronger of the St. Louis Blues. Jagr led the NHL in scoring for the third year in a row and the fourth time overall. He designated a youth hockey program in the Czech Republic as the recipient of the $20,000 that accompanies the award. Both Bure and Pronger received $10,000 to donate to charity.

William M. Jennings Trophy

Jack Adams Award

Bill Masterton Trophy

Lester Patrick Trophy

Lester B. Pearson Award

JACK ADAMS AWARD

An annual award presented by the National Hockey League Broadcasters' Association to "the NHL coach adjudged to have contributed the most to his team's success." Winner selected by a poll among members of the NHL Broadcasters' Association at the end of the regular season. The winner receives $1,000 from the NHLBA.

History: The award was presented by the NHL Broadcasters' Association in 1974 to commemorate the late Jack Adams, coach and general manager of the Detroit Red Wings, whose lifetime dedication to hockey serves as an inspiration to all who aspire to further the game.

1999-2000 Winner: **Joel Quenneville, St. Louis Blues**
Runners-up: **Alain Vigneault, Montreal Canadiens**
Ron Wilson, Washington Capitals

Joel Quenneville of the St. Louis Blues was a first-time recipient of the Jack Adams Award as coach of the year. Quenneville, named on all 79 ballots, polled 61 first-place votes and 355 points overall to outdistance Alain Vigneault of the Montreal Canadiens and Ron Wilson of Washington, who were separated by just one point (117-116) for second place.

Quenneville led the Blues to the Presidents' Trophy for the first time in franchise history by establishing club records with 51 wins and 114 points. St. Louis also posted the NHL's best defensive record, allowing a league-low 165 goals over the 82-game schedule.

BILL MASTERTON MEMORIAL TROPHY

An annual award under the trusteeship of the Professional Hockey Writers' Association to "the National Hockey League player who best exemplifies the qualities of perseverance, sportsmanship and dedication to hockey." Winner selected by a poll among the 28 chapters of the PHWA at the end of the regular season (30 in 2000-01). A $2,500 grant from the PHWA is awarded annually to the Bill Masterton Scholarship Fund, based in Bloomington, MN, in the name of the Masterton Trophy winner.

History: The trophy was presented by the NHL Writers' Association in 1968 to commemorate the late Bill Masterton, a player of the Minnesota North Stars, who exhibited to a high degree the qualities of perseverance, sportsmanship and dedication to hockey, and who died January 15, 1968.

1999-2000 Winner: **Ken Daneyko, New Jersey Devils**

New Jersey Devils defenseman Ken Daneyko was the recipient of the Bill Masterton Memorial Trophy. The 15-year NHL veteran has spent his entire career in New Jersey, and has maintained himself as a key figure in the Devils lineup. He is counted on for his physical presence on defense. Daneyko appeared in his 1,000th NHL game during the 1999-2000 season.

LESTER PATRICK TROPHY

An annual award "for outstanding service to hockey in the United States." Eligible recipients are players, officials, coaches, executives and referees. Winners are selected by an award committee consisting of the president of the NHL, an NHL governor, a representative of the New York Rangers, a member of the Hockey Hall of Fame builder's section, a member of the Hockey Hall of Fame player's section, a member of the U.S. Hockey Hall of Fame, a member of the NHL Broadcasters' Association and a member of the Professional Hockey Writers' Association. Each except the League President is rotated annually. The winner receives a miniature of the trophy.

History: Presented by the New York Rangers in 1966 to honor the late Lester Patrick, longtime general manager and coach of the New York Rangers, whose teams finished out of the playoffs only once in his first 16 years with the club.

1999-2000 Winners: **Mario Lemieux**
Craig Patrick
Lou Vairo

One of hockey's most celebrated talents, Mario Lemieux played 12 seasons with the Pittsburgh Penguins. During his playing career, which ended after the 1996-97 season, Lemieux led the Penguins to two Stanley Cup titles, four division championships, seven consecutive playoff appearances and the NHL's second-best regular-season record during the 1990s. Lemieux won the Art Ross Trophy as the NHL scoring champion six times, the Hart Trophy as most valuable player on three occasions, and the Conn Smythe Trophy as playoff MVP twice.

Despite a battle with cancer and two major back operations, Lemieux finished his NHL career ranked sixth in career goals with 613. He was inducted into the Hockey Hall of Fame in 1997, and returned to the NHL in September, 1999, when he became owner and president of the Penguins. Craig Patrick has been general manager of the Penguins for 10 years, leading the team to nine consecutive playoff appearances and two Stanley Cup championships. Grandson to the award's namesake, he is a member of one of hockey's most famous families, which also includes his father Lynn and uncle Muzz, both former NHL players, coaches and general managers. Craig Patrick played eight seasons in the NHL before retiring in 1979. He was assistant coach and assistant g.m. of the 1980 U.S. Olympic hockey team before joining the New York Rangers organization later that year. After the 1985-86 season, Patrick spent two years as director of athletics at the University of Denver before joining the Penguins.

Lou Vairo has been the director of special projects for USA Hockey since 1992. He has coached hockey from the grassroots level to the Olympics (head coach of the U.S. team in 1984) to the NHL (as an assistant with the New Jersey Devils). From 1978 to 1983, Vairo was coach of the U.S. national junior team, playing a key role in shaping USA Hockey's Coaching Education Program. He has been instrumental in implementing the NHL/USA Hockey Diversity Task Force and is a founder of USA Hockey Summer Select Camps. He also represented USA Hockey on the International Ice Hockey Federation (IIHF) Coaching Committee. He has authored many books and articles on hockey used by coaches around the world.

King Clancy Memorial Trophy

Bud Light Plus-Minus Award

Presidents' Trophy

Maurice "Rocket" Richard Trophy

KING CLANCY MEMORIAL TROPHY

An annual award "to the player who best exemplifies leadership qualities on and off the ice and has made a noteworthy humanitarian contribution in his community."

History: The King Clancy Memorial Trophy was presented to the National Hockey League by the Board of Governors in 1988 to honor the late Frank "King" Clancy.

1999-2000 Winner: Curtis Joseph, Toronto Maple Leafs

Toronto goaltender Curtis Joseph was the 1999-2000 recipient of the King Clancy Memorial Trophy. Since joining the Maple Leafs in 1998, Joseph has had an extraordinary impact on both his team and the community of Toronto through his work with seriously ill children. When Joseph was a member of the Edmonton Oilers, he and his wife Nancy created a program dedicated to patients in local children's hospitals. This commitment continued in Toronto through two programs: "Cujo's Kids," which works exclusively with children's hospitals in Toronto, London and Hamilton, and "Cujo's Crease," a new room for children with cancer at Toronto's world-renowned Hospital for Sick Children. On and off the ice, Curtis Joseph has been a superlative role model and motivator. His community work reflects his generosity and passion for children.

MAURICE "ROCKET" RICHARD TROPHY

An annual award "presented to the player finishing the regular season as the League's goal-scoring leader.

History: A gift to the NHL from the Montreal Canadiens in 1999, the Maurice "Rocket" Richard Trophy honors one of the game's greatest stars. During his 18-year career with the Canadiens from 1942-43 through 1959-60, Richard was the first player in NHL history to score 50 goals in a season and 500 in his career. He played on eight Stanley Cup champions and led the League in goal scoring five times.

1999-2000 Winner: Pavel Bure, Florida Panthers
Runners-up: Owen Nolan, San Jose Sharks
Tony Amonte, Chicago Blackhawks

Florida Panthers right winger Pavel Bure finished the 1999-2000 regular season with 58 goals to earn the Maurice Richard Trophy by a wide margin over Owen Nolan (44 goals) and Tony Amonte (43). Bure tallied goals in 41 of his 74 games played, including a league-leading 14 game-winners. He posted a four-goal performance against Tampa Bay on January 1 and recorded a trio of three-goal games: versus Phoenix on December 8, Buffalo on December 17 and the New York Islanders on March 18.

After missing most of the 1998-99 season due to an injured right knee, Bure accounted for 23.8 percent of the Panthers' goals (58 of 244) while helping Florida to its first playoff appearance since 1997.

PRESIDENTS' TROPHY

An annual award to the club finishing the regular-season with the best overall record. The winner receives $350,000, to be split between the team and its players.

History: Presented to the National Hockey League in 1985-86 by the NHL Board of Governors to recognize the team compiling the top regular-season record.

1999-2000 Winner: St. Louis Blues
Runners-up: Detroit Red Wings
Philadelphia Flyers

The St. Louis Blues finished first in the Central Division and first in the Western Conference with a record of 51-20-11, amassing 114 points (including points for regulation ties) to earn the Presidents' Trophy for the first time in franchise history. The Blues qualified for the playoffs for the 21st consecutive year, the longest active streak among the four major professional sports leagues. The Detroit Red Wings had the NHL's next-best record at 48-24-10 for 108 points. Philadelphia was third overall at 45-25-12 and 105 points.

BUD LIGHT PLUS-MINUS AWARD

An annual award "to the player, having played a minimum of 60 games, who leads the League in plus/minus statistics" at the end of the regular season.
Bud Light will contribute $5,000 on behalf of the winner to the charity of his choice.

History: This award was first presented to the NHL in 1996-97 by Anheuser-Busch Inc. to recognize the League leader in plus-minus statistics. Plus-minus statistics are calculated by giving a player a "plus" when on-ice for an even-strength or shorthand goal scored by his team. He receives a "minus" when on-ice for an even-strength or shorthand goal scored by the opposing team. A plus-minus award has been presented since the 1982-83 season.

1999-2000 Winner: Chris Pronger, St. Louis Blues
Runners-up: Chris Chelios, Detroit Red Wings
Pavol Demitra, St. Louis Blues

Chris Pronger of the St. Louis Blues won his second plus-minus award in three years, leading the NHL with a rating of +52. Pronger helped the Blues post the NHL's best record at 51-20-11 while allowing a league-low 165 goals. Chris Chelios of the Red Wings posted a plus-minus mark of +48, while Pavol Demitra earned a +34.

Roger Crozier MBNA Saving Grace Award

*Bud Light NHL All-Star Game
MVP Award*

ROGER CROZIER MBNA SAVING GRACE AWARD

An award "presented to the goaltender having played a minimum of 25 games with the NHL's best save percentage during the regular season." The winner receives $25,000 to be donated to the youth hockey or educational program of his choice.

History: This award was first presented to the league in 1999-2000 by MBNA Corporation. It is named for Roger Crozier, one of the NHL's top goaltenders during his career. Crozier joined MBNA America Bank in 1983. He passed away on Jan. 11, 1996. Save percentage is calculated by dividing total saves by total shots faced.

1999-2000 Winner: Ed Belfour, Dallas Stars
Runners-up: Jose Theodore, Montreal Canadiens
Dominik Hasek, Buffalo Sabres

Dallas goaltender Ed Belfour is the inaugural winner of the Roger Crozier MBNA Saving Grace Award. In a race that was not decided until overtime of his team's final game, Belfour posted a .919 save percentage to edge Montreal's Jose Theodore by five one-thousandths of one percent (.91916 to .91911). Dominik Hasek of the Buffalo Sabres finished third with a mark of .91880. Belfour allowed just 127 goals on 1,571 shots. He requested that the $25,000 check be divided evenly between the minor hockey program in his hometown of Carman, Manitoba, and Carman Collegiate.

BUD LIGHT NHL ALL-STAR GAME MVP AWARD

1962	Eddie Shack, Tor.	1982	Mike Bossy, NYI
1963	Frank Mahovlich, Tor.	1983	Wayne Gretzky, Edm.
1964	Jean Beliveau, Mtl.	1984	Don Maloney, NYR
1965	Gordie Howe, Det..	1985	Mario Lemieux, Pit.
1967	Henri Richard, Mtl.	1986	Grant Fuhr, Edm.
1968	Bruce Gamble, Tor.	1988	Mario Lemieux, Pit.
1969	Frank Mahovlich, Det.	1989	Wayne Gretzky, L.A.
1970	Bobby Hull, Chi.	1990	Mario Lemieux, Pit.
1971	Bobby Hull, Chi.	1991	Vincent Damphousse, Tor.
1972	Bobby Orr, Bos.	1992	Brett Hull, St.L.
1973	Greg Polis, Pit.	1993	Mike Gartner, NYR
1974	Garry Unger, St.L.	1994	Mike Richter, NYR
1975	Syl Apps Jr., Pit.	1996	Ray Bourque, Bos.
1976	Peter Mahovlich, Mtl.	1997	Mark Recchi, Mtl.
1977	Rick Martin, Buf.	1998	Teemu Selanne, Ana.
1978	Billy Smith, NYI	1999	Wayne Gretzky, NYR
1980	Reggie Leach, Phi.	2000	Pavel Bure, Fla.
1981	Mike Liut, St.L.		

NHL AWARD MONEY BREAKDOWN — 1999-2000

(Players on each club determine how team award money is divided.)

TEAM AWARDS

Stanley Cup Playoffs	Number of Clubs	Share Per Club	Total
Conference Quarter-Final Losers	8	$ 237,500	$1,900,000
Conference Semi-Final Losers	4	412,500	1,650,000
Conference Championship Losers	2	902,500	1,805,000
Stanley Cup Loser	1	1,467,500	1,467,500
Stanley Cup Winners	1	2,142,500	2,142,500
TOTAL PLAYOFF AWARD MONEY			$8,965,000

Final Standings, Regular Season	Number of Clubs	Share Per Club	Total
Presidents' Trophy			
Club's Share	1	$ 100,000	$ 100,000
Players' Share	1	250,000	250,000
Conference First Place*	2	500,000	1,000,000
Conference Second Place*	2	375,000	750,000
Conference Third Place*	2	250,000	500,000
Conference Fourth Place*	2	125,000	250,000
*based on points.			
TOTAL REGULAR-SEASON AWARD MONEY			$2,850,000

INDIVIDUAL AWARDS	Winner	First Runner-up	Second Runner-up
Hart, Calder, Norris, Ross, Vezina, Byng, Selke, Jennings, Masterton Trophies	$10,000	$6,000	$4,000
King Clancy Trophy	$ 3,000	$1,000	
Conn Smythe Trophy	$10,000		
TOTAL INDIVIDUAL AWARD MONEY			$194,000

ALL-STARS	Number of winners	Per Player	Total
First Team All-Stars	6	$10,000	$ 60,000
Second Team All-Stars	6	5,000	$ 30,000
All-Star Game Winners			$250,000
TOTAL ALL-STAR AWARD MONEY			$340,000
TOTAL ALL AWARDS			**$12,349,000**

1999-2000
NHL Player of the Week/Month Award Winners

Player of the Week

Week Ending	Player
Oct. 10	Luc Robitaille, Los Angeles
Oct. 17	Steve Shields, San Jose
Oct. 24	John Vanbiesbrouck, Philadelphia
Oct. 31	Bryan Smolinski, Los Angeles
Nov. 7	Martin Biron, Buffalo
Nov. 14	Jaromir Jagr, Pittsburgh
Nov. 21	Roman Turek, St. Louis
Nov. 28	Jeremy Roenick, Phoenix
Dec. 5	Pierre Turgeon, St. Louis
Dec. 12	Owen Nolan, San Jose
Dec. 19	Pavel Bure, Florida
Dec. 26	Fred Brathwaite, Calgary
Jan. 2	Tomas Vokoun, Nashville
Jan. 9	Martin Brodeur, New Jersey
Jan. 16	Peter Forsberg, Colorado
Jan. 23	Mike Richter, NY Rangers
Jan. 30	Sergei Gonchar, Washington
Feb. 13	Jorgen Jonsson, NY Islanders
Feb. 20	Jean-Sebastien Aubin, Pittsburgh
Feb. 27	Curtis Joseph, Toronto / Jose Theodore, Montreal
Mar. 5	Olaf Kolzig, Washington
Mar. 12	Yanic Perreault, Toronto
Mar. 19	Markus Naslund, Vancouver
Mar. 26	Roman Turek, St. Louis
Apr. 2	Arturs Irbe, Carolina
Apr. 9	Dominik Hasek, Buffalo

Player of the Month

Month	Player
October	Mikhail Shtalenkov, Phoenix
November	Jaromir Jagr, Pittsburgh
December	Pavel Bure, Florida
January	Olaf Kolzig, Washington
February	Jarome Iginla, Calgary
March	Joe Sakic, Colorado

Rookie of the Month

Month	Player
October	Peter Schaefer, Vancouver
November	Scott Gomez, New Jersey
December	Simon Gagne, Philadelphia
January	Trevor Letowski, Phoenix
February	Brian Rafalski, New Jersey
March	Jeff Halpern, Washington

NATIONAL HOCKEY LEAGUE INDIVIDUAL AWARD WINNERS

ART ROSS TROPHY

	Winner	Runner-up
2000	Jaromir Jagr, Pit.	Pavel Bure, Fla.
1999	Jaromir Jagr, Pit.	Teemu Selanne, Ana.
1998	Jaromir Jagr, Pit.	Peter Forsberg, Col.
1997	Mario Lemieux, Pit.	Teemu Selanne, Ana.
1996	Mario Lemieux, Pit.	Jaromir Jagr, Pit.
1995	Jaromir Jagr, Pit.	Eric Lindros, Phi.
1994	Wayne Gretzky, L.A.	Sergei Fedorov, Det.
1993	Mario Lemieux, Pit.	Pat LaFontaine, Buf.
1992	Mario Lemieux, Pit.	Kevin Stevens, Pit.
1991	Wayne Gretzky, L.A.	Brett Hull, St.L.
1990	Wayne Gretzky, L.A.	Mark Messier, Edm.
1989	Mario Lemieux, Pit.	Wayne Gretzky, L.A.
1988	Mario Lemieux, Pit.	Wayne Gretzky, Edm.
1987	Wayne Gretzky, Edm.	Jari Kurri, Edm.
1986	Wayne Gretzky, Edm.	Mario Lemieux, Pit.
1985	Wayne Gretzky, Edm.	Jari Kurri, Edm.
1984	Wayne Gretzky, Edm.	Paul Coffey, Edm.
1983	Wayne Gretzky, Edm.	Peter Stastny, Que.
1982	Wayne Gretzky, Edm.	Mike Bossy, NYI
1981	Wayne Gretzky, Edm.	Marcel Dionne, L.A.
1980	Marcel Dionne, L.A.	Wayne Gretzky, Edm.
1979	Bryan Trottier, NYI	Marcel Dionne, L.A.
1978	Guy Lafleur, Mtl.	Bryan Trottier, NYI
1977	Guy Lafleur, Mtl.	Marcel Dionne, L.A.
1976	Guy Lafleur, Mtl.	Bobby Clarke, Phi.
1975	Bobby Orr, Bos.	Phil Esposito, Bos.
1974	Phil Esposito, Bos.	Bobby Orr, Bos.
1973	Phil Esposito, Bos.	Bobby Clarke, Phi.
1972	Phil Esposito, Bos.	Bobby Orr, Bos.
1971	Phil Esposito, Bos.	Bobby Orr, Bos.
1970	Bobby Orr, Bos.	Phil Esposito, Bos.
1969	Phil Esposito, Bos.	Bobby Hull, Chi.
1968	Stan Mikita, Chi.	Phil Esposito, Bos.
1967	Stan Mikita, Chi.	Bobby Hull, Chi.
1966	Bobby Hull, Chi.	Stan Mikita, Chi.
1965	Stan Mikita, Chi.	Norm Ullman, Det.
1964	Stan Mikita, Chi.	Bobby Hull, Chi.
1963	Gordie Howe, Det.	Andy Bathgate, NYR
1962	Bobby Hull, Chi.	Andy Bathgate, NYR
1961	Bernie Geoffrion, Mtl.	Jean Beliveau, Mtl.
1960	Bobby Hull, Chi.	Bronco Horvath, Bos.
1959	Dickie Moore, Mtl.	Jean Beliveau, Mtl.
1958	Dickie Moore, Mtl.	Henri Richard, Mtl.
1957	Gordie Howe, Det.	Ted Lindsay, Det.
1956	Jean Beliveau, Mtl.	Gordie Howe, Det.
1955	Bernie Geoffrion, Mtl.	Maurice Richard, Mtl.
1954	Gordie Howe, Det.	Maurice Richard, Mtl.
1953	Gordie Howe, Det.	Ted Lindsay, Det.
1952	Gordie Howe, Det.	Ted Lindsay, Det.
1951	Gordie Howe, Det.	Maurice Richard, Mtl.
1950	Ted Lindsay, Det.	Sid Abel, Det.
1949	Roy Conacher, Chi.	Doug Bentley, Chi.
1948*	Elmer Lach, Mtl.	Buddy O'Connor, NYR
1947	Max Bentley, Chi.	Maurice Richard, Mtl.
1946	Max Bentley, Chi.	Gaye Stewart, Tor.
1945	Elmer Lach, Mtl.	Maurice Richard, Mtl.
1944	Herb Cain, Bos.	Doug Bentley, Chi.
1943	Doug Bentley, Chi.	Bill Cowley, Bos.
1942	Bryan Hextall Sr., NYR	Lynn Patrick, NYR
1941	Bill Cowley, Bos.	Bryan Hextall Sr., NYR
1940	Milt Schmidt, Bos.	Woody Dumart, Bos.
1939	Toe Blake, Mtl.	Sweeney Schriner, NYA
1938	Gordie Drillon, Tor.	Syl Apps Sr., Tor.
1937	Sweeney Schriner, NYA	Syl Apps Sr., Tor.
1936	Sweeney Schriner, NYA	Marty Barry, Det.
1935	Charlie Conacher, Tor.	Syd Howe, St.L-Det.
1934	Charlie Conacher, Tor.	Joe Primeau, Tor
1933	Bill Cook, NYR	Harvey Jackson, Tor.
1932	Harvey Jackson, Tor.	Joe Primeau, Tor.
1931	Howie Morenz, Mtl.	Ebbie Goodfellow, Det.
1930	Cooney Weiland, Bos.	Frank Boucher, NYR
1929	Ace Bailey, Tor.	Nels Stewart, Mtl.M
1928	Howie Morenz, Mtl.	Aurel Joliat, Mtl.
1927	Bill Cook, NYR	Dick Irvin, Chi.
1926	Nels Stewart, Mtl.M.	Cy Denneny, Ott.
1925	Babe Dye, Tor.	Cy Denneny, Ott.
1924	Cy Denneny, Ott.	Billy Boucher, Mtl.
1923	Babe Dye, Tor.	Cy Denneny, Ott.
1922	Punch Broadbent, Ott.	Cy Denneny, Ott.
1921	Newsy Lalonde, Mtl.	Babe Dye, Ham., Tor.
1920	Joe Malone, Que.	Newsy Lalonde, Mtl.
1919	Newsy Lalonde, Mtl.	Odie Cleghorn, Mtl.
1918	Joe Malone, Mtl.	Cy Denneny, Ott.

* Trophy first awarded in 1948.
  Scoring leaders listed from 1918 to 1947.

HART TROPHY

	Winner	Runner-up
2000	Chris Pronger, St.L.	Jaromir Jagr, Pit.
1999	Jaromir Jagr, Pit.	Alexei Yashin, Ott.
1998	Dominik Hasek, Buf.	Jaromir Jagr, Pit.
1997	Dominik Hasek, Buf.	Paul Kariya, Ana.
1996	Mario Lemieux, Pit.	Mark Messier, NYR
1995	Eric Lindros, Phi.	Jaromir Jagr, Pit.
1994	Sergei Fedorov, Det.	Dominik Hasek, Buf.
1993	Mario Lemieux, Pit.	Doug Gilmour, Tor.
1992	Mark Messier, NYR	Patrick Roy, Mtl.
1991	Brett Hull, St.L.	Wayne Gretzky, L.A.
1990	Mark Messier, Edm.	Ray Bourque, Bos.
1989	Wayne Gretzky, L.A.	Mario Lemieux, Pit.
1988	Mario Lemieux, Pit.	Grant Fuhr, Edm.
1987	Wayne Gretzky, Edm.	Ray Bourque, Bos.
1986	Wayne Gretzky, Edm.	Mario Lemieux, Pit.
1985	Wayne Gretzky, Edm.	Dale Hawerchuk, Wpg.
1984	Wayne Gretzky, Edm.	Rod Langway, Wsh.
1983	Wayne Gretzky, Edm.	Pete Peeters, Bos.
1982	Wayne Gretzky, Edm.	Bryan Trottier, NYI
1981	Wayne Gretzky, Edm.	Mike Liut, St.L.
1980	Wayne Gretzky, Edm.	Marcel Dionne, L.A.
1979	Bryan Trottier, NYI	Guy Lafleur, Mtl
1978	Guy Lafleur, Mtl.	Bryan Trottier, NYI
1977	Guy Lafleur, Mtl.	Bobby Clarke, Phi.
1976	Bobby Clarke, Phi.	Denis Potvin, NYI
1975	Bobby Clarke, Phi.	Rogie Vachon, L.A.
1974	Phil Esposito, Bos.	Bernie Parent, Phi.
1973	Bobby Clarke, Phi.	Phil Esposito, Bos.
1972	Bobby Orr, Bos.	Ken Dryden, Mtl.
1971	Bobby Orr, Bos.	Phil Esposito, Bos.
1970	Bobby Orr, Bos.	Tony Esposito, Chi.
1969	Phil Esposito, Bos.	Jean Beliveau, Mtl.
1968	Stan Mikita, Chi.	Jean Beliveau, Mtl.
1967	Stan Mikita, Chi.	Ed Giacomin, NYR
1966	Bobby Hull, Chi.	Jean Beliveau, Mtl.
1965	Bobby Hull, Chi.	Norm Ullman, Det.
1964	Jean Beliveau, Mtl.	Bobby Hull, Chi.
1963	Gordie Howe, Det.	Stan Mikita, Chi.
1962	Jacques Plante, Mtl.	Doug Harvey, NYR
1961	Bernie Geoffrion, Mtl.	Johnny Bower, Tor.
1960	Gordie Howe, Det.	Bobby Hull, Chi.
1959	Andy Bathgate, NYR	Gordie Howe, Det.
1958	Gordie Howe, Det.	Andy Bathgate, NYR
1957	Gordie Howe, Det.	Jean Beliveau, Mtl.
1956	Jean Beliveau, Mtl.	Tod Sloan, Tor.
1955	Ted Kennedy, Tor.	Harry Lumley, Tor.
1954	Al Rollins, Chi.	Red Kelly, Det.
1953	Gordie Howe, Det.	Al Rollins, Chi.
1952	Gordie Howe, Det.	Elmer Lach, Mtl.
1951	Milt Schmidt, Bos.	Maurice Richard, Mtl.
1950	Chuck Rayner, NYR	Ted Kennedy, Tor.
1949	Sid Abel, Det.	Bill Durnan, Mtl.
1948	Buddy O'Connor, NYR	Frank Brimsek, Bos.
1947	Maurice Richard, Mtl.	Milt Schmidt, Bos.
1946	Max Bentley, Chi.	Gaye Stewart, Tor.
1945	Elmer Lach, Mtl.	Maurice Richard, Mtl.
1944	Babe Pratt, Tor.	Bill Cowley, Bos.
1943	Bill Cowley, Bos.	Doug Bentley, Chi.
1942	Tom Anderson, Bro.	Syl Apps Sr., Tor.
1941	Bill Cowley, Bos.	Dit Clapper, Bos.
1940	Ebbie Goodfellow, Det.	Syl Apps Sr., Tor.
1939	Toe Blake, Mtl.	Syl Apps Sr., Tor.
1938	Eddie Shore, Bos.	Paul Thompson, Chi.
1937	Babe Siebert, Mtl.	Lionel Conacher, Mtl.M
1936	Eddie Shore, Bos.	Hooley Smith, Mtl.M
1935	Eddie Shore, Bos.	Charlie Conacher, Tor.
1934	Aurel Joliat, Mtl.	Lionel Conacher, Chi.
1933	Eddie Shore, Bos.	Bill Cook, NYR
1932	Howie Morenz, Mtl.	Ching Johnson, NYR
1931	Howie Morenz, Mtl.	Eddie Shore, Bos.
1930	Nels Stewart, Mtl.M.	Lionel Hitchman, Bos.
1929	Roy Worters, NYA	Ace Bailey, Tor.
1928	Howie Morenz, Mtl.	Roy Worters, Pit.
1927	Herb Gardiner, Mtl.	Bill Cook, NYR
1926	Nels Stewart, Mtl.M.	Sprague Cleghorn, Bos.
1925	Billy Burch, Ham.	Howie Morenz, Mtl.
1924	Frank Nighbor, Ott.	Sprague Cleghorn, Mtl.

BILL MASTERTON TROPHY WINNERS

2000	Ken Daneyko	New Jersey
1999	John Cullen	Tampa Bay
1998	Jamie McLennan	St. Louis
1997	Tony Granato	San Jose
1996	Gary Roberts	Calgary
1995	Pat LaFontaine	Buffalo
1994	Cam Neely	Boston
1993	Mario Lemieux	Pittsburgh
1992	Mark Fitzpatrick	NY Islanders
1991	Dave Taylor	Los Angeles
1990	Gord Kluzak	Boston
1989	Tim Kerr	Philadelphia
1988	Bob Bourne	Los Angeles
1987	Doug Jarvis	Hartford
1986	Charlie Simmer	Boston
1985	Anders Hedberg	NY Rangers
1984	Brad Park	Detroit
1983	Lanny McDonald	Calgary
1982	Glenn Resch	Colorado
1981	Blake Dunlop	St. Louis
1980	Al MacAdam	Minnesota
1979	Serge Savard	Montreal
1978	Butch Goring	Los Angeles
1977	Ed Westfall	NY Islanders
1976	Rod Gilbert	NY Rangers
1975	Don Luce	Buffalo
1974	Henri Richard	Montreal
1973	Lowell MacDonald	Pittsburgh
1972	Bobby Clarke	Philadelphia
1971	Jean Ratelle	NY Rangers
1970	Pit Martin	Chicago
1969	Ted Hampson	Oakland
1968	Claude Provost	Montreal

PRESIDENTS' TROPHY

	Winner	Runner-up
2000	St. Louis Blues	Detroit Red Wings
1999	Dallas Stars	New Jersey Devils
1998	Dallas Stars	New Jersey Devils
1997	Colorado Avalanche	Dallas Stars
1996	Detroit Red Wings	Colorado Avalanche
1995	Detroit Red Wings	Quebec Nordiques
1994	New York Rangers	New Jersey Devils
1993	Pittsburgh Penguins	Boston Bruins
1992	New York Rangers	Washington Capitals
1991	Chicago Blackhawks	St. Louis Blues
1990	Boston Bruins	Calgary Flames
1989	Calgary Flames	Montreal Canadiens
1988	Calgary Flames	Montreal Canadiens
1987	Edmonton Oilers	Philadelphia Flyers
1986	Edmonton Oilers	Philadelphia Flyers

LADY BYNG TROPHY

	Winner	Runner-up
2000	Pavol Demitra, St.L.	Nicklas Lidstrom, Det.
1999	Wayne Gretzky, NYR.	Nicklas Lidstrom, Det.
1998	Ron Francis, Pit.	Teemu Selanne, Ana.
1997	Paul Kariya, Ana.	Teemu Selanne, Ana.
1996	Paul Kariya, Ana.	Adam Oates, Bos.
1995	Ron Francis, Pit.	Adam Oates, Bos.
1994	Wayne Gretzky, L.A.	Adam Oates, Bos.
1993	Pierre Turgeon, NYI	Adam Oates, Bos.
1992	Wayne Gretzky, L.A.	Joe Sakic, Que.
1991	Wayne Gretzky, L.A.	Brett Hull, St.L.
1990	Brett Hull, St.L.	Wayne Gretzky, L.A.
1989	Joe Mullen, Cgy.	Wayne Gretzky, L.A.
1988	Mats Naslund, Mtl.	Wayne Gretzky, Edm.
1987	Joe Mullen, Cgy.	Wayne Gretzky, Edm.
1986	Mike Bossy, NYI	Jari Kurri, Edm.
1985	Jari Kurri, Edm.	Joe Mullen, St.L.
1984	Mike Bossy, NYI	Rick Middleton, Bos.
1983	Mike Bossy, NYI	Rick Middleton, Bos.
1982	Rick Middleton, Bos.	Mike Bossy, NYI
1981	Rick Kehoe, Pit.	Wayne Gretzky, Edm.
1980	Wayne Gretzky, Edm.	Marcel Dionne, L.A.
1979	Bob MacMillan, Atl.	Marcel Dionne, L.A.
1978	Butch Goring, L.A.	Peter McNab, Bos.
1977	Marcel Dionne, L.A.	Jean Ratelle, Bos.
1976	Jean Ratelle, NYR-Bos.	Jean Pronovost, Pit.
1975	Marcel Dionne, Det.	John Bucyk, Bos.
1974	John Bucyk, Bos.	Lowell MacDonald, Pit.
1973	Gilbert Perreault, Buf.	Jean Ratelle, NYR
1972	Jean Ratelle, NYR	John Bucyk, Bos.
1971	John Bucyk, Bos.	Dave Keon, Tor.
1970	Phil Goyette, St.L.	John Bucyk, Bos.
1969	Alex Delvecchio, Det.	Ted Hampson, Oak.
1968	Stan Mikita, Chi.	John Bucyk, Bos.
1967	Stan Mikita, Chi.	Dave Keon, Tor.
1966	Alex Delvecchio, Det.	Bobby Rousseau, Mtl.
1965	Bobby Hull, Chi.	Alex Delvecchio, Det.
1964	Ken Wharram, Chi.	Dave Keon, Tor.
1963	Dave Keon, Tor.	Camille Henry, NYR
1962	Dave Keon, Tor.	Claude Provost, Mtl.
1961	Red Kelly, Tor.	Norm Ullman, Det.
1960	Don McKenney, Bos.	Andy Hebenton, NYR
1959	Alex Delvecchio, Det.	Andy Hebenton, NYR
1958	Camille Henry, NYR	Don Marshall, Mtl.
1957	Andy Hebenton, NYR	Earl Reibel, Det.
1956	Earl Reibel, Det.	Floyd Curry, Mtl.
1955	Sid Smith, Tor.	Danny Lewicki, NYR
1954	Red Kelly, Det.	Don Raleigh, NYR
1953	Red Kelly, Det.	Wally Hergesheimer, NYR
1952	Sid Smith, Tor.	Red Kelly, Det.
1951	Red Kelly, Det.	Woody Dumart, Bos.
1950	Edgar Laprade, NYR	Red Kelly, Det.
1949	Bill Quackenbush, Det.	Harry Watson, Tor.
1948	Buddy O'Connor, NYR	Syl Apps Sr., Tor.
1947	Bobby Bauer, Bos.	Syl Apps Sr., Tor.
1946	Toe Blake, Mtl.	Clint Smith, Chi.
1945	Bill Mosienko, Chi.	Syd Howe, Det.
1944	Clint Smith, Chi.	Herb Cain, Bos.
1943	Max Bentley, Chi.	Buddy O'Connor, Mtl.
1942	Syl Apps Sr., Tor.	Gordie Drillon, Tor.
1941	Bobby Bauer, Bos.	Gordie Drillon, Tor.
1940	Bobby Bauer, Bos.	Clint Smith, NYR
1939	Clint Smith, NYR	Marty Barry, Det.
1938	Gordie Drillon, Tor.	Clint Smith, NYR
1937	Marty Barry, Det.	Gordie Drillon, Tor.
1936	Doc Romnes, Chi.	Sweeney Schriner, NYA
1935	Frank Boucher, NYR	Russ Blinco, Mtl.M
1934	Frank Boucher, NYR	Joe Primeau, Tor.
1933	Frank Boucher, NYR	Joe Primeau, Tor.
1932	Joe Primeau, Tor.	Frank Boucher, NYR
1931	Frank Boucher, NYR	Normie Himes, NYA
1930	Frank Boucher, NYR	Normie Himes, NYA
1929	Frank Boucher, NYR	Harry Darragh, Pit.
1928	Frank Boucher, NYR	George Hay, Det.
1927	Billy Burch, NYA	Dick Irvin, Chi.
1926	Frank Nighbor, Ott.	Billy Burch, NYA
1925	Frank Nighbor, Ott.	none

KING CLANCY MEMORIAL TROPHY WINNERS

2000	Curtis Joseph	Toronto
1999	Rob Ray	Buffalo
1998	Kelly Chase	St. Louis
1997	Trevor Linden	Vancouver
1996	Kris King	Winnipeg
1995	Joe Nieuwendyk	Calgary
1994	Adam Graves	NY Rangers
1993	Dave Poulin	Boston
1992	Ray Bourque	Boston
1991	Dave Taylor	Los Angeles
1990	Kevin Lowe	Edmonton
1989	Bryan Trottier	NY Islanders
1988	Lanny McDonald	Calgary

VEZINA TROPHY

	Winner	Runner-up
2000	Olaf Kolzig, Wsh.	Roman Turek, St.L.
1999	Dominik Hasek, Buf.	Curtis Joseph, Tor.
1998	Dominik Hasek, Buf.	Martin Brodeur, N.J.
1997	Dominik Hasek, Buf.	Martin Brodeur, N.J.
1996	Jim Carey, Wsh.	Chris Osgood, Det.
1995	Dominik Hasek, Buf.	Ed Belfour, Chi.
1994	Dominik Hasek, Buf.	John Vanbiesbrouck, Fla.
1993	Ed Belfour, Chi.	Tom Barrasso, Pit.
1992	Patrick Roy, Mtl.	Kirk McLean, Van.
1991	Ed Belfour, Chi.	Patrick Roy, Mtl.
1990	Patrick Roy, Mtl.	Daren Puppa, Buf.
1989	Patrick Roy, Mtl.	Mike Vernon, Cgy.
1988	Grant Fuhr, Edm.	Tom Barrasso, Buf.
1987	Ron Hextall, Phi.	Mike Liut, Hfd.
1986	John Vanbiesbrouck, NYR	Bob Froese, Phi.
1985	Pelle Lindbergh, Phi.	Tom Barrasso, Buf.
1984	Tom Barrasso, Buf.	Rejean Lemelin, Cgy.
1983	Pete Peeters, Bos.	Roland Melanson, NYI
1982	Billy Smith, NYI	Grant Fuhr, Edm.
1981	Richard Sevigny, Mtl.	Pete Peeters, Phi.
	Denis Herron, Mtl.	Rick St. Croix, Phi.
	Michel Larocque, Mtl.	
1980	Bob Sauve, Buf.	Gerry Cheevers, Bos.
	Don Edwards, Buf.	Gilles Gilbert, Bos.
1979	Ken Dryden, Mtl.	Glenn Resch, NYI
	Michel Larocque, Mtl.	Billy Smith, NYI
1978	Ken Dryden, Mtl.	Bernie Parent, Phi.
	Michel Larocque	Wayne Stephenson, Phi.
1977	Ken Dryden, Mtl.	Glenn Resch, NYI
	Michel Larocque, Mtl.	Billy Smith, NYI
1976	Ken Dryden, Mtl.	Glenn Resch, NYI
		Billy Smith, NYI
1975	Bernie Parent, Phi.	Rogie Vachon, L.A.
		Gary Edwards, L.A.
1974	Bernie Parent, Phi. (tie)	Gilles Gilbert, Bos.
	Tony Esposito, Chi. (tie)	
1973	Ken Dryden, Mtl.	Ed Giacomin, NYR
		Gilles Villemure, NYR
1972	Tony Esposito, Chi.	Cesare Maniago, Min.
	Gary Smith, Chi.	Gump Worsley, Min.
1971	Ed Giacomin, NYR	Tony Esposito, Chi.
	Gilles Villemure, NYR	
1970	Tony Esposito, Chi.	Jacques Plante, St.L.
		Ernie Wakely, St.L.
1969	Jacques Plante, St.L.	Ed Giacomin, NYR
	Glenn Hall, St.L.	
1968	Gump Worsley, Mtl.	Johnny Bower, Tor.
	Rogie Vachon, Mtl.	Bruce Gamble, Tor.
1967	Glenn Hall, Chi.	Charlie Hodge, Mtl.
	Denis Dejordy, Chi.	
1966	Gump Worsley, Mtl.	Glenn Hall, Chi.
	Charlie Hodge, Mtl.	
1965	Terry Sawchuk, Tor.	Roger Crozier, Det.
	Johnny Bower, Tor.	
1964	Charlie Hodge, Mtl.	Glenn Hall, Chi.
1963	Glenn Hall, Chi.	Johnny Bower, Tor.
		Don Simmons, Tor.
1962	Jacques Plante, Mtl.	Johnny Bower, Tor.
1961	Johnny Bower, Tor.	Glenn Hall, Chi.
1960	Jacques Plante, Mtl.	Glenn Hall, Chi.
1959	Jacques Plante, Mtl.	Johnny Bower, Tor.
		Ed Chadwick, Tor.
1958	Jacques Plante, Mtl.	Gump Worsley, NYR
		Marcel Paille, NYR
1957	Jacques Plante, Mtl.	Glenn Hall, Det.
1956	Jacques Plante, Mtl.	Glenn Hall, Det.
1955	Terry Sawchuk, Det.	Harry Lumley, Tor.
1954	Harry Lumley, Tor.	Terry Sawchuk, Det.
1953	Terry Sawchuk, Det.	Gerry McNeil, Mtl.
1952	Terry Sawchuk, Det.	Al Rollins, Tor.
1951	Al Rollins, Tor.	Terry Sawchuk, Det.
1950	Bill Durnan, Mtl.	Harry Lumley, Det.
1949	Bill Durnan, Mtl.	Harry Lumley, Det.
1948	Turk Broda, Tor.	Harry Lumley, Det.
1947	Bill Durnan, Mtl.	Turk Broda, Tor.
1946	Bill Durnan, Mtl.	Frank Brimsek, Bos.
1945	Bill Durnan, Mtl.	Frank McCool, Tor. (tie)
		Harry Lumley, Det. (tie)
1944	Bill Durnan, Mtl.	Paul Bibeault, Tor.
1943	Johnny Mowers, Det.	Turk Broda, Tor.
1942	Frank Brimsek, Bos.	Turk Broda, Tor.
1941	Turk Broda, Tor.	Frank Brimsek, Bos. (tie)
		Johnny Mowers, Det. (tie)
1940	Dave Kerr, NYR	Frank Brimsek, Bos.
1939	Frank Brimsek, Bos.	Dave Kerr, NYR
1938	Tiny Thompson, Bos.	Dave Kerr, NYR
1937	Norman Smith, Det.	Dave Kerr, NYR
1936	Tiny Thompson, Bos.	Mike Karakas, Chi.
1935	Lorne Chabot, Chi.	Alex Connell, Mtl.M
1934	Charlie Gardiner, Chi.	Wilf Cude, Det.
1933	Tiny Thompson, Bos.	John Ross Roach, Det.
1932	Charlie Gardiner, Chi.	Alex Connell, Det.
1931	Roy Worters, NYA	Charlie Gardiner, Chi.
1930	Tiny Thompson, Bos.	Charlie Gardiner, Chi.
1929	George Hainsworth, Mtl.	Tiny Thompson, Bos.
1928	George Hainsworth, Mtl.	Alex Connell, Ott.
1927	George Hainsworth, Mtl.	Clint Benedict, Mtl.M

CALDER MEMORIAL TROPHY WINNERS

	Winner	Runner-up
2000	Scott Gomez, N.J.	Brad Stuart, S.J.
1999	Chris Drury, Col.	Marian Hossa, Ott.
1998	Sergei Samsonov, Bos.	Mattias Ohlund, Van.
1997	Bryan Berard, NYI	Jarome Iginla, Cgy.
1996	Daniel Alfredsson, Ott.	Eric Daze, Chi.
1995	Peter Forsberg, Que.	Jim Carey, Wsh.
1994	Martin Brodeur, N.J.	Jason Arnott, Edm.
1993	Teemu Selanne, Wpg.	Joe Juneau, Bos.
1992	Pavel Bure, Van.	Nicklas Lidstrom, Det
1991	Ed Belfour, Chi.	Sergei Fedorov, Det.
1990	Sergei Makarov, Cgy.	Mike Modano, Min.
1989	Brian Leetch, NYR	Trevor Linden, Van.
1988	Joe Nieuwendyk, Cgy.	Ray Sheppard, Buf.
1987	Luc Robitaille, L.A.	Ron Hextall, Phi.
1986	Gary Suter, Cgy.	Wendel Clark, Tor.
1985	Mario Lemieux, Pit.	Chris Chelios, Mtl.
1984	Tom Barrasso, Buf.	Steve Yzerman, Det.
1983	Steve Larmer, Chi.	Phil Housley, Buf.
1982	Dale Hawerchuk, Wpg.	Barry Pederson, Bos.
1981	Peter Stastny, Que.	Larry Murphy, L.A.
1980	Ray Bourque, Bos.	Mike Foligno, Det.
1979	Bobby Smith, Min	Ryan Walter, Wsh.
1978	Mike Bossy, NYI	Barry Beck, Col.
1977	Willi Plett, Atl.	Don Murdoch, NYR
1976	Bryan Trottier, NYI	Glenn Resch, NYI
1975	Eric Vail, Atl.	Pierre Larouche, Pit.
1974	Denis Potvin, NYI	Tom Lysiak, Atl.
1973	Steve Vickers, NYR	Bill Barber, Phi.
1972	Ken Dryden, Mtl.	Rick Martin, Buf.
1971	Gilbert Perreault, Buf.	Jude Drouin, Min.
1970	Tony Esposito, Chi.	Bill Fairbairn, NYR
1969	Danny Grant, Min.	Norm Ferguson, Oak.
1968	Derek Sanderson, Bos.	Jacques Lemaire, Mtl.
1967	Bobby Orr, Bos.	Ed Van Impe, Chi.
1966	Brit Selby, Tor.	Bert Marshall, Det.
1965	Roger Crozier, Det.	Ron Ellis, Tor.
1964	Jacques Laperriere, Mtl.	John Ferguson, Mtl.
1963	Kent Douglas, Tor.	Doug Barkley, Det.
1962	Bobby Rousseau, Mtl.	Cliff Pennington, Bos.
1961	Dave Keon, Tor.	Bob Nevin, Tor.
1960	Bill Hay, Chi.	Murray Oliver, Det.
1959	Ralph Backstrom, Mtl.	Carl Brewer, Tor.
1958	Frank Mahovlich, Tor.	Bobby Hull, Chi.
1957	Larry Regan, Bos.	Ed Chadwick, Tor.
1956	Glenn Hall, Det.	Andy Hebenton, NYR
1955	Ed Litzenberger, Chi.	Don McKenney, Bos.
1954	Camille Henry, NYR	Earl Reibel, Det.
1953	Gump Worsley, NYR	Gord Hannigan, Tor.
1952	Bernie Geoffrion, Mtl.	Hy Buller, NYR
1951	Terry Sawchuk, Det.	Al Rollins, Tor.
1950	Jack Gelineau, Bos.	Phil Maloney, Bos.
1949	Pentti Lund, NYR	Allan Stanley, NYR
1948	Jim McFadden, Det.	Pete Babando, Bos.
1947	Howie Meeker, Tor.	Jimmy Conacher, Det.
1946	Edgar Laprade, NYR	George Gee, Chi.
1945	Frank McCool, Tor.	Ken Smith, Bos.
1944	Gus Bodnar, Tor.	Bill Durnan, Mtl.
1943	Gaye Stewart, Tor.	Glen Harmon, Mtl.
1942	Grant Warwick, NYR	Buddy O'Connor, Mtl.
1941	Johnny Quilty, Mtl.	Johnny Mowers, Det.
1940	Kilby MacDonald, NYR	Wally Stanowski, Tor.
1939	Frank Brimsek, Bos.	Roy Conacher, Bos.
1938	Cully Dahlstrom, Chi.	Murph Chamberlain, Tor.
1937	Syl Apps Sr., Tor.	Gordie Drillon, Tor.
1936	Mike Karakas, Chi.	Bucko McDonald, Det.
1935	Sweeney Schriner, NYA	Bert Connolly, NYR
1934	Russ Blinko, Mtl.M.	none

FRANK J. SELKE TROPHY WINNERS

	Winner	Runner-up
2000	Steve Yzerman, Det.	Michal Handzus, St.L.
1999	Jere Lehtinen, Dal.	Magnus Arvedson, Ott.
1998	Jere Lehtinen, Dal.	Michael Peca, Buf.
1997	Michael Peca, Buf.	Peter Forsberg, Col.
1996	Sergei Fedorov, Det.	Ron Francis, Pit.
1995	Ron Francis, Pit.	Esa Tikkanen, St.L.
1994	Sergei Fedorov, Det.	Doug Gilmour, Tor.
1993	Doug Gilmour, Tor.	Dave Poulin, Bos.
1992	Guy Carbonneau, Mtl.	Sergei Fedorov, Det.
1991	Dirk Graham, Chi.	Esa Tikkanen, Edm.
1990	Rick Meagher, St.L.	Guy Carbonneau, Mtl.
1989	Guy Carbonneau, Mtl.	Esa Tikkanen, Edm.
1988	Guy Carbonneau, Mtl.	Steve Kasper, Bos.
1987	Dave Poulin, Phi.	Guy Carbonneau, Mtl.
1986	Troy Murray, Chi.	Ron Sutter, Phi.
1985	Craig Ramsay, Buf.	Doug Jarvis, Wsh.
1984	Doug Jarvis, Wsh.	Bryan Trottier, NYI
1983	Bobby Clarke, Phi.	Jari Kurri, Edm.
1982	Steve Kasper, Bos.	Bob Gainey, Mtl.
1981	Bob Gainey, Mtl.	Craig Ramsay, Buf.
1980	Bob Gainey, Mtl.	Craig Ramsay, Buf.
1979	Bob Gainey, Mtl.	Don Marcotte, Bos.
1978	Bob Gainey, Mtl.	Craig Ramsay, Buf.

CONN SMYTHE TROPHY WINNERS

Year	Winner	Team
2000	Scott Stevens	New Jersey
1999	Joe Nieuwendyk	Dallas
1998	Steve Yzerman	Detroit
1997	Mike Vernon	Detroit
1996	Joe Sakic	Colorado
1995	Claude Lemieux	New Jersey
1994	Brian Leetch	NY Rangers
1993	Patrick Roy	Montreal
1992	Mario Lemieux	Pittsburgh
1991	Mario Lemieux	Pittsburgh
1990	Bill Ranford	Edmonton
1989	Al MacInnis	Calgary
1988	Wayne Gretzky	Edmonton
1987	Ron Hextall	Philadelphia
1986	Patrick Roy	Montreal
1985	Wayne Gretzky	Edmonton
1984	Mark Messier	Edmonton
1983	Billy Smith	NY Islanders
1982	Mike Bossy	NY Islanders
1981	Butch Goring	NY Islanders
1980	Bryan Trottier	NY Islanders
1979	Bob Gainey	Montreal
1978	Larry Robinson	Montreal
1977	Guy Lafleur	Montreal
1976	Reggie Leach	Philadelphia
1975	Bernie Parent	Philadelphia
1974	Bernie Parent	Philadelphia
1973	Yvan Cournoyer	Montreal
1972	Bobby Orr	Boston
1971	Ken Dryden	Montreal
1970	Bobby Orr	Boston
1969	Serge Savard	Montreal
1968	Glenn Hall	St. Louis
1967	Dave Keon	Toronto
1966	Roger Crozier	Detroit
1965	Jean Béliveau	Montreal

JAMES NORRIS TROPHY WINNERS

Year	Winner	Runner-up
2000	Chris Pronger, St.L.	Nicklas Lidstrom, Det.
1999	Al MacInnis, St.L.	Nicklas Lidstrom, Det.
1998	Rob Blake, L.A.	Nicklas Lidstrom, Det.
1997	Brian Leetch, NYR	V. Konstantinov, Det.
1996	Chris Chelios, Chi.	Ray Bourque, Bos.
1995	Paul Coffey, Det.	Chris Chelios, Chi.
1994	Ray Bourque, Bos.	Scott Stevens, N.J.
1993	Chris Chelios, Chi.	Ray Bourque, Bos.
1992	Brian Leetch, NYR	Ray Bourque, Bos.
1991	Ray Bourque, Bos.	Al MacInnis, Cgy.
1990	Ray Bourque, Bos.	Al MacInnis, Cgy.
1989	Chris Chelios, Mtl	Paul Coffey, Pit.
1988	Ray Bourque, Bos.	Scott Stevens, Wsh.
1987	Ray Bourque, Bos.	Mark Howe, Phi.
1986	Paul Coffey, Edm.	Mark Howe, Phi.
1985	Paul Coffey, Edm.	Ray Bourque, Bos.
1984	Rod Langway, Wsh.	Paul Coffey, Edm.
1983	Rod Langway, Wsh.	Mark Howe, Phi.
1982	Doug Wilson, Chi.	Ray Bourque, Bos.
1981	Randy Carlyle, Pit.	Denis Potvin, NYI
1980	Larry Robinson, Mtl.	Borje Salming, Tor.
1979	Denis Potvin, NYI	Larry Robinson, Mtl.
1978	Denis Potvin, NYI	Brad Park, Bos.
1977	Larry Robinson, Mtl.	Borje Salming, Tor.
1976	Denis Potvin, NYI	Brad Park, NYR-Bos.
1975	Bobby Orr, Bos.	Denis Potvin, NYI
1974	Bobby Orr, Bos.	Brad Park, NYR
1973	Bobby Orr, Bos.	Guy Lapointe, Mtl.
1972	Bobby Orr, Bos.	Brad Park, NYR
1971	Bobby Orr, Bos.	Brad Park, NYR
1970	Bobby Orr, Bos.	Brad Park, NYR
1969	Bobby Orr, Bos.	Tim Horton, Tor.
1968	Bobby Orr, Bos.	J.C. Tremblay, Mtl
1967	Harry Howell, NYR	Pierre Pilote, Chi.
1966	Jacques Laperriere, Mtl.	Pierre Pilote, Chi.
1965	Pierre Pilote, Chi.	Jacques Laperriere, Mtl.
1964	Pierre Pilote, Chi.	Tim Horton, Tor.
1963	Pierre Pilote, Chi.	Carl Brewer, Tor.
1962	Doug Harvey, NYR	Pierre Pilote, Chi.
1961	Doug Harvey, Mtl.	Marcel Pronovost, Det.
1960	Doug Harvey, Mtl.	Allan Stanley, Tor.
1959	Tom Johnson, Mtl.	Bill Gadsby, NYR
1958	Doug Harvey, Mtl.	Bill Gadsby, NYR
1957	Doug Harvey, Mtl.	Red Kelly, Det.
1956	Doug Harvey, Mtl.	Bill Gadsby, NYR
1955	Doug Harvey, Mtl.	Red Kelly, Det.
1954	Red Kelly, Det.	Doug Harvey, Mtl.

MAURICE "ROCKET" RICHARD TROPHY WINNER

Year	Winner	Team
2000	Pavel Bure	Florida
1999	Teemu Selanne	Anaheim

LESTER PATRICK TROPHY WINNERS

Year	Winner
2000	Mario Lemieux
	Craig Patrick
	Lou Vairo
1999	Harry Sinden
	1998 U.S. Olympic Women's Hockey Team
1998	Peter Karmanos
	Neal Broten
	John Mayasich
	Max McNab
1997	Seymour H. Knox III
	Bill Cleary
	Pat LaFontaine
1996	George Gund
	Ken Morrow
	Milt Schmidt
1995	Joe Mullen
	Brian Mullen
	Bob Fleming
1994	Wayne Gretzky
	Robert Ridder
1993	*Frank Boucher
	*Mervyn "Red" Dutton
	Bruce McNall
	Gil Stein
1992	Al Arbour
	Art Berglund
	Lou Lamoriello
1991	Rod Gilbert
	Mike Ilitch
1990	Len Ceglarski
1989	Dan Kelly
	Lou Nanne
	*Lynn Patrick
	Bud Poile
1988	Keith Allen
	Fred Cusick
	Bob Johnson
1987	*Hobey Baker
	Frank Mathers
1986	John MacInnes
	Jack Riley
1985	Jack Butterfield
	Arthur M. Wirtz
1984	John A. Ziegler Jr.
	*Arthur Howie Ross
1983	Bill Torrey
1982	Emile P. Francis
1981	Charles M. Schulz
1980	Bobby Clarke
	Edward M. Snider
	Frederick A. Shero
	1980 U.S. Olympic Hockey Team
1979	Bobby Orr
1978	Phil Esposito
	Tom Fitzgerald
	William T. Tutt
	William W. Wirtz
1977	John P. Bucyk
	Murray A. Armstrong
	John Mariucci
1976	Stanley Mikita
	George A. Leader
	Bruce A. Norris
1975	Donald M. Clark
	William L. Chadwick
	Thomas N. Ivan
1974	Alex Delvecchio
	Murray Murdoch
	*Weston W. Adams, Sr.
	*Charles L. Crovat
1973	Walter L. Bush, Jr.
1972	Clarence S. Campbell
	John A. "Snooks" Kelly
	Ralph "Cooney" Weiland
	*James D. Norris
1971	William M. Jennings
	*John B. Sollenberger
	*Terrance G. Sawchuk
1970	Edward W. Shore
	*James C. V. Hendy
1969	Robert M. Hull
	*Edward J. Jeremiah
1968	Thomas F. Lockhart
	*Walter A. Brown
	*Gen. John R. Kilpatrick
1967	Gordon Howe
	*Charles F. Adams
	*James Norris, Sr.
1966	J.J. "Jack" Adams

* awarded posthumously

BUD LIGHT PLUS-MINUS AWARD WINNERS

Year	Winner	Team
2000	Chris Pronger	St. Louis
1999	John LeClair	Philadelphia
1998	Chris Pronger	St. Louis
1997	John LeClair	Philadelphia

WILLIAM M. JENNINGS TROPHY WINNERS

Year	Winner	Runner-up
2000	Roman Turek, St.L.	John Vanbiesbrouck, Phi.
		Brian Boucher
1999	Ed Belfour, Dal.	Dominik Hasek, Buf.
	Roman Turek	
1998	Martin Brodeur, N.J.	Ed Belfour, Dal.
1997	Martin Brodeur, N.J.	Chris Osgood, Det.
	Mike Dunham	Mike Vernon
1996	Chris Osgood, Det.	Martin Brodeur, N.J.
	Mike Vernon	
1995	Ed Belfour, Chi.	Mike Vernon, Det.
		Chris Osgood
1994	Dominik Hasek, Buf.	Martin Brodeur, N.J.
	Grant Fuhr	Chris Terreri
1993	Ed Belfour, Chi.	Felix Potvin, Tor.
		Grant Fuhr
1992	Patrick Roy, Mtl.	Ed Belfour, Chi.
1991	Ed Belfour, Chi.	Patrick Roy, Mtl.
1990	Andy Moog, Bos.	Patrick Roy, Mtl.
	Rejean Lemelin	Brian Hayward
1989	Patrick Roy, Mtl.	Mike Vernon, Cgy.
	Brian Hayward	Rick Wamsley
1988	Patrick Roy, Mtl.	Clint Malarchuk, Wsh.
	Brian Hayward	Pete Peeters
1987	Patrick Roy, Mtl.	Ron Hextall, Phi.
	Brian Hayward	
1986	Bob Froese, Phi.	Al Jensen, Wsh.
	Darren Jensen	Pete Peeters
1985	Tom Barrasso, Buf.	Pat Riggin, Wsh.
	Bob Sauve	
1984	Al Jensen, Wsh.	Tom Barrasso, Buf.
	Pat Riggin	Bob Sauve
1983	Rollie Melanson, NYI	Pete Peeters, Bos.
	Billy Smith	
1982	Rick Wamsley, Mtl.	Billy Smith, NYI
	Denis Herron	Rollie Melanson

LESTER B. PEARSON AWARD WINNERS

Year	Winner	Team
2000	Jaromir Jagr	Pittsburgh
1999	Jaromir Jagr	Pittsburgh
1998	Dominik Hasek	Buffalo
1997	Dominik Hasek	Buffalo
1996	Mario Lemieux	Pittsburgh
1995	Eric Lindros	Philadelphia
1994	Sergei Fedorov	Detroit
1993	Mario Lemieux	Pittsburgh
1992	Mark Messier	NY Rangers
1991	Brett Hull	St. Louis
1990	Mark Messier	Edmonton
1989	Steve Yzerman	Detroit
1988	Mario Lemieux	Pittsburgh
1987	Wayne Gretzky	Edmonton
1986	Mario Lemieux	Pittsburgh
1985	Wayne Gretzky	Edmonton
1984	Wayne Gretzky	Edmonton
1983	Wayne Gretzky	Edmonton
1982	Wayne Gretzky	Edmonton
1981	Mike Liut	St. Louis
1980	Marcel Dionne	Los Angeles
1979	Marcel Dionne	Los Angeles
1978	Guy Lafleur	Montreal
1977	Guy Lafleur	Montreal
1976	Guy Lafleur	Montreal
1975	Bobby Orr	Boston
1974	Phil Esposito	Boston
1973	Bobby Clarke	Philadelphia
1972	Jean Ratelle	NY Rangers
1971	Phil Esposito	Boston

JACK ADAMS AWARD WINNERS

Year	Winner	Runner-up
2000	Joel Quenneville, St.L.	Alain Vigneault, Mtl.
1999	Jacques Martin, Ott.	Pat Quinn, Tor.
1998	Pat Burns, Bos.	Larry Robinson, L.A.
1997	Ted Nolan, Buf.	Ken Hitchcock, Dal.
1996	Scotty Bowman, Det.	Doug MacLean, Fla.
1995	Marc Crawford, Que.	Scotty Bowman, Det.
1994	Jacques Lemaire, N.J.	Kevin Constantine, S.J.
1993	Pat Burns, Tor.	Brian Sutter, Bos.
1992	Pat Quinn, Van.	Roger Neilson, NYR
1991	Brian Sutter, St.L.	Tom Webster, L.A.
1990	Bob Murdoch, Wpg.	Mike Milbury, Bos.
1989	Pat Burns, Mtl.	Bob McCammon, Van.
1988	Jacques Demers, Det.	Terry Crisp, Cgy.
1987	Jacques Demers, Det.	Jack Evans, Hfd.
1986	Glen Sather, Edm.	Jacques Demers, St.L.
1985	Mike Keenan, Phi.	Barry Long, Wpg.
1984	Bryan Murray, Wsh.	Scotty Bowman, Buf.
1983	Orval Tessier, Chi.	
1982	Tom Watt, Wpg.	
1981	Red Berenson, St.L.	Bob Berry, L.A.
1980	Pat Quinn, Phi.	
1979	Al Arbour, NYI	Fred Shero, NYR
1978	Bobby Kromm, Det.	Don Cherry, Bos.
1977	Scotty Bowman, Mtl.	Tom McVie, Wsh.
1976	Don Cherry, Bos.	
1975	Bob Pulford, L.A.	
1974	Fred Shero, Phi.	

NHL Amateur and Entry Draft

History

Year	Site	Date	Total Players Drafted
1963	Queen Elizabeth Hotel	June 5	21
1964	Queen Elizabeth Hotel	June 11	24
1965	Queen Elizabeth Hotel	April 27	11
1966	Mount Royal Hotel	April 25	24
1967	Queen Elizabeth Hotel	June 7	18
1968	Queen Elizabeth Hotel	June 13	24
1969	Queen Elizabeth Hotel	June 12	84
1970	Queen Elizabeth Hotel	June 11	115
1971	Queen Elizabeth Hotel	June 10	117
1972	Queen Elizabeth Hotel	June 8	152
1973	Mount Royal Hotel	May 15	168
1974	NHL Montreal Office	May 28	247
1975	NHL Montreal Office	June 3	217
1976	NHL Montreal Office	June 1	135
1977	NHL Montreal Office	June 14	185
1978	Queen Elizabeth Hotel	June 15	234
1979	Queen Elizabeth Hotel	August 9	126
1980	Montreal Forum	June 11	210
1981	Montreal Forum	June 10	211
1982	Montreal Forum	June 9	252
1983	Montreal Forum	June 8	242
1984	Montreal Forum	June 9	250
1985	Toronto Convention Centre	June 15	252
1986	Montreal Forum	June 21	252
1987	Joe Louis Sports Arena	June 13	252
1988	Montreal Forum	June 11	252
1989	Metropolitan Sports Center	June 17	252
1990	B. C. Place	June 16	250
1991	Memorial Auditorium	June 9	264
1992	Montreal Forum	June 20	264
1993	Colisée de Québec	June 26	286
1994	Hartford Civic Center	June 28-29	286
1995	Edmonton Coliseum	July 8	234
1996	Kiel Center	June 22	241
1997	Civic Arena	June 21	246
1998	Marine Midland Arena	June 27	258
1999	FleetCenter	June 26	272
2000	Saddledome	June 24-25	293

* The NHL Amateur Draft became the NHL Entry Draft in 1979

First Selections

Year	Player	Pos	Drafted By	Drafted From	Age
1969	Rejean Houle	LW	Montreal	Montreal Jr. Canadiens	19.8
1970	Gilbert Perreault	C	Buffalo	Montreal Jr. Canadiens	19.7
1971	Guy Lafleur	RW	Montreal	Quebec Remparts	19.9
1972	Billy Harris	RW	NY Islanders	Toronto Marlboros	20.4
1973	Denis Potvin	D	NY Islanders	Ottawa 67's	19.7
1974	Greg Joly	D	Washington	Regina Pats	20.0
1975	Mel Bridgman	C	Philadelphia	Victoria Cougars	20.1
1976	Rick Green	D	Washington	London Knights	20.3
1977	Dale McCourt	C	Detroit	St. Catharines Fincups	20.4
1978	Bobby Smith	C	Minnesota	Ottawa 67's	20.4
1979	Rob Ramage	D	Colorado	London Knights	20.5
1980	Doug Wickenheiser	C	Montreal	Regina Pats	19.2
1981	Dale Hawerchuk	C	Winnipeg	Cornwall Royals	18.2
1982	Gord Kluzak	D	Boston	Nanaimo Islanders	18.3
1983	Brian Lawton	C	Minnesota	Mount St. Charles HS	18.11
1984	Mario Lemieux	C	Pittsburgh	Laval Voisins	18.8
1985	Wendel Clark	LW/D	Toronto	Saskatoon Blades	18.7
1986	Joe Murphy	C	Detroit	Michigan State	18.8
1987	Pierre Turgeon	C	Buffalo	Granby Bisons	17.10
1988	Mike Modano	C	Minnesota	Prince Albert Raiders	18.0
1989	Mats Sundin	RW	Quebec	Nacka (Sweden)	18.4
1990	Owen Nolan	RW	Quebec	Cornwall Royals	18.4
1991	Eric Lindros	C	Quebec	Oshawa Generals	18.3
1992	Roman Hamrlik	D	Tampa Bay	ZPS Zlin (Czech.)	18.2
1993	Alexandre Daigle	C	Ottawa	Victoriaville Tigres	18.5
1994	Ed Jovanovski	D	Florida	Windsor Spitfires	18.0
1995	Bryan Berard	D	Ottawa	Detroit Jr. Red Wings	18.4
1996	Chris Phillips	D	Ottawa	Prince Albert Raiders	18.3
1997	Joe Thornton	C	Boston	Sault Ste. Marie	17.11
1998	Vincent Lecavalier	C	Tampa Bay	Rimouski Oceanic	18.2
1999	Patrik Stefan	C	Atlanta	Long Beach Ice Dogs	18.9
2000	Rick DiPietro	G	NY Islanders	Boston University	18.9

Top prospects heading into the 2000 NHL Entry Draft, wearing the jerseys of their 1999-2000 teams: Left to right, front row, Rick DiPietro (Boston University, G, selected 1st overall by NY Islanders), Dany Heatley (U. of Wisconsin, LW, 2nd by Atlanta), Brent Krahn (Calgary Hitmen, G, 9th by Calgary); back row, Brad Boyes (Erie, C, 24th by Toronto), Rostislav Klesla (Brampton, LW, 4th by Columbus), Scott Hartnell (Prince Albert, RW, 6th by Nashville), Brooks Orpik (Boston College, D, 18th by Pittsburgh), Raffi Torres, (Brampton, LW, 5th by NY Islanders).

Draft Summary

Following is a summary of the number of players drafted from the Ontario Hockey League (OHL), Western Hockey League (WHL), Quebec Major Junior Hockey League (QMJHL), United States Colleges, United States High Schools, European Leagues and other Leagues throughout North America since 1969:

	OHL	WHL	QMJHL	US Colleges	US HS	International	Other
1969	36	20	11	7	0	1	9
1970	51	22	13	16	0	0	13
1971	41	28	13	22	0	0	13
1972	46	44	30	21	0	0	11
1973	56	49	24	25	0	0	14
1974	69	66	40	41	0	6	25
1975	55	57	28	59	0	6	12
1976	47	33	18	26	0	8	3
1977	42	44	40	49	0	5	5
1978	59	48	22	73	0	16	16
1979	48	37	19	15	0	6	1
1980	73	41	24	42	7	13	10
1981	59	37	28	21	17	32	17
1982	60	55	17	20	47	35	18
1983	57	41	24	14	35	34	37
1984	55	38	16	22	44	40	36
1985	59	47	15	20	48	31	31
1986	66	32	22	22	40	28	42
1987	32	36	17	40	69	38	20
1988	32	30	22	48	56	39	25
1989	39	44	16	48	47	38	20
1990	39	33	14	38	57	53	16
1991	43	40	25	43	37	55	21
1992	57	45	22	9	25	84	22
1993	60	44	23	17	33	78	31
1994	45	66	28	6	28	80	33
1995	54	55	35	5	2	69	14
1996	51	54	31	25	6	58	16
1997	52	63	19	26	4	63	19
1998	50	44	41	27	7	75	14
1999	52	40	20	36	9	94	21
2000	39	41	21	35	7	123	27
Total	1624	1374	738	918	625	1208	612

Total Drafted, 1969-2000: 7,099

Ontario Hockey League

Club	'69	'70	'71	'72	'73	'74	'75	'76	'77	'78	'79	'80	'81	'82	'83	'84	'85	'86	'87	'88	'89	'90	'91	'92	'93	'94	'95	'96	'97	'98	'99	'00	Total
Peterborough	5	5	4	5	9	4	8	1	4	6	9	10	3	5	7	3	9	2	5	2	2	4	3	4	4	2	5	4	5	1	4	1	145
Oshawa	5	4	3	5	5	7	6	6	1	3	3	2	9	5	5	6	6	6	3	2	4	2	4	4	4	1	10	1	3	4	3	2	134
Kitchener	1	6	2	8	4	13	3	1	3	4	4	4	5	5	8	4	6	3	2	1	7	5	3	1	4	2	4	2	3	5	–	1	124
Ottawa	2	4	3	4	6	5	6	5	5	5	3	8	4	9	2	2	3	3	2	1	–	5	5	6	4	1	1	2	5	2	6	2	121
London	4	9	1	5	6	6	3	5	4	3	6	2	5	5	3	7	1	3	2	6	3	3	1	3	4	1	1	4	1	8	4	1	120
Sudbury	–	–	–	–	6	6	4	5	4	4	3	7	2	4	–	2	5	3	1	–	1	2	8	2	10	2	2	1	3	5	5	–	97
S.S. Marie	–	–	–	–	4	5	2	5	1	5	3	3	8	1	6	4	5	7	1	2	3	1	2	7	3	4	3	4	1	4	1	1	96
Kingston	–	–	–	–	–	4	4	6	4	9	2	8	5	2	1	3	3	4	1	1	–	2	2	3	5	2	3	4	4	1	4	–	87
Niagara Falls	4	2	1	4	–	–	–	–	2	3	5	8	6	6	–	–	–	–	–	–	4	4	4	4	4	3	2	6	–	–	–	–	72
Windsor	–	–	–	–	–	–	–	2	1	4	2	3	5	3	2	2	3	7	–	5	2	1	–	3	–	3	4	1	5	1	2	2	63
Guelph	–	–	–	–	–	–	–	–	–	–	–	–	–	–	1	5	3	8	2	–	4	–	–	2	2	7	5	6	1	5	3	1	55
North Bay	–	–	–	–	–	–	–	–	–	–	–	–	–	–	4	4	3	3	3	3	1	4	2	5	2	7	2	1	1	2	2	2	51
Belleville	–	–	–	–	–	–	–	–	–	–	–	–	–	–	3	4	4	5	2	–	4	2	1	4	–	3	3	–	5	2	5	1	48
Det./Plymouth	–	–	–	–	–	–	–	–	–	–	–	–	–	–	–	–	–	–	–	–	–	–	2	2	7	2	6	3	4	2	2	6	36
Owen Sound	–	–	–	–	–	–	–	–	–	–	–	–	–	–	–	–	–	–	–	–	–	1	1	2	4	3	2	3	2	1	–	1	20
Barrie	–	–	–	–	–	–	–	–	–	–	–	–	–	–	–	–	–	–	–	–	–	–	–	–	–	–	–	2	4	3	6	3	18
Sarnia	–	–	–	–	–	–	–	–	–	–	–	–	–	–	–	–	–	–	–	–	–	–	–	–	–	–	1	7	2	3	1	3	17
Erie	–	–	–	–	–	–	–	–	–	–	–	–	–	–	–	–	–	–	–	–	–	–	–	–	–	–	–	–	3	1	2	3	9
Brampton	–	–	–	–	–	–	–	–	–	–	–	–	–	–	–	–	–	–	–	–	–	–	–	–	–	–	–	–	–	–	2	6	8
Mississauga	–	–	–	–	–	–	–	–	–	–	–	–	–	–	–	–	–	–	–	–	–	–	–	–	–	–	–	–	–	–	–	2	2
St. Michael's	–	–	–	–	–	–	–	–	–	–	–	–	–	–	–	–	–	–	–	–	–	–	–	–	–	–	–	–	–	–	–	1	1

Teams no longer operating

Club	'69	'70	'71	'72	'73	'74	'75	'76	'77	'78	'79	'80	'81	'82	'83	'84	'85	'86	'87	'88	'89	'90	'91	'92	'93	'94	'95	'96	'97	'98	'99	'00	Total
Toronto	3	7	6	5	6	8	4	4	7	5	4	10	2	6	4	4	3	4	1	2	2	–	–	–	–	–	–	–	–	–	–	–	97
Hamilton	2	3	5	4	6	4	7	3	–	8	1	–	–	–	–	–	3	6	4	4	–	–	2	–	–	–	–	–	–	–	–	–	62
St. Catharines	5	5	8	5	4	7	8	4	6	–	–	–	–	–	–	–	–	–	–	–	–	–	–	–	–	–	–	–	–	–	–	–	52
Cornwall	–	–	–	–	–	–	–	–	–	–	–	–	–	7	4	3	2	2	3	3	2	3	3	5	–	–	–	–	–	–	–	–	37
Brantford	–	–	–	–	–	–	–	–	–	–	3	8	5	2	7	2	–	–	–	–	–	–	–	–	–	–	–	–	–	–	–	–	27
Montreal	5	6	8	1	–	–	–	–	–	–	–	–	–	–	–	–	–	–	–	–	–	–	–	–	–	–	–	–	–	–	–	–	20
Newmarket	–	–	–	–	–	–	–	–	–	–	–	–	–	–	–	–	–	–	–	–	–	–	–	–	3	2	–	–	–	–	–	–	5

Year	Total Ontario Drafted	Total Players Drafted	Ontario %
1969	36	84	42.9
1970	51	115	44.3
1971	41	117	35.0
1972	46	152	30.3
1973	56	168	33.3
1974	69	247	27.9
1975	55	217	25.3
1976	47	135	34.8
1977	42	185	22.7
1978	59	234	25.2
1979	48	126	38.1
1980	73	210	34.8
1981	59	211	28.0
1982	60	252	23.8
1983	57	242	23.6
1984	55	250	22.0
1985	59	252	23.4
1986	66	252	26.2
1987	32	252	12.7
1988	32	252	12.7
1989	39	252	15.5
1990	39	250	15.6
1991	43	264	16.3
1992	57	264	21.6
1993	60	286	21.0
1994	45	286	15.7
1995	54	234	23.1
1996	51	241	21.1
1997	52	246	21.1
1998	50	258	19.4
1999	52	272	19.1
2000	39	293	13.3
Total	**1624**	**7099**	**22.8**

Western Hockey League

Club	'69	'70	'71	'72	'73	'74	'75	'76	'77	'78	'79	'80	'81	'82	'83	'84	'85	'86	'87	'88	'89	'90	'91	'92	'93	'94	'95	'96	'97	'98	'99	'00	Total
Regina	–	–	5	5	1	8	5	3	1	4	1	3	5	6	8	4	4	3	2	–	5	1	–	4	–	3	2	4	3	2	4	2	98
Portland	–	–	–	–	–	–	–	–	4	8	7	8	6	7	7	5	2	4	3	1	4	1	1	4	4	3	2	1	3	3	1	6	95
Saskatoon	1	–	1	3	8	4	5	3	4	1	2	2	3	5	5	3	1	5	4	4	3	2	2	3	2	4	2	2	2	2	4	1	93
Medicine Hat	–	–	–	4	6	4	5	3	5	4	–	4	2	1	2	1	6	2	5	1	4	1	3	3	1	6	2	7	2	3	1	–	88
Kamloops	–	–	–	–	–	4	4	4	4	–	–	–	–	2	4	4	4	4	3	1	5	4	6	3	2	9	5	4	3	1	4	4	88
Brandon	–	3	1	5	2	7	4	–	3	1	10	5	2	2	1	3	2	1	3	3	–	1	1	1	2	5	6	2	5	4	–	–	85
Lethbridge	–	–	–	–	–	–	3	2	3	5	4	1	4	7	2	1	5	1	–	3	3	4	7	3	4	3	3	1	5	1	–	3	78
Seattle	–	–	–	–	–	–	–	–	–	4	2	3	–	6	–	1	3	1	2	4	2	6	3	2	4	5	5	1	8	2	6	4	74
Prince Albert	–	–	–	–	–	–	–	–	–	–	–	–	–	4	2	2	6	6	1	3	3	4	6	2	5	3	4	3	5	3	3	2	67
Swift Current	1	–	1	–	3	6	–	–	–	–	–	–	–	–	–	–	–	–	5	2	2	2	1	1	5	4	4	1	2	2	1	3	46
Spokane	–	–	–	–	–	–	–	–	–	–	–	–	1	–	–	–	–	–	1	3	2	1	5	7	4	4	4	5	4	1	1	2	45
Moose Jaw	–	–	–	–	–	–	–	–	–	–	–	–	–	–	–	–	4	1	3	–	3	1	2	3	2	3	4	4	4	2	1	5	42
Tri-City	–	–	–	–	–	–	–	–	–	–	–	–	–	–	–	–	–	–	–	–	4	3	3	5	2	2	6	6	1	4	1	2	39
Red Deer	–	–	–	–	–	–	–	–	–	–	–	–	–	–	–	–	–	–	–	–	–	–	–	–	3	5	2	4	3	5	1	1	24
Kelowna	–	–	–	–	–	–	–	–	–	–	–	–	–	–	–	–	–	–	–	–	–	–	–	–	–	–	–	4	7	2	2	1	16
Calgary	–	–	–	–	–	–	–	–	–	–	–	–	–	–	–	–	–	–	–	–	–	–	–	–	–	–	–	3	–	3	6	4	16
Prince George	–	–	–	–	–	–	–	–	–	–	–	–	–	–	–	–	–	–	–	–	–	–	–	–	–	–	2	2	2	4	2	–	12
Edmonton	–	–	–	–	–	–	–	–	–	–	–	–	–	–	–	–	–	–	–	–	–	–	–	–	–	–	–	–	4	–	–	–	4
Kootenay	–	–	–	–	–	–	–	–	–	–	–	–	–	–	–	–	–	–	–	–	–	–	–	–	–	–	–	–	–	–	2	1	3

Teams no longer operating

Club	'69	'70	'71	'72	'73	'74	'75	'76	'77	'78	'79	'80	'81	'82	'83	'84	'85	'86	'87	'88	'89	'90	'91	'92	'93	'94	'95	'96	'97	'98	'99	'00	Total
Victoria	–	–	–	2	2	5	7	4	3	3	1	8	6	2	3	4	2	1	2	4	4	2	–	1	2	2	–	–	–	–	–	–	70
Calgary	3	5	2	7	4	8	4	4	4	3	–	2	5	4	3	3	3	2	–	–	–	–	–	–	–	–	–	–	–	–	–	–	66
New Westm'r	–	–	–	6	8	7	9	5	8	6	5	1	–	–	–	2	1	1	2	1	–	–	–	–	–	–	–	–	–	–	–	–	62
Flin Flon	4	4	5	2	4	7	4	3	1	5	–	–	–	–	–	–	–	–	–	–	–	–	–	–	–	–	–	–	–	–	–	–	39
Winnipeg	3	2	4	2	5	4	4	–	4	–	–	–	1	4	1	–	–	–	–	–	–	–	–	–	–	–	–	–	–	–	–	–	34
Edmonton	4	4	5	6	6	2	3	2	–	–	2	–	–	–	–	–	–	–	–	–	–	–	–	–	–	–	–	–	–	–	–	–	34
Billings	–	–	–	–	–	–	–	–	–	4	3	4	2	–	–	–	–	–	–	–	–	–	–	–	–	–	–	–	–	–	–	–	13
Estevan	4	4	4	–	–	–	–	–	–	–	–	–	–	–	–	–	–	–	–	–	–	–	–	–	–	–	–	–	–	–	–	–	12
Tacoma	–	–	–	–	–	–	–	–	–	–	–	–	–	–	–	–	–	–	–	–	–	–	–	3	2	5	2	–	–	–	–	–	12
Kelowna	–	–	–	–	–	–	–	–	–	–	–	–	–	–	2	4	5	–	–	–	–	–	–	–	–	–	–	–	–	–	–	–	11
Nanaimo	–	–	–	–	–	–	–	–	–	–	–	–	–	5	1	–	–	–	–	–	–	–	–	–	–	–	–	–	–	–	–	–	6
Vancouver	–	–	–	2	–	–	–	–	–	–	–	–	–	–	–	–	–	–	–	–	–	–	–	–	–	–	–	–	–	–	–	–	2

Year	Total Western Drafted	Total Players Drafted	Western %
1969	20	84	23.8
1970	22	115	19.1
1971	28	117	23.9
1972	44	152	28.9
1973	49	168	29.2
1974	66	247	26.7
1975	57	217	26.3
1976	33	135	24.4
1977	44	185	23.8
1978	48	234	20.5
1979	37	126	29.4
1980	41	210	19.5
1981	37	211	17.5
1982	55	252	21.8
1983	41	242	16.9
1984	37	250	14.8
1985	48	252	19.0
1986	32	252	12.7
1987	36	252	14.3
1988	30	252	11.9
1989	44	252	17.5
1990	33	250	13.2
1991	40	264	15.2
1992	45	264	17.0
1993	44	286	15.4
1994	66	286	23.0
1995	55	234	23.5
1996	54	241	22.4
1997	63	246	25.6
1998	44	258	17.0
1999	40	272	14.7
2000	41	293	14.0
Total	**1374**	**7099**	**19.3**

A first-overall draft choice out of Saskatoon in 1985, Wendel Clark finished up his NHL career back where it began with the Toronto Maple Leafs in 1999-2000. Canucks goalie Felix Potvin is a former Leafs draft choice from the QMJHL.

Quebec Major Junior Hockey League

Club	'69	'70	'71	'72	'73	'74	'75	'76	'77	'78	'79	'80	'81	'82	'83	'84	'85	'86	'87	'88	'89	'90	'91	'92	'93	'94	'95	'96	'97	'98	'99	'00	Total
Shawinigan	3	2	1	6	1	5	3	–	3	–	–	2	2	5	5	2	–	2	1	–	2	–	2	3	1	1	2	4	1	3	1	1	64
Sherbrooke	–	–	2	2	4	3	7	5	6	3	4	1	5	2	–	–	–	–	–	–	–	–	–	–	3	2	4	–	1	5	–	–	59
Hull	–	–	–	–	–	–	3	2	2	3	–	3	1	–	3	1	–	4	3	2	2	3	3	3	3	1	3	3	–	3	4	–	55
Drummondville	2	4	1	4	2	1	–	–	–	–	–	–	–	–	–	1	2	2	2	4	1	–	4	2	2	1	4	3	2	2	–	1	47
Chicoutimi	–	–	–	–	–	1	–	–	5	1	1	3	6	1	3	–	3	1	2	2	1	1	–	1	1	3	2	–	2	1	–	1	42
Granby	–	–	–	–	–	–	–	–	–	–	–	–	–	2	1	3	2	2	4	–	2	–	2	–	1	5	2	3	1	–	–	–	30
Victoriaville	–	–	–	–	–	–	–	–	–	–	–	–	–	–	–	–	–	–	–	4	–	1	–	2	6	1	1	3	2	1	2	3	26
Beauport	–	–	–	–	–	–	–	–	–	–	–	–	–	–	–	–	–	–	–	–	–	–	1	3	1	3	7	3	3	–	–	–	21
St. Hyacinthe	–	–	–	–	–	–	–	–	–	–	–	–	–	–	–	–	–	–	–	–	–	3	1	2	1	4	–	4	–	–	–	–	15
Val D'Or	–	–	–	–	–	–	–	–	–	–	–	–	–	–	–	–	–	–	–	–	–	–	–	–	–	1	2	4	2	–	3	2	14
Halifax	–	–	–	–	–	–	–	–	–	–	–	–	–	–	–	–	–	–	–	–	–	–	–	–	–	–	3	1	3	3	–	2	12
Rimouski	–	–	–	–	–	–	–	–	–	–	–	–	–	–	–	–	–	–	–	–	–	–	–	–	–	–	–	–	–	5	2	2	9
Rouyn-Noranda	–	–	–	–	–	–	–	–	–	–	–	–	–	–	–	–	–	–	–	–	–	–	–	–	–	–	–	–	–	3	1	4	8
Quebec	–	–	–	–	–	–	–	–	–	–	–	–	–	–	–	–	–	–	–	–	–	–	–	–	–	–	–	–	–	4	3	–	7
Moncton	–	–	–	–	–	–	–	–	–	–	–	–	–	–	–	–	–	–	–	–	–	–	–	–	–	–	–	1	1	2	2	–	6
Baie-Comeau	–	–	–	–	–	–	–	–	–	–	–	–	–	–	–	–	–	–	–	–	–	–	–	–	–	–	–	–	–	3	–	2	5
Cape Breton	–	–	–	–	–	–	–	–	–	–	–	–	–	–	–	–	–	–	–	–	–	–	–	–	–	–	–	–	–	3	–	1	4
Acadie-Bathurst	–	–	–	–	–	–	–	–	–	–	–	–	–	–	–	–	–	–	–	–	–	–	–	–	–	–	–	–	–	–	2	–	2
Montreal	–	–	–	–	–	–	–	–	–	–	–	–	–	–	–	–	–	–	–	–	–	–	–	–	–	–	–	–	–	–	–	2	2
Teams no longer operating																																	
Laval	–	–	–	1	–	2	1	1	4	2	1	–	–	2	1	2	–	5	3	1	3	3	4	1	2	5	4	2	1	3	–	–	54
Quebec	1	1	2	4	6	6	1	3	7	1	3	2	2	1	2	2	3	–	–	–	–	–	–	–	–	–	–	–	–	–	–	–	47
Trois Rivieres	–	1	2	2	2	2	3	2	6	3	2	2	2	1	3	–	3	–	1	3	3	1	2	1	–	–	–	–	–	–	–	–	47
Cornwall	2	1	2	6	4	8	1	3	1	6	1	5	5	–	–	–	–	–	–	–	–	–	–	–	–	–	–	–	–	–	–	–	45
Montreal	–	–	–	–	4	4	8	1	3	2	4	3	–	3	–	–	–	–	–	–	–	–	–	–	–	–	–	–	–	–	–	–	32
Sorel	2	3	1	3	1	8	1	1	3	–	–	–	5	–	–	–	–	–	–	–	–	–	–	–	–	–	–	–	–	–	–	–	28
Verdun	–	1	1	2	–	–	–	–	–	1	3	3	–	–	3	3	–	3	0	3	1	–	–	3	–	–	–	–	–	–	–	–	27
St. Jean	–	–	–	–	–	–	–	–	–	–	–	–	–	–	2	–	1	1	0	3	1	–	3	1	2	1	1	–	–	–	–	–	16
Longueuil	–	–	–	–	–	–	–	–	–	–	–	–	–	–	1	2	1	2	1	–	–	2	3	–	–	–	–	–	–	–	–	–	12
St. Jerome	1	–	1	–	–	–	–	–	–	–	–	–	–	–	–	–	–	–	–	–	–	–	–	–	–	–	–	–	–	–	–	–	2

Year	Total Quebec Drafted	Total Players Drafted	Quebec %
1969	11	84	13.1
1970	13	115	11.3
1971	13	117	11.1
1972	30	152	19.7
1973	24	168	14.3
1974	40	247	16.2
1975	28	217	12.9
1976	18	135	13.3
1977	40	185	21.6
1978	22	234	9.4
1979	19	126	15.1
1980	24	210	11.4
1981	28	211	13.3
1982	17	252	6.7
1983	24	242	9.9
1984	16	250	6.4
1985	15	252	5.9
1986	22	252	8.7
1987	17	252	6.7
1988	22	252	8.7
1989	16	252	6.3
1990	14	250	5.6
1991	25	264	9.5
1992	22	264	8.3
1993	23	286	8.0
1994	28	286	9.7
1995	35	234	14.9
1996	31	241	12.8
1997	19	246	7.7
1998	41	258	15.9
1999	20	272	7.3
2000	21	293	7.1
Total	**738**	**7099**	**10.4**

United States Colleges

Club	'69	'70	'71	'72	'73	'74	'75	'76	'77	'78	'79	'80	'81	'82	'83	'84	'85	'86	'87	'88	'89	'90	'91	'92	'93	'94	'95	'96	'97	'98	99	'00	Total
Minnesota	1	3	2	–	–	9	4	4	5	5	2	3	1	1	1	–	–	2	1	1	1	–	–	–	–	–	2	3	2	1	3	3	60
Michigan	1	–	–	–	2	2	3	3	1	6	–	4	–	–	–	1	1	–	1	2	3	5	4	2	1	1	–	3	1	3	2	1	53
Michigan Tech	–	–	3	1	2	5	4	4	1	2	1	4	–	1	–	2	2	2	1	1	2	1	2	–	1	2	–	1	–	–	–	–	45
Boston U.	–	4	–	–	1	1	1	1	4	5	1	–	1	–	–	1	1	2	2	3	1	2	2	1	1	–	1	1	1	2	3	1	44
Denver	1	3	2	4	2	3	1	2	2	2	2	1	–	1	–	–	1	2	4	1	1	–	–	–	–	–	–	–	3	–	1	–	39
Wisconsin	–	1	2	4	5	4	4	2	3	–	1	–	3	2	–	1	1	–	1	–	1	–	1	–	–	–	–	–	–	–	2	3	41
Michigan State	–	–	1	–	1	1	1	1	–	–	–	2	–	2	–	2	–	1	1	4	4	5	4	1	1	1	–	1	1	1	2	2	40
North Dakota	2	3	3	1	4	2	1	–	1	2	3	3	1	–	–	1	–	–	–	–	2	1	1	–	–	–	–	–	2	–	1	1	35
Clarkson	–	–	2	2	1	–	2	–	2	2	1	1	1	1	1	1	–	–	1	1	1	3	2	1	1	–	–	–	–	3	1	1	32
Providence	–	–	–	–	–	–	3	2	3	4	–	5	4	1	2	–	1	1	–	–	–	1	–	–	–	–	–	–	1	2	–	2	32
New Hampshire	–	–	–	1	1	3	6	–	4	1	1	2	1	1	1	2	–	–	–	1	–	–	–	–	–	–	–	–	1	–	1	2	29
Harvard	–	–	2	–	–	–	2	–	2	2	–	–	–	1	1	–	2	–	1	1	2	–	–	–	2	1	–	3	1	2	1	2	28
Cornell	–	–	–	2	1	1	–	1	1	1	–	1	1	1	–	1	2	–	1	2	5	2	–	–	–	–	–	–	1	–	2	2	28
Boston College	–	1	–	–	–	–	1	1	–	5	–	2	1	1	–	–	–	1	2	–	2	–	–	–	–	–	–	2	3	3	–	3	28
Colorado	2	1	–	–	–	1	3	1	2	2	–	1	–	–	–	3	–	1	–	1	–	2	–	–	–	–	1	–	–	3	1	2	27
Bowling Green	–	–	–	–	–	1	3	2	1	1	1	1	–	–	1	–	–	–	–	3	2	1	3	1	–	–	–	–	1	1	1	–	24
Notre Dame	–	–	2	3	–	–	7	2	–	3	1	1	–	–	–	–	–	–	–	–	–	–	–	–	–	–	–	1	2	–	2	1	25
Lake Superior	–	–	–	–	1	1	1	–	–	3	–	–	–	–	–	1	–	3	–	3	2	3	1	–	1	–	–	1	1	–	1	–	23
W. Michigan	–	–	–	–	–	–	–	–	2	–	–	2	–	–	2	2	–	2	1	1	1	1	4	–	2	–	–	–	1	1	–	–	22
St. Lawrence	–	–	–	–	–	–	1	–	1	4	–	–	–	3	–	1	1	1	1	1	1	1	2	–	1	–	–	1	1	–	1	–	22
RPI	–	–	–	–	1	–	–	–	1	3	–	1	2	1	1	–	1	–	2	2	–	–	3	1	–	–	–	–	1	–	2	2	24
Northern Mich.	–	–	–	–	–	–	–	–	–	4	–	1	2	1	–	–	–	–	4	1	2	–	1	–	–	–	–	1	–	–	–	1	18
Vermont	–	–	–	–	1	–	4	–	1	1	–	1	1	–	1	1	2	–	–	1	–	–	1	–	–	1	–	1	–	–	–	–	17
Maine	–	–	–	–	–	–	–	–	–	–	–	–	–	1	1	–	–	1	–	3	2	1	–	–	1	–	–	1	1	1	4	1	18
Ohio State	–	–	–	–	–	–	–	–	2	1	–	–	–	–	–	1	–	–	2	2	–	1	1	1	1	–	–	1	1	–	1	–	15
Miami of Ohio	–	–	–	–	–	–	–	–	–	–	–	–	–	–	–	–	1	–	2	4	2	–	2	1	1	–	–	–	–	1	–	–	14
Minn.-Duluth	–	–	2	1	–	–	–	–	1	1	–	–	1	–	–	–	–	–	–	2	1	2	1	–	–	–	–	–	–	1	–	–	13
Brown	–	–	–	–	1	2	1	–	3	2	–	–	–	1	–	–	–	–	–	–	–	–	1	–	–	–	–	–	–	–	–	1	12
Colgate	–	–	–	–	–	1	–	–	–	2	1	–	–	–	–	–	–	–	–	1	1	2	2	–	–	–	–	–	–	–	–	–	10
Yale	–	–	–	1	–	–	1	–	–	2	–	1	–	–	–	–	–	1	2	–	1	–	–	–	1	–	–	–	–	–	–	–	10
Northeastern	–	–	–	–	–	1	–	–	–	1	–	1	–	–	1	–	1	1	–	–	1	1	–	–	–	–	–	–	–	1	1	–	10

Colleges with fewer than 10 players drafted:

9 - Princeton; **8** - Ferris State; **6** - Illinois-Chicago, St. Louis, Dartmouth, Lowell; **5** - Merrimack, Pennsylvania, Union College; **4** - Alaska-Anchorage, Union College; **3** - Babson College, St. Cloud State; **2** - Alaska-Fairbanks; **1** - American International College, Army, Bemidji State, Greenway, Hamilton, St. Anselen College, St. Thomas, Salem State, San Diego U., Wisconsin-River Falls, Air Force, Nebraska-Omaha

Year	Total College Drafted	Total Players Drafted	College %
1969	7	84	8.3
1970	16	115	13.9
1971	22	117	18.8
1972	21	152	13.8
1973	25	168	14.9
1974	41	247	16.6
1975	59	217	26.7
1976	26	135	19.3
1977	49	185	26.5
1978	73	234	31.2
1979	15	126	11.9
1980	42	210	20.0
1981	21	211	10.0
1982	20	252	7.9
1983	14	242	5.8
1984	22	250	8.8
1985	20	252	7.9
1986	22	252	8.7
1987	40	252	15.9
1988	48	252	19.0
1989	48	252	19.0
1990	38	250	15.2
1991	43	264	16.3
1992	9	264	3.4
1993	17	286	5.9
1994	6	286	2.1
1995	5	234	2.1
1996	25	241	10.4
1997	26	246	10.5
1998	27	258	10.4
1999	36	272	13.2
2000	35	293	11.9
Total	**918**	**7099**	**12.9**

United States High Schools (10 or more players drafted)

Club	'80	'81	'82	'83	'84	'85	'86	'87	'88	'89	'90	'91	'92	'93	'94	'95	'96	'97	'98	'99	'00	Total
Northwood Prep (NY)	–	–	2	1	–	2	2	4	1	1	3	1	–	1	1	–	–	–	–	–	1	20
Belmont Hill (MA)	–	–	–	1	–	2	1	2	1	3	2	1	2	–	1	–	–	–	–	–	–	16
Cushing Acad. (MA)	–	–	–	–	1	–	–	–	3	2	3	1	–	2	2	–	1	1	–	–	–	16
Edina (MN)	–	1	4	2	2	–	–	1	2	2	1	–	1	–	–	–	–	–	–	–	–	16
Hill-Murray (MN)	–	–	–	–	3	–	3	3	–	2	3	–	–	–	1	–	–	–	–	–	–	15
Mount St. Charles (RI)	–	1	–	3	1	–	2	1	2	1	1	–	–	–	–	–	–	–	–	–	–	12
Culver Mil. Acad. (IN)	–	–	–	–	–	–	–	2	1	2	2	1	2	2	–	–	–	–	–	–	–	12
Catholic Memorial (MA)	–	–	–	–	–	2	–	1	1	2	–	–	2	1	2	–	–	–	1	–	–	12
Canterbury (CT)	–	–	–	–	–	–	2	–	3	–	2	–	2	1	–	–	–	–	–	–	–	10
Matignon (MA)	1	1	1	–	3	–	–	3	–	–	–	1	–	–	–	–	–	–	–	–	–	10
Roseau (MN)	1	–	1	1	1	–	1	–	–	1	3	1	–	–	–	–	–	–	–	–	–	10
Deerfield (IL)	–	–	–	–	1	1	–	1	1	2	–	1	–	–	–	–	–	–	–	1	2	10
Choate (CT)	–	–	–	–	–	1	–	2	3	–	1	1	1	–	–	–	–	–	–	–	1	10

Year	Total USHS Drafted	Total Players Drafted	USHS %
1980	7	210	3.3
1981	17	211	8.1
1982	47	252	18.6
1983	35	242	14.5
1984	44	250	17.6
1985	48	252	19.1
1986	40	252	15.9
1987	69	252	27.4
1988	56	252	22.2
1989	47	252	18.7
1990	57	250	22.8
1991	37	264	14.0
1992	25	264	9.5
1993	33	286	11.5
1994	28	286	9.7
1995	2	234	0.9
1996	6	241	2.4
1997	4	246	1.6
1998	7	258	2.7
1999	9	272	3.3
2000	7	293	2.4
Total	**625**	**7099**	**8.8**

International

Country	'69	'70	'71	'72	'73	'74	'75	'76	'77	'78	'79	'80	'81	'82	'83	'84	'85	'86	'87	'88	'89	'90	'91	'92	'93	'94	'95	'96	'97	'98	'99	'00	Total
USSR/CIS	–	–	–	–	–	1	–	–	2	–	–	–	3	5	1	2	1	2	11	18	14	25	45	31	35	27	17	16	22	29	44		351
Sweden	–	–	–	–	–	5	2	5	2	8	5	9	14	14	10	14	16	9	15	14	9	7	11	11	18	17	8	16	14	19	24	24	320
Czech Republic and Slovakia	–	–	–	–	–	–	–	–	–	2	1	–	4	13	8	6	11	5	8	21	9	17	15	18	21	14	17	20	20	28			280
Finland	1	–	–	–	1	3	2	3	2	–	4	12	5	9	10	4	10	6	7	3	9	6	8	9	8	12	7	11	12	17	19		200
Germany	–	–	–	–	–	–	2	–	–	2	–	1	2	1	–	1	2	–	–	1	–	1	3	1	1	3	1	–	–	1	–		24
Switzerland	–	–	–	–	–	–	–	1	–	–	–	–	–	–	–	–	–	–	–	–	1	2	1	–	1	3	2	3	7				21
Norway	–	–	–	–	–	–	–	–	–	–	–	–	–	–	–	2	–	2	1	–	–	–	–	–	1	–	–	–	–	–			6
Denmark	–	–	–	–	–	–	–	–	–	–	–	1	1	–	–	–	–	–	–	–	–	–	–	–	–	–	–	–	–	–			2
Scotland	–	–	–	–	–	–	–	–	–	–	–	–	–	–	1	–	–	–	–	–	–	–	–	–	–	–	–	–	–	–			1
Poland	–	–	–	–	–	–	–	–	–	–	–	–	–	–	–	–	–	–	–	–	1	–	–	–	–	–	–	–	–	–			1
Japan	–	–	–	–	–	–	–	–	–	–	–	–	–	–	–	–	–	–	–	–	–	–	1	–	–	–	–	–	–	–			1
Hungary	–	–	–	–	–	–	–	–	–	–	–	–	–	–	–	–	–	–	–	–	–	–	–	–	–	–	–	–	–	1	–		1

Year	Total Int'l Drafted	Total Players Drafted	Int'l %
1969	1	84	1.2
1970	0	115	0
1971	0	117	0
1972	0	152	0
1973	0	168	0
1974	6	247	2.4
1975	6	217	2.8
1976	8	135	5.9
1977	5	185	2.7
1978	16	234	6.8
1979	6	126	4.8
1980	13	210	6.2
1981	32	211	15.2
1982	35	252	13.9
1983	34	242	14.0
1984	40	250	17.6
1985	31	252	12.3
1986	28	252	11.1
1987	38	252	15.1
1988	39	252	15.5
1989	38	252	15.1
1990	53	250	21.2
1991	55	264	20.8
1992	84	264	31.4
1993	78	286	27.3
1994	80	286	27.9
1995	69	234	29.5
1996	58	241	24.0
1997	63	246	25.6
1998	75	258	29.0
1999	94	272	34.5
2000	123	293	42.0
Total	**1208**	**7099**	**17.0**

Russia/C.I.S.

Club	'74	'75	'76	'77	'78	'79	'80	'81	'82	'83	'84	'85	'86	'87	'88	'89	'90	'91	'92	'93	'94	'95	'96	'97	'98	'99	'00	Total
CSKA Moscow	–	–	–	1	–	–	–	1	4	–	1	1	1	5	8	3	4	7	3	5	2	3	–	1	3	–		53
Dynamo Moscow	–	–	–	–	–	–	–	–	2	3	4	7	10	2	1	7	1	1	1	2	2	1						43
Krylja Sovetov Moscow	–	–	–	–	–	–	–	–	–	1	1	2	4	3	1	5	3	2	1	1	2	1						27
Torpedo-2 Yaroslavl	–	–	–	–	–	–	–	–	–	–	–	–	–	–	–	–	–	1	2	2	4	–	9					18
Spartak Moscow	–	–	–	–	–	–	–	–	–	–	1	4	–	6	1	–	–	1	1	1								16
Torpedo Yaroslavl	–	–	–	–	–	–	–	–	–	1	2	–	1	5	1	1	3	1	1									16
Traktor Chelyabinsk	–	–	–	–	–	–	–	–	2	–	–	2	7	1	1	1	1											15
Dynamo-2 Moscow	–	–	–	–	–	–	–	–	–	–	2	1	2	–	–	3	3	–	4									15
Khimik Voskresensk	–	–	–	–	–	1	–	–	–	1	3	1	2	–	1	1	1											12
Lada Togliatti	–	–	–	–	–	–	–	–	–	–	–	1	2	–	–	1	3	1	2	2								12
Sokol Kiev	–	–	–	–	–	–	–	–	–	1	1	2	3	1	–	2	1											11
Pardaugava Riga[1]	–	1	–	–	–	–	–	–	1	2	–	1	4	1														10
Severstal Cherepoyets[5]	–	–	–	–	–	–	–	–	–	1	1	–	1	1	–	5	1											10
SKA St. Peterburg[2]	–	–	–	1	–	–	–	–	–	2	1	–	1	–	2	1												9
Torpedo Ust Kamenogorsk	–	–	–	–	–	–	–	–	–	1	1	2	1	–	2	1												8
Salavat Yulayev Ufa	–	–	–	–	–	–	–	–	–	–	2	2	1	1	1	–	1											8
HC CSKA Moscow	–	–	–	–	–	–	–	–	–	–	–	–	–	–	–	–	2	5										7
CSKA-2 Moscow	–	–	–	–	–	–	–	–	–	–	–	1	–	2	2	–												5
Avangard Omsk	–	–	–	–	–	–	–	–	–	–	–	3	–	1	–	1												5
Tivali Minsk[3]	–	–	–	–	–	–	–	1	–	–	2	1																4
Kristall Elektrostal	–	–	–	–	–	–	–	–	3	–	–	1																4
Torpedo Nizhny Novgorod[4]	–	–	–	–	–	–	1	–	2	–	–	1																4
Metallurg Novokuznetsk	–	–	–	–	–	–	–	–	–	–	–	–	2	2														4
Avtomobilist Yekaterinburg	–	–	–	–	–	–	–	–	–	–	1	1	1															3
Molot Perm	–	–	–	–	–	–	–	–	–	–	1	1	1															3
AK Bars Kazan	–	–	–	–	–	–	–	–	–	–	–	1	–	1	1													3
Neftekhimik Nizhnekamsk	–	–	–	–	–	–	–	–	–	–	1	–	2															3
Lada-2 Togliatti	–	–	–	–	–	–	–	–	–	–	–	–	1	2														3
CSK VVS Samara	–	–	–	–	–	–	–	–	–	–	–	–	1	1														2
Dizelist Penza	–	–	–	–	–	–	–	–	–	–	–	–	1	1														2
Severstal-2 Cherepovets	–	–	–	–	–	–	–	–	–	–	–	–	1	1														2
Metallurg-2 Novoiwznetsk	–	–	–	–	–	–	–	–	–	–	–	–	–	2														2

Former club names: [1]–Dynamo Riga, HC Riga, [2]–SKA Leningrad, [3]–Dynamo Minsk, [4]–Torpedo Gorky, [5]–Metallurg Cherepovets

Teams with one player selected:
Argus Moscow, Dynamo Kharov, Izorhets St. Petersburg, Khimik Novopolotsk, Kristall Saratov, Krylja Sovetov-2 Moscow, Mechel Chelyabinsk, Salavat Novoil Ufa, Ak-Bars-2 Kazan, Dynamo-81 Riga, Amur Khabarovsk, SKA-2 St. Petersburg.

Sweden

Club	'74	'75	'76	'77	'78	'79	'80	'81	'82	'83	'84	'85	'86	'87	'88	'89	'90	'91	'92	'93	'94	'95	'96	'97	'98	'99	'00	Total
MoDo Hockey Ornskoldsvik	–	–	1	–	–	1	–	–	1	–	2	–	–	1	–	–	–	2	2	5	–	–	3	3	–	7	3	31
Djurgarden Stockholm	1	1	1	–	1	–	1	2	1	–	1	2	1	–	1	2	1	1	–	3	2	2	–	1	4			31
Farjestad Karlstad	–	–	–	2	–	2	2	–	1	2	1	1	2	–	–	–	1	–	1	2	1	–	–	3	6	1	–	29
Leksand	1	–	–	–	1	–	1	–	2	2	1	1	2	1	–	2	–	2	2	–	1	–	2	–	5			26
AIK Solna	–	–	1	1	–	2	3	1	–	4	–	–	–	1	1	1	–	1	–	1	1	3						22
Vastra Frolunda Goteborg	–	–	–	–	–	2	1	–	1	1	1	–	–	–	1	–	3	1	1	–	1	2	4					19
Brynas Gavle	1	–	–	1	1	1	1	–	1	2	–	4	–	–	–	–	1	1	2	1	1							19
HV 71 Jonkoping	–	–	–	–	1	–	–	1	1	–	1	–	–	1	–	2	1	4	3	1	–	1						17
Sodertalje	–	–	–	–	1	–	1	2	2	2	–	2	–	–	1	–	–	–										15
Skelleftea	–	1	1	–	–	1	1	2	1	–	1	–	–	1	–	–	–											10
Lulea	–	–	–	–	–	1	–	–	1	1	–	–	–	–	1	1	2											10
Rogle Angelholm	–	–	–	–	–	1	–	2	–	–	2	2	–	–	1	–												9
Vasteras	–	–	–	–	2	2	1	1	–	1	1	–	–	1														9
Malmo	–	–	–	–	–	1	1	1	–	1	1	1	1	1														8
Sundsvall Timra[1]	–	–	1	2	1	–	–	–	1	1																		7
Bjorkloven Umea	–	–	–	2	1	–	1	1																				5
Orebro	–	–	–	–	1	2	1	1																				5
Hammarby Stockholm	–	–	1	1	1	–	1	–	1																			5
Nacka	–	–	–	–	–	1	–	1	–	1	1																	4
Mora	–	–	–	–	–	1	–	1	1	1																		4
Huddinge	–	–	–	–	–	–	1	1	–	2	–	1																4
Falun	–	–	–	1	–	1	1																					3
Team Kiruna	–	–	–	1	1	–	1																					3
Boden	1	–	–	1	–	1																						3
Pitea	–	–	–	–	1	1	1																					3
Troja	–	–	–	–	1	1	1																					3
Grums	–	–	–	–	–	–	1	1	1																			3
Ostersund	–	–	–	–	–	–	–	2																				2

Former club names: [1]–Timra

Teams with one player selected:
Almtuna, Danderyd Hockey, Fagersta, Karskoga, Stocksund, S/G Hockey 83 Gavle, Talje, Tunabro, Uppsala, Vallentuna, Vita Hasten.

Czech Republic and Slovakia

Club	'69	'70	'71	'72	'73	'74	'75	'76	'77	'78	'79	'80	'81	'82	'83	'84	'85	'86	'87	'88	'89	'90	'91	'92	'93	'94	'95	'96	'97	'98	'99	'00	Total
Chemopetrol Litvinov[1]	-	-	-	-	-	-	-	-	-	-	-	-	-	3	1	2	-	-	-	2	2	1	3	2	4	2	2	2	1	1	-	-	28
Dukla Jihlava	-	-	-	-	-	-	-	-	-	-	-	2	4	3	1	-	3	1	1	3	2	1	1	2	2	-	1	-	-	-	1	-	28
HC Ceske Budejovice[6]	-	-	-	-	-	-	-	-	-	-	-	2	1	1	-	-	1	1	1	2	-	-	1	2	3	1	2	1	1	1	3	-	22
Slovan Bratislava	-	-	-	-	-	-	1	1	-	2	-	-	1	1	1	-	-	1	-	-	3	-	1	1	1	2	2	-	-	-	-	-	18
Dukla Trencin	-	-	-	-	-	-	-	-	-	1	-	-	1	1	1	-	2	2	-	1	2	1	-	2	3	1	-	-	-	-	-	-	18
Sparta Praha	-	-	-	-	-	-	-	-	1	-	2	1	1	2	1	2	1	-	1	1	-	1	1	-	1	1	-	-	-	-	-	-	17
ZPS Zlin[2]	-	-	-	-	-	-	-	-	-	1	-	1	1	1	-	-	2	2	1	-	2	-	1	2	2	-	-	-	-	-	-	-	16
HC Kladno[7]	-	-	-	-	-	-	-	2	1	-	1	-	1	-	-	1	2	1	2	-	2	-	2	-	-	2	1	-	-	-	-	-	16
Slavia Praha	-	-	-	-	-	-	-	-	-	1	-	-	-	1	-	-	1	4	5	2	3	-	-	-	-	-	-	-	-	-	-	-	16
HC Vitkovice[8]	-	-	-	-	1	-	1	-	1	-	-	1	-	1	3	1	1	1	-	1	1	1	-	-	-	-	-	-	-	-	-	-	13
HC Kosice[3]	-	-	-	-	-	-	1	2	-	2	-	1	-	2	-	1	1	1	1	-	-	-	-	-	-	-	-	-	-	-	-	-	12
Interconex Plzen[9]	-	-	-	-	-	-	-	-	-	1	-	1	1	3	1	1	-	1	-	1	-	1	-	-	-	-	-	-	-	-	-	-	10
HC Pardubice[4]	-	-	-	-	-	-	-	2	-	2	-	-	-	-	-	2	1	1	-	-	-	-	-	-	-	-	-	-	-	-	-	-	9
Zetor Brno	-	-	-	-	-	-	-	1	3	-	2	-	1	-	1	-	-	-	-	-	-	-	-	-	-	-	-	-	-	-	-	-	8
HC Olomouc[5]	-	-	-	-	-	-	-	1	-	-	2	-	1	2	-	1	-	-	-	-	-	-	-	-	-	-	-	-	-	-	-	-	7
ZTK Zvolen	-	-	-	-	-	-	-	-	-	1	-	1	1	-	2	2	-	-	-	-	-	-	-	-	-	-	-	-	-	-	-	-	7
AC Nitra	-	-	-	-	-	-	-	-	-	2	-	1	-	1	1	-	-	-	-	-	-	-	-	-	-	-	-	-	-	-	-	-	5
HC Vsetin	-	-	-	-	-	-	-	-	-	-	-	-	-	-	2	1	-	2	-	-	-	-	-	-	-	-	-	-	-	-	-	-	5
ZTS Martin	-	-	-	-	-	-	-	-	-	-	-	1	-	-	-	2	-	-	1	-	-	-	-	-	-	-	-	-	-	-	-	-	4
Zelezarny Trinec	-	-	-	-	-	-	-	-	-	-	-	-	-	-	-	-	-	-	-	-	-	-	-	-	1	1	-	3	-	-	-	-	3
IS Banska Bystrica	-	-	-	-	-	-	-	-	-	-	-	-	-	-	-	1	1	-	-	-	-	-	-	-	-	-	-	-	-	-	-	-	2
ZPA Presov	-	-	-	-	-	-	-	-	-	-	-	-	-	-	-	-	1	-	1	-	-	-	-	-	-	-	-	-	-	-	-	-	2
Partizan Liptovsky Mikulas	-	-	-	-	-	-	-	-	-	-	-	-	1	-	-	-	-	-	-	-	-	-	1	-	-	-	-	-	-	-	-	-	2
VTJ Pisek	-	-	-	-	-	-	-	-	-	-	-	-	-	-	-	1	-	-	-	-	-	-	-	-	-	-	-	-	1	-	-	2
Michalovce	-	-	-	-	-	-	-	-	-	-	-	-	-	-	-	-	-	-	-	-	-	-	-	-	-	-	-	-	-	2	-	2
Ingstav Brno	-	-	-	-	-	-	-	-	-	-	-	-	-	-	-	-	-	-	-	-	-	-	-	-	-	-	-	-	-	-	-	2	2

Former club names: [1]–CHZ Litvinov, [2]–TJ Gottwaldov, TJ Zlin, [3]–VSZ Kosice, [4]–Tesla Pardubice, [5]–DS Olomouc, [6]–Motor Ceske Budejovice, [7]–Poldi Kladno, [8]–TJ Vitkovice, [9]–Skoda Plzen.

Teams with one player selected:
Ingstav Brno, Banik Sokolov, Havlickuv Brod, KLH Chomutov, HC Havirov, HC Karlovy Vary, HC Skalica, HK Trnava, KHM Zvolen.

Finland

Club	'69	'70	'71	'72	'73	'74	'75	'76	'77	'78	'79	'80	'81	'82	'83	'84	'85	'86	'87	'88	'89	'90	'91	'92	'93	'94	'95	'96	'97	'98	'99	'00	Total
TPS Turku	-	-	-	-	-	-	-	-	-	1	6	-	-	1	1	-	-	-	-	-	-	-	3	2	3	1	3	3	1	3	-	-	28
HIFK Helsinki	1	-	-	-	-	1	-	1	-	-	1	1	2	2	1	-	2	1	-	2	-	1	-	1	2	4	2	-	-	-	-	-	25
Ilves Tampere	-	-	-	-	-	1	2	-	2	-	2	2	1	-	1	-	1	1	-	-	2	-	2	1	3	-	-	-	-	-	-	-	21
Jokerit Helsinki	-	-	-	-	-	-	-	2	1	-	1	-	1	1	-	2	3	1	-	1	1	1	3	3	-	-	-	-	-	-	-	-	21
Tappara Tampere	-	-	-	1	-	-	-	-	2	-	4	1	1	1	1	-	1	-	1	2	-	1	-	-	-	-	-	-	-	-	-	-	14
Assat Pori	-	-	-	-	-	2	-	-	1	2	2	-	1	1	-	1	1	-	1	-	-	1	-	-	-	-	-	-	-	-	-	-	13
Lukko Rauma	-	-	-	-	-	2	1	-	2	1	1	1	1	-	2	1	-	-	-	-	-	-	-	-	-	-	-	-	-	-	-	-	12
Karpat Oulu	-	-	-	-	-	-	-	1	1	1	2	2	1	1	1	1	-	-	-	-	-	-	-	-	-	-	-	-	-	-	-	-	11
Kiekko-Espoo	-	-	-	-	-	-	-	-	-	1	1	1	2	-	2	1	1	2	-	-	-	-	-	-	-	-	-	-	-	-	-	-	11
HPK Hameenlinna	-	-	-	-	-	-	-	1	-	2	-	-	1	1	1	3	-	-	-	-	-	-	-	-	-	-	-	-	-	-	-	-	9
Reipas Lahti	-	-	-	-	1	1	1	2	1	1	-	-	-	-	-	-	-	-	-	-	-	-	-	-	-	-	-	-	-	-	-	-	7
JyP HT Jyvaskyla	-	-	-	-	-	-	-	-	2	1	3	-	-	-	-	-	-	-	-	-	-	-	-	-	-	-	-	-	-	-	-	-	7
KalPa Kuopio	-	-	-	-	-	-	-	1	2	1	-	1	-	1	-	-	-	-	-	-	-	-	-	-	-	-	-	-	-	-	-	-	6
Kiekoo-67 Turku	-	-	-	-	-	-	-	-	-	-	-	-	-	3	-	-	-	-	-	-	-	-	-	-	-	-	-	-	-	-	-	-	3
SaiPa Lappeenranta	-	-	-	-	-	-	1	-	-	-	-	-	-	-	-	-	-	-	-	-	-	-	-	1	-	-	-	-	-	-	-	-	3
Sapko Savonlinna	-	-	-	-	-	-	-	1	1	-	-	-	-	-	-	-	-	-	-	-	-	-	-	-	-	-	-	-	-	-	-	-	2
Sport Vaasa	-	-	-	-	-	-	-	-	1	-	1	-	-	-	-	-	-	-	-	-	-	-	-	-	-	-	-	-	-	-	-	-	2

Teams with one player selected:
GrIFK Kauniainen, Koo Koo Kouvola, S-Kiekko Seinajoki, Junkkarit Kalajoki, Hermes Kokkola.

2000 Entry Draft Analysis

Country of Origin

Country	Players Drafted
Canada	96
USA	56
Russia	39
Sweden	23
Czech Republic	24
Finland	19
Slovakia	16
Kazakhstan	6
Switzerland	6
Latvia	2
Austria	1
Ukraine	1
Hungary	1
Slovenia	1
Great Britain	1
Germany	1

Birth Year

Year	Players Drafted
1982	116
1981	86
1980	60
1979	6
1978	2
1977	4
1976	5
1975	3
1974	2
1973	3
1972	3
1971	2
1968	1

Position

Position	Players Drafted
Defense	99
Center	83
Right Wing	42
Left Wing	37
Goaltender	32

Note: Players drafted in the international category played outside North America in their draft year. European-born players drafted from the OHL, QMJHL, WHL or U.S. Colleges are not counted as International players. See Country of Origin, at left.

Notes on 2000 First Round Selections

1. NY ISLANDERS • **RICK DiPIETRO** • G • A strong puckhandler with great agility and balance, Rick DiPietro is the first goalie to be chosen #1 since the draft became universal in 1969. He is an aggressive goalie with a good glove hand who was named Hockey East rookie of the year in 1999-2000 and best goalie at the 2000 World Junior Championships. A graduate of the U.S. National Team Development Program, DiPietro set an NCAA record with 77 saves in one game for Boston University last season.

2. ATLANTA • **DANY HEATLEY** • LW • The top-rated prospect entering the draft, Dany Heatley was fourth in WCHA scoring with the University of Wisconsin in 1999-2000. He was named WCHA rookie of the year and was a First-Team All-Star. Heatley is an upright skater with deceptive speed when carrying the puck. He has a powerful shot with a quick release and is an excellent puckhandler with a long reach.

3. MINNESOTA • **MARIAN GABORIK** • LW • Rated by some teams as a possible #1 pick, Marian Gaborik began playing in the Slovakian senior league as a 16-year-old and has represented his country at the 1999 and 2000 World Junior Championships. With good speed and acceleration, Gaborik is a natural scorer who is very dangerous in the offensive zone. He is a good puckhandler who reads the play very well.

4. COLUMBUS • **ROSTISLAV KLESLA** • D • A native of the Czech Republic who came to North America in 1998, Rostislav Klesla was named to the OHL's First All-Rookie Team with the Brampton Battalion in 1999-2000. "Rusty" was considered the best defenseman available in the draft. He is an excellent two-way player with a good knowledge of the game. At 6'2" and 198 pounds, he is a very agile, solid skater.

5. NY ISLANDERS • **RAFFI TORRES** • LW • The son of a Mexican father and a Peruvian mother, Raffi Torres ranked seventh in the OHL in scoring in 1999-2000 as a member of the Brampton Battalion. He was voted both the player most dangerous in the goal area and the player with the best shot in the Western Conference in the 2000 OHL Coaches Poll. Torres is a shifty skater who is very strong along the boards.

6. NASHVILLE • **SCOTT HARTNELL** • RW • A creative player who excels at the physical part of the game, Scott Hartnell was named captain of the WHL's Prince Albert Raiders as a 17-year-old in 1999-2000. He won the puck control event at the 2000 Top Prospects skills evaluation and is very dangerous around the net. Hartnell is a good team player who can intimidate opponents with his work ethic and physical play.

7. BOSTON • **LARS JONSSON** • D • One of the top-scoring defensemen in junior hockey, Lars Jonsson helped his Leksand team finish in first place in the Swedish junior league in 1999-2000. He is a mobile defenseman who is strong and fast on his skates. He likes to join the offensive rush and has good overall puck skills. Jonsson has an excellent shot from the point and is often used on the power-play.

8. TAMPA BAY • **NIKITA ALEXEEV** • RW • At 6'5" and 215 pounds, Nikita Alexeev is a power forward who excels in a fast-paced game. He was the fastest skater in the 2000 Top Prospects skills evaluation, but needs to improve his physical play. Alexeev played on the Russian Junior Championship team in 1996-97 before coming to North America to join the Erie Otters of the OHL in 1998-99.

9. CALGARY • **BRENT KRAHN** • G • Ranked among the WHL leaders in goals-against average, wins and shutouts in 1999-2000, Brent Krahn is strong in the crease and does not get distracted. Standing 6'4" and weighing 200 pounds, he has excellent body control and good lateral movement. Krahn plays the angles well and uses the paddle-down technique effectively. He has excellent focus and concentration.

10. CHICAGO • **MIKHAIL YAKUBOV** • C • A very good all-around player with a high overall skill level, Mikhail Yakubov was NHL Central Scouting's second-ranked European prospect entering the 2000 draft. An excellent puckhandler, he is a better playmaker than goal scorer and maneuvers well in heavy traffic. He needs to improve his strength and intensity, but Yakubov will take a hit to make the play.

11. CHICAGO • **PAVEL VOROBJEV** • RW • A native of Kazakhstan who played with the Russian team at the Under-18 2000 World Championships, Pavel Vorobjev jumped from 40th on the Mid-Term report to the top-ranked European player in Central Scouting's final rankings. Vorobjev is an aggressive player with good speed and strong balance who maneuvers well in traffic. He has good scoring ability and a good selection of shots, and is also a solid checker.

12. ANAHEIM • **ALEXEI SMIRNOV** • LW • Though he needs to improve his consistency, Alexei Smirnov has the size, strength and skating skill to become a star. Standing 6'3" and weighing 211 pounds, Smirnov is an excellent puckhandler who is a constant scoring threat. He has a good selection of shots plus strong playmaking and passing skills. He is capable of impressive puck control and spectacular goals.

13. MONTREAL • **RON HAINSEY** • D • A confident puckhandler who is capable of creating offense, Ron Hainsey played for Team USA at the 2000 World Junior Championships and was named to the Hockey East All-Rookie Team at the University of Mass-Lowell. He is a very good skater with good lateral quickness and a smooth stride who effectively anticipates the play. Hainsey has a quick, low shot from the point.

14. COLORADO • **VACLAV NEDOROST** • C • A very good skater with good straight-away speed, Vaclav Nedorost was a member of the gold medal-winning Czech team at the 2000 World Junior Championships. A creative playmaker with very strong puckhandling skills, Nedorost excels in a finesse game. Though very aware of his defensive responsibilities, he needs to improve his strength and be more aggressive.

15. BUFFALO • **ARTEM KRYUKOV** • C • A big, fast skater with a powerful shot, Artem Kryukov possesses a high overall skill level with good hockey sense. The 6'3", 187-pound center began 1999-2000 with the Yaroslavl senior team in Russia, but missed most of the season due to injury. He is a good puckhandler with strong passing and playmaking skills and can maneuver well in heavy traffic.

16. MONTREAL • **MARCEL HOSSA** • C • The brother of Marian Hossa, Marcel Hossa was the top scorer with the WHL's Portland Winter Hawks in 1999–2000 and represented Slovakia at the 2000 World Junior Championships. He is a deceptive skater with very good balance who maneuvers well in traffic and is very good at creating room for his linemates. Hossa is very strong on the face-off and is a tough competitor.

17. EDMONTON • **ALEXEI MIKHNOV** • LW • This native of the Ukraine was not seen by many scouts prior to the draft, and was ranked only 19th among Europeans by Central Scouting. At 6'5" and 198 pounds, Alexei Mikhnov has excellent size and uses it effectively along the boards and in the corners. He is a well-balanced, mobile skater and a confident puckhandler with strong passing skills.

18. PITTSBURGH • **BROOKS ORPIK** • D • Named after "Miracle on Ice" coach Herb Brooks, Brooks Orpik stands 6'3" and weighs 217 pounds. He uses his size and long reach to his advantage and can dominate the defensive zone. Orpik is a very good skater with excellent agility and lateral movement. He is a good passer with a good shot from the point and is capable of leading an offensive rush.

19. PHOENIX • **KRYSTOFER KOLANOS** • C • A top scorer in the Alberta Junior Hockey League in 1998-99, Krys Kolanos helped Boston College reach the finals of the 2000 NCAA championships. Kolanos is a strong and agile skater with excellent puck control and strong passing skills. A solid goal scorer with an impressive backhand shot, Kolanos is tough along the boards and behind the net. He reads the play well.

20. LOS ANGELES • **ALEXANDER FROLOV** • LW • With five goals scored in six games at the Under-18 2000 World Championships, Alexander Frolov is a natural scorer with a strong selection of shots. He is an excellent skater with good straight-way speed and excels in a finesse-style game. Frolov has good hockey sense and is aware of his defensive responsibilities. He has good puckhandling skills and is effective at controlling the puck along the boards.

21. OTTAWA • **ANTON VOLCHENKOV** • D • A member of the Central Army team and the son of a former Red Army player, Anton Volchenkov is quick to the puck and is a solid, defensive defenseman. He is a strong, quick skater with good acceleration who is always involved in the game. Volchenkov is a good playmaker with strong passing skills. He has a high overall skill level and a lot of offensive potential.

22. NEW JERSEY • **DAVID HALE** • D • Standing 6'2" and weighing 204 pounds, David Hale is a physical defenseman with a strong work ethic. He was named to the All-USHL First Team as a member of Sioux City in 1999-2000 and was named to the All-Tournament team after helping the U.S. win the 2000 Viking Cup. Hale skates with a wide stance and has a powerful stride. He is agile and well-balanced and reads the play effectively. Hale is a punishing player.

23. VANCOUVER • **NATHAN SMITH** • C • A smooth-skating center with good acceleration, Nathan Smith scored two goals and was named Team Orr Player of the Game at the 2000 Top Prospects Game. An excellent two-way player, Smith is an effective forechecker who is also a creative player with good passing skills. His older brother Jarrett was selected 59th overall by the New York Islanders in the 1997 Entry Draft.

24. TORONTO • **BRAD BOYES** • C • Named Scholastic Player of the Year in 1999-2000, Brad Boyes was also the Erie Otters' top scorer and Most Outstanding Player. He has excellent awareness and hockey sense, and can read the developing play. Boyes is a good puckhandler with strong passing skills who plays an aggressive game with a strong desire to win. He is an offensive-minded player who is a good forechecker and forces turnovers.

25. DALLAS • **STEVE OTT** • C • An in-your-face player who was named Best Checker in the Western Conference in the 2000 OHL Coaches Poll, Steve Ott stands 6' but weighs only 160 pounds. He is an intense competitor with a strong desire to win and was named Player of the Game for Team Cherry at the 2000 Top Prospects Game. Ott is a good skater with excellent puckhandling skills who drives the net.

26. WASHINGTON • **BRIAN SUTHERBY** • C • A very poised and patient player, Brian Sutherby is a tough competitor who enjoys the physical game. He is used in all game situations and is very effective on special teams. Sutherby is an excellent playmaker with good passing skills and takes advantage of his size (6'2", 180 pounds) to control and protect the puck. He is a two-way player who is willing to sacrifice for the team.

27. BOSTON • **MARTIN SAMUELSSON** • LW • A powerful, dynamic skater with very good speed and acceleration, Martin Samuelsson had eight points in six games for Sweden at the Under-18 2000 World Championships, but missed most of the 1999-2000 season because of a shoulder injury. He is a playmaker who creates a lot of scoring chances for his linemates, but needs to take advantage of his size (6'2", 194 pounds) and improve his shot.

28. PHILADELPHIA • **JUSTIN WILLIAMS** • RW • After scoring just four goals as an OHL rookie, Justin Williams scored 37 times for the Plymouth Whalers in 1999-2000. A very good skater with impressive quickness, Williams reads the play effectively and is quick to find open ice. He is a smooth puckhandler with strong playmaking abilities and has a quick, accurate shot.

29. DETROIT • **NIKLAS KRONWALL** • D • Though he stands just 5'11" and weighs only 165 pounds, Niklas Kronwall is a confident puckhandler who is able to rush the puck. He is a well-balanced skater with good mobility who plays a strong positional game. Kronwall is a hard-working defenseman who is very effective on special teams. He helped Djurgarden win the Swedish championship in 1999-2000.

30. ST. LOUIS • **JEFF TAFFE** • C • A Minnesota high-school star who was named rookie of the year with the University of Minnesota in 1999-2000, Jeff Taffe (pronounced TAIF) is a smooth, effortless skater with good speed and acceleration. He is an exceptional puckhandler who excels in one-on-one situations and has a good wrist shot with a quick release. Though not an overly physical player, Taffe is an aggressive forechecker and is very strong on face-offs.

Players selected first through tenth in the 2000 NHL Entry Draft: (All rows left to right):
Top row: 1. Rick DiPietro, G, NY Islanders; 2. Dany Heatley, LW, Atlanta.
Second row: 3. Marian Gaborik, LW, Minnesota; 4. Rostislav Klesla, D, Columbus.
Third row: 5. Raffi Torres, LW, NY Islanders; 6. Scott Hartnell, RW, Nashville.
Fourth row: 7. Lars Jonsson, D, Boston; 8. Nikita Alexeev, RW, Tampa Bay.
Fifth row: 9. Brent Krahn, G, Calgary; 10. Mikhail Yakubov. C, Chicago.

2000 Entry Draft

Transferred draft choice notation:

Example: Col.-Ana. represents a draft choice transferred **from** Colorado **to** Anaheim.

Pick	Player	Claimed By	Amateur Club	Position
ROUND #1				
1	DiPIETRO, Rick	NYI	Boston University	G
2	HEATLEY, Dany	Atl.	U. of Wisconsin	LW
3	GABORIK, Marian	Min.	Dukla Trencin	LW
4	KLESLA, Rostislav	CBJ	Brampton	D
5	TORRES, Raffi	T.B.-NYI	Brampton	LW
6	HARTNELL, Scott	Nsh.	Prince Albert	RW
7	JONSSON, Lars	Bos.	Leksand Jr.	D
8	ALEXEEV, Nikita	NYR-T.B.	Erie	RW
9	KRAHN, Brent	Cgy.	Calgary	G
10	YAKUBOV, Mikhail	Chi.	Lada Togliatti 2	C
11	VOROBJEV, Pavel	Van.-Chi.	Yaroslavl	RW
12	SMIRNOV, Alexei	Ana.	Tver	LW
13	HAINSEY, Ron	Mtl.	Mass.-Lowell	D
14	NEDOROST, Vaclav	Car.-Col.	Budejovice	C
15	KRYUKOV, Artem	Buf.	Yaroslavl 2	C
16	HOSSA, Marcel	S.J.-Mtl.	Portland	C
17	MIKHNOV, Alexei	Edm.	Yaroslavl 2	W
18	ORPIK, Brooks	Pit.	Boston College	D
19	KOLANOS, Krystofer	Phx.	Boston College	C
20	FROLOV, Alexander	L.A.	Yaroslavl 2	LW
21	VOLCHENKOV, Anton	Ott.	HC Moscow	D
22	HALE, David	Col.-N.J.	Sioux City	D
23	SMITH, Nathan	Fla.-Van.	Swift Current	C
24	BOYES, Brad	Tor.	Erie	C
25	OTT, Steve	Dal.	Windsor	C
26	SUTHERBY, Brian	Wsh.	Moose Jaw	C
27	SAMUELSSON, Martin	N.J.-Col.-Bos.	MoDo Jr.	W
28	WILLIAMS, Justin	Phi.	Plymouth	RW
29	KRONWALL, Niklas	Det.	Djurgarden	D
30	TAFFE, Jeff	St.L.	U. of Minnesota	C
ROUND #2				
31	NIKULIN, Ilja	Atl.	Tver	D
32	KURKA, Tomas	CBJ-Col.-Car.	Plymouth	LW
33	SCHULTZ, Nick	Min.	Prince Albert	D
34	ZAINULLAN, Ruslan	T.B.	Kazan	RW
35	WINCHESTER, Brad	NYI-Edm.	U. of Wisconsin	LW
36	WIDING, Daniel	Nsh.	Leksand Jr.	RW
37	HILBERT, Andy	Bos.	U. of Michigan	C
38	KOPECKY, Tomas	NYR-Det.	Dukla Trencin	C
39	LAINE, Teemu	Van.-NYI-N.J.	Jokerit	RW
40	FOSTER, Kurtis	Cgy.	Peterborough	D
41	MAATTA, Tero	Chi-S.J.	Jokerit Jr.	D
42	USTRNUL, Libor	Van.-Atl.	Plymouth	D
43	PETTINGER, Matt	Ana.-Cgy.-Wsh.	Calgary	LW
44	BRYZGALOV, Ilja	Mtl.-Ana.	Lada Togliatti	G
45	CHOUINARD, Mathieu	Ott.	Shawinigan	G
46	STOLL, Jarret	Col.-Cgy.	Kootenay	C
47	AULIN, Jared	Car.-Col.	Kamloops	C
48	DICAIRE, Gerard	Buf.	Seattle	D
49	NORDQVIST, Jonas	S.J.-Chi.	Leksand Jr.	C
50	SOIN, Sergei	Col.	Krylja Sovetov	C
51	VERNARSKY, Kris	Edm.-Tor.	Plymouth	C
52	ENDICOTT, Shane	Pit.	Seattle	C
53	TATARINOV, Alexander	Phx.	Yaroslavl 2	RW
54	LILJA, Andreas	L.A.	Malmo	D
55	VERMETTE, Antoine	Ott.	Victoriaville	C
56	SUGLOBOV, Alexander	N.J.	Yaroslavl 2	C
57	DeMARCHI, Matt	Col.-N.J.	U. of Minnesota	D
58	SAPOZHNIKOV, Vladimir	Fla.	Novokuznetsk 2	D
59	HUML, Ivan	Tor.-Bos.	Langley	LW
60	ELLIS, Dan	Dal.	Omaha	G
61	CUTTA, Jakub	Wsh.	Swift Current	D
62	MARTIN, Paul	N.J.	Elk River High School	D
63	SAVIELS, Argis	Phi.-Car.-Col.	Owen Sound	D
64	NOVAK, Filip	Det.-NYR	Regina	D
65	MORISSET, David	St.L.	Seattle	RW
ROUND #3				
66	MAKELA, Tuukka	Bos.	HIFK Jr.	D
67	BIRBRAER, Maxim	Van.-Atl.-N.J.	Newmarket	LW
68	LUNDQVIST, Joel	Min.-Dal.	V. Frolunda Jr.	C
69	KNOPP, Ben	CBJ	Moose Jaw	RW
70	TELLQVIST, Mikael	T.B.-Tor.	Djurgarden	G
71	BELL, Thatcher	NYI-Van.	Rimouski	C
72	NILSSON, Mattias	Nsh.	MoDo Jr.	D
73	ZINOVJEV, Sergei	Bos.	Novokuznetsk	RW
74	RADULOV, Igor	NYR-T.B.-S.J.-Chi.	Yaroslavl 2	LW
75	PAPINEAU, Justin	Cgy.-St.L.	Belleville	C
76	RUPP, Michael	Chi.-N.J.	Erie	LW
77	FRIED, Robert	Van.-Fla.	Deerfield Acad.	RW
78	BALEJ, Jozef	Ana.-Mtl.	Portland	RW
79	HANCHUK, Tyler	Mtl.	Brampton	D
80	BAYDA, Ryan	Car.	U. of North Dakota	LW
81	KHARITONOV, Alexander	Buf.-T.B.	Dynamo Moscow	RW
82	OCONNOR, Sean	S.J.-Fla.	Moose Jaw	RW
83	LYUBIMOV, Alexander	Edm.	Lada Togliatti	D
84	HAMERLIK, Peter	Pit.	Skalica Jr.	G
85	ABID, Ramzi	Phx.	Halifax	LW
86	LEHOUX, Yanick	L.A.	Baie Comeau	C
87	BOHAC, Jan	Ott.	Slavia Praha	C
88	SAUER, Kurt	Col.	Spokane	D
89	PIVKO, Libor	Fla.-Nsh.	Havirov	LW
90	RACINE, Jean-Francois	Tor.	Drummondville	G
91	TERESCHENKO, Alexei	Dal.	Dynamo Moscow	C
92	KLIAZMINE, Sergei	Wsh.-Col.	Dynamo Moscow 2	LTW
93	BRANHAM, Tim	N.J.-Van.	Barrie	C
94	DROZDETSKY, Alexander	Phi.	SKA St.Petersburg	D
95	MOORE, Dominic	Det.-NYR	Harvard	F
96	BERGERON, Antoine	St.L.	Val D'Or	C
				D

ROUND #4

#	Name	Team	Club/School	Pos
97	WALLIN, Niclas	Atl.-Car.	Brynas	D
98	RONNQVIST, Jonas	NYI-CBJ-Ana.	Lulea	W
99	CAVOSIE, Marc	Min.	Rensselaer	F
100	DELISLE, Miguel	T.B.-Tor.	Ottawa	RW
101	TUKIO, Arto	NYI	Ilves	D
102	LIV, Stefan	Nsh.-Det.	HV 71	G
103	NOWAK, James Brett	Bos.	Harvard	F
104	DISALVATORE, Jon	NYR-S.J.	Providence	RW
105	GORBUNOV, Vladimir	T.B.-Cgy.-NYI	HC Moscow	D
106	BALAN, Scott	Chi.	Regina	D
107	MALLETTE, Carl	Van.-Atl.	Victoriaville	C
108	ROBSON, Blake	Ana.-Car.-Atl.	Portland	LW
109	ENEQVIST, Johan	Mtl.	Leksand Jr.	LW
110	NEWMAN, Jared	Car.	Plymouth	D
111	ROUSSEAU, Ghyslain	Buf.	Baie Comeau	G
112	DUBEN, Premsyl	S.J.-NYR	Dukla Jihlava	D
113	DICKENSON, Lou	Edm.	Mississauga	F
114	LARRIVEE, Christian	Pit.-Mtl.	Chicoutimi	C
115	EADE, Chris	Phx.-Fla.	North Bay	D
116	SZUPER, Levente	Buf.-Wsh.-Cgy.	Ottawa	G
117	MALMIVAARA, Olli	L.A.-Chi.	Jokerit Jr.	D
118	VISNOVSKY, Lubomir	Ott.-L.A.	Bratislava	D
119	FAHEY, Brian	Col.	U. of Wisconsin	D
120	PARLEY, Davis	Fla.	Kamloops	G
121	VANBUSKIRK, Ryan	Tor.-Ana.-Chi.-Wsh.	Sarnia	D
122	BYFUGLIEN, Derrick	Ott.	Fargo	D
123	KHOMITSKY, Vadim	Dal.	HC Moscow	D
124	OUELLET, Michel	Wsh.-Ana.-Mtl.-Pit.	Rimouski	RW
125	COLE, Phil	N.J.	Lethbridge	D
126	HAGGLUND, Johan	Phi.-T.B.	MoDo Jr.	C
127	SEMENOV, Dmitri	Det.	Dynamo Moscow 2	RW
128	SELUYANOV, Alexander	Det.	Ufa	D
129	RIDDLE, Troy	St.L.	Des Moines	F
130	VAN LEUSEN, Aaron	Det.	Brampton	F

ROUND #5

#	Name	Team	Club/School	Pos
131	HENDRICKS, Matt	Atl.-Nsh.	Blaine	C
132	SUCHINSKY, Maxim	Min.	Omsk	RW
133	NUMMELIN, Petteri	CBJ	Davos	D
134	PODHRADSKY, Peter	T.B.-Ana.	Bratislava	D
135	JEFFERSON, Mike	N.J.	Barrie	C
136	UPPER, Dmitri	NYI	Nizhny Novgorod	C
137	STUART, Mike	Nsh.	Colorado College	D
138	HEFFERNAN, Scott	Bos.-CBJ	Sarnia	C
139	BERNIKOV, Ruslan	Dal.	Khabarovsk	RW
140	MARTZ, Nathan	NYR	Chilliwack	C
141	DAVIS, Wade	Cgy.	Calgary	D
142	PINC, Michal	Chi.-S.J.	Rouyn-Noranda	C
143	SNEE, Brandon	S.J.-NYR	Union College	G
144	DUMA, Pavel	Van.	Nizhnekamsk	C
145	GLENN, Ryan	Ana.-Mtl.	Walpole	D
146	KOCI, David	Mtl.-Pit.	Sparta Praha Jr.	D
147	McRAE, Matt	Car.-Atl.	Cornell University	C
148	OTTOSON, Kristofer	Phi.-Car.-NYI	Djurgarden	RW
149	DENISOV, Dennis	Buf.	HC Moscow	D
150	KOLARIK, Tyler	S.J.-Buf.-CBJ	Deerfield	C
151	BARKUNOV, Alexander	L.A.-Wsh.-Chi.	Yaroslavl 2	D
152	FLACHE, Paul	Edm.	Brampton	D
153	CASS, Bill	Ana.-Pit.	Boston College	D
154	KOALSKA, Matt	Phx.-Edm.-Nsh.	Twin Cities	C
155	MOEN, Travis	Cgy.	Kelowna	LW
156	ZANON, Greg	L.A.-Ott.	U. of Nebraska-Omaha	C
157	POTULNY, Grant	L.A.-Ott.	Lincoln	C
158	CONNOLLY, Sean	Ott.	Northern Michigan	D
159	LILES, John-Michael	Col.	Michigan State	D
160	KISER, Nate	Fla.-Phx.	Plymouth	D
161	SEDOV, Pavel	Tor.-T.B.	Khimik	LW
162	CHERNOV, Artem	Dal.	Novokuznetsk	C
163	NEPRYAYEV, Ivan	Wsh.	Yaroslavl 2	C
164	KOSTUR, Matus	N.J.	Zvolen	G
165	MARSTERS, Nathan	Phi.-L.A.	Chilliwack	G
166	SCHAEFER, Nolan	Det.-S.J.	Providence College	G
167	WELLER, Craig	St.L.	Calgary Canucks	D

ROUND #6

#	Name	Team	Club/School	Pos
168	SMID, Zdenek	Atl.	Karlovy Vary	G
169	BENDERA, Shane	CBJ	Red Deer	G
170	REITZ, Erik	Min.	Barrie	D
171	CECHMANEK, Roman	T.B.-Phi.	Vsetin	G
172	SELIG, Scott	Phi.-NYI-Mtl.	Thayer Academy	C/RW
173	HARANT, Tomas	Nsh.	Zilina	D
174	KULTANEN, Jarno	Bos.	HIFK	D
175	HELFENSTEIN, Sven	NYR	Kloten	LW
176	HENTUNEN, Jukka	Cgy.	HPK	RW
177	AYERS, Michael	Chi.	Dubuque	G
178	DWYER, Jeff	Phi.-Van.-Atl.	Choate	D
179	SOZINOV, Vadim	Ana.-Tor.	Novokuznetsk 2	C
180	HORDICHUK, Darcy	Mtl.-Atl.	Saskatoon	LW
181	FORREST, Justin	Car.	US National Under 18	D
182	CHVOJKA, Petr	Buf.-Mtl.	Plzen Jr.	D
183	MACHO, Michal	S.J.	Martin	C
184	NORRIE, Shaun	Edm.	Calgary	RW
185	FOLEY, Patrick	Pit.	New Hampshire	LW
186	GAUVREAU, Brent	Phx.	Oshawa	C
187	BACKER, Per	L.A.-Det.	Grums	RW
188	MALEYKO, Jason	Ott.	Brampton	D
189	BAHEN, Chris	Col.	Clarkson	D
190	OLSON, Josh	Fla.	Omaha	LW
191	GIONET, Aaron	Tor.-T.B.	Kamloops	D
192	VLCEK, Ladislav	Dal.	Kladno	RW
193	MARTIN, Joey	Wsh.-Chi.	Omaha	D
194	ENGELLAND, Deryk	N.J.	Moose Jaw	D
195	SHIELDS, Colin	Phi.	Cleveland	RW
196	BALLANTYNE, Paul	Det.	Sault Ste. Marie	D
197	IRGL, Zbynek	St.L.-Nsh.	Vitkovice	C

ROUND #7

#	Name	Team	Club/School	Pos
198	MAGOWAN, Ken	Atl.-N.J.	Vernon	LW
199	PASSMORE, Brian	Min.	Oshawa	C
200	JOKILA, Janne	CBJ	TPS Jr.	LW
201	FEDEROV, Yevgeny	T.B.-Wsh.-L.A.	Perm	C
202	CALDWELL, Ryan	NYI-T.B.-NYI	Thunder Bay	D
203	PENKO, Jure	Nsh.	Green Bay	C
204	BERTI, Chris	Bos.	Sarnia	C/LW
205	LUNDQVIST, Henrik	NYR	V. Frolunda Jr.	G
206	ERIKSSON, Tim	Cgy.-Wsh.-L.A.	V. Frolunda Jr.	C
207	LOYA, Cliff	Chi.	U. of Maine	C
208	REID, Brandon	Van.	Halifax	C
209	SEIKOLA, Markus	Ana.-Tor.	TPS Jr.	D
210	EICHELBERGER, John	Mtl.-T.B.-Phi.	Green Bay,	C/LW
211	CULLEN, Joe	Edm.	Colorado Coll.	C
212	KAHNBERG, Magnus	Car.	V. Frolunda Jr.	LW
213	BIZYAYEV, Vasili	Buf.	HC Moscow	RW
214	BARTOS, Peter	S.J.-Min.	Budejovice	C
215	LOMBARDI, Matthew	Edm.	Victoriaville	C
216	ABBOTT, Jim	Pit.	U. of New Hampshire	LW
217	SAMOILOV, Igor	Phx.	Yaroslavl 2	D
218	OLYNICK, Craig	L.A.	Seattle	D
219	TUOKKO, Marco	Dal.	TPS	C
220	GAUSTAD, Paul	Ott.-T.B.--Buf.	Portland	C/LW
221	MOLNAR, Aaron	Col.	London	G
222	PRIECHODSKY, Marek	Fla.-T.B.	Trnava	D
223	VELEBNY, Lubos	Tor.	Zvolen Jr.	D
224	MIETTINEN, Antti	Dal.	HPK	C
225	LUCHKIN, Vladislav	Wsh.-Chi.	Cherepovets 2	C
226	EKLUND, Brian	N.J.-T.B.	Brown U.	G
227	LEFEBVRE, Guillaume	Phi.	Rouyn Noranda	C
228	SVENSSON, Jimmie	Det.	Vasteras Jr.	D
229	LUTES, Brett	St.L.	Montreal	LW

ROUND #8

#	Name	Team	Club/School	Pos
230	ISOSALO, Samu	Atl.	North Bay	RW
231	ZINGONI, Peter	CBJ	New England	C
232	SEKERAS, Lubomir	Min.	Trinec	D
233	POLUKEYEV, Alexander	T.B.	SKA St.Petersburg 2	G
234	SPRUKTS, Janis	NYI-Fla.	Lukko Jr.	C
235	KOWALSKI, Craig	Car.	Compuware	G
236	CHRISTEEN, Mats	Nsh.	Sodertalje Jr.	D
237	KUTLAK, Zdenek	Bos.	Budejovice	D
238	EBERLY, Dan	NYR	RPI	D
239	HAJEK, David	Cgy.	Chomutov	D
240	BERKHOEL, Adam	Chi.	Twin Cities	G
241	BARRETT, Nathan	Van.	Lethbridge	C
242	NIELSEN, Evan	Ana.-Atl.	U. of Notre Dame	D
243	PUURULA, Joni	Mtl.	Hermes	G
244	BOWEN, Eric	Car.-Atl.	Portland	RW
245	WELCH, Dan	Buf.-L.A.	U. of Minnesota	RW
246	WISEMAN, Chad	S.J.	Mississauga	LW
247	PLATT, Jason	Edm.	Omaha	D
248	CRAMPTON, Steven	Pit.	Moose Jaw	RW
249	VENALAINEN, Sami	Phx.	Tappara Jr.	RW
250	CONNE, Flavien	L.A.	Fribourg	C
251	JACKSON, Todd	Ott.-Det.	US National Team	RW
252	BOOTLAND, Darryl	Col.	Toronto St. Michael's	RW
253	SOMMERFELD, Matthew	Fla.	Swift Current	LW
254	SHINKAR, Alexander	Tor.	Cherepovets	RW
255	JOHANSSON, Eric	Dal.-Min.	Tri-City	C
256	SAARINEN, Pasi	Wsh.-S.J.	Ilves	D
257	McCUTCHEON, Warren	N.J.	Lethbridge	C
258	McMORROW, Sean	Cgy.-Buf.	Kitchener	RW
259	KELLY, Regan	Phi.	Nipawin	D
260	BUMAGIN, Yevgeni	Det.	Lada Togliatti 2	C
261	DIVIS, Reinhad	St.L.	Leksand	G

ROUND #9

#	Name	Team	Club/School	Pos
262	FLACHE, Peter	Atl.-Chi.	Guelph	C
263	ZIEGLER, Thomas	Min.-N.J.-T.B.	Ambri	RW
264	ALTAREV, Dmitri	CBJ-NYI	Penza	LW
265	COTE, Jean-Phillipe	T.B.-Tor.	Cape Breton	D
266	KOTARY, Sean	NYI-Col.	Northwood Prep	C
267	PETTINEN, Tomi	Nsh.-NYI	Ilves	D
268	KOLARIK, Pavel	Bos.	Slavia Praha	D
269	RICHTER, Martin	NYR	SaiPa	D
270	DUPONT, Micki	Cgy.	Kamloops	D
271	von ARX, Reto	Chi.	Davos	C
272	SMITH, Tim	Van.	Spokane	C
273	SIMICEK, Roman	Ana.-Pit.	HPK	C
274	MURATOV, Yevgeny	Edm.	Nizhnekamsk	LW
275	GAUTHIER, Jonathan	Mtl.	Rouyn Noranda	D
276	FERGUSON, Troy	Car.	Michigan State	F
277	COURTNEY, Ryan	Buf.	Windsor	LW
278	PAROULEK, Martin	S.J.-CBJ	Vsetin	RW
279	LINDSTROM, Andreas	Edm.-Bos.	Lulea Jr.	RW
280	BOUCHER, Nick	Pit.	Dartmouth College	G
281	FABUS, Peter	Phx.	Dukla Trencin	C
282	GRAHN, Carl	L.A.	Kalpa Jr.	G
283	DEMONE, James	Ott.	Portland	D
284	HOHENER, Martin	Nsh.	Kloten	D
285	WARD, Blake	Col.	Tri City	G
286	NEDOROST, Andrej	Fla.-CBJ	Trencin Jr.	C
287	KOPECKY, Milan	Tor.-T.B.-Phi.	Slavia Praha Jr.	LW
288	McRAE, Mark	Dal.-Atl.	Cornell University	D
289	NORD, Bjorn	Cgy.-Wsh.	Djurgarden	D
290	GAMACHE, Simon	N.J.-Atl.	Val D'Or	C
291	RAMHOLT, Arne	Phi.-Chi.	Kloten	D
292	MANDEVILLE, Louie	Det.-CBJ	Rouyn Noranda	D
293	KINOS, Lauri	St.L.	Montreal	D

Draft Choices, 1999-69

1999

FIRST ROUND

	Selection	Claimed By	Amateur Club	
1	STEFAN, Patrik	T.B.-Van.-Atl.	Long Beach	C
2	SEDIN, Daniel	Atl.-Van.	MoDo	LW
3	SEDIN, Henrik	Van.	MoDo	C
4	BRENDL, Pavel	Chi.-Van.-T.B.-NYR	Calgary	RW
5	CONNOLLY, Tim	NYI	Erie	C
6	FINLEY, Brian	Nsh.	Barrie	G
7	BEECH, Kris	Wsh.	Calgary	C
8	PYATT, Taylor	L.A.-NYI	Sudbury	LW
9	LUNDMARK, Jamie	Cgy.-NYR	Moose Jaw	C
10	MEZEI, Branislav	Mtl.-NYI	Belleville	D
11	SAPRYKIN, Oleg	NYR-Cgy.	Seattle	C
12	SHVIDKY, Denis	Fla.	Barrie	RW
13	RITA, Jani	Edm.	Jokerit Helsinki	RW
14	JILLSON, Jeff	S.J.	U. of Michigan	D
15	KELMAN, Scott	Ana.-Phx.	Seattle	D
16	TANABE, David	Car.	U. of Wisconsin	D
17	JACKMAN, Barret	St.L.	Regina	D
18	KOLTSOV, Konstantin	Pit.	Cherepovets	LW
19	SAFRONOV, Kirill	Phx.	St. Petersburg	D
20	HEISTEN, Barrett	Buf.	U. of Maine	LW
21	BOYNTON, Nicholas	Bos.	Ottawa	D
22	OUELLET, Maxime	Phi.	Quebec	G
23	MCCARTHY, Steve	Det.-Chi.	Kootenay	D
24	CEREDA, Luca	Tor.	Ambri	C
25	KULESHOV, Mikhail	Col.	Cherepovets	LW
26	HAVLAT, Martin	Ott.	Trinec	C
27	AHONEN, Ari	N.J.	JyP HT Jr.	G
28	KUDROC, Kristian	Dal.-NYI	Michalovce	D

ROUND #2

29	SIVEK, Michal	T.B.-Wsh.	HC Kladno Jr.	C
30	SELLARS, Luke	Atl.	Ottawa	D
31	STEPHENS, Charlie	Van.-Col.-Wsh.	Guelph	F
32	RYAN, Michael	NYI-Dal.	Boston College H.S.	C
33	ANDERSSON, Jonas	Nsh.	AIK Solna Jr.	RW
34	LUPASCHUK, Ross	Wsh.	Prince Albert	D
35	BARTOVIC, Milan	L.A.-Buf.	Dukla Trencin Jrs.	RW
36	SEMENOV, Alexei	Edm.	Sudbury	D
37	YONKMAN, Nolan	Wsh.	Kelowna	D
38	CAVANAUGH, Dan	Cgy.	Boston University	F
39	BUTURLIN, Alexander	Mtl.	CSKA Moscow Jr.	LW
40	AULD, Alexander	St.L.-Fla.	North Bay	G
41	SALMELAINEN, Tony	Edm.	HIFK Helsinki	LW
42	COMMODORE, Mike	N.J.	U. of North Dakota	D
43	SHEFER, Andrei	L.A.	Cherepovets	LW
44	LEOPOLD, Jordan	NYR-Ott.-Ana.	U. of Minnesota	D
45	GRENIER, Martin	Fla.-Nsh.-Col.	Quebec	D
46	LEVINSKY, Dmitri	Chi.	Cherepovets	RW
47	KEEFE, Sheldon	S.J.-Det.-T.B.	Barrie	RW
48	LAJEUNESSE, Simon	Ana.-Ott.	Moncton	G
49	LYSAK, Brett	Car.	Regina	C
50	CLOUTHIER, Brett	St.L.-NYI	Kingston	LW
51	MURLEY, Matt	Pit.	R.P.I.	LW
52	HALL, Adam	Nsh.	Michigan State	RW
53	RALPH, Brad	Phx.	Oshawa	LW
54	HUTCHINSON, Andrew	Col.-Nsh.	Michigan State	D
55	JANIK, Doug	Buf.	U. of Maine	D
56	ZULTEK, Matt	Bos.	Ottawa	LW
57	VAN HOOF, Jeremy	Pit.	Ottawa	D
58	CARKNER, Matt	Phi.-Mtl.	Peterborough	D
59	INMAN, David	Det.-NYR	U. of Notre Dame	C
60	REYNOLDS, Peter	Tor.	London	D
61	HILL, Ed	Col.-Nsh.	Barrie	D
62	SAINOMAA, Teemu	Ott.	Jokerit Helsinki Jr.	LW
63	MOKHOV, Stepan	N.J.-Chi.	Cherepovets	D
64	ZIGOMANIS, Michael	Dal.-Buf.	Kingston	C
65	LASAK, Jan	Nsh.	ZTK Zvolen Jr.	G
66	JANCEVSKI, Dan	St.L.-Dal.	London	D

1998

FIRST ROUND

	Selection	Claimed By	Amateur Club	
1	LECAVALIER, Vincent	Fla.-S.J.-T.B.	Rimouski	C
2	LEGWAND, David	T.B.-S.J.-Nsh.	Plymouth	C
3	STUART, Brad	Nsh.-S.J.	Regina	D
4	ALLEN, Bryan	Van.	Oshawa	D
5	VISHNEVSKY, Vitaly	Ana.	Torpedo-2 Yaroslavl	D
6	FATA, Rico	Cgy.	London	C
7	MALHOTRA, Manny	NYR	Guelph	C
8	BELL, Mark	Tor.-Chi.	Ottawa	LW
9	RUPP, Michael	NYI	Erie	LW
10	ANTROPOV, Nikolai	Chi.-Tor.	Torpedo Ust-Kamenogorsk	C
11	HEEREMA, Jeff	Car.	Sarnia	RW
12	TANGUAY, Alex	S.J.-Col.	Halifax	C
13	HENRICH, Michael	Edm.	Barrie	RW
14	DESROCHERS, Patrick	Phx.	Sarnia	G
15	CHOUINARD, Mathieu	Ott.	Shawinigan	G
16	CHOUINARD, Eric	Mtl.	Quebec	C
17	SKOULA, Martin	L.A.-Col.	Barrie	D
18	KALININ, Dimitri	Buf.	Traktor Chelyabinsk	D
19	REGEHER, Robyn	Bos.-Col.	Kamloops	D
20	PARKER, Scott	Wsh.-Col.	Kelowna	D
21	BIRON, Mathieu	Col.-L.A.	Shawinigan	D
22	GAGNE, Simon	Phi.-T.B.-Phi.	Quebec	C
23	KRAFT, Milan	T.B.	Keramika Plzen Jr.	C
24	BACKMAN, Christian	St.L.	Vastra Frolunda Jr.	D
25	FISCHER, Jiri	Det.	Hull	D
26	VAN RYN, Mike	N.J.	U. of Michigan	D
27	GOMEZ, Scott	Dal.-N.J.	Tri-City	C

SECOND ROUND

28	ABID, Ramzi	T.B.-Col.	Chicoutimi	LW
29	CHEECHOO, Jonathon	Nsh.-S.J.	Belleville	RW
30	ROSSITER, Kyle	Fla.	Spokane	D
31	CHUBAROV, Artem	Van.	Dynamo Moscow	C
32	PEAT, Stephen	Ana.	Red Deer	D
33	BETTS, Blair	Cgy.	Prince George	C
34	PETERS, Andrew	NYR-Buf.	Oshawa	LW
35	SVOBODA, Petr	Tor.	Havlickuv Brod	D
36	NEILSON, Chris	NYI	Calgary	D
37	BERGLUND, Christian	N.J.	Farjestad Karlstad Jr.	C
38	SAUVE, Philippe	Chi-Col.	Rimouski	G
39	ERSKINE, John	Car.-N.J.-Dal.	London	D
40	COPLEY, Randy	NYR	Cape Breton	RW
41	LINNIK, Maxim	S.J.-Det.-St.L.	St. Thomas Jr. B	D
42	BECKETT, Jason	Edm.-Phi.	Seattle	D
43	VAANANEN, Ossi	Phx.	Jokerit Helsinki Jr.	D
44	FISHER, Mike	Ott.	Sudbury	C
45	RIBEIRO, Mike	Mtl.	Rouyn-Noranda	C
46	PAPINEAU, Justin	L.A.	Belleville	C
47	MILLEY, Norman	Buf.	Sudbury	RW
48	GIRARD, Jonathon	Bos.	Laval	D
49	CRUZ, Jomar	Wsh.	Brandon	G
50	KRISTEK, Jaroslav	Col.-S.J.-Buf.	ZPS Zlin	RW
51	FORBES, Ian	Phi.	Guelph	D
52	ALLEN, Bobby	Bos.	Boston College	D
53	MOORE, Steve	Col.	Harvard	C
54	ZEVAKHIN, Alexander	Pit.	CSKA Moscow	RW
55	BARNES, Ryan	St.L.-Det.	Sudbury	LW
56	VALTONEN, Tomek	Det.	Ilves Tampere Jr.	LW
57	BOUCK, Tyler	N.J.-Dal.	Prince George	RW
58	BALA, Chris	Dal.-Phi.-Ott.	Harvard	LW

1997

FIRST ROUND

	Selection	Claimed By	Amateur Club	
1	THORNTON, Joe	Bos.	Sault Ste. Marie	C
2	MARLEAU, Patrick	S.J.	Seattle	C
3	JOKINEN, Olli	L.A.	HIFK Helsinki	C
4	LUONGO, Roberto	Tor.-NYI	Val D'Or	G
5	BREWER, Eric	NYI	Prince George	D
6	TKACZUK, Daniel	Cgy.	Barrie	C
7	MARA, Paul	T.B.	Sudbury	D
8	SAMSONOV, Sergei	Car.-Bos.	Detroit	LW
9	BOYNTON, Nicholas	Wsh.	Ottawa	D
10	FERENCE, Brad	Van.	Spokane	D
11	WARD, Jason	Mtl.	Erie	C
12	HOSSA, Marian	Ott.	Dukla Trencin	RW
13	CLEARY, Daniel	Chi.	Belleville	LW
14	RIESEN, Michel	Edm.	Biel-Bienne	LW
15	ZULTEK, Matt	St.L.-Edm.-St.L.-L.A.	Ottawa	C
16	JONES, Ty	Pho.-Chi.	Spokane	RW
17	DOME, Robert	Pit.	Long Beach/ Las Vegas	RW
18	HOLMQVIST, Mikael	Ana.	Djurgarden	C
19	CHERNESKI, Stefan	NYR	Brandon	RW
20	BROWN, Mike	Fla.	Red Deer	C
21	NORONEN, Mika	Buf.	Tappara Tampere	G
22	TSELIOS, Nikos	Det.-Car.	Belleville	D
23	HANNAN, Scott	Phi.-Car.-S.J.	Kelowna	D
24	DAMPHOUSSE, J-F	N.J.	Moncton	G
25	MORROW, Brenden	Dal.	Portland	LW
26	GRIMES, Kevin	Col.	Kingston	D

SECOND ROUND

27	CLYMER, Ben	Bos.	U. of Minnesota	D
28	DEFAUW, Brad	S.J.-Car.	U. of North Dakota	LW
29	BARNEY, Scott	L.A.	Peterborough	C
30	PELLETIER, Jean-Marc	Tor.-Phi.	Cornell U.	G
32	ZEHR, Jeff	NYI	Windsor	LW
32	LINDSAY, Evan	Cgy.	Prince Albert	G
34	KOS, Kyle	T.B.	Red Deer	D
34	BONNI, Ryan	Car.-Van.	Saskatoon	D
35	FORTIN, J-F	Wsh.	Sherbrooke	D
36	DRUKEN, Harold	Van.	Detroit	LW
37	BAUMGARTNER, Gregor	Mtl.	Laval	C
38	GRON, Stanislav	Ott.-N.J.	Slovan Bratislava Jr.	C
39	REICH, Jeremy	Chi.	Seattle	C
41	RENNETTE, Tyler	St.L.	North Bay	C
42	DOVIGI, Patrick	Edm.	Erie	G
42	TRIPP, John	St.L.-Cgy.	Oshawa	RW
43	GUSTAFSSON, Juha	Pho.	Kiekko-Espoo Jr.	C
44	GAFFANEY, Brian	Pit.	North Iowa Jr. A	D
46	BALMOCHNYKH, Maxim	Ana.	Lada Togliatti	LW
46	JARVIS, Wes	NYR	Kitchener	D
47	HUSELIUS, Kristian	Fla.	Farjestad Karlstad	LW
48	TALLINDER, Henrik	Buf.	AIK Solna	D
49	BUTSAYEV, Yuri	Det.	Lada Togliatti	C
50	KAVANAGH, Pat	Phi.	Peterborough	RW
51	KOKOREV, Dmitri	N.J.-Car.-Cgy.	Dynamo-2 Moscow	D
52	LYASHENKO, Roman	Dal.	Torpedo Yaroslavl	C
53	BELAK, Graham	Col.	Edmonton	D

Mike Rathje, battling in front of the Nashville bench, was selected third overall by San Jose in 1992. The Sharks have had excellent success with their top draft picks, including Brad Stuart (1998), Patrick Marleau (1997) and Jeff Friesen (1994).

1996

FIRST ROUND

Selection	Claimed By	Amateur Club	
1 PHILLIPS, Chris	Ott.	Prince Albert	D
2 ZYUZIN, Andrei	S.J.	Salavat Yulayev Ufa	D
3 DUMONT, Jean-Pierre	NYI	Val d'Or	RW
4 VOLCHKOV, Alexander	L.A.-Wsh.	Barrie	C
5 JACKMAN, Richard	Dal.	Sault Ste. Marie	D
6 DEVEREAUX, Boyd	Edm.	Kitchener	C
7 RASMUSSEN, Erik	Buf.	U. of Minnesota	C
8 AITKEN, Johnathan	Hfd.-Bos.	Medicine Hat	D
9 SALEI, Ruslan	Ana.	Las Vegas	D
10 WARD, Lance	N.J.	Red Deer	D
11 FOCHT, Dan	Pho.	Tri-City	D
12 HOLDEN, Josh	Van.	Regina	C
13 MORRIS, Derek	Cgy.	Regina	D
14 REASONER, Marty	St.L.-Edm.-St.L.	Boston College	C
15 ZUBRUS, Dainius	Tor.-Phi.	Pembroke	RW
16 LAROCQUE, Mario	T.B.	Hull	D
17 SVEJKOVSKY, Jaroslav	Wsh.	Tri-City	RW
18 HIGGINS, Matt	Mtl.	Moose Jaw	C
19 DESCOTEAUX, Matthieu	Bos.-Edm.	Shawinigan	D
20 NILSON, Marcus	Fla.	Djurgarden Stockholm	C
21 STURM, Marco	Chi.-S.J.	Landshut	C
22 BROWN, Jeff	NYR	Sarnia	D
23 HILLIER, Craig	Pit.	Ottawa	G
24 BRIERE, Daniel	Phi.-Pho.	Drummondville	C
25 RATCHUK, Peter	Col.	Shattuck St. Mary's	D
26 WALLIN, Jesse	Det.	Red Deer	D

SECOND ROUND

Selection	Claimed By	Amateur Club	
27 SARICH, Cory	Ott.-St.L.-Buf.	Saskatoon	D
28 SKRBEK, Pavel	S.J.-N.J.-Pit.	HC Kladno	D
29 LACOUTURE, Dan	NYI	Jr. Whalers	LW
30 GREEN, Josh	L.A.	Medicine Hat	LW
31 ROYER, Remi	Dal.-Pho.-S.J.-Chi.	St-Hyacinthe	D
32 HAJT, Chris	Edm.	Guelph	D
33 VAN OENE, Darren	Buf.	Brandon	LW
34 WASYLUK, Trevor	Hfd.	Medicine Hat	LW
35 CULLEN, Matt	Ana.	St. Cloud State	C
36 POSMYK, Marek	N.J.-Tor.	Dukla Jihlava	D
37 CISAR, Marian	Pho.-L.A.	Slovan Bratislava	W
38 MASON, Wesley	Van.-N.J.	Sarnia	LW
39 BRIGLEY, Travis	Cgy.	Lethbridge	LW
40 BEGIN, Steve	St.L.-Cgy.	Val d'Or	C
41 DEWOLF, Joshua	Tor.-Pit.-N.J.	Twin Cities	D
42 PAUL, Jeff	T.B.-Chi.	Niagara Falls	D
43 BULIS, Jan	Wsh.	Barrie	C
44 GARON, Mathieu	Mtl.	Victoriaville	G
45 KUSTER, Henry	Bos.	Medicine Hat	RW
46 PETERS, Geoff	Fla.-S.J.-Chi.	Niagara Falls	C
47 DAGENAIS, Pierre	Chi.-T.B.-N.J.	Moncton	LW
48 GONEAU, Daniel	NYR	Granby	LW
49 WHITE, Colin	Pit.-N.J.	Hull	D
50 LARIVEE, Francis	Phi.-Tor.	Laval	G
51 BABENKO, Yuri	Col.	Krylja Sovetov	C
52 MILLER, Aren	Det.	Spokane	G

1995

FIRST ROUND

Selection	Claimed By	Amateur Club	
1. BERARD, Bryan	Ott.	Detroit	D
2. REDDEN, Wade	NYI	Brandon	D
3. BERG, Aki-Petteri	L.A.	Kiekko-67 Turku	D
4. KILGER, Chad	Ana.	Kingston	C
5. LANGKOW, Daymond	T.B.	Tri-City	C
6. KELLY, Steve	Edm.	Prince Albert	C
7. DOAN, Shane	Wpg.	Kamloops	RW
8. RYAN, Terry	Mtl.	Tri-City	LW
9. McLAREN, Kyle	Hfd.-Bos.	Tacoma	D
10. DVORAK, Radek	Fla.	HC Ceske Budejovice	W
11. IGINLA, Jarome	Dal.	Kamloops	C
12. RIIHIJARVI, Teemu	S.J.	Kiekko-Espoo Jr.	LW
13. GIGUERE, J-Sebastien	NYR-Hfd.	Halifax	G
14. McKEE, Jay	Van.-Buf.	Niagara Falls	D
15. WARE, Jeff	Tor.	Oshawa	D
16. BIRON, Martin	Buf.	Beauport	G
17. CHURCH, Brad	Wsh.	Prince Albert	LW
18. SYKORA, Petr	N.J.	Detroit	C
19. NABOKOV, Dmitri	Chi.	Krylja Sovetov	C
20. GAUTHIER, Denis Jr.	Cgy.	Drummondville	D
21. BROWN, Sean	Bos.	Belleville	D
22. BOUCHER, Brian	Phi.	Tri-City	G
23. ELOMO, Miika	St.L.-Wsh.	Kiekko-67 Turku	LW
24. MOROZOV, Alexei	Pit.	Krylja Sovetov	RW
25. DENIS, Marc	Col.	Chicoutimi	G
26. KUZNETSOV, Maxim	Det.	Dynamo Moscow	D

SECOND ROUND

Selection	Claimed By	Amateur Club	
27. MORO, Marc	Ott.	Kingston	D
28. HLAVAC, Jan	NYI	Sparta Praha	LW
29. WESENBERG, Brian	Ana.	Guelph	RW
30. McBAIN, Mike	T.B.	Red Deer	D
31. LARAQUE, Georges	Edm.	St-Jean	RW
32. CHOUINARD, Marc	Wpg.	Beauport	C
33. MacLEAN, Donald	L.A.	Beauport	C
34. DOIG, Jason	Mtl.-Wpg.	Laval	D
35. FEDOTOV, Sergei	Hfd.	Dynamo Moscow	D
36. MacDONALD, Aaron	Fla.	Swift Current	G
37. COTE, Patrick	Dal.	Beauport	LW
38. ROED, Peter	S.J.	White Bear Lake	C
39. DUBE, Christian	NYR	Sherbrooke	C
40. McALLISTER, Chris	Van.	Saskatoon	D
41. SMITH, Denis (D.J.)	Tor.-NYI	Windsor	D
42. DUTIAUME, Mark	Buf.	Brandon	LW
43. HAY, Dwayne	Wsh.	Guelph	LW
44. PERROTT, Nathan	N.J.	Oshawa	RW
45. LAFLAMME, Christian	Chi.	Beauport	D
46. SMIRNOV, Pavel	Cgy.	Molot Perm	RW/C
47. SCHAFER, Paxton	Bos.	Medicine Hat	G
48. KENNY, Shane	Phi.	Owen Sound	D
49. HECHT, Jochen	St.L.	Mannheim	C
50. ROSA, Pavel	Pit.-L.A.	Litvinov Jr.	RW
51. BEAUDOIN, Nic	Col.	Detroit	LW
52. AUDET, Philippe	Det.	Granby	LW

1994

FIRST ROUND

Selection	Claimed By	Amateur Club	
1. JOVANOVSKI, Ed	Fla.	Windsor	D
2. TVERDOVSKY, Oleg	Ana.	Soviet Wings	D
3. BONK, Radek	Ott.	Las Vegas	C
4. BONSIGNORE, Jason	Wpg.-Edm.	Niagara Falls	C
5. O'NEILL, Jeff	Hfd.	Guelph	C
6. SMYTH, Ryan	Edm.	Moose Jaw	LW
7. STORR, Jamie	L.A.	Owen Sound	G
8. WIEMER, Jason	T.B.	Portland	LW
9. LINDROS, Brett	Que.-NYI	Kingston	RW
10. BAUMGARTNER, Nolan	Phi.-Que.-Tor.-Wsh.	Kamloops	D
11. FRIESEN, Jeff	S.J.	Regina	LW
12. BELAK, Wade	NYI-Que.	Saskatoon	D
13. OHLUND, Mattias	Van.	Pitea	D
14. MOREAU, Ethan	Chi.	Niagara Falls	LW
15. KHARLAMOV, Alexander	Wsh.	CSKA Moscow	C
16. FICHAUD, Eric	St.L.-Wsh.-Tor.	Chicoutimi	G
17. PRIMEAU, Wayne	Buf.	Owen Sound	C
18. BROWN, Brad	Mtl.	North Bay	C
19. DINGMAN, Chris	Cgy.	Brandon	LW
20. BOTTERILL, Jason	Dal.	U. of Michigan	LW
21. RYABCHIKOV, Evgeni	Bos.	Molot Perm	G
22. KEALTY, Jeffrey	Tor.-Que.	Catholic Memorial	D
23. GOLUBOVSKY, Yan	Det.	CSKA Jr. Moscow	D
24. WELLS, Chris	Pit.	Seattle	G
25. SHARIFIJANOV, Vadim	N.J.	Salavat Yulayev ufa	RW
26. CLOUTIER, Dan	NYR	Sault Ste. Marie	G

SECOND ROUND

Selection	Claimed By	Amateur Club	
27. WARRENER, Rhett	Fla.	Saskatoon	D
28. DAVIDSSON, Johan	Ana.	HV 71	C
29. NECKAR, Stanislav	Ott.	Ceske Budejovice	D
30. QUINT, Deron	Wpg.	Seattle	D
31. PODOLLAN, Jason	Hfd.-Fla.	Spokane	C
32. WATT, Mike	Edm.	Stratford Jr. B	LW
33. JOHNSON, Matt	L.A.	Peterborough	LW
34. CLOUTIER, Colin	T.B.	Brandon	C
35. MARHA, Josef	Que.	Dukla Jihlava	C
36. JOHNSON, Ryan	Phi.-Fla.	Thunder Bay Jr. A	C
37. NIKOLOV, Angel	S.J.	Litvinov	D
38. HOLLAND, Jason	NYI	Kamloops	D
39. GORDON, Robb	Van.	Powell River Jr. A	C
40. LEROUX, Jean-Yves	Chi.	Beauport	LW
41. CHERREY, Scott	Wsh.	North Bay	LW
42. SCATCHARD, Dave	St.L.-Van.	Portland	C
43. BROWN, Curtis	Buf.	Moose Jaw	C
44. THEODORE, Jose	Mtl.	St-Jean	G
45. RYABYKIN, Dmitri	Cgy.	Dynamo-2	D
46. JINMAN, Lee	Dal.	North Bay	C
47. GONEAU, Daniel	Bos.	Laval	LW
48. HAGGERTY, Sean	Tor.	Detroit	LW
49. DANDENAULT, Mathieu	Det.	Sherbrooke	RW
50. PARK, Richard	Pit.	Belleville	C
51. ELIAS, Patrik	N.J.	Kladno	LW
52. VERCIK, Rudolf	NYR	Slovan Bratislava	LW

1993

FIRST ROUND

Selection	Claimed By	Amateur Club	
1. DAIGLE, Alexandre	Ott.	Victoriaville	C
2. PRONGER, Chris	S.J.-Hfd.	Peterborough	D
3. GRATTON, Chris	T.B.	Kingston	C
4. KARIYA, Paul	Ana.	University of Maine	LW
5. NIEDERMAYER, Rob	Fla.	Medicine Hat	C
6. KOZLOV, Viktor	Hfd.-S.J.	Dynamo Moscow	LW
7. ARNOTT, Jason	Edm.	Oshawa	C
8. SUNDSTROM, Niklas	NYR	MoDo	LW
9. HARVEY, Todd	Dal.	Detroit	C
10. THIBAULT, Jocelyn	Phi.-Que.	Sherbrooke	G
11. WITT, Brendan	St. L.-Wsh.	Seattle	D
12. JONSSON, Kenny	Buf.-Tor.	Rogle Angelholm	D
13. PEDERSON, Denis	N.J.	Prince Albert	C
14. DEADMARSH, Adam	NYI-Que.	Portland	C
15. LINDGREN, Mats	Wpg.	Skelleftea	C
16. STAJDUHAR, Nick	L.A.-Edm.	London	D
17. ALLISON, Jason	Wsh.	London	C
18. MATTSSON, Jesper	Cgy.	Malmo	C
19. WILSON, Landon	Tor.	Dubuque Jr. A	RW
20. WILSON, Mike	Van.	Sudbury	D
21. KOIVU, Saku	Mtl.	TPS Turku	C
22. ERIKSSON, Anders	Det.	MoDo	D
23. BERTUZZI, Todd	Que.-NYI	Guelph	C
24. LECOMPTE, Eric	Chi.	Hull	LW
25. ADAMS, Kevyn	Bos.	Miami-Ohio	C
26. BERGQVIST, Stefan	Pit.	Leksand	D

SECOND ROUND

Selection	Claimed By	Amateur Club	
27. BICANEK, Radim	Ott.	Dukla Jihlava	D
28. DONOVAN, Shean	S.J.	Ottawa	RW
29. MOSS, Tyler	T.B.	Kingston	G
30. TSULYGIN, Nikolai	Ana.	Salavat Yulalev Ufa	D
31. LANGKOW, Scott	Fla.-Wpg.	Portland	G
32. PANDOLFO, Jay	Hfd.-N.J.	Boston University	LW
33. VYBORNY, David	Edm.	Sparta Praha	C
34. SOROCHAN, Lee	NYR	Lethbridge	D
35. LANGENBRUNNER, Jamie	Dal.	Cloquet	C
36. NIINIMAA, Janne	Phi.	Karpat Oulu	D
37. BETS, Maxim	St. L.	Spokane	LW
38. TSYGUROV, Denis	Buf.	Lada Togliatti	D
39. MORRISON, Brendan	N.J.	Penticton T-II Jr. A	C
40. McCABE, Bryan	NYI	Spokane	D
41. WEEKES, Kevin	Wpg.-Fla.	Owen Sound	G
42. TOPOROWSKI, Shayne	L.A.	Prince Albert	RW
43. BUDAYEV, Alexei	Wsh.-Wpg.	Kristall Elektrostal	C
44. ALLISON, Jamie	Cgy.	Detroit	D
45. KROUPA, Vlastimil	Tor.-Hfd.-S.J.	Chemopetrol Litvinov	D
46. GIRARD, Rick	Van.	Swift Current	C
47. FITZPATRICK, Rory	Mtl.	Sudbury	D
48. COLEMAN, Jonathan	Det.	Andover Academy	D
49. BUCKBERGER, Ashley	Que.	Swift Current	RW
50. MANLOW, Eric	Chi.	Kitchener	C
51. ALVEY, Matt	Bos.	Springfield Jr. B	RW
52. PITTIS, Domenic	Pit.	Lethbridge	C

1992

FIRST ROUND

Selection	Claimed By	Amateur Club	
1. HAMRLIK, Roman	T.B.	ZPS Zlin	D
2. YASHIN, Alexei	Ott.	Dynamo Moscow	C
3. RATHJE, Mike	S.J.	Medicine Hat	D
4. WARRINER, Todd	Que.	Windsor	LW
5. KASPARAITIS, Darius	Tor.-NYI	Dynamo Moscow	D
6. STILLMAN, Cory	Cgy.	Windsor	C
7. SITTLER, Ryan	Phi.	Nichols	LW
8. CONVERY, Brandon	NYI-Tor.	Sudbury	C
9. PETROVICKY, Robert	Hfd.	Dukla Trencin	C
10. NAZAROV, Andrei	Min.-S.J.	Dynamo Moscow	LW
11. COOPER, David	Buf.	Medicine Hat	D
12. KRIVOKRASOV, Sergei	Wpg.-Chi.	CSKA Moscow	RW
13. HULBIG, Joe	Edm.	St. Sebastian's	LW
14. GONCHAR, Sergei	St.L.-Wsh.	Chelybinsk	D
15. BOWEN, Jason	L.A.-Pit.-Phi.	Tri-City	LW
16. KVARTALNOV, Dmitri	Bos.	San Diego	LW
17. BAUTIN, Sergei	Chi.-Wpg.	Dynamo Moscow	D
18. SMITH, Jason	N.J.	Regina	D
19. STRAKA, Martin	Pit.	Skoda Plzen	C
20. WILKIE, David	Mtl.	Kamloops	D
21. POLASEK, Libor	Van.	TJ Vitkovice	C
22. BOWEN, Curtis	Det.	Ottawa	LW
23. MARSHALL, Grant	Wsh.-Tor.	Ottawa	RW
24. FERRARO, Peter	NYR	Waterloo Jr. A	C

SECOND ROUND

Selection	Claimed By	Amateur Club	
25. PENNEY, Chad	Ott.	North Bay	LW
26. BANNISTER, Drew	T.B.	Sault-Ste-Marie	D
27. MIRONOV, Boris	S.J.-Chi.-Wpg.	CSKA Moscow	D
28. BROUSSEAU, Paul	Que.	Hull	RW
29. GRONMAN, Toumas	Tor.-Que.	Tacoma	D
30. O'SULLIVAN, Chris	Cgy.	Catholic Memorial	D
31. METLYUK, Denis	Phi.	Lada Togliatti	C
32. CAREY, Jim	NYI-Tor.-Wsh.	Catholic Memorial	G
33. BURE, Valeri	Hfd.-Mtl.	Spokane	LW
34. VARVIO, Jarkko	Min.	HPK	RW
35. CIERNY, Jozef	Buf.	ZTK Zvolen	LW
36. SHANTZ, Jeff	Wpg.-Chi.	Regina	C
37. REICHEL, Martin	Edm.	Freiburg	RW
38. KOROLEV, Igor	St.L.	Dynamo Moscow	RW
39. HOCKING, Justin	L.A.	Spokane	D
40. PECA, Mike	Bos.-Van.	Ottawa	C
41. KLIMOVICH, Sergei	Chi.	Dynamo Moscow	C
42. BRYLIN, Sergei	N.J.	CSKA Moscow	C
43. HUSSEY, Marc	Pit.	Moose Jaw	D
44. CORPSE, Keli	Mtl.	Kingston	C
45. FOUNTAIN, Michael	Van.	Oshawa	G
46. McCARTY, Darren	Det.	Belleville	RW
47. NIKOLISHIN, Andrei	Wsh.-Hfd.	Dynamo Moscow	LW
48. NORSTROM, Mattias	NYR	AIK	D

1991

FIRST ROUND

Selection	Claimed By	Amateur Club	
1. LINDROS, Eric	Que.	Oshawa	C
2. FALLOON, Pat	S.J.	Spokane	RW
3. NIEDERMAYER, Scott	Tor.-N.J.	Kamloops	D
4. LACHANCE, Scott	NYI	Boston University	D
5. WARD, Aaron	Wpg.	U. of Michigan	D
6. FORSBERG, Peter	Phi.	MoDo	C
7. STOJANOV, Alex	Van.	Hamilton	RW
8. MATVICHUK, Richard	Min.	Saskatoon	D
9. POULIN, Patrick	Hfd.	St.-Hyacinthe	LW
10. LAPOINTE, Martin	Det.	Laval	RW
11. ROLSTON, Brian	N.J.	Detroit Comp. Jr. A	C
12. WRIGHT, Tyler	Edm.	Swift Current	C
13. BOUCHER, Phillipe	Buf.	Granby	D
14. PEAKE, Pat	Wsh.	Detroit	C
15. KOVALEV, Alexei	NYR	D'amo Moscow	RW
16. NASLUND, Markus	Pit.	MoDo	RW
17. BILODEAU, Brent	Mtl.	Seattle	D
18. MURRAY, Glen	Bos.	Sudbury	RW
19. SUNDBLAD, Niklas	Cgy.	AIK	RW
20. RUCINSKY, Martin	L.A.-Edm.	CHZ Litvinov	LW
21. HALVERSON, Trevor	St.L.-Wsh.	North Bay	LW
22. McAMMOND, Dean	Chi.	Prince Albert	C

SECOND ROUND

Selection	Claimed By	Amateur Club	
23. WHITNEY, Ray	S.J.	Spokane	C
24. CORBET, Rene	Que.	Drummondville	LW
25. LAVIGNE, Eric	Tor.-Que.-Wsh.	Hull	D
26. PALFFY, Zigmund	NYI	AC Nitra	LW
27. STAIOS, Steve	Wpg.-St.L.	Niagara Falls	D
28. CAMPBELL, Jim	Phi.-Mtl.	Northwood Prep	C
29. CULLIMORE, Jassen	Van.	Peterborough	D
30. OZOLINSH, Sandis	Min.-S.J.	Dynamo Riga	D
31. HAMRLIK, Martin	Hfd.	TJ Zin	D
32. PUSHOR, Jamie	Det.	Lethbridge	D
33. HEXTALL, Donevan	N.J.	Prince Albert	LW
34. VERNER, Andrew	Edm.	Peterborough	G
35. DAWE, Jason	Buf.	Peterborough	LW
36. NELSON, Jeff	Wsh.	Prince Albert	C
37. WERENKA, Darcy	NYR	Lethbridge	D
38. FITZGERALD, Rusty	Pit.	Duluth East HS	C
39. POMICHTER, Michael	Mtl.-Chi.	Springfield Jr. B	C
40. STUMPEL, Jozef	Bos.	AC Nitra	RW
41. GROLEAU, Francois	Cgy.	Shawinigan	D
42. LEVEQUE, Guy	L.A.	Cornwall	C
43. DARBY, Craig	St.L.-Mtl.	Albany Academy	C
44. MATTHEWS, Jamie	Chi.	Sudbury	C

1990

FIRST ROUND

Selection	Claimed By	Amateur Club	
1. NOLAN, Owen	Que.	Cornwall	RW
2. NEDVED, Petr	Van.	Seattle	C
3. PRIMEAU, Keith	Det.	Niagara Falls	C
4. RICCI, Mike	Phi.	Peterborough	C
5. JAGR, Jaromir	Pit.	Poldi Kladno	LW
6. SCISSONS, Scott	NYI	Saskatoon	C
7. SYDOR, Darryl	L.A.	Kamloops	D
8. HATCHER, Derian	Min.	North Bay	D
9. SLANEY, John	Wsh.	Cornwall	D
10. BEREHOWSKY, Drake	Tor.	Kingston	D
11. KIDD, Trevor	N.J.-Cgy.	Brandon	G
12. STEVENSON, Turner	St.L.-Mtl.	Seattle	RW
13. STEWART, Michael	NYR	Michigan State	D
14. MAY, Brad	Wpg.-Buf.	Niagara Falls	LW
15. GREIG, Mark	Hfd.	Lethbridge	RW
16. DYKHUIS, Karl	Chi.	Hull	D
17. ALLISON, Scott	Edm.	Prince Albert	C
18. ANTOSKI, Shawn	Mtl.-St.L.-Van.	North Bay	LW
19. TKACHUK, Keith	Buf.-Wpg.	Malden Catholic	LW
20. BRODEUR, Martin	Cgy.-N.J.	St. Hyacinthe	G
21. SMOLINSKI, Bryan	Bos.	Michigan State	C

SECOND ROUND

Selection	Claimed By	Amateur Club	
22. HUGHES, Ryan	Que.	Cornell	C
23. SLEGR, Jiri	Van.	CHZ Litvinov	D
24. HARLOCK, David	Det.-Cgy.-N.J.	U. of Michigan	D
25. SIMON, Chris	Phi.	Ottawa	LW
26. PERREAULT, Nicolas P.	Pit.-Cgy.	Hawkesbury Jr. A	D
27. TAYLOR, Chris	NYI	London	C
28. SEMCHUK, Brandy	L.A.	Canadian National	RW
29. GOTZIAMAN, Chris	Min.-Cgy.-N.J.	Roseau	RW
30. PASMA, Rod	Wsh.	Cornwall	D
31. POTVIN, Felix	Tor.	Chicoutimi	G
32. VIITAKOSKI, Vesa	N.J.-Cgy.	SaiPa	LW
33. JOHNSON, Craig	St.L.	Hill-Murray HS	C
34. WEIGHT, Doug	NYR	Lake Superior	C
35. MULLER, Mike	Wpg.	Wayzata	D
36. SANDERSON, Geoff	Hfd.	Swift Current	C
37. DROPPA, Ivan	Chi.	Partizan	D
38. LEGAULT, Alexandre	Edm.	Boston University	RW
39. KUWABARA, Ryan	Mtl.	Ottawa	RW
40. RENBERG, Mikael	Buf.-Phi.	Pitea	LW
41. BELZILE, Etienne	Cgy.	Cornell	D
42. SANDWITH, Terran	Bos.-Phi.	Tri-City	D

1989

FIRST ROUND

Selection	Claimed By	Amateur Club	
1. SUNDIN, Mats	Que.	Nacka	RW
2. CHYZOWSKI, Dave	NYI	Kamloops	LW
3. THORNTON, Scott	Tor.	Belleville	C
4. BARNES, Stu	Wpg.	Tri-City	C
5. GUERIN, Bill	N.J.	Springfield Jr. B	RW
6. BENNETT, Adam	Chi.	Sudbury	D
7. ZMOLEK, Doug	Min.	John Marshall	D
8. HERTER, Jason	Van.	U. of North Dakota	D
9. MARSHALL, Jason	St.L.	Vernon Jr. A	D
10. HOLIK, Robert	Hfd.	Dukla Jihlava	C
11. SILLINGER, Mike	Det.	Regina	C
12. PEARSON, Rob	Phi.-Tor.	Belleville	RW
13. VALLIS, Lindsay	NYR-Mtl.	Seattle	RW
14. HALLER, Kevin	Buf.	Regina	D
15. SOULES, Jason	Edm.	Niagara Falls	D
16. HEWARD, Jamie	Pit.	Regina	RW
17. STEVENSON, Shayne	Bos.	Kitchener	RW
18. MILLER, Jason	L.A.-Edm.-N.J.	Medicine Hat	C
19. KOLZIG, Olaf	Wsh.	Tri-City	G
20. RICE, Steven	Mtl.-NYR	Kitchener	RW
21. BANCROFT, Steve	Cgy.-Tor.	Belleville	D

SECOND ROUND

Selection	Claimed By	Amateur Club	
22. FOOTE, Adam	Que.	Sault Ste. Marie	D
23. GREEN, Travis	NYI	Spokane	C
24. MANDERVILLE, Kent	Tor.-Cgy.	Notre Dame Jr. A	LW
25. RATUSHNY, Dan	Wpg.	Cornell	D
26. SKALDE, Jarrod	N.J.	Oshawa	C
27. SPEER, Michael	Chi.	Guelph	D
28. CRAIG, Mike	Min.	Oshawa	RW
29. WOODWARD, Robert	Van.	Deerfield	LW
30. BRISEBOIS, Patrice	St.L.-Mtl.	Laval	D
31. CORRIVEAU, Rick	Hfd.-St.L.	London	D
32. BOUGHNER, Bob	Det.	Sault-Ste. Marie	D
33. JOHNSON, Greg	Phi.	Thunder Bay Jr. A	C
34. JUHLIN, Patrik	NYR-Phi.	Vasteras	LW
35. DAFOE, Byron	Buf.-Wsh.	Portland	D
36. BORGO, Richard	Edm.	Kitchener	G
37. LAUS, Paul	Pit.	Niagara Falls	D
38. PARSON, Mike	Bos.	Guelph	G
39. THOMPSON, Brent	L.A.	Medicine Hat	D
40. PROSOFSKY, Jason	Wsh.-NYR	Medicine Hat	RW
41. LAROUCHE, Steve	Mtl.	Trois-Rivieres	C
42. DRURY, Ted	Cgy.	Fairfield Prep	C

1988

FIRST ROUND

Selection	Claimed By	Amateur Club	
1. MODANO, Mike	Min.	Prince Albert	C
2. LINDEN, Trevor	Van.	Medicine Hat	RW
3. LESCHYSHYN, Curtis	Que.	Saskatoon	D
4. SHANNON, Darrin	Pit.	Windsor	LW
5. DORE, Daniel	NYR-Que.	Drummondville	RW
6. PEARSON, Scott	Tor.	Kingston	LW
7. GELINAS, Martin	L.A.	Hull	LW
8. ROENICK, Jeremy	Chi.	Thayer Academy	C
9. BRIND'AMOUR, Rod	St.L.	Notre Dame Jr. A	C
10. SELANNE, Teemu	Wpg.	Jokerit	RW
11. GOVEDARIS, Chris	Hfd.	Toronto	LW
12. FOSTER, Corey	N.J.	Peterborough	D
13. SAVAGE, Joel	Buf.	Victoria	RW
14. BOIVIN, Claude	Phi.	Drummondville	LW
15. SAVAGE, Reginald	Wsh.	Victoriaville	C
16. CHEVELDAYOFF, Kevin	NYI	Brandon	D
17. KOCUR, Kory	Det.	Saskatoon	RW
18. CIMETTA, Robert	Bos.	Toronto	LW
19. LEROUX, Francois	Edm.	St. Jean	D
20. CHARRON, Eric	Mtl.	Trois-Rivieres	D
21. MUZZATTI, Jason	Cgy.	Michigan State	G

SECOND ROUND

Selection	Claimed By	Amateur Club	
22. MALLETTE, Troy	Min.-NYR	Sault Ste. Marie	C
23. CHRISTIAN, Jeff	Van.-N.J.	London	LW
24. FISET, Stephane	Que.	Victoriaville	G
25. MAJOR, Mark	Pit.	North Bay	D
26. DUVAL, Murray	NYR	Spokane	RW
27. DOMI, Tie	Tor.	Peterborough	RW
28. HOLDEN, Paul	L.A.	London	D
29. DOUCET, Wayne	Chi.-NYI	Hamilton	LW
30. PLAVSIC, Adrien	St.L.	U. of New Hampshire	D
31. ROMANIUK, Russell	Wpg.	St. Boniface Jr. A	LW
32. RICHTER, Barry	Hfd.	Culver Academy	D
33. ROHLIN, Leif	N.J.-Van.	Vasteras	D
34. ST. AMOUR, Martin	Buf.-Mtl.	Verdun	LW
35. MURRAY, Pat	Phi.	Michigan State	LW
36. TAYLOR, Tim	Wsh.	London	C
37. LEBRUN, Sean	NYI	New Westminster	LW
38. ANGLEHART, Serge	Det.	Drummondville	D
39. KOIVUNEN, Petro	Bos.-Edm.	Espoo	C
40. GAETZ, Link	Edm.-Min.	Spokane	D
41. BARTLEY, Wade	Mtl.-St.L.-Wsh.	Dauphin Jr. A	D
42. HARKINS, Todd	Cgy.	Miami-Ohio	RW

1987

FIRST ROUND

Selection	Claimed By	Amateur Club	
1. TURGEON, Pierre	Buf.	Granby	C
2. SHANAHAN, Brendan	N.J.	London	C
3. WESLEY, Glen	Van.-Bos.	Portland	D
4. McBEAN, Wayne	Min.-L.A.	Medicine Hat	D
5. JOSEPH, Chris	Pit.	Seattle	D
6. ARCHIBALD, David	L.A.-Min.	Portland	C/LW
7. RICHARDSON, Luke	Tor.	Peterborough	D
8. WAITE, Jimmy	Chi.	Chicoutimi	G
9. FOGARTY, Bryan	Que.	Kingston	D
10. MORE, Jayson	NYR	New Westminster	D
11. RACINE, Yves	Det.	Longueuil	D
12. OSBORNE, Keith	St.L.	North Bay	RW
13. CHYNOWETH, Dean	NYI	Medicine Hat	D
14. QUINTAL, Stephane	Bos.	Granby	D
15. SAKIC, Joe	Wsh.-Que.	Swift Current	C
16. MARCHMENT, Bryan	Wpg.	Belleville	D
17. CASSELS, Andrew	Mtl.	Ottawa	C
18. HULL, Jody	Hfd.	Peterborough	RW
19. DEASLEY, Bryan	Cgy.	U. of Michigan	LW
20. RUMBLE, Darren	Phi.	Kitchener	D
21. SOBERLAK, Peter	Edm.	Swift Current	LW

SECOND ROUND

Selection	Claimed By	Amateur Club	
22. MILLER, Brad	Buf.	Regina	D
23. PERSSON, Rickard	N.J.	Ostersund	D
24. MURPHY, Rob	Van.	Laval	C
25. MATTEAU, Stephane	Min.-Cgy.	Hull	LW
26. TABARACCI, Richard	Pit.	Cornwall	G
27. FITZPATRICK, Mark	L.A.	Medicine Hat	G
28. MAROIS, Daniel	Tor.	Chicoutimi	RW
29. McGILL, Ryan	Chi.	Swift Current	D
30. HARDING, Jeff	Que.-Phi.	St. Michael's Jr. B	LW
31. LACROIX, Daniel	NYR	Granby	LW
32. KRUPPKE, Gordon	Det.	Prince Albert	D
33. LECLAIR, John	St.L.-Mtl.	Bellows Academy	D
34. HACKETT, Jeff	NYI	Oshawa	G
35. McCRADY, Scott	Bos.-Min.	Medicine Hat	D
36. BALLANTYNE, Jeff	Wsh.	Ottawa	D
37. ERICKSSON, Patrik	Wpg.	Brynas	C
38. DESJARDINS, Eric	Mtl.	Granby	D
39. BURT, Adam	Hfd.	North Bay	D
40. GRANT, Kevin	Cgy.	Kitchener	D
41. WILKIE, Bob	Phi.-Det.	Swift Current	D
42. WERENKA, Brad	Edm.	N. Michigan	D

1986

FIRST ROUND

Selection	Claimed By	Amateur Club	
1. MURPHY, Joe	Det.	Michigan State	C
2. CARSON, Jimmy	L.A.	Verdun	C
3. BRADY, Neil	N.J.	Medicine Hat	C
4. ZALAPSKI, Zarley	Pit.	Canadian National	D
5. ANDERSON, Shawn	Buf.	Canadian National	D
6. DAMPHOUSSE, Vincent	Tor.	Laval	LW
7. WOODLEY, Dan	Van.	Portland	C
8. ELYNUIK, Pat	Wpg.	Prince Albert	RW
9. LEETCH, Brian	NYR	Avon Old Farms HS	D
10. LEMIEUX, Jocelyn	St.L.	Laval	RW
11. YOUNG, Scott	Hfd.	Boston University	RW
12. BABE, Warren	Min.	Lethbridge	LW
13. JANNEY, Craig	Bos.	Boston College	C
14. SANIPASS, Everett	Chi.	Verdun	LW
15. PEDERSON, Mark	Mtl.	Medicine Hat	LW
16. PELAWA, George	Cgy.	Bemidji HS	RW
17. FITZGERALD, Tom	NYI	Austin Prep	C
18. McRAE, Ken	Que.	Sudbury	C
19. GREENLAW, Jeff	Wsh.	Canadian National	LW
20. HUFFMAN, Kerry	Phi.	Guelph	D
21. ISSEL, Kim	Edm.	Prince Albert	RW

SECOND ROUND

Selection	Claimed By	Amateur Club	
22. GRAVES, Adam	Det.	Windsor	C
23. SEPPO, Jukka	L.A.-Phi.	Sport	LW
24. COPELAND, Todd	N.J.	Belmont Hill HS	D
25. CAPUANO, Dave	Pit.	Mt. St. Charles HS	C
26. BROWN, Greg	Buf.	St. Mark's	D
27. BRUNET, Benoit	Tor.-Mtl.	Hull	LW
28. HAWLEY, Kent	Van.-Phi.	Ottawa	C
29. NUMMINEN, Teppo	Wpg.	Tappara	D
30. WILKINSON, Neil	NYR-Min.	Selkirk	D
31. POSMA, Mike	St.L.	Buffalo Jr. A	D
32. LaFORGE, Marc	Hfd.	Kingston	D
33. KOLSTAD, Dean	Min.	Prince Albert	D
34. TIRKKONEN, Pekka	Bos.	SaPKo	C
35. KURZAWSKI, Mark	Chi.	Windsor	D
36. SHANNON, Darryl	Mtl.-Tor.	Windsor	D
37. GLYNN, Brian	Cgy.	Saskatoon	D
38. VASKE, Dennis	NYI	Armstrong HS	D
39. ROUTHIER, Jean-Marc	Que.	Hull	RW
40. SEFTEL, Steve	Wsh.	Kingston	LW
41. GUERARD, Stephane	Phi.-Que.	Shawinigan	D
42. NICHOLS, Jamie	Edm.	Portland	LW

1985

FIRST ROUND

Selection	Claimed By	Amateur Club	
1. CLARK, Wendel	Tor.	Saskatoon	D
2. SIMPSON, Craig	Pit.	Michigan State	C
3. WOLANIN, Craig	N.J.	Kitchener	D
4. SANDLAK, Jim	Van.	London	RW
5. MURZYN, Dana	Hfd.	Calgary	D
6. DALGARNO, Brad	Min.-NYI	Hamilton	RW
7. DAHLEN, Ulf	NYR	Ostersund	C
8. FEDYK, Brent	Det.	Regina	RW
9. DUNCANSON, Craig	L.A.	Sudbury	LW
10. GRATTON, Dan	Bos.-L.A.	Oshawa	C
11. MANSON, David	Chi.	Prince Albert	D
12. CHARBONNEAU, Jose	St.L.-Mtl.	Drummondville	RW
13. KING, Derek	NYI	Sault Ste. Marie	LW
14. JOHANSSON, Calle	Buf.	V. Frolunda	D
15. LATTA, Dave	Que.	Kitchener	LW
16. CHORSKE, Tom	Mtl.	Minneapolis SW HS	LW
17. BIOTTI, Chris	Cgy.	Belmont Hill HS	D
18. STEWART, Ryan	Wpg.	Kamloops	C
19. CORRIVEAU, Yvon	Wsh.	Toronto	LW
20. METCALFE, Scott	Edm.	Kingston	LW
21. SEABROOKE, Glen	Phi.	Peterborough	C

SECOND ROUND

Selection	Claimed By	Amateur Club	
22. SPANGLER, Ken	Tor.	Calgary	D
23. GIFFIN, Lee	Pit.	Oshawa	RW
24. BURKE, Sean	N.J.	Toronto	G
25. GAMBLE, Troy	Van.	Medicine Hat	G
26. WHITMORE, Kay	Hfd.	Peterborough	G
27. NIEUWENDYK, Joe	Min.-Cgy.	Cornell	C
28. RICHTER, Mike	NYR	Northwood Prep.	G
29. SHARPLES, Jeff	Det.	Kelowna	D
30. EDLUND, Par	L.A.	Bjorkloven	RW
31. COTE, Alain	Bos.	Quebec	D
32. WEINRICH, Eric	Chi.-N.J.	North Yarmouth	D
33. RICHARD, Todd	Mtl.	Armstrong HS	D
34. LAUER, Brad	NYI	Regina	RW
35. HOGUE, Benoit	Buf.	St-Jean	C
36. LAFRENIERE, Jason	Que.	Hamilton	C
37. RAGLAN, Herb	Mtl.-St.L.	Kingston	RW
38. WENAAS, Jeff	Cgy.	Medicine Hat	C
39. OHMAN, Roger	Wpg.	Leksand	D
40. DRUCE, John	Wsh.	Peterborough	RW
41. CARNELLEY, Todd	Edm.	Kamloops	D
42. RENDALL, Bruce	Phi.	Chatham	LW

1984

FIRST ROUND

Selection	Claimed By	Amateur Club	
1. LEMIEUX, Mario	Pit.	Laval	C
2. MULLER, Kirk	N.J.	Cdn-Nat.-Guelph	C
3. OLCZYK, Ed	L.A.-Chi.	U.S. National	RW
4. IAFRATE, Al	Tor.	U.S. National-Belleville	D
5. SVOBODA, Petr	Hfd.-Mtl.	CHZ	D
6. REDMOND, Craig	Chi.-L.A.	Canadian National	D
7. BURR, Shawn	Det.	Kitchener	C
8. CORSON, Shayne	St.L.-Mtl.	Brantford	C
9. BODGER, Doug	Wpg.-Pit.	Kamloops Jr. A	D
10. DAIGNEAULT, J.J.	Van.	Cdn. Nat.-Longueuil	D
11. COTE, Sylvain	Mtl.-Hfd.	Quebec	D
12. ROBERTS, Gary	Cgy.	Ottawa	LW
13. QUINN, David	Min.	Kent HS	D
14. CARKNER, Terry	NYR	Peterborough	D
15. STIENBURG, Trevor	Que.	Guelph	C
16. BELANGER, Roger	Phi.-Pit.	Kingston	C
17. HATCHER, Kevin	Wsh.	North Bay	D
18. ANDERSSON, Mikael	Buf.	V. Frolunda	C
19. PASIN, Dave	Bos.	Prince Albert	RW
20. MacPHERSON, Duncan	NYI	Saskatoon	D
21. ODELEIN, Selmar	Edm.	Regina	D

SECOND ROUND

Selection	Claimed By	Amateur Club	
22. SMYTH, Greg	Phi.	London	D
23. BILLINGTON, Craig	N.J.	Belleville	G
24. WILKS, Brian	L.A.	Kitchener	C
25. GILL, Todd	Tor.	Windsor	D
26. BENNING, Brian	Hfd.-St.L.	Portland	D
27. MELLANBY, Scott	Chi.-Phi.	Henry Carr Jr. B	RW
28. HOUDA, Doug	Det.	Calgary	D
29. RICHER, Stephane	St.L.-Mtl.	Granby	C
30. DOURIS, Peter	Wpg.	U. of New Hampshire	C
31. ROHLICEK, Jeff	Van.	Portland	LW
32. HRKAC, Anthony	Mtl.-St.L.	Orillia Jr. A	C
33. SABOURIN, Ken	Cgy.	Sault Ste. Marie	D
34. LEACH, Stephen	Min.-Wsh.	Matignon HS	RW
35. HELMINEN, Raimo	NYR	Ilves	C
36. BROWN, Jeff	Que.	Sudbury	D
37. CHYCHRUN, Jeff	Phi.	Kingston	D
38. RANHEIM, Paul	Wsh.-Cgy.	Edina HS	C
39. TRAPP, Doug	Buf.	Regina	LW
40. PODLOSKI, Ray	Bos.	Portland	C
41. MELANSON, Bruce	NYI	Oshawa	RW
42. REAUGH, Daryl	Edm.	Kamloops Jr. A	G

1983

FIRST ROUND

Selection	Claimed By	Amateur Club	
1. LAWTON, Brian	Pit.-Min.	Mount St. Charles HS	C
2. TURGEON, Sylvain	Hfd.	Hull	C
3. LaFONTAINE, Pat	N.J.-NYI	Verdun	C
4. YZERMAN, Steve	Det.	Peterborough	C
5. BARRASSO, Tom	St.L.-L.A.-Buf.	Acton-Boxboro HS	G
6. MacLEAN, John	L.A.-N.J.	Oshawa	RW
7. COURTNALL, Russ	Tor.	Victoria	C
8. McBAIN, Andrew	Wpg.	North Bay	RW
9. NEELY, Cam	Van.	Portland	RW
10. LACOMBE, Normand	Cgy.-Buf.	U. of New Hampshire	RW
11. CREIGHTON, Adam	Que.-Buf.	Ottawa	C
12. GAGNER, Dave	NYR	Brantford	C
13. QUINN, Dan	Buf.-Cgy.	Belleville	C
14. DOLLAS, Bobby	Wsh.-Wpg.	Laval	D
15. ERREY, Bob	Min.-Pit.	Peterborough	LW
16. DIDUCK, Gerald	NYI	Lethbridge	D
17. TURCOTTE, Alfie	Mtl.	Portland	C
18. CASSIDY, Bruce	Chi.	Ottawa	D
19. BEUKEBOOM, Jeff	Edm.	Sault Ste. Marie	D
20. JENSEN, David	Phi.-Hfd.	Lawrence	C
21. MARKWART, Nevin	Bos.	Regina	LW

SECOND ROUND

Selection	Claimed By	Amateur Club	
22. CHARLESWORTH, Todd	Pit.	Oshawa	D
23. SIREN, Ville	Hfd.	Ilves	D
24. EVANS, Shawn	N.J.	Peterborough	D
25. LAMBERT, Lane	Det.	Saskatoon	RW
26. LEMIEUX, Claude	St.L.-Mtl.	Trois-Rivières	RW
27. MOMESSO, Sergio	L.A.-Mtl.	Shawinigan	C
28. JACKSON, Jeff	Tor.	Brantford	LW
29. BERRY, Brad	Wpg.	St. Albert	D
30. BRUCE, Dave	Van.	Kitchener	RW
31. TUCKER, John	Cgy.-Buf.	Kitchener	C
32. HEROUX, Yves	Que.	Chicoutimi	RW
33. HEATH, Randy	NYR	Portland	LW
34. HAJDU, Richard	Wsh.-Buf.	Kamloops Jr. A	LW
35. FRANCIS, Todd	Mtl.	Brantford	RW
36. PARKS, Malcolm	Min.	St. Albert	C
37. McKECHNEY, Garnet	NYI	Kitchener	RW
38. MUSIL, Frantisek	Mtl.-Min.	Tesla	D
39. PRESLEY, Wayne	Chi.	Kitchener	RW
40. GOLDEN, Mike	Edm.	Reading HS	C
41. ZEZEL, Peter	Phi.	Toronto	C
42. JOHNSTON, Greg	Bos.	Toronto	RW

1982

FIRST ROUND

Selection	Claimed By	Amateur Club	
1. KLUZAK, Gord	Col.-Bos.	Nanaimo	D
2. BELLOWS, Brian	Det.-Min.	Kitchener	RW
3. NYLUND, Gary	Tor.	Portland	D
4. SUTTER, Ron	Hfd.-Phi.	Lethbridge	C
5. STEVENS, Scott	L.A.-Wsh.	Kitchener	D
6. HOUSLEY, Phil	Wsh.-Buf.	S. St. Paul HS	D
7. YAREMCHUK, Ken	Chi.	Portland	C
8. TROTTIER, Rocky	St.L.-N.J.	Nanaimo	RW
9. CYR, Paul	Cgy.-Buf.	Victoria	LW
10. SUTTER, Rich	Pit.	Lethbridge	RW
11. PETIT, Michel	Van.	Sherbrooke	D
12. KYTE, Jim	Wpg.	Cornwall	D
13. SHAW, David	Que.	Kitchener	D
14. LAWLESS, Paul	Phi.-Hfd.	Windsor	LW
15. KONTOS, Chris	NYR	Toronto	C
16. ANDREYCHUK, Dave	Buf.	Oshawa	LW
17. CRAVEN, Murray	Min.-Det.	Medicine Hat	C
18. DANEYKO, Ken	Bos.-N.J.	Seattle	D
19. HEROUX, Alain	Mtl.	Chicoutimi	LW
20. PLAYFAIR, Jim	Edm.	Portland	D
21. FLATLEY, Pat	NYI	U. of Wisconsin	RW

SECOND ROUND

Selection	Claimed By	Amateur Club	
22. CURRAN, Brian	Col.-Bos.	Portland	D
23. COURTEAU, Yves	Det.	Laval	RW
24. LEEMAN, Gary	Tor.	Regina	D
25. IHNACAK, Peter	Hfd.-Tor.	Sparta	C
26. ANDERSON, Mike	L.A.-Buf.	N. St. Paul HS	D
27. HEIDT, Mike	Wsh.-L.A.	Calgary	D
28. BADEAU, Rene	St.L.-Chi.	Quebec	D
29. REIERSON, Dave	Cgy.	Prince Albert	D
30. JOHANSSON, Jens	Buf.	Pitea	D
31. GAUVREAU, Jocelyn	Pit.-Mtl.	Granby	D
32. CARLSON, Kent	Van.-Mtl.	St. Lawrence University	D
33. MALEY, David	Wpg.-Mtl.	Edina HS	C
34. GILLIS, Paul	Que.	Niagara Falls	C
35. PATERSON, Mark	Phi.-Hfd.	Ottawa	D
36. SANDSTROM, Tomas	NYR	Farjestads	RW
37. KROMM, Richard	Buf.-Cgy.	Portland	LW
38. HRYNEWICH, Tim	Min.-Pit.	Sudbury	LW
39. BYERS, Lyndon	Bos.	Regina	RW
40. SANDELIN, Scott	Mtl.	Hibbing HS	D
41. GRAVES, Steve	Edm.	Sault Ste. Marie	C
42. SMITH, Vern	NYI	Lethbridge	D

1981

FIRST ROUND

Selection	Claimed By	Amateur Club	
1. HAWERCHUK, Dale	Wpg.	Cornwall	C
2. SMITH, Doug	Det.-L.A.	Ottawa	C
3. CARPENTER, Bobby	Col.-Wsh.	St. John's HS	C
4. FRANCIS, Ron	Hfd.	Sault Ste. Marie	C
5. CIRELLA, Joe	Wsh.-Col.	Oshawa	D
6. BENNING, Jim	Tor.	Portland	D
7. HUNTER, Mark	Pit.-Mtl.	Brantford	RW
8. FUHR, Grant	Edm.	Victoria	G
9. PATRICK, James	NYR	Prince Albert	D
10. BUTCHER, Garth	Van.	Regina	D
11. MOLLER, Randy	Que.	Lethbridge	D
12. TANTI, Tony	Chi.	Oshawa	RW
13. MEIGHAN, Ron	Min.	Niagara Falls	D
14. LEVEILLE, Normand	Bos.	Chicoutimi	LW
15. MacINNIS, Allan	Cgy.	Kitchener	D
16. SMITH, Steve	Phi.	Sault Ste. Marie	D
17. DUDACEK, Jiri	Buf.	Poldi Kladno	RW
18. DELORME, Gilbert	L.A.-Mtl.	Chicoutimi	D
19. INGMAN, Jan	Mtl.	Farjestad	LW
20. RUFF, Marty	St.L.	Lethbridge	D
21. BOUTILIER, Paul	NYI	Sherbrooke	D

SECOND ROUND

Selection	Claimed By	Amateur Club	
22. ARNIEL, Scott	Wpg.	Cornwall	LW
23. LOISELLE, Claude	Det.	Windsor	C
24. YAREMCHUK, Gary	Col.-Tor.	Portland	C
25. GRIFFIN, Kevin	Hfd.-Chi.	Portland	LW
26. CHERNOMAZ, Rich	Wsh.-Col.	Victoria	C
27. DONNELLY, Dave	Tor.-Min.	St. Albert	C
28. GATZOS, Steve	Pit.	Sault Ste. Marie	RW
29. STRUEBY, Todd	Edm.	Regina	LW
30. ERIXON, Jan	NYR	Skelleftea	RW
31. SANDS, Mike	Van.-Min.	Sudbury	G
32. ERIKSSON, Lars	Que.-Mtl.	Brynas	G
33. HIRSCH, Tom	Chi.-Min.	Patrick Henry HS	D
34. PREUSS, Dave	Min.	St. Thomas Academy	RW
35. DUFOUR, Luc	Bos.	Chicoutimi	RW
36. NORDIN, Hakan	Cgy.-St.L.	Farjestad	D
37. COSTELLO, Rich	Phi.	Natick HS	C
38. VIRTA, Hannu	Buf.	TPS	D
39. KENNEDY, Dean	L.A.	Brandon	D
40. CHELIOS, Chris	Mtl.	Moose Jaw	D
41. WAHLSTEN, Jali	St.L.-Min.	TPS	C
42. DINEEN, Gord	NYI	Sault Ste. Marie	D

1980

FIRST ROUND

Selection	Claimed By	Amateur Club	
1. WICKENHEISER, Doug	Col.-Mtl.	Regina	C
2. BABYCH, Dave	Wpg.	Portland	D
3. SAVARD, Denis	Que.-Chi.	Montreal	C
4. MURPHY, Larry	Det.-L.A.	Peterborough	D
5. VEITCH, Darren	Wsh.	Regina	D
6. COFFEY, Paul	Edm.	Kitchener	D
7. LANZ, Rick	Van.	Oshawa	D
8. ARTHUR, Fred	Hfd.	Cornwall	D
9. BULLARD, Mike	Pit.	Brantford	C
10. FOX, Jimmy	L.A.	Ottawa	RW
11. BLAISDELL, Mike	Tor.-Det.	Regina	RW
12. WILSON, Rik	St.L.	Kingston	D
13. CYR, Denis	Cgy.	Montreal	RW
14. MALONE, Jim	NYR	Toronto	C
15. DUPONT, Jerome	Chi.	Toronto	D
16. PALMER, Brad	Min.	Victoria	LW
17. SUTTER, Brent	NYI	Red Deer	C
18. PEDERSON, Barry	Bos.	Victoria	C
19. GAGNE, Paul	Mtl.-Col.	Windsor	LW
20. PATRICK, Steve	Buf.	Brandon	RW
21. STOTHERS, Mike	Phi.	Kingston	D

SECOND ROUND

Selection	Claimed By	Amateur Club	
22. WARD, Joe	Col.	Seattle	C
23. MANTHA, Moe	Wpg.	Toronto	D
24. ROCHEFORT, Normand	Que.	Quebec	D
25. MUNI, Craig	Det.-Tor.	Kingston	D
26. McGILL, Bob	Wsh.-Tor.	Victoria	D
27. NATTRESS, Ric	Edm.-Mtl.	Brantford	D
28. LUDZIK, Steve	Van.-Chi.	Niagara Falls	C
29. GALARNEAU, Michel	Hfd.	Hull	C
30. SOLHEIM, Ken	Pit.-Chi.	Medicine Hat	LW
31. CURTALE, Tony	L.A.-Cgy.	Brantford	D
32. LaVALLEE, Kevin	Tor.-Cgy.	Brantford	LW
33. TERRION, Greg	St.L.-L.A.	Brantford	LW
34. MORRISON, Dave	Cgy.-L.A.	Peterborough	RW
35. ALLISON, Mike	NYR	Sudbury	LW
36. DAWES, Len	Chi.	Victoria	D
37. BEAUPRE, Don	Min.	Sudbury	G
38. HRUDEY, Kelly	NYI	Medicine Hat	G
39. KONROYD, Steve	Cgy.	Oshawa	D
40. CHABOT, John	Mtl.	Hull	C
41. MOLLER, Mike	Buf.	Lethbridge	RW
42. FRASER, Jay	Phi.	Ottawa	LW

1979

FIRST ROUND

Selection	Claimed By	Amateur Club	
1. RAMAGE, Rob	Col.	London	D
2. TURNBULL, Perry	St.L.	Portland	C
3. FOLIGNO, Mike	Det.	Sudbury	RW
4. GARTNER, Mike	Wsh.	Niagara Falls	RW
5. VAIVE, Rick	Van.	Sherbrooke	RW
6. HARTSBURG, Craig	Min.	Sault St. Marie	D
7. BROWN, Keith	Chi.	Portland	D
8. BOURQUE, Raymond	L.A.-Bos.	Verdun	D
9. BOSCHMAN, Laurie	Tor.	Brandon	C
10. McCARTHY, Tom	Wsh.-Min.	Oshawa	LW
11. RAMSEY, Mike	Buf.	U. of Minnesota	D
12. REINHART, Paul	Atl.	Kitchener	D
13. SULLIMAN, Doug	NYR	Kitchener	RW
14. PROPP, Brian	Phi.	Brandon	LW
15. McCRIMMON, Brad	Bos.	Brandon	D
16. WELLS, Jay	Mtl.-L.A.	Kingston	D
17. SUTTER, Duane	NYI	Lethbridge	RW
18. ALLISON, Ray	Hfd.	Brandon	RW
19. MANN, Jimmy	Wpg.	Sherbrooke	RW
20. GOULET, Michel	Que.	Quebec	LW
21. LOWE, Kevin	Edm.	Quebec	D

SECOND ROUND

Selection	Claimed By	Amateur Club	
22. WESLEY, Blake	Col.-Phi.	Portland	D
23. PEROVICH, Mike	St.L.-Atl.	Brandon	D
24. RAUSSE, Errol	Det.-Wsh.	Seattle	LW
25. JONSSON, Tomas	Wsh.-NYI	MoDo AIK	D
26. ASHTON, Brent	Van.	Saskatoon	LW
27. GINGRAS, Gaston	Min.-Mtl.	Hamilton	D
28. TRIMPER, Tim	Chi.	Peterborough	LW
29. HOPKINS, Dean	L.A.	London	RW
30. HARDY, Mark	Tor.-L.A.	Montreal	D
31. MARSHALL, Paul	Wsh.-Pit.	Brantford	LW
32. RUFF, Lindy	Buf.	Lethbridge	D
33. RIGGIN, Pat	Atl.	London	G
34. HOSPODAR, Ed	NYR	Ottawa	D
35. LINDBERGH, Pelle	Phi.	AIK Solna	G
36. MORRISON, Doug	Bos.	Lethbridge	RW
37. NASLUND, Mats	Mtl.	Brynas IFK	LW
38. CARROLL, Billy	NYI	London	C
39. SMITH, Stuart	Hfd.	Peterborough	D
40. CHRISTIAN, Dave	Wpg.	U. of North Dakota	C
41. HUNTER, Dale	Que.	Sudbury	C
42. BROTEN, Neal	Min.	U. of Minnesota	C

1978

FIRST ROUND

Selection	Claimed By	Amateur Club	
1. SMITH, Bobby	Min.	Ottawa	C
2. WALTER, Ryan	Wsh.	Seattle	LW
3. BABYCH, Wayne	St.L.	Portland	RW
4. DERLAGO, Bill	Van.	Brandon	C
5. GILLIS, Mike	Col.	Kingston	LW
6. WILSON, Behn	Pit.-Phi.	Kingston	D
7. LINSEMAN, Ken	NYR-Phi.	Kingston	C
8. GEOFFRION, Danny	L.A.-Mtl.	Cornwall	RW
9. HUBER, Willie	Det.	Hamilton	D
10. HIGGINS, Tim	Chi.	Ottawa	RW
11. MARSH, Brad	Atl.	London	D
12. PETERSON, Brent	Tor.-Det.	Portland	C
13. PLAYFAIR, Larry	Buf.	Portland	D
14. LUCAS, Danny	Phi.	Sault Ste. Marie	RW
15. TAMBELLINI, Steve	NYI	Lethbridge	C
16. SECORD, Al	Bos.	Hamilton	LW
17. HUNTER, Dave	Mtl.	Sudbury	LW
18. COULIS, Tim	Wsh.	Hamilton	LW

SECOND ROUND

Selection	Claimed By	Amateur Club	
19. PAYNE, Steve	Min.	Ottawa	LW
20. MULVEY, Paul	Wsh.	Portland	RW
21. QUENNEVILLE, Joel	Tor.	Windsor	D
22. FRASER, Curt	Van.	Victoria	LW
23. MacKINNON, Paul	Wsh.	Peterborough	D
24. CHRISTOFF, Steve	Min.	U. of Minnesota	C
25. MEEKER, Mike	Pit.	Peterborough	RW
26. MALONEY, Don	NYR	Kitchener	LW
27. MALINOWSKI, Merlin	Col.	Medicine Hat	C
28. HICKS, Glenn	Det.	Flin Flon	LW
29. LECUYER, Doug	Chi.	Portland	LW
30. YAKIWCHUK, Dale	Mtl.	Portland	C
31. JENSEN, Al	Det.	Hamilton	G
32. McKEGNEY, Tony	Buf.	Kingston	LW
33. SIMURDA, Mike	Phi.	Kingston	RW
34. JOHNSTON, Randy	NYI	Peterborough	D
35. NICOLSON, Graeme	Bos.	Cornwall	D
36. CARTER, Ron	Mtl.	Sherbrooke	RW

1977

FIRST ROUND

Selection	Claimed By	Amateur Club	
1. McCOURT, Dale	Det.	St. Catharines	C
2. BECK, Barry	Col.	New Westminster	D
3. PICARD, Robert	Wsh.	Montreal	D
4. GILLIS, Jere	Van.	Sherbrooke	LW
5. CROMBEEN, Mike	Cle.	Kingston	RW
6. WILSON, Doug	Chi.	Ottawa	D
7. MAXWELL, Brad	Min.	New Westminster	D
8. DEBLOIS, Lucien	NYR	Sorel	C
9. CAMPBELL, Scott	St.L.	London	D
10. NAPIER, Mark	Atl.-Mtl.	Toronto	RW
11. ANDERSON, John	Tor.	Toronto	RW
12. JOHANSEN, Trevor	Pit.-Tor.	Toronto	D
13. DUGUAY, Ron	L.A.-NYR	Sudbury	C
14. SEILING, Ric	Buf.	St. Catharines	RW
15. BOSSY, Mike	NYI	Laval	RW
16. FOSTER, Dwight	Bos.	Kitchener	C/RW
17. McCARTHY, Kevin	Phi.	Winnipeg	D
18. DUPONT, Norm	Mtl.	Montreal	C

SECOND ROUND

Selection	Claimed By	Amateur Club	
19. SAVARD, Jean	Det.-Chi.	Quebec	C
20. ZAHARKO, Miles	Col.-Atl.	New Westminster	D
21. LOFTHOUSE, Mark	Wsh.	New Westminster	RW
22. BANDURA, Jeff	Van.	Portland	D
23. CHICOINE, Daniel	Cle.	Sherbrooke	RW
24. GLADNEY, Bob	Chi.-Tor.	Oshawa	D
25. SEMENKO, Dave	Min.	Brandon	LW
26. KEATING, Mike	NYR	St. Catharines	LW
27. LABATTE, Neil	St.L.	Toronto	D
28. LAURENCE, Don	Atl.	Kitchener	C
29. SAGANIUK, Rocky	Tor.	Lethbridge	RW
30. HAMILTON, Jim	Pit.	London	RW
31. HILL, Brian	L.A.-Atl.	Medicine Hat	RW
32. ARESHENKOFF, Ron	Buf.	Medicine Hat	C
33. TONELLI, John	NYI	Toronto	LW
34. PARRO, Dave	Bos.	Saskatoon	G
35. GORENCE, Tom	Phi.	U. of Minnesota	RW
36. LANGWAY, Rod	Mtl.	U. of New Hampshire	D

1976

FIRST ROUND

Selection	Claimed By	Amateur Club	
1. GREEN, Rick	K.C.-Wsh.	London	D
2. CHAPMAN, Blair	Pit.	Saskatoon	RW
3. SHARPLEY, Glen	Min.	Hull	C
4. WILLIAMS, Fred	Det.	Saskatoon	C
5. JOHANSSON, Bjorn	Cal.	Sweden	D
6. MURDOCH, Don	NYR	Medicine Hat	RW
7. FEDERKO, Bernie	St.L.	Saskatoon	C
8. SHAND, Dave	Van.-Atl.	Peterborough	D
9. CLOUTIER, Real	Chi.	Quebec	RW
10. PHILLIPOFF, Harold	Atl.	New Westminster	LW
11. GARDNER, Paul	Pit.-K.C.	Oshawa	C
12. LEE, Peter	Tor.-Mtl.	Ottawa	RW
13. SCHUTT, Rod	L.A.-Mtl.	Sudbury	LW
14. McKENDRY, Alex	NYI	Sudbury	LW
15. CARROLL, Greg	Buf.-Wsh.	Medicine Hat	C
16. PACHAL, Clayton	Bos.	New Westminster	C
17. SUZOR, Mark	Phi.	Kingston	D
18. BAKER, Bruce	Mtl.	Ottawa	RW

SECOND ROUND

Selection	Claimed By	Amateur Club	
19. MALONE, Greg	Wsh.-Pit.	Oshawa	C
20. SUTTER, Brian	K.C.-St.L.	Lethbridge	LW
21. CLIPPINGDALE, Steve	Min.-L.A.	New Westminster	LW
22. LARSON, Reed	Det.	U. of Minnesota	D
23. STENLUND, Vern	Cal.	London	C
24. FARRISH, Dave	NYR	Sudbury	D
25. SMRKE, John	St.L.	Toronto	LW
26. MANNO, Bob	Van.	St. Catharines	D
27. McDILL, Jeff	Chi.	Victoria	RW
28. SIMPSON, Bobby	Atl.	Sherbrooke	LW
29. MARSH, Peter	Pit.	Sherbrooke	RW
30. CARLYLE, Randy	Tor.	Sudbury	D
31. ROBERTS, Jim	L.A.-Min.	Ottawa	LW
32. KASZYCKI, Mike	NYI	Sault Ste. Marie	C
33. KOWAL, Joe	Buf.	Hamilton	LW
34. GLOECKNER, Larry	Bos.	Victoria	D
35. CALLANDER, Drew	Phi.	Regina	C
36. MELROSE, Barry	Mtl.	Kamloops	D

1975

FIRST ROUND

Selection	Claimed By	Amateur Club	
1. BRIDGMAN, Mel	Wsh.-Phi.	Victoria	C
2. DEAN, Barry	K.C.	Medicine Hat	LW
3. KLASSEN, Ralph	Cal.	Saskatoon	C
4. MAXWELL, Brian	Min.	Medicine Hat	D
5. LAPOINTE, Rick	Det.	Victoria	D
6. ASHBY, Don	Tor.	Calgary	C
7. VAYDIK, Greg	Chi.	Medicine Hat	C
8. MULHERN, Richard	Atl.	Sherbrooke	D
9. SADLER, Robin	St.L.-Mtl.	Edmonton	D
10. BLIGHT, Rick	Van.	Brandon	RW
11. PRICE, Pat	NYI	Saskatoon	D
12. DILLON, Wayne	NYR	Toronto	C
13. LAXTON, Gord	Pit.	New Westminster	G
14. HALWARD, Doug	Bos.	Peterborough	D
15. MONDOU, Pierre	L.A.-Mtl.	Montreal	C
16. YOUNG, Tim	Mtl.-L.A.	Ottawa	C
17. SAUVE, Bob	Buf.	Laval	G
18. FORSYTH, Alex	Phi.-Wsh.	Kingston	C

SECOND ROUND

Selection	Claimed By	Amateur Club	
19. SCAMURRA, Peter	Wsh.	Peterborough	D
20. CAIRNS, Don	K.C.	Victoria	LW
21. MARUK, Dennis	Cal.	London	C
22. ENGBLOM, Brian	Min.-Mtl.	U. of Wisconsin	D
23. ROLLINS, Jerry	Det.	Winnipeg	D
24. JARVIS, Doug	Tor.	Peterborough	C
25. ARNDT, Daniel	Chi.	Saskatoon	LW
26. BOWNESS, Rick	Atl.	Montreal	RW
27. STANIOWSKI, Ed	St.L.	Regina	G
28. GASSOFF, Brad	Van.	Kamloops	D
29. SALVIAN, David	NYI	St. Catharines	RW
30. SOETAERT, Doug	NYR	Edmonton	G
31. ANDERSON, Russ	Pit.	U. of Minnesota	D
32. SMITH, Barry	Bos.	New Westminster	C
33. BUCYK, Terry	L.A.	Lethbridge	RW
34. GREENBANK, Kelvin	Mtl.	Winnipeg	RW
35. BREITENBACH, Ken	Buf.	St. Catharines	D
36. MASTERS, Jamie	Phi.-St.L.	Ottawa	D

1974

FIRST ROUND

Selection	Claimed By	Amateur Club	
1. JOLY, Greg	Wsh.	Regina	D
2. PAIEMENT, Wilfred	K.C.	St. Catharines	RW
3. HAMPTON, Rick	Cal.	St. Catharines	D
4. GILLIES, Clark	NYI	Regina	LW
5. CONNOR, Cam	Van.-Mtl.	Flin Flon	RW
6. HICKS, Doug	Min.	Flin Flon	D
7. RISEBROUGH, Doug	St.L.-Mtl.	Kitchener	C
8. LAROUCHE, Pierre	Pit.	Sorel	C
9. LOCHEAD, Bill	Det.	Oshawa	LW
10. CHARTRAW, Rick	Atl.-Mtl.	Kitchener	D
11. FOGOLIN, Lee	Buf.	Oshawa	D
12. TREMBLAY, Mario	L.A.-Mtl.	Montreal	RW
13. VALIQUETTE, Jack	Tor.	Sault Ste. Marie	C
14. MALONEY, Dave	NYR	Kitchener	D
15. McTAVISH, Gord	Mtl.	Sudbury	C
16. MULVEY, Grant	Chi.	Calgary	RW
17. CHIPPERFIELD, Ron	Phi.-Cal.	Brandon	C
18. LARWAY, Don	Bos.	Swift Current	RW

SECOND ROUND

Selection	Claimed By	Amateur Club	
19. MARSON, Mike	Wsh.	Sudbury	LW
20. BURDON, Glen	K.C.	Regina	C
21. AFFLECK, Bruce	Cal.	U. of Denver	D
22. TROTTIER, Bryan	NYI	Swift Current	C
23. SEDLBAUER, Ron	Van.	Kitchener	LW
24. NANTAIS, Rick	Min.	Quebec	LW
25. HOWE, Mark	St.L.-Bos.	Toronto	D
26. HESS, Bob	Pit.-St.L.	New Westminster	D
27. COSSETTE, Jacques	Det.-Pit.	Sorel	RW
28. CHOUINARD, Guy	Atl.	Quebec	C
29. GARE, Danny	Buf.	Calgary	RW
30. MacGREGOR, Gary	L.A.-Atl.	Cornwall	C
31. WILLIAMS, Dave	Tor.	Swift Current	LW
32. GRESCHNER, Ron	NYR	New Westminster	D
33. LUPIEN, Gilles	Mtl.	Montreal	D
34. DAIGLE, Alain	Chi.	Trois-Rivières	RW
35. McLEAN, Don	Phi.	Sudbury	D
36. STURGEON, Peter	Bos.	Kitchener	LW

1973

FIRST ROUND

Selection	Claimed By	Amateur Club	
1. POTVIN, Denis	NYI	Ottawa	D
2. LYSIAK, Tom	Cal.-Mtl.-Atl.	Medicine Hat	C
3. VERVERGAERT, Dennis	Van.	London	RW
4. McDONALD, Lanny	Tor.	Medicine Hat	RW
5. DAVIDSON, John	Atl.-Mtl.-St.L.	Calgary	G
6. SAVARD, Andre	L.A.-Bos.	Quebec	C
7. STOUGHTON, Blaine	Pit.	Flin Flon	RW
8. GAINEY, Bob	St.L.-Mtl.	Peterborough	LW
9. DAILEY, Bob	Min.-Mtl.-Van.	Toronto	D
10. NEELY, Bob	Phi.-Tor.	Peterborough	LW
11. RICHARDSON, Terry	Det.	New Westminster	G
12. TITANIC, Morris	Buf.	Sudbury	LW
13. ROTA, Darcy	Chi.	Edmonton	LW
14. MIDDLETON, Rick	NYR	Oshawa	RW
15. TURNBULL, Ian	Bos.-Tor.	Ottawa	D
16. MERCREDI, Vic	Mtl.-Atl.	New Westminster	C

SECOND ROUND

Selection	Claimed By	Amateur Club	
17. GOLDUP, Glen	NYI-Mtl.	Toronto	RW
18. DUNLOP, Blake	Cal.-Min.	Ottawa	C
19. BORDELEAU, Paulin	Van.	Toronto	RW
20. GOODENOUGH, Larry	Tor.-Phi.	London	D
21. VAIL, Eric	Atl.	Sudbury	LW
22. MARRIN, Peter	L.A.-Mtl.	Toronto	C
23. BIANCHIN, Wayne	Pit.	Flin Flon	LW
24. PESUT, George	St.L.	Saskatoon	D
25. ROGERS, John	Min.	Edmonton	RW
26. LEVINS, Brent	Phi.	Swift Current	
27. CAMPBELL, Colin	Det.-Pit.	Peterborough	D
28. LANDRY, Jean	Buf.	Quebec	D
29. THOMAS, Reg	Chi.	London	LW
30. HICKEY, Pat	NYR	Hamilton	LW
31. KOWAL, Joe	Bos.	Peterborough	RW
32. ANDRUFF, Ron	Mtl.	Flin Flon	C

1972

FIRST ROUND

Selection	Claimed By	Amateur Club	
1. HARRIS, Billy	NYI	Toronto	RW
2. RICHARD, Jacques	Atl.	Quebec	LW
3. LEVER, Don	Van.	Niagara Falls	C
4. SHUTT, Steve	L.A.-Mtl.	Toronto	LW
5. SCHOENFELD, Jim	Buf.	Niagara Falls	D
6. LAROCQUE, Michel	Cal.-Mtl.	Ottawa	G
7. BARBER, Bill	Phi.	Kitchener	LW
8. GARDNER, Dave	Pit.-Min.-Mtl.	Toronto	C
9. MERRICK, Wayne	St.L.	Ottawa	C
10. BLANCHARD, Albert	Det.-NYR	Kitchener	LW
11. FERGUSON, George	Tor.	Toronto	C
12. BYERS, Jerry	Min.	Kitchener	LW
13. RUSSELL, Phil	Chi.	Edmonton	D
14. VAN BOXMEER, John	Mtl.	Guelph	D
15. MacMILLAN, Bobby	NYR	St. Catharines	RW
16. BLOOM, Mike	Bos.	St. Catharines	LW

SECOND ROUND

17. HENNING Lorne	NYI	New Westminster	C
18. BIALOWAS, Dwight	Atl.	Regina	D
19. McSHEFFREY, Brian	Van.	Ottawa	RW
20. KOZAK, Don	L.A.	Edmonton	RW
21. SACHARUK, Larry	Buf.-NYR	Saskatoon	D
22. CASSIDY, Tom	Cal.	Kitchener	C
23. BLADON, Tom	Phi.	Edmonton	D
24. LYNCH, Jack	Pit.	Oshawa	D
25. CARRIERE, Larry	St.L.-Buf.	Loyola College	D
26. GUITE, Pierre	Det.	St. Catharines	LW
27. OSBURN, Randy	Tor.	London	LW
28. WEIR, Stan	Min.-Cal.	Medicine Hat	C
29. OGILVIE, Brian	Chi.	Edmonton	C
30. LUKOWICH, Bernie	Mtl.-Pit.	New Westminster	RW
31. VILLEMURE, Rene	NYR	Shawinigan	LW
32. ELDER, Wayne	Bos.	London	D

1971

FIRST ROUND

Selection	Claimed By	Amateur Club	
1. LAFLEUR, Guy	Cal.-Mtl.	Quebec	RW
2. DIONNE, Marcel	Det.	St. Catharines	C
3. GUEVREMONT, Jocelyn	Van.	Montreal	D
4. CARR, Gene	Pit.-St.L.	Flin Flon	C
5. MARTIN, Rick	Buf.	Montreal	LW
6. JONES, Ron	L.A.-Bos.	Edmonton	D
7. ARNASON, Chuck	Min.-Mtl.	Flin Flon	RW
8. WRIGHT, Larry	Phi.	Regina	C
9. PLANTE, Pierre	Tor.-Phi.	Drummondville	RW
10. VICKERS, Steve	St.L.-NYR	Toronto	LW
11. WILSON, Murray	Mtl.	Ottawa	LW
12. SPRING, Dan	Chi.	Edmonton	C
13. DURBANO, Steve	NYR	Toronto	D
14. O'REILLY, Terry	Bos.	Oshawa	RW

SECOND ROUND

15. BAIRD, Ken	Cal.	Flin Flon	D
16. BOUCHA, Henry	Det.	U.S. Nationals	C
17. LALONDE, Bobby	Van.	Montreal	C
18. McKENZIE, Brian	Pit.	St. Catharines	LW
19. RAMSAY, Craig	Buf.	Peterborough	LW
20. ROBINSON, Larry	L.A.-Mtl.	Kitchener	D
21. NORRISH, Rod	Min.	Regina	LW
22. KEHOE, Rick	Phi.-Tor.	Hamilton	RW
23. FORTIER, Dave	Tor.	St. Catharines	D
24. DEGUISE, Michel	St.L.-Mtl.	Sorel	G
25. FRENCH, Terry	Mtl.	Ottawa	C
26. KRYSKOW, Dave	Chi.	Edmonton	LW
27. WILLIAMS, Tom	NYR	Hamilton	LW
28. RIDLEY, Curt	Bos.	Portage	G

1970

FIRST ROUND

Selection	Claimed By	Amateur Club	
1. PERREAULT, Gilbert	Buf.	Montreal	C
2. TALLON, Dale	Van.	Toronto	D
3. LEACH, Reg	L.A.-Bos.	Flin Flon	LW
4. MacLEISH, Rick	Phi.-Bos.	Peterborough	C
5. MARTINIUK, Ray	Oak.-Mtl.	Flin Flon	G
6. LEFLEY, Chuck	Min.-Mtl.	Canadian Nationals	C
7. POLIS, Greg	Pit.	Estevan	LW
8. SITTLER, Darryl	Tor.	London	C
9. PLUMB, Ron	Bos.	Peterborough	D
10. ODDLEIFSON, Chris	St.L.-Oak.	Winnipeg	C
11. GRATTON, Norm	Mtl.-NYR	Montreal	LW
12. LAJEUNESSE, Serge	Det.	Montreal	RW
13. STEWART, Bob	Bos.	Oshawa	D
14. MALONEY, Dan	Chi.	London	LW

SECOND ROUND

15. DEADMARSH, Butch	Buf.	Brandon	LW
16. HARGREAVES, Jim	Van.	Winnipeg	D
17. HARVEY, Fred	L.A.-Min.	Hamilton	RW
18. CLEMENT, Bill	Phi.	Ottawa	C
19. LAFRAMBOISE, Pete	Oak.	Ottawa	C
20. BARRETT, Fred	Min.	Toronto	D
21. STEWART, John	Pit.	Flin Flon	LW
22. THOMPSON, Errol	Tor.	Charlottetown	LW
23. KEOGAN, Murray	St.L.	U. of Minnesota	C
24. McDONOUGH, Al	Mtl.-L.A.	St. Catharines	RW
25. MURPHY, Mike	NYR	Toronto	RW
26. GUINDON, Bobby	Det.	Montreal	LW
27. BOUCHARD, Dan	Bos.	London	G
28. ARCHAMBAULT, Mike	Chi.	Drummondville	LW

1969

FIRST ROUND

Selection	Claimed By	Amateur Club	
1. HOULE, Rejean	Mtl.	Montreal	LW
2. TARDIF, Marc	Mtl.	Montreal	LW
3. TANNAHILL, Don	Min.-Bos.	Niagara Falls	LW
4. SPRING, Frank	Pit.-Bos.	Edmonton	RW
5. REDMOND, Dick	L.A.-Mtl.-Min.	St. Catharines	D
6. CURRIER, Bob	Phi.	Cornwall	C
7. FEATHERSTONE, Tony	Oak.	Peterborough	RW
8. DUPONT, André	St.L.-NYR	Montreal	D
9. MOSER, Ernie	Det.-Tor.	Estevan	RW
10. RUTHERFORD, Jim	Det.	Hamilton	G
11. BOLDIREV, Ivan	Bos.	Oshawa	C
12. JARRY, Pierre	NYR	Ottawa	LW
13. BORDELEAU, J.-P.	Chi.	Montreal	RW
14. O'BRIEN, Dennis	Min.	St. Catharines	D

SECOND ROUND

15. KESSELL, Rick	Pit.	Oshawa	C
16. HOGANSON, Dale	L.A.	Estevan	D
17. CLARKE, Bobby	Phi.	Flin Flon	C
18. STACKHOUSE, Ron	Oak.	Peterborough	D
19. LOWE, Mike	St.L.	Loyola College	
20. BRINDLEY, Doug	Tor.	Niagara Falls	C
21. GARWASIUK, Ron	Det.	Regina	LW
22. QUOQUOCHI, Art	Bos.	Montreal	
23. WILSON, Bert	NYR	London	LW
24. ROMANCHYCH, Larry	Chi.	Flin Flon	RW
25. GILBERT, Gilles	Min.	London	G
26. BRIERE, Michel	Pit.	Shawinigan Falls	C
27. BODDY, Greg	L.A.	Edmonton	D
28. BROSSART, Bill	Phi.	Estevan	D

Though he did wear a helmet in his early days, the image fans have of Guy Lafleur is that of his blonde hair blowing in the breeze he created as he blazed across the Forum ice. Lafleur was the top pick in the 1971 Amateur Draft.

NHL All-Stars

Active Players' All-Star Selection Records

GOALTENDERS

Player	First Team Selections		Second Team Selections		Total
Dominik Hasek	(5)	1993-94; 1994-95; 1996-97; 1997-98; 1998-99.	(0)		5
Patrick Roy	(3)	1988-89; 1989-90; 1991-92.	(2)	1987-88; 1990-91.	5
Ed Belfour	(2)	1990-91; 1992-93.	(1)	1994-95.	3
Tom Barrasso	(1)	1983-84.	(2)	1984-85; 1992-93.	3
Grant Fuhr	(1)	1987-88.	(1)	1981-82.	2
J.Vanbiesbrouck	(1)	1985-86.	(1)	1993-94.	2
Martin Brodeur	(0)		(2)	1996-97; 1997-98.	2
Olaf Kolzig	(1)	99-2000.	(0)		1
Mike Vernon	(0)		(1)	1988-89.	1
Daren Puppa	(0)		(1)	1989-90.	1
Kirk McLean	(0)		(1)	1991-92.	1
Chris Osgood	(0)		(1)	1995-96.	1
Byron Dafoe	(0)		(1)	1998-99.	1
Roman Turek	(0)		(1)	99-2000.	1

DEFENSEMEN

Player	First Team Selections		Second Team Selections		Total
Ray Bourque	(12)	1979-80; 1981-82; 1983-84; 1984-85; 1986-87; 1987-88; 1989-90; 1990-91; 1991-92; 1992-93; 1993-94; 1995-96.	(6)	1980-81; 1982-83; 1985-86; 1988-89; 1994-95; 1998-99.	18
Paul Coffey	(4)	1984-85; 1985-86; 1988-89; 1994-95.	(4)	1981-82; 1982-83; 1983-84; 1989-90.	8
Chris Chelios	(4)	1988-89; 1992-93; 1994-95; 1995-96.	(2)	1990-91; 1996-97.	6
Al MacInnis	(3)	1989-90; 1990-91; 1998-99.	(3)	1986-87; 1988-89; 1993-94.	6
Brian Leetch	(2)	1991-92; 1996-97.	(3)	1990-91; 1993-94; 1995-96.	5
Scott Stevens	(2)	1987-88; 1993-94.	(2)	1991-92; 1996-97.	4
Nicklas Lidstrom	(3)	1997-98; 1998-99; 99-2000.	(0)		3
Larry Murphy	(0)		(3)	1986-87; 1992-93; 1994-95.	3
Rob Blake	(1)	1997-98.	(1)	99-2000.	2
Chris Pronger	(1)	99-2000.	(1)	1997-98.	2
Eric Desjardins	(0)		(2)	1998-99; 99-2000.	2
Sandis Ozolinsh	(1)	1996-97.	(0)		1
Gary Suter	(0)		(1)	1987-88.	1
Phil Housley	(0)		(1)	1991-92.	1
Scott Niedermayer	(0)		(1)	1997-98.	1

CENTERS

Player	First Team Selections		Second Team Selections		Total
Mark Messier	(2)	1989-90; 1991-92.	(0)		2
Peter Forsberg	(2)	1997-98; 1998-99.	(0)		2
Eric Lindros	(1)	1994-95.	(1)	1995-96.	2
Sergei Fedorov	(1)	1993-94.	(0)		1
Steve Yzerman	(1)	99-2000.	(0)		1
Adam Oates	(0)		(1)	1990-91.	1
Alexei Zhamnov	(0)		(1)	1994-95.	1
Alexei Yashin	(0)		(1)	1998-99.	1
Mike Modano	(0)		(1)	99-2000.	1

RIGHT WINGERS

Player	First Team Selections		Second Team Selections		Total
Jaromir Jagr	(5)	1994-95; 1995-96; 1997-98; 1998-99; 99-2000.	(1)	1996-97.	6
Teemu Selanne	(2)	1992-93; 1996-97.	(2)	1997-98; 1998-99.	4
Brett Hull	(3)	1989-90; 1990-91; 1991-92.	(0)		3
Pavel Bure	(1)	1993-94.	(1)	99-2000	2
Alexander Mogilny	(0)		(2)	1992-93; 1995-96.	2
Mark Recchi	(0)		(1)	1991-92.	1
Theoren Fleury	(0)		(1)	1994-95.	1

LEFT WINGERS

Player	First Team Selections		Second Team Selections		Total
Luc Robitaille	(5)	1987-88; 1988-89; 1989-90; 1990-91; 1992-93.	(2)	1986-87; 1991-92.	7
John LeClair	(2)	1994-95; 1997-98.	(3)	1995-96; 1996-97; 1998-99.	5
Paul Kariya	(3)	1995-96; 1996-97; 1998-99.	(1)	99-2000.	4
Mark Messier	(2)	1981-82; 1982-83.	(1)	1983-84.	3
Kevin Stevens	(1)	1991-92.	(2)	1990-91; 1992-93.	3
Brendan Shanahan	(2)	1993-94; 99-2000.	(0)		2
Keith Tkachuk	(0)		(2)	1994-95; 1997-98.	2
Adam Graves	(0)		(1)	1993-94.	1

Leading NHL All-Stars 1930-31 to 1999-2000

Player	Pos	Team	NHL Seasons	First Team Selections	Second Team Selections	Total Selections
Howe, Gordie	RW	Detroit	26	12	9	21
* Bourque, Ray	D	Boston	21	12	6	18
Gretzky, Wayne	C	Edm., L.A.	20	8	7	15
Richard, Maurice	RW	Montreal	18	8	6	14
Hull, Bobby	LW	Chicago	16	10	2	12
Harvey, Doug	D	Mtl., NYR	19	10	1	11
Hall, Glenn	G	Det., Chi., St.L.	18	7	4	11
Beliveau, Jean	C	Montreal	20	6	4	10
Seibert, Earl	D	NYR, Chi	15	4	6	10
Orr, Bobby	D	Boston	12	8	1	9
Lindsay, Ted	LW	Detroit	17	8	1	9
Mahovlich, Frank	LW	Tor., Det., Mtl.	18	3	6	9
Shore, Eddie	D	Boston	14	7	1	8
Mikita, Stan	C	Chicago	22	6	2	8
Kelly, Red	D	Detroit	20	6	2	8
Esposito, Phil	C	Boston	18	6	2	8
Pilote, Pierre	D	Chicago	14	5	3	8
Lemieux, Mario	C	Pittsburgh	12	5	3	8
Bossy, Mike	RW	NY Islanders	10	5	3	8
* Coffey, Paul	D	Edm., Pit., Det.	20	4	4	8
Brimsek, Frank	G	Boston	10	2	6	8
* Robitaille, Luc	LW	Los Angeles	14	5	2	7
Potvin, Denis	D	NY Islanders	15	5	2	7
Park, Brad	D	NYR, Bos.	17	5	2	7
Plante, Jacques	G	Mtl., Tor.	18	3	4	7
Gadsby, Bill	D	Chi., NYR, Det.	20	3	4	7
Sawchuk, Terry	G	Detroit	21	3	4	7
Durnan, Bill	G	Montreal	7	6	0	6
Lafleur, Guy	RW	Montreal	16	6	0	6
Dryden, Ken	G	Montreal	8	5	1	6
* Jagr, Jaromir	RW	Pittsburgh	10	5	1	6
* Chelios, Chris	D	Mtl., Chi.	17	4	2	6
* MacInnis, Al	D	Cgy., St.L.	19	3	3	6
Clapper, Dit	RW/D	Boston	20	3	3	6
Robinson, Larry	D	Montreal	20	3	3	6
Horton, Tim	D	Toronto	24	3	3	6
Salming, Borje	D	Toronto	17	1	5	6
* Hasek, Dominik	G	Buffalo	10	5	0	5
Cowley, Bill	C	Boston	13	4	1	5
* Messier, Mark	LW/C	Edm., NYR	21	4	1	5
Jackson, Harvey	LW	Toronto	15	4	1	5
Goulet, Michel	LW	Quebec	15	3	2	5
Conacher, Charlie	RW	Toronto	12	3	2	5
Stewart, Jack	D	Detroit	12	3	2	5
Lach, Elmer	C	Montreal	14	3	2	5
Quackenbush, Bill	D	Det., Bos.	14	3	2	5
Blake, Toe	LW	Montreal	15	3	2	5
Esposito, Tony	G	Chicago	16	3	2	5
* Roy, Patrick	G	Montreal	16	2	3	5
Reardon, Ken	D	Montreal	7	2	3	5
Kurri, Jari	RW	Edmonton	16	2	3	5
Apps Sr., Syl	C	Toronto	10	2	3	5
Giacomin, Ed	G	NY Rangers	13	2	3	5
* Leetch, Brian	D	NY Rangers	11	2	3	5
* LeClair, John	LW	Mtl., Phi.	10	2	3	5

* Active

Position Leaders in All-Star Selections

Position	Player	First Team	Second Team	Total
GOAL	Glenn Hall	7	4	11
	Frank Brimsek	2	6	8
	Jacques Plante	3	4	7
	Terry Sawchuk	3	4	7
	Bill Durnan	6	0	6
	Ken Dryden	5	1	6
DEFENSE	* Ray Bourque	12	6	18
	Doug Harvey	10	1	11
	Earl Seibert	4	6	10
	Bobby Orr	8	1	9
	Eddie Shore	7	1	8
	Red Kelly	6	2	8
	Pierre Pilote	5	3	8
	* Paul Coffey	4	4	8

Position	Player	First Team	Second Team	Total
LEFT WING	Bobby Hull	10	2	12
	Ted Lindsay	8	1	9
	Frank Mahovlich	3	6	9
	* Luc Robitaille	5	2	7
	Harvey Jackson	4	1	5
	Michel Goulet	3	2	5
	Toe Blake	3	2	5
RIGHT WING	Gordie Howe	12	9	21
	Maurice Richard	8	6	14
	Mike Bossy	5	3	8
	Guy Lafleur	6	0	6
	* Jaromir Jagr	5	1	6
CENTER	Wayne Gretzky	8	7	15
	Jean Beliveau	6	4	10
	Stan Mikita	6	2	8
	Phil Esposito	6	2	8
	Mario Lemieux	5	3	8

* active player

2001 NHL ALL-STAR GAME COLORADO

All-Star Teams
1930-2000

Voting for the NHL All-Star Team is conducted among the representatives of the Professional Hockey Writers' Association at the end of the season.

Following is a list of the First and Second All-Star Teams since their inception in 1930-31.

First Team		Second Team		First Team		Second Team		First Team		Second Team

1999-2000 | | | | 1992-93 | | | | 1988-89

First Team		Second Team	First Team		Second Team	First Team		Second Team
1999-2000			**1992-93**			**1988-89**		
Kolzig, Olaf, Wsh.	G	Turek, Roman, St. L.	Belfour, Ed, Chi.	G	Barrasso, Tom, Pit.	Roy, Patrick, Mtl.	G	Vernon, Mike, Cgy.
Pronger, Chris, St. L.	D	Blake, Rob, L.A.	Chelios, Chris, Chi.	D	Murphy, Larry, Pit.	Chelios, Chris, Mtl.	D	MacInnis, Al, Cgy.
Lindstrom, Nicklas, Det.	D	Desjardins, Eric, Phi.	Bourque, Ray, Bos.	D	Iafrate, Al, Wsh.	Coffey, Paul, Pit.	D	Bourque, Ray, Bos.
Yzerman, Steve, Det.	C	Modano, Mike, Dal.	Lemieux, Mario, Pit.	C	LaFontaine, Pat, Buf.	Lemieux, Mario, Pit.	C	Gretzky, Wayne, L.A.
Jagr, Jaromir, Pit.	RW	Bure, Pavel, Fla.	Selanne, Teemu, Wpg.	RW	Mogilny, Alexander, Buf.	Mullen, Joe, Cgy.	RW	Kurri, Jari, Edm.
Shanahan, Brendan, Det.	LW	Kariya, Paul, Ana.	Robitaille, Luc, L.A.	LW	Stevens, Kevin, Pit.	Robitaille, Luc, L.A.	LW	Gallant, Gerard, Det.
1998-99			**1991-92**			**1987-88**		
Hasek, Dominik, Buf.	G	Dafoe, Byron, Bos.	Roy, Patrick, Mtl.	G	McLean, Kirk, Van.	Fuhr, Grant, Edm.	G	Roy, Patrick, Mtl.
MacInnis, Al, St. L.	D	Bourque, Ray, Bos.	Leetch, Brian, NYR	D	Housley, Phil, Wpg.	Bourque, Ray, Bos.	D	Suter, Gary, Cgy.
Lindstrom, Nicklas, Det.	D	Desjardins, Eric, Phi.	Bourque, Ray, Bos.	D	Stevens, Scott, N.J.	Stevens, Scott, Wsh.	D	McCrimmon, Brad, Cgy.
Forsberg, Peter, Col.	C	Yashin, Alexei, Ott.	Messier, Mark, NYR	C	Lemieux, Mario, Pit.	Lemieux, Mario, Pit.	C	Gretzky, Wayne, Edm.
Jagr, Jaromir, Pit.	RW	Selanne, Teemu, Ana.	Hull, Brett, St. L.	RW	Recchi, Mark, Pit., Phi.	Loob, Hakan, Cgy.	RW	Neely, Cam, Bos.
Kariya, Paul, Ana.	LW	Le Clair, John, Phi.	Stevens, Kevin, Pit.	LW	Robitaille, Luc, L.A.	Robitaille, Luc, L.A.	LW	Goulet, Michel, Que.
1997-98			**1990-91**			**1986-87**		
Hasek, Dominik, Buf.	G	Brodeur, Martin, N.J.	Belfour, Ed, Chi.	G	Roy, Patrick, Mtl.	Hextall, Ron, Phi.	G	Liut, Mike, Hfd.
Lidstrom, Nicklas, Det.	D	Pronger, Chris, St.L.	Bourque, Ray, Bos.	D	Chelios, Chris, Chi.	Bourque, Ray, Bos.	D	Murphy, Larry, Wsh.
Blake, Rob, L.A.	D	Niedermayer, Scott, N.J.	MacInnis, Al, Cgy.	D	Leetch, Brian, NYR	Howe, Mark, Phi.	D	MacInnis, Al, Cgy.
Forsberg, Peter, Col.	C	Gretzky, Wayne, NYR	Gretzky, Wayne, L.A.	C	Oates, Adam, St. L.	Gretzky, Wayne, Edm.	C	Lemieux, Mario, Pit.
Jagr, Jaromir, Pit.	RW	Selanne, Teemu, Ana.	Hull, Brett, St. L.	RW	Neely, Cam, Bos.	Kurri, Jari, Edm.	RW	Kerr, Tim, Phi.
LeClair, John, Phi.	LW	Tkachuk, Keith, Phx.	Robitaille, Luc, L.A.	LW	Stevens, Kevin, Pit.	Goulet, Michel, Que.	LW	Robitaille, Luc, L.A.
1996-97			**1989-90**			**1985-86**		
Hasek, Dominik, Buf.	G	Brodeur, Martin, N.J.	Roy, Patrick, Mtl.	G	Puppa, Daren, Buf.	Vanbiesbrouck, John, NYR	G	Froese, Bob, Phi.
Leetch, Brian, NYR	D	Chelios, Chris, Chi.	Bourque, Ray, Bos.	D	Coffey, Paul, Pit.	Coffey, Paul, Edm.	D	Robinson, Larry, Mtl.
Ozolinsh, Sandis, Col.	D	Stevens, Scott, N.J.	MacInnis, Al, Cgy.	D	Wilson, Doug, Chi.	Howe, Mark, Phi.	D	Bourque, Ray, Bos.
Lemieux, Mario, Pit.	C	Gretzky, Wayne, NYR	Messier, Mark, Edm.	C	Gretzky, Wayne, L.A.	Gretzky, Wayne, Edm.	C	Lemieux, Mario, Pit.
Selanne, Teemu, Ana.	RW	Jagr, Jaromir, Pit.	Hull, Brett, St. L.	RW	Neely, Cam, Bos.	Bossy, Mike, NYI	RW	Kurri, Jari, Edm.
Kariya, Paul, Ana.	LW	LeClair, John, Phi.	Robitaille, Luc, L.A.	LW	Bellows, Brian, Min.	Goulet, Michel, Que.	LW	Naslund, Mats, Mtl.
1995-96								
Carey, Jim, Wsh.	G	Osgood, Chris, Det.						
Chelios, Chris, Chi.	D	Konstantinov, V., Det.						
Bourque, Ray, Bos.	D	Leetch, Brian, NYR.						
Lemieux, Mario, Pit.	C	Lindros, Eric, Phi.						
Jagr, Jaromir, Pit.	RW	Mogilny, Alexander, Van.						
Kariya, Paul, Ana.	LW	LeClair, John, Phi.						
1994-95								
Hasek, Dominik, Buf.	G	Belfour, Ed, Chi.						
Coffey, Paul, Det.	D	Bourque, Ray, Bos.						
Chelios, Chris, Chi.	D	Murphy, Larry, Pit.						
Lindros, Eric, Phi.	C	Zhamnov, Alexei, Wpg.						
Jagr, Jaromir, Pit.	RW	Fleury, Theoren, Cgy.						
LeClair, John, Mtl., Phi.	LW	Tkachuk, Keith, Wpg.						
1993-94								
Hasek, Dominik, Buf.	G	Vanbiesbrouck, John, Fla.						
Bourque, Ray, Bos.	D	MacInnis, Al, Cgy.						
Stevens, Scott, N.J.	D	Leetch, Brian, NYR						
Fedorov, Sergei, Det.	C	Gretzky, Wayne, L.A.						
Bure, Pavel, Van.	RW	Neely, Cam, Bos.						
Shanahan, Brendan, St. L.	LW	Graves, Adam, NYR						

Until the 1999-2000 season, the best player never elected to an NHL All-Star Team was Steve Yzerman. The Detroit captain finally made the grade, earning a selection to the First Team after his 17th season.

First Team		Second Team

1984-85

First Team	Pos	Second Team
Lindbergh, Pelle, Phi.	G	Barrasso, Tom, Buf.
Coffey, Paul, Edm.	D	Langway, Rod, Wsh.
Bourque, Ray, Bos.	D	Wilson, Doug, Chi.
Gretzky, Wayne, Edm.	C	Hawerchuk, Dale, Wpg.
Kurri, Jari, Edm.	RW	Bossy, Mike, NYI
Ogrodnick, John, Det.	LW	Tonelli, John, NYI

1983-84

First Team	Pos	Second Team
Barrasso, Tom, Buf.	G	Riggin, Pat, Wsh.
Langway, Rod, Wsh.	D	Coffey, Paul, Edm.
Bourque, Ray, Bos.	D	Potvin, Denis, NYI
Gretzky, Wayne, Edm.	C	Trottier, Bryan, NYI
Bossy, Mike, NYI	RW	Kurri, Jari, Edm.
Goulet, Michel, Que.	LW	Messier, Mark, Edm.

1982-83

First Team	Pos	Second Team
Peeters, Pete, Bos.	G	Melanson, Rollie, NYI
Howe, Mark, Phi.	D	Bourque, Ray, Bos.
Langway, Rod, Wsh.	D	Coffey, Paul, Edm.
Gretzky, Wayne, Edm.	C	Savard, Denis, Chi.
Bossy, Mike, NYI	RW	McDonald, Lanny, Cgy.
Messier, Mark, Edm.	LW	Goulet, Michel, Que.

1981-82

First Team	Pos	Second Team
Smith, Billy, NYI	G	Fuhr, Grant, Edm.
Wilson, Doug, Chi.	D	Coffey, Paul, Edm.
Bourque, Ray, Bos.	D	Engblom, Brian, Mtl.
Gretzky, Wayne, Edm.	C	Trottier, Bryan, NYI
Bossy, Mike, NYI	RW	Middleton, Rick, Bos.
Messier, Mark, Edm.	LW	Tonelli, John, NYI

1980-81

First Team	Pos	Second Team
Liut, Mike, St.L.	G	Lessard, Mario, L.A.
Potvin, Denis, NYI	D	Robinson, Larry, Mtl.
Carlyle, Randy, Pit.	D	Bourque, Ray, Bos.
Gretzky, Wayne, Edm.	C	Dionne, Marcel, L.A.
Bossy, Mike, NYI	RW	Taylor, Dave, L.A.
Simmer, Charlie, L.A.	LW	Barber, Bill, Phi.

1979-80

First Team	Pos	Second Team
Esposito, Tony, Chi.	G	Edwards, Don, Buf.
Robinson, Larry, Mtl.	D	Salming, Borje, Tor.
Bourque, Ray, Bos.	D	Schoenfeld, Jim, Buf.
Dionne, Marcel, L.A.	C	Gretzky, Wayne, Edm.
Lafleur, Guy, Mtl.	RW	Gare, Danny, Buf.
Simmer, Charlie, L.A.	LW	Shutt, Steve, Mtl.

1978-79

First Team	Pos	Second Team
Dryden, Ken, Mtl.	G	Resch, Glenn, NYI
Potvin, Denis, NYI	D	Salming, Borje, Tor.
Robinson, Larry, Mtl.	D	Savard, Serge, Mtl.
Trottier, Bryan, NYI	C	Dionne, Marcel, L.A.
Lafleur, Guy, Mtl.	RW	Bossy, Mike, NYI
Gillies, Clark, NYI	LW	Barber, Bill, Phi.

1977-78

First Team	Pos	Second Team
Dryden, Ken, Mtl.	G	Edwards, Don, Buf.
Potvin, Denis, NYI	D	Robinson, Larry, Mtl.
Park, Brad, Bos.	D	Salming, Borje, Tor.
Trottier, Bryan, NYI	C	Sittler, Darryl, Tor.
Lafleur, Guy, Mtl.	RW	Bossy, Mike, NYI
Gillies, Clark, NYI	LW	Shutt, Steve, Mtl.

1976-77

First Team	Pos	Second Team
Dryden, Ken, Mtl.	G	Vachon, Rogie, L.A.
Robinson, Larry, Mtl.	D	Potvin, Denis, NYI
Salming, Borje, Tor.	D	Lapointe, Guy, Mtl.
Dionne, Marcel, L.A.	C	Perreault, Gilbert, Buf.
Lafleur, Guy, Mtl.	RW	McDonald, Lanny, Tor.
Shutt, Steve, Mtl.	LW	Martin, Rick, Buf.

1975-76

First Team	Pos	Second Team
Dryden, Ken, Mtl.	G	Resch, Glenn, NYI
Potvin, Denis, NYI	D	Salming, Borje, Tor.
Park, Brad, Bos.	D	Lapointe, Guy, Mtl.
Clarke, Bobby, Phi.	C	Perreault, Gilbert, Buf.
Lafleur, Guy, Mtl.	RW	Leach, Reggie, Phi.
Barber, Bill, Phi.	LW	Martin, Rick, Buf.

1974-75

First Team	Pos	Second Team
Parent, Bernie, Phi.	G	Vachon, Rogie, L.A.
Orr, Bobby, Bos.	D	Lapointe, Guy, Mtl.
Potvin, Denis, NYI	D	Salming, Borje, Tor.
Clarke, Bobby, Phi.	C	Esposito, Phil, Bos.
Lafleur, Guy, Mtl.	RW	Robert, René, Buf.
Martin, Rick, Buf.	LW	Vickers, Steve, NYR

1973-74

First Team	Pos	Second Team
Parent, Bernie, Phi.	G	Esposito, Tony, Chi.
Orr, Bobby, Bos.	D	White, Bill, Chi.
Park, Brad, NYR	D	Ashbee, Barry, Phi.
Esposito, Phil, Bos.	C	Clarke, Bobby, Phi.
Hodge, Ken, Bos.	RW	Redmond, Mickey, Det.
Martin, Rick, Buf.	LW	Cashman, Wayne, Bos.

1972-73

First Team	Pos	Second Team
Dryden, Ken, Mtl.	G	Esposito, Tony, Chi.
Orr, Bobby, Bos.	D	Park, Brad, NYR
Lapointe, Guy, Mtl.	D	White, Bill, Chi.
Esposito, Phil, Bos.	C	Clarke, Bobby, Phi.
Redmond, Mickey, Det.	RW	Cournoyer, Yvan, Mtl.
Mahovlich, Frank, Mtl.	LW	Hull, Dennis, Chi.

1971-72

First Team	Pos	Second Team
Esposito, Tony, Chi.	G	Dryden, Ken, Mtl.
Orr, Bobby, Bos.	D	White, Bill, Chi.
Park, Brad, NYR	D	Stapleton, Pat, Chi.
Esposito, Phil, Bos.	C	Ratelle, Jean, NYR
Gilbert, Rod, NYR	RW	Cournoyer, Yvan, Mtl.
Hull, Bobby, Chi.	LW	Hadfield, Vic, NYR

1970-71

First Team	Pos	Second Team
Giacomin, Ed, NYR	G	Plante, Jacques, Tor.
Orr, Bobby, Bos.	D	Park, Brad, NYR
Tremblay, J.C., Mtl.	D	Stapleton, Pat, Chi.
Esposito, Phil, Bos.	C	Keon, Dave, Tor.
Hodge, Ken, Bos.	RW	Cournoyer, Yvan, Mtl.
Bucyk, John, Bos.	LW	Hull, Bobby, Chi.

1969-70

First Team	Pos	Second Team
Esposito, Tony, Chi.	G	Giacomin, Ed, NYR
Orr, Bobby, Bos.	D	Brewer, Carl, Det.
Park, Brad, NYR	D	Laperriere, Jacques, Mtl.
Esposito, Phil, Bos.	C	Mikita, Stan, Chi.
Howe, Gordie, Det.	RW	McKenzie, John, Bos.
Hull, Bobby, Chi.	LW	Mahovlich, Frank, Det.

1968-69

First Team	Pos	Second Team
Hall, Glenn, St.L.	G	Giacomin, Ed, NYR
Orr, Bobby, Bos.	D	Green, Ted, Bos.
Horton, Tim, Tor.	D	Harris, Ted, Mtl.
Esposito, Phil, Bos.	C	Béliveau, Jean, Mtl.
Howe, Gordie, Det.	RW	Cournoyer, Yvan, Mtl.
Hull, Bobby, Chi.	LW	Mahovlich, Frank, Det.

1967-68

First Team	Pos	Second Team
Worsley, Gump, Mtl.	G	Giacomin, Ed, NYR
Orr, Bobby, Bos.	D	Tremblay, J.C., Mtl.
Horton, Tim, Tor.	D	Neilson, Jim, NYR
Mikita, Stan, Chi.	C	Esposito, Phil, Bos.
Howe, Gordie, Det.	RW	Gilbert, Rod, NYR
Hull, Bobby, Chi.	LW	Bucyk, John, Bos.

1966-67

First Team	Pos	Second Team
Giacomin, Ed, NYR	G	Hall, Glenn, Chi.
Pilote, Pierre, Chi.	D	Horton, Tim, Tor.
Howell, Harry, NYR	D	Orr, Bobby, Bos.
Mikita, Stan, Chi.	C	Ullman, Norm, Det.
Wharram, Kenny, Chi.	RW	Howe, Gordie, Det.
Hull, Bobby, Chi.	LW	Marshall, Don, NYR

1965-66

First Team	Pos	Second Team
Hall, Glenn, Chi.	G	Worsley, Gump, Mtl.
Laperriere, Jacques, Mtl.	D	Stanley, Allan, Tor.
Pilote, Pierre, Chi.	D	Stapleton, Pat, Chi.
Mikita, Stan, Chi.	C	Béliveau, Jean, Mtl.
Howe, Gordie, Det.	RW	Rousseau, Bobby, Mtl.
Hull, Bobby, Chi.	LW	Mahovlich, Frank, Tor.

1964-65

First Team	Pos	Second Team
Crozier, Roger, Det.	G	Hodge, Charlie, Mtl.
Pilote, Pierre, Chi.	D	Gadsby, Bill, Det.
Laperriere, Jacques, Mtl.	D	Brewer, Carl, Tor.
Ullman, Norm, Det.	C	Mikita, Stan, Chi.
Provost, Claude, Mtl.	RW	Howe, Gordie, Det.
Hull, Bobby, Chi.	LW	Mahovlich, Frank, Tor.

1963-64

First Team	Pos	Second Team
Hall, Glenn, Chi.	G	Hodge, Charlie, Mtl.
Pilote, Pierre, Chi.	D	Vasko, Elmer, Chi.
Horton, Tim, Tor.	D	Laperriere, Jacques, Mtl.
Mikita, Stan, Chi.	C	Béliveau, Jean, Mtl.
Wharram, Kenny, Chi.	RW	Howe, Gordie, Det.
Hull, Bobby, Chi.	LW	Mahovlich, Frank, Tor.

1962-63

First Team	Pos	Second Team
Hall, Glenn, Chi.	G	Sawchuk, Terry, Det.
Pilote, Pierre, Chi.	D	Horton, Tim, Tor.
Brewer, Carl, Tor.	D	Vasko, Elmer, Chi.
Mikita, Stan, Chi.	C	Richard, Henri, Mtl.
Howe, Gordie, Det.	RW	Bathgate, Andy, NYR
Mahovlich, Frank, Tor.	LW	Hull, Bobby, Chi.

1961-62

First Team	Pos	Second Team
Plante, Jacques, Mtl.	G	Hall, Glenn, Chi.
Harvey, Doug, NYR	D	Brewer, Carl, Tor.
Talbot, Jean-Guy, Mtl.	D	Pilote, Pierre, Chi.
Mikita, Stan, Chi.	C	Keon, Dave, Tor.
Bathgate, Andy, NYR	RW	Howe, Gordie, Det.
Hull, Bobby, Chi.	LW	Mahovlich, Frank, Tor.

1960-61

First Team	Pos	Second Team
Bower, Johnny, Tor.	G	Hall, Glenn, Chi.
Harvey, Doug, Mtl.	D	Stanley, Allan, Tor.
Pronovost, Marcel, Det.	D	Pilote, Pierre, Chi.
Béliveau, Jean, Mtl.	C	Richard, Henri, Mtl.
Geoffrion, Bernie, Mtl.	RW	Howe, Gordie, Det.
Mahovlich, Frank, Tor.	LW	Moore, Dickie, Mtl.

1959-60

First Team	Pos	Second Team
Hall, Glenn, Chi.	G	Plante, Jacques, Mtl.
Harvey, Doug, Mtl.	D	Stanley, Allan, Tor.
Pronovost, Marcel, Det.	D	Pilote, Pierre, Chi.
Béliveau, Jean, Mtl.	C	Horvath, Bronco, Bos.
Howe, Gordie, Det.	RW	Geoffrion, Bernie, Mtl.
Hull, Bobby, Chi.	LW	Prentice, Dean, NYR

1958-59

First Team	Pos	Second Team
Plante, Jacques, Mtl.	G	Sawchuk, Terry, Det.
Johnson, Tom, Mtl.	D	Pronovost, Marcel, Det.
Gadsby, Bill, NYR	D	Harvey, Doug, Mtl.
Béliveau, Jean, Mtl.	C	Richard, Henri, Mtl.
Bathgate, Andy, NYR	RW	Howe, Gordie, Det.
Moore, Dickie, Mtl.	LW	Delvecchio, Alex, Det.

Hockey lost three former All-Stars and Honoured Members of the Hockey Hall of Fame during the 1999-2000 season. The death of Rocket Richard on May 27, 2000, was national news for days in Canada and his funeral was broadcast live from coast to coast. Bill Quackenbush and Sid Abel, teammates in Detroit – and of Richard in the 1949 All-Star Game – also passed away in the last year. Quackenbush (above), a great playmaking defenseman with Boston and Detroit, died on September 12, 1999. Sid Abel (left, center), who centered Gordie Howe and Ted Lindsay on Detroit's famed Production Line, passed away on February 7, 2000.

1957-58

First Team		Second Team
Hall, Glenn, Chi.	G	Plante, Jacques, Mtl.
Harvey, Doug, Mtl.	D	Flaman, Fern, Bos.
Gadsby, Bill, NYR	D	Pronovost, Marcel, Det.
Richard, Henri, Mtl.	C	Béliveau, Jean, Mtl.
Howe, Gordie, Det.	RW	Bathgate, Andy, NYR
Moore, Dickie, Mtl.	LW	Henry, Camille, NYR

1956-57

First Team		Second Team
Hall, Glenn, Det.	G	Plante, Jacques, Mtl.
Harvey, Doug, Mtl.	D	Flaman, Fern, Bos.
Kelly, Red, Det.	D	Gadsby, Bill, NYR
Béliveau, Jean, Mtl.	C	Litzenberger, Ed, Chi.
Howe, Gordie, Det.	RW	Richard, Maurice, Mtl.
Lindsay, Ted, Det.	LW	Chevrefils, Real, Bos.

1955-56

First Team		Second Team
Plante, Jacques, Mtl.	G	Hall, Glenn, Det.
Harvey, Doug, Mtl.	D	Kelly, Red, Det.
Gadsby, Bill, NYR	D	Johnson, Tom, Mtl.
Béliveau, Jean, Mtl.	C	Sloan, Tod, Tor.
Richard, Maurice, Mtl.	RW	Howe, Gordie, Det.
Lindsay, Ted, Det.	LW	Olmstead, Bert, Mtl.

1954-55

First Team		Second Team
Lumley, Harry, Tor.	G	Sawchuk, Terry, Det.
Harvey, Doug, Mtl.	D	Goldham, Bob, Det.
Kelly, Red, Det.	D	Flaman, Fern, Bos.
Béliveau, Jean, Mtl.	C	Mosdell, Ken, Mtl.
Richard, Maurice, Mtl.	RW	Geoffrion, Bernie, Mtl.
Smith, Sid, Tor.	LW	Lewicki, Danny, NYR

1953-54

First Team		Second Team
Lumley, Harry, Tor.	G	Sawchuk, Terry, Det.
Kelly, Red, Det.	D	Gadsby, Bill, Chi.
Harvey, Doug, Mtl.	D	Horton, Tim, Tor.
Mosdell, Kenny, Mtl.	C	Kennedy, Ted, Tor.
Howe, Gordie, Det.	RW	Richard, Maurice, Mtl.
Lindsay, Ted, Det.	LW	Sandford, Ed, Bos.

1952-53

First Team		Second Team
Sawchuk, Terry, Det.	G	McNeil, Gerry, Mtl.
Kelly, Red, Det.	D	Quackenbush, Bill, Bos.
Harvey, Doug, Mtl.	D	Gadsby, Bill, Chi.
Mackell, Fleming, Bos.	C	Delvecchio, Alex, Det.
Howe, Gordie, Det.	RW	Richard, Maurice, Mtl.
Lindsay, Ted, Det.	LW	Olmstead, Bert, Mtl.

1951-52

First Team		Second Team
Sawchuk, Terry, Det.	G	Henry, Jim, Bos.
Kelly, Red, Det.	D	Buller, Hy, NYR
Harvey, Doug, Mtl.	D	Thomson, Jimmy, Tor.
Lach, Elmer, Mtl.	C	Schmidt, Milt, Bos.
Howe, Gordie, Det.	RW	Richard, Maurice, Mtl.
Lindsay, Ted, Det.	LW	Smith, Sid, Tor.

1950-51

First Team		Second Team
Sawchuk, Terry, Det.	G	Rayner, Chuck, NYR
Kelly, Red, Det.	D	Thomson, Jim, Tor.
Quackenbush, Bill, Bos.	D	Reise Jr., Leo, Det.
Schmidt, Milt, Bos.	C	Abel, Sid, Det.
	(tied)	Kennedy, Ted, Tor.
Howe, Gordie, Det.	RW	Richard, Maurice, Mtl.
Lindsay, Ted, Det.	LW	Smith, Sid, Tor.

1949-50

First Team		Second Team
Durnan, Bill, Mtl.	G	Rayner, Chuck, NYR
Mortson, Gus, Tor.	D	Reise Jr., Leo, Det.
Reardon, Ken, Mtl.	D	Kelly, Red, Det.
Abel, Sid, Det.	C	Kennedy, Ted, Tor.
Richard, Maurice, Mtl.	RW	Howe, Gordie, Det.
Lindsay, Ted, Det.	LW	Leswick, Tony, NYR

1948-49

First Team		Second Team
Durnan, Bill, Mtl.	G	Rayner, Chuck, NYR
Quackenbush, Bill, Det.	D	Harmon, Glen, Mtl.
Stewart, Jack, Det.	D	Reardon, Ken, Mtl.
Abel, Sid, Det.	C	Bentley, Doug, Chi.
Richard, Maurice, Mtl.	RW	Howe, Gordie, Det.
Conacher, Roy, Chi.	LW	Lindsay, Ted, Det.

1947-48

First Team		Second Team
Broda, Turk, Tor.	G	Brimsek, Frank, Bos.
Quackenbush, Bill, Det.	D	Reardon, Ken, Mtl.
Stewart, Jack, Det.	D	Colville, Neil, NYR
Lach, Elmer, Mtl.	C	O'Connor, Buddy, NYR
Richard, Maurice, Mtl.	RW	Poile, Bud, Chi.
Lindsay, Ted, Det.	LW	Stewart, Gaye, Chi.

1946-47

First Team		Second Team
Durnan, Bill, Mtl.	G	Brimsek, Frank, Bos.
Reardon, Ken, Mtl.	D	Stewart, Jack, Det.
Bouchard, Butch, Mtl.	D	Quackenbush, Bill, Det.
Schmidt, Milt, Bos.	C	Bentley, Max, Chi.
Richard, Maurice, Mtl.	RW	Bauer, Bobby, Bos.
Bentley, Doug, Chi.	LW	Dumart, Woody, Bos.

1945-46

First Team		Second Team
Durnan, Bill, Mtl.	G	Brimsek, Frank, Bos.
Crawford, Jack, Bos.	D	Reardon, Ken, Mtl.
Bouchard, Butch, Mtl.	D	Stewart, Jack, Det.
Bentley, Max, Chi.	C	Lach, Elmer, Mtl.
Richard, Maurice, Mtl.	RW	Mosienko, Bill, Chi.
Stewart, Gaye, Tor.	LW	Blake, Toe, Mtl.
Irvin, Dick, Mtl.	Coach	Gottselig, Johnny, Chi.

1944-45

First Team		Second Team
Durnan, Bill, Mtl.	G	Karakas, Mike, Chi.
Bouchard, Butch, Mtl.	D	Harmon, Glen, Mtl.
Hollett, Flash, Det.	D	Pratt, Babe, Tor.
Lach, Elmer, Mtl.	C	Cowley, Bill, Bos.
Richard, Maurice, Mtl.	RW	Mosienko, Bill, Chi.
Blake, Toe, Mtl.	LW	Howe, Syd, Det.
Irvin, Dick, Mtl.	Coach	Adams, Jack, Det.

1943-44

First Team		Second Team
Durnan, Bill, Mtl.	G	Bibeault, Paul, Tor.
Seibert, Earl, Chi.	D	Bouchard, Butch, Mtl.
Pratt, Babe, Tor.	D	Clapper, Dit, Bos.
Cowley, Bill, Bos.	C	Lach, Elmer, Mtl.
Carr, Lorne, Tor.	RW	Richard, Maurice, Mtl.
Bentley, Doug, Chi.	LW	Cain, Herb, Bos.
Irvin, Dick, Mtl.	Coach	Day, Hap, Tor.

1942-43

First Team		Second Team
Mowers, Johnny, Det.	G	Brimsek, Frank, Bos.
Seibert, Earl, Chi.	D	Crawford, Jack, Bos.
Stewart, Jack, Det.	D	Hollett, Flash, Bos.
Cowley, Bill, Bos.	C	Apps Sr., Syl, Tor.
Carr, Lorne, Tor.	RW	Hextall Sr., Bryan, NYR
Bentley, Doug, Chi.	LW	Patrick, Lynn, NYR
Adams, Jack, Det.	Coach	Ross, Art, Bos.

1941-42

First Team		Second Team
Brimsek, Frank, Bos.	G	Broda, Turk, Tor.
Seibert, Earl, Chi.	D	Egan, Pat, Bro.
Anderson, Tom, Bro.	D	McDonald, Bucko, Tor.
Apps Sr., Syl, Tor.	C	Watson, Phil, NYR
Hextall Sr., Bryan, NYR	RW	Drillon, Gordie, Tor.
Patrick, Lynn, NYR	LW	Abel, Sid, Det.
Boucher, Frank, NYR	Coach	Thompson, Paul, Chi.

1940-41

First Team		Second Team
Broda, Turk, Tor.	G	Brimsek, Frank, Bos.
Clapper, Dit, Bos.	D	Seibert, Earl, Chi.
Stanowski, Wally, Tor.	D	Heller, Ott, NYR
Cowley, Bill, Bos.	C	Apps Sr., Syl, Tor.
Hextall Sr., Bryan, NYR	RW	Bauer, Bobby, Bos.
Schriner, Sweeney, Tor.	LW	Dumart, Woody, Bos.
Weiland, Cooney, Bos.	Coach	Irvin, Dick, Mtl.

1939-40

First Team		Second Team
Kerr, Dave, NYR	G	Brimsek, Frank, Bos.
Clapper, Dit, Bos.	D	Coulter, Art, NYR
Goodfellow, Ebbie, Det.	D	Seibert, Earl, Chi.
Schmidt, Milt, Bos.	C	Colville, Neil, NYR
Hextall Sr., Bryan, NYR	RW	Bauer, Bobby, Bos.
Blake, Toe, Mtl.	LW	Dumart, Woody, Bos.
Thompson, Paul, Chi.	Coach	Boucher, Frank, NYR

1938-39

First Team		Second Team
Brimsek, Frank, Bos.	G	Robertson, Earl, NYA
Shore, Eddie, Bos.	D	Seibert, Earl, Chi.
Clapper, Dit, Bos.	D	Coulter, Art, NYR
Apps Sr., Syl, Tor.	C	Colville, Neil, NYR
Drillon, Gordie, Tor.	RW	Bauer, Bobby, Bos.
Blake, Toe, Mtl.	LW	Gottselig, Johnny, Chi.
Ross, Art, Bos.	Coach	Dutton, Red, NYA

1937-38

First Team		Second Team
Thompson, Tiny, Bos.	G	Kerr, Dave, NYR
Shore, Eddie, Bos.	D	Coulter, Art, NYR
Siebert, Babe, Mtl.	D	Seibert, Earl, Chi.
Cowley, Bill, Bos.	C	Apps Sr., Syl, Tor.
Dillon, Cecil, NYR	RW	
Drillon, Gordie, Tor.	(tied)	
Thompson, Paul, Chi.	LW	Blake, Toe, Mtl.
Patrick, Lester, NYR	Coach	Ross, Art, Bos.

1936-37

First Team		Second Team
Smith, Norman, Det.	G	Cude, Wilf, Mtl.
Siebert, Babe, Mtl.	D	Seibert, Earl, Chi.
Goodfellow, Ebbie, Det.	D	Conacher, Lionel, Mtl. M.
Barry, Marty, Det.	C	Chapman, Art, NYA
Aurie, Larry, Det.	RW	Dillon, Cecil, NYR
Jackson, Harvey, Tor.	LW	Schriner, Sweeney, NYA
Adams, Jack, Det.	Coach	Hart, Cecil, Mtl.

1935-36

First Team		Second Team
Thompson, Tiny, Bos.	G	Cude, Wilf, Mtl.
Shore, Eddie, Bos.	D	Seibert, Earl, Chi.
Siebert, Babe, Bos.	D	Goodfellow, Ebbie, Det.
Smith, Hooley, Mtl. M.	C	Thoms, Bill, Tor.
Conacher, Charlie, Tor.	RW	Dillon, Cecil, NYR
Schriner, Sweeney, NYA	LW	Thompson, Paul, Chi.
Patrick, Lester, NYR	Coach	Gorman, Tommy, Mtl. M.

1934-35

First Team		Second Team
Chabot, Lorne, Chi.	G	Thompson, Tiny, Bos.
Shore, Eddie, Bos.	D	Wentworth, Cy, Mtl. M.
Seibert, Earl, NYR	D	Coulter, Art, Chi.
Boucher, Frank, NYR	C	Weiland, Cooney, Det.
Conacher, Charlie, Tor.	RW	Clapper, Dit, Bos.
Jackson, Harvey, Tor.	LW	Joliat, Aurel, Mtl.
Patrick, Lester, NYR	Coach	Irvin, Dick, Tor.

1933-34

First Team		Second Team
Gardiner, Chuck, Chi.	G	Worters, Roy, NYA
Clancy, King, Tor.	D	Shore, Eddie, Bos.
Conacher, Lionel, Chi.	D	Johnson, Ching, NYR
Boucher, Frank, NYR	C	Primeau, Joe, Tor.
Conacher, Charlie, Tor.	RW	Cook, Bill, NYR
Jackson, Harvey, Tor.	LW	Joliat, Aurel, Mtl.
Patrick, Lester, NYR	Coach	Irvin, Dick, Tor.

1932-33

First Team		Second Team
Roach, John Ross, Det.	G	Gardiner, Chuck, Chi.
Shore, Eddie, Bos.	D	Clancy, King, Tor.
Johnson, Ching, NYR	D	Conacher, Lionel, Mtl. M.
Boucher, Frank, NYR	C	Morenz, Howie, Mtl.
Cook, Bill, NYR	RW	Conacher, Charlie, Tor.
Northcott, Baldy, Mtl M.	LW	Jackson, Harvey, Tor.
Patrick, Lester, NYR	Coach	Irvin, Dick, Tor.

1931-32

First Team		Second Team
Gardiner, Chuck, Chi.	G	Worters, Roy, NYA
Shore, Eddie, Bos.	D	Mantha, Sylvio, Mtl.
Johnson, Ching, NYR	D	Clancy, King, Tor.
Morenz, Howie, Mtl.	C	Smith, Hooley, Mtl. M.
Cook, Bill, NYR	RW	Conacher, Charlie, Tor.
Jackson, Harvey, Tor.	LW	Joliat, Aurel, Mtl.
Patrick, Lester, NYR	Coach	Irvin, Dick, Tor.

1930-31

First Team		Second Team
Gardiner, Chuck, Chi.	G	Thompson, Tiny, Bos.
Shore, Eddie, Bos.	D	Mantha, Sylvio, Mtl.
Clancy, King, Tor.	D	Johnson, Ching, NYR
Morenz, Howie, Mtl.	C	Boucher, Frank, NYR
Cook, Bill, NYR	RW	Clapper, Dit, Bos.
Joliat, Aurel, Mtl.	LW	Cook, Bun, NYR
Patrick, Lester, NYR	Coach	Irvin, Dick, Chi.

All-Star Game Results

Year	Venue	Score	Coaches	Attendance
2000	Toronto	World 9, North America 4	Scotty Bowman, Pat Quinn	19,300
1999	Tampa Bay	North America 8, World 6	Lindy Ruff, Ken Hitchcock	19,758
1998	Vancouver	North America 8, World 7	Jacques Lemaire, Ken Hitchcock	18,422
1997	San Jose	Eastern 11, Western 7	Doug MacLean, Ken Hitchcock	17,422
1996	Boston	Eastern 5, Western 4	Doug MacLean, Scotty Bowman	17,565
1994	NY Rangers	Eastern 9, Western 8	Jacques Demers, Barry Melrose	18,200
1993	Montreal	Wales 16, Campbell 6	Scotty Bowman, Mike Keenan	17,137
1992	Philadelphia	Campbell 10, Wales 6	Bob Gainey, Scotty Bowman	17,380
1991	Chicago	Campbell 11, Wales 5	John Muckler, Mike Milbury	18,472
1990	Pittsburgh	Wales 12, Campbell 7	Pat Burns, Terry Crisp	16,236
1989	Edmonton	Campbell 9, Wales 5	Glen Sather, Terry O'Reilly	17,503
1988	St. Louis	Wales 6, Campbell 5 OT	Mike Keenan, Glen Sather	17,878
1986	Hartford	Wales 4, Campbell 3 OT	Mike Keenan, Glen Sather •	15,100
1985	Calgary	Wales 6, Campbell 4	Al Arbour, Glen Sather	16,825
1984	New Jersey	Wales 7, Campbell 6	Al Arbour, Glen Sather	18,939
1983	NY Islanders	Campbell 9, Wales 3	Roger Neilson, Al Arbour	15,230
1982	Washington	Wales 4, Campbell 2	Al Arbour, Glen Sonmor	18,130
1981	Los Angeles	Campbell 4, Wales 1	Pat Quinn, Scotty Bowman	15,761
1980	Detroit	Wales 6, Campbell 3	Scotty Bowman, Al Arbour	21,002
1978	Buffalo	Wales 3, Campbell 2 OT	Scotty Bowman, Fred Shero	16,433
1977	Vancouver	Wales 4, Campbell 3	Scotty Bowman, Fred Shero	15,607
1976	Philadelphia	Wales 7, Campbell 5	Floyd Smith, Fred Shero	16,436
1975	Montreal	Wales 7, Campbell 1	Bep Guidolin, Fred Shero	16,080
1974	Chicago	West 6, East 4	Billy Reay, Scotty Bowman	16,426
1973	New York	East 5, West 4	Tom Johnson, Billy Reay	16,986
1972	Minnesota	East 3, West 2	Al MacNeil, Billy Reay	15,423
1971	Boston	West 2, East 1	Scotty Bowman, Harry Sinden	14,790
1970	St. Louis	East 4, West 1	Claude Ruel, Scotty Bowman	16,587
1969	Montreal	East 3, West 3	Toe Blake, Scotty Bowman	16,260
1968	Toronto	Toronto 4, All-Stars 3	Punch Imlach, Toe Blake	15,753
1967	Montreal	Montreal 3, All-Stars 0	Toe Blake, Sid Abel	14,284
1965	Montreal	All-Stars 5, Montreal 2	Billy Reay, Toe Blake	13,529
1964	Toronto	All-Stars 3, Toronto 2	Sid Abel, Punch Imlach	14,232
1963	Toronto	All-Stars 3, Toronto 3	Sid Abel, Punch Imlach	14,034
1962	Toronto	Toronto 4, All-Stars 1	Punch Imlach, Rudy Pilous	14,236
1961	Chicago	All-Stars 3, Chicago 1	Sid Abel, Rudy Pilous	14,534
1960	Montreal	All-Stars 2, Montreal 1	Punch Imlach, Toe Blake	13,949
1959	Montreal	Montreal 6, All-Stars 1	Toe Blake, Punch Imlach	13,818
1958	Montreal	Montreal 6, All-Stars 3	Toe Blake, Milt Schmidt	13,989
1957	Montreal	All-Stars 5, Montreal 3	Milt Schmidt, Toe Blake	13,003
1956	Montreal	All-Stars 1, Montreal 1	Jim Skinner, Toe Blake	13,095
1955	Detroit	Detroit 3, All-Stars 1	Jim Skinner, Dick Irvin	10,111
1954	Detroit	All-Stars 2, Detroit 2	King Clancy, Jim Skinner	10,689
1953	Montreal	All-Stars 3, Montreal 1	Lynn Patrick, Dick Irvin	14,153
1952	Detroit	1st team 1, 2nd team 1	Tommy Ivan, Dick Irvin	10,680
1951	Toronto	1st team 2, 2nd team 2	Joe Primeau, Dick Irvin	11,469
1950	Detroit	Detroit 7, All-Stars 1	Tommy Ivan, Lynn Patrick	9,166
1949	Toronto	All-Stars 3, Toronto 1	Tommy Ivan, Hap Day	13,541
1948	Chicago	All-Stars 3, Toronto 1	Tommy Ivan, Hap Day	12,794
1947	Toronto	All-Stars 4, Toronto 3	Dick Irvin, Hap Day	14,169

There was no All-Star contest during the calendar year of 1966 because the game was moved from the start of season to mid-season. In 1979, the Challenge Cup series between the Soviet Union and Team NHL replaced the All-Star Game. In 1987, Rendez-Vous '87, two games between the Soviet Union and Team NHL replaced the All-Star Game. Rendez-Vous '87 scores: game one, NHL All-Stars 4, Soviet Union 3; game two, Soviet Union 5, NHL All-Stars 3. There was no All-Star Game in 1995 due to a labor disruption.

NHL ALL-ROOKIE TEAM

Voting for the NHL All-Rookie Team is conducted among the representatives of the Professional Hockey Writers' Association at the end of the season. The rookie all-star team was first selected for the 1982-83 season.

1999-2000
Brian Boucher, Philadelphia	Goal
Brian Rafalski, New Jersey	Defense
Brad Stuart, San Jose	Defense
Simon Gagne, Philadelphia	Forward
Scott Gomez, New Jersey	Forward
Michael York, NY Rangers	Forward

1997-98
Jamie Storr, Los Angeles	Goal
Mattias Ohlund, Vancouver	Defense
Derek Morris, Calgary	Defense
Sergei Samsonov, Boston	Forward
Patrick Elias, New Jersey	Forward
Mike Johnson, Toronto	Forward

1995-96
Corey Hirsch, Vancouver	Goal
Ed Jovanovski, Florida	Defense
Kyle McLaren, Boston	Defense
Daniel Alfredsson, Ottawa	Forward
Eric Daze, Chicago	Forward
Petr Sykora, New Jersey	Forward

1993-94
Martin Brodeur, New Jersey	Goal
Chris Pronger, Hartford	Defense
Boris Mironov, Wpg./Edm.	Defense
Jason Arnott, Edmonton	Center
Mikael Renberg, Philadelphia	Wing
Oleg Petrov, Montreal	Wing

1991-92
Dominik Hasek, Chicago	Goal
Nicklas Lidstrom, Detroit	Defense
Vladimir Konstantinov, Detroit	Defense
Kevin Todd, New Jersey	Center
Tony Amonte, NY Rangers	Right Wing
Gilbert Dionne, Montreal	Left Wing

1998-99
Jamie Storr, Los Angeles	Goal
Tom Poti, Edmonton	Defense
Sami Salo, Ottawa	Defense
Chris Drury, Colorado	Forward
Milan Hejduk, Colorado	Forward
Marian Hossa, Ottawa	Forward

1996-97
Patrick Lalime, Pittsburgh	Goal
Bryan Berard, NY Islanders	Defense
Janne Niinimaa, Philadelphia	Defense
Jarome Iginla, Calgary	Forward
Jim Campbell, St. Louis	Forward
Sergei Berezin, Toronto	Forward

1994-95
Jim Carey, Washington	Goal
Chris Therien, Philadelphia	Defense
Kenny Jonsson, Toronto	Defense
Peter Forsberg, Quebec	Forward
Jeff Friesen, San Jose	Forward
Paul Kariya, Anaheim	Forward

1992-93
Felix Potvin, Toronto	Goal
Vladimir Malakhov, NY Islanders	Defense
Scott Niedermayer, New Jersey	Defense
Eric Lindros, Philadelphia	
Teemu Selanne, Winnipeg	
Joe Juneau, Boston	

1990-91
Ed Belfour, Chicago	Goal
Eric Weinrich, New Jersey	Defense
Rob Blake, Los Angeles	Defense
Sergei Fedorov, Detroit	Center
Ken Hodge, Boston	
Jaromir Jagr, Pittsburgh	

1999-2000 All-Star Game Summary

February 6, 2000 at Toronto   World 9, North America 4

PLAYERS ON ICE: North America — Joseph, Brodeur, Richter, MacInnis, S. Stevens, Blake, Housley, Chelios, Desjardins, C. Pronger, Bourque, Recchi, Kariya, Amonte, M. Messier, Nolan, Shanahan, Whitney, LeClair, Yzerman, Gomez, Modano, Lindros, Sakic, Roenick.

The World — Turek, Salo, Kolzig, Buzek, Lidstrom, Ozolinsh, Svoboda, Numminen, Yushkevich, Zubov, Selanne, P. Bure, Sundin, Bonk, V. Bure, Hejduk, Kapanen, Viktor Kozlov, Rucinsky, Czerkawski, Elias, Demitra, Jagr, Satan.

SUMMARY
First Period
1. World	Demitra (1)	(Yushkevich, Elias)	3:12
2. World	Jagr (1)	(Rucinsky)	10:50
3. North America	Sakic (1)	(Whitney, Recchi)	13:56
4. World	Yushkevich (1)	(Kozlov, P. Bure)	14:35
5. North America	Roenick (1)	(Modano)	19:30

PENALTIES: None

Second Period
6. World	P. Bure (1)	(V. Bure)	0:33
7. World	P. Bure (2)	(V. Bure, Kozlov)	8:38
8. North America	Amonte (1)	(Modano, Bourque)	12:14
9. North America	Whitney (1)	(Desjardins, Messier)	17:08

PENALTIES: None

Third Period
10. World	Demitra (1)	(Hejduk, Elias)	8:52
11. World	P. Bure (3)	(Lidstrom, Kozlov)	9:31
12. World	Satan (1)	(Czerkawski, Bonk)	10:51
13. World	Bonk (1)	(Jagr, Rucinsky)	19:28

Penalties: Ozolinsh, World (hooking) 5:51

SHOTS ON GOAL BY:

North America	12	11	9	**32**
World	20	13	15	**48**

	Goaltenders:	Time	SA	GA	ENG	Dec
N. America	Joseph	20:00	20	3	0	
N. America	Brodeur	20:00	13	2	0	L
N. America	Richter	20:00	15	4	0	
World	Turek	20:00	13	2	0	
World	Salo	20:00	11	2	0	W
World	Kolzig	20:00	9	0	0	

PP Conversions: North America 0/1; World 0/0.

Referee: Kerry Fraser, Don Koharski   Linesmen: Gerard Gauthier, Ray Scapinello
Attendance: 19,300.

2TORONTO.
NHL ALL-STAR WEEKEND

1989-90
Bob Essensa, Winnipeg	Goal
Brad Shaw, Hartford	Defense
Geoff Smith, Edmonton	Defense
Mike Modano, Minnesota	Center
Sergei Makarov, Calgary	Right Wing
Rod Brind'Amour, St. Louis	Left Wing

1987-88
Darren Pang, Chicago	Goal
Glen Wesley, Boston	Defense
Calle Johansson, Buffalo	Defense
Joe Nieuwendyk, Calgary	Center
Ray Sheppard, Buffalo	Right Wing
Iain Duncan, Winnipeg	Left Wing

1985-86
Patrick Roy, Montreal	Goal
Gary Suter, Calgary	Defense
Dana Murzyn, Hartford	Defense
Mike Ridley, NY Rangers	Center
Kjell Dahlin, Montreal	Right Wing
Wendel Clark, Toronto	Left Wing

1983-84
Tom Barrasso, Buffalo	Goal
Thomas Eriksson, Philadelphia	Defense
Jamie Macoun, Calgary	Defense
Steve Yzerman, Detroit	Center
Hakan Loob, Calgary	Right Wing
Sylvain Turgeon, Hartford	Left Wing

1988-89
Peter Sidorkiewicz, Hartford	
Brian Leetch, NY Rangers	
Zarley Zalapski, Pittsburgh	
Trevor Linden, Vancouver	
Tony Granato, NY Rangers	
David Volek, NY Islanders	

1986-87
Ron Hextall, Philadelphia	
Steve Duchesne, Los Angeles	
Brian Benning, St. Louis	
Jimmy Carson, Los Angeles	
Jim Sandlak, Vancouver	
Luc Robitaille, Los Angeles	

1984-85
Steve Penney, Montreal	
Chris Chelios, Montreal	
Bruce Bell, Quebec	
Mario Lemieux, Pittsburgh	
Tomas Sandstrom, NY Rangers	
Warren Young, Pittsburgh	

1982-83
Pelle Lindbergh, Philadelphia	
Scott Stevens, Washington	
Phil Housley, Buffalo	
Dan Daoust, Mtl./Tor.	
Steve Larmer, Chicago	
Mats Naslund, Montreal	

All-Star Game Records
1947 through 2000

TEAM RECORDS

MOST GOALS, BOTH TEAMS, ONE GAME:
22 — Wales 16, Campbell 6, 1993 at Montreal
19 — Wales 12, Campbell 7, 1990 at Pittsburgh
18 — East 11, West 7, 1997 at San Jose
17 — East 9, West 8, 1994 at NY Rangers
16 — Campbell 11, Wales 5, 1991 at Chicago
— Campbell 10, Wales 6, 1992 at Philadelphia
15 — North America 8, World 7, 1998 at Vancouver
14 — Campbell 9, Wales 5, 1989 at Edmonton
— North America 8, World 6, 1999 at Tampa Bay

FEWEST GOALS, BOTH TEAMS, ONE GAME:
2 — NHL All-Stars 1, Montreal Canadiens 1, 1956 at Montreal
— First Team All-Stars 1, Second Team All-Stars 1, 1952 at Detroit
3 — West 2, East 1, 1971 at Boston
— Montreal Canadiens 3, NHL All-Stars 0, 1967 at Montreal
— NHL All-Stars 2, Montreal Canadiens 1, 1960 at Montreal

MOST GOALS, ONE TEAM, ONE GAME:
16 — Wales 16, Campbell 6, 1993 at Montreal
12 — Wales 12, Campbell 7, 1990 at Pittsburgh
11 — Campbell 11, Wales 5, 1991 at Chicago
— East 11, West 7, 1997 at San Jose
10 — Campbell 10, Wales 6, 1992 at Philadelphia

FEWEST GOALS, ONE TEAM, ONE GAME:
0 — NHL All-Stars 0, Montreal Canadiens 3, 1967 at Montreal
1 — 17 times (1981, 1975, 1971, 1970, 1962, 1961, 1960, 1959, both teams 1956, 1955, 1953, both teams 1952, 1950, 1949, 1948)

MOST SHOTS, BOTH TEAMS, ONE GAME (SINCE 1955):
102 — 1994 at NY Rangers — East 9 (56 shots),
West 8 (46 shots)
90 — 1993 at Montreal — Wales 16 (49 shots),
Campbell 6 (41 shots)
87 — 1990 at Pittsburgh — Wales 12 (45 shots),
Campbell 7 (42 shots)
— 1997 at San Jose — East 11 (41 shots),
West 7 (46 shots)
85 — 1999 at Tampa Bay — North America 8 (49 shots),
World 6 (36 shots)

FEWEST SHOTS, BOTH TEAMS, ONE GAME (SINCE 1955):
52 — 1978 at Buffalo — Campbell 2 (12 shots)
Wales 3 (40 shots)
53 — 1960 at Montreal — NHL All-Stars 2 (27 shots)
Montreal Canadiens 1 (26 shots)
55 — 1956 at Montreal — NHL All-Stars 1 (28 shots)
Montreal Canadiens 1 (27 shots)
— 1971 at Boston — West 2 (28 shots)
East 1 (27 shots)

MOST SHOTS, ONE TEAM, ONE GAME (SINCE 1955):
56 — 1994 at NY Rangers — East (9-8 vs. West)
49 — 1993 at Montreal — Wales (16-6 vs. Campbell)
— 1999 at Tampa Bay — North America (8-6 vs. Campbell)
48 — 2000 at Toronto — World (9-4 vs. North America)
46 — 1994 at NY Rangers — West (8-9 vs. East)
— 1997 at San Jose — West (7-11 vs. East)

FEWEST SHOTS, ONE TEAM, ONE GAME (SINCE 1955):
12 — 1978 at Buffalo — Campbell (2-3 vs. Wales)
17 — 1970 at St. Louis — West (1-4 vs. East)
23 — 1961 at Chicago — Chicago Black Hawks (1-3 vs. NHL All-Stars)
24 — 1976 at Philadelphia — Campbell (5-7 vs. Wales)

MOST POWER-PLAY GOALS, BOTH TEAMS, ONE GAME (SINCE 1950):
3 — 1953 at Montreal — NHL All-Stars 3 (2 power-play goals),
Montreal Canadiens 1 (1 power-play goal)
— 1954 at Detroit — NHL All-Stars 2 (1 power-play goal)
Detroit Red Wings 2 (2 power-play goals)
— 1958 at Montreal — NHL All-Stars 3 (1 power-play goal)
Montreal Canadiens 6 (2 power-play goals)

FEWEST POWER-PLAY GOALS, BOTH TEAMS, ONE GAME (SINCE 1950):
0 — 18 times (1952, 1959, 1960, 1967, 1968, 1969, 1972, 1973, 1976, 1980, 1981, 1984, 1985, 1992, 1994, 1996, 1999, 2000)

FASTEST TWO GOALS, BOTH TEAMS, FROM START OF GAME:
37 seconds — 1970 at St. Louis — Jacques Laperriere of East scored at 20 seconds and Dean Prentice of West scored at 37 seconds. Final score: East 4, West 1.
2:15 — 1998 at Vancouver — Teemu Selanee scored at 0:53 and Jaromir Jagr scored at 2:15 for World. Final score: North America 8, World 7.
3:37 — 1993 at Montreal — Mike Gartner scored at 3:15 and at 3:37 for Wales. Final score: Wales 16, Campbell 6.

FASTEST TWO GOALS, BOTH TEAMS:
8 seconds — 1997 at San Jose — Owen Nolan scored at 18:54 and 19:02 of second period for West. Final Score: East 11, West 7.
10 seconds — 1976 at Philadelphia — Dennis Ververgaert scored at 4:33 and at 4:43 of third period for Campbell. Final score: Wales 7, Campbell 5.
13 seconds — 1998 at Vancouver — Teemu Selanne scored at 4:00 of first period for World and John LeClair scored at 4:13 for North America. Final score: North America 8, World 7.

FASTEST THREE GOALS, BOTH TEAMS:
1:08 — 1993 at Montreal — all by Wales — Mike Gartner scored at 3:15 and at 3:37 of first period; Peter Bondra scored at 4:23. Final score: Wales 16, Campbell 6.
1:14 — 1994 at NY Rangers — Bob Kudelski scored at 9:46 of first period for East; Sergei Fedorov scored at 10:20 for West; Eric Lindros scored at 11:00 for East. Final score: East 9, West 8.
1:23 — 1999 at Tampa Bay — Mats Sundin scored at 2:57 of third period for World; Darryl Sydor scored at 4:02 for North America; Sergei Zubov scored at 4:20 for World. Final score: North America 8, World 6.

FASTEST FOUR GOALS, BOTH TEAMS:
2:24 — 1997 at San Jose — Brendan Shanahan scored at 16:38 of second period for West; Dale Hawerchuk scored at 17:28 for East; Owen Nolan scored at 18:54 and 19:02 for West. Final score: East 11, West 7.
3:04 — 1997 at San Jose — Mark Recchi scored at 15:32 of first period for East; Dale Hawerchuk scored at 16:19 for East; Pavel Bure scored at 17:36 for West; Paul Kariya scored at 18:36 for West. Final score: East 11, West 7.
3:20 — 1998 at Vancouver — Teemu Selanne scored at 0:53 of first period for World; Jaromir Jagr scored at 2:15 for World; Selanne scored at 4:00 for World; John LeClair scored at 4:13 for North America. Final score: North America 8, World 7.

FASTEST TWO GOALS, ONE TEAM, FROM START OF GAME:
2:15 — 1998 at Vancouver — World — Teemu Selanee scored at 0:53 and Jaromir Jagr scored at 2:15. Final score: North America 8, World 7.
3:37 — 1993 at Montreal — Wales — Mike Gartner scored at 3:15 and at 3:37. Final score: Wales 16, Campbell 6.
4:19 — 1980 at Detroit — Wales — Larry Robinson scored at 3:58 and Steve Payne scored at 4:19. Final score: Wales 6, Campbell 3.

FASTEST TWO GOALS, ONE TEAM:
8 seconds — 1997 at San Jose — West — Owen Nolan scored at 18:54 and at 19:02 of second period. Final score: East 11, West 7.
10 seconds — 1976 at Philadelphia — Campbell — Dennis Ververgaert scored at 4:33 and at 4:43 of third period. Final score: Wales 7, Campbell 5.
14 seconds — 1989 at Edmonton — Campbell — Steve Yzerman and Gary Leeman scored at 17:21 and 17:35 of second period. Final score: Campbell 9, Wales 5.

FASTEST THREE GOALS, ONE TEAM:
1:08 — 1993 at Montreal — Wales — Mike Gartner scored at 3:15 and 3:37 of first period; Peter Bondra scored at 4:23. Final score: Wales 16, Campbell 6.
1:32 — 1980 at Detroit — Wales — Ron Stackhouse scored at 11:40 of third period; Craig Hartsburg scored at 12:40; Reed Larson scored at 13:12. Final score: Wales 6, Campbell 3.
1:42 — 1993 at Montreal — Wales — Alexander Mogilny scored at 11:40 of first period; Pierre Turgeon scored at 13:05; Mike Gartner scored at 13:22. Final score: Wales 16, Campbell 6.

FASTEST FOUR GOALS, ONE TEAM:
4:19 — 1992 at Philadelphia — Campbell — Brian Bellows scored at 7:40 of second period; Jeremy Roenick scored at 8:13; Theoren Fleury scored at 11:06, Brett Hull scored at 11:59. Final score: Campbell 10, Wales 6.
4:26 — 1980 at Detroit — Wales — Ron Stackhouse scored at 11:40 of third period; Craig Hartsburg scored at 12:40; Reed Larson scored at 13:12; Real Cloutier scored at 16:06. Final score: Wales 6, Campbell 3.
4:29 — 1999 at Tampa Bay — North America — Paul Kariya scored at 16:45 of first period; Mark Recchi scored at 17:18; Ray Bourque scored at 0:17 of second period; Wayne Gretzky scored at 1:14. Final score: North America 8, World 6.

MOST GOALS, BOTH TEAMS, ONE PERIOD:
10 — 1997 at San Jose — Second period — East (6), West (4). Final score: East 11, West 7.
9 — 1990 at Pittsburgh — First period — Wales (7), Campbell (2). Final score: Wales 12, Campbell 7.
8 — 1992 at Philadelphia — Second period — Campbell (6), Wales (2). Final Score: Campbell 10, Wales 6.
— 1993 at Montreal — Second period — Wales (6), Campbell (2). Final score: Wales 16, Campbell 6.
— 1993 at Montreal — Third period — Wales (4), Campbell (4). Final score: Wales 16, Campbell 6.

MOST GOALS, ONE TEAM, ONE PERIOD:
7 — 1990 at Pittsburgh — First period — Wales. Final score: Wales 12, Campbell 7.
6 — 1983 at NY Islanders — Third period — Campbell. Final score: Campbell 9, Wales 3.
— 1992 at Philadelphia — Second Period — Campbell. Final score: Campbell 10, Wales 6.
— 1993 at Montreal — First period — Wales. Final score: Wales 16, Campbell 6.
— 1993 at Montreal — Second period — Wales. Final score: Wales 16, Campbell 6.
— 1997 at San Jose — Second period — East. Final score: East 11, West 7.

MOST SHOTS, BOTH TEAMS, ONE PERIOD:
39 — 1994 at NY Rangers — Second period — West (21), East (18). Final score: East 9, West 8.
36 — 1990 at Pittsburgh — Third period — Campbell (22), Wales (14). Final score: Wales 12, Campbell 7.
— 1994 at NY Rangers — First period — East (19), West (17). Final score: East 9, West 8.

MOST SHOTS, ONE TEAM, ONE PERIOD:
22 — 1990 at Pittsburgh — Third period — Campbell. Final score: Wales 12, Campbell 7.
— 1991 at Chicago — Third Period — Wales. Final score: Campbell 11, Wales 5.
— 1993 at Montreal — First period — Wales. Final score: Wales 16, Campbell 6.

FEWEST SHOTS, BOTH TEAMS, ONE PERIOD:
9 — 1971 at Boston — Third period — East (2), West (7). Final score: West 2, East 1.
— 1980 at Detroit — Second period — Campbell (4), Wales (5). Final score: Wales 6, Campbell 3.
13 — 1982 at Washington — Third period — Campbell (6), Wales (7). Final score: Wales 4, Campbell 2.
14 — 1978 at Buffalo — First period — Campbell (7), Wales (7). Final score: Wales 3, Campbell 2.
— 1986 at Hartford — First period — Campbell (6), Wales (8). Final score: Wales 4, Campbell 3.

FEWEST SHOTS, ONE TEAM, ONE PERIOD:
2 — 1971 at Boston — Third period — East. Final score: West 2, East 1.
— 1978 at Buffalo — Second period — Campbell. Final score: Wales 3, Campbell 2.
3 — 1978 at Buffalo — Third period — Campbell. Final score: Wales 3, Campbell 2.
4 — 1955 at Detroit — First period — NHL All-Stars. Final score: Detroit Red Wings 3, NHL All-Stars 1.
4 — 1980 at Detroit — Second period — Campbell. Final score: Wales 6, Campbell 3.

INDIVIDUAL RECORDS

Games

MOST GAMES PLAYED:
23 — Gordie Howe from 1948 through 1980
18 — Wayne Gretzky from 1980 through 1999
— Ray Bourque from 1981 through 2000
15 — Frank Mahovlich from 1959 through 1974
14 — Paul Coffey from 1982 through 1997
— Mark Messier from 1982 through 2000

Goals

MOST GOALS (CAREER):
13 — Wayne Gretzky in 18GP
11 — Mario Lemieux in 8GP
10 — Gordie Howe in 23GP
8 — Frank Mahovlich in 15GP
7 — Maurice Richard in 13GP
— Pavel Bure in 5GP

MOST GOALS, ONE GAME:
4 — Wayne Gretzky, Campbell, 1983
— Mario Lemieux, Wales, 1990
— Vince Damphousse, Campbell, 1991
— Mike Gartner, Wales, 1993
3 — Ted Lindsay, Detroit, 1950
— Mario Lemieux, Wales, 1988
— Pierre Turgeon, Wales, 1993
— Mark Recchi, East, 1997
— Owen Nolan, West, 1997
— Teemu Selanne, World, 1998
— Pavel Bure, World, 2000

MOST GOALS, ONE PERIOD:
4 — Wayne Gretzky, Campbell, Third period, 1983
3 — Mario Lemieux, Wales, First period, 1990
— Vince Damphousse, Campbell, Third period, 1991
— Mike Gartner, Wales, First period, 1993

Assists

MOST ASSISTS (CAREER):
13 — Mark Messier in 14GP
— Ray Bourque in 18GP
12 — Adam Oates in 5GP
— Joe Sakic in 8GP
— Wayne Gretzky in 18GP

MOST ASSISTS, ONE GAME:
5 — Mats Naslund, Wales, 1988
4 — Ray Bourque, Wales, 1985
— Adam Oates, Campbell, 1991
— Adam Oates, Wales, 1993
— Mark Recchi, Wales, 1993
— Pierre Turgeon, East, 1994

MOST ASSISTS, ONE PERIOD:
4 — Adam Oates, Wales, First period, 1993
3 — Mark Messier, Campbell, Third period, 1983

Howie Morenz was among those who suited up for the Ace Bailey Benefit Game on February 14, 1934 — a forerunner of the NHL All-Star Game. Another benefit game was played to aid Morenz's family after his tragic death in 1937.

Points

MOST POINTS, CAREER:
25 — Wayne Gretzky (13G-12A in 18GP)
20 — Mario Lemieux (11G-9A in 8GP)
19 — Gordie Howe (10G-9A in 23GP)
18 — Mark Messier (5G-13A in 14GP)
17 — Ray Bourque (4G-13A in 18GP)

MOST POINTS, ONE GAME:
6 — Mario Lemieux, Wales, 1988 (3G-3A)
5 — Mats Naslund, Wales, 1988 (5A)
— Adam Oates, Campbell, 1991 (1G-4A)
— Mike Gartner, Wales, 1993 (4G-1A)
— Mark Recchi, Wales, 1993 (1G-4A)
— Pierre Turgeon, Wales, 1993 (3G-2A)

MOST POINTS, ONE PERIOD:
4 — Wayne Gretzky, Campbell, Third period, 1983 (4G)
— **Mike Gartner,** Wales, First period, 1993 (3G-1A)
— **Adam Oates,** Wales, First period, 1993 (4A)
3 — Gordie Howe, NHL All-Stars, Second period, 1965 (1G-2A)
— Pete Mahovlich, Wales, First period, 1976 (1G-2A)
— Mark Messier, Campbell, Third period, 1983 (3A)
— Mario Lemieux, Wales, Second period, 1988 (1G-2A)
— Mario Lemieux, Wales, First period, 1990 (3G)
— Vince Damphousse, Campbell, Third period, 1991 (3G)
— Mark Recchi, Wales, Second period, 1993 (1G-2A)

Power-Play Goals

MOST POWER-PLAY GOALS, CAREER:
6 — Gordie Howe in 23GP
3 — Bobby Hull in 12GP
— Maurice Richard in 13GP

Fastest Goals

FASTEST GOAL FROM START OF GAME:
19 seconds — Ted Lindsay, Detroit, 1950
20 seconds — Jacques Laperriere, East, 1970
21 seconds — Mario Lemieux, Wales, 1990
36 seconds — Chico Maki, West, 1971
37 seconds — Dean Prentice, West, 1970

FASTEST GOAL FROM START OF A PERIOD:
17 seconds — Ray Bourque, North America, 1999 (second period)
19 seconds — Ted Lindsay, Detroit, 1950 (first period)
— Rick Tocchet, Wales, 1993 (second period)
20 seconds — Jacques Laperriere, East, 1970 (first period)
21 seconds — Mario Lemieux, Wales, 1990 (first period)
26 seconds — Wayne Gretzky, Campbell, 1982 (second period)

FASTEST TWO GOALS (ONE PLAYER) FROM START OF GAME:
3:37 — Mike Gartner, Wales, 1993, at 3:15 and 3:37.
4:00 — Teemu Selanne, World, 1998, at 0:53 and 4:00
5:25 — Wally Hergesheimer, NHL All-Stars, 1953, at 4:06 and 5:25.

FASTEST TWO GOALS (ONE PLAYER) FROM START OF A PERIOD:
3:37 — Mike Gartner, Wales, 1993, at 3:15 and 3:37 of first period.
4:00 — Teemu Selanne, World, 1998, at 0:53 and 4:00 of first period.
4:43 — Dennis Ververgaert, Campbell, 1976, at 4:33 and 4:43 of third period.

FASTEST TWO GOALS (ONE PLAYER):
8 seconds — Owen Nolan, West, 1997. Scored at 18:54 and 19:02 of second period.
10 seconds — Dennis Ververgaert, Campbell, 1976. Scored at 4:33 and 4:43 of third period.
22 seconds — Mike Gartner, Wales, 1993. Scored at 3:15 and 3:37 of first period.

Penalties

MOST PENALTY MINUTES:
25 — Gordie Howe in 23GP
21 — Gus Mortson in 9GP
16 — Harry Howell in 7GP

Goaltenders

MOST GAMES PLAYED:
13 — Glenn Hall from 1955-1969
11 — Terry Sawchuk from 1950-1968
8 — Jacques Plante from 1956-1970
— Patrick Roy from 1988-1998
6 — Tony Esposito from 1970-1980
— Ed Giacomin from 1967-1973
— Grant Fuhr from 1982-1989

MOST MINUTES PLAYED:
540 — Glenn Hall in 13GP
467 — Terry Sawchuk in 11GP
370 — Jacques Plante in 8GP
209 — Turk Broda in 4GP
190 — Patrick Roy in 8GP
182 — Ed Giacomin in 6GP

MOST GOALS AGAINST:
24 — Patrick Roy in 8GP
22 — Glenn Hall in 13GP
21 — Mike Vernon in 5GP
19 — Terry Sawchuk in 11GP
18 — Jacques Plante in 8GP
— Andy Moog in 4GP

BEST GOALS-AGAINST-AVERAGE AMONG THOSE WITH AT LEAST TWO GAMES PLAYED:
0.68 — Gilles Villemure in 3GP
1.49 — Gerry McNeil in 3GP
1.50 — Johnny Bower in 4GP
1.51 — Frank Brimsek in 2GP
1.64 — Gump Worsley in 4GP
2.03 — Don Edwards in 2GP

Ten Edmonton Oilers took part in 1986 All-Star Game: (left to right)
Andy Moog, Wayne Gretzky, Glenn Anderson, Paul Coffey, Kevin Lowe,
Glen Sather, Mark Messier, Lee Fogolin, Jari Kurri and Grant Fuhr.

Hockey Hall of Fame

(Year of induction is listed after each Honoured Members name)

Location: BCE Place, at the corner of Front and Yonge Streets in the heart of downtown Toronto. Easy access from all major highways running into Toronto. Close to TTC and Union Station.

Telephone: administration (416) 360-7735; information (416) 360-7765.

Summer and Christmas/March break hours: Monday to Saturday 9:30 a.m. to 6 p.m.; Sunday 10:00 a.m. to 6 p.m.

Fall/Winter/Spring hours (except Christmas/March break): Monday to Friday 10 a.m. to 5 p.m.; Saturday 9:30 a.m. to 6 p.m.; Sunday 10:30 a.m. to 5 p.m. The Hockey Hall of Fame can be booked for private functions after hours.

Website address: www.hhof.com

History: The Hockey Hall of Fame was established in 1943. Members were first honoured in 1945. On August 26, 1961, the Hockey Hall of Fame opened its doors to the public in a building located on the grounds of the Canadian National Exhibition in Toronto. The Hockey Hall of Fame relocated to its new site at BCE Place and welcomed the hockey world on June 18, 1993.

Honour Roll: There are 319 Honoured Members in the Hockey Hall of Fame. 218 have been inducted as players, 87 as builders and 14 as Referees/Linesmen. In addition, there are 64 media honourees.

Sponsors: Special thanks to Bell Canada, Blockbuster Video, Coca-Cola Ltd., Ford of Canada, Household Financial Services, IBM Corporation, Imperial Oil, International Ice Hockey Federation, Kodak Canada Inc., London Life Insurance Company, Molson Breweries, National Hockey League, The Toronto Sun Publishing Corporation, The Sports Network Inc. (TSN/RDS).

A slick skater and a superior playmaker, Denis Savard scored 473 career goals and set up 865 more for teammates. He enters the Hockey Hall of Fame in 2000 along with Joe Mullen and builder Walter Bush.

PLAYERS

* Abel, Sidney Gerald 1969
* Adams, John James "Jack" 1959
* Apps, Charles Joseph Sylvanus "Syl" 1961
  Armstrong, George Edward 1975
* Bailey, Irvine Wallace "Ace" 1975
* Bain, Donald H. "Dan" 1945
* Baker, Hobart "Hobey" 1945
  Barber, William Charles "Bill" 1990
* Barry, Martin J. "Marty" 1965
  Bathgate, Andrew James "Andy" 1978
* Bauer, Robert Theodore "Bobby" 1996
  Béliveau, Jean Arthur 1972
* Benedict, Clinton S. 1965
* Bentley, Douglas Wagner 1964
* Bentley, Maxwell H. L. 1966
* Blake, Hector Toe 1966
  Boivin, Leo Joseph 1986
* Boon, Richard R. "Dickie" 1952
  Bossy, Michael 1991
  Bouchard, Butch Joseph "Butch" 1966
* Boucher, Frank 1958
* Boucher, George "Buck" 1960
  Bower, John William 1976
* Bowie, Russell 1945
* Brimsek, Francis Charles 1966
* Broadbent, Harry L. "Punch" 1962
* Broda, Walter Edward "Turk" 1967
  Bucyk, John Paul 1981
* Burch, Billy 1974
* Cameron, Harold Hugh "Harry" 1962
  Cheevers, Gerald Michael "Gerry" 1985
* Clancy, Francis Michael "King" 1958
* Clapper, Aubrey "Dit" 1947
  Clarke, Robert "Bobby" 1987
* Cleghorn, Sprague 1958
* Colville, Neil MacNeil 1967
* Conacher, Charles W. 1961
* Conacher, Lionel Pretoria 1994
* Conacher, Roy Gordon 1998
* Connell, Alex 1958
* Cook, Fred "Bun" 1995
* Cook, William Osser 1952
  Coulter, Arthur Edmund 1974
  Cournoyer, Yvan Serge 1982
* Cowley, William Mailes 1968
* Crawford, Samuel Russell "Rusty" 1962
* Darragh, John Proctor "Jack" 1962
  Davidson, Allan M. "Scotty" 1950
* Day, Clarence Henry Hap 1961
  Delvecchio, Alex 1977
* Denneny, Cyril "Cy" 1959
  Dionne, Marcel 1992
* Drillon, Gordon Arthur 1975

* Drinkwater, Charles Graham 1950
  Dryden, Kenneth Wayne 1983
  Dumart, Woodrow "Woody" 1992
* Dunderdale, Thomas 1974
* Durnan, William Ronald 1964
* Dutton, Mervyn A. "Red" 1958
* Dye, Cecil Henry "Babe" 1970
  Esposito, Anthony James "Tony" 1988
  Esposito, Philip Anthony 1984
* Farrell, Arthur F. 1965
  Flaman, Ferdinand Charles "Fern" 1990
* Foyston, Frank 1958
* Fredrickson, Frank 1958
  Gadsby, William Alexander 1970
  Gainey, Bob 1992
* Gardiner, Charles Robert "Chuck" 1945
* Gardiner, Herbert Martin "Herb" 1958
* Gardner, James Henry "Jimmy" 1962
  Geoffrion, Jos. A. Bernard "Boom Boom" 1972
* Gerard, Eddie 1945
  Giacomin, Edward "Eddie" 1987
  Gilbert, Rodrigue Gabriel "Rod" 1982
* Gilmour, Hamilton Livingstone "Billy" 1962
* Goheen, Frank Xavier "Moose" 1952
* Goodfellow, Ebenezer R. "Ebbie" 1963
  Goulet, Michel 1998
* Grant, Michael "Mike" 1950
* Green, Wilfred "Shorty" 1962
  Gretzky, Wayne Douglas 1999
* Griffis, Silas Seth "Si" 1950
* Hainsworth, George 1961
  Hall, Glenn Henry 1975
* Hall, Joseph Henry 1961
* Harvey, Douglas Norman 1973
* Hay, George 1958
* Hern, William Milton "Riley" 1962
* Hextall, Bryan Aldwyn 1969
* Holmes, Harry Hap 1972
* Hooper, Charles Thomas "Tom" 1962
  Horner, George Reginald "Red" 1965
* Horton, Miles Gilbert "Tim" 1977
  Howe, Gordon 1972
* Howe, Sydney Harris 1965
  Howell, Henry Vernon "Harry" 1979
  Hull, Robert Marvin 1983
* Hutton, John Bower "Bouse" 1962
* Hyland, Harry M. 1962
* Irvin, James Dickenson "Dick" 1958
* Jackson, Harvey "Busher" 1971
* Johnson, Ernest "Moose" 1952
* Johnson, Ivan "Ching" 1958
  Johnson, Thomas Christian 1970
* Joliat, Aurel 1947

* Keats, Gordon "Duke" 1958
  Kelly, Leonard Patrick "Red" 1969
  Kennedy, Theodore Samuel "Teeder" 1966
  Keon, David Michael 1986
  Lach, Elmer James 1966
  Lafleur, Guy Damien 1988
* Lalonde, Edouard Charles "Newsy" 1950
  Laperriere, Jacques 1987
  Lapointe, Guy 1993
  Laprade, Edgar 1993
* Laviolette, Jean Baptiste "Jack" 1962
* Lehman, Hugh 1958
  Lemaire, Jacques Gerard 1984
  Lemieux, Mario 1997
* LeSueur, Percy 1961
* Lewis, Herbert A. 1989
  Lindsay, Robert Blake Theodore "Ted" 1966
* Lumley, Harry 1980
* MacKay, Duncan "Mickey" 1952
  Mahovlich, Frank William 1981
* Malone, Joseph "Joe" 1950
* Mantha, Sylvio 1960
* Marshall, John "Jack" 1965
* Maxwell, Fred G. "Steamer" 1962
  McDonald, Lanny 1992
* McGee, Frank 1945
* McGimsie, William George "Billy" 1962
* McNamara, George 1958
  Mikita, Stanley 1983
  Moore, Richard Winston 1974
* Moran, Patrick Joseph "Paddy" 1958
* Morenz, Howie 1945
* Mosienko, William "Billy" 1965
* Mullen, Joseph P. 2000
* Nighbor, Frank 1947
* Noble, Edward Reginald "Reg" 1962
* O'Connor, Herbert William "Buddy" 1988
* Oliver, Harry 1967
  Olmstead, Murray Bert "Bert" 1985
  Orr, Robert Gordon 1979
  Parent, Bernard Marcel 1984
  Park, Douglas Bradford "Brad" 1988
* Patrick, Joseph Lynn 1980
* Patrick, Lester 1947
  Perreault, Gilbert 1990
* Phillips, Tommy 1945
  Pilote, Joseph Albert Pierre Paul 1975
* Pitre, Didier "Pit" 1962
* Plante, Joseph Jacques Omer 1978
  Potvin, Denis 1991
* Pratt, Walter "Babe" 1966
* Primeau, A. Joseph 1963
  Pronovost, Joseph René Marcel 1978

Pulford, Bob 1991
* Pulford, Harvey 1945
* Quackenbush, Hubert George "Bill" 1976
* Rankin, Frank 1961
Ratelle, Joseph Gilbert Yvan Jean "Jean" 1985
Rayner, Claude Earl "Chuck" 1973
Reardon, Kenneth Joseph 1966
Richard, Joseph Henri 1979
* Richard, Joseph Henri Maurice "Rocket" 1961
* Richardson, George Taylor 1950
* Roberts, Gordon 1971
Robinson, Larry 1995
* Ross, Arthur Howie 1945
* Russel, Blair 1965
* Russell, Ernest 1965
* Ruttan, J.D. "Jack" 1962
Salming, Borje Anders 1996
Savard, Denis Joseph 2000
Savard, Serge A. 1986
* Sawchuk, Terrance Gordon "Terry" 1971
* Scanlan, Fred 1965
Schmidt, Milton Conrad "Milt" 1961
* Schriner, David "Sweeney" 1962
* Seibert, Earl Walter 1963
* Seibert, Oliver Levi 1961
* Shore, Edward W. "Eddie" 1947
Shutt, Stephen 1993
* Siebert, Albert C. "Babe" 1964
* Simpson, Harold Edward "Bullet Joe" 1962
Sittler, Darryl Glen 1989
* Smith, Alfred E. 1962
Smith, Clint 1991
* Smith, Reginald "Hooley" 1972
* Smith, Thomas James 1973
Smith, William John "Billy" 1993
Stanley, Allan Herbert 1981
* Stanley, Russell "Barney" 1962
Stastny, Peter 1998
* Stewart, John Sherratt "Black Jack" 1964
* Stewart, Nelson "Nels" 1962
* Stuart, Bruce 1961
* Stuart, Hod 1945
* Taylor, Frederic "Cyclone" (O.B.E.) 1947
* Thompson, Cecil R. "Tiny" 1959
Tretiak, Vladislav 1989
* Trihey, Col. Harry J. 1950
Trottier, Bryan 1997
Ullman, Norman V. Alexander "Norm" 1982
* Vezina, Georges 1945
* Walker, John Phillip "Jack" 1960
* Walsh, Martin "Marty" 1962
* Watson, Harry E. 1962
Watson, Harry 1994
* Weiland, Ralph "Cooney" 1971
* Westwick, Harry 1962
* Whitcroft, Fred 1962
* Wilson, Gordon Allan "Phat" 1962
Worsley, Lorne John "Gump" 1980
* Worters, Roy 1969

BUILDERS

* Adams, Charles 1960
* Adams, Weston W. 1972
* Ahearn, Thomas Franklin "Frank" 1962
* Ahearne, John Francis "Bunny" 1977
* Allan, Sir Montagu (C.V.O.) 1945
Allen, Keith 1992
Arbour, Alger Joseph "Al" 1996
* Ballard, Harold Edwin 1977
* Bauer, Father David 1989
* Bickell, John Paris 1978
Bowman, Scott 1991
* Brown, George V. 1961
* Brown, Walter A. 1962
* Buckland, Frank 1975
Bush, Walter Sr. 2000
Butterfield, Jack Arlington 1980
* Calder, Frank 1947
* Campbell, Angus D. 1964
* Campbell, Clarence Sutherland 1966
* Cattarinich, Joseph 1977
* Dandurand, Joseph Viateur "Leo" 1963
* Dilio, Francis Paul 1964
* Dudley, George S. 1958
* Dunn, James A. 1968
Francis, Emile 1982
* Gibson, Dr. John L. "Jack" 1976
* Gorman, Thomas Patrick "Tommy" 1963

* Griffiths, Frank A. 1993
* Hanley, William 1986
* Hay, Charles 1974
* Hendy, James C. 1968
* Hewitt, Foster 1965
* Hewitt, William Abraham 1947
* Hume, Fred J. 1962
* Imlach, George "Punch" 1984
* Ivan, Thomas N. 1974
* Jennings, William M. 1975
* Johnson, Bob 1992
* Juckes, Gordon W. 1979
* Kilpatrick, Gen. John Reed 1960
* Knox, Seymour H. III 1993
* Leader, George Alfred 1969
* LeBel, Robert 1970
* Lockhart, Thomas F. 1965
* Loicq, Paul 1961
* Mariucci, John 1985
Mathers, Frank 1992
* McLaughlin, Major Frederic 1963
* Milford, John "Jake" 1984
Molson, Hon. Hartland de Montarville 1973
Morrison, Ian "Scotty" 1999
* Murray, Monsignor Athol 1998
* Nelson, Francis 1947
* Norris, Bruce A. 1969
* Norris, Sr., James 1958
* Norris, James Dougan 1962
* Northey, William M. 1947
* O'Brien, John Ambrose 1962
O'Neill, Brian 1994
* Page, Fred 1993
* Patrick, Frank 1958
* Pickard, Allan W. 1958
* Pilous, Rudy 1985
Poile, Norman "Bud" 1990
Pollock, Samuel Patterson Smyth 1978
* Raymond, Sen. Donat 1958
* Robertson, John Ross 1947
* Robinson, Claude C. 1947
* Ross, Philip D. 1976
Sabetzki, Dr. Gunther 1995
Sather, Glen 1997
* Selke, Frank J. 1960
Sinden, Harry James 1983
* Smith, Frank D. 1962
* Smythe, Conn 1958
Snider, Edward M. 1988
* Stanley of Preston, Lord (G.C.B.) 1945
Sutherland, Cap. James T. 1947
* Tarasov, Anatoli V. 1974
Torrey, Bill 1995
* Turner, Lloyd 1958
* Tutt, William Thayer 1978
* Voss, Carl Potter 1974
* Waghorn, Fred C. 1961
* Wirtz, Arthur Michael 1971
Wirtz, William W. "Bill" 1976
Ziegler, John A. Jr. 1987

REFEREES/LINESMEN

Armstrong, Neil 1991
Ashley, John George 1981
Chadwick, William L. 1964
D'Amico, John 1993
* Elliott, Chaucer 1961
* Hayes, George William 1988
* Hewitson, Robert W. 1963
* Ion, Fred J. "Mickey" 1961
Pavelich, Matt 1987
* Rodden, Michael J. "Mike" 1962
* Smeaton, J. Cooper 1961
Storey, Roy Alvin "Red" 1967
Udvari, Frank Joseph 1973
Van Hellemond, Andy 1999

Hockey Hall of Fame Game
Saturday, November 11, 2000
Chicago Blackhawks vs.
Toronto Maple Leafs at
Air Canada Centre in Toronto.

Elmer Ferguson Memorial Award Winners

In recognition of distinguished members of the newspaper profession whose words have brought honor to journalism and to hockey. Selected by the Professional Hockey Writers' Association.

* Barton, Charlie, Buffalo-Courier Express 1985
* Beauchamp, Jacques, Montreal Matin/Journal de Montréal 1984
* Brennan, Bill, Detroit News 1987
* Burchard, Jim, New York World Telegram 1984
* Burnett, Red, Toronto Star 1984
* Carroll, Dink, Montreal Gazette 1984
Coleman, Jim, Southam Newspapers 1984
Conway, Russ, Eagle-Tribune 1999
* Damata, Ted, Chicago Tribune 1984
Delano, Hugh, New York Post 1991
Desjardins, Marcel, Montréal La Presse 1984
* Dulmage, Jack, Windsor Star 1984
Dunnell, Milt, Toronto Star 1984
* Ferguson, Elmer, Montreal Herald/Star 1984
Fisher, Red, Montreal Star/Gazette 1985
* Fitzgerald, Tom, Boston Globe 1984
Frayne, Trent, Toronto Telegram/Globe and Mail/ Sun 1984
Gatecliff, Jack, St. Catherines Standard 1995
Gross, George, Toronto Telegram/Sun 1985
Johnston, Dick, Buffalo News 1986
* Laney, Al, New York Herald-Tribune 1984
Larochelle, Claude, Le Soleil 1989
L'Esperance, Zotique, Journal de Montréal/ le Petit Journal 1985
* MacLeod, Rex, Toronto Globe and Mail/Star 1987
Matheson, Jim, Edmonton Journal 2000
* Mayer, Charles, le Journal de Montréal/la Patrie 1985
McKenzie, Ken, The Hockey News 1997
Monahan, Leo, Boston Daily Record/ Record-American/Herald American 1986
Moriarty, Tim, UPI/Newsday 1986
* Nichols, Joe, New York Times 1984
* O'Brien, Andy, Weekend Magazine 1985
Orr, Frank, Toronto Star 1989
Olan, Ben, New York Associated Press 1987
* O'Meara, Basil, Montreal Star 1984
Pedneault, Yvon, La Presse/Le Journale de Montreal 1998
Proudfoot, Jim, Toronto Star 1988
Raymond, Bertrand, le Journal de Montréal 1990
Rosa, Fran, Boston Globe 1987
Strachan, Al, Globe and Mail/Toronto Sun 1993
* Vipond, Jim, Toronto Globe and Mail 1984
Walter, Lewis, Detroit Times 1984
Young, Scott, Toronto Globe and Mail/Telegram 1988

Foster Hewitt Memorial Award Winners

In recognition of members of the radio and television industry who made outstanding contributions to their profession and the game during their career in hockey broadcasting. Selected by the NHL Broadcasters' Association.

Cole, Bob, Hockey Night in Canada 1996
Cusick, Fred, Boston 1984
* Darling, Ted, Buffalo 1994
* Gallivan, Danny, Montreal 1984
Garneau, Richard, Montreal 1999
* Hart, Gene, Philadelphia 1997
* Hewitt, Foster, Toronto 1984
Irvin, Dick, Montreal 1988
* Kelly, Dan, St. Louis 1989
* Lecavelier, René, Montreal 1984
Lynch, Budd, Detroit 1985
Martyn, Bruce, Detroit 1991
McDonald, Jiggs, Los Angeles, Atlanta, NY Islanders 1990
McFarlane, Brian, Hockey Night in Canada 1995
* McKnight, Wes, Toronto 1986
Meeker, Howie, Hockey Night in Canada 1998
Miller, Bob, Los Angeles 2000
Pettit, Lloyd, Chicago 1986
Robson, Jim, Vancouver 1992
Shaver, Al, Minnesota 1993
* Smith, Doug, Montreal 1985
Wilson, Bob, Boston 1987

* Deceased

United States Hockey Hall of Fame

The United States Hockey Hall of Fame is located in Eveleth, Minnesota, 60 miles north of Duluth, on Highway 53. The facility is open Monday to Saturday 9 a.m. to 5 p.m. and Sundays 10 a.m to 3 p.m.; Individual Admission is $6.00 for adults, $5.00 for Senior Citizens, $5.00 for Youths (13-17), and $4.00 for children (6-12). Call for any further information: 1-800-443-7825 or 218-744-5167. Website address: www.ushockeyhall.com

The Hall was dedicated and opened on June 21, 1973, largely as the result of the work of D. Kelly Campbell, Chairman of the Eveleth Civic Association's Project H Committee. There are now 103 enshrinees consisting of 62 players, 22 coaches, 17 administrators, one player/administrator and one referee. New members are inducted annually in October and must have made a significant contribution toward hockey in the United States during the course of their careers. Support for the Hall comes from sponsorship and membership programs, grants from the hockey community, and government agencies.

PLAYERS

* Abel, Clarence "Taffy" 1973
* Baker, Hobart "Hobey" 1973
  Bartholome, Earl 1977
* Bessone, Peter 1978
  Blake, Robert 1985
  Boucha, Henry 1995
* Brimsek, Frank 1973
  Cavanagh, Joe 1994
* Chaisson, Ray 1974
* Chase, John P. 1973
  Christian, Roger 1989
  Christian, William "Bill" 1984
  Cleary, Robert 1981
  Cleary, William 1976
* Conroy, Anthony 1975
  Curran, Mike 1998
  Dahlstrom, Carl "Cully" 1973
* Desjardins, Victor 1974
* Desmond, Richard 1988
* Dill, Robert 1979
  Everett, Doug 1974
  Ftorek, Robbie 1991
* Garrison, John B. 1973
  Garrity, Jack 1986
* Goheen, Frank "Moose" 1973
  Grant, Wally 1994
* Harding, Austin "Austie" 1975
* Iglehart, Stewart 1975
* Johnson, Virgil 1974
* Karakas, Mike 1973
  Kirrane, Jack 1987
* Lane, Myles J. 1973
  Langevin, David R. 1993
  Langway, Rod 1999
  Larson, Reed 1996
* Linder, Joseph 1975
* LoPresti, Sam L. 1973
* Mariucci, John 1973
  Matchefts, John 1991
  Mather, Bruce 1998
  Mayasich, John 1976
  McCartan, Jack 1983
* Moe, William 1974
  Morrow, Ken 1995
* Moseley, Fred 1975
  Mullen, Joe 1998
* Murray, Sr.Hugh "Muzz" 1987
* Nelson, Hubert "Hub" 1978
* Nyrop, William D. 1997
* Olson , Eddie 1977
* Owen, Jr., George 1973
* Palmer, Winthrop 1973
  Paradise, Robert 1989
  Purpur, Clifford "Fido" 1974
  Riley, William 1977
  Roberts, Gordie 1999
* Romnes, Elwin "Doc" 1973
  Rondeau, Richard 1985
  Sheehy, Timothy K. 1997
* Williams, Thomas 1981
* Winters, Frank "Coddy" 1973
* Yackel, Ken 1986

COACHES

* Almquist, Oscar 1983
  Bessone, Amo 1992
  Brooks, Herbert 1990
  Ceglarski, Len 1992
* Fullerton, James 1992
  Gambucci, Sergio 1996
* Gordon, Malcolm K. 1973
  Harkness, Nevin D. "Ned" 1994
  Heyliger, Victor 1974
* Holt, Jr. Charles E. 1997
  Ikola, Willard 1990
* Jeremiah, Edward J. 1973
* Johnson, Bob 1991
* Kelley, John "Snooks" 1974
  Kelley, John H. "Jack" 1993
  Patrick, Craig 1996
  Pleban, Jon "Connie" 1990
  Riley, Jack 1979
* Ross, Larry 1988
* Thompson, Clifford, R. 1973
* Stewart, William 1982
* Winsor, Alfred "Ralph" 1973

ADMINISTRATORS

* Brown, George V. 1973
* Brown, Walter A. 1973
  Bush, Walter 1980
* Clark, Donald 1978
  Claypool, James 1995
* Gibson, J.C. "Doc" 1973
* Jennings, William M. 1981
* Kahler, Nick 1980
* Lockhart, Thomas F. 1973
  Marvin, Cal 1982
* Ridder, Robert 1976
* Schulz, Charles M. 1993
  Trumble, Harold 1985
* Tutt, William Thayer 1973
  Watson, Sid 1999
  Wirtz, William W. "Bill" 1984
* Wright, Lyle Z.1973

PLAYER/ADMINISTRATOR

Nanne, Lou 1998

REFEREE

Chadwick, William 1974

*Deceased

Rod Langway was born in Formosa (Taiwan) but was raised in Randolph, Massachusetts, and grew up to become the first American to win the Norris Trophy. "The Secretary of Defense" was elected to the U.S. Hockey Hall of Fame in 1999.

Results

2000 Stanley Cup Playoffs

CONFERENCE QUARTER-FINALS
(Best-of-seven series)

Eastern Conference

Series 'A'
Thu Apr 13	Buffalo 2	At	Philadelphia 3
Fri Apr 14	Buffalo 1	At	Philadelphia 2
Sun Apr 16	Philadelphia 2	At	Buffalo 0
Tue Apr 18	Philadelphia 2	At	Buffalo 3*
Thu Apr 20	Buffalo 2	At	Philadelphia 5

*Stu Barnes Scored At 4:42 Of Overtime

(Philadelphia Won Series 4-1)

Series 'B'
Thu Apr 13	Pittsburgh 7	At	Washington 0
Sat Apr 15	Washington 1	At	Pittsburgh 2*
Mon Apr 17	Washington 3	At	Pittsburgh 4
Wed Apr 19	Pittsburgh 2	At	Washington 3
Fri Apr 21	Pittsburgh 2	At	Washington 1

*Jaromir Jagr Scored At 5:49 Of Overtime

(Pittsburgh Won Series 4-1)

Series 'C'
Wed Apr 12	Ottawa 0	At	Toronto 2
Sat Apr 15	Ottawa 1	At	Toronto 5
Mon Apr 17	Toronto 3	At	Ottawa 4
Wed Apr 19	Toronto 1	At	Ottawa 2
Sat Apr 22	Ottawa 1	At	Toronto 2*
Mon Apr 24	Toronto 4	At	Ottawa 2

*Steve Thomas Scored At 14:47 Of Overtime

(Toronto Won Series 4-2)

Series 'D'
Thu Apr 13	Florida 3	At	New Jersey 4
Sun Apr 16	Florida 1	At	New Jersey 2
Tue Apr 18	New Jersey 2	At	Florida 1
Thu Apr 20	New Jersey 4	At	Florida 1

(New Jersey Won Series 4-0)

Western Conference

Series 'E'
Wed Apr 12	San Jose 3	At	St. Louis 5
Sat Apr 15	San Jose 4	At	St. Louis 2
Mon Apr 17	St. Louis 1	At	San Jose 2
Wed Apr 19	St. Louis 3	At	San Jose 3
Fri Apr 21	San Jose 3	At	St. Louis 5
Sun Apr 23	St. Louis 6	At	San Jose 2
Tue Apr 25	San Jose 3	At	St. Louis 1

(San Jose Won Series 4-3)

Series 'F'
Wed Apr 12	Edmonton 1	At	Dallas 2
Thu Apr 13	Edmonton 0	At	Dallas 3
Sun Apr 16	Dallas 2	At	Edmonton 5
Tue Apr 18	Dallas 4	At	Edmonton 3
Fri Apr 21	Edmonton 2	At	Dallas 3

(Dallas Won Series 4-1)

Series 'G'
Thu Apr 13	Phoenix 3	At	Colorado 6
Sat Apr 15	Phoenix 1	At	Colorado 3
Mon Apr 17	Colorado 4	At	Phoenix 2
Wed Apr 19	Colorado 2	At	Phoenix 3
Fri Apr 21	Phoenix 1	At	Colorado 2

(Colorado Won Series 4-1)

Series 'H'
Thu Apr 13	Los Angeles 0	At	Detroit 2
Sat Apr 15	Los Angeles 5	At	Detroit 8
Mon Apr 17	Detroit 2	At	Los Angeles 1
Wed Apr 19	Detroit 3	At	Los Angeles 0

(Detroit Won Series 4-0)

CONFERENCE SEMI-FINALS
(Best-of-seven series)

Eastern Conference

Series 'I'
Thu Apr 27	Pittsburgh 2	At	Philadelphia 0
Sat Apr 29	Pittsburgh 4	At	Philadelphia 1
Tue May 2	Philadelphia 4	At	Pittsburgh 3*
Thu May 4	Philadelphia 2	At	Pittsburgh 1**
Sun May 7	Pittsburgh 3	At	Philadelphia 6
Tue May 9	Philadelphia 2	At	Pittsburgh 1

*Andy Delmore Scored At 11:01 Of Overtime
**Keith Primeau Scored At 92:01 Of Overtime

(Philadelphia Won Series 4-2)

Series 'J'
Thu Apr 27	New Jersey 1	At	Toronto 2
Sat Apr 29	New Jersey 1	At	Toronto 0
Mon May 1	Toronto 1	At	New Jersey 5
Wed May 3	Toronto 3	At	New Jersey 2
Sat May 6	New Jersey 4	At	Toronto 3
Mon May 8	Toronto 0	At	New Jersey 3

(New Jersey Won Series 4-2)

Western Conference

Series 'K'
Fri Apr 28	San Jose 0	At	Dallas 4
Sun Apr 30	San Jose 0	At	Dallas 1
Tue May 2	Dallas 1	At	San Jose 2
Fri May 5	Dallas 5	At	San Jose 4
Sun May 7	San Jose 1	At	Dallas 4

(Dallas Won Series 4-1)

Series 'L'
Thu Apr 27	Detroit 0	At	Colorado 2
Sat Apr 29	Detroit 1	At	Colorado 3
Mon May 1	Colorado 1	At	Detroit 3
Wed May 3	Colorado 3	At	Detroit 2*
Fri May 5	Detroit 2	At	Colorado 4

*Chris Drury Scored At 10:21 Of Overtime

(Colorado Won Series 4-1)

CONFERENCE FINALS
(Best-of-seven series)

Eastern Conference

Series 'M'
Sun May 14	New Jersey 4	At	Philadelphia 1
Tue May 16	New Jersey 3	At	Philadelphia 4
Thu May 18	Philadelphia 4	At	New Jersey 2
Sat May 20	Philadelphia 3	At	New Jersey 1
Mon May 22	New Jersey 4	At	Philadelphia 1
Wed May 24	Philadelphia 1	At	New Jersey 2
Fri May 26	New Jersey 2	At	Philadelphia 1

(New Jersey Won Series 4-3)

Western Conference

Series 'N'
Sat May 13	Colorado 2	At	Dallas 0
Mon May 15	Colorado 2	At	Dallas 3
Fri May 19	Dallas 0	At	Colorado 2
Sun May 21	Dallas 4	At	Colorado 1
Tue May 23	Colorado 2	At	Dallas 3*
Thu May 25	Dallas 1	At	Colorado 2
Sat May 27	Colorado 2	At	Dallas 3

*Joe Nieuwendyk Scored At 12:10 Of Overtime

(Dallas Won Series 4-3)

STANLEY CUP CHAMPIONSHIP
(Best-of-seven series)

Series 'O'
Tue May 30	Dallas 3	At	New Jersey 7
Thu June 1	Dallas 2	At	New Jersey 1
Sat June 3	New Jersey 2	At	Dallas 1
Mon June 5	New Jersey 3	At	Dallas 1
Thu June 8	Dallas 1	At	New Jersey 0*
Sat June10	New Jersey 2	At	Dallas 1**

*Mike Modano Scored At 46:21 Of Overtime
**Jason Arnott Scored At 28:20 Of Overtime

(New Jersey Won Series 4-2)

Team Playoff Records

	GP	W	L	GF	GA	%
New Jersey	23	16	7	61	39	.696
Dallas	23	14	9	52	46	.609
Colorado	17	11	6	43	32	.647
Philadelphia	18	11	7	44	40	.611
Pittsburgh	11	6	5	31	23	.545
Toronto	12	6	6	26	26	.500
Detroit	9	5	4	23	19	.556
San Jose	12	5	7	27	37	.417
St. Louis	7	3	4	22	20	.429
Ottawa	6	2	4	10	17	.333
Edmonton	5	1	4	11	14	.200
Buffalo	5	1	4	8	14	.200
Phoenix	5	1	4	10	17	.200
Washington	5	1	4	8	17	.200
Florida	4	0	4	6	12	.000
Los Angeles	4	0	4	6	15	.000

Individual Leaders

Abbreviations: *– rookie eligible for Calder Trophy; **A** – assists; **G** – goals; **GP** – Games Played; **OT** – overtime goals; **GW** – game-winning goals; **PIM** – penalties in minutes; **PP** – power play goals; **Pts** – points; **S** – shots on goal; **SH** – short-handed goals; **%** – percentage of shots resulting in goals; +/– – difference between Goals For (**GF**) scored when a player is on the ice with his team at even strength or short-handed and Goals Against (**GA**) scored when the same player is on the ice with his team at even strength or on a power play.

Playoff Scoring Leaders

Player	Team	GP	G	A	PTS	+/–	PIM	PP	SH	GW	OT	S	%
Brett Hull	Dallas	23	11	13	24	3	4	3	0	4	0	79	13.9
Mike Modano	Dallas	23	10	13	23	3	10	4	0	2	1	67	14.9
Jason Arnott	New Jersey	23	8	12	20	7	18	3	0	1	1	56	14.3
Patrik Elias	New Jersey	23	7	13	20	9	9	2	1	1	0	60	11.7
Mark Recchi	Philadelphia	18	6	12	18	3	6	2	0	1	0	53	11.3
Petr Sykora	New Jersey	23	9	8	17	8	10	1	0	3	0	45	20.0
Jaromir Jagr	Pittsburgh	11	8	8	16	5	6	2	0	4	1	42	19.0
Peter Forsberg	Colorado	16	7	8	15	9	12	2	1	4	0	54	13.0
Adam Deadmarsh	Colorado	17	4	11	15	7	21	1	0	1	0	41	9.8
Chris Drury	Colorado	17	4	10	14	7	4	1	0	2	1	44	9.1
John LeClair	Philadelphia	18	6	7	13	3	6	4	0	1	0	64	9.4
Keith Primeau	Philadelphia	18	2	11	13	4-	13	0	0	1	1	37	5.4
Jan Hrdina	Pittsburgh	9	4	8	12	9	2	1	0	0	0	9	44.4
Martin Straka	Pittsburgh	11	3	9	12	5	10	1	0	0	0	23	13.0
Eric Desjardins	Philadelphia	18	2	10	12	1	2	1	0	1	0	31	6.5
Rick Tocchet	Philadelphia	18	5	6	11	2-	49	2	0	1	0	46	10.9
Scott Stevens	New Jersey	23	3	8	11	9	6	0	0	2	0	29	10.3

Playoff Defensemen Scoring Leaders

Player	Team	GP	G	A	Pts	+/–	PIM	PP:	SH	GW	OT	S	%
Eric Desjardins	Philadelphia	18	2	10	12	1	2	1	0	1	0	31	6.5
Scott Stevens	New Jersey	23	3	8	11	9	6	0	0	2	0	29	10.3
Sandis Ozolinsh	Colorado	17	5	5	10	1	20	3	0	1	0	42	11.9
Sergei Zubov	Dallas	18	2	7	9	1	6	1	1	0	0	34	5.9
Ray Bourque	Colorado	13	1	8	9	4	8	0	0	0	0	28	3.6
Daniel McGillis	Philadelphia	18	2	6	8	1-	12	0	0	0	0	51	3.9
*Brian Rafalski	New Jersey	23	2	6	8	5	8	0	0	1	0	31	6.5
*Andy Delmore	Philadelphia	18	5	2	7	0	14	1	0	1	1	31	16.1
Scott Niedermayer	New Jersey	22	5	2	7	5	10	0	2	1	0	40	12.5
Chris Pronger	St. Louis	7	3	4	7	0	32	2	0	2	0	22	13.6
Gary Suter	San Jose	12	2	5	7	6-	12	1	0	1	0	33	6.1
Richard Matvichuk	Dallas	23	2	5	7	7	14	0	0	0	0	19	10.5
Darryl Sydor	Dallas	23	1	6	7	1	6	0	0	0	0	39	2.6
Adam Foote	Colorado	16	0	7	7	6	28	0	0	0	0	15	.0

GOALTENDING LEADERS

Goals Against Average

Goaltender	Team	GPI	Mins	GA	Avg.
Martin Brodeur	New Jersey	23	1450	39	1.61
Ron Tugnutt	Pittsburgh	11	746	22	1.77
Patrick Roy	Colorado	17	1039	31	1.79
Ed Belfour	Dallas	23	1443	45	1.87
Chris Osgood	Detroit	9	547	18	1.97

Wins

Goaltender	Team	GPI	Mins	W	L
Martin Brodeur	New Jersey	23	1450	16	7
Ed Belfour	Dallas	23	1443	14	9
Patrick Roy	Colorado	17	1039	11	6
Brian Boucher	Philadelphia	18	1183	11	7
Curtis Joseph	Toronto	12	729	6	6
Ron Tugnutt	Pittsburgh	11	746	6	5

Save Percentage

Goaltender	Team	GPI	Mins	GA	SA	S%	W	L
Ron Tugnutt	Pittsburgh	11	746	22	398	.945	6	5
Curtis Joseph	Toronto	12	729	25	369	.932	6	6
Ed Belfour	Dallas	23	1443	45	651	.931	14	9
Patrick Roy	Colorado	17	1039	31	431	.928	11	6
Martin Brodeur	New Jersey	23	1450	39	537	.927	16	7

Shutouts

Goaltender	Team	GPI	Mins	SO
Ed Belfour	Dallas	23	1443	4
Patrick Roy	Colorado	17	1039	3
Chris Osgood	Detroit	9	547	2
Ron Tugnutt	Pittsburgh	11	746	2
Martin Brodeur	New Jersey	23	1450	2
Curtis Joseph	Toronto	12	729	1
Brian Boucher	Philadelphia	18	1183	1

Goal Scoring

Name	Team	GP	G
Brett Hull	Dallas	23	11
Mike Modano	Dallas	23	10
Petr Sykora	New Jersey	23	9
Owen Nolan	San Jose	10	8
Jaromir Jagr	Pittsburgh	11	8
Jason Arnott	New Jersey	23	8
Peter Forsberg	Colorado	16	7
Joe Nieuwendyk	Dallas	23	7
Patrik Elias	New Jersey	23	7
Scott Young	St. Louis	6	6
Steve Thomas	Toronto	12	6
John LeClair	Philadelphia	18	6
Mark Recchi	Philadelphia	18	6

Assists

Name	Team	GP	A
Brett Hull	Dallas	23	13
Mike Modano	Dallas	23	13
Patrik Elias	New Jersey	23	13
Mark Recchi	Philadelphia	18	12
Jason Arnott	New Jersey	23	12
Adam Deadmarsh	Colorado	17	11
Keith Primeau	Philadelphia	18	11
Chris Drury	Colorado	17	10
Eric Desjardins	Philadelphia	18	10
Martin Straka	Pittsburgh	11	9

Power-play Goals

Name	Team	GP	PP
John LeClair	Philadelphia	18	4
Mike Modano	Dallas	23	4
Scott Young	St. Louis	6	3
Mike Ricci	San Jose	12	3
Sandis Ozolinsh	Colorado	17	3
Milan Hejduk	Colorado	17	3
Brett Hull	Dallas	23	3
Joe Nieuwendyk	Dallas	23	3
Jason Arnott	New Jersey	23	3

Game-winning Goals

Name	Team	GP	GW
Jaromir Jagr	Pittsburgh	11	4
Peter Forsberg	Colorado	16	4
Brett Hull	Dallas	23	4
Owen Nolan	San Jose	10	3
Petr Sykora	New Jersey	23	3

Short-handed Goals

Name	Team	GP	SH
Owen Nolan	San Jose	10	2
Scott Niedermayer	New Jersey	22	2
Steve Konowalchuk	Washington	5	1
Ryan Smyth	Edmonton	5	1
Larry Murphy	Detroit	9	1
*Kevyn Adams	Toronto	12	1
Peter Forsberg	Colorado	16	1
Daymond Langkow	Philadelphia	16	1
Sergei Zubov	Dallas	18	1
*John Madden	New Jersey	20	1
Guy Carbonneau	Dallas	23	1
Patrik Elias	New Jersey	23	1

Overtime Goals

Name	Team	GP	OT
Stu Barnes	Buffalo	5	1
Jaromir Jagr	Pittsburgh	11	1
Steve Thomas	Toronto	12	1
Chris Drury	Colorado	17	1
Keith Primeau	Philadelphia	18	1
*Andy Delmore	Philadelphia	18	1
Mike Modano	Dallas	23	1
Joe Nieuwendyk	Dallas	23	1
Jason Arnott	New Jersey	23	1

Shots

Name	Team	GP	S
Brett Hull	Dallas	23	79
Claude Lemieux	New Jersey	23	78
Bobby Holik	New Jersey	23	73
Mike Modano	Dallas	23	67
John LeClair	Philadelphia	18	64

Plus/Minus

Name	Team	GP	+/–
Jan Hrdina	Pittsburgh	9	9
Peter Forsberg	Colorado	16	9
Scott Stevens	New Jersey	23	9
Patrik Elias	New Jersey	23	9
*Colin White	New Jersey	23	9

TEAMS' PLAYOFF HOME/ROAD RECORD

	HOME						ROAD					
	GP	W	L	GF	GA	%	GP	W	L	GF	GA	%
N.J.	11	6	5	29	22	.545	12	10	2	32	17	.833
DAL	13	9	4	29	19	.692	10	5	5	23	27	.500
COL	9	8	1	25	13	.889	8	3	5	18	19	.375
PHI	10	5	5	24	27	.500	8	6	2	20	13	.750
PIT	5	2	3	11	12	.400	6	4	2	20	11	.667
TOR	6	4	2	14	8	.667	6	2	4	12	18	.333
DET	4	3	1	15	9	.750	5	2	3	8	10	.400
S.J.	5	3	2	13	15	.600	7	2	5	14	22	.286
ST.L.	4	2	2	13	13	.500	3	1	2	9	7	.333
OTT	3	2	1	8	8	.667	3	0	3	2	9	.000
EDM	2	1	1	8	6	.500	3	0	3	3	8	.000
BUF	2	1	1	3	4	.500	3	0	3	5	10	.000
PHX	2	1	1	5	6	.500	3	0	3	5	11	.000
WSH	3	1	2	4	11	.333	2	0	2	4	6	.000
FLA	2	0	2	2	6	.000	2	0	2	4	6	.000
L.A.	2	0	2	1	5	.000	2	0	2	5	10	.000
Total	**83**	**48**	**35**	**204**	**184**	**.578**	**83**	**35**	**48**	**184**	**204**	**.422**

TEAMS' POWER-PLAY RECORD

Abbreviations: Adv-total advantages; **PPGF**-power play goals for; **%** arrived by dividing number of power-play goals by total advantages.

	HOME						ROAD						OVERALL			
TEAM	GP	ADV	PPGF	PCTG		TEAM	GP	ADV	PPGF	PCTG		TEAM	GP	ADV	PPGF	PCTG
1 DET	4	20	6	30.0		WSH	2	8	2	25.0		DET	9	43	10	23.3
2 PHI	10	40	11	27.5		N.J.	12	34	8	23.5		PHI	18	69	15	21.7
3 PHX	2	9	2	22.2		BUF	3	9	2	22.2		ST.L.	7	39	8	20.5
4 ST.L.	4	23	5	21.7		ST.L.	3	16	3	18.8		COL	17	86	15	17.4
5 EDM	2	14	3	21.4		PIT	6	32	6	18.8		N.J.	23	70	12	17.1
6 DAL	13	58	11	19.0		DET	5	23	4	17.4		BUF	5	18	3	16.7
7 S.J.	5	27	5	18.5		COL	8	30	5	16.7		DAL	23	93	15	16.1
8 COL	9	56	10	17.9		S.J.	7	36	5	13.9		S.J.	12	63	10	15.9
9 FLA	2	7	1	14.3		PHI	8	29	4	13.8		PHX	5	19	3	15.8
10 BUF	2	9	1	11.1		DAL	10	35	4	11.4		WSH	5	21	3	14.3
11 N.J.	11	36	4	11.1		OTT	3	10	1	10.0		PIT	11	56	8	14.3
12 OTT	3	12	1	8.3		PHX	3	10	1	10.0		EDM	5	25	3	12.0
13 PIT	5	24	2	8.3		TOR	6	21	1	4.8		OTT	6	22	2	9.1
14 WSH	3	13	1	7.7		FLA	2	7	0	.0		FLA	4	14	1	7.1
15 TOR	6	22	1	4.5		L.A.	2	9	0	.0		TOR	12	43	2	4.7
16 L.A.	2	14	0	.0		EDM	3	11	0	.0		L.A.	4	23	0	.0
Total	**83**	**384**	**64**	**16.7**			**83**	**320**	**46**	**14.4**			**83**	**704**	**110**	**15.6**

TEAMS' PENALTY KILLING RECORD

Abbreviations: TSH – Total times short-handed; **PPGA** – power-play goals against; **%** arrived by dividing times short minus power-play goals against by times short.

	HOME					ROAD					OVERALL			
Team	GP	TSH	PPGA	%		Team	GP	TSH	PPGA	%		Team	GP	TSH	PPGA	%
1 N.J.	11	23	0	100.0		FLA	2	7	0	100.0		N.J.	23	67	5	92.5
2 DET	4	16	1	93.8		PHI	8	24	1	95.8		EDM	5	26	2	92.3
3 EDM	2	13	1	92.3		EDM	3	13	1	92.3		OTT	6	23	2	91.3
4 OTT	3	13	1	92.3		OTT	3	10	1	90.0		DET	9	49	5	89.8
5 DAL	13	48	4	91.7		N.J.	12	44	5	88.6		DAL	23	102	12	88.2
6 COL	9	33	3	90.9		PIT	6	25	3	88.0		FLA	4	16	2	87.5
7 TOR	6	20	3	85.0		DET	5	33	4	87.9		PHI	18	58	8	86.2
8 S.J.	5	25	4	84.0		WSH	2	14	2	85.7		TOR	12	47	7	85.1
9 BUF	2	12	2	83.3		TOR	6	27	4	85.2		PIT	11	50	7	84.4
10 ST.L.	4	22	4	81.8		DAL	10	54	8	85.2		ST.L.	7	35	6	82.9
11 PIT	5	20	4	80.0		ST.L.	3	13	2	84.6		COL	17	68	12	82.4
12 PHI	10	34	7	79.4		L.A.	2	13	3	76.9		WSH	5	29	6	79.3
13 FLA	2	9	2	77.8		PHX	3	20	5	75.0		S.J.	12	61	13	78.7
14 WSH	3	15	4	73.3		S.J.	7	36	9	75.0		PHX	5	27	7	74.1
15 PHX	2	7	2	71.4		COL	8	35	9	74.3		L.A.	4	23	7	69.6
16 L.A.	2	10	4	60.0		BUF	3	16	7	56.3		BUF	5	28	9	67.9
Total	**83**	**320**	**46**	**85.6**			**83**	**384**	**64**	**83.3**			**83**	**704**	**110**	**84.4**

SHORT HAND GOALS FOR

	For				Against	
Team	Games	Goals		Team	Games	Goals
N.J.	23	4		PHI	18	0
S.J.	12	2		DET	9	0
DAL	23	2		OTT	6	0
WSH	5	1		WSH	5	0
EDM	5	1		EDM	5	0
DET	9	1		PHX	5	0
TOR	12	1		L.A.	4	0
COL	17	1		N.J.	23	1
PHI	18	1		COL	17	1
FLA	4	0		TOR	12	1
L.A.	4	0		PIT	11	1
BUF	5	0		ST.L.	7	1
PHX	5	0		BUF	5	1
OTT	6	0		FLA	4	1
ST.L.	7	0		S.J.	12	2
PIT	11	0		DAL	23	5
Total	**83**	**14**		**Total**	**83**	**14**

TEAM PENALTIES

Abbreviations: GP – games played; **PEN** – total penalty minutes, including bench penalties; **BMI** – total bench penalty minutes; **AVG** – average penalty minutes per game.

Team	GP	PEN	BMI	AVG
N.J.	23	192	6	8.3
COL	17	178	2	10.5
DAL	23	291	4	12.7
TOR	12	154	0	12.8
FLA	4	54	0	13.5
L.A.	4	54	0	13.5
OTT	6	81	0	13.5
S.J.	12	164	2	13.7
BUF	5	70	4	14.0
PHI	18	257	2	14.3
DET	9	132	0	14.7
PHX	5	75	0	15.0
PIT	11	173	4	15.7
ST.L.	7	114	0	16.3
WSH	5	83	0	16.6
EDM	5	84	0	16.8
TOT	**83**	**2156**	**26**	**26.0**

Despite his brilliance in regular-season play, Martin Brodeur had been taking the heat for New Jersey's recent run of poor playoff performances. Not any more. Brodeur posted 16 wins and a 1.61 GAA during the Devils' 2000 Stanley Cup triumph.

Stanley Cup Record Book

History: The Stanley Cup, the oldest trophy competed for by professional athletes in North America, was donated by Frederick Arthur, Lord Stanley of Preston and son of the Earl of Derby, in 1893. Lord Stanley purchased the trophy for 10 guineas ($50 at that time) for presentation to the amateur hockey champions of Canada. Since 1910, when the National Hockey Association took possession of the Stanley Cup, the trophy has been the symbol of professional hockey supremacy. It has been competed for only by NHL teams since 1926-27 and has been under the exclusive control of the NHL since 1947.

Stanley Cup Standings

1918-2000
(ranked by Cup wins)

Teams	Cup Wins	Yrs.	Series	Wins	Losses	Games	Wins	Losses	Ties	Goals For	Goals Against	Winning %
Montreal	23[1]	72	134[2]	85	48	638	381	249	8	1977	1591	.603
Toronto	13	60	101	54	47	473	225	244	4	1235	1302	.480
Detroit	9	49	91	51	40	449	233	215	1	1266	1186	.520
Boston	5	59	101	47	54	494	236	252	6	1464	1464	.484
Edmonton	5	17	43	31	12	215	133	82	0	844	666	.617
NY Rangers	4	48	86	42	44	386	183	195	8	1091	1114	.484
NY Islanders	4	17	43	30	13	218	128	90	0	748	650	.587
Chicago	3	52	89	40	49	406	187	214	5	1171	1298	.467
Philadelphia	2	26	57	33	24	298	158	140	0	933	881	.530
Pittsburgh	2	20	36	18	18	190	100	90	0	606	597	.526
New Jersey[3]	2	12	23	13	10	133	73	50	0	380	351	.549
Dallas[4]	1	23	46	24	22	250	129	121	0	760	767	.516
Calgary[5]	1	21	32	12	20	156	69	87	0	529	573	.442
Colorado[6]	1	14	29	16	13	162	86	76	0	501	483	.531
St. Louis	0	30	50	20	30	266	120	146	0	763	861	.451
Buffalo	0	24	40	16	24	196	92	104	0	588	609	.469
Los Angeles	0	21	31	10	21	150	55	95	0	473	599	.367
Vancouver	0	16	25	9	16	124	54	70	0	377	422	.435
Washington	0	16	26	10	16	142	65	77	0	442	450	.458
Phoenix[7]	0	15	17	2	15	87	28	59	0	238	330	.322
Carolina[8]	0	9	10	1	9	55	20	35	0	157	194	.367
San Jose	0	5	8	3	5	49	20	29	0	130	184	.408
Ottawa	0	4	5	1	4	28	10	18	0	49	73	.357
Florida	0	3	6	3	3	31	13	18	0	77	82	.419
Anaheim	0	2	3	1	2	15	4	11	0	31	47	.267
Tampa Bay	0	1	1	0	1	6	2	4	0	13	26	.333

[1] Montreal also won the Stanley Cup in 1916.
[2] 1919 final incomplete due to influenza epidemic.
[3] Includes totals of Colorado Rockies 1976-82.
[4] Includes totals of Minnesota North Stars 1967-93.
[5] Includes totals of Atlanta Flames 1972-80.
[6] Includes totals of Quebec 1979-95.
[7] Includes totals of Winnipeg 1979-96.
[8] Includes totals of Hartford 1979-97.

Stanley Cup Winners Prior to Formation of NHL in 1917

Season	Champions	Manager	Coach
1916-17	Seattle Metropolitans	Pete Muldoon	Pete Muldoon
1915-16	Montreal Canadiens	George Kennedy	George Kennedy
1914-15	Vancouver Millionaires	Frank Patrick	Frank Patrick
1913-14	Toronto Blueshirts	Jack Marshall	Scotty Davidson*
1912-13**	Quebec Bulldogs	M.J. Quinn	Joe Malone*
1911-12	Quebec Bulldogs	M.J. Quinn	C. Nolan
1910-11	Ottawa Senators		Bruce Stuart*
1909-10	Montreal Wanderers	R. R. Boon	Pud Glass*
1908-09	Ottawa Senators		Bruce Stuart*
1907-08	Montreal Wanderers	R. R. Boon	Cecil Blachford
1906-07	Montreal Wanderers (Mar. 1907)	R. R. Boon	Cecil Blachford
1906-07	Kenora Thistles (Jan. 1907)	F.A. Hudson	Tommy Phillips*
1905-06	Montreal Wanderers (Mar. 1906)	Cecil Blachford*	
1905-06	Ottawa Silver Seven (Feb. 1906)		A. T. Smith
1904-05	Ottawa Silver Seven		A. T. Smith
1903-04	Ottawa Silver Seven		A. T. Smith
1902-03	Ottawa Silver Seven (Mar. 1903)		A. T. Smith
1902-03	Montreal A.A.A. (Feb. 1903)		C. McKerrow
1901-02	Montreal A.A.A. (Mar. 1902)		C. McKerrow
1901-02	Winnipeg Victorias (Jan. 1902)		
1900-01	Winnipeg Victorias		D. H. Bain*
1899-1900	Montreal Shamrocks		H.J. Trihey*
1898-99	Montreal Shamrocks (Mar. 1899)		H.J. Trihey*
1898-99	Montreal Victorias (Feb. 1899)		Mike Grant*
1897-98	Montreal Victorias		F. Richardson
1896-97	Montreal Victorias		Mike Grant*
1895-96	Montreal Victorias (Dec. 1896)		Mike Grant*
1895-96	Winnipeg Victorias (Feb. 1896)		J.C. G. Armytage
1894-95	Montreal Victorias		Mike Grant*
1893-94	Montreal A.A.A.		
1892-93	Montreal A.A.A.		

* In the early years the teams were frequently run by the Captain. *Indicates Captain
** Victoria defeated Quebec in challenge series. No official recognition.

Stanley Cup Winners

Year	W-L-T in Finals	Winner	Coach	Finalist	Coach
2000	4-2	New Jersey	Larry Robinson	Dallas	Ken Hitchcock
1999	4-2	Dallas	Ken Hitchcock	Buffalo	Lindy Ruff
1998	4-0	Detroit	Scotty Bowman	Washington	Ron Wilson
1997	4-0	Detroit	Scotty Bowman	Philadelphia	Terry Murray
1996	4-0	Colorado	Marc Crawford	Florida	Doug MacLean
1995	4-0	New Jersey	Jacques Lemaire	Detroit	Scotty Bowman
1994	4-3	NY Rangers	Mike Keenan	Vancouver	Pat Quinn
1993	4-1	Montreal	Jacques Demers	Los Angeles	Barry Melrose
1992	4-0	Pittsburgh	Scotty Bowman	Chicago	Mike Keenan
1991	4-2	Pittsburgh	Bob Johnson	Minnesota	Bob Gainey
1990	4-1	Edmonton	John Muckler	Boston	Mike Milbury
1989	4-2	Calgary	Terry Crisp	Montreal	Pat Burns
1988	4-0	Edmonton	Glen Sather	Boston	Terry O'Reilly
1987	4-3	Edmonton	Glen Sather	Philadelphia	Mike Keenan
1986	4-1	Montreal	Jean Perron	Calgary	Bob Johnson
1985	4-1	Edmonton	Glen Sather	Philadelphia	Mike Keenan
1984	4-1	Edmonton	Glen Sather	NY Islanders	Al Arbour
1983	4-0	NY Islanders	Al Arbour	Edmonton	Glen Sather
1982	4-0	NY Islanders	Al Arbour	Vancouver	Roger Neilson
1981	4-1	NY Islanders	Al Arbour	Minnesota	Glen Sonmor
1980	4-2	NY Islanders	Al Arbour	Philadelphia	Pat Quinn
1979	4-1	Montreal	Scotty Bowman	NY Rangers	Fred Shero
1978	4-2	Montreal	Scotty Bowman	Boston	Don Cherry
1977	4-0	Montreal	Scotty Bowman	Boston	Don Cherry
1976	4-0	Montreal	Scotty Bowman	Philadelphia	Fred Shero
1975	4-2	Philadelphia	Fred Shero	Buffalo	Floyd Smith
1974	4-2	Philadelphia	Fred Shero	Boston	Bep Guidolin
1973	4-2	Montreal	Scotty Bowman	Chicago	Billy Reay
1972	4-2	Boston	Tom Johnson	NY Rangers	Emile Francis
1971	4-3	Montreal	Al MacNeil	Chicago	Billy Reay
1970	4-0	Boston	Harry Sinden	St. Louis	Scotty Bowman
1969	4-0	Montreal	Claude Ruel	St. Louis	Scotty Bowman
1968	4-0	Montreal	Toe Blake	St. Louis	Scotty Bowman
1967	4-2	Toronto	Punch Imlach	Montreal	Toe Blake
1966	4-2	Montreal	Toe Blake	Detroit	Sid Abel
1965	4-3	Montreal	Toe Blake	Chicago	Billy Reay
1964	4-3	Toronto	Punch Imlach	Detroit	Sid Abel
1963	4-1	Toronto	Punch Imlach	Detroit	Sid Abel
1962	4-2	Toronto	Punch Imlach	Chicago	Rudy Pilous
1961	4-2	Chicago	Rudy Pilous	Detroit	Sid Abel
1960	4-0	Montreal	Toe Blake	Toronto	Punch Imlach
1959	4-1	Montreal	Toe Blake	Toronto	Punch Imlach
1958	4-2	Montreal	Toe Blake	Boston	Milt Schmidt
1957	4-1	Montreal	Toe Blake	Boston	Milt Schmidt
1956	4-1	Montreal	Toe Blake	Detroit	Jimmy Skinner
1955	4-3	Detroit	Jimmy Skinner	Montreal	Dick Irvin
1954	4-3	Detroit	Tommy Ivan	Montreal	Dick Irvin
1953	4-1	Montreal	Dick Irvin	Boston	Lynn Patrick
1952	4-0	Detroit	Tommy Ivan	Montreal	Dick Irvin
1951	4-1	Toronto	Joe Primeau	Montreal	Dick Irvin
1950	4-3	Detroit	Tommy Ivan	NY Rangers	Lynn Patrick
1949	4-0	Toronto	Hap Day	Detroit	Tommy Ivan
1948	4-0	Toronto	Hap Day	Detroit	Tommy Ivan
1947	4-2	Toronto	Hap Day	Montreal	Dick Irvin
1946	4-1	Montreal	Dick Irvin	Boston	Dit Clapper
1945	4-3	Toronto	Hap Day	Detroit	Jack Adams
1944	4-0	Montreal	Dick Irvin	Chicago	Paul Thompson
1943	4-0	Detroit	Jack Adams	Boston	Art Ross
1942	4-3	Toronto	Hap Day	Detroit	Jack Adams
1941	4-0	Boston	Cooney Weiland	Detroit	Ebbie Goodfellow
1940	4-2	NY Rangers	Frank Boucher	Toronto	Dick Irvin
1939	4-1	Boston	Art Ross	Toronto	Dick Irvin
1938	3-1	Chicago	Bill Stewart	Toronto	Dick Irvin
1937	3-2	Detroit	Jack Adams	NY Rangers	Lester Patrick
1936	3-1	Detroit	Jack Adams	Toronto	Dick Irvin
1935	3-0	Mtl. Maroons	Tommy Gorman	Toronto	Dick Irvin
1934	3-1	Chicago	Tommy Gorman	Detroit	Herbie Lewis
1933	3-1	NY Rangers	Lester Patrick	Toronto	Dick Irvin
1932	3-0	Toronto	Dick Irvin	NY Rangers	Lester Patrick
1931	3-2	Montreal	Cecil Hart	Chicago	Dick Irvin
1930	2-0	Montreal	Cecil Hart	Boston	Art Ross
1929	2-0	Boston	Cy Denneny	NY Rangers	Lester Patrick
1928	3-2	NY Rangers	Lester Patrick	Mtl. Maroons	Eddie Gerard
1927	2-0-2	Ottawa	Dave Gill	Boston	Art Ross

The National Hockey League assumed control of Stanley Cup competition after 1926

Year	W-L-T in Finals	Winner	Coach	Finalist	Coach
1926	3-1	Mtl. Maroons	Eddie Gerard	Victoria	Lester Patrick
1925	3-1	Victoria	Lester Patrick	Montreal	Leo Dandurand
1924	2-0	Montreal	Leo Dandurand	Cgy. Tigers	—
	2-0			Van. Maroons	—
1923	2-0	Ottawa	Pete Green	Edm. Eskimos	—
	3-1			Van. Maroons	—
1922	3-2	Tor. St. Pats	George O'Donoghue	Van. Millionaires	Frank Patrick
1921	3-2	Ottawa	Pete Green	Van. Millionaires	Frank Patrick
1920	3-2	Ottawa	Pete Green	Seattle	
1919	2-2-1	No decision - series between Montreal and Seattle cancelled due to influenza epidemic			
1918	3-2	Tor. Arenas	Dick Carroll	Van. Millionaires	Frank Patrick

Championship Trophies

PRINCE OF WALES TROPHY

Beginning with the 1993-94 season, the club which advances to the Stanley Cup Finals as the winner of the Eastern Conference Championship is presented with the Prince of Wales Trophy.

History: His Royal Highness, the Prince of Wales, donated the trophy to the National Hockey League in 1924. From 1927-28 through 1937-38, the award was presented to the team finishing first in the American Division of the NHL. From 1938-39, when the NHL reverted to one section, to 1966-67, it was presented to the team winning the NHL regular season championship. With expansion in 1967-68, it again became a divisional trophy, awarded to the regular season champions of the East Division through to the end of the 1973-74 season. Beginning in 1974-75, it was awarded to the regular-season winner of the conference bearing the name of the trophy. From 1981-82 to 1992-93 the trophy was presented to the playoff champion in the Wales Conference. Since 1993-94, the trophy has been presented to the playoff champion in the Eastern Conference.

1999-2000 Winner: New Jersey Devils

The New Jersey Devils won their first Prince of Wales Trophy since 1995 on May 26, 2000 after defeating the Philadelphia Flyers 2-1 in game seven of the Eastern Conference Championship series. Before defeating the Flyers, the Devils had series wins over the Florida Panthers and Toronto Maple Leafs.

PRINCE OF WALES TROPHY WINNERS

99-2000	New Jersey Devils	1961-62	Montreal Canadiens
1998-99	Buffalo Sabres	1960-61	Montreal Canadiens
1997-98	Washington Capitals	1959-60	Montreal Canadiens
1996-97	Philadelphia Flyers	1958-59	Montreal Canadiens
1995-96	Florida Panthers	1957-58	Montreal Canadiens
1994-95	New Jersey Devils	1956-57	Detroit Red Wings
1993-94	New York Rangers	1955-56	Montreal Canadiens
1992-93	Montreal Canadiens	1954-55	Detroit Red Wings
1991-92	Pittsburgh Penguins	1953-54	Detroit Red Wings
1990-91	Pittsburgh Penguins	1952-53	Detroit Red Wings
1989-90	Boston Bruins	1951-52	Detroit Red Wings
1988-89	Montreal Canadiens	1950-51	Detroit Red Wings
1987-88	Boston Bruins	1949-50	Detroit Red Wings
1986-87	Philadelphia Flyers	1948-49	Detroit Red Wings
1985-86	Montreal Canadiens	1947-48	Toronto Maple Leafs
1984-85	Philadelphia Flyers	1946-47	Montreal Canadiens
1983-84	New York Islanders	1945-46	Montreal Canadiens
1982-83	New York Islanders	1944-45	Montreal Canadiens
1981-82	New York Islanders	1943-44	Montreal Canadiens
1980-81	Montreal Canadiens	1942-43	Detroit Red Wings
1979-80	Buffalo Sabres	1941-42	New York Rangers
1978-79	Montreal Canadiens	1940-41	Boston Bruins
1977-78	Montreal Canadiens	1939-40	Boston Bruins
1976-77	Montreal Canadiens	1938-39	Boston Bruins
1975-76	Montreal Canadiens	1937-38	Boston Bruins
1974-75	Buffalo Sabres	1936-37	Detroit Red Wings
1973-74	Boston Bruins	1935-36	Detroit Red Wings
1972-73	Montreal Canadiens	1934-35	Boston Bruins
1971-72	Boston Bruins	1933-34	Detroit Red Wings
1970-71	Boston Bruins	1932-33	Boston Bruins
1969-70	Chicago Blackhawks	1931-32	New York Rangers
1968-69	Montreal Canadiens	1930-31	Boston Bruins
1967-68	Montreal Canadiens	1929-30	Boston Bruins
1966-67	Chicago Blackhawks	1928-29	Boston Bruins
1965-66	Montreal Canadiens	1927-28	Boston Bruins
1964-65	Detroit Red Wings	1926-27	Ottawa Senators
1963-64	Montreal Canadiens	1925-26	Montreal Maroons
1962-63	Toronto Maple Leafs	1924-25	Montreal Canadiens
		1923-24	Montreal Canadiens

Prince of Wales Trophy

Clarence S. Campbell Bowl

Stanley Cup

CLARENCE S. CAMPBELL BOWL

Beginning with the 1993-94 season, the club which advances to the Stanley Cup Finals as the winner of the Western Conference Championship is presented with the Clarence S. Campbell Bowl.

History: Presented by the member clubs in 1968 for perpetual competition by the National Hockey League in recognition of the services of Clarence S. Campbell, President of the NHL from 1946 to 1977. From 1967-68 through 1973-74, the trophy was awarded to the regular season champions of the West Division. Beginning in 1974-75, it was awarded to the regular-season winner of the conference bearing the name of the trophy. From 1981-82 to 1992-93 the trophy was presented to the playoff champion in the Campbell Conference. Since 1993-94, the trophy has been presented to the playoff champion in the Western Conference. The trophy itself is a hallmark piece made of sterling silver and was crafted by a British silversmith in 1878.

1999-2000 Winner: Dallas Stars

The Dallas Stars won their second consecutive Clarence Campbell Bowl after defeating the Colorado Avalanche 3-2 in game seven of the Western Conference Championship series. Before defeating the Avalanche, the Stars had series wins over the San Jose Sharks and Edmonton Oilers.

CLARENCE S. CAMPBELL BOWL WINNERS

99-2000	Dallas Stars	1982-83	Edmonton Oilers
1998-99	Dallas Stars	1981-82	Vancouver Canucks
1997-98	Detroit Red Wings	1980-81	New York Islanders
1996-97	Detroit Red Wings	1979-80	Philadelphia Flyers
1995-96	Colorado Avalanche	1978-79	New York Islanders
1994-95	Detroit Red Wings	1977-78	New York Islanders
1993-94	Vancouver Canucks	1976-77	Philadelphia Flyers
1992-93	Los Angeles Kings	1975-76	Philadelphia Flyers
1991-92	Chicago Blackhawks	1974-75	Philadelphia Flyers
1990-91	Minnesota North Stars	1973-74	Philadelphia Flyers
1989-90	Edmonton Oilers	1972-73	Chicago Blackhawks
1988-89	Calgary Flames	1971-72	Chicago Blackhawks
1987-88	Edmonton Oilers	1970-71	Chicago Blackhawks
1986-87	Edmonton Oilers	1969-70	St. Louis Blues
1985-86	Calgary Flames	1968-69	St. Louis Blues
1984-85	Edmonton Oilers	1967-68	Philadelphia Flyers
1983-84	Edmonton Oilers		

Stanley Cup Winners

Rosters and Final Series Scores

1999-2000 — New Jersey Devils — Scott Stevens (Captain), Jason Arnott, Brad Bombardir, Martin Brodeur, Steve Brule, Sergei Brylin, Ken Daneyko, Patrik Elias, Scott Gomez, Bobby Holik, Steve Kelly, Claude Lemieux, John Madden, Vladimir Malakhov, Randy McKay, Alexander Mogilny, Sergei Nemchinov, Scott Niedermayer, Krzysztof Oliwa, Jay Pandolfo, Brian Rafalski, Ken Sutton, Petr Sykora, Chris Terreri, Colin White, Dr. John J. McMullen Owner/Chairman), Peter S. McMullen (Owner), Lou Lamoriello (President/General Manager), Larry Robinson (Head Coach), Viacheslav Fetisov (Assistant Coach), Bob Carpenter (Assistant Coach), Jacques Caron (Goaltending Coach), John Cunniff (AHL Coach), David Conte (Director of Scouting), Milt Fisher (Scout), Claude Carrier (Assistant Director of Scouting), Dan Labraaten (Scout), Marcel Pronovost (Scout), Bob Hoffmeyer (Pro Scout), Dr. Barry Fisher (Orthopedist), Dennis Gendron (AHL Assistant Coach), Robbie Ftorek (Coach), Vladimir Bure (Consultant), Taran Singleton (Hockey Operations), Marie Carnevale (Hockey Operations), Callie Smith (Hockey Operations), Bill Murray (Medical Trainer), Michael Vasalani (Strength/Conditioning Coordinator), Dana McGuane (Equipment Manager), Juergen Merz (Massage Therapist), Harry Bricker (Assistant Equipment Manager), Lou Centanni (Assistant Equipment Manager).

Scores: May 30, at New Jersey - New Jersey 7, Dallas 3; June 1, at New Jersey - Dallas 2, New Jersey 1; June 3, at Dallas - New Jersey 2, Dallas 1; June 5, at Dallas - New Jersey 3, Dallas 1; June 8, at New Jersey - Dallas 1 - New Jersey 0; at Dallas, New Jersey 2 - Dallas 1.

1998-99 — Dallas Stars — Derian Hatcher (Captain), Ed Belfour, Guy Carbonneau, Shawn Chambers, Benoit Hogue, Tony Hrkac, Brett Hull, Mike Keane, Jamie Langenbrunner, Jere Lehtinen, Craig Ludwig, Grant Marshall, Richard Matvichuk, Mike Modano, Joe Nieuwendyk, Derek Plante, Dave Reid, Jon Sim, Brian Skrudland, Blake Sloan, Darryl Sydor, Roman Turek, Pat Verbeek, Sergei Zubov, Thomas Hicks (Chairman of the Board and Owner), Jim Lites (President), Bob Gainey (Vice President, Hockey Operations and General Manager), Doug Armstrong (Assistant General Manager), Craig Button (Director of Player Personnel), Ken Hitchcock (Head Coach), Doug Jarvis (Assistant Coach), Rick Wilson (Assistant Coach), Rick McLaughlin (Vice President and Chief Financial Officer), Jeff Cogen (Vice President, Marketing and Promotion), Bill Strong (Vice President, Marketing and Broadcasting), Tim Bernhardt (Director of Amateur Scouting), Doug Overton (Director of Pro Scouting), Bob Gernander (Chief Scout), Stu MacGregor (Western Scout), Dave Suprenant (Medical Trainer), Dave Smith (Equipment Manager), Rich Matthews (Equipment Manager), J.J. McQueen (Strength and Conditioning Coach), Rick St. Croix (Goaltending Consultant), Dan Stuchal (Director of Team Services), Larry Kelly (Director of Public Relations).

Scores: June 8, at Dallas - Buffalo 3, Dallas 2; June 10, at Dallas - Dallas 4, Buffalo 2; June 12, at Buffalo - Dallas 2, Buffalo 1; June 15, at Buffalo - Buffalo 2, Dallas 1; June 17, at Dallas - Dallas 2, Buffalo 0; June 19, at Buffalo - Dallas 2, Buffalo 1.

Dandenault, Kris Draper, Anders Eriksson, Sergei Fedorov, Viacheslav Fetisov, Brent Gilchrist, Kevin Hodson, Tomas Holmstrom, Michael Knuble, Joey Kocur, Vladimir Konstantinov, Vyacheslav Kozlov, Martin Lapointe, Igor Larionov, Nicklas Lidstrom, Jamie Macoun, Kirk Maltby, Darren McCarty, Dmitri Mironov, Larry Murphy, Chris Osgood, Bob Rouse, Brendan Shanahan, Aaron Ward, Mike Ilitch, (Owner/Chairman), Marian Ilitch (Owner), Atanas Ilitch (Vice President), Christopher Ilitch (Vice President), Denise Ilitch, Ronald Ilitch, Michael Ilitch Jr., Lisa Ilitch Murray, Carole Ilitch Trepeck, Jim Devellano (Senior Vice President), Scotty Bowman (Head Coach), Ken Holland (General Manager), Don Waddell (Assistant General Manager), Barry Smith (Associate Coach), Dave Lewis (Associate Coach), Jim Bedard (Goaltending Consultant), Jim Nill (Director of Player Development), Dan Belisle (Pro Scout), Mark Howe (Pro Scout), Hakan Andersson (Director of European Scouting), Mark Leach (USA Scout), Moe McDonnell (Eastern Scout), Bruce Haralson (Western Scout), John Wharton (Athletic Trainer), Paul Boyer (Equipment Manager) Tim Abbott (Assistant Equipment Manager), Bob Huddleston (Masseur), Sergei Mnatsakanov (Masseur), Wally Crossman (Dressing Room Assistant).
Scores: June 9, at Detroit — Detroit 2, Washington 1; June 11, at Detroit — Detroit 5, Washington 4; June 13, at Washington — Detroit 2, Washington 1; June 16, at Washington — Detroit 4, Washington 1.

1996-97 — Detroit Red Wings — Steve Yzerman (Captain), Doug Brown, Mathieu Dandenault, Kris Draper, Sergei Fedorov, Viacheslav Fetisov, Kevin Hodson, Tomas Holmstrom, Joe Kocur, Vladimir Konstantinov, Vyacheslav Kozlov, Martin Lapointe, Igor Larionov, Nicklas Lidstrom, Kirk Maltby, Darren McCarty, Larry Murphy, Chris Osgood, Jamie Pushor, Bob Rouse, Tomas Sandstrom, Brendan Shanahan, Tim Taylor, Mike Vernon, Aaron Ward, Mike Ilitch (Owner/Chairman), Marian Ilitch (Owner), Atanas Ilitch (Vice President), Christopher Ilitch (Vice President), Denise Ilitch Lites, Ronald Ilitch, Michael Ilitch, Jr., Lisa Ilitch Murray, Carole Ilitch Trepeck, Jim Devellano (Senior Vice President), Scotty Bowman (Head Coach/Director of Player Personnel), Ken Holland (Assistant General Manager), Barry Smith (Associate Coach), Dave Lewis (Associate Coach), Mike Krushelnyski (Assistant Coach). Jim Nill (Director of Player Development), Dan Belisle (Pro Scout), Mark Howe (Pro Scout), Hakan Andersson (Director of European Scouting), John Wharton (Athletic Trainer), Paul Boyer (Equipment Manager) Tim Abbott (Assistant Equipment Manager), Sergei Mnatsakanov (Masseur).
Scores: May 31, at Philadelphia — Detroit 4, Philadelphia 2; June 3, at Philadelphia — Detroit 4, Philadelphia 2; June 5, at Detroit — Detroit 6, Philadelphia 1; June 7, at Detroit — Detroit 2, Philadelphia 1.

1995-96 — Colorado Avalanche — Joe Sakic (Captain), Rene Corbet, Adam Deadmarsh, Stephane Fiset, Adam Foote, Peter Forsberg, Alexei Gusarov, Dave Hannan, Valeri Kamensky, Mike Keane, Jon Klemm, Uwe Krupp, Sylvain Lefebvre, Claude Lemieux, Curtis Leschyshyn, Troy Murray, Sandis Ozolinsh, Mike Ricci, Patrick Roy, Warren Rychel, Chris Simon, Craig Wolanin, Stephane Yelle, Scott Young, Charlie Lyons (Chairman, CEO), Pierre Lacroix (Exec. V.P., G.M.), Marc Crawford (Head Coach), Joel Quenneville (Assistant Coach), Jacques Cloutier (Assistant Coach), Francois Giguere (Assistant General Manager), Michel Goulet (Director of Player Personnel), Dave Draper (Chief Scout), Jean Martineau (Director of Public Relations), Pat Karns (Trainer), Matthew Sokolowski (Assistant Trainer), Rob McLean (Equipment Manager), Mike Kramer (Assistant Equipment Manager), Brock Gibbins (Assistant Equipment Manager), Skip Allen (Strength and Conditioning Coach), Paul Fixter (Video Coordinator), Leo Vyssokov (Massage Therapist).
Scores: June 4, at Colorado — Colorado 3, Florida 1; June 6, at Colorado — Colorado 8, Florida 1; June 8, at Florida — Colorado 3, Florida 2; June 10, at Florida — Colorado 1, Florida 0.

1994-95 — New Jersey Devils — Scott Stevens (Captain), Tommy Albelin, Martin Brodeur, Neil Broten, Sergei Brylin, Bob Carpenter, Shawn Chambers, Tom Chorske, Danton Cole, Ken Daneyko, Kevin Dean, Jim Dowd, Bruce Driver (Alternate Captain), Bill Guerin, Bobby Holik, Claude Lemieux, John MacLean (Alternate Captain), Chris McAlpine, Randy McKay, Scott Niedermayer, Mike Peluso, Stephane J.J. Richer, Brian Rolston, Chris Terreri, Valeri Zelepukin, Dr. John J. McMullen (Owner/Chairman), Peter S. McMullen (Owner), Lou Lamoriello (President/General Manager), Jacques Lemaire (Head Coach), Jacques Caron (Goaltender Coach), Dennis Gendron (Assistant Coach), Larry Robinson (Assistant Coach), Robbie Ftorek (AHL Coach), Alex Abasto (Assistant Equipment Manager), Bob Huddleston (Massage Therapist), David Nichols (Equipment Manager), Ted Schuch (Medical Trainer), Mike Vasalani (Strength Coach), David Conte (Director of Scouting) Claude Carrier (Scout), Milt Fisher (Scout), Dan Labraaten (Scout), Marcel Pronovost (Scout).
Scores: June 17, at Detroit — New Jersey 2, Detroit 1; June 20, at Detroit — New Jersey 4, Detroit 2; June 22, at New Jersey — New Jersey 5, Detroit 2; June 24, at New Jersey — New Jersey 5, Detroit 2.

1993-94 — New York Rangers — Mark Messier (Captain), Brian Leetch, Kevin Lowe, Adam Graves, Steve Larmer, Glenn Anderson, Jeff Beukeboom, Greg Gilbert, Mike Hartman, Glenn Healy, Mike Hudson, Alexander Karpovtsev, Joe Kocur, Alexei Kovalev, Nick Kypreos, Doug Lidster, Stephane Matteau, Craig MacTavish, Sergei Nemchinov, Brian Noonan, Ed Olczyk, Mike Richter, Esa Tikkanen, Jay Wells, Sergei Zubov, Neil Smith (President, General Manager and Governor), Robert Gutkowski, Stanley Jaffe, Kenneth Munoz (Governors), Larry Pleau (Assistant General Manager), Mike Keenan (Head Coach), Colin Campbell (Associate Coach), Dick Todd (Assistant Coach), Matthew Loughren (Manager, Team Operations), Barry Watkins (Director, Communications), Christer Rockstrom, Tony Feltrin, Martin Madden, Herb Hammond, Darwin Bennett (Scouts), Dave Smith, Joe Murphy, Mike Folga, Bruce Lifrieri (Trainers).
Scores: May 31, at New York — Vancouver 3, NY Rangers 2; June 2, at New York — NY Rangers 3, Vancouver 1; June 4, at Vancouver — NY Rangers 5, Vancouver 1; June 7, at Vancouver — NY Rangers 4, Vancouver 2; June 9, at New York — Vancouver 6, at NY Rangers 3; June 11, at Vancouver — Vancouver 4, NY Rangers 1; June 14, at New York — NY Rangers 3, Vancouver 2.

1992-93 — Montreal Canadiens — Guy Carbonneau (Captain), Patrick Roy, Mike Keane, Eric Desjardins, Stephan Lebeau, Mathieu Schneider, Jean-Jacques Daigneault, Denis Savard, Lyle Odelein, Todd Ewen, Kirk Muller, John LeClair, Gilbert Dionne, Benoit Brunet, Patrice Brisebois, Paul Di Pietro, Andre Racicot, Donald Dufresne, Mario Roberge, Sean Hill, Ed Ronan, Kevin Haller, Vincent Damphousse, Brian Bellows, Gary Leeman, Rob Ramage, Ronald Corey (President), Serge Savard (Managing Director & Vice-President Hockey), Jacques Demers (Head Coach), Jacques Laperriere (Assistant Coach), Charles Thiffault (Assistant Coach), Francois Allaire (Goaltending Instructor), Jean Béliveau (Senior Vice-President, Corporate Affairs), Fred Steer (Vice-President, Finance & Adminstration), Aldo Giampaolo (Vice-President, Operations), Bernard Brisset (Vice-President, Marketing & Communications), André Boudrias (Assistant to the Managing Director & Director of Scouting), Jacques Lemaire (Assistant to the Managing Director), Gaeten Lefebvre (Athletic Trainer), John Shipman (Assistant to the Athletic Trainer), Eddy Palchak (Equipment Manager), Pierre Gervais (Assistant to the Equipment Manager), Robert Boulanger (Assistant to the Equipment Manager), Pierre Ouellete (Assistant to the Equipment Manager).
Scores: June 1, at Montreal — Los Angeles 4, Montreal 1; June 2, at Montreal — Montreal 3, Los Angeles 2; June 5, at Los Angeles — Montreal 4, Los Angeles 3; June 7, at Los Angeles — Montreal 3, Los Angeles 2; June 9, at Montreal — Montreal 4, Los Angeles 1.

1991-92 — Pittsburgh Penguins — Mario Lemieux (Captain), Ron Francis, Bryan Trottier, Kevin Stevens, Bob Errey, Phil Bourque, Troy Loney, Rick Tocchet, Joe Mullen, Jaromir Jagr, Jiri Hrdina, Shawn McEachern, Ulf Samuelsson, Kjell Samuelsson, Larry Murphy, Gord Roberts, Jim Paek, Paul Stanton, Tom Barrasso, Ken Wregget, Jay Caufield, Jamie Leach, Wendell Young, Grant Jennings, Peter Taglianetti, Jock Callander, Dave Michayluk, Mike Needham, Jeff Chychrun, Ken Priestlay, Jeff Daniels, Howard Baldwin (Owner and President), Morris Belzberg (Owner), Thomas Ruta (Owner), Donn Patton (Executive Vice President and Chief Financial Officer), Paul Martha (Executive Vice President and General Counsel), Craig Patrick (Executive Vice President and General Manager), Bob Johnson (Coach), Scotty Bowman (Director of Player Development and Coach), Barry Smith, Rick Kehoe, Pierre McGuire, Gilles Meloche, Rick Paterson (Assistant Coaches), Steve Latin (Equipment Manager), Skip Thayer (Trainer), John Welday (Strength and Conditioning Coach), Greg Malone, Les Binkley, Charlie Hodge, John Gill, Ralph Cox (Scouts).
Scores: May 26, at Pittsburgh — Pittsburgh 5, Chicago 4; May 28, at Pittsburgh — Pittsburgh 3, Chicago 1; May 30, at Chicago — Pittsburgh 1, Chicago 0; June 1, at Chicago — Pittsburgh 6, Chicago 5.

1990-91 — Pittsburgh Penguins — Mario Lemieux (Captain), Paul Coffey, Randy Hillier, Bob Errey, Tom Barrasso, Phil Bourque, Jay Caufield, Ron Francis, Randy Gilhen, Jiri Hrdina, Jaromir Jagr, Grant Jennings, Troy Loney, Joe Mullen, Larry Murphy, Jim Paek, Frank Pietrangelo, Barry Pederson, Mark Recchi, Gordie Roberts, Ulf Samuelsson, Paul Stanton, Kevin Stevens, Peter Taglianetti, Bryan Trottier, Scott Young, Wendell Young, Edward J. DeBartolo, Sr. (Owner), Marie D. DeBartolo York (President), Paul Martha (Vice-President & General Counsel), Craig Patrick (General Manager), Scotty Bowman (Director of Player Development & Recruitment), Bob Johnson (Coach), Rick Kehoe (Assistant Coach), Gilles Meloche (Goaltending Coach & Scout), Rick Paterson (Assistant Coach), Barry Smith (Assistant Coach), Steve Latin (Equipment Manager), Skip Thayer (Trainer), John Welday (Strength & Conditioning Coach), Greg Malone (Scout).
Scores: May 15, at Pittsburgh — Minnesota 5, Pittsburgh 4; May 17, at Pittsburgh — Pittsburgh 4, Minnesota 1; May 19, at Minnesota — Minnesota 3, Pittsburgh 1; May 21, at Minnesota — Pittsburgh 5, Minnesota 3; May 23, at Pittsburgh — Pittsburgh 6, Minnesota 4; May 25, at Minnesota — Pittsburgh 8, Minnesota 0.

1989-90 — Edmonton Oilers — Kevin Lowe, Steve Smith, Jeff Beukeboom, Mark Lamb, Joe Murphy, Glenn Anderson, Mark Messier, Adam Graves, Craig MacTavish, Kelly Buchberger, Jari Kurri, Craig Simpson, Martin Gelinas, Randy Gregg, Charlie Huddy, Geoff Smith, Reijo Ruotsalainen, Craig Muni, Bill Ranford, Dave Brown, Pokey Reddick, Petr Klima, Esa Tikkanen, Grant Fuhr, Peter Pocklington (Owner), Glen Sather (President/General Manager), John Muckler (Coach), Ted Green (Co-Coach), Ron Low (Ass't Coach), Bruce MacGregor (Ass't General Manager), Barry Fraser (Director of Player Personnel), John Blackwell (Director of Operations, AHL), Ace Bailey, Ed Chadwick, Lorne Davis, Harry Howell, Matti Vaisanen and Albert Reeves (Scouts), Bill Tuele (Director of Public Relations), Werner Baum (Controller), Dr. Gordon Cameron (Medical Chief of Staff), Dr. David Reid (Team Physician), Barrie Stafford (Athletic Trainer), Ken Lowe (Athletic Therapist), Stuart Poirier (Massage Therapist), Lyle Kulchisky (Ass't Trainer).
Scores: May 15, at Boston — Edmonton 3, Boston 2; May 18, at Boston — Edmonton 7, Boston 2; May 20, at Edmonton — Boston 2, Edmonton 1; May 22, at Edmonton — Edmonton 5, Boston 1; May 24, at Boston — Edmonton 4, Boston 1.

1988-89 — Calgary Flames — Mike Vernon, Rick Wamsley, Al MacInnis, Brad McCrimmon, Dana Murzyn, Ric Nattress, Joe Mullen, Lanny McDonald (Co-captain), Gary Roberts, Colin Patterson, Hakan Loob, Theoren Fleury, Jiri Hrdina, Tim Hunter (Ass't. captain), Gary Suter, Mark Hunter, Jim Peplinski (Co-captain), Joe Nieuwendyk, Brian MacLellan, Joel Otto, Jamie Macoun, Doug Gilmour, Rob Ramage. Norman Green, Harley Hotchkiss, Norman Kwong, Sonia Scurfield, B.J. Seaman, D.K. Seaman (Owners), Cliff Fletcher (President and General Manager), Al MacNeil (Ass't General Manager), Al Coates (Ass't to the President), Terry Crisp (Head Coach), Doug Risebrough, Tom Watt (Ass't Coaches), Glenn Hall (Goaltending Consultant), Jim Murray (Trainer), Bob Stewart (Equipment Manager), Al Murray (Ass't Trainer).
Scores: May 14, at Calgary — Calgary 3, Montreal 2; May 17, at Calgary— Montreal 4, Calgary 2; May 19, at Montreal — Montreal 4, Calgary 3; May 21, at Montreal — Calgary 4, Montreal 2; May 23, at Calgary — Calgary 3, Montreal 2; May 25, at Montreal — Calgary 4, Montreal 2.

1987-88 — Edmonton Oilers — Keith Acton, Glenn Anderson, Jeff Beukeboom,

Geoff Courtnall, Grant Fuhr, Randy Gregg, Wayne Gretzky, Dave Hannan, Charlie Huddy, Mike Krushelnyski, Jari Kurri, Normand Lacombe, Kevin Lowe, Craig MacTavish, Kevin McClelland, Marty McSorley, Mark Messier, Craig Muni, Bill Ranford, Craig Simpson, Steve Smith, Esa Tikkanen, Peter Pocklington (Owner), Glen Sather (General Manager/Coach), John Muckler (Co-Coach), Ted Green (Ass't Coach), Bruce MacGregor (Ass't General Manager), Barry Fraser (Director of Player Personnel), Bill Tuele (Director of Public Relations), Dr. Gordon Cameron (Team Physician), Peter Millar (Athletic Therapist), Barrie Stafford (Trainer), Juergen Mers (Massage Therapist), Lyle Kulchisky (Ass't Trainer).
Scores: May 18, at Edmonton — Edmonton 2, Boston 1; May 20, at Edmonton — Edmonton 4, Boston 2; May 22, at Boston — Edmonton 6, Boston 3; May 24, at Boston — Boston 3, Edmonton 3 (suspended due to power failure); May 26, at Edmonton — Edmonton 6, Boston 3.

1986-87 — Edmonton Oilers — Glenn Anderson, Jeff Beukeboom, Kelly Buchberger, Paul Coffey, Grant Fuhr, Randy Gregg, Wayne Gretzky, Charlie Huddy, Dave Hunter, Mike Krushelnyski, Jari Kurri, Moe Lemay, Kevin Lowe, Craig MacTavish, Kevin McClelland, Marty McSorley, Mark Messier, Andy Moog, Craig Muni, Kent Nilsson, Jaroslav Pouzar, Reijo Ruotsalainen, Steve Smith, Esa Tikkanen, Peter Pocklington (Owner), Glen Sather (General Manager/Coach), John Muckler (Co-Coach), Ted Green (Ass't. Coach), Ron Low (Ass't. Coach), Bruce MacGregor (Ass't. General Manager), Barry Fraser (Director of Player Personnel), Peter Millar (Athletic Therapist), Barrie Stafford (Trainer), Lyle Kulchisky (Ass't Trainer).
Scores: May 17, at Edmonton — Edmonton 4, Philadelphia 2; May 20, at Edmonton — Edmonton 3, Philadelphia 2; May 22, at Philadelphia — Philadelphia 5, Edmonton 3; May 24, at Philadelphia — Edmonton 4, Philadelphia 1; May 26, at Edmonton — Philadelphia 4, Edmonton 3; May 28, at Philadelphia — Philadelphia 3, Edmonton 2; May 31, at Edmonton — Edmonton 3, Philadelphia 1.

1985-86 — Montreal Canadiens — Bob Gainey, Doug Soetaert, Patrick Roy, Rick Green, David Maley, Ryan Walter, Serge Boisvert, Mario Tremblay, Bobby Smith, Craig Ludwig, Tom Kurvers, Kjell Dahlin, Larry Robinson, Guy Carbonneau, Chris Chelios, Petr Svoboda, Mats Naslund, Lucien DeBlois, Steve Rooney, Gaston Gingras, Mike Lalor, Chris Nilan, John Kordic, Claude Lemieux, Mike McPhee, Brian Skrudland, Stephane Richer, Ronald Corey (President), Serge Savard (General Manager), Jean Perron (Coach), Jacques Laperrière (Ass't. Coach), Jean Béliveau (Vice President), Francois-Xavier Seigneur (Vice President), Fred Steer (Vice President), Jacques Lemaire (Ass't. General Manager), André Boudrias (Ass't. General Manager), Claude Ruel (Scouting), Yves Belanger (Athletic Therapist), Gaetan Lefebvre (Ass't. Athletic Therapist), Eddy Palchak (Trainer), Sylvain Toupin (Ass't. Trainer).
Scores: May 16, at Calgary — Calgary 5, Montreal 2; May 18, at Calgary — Montreal 3, Calgary 2; May 20, at Montreal — Montreal 5, Calgary 3; May 22, at Montreal — Montreal 1, Calgary 0; May 24, at Calgary — Montreal 4, Calgary 3.

1984-85 — Edmonton Oilers — Glenn Anderson, Bill Carroll, Paul Coffey, Lee Fogolin, Grant Fuhr, Randy Gregg, Wayne Gretzky, Charlie Huddy, Pat Hughes, Dave Hunter, Don Jackson, Mike Krushelnyski, Jari Kurri, Willy Lindstrom, Kevin Lowe, Dave Lumley, Kevin McClelland, Larry Melnyk, Mark Messier, Andy Moog, Mark Napier, Jaroslav Pouzar, Dave Semenko, Esa Tikkanen, Peter Pocklington (Owner), Glen Sather (General Manager/Coach), John Muckler (Ass't. Coach), Ted Green (Ass't. Coach), Bruce MacGregor (Ass't. General Manager), Barry Fraser (Director of Player Personnel/Chief Scout), Peter Millar (Athletic Therapist), Barrie Stafford, Lyle Kulchisky (Trainers)
Scores: May 21, at Philadelphia — Philadelphia 4, Edmonton 1; May 23, at Philadelphia — Edmonton 3, Philadelphia 1; May 25, at Edmonton — Edmonton 4, Philadelphia 3; May 28, at Edmonton — Edmonton 5, Philadelphia 3; May 30, at Edmonton — Edmonton 8, Philadelphia 3.

1983-84 — Edmonton Oilers — Glenn Anderson, Paul Coffey, Pat Conacher, Lee Fogolin, Grant Fuhr, Randy Gregg, Wayne Gretzky, Charlie Huddy, Pat Hughes, Dave Hunter, Don Jackson, Jari Kurri, Willy Lindstrom, Ken Linseman, Kevin Lowe, Dave Lumley, Kevin McClelland, Mark Messier, Andy Moog, Jaroslav Pouzar, Dave Semenko, Peter Pocklington (Owner), Glen Sather (General Manager/Coach), John Muckler (Ass't. Coach), Ted Green (Ass't. Coach), Bruce MacGregor (Ass't. General Manager), Barry Fraser (Director of Player Personnel/Chief Scout), Peter Millar (Athletic Therapist), Barrie Stafford (Trainer)
Scores: May 10, at New York — Edmonton 1, NY Islanders 0; May 12, at New York — NY Islanders 6, Edmonton 1; May 15, at Edmonton — Edmonton 7, NY Islanders 2; May 17, at Edmonton — Edmonton 7, NY Islanders 2; May 19, at Edmonton — Edmonton 5, NY Islanders 2.

1982-83 — New York Islanders — Mike Bossy, Bob Bourne, Paul Boutilier, Billy Carroll, Greg Gilbert, Clark Gillies, Butch Goring, Mats Hallin, Tomas Jonsson, Anders Kallur, Gord Lane, Dave Langevin, Mike McEwen, Rollie Melanson, Wayne Merrick, Ken Morrow, Bob Nystrom, Stefan Persson, Denis Potvin, Billy Smith, Brent Sutter, Duane Sutter, John Tonelli, Bryan Trottier, Al Arbour (coach), Lorne Henning (ass't coach), Bill Torrey (general manager), Ron Waske, Jim Pickard (trainers)
Scores: May 10, at Edmonton — NY Islanders 2, Edmonton 0; May 12, at Edmonton — NY Islanders 6, Edmonton 3; May 14, at New York — NY Islanders 5, Edmonton 1; May 17, at New York — NY Islanders 4, Edmonton 2

1981-82 — New York Islanders — Mike Bossy, Bob Bourne, Billy Carroll, Butch Goring, Greg Gilbert, Clark Gillies, Tomas Jonsson, Anders Kallur, Gord Lane, Dave Langevin, Hector Marini, Mike McEwen, Rollie Melanson, Wayne Merrick, Ken Morrow, Bob Nystrom, Stefan Persson, Denis Potvin, Billy Smith, Brent Sutter, Duane Sutter, John Tonelli, Bryan Trottier, Al Arbour (coach), Lorne Henning (ass't coach), Bill Torrey (general manager), Jim Devellano (ass't. general manager/dir. of scouting), Ron Waske, Jim Pickard (trainers)
Scores: May 8, at New York — NY Islanders 6, Vancouver 5; May 11, at New York — NY Islanders 6, Vancouver 4; May 13, at Vancouver — NY Islanders 3, Vancouver 0; May 16, at Vancouver — NY Islanders 3, Vancouver 1

1980-81 — New York Islanders — Denis Potvin, Mike McEwen, Ken Morrow, Gord Lane, Bob Lorimer, Stefan Persson, Dave Langevin, Mike Bossy, Bryan Trottier, Butch Goring, Wayne Merrick, Clark Gillies, John Tonelli, Bob Nystrom, Bill Carroll, Bob Bourne, Hector Marini, Anders Kallur, Duane Sutter, Garry Howatt, Lorne Henning, Billy Smith, Rollie Melanson, Al Arbour (coach), Bill Torrey (general manager), Jim Devellano (chief scout), Ron Waske, Jim Pickard (trainers).
Scores: May 12, at New York — NY Islanders 6, Minnesota 3; May 14, at New York — NY Islanders 6, Minnesota 3; May 17, at Minnesota — NY Islanders 7, Minnesota 5; May 19, at Minnesota— Minnesota 4, NY Islanders 2; May 21, at New York — NY Islanders 5, Minnesota 1.

1979-80 — New York Islanders — Gord Lane, Jean Potvin, Bob Lorimer, Denis Potvin, Stefan Persson, Ken Morrow, Dave Langevin, Duane Sutter, Garry Howatt, Clark Gillies, Lorne Henning, Wayne Merrick, Bob Bourne, Steve Tambellini, Bryan Trottier, Mike Bossy, Bob Nystrom, John Tonelli, Anders Kallur, Butch Goring, Alex McKendry, Glenn Resch, Billy Smith, Al Arbour (coach), Bill Torrey (general manager), Jim Devellano (chief scout), Ron Waske, Jim Pickard (trainers).
Scores: May 13, at Philadelphia — NY Islanders 4, Philadelphia 3; May 15, at Philadelphia — Philadelphia 8, NY Islanders 3; May 17, at New York — NY Islanders 6, Philadelphia 2; May 19, at New York — NY Islanders 5, Philadelphia 2; May 22 at Philadelphia — Philadelphia 6, NY Islanders 3; May 24, at New York — NY Islanders 5, Philadelphia 4.

1978-79 — Montreal Canadiens — Ken Dryden, Larry Robinson, Serge Savard, Guy Lapointe, Brian Engblom, Gilles Lupien, Rick Chartraw, Guy Lafleur, Steve Shutt, Jacques Lemaire, Yvan Cournoyer, Réjean Houle, Pierre Mondou, Bob Gainey, Doug Jarvis, Yvon Lambert, Doug Risebrough, Pierre Larouche, Mario Tremblay, Cam Connor, Pat Hughes, Rod Langway, Mark Napier, Michel Larocque, Richard Sévigny, Scotty Bowman (coach), Irving Grundman (managing director), Eddy Palchak, Pierre Meilleur (trainers).
Scores: May 13, at Montreal — NY Rangers 4, Montreal 1; May 15, at Montreal — Montreal 6, NY Rangers 2; May 17, at New York — Montreal 4, NY Rangers 1; May 19, at New York — Montreal 4, NY Rangers 3; May 21, at Montreal — Montreal 4, NY Rangers 1.

1977-78 — Montreal Canadiens — Ken Dryden, Larry Robinson, Serge Savard, Guy Lapointe, Bill Nyrop, Pierre Bouchard, Brian Engblom, Gilles Lupien, Rick Chartraw, Guy Lafleur, Steve Shutt, Jacques Lemaire, Yvan Cournoyer, Réjean Houle, Pierre Mondou, Bob Gainey, Doug Jarvis, Yvon Lambert, Doug Risebrough, Pierre Larouche, Mario Tremblay, Michel Larocque, Murray Wilson, Scotty Bowman (coach), Sam Pollock (general manager), Eddy Palchak, Pierre Meilleur (trainers).
Scores: May 13, at Montreal — Montreal 4, Boston 1; May 16, at Montreal — Montreal 3, Boston 2; May 18, at Boston — Boston 4, Montreal 0; May 21, at Boston — Boston 4, Montreal 3; May 23, at Montreal — Montreal 4, Boston 1; May 25, at Boston — Montreal 4, Boston 1.

1976-77 — Montreal Canadiens — Ken Dryden, Guy Lapointe, Larry Robinson, Serge Savard, Jimmy Roberts, Rick Chartraw, Bill Nyrop, Pierre Bouchard, Brian Engblom, Yvan Cournoyer, Guy Lafleur, Jacques Lemaire, Steve Shutt, Pete Mahovlich, Murray Wilson, Doug Jarvis, Yvon Lambert, Bob Gainey, Doug Risebrough, Mario Tremblay, Rejean Houle, Pierre Mondou, Mike Polich, Michel Larocque, Scotty Bowman (coach), Sam Pollock (general manager), Eddy Palchak, Pierre Meilleur (trainers).
Scores: May 7, at Montreal — Montreal 7, Boston 3; May 10, at Montreal — Montreal 3, Boston 0; May 12, at Boston — Montreal 4, Boston 2; May 14, at Boston — Montreal 2, Boston 1.

1975-76 — Montreal Canadiens — Ken Dryden, Serge Savard, Guy Lapointe, Larry Robinson, Bill Nyrop, Pierre Bouchard, Jimmy Roberts, Guy Lafleur, Steve Shutt, Pete Mahovlich, Yvan Cournoyer, Jacques Lemaire, Yvon Lambert, Bob Gainey, Doug Jarvis, Doug Risebrough, Murray Wilson, Mario Tremblay, Rick Chartraw, Michel Larocque, Scotty Bowman (coach), Sam Pollock (general manager), Eddy Palchak, Pierre Meilleur (trainers).
Scores: May 9, at Montreal — Montreal 4, Philadelphia 3; May 11, at Montreal — Montreal 2, Philadelphia 1; May 13, at Philadelphia — Montreal 3, Philadelphia 2; May 16, at Philadelphia — Montreal 5, Philadelphia 3.

1974-75 — Philadelphia Flyers — Bernie Parent, Wayne Stephenson, Ed Van Impe, Tom Bladon, André Dupont, Joe Watson, Jimmy Watson, Ted Harris, Larry Goodenough, Rick MacLeish, Bobby Clarke, Bill Barber, Reggie Leach, Gary Dornhoefer, Ross Lonsberry, Bob Kelly, Terry Crisp, Don Saleski, Dave Schultz, Orest Kindrachuk, Bill Clement, Fred Shero (coach), Keith Allen (general manager), Frank Lewis, Jim McKenzie (trainers).
Scores: May 15, at Philadelphia — Philadelphia 4, Buffalo 1; May 18, at Philadelphia — Philadelphia 2, Buffalo 1; May 20, at Buffalo — Buffalo 5, Philadelphia 4; May 22, at Buffalo — Buffalo 4, Philadelphia 2; May 25, at Philadelphia — Philadelphia 5, Buffalo 1; May 27, at Buffalo — Philadelphia 2, Buffalo 0.

1973-74 — Philadelphia Flyers — Bernie Parent, Ed Van Impe, Tom Bladon, André Dupont, Joe Watson, Jimmy Watson, Barry Ashbee, Bill Barber, Dave Schultz, Don Saleski, Gary Dornhoefer, Terry Crisp, Bobby Clarke, Simon Nolet, Ross Lonsberry, Rick MacLeish, Bill Flett, Orest Kindrachuk, Bill Clement, Bob Kelly, Bruce Cowick, Al MacAdam, Bobby Taylor, Fred Shero (coach), Keith Allen (general manager), Frank Lewis, Jim McKenzie (trainers).
Scores: May 7, at Boston — Boston 3, Philadelphia 2; May 9, at Boston — Philadelphia 3, Boston 2; May 12, at Philadelphia — Philadelphia 4, Boston 1; May 14, at Philadelphia — Philadelphia 4, Boston 2; May 16, at Boston — Boston 5, Philadelphia 1; May 19, at Philadelphia — Philadelphia 1, Boston 0.

1972-73 — Montreal Canadiens — Ken Dryden, Guy Lapointe, Serge Savard, Larry Robinson, Jacques Laperrière, Bob Murdoch, Pierre Bouchard, Jimmy Roberts, Yvan Cournoyer, Frank Mahovlich, Jacques Lemaire, Pete Mahovlich, Marc Tardif, Henri Richard, Réjean Houle, Guy Lafleur, Chuck Lefley, Claude Larose, Murray Wilson, Steve Shutt, Michel Plasse, Scotty Bowman (coach), Sam Pollock (general manager), Ed Palchak, Bob Williams (trainers).
Scores: April 29, at Montreal — Montreal 8, Chicago 3; May 1, at Montreal — Montreal 4, Chicago 1; May 3, at Chicago — Chicago 7, Montreal 4; May 6, at Chicago — Montreal 4, Chicago 0; May 8, at Montreal — Chicago 8, Montreal 7; May 10, at Chicago — Montreal 6, Chicago 4.

1971-72 — Boston Bruins — Gerry Cheevers, Eddie Johnston, Bobby Orr, Ted Green, Carol Vadnais, Dallas Smith, Don Awrey, Phil Esposito, Ken Hodge, John Bucyk, Mike Walton, Wayne Cashman, Garnet Bailey, Derek Sanderson, Fred Stanfield, Ed Westfall, John McKenzie, Don Marcotte, Garry Peters, Chris Hayes, Tom Johnson (coach), Milt Schmidt (general manager), Dan Canney, John Forristall (trainers).
Scores: April 30, at Boston — Boston 6, NY Rangers 5; May 2, at Boston — Boston 2, NY Rangers 1; May 4, at New York — NY Rangers 5, Boston 2; May 7, at New York — Boston 3, NY Rangers 2; May 9, at Boston — NY Rangers 3, Boston 2; May 11, at New York — Boston 3, NY Rangers 0.

1970-71 — Montreal Canadiens — Ken Dryden, Rogie Vachon, Jacques Laperrière,

J.C. Tremblay, Guy Lapointe, Terry Harper, Pierre Bouchard, Jean Béliveau, Marc Tardif, Yvan Cournoyer, Réjean Houle, Claude Larose, Henri Richard, Phil Roberto, Pete Mahovlich, Leon Rochefort, John Ferguson, Bobby Sheehan, Jacques Lemaire, Frank Mahovlich, Bob Murdoch, Chuck Lefley, Al MacNeil (coach), Sam Pollock (general manager), Yvon Belanger, Ed Palchak (trainers).
Scores: May 4, at Chicago — Chicago 2, Montreal 1; May 6, at Chicago — Chicago 5, Montreal 3; May 9, at Montreal — Montreal 4, Chicago 2; May 11, at Montreal — Montreal 5, Chicago 2; May 13, at Chicago — Chicago 2, Montreal 0; May 16, at Montreal — Montreal 4, Chicago 3; May 18, at Chicago — Montreal 3, Chicago 2.

1969-70 — Boston Bruins — Gerry Cheevers, Eddie Johnston, Bobby Orr, Rick Smith, Dallas Smith, Bill Speer, Gary Doak, Don Awrey, Phil Esposito, Ken Hodge, John Bucyk, Wayne Carleton, Wayne Cashman, Derek Sanderson, Fred Stanfield, Ed Westfall, John McKenzie, Jim Lorentz, Don Marcotte, Bill Lesuk, Dan Schock, Harry Sinden (coach), Milt Schmidt (general manager), Dan Canney, John Forristall (trainers).
Scores: May 3, at St. Louis — Boston 6, St. Louis 1; May 5, at St. Louis — Boston 6, St. Louis 2; May 7, at Boston — Boston 4, St. Louis 1; May 10, at Boston — Boston 4, St. Louis 3.

1968-69 — Montreal Canadiens — Gump Worsley, Rogie Vachon, Jacques Laperrière, J.C. Tremblay, Ted Harris, Serge Savard, Terry Harper, Larry Hillman, Jean Béliveau, Ralph Backstrom, Dick Duff, Yvan Cournoyer, Claude Provost, Bobby Rousseau, Henri Richard, John Ferguson, Christian Bordeleau, Mickey Redmond, Jacques Lemaire, Lucien Grenier, Tony Esposito, Claude Ruel (coach), Sam Pollock (general manager), Larry Aubut, Eddy Palchak (trainers).
Scores: April 27, at Montreal — Montreal 3, St. Louis 1; April 29, at Montreal — Montreal 3, St. Louis 1; May 1 at St. Louis — Montreal 4, St. Louis 0; May 4, at St. Louis — Montreal 2, St. Louis 1.

1967-68 — Montreal Canadiens — Gump Worsley, Rogie Vachon, Jacques Laperrière, J.C. Tremblay, Ted Harris, Serge Savard, Terry Harper, Carol Vadnais, Jean Béliveau, Gilles Tremblay, Ralph Backstrom, Dick Duff, Claude Larose, Yvan Cournoyer, Claude Provost, Bobby Rousseau, Henri Richard, John Ferguson, Danny Grant, Jacques Lemaire, Mickey Redmond, Toe Blake (coach), Sam Pollock (general manager), Larry Aubut, Eddy Palchak (trainers).
Scores: May 5, at St. Louis — Montreal 3, St. Louis 2; May 7, at St. Louis — Montreal 1, St. Louis 0; May 9, at Montreal — Montreal 4, St. Louis 3; May 11, at Montreal — Montreal 3, St. Louis 2.

1966-67 — Toronto Maple Leafs — Johnny Bower, Terry Sawchuk, Larry Hillman, Marcel Pronovost, Tim Horton, Bob Baun, Aut Erickson, Allan Stanley, Red Kelly, Ron Ellis, George Armstrong, Pete Stemkowski, Dave Keon, Mike Walton, Jim Pappin, Bob Pulford, Brian Conacher, Eddie Shack, Frank Mahovlich, Milan Marcetta, Larry Jeffrey, Bruce Gamble, Punch Imlach (manager-coach), Bob Haggart (trainer).
Scores: April 20, at Montreal — Toronto 2, Montreal 6; April 22, at Montreal — Toronto 3, Montreal 0; April 25, at Toronto — Toronto 3, Montreal 2; April 27, at Toronto — Toronto 2, Montreal 6; April 29, at Montreal — Toronto 4, Montreal 1; May 2, at Toronto — Toronto 3, Montreal 1.

1965-66 — Montreal Canadiens — Gump Worsley, Charlie Hodge, Jean-Claude Tremblay, Ted Harris, Jean-Guy Talbot, Terry Harper, Jacques Làperrière, Noel Price, Jean Béliveau, Ralph Backstrom, Dick Duff, Gilles Tremblay, Claude Larose, Yvan Cournoyer, Claude Provost, Bobby Rousseau, Henri Richard, Dave Balon, John Ferguson, Leon Rochefort, Jim Roberts, Toe Blake (coach), Sam Pollock (general manager), Larry Aubut, Andy Galley (trainers).
Scores: April 24, at Montreal — Detroit 3, Montreal 2; April 26, at Montreal — Detroit 5, Montreal 2; April 28, at Detroit — Montreal 4, Detroit 2; May 1, at Detroit — Montreal 2, Detroit 1; May 3, at Montreal — Montreal 5, Detroit 1; May 5, at Detroit — Montreal 3, Detroit 2.

1964-65 — Montreal Canadiens — Gump Worsley, Charlie Hodge, Jean-Claude Tremblay, Ted Harris, Jean-Guy Talbot, Terry Harper, Jacques Laperrière, Jean Gauthier, Noel Picard, Jean Béliveau, Ralph Backstrom, Dick Duff, Claude Larose, Yvan Cournoyer, Claude Provost, Bobby Rousseau, Henri Richard, Dave Balon, John Ferguson, Red Berenson, Jim Roberts, Toe Blake (coach), Sam Pollock (general manager), Larry Aubut, Andy Galley (trainers).
Scores: April 17, at Montreal — Montreal 3, Chicago 2; April 20, at Montreal — Montreal 2, Chicago 0; April 22, at Chicago — Montreal 1, Chicago 3; April 25, at Chicago — Montreal 1, Chicago 5; April 7, at Montreal — Montreal 6, Chicago 0; April 29, at Chicago — Montreal 1, Chicago 2; May 1, at Montreal — Montreal 4, Chicago 0.

1963-64 — Toronto Maple Leafs — Johnny Bower, Don Simmons, Carl Brewer, Tim Horton, Bob Baun, Allan Stanley, Larry Hillman, Al Arbour, Red Kelly, Gerry Ehman, Andy Bathgate, George Armstrong, Ron Stewart, Dave Keon, Billy Harris, Don McKenney, Jim Pappin, Bob Pulford, Eddie Shack, Frank Mahovlich, Ed Litzenberger, Punch Imlach (manager-coach), Bob Haggert (trainer).
Scores April 11, at Toronto — Toronto 3, Detroit 2; April 14, at Toronto — Toronto 3, Detroit 4; April 16, at Detroit — Toronto 3, Detroit 4; April 18, at Detroit — Toronto 4, Detroit 2; April 21, at Toronto — Toronto 1, Detroit 4; April 23, at Detroit — Toronto 4, Detroit 3; April 25, at Toronto — Toronto 4, Detroit 0.

1962-63 — Toronto Maple Leafs — Johnny Bower, Don Simmons, Carl Brewer, Tim Horton, Kent Douglas, Allan Stanley, Bob Baun, Larry Hillman, Red Kelly, Dick Duff, George Armstrong, Bob Nevin, Ron Stewart, Dave Keon, Billy Harris, Bob Pulford, Eddie Shack, Ed Litzenberger, Frank Mahovlich, John MacMillan, Punch Imlach (manager-coach), Bob Haggert (trainer).
Scores: April 9, at Toronto — Toronto 4, Detroit 2; April 11, at Toronto — Toronto 4, Detroit 2; April 14, at Detroit — Toronto 2, Detroit 3; April 16, at Detroit — Toronto 3, Detroit 1.

1961-62 — Toronto Maple Leafs — Johnny Bower, Don Simmons, Carl Brewer, Tim Horton, Bob Baun, Allan Stanley, Al Arbour, Larry Hillman, Red Kelly, Dick Duff, George Armstrong, Frank Mahovlich, Bob Nevin, Ron Stewart, Billy Harris, Bert Olmstead, Bob Pulford, Eddie Shack, Dave Keon, Ed Litzenberger, John MacMillan, Punch Imlach (manager-coach), Bob Haggert (trainer).
Scores: April 10, at Toronto — Toronto 4, Chicago 1; April 12, at Toronto — Toronto 3, Chicago 2; April 15, at Chicago — Toronto 0, Chicago 3; April 17, at Chicago — Toronto 1, Chicago 4; April 19, at Toronto —Toronto 8, Chicago 4; April 22, at Chicago — Toronto 2, Chicago 1.

1960-61 — Chicago Black Hawks — Glenn Hall, Al Arbour, Pierre Pilote, Elmer Vasko, Jack Evans, Dollard St. Laurent, Reggie Fleming, Tod Sloan, Ron Murphy, Ed Litzenberger, Bill Hay, Bobby Hull, Ab McDonald, Eric Nesterenko, Kenny Wharram, Earl Balfour, Stan Mikita, Murray Balfour, Chico Maki, Wayne Hicks, Tommy Ivan (manager), Rudy Pilous (coach), Nick Garen (trainer).
Scores: April 6, at Chicago — Chicago 3, Detroit 2; April 8, at Detroit — Detroit 3, Chicago 1; April 10, at Chicago — Chicago 3, Detroit 1; April 12, at Detroit — Detroit 2, Chicago 1; April 14, at Chicago — Chicago 6, Detroit 3; April 16, at Detroit — Chicago 5, Detroit 1.

1959-60 — Montreal Canadiens — Jacques Plante, Charlie Hodge, Doug Harvey, Tom Johnson, Bob Turner, Jean-Guy Talbot, Albert Langlois, Bernie Geoffrion, Phil Goyette, Bill Hicke, Don Marshall, Ab McDonald, Dickie Moore, André Pronovost, Claude Provost, Henri Richard, Maurice Richard, Frank Selke (manager), Toe Blake (coach), Hector Dubois, Larry Aubut (trainers).
Scores: April 7, at Montreal — Montreal 4, Toronto 2; April 9, at Montreal — Montreal 2, Toronto 1; April 12, at Toronto — Montreal 5, Toronto 2; April 14, at Toronto — Montreal 4, Toronto 0.

1958-59 — Montreal Canadiens — Jacques Plante, Charlie Hodge, Doug Harvey, Tom Johnson, Bob Turner, Jean-Guy Talbot, Albert Langlois, Bernie Geoffrion, Ralph Backstrom, Bill Hicke, Maurice Richard, Dickie Moore, Claude Provost, Ab McDonald, Henri Richard, Marcel Bonin, Phil Goyette, Don Marshall, André Pronovost, Jean Béliveau, Frank Selke (manager), Toe Blake (coach), Hector Dubois, Larry Aubut (trainers).
Scores: April 9, at Montreal — Montreal 5, Toronto 3; April 11, at Montreal — Montreal 3, Toronto 1; April 14, at Toronto — Toronto 3, Montreal 2; April 16, at Toronto — Montreal 3, Toronto 2; April 18, at Montreal — Montreal 5, Toronto 3.

1957-58 — Montreal Canadiens — Jacques Plante, Gerry McNeil, Doug Harvey, Tom Johnson, Bob Turner, Dollard St-Laurent, Jean-Guy Talbot, Albert Langlois, Jean Béliveau, Bernie Geoffrion, Maurice Richard, Dickie Moore, Claude Provost, Floyd Curry, Bert Olmstead, Henri Richard, Marcel Bonin, Phil Goyette, Don Marshall, André Pronovost, Connie Broden, Frank Selke (manager), Toe Blake (coach), Hector Dubois, Larry Aubut (trainers).
Scores: April 8, at Montreal —Montreal 2, Boston 1; April 10, at Montreal — Boston 5, Montreal 2; April 13, at Boston — Montreal 3, Boston 0; April 15, at Boston — Boston 3, Montreal 1; April 17, at Montreal — Montreal 3, Boston 2; April 20, at Boston — Montreal 5, Boston 3.

It had been 29 years since a Bruins team last posed for a Stanley Cup photo when this picture was taken of the 1970 champions. After a record-breaking 1970-71 season ended in playoff disappointment, the Bruins won the Cup again in 1972.

1956-57 — Montreal Canadiens — Jacques Plante, Gerry McNeil, Doug Harvey, Tom Johnson, Bob Turner, Dollard St. Laurent, Jean-Guy Talbot, Jean Béliveau, Bernie Geoffrion, Floyd Curry, Dickie Moore, Maurice Richard, Claude Provost, Bert Olmstead, Henri Richard, Phil Goyette, Don Marshall, André Pronovost, Connie Broden, Frank Selke (manager), Toe Blake (coach), Hector Dubois, Larry Aubut (trainers).
Scores: April 6, at Montreal — Montreal 5, Boston 1; April 9, at Montreal — Montreal 1, Boston 0; April 11, at Boston — Montreal 4, Boston 2; April 14, at Boston — Boston 2, Montreal 0; April 16, at Montreal — Montreal 5, Boston 1.

1955-56 — Montreal Canadiens — Jacques Plante, Doug Harvey, Butch Bouchard, Bob Turner, Tom Johnson, Jean-Guy Talbot, Dollard St. Laurent, Jean Béliveau, Bernie Geoffrion, Bert Olmstead, Floyd Curry, Jackie Leclair, Maurice Richard, Dickie Moore, Henri Richard, Kenny Mosdell, Don Marshall, Claude Provost, Frank Selke (manager), Toe Blake (coach), Hector Dubois (trainer).
Scores: March 31, at Montreal — Montreal 6, Detroit 4; April 3, at Montreal — Montreal 5, Detroit 1; April 5, at Detroit — Detroit 3, Montreal 1; April 8, at Detroit — Montreal 3, Detroit 0; April 10, at Montreal — Montreal 3, Detroit 1.

1954-55 — Detroit Red Wings — Terry Sawchuk, Red Kelly, Bob Goldham, Marcel Pronovost, Benny Woit, Jim Hay, Larry Hillman, Ted Lindsay, Tony Leswick, Gordie Howe, Alex Delvecchio, Marty Pavelich, Glen Skov, Earl Reibel, John Wilson, Bill Dineen, Vic Stasiuk, Marcel Bonin, Jack Adams (manager), Jimmy Skinner (coach), Carl Mattson (trainer).
Scores: April 3, at Detroit — Detroit 4, Montreal 2; April 5, at Detroit — Detroit 7, Montreal 1, April 7, at Montreal — Montreal 4, Detroit 2; April 9, at Montreal — Montreal 5, Detroit 3; April 10, at Detroit — Detroit 5, Montreal 1; April 12, at Montreal — Montreal 6, Detroit 3; April 14, at Detroit — Detroit 3, Montreal 1.

1953-54 — Detroit Red Wings — Terry Sawchuk, Red Kelly, Bob Goldham, Benny Woit, Marcel Pronovost, Al Arbour, Keith Allen, Ted Lindsay, Tony Leswick, Gordie Howe, Marty Pavelich, Alex Delvecchio, Metro Prystai, Glen Skov, Johnny Wilson, Bill Dineen, Jimmy Peters Sr., Earl Reibel, Vic Stasiuk, Jack Adams (manager), Tommy Ivan (coach), Carl Mattson (trainer).
Scores: April 4, at Detroit — Detroit 3, Montreal 1; April 6, at Detroit — Montreal 3, Detroit 1; April 8, at Montreal — Detroit 5, Montreal 2; April 10, at Montreal — Detroit 2, Montreal 0; April 11, at Detroit — Montreal 1, Detroit 0; April 13, at Montreal — Montreal 4, Detroit 1; April 16, at Detroit — Detroit 2, Montreal 1.

1952-53 — Montreal Canadiens — Gerry McNeil, Jacques Plante, Doug Harvey, Butch Bouchard, Tom Johnson, Dollard St. Laurent, Bud MacPherson, Maurice Richard, Elmer Lach, Bert Olmstead, Bernie Geoffrion, Floyd Curry, Paul Masnick, Billy Reay, Dickie Moore, Kenny Mosdell, Dick Gamble, Johnny McCormack, Lorne Davis, Calum MacKay, Eddie Mazur, Frank Selke (manager), Dick Irvin (coach), Hector Dubois (trainer).
Scores: April 9, at Montreal — Montreal 4, Boston 2; April 11, at Montreal — Boston 4, Montreal 1; April 12, at Boston — Montreal 3, Boston 0; April 14, at Boston — Montreal 7, Boston 3; April 16, at Montreal — Montreal 1, Boston 0.

1951-52 — Detroit Red Wings — Terry Sawchuk, Bob Goldham, Benny Woit, Red Kelly, Leo Reise Jr., Marcel Pronovost, Ted Lindsay, Tony Leswick, Gordie Howe, Metro Prystai, Marty Pavelich, Sid Abel, Glen Skov, Alex Delvecchio, John Wilson, Vic Stasiuk, Larry Zeidel, Jack Adams (manager) Tommy Ivan (coach), Carl Mattson (trainer).
Scores: April 10, at Montreal — Detroit 3, Montreal 1; April 12, at Montreal — Detroit 2, Montreal 1; April 13, at Detroit — Detroit 3, Montreal 0; April 15, at Detroit — Detroit 3, Montreal 0.

1950-51 — Toronto Maple Leafs — Turk Broda, Al Rollins, Jim Thomson, Gus Mortson, Bill Barilko, Bill Juzda, Fern Flaman, Hugh Bolton, Ted Kennedy, Sid Smith, Tod Sloan, Cal Gardner, Howie Meeker, Harry Watson, Max Bentley, Joe Klukay, Danny Lewicki, Ray Timgren, Fleming Mackell, Johnny McCormack, Bob Hassard, Conn Smythe (manager), Joe Primeau (coach), Tim Daly (trainer).
Scores: April 11, at Toronto — Toronto 3, Montreal 2; April 14, at Toronto — Montreal 3, Toronto 2; April 17, at Montreal — Toronto 2, Montreal 1; April 19, at Montreal — Toronto 3, Montreal 2; April 21, at Toronto — Toronto 3, Montreal 2.

1949-50 — Detroit Red Wings — Harry Lumley, Jack Stewart, Leo Reise Jr., Clare Martin, Al Dewsbury, Lee Fogolin, Marcel Pronovost, Red Kelly, Ted Lindsay, Sid Abel, Gordie Howe, George Gee, Jimmy Peters Sr., Marty Pavelich, Jim McFadden, Pete Babando, Max McNab, Gerry Couture, Joe Carveth, John Wilson, Larry Wilson, Jack Adams (manager), Tommy Ivan (coach), Carl Mattson (trainer).
Scores: April 11, at Detroit — Detroit 4, NY Rangers 1; April 13, at Toronto* — NY Rangers 3, Detroit 1; April 15, at Toronto — Detroit 4, NY Rangers 0; April 18, at Detroit — NY Rangers 4, Detroit 3; April 20, at Detroit — NY Rangers 2, Detroit 1; April 22, at Detroit — Detroit 5, NY Rangers 4; April 23, at Detroit — Detroit 4, NY Rangers 3.
* Ice was unavailable in Madison Square Garden and Rangers elected to play second and third games on Toronto ice.

1948-49 — Toronto Maple Leafs — Turk Broda, Jim Thomson, Gus Mortson, Bill Barilko, Garth Boesch, Bill Juzda, Ted Kennedy, Howie Meeker, Vic Lynn, Harry Watson, Bill Ezinicki, Cal Gardner, Max Bentley, Joe Klukay, Sid Smith, Don Metz, Ray Timgren, Fleming Mackell, Harry Taylor, Bob Dawes, Tod Sloan, Conn Smythe (manager), Hap Day (coach), Tim Daly (trainer).
Scores: April 8, at Detroit — Toronto 3, Detroit 2; April 10, at Detroit — Toronto 3, Detroit 1; April 13, at Toronto — Toronto 3, Detroit 1; April 16, at Toronto — Toronto 3, Detroit 1.

1947-48 — Toronto Maple Leafs — Turk Broda, Jim Thomson, Wally Stanowski, Garth Boesch, Bill Barilko, Gus Mortson, Phil Samis, Syl Apps Sr., Bill Ezinicki, Harry Watson, Ted Kennedy, Howie Meeker, Vic Lynn, Nick Metz, Max Bentley, Joe Klukay, Les Costello, Don Metz, Sid Smith, Conn Smythe (manager), Hap Day (coach), Tim Daly (trainer).
Scores: April 7, at Toronto — Toronto 5, Detroit 3; April 10, at Toronto — Toronto 4, Detroit 2; April 11, at Detroit — Toronto 2, Detroit 0; April 14, at Detroit — Toronto 7, Detroit 2.

Nick Metz and Wally Stanowski hug Hap Day and the Stanley Cup after Toronto's third straight championship in 1949. With a previous victory in 1945 and another one to come in 1951, the Leafs won the Stanley Cup five times in seven years.

1946-47 — Toronto Maple Leafs — Turk Broda, Garth Boesch, Gus Mortson, Jim Thomson, Wally Stanowski, Bill Barilko, Harry Watson, Bud Poile, Ted Kennedy, Syl Apps Sr., Don Metz, Nick Metz, Bill Ezinicki, Vic Lynn, Howie Meeker, Gaye Stewart, Joe Klukay, Gus Bodnar, Bob Goldham, Conn Smythe (manager), Hap Day (coach), Tim Daly (trainer).
Scores: April 8, at Montreal — Montreal 6, Toronto 0; April 10, at Montreal — Toronto 4, Montreal 0; April 12, at Toronto — Toronto 4, Montreal 2; April 15, at Toronto — Toronto 2, Montreal 1; April 17, at Montreal — Montreal 3, Toronto 1; April 19, at Toronto — Toronto 2, Montreal 1.

1945-46 — Montreal Canadiens — Elmer Lach, Toe Blake, Maurice Richard, Bob Fillion, Dutch Hiller, Murph Chamberlain, Ken Mosdell, Buddy O'Connor, Glen Harmon, Jimmy Peters Sr., Butch Bouchard, Billy Reay, Ken Reardon, Leo Lamoureux, Frank Eddolls, Gerry Plamondon, Bill Durnan, Tommy Gorman (manager), Dick Irvin (coach), Ernie Cook (trainer).
Scores: March 30, at Montreal — Montreal 4, Boston 3; April 2, at Montreal — Montreal 3, Boston 2; April 4, at Boston — Montreal 4, Boston 2; April 7, at Boston — Boston 3, Montreal 2; April 9, at Montreal — Montreal 6, Boston 3.

1944-45 — Toronto Maple Leafs — Don Metz, Frank McCool, Wally Stanowski, Reg Hamilton, Elwyn Morris, Johnny McCreedy, Tommy O'Neill, Ted Kennedy, Babe Pratt, Gus Bodnar, Art Jackson, Jack McLean, Mel Hill, Nick Metz, Bob Davidson, Sweeney Schriner, Lorne Carr, Conn Smythe (manager), Frank Selke (business manager), Hap Day (coach), Tim Daly (trainer).
Scores: April 6, at Detroit — Toronto 1, Detroit 0; April 8, at Detroit — Toronto 2, Detroit 0; April 12, at Toronto — Toronto 1, Detroit 0; April 14, at Toronto — Detroit 5, Toronto 3; April 19, at Detroit — Detroit 2, Toronto 0; April 21, at Toronto — Detroit 1, Toronto 0; April 22, at Detroit — Toronto 2, Detroit 1.

1943-44 — Montreal Canadiens — Toe Blake, Maurice Richard, Elmer Lach, Ray Getliffe, Murph Chamberlain, Phil Watson, Butch Bouchard, Glen Harmon, Buddy O'Connor, Jerry Heffernan, Mike McMahon Sr., Leo Lamoureux, Fernand Majeau, Bob Fillion, Bill Durnan, Tommy Gorman (manager), Dick Irvin (coach), Ernie Cook (trainer).
Scores: April 4, at Montreal — Montreal 5, Chicago 1; April 6, at Chicago — Montreal 3, Chicago 1; April 9, at Chicago — Montreal 3, Chicago 2; April 13, at Montreal — Montreal 5, Chicago 4.

1942-43 — Detroit Red Wings — Jack Stewart, Jimmy Orlando, Sid Abel, Alex Motter, Harry Watson, Joe Carveth, Mud Bruneteau, Eddie Wares, Johnny Mowers, Cully Simon, Don Grosso, Carl Liscombe, Connie Brown, Syd Howe, Les Douglas, Hal Jackson, Joe Fisher, Jack Adams (manager), Ebbie Goodfellow (playing-coach), Honey Walker (trainer).
Scores: April 1, at Detroit — Detroit 6, Boston 2; April 4, at Detroit — Detroit 4, Boston 3; April 7, at Boston — Detroit 4, Boston 0; April 8, at Boston — Detroit 2, Boston 0.

1941-42 — Toronto Maple Leafs — Wally Stanowski, Syl Apps Sr., Bob Goldham, Gordie Drillon, Hank Goldup, Ernie Dickens, Sweeney Schriner, Bucko McDonald, Bob Davidson, Nick Metz, Bingo Kampman, Don Metz, Gaye Stewart, Turk Broda, Johnny McCreedy, Lorne Carr, Pete Langelle, Billy Taylor, Conn Smythe (manager), Hap Day (coach), Frank Selke (business manager), Tim Daly (trainer).
Scores: April 4, at Toronto — Detroit 3, Toronto 2; April 7, at Toronto — Detroit 4, Toronto 2; April 9, at Detroit — Detroit 5, Toronto 2; April 12, at Detroit — Toronto 4, Detroit 3; April 14, at Toronto — Toronto 9, Detroit 3; April 16, at Detroit — Toronto 3, Detroit 0; April 18, at Toronto — Toronto 3, Detroit 1.

1940-41 — Boston Bruins — Bill Cowley, Des Smith, Dit Clapper, Frank Brimsek, Flash Hollett, John Crawford, Bobby Bauer, Pat McReavy, Herb Cain, Mel Hill, Milt Schmidt, Woody Dumart, Roy Conacher, Terry Reardon, Art Jackson, Eddie Wiseman, Art Ross (manager), Cooney Weiland (coach), Win Green (trainer).
Scores: April 6, at Boston — Detroit 2, Boston 3; April 8, at Boston — Detroit 1, Boston 2; April 10, at Detroit — Boston 4, Detroit 2; April 12, at Detroit — Boston 3, Detroit 1.

1939-40 — New York Rangers — Dave Kerr, Art Coulter, Ott Heller, Alex Shibicky, Mac Colville, Neil Colville, Phil Watson, Lynn Patrick, Clint Smith, Muzz Patrick, Babe Pratt, Bryan Hextall Sr., Kilby Macdonald, Dutch Hiller, Alf Pike, Sanford Smith, Lester Patrick (manager), Frank Boucher (coach), Harry Westerby (trainer).
Scores: April 2, at New York — NY Rangers 2, Toronto 1; April 3, at New York — NY Rangers 6, Toronto 2; April 6, at Toronto — NY Rangers 1, Toronto 2; April 9, at Toronto — NY Rangers 0, Toronto 3; April 11, at Toronto — NY Rangers 2, Toronto 1; April 13, at Toronto — NY Rangers 3, Toronto 2.

1938-39 — Boston Bruins — Bobby Bauer, Mel Hill, Flash Hollett, Roy Conacher, Gord Pettinger, Milt Schmidt, Woody Dumart, Jack Crawford, Ray Getliffe, Frank Brimsek, Eddie Shore, Dit Clapper, Bill Cowley, Jack Portland, Red Hamill, Cooney Weiland, Art Ross (manager-coach), Win Green (trainer).
Scores: April 6, at Boston — Toronto 1, Boston 2; April 9, at Boston — Toronto 3, Boston 2; April 11, at Toronto — Toronto 1, Boston 3; April 13, at Toronto — Toronto 0, Boston 2; April 16, at Boston — Toronto 1, Boston 3.

1937-38 — Chicago Black Hawks — Art Wiebe, Carl Voss, Hal Jackson, Mike Karakas, Mush March, Jack Shill, Earl Seibert, Cully Dahlstrom, Alex Levinsky, Johnny Gottselig, Lou Trudel, Pete Palangio, Bill MacKenzie, Doc Romnes, Paul Thompson, Roger Jenkins, Alf Moore, Bert Connolly, Virgil Johnson, Paul Goodman, Bill Stewart (manager-coach), Eddie Froelich (trainer).
Scores: April 5, at Toronto — Chicago 3, Toronto 1; April 7, at Toronto — Chicago 1, Toronto 5; April 10, at Chicago — Chicago 2, Toronto 1; April 12, at Chicago — Chicago 4, Toronto 1.

1936-37 — Detroit Red Wings — Norman Smith, Pete Kelly, Larry Aurie, Herbie Lewis, Hec Kilrea, Mud Bruneteau, Syd Howe, Wally Kilrea, Jimmy Franks, Bucko McDonald, Gord Pettinger, Ebbie Goodfellow, John Gallagher, Ralph Bowman, John Sorrell, Marty Barry, Earl Robertson, John Sherf, Howard Mackie, Jack Adams (manager-coach), Honey Walker (trainer).
Scores: April 6, at New York — Detroit 1, NY Rangers 5; April 8, at Detroit — Detroit 4, NY Rangers 2; April 11, at Detroit — Detroit 0, NY Rangers 1; April 13, at Detroit — Detroit 1, NY Rangers 0; April 15, at Detroit — Detroit 3, NY Rangers 0.

1935-36 — Detroit Red Wings — John Sorrell, Syd Howe, Marty Barry, Herbie Lewis, Mud Bruneteau, Wally Kilrea, Hec Kilrea, Gord Pettinger, Bucko McDonald, Ralph Bowman, Pete Kelly, Doug Young, Ebbie Goodfellow, Norman Smith, Jack Adams (manager-coach), Honey Walker (trainer).
Scores: April 5, at Detroit — Detroit 3, Toronto 1; April 7, at Detroit — Detroit 9, Toronto 4; April 9, at Toronto — Detroit 3, Toronto 4; April 11, at Toronto — Detroit 3, Toronto 2.

1934-35 — Montreal Maroons — Lionel Conacher, Cy Wentworth, Alex Connell, Toe Blake, Stewart Evans, Earl Robinson, Bill Miller, Dave Trottier, Jimmy Ward, Larry Northcott, Hooley Smith, Russ Blinco, Allan Shields, Sammy McManus, Gus Marker, Bob Gracie, Herb Cain, Tommy Gorman (manager-coach), Bill O'Brien (trainer).
Scores: April 4, at Toronto — Mtl. Maroons 3, Toronto 2; April 6, at Toronto — Mtl. Maroons 3, Toronto 1; April 9, at Montreal — Mtl. Maroons 4, Toronto 1.

1933-34 — Chicago Black Hawks — Clarence Abel, Rosie Couture, Lou Trudel, Lionel Conacher, Paul Thompson, Leroy Goldsworthy, Art Coulter, Roger Jenkins, Don McFayden, Tom Cook, Doc Romnes, Johnny Gottselig, Mush March, Johnny Sheppard, Chuck Gardiner (captain), Bill Kendall, Tommy Gorman (manager-coach), Eddie Froelich (trainer).
Scores: April 3, at Detroit — Chicago 2, Detroit 1; April 5, at Detroit — Chicago 4, Detroit 1; April 8, at Chicago — Detroit 5, Chicago 2; April 10, at Chicago — Chicago 1, Detroit 0.

1932-33 — New York Rangers — Ching Johnson, Butch Keeling, Frank Boucher, Art Somers, Babe Siebert, Bun Cook, Andy Aitkenhead, Ott Heller, Oscar Asmundson, Gord Pettinger, Doug Brennan, Cecil Dillon, Bill Cook (captain), Murray Murdoch, Earl Seibert, Lester Patrick (manager-coach), Harry Westerby (trainer).
Scores: April 4, at New York — NY Rangers 5, Toronto 1; April 8, at Toronto — NY Rangers 3, Toronto 1; April 11, at Toronto — Toronto 3, NY Rangers 2; April 13, at Toronto — NY Rangers 1, Toronto 0.

1931-32 — Toronto Maple Leafs — Charlie Conacher, Harvey Jackson, King Clancy, Andy Blair, Red Horner, Lorne Chabot, Alex Levinsky, Joe Primeau, Hal Darragh, Hal Cotton, Frank Finnigan, Hap Day, Ace Bailey, Bob Gracie, Fred Robertson, Earl Miller, Conn Smythe (manager), Dick Irvin (coach), Tim Daly (trainer).
Scores: April 5, at New York — Toronto 6, NY Rangers 4; April 7, at Boston* — Toronto 6, NY Rangers 2; April 9, at Toronto — Toronto 6, NY Rangers 4.
* Ice was unavailable in Madison Square Garden and Rangers elected to play the second game on neutral ice.

1930-31 — Montreal Canadiens — George Hainsworth, Wildor Larochelle, Marty Burke, Sylvio Mantha, Howie Morenz, Johnny Gagnon, Aurel Joliat, Armand Mondou, Pit Lepine, Albert Leduc, Georges Mantha, Art Lesieur, Nick Wasnie, Bert McCaffrey, Gus Rivers, Jean Pusie, Léo Dandurand (manager), Cecil Hart (coach), Ed Dufour (trainer).
Scores: April 3, at Chicago — Montreal 2, Chicago 1; April 5, at Chicago — Chicago 2, Montreal 1; April 9, at Montreal — Chicago 3, Montreal 2; April 11, at Montreal — Montreal 4, Chicago 2; April 14, at Montreal — Montreal 2, Chicago 0.

1929-30 — Montreal Canadiens — George Hainsworth, Marty Burke, Sylvio Mantha, Howie Morenz, Bert McCaffrey, Aurel Joliat, Albert Leduc, Pit Lepine, Wildor Larochelle, Nick Wasnie, Gerald Carson, Armand Mondou, Georges Mantha, Gus Rivers, Léo Dandurand (manager), Cecil Hart (coach), Ed Dufour (trainer).
Scores: April 1, at Boston — Montreal 3, Boston 0; April 3, at Montreal — Montreal 4, Boston 3.

1928-29 — Boston Bruins — Tiny Thompson, Eddie Shore, Lionel Hitchman, Perk Galbraith, Eric Pettinger, Frank Fredrickson, Mickey Mackay, Red Green, Dutch Gainor, Harry Oliver, Eddie Rodden, Dit Clapper, Cooney Weiland, Lloyd Klein, Cy Denneny, Bill Carson, George Owen, Myles Lane, Art Ross (manager-coach), Win Green (trainer).
Scores: March 28, at Boston — Boston 2, NY Rangers 0; March 29, at New York — Boston 2, NY Rangers 1.

1927-28 — New York Rangers — Lorne Chabot, Clarence Abel, Leon Bourgault, Ching Johnson, Bill Cook, Bun Cook, Frank Boucher, Bill Boyd, Murray Murdoch, Paul Thompson, Alex Gray, Joe Miller, Patsy Callighen, Lester Patrick (manager-coach), Harry Westerby (trainer).
Scores: April 5, at Montreal — Mtl. Maroons 2, NY Rangers 0; April 7, at Montreal — NY Rangers 2, Mtl. Maroons 1; April 10, at Montreal — Mtl. Maroons 2, NY Rangers 0; April 12, at Montreal — NY Rangers 1, Mtl. Maroons 0; April 14, at Montreal — NY Rangers 2, Mtl. Maroons 1.

1926-27 — Ottawa Senators — Alex Connell, King Clancy, George Boucher, Ed Gorman, Frank Finnigan, Alex Smith, Hec Kilrea, Hooley Smith, Cy Denneny, Frank Nighbor, Jack Adams, Milt Halliday, Dave Gill (manager-coach).
Scores: April 7, at Boston — Ottawa 0, Boston 0; April 9, at Boston — Ottawa 3, Boston 1; April 11, at Ottawa — Boston 1, Ottawa 1; April 13, at Ottawa — Ottawa 3, Boston 1.

1925-26 — Montreal Maroons — Clint Benedict, Reg Noble, Frank Carson, Dunc Munro, Nels Stewart, Harry Broadbent, Babe Siebert, Chuck Dinsmore, Bill Phillips, Hobie Kitchen, Sam Rothschield, Albert Holway, George Horne, Bernie Brophy, Eddie Gerard (manager-coach), Bill O'Brien (trainer).
Scores: March 30, at Montreal — Mtl. Maroons 3, Victoria 0; April 1, at Montreal — Mtl. Maroons 3, Victoria 0; April 3, at Montreal — Victoria 3, Mtl. Maroons 2; April 6, at Montreal — Mtl. Maroons 2, Victoria 0.

The series in the spring of 1926 ended the annual playoffs between the champions of the East and the champions of the West. Since 1926-27 the annual playoffs in the National Hockey League have decided the Stanley Cup champions.

1924-25 — Victoria Cougars — Harry Holmes, Clem Loughlin, Gord Fraser, Frank Fredrickson, Jack Walker, Wilf Hart, Harold Halderson, Frank Foyston, Wally Elmer, Harry Meeking, Jocko Anderson, Lester Patrick (manager-coach).
Scores: March 21, at Victoria — Victoria 5, Montreal 2; March 23, at Vancouver — Victoria 3, Montreal 1; March 27, at Victoria — Montreal 4, Victoria 2; March 30, at Victoria — Victoria 6, Montreal 1.

1923-24 — Montreal Canadiens — Georges Vezina, Sprague Cleghorn, Billy Couture, Howie Morenz, Aurel Joliat, Billy Boucher, Odie Cleghorn, Sylvio Mantha, Bobby Boucher, Billy Bell, Billy Cameron, Joe Malone, Charles Fortier, Leo Dandurand (manager-coach).
Scores: March 18, at Montreal — Montreal 3, Van. Maroons 2; March 20, at Montreal — Montreal 2, Van. Maroons 1. March 22, at Montreal — Montreal 6, Cgy. Tigers 1; March 25, at Ottawa* — Montreal 3, Cgy. Tigers 0.
* Game transferred to Ottawa to benefit from artificial ice surface.

1922-23 — Ottawa Senators — George Boucher, Lionel Hitchman, Frank Nighbor, King Clancy, Harry Helman, Clint Benedict, Jack Darragh, Eddie Gerard, Cy Denneny, Harry Broadbent, Tommy Gorman (manager), Pete Green (coach), F. Dolan (trainer).
Scores: March 16, at Vancouver — Ottawa 1, Van. Maroons 0; March 19, at Vancouver — Van. Maroons 4, Ottawa 1; March 23, at Vancouver — Ottawa 3, Van. Maroons 2; March 26, at Vancouver — Ottawa 5, Van. Maroons 1; March 29, at Vancouver — Ottawa 2, Edm. Eskimos 1; March 31, at Vancouver — Ottawa 1, Edm. Eskimos 0.

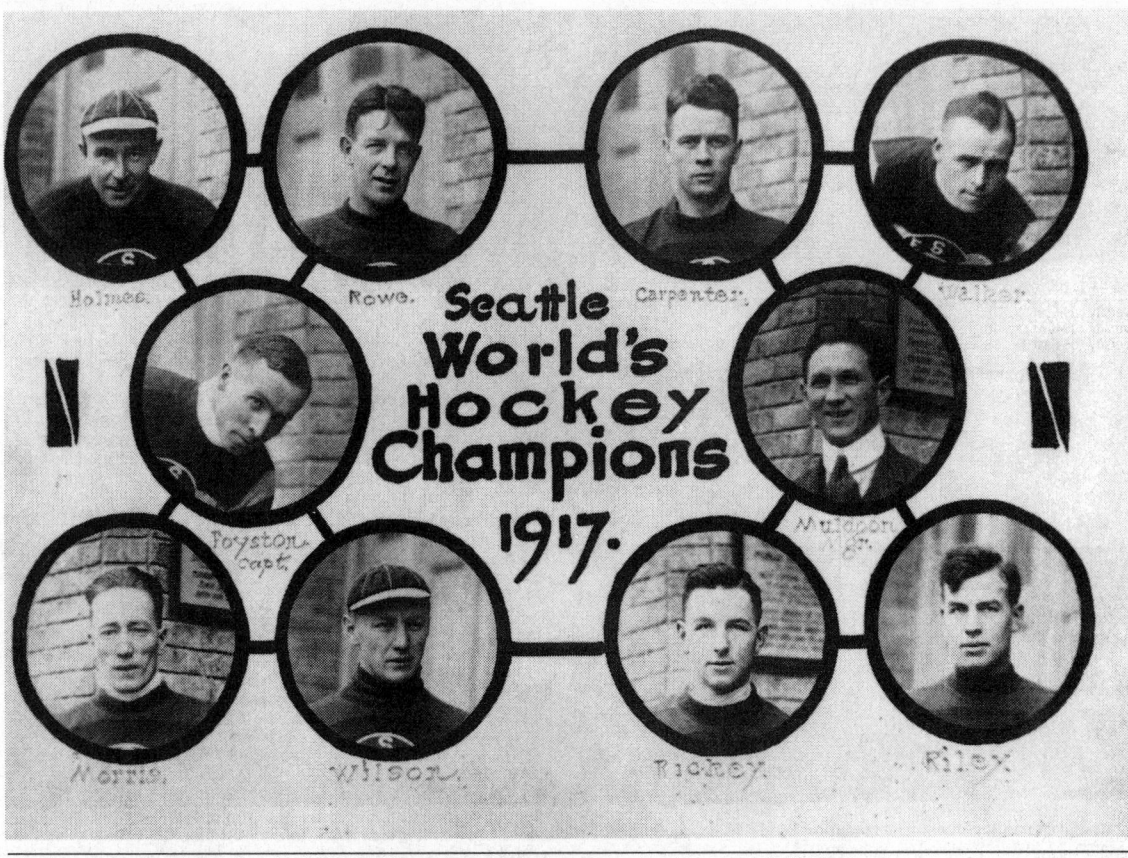

Though the players were all Canadians, the 1917 Seattle Metropolitans were the first American-based team to win the Stanley Cup.
The champions of the Pacific Coast Hockey Association defeated the Montreal Canadiens to win the title.

1921-22 — Toronto St. Pats — Ted Stackhouse, Corb Denneny, Rod Smylie, Lloyd Andrews, John Ross Roach, Harry Cameron, Billy Stuart, Babe Dye, Ken Randall, Reg Noble, Eddie Gerard (borrowed for one game from Ottawa), Stan Jackson, Nolan Mitchell, Charlie Querrie (manager), George O'Donoghue (coach).
Scores: March 17, at Toronto — Van. Millionaires 4, Toronto 3; March 20, at Toronto — Toronto 2, Van. Millionaires 1; March 23, at Toronto — Van. Millionaires 3, Toronto 0; March 25, at Toronto — Toronto 6, Van. Millionaires 0; March 28, at Toronto — Toronto 5, Van. Millionaires 1.

1920-21 — Ottawa Senators — Jack McKell, Jack Darragh, Morley Bruce, George Boucher, Eddie Gerard, Clint Benedict, Sprague Cleghorn, Frank Nighbor, Harry Broadbent, Cy Denneny, Leth Graham, Tommy Gorman (manager),Pete Green (coach), F. Dolan (trainer).
Scores: March 21, at Vancouver — Van. Millionaires 2, Ottawa 1; March 24, at Vancouver — Ottawa 4, Van. Millionaires 3; March 28, at Vancouver — Ottawa 3, Van. Millionaires 2; March 31, at Vancouver — Van. Millionaires 3, Ottawa 2; April 4, at Vancouver — Ottawa 2, Van. Millionaires 1

1919-20 — Ottawa Senators — Jack McKell, Jack Darragh, Morley Bruce, Horrace Merrill, George Boucher, Eddie Gerard, Clint Benedict, Sprague Cleghorn, Frank Nighbor, Harry Broadbent, Cy Denneny, Tommy Gorman (manager), Pete Green (coach).
Scores: March 22, at Ottawa — Ottawa 3, Seattle 2; March 24, at Ottawa — Ottawa 3, Seattle 0; March 27, at Ottawa — Seattle 3, Ottawa 1; March 30, at Toronto* — Seattle 5, Ottawa 2; April 1, at Toronto* — Ottawa 6, Seattle 1.
* Games transferred to Toronto to benefit from artificial ice surface.

1918-19 — No decision, Series halted by Spanish influenza epidemic, illness of several players and death of Joe Hall of Montreal Canadiens from flu. Five games had been played when the series was halted, each team having won two and tied one. The results are shown:
Scores: March 19, at Seattle — Seattle 7, Montreal 0; March 22, at Seattle — Montreal 4, Seattle 2; March 24, at Seattle — Seattle 7, Montreal 2; March 26, at Seattle — Montreal 0, Seattle 0; March 30, at Seattle — Montreal 4, Seattle 3.

1917-18 — Toronto Arenas — Rusty Crawford, Harry Meeking, Ken Randall, Corb Denneny, Harry Cameron, Jack Adams, Alf Skinner, Harry Mummery, Harry Holmes, Reg Noble, Sammy Hebert, Jack Marks, Jack Coughlin, Charlie Querrie (manager), Dick Carroll (coach), Frank Carroll (trainer).
Scores: March 20, at Toronto — Toronto 5, Van. Millionaires 3; March 23, at Toronto — Van. Millionaires 6, Toronto 4; March 26, at Toronto — Toronto 6, Van. Millionaires 3; March 28, at Toronto — Van. Millionaires 8, Toronto 1; March 30, at Toronto — Toronto 2, Van. Millionaires 1.

1916-17 — Seattle Metropolitans — Harry Holmes, Ed Carpenter, Cully Wilson, Jack Walker, Bernie Morris, Frank Foyston, Roy Rickey, Jim Riley, Bobby Rowe (captain), Peter Muldoon (manager).
Scores: March 17, at Seattle — Montreal 8, Seattle 4; March 20, at Seattle — Seattle 6, Montreal 1; March 23, at Seattle — Seattle 4, Montreal 1; March 25, at Seattle — Seattle 9, Montreal 1.

1915-16 — Montreal Canadiens — Georges Vezina, Bert Corbeau, Jack Laviolette, Newsy Lalonde, Louis Berlinguette, Goldie Prodgers, Howard McNamara, Didier Pitre, Skene Ronan, Amos Arbour, Georges Poulin, Jacques Fournier, George Kennedy (manager).
Scores: March 20, at Montreal — Portland 2, Montreal 0; March 22, at Montreal — Montreal 2, Portland 1; March 25, at Montreal — Montreal 6, Portland 3; March 28, at Montreal — Portland 6, Montreal 5; March 30, at Montreal — Montreal 2, Portland 1.

1914-15 — Vancouver Millionaires — Kenny Mallen, Frank Nighbor, Fred (Cyclone) Taylor, Hughie Lehman, Lloyd Cook, Mickey MacKay, Barney Stanley, Jim Seaborn, Si Griffis (captain), Jean Matz, Frank Patrick (playing manager).
Scores: March 22, at Vancouver — Van. Millionaires 6, Ottawa 2; March 24, at Vancouver — Van. Millionaires 8, Ottawa 3; March 26, at Vancouver — Van. Millionaires 12, Ottawa 3.

1913-14 — Toronto Blueshirts — Con Corbeau, F. Roy McGiffen, Jack Walker, George McNamara, Cully Wilson, Frank Foyston, Harry Cameron, Harry Holmes, Alan M. Davidson (captain), Harriston, Jack Marshall (playing-manager), Frank and Dick Carroll (trainers).
Scores: March 14, at Toronto — Toronto 5, Victoria 2; March 17, at Toronto — Toronto 6, Victoria 5; March 19, at Toronto — Toronto 2, Victoria 1.

1912-13 — Quebec Bulldogs — Joe Malone, Joe Hall, Paddy Moran, Harry Mummery, Tommy Smith, Jack Marks, Russell Crawford, Billy Creighton, Jeff Malone, Rocket Power, M.J. Quinn (manager), D. Beland (trainer).
Scores: March 8, at Quebec — Que. Bulldogs 14, Sydney 3; March 10, at Quebec — Que. Bulldogs 6, Sydney 2.

Victoria challenged Quebec but the Bulldogs refused to put the Stanley Cup in competition so the two teams played an exhibition series with Victoria winning two games to one by scores of 7-5, 3-6, 6-1. It was the first meeting between the Eastern champions and the Western champions. The following year, and until the Western Hockey League disbanded after the 1926 playoffs, the Cup went to the winner of the series between East and West.

1911-12 — Quebec Bulldogs — Goldie Prodgers, Joe Hall, Walter Rooney, Paddy Moran, Jack Marks, Jack McDonald, Eddie Oatman, George Leonard, Joe Malone (captain), C. Nolan (coach), M.J. Quinn (manager), D. Beland (trainer).
Scores: March 11, at Quebec — Que. Bulldogs 9, Moncton 3; March 13, at Quebec — Que. Bulldogs 8, Moncton 0.

Prior to 1912, teams could challenge the Stanley Cup champions for the title, thus there was more than one Championship Series played in most of the seasons between 1894 and 1911.

1910-11 — Ottawa Senators — Hamby Shore, Percy LeSueur, Jack Darragh, Bruce Stuart, Marty Walsh, Bruce Ridpath, Fred Lake, Albert (Dubby) Kerr, Alex Currie, Horace Gaul.
Scores: March 13, at Ottawa — Ottawa 7, Galt 4; March 16, at Ottawa — Ottawa 13, Port Arthur 4.

1909-10 — Montreal Wanderers — Cecil W. Blachford, Ernie (Moose) Johnson, Ernie Russell, Riley Hern, Harry Hyland, Jack Marshall, Frank (Pud) Glass (captain), Jimmy Gardner, R. R. Boon (manager).
Scores: March 12, at Montreal — Mtl. Wanderers 7, Berlin (Kitchener) 3.

1908-09 — Ottawa Senators — Fred Lake, Percy LeSueur, Fred (Cyclone) Taylor, H.L. (Billy) Gilmour, Albert Kerr, Edgar Dey, Marty Walsh, Bruce Stuart (captain).
Scores: Ottawa, as champions of the Eastern Canada Hockey Association took over the Stanley Cup in 1909 and, although a challenge was accepted by the Cup trustees from Winnipeg Shamrocks, games could not be arranged because of the lateness of the season. No other challenges were made in 1909. The following season — 1909-10 — however, the Senators accepted two challenges as defending Cup Champions. The first was against Galt in a two-game, total-goals series, and the second against Edmonton, also a two-game, total-goals series. Results: January 5, at Ottawa —Ottawa 12, Galt 3; January 7, at Ottawa — Ottawa 3, Galt 1. January 18, at Ottawa — Ottawa 8,
Edm. Eskimos 4; January 20, at Ottawa — Ottawa 13, Edm. Eskimos 7.

1907-08 — Montreal Wanderers — Riley Hern, Art Ross, Walter Smaill, Frank (Pud) Glass, Bruce Stuart, Ernie Russell, Ernie (Moose) Johnson, Cecil Blachford (captain), Tom Hooper, Larry Gilmour, Ernie Liffiton, R.R. Boon (manager).
Scores: Wanderers accepted four challenges for the Cup: January 9, at Montreal — Mtl. Wanderers 9, Ott. Victorias 3; January 13, at Montreal — Mtl. Wanderers 13, Ott. Victorias 1; March 10, at Montreal — Mtl. Wanderers 11, Wpg. Maple Leafs 5; March 12, at Montreal — Mtl. Wanderers 9, Wpg. Maple Leafs 3; March 14, at Montreal — Mtl. Wanderers 6, Toronto (OPHL) 4. At start of following season, 1908-09, Wanderers were challenged by Edmonton. Results: December 28, at Montreal — Mtl. Wanderers 7, Edm. Eskimos 3; December 30, at Montreal — Edm. Eskimos 7, Mtl. Wanderers 6. Total goals: Mtl. Wanderers 13, Edm. Eskimos 10.

1906-07 — (March) **— Montreal Wanderers** — W. S. (Billy) Strachan, Riley Hern, Lester Patrick, Hod Stuart, Frank (Pud) Glass, Ernie Russell, Cecil Blachford (captain), Ernie (Moose) Johnson, Rod Kennedy, Jack Marshall, R.R. Boon (manager).
Scores: March 23, at Winnipeg — Mtl. Wanderers 7, Kenora 2; March 25, at Winnipeg — Kenora 6, Mtl. Wanderers 5. Total goals: Mtl. Wanderers 12, Kenora 8.

1906-07 — (January) **— Kenora Thistles** — Eddie Geroux, Art Ross, Si Griffis, Tom Hooper, Billy McGimsie, Roxy Beaudro, Tom Phillips.
Scores: January 17, at Montreal — Kenora 4, Mtl. Wanderers 2; Jan. 21, at Montreal — Kenora 8, Mtl. Wanderers 6.

1905-06 — (March) **— Montreal Wanderers** — Henri Menard, Billy Strachan, Rod Kennedy, Lester Patrick, Frank (Pud) Glass, Ernie Russell, Ernie (Moose) Johnson, Cecil Blachford (captain), Josh Arnold, R.R. Boon (manager).
Scores: March 14, at Montreal — Mtl. Wanderers 9, Ottawa 1; March 17, at Ottawa — Ottawa 9, Mtl. Wanderers 3. Total goals: Mtl. Wanderers 12, Ottawa 10. Wanderers accepted a challenge from New Glasgow, N.S., prior to the start of the 1906-07 season. Results: December 27, at Montreal — Mtl. Wanderers 10, New Glasgow 3; December 29, at Montreal — Mtl. Wanderers 7, New Glasgow 2.

1905-06 — (February) **— Ottawa Silver Seven** — Harvey Pulford (captain), Arthur Moore, Harry Westwick, Frank McGee, Alf Smith (playing coach), Billy Gilmour, Billy Hague, Percy LeSueur, Harry Smith, Tommy Smith, Dion, Ebbs.
Scores: February 27, at Ottawa — Ottawa 16, Queen's University 7; February 28, at Ottawa — Ottawa 12, Queen's University 7; March 6, at Ottawa — Ottawa 6, Smiths Falls 5; March 8, at Ottawa — Ottawa 8, Smiths Falls 2.

1904-05 — Ottawa Silver Seven — Dave Finnie, Harvey Pulford (captain), Arthur Moore, Harry Westwick, Frank McGee, Alf Smith (playing coach), Billy Gilmour, Frank White, Horace Gaul, Hamby Shore, Bones Allen.
Scores: January 13, at Ottawa — Ottawa 9, Dawson City 2; January 16, at Ottawa — Ottawa 23, Dawson City 2; March 7, at Ottawa — Rat Portage 9, Ottawa 3; March 9, at Ottawa — Ottawa 4, Rat Portage 2; March 11, at Ottawa — Ottawa 5, Rat Portage 4.

1903-04 — Ottawa Silver Seven — S.C. (Suddy) Gilmour, Arthur Moore, Frank McGee, J.B. (Bouse) Hutton, H.L. (Billy) Gilmour, Jim McGee, Harry Westwick, E. H. (Harvey) Pulford (captain), Scott, Alf Smith (playing coach).
Scores: December 30, at Ottawa — Ottawa 9, Wpg. Rowing Club 1; January 1, at Ottawa — Wpg. Rowing Club 6, Ottawa 2; January 4, at Ottawa — Ottawa 2, Wpg. Rowing Club 0. February 23, at Ottawa — Ottawa 6, Tor. Marlboros 3; February 25, at Ottawa — Ottawa 11, Tor. Marlboros 2; March 2, at Montreal — Ottawa 5, Mtl. Wanderers 5. Following the tie game, a new two-game series was ordered to be played in Ottawa but the Wanderers refused unless the tie game was replayed in Montreal. When no settlement could be reached, the series was abandoned and Ottawa retained the Cup and accepted a two-game challenge from Brandon. Results: (both games at Ottawa), March 9, Ottawa 6, Brandon 3; March 11, Ottawa 9, Brandon 3.

1902-03 — (March) **— Ottawa Silver Seven** — S.C. (Suddy) Gilmour, P.T. (Percy) Sims, J.B. (Bouse) Hutton, D.J. (Dave) Gilmour, H.L. (Billy) Gilmour, Harry Westwick, Frank McGee, F.H. Wood, A.A. Fraser, Charles D. Spittal, E.H. (Harvey) Pulford (captain), Arthur Moore, Alf Smith (coach.)
Scores: March 7, at Montreal — Ottawa 1, Mtl. Victorias 1; March 10, at Ottawa — Ottawa 8, Mtl. Victorias 0. Total goals: Ottawa 9, Mtl. Victorias 1; March 12, at Ottawa — Ottawa 6, Rat Portage 2; March 14, at Ottawa — Ottawa 4, Rat Portage 2.

1902-03 — (February) **— Montreal AAA** — Tom Hodge, R.R. (Dickie) Boon, W.C. (Billy) Nicholson, Tom Phillips, Art Hooper, W.J. (Billy) Bellingham, Charles A. Liffiton, Jack Marshall, Jim Gardner, Cecil Blachford, George Smith.
Scores: January 29, at Montreal — Mtl. AAA 8, Wpg. Victorias 1; January 31, at Montreal — Wpg. Victorias 2, Mtl. AAA 2; February 2, at Montreal — Wpg. Victorias 4, Mtl. AAA 2; February 4, at Montreal — Mtl. AAA 5, Wpg. Victorias 1.

1901-02 — (March) **— Montreal AAA** — Tom Hodge, R.R. (Dickie) Boon, William C. (Billy) Nicholson, Archie Hooper, W.J. (Billy) Bellingham, Charles A. Liffiton, Jack Marshall, Roland Elliott, Jim Gardner.
Scores: March 13, at Winnipeg — Wpg. Victorias 1, Mtl. AAA 0; March 15, at Winnipeg — Mtl. AAA 5, Wpg. Victorias 0; March 17, at Winnipeg — Mtl. AAA 2, Wpg. Victorias 1.

1901-02 — (January) **— Winnipeg Victorias** — Burke Wood, A.B. (Tony) Gingras, Charles W. Johnstone, R.M. (Rod) Flett, Magnus L. Flett, Dan Bain (captain), Fred Scanlon, F. Cadham, G. Brown.
Scores: January 21, at Winnipeg — Wpg. Victorias 5, Tor Wellingtons 3; January 23, at Winnipeg — Wpg. Victorias 5, Tor. Wellingtons 3.

1900-01 — Winnipeg Victorias — Burke Wood, Jack Marshall, A.B. (Tony) Gingras, Charles W. Johnstone, R.M. (Rod) Flett, Magnus L. Flett, Dan Bain (captain), Art Brown.
Scores: January 29, at Montreal — Wpg. Victorias 4, Mtl. Shamrocks 3; January 31, at Montreal — Wpg. Victorias 2, Mtl. Shamrocks 1.

1899-1900 — Montreal Shamrocks — Joe McKenna, Frank Tansey, Frank Wall, Art Farrell, Fred Scanlon, Harry Trihey (captain), Jack Brannen.
Scores: February 12, at Montreal — Mtl. Shamrocks 4, Wpg. Victorias 3; February 14, at Montreal — Wpg. Victorias 3, Mtl. Shamrocks 2; February 16, at Montreal — Mtl. Shamrocks 5, Wpg. Victorias 4; March 5, at Montreal — Mtl. Shamrocks 10, Halifax 2; March 7, at Montreal — Mtl. Shamrocks 11, Halifax 0.

1898-99 — (March) **— Montreal Shamrocks** — Jim McKenna, Frank Tansey, Frank Wall, Harry Trihey (captain), Art Farrell, Fred Scanlon, Jack Brannen, John Dobby, Charles Hoerner.
Scores: March 14, at Montreal — Mtl. Shamrocks 6, Queen's University 2.

1898-99 — (February) **— Montreal Victorias** — Gordon Lewis, Mike Grant, Graham Drinkwater, Cam Davidson, Bob McDougall, Ernie McLea, Frank Richardson, Jack Ewing, Russell Bowie, Douglas Acer, Fred McRobie.
Scores: February 15, at Montreal — Mtl. Victorias 2, Wpg. Victorias 1; February 18, at Montreal — Mtl. Victorias 3, Wpg. Victorias 2.

1897-98 — Montreal Victorias — Gordon Lewis, Hartland McDougall, Mike Grant, Graham Drinkwater, Cam Davidson, Bob McDougall, Ernie McLea, Frank Richardson (captain), Jack Ewing. The Victorias as champions of the Amateur Hockey Association, retained the Cup and were not called upon to defend it.

1896-97 — Montreal Victorias — Gordon Lewis, Harold Henderson, Mike Grant (captain), Cam Davidson, Graham Drinkwater, Robert McDougall, Ernie McLea, Shirley Davidson, Hartland McDougall, Jack Ewing, Percy Molson, David Gillilan, McLellan.
Scores: December 27, at Montreal — Mtl. Victorias 15, Ott. Capitals 2.

1895-96 — (December) **— Montreal Victorias** — Harold Henderson, Mike Grant (captain), Robert McDougall, Graham Drinkwater, Shirley Davidson, Ernie McLea, W. Wallace, Robert Jones, Cam Davidson, David Gillilan, Stanley Willett.
Scores: December 30, at Winnipeg — Mtl. Victorias 6, Wpg. Victorias 5.

1895-96 — (February) **— Winnipeg Victorias** — George "Whitey" Merritt, Rod Flett, Fred Higginbotham, Jack Armitage (captain), Colin "Tote" Campbell, Dan Bain, Bobby Benson, Attie Howard.
Scores: February 14, at Montreal — Wpg. Victorias 2, Mtl. Victorias 0.

1894-95 — Montreal Victorias — Robert Jones, Harold Henderson, Mike Grant (captain), Shirley Davidson, Bob McDougall, Norman Rankin, Graham Drinkwater, Roland Elliot, William Pullan, Hartland McDougall, Jim Fenwick, A. McDougall. Montreal Victorias, as champions of the Amateur Hockey Association, were prepared to defend the Stanley Cup. However, the Stanley Cup trustees had already accepted a challenge match between the 1894 champion Montreal AAA and Queen's University. It was declared that if Montreal AAA defeated Queen's University, Montreal Victorias would be declared Stanley Cup champions. If Queen's University won, the Cup would go to the university club. In a game played March 9, 1895, Montreal AAA defeated Queen's University 5-1. As a result, Montreal Victorias were awarded the Stanley Cup.

1893-94 — Montreal AAA — Herbert Collins, Allan Cameron, George James, Billy Barlow, Clare Mussen, Archie Hodgson, Haviland Routh, Alex Irving, James Stewart, E. O'Brien, A.C. (Toad) Wand, A.B. Kingan.
Scores: March 17, at Mtl. Victorias — Mtl. AAA 3, Mtl. Victorias 2; March 22, at Montreal — Mtl. AAA 3, Ott. Capitals 1.

1892-93 — Montreal AAA — Tom Paton, James Stewart, Allan Cameron, Haviland Routh, Archie Hodgson, Billy Barlow, A.B. Kingan, G.S. Lowe.
In accordance with the terms governing the presentation of the Stanley Cup, it was awarded for the first time to the Montreal AAA as champions of the Amateur Hockey Association in 1893. Once Montreal AAA had been declared holders of the Stanley Cup, any Canadian hockey team could challenge for the trophy.

All-Time NHL Playoff Formats

1917-18 — The regular-season was split into two halves. The winners of both halves faced each other in a two-game, total-goals series for the NHL championship and the right to meet the PCHA champion in the best-of-five Stanley Cup Finals.

1918-19 — Same as 1917-18, except that the Stanley Cup Finals was extended to a best-of-seven series.

1919-20 — Same as 1917-1918, except that Ottawa won both halves of the split regular-season schedule to earn an automatic berth into the best-of-five Stanley Cup Finals against the PCHA champions.

1921-22 — The top two teams at the conclusion of the regular-season faced each other in a two-game, total-goals series for the NHL championship. The NHL champion then moved on to play the winner of the PCHA-WCHL playoff series in the best-of-five Stanley Cup Finals.

1922-23 — The top two teams at the conclusion of the regular-season faced each other in a two-game, total-goals series for the NHL championship. The NHL champion then moved on to play the PCHA champion in the best-of-three Stanley Cup Semi-Finals, and the winner of the Semi-Finals played the WCHL champion, which had been given a bye, in the best-of-three Stanley Cup Finals.

1923-24 — The top two teams at the conclusion of the regular-season faced each other in a two-game, total-goals series for the NHL championship. The NHL champion then moved to play the loser of the PCHA-WCHL playoff (the winner of the PCHA-WCHL playoff earned a bye into the Stanley Cup Finals) in the best-of-three Stanley Cup Semi-Finals. The winner of this series met the PCHA-WCHL playoff winner in the best-of-three Stanley Cup Finals.

1924-25 — The first place team (Hamilton) at the conclusion of the regular-season was supposed to play the winner of a two-game, total goals series between the second (Toronto) and third (Montreal) place clubs. However, Hamilton refused to abide by this new format, demanding greater compensation than offered by the League. Thus, Toronto and Montreal played their two-game, total-goals series, and the winner (Montreal) earned the NHL title and then played the WCHL champion (Victoria) in the best-of-five Stanley Cup Finals.

1925-26 — The format which was intended for 1924-25 went into effect. The winner of the two-game, total-goals series between the second and third place teams squared off against the first place team in the two-game, total-goals NHL championship series. The NHL champion then moved on to play the WHL champion in the best-of-five Stanley Cup Finals.

After the 1925-26 season, the NHL was the only major professional hockey league still in existence and consequently took over sole control of the Stanley Cup competition.

1926-27 — The 10-team league was divided into two divisions — Canadian and American — of five teams apiece. In each division, the winner of the two-game, total-goals series between the second and third place teams faced the first place team in a two-game, total-goals series for the division title. The two division title winners then met in the best-of-five Stanley Cup Finals.

1928-29 — Both first place teams in the two divisions played each other in a best-of-five series. Both second place teams in the two divisions played each other in a two-game, total-goals series as did the two third place teams. The winners of these latter two series then played each other in a best-of-three series for the right to meet the winner of the series between the two first place clubs. This Stanley Cup Final was a best-of-three.

Series A: First in Canadian Division versus first in American (best-of-five)
Series B: Second in Canadian Division versus second in American (two-game, total-goals)
Series C: Third in Canadian Division versus third in American (two-game, total-goals)
Series D: Winner of Series B versus winner of Series C (best-of-three)
Series E: Winner of Series A versus winner of Series D (best of three) for Stanley Cup

1931-32 — Same as 1928-29, except that Series D was changed to a two-game, total-goals format and Series E was changed to best of five.

1936-37 — Same as 1931-32, except that Series B, C, and D were each best-of-three.

1938-39 — With the NHL reduced to seven teams, the two-division system was replaced by one seven-team league. Based on final regular-season standings, the following playoff format was adopted:

Series A: First versus Second (best-of-seven)
Series B: Third versus Fourth (best-of-three)
Series C: Fifth versus Sixth (best-of-three)
Series D: Winner of Series B versus winner of Series C (best-of-three)
Series E: Winner of Series A versus winner of Series D (best-of-seven)

1942-43 — With the NHL reduced to six teams (the "original six"), only the top four finishers qualified for playoff action. The best-of-seven Semi-Finals pitted Team #1 vs Team #3 and Team #2 vs Team #4. The winners of each Semi-Final series met in the best-of-seven Stanley Cup Finals.

1967-68 — When it doubled in size from 6 to 12 teams, the NHL once again was divided into two divisions — East and West — of six teams apiece. The top four clubs in each division qualified for the playoffs (all series were best-of-seven):

Series A; Team #1 (East) vs Team #3 (East)
Series B: Team #2 (East) vs Team #4 (East)
Series C: Team #1 (West) vs Team #3 (West)
Series D: Team #2 (West) vs Team #4 (West)
Series E: Winner of Series A vs winner of Series B
Series F: Winner of Series C vs winner of Series D
Series G: Winner of Series E vs Winner of Series F

1970-71 — Same as 1967-68 except that Series E matched the winners of Series A and D, and Series F matched the winners of Series B and C.

1971-72 — Same as 1970-71, except that Series A and C matched Team #1 vs Team #4, and Series B and D matched Team #2 vs Team #3.

1974-75 — With the League now expanded to 18 teams in four divisions, a completely new playoff format was introduced. First, the #2 and #3 teams in each of the four divisions were pooled together in the Preliminary round. These eight (#2 and #3) clubs were ranked #1 to #8 based on regular-season record:

Series A: Team #1 vs Team #8 (best-of-three)
Series B: Team #2 vs Team #7 (best-of-three)
Series C: Team #3 vs Team #6 (best-of-three)
Series D: Team #4 vs Team #5 (best-of-three)
The winners of this Preliminary round then pooled together with the four division winners, which had received byes into this Quarter-Final round. These eight teams were again ranked #1 to #8 based on regular-season record:
Series E: Team #1 vs Team #8 (best-of-seven)
Series F: Team #2 vs Team #7 (best-of-seven)
Series G: Team #3 vs Team #6 (best-of-seven)
Series H: Team #4 vs Team #5 (best-of-seven)
The four Quarter-Finals winners, which moved on to the Semi-Finals, were then ranked #1 to #4 based on regular season record:
Series I: Team #1 vs Team #4 (best-of-seven)
Series J: Team #2 vs Team #3 (best-of-seven)
Series K: Winner of Series I vs winner of Series J (best-of-seven)

1977-78 — Same as 1974-75, except that the Preliminary round consisted of the #2 teams in the four divisions and the next four teams based on regular-season record (not their standings within their divisions).

1979-80 — With the addition of four WHA franchises, the League expanded its playoff structure to include 16 of its 21 teams. The four first place teams in the four divisions automatically earned playoff berths. Among the 17 other clubs, the top 12, according to regular-season record, also earned berths. All 16 teams were then pooled together and ranked #1 to #16 based on regular-season record:

Series A: Team #1 vs Team #16 (best-of-five)
Series B: Team #2 vs Team #15 (best-of-five)
Series C: Team #3 vs Team #14 (best-of-five)
Series D: Team #4 vs Team #13 (best-of-five)
Series E: Team #5 vs Team #12 (best-of-five)
Series F: Team #6 vs Team #11 (best-of-five)
Series G: Team #7 vs Team #10 (best-of-five)
Series H: Team #8 vs Team # 9 (best-of-five)

The eight Preliminary round winners, ranked #1 to #8 based on regular-season record, moved on to the Quarter-Finals:
Series I: Team #1 vs Team #8 (best-of-seven)
Series J: Team #2 vs Team #7 (best-of-seven)
Series K: Team #3 vs Team #6 (best-of-seven)
Series L: Team #4 vs Team #5 (best-of-seven)
The eight Quarter-Finals winners, ranked #1 to #4 based on regular-season record, moved on to the semi-finals:
Series M: Team #1 vs Team #4 (best-of-seven)
Series N: Team #2 vs Team #3 (best-of-seven)
Series O: Winner of Series M vs winner of Series N (best-of-seven)

1981-82 — The first four teams in each division earned playoff berths. In each division, the first-place team opposed the fourth-place team and the second-place team opposed the third-place team in a best-of-five Division Semi-Final series (DSF). In each division, the two winners of the DSF met in a best-of-seven Division Final series (DF). The two winners in each conference met in a best-of-seven Conference Final series (CF). In the Prince of Wales Conference, the Adams Division winner opposed the Patrick Division winner; in the Clarence Campbell Conference, the Smythe Division winner opposed the Norris Division winner. The two CF winners met in a best-of-seven Stanley Cup Final (F) series.

1986-87 — Division Semi-Final series changed from best-of-five to best-of-seven.

1993-94 — The NHL's playoff draw conference-based rather than division-based. At the conclusion of the regular season, the top eight teams in each of the Eastern and Western Conferences qualify for the playoffs. The teams that finish in first place in each of the League's divisions are seeded first and second in each conference's playoff draw and are assured of home ice advantage in the first two playoff rounds. The remaining teams are seeded based on their regular-season point totals. In each conference, the team seeded #1 plays #8; #2 vs. #7; #3 vs. #6; and #4 vs. #5. All series are best-of-seven with home ice rotating on a 2-2-1-1-1 basis, with the exception of matchups between Central and Pacific Division teams. These matchups will be played on a 2-3-2 basis to reduce travel. In a 2-3-2 series, the team with the most points will have its choice to start the series at home or on the road. The Eastern Conference champion will face the Western Conference champion in the Stanley Cup Final.

1994-95 — Same as 1993-94, except that in first, second or third-round playoff series involving Central and Pacific Division teams, the team with the better record has the choice of using either a 2-3-2 or a 2-2-1-1-1 format. When a 2-3-2 format is selected, the higher-ranked team also has the choice of playing games 1, 2, 6 and 7 at home or playing games 3, 4 and 5 at home. The format for the Stanley Cup Final remains 2-2-1-1-1.

1998-99 — The NHL's clubs are re-aligned into two conferences each consisting of three divisions. The number of teams qualifying for the Stanley Cup Playoffs remains unchanged at 16.

First-round playoff berths will be awarded to the first-place team in each division as well as to the next five best teams based on regular-season point totals in each conference. The three division winners in each conference will be seeded first through third for the playoffs and the next five best teams, in order of points, will be seeded fourth through eighth. In each conference, the team seeded #1 will play #8; #2 vs. #7; #3 vs. #6; and #4 vs. #5 in the quarterfinal round. Home-ice in the Conference Quarterfinals is granted to those teams seeded first through fourth in each conference.

In the Conference Semifinals and Conference Finals, teams will be re-seeded according to the same criteria as the Conference Quarterfinals. Higher seeded teams will have home-ice advantage.

Home-ice advantage for the Stanley Cup Finals will be determined by points.

All series remain best-of-seven.

After losing the 1979 Stanley Cup semifinals to their cross-town rivals, the New York Islanders would go on to win four consecutive Stanley Cup titles and 19 straight playoff series before losing to the Oilers in the 1984 finals.

Team Records

1918-2000

GAMES PLAYED

MOST GAMES PLAYED BY ALL TEAMS, ONE PLAYOFF YEAR:
92 — 1991. There were 51 DSF, 24 DF, 11 CF and 6 F games.
90 — 1994. There were 48 CQF, 23 CSF, 12 CF and 7 F games.
87 — 1987. There were 44 DSF, 25 DF, 11 CF and 7 F games.

MOST GAMES PLAYED, ONE TEAM, ONE PLAYOFF YEAR:
26 — Philadelphia Flyers, 1987. Won DSF 4-2 against NY Rangers, DF 4-3 against NY Islanders, CF 4-2 against Montreal, and lost F 4-3 against Edmonton.
24 — Pittsburgh Penguins,1991. Won DSF 4-3 against New Jersey, DF 4-1 against Washington, CF 4-2 against Boston, and F 4-2 against Minnesota.
— Los Angeles Kings, 1993. Won DSF 4-2 against Calgary, DF 4-2 against Vancouver, CF 4-3 against Toronto, and lost F 4-1 against Montreal.
— Vancouver Canucks, 1994. Won CQF 4-3 against Calgary, CSF 4-1 against Dallas, CF 4-1 against Toronto, and lost F 4-3 against NY Rangers.

PLAYOFF APPEARANCES

MOST STANLEY CUP CHAMPIONSHIPS:
23 — Montreal Canadiens 1924-30-31-44-46-53-56-57-58-59-60-65-66-68-69-71-73-76-77-78-79-86-93
13 — Toronto Maple Leafs 1918-22-32-42-45-47-48-49-51-62-63-64-67
9 — Detroit Red Wings 1936-37-43-50-52-54-55-97-98

MOST CONSECUTIVE STANLEY CUP CHAMPIONSHIPS:
5 — Montreal Canadiens (1956-57-58-59-60)
4 — Montreal Canadiens (1976-77-78-79)
— NY Islanders (1980-81-82-83)

MOST FINAL SERIES APPEARANCES:
32 — Montreal Canadiens in 83-year history.
21 — Toronto Maple Leafs in 83-year history.
— Detroit Red Wings in 73-year history.

MOST CONSECUTIVE FINAL SERIES APPEARANCES:
10 — Montreal Canadiens, (1951-60, inclusive)
5 — Montreal Canadiens, (1965-69, inclusive)
— NY Islanders, (1980-84, inclusive)

MOST YEARS IN PLAYOFFS:
72 — Montreal Canadiens in 83-year history.
60 — Toronto Maple Leafs in 83-year history.
59 — Boston Bruins in 76-year history.

MOST CONSECUTIVE PLAYOFF APPEARANCES:
29 — Boston Bruins (1968-96, inclusive)
28 — Chicago Blackhawks (1970-97, inclusive)
24 — Montreal Canadiens (1971-94, inclusive)
21 — Montreal Canadiens (1949-69, inclusive)
— St. Louis Blues (1980-2000, inclusive)

TEAM WINS

MOST HOME WINS, ONE TEAM, ONE PLAYOFF YEAR:
11 — Edmonton Oilers, 1988 in 11 home-ice games.
10 — Edmonton Oilers, 1985 in 10 home-ice games.
— Montreal Canadiens, 1986 in 11 home-ice games.
— Montreal Canadiens, 1993 in 11 home-ice games.

MOST ROAD WINS, ONE TEAM, ONE PLAYOFF YEAR:
10 — New Jersey Devils, 1995. Won three at Boston in CQF; two at Pittsburgh in CSF; three at Philadelphia in CF; and two at Detroit in F series.
— **New Jersey Devils,** 2000. Won two at Florida in CQF; two at Toronto in CSF; three at Philadelphia in CF; and three at Dallas in F series.
8 — NY Islanders, 1980. Won two at Los Angeles in PR; three at Boston in QF; two at Buffalo in SF; and one at Philadelphia in F series.
— Philadelphia Flyers, 1987. Won two at NY Rangers in DSF; two at NY Islanders in DF; three at Montreal in CF; and one at Edmonton in F series.
— Edmonton Oilers, 1990. Won one at Winnipeg in DSF; two at Los Angeles in DF; two at Chicago in CF and three at Boston in F series.
— Pittsburgh Penguins, 1992. Won two at Washington in DSF; two at NY Rangers in DF; two at Boston in CF; and two at Chicago in F series.
— Vancouver Canucks, 1994. Won three at Calgary in CQF; two at Dallas in CSF; one at Toronto in CF; and two at NY Rangers in F series.
— Colorado Avalanche, 1996. Won two at Vancouver in CQF; two at Chicago in CSF; two at Detroit in CF; and two at Florida in F series.
— Detroit Red Wings, 1998. Won two at Phoenix in CQF; three at St. Louis in CSF; one at Dallas in CF; and two at Washington in F series.
— Colorado Avalanche, 1999. Won three at San Jose in CQF; won three at Detroit in CSF; and won two at Dallas in CF.

MOST ROAD WINS, ALL TEAMS, ONE PLAYOFF YEAR:
46 — 1987. Of 87 games played, road teams won 46 (22 DSF, 14 DF, 8 CF and 2 in Stanley Cup final).

MOST OVERTIME WINS, ONE TEAM, ONE PLAYOFF YEAR:
10 — Montreal Canadiens, 1993. Two against Quebec in DSF; three against Buffalo in DF; two against NY Islanders in CF; and three against Los Angeles in F. Montreal played 20 games.
6 — NY Islanders, 1980. One against Los Angeles in PR; two against Boston in QF; one against Buffalo in SF; and two against Philadelphia in F. Islanders played 21 games.
— Vancouver Canucks, 1994. Three against Calgary in CQF; one against Dallas in CSF; one against Toronto in CF; and one against NY Rangers in F. Vancouver played 24 games.

MOST OVERTIME WINS AT HOME, ONE TEAM, ONE PLAYOFF YEAR:
4 — St. Louis Blues, 1968. Won one vs. Philadelphia in QF and three vs. Minnesota in SF.
— **Montreal Canadiens, 1993.** Won one vs. Quebec in DSF, one vs. Buffalo in DF, one vs. NY Islanders in CF and one vs. Los Angeles in F series.

MOST OVERTIME WINS ON THE ROAD, ONE TEAM, ONE PLAYOFF YEAR:
6 — Montreal Canadiens, 1993. Won one vs. Quebec in DSF, two vs. Buffalo in DF, one vs. NY Islanders in CF and two vs. Los Angeles in F series.

TEAM LOSSES

MOST LOSSES, ONE TEAM, ONE PLAYOFF YEAR:
11 — Philadelphia Flyers, 1987. Lost two vs. NY Rangers in DSF; three vs. NY Islanders in DF; two vs. Montreal in CF; and four vs. Edmonton in F series.

MOST HOME LOSSES, ONE TEAM, ONE PLAYOFF YEAR:
 6 — Philadelphia Flyers, 1987. Lost one vs. NY Rangers in DSF; two vs. NY Islanders in DF; two vs. Montreal in CF; and one vs. Edmonton in F series.
 — Washington Capitals, 1998. Lost two vs. Boston in CQF; two vs. Buffalo in CF; and two vs. Detroit in F series.
 — Colorado Avalanche, 1999. Lost two vs. San Jose in CQF; two vs. Detroit in CSF; and two vs. Dallas in CF series.

MOST ROAD LOSSES, ONE TEAM, ONE PLAYOFF YEAR:
 6 — St. Louis Blues, 1968. Lost two at Philadelphia in QF; two at Minnesota in SF; and two at Montreal in F series.
 — St. Louis Blues, 1970. Lost two at Minnesota in QF; two at Pittsburgh in SF; and two at Boston in F series.
 — NY Islanders, 1984. Lost one at NY Rangers in DSF; two at Montreal in CF; and three at Edmonton in F series.
 — Los Angeles Kings, 1993. Lost one at Calgary in DSF; one at Vancouver in DF; two at Toronto in CF; and two at Montreal in F series.

MOST OVERTIME LOSSES, ONE TEAM, ONE PLAYOFF YEAR:
 4 — Montreal Canadiens, 1951. Lost four vs. Toronto in F series.
 — St. Louis Blues, 1968. Lost one vs. Philadelphia in QF; one vs. Minnesota in SF; and two vs. Montreal in F series.
 — Los Angeles Kings, 1991. Lost one vs. Vancouver in DSF; and three vs. Edmonton in DF series.
 — Los Angeles Kings, 1993. Lost one vs. Toronto in CF; and three vs. Montreal in F series.
 — Philadelphia Flyers, 1996. Lost two vs. Tampa Bay in CQF; and two vs. Florida in CSF series.

MOST OVERTIME LOSSES AT HOME, ONE TEAM, ONE PLAYOFF YEAR:
 2 — Two overtime losses at home by one team in one playoff year has occurred 40 times. The Pittsburgh Penguins are the most recent team to equal this mark when they lost twice in overtime at home to the Philadelphia Flyers in the 2000 Stanley Cup CSF series.

MOST OVERTIME LOSSES ON THE ROAD, ONE TEAM, ONE PLAYOFF YEAR:
 3 — Los Angeles Kings, 1991. Lost one at Vancouver in DSF; and two at Edmonton in DF series.
 — St. Louis Blues, 1996. Lost two at Toronto in CQF; and one at Detroit in CSF series.
 — Dallas Stars, 1999. Lost two at St. Louis in CSF; and one at Colorado in CF series.

PLAYOFF WINNING STREAKS

LONGEST PLAYOFF WINNING STREAK:
14 — Pittsburgh Penguins. Streak started May 9, 1992, at Pittsburgh with a 5-4 win in fourth game of DF series against NY Rangers, won by Pittsburgh 4-2. Continued with a four-game win over Boston in 1992 CF and a four-game sweep of Chicago in 1992 F. Pittsburgh then won the first three games of 1993 DSF versus New Jersey. New Jersey ended the streak April 25, 1993, at New Jersey with a 4-1 win.
12 — Edmonton Oilers. Streak started May 15, 1984, at Edmonton with a 7-2 win in third game of F series against NY Islanders won by Edmonton 4-1. Continued with a three-game sweep of Winnipeg in 1985 DF, Edmonton then won the first two games of 1985 CF versus Chicago. Chicago ended the streak May 9, 1985, at Chicago with a 5-2 win.

MOST CONSECUTIVE WINS, ONE TEAM, ONE PLAYOFF YEAR:
11 — Chicago Blackhawks in 1992. Chicago won last three games of DSF against St. Louis to win series 4-2 and then defeated Detroit 4-0 in DF and Edmonton 4-0 in CF.
 — Pittsburgh Penguins in 1992. Pittsburgh won last three games of DF against NY Rangers to win series 4-2 and then defeated Boston 4-0 in CF and Chicago 4-0 in F.
 — Montreal Canadiens in 1993. Montreal won last four games of DSF against Quebec to win series 4-2, defeated Buffalo 4-0 in DF and won first three games of CF against NY Islanders.

PLAYOFF LOSING STREAKS

LONGEST PLAYOFF LOSING STREAK:
16 Games — Chicago Blackhawks. Streak started in 1975 QF against Buffalo when Chicago lost last two games. Then Chicago lost four games to Montreal in 1976 QF; two games to NY Islanders in 1977 PR; four games to Boston in 1978 QF and four games to NY Islanders in 1979 QF. Streak ended on April 8, 1980 when Chicago defeated St. Louis 3-2 in the opening game of their 1980 PR series.
12 Games — Toronto Maple Leafs. Streak started on April 16, 1979 as Toronto lost four straight games in a QF series against Montreal. Continued with three-game PR defeats versus Philadelphia and NY Islanders in 1980 and 1981 respectively. Toronto failed to qualify for the 1982 playoffs and lost the first two games of a 1983 DSF against Minnesota. Toronto ended the streak with a 6-3 win against the North Stars on April 9, 1983.
 — Los Angeles Kings. Streak started when the Kings lost four consecutive games in the 1993 Stanley Cup Finals against Montreal. The Kings failed to qualify for the playoffs for the next four years. Los Angeles lost four straight games to St. Louis in the 1998 CQF and failed to qualify for the 1999 playoffs. They were defeated in four straight games by Detroit in the 2000 CQF series.

Scott Stevens, who joined New Jersey for the NHL's 75th anniversary season of 1991-92, has captained the Devils to a pair of Stanley Cup championships. Stevens earned the Conn Smythe Trophy as playoff MVP last season.

MOST GOALS IN A SERIES, ONE TEAM

MOST GOALS, ONE TEAM, ONE PLAYOFF SERIES:
44 — **Edmonton Oilers** in 1985 CF. Edmonton won best-of-seven series 4-2, outscoring Chicago 44-25.
35 — Edmonton Oilers in 1983 DF. Edmonton won best-of-seven series 4-1, outscoring Calgary 35-13.
— Calgary Flames in 1995 CQF. Calgary lost best-of-seven series 3-4, outscoring San Jose 35-26.

MOST GOALS, ONE TEAM, TWO-GAME SERIES:
11 — **Buffalo Sabres** in 1977 PR. Buffalo won best-of-three series 2-0, outscoring Minnesota 11-3.
— **Toronto Maple Leafs** in 1978 PR. Toronto won best-of-three series 2-0, outscoring Los Angeles 11-3.
10 — Boston Bruins in 1927 QF. Boston won two-game total goal series 10-5.

MOST GOALS, ONE TEAM, THREE-GAME SERIES:
23 — **Chicago Blackhawks** in 1985 DSF. Chicago won best-of-five series 3-0, outscoring Detroit 23-8.
20 — Minnesota North Stars in 1981 PR. Minnesota won best-of-five series 3-0, outscoring Boston 20-13.
— NY Islanders in 1981 PR. New York won best-of-five series 3-0, outscoring Toronto 20-4.

MOST GOALS, ONE TEAM, FOUR-GAME SERIES:
28 — **Boston Bruins** in 1972 SF. Boston won best-of-seven series 4-0, outscoring St. Louis 28-8.

MOST GOALS, ONE TEAM, FIVE-GAME SERIES:
35 — **Edmonton Oilers** in 1983 DF. Edmonton won best-of-seven series 4-1, outscoring Calgary 35-13.
32 — Edmonton Oilers in 1987 DSF. Edmonton won best-of-seven series 4-1, outscoring Los Angeles 32-20.
28 — NY Rangers in 1979 QF. NY Rangers won best-of-seven series 4-1, outscoring Philadelphia 28-8.
27 — Philadelphia Flyers in 1980 SF. Philadelphia won best-of-seven series 4-1, outscoring Minnesota 27-14.
— Los Angeles Kings, in 1982 DSF. Los Angeles won best-of-five series 3-2, outscoring Edmonton 27-23.

MOST GOALS, ONE TEAM, SIX-GAME SERIES:
44 — **Edmonton Oilers** in 1985 CF. Edmonton won best-of-seven series 4-2, outscoring Chicago 44-25.
33 — Chicago Blackhawks in 1985 DF. Chicago won best-of-seven series 4-2, outscoring Minnesota 33-29.
— Montreal Canadiens in 1973 F. Montreal won best-of-seven series 4-2, outscoring Chicago 33-23.
— Los Angeles Kings in 1993 DSF. Los Angeles won best-of-seven series 4-2, outscoring Calgary 33-28.

MOST GOALS, ONE TEAM, SEVEN-GAME SERIES:
35 — **Calgary Flames** in 1995 CQF. Calgary lost best-of-seven series 3-4, outscoring San Jose 35-26.
33 — Philadelphia Flyers in 1976 QF. Philadelphia won best-of-seven series 4-3, outscoring Toronto 33-23.
— Boston Bruins in 1983 DF. Boston won best-of-seven series 4-3, outscoring Buffalo 33-23.
— Edmonton Oilers in 1984 DF. Edmonton won best-of-seven series 4-3, outscoring Calgary 33-27.

FEWEST GOALS IN A SERIES, ONE TEAM

FEWEST GOALS, ONE TEAM, TWO-GAME SERIES:
0 — **NY Americans** in 1929 SF. Lost two-game total-goal series 1-0 against NY Rangers.
— **Chicago Blackhawks** in 1935 SF. Lost two-game total-goal series 1-0 against Mtl. Maroons.
— **Mtl. Maroons** in 1937 SF. Lost best-of-three series 2-0 to NY Rangers while being outscored 5-0.
— **NY Americans** in 1939 QF. Lost best-of-three series 2-0 to Toronto while being outscored 6-0.

FEWEST GOALS, ONE TEAM, THREE-GAME SERIES:
1 — **Mtl. Maroons** in 1936 SF. Lost best-of-five series 3-0 to Detroit and were outscored 6-1.

FEWEST GOALS, ONE TEAM, FOUR-GAME SERIES:
2 — **Boston Bruins** in 1935 SF. Lost best-of-five series 3-1 to Toronto, while being outscored by Boston 7-2.
— **Montreal Canadiens** in 1952 F. Lost best-of-seven series 4-0 to Detroit, while being outscored by Montreal 11-2.

FEWEST GOALS, ONE TEAM, FIVE-GAME SERIES:
5 — **NY Rangers** in 1928 F. NY Rangers won best-of-five series 3-2, while being outscored by Mtl. Maroons 6-5.
— **Boston Bruins** in 1995 CQF. New Jersey won best-of-seven series 4-1, while outscoring Boston 14-5.
— **New Jersey Devils** in 1997 CSF. NY Rangers won best-of-seven series 4-1, while outscoring New Jersey 10-5.

FEWEST GOALS, ONE TEAM, SIX-GAME SERIES:
5 — **Boston Bruins** in 1951 SF. Toronto won best-of-seven series 4-1 with 1 tie, outscoring Boston 17-5.

FEWEST GOALS, ONE TEAM, SEVEN-GAME SERIES:
9 — **Toronto Maple Leafs,** in 1945 F. Toronto won best-of- seven series 4-3; teams tied in scoring 9-9.
— **Detroit Red Wings,** in 1945 F. Toronto won best-of-seven series 4-3; teams tied in scoring 9-9.

Jari Kurri led the way with 12 goals as the Oilers scored a record 44 times in just six games to oust Chicago from the 1985 Campbell Conference final. The Blackhawks scored 25 times in a losing effort as the two teams combined for 69 goals.

MOST GOALS IN A SERIES, BOTH TEAMS

MOST GOALS, BOTH TEAMS, ONE PLAYOFF SERIES:
69 — **Edmonton Oilers, Chicago Blackhawks** in 1985 CF. Edmonton won best-of-seven series 4-2, outscoring Chicago 44-25.
62 — Chicago Blackhawks, Minnesota North Stars in 1985 DF. Chicago won best-of-seven series 4-2, outscoring Minnesota 33-29.
61 — Los Angeles Kings, Calgary Flames in 1993 DSF. Los Angeles won best-of-seven series 4-2, outscoring Calgary 33-28.
— San Jose Sharks, Calgary Flames in 1995 CQF. San Jose won best-of-seven series 4-3, while being outscored 35-26.

MOST GOALS, BOTH TEAMS, TWO-GAME SERIES:
17 — **Toronto St. Patricks, Montreal Canadiens** in 1918 NHL F. Toronto won two-game total goal series 10-7.
15 — Boston Bruins, Chicago Blackhawks in 1927 QF. Boston won two-game total goal series 10-5.
— Pittsburgh Penguins, St. Louis Blues in 1975 PR. Pittsburgh won best-of-three series 2-0, outscoring St. Louis 9-6.

MOST GOALS, BOTH TEAMS, THREE-GAME SERIES:
33 — **Minnesota North Stars, Boston Bruins** in 1981 PR. Minnesota won best-of-five series 3-0, outscoring Boston 20-13.
31 — Chicago Blackhawks, Detroit Red Wings in 1985 DSF. Chicago won best-of-five series 3-0, outscoring Detroit 23-8.
28 — Toronto Maple Leafs, NY Rangers in 1932 F. Toronto won best-of-five series 3-0, outscoring New York 18-10.

MOST GOALS, BOTH TEAMS, FOUR-GAME SERIES:
36 — **Boston Bruins, St. Louis Blues** in 1972 SF. Boston won best-of-seven series 4-0, outscoring St. Louis 28-8.
— **Minnesota North Stars, Toronto Maple Leafs** in 1983 DSF. Minnesota won best-of-five series 3-1; teams tied in scoring 18-18.
— **Edmonton Oilers, Chicago Blackhawks** in 1983 CF. Edmonton won best-of-seven series 4-0, outscoring Chicago 25-11.
35 — NY Rangers, Los Angeles Kings in 1981 PR. NY Rangers won best-of-five series 3-1, outscoring Los Angeles 23-12.

MOST GOALS, BOTH TEAMS, FIVE-GAME SERIES:
- **52 — Edmonton Oilers, Los Angeles Kings** in 1987 DSF. Edmonton won best-of-seven series 4-1, outscoring Los Angeles 32-20.
- 50 — Los Angeles Kings, Edmonton Oilers in 1982 DSF. Los Angeles won best-of-five series 3-2, outscoring Edmonton 27-23.
- 48 — Edmonton Oilers, Calgary Flames in 1983 DF. Edmonton won best-of-seven series 4-1, outscoring Calgary 35-13.
- — Calgary Flames, Los Angeles Kings in 1988 DSF. Calgary won best-of-seven series 4-1, outscoring Los Angeles 30-18.

MOST GOALS, BOTH TEAMS, SIX-GAME SERIES:
- **69 — Edmonton Oilers, Chicago Blackhawks** in 1985 CF. Edmonton won best-of-seven series 4-2, outscoring Chicago 44-25.
- 62 — Chicago Blackhawks, Minnesota North Stars in 1985 DF. Chicago won best-of-seven series 4-2, outscoring Minnesota 33-29.
- 61 — Los Angeles Kings, Calgary Flames in 1993 DSF. Los Angeles won best-of-seven series 4-2, outscoring Calgary 33-28.

MOST GOALS, BOTH TEAMS, SEVEN-GAME SERIES:
- **61 — San Jose Sharks, Calgary Flames** in 1995 CQF. San Jose won best-of-seven series 4-3, while being outscored 35-26.
- 60 — Edmonton Oilers, Calgary Flames in 1984 DF. Edmonton won best-of-seven series 4-3, outscoring Calgary 33-27.

FEWEST GOALS IN A SERIES, BOTH TEAMS

FEWEST GOALS, BOTH TEAMS, TWO-GAME SERIES:
- **1 — NY Rangers, NY Americans,** in 1929 SF. NY Rangers defeated NY Americans 1-0 in two-game, total-goal series.
- — **Mtl. Maroons, Chicago Blackhawks** in 1935 SF. Mtl. Maroons defeated Chicago 1-0 in two-game, total-goal series.

FEWEST GOALS, BOTH TEAMS, THREE-GAME SERIES:
- **7 — Boston Bruins, Montreal Canadiens** in 1929 SF. Boston won best-of-five series 3-0, outscoring Montreal 5-2.
- — **Detroit Red Wings, Mtl. Maroons** in 1936 SF. Detroit won best-of-five series 3-0, outscoring Mtl. Maroons 6-1.

FEWEST GOALS, BOTH TEAMS, FOUR-GAME SERIES:
- **9 — Toronto Maple Leafs, Boston Bruins** in 1935 SF. Toronto won best-of-five series 3-1, outscoring Boston 7-2.

FEWEST GOALS, BOTH TEAMS, FIVE-GAME SERIES:
- **11 — NY Rangers, Mtl. Maroons** in 1928 F. NY Rangers won best-of-five series 3-2, while being outscored by Mtl. Maroons 6-5.

FEWEST GOALS, BOTH TEAMS, SIX-GAME SERIES:
- **20 — Toronto Maple Leafs, Philadelphia Flyers** in 1999 CQF. Toronto won best-of-seven series 4-2, being outscored by Philadelphia 11-9.

FEWEST GOALS, BOTH TEAMS, SEVEN-GAME SERIES:
- **18 — Toronto Maple Leafs, Detroit Red Wings** in 1945 F. Toronto won best-of-seven series 4-3; teams tied in scoring 9-9.

MOST GOALS IN A GAME OR PERIOD

MOST GOALS, ONE TEAM, ONE GAME:
- **13 — Edmonton Oilers** at Edmonton, April 9, 1987. Edmonton 13, Los Angeles 3. Edmonton won best-of-seven DSF 4-1.
- 12 — Los Angeles Kings at Los Angeles, April 10, 1990. Los Angeles 12, Calgary 4. Los Angeles won best-of-seven DSF 4-2.
- 11 — Montreal Canadiens at Montreal, March 30, 1944. Montreal 11, Toronto 0. Montreal won best-of-seven SF 4-1.
- — Edmonton Oilers at Edmonton, May 4, 1985. Edmonton 11, Chicago 2. Edmonton won best-of-seven CF 4-2.

MOST GOALS, ONE TEAM, ONE PERIOD:
- **7 — Montreal Canadiens,** March 30, 1944, at Montreal in third period, during 11-0 win against Toronto.

MOST GOALS, BOTH TEAMS, ONE GAME:
- **18 — Los Angeles Kings, Edmonton Oilers** at Edmonton, April 7, 1982. Los Angeles 10, Edmonton 8. Los Angeles won best-of-five DSF 3-2.
- 17 — Pittsburgh Penguins, Philadelphia Flyers at Pittsburgh, April 25, 1989. Pittsburgh 10, Philadelphia 7. Philadelphia won best-of-seven DF 4-3.
- 16 — Edmonton Oilers, Los Angeles Kings at Edmonton, April 9, 1987. Edmonton 13, Los Angeles 3. Edmonton won best-of-seven DSF 4-1.
- — Los Angeles Kings, Calgary Flames at Los Angeles, April 10, 1990. Los Angeles 12, Calgary 4. Los Angeles won best-of-seven DF 4-2.

MOST GOALS, BOTH TEAMS, ONE PERIOD:
- **9 — NY Rangers, Philadelphia Flyers,** April 24, 1979, at Philadelphia, third period. NY Rangers won 8-3, scoring six of nine third-period goals.
- — **Los Angeles Kings, Calgary Flames,** at Los Angeles, April 10, 1990, second period. Los Angeles won 12-4, scoring five of nine second-period goals.
- 8 — Chicago Blackhawks, Montreal Canadiens, at Montreal, May 8, 1973, second period. Chicago won 8-7, scoring five of eight second-period goals.
- — Chicago Blackhawks, Edmonton Oilers, at Chicago, May 12, 1985, first period. Chicago won 8-6, scoring five of eight first-period goals.
- — Edmonton Oilers, Winnipeg Jets, at Edmonton, April 6, 1988, third period. Edmonton won 7-4, scoring six of eight third period goals.
- — Hartford Whalers, Montreal Canadiens, at Hartford, April 10, 1988, third period. Hartford won 7-5, scoring five of eight third period goals.
- — Vancouver Canucks, NY Rangers, at New York, June 9, 1994, third period. Vancouver won 6-3, scoring five of eight third period goals.

TEAM POWER-PLAY GOALS

MOST POWER-PLAY GOALS BY ALL TEAMS, ONE PLAYOFF YEAR:
- **199 — 1988** in 83 games.

MOST POWER-PLAY GOALS, ONE TEAM, ONE PLAYOFF YEAR:
- **35 — Minnesota North Stars,** 1991 in 23 games.
- 32 — Edmonton Oilers, 1988 in 18 games.
- 31 — NY Islanders, 1981, in 18 games.

MOST POWER-PLAY GOALS, ONE TEAM, ONE SERIES:
- **15 — NY Islanders** in 1980 F against Philadelphia. NY Islanders won series 4-2.
- — **Minnesota North Stars** in 1991 DSF against Chicago. Minnesota won series 4-2.
- 13 — NY Islanders in 1981 QF against Edmonton. NY Islanders won series 4-2.
- — Calgary Flames in 1986 CF against St. Louis. Calgary won series 4-3.
- 12 — Toronto Maple Leafs in 1976 QF series won by Philadelphia 4-3.

MOST POWER-PLAY GOALS, BOTH TEAMS, ONE SERIES:
- **21 — NY Islanders, Philadelphia Flyers** in 1980 F, won by NY Islanders 4-2. NY Islanders had 15 and Flyers 6.
- — **NY Islanders, Edmonton Oilers** in 1981 QF, won by NY Islanders 4-2. NY Islanders had 13 and Edmonton 8.
- — **Philadelphia Flyers, Pittsburgh Penguins** in 1989 DF, won by Philadelphia 4-3. Philadelphia had 11 and Pittsburgh 10.
- — **Minnesota North Stars, Chicago Blackhawks** in 1991 DSF, won by Minnesota 4-2. Minnesota had 15 and Chicago 6.
- 20 — Toronto Maple Leafs, Philadelphia Flyers in 1976 QF series won by Philadelphia 4-3. Toronto had 12 and Philadelphia 8.

MOST POWER-PLAY GOALS, ONE TEAM, ONE GAME:
- **6 — Boston Bruins,** April 2, 1969, at Boston against Toronto. Boston won 10-0.

MOST POWER-PLAY GOALS, BOTH TEAMS, ONE GAME:
- **8 — Minnesota North Stars, St. Louis Blues,** April 24, 1991 at Minnesota. Minnesota had 4, St. Louis 4. Minnesota won 8-4.
- 7 — Minnesota North Stars, Edmonton Oilers, April 28, 1984 at Minnesota. Minnesota had 4, Edmonton 3. Edmonton won 8-5.
- — Philadelphia Flyers, NY Rangers, April 13, 1985 at New York. Philadelphia had 4, NY Rangers 3. Philadelphia won 6-5.
- — Edmonton Oilers, Chicago Blackhawks, May 14, 1985 at Edmonton. Chicago had 5, Edmonton 2. Edmonton won 10-5.
- — Edmonton Oilers, Los Angeles Kings, April 9, 1987 at Edmonton. Edmonton had 5, Los Angeles 2. Edmonton won 13-3.
- — Vancouver Canucks, Calgary Flames, April 9, 1989 at Vancouver. Vancouver had 4, Calgary 3. Vancouver won 5-3.

MOST POWER-PLAY GOALS, ONE TEAM, ONE PERIOD:
- **4 — Toronto Maple Leafs,** March 26, 1936, second period against Boston at Toronto. Toronto won 8-3.
- — **Minnesota North Stars,** April 28, 1984, second period against Edmonton at Minnesota. Edmonton won 8-5.
- — **Boston Bruins,** April 11, 1991, third period against Hartford at Boston. Boston won 6-1.
- — **Minnesota North Stars,** April 24, 1991, second period against St. Louis at Minnesota. Minnesota won 8-4.
- — **St. Louis Blues,** April 27, 1998, third period at Los Angeles. St. Louis won 4-3.

MOST POWER-PLAY GOALS, BOTH TEAMS, ONE PERIOD:
- **5 — Minnesota North Stars, Edmonton Oilers,** April 28, 1984, second period, at Minnesota. Minnesota had 4 and Edmonton 1. Edmonton won 8-5.
- — **Vancouver Canucks, Calgary Flames,** April 9, 1989, third period at Vancouver. Vancouver had 3 and Calgary 2. Vancouver won 5-3.
- — **Minnesota North Stars, St. Louis Blues,** April 24, 1991, second period, at Minnesota. Minnesota had 4 and St. Louis 1. Minnesota won 8-4.

TEAM SHORTHAND GOALS

MOST SHORTHAND GOALS BY ALL TEAMS, ONE PLAYOFF YEAR:
- **33 — 1988,** in 83 games.

MOST SHORTHAND GOALS, ONE TEAM, ONE PLAYOFF YEAR:
- **10 — Edmonton Oilers,** 1983, in 16 games.
- 9 — NY Islanders, 1981, in 19 games.
- 8 — Philadelphia Flyers, 1989, in 19 games.

MOST SHORTHAND GOALS, ONE TEAM, ONE SERIES:
6 — **Calgary Flames** in 1995 against San Jose in best-of-seven CQF won by San Jose 4-3.
- **Vancouver Canucks** in 1995 against St. Louis in best-of-seven CQF won by Vancouver 4-3.
5 — Edmonton Oilers in 1983 against Calgary in best-of-seven DF won by Edmonton 4-1.
- NY Rangers in 1979 against Philadelphia in best-of-seven QF, won by NY Rangers 4-1.

MOST SHORTHAND GOALS, BOTH TEAMS, ONE SERIES:
7 — **Boston Bruins (4), NY Rangers (3),** in 1958 SF won by Boston 4-2.
- **Edmonton Oilers (5), Calgary Flames (2),** in 1983 DF won by Edmonton 4-1.
- **Vancouver Canucks (6), St. Louis Blues (1),** in 1995 CQF won by Vancouver 4-3.

MOST SHORTHAND GOALS, ONE TEAM, ONE GAME:
3 — **Boston Bruins,** April 11, 1981, at Minnesota. Minnesota won 6-3.
- **NY Islanders,** April 17, 1983, at NY Rangers. NY Rangers won 7-6.
- **Toronto Maple Leafs,** May 8, 1994, at San Jose. Toronto won 8-3.

MOST SHORTHAND GOALS, BOTH TEAMS, ONE GAME:
4 — **NY Islanders, NY Rangers,** April 17, 1983, at NY Rangers. NY Islanders had 3 shorthand goals, NY Rangers 1. NY Rangers won 7-6.
- **Boston Bruins, Minnesota North Stars,** April 11, 1981, at Minnesota. Boston had 3 shorthand goals, Minnesota 1. Minnesota won 6-3.
- **San Jose Sharks, Toronto Maple Leafs,** May 8, 1994, at San Jose. Toronto had 3 shorthand goals, San Jose 1. Toronto won 8-3.
3 — Toronto Maple Leafs, Detroit Red Wings, April 5, 1947, at Toronto. Toronto had 2 shorthand goals, Detroit 1. Toronto won 6-1.
- NY Rangers, Boston Bruins, April 1, 1958, at Boston. NY Rangers had 2 shorthand goals, Boston 1. NY Rangers won 5-2.
- Minnesota North Stars, Philadelphia Flyers, May 4, 1980, at Minnesota. Minnesota had 2 shorthand goals, Philadelphia 1. Philadelphia won 5-3.
- Edmonton Oilers, Winnipeg Jets, April 9, 1988, at Winnipeg. Winnipeg had 2 shorthand goals, Edmonton 1. Winnipeg won 6-4.
- New Jersey Devils, NY Islanders, April 14, 1988, at New Jersey. NY Islanders had 2 shorthand goals, New Jersey 1. New Jersey won 6-5.
- Montreal Canadiens, New Jersey Devils, April 17, 1997, at New Jersey. Montreal had 2 shorthand goals, New Jersey 1. New Jersey won 5-2
- Dallas Stars, San Jose Sharks, May 5, 2000, at San Jose. Dallas had 2 shorthand goals, San Jose 1. Dallas won 5-4.

MOST SHORTHAND GOALS, ONE TEAM, ONE PERIOD:
2 — **Toronto Maple Leafs,** April 5, 1947, at Toronto against Detroit, first period. Toronto won 6-1.
- **Toronto Maple Leafs,** April 13, 1965, at Toronto against Montreal, first period. Montreal won 4-3.
- **Boston Bruins,** April 20, 1969, at Boston against Montreal, first period. Boston won 3-2.
- **Boston Bruins,** April 8, 1970, at Boston against NY Rangers, second period. Boston won 8-2.
- **Boston Bruins,** April 30, 1972, at Boston against NY Rangers, first period. Boston won 6-5.
- **Chicago Blackhawks,** May 3, 1973, at Chicago against Montreal, first period. Chicago won 7-4.
- **Montreal Canadiens,** April 23, 1978, at Detroit, first period. Montreal won 8-0.
- **NY Islanders,** April 8, 1980, at New York against Los Angeles, second period. NY Islanders won 8-1.
- **Los Angeles Kings,** April 9, 1980, at NY Islanders, first period. Los Angeles won 6-3.
- **Boston Bruins,** April 13, 1980, at Pittsburgh, second period. Boston won 8-3.
- **Minnesota North Stars,** May 4, 1980, at Minnesota against Philadelphia, second period. Philadelphia won 5-3.
- **Boston Bruins,** April 11, 1981, at Minnesota, third period. Minnesota won 6-3.
- **NY Islanders,** May 12, 1981, at New York against Minnesota, first period. NY Islanders won 6-3.
- **Montreal Canadiens,** April 7, 1982, at Montreal against Quebec, third period. Montreal won 5-1.
- **Edmonton Oilers,** April 24, 1983, at Edmonton against Chicago, third period. Edmonton won 8-4.
- **Winnipeg Jets,** April 14, 1985, at Calgary, second period. Winnipeg won 5-3.
- **Boston Bruins,** April 6, 1988, at Boston against Buffalo, first period. Boston won 7-3.
- **NY Islanders,** April 14, 1988, at New Jersey, third period. New Jersey won 6-5.
- **Detroit Red Wings,** April 29, 1993, at Toronto, second period. Detroit won 7-3.
- **Toronto Maple Leafs,** May 8, 1994, at San Jose, third period. Toronto won 8-3.
- **Calgary Flames,** May 11, 1995, at San Jose, first period. Calgary won 9-2.
- **Vancouver Canucks,** May 15, 1995 at St. Louis, second period. Vancouver won 6-5.
- **Montreal Canadiens,** April 17, 1997, at New Jersey, second period. New Jersey won 5-2.
- **Philadelphia Flyers,** April 26, 1997, at Philadelphia against Pittsburgh, first period. Philadelphia won 6-3.
- **Phoenix Coyotes,** April 24, 1998, at Detroit, second period. Phoenix won 7-4.
- **Buffalo Sabres,** April 27, 1998, at Buffalo against Philadelphia, second period. Buffalo won 6-3.
- **San Jose Sharks,** April 30, 1999, at Colorado, third period. San Jose won 7-3.

MOST SHORTHAND GOALS, BOTH TEAMS, ONE PERIOD:
3 — **Toronto Maple Leafs, Detroit Red Wings,** April 5, 1947, at Toronto, first period. Toronto had 2 shorthand goals, Detroit 1. Toronto won 6-1.

- **Toronto Maple Leafs, San Jose Sharks,** May 8, 1994, at San Jose, third period. Toronto had 2 shorthand goals, San Jose 1. Toronto won 8-3.

FASTEST GOALS

FASTEST FIVE GOALS, BOTH TEAMS:
3 Minutes, 6 Seconds — **Chicago Blackhawks, Minnesota North Stars,** at Chicago April 21, 1985. Keith Brown scored for Chicago at 1:12, second period; Ken Yaremchuk, Chicago, 1:27; Dino Ciccarelli, Minnesota, 2:48; Tony McKegney, Minnesota, 4:07; and Curt Fraser, Chicago, 4:18. Chicago won 6-2 and best-of-seven DF 4-2.
3 Minutes, 20 Seconds — Minnesota North Stars, Philadelphia Flyers, at Philadelphia, April 29, 1980. Paul Shmyr scored for Minnesota at 13:20, first period; Steve Christoff, Minnesota, 13:59; Ken Linseman, Philadelphia, 14:54; Tom Gorence, Philadelphia, 15:36; and Linseman, 16:40. Minnesota won 6-5. Philadelphia won best-of-seven SF 4-1.
4 Minutes — Detroit Red Wings, Los Angeles Kings, at Detroit, April 15, 2000. Brendan Shanahan scored for Detroit at 0:55, first period; Martin Lapointe, Detroit, 1:33; Luc Robitaille, Los Angeles, 2:04; Kris Draper, Detroit, 3:32; Zigmund Palffy, Los Angeles, 4:55. Detroit won 8-5 and best-of-seven CQF 4-0.

FASTEST FIVE GOALS, ONE TEAM:
3 Minutes, 36 Seconds — **Montreal Canadiens** at Montreal, March 30, 1944, against Toronto. Toe Blake scored at 7:58 of third period and again at 8:37; Maurice Richard, 9:17; Ray Getliffe, 10:33; and Buddy O'Connor, 11:34. Canadiens won 11-0 and best-of-seven SF 4-1.

FASTEST FOUR GOALS, BOTH TEAMS:
1 Minute, 33 Seconds — Philadelphia Flyers, Toronto Maple Leafs at Philadelphia, April 20, 1976. Don Saleski of Philadelphia scored at 10:04 of second period; Bob Neely, Toronto, 10:42; Gary Dornhoefer, Philadelphia, 11:24; and Don Saleski, 11:37. Philadelphia won 7-1 and best-of-seven QF series 4-3.
1 Minute, 34 seconds — Montreal Canadiens, Calgary Flames at Montreal, May 20, 1986. Joel Otto of Calgary scored at 17:59 of first period; Bobby Smith, Montreal, 18:25; Mats Naslund, Montreal, 19:17; and Bob Gainey, Montreal, 19:33. Montreal won 5-3 and best-of-seven F series 4-1.
1 Minute, 38 Seconds — Boston Bruins, Philadelphia Flyers at Philadelphia, April 26, 1977. Gregg Sheppard of Boston scored at 14:01 of second period; Mike Milbury, Boston, 15:01; Gary Dornhoefer, Philadelphia, 15:16; and Jean Ratelle, Boston, 15:39. Boston won 5-4 and best-of-seven SF series 4-0.

FASTEST FOUR GOALS, ONE TEAM:
2 Minutes, 35 Seconds — **Montreal Canadiens** at Montreal, March 30, 1944, against Toronto. Toe Blake scored at 7:58 and 8:37 of third period; Maurice Richard, 9:17; Ray Getliffe, 10:33. Montreal won 11-0 and best-of-seven SF 4-1.

FASTEST THREE GOALS, BOTH TEAMS:
21 Seconds — **Edmonton Oilers, Chicago Blackhawks** at Edmonton, May 7, 1985. Behn Wilson scored for Chicago at 19:22 of third period, Jari Kurri at 19:36 and Glenn Anderson at 19:43 for Edmonton. Edmonton won 7-3 and best-of-seven CF 4-2.
27 Seconds — Phoenix Coyotes, Detroit Red Wings at Detroit, April 24, 1998. Jeremy Roenick scored for Phoenix at 13:24 of the second period. Mathieu Dandenault scored for Detroit at 13:32, and Keith Tkachuk for Phoenix at 13:51. Phoenix won 7-4, Detroit won the best-of-seven CQF 4-2.
30 Seconds — Chicago Blackhawks, Pittsburgh Penguins at Chicago, June 1, 1992. Dirk Graham scored for Chicago at 6:21 of first period, Kevin Stevens for Pittsburgh at 6:33 and Dirk Graham at 6:51. Pittsburgh won 6-5 and best-of-seven F 4-0.

FASTEST THREE GOALS, ONE TEAM:
23 Seconds — **Toronto Maple Leafs** at Toronto, April 12, 1979, against Atlanta. Darryl Sittler scored at 4:04 of first period and again at 4:16 and Ron Ellis at 4:27. Leafs won 7-4 and best-of-five PR 2-0.
38 Seconds — NY Rangers at New York, April 12, 1986 against Philadelphia. Jim Wiemer scored at 12:29 of third period, Bob Brooke at 12:43 and Ron Greschner at 13:07. NY Rangers won 5-2 and best-of-five DSF 3-2.
56 Seconds — Montreal Canadiens at Detroit, April 6, 1954. Dickie Moore scored at 15:03 of first period, Maurice Richard at 15:28 and again at 15:59. Montreal won 3-1. Detroit won best-of-seven F 4-3.

FASTEST TWO GOALS, BOTH TEAMS:
5 Seconds — Pittsburgh Penguins, Buffalo Sabres at Buffalo, April 14, 1979. Gilbert Perreault scored for Buffalo at 12:59 and Jim Hamilton for Pittsburgh at 13:04 of first period. Pittsburgh won 4-3 and best-of-three PR 2-1.
8 Seconds — Minnesota North Stars, St. Louis Blues at Minnesota, April 9, 1989. Bernie Federko scored for St. Louis at 2:28 of third period and Perry Berezan at 2:36 for Minnesota. Minnesota won 5-4. St. Louis won best-of-seven DSF 4-1.
- Phoenix Coyotes, Detroit Red Wings, at Detroit, April 24, 1998. Jeremy Roenick scored for Phoenix at 13:24 of the second period and Mathieu Dandenault for Detroit at 13:32. Phoenix won 7-4, Detroit won the best-of-seven CQF 4-2.
9 Seconds — NY Islanders, Washington Capitals at Washington, April 10, 1986. Bryan Trottier scored for New York at 18:26 of second period and Scott Stevens at 18:35 for Washington. Washington won 5-2, and best-of-five DSF 3-0.
- Buffalo Sabres, Toronto Maple Leafs at Toronto, May 23, 1999. Vaclav Varada scored at 4:23 of first period for Buffalo and Mats Sundin scored at 4:32 for Toronto. Buffalo won 5-4, and best of seven CF 4-1.

FASTEST TWO GOALS, ONE TEAM:
5 Seconds — **Detroit Red Wings** at Detroit, April 11, 1965, against Chicago. Norm Ullman scored at 17:35 and 17:40, second period. Detroit won 4-2. Chicago won best-of-seven SF 4-3.

Though it took him only half the time Mud Bruneteau needed in 1936, Petr Klima's goal at 15:43 of triple overtime (55:43) gave Edmonton a 3-2 win over Boston in the longest game played in the Stanley Cup finals, May 15, 1990.

OVERTIME

SHORTEST OVERTIME:
9 Seconds — Montreal Canadiens, Calgary Flames, at Calgary, May 18, 1986. Montreal won 3-2 on Brian Skrudland's goal and captured the best-of-seven F 4-1.
11 Seconds — NY Islanders, NY Rangers, at NY Rangers, April 11, 1975. NY Islanders won 4-3 on Jean-Paul Parise's goal and captured the best-of-three PR 2-1.

LONGEST OVERTIME:
116 Minutes, 30 Seconds — Detroit Red Wings, Mtl. Maroons at Montreal, March 24, 25, 1936. Detroit 1, Mtl. Maroons 0. Mud Bruneteau scored, assisted by Hec Kilrea, at 16:30 of sixth overtime period, or after 176 minutes, 30 seconds from start of game, which ended at 2:25 a.m. Detroit won best-of-five SF 3-0.

MOST OVERTIME GAMES, ONE PLAYOFF YEAR:
28 — 1993. Of 85 games played, 28 went into overtime.
21 — 1999. Of 86 games played, 21 went into overtime.
19 — 1996. Of 86 games played, 19 went into overtime.
— 1998. Of 82 games played, 19 went into overtime.
18 — 1994. Of 90 games played, 18 went into overtime.
— 1995. Of 81 games played, 18 went into overtime.

FEWEST OVERTIME GAMES, ONE PLAYOFF YEAR:
0 — 1963. None of the 16 games went into overtime, the only year since 1926 that no overtime was required in any playoff series.

MOST OVERTIME GAMES, ONE SERIES:
5 — Toronto Maple Leafs, Montreal Canadiens in 1951. Toronto won best-of-seven F 4-1.
4 — Toronto Maple Leafs, Boston Bruins in 1933. Toronto won best-of-five SF 3-2.
— Boston Bruins, NY Rangers in 1939. Boston won best-of-seven SF 4-3.
— St. Louis Blues, Minnesota North Stars in 1968. St. Louis won best-of-seven SF 4-3.
— Dallas Stars, St. Louis Blues in 1999. Dallas won best-of-seven CSF 4-2.

THREE-OR-MORE GOAL GAMES

MOST THREE-OR-MORE GOAL GAMES BY ALL TEAMS, ONE PLAYOFF YEAR:
12 — 1983 in 66 games.
— 1988 in 83 games.
11 — 1985 in 70 games.
— 1992 in 86 games.

MOST THREE-OR-MORE GOAL GAMES, ONE TEAM, ONE PLAYOFF YEAR:
6 — Edmonton Oilers in 16 games, 1983.
— Edmonton Oilers in 18 games, 1985.

SHUTOUTS

MOST SHUTOUTS, ONE PLAYOFF YEAR, ALL TEAMS:
18 — 1997. Of 82 games played, Colorado and NY Rangers had 3 each, Edmonton, New Jersey, and St. Louis had 2 each, while Anaheim, Buffalo, Detroit, Florida, Ottawa and Phoenix had 1 each.
16 — 1994. Of 90 games played, NY Rangers and Vancouver had 4 each, Toronto had 3, Buffalo had 2, while Washington, Detroit and New Jersey had 1 each.

FEWEST SHUTOUTS, ONE PLAYOFF YEAR, ALL TEAMS:
0 — 1959. 18 games played.

MOST SHUTOUTS, BOTH TEAMS, ONE SERIES:
5 — 1945 F, Toronto Maple Leafs, Detroit Red Wings. Toronto had 3 shutouts, Detroit 2. Toronto won best-of-seven series 4-3.
— 1950 SF, Toronto Maple Leafs, Detroit Red Wings. Toronto had 3 shutouts, Detroit 2. Detroit won best-of-seven series 4-3.

TEAM PENALTIES

FEWEST PENALTIES, BOTH TEAMS, BEST-OF-SEVEN SERIES:
19 — Detroit Red Wings, Toronto Maple Leafs in 1945 F, won by Toronto 4-3. Detroit received 10 minors, Toronto had 9 minors.

FEWEST PENALTIES, ONE TEAM, BEST-OF-SEVEN SERIES:
9 — Toronto Maple Leafs in 1945 F, won by Toronto 4-3 against Detroit.

MOST PENALTIES, BOTH TEAMS, ONE SERIES:
219 — New Jersey Devils, Washington Capitals in 1988 DF won by New Jersey 4-3. New Jersey received 98 minors, 11 majors, 9 misconducts and 1 match penalty. Washington received 80 minors, 11 majors, 8 misconducts and 1 match penalty.

MOST PENALTY MINUTES, BOTH TEAMS, ONE SERIES:
656 — New Jersey Devils, Washington Capitals in 1988 DF won by New Jersey 4-3. New Jersey had 351 minutes; Washington 305.

MOST PENALTIES, ONE TEAM, ONE SERIES:
119 — New Jersey Devils in 1988 DF versus Washington. New Jersey received 98 minors, 11 majors, 9 misconducts and 1 match penalty.

MOST PENALTY MINUTES, ONE TEAM, ONE SERIES:
351 — New Jersey Devils in 1988 DF versus Washington. Series won by New Jersey 4-3.

MOST PENALTIES, BOTH TEAMS, ONE GAME:
66 — Detroit Red Wings, St. Louis Blues, at St. Louis, April 12, 1991. Detroit received 33 penalties; St. Louis 33. St. Louis won 6-1.
62 — New Jersey Devils, Washington Capitals, at New Jersey, April 22, 1988. New Jersey received 32 penalties; Washington 30. New Jersey won 10-4.

MOST PENALTY MINUTES, BOTH TEAMS, ONE GAME:
298 Minutes — Detroit Red Wings, St. Louis Blues, at St. Louis, April 12, 1991. Detroit received 33 penalties for 152 minutes; St. Louis 33 penalties for 146 minutes. St. Louis won 6-1.
267 Minutes — NY Rangers, Los Angeles Kings, at Los Angeles, April 9, 1981. NY Rangers received 31 penalties for 142 minutes; Los Angeles 28 penalties for 125 minutes. Los Angeles won 5-4.

MOST PENALTIES, ONE TEAM, ONE GAME:
33 — Detroit Red Wings, at St. Louis, April 12,1991. St. Louis won 6-1.
— St. Louis Blues, at St. Louis, April 12, 1991. St. Louis won 6-1.
32 — New Jersey Devils, at Washington, April 22,1988. New Jersey won 10-4.
31 — NY Rangers, at Los Angeles, April 9, 1981. Los Angeles won 5-4.
30 — Philadelphia Flyers, at Toronto, April 15, 1976. Toronto won 5-4.

MOST PENALTY MINUTES, ONE TEAM, ONE GAME:
152 — Detroit Red Wings, at St. Louis, April 12, 1991. St. Louis won 6-1.
146 — St. Louis Blues, at St. Louis, April 12, 1991. St. Louis won 6-1.
142 — NY Rangers, at Los Angeles, April 9, 1981. Los Angeles won 5-4.

MOST PENALTIES, BOTH TEAMS, ONE PERIOD:
43 — NY Rangers, Los Angeles Kings, at Los Angeles, April 9, 1981, first period. NY Rangers had 24 penalties; Los Angeles 19. Los Angeles won 5-4.

MOST PENALTY MINUTES, BOTH TEAMS, ONE PERIOD:
248 — NY Islanders, Boston Bruins, at Boston, April 17, 1980, first period. Each team received 124 minutes. Islanders won 5-4.

MOST PENALTIES, ONE TEAM, ONE PERIOD:
24 — NY Rangers, at Los Angeles, April 9, 1981, first period. Los Angeles won 5-4.

MOST PENALTY MINUTES, ONE TEAM, ONE PERIOD:
125 — NY Rangers, at Los Angeles, April 9, 1981, first period. Los Angeles won 5-4.

Individual Records

GAMES PLAYED

MOST YEARS IN PLAYOFFS:
20 — Gordie Howe, Detroit, Hartford (1947-58 incl.; 60-61; 63-66 incl.; 70 & 80)
— **Larry Robinson, Montreal, Los Angeles** (1973-92 incl.)
— **Ray Bourque, Boston, Colorado** (1980-96 incl.; 98-00 incl.)
19 — Red Kelly, Detroit, Toronto
— Larry Murphy, Los Angeles, Washington, Minnesota, Pittsburgh, Toronto, Detroit

MOST CONSECUTIVE YEARS IN PLAYOFFS:
20 — Larry Robinson, Montreal, Los Angeles (1973-1992, inclusive).
17 — Brad Park, NY Rangers, Boston, Detroit (1969-1985, inclusive).
— Ray Bourque, Boston (1980-96, inclusive).
— Larry Murphy, Los Angeles, Washington, Minnesota, Pittsburgh, Toronto, Detroit (1984-2000, inclusive).
16 — Jean Beliveau, Montreal (1954-69, inclusive).
— Bob Gainey, Montreal (1974-89, inclusive).
— Dale Hunter, Quebec, Washington (1981-96, inclusive)

MOST PLAYOFF GAMES:
236 — Mark Messier, Edmonton, NY Rangers
231 — Guy Carbonneau, Montreal, St. Louis, Dallas
227 — Larry Robinson, Montreal, Los Angeles
225 — Glenn Anderson, Edmonton, Toronto, NY Rangers, St. Louis
221 — Bryan Trottier, NY Islanders, Pittsburgh
— Claude Lemieux, Montreal, New Jersey, Colorado

GOALS

MOST GOALS IN PLAYOFFS (CAREER):
122 — Wayne Gretzky, Edmonton, Los Angeles, St. Louis, NY Rangers
109 — Mark Messier, Edmonton, NY Rangers
106 — Jari Kurri, Edmonton, Los Angeles, NY Rangers, Anaheim
93 — Glenn Anderson, Edmonton, Toronto, NY Rangers, St. Louis
88 — Brett Hull, Calgary, St. Louis, Dallas

MOST GOALS, ONE PLAYOFF YEAR:
19 — Reggie Leach, Philadelphia, 1976. 16 games.
— **Jari Kurri, Edmonton,** 1985. 18 games.
18 — Joe Sakic, Colorado, 1996. 22 games.
17 — Newsy Lalonde, Montreal, 1919. 10 games.
— Mike Bossy, NY Islanders, 1981. 18 games.
— Steve Payne, Minnesota, 1981. 19 games.
— Mike Bossy, NY Islanders, 1982. 19 games.
— Mike Bossy, NY Islanders, 1983. 19 games
— Wayne Gretzky, Edmonton, 1985. 18 games.
— Kevin Stevens, Pittsburgh, 1991. 24 games.

MOST GOALS IN ONE SERIES (OTHER THAN FINAL):
12 — Jari Kurri, Edmonton, in 1985 CF, 6 games vs. Chicago.
11 — Newsy Lalonde, Montreal, in 1919 NHL F, 5 games vs. Ottawa.
10 — Tim Kerr, Philadelphia, in 1989 DF, 7 games vs. Pittsburgh.
9 — Reggie Leach, Philadelphia, in 1976 SF, 5 games vs. Boston.
— Bill Barber, Philadelphia, in 1980 SF, 5 games vs. Minnesota.
— Mike Bossy, NY Islanders, in 1983 CF, 6 games vs. Boston.
— Mario Lemieux, Pittsburgh, in 1989 DF, 7 games vs. Philadelphia.

MOST GOALS IN FINAL SERIES:
9 — Babe Dye, Toronto, in 1922, 5 games vs. Van. Millionaires.
8 — Alf Skinner, Toronto, in 1918, 5 games vs. Van. Millionaires.
7 — Jean Beliveau, Montreal, in 1956, 5 games vs. Detroit.
— Mike Bossy, NY Islanders, in 1982, 4 games vs. Vancouver.
— Wayne Gretzky, Edmonton, in 1985, 5 games vs. Philadelphia.

MOST GOALS, ONE GAME:
5 — Newsy Lalonde, Montreal, March 1, 1919, at Montreal. Final score: Montreal 6, Ottawa 3.
— **Maurice Richard, Montreal,** March 23, 1944, at Montreal. Final score: Montreal 5, Toronto 1.
— **Darryl Sittler, Toronto,** April 22, 1976, at Toronto. Final score: Toronto 8, Philadelphia 5.
— **Reggie Leach, Philadelphia,** May 6, 1976, at Philadelphia. Final score: Philadelphia 6, Boston 3.
— **Mario Lemieux, Pittsburgh,** April 25, 1989, at Pittsburgh. Final score: Pittsburgh 10, Philadelphia 7.

MOST GOALS, ONE PERIOD:
4 — Tim Kerr, Philadelphia, April 13, 1985, at New York vs. NY Rangers, second period. Final score: Philadelphia 6, NY Rangers 5.
— **Mario Lemieux, Pittsburgh,** April 25, 1989, at Pittsburgh vs. Philadelphia, first period. Final score: Pittsburgh 10, Philadelphia 7.

ASSISTS

MOST ASSISTS IN PLAYOFFS (CAREER):
260 — Wayne Gretzky, Edmonton, Los Angeles, St. Louis, NY Rangers
186 — Mark Messier, Edmonton, NY Rangers
137 — Paul Coffey, Edmonton, Pittsburgh, Los Angeles, Detroit, Philadelphia, Carolina
133 — Ray Bourque, Boston, Colorado
127 — Jari Kurri, Edmonton, Los Angeles, NY Rangers, Anaheim

MOST ASSISTS, ONE PLAYOFF YEAR:
31 — Wayne Gretzky, Edmonton, 1988. 19 games.
30 — Wayne Gretzky, Edmonton, 1985. 18 games.
29 — Wayne Gretzky, Edmonton, 1987. 21 games.
28 — Mario Lemieux, Pittsburgh, 1991. 23 games.
26 — Wayne Gretzky, Edmonton, 1983. 16 games.

MOST ASSISTS IN ONE SERIES (OTHER THAN FINAL):
14 — Rick Middleton, Boston, in 1983 DF, 7 games vs. Buffalo.
— **Wayne Gretzky, Edmonton,** in 1985 CF, 6 games vs. Chicago.
13 — Wayne Gretzky, Edmonton, in 1987 DSF, 5 games vs. Los Angeles.
— Doug Gilmour, Toronto, in 1994 CSF, 7 games vs. San Jose.
11 — Mark Messier, Edmonton, in 1989 DSF, 7 games vs. Los Angeles.
— Al MacInnis, Calgary, in 1984 DF, 7 games vs. Edmonton.
— Mike Ridley, Washington, in 1992 DSF, 7 games vs. Pittsburgh.
— Ron Francis, Pittsburgh, in 1995 CQF, 7 games vs. Washington.
10 — Fleming Mackell, Boston, in 1958 SF, 6 games vs. NY Rangers.
— Stan Mikita, Chicago, in 1962 SF, 6 games vs. Montreal.
— Bob Bourne, NY Islanders, in 1983 DF, 6 games vs. NY Rangers.
— Wayne Gretzky, Edmonton, in 1988 DSF, 5 games vs. Winnipeg.
— Mario Lemieux, Pittsburgh, in 1992 DSF, 6 games vs. Washington.

MOST ASSISTS IN FINAL SERIES:
10 — Wayne Gretzky, Edmonton, in 1988, 4 games plus suspended game vs. Boston.
9 — Jacques Lemaire, Montreal, in 1973, 6 games vs. Chicago.
— Wayne Gretzky, Edmonton, in 1987, 7 games vs. Philadelphia.
— Larry Murphy, Pittsburgh, in 1991, 6 games vs. Minnesota.

MOST ASSISTS, ONE GAME:
6 — Mikko Leinonen, NY Rangers, April 8, 1982, at New York. Final score: NY Rangers 7, Philadelphia 3.
— **Wayne Gretzky, Edmonton,** April 9, 1987, at Edmonton. Final score: Edmonton 13, Los Angeles 3.
5 — Toe Blake, Montreal, March 23, 1944, at Montreal. Final score: Montreal 5, Toronto 1.
— Maurice Richard, Montreal, March 27, 1956, at Montreal. Final score: Montreal 7, NY Rangers 0.
— Bert Olmstead, Montreal, March 30, 1957, at Montreal. Final score: Montreal 8, NY Rangers 3.
— Don McKenney, Boston, April 5, 1958, at Boston. Final score: Boston 8, NY Rangers 2.
— Stan Mikita, Chicago, April 4, 1973, at Chicago. Final score: Chicago 7, St. Louis 1.
— Wayne Gretzky, Edmonton, April 8, 1981, at Montreal. Final score: Edmonton 6, Montreal 3.
— Paul Coffey, Edmonton, May 14, 1985, at Edmonton. Final score: Edmonton 10, Chicago 5.
— Doug Gilmour, St. Louis, April 15, 1986, at Minnesota. Final score: St. Louis 6, Minnesota 3.
— Risto Siltanen, Quebec, April 14, 1987, at Hartford. Final score: Quebec 7, Hartford 5.
— Patrik Sundstrom, New Jersey, April 22, 1988, at New Jersey. Final score: New Jersey 10, Washington 4.
— Geoff Courtnall, St. Louis Blues, April 23, 1998, at St. Louis. Final score: St. Louis 8, Los Angeles 3.

MOST ASSISTS, ONE PERIOD:
3 — Three assists by one player in one period of a playoff game has been recorded on 71 occasions. Mike Ricci of the San Jose Sharks is the most recent to equal this mark with 3 assists in the third period at Colorado, April 28, 1999. Final score: San Jose 4, Colorado 3.
— Wayne Gretzky has had 3 assists in one period 5 times; Ray Bourque, 3 times; Toe Blake, Jean Beliveau, Doug Harvey and Bobby Orr, twice. Nick Metz of Toronto was the first player to be credited with 3 assists in one period of a playoff game Mar. 21, 1941 at Toronto vs. Boston.

POINTS

MOST POINTS IN PLAYOFFS (CAREER):
382 — Wayne Gretzky, Edmonton, Los Angeles, St. Louis, NY Rangers, 122G, 260A
295 — Mark Messier, Edmonton, NY Rangers, 109G, 186A
233 — Jari Kurri, Edmonton, Los Angeles, NY Rangers, Anaheim, 106G, 127A
214 — Glenn Anderson, Edmonton, Toronto, NY Rangers, St. Louis, 93G, 121A
196 — Paul Coffey, Edmonton, Pittsburgh, Los Angeles, Detroit, Philadelphia, Carolina, 59G, 137A

MOST POINTS, ONE PLAYOFF YEAR:
47 — Wayne Gretzky, Edmonton, in 1985. 17 goals, 30 assists in 18 games.
44 — Mario Lemieux, Pittsburgh, in 1991. 16 goals, 28 assists in 23 games.
43 — Wayne Gretzky, Edmonton, in 1988. 12 goals, 31 assists in 19 games.
40 — Wayne Gretzky, Los Angeles, in 1993. 15 goals, 25 assists in 24 games.
38 — Wayne Gretzky, Edmonton, in 1983. 12 goals, 26 assists in 16 games.

MOST POINTS IN ONE SERIES (OTHER THAN FINAL):
19 — Rick Middleton, Boston, in 1983 DF, 7 games vs. Buffalo. 5 goals, 14 assists.
18 — Wayne Gretzky, Edmonton, in 1985 CF, 6 games vs. Chicago. 4 goals, 14 assists.
17 — Mario Lemieux, Pittsburgh, in 1992 DSF, 6 games vs. Washington. 7 goals, 10 assists.
16 — Barry Pederson, Boston, in 1983 DF, 7 games vs. Buffalo. 7 goals, 9 assists.
  — Doug Gilmour, Toronto, in 1994 CSF, 7 games vs. San Jose. 3 goals, 13 assists.
15 — Jari Kurri, Edmonton, in 1985 CF, 6 games vs. Chicago. 12 goals, 3 assists.
  — Wayne Gretzky, Edmonton, in 1987 DSF, 5 games vs. Los Angeles. 2 goals, 13 assists.
  — Tim Kerr, Philadelphia, in 1989 DF, 7 games vs. Pittsburgh. 10 goals, 5 assists.
  — Mario Lemieux, Pittsburgh, in 1991 CF, 6 games vs. Boston. 6 goals, 9 assists.

MOST POINTS IN FINAL SERIES:
13 — Wayne Gretzky, Edmonton, in 1988, 4 games plus suspended game vs. Boston. 3 goals, 10 assists.
12 — Gordie Howe, Detroit, in 1955, 7 games vs. Montreal. 5 goals, 7 assists.
  — Yvan Cournoyer, Montreal, in 1973, 6 games vs. Chicago. 6 goals, 6 assists.
  — Jacques Lemaire, Montreal, in 1973, 6 games vs. Chicago. 3 goals, 9 assists.
  — Mario Lemieux, Pittsburgh, in 1991, 5 games vs. Minnesota. 5 goals, 7 assists.

MOST POINTS, ONE GAME:
8 — Patrik Sundstrom, New Jersey, April 22, 1988 at New Jersey during 10-4 win over Washington. Sundstrom had 3 goals, 5 assists.
  — **Mario Lemieux, Pittsburgh,** April 25, 1989 at Pittsburgh during 10-7 win over Philadelphia. Lemieux had 5 goals, 3 assists.
7 — Wayne Gretzky, Edmonton, April 17, 1983 at Calgary during 10-2 win. Gretzky had 4 goals, 3 assists.
  — Wayne Gretzky, Edmonton, April 25, 1985 at Winnipeg during 8-3 win. Gretzky had 3 goals, 4 assists.
  — Wayne Gretzky, Edmonton, April 9, 1987, at Edmonton during 13-3 win over Los Angeles. Gretzky had 1 goal, 6 assists.
6 — Dickie Moore, Montreal, March 25, 1954, at Montreal during 8-1 win over Boston. Moore had 2 goals, 4 assists.
  — Phil Esposito, Boston, April 2, 1969, at Boston during 10-0 win over Toronto. Esposito had 4 goals, 2 assists.
  — Darryl Sittler, Toronto, April 22, 1976, at Toronto during 8-5 win over Philadelphia. Sittler had 5 goals, 1 assist.
  — Guy Lafleur, Montreal, April 11, 1977, at Montreal during 7-2 win over St. Louis. Lafleur had 3 goals, 3 assists.
  — Mikko Leinonen, NY Rangers, April 8, 1982, at New York during 7-3 win over Philadelphia. Leinonen had 6 assists.
  — Paul Coffey, Edmonton, May 14, 1985 at Edmonton during 10-5 win over Chicago. Coffey had 1 goal, 5 assists.
  — John Anderson, Hartford, April 12, 1986 at Hartford during 9-4 win over Quebec. Anderson had 2 goals, 4 assists.
  — Mario Lemieux, Pittsburgh, April 23, 1992 at Pittsburgh during 6-4 win over Washington. Lemieux had 3 goals, 3 assists.
  — Geoff Courtnall, St. Louis Blues, April 23, 1998 at St. Louis during 8-3 win over Los Angeles. Courtnall had 1 goal, 5 assists.

MOST POINTS, ONE PERIOD:
4 — Maurice Richard, Montreal, March 29, 1945, at Montreal vs. Toronto. Third period, 3 goals, 1 assist. Final score: Montreal 10, Toronto 3.
  — **Dickie Moore, Montreal,** March 25, 1954, at Montreal vs. Boston. First period, 2 goals, 2 assists. Final score: Montreal 8, Boston 1.
  — **Barry Pederson, Boston,** April 8, 1982, at Boston vs. Buffalo. Second period, 3 goals, 1 assist. Final score: Boston 7, Buffalo 3.
  — **Peter McNab, Boston,** April 11, 1982, at Buffalo. Second period, 1 goal, 3 assists. Final score: Boston 5, Buffalo 2.
  — **Tim Kerr, Philadelphia,** April 13, 1985 at New York. Second period, 4 goals. Final score: Philadelphia 6, Rangers 5.
  — **Ken Linseman, Boston,** April 14, 1985 at Boston vs. Montreal. Second period, 2 goals, 2 assists. Final score: Boston 7, Montreal 6.
  — **Wayne Gretzky, Edmonton,** April 12, 1987, at Los Angeles. Third period, 1 goal, 3 assists. Final score: Edmonton 6, Los Angeles 3.
  — **Glenn Anderson, Edmonton,** April 6, 1988, at Edmonton vs. Winnipeg. Third period, 3 goals, 1 assist. Final score: Edmonton 7, Winnipeg 4.
  — **Mario Lemieux, Pittsburgh,** April 25, 1989, at Pittsburgh vs. Philadelphia. First period, 4 goals. Final score: Pittsburgh 10, Philadelphia 7.
  — **Dave Gagner, Minnesota,** April 8, 1991, at Minnesota vs. Chicago. First period, 2 goals, 2 assists. Final score: Chicago 6, Minnesota 5.
  — **Mario Lemieux, Pittsburgh,** April 23, 1992, at Pittsburgh vs. Washington. Second period, 2 goals, 2 assists. Final score: Pittsburgh 6, Washington 4.

POWER-PLAY GOALS

MOST POWER-PLAY GOALS IN PLAYOFFS (CAREER):
35 — Mike Bossy, NY Islanders
34 — Dino Ciccarelli, Minnesota, Washington, Detroit
  — Wayne Gretzky, Edmonton, Los Angeles, St. Louis, NY Rangers
33 — Brett Hull, St. Louis, Dallas
28 — Mario Lemieux, Pittsburgh

MOST POWER-PLAY GOALS, ONE PLAYOFF YEAR:
9 — Mike Bossy, NY Islanders, 1981. 18 games against Toronto, Edmonton, NY Rangers and Minnesota.
  — **Cam Neely, Boston,** 1991. 19 games against Hartford, Montreal and Pittsburgh.
8 — Tim Kerr, Philadelphia, 1989. 19 games.
  — John Druce, Washington, 1990. 15 games.
  — Brian Propp, Minnesota, 1991. 23 games.
  — Mario Lemieux, Pittsburgh, 1992. 15 games.

MOST POWER-PLAY GOALS, ONE PLAYOFF SERIES:
6 — Chris Kontos, Los Angeles, 1989, DSF vs. Edmonton, won by Los Angeles 4-3.
5 — Andy Bathgate, Detroit, 1966, SF vs. Chicago, won by Detroit 4-2.
  — Denis Potvin, NY Islanders, 1981, QF vs. Edmonton, won by NY Islanders 4-2.
  — Ken Houston, Calgary, 1981, QF vs. Philadelphia, won by Calgary 4-3.
  — Rick Vaive, Chicago, 1988, DSF vs. St. Louis, won by St. Louis 4-1.
  — Tim Kerr, Philadelphia, 1989, DF vs. Pittsburgh, won by Philadelphia 4-3.
  — Mario Lemieux, Pittsburgh, 1989, DF vs. Philadelphia won by Philadelphia 4-3.
  — John Druce, Washington, 1990, DF vs. NY Rangers won by Washington 4-1.
  — Pat LaFontaine, Buffalo, 1992, DSF vs. Boston won by Boston 4-3.
  — Adam Graves, NY Rangers, 1996, CQF vs Montreal, won by NY Rangers 4-2.

MOST POWER-PLAY GOALS, ONE GAME:
3 — Syd Howe, Detroit, March 23, 1939, at Detroit vs. Montreal. Detroit won 7-3.
  — **Sid Smith, Toronto,** April 10, 1949, at Detroit. Toronto won 3-1.
  — **Phil Esposito, Boston,** April 2, 1969, at Boston vs. Toronto. Boston won 10-0.
  — **John Bucyk, Boston,** April 21, 1974, at Boston vs. Chicago. Boston won 8-6.
  — **Denis Potvin, NY Islanders,** April 17, 1981, at New York vs. Edmonton. NY Islanders won 6-3.
  — **Tim Kerr, Philadelphia,** April 13, 1985, at NY Rangers. Philadelphia won 6-5.
  — **Jari Kurri, Edmonton,** April 9, 1987, at Edmonton vs. Los Angeles. Edmonton won 13-3.
  — **Mark Johnson, New Jersey,** April 22, 1988, at New Jersey vs. Washington. New Jersey won 10-4.
  — **Dino Ciccarelli, Detroit,** April 29, 1993, at Toronto. Detroit won 7-3.
  — **Dino Ciccarelli, Detroit,** May 11, 1995, at Dallas. Detroit won 5-1.
  — **Valeri Kamensky, Colorado,** April 24, 1997, at Colorado vs. Chicago. Colorado won 7-0.

MOST POWER-PLAY GOALS, ONE PERIOD:
3 — Tim Kerr, Philadelphia, April 13, 1985 at New York, second period in 6-5 win vs. NY Rangers.
2 — Two power-play goals have been scored by one player in one period on 53 occasions. Charlie Conacher of Toronto was the first to score two power-play goals in one period, setting the mark on March 26, 1936. Brendan Shanahan of the Detroit Red Wings is the most recent to equal this mark with two power-play goals in the first period at Phoenix, May 3, 1998. Final score: Detroit 5, Phoenix 2.

SHORTHAND GOALS

MOST SHORTHAND GOALS IN PLAYOFFS (CAREER):
14 — Mark Messier, Edmonton, NY Rangers
11 — Wayne Gretzky, Edmonton, Los Angeles, St. Louis
10 — Jari Kurri, Edmonton, Los Angeles, NY Rangers
8 — Ed Westfall, Boston, NY Islanders
  — Hakan Loob, Calgary

MOST SHORTHAND GOALS, ONE PLAYOFF YEAR:
3 — Derek Sanderson, Boston, 1969. 1 against Toronto in QF, won by Boston 4-0; 2 against Montreal in SF, won by Montreal, 4-2.
  — **Bill Barber, Philadelphia,** 1980. All against Minnesota in SF, won by Philadelphia 4-1.
  — **Lorne Henning, NY Islanders,** 1980. 1 against Boston in QF won by NY Islanders 4-1; 1 against Buffalo in SF, won by NY Islanders 4-2, 1 against Philadelphia in F, won by NY Islanders 4-2.
  — **Wayne Gretzky, Edmonton,** 1983. 2 against Winnipeg in DSF won by Edmonton 3-0; 1 against Calgary in DF, won by Edmonton 4-1.
  — **Wayne Presley, Chicago,** 1989. All against Detroit in DSF won by Chicago 4-2.
  — **Todd Marchant, Edmonton,** 1997. 1 against Dallas in CQF won by Edmonton 4-3; 2 against Colorado in CSF won by Colorado 4-1.

MOST SHORTHAND GOALS, ONE PLAYOFF SERIES:
3 — Bill Barber, Philadelphia, 1980, SF vs. Minnesota, won by Philadelphia 4-1.
  — **Wayne Presley, Chicago,** 1989, DSF vs. Detroit, won by Chicago 4-2.
2 — Mac Colville, NY Rangers, 1940, SF vs. Boston, won by NY Rangers 4-2.
  — Jerry Toppazzini, Boston, 1958, SF vs. NY Rangers, won by Boston 4-2.
  — Dave Keon, Toronto, 1963, F vs. Detroit, won by Toronto 4-1.
  — Bob Pulford, Toronto, 1964, F vs. Detroit, won by Toronto 4-3.
  — Serge Savard, Montreal, 1968, SF vs. St. Louis, won by Montreal 4-0.
  — Derek Sanderson, Boston, 1969, SF vs. Montreal, won by Montreal 4-2.
  — Bryan Trottier, NY Islanders, 1980, PR vs. Los Angeles, won by NY Islanders 3-1.
  — Bobby Lalonde, Boston, 1981, PR vs. Minnesota, won by Minnesota 3-0.
  — Butch Goring, NY Islanders, 1981, SF vs. NY Rangers, won by NY Islanders 4-0.
  — Wayne Gretzky, Edmonton, 1983, DSF vs. Winnipeg, won by Edmonton 3-0.
  — Mark Messier, Edmonton, 1983, DF vs. Calgary, won by Edmonton 4-1.
  — Jari Kurri, Edmonton, 1983, CF vs. Chicago, won by Edmonton 4-0.
  — Wayne Gretzky, Edmonton, 1985, DF vs. Winnipeg, won by Edmonton 4-0.
  — Kevin Lowe, Edmonton, 1987, F vs. Philadelphia, won by Edmonton 4-3.
  — Bob Gould, Washington, 1988, DSF vs. Philadelphia, won by Washington 4-3.
  — Dave Poulin, Philadelphia, 1989, DF vs. Pittsburgh, won by Philadelphia 4-3.
  — Russ Courtnall, Montreal, 1991, DF vs. Boston, won by Boston 4-3.
  — Sergei Fedorov, Detroit, 1992, DSF vs. Minnesota, won by Detroit 4-3.
  — Mark Messier, NY Rangers, 1992, DSF vs. New Jersey, won by NY Rangers 4-3.
  — Tom Fitzgerald, NY Islanders, 1993, DF vs. Pittsburgh, won by NY Islanders 4-3.
  — Mark Osborne, Toronto, 1994, CSF vs. San Jose, won by Toronto 4-3.
  — Tony Amonte, Chicago, 1997, CQF vs. Colorado, won by Colorado 4-2.
  — Brian Rolston, New Jersey, 1997, CQF vs. Montreal, won by New Jersey 4-1.
  — Rod Brind'Amour, Philadelphia, 1997, CQF vs. Pittsburgh, won by Philadelphia 4-1.
  — Todd Marchant, Edmonton, 1997, CSF vs. Colorado, won by Colorado 4-1.
  — Jeremy Roenick, Phoenix, 1998, CQF vs. Detroit, won by Detroit 4-2.
  — Vincent Damphousse, San Jose, 1999, CQF vs. Colorado, won by Colorado 4-2.
  — Dixon Ward, Buffalo, 1999, CF vs. Toronto, won by Buffalo 4-1.

MOST SHORTHAND GOALS, ONE GAME:

2 — **Dave Keon, Toronto,** April 18, 1963, at Toronto, in 3-1 win vs. Detroit.
— **Bryan Trottier, NY Islanders,** April 8, 1980 at New York, in 8-1 win vs. Los Angeles.
— **Bobby Lalonde, Boston,** April 11, 1981 at Minnesota, in 6-3 win by Minnesota.
— **Wayne Gretzky, Edmonton,** April 6, 1983 at Edmonton, in 6-3 win vs. Winnipeg.
— **Jari Kurri, Edmonton,** April 24, 1983, at Edmonton, in 8-3 win vs. Chicago.
— **Mark Messier, NY Rangers,** April 21, 1992, at New York, in 7-3 loss vs. New Jersey.
— **Tom Fitzgerald, NY Islanders,** May 8, 1993, at New York, in 6-5 win vs. Pittsburgh.
— **Rod Brind'Amour, Philadelphia,** April 26, 1997, at Philadelphia, in 6-3 win vs. Pittsburgh.
— **Jeremy Roenick, Phoenix,** April 24, 1998, at Detroit, in 7-4 win by Phoenix.
— **Vincent Damphousse, San Jose,** April 30, 1999, at Colorado, in 7-3 win by San Jose.

MOST SHORTHAND GOALS, ONE PERIOD:

2 — **Bryan Trottier, NY Islanders,** April 8, 1980, second period at New York in 8-1 win vs. Los Angeles.
— **Bobby Lalonde, Boston,** April 11, 1981, third period at Minnesota in 6-3 win by Minnesota.
— **Jari Kurri, Edmonton,** April 24, 1983, third period at Edmonton in 8-4 win vs. Chicago.
— **Rod Brind'Amour, Philadelphia,** April 26, 1997, first period at Philadelphia in 6-3 win vs. Pittsburgh.
— **Jeremy Roenick, Phoenix,** April 24, 1998, second period at Detroit in 7-4 win by Phoenix.
— **Vincent Damphousse, San Jose,** April 30, 1999, third period at Colorado in 7-3 win by San Jose.

GAME-WINNING GOALS

MOST GAME-WINNING GOALS IN PLAYOFFS (CAREER):

24 — **Wayne Gretzky, Edmonton, Los Angeles, St. Louis, NY Rangers**
21 — Brett Hull, St. Louis, Dallas
19 — Claude Lemieux, Montreal, New Jersey, Colorado
18 — Maurice Richard, Montreal
17 — Mike Bossy, NY Islanders
— Glenn Anderson, Edmonton, Toronto, NY Rangers, St. Louis

MOST GAME-WINNING GOALS, ONE PLAYOFF YEAR:

6 — **Joe Sakic, Colorado,** 1996. 22 games.
— **Joe Nieuwendyk, Dallas,** 1999. 23 games.
5 — Mike Bossy, NY Islanders, 1983. 19 games.
— Jari Kurri, Edmonton, 1987. 21 games.
— Bobby Smith, Minnesota, 1991. 23 games.
— Mario Lemieux, Pittsburgh, 1992. 15 games.

MOST GAME-WINNING GOALS, ONE PLAYOFF SERIES:

4 — **Mike Bossy, NY Islanders,** 1983, CF vs. Boston, won by NY Islanders 4-2.

OVERTIME GOALS

MOST OVERTIME GOALS IN PLAYOFFS (CAREER):

6 — **Maurice Richard, Montreal** (1 in 1946; 3 in 1951; 1 in 1957; 1 in 1958.)
5 — Glenn Anderson, Edmonton, Toronto, NY Rangers, St. Louis
4 — Bob Nystrom, NY Islanders
— Dale Hunter, Quebec, Washington
— Wayne Gretzky, Edmonton, Los Angeles
— Stephane Richer, Montreal, New Jersey
— Joe Murphy, Edmonton, Chicago
— Esa Tikkanen, Edmonton, NY Rangers
— Jaromir Jagr, Pittsburgh
3 — Mel Hill, Boston
— Rene Robert, Buffalo
— Danny Gare, Buffalo
— Jacques Lemaire, Montreal
— Bobby Clarke, Philadelphia
— Terry O'Reilly, Boston
— Mike Bossy, NY Islanders
— Steve Payne, Minnesota
— Ken Morrow, NY Islanders
— Lanny McDonald, Toronto, Calgary
— Peter Stastny, Quebec
— Dino Ciccarelli, Minnesota, Washington
— Russ Courtnall, Montreal
— Kirk Muller, Montreal
— Doug Gilmour, St. Louis, Calgary, Toronto
— Greg Adams, Vancouver
— Claude Lemieux, Montreal, Colorado
— Mike Gartner, Washington, Toronto
— Jeremy Roenick, Chicago, Phoenix
— Joe Sakic, Colorado

MOST OVERTIME GOALS, ONE PLAYOFF YEAR:

3 — **Mel Hill, Boston,** 1939. All against NY Rangers in best-of-seven SF, won by Boston 4-3.
— **Maurice Richard, Montreal,** 1951. 2 against Detroit in best-of-seven SF, won by Montreal 4-2; 1 against Toronto best-of-seven F, won by Toronto 4-1.

MOST OVERTIME GOALS, ONE PLAYOFF SERIES:

3 — **Mel Hill, Boston,** 1939, SF vs. NY Rangers, won by Boston 4-3. Hill scored at 59:25 of overtime March 21 for a 2-1 win; at 8:24, March 23 for a 3-2 win; and at 48:00, April 2 for a 2-1 win.

Captain Butch Bouchard celebrates with Maurice Richard after the Rocket scored the overtime winner in game two of the 1951 Stanley Cup finals at Maple Leaf Gardens. Richard scored three of his record six career overtime goals in 1951.

SCORING BY A DEFENSEMAN

MOST GOALS BY A DEFENSEMAN, ONE PLAYOFF YEAR:
12 — Paul Coffey, Edmonton, 1985. 18 games.
11 — Brian Leetch, NY Rangers, 1994. 23 games.
 9 — Bobby Orr, Boston, 1970. 14 games.
   — Brad Park, Boston, 1978. 15 games.
 8 — Denis Potvin, NY Islanders, 1981. 18 games.
   — Ray Bourque, Boston, 1983. 17 games.
   — Denis Potvin, NY Islanders, 1983. 20 games.
   — Paul Coffey, Edmonton, 1984. 19 games.

MOST GOALS BY A DEFENSEMAN, ONE GAME:
3 — Bobby Orr, Boston, April 11, 1971 at Montreal. Final score: Boston 5, Montreal 2.
   — **Dick Redmond, Chicago,** April 4, 1973 at Chicago. Final score: Chicago 7, St. Louis 1.
   — **Denis Potvin, NY Islanders,** April 17, 1981 at New York. Final score: NY Islanders 6, Edmonton 3.
   — **Paul Reinhart, Calgary,** April 14, 1983 at Edmonton. Final score: Edmonton 6, Calgary 3.
   — **Doug Halward, Vancouver,** April 7, 1984 at Vancouver. Final score: Vancouver 7, Calgary 0.
   — **Paul Reinhart, Calgary,** April 8, 1984 at Vancouver. Final score: Calgary 5, Vancouver 1.
   — **Al Iafrate, Washington,** April 26, 1993 at Washington. Final score: Washington 6, NY Islanders 4.
   — **Eric Desjardins, Montreal,** June 3, 1993 at Montreal. Final score: Montreal 3, Los Angeles 2.
   — **Gary Suter, Chicago,** April 24, 1994, at Chicago. Final score: Chicago 4, Toronto 3.
   — **Brian Leetch, NY Rangers,** May 22, 1995 at Philadelphia. Final score: Philadelphia 4, NY Rangers 3.
   — **Andy Delmore, Philadelphia,** May 7, 2000, at Philadelphia. Final score: Philadelphia 6, Pittsburgh 3.

MOST ASSISTS BY A DEFENSEMAN, ONE PLAYOFF YEAR:
25 — Paul Coffey, Edmonton, 1985. 18 games.
24 — Al MacInnis, Calgary, 1989. 22 games.
23 — Brian Leetch, NY Rangers, 1994. 23 games.
19 — Bobby Orr, Boston, 1972. 15 games.
18 — Ray Bourque, Boston, 1988. 23 games.
   — Ray Bourque, Boston, 1991. 23 games.
   — Larry Murphy, Pittsburgh, 1991. 23 games.

MOST ASSISTS BY A DEFENSEMAN, ONE GAME:
5 — Paul Coffey, Edmonton, May 14, 1985 at Edmonton vs. Chicago. Edmonton won 10-5.
   — **Risto Siltanen, Quebec,** April 14, 1987 at Hartford. Quebec won 7-5.

MOST POINTS BY A DEFENSEMAN, ONE PLAYOFF YEAR:
37 — Paul Coffey, Edmonton, in 1985. 12 goals, 25 assists in 18 games.
34 — Brian Leetch, NY Rangers, in 1994. 11 goals, 23 assists in 23 games.
31 — Al MacInnis, Calgary, in 1989. 7 goals, 24 assists in 22 games.
25 — Denis Potvin, NY Islanders, in 1981. 8 goals, 17 assists in 18 games.
   — Ray Bourque, Boston, in 1991. 7 goals, 18 assists in 19 games.

MOST POINTS BY A DEFENSEMAN, ONE GAME:
6 — Paul Coffey, Edmonton, May 14, 1985 at Edmonton vs. Chicago. 1 goal, 5 assists. Edmonton won 10-5.
5 — Eddie Bush, Detroit, April 9, 1942, at Detroit vs. Toronto. 1 goal, 4 assists. Detroit won 5-2.
   — Bob Dailey, Philadelphia, May 1, 1980, at Philadelphia vs. Minnesota. 1 goal, 4 assists. Philadelphia won 7-0.
   — Denis Potvin, NY Islanders, April 17, 1981, at New York vs. Edmonton. 3 goals, 2 assists. NY Islanders won 6-3.
   — Risto Siltanen, Quebec, April 14, 1987, at Hartford. 5 assists. Quebec won 7-5.

SCORING BY A ROOKIE

MOST GOALS BY A ROOKIE, ONE PLAYOFF YEAR:
14 — Dino Ciccarelli, Minnesota, 1981. 19 games.
11 — Jeremy Roenick, Chicago, 1990. 20 games.
10 — Claude Lemieux, Montreal, 1986. 20 games.
 9 — Pat Flatley, NY Islanders, 1984. 21 games
 8 — Steve Christoff, Minnesota, 1980. 14 games.
   — Brad Palmer, Minnesota, 1981. 19 games.
   — Mike Krushelnyski, Boston, 1983. 17 games.
   — Bob Joyce, Boston, 1988. 23 games.

MOST POINTS BY A ROOKIE, ONE PLAYOFF YEAR:
21 — Dino Ciccarelli, Minnesota, in 1981. 14 goals, 7 assists in 19 games.
20 — Don Maloney, NY Rangers, in 1979. 7 goals, 13 assists in 18 games.

THREE-OR-MORE-GOAL GAMES

MOST THREE-OR-MORE-GOAL GAMES IN PLAYOFFS (CAREER):
10 — Wayne Gretzky, Edmonton, Los Angeles, St. Louis, NY Rangers. Eight three-goal games; two four-goal games.
 7 — Maurice Richard, Montreal. Four three-goal games; two four-goal games; one five-goal game.
   — Jari Kurri, Edmonton, Los Angeles, NY Rangers. Six three-goal games; one four-goal game.
 6 — Dino Ciccarelli, Minnesota, Washington, Detroit. Five three-goal games; one four-goal game.
 5 — Mike Bossy, NY Islanders. Four three-goal games; one four-goal game.

MOST THREE-OR-MORE-GOAL GAMES, ONE PLAYOFF YEAR:
4 — Jari Kurri, Edmonton, 1985. 1 four-goal game, 3 three-goal games.
3 — Mark Messier, Edmonton, 1983. 3 three-goal games.
   — Mike Bossy, NY Islanders, 1983. 1 four-goal game, 2 three-goal games
2 — Newsy Lalonde, Montreal, 1919. 1 five-goal game, 1 four-goal game.
   — Maurice Richard, Montreal, 1944. 1 five-goal game; 1 three-goal game.
   — Doug Bentley, Chicago, 1944. 2 three-goal games.
   — Norm Ullman, Detroit, 1964. 2 three-goal games.
   — Phil Esposito, Boston, 1970. 2 three-goal games.
   — Pit Martin, Chicago, 1973. 2 three-goal games.
   — Rick MacLeish, Philadelphia, 1975. 2 three-goal games.
   — Lanny McDonald, Toronto, 1977. 1 three-goal game; 1 four-goal game.
   — Wayne Gretzky, Edmonton, 1981. 2 three-goal games.
   — Wayne Gretzky, Edmonton, 1983. 2 four-goal games.
   — Wayne Gretzky, Edmonton, 1985. 2 three-goal games.
   — Petr Klima, Detroit, 1988. 2 three-goal games.
   — Cam Neely, Boston, 1991. 2 three-goal games.
   — Wayne Gretzky, NY Rangers, 1997. 2 three-goal games.
   — Daniel Alfredsson, Ottawa, 1998. 2 three-goal games.

MOST THREE-OR-MORE-GOAL GAMES, ONE PLAYOFF SERIES:
3 — Jari Kurri, Edmonton 1985, CF vs. Chicago won by Edmonton 4-2. Kurri scored 3 G May 7 at Edmonton in 7-3 win, 3 G May 14 at Edmonton in 10-5 win and 4 G May 16 at Chicago in 8-2 win.
2 — Doug Bentley, Chicago, 1944, SF vs. Detroit, won by Chicago 4-1. Bentley scored 3 G Mar. 28 at Chicago in 7-1 win and 3 G Mar. 30 at Detroit in 5-2 win.
   — Norm Ullman, Detroit, 1964, SF vs. Chicago, won by Detroit 4-3. Ullman scored 3 G Mar. 29 at Chicago in 7-1 win and 3 G April 7 at Detroit in 7-2 win.
   — Mark Messier, Edmonton, 1983, DF vs. Calgary won by Edmonton 4-1. Messier scored 4 G April 14 at Edmonton in 6-3 win and 3 G April 17 at Calgary in 10-2 win.
   — Mike Bossy, NY Islanders, 1983, CF vs. Boston won by NY Islanders 4-2. Bossy scored 3 G May 3 at New York in 8-3 win and 4 G May 7 at New York in 8-4 win.

SCORING STREAKS

LONGEST CONSECUTIVE GOAL-SCORING STREAK, ONE PLAYOFF YEAR:
10 Games — Reggie Leach, Philadelphia, 1976. Streak started April 17 at Toronto and ended May 9 at Montreal. He scored one goal in each of eight games; two in one game; and five in another; a total of 15 goals.

LONGEST CONSECUTIVE POINT-SCORING STREAK, ONE PLAYOFF YEAR:
18 games — Bryan Trottier, NY Islanders, 1981. 11 goals, 18 assists, 29 points.
17 games — Wayne Gretzky, Edmonton, 1988. 12 goals, 29 assists, 41 points.
   — Al MacInnis, Calgary, 1989. 7 goals, 19 assists, 26 points.

LONGEST CONSECUTIVE POINT-SCORING STREAK, MORE THAN ONE PLAYOFF YEAR:
27 games — Bryan Trottier, NY Islanders, 1980, 1981 and 1982. 7 games in 1980 (3 G, 5 A, 8 PTS), 18 games in 1981 (11 G, 18 A, 29 PTS), and two games in 1982 (2 G, 3 A, 5 PTS). Total points, 42.
19 games — Wayne Gretzky, Edmonton, Los Angeles, 1988 and 1989. 17 games in 1988 (12 G, 29 A, 41 PTS with Edmonton), 2 games in 1989 (1 G, 2 A, 3 PTS with Los Angeles). Total points, 44.

FASTEST GOALS

FASTEST GOAL FROM START OF GAME:
6 Seconds — Don Kozak, Los Angeles, April 17, 1977, at Los Angeles vs. Boston and goaltender Gerry Cheevers. Los Angeles won 7-4.
7 Seconds — Bob Gainey, Montreal, May 5, 1977, at New York vs. NY Islanders and goaltender Glenn Resch. Montreal won 2-1.
   — Terry Murray, Philadelphia, April 12, 1981, at Quebec vs. goaltender Dan Bouchard. Quebec won 4-3 in overtime.
8 Seconds — Stan Smyl, Vancouver, April 7, 1982, at Vancouver vs. Calgary and goaltender Pat Riggin. Vancouver won 5-3.

FASTEST GOAL FROM START OF PERIOD (OTHER THAN FIRST):
6 Seconds — Pelle Eklund, Philadelphia, April 25, 1989, at Pittsburgh vs. goaltender Tom Barrasso, second period. Pittsburgh won 10-7.
9 Seconds — Bill Collins, Minnesota, April 9, 1968, at Minnesota vs. Los Angeles and goaltender Wayne Rutledge, third period. Minnesota won 7-5.
   — Dave Balon, Minnesota, April 25, 1968, at St. Louis vs. goaltender Glenn Hall, third period. Minnesota won 5-1.
   — Murray Oliver, Minnesota, April 8, 1971, at St. Louis vs. goaltender Ernie Wakely, third period. St. Louis won 4-2.
   — Clark Gillies, NY Islanders, April 15, 1977, at Buffalo vs. goaltender Don Edwards, third period. NY Islanders won 4-3.
   — Eric Vail, Atlanta, April 11, 1978, at Atlanta vs. Detroit and goaltender Ron Low, third period. Detroit won 5-3.
   — Stan Smyl, Vancouver, April 10, 1979, at Philadelphia vs. goaltender Wayne Stephenson, third period. Vancouver won 3-2.
   — Wayne Gretzky, Edmonton, April 6, 1983, at Edmonton vs. Winnipeg and goaltender Brian Hayward, second period. Edmonton won 6-3.
   — Mark Messier, Edmonton, April 16, 1984, at Calgary vs. goaltender Don Edwards, third period. Edmonton won 5-3.
   — Brian Skrudland, Montreal, May 18, 1986 at Calgary vs. goaltender Mike Vernon, overtime. Montreal won 3-2.

FASTEST TWO GOALS:
5 Seconds — Norm Ullman, Detroit, at Detroit, April 11, 1965, vs. Chicago and goaltender Glenn Hall. Ullman scored at 17:35 and 17:40 of second period. Detroit won 4-2.

FASTEST TWO GOALS FROM START OF A GAME:
1 Minute, 8 Seconds — Dick Duff, Toronto, April 9, 1963 at Toronto vs. Detroit and goaltender Terry Sawchuk. Duff scored at 49 seconds and 1:08. Final score: Toronto 4, Detroit 2.

FASTEST TWO GOALS FROM START OF A PERIOD:
35 Seconds — Pat LaFontaine, NY Islanders, May 19, 1984 at Edmonton vs. goaltender Andy Moog. LaFontaine scored at 13 and 35 seconds of third period. Final score: Edmonton 5, NY Islanders 2.

PENALTIES

MOST PENALTY MINUTES IN PLAYOFFS (CAREER):
729 — Dale Hunter, Quebec, Washington, Colorado
541 — Chris Nilan, Montreal, NY Rangers, Boston
517 — Claude Lemieux, Montreal, New Jersey, Colorado
466 — Willi Plett, Atlanta, Calgary, Minnesota, Boston
465 — Rick Tocchet, Philadelphia, Pittsburgh, Boston, Phoenix

MOST PENALTIES, ONE GAME:
8 — Forbes Kennedy, Toronto, April 2, 1969, at Boston. Four minors, 2 majors, 1 10-minute misconduct, 1 game misconduct. Final score: Boston 10, Toronto 0.
— Kim Clackson, Pittsburgh, April 14, 1980, at Boston. Five minors, 2 majors, 1 10-minute misconduct. Final score: Boston 6, Pittsburgh 2

MOST PENALTY MINUTES, ONE GAME:
42 — Dave Schultz, Philadelphia, April 22, 1976, at Toronto. One minor, 2 majors, 1 10-minute misconduct and 2 game-misconducts. Final score: Toronto 8, Philadelphia 5.

MOST PENALTIES, ONE PERIOD AND MOST PENALTY MINUTES, ONE PERIOD:
6 Penalties; 39 Minutes — Ed Hospodar, NY Rangers, April 9, 1981, at Los Angeles, first period. Two minors, 1 major, 1 10-minute misconduct, 2 game misconducts. Final score: Los Angeles 5, NY Rangers 4.

GOALTENDING

MOST PLAYOFF GAMES APPEARED IN BY A GOALTENDER (CAREER):
196 — Patrick Roy, Montreal, Colorado
150 — Grant Fuhr, Edmonton, Toronto, Buffalo, Los Angeles, St. Louis
138 — Mike Vernon, Calgary, Detroit, San Jose, Florida
132 — Billy Smith, Los Angeles, NY Islanders
— Andy Moog, Edmonton, Boston, Dallas, Montreal

MOST MINUTES PLAYED BY A GOALTENDER (CAREER):
12,094 — Patrick Roy, Montreal, Colorado
8,834 — Grant Fuhr, Edmonton, Toronto, Buffalo, Los Angeles, St. Louis
8,214 — Mike Vernon, Calgary, Detroit, San Jose, Florida
7,645 — Billy Smith, Los Angeles, NY Islanders
7,452 — Andy Moog, Edmonton, Boston, Dallas, Montreal

MOST MINUTES PLAYED BY A GOALTENDER, ONE PLAYOFF YEAR:
1,544 — Kirk McLean, Vancouver, 1994. 24 games.
— Ed Belfour, Dallas, 1999. 23 games.
1,540 — Ron Hextall, Philadelphia, 1987. 26 games.
1,477 — Mike Richter, NY Rangers, 1994. 23 games.
1,454 — Patrick Roy, Colorado, 1996. 22 games.

MOST SHUTOUTS IN PLAYOFFS (CAREER):
15 — Clint Benedict, Ottawa, Mtl. Maroons
— Patrick Roy, Montreal, Colorado
14 — Jacques Plante, Montreal, St. Louis
13 — Turk Broda, Toronto
12 — Terry Sawchuk, Detroit, Los Angeles

MOST SHUTOUTS, ONE PLAYOFF YEAR:
4 — Clint Benedict, Mtl. Maroons, 1926. 8 games.
— Clint Benedict, Mtl. Maroons, 1928. 9 games.
— Dave Kerr, NY Rangers, 1937. 9 games.
— Frank McCool, Toronto, 1945. 13 games.
— Terry Sawchuk, Detroit, 1952. 8 games.
— Bernie Parent, Philadelphia, 1975. 17 games.
— Ken Dryden, Montreal, 1977. 14 games.
— Mike Richter, NY Rangers, 1994. 23 games.
— Kirk McLean, Vancouver, 1994. 24 games.
— Olaf Kolzig, Washington, 1998. 21 games.
— Ed Belfour, Dallas, 2000. 23 games.

MOST SHUTOUTS, ONE PLAYOFF SERIES:
3 — Clint Benedict, Mtl. Maroons, in 1926 F, 4 games vs. Victoria.
— Dave Kerr, NY Rangers, in 1940 SF, 6 games vs. Boston.
— Frank McCool, Toronto, in 1945 F, 7 games vs. Detroit.
— Turk Broda, Toronto, in 1950 SF, 7 games vs. Detroit.
— Felix Potvin, Toronto, in 1994 CQF, 6 games vs. Chicago.
— Martin Brodeur, New Jersey, in 1995 CQF, 5 games vs. Boston.

MOST WINS BY A GOALTENDER, (CAREER):
121 — Patrick Roy, Montreal, Colorado
92 — Grant Fuhr, Edmonton, Buffalo, St. Louis
88 — Billy Smith, Los Angeles, NY Islanders
80 — Ken Dryden, Montreal
77 — Mike Vernon, Calgary, Detroit, San Jose, Florida

MOST WINS BY A GOALTENDER, ONE PLAYOFF YEAR:
16 — Grant Fuhr, Edmonton, 1988. 19 games.
— Mike Vernon, Calgary, 1989. 22 games.
— Bill Ranford, Edmonton, 1990. 22 games.
— Tom Barrasso, Pittsburgh, 1992. 21 games.
— Patrick Roy, Montreal, 1993. 20 games.
— Mike Richter, NY Rangers, 1994. 23 games.
— Martin Brodeur, New Jersey, 1995. 20 games.
— Patrick Roy, Colorado, 1996. 22 games.
— Mike Vernon, Detroit, 1997. 20 games.
— Chris Osgood, Detroit, 1998. 22 games.
— Ed Belfour, Dallas, 1999. 23 games.
— Martin Brodeur, New Jersey, 2000. 23 games.

MOST CONSECUTIVE WINS BY A GOALTENDER, MORE THAN ONE PLAYOFF YEAR:
14 — Tom Barrasso, Pittsburgh, 1992, 1993; 3 wins against NY Rangers in 1992 DF, won by Pittsburgh 4-2; 4 wins against Boston in 1992 CF, won by Pittsburgh 4-0; 4 wins against Chicago in 1992 F, won by Pittsburgh 4-0; 3 wins against New Jersey in 1993 DSF, won by Pittsburgh 4-1.

MOST CONSECUTIVE WINS BY A GOALTENDER, ONE PLAYOFF YEAR:
11 — Ed Belfour, Chicago, 1992. 3 wins against St. Louis in DSF, won by Chicago 4-2; 4 wins against Detroit in DF, won by Chicago 4-0; and 4 wins against Edmonton in CF, won by Chicago 4-0.
— Tom Barrasso, Pittsburgh, 1992. 3 wins against NY Rangers in DF, won by Pittsburgh 4-2; 4 wins against Boston in CF, won by Pittsburgh 4-0; and 4 wins against Chicago in F, won by Pittsburgh 4-0.
— Patrick Roy, Montreal, 1993. 4 wins against Quebec in DSF, won by Montreal 4-2; 4 wins against Buffalo in DF, won by Montreal 4-0; and 3 wins against NY Islanders in CF, won by Montreal 4-1.

LONGEST SHUTOUT SEQUENCE:
248 Minutes, 32 Seconds — Normie Smith, Detroit, 1936. In best-of-five SF, Smith shut out Mtl. Maroons 1-0, March 24, in 116:30 overtime; shut out Maroons 3-0 in second game, March 26; and was scored against at 12:02 of first period, March 29, by Gus Marker. Detroit won SF 3-0.

MOST CONSECUTIVE SHUTOUTS:
3 — Clint Benedict, Mtl. Maroons, 1926. Benedict shut out Ottawa 1-0, Mar. 27; he then shut out Victoria twice, 3-0, Mar. 30; 3-0, Apr. 1. Mtl. Maroons won NHL F vs. Ottawa 2 goals to 1 and won the best-of-five F vs. Victoria 3-1.
— John Roach, NY Rangers, 1929. Roach shut out NY Americans twice, 0-0, Mar. 19; 1-0, Mar. 21; he then shut out Toronto 1-0, Mar. 24. NY Rangers won QF vs. NY Americans 1 goal to 0 and won the best-of-three SF vs. Toronto 2-0.
— Frank McCool, Toronto, 1945. McCool shut out Detroit 1-0, April 6; 2-0, April 8; 1-0, April 12. Toronto won the best-of-seven F 4-3.

Early Playoff Records

1893-1918
Team Records

MOST GOALS, BOTH TEAMS, ONE GAME:
25 — Ottawa Silver Seven, Dawson City at Ottawa, Jan. 16, 1905. Ottawa 23, Dawson City 2. Ottawa won best-of-three series 2-0.

MOST GOALS, ONE TEAM, ONE GAME:
23 — Ottawa Silver Seven at Ottawa, Jan. 16, 1905. Ottawa defeated Dawson City 23-2.

MOST GOALS, BOTH TEAMS, BEST-OF-THREE SERIES:
42 — Ottawa Silver Seven, Queen's University at Ottawa, 1906. Ottawa defeated Queen's 16-7, Feb. 27, and 12-7, Feb. 28.

MOST GOALS, ONE TEAM, BEST-OF-THREE SERIES:
32 — Ottawa Silver Seven in 1905 at Ottawa. Defeated Dawson City 9-2, Jan. 13, and 23-2, Jan. 16.

MOST GOALS, BOTH TEAMS, BEST-OF-FIVE SERIES:
39 — Toronto Arenas, Vancouver Millionaires at Toronto, 1918. Toronto won 5-3, Mar. 20; 6-3, Mar. 26; 2-1, Mar. 30. Vancouver won 6-4, Mar. 23, and 8-1, Mar. 28. Toronto scored 18 goals; Vancouver 21.

MOST GOALS, ONE TEAM, BEST-OF-FIVE SERIES:
26 — Vancouver Millionaires in 1915 at Vancouver. Defeated Ottawa Senators 6-2, Mar. 22; 8-3, Mar. 24; and 12-3 Mar. 26.

Individual Records

MOST GOALS IN PLAYOFFS:
63 — Frank McGee, Ottawa Silver Seven, in 22 playoff games. Seven goals in four games, 1903; 21 goals in eight games, 1904; 18 goals in four games, 1905; 17 goals in six games, 1906.

MOST GOALS, ONE PLAYOFF SERIES:
15 — Frank McGee, Ottawa Silver Seven, in two games in 1905 at Ottawa. Scored one goal, Jan. 13, in 9-2 victory over Dawson City and 14 goals, Jan. 16, in 23-2 victory.

MOST GOALS, ONE PLAYOFF GAME:
14 — Frank McGee, Ottawa Silver Seven, Jan. 16, 1905 at Ottawa in 23-2 victory over Dawson City.

FASTEST THREE GOALS:
40 Seconds — Marty Walsh, Ottawa Senators, at Ottawa, March 16, 1911, at 3:00, 3:10, and 3:40 of third period. Ottawa defeated Port Arthur 13-4.

All-Time Playoff Goal Leaders since 1918
(40 or more goals)

Player	Teams	Yrs.	GP	G
Wayne Gretzky	Edm., L.A., St.L., NYR	16	208	122
* Mark Messier	Edm., NYR, Van.	17	236	109
Jari Kurri	Edm., L.A., NYR, Ana., Col.	15	200	106
Glenn Anderson	Edm., Tor., NYR, St.L.	15	225	93
* Brett Hull	Cgy., St.L., Dal.	15	153	88
Mike Bossy	NYI	10	129	85
Maurice Richard	Mtl.	15	133	82
* Claude Lemieux	Mtl., N.J., Col.	15	221	80
Jean Beliveau	Mtl.	17	162	79
Dino Ciccarelli	Min., Wsh., Det., T.B., Fla.	14	141	73
* Esa Tikkanen	Edm., NYR, St.L., N.J., Van., Fla., Wsh.	13	186	72
Bryan Trottier	NYI, Pit.	17	221	71
Mario Lemieux	Pit.	7	89	70
Gordie Howe	Det., Hfd.	20	157	68
Denis Savard	Chi., Mtl., T.B.	16	169	66
Yvan Cournoyer	Mtl.	12	147	64
Brian Propp	Phi., Bos., Min., Hfd.	13	160	64
Bobby Smith	Min., Mtl.	13	184	64
* Jaromir Jagr	Pit.	10	124	63
Bobby Hull	Chi., Wpg., Hfd.	14	119	62
Phil Esposito	Chi., Bos., NYR	15	130	61
Jacques Lemaire	Mtl.	11	145	61
* Steve Yzerman	Det.	15	153	61
Joe Mullen	St.L., Cgy., Pit., Bos.	15	143	60
Stan Mikita	Chi.	18	155	59
* Paul Coffey	Edm., Pit., L.A., Det., Hfd., Phi., Chi., Car.	16	194	59
Guy Lafleur	Mtl., NYR, Que.	14	128	58
Bernie Geoffrion	Mtl., NYR	16	132	58
Cam Neely	Van., Bos.	9	93	57
Steve Larmer	Chi., NYR	13	140	56
Denis Potvin	NYI	14	185	56
Rick MacLeish	Phi., Hfd., Pit., Det.	11	114	54
* Doug Gilmour	St.L., Cgy., Tor., N.J., Chi., Buf.	15	157	54
* Joe Nieuwendyk	Cgy., Dal.	12	120	53
Bill Barber	Phi.	11	129	53
* Stephane Richer	Mtl., N.J., T.B., St.L.	12	131	53
* Rick Tocchet	Phi., Pit., L.A., Bos., Wsh., Phx.	12	139	52
Frank Mahovlich	Tor., Det., Mtl.	14	137	51
Brian Bellows	Min., Mtl., T.B., Ana., Wsh.	13	143	51
Steve Shutt	Mtl., L.A.	12	99	50
* Luc Robitaille	L.A., Pit., NYR	12	119	49
Henri Richard	Mtl.	18	180	49
Reggie Leach	Bos., Cal., Phi., Det.	8	94	47
Ted Lindsay	Det., Chi.	16	133	47
Clark Gillies	NYI, Buf.	13	164	47
Dickie Moore	Mtl., Tor., St.L.	14	135	46
Rick Middleton	NYR, Bos.	12	114	45
* Jeremy Roenick	Chi., Phx.	12	100	44
Lanny McDonald	Tor., Col., Cgy.	13	117	44
* Kevin Stevens	Pit., Bos., L.A., NYR	6	86	43
* Joe Sakic	Que., Col.	7	93	43
Ken Linseman	Phi., Edm., Bos., Tor.	11	113	43
Mike Gartner	Wsh., Min., NYR, Tor., Phx.	15	122	43
* Steve Thomas	Tor., Chi., NYI, N.J.	12	131	43
* Mike Modano	Min., Dal.	9	118	42
Bernie Nicholls	L.A., NYR, Edm., N.J., Chi., S.J.	13	118	42
* Sergei Fedorov	Det.	10	129	42
Bobby Clarke	Phi.	13	136	42
Dale Hunter	Que., Wsh., Col.	18	186	42
John Bucyk	Det., Bos.	14	124	41
Tim Kerr	Phi., NYR, Hfd.	10	81	40
Peter McNab	Buf., Bos., Van., N.J.	10	107	40
* Brendan Shanahan	N.J., St.L., Hfd., Det.	11	110	40
* Ron Francis	Hfd., Pit., Car.	14	133	40
Bob Bourne	NYI, L.A.	13	139	40
John Tonelli	NYI, Cgy., L.A., Chi., Que.	13	172	40

All-Time Playoff Assist Leaders since 1918
(60 or more assists)

Player	Teams	Yrs.	GP	A
Wayne Gretzky	Edm., L.A., St.L., NYR	16	208	260
* Mark Messier	Edm., NYR, Van.	17	236	186
* Paul Coffey	Edm., Pit., L.A., Det., Hfd., Phi., Chi., Car.	16	194	137
* Ray Bourque	Bos., Col.	20	193	133
Jari Kurri	Edm., L.A., NYR, Ana., Col.	15	200	127
Glenn Anderson	Edm., Tor., NYR, St.L.	15	225	121
* Doug Gilmour	St.L., Cgy., Tor., N.J., Chi., Buf.	15	157	118
Larry Robinson	Mtl., L.A.	20	227	116
* Larry Murphy	L.A., Wsh., Min., Pit., Tor., Det.	19	209	114
Bryan Trottier	NYI, Pit.	17	221	113
Denis Savard	Chi., Mtl., T.B.	16	169	109
Denis Potvin	NYI	14	185	108
* Al MacInnis	Cgy., St.L.	16	149	105
* Adam Oates	Det., St.L., Bos., Wsh.	12	131	103
Jean Beliveau	Mtl.	17	162	97
Bobby Smith	Min., Mtl.	13	184	96
* Chris Chelios	Mtl., Chi., Det.	16	182	93
* Sergei Fedorov	Det.	10	129	92
Gordie Howe	Det., Hfd.	20	157	92
* Steve Yzerman	Det.	15	153	91
Stan Mikita	Chi.	18	155	91
Brad Park	NYR, Bos., Det.	17	161	90
Craig Janney	Bos., St.L., S.J., Wpg., Phx., T.B., NYI	11	120	86
Mario Lemieux	Pit.	7	89	85
Brian Propp	Phi., Bos., Min., Hfd.	13	160	84
* Ron Francis	Hfd., Pit., Car.	14	133	83
Henri Richard	Mtl.	18	180	80
* Scott Stevens	Wsh., St.L., N.J.	17	178	79
Jacques Lemaire	Mtl.	11	145	78
Ken Linseman	Phi., Edm., Bos., Tor.	11	113	77
Bobby Clarke	Phi.	13	136	77
* Claude Lemieux	Mtl., N.J., Col.	15	221	77
Guy Lafleur	Mtl., NYR, Que.	14	128	76
Phil Esposito	Chi., Bos., NYR	15	130	76
Dale Hunter	Que., Wsh., Col.	18	186	76
Mike Bossy	NYI	10	129	75
Steve Larmer	Chi., NYR	13	140	75
John Tonelli	NYI, Cgy., L.A., Chi., Que.	13	172	75
Peter Stastny	Que., N.J., St.L.	12	93	72
Bernie Nicholls	L.A., NYR, Edm., N.J., Chi., S.J.	13	118	72
* Jaromir Jagr	Pit.	10	124	72
Brian Bellows	Min., Mtl., T.B., Ana., Wsh.	13	143	71
* Brett Hull	Cgy., St.L., Dal.	15	153	71
Gilbert Perreault	Buf.	11	90	70
* Geoff Courtnall	Bos., Edm., Wsh., St.L., Van.	15	156	70
Dale Hawerchuk	Wpg., Buf., St.L., Phi.	15	97	69
Alex Delvecchio	Det.	14	121	69
Bobby Hull	Chi., Wpg., Hfd.	14	119	67
Frank Mahovlich	Tor., Det., Mtl.	14	137	67
Bobby Orr	Bos., Chi.	8	74	66
Bernie Federko	St.L., Det.	11	91	66
Jean Ratelle	NYR, Bos.	15	123	66
Charlie Huddy	Edm., L.A., Buf., St.L.	14	183	66
Dickie Moore	Mtl., Tor., St.L.	14	135	64
Doug Harvey	Mtl., NYR, Det., St.L.	15	137	64
* Sergei Zubov	NYR, Pit., Dal.	7	115	63
Neal Broten	Min., Dal., N.J., L.A.	13	135	63
Yvan Cournoyer	Mtl.	12	147	63
John Bucyk	Det., Bos.	14	124	62
* Brian Leetch	NYR	7	82	61
Doug Wilson	Chi., S.J.	12	95	61
* Luc Robitaille	L.A., Pit., NYR	12	119	61
* Joe Sakic	Que., Col.	7	93	60
* Mike Modano	Min., Dal.	9	118	60
Bernie Geoffrion	Mtl., NYR	16	132	60
* Esa Tikkanen	Edm., NYR, St.L., N.J., Van., Fla., Wsh.	13	186	60

All-Time Playoff Point Leaders since 1918
(100 or more points)

Player	Teams	Yrs.	GP	G	A	Pts.
Wayne Gretzky	Edm., L.A., St.L., NYR	16	208	122	260	382
* Mark Messier	Edm., NYR, Van.	17	236	109	186	295
Jari Kurri	Edm., L.A., NYR, Ana., Col.	15	200	106	127	233
Glenn Anderson	Edm., Tor., NYR, St.L.	15	225	93	121	214
* Paul Coffey	Edm., Pit., L.A., Det., Hfd., Phi., Chi., Car.	16	194	59	137	196
Bryan Trottier	NYI, Pit.	17	221	71	113	184
Jean Beliveau	Mtl.	17	162	79	97	176
Denis Savard	Chi., Mtl., T.B.	16	169	66	109	175
* Doug Gilmour	St.L., Cgy., Tor., N.J., Chi., Buf.	15	157	54	118	172
* Ray Bourque	Bos., Col.	20	193	37	133	170
Denis Potvin	NYI	14	185	56	108	164
Mike Bossy	NYI	10	129	85	75	160
Gordie Howe	Det., Hfd.	20	157	68	92	160
Bobby Smith	Min., Mtl.	13	184	64	96	160
* Brett Hull	Cgy., St.L., Dal.	15	153	88	71	159
* Claude Lemieux	Mtl., N.J., Col.	15	221	80	77	157
Mario Lemieux	Pit.	7	89	70	85	155
* Steve Yzerman	Det.	15	153	61	91	152
* Larry Murphy	L.A., Wsh., Min., Pit., Tor., Det.	19	209	37	114	151
Stan Mikita	Chi.	18	155	59	91	150
Brian Propp	Phi., Bos., Min., Hfd.	13	160	64	84	148
Larry Robinson	Mtl., L.A.	20	227	28	116	144
* Al MacInnis	Cgy., St.L.	16	149	37	105	142
* Adam Oates	Det., St.L., Bos., Wsh.	12	131	38	103	141
Jacques Lemaire	Mtl.	11	145	61	78	139
Phil Esposito	Chi., Bos., NYR	15	130	61	76	137
* Jaromir Jagr	Pit.	10	124	63	72	135
Guy Lafleur	Mtl., NYR, Que.	14	128	58	76	134
* Sergei Fedorov	Det.	10	129	42	92	134
* Esa Tikkanen	Edm., NYR, St.L., N.J., Van., Fla., Wsh.	13	186	72	60	132
Steve Larmer	Chi., NYR	13	140	56	75	131
Bobby Hull	Chi., Wpg., Hfd.	14	119	62	67	129
Henri Richard	Mtl.	18	180	49	80	129
Yvan Cournoyer	Mtl.	12	147	64	63	127
Maurice Richard	Mtl.	15	133	82	44	126
Brad Park	NYR, Bos., Det.	17	161	35	90	125
* Ron Francis	Hfd., Pit., Car.	14	133	40	83	123
Brian Bellows	Min., Mtl., T.B., Ana., Wsh.	13	143	51	71	122
* Chris Chelios	Mtl., Chi., Det.	16	182	28	93	121
Ken Linseman	Phi., Edm., Bos., Tor.	11	113	43	77	120
Bobby Clarke	Phi.	13	136	42	77	119
Bernie Geoffrion	Mtl., NYR	16	132	58	60	118
Frank Mahovlich	Tor., Det., Mtl.	14	137	51	67	118
Dino Ciccarelli	Min., Wsh., Det., T.B., Fla.	14	141	73	45	118
Dale Hunter	Que., Wsh., Col.	18	186	42	76	118
John Tonelli	NYI, Cgy., L.A., Chi., Que.	13	172	40	75	115
Bernie Nicholls	L.A., NYR, Edm., N.J., Chi., S.J.	13	118	42	72	114
* Rick Tocchet	Phi., Pit., L.A., Bos., Wsh., Phx.	12	139	52	59	111
* Luc Robitaille	L.A., Pit., NYR	12	119	49	61	110
Craig Janney	Bos., St.L., S.J., Wpg., Phx., T.B., NYI	11	120	24	86	110
Dickie Moore	Mtl., Tor., St.L.	14	135	46	64	110
* Geoff Courtnall	Bos., Edm., Wsh., St.L., Van.	15	156	39	70	109
Bill Barber	Phi.	11	129	53	55	108
Rick MacLeish	Phi., Hfd., Pit., Det.	11	114	54	53	107
Joe Mullen	St.L., Cgy., Pit., Bos.	15	143	60	46	106
Peter Stastny	Que., N.J., St.L.	12	93	33	72	105
Alex Delvecchio	Det.	14	121	35	69	104
Gilbert Perreault	Buf.	11	90	33	70	103
* Joe Sakic	Que., Col.	7	93	43	60	103
John Bucyk	Det., Bos.	14	124	41	62	103
* Mike Modano	Min., Dal.	9	118	42	60	102
Bernie Federko	St.L., Det.	11	91	35	66	101
* Scott Stevens	Wsh., St.L., N.J.	17	178	22	79	101
* Kevin Stevens	Pit., Bos., L.A., NYR	6	86	43	57	100
Rick Middleton	NYR, Bos.	12	114	45	55	100

* Active

Three-or-more-Goal Games, Playoffs 1918–2000

Player	Team	Date	City	Total Goals	Opposing Goaltender	Score	
Wayne Gretzky (10)	Edm.	Apr. 11/81	Edm.	3	Richard Sevigny	Edm. 6	Mtl. 2
		Apr. 19/81	Edm.	3	Billy Smith	Edm. 5	NYI 2
		Apr. 6/83	Edm.	4	Brian Hayward	Edm. 6	Wpg. 3
		Apr. 17/83	Cgy.	4	Rejean Lemelin	Edm. 10	Cgy. 2
		Apr. 25/85	Wpg.	3	Bryan Hayward (2)		
					Marc Behrend (1)	Edm. 8	Wpg. 3
		May 25/85	Edm.	3	Pelle Lindbergh	Edm. 4	Phi. 3
		Apr. 24/86	Cgy.	3	Mike Vernon	Edm. 7	Cgy. 4
	L.A.	May 29/93	Tor.	3	Felix Potvin	L.A. 5	Tor. 4
	NYR	Apr. 23/97	NYR	3	John Vanbiesbrouck	NYR 3	Fla. 2
		May 18/97	Phi.	3	Garth Snow	NYR 5	Phi. 4
Maurice Richard (7)	Mtl.	Mar. 23/44	Mtl.	5	Paul Bibeault	Mtl. 5	Tor. 1
		Apr. 7/44	Chi.	3	Mike Karakas	Mtl. 3	Chi. 1
		Mar. 29/45	Mtl.	4	Frank McCool	Mtl. 10	Tor. 3
		Apr. 14/53	Bos.	3	Gord Henry	Mtl. 7	Bos. 3
		Mar. 20/56	Mtl.	3	Gump Worsley	Mtl. 7	NYR 1
		Apr. 6/57	Mtl.	4	Don Simmons	Mtl. 5	Bos. 1
		Apr. 1/58	Det.	3	Terry Sawchuk	Mtl. 4	Det. 3
Jari Kurri (7)	Edm.	Apr. 4/84	Edm.	3	Doug Soetaert (1)		
					Mike Veisor (2)	Edm. 9	Wpg. 2
		Apr. 25/85	Wpg.	3	Bryan Hayward (2)		
					Marc Behrend (1)	Edm. 8	Wpg. 3
		May 7/85	Edm.	3	Murray Bannerman	Edm. 7	Chi. 3
		May 14/85	Edm.	3	Murray Bannerman	Edm. 10	Chi. 5
		May 16/85	Chi.	4	Murray Bannerman	Edm. 8	Chi. 2
		Apr. 9/87	Edm.	4	Rollie Melanson (2)		
					Daren Eliot (2)	Edm. 13	L.A. 3
		May 18/90	Bos.	3	Andy Moog (2)		
					Rejean Lemelin (1)	Edm. 7	Bos. 2
Dino Ciccarelli (6)	Min.	May 5/81	Min.	3	Pat Riggin	Min. 7	Cgy. 4
		Apr. 10/82	Min.	3	Murray Bannerman	Min. 7	Chi. 1
	Wsh.	Apr. 5/90	N.J.	3	Sean Burke	Wsh. 5	N.J. 4
		Apr. 25/92	Pit.	4	Tom Barrasso (1)		
					Ken Wregget (3)	Wsh. 7	Pit. 2
	Det.	Apr. 29/93	Tor.	3	Felix Potvin (2)		
					Daren Puppa (1)	Det. 7	Tor. 3
		May 11/95	Dal.	3	Andy Moog (2)		
					Darcy Wakaluk (1)	Det. 5	Dal. 1
Mike Bossy (5)	NYI	Apr. 16/79	NYI	3	Tony Esposito	NYI 6	Chi. 2
		May 8/82	NYI	3	Richard Brodeur	NYI 6	Van. 5
		Apr. 10/83	Wsh.	3	Al Jensen	NYI 6	Wsh. 3
		May 3/83	NYI	3	Pete Peeters	NYI 8	Bos. 3
		May 7/83	NYI	4	Pete Peeters	NYI 8	Bos. 4
Phil Esposito (4)	Bos.	Apr. 2/69	Bos.	4	Bruce Gamble	Bos. 10	Tor. 0
		Apr. 8/70	Bos.	3	Ed Giacomin	Bos. 8	NYR 2
		Apr. 19/70	Chi.	3	Tony Esposito	Bos. 6	Chi. 3
		Apr. 8/75	Bos.	3	Tony Esposito (2)		
					Michel Dumas (1)	Bos. 8	Chi. 2
Mark Messier (4)	Edm.	Apr. 14/83	Edm.	4	Rejean Lemelin	Edm. 6	Cgy. 3
		Apr. 17/83	Cgy.	3	Rejean Lemelin (1)	Edm. 10	Cgy. 2
					Don Edwards (2)		
		Apr. 26/83	Edm.	3	Murray Bannerman	Edm. 8	Chi. 2
	NYR	May 25/94	N.J.	3	Martin Brodeur (2)	NYR 4	N.J. 2
					ENG (1)		
Steve Yzerman (4)	Det.	Apr. 6/89	Det.	3	Alain Chevrier	Chi. 5	Det. 4
		Apr. 4/91	St. L.	3	Vincent Riendeau (2)	Det. 6	St. L. 3
		May 8/96	St. L.	3	Jon Casey	St.L. 5	Det. 4
		Apr. 21/99	Det.	3	Guy Hebert (2)	Det.. 5	Ana. 3
					Pat Jablonski (1)		
Bernie Geoffrion (3)	Mtl.	Mar. 27/52	Mtl.	3	Jim Henry	Mtl. 4	Bos. 0
		Apr. 7/55	Mtl.	3	Terry Sawchuk	Mtl. 4	Det. 2
		Mar. 30/57	Mtl.	3	Gump Worsley	Mtl. 8	NYR 3
Norm Ullman (3)	Det.	Mar. 29/64	Chi.	3	Glenn Hall	Det. 5	Chi. 4
		Apr. 7/64	Det.	3	Glenn Hall (2)		
					Denis DeJordy (1)	Det. 7	Chi. 2
		Apr. 11/65	Det.	3	Glenn Hall	Det. 4	Chi. 2
John Bucyk (3)	Bos.	May 3/70	St. L.	3	Jacques Plante (1)		
					Ernie Wakely (2)	Bos. 6	St. L. 1
		Apr. 20/72	Bos.	3	Jacques Caron (1)		
					Ernie Wakely (2)	Bos. 10	St. L. 2
		Apr. 21/74	Bos.	3	Tony Esposito	Bos. 8	Chi. 6
Rick MacLeish (3)	Phi.	Apr. 11/74	Phi.	3	Phil Myre	Phi. 5	Atl. 1
		Apr. 13/75	Phi.	3	Gord McRae	Phi. 6	Tor. 3
		May 13/75	Phi.	3	Glenn Resch	Phi. 4	NYI 1
Denis Savard (3)	Chi.	Apr. 19/82	Chi.	3	Mike Liut	Chi. 7	StL. 4
		Apr. 10/86	Chi.	4	Ken Wregget	Tor. 6	Chi. 4
		Apr. 9/88	St. L.	3	Greg Millen	Chi. 6	St. L. 3
Tim Kerr (3)	Phi.	Apr. 13/85	NYR	4	Glen Hanlon	Phi. 6	NYR 5
		Apr. 20/87	Phi.	3	Kelly Hrudey	Phi. 4	NYI 2
		Apr. 19/89	Pit.	3	Tom Barrasso	Phi. 4	Pit. 2
Cam Neely (3)	Bos.	Apr. 9/87	Mtl.	3	Patrick Roy	Mtl. 4	Bos. 3
		Apr. 5/91	Bos.	3	Peter Sidorkiewicz	Bos. 4	Hfd. 3
		Apr. 25/91	Bos.	3	Patrick Roy	Bos. 4	Mtl. 1
Petr Klima (3)	Det.	Apr. 7/88	Tor.	3	Alan Bester (2)		
					Ken Wregett (1)	Det. 6	Tor. 2
		Apr. 21/88	St. L.	3	Greg Millen	Det. 6	St. L. 0
	Edm.	May 4/91	Edm.	3	Jon Casey	Edm. 7	Min. 2
Esa Tikkanen (3)	Edm.	May 22/88	Edm.	3	Rejean Lemelin	Edm. 6	Bos. 3
		Apr. 16/91	Cgy.	3	Mike Vernon	Edm. 5	Cgy. 4
		Apr. 26/92	L.A.	3	Kelly Hrudey	Edm. 5	L.A. 2
					Tom Askey (1)		
Mario Lemieux (3)	Pit.	Apr. 25/89	Pit.	5	Ron Hextall	Pit. 10	Phi. 7
		Apr. 23/92	Pit.	3	Don Beaupre	Pit. 6	Wsh. 4
		May 11/96	Pit.	3	Mike Richter	Pit. 7	NYR 3

Player	Team	Date	City	Total Goals	Opposing Goaltender	Score	
Mike Gartner (3)	NYR	Apr. 13/90	NYR	3	Mark Fitzpatrick (2)		
					Glenn Healy (1)	NYR 6	NYI 5
		Apr. 27/92	NYR	3	Chris Terreri	NYR 8	N.J. 5
	Tor.	Apr. 25/96	Tor.	3	Jon Casey	Tor. 5	St.L. 4
Newsy Lalonde (2)	Mtl.	Mar. 1/19	Mtl.	5	Clint Benedict	Mtl. 6	Ott. 3
		Mar. 22/19	Sea.	4	Harry Holmes	Mtl. 4	Sea. 2
Howie Morenz (2)	Mtl.	Mar. 22/24	Mtl.	3	Charles Reid	Mtl. 6	Cgy.T. 1
		Mar. 27/25	Mtl.	3	Harry Holmes	Mtl. 4	Vic. 2
Toe Blake (2)	Mtl.	Mar. 22/38	Mtl.	3	Mike Karakas	Mtl. 6	Chi. 4
		Mar. 26/46	Chi.	3	Mike Karakas	Mtl. 7	Chi. 2
Doug Bentley (2)	Chi.	Mar. 28/44	Chi.	3	Connie Dion	Chi. 7	Det. 1
		Mar. 30/44	Det.	3	Connie Dion	Chi. 5	Det. 2
Ted Kennedy (2)	Tor.	Apr. 14/45	Tor.	3	Harry Lumley	Det. 5	Tor. 3
		Mar. 27/48	Tor.	4	Frank Brimsek	Tor. 5	Bos. 3
Bobby Hull (2)	Chi.	Apr. 7/63	Det.	3	Terry Sawchuk	Det. 7	Chi. 4
		Apr. 9/72	Pit.	3	Jim Rutherford	Chi. 6	Pit. 5
F. St. Marseille (2)	St. L.	Apr. 28/70	St. L.	3	Al Smith	St. L. 5	Pit. 0
		Apr. 6/72	Min.	3	Cesare Maniago	Min. 6	St. L. 5
Pit Martin (2)	Chi.	Apr. 4/73	Chi.	3	Wayne Stephenson	Chi. 7	St. L. 1
		May 10/73	Chi.	3	Ken Dryden	Mtl. 6	Chi. 4
Yvan Cournoyer (2)	Mtl.	Apr. 5/73	Mtl.	3	Dave Dryden	Mtl. 7	Buf. 3
		Apr. 11/74	Mtl.	3	Ed Giacomin	Mtl. 4	NYR 1
Guy Lafleur (2)	Mtl.	May 1/75	Mtl.	3	Roger Crozier (1)		
					Gerry Desjardins (2)	Mtl. 7	Buf. 0
		Apr. 11/77	Mtl.	3	Ed Staniowski	Mtl. 7	St. L. 2
Lanny McDonald (2)	Tor.	Apr. 9/77	Pit.	3	Denis Herron	Tor. 5	Pit. 2
		Apr. 17/77	Tor.	4	Wayne Stephenson	Phi. 6	Tor. 5
Butch Goring (2)	L.A.	Apr. 9/77	L.A.	3	Phil Myre	L.A. 4	Atl. 2
	NYI	May 17/81	Min.	3	Gilles Meloche	NYI 7	Min. 5
Bryan Trottier (2)	NYI	Apr. 8/80	NYI	3	Doug Keans	NYI 8	L.A. 1
		Apr. 9/81	NYI	3	Michel Larocque	NYI 5	Tor. 1
Bill Barber (2)	Phi.	May 4/80	Min.	4	Gilles Meloche	Phi. 5	Min. 3
		Apr. 9/81	Phi.	3	Dan Bouchard	Phi. 8	Que. 5
Brian Propp (2)	Phi.	Apr. 22/81	Phi.	3	Pat Riggin	Phi. 9	Cgy. 4
		Apr. 21/85	Phi.	3	Billy Smith	Phi. 5	NYI 2
Paul Reinhart (2)	Cgy	Apr. 14/83	Edm.	3	Andy Moog	Edm. 6	Cgy. 3
		Apr. 8/84	Van	3	Richard Brodeur	Cgy. 5	Van. 1
Peter Stastny (2)	Que.	Apr. 5/83	Bos.	3	Pete Peeters	Bos. 4	Que. 3
		Apr. 11/87	Que.	3	Mike Liut (2)		
					Steve Weeks (1)	Que. 5	Hfd. 1
Glenn Anderson (2)	Edm.	Apr. 26/83	Edm.	4	Murray Bannerman	Edm. 8	Chi. 2
		Apr. 6/88	Wpg.	3	Daniel Berthiaume	Edm. 7	Wpg. 4
Michel Goulet (2)	Que.	Apr. 23/85	Que.	3	Steve Penney	Que. 7	Mtl. 6
		Apr. 12/87	Que.	3	Mike Liut	Que. 4	Hfd. 1
Peter Zezel (2)	Phi.	Apr. 13/86	NYR	3	John Vanbiesbrouck	Phi. 7	NYR 1
	St. L.	Apr. 11/89	St. L.	3	Jon Casey (2)		
					Kari Takko (1)	St. L. 6	Min. 1
Geoff Courtnall (2)	Van.	Apr. 4/91	L.A.	3	Kelly Hrudey	Van. 6	L.A. 5
		Apr. 30/92	Van.	3	Rick Tabaracci	Van. 5	Win. 0
Joe Sakic (2)	Que.	May 6/95	Que.	3	Mike Richter	Que. 5	NYR 4
	Col.	Apr. 25/96	Col.	3	Corey Hirsch	Col. 5	Van. 4
Daniel Alfredsson (2)	Ott.	Apr. 28/98	Ott.	3	Martin Brodeur	Ott. 4	N.J. 3
		May 11/98	Ott.	3	Olaf Kolzig	Ott. 4	Wsh. 3
Harry Meeking	Tor.	Mar. 11/18	Tor.	3	Georges Vezina	Tor. 7	Mtl. 3
Alf Skinner	Tor.	Mar. 23/18	Tor.	3	Hugh Lehman	Van.M. 6	Tor. 4
Joe Malone	Mtl.	Feb. 23/19	Mtl.	3	Clint Benedict	Mtl. 8	Ott. 4
Odie Cleghorn	Mtl.	Feb. 27/19	Ott.	3	Clint Benedict	Mtl. 5	Ott. 3
Jack Darragh	Ott.	Apr. 1/20	Tor.	3	Harry Holmes	Ott. 6	Sea. 1
George Boucher	Ott.	Mar. 10/21	Ott.	3	Jake Forbes	Ott. 5	Tor. 0
Babe Dye	Tor.	Mar. 28/22	Tor.	4	Hugh Lehman	Tor. 5	Van.M. 1
Percy Galbraith	Bos.	Mar. 31/27	Bos.	3	Hugh Lehman	Bos. 4	Chi. 4
Harvey Jackson	Tor.	Apr. 5/32	NYR	3	John Ross Roach	Tor. 6	NYR 4
Frank Boucher	NYR	Apr. 9/32	Tor.	3	Lorne Chabot	Tor. 6	NYR 4
Charlie Conacher	Tor.	Mar. 26/36	Tor.	3	Tiny Thompson	Tor. 8	Bos. 3
Syd Howe	Det.	Mar. 23/39	Det.	3	Claude Bourque	Det. 7	Mtl. 3
Bryan Hextall Sr.	NYR	Apr. 3/40	NYR	3	Turk Broda	NYR 6	Tor. 2
Joe Benoit	Mtl.	Mar. 22/41	Mtl.	3	Sam LoPresti	Mtl. 4	Chi. 3
Syl Apps Sr.	Tor.	Mar. 25/41	Tor.	3	Frank Brimsek	Tor. 7	Bos. 2
Jack McGill	Bos.	Mar. 29/42	Bos.	3	Johnny Mowers	Det. 6	Bos. 4
Don Metz	Tor.	Apr. 14/42	Tor.	3	Johnny Mowers	Tor. 9	Det. 3
Mud Bruneteau	Det.	Apr. 1/43	Det.	3	Frank Brimsek	Det. 6	Bos. 2
Don Grosso	Det.	Apr. 7/43	Bos.	3	Frank Brimsek	Det. 4	Bos. 0
Carl Liscombe	Det.	Apr. 3/45	Bos.	4	Paul Bibeault	Det. 5	Bos. 3
Billy Reay	Mtl.	Apr. 1/47	Bos.	4	Frank Brimsek	Mtl. 5	Bos. 1
Gerry Plamondon	Mtl.	Mar. 24/49	Det.	3	Harry Lumley	Mtl. 4	Det. 3
Sid Smith	Tor.	Apr. 10/49	Det.	3	Harry Lumley	Tor. 3	Det. 1
Pentti Lund	NYR	Apr. 2/50	NYR	3	Bill Durnan	NYR 4	Mtl. 1
Ted Lindsay	Det.	Apr. 5/55	Det.	4	Charlie Hodge (1)		
					Jacques Plante (3)	Det. 7	Mtl. 1
Gordie Howe	Det.	Apr. 10/55	Det.	3	Jacques Plante	Det. 5	Mtl. 1
Phil Goyette	Mtl.	Mar. 25/58	Mtl.	3	Terry Sawchuk	Mtl. 8	Det. 1
Jerry Toppazzini	Bos.	Apr. 5/58	Bos.	3	Gump Worsley	Bos. 8	NYR 2
Bob Pulford	Tor.	Apr. 19/62	Tor.	3	Glenn Hall	Tor. 8	Chi. 4
Dave Keon	Tor.	Apr. 9/64	Mtl.	3	Charlie Hodge	Tor. 3	Mtl. 1
Henri Richard	Mtl.	Apr. 20/67	Mtl.	3	Terry Sawchuk (2)		
					Johnny Bower (1)	Mtl. 6	Tor. 2
Rosaire Paiement	Phi.	Apr. 13/68	Phi.	3	Glenn Hall (1)		
					Seth Martin (2)	Phi. 6	St. L. 1
Jean Beliveau	Mtl.	Apr. 20/68	Mtl.	3	Denis DeJordy	Mtl. 4	Chi. 1
Red Berenson	St. L.	Apr. 15/69	St. L.	3	Gerry Desjardins	St. L. 4	L.A. 0
Ken Schinkel	Pit.	Apr. 11/70	Oak.	3	Gary Smith	Pit. 5	Oak. 2
Jim Pappin	Chi.	Apr. 11/71	Phi.	3	Bruce Gamble	Chi. 6	Phi. 2
Bobby Orr	Bos.	Apr. 11/71	Mtl.	3	Ken Dryden	Bos. 5	Mtl. 2
Jacques Lemaire	Mtl.	Apr. 20/71	Mtl.	3	Gump Worsley	Mtl. 7	Min. 2
Vic Hadfield	NYR	Apr. 22/71	NYR	3	Tony Esposito	NYR 4	Chi. 1
Fred Stanfield	Bos.	Apr. 18/72	Bos.	3	Jacques Caron	Bos. 6	St. L. 1

Player	Team	Date	City	Total Goals	Opposing Goaltender	Score	
Ken Hodge	Bos.	Apr. 30/72	Bos.	3	Eddie Giacomin	Bos. 6	NYR 5
Steve Vickers	NYR	Apr. 10/73	Bos.	3	Ross Brooks (2)		
					Eddie Johnston (1)	NYR 6	Bos. 3
Dick Redmond	Chi.	Apr. 4/73	Chi.	3	Wayne Stephenson	Chi. 7	St. L. 1
Tom Williams	L.A.	Apr. 14/74	L.A.	3	Mike Veisor	L.A. 5	Chi. 1
Marcel Dionne	L.A.	Apr. 15/76	L.A.	3	Gilles Gilbert	L.A. 6	Bos. 4
Don Saleski	Phi.	Apr. 20/76	Phi.	3	Wayne Thomas	Phi. 7	Tor. 1
Darryl Sittler	Tor.	Apr. 22/76	Tor.	5	Bernie Parent	Tor. 8	Phi. 5
Reggie Leach	Phi.	May 6/76	Phi.	5	Gilles Gilbert	Phi. 6	Bos. 3
Jim Lorentz	Buf.	Apr. 7/77	Min.	3	Pete LoPresti (2)		
					Gary Smith (1)	Buf. 7	Min. 1
Bobby Schmautz	Bos.	Apr. 11/77	Bos.	3	Rogie Vachon	Bos. 8	L.A. 3
Billy Harris	NYI	Apr. 23/77	Mtl.	3	Ken Dryden	Mtl. 4	NYI 3
George Ferguson	Tor.	Apr. 11/78	Tor.	3	Rogie Vachon	Tor. 7	L.A. 3
Jean Ratelle	Bos.	May 3/79	Bos.	3	Ken Dryden	Bos. 4	Mtl. 3
Stan Jonathan	Bos.	May 8/79	Bos.	3	Ken Dryden	Bos. 5	Mtl. 2
Ron Duguay	NYR	Apr. 20/80	NYR	3	Pete Peeters	NYR 4	Phi. 2
Steve Shutt	Mtl.	Apr. 22/80	Mtl.	3	Gilles Meloche	Mtl. 6	Min. 2
Gilbert Perreault	Buf.	May 6/80	NYI	3	Billy Smith (2)		
					ENG (1)	Buf. 7	NYI 4
Paul Holmgren	Phi.	May 15/80	Phil	3	Billy Smith	Phi. 8	NYI 3
Steve Payne	Min.	Apr. 8/81	Bos.	3	Rogie Vachon	Min. 5	Bos. 4
Denis Potvin	NYI	Apr. 17/81	NYI	3	Andy Moog	NYI 6	Edm. 3
Barry Pederson	Bos.	Apr. 8/82	Bos.	3	Don Edwards	Bos. 7	Buf. 3
Duane Sutter	NYI	Apr. 15/83	NYI	3	Glen Hanlon	NYI 5	NYR 0
Doug Halward	Van.	Apr. 7/84	Van.	3	Rejean Lemelin (2)		
					Don Edwards (1)	Van. 7	Cgy. 0
Jorgen Pettersson	St. L.	Apr. 8/84	Det.	3	Eddie Mio	St. L. 3	Det. 2
Clark Gillies	NYI	May 12/84	NYI	3	Grant Fuhr	NYI 6	Edm. 1
Ken Linseman	Bos.	Apr. 14/85	Bos.	3	Steve Penney	Bos. 7	Mtl. 6
Dave Andreychuk	Buf.	Apr. 14/85	Buf.	3	Dan Bouchard	Buf. 7	Que. 4
Greg Paslawski	St. L.	Apr. 15/86	Min.	3	Don Beaupre	St. L. 6	Min. 3
Doug Risebrough	Cgy.	May 4/86	Cgy.	3	Rick Wamsley	Cgy. 8	St. L. 2
Mike McPhee	Mtl.	Apr. 11/87	Bos.	3	Doug Keans	Mtl. 5	Bos. 4
John Ogrodnick	Que.	Apr. 14/87	Hfd.	3	Mike Liut	Que. 7	Hfd. 5
Pelle Eklund	Phi.	May 10/87	Mtl.	3	Patrick Roy (1)		
					Bryan Hayward (2)	Phi. 6	Mtl. 3
John Tucker	Buf.	Apr. 9/88	Bos.	4	Andy Moog	Buf. 6	Bos. 2
Tony Hrkac	St. L.	Apr. 10/88	St. L.	4	Darren Pang	St. L. 6	Chi. 5
Hakan Loob	Cgy.	Apr. 10/88	Cgy.	3	Glenn Healy	Cgy. 7	L.A. 3
Ed Olczyk	Tor.	Apr. 12/88	Tor.	3	Greg Stefan (2)		
					Glen Hanlon (1)	Tor. 6	Det. 5
Aaron Broten	N.J.	Apr. 20/88	N.J.	3	Pete Peeters	N.J. 5	Wsh. 2
Mark Johnson	N.J.	Apr. 22/88	Wsh.	4	Pete Peeters	N.J. 10	Wsh. 4
Patrik Sundstrom	N.J.	Apr. 22/88	Wsh.	3	Pete Peeters (2)		
					Clint Malarchuk (1)	N.J. 10	Wsh. 4
Bob Brooke	Min.	Apr. 5/89	St. L.	3	Greg Millen	St. L. 4	Min. 3
Chris Kontos	L.A.	Apr. 6/89	L.A.	3	Grant Fuhr	L.A. 5	Edm. 2
Wayne Presley	Chi.	Apr. 13/89	Chi.	3	Greg Stefan (1)		
					Glen Hanlon (2)	Chi. 7	Det. 1
Tony Granato	L.A.	Apr. 10/90	L.A.	3	Mike Vernon (1)		
					Rick Wamsley (2)	L.A. 12	Cgy. 4
Tomas Sandstrom	L.A.	Apr. 10/90	L.A.	3	Mike Vernon (1)		
					Rick Wamsley (2)	L.A. 12	Cgy. 4
Dave Taylor	L.A.	Apr. 10/90	L.A.	3	Mike Vernon (1)		
					Rick Wamsley (2)	L.A. 12	Cgy. 4
Bernie Nicholls	NYR	Apr. 19/90	NYR	3	Mike Liut	NYR 7	Wsh. 3
John Druce	Wsh.	Apr. 21/90	NYR	3	John Vanbiesbrouck	Wsh. 6	NYR 3
Adam Oates	St. L.	Apr. 12/91	St. L.	3	Tim Chevaldae	St. L. 6	Det. 1
Luc Robitaille	L.A.	Apr. 26/91	L.A.	3	Grant Fuhr	L.A. 5	Edm. 2
Ron Francis	Pit.	May 9/92	Pit.	3	Mike Richter (2)		
					John V'brouck (1)	Pit. 5	NYR 4
Dirk Graham	Chi.	June 1/92	Chi.	3	Tom Barrasso	Pit. 5	Chi. 2
Joe Murphy	Edm.	May 6/92	Edm.	3	Kirk McLean	Edm. 5	Van. 2
Ray Sheppard	Det.	Apr. 24/92	Min.	3	Jon Casey	Min. 5	Det. 2
Kevin Stevens	Pit.	May 21/92	Bos.	4	Andy Moog	Pit. 5	Bos. 2
Pavel Bure	Van.	Apr. 28/92	Wpg.	3	Rick Tabaracci	Van. 8	Wpg. 3
Brian Noonan	Chi.	Apr. 18/93	Chi.	3	Curtis Joseph	St. L. 4	Chi. 3
Dale Hunter	Wsh.	Apr. 20/93	Wsh.	3	Glenn Healy	NYI 5	Wsh. 4
Teemu Selanne	Wpg.	Apr. 23/93	Wpg.	3	Kirk McLean	Wpg. 5	Van. 4
Ray Ferraro	NYI	Apr. 26/93	Wsh.	4	Don Beaupre	Wsh. 6	NYI 4
Al Iafrate	Wsh.	Apr. 26/93	Wsh.	3	Glenn Healy (2)		
					Mark Fitzpatrick (1)	Wsh. 6	NYI 4
Paul Di Pietro	Mtl.	Apr. 28/93	Mtl.	3	Ron Hextall	Mtl. 6	Que. 2
Wendel Clark	Tor.	May 27/93	L.A.	3	Kelly Hrudey	L.A. 5	Tor. 4
Eric Desjardins	Mtl.	Jun. 3/93	Mtl.	3	Kelly Hrudey	Mtl. 3	L.A. 2
Tony Amonte	Chi.	Apr. 23/94	Chi.	4	Felix Potvin	Chi. 5	Tor. 4
Gary Suter	Chi.	Apr. 24/94	Chi.	3	Felix Potvin	Chi. 4	Tor. 3
Ulf Dahlen	S.J.	May 6/94	S.J.	3	Felix Potvin	S.J. 5	Tor. 2
Mike Sullivan	Cgy.	May 11/95	S.J.	3	Arturs Irbe (2)		
					Wade Flaherty (1)	Cgy. 9	S.J. 2
Theoren Fleury	Cgy.	May 13/95	S.J.	4	Arturs Irbe (3)		
					ENG (1)	Cgy. 6	S.J. 4
Brendan Shanahan	St. L.	May 13/95	Van.	3	Kirk McLean	St. L. 5	Van. 2
John LeClair	Phi.	May 21/95	Phi.	3	Mike Richter	Phi. 5	NYR 4
Brian Leetch	NYR	May 22/95	Phi.	3	Ron Hextall	Phi. 4	NYR 3
Trevor Linden	Van.	Apr. 25/96	Col.	3	Patrick Roy	Col. 5	Van. 4
Jaromir Jagr	Pit.	May 11/96	Pit.	3	Mike Richter	Pit. 7	NYR 3
Peter Forsberg	Col.	Jun. 6/96	Col.	3	John Vanbiesbrouck	Col. 8	Fla. 1
Valeri Zelepukin	N.J.	Apr. 22/97	Mtl.	3	Jocelyn Thibault	N.J. 6	Mtl. 4
Valeri Kamensky	Col.	Apr. 24/97	Col.	3	Jeff Hackett (2)		
					Chris Terreri (1)	Col. 7	Chi. 0
Eric Lindros	Phi.	May 20/97	NYR	3	Mike Richter	Phi. 6	NYR 3
Matthew Barnaby	Buf.	May 10/98	Buf.	3	Andy Moog (2)	Buf. 6	Mtl. 3
					ENG (1)		
Martin Straka	Pit.	Apr. 25/99	Pit.	3	Martin Brodeur	Pit. 4	N.J. 2
Martin Lapointe	Det.	Apr. 15/00	Det.	3	Stephane Fiset (2)	Det. 8	L.A. 5
					Jamie Storr (1)		
Doug Weight	Edm.	Apr. 16/00	Edm.	3	Ed Belfour	Edm. 5	Dal. 2
Bill Guerin	Edm.	Apr. 18/00	Edm.	3	Ed Belfour	Dal. 4	Edm. 3
Scott Young	St. L.	Apr. 23/00	S.J.	3	Steve Shields	St. L. 6	S.J. 2
Andy Delmore	Phi.	May 7/00	Phi.	3	Ron Tugnutt (2)	Phi. 6	Pit. 3
					Peter Skudra (1)		

Leading Playoff Scorers, 1918–2000

Season	Player and Club	Games Played	Goals	Assists	Points
99-2000	Brett Hull, Dallas	23	11	13	24
1998-99	Peter Forsberg, Colorado	19	8	16	24
1997-98	Steve Yzerman, Detroit	22	6	18	24
1996-97	Eric Lindros, Philadelphia	19	12	14	26
1995-96	Joe Sakic, Colorado	22	18	16	34
1994-95	Sergei Fedorov, Detroit	17	7	17	24
1993-94	Brian Leetch, NY Rangers	23	11	23	34
1992-93	Wayne Gretzky, Los Angeles	24	15	25	40
1991-92	Mario Lemieux, Pittsburgh	15	16	18	34
1990-91	Mario Lemieux, Pittsburgh	23	16	28	44
1989-90	Craig Simpson, Edmonton	22	16	15	31
	Mark Messier, Edmonton	22	9	22	31
1988-89	Al MacInnis, Calgary	22	7	24	31
1987-88	Wayne Gretzky, Edmonton	19	12	31	43
1986-87	Wayne Gretzky, Edmonton	21	5	29	34
1985-86	Doug Gilmour, St. Louis	19	9	12	21
	Bernie Federko, St. Louis	19	7	14	21
1984-85	Wayne Gretzky, Edmonton	18	17	30	47
1983-84	Wayne Gretzky, Edmonton	19	13	22	35
1982-83	Wayne Gretzky, Edmonton	16	12	26	38
1981-82	Bryan Trottier, NY Islanders	19	6	23	29
1980-81	Mike Bossy, NY Islanders	18	17	18	35
1979-80	Bryan Trottier, NY Islanders	21	12	17	29
1978-79	Jacques Lemaire, Montreal	16	11	12	23
	Guy Lafleur, Montreal	16	10	13	23
1977-78	Guy Lafleur, Montreal	15	10	11	21
	Larry Robinson, Montreal	15	4	17	21
1976-77	Guy Lafleur, Montreal	14	9	17	26
1975-76	Reggie Leach, Philadelphia	16	19	5	24
1974-75	Rick MacLeish, Philadelphia	17	11	9	20
1973-74	Rick MacLeish, Philadelphia	17	13	9	22
1972-73	Yvan Cournoyer, Montreal	17	15	10	25
1971-72	Phil Esposito, Boston	15	9	15	24
	Bobby Orr, Boston	15	5	19	24
1970-71	Frank Mahovlich, Montreal	20	14	13	27
1969-70	Phil Esposito, Boston	14	13	14	27
1968-69	Phil Esposito, Boston	10	8	10	18
1967-68	Bill Goldsworthy, Minnesota	14	8	7	15
1966-67	Jim Pappin, Toronto	12	7	8	15
1965-66	Norm Ullman, Detroit	12	6	9	15
1964-65	Bobby Hull, Chicago	14	10	7	17
1963-64	Gordie Howe, Detroit	14	9	10	19
1962-63	Gordie Howe, Detroit	11	7	9	16
	Norm Ullman, Detroit	11	4	12	16
1961-62	Stan Mikita, Chicago	12	6	15	21
1960-61	Gordie Howe, Detroit	11	4	11	15
	Pierre Pilote, Chicago	12	3	12	15
1959-60	Henri Richard, Montreal	8	3	9	12
	Bernie Geoffrion, Montreal	8	2	10	12
1958-59	Dickie Moore, Montreal	11	5	12	17
1957-58	Fleming Mackell, Boston	12	5	14	19
1956-57	Bernie Geoffrion, Montreal	11	11	7	18
1955-56	Jean Béliveau, Montreal	10	12	7	19
1954-55	Gordie Howe, Detroit	11	9	11	20
1953-54	Dickie Moore, Montreal	11	5	8	13
1952-53	Ed Sanford, Boston	11	8	3	11
1951-52	Ted Lindsay, Detroit	8	5	2	7
	Floyd Curry, Montreal	11	4	3	7
	Metro Prystai, Detroit	8	2	5	7
	Gordie Howe, Detroit	8	2	5	7
1950-51	Maurice Richard, Montreal	11	9	4	13
	Max Bentley, Toronto	11	2	11	13
1949-50	Pentti Lund, NY Rangers	12	6	5	11
1948-49	Gordie Howe, Detroit	11	8	3	11
1947-48	Ted Kennedy, Toronto	9	8	6	14
1946-47	Maurice Richard, Montreal	10	6	5	11
1945-46	Elmer Lach, Montreal	9	5	12	17
1944-45	Joe Carveth, Detroit	14	5	6	11
1943-44	Toe Blake, Montreal	9	7	11	18
1942-43	Carl Liscombe, Detroit	10	6	8	14
1941-42	Don Grosso, Detroit	12	8	6	14
1940-41	Milt Schmidt, Boston	11	5	6	11
1939-40	Phil Watson, NY Rangers	12	3	6	9
	Neil Colville, NY Rangers	12	2	7	9
1938-39	Bill Cowley, Boston	12	3	11	14
1937-38	Johnny Gottselig, Chicago	10	5	3	8
1936-37	Marty Barry, Detroit	10	4	7	11
1935-36	Frank Boll, Toronto	9	7	3	10
1934-35	Baldy Northcott, Mtl. Maroons	7	4	1	5
	Harvey Jackson, Toronto	7	3	2	5
	Cy Wentworth, Mtl. Maroons	7	3	2	5
1933-34	Larry Aurie, Detroit	9	3	7	10
1932-33	Cecil Dillon, NY Rangers	8	8	2	10
1931-32	Frank Boucher, NY Rangers	7	3	6	9
1930-31	Cooney Weiland, Boston	5	6	3	9
1929-30	Marty Barry, Boston	6	3	3	6
	Cooney Weiland, Boston	6	1	5	6
1928-29	Andy Blair, Toronto	4	3	0	3
	Butch Keeling, NY Rangers	6	3	0	3
	Ace Bailey, Toronto	4	1	2	3
1927-28	Frank Boucher, NY Rangers	9	7	3	10
1926-27	Harry Oliver, Boston	8	4	2	6
	Percy Galbraith, Boston	8	3	3	6
	Frank Fredrickson, Boston	8	2	4	6
1925-26	Nels Stewart, Mtl. Maroons	8	6	3	9
1924-25	Howie Morenz, Montreal	6	7	1	8
1923-24	Howie Morenz, Montreal	6	7	2	9
1922-23	Punch Broadbent, Ottawa	8	6	1	7
1921-22	Babe Dye, Toronto	7	11	2	13
1920-21	Cy Denneny, Ottawa	7	4	2	6
1919-20	Frank Nighbor, Ottawa	5	6	1	7
	Jack Darragh, Ottawa	5	5	2	7
1918-19	Newsy Lalonde, Montreal	10	17	1	18
1917-18	Alf Skinner, Toronto	7	8	1	9

Overtime Games since 1918

Abbreviations: Teams/Cities: — **Ana.** - Anaheim; **Atl.** - Atlanta; **Bos.** - Boston; **Buf.** - Buffalo; **Cgy.** - Calgary; **Cgy. T.** - Calgary Tigers (Western Canada Hockey League); **Chi.** - Chicago; **Col.** - Colorado; **Dal.** - Dallas; **Det.** - Detroit; **Edm.** - Edmonton; **Edm. E.** - Edmonton Eskimos (WCHL); **Fla.** - Florida; **Hfd.** - Hartford; **K.C.** - Kansas City; **L.A.** - Los Angeles; **Min.** - Minnesota; **Mtl.** - Montreal; **Mtl.M.** - Montreal Maroons; **N.J.** - New Jersey; **NYA** - NY Americans; **NYI** - New York Islanders; **NYR** - New York Rangers; **Oak.** - Oakland; **Ott.** - Ottawa; **Phi.** - Philadelphia; **Phx.** - Phoenix; **Pit.** - Pittsburgh; **Que.** - Quebec; **St. L.** - St. Louis; **Sea.** - Seattle Metropolitans (Pacific Coast Hockey Association); **S.J.** - San Jose; **T.B.** - Tampa Bay; **Tor.** - Toronto; **Van.** - Vancouver; **Van. M** - Vancouver Millionaires (PCHA); **Vic.** - Victoria Cougars (WCHL); **Wpg.** - Winnipeg; **Wsh.** - Washington.

SERIES — **CF** - conference final; **CSF** - conference semi-final; **CQF** - conference quarter-final; **DF** - division final; **DSF** - division semi-final; **F** - final; **PR** - preliminary round; **QF** - quarter final; **SF** - semi-final.

Date	City	Series	Score		Scorer	Overtime	Series Winner
Mar. 26/19	Sea.	F	Mtl. 0	Sea. 0	no scorer	20:00	
Mar. 30/19	Sea.	F	Mtl. 4	Sea. 3	Odie Cleghorn	15:57	
Mar. 20/22	Tor.	F	Tor 2	Van.M. 1	Babe Dye	4:50	Tor.
Mar. 29/23	Van.	F	Ott. 2	Edm.E. 1	Cy Denneny	2:08	Ott.
Mar. 31/27	Mtl.	QF	Mtl. 1	Mtl. M. 0	Howie Morenz	12:05	Mtl.
Apr. 7/27	Bos.	F	Ott. 0	Bos. 0	no scorer	20:00	Ott.
Apr. 11/27	Ott.	F	Bos. 1	Ott. 1	no scorer	20:00	Ott.
Apr. 3/28	Mtl.	QF	Mtl. M. 1	Mtl. 0	Russ Oatman	8:20	Mtl. M.
Apr. 7/28	Mtl.	F	NYR 2	Mtl. M. 1	Frank Boucher	7:05	NYR
Mar. 21/29	NYR	QF	NYR 1	NYA 0	Butch Keeling	29:50	NYR
Mar. 26/29	Tor.	SF	NYR 2	Tor. 1	Frank Boucher	2:03	NYR
Mar. 20/30	Mtl.	SF	Bos. 2	Mtl. M. 1	Harry Oliver	45:35	Bos.
Mar. 25/30	Bos.	SF	Mtl. M. 1	Bos. 0	Archie Wilcox	26:27	Bos.
Mar. 26/30	Mtl.	QF	Chi. 2	Mtl. 2	Howie Morenz (Mtl.)	51:43	Mtl.
Mar. 28/30	Mtl.	SF	Mtl. 2	NYR 1	Gus Rivers	68:52	Mtl.
Mar. 24/31	Bos.	SF	Bos. 5	Mtl. 4	Cooney Weiland	18:56	Mtl.
Mar. 26/31	Chi.	QF	Chi. 2	Tor. 1	Stew Adams	19:20	Chi.
Mar. 28/31	Mtl.	SF	Mtl. 4	Bos. 3	Georges Mantha	5:10	Mtl.
Apr. 1/31	Mtl.	SF	Mtl. 3	Bos. 2	Wildor Larochelle	19:00	Mtl.
Apr. 5/31	Chi.	F	Chi. 2	Mtl. 1	Johnny Gottselig	24:50	Mtl.
Apr. 9/31	Mtl.	F	Chi. 3	Mtl. 2	Cy Wentworth	53:50	Mtl.
Mar. 26/32	Mtl.	SF	NYR 4	Mtl. 3	Fred Cook	59:32	NYR
Apr. 2/32	Tor.	SF	Tor. 3	Mtl. M. 2	Bob Gracie	17:59	Tor.
Mar. 25/33	Bos.	SF	Bos. 2	Tor. 1	Marty Barry	14:14	Tor.
Mar. 28/33	Bos.	SF	Tor. 1	Bos. 0	Busher Jackson	15:03	Tor.
Mar. 30/33	Tor.	SF	Bos. 2	Tor. 1	Eddie Shore	4:23	Tor.
Apr. 3/33	Tor.	SF	Tor. 1	Bos. 0	Ken Doraty	104:46	Tor.
Apr. 13/33	Tor.	F	NYR 1	Tor. 0	Bill Cook	7:33	NYR
Mar. 22/34	Tor.	SF	Det. 2	Tor. 1	Herbie Lewis	1:33	Det.
Mar. 25/34	Chi.	QF	Chi. 1	Mtl. 1	Mush March (Chi)	11:05	Chi.
Apr. 3/34	Det.	F	Chi. 2	Det. 1	Paul Thompson	21:10	Chi.
Apr. 10/34	Chi.	F	Chi. 1	Det. 0	Mush March	30:05	Chi.
Mar. 23/35	Bos.	SF	Bos. 1	Tor. 0	Dit Clapper	33:26	Tor.
Mar. 26/35	Chi.	QF	Mtl. M. 1	Chi. 0	Baldy Northcott	4:02	Mtl. M.
Mar. 30/35	Tor.	SF	Tor. 2	Bos. 1	Pep Kelly	1:36	Tor.
Apr. 4/35	Tor.	F	Mtl. M. 3	Tor. 2	Dave Trottier	5:28	Mtl. M.
Mar. 24/36	Mtl.	SF	Det. 1	Mtl. M. 0	Mud Bruneteau	116:30	Det.
Apr. 9/36	Tor.	F	Tor. 4	Det. 3	Buzz Boll	0:31	Det.
Mar. 25/37	NYR	QF	NYR 2	Tor. 1	Babe Pratt	13:05	NYR
Apr. 1/37	Mtl.	SF	Det. 2	Mtl. 1	Hec Kilrea	51:49	Det.
Mar. 22/38	NYR	QF	NYA 2	NYR 1	Johnny Sorrell	21:25	NYA
Mar. 24/38	Tor.	SF	Tor. 1	Bos. 0	George Parsons	21:31	Tor.
Mar. 26/38	Mtl.	QF	Chi. 3	Mtl. 2	Paul Thompson	11:49	Chi.
Mar. 27/38	NYR	QF	NYA 3	NYR 2	Lorne Carr	60:40	NYA
Mar. 29/38	Bos.	SF	Tor. 3	Bos. 2	Gordie Drillon	10:04	Tor.
Mar. 31/38	Chi.	SF	Chi. 1	NYA 0	Cully Dahlstrom	33:01	Chi.
Mar. 21/39	NYR	SF	Bos. 2	NYR 1	Mel Hill	59:25	Bos.
Mar. 23/39	Bos.	SF	Bos. 3	NYR 2	Mel Hill	8:24	Bos.
Mar. 26/39	Det.	QF	Det. 1	Mtl. 0	Marty Barry	7:47	Det.
Mar. 30/39	Bos.	SF	NYR 2	Bos. 1	Clint Smith	17:19	Bos.
Apr. 1/39	Tor.	SF	Tor. 5	Det. 4	Gordie Drillon	5:42	Tor.
Apr. 2/39	Bos.	SF	Bos. 2	NYR 1	Mel Hill	48:00	Bos.
Apr. 9/39	Bos.	F	Tor. 3	Bos. 2	Doc Romnes	10:38	Bos.
Mar. 19/40	Det.	QF	Det. 2	NYA 1	Syd Howe	0:25	Det.
Mar. 19/40	Tor.	QF	Tor. 3	Chi. 2	Syl Apps Sr.	6:35	Tor.
Apr. 2/40	NYR	F	NYR 2	Tor. 1	Alf Pike	15:30	NYR
Apr. 11/40	Tor.	F	NYR 2	Tor. 1	Muzz Patrick	31:43	NYR
Apr. 13/40	Tor.	F	NYR 3	Tor. 2	Bryan Hextall Sr.	2:07	NYR
Mar. 20/41	Det.	QF	Det. 2	NYR 1	Gus Giesebrecht	12:01	Det.
Mar. 22/41	Mtl.	QF	Mtl. 4	Chi. 3	Charlie Sands	34:04	Chi.
Mar. 29/41	Bos.	SF	Tor. 2	Bos. 1	Pete Langelle	17:31	Bos.
Mar. 30/41	Chi.	SF	Det. 2	Chi. 1	Gus Giesebrecht	9:15	Det.
Mar. 22/42	Chi.	QF	Bos. 2	Chi. 1	Des Smith	6:51	Bos.
Mar. 21/43	Bos.	SF	Bos. 5	Mtl. 4	Don Gallinger	12:30	Bos.
Mar. 23/43	Det.	SF	Tor. 3	Det. 2	Jack McLean	70:18	Det.
Mar. 25/43	Mtl.	SF	Bos. 3	Mtl. 2	Harvey Jackson	3:20	Bos.
Mar. 30/43	Tor.	SF	Det. 3	Tor. 2	Adam Brown	9:21	Det.
Mar. 30/43	Bos.	SF	Bos. 5	Mtl. 4	Ab DeMarco	3:41	Bos.
Apr. 13/44	Mtl.	F	Mtl. 5	Chi. 4	Toe Blake	9:12	Mtl.
Mar. 27/45	Tor.	SF	Tor. 4	Mtl. 3	Gus Bodnar	12:36	Tor.
Mar. 29/45	Det.	SF	Det. 3	Bos. 2	Mud Bruneteau	17:12	Det.
Apr. 21/45	Tor.	F	Det. 1	Tor. 0	Ed Bruneteau	14:16	Tor.
Mar. 28/46	Bos.	SF	Bos. 4	Det. 3	Don Gallinger	9:51	Bos.
Mar. 30/46	Mtl.	F	Mtl. 4	Bos. 3	Maurice Richard	9:08	Mtl.
Apr. 2/46	Mtl.	F	Mtl. 3	Bos. 2	Jim Peters	16:55	Mtl.
Apr. 7/46	Bos.	F	Bos. 3	Mtl. 2	Terry Reardon	15:13	Mtl.
Mar. 26/47	Tor.	SF	Tor. 3	Det. 2	Howie Meeker	3:05	Tor.
Mar. 27/47	Mtl.	SF	Mtl. 2	Bos. 1	Kenny Mosdell	5:38	Mtl.
Apr. 3/47	Mtl.	SF	Mtl. 4	Bos. 3	John Quilty	36:40	Mtl.
Apr. 15/47	Tor.	F	Tor. 2	Mtl. 1	Syl Apps Sr.	16:36	Tor.
Mar. 24/48	Tor.	SF	Tor. 5	Bos. 4	Nick Metz	17:03	Tor.
Mar. 22/49	Det.	SF	Det. 2	Mtl. 1	Max McNab	44:52	Det.
Mar. 24/49	Det.	SF	Mtl. 4	Det. 3	Gerry Plamondon	2:59	Det.
Mar. 26/49	Tor.	SF	Bos. 5	Tor. 4	Woody Dumart	16:14	Tor.
Apr. 8/49	Det.	F	Tor. 3	Det. 2	Joe Klukay	17:31	Tor.
Apr. 4/50	Tor.	SF	Det. 2	Tor. 1	Leo Reise Sr.	20:38	Det.
Apr. 4/50	Mtl.	SF	Mtl. 3	NYR 2	Elmer Lach	15:19	NYR
Apr. 9/50	Det.	SF	Det. 1	Tor. 0	Leo Reise	8:39	Det.
Apr. 18/50	Det.	F	NYR 4	Det. 3	Don Raleigh	8:34	Det.
Apr. 20/50	Det.	F	NYR 2	Det. 1	Don Raleigh	1:38	Det.
Apr. 23/50	Det.	F	Det. 4	NYR 3	Pete Babando	28:31	Det.
Mar. 27/51	Det.	SF	Mtl. 3	Det. 2	Maurice Richard	61:09	Mtl.
Mar. 29/51	Det.	SF	Mtl. 1	Det. 0	Maurice Richard	42:20	Mtl.
Mar. 31/51	Tor.	SF	Bos. 1	Tor. 1	no scorer	20:00	Tor.
Apr. 11/51	Tor.	F	Tor. 3	Mtl. 2	Sid Smith	5:51	Tor.
Apr. 14/51	Tor.	F	Mtl. 3	Tor. 2	Maurice Richard	2:55	Tor.
Apr. 17/51	Mtl.	F	Tor. 2	Mtl. 1	Ted Kennedy	4:47	Tor.
Apr. 19/51	Mtl.	F	Tor. 3	Mtl. 2	Harry Watson	5:15	Tor.
Apr. 21/51	Tor.	F	Tor. 3	Mtl. 2	Bill Barilko	2:53	Tor.
Apr. 6/52	Bos.	SF	Mtl. 3	Bos. 2	Paul Masnick	27:49	Mtl.
Mar. 29/53	Bos.	SF	Bos. 2	Det. 1	Jack McIntyre	12:29	Bos.
Mar. 29/53	Chi.	SF	Chi. 2	Mtl. 1	Al Dewsbury	5:18	Mtl.
Apr. 16/53	Mtl.	F	Mtl. 1	Bos. 0	Elmer Lach	1:22	Mtl.
Apr. 1/54	Det.	SF	Det. 4	Tor. 3	Ted Lindsay	21:01	Det.
Apr. 11/54	Det.	F	Mtl. 1	Det. 0	Kenny Mosdell	5:45	Det.
Apr. 16/54	Det.	F	Det. 2	Mtl. 1	Tony Leswick	4:29	Det.
Mar. 29/55	Bos.	SF	Mtl. 4	Bos. 3	Don Marshall	3:05	Mtl.
Mar. 24/56	Tor.	SF	Det. 5	Tor. 4	Ted Lindsay	4:22	Det.
Mar. 28/57	NYR	SF	NYR 4	Mtl. 3	Andy Hebenton	13:38	Mtl.
Apr. 4/57	Mtl.	SF	Mtl. 4	NYR 3	Maurice Richard	1:11	Mtl.
Mar. 27/58	NYR	SF	Bos. 4	NYR 3	Jerry Toppazzini	4:46	Bos.
Mar. 30/58	Det.	SF	Mtl. 2	Det. 1	André Pronovost	11:52	Mtl.
Apr. 17/58	Mtl.	F	Mtl. 3	Bos. 2	Maurice Richard	5:45	Mtl.
Mar. 28/59	Tor.	SF	Tor. 3	Bos. 2	Gerry Ehman	5:02	Tor.
Mar. 31/59	Tor.	SF	Tor. 3	Bos. 2	Frank Mahovlich	11:21	Tor.
Apr. 14/59	Tor.	F	Tor. 3	Mtl. 2	Dick Duff	10:06	Mtl.
Mar. 26/60	Mtl.	SF	Mtl. 4	Chi. 3	Doug Harvey	8:38	Mtl.
Mar. 27/60	Det.	SF	Tor. 5	Det. 4	Frank Mahovlich	43:00	Tor.
Mar. 29/60	Det.	SF	Det. 2	Tor. 1	Gerry Melnyk	1:54	Tor.
Mar. 22/61	Tor.	SF	Tor. 3	Det. 2	George Armstrong	24:51	Det.
Mar. 26/61	Chi.	SF	Chi. 2	Mtl. 1	Murray Balfour	52:12	Chi.
Apr. 5/62	Tor.	SF	Tor. 3	NYR 2	Red Kelly	24:23	Tor.
Apr. 2/64	Det.	SF	Chi. 3	Det. 2	Murray Balfour	8:21	Det.
Apr. 14/64	Tor.	F	Det. 4	Tor. 3	Larry Jeffrey	7:52	Tor.
Apr. 23/64	Det.	F	Tor. 4	Det. 3	Bob Baun	1:43	Tor.
Apr. 6/65	Tor.	SF	Tor. 3	Mtl. 2	Dave Keon	4:17	Mtl.
Apr. 13/65	Tor.	SF	Mtl. 4	Tor. 3	Claude Provost	16:33	Mtl.
May 5/66	Det.	F	Mtl. 3	Det. 2	Henri Richard	2:20	Mtl.
Apr. 13/67	NYR	SF	Mtl. 2	NYR 1	John Ferguson	6:28	Mtl.
Apr. 25/67	Tor.	F	Tor. 3	Mtl. 2	Bob Pulford	28:26	Tor.
Apr. 10/68	St. L.	QF	St. L. 3	Phi. 2	Larry Keenan	24:10	St. L.
Apr. 16/68	St. L.	QF	Phi. 2	St. L. 1	Don Blackburn	31:18	St. L.
Apr. 16/68	Min.	QF	Min. 4	L.A. 3	Milan Marcetta	9:11	Min.
Apr. 22/68	Min.	SF	Min. 3	St. L. 2	Parker MacDonald	3:41	St. L.
Apr. 27/68	St. L.	SF	St. L. 4	Min. 3	Gary Sabourin	1:32	St. L.
Apr. 28/68	Mtl.	SF	Mtl. 4	Chi. 3	Jacques Lemaire	2:14	Mtl.
Apr. 29/68	St. L.	SF	St. L. 3	Min. 2	Bill McCreary	17:27	St. L.
May 3/68	St. L.	SF	St. L. 2	Min. 1	Ron Schock	22:50	St. L.
May 5/68	St. L.	F	Mtl. 3	St. L. 2	Jacques Lemaire	1:41	Mtl.
May 9/68	Mtl.	F	Mtl. 4	St. L. 3	Bobby Rousseau	1:13	Mtl.
Apr. 2/69	Oak.	QF	L.A. 5	Oak. 4	Ted Irvine	0:19	L.A.
Apr. 10/69	Mtl.	SF	Mtl. 3	Bos. 2	Ralph Backstrom	0:42	Mtl.
Apr. 13/69	Mtl.	SF	Mtl. 4	Bos. 3	Mickey Redmond	4:55	Mtl.
Apr. 24/69	Bos.	SF	Mtl. 2	Bos. 1	Jean Béliveau	31:28	Mtl.
Apr. 12/70	Oak.	QF	Pit. 3	Oak. 2	Michel Briere	8:28	Pit.
May 10/70	Bos.	F	Bos. 4	St. L. 3	Bobby Orr	0:40	Bos.
Apr. 15/71	Tor.	QF	NYR 2	Tor. 1	Bob Nevin	9:07	NYR
Apr. 18/71	Chi.	SF	NYR 2	Chi. 1	Pete Stemkowski	1:37	Chi.
Apr. 27/71	Chi.	SF	Chi. 3	NYR 2	Bobby Hull	6:35	Chi.
Apr. 29/71	NYR	SF	NYR 3	Chi. 2	Pete Stemkowski	41:29	Chi.
May 4/71	Chi.	F	Chi. 2	Mtl. 1	Jim Pappin	21:11	Mtl.
Apr. 6/72	Bos.	QF	Tor. 4	Bos. 3	Jim Harrison	2:58	Bos.
Apr. 6/72	Min.	QF	Min. 6	St. L. 5	Bill Goldsworthy	1:36	St. L.
Apr. 9/72	Pit.	QF	Chi. 6	Pit. 5	Pit Martin	0:12	Chi.
Apr. 16/72	Min.	QF	St. L. 2	Min. 1	Kevin O'Shea	10:07	St. L.
Apr. 1/73	Mtl.	QF	Buf. 3	Mtl. 2	René Robert	9:18	Mtl.
Apr. 10/73	Phi.	QF	Phi. 3	Min. 2	Gary Dornhoefer	8:35	Phi.
Apr. 14/73	Mtl.	SF	Phi. 5	Mtl. 4	Rick MacLeish	2:56	Mtl.
Apr. 17/73	Mtl.	SF	Mtl. 4	Phi. 3	Larry Robinson	6:45	Mtl.
Apr. 14/74	Tor.	QF	Bos. 4	Tor. 3	Ken Hodge	1:27	Bos.
Apr. 14/74	Atl.	QF	Phi. 4	Atl. 3	Dave Schultz	5:40	Phi.
Apr. 16/74	Mtl.	QF	NYR 3	Mtl. 2	Ron Harris	4:07	NYR
Apr. 23/74	Chi.	SF	Chi. 4	Bos. 3	Jim Pappin	3:48	Bos.
Apr. 28/74	NYR	SF	NYR 2	Phi. 1	Rod Gilbert	4:20	Phi.
May 9/74	Bos.	F	Phi. 3	Bos. 2	Bobby Clarke	12:01	Phi.
Apr. 8/75	L.A.	PR	L.A. 3	Tor. 2	Mike Murphy	8:53	Tor.
Apr. 10/75	Tor.	PR	Tor. 3	L.A. 2	Blaine Stoughton	10:19	Tor.
Apr. 10/75	Chi.	PR	Chi. 4	Bos. 3	Ivan Boldirev	7:33	Chi.
Apr. 11/75	NYR	PR	NYI 4	NYR 3	Jean-Paul Parise	0:11	NYI
Apr. 19/75	Tor.	QF	Phi. 4	Tor. 3	André Dupont	1:45	Phi.
Apr. 17/75	Chi.	QF	Chi. 5	Buf. 4	Stan Mikita	2:31	Buf.
Apr. 22/75	Mtl.	QF	Mtl. 5	Van. 4	Guy Lafleur	17:06	Mtl.
May 1/75	Phi.	SF	Phi. 5	NYI 4	Bobby Clarke	2:56	Phi.
May 7/75	NYI	SF	NYI 4	Phi. 3	Jude Drouin	1:53	Phi.
Apr. 27/75	Buf.	SF	Buf. 6	Mtl. 5	Danny Gare	4:42	Buf.
May 6/75	Buf.	SF	Buf. 5	Mtl. 4	René Robert	5:56	Buf.
May 20/75	Buf.	F	Buf. 5	Phi. 4	René Robert	18:29	Phi.
Apr. 8/76	Buf.	PR	Buf. 3	St. L. 2	Danny Gare	11:43	Buf.
Apr. 9/76	Buf.	PR	Buf. 2	St. L. 1	Don Luce	14:27	Buf.
Apr. 13/76	Bos.	QF	L.A. 3	Bos. 2	Butch Goring	0:27	Bos.
Apr. 13/76	Buf.	QF	Buf. 3	NYI 2	Danny Gare	14:04	NYI
Apr. 22/76	L.A.	QF	L.A. 4	Bos. 3	Butch Goring	18:28	Bos.
Apr. 29/76	Phi.	SF	Phi. 2	Bos. 1	Reggie Leach	13:38	Phi.
Apr. 15/77	Tor.	QF	Phi. 4	Tor. 3	Rick MacLeish	2:55	Phi.
Apr. 17/77	Tor.	QF	Phi. 6	Tor. 5	Reggie Leach	19:10	Phi.
Apr. 24/77	Phi.	SF	Bos. 4	Phi. 3	Rick Middleton	2:57	Bos.
Apr. 26/77	Phi.	SF	Bos. 5	Phi. 4	Terry O'Reilly	30:07	Bos.
May 3/77	Mtl.	SF	NYI 4	Mtl. 3	Billy Harris	3:58	Mtl.

Date	City	Series	Score	Scorer	Overtime	Series Winner
May 14/77	Bos.	F	Mtl. 2 Bos. 1	Jacques Lemaire	4:32	Mtl.
Apr. 11/78	Phi.	PR	Phi. 3 Col. 2	Mel Bridgman	0:23	Phi.
Apr. 13/78	NYR	PR	NYR 4 Buf. 3	Don Murdoch	1:37	Buf.
Apr. 19/78	Bos.	QF	Bos. 4 Chi. 3	Terry O'Reilly	1:50	Bos.
Apr. 19/78	NYI	QF	NYI 3 Tor. 2	Mike Bossy	2:50	Tor.
Apr. 21/78	Chi.	QF	Bos. 4 Chi. 3	Peter McNab	10:17	Bos.
Apr. 25/78	NYI	QF	NYI 2 Tor. 1	Bob Nystrom	8:02	Tor.
Apr. 29/78	NYI	QF	Tor. 2 NYI 1	Lanny McDonald	4:13	Tor.
May 2/78	Bos.	SF	Bos. 3 Phi. 2	Rick Middleton	1:43	Bos.
May 16/78	Mtl.	F	Mtl. 3 Bos. 2	Guy Lafleur	13:09	Mtl.
May 21/78	Bos.	F	Bos. 4 Mtl. 3	Bobby Schmautz	6:22	Mtl.
Apr. 12/79	L.A.	PR	NYR 2 L.A. 1	Phil Esposito	6:11	NYR
Apr. 14/79	Buf.	PR	Pit. 4 Buf. 3	George Ferguson	0:47	Pit.
Apr. 16/79	Phi.	QF	Phi. 3 NYR 2	Ken Linseman	0:44	NYR
Apr. 18/79	NYI	QF	NYI 1 Chi. 0	Mike Bossy	2:31	NYI
Apr. 21/79	Tor.	QF	Mtl. 4 Tor. 3	Cam Connor	25:25	Mtl.
Apr. 22/79	Tor.	QF	Mtl. 5 Tor. 4	Larry Robinson	4:14	Mtl.
Apr. 28/79	NYR	SF	NYR 4 NYI 3	Denis Potvin	8:02	NYR
May 3/79	NYR	SF	NYI 3 NYR 2	Bob Nystrom	3:40	NYR
May 3/79	Bos.	SF	Bos. 4 Mtl. 3	Jean Ratelle	3:46	Mtl.
May 10/79	Mtl.	SF	Mtl. 5 Bos. 4	Yvon Lambert	9:33	Mtl.
May 19/79	NYR	F	Mtl. 4 NYR 3	Serge Savard	7:25	Mtl.
Apr. 8/80	NYR	PR	NYR 2 Atl. 1	Steve Vickers	0:33	NYR
Apr. 8/80	Phi.	PR	Phi. 4 Edm. 3	Bobby Clarke	8:06	Phi.
Apr. 8/80	Chi.	PR	Chi. 3 St. L. 2	Doug Lecuyer	12:34	Chi.
Apr. 11/80	Hfd.	PR	Mtl. 4 Hfd. 3	Yvon Lambert	0:29	Mtl.
Apr. 11/80	Tor.	PR	Min. 4 Tor. 3	Al MacAdam	0:32	Min.
Apr. 11/80	L.A.	PR	NYI 4 L.A. 3	Ken Morrow	6:55	NYI
Apr. 11/80	Edm.	PR	Phi. 3 Edm. 2	Ken Linseman	23:56	Phi.
Apr. 16/80	Bos.	QF	NYI 2 Bos. 1	Clark Gillies	1:02	NYI
Apr. 17/80	Bos.	QF	NYI 5 Bos. 4	Bob Bourne	1:24	NYI
Apr. 21/80	NYI	QF	Bos. 4 NYI 3	Terry O'Reilly	17:13	NYI
May 1/80	Buf.	SF	NYI 2 Buf. 1	Bob Nystrom	21:20	NYI
May 13/80	Phi.	F	NYI 4 Phi. 3	Denis Potvin	4:07	NYI
May 24/80	NYI	F	NYI 5 Phi. 4	Bob Nystrom	7:11	NYI
Apr. 8/81	Buf.	PR	Buf. 3 Van. 2	Alan Haworth	5:00	Buf.
Apr. 8/81	Bos.	PR	Min. 5 Bos. 4	Steve Payne	3:34	Min.
Apr. 11/81	Chi.	PR	Cgy. 5 Chi. 4	Willi Plett	35:17	Cgy.
Apr. 12/81	Que.	PR	Que. 4 Phi. 3	Dale Hunter	0:37	Phi.
Apr. 14/81	St. L.	PR	St. L. 4 Pit. 3	Mike Crombeen	25:16	St. L.
Apr. 16/81	Buf.	QF	Min. 4 Buf. 3	Steve Payne	0:22	Min.
Apr. 20/81	Min.	QF	Buf. 5 Min. 4	Craig Ramsay	16:32	Min.
Apr. 20/81	Min.	QF	NYI 5 Edm. 4	Ken Morrow	5:41	NYI
Apr. 7/82	Min.	DSF	Chi. 3 Min. 2	Greg Fox	3:34	Chi.
Apr. 8/82	Edm.	DSF	Edm. 3 L.A. 2	Wayne Gretzky	6:20	L.A.
Apr. 8/82	Van.	DSF	Van. 2 Cgy. 1	Dave Williams	14:20	Van.
Apr. 10/82	Pit.	DSF	Pit. 2 NYI 1	Rick Kehoe	4:14	NYI
Apr. 10/82	L.A.	DSF	L.A. 6 Edm. 5	Daryl Evans	2:35	L.A.
Apr. 13/82	Mtl.	DSF	Que. 3 Mtl. 2	Dale Hunter	0:22	Que.
Apr. 13/82	NYI	DSF	NYI 4 Pit. 3	John Tonelli	6:19	NYI
Apr. 16/82	Van.	DF	L.A. 3 Van. 2	Steve Bozek	4:33	Van.
Apr. 18/82	Que.	DF	Que. 3 Bos. 2	Wilf Paiement	11:44	Bos.
Apr. 18/82	NYR	DF	NYI 4 NYR 3	Bryan Trottier	3:00	NYI
Apr. 18/82	L.A.	DF	Van. 4 L.A. 3	Colin Campbell	1:23	Van.
Apr. 21/82	St. L.	DF	St. L. 3 Chi. 2	Bernie Federko	3:28	Chi.
Apr. 23/82	Que.	DF	Bos. 6 Que. 5	Peter McNab	10:54	Que.
Apr. 27/82	Chi.	CF	Van. 2 Chi. 1	Jim Nill	28:58	Van.
May 1/82	Que.	CF	NYI 5 Que. 4	Wayne Merrick	16:52	NYI
May 8/82	NYI	F	NYI 6 Van. 5	Mike Bossy	19:58	NYI
Apr. 5/83	Bos.	DSF	Bos. 4 Que. 3	Barry Pederson	1:46	Bos.
Apr. 6/83	Cgy.	DSF	Cgy. 4 Van. 3	Eddy Beers	12:27	Cgy.
Apr. 7/83	Min.	DSF	Min. 5 Tor. 4	Bobby Smith	5:03	Min.
Apr. 10/83	Tor.	DSF	Min. 5 Tor. 4	Dino Ciccarelli	8:05	Min.
Apr. 10/83	Van.	DSF	Cgy. 4 Van. 3	Greg Meredith	1:06	Cgy.
Apr. 18/83	Min.	DF	Chi. 4 Min. 3	Rich Preston	10:34	Chi.
Apr. 24/83	Bos.	DF	Bos. 3 Buf. 2	Brad Park	1:52	Bos.
Apr. 5/84	Edm.	DSF	Edm. 5 Wpg. 4	Randy Gregg	0:21	Edm.
Apr. 7/84	Det.	DSF	St. L. 4 Det. 3	Mark Reeds	37:07	St. L.
Apr. 8/84	Det.	DSF	St. L. 4 Det. 2	Jorgen Pettersson	2:42	St. L.
Apr. 10/84	NYI	DSF	NYI 3 NYR 2	Ken Morrow	8:56	NYI
Apr. 13/84	Min.	DF	St. L. 4 Min. 3	Doug Gilmour	16:16	Min.
Apr. 13/84	Edm.	DF	Cgy. 6 Edm. 5	Carey Wilson	3:42	Edm.
Apr. 13/84	NYI	DF	NYI 5 Wsh. 4	Anders Kallur	7:35	NYI
Apr. 16/84	Mtl.	DF	Que. 4 Mtl. 3	Bo Berglund	3:00	Mtl.
Apr. 20/84	Cgy.	DF	Cgy. 5 Edm. 4	Lanny McDonald	1:04	Edm.
Apr. 22/84	Min.	DF	Min. 4 St. L. 3	Steve Payne	6:00	Min.
Apr. 10/85	Phi.	DSF	Phi. 5 NYR 4	Mark Howe	8:01	Phi.
Apr. 10/85	Wsh.	DSF	Wsh. 4 NYI 3	Alan Haworth	2:28	NYI
Apr. 10/85	Edm.	DSF	Edm. 3 L.A. 2	Lee Fogolin	3:01	Edm.
Apr. 10/85	Wpg.	DSF	Wpg. 5 Cgy. 4	Brian Mullen	7:56	Wpg.
Apr. 11/85	Wsh.	DSF	Wsh. 2 NYI 1	Mike Gartner	21:23	NYI
Apr. 13/85	L.A.	DF	Edm. 4 L.A. 3	Glenn Anderson	0:46	Edm.
Apr. 18/85	Mtl.	DF	Que. 2 Mtl. 1	Mark Kumpel	12:23	Que.
Apr. 23/85	Que.	DF	Que. 7 Mtl. 6	Dale Hunter	18:36	Que.
May 2/85	Mtl.	DF	Que. 3 Mtl. 2	Peter Stastny	2:22	Que.
Apr. 25/85	Min.	DF	Chi. 7 Min. 6	Darryl Sutter	21:57	Chi.
Apr. 28/85	Chi.	DF	Min. 5 Chi. 4	Dennis Maruk	1:14	Chi.
Apr. 30/85	Chi.	DF	Chi. 6 Min. 5	Darryl Sutter	15:41	Chi.
May 5/85	Que.	CF	Que. 2 Phi. 1	Peter Stastny	6:20	Phi.
Apr. 9/86	Que.	DSF	Hfd. 3 Que. 2	Sylvain Turgeon	2:36	Hfd.
Apr. 12/86	Wpg.	DSF	Cgy. 4 Wpg. 3	Lanny McDonald	8:25	Cgy.
Apr. 17/86	Wsh.	DSF	NYR 4 Wsh. 3	Brian MacLellan	1:16	NYR
Apr. 20/86	Edm.	DF	Edm. 6 Cgy. 5	Glenn Anderson	1:04	Cgy.
Apr. 23/86	Hfd.	DF	Hfd. 2 Mtl. 1	Kevin Dineen	1:07	Mtl.
Apr. 23/86	NYR	DF	NYR 6 Wsh. 5	Bob Brooke	2:40	NYR
Apr. 26/86	St L.	DF	St L. 4 Tor. 3	Mark Reeds	7:11	St L.
Apr. 29/86	Mtl.	DF	Mtl. 2 Hfd. 1	Claude Lemieux	5:55	Mtl.
May 5/86	NYR	CF	Mtl. 4 NYR 3	Claude Lemieux	9:41	Mtl.
May 12/86	St L.	F	St L. 6 Cgy. 5	Doug Wickenheiser	7:30	Cgy.
May 18/86	Cgy.	F	Mtl. 3 Cgy. 2	Brian Skrudland	0:09	Mtl.
Apr. 8/87	Hfd.	DSF	Hfd. 3 Que. 2	Paul MacDermid	2:20	Que.
Apr. 9/87	Mtl.	DSF	Mtl. 4 Bos. 3	Mats Naslund	2:38	Mtl.
Apr. 9/87	St. L.	DSF	Tor. 3 St. L. 2	Rick Lanz	10:17	Tor.
Apr. 11/87	Wpg.	DSF	Cgy. 3 Wpg. 2	Mike Bullard	3:53	Wpg.
Apr. 11/87	Chi.	DSF	Det. 4 Chi. 3	Shawn Burr	4:51	Det.
Apr. 16/87	Que.	DSF	Que. 5 Hfd. 4	Peter Stastny	6:05	Que.
Apr. 18/87	Wsh.	DSF	NYI 3 Wsh. 2	Pat LaFontaine	68:47	NYI
Apr. 21/87	Edm.	DF	Edm. 3 Wpg. 2	Glenn Anderson	0:36	Edm.
Apr. 26/87	Que.	DF	Mtl. 3 Que. 2	Mats Naslund	5:30	Mtl.
Apr. 27/87	Tor.	DF	Tor. 3 Det. 2	Mike Allison	9:31	Det.
May 4/87	Phi.	CF	Phi. 4 Mtl. 3	Ilkka Sinislao	9:11	Phi.
May 20/87	Edm.	F	Edm. 3 Phi. 2	Jari Kurri	6:50	Edm.
Apr. 6/88	NYI	DSF	NYI 4 N.J. 3	Pat LaFontaine	6:11	N.J.
Apr. 10/88	Phi.	DSF	Phi. 5 Wsh. 4	Murray Craven	1:18	Wsh.
Apr. 10/88	N.J.	DSF	NYI 5 N.J. 4	Brent Sutter	15:07	N.J.
Apr. 10/88	Buf.	DSF	Buf. 6 Bos. 5	John Tucker	5:32	Bos.
Apr. 12/88	Det.	DSF	Tor. 6 Det. 5	Ed Olczyk	0:34	Det.
Apr. 16/88	Wsh.	DSF	Wsh. 5 Phi. 4	Dale Hunter	5:57	Wsh.
Apr. 21/88	Cgy.	DF	Edm. 5 Cgy. 4	Wayne Gretzky	7:54	Edm.
May 4/88	Bos.	CF	N.J. 3 Bos. 2	Doug Brown	17:46	Bos.
May 9/88	Det.	CF	Edm. 4 Det. 3	Jari Kurri	11:02	Edm.
Apr. 5/89	St. L.	DSF	St. L. 4 Min. 3	Brett Hull	11:55	St. L.

The Islanders celebrate their victory in the longest game seven in NHL history. Pat LaFontaine's goal against Bob Mason saw the Islanders eliminate the Washington Capitals on April 18, 1987.

Date	City	Series	Score	Scorer		Overtime	Series Winner
Apr. 5/89	Cgy.	DSF	Van. 4	Cgy. 3	Paul Reinhart	2:47	Cgy.
Apr. 6/89	St. L.	DSF	St. L. 4	Min. 3	Rick Meagher	5:30	St. L.
Apr. 6/89	Det.	DSF	Chi. 5	Det. 4	Duane Sutter	14:36	Chi.
Apr. 8/89	Hfd.	DSF	Mtl. 5	Hfd. 4	Stephane Richer	5:01	Mtl.
Apr. 8/89	Phi.	DSF	Wsh. 4	Phi. 3	Kelly Miller	0:51	Phi.
Apr. 9/89	Hfd.	DSF	Mtl. 4	Hfd. 3	Russ Courtnall	15:12	Mtl.
Apr. 15/89	Cgy.	DSF	Cgy. 4	Van. 3	Joel Otto	19:21	Cgy.
Apr. 18/89	Cgy.	DF	Cgy. 4	L.A. 3	Doug Gilmour	7:47	Cgy.
Apr. 19/89	Mtl.	DF	Mtl. 3	Bos. 2	Bobby Smith	12:24	Mtl.
Apr. 20/89	St. L.	DF	St. L. 5	Chi. 4	Tony Hrkac	33:49	Chi.
Apr. 21/89	Phi.	DF	Pit. 4	Phi. 3	Phil Bourque	12:08	Phi.
May 8/89	Chi.	CF	Cgy. 2	Chi. 1	Al MacInnis	15:05	Cgy.
May 9/89	Mtl.	CF	Phi. 2	Mtl. 1	Dave Poulin	5:02	Mtl.
May 19/89	Mtl.	F	Mtl. 4	Cgy. 3	Ryan Walter	38:08	Cgy.
Apr. 5/90	N.J.	DSF	Wsh. 5	N.J. 4	Dino Ciccarelli	5:34	Wsh.
Apr. 6/90	Edm.	DSF	Edm. 3	Wpg. 2	Mark Lamb	4:21	Edm.
Apr. 8/90	Tor.	DSF	St. L. 6	Tor. 5	Sergio Momesso	6:04	St. L.
Apr. 8/90	L.A.	DSF	L.A. 2	Cgy. 1	Tony Granato	8:37	L.A.
Apr. 9/90	Mtl.	DSF	Mtl. 2	Buf. 1	Brian Skrudland	12:35	Mtl.
Apr. 9/90	NYI	DSF	NYI 4	NYR 3	Brent Sutter	20:59	NYR
Apr. 10/90	Wpg.	DSF	Wpg. 4	Edm. 3	Dave Ellett	21:08	Edm.
Apr. 14/90	L.A.	DSF	L.A. 4	Cgy. 3	Mike Krushelnyski	23:14	L.A.
Apr. 15/90	Hfd.	DSF	Hfd. 3	Bos. 2	Kevin Dineen	12:30	Bos.
Apr. 21/90	Bos.	DF	Bos. 5	Mtl. 4	Garry Galley	3:42	Bos.
Apr. 24/90	L.A.	DF	Edm. 6	L.A. 5	Joe Murphy	4:42	Edm.
Apr. 25/90	Wsh.	DF	Wsh. 4	NYR 3	Rod Langway	0:34	Wsh.
Apr. 27/90	NYR	DF	Wsh. 2	NYR 1	John Druce	6:48	Wsh.
May 15/90	Bos.	F	Edm. 3	Bos. 2	Petr Klima	55:13	Edm.
Apr. 4/91	Chi.	DSF	Min. 4	Chi. 3	Brian Propp	4:14	Min.
Apr. 5/91	Pit.	DSF	Pit. 5	N.J. 4	Jaromir Jagr	8:52	Pit.
Apr. 6/91	L.A.	DSF	L.A. 3	Van. 2	Wayne Gretzky	11:08	L.A.
Apr. 8/91	Van.	DSF	Van. 2	L.A. 1	Cliff Ronning	3:12	L.A.
Apr. 11/91	NYR	DSF	Wsh. 5	NYR 4	Dino Ciccarelli	6:44	Wsh.
Apr. 11/91	Mtl.	DSF	Mtl. 4	Buf. 3	Russ Courtnall	5:56	Mtl.
Apr. 14/91	Edm.	DSF	Cgy. 2	Edm. 1	Theoren Fleury	4:40	Edm.
Apr. 16/91	Cgy.	DSF	Edm. 5	Cgy. 4	Esa Tikkanen	6:58	Edm.
Apr. 18/91	L.A.	DF	L.A. 4	Edm. 3	Luc Robitaille	2:13	Edm.
Apr. 19/91	Bos.	DF	Mtl. 4	Bos. 3	Stephane Richer	0:27	Bos.
Apr. 19/91	Pit.	DF	Pit. 7	Wsh. 6	Kevin Stevens	8:10	Pit.
Apr. 20/91	L.A.	DF	Edm. 4	L.A. 3	Petr Klima	24:48	Edm.
Apr. 22/91	Edm.	DF	Edm. 4	L.A. 3	Esa Tikkanen	20:48	Edm.
Apr. 27/91	Mtl.	DF	Mtl. 3	Bos. 2	Shayne Corson	17:47	Bos.
Apr. 28/91	Edm.	DF	Edm. 4	L.A. 3	Craig MacTavish	16:57	Edm.
May 3/91	Bos.	CF	Bos. 5	Pit. 4	Vladimir Ruzicka	8:14	Pit.
Apr. 21/92	Bos.	DSF	Bos. 3	Buf. 2	Adam Oates	11:14	Bos.
Apr. 22/92	Min.	DSF	Det. 5	Min. 4	Yves Racine	1:15	Det.
Apr. 22/92	St. L.	DSF	St. L. 5	Chi. 4	Brett Hull	23:33	Chi.
Apr. 25/92	Buf.	DSF	Bos. 5	Buf. 4	Ted Donato	2:08	Bos.
Apr. 28/92	Min.	DSF	Det. 1	Min. 0	Sergei Fedorov	16:13	Det.
Apr. 29/92	Hfd.	DSF	Hfd. 2	Mtl. 1	Yvon Corriveau	0:24	Mtl.
May 1/92	Mtl.	DSF	Mtl. 3	Hfd. 2	Russ Courtnall	25:26	Mtl.
May 3/92	Van.	DF	Edm. 4	Van. 3	Joe Murphy	8:36	Edm.
May 5/92	Mtl.	DF	Bos. 3	Mtl. 2	Peter Douris	3:12	Bos.
May 7/92	Pit.	DF	NYR 6	Pit. 5	Kris King	1:29	Pit.
May 9/92	Pit.	DF	Pit. 5	NYR 4	Ron Francis	2:47	Pit.
May 17/92	Pit.	CF	Pit. 4	Bos. 3	Jaromir Jagr	9:44	Pit.
May 20/92	Edm.	CF	Chi. 4	Edm. 3	Jeremy Roenick	2:45	Chi.
Apr. 18/93	Bos.	DSF	Buf. 5	Bos. 4	Bob Sweeney	11:03	Buf.
Apr. 18/93	Que.	DSF	Que. 3	Mtl. 2	Scott Young	16:49	Mtl.
Apr. 20/93	Wsh.	DSF	NYI 5	Wsh. 4	Brian Mullen	34:50	NYI
Apr. 22/93	Mtl.	DSF	Mtl. 2	Que. 1	Vincent Damphousse	10:30	Mtl.
Apr. 22/93	Buf.	DSF	Buf. 4	Bos. 3	Yuri Khmylev	1:05	Buf.
Apr. 22/93	NYI	DSF	NYI 4	Wsh. 3	Ray Ferraro	4:46	NYI
Apr. 24/93	Buf.	DSF	Buf. 6	Bos. 5	Brad May	4:48	Buf.
Apr. 24/93	NYI	DSF	NYI 4	Wsh. 3	Ray Ferraro	25:40	NYI
Apr. 25/93	St. L.	DSF	St. L. 4	Chi. 3	Craig Janney	10:43	St. L.
Apr. 26/93	Que.	DSF	Mtl. 5	Que. 4	Kirk Muller	8:17	Mtl.
Apr. 27/93	Det.	DSF	Tor. 5	Det. 4	Mike Foligno	2:05	Tor.
Apr. 27/93	Van.	DSF	Wpg. 4	Van. 3	Teemu Selanne	6:18	Van.
Apr. 29/93	Wpg.	DSF	Van. 4	Wpg. 3	Greg Adams	4:30	Van.
May 1/93	Det.	DSF	Tor. 4	Det. 3	Nikolai Borschevsky	2:35	Tor.
May 3/93	Tor.	DF	Tor. 2	St. L. 1	Doug Gilmour	23:16	Tor.
May 4/93	Mtl.	DF	Mtl. 4	Buf. 3	Guy Carbonneau	2:50	Mtl.
May 5/93	Tor.	DF	St. L. 2	Tor. 1	Jeff Brown	23:03	Tor.
May 6/93	Buf.	DF	Mtl. 4	Buf. 3	Gilbert Dionne	8:28	Mtl.
May 8/93	Buf.	DF	Mtl. 4	Buf. 3	Kirk Muller	11:37	Mtl.
May 11/93	Van.	DF	L.A. 4	Van. 3	Gary Shuchuk	26:31	L.A.
May 14/93	Pit.	DF	NYI 4	Pit. 3	Dave Volek	5:16	NYI
May 18/93	Mtl.	CF	Mtl. 4	NYI 3	Stephan Lebeau	26:21	Mtl.
May 20/93	NYI	CF	Mtl. 2	NYI 1	Guy Carbonneau	12:34	Mtl.
May 25/93	Tor.	CF	Tor. 3	L.A. 2	Glenn Anderson	19:20	L.A.
May 27/93	L.A.	CF	L.A. 5	Tor. 4	Wayne Gretzky	1:41	L.A.
Jun. 3/93	Mtl.	F	Mtl. 3	L.A. 2	Eric Desjardins	0:51	Mtl.
Jun. 5/93	L.A.	F	Mtl. 4	L.A. 3	John LeClair	0:34	Mtl.
Jun. 7/93	L.A.	F	Mtl. 3	L.A. 2	John LeClair	14:37	Mtl.
Apr. 20/94	Tor.	CQF	Tor. 1	Chi. 0	Todd Gill	2:15	Tor.
Apr. 22/94	St. L.	CQF	Dal. 5	St. L. 4	Paul Cavallini	8:34	Dal.
Apr. 24/94	Chi.	CQF	Chi. 4	Tor. 3	Jeremy Roenick	1:23	Tor.
Apr. 25/94	Bos.	CQF	Mtl. 2	Bos. 1	Kirk Muller	17:18	Bos.
Apr. 26/94	Cgy.	CQF	Van. 2	Cgy. 1	Geoff Courtnall	7:15	Van.
Apr. 27/94	Buf.	CQF	Buf. 1	N.J. 0	Dave Hannan	65:43	N.J.
Apr. 28/94	Van.	CQF	Van. 3	Cgy. 2	Trevor Linden	16:43	Van.
Apr. 30/94	Cgy.	CQF	Van. 4	Cgy. 3	Pavel Bure	22:20	Van.
May 3/94	N.J.	CSF	Bos. 6	N.J. 5	Don Sweeney	9:08	N.J.
May 7/94	Bos.	CSF	N.J. 5	Bos. 4	Stephane Richer	14:19	N.J.
May 8/94	Van.	CSF	Van. 2	Dal. 1	Sergio Momesso	11:01	Van.
May 12/94	Tor.	CSF	Tor. 3	S.J. 2	Mike Gartner	8:53	Tor.
May 15/94	NYR	CF	N.J. 4	NYR 3	Stephane Richer	35:23	NYR
May 16/94	Tor.	CF	Tor. 3	Van. 2	Peter Zezel	16:55	Van.
May 19/94	N.J.	CF	NYR 3	N.J. 2	Stephane Matteau	26:13	NYR
May 24/94	Van.	CF	Van. 4	Tor. 3	Greg Adams	20:14	Van.
May 27/94	NYR	CF	NYR 2	N.J. 1	Stephane Matteau	24:24	NYR
May 31/94	NYR	F	Van. 3	NYR 2	Greg Adams	19:26	NYR

Date	City	Series	Score	Scorer		Overtime	Series Winner
May 7/95	Phi.	CQF	Phi. 4	Buf. 3	Karl Dykhuis	10:06	Phi.
May 9/95	Cgy.	CQF	S.J. 5	Cgy. 4	Ulf Dahlen	12:21	S.J.
May 12/95	NYR	CQF	NYR 3	Que. 2	Steve Larmer	8:09	NYR
May 12/95	N.J.	CQF	N.J. 1	Bos. 0	Randy McKay	8:51	N.J.
May 14/95	Pit.	CQF	Pit. 6	Wsh. 5	Luc Robitaille	4:30	Pit.
May 15/95	St. L.	CQF	Van. 6	St. L. 5	Cliff Ronning	1:48	Van.
May 17/95	Tor.	CQF	Tor. 5	Chi. 4	Randy Wood	10:00	Chi.
May 19/95	Cgy.	CQF	S.J. 5	Cgy. 4	Ray Whitney	21:54	S.J.
May 21/95	Phi.	CSF	Phi. 5	NYR 4	Eric Desjardins	7:03	Phi.
May 21/95	Chi.	CSF	Chi. 2	Van. 1	Joe Murphy	9:04	Chi.
May 22/95	Phi.	CSF	Phi. 4	NYR 3	Kevin Haller	0:25	Phi.
May 25/95	Van.	CSF	Chi. 3	Van. 2	Chris Chelios	6:22	Chi.
May 26/95	N.J.	CSF	N.J. 2	Pit. 1	Neal Broten	18:36	N.J.
May 27/95	Van.	CSF	Chi. 4	Van. 3	Chris Chelios	5:35	Chi.
Jun. 1/95	Det.	CF	Det. 2	Chi. 1	Nicklas Lidstrom	1:01	Det.
Jun. 6/95	Chi.	CF	Det. 4	Chi. 3	Vladimir Konstantinov	29:25	Det.
Jun. 7/95	N.J.	CF	Phi. 3	N.J. 2	Eric Lindros	4:19	N.J.
Jun. 11/95	Det.	CF	Det. 2	Chi. 1	Vyacheslav Kozlov	22:25	Det.
Apr. 16/96	NYR	CQF	Mtl. 3	NYR 2	Vincent Damphousse	5:04	NYR
Apr. 18/96	Tor.	CQF	Tor. 5	St. L. 4	Mats Sundin	4:02	St. L.
Apr. 18/96	Phi.	CQF	T.B. 2	Phi. 1	Brian Bellows	9:05	Phi.
Apr. 21/96	St. L.	CQF	St. L. 3	Tor. 2	Glenn Anderson	1:24	St. L.
Apr. 21/96	T.B.	CQF	T.B. 5	Phi. 4	Alexander Selivanov	2:04	Phi.
Apr. 23/96	Cgy.	CQF	Chi. 2	Cgy. 1	Joe Murphy	50:02	Chi.
Apr. 24/96	Wsh.	CQF	Pit. 3	Wsh. 2	Petr Nedved	79:15	Pit.
Apr. 25/96	Col.	CQF	Col. 5	Van. 4	Joe Sakic	0:51	Col.
Apr. 25/96	Tor.	CQF	Tor. 5	St. L. 4	Mike Gartner	7:31	St. L.
May 2/96	Col.	CSF	Chi. 3	Col. 2	Jeremy Roenick	6:29	Col.
May 6/96	Chi.	CSF	Chi. 4	Col. 3	Sergei Krivokrasov	0:46	Col.
May 8/96	St. L.	CSF	St. L. 5	Det. 4	Igor Kravchuk	3:23	Det.
May 8/96	Chi.	CSF	Col. 3	Chi. 2	Joe Sakic	44:33	Col.
May 9/96	Fla.	CSF	Fla. 4	Phi. 3	Dave Lowry	4:06	Fla.
May 12/96	Phi.	CSF	Fla. 2	Phi. 1	Mike Hough	28:05	Fla.
May 13/96	Chi.	CSF	Col. 4	Chi. 3	Sandis Ozolinsh	25:18	Col.
May 16/96	Det.	CSF	Det. 1	St. L. 0	Steve Yzerman	21:15	Det.
May 19/96	Det.	CF	Col. 3	Det. 2	Mike Keane	17:31	Col.
Jun. 10/96	Fla.	F	Col. 1	Fla. 0	Uwe Krupp	44:31	Col.
Apr. 20/97	Chi.	CQF	Chi. 4	Col. 3	Sergei Krivokrasov	31:03	Col.
Apr. 20/97	Edm.	CQF	Edm. 4	Dal. 3	Kelly Buchberger	9:15	Edm.
Apr. 22/97	NYR	CQF	NYR 4	Fla. 3	Esa Tikkanen	16:29	NYR
Apr. 23/97	Ott.	CQF	Ott. 1	Buf. 0	Daniel Alfredsson	2:34	Buf.
Apr. 24/97	Mtl.	CQF	Mtl. 4	N.J. 3	Patrice Brisebois	47:37	N.J.
Apr. 25/97	Fla.	CQF	NYR 3	Fla. 2	Esa Tikkanen	12:02	NYR
Apr. 25/97	Dal.	CQF	Edm. 1	Dal. 0	Ryan Smyth	20:22	Edm.
Apr. 27/97	Phx.	CQF	Ana. 3	Phx. 2	Paul Kariya	7:29	Ana.
Apr. 29/97	Buf.	CQF	Buf. 3	Ott. 2	Derek Plante	5:24	Buf.
Apr. 29/97	Dal.	CQF	Edm. 4	Dal. 3	Todd Marchant	12:26	Edm.
May 2/97	Det.	CSF	Det. 2	Ana. 1	Martin Lapointe	0:59	Det.
May 4/97	Det.	CSF	Det. 3	Ana. 2	Vyacheslav Kozlov	41:31	Det.
May 8/97	Ana.	CSF	Det. 3	Ana. 2	Brendan Shanahan	37:03	Det.
May 9/97	Phi.	CSF	Buf. 5	Phi. 4	Ed Ronan	6:24	Phi.
May 9/97	Edm.	CSF	Col. 3	Edm. 2	Claude Lemieux	8:35	Col.
May 11/97	N.J.	CSF	NYR 2	N.J. 1	Adam Graves	14:08	NYR
Apr. 22/98	N.J.	CQF	OTT. 2	N.J. 1	Bruce Gardiner	5:58	Ott.
Apr. 23/98	Pit.	CQF	Mtl. 3	Pit. 2	Benoit Brunet	18:43	Mtl.
Apr. 24/98	Wsh.	CQF	Bos. 4	Wsh. 3	Darren Van Impe	20:54	Wsh.
Apr. 26/98	Ott.	CQF	Ott. 2	N.J. 1	Alexei Yashin	2:47	Ott.
Apr. 26/98	Bos.	CQF	Wsh. 3	Bos. 2	Joe Juneau	26:31	Wsh.
Apr. 26/98	Edm.	CQF	Col. 5	Edm. 4	Joe Sakic	15:25	Edm.
Apr. 28/98	S.J.	CQF	S.J. 1	Dal. 0	Andrei Zyuzin	6:31	Dal.
May 1/98	Phi.	CQF	Buf. 3	Phi. 2	Michal Grosek	5:40	Buf.
May 2/98	S.J.	CQF	Dal. 3	S.J. 2	Mike Keane	3:43	Dal.
May 3/98	Bos.	CQF	Wsh. 3	Bos. 2	Brian Bellows	15:24	Wsh.
May 3/98	Buf.	CSF	Buf. 3	Mtl. 2	Geoff Sanderson	2:37	Buf.
May 11/98	Edm.	CSF	Dal. 1	Edm. 0	Benoit Hogue	13:07	Dal.
May 12/98	Mtl.	CSF	Buf. 5	Mtl. 4	Michael Peca	21:24	Buf.
May 12/98	St.L.	CSF	Det. 3	St.L. 2	Brendan Shanahan	31:12	Det.
May 25/98	Wsh.	CF	Wsh. 3	Buf. 2	Todd Krygier	3:01	Wsh.
May 28/98	Buf.	CF	Wsh. 4	Buf. 3	Peter Bondra	9:37	Wsh.
Jun. 3/98	Dal.	CF	Dal. 3	Det. 2	Jamie Langenbrunner	0:46	Det.
Jun. 4/98	Buf.	CF	Wsh. 3	Buf. 2	Joe Juneau	6:24	Wsh.
Jun. 11/98	Det.	F	Det. 5	Wsh. 4	Kris Draper	15:24	Det.
Apr. 23/99	Ott.	CQF	Buf. 3	Ott. 2	Miroslav Satan	30:35	Buf.
Apr. 24/99	Car.	CQF	Car. 3	Bos. 2	Ray Sheppard	17:05	Bos.
Apr. 24/99	Phx.	CQF	Phx. 4	St. L. 3	Shane Doan	8:58	St. L.
Apr. 26/99	S.J.	CQF	Col. 2	S.J. 1	Milan Hejduk	7:53	Col.
Apr. 27/99	Edm.	CQF	Dal. 3	Edm. 2	Joe Nieuwendyk	57:34	Dal.
Apr. 30/99	Tor.	CQF	Tor. 2	Phi. 1	Yanic Perreault	11:51	Tor.
Apr. 30/99	Car.	CQF	Bos. 4	Car. 3	Anson Carter	34:45	Bos.
Apr. 30/99	Phx..	CQF	St.L. 2	Phx. 1	Scott Young	5:43	St.L.
May 2/99	Pit.	CQF	Pit. 3	N.J. 2	Jaromir Jagr	8:59	Pit.
May 3/99	S.J.	CQF	Col. 3	S.J. 2	Milan Hejduk	13:12	Col.
May 4/99	Phx.	CQF	St. L. 1	Phx. 0	Pierre Turgeon	17:59	St. L.
May 7/99	Col.	CSF	Det. 3	Col. 2	Kirk Maltby	4:18	Col.
May 8/99	Dal.	CSF	Dal. 5	St. L. 4	Joe Nieuwendyk	8:22	Dal.
May 10/99	St.L.	CSF	St. L. 3	Dal. 2	Pavol Demitra	2:43	Dal.
May 12/99	St.L.	CSF	St. L. 3	Dal. 2	Pierre Turgeon	5:52	Dal.
May 13/99	Pit.	CSF	Tor. 3	Pit. 2	Sergei Berezin	2:18	Tor.
May 17/99	Pit.	CSF	Tor. 4	Pit. 3	Garry Valk	1:57	Tor.
May 17/99	St.L.	CSF	Dal. 2	St. L. 1	Mike Mondano	2:21	Dal.
May 28/99	Col.	CF	Col. 3	Dal. 2	Chris Drury	19:29	Dal.
Jun. 8/99	Dal.	F	Buf. 3	Dal. 2	Jason Woolley	15:30	Dal.
Jun. 19/99	Buf.	F	Dal. 2	Buf. 1	Brett Hull	54:51	Dal.
Apr. 15/00	Pit.	CQF	Pit. 2	Wsh. 1	Jaromir Jagr	5:49	Pit.
Apr. 18/00	Buf.	CQF	Buf. 3	Phi. 2	Stu Barnes	4:42	Phi.
Apr. 22/00	Tor.	CQF	Tor. 2	Ott. 1	Steve Thomas	14:47	Tor.
May 2/00	Pit.	CSF	Phi. 4	Pit. 3	Andy Delmore	11:01	Phi.
May 3/00	Det.	CSF	Col. 3	Det. 2	Chris Drury	10:21	Col.
May 4/00	Pit.	CSF	Pit. 2	Pit. 1	Keith Primeau	92:01	Phi.
May 23/00	Dal.	CF	Dal. 3	Col. 2	Joe Nieuwendyk	12:10	Dal.
Jun. 8/00	N.J.	F	Dal. 1	N.J. 0	Mike Modano	46:21	N.J.
Jun. 10/00	Dal.	F	N.J. 2	Dal. 1	Jason Arnott	28:20	N.J.

NHL Playoff Coaching Records

Coach	Team	Games Coached	Wins	Losses	Ties	%Wins	Playoff Years	Cup Wins	Career
Abel, Sid	Chicago	7	3	4	0	.429	1		
	Detroit	69	29	40	0	.420	8		
	Total	76	32	44	0	.421	9		1952-76
Adams, Jack	Detroit	105	52	52	1	.500	15	3	1927-46
Allen, Keith	Philadelphia	11	3	8	0	.273	2		1967-69
Arbour, Al	St. Louis	11	4	7	0	.364	1		
	NY Islanders	198	119	79	0	.601	15	4	
	Total	209	123	86	0	.589	16	4	1970-94
Berenson, Red	St. Louis	14	5	9	0	.357	2		1979-82
Bergeron, Michel	Quebec	68	31	37	0	.456	7		1980-90
Berry, Bob	Los Angeles	10	2	8	0	.200	3		
	Montreal	8	2	6	0	.250	2		
	St. Louis	15	7	8	0	.467	2		
	Total	33	11	22	0	.333	7		1978-94
Beverley, Nick	Toronto	6	2	4	0	.333	1		1995-96
Blackburn, Don	Hartford	3	0	3	0	.000	1		1979-81
Blair, Wren	Minnesota	14	7	7	0	.500	1		1967-70
Blake, Toe	Montreal	119	82	37	0	.689	13	8	1955-68
Boileau, Marc	Pittsburgh	9	5	4	0	.556	1		1973-76
Boivin, Leo	St. Louis	3	1	2	0	.333	1		1975-78
Boucher, Frank	NY Rangers	27	13	14	0	.481	4	1	1939-54
Boucher, George	Mtl. Maroons	2	0	2	0	.000	1		1930-50
Bowman, Scotty	St. Louis	52	26	26	0	.500	4		
	Montreal	98	70	28	0	.714	8	5	
	Buffalo	36	18	18	0	.500	5		
	Pittsburgh	33	23	10	0	.697	2	1	
	Detroit	105	68	37	0	.648	7	2	
	Total	324	205	119	0	.633	26	8	1967-00
Bowness, Rick	Boston	15	8	7	0	.533	1		1988-98
Brooks, Herb	NY Rangers	24	12	12	0	.500	3		
	New Jersey	5	1	4	0	.200	1		
	Pittsburgh	11	6	5	0	.545	1		
	Total	40	19	21	0	.475	5		1981-00
Brophy, John	Toronto	19	9	10	0	.474	2		1986-89
Burns, Charlie	Minnesota	6	2	4	0	.333	1		1969-75
Burns, Pat	Montreal	56	30	26	0	.536	4		
	Toronto	46	23	23	0	.500	3		
	Boston	18	8	10	0	.444	3		
	Total	120	61	59	0	.508	9		1988-00
Campbell, Colin	NY Rangers	36	18	18	0	.500	3		1994-98
Carpenter, Doug	Toronto	5	1	4	0	.200	1		1984-91
Carroll, Dick	Toronto	9	4	5	0	.444	2	1	1917-19
Cheevers, Gerry	Boston	34	15	19	0	.441	4		1980-85
Cherry, Don	Boston	55	31	24	0	.564	5		1974-80
Clancy, King	Toronto	14	2	12	0	.143	3		1937-56
Clapper, Dit	Boston	25	8	17	0	.320	4		1945-49
Cleghorn, Odie	Pittsburgh	4	1	2	1	.375	2		1925-29
Cleghorn, Sprague	Mtl. Maroons	4	1	1	2	.500	1		1931-32
Constantine, Kevin	San Jose	25	11	14	0	.440	2		
	Pittsburgh	19	8	11	0	.421	2		
	Total	44	19	25	0	.432	4		1993-00
Crawford, Marc	Quebec	6	2	4	0	.333	1		
	Colorado	46	29	17	0	.630	3	1	
	Total	52	31	21	0	.596	4	1	1994-00
Creighton, Fred	Atlanta	9	2	7	0	.222	4		1974-80
Crisp, Terry	Calgary	37	22	15	0	.595	3	1	
	Tampa Bay	6	2	4	0	.333	1		
	Total	43	24	19	0	.558	4	1	1987-98
Crozier, Joe	Buffalo	6	2	4	0	.333	1		1971-81
Cunniff, John	New Jersey	6	2	4	0	.333	1		1982-91
Curry, Alex	Ottawa	2	0	1	1	.250	1		1925-26
Dandurand, Leo	Montreal	16	10	6	0	.625	4	1	1921-35
Day, Hap	Toronto	80	49	31	0	.613	9	5	1940-50
Demers, Jacques	St. Louis	33	16	17	0	.485	3		
	Detroit	38	20	18	0	.526	3		
	Montreal	27	19	8	0	.704	2	1	
	Total	98	55	43	0	.561	8	1	1979-98
Denneny, Cy	Boston	5	5	0	0	1.000	1	1	1928-33
Dudley, Rick	Buffalo	12	4	8	0	.333	1		1989-92
Dugal, Jules	Montreal	3	1	2	0	.333	1		1938-39
Duncan, Art	Toronto	2	0	1	1	.250	1	1	1926-32
Dutton, Red	NY Americans	16	6	10	0	.375	4		1935-42
Esposito, Phil	NY Rangers	10	2	8	0	.200	2		1986-89
Evans, Jack	Hartford	16	8	8	0	.500	3		1975-88
Ferguson, John	Winnipeg	3	0	3	0	.000	1		1975-86
Francis, Bob	Phoenix	5	1	4	0	.200	1		1999-00
Francis, Emile	NY Rangers	75	34	41	0	.453	9		
	St. Louis	14	5	9	0	.357	2		
	Total	89	39	50	0	.438	11		1965-83
Ftorek, Robbie	Los Angeles	16	5	11	0	.313	2		
	New Jersey	7	3	4	0	.429	1		
	Total	23	8	15	0	.348	3		1987-00
Gainey, Bob	Minnesota	30	17	13	0	.567	2		
	Dallas	14	6	8	0	.429	2		
	Total	44	23	21	0	.523	4		1990-96
Geoffrion, Bernie	Atlanta	4	0	4	0	.000	1		1968-80
Gerard, Eddie	Mtl. Maroons	25	11	9	5	.540	1	1	1917-35
Gill, David	Ottawa	8	3	2	3	.563	2	1	1926-29
Glover, Fred	Oakland	11	3	8	0	.273	1		1968-74
Gordon, Jackie	Minnesota	25	11	14	0	.440	3		1970-75
Goring, Butch	Boston	3	0	3	0	.000	1		1985-98

Coach	Team	Games Coached	Wins	Losses	Ties	%Wins	Playoff Years	Cup Wins	Career
Gorman, Tommy	NY Americans	2	0	1	1	.250	1		
	Chicago	8	6	1	1	.813	1	1	
	Mtl. Maroons	15	7	6	2	.533	3	1	
	Total	25	13	8	4	.600	5	2	1925-38
Gottselig, Johnny	Chicago	4	0	4	0	.000	1		1944-48
Green, Pete	Ottawa	26	14	9	3	.596	6	3	1919-25
Green, Ted	Edmonton	16	8	8	0	.500	1		1991-94
Guidolin, Bep	Boston	21	11	10	0	.524	2		1972-76
Harris, Ted	Minnesota	2	0	2	0	.000	1		1975-78
Hart, Cecil	Montreal	37	16	17	4	.486	8	2	1926-39
Hartley, Bob	Colorado	36	22	14	0	.611	2		1998-00
Hartsburg, Craig	Chicago	16	8	8	0	.500	2		
	Anaheim	4	0	4	0	.000	1		
	Total	20	8	12	0	.400	3		1995-00
Harvey, Doug	NY Rangers	6	2	4	0	.333	1		1961-62
Hay, Don	Phoenix	7	3	4	0	.429	1		1996-97
Henning, Lorne	Minnesota	5	2	3	0	.400	1		1985-95
Hitchcock, Ken	Dallas	70	43	27	0	.614	4	1	1995-00
Holmgren, Paul	Philadelphia	19	10	9	0	.526	1		1988-96
Imlach, Punch	Toronto	92	44	48	0	.478	11	4	1958-80
Inglis, Bill	Buffalo	3	1	2	0	.333	1		1978-79
Irvin, Dick	Chicago	9	5	3	1	.611	1		
	Toronto	66	33	32	1	.508	9	1	
	Montreal	115	62	53	0	.539	14	3	
	Total	190	100	88	2	.532	24	4	1928-56
Ivan, Tommy	Detroit	67	36	31	0	.537	7	3	1947-58
Johnson, Bob	Calgary	52	25	27	0	.481	5		
	Pittsburgh	24	16	8	0	.667	1	1	
	Total	76	41	35	0	.539	6	1	1982-91
Johnson, Tom	Boston	22	15	7	0	.682	2	1	1970-73
Johnston, Eddie	Chicago	7	3	4	0	.429	1		
	Pittsburgh	46	22	24	0	.478	5		
	Total	53	25	28	0	.472	6		1979-97
Kasper, Steve	Boston	5	1	4	0	.200	1		1995-97
Keenan, Mike	Philadelphia	57	32	25	0	.561	4		
	Chicago	60	33	27	0	.550	4		
	NY Rangers	23	16	7	0	.696	1	1	
	St. Louis	20	10	10	0	.500	2		
	Total	160	91	69	0	.569	11	1	1984-99
Kelly, Pat	Colorado	2	0	2	0	.000	1		1977-79
Kelly, Red	Los Angeles	18	7	11	0	.389	2		
	Pittsburgh	14	6	8	0	.429	2		
	Toronto	30	11	19	0	.367	4		
	Total	62	24	38	0	.387	8		1967-77
King, Dave	Calgary	20	8	12	0	.400	3		1992-95
Kromm, Bobby	Detroit	7	3	4	0	.429	1		1977-80
Lalonde, Newsy	Montreal	16	7	6	3	.531	4		
	Ottawa	2	0	1	1	.250	1		
	Total	18	7	7	4	.500	5		1917-35
Lemaire, Jacques	Montreal	27	15	12	0	.556	2		
	New Jersey	56	34	22	0	.607	4	1	
	Total	83	49	34	0	.590	6	1	1983-98
Ley, Rick	Hartford	13	5	8	0	.385	2		
	Vancouver	11	4	7	0	.364	1		
	Total	24	9	15	0	.375	3		1989-96
Long, Barry	Winnipeg	11	3	8	0	.273	2		1983-86
Loughlin, Clem	Chicago	4	1	2	1	.375	2		1934-37
Low, Ron	Edmonton	28	10	18	0	.357	2		1994-99
Lowe, Kevin	Edmonton	5	1	4	0	.200	1		1999-00
MacLean, Doug	Florida	27	13	14	0	.481	2		1995-98
MacNeil, Al	Montreal	20	12	8	0	.600	1	1	
	Atlanta	4	1	3	0	.250	1		
	Calgary	19	9	10	0	.474	2		
	Total	43	22	21	0	.512	4	1	1970-82
Magnuson, Keith	Chicago	3	0	3	0	.000	1		1980-82
Mahoney, Bill	Minnesota	16	7	9	0	.438	1		1983-85
Maloney, Dan	Toronto	10	6	4	0	.600	1		
	Winnipeg	15	5	10	0	.333	2		
	Total	25	11	14	0	.440	3		1984-89
Maloney, Phil	Vancouver	7	1	6	0	.143	2		1973-77
Martin, Jacques	St. Louis	16	7	9	0	.438	2		
	Ottawa	28	10	18	0	.357	4		
	Total	44	17	27	0	.386	6		1986-00
Maurice, Paul	Carolina	6	2	4	0	.333	1		1995-00
McCammon, Bob	Philadelphia	10	1	9	0	.100	1		
	Vancouver	7	3	4	0	.429	1		
	Total	17	4	13	0	.235	4		1978-91
McLellan, John	Toronto	11	3	8	0	.273	2		1969-73
McVie, Tom	New Jersey	14	6	8	0	.429	2		1975-92
Melrose, Barry	Los Angeles	24	13	11	0	.542	1		1992-95
Milbury, Mike	Boston	40	23	17	0	.575	2		1989-98
Muckler, John	Edmonton	40	25	15	0	.625	2	1	
	Buffalo	27	11	16	0	.407	4		
	Total	67	36	31	0	.537	6	1	1968-00
Muldoon, Pete	Chicago	2	0	1	1	.250	1		1926-27
Munro, Dunc	Mtl. Maroons	4	1	3	0	.250	1		1929-31
Murdoch, Bob	Chicago	5	1	4	0	.200	1		
	Winnipeg	7	3	4	0	.429	1		
	Total	12	4	8	0	.333	2		1987-91
Murphy, Mike	Los Angeles	5	1	4	0	.200	1		1986-98
Murray, Andy	Los Angeles	4	0	4	0	.000	1		1999-00
Murray, Bryan	Washington	53	24	29	0	.453	7		
	Detroit	25	10	15	0	.400	3		
	Total	78	34	44	0	.436	10		1981-98

Coach	Team	Games Coached	Wins	Losses	Ties	%Wins	Playoff Years	Cup Wins	Career
Murray, Terry	Washington	39	18	21	0	.462	4		
	Philadelphia	46	28	18	0	.609	3		
	Florida	4	0	4	0	.000	1		
	Total	89	46	43	0	.517	8		1989-00
Neale, Harry	**Vancouver**	14	3	11	0	.214	4		1978-86
Neilson, Roger	Toronto	19	8	11	0	.421	2		
	Buffalo	8	4	4	0	.500	1		
	Vancouver	21	12	9	0	.571	2		
	NY Rangers	29	13	16	0	.448	3		
	Philadelphia	29	14	15	0	.483	3		
	Total	106	51	55	0	.481	11		1977-00
Nolan, Ted	**Buffalo**	12	5	7	0	.417	1		1995-97
Nykoluk, Mike	**Toronto**	7	1	6	0	.143	2		1980-84
O'Donoghue, George	**Toronto**	7	4	2	1	.773	1		1921-23
O'Reilly, Terry	**Boston**	37	17	19	1	.473	3		1986-89
Oliver, Murray	**Minnesota**	13	5	8	0	.385	2		1981-83
Paddock, John	**Winnipeg**	13	5	8	0	.385	2		1991-95
Page, Pierre	Minnesota	12	4	8	0	.333	2		
	Quebec	6	2	4	0	.333	1		
	Calgary	4	0	4	0	.000	1		
	Total	22	6	16	0	.273	4		1988-98
Patrick, Craig	NY Rangers	17	7	10	0	.412	2		
	Pittsburgh	5	1	4	0	.200	1		
	Total	22	8	14	0	.364	3		1980-97
Patrick, Frank	**Boston**	6	2	4	0	.333	2		1934-36
Patrick, Lester	**NY Rangers**	65	32	26	7	.546	12	2	1926-39
Patrick, Lynn	NY Rangers	12	7	5	0	.583	1		
	Boston	28	9	18	1	.339	4		
	Total	40	16	23	1	.413	5		1948-76
Perron, Jean	**Montreal**	48	30	18	0	.625	3	1	1985-89
Perry, Don	**Los Angeles**	10	4	6	0	.400	1		1981-84
Pilous, Rudy	**Chicago**	41	19	22	0	.463	5	1	1957-63
Plager, Barclay	**St. Louis**	4	1	3	0	.250	1		1977-83
Pleau, Larry	**Hartford**	10	2	8	0	.200	2		1980-89
Polano, Nick	**Detroit**	7	1	6	0	.143	2		1982-85
Powers, Eddie	**Toronto**	2	0	2	0	.000	1		1924-26
Primeau, Joe	**Toronto**	15	8	6	1	.567	2	1	1950-53
Pronovost, Marcel	**Buffalo**	8	3	5	0	.375	1		1977-79
Pulford, Bob	Los Angeles	26	10	16	0	.385	4		
	Chicago	45	17	28	0	.378	6		
	Total	71	27	44	0	.380	10		1972-00
Quenneville, Joel	**St. Louis**	36	17	19	0	.472	4		1996-00
Quinn, Pat	Philadelphia	39	22	17	0	.564	3		
	Los Angeles	3	0	3	0	.000	1		
	Vancouver	61	31	30	0	.508	5		
	Toronto	29	15	14	0	.517	2		
	Total	132	68	64	0	.515	11		1978-00
Reay, Billy	**Chicago**	116	56	60	0	.483	12		1957-77
Risebrough, Doug	**Calgary**	7	3	4	0	.429	1		1990-00
Roberts, Jim	**Hartford**	7	3	4	0	.429	1		1981-97
Robinson, Larry	Los Angeles	4	0	4	0	.000	1		
	New Jersey	23	16	7	0	.696	1	1	
	Total	27	16	11	0	.593	2	1	1996-00
Ross, Art	**Boston**	65	27	33	5	.454	11	1	1917-45
Ruel, Claude	**Montreal**	27	18	9	0	.667	3	2	1968-81
Ruff, Lindy	**Buffalo**	41	25	16	0	.610	3		1997-00
Sather, Glen	**Edmonton**	127	89	37	1	.705	10	4	1979-94
Sator, Ted	NY Rangers	16	8	8	0	.500	1		
	Buffalo	11	3	8	0	.273	2		
	Total	27	11	16	0	.407	3		1985-89
Schinkel, Ken	**Pittsburgh**	6	2	4	0	.333	2		1972-77
Schmidt, Milt	**Boston**	34	15	19	0	.441	4		1954-76
Schoenfeld, Jim	New Jersey	20	11	9	0	.550	1		
	Washington	24	10	14	0	.417	3		
	Phoenix	13	5	8	0	.385	2		
	Total	57	26	31	0	.456	6		1985-99
Shero, Fred	Philadelphia	83	48	35	0	.578	6	2	
	NY Rangers	27	15	12	0	.556	2		
	Total	110	63	47	0	.573	8	2	1971-81
Simpson, Terry	NY Islanders	20	9	11	0	.450	2		
	Winnipeg	6	2	4	0	.333	1		
	Total	26	11	15	0	.423	3		1986-96
Sinden, Harry	**Boston**	43	24	19	0	.558	5	1	1966-85
Skinner, Jimmy	**Detroit**	26	14	12	0	.538	3	1	1954-58
Smith, Alf	**Ottawa**	5	1	4	0	.200	1		1918-19
Smith, Floyd	**Buffalo**	32	16	16	0	.500	3		1971-80
Smythe, Conn	**Toronto**	4	2	2	0	.500	1		1927-31
Sonmor, Glen	**Minnesota**	43	25	18	0	.581	3		1978-87
Stasiuk, Vic	**Philadelphia**	4	0	4	0	.000	1		1969-73
Stewart, Bill	**Chicago**	10	7	3	0	.700	1	1	1937-39
Stewart, Ron	**Los Angeles**	2	0	2	0	.000	1		1975-78
Sutter, Brian	St. Louis	41	20	21	0	.488	4		
	Boston	22	7	15	0	.318	3		
	Total	63	27	36	0	.429	7		1988-00
Sutter, Darryl	Chicago	26	11	15	0	.423	3		
	San Jose	24	9	15	0	.375	3		
	Total	50	20	30	0	.400	6		1992-00
Talbot, Jean-Guy	St. Louis	5	1	4	0	.200	1		
	NY Rangers	3	1	2	0	.333	1		
	Total	8	2	6	0	.250	2		1972-78
Tessier, Orval	**Chicago**	18	9	9	0	.500	2		1982-85
Thompson, Paul	**Chicago**	19	7	12	0	.368	4		1938-45
Tobin, Bill	**Chicago**	4	1	2	1	.375	2		1929-32
Tremblay, Mario	**Montreal**	11	3	8	0	.273	2		1995-97
Ubriaco, Gene	**Pittsburgh**	11	7	4	0	.636	1		1988-90
Vigneault, Alain	**Montreal**	10	4	6	0	.400	1		1997-00
Watson, Phil	**NY Rangers**	16	4	12	0	.250	3		1955-63
Watt, Tom	Winnipeg	7	1	6	0	.143	2		
	Vancouver	3	0	3	0	.000	1		
	Total	10	1	9	0	.100	3		1981-92
Webster, Tom	**Los Angeles**	28	12	16	0	.429	3		1986-92
Weiland, Cooney	**Boston**	17	10	7	0	.588	2	1	1939-41
White, Bill	**Chicago**	2	0	2	0	.000	1		1976-77
Wilson, Johnny	**Pittsburgh**	12	4	8	0	.333	2		1969-80
Wilson, Ron	Anaheim	11	4	7	0	.364	1		
	Washington	26	13	13	0	.500	2		
	Total	37	17	20	0	.448	3		1993-00
Young, Garry	**St. Louis**	2	0	2	0	.000	1		1972-76

Lester Patrick donned the pads to help the Rangers win their first Stanley Cup title in 1928. He coached them to another title in 1933. Mike Keenan helped the team end a 54-year Stanley Cup jinx when he guided the Rangers to victory in 1994.

Penalty Shots in Stanley Cup Playoff Games

Date	Player	Goaltender	Scored	Final Score				Series
Mar. 25/37	Lionel Conacher, Mtl. Maroons	Tiny Thompson, Boston	No	Mtl. M.	0	at	Bos. 4	QF
Apr. 15/37	Alex Shibicky, NY Rangers	Earl Robertson, Detroit	No	NYR	0	at	Det. 3	F
Apr. 13/44	Virgil Johnson, Chicago	Bill Durnan, Montreal	No	Chi.	4	at	Mtl. 5*	F
Apr. 9/68	Wayne Connelly, Minnesota	Terry Sawchuk, Los Angeles	Yes	L.A.	4	at	Min. 7	QF
Apr. 27/68	Jim Roberts, St. Louis	Cesare Maniago, Minnesota	No	St. L.	4	at	Min. 3	SF
May 16/71	Frank Mahovlich, Montreal	Tony Esposito, Chicago	No	Chi.	3	at	Mtl. 4	F
May 7/75	Bill Barber, Philadelphia	Glenn Resch, NY Islanders	No	Phi.	3	at	NYI 4*	SF
Apr. 20/79	Mike Walton, Chicago	Glenn Resch, NY Islanders	No	NYI	4	at	Chi. 0	QF
Apr. 9/81	Peter McNab, Boston	Don Beaupre, Minnesota	No	Min.	5	at	Bos. 4*	PR
Apr. 17/81	Anders Hedberg, NY Rangers	Mike Liut, St. Louis	Yes	NYR	6	at	St. L. 4	SF
Apr. 9/83	Denis Potvin, NY Islanders	Pat Riggin, Washington	No	NYI	6	at	Wsh. 2	DSF
Apr. 28/84	Wayne Gretzky, Edmonton	Don Beaupre, Minnesota	Yes	Edm.	8	at	Min. 5	CF
May 1/84	Mats Naslund, Montreal	Billy Smith, NY Islanders	No	Mtl.	1	at	NYI 3	CF
Apr. 14/85	Bob Carpenter, Washington	Billy Smith, NY Islanders	No	Wsh.	4	at	NYI. 6	DF
May 28/85	Ron Sutter, Philadelphia	Grant Fuhr, Edmonton	No	Phi.	3	at	Edm. 5	F
May 30/85	Dave Poulin, Philadelphia	Grant Fuhr, Edmonton	No	Phi.	3	at	Edm. 8	F
Apr. 9/88	John Tucker, Buffalo	Andy Moog, Boston	Yes	Bos.	2	at	Buf. 6	DSF
Apr. 9/88	Petr Klima, Detroit	Allan Bester, Toronto	Yes	Det.	6	at	Tor. 3	DSF
Apr. 8/89	Neal Broten, Minnesota	Greg Millen, St. Louis	Yes	St. L.	5	at	Min. 3	DSF
Apr. 4/90	Al MacInnis, Calgary	Kelly Hrudey, Los Angeles	Yes	L.A.	5	at	Cgy. 3	DSF
Apr. 5/90	Randy Wood, NY Islanders	Mike Richter, NY Rangers	No	NYI	1	at	NYR 2	DSF
May 3/90	Kelly Miller, Washington	Andy Moog, Boston	No	Wsh.	3	at	Bos. 5	CF
May 18/90	Petr Klima, Edmonton	Rejean Lemelin, Boston	No	Edm.	7	at	Bos. 2	F
Apr. 6/91	Basil McRae, Minnesota	Ed Belfour, Chicago	Yes	Min.	2	at	Chi. 5	DSF
Apr. 10/91	Steve Duchesne, Los Angeles	Kirk McLean, Vancouver	Yes	L.A.	6	at	Van. 1	DSF
May 11/92	Jaromir Jagr, Pittsburgh	John Vanbiesbrouck, NYR	Yes	Pit.	3	at	NYR 2	DF
May 13/92	Shawn McEachern, Pittsburgh	John Vanbiesbrouck, NYR	No	NYR	1	at	Pit. 5	DF
June 7/94	Pavel Bure, Vancouver	Mike Richter, NYR	No	NYR	4	at	Van. 2	F
May 9/95	Patrick Poulin, Chicago	Felix Potvin, Toronto	No	Tor.	3	at	Chi. 0	CQF
May 10/95	Michal Pivonka, Washington	Tom Barrasso, Pittsburgh	No	Pit.	2	at	Wsh. 6	CQF
Apr. 24/96	Joe Juneau, Washington	Ken Wregget, Pittsburgh	No	Pit.	3	at	Wsh. 2**CQF	
May 11/97	Eric Lindros, Philadelphia	Steve Shields, Buffalo	Yes	Phi.	6	at	Buf. 3	CSF
Apr. 23/98	Alexei Morozov, Pittsburgh	Andy Moog, Montreal	No	Mtl.	3	at	Pit. 2**CQF	
Apr. 22/99	Mats Sundin, Toronto	John Vanbiesbrouck, Phi.	No	Phi.	3	at	Tor. 0	CQF
May 29/99	Mats Sundin, Toronto	Dominik Hasek, Buffalo	Yes	Tor.	2	at	Buf. 5	CF
Apr. 16/00	Eric Desjardins, Philadelphia	Dominik Hasek, Buffalo	No	Phi.	2	at	Buf. 0	CQF

* Game was decided in overtime, but shot taken during regulation time.
** Shot taken in overtime.

Keith Primeau scored at 12:01 of the fifth overtime period to end the longest hockey game since the days of the Great Depression. Primeau's goal gave Philadelphia a 2-1 win over Pittsburgh in game four of their series on May 4, 2000.

Ten Longest Overtime Games

Date	City	Series	Score				Scorer	Overtime	Series Winner
Mar. 24/36	Mtl.	SF	Det. 1	Mtl. M.	0		Mud Bruneteau	116:30	Det.
Apr. 3/33	Tor.	SF	Tor. 1	Bos.	0		Ken Doraty	104:46	Tor.
May 4/00	**Pit.**	**CSF**	**Phi. 2**	**Pit.**	**1**		**Keith Primeau**	**92:01**	**Phi.**
Apr. 24/96	Wsh.	CQF	Pit. 3	Wsh.	2		Petr Nedved	79:15	Pit.
Mar. 23/43	Det.	SF	Tor. 3	Det.	2		Jack McLean	70:18	Det.
Mar. 28/30	Mtl.	SF	Mtl. 2	NYR	1		Gus Rivers	68:52	Mtl.
Apr. 18/87	Wsh.	DSF	NYI 3	Wsh.	2		Pat LaFontaine	68:47	NYI
Apr. 27/94	Buf.	CQF	Buf. 1	N.J.	0		Dave Hannan	65:43	N.J.
Mar. 27/51	Det.	SF	Mtl. 3	Det.	2		Maurice Richard	61:09	Mtl.
Mar. 27/38	NY	QF	NYA 3	NYR	2		Lorne Carr	60:40	NYA

Overtime Record of Current Teams

(Listed by number of OT games played)

Team	Overall				Home				Last OT Game	Road				Last OT Game
	GP	W	L	T	GP	W	L	T		GP	W	L	T	
Montreal	120	69	49	2	55	36	18	1	May 12/98	65	33	31	1	May 8/98
Boston	98	38	57	3	45	20	24	1	May 3/98	53	18	33	2	Apr. 30/99
Toronto	93	49	43	1	59	32	26	1	Apr. 22/00	34	17	17	0	May 13/99
Detroit	64	31	33	0	39	16	23	0	May 3/00	25	15	10	0	Jun. 3/98
NY Rangers	63	30	33	0	27	12	15	0	Apr. 22/97	36	18	18	0	May 11/97
Chicago	62	30	30	2	30	16	13	1	Apr. 20/97	32	14	17	1	May 2/96
Philadelphia	48	24	24	0	20	11	9	0	May 1/98	28	13	15	0	May 4/00
Dallas[1]	45	20	25	0	21	8	13	0	Jun. 10/00	24	12	12	0	Jun. 8/00
St. Louis	44	24	20	0	22	17	5	0	May 12/99	22	7	15	0	May 8/99
Buffalo	41	22	19	0	23	14	9	0	Apr. 18/00	18	8	10	0	Jun. 8/99
NY Islanders	38	29	9	0	17	14	3	0	May 20/93	21	15	6	0	May 18/93
Edmonton	34	20	14	0	19	10	9	0	Apr. 27/99	15	10	5	0	Apr. 29/97
Colorado[2]	34	21	13	0	14	8	6	0	May 28/99	20	13	7	0	May 23/00
Los Angeles	30	12	18	0	16	8	8	0	Jun. 7/93	14	4	10	0	Jun. 3/93
Calgary[3]	30	11	19	0	14	4	10	0	Apr. 23/96	16	7	9	0	Apr. 28/94
Vancouver	29	13	16	0	12	5	7	0	May 27/95	17	8	9	0	Apr. 25/96
Washington	27	13	14	0	10	5	5	0	May 25/98	17	8	9	0	Apr. 15/00
Pittsburgh	23	12	11	0	15	8	7	0	May 4/00	8	4	4	0	Apr. 24/96
New Jersey[4]	22	6	16	0	10	2	8	0	Jun. 8/00	12	4	8	0	Jun. 10/00
Carolina[5]	13	6	7	0	9	5	4	0	Apr. 30/99	4	1	3	0	May 1/92
Phoenix[6]	12	5	7	0	8	3	5	0	May 4/99	4	2	2	0	Apr. 27/93
San Jose	7	3	4	0	4	1	3	0	May 3/99	3	2	1	0	May 19/95
Florida	5	2	3	0	3	1	2	0	Apr. 25/97	2	1	1	0	Apr. 22/97
Anaheim	4	1	3	0	1	0	1	0	May 8/97	3	1	2	0	May 4/97
Ottawa	4	2	2	0	2	1	1	0	Apr. 23/99	2	1	1	0	Apr. 22/00
Tampa Bay	2	2	0	0	1	1	0	0	Apr. 21/96	1	1	0	0	Apr. 18/96

[1] Totals include those of Minnesota North Stars 1967-93.
[2] Totals include those of Quebec 1979-95.
[3] Totals include those of Atlanta Flames 1972-80.
[4] Totals include those of Kansas City and Colorado Rockies 1974-82.
[5] Totals include those of Hartford 1979-97.
[6] Totals include those of Winnipeg 1979-96.

During their run to the Stanley Cup, the New Jersey Devils did not require overtime until game five of the Finals. After suffering a triple-overtime defeat, the Devils bounced back to win the series on a double-overtime goal by Jason Arnott.

Late Additions to Player Register

JOHAN DAVIDSSON signed as a free agent by Vancouver, September 6, 2000.

GRANT FUHR officially announced retirement, September 6, 2000.

NICK NAUMENKO signed as a free agent by Minnesota, September 6, 2000.

DAVE ELLETT officially announced retirement, September 7, 2000.

PAUL KRUSE signed as a free agent by San Jose, September 10, 2000.

BARTOS, Peter (bahr-TOHSH) **MIN.**

Left Wing. Shoots right. 6', 183 lbs.   Born, Martin, Czech., September 5, 1973.
(Minnesota's 7th choice, 214th overall, in 2000 Entry Draft).

				Regular Season						Playoffs		
Season	Club	League	GP	G	A	TP	PIM	GP	G	A	TP	PIM
1991-92	HC Martin	Czech-2	33	13	8	21	16	....	....	....	....	....
1992-93	HC Martin	Czech-2	22	6	5	11	4	....	....	....	....	....
	Dukla Trencin	Czech.	28	1	2	3		10	1	1	2	....
1993-94	ZTS Martin	Slovakia	36	12	9	21	10	6	2	1	3	8
1994-95	ZTS Martin	Slovakia	34	14	20	34	20	3	0	0	0	0
1995-96	ZTS Martin	Slovakia	36	23	16	39	8	13	4	4	8	4
1996-97	ZTS Martin	Slovakia	46	22	15	37	....	5	1	5	6	....
1997-98	ZTS Martin	Slovakia	36	20	26	46	20	3	0	2	2	0
1998-99	HC Budejovice	Cze-Rep	52	22	26	48	24	3	3	0	3	....
1999-00	HC Budejovice	Cze-Rep	52	23	25	48	24	3	0	1	1	6

SEKERAS, Lubomir (SEH-kuhr-ahsh, LOO-buh-meer) **MIN.**

Defense. Shoots left. 6', 176 lbs.   Born, Trencin, Czech., November 18, 1968.
(Minnesota's 8th choice, 232nd overall, in 2000 Entry Draft).

				Regular Season						Playoffs		
Season	Club	League	GP	G	A	TP	PIM	GP	G	A	TP	PIM
1988-89	Dukla Trencin	Czech.	16	2	5	7	22	11	0	4	4	0
1989-90	Dukla Trencin	Czech.	44	6	8	14	....	9	0	2	2	....
1990-91	Dukla Trencin	Czech.	52	6	16	22	....	6	0	1	1	....
1991-92	Dukla Trencin	Czech.	30	2	6	8	32	13	1	1	2	0
1992-93	Dukla Trencin	Czech.	40	5	19	24	48	11	4	9	13	0
1993-94	Dukla Trencin	Slovakia	36	9	12	21	46	9	2	4	6	10
1994-95	Dukla Trencin	Slovakia	36	11	11	22	24	9	2	7	9	8
1995-96	HC Trinec	Cze-Rep	40	11	13	24	44	3	0	0	0	0
1996-97	HC Trinec	Cze-Rep	52	14	21	35	56	4	1	0	1	2
1997-98	HC Trinec	Cze-Rep	50	11	33	44	42	13	2	10	12	4
1998-99	HC Trinec	Cze-Rep	50	8	15	23	38	10	2	6	8	....
1999-00	HC Trinec	Cze-Rep	52	7	24	31	36	4	0	2	2	2

League Abbreviations

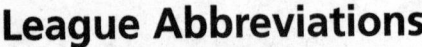

AAHA	Alberta Amateur Hockey Association
ACHL	Atlantic Coast Hockey League
AFHL	American Frontier Hockey League
AJHL	Alberta Junior Hockey Leagues
Alpenliga	Alpenliga (Austria, Italy, Slovenia 1994-1999)
AMHA	Alberta Minor Hockey Association
AUAA	Atlantic University Athletic Association
BCAHA	British Columbia Amateur Hockey Association
BCJHL	British Columbia Junior Hockey League
CCHA	Central Collegiate Hockey Association
CEGEP	Quebec College Prep
CHA	College Hockey America
CIS	Commonwealth of Independent States
ColHL	Colonial Hockey League
CWUAA	Canadian Western University Athletic Association
DEB	Deutsche Eishockey Bundesliga
DEL	Deutsche Eishockey Liga
ECAC	Eastern College Athletic Conference
ECHL	East Coast Hockey League
EJHL	Eastern Junior Hockey League
EuroHL	European Hockey League
Finland-Q	Finland Ice Hockey League Qualification Round
G.N.	Great Northern
GPAC	Great Plains Athletic Conference
H-East	Hockey East
HJHL	Heritage Junior Hockey League
Hi-School	High School (also H.S.)

IEL	Internationale Eishockey Liga
IHL	International Hockey League
IJHL	Interstate Junior Hockey League
KIDHL	Kootenay International Jr.B Hockey League
MAHA	Manitoba Amateur Hockey Association
MBHL	Metropolitan Boston Hockey League
MEHL	Midwest Elite Hockey League
MIAC	Minnesota Intercollegiate Athletic Conference
MJHL	Manitoba Junior Hockey League
MJrHL	Maritime Junior Major Hockey League
MNHL	Michigan National Hockey League
MTHL	Metro Toronto Hockey League
NAJHL	North American Junior Hockey League
Nat-Team	National Team (also Nt.-Team)
NBAHA	New Brunswick Amateur Hockey Association
NCAA	National Collegiate Athletic Association
NEJHL	New England Junior Hockey League
NFAHA	Newfoundland Amateur Hockey Association
NHL	National Hockey League
NOHA	Northern Ontario Hockey Association
NOJHL	Northern Ontario Junior Hockey League
OHL	Ontario Hockey League
OJHL	Ontario Junior Hockey Leagues
OMHA	Ontario Minor Hockey Association
OMJHL	Ontario Major Junior Hockey League
OUAA	Ontario Universities Athletic Association
QAAA	Quebec Amateur Athletic Association

QJHL	Quebec Junior Hockey League
QMJHL	Quebec Major Junior Hockey League
PCJHL	Pacific Coast Junior Hockey League
PIJHL	Pacific International Junior Hockey League
RMJHL	Rocky Mountain Junior Hockey League
Russia-Q	Russian National League Qualification Round
SAHA	Saskatchewan Amateur Hockey Association
SunHL	Sunshine Hockey League
Sweden-Q	Swedish Elitserien Qualification Round
TBAHA	Thunder Bay Amateur Hockey Association
TBJHL	Thunder Bay Junior Hockey League
UHL	United Hockey League
Under-18	U.S. under 18 Hockey Development Program
Under-17	U.S. under 17 Hockey Development Program
USAHA	United States Amateur Hockey Association
USHL	United States (Jr. A) Hockey League
VIJHL	Vancouver Island Junior Hockey League
WCHA	Western Collegiate Hockey Association
WCHL	West Coast Hockey League
WHA	World Hockey Association
WHL	Western Hockey League
WNYHA	Western New York Hockey Association
WPHL	Western Professional Hockey League
WSJHL	Western States Junior Hockey League
X-Games	Exhibition Games, Series or Season

2000-01 Prospect Register

Note: The 2000-01 Prospect Register lists forwards and defensemen only. Goaltenders are listed separately. The Prospect Register lists every player drafted in the first five rounds of the 2000 Entry Draft, players on NHL Reserve Lists and other players who have not yet played in the NHL. Trades and roster changes are current as of September 5, 2000.

Abbreviations: A – assists; **G** – goals; **GP** – games played; **Lea** – league; **PIM** – penalties in minutes; **TP** – total points; ***** – league-leading total.

NHL Player Register begins on page 323.

Goaltender Register begins on page 559.

League Abbreviations are listed on page 264.

ABID, Ramzi
(a-BIHD, RAM-zee) **PHX.**

Left wing. Shoots left. 6'2", 210 lbs.   Born, Montreal, Que., March 24, 1980.
(Phoenix's 3rd choice, 85th overall, in 2000 Entry Draft).

Season	Club	Lea	GP	G	A	TP	PIM	GP	G	A	TP	PIM
					Regular Season					Playoffs		
1995-96	Richelieu Selectes	QAAA	42	10	14	24	18	4	1	2	3	2
1996-97	Chicoutimi	QMJHL	65	13	24	37	141	21	2	12	14	28
1997-98	Chicoutimi	QMJHL	68	50	*85	*135	266	6	3	4	7	10
1998-99	Chicoutimi	QMJHL	21	11	15	26	97	....	....	....	....	....
	Acadie-Bathurst	QMJHL	24	14	22	36	102	23	14	20	34	*84
99-2000	Acadie-Bathurst	QMJHL	13	10	11	21	61	....	....	....	....	....
	Halifax	QMJHL	59	57	80	137	148	10	10	13	23	18

• Re-entered NHL draft. Originally Colorado's 5th choice, 28th overall, in 1998 Entry Draft.
QMJHL First All-Star Team (1998, 2000) • Canadian Major Junior First All-Star Team (2000) • Won Ed Chynoweth Trophy (Memorial Cup Tournament Leading Scorer) (2000)

ABRAHAMSSON, Elias
(AH-brah-ham-suhn, eh-LEE-ahs) **BOS.**

Defense. Shoots left. 6'3", 240 lbs.   Born, Uppsala, Sweden, June 15, 1977.
(Boston's 6th choice, 132nd overall, in 1996 Entry Draft).

Season	Club	Lea	GP	G	A	TP	PIM	GP	G	A	TP	PIM
					Regular Season					Playoffs		
1994-95	Halifax	QMJHL	25	0	3	3	41	....	....	....	....	....
1995-96	Halifax	QMJHL	64	3	11	14	268	6	2	2	4	8
1996-97	Halifax	QMJHL	30	4	10	14	231	18	4	9	13	74
1997-98	Providence Bruins	AHL	29	0	1	1	47	....	....	....	....	....
1998-99	Providence Bruins	AHL	75	2	9	11	184	4	0	0	0	7
99-2000	Providence Bruins	AHL	19	1	1	2	45	....	....	....	....	....
	Hamilton Bulldogs	AHL	56	1	3	4	90	10	0	1	1	4

ADAMS, Craig
(A-dams, KRAYG) **CAR.**

Right wing. Shoots right. 6', 200 lbs.   Born, Calgary, Alta., April 26, 1977.
(Hartford's 9th choice, 223rd overall, in 1996 Entry Draft).

Season	Club	Lea	GP	G	A	TP	PIM	GP	G	A	TP	PIM
					Regular Season					Playoffs		
1995-96	Harvard University	ECAC	34	8	9	17	56	....	....	....	....	....
1996-97	Harvard University	ECAC	32	6	4	10	36	....	....	....	....	....
1997-98	Harvard University	ECAC	12	6	6	12	12	....	....	....	....	....
1998-99	Harvard University	ECAC	31	9	14	23	53	....	....	....	....	....
99-2000	Cincinnati	IHL	73	12	12	24	124	8	0	1	1	14

Rights transferred to **Carolina** after **Hartford** franchise relocated, June 25, 1997.

ADDUONO, Jeremy
(uh-DOO-noh, JAIR-eh-mee) **BUF.**

Right wing. Shoots right. 6', 183 lbs.   Born, Thunder Bay, Ont., August 4, 1978.
(Buffalo's 8th choice, 184th overall, in 1997 Entry Draft).

Season	Club	Lea	GP	G	A	TP	PIM	GP	G	A	TP	PIM
					Regular Season					Playoffs		
1994-95	Thunder Bay	USHL	40	11	10	21	8	....	....	....	....	....
1995-96	Sudbury Wolves	OHL	66	15	22	37	14	....	....	....	....	....
1996-97	Sudbury Wolves	OHL	66	29	40	69	24	....	....	....	....	....
1997-98	Sudbury Wolves	OHL	66	37	69	106	40	10	5	5	10	10
1998-99	Canada	Nat-Team	44	10	18	28	10	....	....	....	....	....
99-2000	Rochester	AHL	51	23	22	45	20	21	6	11	17	2

AFANASENKOV, Dmitry
(ah-fahn-AH-sehn-kahv, D-mee-tree) **T.B.**

Left wing. Shoots right. 6'2", 200 lbs.   Born, Arkhangelsk, USSR, May 12, 1980.
(Tampa Bay's 3rd choice, 72nd overall, in 1998 Entry Draft).

Season	Club	Lea	GP	G	A	TP	PIM	GP	G	A	TP	PIM
					Regular Season					Playoffs		
1995-96	Torpedo Yaroslavl	Russia-2	25	10	5	15	10	....	....	....	....	....
	Torpedo Yaroslavl	Russia-Jr.	35	28	16	44	8	....	....	....	....	....
1996-97	Torpedo Yaroslavl	Russia-3	45	20	15	35	14	....	....	....	....	....
1997-98	Torpedo Yaroslavl	Russia-2	48	14	7	21	20	....	....	....	....	....
1998-99	Moncton Wildcats	QMJHL	15	5	5	10	12	....	....	....	....	....
	Sherbrooke	QMJHL	51	23	30	53	22	13	10	6	16	6
99-2000	Sherbrooke	QMJHL	60	56	43	99	70	5	3	2	5	4

AHMAOJA, Timo
(ahkh-mah-OH-yah, TIH-moo) **ANA.**

Defense. Shoots right. 6'1", 180 lbs.   Born, Jyvaskyla, Finland, August 8, 1978.
(Anaheim's 5th choice, 172nd overall, in 1996 Entry Draft).

Season	Club	Lea	GP	G	A	TP	PIM	GP	G	A	TP	PIM
					Regular Season					Playoffs		
1993-94	JyP Jyvaskyla-C	Finn-Jr.	32	6	9	15	34	6	2	0	2	4
1994-95	JyP Jyvaskyla-B	Finn-Jr.	6	1	3	4	8	....	....	....	....	....
	JyP Jyvaskyla	Finn-Jr.	30	1	1	2	2	7	0	0	0	0
1995-96	JyP Jyvaskyla	Finn-Jr.	28	0	7	7	16	6	1	0	1	2
	JyP Jyvaskyla	Finland	4	0	0	0	4	....	....	....	....	....
1996-97	JyP Jyvaskyla	Finland	35	0	4	4	8	....	....	....	....	....
	JyP Jyvaskyla	Finn-Jr.	19	4	5	9	24	....	....	....	....	....
1997-98	JyP Jyvaskyla	Finland	10	0	0	0	0	....	....	....	....	....
	Lukko Rauma	Finland	10	0	0	0	0	....	....	....	....	....
	Diskos Jyvaskyla	Finland-2	23	1	2	3	14	....	....	....	....	....
1998-99	KalPa Kuopio	Finn-Jr.	3	0	1	1	10	....	....	....	....	....
	KalPa Kuopio	Finland	52	0	1	1	16	....	....	....	....	....
99-2000	Pelicans Lahti	Finland	29	0	0	0	4	....	....	....	....	....

AHOSILTA, Marko
(ah-hoh-SIHL-tuh, mahr-KOH) **N.J.**

Center. Shoots left. 5'8", 165 lbs.   Born, Kuopio, Finland, January 24, 1980.
(New Jersey's 11th choice, 227th overall, in 1998 Entry Draft).

Season	Club	Lea	GP	G	A	TP	PIM	GP	G	A	TP	PIM
					Regular Season					Playoffs		
1994-95	KalPa Kuopio-C	Finn-Jr.	13	4	6	10	10	....	....	....	....	....
1995-96	KalPa Kuopio	Finn-Jr.	12	4	8	12	10	....	....	....	....	....
1996-97	KalPa Kuopio	Finn-Jr.	35	15	21	36	36	5	2	0	2	2
1997-98	KalPa Kuopio	Finn-Jr.	14	14	13	27	10	....	....	....	....	....
	KalPa Kuopio	Finland	2	0	0	0	0	....	....	....	....	....
1998-99	KalPa Kuopio	Finland	1	0	0	0	0	....	....	....	....	....
	KalPa Kuopio	Finn-Jr.	24	7	7	14	10	....	....	....	....	....
99-2000	KalPa Kuopio	Finn-Jr.	10	6	4	10	8	....	....	....	....	....
	KJT-Jarvenpaa	Finland-2	30	19	5	24	14	....	....	....	....	....

ALBERT, Chris
(AHL-buhrt, KRIHS)

Center. Shoots right. 5'11", 195 lbs.   Born, Ottawa, Ont., October 12, 1972.

Season	Club	Lea	GP	G	A	TP	PIM	GP	G	A	TP	PIM
					Regular Season					Playoffs		
1991-92	Union College	ECAC	21	5	7	12	16	....	....	....	....	....
1992-93	Union College	ECAC	25	9	11	20	56	....	....	....	....	....
1993-94	Union College	ECAC	30	11	18	29	48	....	....	....	....	....
1994-95	Union College	ECAC	29	17	15	32	44	....	....	....	....	....
1995-96	San Antonio	CHL	37	8	12	20	54	13	3	1	4	35
1996-97	San Antonio	CHL	55	19	29	48	48	....	....	....	....	....
1997-98	Fort Worth Bulls	WPHL	68	21	29	50	205	13	7	5	12	20
	Detroit Vipers	IHL	2	0	0	0	2	....	....	....	....	....
1998-99	Cincinnati Ducks	AHL	17	4	3	7	109	....	....	....	....	....
	Michigan K-Wings	IHL	23	3	3	6	44	....	....	....	....	....
	Philadelphia	AHL	22	1	3	4	88	15	5	5	10	22
99-2000	Philadelphia	AHL	57	6	10	16	240	....	....	....	....	....
	Quebec Citadelles	AHL	15	4	4	8	51	3	0	0	0	0

Signed as a free agent by **Philadelphia**, July 14, 1999.

ALEXEEV, Nikita
(uh-LEHX-ee-ehv, nih-KEE-tuh) **T.B.**

Right wing. Shoots left. 6'5", 215 lbs.   Born, Murmansk, USSR, December 27, 1981.
(Tampa Bay's 1st choice, 8th overall, in 2000 Entry Draft).

Season	Club	Lea	GP	G	A	TP	PIM	GP	G	A	TP	PIM
					Regular Season					Playoffs		
1997-98	Krylja Sovetov-2	Russia-3	61	11	4	15	36	....	....	....	....	....
1998-99	Erie Otters	OHL	61	17	18	35	14	5	1	1	2	4
99-2000	Erie Otters	OHL	64	24	29	53	42	13	4	3	7	6

ALINC, Jan (AHL-lihnch, YAHN) PIT.

Center. Shoots left. 6'2", 190 lbs. Born, Louny, Czech., May 27, 1972.
(Pittsburgh's 7th choice, 163rd overall, in 1992 Entry Draft).

			Regular Season					Playoffs				
Season	Club	Lea	GP	G	A	TP	PIM	GP	G	A	TP	PIM
1990-91	CHZ Litvinov	Czech.	7	1	1	2	....	....	....	....	....	....
1991-92	CHZ Litvinov	Czech.	45	21	16	37	24	....	....	....	....	....
1992-93	CHZ Litvinov	Czech.	36	16	13	29	....	....	....	....	....	....
1993-94	CHZ Litvinov	Cze-Rep	36	16	25	41	....	4	1	4	5	....
	Czech-Republic	Olympics	6	2	0	2	4	....	....	....	....	....
1994-95	CHZ Litvinov	Cze-Rep	42	16	32	48	50	4	3	2	5	2
1995-96	CHZ Litvinov	Cze-Rep	38	15	29	44	....	16	2	5	7	....
1996-97	Assat-Pori	Finland	47	9	16	25	16	4	0	4	4	2
1997-98	Assat-Pori	Finland	15	2	8	10	10	....	....	....	....	....
	CHZ Litvinov	Cze-Rep	33	12	32	44	14	4	1	2	3	12
1998-99	MoDo Hockey	Sweden	48	7	11	18	22	9	1	0	1	0
99-2000	CHZ Litvinov	Cze-Rep	48	19	15	34	72	6	0	1	1	25

ALLAN, Chad (AHL-lan, CHAD)

Defense. Shoots left. 6'1", 200 lbs. Born, Saskatoon, Sask., July 12, 1976.
(Vancouver's 4th choice, 65th overall, in 1994 Entry Draft).

			Regular Season					Playoffs				
Season	Club	Lea	GP	G	A	TP	PIM	GP	G	A	TP	PIM
1991-92	Saskatoon SSAK	AAHA	36	5	16	21	64	....	....	....	....	....
	Saskatoon Blades	WHL	1	0	0	0	2	....	....	....	....	....
1992-93	Saskatoon Blades	WHL	69	2	10	12	67	9	0	0	0	25
1993-94	Saskatoon Blades	WHL	70	6	16	22	123	16	1	1	2	21
1994-95	Saskatoon Blades	WHL	63	14	29	43	95	9	0	3	3	2
1995-96	Saskatoon Blades	WHL	57	8	30	38	106	4	0	0	0	5
1996-97	Syracuse Crunch	AHL	73	3	10	13	83	3	0	1	1	0
1997-98	Syracuse Crunch	AHL	73	2	10	12	121	5	0	0	0	4
1998-99	Syracuse Crunch	AHL	60	2	8	10	98	....	....	....	....	....
99-2000	Syracuse Crunch	AHL	76	3	18	21	100	4	0	0	0	0

WHL East First All-Star Team (1995) • WHL East Second All-Star Team (1996)

ALLEN, Bobby (AHL-lehn, BAW-bee) BOS.

Defense. Shoots left. 6'1", 198 lbs. Born, Braintree, MA, November 14, 1978.
(Boston's 2nd choice, 52nd overall, in 1998 Entry Draft).

			Regular Season					Playoffs				
Season	Club	Lea	GP	G	A	TP	PIM	GP	G	A	TP	PIM
1996-97	Cushing Academy	Hi-School	36	11	33	44	28	....	....	....	....	....
1997-98	Boston College	H-East	40	7	21	28	49	....	....	....	....	....
1998-99	Boston College	H-East	43	9	23	32	34	....	....	....	....	....
99-2000	Boston College	H-East	42	4	23	27	40	....	....	....	....	....

Hockey East Second All-Star Team (2000)

ALLEN, Bryan (AHL-lehn, BRIGH-an) VAN.

Defense. Shoots left. 6'4", 215 lbs. Born, Kingston, Ont., August 21, 1980.
(Vancouver's 1st choice, 4th overall, in 1998 Entry Draft).

			Regular Season					Playoffs				
Season	Club	Lea	GP	G	A	TP	PIM	GP	G	A	TP	PIM
1995-96	Ernestown Jets	OJHL-C	36	1	16	17	71	....	....	....	....	....
1996-97	Oshawa Generals	OHL	60	2	4	6	76	18	1	3	4	26
1997-98	Oshawa Generals	OHL	48	6	13	19	126	5	0	5	5	18
1998-99	Oshawa Generals	OHL	37	7	15	22	77	15	0	3	3	26
99-2000	Oshawa Generals	OHL	3	0	2	2	12	3	0	0	0	13
	Syracuse Crunch	AHL	9	1	1	2	11	2	0	0	0	2

OHL First All-Star Team (1999) • Missed majority of 1999-2000 season recovering from knee injury suffered in training camp, September 21, 1999.

ANDERSSON, Jonas (AN-duhr-suhn, JOH-nas) NSH.

Right wing. Shoots left. 6'3", 200 lbs. Born, Stockholm, Sweden, February 24, 1981.
(Nashville's 2nd choice, 33rd overall, in 1999 Entry Draft).

			Regular Season					Playoffs				
Season	Club	Lea	GP	G	A	TP	PIM	GP	G	A	TP	PIM
1997-98	AIK Solna	Swede-Jr.	33	14	16	30	32	....	....	....	....	....
1998-99	AIK Solna	Swede-Jr.	16	3	7	10	18	....	....	....	....	....
99-2000	North Bay	OHL	67	31	36	67	27	6	2	2	4	2
	Milwaukee	IHL	2	1	0	1	0	2	0	0	0	2

ANDERSSON-JUNKKA, Jonas (AN-duhr-suhn-JUHNK-ka, JOH-nuh) CBJ

Defense. Shoots right. 6'2", 170 lbs. Born, Kiruna, Sweden, May 4, 1975.
(Pittsburgh's 4th choice, 104th overall, in 1993 Entry Draft).

			Regular Season					Playoffs				
Season	Club	Lea	GP	G	A	TP	PIM	GP	G	A	TP	PIM
1991-92	Kiruna IK	Swede-2	1	0	0	0	0	....	....	....	....	....
1992-93	Kiruna IK	Swede-2	30	3	7	10	32	....	....	....	....	....
1993-94	Kiruna IK	Swede-2	32	6	10	16	84	....	....	....	....	....
1994-95	Vastra Frolunda	Sweden	19	0	2	2	2	....	....	....	....	....
1995-96	Vastra Frolunda	Sweden	31	3	1	4	20	13	1	0	1	6
1996-97	MoDo Hockey	Sweden	12	1	3	4	10	....	....	....	....	....
1997-98	MoDo Hockey	Sweden	35	5	5	10	12	1	0	0	0	0
1998-99	Kiekko-Espoo	Finland	34	4	4	8	20	....	....	....	....	....
	HPK Hameenlinna	Finland	16	1	5	6	16	8	3	1	4	8
99-2000	HPK Hameenlinna	Finland	54	13	18	31	72	8	1	4	5	20

Selected by **Columbus** from **Pittsburgh** in Expansion Draft, June 23, 2000.

ANDREWS, Daryl (AN-drews, DAI-rihl) N.J.

Defense. Shoots left. 6'2", 205 lbs. Born, Campbell River, B.C., April 27, 1977.
(New Jersey's 11th choice, 173rd overall, in 1996 Entry Draft).

			Regular Season					Playoffs				
Season	Club	Lea	GP	G	A	TP	PIM	GP	G	A	TP	PIM
1995-96	Melfort Mustangs	SJHL	55	2	12	14	51	....	....	....	....	....
1996-97	Western Michigan	CCHA	37	6	20	26	86	....	....	....	....	....
1997-98	Western Michigan	CCHA	36	3	0	3	81	....	....	....	....	....
1998-99	Western Michigan	CCHA	33	3	11	14	42	....	....	....	....	....
99-2000	Western Michigan	CCHA	36	3	16	19	52	....	....	....	....	....
	Albany River Rats	AHL	9	0	2	2	9	5	0	0	0	0

ANDREYEV, Alexander (an-DRAY-ehv, AHL-ihx-ander) PHX.

Defense. Shoots left. 6'4", 220 lbs. Born, Riga, Latvia, September 14, 1979.
(Phoenix's 5th choice, 207th overall, in 1997 Entry Draft).

			Regular Season					Playoffs				
Season	Club	Lea	GP	G	A	TP	PIM	GP	G	A	TP	PIM
1996-97	Essamika Riga	Latvia	5	0	0	0	6	....	....	....	....	....
	Weyburn Wings	SJHL	13	0	1	1	81	....	....	....	....	....
1997-98	Prince George	WHL	23	0	1	1	30	....	....	....	....	....
1998-99	Moose Jaw	WHL	60	11	11	22	80	5	0	0	0	4
99-2000	Mississippi	ECHL	21	1	2	3	43	....	....	....	....	....
	B.C. Icemen	UHL	21	1	3	4	80	6	0	0	0	4

ANGEL, Brett (AN-gehl, BREHT) NSH.

Defense. Shoots left. 6'6", 228 lbs. Born, Kingston, Ont., April 29, 1981.
(Nashville's 6th choice, 72nd overall, in 1999 Entry Draft).

			Regular Season					Playoffs				
Season	Club	Lea	GP	G	A	TP	PIM	GP	G	A	TP	PIM
1996-97	Kingston	OJHL	38	4	9	13	94	....	....	....	....	....
1997-98	North Bay	OHL	61	1	3	4	131	....	....	....	....	....
1998-99	North Bay	OHL	55	5	9	14	139	4	0	0	0	7
99-2000	North Bay	OHL	2	0	0	0	4	....	....	....	....	....
	London Knights	OHL	62	3	5	8	119	....	....	....	....	....

ANGELSTAD, Mel (AN-gehl-stahd, MEHL)

Left wing. Shoots left. 6'2", 214 lbs. Born, Saskatoon, Sask., October 31, 1972.

			Regular Season					Playoffs				
Season	Club	Lea	GP	G	A	TP	PIM	GP	G	A	TP	PIM
1988-89	Allan Legionaires	MAHA	35	15	23	38	256	....	....	....	....	....
1989-90	Warman Valley	MJHL	38	1	5	6	411	....	....	....	....	....
1990-91	Flin Flon Bombers	MJHL	62	6	11	17	463	....	....	....	....	....
1991-92	Dauphin Kings	MJHL	44	8	29	37	*296	....	....	....	....	....
1992-93	Thunder Bay	ColHL	45	2	5	7	256	5	0	0	0	10
	Nashville Knights	ECHL	1	0	0	0	14	....	....	....	....	....
1993-94	Thunder Bay	ColHL	58	1	20	21	374	9	1	2	3	65
	P.E.I. Senators	AHL	1	0	0	0	5	....	....	....	....	....
1994-95	Thunder Bay	ColHL	46	0	8	8	317	7	0	3	3	62
	P.E.I. Senators	AHL	3	0	0	0	16	....	....	....	....	....
1995-96	Thunder Bay	ColHL	51	3	3	6	335	16	0	6	6	94
	Phoenix	IHL	5	0	0	0	43	....	....	....	....	....
1996-97	Thunder Bay	ColHL	66	10	21	31	422	7	0	1	1	21
1997-98	Fort Worth	WPHL	19	1	6	7	102	....	....	....	....	....
	Las Vegas	IHL	3	0	0	0	5	....	....	....	....	....
	Orlando	IHL	63	1	3	4	321	8	0	0	0	29
1998-99	Michigan K-Wings	IHL	78	3	5	8	421	5	1	0	1	16
99-2000	Michigan K-Wings	IHL	33	3	4	7	144	....	....	....	....	....

Signed as a free agent by **Dallas**, July 29, 1998. • Played w/ RHI's New Jersey R@R in 1995 (4-2-0-2-40)

ANGER, Niklas (AN-guhr, NIHK-lahs) MTL.

Right wing. Shoots left. 6'1", 185 lbs. Born, Gavle, Sweden, July 31, 1977.
(Montreal's 5th choice, 112th overall, in 1995 Entry Draft).

			Regular Season					Playoffs				
Season	Club	Lea	GP	G	A	TP	PIM	GP	G	A	TP	PIM
1994-95	Djurgardens IF	Swede-Jr.	30	14	12	26	26	....	....	....	....	....
	Djurgardens IF	Sweden	1	0	0	0	0	....	....	....	....	....
1995-96	Djurgardens IF	Sweden	10	0	0	0	2	....	....	....	....	....
1996-97	Djurgardens IF	Sweden	4	0	0	0	0	....	....	....	....	....
	Arlanda HK	Swede-2	16	5	9	14	6	....	....	....	....	....
	Linkopings HC	Swede-2	7	2	1	3	10	....	....	....	....	....
1997-98	Djurgardens IF	Sweden	45	2	5	7	37	12	0	1	1	2
1998-99	AIK Solna	Sweden	47	6	6	12	16	....	....	....	....	....
99-2000	AIK Solna	Sweden	50	11	13	24	14	....	....	....	....	....

ANISIMOV, Artem (ah-NIH-sih-mohv) MIN.

Defense. Shoots left. 6'1", 187 lbs. Born, Kazan, USSR, July 27, 1976.
(Philadelphia's 1st choice, 62nd overall, in 1994 Entry Draft).

			Regular Season					Playoffs				
Season	Club	Lea	GP	G	A	TP	PIM	GP	G	A	TP	PIM
1993-94	Ak Bars Kazan	CIS	38	0	1	1	12	5	0	0	0	0
1994-95	Ak Bars Kazan	CIS	46	3	2	5	55	1	0	0	0	0
1995-96	Ak Bars Kazan	CIS	30	0	2	2	8	....	....	....	....	....
1996-97	Ak Bars Kazan	Russia	5	0	1	1	2	....	....	....	....	....
1997-98	Ak Bars Kazan	Russia	44	0	0	0	26	....	....	....	....	....
1998-99	Ak Bars Kazan	Russia	39	0	4	4	10	9	0	0	0	2
99-2000	Ak Bars Kazan	Russia	11	0	1	1	2	5	1	1	2	4

Selected by **Minnesota** from **Philadelphia** in Expansion Draft, June 23, 2000.

ANTIPOV, Vladimir (an-TIH-pahv) TOR.

Right wing. Shoots left. 5'11", 180 lbs. Born, Appatity, USSR, January 17, 1978.
(Toronto's 6th choice, 103rd overall, in 1996 Entry Draft).

			Regular Season					Playoffs				
Season	Club	Lea	GP	G	A	TP	PIM	GP	G	A	TP	PIM
1995-96	Torpedo Yaroslavl	CIS-2	39	14	11	25	....	....	....	....	....	....
1996-97	Torpedo Yaroslavl	Russia	27	6	4	10	22	2	0	0	0	0
	Torpedo Yaroslavl	Russia-3	14	3	4	7	26	....	....	....	....	....
1997-98	Torpedo Yaroslavl	Russia	41	9	3	12	57	....	....	....	....	....
	Torpedo Yaroslavl	EuroHL	7	0	2	2	2	....	....	....	....	....
1998-99	Torpedo Yaroslavl	Russia	42	7	13	20	30	10	2	2	4	10
99-2000	St. John's Leafs	AHL	45	6	7	13	14	....	....	....	....	....
	South Carolina	ECHL	4	0	4	4	2	....	....	....	....	....
	Long Beach	IHL	16	3	3	6	18	1	0	0	0	0

APPS, Syl (APPS, sihl) TOR.

Center. Shoots right. 6', 195 lbs. Born, Pittsburgh, PA, June 2, 1976.

			Regular Season					Playoffs				
Season	Club	Lea	GP	G	A	TP	PIM	GP	G	A	TP	PIM
1994-95	St. Michael's	OJHL	6	3	1	4	2	....	....	....	....	....
1995-96	Princeton	ECAC	26	4	6	10	30	....	....	....	....	....
1996-97	Princeton	ECAC	27	3	6	9	40	....	....	....	....	....
1997-98	Princeton	ECAC	35	10	8	18	65	....	....	....	....	....
1998-99	Princeton	ECAC	34	13	21	34	45	....	....	....	....	....
99-2000	St. John's Leafs	AHL	58	5	7	12	87	....	....	....	....	....

Signed as a free agent by **Toronto**, July 22, 1999.

ARKHIPOV, Denis (ahr-KHEE-pahv, DIHN-ihs) **NSH.**

Right wing. Shoots left. 6'3", 210 lbs. Born, Kazan, USSR, May 19, 1979.
(Nashville's 2nd choice, 60th overall, in 1998 Entry Draft).

			Regular Season					Playoffs				
Season	Club	Lea	GP	G	A	TP	PIM	GP	G	A	TP	PIM
1994-95	Ak Bars Kazan	Russia-Jr	40	20	12	32	10	....	....	....	....	....
1995-96	Ak Bars Kazan	Russia-Jr.	40	15	8	23	30	....	....	....	....	....
	Ak Bars Kazan-2	Russia-2	15	10	8	18	10	....	....	....	....	....
1996-97	Ak Bars Kazan-2	Russia-3	50	17	23	40	20	....	....	....	....	....
	Ak Bars Kazan	Russia	1	1	0	1	0	....	....	....	....	....
1997-98	Ak Bars Kazan	Russia	29	2	2	4	2	....	....	....	....	....
1998-99	Ak Bars Kazan	Russia	34	12	1	13	22	9	2	3	5	6
99-2000	Ak Bars Kazan	Russia	32	7	9	16	14	18	5	5	10	6

ARMSTRONG, Chris (ahrm-STRAWG, KRIHS) **MIN.**

Defense. Shoots left. 6', 205 lbs. Born, Regina, Sask., June 26, 1975.
(Florida's 3rd choice, 57th overall, in 1993 Entry Draft).

			Regular Season					Playoffs				
Season	Club	Lea	GP	G	A	TP	PIM	GP	G	A	TP	PIM
1990-91	Whitewood Mites	SAHA	40	25	30	55	40	....	....	....	....	....
1991-92	Moose Jaw	WHL	43	2	7	9	19	4	0	0	0	0
1992-93	Moose Jaw	WHL	67	9	35	44	104	....	....	....	....	....
1993-94	Moose Jaw	WHL	64	13	55	68	54	....	....	....	....	....
	Cincinnati	IHL	1	0	0	0	0	10	1	3	4	2
1994-95	Moose Jaw	WHL	66	17	54	71	61	10	2	12	14	22
	Cincinnati	IHL	....	....	....	....	....	9	1	3	4	10
1995-96	Carolina	AHL	78	9	33	42	65	....	....	....	....	....
1996-97	Carolina	AHL	66	9	23	32	38	....	....	....	....	....
1997-98	Fort Wayne	IHL	79	8	36	44	66	4	0	2	2	4
1998-99	Milwaukee	IHL	5	0	3	3	4	....	....	....	....	....
	Hershey Bears	AHL	65	12	32	44	30	5	0	1	1	0
99-2000	Kentucky	AHL	78	9	48	57	77	9	1	5	6	4

WHL East First All-Star Team (1994) • Canadian Major Junior Second All-Star Team (1994) • WHL East Second All-Star Team (1995)

Claimed by **Nashville** from **Florida** in Expansion Draft, June 26, 1998. Signed as a free agent by **San Jose**, September 2, 1999. Selected by **Minnesota** from **San Jose** in Expansion Draft, June 23, 2000.

ARNASON, Tyler (AHR-na-suhn, TIGH-luhr) **CHI.**

Center. Shoots left. 5'11", 185 lbs. Born, Oklahoma City, OK, March 16, 1979.
(Chicago's 6th choice, 183rd overall, in 1998 Entry Draft).

			Regular Season					Playoffs				
Season	Club	Lea	GP	G	A	TP	PIM	GP	G	A	TP	PIM
1997-98	Fargo-Moorhead	USHL	52	37	45	82	16	4	1	1	2	2
1998-99	St. Cloud State	WCHA	38	14	17	31	16	....	....	....	....	....
99-2000	St. Cloud State	WCHA	39	19	30	49	18	....	....	....	....	....

WCHA Second All-Star Team (2000)

ARONSON, Steve **MIN.**

Right wing. Shoots right. 6'1", 205 lbs. Born, Minnetonka, MN, July 15, 1978.

			Regular Season					Playoffs				
Season	Club	Lea	GP	G	A	TP	PIM	GP	G	A	TP	PIM
1996-97	U. of St. Thomas	MIAC	27	11	25	36	44	....	....	....	....	....
1997-98	U. of St. Thomas	MIAC	28	32	25	57	41	....	....	....	....	....
1998-99	U. of St. Thomas	MIAC	31	23	37	60	73	....	....	....	....	....
99-2000	U. of St. Thomas	MIAC	33	38	53	91	72	....	....	....	....	....

MIAC All-Conference Team (1997, 1998, 1999, 2000) • NCAA-3 First Team All-American (1998, 1999, 2000) • Named MIAC Most Valuable Player (1999, 2000) • Named NCAA-3 Player-of-the-Year (2000)

Signed as a free agent by **Minnesota**, May 4, 2000.

AUFIERO, Patrick (ow-fee-AIR-oh, PAT-rihk) **NYR**

Defense. Shoots right. 6'2", 186 lbs. Born, Winchester, MA, July 1, 1980.
(NY Rangers' 5th choice, 90th overall, in 1999 Entry Draft).

			Regular Season					Playoffs				
Season	Club	Lea	GP	G	A	TP	PIM	GP	G	A	TP	PIM
1997-98	Team USA	Under-18	56	10	11	21	111	....	....	....	....	....
1998-99	Boston University	H-East	22	3	4	7	14	....	....	....	....	....
99-2000	Boston University	H-East	38	3	20	23	37	....	....	....	....	....

Hockey East Second All-Star Team (2000)

AULIN, Jared (AW-lihn) **COL.**

Center. Shoots right. 6', 180 lbs. Born, Calgary, Alta., March 15, 1982.
(Colorado's 2nd choice, 47th overall, in 2000 Entry Draft).

			Regular Season					Playoffs				
Season	Club	Lea	GP	G	A	TP	PIM	GP	G	A	TP	PIM
1997-98	Airdrie Xtreme	AAHA	55	42	61	103	60	....	....	....	....	....
1998-99	Kamloops Blazers	WHL	55	7	19	26	23	13	1	3	4	2
99-2000	Kamloops Blazers	WHL	57	17	38	55	70	4	0	1	1	6

AWADA, George

Right wing. Shoots right. 6'2", 215 lbs. Born, Mendota Heights, MN, June 2, 1975.

			Regular Season					Playoffs				
Season	Club	Lea	GP	G	A	TP	PIM	GP	G	A	TP	PIM
1995-96	St. Cloud State	WCHA	21	6	2	8	16	....	....	....	....	....
1996-97	St. Cloud State	WCHA	35	3	2	5	26	....	....	....	....	....
1997-98	St. Cloud State	WCHA	38	15	14	29	74	....	....	....	....	....
1998-99	St. Cloud State	WCHA	39	14	16	30	38	....	....	....	....	....
	Albany River Rats	AHL	10	1	1	2	8	1	0	0	0	0
99-2000	Albany River Rats	AHL	63	8	8	16	29	4	0	0	0	0

Signed as a free agent by **New Jersey**, May 12, 1999.

BABENKO, Yuri (bah-BEHN-koh, EW-ree) **COL.**

Center. Shoots left. 6'1", 200 lbs. Born, Penza, USSR, January 2, 1978.
(Colorado's 2nd choice, 51st overall, in 1996 Entry Draft).

			Regular Season					Playoffs				
Season	Club	Lea	GP	G	A	TP	PIM	GP	G	A	TP	PIM
1995-96	Krylja Sovetov	CIS	21	0	0	0	16	....	....	....	....	....
1996-97	Krylja Sovetov	Russia	4	1	0	1	4	....	....	....	....	....
	Krylja Sovetov-2	Russia-3	26	8	10	18	24	....	....	....	....	....
	CSKA Moscow	Russia-2	24	3	3	6	12	....	....	....	....	....
1997-98	Plymouth Whalers	OHL	59	22	34	56	22	15	3	7	10	24
1998-99	Hershey Bears	AHL	74	11	15	26	47	2	0	1	1	0
99-2000	Hershey Bears	AHL	75	20	25	45	53	14	4	3	7	37

BABY, Stephan (BAY-bee) **ATL.**

Right wing. Shoots right. 6'5", 225 lbs. Born, Chicago, IL, January 31, 1980.
(Atlanta's 8th choice, 188th overall, in 1999 Entry Draft).

			Regular Season					Playoffs				
Season	Club	Lea	GP	G	A	TP	PIM	GP	G	A	TP	PIM
1997-98	Green Bay	USHL	56	17	17	34	85	4	1	3	4	8
1998-99	Green Bay	USHL	55	23	24	47	83	6	1	1	2	4
99-2000	Cornell Big Red	ECAC	31	4	10	14	52	....	....	....	....	....

BACKMAN, Christian (BAK-man, KRIH-stan) **ST.L.**

Defense. Shoots left. 6'2", 187 lbs. Born, Alingsas, Sweden, April 28, 1980.
(St. Louis' 1st choice, 24th overall, in 1998 Entry Draft).

			Regular Season					Playoffs				
Season	Club	Lea	GP	G	A	TP	PIM	GP	G	A	TP	PIM
1996-97	Vastra Frolunda	Swede-Jr.	26	2	5	7	16	....	....	....	....	....
1997-98	Vastra Frolunda	Swede-Jr.	28	5	14	19	12	2	0	1	1	4
1998-99	Vastra Frolunda	Swede-Jr.	4	0	2	2	4	....	....	....	....	....
	Vastra Frolunda	Sweden	49	0	4	4	4	4	0	0	0	0
99-2000	Vastra Frolunda	Sweden	27	1	0	1	14	5	0	0	0	0

BAKER, Kevin (BAY-kuhr) **L.A.**

Right wing. Shoots right. 6'1", 206 lbs. Born, Kingston, Ont., June 15, 1979.
(Los Angeles' 8th choice, 193rd overall, in 1999 Entry Draft).

			Regular Season					Playoffs				
Season	Club	Lea	GP	G	A	TP	PIM	GP	G	A	TP	PIM
1997-98	Belleville Bulls	OHL	63	21	21	42	62	9	4	5	9	11
1998-99	Belleville Bulls	OHL	68	44	37	81	66	12	12	5	17	12
99-2000	Belleville Bulls	OHL	60	28	31	59	90	16	11	5	16	22

BALA, Chris (BA-la, KRIHS) **OTT.**

Left wing. Shoots left. 6'1", 180 lbs. Born, Alexandria, VA, September 24, 1978.
(Ottawa's 3rd choice, 58th overall, in 1998 Entry Draft).

			Regular Season					Playoffs				
Season	Club	Lea	GP	G	A	TP	PIM	GP	G	A	TP	PIM
1996-97	Hill-Murray	Hi-School	23	28	33	61	36	....	....	....	....	....
1997-98	Harvard University	ECAC	33	16	14	30	23	....	....	....	....	....
1998-99	Harvard University	ECAC	28	5	10	15	16	....	....	....	....	....
99-2000	Harvard University	ECAC	30	10	14	24	18	....	....	....	....	....

BALAN, Scott (BAY-luhn) **CHI.**

Defense. Shoots right. 6'2", 194 lbs. Born, Medicine Hat, Alta., May 29, 1982.
(Chicago's 5th choice, 106th overall, in 2000 Entry Draft).

			Regular Season					Playoffs				
Season	Club	Lea	GP	G	A	TP	PIM	GP	G	A	TP	PIM
1997-98	Regina Chiefs	AAHA	56	6	25	31	139	....	....	....	....	....
1998-99	Regina Pats	WHL	63	1	8	9	42	....	....	....	....	....
99-2000	Regina Pats	WHL	67	3	11	14	157	7	0	1	1	17

BALEJ, Jozef (BAH-lay, YOH-zehf) **MTL.**

Right wing. Shoots right. 5'11", 170 lbs. Born, Myjava, Czech., February 22, 1982.
(Montreal's 3rd choice, 78th overall, in 2000 Entry Draft).

			Regular Season					Playoffs				
Season	Club	Lea	GP	G	A	TP	PIM	GP	G	A	TP	PIM
1997-98	Dukla Trencin	Slovak-Jr.	52	57	40	97	60	....	....	....	....	....
1998-99	Thunder Bay	USHL	38	8	7	15	9	....	....	....	....	....
	Rochester	USHL	17	0	1	1	2	....	....	....	....	....
99-2000	Portland	WHL	65	22	23	45	33	....	....	....	....	....

BARBER, Greg (BAHR-buhr) **BOS.**

Right wing. Shoots right. 6', 185 lbs. Born, Dawson Creek, B.C., May 26, 1980.
(Boston's 7th choice, 207th overall, in 1999 Entry Draft).

			Regular Season					Playoffs				
Season	Club	Lea	GP	G	A	TP	PIM	GP	G	A	TP	PIM
1996-97	Kelowna	BCAHA	54	36	48	84	90	....	....	....	....	....
1997-98	Victoria Salsa	BCJHL	60	15	22	37	24	7	2	2	4	4
1998-99	Victoria Salsa	BCJHL	60	41	41	82	95	....	....	....	....	....
99-2000	U. of Denver	WCHA	40	7	8	15	24	....	....	....	....	....

BARCH, Krys (BAHR-ch, KRIHS) **WSH.**

Left wing. Shoots left. 6'2", 200 lbs. Born, Guelph, Ont., March 26, 1980.
(Washington's 3rd choice, 106th overall, in 1998 Entry Draft).

			Regular Season					Playoffs				
Season	Club	Lea	GP	G	A	TP	PIM	GP	G	A	TP	PIM
1996-97	Georgetown	OJHL	51	18	26	44	58	....	....	....	....	....
1997-98	London Knights	OHL	65	9	27	36	62	16	4	3	7	16
1998-99	London Knights	OHL	66	18	20	38	66	25	9	17	26	15
99-2000	London Knights	OHL	56	23	26	49	78	....	....	....	....	....

BARKUNOV, Alexander (bahr-koo-NAHF) **CHI.**

Defense. Shoots right. 6'1", 190 lbs. Born, Novosibirsk, USSR, May 13, 1981.
(Chicago's 7th choice, 151st overall, in 2000 Entry Draft).

			Regular Season					Playoffs				
Season	Club	Lea	GP	G	A	TP	PIM	GP	G	A	TP	PIM
1996-97	Torpedo Yaroslavl	Russia-3	1	0	0	0	0	....	....	....	....	....
1997-98	Torpedo Yaroslavl	Russia-2	20	1	1	2	6	....	....	....	....	....
1998-99	Torpedo Yaroslavl	Russia-3	19	0	3	3	8	....	....	....	....	....
99-2000	Torpedo Yaroslavl	Russia-3	38	5	9	14	....	....	....	....	....	....

BARNES, Ryan (BAHR-nz, Rih-YAN) **DET.**

Left wing. Shoots left. 6'1", 201 lbs. Born, Dunnville, Ont., January 30, 1980.
(Detroit's 2nd choice, 55th overall, in 1998 Entry Draft).

			Regular Season					Playoffs				
Season	Club	Lea	GP	G	A	TP	PIM	GP	G	A	TP	PIM
1996-97	Quinte Hawks	OJHL	46	15	19	34	245	....	....	....	....	....
1997-98	Sudbury Wolves	OHL	46	13	18	31	111	10	0	2	2	24
1998-99	Sudbury Wolves	OHL	8	2	0	2	*23	....	....	....	....	....
	St. Michael's	OHL	31	11	14	25	*215	....	....	....	....	....
	Barrie Colts	OHL	24	16	14	30	*161	12	2	4	6	40
99-2000	Barrie Colts	OHL	31	17	12	29	98	25	7	7	14	49

BARNEY, Scott (BAHR-nee, SKAWT) L.A.

Center. Shoots right. 6'4", 198 lbs. Born, Oshawa, Ont., March 27, 1979.
(Los Angeles' 3rd choice, 29th overall, in 1997 Entry Draft).

			Regular Season					Playoffs				
Season	Club	Lea	GP	G	A	TP	PIM	GP	G	A	TP	PIM
1994-95	North York	OJHL	41	16	19	35	88	....	....	....	....	....
1995-96	Peterborough	OHL	60	22	24	46	52	24	6	8	14	38
1996-97	Peterborough	OHL	64	21	33	54	110	9	0	3	3	16
1997-98	Peterborough	OHL	62	44	32	76	60	4	1	0	1	6
1998-99	Peterborough	OHL	44	41	26	67	80	5	4	1	5	4
	Springfield	AHL	5	0	0	0	2	1	0	0	0	2
99-2000	Lowell	AHL	DID NOT PLAY – INJURED									

• Missed entire 1999-2000 season recovering from back injury suffered in training camp, September 28, 2000.

BARTEK, Martin (BAHR-tehk, MAHR-tehn) NSH.

Center. Shoots right. 6'1", 200 lbs. Born, Kindgssed Jill, Czech., July 17, 1980.
(Nashville's 7th choice, 202nd overall, in 1998 Entry Draft).

			Regular Season					Playoffs				
Season	Club	Lea	GP	G	A	TP	PIM	GP	G	A	TP	PIM
1995-96	HKm Zvolen	Slovak-Jr.	46	75	43	118	....	....	....	....	....	....
1996-97	Kings Edgehill	Hi-School	35	45	40	85	32	....	....	....	....	....
1997-98	Rouyn-Noranda	QMJHL	28	9	19	28	12	....	....	....	....	....
	Rimouski Oceanic	QMJHL	13	3	4	7	6	....	....	....	....	....
	Sherbrooke	QMJHL	25	11	12	23	38	....	....	....	....	....
1998-99	HKm Zvolen	Slovak-Jr.	17	14	17	31	89	....	....	....	....	....
	HKm Zvolen	Slovakia	28	10	8	18	18	2	1	0	1	0
99-2000	Moncton Wildcats	QMJHL	69	32	44	76	36	16	10	13	23	24

BARTLETT, Russ TOR.

Center. Shoots left. 6'2", 185 lbs. Born, Windham, NH, February 10, 1978.
(Toronto's 7th choice, 194th overall, in 1997 Entry Draft).

			Regular Season					Playoffs				
Season	Club	Lea	GP	G	A	TP	PIM	GP	G	A	TP	PIM
1996-97	Phillips-Exeter	Hi-School	31	27	63	90	24	....	....	....	....	....
1997-98	Boston University	H-East	38	8	11	19	44	....	....	....	....	....
1998-99	Boston University	H-East	35	12	20	32	18	....	....	....	....	....
99-2000	St. Lawrence	ECAC	DID NOT PLAY – TRANSFERRED COLLEGES									

BARTOVIC, Milan (BAHR-tuh-vihch, MIH-lan) BUF.

Right wing. Shoots left. 6', 194 lbs. Born, Trencin, Czech., April 9, 1981.
(Buffalo's 2nd choice, 35th overall, in 1999 Entry Draft).

			Regular Season					Playoffs				
Season	Club	Lea	GP	G	A	TP	PIM	GP	G	A	TP	PIM
1997-98	Dukla Trencin	Slovak-Jr.	26	2	6	8	27	....	....	....	....	....
1998-99	Dukla Trencin	Slovak-Jr.	46	36	35	71	62	6	9	3	12	10
99-2000	Tri-City Americans	WHL	18	8	9	17	12	....	....	....	....	....
	Brandon	WHL	38	18	22	40	28	....	....	....	....	....

BATEMAN, Jeff (BAYT-mahn, JEHF) DAL.

Center. Shoots left. 5'11", 179 lbs. Born, Belleville, Ont., August 29, 1981.
(Dallas' 4th choice, 126th overall, in 1999 Entry Draft).

			Regular Season					Playoffs				
Season	Club	Lea	GP	G	A	TP	PIM	GP	G	A	TP	PIM
1997-98	Wellington Dukes	OJHL	50	26	35	61	68	....	....	....	....	....
1998-99	Brampton	OHL	68	23	35	58	27	....	....	....	....	....
99-2000	Brampton	OHL	64	23	41	64	62	6	2	1	3	4

BATOVSKY, Zoltan S.J.

Right wing. Shoots left. 5'11", 186 lbs. Born, Slovad, Czech., March 27, 1979.

			Regular Season					Playoffs				
Season	Club	Lea	GP	G	A	TP	PIM	GP	G	A	TP	PIM
1997-98	Drummondville	QMJHL	69	22	43	65	112	....	....	....	....	....
1998-99	Drummondville	QMJHL	62	29	42	71	126	....	....	....	....	....
99-2000	Drummondville	QMJHL	63	27	60	87	151	16	10	19	29	12

Signed as a free agent by **San Jose**, June 24, 2000.

BAUMGARTNER, Gregor (BAWM-gahr-nuhr, GREHG-oor) DAL.

Left wing. Shoots left. 6'2", 185 lbs. Born, Kapfenberg, Austria, July 13, 1979.
(Dallas' 5th choice, 156th overall, in 1999 Entry Draft).

			Regular Season					Playoffs				
Season	Club	Lea	GP	G	A	TP	PIM	GP	G	A	TP	PIM
1994-95	Ste-Foy Governors	QAAA	43	28	29	57	2	....	....	....	....	....
1995-96	Clarkson	ECAC	7	0	1	1	0	....	....	....	....	....
	Gatineau	QAAA	15	8	11	19	6	....	....	....	....	....
1996-97	Laval Titan	QMJHL	68	19	45	64	15	3	0	0	0	0
1997-98	Laval Titan	QMJHL	68	31	51	82	10	16	5	12	17	6
1998-99	Acadie-Bathurst	QMJHL	68	33	58	91	14	23	8	8	16	8
99-2000	Michigan K-Wings	IHL	59	6	9	15	11	....	....	....	....	....

• Re-entered NHL draft. Originally Montreal's 2nd choice, 37th overall, in 1997 Entry Draft.

BAYDA, Ryan (BAY-duh) CAR.

Left wing. Shoots left. 5'11", 185 lbs. Born, Saskatoon, Sask., December 9, 1980.
(Carolina's 2nd choice, 80th overall, in 2000 Entry Draft).

			Regular Season					Playoffs				
Season	Club	Lea	GP	G	A	TP	PIM	GP	G	A	TP	PIM
1995-96	Saskatoon Flyers	SAHA	60	85	74	159	85	....	....	....	....	....
1996-97	Saskatoon	SAHA	44	22	23	45	18	....	....	....	....	....
1997-98	Saskatoon	SAHA	41	29	49	78	103	....	....	....	....	....
1998-99	Vernon Vipers	BCJHL	45	24	58	82	15	....	....	....	....	....
99-2000	North Dakota	WCHA	44	17	23	40	30	....	....	....	....	....

BCJHL Rookie-of-the-Year (1999) • WCHA All-Rookie Team (2000)

BEAUCHEMIN, Francois (boh-sheh-MEH, frahn-SWUH) MTL.

Defense. Shoots left. 6', 195 lbs. Born, Sorel, Que., June 4, 1980.
(Montreal's 3rd choice, 75th overall, in 1998 Entry Draft).

			Regular Season					Playoffs				
Season	Club	Lea	GP	G	A	TP	PIM	GP	G	A	TP	PIM
1995-96	Richelieu Regents	QAAA	40	9	23	32	59	....	....	....	....	....
1996-97	Laval Titan	QMJHL	66	7	21	28	132	3	0	0	0	2
1997-98	Laval Titan	QMJHL	70	12	35	47	132	16	1	3	4	23
1998-99	Acadie-Bathurst	QMJHL	31	4	17	21	53	23	2	16	18	55
99-2000	Acadie-Bathurst	QMJHL	38	11	36	47	64	....	....	....	....	....
	Moncton Wildcats	QMJHL	33	8	31	39	35	16	2	11	13	14

QMJHL Second All-Star Team (2000)

BEAUDOIN, Eric (boh-DWEH, ERIHK) FLA.

Left wing. Shoots left. 6'5", 204 lbs. Born, Ottawa, Ont., May 3, 1980.
(Tampa Bay's 4th choice, 92nd overall, in 1998 Entry Draft).

			Regular Season					Playoffs				
Season	Club	Lea	GP	G	A	TP	PIM	GP	G	A	TP	PIM
1996-97	Ottawa	OJHL	54	12	19	31	55	....	....	....	....	....
1997-98	Guelph Storm	OHL	62	9	13	22	43	12	3	2	5	4
1998-99	Guelph Storm	OHL	66	28	43	71	79	11	5	3	8	12
99-2000	Guelph Storm	OHL	68	38	34	72	126	6	3	0	3	2

Traded to **Florida** by **Tampa Bay** for Florida's 7th round choice (Marek Priechodsky) in 2000 Entry Draft, June 1, 2000.

BECKETT, Jason (Beh-keht, JAY-suhn) PHI.

Defense. Shoots right. 6'2", 203 lbs. Born, Lethbridge, Alta., July 23, 1980.
(Philadelphia's 2nd choice, 42nd overall, in 1998 Entry Draft).

			Regular Season					Playoffs				
Season	Club	Lea	GP	G	A	TP	PIM	GP	G	A	TP	PIM
1996-97	Lethbridge	AAHA	34	7	10	17	118	....	....	....	....	....
1997-98	Seattle T-Birds	WHL	71	1	11	12	241	5	0	0	0	16
1998-99	Seattle T-Birds	WHL	70	4	26	30	195	11	0	1	1	40
99-2000	Seattle T-Birds	WHL	70	3	15	18	183	7	1	1	2	12

BEECH, Kris (BEECH, KRIHS) WSH.

Center. Shoots left. 6'2", 178 lbs. Born, Salmon Arm, B.C., February 5, 1981.
(Washington's 1st choice, 7th overall, in 1999 Entry Draft).

			Regular Season					Playoffs				
Season	Club	Lea	GP	G	A	TP	PIM	GP	G	A	TP	PIM
1996-97	Sicamous Eagles	KIJHL	49	34	36	70	80	....	....	....	....	....
	Calgary Hitmen	WHL	8	1	1	2	0	....	....	....	....	....
1997-98	Calgary Hitmen	WHL	58	10	25	35	24	12	4	5	9	32
1998-99	Calgary Hitmen	WHL	68	26	41	67	103	6	1	4	5	8
99-2000	Calgary Hitmen	WHL	66	32	54	86	99	5	3	5	8	16

BELANGER, Eric (buh-LAWN-zhay, EHRIK) L.A.

Center. Shoots left. 6', 177 lbs. Born, Sherbrooke, Que., December 16, 1977.
(Los Angeles' 5th choice, 96th overall, in 1996 Entry Draft).

			Regular Season					Playoffs				
Season	Club	Lea	GP	G	A	TP	PIM	GP	G	A	TP	PIM
1994-95	Beauport	QMJHL	71	12	28	40	24	18	5	9	14	25
1995-96	Beauport	QMJHL	59	35	48	83	18	20	13	14	27	6
1996-97	Beauport	QMJHL	31	13	37	50	30	....	....	....	....	....
	Rimouski Oceanic	QMJHL	31	26	41	67	36	4	2	3	5	10
1997-98	Fredericton	AHL	56	17	34	51	28	4	2	1	3	2
1998-99	Springfield	AHL	33	8	18	26	10	3	0	1	1	2
	Long Beach	IHL	1	0	0	0	0	....	....	....	....	....
99-2000	Lowell	AHL	65	15	25	40	20	7	3	3	6	2

BELANGER, Francis (buh-LAWN-zhay, FRAN-sihs) PHI.

Left wing. Shoots left. 6'2", 216 lbs. Born, Bellefeuille, Que., January 15, 1978.
(Philadelphia's 5th choice, 124th overall, in 1998 Entry Draft).

			Regular Season					Playoffs				
Season	Club	Lea	GP	G	A	TP	PIM	GP	G	A	TP	PIM
1994-95	Laval Regents	QAAA	25	11	8	19	78	....	....	....	....	....
1995-96	Hull Olympiques	QMJHL	1	0	0	0	0	....	....	....	....	....
1996-97	Hull Olympiques	QMJHL	53	13	13	26	134	8	2	2	4	57
1997-98	Hull Olympiques	QMJHL	33	22	23	45	133	....	....	....	....	....
	Rimouski Oceanic	QMJHL	30	18	10	28	248	17	14	8	22	61
1998-99	Philadelphia	AHL	58	13	13	26	242	16	4	3	7	16
99-2000	Philadelphia	AHL	35	5	6	11	112	....	....	....	....	....
	Trenton Titans	ECHL	9	1	1	2	29	....	....	....	....	....

BELL, Mark (BEHL, MAWRK) CHI.

Center. Shoots left. 6'3", 198 lbs. Born, St. Paul's, Ont., August 5, 1980.
(Chicago's 1st choice, 8th overall, in 1998 Entry Draft).

			Regular Season					Playoffs				
Season	Club	Lea	GP	G	A	TP	PIM	GP	G	A	TP	PIM
1995-96	Stratford Cullitons	OJHL-B	47	8	15	23	32	....	....	....	....	....
1996-97	Ottawa 67's	OHL	65	8	12	20	40	24	4	7	11	13
1997-98	Ottawa 67's	OHL	55	34	26	60	87	13	6	5	11	14
1998-99	Ottawa 67's	OHL	44	29	26	55	69	9	6	5	11	8
99-2000	Ottawa 67's	OHL	48	34	38	72	95	2	0	1	1	0

BELL, Thatcher (BEHL) VAN.

Center. Shoots left. 6', 172 lbs. Born, Charlottetown, P.E.I., February 1, 1982.
(Vancouver's 2nd choice, 71st overall, in 2000 Entry Draft).

			Regular Season					Playoffs				
Season	Club	Lea	GP	G	A	TP	PIM	GP	G	A	TP	PIM
1997-98	U.C.C. Blues	Hi-School	44	35	50	85	....	....	....	....	....	....
1998-99	Rimouski Oceanic	QMJHL	64	16	38	54	67	11	3	1	4	0
99-2000	Rimouski Oceanic	QMJHL	53	26	43	69	61	5	0	0	0	15

BELLEFEUILLE, Blake CBJ

Right wing. Shoots right. 5'10", 208 lbs. Born, Framingham, MA, December 27, 1977.

			Regular Season					Playoffs				
Season	Club	Lea	GP	G	A	TP	PIM	GP	G	A	TP	PIM
1994-95	Framingham High	Hi-School	20	42	50	92	....	....	....	....	....	....
1995-96	Framingham High	Hi-School	20	31	60	91	....	....	....	....	....	....
1996-97	Boston College	H-East	34	16	19	35	20	....	....	....	....	....
1997-98	Boston College	H-East	41	19	20	39	35	....	....	....	....	....
1998-99	Boston College	H-East	43	24	25	49	80	....	....	....	....	....
99-2000	Boston College	H-East	39	18	31	49	28	....	....	....	....	....

Signed as a free agent by **Columbus**, May 26, 2000.

BELTER, Shane — BOS.

Defense. Shoots right. 6'1", 205 lbs. Born, Swift Current, Sask., October 5, 1977.

			Regular Season					Playoffs				
Season	Club	Lea	GP	G	A	TP	PIM	GP	G	A	TP	PIM
1993-94	Swift Current	SAHA	32	7	19	26	192	....	....	....	....	....
1994-95	Swift Current	SAHA	6	0	1	1	11	....	....	....	....	....
	Swift Current	WHL	55	3	12	15	72	4	0	0	0	6
1995-96	Seattle T-Birds	WHL	63	9	22	31	133	5	0	0	0	11
1996-97	Seattle T-Birds	WHL	13	1	4	5	29	....	....	....	....	....
	Lethbridge	WHL	34	4	24	28	30	17	2	9	11	18
1997-98	Lethbridge	WHL	8	1	4	5	14	....	....	....	....	....
	Kamloops Blazers	WHL	57	21	35	56	69	4	0	1	1	8
1998-99	Providence Bruins	AHL	5	0	0	0	0	....	....	....	....	....
	Greenville Growl	ECHL	54	5	17	22	59	....	....	....	....	....
99-2000	Providence Bruins	AHL	51	4	9	13	77	....	....	....	....	....

Signed as a free agent by **Boston**, April 20, 1998.

BEMBRIDGE, Garrett (bem-BRIHDJ, GAHR-reht) — NYR

Right wing. Shoots right. 6', 180 lbs. Born, Melfort, Sask., July 6, 1981.
(NY Rangers' 6th choice, 137th overall, in 1999 Entry Draft).

			Regular Season					Playoffs				
Season	Club	Lea	GP	G	A	TP	PIM	GP	G	A	TP	PIM
1997-98	Saskatoon Blazers	SAHA	44	29	45	74	74	....	....	....	....	....
	Saskatoon Blades	WHL	6	1	1	2	0	1	0	0	0	0
1998-99	Saskatoon Blades	WHL	68	23	27	50	30	....	....	....	....	....
99-2000	Saskatoon Blades	WHL	72	27	31	58	41	11	5	5	10	2

BENOIT, Mathieu (behn-WAH, MAT-hew)

Right wing. Shoots right. 5'11", 200 lbs. Born, St. Clec, Que., July 12, 1979.
(New Jersey's 6th choice, 188th overall, in 1997 Entry Draft).

			Regular Season					Playoffs				
Season	Club	Lea	GP	G	A	TP	PIM	GP	G	A	TP	PIM
1993-94	Salaberry Lions	QAAA	32	72	42	114	22	....	....	....	....	....
1994-95	Lac St-Louis	QAAA	44	21	33	54	34	....	....	....	....	....
1995-96	Chicoutimi	QMJHL	61	6	14	20	17	17	0	0	0	0
1996-97	Chicoutimi	QMJHL	64	35	36	71	22	9	2	2	4	0
1997-98	Chicoutimi	QMJHL	59	56	61	117	32	6	2	3	5	2
1998-99	Chicoutimi	QMJHL	36	39	14	53	28	....	....	....	....	....
	Acadie-Bathurst	QMJHL	32	23	33	56	6	23	*20	*21	*41	16
99-2000	Acadie-Bathurst	QMJHL	20	29	10	39	38	....	....	....	....	....
	Moncton Wildcats	QMJHL	33	28	34	62	21	16	15	15	30	6
	Albany River Rats	AHL	1	0	0	0	0	....	....	....	....	....

QMJHL First All-Star Team (1998) • QMJHL Second All-Star Team (1999, 2000)

BERG, Reggie (BUHRG, REH-jee) — CAR.

Center. Shoots left. 5'10", 180 lbs. Born, Coon Rapids, MN, September 18, 1976.
(Toronto's 12th choice, 178th overall, in 1996 Entry Draft).

			Regular Season					Playoffs				
Season	Club	Lea	GP	G	A	TP	PIM	GP	G	A	TP	PIM
1993-94	Des Moines	USHL	27	13	24	37	48	....	....	....	....	....
1994-95	Des Moines	USHL	35	30	35	65	75	....	....	....	....	....
1995-96	U. of Minnesota	WCHA	40	23	11	34	69	....	....	....	....	....
1996-97	U. of Minnesota	WCHA	38	11	26	37	48	....	....	....	....	....
1997-98	U. of Minnesota	WCHA	39	20	19	39	53	....	....	....	....	....
1998-99	U. of Minnesota	WCHA	43	20	28	48	64	....	....	....	....	....
99-2000	Florida	ECHL	52	27	25	52	64	5	2	1	3	6
	Orlando	IHL	2	0	0	0	0	....	....	....	....	....

WCHA Second All-Star Team (1998)

Signed as a free agent by **Carolina**, August 21, 2000.

BERGERON, Antoine (BAIR-zhuhr-uhn, ahn-TWAHN) — ST.L.

Defense. Shoots left. 6'2", 202 lbs. Born, Valcourt, Que., December 14, 1981.
(St. Louis' 4th choice, 96th overall, in 2000 Entry Draft).

			Regular Season					Playoffs				
Season	Club	Lea	GP	G	A	TP	PIM	GP	G	A	TP	PIM
1996-97	Magog Selectes	QAAA	34	4	11	15	20	....	....	....	....	....
1997-98	Magog Selectes	QAAA	17	7	10	17	39	10	3	4	7	12
1998-99	Rimouski Oceanic	QMJHL	20	0	4	4	28	....	....	....	....	....
	Victoriaville Tigres	QMJHL	30	3	6	9	73	2	0	0	0	0
99-2000	Victoriaville Tigres	QMJHL	24	2	8	10	30	....	....	....	....	....
	Val-d'Or Foreurs	QMJHL	8	3	1	4	10	....	....	....	....	....

BERGLUND, Christian (BUHRG-luhnd, KRIH-stan) — N.J.

Right wing. Shoots left. 5'11", 185 lbs. Born, Orebro, Sweden, March 12, 1980.
(New Jersey's 3rd choice, 37th overall, in 1998 Entry Draft).

			Regular Season					Playoffs				
Season	Club	Lea	GP	G	A	TP	PIM	GP	G	A	TP	PIM
1994-95	Kariskoga IK	Sweden-4	20	14	13	27	....	....	....	....	....	....
1995-96	Kristinehamn	Sweden-3	23	8	8	16	12	....	....	....	....	....
1996-97	Farjestads BK	Swede-Jr.	21	2	3	5	24	....	....	....	....	....
1997-98	Farjestads BK	Swede-Jr.	29	23	19	42	88	2	0	0	0	0
	Farjestads BK	Sweden	1	0	0	0	0	....	....	....	....	....
1998-99	Farjestads BK	Swede-Jr.	5	3	4	7	22	....	....	....	....	....
	Farjestads BK	Sweden	37	2	4	6	37	4	1	0	1	4
99-2000	Farjestads BK	Sweden	43	8	6	14	44	7	2	1	3	10
	Bofors IK	Sweden-2	6	2	0	2	12	....	....	....	....	....

BERNIKOV, Ruslan (BAIR-nih-kahf, roos-LAHN) — DAL.

Right wing. Shoots left. 6'3", 198 lbs. Born, Vidnoye, USSR, December 4, 1977.
(Dallas' 6th choice, 139th overall, in 2000 Entry Draft).

			Regular Season					Playoffs				
Season	Club	Lea	GP	G	A	TP	PIM	GP	G	A	TP	PIM
1996-97	Dynamo Moscow	Russia-3	32	11	4	15	20	....	....	....	....	....
	Dynamo Moscow	Russia	2	0	0	0	0	....	....	....	....	....
1997-98	SK Yekaterinburg	Russia	23	4	4	8	39	....	....	....	....	....
	SK Yekaterinburg	Russia-Q	20	3	3	6	16	....	....	....	....	....
	SK Yekaterinburg	Russia-3	2	1	1	2	0	....	....	....	....	....
1998-99	Dynamo Moscow	Russia	6	0	1	1	2	....	....	....	....	....
	Krylja Sovetov	Russia	20	3	1	4	24	....	....	....	....	....
	CSKA Moscow	Russia	1	0	0	0	0	....	....	....	....	....
	HC Cherepovets	Russia	5	0	0	0	0	1	0	0	0	0
99-2000	Dynamo Moscow	Russia	6	2	1	3	2	....	....	....	....	....
	Amur Khabarovsk	Russia	14	3	6	9	10	5	3	1	4	2

BERRY, Rick (BAIR-ree, RIHK) — COL.

Defense. Shoots left. 6'2", 210 lbs. Born, Brandon, Man., November 4, 1978.
(Colorado's 3rd choice, 55th overall, in 1997 Entry Draft).

			Regular Season					Playoffs				
Season	Club	Lea	GP	G	A	TP	PIM	GP	G	A	TP	PIM
1994-95	Yellowhead	MAHA	33	12	19	31	90	....	....	....	....	....
1995-96	Seattle T-Birds	WHL	59	4	9	13	103	1	0	0	0	0
1996-97	Seattle T-Birds	WHL	72	12	21	33	125	15	3	7	10	23
1997-98	Seattle T-Birds	WHL	37	5	12	17	100	....	....	....	....	....
	Spokane Chiefs	WHL	22	4	9	13	31	17	1	4	5	26
1998-99	Hershey Bears	AHL	62	2	6	8	153	....	....	....	....	....
99-2000	Hershey Bears	AHL	64	9	16	25	148	13	2	3	5	24

BETOURNAY, Eric (buh-TOOR-nay) — S.J.

Center. Shoots left. 6'1", 190 lbs. Born, Ormstown, Que., April 30, 1981.
(San Jose's 5th choice, 229th overall, in 1999 Entry Draft).

			Regular Season					Playoffs				
Season	Club	Lea	GP	G	A	TP	PIM	GP	G	A	TP	PIM
1997-98	Laval Titan	QMJHL	66	6	15	21	10	16	2	3	5	8
1998-99	Acadie-Bathurst	QMJHL	70	16	29	45	57	23	2	6	8	18
99-2000	Chicoutimi	QMJHL	72	13	33	46	40	....	....	....	....	....

BETTS, Blair (BEHTS, BLAIR) — CGY.

Center. Shoots left. 6'1", 204 lbs. Born, Edmonton, Alta., February 16, 1980.
(Calgary's 2nd choice, 33rd overall, in 1998 Entry Draft).

			Regular Season					Playoffs				
Season	Club	Lea	GP	G	A	TP	PIM	GP	G	A	TP	PIM
1995-96	Sherwood Park	AAHA	34	22	19	41	69	....	....	....	....	....
1996-97	Prince George	WHL	58	12	18	30	19	15	2	2	4	6
1997-98	Prince George	WHL	71	35	41	76	38	11	4	6	10	8
1998-99	Prince George	WHL	42	20	22	42	39	7	3	2	5	8
99-2000	Prince George	WHL	44	24	35	59	38	13	11	11	22	6

BEZINA, Goran (BEH-zee-nuh, GOH-ran) — PHX.

Defense. Shoots left. 6'3", 203 lbs. Born, Split, Yugoslavia, March 21, 1980.
(Phoenix's 8th choice, 234th overall, in 1999 Entry Draft).

			Regular Season					Playoffs				
Season	Club	Lea	GP	G	A	TP	PIM	GP	G	A	TP	PIM
1998-99	Fribourg-Gotteron	Switz-Jr.	22	11	6	17	64	....	....	....	....	....
	Fribourg-Gotteron	Switz.	38	0	0	0	14	4	0	0	0	2
99-2000	Fribourg-Gotteron	Switz.	44	3	6	9	10	4	0	0	0	6

BICEK, Jiri (bee-CHEHK, YEH-ree) — N.J.

Left wing. Shoots left. 5'10", 195 lbs. Born, Kosice, Czech., December 3, 1978.
(New Jersey's 4th choice, 131st overall, in 1997 Entry Draft).

			Regular Season					Playoffs				
Season	Club	Lea	GP	G	A	TP	PIM	GP	G	A	TP	PIM
1994-95	HC Kosice	Slovak-Jr.	42	38	36	74	18	....	....	....	....	....
1995-96	HC Kosice	Slovakia	30	10	15	25	16	9	2	4	6	0
1996-97	HC Kosice	Slovakia	44	11	14	25	20	7	1	3	4	....
1997-98	Albany River Rats	AHL	50	10	10	20	22	13	1	6	7	4
1998-99	Albany River Rats	AHL	79	15	45	60	102	5	2	2	4	2
99-2000	Albany River Rats	AHL	80	7	36	43	51	4	0	2	2	0

BIRBRAER, Maxim (beer-BRIEGH-uhr, max-EEM) — N.J.

Left wing. Shoots left. 6'2", 185 lbs. Born, Ust-Kamenogorsk, USSR, December 15, 1980.
(New Jersey's 6th choice, 67th overall, in 2000 Entry Draft).

			Regular Season					Playoffs				
Season	Club	Lea	GP	G	A	TP	PIM	GP	G	A	TP	PIM
1997-98	Shelburne	OJHL	12	7	11	18	8	....	....	....	....	....
1998-99	Shelburne	OJHL	35	20	22	42	25	....	....	....	....	....
99-2000	Newmarket	OJHL	47	50	32	82	52	....	....	....	....	....

BLANCHARD, Sean (BLAN-chard, SHAWN) — L.A.

Defense. Shoots left. 5'11", 194 lbs. Born, Sudbury, Ont., March 29, 1978.
(Los Angeles' 5th choice, 99th overall, in 1997 Entry Draft).

			Regular Season					Playoffs				
Season	Club	Lea	GP	G	A	TP	PIM	GP	G	A	TP	PIM
1993-94	Valley East Metros	NOHA	35	15	17	32	145	....	....	....	....	....
1994-95	Ottawa 67's	OHL	59	2	5	7	24	....	....	....	....	....
1995-96	Ottawa 67's	OHL	64	7	29	36	49	4	1	3	4	7
1996-97	Ottawa 67's	OHL	66	11	57	68	64	24	3	15	18	34
1997-98	Ottawa 67's	OHL	57	13	51	64	43	13	0	5	5	27
1998-99	Springfield	AHL	10	0	1	1	4	....	....	....	....	....
	Mississippi	ECHL	58	5	24	29	30	17	0	8	8	4
99-2000	Lowell	AHL	54	1	5	6	28	3	0	0	0	2
	Trenton Titans	ECHL	2	0	0	0	0	....	....	....	....	....

OHL First All-Star Team (1997, 1998) • Canadian Major Junior First All-Star Team (1997)
• Canadian Major Junior Defenseman of the Year (1997)

BLATNY, Zdenek (BLAT-nee, z-DEHN-ehk) — ATL.

Center. Shoots left. 6'1", 187 lbs. Born, Brno, Czech., January 14, 1981.
(Atlanta's 3rd choice, 68th overall, in 1999 Entry Draft).

			Regular Season					Playoffs				
Season	Club	Lea	GP	G	A	TP	PIM	GP	G	A	TP	PIM
1997-98	Kometa Brno-Jr.	Cze-Rep	42	22	21	43	40	....	....	....	....	....
1998-99	Seattle T-Birds	WHL	44	18	15	33	25	11	4	0	4	24
99-2000	Seattle T-Birds	WHL	7	4	5	9	12	....	....	....	....	....
	Kootenay Ice	WHL	61	43	39	82	119	21	10	*17	27	46

WHL East Second All-star Team (2000)

BOHAC, Jan (BOH-hach, YAHN) — OTT.

Center. Shoots left. 6'3", 189 lbs. Born, Tabor, Czech., February 3, 1982.
(Ottawa's 4th choice, 87th overall, in 2000 Entry Draft).

			Regular Season					Playoffs				
Season	Club	Lea	GP	G	A	TP	PIM	GP	G	A	TP	PIM
1997-98	Slavia Praha-Jr.	Cze-Rep	39	8	12	20	12	....	....	....	....	....
1998-99	Slavia Praha-Jr.	Cze-Rep	35	6	6	12	10	....	....	....	....	....
	Slavia Praha	Cze-Rep	2	0	0	0	0	....	....	....	....	....
99-2000	Slavia Praha-Jr.	Cze-Rep	25	1	2	3	4	....	....	....	....	....
	Slavia Praha	Cze-Rep	22	7	8	15	6	7	0	1	1	4

BOISVERT, Hugo (bwuh-VAIR, HEW-goh) ATL.

Center. Shoots left. 6', 200 lbs. Born, St-Eustache, Que., February 11, 1976.

			Regular Season					Playoffs				
Season	Club	Lea	GP	G	A	TP	PIM	GP	G	A	TP	PIM
1994-95	Cornwall Colts	OJHL	27	13	19	32	26	....	....	....	....	....
1995-96	Cornwall Colts	OJHL	54	40	90	130	102	15	15	20	35	44
1996-97	Ohio State	CCHA	38	11	27	38	44	....	....	....	....	....
1997-98	Ohio State	CCHA	42	23	*35	58	70	....	....	....	....	....
1998-99	Ohio State	CCHA	41	24	27	51	54	....	....	....	....	....
99-2000	Canada	Nat-Team	39	10	14	24	12	....	....	....	....	....

CCHA First All-Star Team (1998, 1999) • NCAA West First All-American Team (1998) • NCAA West Second All-American Team (1999)

Signed as a free agent by **Atlanta**, June 25, 1999.

BOLIBRUCK, Kevin (BOH-lee-bruhk, KEH-vihn)

Defense. Shoots left. 6'1", 200 lbs. Born, Peterborough, Ont., February 8, 1977.
(Edmonton's 7th choice, 176th overall, in 1997 Entry Draft).

			Regular Season					Playoffs				
Season	Club	Lea	GP	G	A	TP	PIM	GP	G	A	TP	PIM
1993-94	Thorold Hawks	OJHL-B	38	6	18	24	78	....	....	....	....	....
1994-95	Peterborough	OHL	66	2	16	18	88	11	1	1	2	14
1995-96	Peterborough	OHL	57	6	21	27	105	24	3	6	9	46
1996-97	Peterborough	OHL	46	4	26	30	63	11	3	3	6	14
1997-98	Canada	Nat-Team	49	2	5	7	65	....	....	....	....	....
1998-99	Hamilton Bulldogs	AHL	64	1	6	7	42	11	0	1	1	4
99-2000	Hamilton Bulldogs	AHL	54	1	4	5	67	10	0	1	1	4

OHL First All-Star Team (1996)

Re-entered NHL Entry Draft. Originally Ottawa's 4th choice, 89th overall, in 1995 Entry Draft.

Rights traded to **Chicago** by **Ottawa** with Denis Chasse and Ottawa's 6th round choice (later traded back to Ottawa - Ottawa selected Christopher Neil) in 1998 Entry Draft for Mike Prokopec, March 18, 1997.

BOOTLAND, Nick (BOOT-land, NIHK) COL.

Left wing. Shoots left. 6'3", 215 lbs. Born, Shelbourne, Ont., July 31, 1978.
(Dallas' 8th choice, 220th overall, in 1996 Entry Draft).

			Regular Season					Playoffs				
Season	Club	Lea	GP	G	A	TP	PIM	GP	G	A	TP	PIM
1994-95	Orangeville	OJHL	47	11	10	21	57	....	....	....	....	....
1995-96	Guelph Storm	OHL	64	8	7	15	90	16	1	0	1	21
1996-97	Guelph Storm	OHL	64	35	23	58	117	18	11	7	18	36
1997-98	Guelph Storm	OHL	64	23	37	60	128	12	7	6	13	22
1998-99	Hershey Bears	AHL	62	3	6	9	122	....	....	....	....	....
99-2000	Hershey Bears	AHL	59	5	13	18	108	14	2	2	4	26

Signed as a free agent by **Colorado**, August 6, 1998.

BORODKIN, Anton (boh-ROHD-kihn, an-TAWN) DET.

Left wing. Shoots left. 5'11", 177 lbs. Born, Chelyabinsk, USSR, January 26, 1981.
(Detroit's 5th choice, 238th overall, in 1999 Entry Draft).

			Regular Season					Playoffs				
Season	Club	Lea	GP	G	A	TP	PIM	GP	G	A	TP	PIM
1997-98	HC Nadezhda	Russia-3	30	18	10	28	65	....	....	....	....	....
1998-99	Kamloops Blazers	WHL	71	8	29	37	98	12	0	1	1	8
99-2000	Kamloops Blazers	WHL	55	6	19	25	77	4	1	1	2	6

BOUCK, Tyler (BOWK, TIGH-luhr) DAL.

Right wing. Shoots left. 6', 185 lbs. Born, Camrose, Alta., January 13, 1980.
(Dallas' 2nd choice, 57th overall, in 1998 Entry Draft).

			Regular Season					Playoffs				
Season	Club	Lea	GP	G	A	TP	PIM	GP	G	A	TP	PIM
1995-96	Sherwood Park	AMHL	22	10	21	31	58	....	....	....	....	....
1996-97	Prince George	WHL	12	0	2	2	11	....	....	....	....	....
1997-98	Prince George	WHL	65	11	26	37	90	11	1	0	1	21
1998-99	Prince George	WHL	56	22	25	47	178	2	0	2	2	10
99-2000	Prince George	WHL	57	30	33	63	183	13	6	13	19	36

WHL West First All-Star Team (2000)

BOULERICE, Jesse (BOO-luhr-ighs, JEHS-see) PHI.

Left wing. Shoots right. 6'1", 200 lbs. Born, Plattsburgh, NY, August 10, 1978.
(Philadelphia's 4th choice, 133rd overall, in 1996 Entry Draft).

			Regular Season					Playoffs				
Season	Club	Lea	GP	G	A	TP	PIM	GP	G	A	TP	PIM
1994-95	Hawkesbury	OJHL	46	1	8	9	160	....	....	....	....	....
1995-96	Detroit Whalers	OHL	64	2	5	7	150	16	0	0	0	12
1996-97	Detroit Whalers	OHL	33	10	14	24	209	....	....	....	....	....
1997-98	Plymouth Whalers	OHL	53	20	23	43	170	13	2	4	6	35
1998-99	Philadelphia	AHL	24	1	2	3	82	....	....	....	....	....
	New Orleans	ECHL	12	0	1	1	38	....	....	....	....	....
99-2000	Philadelphia	AHL	40	3	4	7	85	4	0	2	2	4
	Trenton Titans	ECHL	25	8	8	16	90	....	....	....	....	....

BOULTON, Eric BUF.

Left wing. Shoots left. 6'1", 215 lbs. Born, Halifax, N.S., August 17, 1976.
(NY Rangers' 12th choice, 234th overall, in 1994 Entry Draft).

			Regular Season					Playoffs				
Season	Club	Lea	GP	G	A	TP	PIM	GP	G	A	TP	PIM
1992-93	Cole Harbour	MJrHL	44	12	15	27	212	....	....	....	....	....
1993-94	Oshawa Generals	OHL	45	4	3	7	149	5	0	0	0	16
1994-95	Oshawa Generals	OHL	27	7	5	12	125	....	....	....	....	....
	Sarnia Sting	OHL	24	3	7	10	134	4	0	1	1	10
1995-96	Sarnia Sting	OHL	66	14	29	43	243	9	0	3	3	29
1996-97	Binghamton	AHL	23	2	3	5	67	3	0	0	0	4
	Charlotte	ECHL	44	14	11	25	325	3	0	1	1	6
1997-98	Charlotte	ECHL	53	11	16	27	202	4	1	0	1	0
	Fort Wayne	IHL	8	0	2	2	42	....	....	....	....	....
1998-99	Florida Everblades	ECHL	26	9	13	22	143	....	....	....	....	....
	Kentucky	AHL	34	3	3	6	154	10	0	1	1	36
	Houston Aeros	IHL	7	1	0	1	41	....	....	....	....	....
99-2000	Rochester	AHL	76	2	2	4	276	18	2	1	3	53

Signed as a free agent by **Buffalo**, September 14, 1999.

BOUMEDIENNE, Josef (BOO-mih-dyehn, JOH-sehf) N.J.

Defense. Shoots left. 6'1", 190 lbs. Born, Stockholm, Sweden, January 12, 1978.
(New Jersey's 7th choice, 91st overall, in 1996 Entry Draft).

			Regular Season					Playoffs				
Season	Club	Lea	GP	G	A	TP	PIM	GP	G	A	TP	PIM
1994-95	Huddinge IF	Swede-Jr.	10	0	2	2	57	....	....	....	....	....
1995-96	Huddinge IK	Swede-Jr.	25	2	4	6	66	....	....	....	....	....
	Huddinge IK	Swede-Jr.	7	0	0	0	14	....	....	....	....	....
1996-97	Sodertalje SK	Sweden	32	1	1	2	32	....	....	....	....	....
1997-98	Sodertalje SK	Sweden	26	3	3	6	28	....	....	....	....	....
1998-99	Tappara Tampere	Finland	51	6	8	14	119	....	....	....	....	....
99-2000	Tappara Tampere	Finland	50	8	24	32	160	4	1	2	3	10

BOWLER, Bill CBJ

Center. Shoots left. 5'9", 180 lbs. Born, Toronto, Ont., September 25, 1974.

			Regular Season					Playoffs				
Season	Club	Lea	GP	G	A	TP	PIM	GP	G	A	TP	PIM
1990-91	Toronto Wings	MTHL	69	58	99	157	....	....	....	....	....	....
1991-92	Windsor Spitfires	OHL	66	25	63	88	28	....	....	....	....	....
1992-93	Windsor Spitfires	OHL	57	44	77	121	41	....	....	....	....	....
1993-94	Windsor Spitfires	OHL	66	47	76	123	39	....	....	....	....	....
1994-95	Windsor Spitfires	OHL	61	33	102	135	63	10	7	15	22	13
	Las Vegas	IHL	....	....	....	....	....	1	0	0	0	0
1995-96	Las Vegas	IHL	75	31	55	86	26	14	3	5	8	22
1996-97	Houston Aeros	IHL	78	22	43	65	79	13	2	5	7	6
1997-98	Hamilton Bulldogs	AHL	46	7	24	31	22	....	....	....	....	....
	Manitoba Moose	IHL	30	9	26	34	30	3	0	2	2	4
1998-99	Manitoba Moose	IHL	82	26	67	93	59	5	6	5	11	6
99-2000	Manitoba Moose	IHL	75	20	42	62	59	2	1	2	3	6

IHL Second All-Star Team (1999)

Signed as a free agent by **Columbus**, August 3, 2000.

BOYES, Brad (BOIZ) TOR.

Center. Shoots right. 6', 181 lbs. Born, Mississauga, Ont., April 17, 1982.
(Toronto's 1st choice, 24th overall, in 2000 Entry Draft).

			Regular Season					Playoffs				
Season	Club	Lea	GP	G	A	TP	PIM	GP	G	A	TP	PIM
1997-98	Mississauga Reps	MTHL	44	27	50	77	....	....	....	....	....	....
1998-99	Erie Otters	OHL	59	24	36	60	30	5	1	2	3	10
99-2000	Erie Otters	OHL	68	36	46	82	38	13	6	8	14	10

BRADLEY, Matt (BRAD-lee, MAT) S.J.

Right wing. Shoots right. 6'2", 195 lbs. Born, Stittsville, Ont., June 13, 1978.
(San Jose's 4th choice, 102nd overall, in 1996 Entry Draft).

			Regular Season					Playoffs				
Season	Club	Lea	GP	G	A	TP	PIM	GP	G	A	TP	PIM
1994-95	Cumberland	OJHL	49	13	20	33	18	....	....	....	....	....
1995-96	Kingston	OHL	55	10	14	24	17	6	0	1	1	6
1996-97	Kingston	OHL	65	24	24	48	41	5	0	4	4	2
	Kentucky	AHL	1	0	1	1	0	....	....	....	....	....
1997-98	Kingston	OHL	55	33	50	83	24	8	3	4	7	7
1998-99	Kentucky	AHL	79	23	20	43	57	10	1	4	5	4
99-2000	Kentucky	AHL	80	22	19	41	81	9	6	3	9	9

BRAND, Aaron (BR-and, AIR-rohn) TOR.

Center. Shoots left. 6', 190 lbs. Born, Toronto, Ont., June 14, 1975.

			Regular Season					Playoffs				
Season	Club	Lea	GP	G	A	TP	PIM	GP	G	A	TP	PIM
1992-93	Pickering Panthers	OJHL	15	7	15	22	4	....	....	....	....	....
	St. Michael's	OJHL	30	15	21	36	16	15	5	18	23	12
1993-94	Newmarket	OHL	65	19	45	64	55	....	....	....	....	....
1994-95	Sarnia Sting	OHL	66	33	42	75	58	3	0	2	2	4
1995-96	Sarnia Sting	OHL	66	46	*73	*119	110	10	7	11	18	18
	St. John's Leafs	AHL	1	0	1	1	0	4	0	0	0	4
1996-97	St. John's Leafs	AHL	75	15	25	40	80	11	3	2	5	2
1997-98	St. John's Leafs	AHL	79	10	20	30	107	4	2	2	4	6
1998-99	St. John's Leafs	AHL	80	7	26	33	88	5	1	2	3	8
99-2000	St. John's Leafs	AHL	80	12	25	37	68	....	....	....	....	....

OHL Second All-Star Team (1996)

Signed as a free agent by **Toronto**, March 21, 1996.

BRANHAM, Tim (BRA-nuhm) VAN.

Defense. Shoots left. 6'2", 185 lbs. Born, Minoqua, WI, May 10, 1981.
(Vancouver's 3rd choice, 93rd overall, in 2000 Entry Draft).

			Regular Season					Playoffs				
Season	Club	Lea	GP	G	A	TP	PIM	GP	G	A	TP	PIM
1997-98	Danville Wings	NAJHL	54	2	7	9	72	....	....	....	....	....
1998-99	Soo Indians	NAJHL	19	2	2	4	30	....	....	....	....	....
99-2000	Soo Indians	NAJHL	22	5	11	16	32	....	....	....	....	....
	Barrie Colts	OHL	38	3	16	19	46	25	4	7	11	17

BRENDL, Pavel (BREHN-duhl, PA-vehl) NYR

Right wing. Shoots right. 6'1", 204 lbs. Born, Opocno, Czech., March 23, 1981.
(NY Rangers' 1st choice, 4th overall, in 1999 Entry Draft).

			Regular Season					Playoffs				
Season	Club	Lea	GP	G	A	TP	PIM	GP	G	A	TP	PIM
1996-97	HC Olomouc-Jr.	Cze-Rep	40	35	17	52	....	....	....	....	....	....
1997-98	HC Olomouc-Jr.	Cze-Rep	38	29	23	52	....	....	....	....	....	....
	HC Olomouc-2	Cze-Rep	12	1	1	2	....	....	....	....	....	....
1998-99	Calgary Hitmen	WHL	68	*73	61	*134	40	20	*21	*25	*46	18
99-2000	Calgary Hitmen	WHL	61	*59	52	111	94	10	7	12	19	8

WHL East First All-Star Team (1999) • Canadian Major Junior First All-Star Team (1999) • Canadian Major Junior Rookie of the Year (1999) • Memorial Cup All-Star Team (1999) • WHL East Second All-Star Team (2000)

BRENNAN, Kip (BREHN-nan, KIHP) L.A.

Left wing. Shoots left. 6'4", 210 lbs. Born, Kingston, Ont., August 27, 1980.
(Los Angeles' 4th choice, 103rd overall, in 1998 Entry Draft).

			Regular Season					Playoffs				
Season	Club	Lea	GP	G	A	TP	PIM	GP	G	A	TP	PIM
1995-96	St. Michael's	OJHL	40	0	11	11	155	....	....	....	....	....
1996-97	Windsor Spitfires	OHL	42	0	10	10	156	5	0	1	1	16
1997-98	Windsor Spitfires	OHL	24	0	7	7	103	....	....	....	....	....
	Sudbury Wolves	OHL	24	0	3	3	85	....	....	....	....	....
1998-99	Sudbury Wolves	OHL	38	9	12	21	160	....	....	....	....	....
99-2000	Sudbury Wolves	OHL	55	16	16	32	228	12	3	3	6	67

BROS, Michal (BROHSH, MEE-khahl) **MIN.**

Center. Shoots right. 6'1", 195 lbs. Born, Olomouc, Czech., January 25, 1976.
(San Jose's 6th choice, 130th overall, in 1995 Entry Draft).

			Regular Season					Playoffs				
Season	**Club**	**Lea**	**GP**	**G**	**A**	**TP**	**PIM**	**GP**	**G**	**A**	**TP**	**PIM**
1994-95	HC Olomouc-Jr.	Cze-Rep	34	29	32	61	....	....	....	....	....	....
1995-96	HC Olomouc	Cze-Rep	35	8	11	19	....	4	2	0	2	....
1996-97	HC Olomouc	Cze-Rep	50	13	14	27	28	....	....	....	....	....
1997-98	Petra Vsetin	Cze-Rep	47	14	18	32	28	10	3	1	4	2
	Petra Vsetin	EuroHL	9	3	0	3	2	....	....	....	....	....
1998-99	Slovnaft Vsetin	Cze-Rep	42	10	18	28	18	12	1	3	4	....
99-2000	Sparta Praha	Cze-Rep	49	6	30	36	49	9	1	3	4	4

Selected by **Minnesota** from **San Jose** in Expansion Draft, June 23, 2000.

BROWN, Jeff (BR-own, JEHF) **NYR**

Defense. Shoots right. 6'2", 218 lbs. Born, Mississauga, Ont., April 24, 1978.
(NY Rangers' 1st choice, 22nd overall, in 1996 Entry Draft).

			Regular Season					Playoffs				
Season	**Club**	**Lea**	**GP**	**G**	**A**	**TP**	**PIM**	**GP**	**G**	**A**	**TP**	**PIM**
1993-94	Thornhill Islanders	OJHL	47	6	18	24	96	....	....	....	....	....
1994-95	Sarnia Sting	OHL	58	2	14	16	52	4	0	2	2	2
1995-96	Sarnia Sting	OHL	65	8	20	28	111	10	1	2	3	12
1996-97	Sarnia Sting	OHL	35	5	14	19	60	....	....	....	....	....
	London Knights	OHL	28	1	17	18	32	....	....	....	....	....
1997-98	London Knights	OHL	63	12	42	54	96	15	1	4	5	26
1998-99	Charlotte	ECHL	12	1	2	3	20	....	....	....	....	....
	Hartford	AHL	9	0	2	2	21	....	....	....	....	....
	Canada	Nat-Team	13	0	2	2	8	....	....	....	....	....
99-2000	Hartford	AHL	6	0	0	0	2	....	....	....	....	....
	Charlotte	ECHL	51	7	18	25	107	....	....	....	....	....

BROWN, Mike (BR-own, MIGHK) **VAN.**

Left wing. Shoots left. 6'5", 185 lbs. Born, Surrey, B.C., April 27, 1979.
(Florida's 1st choice, 20th overall, in 1997 Entry Draft).

			Regular Season					Playoffs				
Season	**Club**	**Lea**	**GP**	**G**	**A**	**TP**	**PIM**	**GP**	**G**	**A**	**TP**	**PIM**
1993-94	Penticton	BCJHL	50	52	48	100	100	....	....	....	....	....
1994-95	Merritt Luckies	BCJHL	45	3	4	7	145	....	....	....	....	....
1995-96	Red Deer Rebels	WHL	62	4	5	9	125	10	0	0	0	18
1996-97	Red Deer Rebels	WHL	70	19	13	32	243	16	1	2	3	47
1997-98	Kamloops Blazers	WHL	72	23	33	56	305	7	2	1	3	22
1998-99	Kamloops Blazers	WHL	69	28	16	44	*285	15	3	7	10	*68
99-2000	Syracuse Crunch	AHL	71	13	18	31	284	4	0	0	0	0

Traded to **Vancouver** by **Florida** with Ed Jovanovski, Dave Gagner, Kevin Weekes and Florida's 1st round choice (Nathan Smith) in 2000 Entry Draft for Pavel Bure, Bret Hedican, Brad Ference and Vancouver's 3rd round choice (Robert Fried) in 2000 Entry Draft, January 17, 1999.

BRUNEL, Craig (broo-NEHL) **BUF.**

Right wing. Shoots right. 6', 200 lbs. Born, Winnipeg, Man., November 12, 1979.
(Buffalo's 12th choice, 263rd overall, in 1999 Entry Draft).

			Regular Season					Playoffs				
Season	**Club**	**Lea**	**GP**	**G**	**A**	**TP**	**PIM**	**GP**	**G**	**A**	**TP**	**PIM**
1995-96	Notre Dame	SAHA	36	4	9	13	79	....	....	....	....	....
1996-97	Prince Albert	WHL	57	5	2	7	208	4	0	0	0	13
1997-98	Prince Albert	WHL	58	6	12	18	247	....	....	....	....	....
1998-99	Prince Albert	WHL	50	10	8	18	173	14	4	2	6	48
99-2000	Prince Albert	WHL	17	0	2	2	59	....	....	....	....	....
	Red Deer Rebels	WHL	35	3	2	5	140	4	0	1	1	22

• Re-entered NHL draft. Originally Nashville's 6th choice, 147th overall, in 1998 Entry Draft.

BULATOV, Alexei (boo-LA-tahf) **NYR**

Right wing. Shoots left. 6'1", 185 lbs. Born, Sverdlovsk, USSR, January 24, 1978.
(NY Rangers' 11th choice, 254th overall, in 1999 Entry Draft).

			Regular Season					Playoffs				
Season	**Club**	**Lea**	**GP**	**G**	**A**	**TP**	**PIM**	**GP**	**G**	**A**	**TP**	**PIM**
1996-97	HC Yekaterinburg	Russia	20	2	4	6	2	....	....	....	....	....
	HC Yekaterinburg	Russia-2	22	6	6	12	10	....	....	....	....	....
1997-98	HC Yekaterinburg	Russia	15	5	3	8	10	....	....	....	....	....
	HC Yekaterinburg	Russia-2	22	7	6	13	14	....	....	....	....	....
1998-99	HC Yekaterinburg	Russia-2	47	21	16	37	24	....	....	....	....	....
99-2000	HC Cherepovets	Russia	9	1	0	1	0	....	....	....	....	....
	Salavat Ufa	Russia	6	0	3	3	2	....	....	....	....	....
	CSK Samara	Russia	6	0	0	0	2	....	....	....	....	....

BURNETT, Garrett (BURH-neht, gair-RHET)

Left wing. Shoots left. 6'3", 230 lbs. Born, Coquitlam, B.C., September 23, 1975.

			Regular Season					Playoffs				
Season	**Club**	**Lea**	**GP**	**G**	**A**	**TP**	**PIM**	**GP**	**G**	**A**	**TP**	**PIM**
1993-94	Trail Smokies	RIJHL	26	2	1	3	248	....	....	....	....	....
1994-95	Sault Ste. Marie	OHL	14	0	1	1	78	....	....	....	....	....
	Kitchener	OHL	22	0	1	1	74	3	0	1	1	23
1995-96	Utica Blizzard	ColHL	15	0	1	1	78	....	....	....	....	....
	Oklahoma City	CHL	3	0	0	0	20	....	....	....	....	....
	Tulsa Oilers	CHL	6	1	0	1	94	....	....	....	....	....
	Nashville Knights	ECHL	3	0	0	0	22	....	....	....	....	....
	Jacksonville	ECHL	8	0	1	1	38	1	0	0	0	0
1996-97	Knoxville	ECHL	50	5	11	16	321	....	....	....	....	....
1997-98	Johnstown Chiefs	ECHL	34	1	1	2	331	....	....	....	....	....
	Philadelphia	AHL	14	1	2	3	129	....	....	....	....	....
1998-99	Kentucky	AHL	31	1	0	1	186	....	....	....	....	....
99-2000	Kentucky	AHL	58	3	3	6	*506	4	0	0	0	31

Signed as a free agent by **San Jose**, July 2, 1998.

BUT, Anton (BOOT, AN-tawn) **N.J.**

Left wing. Shoots left. 6'1", 190 lbs. Born, Kharkov, USSR, July 3, 1980.
(New Jersey's 7th choice, 119th overall, in 1998 Entry Draft).

			Regular Season					Playoffs				
Season	**Club**	**Lea**	**GP**	**G**	**A**	**TP**	**PIM**	**GP**	**G**	**A**	**TP**	**PIM**
1995-96	Torpedo Yaroslavl	Russia-2	60	30	12	42	10	....	....	....	....	....
1996-97	Torpedo Yaroslavl	Russia-3	70	30	20	50	20	....	....	....	....	....
1997-98	Torpedo Yaroslavl	Russia-2	48	12	5	17	28	....	....	....	....	....
1998-99	Torpedo Yaroslavl	Russia	5	0	0	0	0	....	....	....	....	....
99-2000	Torpedo Yaroslavl	Russia	26	2	5	7	16	8	2	1	3	0

BUTURLIN, Alexander (boo-tuhr-LIHN, AL-ehx-an-DEHR) **MTL.**

Right wing. Shoots left. 5'11", 182 lbs. Born, Moscow, USSR, September 3, 1981.
(Montreal's 1st choice, 39th overall, in 1999 Entry Draft).

			Regular Season					Playoffs				
Season	**Club**	**Lea**	**GP**	**G**	**A**	**TP**	**PIM**	**GP**	**G**	**A**	**TP**	**PIM**
1997-98	CSKA Moscow-2	Russia-3	50	12	15	27	46	....	....	....	....	....
	CSKA Moscow	Russia	2	0	0	0	0	....	....	....	....	....
1998-99	CSKA Moscow	Russia	16	1	0	1	6	3	1	0	1	2
	CSKA Moscow-2	Russia-3	STATISTICS NOT AVAILABLE									
99-2000	Sarnia Sting	OHL	57	20	27	47	46	7	4	2	6	12

BYFUGLIEN, Derrick (bigh-FEWG-lehn) **OTT.**

Defense. Shoots left. 6'1", 202 lbs. Born, Roseau, MN, December 23, 1980.
(Ottawa's 5th choice, 122nd overall, in 2000 Entry Draft).

			Regular Season					Playoffs				
Season	**Club**	**Lea**	**GP**	**G**	**A**	**TP**	**PIM**	**GP**	**G**	**A**	**TP**	**PIM**
1998-99	Fargo-Moorhead	USHL	12	2	3	5	71	....	....	....	....	....
99-2000	Fargo-Moorhead	USHL	50	5	11	16	106	....	....	....	....	....

BYRNE, Trevor (BUHR-ne, TREH-vohr) **ST.L.**

Defense. Shoots left. 6'3", 200 lbs. Born, Hingham, MA, May 7, 1980.
(St. Louis' 4th choice, 143rd overall, in 1999 Entry Draft).

			Regular Season					Playoffs				
Season	**Club**	**Lea**	**GP**	**G**	**A**	**TP**	**PIM**	**GP**	**G**	**A**	**TP**	**PIM**
1997-98	Deerfield Academy	Hi-School	25	5	14	19	16	....	....	....	....	....
1998-99	Deerfield Academy	Hi-School	25	9	19	28	22	....	....	....	....	....
99-2000	Dartmouth	ECAC	30	3	9	12	40	....	....	....	....	....

CABANA, Chad (CA-ba-NA, CHAD)

Left wing. Shoots left. 6'1", 205 lbs. Born, Bonnyville, Alta., October 1, 1974.
(Florida's 11th choice, 213th overall, in 1993 Entry Draft).

			Regular Season					Playoffs				
Season	**Club**	**Lea**	**GP**	**G**	**A**	**TP**	**PIM**	**GP**	**G**	**A**	**TP**	**PIM**
1990-91	Bonneyville	AJHL	65	28	42	70	150	....	....	....	....	....
1991-92	Tri-City Americans	WHL	57	5	8	13	145	4	0	1	1	21
1992-93	Tri-City Americans	WHL	68	19	23	42	104	4	1	0	1	10
1993-94	Tri-City Americans	WHL	67	27	33	60	201	4	2	0	2	24
1994-95	Tri-City Americans	WHL	68	25	34	59	252	17	10	11	21	47
1995-96	Carolina	AHL	54	4	9	13	159	....	....	....	....	....
1996-97	Carolina	AHL	55	8	5	13	221	....	....	....	....	....
	Port Huron	ColHL	14	7	9	16	49	....	....	....	....	....
1997-98	New Haven	AHL	34	5	5	10	163	2	0	0	0	7
	Fort Wayne	IHL	6	0	0	0	22	....	....	....	....	....
1998-99	New Haven	AHL	66	6	5	11	251	....	....	....	....	....
99-2000	Louisville	AHL	65	10	17	27	173	4	0	0	0	26

CABANA, Clint (CA-ba-NA, CLIHNT) **VAN.**

Defense. Shoots right. 6'2", 195 lbs. Born, Bonnyville, Alta., April 28, 1978.
(Vancouver's 6th choice, 175th overall, in 1996 Entry Draft).

			Regular Season					Playoffs				
Season	**Club**	**Lea**	**GP**	**G**	**A**	**TP**	**PIM**	**GP**	**G**	**A**	**TP**	**PIM**
1993-94	Bonneyville	AJHL	7	1	0	1	4	....	....	....	....	....
1994-95	Medicine Hat	WHL	49	0	1	1	68	....	....	....	....	....
1995-96	Medicine Hat	WHL	71	1	11	12	156	5	0	1	1	35
1996-97	Medicine Hat	WHL	4	0	1	1	10	....	....	....	....	....
	Edmonton Ice	WHL	67	3	12	15	302	....	....	....	....	....
	Syracuse Crunch	AHL	2	0	0	0	2	....	....	....	....	....
1997-98	Edmonton Ice	WHL	17	1	5	6	60	....	....	....	....	....
	Regina Pats	WHL	34	1	1	2	140	8	1	0	1	16
1998-99	Syracuse Crunch	AHL	19	0	1	1	86	....	....	....	....	....
	Augusta Lynx	ECHL	6	0	0	0	37	2	0	0	0	2
99-2000	Syracuse Crunch	AHL	15	0	3	3	79	....	....	....	....	....
	Augusta Lynx	ECHL	31	2	5	7	124	12	0	0	0	36

CABANA, Paul (CA-ba-NA, PAWL) **VAN.**

Right wing. Shoots right. 6'1", 185 lbs. Born, Calgary, Alta., September 28, 1978.
(Vancouver's 8th choice, 149th overall, in 1998 Entry Draft).

			Regular Season					Playoffs				
Season	**Club**	**Lea**	**GP**	**G**	**A**	**TP**	**PIM**	**GP**	**G**	**A**	**TP**	**PIM**
1996-97	Fort McMurray	AJHL	58	24	22	46	....	3	1	3	4	2
1997-98	Fort McMurray	AJHL	52	48	32	80	111	....	....	....	....	....
1998-99	Michigan Tech	WCHA	38	12	9	21	50	....	....	....	....	....
99-2000	Michigan Tech	WCHA	36	10	5	15	94	....	....	....	....	....

AJHL All-Rookie Team (1997) • AJHL First All-Star Team (1998)

CAMERON, Scott (KAM-erh-RAWN, SCAWT) **N.J.**

Center. Shoots left. 6', 180 lbs. Born, Sudbury, Ont., April 11, 1981.
(New Jersey's 6th choice, 185th overall, in 1999 Entry Draft).

			Regular Season					Playoffs				
Season	**Club**	**Lea**	**GP**	**G**	**A**	**TP**	**PIM**	**GP**	**G**	**A**	**TP**	**PIM**
1997-98	Port Colborne	OJHL	40	16	35	51	73	....	....	....	....	....
1998-99	Barrie Colts	OHL	66	10	32	42	14	12	2	2	4	2
99-2000	Barrie Colts	OHL	21	2	4	6	19	....	....	....	....	....
	North Bay	OHL	49	26	28	54	13	6	3	0	3	4
	Albany River Rats	AHL	3	1	0	1	0	1	0	0	0	0

CARKNER, Matt (KARK-nehr, MAT) **MTL.**

Defense. Shoots right. 6'4", 229 lbs. Born, Winchester, Ont., November 3, 1980.
(Montreal's 2nd choice, 58th overall, in 1999 Entry Draft).

			Regular Season					Playoffs				
Season	**Club**	**Lea**	**GP**	**G**	**A**	**TP**	**PIM**	**GP**	**G**	**A**	**TP**	**PIM**
1996-97	Winchester	OJHL-B	29	1	18	19	....	....	....	....	....	....
1997-98	Peterborough	OHL	57	0	6	6	121	4	0	0	0	2
1998-99	Peterborough	OHL	60	2	16	18	173	5	0	0	0	20
99-2000	Peterborough	OHL	62	3	13	16	177	5	0	1	1	6

CARPENTIER, Benjamin (kar-PAWN-tyay, BEHN-ja-mehn) **NYR**

Defense. Shoots left. 6'2", 195 lbs. Born, Grand-Mere, Que., June 13, 1978.

			Regular Season					Playoffs				
Season	**Club**	**Lea**	**GP**	**G**	**A**	**TP**	**PIM**	**GP**	**G**	**A**	**TP**	**PIM**
1995-96	Shawinigan	QMJHL	65	0	3	3	197	6	0	0	0	2
1996-97	Shawinigan	QMJHL	63	2	4	6	275	7	0	0	0	12
1997-98	Laval Titan	QMJHL	64	1	8	9	279	14	1	3	4	30
1998-99	Charlotte	ECHL	23	4	6	10	68	....	....	....	....	....
	Hartford	AHL	21	0	1	1	31	....	....	....	....	....
99-2000	Hartford	AHL	54	1	1	2	89	2	0	0	0	2

Signed as a free agent by **NY Rangers**, October 3, 1996.

CARTER, Shawn (KAR-tuhr, SHAWN)

Center. Shoots left. 6'2", 210 lbs. Born, Eagle River, WI, April 16, 1973.

			Regular Season					Playoffs				
Season	Club	Lea	GP	G	A	TP	PIM	GP	G	A	TP	PIM
1992-93	U. of Wisconsin	WCHA	5	1	0	1	4	....	....	....	....	....
1993-94	U. of Wisconsin	WCHA	16	2	2	4	24	....	....	....	....	....
1994-95	U. of Wisconsin	WCHA	43	15	13	28	98	....	....	....	....	....
1995-96	U. of Wisconsin	WCHA	40	17	28	45	50	....	....	....	....	....
1996-97	Orlando	IHL	53	22	25	47	40	....	....	....	....	....
	St. John's Leafs	AHL	18	5	6	11	15	7	1	2	3	6
1997-98	St. John's Leafs	AHL	80	14	16	30	117	4	1	0	1	4
1998-99	Orlando	IHL	79	13	26	39	103	17	1	4	5	10
99-2000	Orlando	IHL	81	20	30	50	120	6	0	2	2	4

Signed as a free agent by **Toronto**, February 14, 1997. Signed as a free agent by **Orlando** (IHL), September 10, 1998.

CARVER, Andrew (KAHR-vuhr) **CHI.**

Defense. Shoots left. 6'2", 205 lbs. Born, Halifax, N.S., May 10, 1981.
(Chicago's 8th choice, 223rd overall, in 1999 Entry Draft).

			Regular Season					Playoffs				
Season	Club	Lea	GP	G	A	TP	PIM	GP	G	A	TP	PIM
1997-98	Qunite Hawks	OJHL	41	2	18	20	43	....	....	....	....	....
1998-99	Hull Olympiques	QMJHL	65	2	15	17	104	23	0	1	1	22
99-2000	Hull Olympiques	QMJHL	61	1	18	19	88	15	0	3	3	22

CASS, Bill (KAS) **ANA.**

Defense. Shoots left. 6', 208 lbs. Born, Hingham, MA, September 30, 1980.
(Anaheim's 5th choice, 153rd overall, in 2000 Entry Draft).

			Regular Season					Playoffs				
Season	Club	Lea	GP	G	A	TP	PIM	GP	G	A	TP	PIM
1997-98	Team USA	Under-18	38	4	9	13	75	....	....	....	....	....
1998-99	Team USA	Under-18	41	0	6	6	22	....	....	....	....	....
99-2000	Boston College	H-East	41	1	8	9	26	....	....	....	....	....

CAULFIELD, Kevin (KAW-fihld, KEH-vihn) **WSH.**

Right wing. Shoots right. 6'2", 210 lbs. Born, Boston, MA, January 7, 1978.
(Washington's 4th choice, 116th overall, in 1997 Entry Draft).

			Regular Season					Playoffs				
Season	Club	Lea	GP	G	A	TP	PIM	GP	G	A	TP	PIM
1995-96	Thayer Academy	Hi-School	31	12	23	35	45	....	....	....	....	....
1996-97	Boston College	H-East	38	5	10	15	90	....	....	....	....	....
1997-98	Boston College	H-East	41	9	6	15	82	....	....	....	....	....
1998-99	Boston College	H-East	41	8	8	16	81	....	....	....	....	....
99-2000	Boston College	H-East	42	5	14	19	88	....	....	....	....	....

CAVANAUGH, Dan (KAV-a-NAW, DAN) **MIN.**

Center. Shoots right. 6'1", 190 lbs. Born, Springfield, MA, March 3, 1980.
(Calgary's 2nd choice, 38th overall, in 1999 Entry Draft).

			Regular Season					Playoffs				
Season	Club	Lea	GP	G	A	TP	PIM	GP	G	A	TP	PIM
1997-98	New England	EJHL	51	39	59	98	58	....	....	....	....	....
1998-99	Boston University	H-East	36	6	8	14	60	....	....	....	....	....
99-2000	Boston University	H-East	40	9	25	34	62	....	....	....	....	....

Rights traded to **Minnesota** by **Calgary** with Calgary's 8th round choice in 2001 Entry Draft for Mike Vernon, June 23, 2000.

CAVOSIE, Marc (kuh-VOI-see) **MIN.**

Left wing. Shoots left. 6', 173 lbs. Born, Albany, NY, August 6, 1981.
(Minnesota's 3rd choice, 99th overall, in 2000 Entry Draft).

			Regular Season					Playoffs				
Season	Club	Lea	GP	G	A	TP	PIM	GP	G	A	TP	PIM
1998-99	Albany Academy	Hi-School	28	23	20	43	32	....	....	....	....	....
99-2000	RPI Engineers	ECAC	29	11	17	28	10	4	1	1	2	10

CECH, Vratislav (CHEHKH, VUHR-atih-SLAV) **BOS.**

Defense. Shoots left. 6'3", 196 lbs. Born, Tabor, Czech., January 28, 1979.
(Florida's 3rd choice, 56th overall, in 1997 Entry Draft).

			Regular Season					Playoffs				
Season	Club	Lea	GP	G	A	TP	PIM	GP	G	A	TP	PIM
1995-96	HC Brno-Jr.	Cze-Rep	37	10	13	23	....	....	....	....	....	....
1996-97	Kitchener	OHL	57	5	19	24	72	13	1	2	3	12
1997-98	Kitchener	OHL	63	9	33	42	66	6	2	2	4	13
1998-99	Kitchener	OHL	66	6	21	27	73	1	0	1	1	4
99-2000	Providence Bruins	AHL	3	0	1	1	0	....	....	....	....	....
	Greenville Growl	ECHL	55	7	15	22	51	15	0	5	5	16

Signed as a free agent by **Boston**, July 22, 1999.

CEREDA, Luca (suh-REH-duh, LOO-ka) **TOR.**

Center. Shoots left. 6'2", 202 lbs. Born, Lugano, Switzerland, September 7, 1981.
(Toronto's 1st choice, 24th overall, in 1999 Entry Draft).

			Regular Season					Playoffs				
Season	Club	Lea	GP	G	A	TP	PIM	GP	G	A	TP	PIM
1996-97	Ambri-Piotta	Switz-Jr.	35	13	8	21	....	....	....	....	....	....
1997-98	Ambri-Piotta	Switz-Jr.	28	17	27	44	24	....	....	....	....	....
1998-99	Ambri-Piotta	Switz-Jr.	3	4	3	7	20	....	....	....	....	....
	Ambri-Piotta	Switz.	38	6	10	16	8	15	0	6	6	4
99-2000	Ambri-Piotta	Switz.	44	1	5	6	14	9	0	1	1	2

CHAGODAYEV, Alexander (cheh-goh-digh-ehv, al-ehx-AN-duhr) **ANA.**

Center. Shoots left. 6'1", 180 lbs. Born, Moscow, USSR, January 15, 1981.
(Anaheim's 3rd choice, 105th overall, in 1999 Entry Draft).

			Regular Season					Playoffs				
Season	Club	Lea	GP	G	A	TP	PIM	GP	G	A	TP	PIM
1997-98	CSKA Moscow	Russia	1	0	0	0	0	....	....	....	....	....
	CSKA Moscow	Russia-2	5	1	0	1	0	....	....	....	....	....
1998-99	CSKA Moscow	Russia-2	35	9	9	18	16	....	....	....	....	....
99-2000	HC Moscow	Russia-2	40	5	7	12	....	....	....	....	....	....

CHAMBERLAIN, Jamie (CHAYM-buhr-lihn) **DAL.**

Right wing. Shoots right. 6', 195 lbs. Born, Sarnia, Ont., August 2, 1981.
(Dallas' 10th choice, 265th overall, in 1999 Entry Draft).

			Regular Season					Playoffs				
Season	Club	Lea	GP	G	A	TP	PIM	GP	G	A	TP	PIM
1998-99	Peterborough	OHL	68	15	24	39	26	4	0	1	1	4
99-2000	Peterborough	OHL	65	12	29	41	53	5	2	0	2	6

CHARRON, Craig (shah-ROHN, KRAYG) **L.A.**

Center. Shoots right. 5'10", 175 lbs. Born, North Easton, MA, November 15, 1967.
(Montreal's 1st choice, 25th overall, in 1989 Supplemental Draft).

			Regular Season					Playoffs				
Season	Club	Lea	GP	G	A	TP	PIM	GP	G	A	TP	PIM
1986-87	U. Mass-Lowell	H-East	36	11	16	27	48	....	....	....	....	....
1987-88	U. Mass-Lowell	H-East	39	22	18	40	32	....	....	....	....	....
1988-89	U. Mass-Lowell	H-East	32	14	21	35	32	....	....	....	....	....
1989-90	U. Mass-Lowell	H-East	35	17	29	46	10	....	....	....	....	....
1990-91	Winston-Salem	ECHL	30	11	16	27	10	....	....	....	....	....
	Albany Choppers	IHL	5	0	2	2	0	....	....	....	....	....
	Fredericton	AHL	24	2	5	7	4	5	0	3	3	0
1991-92	Cincinnati	ECHL	64	41	55	96	97	9	5	5	10	10
1992-93	Birmingham Bulls	ECHL	23	9	17	26	18	....	....	....	....	....
	Cincinnati	IHL	27	6	8	14	8	....	....	....	....	....
1993-94	Holje BK	Sweden-2	33	49	40	89	....	....	....	....	....	....
1994-95	Dayton Bombers	ECHL	48	35	47	82	82	9	9	13	22	10
	Kalamazoo Wings	IHL	2	0	0	0	0	....	....	....	....	....
	Fort Wayne	IHL	2	1	0	1	4	....	....	....	....	....
	Cornwall Aces	AHL	6	5	0	5	0	2	0	0	0	0
1995-96	Rochester	AHL	72	43	52	95	79	19	7	10	17	12
1996-97	Rochester	AHL	72	24	41	65	42	10	8	8	16	2
1997-98	Rochester	AHL	75	25	53	78	51	4	1	1	2	0
1998-99	Lowell	AHL	71	22	39	61	41	3	1	2	3	8
99-2000	St. John's Leafs	AHL	32	11	18	29	14	....	....	....	....	....
	Lowell	AHL	22	8	13	21	14	7	2	3	5	4

Signed as a free agent by **NY Islanders**, September 3, 1998. Traded to **Toronto** by **NY Islanders** for Niklas Andersson, August 17, 1999. Traded to **Los Angeles** by **Toronto** for Donald MacLean, February 23, 2000.

CHARTIER, Christian (SHAR-tee-yay, KRIHS-t'yehn) **EDM.**

Defense. Shoots left. 6', 219 lbs. Born, Russell, Man., December 29, 1980.
(Edmonton's 8th choice, 199th overall, in 1999 Entry Draft).

			Regular Season					Playoffs				
Season	Club	Lea	GP	G	A	TP	PIM	GP	G	A	TP	PIM
1996-97	Saskatoon Blades	WHL	64	2	23	25	32	....	....	....	....	....
1997-98	Saskatoon Blades	WHL	68	8	33	41	43	6	0	3	3	12
1998-99	Saskatoon Blades	WHL	62	2	14	16	71	....	....	....	....	....
99-2000	Saskatoon Blades	WHL	11	2	2	4	4	....	....	....	....	....
	Prince George	WHL	57	16	36	52	60	13	4	9	13	12

WHL West Second All-Star Team (2000)

CHEECHOO, Jonathan (CHEE-choo, JOHN-a-THOHN) **S.J.**

Right wing. Shoots right. 6', 200 lbs. Born, Moose Factory, Ont., July 15, 1980.
(San Jose's 2nd choice, 29th overall, in 1998 Entry Draft).

			Regular Season					Playoffs				
Season	Club	Lea	GP	G	A	TP	PIM	GP	G	A	TP	PIM
1996-97	Kitchener	OJHL	43	35	41	76	33	....	....	....	....	....
1997-98	Belleville Bulls	OHL	64	31	45	76	62	10	4	2	6	10
1998-99	Belleville Bulls	OHL	63	35	47	82	74	21	15	15	30	27
99-2000	Belleville Bulls	OHL	66	45	46	91	102	16	5	12	17	16

CHERNESKI, Stefan (chuhr-NEHS-kee, STEHF-an) **NYR**

Right wing. Shoots right. 6', 195 lbs. Born, Winnipeg, Man., September 19, 1978.
(NY Rangers' 1st choice, 19th overall, in 1997 Entry Draft).

			Regular Season					Playoffs				
Season	Club	Lea	GP	G	A	TP	PIM	GP	G	A	TP	PIM
1994-95	Norman Lions	MAHA	36	35	29	64	....	....	....	....	....	....
1995-96	Brandon	WHL	58	8	21	29	62	19	3	1	4	11
1996-97	Brandon	WHL	56	39	29	68	83	....	....	....	....	....
1997-98	Brandon	WHL	65	43	38	81	127	18	*15	8	23	21
1998-99	Hartford	AHL	11	1	2	3	41	....	....	....	....	....
99-2000	Hartford	AHL	1	0	0	0	0	....	....	....	....	....

Canadian Major Junior Scholastic Player of the Year (1997)

• Missed majority of 1998-99 and 1999-2000 seasons recovering from knee injury suffered in game vs. Springfield (AHL), November 13, 1998.

CHERNOV, Artem (chair-NAHF, AR-tehm) **DAL.**

Center. Shoots left. 5'10", 176 lbs. Born, Novokuznetsk, USSR, April 28, 1982.
(Dallas' 7th choice, 162nd overall, in 2000 Entry Draft).

			Regular Season					Playoffs				
Season	Club	Lea	GP	G	A	TP	PIM	GP	G	A	TP	PIM
1997-98	HC Novokuznetsk	Russia-3	4	0	0	0	0	....	....	....	....	....
1998-99	HC Novokuznetsk	Russia-4	32	9	7	16	14	....	....	....	....	....
99-2000	HC Novokuznetsk	Russia	10	2	3	5	0	5	0	0	0	0

CHERNOV, Mikhail (chair-NAHF, MIHK-ayl) **PHI.**

Defense. Shoots right. 6'2", 205 lbs. Born, Prokopjevsk, USSR, November 11, 1978.
(Philadelphia's 4th choice, 103rd overall, in 1997 Entry Draft).

			Regular Season					Playoffs				
Season	Club	Lea	GP	G	A	TP	PIM	GP	G	A	TP	PIM
1995-96	Novisibirsk	CIS-2	40	2	7	9	10	....	....	....	....	....
1996-97	Torpedo Yaroslavl	Russia-3	33	4	2	6	40	....	....	....	....	....
	Torpedo Yaroslavl	Russia	5	0	0	0	0	....	....	....	....	....
1997-98	Torpedo Yaroslavl	Russia	7	0	0	0	4	....	....	....	....	....
1998-99	Philadelphia	AHL	56	4	3	7	98	14	1	0	1	8
99-2000	Philadelphia	AHL	67	10	6	16	54	5	1	2	3	22

CHIMERA, Jason (CHIHM-air-a, JAY-suhn) **EDM.**

Center. Shoots left. 6', 180 lbs. Born, Edmonton, Alta., May 2, 1979.
(Edmonton's 5th choice, 121st overall, in 1997 Entry Draft).

			Regular Season					Playoffs				
Season	Club	Lea	GP	G	A	TP	PIM	GP	G	A	TP	PIM
1994-95	Edmonton Pats	AAHA	33	27	31	58	42	....	....	....	....	....
1995-96	Edmonton Pats	AAHA	34	23	24	47	44	....	....	....	....	....
1996-97	Medicine Hat	WHL	71	16	23	39	64	4	0	1	1	4
1997-98	Medicine Hat	WHL	72	34	32	66	93	....	....	....	....	....
	Hamilton Bulldogs	AHL	4	0	0	0	8	....	....	....	....	....
1998-99	Medicine Hat	WHL	37	18	22	40	84	....	....	....	....	....
	Brandon	WHL	21	14	12	26	32	5	4	1	5	8
99-2000	Hamilton Bulldogs	AHL	78	15	13	28	77	10	0	2	2	12

CHOUINARD, Eric (shwee-NAHR, ERIHK) MTL.

Center. Shoots left. 6'3", 202 lbs. Born, Atlanta, GA, July 8, 1980.
(Montreal's 1st choice, 16th overall, in 1998 Entry Draft).

			Regular Season					Playoffs				
Season	Club	Lea	GP	G	A	TP	PIM	GP	G	A	TP	PIM
1996-97	Ste-Foy Governors	QAAA	40	29	41	70	40	....	....	....	....	....
1997-98	Quebec Remparts	QMJHL	68	41	42	83	18	14	7	10	17	6
1998-99	Quebec Remparts	QMJHL	62	50	59	109	56	13	8	10	18	8
	Fredericton	AHL	....	....	....	....	....	6	3	2	5	0
99-2000	Quebec Remparts	QMJHL	50	57	47	104	105	11	14	4	18	8

CHOUINARD, Marc (shwee-NAHR, MAHRK) ANA.

Center. Shoots right. 6'5", 204 lbs. Born, Charlesbourg, Que., May 6, 1977.
(Winnipeg's 2nd choice, 32nd overall, in 1995 Entry Draft).

			Regular Season					Playoffs				
Season	Club	Lea	GP	G	A	TP	PIM	GP	G	A	TP	PIM
1993-94	Beauport	QMJHL	62	11	19	30	23	13	2	5	7	2
1994-95	Beauport	QMJHL	68	24	40	64	32	18	1	6	7	4
1995-96	Beauport	QMJHL	30	14	21	35	19	....	....	....	....	....
	Halifax	QMJHL	24	6	12	18	17	6	2	1	3	2
1996-97	Halifax	QMJHL	63	24	49	73	74	18	9	16	25	12
1997-98	Cincinnati Ducks	AHL	8	1	2	3	4	....	....	....	....	....
1998-99	Cincinnati Ducks	AHL	69	7	8	15	20	3	0	0	0	4
99-2000	Cincinnati Ducks	AHL	70	17	16	33	29	....	....	....	....	....

Traded to **Anaheim** by **Winnipeg** with Teemu Selanne and Winnipeg's 4th round choice (later traded to Toronto - later traded to Montreal - Montreal selected Kim Staal) in 1996 Entry Draft for Chad Kilger, Oleg Tverdovsky and Anaheim's 3rd round choice (Per-Anton Ludstrom) in 1996 Entry Draft, February 7, 1996.

CHVOJKA, Petr (CHVOI-kuh) MTL.

Defense. Shoots left. 6', 189 lbs. Born, Slany, Czech., May 27, 1982.
(Montreal's 9th choice, 182nd overall, in 2000 Entry Draft).

			Regular Season					Playoffs				
Season	Club	Lea	GP	G	A	TP	PIM	GP	G	A	TP	PIM
1997-98	HC Plzen-Jr.	Cze-Rep	35	5	9	14	....	....	....	....	....	....
1998-99	HC Plzen-Jr.	Cze-Rep	49	19	25	44	....	....	....	....	....	....
99-2000	HC Plzen-Jr.	Cze-Rep	40	7	15	22	104	....	....	....	....	....
	HC Plzen	Cze-Rep	4	0	0	0	2	1	0	0	0	0

CIBAK, Martin (TSEE-bak, MAHR-tihn) T.B.

Center. Shoots left. 6', 183 lbs. Born, Liptovmikulas, Czech., May 17, 1980.
(Tampa Bay's 11th choice, 252nd overall, in 1998 Entry Draft).

			Regular Season					Playoffs				
Season	Club	Lea	GP	G	A	TP	PIM	GP	G	A	TP	PIM
1995-96	HK Liptovsky	Slovak-Jr.	48	38	35	73	....	....	....	....	....	....
1996-97	HK Liptovsky	Slovak-Jr.	45	22	18	40	....	....	....	....	....	....
1997-98	HK Liptovsky	Slovak-Jr.	42	31	21	52	....	....	....	....	....	....
	HK Liptovsky	Slovakia	28	1	3	4	10	....	....	....	....	....
1998-99	Medicine Hat	WHL	66	21	26	47	72	....	....	....	....	....
99-2000	Medicine Hat	WHL	58	16	29	45	77	....	....	....	....	....

CLARK, Kyle (KLAHRK, KIGHLE) WSH.

Right wing. Shoots right. 6'7", 210 lbs. Born, Burlington, VT, February 14, 1980.
(Washington's 7th choice, 175th overall, in 1999 Entry Draft).

			Regular Season					Playoffs				
Season	Club	Lea	GP	G	A	TP	PIM	GP	G	A	TP	PIM
1997-98	Team USA	Under-18	65	14	11	25	287	....	....	....	....	....
1998-99	Harvard University	ECAC	20	0	2	2	30	....	....	....	....	....
99-2000	Harvard University	ECAC	22	0	3	3	30	....	....	....	....	....

CLARK, Ryan (KLAHRK, RIGH-yan) NYI

Defense. Shoots left. 6'3", 205 lbs. Born, Edmonton, Alta., October 30, 1977.
(NY Islanders' 11th choice, 222nd overall, in 1997 Entry Draft).

			Regular Season					Playoffs				
Season	Club	Lea	GP	G	A	TP	PIM	GP	G	A	TP	PIM
1996-97	Lincoln Stars	USHL	35	6	7	13	94	....	....	....	....	....
1997-98	Notre Dame	CCHA	38	0	6	6	22	....	....	....	....	....
1998-99	Notre Dame	CCHA	14	1	2	3	26	....	....	....	....	....
99-2000	Notre Dame	CCHA	36	1	3	4	60	....	....	....	....	....

CLARKE, Noah (KLAHRK) L.A.

Left wing. Shoots left. 5'9", 175 lbs. Born, LaVerne, CA, June 11, 1979.
(Los Angeles' 10th choice, 250th overall, in 1999 Entry Draft).

			Regular Season					Playoffs				
Season	Club	Lea	GP	G	A	TP	PIM	GP	G	A	TP	PIM
1997-98	Des Moines	USHL	54	19	30	49	29	12	2	9	11	23
1998-99	Des Moines	USHL	52	31	32	63	47	13	8	2	10	16
99-2000	Colorado	WCHA	39	17	20	37	30	....	....	....	....	....

CLASSEN, Greg NSH.

Center. Shoots left. 6'1", 194 lbs. Born, Aylsham, Sask., August 24, 1977.

			Regular Season					Playoffs				
Season	Club	Lea	GP	G	A	TP	PIM	GP	G	A	TP	PIM
1997-98	Nipawin Hawks	SJHL	59	32	50	82	50	....	....	....	....	....
1998-99	Merrimack College	H-East	36	14	11	25	28	....	....	....	....	....
99-2000	Merrimack College	H-East	36	14	16	30	16	....	....	....	....	....
	Milwaukee	IHL	11	1	0	1	2	2	0	0	0	2

Signed as a free agent by **Nashville**, March 27, 2000.

CLAUSON, Kevin (KLAW-sohn, KEH-vihn) NYI

Defense. Shoots left. 6'5", 210 lbs. Born, Lebanon, NH, November 13, 1978.
(NY Islanders' 5th choice, 155th overall, in 1998 Entry Draft).

			Regular Season					Playoffs				
Season	Club	Lea	GP	G	A	TP	PIM	GP	G	A	TP	PIM
1996-97	Boston Bulldogs	MBAHL	60	17	41	58	....	....	....	....	....	....
1997-98	Western Michigan	CCHA	36	1	1	2	56	....	....	....	....	....
1998-99	Western Michigan	CCHA	12	0	1	1	14	....	....	....	....	....
99-2000	U. of Maine	H-East	7	0	0	0	2	....	....	....	....	....

• Eligible to play second semester of 1999-2000 season only under NCAA transfer rules.

CLOUTHIER, Brett (KLOO-tyay, BREHT) N.J.

Left wing. Shoots left. 6'4", 220 lbs. Born, Ottawa, Ont., June 9, 1981.
(New Jersey's 3rd choice, 50th overall, in 1999 Entry Draft).

			Regular Season					Playoffs				
Season	Club	Lea	GP	G	A	TP	PIM	GP	G	A	TP	PIM
1997-98	Kanata Lasers	OJHL	50	12	10	22	135	....	....	....	....	....
1998-99	Kingston	OHL	64	8	14	22	227	5	1	1	2	4
99-2000	Kingston	OHL	65	13	26	39	266	5	2	0	2	17

COLAGIACOMO, Adam (coh-lah-JAH-coh-moh, A-dam) S.J.

Right wing. Shoots right. 6'2", 200 lbs. Born, Toronto, Ont., March 17, 1979.
(San Jose's 3rd choice, 82nd overall, in 1997 Entry Draft).

			Regular Season					Playoffs				
Season	Club	Lea	GP	G	A	TP	PIM	GP	G	A	TP	PIM
1994-95	Royal York	OJHL	33	39	20	59	48	....	....	....	....	....
1995-96	London Knights	OHL	66	28	38	66	88	....	....	....	....	....
1996-97	London Knights	OHL	26	11	11	22	37	....	....	....	....	....
	Oshawa 67's	OHL	23	14	10	24	32	13	1	5	6	4
1997-98	Oshawa 67's	OHL	58	25	31	56	80	7	1	0	1	2
1998-99	Plymouth Whalers	OHL	67	40	68	108	89	10	6	9	15	14
99-2000	Kentucky	AHL	42	5	8	13	27	1	1	0	1	0
	New Orleans	ECHL	18	7	7	14	12	3	0	2	2	2

COLE, Erik (COH-leh, ERIHK) CAR.

Left wing. Shoots left. 6'1", 200 lbs. Born, Oswego, NY, November 6, 1978.
(Carolina's 3rd choice, 71st overall, in 1998 Entry Draft).

			Regular Season					Playoffs				
Season	Club	Lea	GP	G	A	TP	PIM	GP	G	A	TP	PIM
1996-97	Des Moines	USHL	48	30	34	64	140	....	....	....	....	....
1997-98	Clarkson	ECAC	34	11	20	31	55	....	....	....	....	....
1998-99	Clarkson	ECAC	36	*22	20	42	50	....	....	....	....	....
99-2000	Clarkson	ECAC	33	19	11	30	46	....	....	....	....	....
	Cincinnati	IHL	9	4	3	7	2	7	1	1	2	2

ECAC First All-Star Team (1999) • NCAA East Second All-American Team (1999) • ECAC Second All-Star Team (2000)

COLE, Phil (KOHL, fihl) N.J.

Defense. Shoots left. 6'4", 190 lbs. Born, Winnipeg, Man., September 6, 1982.
(New Jersey's 8th choice, 125th overall, in 2000 Entry Draft).

			Regular Season					Playoffs				
Season	Club	Lea	GP	G	A	TP	PIM	GP	G	A	TP	PIM
1997-98	Winnipeg Sharks	MAHA	45	0	18	18	68	5	0	4	4	2
1998-99	Lethbridge	WHL	45	2	1	3	64	4	0	0	0	0
99-2000	Lethbridge	WHL	51	1	6	7	112	....	....	....	....	....

COLEMAN, Jon (KOHL-man, JAWN)

Defense. Shoots right. 6'1", 205 lbs. Born, Boston, MA, March 9, 1975.
(Detroit's 2nd choice, 48th overall, in 1993 Entry Draft).

			Regular Season					Playoffs				
Season	Club	Lea	GP	G	A	TP	PIM	GP	G	A	TP	PIM
1992-93	Phillips Academy	Hi-School	24	14	33	47	40	....	....	....	....	....
1993-94	Boston University	H-East	29	1	14	15	26	....	....	....	....	....
1994-95	Boston University	H-East	40	5	23	28	42	....	....	....	....	....
1995-96	Boston University	H-East	40	7	31	38	58	....	....	....	....	....
1996-97	Boston University	H-East	39	5	27	32	20	....	....	....	....	....
1997-98	Detroit Vipers	IHL	1	0	0	0	0	....	....	....	....	....
	Adirondack	AHL	54	2	29	31	23	2	0	0	0	0
1998-99	Adirondack	AHL	72	12	26	38	32	3	0	0	0	0
99-2000	Kentucky	AHL	66	1	14	15	43	9	2	4	6	2

Hockey East Second All-Star Team (1996, 1997) • NCAA East Second All-American Team (1996) • NCAA East First All-American Team (1997)

Signed as a free agent by **San Jose**, August 26, 1999.

COLLINS, Brian (kAW-lihns, BRIGH-an) NYI

Center. Shoots left. 6'1", 190 lbs. Born, Worcester, MA, September 13, 1980.
(NY Islanders' 6th choice, 87th overall, in 1999 Entry Draft).

			Regular Season					Playoffs				
Season	Club	Lea	GP	G	A	TP	PIM	GP	G	A	TP	PIM
1998-99	St. John's Prep	Hi-School	28	38	35	73	20	....	....	....	....	....
99-2000	Boston University	H-East	42	13	11	24	61	....	....	....	....	....

COMMODORE, Mike (kAWM-uh-dohr, MIGHK) N.J.

Defense. Shoots right. 6'4", 225 lbs. Born, Fort Saskatchewan, Alta., November 7, 1979.
(New Jersey's 2nd choice, 42nd overall, in 1999 Entry Draft).

			Regular Season					Playoffs				
Season	Club	Lea	GP	G	A	TP	PIM	GP	G	A	TP	PIM
1996-97	Ft-Saskatchewan	AJHL	51	3	8	11	244	....	....	....	....	....
1997-98	North Dakota	WCHA	29	0	5	5	74	....	....	....	....	....
1998-99	North Dakota	WCHA	39	5	8	13	154	....	....	....	....	....
99-2000	North Dakota	WCHA	38	5	7	12	*154	....	....	....	....	....

NCAA Championship All-Tournament Team (2000)

COMRIE, Mike (kAWM-ree, MIGHK) EDM.

Center. Shoots left. 5'9", 172 lbs. Born, Edmonton, Alta., September 11, 1980.
(Edmonton's 5th choice, 91st overall, in 1999 Entry Draft).

			Regular Season					Playoffs				
Season	Club	Lea	GP	G	A	TP	PIM	GP	G	A	TP	PIM
1995-96	Edmonton SSAC	AAHA	33	51	52	103	....	....	....	....	....	....
1996-97	St. Albert Saints	AJHL	63	37	41	78	44	....	....	....	....	....
1997-98	St. Albert Saints	AJHL	58	*60	*78	*138	134	19	*24	*24	*48	51
1998-99	U. of Michigan	CCHA	42	19	25	44	38	....	....	....	....	....
99-2000	U. of Michigan	CCHA	40	24	35	59	95	....	....	....	....	....

AJHL Rookie-of-the-Year (1997) • AJHL MVP (1998) • Canadian Junior "A" Player-of-the-Year (1998) • CCHA First All-Star Team (2000) • NCAA West Second All-American Team (2000)

CONCANNON, Mark (KAHN-kan-nuhn, MAHRK) S.J.

Left wing. Shoots left. 6', 200 lbs. Born, Boston, MA, June 12, 1980.
(San Jose's 2nd choice, 82nd overall, in 1999 Entry Draft).

			Regular Season					Playoffs				
Season	Club	Lea	GP	G	A	TP	PIM	GP	G	A	TP	PIM
1998-99	Winchendon	Hi-School	26	23	38	61	11	....	....	....	....	....
99-2000	U. Mass-Lowell	H-East	23	4	3	7	8	....	....	....	....	....

CONNOLLY, Sean (KAW-nuhl-lee, SHAWN) OTT.

Defense. Shoots right. 6'1", 187 lbs. Born, Dearborn, MI, October 8, 1980.
(Ottawa's 8th choice, 158th overall, in 2000 Entry Draft).

			Regular Season					Playoffs				
Season	Club	Lea	GP	G	A	TP	PIM	GP	G	A	TP	PIM
1997-98	Markham Waxers	OJHL	45	10	28	38	181	....	....	....	....	....
1998-99	North-Michigan	CCHA	33	4	18	22	62	....	....	....	....	....
99-2000	North-Michigan	CCHA	35	2	14	16	64	....	....	....	....	....

COOK, Jesse (KOOK, JEH-see) CGY.

Defense. Shoots right. 6'6", 210 lbs. Born, Denver, CO, October 11, 1979.
(Calgary's 6th choice, 153rd overall, in 1999 Entry Draft).

			Regular Season					Playoffs				
Season	Club	Lea	GP	G	A	TP	PIM	GP	G	A	TP	PIM
1997-98	Calgary Royals	AJHL	34	5	24	29	35	3	1	2	3	4
1998-99	U. of Denver	WCHA	33	0	10	10	22	....	....	....	....	....
99-2000	U. of Denver	WCHA	41	2	12	14	40	....	....	....	....	....

COPLEY, Randy (COHP-lee, RAN-dee)

Right wing. Shoots right. 6'1", 205 lbs. Born, Inverness, N.S., October 4, 1979.
(NY Rangers' 2nd choice, 40th overall, in 1998 Entry Draft).

			Regular Season					Playoffs				
Season	Club	Lea	GP	G	A	TP	PIM	GP	G	A	TP	PIM
1996-97	Granby Bisons	QMJHL	70	7	14	21	114	5	0	0	0	5
1997-98	Cape Breton	QMJHL	69	34	42	76	194	4	0	0	0	16
1998-99	Cape Breton	QMJHL	25	8	22	30	60	....	....	....	....	....
	Rouyn-Noranda	QMJHL	38	7	25	32	87	11	3	5	8	14
99-2000	Montreal Rockets	QMJHL	54	34	47	81	70	5	1	1	2	20

CORRINET, Chris (KOHR-rih-neht, KRIHS) WSH.

Right wing. Shoots right. 6'3", 220 lbs. Born, Derby, CT, October 29, 1978.
(Washington's 4th choice, 107th overall, in 1998 Entry Draft).

			Regular Season					Playoffs				
Season	Club	Lea	GP	G	A	TP	PIM	GP	G	A	TP	PIM
1996-97	Deerfield Academy	Hi-School	16	6	15	21	10	....	....	....	....	....
1997-98	Princeton	ECAC	31	3	6	9	22	....	....	....	....	....
1998-99	Princeton	ECAC	32	10	6	16	38	....	....	....	....	....
99-2000	Princeton	ECAC	30	10	14	24	41	....	....	....	....	....

CORSO, Daniel (KOHR-soh, DAN-yehl) ST.L.

Center. Shoots left. 5'10", 183 lbs. Born, Montreal, Que., April 3, 1978.
(St. Louis' 6th choice, 169th overall, in 1996 Entry Draft).

			Regular Season					Playoffs				
Season	Club	Lea	GP	G	A	TP	PIM	GP	G	A	TP	PIM
1994-95	Victoriaville Tigres	QMJHL	65	27	26	53	6	4	2	5	7	2
1995-96	Victoriaville Tigres	QMJHL	65	49	65	114	77	12	6	7	13	4
1996-97	Victoriaville Tigres	QMJHL	54	51	68	119	50	....	....	....	....	....
1997-98	Victoriaville Tigres	QMJHL	35	24	51	75	20	3	1	1	2	2
1998-99	Worcester	AHL	63	14	14	28	26	....	....	....	....	....
99-2000	Worcester	AHL	71	21	34	55	19	9	2	3	5	10

QMJHL First All-Star Team (1997)

CORVO, Joseph (KOHR-voh, JOH-sehf) L.A.

Defense. Shoots right. 6', 205 lbs. Born, Oak Park, IL, June 20, 1977.
(Los Angeles' 4th choice, 83rd overall, in 1997 Entry Draft).

			Regular Season					Playoffs				
Season	Club	Lea	GP	G	A	TP	PIM	GP	G	A	TP	PIM
1995-96	Western Michigan	CCHA	41	5	25	30	38	....	....	....	....	....
1996-97	Western Michigan	CCHA	32	12	21	33	85	....	....	....	....	....
1997-98	Western Michigan	CCHA	32	5	12	17	93	....	....	....	....	....
1998-99	Springfield	AHL	50	5	15	20	32	....	....	....	....	....
	Hampton Roads	ECHL	5	0	0	0	15	4	0	1	1	0
99-2000			DID NOT PLAY									

CCHA Second All-Star Team (1997)

• Sat out entire 1999-2000 season after failing to come to contract terms with **LA Kings**. Re-signed with LA Kings, June 8, 2000.

COX, Justin (KAWKS, JUH-stihn) DAL.

Right wing. Shoots right. 6', 160 lbs. Born, Merritt, B.C., March 13, 1981.
(Dallas' 6th choice, 184th overall, in 1999 Entry Draft).

			Regular Season					Playoffs				
Season	Club	Lea	GP	G	A	TP	PIM	GP	G	A	TP	PIM
1996-97	Spruce Grove	AMHL	78	57	92	149	86	....	....	....	....	....
1997-98	Prince George	WHL	40	1	4	5	15	2	0	0	0	0
1998-99	Prince George	WHL	72	9	13	22	51	7	1	0	1	13
99-2000	Prince George	WHL	71	33	38	71	74	13	2	4	6	16

CRAIN, Jason (KRAYN, JAY-suhn) L.A.

Defense. Shoots left. 6'3", 190 lbs. Born, Pittsburgh, PA, January 3, 1980.
(Los Angeles' 2nd choice, 74th overall, in 1999 Entry Draft).

			Regular Season					Playoffs				
Season	Club	Lea	GP	G	A	TP	PIM	GP	G	A	TP	PIM
1996-97	St. Thomas Stars	OJHL-B	50	9	18	27	67	....	....	....	....	....
1997-98	St. Thomas Stars	OJHL-B	43	6	33	39	49	....	....	....	....	....
1998-99	Ohio State	CCHA	41	3	14	17	18	....	....	....	....	....
99-2000	Ohio State	CCHA	35	2	9	11	32	....	....	....	....	....

CRONIN, John (KROH-nihhn) BOS.

Defense. Shoots right. 6'2", 200 lbs. Born, Duxbury, MA, May 1, 1980.
(Boston's 8th choice, 236th overall, in 1999 Entry Draft).

			Regular Season					Playoffs				
Season	Club	Lea	GP	G	A	TP	PIM	GP	G	A	TP	PIM
1997-98	Nobles-Greenough	Hi-School	30	8	22	30	14	....	....	....	....	....
1998-99	Nobles-Greenough	Hi-School	30	8	26	34	24	....	....	....	....	....
99-2000	Boston University	H-East	28	3	5	8	26	....	....	....	....	....

CROZIER, Greg (KROH-zuhr, GREHG) PIT.

Left wing. Shoots left. 6'3", 200 lbs. Born, Calgary, Alta., July 6, 1976.
(Pittsburgh's 4th choice, 73rd overall, in 1994 Entry Draft).

			Regular Season					Playoffs				
Season	Club	Lea	GP	G	A	TP	PIM	GP	G	A	TP	PIM
1991-92	Amherst	Hi-School	46	61	47	108	47	....	....	....	....	....
1992-93	Lawrence Prep	Hi-School	22	22	14	36	....	....	....	....	....	....
1993-94	Lawrence Prep	Hi-School	18	22	26	48	12	....	....	....	....	....
1994-95	Lawrence Prep	Hi-School	31	45	32	77	22	....	....	....	....	....
1995-96	U. of Michigan	CCHA	42	14	10	24	46	....	....	....	....	....
1996-97	U. of Michigan	CCHA	31	5	15	20	45	....	....	....	....	....
1997-98	U. of Michigan	CCHA	45	12	10	22	26	....	....	....	....	....
1998-99	U. of Michigan	CCHA	39	7	6	13	63	....	....	....	....	....
99-2000	Wilkes-Barre	AHL	71	22	22	44	33	....	....	....	....	....

CULL, Trent PIT.

Defense. Shoots left. 6'2", 215 lbs. Born, Brampton, Ont., September 27, 1973.

			Regular Season					Playoffs				
Season	Club	Lea	GP	G	A	TP	PIM	GP	G	A	TP	PIM
1988-89	Georgetown	OJHL-B	36	1	5	6	51	....	....	....	....	....
1989-90	Owen Sound	OHL	57	0	5	5	53	12	0	2	2	11
1990-91	Owen Sound	OHL	24	1	2	3	19	....	....	....	....	....
	Windsor Spitfires	OHL	33	1	6	7	34	11	0	0	0	8
1991-92	Windsor Spitfires	OHL	32	0	6	6	66	....	....	....	....	....
	Kingston	OHL	18	0	0	0	31	....	....	....	....	....
1992-93	Kingston	OHL	60	11	28	39	144	16	2	8	10	37
1993-94	Kingston	OHL	50	2	30	32	147	6	0	1	1	6
1994-95	St. John's Leafs	AHL	43	0	1	1	53	....	....	....	....	....
	Brantford Smoke	ColHL	4	0	0	0	14	....	....	....	....	....
1995-96	St. John's Leafs	AHL	46	2	1	3	118	4	0	0	0	6
1996-97	St. John's Leafs	AHL	75	4	5	9	219	8	0	1	1	18
1997-98	Houston Aeros	IHL	72	4	8	12	201	4	0	0	0	4
1998-99	Houston Aeros	IHL	72	2	14	16	232	19	0	2	2	34
99-2000	Springfield	AHL	28	0	2	2	74	....	....	....	....	....
	Houston Aeros	IHL	35	2	7	9	133	5	0	0	0	24

Signed as a free agent by **Toronto**, June 4, 1994. Signed as a free agent by **Phoenix**, August 26, 1999. Signed as a free agent by **Pittsburgh**, August 28, 2000.

CULLEN, David (KUH-lehn, DAY-vihd) PHX.

Defense. Shoots right. 6'2", 209 lbs. Born, St. Catharines, Ont., December 30, 1976.

			Regular Season					Playoffs				
Season	Club	Lea	GP	G	A	TP	PIM	GP	G	A	TP	PIM
1992-93	Thorold Hawks	OJHL-B	34	4	6	10	28	....	....	....	....	....
1993-94	Thorold Hawks	OJHL	40	10	35	45	26	....	....	....	....	....
1994-95	Thorold Hawks	OJHL-B	36	16	30	46	12	....	....	....	....	....
1995-96	U. of Maine	H-East	34	2	4	6	22	....	....	....	....	....
1996-97	U. of Maine	H-East	35	5	25	30	8	....	....	....	....	....
1997-98	U. of Maine	H-East	36	10	27	37	24	....	....	....	....	....
1998-99	U. of Maine	H-East	41	11	33	44	24	....	....	....	....	....
99-2000	Springfield	AHL	78	10	21	31	57	2	0	0	0	2

Hockey East First All-Star Team (1999) • NCAA East First All-American Team (1999) • NCAA Championship All-Tournament Team (1999)

Signed as a free agent by **Phoenix**, April 16, 1999.

CUNNIFF, David (KUH-nihf, DAY-vihd)

Left wing. Shoots left. 5'9", 185 lbs. Born, South Boston, MA, October 9, 1973.

			Regular Season					Playoffs				
Season	Club	Lea	GP	G	A	TP	PIM	GP	G	A	TP	PIM
1995-96	Salem State	ECAC-2	27	12	17	29	62	....	....	....	....	....
1996-97	Jacksonville	ECHL	16	4	5	9	75	....	....	....	....	....
	Raleigh IceCaps	ECHL	46	14	6	20	67	....	....	....	....	....
1997-98	Raleigh IceCaps	ECHL	62	12	12	24	168	....	....	....	....	....
	Albany River Rats	AHL	4	0	0	0	13	....	....	....	....	....
1998-99	Albany River Rats	AHL	48	2	9	11	118	5	0	1	1	4
99-2000	Albany River Rats	AHL	68	3	11	14	88	5	0	0	0	4

Signed as a free agent by **New Jersey**, October 1, 1997.

CUTTA, Jakub (KOO-tuh, YA-kuhb) WSH.

Defense. Shoots left. 6'2", 195 lbs. Born, Jablonec nad Nisou, Czech., December 29, 1981.
(Washington's 3rd choice, 61st overall, in 2000 Entry Draft).

			Regular Season					Playoffs				
Season	Club	Lea	GP	G	A	TP	PIM	GP	G	A	TP	PIM
1997-98	Stadion Liberec-Jr.	Cze-Rep	29	3	13	16	70	....	....	....	....	....
1998-99	Swift Current	WHL	59	3	3	6	63	....	....	....	....	....
99-2000	Swift Current	WHL	71	2	12	14	114	12	0	2	2	24

DAGENAIS, Pierre (da-ZHUH-nay, PEE-air) N.J.

Right wing. Shoots left. 6'4", 210 lbs. Born, Blainville, Que., March 4, 1978.
(New Jersey's 6th choice, 105th overall, in 1998 Entry Draft).

			Regular Season					Playoffs				
Season	Club	Lea	GP	G	A	TP	PIM	GP	G	A	TP	PIM
1994-95	Laval Regents	QAAA	34	28	14	42	68	....	....	....	....	....
1995-96	Moncton Alpines	QMJHL	67	43	25	68	59	....	....	....	....	....
1996-97	Moncton Wildcats	QMJHL	6	4	2	6	0	....	....	....	....	....
	Laval Titan	QMJHL	37	16	14	30	40	....	....	....	....	....
	Rouyn-Noranda	QMJHL	27	21	8	29	22	....	....	....	....	....
1997-98	Rouyn-Noranda	QMJHL	60	*66	67	133	50	6	6	2	8	2
1998-99	Albany River Rats	AHL	69	17	13	30	37	4	0	0	0	0
99-2000	Albany River Rats	AHL	80	35	30	65	47	5	1	0	1	14

• Re-entered NHL draft. Originally New Jersey's 4th choice, 47th overall, in 1996 Entry Draft.

QMJHL Second All-Star Team (1998)

DANDENAULT, Eric

Defense. Shoots right. 6', 195 lbs. Born, Sherbrooke, Que., March 10, 1970.

			Regular Season					Playoffs				
Season	Club	Lea	GP	G	A	TP	PIM	GP	G	A	TP	PIM
1988-89	Drummondville	QMJHL	66	5	24	29	64	4	0	1	1	0
1989-90	Drummondville	QMJHL	53	12	29	41	188	....	....	....	....	....
	Chicoutimi	QMJHL	14	2	9	11	50	5	0	2	2	55
1990-91	Drummondville	QMJHL	67	14	33	47	215	14	5	6	11	84
1991-92	Hershey Bears	AHL	69	6	13	19	149	3	0	0	0	4
1992-93	Hershey Bears	AHL	72	20	19	39	118	....	....	....	....	....
1993-94	Hershey Bears	AHL	14	2	1	3	49	....	....	....	....	....
	Johnstown Chiefs	ECHL	2	1	1	2	6	....	....	....	....	....
1994-95	HC Fassa	Italy	31	14	17	31	87	....	....	....	....	....
	STIJ Geleen	Holland	5	7	6	13	18	....	....	....	....	....
1995-96	Saginaw Wheels	ColHL	61	5	30	35	160	....	....	....	....	....
	Cincinnati	IHL	16	1	2	3	49	17	1	6	7	30
1996-97	Cincinnati	IHL	77	5	14	19	240	3	0	0	0	7
1997-98	Cincinnati	IHL	81	2	11	13	230	9	0	2	2	18
1998-99	Cincinnati	IHL	63	4	13	17	180	3	0	0	0	2
99-2000	Cincinnati	IHL	62	4	5	9	201	3	0	0	0	29

Signed as a free agent by **Philadelphia**, December 4, 1991. • Missed majority of 1993-94 season recovering from hernia injury suffered in practice, October 31, 1993. Signed as a free agent by **Cincinnati** (IHL), March 11, 1996. Signed as a free agent by **Carolina**, August 31, 1999.

DARBY, Regan (DAHR-bee, REE-gan) VAN.

Defense. Shoots left. 6'2", 200 lbs. Born, Estevan, Sask., July 17, 1980.
(Vancouver's 5th choice, 90th overall, in 1998 Entry Draft).

			Regular Season					Playoffs				
Season	Club	Lea	GP	G	A	TP	PIM	GP	G	A	TP	PIM
1997-98	Spokane Chiefs	WHL	7	0	1	1	28	....	....	....	....	....
	Tri-City Americans	WHL	32	1	2	3	125	....	....	....	....	....
1998-99	Tri-City Americans	WHL	38	2	4	6	152	....	....	....	....	....
	Red Deer Rebels	WHL	19	1	6	7	90	9	0	1	1	18
99-2000	Red Deer Rebels	WHL	18	3	6	9	79	....	....	....	....	....
	Prince Albert	WHL	44	1	9	10	143	6	0	1	1	23

DARCHE, Mathieu CBJ

Left wing. Shoots left. 6'1", 225 lbs. Born, St-Laurent, Que., November 26, 1976.

			Regular Season					Playoffs				
Season	Club	Lea	GP	G	A	TP	PIM	GP	G	A	TP	PIM
1996-97	McGill University	OUAA	23	1	2	3	27	....	....	....	....	....
1997-98	McGill University	OUAA	40	28	17	45	69	....	....	....	....	....
1998-99	McGill University	OUAA	32	16	24	40	60	....	....	....	....	....
99-2000	McGill University	OUAA	33	31	41	72	38	5	2	8	10	16

OUAA First All-Star Team (2000) • CIAU All-Canadian Team (2000)

Signed as a free agent by **Columbus**, May 16, 2000.

DARDIS, Jay (DAHR-dihs, JAY) NYR

Center. Shoots right. 6'3", 190 lbs. Born, Proctor, MN, July 4, 1981.
(NY Rangers' 7th choice, 177th overall, in 1999 Entry Draft).

			Regular Season					Playoffs				
Season	Club	Lea	GP	G	A	TP	PIM	GP	G	A	TP	PIM
1998-99	Proctor High	Hi-School	26	23	36	59	32	....	....	....	....	....
99-2000	Waterloo Hawks	USHL	17	3	4	7	18	....	....	....	....	....
	Rochester	USHL	22	4	4	8	10	....	....	....	....	....

DATSYUK, Pavel (daht-SOOK, PA-vehl) DET.

Center. Shoots left. 5'11", 180 lbs. Born, Sverdlovsk, USSR, July 20, 1978.
(Detroit's 8th choice, 171st overall, in 1998 Entry Draft).

			Regular Season					Playoffs				
Season	Club	Lea	GP	G	A	TP	PIM	GP	G	A	TP	PIM
1996-97	SK Yekaterinburg	Russia	18	2	2	4	4	....	....	....	....	....
	SK Yekaterinburg	Russia-2	36	12	10	22	12	....	....	....	....	....
1997-98	SK Yekaterinburg	Russia	24	3	5	8	4	....	....	....	....	....
	SK Yekaterinburg	Russia-2	22	7	8	15	4	....	....	....	....	....
1998-99	Yekaterinburg-2	Russia-3	22	12	15	27	12	....	....	....	....	....
	SK Yekaterinburg	Russia-2	13	9	8	17	2	9	3	7	10	10
99-2000	SK Yekaterinburg	Russia	15	1	3	4	4	....	....	....	....	....

DAVIDSON, Matt (DAY-vihd-SOHN, MAT) CBJ

Right wing. Shoots right. 6'2", 190 lbs. Born, Flin Flon, Man., August 9, 1977.
(Buffalo's 5th choice, 94th overall, in 1995 Entry Draft).

			Regular Season					Playoffs				
Season	Club	Lea	GP	G	A	TP	PIM	GP	G	A	TP	PIM
1992-93	Saskatoon	SAHA	36	14	18	32	36	....	....	....	....	....
1993-94	Portland	WHL	59	4	12	16	18	10	0	0	0	4
1994-95	Portland	WHL	72	17	20	37	51	9	1	3	4	0
1995-96	Portland	WHL	70	24	26	50	96	7	2	2	4	2
1996-97	Portland	WHL	72	44	27	71	47	6	0	1	1	2
1997-98	Rochester	AHL	72	15	12	27	12	3	1	0	1	2
1998-99	Rochester	AHL	80	26	15	41	44	18	2	1	3	6
99-2000	Rochester	AHL	80	12	20	32	30	19	4	2	6	8

Traded to **Columbus** by **Buffalo** with Jean-Luc Grand-Pierre, San Jose's 5th round choice (previously acquired, Columbus selected Tyler Kolarik) in 2000 Entry Draft and Buffalo's 5th round choice in 2001 Entry Draft to complete Expansion Draft agreement which had Columbus select Geoff Sanderson and Dwayne Roloson from Buffalo, June 23, 2000.

DAVIS, Ken (DAY-vihs) DET.

Right wing. Shoots right. 6'4", 210 lbs. Born, Calgary, Alta., March 20, 1981.
(Detroit's 6th choice, 266th overall, in 1999 Entry Draft).

			Regular Season					Playoffs				
Season	Club	Lea	GP	G	A	TP	PIM	GP	G	A	TP	PIM
1998-99	Portland	WHL	72	13	14	27	76	4	0	1	1	11
99-2000	Portland	WHL	6	1	2	3	18	....	....	....	....	....
	Medicine Hat	WHL	61	23	10	33	86	....	....	....	....	....

DAVIS, Wade (DAY-vihs) CGY.

Defense. Shoots right. 6'4", 185 lbs. Born, Kamloops, B.C., April 13, 1982.
(Calgary's 5th choice, 141st overall, in 2000 Entry Draft).

			Regular Season					Playoffs				
Season	Club	Lea	GP	G	A	TP	PIM	GP	G	A	TP	PIM
1997-98	Fernie Ghostriders	RMJHL	42	8	17	25	19	....	....	....	....	....
1998-99	Calgary Hitmen	WHL	38	0	2	2	21	2	0	0	0	0
99-2000	Calgary Hitmen	WHL	61	3	15	18	59	13	0	2	2	15

DAVISON, Rob (DAY-vihs-ohn, RAWB) S.J.

Defense. Shoots left. 6'2", 220 lbs. Born, St. Catharines, Ont., May 1, 1980.
(San Jose's 4th choice, 98th overall, in 1998 Entry Draft).

			Regular Season					Playoffs				
Season	Club	Lea	GP	G	A	TP	PIM	GP	G	A	TP	PIM
1996-97	St. Michaels	OJHL	45	2	6	8	93	....	....	....	....	....
1997-98	North Bay	OHL	59	0	11	11	200	....	....	....	....	....
1998-99	North Bay	OHL	59	2	17	19	150	4	0	1	1	12
99-2000	North Bay	OHL	67	4	6	10	194	6	0	1	1	8

DAW, Jeff (DAW, JEHF) MIN.

Center. Shoots right. 6'3", 190 lbs. Born, Carlisle, Ont., February 28, 1972.

			Regular Season					Playoffs				
Season	Club	Lea	GP	G	A	TP	PIM	GP	G	A	TP	PIM
1992-93	U. Mass-Lowell	H-East	37	12	18	30	14	....	....	....	....	....
1993-94	U. Mass-Lowell	H-East	40	6	12	18	12	....	....	....	....	....
1994-95	U. Mass-Lowell	H-East	40	27	15	42	24	....	....	....	....	....
1995-96	U. Mass-Lowell	H-East	40	23	28	51	10	....	....	....	....	....
1996-97	Wheeling Nailers	ECHL	13	3	8	11	26	....	....	....	....	....
	Hamilton Bulldogs	AHL	56	11	8	19	39	19	4	5	9	0
1997-98	Hamilton Bulldogs	AHL	79	28	35	63	20	9	6	3	9	0
1998-99	Hamilton Bulldogs	AHL	66	18	29	47	10	11	0	3	3	4
99-2000	Cleveland	IHL	9	4	1	5	2	....	....	....	....	....
	Houston Aeros	IHL	44	9	8	17	12	....	....	....	....	....
	Lowell	AHL	10	0	5	5	4	7	1	2	3	6

Signed as a free agent by **Edmonton**, August 1, 1996. Signed as a free agent by **Chicago**, July 22, 1999. Traded to **Lowell** (AHL) by **Houston** (IHL) with Chicago retaining NHL rights for Dave Hymotitz, March 17, 2000. Selected by **Minnesota** from **Chicago** in Expansion Draft, June 23, 2000.

DECECCO, Bret (duh-CHEHK-oh) BUF.

Right wing. Shoots right. 5'10", 189 lbs. Born, Edmonton, Alta., May 20, 1980.
(Buffalo's 10th choice, 206th overall, in 1999 Entry Draft).

			Regular Season					Playoffs				
Season	Club	Lea	GP	G	A	TP	PIM	GP	G	A	TP	PIM
1996-97	Seattle T-Birds	WHL	54	17	19	36	40	15	7	1	8	9
1997-98	Seattle T-Birds	WHL	71	36	56	92	84	3	0	0	0	0
1998-99	Seattle T-Birds	WHL	72	57	43	100	81	11	1	4	5	21
99-2000	Seattle T-Birds	WHL	51	29	26	55	56	4	4	2	6	4

WHL West Second All-Star Team (1999)

DEFAUW, Brad (duh-FOU, BRAD) CAR.

Left wing. Shoots left. 6'2", 210 lbs. Born, Edina, MN, November 10, 1977.
(Carolina's 2nd choice, 28th overall, in 1997 Entry Draft).

			Regular Season					Playoffs				
Season	Club	Lea	GP	G	A	TP	PIM	GP	G	A	TP	PIM
1995-96	Apple Collegiate	Hi-School	28	21	34	55	14	....	....	....	....	....
1996-97	North Dakota	WCHA	37	7	6	13	39	....	....	....	....	....
1997-98	North Dakota	WCHA	36	9	11	20	34	....	....	....	....	....
1998-99	North Dakota	WCHA	34	11	12	23	64	....	....	....	....	....
99-2000	North Dakota	WCHA	43	13	9	22	52	....	....	....	....	....

DEGERMAN, Tommi (DEH-guhr-mahn, TAWM-mee) ANA.

Left wing. Shoots left. 6'2", 200 lbs. Born, Vihti, Finland, February 23, 1976.
(Anaheim's 8th choice, 235th overall, in 1997 Entry Draft).

			Regular Season					Playoffs				
Season	Club	Lea	GP	G	A	TP	PIM	GP	G	A	TP	PIM
1992-93	Kiekko-Espoo-B	Finn-Jr.	35	14	17	31	4	5	3	4	*7	0
1993-94	Kiekko-Espoo-B	Finn-Jr.	13	8	5	13	14	....	....	....	....	....
	Kiekko-Espoo	Finn-Jr.	34	2	6	8	14	....	....	....	....	....
1994-95	Kiekko-Espoo	Finn-Jr.	26	4	7	11	14	5	1	0	1	4
1995-96	Kiekko-Espoo	Finn-Jr.	36	11	15	26	14	....	....	....	....	....
1996-97	Kiekko-Espoo	Finn-Jr.	3	3	0	3	0	....	....	....	....	....
	Pelicans Lahti	Finland-2	4	0	4	4	0	....	....	....	....	....
	Kiekko-Espoo	Finland	23	2	0	2	2	....	....	....	....	....
	Boston University	H-East	17	6	10	16	19	....	....	....	....	....
1997-98	Boston University	H-East	35	12	20	32	37	....	....	....	....	....
1998-99	Boston University	H-East	27	12	9	21	24	....	....	....	....	....
99-2000	Boston University	H-East	42	19	24	43	18	....	....	....	....	....

DELEEUW, Adam (DEH-lee-EW, A-dam) DET.

Left wing. Shoots left. 6', 206 lbs. Born, Brampton, Ont., February 29, 1980.
(Detroit's 7th choice, 151st overall, in 1998 Entry Draft).

			Regular Season					Playoffs				
Season	Club	Lea	GP	G	A	TP	PIM	GP	G	A	TP	PIM
1996-97	Brampton Capitals	OJHL	45	11	17	28	97	....	....	....	....	....
1997-98	Barrie Colts	OHL	56	10	6	16	224	....	....	....	....	....
1998-99	Barrie Colts	OHL	39	15	16	31	146	....	....	....	....	....
	St. Michael's	OHL	29	10	5	15	55	....	....	....	....	....
99-2000	St. Michael's	OHL	45	11	19	30	107	....	....	....	....	....
	Dayton Bombers	ECHL	2	0	0	0	2	3	0	0	0	2

DELISLE, Miguel (duh-LIGHL, mih-GEHL) TOR.

Right wing. Shoots right. 6'2", 202 lbs. Born, Cornwall, Ont., April 6, 1982.
(Toronto's 5th choice, 100th overall, in 2000 Entry Draft).

			Regular Season					Playoffs				
Season	Club	Lea	GP	G	A	TP	PIM	GP	G	A	TP	PIM
1997-98	Caledon	OJHL	46	20	24	44	142	....	....	....	....	....
1998-99	Ottawa 67's	OHL	57	16	17	33	34	9	1	0	1	4
99-2000	Ottawa 67's	OHL	54	20	29	49	73	11	4	1	5	28

DeMARCHI, Matt (dih-MAHR-shee) N.J.

Defense. Shoots left. 6'3", 180 lbs. Born, Bemidji, MN, May 4, 1981.
(New Jersey's 4th choice, 57th overall, in 2000 Entry Draft).

			Regular Season					Playoffs				
Season	Club	Lea	GP	G	A	TP	PIM	GP	G	A	TP	PIM
1997-98	North Iowa	USHL	34	1	2	3	66	10	0	1	1	19
1998-99	North Iowa	USHL	53	4	14	18	131	....	....	....	....	....
99-2000	U. of Minnesota	WCHA	39	1	6	7	82	....	....	....	....	....

DEMIDOV, Ilja (deh-MEE-dahf, ihl-YA) **OTT.**

Defense. Shoots left. 6'3", 185 lbs. Born, Moscow, USSR, April 14, 1979.
(Calgary's 10th choice, 140th overall, in 1997 Entry Draft).

			Regular Season					Playoffs				
Season	**Club**	**Lea**	**GP**	**G**	**A**	**TP**	**PIM**	**GP**	**G**	**A**	**TP**	**PIM**
1995-96	D'amo Moscow-2	CIS-2	10	0	14	14	....	....	....	....	....	....
1996-97	D'amo Moscow-2	Russia-3	32	1	0	1	60	....	....	....	....	....
1997-98	Oshawa Generals	OHL	61	4	16	20	67	7	0	1	1	2
1998-99	Oshawa Generals	OHL	62	4	23	27	72	15	2	5	7	24
99-2000	Oshawa Generals	OHL	62	11	37	48	105	5	0	2	2	24

Signed as a free agent by **Ottawa**, February 25, 2000.

DENISOV, Denis (den-NEES-ahf, deh-NEES) **BUF.**

Left wing. Shoots left. 6', 183 lbs. Born, Kalinin, USSR, December 31, 1981.
(Buffalo's 4th choice, 149th overall, in 2000 Entry Draft).

			Regular Season					Playoffs				
Season	**Club**	**Lea**	**GP**	**G**	**A**	**TP**	**PIM**	**GP**	**G**	**A**	**TP**	**PIM**
1997-98	CSKA Moscow	Russia	7	0	0	0	4	....	....	....	....	....
1998-99	CSKA Moscow	Russia-2	42	1	6	7	16	....	....	....	....	....
99-2000	CSKA Moscow	Russia-2	39	1	8	9	16	....	....	....	....	....

DESCOTEAUX, Matthieu (DAY-koh-toh, MAT-yoo) **MTL.**

Defense. Shoots left. 6'3", 220 lbs. Born, Pierreville, Que., September 23, 1977.
(Edmonton's 2nd choice, 19th overall, in 1996 Entry Draft).

			Regular Season					Playoffs				
Season	**Club**	**Lea**	**GP**	**G**	**A**	**TP**	**PIM**	**GP**	**G**	**A**	**TP**	**PIM**
1994-95	Shawinigan	QMJHL	50	3	2	5	28	15	1	1	2	19
1995-96	Shawinigan	QMJHL	69	2	13	15	129	6	0	0	0	6
1996-97	Shawinigan	QMJHL	38	6	18	24	121	....	....	....	....	....
	Hull Olympiques	QMJHL	32	6	19	25	34	14	1	8	9	29
1997-98	Hamilton Bulldogs	AHL	67	2	8	10	70	2	0	0	0	0
1998-99	Hamilton Bulldogs	AHL	74	6	12	18	49	4	0	0	0	0
99-2000	Hamilton Bulldogs	AHL	49	5	7	12	29	....	....	....	....	....
	Quebec Citadelles	AHL	12	0	6	6	6	2	0	1	1	0

Traded to **Montreal** by **Edmonton** with Christian Laflamme for Igor Ulanov and Alain Nasreddine, March 9, 2000.

DESMARAIS, James (deh-mahr-AY) **ST.L.**

Center. Shoots right. 5'10", 170 lbs. Born, Montreal, Que., May 4, 1979.
(St. Louis' 10th choice, 270th overall, in 1999 Entry Draft).

			Regular Season					Playoffs				
Season	**Club**	**Lea**	**GP**	**G**	**A**	**TP**	**PIM**	**GP**	**G**	**A**	**TP**	**PIM**
1996-97	Laval Titan	QMJHL	67	12	21	33	32	3	0	0	0	4
1997-98	Laval Titan	QMJHL	68	33	40	73	56	15	6	5	11	12
1998-99	Rouyn-Noranda	QMJHL	66	62	73	135	127	11	6	7	13	14
99-2000	Peoria	ECHL	59	26	33	59	51	....	....	....	....	....
	Worcester	AHL	8	0	2	2	0	....	....	....	....	....

QMJHL First All-Star Team (1999)

DESSNER, Jeff (DEHS-nehr, JEHF) **NYR**

Defense. Shoots left. 6'2", 177 lbs. Born, Skokie, IL, April 16, 1977.
(NY Rangers' 6th choice, 185th overall, in 1996 Entry Draft).

			Regular Season					Playoffs				
Season	**Club**	**Lea**	**GP**	**G**	**A**	**TP**	**PIM**	**GP**	**G**	**A**	**TP**	**PIM**
1995-96	Taft High	Hi-School	25	12	18	30	....	....	....	....	....	....
1996-97	U. of Wisconsin	WCHA			Did Not Play – Injured							
1997-98	U. of Wisconsin	WCHA	19	1	3	4	43	....	....	....	....	....
1998-99	U. of Wisconsin	WCHA	37	7	14	21	46	....	....	....	....	....
99-2000	U. of Wisconsin	WCHA	40	11	15	26	59	....	....	....	....	....

WCHA First All-Star Team (2000) • NCAA West First All-American Team (2000)

• Missed entire 1996-97 season recovering from back surgery, June, 1996.

DeWOLF, Josh (duh-WOOLF, JAWSH) **MTL.**

Defense. Shoots left. 6'2", 200 lbs. Born, Bloomington, MN, July 25, 1977.
(New Jersey's 3rd choice, 41st overall, in 1996 Entry Draft).

			Regular Season					Playoffs				
Season	**Club**	**Lea**	**GP**	**G**	**A**	**TP**	**PIM**	**GP**	**G**	**A**	**TP**	**PIM**
1993-94	Bloomington High	Hi-School	25	1	14	15	32	....	....	....	....	....
1994-95	Bloomington High	Hi-School	28	6	22	28	52	....	....	....	....	....
1995-96	Twin Cities	USHL	40	11	15	26	38	....	....	....	....	....
1996-97	St. Cloud State	WCHA	31	3	11	14	62	....	....	....	....	....
1997-98	St. Cloud State	WCHA	37	9	9	18	78	....	....	....	....	....
	Albany River Rats	AHL	2	0	0	0	0	....	....	....	....	....
1998-99	Albany River Rats	AHL	75	1	17	18	111	5	0	0	0	2
99-2000	Albany River Rats	AHL	58	3	11	14	38	....	....	....	....	....
	Quebec Citadelles	AHL	15	1	0	1	17	3	0	1	1	0

Traded to **Montreal** by **New Jersey** with Sheldon Souray and New Jersey's 2nd round choice in 2001 Entry Draft for Vladimir Malakhov, March 1, 2000.

DEYELL, Mark (digh-EHL, MAHRK)

Center. Shoots right. 6', 180 lbs. Born, Regina, Sask., March 26, 1976.
(Toronto's 4th choice, 126th overall, in 1994 Entry Draft).

			Regular Season					Playoffs				
Season	**Club**	**Lea**	**GP**	**G**	**A**	**TP**	**PIM**	**GP**	**G**	**A**	**TP**	**PIM**
1992-93	Winnipeg	MAHA	35	45	56	101	125	....	....	....	....	....
1993-94	Saskatoon Blades	WHL	66	17	36	53	52	16	5	2	7	20
1994-95	Saskatoon Blades	WHL	70	34	68	102	56	10	2	5	7	14
1995-96	Saskatoon Blades	WHL	69	61	*98	*159	122	4	0	5	5	8
1996-97	St. John's Leafs	AHL	58	15	27	42	30	10	1	5	6	6
1997-98	St. John's Leafs	AHL	72	20	43	63	75	4	1	1	2	4
1998-99	St. John's Leafs	AHL	44	20	27	47	39	3	0	3	3	0
99-2000	St. John's Leafs	AHL			Did Not Play – Injured							

WHL East First All-Star Team (1996)

• Missed remainder of 1998-99 season and entire 1999-2000 season recovering from eye injury suffered in game vs. Fredericton (AHL), April 27, 1999.

DICAIRE, Gerard (dih-KAIR, zhehr-AHR)) **BUF.**

Defense. Shoots left. 6'2", 198 lbs. Born, Faro, Yukon, September 14, 1982.
(Buffalo's 2nd choice, 48th overall, in 2000 Entry Draft).

			Regular Season					Playoffs				
Season	**Club**	**Lea**	**GP**	**G**	**A**	**TP**	**PIM**	**GP**	**G**	**A**	**TP**	**PIM**
1998-99	Prince George	BCJHL	51	6	22	28	28	....	....	....	....	....
99-2000	Seattle T-Birds	WHL	68	11	25	36	38	7	0	1	1	6

DICKENSON, Lou (DIH-kehn-suhn) **EDM.**

Center. Shoots left. 6'1", 192 lbs. Born, Ottawa, Ont., August 15, 1982.
(Edmonton's 4th choice, 113th overall, in 2000 Entry Draft).

			Regular Season					Playoffs				
Season	**Club**	**Lea**	**GP**	**G**	**A**	**TP**	**PIM**	**GP**	**G**	**A**	**TP**	**PIM**
1997-98	South Ottawa	OMHA	36	37	37	74	40	....	....	....	....	....
1998-99	Mississauga	OHL	62	19	27	46	12	....	....	....	....	....
99-2000	Mississauga	OHL	66	21	25	46	46	....	....	....	....	....

DIETRICH, Brandon **NYR**

Right wing. Shoots right. 6', 190 lbs. Born, Waterloo, Ont., March 22, 1978.

			Regular Season					Playoffs				
Season	**Club**	**Lea**	**GP**	**G**	**A**	**TP**	**PIM**	**GP**	**G**	**A**	**TP**	**PIM**
1998-99	St. Lawrence	ECAC	39	20	19	39	22	....	....	....	....	....
99-2000	St. Lawrence	ECAC	36	15	26	41	20	....	....	....	....	....

ECAC First All-Star Team (2000) • NCAA East Second All-American Team (2000)

Signed as a free agent by **NY Rangers**, June 29, 2000.

DiLAURO, Raymond (dih-LAW-roh) **ATL.**

Defense. Shoots right. 6'2", 220 lbs. Born, Bensalem, PA, July 13, 1979.
(Atlanta's 11th choice, 246th overall, in 1999 Entry Draft).

			Regular Season					Playoffs				
Season	**Club**	**Lea**	**GP**	**G**	**A**	**TP**	**PIM**	**GP**	**G**	**A**	**TP**	**PIM**
1997-98	Sports Academy	X-Games	32	17	50	67	....	....	....	....	....	....
1998-99	St. Lawrence	ECAC	35	4	8	12	12	....	....	....	....	....
99-2000	St. Lawrence	ECAC	37	3	9	12	22	....	....	....	....	....

DIMITRAKOS, Nicholas (DIH-mih-tra-kohs, NIK-oh-lahs) **S.J.**

Right wing. Shoots right. 5'11", 190 lbs. Born, Boston, MA, May 21, 1979.
(San Jose's 4th choice, 155th overall, in 1999 Entry Draft).

			Regular Season					Playoffs				
Season	**Club**	**Lea**	**GP**	**G**	**A**	**TP**	**PIM**	**GP**	**G**	**A**	**TP**	**PIM**
1997-98	Avon Old Farms	Hi-School	26	27	28	55	....	....	....	....	....	....
1998-99	U. of Maine	H-East	35	8	19	27	33	....	....	....	....	....
99-2000	U. of Maine	H-East	32	11	16	27	16	....	....	....	....	....

NCAA Championship All-Tournament Team (1999)

DIPENTA, Joe (DIH-pehn-tah, JOW)

Defense. Shoots left. 6'2", 221 lbs. Born, Barrie, Ont., February 25, 1979.
(Florida's 2nd choice, 61st overall, in 1998 Entry Draft).

			Regular Season					Playoffs				
Season	**Club**	**Lea**	**GP**	**G**	**A**	**TP**	**PIM**	**GP**	**G**	**A**	**TP**	**PIM**
1996-97	Smiths Falls	OJHL	54	13	22	35	92	....	....	....	....	....
1997-98	Boston University	H-East	38	2	16	18	50	....	....	....	....	....
1998-99	Boston University	H-East	36	2	15	17	72	....	....	....	....	....
99-2000	Halifax	QMJHL	63	13	43	56	83	10	3	4	7	26

DIROBERTO, Torrey (DIH-raw-buhr-toh, TOHR-ree) **ANA.**

Center. Shoots left. 5'11", 186 lbs. Born, Utica, NY, April 17, 1978.
(Buffalo's 6th choice, 128th overall, in 1997 Entry Draft).

			Regular Season					Playoffs				
Season	**Club**	**Lea**	**GP**	**G**	**A**	**TP**	**PIM**	**GP**	**G**	**A**	**TP**	**PIM**
1994-95	Indianapolis Colts	MEHL	56	38	52	90	36	....	....	....	....	....
1995-96	Seattle T-Birds	WHL	70	16	19	35	118	5	0	2	2	8
1996-97	Seattle T-Birds	WHL	72	37	44	81	91	15	9	5	14	8
1997-98	Seattle T-Birds	WHL	43	14	21	35	48	5	0	2	2	14
1998-99	Seattle T-Birds	WHL	66	25	42	67	100	11	4	4	8	14
99-2000	Cincinnati Ducks	AHL	73	18	16	34	41	....	....	....	....	....
	Huntington	ECHL	3	1	1	2	6	....	....	....	....	....
	Dayton Bombers	ECHL	1	0	1	1	0	....	....	....	....	....

Signed as a free agent by **Anaheim**, July 1, 1999.

DISALVATORE, Jon (dih-sal-vuh-TOH-ray) **S.J.**

Right wing. Shoots right. 6'1", 180 lbs. Born, Bangor, ME, March 30, 1981.
(San Jose's 2nd choice, 104th overall, in 2000 Entry Draft).

			Regular Season					Playoffs				
Season	**Club**	**Lea**	**GP**	**G**	**A**	**TP**	**PIM**	**GP**	**G**	**A**	**TP**	**PIM**
1997-98	New England	EJHL	38	24	41	65	....	....	....	....	....	....
1998-99	New England	EJHL	48	44	76	*120	38	....	....	....	....	....
99-2000	Providence	H-East	38	15	12	27	12	....	....	....	....	....

Named EJHL MVP (1999) • EJHL First All-Star Team (1999)

DIVISEK, Tomas (DIH-vih-sehk, TOH-mahs) **PHI.**

Left wing. Shoots left. 6'2", 194 lbs. Born, Most, Czech., July 19, 1979.
(Philadelphia's 9th choice, 195th overall, in 1998 Entry Draft).

			Regular Season					Playoffs				
Season	**Club**	**Lea**	**GP**	**G**	**A**	**TP**	**PIM**	**GP**	**G**	**A**	**TP**	**PIM**
1995-96	Slavia Praha-Jr.	Cze-Rep	36	20	27	47	12	....	....	....	....	....
1996-97	Slavia Praha-Jr.	Cze-Rep	41	17	25	42	18	....	....	....	....	....
	Slavia Praha	Cze-Rep	1	0	0	0	0	....	....	....	....	....
1997-98	Slavia Praha-Jr.	Cze-Rep	27	20	16	36	12	....	....	....	....	....
	Slavia Praha	Cze-Rep	22	2	0	2	8	....	....	....	....	....
1998-99	Slavia Praha	Cze-Rep	45	8	4	12	26	....	....	....	....	....
99-2000	Philadelphia	AHL	59	18	31	49	30	5	0	3	3	2

DIXON, Sean (DIHX-on, SHAWN) **MTL.**

Defense. Shoots left. 6'4", 183 lbs. Born, Kitchener, Ont., February 22, 1981.
(Montreal's 8th choice, 167th overall, in 1999 Entry Draft).

			Regular Season					Playoffs				
Season	**Club**	**Lea**	**GP**	**G**	**A**	**TP**	**PIM**	**GP**	**G**	**A**	**TP**	**PIM**
1996-97	Waterloo Lions	OMHA	24	7	16	23	40	....	....	....	....	....
	Waterloo Hawks	OJHL-B	6	0	1	1	4	....	....	....	....	....
1997-98	Erie Otters	OHL	58	0	8	8	22	4	0	2	2	0
1998-99	Erie Otters	OHL	55	2	12	14	57	....	....	....	....	....
99-2000	Erie Otters	OHL	68	5	11	16	56	13	0	2	2	10

DOBRYSHKIN, Yuri (doh-BRIHSH-kihn, yew-REE) ATL.

Left wing. Shoots right. 6', 189 lbs. Born, Penza, USSR, July 19, 1979.
(Atlanta's 7th choice, 159th overall, in 1999 Entry Draft).

			Regular Season					Playoffs				
Season	Club	Lea	GP	G	A	TP	PIM	GP	G	A	TP	PIM
1996-97	Krylja Sovetov-2	Russia-3	35	13	5	18	42	....	....	....	....	....
	Krylja Sovetov	Russia	2	0	0	0	0	2	0	0	0	0
1997-98	Krylja Sovetov-2	Russia-3	26	12	5	17	68	....	....	....	....	....
	Krylja Sovetov	Russia	22	4	0	4	12	....	....	....	....	....
1998-99	Krylja Sovetov	Russia	37	6	4	10	30	....	....	....	....	....
	Krylja Sovetov	Russia-Q	13	5	1	6	56	....	....	....	....	....
99-2000	Ak Bars Kazan	Russia	27	6	9	15	24	17	2	0	2	10

DODGINGHORSE, Brent (daw-JIHN-HOHR-she, BREHNT)

Center. Shoots left. 6', 180 lbs. Born, Calgary, Alta., February 17, 1978.

			Regular Season					Playoffs				
Season	Club	Lea	GP	G	A	TP	PIM	GP	G	A	TP	PIM
1996-97	Vernon Lakers	BCJHL	58	34	57	91	137	....	....	....	....	....
1997-98	Omaha Lancers	USHL	12	7	5	12	55	....	....	....	....	....
	Calgary Hitmen	WHL	53	14	23	37	78	12	2	6	8	42
1998-99	Calgary Hitmen	WHL	50	13	31	44	153	21	10	15	25	72
99-2000	Johnstown Chiefs	ECHL	17	1	2	3	62	....	....	....	....	....

Signed as a free agent by **Calgary**, June 18, 1999.

DOELL, Curtis (DOW-ehl, KUHR-tihs) FLA.

Defense. Shoots right. 5'11", 209 lbs. Born, Saskatoon, Sask., October 3, 1976.

			Regular Season					Playoffs				
Season	Club	Lea	GP	G	A	TP	PIM	GP	G	A	TP	PIM
1996-97	Minnesota-Duluth	WCHA	37	6	20	26	114	....	....	....	....	....
1997-98	Minnesota-Duluth	WCHA	39	9	23	32	120	....	....	....	....	....
1998-99	Kentucky	AHL	53	2	8	10	166	....	....	....	....	....
99-2000	Louisville	AHL	33	2	7	9	85	....	....	....	....	....

Signed as a free agent by **Florida**, June 5, 1998.

DOMAN, Matt (DOH-man, MAT) CGY.

Right wing. Shoots right. 6'1", 218 lbs. Born, St. Cloud, MN, February 10, 1980.
(Calgary's 5th choice, 135th overall, in 1999 Entry Draft).

			Regular Season					Playoffs				
Season	Club	Lea	GP	G	A	TP	PIM	GP	G	A	TP	PIM
1997-98	Team USA	Under-18	55	24	22	46	208	....	....	....	....	....
1998-99	U. of Wisconsin	WCHA	34	5	5	10	52	....	....	....	....	....
99-2000	U. of Wisconsin	WCHA	22	1	12	13	53	....	....	....	....	....

DONIKA, Mikhail (DAW-nih-ka) DAL.

Defense. Shoots left. 6', 185 lbs. Born, Yaroslavl, USSR, May 15, 1979.
(Dallas' 11th choice, 272nd overall, in 1999 Entry Draft).

			Regular Season					Playoffs				
Season	Club	Lea	GP	G	A	TP	PIM	GP	G	A	TP	PIM
1996-97	Torpedo Yaroslavl	Russia-3	15	3	5	8	6	....	....	....	....	....
	Torpedo Yaroslavl	Russia	22	1	0	1	6	2	0	0	0	0
1997-98	Torpedo Yaroslavl	Russia-2	19	1	2	3	32	....	....	....	....	....
	Torpedo Yaroslavl	Russia	30	0	2	2	14	....	....	....	....	....
1998-99	Torpedo Yaroslavl	Russia	37	0	1	1	10	....	....	....	....	....
	Torpedo Yaroslavl	Russia-3	6	2	1	3	4	....	....	....	....	....
99-2000	Torpedo Yaroslavl	Russia	35	0	1	1	22	10	0	0	0	4

DOYLE, Jason (DOIL, JAY-suhn)

Right wing. Shoots right. 6'1", 200 lbs. Born, Toronto, Ont., May 15, 1978.
(NY Islanders' 9th choice, 242nd overall, in 1998 Entry Draft).

			Regular Season					Playoffs				
Season	Club	Lea	GP	G	A	TP	PIM	GP	G	A	TP	PIM
1993-94	Wexford Hawks	MAHA	29	28	35	63	50	....	....	....	....	....
1994-95	London Knights	OHL	45	4	10	14	7	4	1	1	2	0
1995-96	London Knights	OHL	21	11	5	16	24	....	....	....	....	....
	Sault Ste. Marie	OHL	44	17	17	34	30	4	1	1	2	6
1996-97	Sault Ste. Marie	OHL	5	....	1	1	5	....	....	....	....	....
	Owen Sound	OHL	58	13	15	28	33	4	1	1	2	4
1997-98	Owen Sound	OHL	46	15	22	37	70	10	7	4	11	11
1998-99	Brampton	OHL	4	2	1	3	7	....	....	....	....	....
	London Knights	OHL	54	20	31	51	61	25	12	22	34	24
99-2000	UNB Varsity Reds	AUAA	21	4	4	8	12	7	2	1	3	2

• Re-entered NHL draft. Originally Boston's 4th choice, 80th overall, in 1996 Entry Draft.

DOYLE, Trevor (DOIL, TREH-vuhr)

Defense. Shoots right. 6'3", 216 lbs. Born, Ottawa, Ont., January 1, 1974.
(Florida's 9th choice, 161st overall, in 1993 Entry Draft).

			Regular Season					Playoffs				
Season	Club	Lea	GP	G	A	TP	PIM	GP	G	A	TP	PIM
1989-90	Nepean Raiders	OJHL	54	2	5	7	10	....	....	....	....	....
1990-91						DID NOT PLAY						
1991-92	Nepean Raiders	OJHL	1	0	1	1	2	....	....	....	....	....
	Kingston	OHL	26	0	1	1	19	....	....	....	....	....
1992-93	Kingston	OHL	62	1	8	9	148	16	2	3	5	25
1993-94	Kingston	OHL	53	2	12	14	246	3	0	0	0	4
1994-95	Cincinnati	IHL	52	0	3	3	139	6	0	0	0	13
1995-96	Carolina	AHL	48	1	2	3	117	....	....	....	....	....
1996-97	Carolina	AHL	47	3	10	13	288	....	....	....	....	....
1997-98	Fort Wayne	IHL	36	1	1	2	201	4	0	0	0	23
1998-99	Eisbaren Berlin	DEL	15	1	5	6	8	....	....	....	....	....
	Saint John Flames	AHL	2	0	0	0	5	....	....	....	....	....
	Michigan K-Wings	IHL	4	0	0	0	2	....	....	....	....	....
99-2000	Syracuse Crunch	AHL	77	2	6	8	235	....	....	....	....	....

DRANEY, Brett (DRAY-nee, BREHT) DAL.

Left wing. Shoots left. 6'1", 179 lbs. Born, Merritt, B.C., March 12, 1981.
(Dallas' 7th choice, 186th overall, in 1999 Entry Draft).

			Regular Season					Playoffs				
Season	Club	Lea	GP	G	A	TP	PIM	GP	G	A	TP	PIM
1996-97	Kamloops JV's	BCAHA	43	69	73	132	54	....	....	....	....	....
1997-98	Kamloops Blazers	WHL	42	2	2	4	16	7	0	0	0	0
1998-99	Kamloops Blazers	WHL	58	7	10	17	48	15	1	1	2	8
99-2000	Kamloops Blazers	WHL	62	18	27	45	63	4	1	1	2	11

DROZDETSKY, Alexander (drawz-DEHT-skee) PHI.

Right wing. Shoots left. 6', 174 lbs. Born, Moscow, USSR, October 11, 1981.
(Philadelphia's 2nd choice, 94th overall, in 2000 Entry Draft).

			Regular Season					Playoffs				
Season	Club	Lea	GP	G	A	TP	PIM	GP	G	A	TP	PIM
1997-98	St. Petersburg-2	Russia-3	19	0	1	1	0	....	....	....	....	....
1998-99	St. Petersburg-2	Russia-4	24	5	3	8	12	....	....	....	....	....
99-2000	St. Petersburg-2	Russia-3	4	4	1	5	2	....	....	....	....	....
	St. Petersburg	Russia	32	2	0	2	10	4	0	0	0	0

DUBEN, Premysl (DUH-behn, PREHM-uh-suhl) NYR

Defense. Shoots left. 6'3", 220 lbs. Born, Jihlava, Czech., October 5, 1981.
(NY Rangers' 3rd choice, 112th overall, in 2000 Entry Draft).

			Regular Season					Playoffs				
Season	Club	Lea	GP	G	A	TP	PIM	GP	G	A	TP	PIM
1997-98	Dukla Jihlava-Jr.	Cze-Rep	25	1	6	7	34	....	....	....	....	....
1998-99	Dukla Jihlava-Jr.	Cze-Rep	41	1	5	6	18	....	....	....	....	....
99-2000	Dukla Jihlava-Jr.	Cze-Rep	27	4	2	6	36	....	....	....	....	....
	Dukla Jihlava-2	Cze-Rep	19	0	1	1	10	14	0	1	1	4

DUCE, Bryan (DEWSE, BRIGH-an) N.J.

Right wing. Shoots right. 6', 200 lbs. Born, Thunder Bay, Ont., January 15, 1978.

			Regular Season					Playoffs				
Season	Club	Lea	GP	G	A	TP	PIM	GP	G	A	TP	PIM
1994-95	Thunder Bay	TBAHA	60	39	41	80	55	....	....	....	....	....
1995-96	Kitchener	OHL	55	14	9	23	16	11	0	0	0	2
1996-97	Kitchener	OHL	62	27	30	57	36	11	5	3	8	2
1997-98	Kitchener	OHL	37	9	20	29	12	....	....	....	....	....
	Sault Ste. Marie	OHL	21	3	2	5	4	....	....	....	....	....
1998-99	Albany River Rats	AHL	2	0	0	0	2	....	....	....	....	....
	Augusta Lynx	ECHL	68	17	27	44	33	2	0	0	0	0
99-2000	Augusta Lynx	ECHL	50	3	15	18	26	3	0	0	0	0

Signed as a free agent by **New Jersey**, August 12, 1997.

DUDA, Radek (DOO-duh, RA-dehk) CGY.

Right wing. Shoots left. 6'1", 193 lbs. Born, Skolov, Czech., January 28, 1979.
(Calgary's 7th choice, 192nd overall, in 1998 Entry Draft).

			Regular Season					Playoffs				
Season	Club	Lea	GP	G	A	TP	PIM	GP	G	A	TP	PIM
1994-95	Sokolov Praha-Jr.	Cze-Rep	36	67	37	104	....	....	....	....	....	....
1995-96	Sparta Praha-Jr.	Cze-Rep	39	15	10	25	....	....	....	....	....	....
1996-97	Sparta Praha-Jr.	Cze-Rep	21	9	14	23	....	....	....	....	....	....
	Sparta Praha-2	Cze-Rep	1	0	0	0	....	....	....	....	....	....
	Sparta Praha	Cze-Rep	....	....	....	....	....	1	0	0	0	0
1997-98	Sparta Praha	Cze-Rep	39	3	3	6	41	10	0	2	2	6
1998-99	Regina Pats	WHL	65	24	31	55	139	....	....	....	....	....
99-2000	Lethbridge	WHL	69	42	64	106	193	....	....	....	....	....

DUMA, Pavel (DOO-muh) VAN.

Center. Shoots left. 6'1", 183 lbs. Born, Karaganda, USSR, June 20, 1981.
(Vancouver's 4th choice, 144th overall, in 2000 Entry Draft).

			Regular Season					Playoffs				
Season	Club	Lea	GP	G	A	TP	PIM	GP	G	A	TP	PIM
1997-98	SK Nizhnekamsk	Russia-3	36	6	2	8	18	....	....	....	....	....
1998-99	SK Nizhnekamsk	Russia-4	34	13	12	25	20	....	....	....	....	....
	SK Nizhnekamsk	Russia	4	0	0	0	2	3	0	2	2	2
99-2000	SK Nizhnekamsk	Russia	29	2	5	7	14	....	....	....	....	....
	Ak Bars Kazan	Russia	8	0	1	1	2	7	0	0	0	2

DURAK, Miroslav (DOO-rak) NSH.

Defense. Shoots right. 6'4", 211 lbs. Born, Topolcany, Czech., June 9, 1981.
(Nashville's 14th choice, 220th overall, in 1999 Entry Draft).

			Regular Season					Playoffs				
Season	Club	Lea	GP	G	A	TP	PIM	GP	G	A	TP	PIM
1997-98	Slovan Bratislava	Slovak-Jr.	36	4	10	14	34	....	....	....	....	....
1998-99	Slovan Bratislava	Slovak-Jr.	38	1	7	8	48	....	....	....	....	....
99-2000	Des Moines	USHL	55	5	6	11	93	9	2	1	3	12

DUSBABEK, Joe (doo-sa-BEHK, JOH) S.J.

Right wing. Shoots right. 6'1", 200 lbs. Born, Fairbault, MN, May 1, 1978.
(San Jose's 5th choice, 163rd overall, in 1997 Entry Draft).

			Regular Season					Playoffs				
Season	Club	Lea	GP	G	A	TP	PIM	GP	G	A	TP	PIM
1996-97	Notre Dame	CCHA	35	13	12	25	74	....	....	....	....	....
1997-98	Notre Dame	CCHA	21	1	8	9	32	....	....	....	....	....
1998-99	Notre Dame	CCHA	34	4	10	14	36	....	....	....	....	....
99-2000	Notre Dame	CCHA	37	8	19	27	30	....	....	....	....	....

DYMENT, Chris (DIGH-mehnt, KRIHS) MTL.

Defense. Shoots right. 6'3", 201 lbs. Born, Stoneham, MA, October 24, 1979.
(Montreal's 3rd choice, 97th overall, in 1999 Entry Draft).

			Regular Season					Playoffs				
Season	Club	Lea	GP	G	A	TP	PIM	GP	G	A	TP	PIM
1997-98	Reading High	Hi-School	22	22	22	44	15	....	....	....	....	....
1998-99	Boston University	H-East	25	1	5	6	16	....	....	....	....	....
99-2000	Boston University	H-East	42	11	20	31	42	....	....	....	....	....

Hockey East First All-Star Team (2000) • NCAA East Second All-American Team (2000)

EADE, Chris (EE-dee) FLA.

Defense. Shoots right. 6'1", 196 lbs. Born, Etobicoke, Ont., April 20, 1982.
(Florida's 4th choice, 115th overall, in 2000 Entry Draft).

			Regular Season					Playoffs				
Season	Club	Lea	GP	G	A	TP	PIM	GP	G	A	TP	PIM
1997-98	Oshawa Legion	OJHL	45	10	13	23	186	....	....	....	....	....
1998-99	North Bay	OHL	46	1	6	7	32	4	0	0	0	0
99-2000	North Bay	OHL	58	5	25	30	64	3	0	0	0	4

EAGLES, Travis (EE-guhls) FLA.

Right wing. Shoots right. 6'3", 208 lbs. Born, Estevan, Sask., May 5, 1981.
(Florida's 8th choice, 198th overall, in 1999 Entry Draft).

			Regular Season					Playoffs				
Season	Club	Lea	GP	G	A	TP	PIM	GP	G	A	TP	PIM
1997-98	Saskatoon Blazers	SAHA	28	13	25	38	16	....	....	....	....	....
1998-99	Prince George	WHL	48	1	9	10	66	5	0	0	0	8
99-2000	Prince George	WHL	59	8	15	23	81	13	4	0	4	17

EDINGER, Adam (EH-dihn-juhr, A-dam) NYI

Center. Shoots left. 6'2", 210 lbs. Born, Toledo, OH, September 21, 1977.
(NY Islanders' 7th choice, 115th overall, in 1997 Entry Draft).

			Regular Season					Playoffs				
Season	Club	Lea	GP	G	A	TP	PIM	GP	G	A	TP	PIM
1994-95	Leamington Flyers	OJHL	38	19	62	81	100	....	....	....	....	....
1995-96	Leamington Flyers	OJHL	45	45	50	95	120	....	....	....	....	....
1996-97	Bowling Green	CCHA	34	11	18	29	42	....	....	....	....	....
1997-98	Bowling Green	CCHA	27	9	13	22	62	....	....	....	....	....
1998-99	Bowling Green	CCHA	38	23	25	48	36	....	....	....	....	....
99-2000	Bowling Green	CCHA	36	14	18	32	34	....	....	....	....	....
	Trenton Titans	ECHL	3	3	1	4	0	....	....	....	....	....

CCHA First All-Star Team (1999)

ELOFSSON, Jonas (EHL-uhf-suhn, YEW-nuhs) CHI.

Defense. Shoots left. 6'1", 180 lbs. Born, Ulricehamn, Sweden, January 31, 1979.
(Edmonton's 4th choice, 94th overall, in 1997 Entry Draft).

			Regular Season					Playoffs				
Season	Club	Lea	GP	G	A	TP	PIM	GP	G	A	TP	PIM
1995-96	Farjestads BK	Swede-Jr.	26	6	11	17	18	....	....	....	....	....
1996-97	Farjestads BK	Sweden	3	0	0	0	0	5	0	1	1	0
	Farjestads BK	EuroHL	2	1	1	2	0	....	....	....	....	....
1997-98	Farjestads BK	Sweden	29	3	2	5	14	12	0	1	1	6
	Farjestads BK	EuroHL	7	1	1	2	4	....	....	....	....	....
1998-99	Farjestads BK	Sweden	40	2	7	9	18	4	0	0	0	0
	Farjestads BK	EuroHL	5	1	0	1	4	....	....	....	....	....
99-2000	Farjestads BK	Sweden	47	3	6	9	44	4	0	0	0	6

Traded to **Chicago** by **Edmonton** with Boris Mironov and Dean McAmmond for Chad Kilger, Daniel Cleary, Ethan Moreau and Christian Laflamme, March 20, 1999.

ELOMO, Teemu (eh-LOH-moh, TEE-moo) DAL.

Left wing. Shoots left. 5'11", 176 lbs. Born, Turku, Finland, January 13, 1979.
(Dallas' 5th choice, 132nd overall, in 1997 Entry Draft).

			Regular Season					Playoffs				
Season	Club	Lea	GP	G	A	TP	PIM	GP	G	A	TP	PIM
1993-94	TPS Turku-C	Finn-Jr.	34	7	25	32	56	....	....	....	....	....
1994-95	TPS Turku-C	Finn-Jr.	24	19	22	41	82	....	....	....	....	....
	TPS Turku-B	Finn-Jr.	8	5	2	7	12	2	1	0	1	0
1995-96	TPS Turku-B	Finn-Jr.	17	9	8	17	28	....	....	....	....	....
	TPS Turku	Finn-Jr.	2	0	0	0	0	....	....	....	....	....
	Kiekko-67	Finland-2	11	1	0	1	14	6	2	0	2	8
1996-97	TPS Turku	Finn-Jr.	9	6	2	8	16	....	....	....	....	....
	Kiekko-67	Finland-2	15	4	3	7	24	....	....	....	....	....
	TPS Turku	Finland	6	0	1	1	0	3	0	0	0	2
1997-98	TPS Turku	Finland	26	3	3	6	14	3	1	0	1	2
	TPS Turku	EuroHL	3	0	0	0	2	....	....	....	....	....
1998-99	TPS Turku	Finland	34	4	8	12	16	5	0	0	0	2
99-2000	TPS Turku	Finland	52	9	7	16	28	11	3	2	5	0

ENDICOTT, Shane (ehn-DIH-kawt) PIT.

Center. Shoots left. 6'4", 200 lbs. Born, Saskatoon, Sask., December 21, 1981.
(Pittsburgh's 2nd choice, 52nd overall, in 2000 Entry Draft).

			Regular Season					Playoffs				
Season	Club	Lea	GP	G	A	TP	PIM	GP	G	A	TP	PIM
1997-98	Saskatoon Blazers	SAHA	43	31	32	63	42	....	....	....	....	....
	Seattle T-Birds	WHL	5	0	0	0	0	....	....	....	....	....
1998-99	Seattle T-Birds	WHL	72	13	26	39	27	11	0	1	1	0
99-2000	Seattle T-Birds	WHL	70	23	32	55	62	7	1	6	7	6

ENEQVIST, Johan (EHN-uh-kvist, YOH-han) MTL.

Center. Shoots left. 6', 183 lbs. Born, Nacka, Sweden, January 21, 1982.
(Montreal's 5th choice, 109th overall, in 2000 Entry Draft).

			Regular Season					Playoffs				
Season	Club	Lea	GP	G	A	TP	PIM	GP	G	A	TP	PIM
99-2000	Leksands IF	Swede-Jr.	36	10	13	23	36	2	0	0	0	0

ERAT, Martin (AIR-at) NSH.

Left wing. Shoots left. 6', 197 lbs. Born, Trebic, Czech., August 28, 1981.
(Nashville's 12th choice, 191st overall, in 1999 Entry Draft).

			Regular Season					Playoffs				
Season	Club	Lea	GP	G	A	TP	PIM	GP	G	A	TP	PIM
1997-98	ZPS Zlin-Jr.	Cze-Rep	46	35	30	65	....	....	....	....	....	....
1998-99	ZPS Zlin-Jr.	Cze-Rep	35	21	23	44	....	....	....	....	....	....
	ZPS Zlin	Cze-Rep	5	0	0	0	2	....	....	....	....	....
99-2000	Saskatoon Blades	WHL	66	27	26	53	82	11	4	8	12	16

ERSKINE, John (AIR-skign, JAWN) DAL.

Defense. Shoots left. 6'4", 211 lbs. Born, Kingston, Ont., June 26, 1980.
(Dallas' 1st choice, 39th overall, in 1998 Entry Draft).

			Regular Season					Playoffs				
Season	Club	Lea	GP	G	A	TP	PIM	GP	G	A	TP	PIM
1996-97	Quinte Hawks	OJHL	48	4	16	20	241	....	....	....	....	....
1997-98	London Knights	OHL	55	0	9	9	205	16	0	5	5	25
1998-99	London Knights	OHL	57	8	12	20	208	25	5	10	15	38
99-2000	London Knights	OHL	58	12	31	43	177	....	....	....	....	....

OHL First All-Star Team (2000)

EVANS, Blake (EH-vans, BLAYK) WSH.

Center. Shoots right. 6'1", 221 lbs. Born, Kindersley, Sask., July 2, 1980.
(Washington's 10th choice, 251st overall, in 1998 Entry Draft).

			Regular Season					Playoffs				
Season	Club	Lea	GP	G	A	TP	PIM	GP	G	A	TP	PIM
1995-96	Saskatoon	SAHA	41	15	23	38	84	....	....	....	....	....
1996-97	Spokane Chiefs	WHL	53	4	7	11	19	7	0	0	0	0
1997-98	Spokane Chiefs	WHL	16	6	5	11	29	....	....	....	....	....
	Tri-City Americans	WHL	57	13	29	42	102	....	....	....	....	....
1998-99	Tri-City Americans	WHL	72	18	29	47	131	12	0	4	4	16
99-2000	Tri-City Americans	WHL	72	27	43	70	110	4	1	0	1	6

EVANS, David (EHV-vuhns) CAR.

Center. Shoots right. 6'3", 185 lbs. Born, Albany, NY, February 17, 1980.
(Carolina's 7th choice, 231st overall, in 1999 Entry Draft).

			Regular Season					Playoffs				
Season	Club	Lea	GP	G	A	TP	PIM	GP	G	A	TP	PIM
1997-98	Capital District	X-Games	51	53	60	113	....	....	....	....	....	....
1998-99	Clarkson	ECAC	33	6	10	16	6	....	....	....	....	....
99-2000	Clarkson	ECAC	34	11	17	28	18	....	....	....	....	....

EXELBY, Garnet (EHX-uhl-bee) ATL.

Defense. Shoots left. 6'1", 194 lbs. Born, Craik, Sask., August 16, 1981.
(Atlanta's 9th choice, 217th overall, in 1999 Entry Draft).

			Regular Season					Playoffs				
Season	Club	Lea	GP	G	A	TP	PIM	GP	G	A	TP	PIM
1997-98	Winnipeg Blues	MJHL	46	5	11	16	110	....	....	....	....	....
1998-99	Saskatoon Blades	WHL	61	5	3	8	91	....	....	....	....	....
99-2000	Saskatoon Blades	WHL	63	1	8	9	79	11	0	2	2	21

FADRNY, Jan (FAHD-uhr-nee, YAN) PIT.

Center. Shoots right. 6', 182 lbs. Born, Brno, Czech., June 14, 1980.
(Pittsburgh's 6th choice, 169th overall, in 1998 Entry Draft).

			Regular Season					Playoffs				
Season	Club	Lea	GP	G	A	TP	PIM	GP	G	A	TP	PIM
1995-96	Kometa Brno-Jr.	Cze-Rep	36	22	15	37	26	....	....	....	....	....
1996-97	HC Olomouc-Jr.	Cze-Rep	38	16	24	40	32	....	....	....	....	....
1997-98	Slavia Praha-Jr.	Cze-Rep	14	7	4	11	12	....	....	....	....	....
	Slavia Praha	Cze-Rep	18	1	1	2	2	3	0	0	0	4
1998-99	Brandon	WHL	45	4	17	21	36	5	1	2	3	4
99-2000	Brandon	WHL	55	26	25	51	56	....	....	....	....	....

FAHEY, Brian (FAY-hee) COL.

Defense. Shoots right. 6', 200 lbs. Born, Des Plaines, IL, March 2, 1981.
(Colorado's 7th choice, 119th overall, in 2000 Entry Draft).

			Regular Season					Playoffs				
Season	Club	Lea	GP	G	A	TP	PIM	GP	G	A	TP	PIM
1997-98	Team USA	Under-18	52	9	9	18	....	....	....	....	....	....
1998-99	Team USA	Under-18	68	7	21	28	....	....	....	....	....	....
99-2000	U. of Wisconsin	WCHA	41	6	11	17	42	1	0	0	0	2

WCHA All-Rookie Team (2000)

FAHEY, Jim (FA-hee, JIHM) S.J.

Defense. Shoots right. 6', 215 lbs. Born, Boston, MA, May 11, 1979.
(San Jose's 9th choice, 212th overall, in 1998 Entry Draft).

			Regular Season					Playoffs				
Season	Club	Lea	GP	G	A	TP	PIM	GP	G	A	TP	PIM
1997-98	Catholic Memorial	Hi-School	24	12	32	44	28	....	....	....	....	....
1998-99	Northeastern	H-East	32	5	13	18	34	....	....	....	....	....
99-2000	Northeastern	H-East	36	3	17	20	62	....	....	....	....	....

FARRELL, Michael (FAHR-ehl, MIHK-ehl) WSH.

Defense. Shoots right. 6'1", 205 lbs. Born, Edina, MN, October 20, 1978.
(Washington's 9th choice, 220th overall, in 1998 Entry Draft).

			Regular Season					Playoffs				
Season	Club	Lea	GP	G	A	TP	PIM	GP	G	A	TP	PIM
1997-98	Providence	H-East	33	5	8	13	32	....	....	....	....	....
1998-99	Providence	H-East	29	3	12	15	51	....	....	....	....	....
99-2000	Providence	H-East	36	3	6	9	71	....	....	....	....	....
	Portland Pirates	AHL	7	2	0	2	0	4	0	1	1	0

FAST, Brad (FAST, BRAD) CAR.

Defense. Shoots left. 6', 185 lbs. Born, Fort St. John, B.C., February 21, 1980.
(Carolina's 2nd choice, 84th overall, in 1999 Entry Draft).

			Regular Season					Playoffs				
Season	Club	Lea	GP	G	A	TP	PIM	GP	G	A	TP	PIM
1994-95	Fort St. John	BCAHA	40	9	26	35	40	....	....	....	....	....
1995-96	Fort St. John	BCAHA	60	53	52	105	70	....	....	....	....	....
1996-97	Prince George	BCJHL	49	3	7	10	19	....	....	....	....	....
1997-98	Prince George	BCJHL	59	10	33	43	22	....	....	....	....	....
1998-99	Prince George	BCJHL	59	27	46	73	....	....	....	....	....	....
99-2000	Michigan State	CCHA	42	5	9	14	20	....	....	....	....	....

FAUTEUX, Jonathan (foh-TOH, JOHN-a-THAN) EDM.

Defense. Shoots right. 6'2", 232 lbs. Born, Terrebone, Que., December 3, 1980.
(Edmonton's 6th choice, 139th overall, in 1999 Entry Draft).

			Regular Season					Playoffs				
Season	Club	Lea	GP	G	A	TP	PIM	GP	G	A	TP	PIM
1995-96	Cap-d-Madelaine	QAAA	37	0	6	6	52	....	....	....	....	....
1996-97	Val-d'Or Foreurs	QMJHL	62	1	2	3	26	13	1	0	1	4
1997-98	Val-d'Or Foreurs	QMJHL	56	4	10	14	74	4	0	1	1	4
1998-99	Val-d'Or Foreurs	QMJHL	59	15	33	48	139	6	1	2	3	8
99-2000	Val-d'Or Foreurs	QMJHL	19	6	7	13	34	....	....	....	....	....
	Victoriaville Tigres	QMJHL	18	4	1	5	36	6	2	2	4	12

FEDOROV, Fedor (FEH-duh-rahf, feh-DUHR) T.B.

Center. Shoots left. 6'3", 187 lbs. Born, Moscow, USSR, June 11, 1981.
(Tampa Bay's 7th choice, 182nd overall, in 1999 Entry Draft).

			Regular Season					Playoffs				
Season	Club	Lea	GP	G	A	TP	PIM	GP	G	A	TP	PIM
1997-98	Detroit Caesars	MNHL	13	3	7	10	18	....	....	....	....	....
1998-99	Port Huron	UHL	42	2	5	7	20	....	....	....	....	....
99-2000	Windsor	OHL	60	7	10	17	115	12	1	0	1	4

FEDORUK, Todd (FEH-duh-ruhk, TAWD) PHI.

Left wing. Shoots left. 6'1", 205 lbs. Born, Redwater, Alta., February 13, 1979.
(Philadelphia's 6th choice, 164th overall, in 1997 Entry Draft).

			Regular Season					Playoffs				
Season	Club	Lea	GP	G	A	TP	PIM	GP	G	A	TP	PIM
1995-96	Kelowna Rockets	WHL	44	1	1	2	83	4	0	0	0	6
1996-97	Kelowna Rockets	WHL	31	1	5	6	87	6	0	0	0	13
1997-98	Kelowna Rockets	WHL	31	3	5	8	120	....	....	....	....	....
	Regina Pats	WHL	21	4	3	7	80	9	1	2	3	23
1998-99	Regina Pats	WHL	39	12	12	24	107	....	....	....	....	....
	Prince Albert	WHL	28	6	4	10	75	13	1	6	7	49
99-2000	Philadelphia	AHL	19	1	2	3	40	5	0	1	1	2
	Trenton Titans	ECHL	18	2	5	7	118	....	....	....	....	....

FEDOTENKO, Ruslan PHI.

Center. Shoots left. 6'2", 191 lbs. Born, Kiev, Ukraine, January 18, 1970.

			Regular Season					Playoffs				
Season	Club	Lea	GP	G	A	TP	PIM	GP	G	A	TP	PIM
1997-98	Melfort Mustangs	SJHL	68	35	31	66	....	....	....	....	....	....
1998-99	Sioux City	USHL	55	43	34	77	139	5	5	1	6	9
99-2000	Trenton Titans	ECHL	8	5	3	8	9	....	....	....	....	....
	Philadelphia	AHL	67	16	34	50	42	2	0	0	0	0

Signed as a free agent by **Philadelphia**, August 3, 1999.

FEIL, Chris (FEHL, KRIHS) CHI.

Defense. Shoots left. 6'2", 202 lbs. Born, Orland Park, IL, April 25, 1978.
(Chicago's 11th choice, 230th overall, in 1997 Entry Draft).

			Regular Season					Playoffs				
Season	**Club**	**Lea**	**GP**	**G**	**A**	**TP**	**PIM**	**GP**	**G**	**A**	**TP**	**PIM**
1996-97	Ohio State	CCHA	33	5	4	9	119	....	....	....	....	....
1997-98	Barrie Colts	OHL	40	3	16	19	51	6	0	0	0	15
1998-99	Barrie Colts	OHL	67	10	31	41	158	12	1	6	7	25
99-2000	Trenton Titans	ECHL	43	2	2	4	70	....	....	....	....	....
	Cleveland	IHL	3	0	0	0	2	....	....	....	....	....

FENIAK, Jeff (FEH-nee-ak) PHI.

Defense. Shoots left. 6'5", 210 lbs. Born, Edmonton, Alta., January 31, 1981.
(Philadelphia's 2nd choice, 119th overall, in 1999 Entry Draft).

			Regular Season					Playoffs				
Season	**Club**	**Lea**	**GP**	**G**	**A**	**TP**	**PIM**	**GP**	**G**	**A**	**TP**	**PIM**
1997-98	Calgary Hitmen	WHL	48	0	2	2	25	4	0	0	0	0
1998-99	Calgary Hitmen	WHL	39	1	4	5	81	17	0	1	1	16
99-2000	Calgary Hitmen	WHL	29	0	6	6	106	....	....	....	....	....
	Tri-City Americans	WHL	45	1	7	8	106	4	0	0	0	12

FIBIGER, Jesse (feh-BEH-gehr, JEH-see) ANA.

Defense. Shoots left. 6'3", 205 lbs. Born, Victoria, B.C., April 4, 1978.
(Anaheim's 5th choice, 178th overall, in 1998 Entry Draft).

			Regular Season					Playoffs				
Season	**Club**	**Lea**	**GP**	**G**	**A**	**TP**	**PIM**	**GP**	**G**	**A**	**TP**	**PIM**
1996-97	Victoria Salsa	BCJHL	53	6	18	24	88	....	....	....	....	....
1997-98	Minnesota-Duluth	WCHA	40	3	6	9	82	....	....	....	....	....
1998-99	Minnesota-Duluth	WCHA	36	4	16	20	61	....	....	....	....	....
99-2000	Minnesota-Duluth	WCHA	37	4	6	10	83	....	....	....	....	....

FILIPOWICZ, Jayme (fihl-ih-POW-its) NSH.

Defense. Shoots left. 6'2", 215 lbs. Born, Arlington Heights, IL, June 15, 1976.

			Regular Season					Playoffs				
Season	**Club**	**Lea**	**GP**	**G**	**A**	**TP**	**PIM**	**GP**	**G**	**A**	**TP**	**PIM**
1996-97	New Hampshire	H-East	35	3	16	19	43	....	....	....	....	....
1997-98	New Hampshire	H-East	38	3	28	31	47	....	....	....	....	....
1998-99	New Hampshire	H-East	41	8	30	38	56	....	....	....	....	....
99-2000	Milwaukee	IHL	76	9	23	32	118	3	0	1	1	0

Hockey East First All-Star Team (1999) • NCAA East Second All-American Team (1999) • NCAA Championship All-Tournament Team (1999)

Signed as a free agent by **Nashville**, June 17, 1999.

FINGER, Jeff (FIHN-guhr) COL.

Defense. Shoots right. 6'1", 195 lbs. Born, Hancock, MI, December 18, 1979.
(Colorado's 11th choice, 240th overall, in 1999 Entry Draft).

			Regular Season					Playoffs				
Season	**Club**	**Lea**	**GP**	**G**	**A**	**TP**	**PIM**	**GP**	**G**	**A**	**TP**	**PIM**
1997-98	Green Bay	USHL	51	5	9	14	208	4	0	0	0	18
1998-99	Green Bay	USHL	54	11	28	39	199	6	0	3	3	14
99-2000	Green Bay	USHL	55	13	35	48	15	5	1	6	7	22

FINNSTROM, Johan (FIHN-struhm, YOH-hahn) CGY.

Defense. Shoots left. 6'3", 205 lbs. Born, Broby, Sweden, March 27, 1976.
(Calgary's 5th choice, 97th overall, in 1994 Entry Draft).

			Regular Season					Playoffs				
Season	**Club**	**Lea**	**GP**	**G**	**A**	**TP**	**PIM**	**GP**	**G**	**A**	**TP**	**PIM**
1993-94	Rogle Angelholm	Sweden	7	1	1	2	2	....	....	....	....	....
1994-95	Rogle Angelholm	Sweden	19	0	0	0	10	....	....	....	....	....
1995-96	Rogle Angelholm	Sweden	18	0	0	0	10	....	....	....	....	....
1996-97	Rogle Angelholm	Swede-2	31	1	5	6	59	....	....	....	....	....
1997-98	Lulea HF	Sweden	45	0	1	1	17	3	0	0	0	0
	Lulea HF	EuroHL	6	0	0	0	4	....	....	....	....	....
1998-99	Lulea HF	Sweden	49	1	8	9	63	9	0	4	4	12
99-2000	Lulea HF	Sweden	46	1	4	5	71	9	0	0	0	4

FITZGERALD, Randy (FIHTZ-jer-awld, RAN-dee) MIN.

Left wing. Shoots left. 5'11", 174 lbs. Born, Toronto, Ont., September 5, 1979.
(Carolina's 8th choice, 199th overall, in 1997 Entry Draft).

			Regular Season					Playoffs				
Season	**Club**	**Lea**	**GP**	**G**	**A**	**TP**	**PIM**	**GP**	**G**	**A**	**TP**	**PIM**
1995-96	Markham Waxers	OJHL	46	17	17	34	79	....	....	....	....	....
1996-97	Detroit Whalers	OHL	65	12	18	30	123	5	0	1	1	13
1997-98	Plymouth Whalers	OHL	54	11	24	35	104	15	6	3	9	46
1998-99	Plymouth Whalers	OHL	64	15	34	49	144	11	3	7	10	16
99-2000	Plymouth Whalers	OHL	50	18	24	42	89	23	13	10	23	47

Signed as a free agent by **Minnesota**, June 14, 2000.

FLACHE, Paul (FLACH) EDM.

Defense. Shoots right. 6'5", 195 lbs. Born, Toronto, Ont., March 4, 1982.
(Edmonton's 5th choice, 152nd overall, in 2000 Entry Draft).

			Regular Season					Playoffs				
Season	**Club**	**Lea**	**GP**	**G**	**A**	**TP**	**PIM**	**GP**	**G**	**A**	**TP**	**PIM**
1998-99	Cobourg	OJHL-B	41	1	6	7	50	....	....	....	....	....
99-2000	Brampton	OHL	54	1	0	1	59	6	0	0	0	8

FLINN, Ryan (FLIHN, RIGH-yan)

Left wing. Shoots left. 6'4", 210 lbs. Born, Halifax, N.S., April 20, 1980.
(New Jersey's 8th choice, 143rd overall, in 1998 Entry Draft).

			Regular Season					Playoffs				
Season	**Club**	**Lea**	**GP**	**G**	**A**	**TP**	**PIM**	**GP**	**G**	**A**	**TP**	**PIM**
1996-97	Laval Titan	QMJHL	23	3	2	5	56	2	0	0	0	0
1997-98	Laval Titan	QMJHL	59	4	12	16	217	15	1	0	1	63
1998-99	Acadie-Bathurst	QMJHL	44	3	4	7	195	23	2	0	2	37
99-2000	Halifax	QMJHL	67	14	19	33	365	....	....	....	....	....

FOCHT, Dan (FOHKT, DAN) PHX.

Defense. Shoots left. 6'6", 240 lbs. Born, Regina, Sask., December 31, 1977.
(Phoenix's 1st choice, 11th overall, in 1996 Entry Draft).

			Regular Season					Playoffs				
Season	**Club**	**Lea**	**GP**	**G**	**A**	**TP**	**PIM**	**GP**	**G**	**A**	**TP**	**PIM**
1994-95	Saskatoon Blazers	SAHA	33	6	12	18	98	....	....	....	....	....
1995-96	Tri-City Americans	WHL	63	6	12	18	161	11	1	1	2	23
1996-97	Tri-City Americans	WHL	28	0	5	5	92	....	....	....	....	....
	Regina Pats	WHL	22	2	2	4	59	5	0	2	2	8
	Springfield	AHL	1	0	0	0	2	....	....	....	....	....
1997-98	Springfield	AHL	61	2	5	7	125	3	0	0	0	4
1998-99	Mississippi	ECHL	2	0	0	0	6	....	....	....	....	....
	Springfield	AHL	30	0	2	2	58	3	1	0	1	10
99-2000	Jokerit Helsinki	Finland	2	0	0	0	0	....	....	....	....	....
	Mississippi	ECHL	4	0	1	1	0	....	....	....	....	....
	Springfield	AHL	44	2	9	11	86	5	0	1	1	2

FORBES, Ian (FOHRBS, EE-an) PHI.

Defense. Shoots left. 6'6", 180 lbs. Born, Brampton, Ont., August 2, 1980.
(Philadelphia's 3rd choice, 51st overall, in 1998 Entry Draft).

			Regular Season					Playoffs				
Season	**Club**	**Lea**	**GP**	**G**	**A**	**TP**	**PIM**	**GP**	**G**	**A**	**TP**	**PIM**
1996-97	Mississauga Reps	MTHL	39	10	32	42	178	....	....	....	....	....
1997-98	Guelph Platers	OJHL-B	3	0	1	1	19	....	....	....	....	....
	Guelph Storm	OHL	61	2	3	5	164	12	0	0	0	16
1998-99	Guelph Storm	OHL	60	1	8	9	182	5	0	1	1	8
99-2000	Guelph Storm	OHL	62	2	7	9	143	6	0	0	0	11

FORSANDER, Johan (fohr-SAHN-duhr, YOH-hahn) DET.

Left wing. Shoots left. 6'1", 174 lbs. Born, Jonkoping, Sweden, April 28, 1978.
(Detroit's 3rd choice, 108th overall, in 1996 Entry Draft).

			Regular Season					Playoffs				
Season	**Club**	**Lea**	**GP**	**G**	**A**	**TP**	**PIM**	**GP**	**G**	**A**	**TP**	**PIM**
1995-96	HV Jonkoping	Swede-Jr.	27	15	8	23	12	....	....	....	....	....
	HV Jonkoping	Sweden	6	0	0	0	0	3	0	0	0	2
1996-97	HV Jonkoping	Sweden	44	3	2	5	6	5	0	0	0	0
1997-98	HV Jonkoping	Sweden	46	3	2	5	12	5	0	0	0	0
1998-99	HV Jonkoping	Sweden	48	5	4	9	6	....	....	....	....	....
99-2000	HV Jonkoping	Sweden	48	9	9	18	6	6	0	0	0	4

FORSTER, Nathan (FOHRS-tuhr, NAY-than) WSH.

Defense. Shoots right. 6'1", 195 lbs. Born, Vancouver, B.C., July 3, 1980.
(Washington's 7th choice, 179th overall, in 1998 Entry Draft).

			Regular Season					Playoffs				
Season	**Club**	**Lea**	**GP**	**G**	**A**	**TP**	**PIM**	**GP**	**G**	**A**	**TP**	**PIM**
1995-96	Victoria Lions	BCAHA	49	25	48	73	122	....	....	....	....	....
1996-97	Seattle T-Birds	WHL	22	1	2	3	39	4	0	0	0	0
1997-98	Seattle T-Birds	WHL	68	1	12	13	153	5	0	1	1	8
1998-99	Seattle T-Birds	WHL	65	5	17	22	153	10	0	2	2	26
99-2000	Seattle T-Birds	WHL	51	9	28	37	104	7	1	4	5	30

FORTIER, Francois (FOHR-tay, FRAN-swaw) NYR

Left wing. Shoots left. 5'11", 194 lbs. Born, Beauport, Que., June 13, 1979.

			Regular Season					Playoffs				
Season	**Club**	**Lea**	**GP**	**G**	**A**	**TP**	**PIM**	**GP**	**G**	**A**	**TP**	**PIM**
1995-96	Ste-Foy Governors	QAAA	41	16	17	33	36	....	....	....	....	....
1996-97	Sherbrooke	QMJHL	62	21	16	37	74	3	0	2	2	2
1997-98	Sherbrooke	QMJHL	70	36	52	88	42	....	....	....	....	....
1998-99	Sherbrooke	QMJHL	48	36	40	76	8	13	6	9	15	4
	Hartford	AHL	1	0	0	0	0	....	....	....	....	....
99-2000	Hartford	AHL	63	6	9	15	14	....	....	....	....	....

Signed as a free agent by **NY Rangers**, October 5, 1998.

FORTIN, Jean-Francois (fohr-TEHN, JEHN-fran-SWUH) WSH.

Defense. Shoots right. 6'2", 200 lbs. Born, Laval, Que., March 15, 1979.
(Washington's 2nd choice, 35th overall, in 1997 Entry Draft).

			Regular Season					Playoffs				
Season	**Club**	**Lea**	**GP**	**G**	**A**	**TP**	**PIM**	**GP**	**G**	**A**	**TP**	**PIM**
1993-94	Laval Regents	QAAA	31	8	20	28	32	....	....	....	....	....
1994-95	Amos Regents	QAAA	44	2	14	16	34	....	....	....	....	....
1995-96	Sherbrooke	QMJHL	69	7	15	22	40	7	2	6	8	2
1996-97	Sherbrooke	QMJHL	59	7	30	37	89	2	0	1	1	14
1997-98	Sherbrooke	QMJHL	55	12	25	37	37	....	....	....	....	....
1998-99	Sherbrooke	QMJHL	64	17	33	50	78	12	5	13	18	20
99-2000	Portland	AHL	43	3	5	8	44	2	0	0	0	0
	Hampton Roads	ECHL	7	0	2	2	0	....	....	....	....	....

FOSTER, Kurtis (FAW-stuhr) CGY.

Defense. Shoots right. 6'5", 205 lbs. Born, Carp, Ont., November 24, 1981.
(Calgary's 2nd choice, 40th overall, in 2000 Entry Draft).

			Regular Season					Playoffs				
Season	**Club**	**Lea**	**GP**	**G**	**A**	**TP**	**PIM**	**GP**	**G**	**A**	**TP**	**PIM**
1997-98	Ottawa Valley	OMHA	36	7	18	25	88	....	....	....	....	....
1998-99	Peterborough	OHL	54	2	13	15	59	5	0	0	0	6
99-2000	Peterborough	OHL	68	6	18	24	116	5	1	2	3	4

FRANCZ, Robert (FRANZ, RAW-behrt) PHX.

Left wing. Shoots left. 6'2", 210 lbs. Born, Bad Muskau, East Germany, March 30, 1978.
(Phoenix's 4th choice, 151st overall, in 1997 Entry Draft).

			Regular Season					Playoffs				
Season	**Club**	**Lea**	**GP**	**G**	**A**	**TP**	**PIM**	**GP**	**G**	**A**	**TP**	**PIM**
1995-96	Augsburger EV	DEL-Jr.	7	1	1	2	62	....	....	....	....	....
	Augsburger EV	DEL	36	0	1	1	43	6	0	0	0	0
1996-97	Peterborough	OHL	60	9	21	30	149	8	1	1	2	17
1997-98	Peterborough	OHL	60	24	27	51	135	4	1	0	1	10
1998-99	Peterborough	OHL	65	25	32	57	171	5	0	2	2	12
	Springfield	AHL	2	1	0	1	4	1	0	0	0	0
99-2000	Springfield	AHL	36	0	3	3	89	2	0	0	0	0
	Mississippi	ECHL	16	7	4	11	56	....	....	....	....	....

FRIED, Robert (FREED) FLA.

Right wing. Shoots right. 6'3", 200 lbs. Born, Philadelphia, PA, March 8, 1981.
(Florida's 2nd choice, 77th overall, in 2000 Entry Draft).

			Regular Season					Playoffs				
Season	**Club**	**Lea**	**GP**	**G**	**A**	**TP**	**PIM**	**GP**	**G**	**A**	**TP**	**PIM**
1998-99	Deerfield Academy	Hi-School	24	13	20	33	28	....	....	....	....	....
99-2000	Deerfield Academy	Hi-School	26	25	20	45	35	....	....	....	....	....

FROGREN, Jonas (FREW-grehn, YOH-nuhs) CGY.

Defense. Shoots left. 6'1", 190 lbs. Born, Falun, Sweden, August 28, 1980.
(Calgary's 8th choice, 206th overall, in 1998 Entry Draft).

			Regular Season					Playoffs				
Season	Club	Lea	GP	G	A	TP	PIM	GP	G	A	TP	PIM
1996-97	Farjestads BK	Swede-Jr.	20	2	7	9	4	....	....	....	....	....
1997-98	Farjestads BK	Swede-Jr.	28	5	6	11	12	2	1	0	1	0
1998-99	Farjestads BK	Swede-Jr.	14	1	5	6	12	....	....	....	....	....
	Farjestads BK	Sweden	22	0	0	0	2	....	....	....	....	....
99-2000	Bofors IF	Swede-2	43	2	7	9	40	....	....	....	....	....

FROLOV, Alexander (froh-LAHF) L.A.

Left wing. Shoots right. 6'4", 191 lbs. Born, Moscow, USSR, June 19, 1982.
(Los Angeles' 1st choice, 20th overall, in 2000 Entry Draft).

			Regular Season					Playoffs				
Season	Club	Lea	GP	G	A	TP	PIM	GP	G	A	TP	PIM
1998-99	Spartak Moscow	Russia-Q	1	0	0	0	0	....	....	....	....	....
99-2000	Torpedo Yaroslavl	Russia-3	36	27	13	40	30	....	....	....	....	....

FRYLEN, Edvin (FREE-ew-lihn, EHD-vihn) ST.L.

Defense. Shoots left. 6', 211 lbs. Born, Jarfalla, Sweden, December 23, 1975.
(St. Louis' 3rd choice, 120th overall, in 1994 Entry Draft).

			Regular Season					Playoffs				
Season	Club	Lea	GP	G	A	TP	PIM	GP	G	A	TP	PIM
1991-92	Vasteras IK	Sweden	2	0	0	0	0	....	....	....	....	....
1992-93	Vasteras IK	Sweden	29	0	2	2	14	3	0	0	0	0
1993-94	Vasteras IK	Sweden	32	1	0	1	26	....	....	....	....	....
1994-95	Vasteras IK	Sweden	25	2	1	3	14	4	0	0	0	4
1995-96	Vasteras IK	Sweden	39	8	5	13	16	....	....	....	....	....
1996-97	Vasteras IK	Sweden	47	8	3	11	32	....	....	....	....	....
1997-98	Vasteras IK	Sweden	46	4	7	11	36	....	....	....	....	....
1998-99	Vasteras IK	Sweden	50	6	20	26	36	....	....	....	....	....
99-2000	Linkopings HC	Sweden	45	10	6	16	30	....	....	....	....	....

GABORIK, Marian (guh-BOHR-ihk, MAIR-ee-uhn) MIN.

Left wing. Shoots left. 6'1", 183 lbs. Born, Trencin, Czech., February 14, 1982.
(Minnesota's 1st choice, 3rd overall, in 2000 Entry Draft).

			Regular Season					Playoffs				
Season	Club	Lea	GP	G	A	TP	PIM	GP	G	A	TP	PIM
1997-98	Dukla Trencin	Slovak-Jr.	36	37	22	59	28	....	....	....	....	....
	Dukla Trencin	Slovakia	1	1	0	1	0	....	....	....	....	....
1998-99	Dukla Trencin	Slovakia	33	11	9	20	6	3	1	0	1	2
99-2000	Dukla Trencin	Slovakia	50	25	21	46	34	5	1	2	3	2

GAFFANEY, Brian (GAF-an-nee, BRIGH-an) PIT.

Defense. Shoots left. 6'5", 205 lbs. Born, Alexandria, MN, October 4, 1977.
(Pittsburgh's 2nd choice, 44th overall, in 1997 Entry Draft).

			Regular Season					Playoffs				
Season	Club	Lea	GP	G	A	TP	PIM	GP	G	A	TP	PIM
1996-97	North Iowa	USHL	48	8	13	21	49	....	....	....	....	....
1997-98	St. Cloud State	WCHA	26	0	2	2	37	....	....	....	....	....
1998-99	St. Cloud State	WCHA	37	3	5	8	45	....	....	....	....	....
99-2000	St. Cloud State	WCHA	38	1	4	5	51	....	....	....	....	....

GAGNON, Jonathan (GAN-YAW, JOHN-a-THAN) TOR.

Center. Shoots left. 6'1", 190 lbs. Born, Montreal, Que., May 20, 1980.
(Toronto's 7th choice, 181st overall, in 1998 Entry Draft).

			Regular Season					Playoffs				
Season	Club	Lea	GP	G	A	TP	PIM	GP	G	A	TP	PIM
1996-97	Val-d'Or Foreurs	QMJHL	65	5	15	20	35	13	1	0	1	2
1997-98	Val-d'Or Foreurs	QMJHL	40	9	19	28	54	....	....	....	....	....
	Cape Breton	QMJHL	29	6	7	13	25	4	2	3	5	12
1998-99	Cape Breton	QMJHL	68	27	37	64	39	5	2	4	6	2
99-2000	Rouyn-Noranda	QMJHL	10	0	1	1	14	....	....	....	....	....
	Cape Breton	QMJHL	26	8	12	20	25	....	....	....	....	....
	Halifax	QMJHL	19	11	4	15	37	....	....	....	....	....
	Drummondville	QMJHL	27	16	21	37	38	14	4	12	16	8

GAINEY, Steve (GAY-nee, STEEV) DAL.

Left wing. Shoots left. 6', 180 lbs. Born, Montreal, Que., January 26, 1979.
(Dallas' 3rd choice, 77th overall, in 1997 Entry Draft).

			Regular Season					Playoffs				
Season	Club	Lea	GP	G	A	TP	PIM	GP	G	A	TP	PIM
1995-96	Kamloops Blazers	WHL	49	1	4	5	40	3	0	0	0	0
1996-97	Kamloops Blazers	WHL	60	9	18	27	60	2	0	0	0	9
1997-98	Kamloops Blazers	WHL	68	21	34	55	93	7	1	7	8	15
1998-99	Kamloops Blazers	WHL	68	30	34	64	155	15	5	4	9	38
99-2000	Michigan K-Wings	IHL	58	8	10	18	41	....	....	....	....	....
	Fort Wayne	UHL	1	0	0	0	0	....	....	....	....	....

GARDINER, Peter (GAHR-din-uhr, PEE-tuhr) MIN.

Right wing. Shoots right. 6'5", 220 lbs. Born, Toronto, Ont., September 29, 1977.
(Chicago's 6th choice, 120th overall, in 1997 Entry Draft).

			Regular Season					Playoffs				
Season	Club	Lea	GP	G	A	TP	PIM	GP	G	A	TP	PIM
1993-94	Wexford Raiders	OJHL	2	1	1	2	0	....	....	....	....	....
1994-95	Wexford Raiders	OJHL	44	7	15	22	34	....	....	....	....	....
1995-96	Wexford Raiders	OJHL	44	18	28	46	113	....	....	....	....	....
1996-97	RPI Engineers	ECAC	36	10	21	31	47	....	....	....	....	....
1997-98	RPI Engineers	ECAC	35	10	9	19	52	....	....	....	....	....
1998-99	RPI Engineers	ECAC	37	17	21	38	76	....	....	....	....	....
99-2000	RPI Engineers	ECAC	36	11	13	24	62	....	....	....	....	....

Signed as a free agent by **Minnesota**, June 7, 2000.

GILLIS, Nick (GIHL-LIHS, NIHK) OTT.

Right wing. Shoots right. 6', 188 lbs. Born, Cambridge, MA, February 20, 1978.
(Ottawa's 7th choice, 203rd overall, in 1997 Entry Draft).

			Regular Season					Playoffs				
Season	Club	Lea	GP	G	A	TP	PIM	GP	G	A	TP	PIM
1993-94	Boston Terriers	X-Games	60	58	70	128	112	....	....	....	....	....
1994-95	Cushing Academy	Hi-School	28	15	38	53	62	....	....	....	....	....
	Central-Mass	MBHL	8	14	10	24	....	....	....	....	....	....
1995-96	Cushing Academy	Hi-School	34	34	58	92	47	....	....	....	....	....
1996-97	Cushing Academy	Hi-School	32	30	54	84	27	....	....	....	....	....
1997-98	Boston University	H-East	34	8	12	20	43	....	....	....	....	....
1998-99	Boston University	H-East	33	3	16	19	37	....	....	....	....	....
99-2000	Boston University	H-East	42	8	18	26	26	....	....	....	....	....

GIONTA, Brian (jee-OHN-tuh, BRIGH-an) N.J.

Right wing. Shoots right. 5'7", 160 lbs. Born, Rochester, NY, January 18, 1979.
(New Jersey's 4th choice, 82nd overall, in 1998 Entry Draft).

			Regular Season					Playoffs				
Season	Club	Lea	GP	G	A	TP	PIM	GP	G	A	TP	PIM
1994-95	Rochester	EJHL-B	28	*52	37	*89	....	....	....	....	....	....
1995-96	Niagara Scenics	OJHL	51	47	44	91	59	....	....	....	....	....
1996-97	Niagara Scenics	OJHL	50	57	70	127	101	6	6	11	17	21
1997-98	Boston College	H-East	40	30	32	62	44	....	....	....	....	....
1998-99	Boston College	H-East	39	27	33	60	46	....	....	....	....	....
99-2000	Boston College	H-East	42	*33	23	56	66	....	....	....	....	....

Metro Jr. "A" Player-of-the-Year (1996) • Hockey East Rookie-of-the-Year (1997) • Hockey East Second All-Star Team (1998) • NCAA East Second All-American Team (1998) • Hockey East First All-Star Team (1999, 2000) • NCAA East First All-American Team (1999, 2000)

GIROUX, Alexandre (ZHIH-roo) OTT.

Center. Shoots left. 6'2", 165 lbs. Born, Quebec, Que., June 16, 1981.
(Ottawa's 9th choice, 213th overall, in 1999 Entry Draft).

			Regular Season					Playoffs				
Season	Club	Lea	GP	G	A	TP	PIM	GP	G	A	TP	PIM
1997-98	Ste-Foy Governors	QAAA	42	28	30	58	96	....	....	....	....	....
1998-99	Hull Olympiques	QMJHL	67	15	22	37	124	22	2	2	4	8
99-2000	Hull Olympiques	QMJHL	72	52	47	99	117	15	12	6	18	30

GLENN, Ryan (GLEHN) MTL.

Defense. Shoots left. 6'3", 210 lbs. Born, New Westminster, B.C., June 7, 1980.
(Montreal's 7th choice, 145th overall, in 2000 Entry Draft).

			Regular Season					Playoffs				
Season	Club	Lea	GP	G	A	TP	PIM	GP	G	A	TP	PIM
99-2000	Walpole Stars	EJHL	42	19	40	59	54	....	....	....	....	....

GOC, Sascha (GAWCH, SA-shah) N.J.

Defense. Shoots right. 6'2", 220 lbs. Born, Calw, West Germany, April 17, 1979.
(New Jersey's 5th choice, 159th overall, in 1997 Entry Draft).

			Regular Season					Playoffs				
Season	Club	Lea	GP	G	A	TP	PIM	GP	G	A	TP	PIM
1995-96	Schwenningen	DEL-Jr.	11	3	6	9	77	....	....	....	....	....
	Schwenningen	DEL	1	0	0	0	0	....	....	....	....	....
1996-97	Schwenningen	DEL	41	3	1	4	28	5	0	0	0	0
1997-98	Schwenningen	DEL	49	5	5	10	45	....	....	....	....	....
1998-99	Albany River Rats	AHL	55	1	12	13	24	2	0	0	0	0
99-2000	Albany River Rats	AHL	64	9	22	31	35	5	2	0	2	6

GODARD, Eric FLA.

Right wing. Shoots right. 6'4", 215 lbs. Born, Vernon, B.C., March 7, 1980.

			Regular Season					Playoffs				
Season	Club	Lea	GP	G	A	TP	PIM	GP	G	A	TP	PIM
1997-98	Lethbridge	WHL	7	0	0	0	26	2	0	0	0	0
1998-99	Lethbridge	WHL	66	2	5	7	213	4	0	0	0	14
99-2000	Lethbridge	WHL	60	3	5	8	310	....	....	....	....	....
	Louisville	AHL	4	0	1	1	16	....	....	....	....	....

Signed as a free agent by **Florida**, September 24, 1999.

GOLDADE, Aaron (GOHLD-ayd, AIR-rohn) BUF.

Center. Shoots left. 6', 180 lbs. Born, Prince Albert, Sask., July 30, 1980.
(Buffalo's 6th choice, 137th overall, in 1998 Entry Draft).

			Regular Season					Playoffs				
Season	Club	Lea	GP	G	A	TP	PIM	GP	G	A	TP	PIM
1995-96	Prince Albert	AMHL	44	31	38	69	26	....	....	....	....	....
1996-97	Brandon	WHL	59	4	10	14	51	6	0	1	1	0
1997-98	Brandon	WHL	66	19	16	35	58	16	0	2	2	22
1998-99	Brandon	WHL	64	27	33	60	56	5	0	1	1	8
99-2000	Brandon	WHL	56	14	28	42	33	....	....	....	....	....

GORBUNOV, Vladimir (gohr-buh-NAHF) NYI

Center. Shoots left. 6', 174 lbs. Born, Moscow, USSR, April 22, 1982.
(NY Islanders' 4th choice, 105th overall, in 2000 Entry Draft).

			Regular Season					Playoffs				
Season	Club	Lea	GP	G	A	TP	PIM	GP	G	A	TP	PIM
99-2000	CSKA Moscow	Russia-2			STATISTICS NOT AVAILABLE							

GORDON, Heath (GOHR-dohn, HEETH) CHI.

Right wing. Shoots left. 6'2", 197 lbs. Born, Boston, MA, May 28, 1978.
(Chicago's 8th choice, 147th overall, in 1997 Entry Draft).

			Regular Season					Playoffs				
Season	Club	Lea	GP	G	A	TP	PIM	GP	G	A	TP	PIM
1996-97	Green Bay	USHL	52	16	28	44	71	17	7	12	19	28
1997-98	Providence	H-East	18	2	2	4	22	....	....	....	....	....
1998-99	Providence	H-East	30	7	10	17	16	....	....	....	....	....
99-2000	Providence	H-East	29	4	3	7	26	....	....	....	....	....

GOREN, Lee (GOH-rehn, LEE) BOS.

Right wing. Shoots right. 6'3", 200 lbs. Born, Winnipeg, Man., December 26, 1977.
(Boston's 5th choice, 63rd overall, in 1997 Entry Draft).

			Regular Season					Playoffs				
Season	Club	Lea	GP	G	A	TP	PIM	GP	G	A	TP	PIM
1995-96	Minot Top Guns	SJHL	64	31	55	86	....	....	....	....	....	....
	Saskatoon Blades	WHL	2	0	0	0	2	....	....	....	....	....
1996-97	North Dakota	WCHA			DID NOT PLAY – FRESHMAN							
1997-98	North Dakota	WCHA	29	3	13	16	26	....	....	....	....	....
1998-99	North Dakota	WCHA	38	26	19	45	20	....	....	....	....	....
99-2000	North Dakota	WCHA	44	*34	29	63	42	....	....	....	....	....

WCHA Second All-Star Team (2000) • NCAA West Second All-American Team (2000) • NCAA Championship All-Tournament Team (2000) • NCAA Championship Tournament MVP (2000)

GORNICK, Brian (GOHR-nihk) ANA.

Center. Shoots left. 6'4", 200 lbs. Born, St. Paul, MN, March 17, 1980.
(Anaheim's 7th choice, 258th overall, in 1999 Entry Draft).

			Regular Season					Playoffs				
Season	Club	Lea	GP	G	A	TP	PIM	GP	G	A	TP	PIM
1998-99	Air Force Falcons	CHA	34	10	11	21	20	....	....	....	....	....
99-2000	Air Force Falcons	CHA	39	13	25	38	26	....	....	....	....	....

GOROVIKOV, Konstantin (goh-roh-vih-KAHF, kawn-stehn-TEEN) OTT.

Center. Shoots left. 5'11", 172 lbs. Born, Novosibirsk, USSR, August 31, 1977.
(Ottawa's 10th choice, 269th overall, in 1999 Entry Draft).

			Regular Season					Playoffs				
Season	**Club**	**Lea**	**GP**	**G**	**A**	**TP**	**PIM**	**GP**	**G**	**A**	**TP**	**PIM**
1994-95	St. Petersburg	CIS-3	38	6	5	11	22	....	....	....	....	....
	St. Petersburg	CIS	13	1	0	1	4	2	0	0	0	0
1995-96	St. Petersburg	CIS	45	2	4	6	18	2	0	0	0	0
	St. Petersburg	CIS-3	3	2	0	2	0	....	....	....	....	....
1996-97	St. Petersburg	Russia	37	4	2	6	20	....	....	....	....	....
1997-98	St. Petersburg	Russia	44	6	12	18	22	....	....	....	....	....
1998-99	St. Petersburg	Russia	42	12	7	19	14	....	....	....	....	....
99-2000	Grand Rapids	IHL	57	9	14	23	30	8	1	0	1	4

GOSSELIN, Christian (gawz-LEH, KRIHST-an) S.J.

Defense. Shoots right. 6'5", 235 lbs. Born, Laval, Que., August 21, 1976.
(New Jersey's 5th choice, 129th overall, in 1994 Entry Draft).

			Regular Season					Playoffs				
Season	**Club**	**Lea**	**GP**	**G**	**A**	**TP**	**PIM**	**GP**	**G**	**A**	**TP**	**PIM**
1992-93	Hull Olympiques	QMJHL	49	1	3	4	24	....	....	....	....	....
1993-94	St-Hyacinthe	QMJHL	12	3	2	5	16	....	....	....	....	....
1994-95	St-Hyacinthe	QMJHL	60	5	10	15	202	5	0	0	0	11
1995-96	Laval Titan	QMJHL	21	1	8	9	69	....	....	....	....	....
1996-97	Macon Whoopies	CHL	63	8	10	18	229	5	0	0	0	29
1997-98	Pensacola	ECHL	42	6	5	11	181	18	0	1	1	52
	Fredericton	AHL	6	0	0	0	17	....	....	....	....	....
1998-99	Kentucky	AHL	31	1	1	2	107	....	....	....	....	....
99-2000	Kentucky	AHL	68	0	4	4	266	9	0	0	0	34

Signed as a free agent by **San Jose**, July 15, 1998.

GREEN, Mike FLA.

Center/Right wing. Shoots right. 5'11", 192 lbs. Born, Calgary, AB, August 23, 1979.

			Regular Season					Playoffs				
Season	**Club**	**Lea**	**GP**	**G**	**A**	**TP**	**PIM**	**GP**	**G**	**A**	**TP**	**PIM**
1996-97	Calgary Stars	AHAA	35	34	27	61	78	....	....	....	....	....
	Edmonton Ice	WHL	7	0	2	2	0	....	....	....	....	....
1997-98	Edmonton Ice	WHL	71	15	26	41	16	....	....	....	....	....
1998-99	Kootenay Ice	WHL	71	35	45	80	37	7	2	2	4	4
99-2000	Kootenay Ice	WHL	69	43	49	92	63	21	9	16	25	20

WHL East Second All-Star Team (2000)

Signed as a free agent by **Florida**, April 7, 2000.

GRENIER, Martin (GREH-nyay, MAHR-tihn) BOS.

Defense. Shoots left. 6'5", 231 lbs. Born, Laval, Que., November 2, 1980.
(Colorado's 2nd choice, 45th overall, in 1999 Entry Draft).

			Regular Season					Playoffs				
Season	**Club**	**Lea**	**GP**	**G**	**A**	**TP**	**PIM**	**GP**	**G**	**A**	**TP**	**PIM**
1996-97	St-Jerome	QAAA	34	3	16	19	117	....	....	....	....	....
1997-98	Quebec Remparts	QMJHL	61	4	11	15	202	14	0	2	2	36
1998-99	Quebec Remparts	QMJHL	60	7	18	25	*479	13	0	4	4	29
99-2000	Quebec Remparts	QMJHL	67	11	35	46	302	7	1	4	5	27

Traded to **Boston** by **Colorado** with Brian Rolston, Sami Pahlsson and New Jersey's 1st round choice (previously acquired, Boston selected Martin Samuelsson) in 2000 Entry Draft for Ray Bourque and Dave Andreychuk, March 6, 2000.

GRIMES, Kevin (GRIGHMS, KEH-vihn) OTT.

Defense. Shoots left. 6'3", 218 lbs. Born, Ottawa, Ont., August 19, 1979.
(Colorado's 1st choice, 26th overall, in 1997 Entry Draft).

			Regular Season					Playoffs				
Season	**Club**	**Lea**	**GP**	**G**	**A**	**TP**	**PIM**	**GP**	**G**	**A**	**TP**	**PIM**
1995-96	Cumberland	OJHL-B	51	2	10	12	220	....	....	....	....	....
1996-97	Kingston	OHL	57	2	12	14	188	1	0	0	0	0
1997-98	Kingston	OHL	62	1	27	28	179	12	0	1	1	16
1998-99	Kingston	OHL	56	5	20	25	184	5	2	3	5	12
99-2000	Pee Dee Pride	ECHL	41	1	2	3	87	....	....	....	....	....
	Grand Rapids	IHL	4	0	0	0	13	....	....	....	....	....

Signed as a free agent by **Ottawa**, August 24, 1999.

GRON, Stanislav (GRAHN, Stan-ih-slav) N.J.

Right wing. Shoots left. 6'2", 210 lbs. Born, Bratislava, Czech., October 28, 1978.
(New Jersey's 2nd choice, 38th overall, in 1997 Entry Draft).

			Regular Season					Playoffs				
Season	**Club**	**Lea**	**GP**	**G**	**A**	**TP**	**PIM**	**GP**	***G**	**A**	**TP**	**PIM**
1994-95	Slovan Bratislava	Slovak-Jr.	40	49	26	75	20	....	....	....	....	....
1995-96	Slovan Bratislava	Slovak-Jr.	43	33	25	58	14	....	....	....	....	....
	Slovan Bratislava	Slovakia	....	....	....	....	....	1	0	0	0	0
1996-97	Slovan Bratislava	Slovak-Jr.	22	20	16	36	....	....	....	....	....	....
	Slovan Bratislava	Slovakia	7	0	0	0	....	....	....	....	....	....
1997-98	Seattle T-Birds	WHL	61	9	29	38	21	5	1	5	6	0
1998-99	Kootenay Ice	WHL	49	28	18	46	18	7	3	8	11	12
	Utah Grizzlies	IHL	4	0	3	3	0	....	....	....	....	....
99-2000	Albany River Rats	AHL	65	19	10	29	17	5	1	1	2	2

GROSCHL, Tamas (GROH-shuhl, TAW-mahsh) EDM.

Right wing. Shoots left. 6'2", 183 lbs. Born, Budapest, Hungary, August 21, 1980.
(Edmonton's 9th choice, 256th overall, in 1999 Entry Draft).

			Regular Season					Playoffs				
Season	**Club**	**Lea**	**GP**	**G**	**A**	**TP**	**PIM**	**GP**	**G**	**A**	**TP**	**PIM**
1998-99	UTE Budapest	Hungary				STATISTICS NOT AVAILABLE						
99-2000	Team Hungary	Nat-Team	11	4	5	9	35	....	....	....	....	....
	Leksands IF	Sweden	2	0	0	0	0	....	....	....	....	....

GUITE, Ben (GWIGHT, BEHN) MTL.

Right wing. Shoots right. 6', 202 lbs. Born, Montreal, Que., July 17, 1978.
(Montreal's 8th choice, 172nd overall, in 1997 Entry Draft).

			Regular Season					Playoffs				
Season	**Club**	**Lea**	**GP**	**G**	**A**	**TP**	**PIM**	**GP**	**G**	**A**	**TP**	**PIM**
1996-97	U. of Maine	H-East	34	7	7	14	21	....	....	....	....	....
1997-98	U. of Maine	H-East	32	6	12	18	20	....	....	....	....	....
1998-99	U. of Maine	H-East	40	12	16	28	30	....	....	....	....	....
99-2000	U. of Maine	H-East	40	22	14	36	36	....	....	....	....	....

GUSAKOV, Yevgeny (goo-sawk-KAHF) NYR

Right wing. Shoots left. 6'6", 225 lbs. Born, Togliatti, USSR, March 6, 1981.
(NY Rangers' 9th choice, 226th overall, in 1999 Entry Draft).

			Regular Season					Playoffs				
Season	**Club**	**Lea**	**GP**	**G**	**A**	**TP**	**PIM**	**GP**	**G**	**A**	**TP**	**PIM**
1997-98	Lada Togliatti-2	Russia-3	24	4	2	6	10	....	....	....	....	....
1998-99	Lada Togliatti-2	Russia-4	42	12	3	15	28	....	....	....	....	....
99-2000	Baie-Comeau	QMJHL	61	25	22	47	135	6	5	1	6	10

GUSTAFSSON, Juha (GOOS-tahf-suhn, YOO-huh) PHX.

Defense. Shoots left. 6'3", 200 lbs. Born, Helsinki, Finland, April 26, 1979.
(Phoenix's 1st choice, 43rd overall, in 1997 Entry Draft).

			Regular Season					Playoffs				
Season	**Club**	**Lea**	**GP**	**G**	**A**	**TP**	**PIM**	**GP**	**G**	**A**	**TP**	**PIM**
1994-95	Kiekko-Espoo-B	Finn-Jr.	24	1	4	5	26	....	....	....	....	....
	Kiekko-Espoo	Finn-Jr.	2	0	0	0	0	4	0	0	0	4
1995-96	Kiekko-Espoo	Finn-Jr.	33	1	5	6	28	4	0	0	0	2
	Kiekko-Espoo	Finland	1	0	0	0	0	....	....	....	....	....
1996-97	Kiekko-Espoo	Finn-Jr.	32	1	3	4	30	....	....	....	....	....
	Kiekko-Espoo	Finland	3	0	0	0	0	3	0	0	0	0
1997-98	Kiekko-Espoo	Finn-Jr.	33	3	3	6	18	....	....	....	....	....
	Kiekko-Espoo	Finland	2	0	0	0	0	....	....	....	....	....
1998-99	Ahmat Hyvinkaa	Finland-2	37	3	7	10	36	....	....	....	....	....
99-2000	Blues Espoo	Finland	33	1	4	5	26	....	....	....	....	....

GYORI, Dylan PIT.

Center. Shoots left. 5'11", 190 lbs. Born, Rimbey, Alta., February 20, 1979.

			Regular Season					Playoffs				
Season	**Club**	**Lea**	**GP**	**G**	**A**	**TP**	**PIM**	**GP**	**G**	**A**	**TP**	**PIM**
1994-95	Red Deer Chiefs	AMHL	36	36	27	63	61	....	....	....	....	....
	Tri-City Americans	WHL	3	0	0	0	0	....	....	....	....	....
1995-96	Tri-City Americans	WHL	50	12	13	25	26	10	0	0	0	2
1996-97	Tri-City Americans	WHL	72	29	27	56	95	....	....	....	....	....
1997-98	Tri-City Americans	WHL	72	33	54	87	81	....	....	....	....	....
1998-99	Tri-City Americans	WHL	69	53	65	118	112	12	7	11	18	25
99-2000	Wilkes-Barre	AHL	36	2	2	4	23	....	....	....	....	....
	Richmond	ECHL	29	11	20	31	50	3	1	0	1	6

WHL West First All-Star Team (1999)

Signed as a free agent by **Pittsburgh**, August 19, 1999.

HAGGLUND, Johan (HAG-luhnd, YOH-hahn) T.B.

Center. Shoots left. 6'2", 196 lbs. Born, Ornskoldsvik, Sweden, June 9, 1982.
(Tampa Bay's 4th choice, 126th overall, in 2000 Entry Draft).

			Regular Season					Playoffs				
Season	**Club**	**Lea**	**GP**	**G**	**A**	**TP**	**PIM**	**GP**	**G**	**A**	**TP**	**PIM**
1998-99	Modo Hockey	Swede-Jr.	28	16	22	38	52	....	....	....	....	....
99-2000	Modo Hockey	Swede-Jr.	35	7	10	17	75	2	1	0	1	0

HAGLUND, Bobby (HAG-luhnd, BAWB-bee) ST.L.

Left wing. Shoots left. 5'11", 195 lbs. Born, Worcester, MA, November 17, 1977.
(St. Louis' 7th choice, 206th overall, in 1997 Entry Draft).

			Regular Season					Playoffs				
Season	**Club**	**Lea**	**GP**	**G**	**A**	**TP**	**PIM**	**GP**	**G**	**A**	**TP**	**PIM**
1995-96	St. Peter-Marian	Hi-School	23	38	29	67	....	....	....	....	....	....
1996-97	Des Moines	USHL	45	18	14	32	86	4	0	0	0	0
1997-98	Northeastern	H-East	29	5	7	12	24	....	....	....	....	....
1998-99	Northeastern	H-East	27	3	5	8	31	....	....	....	....	....
99-2000	Northeastern	H-East	1	0	0	0	0	....	....	....	....	....

• Missed remainder of 1998-99 season and majority of 1999-2000 season recovering from head injury suffered in game vs. Providence (H-East), March 7, 1999.

HAGMAN, Niklas (HAG-muhn, NIHK-las) FLA.

Left wing. Shoots left. 5'11", 183 lbs. Born, Espoo, Finland, December 5, 1979.
(Florida's 3rd choice, 70th overall, in 1999 Entry Draft).

			Regular Season					Playoffs				
Season	**Club**	**Lea**	**GP**	**G**	**A**	**TP**	**PIM**	**GP**	**G**	**A**	**TP**	**PIM**
1994-95	HIFK Helsinki-C	Finn-Jr.	28	30	15	45	40	4	2	0	2	6
1995-96	HIFK Helsinki-B	Finn-Jr.	26	12	21	33	32	4	3	0	3	2
	HIFK Helsinki	Finn-Jr.	12	3	1	4	0	....	....	....	....	....
1996-97	HIFK Helsinki	Finn-Jr.	30	13	12	25	30	4	1	1	2	0
1997-98	HIFK Helsinki	Finn-Jr.	26	9	5	14	16	....	....	....	....	....
	HIFK Helsinki	Finland	8	1	0	1	0	....	....	....	....	....
1998-99	HIFK Helsinki	Finn-Jr.	14	4	9	13	43	....	....	....	....	....
	HIFK Helsinki	EuroHL	1	0	1	1	0	....	....	....	....	....
	HIFK Helsinki	Finland	17	1	1	2	14	....	....	....	....	....
	Kiekko-Espoo	Finland	14	1	1	2	2	4	1	0	1	0
99-2000	Karpat Oulu	Finland-2	41	17	18	35	12	7	4	2	6	....

HAHL, Riku (HAHL, REE-koo) COL.

Center. Shoots left. 6', 187 lbs. Born, Hameenlinna, Finland, November 1, 1980.
(Colorado's 9th choice, 183rd overall, in 1999 Entry Draft).

			Regular Season					Playoffs				
Season	**Club**	**Lea**	**GP**	**G**	**A**	**TP**	**PIM**	**GP**	**G**	**A**	**TP**	**PIM**
1995-96	HPK Hameenlinna	Finn-Jr.	32	18	30	48	28	....	....	....	....	....
1996-97	HPK Hameenlinna	Finn-Jr.	2	0	1	1	2	6	2	0	2	2
1997-98	HPK Hameenlinna	Finn-Jr.	35	13	6	19	12	....	....	....	....	....
1998-99	HPK Hameenlinna	Finn-Jr.	6	0	2	2	6	....	....	....	....	....
	HPK Hameenlinna	Finland	28	0	1	1	0	8	0	0	0	2
99-2000	HPK Hameenlinna	Finland	50	4	3	7	18	8	0	0	0	2

HAINSEY, Ron (HAYN-zee) MTL.

Defense. Shoots left. 6'3", 187 lbs. Born, Bolton, CT, March 24, 1981.
(Montreal's 1st choice, 13th overall, in 2000 Entry Draft).

			Regular Season					Playoffs				
Season	**Club**	**Lea**	**GP**	**G**	**A**	**TP**	**PIM**	**GP**	**G**	**A**	**TP**	**PIM**
1997-98	Team USA	Under-18	66	6	15	21	44	....	....	....	....	....
1998-99	Team USA	Under-18	48	5	12	17	45	....	....	....	....	....
99-2000	U. Mass-Lowell	H-East	30	3	8	11	20	....	....	....	....	....

HAJT, Chris (HIGHT, KRIHS) **EDM.**

Defense. Shoots left. 6'3", 206 lbs. Born, Saskatoon, Sask., July 5, 1978.
(Edmonton's 3rd choice, 32nd overall, in 1996 Entry Draft).

			Regular Season					Playoffs				
Season	Club	Lea	GP	G	A	TP	PIM	GP	G	A	TP	PIM
1993-94	Amherst Knights	WNYHA	38	8	20	28	16	....	....	....	....	....
1994-95	Guelph Storm	OHL	57	1	7	8	35	14	0	2	2	9
1995-96	Guelph Storm	OHL	63	8	27	35	69	16	0	6	6	13
1996-97	Guelph Storm	OHL	58	11	15	26	62	18	0	8	8	25
1997-98	Guelph Storm	OHL	44	2	21	23	46	12	1	5	6	11
1998-99	Hamilton Bulldogs	AHL	64	0	4	4	36	....	....	....	....	....
99-2000	Hamilton Bulldogs	AHL	54	0	8	8	30	10	0	2	2	0

OHL Second All-Star Team (1998)

HAKANSSON, Mikael (HAK-ahn-suhn) **TOR.**

Center. Shoots left. 6'2", 204 lbs. Born, Stockholm, Sweden, May 31, 1974.
(Toronto's 7th choice, 125th overall, in 1992 Entry Draft).

			Regular Season					Playoffs				
Season	Club	Lea	GP	G	A	TP	PIM	GP	G	A	TP	PIM
1990-91	Nacka IK	Sweden-2	27	2	5	7	6	....	....	....	....	....
1991-92	Nacka IK	Sweden-2	29	3	15	18	24	....	....	....	....	....
1992-93	Djurgardens IF	Sweden	40	0	1	1	6	3	0	0	0	0
1993-94	Djurgardens IF	Sweden	37	3	3	6	12	4	0	0	0	0
1994-95	MoDo Hockey	Sweden	37	3	7	10	16	....	....	....	....	....
1995-96	MoDo Hockey	Sweden	40	8	4	12	18	8	2	0	2	0
1996-97	Djurgardens IF	Sweden	48	8	12	20	12	4	0	0	0	0
1997-98	Djurgardens IF	Sweden	43	9	2	11	8	15	3	0	3	14
1998-99	Djurgardens IF	Sweden	48	13	12	25	14	4	1	0	1	0
	Djurgardens IF	EuroHL	6	0	1	1	20	....	....	....	....	....
99-2000	Djurgardens IF	Sweden	48	17	17	34	26	13	3	8	11	12

HALE, David (HAYL) **N.J.**

Defense. Shoots left. 6'2", 204 lbs. Born, Colorado Springs, CO, June 18, 1981.
(New Jersey's 1st choice, 22nd overall, in 2000 Entry Draft).

			Regular Season					Playoffs				
Season	Club	Lea	GP	G	A	TP	PIM	GP	G	A	TP	PIM
1998-99	Sioux City	USHL	56	3	15	18	127	5	0	0	0	18
99-2000	Sioux City	USHL	54	6	18	24	187	5	0	2	2	6

HALL, Adam (HAWL, A-dam) **NSH.**

Right wing. Shoots right. 6'3", 200 lbs. Born, Kalamazoo, MI, August 14, 1980.
(Nashville's 3rd choice, 52nd overall, in 1999 Entry Draft).

			Regular Season					Playoffs				
Season	Club	Lea	GP	G	A	TP	PIM	GP	G	A	TP	PIM
1996-97	Bramalea Blues	OJHL	43	9	14	23	92	....	....	....	....	....
1997-98	Team USA	Under-18	71	42	23	65	63	....	....	....	....	....
1998-99	Michigan State	CCHA	36	16	7	23	74	....	....	....	....	....
99-2000	Michigan State	CCHA	40	26	13	39	38	....	....	....	....	....

CCHA Second All-Star Team (2000)

HALL, Todd (HAWL, TODD) **NYR**

Left wing. Shoots left. 6'1", 200 lbs. Born, Hamden, CT, January 22, 1973.
(Hartford's 3rd choice, 53rd overall, in 1991 Entry Draft).

			Regular Season					Playoffs				
Season	Club	Lea	GP	G	A	TP	PIM	GP	G	A	TP	PIM
1990-91	Hamden High	Hi-School	23	10	15	25	12	....	....	....	....	....
1991-92	Boston College	H-East	33	2	10	12	14	....	....	....	....	....
1992-93	Boston College	H-East	34	2	10	12	22	....	....	....	....	....
1993-94	New Hampshire	H-East	DID NOT PLAY – TRANSFERRED COLLEGES									
1994-95	New Hampshire	H-East	36	8	18	26	16	....	....	....	....	....
1995-96	New Hampshire	H-East	31	4	26	30	10	....	....	....	....	....
1996-97	Binghamton	AHL	40	3	7	10	12	4	0	1	1	0
	Charlotte	ECHL	13	0	2	2	8	....	....	....	....	....
1997-98	Hartford	AHL	73	7	18	25	26	8	0	1	1	8
1998-99	Hartford	AHL	72	14	15	29	12	1	0	0	0	0
99-2000	Hartford	AHL	74	11	34	45	14	23	2	6	8	8

Hockey East Second All-Star Team (1996)

Signed as a free agent by **NY Rangers**, July 28, 1997.

HALVARDSSON, Johan (HAL-vahrds-sohn, YOH-hahn) **NYI**

Defense. Shoots left. 6'3", 198 lbs. Born, Jonkoping, Sweden, December 26, 1979.
(NY Islanders' 8th choice, 102nd overall, in 1999 Entry Draft).

			Regular Season					Playoffs				
Season	Club	Lea	GP	G	A	TP	PIM	GP	G	A	TP	PIM
1997-98	HV Jonkoping	Swede-Jr.	28	5	5	10	65	....	....	....	....	....
1998-99	HV Jonkoping	Sweden	17	1	2	3	33	....	....	....	....	....
99-2000	HV Jonkoping	Sweden	46	0	3	3	75	5	0	0	0	8

HAMILTON, Jason (Ham-ihl-TOHN, JAY-suhn) **CHI.**

Defense. Shoots right. 6'2", 218 lbs. Born, Montreal, Que., January 25, 1977.

			Regular Season					Playoffs				
Season	Club	Lea	GP	G	A	TP	PIM	GP	G	A	TP	PIM
1994-95	Gloucester	OMHA	13	6	8	14	91	....	....	....	....	....
1995-96	Shawinigan	QMJHL	62	3	6	9	240	6	0	0	0	15
1996-97	Shawinigan	QMJHL	67	2	5	7	254	7	0	1	1	8
1997-98	Shawinigan	QMJHL	59	2	9	11	358	6	0	1	1	55
1998-99	Portland Pirates	AHL	4	0	0	0	0	....	....	....	....	....
	Greenville Growl	ECHL	45	2	6	8	206	....	....	....	....	....
99-2000	Hampton Roads	ECHL	2	0	1	1	20	....	....	....	....	....
	Baton Rouge	ECHL	46	1	2	3	291	....	....	....	....	....

Signed as a free agent by **Chicago**, July 18, 1998.

HANCHUCK, Tyler (HAN-chuhk) **MTL.**

Defense. Shoots left. 6'3", 210 lbs. Born, Sault Ste. Marie, Ont., February 7, 1982.
(Montreal's 4th choice, 79th overall, in 2000 Entry Draft).

			Regular Season					Playoffs				
Season	Club	Lea	GP	G	A	TP	PIM	GP	G	A	TP	PIM
1997-98	S.S. Marie Minelli	NOHA	67	9	25	34	110	....	....	....	....	....
1998-99	Brampton	OHL	57	0	3	3	87	....	....	....	....	....
99-2000	Brampton	OHL	58	0	8	8	81	6	0	0	0	8

HANKINSON, Casey (HAN-kihn-suhn, KAY-see) **CHI.**

Left wing. Shoots left. 6'1", 187 lbs. Born, Edina, MN, May 8, 1976.
(Chicago's 9th choice, 201st overall, in 1995 Entry Draft).

			Regular Season					Playoffs				
Season	Club	Lea	GP	G	A	TP	PIM	GP	G	A	TP	PIM
1992-93	Edina High	Hi-School	25	20	26	46	....	....	....	....	....	....
1993-94	Edina High	Hi-School	24	21	20	41	50	....	....	....	....	....
1994-95	U. of Minnesota	WCHA	33	7	1	8	86	....	....	....	....	....
1995-96	U. of Minnesota	WCHA	39	16	19	35	101	....	....	....	....	....
1996-97	U. of Minnesota	WCHA	42	17	24	41	79	....	....	....	....	....
1997-98	U. of Minnesota	WCHA	35	10	12	22	81	....	....	....	....	....
1998-99	Portland	AHL	72	10	13	23	106	....	....	....	....	....
99-2000	Cleveland	IHL	82	7	22	29	140	2	0	0	0	2

HANNUS, Tommi (HA-nuhs, TAW-mee) **L.A.**

Center. Shoots right. 6', 180 lbs. Born, Vantaa, Finland, June 27, 1980.
(Los Angeles' 7th choice, 190th overall, in 1998 Entry Draft).

			Regular Season					Playoffs				
Season	Club	Lea	GP	G	A	TP	PIM	GP	G	A	TP	PIM
1994-95	TPS Turku-C	Finn-Jr.	27	24	13	37	43	....	....	....	....	....
1995-96	TPS Turku-C	Finn-Jr.	29	34	22	56	67	....	....	....	....	....
	TPS Turku-B	Finn-Jr.	1	1	0	1	2	....	....	....	....	....
1996-97	TPS Turku	Finn-Jr.	45	14	13	27	10	6	4	2	6	10
1997-98	TPS Turku	Finn-Jr.	19	6	3	9	4	....	....	....	....	....
1998-99	TPS Turku	Finn-Jr.	8	5	4	9	22	....	....	....	....	....
	TuTo Turku	Finland-2	18	6	4	10	16	8	0	2	2	8
99-2000	TPS Turku	Finn-Jr.	3	4	3	7	6	....	....	....	....	....
	TuTo Turku	Finland-2	27	11	6	17	20	....	....	....	....	....
	Assat-Pori	Finland	13	1	0	1	4	....	....	....	....	....

HARDER, Mike (HAHR-duhr, MIGHK) **NYR**

Center. Shoots right. 6', 185 lbs. Born, Winnipeg, Man., February 8, 1973.

			Regular Season					Playoffs				
Season	Club	Lea	GP	G	A	TP	PIM	GP	G	A	TP	PIM
1993-94	Colgate University	ECAC	33	21	25	46	14	....	....	....	....	....
1994-95	Colgate University	ECAC	36	22	36	58	13	....	....	....	....	....
1995-96	Colgate University	ECAC	32	23	32	55	26	....	....	....	....	....
1996-97	Colgate University	ECAC	33	22	33	55	20	....	....	....	....	....
	Hamilton Bulldogs	AHL	2	0	1	1	0	....	....	....	....	....
	Milwaukee	IHL	7	1	3	4	6	2	0	1	1	0
1997-98	Milwaukee	IHL	62	20	17	37	32	....	....	....	....	....
	Springfield	AHL	3	2	0	2	2	....	....	....	....	....
	Rochester	AHL	8	4	2	6	0	4	3	2	5	8
1998-99	Rochester	AHL	79	31	48	79	39	20	2	9	11	23
99-2000	Hartford	AHL	56	18	21	39	33	12	0	4	4	4

ECAC Second All-Star Team (1995, 1996) • ECAC First All-Star Team (1997) • NCAA East Second All-American Team (1997)

Signed as a free agent by **NY Rangers**, August 2, 1999.

HARIKKALA, Jaakko (HAHR-ee-kuh-lah, YAH-koh) **BOS.**

Defense. Shoots left. 6'2", 215 lbs. Born, Kalanti, Finland, March 30, 1981.
(Boston's 4th choice, 118th overall, in 1999 Entry Draft).

			Regular Season					Playoffs				
Season	Club	Lea	GP	G	A	TP	PIM	GP	G	A	TP	PIM
1997-98	Jaa-Kotkat	Finland-2	45	2	6	8	65	....	....	....	....	....
1998-99	Lukko Rauma	Finn-Jr.	11	1	3	4	22	....	....	....	....	....
	Lukko Rauma	Finland	35	0	0	0	10	....	....	....	....	....
99-2000	Lukko Rauma	Finland	24	0	0	0	2	....	....	....	....	....

HARLTON, Tyler (HAHRL-tawn, TIGH-luhr) **TOR.**

Defense. Shoots left. 6'2", 212 lbs. Born, Pense, Sask., January 11, 1976.
(St. Louis' 2nd choice, 94th overall, in 1994 Entry Draft).

			Regular Season					Playoffs				
Season	Club	Lea	GP	G	A	TP	PIM	GP	G	A	TP	PIM
1993-94	Vernon Vipers	BCJHL	60	3	18	21	102	....	....	....	....	....
1994-95	Michigan State	CCHA	39	1	3	4	55	....	....	....	....	....
1995-96	Michigan State	CCHA	39	1	6	7	51	....	....	....	....	....
1996-97	Michigan State	CCHA	39	2	9	11	75	....	....	....	....	....
1997-98	Michigan State	CCHA	44	1	12	13	68	....	....	....	....	....
1998-99	Worcester	AHL	58	2	5	7	94	....	....	....	....	....
	Peoria Riverman	ECHL	6	0	2	2	40	....	....	....	....	....
99-2000	Worcester	AHL	3	0	0	0	4	....	....	....	....	....
	St. John's Leafs	AHL	56	2	6	8	62	....	....	....	....	....

CCHA First All-Star Team (1998) • NCAA West Second All-American Team (1998)

Traded to **Toronto** by **St. Louis** with a conditional choice in 2000 Entry Draft for Derek King and a conditional choice in 2000 Entry Draft, October 20, 1999.

HARRIS, Darcy (HAIR-rihs, DAHR-see) **MTL.**

Right wing. Shoots right. 6'2", 196 lbs. Born, O'Leary, P.E.I., December 22, 1978.
(Montreal's 10th choice, 247th overall, in 1998 Entry Draft).

			Regular Season					Playoffs				
Season	Club	Lea	GP	G	A	TP	PIM	GP	G	A	TP	PIM
1995-96	Summerside	MJrHL	48	13	13	26	168	....	....	....	....	....
1996-97	Kitchener Rangers	OHL	55	4	8	12	134	4	0	0	0	4
1997-98	Kitchener Rangers	OHL	61	21	19	40	200	6	2	4	6	28
1998-99	Fredericton	AHL	31	3	3	6	97	3	0	0	0	0
99-2000	Quebec Citadelles	AHL	36	0	1	1	94	....	....	....	....	....

HARTNELL, Scott (HAHRT-nuhl) **NSH.**

Right wing. Shoots left. 6'3", 198 lbs. Born, Regina, Sask., April 18, 1982.
(Nashville's 1st choice, 6th overall, in 2000 Entry Draft).

			Regular Season					Playoffs				
Season	Club	Lea	GP	G	A	TP	PIM	GP	G	A	TP	PIM
1997-98	Lloydminster	AJHL	56	9	25	34	82	4	2	1	3	8
	Prince Albert	WHL	1	0	1	1	2	....	....	....	....	....
1998-99	Prince Albert	WHL	65	10	34	44	104	14	0	5	5	22
99-2000	Prince Albert	WHL	62	27	55	82	124	6	3	2	5	6

HARTSBURG, Chris (HAHRTZ-buhrg) **N.J.**

Center. Shoots right. 6', 190 lbs. Born, Edina, MN, May 30, 1980.
(New Jersey's 7th choice, 214th overall, in 1999 Entry Draft).

			Regular Season					Playoffs				
Season	Club	Lea	GP	G	A	TP	PIM	GP	G	A	TP	PIM
1995-96	Cambridge Hawks	OJHL	46	12	15	27	10	....	....	....	....	....
1996-97	Cambridge Hawks	OJHL	47	14	19	33	29	....	....	....	....	....
1997-98	Omaha Lancers	USHL	54	16	19	35	58	12	2	2	4	20
1998-99	Colorado College	WCHA	34	6	4	10	60	....	....	....	....	....
99-2000	Colorado College	WCHA	33	3	2	5	50	....	....	....	....	....

HARVEY, Paul (HAHR-vee, PAWL) FLA.

Right wing. Shoots right. 6'4", 196 lbs. Born, South Boston, MA, August 8, 1978.

			Regular Season					Playoffs				
Season	Club	Lea	GP	G	A	TP	PIM	GP	G	A	TP	PIM
1996-97	Syracuse Crunch	OJHL	23	18	31	49	196	....	....	....	....	....
1997-98	Erie Otters	OHL	31	3	6	9	64	6	0	1	1	0
1998-99	Erie Otters	OHL	61	16	17	33	132	5	1	0	1	15
99-2000	Louisville	AHL	34	2	7	9	50	2	0	0	0	0
	Port Huron Cats	UHL	16	1	5	6	22	3	1	0	1	2

Signed as a free agent by **Florida**, June 16, 1999

HAVELKA, Petr (huh-VEHL-kah, PEE-tuhr) PIT.

Left wing. Shoots left. 6'2", 187 lbs. Born, Most, Czech., March 4, 1979.
(Pittsburgh's 6th choice, 152nd overall, in 1997 Entry Draft).

			Regular Season					Playoffs				
Season	Club	Lea	GP	G	A	TP	PIM	GP	G	A	TP	PIM
1995-96	Sparta Praha-Jr.	Cze-Rep	40	15	10	25	....	....	....	....	....	....
1996-97	Sparta Praha-Jr.	Cze-Rep	22	14	13	27	....	....	....	....	....	....
	Sparta Praha	Cze-Rep	....	....	....	....	....	1	0	0	0	0
1997-98	Sparta Praha-Jr.	Cze-Rep	DID NOT PLAY – INJURED									
1998-99	Sparta Praha-Jr.	Cze-Rep	5	7	3	10	....	4	1	1	2	....
	Velvana Kladno	Cze-Rep	5	0	0	0	0	....	....	....	....	....
99-2000	Velvana Kladno	Cze-Rep	6	1	2	3	2	....	....	....	....	....
	Sparta Praha	Cze-Rep	10	0	1	1	0	3	0	0	0	0

HAVLAT, Martin (hahv-lat, MAHR-tihn) OTT.

Center. Shoots left. 6'1", 178 lbs. Born, Mlada Boleslav, Czech., April 19, 1981.
(Ottawa's 1st choice, 26th overall, in 1999 Entry Draft).

			Regular Season					Playoffs				
Season	Club	Lea	GP	G	A	TP	PIM	GP	G	A	TP	PIM
1997-98	Ytong Brno-Jr.	Cze-Rep	32	38	29	67	....	....	....	....	....	....
1998-99	HC Trinec-Jr.	Cze-Rep	31	28	23	51	....	....	....	....	....	....
	HC Trinec	Cze-Rep	24	2	3	5	4	8	0	0	0	....
99-2000	HC Trinec	Cze-Rep	46	13	29	42	42	4	0	2	2	8

HAY, Darrell (HAY) VAN.

Defense. Shoots right. 6', 190 lbs. Born, Kamloops, B.C, April 2, 1980.
(Vancouver's 8th choice, 271st overall, in 1999 Entry Draft).

			Regular Season					Playoffs				
Season	Club	Lea	GP	G	A	TP	PIM	GP	G	A	TP	PIM
1995-96	Kamloops Lions	BCAHA	65	34	57	91	155	....	....	....	....	....
1996-97	Tri-City Americans	WHL	61	0	10	10	41	....	....	....	....	....
1997-98	Tri-City Americans	WHL	71	5	33	38	90	....	....	....	....	....
1998-99	Tri-City Americans	WHL	72	13	49	62	87	12	2	10	12	22
99-2000	Tri-City Americans	WHL	64	15	36	51	85	4	0	1	1	8

WHL West Second All-Star Team (2000)

HAYDAR, Darren (HAY-duhr) NSH.

Right wing. Shoots left. 5'9", 160 lbs. Born, Toronto, Ont., October 22, 1979.
(Nashville's 14th choice, 248th overall, in 1999 Entry Draft).

			Regular Season					Playoffs				
Season	Club	Lea	GP	G	A	TP	PIM	GP	G	A	TP	PIM
1996-97	Milton Merchants	OJHL	51	32	68	100	....	....	....	....	....	....
1997-98	Milton Merchants	OJHL	51	*71	*69	*140	65	....	....	....	....	....
1998-99	New Hampshire	H-East	41	31	30	61	34	....	....	....	....	....
99-2000	New Hampshire	H-East	38	22	19	41	42	....	....	....	....	....

OJHL Player-of-the-Year (1998) • OJHL First All-Star Team (1998) • Hockey East Second All-Star Team (1999, 2000)

HEALEY, Eric PHX.

Left wing. Shoots left. 5'11", 196 lbs. Born, Hull, MA, January 20, 1975.

			Regular Season					Playoffs				
Season	Club	Lea	GP	G	A	TP	PIM	GP	G	A	TP	PIM
1993-94	New England	NEJHL	37	61	76	137	....	....	....	....	....	....
1994-95	RPI Engineers	ECAC	37	13	11	24	35	....	....	....	....	....
1995-96	RPI Engineers	ECAC	35	18	22	40	57	....	....	....	....	....
1996-97	RPI Engineers	ECAC	36	30	26	56	63	....	....	....	....	....
1997-98	RPI Engineers	ECAC	35	21	27	48	42	....	....	....	....	....
1998-99	Saint John Flames	AHL	64	14	24	38	77	....	....	....	....	....
	Orlando	IHL	13	5	4	9	13	8	1	0	1	12
99-2000	Springfield	AHL	32	14	15	29	51	1	0	0	0	2

ECAC Second All-Star Team (1997) • NCAA East Second All-American Team (1997, 1998) • ECAC First All-Star Team (1998)

Signed as a free agent by **Calgary**, September 22, 1998. Signed as a free agent by **Phoenix**, July 26, 1999.

HEATLEY, Dany (HEET-lee) ATL.

Left wing. Shoots left. 6'1", 200 lbs. Born, Freiburg, Germany, January 21, 1981.
(Atlanta's 1st choice, 2nd overall, in 2000 Entry Draft).

			Regular Season					Playoffs				
Season	Club	Lea	GP	G	A	TP	PIM	GP	G	A	TP	PIM
1996-97	Calgary Blazers	AAHA	25	30	42	72	26	....	....	....	....	....
1997-98	Calgary Buffaloes	AMHL	36	39	42	*91	34	10	10	12	*22	30
1998-99	Calgary Canucks	AJHL	60	*70	56	*126	91	13	*22	13	*35	6
99-2000	U. of Wisconsin	WCHA	38	28	28	56	32	....	....	....	....	....

Air Canada Cup MVP (1997) • AJHL Player-of-the-Year (1999) • Canadian Junior "A" Player-of-the-Year (1999) • WCHA Rookie-of-the-Year (2000) • WCHA First All-Star Team (2000) • NCAA Second All-American Team (2000)

HEDIN, Pierre (heh-DEEN) TOR.

Defense. Shoots left. 6'1", 198 lbs. Born, Ornskoldsvik, Sweden, February 19, 1978.
(Toronto's 8th choice, 239th overall, in 1999 Entry Draft).

			Regular Season					Playoffs				
Season	Club	Lea	GP	G	A	TP	PIM	GP	G	A	TP	PIM
1994-95	MoDo Hockey	Swede-Jr.	21	0	3	3	20	....	....	....	....	....
1996-97	MoDo Hockey	Sweden	19	1	2	3	6	....	....	....	....	....
1997-98	MoDo Hockey	Sweden	29	2	1	3	26	9	1	1	2	4
1998-99	MoDo Hockey	Sweden	41	6	5	11	28	13	1	1	2	12
99-2000	MoDo Hockey	Sweden	48	9	5	14	36	13	0	2	2	8

HEDSTROM, Jonathan (HEHD-struhm, JOHN-a-THOHN) ANA.

Right wing. Shoots left. 6', 200 lbs. Born, Skelleftea, Sweden, December 27, 1977.
(Toronto's 8th choice, 221st overall, in 1997 Entry Draft).

			Regular Season					Playoffs				
Season	Club	Lea	GP	G	A	TP	PIM	GP	G	A	TP	PIM
1995-96	HV Skelleftea	Swede-2	7	0	0	0	0	....	....	....	....	....
1996-97	HV Skelleftea	Swede-2	12	1	1	2	10	6	0	0	0	2
	HV Skelleftea	Swede-Jr.	9	4	4	8	....	....	....	....	....	....
1997-98	HV Skelleftea	Swede-2	16	2	3	5	....	....	....	....	....	....
	HV Skelleftea	Swede-Jr.	1	0	0	0	2	....	....	....	....	....
1998-99	Skelleftea AIK	Swede-2	36	15	28	43	74	....	....	....	....	....
99-2000	Lulea HF	Sweden	48	9	17	26	46	9	2	1	3	12

Rights traded to **Anaheim** by **Toronto** for Anaheim's 6th (Vadim Sozinov) and 7th (Markus Seikola) round choices in 2000 Entry Draft, June 25, 2000.

HEEREMA, Jeff (HEER-eh-muh, JEHF) CAR.

Right wing. Shoots right. 6'1", 190 lbs. Born, Thunder Bay, Ont., January 17, 1980.
(Carolina's 1st choice, 11th overall, in 1998 Entry Draft).

			Regular Season					Playoffs				
Season	Club	Lea	GP	G	A	TP	PIM	GP	G	A	TP	PIM
1996-97	Thunder Bay	TBAHA	54	42	29	71	112	....	....	....	....	....
1997-98	Sarnia Sting	OHL	63	32	40	72	88	5	4	1	5	10
1998-99	Sarnia Sting	OHL	62	31	39	70	113	6	5	1	6	0
99-2000	Sarnia Sting	OHL	67	36	41	77	62	7	4	2	6	10

HEFFERNAN, Scott (HEH-fuhr-nuhn) CBJ

Defense. Shoots left. 6'5", 187 lbs. Born, Montreal, Que., March 9, 1982.
(Columbus' 4th choice, 138th overall, in 2000 Entry Draft).

			Regular Season					Playoffs				
Season	Club	Lea	GP	G	A	TP	PIM	GP	G	A	TP	PIM
1998-99	Pembroke	OJHL	44	3	5	8	51	....	....	....	....	....
99-2000	Sarnia Sting	OHL	55	5	10	15	24	7	0	1	1	4

HEISTEN, Barrett (HIGH-stehn, BAIR-reht) BUF.

Left wing. Shoots left. 6'1", 189 lbs. Born, Anchorage, AK, March 19, 1980.
(Buffalo's 1st choice, 20th overall, in 1999 Entry Draft).

			Regular Season					Playoffs				
Season	Club	Lea	GP	G	A	TP	PIM	GP	G	A	TP	PIM
1996-97	Anchorage Stars	AAHL	39	35	29	64	....	....	....	....	....	....
1997-98	Team USA	Under-18	50	11	26	37	245	....	....	....	....	....
1998-99	U. of Maine	H-East	34	12	16	28	72	....	....	....	....	....
99-2000	U. of Maine	H-East	37	13	24	37	86	....	....	....	....	....

HELBLING, Timo (HEHL-blihng, TEE-moh) NSH.

Defense. Shoots right. 6'2", 187 lbs. Born, Basel, Switzerland, July 21, 1981.
(Nashville's 11th choice, 162nd overall, in 1999 Entry Draft).

			Regular Season					Playoffs				
Season	Club	Lea	GP	G	A	TP	PIM	GP	G	A	TP	PIM
1997-98	HC Davos	Switz-Jr.	34	6	6	12	38	....	....	....	....	....
1998-99	HC Davos	Switz-Jr.	28	5	10	15	116	2	1	3	4	35
	HC Davos	Switz.	44	0	0	0	8	4	0	0	0	0
99-2000	HC Davos	Switz.	44	0	0	0	49	5	0	0	0	0

HEMINGWAY, Colin (HEH-mihng-way) ST.L.

Right wing. Shoots right. 6', 190 lbs. Born, Regina, Sask., August 12, 1980.
(St. Louis' 7th choice, 221st overall, in 1999 Entry Draft).

			Regular Season					Playoffs				
Season	Club	Lea	GP	G	A	TP	PIM	GP	G	A	TP	PIM
1997-98	South Surrey	BCJHL	58	12	16	28	46	....	....	....	....	....
1998-99	South Surrey	BCJHL	59	40	64	104	52	....	....	....	....	....
99-2000	New Hampshire	H-East	22	3	5	8	6	....	....	....	....	....

HENDRICKS, Matt (HEHN-drihks) NSH.

Center. Shoots left. 6', 195 lbs. Born, Blaine, MN, June 17, 1981.
(Nashville's 5th choice, 131st overall, in 2000 Entry Draft).

			Regular Season					Playoffs				
Season	Club	Lea	GP	G	A	TP	PIM	GP	G	A	TP	PIM
1998-99	Blaine High	Hi-School	22	23	34	57	42	....	....	....	....	....
99-2000	Blaine High	Hi-School	21	23	30	53	28	....	....	....	....	....

HENKEL, Jim (HEHN-kehl, JIHM) L.A.

Center. Shoots left. 6'2", 180 lbs. Born, Red Bank, NJ, May 25, 1979.
(Los Angeles' 8th choice, 217th overall, in 1998 Entry Draft).

			Regular Season					Playoffs				
Season	Club	Lea	GP	G	A	TP	PIM	GP	G	A	TP	PIM
1997-98	New England	EJHL	37	34	37	71	....	11	7	17	24	....
1998-99	RPI Engineers	ECAC	20	0	4	4	14	....	....	....	....	....
99-2000	RPI Engineers	ECAC	34	2	5	7	28	....	....	....	....	....

HENNING, Brett (HEH-nihng) NYI

Center. Shoots left. 6'1", 203 lbs. Born, Huntington, NY, May 7, 1980.
(NY Islanders' 13th choice, 255th overall, in 1999 Entry Draft).

			Regular Season					Playoffs				
Season	Club	Lea	GP	G	A	TP	PIM	GP	G	A	TP	PIM
1995-96	Cambridge Hawks	OJHL	46	8	26	34	49	....	....	....	....	....
1996-97	Cambridge Hawks	OJHL	43	11	21	32	70	....	....	....	....	....
1997-98	Team USA	Under-18	71	13	31	44	96	....	....	....	....	....
1998-99	Notre Dame	CCHA	38	4	6	10	30	....	....	....	....	....
99-2000	Notre Dame	CCHA	36	3	7	10	16	....	....	....	....	....

HENNING, Petter (HEH-nihng) NYR

Right wing. Shoots left. 6', 209 lbs. Born, Ornskoldsvik, Sweden, September 15, 1980.
(NY Rangers' 10th choice, 251st overall, in 1999 Entry Draft).

			Regular Season					Playoffs				
Season	Club	Lea	GP	G	A	TP	PIM	GP	G	A	TP	PIM
1997-98	MoDo Hockey	Swede-Jr.	27	7	6	13	12	....	....	....	....	....
1998-99	MoDo Hockey	Swede-Jr.	38	10	10	20	74	....	....	....	....	....
	MoDo Hockey	Sweden	1	0	0	0	0	....	....	....	....	....
99-2000	Skelleftea AIK	Sweden	8	0	0	0	2	....	....	....	....	....

HENRICH, Michael (HEHN-rihch, MIGH-kuhl) EDM.

Right wing. Shoots right. 6'2", 206 lbs. Born, Thornhill, Ont., March 3, 1980.
(Edmonton's 1st choice, 13th overall, in 1998 Entry Draft).

			Regular Season					Playoffs				
Season	Club	Lea	GP	G	A	TP	PIM	GP	G	A	TP	PIM
1995-96	Wexford Raiders	OJHL	4	1	0	1	0	....	....	....	....	....
1996-97	Barrie Colts	OHL	52	9	15	24	19	9	0	5	5	0
1997-98	Barrie Colts	OHL	66	41	22	63	75	5	1	3	4	0
1998-99	Barrie Colts	OHL	62	38	33	71	42	12	0	2	2	4
99-2000	Barrie Colts	OHL	66	38	48	86	69	25	10	18	28	30

HENRY, Alex EDM.

Defense. Shoots left. 6'5", 220 lbs. Born, Elliot Lake, Ont., October 18, 1979.
(Edmonton's 2nd choice, 67th overall, in 1998 Entry Draft).

			Regular Season					Playoffs				
Season	Club	Lea	GP	G	A	TP	PIM	GP	G	A	TP	PIM
1995-96	Timmins Titans	NOHA	30	2	4	11	15	....	....	....	....	....
	Timmins Bears	NOJHA	2	0	0	0	0	....	....	....	....	....
1996-97	London Knights	OHL	61	1	10	11	65	....	....	....	....	....
1997-98	London Knights	OHL	62	5	9	14	97	16	0	3	3	14
1998-99	London Knights	OHL	68	5	23	28	105	25	3	10	13	22
99-2000	Hamilton Bulldogs	AHL	60	1	0	1	69	....	....	....	....	....

HENRY, Burke (HEHN-ree, BUHRK) NYR

Defense. Shoots left. 6'3", 190 lbs. Born, Ste. Rose, Man., January 21, 1979.
(NY Rangers' 3rd choice, 73rd overall, in 1997 Entry Draft).

			Regular Season					Playoffs				
Season	Club	Lea	GP	G	A	TP	PIM	GP	G	A	TP	PIM
1995-96	Brandon	WHL	50	6	11	17	58	19	0	4	4	19
1996-97	Brandon	WHL	55	6	25	31	81	6	1	3	4	4
1997-98	Brandon	WHL	72	18	65	83	153	18	3	16	19	37
1998-99	Brandon	WHL	68	18	58	76	151	5	1	6	7	9
99-2000	Hartford	AHL	64	3	12	15	47	5	0	0	0	2

WHL East First All-Star Team (1998) • WHL East Second All-Star Team (1999)

HILBERT, Andy (HIHL-buhrt) BOS.

Center. Shoots left. 5'11", 190 lbs. Born, Howell, MI, February 6, 1981.
(Boston's 3rd choice, 37th overall, in 2000 Entry Draft).

			Regular Season					Playoffs				
Season	Club	Lea	GP	G	A	TP	PIM	GP	G	A	TP	PIM
1997-98	Team USA	Under-18	75	34	30	64	148	....	....	....	....	....
1998-99	Team USA	Under-18	46	23	35	58	140	....	....	....	....	....
99-2000	U. of Michigan	CCHA	35	17	15	32	39	....	....	....	....	....

HILL, Ed (HIHL, EHD) NSH.

Defense. Shoots left. 6'3", 215 lbs. Born, Newburyport, MA, October 24, 1980.
(Nashville's 5th choice, 61st overall, in 1999 Entry Draft).

			Regular Season					Playoffs				
Season	Club	Lea	GP	G	A	TP	PIM	GP	G	A	TP	PIM
1996-97	Green Bay	USHL	61	4	11	15	36	17	0	1	1	14
1997-98	Green Bay	USHL	51	1	16	17	76	3	0	0	0	0
1998-99	Barrie Colts	OHL	53	7	17	24	42	12	0	2	2	8
99-2000	Barrie Colts	OHL	66	1	18	19	63	25	1	3	4	14

HINZ, Chad (HIHNZ, CHAD) EDM.

Right wing. Shoots right. 5'10", 190 lbs. Born, Saskatoon, Sask., March 21, 1979.
(Edmonton's 8th choice, 187th overall, in 1997 Entry Draft).

			Regular Season					Playoffs				
Season	Club	Lea	GP	G	A	TP	PIM	GP	G	A	TP	PIM
1994-95	Saskatoon	SAHA	29	25	21	46	41	....	....	....	....	....
1995-96	Moose Jaw	WHL	70	22	32	54	65	....	....	....	....	....
1996-97	Moose Jaw	WHL	72	37	47	84	47	12	4	1	5	11
1997-98	Moose Jaw	WHL	72	20	57	77	45	4	1	2	3	2
1998-99	Moose Jaw	WHL	71	42	*75	117	40	11	4	12	16	12
	Hamilton Bulldogs	AHL	3	0	0	0	2	....	....	....	....	....
99-2000	Hamilton Bulldogs	AHL	18	1	4	5	2	5	1	0	1	0
	Tallahassee	ECHL	49	15	25	40	35	....	....	....	....	....

WHL East First All-Star Team (1999)

HIRVONEN, Tomi (HIHR-voh-nehn, TAW-mee) COL.

Center. Shoots left. 5'11", 185 lbs. Born, Tampere, Finland, January 11, 1977.
(Colorado's 8th choice, 207th overall, in 1995 Entry Draft).

			Regular Season					Playoffs				
Season	Club	Lea	GP	G	A	TP	PIM	GP	G	A	TP	PIM
1992-93	Ilves Tampere-C	Finn-Jr	34	32	20	52	71	....	....	....	....	....
1993-94	Ilves Tampere-B	Finn-Jr	28	13	14	27	96	....	....	....	....	....
	Ilves Tampere	Finn-Jr.	1	0	0	0	0	....	....	....	....	....
1994-95	Ilves Tampere-B	Finn-Jr.	6	1	5	6	14	....	....	....	....	....
	Ilves Tampere	Finn-Jr.	28	9	13	22	30	8	4	2	6	14
1995-96	Ilves Tampere	Finn-Jr.	5	2	2	4	37	7	5	10	15	8
	KooVee Tampere	Finland-2	7	4	1	5	26	....	....	....	....	....
	Ilves Tampere	Finland	28	1	0	1	24	....	....	....	....	....
1996-97	Ilves Tampere	Finn-Jr.	5	2	2	4	37	4	1	3	4	8
	Ilves Tampere	Finland	40	0	7	7	22	6	0	0	0	4
1997-98	Ilves Tampere	Finland	48	10	12	22	54	9	0	0	0	2
	Ilves Tampere	Finn-Jr.	....	....	....	....	....	2	5	0	5	4
1998-99	Ilves Tampere	Finland	50	5	15	20	94	4	0	0	0	8
	Ilves Tampere	EuroHL	6	1	3	4	2	....	....	....	....	....
99-2000	Ilves Tampere	Finland	45	4	7	11	62	3	0	1	1	6

HNIDY, Shane OTT.

Defense. Shoots right. 6'2", 210 lbs. Born, Neepawa, Man., November 8, 1975.
(Buffalo's 7th choice, 173rd overall, in 1994 Entry Draft).

			Regular Season					Playoffs				
Season	Club	Lea	GP	G	A	TP	PIM	GP	G	A	TP	PIM
1991-92	Swift Current	WHL	56	1	3	4	11	4	0	0	0	0
1992-93	Swift Current	WHL	45	5	12	17	62	....	....	....	....	....
	Prince Albert	WHL	27	2	10	12	43	....	....	....	....	....
1993-94	Prince Albert	WHL	69	7	26	33	113	....	....	....	....	....
1994-95	Prince Albert	WHL	72	5	29	34	169	15	4	7	11	29
1995-96	Prince Albert	WHL	58	11	42	53	100	18	4	11	15	34
1996-97	Baton Rouge	ECHL	21	3	10	13	50	....	....	....	....	....
	Saint John Flames	AHL	44	2	12	14	112	....	....	....	....	....
1997-98	Grand Rapids	IHL	77	6	12	18	210	3	0	2	2	23
1998-99	Adirondack	AHL	68	9	20	29	121	3	0	1	1	0
99-2000	Cincinnati Ducks	AHL	68	9	19	28	153	....	....	....	....	....

Signed as a free agent by **Detroit**, August 6, 1998. Traded to **Ottawa** by **Detroit** for Ottawa's 8th round choice (Todd Jackson) in 2000 Entry Draft, June 25, 2000.

HOGAN, Peter (HOH-gan, PEE-tuhr) L.A.

Defense. Shoots right. 6'3", 195 lbs. Born, Oshawa, Ont., January 10, 1978.
(Los Angeles' 7th choice, 123rd overall, in 1996 Entry Draft).

			Regular Season					Playoffs				
Season	Club	Lea	GP	G	A	TP	PIM	GP	G	A	TP	PIM
1994-95	Wexford Hawks	MTHL	36	5	16	21	....	....	....	....	....	....
	Wexford Raiders	OJHL	5	0	1	1	0	....	....	....	....	....
1995-96	Oshawa Generals	OHL	66	3	25	28	54	5	2	0	2	2
1996-97	Oshawa Generals	OHL	65	13	37	50	56	18	1	11	12	22
1997-98	Oshawa Generals	OHL	63	10	28	38	104	....	....	....	....	....
1998-99	Springfield	AHL	71	1	14	15	41	2	0	0	0	0
99-2000	Canada	Nat-Team	23	1	4	5	12	....	....	....	....	....
	Lowell	AHL	23	1	4	5	16	....	....	....	....	....

HOLLIS, Scott CBJ

Right wing. Shoots right. 6', 185 lbs. Born, Kingston, Ont., September 18, 1972.
(Vancouver's 9th choice, 165th overall, in 1992 Entry Draft).

			Regular Season					Playoffs				
Season	Club	Lea	GP	G	A	TP	PIM	GP	G	A	TP	PIM
1988-89	Kingston Lions	OMHA	14	14	14	28	15	....	....	....	....	....
1989-90	Oshawa Generals	OHL	50	4	6	10	33	....	....	....	....	....
1990-91	Oshawa Generals	OHL	66	24	33	57	91	16	5	3	8	20
1991-92	Oshawa Generals	OHL	66	47	54	101	183	....	....	....	....	....
1992-93	Oshawa Generals	OHL	62	49	53	102	148	....	....	....	....	....
1993-94	Las Vegas	IHL	23	3	1	4	65	....	....	....	....	....
	Knoxville	ECHL	29	20	16	36	99	3	3	1	4	8
1994-95	Adirondack	AHL	48	12	15	27	118	....	....	....	....	....
1995-96	Toledo Storm	ECHL	7	7	11	18	5	....	....	....	....	....
	Adirondack	AHL	55	18	17	37	111	3	0	1	1	4
1996-97	San Antonio	IHL	73	17	17	34	187	9	1	1	2	6
1997-98	San Antonio	IHL	19	15	6	21	21	....	....	....	....	....
	Orlando	IHL	48	16	23	39	68	17	5	4	9	30
1998-99	Orlando	IHL	3	1	1	2	6	....	....	....	....	....
	Long Beach	IHL	13	2	5	7	21	....	....	....	....	....
	Las Vegas	IHL	53	20	25	45	67	....	....	....	....	....
99-2000	SB Rosenheim	DEL	63	21	16	37	80	....	....	....	....	....

Signed as a free agent by **Columbus**, August 7, 2000.

HOLMQVIST, Mikael (HOHLM-kvihst, MIHK-al) ANA.

Center. Shoots left. 6'3", 189 lbs. Born, Stockholm, Sweden, June 8, 1979.
(Anaheim's 1st choice, 18th overall, in 1997 Entry Draft).

			Regular Season					Playoffs				
Season	Club	Lea	GP	G	A	TP	PIM	GP	G	A	TP	PIM
1995-96	Djurgardens IF	Swede-Jr.	24	7	2	9	4	....	....	....	....	....
1996-97	Djurgardens IF	Swede-Jr.	39	29	35	64	110	....	....	....	....	....
	Djurgardens IF	Sweden	9	0	0	0	0	....	....	....	....	....
1997-98	Farjestads BK	Sweden	41	2	3	5	6	7	0	0	0	0
	Farjestads BK	EuroHL	5	2	2	4	2	....	....	....	....	....
1998-99	Farjestads BK	Sweden	15	0	0	0	6	....	....	....	....	....
	Farjestads BK	EuroHL	3	0	0	0	0	1	0	0	0	0
	Farjestads BK	Swede-Jr.	2	2	2	4	2	....	....	....	....	....
	Hammarby IF	Swede-2	3	2	0	2	0	....	....	....	....	....
99-2000	TPS Turku	Finland	54	12	3	15	14	11	2	3	5	4

HORACEK, Jan (HOHR-uh-chehk, YAN) ST.L.

Defense. Shoots right. 6'4", 206 lbs. Born, Benesov, Czech., May 22, 1979.
(St. Louis' 3rd choice, 98th overall, in 1997 Entry Draft).

			Regular Season					Playoffs				
Season	Club	Lea	GP	G	A	TP	PIM	GP	G	A	TP	PIM
1995-96	Slavia Praha	Cze-Rep	8	0	1	1	4	....	....	....	....	....
	Slavia Praha-Jr.	Cze-Rep	18	1	5	6	0	....	....	....	....	....
	HC Karlovy	Cze-Rep-2	11	0	0	0	0	....	....	....	....	....
1996-97	Slavia Praha-Jr.	Cze-Rep	25	4	14	18	....	....	....	....	....	....
	Slavia Praha	Cze-Rep	9	0	0	0	6	3	0	0	0	0
	HC Beroun-2	Cze-Rep	2	0	0	0	....	....	....	....	....	....
1997-98	Moncton Wildcats	QMJHL	54	3	18	21	146	10	1	5	6	20
1998-99	Slavia Praha	Cze-Rep	1	0	0	0	2	....	....	....	....	....
	Worcester	AHL	53	1	13	14	119	4	0	0	0	6
99-2000	Worcester	AHL	68	1	8	9	145	9	0	0	0	2

HORCOFF, Shawn (HOHR-cuhf, SHAWN) EDM.

Center. Shoots left. 6'1", 202 lbs. Born, Trail, B.C., September 17, 1978.
(Edmonton's 3rd choice, 99th overall, in 1998 Entry Draft).

			Regular Season					Playoffs				
Season	Club	Lea	GP	G	A	TP	PIM	GP	G	A	TP	PIM
1995-96	Chilliwack Chiefs	BCJHL	58	49	96	*146	44	....	....	....	....	....
1996-97	Michigan State	CCHA	40	10	13	23	20	....	....	....	....	....
1997-98	Michigan State	CCHA	34	14	13	27	50	....	....	....	....	....
1998-99	Michigan State	CCHA	39	12	25	37	70	....	....	....	....	....
99-2000	Michigan State	CCHA	42	14	51	65	50	....	....	....	....	....

BCJHL Subway Player-of-the-Year (1996) • Won Brett Hull Trophy (BCJHL Scoring Leader) (1996) • BCJHL First All-Star Team (1996) • CCHA First All-Star Team (2000) • NCAA West First All-American Team (2000)

HORNUNG, Todd (HOHR-nuhng, TAWD) WSH.

Center. Shoots left. 6', 200 lbs. Born, Swift Current, Sask., September 3, 1980.
(Washington's 2nd choice, 59th overall, in 1998 Entry Draft).

			Regular Season					Playoffs				
Season	Club	Lea	GP	G	A	TP	PIM	GP	G	A	TP	PIM
1995-96	Swift Current	SAHA	59	71	55	126	276	....	....	....	....	....
	Portland	WHL	1	0	0	0	0	....	....	....	....	....
1996-97	Portland	WHL	59	3	3	6	51	6	0	0	0	0
1997-98	Portland	WHL	64	19	18	37	96	16	6	6	12	26
1998-99	Portland	WHL	45	15	15	30	86	....	....	....	....	....
	Lethbridge	WHL	13	1	1	2	26	....	....	....	....	....
99-2000	Swift Current	WHL	22	3	2	5	28	11	2	1	3	11

HOSSA, Marcel (HOH-sah) MTL.

Center. Shoots left. 6'1", 200 lbs. Born, Ilava, Czech., October 12, 1981.
(Montreal's 2nd choice, 16th overall, in 2000 Entry Draft).

			Regular Season					Playoffs				
Season	Club	Lea	GP	G	A	TP	PIM	GP	G	A	TP	PIM
1996-97	Dukla Trencin	Slovak-Jr.	45	30	21	51	30	....	....	....	....	....
1997-98	Dukla Trencin	Slovak-Jr.	39	11	38	49	44	....	....	....	....	....
1998-99	Portland	WHL	70	7	14	21	66	2	0	0	0	2
99-2000	Portland	WHL	60	24	29	53	58	....	....	....	....	....

HOUSE, Bobby (HOWSE, BAW-bee) TOR.

Right wing. Shoots right. 6'1", 205 lbs. Born, Whitehorse, Yukon, January 7, 1973.
(Chicago's 4th choice, 66th overall, in 1991 Entry Draft).

			Regular Season					Playoffs				
Season	Club	Lea	GP	G	A	TP	PIM	GP	G	A	TP	PIM
1988-89	Whitehorse Elks	AAHL	28	36	27	63	28	....	....	....	....	....
1989-90	Spokane Chiefs	WHL	64	18	16	34	74	5	0	0	0	6
1990-91	Spokane Chiefs	WHL	38	11	19	30	63	....	....	....	....	....
	Brandon	WHL	23	18	7	25	14	....	....	....	....	....
1991-92	Brandon	WHL	71	35	42	77	133	....	....	....	....	....
1992-93	Brandon	WHL	61	57	39	96	87	4	2	2	4	0
1993-94	Indianapolis Ice	IHL	42	10	8	18	51	....	....	....	....	....
	Flint Generals	ColHL	4	3	3	6	0	....	....	....	....	....
1994-95	Columbus Chill	ECHL	9	11	6	17	2	....	....	....	....	....
	Indianapolis Ice	IHL	26	2	3	5	26	....	....	....	....	....
	Albany River Rats	AHL	26	4	7	11	12	8	1	1	2	0
1995-96	Albany River Rats	AHL	77	37	49	86	57	4	0	0	0	4
1996-97	Albany River Rats	AHL	68	18	16	34	65	16	3	2	5	23
1997-98	Albany River Rats	AHL	19	10	10	20	10	....	....	....	....	....
	Hershey Bears	AHL	20	2	6	8	8	....	....	....	....	....
	Quebec Rafales	IHL	24	5	7	12	12	....	....	....	....	....
	Syracuse Crunch	AHL	9	5	6	11	6	5	2	0	2	4
1998-99	Augusta Lynx	ECHL	5	1	0	1	15	....	....	....	....	....
	Albany River Rats	AHL	1	0	0	0	0	....	....	....	....	....
	Springfield	AHL	56	11	18	29	27	3	1	0	1	2
99-2000	St. John's Leafs	AHL	68	24	29	53	46	....	....	....	....	....

WHL East Second All-Star Team (1993)

Traded to **New Jersey** by **Chicago** for cash, May 21, 1996. Signed as a free agent by **Toronto**, August 20, 1999.

HUBACEK, Petr (HOO-buh-chehk, PEE-tuhr) PHI.

Center. Shoots right. 6'2", 183 lbs. Born, Brno, Czech., September 2, 1979.
(Philadelphia's 11th choice, 243rd overall, in 1998 Entry Draft).

			Regular Season					Playoffs				
Season	Club	Lea	GP	G	A	TP	PIM	GP	G	A	TP	PIM
1997-98	HC Brno-Jr.	Cze-Rep	17	9	5	14	....	....	....	....	....	....
	Zetor Brno-Jr.	Cze-Rep	48	6	10	16	....	....	....	....	....	....
1998-99	HC Vitkovice	Cze-Rep	25	0	4	4	2	4	0	0	0	0
99-2000	HC Vitkovice	Cze-Rep	48	11	12	23	81	....	....	....	....	....

HUML, Ivan (HUH-muhl, ee-VAHN) BOS.

Left wing. Shoots left. 6'2", 183 lbs. Born, Kladno, Czech., September 6, 1981.
(Boston's 4th choice, 59th overall, in 2000 Entry Draft).

			Regular Season					Playoffs				
Season	Club	Lea	GP	G	A	TP	PIM	GP	G	A	TP	PIM
1996-97	HC Kladno-Jr.	Cze-Rep	37	16	3	19	....	....	....	....	....	....
1997-98	HC Kladno-Jr.	Cze-Rep	46	37	24	61	....	....	....	....	....	....
	HC Kladno	Cze-Rep	1	0	0	0	0	....	....	....	....	....
1998-99	HC Kladno-Jr.	Cze-Rep	18	6	6	12	....	....	....	....	....	....
	Langley Hornets	BCJHL	33	23	17	40	41	....	....	....	....	....
99-2000	Langley Hornets	BCJHL	49	53	51	104	72	....	....	....	....	....

HUNTER, Trent (HUHN-tuhr, TREHNT) NYI

Right wing. Shoots right. 6'3", 191 lbs. Born, Red Deer, Alta., July 5, 1980.
(Anaheim's 4th choice, 150th overall, in 1998 Entry Draft).

			Regular Season					Playoffs				
Season	Club	Lea	GP	G	A	TP	PIM	GP	G	A	TP	PIM
1996-97	Red Deer Chiefs	AMHL	42	30	25	55	50	....	....	....	....	....
1997-98	Prince George	WHL	60	13	14	27	34	8	1	0	1	4
1998-99	Prince George	WHL	50	18	20	38	34	7	2	5	7	2
99-2000	Prince George	WHL	67	46	49	95	47	13	7	15	22	6

WHL West First All-Star Team (2000)

Traded to **NY Islanders** by **Anaheim** for Columbus' 4th round choice (previously acquired, Anaheim selected Jonas Ronnqvist) in 2000 Entry Draft, May 23, 2000.

HUSELIUS, Kristian (hoo-SAY-lee-oos, KRIHST-yan) FLA.

Right wing. Shoots left. 6'1", 183 lbs. Born, Haninge, Sweden, November 10, 1978.
(Florida's 2nd choice, 47th overall, in 1997 Entry Draft).

			Regular Season					Playoffs				
Season	Club	Lea	GP	G	A	TP	PIM	GP	G	A	TP	PIM
1995-96	Hammarby IF	Swede-Jr.	25	13	8	21	14	....	....	....	....	....
	Hammarby IF	Sweden	6	1	0	1	0	....	....	....	....	....
1996-97	Farjestads BK	Sweden	13	2	0	2	4	5	1	0	1	0
1997-98	Farjestads BK	Sweden	34	2	1	3	2	11	0	0	0	0
	Farjestads BK	EuroHL	5	2	3	5	0	....	....	....	....	....
1998-99	Farjestads BK	Sweden	28	4	4	8	4	....	....	....	....	....
	Farjestads BK	EuroHL	6	2	2	4	8	1	0	0	0	0
	Vastra Frolunda	Sweden	20	2	2	4	2	4	1	0	1	0
99-2000	Vastra Frolunda	Sweden	50	21	23	44	20	5	2	2	4	8

HUSKINS, Kent (HUHS-kihns, KEHNT) CHI.

Defense. Shoots left. 6'2", 190 lbs. Born, Ottawa, Ont., May 4, 1979.
(Chicago's 3rd choice, 156th overall, in 1998 Entry Draft).

			Regular Season					Playoffs				
Season	Club	Lea	GP	G	A	TP	PIM	GP	G	A	TP	PIM
1995-96	Kanata Lasers	OJHL	49	6	21	27	18	....	....	....	....	....
1996-97	Kanata Lasers	OJHL	53	11	36	47	89	....	....	....	....	....
1997-98	Clarkson	ECAC	35	2	8	10	46	....	....	....	....	....
1998-99	Clarkson	ECAC	37	5	11	16	28	....	....	....	....	....
99-2000	Clarkson	ECAC	28	2	16	18	30	....	....	....	....	....

ECAC First All-Star Team (2000)

HUSSEY, Matt (HUH-see, MAT) PIT.

Center. Shoots left. 6'2", 195 lbs. Born, New Haven, CT, May 28, 1979.
(Pittsburgh's 10th choice, 254th overall, in 1998 Entry Draft).

			Regular Season					Playoffs				
Season	Club	Lea	GP	G	A	TP	PIM	GP	G	A	TP	PIM
1997-98	Avon Old Farms	Hi-School	26	26	23	49	20	....	....	....	....	....
1998-99	U. of Wisconsin	WCHA	37	10	5	15	18	....	....	....	....	....
99-2000	U. of Wisconsin	WCHA	35	5	11	16	8	....	....	....	....	....

HUTCHINS, Tony (HUHT-chihns, TOH-nee) ST.L.

Center. Shoots left. 6', 196 lbs. Born, Wolfeboro, NH, January 11, 1977.
(St. Louis' 9th choice, 203rd overall, in 1996 Entry Draft).

			Regular Season					Playoffs				
Season	Club	Lea	GP	G	A	TP	PIM	GP	G	A	TP	PIM
1995-96	Lawrence Prep	Hi-School	27	18	20	38	22	....	....	....	....	....
1996-97	Boston College	H-East	26	8	0	8	10	....	....	....	....	....
1997-98	Boston College	H-East	39	12	5	17	52	....	....	....	....	....
1998-99	Boston College	H-East	39	4	9	13	42	....	....	....	....	....
99-2000	Boston College	H-East	18	2	2	4	8	....	....	....	....	....

HUTCHINSON, Andrew (HUHT-chihn-SOHN, AN-drew) NSH.

Defense. Shoots right. 6'2", 190 lbs. Born, Evanston, IL, March 24, 1980.
(Nashville's 4th choice, 54th overall, in 1999 Entry Draft).

			Regular Season					Playoffs				
Season	Club	Lea	GP	G	A	TP	PIM	GP	G	A	TP	PIM
1997-98	Team USA	Under-18	59	7	21	28	53	....	....	....	....	....
1998-99	Michigan State	CCHA	37	3	12	15	26	....	....	....	....	....
99-2000	Michigan State	CCHA	42	5	12	17	64	....	....	....	....	....

HYACINTHE, Seneque (SEH-nehk, high-a-SIHNT) BUF.

Left wing. Shoots left. 5'11", 180 lbs. Born, Montreal, Que., February 22, 1981.
(Buffalo's 9th choice, 178th overall, in 1999 Entry Draft).

			Regular Season					Playoffs				
Season	Club	Lea	GP	G	A	TP	PIM	GP	G	A	TP	PIM
1997-98	Laval Titan	QMJHL	65	10	8	18	37	8	3	2	5	2
1998-99	Acadie-Bathurst	QMJHL	31	13	17	30	70	....	....	....	....	....
	Val-d'Or Foreurs	QMJHL	32	11	16	27	36	4	0	2	2	2
99-2000	Val-d'Or Foreurs	QMJHL	49	15	30	45	43	....	....	....	....	....

HYMOVITZ, David (HIH-moh-vihtz, DAY-vihd) L.A.

Left wing. Shoots left. 5'11", 191 lbs. Born, Boston, MA, May 30, 1973.
(Chicago's 9th choice, 209th overall, in 1992 Entry Draft).

			Regular Season					Playoffs				
Season	Club	Lea	GP	G	A	TP	PIM	GP	G	A	TP	PIM
1991-92	Thayer Academy	Hi-School	26	28	21	49	22	....	....	....	....	....
1992-93	Boston College	H-East	37	7	6	13	6	....	....	....	....	....
1993-94	Boston College	H-East	36	18	14	32	18	....	....	....	....	....
1994-95	Boston College	H-East	35	21	19	40	22	....	....	....	....	....
1995-96	Boston College	H-East	36	26	18	44	32	....	....	....	....	....
1996-97	Columbus Chill	ECHL	58	39	32	71	29	5	4	1	5	2
	Indianapolis Ice	IHL	6	0	1	1	0	1	0	0	0	0
1997-98	Indianapolis Ice	IHL	63	11	15	26	20	5	1	1	2	6
1998-99	Indianapolis Ice	IHL	78	46	30	76	42	5	2	3	5	2
99-2000	Lowell	AHL	67	19	17	36	30	....	....	....	....	....
	Houston Aeros	IHL	18	10	3	13	16	11	3	4	7	8

IHL Second All-Star Team (1999)

Signed as a free agent by **Los Angeles**, June 10, 1999. Traded to **Houston** (IHL) by **Lowell** (AHL) with LA Kings retaining NHL rights for Jeff Daw , March 17, 2000.

HYVONEN, Hannes (HOO-voh-nuhn, HAH-nuhs) S.J.

Right wing. Shoots right. 6'2", 200 lbs. Born, Oulu, Finland, August 29, 1975.
(San Jose's 7th choice, 257th overall, in 1999 Entry Draft).

			Regular Season					Playoffs				
Season	Club	Lea	GP	G	A	TP	PIM	GP	G	A	TP	PIM
1993-94	Karpat Oulu	Finn-Jr.	35	15	13	28	26	3	0	0	0	0
	Karpat Oulu	Finland-2	3	3	1	4	2	....	....	....	....	....
1994-95	TPS Turku	Finn-Jr.	10	8	2	10	64	....	....	....	....	....
	Kiekko-67	Finn-Jr.	1	1	0	1	0	....	....	....	....	....
	Kiekko-67	Finland-2	16	4	2	6	10	....	....	....	....	....
	TPS Turku	Finland	9	4	3	7	16	5	0	0	0	7
1995-96	Kiekko-67	Finland-2	2	1	0	1	8	....	....	....	....	....
	TPS Turku	Finland	30	11	5	16	49	7	0	1	1	28
1996-97	TPS Turku	Finland	41	10	5	15	48	10	4	2	6	14
1997-98	TPS Turku	Finland	29	2	6	8	71	2	0	0	0	0
1998-99	Blues Espoo	Finland	52	23	18	41	74	4	2	1	3	2
99-2000	Blues Espoo	Finland	18	5	2	7	*89	....	....	....	....	....
	HIFK Helsinki	Finland	22	2	2	4	*100	9	4	0	4	8

HYYTIA, Mikko (HOO-tee-a, MEE-koh) MTL.

Center. Shoots left. 6', 180 lbs. Born, Jyvaskyla, Finland, July 12, 1981.
(Montreal's 10th choice, 225th overall, in 1999 Entry Draft).

			Regular Season					Playoffs				
Season	Club	Lea	GP	G	A	TP	PIM	GP	G	A	TP	PIM
1997-98	JyP Jyvaskyla	Finn-Jr.	36	11	15	26	14	5	2	1	3	2
1998-99	JyP Jyvaskyla	Finn-Jr.	12	2	7	9	4	....	....	....	....	....
	JyP Jyvaskyla-B	Finn-Jr.	27	32	15	47	53	....	....	....	....	....
99-2000	JyP Jyvaskyla-B	Finn-Jr.	7	3	3	6	4	....	....	....	....	....
	JyP Jyvaskyla	Finn-Jr.	1	0	0	0	0	....	....	....	....	....

IANIERO, Andrew (juh-NAIR-oh, AN-drew) OTT.

Left wing. Shoots left. 6', 197 lbs. Born, St. Catharines, Ont., January 10, 1981.
(Ottawa's 5th choice, 154th overall, in 1999 Entry Draft).

			Regular Season					Playoffs				
Season	Club	Lea	GP	G	A	TP	PIM	GP	G	A	TP	PIM
1997-98	Brampton Capitals	OJHL	45	6	14	20	75	....	....	....	....	....
1998-99	Kingston	OHL	68	21	26	47	81	5	5	3	8	15
99-2000	Kingston	OHL	67	23	33	56	42	5	5	0	5	4

INMAN, David (IHN-man, DAY-vihd) NYR

Center. Shoots left. 6'1", 180 lbs. Born, New York, NY, June 13, 1980.
(NY Rangers' 3rd choice, 59th overall, in 1999 Entry Draft).

			Regular Season					Playoffs				
Season	Club	Lea	GP	G	A	TP	PIM	GP	G	A	TP	PIM
1995-96	Wexford Raiders	OJHL	4	2	1	3	0	....	....	....	....	....
1996-97	Wexford Raiders	OJHL	43	32	56	88	59	....	....	....	....	....
1997-98	Wexford Raiders	OJHL	37	36	44	80	82	....	....	....	....	....
1998-99	Notre Dame	CCHA	38	10	10	20	74	....	....	....	....	....
99-2000	Notre Dame	CCHA	32	13	7	20	12	....	....	....	....	....

IRVING, Joel (UHR-vihng, JOHL)

Center. Shoots right. 6'4", 210 lbs. Born, Lumsden, Sask., January 2, 1976.
(Montreal's 8th choice, 148th overall, in 1994 Entry Draft).

			Regular Season					Playoffs				
Season	**Club**	**Lea**	**GP**	**G**	**A**	**TP**	**PIM**	**GP**	**G**	**A**	**TP**	**PIM**
1993-94	Regina Capitals	AJHL	32	16	46	62	22	....	....	....	....	....
1994-95	Western Michigan	CCHA	30	2	3	5	20	....	....	....	....	....
1995-96	Western Michigan	CCHA	39	7	6	13	58	....	....	....	....	....
1996-97	Western Michigan	CCHA	34	8	11	19	62	....	....	....	....	....
1997-98	Western Michigan	CCHA	36	8	10	18	82	....	....	....	....	....
1998-99	Saint John Flames	AHL	5	0	0	0	2	....	....	....	....	....
	Johnstown Chiefs	ECHL	65	26	20	46	112	....	....	....	....	....
99-2000	Saint John Flames	AHL	7	1	2	3	5	....	....	....	....	....
	Orlando	IHL	2	0	0	0	2	....	....	....	....	....
	Johnstown Chiefs	ECHL	61	25	26	51	152	7	2	2	4	20

Signed as a free agent by **Calgary**, July 28, 1998. Traded to **Atlanta** by **Calgary** for future considerations, February 18, 2000.

JACKMAN, Barret (JAK-man, BAIR-reht) ST.L.

Defense. Shoots left. 6'1", 200 lbs. Born, Trail, B.C., March 5, 1981.
(St. Louis' 1st choice, 17th overall, in 1999 Entry Draft).

			Regular Season					Playoffs				
Season	**Club**	**Lea**	**GP**	**G**	**A**	**TP**	**PIM**	**GP**	**G**	**A**	**TP**	**PIM**
1996-97	Beaver Valley	VIJHL	32	22	25	47	180	....	....	....	....	....
1997-98	Regina Pats	WHL	68	2	11	13	224	9	0	3	3	32
1998-99	Regina Pats	WHL	70	8	36	44	259	....	....	....	....	....
99-2000	Regina Pats	WHL	53	9	37	46	175	6	1	1	2	19
	Worcester	AHL	....	....	....	....	....	2	0	0	0	13

WHL East Second All-Star Team (2000)

JACOBS, Ian (JAY-cawbs, EE-an) FLA.

Right wing. Shoots right. 6'4", 207 lbs. Born, Walpole Island, Ont., May 16, 1980.
(Florida's 8th choice, 203rd overall, in 1998 Entry Draft).

			Regular Season					Playoffs				
Season	**Club**	**Lea**	**GP**	**G**	**A**	**TP**	**PIM**	**GP**	**G**	**A**	**TP**	**PIM**
1996-97	Chatham Macs	OJHL-B	48	15	16	31	85	....	....	....	....	....
1997-98	Ottawa 67's	OHL	61	7	8	15	23	9	0	0	0	4
1998-99	Ottawa 67's	OHL	63	7	17	24	46	9	1	2	3	7
99-2000	Ottawa 67's	OHL	59	13	26	39	56	11	1	3	4	11

JACOBSEN, Michael (JAY-cawbs, MIGH-kuhl) CHI.

Defense. Shoots left. 6'1", 207 lbs. Born, Thunder Bay, Ont., July 24, 1981.
(Chicago's 4th choice, 134th overall, in 1999 Entry Draft).

			Regular Season					Playoffs				
Season	**Club**	**Lea**	**GP**	**G**	**A**	**TP**	**PIM**	**GP**	**G**	**A**	**TP**	**PIM**
1996-97	Thunder Bay	TBAHA	71	28	42	70	40	....	....	....	....	....
1997-98	Belleville Bulls	OHL	56	7	14	21	14	10	0	3	3	0
1998-99	Belleville Bulls	OHL	68	5	27	32	33	21	0	4	4	10
99-2000	Belleville Bulls	OHL	68	9	40	49	18	16	2	5	7	7

JAMIESON, Dusty (JAY-mih-suhn, DUHS-tee) MTL.

Left wing. Shoots left. 6'3", 176 lbs. Born, Sarnia, Ont., May 26, 1981.
(Montreal's 5th choice, 136th overall, in 1999 Entry Draft).

			Regular Season					Playoffs				
Season	**Club**	**Lea**	**GP**	**G**	**A**	**TP**	**PIM**	**GP**	**G**	**A**	**TP**	**PIM**
1996-97	St. Thomas Stars	OJHL-B	50	15	16	31	19	....	....	....	....	....
1997-98	Guelph Storm	OHL	48	3	4	7	0	12	0	1	1	0
1998-99	Guelph Storm	OHL	12	2	7	9	0	....	....	....	....	....
	Sarnia Sting	OHL	54	14	21	35	10	6	1	0	1	2
99-2000	Sarnia Sting	OHL	50	15	17	32	15	7	3	2	5	0

JANCEVSKI, Dan DAL.

Defense. Shoots left. 6'3", 222 lbs. Born, Windsor, Ont., June 15, 1981.
(Dallas' 2nd choice, 66th overall, in 1999 Entry Draft).

			Regular Season					Playoffs				
Season	**Club**	**Lea**	**GP**	**G**	**A**	**TP**	**PIM**	**GP**	**G**	**A**	**TP**	**PIM**
1995-96	Riverside Regents	OMHA	59	9	22	31	67	....	....	....	....	....
1996-97	Windsor Lions	OMHA	47	6	20	26	99	....	....	....	....	....
1997-98	Tecumseh	OJHL-B	49	3	11	14	145	....	....	....	....	....
1998-99	London Knights	OHL	68	2	12	14	115	25	1	7	8	24
99-2000	London Knights	OHL	59	8	15	23	138	....	....	....	....	....

JANIK, Doug (JAN-nihk, DUHG) BUF.

Defense. Shoots left. 6'1", 198 lbs. Born, Agawam, MA, March 26, 1980.
(Buffalo's 3rd choice, 55th overall, in 1999 Entry Draft).

			Regular Season					Playoffs				
Season	**Club**	**Lea**	**GP**	**G**	**A**	**TP**	**PIM**	**GP**	**G**	**A**	**TP**	**PIM**
1996-97	Springfield Pics	EJHL	39	12	24	36	22	11	5	9	14	10
1997-98	Team USA	Under-18	65	8	26	34	105	....	....	....	....	....
1998-99	U. of Maine	H-East	35	3	13	16	44	....	....	....	....	....
99-2000	U. of Maine	H-East	36	6	14	20	54	....	....	....	....	....

JARDINE, Ryan (JAHR-dighn, RIGH-yan) FLA.

Left wing. Shoots left. 6', 210 lbs. Born, Ottawa, Ont., March 15, 1980.
(Florida's 4th choice, 89th overall, in 1998 Entry Draft).

			Regular Season					Playoffs				
Season	**Club**	**Lea**	**GP**	**G**	**A**	**TP**	**PIM**	**GP**	**G**	**A**	**TP**	**PIM**
1996-97	Kanata Lasers	OJHL	52	30	27	57	76	....	....	....	....	....
1997-98	Sault Ste. Marie	OHL	65	28	32	60	16	....	....	....	....	....
1998-99	Sault Ste. Marie	OHL	68	27	34	61	56	5	0	1	1	6
99-2000	Sault Ste. Marie	OHL	65	43	34	77	58	17	11	8	19	16

JARVIS, Wes NYR

Defense. Shoots left. 6'5", 215 lbs. Born, Toronto, Ont., April 16, 1979.
(NY Rangers' 2nd choice, 46th overall, in 1997 Entry Draft).

			Regular Season					Playoffs				
Season	**Club**	**Lea**	**GP**	**G**	**A**	**TP**	**PIM**	**GP**	**G**	**A**	**TP**	**PIM**
1993-94	Ottawa	OJHL	42	22	43	65	52	....	....	....	....	....
1994-95	Ottawa	OJHL	45	23	48	71	48	....	....	....	....	....
1995-96	Gloucester	OJHL	43	3	6	9	73	....	....	....	....	....
1996-97	Kitchener	OHL	56	4	8	12	108	13	0	4	4	25
1997-98	Kitchener	OHL	47	10	18	28	112	1	0	0	0	2
1998-99	Kitchener	OHL	52	5	18	23	80	1	0	0	0	2
	Canada	Nat-Team	7	1	0	1	4	....	....	....	....	....
99-2000	Canada	Nat-Team	43	2	5	7	50	....	....	....	....	....

JASPERS, Jason (JAS-puhrs, JAY-suhn) PHX.

Center/Left wing. Shoots left. 5'11", 185 lbs. Born, Thunder Bay, Ont., April 8, 1981.
(Phoenix's 4th choice, 71st overall, in 1999 Entry Draft).

			Regular Season					Playoffs				
Season	**Club**	**Lea**	**GP**	**G**	**A**	**TP**	**PIM**	**GP**	**G**	**A**	**TP**	**PIM**
1997-98	Thunder Bay	TBAHA	72	45	75	120	90	....	....	....	....	....
1998-99	Sudbury Wolves	OHL	68	28	33	61	81	4	2	1	3	13
99-2000	Sudbury Wolves	OHL	68	46	61	107	107	12	4	6	10	27

OHL Second All-Star Team (2000)

JEFFERSON, Mike (JEH-fuhr-suhn) N.J.

Center. Shoots right. 5'9", 190 lbs. Born, Brampton, Ont., October 21, 1980.
(New Jersey's 8th choice, 135th overall, in 2000 Entry Draft).

			Regular Season					Playoffs				
Season	**Club**	**Lea**	**GP**	**G**	**A**	**TP**	**PIM**	**GP**	**G**	**A**	**TP**	**PIM**
1998-99	St. Michael's	OHL	27	18	22	40	116	....	....	....	....	....
	Barrie Colts	OHL	26	15	20	35	62	9	6	5	11	38
99-2000	Barrie Colts	OHL	58	34	53	87	203	25	7	16	23	107

JENSEN, Erik (JEHN-sehn, AIR-ihk) N.J.

Right wing. Shoots right. 6'1", 195 lbs. Born, Madison, WI, September 4, 1979.
(New Jersey's 10th choice, 199th overall, in 1998 Entry Draft).

			Regular Season					Playoffs				
Season	**Club**	**Lea**	**GP**	**G**	**A**	**TP**	**PIM**	**GP**	**G**	**A**	**TP**	**PIM**
1997-98	Des Moines	USHL	41	12	14	26	90	....	....	....	....	....
1998-99	Des Moines	USHL	26	5	11	16	62	14	4	3	7	35
99-2000	U. of Wisconsin	WCHA	22	3	3	6	30	....	....	....	....	....

JILLSON, Jeff (JIHL-sohn, JEHF) S.J.

Defense. Shoots right. 6'3", 220 lbs. Born, Providence, RI, July 24, 1980.
(San Jose's 1st choice, 14th overall, in 1999 Entry Draft).

			Regular Season					Playoffs				
Season	**Club**	**Lea**	**GP**	**G**	**A**	**TP**	**PIM**	**GP**	**G**	**A**	**TP**	**PIM**
1996-97	Mount St. Charles	Hi-School	15	16	14	30	20	4	0	4	4	3
1997-98	Mount St. Charles	Hi-School	15	10	13	23	32	5	4	5	9	4.5
1998-99	U. of Michigan	CCHA	38	5	19	24	71	....	....	....	....	....
99-2000	U. of Michigan	CCHA	38	8	26	34	115	....	....	....	....	....

CCHA First All-Star Team (2000) • NCAA West First All-American Team (2000)

JINDRICH, Robert (IHN-drihkh, RAW-buhrt) S.J.

Defense. Shoots left. 5'11", 190 lbs. Born, Plzen, Czech., October 14, 1976.
(San Jose's 10th choice, 168th overall, in 1995 Entry Draft).

			Regular Season					Playoffs				
Season	**Club**	**Lea**	**GP**	**G**	**A**	**TP**	**PIM**	**GP**	**G**	**A**	**TP**	**PIM**
1993-94	ZKZ Plzen	Cze-Rep	18	0	2	2	....	....	....	....	....	....
1994-95	ZKZ Plzen	Cze-Rep	11	1	0	1	4	....	....	....	....	....
1995-96	ZKZ Plzen	Cze-Rep	37	1	3	4	....	3	0	0	0	....
1996-97	ZKZ Plzen	Cze-Rep	49	7	9	16	44	....	....	....	....	....
1997-98	ZKZ Plzen	Cze-Rep	39	1	6	7	18	4	0	0	0	0
1998-99	ZKZ Plzen	Cze-Rep	52	6	12	18	24	5	1	0	1	....
99-2000	Kentucky	AHL	78	2	21	23	51	9	0	4	4	6

JOHANSSON, Daniel (yoh-HAN-suhn, DAN-yehl) L.A.

Center. Shoots left. 5'11", 176 lbs. Born, Ornskoldsvik, Sweden, July 5, 1981.
(Los Angeles' 6th choice, 125th overall, in 1999 Entry Draft).

			Regular Season					Playoffs				
Season	**Club**	**Lea**	**GP**	**G**	**A**	**TP**	**PIM**	**GP**	**G**	**A**	**TP**	**PIM**
1997-98	MoDo Hockey	Swede-Jr.	6	0	0	0	0	....	....	....	....	....
1998-99	MoDo Hockey	Swede-Jr.	43	10	19	29	....	....	....	....	....	....
99-2000	MoDo Hockey	Swede-Jr.	35	11	21	32	34	....	....	....	....	....

JOHANSSON, David (yoh-HAHN-suhn) WSH.

Defense. Shoots left. 6', 176 lbs. Born, Lidingo, Sweden, June 15, 1981.
(Washington's 8th choice, 192nd overall, in 1999 Entry Draft).

			Regular Season					Playoffs				
Season	**Club**	**Lea**	**GP**	**G**	**A**	**TP**	**PIM**	**GP**	**G**	**A**	**TP**	**PIM**
1997-98	AIK Solna	Swede-Jr.	13	0	1	1	10	....	....	....	....	....
1998-99	AIK Solna	Swede-Jr.	33	5	5	10	30	....	....	....	....	....
99-2000	Kelowna Rockets	WHL	62	3	24	27	36	2	0	0	0	0

JOHANSSON, Mikael (yoh-HAHN-suhn) COL.

Center. Shoots left. 5'10", 180 lbs. Born, Stockholm, Swe., June 12, 1966.
(Quebec's 7th choice, 134th overall, in 1991 Entry Draft).

			Regular Season					Playoffs				
Season	**Club**	**Lea**	**GP**	**G**	**A**	**TP**	**PIM**	**GP**	**G**	**A**	**TP**	**PIM**
1986-87	Djurgardens IF	Sweden	32	9	16	25	8	....	....	....	....	....
1987-88	Djurgardens IF	Sweden	38	11	22	33	10	3	1	1	2	0
1988-89	Djurgardens IF	Sweden	29	6	15	21	10	....	....	....	....	....
1989-90	Djurgardens IF	Sweden	37	14	20	34	12	8	5	4	9	0
1990-91	Djurgardens IF	Sweden	39	13	27	40	21	7	2	7	9	0
1991-92	Djurgardens IF	Sweden	30	15	21	36	12	9	1	5	6	4
1992-93	EHC Kloten	Switz.	36	18	30	48	2	....	....	....	....	....
1993-94	EHC Kloten	Switz.	36	22	29	51	24	12	9	14	23	8
1994-95	EHC Kloten	Switz.	35	14	36	50	8	12	4	9	13	8
1995-96	EHC Kloten	Switz.	35	13	20	33	10	10	5	13	18	2
1996-97	EHC Kloten	Switz.	46	17	27	44	10	4	1	2	3	2
1997-98	Djurgardens IF	Sweden	43	15	23	38	18	15	6	6	*12	4
1998-99	Djurgardens IF	Sweden	39	5	12	17	20	4	0	0	0	0
	Djurgardens IF	EuroHL	5	0	4	4	4	....	....	....	....	....
99-2000	Djurgardens IF	Sweden	49	17	22	39	16	13	8	8	16	0

JOHANSSON, Tobias (yoh-HAHN-suhn, TOH-bigh-as) ANA.

Left wing. Shoots left. 5'11", 180 lbs. Born, Malmo, Sweden, October 22, 1977.
(Anaheim's 7th choice, 224th overall, in 1996 Entry Draft).

			Regular Season					Playoffs				
Season	**Club**	**Lea**	**GP**	**G**	**A**	**TP**	**PIM**	**GP**	**G**	**A**	**TP**	**PIM**
1995-96	Malmo IF	Swede-Jr.	30	7	13	20	38	....	....	....	....	....
1996-97	Malmo IF	Swede-Jr.	15	6	8	14	63	....	....	....	....	....
1997-98	Tranas AIF	Swede-2	31	7	2	9	18	....	....	....	....	....
1998-99	Tranas AIF	Swede-2	32	11	5	16	28	....	....	....	....	....
99-2000	Tranas AIF	Swede-2	30	8	5	13	73	....	....	....	....	....
	Tranas AIF	Sweden	14	2	3	5	10	....	....	....	....	....

JOHNSON, Adam (JAWN-sohn, A-dam) NYI

Defense. Shoots left. 6'6", 220 lbs. Born, Minneapolis, MN, August 2, 1980.
(NY Islanders' 10th choice, 140th overall, in 1999 Entry Draft).

			Regular Season					Playoffs				
Season	Club	Lea	GP	G	A	TP	PIM	GP	G	A	TP	PIM
1998-99	Greenway High	Hi-School	17	5	13	18	32	....	....	....	....	....
99-2000	Tri-City Americans	WHL	52	0	3	3	90	4	0	1	1	4

JOHNSTONE, Alex (JAWN-stohn, AL-ehx) N.J.

Defense. Shoots left. 6'1", 200 lbs. Born, Halifax, N.S., December 28, 1979.

			Regular Season					Playoffs				
Season	Club	Lea	GP	G	A	TP	PIM	GP	G	A	TP	PIM
1996-97	Halifax	QMJHL	39	1	5	6	213	18	1	0	1	48
1997-98	Halifax	QMJHL	66	3	10	13	390	5	0	2	2	8
1998-99	Halifax	QMJHL	60	1	8	9	248	5	0	1	1	4
99-2000	Albany River Rats	AHL	13	0	0	0	22	....	....	....	....	....
	Augusta Lynx	ECHL	21	0	2	2	88	....	....	....	....	....

Signed as a free agent by **New Jersey**, August 8, 1998.

JOKELA, Mikko (YOH-kih-lah, MIH-koh) N.J.

Defense. Shoots right. 6'1", 215 lbs. Born, Lappeenranta, Finland, March 4, 1980.
(New Jersey's 5th choice, 96th overall, in 1998 Entry Draft).

			Regular Season					Playoffs				
Season	Club	Lea	GP	G	A	TP	PIM	GP	G	A	TP	PIM
1994-95	KalPa Kuopio-C	Finn-Jr.	29	7	12	19	36	....	....	....	....	....
1995-96	KalPa Kuopio-C	Finn-Jr.	23	10	19	29	103	6	3	5	8	4
	KalPa Kuopio-B	Finn-Jr.	9	2	1	3	20	....	....	....	....	....
	KalPa Kuopio	Finn-Jr.	11	2	1	3	20	....	....	....	....	....
1996-97	KalPa Kuopio	Finn-Jr.	45	5	7	12	26	5	1	1	2	4
1997-98	HIFK Helsinki	Finn-Jr.	22	2	5	7	14	....	....	....	....	....
	HIFK Helsinki	Finland	16	0	0	0	0	....	....	....	....	....
	Hermes HT	Finland-2	6	0	1	1	2	....	....	....	....	....
1998-99	HIFK Helsinki	Finland	3	0	0	0	2	....	....	....	....	....
	KalPa Kuopio	Finland	42	1	2	3	18	....	....	....	....	....
99-2000	SaiPa	Finland	48	0	5	5	50	....	....	....	....	....

JONES, Mike T.B.

Defense. Shoots left. 6'3", 190 lbs. Born, Toledo, OH, May 18, 1976.

			Regular Season					Playoffs				
Season	Club	Lea	GP	G	A	TP	PIM	GP	G	A	TP	PIM
1995-96	Cleveland Barons	NAJHL	46	25	*45	70	....	....	....	....	....	....
1996-97	Bowling Green	CCHA	27	1	6	7	47	....	....	....	....	....
1997-98	Bowling Green	CCHA	28	3	12	15	69	....	....	....	....	....
1998-99	Bowling Green	CCHA	38	8	21	29	80	....	....	....	....	....
99-2000	Bowling Green	CCHA	34	6	13	19	71	....	....	....	....	....

NAJHL Defenseman-of-the-Year (1995) • CCHA Second All-Star Team (1999)

Signed as a free agent by **Tampa Bay**, April 13, 2000.

JONSSON, Lars (YAWN-suhn) BOS.

Defense. Shoots left. 6'1", 198 lbs. Born, Borlange, Sweden, January 2, 1982.
(Boston's 1st choice, 7th overall, in 2000 Entry Draft).

			Regular Season					Playoffs				
Season	Club	Lea	GP	G	A	TP	PIM	GP	G	A	TP	PIM
1998-99	Leksands IF	Swede-Jr.	40	4	8	12	42	....	....	....	....	....
99-2000	Leksands IF	Swede-Jr.	34	16	22	38	50	2	0	0	0	0
	Leksands IF	Sweden	5	0	0	0	4	....	....	....	....	....

KACZOWKA, David (kuh-ZOW-kuh, DAY-vihd) ATL.

Left wing. Shoots left. 6'2", 205 lbs. Born, Regina, Sask., July 5, 1981.
(Atlanta's 4th choice, 98th overall, in 1999 Entry Draft).

			Regular Season					Playoffs				
Season	Club	Lea	GP	G	A	TP	PIM	GP	G	A	TP	PIM
1997-98	Prince Albert	SAHA	56	5	13	18	334	....	....	....	....	....
1998-99	Seattle T-Birds	WHL	60	3	2	5	247	9	0	0	0	24
99-2000	Seattle T-Birds	WHL	63	3	3	6	211	1	0	0	0	0

KALLARSSON, Tomi (KAL-ahr-suhn, TAW-mee) NYR

Defense. Shoots left. 6'3", 194 lbs. Born, Lempaala, Finland, March 15, 1979.
(NY Rangers' 4th choice, 93rd overall, in 1997 Entry Draft).

			Regular Season					Playoffs				
Season	Club	Lea	GP	G	A	TP	PIM	GP	G	A	TP	PIM
1994-95	Tappara Tampere	Finn-Jr.	22	9	4	13	26	....	....	....	....	....
1995-96	Tappara Tampere	Finn-Jr.	31	3	5	8	24	6	0	0	0	0
1996-97	HPK Hameenlinna	Finn-Jr.	31	1	3	4	26	6	0	0	0	2
1997-98	HPK Hameenlinna	Finn-Jr.	32	5	9	14	71	....	....	....	....	....
	Pelicans Lahti	Finland-2	3	0	0	0	0	....	....	....	....	....
	HPK Hameenlinna	Finland	12	0	0	0	2	....	....	....	....	....
1998-99	HPK Hameenlinna	Finn-Jr.	2	0	1	1	6	....	....	....	....	....
	HPK Hameenlinna	Finland	25	0	0	0	22	8	0	0	0	8
	Ahmat Hyvinkaa	Finland-2	21	2	7	9	52	....	....	....	....	....
99-2000	HPK Hameenlinna	Finland	50	0	5	5	58	8	0	0	0	4
	HPK Hameenlinna	Finn-Jr.	3	2	2	4	4	....	....	....	....	....

KALLIO, Tomi (KAL-ee-oh, TAW-mee) ATL.

Left wing. Shoots left. 6'1", 180 lbs. Born, Turku, Finland, January 27, 1977.
(Colorado's 4th choice, 81st overall, in 1995 Entry Draft).

			Regular Season					Playoffs				
Season	Club	Lea	GP	G	A	TP	PIM	GP	G	A	TP	PIM
1992-93	TPS Turku-C	Finn-Jr.	39	39	34	73	18	....	....	....	....	....
1993-94	TPS Turku-B	Finn-Jr.	10	5	6	11	14	1	0	1	1	0
	TPS Turku	Finn-Jr.	33	9	7	16	16	6	0	1	1	2
1994-95	TPS Turku	Finn-Jr.	14	5	12	17	24	....	....	....	....	....
	TPS Turku-B	Finn-Jr.	1	2	0	2	0	....	....	....	....	....
	Kiekko-67	Finland-2	25	8	5	13	16	7	3	1	4	6
1995-96	TPS Turku	Finn-Jr.	8	8	3	11	14	....	....	....	....	....
	Kiekko-67	Finland-2	29	10	11	21	28	....	....	....	....	....
	TPS Turku	Finland	8	2	3	5	10	4	0	0	0	2
1996-97	TPS Turku	Finland	47	9	10	19	18	8	2	0	2	2
	TPS Turku	EuroHL	6	2	0	2	25	4	0	0	0	0
1997-98	TPS Turku	Finland	47	10	10	20	8	4	0	2	2	0
	TPS Turku	EuroHL	6	0	1	1	2	....	....	....	....	....
1998-99	TPS Turku	Finland	54	15	21	36	20	10	3	4	7	6
99-2000	TPS Turku	Finland	50	26	27	53	40	11	4	*9	13	4

Claimed by **Atlanta** from **Colorado** in Expansion Draft, June 25, 1999.

KALMIKOV, Konstantin (kahl-mih-KAHV, KAWN-stan-tihn) TOR.

Left wing. Shoots right. 6'4", 205 lbs. Born, Kharkov, USSR, June 14, 1978.
(Toronto's 4th choice, 68th overall, in 1996 Entry Draft).

			Regular Season					Playoffs				
Season	Club	Lea	GP	G	A	TP	PIM	GP	G	A	TP	PIM
1994-95	Druzhba-78	Russia	65	51	55	106	45	....	....	....	....	....
1995-96	Flint Generals	ColHL	38	4	12	16	16	....	....	....	....	....
	Detroit Falcons	ColHL	5	0	1	1	0	....	....	....	....	....
1996-97	Sudbury Wolves	OHL	66	22	34	56	25	....	....	....	....	....
	St. John's Leafs	AHL	2	0	0	0	0	....	....	....	....	....
1997-98	Sudbury Wolves	OHL	66	32	32	64	21	10	7	2	9	2
1998-99	St. John's Leafs	AHL	52	3	4	7	4	....	....	....	....	....
99-2000	St. John's Leafs	AHL	76	8	20	28	21	....	....	....	....	....

KANE, Boyd (KAYN, BOIYD) NYR

Left wing. Shoots left. 6'2", 218 lbs. Born, Swift Current, Sask., April 18, 1978.
(NY Rangers' 4th choice, 114th overall, in 1998 Entry Draft).

			Regular Season					Playoffs				
Season	Club	Lea	GP	G	A	TP	PIM	GP	G	A	TP	PIM
1994-95	Regina Pats	WHL	25	6	5	11	6	4	0	0	0	0
1995-96	Regina Pats	WHL	72	21	42	63	155	11	5	7	12	12
1996-97	Regina Pats	WHL	66	25	50	75	154	5	1	1	2	15
1997-98	Regina Pats	WHL	68	48	45	93	133	9	5	7	12	29
1998-99	Hartford	AHL	56	3	5	8	23	....	....	....	....	....
	Charlotte	ECHL	12	5	6	11	14	....	....	....	....	....
99-2000	Charlotte	ECHL	47	10	19	29	110	....	....	....	....	....
	Hartford	AHL	8	0	0	0	9	....	....	....	....	....
	B.C. Icemen	UHL	3	0	2	2	4	1	0	0	0	0

• Re-entered NHL draft. Originally Pittsburgh's 3rd choice, 72nd overall, in 1996 Entry Draft.

KANKAANPERA, Markus (kan-kahn-PEHR-a) VAN.

Defense. Shoots left. 6'1", 191 lbs. Born, Skelleftea, Sweden, April 27, 1980.
(Vancouver's 7th choice, 218th overall, in 1999 Entry Draft).

			Regular Season					Playoffs				
Season	Club	Lea	GP	G	A	TP	PIM	GP	G	A	TP	PIM
1996-97	JyP Jyvaskyla	Finn-Jr.	33	3	5	8	83	....	....	....	....	....
1997-98	JyP Jyvaskyla-B	Finn-Jr.	13	4	10	14	18	5	3	2	5	6
	JyP Jyvaskyla	Finn-Jr.	32	0	0	0	2	....	....	....	....	....
1998-99	JyP Jyvaskyla	Finn-Jr.	1	0	0	0	4	....	....	....	....	....
	JyP Jyvaskyla	Finland	50	0	2	2	85	3	0	0	0	0
99-2000	JyP Jyvaskyla	Finland	47	0	5	5	87	....	....	....	....	....
	JyP Jyvaskyla	Finn-Jr.	3	1	1	2	2	3	0	1	1	6

KAPANEN, Niko (KA-pah-nehn, NEE-KOH) DAL.

Center. Shoots left. 5'9", 180 lbs. Born, Hattula, Finland, April 29, 1978.
(Dallas' 5th choice, 173rd overall, in 1998 Entry Draft).

			Regular Season					Playoffs				
Season	Club	Lea	GP	G	A	TP	PIM	GP	G	A	TP	PIM
1992-93	HK Hameenlinna	Finn-Jr.	14	14	6	20	2	....	....	....	....	....
1993-94	Hameenlinna-C	Finn-Jr.	2	0	1	1	0	....	....	....	....	....
	HPK Hameenlinna	Finn-Jr.	31	17	33	50	34	....	....	....	....	....
1994-95	HK Hameenlinna	Finn-Jr.	37	19	44	63	40	....	....	....	....	....
1995-96	HPK Hameenlinna	Finn-Jr.	26	15	22	37	34	....	....	....	....	....
	Hameenlinna-B	Finn-Jr.	10	6	6	12	8	....	....	....	....	....
	HPK Hameenlinna	Finland	7	1	0	1	0	....	....	....	....	....
1996-97	HPK Hameenlinna	Finn-Jr.	5	1	7	8	2	2	0	1	1	2
	HPK Hameenlinna	Finland	41	6	9	15	12	10	4	5	9	2
	HPK Hameenlinna	EuroHL	6	3	0	3	4	1	0	0	0	0
1997-98	HPK Hameenlinna	Finn-Jr.	2	1	1	2	0	....	....	....	....	....
	HPK Hameenlinna	Finland	48	8	18	26	44	....	....	....	....	....
1998-99	HPK Hameenlinna	Finland	53	14	29	43	49	8	3	4	7	4
99-2000	HPK Hameenlinna	Finland	53	20	28	48	40	8	1	9	10	4

KARLIN, Mattias (KAR-lihn, MAT-teeuhs) BOS.

Center/Right wing. Shoots left. 5'11", 183 lbs. Born, Ornskoldsvik, Sweden, July 4, 1979.
(Boston's 4th choice, 54th overall, in 1997 Entry Draft).

			Regular Season					Playoffs				
Season	Club	Lea	GP	G	A	TP	PIM	GP	G	A	TP	PIM
1995-96	MoDo Hockey	Swede-Jr.	30	12	23	35	16	....	....	....	....	....
1996-97	MoDo Hockey	Sweden	6	0	0	0	0	....	....	....	....	....
1997-98	MoDo Hockey	Sweden	32	0	2	2	8	1	0	0	0	0
1998-99	MoDo Hockey	Sweden	50	2	5	7	14	13	1	1	2	4
99-2000	MoDo Hockey	Sweden	42	0	5	5	10	12	0	0	0	2

KARLSSON, Gabriel (KARLS-sohn, ga-BREE-ehl) DAL.

Center. Shoots left. 6'1", 189 lbs. Born, Borlange, Sweden, January 22, 1980.
(Dallas' 3rd choice, 86th overall, in 1998 Entry Draft).

			Regular Season					Playoffs				
Season	Club	Lea	GP	G	A	TP	PIM	GP	G	A	TP	PIM
1996-97	HV Jonkoping	Swede-Jr.	25	7	9	16	....	....	....	....	....	....
1997-98	HV Jonkoping	Swede-Jr.	27	11	15	26	32	....	....	....	....	....
	HV Jonkoping	Sweden	1	0	0	0	0	....	....	....	....	....
1998-99	HV Jonkoping	Swede-Jr.	12	4	9	13	4	....	....	....	....	....
	HV Jonkoping	Sweden	33	2	1	3	2	....	....	....	....	....
99-2000	HV Jonkoping	Sweden	50	5	3	8	12	6	0	0	0	2

KASPARIK, Pavel (kas-PAHR-ihk) PHI.

Center. Shoots left. 6'2", 198 lbs. Born, Pisek, Czech., January 11, 1979.
(Philadelphia's 4th choice, 200th overall, in 1999 Entry Draft).

			Regular Season					Playoffs				
Season	Club	Lea	GP	G	A	TP	PIM	GP	G	A	TP	PIM
1996-97	IHC Pisek-Jr.	Cze-Rep	36	12	5	17	....	....	....	....	....	....
1997-98	IHC Pisek-Jr.	Cze-Rep	39	21	19	40	....	....	....	....	....	....
	IHC Pisek-2	Cze-Rep	15	3	3	6	....	....	....	....	....	....
1998-99	IHC Pisek-Jr.	Cze-Rep	7	2	3	5	....	....	....	....	....	....
	IHC Pisek-2	Cze-Rep	51	20	23	43	....	....	....	....	....	....
99-2000	IHC Pisek-2	Cze-Rep	24	6	9	15	....	....	....	....	....	....
	HC Havirov	Cze-Rep	1	0	0	0	0	....	....	....	....	....
	Sparta Praha	Cze-Rep	22	1	1	2	0	....	....	....	....	....

KAUPPINEN, Marko (KOW-pih-nehn, MAHR-koh) PHI.

Defense. Shoots left. 6', 178 lbs. Born, Mikkeli, Finland, March 23, 1979.
(Philadelphia's 7th choice, 214th overall, in 1997 Entry Draft).

			Regular Season					Playoffs				
Season	Club	Lea	GP	G	A	TP	PIM	GP	G	A	TP	PIM
1994-95	Jukurit Mikkeli-C	Finn-Jr.	31	12	11	23	48	....	....	....	....	....
1995-96	Jukurit Mikkeli	Finland-3	19	1	5	6	10	3	0	0	0	0
1996-97	JyP Jyvaskyla	Finn-Jr.	29	2	3	5	14	7	0	0	0	29
1997-98	JyP Jyvaskyla	Finn-Jr.	16	2	4	6	16	....	....	....	....	....
	Diskos Jyvaskyla	Finland-2	2	2	1	3	0	....	....	....	....	....
	JyP Jyvaskyla	Finland	33	2	6	8	26	....	....	....	....	....
1998-99	JyP Jyvaskyla	Finn-Jr.	3	2	1	3	6	....	....	....	....	....
	JyP Jyvaskyla	Finland	49	5	7	12	56	3	0	0	0	6
99-2000	Jokerit Helsinki	Finn-Jr.	5	0	3	3	8	1	1	0	1	4
	Jokerit Helsinki	Finland	47	4	9	13	16	10	1	3	4	2

KAVANAGH, Pat (KA-vuh-naw, PAT) VAN.

Right wing. Shoots right. 6'3", 192 lbs. Born, Ottawa, Ont., March 14, 1979.
(Philadelphia's 2nd choice, 50th overall, in 1997 Entry Draft).

			Regular Season					Playoffs				
Season	Club	Lea	GP	G	A	TP	PIM	GP	G	A	TP	PIM
1995-96	Kanata Lasers	OJHL	54	19	16	35	99	....	....	....	....	....
1996-97	Peterborough	OHL	43	6	8	14	53	11	1	1	2	12
1997-98	Peterborough	OHL	66	10	16	26	85	4	1	0	1	6
1998-99	Peterborough	OHL	68	26	43	69	118	5	0	5	5	10
99-2000	Syracuse Crunch	AHL	68	12	8	20	56	4	0	0	0	0

Traded to **Vancouver** by **Philadelphia** for Vancouver's 6th round choice (Konstantin Rudenko) in 1999 Entry Draft, June 1, 1999.

KAZAKEVICH, Mikhail (kah-zak-KAY-vihch, MIHK-hayl) PIT.

Left wing. Shoots left. 6'1", 187 lbs. Born, Murmansk, USSR, April 17, 1981.
(Pittsburgh's 13th choice, 258th overall, in 1994 Entry Draft).

			Regular Season					Playoffs				
Season	Club	Lea	GP	G	A	TP	PIM	GP	G	A	TP	PIM
1992-93	Torpedo Yaroslavl	CIS	7	0	1	1	0	3	0	0	0	0
1993-94	Torpedo Yaroslavl	CIS	4	0	0	0	2	....	....	....	....	....
1994-95	Torpedo Yaroslavl	CIS	11	1	3	4	2	....	....	....	....	....
1995-96	Moncton Alpines	QMJHL	41	7	13	20	16	....	....	....	....	....
	Shawinigan	QMJHL	14	1	3	4	8	4	0	1	1	2
1996-97	HK Khimik	Russia	1	0	0	0	0	....	....	....	....	....
1997-98	Kristall Saratov	Russia	10	0	1	1	8	....	....	....	....	....
1998-99	St. Petersburg	Russia	2	0	0	0	0	....	....	....	....	....

KEALTY, Jeff NSH.

Defense. Shoots left. 6'4", 220 lbs. Born, Boston, MA, April 9, 1976.
(Quebec's 2nd choice, 22nd overall, in 1994 Entry Draft).

			Regular Season					Playoffs				
Season	Club	Lea	GP	G	A	TP	PIM	GP	G	A	TP	PIM
1993-94	Catholic Memorial	Hi-School	25	10	22	32	....	....	....	....	....	....
1994-95	Boston University	H-East	25	0	5	5	29	....	....	....	....	....
1995-96	Boston University	H-East	35	4	14	18	38	....	....	....	....	....
1996-97	Boston University	H-East	40	4	9	13	42	....	....	....	....	....
1997-98	Boston University	H-East	38	11	15	26	53	....	....	....	....	....
1998-99	Milwaukee	IHL	70	8	14	22	134	2	0	1	1	4
99-2000	Milwaukee	IHL	1	0	0	0	2	....	....	....	....	....

Signed as a free agent by **Nashville**, October 12, 1998. • Missed majority of 1999-2000 season recovering from head injury suffered in training camp, September, 1999.

KEEFE, Sheldon (KEE-feh, SHEHL-dohn) T.B.

Right wing. Shoots right. 5'11", 185 lbs. Born, Brampton, Ont., September 17, 1980.
(Tampa Bay's 1st choice, 47th overall, in 1999 Entry Draft).

			Regular Season					Playoffs				
Season	Club	Lea	GP	G	A	TP	PIM	GP	G	A	TP	PIM
1995-96	Toronto Nats	MTHL	45	66	71	137	....	....	....	....	....	....
1996-97	Quinte Hawks	OJHL	44	21	23	44	....	....	....	....	....	....
1997-98	Caledon Canucks	OJHL	43	41	40	81	117	....	....	....	....	....
1998-99	St. Michael's	OHL	38	37	37	74	80	....	....	....	....	....
	Barrie Colts	OHL	28	14	28	42	60	10	5	5	10	31
99-2000	Barrie Colts	OHL	66	48	*73	*121	95	25	10	13	23	41

OHL Second All-Star Team (2000) • Memorial Cup All-Star Team (2000)

KELLEHER, Chris (KEH-leh-huhr, KRIHS) PIT.

Defense. Shoots left. 6'1", 210 lbs. Born, Cambridge, MA, March 23, 1975.
(Pittsburgh's 5th choice, 130th overall, in 1993 Entry Draft).

			Regular Season					Playoffs				
Season	Club	Lea	GP	G	A	TP	PIM	GP	G	A	TP	PIM
1990-91	Belmont Hill	Hi-School	20	4	23	27	14	....	....	....	....	....
1991-92	St. Sebastien's	Hi-School	28	7	27	34	12	....	....	....	....	....
1992-93	St. Sebastien's	Hi-School	25	8	30	38	16	....	....	....	....	....
1993-94	St. Sebastian's	Hi-School	24	10	21	31	....	....	....	....	....	....
1994-95	Boston University	H-East	35	3	17	20	62	....	....	....	....	....
1995-96	Boston University	H-East	37	7	18	25	43	....	....	....	....	....
1996-97	Boston University	H-East	39	10	24	34	54	....	....	....	....	....
1997-98	Boston University	H-East	37	4	26	30	40	....	....	....	....	....
1998-99	Syracuse Crunch	AHL	45	1	4	5	43	....	....	....	....	....
99-2000	Wilkes-Barre	AHL	67	0	12	12	40	....	....	....	....	....

NCAA East Second All-American Team (1997, 1998) • Hockey East Second All-Star Team (1998)

KELLY, Chris (KEHL-lee, KRIHS) OTT.

Center/Left wing. Shoots left. 6', 179 lbs. Born, Toronto, Ont., November 11, 1980.
(Ottawa's 4th choice, 94th overall, in 1999 Entry Draft).

			Regular Season					Playoffs				
Season	Club	Lea	GP	G	A	TP	PIM	GP	G	A	TP	PIM
1995-96	Toronto Marlies	MTHL	42	25	45	70	25	....	....	....	....	....
1996-97	Aurora Tigers	OJHL	49	14	20	34	11	....	....	....	....	....
1997-98	London Knights	OHL	54	15	14	29	4	16	4	5	9	12
1998-99	London Knights	OHL	68	36	41	77	60	25	9	17	26	22
99-2000	London Knights	OHL	63	29	43	72	57	....	....	....	....	....

KELMAN, Scott (KEHL-man, SCAWT) PHX.

Center. Shoots left. 6'3", 197 lbs. Born, Winnipeg, Man., May 7, 1981.
(Phoenix's 1st choice, 15th overall, in 1999 Entry Draft).

			Regular Season					Playoffs				
Season	Club	Lea	GP	G	A	TP	PIM	GP	G	A	TP	PIM
1996-97	Winnipeg Legion	MAHA	35	21	44	65	78	....	....	....	....	....
	Seattle T-Birds	WHL	5	0	1	1	0	....	....	....	....	....
1997-98	Seattle T-Birds	WHL	61	13	17	30	35	5	0	0	0	4
1998-99	Seattle T-Birds	WHL	66	19	54	73	95	11	4	3	7	37
99-2000	Seattle T-Birds	WHL	64	13	42	55	104	2	0	0	0	2

KESA, Teemu (KEH-sah, TEE-moo) N.J.

Defense. Shoots right. 6', 185 lbs. Born, Helsinki, Finland, June 7, 1981.
(New Jersey's 5th choice, 100th overall, in 1999 Entry Draft).

			Regular Season					Playoffs				
Season	Club	Lea	GP	G	A	TP	PIM	GP	G	A	TP	PIM
1996-97	Tappara Tampere	Finn-Jr.	32	1	5	6	58	4	1	0	4	29
1997-98	Ilves Tampere-B	Finn-Jr.	33	8	1	9	78	....	....	....	....	....
1998-99	Ilves Tampere-B	Finn-Jr.	24	4	5	9	146	....	....	....	....	....
	Ilves Tampere	Finn-Jr.	6	0	1	1	10	....	....	....	....	....
99-2000	Ilves Tampere	Finn-Jr.	31	1	7	8	92	....	....	....	....	....
	Ilves Tampere	Finland	5	0	0	0	8	....	....	....	....	....

KHARITONOV, Alexander (khar-ih-TOH-nahf) T.B.

Left wing. Shoots right. 5'9", 169 lbs. Born, Moscow, USSR, March 30, 1976.
(Tampa Bay's 3rd choice, 81st overall, in 2000 Entry Draft).

			Regular Season					Playoffs				
Season	Club	Lea	GP	G	A	TP	PIM	GP	G	A	TP	PIM
1996-97	D'amo Moscow-2	Russia-3	3	1	1	2	0	....	....	....	....	....
	Dynamo Moscow	Russia	36	11	9	20	12	4	2	0	2	2
1997-98	Dynamo Moscow	Russia	44	19	16	35	20	....	....	....	....	....
1998-99	Dynamo Moscow	Russia	42	8	6	14	24	16	4	3	7	2
99-2000	Dynamo Moscow	Russia	35	14	20	34	26	17	*8	4	12	10

KHAVANOV, Alexander (khuh-VAN-ahf) ST.L.

Defense. Shoots left. 6', 187 lbs. Born, Ryazan, USSR, January 30, 1972.
(St. Louis' 8th choice, 232nd overall, in 1999 Entry Draft).

			Regular Season					Playoffs				
Season	Club	Lea	GP	G	A	TP	PIM	GP	G	A	TP	PIM
1992-93	Birmingham Bulls	ECHL	19	0	3	3	14	....	....	....	....	....
	Raleigh Icecaps	ECHL	17	0	6	6	8	....	....	....	....	....
1993-94	St. Petersburg	CIS	41	1	2	3	24	....	....	....	....	....
1994-95	St. Petersburg	CIS	49	7	0	7	32	3	0	0	0	0
1995-96	St. Petersburg	CIS	32	1	5	6	41	....	....	....	....	....
	HPK Hameenlinna	Finland	16	0	2	2	4	9	0	0	0	0
1996-97	HK Cherepovets	Russia	39	3	8	11	56	3	1	0	1	4
1997-98	HK Cherepovets	Russia	44	3	5	8	46	....	....	....	....	....
1998-99	Dynamo Moscow	Russia	40	2	7	9	14	16	1	5	6	35
99-2000	Dynamo Moscow	Russia	38	5	12	17	49	17	0	3	3	4

KHOMITSKY, Vadim (khoh-MIHT-skee, va-DEEM) DAL.

Defense. Shoots left. 6'1", 185 lbs. Born, Voskresensk, USSR, July 21, 1982.
(Dallas' 5th choice, 123rd overall, in 2000 Entry Draft).

			Regular Season					Playoffs				
Season	Club	Lea	GP	G	A	TP	PIM	GP	G	A	TP	PIM
1998-99	HK Voskresensk	Russia-2	9	0	0	0	10	....	....	....	....	....
99-2000	HK Voskresensk	Russia-2	17	0	0	0	31	....	....	....	....	....
	CSKA Moscow	Russia-2	11	0	1	1	10	....	....	....	....	....

KIDNEY, Kyle (KIHD-nee, KIGHL) COL.

Left wing. Shoots left. 6'2", 223 lbs. Born, Ithaca, NY, January 11, 1978.
(Colorado's 9th choice, 243rd overall, in 1997 Entry Draft).

			Regular Season					Playoffs				
Season	Club	Lea	GP	G	A	TP	PIM	GP	G	A	TP	PIM
1996-97	Salisbury High	Hi-School	28	27	35	62	....	....	....	....	....	....
1997-98	U. Mass-Lowell	H-East	33	3	8	11	38	....	....	....	....	....
1998-99	U. Mass-Lowell	H-East	30	3	7	10	58	....	....	....	....	....
99-2000	U. Mass-Lowell	H-East	28	4	7	11	26	....	....	....	....	....

KINCH, Matthew (KIHNCH, MAT-thew) BUF.

Defense. Shoots left. 6', 195 lbs. Born, Red Deer, Alta., February 17, 1980.
(Buffalo's 8th choice, 146th overall, in 1999 Entry Draft).

			Regular Season					Playoffs				
Season	Club	Lea	GP	G	A	TP	PIM	GP	G	A	TP	PIM
1995-96	Red Deer Chiefs	AAHA	35	6	17	23	31	....	....	....	....	....
	Calgary Hitmen	WHL	1	0	1	1	2	....	....	....	....	....
1996-97	Calgary Hitmen	WHL	64	10	22	32	31	....	....	....	....	....
1997-98	Calgary Hitmen	WHL	55	7	24	31	13	18	3	2	5	4
1998-99	Calgary Hitmen	WHL	68	14	69	83	16	21	8	15	23	59
99-2000	Calgary Hitmen	WHL	62	14	61	75	24	13	2	12	14	8

WHL East First All-Star Team (1999) • Memorial Cup All-Star Team (1999) • WHL East Second All-Star Team (2000)

KIRILENKO, Dmitri (kih-reh-LEHN-koh) CGY.

Center. Shoots left. 5'11", 183 lbs. Born, Moscow, USSR, August 4, 1979.
(Calgary's 10th choice, 252nd overall, in 1999 Entry Draft).

			Regular Season					Playoffs				
Season	Club	Lea	GP	G	A	TP	PIM	GP	G	A	TP	PIM
1995-96	Spartak Moscow	Russia-Jr.	40	30	35	65	120	....	....	....	....	....
1996-97	Spartak Moscow	Russia-3	22	1	2	3	4	....	....	....	....	....
1997-98	CSKA Moscow	Russia	16	0	0	0	10	....	....	....	....	....
	CSKA Moscow	Russia-3	47	18	10	28	58	....	....	....	....	....
1998-99	CSKA Moscow	Russia	37	4	4	8	22	3	0	0	0	0
99-2000	CSKA Moscow	Russia	26	5	0	5	26	2	0	0	0	2

KISER, Nate (KIGH-zuhr) PHX.

Defense. Shoots right. 6'1", 190 lbs. Born, Southgate, MI, May 4, 1982.
(Phoenix's 4th choice, 160th overall, in 2000 Entry Draft).

			Regular Season					Playoffs				
Season	Club	Lea	GP	G	A	TP	PIM	GP	G	A	TP	PIM
1998-99	Compuware	NAJHL	32	2	3	5	42	....	....	....	....	....
99-2000	Plymouth Whalers	OHL	63	3	5	8	102	23	1	1	2	18

KLESLA, Rostislav (KLEHS-luh, RAHS-tih-slav) **CBJ**

Defense. Shoots left. 6'2", 198 lbs. Born, Novy Jicin, Czech., March 21, 1982.
(Columbus' 1st choice, 4th overall, in 2000 Entry Draft).

			Regular Season					Playoffs				
Season	Club	Lea	GP	G	A	TP	PIM	GP	G	A	TP	PIM
1997-98	HC Opava-Jr.	Cze-Rep	38	11	18	29	87	....	....	....	....	....
1998-99	Sioux City	USHL	54	4	12	16	100	5	2	0	2	2
99-2000	Brampton	OHL	67	16	29	45	174	6	1	1	2	21

KLIAZMINE, Sergei (klee-YAZ-mihn) **COL.**

Left wing. Shoots left. 6'3", 190 lbs. Born, Mozhajsk, USSR, January 3, 1982.
(Colorado's 6th choice, 92nd overall, in 2000 Entry Draft).

			Regular Season					Playoffs				
Season	Club	Lea	GP	G	A	TP	PIM	GP	G	A	TP	PIM
1998-99	SKA Spartak-2	Russia-4	2	0	1	1	2	....	....	....	....	....
	Krylja Sovetov	Russia-Q	19	1	3	4	12	....	....	....	....	....
99-2000	D'amo Moscow-2	Russia-3	16	3	2	5	18	....	....	....	....	....

KLIMENTIEV, Sergei (klih-MEHN-tyehv, SAIR-gay) **CBJ**

Defense. Shoots left. 5'11", 200 lbs. Born, Kiev, USSR, April 5, 1975.
(Buffalo's 4th choice, 121st overall, in 1994 Entry Draft).

			Regular Season					Playoffs				
Season	Club	Lea	GP	G	A	TP	PIM	GP	G	A	TP	PIM
1991-92	SVSM Kiev	CIS-3	42	4	15	19	....	....	....	....	....	....
1992-93	Sokol Kiev	CIS	3	0	0	0	4	1	0	0	0	0
1993-94	Medicine Hat	WHL	72	16	26	42	165	3	0	0	0	4
1994-95	Medicine Hat	WHL	71	19	45	64	146	5	4	2	6	14
	Rochester	AHL	7	0	0	0	8	1	0	0	0	0
1995-96	Rochester	AHL	70	7	29	36	74	19	2	8	10	16
1996-97	Rochester	AHL	77	14	28	42	114	10	1	4	5	28
1997-98	Rochester	AHL	57	4	22	26	94	....	....	....	....	....
1998-99	Philadelphia	AHL	43	5	12	17	99	....	....	....	....	....
	Milwaukee	IHL	35	4	11	15	59	2	0	0	0	6
99-2000	Ak Bars Kazan	Russia	33	5	7	12	52	17	2	2	4	28

Signed as a free agent by **Philadelphia**, July 9, 1998. Traded to **Nashville** by **Philadelphia** for cash, January 26, 1999. Signed as a free agent by **Columbus**, August 7, 2000.

KLOUCEK, Tomas (KLOH-chehk, TAW-mahsh) **NYR**

Defense. Shoots left. 6'3", 203 lbs. Born, Prague, Czech., March 7, 1980.
(NY Rangers' 6th choice, 131st overall, in 1998 Entry Draft).

			Regular Season					Playoffs				
Season	Club	Lea	GP	G	A	TP	PIM	GP	G	A	TP	PIM
1995-96	Slavia Praha-Jr.	Cze-Rep	40	2	8	10	....	....	....	....	....	....
1996-97	Slavia Praha-Jr.	Cze-Rep	43	4	14	18	44	....	....	....	....	....
1997-98	Slavia Praha-Jr.	Cze-Rep	43	1	9	10	....	....	....	....	....	....
1998-99	Cape Breton	QMJHL	59	4	17	21	162	2	0	0	0	4
99-2000	Hartford	AHL	73	2	8	10	113	23	0	4	4	18

KNOPP, Ben (KUH-nawp) **CBJ**

Right wing. Shoots right. 6', 185 lbs. Born, Calgary, Alta., April 8, 1982.
(Columbus' 2nd choice, 69th overall, in 2000 Entry Draft).

			Regular Season					Playoffs				
Season	Club	Lea	GP	G	A	TP	PIM	GP	G	A	TP	PIM
1997-98	Calgary Buffaloes	AMHL	35	28	48	76	34	10	10	6	16	30
1998-99	Calgary Canucks	AJHL	55	37	45	82	161	....	....	....	....	....
99-2000	Moose Jaw	WHL	72	30	30	60	101	4	2	2	4	4

KOALSKA, Matt (KOHL-skuh) **NSH.**

Center. Shoots left. 6'1", 190 lbs. Born, St. Paul, MN, May 16, 1980.
(Nashville's 7th choice, 154th overall, in 2000 Entry Draft).

			Regular Season					Playoffs				
Season	Club	Lea	GP	G	A	TP	PIM	GP	G	A	TP	PIM
1998-99	Hill-Murray	Hi-School	26	19	44	63	18	....	....	....	....	....
99-2000	Twin Cities	USHL	57	24	34	58	19	13	5	5	10	4

First All-State Schoolboy Team (1999) • First All-Conference Schoolboy Team (1999)

KOCH, Geoff (KAWCH, JEHF) **NSH.**

Left wing. Shoots left. 6'1", 190 lbs. Born, Exeter, NH, June 27, 1979.
(Nashville's 3rd choice, 85th overall, in 1998 Entry Draft).

			Regular Season					Playoffs				
Season	Club	Lea	GP	G	A	TP	PIM	GP	G	A	TP	PIM
1994-95	Exeter Academy	Hi-School	24	32	20	52	51	....	....	....	....	....
1995-96	Exeter Academy	Hi-School	28	37	40	77	48	....	....	....	....	....
1996-97	Exeter Academy	Hi-School	22	30	30	60	62	....	....	....	....	....
1997-98	U. of Michigan	CCHA	43	5	6	11	51	....	....	....	....	....
1998-99	U. of Michigan	CCHA	40	4	12	16	101	....	....	....	....	....
99-2000	U. of Michigan	CCHA	36	12	16	28	56	....	....	....	....	....

KOCI, David (KOH-chee) **PIT.**

Defense. Shoots left. 6'6", 216 lbs. Born, Prague, Czech., May 12, 1981.
(Pittsburgh's 5th choice, 146th overall, in 2000 Entry Draft).

			Regular Season					Playoffs				
Season	Club	Lea	GP	G	A	TP	PIM	GP	G	A	TP	PIM
1997-98	Sparta Praha-Jr.	Cze-Rep	41	2	9	11	105	....	....	....	....	....
1998-99	HC Hvezda-Jr.	Cze-Rep	22	1	3	4	36	....	....	....	....	....
	Sparta Praha-Jr.	Cze-Rep	7	0	0	0	4	....	....	....	....	....
99-2000	Sparta Praha-Jr.	Cze-Rep	47	0	6	6	124	....	....	....	....	....

KOEHLER, Greg (KOH-luhr, GREHG) **CAR.**

Center. Shoots left. 6'2", 195 lbs. Born, Scarborough, Ont., February 27, 1975.

			Regular Season					Playoffs				
Season	Club	Lea	GP	G	A	TP	PIM	GP	G	A	TP	PIM
1992-93	Niagara Falls	OJHL-B	40	24	19	43	125	....	....	....	....	....
1993-94	North York	OJHL	49	27	47	74	179	....	....	....	....	....
1994-95	North York	OJHL	47	28	43	71	126	....	....	....	....	....
1995-96	Brampton	OJHL	49	33	64	97	87	....	....	....	....	....
1996-97	U. Mass-Lowell	H-East	37	16	20	36	49	....	....	....	....	....
1997-98	U. Mass-Lowell	H-East	33	20	17	37	62	....	....	....	....	....
	New Haven	AHL	3	0	0	0	2	....	....	....	....	....
1998-99	New Haven	AHL	26	4	0	4	29	....	....	....	....	....
	Florida	ECHL	29	13	14	27	62	6	2	3	5	12
99-2000	Cincinnati	IHL	74	12	13	25	157	8	0	3	3	14

Signed as a free agent by **Carolina**, March 31, 1998.

KOKOREV, Dmitri (KOH-koh-rehf, DEH-mee-tree) **CGY.**

Defense. Shoots left. 6'3", 198 lbs. Born, Moscow, USSR, January 9, 1979.
(Calgary's 4th choice, 51st overall, in 1997 Entry Draft).

			Regular Season					Playoffs				
Season	Club	Lea	GP	G	A	TP	PIM	GP	G	A	TP	PIM
1996-97	Dynamo Moscow	Russia-3	27	2	4	6	24	....	....	....	....	....
	Dynamo Moscow	Russia	1	0	0	0	0	....	....	....	....	....
1997-98	Dynamo Moscow	Russia-2	24	1	2	3	20	....	....	....	....	....
1998-99	Dynamo Moscow	Russia	26	0	1	1	20	8	1	0	1	0
99-2000	Dynamo Moscow	Russia	22	0	1	1	14	1	0	0	0	0

KOLANOS, Krys (koh-LA-nohs) **PHX.**

Center. Shoots right. 6'2", 196 lbs. Born, Calgary, Alta., July 27, 1981.
(Phoenix's 1st choice, 19th overall, in 2000 Entry Draft).

			Regular Season					Playoffs				
Season	Club	Lea	GP	G	A	TP	PIM	GP	G	A	TP	PIM
1996-97	Calgary Majors	AAHA	24	24	35	59	....	....	....	....	....	....
1997-98	Calgary Buffaloes	AMHL	34	34	43	77	29	....	....	....	....	....
1998-99	Calgary Royals	AJHL	58	43	67	110	98	....	....	....	....	....
99-2000	Boston College	H-East	42	16	16	32	48	....	....	....	....	....

AJHL Rookie-of-the-Year (1999) • AJHL First All-Star Team (1999) • Hockey East All-Rookie Team (2000)

KOLARIK, Pavel **BOS.**

Defense. Shoots left. 6'1", 207 lbs. Born, Vyskov, Czech., October 24, 1972.
(Boston's 11th choice, 268th overall, in 2000 Entry Draft).

			Regular Season					Playoffs				
Season	Club	Lea	GP	G	A	TP	PIM	GP	G	A	TP	PIM
1996-97	Slavia Praha	Cze-Rep	27	1	2	3	10	3	0	0	0	2
1997-98	Slavia Praha	Cze-Rep	51	0	4	4	24	5	0	0	0	2
1998-99	Slavia Praha	Cze-Rep	51	1	8	9	44	....	....	....	....	....
99-2000	Slavia Praha	Cze-Rep	52	5	3	8	38	....	....	....	....	....

KOLARIK, Tyler (koh-LAHR-ihk) **CBJ**

Center. Shoots right. 5'10", 190 lbs. Born, Philadelphia, PA, January 26, 1981.
(Columbus' 5th choice, 150th overall, in 2000 Entry Draft).

			Regular Season					Playoffs				
Season	Club	Lea	GP	G	A	TP	PIM	GP	G	A	TP	PIM
99-2000	Deerfield Academy	Hi-School	26	31	22	53	8	....	....	....	....	....
	NY/Mid-Atlantic	MBHL	3	4	3	7	0	....	....	....	....	....

KOLKUNOV, Alexei (kohl-koo-NAHV, al-EHX-ay) **PIT.**

Center. Shoots left. 6', 201 lbs. Born, Belgorod, USSR, February 3, 1977.
(Pittsburgh's 5th choice, 154th overall, in 1995 Entry Draft).

			Regular Season					Playoffs				
Season	Club	Lea	GP	G	A	TP	PIM	GP	G	A	TP	PIM
1994-95	Krylja Sovetov	CIS-Jr.	44	9	16	25	36	2	0	0	0	4
	Krylja Sovetov	CIS	7	0	0	0	0	4	1	0	1	0
1995-96	Krylja Sovetov	CIS	43	9	3	12	35	....	....	....	....	....
1996-97	Krylja Sovetov	Russia	44	9	16	25	36	2	0	0	0	4
1997-98	Krylja Sovetov	Russia	20	6	4	10	22	....	....	....	....	....
1998-99	Syracuse Crunch	AHL	55	5	13	18	20	....	....	....	....	....
99-2000	Wilkes-Barre	AHL	75	12	25	37	33	....	....	....	....	....

KOLNIK, Juraj (KOHL-nihk, YEW-igh) **NYI**

Right wing. Shoots right. 5'10", 182 lbs. Born, Nitra, Czech., November 13, 1980.
(NY Islanders' 7th choice, 101st overall, in 1999 Entry Draft).

			Regular Season					Playoffs				
Season	Club	Lea	GP	G	A	TP	PIM	GP	G	A	TP	PIM
1997-98	MHC Nitra	Slovak-Jr.	26	28	16	44	50	....	....	....	....	....
	MHC Nitra	Slovakia	28	1	3	4	6	....	....	....	....	....
1998-99	Quebec Remparts	QMJHL	12	6	5	11	6	....	....	....	....	....
	Rimouski Oceanic	QMJHL	50	36	37	73	34	11	9	6	15	6
99-2000	Rimouski Oceanic	QMJHL	47	53	53	106	53	14	10	17	27	16

Memorial Cup All-Star Team (2000)

KOLTSOV, Konstantin (KOHLT-sahv, KOHN-stan-tihn) **PIT.**

Right wing. Shoots left. 6', 187 lbs. Born, Minsk, USSR, April 17, 1981.
(Pittsburgh's 1st choice, 18th overall, in 1999 Entry Draft).

			Regular Season					Playoffs				
Season	Club	Lea	GP	G	A	TP	PIM	GP	G	A	TP	PIM
1997-98	HC Cherepovets-2	Russia-3	44	11	12	23	16	....	....	....	....	....
	HC Cherepovets	Russia	2	0	0	0	2	....	....	....	....	....
1998-99	HC Cherepovets-2	Russia-3	11	1	4	5	18	....	....	....	....	....
	HC Cherepovets-3	Russia-4	2	0	1	1	2	....	....	....	....	....
	HC Cherepovets	Russia	33	3	0	3	8	1	0	0	0	2
99-2000	SK Novokuznetsk	Russia	30	3	4	7	12	11	1	1	2	6

KOMAROV, Alexei (KOH-muh-rahf, al-EHX-ay) **DAL.**

Defense. Shoots left. 6'4", 194 lbs. Born, Moscow, USSR, June 11, 1978.
(Dallas' 8th choice, 216th overall, in 1997 Entry Draft).

			Regular Season					Playoffs				
Season	Club	Lea	GP	G	A	TP	PIM	GP	G	A	TP	PIM
1996-97	D'amo Moscow-2	Russia-3	32	2	3	5	12	....	....	....	....	....
1997-98	HC Yekaterinburg	Russia-2	22	0	1	1	14	....	....	....	....	....
	HC Yekaterinburg	Russia	19	0	0	0	6	....	....	....	....	....
1998-99	Spartak Moscow	Russia	21	1	0	1	6	....	....	....	....	....

KOPECKY, Tomas (koh-PEHTS-kee, TAW-mahsh) **DET.**

Center. Shoots left. 6'3", 187 lbs. Born, Ilava, Czech., February 5, 1982.
(Detroit's 2nd choice, 38th overall, in 2000 Entry Draft).

			Regular Season					Playoffs				
Season	Club	Lea	GP	G	A	TP	PIM	GP	G	A	TP	PIM
1997-98	Dukla Trencin	Slovak-Jr.	41	19	22	41	....	....	....	....	....	....
1998-99	Dukla Trencin	Slovak-Jr.	44	13	16	29	18	....	....	....	....	....
99-2000	Dukla Trencin	Slovak-Jr.	14	8	9	17	36	....	....	....	....	....
	Dukla Trencin	Slovakia	52	3	4	7	24	5	0	0	0	0

KOPISCHKE, Jay (koh-PIHSH-kee, JAY) L.A.

Left wing. Shoots left. 6'3", 210 lbs. Born, Alexandria, MN, February 7, 1978.
(Los Angeles' 8th choice, 193rd overall, in 1997 Entry Draft).

			Regular Season					Playoffs				
Season	Club	Lea	GP	G	A	TP	PIM	GP	G	A	TP	PIM
1996-97	North Iowa	USHL	53	14	17	31	97	12	4	3	7	47
1997-98	Notre Dame	CCHA	40	2	4	6	24	....	....	....	....	....
1998-99	Notre Dame	CCHA	29	0	3	3	30	....	....	....	....	....
99-2000	Notre Dame	CCHA	33	6	5	11	34	....	....	....	....	....

KOS, Kyle (KOHS, KIGHL) T.B.

Defense. Shoots left. 6'3", 184 lbs. Born, Hope, B.C., May 25, 1979.
(Tampa Bay's 2nd choice, 33rd overall, in 1997 Entry Draft).

			Regular Season					Playoffs				
Season	Club	Lea	GP	G	A	TP	PIM	GP	G	A	TP	PIM
1994-95	Notre Dame	SAHA	35	15	25	40	25	....	....	....	....	....
1995-96	Notre Dame	SJHL	40	2	10	12	22	....	....	....	....	....
1996-97	Red Deer Rebels	WHL	64	2	18	20	40	10	0	0	0	8
1997-98	Red Deer Rebels	WHL	71	7	33	40	102	5	0	3	3	4
1998-99	Red Deer Rebels	WHL	37	3	17	20	56	....	....	....	....	....
	Kamloops Blazers	WHL	28	6	14	20	42	9	0	0	0	8
99-2000	Detroit Vipers	IHL	44	1	2	3	77	....	....	....	....	....
	Utah Grizzlies	IHL	12	0	1	1	24	2	0	1	1	0

KOSICK, Mark (KOHS-ihk, MAHRK) CAR.

Center. Shoots left. 5'11", 190 lbs. Born, Victoria, B.C., March 25, 1979.
(Carolina's 9th choice, 211th overall, in 1998 Entry Draft).

			Regular Season					Playoffs				
Season	Club	Lea	GP	G	A	TP	PIM	GP	G	A	TP	PIM
1996-97	Victoria Salsa	BCJHL	54	21	37	58	12	....	....	....	....	....
1997-98	U. of Michigan	CCHA	45	14	32	46	18	....	....	....	....	....
1998-99	U. of Michigan	CCHA	42	12	23	35	14	....	....	....	....	....
99-2000	U. of Michigan	CCHA	37	18	16	34	16	....	....	....	....	....

NCAA Championship All-Tournament Team (2000)

KOSTOPOULOS, Tom (kaw-STAWP-oh-lihs) PIT.

Right wing. Shoots right. 6', 205 lbs. Born, Mississauga, Ont., January 24, 1979.
(Pittsburgh's 9th choice, 204th overall, in 1999 Entry Draft).

			Regular Season					Playoffs				
Season	Club	Lea	GP	G	A	TP	PIM	GP	G	A	TP	PIM
1995-96	Brampton Blues	OJHL	24	9	9	18	28	....	....	....	....	....
1996-97	London Knights	OHL	64	13	12	25	67	....	....	....	....	....
1997-98	London Knights	OHL	66	24	26	50	108	16	6	4	10	26
1998-99	London Knights	OHL	66	27	60	87	114	25	19	16	35	32
99-2000	Wilkes-Barre	AHL	76	26	32	58	121	....	....	....	....	....

KOTALIK, Ales (KOH-tuh-lihk, AH-lehsh) BUF.

Right wing. Shoots right. 6'1", 198 lbs. Born, Jindrichuv Hradec, Czech., December 23, 1978.
(Buffalo's 7th choice, 164th overall, in 1998 Entry Draft).

			Regular Season					Playoffs				
Season	Club	Lea	GP	G	A	TP	PIM	GP	G	A	TP	PIM
1993-94	HC Budejovice-Jr.	Cze-Rep	28	12	12	24	....	....	....	....	....	....
1994-95	HC Budejovice-Jr.	Cze-Rep	36	26	17	43	....	....	....	....	....	....
1995-96	HC Budejovice-Jr.	Cze-Rep	28	6	7	13	....	....	....	....	....	....
1996-97	HC Budejovice-Jr.	Cze-Rep	36	15	16	31	24	....	....	....	....	....
1997-98	HC Budejovice	Cze-Rep	47	9	7	16	14	....	....	....	....	....
1998-99	HC Budejovice	Cze-Rep	41	8	13	21	16	3	0	0	0	....
99-2000	HC Budejovice	Cze-Rep	43	7	12	19	34	3	0	1	1	6

KOVAC, Kristian (KOH-vach, KRIHST-yan) COL.

Right wing. Shoots right. 6'2", 205 lbs. Born, Kosice, Czech., January 1, 1981.
(Colorado's 5th choice, 122nd overall, in 1999 Entry Draft).

			Regular Season					Playoffs				
Season	Club	Lea	GP	G	A	TP	PIM	GP	G	A	TP	PIM
1997-98	HC Kosice	Slovak-Jr.	47	22	11	33	103	....	....	....	....	....
1998-99	HC Kosice	Slovak-Jr.	39	30	20	50	73	2	1	0	1	2
	HC Kosice	Slovakia	6	0	0	0	2	....	....	....	....	....
99-2000	Victoriaville Tigres	QMJHL	65	11	18	29	50	5	0	0	0	4

KRAFT, Milan (KRAFT, MIH-lan) PIT.

Center. Shoots right. 6'3", 195 lbs. Born, Plzen, Czech., January 17, 1980.
(Pittsburgh's 1st choice, 23rd overall, in 1998 Entry Draft).

			Regular Season					Playoffs				
Season	Club	Lea	GP	G	A	TP	PIM	GP	G	A	TP	PIM
1995-96	ZKZ Plzen-Jr.	Cze-Rep	49	54	41	95	....	....	....	....	....	....
1996-97	ZKZ Plzen-Jr.	Cze-Rep	29	24	12	36	....	....	....	....	....	....
	ZKZ Plzen	Cze-Rep	9	0	1	1	2	....	....	....	....	....
1997-98	Keramika Plzen	Cze-Rep	24	22	21	43	12	....	....	....	....	....
	Keramika Plzen	Cze-Rep	16	0	5	5	0	1	0	0	0	0
1998-99	Prince Albert	WHL	68	40	46	86	32	14	7	13	20	6
99-2000	Prince Albert	WHL	56	34	35	69	42	6	4	1	5	4

KRAFT, Ryan S.J.

Center. Shoots left. 5'9", 181 lbs. Born, Bottineau, ND, November 7, 1975.
(San Jose's 11th choice, 194th overall, in 1995 Entry Draft).

			Regular Season					Playoffs				
Season	Club	Lea	GP	G	A	TP	PIM	GP	G	A	TP	PIM
1994-95	U. of Minnesota	WCHA	44	13	33	46	44	....	....	....	....	....
1995-96	U. of Minnesota	WCHA	41	13	24	37	24	....	....	....	....	....
1996-97	U. of Minnesota	WCHA	42	25	21	46	37	....	....	....	....	....
1997-98	U. of Minnesota	WCHA	32	11	26	37	16	....	....	....	....	....
1998-99	Richmond	ECHL	63	28	36	64	35	18	10	10	20	4
99-2000	Richmond	ECHL	44	32	35	67	32	....	....	....	....	....
	Cleveland	IHL	1	0	1	1	0	....	....	....	....	....
	Kentucky	AHL	15	7	6	13	2	5	3	1	4	0

KRESTANOVICH, Jordan (KREH-sta-noh-vihtch, JOHR-dan) COL.

Left wing. Shoots left. 6', 168 lbs. Born, Surrey, B.C., June 14, 1981.
(Colorado's 7th choice, 152nd overall, in 1999 Entry Draft).

			Regular Season					Playoffs				
Season	Club	Lea	GP	G	A	TP	PIM	GP	G	A	TP	PIM
1996-97	Surrey Chiefs	BCAHA	55	79	81	160	....	....	....	....	....	....
1997-98	Calgary Hitmen	WHL	22	1	0	1	0	13	0	0	0	0
1998-99	Calgary Hitmen	WHL	62	6	13	19	10	20	3	8	11	4
99-2000	Calgary Hitmen	WHL	72	19	24	43	22	13	7	7	14	4
	Hershey Bears	AHL	....	....	....	....	....	1	0	0	0	0

KREVSUN, Alexander (KREHV-sihn, al-ehx-AN-duhr) NSH.

Right wing. Shoots left. 6'1", 210 lbs. Born, Togliatti, USSR, June 2, 1980.
(Nashville's 9th choice, 124th overall, in 1999 Entry Draft).

			Regular Season					Playoffs				
Season	Club	Lea	GP	G	A	TP	PIM	GP	G	A	TP	PIM
1996-97	Lada Togliatti	Russia	2	0	0	0	0	....	....	....	....	....
1997-98	Lada Togliatti-2	Russia-3	37	10	5	15	24	....	....	....	....	....
1998-99	Lada Togliatti-2	Russia-4	24	10	4	14	30	....	....	....	....	....
	CSK Samara-2	Russia-4	8	4	0	4	4	....	....	....	....	....
	CSK Samara	Russia	5	0	2	2	4	2	0	0	0	0
99-2000	Krylja Sovetov	Russia-2	14	1	1	2	16	....	....	....	....	....
	CSK Samara-2	Russia-4	1	0	0	0	0	....	....	....	....	....

KRISTEK, Jaroslav (KRIHSH-tehk, YAH-roh-slahv) BUF.

Right wing. Shoots left. 6'2", 190 lbs. Born, Zlin, Czech., March 16, 1980.
(Buffalo's 4th choice, 50th overall, in 1998 Entry Draft).

			Regular Season					Playoffs				
Season	Club	Lea	GP	G	A	TP	PIM	GP	G	A	TP	PIM
1995-96	ZPS Zlin-Jr.	Cze-Rep	34	33	20	53	....	....	....	....	....	....
1996-97	ZPS Zlin-Jr.	Cze-Rep	44	28	27	55	....	....	....	....	....	....
1997-98	ZPS Zlin-Jr.	Cze-Rep	7	8	5	13	....	....	....	....	....	....
	HC Prostejov-2	Cze-Rep	4	0	0	0	....	....	....	....	....	....
	ZPS Zlin	Cze-Rep	37	2	8	10	20	....	....	....	....	....
1998-99	Tri-City Americans	WHL	70	38	48	86	55	12	4	3	7	2
99-2000	Tri-City Americans	WHL	45	26	25	51	16	2	0	0	0	0

KRISTOFFERSON, Marc (KRIHST-aw-fuhr-SOHN, MAHRK) DAL.

Right wing. Shoots left. 6'3", 200 lbs. Born, Ostersund, Sweden, January 22, 1979.
(Dallas' 4th choice, 105th overall, in 1997 Entry Draft).

			Regular Season					Playoffs				
Season	Club	Lea	GP	G	A	TP	PIM	GP	G	A	TP	PIM
1995-96	Mora IK	Swede-Jr.	16	2	2	4	28	....	....	....	....	....
	Mora IK	Sweden-2	26	1	0	1	20	5	0	0	0	2
1996-97	Mora IK	Swede-2	33	1	5	6	26	....	....	....	....	....
1997-98	Mora IK	Swede-2	27	7	6	13	40	....	....	....	....	....
1998-99	HV Jonkoping	Swede-Jr.	3	0	1	1	27	....	....	....	....	....
	HV Jonkoping	Sweden	34	0	1	1	65	....	....	....	....	....
99-2000	HV Jonkoping	Sweden	10	0	0	0	0	....	....	....	....	....
	Blues Espoo	Finland	29	7	4	11	42	1	1	0	1	0

KRONWALL, Niklas (KRAHN-wuhl) DET.

Defense. Shoots left. 5'11", 165 lbs. Born, Stockholm, Sweden, January 12, 1981.
(Detroit's 1st choice, 29th overall, in 2000 Entry Draft).

			Regular Season					Playoffs				
Season	Club	Lea	GP	G	A	TP	PIM	GP	G	A	TP	PIM
1996-97	Djurgardens IF	Swede-Jr.	1	0	0	0	0	....	....	....	....	....
1997-98	Djurgardens IF	Swede-Jr.	27	4	3	7	71	2	0	0	0	2
1998-99	Huddinge IK	Swede-2	24	1	1	2	24	....	....	....	....	....
99-2000	Djurgardens IF	Sweden	37	1	4	5	16	8	0	0	0	8

KRUCHININ, Andrei (kroo-CHIHN-ihn, AWN-dray) MTL.

Defense. Shoots left. 5'11", 176 lbs. Born, Karaganda, USSR, May 18, 1978.
(Montreal's 7th choice, 189th overall, in 1998 Entry Draft).

			Regular Season					Playoffs				
Season	Club	Lea	GP	G	A	TP	PIM	GP	G	A	TP	PIM
1996-97	Lada Togliatti	Russia	19	0	1	1	8	11	0	0	0	0
1997-98	Lada Togliatti	Russia	43	0	4	4	73	....	....	....	....	....
1998-99	Lada Togliatti	Russia	41	1	4	5	56	6	0	1	1	2
99-2000	CSK Samara	Russia	6	1	0	1	0	....	....	....	....	....
	Lada Togliatti	Russia	25	1	2	3	24	6	1	0	1	4

KRYUKOV, Artem (KREE-oo-kahf, AHR-tehm) BUF.

Center. Shoots left. 6'3", 187 lbs. Born, Novosibirsk, USSR, March 5, 1982.
(Buffalo's 1st choice, 15th overall, in 2000 Entry Draft).

			Regular Season					Playoffs				
Season	Club	Lea	GP	G	A	TP	PIM	GP	G	A	TP	PIM
1997-98	Torpedo Yaroslavl	Russia-2	7	0	0	0	2	....	....	....	....	....
1998-99	Torpedo Yaroslavl	Russia-3	20	2	2	4	6	....	....	....	....	....
99-2000	Torpedo Yaroslavl	Russia-3	14	1	1	2	12	....	....	....	....	....
	Torpedo Yaroslavl	Russia	3	0	0	0	4	....	....	....	....	....

KUCERA, Jiri (kuh-CHEH-rah, YUHREE) PIT.

Center. Shoots left. 5'11", 180 lbs. Born, Bratislava, Czech., March 28, 1966.
(Pittsburgh's 8th choice, 152nd overall, in 1987 Entry Draft).

			Regular Season					Playoffs				
Season	Club	Lea	GP	G	A	TP	PIM	GP	G	A	TP	PIM
1984-85	Skoda Pizen	Czech.	40	6	6	12	4	....	....	....	....	....
1985-86	Dukla Jihlava	Czech.	30	6	4	10	....	....	....	....	....	....
1986-87	Dukla Jihlava	Czech.	43	13	12	25	18	....	....	....	....	....
1987-88	Skoda Plzen	Czech.	41	21	24	45	22	....	....	....	....	....
1988-89	Skoda Plzen	Czech.	40	20	15	35	22	....	....	....	....	....
1989-90	Skoda Plzen	Czech.	47	13	24	37	....	....	....	....	....	....
1990-91	Tappara Tampere	Finland	44	23	34	57	26	3	0	2	2	4
1991-92	Tappara Tampere	Finland	44	22	20	42	8	....	....	....	....	....
1992-93	Tappara Tampere	Finland	48	22	32	54	20	....	....	....	....	....
1993-94	Tappara Tampere	Finland	47	16	26	42	37	10	7	5	12	4
	Olympics	Cze-Rep	8	6	2	8	4	....	....	....	....	....
1994-95	Lulea HF	Sweden	40	15	12	27	24	9	2	7	9	8
1995-96	Lulea HF	Sweden	39	15	19	34	38	12	4	6	10	6
1996-97	ZKZ Plzen	Cze-Rep	43	10	23	33	28	....	....	....	....	....
1997-98	EHC Kloten	Switz.	38	8	22	30	18	7	1	2	3	2
1998-99	Lulea HF	Sweden	44	7	21	28	52	5	2	1	3	4
99-2000	Lulea HF	Sweden	47	13	21	34	34	9	1	1	2	6

KUDROC, Kristian (KOO-drawch, KRIHS-tan) T.B.

Defense. Shoots right. 6'6", 229 lbs. Born, Michalovce, Czech., May 21, 1981.
(NY Islanders' 4th choice, 28th overall, in 1999 Entry Draft).

			Regular Season					Playoffs				
Season	Club	Lea	GP	G	A	TP	PIM	GP	G	A	TP	PIM
1997-98	HK Michalovce	Slovak-Jr.	47	7	4	11	66	....	....	....	....	....
	HK Michalovce	Slovak-2	4	0	0	0	0	....	....	....	....	....
1998-99	HK Michalovce	Slovak-2	17	0	3	3	12	....	....	....	....	....
99-2000	Quebec Remparts	QMJHL	57	9	22	31	172	11	2	5	7	29

Traded to **Tampa Bay** by **NY Islanders** with Kevin Weekes and NY Islanders' 2nd round choice in 2001 Entry Draft for Tampa Bay's 1st round choice (Raffi Torres) in 2000 Entry Draft, Calgary's 4th round choice (previously acquired, NY Islanders selected Vladimir Gorbunov) in 2000 Entry Draft and NY Islanders' 7th round choice (previously acquired, NY Islanders selected Ryan Caldwell) in 2000 Entry Draft, June 24, 2000.

KUKI, Arto (KUH-kee, AHR-toh) **MTL.**

Center. Shoots left. 6'3", 205 lbs. Born, Espoo, Finland, February 22, 1976.
(Montreal's 6th choice, 96th overall, in 1994 Entry Draft).

			Regular Season					Playoffs				
Season	**Club**	**Lea**	**GP**	**G**	**A**	**TP**	**PIM**	**GP**	**G**	**A**	**TP**	**PIM**
1992-93	Kiekko-Espoo-B	Finn-Jr.	37	11	6	17	22	....	....	....	....	....
1993-94	Kiekko-Espoo	Finn-Jr.	26	1	10	11	28	....	....	....	....	....
1994-95	Kiekko-Espoo	Finn-Jr.	33	7	10	17	36	5	0	0	0	2
	Kiekko-Espoo	Finland	4	0	1	1	0	....	....	....	....	....
1995-96	Kiekko-Espoo	Finn-Jr.	2	1	0	1	2	4	2	1	3	2
	Kiekko-Espoo	Finland	47	6	3	9	16	....	....	....	....	....
1996-97	Kiekko-Espoo	Finland	50	6	15	21	20	4	0	1	1	2
1997-98	Kiekko-Espoo	Finland	17	2	1	3	0	8	1	1	2	2
1998-99	Ahmat Hyvinkaa	Finland-2	5	0	3	3	2	....	....	....	....	....
	Kiekko-Espoo	Finland	27	2	1	3	22	4	0	1	1	0
99-2000	Blues Espoo	Finland	42	2	9	11	33	4	0	0	0	8

KULESHOV, Mikhail (koo-leh-SHAWV, MIHK-ayl) **COL.**

Left wing. Shoots right. 6'2", 200 lbs. Born, Perm, USSR, January 7, 1981.
(Colorado's 1st choice, 25th overall, in 1999 Entry Draft).

			Regular Season					Playoffs				
Season	**Club**	**Lea**	**GP**	**G**	**A**	**TP**	**PIM**	**GP**	**G**	**A**	**TP**	**PIM**
1997-98	Avangard Omsk	Russia-3	12	12	3	15	12	....	....	....	....	....
	Avangard Omsk	Russia	4	1	0	1	4	....	....	....	....	....
1998-99	HC Cherepovets-3	Russia-4	3	2	1	3	32	....	....	....	....	....
	HC Cherepovets-2	Russia-3	25	7	5	12	12	....	....	....	....	....
	HC Cherepovets	Russia	15	2	0	2	8	3	0	0	0	4
99-2000	HC Cherepovets	Russia	8	0	0	0	4	3	0	0	0	2

KULTANEN, Jarno (kuhl-TAH-nuhn, YAR-noh) **BOS.**

Defense. Shoots left. 6'2", 198 lbs. Born, Luumaki, Finland, January 8, 1973.
(Boston's 8th choice, 174th overall, in 2000 Entry Draft).

			Regular Season					Playoffs				
Season	**Club**	**Lea**	**GP**	**G**	**A**	**TP**	**PIM**	**GP**	**G**	**A**	**TP**	**PIM**
1991-92	KooKoo Kouvola	Finn-Jr.	22	7	17	24	28	....	....	....	....	....
	KooKoo Kouvola	Finland-2	1	0	0	0	0	....	....	....	....	....
1992-93	KooKoo Kouvola	Finn-Jr.	11	6	5	11	8	....	....	....	....	....
	KooKoo Kouvola	Finland-2	27	1	1	2	33	....	....	....	....	....
	Centers Pietarssari	Finland-2	1	1	0	1	0	....	....	....	....	....
1993-94	KooKoo Kouvola	Finn-Jr.	3	1	0	1	2	....	....	....	....	....
	KooKoo Kouvola	Finland-2	45	7	10	17	42	....	....	....	....	....
1994-95	KalPa Kuopio	Finland	47	5	12	17	26	3	0	0	0	8
1995-96	KalPa Kuopio	Finland	49	4	10	14	42	....	....	....	....	....
1996-97	HIFK Helsinki	Finland	24	1	3	4	6	....	....	....	....	....
1997-98	HIFK Helsinki	Finland	25	0	1	1	20	8	0	1	1	2
1998-99	HIFK Helsinki	Finland	51	6	6	12	53	10	1	0	1	27
99-2000	HIFK Helsinki	Finland	46	6	8	14	51	9	0	0	0	6

KUPARINEN, Mikko (koo-PAHR-ai-nehn, MEE-koh) **T.B.**

Defense. Shoots left. 6'3", 213 lbs. Born, Kerava, Finland, March 29, 1977.
(Tampa Bay's 10th choice, 244th overall, in 1999 Entry Draft).

			Regular Season					Playoffs				
Season	**Club**	**Lea**	**GP**	**G**	**A**	**TP**	**PIM**	**GP**	**G**	**A**	**TP**	**PIM**
1994-95	Hameenlinna-B	Finn-Jr.	31	4	7	11	16	....	....	....	....	....
1995-96	Hameenlinna-B	Finn-Jr.	19	5	6	11	8	....	....	....	....	....
1996-97	HPK Hameenlinna	Finn-Jr.	35	0	6	6	38	4	0	0	0	2
	HPK Hameenlinna	Finland	1	0	1	1	2	....	....	....	....	....
1997-98	HPK Hameenlinna	Finn-Jr.	28	2	4	6	18	....	....	....	....	....
1998-99	Ahmat Hyvinkas	Finland-2	3	0	0	0	2	....	....	....	....	....
	HPK Hameenlinna	Finland	33	0	3	3	52	....	....	....	....	....
	Grand Rapids	IHL	19	0	2	2	35	....	....	....	....	....
99-2000	HIFK Helsinki	Finland	28	0	2	2	49	9	0	0	0	0
	Detroit Vipers	IHL	5	0	0	0	2	....	....	....	....	....
	Long Beach	IHL	4	0	0	0	4	....	....	....	....	....

Traded to **Atlanta** by **Tampa Bay** for future considerations, October 29, 1999. Traded to **Tampa Bay** by **Atlanta** for Chris McAlpine, March 11, 2000.

KURKA, Tomas (KUHR-kuh, TAW-mahsh) **CAR.**

Left wing. Shoots left. 5'11", 190 lbs. Born, Most, Czech., December 14, 1981.
(Carolina's 1st choice, 32nd overall, in 2000 Entry Draft).

			Regular Season					Playoffs				
Season	**Club**	**Lea**	**GP**	**G**	**A**	**TP**	**PIM**	**GP**	**G**	**A**	**TP**	**PIM**
1996-97	CHZ Litvinov-Jr.	Cze-Rep	38	25	20	45	20	....	....	....	....	....
1997-98	CHZ Litvinov-Jr.	Cze-Rep	44	38	23	61	90	....	....	....	....	....
1998-99	CHZ Litvinov-Jr.	Cze-Rep	42	23	16	39	47	....	....	....	....	....
	CHZ Litvinov	Cze-Rep	6	0	0	0	0	....	....	....	....	....
99-2000	Plymouth Whalers	OHL	64	36	28	64	37	17	7	6	13	6

KUTLAK, Zdenek **BOS.**

Defense. Shoots left. 6'3", 207 lbs. Born, Budejovice, Czech., February 13, 1980.
(Boston's 10th choice, 237th overall, in 2000 Entry Draft).

			Regular Season					Playoffs				
Season	**Club**	**Lea**	**GP**	**G**	**A**	**TP**	**PIM**	**GP**	**G**	**A**	**TP**	**PIM**
1996-97	HC Budejovice-Jr.	Cze-Rep	45	8	11	19	20	....	....	....	....	....
1997-98	HC Budejovice-Jr.	Cze-Rep	43	1	6	7	30	....	....	....	....	....
1998-99	HC Budejovice-Jr.	C-Rep-Jr.	31	6	14	20	20	....	....	....	....	....
	HC Budejovice	Cze-Rep	22	1	3	4	4	3	0	0	0	0
99-2000	HC Budejovice-Jr.	Cze-Rep	8	4	2	6	26	....	....	....	....	....
	SHC Hradec	Cze-Rep	4	1	1	2	0	....	....	....	....	....
	IHC Pisek	Cze-Rep	3	1	0	1	0	2	0	0	0	2
	HC Budejovice	Cze-Rep	28	1	0	1	2	1	0	0	0	0

KUZNETSOV, Maxim (kooz-NEHT-zahv, MAX-ihm) **DET.**

Defense. Shoots left. 6'5", 198 lbs. Born, Pavlodar, USSR, March 24, 1977.
(Detroit's 1st choice, 26th overall, in 1995 Entry Draft).

			Regular Season					Playoffs				
Season	**Club**	**Lea**	**GP**	**G**	**A**	**TP**	**PIM**	**GP**	**G**	**A**	**TP**	**PIM**
1994-95	Dynamo Moscow	CIS	11	0	0	0	8	....	....	....	....	....
1995-96	Dynamo Moscow	CIS	9	1	1	2	22	4	0	0	0	0
1996-97	Dynamo Moscow	Russia	23	0	2	2	16	....	....	....	....	....
	Adirondack	AHL	2	0	1	1	6	2	0	0	0	0
1997-98	Adirondack	AHL	51	5	5	10	43	3	0	1	1	4
1998-99	Adirondack	AHL	60	0	4	4	30	3	0	0	0	0
99-2000	Cincinnati Ducks	AHL	47	2	9	11	36	....	....	....	....	....

KUZNIK, Greg (kooz-NIHK, GREHG) **CAR.**

Defense. Shoots left. 6', 182 lbs. Born, Prince George, B.C., June 12, 1978.
(Hartford's 7th choice, 171st overall, in 1996 Entry Draft).

			Regular Season					Playoffs				
Season	**Club**	**Lea**	**GP**	**G**	**A**	**TP**	**PIM**	**GP**	**G**	**A**	**TP**	**PIM**
1994-95	New Westminster	PCJHL	45	2	13	15	83	....	....	....	....	....
1995-96	Seattle T-Birds	WHL	70	2	13	15	149	5	0	0	0	6
1996-97	Seattle T-Birds	WHL	70	4	9	13	161	14	0	2	2	26
1997-98	Seattle T-Birds	WHL	72	5	12	17	197	5	0	0	0	4
1998-99	New Haven	AHL	27	1	0	1	33	....	....	....	....	....
	Florida Everblades	ECHL	50	6	8	14	110	5	1	0	1	0
99-2000	Cincinnati	IHL	46	0	3	3	53	4	0	0	0	4
	Dayton Bombers	ECHL	7	1	0	1	16	....	....	....	....	....
	Florida Everblades	ECHL	9	1	4	5	6	3	0	0	0	2

KWIATKOWSKI, Joel (KWEE-at-KOW-skee, JOHL) **OTT.**

Defense. Shoots left. 6'2", 206 lbs. Born, Kindersley, Sask., March 22, 1977.
(Dallas' 7th choice, 194th overall, in 1996 Entry Draft).

			Regular Season					Playoffs				
Season	**Club**	**Lea**	**GP**	**G**	**A**	**TP**	**PIM**	**GP**	**G**	**A**	**TP**	**PIM**
1994-95	North Battleford	SJHL	51	3	14	17	89	....	....	....	....	....
	Tacoma Rockets	WHL	70	4	13	17	66	4	0	0	0	2
1995-96	Kelowna Rockets	WHL	40	6	17	23	85	....	....	....	....	....
	Prince George	WHL	32	6	11	17	48	....	....	....	....	....
1996-97	Prince George	WHL	72	15	37	52	94	15	4	2	6	24
1997-98	Prince George	WHL	62	21	43	64	65	11	3	6	9	6
1998-99	Cincinnati Ducks	AHL	80	12	21	33	48	3	2	0	2	0
99-2000	Cincinnati Ducks	AHL	70	4	22	26	28	....	....	....	....	....

WHL West Second All-Star Team (1997) • WHL West First All-Star Team (1998)

Signed as a free agent by **Anaheim**, June 18, 1998. Traded to **Ottawa** by **Anaheim** for Patrick Traverse, June 12, 2000.

LAATIKAINEN, Arto (lah-tee-KIGH-nuhn) **NYR**

Defense. Shoots left. 6', 187 lbs. Born, Espoo, Finland, May 24, 1980.
(NY Rangers' 8th choice, 197th overall, in 1999 Entry Draft).

			Regular Season					Playoffs				
Season	**Club**	**Lea**	**GP**	**G**	**A**	**TP**	**PIM**	**GP**	**G**	**A**	**TP**	**PIM**
1996-97	Blues Espoo	Finn-Jr.	34	2	9	11	34	....	....	....	....	....
1997-98	Blues Espoo-B	Finn-Jr.	7	2	1	3	6	....	....	....	....	....
	Blues Espoo	Finn-Jr.	35	7	9	16	24	5	2	0	2	2
1998-99	Blues Espoo	Finn-Jr.	3	0	1	1	4	1	1	1	2	0
	Blues Espoo	Finland	48	0	6	6	14	4	0	2	2	2
99-2000	Blues Espoo	Finland	51	6	5	11	12	4	1	0	1	4
	Blues Espoo	Finn-Jr.	1	0	0	0	2	....	....	....	....	....

LABRAATEN, Jan (la-BRA-tuhn, YAN) **CGY.**

Left wing. Shoots right. 6'2", 198 lbs. Born, Karlstad, Sweden, February 17, 1977.
(Calgary's 4th choice, 98th overall, in 1995 Entry Draft).

			Regular Season					Playoffs				
Season	**Club**	**Lea**	**GP**	**G**	**A**	**TP**	**PIM**	**GP**	**G**	**A**	**TP**	**PIM**
1994-95	Farjestads BK	Swede-Jr.	25	10	6	16	20	....	....	....	....	....
	Farjestads BK	Sweden	2	0	1	1	2	1	0	0	0	0
1995-96	Farjestads BK	Sweden	4	0	0	0	0	....	....	....	....	....
1996-97	Orebro IK	Swede-2	30	9	6	15	51	....	....	....	....	....
1997-98	Raleigh IceCaps	ECHL	41	5	12	17	26	....	....	....	....	....
1998-99	Jacksonville	ECHL	1	0	0	0	0	....	....	....	....	....
	Monroe	WPHL	54	11	21	32	39	6	0	0	0	0
99-2000	Grums BK	Swede-2	46	6	16	22	69	....	....	....	....	....

LACHANCE, Bob (lah-CHANTS, BAWB)

Right wing. Shoots right. 5'11", 180 lbs. Born, Northampton, MA, February 1, 1974.
(St. Louis' 5th choice, 134th overall, in 1992 Entry Draft).

			Regular Season					Playoffs				
Season	**Club**	**Lea**	**GP**	**G**	**A**	**TP**	**PIM**	**GP**	**G**	**A**	**TP**	**PIM**
1991-92	Springfield Pics	NAJHL	46	40	98	138	87	....	....	....	....	....
1992-93	Boston University	H-East	33	4	10	14	24	....	....	....	....	....
1993-94	Boston University	H-East	32	13	19	32	42	....	....	....	....	....
1994-95	Boston University	H-East	37	12	29	41	51	....	....	....	....	....
1995-96	Boston University	H-East	39	15	37	52	67	....	....	....	....	....
	Worcester	AHL	7	1	0	1	6	....	....	....	....	....
1996-97	Worcester	AHL	74	21	35	56	66	5	0	2	2	4
1997-98	Worcester	AHL	70	15	33	48	56	11	6	10	16	12
1998-99	Indianapolis Ice	IHL	70	17	46	63	59	7	1	5	6	16
99-2000	Orlando	IHL	76	13	38	51	112	4	0	1	1	16

Signed as a free agent by **Atlanta**, June 21, 1999.

LAINE, Teemu (LIGH-neh, TEE-moo) **N.J.**

Right wing. Shoots left. 6', 200 lbs. Born, Helsinki, Finland, August 9, 1982.
(New Jersey's 2nd choice, 39th overall, in 2000 Entry Draft).

			Regular Season					Playoffs				
Season	**Club**	**Lea**	**GP**	**G**	**A**	**TP**	**PIM**	**GP**	**G**	**A**	**TP**	**PIM**
1998-99	Jokerit Helsinki	Finn-Jr.	29	20	17	37	83	6	0	2	2	6
99-2000	Jokerit Helsinki	Finn-Jr.	23	5	9	14	42	....	....	....	....	....
	Jokerit Helsinki	Finland	14	1	1	2	8	....	....	....	....	....

LAKOS, Andre (LA-kaws, AWN-dray) **N.J.**

Defense. Shoots right. 6'6", 230 lbs. Born, Vienna, Austria, July 29, 1979.
(New Jersey's 4th choice, 95th overall, in 1999 Entry Draft).

			Regular Season					Playoffs				
Season	**Club**	**Lea**	**GP**	**G**	**A**	**TP**	**PIM**	**GP**	**G**	**A**	**TP**	**PIM**
1995-96	Mtl-Bourassa	QAAA	40	2	13	15	68	....	....	....	....	....
1996-97	Shelburne Wolves	OJHL	36	5	12	17	47	....	....	....	....	....
1997-98	St. Michael's	OHL	49	2	10	12	54	....	....	....	....	....
1998-99	Barrie Colts	OHL	62	4	23	27	40	12	3	3	6	8
99-2000	Albany River Rats	AHL	65	1	7	8	41	5	0	2	2	4

LANGFELD, Josh (LANG-fehld, JAWSH) **OTT.**

Right wing. Shoots right. 6'3", 205 lbs. Born, Fridley, MN, July 17, 1977.
(Ottawa's 3rd choice, 66th overall, in 1997 Entry Draft).

			Regular Season					Playoffs				
Season	**Club**	**Lea**	**GP**	**G**	**A**	**TP**	**PIM**	**GP**	**G**	**A**	**TP**	**PIM**
1995-96	Great Falls	AFJHL	45	45	40	85	105	....	....	....	....	....
1996-97	Lincoln Stars	USHL	38	35	23	58	100	14	8	*13	*21	42
1997-98	U. of Michigan	CCHA	46	19	17	36	66	....	....	....	....	....
1998-99	U. of Michigan	CCHA	41	21	14	35	84	....	....	....	....	....
99-2000	U. of Michigan	CCHA	39	9	21	30	56	....	....	....	....	....

NCAA Championship All-Tournament Team (1998)

LAPLANTE, Eric (LA-plawnt, AIR-ihk) S.J.

Left wing. Shoots left. 6', 195 lbs. Born, St. Maurice, Que., December 1, 1979.
(San Jose's 3rd choice, 65th overall, in 1998 Entry Draft).

			Regular Season					Playoffs				
Season	Club	Lea	GP	G	A	TP	PIM	GP	G	A	TP	PIM
1995-96	Cap-d-Madelaine	QAAA	41	13	18	31	138	....	....	....	....	....
1996-97	Halifax	QMJHL	68	20	30	50	245	18	3	11	14	28
1997-98	Halifax	QMJHL	40	19	22	41	193	....	....	....	....	....
1998-99	Drummondville	QMJHL	42	14	25	39	258	....	....	....	....	....
	Quebec Remparts	QMJHL	23	4	17	21	58	13	8	7	15	45
99-2000	Quebec Remparts	QMJHL	47	24	35	59	234	10	3	5	8	*83

LARIVIERE, Jacques (la-RIHV-air, JAW-kehs) TOR.

Left wing. Shoots left. 6'4", 218 lbs. Born, Sorel, Que., December 18, 1979.
(New Jersey's 9th choice, 172nd overall, in 1998 Entry Draft).

			Regular Season					Playoffs				
Season	Club	Lea	GP	G	A	TP	PIM	GP	G	A	TP	PIM
1996-97	Gatineau	QAAA	53	35	20	55	95	....	....	....	....	....
	Moncton Wildcats	QMJHL	3	0	0	0	5	....	....	....	....	....
1997-98	Moncton Wildcats	QMJHL	68	3	1	4	249	9	0	0	0	15
1998-99	Moncton Wildcats	QMJHL	66	5	5	10	306	4	0	1	1	12
99-2000	Rimouski Oceanic	QMJHL	61	12	24	36	309	14	4	3	7	50

Signed as a free agent by **Toronto**, October 25, 1999.

LAROSE, Cory MIN.

Left wing. Shoots left. 6', 188 lbs. Born, Campbellton, N.B., May 14, 1975.

			Regular Season					Playoffs				
Season	Club	Lea	GP	G	A	TP	PIM	GP	G	A	TP	PIM
1995-96	Langley Thunder	BCJHL	54	28	46	74	61	....	....	....	....	....
1996-97	U. of Maine	H-East	35	10	27	37	32	....	....	....	....	....
1997-98	U. of Maine	H-East	34	15	25	40	22	....	....	....	....	....
1998-99	U. of Maine	H-East	38	21	31	52	34	....	....	....	....	....
99-2000	U. of Maine	H-East	39	15	*36	51	45	....	....	....	....	....

BCJHL Playoff MVP (1996) • Hockey East First All-Star Team (2000) • NCAA East Second All-American Team (2000)

Signed as a free agent by **Minnesota**, May 10, 2000.

LARRIVEE, Christian (la-ree-VAY, krihs-TYEH) MTL.

Center. Shoots left. 6'3", 185 lbs. Born, Gaspe, Que., August 25, 1982.
(Montreal's 6th choice, 114th overall, in 2000 Entry Draft).

			Regular Season					Playoffs				
Season	Club	Lea	GP	G	A	TP	PIM	GP	G	A	TP	PIM
1998-99	Jonquiere Aces	QAAA	42	26	36	62	10	....	....	....	....	....
99-2000	Chicoutimi	QMJHL	69	8	15	23	18	....	....	....	....	....

LAUZON, Ryan (LOH-zohn, RIGH-yan) PHX.

Center. Shoots left. 5'9", 182 lbs. Born, Halifax, N.S., October 8, 1980.
(Phoenix's 5th choice, 116th overall, in 1999 Entry Draft).

			Regular Season					Playoffs				
Season	Club	Lea	GP	G	A	TP	PIM	GP	G	A	TP	PIM
1996-97	Hull Olympiques	QMJHL	65	8	10	18	16	14	1	0	1	0
1997-98	Hull Olympiques	QMJHL	64	33	56	89	37	11	8	13	21	2
1998-99	Hull Olympiques	QMJHL	57	21	47	68	36	23	3	20	23	10
99-2000	Hull Olympiques	QMJHL	49	24	35	59	37	15	6	8	14	8

LAW, Kirby (LAW, KUHR-bee) PHI.

Right wing. Shoots right. 6'1", 180 lbs. Born, McCreary, Man., March 11, 1977.

			Regular Season					Playoffs				
Season	Club	Lea	GP	G	A	TP	PIM	GP	G	A	TP	PIM
1992-93	Dauphin Selects	MAHA	48	20	15	35	8	....	....	....	....	....
1993-94	Saskatoon Blades	WHL	66	9	11	20	39	16	0	0	0	6
1994-95	Saskatoon Blades	WHL	46	10	15	25	44	....	....	....	....	....
	Lethbridge	WHL	24	4	10	14	38	....	....	....	....	....
1995-96	Lethbridge	WHL	71	17	45	62	133	4	0	0	0	12
1996-97	Lethbridge	WHL	72	39	52	91	200	19	4	14	18	60
1997-98	Brandon	WHL	49	34	44	78	153	9	3	3	6	41
1998-99	Orlando	IHL	67	18	13	31	136	....	....	....	....	....
	Adirondack	AHL	11	2	3	5	40	3	1	0	1	2
99-2000	Louisville	AHL	66	31	21	52	173	....	....	....	....	....
	Orlando	IHL	1	1	0	1	0	....	....	....	....	....
	Philadelphia	AHL	12	1	4	5	6	5	2	0	2	2

Signed as a free agent by **Atlanta**, July 27, 1999. Traded to **Philadelphia** by **Atlanta** for Vancouver's 6th round choice (previously acquired, Atlanta selected Jeff Dwyer) in 2000 Entry Draft and a conditional choice in 2001 Entry Draft, March 14, 2000.

LAZAREV, Yevgeny (LA-zahr-ehv, YEHV-geh-nee) COL.

Right wing. Shoots left. 6'2", 205 lbs. Born, Kharkov, USSR, April 25, 1980.
(Colorado's 8th choice, 79th overall, in 1998 Entry Draft).

			Regular Season					Playoffs				
Season	Club	Lea	GP	G	A	TP	PIM	GP	G	A	TP	PIM
1995-96	Torpedo Yaroslavl	Russia-2	60	32	30	62	45	....	....	....	....	....
1996-97	Torpedo Yaroslavl	Russia-3	44	18	15	33	38	16	23	21	44	22
	Torpedo Yaroslavl	Russia	1	0	0	0	0	....	....	....	....	....
1997-98	Kitchener	OJHL	11	9	13	22	19	5	5	2	7	17
1998-99	Hershey Bears	AHL	53	6	15	21	18	....	....	....	....	....
99-2000	Hershey Bears	AHL	46	2	11	13	44	8	0	1	1	2

LEACH, Jay (LEECH, JAY) PHX.

Defense. Shoots left. 6'4", 215 lbs. Born, Syracuse, NY, September 2, 1979.
(Phoenix's 5th choice, 115th overall, in 1998 Entry Draft).

			Regular Season					Playoffs				
Season	Club	Lea	GP	G	A	TP	PIM	GP	G	A	TP	PIM
1996-97	Capital District	NAJHL	57	8	50	58	140	....	....	....	....	....
1997-98	Providence	H-East	32	0	8	8	29	....	....	....	....	....
1998-99	Providence	H-East	33	1	8	9	42	....	....	....	....	....
99-2000	Providence	H-East	37	1	9	10	101	....	....	....	....	....

LEAHY, Patrick (LEH-hey, PAT-rihk) NYR

Right wing. Shoots right. 6'3", 190 lbs. Born, Brighton, MA, June 9, 1979.
(NY Rangers' 5th choice, 122nd overall, in 1998 Entry Draft).

			Regular Season					Playoffs				
Season	Club	Lea	GP	G	A	TP	PIM	GP	G	A	TP	PIM
1996-97	Boston Prep	Hi-School	25	24	24	48	....	....	....	....	....	....
1997-98	U. of Miami-Ohio	CCHA	28	0	1	1	24	....	....	....	....	....
1998-99	U. of Miami-Ohio	CCHA	34	10	20	30	40	....	....	....	....	....
99-2000	U. of Miami-Ohio	CCHA	36	16	22	38	89	....	....	....	....	....

LEEB, Greg (LEEB, GREHG) DAL.

Center. Shoots left. 5'9", 160 lbs. Born, Red Deer, Alta., May 31, 1977.

			Regular Season					Playoffs				
Season	Club	Lea	GP	G	A	TP	PIM	GP	G	A	TP	PIM
1993-94	Red Deer Royals	AAHA	36	19	30	49	24	....	....	....	....	....
1994-95	Spokane Chiefs	WHL	72	21	34	55	48	11	5	10	15	10
1995-96	Spokane Chiefs	WHL	64	33	21	54	54	18	1	7	8	16
1996-97	Spokane Chiefs	WHL	72	27	59	86	69	9	3	3	6	4
1997-98	Spokane Chiefs	WHL	68	46	50	96	54	18	10	10	20	10
1998-99	Michigan K-Wings	IHL	77	16	27	43	18	5	0	3	3	4
99-2000	Michigan K-Wings	IHL	73	9	17	26	76	....	....	....	....	....

WHL West Second All-Star Team (1998)

Signed as a free agent by **Dallas**, July 24, 1998.

LEGAULT, Jay (LEH-goh, JAY) ANA.

Left wing. Shoots left. 6'4", 205 lbs. Born, Peterborough, Ont., May 15, 1979.
(Anaheim's 3rd choice, 72nd overall, in 1997 Entry Draft).

			Regular Season					Playoffs				
Season	Club	Lea	GP	G	A	TP	PIM	GP	G	A	TP	PIM
1994-95	Peterborough B's	OMHA	34	41	70	111	68	....	....	....	....	....
1995-96	Oshawa 67's	OHL	61	2	11	13	37	5	0	1	1	8
1996-97	Oshawa 67's	OHL	39	13	26	39	50	....	....	....	....	....
	London Knights	OHL	28	6	13	19	37	....	....	....	....	....
1997-98	London Knights	OHL	61	39	56	95	87	16	1	8	9	34
1998-99	London Knights	OHL	65	43	51	94	99	25	8	18	26	40
99-2000	Cincinnati Ducks	AHL	70	15	19	34	75	....	....	....	....	....
	Dayton Bombers	ECHL	2	0	0	0	2	....	....	....	....	....

LEGG, Chris (LEHG, KRIHS) EDM.

Center. Shoots left. 5'11", 177 lbs. Born, London, Ont., February 19, 1980.
(Edmonton's 7th choice, 171st overall, in 1999 Entry Draft).

			Regular Season					Playoffs				
Season	Club	Lea	GP	G	A	TP	PIM	GP	G	A	TP	PIM
1997-98	London Nationals	OJHL-B	50	36	32	68	45	....	....	....	....	....
1998-99	London Nationals	OJHL-B	52	38	40	78	28	....	....	....	....	....
99-2000	Brown University	ECAC	23	2	3	5	4	....	....	....	....	....

LEHOUX, Jason N.J.

Right wing. Shoots left. 6'2", 227 lbs. Born, Ste-Marie-Beauce, Que., July 21, 1979.

			Regular Season					Playoffs				
Season	Club	Lea	GP	G	A	TP	PIM	GP	G	A	TP	PIM
1996-97	Rimouski Oceanic	QMJHL	16	1	2	3	111	....	....	....	....	....
1997-98	Rouyn-Noranda	QMJHL	28	6	1	7	95	6	3	1	4	6
1998-99	Rouyn-Noranda	QMJHL	64	13	20	33	288	6	1	2	3	49
99-2000	Rouyn-Noranda	QMJHL	14	4	7	11	54	....	....	....	....	....
	Hull Olympiques	QMJHL	29	11	7	18	109	15	6	4	10	14

Signed as a free agent by **New Jersey**, June 27, 2000.

LEHOUX, Yanick (luh-HOO) L.A.

Center. Shoots right. 6', 170 lbs. Born, Montreal, Que., April 8, 1982.
(Los Angeles' 3rd choice, 86th overall, in 2000 Entry Draft).

			Regular Season					Playoffs				
Season	Club	Lea	GP	G	A	TP	PIM	GP	G	A	TP	PIM
1997-98	Cap-d-Madelaine	QAAA	42	29	50	79	26	....	....	....	....	....
1998-99	Baie-Comeau	QMJHL	63	10	20	30	31	....	....	....	....	....
99-2000	Baie-Comeau	QMJHL	67	31	61	92	14	6	1	2	3	2

LEOPOLD, Jordan (LEE-oh-pohld, JOHR-dan) ANA.

Defense. Shoots left. 6', 193 lbs. Born, Golden Valley, MN, August 3, 1980.
(Anaheim's 1st choice, 44th overall, in 1999 Entry Draft).

			Regular Season					Playoffs				
Season	Club	Lea	GP	G	A	TP	PIM	GP	G	A	TP	PIM
1995-96	Armstrong High	Hi-School	19	11	14	25	30	....	....	....	....	....
1996-97	Armstrong High	Hi-School	30	24	36	60	....	....	....	....	....	....
1997-98	Team USA	Under-18	60	11	12	23	16	....	....	....	....	....
1998-99	U. of Minnesota	WCHA	39	7	16	23	20	....	....	....	....	....
99-2000	U. of Minnesota	WCHA	39	6	18	24	20	....	....	....	....	....

WCHA Second All-Star Team (2000)

LESSARD, Francis (leh-SAHR, FRAN-sihs) PHI.

Defense. Shoots right. 6'2", 184 lbs. Born, Montreal, Que., May 30, 1979.
(Carolina's 3rd choice, 80th overall, in 1997 Entry Draft).

			Regular Season					Playoffs				
Season	Club	Lea	GP	G	A	TP	PIM	GP	G	A	TP	PIM
1995-96	Laval Regents	QAAA	41	5	7	12	73	....	....	....	....	....
1996-97	Val-d'Or Foreurs	QMJHL	66	1	9	10	287	....	....	....	....	....
1997-98	Val-d'Or Foreurs	QMJHL	63	3	20	23	338	19	1	6	7	*101
1998-99	Drummondville	QMJHL	53	12	36	48	295	....	....	....	....	....
99-2000	Philadelphia	AHL	78	4	8	12	416	5	0	1	1	7

Memorial Cup All-Star Team (1998)

Traded to **Philadelphia** by **Carolina** for Philadelphia's 8th round choice (Antti Jokela) in 1999 Entry Draft, May 25, 1999.

LEVESQUE, Willie (luh-VEHK, WIHL-lee) S.J.

Right wing. Shoots right. 6', 195 lbs. Born, Oak Bluffs, MA, January 22, 1980.
(San Jose's 3rd choice, 111th overall, in 1999 Entry Draft).

			Regular Season					Playoffs				
Season	Club	Lea	GP	G	A	TP	PIM	GP	G	A	TP	PIM
1997-98	Team USA	Under-18	60	12	24	36	118	....	....	....	....	....
1998-99	Northeastern	H-East	34	12	10	22	38	....	....	....	....	....
99-2000	Northeastern	H-East	33	9	13	22	45	....	....	....	....	....

LEVINSKI, Dimitri (leh-VOHN-skee, DEH-mih-TREE) CHI.

Right wing. Shoots left. 6'1", 183 lbs. Born, Ust-Kamenogorsk, USSR, June 23, 1981.
(Chicago's 2nd choice, 46th overall, in 1999 Entry Draft).

			Regular Season					Playoffs				
Season	Club	Lea	GP	G	A	TP	PIM	GP	G	A	TP	PIM
1997-98	Avangard Omsk	Russia-3	18	5	2	7	8	....	....	....	....	....
1998-99	HC Cherepovets-3	Russia-4	3	2	0	2	2	....	....	....	....	....
	HC Cherepovets-2	Russia-3	26	4	2	6	39	....	....	....	....	....
	HC Cherepovets	Russia	1	0	0	0	0	....	....	....	....	....
99-2000	St. Petersburg	Russia	25	0	2	2	4	4	0	0	0	0

LEWERSTROM, Erik (LEH-vuhr-struhm, AIR-ihk) PHX.

Defense. Shoots left. 6'2", 198 lbs. Born, Grums, Sweden, May 28, 1980.
(Phoenix's 7th choice, 168th overall, in 1999 Entry Draft).

			Regular Season					Playoffs				
Season	Club	Lea	GP	G	A	TP	PIM	GP	G	A	TP	PIM
1996-97	Grums IK	Swede-2	1	0	0	0	0	....	....	....	....	....
1997-98	Grums IK	Swede-2	4	0	0	0	2	....	....	....	....	....
1998-99	Grums IK	Swede-2	29	3	9	12	42	....	....	....	....	....
99-2000	Grums IK	Swede-2	37	5	7	12	88	....	....	....	....	....

LEWIS, Carlyle N.J.

Right wing. Shoots right. 6'3", 230 lbs. Born, Middleton, N.S., March 1, 1978.

			Regular Season					Playoffs				
Season	Club	Lea	GP	G	A	TP	PIM	GP	G	A	TP	PIM
1994-95	Summerside	MJrHL	20	3	5	8	63	....	....	....	....	....
1995-96	Beaufort Harfangs	QMJHL	30	0	2	2	90	....	....	....	....	....
1996-97	Beaufort Harfangs	QMJHL	66	7	8	15	353	....	....	....	....	....
1997-98	Laval Titans	QMJHL	59	9	13	22	310	16	1	3	4	53
1998-99	Halifax	QMJHL	65	20	27	47	425	5	1	1	2	18
99-2000	Albany River Rats	AHL	69	1	2	3	181	4	0	0	0	0

Signed as a free agent by **New Jersey**, January 26, 1999.

LILES, John-Michael (LIGH-uhls) COL.

Defense. Shoots left. 6', 183 lbs. Born, Zionsville, IN, November 25, 1980.
(Colorado's 8th choice, 159th overall, in 2000 Entry Draft).

			Regular Season					Playoffs				
Season	Club	Lea	GP	G	A	TP	PIM	GP	G	A	TP	PIM
1997-98	Team USA	Under-18	67	6	14	20	44	....	....	....	....	....
1998-99	Team USA	Under-17	13	2	5	7	6	....	....	....	....	....
	Team USA	Under-18	46	4	14	18	47	....	....	....	....	....
99-2000	Michigan State	CCHA	40	8	20	28	26	....	....	....	....	....

LILJA, Andreas (LIHL-yuh, an-DRAY-uhs) L.A.

Defense. Shoots left. 6'3", 222 lbs. Born, Landskrona, Sweden, July 13, 1975.
(Los Angeles' 2nd choice, 54th overall, in 2000 Entry Draft).

			Regular Season					Playoffs				
Season	Club	Lea	GP	G	A	TP	PIM	GP	G	A	TP	PIM
1995-96	Malmo IF	Sweden	40	1	5	6	63	5	0	1	1	2
1996-97	Malmo IF	Sweden	47	1	0	1	22	4	0	0	0	10
1997-98	Malmo IF	Sweden	10	0	0	0	0	....	....	....	....	....
1998-99	Malmo IF	Sweden	41	0	3	3	14	1	0	0	0	4
99-2000	Malmo IF	Sweden	49	8	11	19	88	6	0	0	0	8

LIND, Eric (LIHND, AIR-ihk) PIT.

Defense. Shoots right. 6'1", 198 lbs. Born, New Canaan, CT, March 12, 1978.
(Pittsburgh's 9th choice, 234th overall, in 1997 Entry Draft).

			Regular Season					Playoffs				
Season	Club	Lea	GP	G	A	TP	PIM	GP	G	A	TP	PIM
1996-97	Avon Old Farms	Hi-School	55	18	39	57	50	....	....	....	....	....
1997-98	New Hampshire	H-East	33	1	11	12	63	....	....	....	....	....
1998-99	New Hampshire	H-East	41	3	9	12	20	....	....	....	....	....
99-2000	New Hampshire	H-East	38	1	3	4	18	....	....	....	....	....

LINDSTROM, Sanny (LIHND-struhm, SAN-nee) COL.

Defense. Shoots left. 6'2", 205 lbs. Born, Huddinge, Sweden, December 24, 1979.
(Colorado's 4th choice, 112th overall, in 1999 Entry Draft).

			Regular Season					Playoffs				
Season	Club	Lea	GP	G	A	TP	PIM	GP	G	A	TP	PIM
1997-98	Huddinge IK	Swede-2	32	6	6	12	46	....	....	....	....	....
1998-99	Huddinge IK	Swede-2	37	4	4	8	65	....	....	....	....	....
99-2000	Hershey Bears	AHL	42	1	2	3	57	....	....	....	....	....
	Baton Rouge	ECHL	11	1	2	3	16	....	....	....	....	....

LINGREN, Steve (LIHN-grehn, STEEV)

Defense. Shoots left. 6', 193 lbs. Born, Lake Cowachin, B.C., July 23, 1973.

			Regular Season					Playoffs				
Season	Club	Lea	GP	G	A	TP	PIM	GP	G	A	TP	PIM
1991-92	Victoria Cougars	WHL	70	4	14	18	103	....	....	....	....	....
1992-93	Victoria Cougars	WHL	72	10	43	53	148	....	....	....	....	....
1993-94	Victoria Cougars	WHL	56	14	21	35	118	....	....	....	....	....
	Kalamazoo Wings	IHL	2	0	0	0	0	....	....	....	....	....
1994-95	Dayton Bombers	ECHL	64	11	23	34	128	9	2	8	10	16
	Kalamazoo	IHL	4	0	0	0	0	....	....	....	....	....
1995-96	Dayton Bombers	ECHL	51	15	28	43	83	....	....	....	....	....
	Cornwall Aces	AHL	1	0	1	1	0	....	....	....	....	....
	Michigan K-Wings	IHL	2	0	0	0	0	....	....	....	....	....
1996-97	Dayton Bombers	ECHL	9	2	5	7	15	....	....	....	....	....
	Hershey Bears	AHL	40	3	10	13	67	12	1	2	3	8
1997-98	Hershey Bears	AHL	63	12	18	30	89	....	....	....	....	....
1998-99	Kentucky	AHL	74	11	19	30	60	12	0	4	4	0
99-2000	Kansas City	IHL	75	10	15	25	54	....	....	....	....	....

ECHL First All-Star Team (1996)

Signed as a free agent by **San Jose**, August 3, 1998.

LITVINENKO, Alexei (liht-vihn-EHN-koh) PHX.

Defense. Shoots left. 6'4", 180 lbs. Born, Ust-Kamenogorsk, USSR, March 7, 1980.
(Phoenix's 9th choice, 262nd overall, in 1999 Entry Draft).

			Regular Season					Playoffs				
Season	Club	Lea	GP	G	A	TP	PIM	GP	G	A	TP	PIM
1997-98	Ust-Kamenogorsk	Russia-3	12	0	0	0	8	....	....	....	....	....
	Ust-Kamenogorsk	Russia-2	2	0	0	0	0	....	....	....	....	....
1998-99	Ust-Kamenogorsk	Russia-4	31	3	4	7	52	....	....	....	....	....
	Ust-Kamenogorsk	Russia-3	16	0	4	4	14	....	....	....	....	....
99-2000	Dynamo Moscow	Russia	7	0	0	0	4	....	....	....	....	....

LOVDAHL, Anders (LUHV-duhl, AN-duhrs) COL.

Center. Shoots left. 6'4", 189 lbs. Born, Borlange, Sweden, February 4, 1981.
(Colorado's 8th choice, 158th overall, in 1999 Entry Draft).

			Regular Season					Playoffs				
Season	Club	Lea	GP	G	A	TP	PIM	GP	G	A	TP	PIM
1997-98	HV Jonkoping	Swede-Jr.	26	5	5	10	18	....	....	....	....	....
1998-99	HV Jonkoping	Swede-Jr.	DID NOT PLAY – INJURED									
99-2000	Calgary Hitmen	WHL	36	5	9	14	28	....	....	....	....	....
	Moose Jaw	WHL	31	3	0	3	8	4	0	0	0	2

LOVEN, Fredrik (LUH-vehn, FREHD-rihk) PHX.

Center. Shoots left. 6'2", 183 lbs. Born, Stockholm, Sweden, March 14, 1977.
(Winnipeg's 10th choice, 189th overall, in 1995 Entry Draft).

			Regular Season					Playoffs				
Season	Club	Lea	GP	G	A	TP	PIM	GP	G	A	TP	PIM
1994-95	Djurgardens IF	Swede-Jr.	29	6	10	16	14	....	....	....	....	....
1995-96	Djurgardens IF	Sweden	4	0	0	0	0	4	0	0	0	0
1996-97	Djurgardens IF	Swede-Jr.	4	2	2	4	8	....	....	....	....	....
	Arlanda IK	Swede-2	5	0	3	3	4	....	....	....	....	....
	Djurgardens IF	Sweden	7	0	0	0	0	....	....	....	....	....
1997-98	Bjorkloven IF	Swede-2	32	5	6	11	8	14	0	2	2	10
1998-99	Hammarby IF	Swede-2	37	8	17	25	47	5	2	0	2	4
99-2000	Hammarby IF	Swede-2	45	2	8	10	34	2	0	0	0	0

LOW, Reed (LOH, REED) ST.L.

Right wing. Shoots right. 6'3", 220 lbs. Born, Moose Jaw, Sask., June 21, 1976.
(St. Louis' 7th choice, 177th overall, in 1996 Entry Draft).

			Regular Season					Playoffs				
Season	Club	Lea	GP	G	A	TP	PIM	GP	G	A	TP	PIM
1995-96	Moose Jaw	WHL	61	12	7	19	221	....	....	....	....	....
1996-97	Moose Jaw	WHL	62	16	11	27	228	12	2	1	3	50
1997-98	Worcester	AHL	17	1	1	2	75	3	0	0	0	0
	Baton Rouge	ECHL	39	4	2	6	145	....	....	....	....	....
1998-99	Worcester	AHL	77	5	6	11	239	4	0	0	0	2
99-2000	Worcester	AHL	80	12	16	28	203	9	1	3	4	16

LUCHINKIN, Sergei (loo-CHIHN-kihn, SAIR-gay) CBJ

Left wing. Shoots left. 5'11", 172 lbs. Born, Dmitrov, USSR, October 16, 1976.
(Dallas' 9th choice, 202nd overall, in 1995 Entry Draft).

			Regular Season					Playoffs				
Season	Club	Lea	GP	G	A	TP	PIM	GP	G	A	TP	PIM
1994-95	Dynamo Moscow	CIS	6	1	0	1	4	....	....	....	....	....
1995-96	Dynamo Moscow	CIS	21	6	2	8	14	10	0	1	1	6
1996-97	Dynamo Moscow	Russia	18	1	5	6	4	....	....	....	....	....
1997-98	Dynamo Moscow	EuroHL	1	0	0	0	0	....	....	....	....	....
	Dynamo Moscow	Russia	6	0	1	1	0	....	....	....	....	....
	Spartak Moscow	Russia	10	0	1	1	4	....	....	....	....	....
1998-99	Spartak Moscow	Russia	33	4	5	9	18	....	....	....	....	....

Selected by **Columbus** from **Boston** in Expansion Draft, June 23, 2000.

LUNDBOHM, Andy (LUHND-bawm, AN-dee) S.J.

Center. Shoots left. 6'3", 225 lbs. Born, Roseau, MN, March 24, 1977.

			Regular Season					Playoffs				
Season	Club	Lea	GP	G	A	TP	PIM	GP	G	A	TP	PIM
1995-96	Army Knights	NCAA	37	21	25	46	....	....	....	....	....	....
1996-97	Army Knights	NCAA	29	19	27	46	16	....	....	....	....	....
1997-98	Army Knights	NCAA	31	19	25	44	....	....	....	....	....	....
1998-99	Army Knights	NCAA	26	17	15	32	30	....	....	....	....	....
99-2000	New Orleans	ECHL	12	2	2	4	4	....	....	....	....	....
	Kentucky	AHL	22	2	1	3	8	2	0	0	0	5

Signed as a free agent by **San Jose**, June 11, 1999.

LUNDMARK, Jamie (LUHND-mahrk, JAY-mee) NYR

Center. Shoots right. 6', 174 lbs. Born, Edmonton, Alta., January 16, 1981.
(NY Rangers' 2nd choice, 9th overall, in 1999 Entry Draft).

			Regular Season					Playoffs				
Season	Club	Lea	GP	G	A	TP	PIM	GP	G	A	TP	PIM
1996-97	St. Albert Saints	AJHL	35	10	9	19	8	....	....	....	....	....
1997-98	St. Albert Saints	AJHL	57	33	58	91	176	19	12	19	31	....
1998-99	Moose Jaw	WHL	70	40	51	91	121	11	5	4	9	24
99-2000	Moose Jaw	WHL	37	21	27	48	33	....	....	....	....	....

WHL East Second All-Star Team (1999)

LUNDQVIST, Joel (LOOND-kvihst) DAL.

Center. Shoots left. 6', 180 lbs. Born, Are, Sweden, March 2, 1982.
(Dallas' 3rd choice, 68th overall, in 2000 Entry Draft).

			Regular Season					Playoffs				
Season	Club	Lea	GP	G	A	TP	PIM	GP	G	A	TP	PIM
1997-98	Rogle BK	Swede-Jr.	59	36	40	76	....	....	....	....	....	....
1998-99	Vasta Frolunda	Swede-Jr.	32	26	38	64	37	4	3	1	4	2
99-2000	Vasta Frolunda	Swede-Jr.	25	7	12	19	2	6	2	3	5	2

LUNDQVIST, Stefan (LUHND-kvihst, STEH-fan) NYR

Right wing. Shoots left. 6'3", 209 lbs. Born, Gavle, Sweden, February 18, 1978.
(NY Rangers' 7th choice, 180th overall, in 1998 Entry Draft).

			Regular Season					Playoffs				
Season	Club	Lea	GP	G	A	TP	PIM	GP	G	A	TP	PIM
1994-95	Avesta BK	Swede-2	3	0	1	1	0	....	....	....	....	....
1995-96	Avesta BK	Swede-3	27	24	13	37	10	....	....	....	....	....
1996-97	Avesta BK	Swede-3	31	37	29	66	....	....	....	....	....	....
1997-98	Brynas IF	Swede-Jr.	21	23	15	38	2	....	....	....	....	....
	Brynas IF	Sweden	27	2	2	4	0	1	0	0	0	0
1998-99	Brynas IF	Sweden	13	0	0	0	0	....	....	....	....	....
	Uppsala ALF	Swede-2	15	7	8	15	0	....	....	....	....	....
	Mora IK	Swede-2	23	10	7	17	22	4	2	2	4	2
99-2000	Brynas IF	Sweden	48	6	4	10	12	11	1	0	1	0

LUNDSTROM, Per-Anton (LUHND-struhm, PAIR-AN-tawn) PHX.

Defense. Shoots left. 6'2", 185 lbs. Born, Umea, Sweden, September 29, 1977.
(Phoenix's 3rd choice, 62nd overall, in 1996 Entry Draft).

			Regular Season					Playoffs				
Season	Club	Lea	GP	G	A	TP	PIM	GP	G	A	TP	PIM
1994-95	MoDo Hockey	Swede-Jr.	20	3	4	7	18	....	....	....	....	....
1995-96	MoDo Hockey	Swede-Jr.	25	3	3	6	28	2	1	0	1	4
	MoDo Hockey	Sweden	19	1	1	2	29	4	0	0	0	2
1996-97	MoDo Hockey	Sweden	35	0	0	0	42	....	....	....	....	....
1997-98	Bjorkloven IF	Swede-2	31	6	13	19	71	....	....	....	....	....
1998-99	Bjorkloven IF	Sweden	39	1	2	3	36	....	....	....	....	....
99-2000	AIK Solna	Sweden	50	4	5	9	48	....	....	....	....	....

LUPASCHUK, Ross (LOO-puhs-chuhk, RAWS) **WSH.**

Defense. Shoots right. 6'1", 211 lbs. Born, Edmonton, Alta., January 19, 1981.
(Washington's 4th choice, 34th overall, in 1999 Entry Draft).

			Regular Season					Playoffs				
Season	Club	Lea	GP	G	A	TP	PIM	GP	G	A	TP	PIM
1996-97	Edmonton Mets	AAHA	65	5	22	27	87	....	....	....	....	....
1997-98	Prince Albert	WHL	67	6	12	18	170	....	....	....	....	....
1998-99	Prince Albert	WHL	67	8	20	28	127	14	4	9	13	16
99-2000	Prince Albert	WHL	22	8	8	16	42	....	....	....	....	....
	Red Deer Rebels	WHL	46	13	27	40	116	4	0	1	1	10

LYDMAN, Toni (LEED-man, TOH-nee) **CGY.**

Defense. Shoots left. 6'1", 200 lbs. Born, Lahti, Finland, September 25, 1977.
(Calgary's 5th choice, 89th overall, in 1996 Entry Draft).

			Regular Season					Playoffs				
Season	Club	Lea	GP	G	A	TP	PIM	GP	G	A	TP	PIM
1992-93	Kiekko Reipas-C	Finn-Jr.	36	10	9	19	22	....	....	....	....	....
1993-94	Kiekko Reipas-B	Finn-Jr.	9	3	1	4	4	....	....	....	....	....
	Reipas Lahti	Finn-Jr.	1	0	0	0	0	....	....	....	....	....
1994-95	Kiekko Reipas-B	Finn-Jr.	9	7	4	11	12	....	....	....	....	....
	Reipas Lahti-2	Finn-Jr.	26	6	4	10	10	....	....	....	....	....
1995-96	Reipas Lahti	Finn-Jr.	9	2	2	4	6	....	....	....	....	....
	Reipas Lahti	Finland	39	5	2	7	30	3	0	1	1	0
1996-97	Tappara Tampere	Finland	49	1	2	3	65	3	0	0	0	6
1997-98	Tappara Tampere	Finland	48	4	10	14	48	4	0	2	2	0
1998-99	HIFK Helsinki	Finland	42	4	7	11	36	11	0	3	3	2
	HIFK Finland	EuroHL	6	0	2	2	29	4	1	....	....	....
99-2000	HIFK Helsinki	Finland	46	4	18	22	36	9	0	4	4	6

LYSAK, Brett (LIGH-sak, BREHT) **CAR.**

Center. Shoots left. 6', 190 lbs. Born, Edmonton, Alta., December 30, 1980.
(Carolina's 2nd choice, 49th overall, in 1999 Entry Draft).

			Regular Season					Playoffs				
Season	Club	Lea	GP	G	A	TP	PIM	GP	G	A	TP	PIM
1995-96	St. Albert Saints	AAHA	35	20	23	43	68	....	....	....	....	....
1996-97	Regina Pats	WHL	66	11	14	25	41	5	0	1	1	5
1997-98	Regina Pats	WHL	70	22	38	60	82	9	6	2	8	8
1998-99	Regina Pats	WHL	61	39	49	88	84	....	....	....	....	....
99-2000	Regina Pats	WHL	70	38	40	78	24	7	5	4	9	2

WHL East Second All-Star Team (1999)

LYUBIMOV, Alexander (loo-BEE-mahf) **EDM.**

Defense. Shoots left. 6'3", 196 lbs. Born, Ust-Kamenogorsk, USSR, February 15, 1980.
(Edmonton's 3rd choice, 83rd overall, in 2000 Entry Draft).

			Regular Season					Playoffs				
Season	Club	Lea	GP	G	A	TP	PIM	GP	G	A	TP	PIM
1997-98	Lada Togliatti-2	Russia-3	38	7	6	13	63	....	....	....	....	....
1998-99	Lada Togliatti-2	Russia-4	44	5	4	9	36	....	....	....	....	....
99-2000	CSK Samara	Russia	17	0	1	1	14	....	....	....	....	....
	Lada Togliatti	Russia	8	0	0	0	6	7	0	1	1	2

MAATTA, Tero (MAH-tuh, TEH-roh) **S.J.**

Defense. Shoots left. 6'1", 205 lbs. Born, Vantaa, Finland, January 2, 1982.
(San Jose's 1st choice, 41st overall, in 2000 Entry Draft).

			Regular Season					Playoffs				
Season	Club	Lea	GP	G	A	TP	PIM	GP	G	A	TP	PIM
1997-98	Jokerit Helsinki	Finn-Jr.	28	4	7	11	10	2	0	0	0	2
1998-99	Jokerit Helsinki	Finn-Jr.	38	4	8	12	75	8	1	3	4	6
99-2000	Jokerit Helsinki	Finn-Jr.	31	4	4	8	53	....	....	....	....	....

MacINTYRE, Dave **PHX.**

Defense. Shoots left. 5'11", 190 lbs. Born, New Glascow, N.S., October 20, 1968.

			Regular Season					Playoffs				
Season	Club	Lea	GP	G	A	TP	PIM	GP	G	A	TP	PIM
1987-88	New Hampshire	H-East	30	5	5	10	30	....	....	....	....	....
1988-89	New Hampshire	H-East	33	0	4	4	24	....	....	....	....	....
1989-90	New Hampshire	H-East	37	5	15	20	20	....	....	....	....	....
1990-91	New Hampshire	H-East	34	4	14	18	10	....	....	....	....	....
	Johnstown Chiefs	ECHL	....	....	....	....	....	7	0	4	4	0
1991-92	Johnstown Chiefs	ECHL	63	21	37	58	84	6	1	2	3	4
	Moncton Hawks	AHL	6	0	1	1	0	11	2	2	4	16
1992-93	Dayton Bombers	ECHL	6	2	4	6	10	....	....	....	....	....
	Moncton Hawks	AHL	50	5	17	22	37	2	0	0	0	0
1993-94	Salt Lake City	IHL	71	9	27	36	69	....	....	....	....	....
1994-95	Peoria Rivermen	IHL	71	10	31	41	52	8	2	3	5	0
1995-96	Peoria Rivermen	IHL	74	11	35	46	60	6	0	0	0	8
1996-97	San Antonio	IHL	76	17	36	53	104	8	1	4	5	2
1997-98	San Antonio	IHL	19	4	10	14	12	....	....	....	....	....
	Milwaukee	IHL	12	6	2	8	8	....	....	....	....	....
	Orlando	IHL	19	0	10	10	25	....	....	....	....	....
1998-99	Berlin Capitals	DEL	12	1	3	4	8	....	....	....	....	....
99-2000	JyP Jyvaskyla	Finland	31	2	6	8	70	....	....	....	....	....

Signed as a free agent by **Phoenix**, August 3, 2000.

MacISAAC, Dave (muh-KIGH-zuhk, DAYV) **S.J.**

Defense. Shoots left. 6'2", 225 lbs. Born, Cambridge, MA, April 23, 1972.

			Regular Season					Playoffs				
Season	Club	Lea	GP	G	A	TP	PIM	GP	G	A	TP	PIM
1992-93	U. of Maine	H-East	35	5	32	37	14	....	....	....	....	....
1993-94	U. of Maine	H-East	31	4	20	24	22	....	....	....	....	....
1994-95	U. of Maine	H-East	44	5	13	18	44	....	....	....	....	....
	Milwaukee	IHL	2	0	0	0	5	9	0	2	2	2
1995-96	Milwaukee	IHL	71	7	16	23	165	....	....	....	....	....
1996-97	Philadelphia	AHL	61	3	15	18	187	10	0	1	1	31
1997-98	Philadelphia	AHL	80	7	21	28	241	18	5	13	18	20
1998-99	Philadelphia	AHL	47	6	15	21	98	16	2	5	7	50
99-2000	Lowell	AHL	77	1	25	26	179	7	0	1	1	4

Signed as a free agent by **Philadelphia**, July 30, 1996. Signed as a free agent by **LA Kings**, August 25, 1999. Signed as a free agent by **San Jose**, August 10, 2000.

MACKENZIE, Derek (muh-KEHN-zee, DAIR-ehk) **ATL.**

Center. Shoots left. 5'11", 169 lbs. Born, Sudbury, Ont., June 11, 1981.
(Atlanta's 6th choice, 128th overall, in 1999 Entry Draft).

			Regular Season					Playoffs				
Season	Club	Lea	GP	G	A	TP	PIM	GP	G	A	TP	PIM
1996-97	Rayside-Balfour	NOJHA	40	23	32	55	40	....	....	....	....	....
1997-98	Sudbury Wolves	OHL	59	9	11	20	26	....	....	....	....	....
1998-99	Sudbury Wolves	OHL	68	22	65	87	74	4	2	4	6	2
99-2000	Sudbury Wolves	OHL	68	24	33	57	110	12	5	9	14	16

MacMILLAN, Jeff (muhk-MIHL-uhn) **DAL.**

Defense. Shoots left. 6'3", 202 lbs. Born, Durham, Ont., March 30, 1979.
(Dallas' 8th choice, 215th overall, in 1999 Entry Draft).

			Regular Season					Playoffs				
Season	Club	Lea	GP	G	A	TP	PIM	GP	G	A	TP	PIM
1996-97	Oshawa Generals	OHL	39	0	4	4	15	15	0	0	0	4
1997-98	Oshawa Generals	OHL	64	3	12	15	72	7	0	3	3	11
1998-99	Oshawa Generals	OHL	65	3	18	21	109	15	3	6	9	28
99-2000	Michigan K-Wings	IHL	53	0	3	3	54	....	....	....	....	....
	Fort Wayne	UHL	7	1	1	2	25	9	0	2	2	10

MacNEIL, Ian (muhk-NEEL, EE-an) **CAR.**

Center. Shoots left. 6'2", 190 lbs. Born, Halifax, N.S., April 27, 1977.
(Hartford's 3rd choice, 85th overall, in 1995 Entry Draft).

			Regular Season					Playoffs				
Season	Club	Lea	GP	G	A	TP	PIM	GP	G	A	TP	PIM
1993-94	Whitby Lions	OMHA	50	30	22	52	102	....	....	....	....	....
1994-95	Oshawa 67's	OHL	60	7	21	28	62	7	0	2	2	0
1995-96	Oshawa 67's	OHL	49	15	17	32	54	5	1	2	3	8
1996-97	Oshawa 67's	OHL	64	23	20	43	96	18	2	3	5	37
1997-98	New Haven	AHL	68	12	21	33	67	3	1	0	1	10
1998-99	New Haven	AHL	47	6	4	10	62	....	....	....	....	....
99-2000	Cincinnati	IHL	81	19	18	37	100	11	3	2	5	25

Rights transferred to **Carolina** after **Hartford** franchise relocated, June 25, 1997.

MAGNUSON, William (MAG-nuh-sohn, Wihl-ee-am) **COL.**

Defense. Shoots right. 6'5", 232 lbs. Born, Anchorage, AK, February 19, 1980.
(Colorado's 6th choice, 142nd overall, in 1999 Entry Draft).

			Regular Season					Playoffs				
Season	Club	Lea	GP	G	A	TP	PIM	GP	G	A	TP	PIM
1997-98	Team USA	Under-18	69	2	15	17	62	....	....	....	....	....
1998-99	Lake Superior	CCHA	32	0	1	1	44	....	....	....	....	....
99-2000	Lake Superior	CCHA	27	0	2	2	38	....	....	....	....	....

MAKELA, Tuukka (MA-kuh-luh TUH-kuh) **BOS.**

Defense. Shoots left. 6'2", 202 lbs. Born, Helsinki, Finland, May 24, 1982.
(Boston's 5th choice, 66th overall, in 2000 Entry Draft).

			Regular Season					Playoffs				
Season	Club	Lea	GP	G	A	TP	PIM	GP	G	A	TP	PIM
1998-99	HIFK Helsinki	Finn-Jr.	32	1	1	2	20	3	0	1	1	0
99-2000	HIFK Helsinki	Finn-Jr.	36	2	5	7	22	....	....	....	....	....

MALENKIKH, Vladimir (MAH-lihn-keh) **PIT.**

Defense. Shoots left. 6'1", 187 lbs. Born, Togliatti, USSR, October 1, 1980.
(Pittsburgh's 7th choice, 157th overall, in 1999 Entry Draft).

			Regular Season					Playoffs				
Season	Club	Lea	GP	G	A	TP	PIM	GP	G	A	TP	PIM
1997-98	Lada Togliatti-2	Russia-3	39	6	4	10	112	....	....	....	....	....
1998-99	Lada Togliatti-2	Russia-4	38	6	3	9	68	....	....	....	....	....
	Lada Togliatti	Russia	9	0	0	0	2	....	....	....	....	....
99-2000	CSK Samara	Russia	7	0	1	1	14	....	....	....	....	....

MALLETTE, Carl (muh-LEHT) **ATL.**

Center. Shoots right. 6'1", 188 lbs. Born, Pointe-Claire, Que., November 17, 1981.
(Atlanta's 4th choice, 107th overall, in 2000 Entry Draft).

			Regular Season					Playoffs				
Season	Club	Lea	GP	G	A	TP	PIM	GP	G	A	TP	PIM
1996-97	Rive-Sud Express	QAAA	32	14	22	36	35	7	2	6	8	16
1997-98	Victoriaville Tigres	QMJHL	55	8	7	15	30	6	1	1	2	4
1998-99	Victoriaville Tigres	QMJHL	62	27	46	73	51	6	1	2	3	2
99-2000	Victoriaville Tigres	QMJHL	69	49	76	125	97	6	6	3	9	28

MALMIVAARA, Olli (mal-MIH-vah-ruh, OH-lee) **CHI.**

Defense. Shoots left. 6'4", 205 lbs. Born, Kajaani, Finland, March 13, 1982.
(Chicago's 6th choice, 117th overall, in 2000 Entry Draft).

			Regular Season					Playoffs				
Season	Club	Lea	GP	G	A	TP	PIM	GP	G	A	TP	PIM
1998-99	Jokerit Helsinki	Finn-Jr.	35	1	8	9	10	7	0	0	0	2
99-2000	Jokerit Helsinki	Finn-Jr.	27	3	3	6	12	....	....	....	....	....

MALONE, Ryan (MA-lohne, RIGH-yan) **PIT.**

Left wing. Shoots left. 6'3", 190 lbs. Born, Pittsburgh, PA, December 1, 1979.
(Pittsburgh's 5th choice, 115th overall, in 1999 Entry Draft).

			Regular Season					Playoffs				
Season	Club	Lea	GP	G	A	TP	PIM	GP	G	A	TP	PIM
1997-98	Shattuck High	Hi-School	50	41	44	85	69	....	....	....	....	....
1998-99	Omaha Lancers	USHL	51	14	22	36	81	....	....	....	....	....
99-2000	St. Cloud State	WCHA	38	9	21	30	68	....	....	....	....	....

MANLOW, Eric **BOS.**

Center. Shoots left. 6', 190 lbs. Born, Belleville, Ont., April 7, 1975.
(Chicago's 2nd choice, 50th overall, in 1993 Entry Draft).

			Regular Season					Playoffs				
Season	Club	Lea	GP	G	A	TP	PIM	GP	G	A	TP	PIM
1990-91	Peterborough	OMHA	59	67	51	118	90	....	....	....	....	....
	Peterborough B's	OJHL	1	0	0	0	0	....	....	....	....	....
1991-92	Kitchener	OHL	59	12	20	32	17	14	2	5	7	10
1992-93	Kitchener	OHL	53	26	21	47	31	4	0	1	1	2
1993-94	Kitchener	OHL	49	28	32	60	25	3	0	1	1	4
1994-95	Kitchener	OHL	44	25	29	54	26	....	....	....	....	....
	Detroit Whalers	OHL	16	4	16	20	11	21	11	10	21	18
1995-96	Indianapolis Ice	IHL	75	6	11	17	32	4	0	1	1	4
1996-97	Baltimore Bandits	AHL	36	6	6	12	13	3	0	0	0	0
	Columbus Chill	ECHL	32	18	18	36	20	....	....	....	....	....
1997-98	Indianapolis Ice	IHL	60	8	11	19	25	3	1	0	1	0
1998-99	Long Beach	IHL	51	9	19	28	30	8	0	0	0	8
	Florida Everblades	ECHL	18	8	15	23	11	....	....	....	....	....
99-2000	Florida Everblades	ECHL	26	14	24	38	24	....	....	....	....	....
	Providence Bruins	AHL	46	17	16	33	14	14	6	8	14	8

Signed as a free agent by **Providence** (AHL), January 24, 2000. Signed as a free agent by **Boston**, July 11, 2000.

MANNING, Paul (MAN-nihng, PAWL) **CGY.**

Defense. Shoots left. 6'4", 193 lbs. Born, Red Deer, Alta., April 15, 1979.
(Calgary's 3rd choice, 62nd overall, in 1998 Entry Draft).

			Regular Season					Playoffs				
Season	Club	Lea	GP	G	A	TP	PIM	GP	G	A	TP	PIM
1996-97	Red Deer Vipers	HJHL	36	9	33	42	....	....	....	....	....	....
1997-98	Colorado College	WCHA	30	1	5	6	16	....	....	....	....	....
1998-99	Colorado College	WCHA	41	3	10	13	75	....	....	....	....	....
99-2000	Colorado College	WCHA	39	6	17	23	26	....	....	....	....	....

MAPLETOFT, Justin (MAPLE-tawft, JUH-stihn) **NYI**

Center. Shoots left. 6'1", 180 lbs. Born, Lloydminster, Sask., January 11, 1981.
(NY Islanders' 9th choice, 130th overall, in 1999 Entry Draft).

			Regular Season					Playoffs				
Season	Club	Lea	GP	G	A	TP	PIM	GP	G	A	TP	PIM
1997-98	Red Deer Rebels	WHL	65	9	4	13	41	....	....	....	....	....
1998-99	Red Deer Rebels	WHL	72	24	22	46	81	....	....	....	....	....
99-2000	Red Deer Rebels	WHL	72	39	57	96	135	4	2	1	3	28

WHL East First All-Star Team (2000)

MARCHANT, Terry (mahr-SHAHNT, TAIR-ree)

Left wing. Shoots left. 6'2", 205 lbs. Born, Buffalo, NY, February 24, 1976.
(Edmonton's 9th choice, 136th overall, in 1994 Entry Draft).

			Regular Season					Playoffs				
Season	Club	Lea	GP	G	A	TP	PIM	GP	G	A	TP	PIM
1993-94	Niagara Scenics	NAJHL	42	27	40	67	43	....	....	....	....	....
1994-95	Lake Superior	CCHA	23	2	5	7	12	....	....	....	....	....
1995-96	Lake Superior	CCHA	36	8	5	13	15	....	....	....	....	....
1996-97	Lake Superior	CCHA	38	12	14	26	26	....	....	....	....	....
1997-98	Lake Superior	CCHA	36	17	22	39	24	....	....	....	....	....
1998-99	Hamilton Bulldogs	AHL	47	12	8	20	10	2	1	0	1	0
99-2000	Houston Aeros	IHL	66	11	13	24	41	11	4	2	6	4

CCHA Second All-Star Team (1998)

MARKOV, Andrei (MAHR-kahf, AN-dray) **MTL.**

Defense. Shoots left. 6', 185 lbs. Born, Voskresensk, USSR, December 20, 1978.
(Montreal's 6th choice, 162nd overall, in 1998 Entry Draft).

			Regular Season					Playoffs				
Season	Club	Lea	GP	G	A	TP	PIM	GP	G	A	TP	PIM
1995-96	HK Khimik	CIS	38	0	0	0	14	....	....	....	....	....
1996-97	HK Khimik	Russia	43	8	4	12	32	2	1	1	2	0
1997-98	HK Khimik	Russia	43	10	5	15	83	....	....	....	....	....
1998-99	Dynamo Moscow	Russia	38	10	11	21	32	16	3	6	9	6
99-2000	Dynamo Moscow	Russia	29	11	12	23	28	17	4	3	7	8

MAROIS, Jerome (MAIR-wuh, jair-OHM) **MTL.**

Left wing. Shoots left. 6', 188 lbs. Born, Quebec, Que., January 27, 1981.
(Montreal's 11th choice, 253rd overall, in 1999 Entry Draft).

			Regular Season					Playoffs				
Season	Club	Lea	GP	G	A	TP	PIM	GP	G	A	TP	PIM
1997-98	Quebec	QMJHL	55	5	12	17	12	12	2	0	2	2
1998-99	Quebec	QMJHL	52	8	15	23	48	12	0	4	4	13
99-2000	Cape Breton	QMJHL	66	28	34	62	95	4	2	1	3	14

MARTIN, Mike **CGY.**

Defense. Shoots right. 6'2", 205 lbs. Born, Stratford, Ont., October 27, 1976.
(NY Rangers' 2nd choice, 65th overall, in 1995 Entry Draft).

			Regular Season					Playoffs				
Season	Club	Lea	GP	G	A	TP	PIM	GP	G	A	TP	PIM
1992-93	Windsor	OHL	61	2	7	9	80	....	....	....	....	....
1993-94	Windsor	OHL	64	2	29	31	94	4	1	2	3	4
1994-95	Windsor	OHL	53	9	28	37	79	10	1	3	4	21
1995-96	Windsor	OHL	65	19	48	67	128	7	0	6	6	14
1996-97	Binghamton	AHL	62	2	7	9	45	3	0	1	1	2
1997-98	Hartford	AHL	60	4	11	15	70	4	0	0	0	2
1998-99	Fort Wayne	IHL	75	6	20	26	89	2	0	0	0	4
99-2000	Michigan	IHL	74	8	15	23	99	....	....	....	....	....

Signed as a free agent by **Calgary**, August, 2000.

MARTIN, Paul (MAHR-tihn) **N.J.**

Defense. Shoots left. 6'1", 170 lbs. Born, Minneapolis, MN, March 5, 1981.
(New Jersey's 5th choice, 62nd overall, in 2000 Entry Draft).

			Regular Season					Playoffs				
Season	Club	Lea	GP	G	A	TP	PIM	GP	G	A	TP	PIM
99-2000	Elk River High	Hi-School	24	15	35	50	26	....	....	....	....	....

MARTINEK, Radek (MAHR-tih-nehk) **NYI**

Defense. Shoots right. 6', 196 lbs. Born, Havlickuv Brod, Czech., August 31, 1976.
(NY Islanders' 12th choice, 228th overall, in 1999 Entry Draft).

			Regular Season					Playoffs				
Season	Club	Lea	GP	G	A	TP	PIM	GP	G	A	TP	PIM
1996-97	HC Budejovice	Cze-Rep	52	3	5	8	40	5	0	1	1	2
1997-98	HC Budejovice	Cze-Rep	42	2	7	9	36	....	....	....	....	....
1998-99	HC Budejovice	Cze-Rep	52	12	13	25	50	3	0	2	2	....
99-2000	HC Budejovice	Cze-Rep	45	5	18	23	24	3	0	0	0	6

MARTONE, Mike (mahr-TOHN, MIGHK) **PHX.**

Defense. Shoots right. 6'2", 203 lbs. Born, Sault Ste. Marie, Ont., September 26, 1977.
(Buffalo's 6th choice, 106th overall, in 1996 Entry Draft).

			Regular Season					Playoffs				
Season	Club	Lea	GP	G	A	TP	PIM	GP	G	A	TP	PIM
1993-94	S.S. Marie Legion	NOHA	35	5	16	21	78	....	....	....	....	....
1994-95	Peterborough	OHL	62	3	9	12	99	10	0	2	2	4
1995-96	Peterborough	OHL	64	3	12	15	127	24	7	5	12	37
1996-97	Peterborough	OHL	50	9	21	30	104	10	0	6	6	30
1997-98	Peterborough	OHL	48	5	17	22	88	4	0	2	2	10
1998-99	Springfield	AHL	2	0	0	0	2	....	....	....	....	....
	Mississippi	ECHL	44	5	11	16	59	18	0	3	3	40
99-2000	Mississippi	ECHL	62	3	9	12	133	7	1	1	2	23

Signed as a free agent by **Phoenix**, August 12, 1998.

MARTYNYUK, Denis (mahr-tih-nyook, DEH-nihs) **VAN.**

Left wing. Shoots left. 6'3", 190 lbs. Born, Kapfenberg, Austria, July 26, 1979.
(Vancouver's 11th choice, 201st overall, in 1997 Entry Draft).

			Regular Season					Playoffs				
Season	Club	Lea	GP	G	A	TP	PIM	GP	G	A	TP	PIM
1994-95	CSKA Moscow	Russia-Jr.	34	25	25	50	20	....	....	....	....	....
1995-96	CSKA Moscow	Russia-Jr.	36	10	15	25	20	....	....	....	....	....
	CSKA Moscow	Russia-2	25	2	5	7	20	....	....	....	....	....
1996-97	CSKA Moscow	Russia-3	41	7	4	11	12	....	....	....	....	....
	CSKA Moscow	Russia	3	1	0	1	0	....	....	....	....	....
1997-98	Spartak Moscow	Russia-3	45	9	5	14	34	....	....	....	....	....
1998-99	Spartak Moscow	Russia	17	0	0	0	8	....	....	....	....	....
99-2000	Spartak Moscow	Russia-2	STATISTICS NOT AVAILABLE									

MARTZ, Nathan (MAHRTZ) **NYR**

Center. Shoots left. 6'3", 169 lbs. Born, Chilliwack, B.C., March 4, 1981.
(NY Rangers' 4th choice, 140th overall, in 2000 Entry Draft).

			Regular Season					Playoffs				
Season	Club	Lea	GP	G	A	TP	PIM	GP	G	A	TP	PIM
99-2000	Chilliwack	BCJHL	59	35	75	110	97	....	....	....	....	....

MASON, Wes **ATL.**

Left wing. Shoots left. 6'2", 180 lbs. Born, Windsor, Ont., December 12, 1977.
(New Jersey's 2nd choice, 38th overall, in 1996 Entry Draft).

			Regular Season					Playoffs				
Season	Club	Lea	GP	G	A	TP	PIM	GP	G	A	TP	PIM
1992-93	Port Stanley	OJHL-D	38	19	39	58	88	....	....	....	....	....
1993-94	Chatham Maroons	OJHL-B	52	26	47	73	123	....	....	....	....	....
1994-95	Sarnia Sting	OHL	38	1	8	9	50	2	0	0	0	9
1995-96	Sarnia Sting	OHL	63	23	45	68	97	10	3	2	5	16
1996-97	Sarnia Sting	OHL	66	45	46	91	72	12	7	11	18	10
1997-98	Sarnia Sting	OHL	2	1	0	1	4	....	....	....	....	....
	Sudbury Wolves	OHL	9	3	8	11	12	....	....	....	....	....
	Kingston	OHL	38	10	19	29	38	10	0	2	2	4
1998-99	Albany River Rats	AHL	27	4	4	8	36	....	....	....	....	....
	Augusta Lynx	ECHL	30	13	14	27	75	2	1	0	1	6
99-2000	Augusta Lynx	ECHL	28	18	20	38	41	....	....	....	....	....
	Orlando	IHL	33	11	15	26	30	....	....	....	....	....
	Louisville	AHL	8	1	2	3	2	3	0	0	0	0

Traded to **Atlanta** by **New Jersey** with Eric Bertrand for Sylvain Cloutier, Jeff Williams and Atlanta's 7th round choice (Ken Magovan) in 2000 Entry Draft, November 1, 1999.

MATEJOVSKY, Radek (ma-teh-YAHV-skee, ra-DEHK) **NYI**

Right wing. Shoots right. 6'1", 187 lbs. Born, Praha, Czech., November 17, 1977.
(NY Islanders' 9th choice, 250th overall, in 1998 Entry Draft).

			Regular Season					Playoffs				
Season	Club	Lea	GP	G	A	TP	PIM	GP	G	A	TP	PIM
1992-93	HC Budejovice-Jr.	Cze-Rep	25	38	24	62	....	....	....	....	....	....
1993-94	Slavia Praha-Jr.	Cze-Rep	45	30	26	56	....	....	....	....	....	....
1994-95	Slavia Praha-Jr.	Cze-Rep	28	7	8	15	12	....	....	....	....	....
1995-96	Slavia Praha-Jr.	Cze-Rep	47	37	21	58	24	....	....	....	....	....
1996-97	Slavia Praha-Jr.	Cze-Rep	4	1	1	2	....	....	....	....	....	....
	HC Beroun-2	Cze-Rep	12	3	1	4	18	....	....	....	....	....
	Slavia Praha	Cze-Rep	41	3	4	7	10	3	0	0	0	0
1997-98	Slavia Praha	Cze-Rep	52	9	4	13	24	3	0	0	0	0
1998-99	Dukla Jihlava	Cze-Rep	52	12	10	22	57	....	....	....	....	....
99-2000	Slavia Praha	Cze-Rep	25	4	3	7	22	....	....	....	....	....
	HC Pardubice	Cze-Rep	25	2	4	6	18	3	0	0	0	0

MATHIEU, Alexandre (mah-TYOO, al-ehx-AN-duhr) **PIT.**

Left wing. Shoots left. 6'2", 177 lbs. Born, Repentigny, Que., February 12, 1979.
(Pittsburgh's 4th choice, 97th overall, in 1997 Entry Draft).

			Regular Season					Playoffs				
Season	Club	Lea	GP	G	A	TP	PIM	GP	G	A	TP	PIM
1996-97	Halifax	QMJHL	70	12	22	34	16	18	2	5	7	2
1997-98	Halifax	QMJHL	68	35	41	76	52	5	1	1	2	4
1998-99	Halifax	QMJHL	69	21	27	48	90	5	0	1	1	4
99-2000	Wilkes-Barre	AHL	52	4	4	8	18	....	....	....	....	....

MATTEUCCI, Mike — MIN.

Defense. Shoots left. 6'2", 210 lbs. Born, Trail, B.C., December 27, 1971.

			Regular Season					Playoffs				
Season	Club	Lea	GP	G	A	TP	PIM	GP	G	A	TP	PIM
1992-93	Lake Superior	CCHA	19	1	3	4	16	....	....	....	....	....
1993-94	Lake Superior	CCHA	45	6	11	17	64	....	....	....	....	....
1994-95	Lake Superior	CCHA	38	3	11	14	52	....	....	....	....	....
1995-96	Lake Superior	CCHA	40	3	13	16	82	....	....	....	....	....
	Los Angeles	IHL	4	0	0	0	7	....	....	....	....	....
1996-97	Long Beach	IHL	81	4	4	8	254	18	0	1	1	42
1997-98	Long Beach	IHL	79	1	7	8	258	17	0	2	2	57
1998-99	Long Beach	IHL	79	3	9	12	253	8	0	1	1	12
99-2000	Long Beach	IHL	64	0	4	4	170	6	0	0	0	16

Signed as a free agent by **Edmonton**, September 10, 1998. Traded to **Boston** by **Edmonton** for Kay Whitmore, December 29, 1999. Signed as a free agent by **Minnesota**, July 20, 2000. • Played w/ RHI's San Jose Rhinos in 1996 (14-2-3-5-12)

MAXIMENKO, Andrei (max-EE-mehn-koh, AWN-dray) — DET.

Left wing. Shoots right. 5'11", 172 lbs. Born, Moscow, USSR, January 10, 1981.
(Detroit's 2nd choice, 149th overall, in 1999 Entry Draft).

			Regular Season					Playoffs				
Season	Club	Lea	GP	G	A	TP	PIM	GP	G	A	TP	PIM
1997-98	Krylja Sovetov	Russia-3	42	2	4	6	12	....	....	....	....	....
1998-99	Krylja Sovetov	Russia-Q	13	1	1	2	8	....	....	....	....	....
	Krylja Sovetov	Russia	15	0	1	1	16	....	....	....	....	....
99-2000	Krylja Sovetov	Russia-2	STATISTICS NOT AVAILABLE									

MAXWELL, Dennis (max-WEHL, DEHN-ihs)

Center. Shoots right. 6'2", 210 lbs. Born, Dauphin, Man., June 4, 1974.
(Tampa Bay's 8th choice, 170th overall, in 1992 Entry Draft).

			Regular Season					Playoffs				
Season	Club	Lea	GP	G	A	TP	PIM	GP	G	A	TP	PIM
1990-91	Hamilton Kilty B's	OJHL-B	42	8	29	37	161	....	....	....	....	....
1991-92	Niagara Falls	OHL	66	20	26	46	139	17	4	9	13	32
1992-93	Niagara Falls	OHL	12	5	9	14	21	....	....	....	....	....
	Sudbury Wolves	OHL	52	15	24	39	116	14	3	4	7	42
1993-94	Niagara Falls	OHL	17	2	14	16	41	....	....	....	....	....
	Newmarket	OHL	41	12	24	36	113	....	....	....	....	....
1994-95	Sarnia Sting	OHL	55	16	30	46	227	3	0	0	0	18
	Saginaw Wheels	ColHL	....	....	....	....	....	10	0	1	1	36
1995-96	Binghamton	AHL	8	1	0	1	7	....	....	....	....	....
	Charlotte	ECHL	51	25	19	44	291	14	5	5	10	78
1996-97	Tallahassee	ECHL	30	13	22	35	175	....	....	....	....	....
	Carolina	AHL	2	0	0	0	2	....	....	....	....	....
	St. John's Leafs	AHL	20	2	2	4	97	....	....	....	....	....
	San Antonio	IHL	14	1	4	5	32	4	1	0	1	41
1997-98	San Antonio	IHL	6	0	0	0	49	....	....	....	....	....
	Quebec Rafales	IHL	55	9	13	22	249	....	....	....	....	....
1998-99	St. John's Leafs	AHL	41	9	16	25	212	5	0	3	3	8
99-2000	St. John's Leafs	AHL	36	5	14	19	171	....	....	....	....	....
	Greenville Growl	ECHL	12	5	8	13	29	4	2	0	2	34

Signed as a free agent by **Toronto**, September 28, 1998.

McCAMBRIDGE, Keith (muh-KAYM-brihdj, KEETH) — BOS.

Defense. Shoots left. 6'2", 205 lbs. Born, Thompson, Man., February 1, 1974.
(Calgary's 10th choice, 201st overall, in 1994 Entry Draft).

			Regular Season					Playoffs				
Season	Club	Lea	GP	G	A	TP	PIM	GP	G	A	TP	PIM
1991-92	Swift Current	WHL	72	1	4	5	84	8	0	0	0	2
1992-93	Swift Current	WHL	70	0	6	6	87	17	0	1	1	27
1993-94	Swift Current	WHL	71	0	10	10	179	7	0	0	0	4
1994-95	Swift Current	WHL	48	5	7	12	120	....	....	....	....	....
	Kamloops Blazers	WHL	21	0	6	6	90	21	0	5	5	49
1995-96	Saint John Flames	AHL	48	1	3	4	89	16	0	0	0	6
1996-97	Saint John Flames	AHL	56	2	1	3	109	....	....	....	....	....
1997-98	Saint John Flames	AHL	56	4	4	8	118	....	....	....	....	....
	Las Vegas	IHL	10	0	1	1	16	4	0	0	0	9
1998-99	Las Vegas	IHL	18	1	2	3	56	....	....	....	....	....
	Long Beach	IHL	52	2	5	7	200	8	0	0	0	20
99-2000	Providence Bruins	AHL	47	0	2	2	135	....	....	....	....	....
	Manitoba Moose	IHL	3	0	1	1	4	....	....	....	....	....

Signed as free agent by **Boston**, August 20, 1999.

McCANN, Sean — ATL.

Defense. Shoots right. 6', 195 lbs. Born, North York, Ont., September 18, 1971.
(Florida's 1st choice, 1st overall, in 1994 Supplemental Draft).

			Regular Season					Playoffs				
Season	Club	Lea	GP	G	A	TP	PIM	GP	G	A	TP	PIM
1988-89	Thornhill T-Birds	OJHL-B	37	2	12	14	153	....	....	....	....	....
1989-90	Thornhill T-Birds	OJHL-B	42	12	19	31	111	....	....	....	....	....
1990-91	Harvard University	ECAC	28	2	9	11	88	....	....	....	....	....
1991-92	Harvard University	ECAC	27	4	10	14	51	....	....	....	....	....
1992-93	Harvard University	ECAC	31	4	5	9	38	....	....	....	....	....
1993-94	Harvard University	ECAC	33	22	17	39	82	....	....	....	....	....
1994-95	Cincinnati	IHL	76	10	12	22	58	10	0	2	2	8
1995-96	Carolina	AHL	80	14	33	47	61	....	....	....	....	....
1996-97	Grand Rapids	IHL	76	8	26	34	46	5	0	0	0	2
1997-98	Milwaukee	IHL	33	6	11	17	37	....	....	....	....	....
	Orlando	IHL	26	5	3	8	30	....	....	....	....	....
1998-99	Orlando	IHL	42	4	9	13	28	....	....	....	....	....
	Springfield	AHL	31	8	15	23	31	3	0	1	1	4
99-2000	Springfield	AHL	62	5	38	43	77	....	....	....	....	....
	Syracuse Crunch	AHL	11	0	9	9	12	4	0	2	2	0

ECAC First All-Star Team (1994) • NCAA East First All-American Team (1994) • NCAA Final Four All-Tournament Team (1994) • NCAA Final Four Tournament Most Valuable Player (1994)

Signed as a free agent by **Phoenix**, August, 1999. Loaned to **Syracuse** (AHL) by **Springfield** (AHL) for loan of Martin Gendron, March 15, 2000. Signed as a free agent by **Atlanta**, July 19, 2000.

McCORMICK, Morgan (muh-KOHR-mihk, MOHR-gahn) — FLA.

Right wing. Shoots right. 6'4", 210 lbs. Born, Guelph, Ont., February 21, 1981.
(Florida's 5th choice, 103rd overall, in 1999 Entry Draft).

			Regular Season					Playoffs				
Season	Club	Lea	GP	G	A	TP	PIM	GP	G	A	TP	PIM
1997-98	Georgetown	OJHL	46	8	15	23	93	....	....	....	....	....
1998-99	Kingston	OHL	34	6	5	11	43	5	0	0	0	13
99-2000	Kingston	OHL	8	1	0	1	13	....	....	....	....	....
	Guelph Storm	OHL	59	8	21	29	105	6	0	1	1	7

McDONALD, Andy (mihk-DAW-nuhld, AN-dee) — ANA.

Center. Shoots left. 5'10", 185 lbs. Born, Strathroy, Ont., August 25, 1977.

			Regular Season					Playoffs				
Season	Club	Lea	GP	G	A	TP	PIM	GP	G	A	TP	PIM
1995-96	Strathroy Blades	OJHL-B	52	31	56	87	103	....	....	....	....	....
1996-97	Colgate	ECAC	33	9	10	19	16	....	....	....	....	....
1997-98	Colgate	ECAC	35	13	19	32	26	....	....	....	....	....
1998-99	Colgate	ECAC	35	20	26	46	42	....	....	....	....	....
99-2000	Colgate	ECAC	34	25	*33	*58	49	....	....	....	....	....

ECAC Second All-Star Team (1999) • ECAC First All-Star Team (2000) • NCAA East First All-American Team (2000)

Signed as a free agent by **Anaheim**, April 3, 2000.

McDONALD, Brent (muhk-DAW-nuhld, BREHNT) — CAR.

Center. Shoots right. 5'11", 180 lbs. Born, Olds, Alta., October 7, 1979.
(Carolina's 10th choice, 239th overall, in 1998 Entry Draft).

			Regular Season					Playoffs				
Season	Club	Lea	GP	G	A	TP	PIM	GP	G	A	TP	PIM
1995-96	Red Deer Rebels	WHL	68	1	7	8	55	6	0	1	1	2
1996-97	Red Deer Rebels	WHL	69	11	17	28	94	16	4	3	7	38
1997-98	Red Deer Rebels	WHL	69	18	27	45	93	5	0	2	2	4
1998-99	Red Deer Rebels	WHL	38	17	18	35	64	....	....	....	....	....
	Prince George	WHL	34	13	13	26	40	7	1	1	2	18
99-2000	Prince George	WHL	7	1	3	4	6	....	....	....	....	....
	Spokane Chiefs	WHL	61	28	30	58	77	15	5	8	13	42

McDONELL, Kent (MUHK-dawn-EHL, KEHNT) — CBJ

Right wing. Shoots right. 6', 200 lbs. Born, Williamstown, Ont., March 1, 1979.
(Detroit's 3rd choice, 181st overall, in 1999 Entry Draft).

			Regular Season					Playoffs				
Season	Club	Lea	GP	G	A	TP	PIM	GP	G	A	TP	PIM
1995-96	Cornwall	OJHL	33	21	14	35	64	....	....	....	....	....
1996-97	Guelph Storm	OHL	56	7	5	12	57	16	0	2	2	4
1997-98	Guelph Storm	OHL	64	28	23	51	76	12	7	4	11	18
1998-99	Guelph Storm	OHL	60	31	38	69	110	11	4	3	7	36
99-2000	Guelph Storm	OHL	56	35	35	70	100	6	1	4	5	6

• Re-entered NHL draft. Originally Carolina's 9th choice, 225th overall, in 1997 Entry Draft.

Traded to **Columbus** by **Detroit** for future considerations, August 14, 2000.

McGRATTAN, Brian (muhk-GRA-tuhn, BRIGH-an) — L.A.

Right wing. Shoots right. 6'3", 210 lbs. Born, Hamilton, Ont., September 2, 1981.
(Los Angeles' 5th choice, 104th overall, in 1999 Entry Draft).

			Regular Season					Playoffs				
Season	Club	Lea	GP	G	A	TP	PIM	GP	G	A	TP	PIM
1997-98	Guelph Royals	OJHL-B	15	4	3	7	94	....	....	....	....	....
	Guelph Storm	OHL	25	3	2	5	11	....	....	....	....	....
1998-99	Guelph Storm	OHL	6	1	3	4	15	....	....	....	....	....
	Sudbury Wolves	OHL	53	7	10	17	153	4	0	0	0	8
99-2000	Sudbury Wolves	OHL	25	2	8	10	79	....	....	....	....	....
	Mississauga	OHL	42	9	13	22	166	....	....	....	....	....

McKERCHER, Jeff (muh-KUHR-chur, JEHF) — DAL.

Defense. Shoots right. 6'2", 218 lbs. Born, Cornwall, Ont., January 14, 1979.
(Dallas' 7th choice, 189th overall, in 1997 Entry Draft).

			Regular Season					Playoffs				
Season	Club	Lea	GP	G	A	TP	PIM	GP	G	A	TP	PIM
1995-96	Cornwall Royals	OJHL	53	1	16	17	33	....	....	....	....	....
1996-97	Barrie Colts	OHL	60	1	4	5	32	9	0	1	1	13
1997-98	Barrie Colts	OHL	51	0	2	2	21	6	0	0	0	2
1998-99	Sault Ste. Marie	OHL	8	0	0	0	0	....	....	....	....	....
	Peterborough	OHL	57	1	7	8	22	5	0	0	0	4
99-2000	Fort Wayne	UHL	72	2	7	9	55	11	0	4	4	4

McLAREN, Steve (muh-KLAIR-uhn, STEEV) — PHI.

Left wing. Shoots left. 6', 200 lbs. Born, Owen Sound, Ont., February 3, 1975.
(Chicago's 3rd choice, 85th overall, in 1994 Entry Draft).

			Regular Season					Playoffs				
Season	Club	Lea	GP	G	A	TP	PIM	GP	G	A	TP	PIM
1993-94	North Bay	OHL	55	2	15	17	130	18	0	3	3	50
1994-95	North Bay	OHL	27	3	10	13	119	6	2	1	3	23
1995-96	Indianapolis Ice	IHL	54	1	2	3	170	3	0	0	0	2
1996-97	Indianapolis Ice	IHL	63	2	5	7	309	4	0	0	0	10
1997-98	Indianapolis Ice	IHL	61	3	5	8	208	5	0	0	0	24
1998-99	Philadelphia	AHL	52	4	3	7	216	7	0	0	0	2
99-2000	Philadelphia	AHL	64	1	2	3	247	....	....	....	....	....

Signed as a free agent by **Philadelphia**, August 24, 1998.

McLEAN, Brett (muh-CLAYN, BREHT) — MIN.

Center. Shoots left. 5'11", 194 lbs. Born, Comox, B.C., August 14, 1978.
(Dallas' 9th choice, 242nd overall, in 1997 Entry Draft).

			Regular Season					Playoffs				
Season	Club	Lea	GP	G	A	TP	PIM	GP	G	A	TP	PIM
1993-94	Notre Dame	SAHA	71	109	124	233	70	....	....	....	....	....
1994-95	Tacoma Rockets	WHL	67	11	23	34	33	4	0	1	1	0
1995-96	Kelowna Rockets	WHL	71	37	42	79	60	6	2	2	4	6
1996-97	Kelowna Rockets	WHL	72	44	60	104	98	6	4	2	6	12
1997-98	Kelowna Rockets	WHL	54	42	45	87	91	7	4	5	9	17
1998-99	Kelowna Rockets	WHL	44	32	38	70	46	....	....	....	....	....
	Brandon	WHL	21	15	16	31	20	5	1	6	7	8
99-2000	Johnstown Chiefs	ECHL	8	4	7	11	6	....	....	....	....	....
	Saint John Flames	AHL	72	15	23	38	115	3	0	1	1	2

Signed as a free agent by **Calgary**, September, 1999. Signed as a free agent by **Minnesota**, July 13, 2000.

McMAHON, Mark (muhk-MAN, MAHRK) CAR.

Defense. Shoots left. 6'1", 185 lbs. Born, Geralton, Ont., February 10, 1978.
(Hartford's 5th choice, 116th overall, in 1996 Entry Draft).

			Regular Season					Playoffs				
Season	Club	Lea	GP	G	A	TP	PIM	GP	G	A	TP	PIM
1994-95	Elmira Kings	OJHL-B	41	3	10	13	91	....	....	....	....	....
1995-96	Kitchener	OHL	55	1	8	9	105	5	0	1	1	17
1996-97	Kitchener	OHL	63	4	18	22	155	13	0	6	6	31
1997-98	Kitchener	OHL	61	12	38	50	175	6	1	5	6	27
	New Haven	AHL	4	0	1	1	6	2	0	0	0	16
1998-99	Plymouth	OHL	34	2	12	14	91	11	0	1	1	25
	Florida Everblades	ECHL	13	1	4	5	59	....	....	....	....	....
99-2000	Arkansas Blades	ECHL	35	4	10	14	149	....	....	....	....	....
	Jacksonville	ECHL	5	0	0	0	2	....	....	....	....	....
	Cincinnati	IHL	1	0	0	0	4	....	....	....	....	....
	Dayton Bombers	ECHL	21	2	3	5	71	3	0	0	0	8

Rights transferred to **Carolina** after **Hartford** franchise relocated, June 25, 1997.

McMEEKIN, Brian (muhk-MEE-khin) ST.L.

Defense. Shoots right. 6'4", 205 lbs. Born, Trail, B.C., June 20, 1979.
(St. Louis' 9th choice, 260th overall, in 1999 Entry Draft).

			Regular Season					Playoffs				
Season	Club	Lea	GP	G	A	TP	PIM	GP	G	A	TP	PIM
1997-98	Trail Smokies	BCJHL	49	4	7	11	66	10	0	1	1	10
1998-99	Cornell Big Red	ECAC	26	0	1	1	12	....	....	....	....	....
99-2000	Cornell Big Red	ECAC	11	0	1	1	8	....	....	....	....	....

McPHERSON, Andrew (muhk-FUHR-suhn) PIT.

Left wing. Shoots left. 6'2", 175 lbs. Born, Ottawa, Ont., April 28, 1979.
(Pittsburgh's 11th choice, 261st overall, in 1999 Entry Draft).

			Regular Season					Playoffs				
Season	Club	Lea	GP	G	A	TP	PIM	GP	G	A	TP	PIM
1997-98	Dauphin Kings	MJHL	61	24	37	61	132	....	....	....	....	....
1998-99	RPI Engineers	ECAC	29	5	4	9	12	....	....	....	....	....
99-2000	RPI Engineers	ECAC	37	10	6	16	22	....	....	....	....	....

McRAE, Matt (muh-KRAY) ATL.

Center. Shoots right. 6', 180 lbs. Born, Toronto, Ont., April 29, 1981.
(Atlanta's 6th choice, 147th overall, in 2000 Entry Draft).

			Regular Season					Playoffs				
Season	Club	Lea	GP	G	A	TP	PIM	GP	G	A	TP	PIM
1998-99	Brampton Capitals	OJHL	50	34	40	74	29	....	....	....	....	....
99-2000	Cornell Big Red	ECAC	31	8	16	24	22	....	....	....	....	....

MELENOVSKY, Marek (meh-leh-NAHF-skee, MAIR-ehk) TOR.

Center. Shoots left. 5'10", 180 lbs. Born, Humpolec, Czech., March 30, 1977.
(Toronto's 5th choice, 171st overall, in 1995 Entry Draft).

			Regular Season					Playoffs				
Season	Club	Lea	GP	G	A	TP	PIM	GP	G	A	TP	PIM
1994-95	Dukla Jihlava-Jr.	Cze-Rep	28	23	11	34	....	....	....	....	....	....
	Dukla Jihlava	Cze-Rep	3	0	0	0	0	5	1	3	4	0
1995-96	Dukla Jihlava	Cze-Rep	33	3	3	6	....	5	1	2	3	....
1996-97	Dukla Jihlava	Cze-Rep	46	5	13	18	22	....	....	....	....	....
	St. John's Leafs	AHL	2	1	2	3	0	2	0	0	0	0
1997-98	Dukla Jihlava	Cze-Rep	18	10	14	24	30	....	....	....	....	....
1998-99	Dukla Jihlava	Cze-Rep	52	7	10	17	26	....	....	....	....	....
	Dukla Jihlava	EuroHL	6	0	2	2	2	....	....	....	....	....
99-2000	HC Havirov	Cze-Rep	49	12	12	24	32	....	....	....	....	....

MELICHAR, Josef (mehl-ee-KHAHR, YOH-sehf) PIT.

Defense. Shoots left. 6'2", 214 lbs. Born, Ceske Budejovice, Czech., January 20, 1979.
(Pittsburgh's 3rd choice, 71st overall, in 1997 Entry Draft).

			Regular Season					Playoffs				
Season	Club	Lea	GP	G	A	TP	PIM	GP	G	A	TP	PIM
1995-96	HC Budejovice-Jr.	Cze-Rep	38	3	4	7	....	....	....	....	....	....
1996-97	HC Budejovice-Jr.	Cze-Rep	41	2	3	5	10	....	....	....	....	....
1997-98	Tri-City Americans	WHL	67	9	24	33	154	....	....	....	....	....
1998-99	Tri-City Americans	WHL	65	8	28	36	125	11	1	0	1	15
99-2000	Wilkes-Barre	AHL	80	3	9	12	126	....	....	....	....	....

MELIN, Bjorn (MEH-lihn, b-YUHRN) NYI

Right wing. Shoots right. 6'1", 178 lbs. Born, Jonkoping, Sweden, July 4, 1981.
(NY Islanders' 11th choice, 163rd overall, in 1999 Entry Draft).

			Regular Season					Playoffs				
Season	Club	Lea	GP	G	A	TP	PIM	GP	G	A	TP	PIM
1997-98	HV Jonkoping	Swede-Jr.	8	0	3	3	2	....	....	....	....	....
1998-99	HV Jonkoping	Swede-Jr.	30	12	7	19	50	....	....	....	....	....
99-2000	HV Jonkoping	Sweden	23	3	0	3	2	5	0	0	0	0

MELOCHE, Eric (muh-LAWSH, AIR-ihk) PIT.

Right wing. Shoots right. 5'11", 195 lbs. Born, Montreal, Que., May 1, 1976.
(Pittsburgh's 7th choice, 186th overall, in 1996 Entry Draft).

			Regular Season					Playoffs				
Season	Club	Lea	GP	G	A	TP	PIM	GP	G	A	TP	PIM
1994-95	Cornwall Colts	OJHL	40	7	15	22	51	....	....	....	....	....
1995-96	Cornwall Colts	OJHL	64	68	53	121	162	....	....	....	....	....
1996-97	Ohio State	CCHA	39	12	11	23	78	....	....	....	....	....
1997-98	Ohio State	CCHA	42	26	22	48	86	....	....	....	....	....
1998-99	Ohio State	CCHA	35	11	16	27	87	....	....	....	....	....
99-2000	Ohio State	CCHA	36	20	11	31	*138	....	....	....	....	....

MERRICK, Andrew (MEHR-rihk, AN-drew) CAR.

Center. Shoots left. 5'11", 202 lbs. Born, Syosset, NY, March 23, 1978.
(Carolina's 6th choice, 169th overall, in 1997 Entry Draft).

			Regular Season					Playoffs				
Season	Club	Lea	GP	G	A	TP	PIM	GP	G	A	TP	PIM
1994-95	Sarnia	OJHL-B	47	25	37	62	161	....	....	....	....	....
1995-96	Sarnia	OJHL-B	49	29	27	56	116	....	....	....	....	....
1996-97	U. of Michigan	CCHA	36	3	10	13	42	....	....	....	....	....
1997-98	U. of Michigan	CCHA	33	4	3	7	74	....	....	....	....	....
1998-99	U. of Michigan	CCHA	32	1	3	4	61	....	....	....	....	....
99-2000	U. of Michigan	CCHA	16	2	3	5	36	....	....	....	....	....

METCALF, Peter (MEHT-kaf) TOR.

Defense. Shoots left. 6', 190 lbs. Born, Colorado Springs, CO, February 25, 1979.
(Toronto's 9th choice, 267th overall, in 1999 Entry Draft).

			Regular Season					Playoffs				
Season	Club	Lea	GP	G	A	TP	PIM	GP	G	A	TP	PIM
1997-98	Cushing Academy	Hi-School	25	18	48	66	....	....	....	....	....	....
1998-99	U. of Maine	H-East	33	6	17	23	34	....	....	....	....	....
99-2000	U. of Maine	H-East	40	4	17	21	56	....	....	....	....	....

METHOT, Francois (meh-THOH, FRAN-swaw) BUF.

Center. Shoots right. 6', 184 lbs. Born, Montreal, Que., April 26, 1978.
(Buffalo's 4th choice, 54th overall, in 1996 Entry Draft).

			Regular Season					Playoffs				
Season	Club	Lea	GP	G	A	TP	PIM	GP	G	A	TP	PIM
1994-95	St-Hyacinthe	QMJHL	60	14	38	52	22	5	0	1	1	0
1995-96	St-Hyacinthe	QMJHL	68	32	62	94	22	12	6	6	12	4
1996-97	Rouyn-Noranda	QMJHL	47	21	30	51	22	....	....	....	....	....
	Shawinigan	QMJHL	18	8	17	25	2	7	2	6	8	2
1997-98	Shawinigan	QMJHL	36	23	42	65	10	6	1	3	4	5
1998-99	Rochester	AHL	58	5	8	13	8	9	0	1	1	0
99-2000	Rochester	AHL	80	14	18	32	20	21	2	4	6	16

MEYER, Doug (MIGH-yuhr, DUHG) PIT.

Left wing. Shoots left. 6'1", 197 lbs. Born, Bloomington, MN, February 21, 1980.
(Pittsburgh's 8th choice, 176th overall, in 1999 Entry Draft).

			Regular Season					Playoffs				
Season	Club	Lea	GP	G	A	TP	PIM	GP	G	A	TP	PIM
1998-99	U. of Minnesota	WCHA	36	4	4	8	18	....	....	....	....	....
99-2000	U. of Minnesota	WCHA	26	1	3	4	18	....	....	....	....	....

MEZEI, Branislav (MEH-zay, BRAN-ih-slav) NYI

Defense. Shoots left. 6'4", 221 lbs. Born, Nitra, Czech., October 8, 1980.
(NY Islanders' 3rd choice, 10th overall, in 1999 Entry Draft).

			Regular Season					Playoffs				
Season	Club	Lea	GP	G	A	TP	PIM	GP	G	A	TP	PIM
1996-97	MHC Nitra	Slovak-Jr.	40	8	17	25	42	....	....	....	....	....
1997-98	Belleville Bulls	OHL	53	3	5	8	58	8	0	2	2	8
1998-99	Belleville Bulls	OHL	60	5	18	23	90	18	0	4	4	29
99-2000	Belleville Bulls	OHL	58	7	21	28	99	6	0	3	3	10

OHL First All-Star Team (2000)

MIETTINEN, Tommi (mih-EHT-tih-nehn, TAWM-mee) ANA.

Center. Shoots left. 5'10", 165 lbs. Born, Kuopio, Finland, December 3, 1975.
(Anaheim's 9th choice, 236th overall, in 1994 Entry Draft).

			Regular Season					Playoffs				
Season	Club	Lea	GP	G	A	TP	PIM	GP	G	A	TP	PIM
1991-92	KalPa Kuopio	Finn-Jr.	37	9	16	25	12	....	....	....	....	....
1992-93	KalPa Kuopio-B	Finn-Jr.	7	3	8	11	2	....	....	....	....	....
	KalPa Kuopio	Finn-Jr.	26	16	27	43	14	....	....	....	....	....
	KalPa Kuopio	Finland	14	0	0	0	0	....	....	....	....	....
1993-94	KalPa Kuopio	Finn-Jr.	9	5	9	14	10	....	....	....	....	....
	KalPa Kuopio	Finland	47	5	7	12	14	....	....	....	....	....
1994-95	KalPa Kuopio	Finn-Jr.	2	1	3	4	2	....	....	....	....	....
	KalPa Kuopio	Finland	48	13	16	29	26	3	1	1	2	2
1995-96	TPS Turku	Finland	36	3	10	13	10	10	2	1	3	29
1996-97	TPS Turku	Finland	41	6	15	21	6	12	3	4	7	8
1997-98	TPS Turku	Finland	42	8	6	14	26	4	0	0	0	0
	TPS Turku	EuroHL	3	0	0	0	2	....	....	....	....	....
1998-99	TPS Turku	Finland	54	10	17	27	26	10	4	4	8	0
99-2000	Ilves-Tampere	Finland	54	13	20	33	24	....	....	....	....	....

MIKHNOV, Alexei (MIHKH-nahf) EDM.

Wing. Shoots left. 6'5", 198 lbs. Born, Kiev, USSR, August 31, 1982.
(Edmonton's 1st choice, 17th overall, in 2000 Entry Draft).

			Regular Season					Playoffs				
Season	Club	Lea	GP	G	A	TP	PIM	GP	G	A	TP	PIM
1997-98	Torpedo Yaroslavl	Russia-2	6	0	0	0	0	....	....	....	....	....
1998-99	Torpedo Yaroslavl	Russia-3	14	2	2	4	4	....	....	....	....	....
99-2000	Torpedo Yaroslavl	Russia-3	53	24	17	41	10	....	....	....	....	....

MIKKOLA, Ilkka (mih-KOHLA, IHL-ka) MTL.

Defense. Shoots left. 6', 189 lbs. Born, Oulu, Finland, January 18, 1979.
(Montreal's 3rd choice, 65th overall, in 1997 Entry Draft).

			Regular Season					Playoffs				
Season	Club	Lea	GP	G	A	TP	PIM	GP	G	A	TP	PIM
1993-94	Karpat Oulu-C	Finn-Jr.	22	3	6	9	4	4	0	1	1	4
1994-95	Karpat Oulu-C	Finn-Jr.	31	17	27	44	24	3	0	0	0	8
1995-96	Karpat Oulu-B	Finn-Jr.	4	2	0	2	0	....	....	....	....	....
	Karpat Oulu	Finn-Jr.	21	2	3	5	20	....	....	....	....	....
	Karpat Oulu	Finland-2	10	0	4	4	29	2	0	0	0	2
1996-97	Karpat Oulu	Finn-Jr.	40	7	12	19	32	6	0	0	0	4
1997-98	Karpat Oulu	Finland-2	27	7	2	9	34	....	....	....	....	....
	Karpat Oulu	Finn-Jr.	8	4	2	6	10	....	....	....	....	....
1998-99	TPS Turku	Finland	42	1	3	4	41	10	1	0	1	6
99-2000	TPS Turku	Finland	54	2	6	8	48	11	0	0	0	6

MILLER, Nate L.A.

Right wing. Shoots left. 6'3", 192 lbs. Born, Anoka, MN, June 3, 1976.

			Regular Season					Playoffs				
Season	Club	Lea	GP	G	A	TP	PIM	GP	G	A	TP	PIM
1995-96	Twin Cities	USHL	53	25	34	59	91	....	....	....	....	....
1996-97	U. of Minnesota	WCHA	40	5	9	14	36	....	....	....	....	....
1997-98	U. of Minnesota	WCHA	39	8	6	14	42	....	....	....	....	....
1998-99	U. of Minnesota	WCHA	43	6	8	14	70	....	....	....	....	....
99-2000	U. of Minnesota	WCHA	41	16	19	35	38	....	....	....	....	....

Signed as a free agent by **LA Kings**, August 11, 2000.

MILLEY, Norman (MIHL-lee, NOHR-man) BUF.

Right wing. Shoots right. 6', 200 lbs. Born, Toronto, Ont., February 14, 1980.
(Buffalo's 3rd choice, 47th overall, in 1998 Entry Draft).

			Regular Season					Playoffs				
Season	Club	Lea	GP	G	A	TP	PIM	GP	G	A	TP	PIM
1995-96	Toronto Wings	MTHL	42	42	36	78	....	....	....	....	....	....
	St. Michael's	OJHL	5	2	1	3	0	....	....	....	....	....
1996-97	Sudbury Wolves	OHL	61	30	32	62	15	....	....	....	....	....
1997-98	Sudbury Wolves	OHL	62	33	41	74	48	10	0	1	1	4
1998-99	Sudbury Wolves	OHL	68	52	68	120	47	4	2	3	5	4
99-2000	Sudbury Wolves	OHL	68	*52	60	112	47	12	8	11	19	6

OHL Second All-Star Team (1999) • OHL First All-Star Team (2000) • Canadian Major Junior First All-Star Team (2000)

MISCHLER, Graig (MIH-schluhr, GREHG) VAN.

Center. Shoots left. 6'3", 174 lbs. Born, Holbrook, NY, September 15, 1978.
(Vancouver's 10th choice, 204th overall, in 1998 Entry Draft).

			Regular Season					Playoffs				
Season	Club	Lea	GP	G	A	TP	PIM	GP	G	A	TP	PIM
1997-98	Northeastern	H-East	39	7	13	20	22	....	....	....	....	....
1998-99	Northeastern	H-East	33	8	15	23	36	....	....	....	....	....
99-2000	Northeastern	H-East	34	9	14	23	22	....	....	....	....	....

MISKOVICH, Aaron (MIHS-kuh-vihch, AIR-ohn) COL.

Center. Shoots left. 5'10", 185 lbs. Born, Grand Rapids, MN, April 28, 1978.
(Colorado's 6th choice, 133rd overall, in 1997 Entry Draft).

			Regular Season					Playoffs				
Season	Club	Lea	GP	G	A	TP	PIM	GP	G	A	TP	PIM
1996-97	Green Bay	USHL	14	4	9	13	14	....	....	....	....	....
1997-98	U. of Minnesota	WCHA	28	4	8	12	14	....	....	....	....	....
1998-99	U. of Minnesota	WCHA	42	11	11	22	36	....	....	....	....	....
99-2000	U. of Minnesota	WCHA	41	16	16	32	24	....	....	....	....	....

MITCHELL, Kevin (MIHT-chehl, KEH-vihn) CGY.

Defense. Shoots left. 5'11", 190 lbs. Born, Bronx, NY, June 5, 1980.
(Calgary's 9th choice, 234th overall, in 1998 Entry Draft).

			Regular Season					Playoffs				
Season	Club	Lea	GP	G	A	TP	PIM	GP	G	A	TP	PIM
1996-97	Cambridge Hawks	OJHL-B	47	30	28	58	140	....	....	....	....	....
1997-98	Guelph Storm	OHL	65	10	46	56	73	12	1	7	8	14
1998-99	Guelph Storm	OHL	68	26	52	78	107	11	3	10	13	29
99-2000	Guelph Storm	OHL	68	19	58	77	94	6	1	2	3	10

OHL Second All-Star Team (1999, 2000)

MIZZI, Preston (MIHZ-zee, PREH-stohn) PHX.

Center. Shoots left. 5'11", 191 lbs. Born, Sault Ste. Marie, Ont., December 22, 1980.
(Phoenix's 6th choice, 123rd overall, in 1999 Entry Draft).

			Regular Season					Playoffs				
Season	Club	Lea	GP	G	A	TP	PIM	GP	G	A	TP	PIM
1996-97	Newmarket	OJHL	42	26	26	52	78	....	....	....	....	....
1997-98	Peterborough	OHL	66	17	32	49	37	4	0	3	3	12
1998-99	Peterborough	OHL	67	29	29	58	74	5	2	3	5	15
99-2000	Peterborough	OHL	67	27	35	62	80	5	1	1	2	6

MOEN, Travis (MOH-ehn) CGY.

Left wing. Shoots left. 6'2", 198 lbs. Born, Swift Current, Sask., April 6, 1982.
(Calgary's 6th choice, 155th overall, in 2000 Entry Draft).

			Regular Season					Playoffs				
Season	Club	Lea	GP	G	A	TP	PIM	GP	G	A	TP	PIM
1998-99	Kelowna Rockets	WHL	4	0	0	0	0	....	....	....	....	....
99-2000	Kelowna Rockets	WHL	66	9	6	15	96	5	1	1	2	2

MOKHOV, Stepan (MOH-khohv, STEH-pan) CHI.

Defense. Shoots left. 6'1", 183 lbs. Born, Ust-Kamenogorsk, USSR, January 22, 1981.
(Chicago's 3rd choice, 63rd overall, in 1999 Entry Draft).

			Regular Season					Playoffs				
Season	Club	Lea	GP	G	A	TP	PIM	GP	G	A	TP	PIM
1997-98	Avangard Omsk	Russia-3	18	0	1	1	8	....	....	....	....	....
1998-99	HC Cherepovets	Russia-3	25	2	0	2	34	....	....	....	....	....
	HC Cherepovets	Russia-4	3	0	0	0	6	....	....	....	....	....
	HC Cherepovets	Russia	1	0	0	0	0	....	....	....	....	....
99-2000	HC Novokuznetsk	Russia	18	0	1	1	6	14	1	0	1	4

MOORE, Dominic (MOOR) NYR

Center. Shoots left. 6', 180 lbs. Born, Thornhill, Ont., August 3, 1980.
(NY Rangers' 2nd choice, 95th overall, in 2000 Entry Draft).

			Regular Season					Playoffs				
Season	Club	Lea	GP	G	A	TP	PIM	GP	G	A	TP	PIM
1998-99	Aurora Tigers	OJHL	51	34	53	87	70	....	....	....	....	....
99-2000	Harvard University	ECAC	30	12	24	28	16	....	....	....	....	....

ECAC All-Rookie Team (2000)

MOORE, Mark (MOOR, MAHRK) PIT.

Defense. Shoots right. 6'3", 185 lbs. Born, Windsor, Ont., February 18, 1977.
(Pittsburgh's 7th choice, 179th overall, in 1997 Entry Draft).

			Regular Season					Playoffs				
Season	Club	Lea	GP	G	A	TP	PIM	GP	G	A	TP	PIM
1995-96	Thornhill Rattlers	OJHL	50	12	18	30	51	....	....	....	....	....
1996-97	Harvard University	ECAC	22	5	2	7	16	....	....	....	....	....
1997-98	Harvard University	ECAC	32	1	3	4	90	....	....	....	....	....
1998-99	Harvard University	ECAC	32	1	2	3	82	....	....	....	....	....
99-2000	Harvard University	ECAC	28	0	2	2	48	....	....	....	....	....

MOORE, Steve COL.

Center. Shoots right. 6'2", 190 lbs. Born, Windsor, Ont., September 22, 1978.
(Colorado's 7th choice, 53rd overall, in 1998 Entry Draft).

			Regular Season					Playoffs				
Season	Club	Lea	GP	G	A	TP	PIM	GP	G	A	TP	PIM
1995-96	Thornhill Rattlers	OJHL	50	25	27	52	57	....	....	....	....	....
1996-97	Thornhill Rattlers	OJHL	50	34	52	86	52	....	....	....	....	....
1997-98	Harvard University	ECAC	33	10	23	33	46	....	....	....	....	....
1998-99	Harvard University	ECAC	30	18	13	31	34	....	....	....	....	....
99-2000	Harvard University	ECAC	27	10	16	26	53	....	....	....	....	....

MORAN, Brad (moh-RAN, BRAD) CBJ

Center. Shoots left. 5'11", 180 lbs. Born, Abbotsford, B.C., March 20, 1979.
(Buffalo's 8th choice, 191st overall, in 1998 Entry Draft).

			Regular Season					Playoffs				
Season	Club	Lea	GP	G	A	TP	PIM	GP	G	A	TP	PIM
1994-95	Abbotsford	BCAHA	56	66	93	159	40	....	....	....	....	....
1995-96	Calgary Hitmen	WHL	70	13	31	44	28	....	....	....	....	....
1996-97	Calgary Hitmen	WHL	72	30	36	66	61	....	....	....	....	....
1997-98	Calgary Hitmen	WHL	72	53	49	102	64	18	10	8	18	20
1998-99	Calgary Hitmen	WHL	71	60	58	118	96	21	17	*25	42	26
99-2000	Calgary Hitmen	WHL	72	48	*72	*120	84	13	7	15	22	18

WHL East First All-Star Team (1999, 2000)

Signed as a free agent by **Columbus**, June 5, 2000.

MORIN, Olivier (moh-REH, AWL-ih-vuhr) MTL.

Right wing. Shoots right. 6', 184 lbs. Born, Montreal, Que., April 2, 1978.

			Regular Season					Playoffs				
Season	Club	Lea	GP	G	A	TP	PIM	GP	G	A	TP	PIM
1995-96	Chicoutimi	QMJHL	68	17	32	49	102	17	6	5	11	51
1996-97	Chicoutimi	QMJHL	70	22	44	66	152	21	5	8	13	24
1997-98	Val-d'Or Foreurs	QMJHL	56	20	31	51	73	4	4	3	7	4
1998-99	New Orleans	ECHL	54	9	8	17	61	9	0	0	0	2
99-2000	Tallahassee	ECHL	53	29	26	55	113	....	....	....	....	....
	Quebec Citadelles	AHL	10	1	0	1	5	....	....	....	....	....

Signed as a free agent by **Montreal**, October 3, 1996.

MORISSET, David (moh-rih-SEHT) ST.L.

Right wing. Shoots right. 6'2", 195 lbs. Born, Langley, B.C., April 6, 1981.
(St. Louis' 2nd choice, 65th overall, in 2000 Entry Draft).

			Regular Season					Playoffs				
Season	Club	Lea	GP	G	A	TP	PIM	GP	G	A	TP	PIM
1997-98	Seattle T-Birds	WHL	58	6	2	8	104	5	1	0	1	6
1998-99	Seattle T-Birds	WHL	17	4	0	4	31	11	1	1	2	22
99-2000	Seattle T-Birds	WHL	60	23	34	57	69	7	3	4	7	12

MOROZOV, Valentin (moh-ROH-zohv, VA-lehn-TIHN)

Center. Shoots left. 5'11", 196 lbs. Born, Moscow, USSR, June 1, 1975.
(Pittsburgh's 8th choice, 154th overall, in 1994 Entry Draft).

			Regular Season					Playoffs				
Season	Club	Lea	GP	G	A	TP	PIM	GP	G	A	TP	PIM
1992-93	CSKA Moscow	CIS	17	0	0	0	6	....	....	....	....	....
1993-94	CSKA Moscow	CIS	18	4	1	5	8	3	0	1	1	0
1994-95	CSKA Moscow	CIS	47	9	4	13	10	2	2	0	2	0
1995-96	CSKA Moscow	CIS	51	30	11	41	28	3	1	0	1	2
1996-97	CSKA Moscow	Russia	22	8	5	13	8	....	....	....	....	....
	CSKA Moscow	EuroHL	4	2	1	3	0	....	....	....	....	....
1997-98	Krylja Sovetov	Russia	34	5	15	20	8	....	....	....	....	....
1998-99	Syracuse Crunch	AHL	63	17	23	40	10	....	....	....	....	....
99-2000	Wilkes-Barre	AHL	59	14	25	39	4	....	....	....	....	....

MORRISON, Justin (MOHR-rihs-OHN, JUHS-tihn) VAN.

Right wing. Shoots right. 6'3", 205 lbs. Born, Los Angeles, CA, September 10, 1979.
(Vancouver's 4th choice, 81st overall, in 1998 Entry Draft).

			Regular Season					Playoffs				
Season	Club	Lea	GP	G	A	TP	PIM	GP	G	A	TP	PIM
1996-97	Omaha Lancers	USHL	62	12	24	36	44	10	2	4	6	8
1997-98	Colorado College	WCHA	42	4	9	13	8	....	....	....	....	....
1998-99	Colorado College	WCHA	38	23	15	38	33	....	....	....	....	....
99-2000	Colorado College	WCHA	38	7	19	26	28	....	....	....	....	....

MOSOVSKY, Karel (moh-SAWV-skee, KA-rehl) BUF.

Left wing. Shoots right. 6'3", 201 lbs. Born, Piesk, Czech., August 22, 1981.
(Buffalo's 6th choice, 117th overall, in 1999 Entry Draft).

			Regular Season					Playoffs				
Season	Club	Lea	GP	G	A	TP	PIM	GP	G	A	TP	PIM
1997-98	HC Budejovice-Jr.	Cze-Rep	36	15	17	32	52	....	....	....	....	....
1998-99	Regina Pats	WHL	68	26	25	51	58	....	....	....	....	....
99-2000	Regina Pats	WHL	56	24	34	58	80	7	3	1	4	12

MOTTAU, Mike (MAW-tuh, MIGHK) NYR

Defense. Shoots left. 6', 192 lbs. Born, Quincy, MA, March 19, 1978.
(NY Rangers' 10th choice, 182nd overall, in 1997 Entry Draft).

			Regular Season					Playoffs				
Season	Club	Lea	GP	G	A	TP	PIM	GP	G	A	TP	PIM
1994-95	Thayer Academy	Hi-School	29	7	19	26	....	....	....	....	....	....
1995-96	Thayer Academy	Hi-School	31	6	20	26	....	....	....	....	....	....
1996-97	Boston College	H-East	38	5	18	23	77	....	....	....	....	....
1997-98	Boston College	H-East	40	13	36	49	50	....	....	....	....	....
1998-99	Boston College	H-East	43	3	39	42	44	....	....	....	....	....
99-2000	Boston College	H-East	42	6	37	43	61	....	....	....	....	....

Boston Independent School League MVP (1996) • Hockey East First All-Star Team (1998, 2000) • NCAA East Second All-American Team (1998) • NCAA Championship All-Tournament Team (1998, 2000) • Hockey East Second All-Star Team (1999) • NCAA East First All-American Team (1999, 2000) • Won Hobey Baker Memorial Award (Top U.S. Collegiate Player) (2000)

MRAZEK, Frantisek (muh-RA-zehk, FRAN-tih-SEHK) TOR.

Left wing. Shoots left. 6'4", 211 lbs. Born, Ceske-Budejovice, Czech., May 16, 1979.
(Toronto's 3rd choice, 111th overall, in 1997 Entry Draft).

			Regular Season					Playoffs				
Season	Club	Lea	GP	G	A	TP	PIM	GP	G	A	TP	PIM
1995-96	HC Budejovice-Jr.	Cze-Rep	19	8	3	11	....	....	....	....	....	....
1996-97	HC Budejovice-Jr.	Cze-Rep	40	18	15	33	....	....	....	....	....	....
1997-98	Red Deer Rebels	WHL	65	30	24	54	71	5	1	0	1	2
1998-99	Red Deer Rebels	WHL	60	34	42	76	79	9	6	4	10	16
99-2000	St. John's Leafs	AHL	1	0	0	0	0	....	....	....	....	....

• Missed majority of 1999-2000 season recovering from knee injury suffered in training camp, October 1, 1999.

MULICK, Robert (muhl-LIHK, RAW-buhrt) S.J.

Defense. Shoots right. 6'2", 205 lbs. Born, Toronto, Ont., October 23, 1979.
(San Jose's 8th choice, 185th overall, in 1998 Entry Draft).

			Regular Season					Playoffs				
Season	Club	Lea	GP	G	A	TP	PIM	GP	G	A	TP	PIM
1994-95	Mississauga Reps	MTHL	52	8	23	31	80	....	....	....	....	....
1995-96	Sault Ste. Marie	OHL	54	0	3	3	58	3	0	0	0	0
1996-97	Sault Ste. Marie	OHL	60	2	8	10	49	11	0	1	1	12
1997-98	Sault Ste. Marie	OHL	61	0	10	10	109	....	....	....	....	....
1998-99	Sault Ste. Marie	OHL	66	1	12	13	83	5	0	1	1	10
99-2000	Kentucky	AHL	52	0	0	0	52	9	0	0	0	10

MURLEY, Matt (MUHR-lee, MAT) PIT.

Left wing. Shoots left. 6'1", 192 lbs. Born, Troy, NY, December 17, 1979.
(Pittsburgh's 2nd choice, 51st overall, in 1999 Entry Draft).

			Regular Season					Playoffs				
Season	Club	Lea	GP	G	A	TP	PIM	GP	G	A	TP	PIM
1996-97	Syracuse	OJHL	48	52	58	110	111	....	....	....	....	....
1997-98	Syracuse	OJHL	49	56	70	126	103	....	....	....	....	....
1998-99	RPI Engineers	ECAC	36	17	32	49	32	....	....	....	....	....
99-2000	RPI Engineers	ECAC	35	9	29	38	42	....	....	....	....	....

MUROVIC, Mirko (MUHR-roh-VIHK, MEER-koh) TOR.

Left wing. Shoots left. 6'3", 190 lbs. Born, Montreal, Que., February 2, 1981.
(Toronto's 3rd choice, 108th overall, in 1999 Entry Draft).

			Regular Season					Playoffs				
Season	Club	Lea	GP	G	A	TP	PIM	GP	G	A	TP	PIM
1996-97	Gatineau Lions	QAAA	37	5	12	17	12	....	....	....	....	....
1997-98	Moncton Alpines	QMJHL	54	10	15	25	10	....	....	....	....	....
1998-99	Moncton Wildcats	QMJHL	69	21	33	54	60	4	0	1	1	2
99-2000	Moncton Wildcats	QMJHL	72	19	51	70	113	7	2	4	6	2

MURPHY, Mark (MUHR-fee, MAHRK) WSH.

Left wing. Shoots left. 5'11", 200 lbs. Born, Stoughton, MA, August 6, 1976.
(Toronto's 6th choice, 197th overall, in 1995 Entry Draft).

			Regular Season					Playoffs				
Season	Club	Lea	GP	G	A	TP	PIM	GP	G	A	TP	PIM
1994-95	Stratford Cullitons	OJHL-B	47	52	56	108	64	....	....	....	....	....
1995-96	Stratford Cullitons	OJHL-B	1	0	0	0	0	....	....	....	....	....
	RPI Engineers	ECAC	32	1	1	2	50	....	....	....	....	....
1996-97	RPI Engineers	ECAC	34	9	18	27	56	....	....	....	....	....
1997-98	RPI Engineers	ECAC	35	8	27	35	63	....	....	....	....	....
1998-99	RPI Engineers	ECAC	37	11	30	41	76	....	....	....	....	....
99-2000	Wilkes-Barre	AHL	38	11	22	33	35	....	....	....	....	....
	Trenton Titans	ECHL	37	21	18	39	60	12	2	8	10	17
	Philadelphia	AHL	....	....	....	....	....	2	0	0	0	0

Signed as a free agent by **Washington**, July 13, 2000.

MURPHY, Ryan (MUHR-fee, RIGH-yan) CAR.

Left wing. Shoots left. 6'1", 192 lbs. Born, Van Nuys, CA, March 21, 1979.
(Carolina's 4th choice, 113th overall, in 1999 Entry Draft).

			Regular Season					Playoffs				
Season	Club	Lea	GP	G	A	TP	PIM	GP	G	A	TP	PIM
1995-96	Thornhill Rattlers	OJHL	32	13	16	29	49	....	....	....	....	....
1996-97	Thornhill Rattlers	OJHL	41	22	32	54	36	....	....	....	....	....
1997-98	Bowling Green	CCHA	36	3	9	12	27	....	....	....	....	....
1998-99	Bowling Green	CCHA	34	10	23	33	38	....	....	....	....	....
99-2000	Bowling Green	CCHA	36	9	10	19	63	....	....	....	....	....

MURRAY, Craig (MUHR-ray, KRAYG) MTL.

Center. Shoots left. 6', 175 lbs. Born, Souris, Man., February 22, 1979.
(Montreal's 8th choice, 201st overall, in 1998 Entry Draft).

			Regular Season					Playoffs				
Season	Club	Lea	GP	G	A	TP	PIM	GP	G	A	TP	PIM
1994-95	Penticton Pats	BCAHA	60	74	76	150	42	....	....	....	....	....
1995-96	Penticton	BCJHL	55	14	6	20	54	....	....	....	....	....
1996-97	Penticton	BCJHL	45	25	31	56	39	....	....	....	....	....
1997-98	Penticton	BCJHL	57	45	52	97	50	7	6	8	14	14
1998-99	U. of Michigan	CCHA	16	0	1	1	6	....	....	....	....	....
99-2000	U. of Michigan	CCHA	23	2	1	3	12	....	....	....	....	....

MURRAY, Doug (MUH-ree) S.J.

Defense. Shoots left. 6'3", 220 lbs. Born, Bromma, Sweden, March 12, 1980.
(San Jose's 6th choice, 241st overall, in 1999 Entry Draft).

			Regular Season					Playoffs				
Season	Club	Lea	GP	G	A	TP	PIM	GP	G	A	TP	PIM
1998-99	NY Apple Core	EJHL	60	17	47	64	62	....	....	....	....	....
99-2000	Cornell Big Red	ECAC	32	3	6	9	38	....	....	....	....	....

NAUMENKO, Nick (NAH-mehn-koh, NIHK) MIN.

Defense. Shoots right. 5'11", 185 lbs. Born, Chicago, IL, July 7, 1974.
(St. Louis' 9th choice, 182nd overall, in 1992 Entry Draft).

			Regular Season					Playoffs				
Season	Club	Lea	GP	G	A	TP	PIM	GP	G	A	TP	PIM
1991-92	Dubuque Saints	USHL	24	6	19	25	4	....	....	....	....	....
1992-93	North Dakota	WCHA	38	10	24	34	26	....	....	....	....	....
1993-94	North Dakota	WCHA	32	4	22	26	22	....	....	....	....	....
1994-95	North Dakota	WCHA	39	13	26	39	78	....	....	....	....	....
1995-96	North Dakota	WCHA	37	11	30	41	32	....	....	....	....	....
1996-97	Worcester	AHL	54	6	22	28	72	1	0	0	0	0
1997-98	Worcester	AHL	71	12	34	46	63	11	1	7	8	8
1998-99	Utah Grizzlies	IHL	20	4	3	7	20	....	....	....	....	....
	Las Vegas	IHL	34	5	16	21	37	....	....	....	....	....
	Kansas City	IHL	21	3	8	11	4	3	1	2	3	4
99-2000	Kansas City	IHL	54	9	27	36	79	....	....	....	....	....

WCHA First All-Star Team (1995, 1996)

NEDOROST, Vaclav (neh-DOHR-uhst, VA-tslav) COL.

Center. Shoots left. 6'1", 187 lbs. Born, Ceske Budejovice, Czech., March 16, 1982.
(Colorado's 1st choice, 14th overall, in 2000 Entry Draft).

			Regular Season					Playoffs				
Season	Club	Lea	GP	G	A	TP	PIM	GP	G	A	TP	PIM
1997-98	HC Budejovice-Jr.	Cze-Rep	43	30	23	53	20	....	....	....	....	....
1998-99	HC Budejovice-Jr.	Cze-Rep	39	6	15	21	20	....	....	....	....	....
	HC Budejovice	Cze-Rep	7	0	2	2	0	....	....	....	....	....
99-2000	HC Budejovice-Jr.	Cze-Rep	14	4	7	11	4	....	....	....	....	....
	HC Budejovice	Cze-Rep	38	8	6	14	6	3	0	0	0	0

NEHRLING, Lucas (NEHR-lihng, LEW-cas) N.J.

Defense. Shoots right. 6'5", 225 lbs. Born, Peterborough, Ont., August 14, 1979.
(New Jersey's 3rd choice, 104th overall, in 1997 Entry Draft).

			Regular Season					Playoffs				
Season	Club	Lea	GP	G	A	TP	PIM	GP	G	A	TP	PIM
1995-96	Quinte Hawks	OMHA	25	0	9	9	59	....	....	....	....	....
1996-97	Sarnia Sting	OHL	63	3	12	15	74	12	0	2	2	23
1997-98	Sarnia Sting	OHL	22	0	2	2	46	....	....	....	....	....
	Kingston	OHL	39	1	8	9	83	12	0	1	1	19
1998-99	Kingston	OHL	2	0	1	1	13	....	....	....	....	....
	Guelph Storm	OHL	60	5	14	19	131	11	0	1	1	35
99-2000	Augusta Lynx	ECHL	9	1	0	1	12	....	....	....	....	....
	Arkansas	ECHL	16	0	1	1	51	....	....	....	....	....
	Muskegon Fury	UHL	22	1	2	3	86	2	0	0	0	2
	Albany River Rats	AHL	18	0	0	0	27	4	0	0	0	0

NEIL, Christopher (NEEL, KRIHS-toh-fuhr) OTT.

Right wing. Shoots right. 6'1", 213 lbs. Born, Markdale, Ont., June 18, 1979.
(Ottawa's 7th choice, 161st overall, in 1998 Entry Draft).

			Regular Season					Playoffs				
Season	Club	Lea	GP	G	A	TP	PIM	GP	G	A	TP	PIM
1995-96	Orangeville	OJHL-B	43	15	15	30	50	....	....	....	....	....
1996-97	North Bay	OHL	65	13	16	29	150	....	....	....	....	....
1997-98	North Bay	OHL	59	26	29	55	231	....	....	....	....	....
1998-99	North Bay	OHL	66	26	46	72	215	4	1	0	1	15
99-2000	Mobile Mysticks	ECHL	4	0	2	2	39	....	....	....	....	....
	Grand Rapids	IHL	51	9	10	19	301	8	0	2	2	24

NEPRYAYEV, Ivan (neh-pree-YIGH-ehv) WSH.

Center. Shoots left. 6'1", 178 lbs. Born, Yaroslavl, USSR, February 4, 1982.
(Washington's 5th choice, 163rd overall, in 2000 Entry Draft).

			Regular Season					Playoffs				
Season	Club	Lea	GP	G	A	TP	PIM	GP	G	A	TP	PIM
1997-98	Torpedo Yaroslavl	Russia-2	6	0	0	0	0	....	....	....	....	....
1998-99	Torpedo Yaroslavl	Russia-3	15	1	0	1	0	....	....	....	....	....
99-2000	Torpedo Yaroslavl	Russia-3	40	8	14	22	....	....	....	....	....	....

NEWMAN, Jared (NOO-muhn) CAR.

Defense. Shoots right. 6'2", 201 lbs. Born, Detroit, MI, March 7, 1982.
(Carolina's 4th choice, 110th overall, in 2000 Entry Draft).

			Regular Season					Playoffs				
Season	Club	Lea	GP	G	A	TP	PIM	GP	G	A	TP	PIM
1997-98	Plymouth B's	NAJHL	49	1	4	5	69	....	....	....	....	....
1998-99	Plymouth Whalers	OHL	66	2	15	17	57	11	1	2	3	9
99-2000	Plymouth Whalers	OHL	50	1	15	16	123	23	0	5	5	34

NIELSEN, Chris (NEEL-sehn, KRIHS) CBJ

Center. Shoots right. 6'1", 190 lbs. Born, Moshi, Tanzania, February 16, 1980.
(NY Islanders' 2nd choice, 36th overall, in 1998 Entry Draft).

			Regular Season					Playoffs				
Season	Club	Lea	GP	G	A	TP	PIM	GP	G	A	TP	PIM
1995-96	S-W Cougars	MAHA	39	37	35	72	59	....	....	....	....	....
	Calgary Hitmen	WHL	6	0	0	0	0	....	....	....	....	....
1996-97	Calgary Hitmen	WHL	62	11	19	30	39	....	....	....	....	....
1997-98	Calgary Hitmen	WHL	68	22	29	51	31	18	2	4	6	10
1998-99	Calgary Hitmen	WHL	70	22	24	46	45	21	11	5	16	28
99-2000	Calgary Hitmen	WHL	62	38	31	69	86	13	14	9	23	20

Traded to **Columbus** by **NY Islanders** for Columbus' 4th (later traded to Anaheim - Anaheim selected Jonas Ronnqvist) and 9th (Dmitri Altarev) rouind choices in 2000 Entry Draft, May 11, 2000.

NIEMI, Antti-Jussi (nee-mee, AN-tee-YOO-see) ANA.

Defense. Shoots left. 6'1", 183 lbs. Born, Vantaa, Finland, September 22, 1977.
(Ottawa's 2nd choice, 81st overall, in 1996 Entry Draft).

			Regular Season					Playoffs				
Season	Club	Lea	GP	G	A	TP	PIM	GP	G	A	TP	PIM
1992-93	Jokerit Helsinki-C	Finn-Jr.	38	9	23	32	54	....	....	....	....	....
	Jokerit Helsinki-B	Finn-Jr.	2	0	0	0	2	....	....	....	....	....
1993-94	Jokerit Helsinki-B	Finn-Jr.	13	1	1	2	8	....	....	....	....	....
	Jokerit Helsinki	Finn-Jr.	33	0	3	3	26	....	....	....	....	....
1994-95	Jokerit Helsinki-B	Finn-Jr.	10	3	5	8	42	....	....	....	....	....
	Jokerit Helsinki	Finn-Jr.	24	4	8	12	74	....	....	....	....	....
1995-96	Jokerit Helsinki	Finn-Jr.	34	11	18	29	56	8	0	4	4	39
	Jarvenpaa HT	Finland-2	4	0	2	2	8	....	....	....	....	....
	Jokerit Helsinki	Finland	6	0	2	2	6	1	0	0	0	0
1996-97	Jokerit Helsinki	Finland	44	2	9	11	38	9	0	2	2	2
1997-98	Jokerit Helsinki	Finland	46	2	6	8	24	8	0	1	1	0
	Jokerit Helsinki	EuroHL	6	0	1	1	6	....	....	....	....	....
1998-99	Jokerit Helsinki	Finland	53	3	7	10	107	3	0	0	0	2
	Jokerit Helsinki	EuroHL	6	2	2	4	4	2	0	1	1	0
99-2000	Jokerit Helsinki	Finland	53	8	8	16	79	11	0	3	3	6

Rights traded to **Anaheim** by **Ottawa** with Ted Donato for Patrick Lalime, June 18, 1999.

NIKOLOV, Angel (NIH-koh-lohv, AYN-jehl) S.J.

Defense. Shoots left. 6'2", 205 lbs. Born, Most, Czech., November 18, 1975.
(San Jose's 2nd choice, 37th overall, in 1994 Entry Draft).

			Regular Season					Playoffs				
Season	Club	Lea	GP	G	A	TP	PIM	GP	G	A	TP	PIM
1993-94	CHZ Litvinov	Cze-Rep	10	2	2	4	....	3	0	0	0	....
1994-95	CHZ Litvinov	Cze-Rep	41	1	4	5	18	4	0	0	0	27
1995-96	CHZ Litvinov	Cze-Rep	40	1	7	8	....	10	0	1	1	....
1996-97	CHZ Litvinov	Cze-Rep	47	0	9	9	44	....	....	....	....	....
1997-98	CHZ Litvinov	Cze-Rep	51	1	4	5	53	4	0	3	3	27
1998-99	CHZ Litvinov	Cze-Rep	51	5	12	17	54	....	....	....	....	....
99-2000	CHZ Litvinov	Cze-Rep	51	6	15	21	32	7	1	2	3	2

NIKULIN, Ilja (nij-KOO-lihn, ihl-YUH) ATL.

Defense. Shoots left. 6'3", 205 lbs. Born, Moscow, USSR, March 12, 1982.
(Atlanta's 2nd choice, 31st overall, in 2000 Entry Draft).

			Regular Season					Playoffs				
Season	Club	Lea	GP	G	A	TP	PIM	GP	G	A	TP	PIM
1998-99	D'amo Moscow-2	Russia-3	23	0	2	2	18	....	....	....	....	....
99-2000	D'amo Moscow-2	Russia-3	13	3	3	6	22	....	....	....	....	....
	THC Tver	Russia-2	10	7	9	16	40	....	....	....	....	....

NILSSON, Magnus (NIHL-suhn, MAG-nuhs) **DET.**

Right wing. Shoots left. 6'1", 187 lbs. Born, Finspang, Sweden, February 1, 1978.
(Detroit's 5th choice, 144th overall, in 1996 Entry Draft).

			Regular Season					Playoffs				
Season	Club	Lea	GP	G	A	TP	PIM	GP	G	A	TP	PIM
1995-96	Vita Hasten	Swede-2	28	3	3	6	16	....	....	....	....	....
1996-97	Malmo IF	Swede-Jr.	14	10	9	19	45	....	....	....	....	....
	Malmo IF	Sweden	12	0	0	0	0	....	....	....	....	....
1997-98	Malmo IF	Sweden	45	6	1	7	6	....	....	....	....	....
1998-99	Malmo IF	Sweden	42	0	0	0	10	4	0	0	0	0
99-2000	Malmo IF	Sweden	44	5	5	10	63	6	0	0	0	25

NILSSON, Mattias (NIHL-suhn, MA-tee-uhs) **NSH.**

Defense. Shoots left. 6'4", 184 lbs. Born, Ornskoldsvik, Sweden, February 6, 1982.
(Nashville's 3rd choice, 72nd overall, in 2000 Entry Draft).

			Regular Season					Playoffs				
Season	Club	Lea	GP	G	A	TP	PIM	GP	G	A	TP	PIM
1997-98	Modo Hockey	Swede-Jr.	40	20	14	34	34	....	....	....	....	....
1998-99	Modo Hockey	Swede-Jr.	30	7	7	14	26	....	....	....	....	....
99-2000	Modo Hockey	Swede-Jr.	33	5	5	10	56	2	0	0	0	0

NITTEL, Adam (nih-TEHL, A-dam) **S.J.**

Right wing. Shoots right. 6'2", 225 lbs. Born, Kitchener, Ont., July 17, 1978.
(San Jose's 4th choice, 107th overall, in 1997 Entry Draft).

			Regular Season					Playoffs				
Season	Club	Lea	GP	G	A	TP	PIM	GP	G	A	TP	PIM
1994-95	Guelph Platers	OJHL-B	36	1	8	9	92	....	....	....	....	....
1995-96	Royal York	OJHL	32	8	8	16	93	....	....	....	....	....
	Niagara Falls	OHL	39	3	3	6	74	10	0	3	3	39
1996-97	Erie Otters	OHL	46	8	11	19	194	....	....	....	....	....
1997-98	Erie Otters	OHL	48	11	17	28	*309	7	0	0	0	19
1998-99	Mississauga	OHL	34	15	16	31	235	....	....	....	....	....
	Sault Ste. Marie	OHL	21	3	8	11	101	5	1	2	3	30
99-2000	Kentucky	AHL	29	2	4	6	116	....	....	....	....	....
	New Orleans	ECHL	26	2	3	5	96	3	0	1	1	28

NORD, Bjorn **WSH.**

Defense. Shoots right. 6', 196 lbs. Born, Huddinge, Sweden, April 5, 1972.
(Washington's 6th choice, 289th overall, in 2000 Entry Draft).

			Regular Season					Playoffs				
Season	Club	Lea	GP	G	A	TP	PIM	GP	G	A	TP	PIM
1991-92	Huddinge IK	Sweden-2	33	12	10	22	64	4	1	1	2	6
1992-93	Djurgardens IF	Sweden	35	2	2	4	42	6	0	2	2	10
1993-94	Djurgardens IF	Sweden	39	6	11	17	20	6	0	3	3	4
1994-95	Djurgardens IF	Sweden	39	7	7	14	42	3	0	0	0	2
1995-96	Djurgardens IF	Sweden	40	8	10	18	50	4	0	0	0	6
1996-97	Djurgardens IF	Sweden	50	11	14	25	50	4	1	1	2	4
1997-98	Djurgardens IF	Sweden	43	6	11	17	65	15	5	6	11	28
1998-99	Djurgardens IF	Sweden	50	12	20	32	50	4	0	2	2	2
99-2000	Djurgardens IF	Sweden	49	17	11	28	62	13	4	2	6	8

NORDGREN, Niklas (NOHD-grehn, NIHK-lahs) **CAR.**

Left wing. Shoots right. 5'11", 190 lbs. Born, Ornskoldsvik, Sweden, June 28, 1979.
(Carolina's 7th choice, 195th overall, in 1997 Entry Draft).

			Regular Season					Playoffs				
Season	Club	Lea	GP	G	A	TP	PIM	GP	G	A	TP	PIM
1995-96	MoDo Hockey-B	Swede-Jr.	30	37	27	64	....	....	....	....	....	....
1996-97	MoDo Hockey	Swede-Jr.	22	14	6	20	....	....	....	....	....	....
	MoDo Hockey	Sweden	5	0	0	0	0	....	....	....	....	....
1997-98	MoDo Hockey	Swede-Jr.	28	15	15	30	52	....	....	....	....	....
1998-99	MoDo Hockey	Sweden	7	0	0	0	2	....	....	....	....	....
	MoDo Hockey	Swede-2	22	7	4	11	22	....	....	....	....	....
99-2000	Sundsvall IK	Swede-2	27	21	11	32	58	....	....	....	....	....
	MoDo Hockey	EuroHL	1	0	0	0	0	1	0	0	0	0

NORDQVIST, Jonas (NAWRD-kvihst, YOH-nuhs) **CHI.**

Center. Shoots left. 6'2", 196 lbs. Born, Leksand, Sweden, April 26, 1982.
(Chicago's 3rd choice, 49th overall, in 2000 Entry Draft).

			Regular Season					Playoffs				
Season	Club	Lea	GP	G	A	TP	PIM	GP	G	A	TP	PIM
1997-98	Leksands IF	Swede-Jr.	42	26	35	61	....	....	....	....	....	....
1998-99	Leksands IF	Swede-Jr.	32	14	25	39	....	....	....	....	....	....
99-2000	Leksands IF	Swede-Jr.	34	15	24	39	32	2	0	0	0	2
	Leksands IF	Sweden	3	0	0	0	0	....	....	....	....	....

NORTON, Brad (NOHR-tohn, BRAD) **EDM.**

Defense. Shoots left. 6'4", 225 lbs. Born, Cambridge, MA, February 13, 1975.
(Edmonton's 9th choice, 215th overall, in 1993 Entry Draft).

			Regular Season					Playoffs				
Season	Club	Lea	GP	G	A	TP	PIM	GP	G	A	TP	PIM
1994-95	U. Mass-Amherst	H-East	30	0	6	6	89	....	....	....	....	....
1995-96	U. Mass-Amherst	H-East	34	4	12	16	99	....	....	....	....	....
1996-97	U. Mass-Amherst	H-East	35	2	16	18	88	....	....	....	....	....
1997-98	U. Mass-Amherst	H-East	20	2	13	15	28	....	....	....	....	....
	Detroit Vipers	IHL	33	1	4	5	56	22	0	2	2	87
1998-99	Hamilton Bulldogs	AHL	58	1	8	9	134	11	0	1	1	6
99-2000	Hamilton Bulldogs	AHL	40	5	12	17	104	10	1	4	5	26

NOVAK, Filip (NOH-vak, FIH-lihp) **NYR**

Defense. Shoots left. 6', 174 lbs. Born, Ceske Budejovice, Czech., May 7, 1982.
(NY Rangers' 1st choice, 64th overall, in 2000 Entry Draft).

			Regular Season					Playoffs				
Season	Club	Lea	GP	G	A	TP	PIM	GP	G	A	TP	PIM
1998-99	HC Budejovice-Jr.	Cze-Rep	68	8	10	18	34	....	....	....	....	....
99-2000	Regina Pats	WHL	47	7	32	39	70	7	1	4	5	5

NOWAK, Brett (NOH-wak) **BOS.**

Center. Shoots left. 6'2", 192 lbs. Born, New Haven, CT, May 20, 1981.
(Boston's 7th choice, 102nd overall, in 2000 Entry Draft).

			Regular Season					Playoffs				
Season	Club	Lea	GP	G	A	TP	PIM	GP	G	A	TP	PIM
1997-98	Hotchkiss Prep	Hi-School	21	24	42	66	42	....	....	....	....	....
1998-99	Harvard University	ECAC	30	1	2	3	6	....	....	....	....	....
99-2000	Harvard University	ECAC	23	0	3	3	6	....	....	....	....	....

NUMMELIN, Petteri (NOO-muh-lihn, PEH-tuh-ree) **CBJ**

Defense. Shoots left. 5'10", 196 lbs. Born, Turku, Finland, November 25, 1972.
(Columbus' 3rd choice, 133rd overall, in 2000 Entry Draft).

			Regular Season					Playoffs				
Season	Club	Lea	GP	G	A	TP	PIM	GP	G	A	TP	PIM
1988-89	TPS Turku	Finn-Jr.	11	2	3	5	2	....	....	....	....	....
1989-90	TPS Turku	Finn-Jr.	33	6	14	20	45	....	....	....	....	....
1990-91	Kiekko-67	Finland-2	2	0	2	2	4	....	....	....	....	....
	TPS Turku	Finn-Jr.	35	20	16	36	28	....	....	....	....	....
1991-92	Kiekko-67	Finland-2	41	12	24	36	36	....	....	....	....	....
1992-93	TPS Turku	Finn-Jr.	1	1	0	1	0	....	....	....	....	....
	TPS Turku	Finland	3	0	0	0	8	....	....	....	....	....
	Reipas Lahti	Finland	14	3	4	7	18	....	....	....	....	....
	Reipas Lahti	Finland-Q	6	2	4	6	2	....	....	....	....	....
	Kiekko-67	Finland-2	28	14	15	29	18	....	....	....	....	....
1993-94	TPS Turku	Finland	44	14	24	38	20	11	0	3	3	4
1994-95	TPS Turku	Finland	48	10	17	27	32	11	4	3	7	0
1995-96	Vastra Frolunda	Sweden	32	7	11	18	26	12	2	7	9	4
1996-97	Vastra Frolunda	Sweden	44	20	14	34	39	2	0	1	1	0
1997-98	HC Davos	Switz.	33	13	17	30	24	17	8	14	22	2
1998-99	HC Davos	Switz.	44	11	42	53	22	4	0	2	2	2
99-2000	HC Davos	Switz.	40	15	23	38	20	5	0	3	3	0

NUUTINEN, Sami (NOO-tih-nehn, SA-mee) **EDM.**

Defense. Shoots left. 6'1", 189 lbs. Born, Espoo, Finland, June 11, 1971.
(Edmonton's 12th choice, 248th overall, in 1990 Entry Draft).

			Regular Season					Playoffs				
Season	Club	Lea	GP	G	A	TP	PIM	GP	G	A	TP	PIM
1988-89	Kiekko Espoo	Finn-Jr.	6	1	7	8	10	4	2	4	6	2
	Kiekko Espoo	Finland-2	39	18	10	28	46	....	....	....	....	....
1989-90	Kiekko Espoo	Finland-2	40	8	15	23	....	....	....	....	....	....
	Kiekko Espoo	Finn-Jr.	8	3	5	8	6	5	3	1	4	8
1990-91	K-Kissat	Finland-2	3	1	0	1	0	....	....	....	....	....
	HIFK Helsinki	Finland	27	1	3	4	6	3	0	0	0	0
1991-92	HIFK Helsinki	Finland	44	5	6	11	10	9	0	1	1	4
1992-93	Kiekko Espoo	Finland	48	7	11	18	59	....	....	....	....	....
1993-94	Kiekko Espoo	Finland	46	9	15	24	36	....	....	....	....	....
1994-95	Kiekko Espoo	Finland	50	8	24	32	38	4	0	1	1	0
1995-96	Kiekko Espoo	Finland	49	7	7	14	54	....	....	....	....	....
1996-97	Vasteras IK	Sweden	50	7	7	14	22	....	....	....	....	....
1997-98	Kiekko Espoo	Finland	48	4	17	21	51	8	0	2	2	6
1998-99	Jokerit Helsinki	Finland	54	10	18	28	22	3	0	2	2	0
99-2000	SB Rosenheim	DEL	52	2	11	13	16	....	....	....	....	....

NYCHOLAT, Lawrence **MIN.**

Defense. Shoots left. 6', 192 lbs. Born, Calgary, Alta., May 7, 1979.

			Regular Season					Playoffs				
Season	Club	Lea	GP	G	A	TP	PIM	GP	G	A	TP	PIM
1995-96	Notre Dame	SAHA	42	10	36	46	66	....	....	....	....	....
1996-97	Swift Current	WHL	67	8	13	21	82	....	....	....	....	....
1997-98	Swift Current	WHL	71	13	35	48	108	....	....	....	....	....
1998-99	Swift Current	WHL	72	16	44	60	125	6	2	2	4	12
99-2000	Swift Current	WHL	70	22	58	80	92	2	0	0	0	0

Signed as a free agent by **Minnesota**, August 31, 2000.

NYSTROM, David (NEW-strawm) **PHI.**

Left wing. Shoots right. 6', 174 lbs. Born, Hagersten, Sweden, February 21, 1980.
(Philadelphia's 6th choice, 224th overall, in 1999 Entry Draft).

			Regular Season					Playoffs				
Season	Club	Lea	GP	G	A	TP	PIM	GP	G	A	TP	PIM
1996-97	Vastra Frolunda	Swede-Jr.	23	6	2	8	....	....	....	....	....	....
1997-98	Vastra Frolunda	Swede-Jr.	29	17	18	35	26	2	0	0	0	0
1998-99	Vastra Frolunda	Swede-Jr.	28	15	16	31	20	....	....	....	....	....
99-2000	Troja IF	Swede-2	32	12	10	22	28	....	....	....	....	....

O'CONNOR, Sean (oh-KAW-nuhr, SHAWN) **FLA.**

Right wing. Shoots right. 6'3", 220 lbs. Born, Victoria, B.C., October 19, 1981.
(Florida's 3rd choice, 82nd overall, in 2000 Entry Draft).

			Regular Season					Playoffs				
Season	Club	Lea	GP	G	A	TP	PIM	GP	G	A	TP	PIM
1995-96	Victoria RRC	BCAHA	60	23	45	68	70	....	....	....	....	....
1996-97	Victoria RRC	BCAHA	50	59	73	132	190	....	....	....	....	....
1997-98	Victoria Salsa	BCJHL	50	9	17	26	145	....	....	....	....	....
1998-99	Victoria Salsa	BCJHL	53	17	18	35	197	....	....	....	....	....
99-2000	Moose Jaw	WHL	51	5	8	13	166	2	0	0	0	2

O'BRIEN, Sean (OH-BRI-ehn, SHAWN)

Left wing. Shoots left. 6', 200 lbs. Born, Belmont, MA, February 9, 1972.

			Regular Season					Playoffs				
Season	Club	Lea	GP	G	A	TP	PIM	GP	G	A	TP	PIM
1990-91	Princeton	ECAC	24	0	6	6	12	....	....	....	....	....
1991-92	Princeton	ECAC	27	3	10	13	38	....	....	....	....	....
1992-93	Princeton	ECAC	29	2	22	24	54	....	....	....	....	....
1993-94	Princeton	ECAC	28	8	15	23	40	....	....	....	....	....
1994-95	Richmond	ECHL	52	5	•18	23	147	17	2	5	7	77
	Houston Aeros	IHL	13	2	1	3	23	....	....	....	....	....
1995-96	Las Vegas	IHL	1	0	....	0	2	....	....	....	....	....
	Utah Grizzlies	IHL	7	2	2	4	12	....	....	....	....	....
	Houston Aeros	IHL	4	0	1	1	12	....	....	....	....	....
	Tallahasee	ECHL	54	9	19	28	179	8	0	2	2	23
1996-97	Tallahasee	ECHL	10	7	3	10	29	....	....	....	....	....
	Utah Grizzlies	IHL	50	21	10	31	135	....	....	....	....	....
	Phoenix	IHL	10	3	3	6	20	....	....	....	....	....
1997-98	Fayetteville Force	CHL	1	0	0	0	0	....	....	....	....	....
	Philadelphia	AHL	33	7	10	17	88	20	4	2	6	48
	Utah Grizzlies	IHL	36	3	8	11	77	....	....	....	....	....
1998-99	Syracuse Crunch	AHL	45	5	11	16	155	....	....	....	....	....
	Philadelphia	AHL	18	1	2	3	60	16	3	4	7	24
99-2000	Philadelphia	AHL	61	6	11	17	139	5	0	0	0	2

ECAC Second All-Star Team (1994)

Signed as a free agent by **LA Kings**, June 26, 1997. Signed as a free agent by **Pittsburgh**, August 11, 1998. Traded to **Philadelphia** by **Pittsburgh** for future considerations, February 10, 1999.

OBSUT, Jaroslav (OHB-suht, YAHR-oh-slahv) ST.L.

Defense. Shoots left. 6'1", 200 lbs. Born, Presov, Czech., September 3, 1976.
(Winnipeg's 9th choice, 188th overall, in 1995 Entry Draft).

			Regular Season					Playoffs				
Season	**Club**	**Lea**	**GP**	**G**	**A**	**TP**	**PIM**	**GP**	**G**	**A**	**TP**	**PIM**
1994-95	North Battleford	SJHL	55	21	30	51	126	....	....	....	....	....
1995-96	Swift Current	WHL	72	10	11	21	57	6	0	0	0	2
1996-97	Edmonton Ice	WHL	13	2	9	11	4	....	....	....	....	....
	Medicine Hat	WHL	50	8	26	34	42	4	0	2	2	2
	Toledo Storm	ECHL	3	1	0	1	0	5	0	1	1	6
1997-98	Raleigh Icecaps	ECHL	60	6	26	32	46	....	....	....	....	....
	Syracuse Crunch	AHL	4	0	1	1	4	....	....	....	....	....
1998-99	Augusta Lynx	ECHL	41	11	25	36	42	....	....	....	....	....
	Manitoba Moose	IHL	2	0	0	0	0	....	....	....	....	....
	Worcester	AHL	31	2	8	10	14	4	0	1	1	2
99-2000	Worcester	AHL	7	0	2	2	4	....	....	....	....	....

Signed as a free agent by **St. Louis**, April 26, 1999. • Missed majority of 1999-2000 season recovering from knee injury suffered in practice, October, 1999.

O'DETTE, Matt CGY.

Defense. Shoots right. 6'5", 228 lbs. Born, Oshawa, Ont., November 9, 1975.
(Florida's 7th choice, 157th overall, in 1994 Entry Draft).

			Regular Season					Playoffs				
Season	**Club**	**Lea**	**GP**	**G**	**A**	**TP**	**PIM**	**GP**	**G**	**A**	**TP**	**PIM**
1992-93	Kitchener	OHL	28	0	0	0	6	....	....	....	....	....
1993-94	Kitchener	OHL	46	1	3	4	107	....	....	....	....	....
1994-95	Kitchener	OHL	10	1	2	3	29	....	....	....	....	....
	Sault Ste. Marie	OHL	42	3	12	15	94	....	....	....	....	....
1995-96	Kitchener	OHL	57	6	7	13	146	4	0	0	0	2
1996-97	Roanoke Express	ECHL	69	6	16	22	139	4	0	0	0	10
1997-98	Saint John Flames	AHL	58	0	5	5	92	15	0	1	1	10
	Roanoke Express	ECHL	5	0	0	0	29	....	....	....	....	....
1998-99	Saint John Flames	AHL	42	0	1	1	82	2	0	0	0	14
99-2000	Saint John Flames	AHL	69	1	4	5	177	3	0	0	0	0

Signed as a free agent by **Calgary**, September, 1999.

ODUYA, Fredrik (oh-DOO-yuh, FRED-rihk) CGY.

Left wing. Shoots left. 6'3", 220 lbs. Born, Stockholm, Sweden, May 31, 1975.
(San Jose's 8th choice, 154th overall, in 1993 Entry Draft).

			Regular Season					Playoffs				
Season	**Club**	**Lea**	**GP**	**G**	**A**	**TP**	**PIM**	**GP**	**G**	**A**	**TP**	**PIM**
1991-92	Windsor Bulldogs	OJHL-B	43	2	8	10	24	....	....	....	....	....
1992-93	Guelph Storm	OHL	23	2	4	6	29	....	....	....	....	....
	Ottawa 67's	OHL	17	0	3	3	70	....	....	....	....	....
1993-94	Ottawa 67's	OHL	51	11	12	23	181	17	0	3	3	22
1994-95	Ottawa 67's	OHL	61	2	13	15	175	....	....	....	....	....
1995-96	Kansas City	IHL	56	2	6	8	235	3	0	0	0	2
1996-97	Kentucky	AHL	69	2	9	11	241	....	....	....	....	....
1997-98	Kentucky	AHL	72	6	10	16	300	....	....	....	....	....
1998-99	Orlando	IHL	64	2	14	16	259	....	....	....	....	....
	Saint John Flames	AHL	12	0	2	2	48	6	0	0	0	22
99-2000	Saint John Flames	AHL	10	0	0	0	42	....	....	....	....	....

Traded to **Calgary** by **San Jose** for Eric Landry, July 12, 1999. • Missed majority of 1999-2000 season recovering from back injury suffered in practice, October, 1999.

O'LEARY, Pat (OH-leer-ree, PAT) PHX.

Center. Shoots left. 6'2", 190 lbs. Born, Minneapolis, MN, September 2, 1979.
(Phoenix's 3rd choice, 73rd overall, in 1998 Entry Draft).

			Regular Season					Playoffs				
Season	**Club**	**Lea**	**GP**	**G**	**A**	**TP**	**PIM**	**GP**	**G**	**A**	**TP**	**PIM**
1996-97	Robbinsdale	Hi-School	22	28	27	55	42	....	....	....	....	....
1997-98	Robbinsdale	Hi-School	24	22	27	49	28	....	....	....	....	....
1998-99	U. of Minnesota	WCHA	17	0	2	2	8	....	....	....	....	....
99-2000	U. of Minnesota	WCHA	25	6	1	7	8	....	....	....	....	....

OLVESTAD, Jimmie (OHL-vuh-stahd, JIHM-mee) T.B.

Left wing. Shoots left. 6'1", 194 lbs. Born, Stockholm, Sweden, February 16, 1980.
(Tampa Bay's 4th choice, 88th overall, in 1999 Entry Draft).

			Regular Season					Playoffs				
Season	**Club**	**Lea**	**GP**	**G**	**A**	**TP**	**PIM**	**GP**	**G**	**A**	**TP**	**PIM**
1996-97	Huddinge IF	Swede-Jr.	40	15	16	31	....	....	....	....	....	....
1997-98	Djurgardens IF	Swede-Jr.	10	3	3	6	10	....	....	....	....	....
	Huddinge IF	Swede-2	11	0	0	0	6	....	....	....	....	....
1998-99	Djurgardens IF	Sweden	44	2	4	6	18	4	0	0	0	8
99-2000	Djurgardens IF	Sweden	50	6	3	9	34	13	1	2	3	12

OREKHOVSKY, Oleg (oh-reh-KHOHV-skee, OH-lehg) MIN.

Defense. Shoots right. 6', 183 lbs. Born, Krasnoyarsk, USSR, November 3, 1977.
(Washington's 11th choice, 206th overall, in 1996 Entry Draft).

			Regular Season					Playoffs				
Season	**Club**	**Lea**	**GP**	**G**	**A**	**TP**	**PIM**	**GP**	**G**	**A**	**TP**	**PIM**
1994-95	Dynamo Moscow	CIS	30	0	1	1	18	....	....	....	....	....
1995-96	Dynamo Moscow	CIS	22	1	2	3	14	8	0	0	0	6
1996-97	Dynamo Moscow	Russia	32	4	2	6	16	4	2	1	3	2
1997-98	Dynamo Moscow	EuroHL	7	2	1	3	12	....	....	....	....	....
	Dynamo Moscow	Russia	40	4	5	9	34	....	....	....	....	....
1998-99	Dynamo Moscow	Russia	42	1	1	2	22	16	1	2	3	6
99-2000	Dynamo Moscow	Russia	37	3	6	9	38	15	1	0	1	4

Selected by **Minnesota** from **Washington** in Expansion Draft, June 23, 2000.

ORLOV, Maxim (ohr-LAHF, max-EEM) WSH.

Center. Shoots left. 6', 176 lbs. Born, Moscow, USSR, March 31, 1981.
(Washington's 9th choice, 219th overall, in 1999 Entry Draft).

			Regular Season					Playoffs				
Season	**Club**	**Lea**	**GP**	**G**	**A**	**TP**	**PIM**	**GP**	**G**	**A**	**TP**	**PIM**
1998-99	CSKA Moscow	Russia	2	0	0	0	2	1	0	0	0	0
99-2000	CSKA Moscow	Russia	25	0	0	0	2	2	0	0	0	2

ORPIK, Brooks (OHR-pihk) PIT.

Defense. Shoots left. 6'3", 217 lbs. Born, Amherst, NY, September 26, 1980.
(Pittsburgh's 1st choice, 18th overall, in 2000 Entry Draft).

			Regular Season					Playoffs				
Season	**Club**	**Lea**	**GP**	**G**	**A**	**TP**	**PIM**	**GP**	**G**	**A**	**TP**	**PIM**
1997-98	Thayer Academy	Hi-School	22	0	7	7	....	....	....	....	....	....
1998-99	Boston College	H-East	41	1	10	11	*96	....	....	....	....	....
99-2000	Boston College	H-East	38	1	9	10	102	....	....	....	....	....

OTT, Steve (AHT) DAL.

Center. Shoots left. 6', 160 lbs. Born, Summerside, P.E.I., August 19, 1982.
(Dallas' 1st choice, 25th overall, in 2000 Entry Draft).

			Regular Season					Playoffs				
Season	**Club**	**Lea**	**GP**	**G**	**A**	**TP**	**PIM**	**GP**	**G**	**A**	**TP**	**PIM**
1998-99	Leamington Flyers	OJHL-B	48	14	30	44	110	....	....	....	....	....
99-2000	Windsor Spitfires	OHL	66	23	39	62	131	12	3	5	8	21

OTTOSSON, Kristofer (AW-toh-suhn) NYI

Right wing. Shoots left. 5'10", 187 lbs. Born, Stockholm, Sweden, January 9, 1976.
(NY Islanders' 6th choice, 148th overall, in 2000 Entry Draft).

			Regular Season					Playoffs				
Season	**Club**	**Lea**	**GP**	**G**	**A**	**TP**	**PIM**	**GP**	**G**	**A**	**TP**	**PIM**
1993-94	Djurgardens IF	Swede-Jr.	13	3	6	9	4	....	....	....	....	....
1994-95	Djurgardens IF	Sweden	30	0	0	0	2	3	0	0	0	0
1995-96	Djurgardens IF	Sweden	32	1	0	1	2	2	0	0	0	0
1996-97	Djurgardens IF	Sweden	20	0	0	0	2	....	....	....	....	....
	Arlanda HC	Sweden-2	6	6	0	6	0	....	....	....	....	....
	Huddinge IF	Sweden-2	13	1	3	4	2	2	0	1	1	0
1997-98	Huddinge IF	Sweden-2	30	17	20	37	14	....	....	....	....	....
1998-99	Huddinge IF	Sweden-2	41	15	19	34	16	....	....	....	....	....
99-2000	Djurgardens IF	Sweden	47	25	15	40	12	13	7	2	9	2

OUELLET, Michel (oo-LEHT, mih-SHEHL) PIT.

Right wing. Shoots right. 6'1", 182 lbs. Born, Rimouski, Que., March 5, 1982.
(Pittsburgh's 4th choice, 124th overall, in 2000 Entry Draft).

			Regular Season					Playoffs				
Season	**Club**	**Lea**	**GP**	**G**	**A**	**TP**	**PIM**	**GP**	**G**	**A**	**TP**	**PIM**
1998-99	Rimouski Oceanic	QMJHL	28	7	13	20	10	11	0	1	1	6
99-2000	Rimouski Oceanic	QMJHL	72	36	53	89	38	14	4	5	9	14

PAHLSSON, Samuel (PAWL-suhn, SAM-yew-al) BOS.

Center. Shoots left. 5'11", 190 lbs. Born, Ornskoldsvik, Sweden, December 17, 1977.
(Colorado's 10th choice, 176th overall, in 1996 Entry Draft).

			Regular Season					Playoffs				
Season	**Club**	**Lea**	**GP**	**G**	**A**	**TP**	**PIM**	**GP**	**G**	**A**	**TP**	**PIM**
1994-95	MoDo Hockey	Swede-Jr.	30	10	11	21	26	....	....	....	....	....
	MoDo Hockey	Sweden	1	0	0	0	0	....	....	....	....	....
1995-96	MoDo Hockey	Swede-Jr.	5	2	6	8	2	....	....	....	....	....
	MoDo Hockey	Sweden	36	1	3	4	8	4	0	0	0	0
1996-97	MoDo Hockey	Sweden	49	8	9	17	83	....	....	....	....	....
1997-98	MoDo Hockey	Sweden	23	6	11	17	24	9	3	0	3	6
1998-99	MoDo Hockey	Sweden	50	17	17	34	44	13	3	3	6	10
99-2000	MoDo Hockey	Sweden	47	16	11	27	67	13	3	3	6	8
	MoDo Hockey	EuroHL	4	1	0	1	0	3	1	1	2	2

Traded to **Boston** by **Philadelphia** with Brian Rolston, Martin Grenier and New Jersey's 1st round choice (previously acquired, Boston selected Martin Samuelsson) in 2000 Entry Draft for Ray Bourque and Dave Andreychuk, March 6, 2000.

PANDOLFO, Mike (pan-DAHL-foh, MIGHK) BUF.

Left wing. Shoots left. 6'3", 226 lbs. Born, Winchester, MA, September 15, 1979.
(Buffalo's 5th choice, 77th overall, in 1998 Entry Draft).

			Regular Season					Playoffs				
Season	**Club**	**Lea**	**GP**	**G**	**A**	**TP**	**PIM**	**GP**	**G**	**A**	**TP**	**PIM**
1996-97	St. Sebastians	Hi-School	32	27	28	55	30	....	....	....	....	....
1997-98	St. Sebastians	Hi-School	28	29	23	52	18	....	....	....	....	....
1998-99	Boston University	H-East	34	13	4	17	26	....	....	....	....	....
99-2000	Boston University	H-East	41	13	10	23	37	....	....	....	....	....

PANOV, Konstantin (PAN-ahv, KAWN-stan-tihn) NSH.

Right wing. Shoots left. 6', 188 lbs. Born, Chelyabinsk, USSR, June 29, 1980.
(Nashville's 10th choice, 131st overall, in 1999 Entry Draft).

			Regular Season					Playoffs				
Season	**Club**	**Lea**	**GP**	**G**	**A**	**TP**	**PIM**	**GP**	**G**	**A**	**TP**	**PIM**
1996-97	HC Nadezhda	Russia-3	25	18	30	48	22	....	....	....	....	....
1997-98	Yunior-T Kurgan	Russia-3	20	7	3	10	6	....	....	....	....	....
	HC Chelyabinsk	Russia	6	2	0	2	4	2	0	0	0	0
1998-99	Kamloops Blazers	WHL	62	33	30	63	62	13	5	3	8	10
99-2000	Kamloops Blazers	WHL	64	43	30	73	47	....	....	....	....	....

WHL West Second All-Star Team (2000)

PAPINEAU, Justin (PA-pee-noh) ST.L.

Center. Shoots left. 5'10", 180 lbs. Born, Ottawa, Ont., January 15, 1980.
(St. Louis' 3rd choice, 75th overall, in 2000 Entry Draft).

			Regular Season					Playoffs				
Season	**Club**	**Lea**	**GP**	**G**	**A**	**TP**	**PIM**	**GP**	**G**	**A**	**TP**	**PIM**
1995-96	Ottawa	OJHL	52	31	19	50	51	....	....	....	....	....
1996-97	Belleville Bulls	OHL	50	10	32	42	32	....	....	....	....	....
1997-98	Belleville Bulls	OHL	66	41	53	94	34	10	5	9	14	6
1998-99	Belleville Bulls	OHL	68	52	47	99	28	21	*21	*30	*51	20
99-2000	Belleville Bulls	OHL	60	40	36	76	52	16	4	12	16	16

• Re-entered NHL draft. Originally Los Angeles' 2nd choice, 46th overall, in 1998 Entry Draft.

PARROS, George (PAIR-ohs) L.A.

Right wing. Shoots right. 6'4", 210 lbs. Born, Washington, PA, December 29, 1979.
(Los Angeles' 9th choice, 222nd overall, in 1999 Entry Draft).

			Regular Season					Playoffs				
Season	**Club**	**Lea**	**GP**	**G**	**A**	**TP**	**PIM**	**GP**	**G**	**A**	**TP**	**PIM**
1998-99	Chicago Freeze	NAJHL	54	30	20	50	126	....	....	....	....	....
99-2000	Princeton Tigers	ECAC	27	4	2	6	14	....	....	....	....	....

NAJHL Rookie-of-the-Year (1999) • NAJHL All-Rookie Team (1999)

PASTUKH, Yevgeny (pas-TOOKH, YEHV-jehn-ee) ST.L.

Left wing. Shoots left. 5'11", 178 lbs. Born, Kharkov, USSR, January 18, 1979.
(St. Louis' 7th choice, 225th overall, in 1998 Entry Draft).

			Regular Season					Playoffs				
Season	**Club**	**Lea**	**GP**	**G**	**A**	**TP**	**PIM**	**GP**	**G**	**A**	**TP**	**PIM**
1995-96	Torpedo Yaroslavl	Russia-2	4	0	0	0	0	....	....	....	....	....
1996-97	Torpedo Yaroslavl	Russia-3	34	3	5	8	6	....	....	....	....	....
1997-98	Torpedo Yaroslavl	Russia-2	26	6	6	12	14	....	....	....	....	....
	Torpedo Yaroslavl	Russia	3	0	0	0	0	....	....	....	....	....
	HK Khimik	Russia	3	0	0	0	2	....	....	....	....	....
1998-99	HK Khimik	Russia	8	0	0	0	0	....	....	....	....	....
99-2000	HK Khimik	Russia-2	STATISTICS NOT AVAILABLE									

PAUL, Jeff (PAWL, JEHF) CHI.

Defense. Shoots right. 6'3", 196 lbs. Born, London, Ont., March 1, 1978.
(Chicago's 2nd choice, 42nd overall, in 1996 Entry Draft).

			Regular Season					Playoffs				
Season	**Club**	**Lea**	**GP**	**G**	**A**	**TP**	**PIM**	**GP**	**G**	**A**	**TP**	**PIM**
1993-94	Woodstock	OJHL-C	36	1	6	7	73	....	....	....	....	....
1994-95	Niagara Falls	OHL	57	3	10	13	64	6	0	2	2	0
1995-96	Niagara Falls	OHL	48	1	7	8	81	10	0	4	4	37
1996-97	Erie Otters	OHL	60	4	23	27	152	5	2	0	2	12
1997-98	Erie Otters	OHL	48	3	17	20	108	7	0	2	2	13
1998-99	Portland Pirates	AHL	6	0	0	0	4	....	....	....	....	....
	Indianapolis Ice	IHL	55	0	7	7	120	7	0	2	2	12
99-2000	Cleveland	IHL	69	6	6	12	210	9	1	0	1	12

PAVLIKOVSKY, Rastislav (pahv-lih-KAWV-skee, RA-this-LAHV) OTT.

Center. Shoots left. 5'11", 193 lbs. Born, Dubnica, Czech., September 8, 1979.
(Ottawa's 10th choice, 246th overall, in 1998 Entry Draft).

			Regular Season					Playoffs				
Season	**Club**	**Lea**	**GP**	**G**	**A**	**TP**	**PIM**	**GP**	**G**	**A**	**TP**	**PIM**
1993-94	Dukla Trencin	Slovakia	3	0	1	1	0	....	....	....	....	....
1994-95	Dukla Trencin	Slovakia	14	0	7	7	4	6	1	1	2	0
1995-96	Sault Ste. Marie	OHL	13	0	3	3	6	....	....	....	....	....
	Dukla Trencin	Slovakia	10	1	1	2	6	12	4	1	5	....
1996-97	Dukla Trencin	Slovakia	35	9	11	20	....	7	1	2	3	....
1997-98	Dukla Trencin	Slovakia	3	2	1	3	0	....	....	....	....	....
	Las Vegas	IHL	1	0	0	0	0	....	....	....	....	....
	Utah Grizzlies	IHL	74	17	29	46	54	2	0	0	0	6
1998-99	Cincinnati	IHL	31	4	12	16	28	....	....	....	....	....
	Cincinnati Ducks	AHL	36	12	23	35	59	2	0	1	1	4
99-2000	Grand Rapids	IHL	15	0	5	5	24	....	....	....	....	....
	Philadelphia	AHL	12	4	7	11	8	....	....	....	....	....
	Cincinnati Ducks	AHL	17	3	5	8	10	....	....	....	....	....

PAVLOV, Yevgeny (pahv-lohv, YEHV-jeh-nee) NSH.

Left wing. Shoots right. 6'1", 195 lbs. Born, Togliatti, USSR, January 10, 1981.
(Nashville's 8th choice, 121st overall, in 1999 Entry Draft).

			Regular Season					Playoffs				
Season	**Club**	**Lea**	**GP**	**G**	**A**	**TP**	**PIM**	**GP**	**G**	**A**	**TP**	**PIM**
1997-98	Lada Togliatti-2	Russia-3	27	8	1	9	4	....	....	....	....	....
1998-99	Lada Togliatti-2	Russia-4	33	17	3	20	8	....	....	....	....	....
	Lada Togliatti	Russia	9	0	1	1	2	....	....	....	....	....
99-2000	Lada Togliatti-2	Russia-3	55	30	17	47	18	....	....	....	....	....
	Salavat Ufa	Russia	5	1	0	1	10	....	....	....	....	....
	Lada Togliatti	Russia	2	0	0	0	0	1	0	0	0	0

PAYER, Serge (PAY-uhr, SAIRZH) FLA.

Center. Shoots left. 6', 192 lbs. Born, Rockland, Ont., May 7, 1979.

			Regular Season					Playoffs				
Season	**Club**	**Lea**	**GP**	**G**	**A**	**TP**	**PIM**	**GP**	**G**	**A**	**TP**	**PIM**
1994-95	Cumberland	OMHA	42	37	46	83	55	....	....	....	....	....
1995-96	Kitchener	OHL	66	8	16	24	18	12	0	2	2	2
1996-97	Kitchener	OHL	63	7	16	23	27	13	1	3	4	2
1997-98	Kitchener	OHL	44	20	21	41	51	6	3	0	3	7
1998-99	Kitchener	OHL	40	18	19	37	22	....	....	....	....	....
99-2000	Kitchener	OHL	44	10	26	36	53	5	0	3	3	6

Signed as a free agent by **Florida**, September 30, 1997.

PAYETTE, Andre (PAY-ehteh, AN-dray)

Center. Shoots left. 6'2", 205 lbs. Born, Cornwall, Ont., July 29, 1976.
(Philadelphia's 9th choice, 244th overall, in 1994 Entry Draft).

			Regular Season					Playoffs				
Season	**Club**	**Lea**	**GP**	**G**	**A**	**TP**	**PIM**	**GP**	**G**	**A**	**TP**	**PIM**
1992-93	Cumberland	OJHL	54	6	8	14	122	....	....	....	....	....
1993-94	Sault Ste. Marie	OHL	40	2	3	5	98	....	....	....	....	....
1994-95	Sault Ste. Marie	OHL	50	15	15	30	177	....	....	....	....	....
1995-96	Sault Ste. Marie	OHL	57	20	19	39	257	4	0	0	0	5
1996-97	Sault Ste. Marie	OHL	4	3	0	3	19	....	....	....	....	....
	Kingston	OHL	29	10	13	23	143	2	0	0	0	2
1997-98	Philadelphia	AHL	56	5	5	10	209	4	0	0	0	9
1998-99	Philadelphia	AHL	12	0	1	1	34	....	....	....	....	....
	Mohawk Valley	UHL	51	9	21	30	241	....	....	....	....	....
99-2000	Mohawk Valley	UHL	58	9	23	32	160	7	4	1	5	33
	Rochester	AHL	2	0	0	0	0	....	....	....	....	....

PEAT, Stephen (PEET, STEEV-vuhn) WSH.

Defense. Shoots right. 6'3", 210 lbs. Born, Princeton, B.C., March 10, 1980.
(Anaheim's 2nd choice, 32nd overall, in 1998 Entry Draft).

			Regular Season					Playoffs				
Season	**Club**	**Lea**	**GP**	**G**	**A**	**TP**	**PIM**	**GP**	**G**	**A**	**TP**	**PIM**
1995-96	Langley Thunder	BCJHL	59	5	15	20	112	....	....	....	....	....
	Red Deer Rebels	WHL	1	0	0	0	0	....	....	....	....	....
1996-97	Red Deer Rebels	WHL	68	3	14	17	161	16	0	2	2	22
1997-98	Red Deer Rebels	WHL	63	6	12	18	189	5	0	0	0	8
1998-99	Red Deer Rebels	WHL	31	2	6	8	98	....	....	....	....	....
	Tri-City Americans	WHL	5	0	0	0	19	....	....	....	....	....
99-2000	Tri-City Americans	WHL	12	0	2	2	48	....	....	....	....	....
	Calgary Hitmen	WHL	23	0	8	8	100	13	0	1	1	33

Rights traded to **Washington** by **Anaheim** for Washington's 4th round choice (later traded to Montreal - later traded to Pittsburgh - Pittsburgh selected Michel Ouellet) in 2000 Entry Draft, June 1, 2000.

PECKER, Cory (PEH-kuhr, KOH-ree) CGY.

Center. Shoots right. 6', 190 lbs. Born, Montreal, Que., March 20, 1981.
(Calgary's 7th choice, 166th overall, in 1999 Entry Draft).

			Regular Season					Playoffs				
Season	**Club**	**Lea**	**GP**	**G**	**A**	**TP**	**PIM**	**GP**	**G**	**A**	**TP**	**PIM**
1996-97	Lac St-Louis	QAAA	40	30	40	70	....	....	....	....	....	....
1997-98	Sault Ste. Marie	OHL	29	3	4	7	15	....	....	....	....	....
1998-99	Sault Ste. Marie	OHL	68	25	34	59	24	5	1	2	3	2
99-2000	Sault Ste. Marie	OHL	65	33	36	69	38	12	6	8	14	8

PELUSO, Mike (puh-LOO-soh, MIGHK) WSH.

Right wing. Shoots right. 6'1", 208 lbs. Born, Bismark, ND, September 2, 1974.
(Calgary's 12th choice, 253rd overall, in 1994 Entry Draft).

			Regular Season					Playoffs				
Season	**Club**	**Lea**	**GP**	**G**	**A**	**TP**	**PIM**	**GP**	**G**	**A**	**TP**	**PIM**
1993-94	Omaha Lancers	USHL	48	36	29	65	77	....	....	....	....	....
1994-95	Minnesota-Duluth	WCHA	38	11	23	34	38	....	....	....	....	....
1995-96	Minnesota-Duluth	WCHA	38	25	19	44	64	....	....	....	....	....
1996-97	Minnesota-Duluth	WCHA	37	20	20	40	53	....	....	....	....	....
1997-98	Minnesota-Duluth	WCHA	40	24	21	45	100	....	....	....	....	....
1998-99	Portland Pirates	AHL	26	7	6	13	6	....	....	....	....	....
99-2000	Portland Pirates	AHL	71	25	29	54	86	4	2	0	2	0

WCHA Second All-Star Team (1997)

Signed as a free agent by **Washington**, October 9, 1998.

PEPPERALL, Colin (PEH-puhr-awl, CAWL-ihn) CHI.

Left wing. Shoots left. 5'11", 160 lbs. Born, Niagara Falls, Ont., April 28, 1978.
(NY Rangers' 4th choice, 131st overall, in 1996 Entry Draft).

			Regular Season					Playoffs				
Season	**Club**	**Lea**	**GP**	**G**	**A**	**TP**	**PIM**	**GP**	**G**	**A**	**TP**	**PIM**
1993-94	Chippawa	OJHL-C	40	18	32	50	78	....	....	....	....	....
	Niagara Falls	OJHL-B	4	0	0	0	2	....	....	....	....	....
1994-95	Niagara Falls	OJHL-B	36	22	27	49	86	....	....	....	....	....
1995-96	Niagara Falls	OHL	66	26	26	52	47	10	3	4	7	8
1996-97	Erie Otters	OHL	66	36	36	72	39	5	3	2	5	2
1997-98	Erie Otters	OHL	60	31	60	91	151	7	4	4	8	16
	Hartford	AHL	3	1	0	1	2	....	....	....	....	....
1998-99	Portland Pirates	AHL	4	0	0	0	6	....	....	....	....	....
	Greenville Growl	ECHL	55	15	20	35	128	....	....	....	....	....
	Indianapolis Ice	IHL	9	2	2	4	12	....	....	....	....	....
99-2000	Hampton Roads	ECHL	45	14	22	36	157	9	1	5	6	43
	Cleveland	IHL	22	0	2	2	16	....	....	....	....	....

OHL Second All-Star Team (1998)

Traded to **Chicago** by **NY Rangers** for future considerations, June 2, 1998.

PEPPERALL, Ryan (PEH-puhr-awl, RIGH-yan)

Right wing. Shoots right. 6'1", 185 lbs. Born, Niagara Falls, Ont., January 26, 1977.
(Toronto's 2nd choice, 54th overall, in 1995 Entry Draft).

			Regular Season					Playoffs				
Season	**Club**	**Lea**	**GP**	**G**	**A**	**TP**	**PIM**	**GP**	**G**	**A**	**TP**	**PIM**
1993-94	Chippawa	OJHL-C	8	4	8	12	39	....	....	....	....	....
	Niagara Falls	OJHL-B	37	14	20	34	156	....	....	....	....	....
1994-95	Kitchener	OHL	62	17	16	33	86	5	2	2	4	8
1995-96	Kitchener	OHL	66	31	26	57	173	12	3	4	7	34
1996-97	Kitchener	OHL	65	35	36	71	201	13	9	6	15	17
1997-98	St. John's Leafs	AHL	63	3	4	7	50	1	0	0	0	0
1998-99	St. John's Leafs	AHL	79	16	8	24	70	5	1	0	1	2
99-2000	St. John's Leafs	AHL	77	11	7	18	83	....	....	....	....	....

PERIARD, Michel (pair-EE-ahr, MIHK-al) FLA.

Defense. Shoots left. 5'11", 183 lbs. Born, Montreal, Que., November 10, 1979.
(Ottawa's 8th choice, 188th overall, in 1998 Entry Draft).

			Regular Season					Playoffs				
Season	**Club**	**Lea**	**GP**	**G**	**A**	**TP**	**PIM**	**GP**	**G**	**A**	**TP**	**PIM**
1997-98	Shawinigan	QMJHL	68	14	30	44	64	5	0	0	0	18
1998-99	Shawinigan	QMJHL	64	14	40	54	90	6	1	2	3	4
99-2000	Rimouski Oceanic	QMJHL	70	25	75	100	58	14	5	17	22	16

QMJHL First All-Star Team (2000) • Canadian Major Junior First All-Star Team (2000) • Memorial Cup All-Star Team (2000)

Signed as a free agent by **Florida**, August 1, 2000.

PERROTT, Nathan (PEHR-roht, NAY-than) CHI.

Right wing. Shoots right. 6', 215 lbs. Born, Owen Sound, Ont., December 8, 1976.
(New Jersey's 2nd choice, 44th overall, in 1995 Entry Draft).

			Regular Season					Playoffs				
Season	**Club**	**Lea**	**GP**	**G**	**A**	**TP**	**PIM**	**GP**	**G**	**A**	**TP**	**PIM**
1992-93	Walkerton	OJHL-C	25	6	13	19	45	....	....	....	....	....
1993-94	St. Mary's	OJHL-B	41	11	26	37	249	....	....	....	....	....
1994-95	Oshawa Generals	OHL	63	18	28	46	233	2	1	1	2	9
1995-96	Oshawa Generals	OHL	59	30	32	62	158	5	2	3	5	8
	Albany River Rats	AHL	4	0	0	0	12	....	....	....	....	....
1996-97	Oshawa Generals	OHL	5	1	0	1	17	....	....	....	....	....
	Sault Ste. Marie	OHL	37	18	23	41	120	11	5	5	10	60
1997-98	Indianapolis Ice	IHL	31	4	3	7	76	....	....	....	....	....
	Jacksonville	ECHL	30	6	8	14	135	....	....	....	....	....
1998-99	Indianapolis Ice	IHL	72	14	11	25	307	7	3	1	4	45
99-2000	Cleveland	IHL	65	12	9	21	248	9	2	1	3	19

Signed as a free agent by **Chicago**, August 27, 1997.

PERRY, Scott (PEHR-ree, SCAWT) DAL.

Center. Shoots left. 6', 180 lbs. Born, Boston, MA, October 12, 1978.
(Dallas' 6th choice, 200th overall, in 1998 Entry Draft).

			Regular Season					Playoffs				
Season	**Club**	**Lea**	**GP**	**G**	**A**	**TP**	**PIM**	**GP**	**G**	**A**	**TP**	**PIM**
1997-98	Boston University	H-East	38	5	12	17	18	....	....	....	....	....
1998-99	Boston University	H-East	33	4	8	12	26	....	....	....	....	....
99-2000	Boston University	H-East	40	0	3	3	18	....	....	....	....	....

PETERS, Andrew (PEE-tuhrs, AN-drew) BUF.

Left wing. Shoots left. 6'4", 213 lbs. Born, St. Catharines, Ont., May 5, 1980.
(Buffalo's 2nd choice, 34th overall, in 1998 Entry Draft).

			Regular Season					Playoffs				
Season	**Club**	**Lea**	**GP**	**G**	**A**	**TP**	**PIM**	**GP**	**G**	**A**	**TP**	**PIM**
1996-97	Georgetown	OJHL	46	11	16	27	65	....	....	....	....	....
1997-98	Oshawa Generals	OHL	60	11	7	18	220	7	2	0	2	19
1998-99	Oshawa Generals	OHL	54	14	10	24	137	15	2	7	9	36
99-2000	Kitchener	OHL	42	6	13	19	95	4	0	1	1	14

PETERS, Dan **PHI.**

Defense. Shoots left. 5'10", 183 lbs. Born, Cottage Grove, MN, November 24, 1977.

			Regular Season					Playoffs				
Season	Club	Lea	GP	G	A	TP	PIM	GP	G	A	TP	PIM
1995-96	Omaha Lancers	USHL	54	11	36	47	....	....	....	....	....	....
1996-97	Colorado College	WCHA	36	4	12	16	62	....	....	....	....	....
1997-98	Colorado College	WCHA	37	5	16	21	108	....	....	....	....	....
1998-99	Colorado College	WCHA	36	8	21	29	82	....	....	....	....	....
99-2000	Colorado College	WCHA	27	2	8	10	58	....	....	....	....	....

WCHA Second All-Star Team (1999)

Signed as a free agent by **Philadelphia**, May 5, 2000.

PETERS, Geoff (PEE-tuhrs, JEHF) **CHI.**

Center. Shoots left. 6'1", 185 lbs. Born, Hamilton, Ont., April 30, 1978.
(Chicago's 3rd choice, 46th overall, in 1996 Entry Draft).

			Regular Season					Playoffs				
Season	Club	Lea	GP	G	A	TP	PIM	GP	G	A	TP	PIM
1993-94	Wexford Hawks	MTHL	34	39	26	65	26	....	....	....	....	....
1994-95	Niagara Falls	OHL	57	11	9	20	37	6	2	0	2	4
1995-96	Niagara Falls	OHL	64	25	34	59	51	10	4	4	8	8
1996-97	Erie Otters	OHL	28	12	10	22	39	5	1	3	4	7
1997-98	Erie Otters	OHL	31	15	11	26	36	....	....	....	....	....
	North Bay	OHL	20	11	14	25	22	....	....	....	....	....
	Indianapolis Ice	IHL	2	0	0	0	10	....	....	....	....	....
1998-99	Canada	Nat-Team	38	9	4	13	50	....	....	....	....	....
	Portland Pirates	AHL	4	1	1	2	9	....	....	....	....	....
99-2000	Cleveland	IHL	68	10	4	14	87	7	0	3	3	4

PETERSEN, Toby (PEE-tuhr-sohn, TOH-bee) **PIT.**

Center. Shoots left. 5'10", 196 lbs. Born, Minneapolis, MN, October 27, 1978.
(Pittsburgh's 9th choice, 244th overall, in 1998 Entry Draft).

			Regular Season					Playoffs				
Season	Club	Lea	GP	G	A	TP	PIM	GP	G	A	TP	PIM
1995-96	Jefferson High	Hi-School	25	29	30	59	....	....	....	....	....	....
1996-97	Colorado College	WCHA	40	17	21	38	18	....	....	....	....	....
1997-98	Colorado College	WCHA	40	16	17	33	34	....	....	....	....	....
1998-99	Colorado College	WCHA	21	12	12	24	2	....	....	....	....	....
99-2000	Colorado College	WCHA	37	14	19	33	8	....	....	....	....	....

PETRAKOV, Andrei (peh-trah-KAHF) **ST.L.**

Right wing. Shoots left. 6', 204 lbs. Born, Sverdlovsk, USSR, April 26, 1976.
(St. Louis' 4th choice, 97th overall, in 1996 Entry Draft).

			Regular Season					Playoffs				
Season	Club	Lea	GP	G	A	TP	PIM	GP	G	A	TP	PIM
1992-93	SK Yekaterinburg	CIS	5	0	0	0	0	1	0	0	0	0
1993-94	SK Yekaterinburg	CIS	35	4	2	6	10	....	....	....	....	....
1994-95	SK Yekaterinburg	CIS	11	1	1	2	6	1	0	0	0	0
1995-96	SK Yekaterinburg	CIS-2	52	17	6	23	14	....	....	....	....	....
1996-97	SK Yekaterinburg	Russia	14	6	1	7	6	....	....	....	....	....
	MC Magnitogorsk	Russia	18	4	0	4	8	6	0	0	0	0
1997-98	CSK Samara	Russia	9	0	0	0	4	....	....	....	....	....
	MC Magnitogorsk	Russia	29	9	11	20	0	....	....	....	....	....
1998-99	MC Magnitogorsk	Russia	10	4	4	8	8	15	4	8	12	4
	Worcester	AHL	4	0	1	1	2	....	....	....	....	....
	Muskegon Fury	UHL	5	4	3	7	0	....	....	....	....	....
	Fort Wayne	IHL	11	2	4	6	0	....	....	....	....	....
99-2000	MC Magnitogorsk	Russia	27	9	12	21	20	2	0	1	1	2

PETRASEK, David (PEH-truh-sehk) **DET.**

Defense. Shoots right. 6', 187 lbs. Born, Jonkoping, Sweden, February 1, 1976.
(Detroit's 10th choice, 226th overall, in 1998 Entry Draft).

			Regular Season					Playoffs				
Season	Club	Lea	GP	G	A	TP	PIM	GP	G	A	TP	PIM
1993-94	HV Jonkoping	Swede-Jr.	14	3	3	6	26	....	....	....	....	....
1994-95	HV Jonkoping	Sweden	30	0	1	1	6	11	0	0	0	0
	HV Jonkoping	Swede-Jr.	19	8	9	17	55	....	....	....	....	....
1995-96	HV Jonkoping	Swede-Jr.	12	1	5	6	16	....	....	....	....	....
	HV Jonkoping	Sweden	36	0	1	1	14	1	0	0	0	0
1996-97	HV Jonkoping	Swede-Jr.	3	0	0	0	....	....	....	....	....	....
	HV Jonkoping	Sweden	49	2	4	6	14	5	0	0	0	4
1997-98	HV Jonkoping	Sweden	43	6	7	13	80	5	2	2	4	14
1998-99	HV Jonkoping	Sweden	45	3	4	7	48	....	....	....	....	....
99-2000	HV Jonkoping	Sweden	46	4	6	10	54	5	1	1	2	41

PETRE, Henrik (PEH-truh, HEHN-rihk) **WSH.**

Defense. Shoots left. 6'1", 187 lbs. Born, Stockholm, Sweden, April 9, 1979.
(Washington's 5th choice, 143rd overall, in 1997 Entry Draft).

			Regular Season					Playoffs				
Season	Club	Lea	GP	G	A	TP	PIM	GP	G	A	TP	PIM
1995-96	Djurgardens IF	Swede-Jr.	21	6	4	10	8	....	....	....	....	....
1996-97	Djurgardens IF	Swede-Jr.	20	7	6	13	....	....	....	....	....	....
1997-98	Huddinge IF	Swede-2	30	4	4	8	30	....	....	....	....	....
1998-99	Djurgardens IF	Sweden	9	0	0	0	10	....	....	....	....	....
	Huddinge IF	Swede-2	14	0	1	1	20	....	....	....	....	....
99-2000	Brynas IF	Sweden	47	3	3	6	73	11	1	0	1	12

PETRILAINEN, Pasi (peh-trih-LAI-nehn, PAH-see) **N.J.**

Defense. Shoots left. 5'10", 185 lbs. Born, Tampere, Finland, May 5, 1978.
(New Jersey's 14th choice, 225th overall, in 1996 Entry Draft).

			Regular Season					Playoffs				
Season	Club	Lea	GP	G	A	TP	PIM	GP	G	A	TP	PIM
1992-93	Tappara Tampere	Finn-Jr.	1	0	0	0	2	....	....	....	....	....
1993-94	HC Tampere-C	Finn-Jr.	30	6	20	26	36	7	2	4	6	4
	Tappara Tampere	Finn-Jr.	2	0	0	0	0	....	....	....	....	....
1994-95	HC Tampere-B	Finn-Jr.	8	1	5	6	4	7	1	3	4	2
	Tappara Tampere	Finn-Jr.	14	3	4	7	6	....	....	....	....	....
	Tappara Tampere	Finland	25	3	0	3	14	....	....	....	....	....
1995-96	Tappara Tampere	Finn-Jr.	5	0	2	2	4	....	....	....	....	....
	Tappara Tampere	Finland	40	0	4	4	18	4	0	0	0	2
	HC Tampere-B	Finn-Jr.	....	....	....	....	....	1	1	1	2	2
1996-97	Tappara Tampere	Finland	43	2	9	11	46	3	0	0	0	2
1997-98	Tappara Tampere	Finland	48	4	7	11	34	4	0	0	0	4
1998-99	Tappara Tampere	Finland	35	3	3	6	26	....	....	....	....	....
99-2000	Tappara Tampere	Finland	39	1	9	10	22	4	0	1	1	0

PETROCHININ, Evgeny (peht-roh-CHIH-nihn) **DAL.**

Defense. Shoots left. 6'2", 190 lbs. Born, Murmansk, USSR, February 7, 1976.
(Dallas' 5th choice, 150th overall, in 1994 Entry Draft).

			Regular Season					Playoffs				
Season	Club	Lea	GP	G	A	TP	PIM	GP	G	A	TP	PIM
1993-94	Spartak Moscow	CIS	2	0	0	0	0	....	....	....	....	....
1994-95	Spartak Moscow	CIS	45	0	2	2	14	....	....	....	....	....
1995-96	Spartak Moscow	CIS	50	5	17	22	18	5	3	0	3	0
1996-97	Spartak Moscow	Russia	32	5	6	11	52	....	....	....	....	....
1997-98	Spartak Moscow	Russia	46	12	6	18	100	....	....	....	....	....
1998-99	Spartak Moscow	Russia	21	4	6	10	14	....	....	....	....	....
	Ak Bars Kazan	Russia	6	0	2	2	2	9	1	1	2	24
99-2000	MC Novokuznetsk	Russia	33	7	10	17	38	14	2	1	3	26

PETROVICKY, Ronald (PEHT-roh-vih-kee, RAW-nohld) **CGY.**

Right wing. Shoots right. 5'11", 188 lbs. Born, Zilina, Czech., February 15, 1977.
(Calgary's 9th choice, 228th overall, in 1996 Entry Draft).

			Regular Season					Playoffs				
Season	Club	Lea	GP	G	A	TP	PIM	GP	G	A	TP	PIM
1993-94	Dukla Trencin	Slovak-Jr.	36	28	27	55	42	....	....	....	....	....
	Dukla Trencin	Slovakia	1	0	0	0	0	....	....	....	....	....
1994-95	Tri-City Americans	WHL	39	4	11	15	86	....	....	....	....	....
	Prince George	WHL	21	4	6	10	37	....	....	....	....	....
1995-96	Prince George	WHL	39	19	21	40	61	....	....	....	....	....
1996-97	Prince George	WHL	72	32	37	69	119	15	4	9	13	31
1997-98	Regina Pats	WHL	71	64	49	113	168	9	2	4	6	11
1998-99	Saint John Flames	AHL	78	12	21	33	114	7	1	2	3	19
99-2000	Saint John Flames	AHL	67	23	33	56	131	3	1	1	2	6

WHL East Second All-Star Team (1998)

PETTINGER, Matt (PEH-tihn-juhr) **WSH.**

Left wing. Shoots left. 6'1", 205 lbs. Born, Edmonton, Alta, October 22, 1980.
(Washington's 2nd choice, 43rd overall, in 2000 Entry Draft).

			Regular Season					Playoffs				
Season	Club	Lea	GP	G	A	TP	PIM	GP	G	A	TP	PIM
1997-98	Victoria Salsa	BCJHL	55	22	20	42	56	7	5	1	6	8
1998-99	U. of Denver	WCHA	33	6	14	20	44	....	....	....	....	....
99-2000	U. of Denver	WCHA	19	2	6	8	49	....	....	....	....	....
	Calgary Hitman	WHL	27	14	6	20	41	11	2	6	8	30

PHILLIPS, Greg (FIHL-ihps, GREHG) **L.A.**

Right wing. Shoots right. 6'2", 205 lbs. Born, Winnipeg, Man., March 27, 1978.
(Los Angeles' 3rd choice, 57th overall, in 1996 Entry Draft).

			Regular Season					Playoffs				
Season	Club	Lea	GP	G	A	TP	PIM	GP	G	A	TP	PIM
1993-94	Winnipeg Lions	MAHA	21	12	4	16	51	....	....	....	....	....
1994-95	Saskatoon Blades	WHL	64	3	5	8	94	10	0	0	0	4
1995-96	Saskatoon Blades	WHL	67	21	24	45	132	4	1	2	3	2
1996-97	Saskatoon Blades	WHL	34	17	19	36	64	....	....	....	....	....
1997-98	Saskatoon Blades	WHL	47	24	28	52	116	....	....	....	....	....
	Brandon	WHL	22	10	21	31	49	18	11	11	22	58
1998-99	Springfield	AHL	63	16	13	29	74	3	0	0	0	4
99-2000	Lowell	AHL	62	20	10	30	140	7	3	0	3	10

PINC, Michal (PIHNTS, MIH-khuhl) **S.J.**

Center. Shoots left. 5'11", 180 lbs. Born, Litvinov, Czech., December 2, 1981.
(San Jose's 3rd choice, 142nd overall, in 2000 Entry Draft).

			Regular Season					Playoffs				
Season	Club	Lea	GP	G	A	TP	PIM	GP	G	A	TP	PIM
1997-98	CHZ Litvinov-Jr	Cze-Rep	47	18	36	54	....	....	....	....	....	....
1998-99	CHZ Litvinov-Jr	Cze-Rep	41	24	17	41	....	....	....	....	....	....
	CHZ Litvinov	Cze-Rep	7	0	0	0	4	....	....	....	....	....
99-2000	Hull Olympiques	QMJHL	31	11	27	38	67	....	....	....	....	....
	Rouyn-Noranda	QMJHL	27	8	16	24	64	11	0	5	5	18

PIROS, Kamil (PIH-ruhsh, KA-mihl) **BUF.**

Center. Shoots left. 6'1", 183 lbs. Born, Most, Czech., November 20, 1978.
(Buffalo's 9th choice, 212th overall, in 1997 Entry Draft).

			Regular Season					Playoffs				
Season	Club	Lea	GP	G	A	TP	PIM	GP	G	A	TP	PIM
1993-94	HC Most-Jr.	Cze-Rep	16	12	10	22	....	....	....	....	....	....
	CHZ Litvinov-Jr.	Cze-Rep	22	6	13	19	....	....	....	....	....	....
1994-95	CHZ Litvinov-Jr.	Cze-Rep	40	27	16	43	....	....	....	....	....	....
1995-96	CHZ Litvinov-Jr.	Cze-Rep	42	16	13	29	....	....	....	....	....	....
1996-97	CHZ Litvinov	Cze-Rep	3	2	1	3	....	....	....	....	....	....
	CHZ Litvinov	Cze-Rep	38	4	9	13	10	....	....	....	....	....
1997-98	CHZ Litvinov	Cze-Rep	14	0	1	1	2	....	....	....	....	....
	HC Vitkovice	Cze-Rep	26	2	9	11	14	....	....	....	....	....
1998-99	CHZ Litvinov	Cze-Rep	41	7	9	16	10	....	....	....	....	....
99-2000	CHZ Litvinov	Cze-Rep	40	8	8	16	18	7	0	3	3	2

PISANI, Fernando (pih-ZAN-ee, FUHR-nan-DOH) **EDM.**

Center/Left wing. Shoots left. 6'1", 185 lbs. Born, Edmonton, Alta., December 27, 1976.
(Edmonton's 9th choice, 195th overall, in 1996 Entry Draft).

			Regular Season					Playoffs				
Season	Club	Lea	GP	G	A	TP	PIM	GP	G	A	TP	PIM
1995-96	St. Albert Saints	AJHL	58	40	63	103	134	18	7	22	29	28
1996-97	Providence	H-East	35	12	18	30	36	....	....	....	....	....
1997-98	Providence	H-East	36	16	18	34	20	....	....	....	....	....
1998-99	Providence	H-East	38	14	37	51	42	....	....	....	....	....
99-2000	Providence	H-East	38	14	24	38	56	....	....	....	....	....

PIVKO, Libor (PIHV-koh, LEE-bohr) **NSH.**

Left wing. Shoots left. 6'2", 176 lbs. Born, Novy Jicin, Czech., March 29, 1980.
(Nashville's 4th choice, 89th overall, in 2000 Entry Draft).

			Regular Season					Playoffs				
Season	Club	Lea	GP	G	A	TP	PIM	GP	G	A	TP	PIM
1995-96	HC Opava-Jr.	Cze-Rep	37	19	14	33	30	....	....	....	....	....
1996-97	HC Opava-Jr.	Cze-Rep	16	12	9	21	22	....	....	....	....	....
1997-98	HC Opava-Jr.	Cze-Rep	37	15	11	26	36	....	....	....	....	....
1998-99	HC Opava-Jr.	Cze-Rep	38	21	14	35	....	....	....	....	....	....
	HC Opava	Cze-Rep	5	0	1	1	0	....	....	....	....	....
99-2000	HC Havirov-Jr.	Cze-Rep	5	1	3	4	4	....	....	....	....	....
	HC Havirov	Cze-Rep	40	11	11	22	41	....	....	....	....	....
	HC Brno-3	Cze-Rep	....	....	....	....	....	4	3	4	7	0

PLEKHANOV, Dmitri (plih-KHAH-nahv, dih-MEE-tree) ST.L.

Defense. Shoots left. 6'2", 176 lbs. Born, Nizhnekamsk, USSR, March 13, 1978.
(St. Louis' 8th choice, 232nd overall, in 1997 Entry Draft).

			Regular Season					Playoffs				
Season	Club	Lea	GP	G	A	TP	PIM	GP	G	A	TP	PIM
1995-96	HC Nizhnekamsk	CIS	30	1	2	3	28	....	....	....	....	....
1996-97	HC Nizhnekamsk	Russia	26	0	0	0	18	2	0	0	0	2
1997-98	HC Nizhnekamsk	Russia	18	0	0	0	6	....	....	....	....	....
1998-99	HC Nizhnekamsk	Russia	3	0	0	0	2	....	....	....	....	....
99-2000	HC Nizhnekamsk	Russia	3	0	0	0	0	....	....	....	....	....

PLETKA, Vaclav (PLEHT-kuh, VA-tslav) PHI.

Right wing. Shoots left. 5'10", 176 lbs. Born, Mlada Boleslav, Czech., June 8, 1979.
(Philadelphia's 5th choice, 208th overall, in 1999 Entry Draft).

			Regular Season					Playoffs				
Season	Club	Lea	GP	G	A	TP	PIM	GP	G	A	TP	PIM
1995-96	Mlada Boleslav-Jr.	Cze-Rep	35	22	17	39	....	....	....	....	....	....
1996-97	Mlada Boleslav-Jr.	Cze-Rep	37	28	13	41	....	....	....	....	....	....
1997-98	Mlada Boleslav-Jr.	Cze-Rep	36	23	25	48	....	....	....	....	....	....
1998-99	HC Trinec-Jr.	Cze-Rep	20	11	5	16	....	....	....	....	....	....
	HC Trinec	Cze-Rep	50	15	11	26	20	10	2	1	3	....
99-2000	HC Trinec	Cze-Rep	51	28	21	49	62	4	2	2	4	2

PODHRADSKY, Peter (pohd-RAD-skee) ANA.

Defense. Shoots right. 6'2", 194 lbs. Born, Bratislava, Czech., December 10, 1979.
(Anaheim's 4th choice, 134th overall, in 2000 Entry Draft).

			Regular Season					Playoffs				
Season	Club	Lea	GP	G	A	TP	PIM	GP	G	A	TP	PIM
1995-96	HC Bratislava-Jr.	Slovakia	50	14	17	31	....	....	....	....	....	....
1996-97	HC Bratislava-Jr.	Slovakia	41	2	6	8	28	....	....	....	....	....
1997-98	HC Bratislava-Jr.	Slovakia	48	11	13	24	58	....	....	....	....	....
1998-99	HC Bratislava-Jr.	Slovakia	25	9	14	23	57	2	0	1	1	0
	HC Bratislava	Slovakia	23	1	4	5	37	4	0	0	0	0
99-2000	HK Trnava-2	Slovakia	1	0	0	0	0	....	....	....	....	....
	HC Bratislava	Slovakia	40	4	11	15	63	8	1	0	1	2

PODKONICKY, Andrei (pohd-koh-NIHTZ-kee, AWN-dray) ST.L.

Center. Shoots left. 6'2", 202 lbs. Born, Zvolen, Czech., May 9, 1978.
(St. Louis' 8th choice, 196th overall, in 1996 Entry Draft).

			Regular Season					Playoffs				
Season	Club	Lea	GP	G	A	TP	PIM	GP	G	A	TP	PIM
1994-95	HKM Zvolen	Slovak-2	17	0	4	4	6	....	....	....	....	....
1995-96	HKM Zvolen	Slovak-2	38	18	12	30	18	....	....	....	....	....
1996-97	Portland	WHL	71	25	46	71	127	6	1	1	2	8
1997-98	Portland	WHL	64	30	44	74	81	16	4	12	16	20
1998-99	Worcester	AHL	61	19	24	43	52	4	0	0	0	4
99-2000	Worcester	AHL	77	16	25	41	68	9	2	5	7	6

Memorial Cup All-Star Team (1998) • Won Ed Chynoweth Award (Memorial Cup Tournament Top Scorer) (1998)

POHL, John (PAWL, JAWN) ST.L.

Center. Shoots right. 6', 173 lbs. Born, Rochester, MN, June 29, 1979.
(St. Louis' 8th choice, 255th overall, in 1998 Entry Draft).

			Regular Season					Playoffs				
Season	Club	Lea	GP	G	A	TP	PIM	GP	G	A	TP	PIM
1997-98	Red Wing High	Hi-School	28	30	77	107	18	....	....	....	....	....
1998-99	U. of Minnesota	WCHA	42	7	10	17	18	....	....	....	....	....
99-2000	U. of Minnesota	WCHA	41	18	41	59	26	....	....	....	....	....

WCHA Second All-Star Team (2000)

POLLOCK, Jame (PAWL-lawk, JAYM) ST.L.

Defense. Shoots right. 6'3", 202 lbs. Born, Quebec City, Que., June 16, 1979.
(St. Louis' 4th choice, 106th overall, in 1997 Entry Draft).

			Regular Season					Playoffs				
Season	Club	Lea	GP	G	A	TP	PIM	GP	G	A	TP	PIM
1994-95	Victoria Legion	BCAHA	43	22	56	78	96	....	....	....	....	....
1995-96	Seattle T-Birds	WHL	32	0	1	1	15	....	....	....	....	....
1996-97	Seattle T-Birds	WHL	66	15	19	34	94	15	3	5	8	16
1997-98	Seattle T-Birds	WHL	66	11	36	47	78	5	0	1	1	17
1998-99	Seattle T-Birds	WHL	59	10	32	42	78	11	3	4	7	8
99-2000	Worcester	AHL	56	12	12	24	50	9	5	3	8	6

PONIKAROVSKY, Alexei (poh-NIH-kahr-ohv-skee, al-EHX-ay) TOR.

Right wing. Shoots left. 6'4", 196 lbs. Born, Kiev, USSR, April 9, 1980.
(Toronto's 4th choice, 87th overall, in 1998 Entry Draft).

			Regular Season					Playoffs				
Season	Club	Lea	GP	G	A	TP	PIM	GP	G	A	TP	PIM
1995-96	Dynamo Moscow	Russia-Jr.	70	14	10	24	20	....	....	....	....	....
1996-97	Dynamo Moscow	Russia-Jr.	60	12	15	27	30	....	....	....	....	....
	Dynamo Moscow	Russia-3	2	0	0	0	2	....	....	....	....	....
1997-98	Dynamo Moscow	Russia-2	24	1	2	3	30	....	....	....	....	....
1998-99	Krylja Sovetov	Russia	13	2	1	3	2	....	....	....	....	....
	Dynamo Moscow	Russia	....	....	....	....	....	3	0	0	0	2
99-2000	Dynamo Moscow	Russia	19	1	0	1	8	1	0	0	0	0

POTHIER, Brian ATL.

Defense. Shoots right. 6'1", 195 lbs. Born, New Bedford, MA, April 15, 1977.

			Regular Season					Playoffs				
Season	Club	Lea	GP	G	A	TP	PIM	GP	G	A	TP	PIM
1995-96	Northfield High	Hi-School	20	1	11	12	....	....	....	....	....	....
1996-97	RPI Engineers	ECAC	34	1	11	12	42	....	....	....	....	....
1997-98	RPI Engineers	ECAC	35	2	9	11	28	....	....	....	....	....
1998-99	RPI Engineers	ECAC	37	5	13	18	36	....	....	....	....	....
99-2000	RPI Engineers	ECAC	36	9	24	33	44	....	....	....	....	....

ECAC Second All-Star Team (2000) • NCAA East Second All-American Team (2000)

Signed as a free agent by **Atlanta**, April 8, 2000.

POTULNY, Grant (puh-TUHL-nee) OTT.

Center. Shoots left. 6'2", 194 lbs. Born, Grand Forks, ND, March 4, 1980.
(Ottawa's 7th choice, 157th overall, in 2000 Entry Draft).

			Regular Season					Playoffs				
Season	Club	Lea	GP	G	A	TP	PIM	GP	G	A	TP	PIM
1998-99	Lincoln Stars	USHL	46	7	11	18	76	10	2	1	3	7
99-2000	Lincoln Stars	USHL	56	25	30	55	85	10	3	4	7	4

PRATT, Harlan CAR.

Defense. Shoots left. 6'1", 195 lbs. Born, Fort McMurray, Alta., December 10, 1978.
(Pittsburgh's 5th choice, 124th overall, in 1997 Entry Draft).

			Regular Season					Playoffs				
Season	Club	Lea	GP	G	A	TP	PIM	GP	G	A	TP	PIM
1994-95	Seattle T-Birds	WHL	33	1	0	1	17	1	0	0	0	0
1995-96	Red Deer Rebels	WHL	60	2	3	5	22	10	0	0	0	4
1996-97	Red Deer Rebels	WHL	2	0	0	0	2	....	....	....	....	....
	Prince Albert	WHL	65	7	26	33	49	4	1	1	2	4
1997-98	Prince Albert	WHL	37	6	14	20	12	....	....	....	....	....
	Regina Pats	WHL	24	2	6	8	23	9	2	2	4	2
1998-99	Portland	WHL	10	1	3	4	10	....	....	....	....	....
	Toledo Storm	ECHL	61	4	35	39	32	3	0	0	0	0
99-2000	Florida Everblades	ECHL	68	4	29	33	38	5	0	1	1	2

Signed as a free agent by **Carolina**, August 21, 2000.

PRESTBERG, Pelle (PEHST-buhrg, PEHL-lee) ANA.

Left wing. Shoots left. 5'10", 170 lbs. Born, Jonkoping, Sweden, February 5, 1975.
(Anaheim's 7th choice, 233rd overall, in 1998 Entry Draft).

			Regular Season					Playoffs				
Season	Club	Lea	GP	G	A	TP	PIM	GP	G	A	TP	PIM
1990-91	IFK Munkfors	Swede-3	3	0	3	3	....	....	....	....	....	....
1991-92	IFK Munkfors	Swede-3	26	6	10	16	18	....	....	....	....	....
1992-93	IFK Munkfors	Swede-3	36	8	8	16	20	....	....	....	....	....
1993-94	Sunne IK	Swede-3	32	8	6	14	16	....	....	....	....	....
1994-95	IFK Munkfors	Swede-3	27	13	9	22	44	....	....	....	....	....
1995-96	IFK Munkfors	Swede-3	30	20	11	31	32	....	....	....	....	....
1996-97	IFK Munkfors	Swede-3	32	28	10	38	50	....	....	....	....	....
1997-98	Farjestads BK	Sweden	45	29	15	44	22	12	*9	2	11	8
1998-99	Farjestads BK	Sweden	48	18	15	33	28	4	0	1	1	4
99-2000	Farjestads BK	Sweden	48	13	9	22	26	7	1	1	2	18

PRESTON, Tim (PREH-stohn, TIHM) BUF.

Left wing. Shoots left. 6'1", 190 lbs. Born, Vancouver, B.C., June 30, 1981.
(Buffalo's 5th choice, 73rd overall, in 1999 Entry Draft).

			Regular Season					Playoffs				
Season	Club	Lea	GP	G	A	TP	PIM	GP	G	A	TP	PIM
1996-97	Langley Lions	BCAHA	75	80	105	185	75	....	....	....	....	....
1997-98	Seattle T-Birds	WHL	55	11	5	16	49	5	0	0	0	0
1998-99	Seattle T-Birds	WHL	60	12	15	27	98	11	0	1	1	11
99-2000	Seattle T-Birds	WHL	68	16	17	33	62	7	2	2	4	4

PROCHAZKA, Libor (proh-HAHZ-kah, lih-BOHR)

Defense. Shoots right. 6', 185 lbs. Born, Vlasim, Czech., April 25, 1974.
(St. Louis' 8th choice, 245th overall, in 1993 Entry Draft).

			Regular Season					Playoffs				
Season	Club	Lea	GP	G	A	TP	PIM	GP	G	A	TP	PIM
1991-92	Poldi Kladno	Czech.	7	0	0	0	0	....	....	....	....	....
1992-93	Poldi Kladno	Czech.	34	2	2	4	....	....	....	....	....	....
1993-94	Poldi Kladno	Cze-Rep	41	4	7	11	....	8	0	3	3	....
1994-95	Poldi Kladno	Cze-Rep	40	4	16	20	81	11	2	1	3	14
1995-96	Poldi Kladno	Cze-Rep	38	6	10	16	....	8	2	1	3	....
1996-97	Poldi Kladno	Cze-Rep	49	4	15	19	108	3	0	0	0	4
1997-98	AIK Solna	Sweden	43	3	4	7	92	....	....	....	....	....
	Czech-Republic	Olympics	1	0	0	0	0	....	....	....	....	....
1998-99	HC Trinec	Cze-Rep	51	9	28	37	112	7	1	5	6	....
99-2000	Worcester	AHL	36	2	6	8	32	3	0	0	0	2

PROSOFSKY, Garrett (proh-SAWF-skee, GAHR-reht) PHI.

Center. Shoots left. 5'11", 180 lbs. Born, Saskatoon, Sask., May 19, 1980.
(Philadelphia's 6th choice, 139th overall, in 1998 Entry Draft).

			Regular Season					Playoffs				
Season	Club	Lea	GP	G	A	TP	PIM	GP	G	A	TP	PIM
1995-96	Saskatoon AAA	SAHA	42	30	51	81	35	....	....	....	....	....
	Saskatoon Blades	WHL	4	0	0	0	0	....	....	....	....	....
1996-97	Saskatoon Blades	WHL	66	20	45	65	67	....	....	....	....	....
1997-98	Saskatoon Blades	WHL	71	28	42	70	76	6	6	3	9	4
1998-99	Saskatoon Blades	WHL	25	8	7	15	21	....	....	....	....	....
	Prince Albert	WHL	24	15	16	31	21	14	7	8	15	20
99-2000	Prince Albert	WHL	70	26	38	64	58	6	1	2	3	10

PROTSENKO, Boris (proht-SEHN-koh, BOH-rihs) PIT.

Right wing. Shoots right. 5'11", 192 lbs. Born, Kiev, USSR, August 21, 1978.
(Pittsburgh's 4th choice, 77th overall, in 1996 Entry Draft).

			Regular Season					Playoffs				
Season	Club	Lea	GP	G	A	TP	PIM	GP	G	A	TP	PIM
1994-95	Fernie Riders	RMJHL	47	27	25	52	199	....	....	....	....	....
1995-96	Calgary Hitmen	WHL	71	46	29	75	68	....	....	....	....	....
1996-97	Calgary Hitmen	WHL	67	35	32	67	136	....	....	....	....	....
1997-98	Calgary Hitmen	WHL	70	40	47	87	124	18	6	8	14	30
1998-99	Syracuse Crunch	AHL	65	24	24	48	84	....	....	....	....	....
99-2000	Wilkes-Barre	AHL	64	15	21	36	41	....	....	....	....	....

PUDLICK, Michael L.A.

Defense. Shoots left. 6'3", 190 lbs. Born, Blaine, MN, February 24, 1978.

			Regular Season					Playoffs				
Season	Club	Lea	GP	G	A	TP	PIM	GP	G	A	TP	PIM
1995-96	Blaine High	Hi-School	25	9	30	39	....	....	....	....	....	....
1996-97	Twin Cities	USHL	49	10	19	29	93	5	0	2	2	4
1997-98	Twin Cities	USHL	50	3	14	17	138	....	....	....	....	....
1998-99	St. Cloud State	WCHA	37	13	12	25	74	....	....	....	....	....
99-2000	St. Cloud State	WCHA	40	8	22	30	65	....	....	....	....	....

WCHA First All-Star Team (2000) • NCAA West Second All-American Team (2000)

Signed as a free agent by **LA Kings**, April 5, 2000.

PYATT, Taylor (PIGH-at, TAY-lohr) NYI

Left wing. Shoots left. 6'4", 220 lbs. Born, Thunder Bay, Ont., August 19, 1981.
(NY Islanders' 2nd choice, 8th overall, in 1999 Entry Draft).

			Regular Season					Playoffs				
Season	Club	Lea	GP	G	A	TP	PIM	GP	G	A	TP	PIM
1996-97	Thunder Bay	TBAHA	60	52	61	113	72	....	....	....	....	....
1997-98	Sudbury Wolves	OHL	58	14	17	31	104	10	3	1	4	8
1998-99	Sudbury Wolves	OHL	68	37	38	75	95	4	0	4	4	6
99-2000	Sudbury Wolves	OHL	68	40	49	89	98	12	8	7	15	25

OHL First All-Star Team (2000)

RACHUNEK, Ivan (ra-KHOO-nuhk) **T.B.**

Right wing. Shoots left. 5'10", 172 lbs. Born, Gottwaldov, Czech., July 6, 1981.
(Tampa Bay's 8th choice, 187th overall, in 1999 Entry Draft).

			Regular Season					Playoffs				
Season	**Club**	**Lea**	**GP**	**G**	**A**	**TP**	**PIM**	**GP**	**G**	**A**	**TP**	**PIM**
1997-98	Barum Zlin-Jr.	Cze-Rep	48	15	25	40	172	....	....	....	....	....
1998-99	Barum Zlin-Jr.	Cze-Rep	40	37	22	59	70	....	....	....	....	....
	Barum Zlin	Cze-Rep	5	0	0	0	0	....	....	....	....	....
99-2000	Barum Zlin	Cze-Rep	5	0	1	1	2	....	....	....	....	....
	Windsor Spitfires	OHL	15	2	2	4	21	....	....	....	....	....

RADIVOJEVIC, Branko (ra-dih-VOI-uh-vihch, BRAN-koh) **COL.**

Right wing. Shoots right. 6'1", 200 lbs. Born, Piestany, Czech., November 24, 1980.
(Colorado's 3rd choice, 93rd overall, in 1999 Entry Draft).

			Regular Season					Playoffs				
Season	**Club**	**Lea**	**GP**	**G**	**A**	**TP**	**PIM**	**GP**	**G**	**A**	**TP**	**PIM**
1997-98	Dukla Trencin	Slovak-Jr.	52	30	31	61	50	....	....	....	....	....
	Dukla Trencin	Slovakia	1	0	0	0	2	....	....	....	....	....
1998-99	Belleville Bulls	OHL	68	20	38	58	61	21	7	17	24	18
99-2000	Belleville Bulls	OHL	59	23	49	72	86	16	5	8	13	32

RADULOV, Igor (rah-DOO-lahf) **CHI.**

Left wing. Shoots left. 6', 194 lbs. Born, Nizhny Tagil, USSR, August 23, 1982.
(Chicago's 4th choice, 74th overall, in 2000 Entry Draft).

			Regular Season					Playoffs				
Season	**Club**	**Lea**	**GP**	**G**	**A**	**TP**	**PIM**	**GP**	**G**	**A**	**TP**	**PIM**
1997-98	Torpedo Yaroslavl	Russia-2	5	0	2	2	4	....	....	....	....	....
1998-99	Torpedo Yaroslavl	Russia-3	21	2	3	5	4	....	....	....	....	....
99-2000	Torpedo Yaroslavl	Russia-3	31	17	16	33		....	....	....	....	....

RAJAMAKI, Erkki (righ-ya-MA-kee, UHR-kee) **T.B.**

Left wing. Shoots left. 6'2", 205 lbs. Born, Vantaa, Finland, October 30, 1978.
(Tampa Bay's 9th choice, 216th overall, in 1999 Entry Draft).

			Regular Season					Playoffs				
Season	**Club**	**Lea**	**GP**	**G**	**A**	**TP**	**PIM**	**GP**	**G**	**A**	**TP**	**PIM**
1996-97	Kiekko-Vantaa-2	Finn-Jr.	33	14	19	33	32	....	....	....	....	....
1997-98	HIFK Helsinki	Finn-Jr.	14	1	2	3	2	....	....	....	....	....
	Kiekko-Vantaa-2	Finn-Jr.	....	....	....	....	....	10	3	0	3	2
1998-99	HIFK Helsinki-2	Finn-Jr.	14	2	2	4	8	....	....	....	....	....
	HIFK Helsinki	Finland	14	0	0	0	2	....	....	....	....	....
	HIFK Helsinki	Finn-Jr.	....	....	....	....	....	13	7	3	10	45
99-2000	Colgate University	ECAC	31	1	6	7	20	....	....	....	....	....

RAJAMAKI, Tommi (righ-YAH-ma-kee) **CBJ**

Defense. Shoots left. 6'2", 205 lbs. Born, Pori, Finland, February 29, 1976.
(Toronto's 6th choice, 178th overall, in 1994 Entry Draft).

			Regular Season					Playoffs				
Season	**Club**	**Lea**	**GP**	**G**	**A**	**TP**	**PIM**	**GP**	**G**	**A**	**TP**	**PIM**
1994-95	Assat-Pori	Finn-Jr.	29	11	17	28	30	....	....	....	....	....
	Assat-Pori	Finland	12	4	1	5	8	7	0	1	1	2
1995-96	Assat-Pori	Finland	45	5	2	7	26	3	0	0	0	6
1996-97	Assat-Pori	Finland	46	0	1	1	16	4	0	0	0	2
1997-98	TPS Turku	Finland	46	1	1	2	24	4	0	0	0	0
1998-99	TPS Turku	Finland	53	3	3	6	24	10	0	0	0	6
99-2000	TPS Turku	Finland	53	2	6	8	51	11	0	1	1	2
	TPS Turku	EuroHL	6	0	3	3	0	5	0	0	0	0

Selected by **Columbus** from **Toronto** in Expansion Draft, June 23, 2000.

RAJNOHA, Pavel (righ-NOH-kha, PAH-vehl)) **CGY.**

Defense. Shoots right. 6', 185 lbs. Born, Gottwaldov, Czech., February 23, 1974.
(Calgary's 8th choice, 150th overall, in 1992 Entry Draft).

			Regular Season					Playoffs				
Season	**Club**	**Lea**	**GP**	**G**	**A**	**TP**	**PIM**	**GP**	**G**	**A**	**TP**	**PIM**
1990-91	TJ Zlin	Czech.	6	0	0	0	4	....	....	....	....	....
1991-92	ZPS Zlin	Czech.	24	0	1	1	4	....	....	....	....	....
1992-93	ZPS Zlin	Czech.	26	2	1	3		....	....	....	....	....
1993-94	ZPS Zlin	Cze-Rep	28	2	1	3	0	3	0	4	4	....
1994-95	ZPS Zlin	Cze-Rep	29	0	6	6	22	....	....	....	....	....
1995-96	Dukla Jihlava	Cze-Rep	38	0	2	2	....	8	0	0	0	....
1996-97	ZPS Zlin	Cze-Rep	32	6	5	11	4	....	....	....	....	....
1997-98	ZPS Zlin	Cze-Rep	15	1	2	3	12	....	....	....	....	....
1998-99	Dukla Jihlava	Cze-Rep	18	1	3	4	8	....	....	....	....	....

RALPH, Brad (RALF, BRAD) **PHX.**

Left wing. Shoots left. 6'2", 198 lbs. Born, Ottawa, Ont., October 17, 1980.
(Phoenix's 3rd choice, 53rd overall, in 1999 Entry Draft).

			Regular Season					Playoffs				
Season	**Club**	**Lea**	**GP**	**G**	**A**	**TP**	**PIM**	**GP**	**G**	**A**	**TP**	**PIM**
1996-97	Kanata Valley	OJHL	44	13	13	26	63	....	....	....	....	....
1997-98	Oshawa Generals	OHL	59	20	17	37	45	7	2	1	3	8
1998-99	Oshawa Generals	OHL	67	31	44	75	93	14	7	7	14	10
99-2000	Oshawa Generals	OHL	56	28	35	63	68	5	1	1	2	4

RAZIN, Gennady (RAH-zihn, gen-AH-dee) **MTL.**

Defense. Shoots left. 6'4", 200 lbs. Born, Kharkov, USSR, February 3, 1978.
(Montreal's 6th choice, 122nd overall, in 1997 Entry Draft).

			Regular Season					Playoffs				
Season	**Club**	**Lea**	**GP**	**G**	**A**	**TP**	**PIM**	**GP**	**G**	**A**	**TP**	**PIM**
1995-96	St. Albert Saints	AJHL	52	3	16	19	113	18	1	10	11	8
1996-97	Kamloops Blazers	WHL	63	7	19	26	56	3	0	0	0	4
1997-98	Kamloops Blazers	WHL	70	2	11	13	64	7	0	0	0	4
1998-99	Fredericton	AHL	48	0	3	3	16	4	0	0	0	2
99-2000	Quebec Citadelles	AHL	66	2	9	11	29	3	0	0	0	0

READY, Ryan (REH-dee, RIGH-yan) **VAN.**

Left wing. Shoots left. 6'2", 195 lbs. Born, Peterborough, Ont., November 7, 1978.
(Calgary's 8th choice, 100th overall, in 1997 Entry Draft).

			Regular Season					Playoffs				
Season	**Club**	**Lea**	**GP**	**G**	**A**	**TP**	**PIM**	**GP**	**G**	**A**	**TP**	**PIM**
1994-95	Peterborough B's	OJHL	48	20	33	53	65	....	....	....	....	....
1995-96	Belleville Bulls	OHL	63	5	13	18	54	10	0	2	2	2
1996-97	Belleville Bulls	OHL	66	23	24	47	102	6	1	3	4	4
1997-98	Belleville Bulls	OHL	66	33	39	72	80	10	5	2	7	12
1998-99	Belleville Bulls	OHL	63	33	59	92	73	21	10	28	38	22
99-2000	Syracuse Crunch	AHL	70	4	12	16	59	2	0	0	0	0

OHL First All-Star Team (1999)

Signed as a free agent by **Vancouver**, June 16, 1999.

REED, Josh (REED, JAWSH) **VAN.**

Defense. Shoots right. 6'2", 204 lbs. Born, Vernon, B.C., May 21, 1979.
(Vancouver's 5th choice, 172nd overall, in 1999 Entry Draft).

			Regular Season					Playoffs				
Season	**Club**	**Lea**	**GP**	**G**	**A**	**TP**	**PIM**	**GP**	**G**	**A**	**TP**	**PIM**
1994-95	Vernon Leafs	BCAHA	56	13	41	54	136	....	....	....	....	....
1995-96	Vernon Vikings	BCAHA	50	9	43	52	150	....	....	....	....	....
1996-97	Cowichan Valley	BCJHL	42	3	3	6	61	....	....	....	....	....
1997-98	Cowichan Valley	BCJHL	50	5	20	25	115	....	....	....	....	....
1998-99	Vernon Vipers	BCJHL	54	16	38	54	110	....	....	....	....	....
99-2000	U. of Mass-Lowell	H-East	30	2	10	12	24	....	....	....	....	....

REHNBERG, Henrik (REHN-buhrg) **N.J.**

Defense. Shoots left. 6'2", 195 lbs. Born, Grava, Sweden, July 20, 1977.
(New Jersey's 6th choice, 96th overall, in 1995 Entry Draft).

			Regular Season					Playoffs				
Season	**Club**	**Lea**	**GP**	**G**	**A**	**TP**	**PIM**	**GP**	**G**	**A**	**TP**	**PIM**
1994-95	Farjestads BK	Swede-Jr.	24	1	2	3	62	....	....	....	....	....
1995-96	Farjestads BK	Swede-Jr.	21	1	4	5	38	....	....	....	....	....
	Farjestads BK	Sweden	4	0	0	0	0	....	....	....	....	....
1996-97	Farjestads BK	Sweden	42	2	3	5	38	14	1	1	2	16
1997-98	Farjestads BK	Sweden	32	0	1	1	24	10	0	0	0	12
	Farjestads BK	EuroHL	6	0	0	0	39	....	....	....	....	....
1998-99	Albany River Rats	AHL	55	1	4	5	49	2	0	0	0	0
99-2000	Farjestads BK	Sweden	46	1	3	4	66	7	0	1	1	18

REICH, Jeremy (RIGHK, JAIR-eh-MEE) **CBJ**

Center. Shoots left. 6'1", 190 lbs. Born, Craik, Sask., February 11, 1979.
(Chicago's 3rd choice, 39th overall, in 1997 Entry Draft).

			Regular Season					Playoffs				
Season	**Club**	**Lea**	**GP**	**G**	**A**	**TP**	**PIM**	**GP**	**G**	**A**	**TP**	**PIM**
1993-94	Pilote Butte	SAHA	80	70	65	135	120	....	....	....	....	....
1994-95	Saskatoon AAA	SMHL	35	13	20	33	81	....	....	....	....	....
1995-96	Seattle T-Birds	WHL	65	11	11	22	88	5	0	1	1	10
1996-97	Seattle T-Birds	WHL	62	19	31	50	134	15	2	5	7	36
1997-98	Seattle T-Birds	WHL	43	24	23	47	121	....	....	....	....	....
	Swift Current	WHL	22	8	8	16	47	12	5	6	11	37
1998-99	Swift Current	WHL	67	21	28	49	220	6	0	3	3	26
99-2000	Swift Current	WHL	72	33	58	91	167	12	2	10	12	19

Signed as a free agent by **Columbus**, May 17, 2000.

RENNETTE, Tyler (REHN-neht, TIGH-luhr) **ST.L.**

Center. Shoots right. 6'1", 175 lbs. Born, North Bay, Ont., April 16, 1979.
(St. Louis' 1st choice, 40th overall, in 1997 Entry Draft).

			Regular Season					Playoffs				
Season	**Club**	**Lea**	**GP**	**G**	**A**	**TP**	**PIM**	**GP**	**G**	**A**	**TP**	**PIM**
1994-95	North Bay	NOHA	52	24	42	66	72	....	....	....	....	....
1995-96	Waterloo Hawks	OJHL-B	45	27	47	74	64	....	....	....	....	....
1996-97	North Bay	OHL	63	24	34	58	42	....	....	....	....	....
1997-98	North Bay	OHL	31	17	14	31	37	....	....	....	....	....
	Erie Otters	OHL	24	16	17	33	20	6	3	3	6	2
1998-99	Erie Otters	OHL	61	30	37	67	40	5	6	1	7	8
99-2000	Worcester	AHL	55	8	17	25	16	7	2	3	5	4

REYNOLDS, Peter (REH-nolds, PEE-tuhr) **TOR.**

Defense. Shoots right. 6'3", 195 lbs. Born, Waterloo, Ont., April 27, 1981.
(Toronto's 2nd choice, 60th overall, in 1999 Entry Draft).

			Regular Season					Playoffs				
Season	**Club**	**Lea**	**GP**	**G**	**A**	**TP**	**PIM**	**GP**	**G**	**A**	**TP**	**PIM**
1996-97	Caledon Canucks	OJHL	45	1	10	11	69	....	....	....	....	....
1997-98	London Knights	OHL	55	0	8	8	30	16	0	0	0	10
1998-99	London Knights	OHL	59	2	25	27	55	23	2	3	5	24
99-2000	North Bay	OHL	61	3	29	32	53	6	1	3	4	10

RIAZANTSEV, Alexander (ree-ZAHNT-sehv, al-ehx-AN-duhr) **COL.**

Defense. Shoots right. 6', 210 lbs. Born, Moscow, USSR, March 15, 1980.
(Colorado's 10th choice, 167th overall, in 1998 Entry Draft).

			Regular Season					Playoffs				
Season	**Club**	**Lea**	**GP**	**G**	**A**	**TP**	**PIM**	**GP**	**G**	**A**	**TP**	**PIM**
1996-97	Spartak Moscow	Russia	20	1	2	3	4	....	....	....	....	....
	Spartak Moscow	Russia-3	18	0	0	0	8	....	....	....	....	....
1997-98	Spartak Moscow-2	Russia-3	31	3	8	11	26	....	....	....	....	....
	Victoriaville Tigres	QMJHL	22	6	9	15	14	4	0	0	0	0
1998-99	Victoriaville Tigres	QMJHL	64	17	40	57	57	6	0	3	3	10
	Hershey Bears	AHL	2	0	0	0	0	....	....	....	....	....
99-2000	Victoriaville Tigres	QMJHL	48	17	45	62	45	6	2	5	7	20
	Hershey Bears	AHL	2	0	1	1	2	6	1	1	2	0

RICHARDS, Brad (RIH-chahrds, BRAD) **T.B.**

Left wing. Shoots left. 6'1", 187 lbs. Born, Montague, P.E.I., May 2, 1980.
(Tampa Bay's 2nd choice, 64th overall, in 1998 Entry Draft).

			Regular Season					Playoffs				
Season	**Club**	**Lea**	**GP**	**G**	**A**	**TP**	**PIM**	**GP**	**G**	**A**	**TP**	**PIM**
1996-97	Notre Dame	SJHL	63	39	48	87	73	....	....	....	....	....
1997-98	Rimouski Oceanic	QMJHL	68	33	82	115	44	19	8	24	32	2
1998-99	Rimouski Oceanic	QMJHL	59	39	92	131	55	11	9	12	21	6
99-2000	Rimouski Oceanic	QMJHL	63	*71	*115	*186	69	12	13	*24	*37	16

QMJHL First All-Star Team (2000) • Canadian Major Junior First All-Star Team (2000) • Canadian Major Junior Player of the Year (2000) • Memorial Cup All-Star Team (2000) • Won Stafford Smythe Memorial Trophy (Memorial Cup Tournament MVP) (2000)

RICHTER, Martin **NYR**

Defense. Shoots right. 6'1", 196 lbs. Born, Prostejov, Czech., December 6, 1977.
(NY Rangers' 9th choice, 269th overall, in 2000 Entry Draft).

			Regular Season					Playoffs				
Season	**Club**	**Lea**	**GP**	**G**	**A**	**TP**	**PIM**	**GP**	**G**	**A**	**TP**	**PIM**
1997-98	HC Olomouc	Cze-Rep	17	1	0	1	26	....	....	....	....	....
1998-99	HC Karlovy Vary	Cze-Rep	51	3	6	9	44	....	....	....	....	....
99-2000	SaiPa	Finland	26	1	3	4	54	....	....	....	....	....

RIDDLE, Troy (RIH-duhl) **ST.L.**

Center. Shoots right. 6', 172 lbs. Born, Minneapolis, MN, August 24, 1981.
(St. Louis' 5th choice, 129th overall, in 2000 Entry Draft).

			Regular Season					Playoffs				
Season	**Club**	**Lea**	**GP**	**G**	**A**	**TP**	**PIM**	**GP**	**G**	**A**	**TP**	**PIM**
99-2000	Des Moines	USHL	53	36	30	66	95	8	2	2	4	31

RIESEN, Michel — (REE-sehn, MEE-shehl) **EDM.**

Right wing. Shoots right. 6'2", 190 lbs. Born, Oberbalm, Switzerland, April 11, 1979.
(Edmonton's 1st choice, 14th overall, in 1997 Entry Draft).

			Regular Season					Playoffs				
Season	Club	Lea	GP	G	A	TP	PIM	GP	G	A	TP	PIM
1994-95	EHC Biel	Switz.	12	0	2	2	0	6	2	0	2	0
1995-96	EHC Biel	Switz-2	34	9	6	15	2	3	1	0	1	0
1996-97	EHC Biel	Switz-2	38	16	16	32	49	....	....	....	....	....
1997-98	HC Davos	Switz.	32	16	9	25	8	18	5	5	10	4
1998-99	Hamilton Bulldogs	AHL	60	6	17	23	6	3	0	0	0	0
99-2000	Hamilton Bulldogs	AHL	73	29	31	60	20	10	3	5	8	4

RITA, Jani — (REETA, YA-nee) **EDM.**

Right wing. Shoots right. 6'1", 206 lbs. Born, Helsinki, Finland, July 25, 1981.
(Edmonton's 1st choice, 13th overall, in 1999 Entry Draft).

			Regular Season					Playoffs				
Season	Club	Lea	GP	G	A	TP	PIM	GP	G	A	TP	PIM
1994-95	Jokerit Helsinki-C	Finn-Jr.	7	3	0	3	0	6	1	0	1	0
1995-96	Jokerit Helsinki-C	Finn-Jr.	12	10	3	13	2	....	....	....	....	....
	Jokerit Helsinki-B	Finn-Jr.	5	0	0	0	0	....	....	....	....	....
1997-98	Jokerit Helsinki	Finn-Jr.	36	15	9	24	2	8	4	1	5	0
	Jokerit Helsinki	Finland	....	....	....	....	....	1	0	0	0	0
1998-99	Jokerit Helsinki	Finn-Jr.	20	9	13	22	8	....	....	....	....	....
	Jokerit Helsinki	Finland	41	3	2	5	39	....	....	....	....	....
99-2000	Jokerit Helsinki	Finland	49	6	3	9	10	11	1	0	1	0

RITCHLIN, Sean — (RIHCH-lihn, SHAWN) **ATL.**

Right wing. Shoots right. 6', 200 lbs. Born, Rochester, NY, June 14, 1977.
(New Jersey's 10th choice, 145th overall, in 1996 Entry Draft).

			Regular Season					Playoffs				
Season	Club	Lea	GP	G	A	TP	PIM	GP	G	A	TP	PIM
1994-95	Hotchkiss Prep	Hi-School	25	*28	*31	*59	26	....	....	....	....	....
1995-96	U. of Michigan	CCHA	27	7	7	14	24	....	....	....	....	....
1996-97	U. of Michigan	CCHA	38	10	10	20	48	....	....	....	....	....
1997-98	U. of Michigan	CCHA	27	3	3	6	29	1	0	0	0	2
1998-99	U. of Michigan	CCHA	42	12	5	17	55	4	2	2	4	8
99-2000	Greenville	ECHL	39	13	13	26	19	15	8	4	12	18
	Orlando	IHL	19	0	0	0	6	....	....	....	....	....

Signed as a free agent by **Atlanta**, August 12, 1999.

RIVA, Danny — (REE-vuh, DAN-nee) **NSH.**

Center. Shoots right. 6', 190 lbs. Born, Framingham, MA, September 17, 1975.

			Regular Season					Playoffs				
Season	Club	Lea	GP	G	A	TP	PIM	GP	G	A	TP	PIM
1995-96	RPI Engineers	ECAC	35	3	7	10	30	....	....	....	....	....
1996-97	RPI Engineers	ECAC	36	12	14	26	30	....	....	....	....	....
1997-98	RPI Engineers	ECAC	35	10	18	28	16	....	....	....	....	....
1998-99	RPI Engineers	ECAC	36	*22	*35	*57	35	....	....	....	....	....
	Milwaukee	IHL	8	0	2	2	4	1	0	1	1	0
99-2000	Milwaukee	IHL	67	8	12	20	18	3	0	0	0	2

ECAC First All-Star Team (1999)

Signed as a free agent by **Nashville**, May 4, 1999.

ROBINSON, Darcy — (RAW-bihn-suhn) **PIT.**

Defense. Shoots right. 6'3", 229 lbs. Born, Kamloops, B.C., May 3, 1981.
(Pittsburgh's 10th choice, 233rd overall, in 1999 Entry Draft).

			Regular Season					Playoffs				
Season	Club	Lea	GP	G	A	TP	PIM	GP	G	A	TP	PIM
1997-98	Saskatoon Blades	WHL	62	1	2	3	84	4	0	0	0	2
1998-99	Saskatoon Blades	WHL	48	3	6	9	86	....	....	....	....	....
99-2000	Saskatoon Blades	WHL	59	5	9	14	91	10	1	3	4	13

ROBSON, Blake — (ROHB-suhn) **ATL.**

Center. Shoots left. 6', 190 lbs. Born, Calgary, Alta., March 31, 1982.
(Atlanta's 5th choice, 108th overall, in 2000 Entry Draft).

			Regular Season					Playoffs				
Season	Club	Lea	GP	G	A	TP	PIM	GP	G	A	TP	PIM
1998-99	Portland	WHL	61	14	18	32	54	4	0	0	0	4
99-2000	Portland	WHL	70	20	27	47	96	....	....	....	....	....

ROCHEFORT, Richard — (ROHSH-fohr, RIH-chahrd) **N.J.**

Center. Shoots right. 5'10", 195 lbs. Born, North Bay, Ont., January 7, 1977.
(New Jersey's 9th choice, 174th overall, in 1995 Entry Draft).

			Regular Season					Playoffs				
Season	Club	Lea	GP	G	A	TP	PIM	GP	G	A	TP	PIM
1993-94	Waterloo Hawks	OJHL	45	21	32	53	41	....	....	....	....	....
1994-95	Sudbury Wolves	OHL	57	21	44	65	26	13	3	7	10	6
1995-96	Sudbury Wolves	OHL	56	25	40	65	38	....	....	....	....	....
1996-97	Sudbury Wolves	OHL	28	18	24	42	40	....	....	....	....	....
	Sarnia Sting	OHL	18	5	23	28	23	12	3	9	12	8
1997-98	Albany River Rats	AHL	59	7	14	21	16	13	1	0	1	4
1998-99	Albany River Rats	AHL	70	16	10	26	26	5	1	0	1	0
99-2000	Albany River Rats	AHL	55	12	12	24	22	5	0	0	0	0

ROED, Peter — (ROHD, PEE-tuhr)

Center. Shoots left. 5'11", 190 lbs. Born, St. Paul, MN, November 15, 1976.
(San Jose's 2nd choice, 38th overall, in 1995 Entry Draft).

			Regular Season					Playoffs				
Season	Club	Lea	GP	G	A	TP	PIM	GP	G	A	TP	PIM
1994-95	White Bear Lake	Hi-School	28	20	39	59	22	....	....	....	....	....
1995-96	Prince George	WHL	66	18	19	37	36	....	....	....	....	....
1996-97	Prince George	WHL	51	21	16	37	8	14	5	2	7	9
	Louisville	ECHL	7	1	0	1	4	....	....	....	....	....
1997-98	Kentucky	AHL	67	6	7	13	44	....	....	....	....	....
	Louisville	ECHL	4	0	2	2	10	....	....	....	....	....
1998-99	Richmond	ECHL	60	26	24	50	68	18	6	10	16	14
99-2000	Kentucky	AHL	75	13	19	32	54	9	3	2	5	2

ROHLOFF, Todd — (ROH-lawf, TAWD) **WSH.**

Defense. Shoots left. 6'3", 213 lbs. Born, Grand Rapids, IL, January 16, 1974.

			Regular Season					Playoffs				
Season	Club	Lea	GP	G	A	TP	PIM	GP	G	A	TP	PIM
1993-94	St. Paul Vulcans	USHL	47	4	22	26	....	....	....	....	....	....
1994-95	U. of Miami-Ohio	CCHA	38	1	6	7	22	....	....	....	....	....
1995-96	U. of Miami-Ohio	CCHA	23	2	4	6	24	....	....	....	....	....
1996-97	U. of Miami-Ohio	CCHA	38	2	12	14	48	....	....	....	....	....
1997-98	U. of Miami-Ohio	CCHA	17	2	5	7	38	....	....	....	....	....
	Indianapolis Ice	IHL	5	0	1	1	6	1	0	0	0	0
1998-99	Portland Pirates	AHL	58	1	6	7	58	....	....	....	....	....
	Indianapolis Ice	IHL	12	2	0	2	8	5	1	1	2	6
99-2000	Cleveland	IHL	77	1	13	14	88	9	0	0	0	6

Signed as a free agent by **Chicago**, March 24, 1998. Signed as a free agent by **Washington**, July 21, 2000.

RONNQVIST, Jonas — (RAWN-kvihst, YOH-nuhs) **ANA.**

Right wing. Shoots right. 6'1", 200 lbs. Born, Kalix, Sweden, August 22, 1973.
(Anaheim's 3rd choice, 98th overall, in 2000 Entry Draft).

			Regular Season					Playoffs				
Season	Club	Lea	GP	G	A	TP	PIM	GP	G	A	TP	PIM
1992-93	Bodens IK	Swede-2	35	10	4	14	16	....	....	....	....	....
1993-94	Bodens IK	Swede-2	34	15	10	25	24	9	1	1	2	6
1994-95	Bodens IK	Swede-2	35	10	5	15	20	8	1	0	1	0
1995-96	Bodens IK	Swede-2	26	12	10	22	26	....	....	....	....	....
1996-97	Bodens IK	Swede-2	32	15	14	29	48	....	....	....	....	....
1997-98	Lulea HF	Sweden	40	6	8	14	18	3	0	0	0	2
1998-99	Lulea HF	Sweden	41	5	8	13	30	3	0	2	2	29
99-2000	Lulea HF	Sweden	49	15	24	39	42	8	3	3	6	4

ROSSITER, Kyle — (RAWS-ih-tuhr, KIGHL) **FLA.**

Defense. Shoots left. 6'3", 217 lbs. Born, Edmonton, Alta., June 9, 1980.
(Florida's 1st choice, 30th overall, in 1998 Entry Draft).

			Regular Season					Playoffs				
Season	Club	Lea	GP	G	A	TP	PIM	GP	G	A	TP	PIM
1995-96	Edmonton South	AMHL	34	5	19	24	116	....	....	....	....	....
1996-97	Spokane Chiefs	WHL	50	0	2	2	65	9	0	0	0	6
1997-98	Spokane Chiefs	WHL	61	6	16	22	190	15	0	3	3	28
1998-99	Spokane Chiefs	WHL	71	4	17	21	206	....	....	....	....	....
99-2000	Spokane Chiefs	WHL	63	11	22	33	155	15	1	4	5	25

Canadian Major Junior Scholastic Player of the Year (1998)

ROSTOV, Sergei — (roh-STOHV, SAIR-gay) **TOR.**

Defense. Shoots left. 6'3", 194 lbs. Born, Murmansk, USSR, March 29, 1980.
(Toronto's 10th choice, 236th overall, in 1998 Entry Draft).

			Regular Season					Playoffs				
Season	Club	Lea	GP	G	A	TP	PIM	GP	G	A	TP	PIM
1995-96	Torpedo Yaroslavl	Russia-2	80	1	3	4	60	....	....	....	....	....
1996-97	CSKA Moscow	Russia-Jr.	45	8	10	18	70	....	....	....	....	....
	Torpedo Yaroslavl	Russia-3	8	0	0	0	0	....	....	....	....	....
1997-98	Dynamo Moscow	Russia-2	32	1	1	2	51	....	....	....	....	....
1998-99	HC Tverskoi Tver	Russia-2	11	3	1	4	8	....	....	....	....	....
99-2000	STATISTICS NOT AVAILABLE											

ROURKE, Allan — (RAWRK, AL-lan) **TOR.**

Defense. Shoots left. 6'1", 214 lbs. Born, Mississauga, Ont., March 6, 1980.
(Toronto's 6th choice, 154th overall, in 1998 Entry Draft).

			Regular Season					Playoffs				
Season	Club	Lea	GP	G	A	TP	PIM	GP	G	A	TP	PIM
1995-96	Mississauga Reps	MTHL	38	15	25	40	173	....	....	....	....	....
1996-97	Kitchener	OHL	25	1	1	2	12	6	0	0	0	0
1997-98	Kitchener	OHL	48	5	17	22	59	6	1	1	2	6
1998-99	Kitchener	OHL	66	11	28	39	79	1	0	0	0	2
99-2000	Kitchener	OHL	67	31	43	74	57	5	0	6	6	13

OHL Second All-Star Team (2000)

ROY, Jimmy — (ROI, JIHM-mee)

Center. Shoots right. 5'11", 170 lbs. Born, Sioux Lookout, Ont., September 22, 1975.
(Dallas' 7th choice, 254th overall, in 1994 Entry Draft).

			Regular Season					Playoffs				
Season	Club	Lea	GP	G	A	TP	PIM	GP	G	A	TP	PIM
1993-94	Thunder Bay	USHL	46	21	33	54	101	....	....	....	....	....
1994-95	Michigan Tech	WCHA	38	5	11	16	62	....	....	....	....	....
1995-96	Michigan Tech	WCHA	42	17	17	34	84	....	....	....	....	....
1996-97	Canada	Nat-Team	55	10	17	27	82	....	....	....	....	....
1997-98	Manitoba Moose	IHL	61	8	10	18	133	3	0	0	0	6
1998-99	Manitoba Moose	IHL	78	10	16	26	185	5	0	1	1	6
99-2000	Manitoba Moose	IHL	74	12	9	21	187	1	0	0	0	16

ROY, Stephane — (WAH, STEH-fan)

Center. Shoots left. 5'11", 191 lbs. Born, Ste-Martine, Que., January 26, 1976.
(St. Louis' 1st choice, 68th overall, in 1994 Entry Draft).

			Regular Season					Playoffs				
Season	Club	Lea	GP	G	A	TP	PIM	GP	G	A	TP	PIM
1993-94	Val-d'Or Foreurs	QMJHL	72	25	28	53	116	....	....	....	....	....
1994-95	Val-d'Or Foreurs	QMJHL	68	19	52	71	113	....	....	....	....	....
1995-96	Val-d'Or Foreurs	QMJHL	62	43	72	115	89	13	9	15	24	10
	Worcester	AHL	1	0	0	0	2	....	....	....	....	....
1996-97	Worcester	AHL	66	24	23	47	57	5	2	0	2	4
1997-98	Worcester	AHL	77	21	27	48	95	10	4	4	8	10
1998-99	Worcester	AHL	64	16	28	44	41	4	0	2	2	2
99-2000	Quebec Citadelles	AHL	73	13	28	41	43	3	1	1	2	0

Canadian Major Junior Humanitarian Player of the Year (1994)

Signed as a free agent by **Quebec** (AHL), September 6, 1999.

ROZAKOV, Rail — (roh-zah-KAWF, righ-EEL) **CGY.**

Defense. Shoots left. 6'1", 198 lbs. Born, Murmansk, USSR, March 29, 1981.
(Calgary's 4th choice, 106th overall, in 1999 Entry Draft).

			Regular Season					Playoffs				
Season	Club	Lea	GP	G	A	TP	PIM	GP	G	A	TP	PIM
1997-98	Lada Togliatti-2	Russia-3	36	0	2	2	43	....	....	....	....	....
1998-99	Lada Togliatti-2	Russia-4	30	0	0	0	14	....	....	....	....	....
99-2000	STATISTICS NOT AVAILABLE											

RUDENKO, Konstantin (roo-DEHN-koh, KOHN-stan-tihn) PHI.

Left wing. Shoots right. 5'10", 163 lbs. Born, Ust-Kamenogorsk, USSR, July 23, 1981.
(Philadelphia's 3rd choice, 160th overall, in 1999 Entry Draft).

			Regular Season					Playoffs				
Season	Club	Lea	GP	G	A	TP	PIM	GP	G	A	TP	PIM
1997-98	Avangard Omsk	Russia-3	22	7	8	15	4	....	....	....	....	....
1998-99	HC Cherepovets	Russia-3	28	15	9	24	67	....	....	....	....	....
	HC Cherepovets	Russia-4	3	0	1	1	4	....	....	....	....	....
99-2000	St. Petersburg	Russia	19	1	1	2	10	1	0	0	0	0

RULLIER, Joe (ROO-yay, JOH) L.A.

Defense. Shoots right. 6'3", 200 lbs. Born, Montreal, Que., January 28, 1980.
(Los Angeles' 5th choice, 133rd overall, in 1998 Entry Draft).

			Regular Season					Playoffs				
Season	Club	Lea	GP	G	A	TP	PIM	GP	G	A	TP	PIM
1996-97	Rimouski Oceanic	QMJHL	23	0	3	3	87	4	0	0	0	11
1997-98	Rimouski Oceanic	QMJHL	55	1	10	11	176	16	1	4	5	34
1998-99	Rimouski Oceanic	QMJHL	54	7	32	39	202	11	2	3	5	26
99-2000	Rimouski Oceanic	QMJHL	49	3	32	35	161	14	1	8	9	34

RUPP, Michael (RUHP) N.J.

Left wing. Shoots left. 6'5", 230 lbs. Born, Cleveland, OH, January 13, 1980.
(New Jersey's 7th choice, 76th overall, in 2000 Entry Draft).

			Regular Season					Playoffs				
Season	Club	Lea	GP	G	A	TP	PIM	GP	G	A	TP	PIM
1996-97	St. Edwards	H.S	20	26	24	50	....	....	....	....	....	....
1997-98	Windsor Spitfires	OHL	38	9	8	17	60	....	....	....	....	....
	Erie Otters	OHL	26	7	3	10	57	7	3	1	4	6
1998-99	Erie Otters	OHL	63	22	25	47	102	5	0	2	2	25
99-2000	Erie Otters	OHL	58	32	21	53	134	13	5	5	10	22

• Re-entered NHL draft. Originally NY Islanders' 1st choice, 9th overall, in 1998 Entry Draft.

RUUTU, Mikko (ROO-too, MIH-koh) OTT.

Left wing. Shoots left. 6'4", 183 lbs. Born, Vantaa, Finland, September 10, 1978.
(Ottawa's 7th choice, 201st overall, in 1999 Entry Draft).

			Regular Season					Playoffs				
Season	Club	Lea	GP	G	A	TP	PIM	GP	G	A	TP	PIM
1997-98	HIFK Helsinki	Finn-Jr.	24	4	2	6	37	....	....	....	....	....
1998-99	HIFK Helsinki	Finn-Jr.	23	13	8	21	30	....	....	....	....	....
	HIFK Helsinki	Finland	31	3	1	4	12	4	0	0	0	2
99-2000	Clarkson	ECAC	33	5	6	11	26	....	....	....	....	....

RYAN, Michael (RIGH-yan, MIGH-kuhl) DAL.

Center. Shoots left. 6'1", 170 lbs. Born, Milton, MA, May 16, 1980.
(Dallas' 1st choice, 32nd overall, in 1999 Entry Draft).

			Regular Season					Playoffs				
Season	Club	Lea	GP	G	A	TP	PIM	GP	G	A	TP	PIM
1997-98	Boston College	Hi-School	23	22	14	36	28	....	....	....	....	....
1998-99	Boston College	Hi-School	21	20	24	44	22	....	....	....	....	....
99-2000	Northeastern	H-East	32	4	9	13	47	....	....	....	....	....

RYBIN, Maxim (ray-bihn, max-EEM) ANA.

Left wing. Shoots right. 5'9", 180 lbs. Born, Moscow, USSR, June 15, 1981.
(Anaheim's 4th choice, 141st overall, in 1999 Entry Draft).

			Regular Season					Playoffs				
Season	Club	Lea	GP	G	A	TP	PIM	GP	G	A	TP	PIM
1996-97	Spartak Moscow-2	Russia-3	5	0	0	0	4	....	....	....	....	....
	Spartak Moscow	Russia	6	0	0	0	0	....	....	....	....	....
1997-98	Spartak Moscow-2	Russia-3	25	13	5	18	26	....	....	....	....	....
	Spartak Moscow	Russia	5	0	0	0	2	....	....	....	....	....
1998-99	Spartak Moscow	Russia	41	13	8	21	52	....	....	....	....	....
	Spartak Moscow	Russia-Q	12	2	4	6	31	....	....	....	....	....
99-2000	Sarnia Sting	OHL	66	29	27	56	47	7	4	1	5	2

RYCROFT, Mark ST.L.

Right wing. Shoots right. 6', 197 lbs. Born, Nanaimo, B.C., July 12, 1978.

			Regular Season					Playoffs				
Season	Club	Lea	GP	G	A	TP	PIM	GP	G	A	TP	PIM
1997-98	U. of Denver	WCHA	35	15	17	32	28	....	....	....	....	....
1998-99	U. of Denver	WCHA	41	19	18	37	36	....	....	....	....	....
99-2000	U. of Denver	WCHA	41	17	17	34	87	....	....	....	....	....

WCHA All-Rookie Team (1998) • Signed as a free agent by **St. Louis**, May 15, 2000.

RYDER, Michael (RIGH-duhr, MIGH-kuhl) MTL.

Center. Shoots right. 6', 187 lbs. Born, St. John's, Nfld., March 31, 1980.
(Montreal's 9th choice, 216th overall, in 1998 Entry Draft).

			Regular Season					Playoffs				
Season	Club	Lea	GP	G	A	TP	PIM	GP	G	A	TP	PIM
1996-97	Bonavista Saints	NFAHA	23	31	17	48	....	....	....	....	....	....
1997-98	Hull Olympiques	QMJHL	69	34	28	62	41	10	4	2	6	4
1998-99	Hull Olympiques	QMJHL	69	44	43	87	65	23	*20	16	36	39
99-2000	Hull Olympiques	QMJHL	63	50	58	108	50	15	11	17	28	28

SACHL, Peter (SAH-khuhl) NSH.

Left wing. Shoots left. 6'2", 205 lbs. Born, Jindrichuv Hradec, Czech., December 2, 1977.
(NY Islanders' 6th choice, 128th overall, in 1996 Entry Draft).

			Regular Season					Playoffs				
Season	Club	Lea	GP	G	A	TP	PIM	GP	G	A	TP	PIM
1994-95	HC Budejovice-Jr.	Cze-Rep	40	6	8	14	....	....	....	....	....	....
1995-96	HC Budejovice-Jr.	Cze-Rep	39	19	17	36	....	....	....	....	....	....
	HC Budejovice	Cze-Rep	....	....	....	....	....	2	0	0	0	....
1996-97	HC Budejovice	Cze-Rep	2	0	0	0	0	....	....	....	....	....
	Tri-City Americans	WHL	63	13	24	37	32	....	....	....	....	....
1997-98	HC Budejovice	Cze-Rep	20	1	3	4	4	....	....	....	....	....
1998-99	HC Budejovice	Cze-Rep	4	0	1	1	2	....	....	....	....	....
99-2000	Tacoma Sabercats	WCHL	1	0	0	0	0	....	....	....	....	....
	Asheville Smoke	UHL	3	0	1	1	4	....	....	....	....	....
	Fort Wayne	UHL	55	30	24	54	28	10	4	7	11	8

Traded to **Nashville** by **NY Islanders** for Nashville's 9th round choice (Tomi Pettinen) in 2000 Entry Draft, March 14, 2000.

SAFRONOV, Kirill (sah-FRAW-nawf, kih-RIHL) PHX.

Defense. Shoots left. 6'2", 209 lbs. Born, Leningrad, USSR, February 26, 1981.
(Phoenix's 2nd choice, 19th overall, in 1999 Entry Draft).

			Regular Season					Playoffs				
Season	Club	Lea	GP	G	A	TP	PIM	GP	G	A	TP	PIM
1996-97	St. Petersburg-2	Russia-3	9	0	0	0	6	....	....	....	....	....
	St. Petersburg	Russia	1	0	0	0	0	....	....	....	....	....
1997-98	St. Petersburg-2	Russia-3	34	4	3	7	36	....	....	....	....	....
	St. Petersburg	Russia	9	0	1	1	4	1	0	0	0	0
1998-99	St. Petersburg-2	Russia-4	4	2	1	3	2	....	....	....	....	....
	St. Petersburg	Russia	35	1	1	2	26	....	....	....	....	....
	St. Petersburg	Russia-Q	10	0	2	2	6	....	....	....	....	....
99-2000	Quebec Remparts	QMJHL	55	11	32	43	95	11	2	4	6	14

SAINOMAA, Teemu (SIGH-noh-muh, TEE-moo) OTT.

Left wing. Shoots left. 6'3", 202 lbs. Born, Helsinki, Finland, May 15, 1981.
(Ottawa's 3rd choice, 62nd overall, in 1999 Entry Draft).

			Regular Season					Playoffs				
Season	Club	Lea	GP	G	A	TP	PIM	GP	G	A	TP	PIM
1997-98	Jokerit Helsinki-B	Finn-Jr.	12	3	5	8	8	3	1	1	2	6
1998-99	Jokerit Helsinki	Finn-Jr.	11	4	5	9	0	....	....	....	....	....
99-2000	Jokerit Helsinki	Finn-Jr.	30	6	7	13	59	11	6	2	8	20
	Jokerit Helsinki	Finland	6	0	0	0	0					

ST. CROIX, Chris (SAINT KWAH, KRIHS) CGY.

Defense. Shoots right. 6'1", 199 lbs. Born, Voorhees, NJ, May 2, 1979.
(Calgary's 7th choice, 92nd overall, in 1997 Entry Draft).

			Regular Season					Playoffs				
Season	Club	Lea	GP	G	A	TP	PIM	GP	G	A	TP	PIM
1993-94	Winnipeg Blues	MAHA	35	2	40	42	30	....	....	....	....	....
1994-95	Winnipeg Blues	MAHA	40	9	32	41	20	....	....	....	....	....
1995-96	Kamloops Blazers	WHL	61	4	5	9	29	13	0	2	2	4
1996-97	Kamloops Blazers	WHL	67	11	39	50	67	5	0	1	1	2
1997-98	Kamloops Blazers	WHL	46	3	13	16	51	7	1	1	2	6
1998-99	Kamloops Blazers	WHL	64	8	27	35	123	14	0	4	4	16
99-2000	Saint John Flames	AHL	75	5	16	21	51	3	0	1	1	2

ST. JACQUES, Bruno (SAINT ZHAWK, BREW-noh) PHI.

Defense. Shoots left. 6'2", 195 lbs. Born, Montreal, Que., August 22, 1980.
(Philadelphia's 12th choice, 253rd overall, in 1998 Entry Draft).

			Regular Season					Playoffs				
Season	Club	Lea	GP	G	A	TP	PIM	GP	G	A	TP	PIM
1997-98	Baie-Comeau	QMJHL	63	1	11	12	140	....	....	....	....	....
1998-99	Baie-Comeau	QMJHL	49	8	13	21	85	....	....	....	....	....
99-2000	Baie-Comeau	QMJHL	60	8	28	36	120	6	0	2	2	10
	Philadelphia	AHL	3	0	1	1	0	1	0	0	0	0

ST. PIERRE, Samuel T.B.

Right wing. Shoots right. 6'2", 201 lbs. Born, Laurierville, Que., June 28, 1979.
(Tampa Bay's 10th choice, 185th overall, in 1997 Entry Draft).

			Regular Season					Playoffs				
Season	Club	Lea	GP	G	A	TP	PIM	GP	G	A	TP	PIM
1996-97	Victoriaville Tigres	QMJHL	61	13	10	23	24	6	0	1	1	2
1997-98	Victoriaville Tigres	QMJHL	34	8	10	18	32	....	....	....	....	....
	Drummondville	QMJHL	35	28	15	43	16	....	....	....	....	....
1998-99	Drummondville	QMJHL	68	47	28	75	65	....	....	....	....	....
	Cleveland	IHL	13	2	5	7	4	....	....	....	....	....
99-2000	Detroit Vipers	IHL	47	11	4	15	25	....	....	....	....	....

SALMELAINEN, Tony (sal-meh-LIGH-nehn, TOH-nee) EDM.

Left wing. Shoots right. 5'9", 176 lbs. Born, Espoo, Finland, August 8, 1981.
(Edmonton's 3rd choice, 41st overall, in 1999 Entry Draft).

			Regular Season					Playoffs				
Season	Club	Lea	GP	G	A	TP	PIM	GP	G	A	TP	PIM
1997-98	Blues Espoo-B	Finn-Jr.	5	2	2	4	10	....	....	....	....	....
	HIFK Helsinki-B	Finn-Jr.	28	23	16	39	30	....	....	....	....	....
	HIFK Helsinki	Finn-Jr.	5	0	0	0	0	....	....	....	....	....
1998-99	HIFK Helsinki-2	Finn-Jr.	21	13	10	23	45	....	....	....	....	....
	HIFK Helsinki	Finn-Jr.	....	....	....	....	....	10	10	8	18	10
99-2000	HIFK Helsinki	Finn-Jr.	1	0	1	1	0	....	....	....	....	....
	HIFK Helsinki	Finland	1	1	0	1	0	....	....	....	....	....

SALVADOR, Bryce (SAL-vuh-dohr, BRIGHS) ST.L.

Defense. Shoots left. 6'2", 215 lbs. Born, Brandon, Man., February 11, 1976.
(Tampa Bay's 6th choice, 138th overall, in 1994 Entry Draft).

			Regular Season					Playoffs				
Season	Club	Lea	GP	G	A	TP	PIM	GP	G	A	TP	PIM
1992-93	Lethbridge	WHL	64	1	4	5	29	4	0	0	0	0
1993-94	Lethbridge	WHL	61	4	14	18	36	9	0	1	1	2
1994-95	Lethbridge	WHL	67	1	9	10	88	....	....	....	....	....
1995-96	Lethbridge	WHL	56	4	12	16	75	3	0	1	1	2
1996-97	Lethbridge	WHL	63	8	32	40	81	19	0	7	7	14
1997-98	Worcester	AHL	46	2	8	10	74	11	0	1	1	45
1998-99	Worcester	AHL	69	5	13	18	129	4	0	1	1	2
99-2000	Worcester	AHL	55	0	13	13	53	9	0	1	1	2

Signed as a free agent by **St. Louis**, December 16, 1996.

SAMUELSSON, Martin (SAM-yuhl-suhn) BOS.

Right wing. Shoots left. 6'2", 194 lbs. Born, Upplands Vasby, Sweden, January 25, 1982.
(Boston's 2nd choice, 27th overall, in 2000 Entry Draft).

			Regular Season					Playoffs				
Season	Club	Lea	GP	G	A	TP	PIM	GP	G	A	TP	PIM
1997-98	Hammarby IF	Swede-Jr.	20	13	12	25	....	....	....	....	....	....
	Hammarby IF	Swede-2	2	0	0	0	0	....	....	....	....	....
1998-99	MoDo Hockey	Swede-Jr.	31	18	13	31	10	....	....	....	....	....
99-2000	MoDo Hockey	Swede-Jr.	19	9	8	17	18	2	1	0	1	2

SAMUELSSON, Mikael (SAM-yuhl-suhn, MIH-kigh-ehl) S.J.

Right wing. Shoots left. 6'1", 195 lbs. Born, Mariefred, Sweden, December 23, 1976.
(San Jose's 7th choice, 145th overall, in 1998 Entry Draft).

			Regular Season					Playoffs				
Season	Club	Lea	GP	G	A	TP	PIM	GP	G	A	TP	PIM
1994-95	Sodertalje SK	Swede-Jr.	30	8	6	14	12	....	....	....	....	....
1995-96	Sodertalje SK	Swede-Jr.	22	13	12	25	20	....	....	....	....	....
	Sodertalje SK	Swede-2	18	5	1	6	0	4	0	0	0	0
1996-97	Sodertalje SK	Swede-Jr.	2	2	1	3	....	....	....	....	....	....
	Sodertalje SK	Sweden	29	3	2	5	10	....	....	....	....	....
1997-98	IK Nykopings	Swede-2	10	5	1	6	14	....	....	....	....	....
	Sodertalje SK	Swede-Q	10	3	1	4	16	....	....	....	....	....
	Sodertalje SK	Sweden	31	8	8	16	47	....	....	....	....	....
1998-99	Sodertalje SK	Swede-2	18	13	10	23	26	10	2	2	4	12
	Vastra Frolunda	Sweden	27	0	5	5	10	....	....	....	....	....
99-2000	Brynas IF	Sweden	40	4	3	7	76	11	7	2	9	6

SANDSTROM, Jan (SAND-struhm, YAN) ANA.

Defense. Shoots left. 6', 190 lbs. Born, Pitea, Sweden, January 24, 1978.
(Anaheim's 5th choice, 173rd overall, in 1999 Entry Draft).

			Regular Season					Playoffs				
Season	Club	Lea	GP	G	A	TP	PIM	GP	G	A	TP	PIM
1994-95	Pitea HC	Swede-2	12	1	0	1	4	....	....	....	....	....
1995-96	Pitea HC	Swede-2	29	1	11	12	18	....	....	....	....	....
1996-97	Pitea HC	Swede-2	28	3	4	7	28	....	....	....	....	....
1997-98	AIK Solna	Sweden	38	0	2	2	16	....	....	....	....	....
1998-99	AIK Solna	Sweden	47	2	7	9	18	....	....	....	....	....
99-2000	AIK Solna	Sweden	49	2	6	8	22	....	....	....	....	....

SANTALA, Tommi (SAHN-tah-luh) ATL.

Center. Shoots right. 6'2", 198 lbs. Born, Helsinki, Finland, June 27, 1979.
(Atlanta's 10th choice, 245th overall, in 1999 Entry Draft).

			Regular Season					Playoffs				
Season	Club	Lea	GP	G	A	TP	PIM	GP	G	A	TP	PIM
1995-96	Jokerit Helsinki	Finn-Jr.	25	8	4	12	12	6	1	2	3	4
1996-97	Jokerit Helsinki	Finn-Jr.	20	0	2	2	10	5	0	0	0	0
1997-98	Jokerit Helsinki	Finn-Jr.	36	10	28	38	48	8	0	1	1	4
1998-99	Jokerit Helsinki	Finn-Jr.	30	20	24	44	20	8	1	3	4	22
	Jokerit Helsinki	Finland	30	0	0	0	14	3	0	0	0	0
99-2000	Jokerit Helsinki	Finn-Jr.	5	6	4	10	4	....	....	....	....	....
	Jokerit Helsinki	Finland	14	0	1	1	0	....	....	....	....	....
	HPK Hameenlinna	Finn-Jr.	2	3	1	4	2	....	....	....	....	....
	HPK Hameenlinna	Finland	38	8	19	27	65	8	3	4	7	10

SAPOZHNIKOV, Vladimir (suh-POHZH-nih-kahf) FLA.

Defense. Shoots left. 6'3", 205 lbs. Born, Seversk, USSR, August 2, 1982.
(Florida's 1st choice, 58th overall, in 2000 Entry Draft).

			Regular Season					Playoffs				
Season	Club	Lea	GP	G	A	TP	PIM	GP	G	A	TP	PIM
1997-98	Sibir Novosibirsk	Russia-3	15	0	0	0	2	....	....	....	....	....
1998-99	HC Novokuznetsk	Russia-3	STATISTICS NOT AVAILABLE									
99-2000	HC Novokuznetsk	Russia-3	STATISTICS NOT AVAILABLE									

SARICH, Rod (SAHR-ihch, RAWD) FLA.

Defense. Shoots right. 6'3", 191 lbs. Born, Davidson, Sask., March 3, 1981.
(Florida's 6th choice, 109th overall, in 1999 Entry Draft).

			Regular Season					Playoffs				
Season	Club	Lea	GP	G	A	TP	PIM	GP	G	A	TP	PIM
1997-98	Saskatoon Blazers	SAHA	36	1	38	39	50	....	....	....	....	....
	Calgary Hitmen	WHL	9	0	1	1	2	17	0	0	0	0
1998-99	Calgary Hitmen	WHL	65	3	15	18	22	21	1	2	3	8
99-2000	Calgary Hitmen	WHL	70	3	11	14	76	13	0	2	2	8

SARNO, Peter (SAHR-noh, PEE-tuhr) EDM.

Center. Shoots left. 5'11", 185 lbs. Born, Toronto, Ont., July 26, 1979.
(Edmonton's 6th choice, 141st overall, in 1997 Entry Draft).

			Regular Season					Playoffs				
Season	Club	Lea	GP	G	A	TP	PIM	GP	G	A	TP	PIM
1995-96	North York	OJHL	52	39	57	96	27	....	....	....	....	....
1996-97	Windsor Spitfires	OHL	66	20	63	83	59	5	0	3	3	6
1997-98	Windsor Spitfires	OHL	64	33	88	121	18	....	....	....	....	....
	Hamilton Bulldogs	AHL	8	1	1	2	2	....	....	....	....	....
1998-99	Sarnia Sting	OHL	68	37	*93	*130	49	6	1	7	8	2
99-2000	Hamilton Bulldogs	AHL	67	10	36	46	31	....	....	....	....	....

SAUER, Kent (SAW-uhr, KEHNT) NSH.

Defense. Shoots right. 6'2", 230 lbs. Born, St. Cloud, MN, May 10, 1979.
(Nashville's 4th choice, 88th overall, in 1998 Entry Draft).

			Regular Season					Playoffs				
Season	Club	Lea	GP	G	A	TP	PIM	GP	G	A	TP	PIM
1996-97	St. Cloud-Apollo	Hi-School	23	14	15	29	20	....	....	....	....	....
1997-98	North Iowa	USHL	54	4	19	23	99	10	1	2	3	18
1998-99	Minnesota-Duluth	WCHA	38	1	3	4	50	....	....	....	....	....
99-2000	Portland	WHL	65	12	13	25	116	....	....	....	....	....
	Milwaukee	IHL	6	0	0	0	0	....	....	....	....	....

SAUER, Kurt (SOW-uhr) COL.

Defense. Shoots left. 6'4", 220 lbs. Born, St. Cloud, MN, January 16, 1981.
(Colorado's 5th choice, 88th overall, in 2000 Entry Draft).

			Regular Season					Playoffs				
Season	Club	Lea	GP	G	A	TP	PIM	GP	G	A	TP	PIM
1998-99	North Iowa	USHL	52	1	4	5	67	....	....	....	....	....
99-2000	Spokane Chiefs	WHL	71	3	12	15	48	15	2	1	3	8

SAVIELS, Agris (sah-VEE-ehls, AG-rihs) COL.

Defense. Shoots left. 6'2", 200 lbs. Born, Riga, Latvia, January 15, 1982.
(Colorado's 4th choice, 63rd overall, in 2000 Entry Draft).

			Regular Season					Playoffs				
Season	Club	Lea	GP	G	A	TP	PIM	GP	G	A	TP	PIM
1996-97	HK Lido-Nafta	Latvia	40	4	15	19	40	....	....	....	....	....
	Dynamo Riga	Latvia-Jr.	15	1	2	3	4	....	....	....	....	....
1997-98	HK Lido-Nafta	Latvia	40	7	21	28	30	....	....	....	....	....
	Dynamo Riga	Latvia-Jr.	15	1	2	3	4	....	....	....	....	....
1998-99	Notre Dame	SAHA	18	6	9	15	25	....	....	....	....	....
	Notre Dame	SJHL	30	6	13	19	....	....	....	....	....	....
99-2000	Owen Sound	OHL	65	7	25	32	56	....	....	....	....	....

SCHADILOV, Igor (sha-DEE-lahf) WSH.

Defense. Shoots left. 6'2", 189 lbs. Born, Moscow, USSR, June 7, 1980.
(Washington's 10th choice, 249th overall, in 1999 Entry Draft).

			Regular Season					Playoffs				
Season	Club	Lea	GP	G	A	TP	PIM	GP	G	A	TP	PIM
1996-97	Dynamo Moscow	Russia-Jr.	30	3	7	10	30	....	....	....	....	....
1997-98	D'amo Moscow-2	Russia-2	38	1	0	1	6	....	....	....	....	....
1998-99	D'amo Moscow-3	Russia-3	28	2	9	11	15	....	....	....	....	....
	Dynamo Moscow	Russia	2	0	0	0	0	....	....	....	....	....
	Krylja Sovetov	Russia	7	0	0	0	0	....	....	....	....	....
99-2000	Dynamo Moscow	Russia	26	0	2	2	8	16	0	0	0	2

SCHEFFELMAIER, Brett (sch-EHFEHL-mai-uhr, BREHT) T.B.

Defense. Shoots right. 6'5", 200 lbs. Born, Coronation, Alta., March 31, 1981.
(Tampa Bay's 3rd choice, 75th overall, in 1999 Entry Draft).

			Regular Season					Playoffs				
Season	Club	Lea	GP	G	A	TP	PIM	GP	G	A	TP	PIM
1997-98	Medicine Hat	WHL	25	0	1	1	69	....	....	....	....	....
1998-99	Medicine Hat	WHL	69	3	10	13	252	....	....	....	....	....
99-2000	Medicine Hat	WHL	71	1	9	10	281	....	....	....	....	....

SCHILL, Jonathan CBJ

Left wing. Shoots left. 6'1", 201 lbs. Born, Kitchener, Ont., June 28, 1979.

			Regular Season					Playoffs				
Season	Club	Lea	GP	G	A	TP	PIM	GP	G	A	TP	PIM
1995-96	Kitchener Lions	OMHA	30	17	12	29	100	....	....	....	....	....
	Kitchener B's	OJHL-B	1	0	0	0	0	....	....	....	....	....
1996-97	Kingston	OHL	52	3	7	10	16	....	....	....	....	....
1997-98	Kingston	OHL	64	14	17	31	34	12	1	1	2	4
1998-99	Kingston	OHL	68	32	27	59	93	5	2	1	3	6
99-2000	Kingston	OHL	65	39	48	87	79	3	1	1	2	6

Signed as a free agent by **Columbus**, May 8, 2000.

SCHNABEL, Robert (SHNAH-buhl, RAW-buhrt) PHX.

Defense. Shoots left. 6'6", 234 lbs. Born, Prague, Czech., November 10, 1978.
(Phoenix's 7th choice, 129th overall, in 1998 Entry Draft).

			Regular Season					Playoffs				
Season	Club	Lea	GP	G	A	TP	PIM	GP	G	A	TP	PIM
1994-95	Slavia Praha-Jr.	Cze-Rep	35	11	6	17	14	....	....	....	....	....
1995-96	Slavia Praha-Jr.	Cze-Rep	38	3	5	8	....	....	....	....	....	....
1996-97	Slavia Praha-Jr.	Cze-Rep	36	5	2	7	....	....	....	....	....	....
	Slavia Praha	Cze-Rep	4	0	0	0	4	1	0	0	0	0
1997-98	Red Deer Rebels	WHL	61	1	22	23	143	5	0	0	0	16
1998-99	Red Deer Rebels	WHL	1	0	0	0	2	....	....	....	....	....
	Springfield	AHL	77	1	7	8	155	3	1	0	1	4
99-2000	Springfield	AHL	40	2	8	10	133	5	0	0	0	4

• Re-entered NHL draft. Originally NY Islanders' 5th choice, 79th overall, in 1997 Entry Draft.

SCHUELLER, Doug FLA.

Defense. Shoots right. 6'1", 210 lbs. Born, Inver Grove Heights, MN, March 30, 1977.
(Florida's 9th choice, 211th overall, in 1997 Entry Draft).

			Regular Season					Playoffs				
Season	Club	Lea	GP	G	A	TP	PIM	GP	G	A	TP	PIM
1997-98	Bowling Green	CCHA	36	5	14	19	62	....	....	....	....	....
1998-99	Bowling Green	CCHA	37	7	5	12	54	....	....	....	....	....
99-2000	Bowling Green	CCHA	32	2	5	7	85	....	....	....	....	....

SCHULTZ, Nick (SHULTZ) MIN.

Defense. Shoots left. 6', 187 lbs. Born, Regina, Sask., August 25, 1982.
(Minnesota's 2nd choice, 33rd overall, in 2000 Entry Draft).

			Regular Season					Playoffs				
Season	Club	Lea	GP	G	A	TP	PIM	GP	G	A	TP	PIM
1998-99	Prince Albert	WHL	58	5	18	23	37	14	0	7	7	0
99-2000	Prince Albert	WHL	72	11	33	44	38	6	0	3	3	2

SCISSONS, Jeff (SKIH-zuhns, JEHF) VAN.

Center. Shoots left. 6'1", 190 lbs. Born, Saskatoon, Sask., November 24, 1976.
(Vancouver's 7th choice, 201st overall, in 1996 Entry Draft).

			Regular Season					Playoffs				
Season	Club	Lea	GP	G	A	TP	PIM	GP	G	A	TP	PIM
1992-93	Saskatoon	SAHA	35	8	11	19	32	....	....	....	....	....
1993-94	Saskatoon	SAHA	35	20	37	57	42	....	....	....	....	....
1994-95	Vernon Lakers	BCJHL	50	10	20	30	....	....	....	....	....	....
1995-96	Vernon Vipers	BCJHL	60	26	48	74	28	30	14	18	32	....
1996-97	Minnesota-Duluth	WCHA	38	3	14	17	30	....	....	....	....	....
1997-98	Minnesota-Duluth	WCHA	40	17	24	41	50	....	....	....	....	....
1998-99	Minnesota-Duluth	WCHA	38	18	19	37	42	....	....	....	....	....
99-2000	Minnesota-Duluth	WCHA	37	14	19	33	32	....	....	....	....	....

WCHA Student Athlete-of-the-Year Award (2000) • Established Minnesota-Duluth record by appearing in 153 consecutive games, March 23, 2000.

SCORSUNE, Matthew (SKOHR-soon, MAT-thew) COL.

Defense. Shoots right. 6'2", 210 lbs. Born, Morristown, NJ, June 27, 1977.
(Colorado's 12th choice, 214th overall, in 1996 Entry Draft).

			Regular Season					Playoffs				
Season	Club	Lea	GP	G	A	TP	PIM	GP	G	A	TP	PIM
1995-96	Hotchkiss High	Hi-School	24	7	22	29	24	....	....	....	....	....
1996-97	Harvard University	ECAC	30	3	8	11	28	....	....	....	....	....
1997-98	Harvard University	ECAC	33	9	10	19	30	....	....	....	....	....
1998-99	Harvard University	ECAC	31	8	9	17	34	....	....	....	....	....
99-2000	Harvard University	ECAC	30	5	8	13	38	....	....	....	....	....

SCUDERI, Robert (SKUD-uhree, RAW-buhrt) PIT.

Defense. Shoots left. 6'2", 194 lbs. Born, Syosset, NY, December 30, 1978.
(Pittsburgh's 5th choice, 134th overall, in 1998 Entry Draft).

			Regular Season					Playoffs				
Season	Club	Lea	GP	G	A	TP	PIM	GP	G	A	TP	PIM
1996-97	St. Anthony's	Hi-School	32	25	47	72	....	....	....	....	....	....
	NY Apple Core	MJHL-B	30	22	30	52	64	....	....	....	....	....
1997-98	Boston College	H-East	42	0	24	24	12	....	....	....	....	....
1998-99	Boston College	H-East	41	2	8	10	20	....	....	....	....	....
99-2000	Boston College	H-East	42	1	12	13	22	....	....	....	....	....

SEDIN, Daniel (suh-DEEN, DAN-yehl) VAN.

Left wing. Shoots left. 6'1", 200 lbs. Born, Ornskoldsvik, Sweden, September 26, 1980.
(Vancouver's 1st choice, 2nd overall, in 1999 Entry Draft).

			Regular Season					Playoffs				
Season	Club	Lea	GP	G	A	TP	PIM	GP	G	A	TP	PIM
1996-97	MoDo Hockey	Swede-Jr.	26	26	14	40	....	....	....	....	....	....
1997-98	MoDo Hockey	Swede-Jr.	4	3	3	6	4	....	....	....	....	....
	MoDo Hockey	Sweden	45	4	8	12	26	9	0	0	0	2
1998-99	MoDo Hockey	Sweden	50	21	21	42	20	13	4	8	12	14
99-2000	MoDo Hockey	Sweden	50	19	26	45	28	13	*8	6	14	18

SEDIN, Henrik (suh-DEEN, HEHN-rihk) VAN.

Center. Shoots left. 6'2", 200 lbs. Born, Ornskoldsvik, Sweden, September 26, 1980.
(Vancouver's 2nd choice, 3rd overall, in 1999 Entry Draft).

			Regular Season					Playoffs				
Season	Club	Lea	GP	G	A	TP	PIM	GP	G	A	TP	PIM
1996-97	MoDo Hockey	Swede-Jr.	26	14	22	36	....	....	....	....	....	....
1997-98	MoDo Hockey	Swede-Jr.	8	4	7	11	6	....	....	....	....	....
	MoDo Hockey	Sweden	39	1	4	5	8	7	0	0	0	0
1998-99	MoDo Hockey	Sweden	49	12	22	34	32	13	2	8	10	6
99-2000	MoDo Hockey	Sweden	50	9	38	47	22	13	5	9	14	2

SEDOV, Pavel (she-DAHF) T.B.

Left wing. Shoots left. 6'3", 185 lbs. Born, Voskresensk, USSR, January 12, 1982.
(Tampa Bay's 5th choice, 161st overall, in 2000 Entry Draft).

			Regular Season					Playoffs				
Season	Club	Lea	GP	G	A	TP	PIM	GP	G	A	TP	PIM
99-2000	Khimik	Russia-2	STATISTICS NOT AVAILABLE									

SEELEY, Richard (SEE-lee, RIH-chahrd) L.A.

Defense. Shoots left. 6'2", 205 lbs. Born, Powell River, B.C., April 30, 1979.
(Los Angeles' 6th choice, 137th overall, in 1997 Entry Draft).

			Regular Season					Playoffs				
Season	Club	Lea	GP	G	A	TP	PIM	GP	G	A	TP	PIM
1995-96	Powell River	BCJHL	44	1	8	9	42	....	....	....	....	....
1996-97	Lethbridge	WHL	3	0	0	0	11	....	....	....	....	....
	Prince Albert	WHL	18	0	1	1	9	4	0	0	0	2
1997-98	Prince Albert	WHL	65	8	21	29	114	....	....	....	....	....
1998-99	Prince Albert	WHL	61	10	48	58	110	14	1	11	12	14
99-2000	Lowell	AHL	36	5	1	6	37	....	....	....	....	....

SEIKKULA, Timo (SAY-koo-lah, TEE-moh) PIT.

Center. Shoots left. 6'2", 183 lbs. Born, Kalajoki, Finland, May 27, 1978.
(Pittsburgh's 8th choice, 238th overall, in 1996 Entry Draft).

			Regular Season					Playoffs				
Season	Club	Lea	GP	G	A	TP	PIM	GP	G	A	TP	PIM
1994-95	Junkkarit HT	Finland-2	44	1	2	3	8	....	....	....	....	....
1995-96	Junkkarit HT	Finland-2	41	9	9	18	58	....	....	....	....	....
	Junkkarit HT	Finland-3	....	....	....	....	....	5	1	2	3	22
1996-97	TPS Turku	Finn-Jr.	4	1	0	1	4	....	....	....	....	....
	Kiekko-67	Finland-2	43	5	5	10	38	....	....	....	....	....
	Kiekko-67	Finland-3	....	....	....	....	....	3	1	0	1	4
1997-98	TPS Turku	Finn-Jr.	12	6	2	8	10	7	3	4	7	12
	TuTo Turku	Finland-2	17	4	4	8	29	....	....	....	....	....
	TPS Turku	Finland	1	0	1	1	0	....	....	....	....	....
1998-99	KalPa Kuopio	Finn-Jr.	1	1	0	1	4	....	....	....	....	....
	KalPa Kuopio	Finland	52	3	8	11	40	....	....	....	....	....
	KalPa Kuopio	Finland-2	....	....	....	....	....	6	0	0	0	0
	KalPa Kuopio-2	Finn-Jr.	....	....	....	....	....	1	0	0	0	0
99-2000	Hermes Kokkola	Finland-2	48	3	11	14	34	3	1	0	1	2

SELF, Brad (SEHLF) BUF.

Center. Shoots left. 5'10", 165 lbs. Born, Peterborough, Ont., February 27, 1981.
(Buffalo's 11th choice, 235th overall, in 1999 Entry Draft).

			Regular Season					Playoffs				
Season	Club	Lea	GP	G	A	TP	PIM	GP	G	A	TP	PIM
1998-99	Peterborough	OHL	48	17	12	29	8	5	1	0	1	4
99-2000	Peterborough	OHL	68	18	16	34	18	5	2	0	2	0

SELLARS, Luke (SEHL-lahrs, LEWK) ATL.

Defense. Shoots left. 6'1", 195 lbs. Born, Toronto, Ont., May 21, 1981.
(Atlanta's 2nd choice, 30th overall, in 1999 Entry Draft).

			Regular Season					Playoffs				
Season	Club	Lea	GP	G	A	TP	PIM	GP	G	A	TP	PIM
1997-98	Wexford Raiders	OJHL	46	2	18	20	155	....	....	....	....	....
1998-99	Ottawa 67's	OHL	56	4	19	23	87	9	1	2	3	7
99-2000	Ottawa 67's	OHL	56	8	34	42	147	11	4	6	10	28

SELMSER, Sean CBJ

Left wing. Shoots left. 6'1", 195 lbs. Born, Calgary, Alta., November 10, 1974.
(Pittsburgh's 7th choice, 182nd overall, in 1993 Entry Draft).

			Regular Season					Playoffs				
Season	Club	Lea	GP	G	A	TP	PIM	GP	G	A	TP	PIM
1991-92	Calgary Buffaloes	AMHL	32	21	24	45	131	....	....	....	....	....
1992-93	Red Deer Rebels	WHL	70	13	27	40	216	4	0	0	0	10
1993-94	Red Deer Rebels	WHL	71	25	25	50	201	4	1	0	1	14
1994-95	Red Deer Rebels	WHL	33	11	17	28	65	....	....	....	....	....
1995-96	Hampton Roads	ECHL	70	23	31	54	211	3	2	0	2	8
	Portland Pirates	AHL	6	4	1	5	28	5	2	3	5	11
1996-97	Canada	Nat-Team	59	20	18	38	150	....	....	....	....	....
	Manitoba Moose	IHL	4	0	2	2	12	....	....	....	....	....
1997-98	Canada	Nat-Team	52	8	22	30	122	....	....	....	....	....
	Portland Pirates	AHL	....	....	....	....	....	1	0	1	1	0
1998-99	Fort Wayne	IHL	80	9	15	24	200	2	0	0	0	2
99-2000	Hamilton Bulldogs	AHL	72	14	12	26	151	10	3	4	7	10

Signed as a free agent by **Columbus**, August 3, 2000.

SELUYANOV, Alexander (sehl-oo-YA-nahf) DET.

Defense. Shoots right. 5'11", 172 lbs. Born, Ufa, USSR, March 24, 1982.
(Detroit's 5th choice, 128th overall, in 2000 Entry Draft).

			Regular Season					Playoffs				
Season	Club	Lea	GP	G	A	TP	PIM	GP	G	A	TP	PIM
1997-98	Novoil Ufa	Russia-3	19	0	1	1	8	....	....	....	....	....
1998-99	Novoil Ufa	Russia-4	20	3	3	6	8	....	....	....	....	....
99-2000	Ufa Salavat-2	Russia-3	18	3	4	7	10	....	....	....	....	....
	Ufa Salavat	Russia	13	1	2	3	4	....	....	....	....	....

SEMENOV, Alexei (seh-MEH-nahv, al-EHX-ay) EDM.

Defense. Shoots left. 6'6", 210 lbs. Born, Murmansk, USSR, April 10, 1981.
(Edmonton's 2nd choice, 36th overall, in 1999 Entry Draft).

			Regular Season					Playoffs				
Season	Club	Lea	GP	G	A	TP	PIM	GP	G	A	TP	PIM
1997-98	Krylja Sovetov	Russia-3	52	1	2	3	48	....	....	....	....	....
1998-99	St. Petersburg-2	Russia-4	19	0	1	1	20	....	....	....	....	....
	Sudbury Wolves	OHL	28	0	3	3	28	2	0	0	0	4
99-2000	Sudbury Wolves	OHL	65	9	35	44	135	12	1	3	4	23
	Hamilton Bulldogs	AHL	....	....	....	....	....	3	0	0	0	0

SEMENOV, Dmitri (she-MEH-nahv, dih-MEE-tree) DET.

Right wing. Shoots left. 5'10", 178 lbs. Born, Moscow, USSR, April 19, 1982.
(Detroit's 4th choice, 127th overall, in 2000 Entry Draft).

			Regular Season					Playoffs				
Season	Club	Lea	GP	G	A	TP	PIM	GP	G	A	TP	PIM
1997-98	Dynamo Moscow	Russia-2	13	2	1	3	2	....	....	....	....	....
1998-99	Dynamo Moscow	Russia-3	26	14	4	18	16	....	....	....	....	....
99-2000	Dynamo Moscow	Russia-3	STATISTICS NOT AVAILABLE									
	THC Tver	Russia-2	STATISTICS NOT AVAILABLE									

SESSA, Jason (SEH-sa, JAY-suhn) TOR.

Right wing. Shoots right. 6'1", 190 lbs. Born, Long Island, NY, July 17, 1977.
(Toronto's 5th choice, 86th overall, in 1996 Entry Draft).

			Regular Season					Playoffs				
Season	Club	Lea	GP	G	A	TP	PIM	GP	G	A	TP	PIM
1994-95	Rochester	USHL	47	45	22	67	81	....	....	....	....	....
1995-96	Lake Superior	CCHA	30	9	5	14	12	....	....	....	....	....
1996-97	Lake Superior	CCHA	34	22	22	44	91	....	....	....	....	....
1997-98	Lake Superior	CCHA	32	16	13	29	55	....	....	....	....	....
	St. John's Leafs	AHL	5	0	0	0	6	....	....	....	....	....
1998-99	St. John's Leafs	AHL	56	9	4	13	25	....	....	....	....	....
99-2000	St. John's Leafs	AHL	30	7	14	21	54	....	....	....	....	....
	Louisiana Gators	ECHL	17	1	4	5	14	....	....	....	....	....
	South Carolina	ECHL	15	10	8	18	30	7	4	1	5	2

CCHA Second All-Star Team (1997)

SHAFIKOV, Ruslan (SHAH-fee-kahv, roos-LAHN) PHI.

Center. Shoots right. 6'1", 176 lbs. Born, Ufa, USSR, May 11, 1976.
(Philadelphia's 8th choice, 204th overall, in 1995 Entry Draft).

			Regular Season					Playoffs				
Season	Club	Lea	GP	G	A	TP	PIM	GP	G	A	TP	PIM
1994-95	Ufa Salavat	CIS	30	2	0	2	10	7	1	1	2	4
1995-96	Ufa Salavat	CIS	51	9	2	11	18	3	0	0	0	4
1996-97	Ufa Salavat	Russia	31	11	7	18	22	10	3	2	5	12
1997-98	Ufa Salavat	Russia	40	12	4	16	16	....	....	....	....	....
1998-99	Ufa Salavat	Russia	41	4	10	14	26	4	1	1	2	2
99-2000	St. Petersburg	Russia	35	5	7	12	6	3	0	0	0	2

SHAPLEY, Larry (SHAP-lee, LAIR-ree) VAN.

Defense. Shoots right. 6'6", 215 lbs. Born, Dunnville, Ont., February 6, 1978.
(Vancouver's 9th choice, 148th overall, in 1997 Entry Draft).

			Regular Season					Playoffs				
Season	Club	Lea	GP	G	A	TP	PIM	GP	G	A	TP	PIM
1996-97	Welland Cougars	OJHL-B	35	3	10	13	270	....	....	....	....	....
	Peterborough	OJHL	8	0	0	0	30	....	....	....	....	....
1997-98	Peterborough	OHL	63	1	1	2	211	4	0	0	0	0
1998-99	Syracuse Crunch	AHL	50	1	1	2	254	....	....	....	....	....
99-2000	Tallahassee	ECHL	11	0	0	0	48	....	....	....	....	....
	Manitoba Moose	IHL	18	0	0	0	83	....	....	....	....	....

SHASBY, Matt (SHAS-bee, MAT) MTL.

Defense. Shoots left. 6'3", 188 lbs. Born, Sioux Falls, SD, July 2, 1980.
(Montreal's 7th choice, 150th overall, in 1999 Entry Draft).

			Regular Season					Playoffs				
Season	Club	Lea	GP	G	A	TP	PIM	GP	G	A	TP	PIM
1997-98	Lincoln Stars	USHL	43	1	15	16	30	8	0	0	0	2
1998-99	Des Moines	USHL	49	4	22	26	34	11	0	1	1	12
99-2000	Alaska-Anchorage	WCHA	32	1	8	9	36	....	....	....	....	....

SHAW, Lloyd (SHAW, LOID)

Defense. Shoots right. 6'3", 220 lbs. Born, Regina, Sask., September 26, 1976.
(Vancouver's 4th choice, 92nd overall, in 1995 Entry Draft).

			Regular Season					Playoffs				
Season	Club	Lea	GP	G	A	TP	PIM	GP	G	A	TP	PIM
1992-93	Regina Canucks	SAHA	36	11	24	35	60	....	....	....	....	....
1993-94	Seattle T-Birds	WHL	47	0	4	4	107	8	0	0	0	23
1994-95	Seattle T-Birds	WHL	66	3	12	15	313	3	0	0	0	13
1995-96	Seattle T-Birds	WHL	27	0	1	1	92	....	....	....	....	....
	Red Deer Rebels	WHL	37	2	4	6	120	10	0	2	2	25
1996-97	Red Deer Rebels	WHL	66	8	16	24	257	16	0	6	6	60
1997-98	Cincinnati Ducks	AHL	60	1	2	3	138	....	....	....	....	....
	Columbus Chill	ECHL	4	0	0	0	7	....	....	....	....	....
1998-99	Cincinnati Ducks	AHL	50	2	0	2	170	....	....	....	....	....
	Huntington	ECHL	2	0	0	0	4	....	....	....	....	....
99-2000	Cincinnati Ducks	AHL	57	1	6	7	155	....	....	....	....	....

Signed as a free agent by **Anaheim**, July 7, 1997.

SHEARER, Rob (SHEER-uhr, RAWB) COL.

Center. Shoots right. 5'10", 190 lbs. Born, Kitchener, Ont., October 19, 1976.

			Regular Season					Playoffs				
Season	Club	Lea	GP	G	A	TP	PIM	GP	G	A	TP	PIM
1992-93	Kitchener Lions	OMHA	27	27	24	51	....	....	....	....	....	....
1993-94	Windsor Spitfires	OHL	66	17	25	42	46	4	0	2	2	6
1994-95	Windsor Spitfires	OHL	59	28	28	56	48	10	4	4	8	10
1995-96	Windsor Spitfires	OHL	63	40	53	93	74	7	6	3	9	8
1996-97	Hershey Bears	AHL	78	12	16	28	88	23	0	4	4	9
1997-98	Hershey Bears	AHL	79	30	30	60	44	7	0	5	5	6
1998-99	Hershey Bears	AHL	77	24	42	66	43	3	0	0	0	6
99-2000	Hershey Bears	AHL	70	21	46	67	55	14	1	7	8	10

Signed as a free agent by **Colorado**, October 5, 1995.

SHEFER, Andrei (SHEH-fuhr, AN-dray) **L.A.**

Right wing. Shoots left. 6'1", 194 lbs. Born, Sverdlovsk, USSR, July 26, 1981.
(Los Angeles' 1st choice, 43rd overall, in 1999 Entry Draft).

			Regular Season					Playoffs				
Season	Club	Lea	GP	G	A	TP	PIM	GP	G	A	TP	PIM
1997-98	DM Yekaterinburg	Russia-3	16	3	3	6	18	....	....	....	....	....
1998-99	HC Cherepovets	Russia-3	21	6	5	11	20	....	....	....	....	....
	HC Cherepovets	Russia-4	6	2	2	4	18	....	....	....	....	....
	HC Cherepovets	Russia	8	1	0	1	4	....	....	....	....	....
99-2000	Halifax Moose	QMJHL	72	34	42	76	30	10	0	5	5	4

SHELLEY, Jody (SHEH-lee, JOH-dee)

Left wing. Shoots left. 6'3", 228 lbs. Born, Yarmouth, N.S., February 7, 1976.

			Regular Season					Playoffs				
Season	Club	Lea	GP	G	A	TP	PIM	GP	G	A	TP	PIM
1994-95	Halifax Moose	QMJHL	72	10	12	22	194	7	0	1	1	12
1995-96	Halifax Moose	QMJHL	50	13	19	32	319	6	0	2	2	36
1996-97	Halifax Moose	QMJHL	58	25	19	44	*448	17	6	6	12	*123
1997-98	Dalhousie Tigers	AUAA	19	6	11	17	145	....	....	....	....	....
	Saint John Flames	AHL	18	1	1	2	50	....	....	....	....	....
1998-99	Saint John Flames	AHL	8	0	0	0	46	....	....	....	....	....
	Johnstown Chiefs	ECHL	52	12	17	29	325	....	....	....	....	....
99-2000	Johnstown Chiefs	ECHL	36	9	17	26	256	....	....	....	....	....
	Saint John Flames	AHL	22	1	4	5	93	3	0	0	0	2

Signed as a free agent by **Calgary**, September 1, 1998.

SHIKHANOV, Sergei (shih-KHAHN-ohf, SAIR-gay) **CHI.**

Right wing. Shoots left. 6'2", 190 lbs. Born, Togliatti, USSR, April 8, 1978.
(Chicago's 10th choice, 204th overall, in 1997 Entry Draft).

			Regular Season					Playoffs				
Season	Club	Lea	GP	G	A	TP	PIM	GP	G	A	TP	PIM
1996-97	Lada Togliatti	Russia	19	4	4	8	20	8	1	0	1	10
	HK Neftekhimik	Russia	5	1	1	2	2	....	....	....	....	....
1997-98	Lada Togliatti	Russia	19	3	0	3	4	....	....	....	....	....
1998-99	Lada Togliatti	Russia	29	4	5	9	65	3	0	0	0	2
	CSK Samara	Russia	11	3	4	7	10	3	1	0	1	2
99-2000	Torpedo Yaroslavl	Russia	31	2	3	5	24	7	0	2	2	4

SHIRREFFS, Steve (SHUHR-ehfs, STEEV) **WSH.**

Defense. Shoots right. 6'3", 220 lbs. Born, Norwich, VT, February 18, 1976.
(Calgary's 7th choice, 233rd overall, in 1995 Entry Draft).

			Regular Season					Playoffs				
Season	Club	Lea	GP	G	A	TP	PIM	GP	G	A	TP	PIM
1995-96	Princeton	ECAC	25	0	3	3	6	....	....	....	....	....
1996-97	Princeton	ECAC	34	5	4	9	12	....	....	....	....	....
1997-98	Princeton	ECAC	36	9	24	33	54	....	....	....	....	....
1998-99	Princeton	ECAC	27	2	17	19	39	....	....	....	....	....
99-2000	Portland	AHL	44	3	5	8	14	....	....	....	....	....
	Hampton Roads	ECHL	14	3	3	6	8	10	0	1	1	25

ECAC First All-Star Team (1998) • NCAA East Second All-American Team (1998) • ECAC Second All-Star Team (1999)

Traded to **Washington** by **Calgary** for Benoit Gratton, August 18, 1999.

SHMYR, Jason (SHMEER, JAY-suhn) **WSH.**

Left wing. Shoots left. 6'4", 220 lbs. Born, Fairview, Alta., July 27, 1975.

			Regular Season					Playoffs				
Season	Club	Lea	GP	G	A	TP	PIM	GP	G	A	TP	PIM
1995-96	Bonneyville	AJHL	42	10	22	32	270	....	....	....	....	....
1996-97	Anchorage Aces	WCHL	51	8	12	20	388	9	1	1	2	50
	Pensacola	ECHL	1	0	0	0	2	....	....	....	....	....
1997-98	Anchorage Aces	WCHL	31	4	6	10	177	....	....	....	....	....
	Utah Grizzlies	IHL	3	0	0	0	7	....	....	....	....	....
	San Diego Gulls	WCHL	14	0	3	3	50	11	3	3	6	78
1998-99	Long Beach	IHL	8	0	0	0	35	....	....	....	....	....
	San Diego Gulls	WCHL	2	0	0	0	7	....	....	....	....	....
	Manitoba Moose	IHL	57	1	1	2	227	3	0	0	0	0
99-2000	Portland Pirates	AHL	53	3	4	7	170	2	0	0	0	2

Signed as a free agent by **Washington**, April 27, 1999.

SHVIDKI, Denis (SHVIHD-kee, DEH-nihs) **FLA.**

Right wing. Shoots left. 6', 195 lbs. Born, Kharkov, USSR, November 21, 1980.
(Florida's 1st choice, 12th overall, in 1999 Entry Draft).

			Regular Season					Playoffs				
Season	Club	Lea	GP	G	A	TP	PIM	GP	G	A	TP	PIM
1996-97	Torpedo Yaroslavl	Russia-3	35	21	12	33	32	....	....	....	....	....
	Torpedo Yaroslavl	Russia	17	3	2	5	6	....	....	....	....	....
1997-98	Torpedo Yaroslavl	Russia-2	32	20	13	33	20	....	....	....	....	....
	Torpedo Yaroslavl	Russia	15	1	1	2	2	....	....	....	....	....
1998-99	Barrie Colts	OHL	61	35	59	94	8	12	7	9	16	2
99-2000	Barrie Colts	OHL	61	41	65	106	55	9	3	1	4	2

OHL Second All-Star Team (1999)

SICAK, Vladimir **ATL.**

Defense. Shoots left. 5'11", 192 lbs. Born, Jindrichuv Hradec, Czech., January 12, 1980.

			Regular Season					Playoffs				
Season	Club	Lea	GP	G	A	TP	PIM	GP	G	A	TP	PIM
1998-99	Medicine Hat	WHL	35	1	9	10	71	....	....	....	....	....
99-2000	Medicine Hat	WHL	72	7	27	34	73	....	....	....	....	....

Signed as a free agent by **Atlanta**, September 24, 1999.

SIDYAKIN, Andrei (sihd-YA-kihn, AN-dray) **MTL.**

Right wing. Shoots left. 5'11", 169 lbs. Born, Ufa, USSR, January 20, 1979.
(Montreal's 10th choice, 202nd overall, in 1997 Entry Draft).

			Regular Season					Playoffs				
Season	Club	Lea	GP	G	A	TP	PIM	GP	G	A	TP	PIM
1994-95	Ufa Salavat	CIS	7	0	1	1	0	....	....	....	....	....
1995-96	Ufa Salavat	CIS	25	1	0	1	4	3	0	0	0	2
1996-97	Ufa Salavat	Russia	29	3	5	8	4	....	....	....	....	....
1997-98	Ufa Salavat	Russia	42	5	4	9	32	....	....	....	....	....
1998-99	Ufa Salavat	Russia	36	6	4	10	14	2	0	0	0	2
99-2000	Ufa Salavat	Russia	38	7	2	9	32	....	....	....	....	....

SIKLENKA, Mike (sih-KLEHN-kuh, MIGHK) **WSH.**

Defense. Shoots right. 6'5", 224 lbs. Born, Meadow Lake, Sask., December 18, 1979.
(Washington's 5th choice, 118th overall, in 1998 Entry Draft).

			Regular Season					Playoffs				
Season	Club	Lea	GP	G	A	TP	PIM	GP	G	A	TP	PIM
1997-98	Lloydminster	SJHL	54	10	17	27	120	....	....	....	....	....
1998-99	Seattle T-Birds	WHL	68	19	13	32	115	11	6	6	12	24
99-2000	Portland Pirates	AHL	9	0	0	0	14	....	....	....	....	....
	Hampton Roads	ECHL	58	7	4	11	62	8	1	0	1	15

SIMICEK, Roman **PIT.**

Center. Shoots left. 6'3", 210 lbs. Born, Ostrava, Czech., November 4, 1971.
(Pittsburgh's 9th choice, 273rd overall, in 2000 Entry Draft).

			Regular Season					Playoffs				
Season	Club	Lea	GP	G	A	TP	PIM	GP	G	A	TP	PIM
1990-91	TJ Vitkovice	Czech.	35	2	4	6	....	....	....	....	....	....
1991-92	TJ Vitkovice	Czech.	33	6	12	18	34	12	2	7	9	....
1992-93	TJ Vitkovice	Czech.	38	8	15	23	52	14	5	8	13	....
1993-94	HC Vitkovice	Cze-Rep	40	18	16	34	78	5	0	2	2	....
1994-95	HC Vitkovice	Cze-Rep	41	11	14	25	100	6	1	3	4	8
1995-96	HC Vitkovice	Cze-Rep	39	9	11	20	38	4	2	0	2	8
1996-97	HC Vitkovice	Cze-Rep	49	18	19	37	48	9	4	4	8	22
1997-98	HC Vitkovice	Cze-Rep	40	16	27	43	71	9	2	4	6	6
1998-99	HPK Hameenlinna	Finland	49	24	27	51	75	8	2	5	7	18
99-2000	HPK Hameenlinna	Finland	23	10	17	27	50	8	2	4	6	10

SIMON, Benjamin (SIGH-mohn, BEN-ja-mihn) **ATL.**

Center. Shoots left. 5'11", 178 lbs. Born, Shaker Heights, OH, June 14, 1978.
(Chicago's 5th choice, 110th overall, in 1997 Entry Draft).

			Regular Season					Playoffs				
Season	Club	Lea	GP	G	A	TP	PIM	GP	G	A	TP	PIM
1992-93	Shaker High	Hi-School	25	15	21	36	....	....	....	....	....	....
1993-94	Shaker High	Hi-School	24	45	41	86	....	....	....	....	....	....
1994-95	Shaker High	Hi-School	25	61	68	129	....	....	....	....	....	....
1995-96	Cleveland Barons	NAJHL	45	38	33	71	....	5	7	13	20	....
1996-97	Notre Dame	CCHA	30	4	15	19	79	....	....	....	....	....
1997-98	Notre Dame	CCHA	37	9	28	37	91	....	....	....	....	....
1998-99	Notre Dame	CCHA	37	18	24	42	65	....	....	....	....	....
99-2000	Notre Dame	CCHA	40	13	19	32	53	....	....	....	....	....

CCHA Second All-Star Team (1999)

Rights traded to **Atlanta** by **Chicago** for Atlanta's 9th round choice (Peter Flache) in 2000 Entry Draft, June 25, 2000.

SIMONS, Mikael (SIH-mawns, mih-KIGHL) **L.A.**

Center. Shoots left. 6'2", 194 lbs. Born, Falun, Sweden, January 15, 1978.
(Los Angeles' 4th choice, 84th overall, in 1996 Entry Draft).

			Regular Season					Playoffs				
Season	Club	Lea	GP	G	A	TP	PIM	GP	G	A	TP	PIM
1994-95	Mora IK	Finn-Jr.	26	5	3	8	57	....	....	....	....	....
1995-96	Mora IK	Swede-Jr.	10	4	4	8	12	....	....	....	....	....
	Mora IK	Swede-2	33	6	3	9	22	6	0	2	2	2
1996-97	Mora IK	Swede-Jr.	1	0	0	0	0	....	....	....	....	....
	Mora IK	Swede-2	33	6	3	9	22	6	0	2	2	2
1997-98	Mora IK	Swede-2	30	16	9	25	88	4	3	0	3	2
1998-99	Mora IK	Swede-2	41	14	9	23	36	14	4	3	7	14
99-2000	Mora IK	Swede-2	32	11	7	18	28	....	....	....	....	....
	Mora IK	Swede-Q	14	2	3	5	28	5	0	1	1	4

SIVEK, Michal (sih-VIHK, mee-KHAHL) **WSH.**

Center. Shoots left. 6'3", 209 lbs. Born, Nachod, Czech., January 21, 1981.
(Washington's 2nd choice, 29th overall, in 1999 Entry Draft).

			Regular Season					Playoffs				
Season	Club	Lea	GP	G	A	TP	PIM	GP	G	A	TP	PIM
1997-98	Sparta Praha-Jr.	Cze-Rep	31	13	8	21	....	....	....	....	....	....
	Sparta Praha	Cze-Rep	25	1	1	2	10	5	1	0	1	0
1998-99	Sparta Praha	Cze-Rep	1	1	0	1	....	....	....	....	....	....
	Velvana Kladno	Cze-Rep	34	3	8	11	24	....	....	....	....	....
99-2000	Prince Albert	WHL	53	23	37	60	65	6	1	4	5	10

SKRLAC, Rob (SKUHR-lak, RAWB) **N.J.**

Left wing. Shoots left. 6'5", 240 lbs. Born, Campbell, B.C., June 10, 1976.
(Buffalo's 11th choice, 224th overall, in 1995 Entry Draft).

			Regular Season					Playoffs				
Season	Club	Lea	GP	G	A	TP	PIM	GP	G	A	TP	PIM
1993-94	Kamloops BB's	BCAHA	49	44	55	99	56	....	....	....	....	....
1994-95	Kamloops Blazers	WHL	23	0	1	1	177	....	....	....	....	....
1995-96	Kamloops Blazers	WHL	63	1	4	5	216	13	0	0	0	52
1996-97	Kamloops Blazers	WHL	61	8	10	18	278	5	0	0	0	35
1997-98	Albany River Rats	AHL	53	0	2	2	256	....	....	....	....	....
1998-99	Albany River Rats	AHL	61	1	1	2	213	1	0	0	0	0
99-2000	Albany River Rats	AHL	37	0	0	0	115	....	....	....	....	....

Signed as a free agent by **New Jersey**, June 17, 1997.

SKROBOT, Sergei (SKROH-bawt, SAIR-gay) **PHI.**

Defense. Shoots right. 6'3", 191 lbs. Born, Most, Czech, March 9, 1980.
(Philadelphia's 13th choice, 258th overall, in 1998 Entry Draft).

			Regular Season					Playoffs				
Season	Club	Lea	GP	G	A	TP	PIM	GP	G	A	TP	PIM
1995-96	Dynamo Moscow	Russia-Jr.	30	4	10	14	8	....	....	....	....	....
1996-97	D'amo Moscow-2	Russia-3	70	5	10	15	10	....	....	....	....	....
1997-98	D'amo Moscow-2	Russia-2	44	2	4	6	10	....	....	....	....	....
1998-99	Tverskoi Tver	Russia-2	11	2	3	5	0	....	....	....	....	....
99-2000	Philadelphia	AHL	5	0	0	0	2	....	....	....	....	....
	Trenton Titans	ECHL	58	4	17	21	24	14	3	5	8	6

SKVARIDLO, Tomas (SHKVAHR-ihd-loh, TOH-mas) **PIT.**

Left wing. Shoots left. 6'1", 180 lbs. Born, Zvolen, Czech., June 19, 1981.
(Pittsburgh's 6th choice, 144th overall, in 1999 Entry Draft).

			Regular Season					Playoffs				
Season	Club	Lea	GP	G	A	TP	PIM	GP	G	A	TP	PIM
1997-98	HKM Zvolen	Slovak-Jr.	51	11	11	22	22	....	....	....	....	....
1998-99	HKM Zvolen	Slovak-Jr.	35	21	11	32	18	6	0	4	4	2
	HKM Zvolen	Slovak-2	9	1	1	2	2	....	....	....	....	....
	HKM Zvolen	Slovakia	1	0	0	0	0	....	....	....	....	....
99-2000	Kingston	OHL	66	19	25	44	14	5	0	0	0	2

SMIRNOV, Alexei (smihr-NAHV) ANA.

Left wing. Shoots left. 6'3", 211 lbs. Born, Tver, USSR, January 28, 1982.
(Anaheim's 1st choice, 12th overall, in 2000 Entry Draft).

			Regular Season					Playoffs				
Season	**Club**	**Lea**	**GP**	**G**	**A**	**TP**	**PIM**	**GP**	**G**	**A**	**TP**	**PIM**
1997-98	D'amo Moscow-2	Russia-2	11	1	1	2	4	....	....	....	....	....
1998-99	D'amo Moscow-2	Russia-3	27	9	3	12	24	....	....	....	....	....
99-2000	Dynamo Moscow	Russia	1	0	0	0	0	....	....	....	....	....
	D'amo Moscow-2	Russia-3	12	5	3	8	34	....	....	....	....	....
	THC Tver	Russia-2	35	3	5	8	24	....	....	....	....	....

SMIRNOV, Oleg (smihr-NOHF, OH-lehg) EDM.

Left wing. Shoots right. 5'11", 176 lbs. Born, Elektrostal, USSR, April 8, 1980.
(Edmonton's 6th choice, 144th overall, in 1998 Entry Draft).

			Regular Season					Playoffs				
Season	**Club**	**Lea**	**GP**	**G**	**A**	**TP**	**PIM**	**GP**	**G**	**A**	**TP**	**PIM**
1996-97	Kristall Elektrostal	Russia-3	38	2	2	4	8	....	....	....	....	....
1997-98	Kristall Elektrostal	Russia	6	0	2	2	0	....	....	....	....	....
	Kristall Elektrostal	Russia-2	10	0	0	0	2	....	....	....	....	....
1998-99	HC Chelyabinsk	Russia	27	0	3	3	6	....	....	....	....	....
	HC Lipetsk	Russia	3	0	0	0	0	....	....	....	....	....
	Spartak Moscow	Russia	14	4	0	4	4	....	....	....	....	....
99-2000	Spartak Moscow	Russia	STATISTICS NOT AVAILABLE									

SMITH, Donald (SMIHTH, DAW-nohld) CAR.

Center. Shoots left. 6'3", 195 lbs. Born, Buffalo, NY, March 17, 1979.
(Carolina's 7th choice, 184th overall, in 1998 Entry Draft).

			Regular Season					Playoffs				
Season	**Club**	**Lea**	**GP**	**G**	**A**	**TP**	**PIM**	**GP**	**G**	**A**	**TP**	**PIM**
1996-97	Nichols High	Hi-School	31	25	29	54	....	....	....	....	....	....
1997-98	Clarkson	ECAC	30	4	6	10	8	....	....	....	....	....
1998-99	Clarkson	ECAC	37	9	12	21	18	....	....	....	....	....
99-2000	Clarkson	ECAC	35	7	9	16	20	....	....	....	....	....

SMITH, Jarrett (SMIHTH, JAHR-reht) ANA.

Center. Shoots left. 6'1", 190 lbs. Born, Edmonton, Alta., June 15, 1979.
(NY Islanders' 4th choice, 59th overall, in 1997 Entry Draft).

			Regular Season					Playoffs				
Season	**Club**	**Lea**	**GP**	**G**	**A**	**TP**	**PIM**	**GP**	**G**	**A**	**TP**	**PIM**
1994-95	Sherwood Park	AMHL	34	21	26	47	45	....	....	....	....	....
1995-96	Prince George	WHL	18	2	0	2	6	....	....	....	....	....
1996-97	Prince George	WHL	67	20	22	42	58	15	2	2	4	5
1997-98	Prince George	WHL	42	12	22	34	21	11	3	1	4	8
1998-99	Prince George	WHL	49	20	37	57	54	3	0	2	2	2
99-2000	Prince Albert	WHL	72	27	32	59	53	6	2	4	6	20

Signed as a free agent by **Anaheim**, June 13, 2000.

SMITH, Kenton T.B.

Forward/defense. Shoots left. 5'11", 177 lbs. Born, Edmonton, AB, September 10, 1979.

			Regular Season					Playoffs				
Season	**Club**	**Lea**	**GP**	**G**	**A**	**TP**	**PIM**	**GP**	**G**	**A**	**TP**	**PIM**
1994-95	Edmonton SSA	AMHL	33	20	25	45	30	....	....	....	....	....
1995-96	Calgary Hitmen	WHL	53	3	17	20	32	....	....	....	....	....
1996-97	Calgary Hitmen	WHL	72	7	26	33	63	....	....	....	....	....
1997-98	Calgary Hitmen	WHL	69	7	26	33	81	18	1	6	7	26
1998-99	Calgary Hitmen	WHL	69	19	35	54	138	21	1	14	15	34
99-2000	Calgary Hitmen	WHL	71	7	46	53	128	13	3	8	11	25

Signed as a free agent by **Tampa Bay**, March 30, 2000.

SMITH, Mark (SMIHTH, MAHRK) S.J.

Center. Shoots left. 5'10", 200 lbs. Born, Eyebrow, Sask., October 24, 1977.
(San Jose's 7th choice, 219th overall, in 1997 Entry Draft).

			Regular Season					Playoffs				
Season	**Club**	**Lea**	**GP**	**G**	**A**	**TP**	**PIM**	**GP**	**G**	**A**	**TP**	**PIM**
1993-94	Nipawin Hawks	SJHL	62	14	12	26	44	....	....	....	....	....
1994-95	Lethbridge	WHL	49	3	4	7	25	....	....	....	....	....
1995-96	Lethbridge	WHL	71	11	24	35	59	4	2	0	2	2
1996-97	Lethbridge	WHL	62	19	38	57	125	19	7	13	20	51
1997-98	Lethbridge	WHL	70	42	67	109	206	3	0	2	2	18
	Kentucky	AHL	2	0	0	0	0	....	....	....	....	....
1998-99	Kentucky	AHL	78	18	21	39	101	12	2	7	9	16
99-2000	Kentucky	AHL	79	21	45	66	153	9	0	5	5	22

WHL East Second All-Star Team (1998)

SMITH, Matt (SMIHTH, MAT) ST.L.

Defense. Shoots right. 6'6", 229 lbs. Born, Kent, England, December 23, 1976.

			Regular Season					Playoffs				
Season	**Club**	**Lea**	**GP**	**G**	**A**	**TP**	**PIM**	**GP**	**G**	**A**	**TP**	**PIM**
1997-98	U. Mass-Amherst	H-East	33	5	8	13	48	....	....	....	....	....
	Worcester	AHL	4	1	0	1	4	3	0	0	0	10
1998-99	Worcester	AHL	44	3	8	11	81	....	....	....	....	....
	Peoria Riverman	ECHL	6	0	3	3	6	4	1	1	2	6
99-2000	Worcester	AHL	6	0	0	0	6	....	....	....	....	....
	Peoria Riverman	ECHL	57	11	15	26	101	13	2	3	5	11

Signed as a free agent by **St. Louis**, March 27, 1998.

SMITH, Nathan (SMIHTH, NAY-thun) VAN.

Center. Shoots left. 6'2", 192 lbs. Born, Edmonton, Alta., February 9, 1982.
(Vancouver's 1st choice, 23rd overall, in 2000 Entry Draft).

			Regular Season					Playoffs				
Season	**Club**	**Lea**	**GP**	**G**	**A**	**TP**	**PIM**	**GP**	**G**	**A**	**TP**	**PIM**
1997-98	Sherwood Park	AMHL	35	15	13	28	24	....	....	....	....	....
1998-99	Swift Current	WHL	47	5	8	13	26	....	....	....	....	....
99-2000	Swift Current	WHL	70	21	28	49	72	12	1	6	7	4

SMITH, Nick (SMIHTH, NIHK) FLA.

Center. Shoots left. 6'2", 180 lbs. Born, Hamilton, Ont., March 23, 1979.
(Florida's 4th choice, 74th overall, in 1997 Entry Draft).

			Regular Season					Playoffs				
Season	**Club**	**Lea**	**GP**	**G**	**A**	**TP**	**PIM**	**GP**	**G**	**A**	**TP**	**PIM**
1995-96	Shelburne Wolves	OJHL-B	42	13	18	31	12	....	....	....	....	....
1996-97	Barrie Colts	OHL	63	10	18	28	15	9	3	8	11	13
1997-98	Barrie Colts	OHL	63	13	21	34	21	6	1	2	3	4
1998-99	Barrie Colts	OHL	68	19	34	53	18	12	3	8	11	8
99-2000	Louisville Panthers	AHL	53	8	4	12	8	4	0	0	0	0
	Port Huron	UHL	2	1	1	2	0	....	....	....	....	....

SMITHSON, Jerred L.A.

Right wing. Shoots right. 6'2", 190 lbs. Born, Vernon, B.C., February 4, 1979.

			Regular Season					Playoffs				
Season	**Club**	**Lea**	**GP**	**G**	**A**	**TP**	**PIM**	**GP**	**G**	**A**	**TP**	**PIM**
1994-95	Vernon Leafs	BCAHA	64	39	46	85	120	....	....	....	....	....
1995-96	Calgary Hitmen	WHL	60	4	2	6	16	....	....	....	....	....
1996-97	Calgary Hitmen	WHL	65	3	6	9	49	....	....	....	....	....
1997-98	Calgary Hitmen	WHL	65	12	9	21	65	18	0	2	2	25
1998-99	Calgary Hitmen	WHL	63	14	22	36	108	21	3	7	10	17
99-2000	Calgary Hitmen	WHL	66	14	25	39	111	10	1	1	2	16

Signed as a free agent by **LA Kings**, February 18, 2000.

SMREK, Peter (SMUHR-ehk, PEE-tuhr) ST.L.

Defense. Shoots left. 6'1", 215 lbs. Born, Martin, Czech., February 16, 1979.
(St. Louis' 2nd choice, 85th overall, in 1999 Entry Draft).

			Regular Season					Playoffs				
Season	**Club**	**Lea**	**GP**	**G**	**A**	**TP**	**PIM**	**GP**	**G**	**A**	**TP**	**PIM**
1996-97	ZTS Martin	Slovakia	12	1	0	1	....	3	0	0	0	....
1997-98	ZTS Martin	Slovak-Jr.	19	7	6	13	32	....	....	....	....	....
	ZTS Martin	Slovakia	23	0	5	5	24	1	0	0	0	0
1998-99	Des Moines	USHL	52	6	26	32	59	14	2	7	9	8
99-2000	Peoria Rivermen	ECHL	4	1	1	2	2	....	....	....	....	....
	Worcester	AHL	64	5	19	24	26	2	0	0	0	4

SNESRUD, Mat (SHEHS-rud, MAT) ANA.

Defense. Shoots right. 6'1", 205 lbs. Born, Minneapolis, MN, January 28, 1977.
(Anaheim's 6th choice, 181st overall, in 1997 Entry Draft).

			Regular Season					Playoffs				
Season	**Club**	**Lea**	**GP**	**G**	**A**	**TP**	**PIM**	**GP**	**G**	**A**	**TP**	**PIM**
1995-96	North Iowa	USHL	43	0	6	6	30	....	....	....	....	....
1996-97	North Iowa	USHL	50	12	22	34	76	....	....	....	....	....
1997-98	Michigan Tech	WCHA	39	0	18	18	44	....	....	....	....	....
1998-99	Michigan Tech	WCHA	37	3	8	11	22	....	....	....	....	....
99-2000	Michigan Tech	WCHA	38	3	7	10	44	....	....	....	....	....

SNYDER, Dan (SHNIGH-duhr, DAN) ATL.

Center. Shoots left. 6', 185 lbs. Born, Elmira, Ont., February 23, 1978.

			Regular Season					Playoffs				
Season	**Club**	**Lea**	**GP**	**G**	**A**	**TP**	**PIM**	**GP**	**G**	**A**	**TP**	**PIM**
1994-95	Elmira Kings	OJHL-B	43	8	17	25	46	....	....	....	....	....
1995-96	Owen Sound	OHL	63	8	17	25	78	6	1	2	3	4
1996-97	Owen Sound	OHL	57	17	29	46	96	4	2	3	5	8
1997-98	Owen Sound	OHL	46	23	33	56	74	10	2	3	5	16
1998-99	Owen Sound	OHL	64	27	67	94	110	16	8	5	13	30
99-2000	Orlando Bears	IHL	71	12	13	25	123	6	1	2	3	4

Signed as a free agent by **Atlanta**, June 28, 1999.

SOCHOR, Jan (soh-KHAWR, YAN) TOR.

Left wing. Shoots right. 6', 198 lbs. Born, Usti nad Labem, Czech., January 17, 1980.
(Toronto's 6th choice, 161st overall, in 1999 Entry Draft).

			Regular Season					Playoffs				
Season	**Club**	**Lea**	**GP**	**G**	**A**	**TP**	**PIM**	**GP**	**G**	**A**	**TP**	**PIM**
1996-97	Slavia Praha-Jr.	Cze-Rep	26	11	12	23	....	....	....	....	....	....
1997-98	Slavia Praha-Jr.	Cze-Rep	33	26	12	38	....	....	....	....	....	....
	Slavia Praha	Cze-Rep	14	1	1	2	2	1	0	0	0	0
1998-99	Slavia Praha-Jr.	Cze-Rep	7	2	1	3	2	....	....	....	....	....
	Slavia Praha	Cze-Rep	47	10	10	20	14	....	....	....	....	....
99-2000	Slavia Praha	Cze-Rep	39	7	11	18	37	....	....	....	....	....

SODERBERG, Anders (SOH-dehr-buhrg, AN-duhrs) BOS.

Right wing. Shoots right. 5'6", 161 lbs. Born, Ornskoldsvik, Sweden, October 7, 1975.
(Boston's 10th choice, 234th overall, in 1996 Entry Draft).

			Regular Season					Playoffs				
Season	**Club**	**Lea**	**GP**	**G**	**A**	**TP**	**PIM**	**GP**	**G**	**A**	**TP**	**PIM**
1992-93	MoDo Hockey	Swede-Jr.	13	6	12	18	2	....	....	....	....	....
	MoDo Hockey	Sweden	1	0	0	0	0	....	....	....	....	....
1993-94	MoDo Hockey	Swede-Jr.	9	8	5	13	10	....	....	....	....	....
	MoDo Hockey	Sweden	19	0	0	0	2	9	0	0	0	0
1994-95	MoDo Hockey	Sweden	38	9	14	23	2	....	....	....	....	....
1995-96	MoDo Hockey	Sweden	40	10	18	28	10	8	3	3	6	0
1996-97	MoDo Hockey	Sweden	39	9	13	22	16	....	....	....	....	....
1997-98	MoDo Hockey	Sweden	44	15	10	25	4	9	5	1	6	2
1998-99	MoDo Hockey	Sweden	49	6	15	21	18	13	3	6	9	4
99-2000	MoDo Hockey	Sweden	43	15	10	25	18	9	1	2	3	0

SOIN, Sergei (SOY-ihn) COL.

Center. Shoots left. 6'1", 183 lbs. Born, Moscow, USSR, March 31, 1982.
(Colorado's 3rd choice, 50th overall, in 2000 Entry Draft).

			Regular Season					Playoffs				
Season	**Club**	**Lea**	**GP**	**G**	**A**	**TP**	**PIM**	**GP**	**G**	**A**	**TP**	**PIM**
1997-98	Krylja Sovetov-2	Russia-3	2	0	0	0	0	....	....	....	....	....
1998-99	Krylja Sovetov	Russia	20	1	2	3	6	....	....	....	....	....
	Krylja Sovetov	Russia-Q	14	0	2	2	6	....	....	....	....	....
99-2000	Krylja Sovetov	Russia-2	33	8	7	5	24	....	....	....	....	....

SOLING, Jonas (SOH-lihng, YOH-nahs) VAN.

Right wing. Shoots left. 6'4", 192 lbs. Born, Stockholm, Sweden, September 7, 1978.
(Vancouver's 3rd choice, 93rd overall, in 1996 Entry Draft).

			Regular Season					Playoffs				
Season	**Club**	**Lea**	**GP**	**G**	**A**	**TP**	**PIM**	**GP**	**G**	**A**	**TP**	**PIM**
1995-96	Huddinge IK	Swede-Jr.	24	8	4	12	18	....	....	....	....	....
	Huddinge IK	Swede-2	5	0	0	0	0	....	....	....	....	....
1996-97	Sudbury Wolves	OHL	66	18	22	40	60	....	....	....	....	....
1997-98	Sudbury Wolves	OHL	56	9	25	34	67	10	0	7	7	10
1998-99	Syracuse Crunch	AHL	29	2	2	4	4	....	....	....	....	....
	Augusta Lynx	ECHL	50	27	20	47	71	....	....	....	....	....
99-2000	Syracuse Crunch	AHL	4	0	0	0	0	....	....	....	....	....
	Augusta Lynx	ECHL	66	22	31	53	49	12	4	0	4	6

SOMERVUORI, Eero (soh-muhr-VOH-ree, ai-AIR-oh) T.B.

Right wing. Shoots right. 5'10", 167 lbs. Born, Jarvenpaa, Finland, February 7, 1979.
(Tampa Bay's 9th choice, 170th overall, in 1997 Entry Draft).

			Regular Season					Playoffs				
Season	Club	Lea	GP	G	A	TP	PIM	GP	G	A	TP	PIM
1993-94	Jokerit Helsinki-C	Finn-Jr.	29	23	31	54	16	....	....	....	....	....
1994-95	Jokerit Helsinki-C	Finn-Jr.	17	23	16	39	8	6	7	3	10	2
	Jokerit Helsinki-B	Finn-Jr.	15	8	10	18	4	....	....	....	....	....
	Jokerit Helsinki	Finn-Jr.	11	1	2	3	2	....	....	....	....	....
1995-96	Jokerit Helsinki	Finn-Jr.	28	14	12	26	10	9	4	1	5	4
	Jokerit Helsinki	Finland	6	1	2	3	0	....	....	....	....	....
	KJT Jarvenpaa	Finland-2	1	0	0	0	0	....	....	....	....	....
1996-97	Jokerit Helsinki	Finn-Jr.	28	20	19	39	30	5	3	0	3	4
	Jokerit Helsinki	EuroHL	3	0	0	0	0	2	2	0	0	0
	Jokerit Helsinki	Finland	35	1	1	2	2	5	0	0	0	0
1997-98	Jokerit Helsinki	Finn-Jr.	14	4	8	12	2	....	....	....	....	....
	Jokerit Helsinki	EuroHL	5	0	0	0	0	....	....	....	....	....
	Jokerit Helsinki	Finland	42	3	7	10	46	8	2	1	3	6
1998-99	Jokerit Helsinki	Finn-Jr.	4	1	1	2	2	....	....	....	....	....
	Jokerit Helsinki	EuroHL	6	0	0	0	0	1	0	0	0	0
	Jokerit Helsinki	Finland	50	7	8	15	24	3	1	0	1	6
99-2000	Jokerit Helsinki	Finland	54	6	6	12	10	11	1	0	1	0

SOMIK, Radovan (SAW-mihk, RAH-doh-vahn) PHI.

Right wing. Shoots right. 6'2", 194 lbs. Born, Martin, Czech., May 5, 1977.
(Philadelphia's 3rd choice, 100th overall, in 1995 Entry Draft).

			Regular Season					Playoffs				
Season	Club	Lea	GP	G	A	TP	PIM	GP	G	A	TP	PIM
1993-94	ZTS Martin	Slovakia	1	0	0	0	0	....	....	....	....	....
1994-95	ZTS Martin	Slovakia	25	3	0	3	39	3	1	0	1	2
1995-96	ZTS Martin	Slovakia	25	3	6	9	8	9	1	0	1	....
1996-97	ZTS Martin	Slovakia	35	3	5	8	....	3	0	0	0	....
1997-98	ZTS Martin	Slovakia	26	6	9	15	10	3	0	0	0	0
1998-99	Dukla Trencin	Slovakia	26	1	4	5	6	....	....	....	....	....
99-2000	ZTS Martin	Slovak-2	40	38	28	66	32	....	....	....	....	....

SOUZA, Mike (SOO-zah, MIGHK) CHI.

Left wing. Shoots left. 6'1", 190 lbs. Born, Melrose, MA, January 28, 1978.
(Chicago's 4th choice, 67th overall, in 1997 Entry Draft).

			Regular Season					Playoffs				
Season	Club	Lea	GP	G	A	TP	PIM	GP	G	A	TP	PIM
1992-93	Wakefield High	Hi-School	20	22	13	35	....	....	....	....	....	....
1993-94	Wakefield High	Hi-School	22	28	34	62	....	....	....	....	....	....
1994-95	Wakefield High	Hi-School	21	22	31	53	....	....	....	....	....	....
1995-96	Wakefield High	Hi-School	21	25	31	56	....	....	....	....	....	....
1996-97	New Hampshire	H-East	39	15	11	26	20	....	....	....	....	....
1997-98	New Hampshire	H-East	38	13	12	25	36	....	....	....	....	....
1998-99	New Hampshire	H-East	41	23	42	65	38	....	....	....	....	....
99-2000	New Hampshire	H-East	38	15	25	40	58	....	....	....	....	....

NCAA Championship All-Tournament Team (1999) • Hockey East Second All-Star Team (2000)

SPANHEL, Martin CBJ

Right wing. Shoots left. 6'2", 202 lbs. Born, Zlin, Czech., July 1, 1977.
(Philadelphia's 6th choice, 152nd overall, in 1995 Entry Draft).

			Regular Season					Playoffs				
Season	Club	Lea	GP	G	A	TP	PIM	GP	G	A	TP	PIM
1994-95	ZPS Zlin-Jr.	Cze-Rep	33	25	16	41	0	....	....	....	....	....
	ZPS Zlin	Cze-Rep	1	0	0	0	0	....	....	....	....	....
1995-96	Lethbridge	WHL	6	1	0	1	0	....	....	....	....	....
	Moose Jaw	WHL	61	4	12	16	33	....	....	....	....	....
1996-97	ZPS Zlin	Cze-Rep	22	3	6	9	20	....	....	....	....	....
1997-98	ZPS Zlin	Cze-Rep	40	7	9	16	70	....	....	....	....	....
1998-99	HCK Plzen	Cze-Rep	49	12	12	24	60	5	2	1	3	27
99-2000	HCK Plzen	Cze-Rep	52	21	27	48	86	7	1	4	5	12

Traded to **San Jose** by **Philadelphia** with Philadelphia's 1st round choice (later traded to Phoenix - Phoenix selected Daniel Briere) in 1996 Entry Draft and Philadelphia's 4th round choice (later traded to Buffalo - Buffalo selected Mike Martone) in 1996 Entry Draft for Pat Falloon, November 16, 1995. Traded to **Buffalo** by **San Jose** with Vaclav Varada and Philadelphia's 1st (previously acquired by San Jose - later traded to Phoenix - Phoenix selected Daniel Briere) and 4th (previously acquired, Buffalo selected Mike Martone) round choices in 1996 Entry Draft for Doug Bodger, November 16, 1995. Signed as a free agent by **Columbus**, May 30, 2000.

SPIRIDONOV, Maxim (spih-rih-DAWN-uhv, max-EEM) EDM.

Left wing. Shoots left. 5'10", 185 lbs. Born, Moscow, USSR, April 7, 1978.
(Edmonton's 10th choice, 241st overall, in 1998 Entry Draft).

			Regular Season					Playoffs				
Season	Club	Lea	GP	G	A	TP	PIM	GP	G	A	TP	PIM
1993-94	CSKA Moscow	Russia-Jr.	35	20	20	40	16	....	....	....	....	....
1994-95	CSKA Moscow	Russia-Jr.	68	60	31	91	34	....	....	....	....	....
1995-96	Smiths Falls Bears	OJHL	51	52	36	88	71	....	....	....	....	....
1996-97	London Knights	OHL	55	31	22	53	99	....	....	....	....	....
1997-98	London Knights	OHL	66	54	44	98	52	16	3	4	7	4
	Grand Rapids	IHL	....	....	....	....	....	3	0	0	0	0
1998-99	Grand Rapids	IHL	41	11	17	28	12	....	....	....	....	....
	Springfield	AHL	23	8	8	16	2	2	0	0	0	2
99-2000	Tallahassee	ECHL	57	22	30	52	67	....	....	....	....	....
	Hamilton Bulldogs	AHL	10	5	2	7	2	4	1	1	2	0

OHL Second All-Star Team (1998)

SRDINKO, Jan (suhr-DIHN-koh, YAN) N.J.

Defense. Shoots left. 5'11", 195 lbs. Born, Vsetin, Czech., February 22, 1974.
(New Jersey's 8th choice, 241st overall, in 1997 Entry Draft).

			Regular Season					Playoffs				
Season	Club	Lea	GP	G	A	TP	PIM	GP	G	A	TP	PIM
1995-96	Petra Vsetin	Cze-Rep	31	0	3	3	....	9	0	0	0	....
1996-97	Petra Vsetin	Cze-Rep	49	2	8	10	71	10	0	3	3	29
1997-98	Petra Vsetin	Cze-Rep	47	1	4	5	95	10	0	3	3	4
	Petra Vsetin	EuroHL	9	0	1	1	4	....	....	....	....	....
1998-99	Slovnaft Vsetin	Cze-Rep	50	2	7	9	58	12	0	1	1	....
99-2000	Slovnaft Vsetin	Cze-Rep	48	3	10	13	50	9	2	0	2	29

SRYUBKO, Andrei (SHROOB-koh) CBJ

Defense. Shoots left. 6'3", 205 lbs. Born, Kiev, USSR, October 21, 1975.

			Regular Season					Playoffs				
Season	Club	Lea	GP	G	A	TP	PIM	GP	G	A	TP	PIM
1996-97	Toledo Storm	ECHL	62	0	8	8	238	5	0	0	0	4
1997-98	Toledo Storm	ECHL	50	1	12	13	165	7	0	0	0	8
	Las Vegas	IHL	13	0	0	0	57	....	....	....	....	....
1998-99	Port Huron	UHL	22	2	2	4	78	2	0	0	0	4
	Fort Wayne	IHL	1	0	0	0	0	....	....	....	....	....
	Las Vegas	IHL	51	0	8	8	164	....	....	....	....	....
99-2000	Port Huron	UHL	2	0	0	0	7	....	....	....	....	....
	Utah Grizzlies	IHL	5	1	1	2	32	....	....	....	....	....
	Grand Rapids	IHL	28	0	1	1	109	2	0	0	0	9

Signed as a free agent by **Columbus**, August 3, 2000.

STAAL, Kim (STOHL, KIHM) MTL.

Center. Shoots right. 6', 185 lbs. Born, Herlev, Denmark, March 10, 1978.
(Montreal's 4th choice, 92nd overall, in 1996 Entry Draft).

			Regular Season					Playoffs				
Season	Club	Lea	GP	G	A	TP	PIM	GP	G	A	TP	PIM
1994-95	Malmo IF	Swede-Jr.	17	4	2	6	4	....	....	....	....	....
1995-96	Malmo IF	Swede-Jr.	30	24	20	44	14	....	....	....	....	....
1996-97	Malmo IF	Sweden	4	0	1	1	2	....	....	....	....	....
	Malmo IF	Swede-Jr.	3	6	4	10	2	....	....	....	....	....
1997-98	Malmo IF	Swede-Jr.	20	13	11	24	36	....	....	....	....	....
	Malmo IF	Sweden	13	0	1	1	1	....	....	....	....	....
1998-99	Malmo IF	Sweden	48	1	5	6	14	4	0	0	0	0
99-2000	Malmo IF	Sweden	50	14	10	24	24	6	1	1	2	4

STARLING, Chad (STAHR-lihng, CHAD) ST.L.

Defense. Shoots left. 6'6", 210 lbs. Born, Saskatoon, Sask., September 16, 1980.
(St. Louis' 3rd choice, 114th overall, in 1999 Entry Draft).

			Regular Season					Playoffs				
Season	Club	Lea	GP	G	A	TP	PIM	GP	G	A	TP	PIM
1997-98	Saskatoon Legion	SAHA	60	15	49	64	172	....	....	....	....	....
	Kamloops Blazers	WHL	1	0	0	0	0	....	....	....	....	....
1998-99	Kamloops Blazers	WHL	65	4	13	17	101	14	0	0	0	8
99-2000	Kamloops Blazers	WHL	51	4	7	11	87	4	0	0	0	6

STAYZER, Blair (STAY-zuhr) CGY.

Left wing. Shoots left. 6'3", 205 lbs. Born, Dunnville, Ont., October 4, 1980.
(Calgary's 9th choice, 190th overall, in 1999 Entry Draft).

			Regular Season					Playoffs				
Season	Club	Lea	GP	G	A	TP	PIM	GP	G	A	TP	PIM
1997-98	Windsor	OHL	57	4	8	12	132	....	....	....	....	....
1998-99	Windsor	OHL	62	12	19	31	140	5	2	0	2	14
99-2000	Windsor	OHL	44	14	5	19	100	11	1	3	4	14

STEEN, Calle (STEEN, CAL-lee) DET.

Right wing. Shoots left. 5'11", 198 lbs. Born, Stockholm, Sweden, May 16, 1980.
(Detroit's 6th choice, 142nd overall, in 1998 Entry Draft).

			Regular Season					Playoffs				
Season	Club	Lea	GP	G	A	TP	PIM	GP	G	A	TP	PIM
1995-96	Hammarby IF	Swede-Jr.	5	0	0	0	0	....	....	....	....	....
1996-97	Hammarby IF	Swede-Jr.	24	4	9	13	....	....	....	....	....	....
1997-98	Hammarby IF	Swede-2	21	1	3	4	22	....	....	....	....	....
1998-99	Hammarby IF	Swede-2	33	4	16	20	28	5	0	2	2	6
99-2000	Mora IK	Swede-Q	22	4	2	6	42	....	....	....	....	....
	Mora IK	Swede-2	10	0	2	2	6	9	0	2	2	10

STEPHENS, Charlie (STEE-vuhns, CHAHR-lee) WSH.

Center/Right wing. Shoots right. 6'4", 225 lbs. Born, Nilestown, Ont., April 5, 1981.
(Washington's 3rd choice, 31st overall, in 1999 Entry Draft).

			Regular Season					Playoffs				
Season	Club	Lea	GP	G	A	TP	PIM	GP	G	A	TP	PIM
1995-96	Elgin/Middlesex	OMHA	60	25	29	54	60	....	....	....	....	....
1996-97	Leamington	OJHL-B	50	26	36	62	103	....	....	....	....	....
1997-98	St. Michael's	OHL	58	9	21	30	38	....	....	....	....	....
1998-99	St. Michael's	OHL	7	2	4	6	8	....	....	....	....	....
	Guelph Storm	OHL	61	24	28	52	72	11	3	5	8	19
99-2000	Guelph Storm	OHL	56	16	34	50	87	6	1	3	4	15

STIENSTRA, Doug N.J.

Left wing. Shoots left. 6'1", 210 lbs. Born, Kelowna, B.C., June 18, 1976.

			Regular Season					Playoffs				
Season	Club	Lea	GP	G	A	TP	PIM	GP	G	A	TP	PIM
1992-93	Columbia Valley	KIJHL	38	30	32	62	20	....	....	....	....	....
1993-94	Prince George	RMJHL	51	15	29	44	16	....	....	....	....	....
1994-95	Cowichan Valley	BCJHL	58	38	33	71	....	....	....	....	....	....
1996-97	Cornell Big Red	ECAC	35	6	10	16	35	....	....	....	....	....
1997-98	Cornell Big Red	ECAC	32	13	15	28	56	....	....	....	....	....
1998-99	Cornell Big Red	ECAC	31	12	11	23	30	....	....	....	....	....
99-2000	Cornell Big Red	ECAC	28	15	17	32	44	....	....	....	....	....

All-Ivy Second All-StarTeam (2000) • Named ECAC Best Defenseman (2000) • Signed as a free agent by **New Jersey**, May 4, 2000.

STOLL, Jarret (STOHL) CGY.

Center. Shoots right. 6'1", 199 lbs. Born, Melville, Sask., June 25, 1982.
(Calgary's 3rd choice, 46th overall, in 2000 Entry Draft).

			Regular Season					Playoffs				
Season	Club	Lea	GP	G	A	TP	PIM	GP	G	A	TP	PIM
1997-98	Saskatoon Blazers	SAHA	44	45	44	89	78	....	....	....	....	....
1998-99	Kootenay Ice	WHL	57	13	21	34	38	4	0	0	0	2
99-2000	Kootenay Ice	WHL	71	37	38	75	64	20	7	9	16	24

STOREY, Ben (STOY-ree, BEHN) COL.

Defense. Shoots left. 6'2", 200 lbs. Born, Ottawa, Ont., June 22, 1977.
(Colorado's 4th choice, 98th overall, in 1996 Entry Draft).

			Regular Season					Playoffs				
Season	Club	Lea	GP	G	A	TP	PIM	GP	G	A	TP	PIM
1993-94	Ottawa	OJHL	57	5	30	35	86	....	....	....	....	....
1994-95	Ottawa	OJHL	51	6	33	39	83	....	....	....	....	....
1995-96	Harvard University	ECAC	33	2	11	13	44	....	....	....	....	....
1996-97	Harvard University	ECAC	25	0	6	6	40	....	....	....	....	....
1997-98	Harvard University	ECAC	33	9	16	25	56	....	....	....	....	....
1998-99	Harvard University	ECAC	23	4	11	15	30	....	....	....	....	....
	Hershey Bears	AHL	5	0	0	0	0	....	....	....	....	....
99-2000	Hershey Bears	AHL	65	6	18	24	69	14	2	2	4	8

STORK, Dean (STOHRK, DEEN) WSH.

Defense. Shoots left. 6'3", 223 lbs. Born, Edmonton, Alta., October 2, 1975.

			Regular Season					Playoffs				
Season	Club	Lea	GP	G	A	TP	PIM	GP	G	A	TP	PIM
1991-92	Penticton Sky	BCAHA	48	28	22	50	168	....	....	....	....	....
1992-93	Bellingham	BCJHL	58	2	8	10	69	....	....	....	....	....
1993-94	Bellingham	BCJHL	38	2	9	11	57	....	....	....	....	....
	Penticton	BCJHL	25	0	3	3	52	....	....	....	....	....
1994-95	Penticton	BCJHL	STATISTICS NOT AVAILABLE									
1995-96	Penticton	BCJHL	45	24	30	54	....	....	....	....	....	....
1996-97	U. Mass-Amherst	H-East	34	1	4	5	54	....	....	....	....	....
1997-98	U. Mass-Amherst	H-East	33	3	6	9	66	....	....	....	....	....
1998-99	U. Mass-Amherst	H-East	34	9	7	16	44	....	....	....	....	....
	Portland Pirates	AHL	10	0	2	2	13	....	....	....	....	....
99-2000	Portland Pirates	AHL	3	0	0	0	2	....	....	....	....	....
	Hampton Roads	ECHL	52	5	13	18	69	8	0	3	3	2

Signed as a free agent by **Washington**, March 24, 1999.

STRAKA, Josef (STRAH-kuh, JOH-sehf) CGY.

Center. Shoots right. 5'11", 183 lbs. Born, Jindrichuv Hradec, Czech., February 11, 1978.
(Calgary's 7th choice, 122nd overall, in 1996 Entry Draft).

			Regular Season					Playoffs				
Season	Club	Lea	GP	G	A	TP	PIM	GP	G	A	TP	PIM
1994-95	CHZ Litvinov-Jr.	Cze-Rep	40	33	42	75	....	....	....	....	....	....
1995-96	CHZ Litvinov	Cze-Rep	33	5	6	11	14	15	3	1	4	....
1996-97	CHZ Litvinov	Cze-Rep	52	14	16	30	32	....	....	....	....	....
1997-98	CHZ Litvinov	Cze-Rep	17	2	4	6	8	....	....	....	....	....
1998-99	CHZ Litvinov	Cze-Rep	50	5	17	22	48	....	....	....	....	....
99-2000	CHZ Litvinov	Cze-Rep	11	1	1	2	6	....	....	....	....	....
	HC Plzen	Cze-Rep	26	5	4	9	6	7	0	2	2	0

STREIT, Martin (STRIGHT, MAHR-tihn) CBJ

Left wing. Shoots right. 6'2", 191 lbs. Born, Vyskov, Czech., February 2, 1977.
(Philadelphia's 7th choice, 178th overall, in 1995 Entry Draft).

			Regular Season					Playoffs				
Season	Club	Lea	GP	G	A	TP	PIM	GP	G	A	TP	PIM
1995-96	HC Olomouc-Jr.	Cze-Rep	19	10	6	16	....	....	....	....	....	....
	HC Olomouc	Cze-Rep	10	0	0	0	....	....	....	....	....	....
1996-97	HC Olomouc	Cze-Rep	18	1	2	3	14	....	....	....	....	....
1997-98	Karlovy Vary	Cze-Rep	48	5	13	18	24	....	....	....	....	....
1998-99	Karlovy Vary	Cze-Rep	48	9	4	13	34	....	....	....	....	....
99-2000	Karlovy Vary	Cze-Rep	18	0	2	2	20	....	....	....	....	....
	HC Vitkovice	Cze-Rep	31	3	6	9	28	....	....	....	....	....

Selected by **Columbus** from **Philadelphia** in Expansion Draft, June 23, 2000.

STRINGER, Rejean (STRAHN-jay) S.J.

Center. Shoots left. 5'11", 205 lbs. Born, Gravelbourg, Sask., August 21, 1974.

			Regular Season					Playoffs				
Season	Club	Lea	GP	G	A	TP	PIM	GP	G	A	TP	PIM
1995-96	Merrimack	H-East	32	8	7	15	16	....	....	....	....	....
1996-97	Merrimack	H-East	34	18	18	36	14	....	....	....	....	....
1997-98	Merrimack	H-East	38	11	46	57	44	....	....	....	....	....
1998-99	Merrimack	H-East	36	17	39	56	44	....	....	....	....	....
99-2000	New Orleans Brass	ECHL	30	6	13	19	6	3	0	0	0	0
	Kentucky	AHL	40	6	13	19	12	2	0	0	0	0

Hockey East Second All-Star Team (1999) • NCAA East Second All-American Team (1999)

Signed as a free agent by **San Jose**, August 27, 1999.

STROM, Peter (STRUHM, PEE-tuhr) MTL.

Left wing. Shoots right. 6', 178 lbs. Born, Snotorp, Sweden, January 14, 1975.
(Montreal's 10th choice, 200th overall, in 1994 Entry Draft).

			Regular Season					Playoffs				
Season	Club	Lea	GP	G	A	TP	PIM	GP	G	A	TP	PIM
1993-94	Vastra Frolunda	Sweden	29	0	0	0	8	....	....	....	....	....
1994-95	Vastra Frolunda	Sweden	16	0	3	3	10	....	....	....	....	....
	Vastra Frolunda	Swede-2	12	8	10	18	10	....	....	....	....	....
1995-96	Vastra Frolunda	Sweden	35	7	8	15	10	13	0	3	3	0
1996-97	Vastra Frolunda	Sweden	49	7	16	23	24	3	0	0	0	2
1997-98	Vastra Frolunda	Sweden	46	6	15	21	22	7	0	4	4	0
1998-99	Vastra Frolunda	Sweden	49	17	15	32	18	4	0	2	2	0
99-2000	Vastra Frolunda	Sweden	50	12	26	38	20	5	0	1	1	2

STUART, Mike (STOO-uhrt) NSH.

Defense. Shoots right. 6'1", 193 lbs. Born, Rochester, MN, August 31, 1980.
(Nashville's 6th choice, 137th overall, in 2000 Entry Draft).

			Regular Season					Playoffs				
Season	Club	Lea	GP	G	A	TP	PIM	GP	G	A	TP	PIM
1996-97	Rochester	USHL	46	4	9	13	22	....	....	....	....	....
1997-98	Rochester	USHL	50	4	15	19	40	....	....	....	....	....
1998-99	Colorado College	WCHA	40	2	12	14	44	....	....	....	....	....
99-2000	Colorado College	WCHA	32	2	5	7	26	....	....	....	....	....

USHL All-Rookie Team (1997)

STUSSI, Rene (SHTOO-see, REH-nay) ANA.

Center. Shoots right. 5'11", 183 lbs. Born, Muri, Switzerland, December 13, 1978.
(Anaheim's 7th choice, 209th overall, in 1997 Entry Draft).

			Regular Season					Playoffs				
Season	Club	Lea	GP	G	A	TP	PIM	GP	G	A	TP	PIM
1995-96	HC Thurgau	Switz-2	34	2	4	6	10	7	3	0	3	2
1996-97	HC Thurgau	Switz-2	42	20	31	51	24	8	5	4	9	4
1997-98	HC Kloten	Switz.	38	9	8	17	10	7	1	0	1	4
1998-99	EHC Kloten	Switz.	36	5	5	10	14	....	....	....	....	....
	ZSC Zurich	Switz.	7	1	1	2	6	7	1	1	2	4
99-2000	EV Zug	Switz.	45	7	5	12	13	9	0	1	1	0

STYF, Par (STOOF, PAHR) PHI.

Defense. Shoots left. 6', 187 lbs. Born, Harnosand, Sweden, April 11, 1979.
(Philadelphia's 8th choice, 240th overall, in 1997 Entry Draft).

			Regular Season					Playoffs				
Season	Club	Lea	GP	G	A	TP	PIM	GP	G	A	TP	PIM
1996-97	MoDo Hockey	Swede-Jr.	11	2	4	6	....	....	....	....	....	....
1997-98	MoDo Hockey	Swede-Jr.	17	7	5	12	60	....	....	....	....	....
1998-99	Ornskoldsvik SK	Swede-2	18	2	5	7	63	....	....	....	....	....
99-2000	Timra IF	Swede-2	27	0	2	2	49	....	....	....	....	....

SUBBOTIN, Dmitri (soo-BOH-tihn, DIH-mih-TREE) CBJ

Left wing. Shoots left. 6'1", 183 lbs. Born, Tomsk, USSR, October 20, 1977.
(NY Rangers' 3rd choice, 76th overall, in 1996 Entry Draft).

			Regular Season					Playoffs				
Season	Club	Lea	GP	G	A	TP	PIM	GP	G	A	TP	PIM
1993-94	HC Yekaterinburg	CIS	12	0	3	3	4	....	....	....	....	....
1994-95	HC Yekaterinburg	CIS	52	9	6	15	75	2	0	0	0	2
1995-96	CSKA Moscow	CIS	41	6	5	11	62	3	0	0	0	0
1996-97	CSKA Moscow	Russia	17	5	3	8	22	2	0	0	0	2
	CSKA Moscow	Russia-2	8	1	0	1	8	....	....	....	....	....
1997-98	CSKA Moscow	Russia	16	1	1	2	47	....	....	....	....	....
1998-99	Dynamo Moscow	Russia	1	0	1	1	0	....	....	....	....	....
	Lada Togliatti	Russia	31	8	3	11	47	7	0	0	0	4
99-2000	Lada Togliatti	Russia	27	10	4	14	26	7	1	1	2	4

Selected by **Columbus** from **NY Rangers** in Expansion Draft, June 23, 2000.

SUGDEN, Brandon (SUHG-duhn) ST.L.

Defense. Shoots right. 6'2", 178 lbs. Born, Toronto, Ont., June 23, 1978.
(Toronto's 8th choice, 111th overall, in 1996 Entry Draft).

			Regular Season					Playoffs				
Season	Club	Lea	GP	G	A	TP	PIM	GP	G	A	TP	PIM
1995-96	London Knights	OHL	55	2	7	9	*264	....	....	....	....	....
1996-97	London Knights	OHL	31	4	10	14	158	....	....	....	....	....
	Sudbury Wolves	OHL	20	....	4	4	70	....	....	....	....	....
1997-98	Sudbury Wolves	OHL	11	2	3	5	62	....	....	....	....	....
	Barrie Colts	OHL	49	6	21	27	191	6	0	0	0	18
1998-99	Cincinnati	IHL	6	0	2	2	51	....	....	....	....	....
	Dayton Bombers	ECHL	44	0	1	1	233	1	0	0	0	17
99-2000	Dayton Bombers	ECHL	13	0	1	1	110	....	....	....	....	....

Signed as a free agent by **St. Louis**, June 29, 1998.

SUGLOBOV, Alexander (suh-GLOH-bahf) N.J.

Right wing. Shoots left. 6', 176 lbs. Born, Elektrostal, USSR, January 15, 1982.
(New Jersey's 3rd choice, 56th overall, in 2000 Entry Draft).

			Regular Season					Playoffs				
Season	Club	Lea	GP	G	A	TP	PIM	GP	G	A	TP	PIM
1998-99	Spartak Moscow-2	Russia-4	1	0	0	0	0	....	....	....	....	....
	Spartak Moscow	Russia	1	0	0	0	0	....	....	....	....	....
99-2000	Torpedo Yaroslavl	Russia-3	38	23	10	33		....	....	....	....	....

SULC, Jan (SOOLTZ, YAN) T.B.

Center. Shoots right. 6'3", 190 lbs. Born, Litvinov, Czech., February 17, 1979.
(Tampa Bay's 5th choice, 109th overall, in 1997 Entry Draft).

			Regular Season					Playoffs				
Season	Club	Lea	GP	G	A	TP	PIM	GP	G	A	TP	PIM
1996-97	CHZ Litvinov-Jr.	Cze-Rep	37	14	17	31	....	....	....	....	....	....
1997-98	St. Michael's	OHL	34	3	10	13	11	....	....	....	....	....
	Kingston	OHL	29	6	8	14	7	12	0	0	0	0
1998-99	Kingston	OHL	13	4	4	8	6	....	....	....	....	....
	Owen Sound	OHL	53	20	29	49	59	16	4	8	12	18
99-2000	Toledo Storm	ECHL	51	10	11	21	40	....	....	....	....	....
	Detroit Vipers	IHL	21	0	3	3	15	....	....	....	....	....

SULLIVAN, Brian (suh-LIH-vuhn) DAL.

Defense. Shoots left. 6'3", 185 lbs. Born, Marshfield, MA, June 27, 1980.
(Dallas' 9th choice, 243rd overall, in 1999 Entry Draft).

			Regular Season					Playoffs				
Season	Club	Lea	GP	G	A	TP	PIM	GP	G	A	TP	PIM
1997-98	Thayer Academy	Hi-School	26	0	5	5	17	....	....	....	....	....
1998-99	Thayer Academy	Hi-School	21	0	7	7	10	....	....	....	....	....
99-2000	Northeastern	H-East	23	0	1	1	8	....	....	....	....	....

SULLIVAN, Jeff (SUHL-lih-vahn, JEHF)

Defense. Shoots left. 6'1", 185 lbs. Born, St. John's, Nfld., September 18, 1978.
(Ottawa's 5th choice, 146th overall, in 1997 Entry Draft).

			Regular Season					Playoffs				
Season	Club	Lea	GP	G	A	TP	PIM	GP	G	A	TP	PIM
1994-95	St. John's Caps	NFAHA	40	10	15	25	120	....	....	....	....	....
1995-96	East Hants	MJrHL	52	15	20	35	270	....	....	....	....	....
1996-97	Granby Bisons	QMJHL	25	4	8	12	47	....	....	....	....	....
	Halifax	QMJHL	45	4	23	27	200	18	0	5	5	96
1997-98	Halifax	QMJHL	69	9	27	36	377	5	0	1	1	21
1998-99	Halifax	QMJHL	69	7	30	37	320	5	1	1	2	14
99-2000	Saint John Flames	AHL	9	0	3	3	16	....	....	....	....	....
	Johnstown Chiefs	ECHL	58	2	8	10	181	7	0	2	2	32

SURMA, Damian (SUHR-ma, DAY-mee-an) CAR.

Left wing. Shoots left. 5'9", 200 lbs. Born, Lincoln Park, MI, June 22, 1981.
(Carolina's 5th choice, 174th overall, in 1999 Entry Draft).

			Regular Season					Playoffs				
Season	Club	Lea	GP	G	A	TP	PIM	GP	G	A	TP	PIM
1997-98	Compuware	NAJHL	50	12	17	29	50	6	3	1	4	4
1998-99	Plymouth Whalers	OHL	65	17	15	32	62	11	3	6	9	15
99-2000	Plymouth Whalers	OHL	66	34	44	78	114	20	9	8	17	10

SUSHINSKY, Maxim (soo-SHIHN-skee, max-EEM) **MIN.**

Right wing. Shoots left. 5'8", 165 lbs. Born, Leningrad, USSR, June 1, 1974.
(Minnesota's 4th choice, 132nd overall, in 2000 Entry Draft).

			Regular Season					Playoffs				
Season	Club	Lea	GP	G	A	TP	PIM	GP	G	A	TP	PIM
1990-91	SKA Leningrad-2	USSR-3	8	1	0	1	0	....	....	....	....	....
	SKA Leningrad	USSR	3	0	1	1	0	....	....	....	....	....
	SKA Leningrad	USSR-Q	1	0	0	0	0	....	....	....	....	....
1991-92	St. Petersburg-2	CIS-3	20	14	1	15	38	....	....	....	....	....
	St. Petersburg	CIS-2	45	5	3	8	16	....	....	....	....	....
1992-93	St. Petersburg	CIS	23	2	3	5	22	6	2	1	3	2
1993-94	St. Petersburg	CIS	45	7	4	11	26	....	....	....	....	....
1994-95	St. Petersburg	CIS	52	11	11	22	57	3	1	0	1	6
1995-96	St. Petersburg	CIS	49	21	15	36	43	2	0	0	0	0
1996-97	Avangard Omsk	Russia	39	20	16	36	24	5	3	1	4	0
1997-98	Avangard Omsk	Russia	20	6	11	17	6	....	....	....	....	....
1998-99	Avangard Omsk	Russia	41	15	16	31	46	5	3	1	4	10
99-2000	Avangard Omsk	Russia	37	19	24	43	58	8	2	5	7	6

SUTHERBY, Brian (SUH-thur-bee) **WSH.**

Center. Shoots left. 6'2", 180 lbs. Born, Edmonton, Alta., March 1, 1982.
(Washington's 1st choice, 26th overall, in 2000 Entry Draft).

			Regular Season					Playoffs				
Season	Club	Lea	GP	G	A	TP	PIM	GP	G	A	TP	PIM
1997-98	CAC Cement	AMHL	36	36	23	59	60	....	....	....	....	....
1998-99	Moose Jaw	WHL	66	9	12	21	47	11	0	1	1	0
99-2000	Moose Jaw	WHL	47	18	17	35	102	4	1	1	2	12

SUTTER, Shaun (SUH-tuhr, SHAWN) **CGY.**

Center. Shoots right. 6'1", 175 lbs. Born, Red Deer, Alta., June 2, 1980.
(Calgary's 4th choice, 102nd overall, in 1998 Entry Draft).

			Regular Season					Playoffs				
Season	Club	Lea	GP	G	A	TP	PIM	GP	G	A	TP	PIM
1995-96	Red Deer Chiefs	AAHA	23	4	6	10	62	....	....	....	....	....
1996-97	Red Deer Chiefs	AAHA	33	15	24	39	143	....	....	....	....	....
	Lethbridge	WHL	1	0	0	0	0	....	....	....	....	....
1997-98	Lethbridge	WHL	69	11	9	20	146	4	0	0	0	4
1998-99	Lethbridge	WHL	35	8	4	12	43	....	....	....	....	....
	Medicine Hat	WHL	23	9	5	14	38	....	....	....	....	....
99-2000	Medicine Hat	WHL	29	1	7	8	43	....	....	....	....	....
	Calgary Hitmen	WHL	6	0	1	1	8	....	....	....	....	....

SUURSOO, Toivo (SUH-uhr-soh-oh, TOI-voh) **DET.**

Left wing. Shoots right. 6', 175 lbs. Born, Tallinn, USSR, November 23, 1975.
(Detroit's 10th choice, 283rd overall, in 1994 Entry Draft).

			Regular Season					Playoffs				
Season	Club	Lea	GP	G	A	TP	PIM	GP	G	A	TP	PIM
1993-94	Krylja Sovetov	CIS	33	3	0	3	8	....	....	....	....	....
1994-95	Krylja Sovetov	CIS	47	10	5	15	36	4	0	0	0	4
1995-96	Krylja Sovetov	CIS	47	6	4	10	36	....	....	....	....	....
1996-97	TPS Turku	Finland	50	11	8	19	64	12	2	3	5	4
1997-98	TPS Turku	Finland	38	17	5	22	46	4	2	1	3	2
	TPS Turku	EuroHL	4	2	0	2	0	....	....	....	....	....
1998-99	Malmo IF	Sweden	29	8	6	14	57	8	4	3	7	12
	Adirondack	AHL	2	0	0	0	0	....	....	....	....	....
99-2000	Malmo IF	Sweden	32	6	5	11	24	1	0	0	0	0

SVOBODA, Jaroslav (svah-BOH-duh) **CAR.**

Left wing. Shoots left. 6'2", 190 lbs. Born, Cervenka, Czech., June 1, 1980.
(Carolina's 8th choice, 208th overall, in 1998 Entry Draft).

			Regular Season					Playoffs				
Season	Club	Lea	GP	G	A	TP	PIM	GP	G	A	TP	PIM
1995-96	HC Olomouc-Jr.	Cze-Rep	40	13	15	28	....	....	....	....	....	....
1996-97	HC Olomouc-Jr.	Cze-Rep	39	19	14	33	....	....	....	....	....	....
1997-98	HC Olomouc-Jr.	Cze-Rep	36	14	21	35	....	....	....	....	....	....
	HC Olomouc-2	Cze-Rep	13	0	1	1	....	....	....	....	....	....
1998-99	Kootenay Ice	WHL	54	26	33	59	46	7	2	2	4	11
99-2000	Kootenay Ice	WHL	56	23	43	66	97	21	*15	13	*28	51

SVOBODA, Petr (svah-BOH-duh, PEE-tuhr) **TOR.**

Defense. Shoots right. 6'3", 200 lbs. Born, Jihlava, Czech., June 20, 1980.
(Toronto's 2nd choice, 35th overall, in 1998 Entry Draft).

			Regular Season					Playoffs				
Season	Club	Lea	GP	G	A	TP	PIM	GP	G	A	TP	PIM
1995-96	SK Jihlava-Jr.	Cze-Rep	38	4	12	16	50	....	....	....	....	....
1996-97	SK Jihlava-Jr.	Cze-Rep	29	1	3	4	....	....	....	....	....	....
1997-98	Dukla Jihlava	Cze-Rep	1	0	0	0	0	....	....	....	....	....
	Havlickuv Brod-2	Cze-Rep	18	1	2	3	16	....	....	....	....	....
	SK Jihlava-Jr.	Cze-Rep	12	0	2	2	....	....	....	....	....	....
1998-99	Dukla Jihlava	Cze-Rep	40	1	5	6	28	....	....	....	....	....
99-2000	HC Ocelari Trinec	Cze-Rep	46	1	2	3	44	3	0	0	0	0

SWANSON, Brian (SWAHN-sohn, BRIGH-an)

Center. Shoots left. 5'10", 180 lbs. Born, Anchorage, AK, March 24, 1976.
(San Jose's 5th choice, 115th overall, in 1994 Entry Draft).

			Regular Season					Playoffs				
Season	Club	Lea	GP	G	A	TP	PIM	GP	G	A	TP	PIM
1991-92	Anchorage Stars	AAHL	50	35	40	75	10	....	....	....	....	....
1992-93	Anchorage Stars	AAHL	45	40	50	90	12	....	....	....	....	....
1993-94	Omaha Lancers	USHL	47	38	42	80	40	....	....	....	....	....
1994-95	Omaha Lancers	USHL	33	14	35	49	12	....	....	....	....	....
1995-96	Colorado College	WCHA	40	26	33	59	24	....	....	....	....	....
1996-97	Colorado College	WCHA	43	19	32	51	47	....	....	....	....	....
1997-98	Colorado College	WCHA	42	18	*38	*56	26	....	....	....	....	....
1998-99	Colorado College	WCHA	42	25	*41	66	28	....	....	....	....	....
	Hartford	AHL	4	0	0	0	4	....	....	....	....	....
99-2000	Hamilton Bulldogs	AHL	69	19	40	59	18	10	2	5	7	6

WCHA Second All-Star Team (1996) • WCHA First All-Star Team (1997, 1998, 1999) • NCAA West Second All-American Team (1998) • NCAA West First All-American Team (1999)

Traded to **NY Rangers** by **San Jose** with Jayson More and San Jose's 4th round choice (later traded back to San Jose - San Jose selected Adam Colagiacomo) in 1997 Entry Draft for Marty McSorley, August 20, 1996. Signed as a free agent by **Edmonton**, August 19, 1999.

SWANSON, Scott (SWAHN-sohn, SCAWT) **WSH.**

Defense. Shoots left. 6'2", 190 lbs. Born, St. Paul, MN, February 15, 1975.
(Washington's 10th choice, 225th overall, in 1995 Entry Draft).

			Regular Season					Playoffs				
Season	Club	Lea	GP	G	A	TP	PIM	GP	G	A	TP	PIM
1994-95	Omaha Lancers	USHL	48	14	46	60	22	....	....	....	....	....
1995-96	Omaha Lancers	USHL	1	0	0	0	0	....	....	....	....	....
	Colorado College	WCHA	42	13	35	48	16	....	....	....	....	....
1996-97	Colorado College	WCHA	44	4	16	20	22	....	....	....	....	....
1997-98	Colorado College	WCHA	42	7	32	39	24	....	....	....	....	....
1998-99	Colorado College	WCHA	42	11	*41	52	16	....	....	....	....	....
99-2000	Houston Aeros	IHL	67	6	7	13	38	6	0	1	1	6

WCHA Second All-Star Team (1996) • NCAA Championship All-Tournament Team (1996) • WCHA First All-Star Team (1999) • NCAA West First All-American Team (1999)

SZYSKY, Chris (SHIHS-kee, KRIHS) **OTT.**

Right wing. Shoots right. 6', 208 lbs. Born, White City, Sask., June 8, 1976.
(Dallas' 8th choice, 280th overall, in 1994 Entry Draft).

			Regular Season					Playoffs				
Season	Club	Lea	GP	G	A	TP	PIM	GP	G	A	TP	PIM
1993-94	Swift Current	WHL	60	6	10	16	82	7	0	1	1	12
1994-95	Swift Current	WHL	61	6	6	12	105	6	2	0	2	10
1995-96	Swift Current	WHL	63	19	16	35	115	6	3	2	5	21
1996-97	Swift Current	WHL	66	28	30	58	181	10	5	10	15	18
1997-98	Canada	Nat-Team	50	9	20	29	111	....	....	....	....	....
1998-99	Canada	Nat-Team	41	9	13	22	56	....	....	....	....	....
	Grand Rapids	IHL	6	1	1	2	10	....	....	....	....	....
99-2000	Grand Rapids	IHL	32	5	4	9	44	15	2	3	5	45

Signed as a free agent by **Ottawa**, June 20, 1999.

TAFFE, Jeff (TAYF) **ST.L.**

Center. Shoots left. 6'2", 180 lbs. Born, Hastings, MN, February 19, 1981.
(St. Louis' 1st choice, 30th overall, in 2000 Entry Draft).

			Regular Season					Playoffs				
Season	Club	Lea	GP	G	A	TP	PIM	GP	G	A	TP	PIM
1996-97	Hastings High	Hi-School	25	21	37	58	....	....	....	....	....	....
1997-98	Hastings High	Hi-School	28	37	29	66	....	....	....	....	....	....
1998-99	Hastings High	Hi-School	28	39	51	90	....	....	....	....	....	....
99-2000	U. of Minnesota	WCHA	39	10	10	20	22	....	....	....	....	....

TALLINDER, Henrik (tah-LIHN-duhr, HEHN-rihk) **BUF.**

Defense. Shoots left. 6'3", 194 lbs. Born, Stockholm, Sweden, January 10, 1979.
(Buffalo's 2nd choice, 48th overall, in 1997 Entry Draft).

			Regular Season					Playoffs				
Season	Club	Lea	GP	G	A	TP	PIM	GP	G	A	TP	PIM
1996-97	AIK Solna	Swede-Jr.	40	4	13	17	55	....	....	....	....	....
	AIK Solna	Sweden	1	0	0	0	0	....	....	....	....	....
1997-98	AIK Solna	Sweden	34	0	0	0	26	....	....	....	....	....
1998-99	AIK Solna	Sweden	36	0	0	0	30	....	....	....	....	....
99-2000	AIK Solna	Sweden	50	0	2	2	59	....	....	....	....	....

TAPPER, Brad **ATL.**

Center. Shoots right. 6', 175 lbs. Born, Scarborough, Ont., April 28, 1978.

			Regular Season					Playoffs				
Season	Club	Lea	GP	G	A	TP	PIM	GP	G	A	TP	PIM
1996-97	Wexford Raiders	OJHL	50	42	70	112	169	....	....	....	....	....
1997-98	RPI Engineers	ECAC	34	14	11	25	62	....	....	....	....	....
1998-99	RPI Engineers	ECAC	35	20	20	40	60	....	....	....	....	....
99-2000	RPI Engineers	ECAC	37	*31	20	51	81	....	....	....	....	....

ECAC First All-Star Team (2000) • NCAA East Second All-American Team (2000)

Signed as a free agent by **Atlanta**, April 11, 2000.

TARVAINEN, Jussi (tahr-VIGH-nehn, YU-see) **EDM.**

Right wing. Shoots right. 6'3", 215 lbs. Born, Lahti, Finland, May 31, 1976.
(Edmonton's 7th choice, 95th overall, in 1994 Entry Draft).

			Regular Season					Playoffs				
Season	Club	Lea	GP	G	A	TP	PIM	GP	G	A	TP	PIM
1992-93	KalPa Kuopio-B	Finn-Jr.	18	13	9	22	38	....	....	....	....	....
	KalPa Kuopio	Finn-Jr.	17	3	6	9	35	....	....	....	....	....
1993-94	Junkkarit HT-2	Finn-Jr.	1	0	0	0	0	....	....	....	....	....
	KalPa Kuopio	Finn-Jr.	16	9	14	23	12	....	....	....	....	....
	KalPa Kuopio	Finland	42	3	4	7	20	....	....	....	....	....
1994-95	KalPa Kuopio	Finn-Jr.	3	4	0	4	2	....	....	....	....	....
	KalPa Kuopio	Finland	45	10	7	17	34	3	0	0	0	2
1995-96	KalPa Kuopio	Finn-Jr.	3	2	3	5	10	7	3	4	7	12
	KalPa Kuopio	Finland	47	8	11	19	50	....	....	....	....	....
1996-97	KalPa Kuopio	Finland	49	14	26	40	62	....	....	....	....	....
	KalPa Kuopio	Finn-Jr.	....	....	....	....	....	1	0	0	0	2
	KalPa Kuopio	Finland-2	....	....	....	....	....	6	4	3	7	4
1997-98	JyP Jyvaskyla	Finland	43	12	26	38	59	....	....	....	....	....
1998-99	JyP Jyvaskyla	Finland	54	17	24	41	84	3	0	0	0	8
99-2000	Tappara Tampere	Finland	52	20	27	47	91	4	1	0	1	2

TATARINOV, Alexander (ta-TAHR-ee-nahf) **PHX.**

Right wing. Shoots left. 5'11", 176 lbs. Born, Sverdlovsk, USSR, April 14, 1982.
(Phoenix's 2nd choice, 53rd overall, in 2000 Entry Draft).

			Regular Season					Playoffs				
Season	Club	Lea	GP	G	A	TP	PIM	GP	G	A	TP	PIM
1998-99	Spartak Moscow	Russia	2	0	0	0	0	....	....	....	....	....
	Spartak Moscow	Russia-Q	1	0	0	0	0	....	....	....	....	....
99-2000	Torpedo Yaroslavl	Russia-3	35	12	12	24	36	....	....	....	....	....

TENKRAT, Petr (TEHN-krat) **ANA.**

Right wing. Shoots right. 6'1", 185 lbs. Born, Kladno, Czech., May 31, 1977.
(Anaheim's 6th choice, 230th overall, in 1999 Entry Draft).

			Regular Season					Playoffs				
Season	Club	Lea	GP	G	A	TP	PIM	GP	G	A	TP	PIM
1996-97	Poldi Kladno	Cze-Rep	43	5	9	14	6	3	0	1	1	0
1997-98	Poldi Kladno	Cze-Rep	52	9	10	19	24	....	....	....	....	....
1998-99	HC Velvana	Cze-Rep	50	21	14	35	32	....	....	....	....	....
99-2000	HPK Hameenlinna	Finland	32	20	9	29	31	....	....	....	....	....
	Ilves Tampere	Finland	22	15	5	20	44	3	1	1	2	14

TERESCHENKO, Alexei (teh-REH-shehn-koh) DAL.

Center. Shoots left. 5'11", 176 lbs. Born, Mozhaisk, USSR, December 16, 1980.
(Dallas' 4th choice, 91st overall, in 2000 Entry Draft).

			Regular Season					Playoffs				
Season	Club	Lea	GP	G	A	TP	PIM	GP	G	A	TP	PIM
1997-98	D'amo Moscow-2	Russia-2	26	6	7	13	30	....	....	....	....	....
1998-99	D'amo Moscow-2	Russia-3	28	4	17	21	20	....	....	....	....	....
	THC Tver	Russia-2	12	3	4	7	4	....	....	....	....	....
	Dynamo Moscow	Russia	1	0	1	1	0	2	0	0	0	0
99-2000	Dynamo Moscow	Russia	27	1	1	2	10	17	1	1	2	8

TETARENKO, Joey (teh-tar-EHN-koh, JOH-ee) FLA.

Defense. Shoots right. 6'2", 212 lbs. Born, Prince Albert, Sask., March 3, 1978.
(Florida's 4th choice, 82nd overall, in 1996 Entry Draft).

			Regular Season					Playoffs				
Season	Club	Lea	GP	G	A	TP	PIM	GP	G	A	TP	PIM
1994-95	Portland	WHL	59	0	1	1	134	9	0	0	0	8
1995-96	Portland	WHL	71	4	11	15	190	7	0	1	1	17
1996-97	Portland	WHL	68	8	18	26	182	2	0	0	0	2
1997-98	Portland	WHL	49	2	12	14	148	16	0	2	2	30
1998-99	New Haven	AHL	65	4	10	14	154	....	....	....	....	....
99-2000	Louisville	AHL	57	3	11	14	136	4	0	0	0	2

TETRAULT, Daniel (teh-TROH, DAN-yehl)

Defense. Shoots right. 6', 198 lbs. Born, St. Boniface, Man., September 4, 1979.
(Montreal's 4th choice, 91st overall, in 1997 Entry Draft).

			Regular Season					Playoffs				
Season	Club	Lea	GP	G	A	TP	PIM	GP	G	A	TP	PIM
1994-95	Eastman Selects	MAHA	34	11	20	31	82	....	....	....	....	....
1995-96	Brandon	WHL	72	6	13	19	91	19	1	1	2	25
1996-97	Brandon	WHL	64	5	24	29	136	6	0	0	0	14
1997-98	Brandon	WHL	16	2	3	5	32	18	0	5	5	25
1998-99	Brandon	WHL	57	10	36	46	91	4	0	0	0	9
99-2000	Brandon	WHL	31	4	10	14	43	....	....	....	....	....

THEORET, Luc (THEE-ohr-eht, LEWK) BUF.

Defense. Shoots left. 6'2", 192 lbs. Born, Winnipeg, Man., July 30, 1979.
(Buffalo's 5th choice, 101st overall, in 1997 Entry Draft).

			Regular Season					Playoffs				
Season	Club	Lea	GP	G	A	TP	PIM	GP	G	A	TP	PIM
1995-96	Lethbridge	WHL	47	4	13	17	41	4	0	0	0	6
1996-97	Lethbridge	WHL	43	3	7	10	51	19	1	5	6	8
1997-98	Lethbridge	WHL	65	12	37	49	98	4	0	1	1	8
1998-99	Lethbridge	WHL	46	13	39	52	92	....	....	....	....	....
	Portland	WHL	3	0	0	0	10	....	....	....	....	....
99-2000	South Carolina	ECHL	48	9	10	19	74	10	2	2	4	10

THINEL, Marc-Andre (tih-nehl, MAHRK-AWN-dray) MTL.

Right wing. Shoots left. 6', 160 lbs. Born, St. Jerome, Que., March 24, 1981.
(Montreal's 6th choice, 145th overall, in 1999 Entry Draft).

			Regular Season					Playoffs				
Season	Club	Lea	GP	G	A	TP	PIM	GP	G	A	TP	PIM
1997-98	Victoriaville Tigres	QMJHL	58	7	10	17	20	6	0	3	3	4
1998-99	Victoriaville Tigres	QMJHL	66	45	58	103	16	6	5	3	8	4
99-2000	Victoriaville Tigres	QMJHL	71	59	73	132	55	6	5	6	11	18

QMJHL First All-Star Team (2000)

THOMPSON, Chris (THOHMP-sohn, KRIHS) N.J.

Right wing. Shoots left. 6'1", 200 lbs. Born, Prince Albert, Sask., April 10, 1978.

			Regular Season					Playoffs				
Season	Club	Lea	GP	G	A	TP	PIM	GP	G	A	TP	PIM
1994-95	Prince Albert	SAHA	36	13	16	29	82	....	....	....	....	....
1995-96	Seattle T-Birds	WHL	56	8	5	13	86	5	0	0	0	21
1996-97	Seattle T-Birds	WHL	65	3	14	17	191	15	1	1	2	67
1997-98	Seattle T-Birds	WHL	70	16	32	48	339	5	0	0	0	18
1998-99	Albany River Rats	AHL	9	0	0	0	14	....	....	....	....	....
	Augusta Lynx	ECHL	57	16	14	30	221	2	0	0	0	4
99-2000	Augusta Lynx	ECHL	65	23	30	53	184	9	0	6	6	38

Signed as a free agent by **New Jersey**, July 23, 1998.

THOMPSON, Mark (THOHMP-sohn, MAHRK) T.B.

Defense. Shoots right. 6'8", 234 lbs. Born, St. Albert, Alta., April 26, 1979.
(Tampa Bay's 4th choice, 108th overall, in 1997 Entry Draft).

			Regular Season					Playoffs				
Season	Club	Lea	GP	G	A	TP	PIM	GP	G	A	TP	PIM
1994-95	St. Albert Raiders	AMHL	35	4	11	15	90	....	....	....	....	....
1996-97	Regina Pats	WHL	32	1	5	6	20	3	0	1	1	2
1997-98	Regina Pats	WHL	46	0	2	2	44	2	0	0	0	0
1998-99	Kootenay Ice	WHL	36	2	7	9	76	4	0	0	0	2
99-2000	Detroit Vipers	IHL	19	1	0	1	14	....	....	....	....	....
	Toledo Storm	ECHL	53	1	2	3	122	....	....	....	....	....

THORNTON, Shawn (THOHR-tohn, SHAWN) TOR.

Right wing. Shoots right. 6'1", 196 lbs. Born, Oshawa, Ont., July 23, 1979.
(Toronto's 6th choice, 190th overall, in 1997 Entry Draft).

			Regular Season					Playoffs				
Season	Club	Lea	GP	G	A	TP	PIM	GP	G	A	TP	PIM
1995-96	Peterborough	OHL	63	4	10	14	192	24	3	0	3	25
1996-97	Peterborough	OHL	61	19	10	29	204	11	2	4	6	20
1997-98	St. John's Leafs	AHL	59	0	3	3	225	....	....	....	....	....
1998-99	St. John's Leafs	AHL	78	8	11	19	354	5	0	0	0	9
99-2000	St. John's Leafs	AHL	60	4	12	16	316	....	....	....	....	....

THORPE, Ryan (THOHRP, RIGH-yan) VAN.

Left wing. Shoots left. 6'4", 202 lbs. Born, Vancouver, B.C., February 6, 1981.
(Vancouver's 4th choice, 129th overall, in 1999 Entry Draft).

			Regular Season					Playoffs				
Season	Club	Lea	GP	G	A	TP	PIM	GP	G	A	TP	PIM
1995-96	Semiahmoo	BCAHA	29	15	29	44	71	....	....	....	....	....
1997-98	Kamloops Blazers	WHL	43	2	1	3	19	7	0	0	0	2
1998-99	Kamloops Blazers	WHL	22	2	1	3	68	....	....	....	....	....
	Spokane Chiefs	WHL	19	10	3	13	21	....	....	....	....	....
99-2000	Spokane Chiefs	WHL	51	3	9	12	31	6	0	0	0	4

TIBBETTS, Billy PIT.

Right wing. Shoots right. 6'2", 215 lbs. Born, Boston, MA, October 14, 1974.

			Regular Season					Playoffs				
Season	Club	Lea	GP	G	A	TP	PIM	GP	G	A	TP	PIM
1993-94	Tri-City Americans	WHL	9	0	2	2	39	....	....	....	....	....
1994-95	Birmingham Bulls	ECHL	2	0	1	1	18	....	....	....	....	....
1995-96	Johnstown Chiefs	ECHL	58	57	31	68	300	....	....	....	....	....
1996/00			DID NOT PLAY									

• Missed entire 1996-97 through 1999-2000 seasons serving prison sentence for parole violations and assault and battery charges, July 12, 1996. Signed as a free agent by **Pittsburgh**, April 10, 2000.

TIILIKAINEN, Jukka (TEE-ee-lee-kigh-nehn, yoo-KUH) L.A.

Left wing. Shoots left. 6', 190 lbs. Born, Espoo, Finland, April 4, 1974.
(Los Angeles' 8th choice, 255th overall, in 1992 Entry Draft).

			Regular Season					Playoffs				
Season	Club	Lea	GP	G	A	TP	PIM	GP	G	A	TP	PIM
1992-93	Vantaa HT	Finland-2	18	7	3	10	10	....	....	....	....	....
	Kiekko Espoo	Finland	5	0	0	0	4	....	....	....	....	....
1993-94	Kiekko Espoo	Finland	33	2	4	6	12	....	....	....	....	....
1994-95	TPS Turku	Finland	38	5	4	9	8	11	1	0	1	8
1995-96	TPS Turku	Finland	38	6	13	19	28	10	0	2	2	2
1996-97	Lukko Rauma	Finland	49	15	12	27	42	....	....	....	....	....
1997-98	Assat-Pori	Finland	48	13	13	26	18	3	0	2	2	0
1998-99	Jokerit Helsinki	Finland	51	7	8	15	52	2	0	0	0	4
99-2000	Jokerit Helsinki	Finland	19	1	2	3	31	....	....	....	....	....
	AIK Solna	Sweden	29	8	6	14	22	....	....	....	....	....

TIMKIN, Alexei (TIHM-kihn, al-EHX-ay) DAL.

Right wing. Shoots left. 6'2", 194 lbs. Born, Kirov, USSR, April 21, 1979.
(Dallas' 6th choice, 160th overall, in 1997 Entry Draft).

			Regular Season					Playoffs				
Season	Club	Lea	GP	G	A	TP	PIM	GP	G	A	TP	PIM
1996-97	Torpedo Yaroslavl	Russia-3	47	16	6	22	54	....	....	....	....	....
	Torpedo Yaroslavl	Russia	3	0	1	1	0	....	....	....	....	....
1997-98	Torpedo Yaroslavl	Russia-2	16	4	5	9	14	....	....	....	....	....
1998-99			STATISTICS NOT AVAILABLE									
99-2000			STATISTICS NOT AVAILABLE									

TIMMONS, K.C. (TIHM-mohns, KAY-SEE) COL.

Left wing. Shoots left. 6'4", 215 lbs. Born, Victoria, B.C., April 6, 1980.
(Colorado's 9th choice, 141st overall, in 1998 Entry Draft).

			Regular Season					Playoffs				
Season	Club	Lea	GP	G	A	TP	PIM	GP	G	A	TP	PIM
1995-96	Victoria Lions	BCAHA	68	82	101	183	190	....	....	....	....	....
1996-97	Tri-City Americans	WHL	52	0	5	5	27	....	....	....	....	....
1997-98	Tri-City Americans	WHL	72	11	7	18	139	....	....	....	....	....
1998-99	Tri-City Americans	WHL	69	13	11	24	113	12	1	1	2	36
99-2000	Tri-City Americans	WHL	69	24	24	48	193	4	0	0	0	4
	Hershey Bears	AHL	....	....	....	....	....	4	0	0	0	15

TIMOFEEV, Denis (teh-moh-FAY-ehf) BOS.

Defense. Shoots left. 6'6", 190 lbs. Born, Moscow, USSR, January 14, 1979.
(Boston's 7th choice, 135th overall, in 1997 Entry Draft).

			Regular Season					Playoffs				
Season	Club	Lea	GP	G	A	TP	PIM	GP	G	A	TP	PIM
1996-97	CSKA Moscow	Russia	41	6	8	14	....	....	....	....	....	....
	CSKA Moscow	Russia-3	11	0	0	0	2	....	....	....	....	....
1997-98	CSKA Moscow	Russia-Jr.	STATISTICS NOT AVAILABLE									
1998-99	CSKA Moscow	Russia-Jr.	31	4	12	16	16	....	....	....	....	....
99-2000	Providence Bruins	AHL	16	0	1	1	14	....	....	....	....	....
	Greenville Growl	ECHL	24	2	3	5	30	10	0	1	1	24

TJARNQVIST, Daniel (TUH-yahrn-kvihst, DAN-yehl) ATL.

Defense. Shoots left. 6'2", 180 lbs. Born, Umea, Sweden, October 14, 1976.
(Florida's 5th choice, 88th overall, in 1995 Entry Draft).

			Regular Season					Playoffs				
Season	Club	Lea	GP	G	A	TP	PIM	GP	G	A	TP	PIM
1994-95	Rogle BK	Sweden	18	0	1	1	2	....	....	....	....	....
	Rogle BK	Swede-2	15	2	3	5	0	....	....	....	....	....
1995-96	Rogle BK	Sweden	22	1	7	8	6	....	....	....	....	....
1996-97	Jokerit Helsinki	Finland	44	3	8	11	4	9	0	3	3	4
	Jokerit Helsinki	EuroHL	6	1	1	2	2	....	....	....	....	....
1997-98	Djurgardens IF	Sweden	40	5	9	14	12	15	1	1	2	2
1998-99	Djurgardens IF	Sweden	40	4	3	7	16	4	0	0	0	2
99-2000	Djurgardens IF	Sweden	42	3	16	19	8	5	0	0	0	2

Traded to **Atlanta** by **Florida** with Gord Murphy, Herbert Vasiljevs and Ottawa's 6th round choice (previously acquired, later traded to Dallas - Dallas selected Justin Cox) in 1999 Entry Draft for Trevor Kidd, June 25, 1999.

TJARNQVIST, Mathias (TUH-yahrn-kvihst, MAT-ee-uhs) DAL.

Right wing. Shoots left. 6'1", 183 lbs. Born, Umea, Sweden, April 15, 1979.
(Dallas' 3rd choice, 96th overall, in 1999 Entry Draft).

			Regular Season					Playoffs				
Season	Club	Lea	GP	G	A	TP	PIM	GP	G	A	TP	PIM
1995-96	Rogle BK	Swede-Jr.	4	2	0	2	0	....	....	....	....	....
1996-97	Rogle BK	Swede-Jr.	18	5	8	13	....	....	....	....	....	....
	Rogle BK	Swede-2	15	1	4	5	4	....	....	....	....	....
1997-98	Rogle BK	Swede-2	31	12	11	23	30	....	....	....	....	....
1998-99	Rogle BK	Swede-2	34	18	16	34	44	5	4	1	5	4
99-2000	Djurgardens IF	Sweden	50	12	12	24	20	13	3	2	5	16

TKACZUK, Daniel (kuh-CHUK, DAN-yehl) CGY.

Center. Shoots left. 6'1", 197 lbs. Born, Toronto, Ont., June 10, 1979.
(Calgary's 1st choice, 6th overall, in 1997 Entry Draft).

			Regular Season					Playoffs				
Season	Club	Lea	GP	G	A	TP	PIM	GP	G	A	TP	PIM
1994-95	Mississauga Reps	MTHL	53	65	66	131	20	....	....	....	....	....
1995-96	Barrie Colts	OHL	61	22	39	61	38	7	1	2	3	8
1996-97	Barrie Colts	OHL	62	45	48	93	49	9	7	2	9	2
1997-98	Barrie Colts	OHL	57	35	40	75	38	6	2	3	5	8
1998-99	Barrie Colts	OHL	58	43	62	105	58	12	7	8	15	10
99-2000	Saint John Flames	AHL	80	25	41	66	56	3	0	0	0	0

OHL First All-Star Team (1999)

TOBLER, Ryan — NSH.

Left wing. Shoots left. 6'3", 222 lbs. Born, Calgary, Alta., May 13, 1976.

			Regular Season					Playoffs				
Season	Club	Lea	GP	G	A	TP	PIM	GP	G	A	TP	PIM
1994-95	Saskatoon Blades	WHL	61	11	19	30	81	10	1	2	3	8
1995-96	Calgary Hitmen	WHL	16	10	3	13	8	....	....	....	....	....
	Swift Current	WHL	25	17	11	28	31	6	1	1	2	2
1996-97	Swift Current	WHL	39	10	17	27	40	....	....	....	....	....
	Moose Jaw	WHL	24	6	15	21	16	12	1	6	7	16
1997-98	Lake Charles	WPHL	66	22	34	56	204	4	2	3	5	18
	Utah Grizzlies	IHL	3	1	0	1	2	....	....	....	....	....
1998-99	Adirondack	AHL	64	9	18	27	157	3	0	0	0	2
99-2000	Milwaukee	IHL	78	19	28	47	293	2	0	0	0	0

Signed as a free agent by **Nashville**, May 1, 2000.

TOLKUNOV, Dmitri — CHI.

Defense. Shoots right. 6'2", 190 lbs. Born, Kiev, USSR, May 5, 1979.

			Regular Season					Playoffs				
Season	Club	Lea	GP	G	A	TP	PIM	GP	G	A	TP	PIM
1996-97	Hull Olympiques	QMJHL	34	3	8	11	99	....	....	....	....	....
	Beauport	QMJHL	27	3	7	10	18	4	0	1	1	4
1997-98	Quebec Rafales	QMJHL	66	10	25	35	81	14	3	9	12	22
1998-99	Quebec Rafales	QMJHL	69	11	57	68	110	13	2	7	9	22
99-2000	Cleveland	IHL	65	3	12	15	54	8	0	0	0	2

QMJHL Second All-Star Team (1999)

Signed as a free agent by **Chicago**, October 8, 1998.

TOLSA, Jari — (TOHL-suh, YA-ree) DET.

Center. Shoots left. 6', 172 lbs. Born, Goteborg, Sweden, April 20, 1981.
(Detroit's 1st choice, 120th overall, in 1999 Entry Draft).

			Regular Season					Playoffs				
Season	Club	Lea	GP	G	A	TP	PIM	GP	G	A	TP	PIM
1997-98	Vastra Frolunda	Swede-Jr.	26	18	25	43	30	....	....	....	....	....
1998-99	Vastra Frolunda	Swede-Jr.	35	16	21	37	51	....	....	....	....	....
99-2000	Vastra Frolunda	Sweden	10	0	0	0	0	....	....	....	....	....

TORRES, Raffi — (TAW-rehs, RA-fee) NYI

Left wing. Shoots left. 5'11", 207 lbs. Born, Toronto, Ont., October 8, 1981.
(NY Islanders' 2nd choice, 5th overall, in 2000 Entry Draft).

			Regular Season					Playoffs				
Season	Club	Lea	GP	G	A	TP	PIM	GP	G	A	TP	PIM
1997-98	Thornhill Rattlers	OJHL	46	17	16	33	90	....	....	....	....	....
1998-99	Brampton	OHL	62	35	27	62	32	....	....	....	....	....
99-2000	Brampton	OHL	68	43	48	91	40	6	5	2	7	23

OHL Second All-Star Team (2000)

TORY, Jeff — (TOH-ree, JEHF) DAL.

Defense. Shoots right. 5'11", 190 lbs. Born, Burnaby, B.C., May 9, 1973.

			Regular Season					Playoffs				
Season	Club	Lea	GP	G	A	TP	PIM	GP	G	A	TP	PIM
1993-94	U. of Maine	H-East	3	0	0	0	4	....	....	....	....	....
1994-95	U. of Maine	H-East	40	13	42	55	22	....	....	....	....	....
1995-96	U. of Maine	H-East	37	4	36	40	36	....	....	....	....	....
1996-97	Canada	Nt-Team	54	8	37	45	30	....	....	....	....	....
	Kentucky	AHL	3	0	2	2	0	4	0	0	0	2
1997-98	Houston Aeros	IHL	74	11	27	38	35	4	0	1	1	2
1998-99	Houston Aeros	IHL	79	19	36	55	46	18	2	6	8	8
99-2000	Philadelphia	AHL	76	17	41	58	44	5	1	3	4	4

Hockey East First All-Star Team (1995) • NCAA East Second All-American Team (1995) • Hockey East All-Star Team (1996) • NCAA East First All-American Team (1996)

Signed as a free agent by **Philadelphia**, July 27, 1999. Signed as a free agent by **Dallas**, July 26, 2000.

TRATTNIG, Matthias — (TRAT-nihg, MAH-tee-uhs) CHI.

Center. Shoots left. 6'1", 208 lbs. Born, Graz, Austria, April 22, 1979.
(Chicago's 2nd choice, 94th overall, in 1998 Entry Draft).

			Regular Season					Playoffs				
Season	Club	Lea	GP	G	A	TP	PIM	GP	G	A	TP	PIM
1995-96	EC Graz	Austria	17	0	1	1	0	....	....	....	....	....
1996-97	Capital District	NYJHL	51	30	54	84	64	....	....	....	....	....
1997-98	U. of Maine	H-East	34	8	9	17	30	....	....	....	....	....
1998-99	U. of Maine	H-East	39	5	5	10	32	....	....	....	....	....
99-2000	U. of Maine	H-East	39	8	11	19	26	....	....	....	....	....

TRAVNICEK, Michal — (TRAV-nih-chehk, MEE-khuhl) TOR.

Right wing. Shoots left. 6'1", 198 lbs. Born, Decin, Czech., March 14, 1980.
(Toronto's 9th choice, 228th overall, in 1998 Entry Draft).

			Regular Season					Playoffs				
Season	Club	Lea	GP	G	A	TP	PIM	GP	G	A	TP	PIM
1996-97	CHZ Litvinov	Czech-Jr.	45	35	22	57	....	....	....	....	....	....
1997-98	CHZ Litvinov	Czech-Jr.	43	18	20	38	....	....	....	....	....	....
1998-99	CHZ Litvinov	Cze-Rep	49	7	7	14	65	....	....	....	....	....
99-2000	CHZ Litvinov	Cze-Rep	51	3	6	9	28	7	0	0	0	0

TREILLE, Yorick — (TRAYL, YOH-rihk) CHI.

Right wing. Shoots right. 6'3", 185 lbs. Born, Cannes, France, July 15, 1980.
(Chicago's 7th choice, 195th overall, in 1999 Entry Draft).

			Regular Season					Playoffs				
Season	Club	Lea	GP	G	A	TP	PIM	GP	G	A	TP	PIM
1997-98	Notre Dame	SJHL	54	18	28	46	42	....	....	....	....	....
1998-99	U. Mass-Lowell	H-East	30	6	5	11	24	....	....	....	....	....
99-2000	U. Mass-Lowell	H-East	33	10	12	22	34	....	....	....	....	....

TREMBLAY, Didier — (TRAHM-blay, DEE-duhr) ST.L.

Defense. Shoots left. 6'1", 190 lbs. Born, Laval, Que., May 4, 1979.
(St. Louis' 2nd choice, 86th overall, in 1997 Entry Draft).

			Regular Season					Playoffs				
Season	Club	Lea	GP	G	A	TP	PIM	GP	G	A	TP	PIM
1993-94	Rive-Nord	QAAA	31	11	20	31	44	....	....	....	....	....
1994-95	Laval Regents	QAAA	44	3	22	25	52	....	....	....	....	....
1995-96	Halifax	QMJHL	56	4	10	14	80	6	0	3	3	4
1996-97	Halifax	QMJHL	68	11	26	37	79	12	1	3	4	6
1997-98	Halifax	QMJHL	39	6	19	25	26	....	....	....	....	....
	Val-d'Or Foreurs	QMJHL	31	6	24	30	43	19	5	13	18	8
1998-99	Val-d'Or Foreurs	QMJHL	63	23	51	74	56	6	1	4	5	4
99-2000	Worcester	AHL	27	1	6	7	8	....	....	....	....	....
	Peoria Rivermen	ECHL	36	5	16	21	14	18	6	7	13	18

TRIPP, John — (TRIHP, JAWN)

Right wing. Shoots right. 6'2", 215 lbs. Born, Kingston, Ont., May 4, 1977.
(Calgary's 3rd choice, 42nd overall, in 1997 Entry Draft).

			Regular Season					Playoffs				
Season	Club	Lea	GP	G	A	TP	PIM	GP	G	A	TP	PIM
1993-94	St. Marys Lincolns	OJHL-B	42	15	29	44	116	....	....	....	....	....
1994-95	Oshawa Generals	OHL	58	6	11	17	53	7	0	1	1	4
1995-96	Oshawa Generals	OHL	56	13	14	27	95	5	1	1	2	13
1996-97	Oshawa Generals	OHL	59	28	20	48	126	18	*16	10	26	42
1997-98	Roanoke Express	ECHL	9	0	2	2	22	....	....	....	....	....
	Saint John Flames	AHL	61	1	11	12	66	2	0	1	1	0
1998-99	Saint John Flames	AHL	2	0	0	0	10	....	....	....	....	....
	Johnstown Chiefs	ECHL	7	2	0	2	12	....	....	....	....	....
99-2000	Johnstown Chiefs	ECHL	38	13	11	24	64	....	....	....	....	....
	Saint John Flames	AHL	29	8	7	15	38	3	0	0	0	2

• Re-entered NHL draft. Originally Colorado's 3rd choice, 77th overall, in 1995 Entry Draft.

TROCHINSKY, Andrei — (troh-SCHIHN-skee, AN-dray) ST.L.

Center. Shoots left. 6'5", 187 lbs. Born, Ust-Kamenogorsk, USSR, February 14, 1978.
(St. Louis' 5th choice, 170th overall, in 1998 Entry Draft).

			Regular Season					Playoffs				
Season	Club	Lea	GP	G	A	TP	PIM	GP	G	A	TP	PIM
1996-97	Ust-Kamenogorsk	Russia-2	9	1	1	2	8	....	....	....	....	....
1997-98	Ust-Kamenogorsk	Russia-2	47	10	16	26	34	....	....	....	....	....
1998-99	Ust-Kamenogorsk	Russia-4	4	4	4	8	6	....	....	....	....	....
	Ust-Kamenogorsk	Russia-3	42	11	21	32	62	....	....	....	....	....
99-2000	Ust-Kamenogorsk	Russia-3	50	20	46	66	....	....	....	....	....	....

TROTTIER, Joel — (TRAH-chay, JOHL) BOS.

Right wing. Shoots right. 6', 200 lbs. Born, Alexandria, Ont., February 11, 1977.
(Boston's 8th choice, 162nd overall, in 1997 Entry Draft).

			Regular Season					Playoffs				
Season	Club	Lea	GP	G	A	TP	PIM	GP	G	A	TP	PIM
1993-94	Cornwall Royals	OJHL	55	13	17	30	78	....	....	....	....	....
1994-95	Ottawa 67's	OHL	53	7	10	17	13	....	....	....	....	....
1995-96	Ottawa 67's	OHL	63	25	19	44	57	4	4	1	5	7
1996-97	Ottawa 67's	OHL	56	41	39	80	57	22	14	12	26	23
1997-98	Plymouth Whalers	OHL	10	4	6	10	17	....	....	....	....	....
	Belleville Bulls	OHL	43	23	32	55	51	10	5	6	11	9
1998-99	Providence Bruins	AHL	7	3	0	3	17	....	....	....	....	....
	Greenville Growl	ECHL	53	15	15	30	49	....	....	....	....	....
99-2000	Greenville Growl	ECHL	49	10	20	30	53	....	....	....	....	....
	Providence Bruins	AHL	6	0	1	1	2	....	....	....	....	....

TRUDEAU, Roger — ST.L.

Left wing. Shoots left. 6'3", 205 lbs. Born, Marquette, MI, April 22, 1976.

			Regular Season					Playoffs				
Season	Club	Lea	GP	G	A	TP	PIM	GP	G	A	TP	PIM
1995-96	Waterloo Hawks	USHL	27	12	23	35	....	....	....	....	....	....
1996-97	North-Michigan	CCHA	38	12	6	18	14	....	....	....	....	....
1997-98	North-Michigan	CCHA	33	16	12	28	28	....	....	....	....	....
1998-99	North-Michigan	CCHA	42	19	14	33	42	....	....	....	....	....
99-2000	North-Michigan	CCHA	39	21	15	36	48	....	....	....	....	....

CCHA First All-Star Team (2000)

Signed as a free agent by **St. Louis**, March 20, 2000.

TSELIOS, Nikos — (TSEHL-ee-ohs, NEE-kohs) CAR.

Defense. Shoots left. 6'5", 210 lbs. Born, Oak Park, IL, January 20, 1979.
(Carolina's 1st choice, 22nd overall, in 1997 Entry Draft).

			Regular Season					Playoffs				
Season	Club	Lea	GP	G	A	TP	PIM	GP	G	A	TP	PIM
1995-96	Chicago Amerks	MEHL	27	5	8	13	40	....	....	....	....	....
1996-97	Belleville Bulls	OHL	64	9	37	46	61	6	1	1	2	2
1997-98	Belleville Bulls	OHL	20	2	10	12	16	....	....	....	....	....
	Plymouth Whalers	OHL	41	8	20	28	27	15	1	8	9	27
1998-99	Plymouth Whalers	OHL	60	21	39	60	60	11	4	10	14	8
99-2000	Cincinnati	IHL	80	3	19	22	75	10	0	2	2	4

TSYBUK, Yevgeny — (tsee-BUHK, YEHV-jeh-nee) DAL.

Defense. Shoots left. 6', 196 lbs. Born, Chebarkul, USSR, February 2, 1978.
(Dallas' 5th choice, 113th overall, in 1996 Entry Draft).

			Regular Season					Playoffs				
Season	Club	Lea	GP	G	A	TP	PIM	GP	G	A	TP	PIM
1996-97	Lethbridge	WHL	10	0	1	1	13	....	....	....	....	....
1997-98	Lethbridge	WHL	41	5	13	18	129	4	1	1	2	12
1998-99	Michigan K-Wings	IHL	42	1	3	4	69	2	0	0	0	2
99-2000	Michigan K-Wings	IHL	50	0	2	2	82	....	....	....	....	....

TUKIO, Arto — (TOO-kee-oh, AHR-toh) NYI

Defense. Shoots left. 5'10", 176 lbs. Born, Tampere, Finland, April 4, 1981.
(NY Islanders' 3rd choice, 101st overall, in 2000 Entry Draft).

			Regular Season					Playoffs				
Season	Club	Lea	GP	G	A	TP	PIM	GP	G	A	TP	PIM
1996-97	Ilves Tampere-B	Finn-Jr.	20	0	2	2	6	1	1	0	1	0
	Ilves Tampere-C	Finn-Jr.	6	1	3	4	4	....	....	....	....	....
1997-98	Ilves Tampere-B	Finn-Jr.	39	7	7	14	64	....	....	....	....	....
1998-99	Ilves Tampere-B	Finn-Jr.	10	1	5	6	18	....	....	....	....	....
	Ilves Tampere	Finn-Jr.	18	1	4	5	12	10	0	0	0	2
99-2000	Ilves Tampere	Finn-Jr.	11	2	1	3	24	....	....	....	....	....
	Hermes Kokkola	Finland-2	1	0	0	0	0	....	....	....	....	....
	Ilves Tampere	Finland	42	2	1	3	20	3	0	0	0	0

TVRDON, Roman (t-vahr-DAWN) WSH.

Center. Shoots left. 6'1", 189 lbs. Born, Trencin, Czech., January 29, 1981.
(Washington's 6th choice, 132nd overall, in 1999 Entry Draft).

			Regular Season					Playoffs				
Season	Club	Lea	GP	G	A	TP	PIM	GP	G	A	TP	PIM
1997-98	Dukla Trencin	Slovak-Jr.	48	4	12	16	39	....	....	....	....	....
1998-99	Dukla Trencin	Slovak-Jr.	49	23	23	46	20	6	4	4	8	4
99-2000	Spokane Chiefs	WHL	69	26	44	70	40	15	4	7	11	16

TWORDIK, Brad (TWOHR-dihk, BRAD)

Center. Shoots left. 5'10", 201 lbs. Born, Saskatoon, Sask., November 20, 1979.
(St. Louis' 6th choice, 197th overall, in 1998 Entry Draft).

			Regular Season					Playoffs				
Season	Club	Lea	GP	G	A	TP	PIM	GP	G	A	TP	PIM
1995-96	Saskatoon Blazers	SAHA	42	42	49	91	62	....	....	....	....	....
	Brandon	WHL	3	0	0	0	2	....	....	....	....	....
1996-97	Brandon	WHL	71	23	33	56	77	6	1	1	2	17
1997-98	Brandon	WHL	69	23	49	72	81	18	5	11	16	35
1998-99	Brandon	WHL	57	29	45	74	67	5	2	1	3	9
99-2000	Brandon	WHL	72	24	45	69	57	....	....	....	....	....
	Idaho Steelheads	WCHL	4	3	5	8	0	3	0	1	1	0

ULMER, Jeff NYR

Right wing. Shoots right. 5'11", 190 lbs. Born, Wilcox, Sask., April 27, 1977.

			Regular Season					Playoffs				
Season	Club	Lea	GP	G	A	TP	PIM	GP	G	A	TP	PIM
1994-95	Notre Dame	AJHL	63	25	35	60	....	....	....	....	....	....
1995-96	North Dakota	WCHA	29	5	3	8	26	....	....	....	....	....
1996-97	North Dakota	WCHA	26	6	11	17	16	....	....	....	....	....
1997-98	North Dakota	WCHA	32	12	12	24	44	....	....	....	....	....
1998-99	North Dakota	WCHA	38	16	20	36	46	....	....	....	....	....
99-2000	Team Canada	Nt-Team	48	14	25	39	20	....	....	....	....	....
	Houston Aeros	IHL	5	1	0	1	0	11	2	4	6	6

Signed as a free agent by **Houston** (IHL), March 30, 2000. Signed as a free agent by **NY Rangers**, July 27, 2000.

ULMER, Layne (UHL-muhr) OTT.

Center. Shoots left. 6', 193 lbs. Born, North Battleford, Sask., September 14, 1980.
(Ottawa's 8th choice, 209th overall, in 1999 Entry Draft).

			Regular Season					Playoffs				
Season	Club	Lea	GP	G	A	TP	PIM	GP	G	A	TP	PIM
1996-97	Swift Current	SAHA	43	35	49	84	31	....	....	....	....	....
1997-98	Swift Current	WHL	50	8	9	17	23	12	3	1	4	0
1998-99	Swift Current	WHL	72	40	35	75	34	6	2	1	3	4
99-2000	Swift Current	WHL	71	50	54	104	66	12	12	6	18	16

WHL East First All-Star Team (2000)

UPPER, Dmitri (OO-puhr, dih-MEE-tree) NYI

Center. Shoots right. 6', 185 lbs. Born, Ust-Kamenogorsk, USSR, July 27, 1978.
(NY Islanders' 5th choice, 136th overall, in 2000 Entry Draft).

			Regular Season					Playoffs				
Season	Club	Lea	GP	G	A	TP	PIM	GP	G	A	TP	PIM
1997-98	Ust-Kamenogorsk	Russia-2	47	16	12	28	44	....	....	....	....	....
1998-99	Ust-Kamenogorsk	Russia-3	29	10	11	21	44	....	....	....	....	....
	Torpedo Nizhny	Russia-2	28	10	16	26	65	....	....	....	....	....
99-2000	Torpedo Nizhny	Russia	36	14	6	20	50	5	1	1	2	4

URICK, Brian (YOOR-ihk, BRIGH-an) EDM.

Right wing. Shoots right. 6'1", 195 lbs. Born, Minneapolis, MN, January 25, 1977.
(Edmonton's 5th choice, 114th overall, in 1996 Entry Draft).

			Regular Season					Playoffs				
Season	Club	Lea	GP	G	A	TP	PIM	GP	G	A	TP	PIM
1994-95	Minnetonka High	Hi-School	24	30	29	59	28	....	....	....	....	....
1995-96	Notre Dame	CCHA	36	12	15	27	66	....	....	....	....	....
1996-97	Notre Dame	CCHA	34	13	12	25	88	....	....	....	....	....
1997-98	Notre Dame	CCHA	41	16	18	34	40	....	....	....	....	....
1998-99	Notre Dame	CCHA	35	16	25	41	45	....	....	....	....	....
99-2000	Hamilton Bulldogs	AHL	14	2	1	3	2	6	1	0	1	0
	Tallahassee	ECHL	45	21	20	41	14	....	....	....	....	....

USTRNUL, Libor (OOS-tuhr-nuhl, LEE-bohr) ATL.

Defense. Shoots left. 6'4", 228 lbs. Born, Steruberk, Czech., February 20, 1982.
(Atlanta's 3rd choice, 42nd overall, in 2000 Entry Draft).

			Regular Season					Playoffs				
Season	Club	Lea	GP	G	A	TP	PIM	GP	G	A	TP	PIM
1997-98	HC Olomouc-Jr.	Cze-Rep	45	2	11	13	54	....	....	....	....	....
1998-99	Thunder Bay	USHL	52	2	5	7	65	18	1	4	5	95
99-2000	Plymouth Whalers	OHL	68	0	15	15	208	23	0	3	3	29

VAANANEN, Ossi (VAN-ih-nehn, AW-see) PHX.

Defense. Shoots left. 6'4", 205 lbs. Born, Vantaa, Finland, August 18, 1980.
(Phoenix's 2nd choice, 43rd overall, in 1998 Entry Draft).

			Regular Season					Playoffs				
Season	Club	Lea	GP	G	A	TP	PIM	GP	G	A	TP	PIM
1994-95	Jokerit Helsinki-C	Finn-Jr.	23	0	1	1	10	6	0	0	0	8
1995-96	Jokerit Helsinki-C	Finn-Jr.	12	0	0	0	10	....	....	....	....	....
	Jokerit Helsinki-B	Finn-Jr.	1	0	0	0	0	1	0	0	0	0
1996-97	Jokerit Helsinki	Finn-Jr.	17	1	2	3	43	....	....	....	....	....
1997-98	Jokerit Helsinki	Finn-Jr.	31	0	6	6	24	....	....	....	....	....
1998-99	Jokerit Helsinki	Finn-Jr.	12	1	6	7	16	....	....	....	....	....
	Jokerit Helsinki	EuroHL	5	0	0	0	2	1	0	1	1	2
	Jokerit Helsinki	Finland	48	0	1	1	42	3	0	1	1	2
99-2000	Jokerit Helsinki	Finland	49	1	6	7	46	11	1	1	2	2

VALENTINE, Curtis (VAL-lehn-tighn, KUHR-tihs) VAN.

Left wing. Shoots left. 6'5", 195 lbs. Born, Haileybury, Ont., July 22, 1979.
(Vancouver's 11th choice, 219th overall, in 1998 Entry Draft).

			Regular Season					Playoffs				
Season	Club	Lea	GP	G	A	TP	PIM	GP	G	A	TP	PIM
1996-97	Capital District	X-Games	56	53	60	113	28	....	....	....	....	....
1997-98	Bowling Green	CCHA	38	7	8	15	34	....	....	....	....	....
1998-99	Bowling Green	CCHA	38	4	8	12	40	....	....	....	....	....
99-2000	Bowling Green	CCHA	37	5	7	12	24	....	....	....	....	....

VALTONEN, Tomek (VAL-tuh-nehn, Toh-MEHK) DET.

Left wing. Shoots left. 6'1", 198 lbs. Born, Piotrkow Trybunalski, Poland, January 8, 1980.
(Detroit's 3rd choice, 56th overall, in 1998 Entry Draft).

			Regular Season					Playoffs				
Season	Club	Lea	GP	G	A	TP	PIM	GP	G	A	TP	PIM
1995-96	Ilves Tampere-C	Finn-Jr.	9	3	3	6	24	....	....	....	....	....
	Ilves Tampere-B	Finn-Jr.	11	7	7	14	28	....	....	....	....	....
	Ilves Tampere	Finn-Jr.	....	....	....	....	....	1	0	0	0	0
1996-97	Ilves Tampere-B	Finn-Jr.	26	10	9	19	82	3	0	1	1	6
	Ilves Tampere	Finn-Jr.	1	0	0	0	0	....	....	....	....	....
1997-98	JyP Joensuu	Finn-Jr.	3	0	0	0	12	....	....	....	....	....
	JyP Joensuu	Finland-2	6	1	2	3	39	....	....	....	....	....
	Ilves Tampere	Finn-Jr.	13	3	2	5	36	....	....	....	....	....
	Ilves Tampere	Finland	19	1	0	1	14	3	0	0	0	0
	Ilves Tampere-2	Finn-Jr.	....	....	....	....	....	7	0	2	2	16
1998-99	Plymouth Whalers	OHL	43	8	16	24	53	7	1	0	1	0
99-2000	Jokerit Helsinki	Finland	41	0	3	3	63	9	1	0	1	8

VAN LEUSEN, Aaron (VAN LOO-suhn) DET.

Center. Shoots right. 6', 196 lbs. Born, Barrie, Ont., October 28, 1981.
(Detroit's 6th choice, 130th overall, in 2000 Entry Draft).

			Regular Season					Playoffs				
Season	Club	Lea	GP	G	A	TP	PIM	GP	G	A	TP	PIM
1997-98	Barrie Lions	OMHA	50	26	36	62	45	....	....	....	....	....
1998-99	Brampton	OHL	58	7	8	15	15	....	....	....	....	....
99-2000	Brampton	OHL	57	17	20	37	24	6	2	1	3	6

VAN ACKER, Eric (VAN-akuhr, EH-rihk) BOS.

Defense. Shoots left. 6'5", 246 lbs. Born, St-Jean, Que., March 1, 1979.
(Boston's 11th choice, 218th overall, in 1997 Entry Draft).

			Regular Season					Playoffs				
Season	Club	Lea	GP	G	A	TP	PIM	GP	G	A	TP	PIM
1996-97	Chicoutimi	QMJHL	69	2	5	7	153	16	0	0	0	4
	Richilieu Regents	QAAA	52	3	7	10	84	....	....	....	....	....
1997-98	Chicoutimi	QMJHL	49	1	5	6	136	6	0	0	0	14
1998-99	Baie-Comeau	QMJHL	65	1	6	7	192	....	....	....	....	....
99-2000	Greenville Growl	ECHL	46	0	8	8	112	13	1	0	1	37
	Providence Bruins	AHL	4	0	0	0	2	....	....	....	....	....

VanBUSKIRK, Ryan (van-BUHS-kuhrk) WSH.

Defense. Shoots left. 6'1", 190 lbs. Born, Sault Ste. Marie, MI, January 12, 1980.
(Washington's 4th choice, 121st overall, in 2000 Entry Draft).

			Regular Season					Playoffs				
Season	Club	Lea	GP	G	A	TP	PIM	GP	G	A	TP	PIM
1996-97	Petrolia Jets	OJHL	43	7	28	35	133	....	....	....	....	....
1997-98	Sarnia Sting	OHL	61	8	17	25	84	5	1	2	3	4
1998-99	Sarnia Sting	OHL	66	15	33	48	85	6	1	2	3	4
99-2000	Sarnia Sting	OHL	45	8	20	28	62	7	1	2	3	16

• Re-entered NHL draft. Originally Phoenix's 4th choice, 100th overall, in 1998 Entry Draft.

VAN HOOF, Jeremy (van-HOOF, JAIR-reh-mee) PIT.

Defense. Shoots left. 6'2", 208 lbs. Born, Lindsay, Ont., August 12, 1981.
(Pittsburgh's 3rd choice, 57th overall, in 1999 Entry Draft).

			Regular Season					Playoffs				
Season	Club	Lea	GP	G	A	TP	PIM	GP	G	A	TP	PIM
1997-98	Lindsay Muskies	OJHL	50	2	8	10	40	....	....	....	....	....
1998-99	Ottawa 67's	OHL	54	0	13	13	46	5	1	0	1	2
99-2000	Ottawa 67's	OHL	66	4	14	18	71	11	1	0	1	12

VAN OENE, Darren (van OH-uhn, DAIR-rehn) BUF.

Left wing. Shoots left. 6'4", 216 lbs. Born, Edmonton, Alta., January 18, 1978.
(Buffalo's 3rd choice, 33rd overall, in 1996 Entry Draft).

			Regular Season					Playoffs				
Season	Club	Lea	GP	G	A	TP	PIM	GP	G	A	TP	PIM
1993-94	Edmonton SSAC	AMHL	34	15	16	31	121	....	....	....	....	....
1994-95	Brandon	WHL	58	5	13	18	106	18	1	1	2	34
1995-96	Brandon	WHL	47	10	18	28	126	18	1	6	7	*78
1996-97	Brandon	WHL	56	21	27	48	139	6	2	3	5	19
1997-98	Brandon	WHL	51	23	24	47	161	18	6	8	14	51
1998-99	Rochester	AHL	73	11	20	31	143	12	2	4	6	8
99-2000	Rochester	AHL	80	20	18	38	153	21	1	3	4	24

VAN RYN, Mike (VAN RIHN, MIGHK) ST.L.

Defense. Shoots right. 6'1", 190 lbs. Born, London, Ont., May 14, 1979.
(New Jersey's 1st choice, 26th overall, in 1998 Entry Draft).

			Regular Season					Playoffs				
Season	Club	Lea	GP	G	A	TP	PIM	GP	G	A	TP	PIM
1996-97	London Diamonds	OJHL-B	46	14	31	45	32	....	....	....	....	....
1997-98	U. of Michigan	CCHA	38	4	14	18	44	....	....	....	....	....
1998-99	U. of Michigan	CCHA	37	10	13	23	52	....	....	....	....	....
99-2000	Sarnia Sting	OHL	61	6	35	41	34	7	0	5	5	4

Signed as a free agent by **St. Louis**, June 30, 2000.

VASICEK, Josef (VAHSH-ih-chehk, YOH-zehf) CAR.

Center. Shoots left. 6'4", 200 lbs. Born, Havlickuv Brod, Czech., September 12, 1980.
(Carolina's 4th choice, 91st overall, in 1998 Entry Draft).

			Regular Season					Playoffs				
Season	Club	Lea	GP	G	A	TP	PIM	GP	G	A	TP	PIM
1995-96	HK Brod-Jr.	Cze-Rep	36	25	25	50	....	....	....	....	....	....
1996-97	Slavia Praha-Jr.	Cze-Rep	37	20	40	60	....	....	....	....	....	....
1997-98	Slavia Praha-Jr.	Cze-Rep	34	13	20	33	....	....	....	....	....	....
1998-99	Sault Ste. Marie	OHL	66	21	35	56	30	5	3	0	3	10
99-2000	Sault Ste. Marie	OHL	54	26	46	72	49	17	5	15	20	8

VAUCLAIR, Julien (voh-KLAIR, JEW-lee-ehn) OTT.

Defense. Shoots left. 6'1", 198 lbs. Born, Delemont, Switzerland, October 2, 1979.
(Ottawa's 4th choice, 74th overall, in 1998 Entry Draft).

			Regular Season					Playoffs				
Season	Club	Lea	GP	G	A	TP	PIM	GP	G	A	TP	PIM
1995-96	HC Ajoie	Switz-3	20	4	10	14	....	....	....	....	....	....
1996-97	HC Ajoie	Switz-2	40	0	6	6	24	9	0	2	2	8
1997-98	HC Lugano	Switz.	36	1	2	3	12	7	0	0	0	25
1998-99	HC Lugano	Switz.	38	0	3	3	8	....	....	....	....	....
99-2000	HC Lugano	Switz.	45	3	3	6	16	14	0	0	0	0

VELLINGA, Mike (VEHL-ihn-GA, MIGHK) **CGY.**

Defense. Shoots right. 6'2", 212 lbs. Born, Chatham, Ont., August 19, 1978.
(Chicago's 5th choice, 184th overall, in 1996 Entry Draft).

			Regular Season					Playoffs				
Season	Club	Lea	GP	G	A	TP	PIM	GP	G	A	TP	PIM
1994-95	Chatham	OJHL-B	50	6	14	20	79	....	....	....	....	....
1995-96	Guelph Storm	OHL	57	3	8	11	32	16	2	6	8	6
1996-97	Guelph Storm	OHL	66	6	30	36	73	18	1	9	10	34
1997-98	Guelph Storm	OHL	63	6	22	28	101	12	1	8	9	28
1998-99	Saint John Flames	AHL	15	0	1	1	6	....	....	....	....	....
	Orlando	IHL	1	0	0	0	4	....	....	....	....	....
	Johnstown	ECHL	45	1	14	15	22	....	....	....	....	....
99-2000	Saint John Flames	AHL	2	0	0	0	0	....	....	....	....	....
	Johnstown	ECHL	69	2	17	19	144	7	0	1	1	18

Signed as a free agent by **Calgary**, July 21, 1998.

VERCIK, Rudolf (VEHR-chihk, ROO-dawlf) **NYR**

Left wing. Shoots left. 6'1", 189 lbs. Born, Bratislava, Czech., March 19, 1976.
(NY Rangers' 2nd choice, 52nd overall, in 1994 Entry Draft).

			Regular Season					Playoffs				
Season	Club	Lea	GP	G	A	TP	PIM	GP	G	A	TP	PIM
1993-94	HC Bratislava	Slovakia	17	1	4	5	14	....	....	....	....	....
1994-95	HC Bratislava	Slovakia	33	14	9	23	22	....	....	....	....	....
1995-96	HC Bratislava	Slovakia	28	7	3	10	61	13	1	0	1	....
1996-97	HC Bratislava	Slovakia	40	8	3	11	....	2	0	0	0	....
1997-98	Nova Ves	Slovakia	36	8	5	13	36	3	1	1	2	0
1998-99	HC Bratislava	Slovakia	35	6	7	13	53	7	1	0	1	4
99-2000	HC Bratislava	Slovakia	51	8	15	23	36	3	1	1	2	0

VERENIKIN, Sergei (veh-rih-NEE-kihn, SAIR-gay) **OTT.**

Right wing. Shoots left. 5'11", 187 lbs. Born, Yaroslavl, USSR, September 8, 1979.
(Ottawa's 9th choice, 223rd overall, in 1998 Entry Draft).

			Regular Season					Playoffs				
Season	Club	Lea	GP	G	A	TP	PIM	GP	G	A	TP	PIM
1997-98	Torpedo Yaroslavl	Russia-2	44	11	4	15	100	....	....	....	....	....
	Torpedo Yaroslavl	Russia	3	0	0	0	0	....	....	....	....	....
1998-99	Torpedo Yaroslavl	Russia	37	2	5	7	16	8	0	0	0	18
99-2000	Torpedo Yaroslavl	Russia	25	4	1	5	18	4	0	0	0	2

VERMETTE, Antoine (vuhr-MEHT, AN-twuhn) **OTT.**

Center. Shoots left. 6', 184 lbs. Born, St-Agapit, Quebec, July 20, 1982.
(Ottawa's 3rd choice, 55th overall, in 2000 Entry Draft).

			Regular Season					Playoffs				
Season	Club	Lea	GP	G	A	TP	PIM	GP	G	A	TP	PIM
1997-98	Levis Commanders	QAAA	8	1	1	2	4	1	0	0	0	0
1998-99	Quebec Remparts	QMJHL	57	9	17	26	32	13	0	0	0	2
99-2000	Victoriaville Tigres	QMJHL	71	30	41	71	87	6	0	1	1	6

VERNARSKY, Kris (veh-NAHR-skee) **TOR.**

Center. Shoots left. 6'3", 201 lbs. Born, Detroit, MI, April 5, 1982.
(Toronto's 2nd choice, 51st overall, in 2000 Entry Draft).

			Regular Season					Playoffs				
Season	Club	Lea	GP	G	A	TP	PIM	GP	G	A	TP	PIM
1997-98	Team USA	Under-18	69	11	18	29	97	....	....	....	....	....
1998-99	Plymouth Whalers	OHL	45	3	14	17	30	11	0	0	0	2
99-2000	Plymouth Whalers	OHL	64	16	22	38	63	19	3	6	9	24

VEROT, Darcy **PIT.**

Defense. Shoots left. 6', 190 lbs. Born, Radville, Sask., July 13, 1976.

			Regular Season					Playoffs				
Season	Club	Lea	GP	G	A	TP	PIM	GP	G	A	TP	PIM
1997-98	Lake Charles	WPHL	68	11	26	37	269	4	0	1	1	25
1998-99	Lake Charles	WPHL	68	17	23	40	236	9	2	4	6	53
99-2000	Wheeling Nailers	ECHL	44	7	12	19	240	....	....	....	....	....
	Wilkes-Barre	AHL	23	5	5	10	96	....	....	....	....	....

Signed as a free agent by **Wilkes-Barre** (AHL), February 25, 2000. Signed as a free agent by **Pittsburgh**, July 28, 2000.

VERTALA, Timo (vehr-TAH-lah, TEE-moh) **MTL.**

Left wing. Shoots left. 6'1", 180 lbs. Born, Jyvaskyla, Finland, May 2, 1978.
(Montreal's 8th choice, 181st overall, in 1996 Entry Draft).

			Regular Season					Playoffs				
Season	Club	Lea	GP	G	A	TP	PIM	GP	G	A	TP	PIM
1993-94	JyP Jyvaskyla-C	Finn-Jr.	26	24	13	37	60	6	2	4	6	*28
	JyP Jyvaskyla-B	Finn-Jr.	6	0	0	0	0	....	....	....	....	....
1994-95	JyP Jyvaskyla-B	Finn-Jr.	16	3	5	8	46	....	....	....	....	....
	JyP Jyvaskyla	Finn-Jr.	30	2	8	10	18	8	0	1	1	10
1995-96	JyP Jyvaskyla	Finn-Jr.	35	15	10	25	54	6	1	1	2	6
	JyP Jyvaskyla	Finland	3	0	1	1	2	....	....	....	....	....
1996-97	JyP Jyvaskyla	Finn-Jr.	7	4	4	8	12	....	....	....	....	....
	JyP Jyvaskyla	Finland	46	8	5	13	39	4	0	0	0	0
1997-98	JyP Jyvaskyla	Finn-Jr.	2	2	1	3	4	....	....	....	....	....
	JyP Jyvaskyla	Finland	43	4	8	12	34	....	....	....	....	....
1998-99	JyP Jyvaskyla	Finland	48	5	5	10	60	3	0	0	0	2
99-2000	Tappara Tampere	Finland	50	24	18	42	82	4	0	2	2	0

VIGIER, J.P. **ATL.**

Right wing. Shoots right. 6', 195 lbs. Born, Notre Dame de Lourdes, Man., September 11, 1976.

			Regular Season					Playoffs				
Season	Club	Lea	GP	G	A	TP	PIM	GP	G	A	TP	PIM
1995-96	Portage	MJHL	56	32	49	81	....	....	....	....	....	....
1996-97	North-Michigan	WCHA	36	10	14	24	54	....	....	....	....	....
1997-98	North-Michigan	WCHA	36	12	15	27	60	....	....	....	....	....
1998-99	North-Michigan	WCHA	42	21	18	39	80	....	....	....	....	....
99-2000	North-Michigan	CCHA	39	18	17	35	72	....	....	....	....	....
	Orlando	IHL	3	1	0	1	0	....	....	....	....	....

CCHA Second All-Star Team (1999)

Signed as a free agent by **Atlanta**, April 20, 2000.

VIKINGSTAD, Tore (VIH-kihng-stahd, TOO-reh) **ST.L.**

Center. Shoots left. 6'4", 202 lbs. Born, Stavenger, Norway, October 8, 1975.
(St. Louis' 5th choice, 180th overall, in 1999 Entry Draft).

			Regular Season					Playoffs				
Season	Club	Lea	GP	G	A	TP	PIM	GP	G	A	TP	PIM
1994-95	Viking IHK	Norway	28	5	3	8	8	....	....	....	....	....
1995-96	Viking IHK	Norway	27	12	11	23	....	....	....	....	....	....
1996-97	IL Stjernen	Norway	42	23	35	58	20	....	....	....	....	....
1997-98	IL Stjernen	Norway	42	26	31	57	18	....	....	....	....	....
1998-99	Farjestads BK	Sweden	49	9	11	20	18	4	2	3	5	0
99-2000	Farjestads BK	Sweden	47	8	19	27	26	7	3	0	3	6

VISNOVSKY, Lubomir (vihsh-NAWV-skee) **L.A.**

Defense. Shoots left. 5'10", 183 lbs. Born, Topolcany, Czech., August 11, 1976.
(Los Angeles' 4th choice, 118th overall, in 2000 Entry Draft).

			Regular Season					Playoffs				
Season	Club	Lea	GP	G	A	TP	PIM	GP	G	A	TP	PIM
1994-95	Slovan Bratislava	Slovakia	36	11	12	23	10	9	1	3	4	2
1995-96	Slovan Bratislava	Slovakia	35	8	6	14	22	13	1	5	6	2
1996-97	Slovan Bratislava	Slovakia	44	11	12	23	....	2	0	1	1	....
1997-98	Slovan Bratislava	Slovakia	36	7	9	16	16	11	2	4	6	8
1998-99	Slovan Bratislava	Slovakia	40	9	10	19	31	10	5	5	10	0
99-2000	Slovan Bratislava	Slovakia	52	21	24	45	38	8	5	3	8	16

VLASAK, Tomas (VLAH-sahk) **L.A.**

Center. Shoots right. 5'10", 175 lbs. Born, Prague, Czech., February 1, 1975.
(Los Angeles' 6th choice, 120th overall, in 1993 Entry Draft).

			Regular Season					Playoffs				
Season	Club	Lea	GP	G	A	TP	PIM	GP	G	A	TP	PIM
1992-93	Slavia Praha	Czech-2	31	17	6	23	....	....	....	....	....	....
1993-94	CHZ Litvinov	Cze-Rep	41	16	11	27	0	4	0	1	1	....
1994-95	CHZ Litvinov	Cze-Rep	35	6	14	20	4	4	0	0	0	4
1995-96	CHZ Litvinov	Cze-Rep	35	10	22	32	....	15	5	5	10	....
1996-97	CHZ Litvinov	Cze-Rep	52	26	34	60	16	....	....	....	....	....
1997-98	CHZ Litvinov	Cze-Rep	51	22	44	66	40	4	1	2	3	2
1998-99	HPK Hameenlinna	Finland	54	28	29	57	36	8	2	*9	11	0
99-2000	HPK Hameenlinna	Finland	48	24	39	63	63	8	3	4	7	6

VLASENKOV, Dmitri (vlah-SEHN-khahf, dih-MEE-tree) **ATL.**

Left wing. Shoots left. 5'11", 183 lbs. Born, Safonovo, USSR, January 1, 1978.
(Calgary's 4th choice, 73rd overall, in 1996 Entry Draft).

			Regular Season					Playoffs				
Season	Club	Lea	GP	G	A	TP	PIM	GP	G	A	TP	PIM
1995-96	Torpedo Yaroslavl	CIS	17	1	1	2	4	1	0	0	0	0
1996-97	Torpedo Yaroslavl	Russia-3	18	10	2	12	6	....	....	....	....	....
	Torpedo Yaroslavl	Russia	28	3	2	5	10	8	1	1	2	2
1997-98	Torpedo Yaroslavl	EuroHL	6	0	0	0	2	....	....	....	....	....
	Torpedo Yaroslavl	Russia	44	10	3	13	12	....	....	....	....	....
1998-99	Torpedo Yaroslavl	Russia	41	11	5	16	26	10	1	2	3	6
99-2000	Torpedo Yaroslavl	Russia	38	15	20	35	10	10	3	4	7	6

Traded to **Atlanta** by **Calgary** with Hnat Domenichelli for Darryl Shannon and Jason Botterill, February 11, 2000.

VOLCHENKOV, Anton (vohl-chen-KAHF, an-TUHN) **OTT.**

Defense. Shoots left. 6'1", 209 lbs. Born, Moscow, USSR, February 25, 1982.
(Ottawa's 1st choice, 21st overall, in 2000 Entry Draft).

			Regular Season					Playoffs				
Season	Club	Lea	GP	G	A	TP	PIM	GP	G	A	TP	PIM
99-2000	CSKA Moscow	Russia-2	30	2	9	11	36	....	....	....	....	....

VOROBJEV, Pavel (voh-roh-BEE-ehf) **CHI.**

Right wing. Shoots left. 6', 183 lbs. Born, Karaganda, USSR, May 5, 1982.
(Chicago's 2nd choice, 11th overall, in 2000 Entry Draft).

			Regular Season					Playoffs				
Season	Club	Lea	GP	G	A	TP	PIM	GP	G	A	TP	PIM
1997-98	Torpedo Yaroslavl	Russia-2	16	2	0	2	6	....	....	....	....	....
1998-99	Torpedo Yaroslavl	Russia-3	17	0	1	1	0	....	....	....	....	....
99-2000	Torpedo Yaroslavl	Russia-3	40	19	15	34	20	....	....	....	....	....
	Torpedo Yaroslavl	Russia	8	2	0	2	4	10	2	2	4	0

VOTH, Brad (VOHTH, BRAD)

Defense. Shoots right. 6'4", 223 lbs. Born, Saskatoon, Sask., February 25, 1980.
(St. Louis' 4th choice, 157th overall, in 1998 Entry Draft).

			Regular Season					Playoffs				
Season	Club	Lea	GP	G	A	TP	PIM	GP	G	A	TP	PIM
1996-97	Calgary Stars	AMHL	30	3	10	13	190	....	....	....	....	....
	Medicine Hat	WHL	2	0	0	0	2	....	....	....	....	....
1997-98	Medicine Hat	WHL	70	8	5	13	244	....	....	....	....	....
1998-99	Medicine Hat	WHL	40	4	6	10	102	....	....	....	....	....
99-2000	Medicine Hat	WHL	58	9	7	16	222	....	....	....	....	....

VRBATA, Radim (vuhr-BA-tuh, ra-DEEM) **COL.**

Right wing. Shoots right. 6'1", 185 lbs. Born, Mlada Boleslav, Czech., June 13, 1981.
(Colorado's 10th choice, 212th overall, in 1999 Entry Draft).

			Regular Season					Playoffs				
Season	Club	Lea	GP	G	A	TP	PIM	GP	G	A	TP	PIM
1997-98	Mlada Boleslav	Cze-Rep	35	42	31	73	4	....	....	....	....	....
1998-99	Hull Olympiques	QMJHL	54	22	38	60	16	23	6	13	19	6
99-2000	Hull Olympiques	QMJHL	58	29	45	74	26	15	3	9	12	8

VUORIVIRTA, Juha (voh-RIH-vihr-tah, YOO-hah) **L.A.**

Center. Shoots left. 6'3", 189 lbs. Born, Oulu, Finland, May 3, 1976.
(Los Angeles' 8th choice, 163rd overall, in 1995 Entry Draft).

			Regular Season					Playoffs				
Season	Club	Lea	GP	G	A	TP	PIM	GP	G	A	TP	PIM
1994-95	Tappara Tampere	Finland	39	2	3	5	12	....	....	....	....	....
1995-96	Tappara Tampere	Finland	4	2	5	7	0	....	....	....	....	....
	Tappara Tampere	Finland	47	6	3	9	20	4	0	0	0	0
1996-97	Tappara Tampere	Finland	49	5	3	8	20	3	0	0	0	0
1997-98	Tappara Tampere	Finland	46	6	9	15	16	3	0	1	1	2
1998-99	Karpat Oulu	Finland-2	15	3	5	8	4	2	1	0	1	0
	Tappara Tampere	Finland	26	0	1	1	4	....	....	....	....	....
99-2000	Tappara Tampere	Finland	DID NOT PLAY – INJURED									

• Missed entire 1999-2000 season recovering from knee injury suffered in training camp, August, 1999.

VYBORNY, David — CBJ

Right wing. Shoots right. 5'10", 183 lbs. Born, Jihlava, Czech., June 2, 1975.
(Edmonton's 3rd choice, 33rd overall, in 1993 Entry Draft).

			Regular Season					Playoffs				
Season	Club	Lea	GP	G	A	TP	PIM	GP	G	A	TP	PIM
1991-92	Sparta Praha	Czech.	32	6	9	15	2	....	....	....	....	....
1992-93	Sparta Praha	Czech.	52	20	24	44	....	....	....	....	....	....
1993-94	Sparta Praha	Cze-Rep	44	15	20	35	0	6	4	7	11	0
1994-95	Cape Breton	AHL	76	23	38	61	30	....	....	....	....	....
1995-96	Sparta Praha	Cze-Rep	40	12	18	30	....	12	6	5	11	....
1996-97	Sparta Praha	Cze-Rep	47	20	29	49	14	10	7	7	14	6
1997-98	MoDo Hockey	Sweden	45	16	21	37	34	9	0	2	2	2
1998-99	Sparta Praha	Cze-Rep	52	24	*46	*70	22	8	1	3	4	....
99-2000	Sparta Praha	Cze-Rep	50	25	38	63	30	9	3	*8	*11	4

Signed as a free agent by **Columbus**, June 8, 2000.

VYDARENY, Rene — (vih-DAH-reh-nay, REH-nay) — VAN.

Defense. Shoots left. 6'1", 198 lbs. Born, Bratislava, Czech., May 6, 1981.
(Vancouver's 3rd choice, 69th overall, in 1999 Entry Draft).

			Regular Season					Playoffs				
Season	Club	Lea	GP	G	A	TP	PIM	GP	G	A	TP	PIM
1997-98	Slovan Bratislava	Slovak-Jr.	50	5	14	19	26	....	....	....	....	....
1998-99	Slovan Bratislava	Slovak-Jr.	42	4	7	11	65	2	0	0	0	2
	HC Trnava	Slovak-2	20	1	6	7	6	....	....	....	....	....
99-2000	Rimouski Oceanic	QMJHL	51	7	23	30	41	14	2	2	4	20

WALBY, Steffon — (WAHL-bee, STEH-fohn)

Right wing. Shoots right. 6'1", 198 lbs. Born, Madison, WI, November 22, 1972.

			Regular Season					Playoffs				
Season	Club	Lea	GP	G	A	TP	PIM	GP	G	A	TP	PIM
1991-92	Kelowna Spartans	BCJHL	24	18	13	31	10	....	....	....	....	....
1992-93	Kelowna Spartans	BCJHL	59	53	68	121	76	....	....	....	....	....
1993-94	St. John's Leafs	AHL	63	15	22	37	79	2	0	0	0	2
1994-95	St. John's Leafs	AHL	70	23	23	46	30	5	1	1	2	4
1995-96	St. John's Leafs	AHL	57	23	31	54	61	4	2	2	4	17
1996-97	Hershey Bears	AHL	74	24	23	47	61	19	7	3	10	34
1997-98	Fort Wayne	IHL	77	28	26	54	53	4	1	1	2	6
1998-99	Rochester	AHL	48	15	13	28	52	....	....	....	....	....
	Kentucky	AHL	11	8	4	12	6	12	3	2	5	14
99-2000	Hershey Bears	AHL	49	19	13	32	50	14	3	9	12	11

Signed as a free agent by **Toronto**, August 20, 1993. Signed as a free agent by **Buffalo**, August 31, 1998. Signed as a free agent by **Colorado**, September, 1999.

WALKER, Matt — (WAHL-kuhr, MAT) — ST.L.

Defense. Shoots right. 6'2", 222 lbs. Born, Beaverlodge, Alta., April 7, 1980.
(St. Louis' 3rd choice, 83rd overall, in 1998 Entry Draft).

			Regular Season					Playoffs				
Season	Club	Lea	GP	G	A	TP	PIM	GP	G	A	TP	PIM
1996-97	Grand Prairie	AAHA	68	22	62	74	186	....	....	....	....	....
1997-98	Portland	WHL	64	2	13	15	124	16	0	0	0	21
1998-99	Portland	WHL	64	1	10	11	151	4	0	1	1	6
99-2000	Portland	WHL	38	2	7	9	97	....	....	....	....	....
	Kootenay Ice	WHL	31	4	19	23	53	21	5	13	18	24

WALLIN, Niclas — (VAH-lihn) — CAR.

Defense. Shoots left. 6'3", 220 lbs. Born, Boden, Sweden, February 20, 1975.
(Carolina's 3rd choice, 97th overall, in 2000 Entry Draft).

			Regular Season					Playoffs				
Season	Club	Lea	GP	G	A	TP	PIM	GP	G	A	TP	PIM
1995-96	Bodens IK	Swede-2	30	2	7	9	26	2	0	1	1	2
1996-97	Brynas IF	Sweden	47	1	1	2	14	....	....	....	....	....
1997-98	Brynas IF	Sweden	44	2	3	5	57	3	0	1	1	4
1998-99	Brynas IF	Sweden	46	2	4	6	52	14	0	1	1	8
99-2000	Brynas IF	Sweden	48	7	9	16	73	11	2	1	3	14

WALLIN, Viktor — (WAHL-in, VIHK-tohr) — ANA.

Defense. Shoots left. 6'3", 200 lbs. Born, Jonkoping, Sweden, January 17, 1980.
(Anaheim's 3rd choice, 112th overall, in 1998 Entry Draft).

			Regular Season					Playoffs				
Season	Club	Lea	GP	G	A	TP	PIM	GP	G	A	TP	PIM
1996-97	HV Jonkoping	Swede-Jr.	16	1	2	3	....	....	....	....	....	....
1997-98	HV Jonkoping	Swede-Jr.	28	9	15	24	42	....	....	....	....	....
1998-99	HV Jonkoping	Sweden	STATISTICS NOT AVAILABLE									
99-2000	HV Jonkoping	Sweden	43	2	2	4	16	6	1	1	2	4

WALSER, Derrick — CGY.

Defense. Shoots left. 5'10", 190 lbs. Born, New Glasgow, N.S., May 12, 1978.

			Regular Season					Playoffs				
Season	Club	Lea	GP	G	A	TP	PIM	GP	G	A	TP	PIM
1994-95	Beauport	QMJHL	48	4	18	22	34	12	2	5	7	2
1995-96	Beauport	QMJHL	69	9	31	40	56	20	2	11	13	16
1996-97	Beauport	QMJHL	37	13	25	38	26	....	....	....	....	....
	Rimouski Oceanic	QMJHL	31	15	30	45	44	4	2	2	4	6
1997-98	Rimouski Oceanic	QMJHL	70	41	69	110	135	18	10	*26	36	49
1998-99	Saint John Flames	AHL	40	3	7	10	24	....	....	....	....	....
	Johnstown Chiefs	ECHL	24	8	12	20	29	....	....	....	....	....
99-2000	Saint John Flames	AHL	14	2	3	5	10	....	....	....	....	....
	Johnstown Chiefs	ECHL	54	17	26	43	104	7	3	3	6	8

QMJHL First All-Star Team (1998) • Canadian Major Junior First All-Star Team (1998) • Canadian Major Junior Defenseman of the Year (1998)

Signed as a free agent by **Calgary**, October 16, 1998.

WALSH, Brendan — MIN.

Right wing. Shoots right. 5'9", 181 lbs. Born, Dorchester, MA, October 22, 1974.

			Regular Season					Playoffs				
Season	Club	Lea	GP	G	A	TP	PIM	GP	G	A	TP	PIM
1995-96	Boston University	H-East	38	8	16	24	90	....	....	....	....	....
1996-97	Boston University	H-East	27	5	8	13	83	....	....	....	....	....
1997-98	U. of Maine	H-East	DID NOT PLAY – TRANSFERRED COLLEGES									
1998-99	U. of Maine	H-East	30	7	13	20	58	....	....	....	....	....
99-2000	U. of Maine	H-East	39	9	21	30	*106	....	....	....	....	....

Signed as a free agent by **Minnesota**, May 18, 2000.

WANVIG, Kyle — (WEHN-vihg, KIGHL) — BOS.

Right wing. Shoots right. 6'2", 197 lbs. Born, Calgary, Alta., January 29, 1981.
(Boston's 3rd choice, 89th overall, in 1999 Entry Draft).

			Regular Season					Playoffs				
Season	Club	Lea	GP	G	A	TP	PIM	GP	G	A	TP	PIM
1996-97	Calgary Blazers	AAHA	26	31	48	79	85	....	....	....	....	....
1997-98	Edmonton Ice	WHL	62	17	12	29	69	....	....	....	....	....
1998-99	Kootenay Ice	WHL	71	12	20	32	119	7	1	3	4	18
99-2000	Kootenay Ice	WHL	6	2	2	4	12	....	....	....	....	....
	Red Deer Rebels	WHL	58	21	18	39	123	4	1	0	1	4

WARD, Lance — (WOHRD, LAN-seh) — FLA.

Defense. Shoots left. 6'3", 215 lbs. Born, Lloydminster, Alta., June 2, 1978.
(Florida's 3rd choice, 63rd overall, in 1998 Entry Draft).

			Regular Season					Playoffs				
Season	Club	Lea	GP	G	A	TP	PIM	GP	G	A	TP	PIM
1993-94	Lloydminister	AAHA	20	8	12	20	68	....	....	....	....	....
1994-95	Red Deer Rebels	WHL	28	0	0	0	57	....	....	....	....	....
1995-96	Red Deer Rebels	WHL	72	4	13	17	127	10	0	4	4	10
1996-97	Red Deer Rebels	WHL	70	5	34	39	229	16	0	3	3	36
1997-98	Red Deer Rebels	WHL	71	8	25	33	233	5	0	0	0	16
1998-99	Miami Matadors	ECHL	6	1	0	1	12	....	....	....	....	....
	Fort Wayne	IHL	13	0	2	2	28	....	....	....	....	....
	New Haven	AHL	43	2	5	7	51	....	....	....	....	....
99-2000	Louisville	AHL	80	4	16	20	190	4	0	0	0	6

• Re-entered NHL draft. Originally New Jersey's 1st choice, 10th overall, in 1996 Entry Draft.

WARREN, Morgan — (WAHR-ihn, MOHR-gan) — TOR.

Right wing. Shoots right. 6'2", 193 lbs. Born, Summerside, P.E.I., March 6, 1980.
(Toronto's 5th choice, 126th overall, in 1998 Entry Draft).

			Regular Season					Playoffs				
Season	Club	Lea	GP	G	A	TP	PIM	GP	G	A	TP	PIM
1996-97	Quinte Hawks	OJHL	49	32	38	70	65	....	....	....	....	....
1997-98	Moncton Wildcats	QMJHL	58	11	10	21	80	10	2	2	4	2
1998-99	Moncton Wildcats	QMJHL	48	20	16	36	68	1	0	0	0	2
99-2000	Moncton Wildcats	QMJHL	65	29	36	65	53	16	7	5	12	4

WATSON, Dan — CBJ

Defense. Shoots right. 6'2", 221 lbs. Born, Glencoe, Ont., October 5, 1979.

			Regular Season					Playoffs				
Season	Club	Lea	GP	G	A	TP	PIM	GP	G	A	TP	PIM
1995-96	Strathroy	OJHL-B	46	6	13	19	12	....	....	....	....	....
1996-97	Strathroy	OJHL-B	49	5	25	30	33	....	....	....	....	....
	Sarnia Sting	OHL	10	0	2	2	7	....	....	....	....	....
1997-98	Sarnia Sting	OHL	66	6	15	21	19	5	0	1	1	4
1998-99	Sarnia Sting	OHL	68	2	18	20	27	6	0	0	0	4
99-2000	Sarnia Sting	OHL	68	1	15	16	40	7	0	0	0	4

Signed as a free agent by **Columbus**, May 29, 2000.

WEAVER, Mike — ATL.

Defense. Shoots right. 5'10", 182 lbs. Born, Bramalea, Ont., May 2, 1978.

			Regular Season					Playoffs				
Season	Club	Lea	GP	G	A	TP	PIM	GP	G	A	TP	PIM
1995-96	Bramalea	OJHL	48	10	39	49	....	....	....	....	....	....
1996-97	Michigan State	CCHA	39	0	7	7	46	....	....	....	....	....
1997-98	Michigan State	CCHA	44	4	22	26	68	....	....	....	....	....
1998-99	Michigan State	CCHA	42	1	6	7	54	....	....	....	....	....
99-2000	Michigan State	CCHA	26	0	7	7	20	....	....	....	....	....

OJHL's Best Defenseman (1996) • CCHA All-Tournament Team (1997) • CCHA First All-Star Team (1999, 2000) • NCAA West Second Team All-American (1999, 2000) • CCHA's Best Defensive Defenseman (1999, 2000)

Signed as a free agent by **Atlanta**, June 15, 2000.

WEINHANDL, Mattias — (vayn-hanh-duhl, mah-TEE-uhs) — NYI

Right wing. Shoots right. 6', 183 lbs. Born, Ljungby, Sweden, June 1, 1980.
(NY Islanders' 5th choice, 78th overall, in 1999 Entry Draft).

			Regular Season					Playoffs				
Season	Club	Lea	GP	G	A	TP	PIM	GP	G	A	TP	PIM
1995-96	Troja-Ljungby	Swede-Jr.	28	38	40	78	....	....	....	....	....	....
1996-97	Troja-Ljungby	Swede-Jr.	48	61	69	130	46	....	....	....	....	....
1997-98	Troja-Ljungby	Swede-2	28	3	2	5	2	5	0	0	0	2
1998-99	Troja-Ljungby	Swede-2	38	20	20	40	30	5	4	3	7	4
99-2000	MoDo Hockey	Sweden	32	15	9	24	6	13	5	3	8	8

WELLER, Craig — (WEH-luhr) — ST.L.

Defense. Shoots right. 6'3", 195 lbs. Born, Calgary, Alta., January 17, 1981.
(St. Louis' 6th choice, 167th overall, in 2000 Entry Draft).

			Regular Season					Playoffs				
Season	Club	Lea	GP	G	A	TP	PIM	GP	G	A	TP	PIM
1998-99	Calgary Canucks	AJHL	49	4	14	18	80	13	0	1	1	10
99-2000	Calgary Canucks	AJHL	53	3	14	17	100	4	0	0	0	4

WENDELL, Erik — (WEHN-dehl, AIR-ihk) — WSH.

Center. Shoots left. 6'1", 197 lbs. Born, Minneapolis, MN, August 23, 1979.
(Washington's 6th choice, 125th overall, in 1998 Entry Draft).

			Regular Season					Playoffs				
Season	Club	Lea	GP	G	A	TP	PIM	GP	G	A	TP	PIM
1997-98	Maple Grove	Hi-School	24	24	23	47	38	....	....	....	....	....
1998-99	U. of Minnesota	WCHA	41	7	7	14	46	....	....	....	....	....
99-2000	U. of Minnesota	WCHA	32	4	2	6	26	....	....	....	....	....

WENNERBERG, Mattias — (VEH-nuhr-buhrg, MA-tee-uhs) — CHI.

Center. Shoots left. 5'11", 176 lbs. Born, Uma, Sweden, August 6, 1981.
(Chicago's 6th choice, 194th overall, in 1999 Entry Draft).

			Regular Season					Playoffs				
Season	Club	Lea	GP	G	A	TP	PIM	GP	G	A	TP	PIM
1996-97	Vilhelmina HC	Swede-4	20	7	12	19	14	....	....	....	....	....
1997-98	MoDo Hockey	Swede-Jr.	30	10	17	27	....	....	....	....	....	....
1998-99	MoDo Hockey	Swede-Jr.	43	13	12	25	....	....	....	....	....	....
99-2000	MoDo Hockey	Swede-Jr.	32	14	6	20	102	....	....	....	....	....

WESTRUM, Erik (WEHST-ruhm, AIR-ihk) PHX.

Center. Shoots left. 5'11", 194 lbs. Born, Minneapolis, MN, July 26, 1979.
(Phoenix's 9th choice, 187th overall, in 1998 Entry Draft).

			Regular Season					Playoffs				
Season	Club	Lea	GP	G	A	TP	PIM	GP	G	A	TP	PIM
1996-97	Apple Valley High	Hi-School	25	23	33	56	....	....	....	....	....	....
1997-98	U. of Minnesota	WCHA	39	6	12	18	43	....	....	....	....	....
1998-99	U. of Minnesota	WCHA	41	10	26	36	81	....	....	....	....	....
99-2000	U. of Minnesota	WCHA	39	27	26	53	99	....	....	....	....	....

WICHSER, Adrian FLA.

Center. Shoots left. 6', 180 lbs. Born, Winterthor, Switz., March 18, 1980.
(Florida's 9th choice, 231st overall, in 1998 Entry Draft).

			Regular Season					Playoffs				
Season	Club	Lea	GP	G	A	TP	PIM	GP	G	A	TP	PIM
1997-98	EHC Kloten	Switz.	35	6	5	11	31	7	0	1	1	8
1998-99	EHC Kloten	Switz.	40	11	14	25	14	9	7	0	7	8
99-2000	EHC Kloten	Switz.	33	8	15	23	12	6	2	1	3	0

WIDING, Daniel (VEE-dihng) NSH.

Right wing. Shoots right. 6'1", 186 lbs. Born, Gavle, Sweden, April 13, 1982.
(Nashville's 2nd choice, 36th overall, in 2000 Entry Draft).

			Regular Season					Playoffs				
Season	Club	Lea	GP	G	A	TP	PIM	GP	G	A	TP	PIM
99-2000	Leksands IF	Swede-Jr.	34	15	12	27	65	2	1	0	1	4
	Leksands IF	Sweden	3	0	0	0	2	....	....	....	....	....

WIKSTROM, John (WIHK-strohm, JAWN) DET.

Defense. Shoots left. 6'3", 200 lbs. Born, Lulea, Sweden, January 30, 1979.
(Detroit's 4th choice, 129th overall, in 1997 Entry Draft).

			Regular Season					Playoffs				
Season	Club	Lea	GP	G	A	TP	PIM	GP	G	A	TP	PIM
1995-96	Lulea HF	Sweden	9	0	0	0	2	....	....	....	....	....
1996-97	Lulea HF	Sweden	9	0	0	0	0	3	0	0	0	0
1997-98	Lulea HF	Sweden	1	0	0	0	0	....	....	....	....	....
	Lulea HF	EuroHL	1	0	0	0	0	....	....	....	....	....
	Pitea IK	Swede-2	4	0	0	0	0	....	....	....	....	....
1998-99	Morrum IS	Swede-2	23	0	1	1	28	....	....	....	....	....
99-2000	Louisiana Gators	ECHL	10	0	0	0	4	....	....	....	....	....
	Wheeling Nailers	ECHL	48	4	4	8	23	....	....	....	....	....

WILFORD, Marty (WIHL-fohrd, MAHR-tee) CHI.

Defense. Shoots left. 6', 216 lbs. Born, Cobourg, Ont., April 17, 1977.
(Chicago's 7th choice, 149th overall, in 1995 Entry Draft).

			Regular Season					Playoffs				
Season	Club	Lea	GP	G	A	TP	PIM	GP	G	A	TP	PIM
1993-94	Peterborough B's	OJHL	40	3	19	22	*107	....	....	....	....	....
1994-95	Oshawa Generals	OHL	63	1	6	7	95	7	1	1	2	4
1995-96	Oshawa Generals	OHL	65	3	24	27	107	5	0	1	1	4
1996-97	Oshawa Generals	OHL	62	19	43	62	126	16	2	18	20	28
1997-98	Columbus Chill	ECHL	46	8	27	35	123	....	....	....	....	....
	Indianapolis Ice	IHL	26	0	4	4	16	....	....	....	....	....
1998-99	Indianapolis Ice	IHL	80	3	13	16	116	7	0	1	1	16
99-2000	Cleveland	IHL	7	0	3	3	24	....	....	....	....	....
	Houston Aeros	IHL	45	0	9	9	30	11	2	2	4	18

OHL Second All-Star Team (1997)

WILLIAMS, Jeff (WIHL-lee-ams, JEHF) CBJ

Center. Shoots left. 6'1", 200 lbs. Born, Pointe-Claire, Que., February 11, 1976.
(New Jersey's 8th choice, 181st overall, in 1994 Entry Draft).

			Regular Season					Playoffs				
Season	Club	Lea	GP	G	A	TP	PIM	GP	G	A	TP	PIM
1991-92	North York	MTHL	56	53	51	104	23	....	....	....	....	....
	Newmarket	OJHL-B	4	1	1	2	4	....	....	....	....	....
1992-93	Newmarket	OJHL-B	45	28	35	63	18	....	....	....	....	....
1993-94	Newmarket	OJHL-B	4	1	1	2	4	....	....	....	....	....
	Guelph Storm	OHL	62	14	12	26	19	9	2	1	3	4
1994-95	Guelph Storm	OHL	52	15	32	47	21	14	5	5	10	0
1995-96	Guelph Storm	OHL	63	15	49	64	42	16	13	15	28	10
1996-97	Raleigh IceCaps	ECHL	20	4	8	12	8	....	....	....	....	....
	Albany River Rats	AHL	46	13	20	33	12	15	1	2	3	15
1997-98	Albany River Rats	AHL	58	13	12	25	20	12	5	6	11	2
1998-99	Albany River Rats	AHL	74	*46	27	73	39	5	1	2	3	0
99-2000	Orlando	IHL	6	2	4	6	0	....	....	....	....	....
	Albany River Rats	AHL	71	29	20	49	24	5	0	0	0	2

Canadian Major Junior Most Sportsmanlike Player of the Year (1996) • AHL Second All-Star Team (1999)

Traded to **New Jersey** by **Atlanta** with Sylvain Cloutier and Atlanta's 7th round choice (Ken Magovan) in 2000 Entry Draft for Wes Mason and Eric Bertrand, November 1, 1999. Selected by **Columbus** from **New Jersey** in Expansion Draft, June 23, 2000.

WILLIAMS, Justin (WIHL-yuhms) PHI.

Right wing. Shoots right. 6'1", 176 lbs. Born, Coburg, Ont., October 4, 1981.
(Philadelphia's 1st choice, 28th overall, in 2000 Entry Draft).

			Regular Season					Playoffs				
Season	Club	Lea	GP	G	A	TP	PIM	GP	G	A	TP	PIM
1997-98	Cobourne Colts	OJHL-C	36	32	35	67	26	....	....	....	....	....
	Colbourg Cougars	OJHL-B	17	0	3	3	5	....	....	....	....	....
1998-99	Plymouth Whalers	OHL	47	4	8	12	28	7	1	2	3	0
99-2000	Plymouth Whalers	OHL	68	37	46	83	46	23	*14	16	*30	10

WILLIS, Tyler (WHIL-lihs, TIGH-luhr)

Right wing. Shoots right. 5'9", 171 lbs. Born, Princeton, B.C., April 8, 1977.
(Vancouver's 8th choice, 196th overall, in 1995 Entry Draft).

			Regular Season					Playoffs				
Season	Club	Lea	GP	G	A	TP	PIM	GP	G	A	TP	PIM
1993-94	Swift Current	WHL	71	19	26	45	263	....	....	....	....	....
1994-95	Swift Current	WHL	71	21	29	50	284	6	0	0	0	20
1995-96	Swift Current	WHL	40	9	38	47	196	....	....	....	....	....
	Seattle T-Birds	WHL	15	1	3	4	71	5	1	5	6	13
1996-97	Seattle T-Birds	WHL	72	12	40	52	302	15	1	7	8	68
1997-98	Worcester	AHL	24	2	1	3	140	....	....	....	....	....
	Baton Rouge	ECHL	21	4	10	14	112	....	....	....	....	....
1998-99	Worcester	AHL	55	8	10	18	227	....	....	....	....	....
99-2000	Worcester	AHL	32	3	10	13	98	9	1	2	3	8
	Peoria Rivermen	ECHL	19	5	6	11	89	....	....	....	....	....

Signed as a free agent by **St. Louis**, October 3, 1997.

WINCHESTER, Brad (WIHN-chehst-uhr) EDM.

Left wing. Shoots left. 6'5", 208 lbs. Born, Madison, WI, March 1, 1981.
(Edmonton's 2nd choice, 35th overall, in 2000 Entry Draft).

			Regular Season					Playoffs				
Season	Club	Lea	GP	G	A	TP	PIM	GP	G	A	TP	PIM
1997-98	Team USA	Under-18	74	22	23	45	162	....	....	....	....	....
1998-99	Team USA	Under-18	65	21	23	44	103	....	....	....	....	....
99-2000	U. of Wisconsin	WCHA	33	9	9	18	48	....	....	....	....	....

WOODS, Brad (WUHDS, BRAD) FLA.

Defense. Shoots right. 6'4", 200 lbs. Born, Cambridge, Ont., March 4, 1981.
(Florida's 7th choice, 169th overall, in 1999 Entry Draft).

			Regular Season					Playoffs				
Season	Club	Lea	GP	G	A	TP	PIM	GP	G	A	TP	PIM
1997-98	Cambridge Hawks	OMHA	54	6	18	24	145	....	....	....	....	....
1998-99	Brampton	OHL	58	1	5	6	42	....	....	....	....	....
99-2000	Brampton	OHL	68	5	11	16	30	6	0	0	0	8

YAKUBOV, Mikhail (yuh-KOO-bahf, mih-KIGH-eel) CHI.

Center. Shoots left. 6'3", 185 lbs. Born, Barnaul, USSR, February 16, 1982.
(Chicago's 1st choice, 10th overall, in 2000 Entry Draft).

			Regular Season					Playoffs				
Season	Club	Lea	GP	G	A	TP	PIM	GP	G	A	TP	PIM
1997-98	Lada Togliatti-2	Russia-3	7	0	0	0	0	....	....	....	....	....
1998-99	Lada Togliatti-2	Russia-4	38	11	4	15	32	....	....	....	....	....
99-2000	Lada Togliatti-2	Russia-3	26	12	19	31	14	....	....	....	....	....

YERKOVICH, Sergei (yehr-KOH-vihch, SAIR-gay)

Defense. Shoots left. 6'3", 210 lbs. Born, Minsk, USSR, September 3, 1974.
(Edmonton's 3rd choice, 68th overall, in 1997 Entry Draft).

			Regular Season					Playoffs				
Season	Club	Lea	GP	G	A	TP	PIM	GP	G	A	TP	PIM
1993-94	Tivali Minsk	CIS	39	2	1	3	34	....	....	....	....	....
1994-95	Tivali Minsk	CIS	45	3	1	4	52	....	....	....	....	....
1995-96	Tivali Minsk	CIS	41	5	3	8	30	....	....	....	....	....
1996-97	Las Vegas	IHL	76	6	19	25	167	....	....	....	....	....
1997-98	Las Vegas	IHL	69	7	15	22	130	4	0	0	0	6
	Belarus	Olympics	6	2	0	2	16	....	....	....	....	....
1998-99	Hamilton Bulldogs	AHL	69	7	11	18	103	8	0	2	2	2
99-2000	Hamilton Bulldogs	AHL	72	2	28	30	64	10	1	3	4	16

YERSHOV, Andrei (yuhr-SHAWF, AWN-dray) CHI.

Defense. Shoots left. 6', 176 lbs. Born, Voskresensk, USSR, August 22, 1976.
(Chicago's 9th choice, 240th overall, in 1998 Entry Draft).

			Regular Season					Playoffs				
Season	Club	Lea	GP	G	A	TP	PIM	GP	G	A	TP	PIM
1994-95	HK Khimik	CIS	16	0	0	0	6	....	....	....	....	....
1995-96	HK Khimik	CIS	18	1	0	1	28	....	....	....	....	....
1996-97	HK Khimik	Russia	23	3	1	4	32	2	0	0	0	2
1997-98	HK Khimik	Russia	45	5	8	13	60	....	....	....	....	....
1998-99	HK Khimik	Russia	33	6	6	12	88	....	....	....	....	....
99-2000	Lada Togliatti	Russia	10	0	1	1	12	4	0	0	0	6

YONKMAN, Nolan (YAWK-man, NOH-lan) WSH.

Defense. Shoots right. 6'5", 218 lbs. Born, Punnicht, Sask., April 1, 1981.
(Washington's 5th choice, 37th overall, in 1999 Entry Draft).

			Regular Season					Playoffs				
Season	Club	Lea	GP	G	A	TP	PIM	GP	G	A	TP	PIM
1996-97	Naicam Lions	SAHA	64	15	23	38	36	....	....	....	....	....
	Kelowna Rockets	WHL	4	0	0	0	0	....	....	....	....	....
1997-98	Kelowna Rockets	WHL	65	0	2	2	36	7	0	0	0	2
1998-99	Kelowna Rockets	WHL	61	1	6	7	129	6	0	0	0	6
99-2000	Kelowna Rockets	WHL	71	5	7	12	153	5	0	0	0	8

YTFELDT, David (YOOT-fehld, DAY-vihd) VAN.

Defense. Shoots left. 6'1", 187 lbs. Born, Ornskoldsvik, Sweden, September 29, 1979.
(Vancouver's 6th choice, 136th overall, in 1998 Entry Draft).

			Regular Season					Playoffs				
Season	Club	Lea	GP	G	A	TP	PIM	GP	G	A	TP	PIM
1996-97	Leksands IF	Swede-Jr.	25	3	5	8		....	....	....	....	....
1997-98	Leksands IF	Sweden	10	0	0	0	2	....	....	....	....	....
	Leksands IF	Swede-Jr.	23	13	10	23	101	....	....	....	....	....
1998-99	Leksands IF	Sweden	39	0	4	4	65	4	0	1	1	4
99-2000	Leksands IF	Sweden	50	3	9	12	72	....	....	....	....	....

• Name when drafted was David Jonsson. His last name was legally changed to Ytfeldt.

ZAINULLIN, Ruslan (zihj-NOO-luhn, eoos-LAHN) T.B.

Right wing. Shoots left. 6'2", 202 lbs. Born, Kazan, USSR, February 14, 1982.
(Tampa Bay's 2nd choice, 34th overall, in 2000 Entry Draft).

			Regular Season					Playoffs				
Season	Club	Lea	GP	G	A	TP	PIM	GP	G	A	TP	PIM
1997-98	Ak Bars Kazan-2	Russia-3	27	0	1	1	2	....	....	....	....	....
1998-99	Ak Bars Kazan-2	Russia-4	36	13	8	21	22	....	....	....	....	....
99-2000	Ak Bars Kazan-2	Russia-3	12	13	6	19		....	....	....	....	....
	Ak Bars Kazan	Russia	14	1	1	2	4	....	....	....	....	....

ZALESAK, Miroslav (zah-LIH-sahk, MEER-oh-slav) S.J.

Right wing. Shoots left. 6', 185 lbs. Born, Skalica, Czech., January 2, 1980.
(San Jose's 5th choice, 104th overall, in 1998 Entry Draft).

			Regular Season					Playoffs				
Season	Club	Lea	GP	G	A	TP	PIM	GP	G	A	TP	PIM
1995-96	MHC Nitra	Slovak-Jr.	49	53	29	82	....	....	....	....	....	....
1996-97	MHC Nitra	Slovak-Jr.	58	51	31	82	....	....	....	....	....	....
1997-98	MHC Nitra	Slovak-Jr.	27	32	29	61	30	....	....	....	....	....
	MHC Nitra	Slovakia	30	8	6	14	0	....	....	....	....	....
1998-99	MHC Nitra	Slovakia	15	4	3	7	10	....	....	....	....	....
	Drummondville	QMJHL	45	24	27	51	18	....	....	....	....	....
99-2000	Drummondville	QMJHL	60	50	61	111	40	16	7	11	18	4

ZANON, Greg   (ZA-nuhn)   OTT.

Defense. Shoots left. 5'11", 200 lbs.   Born, Burnaby, B.C., June 5, 1980.
(Ottawa's 6th choice, 156th overall, in 2000 Entry Draft).

			Regular Season						Playoffs			
Season	Club	Lea	GP	G	A	TP	PIM	GP	G	A	TP	PIM
1995-96	Burnaby WCC	BCAHA	49	16	27	43	142	....	....	....	....	....
1996-97	Victoria Salsa	BCJHL	53	4	13	17	124	....	....	....	....	....
1997-98	Victoria Salsa	BCJHL	59	11	21	32	108	7	0	2	2	10
1998-99	Surrey Eagles	BCJHL	59	17	54	71	154	....	....	....	....	....
99-2000	Nebraska-Omaha	CCHA	42	3	26	29	56	....	....	....	....	....

ZAVORAL, Vaclav   (ZA-vohr-uhl, VATS-lahf)   TOR.

Defense. Shoots left. 6'3", 207 lbs.   Born, Teplice, Czech., May 22, 1981.
(Toronto's 5th choice, 151st overall, in 1999 Entry Draft).

			Regular Season						Playoffs			
Season	Club	Lea	GP	G	A	TP	PIM	GP	G	A	TP	PIM
1997-98	HC Litvinov-Jr.	Cze-Rep	46	0	5	5	....	....	....	....	....	....
1998-99	HC Litvinov-Jr.	Cze-Rep	43	2	10	12	....	....	....	....	....	....
	HC Litvinov	Cze-Rep	1	0	1	1	2	....	....	....	....	....
99-2000	Sault Ste. Marie	OHL	57	3	11	14	89	14	0	2	2	28

ZETTERBERG, Henrik   (ZEH-tuhr-buhrg)   DET.

Left wing. Shoots left. 5'11", 176 lbs.   Born, Njurunda, Sweden, October 9, 1980.
(Detroit's 4th choice, 210th overall, in 1999 Entry Draft).

			Regular Season						Playoffs			
Season	Club	Lea	GP	G	A	TP	PIM	GP	G	A	TP	PIM
1997-98	Timra IK	Swede-Jr.	18	9	5	14	4	....	....	....	....	....
	Timra IK	Swede-2	16	1	2	3	4	4	0	1	1	0
1998-99	Timra IK	Swede-2	37	15	13	28	2	4	2	1	3	2
99-2000	Timra IK	Swede-Q	31	16	8	24	20	....	....	....	....	....
	Timra IK	Swede-2	11	4	6	10	0	10	10	4	14	4

ZEVAKHIN, Alexander   (zeh-VAH-khin, al-ehx-AN-duhr))   PIT.

Right wing. Shoots left. 6', 187 lbs.   Born, Perm, USSR, December 30, 1978.
(Pittsburgh's 2nd choice, 54th overall, in 1998 Entry Draft).

			Regular Season						Playoffs			
Season	Club	Lea	GP	G	A	TP	PIM	GP	G	A	TP	PIM
1995-96	CSKA Moscow	Russia-Jr.	65	52	30	82	30	....	....	....	....	....
1996-97	CSKA Moscow	Russia	29	7	3	10	10	....	....	....	....	....
	CSKA Moscow-2	Russia-3	30	15	18	33	10	....	....	....	....	....
1997-98	CSKA Moscow-2	Russia-3	32	13	14	27	20	....	....	....	....	....
	CSKA Moscow	Russia	10	1	0	1	0	....	....	....	....	....
1998-99	CSKA Moscow	Russia	42	7	4	11	16	3	0	0	0	0
99-2000	CSKA Moscow	Russia	15	1	0	1	6	....	....	....	....	....

ZHURIK, Alexander   (ZHUH-rihk, al-ehx-AN-duhr)

Defense. Shoots left. 6'3", 195 lbs.   Born, Minsk, USSR, May 29, 1975.
(Edmonton's 7th choice, 163rd overall, in 1993 Entry Draft).

			Regular Season						Playoffs			
Season	Club	Lea	GP	G	A	TP	PIM	GP	G	A	TP	PIM
1993-94	Kingston	OHL	59	7	23	30	92	6	0	0	0	4
1994-95	Kingston	OHL	54	3	21	24	51	6	0	0	0	0
1995-96	Cape Breton	AHL	80	5	36	41	85	....	....	....	....	....
1996-97	Hamilton Bulldogs	AHL	72	5	16	21	49	22	2	11	13	14
1997-98	Hamilton Bulldogs	AHL	63	1	23	24	84	9	0	4	4	8
	Belarus	Olympics	4	0	0	0	10	....	....	....	....	....
1998-99	Dynamo Moscow	Russia	42	1	7	8	88	15	0	0	0	0
99-2000	Hamilton Bulldogs	AHL	54	2	16	18	54	10	0	3	3	10

ZIB, Lukas   (ZIHB, LOO-kahsh)   EDM.

Defense. Shoots right. 6'1", 200 lbs.   Born, Ceske Budejovice, Czech., February 24, 1977.
(Edmonton's 3rd choice, 57th overall, in 1995 Entry Draft).

			Regular Season						Playoffs			
Season	Club	Lea	GP	G	A	TP	PIM	GP	G	A	TP	PIM
1994-95	HC Budejovice	Cze-Rep	13	2	0	2	16	9	1	0	1	6
1995-96	HC Budejovice-Jr.	Cze-Rep	11	5	1	6	....	....	....	....	....	....
	HC Budejovice	Cze-Rep	10	1	0	1	....	2	0	0	0	....
1996-97	HC Budejovice	Cze-Rep	13	0	0	0	4	2	0	0	0	0
1997-98	HC Budejovice	Cze-Rep	47	5	6	11	22	....	....	....	....	....
1998-99	HC Budejovice	Cze-Rep	24	1	4	5	18	....	....	....	....	....
99-2000	HC Budejovice	Cze-Rep	38	3	6	9	10	1	0	0	0	0

ZIEGLER, Thomas   T.B.

Right wing. Shoots left. 5'11", 174 lbs.   Born, Zurich, Switz., June 9, 1978.
(Tampa Bay's 10th choice, 263rd overall, in 2000 Entry Draft).

			Regular Season						Playoffs			
Season	Club	Lea	GP	G	A	TP	PIM	GP	G	A	TP	PIM
1996-97	GC Zurich	Switz-Jr.	34	19	11	30	....	....	....	....	....	....
	GC Zurich	Switz-2	11	0	1	1	2	....	....	....	....	....
1997-98	GC Zurich	Switz-Jr.	13	9	3	12	32	....	....	....	....	....
	GC Zurich	Switz-2	25	5	4	9	22	....	....	....	....	....
	ZSC Zurich	Switz.	10	0	0	0	0	....	....	....	....	....
	ZSC Zurich	Switz-Q	8	0	2	2	2	....	....	....	....	....
1998-99	Ambri-Piotta	Switz.	38	2	4	6	18	12	0	0	0	8
	HC Sierre	Switz-2	4	1	2	3	2	....	....	....	....	....
99-2000	Ambri-Piotta	Switz.	45	7	7	14	24	9	1	5	6	16

ZIGOMANIS, Michael   (zih-goh-MAN-his, MIGH-kuhl)   BUF.

Center. Shoots right. 6'1", 189 lbs.   Born, North York, Ont., January 17, 1981.
(Buffalo's 4th choice, 64th overall, in 1999 Entry Draft).

			Regular Season						Playoffs			
Season	Club	Lea	GP	G	A	TP	PIM	GP	G	A	TP	PIM
1996-97	Wexford Hawks	MTHL	40	37	48	85	23	....	....	....	....	....
	Wexford Raiders	OJHL	8	2	5	7	2	....	....	....	....	....
1997-98	Kingston	OHL	62	23	51	74	30	12	1	6	7	2
1998-99	Kingston	OHL	67	29	56	85	36	5	1	7	8	2
99-2000	Kingston	OHL	59	40	54	94	49	5	0	4	4	0

ZIMAKOV, Sergei   (zih-MAH-kahv, SAIR-gay)   WSH.

Defense. Shoots left. 6'1", 194 lbs.   Born, Moscow, USSR, January 15, 1978.
(Washington's 4th choice, 58th overall, in 1996 Entry Draft).

			Regular Season						Playoffs			
Season	Club	Lea	GP	G	A	TP	PIM	GP	G	A	TP	PIM
1994-95	Omaha Lancers	USHL	48	14	46	60	22	....	....	....	....	....
1995-96	Krylja Sovetov	CIS	49	2	7	9	36	....	....	....	....	....
1996-97	Krylja Sovetov	Russia	39	4	3	7	57	2	0	0	0	0
1997-98	Krylja Sovetov	Russia	42	4	1	5	48	....	....	....	....	....
1998-99	Ak Bars Kazan	Russia	28	1	0	1	6	8	0	1	1	6
99-2000	Molot-Perm	Russia	31	1	2	3	34	8	0	1	1	0

ZINOVJEV, Sergei   (zih-NOH-vee-ehv)   BOS.

Center/Left wing. Shoots left. 5'11", 176 lbs.   Born, Novokuznetsk, USSR, March 4, 1980.
(Boston's 6th choice, 73rd overall, in 2000 Entry Draft).

			Regular Season						Playoffs			
Season	Club	Lea	GP	G	A	TP	PIM	GP	G	A	TP	PIM
1997-98	Ust-Novokuznetsk	Russia-3	40	7	7	14	36	....	....	....	....	....
1998-99	Ust-Novokuznetsk	Russia-4	4	0	1	1	8	....	....	....	....	....
	Ust-Novokuznetsk	Russia	31	2	4	6	14	3	0	0	0	0
99-2000	Ust-Novokuznetsk	Russia	28	0	2	2	16	....	....	....	....	....

ZION, Jonathon   (ZIGH-awn, JOHN-a-THAN)   TOR.

Defense. Shoots left. 6', 198 lbs.   Born, Nepean, Ont., May 21, 1981.
(Toronto's 4th choice, 110th overall, in 1999 Entry Draft).

			Regular Season						Playoffs			
Season	Club	Lea	GP	G	A	TP	PIM	GP	G	A	TP	PIM
1996-97	Nepean Raiders	OJHL	47	8	26	34	14	....	....	....	....	....
1997-98	Ottawa 67's	OHL	53	4	19	23	20	13	3	12	15	2
1998-99	Ottawa 67's	OHL	60	8	33	41	10	9	2	3	5	8
99-2000	Ottawa 67's	OHL	66	7	52	59	16	11	3	10	13	8

ZIZKA, Tomas   (ZHIHZH-kuh, TAW-mahsh)   L.A.

Defense. Shoots left. 6'1", 198 lbs.   Born, Sternberk, Czech., October 10, 1979.
(Los Angeles' 6th choice, 163rd overall, in 1998 Entry Draft).

			Regular Season						Playoffs			
Season	Club	Lea	GP	G	A	TP	PIM	GP	G	A	TP	PIM
1994-95	ZPS Zlin-Jr.	Cze-Rep	39	1	10	11	....	....	....	....	....	....
1995-96	ZPS Zlin-Jr.	Cze-Rep	47	2	8	10	....	....	....	....	....	....
1996-97	ZPS Zlin-Jr.	Cze-Rep	14	1	0	1	....	....	....	....	....	....
1997-98	ZPS Zlin-Jr.	Cze-Rep	11	3	4	7	....	....	....	....	....	....
	ZPS Zlin	Cze-Rep	33	0	3	3	2	....	....	....	....	....
1998-99	ZPS Zlin	Cze-Rep	44	3	7	10	14	11	1	2	3	....
99-2000	HC Barum Zlin	Cze-Rep	46	4	6	10	30	4	1	0	1	4

ZULTEK, Matt   (ZUHL-tehk, MAT)   BOS.

Center. Shoots left. 6'4", 222 lbs.   Born, Windsor, Ont., March 12, 1979.
(Boston's 2nd choice, 56th overall, in 1999 Entry Draft).

			Regular Season						Playoffs			
Season	Club	Lea	GP	G	A	TP	PIM	GP	G	A	TP	PIM
1994-95	Toronto Marlies	MTHL	94	45	36	81	110	....	....	....	....	....
1995-96	Caledon Cunucks	OJHL	50	19	14	33	40	....	....	....	....	....
1996-97	Ottawa 67's	OHL	63	27	13	40	76	21	7	6	13	27
1997-98	Ottawa 67's	OHL	62	28	28	56	156	13	6	12	18	20
1998-99	Ottawa 67's	OHL	56	33	33	66	71	9	6	2	8	4
99-2000	Ottawa 67's	OHL	28	9	6	15	34	11	3	5	8	12

• Re-entered NHL draft. Originally Los Angeles' 2nd choice, 15th overall, in 1997 Entry Draft.

Key to Prospect, NHL Player and Goaltender Registers

Demographics: Position, shooting side (catching hand for goaltenders), height, weight, place and date of birth as well as draft information, if any, is located on this line.

Major Junior, NCAA, minor pro, senior European and NHL clubs form a permanent part of each player's data panel. If a player sees action with more than one club in any of the above categories, a separate line is included for each one.

Olympic Team statistics are also listed.

Player's NHL organization as of September 5, 2000. This includes players under contract, unsigned draft choices and other players on reserve lists. Free agents as of September 5, 2000 show a blank here.

The complete career data panels of players with NHL experience who announced their retirement before the start of the 2000-01 season are included in the 2000-01 Player Register. These newly-retired players also show a blank here.

Each NHL club's minor-pro affiliates are listed on page 129.

								Regular Season												Playoffs						
Season	Club	League	GP	G	A	Pts	PIM	PP	SH	GW	S	%	+/–	TF	F%	H	SB	Min	GP	G	A	Pts	PIM	PP	H	GW

NIEUWENDYK, Joe (NOO-ihn-DIGHK, JOH) **DAL.**

Center. Shoots left. 6'1", 205 lbs.   Born, Oshawa, Ont., September 10, 1966. Calgary's 2nd choice, 27th overall, in 1985 Entry Draft.

Season	Club	League	GP	G	A	Pts	PIM	PP	SH	GW	S	%	+/–	TF	F%	H	SB	Min	GP	G	A	Pts	PIM	PP	H	GW
1983-84	Pickering	OJHL-B	38	30	28	58	35	....	....	....	....	....	....	....	....	....	....	....	....	....	....	....	....	....	....	....
1984-85	Cornell Big Red	ECAC	29	21	24	45	30	....	....	....	....	....	....	....	....	....	....	....	....	....	....	....	....	....	....	....
1985-86	Cornell Big Red	ECAC	29	26	28	54	67	....	....	....	....	....	....	....	....	....	....	....	....	....	....	....	....	....	....	....
1986-87	Cornell Big Red	ECAC	23	26	26	52	26	....	....	....	....	....	....	....	....	....	....	....	....	....	....	....	....	....	....	....
	Canada	Nat-Team	5	2	0	2	0	....	....	....	....	....	....	....	....	....	....	....	....	....	....	....	....	....	....	....
	Calgary	NHL	9	5	1	6	0	2	0	1	16	31.3	0	....	....	....	....	....	6	2	2	4	0	0	0	0
1987-88	Calgary	NHL	75	51	41	92	23	31	3	8	212	24.1	20	....	....	....	....	....	8	3	4	7	2	1	0	0
1988-89♦	Calgary	NHL	77	51	31	82	40	19	3	11	215	23.7	26	....	....	....	....	....	22	10	4	14	10	6	0	1
1989-90	Calgary	NHL	79	45	50	95	40	18	0	3	226	19.9	32	....	....	....	....	....	6	4	6	10	4	1	0	0
1990-91	Calgary	NHL	79	45	40	85	36	22	4	1	222	20.3	19	....	....	....	....	....	7	4	1	5	10	2	0	0
1991-92	Calgary	NHL	69	22	34	56	55	7	0	2	137	16.1	–1	....	....	....	....	....	....	....	....	....	....	....	....	....
1992-93	Calgary	NHL	79	38	37	75	52	14	0	6	208	18.3	9	....	....	....	....	....	6	3	6	9	10	1	0	0
1993-94	Calgary	NHL	64	36	39	75	51	14	1	7	191	18.8	19	....	....	....	....	....	6	2	2	4	0	1	0	0
1994-95	Calgary	NHL	46	21	29	50	33	3	0	4	122	17.2	11	....	....	....	....	....	5	4	3	7	0	2	0	1
1995-96	Dallas	NHL	52	14	18	32	41	8	0	3	138	10.1	–17	....	....	....	....	....	....	....	....	....	....	....	....	....
1996-97	Dallas	NHL	66	30	21	51	32	8	0	5	173	17.3	–5	....	....	....	....	....	7	2	2	4	0	0	0	0
1997-98	Dallas	NHL	73	39	30	69	30	14	0	11	203	19.2	16	....	....	....	....	....	....	1	0	1	....	0	0	0
	Canada	Olympics	6	2	3	5	2	....	....	....	....	....	....	....	....	....	....	....	....	....	....	....	....	....	....	....
1998-99♦	Dallas	NHL	67	28	27	55	34	8	0	8	157	17.8	11	1170	63.2	42	9	15:33	23	*11	10	21	19	3	0	6
99-2000	Dallas	NHL	48	15	19	34	26	7	0	2	110	13.6	–1	924	59.1	17	8	16:15	23	7	3	10	18	3	0	2
	NHL Totals		883	440	417	857	493	175	11	69	2330	18.9		2094	61.4	59	17	15:51	120	53	43	96	79	20	0	10

ECAC First All-Star Team (1986, 1987) • NCAA East First All-American Team (1986, 1987) • NHL All-Rookie Team (1988) • Won Calder Memorial Trophy (1988) • Won Dodge Ram Tough Award (1988) • Won King Clancy Memorial Trophy (1995) • Won Conn Smythe Trophy (1999) • Played in NHL All-Star Game (1988, 1989, 1990, 1994)
Traded to **Dallas** by **Calgary** for Corey Millen and Jarome Iginla, December 19, 1995.

Diamond (♦) indicates Member of Stanley Cup-winning team.

Asterisk (*) indicates league leader in this statistical category.

Trade and free agent signing dates are based on when the player's contract is filed with NHL Central Registry. This date often differs from the date when the club announces that it has made a trade or come to terms with a free agent.

All-star team selections and awards are listed below player's year-by-year data.

NHL All-Star Game appearances are listed above trade notes.

All trades, free agent signings and other transactions involving NHL clubs are listed in chronological order. First draft selection for players who re-enter the NHL Entry Draft is noted here. Other special notes are also listed here. These are highlighted with a bullet (•).

BEGINNING WITH THE 1999-2000 EDITION OF THE *NHL Official Guide & Record Book*, additional statistical categories have been included for forwards and defensemen in the National Hockey League. These new categories are, from left to right in the sample panel above, power-play goals (PP), shorthand goals (SH), game-winning goals (GW), shots on goal (S), percentage of shots that score (%), plus-minus rating (+/–), total faceoffs taken (TF), faceoff winning percentage (F%), hits (H), shots blocked (SB) and average time-on-ice per game played (Min).

To integrate this new data, the Player Register has been has been split into two sections. The Prospect Register presents data on players who have yet to play in the NHL. The NHL Player Register, containing more information and a photo of each player, lists all active players who have appeared in an NHL regular-season or playoff game at any time.

The Goaltender and Retired Player registers follow the NHL Player Register. The order of the Registers is as follows: Prospect, NHL Player, Goaltender, Retired Player and Retired Goaltender.

Pronunciation of Player Names

United Press International phonetic style.

AY	long A as in mate
A	short A as in cat
AI	nasal A as on air
AH	short A as in father
AW	broad A as in talk
EE	long E as in meat
EH	short E as in get
UH	hollow E as in "the"
AY	French long E with acute accent as in Pathe
IH	middle E as in pretty
EW	EW dipthong as in few
IGH	long I as in time
EE	French long I as in machine
IH	short I as in pity
OH	long O as in note
AH	short O as in hot
AW	broad O as in fought
OI	OI dipthong as in noise
OO	long double OO as in fool
UH	short double O as in ouch
OW	OW dipthong as in how
EW	long U as in mule
OO	long U as in rule
U	middle U as in put
UH	short U as in shut or hurt
K	hard C as in cat
S	soft C as in cease
SH	soft CH as in machine
CH	hard CH or TCH as in catch
Z	hard S as in bells
S	soft S as in sun
G	hard G as in gang
J	soft G as in general
ZH	soft J as in French version of Joliet
KH	gutteral CH as in Scottish version of Loch

Some information is unavailable at press time. Readers are encouraged to contribute.
See page 5 for contact names and addresses.

2000-01
NHL Player
Register

Note: The 2000-01 NHL Player Register lists forwards and defensemen only. Goaltenders are listed separately. The NHL Player Register lists every skater who has played in the NHL. Trades and roster changes are current as of September 5, 2000.

Abbreviations: A – assists; **F%** – faceoff winning percentage; **G** – goals; **GP** – games played; **GT** – game-tying goals scored; **GW** – game-winning goals scored; **H** – HITS: any legal contact by one player on an opposing player that impedes the opposing player's progress; **Lea** – league; **MIN** – average time on ice; **PIM** – penalties in minutes; **+/–** – plus/minus rating; **PP** – powerplay goals scored; **Pts** – points; **S** – shots on goal; **S%** – shooting percentage; **SB** – shots blocked; **SH** – shorthand goal scored; **TF** – Total faceoffs taken; ***** – league-leading total; **♦** – member of Stanley Cup-winning team.

Prospect Register begins on page 265.

Goaltender Register begins on page 559.

League abbreviations are listed on page 264.

Season	Club	League	GP	G	A	Pts	PIM	PP	SH	GW	S	%	+/–	TF	F%	H	SB	Min	GP	G	A	Pts	PIM	PP	SH	GW

AALTO, Antti
(AL-toh, AN-tee) **ANA.**

Center. Shoots left. 6'2", 210 lbs. Born, Lappeenranta, Finland, March 4, 1975. Anaheim's 6th choice, 134th overall, in 1993 Entry Draft.

Season	Club	League	GP	G	A	Pts	PIM	PP	SH	GW	S	%	+/–	TF	F%	H	SB	Min	GP	G	A	Pts	PIM	PP	SH	GW
1991-92	SaiPa	Finn-Jr.	13	7	9	16	38												6	3	1	4	6			
	SaiPa	Finland-2	20	6	6	12	20																			
1992-93	SaiPa-B	Finn-Jr.	3	0	1	1	2																			
	SaiPa-2	Finn-Jr.	3	4	2	6	2												6	2	2	4	8			
	TPS Turku	Finn-Jr.	14	6	8	14	18																			
	TPS Turku	Finland	1	0	0	0	0																			
	SaiPa	Finland-2	23	6	8	14	14																			
1993-94	TPS Turku	Finn-Jr.	10	3	8	11	14												5	1	4	5	12			
	Kiekko-67 Turku	Finland-2	4	2	2	4	27																			
	TPS Turku	Finland	33	5	9	14	16												10	1	1	2	4			
1994-95	Kiekko-67 Turku	Finn-Jr.	2	1	2	3	2																			
	Kiekko-67 Turku	Finland-2	1	1	0	1	29																			
	TPS Turku	Finland	44	11	7	18	18												5	0	1	1	2			
1995-96	Kiekko-67 Turku	Finland-2	2	0	2	2	2																			
	TPS Turku	Finland	40	15	16	31	22												11	3	5	8	14			
1996-97	TPS Turku	Finland	44	15	19	34	60												11	5	6	11	31			
	TPS Turku	EuroHL	5	3	3	6	2												2	1	1	2	0			
1997-98	**Anaheim**	**NHL**	**3**	**0**	**0**	**0**	**0**	0	0	0	1	0.0	–1													
	Cincinnati Ducks	AHL	29	4	9	13	30																			
1998-99	**Anaheim**	**NHL**	**73**	**3**	**5**	**8**	**24**	2	0	0	61	4.9	–12	22	22.7	64	12	9:23	4	0	0	0	2	0	0	0
99-2000	**Anaheim**	**NHL**	**63**	**7**	**11**	**18**	**26**	1	0	1	102	6.9	–13	827	51.0	83	12	13:11								
	NHL Totals		**139**	**10**	**16**	**26**	**50**	3	0	1	164	6.1		849	50.3	147	24	11:09	4	0	0	0	2	0	0	0

ADAMS, Bryan
(A-dams, BRIGH-an) **ATL.**

Left wing. Shoots left. 6', 185 lbs. Born, Fort St. James, B.C., March 20, 1977.

Season	Club	League	GP	G	A	Pts	PIM	PP	SH	GW	S	%	+/–	TF	F%	H	SB	Min	GP	G	A	Pts	PIM	PP	SH	GW
1994-95	Prince George	RMJHL	48	37	53	90																				
1995-96	Michigan State	CCHA	42	3	8	11	12																			
1996-97	Michigan State	CCHA	29	7	7	14	51																			
1997-98	Michigan State	CCHA	31	9	21	30	39																			
1998-99	Michigan State	CCHA	42	21	16	37	56																			
99-2000	**Atlanta**	**NHL**	**2**	**0**	**0**	**0**	**0**	0	0	0	1	0.0	–1	0	0.0	5	0	10:57								
	Orlando	IHL	64	16	18	34	27												4	0	1	1	6			
	NHL Totals		**2**	**0**	**0**	**0**	**0**	0	0	0	1	0.0		0	0.0	5	0	10:56								

Signed as a free agent by **Atlanta**, July 6, 1999.

ADAMS, Greg
(A-dams, GREHG)

Left wing. Shoots left. 6'3", 195 lbs. Born, Nelson, B.C., August 15, 1963.

Season	Club	League	GP	G	A	Pts	PIM	PP	SH	GW	S	%	+/–	TF	F%	H	SB	Min	GP	G	A	Pts	PIM	PP	SH	GW
1980-81	Kelowna Bucks	BCJHL	48	40	50	90	16																			
1981-82	Kelowna Bucks	BCJHL	45	31	42	73	24																			
1982-83	North Arizona	ACHA	29	14	21	35	46																			
1983-84	North Arizona	ACHA	26	44	29	73	24																			
1984-85	**New Jersey**	**NHL**	**36**	**12**	**9**	**21**	**14**	5	0	0	63	19.0	–14													
	Maine Mariners	AHL	41	15	20	35	12												11	3	4	7	0			
1985-86	**New Jersey**	**NHL**	**78**	**35**	**42**	**77**	**30**	10	0	2	202	17.3	–7													
1986-87	**New Jersey**	**NHL**	**72**	**20**	**27**	**47**	**19**	6	0	1	143	14.0	–16													
1987-88	**Vancouver**	**NHL**	**80**	**36**	**40**	**76**	**30**	12	0	5	227	15.9	–24													
1988-89	**Vancouver**	**NHL**	**61**	**19**	**14**	**33**	**24**	9	0	2	144	13.2	–21						7	2	3	5	2	0	0	0
1989-90	**Vancouver**	**NHL**	**65**	**30**	**20**	**50**	**18**	13	0	1	181	16.6	–8													
1990-91	**Vancouver**	**NHL**	**55**	**21**	**24**	**45**	**10**	5	1	2	148	14.2	–5						5	0	0	0	2	0	0	0
1991-92	**Vancouver**	**NHL**	**76**	**30**	**27**	**57**	**26**	13	1	5	184	16.3	8						6	0	2	2	4	0	0	0
1992-93	**Vancouver**	**NHL**	**53**	**25**	**31**	**56**	**14**	6	1	3	124	20.2	31						12	7	6	13	6	5	0	1
1993-94	**Vancouver**	**NHL**	**68**	**13**	**24**	**37**	**20**	5	1	2	139	9.4	–1						23	6	8	14	2	2	0	2
1994-95	**Vancouver**	**NHL**	**31**	**5**	**10**	**15**	**12**	2	2	0	56	8.9	1													
	Dallas	**NHL**	**12**	**3**	**3**	**6**	**4**	1	0	0	16	18.8	–4						5	2	0	2	0	0	0	0

			Regular Season																	Playoffs							
Season	Club	League	GP	G	A	Pts	PIM	PP	SH	GW	S	%	+/-	TF	F%	H	SB	Min	GP	G	A	Pts	PIM	PP	SH	GW
1995-96	Dallas	NHL	66	22	21	43	33	11	1	1	140	15.7	-21	....	....	....	....	....	3	0	1	1	0	0	0	0
1996-97	Dallas	NHL	50	21	15	36	2	5	0	4	113	18.6	27	....	....	....	....	....	12	2	2	4	0	0	0	2
1997-98	Dallas	NHL	49	14	18	32	20	7	0	1	75	18.7	11	....	....	....	....	....	3	0	1	1	0	0	0	0
1998-99	Phoenix	NHL	75	19	24	43	26	5	0	3	176	10.8	-1	295	52.9	26	15	17:22	5	0	0	0	0	0	0	0
99-2000	Phoenix	NHL	69	19	27	46	14	5	0	0	129	14.7	-1	141	45.4	27	15	16:58	....							
	NHL Totals		996	344	376	720	316	120	7	30	2260	15.2		436	50.5	53	30	17:10	81	19	23	42	16	7	0	5

Played in NHL All-Star Game (1988) • Family name originally Adamakos
Signed as a free agent by **New Jersey**, June 25, 1984. Traded to **Vancouver** by **New Jersey** with Kirk McLean and New Jersey's 2nd round choice (Leif Rohlin) in 1988 Entry Draft for Patrik Sundstrom and Vancouver's 2nd (Jeff Christian) and 4th (Matt Ruchty) round choices in 1988 Entry Draft, September 15, 1987. Traded to **Dallas** by **Vancouver** with Dan Kesa and Vancouver's 5th round choice (later traded to LA Kings - LA Kings selected Jason Morgan) in 1995 Entry Draft for Russ Courtnall, April 7, 1995. Signed as a free agent by **Phoenix**, September 1, 1998.

ADAMS, Kevyn

(A-dams, KEH-vihn)   **CBJ**

Center. Shoots right. 6'1", 195 lbs.   Born, Washington, D.C., October 8, 1974. Boston's 1st choice, 25th overall, in 1993 Entry Draft.

Season	Club	League	GP	G	A	Pts	PIM	PP	SH	GW	S	%	+/-	TF	F%	H	SB	Min	GP	G	A	Pts	PIM	PP	SH	GW
1990-91	Niagara Scenics	NAJHL	55	17	20	37	24	....	....	....	....	....	....	....	....	....	....	....	....	....	....	....	....	....	....	....
1991-92	Niagara Scenics	NAJHL	40	25	33	58	51	....	....	....	....	....	....	....	....	....	....	....	....	....	....	....	....	....	....	....
1992-93	U. of Miami-Ohio	CCHA	40	17	15	32	18	....	....	....	....	....	....	....	....	....	....	....	....	....	....	....	....	....	....	....
1993-94	U. of Miami-Ohio	CCHA	36	15	28	43	24	....	....	....	....	....	....	....	....	....	....	....	....	....	....	....	....	....	....	....
1994-95	U. of Miami-Ohio	CCHA	38	20	29	49	30	....	....	....	....	....	....	....	....	....	....	....	....	....	....	....	....	....	....	....
1995-96	U. of Miami-Ohio	CCHA	36	17	30	47	30	....	....	....	....	....	....	....	....	....	....	....	5	1	1	2	4	....	....	....
1996-97	Grand Rapids	IHL	82	22	25	47	47	....	....	....	....	....	....	....	....	....	....	....	....	....	....	....	....	....	....	....
1997-98	**Toronto**	**NHL**	**5**	**0**	**0**	**0**	**7**	0	0	0	3	0.0	0	....	....	....	....	....	4	0	0	0	4	....	....	....
	St. John's Leafs	AHL	59	17	20	37	99	....	....	....	....	....	....	....	9	44.4	2	0	7:56	7	0	2	2	14	0	0	0
1998-99	**Toronto**	**NHL**	**1**	**0**	**0**	**0**	**0**	0	0	0	1	0.0	0	....	....	....	....	....	5	2	0	2	4	....	....	....
	St. John's Leafs	AHL	80	15	35	50	85	....	....	....	....	....	....	....	....	....	....	....	....	....	....	....	....	....	....	....
99-2000	**Toronto**	**NHL**	**52**	**5**	**8**	**13**	**39**	0	0	0	70	7.1	-7	604	56.5	78	13	12:23	12	1	0	1	7	0	1	0
	St. John's Leafs	AHL	23	6	11	17	24	....	....	....	....	....	....	....	....	....	....	....	....	....	....	....	....	....	....	....
	NHL Totals		**58**	**5**	**8**	**13**	**46**	0	0	0	74	6.8		613	56.3	80	13	12:18	19	1	2	3	21	0	1	0

CCHA Second All-Star Team (1995)
Signed as a free agent by **Toronto**, August 7, 1997. Selected by **Columbus** from **Toronto** in Expansion Draft, June 23, 2000.

AFINOGENOV, Maxim

(ah-fihn-ah-GEHN-ahf, mahx-EEM)   **BUF.**

Right wing. Shoots left. 6', 195 lbs.   Born, Moscow, USSR, September 4, 1979. Buffalo's 3rd choice, 69th overall, in 1997 Entry Draft.

Season	Club	League	GP	G	A	Pts	PIM	PP	SH	GW	S	%	+/-	TF	F%	H	SB	Min	GP	G	A	Pts	PIM	PP	SH	GW
1996-97	Dynamo Moscow	Russia	29	6	5	11	10	....	....	....	....	....	....	....	....	....	....	....	4	0	2	2	0	....	....	....
	Dynamo Moscow	EuroHL	3	0	0	0	0	....	....	....	....	....	....	....	....	....	....	....	3	1	0	1	4	....	....	....
1997-98	Dynamo Moscow	Russia	35	10	5	15	53	....	....	....	....	....	....	....	....	....	....	....	....	....	....	....	....	....	....	....
	Dynamo Moscow	EuroHL	6	3	1	4	27	....	....	....	....	....	....	....	....	....	....	....	16	*10	6	*16	14	....	....	....
1998-99	Dynamo Moscow	Russia	38	8	13	21	24	....	....	....	....	....	....	....	....	....	....	....	4	1	3	7	27	....	....	....
	Dynamo Moscow	EuroHL	5	3	5	8	29	....	....	....	....	....	....	....	....	....	....	....	5	0	1	1	2	0	0	0
99-2000	**Buffalo**	**NHL**	**65**	**16**	**18**	**34**	**41**	2	0	2	128	12.5	-4	0	0.0	32	10	13:09	5	0	1	1	2	0	0	0
	Rochester	AHL	15	6	12	18	8	....	....	....	....	....	....	....	....	....	....	....	8	3	1	4	4	....	....	....
	NHL Totals		**65**	**16**	**18**	**34**	**41**	2	0	2	128	12.5		0	0.0	32	10	13:09	5	0	1	1	2	0	0	0

AITKEN, Johnathan

(ATE-kin, JOHN-a-than)   **BOS.**

Defense. Shoots left. 6'4", 215 lbs.   Born, Edmonton, Alta., May 24, 1978. Boston's 1st choice, 8th overall, in 1996 Entry Draft.

Season	Club	League	GP	G	A	Pts	PIM	PP	SH	GW	S	%	+/-	TF	F%	H	SB	Min	GP	G	A	Pts	PIM	PP	SH	GW
1993-94	Sherwood Park	AAHA	31	4	9	13	54	....	....	....	....	....	....	....	....	....	....	....	5	0	0	0	0	....	....	....
1994-95	Medicine Hat	WHL	53	0	5	5	71	....	....	....	....	....	....	....	....	....	....	....	5	1	0	1	6	....	....	....
1995-96	Medicine Hat	WHL	71	6	14	20	131	....	....	....	....	....	....	....	....	....	....	....	6	0	0	0	4	....	....	....
1996-97	Brandon	WHL	65	4	18	22	211	....	....	....	....	....	....	....	....	....	....	....	18	0	8	8	67	....	....	....
1997-98	Brandon	WHL	69	9	25	34	183	....	....	....	....	....	....	....	....	....	....	....	13	0	0	0	17	....	....	....
1998-99	Providence Bruins	AHL	65	2	9	11	92	....	....	....	....	....	....	....	....	....	....	....	....	....	....	....	....	....	....	....
99-2000	**Boston**	**NHL**	**3**	**0**	**0**	**0**	**0**	0	0	0	2	0.0	-3	0	0.0	5	3	18:57	....	....	....	....	....	....	....	....
	Providence Bruins	AHL	70	2	12	14	121	....	....	....	....	....	....	....	....	....	....	....	11	1	0	1	26	....	....	....
	NHL Totals		**3**	**0**	**0**	**0**	**0**	0	0	0	2	0.0		0	0.0	5	3	18:57	....	....	....	....	....	....	....	....

WHL East Second All-Star Team (1998)

AIVAZOFF, Micah

(A-vuh-zahf, MIGH-kuh)

Center. Shoots left. 6', 195 lbs.   Born, Powell River, B.C., May 4, 1969. Los Angeles' 6th choice, 109th overall, in 1988 Entry Draft.

Season	Club	League	GP	G	A	Pts	PIM	PP	SH	GW	S	%	+/-	TF	F%	H	SB	Min	GP	G	A	Pts	PIM	PP	SH	GW
1985-86	Victoria Cougars	WHL	25	3	4	7	25	....	....	....	....	....	....	....	....	....	....	....	5	1	0	1	2	....	....	....
1986-87	Victoria Cougars	WHL	72	18	39	57	112	....	....	....	....	....	....	....	....	....	....	....	8	3	4	7	14	....	....	....
1987-88	Victoria Cougars	WHL	69	26	57	83	79	....	....	....	....	....	....	....	....	....	....	....	8	5	7	12	2	....	....	....
1988-89	Victoria Cougars	WHL	70	35	65	100	136	....	....	....	....	....	....	....	....	....	....	....	....	....	....	....	....	....	....	....
1989-90	New Haven	AHL	77	20	39	59	71	....	....	....	....	....	....	....	....	....	....	....	....	....	....	....	....	....	....	....
1990-91	New Haven	AHL	79	11	29	40	84	....	....	....	....	....	....	....	....	....	....	....	19	2	8	10	25	....	....	....
1991-92	Adirondack	AHL	61	9	20	29	50	....	....	....	....	....	....	....	....	....	....	....	11	8	6	14	10	....	....	....
1992-93	Adirondack	AHL	79	32	53	85	100	....	....	....	....	....	....	....	....	....	....	....	....	....	....	....	....	....	....	....
1993-94	**Detroit**	**NHL**	**59**	**4**	**4**	**8**	**38**	0	0	0	52	7.7	-1	....	....	....	....	....	....	....	....	....	....	....	....	....
1994-95	**Edmonton**	**NHL**	**21**	**0**	**1**	**1**	**2**	0	0	0	6	0.0	-2	....	....	....	....	....	....	....	....	....	....	....	....	....
1995-96	**NY Islanders**	**NHL**	**12**	**0**	**1**	**1**	**6**	0	0	0	8	0.0	-6	....	....	....	....	....	....	....	....	....	....	....	....	....
	Utah Grizzlies	IHL	59	14	21	35	58	....	....	....	....	....	....	....	....	....	....	....	22	3	5	8	33	....	....	....
1996-97	Binghamton	AHL	75	12	36	48	70	....	....	....	....	....	....	....	....	....	....	....	4	1	1	2	0	....	....	....
1997-98	ERC Ingolstadt	DEB-2	19	9	19	28	59	....	....	....	....	....	....	....	....	....	....	....	....	....	....	....	....	....	....	....
	San Antonio		54	13	33	46	33	....	....	....	....	....	....	....	....	....	....	....	....	....	....	....	....	....	....	....
1998-99	Utah Grizzlies	IHL	79	25	22	47	67	....	....	....	....	....	....	....	....	....	....	....	5	0	0	0	4	....	....	....
99-2000	Utah Grizzlies	IHL	80	15	31	46	81	....	....	....	....	....	....	....	....	....	....	....	....	....	....	....	....	....	....	....
	NHL Totals		**92**	**4**	**6**	**10**	**46**	0	0	0	66	6.1		....	....	....	....	....	....	....	....	....	....	....	....	....

Signed as a free agent by **Detroit**, March 18, 1993. Claimed by **Pittsburgh** from **Detroit** in Waiver Draft, January 18, 1995. Claimed by **Edmonton** from **Pittsburgh** in Waiver Draft, January 18, 1995. Signed as a free agent by **NY Islanders**, August 23, 1995. Signed as a free agent by **NY Rangers**, August 23, 1996.

ALATALO, Mika

(a-luh-TAH-loh, MEE-kuh)   **PHX.**

Left wing. Shoots left. 6', 202 lbs.   Born, Oulu, Finland, June 11, 1971. Winnipeg's 11th choice, 203rd overall, in 1990 Entry Draft.

Season	Club	League	GP	G	A	Pts	PIM	PP	SH	GW	S	%	+/-	TF	F%	H	SB	Min	GP	G	A	Pts	PIM	PP	SH	GW
1988-89	KooKoo Kouvola	Finland	34	8	6	14	10	....	....	....	....	....	....	....	....	....	....	....	....	....	....	....	....	....	....	....
1989-90	KooKoo Kouvola	Finland	41	3	5	8	22	....	....	....	....	....	....	....	....	....	....	....	....	....	....	....	....	....	....	....
1990-91	Lukko Rauma	Finland	39	10	1	11	10	....	....	....	....	....	....	....	....	....	....	....	2	0	0	0	0	....	....	....
1991-92	Lukko Rauma	Finland	43	20	17	37	32	....	....	....	....	....	....	....	....	....	....	....	3	0	0	0	0	....	....	....
1992-93	Lukko Rauma	Finland	48	16	19	35	38	....	....	....	....	....	....	....	....	....	....	....	9	2	2	4	4	....	....	....
1993-94	Lukko Rauma	Finland	45	19	15	34	77	....	....	....	....	....	....	....	....	....	....	....	....	....	....	....	....	....	....	....
	Finland	Olympics	7	2	1	3	2	....	....	....	....	....	....	....	....	....	....	....	....	....	....	....	....	....	....	....
1994-95	TPS Turku	Finland	44	23	13	36	79	....	....	....	....	....	....	....	....	....	....	....	13	2	5	7	8	....	....	....
1995-96	TPS Turku	Finland	49	19	18	37	44	....	....	....	....	....	....	....	....	....	....	....	11	3	4	7	8	....	....	....
1996-97	Lulea HF	Sweden	50	19	18	37	54	....	....	....	....	....	....	....	....	....	....	....	10	2	3	5	22	....	....	....
1997-98	Lulea HF	Sweden	45	14	10	24	22	....	....	....	....	....	....	....	....	....	....	....	2	0	0	0	0	....	....	....
1998-99	TPS Turku	Finland	53	14	23	37	44	....	....	....	....	....	....	....	....	....	....	....	10	6	3	9	6	....	....	....
99-2000	**Phoenix**	**NHL**	**82**	**10**	**17**	**27**	**36**	1	0	1	107	9.3	-3	3	0.0	92	17	12:37	5	0	0	0	2	0	0	0
	NHL Totals		**82**	**10**	**17**	**27**	**36**	1	0	1	107	9.3		3	0.0	92	17	12:37	5	0	0	0	2	0	0	0

Transferred to **Phoenix** after **Winnipeg** franchise relocated, July 1, 1996.

ALBELIN, Tommy

(AHL-buh-LEEN, TAWM-mee) **CGY.**

Defense. Shoots left. 6'1", 194 lbs. Born, Stockholm, Sweden, May 21, 1964. Quebec's 7th choice, 158th overall, in 1983 Entry Draft.

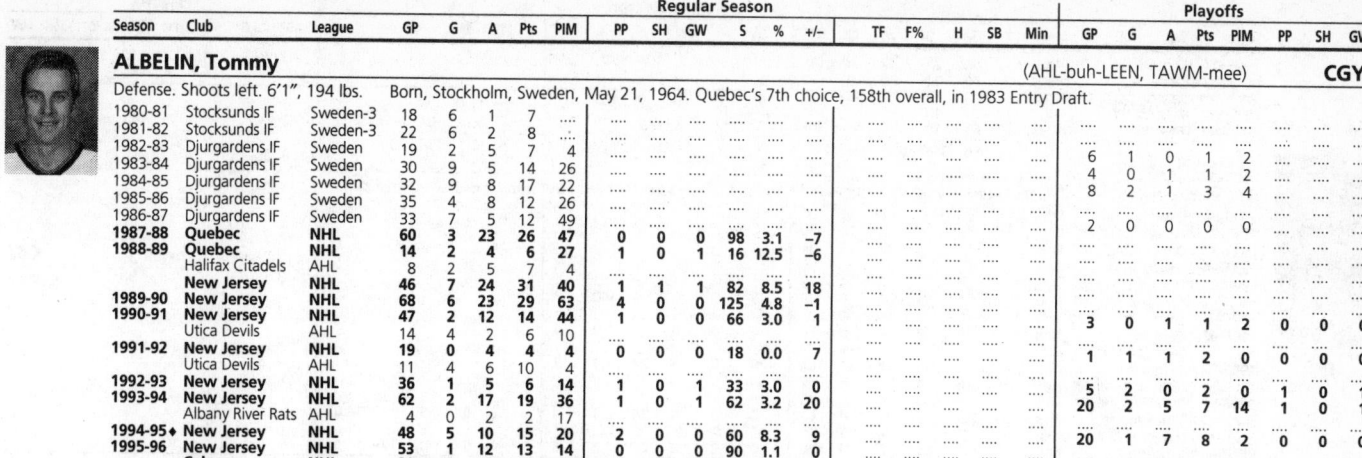

			Regular Season																Playoffs							
Season	Club	League	GP	G	A	Pts	PIM	PP	SH	GW	S	%	+/–	TF	F%	H	SB	Min	GP	G	A	Pts	PIM	PP	SH	GW
1980-81	Stocksunds IF	Sweden-3	18	6	1	7	....	....	....	....	....	....	....	....	....	....	....	....	....	....	....	....	....	....	....	....
1981-82	Stocksunds IF	Sweden-3	22	6	2	8	....	....	....	....	....	....	....	....	....	....	....	....	....	....	....	....	....	....	....	....
1982-83	Djurgardens IF	Sweden	19	2	5	7	4	....	....	....	....	....	....	....	....	....	....	....	6	1	0	1	2	....	....	....
1983-84	Djurgardens IF	Sweden	30	9	5	14	26	....	....	....	....	....	....	....	....	....	....	....	4	0	1	1	2	....	....	....
1984-85	Djurgardens IF	Sweden	32	9	8	17	22	....	....	....	....	....	....	....	....	....	....	....	8	2	1	3	4	....	....	....
1985-86	Djurgardens IF	Sweden	35	4	8	12	26	....	....	....	....	....	....	....	....	....	....	....	....	....	....	....	....	....	....	....
1986-87	Djurgardens IF	Sweden	33	7	5	12	49	....	....	....	....	....	....	....	....	....	....	....	2	0	0	0	0	....	....	....
1987-88	**Quebec**	**NHL**	**60**	**3**	**23**	**26**	**47**	**0**	**0**	**0**	**98**	**3.1**	**–7**	....	....	....	....	....	....	....	....	....	....	....	....	....
1988-89	**Quebec**	**NHL**	**14**	**2**	**4**	**6**	**27**	**1**	**0**	**1**	**16**	**12.5**	**–6**	....	....	....	....	....	....	....	....	....	....	....	....	....
	Halifax Citadels	AHL	8	2	5	7	4	....	....	....	....	....	....	....	....	....	....	....	....	....	....	....	....	....	....	....
	New Jersey	**NHL**	**46**	**7**	**24**	**31**	**40**	**1**	**1**	**1**	**82**	**8.5**	**18**	....	....	....	....	....	....	....	....	....	....	....	....	....
1989-90	**New Jersey**	**NHL**	**68**	**6**	**23**	**29**	**63**	**4**	**0**	**0**	**125**	**4.8**	**–1**	....	....	....	....	....	....	....	....	....	....	....	....	....
1990-91	**New Jersey**	**NHL**	**47**	**2**	**12**	**14**	**44**	**1**	**0**	**0**	**66**	**3.0**	**1**	....	....	....	....	....	**3**	**0**	**1**	**1**	**2**	**0**	**0**	**0**
	Utica Devils	AHL	14	4	2	6	10	....	....	....	....	....	....	....	....	....	....	....	....	....	....	....	....	....	....	....
1991-92	**New Jersey**	**NHL**	**19**	**0**	**4**	**4**	**4**	**0**	**0**	**0**	**18**	**0.0**	**7**	....	....	....	....	....	**1**	**1**	**1**	**2**	**0**	**0**	**0**	**0**
	Utica Devils	AHL	11	4	6	10	4	....	....	....	....	....	....	....	....	....	....	....	....	....	....	....	....	....	....	....
1992-93	**New Jersey**	**NHL**	**36**	**1**	**5**	**6**	**14**	**1**	**0**	**1**	**33**	**3.0**	**0**	....	....	....	....	....	**5**	**2**	**0**	**2**	**0**	**1**	**0**	**1**
1993-94	**New Jersey**	**NHL**	**62**	**2**	**17**	**19**	**36**	**1**	**0**	**1**	**62**	**3.2**	**20**	....	....	....	....	....	**20**	**2**	**5**	**7**	**14**	**1**	**0**	**1**
	Albany River Rats	AHL	4	0	2	2	17	....	....	....	....	....	....	....	....	....	....	....	....	....	....	....	....	....	....	....
1994-95♦	**New Jersey**	**NHL**	**48**	**5**	**10**	**15**	**20**	**2**	**0**	**0**	**60**	**8.3**	**9**	....	....	....	....	....	**20**	**1**	**7**	**8**	**2**	**0**	**0**	**0**
1995-96	**New Jersey**	**NHL**	**53**	**1**	**12**	**13**	**14**	**0**	**0**	**0**	**90**	**1.1**	**0**	....	....	....	....	....	....	....	....	....	....	....	....	....
	Calgary	**NHL**	**20**	**0**	**1**	**1**	**4**	**0**	**0**	**0**	**31**	**0.0**	**1**	....	....	....	....	....	**4**	**0**	**0**	**0**	**0**	**0**	**0**	**0**
1996-97	**Calgary**	**NHL**	**72**	**4**	**11**	**15**	**14**	**2**	**0**	**0**	**103**	**3.9**	**–8**	....	....	....	....	....	....	....	....	....	....	....	....	....
1997-98	**Calgary**	**NHL**	**69**	**2**	**17**	**19**	**32**	**1**	**0**	**2**	**88**	**2.3**	**9**	....	....	....	....	....	....	....	....	....	....	....	....	....
	Sweden	Olympics	3	0	0	0	4	....	....	....	....	....	....	....	....	....	....	....	....	....	....	....	....	....	....	....
1998-99	**Calgary**	**NHL**	**60**	**1**	**5**	**6**	**8**	**0**	**0**	**0**	**54**	**1.9**	**–11**	**1**	**0.0**	**34**	**55**	**19:08**	....	....	....	....	....	....	....	....
99-2000	**Calgary**	**NHL**	**41**	**4**	**6**	**10**	**12**	**1**	**1**	**1**	**37**	**10.8**	**–3**	**0**	**0.0**	**21**	**60**	**21:35**	....	....	....	....	....	....	....	....
	NHL Totals		**715**	**40**	**174**	**214**	**379**	**15**	**2**	**7**	**963**	**4.2**		**1**	**0.0**	**55**	**115**	**20:08**	**53**	**6**	**14**	**20**	**18**	**2**	**0**	**2**

Swedish World All-Star Team (1987, 1997)

Traded to **New Jersey** by **Quebec** for New Jersey's 4th round choice (Niclas Andersson) in 1989 Entry Draft, December 12, 1988. Traded to **Calgary** by **New Jersey** with Cale Hulse and Jocelyn Lemieux for Phil Housley and Dan Keczmer, February 26, 1996.

ALDRIDGE, Keith

Defense. Shoots right. 5'11", 185 lbs. Born, Detroit, MI, July 20, 1973.

1992-93	Lake Superior	CCHA	37	3	11	14	30	....	....	....	....	....	....	....	....	....	....	....	....	....	....	....	....	....	....	....
1993-94	Lake Superior	CCHA	45	10	24	34	86	....	....	....	....	....	....	....	....	....	....	....	....	....	....	....	....	....	....	....
1994-95	Lake Superior	CCHA	40	10	31	41	89	....	....	....	....	....	....	....	....	....	....	....	....	....	....	....	....	....	....	....
1995-96	Lake Superior	CCHA	38	14	36	50	88	....	....	....	....	....	....	....	....	....	....	....	....	....	....	....	....	....	....	....
	Baltimore Bandits	AHL	7	0	2	2	2	....	....	....	....	....	....	....	....	....	....	....	....	....	....	....	....	....	....	....
1996-97	Baltimore Bandits	AHL	51	4	9	13	92	....	....	....	....	....	....	....	....	....	....	....	3	0	0	0	4	....	....	....
1997-98	Detroit Vipers	IHL	79	13	21	34	89	....	....	....	....	....	....	....	....	....	....	....	23	1	9	10	67	....	....	....
1998-99	Detroit Vipers	IHL	66	15	28	43	130	....	....	....	....	....	....	....	....	....	....	....	11	2	7	9	49	....	....	....
99-2000	**Dallas**	**NHL**	**4**	**0**	**0**	**0**	**0**	**0**	**0**	**0**	**6**	**0.0**	**1**	**1**	**100.0**	**9**	**1**	**11:05**	....	....	....	....	....	....	....	....
	Michigan K-Wings	IHL	55	2	10	12	55	....	....	....	....	....	....	....	....	....	....	....	....	....	....	....	....	....	....	....
	NHL Totals		**4**	**0**	**0**	**0**	**0**	**0**	**0**	**0**	**6**	**0.0**		**1**	**100.0**	**9**	**1**	**11:05**	....	....	....	....	....	....	....	....

CCHA Second All-Star Team (1994) • CCHA First All-Star Team (1995, 1996) • NCAA West Second All-American Team (1995) • NCAA West First All-American Team (1996)

Signed as a free agent by **Dallas**, September 1, 1999.

ALFREDSSON, Daniel

(AHL-frehd-suhn, DAN-yehl) **OTT.**

Right wing. Shoots right. 5'11", 195 lbs. Born, Gothenburg, Sweden, December 11, 1972. Ottawa's 5th choice, 133rd overall, in 1994 Entry Draft.

1990-91	IF Molndal	Sweden-2	3	0	0	0	2	....	....	....	....	....	....	....	....	....	....	....	8	4	4	8	4	....	....	....
1991-92	IF Molndal	Sweden-2	32	12	8	20	43	....	....	....	....	....	....	....	....	....	....	....	....	....	....	....	....	....	....	....
1992-93	Vastra Frolunda	Sweden	20	1	5	6	8	....	....	....	....	....	....	....	....	....	....	....	....	....	....	....	....	....	....	....
1993-94	Vastra Frolunda	Sweden	39	20	10	30	18	....	....	....	....	....	....	....	....	....	....	....	4	1	1	2	....	....	....	....
1994-95	Vastra Frolunda	Sweden	22	7	11	18	22	....	....	....	....	....	....	....	....	....	....	....	....	....	....	....	....	....	....	....
1995-96	**Ottawa**	**NHL**	**82**	**26**	**35**	**61**	**28**	**8**	**2**	**3**	**212**	**12.3**	**–18**	....	....	....	....	....	....	....	....	....	....	....	....	....
1996-97	**Ottawa**	**NHL**	**76**	**24**	**47**	**71**	**30**	**11**	**1**	**1**	**247**	**9.7**	**5**	....	....	....	....	....	**7**	**5**	**2**	**7**	**6**	**3**	**0**	**2**
1997-98	**Ottawa**	**NHL**	**55**	**17**	**28**	**45**	**18**	**7**	**0**	**7**	**149**	**11.4**	**7**	....	....	....	....	....	**11**	**7**	**2**	**9**	**20**	**2**	**1**	**1**
	Sweden	Olympics	4	2	3	5	2	....	....	....	....	....	....	....	....	....	....	....	....	....	....	....	....	....	....	....
1998-99	**Ottawa**	**NHL**	**58**	**11**	**22**	**33**	**14**	**3**	**0**	**5**	**163**	**6.7**	**8**	**7**	**57.1**	**67**	**21**	**17:22**	**4**	**1**	**2**	**3**	**4**	**1**	**0**	**0**
99-2000	**Ottawa**	**NHL**	**57**	**21**	**38**	**59**	**28**	**4**	**2**	**0**	**164**	**12.8**	**11**	**3**	**66.7**	**58**	**29**	**18:45**	**6**	**1**	**3**	**4**	**2**	**1**	**0**	**0**
	NHL Totals		**328**	**99**	**170**	**269**	**118**	**33**	**5**	**16**	**935**	**10.6**		**10**	**60.0**	**125**	**50**	**18:03**	**28**	**14**	**9**	**23**	**32**	**7**	**1**	**3**

NHL All-Rookie Team (1996) • Won Calder Memorial Trophy (1996) • Played in NHL All-Star Game (1996, 1997, 1998)

ALLEN, Chris

(AHL-lehn, KRIHS) **FLA.**

Defense. Shoots right. 6'2", 197 lbs. Born, Chatham, Ont., May 8, 1978. Florida's 2nd choice, 60th overall, in 1996 Entry Draft.

1992-93	Blenheim	OJHL-C	3	0	0	0	0	....	....	....	....	....	....	....	....	....	....	....	....	....	....	....	....	....	....	....
1993-94	Leamington	OJHL-B	52	6	20	26	38	....	....	....	....	....	....	....	....	....	....	....	....	....	....	....	....	....	....	....
1994-95	Kingston	OHL	43	3	5	8	15	....	....	....	....	....	....	....	....	....	....	....	2	0	0	0	0	....	....	....
1995-96	Kingston	OHL	55	21	18	39	58	....	....	....	....	....	....	....	....	....	....	....	6	0	2	2	8	....	....	....
1996-97	Kingston	OHL	61	14	29	43	81	....	....	....	....	....	....	....	....	....	....	....	5	1	2	3	4	....	....	....
	Carolina	AHL	9	0	0	0	2	....	....	....	....	....	....	....	....	....	....	....	....	....	....	....	....	....	....	....
1997-98	Kingston	OHL	66	38	57	95	91	....	....	....	....	....	....	....	....	....	....	....	10	4	2	6	6	....	....	....
	Florida	**NHL**	**1**	**0**	**0**	**0**	**2**	**0**	**0**	**0**	**1**	**0.0**	**0**	....	....	....	....	....	....	....	....	....	....	....	....	....
1998-99	**Florida**	**NHL**	**1**	**0**	**0**	**0**	**0**	**0**	**0**	**0**	**0**	**0.0**	**1**	**0**	**0.0**	**0**	**0**	**12:35**	....	....	....	....	....	....	....	....
	New Haven	AHL	58	8	27	35	43	....	....	....	....	....	....	....	....	....	....	....	....	....	....	....	....	....	....	....
99-2000	Louisville	AHL	36	5	6	11	12	....	....	....	....	....	....	....	....	....	....	....	....	....	....	....	....	....	....	....
	Port Huron	UHL	6	2	1	3	4	....	....	....	....	....	....	....	....	....	....	....	....	....	....	....	....	....	....	....
	NHL Totals		**2**	**0**	**0**	**0**	**2**	**0**	**0**	**0**	**1**	**0.0**		**0**	**0.0**	**0**	**0**	**12:35**	....	....	....	....	....	....	....	....

OHL First All-Star Team (1998) • Canadian Major Junior First All-Star Team (1998)

ALLEN, Peter

(AHL-lehn, PEE-tuhr)

Defense. Shoots right. 6'2", 200 lbs. Born, Calgary, Alta., March 6, 1970. Boston's 1st choice, 24th overall, in 1991 Supplemental Draft.

1988-89	Calgary College	ACAC	24	7	30	37	....	....	....	....	....	....	....	....	....	....	....	....	....	....	....	....	....	....	....	....
1989-90	Yale University	ECAC	26	2	4	6	16	....	....	....	....	....	....	....	....	....	....	....	....	....	....	....	....	....	....	....
1990-91	Yale University	ECAC	17	0	6	6	14	....	....	....	....	....	....	....	....	....	....	....	....	....	....	....	....	....	....	....
1991-92	Yale University	ECAC	26	5	13	18	26	....	....	....	....	....	....	....	....	....	....	....	....	....	....	....	....	....	....	....
1992-93	Yale University	ECAC	30	3	15	18	32	....	....	....	....	....	....	....	....	....	....	....	....	....	....	....	....	....	....	....
1993-94	Richmond	ECHL	52	2	16	18	62	....	....	....	....	....	....	....	....	....	....	....	....	....	....	....	....	....	....	....
	P.E.I. Senators	AHL	6	0	1	1	6	....	....	....	....	....	....	....	....	....	....	....	....	....	....	....	....	....	....	....
1994-95	Canada	Nat-Team	52	5	15	20	36	....	....	....	....	....	....	....	....	....	....	....	....	....	....	....	....	....	....	....
1995-96	**Pittsburgh**	**NHL**	**8**	**0**	**0**	**0**	**8**	**0**	**0**	**0**	**2**	**0.0**	**2**	....	....	....	....	....	....	....	....	....	....	....	....	....
	Cleveland	IHL	65	3	45	48	55	....	....	....	....	....	....	....	....	....	....	....	3	0	0	0	2	....	....	....
1996-97	Cleveland	IHL	81	14	31	45	75	....	....	....	....	....	....	....	....	....	....	....	14	0	6	6	24	....	....	....
1997-98	Kentucky	AHL	72	0	18	18	73	....	....	....	....	....	....	....	....	....	....	....	3	0	1	1	4	....	....	....

			Regular Season																Playoffs							
Season	Club	League	GP	G	A	Pts	PIM	PP	SH	GW	S	%	+/-	TF	F%	H	SB	Min	GP	G	A	Pts	PIM	PP	SH	GW
1998-99	Kentucky	AHL	72	3	17	20	48	....	....	....	....	....	....	....	....	....	....	....	12	1	1	2	8	....	....	....
99-2000	Canada	Nat-Team	49	5	20	25	30	....	....	....	....	....	....	....	....	....	....	....	....	....	....	....	....	....	....	....
	NHL Totals		8	0	0	0	8	0	0	0	2	0.0		....	....	....	....	....	....	....	....	....	....	....	....	....

Signed as a free agent by **Pittsburgh**, August 10, 1995. Signed as a free agent by **San Jose**, August 19, 1997.

ALLISON, Jamie

(AHL-lih-sohn, JAY-mee) **CHI.**

Defense. Shoots left. 6'1", 200 lbs. Born, Lindsay, Ont., May 13, 1975. Calgary's 2nd choice, 44th overall, in 1993 Entry Draft.

			Regular Season																Playoffs							
Season	Club	League	GP	G	A	Pts	PIM	PP	SH	GW	S	%	+/-	TF	F%	H	SB	Min	GP	G	A	Pts	PIM	PP	SH	GW
1990-91	Waterloo Siskins	OJHL-B	38	3	8	11	91	....	....	....	....	....	....	....	....	....	....	....	....	....	....	....	....	....	....	....
1991-92	Windsor Spitfires	OHL	59	4	8	12	70	....	....	....	....	....	....	....	....	....	....	....	4	1	1	2	2	....	....	....
1992-93	Detroit Jr. Wings	OHL	61	0	13	13	64	....	....	....	....	....	....	....	....	....	....	....	15	2	5	7	23	....	....	....
1993-94	Detroit Jr. Wings	OHL	40	2	22	24	69	....	....	....	....	....	....	....	....	....	....	....	17	2	9	11	35	....	....	....
1994-95	Detroit Jr. Wings	OHL	50	1	14	15	119	....	....	....	....	....	....	....	....	....	....	....	18	2	7	9	35	....	....	....
	Calgary	NHL	1	0	0	0	0	0	0	0	0	0.0	0	....	....	....	....	....	....	....	....	....	....	....	....	....
1995-96	Saint John Flames	AHL	71	3	16	19	223	....	....	....	....	....	....	....	....	....	....	....	14	0	2	2	16	....	....	....
1996-97	Calgary	NHL	20	0	0	0	35	0	0	0	8	0.0	–4	....	....	....	....	....	....	....	....	....	....	....	....	....
	Saint John Flames	AHL	46	3	6	9	139	....	....	....	....	....	....	....	....	....	....	....	5	0	1	1	4	....	....	....
1997-98	Calgary	NHL	43	3	8	11	104	0	0	1	27	11.1	3	....	....	....	....	....	....	....	....	....	....	....	....	....
	Saint John Flames	AHL	16	0	5	5	49	....	....	....	....	....	....	....	....	....	....	....	....	....	....	....	....	....	....	....
1998-99	Saint John Flames	AHL	5	0	0	0	23	....	....	....	....	....	....	....	....	....	....	....	....	....	....	....	....	....	....	....
	Chicago	NHL	39	2	2	4	62	0	0	0	24	8.3	0	0	0.0	50	12	14:01	....	....	....	....	....	....	....	....
	Indianapolis Ice	IHL	3	1	0	1	10	....	....	....	....	....	....	....	....	....	....	....	....	....	....	....	....	....	....	....
99-2000	Chicago	NHL	59	1	3	4	102	0	0	0	24	4.2	–5	0	0.0	87	29	14:14	....	....	....	....	....	....	....	....
	NHL Totals		162	6	13	19	303	0	0	1	83	7.2		0	0.0	137	41	14:09	....	....	....	....	....	....	....	....

Traded to **Chicago** by **Calgary** with Marty McInnis and Eric Andersson for Jeff Shantz and Steve Dubinsky, October 27, 1998.

ALLISON, Jason

(AHL-lih-sohn, JAY-suhn) **BOS.**

Center. Shoots right. 6'3", 218 lbs. Born, North York, Ont., May 29, 1975. Washington's 2nd choice, 17th overall, in 1993 Entry Draft.

			Regular Season																Playoffs							
Season	Club	League	GP	G	A	Pts	PIM	PP	SH	GW	S	%	+/-	TF	F%	H	SB	Min	GP	G	A	Pts	PIM	PP	SH	GW
1990-91	North York	MTHL	63	53	41	94	....	....	....	....	....	....	....	....	....	....	....	....	....	....	....	....	....	....	....	....
1991-92	London Knights	OHL	65	11	19	30	15	....	....	....	....	....	....	....	....	....	....	....	7	0	0	0	0	....	....	....
1992-93	London Knights	OHL	66	42	76	118	50	....	....	....	....	....	....	....	....	....	....	....	12	7	13	20	8	....	....	....
1993-94	London Knights	OHL	56	55	87	*142	68	....	....	....	....	....	....	....	....	....	....	....	5	2	13	15	13	....	....	....
	Washington	NHL	2	0	1	1	0	0	0	0	5	0.0	1	....	....	....	....	....	....	....	....	....	....	....	....	....
	Portland Pirates	AHL	....	....	....	....	....	....	....	....	....	....	....	....	....	....	....	....	6	2	1	3	0	....	....	....
1994-95	London Knights	OHL	15	15	21	36	43	....	....	....	....	....	....	....	....	....	....	....	....	....	....	....	....	....	....	....
	Washington	NHL	12	2	1	3	6	2	0	0	9	22.2	–3	....	....	....	....	....	....	....	....	....	....	....	....	....
	Portland Pirates	AHL	8	5	4	9	2	....	....	....	....	....	....	....	....	....	....	....	7	3	8	11	2	....	....	....
1995-96	Washington	NHL	19	0	3	3	2	0	0	0	18	0.0	–3	....	....	....	....	....	....	....	....	....	....	....	....	....
	Portland Pirates	AHL	57	28	41	69	42	....	....	....	....	....	....	....	....	....	....	....	6	1	6	7	9	....	....	....
1996-97	Washington	NHL	53	5	17	22	25	1	0	1	71	7.0	–3	....	....	....	....	....	....	....	....	....	....	....	....	....
	Boston	NHL	19	3	9	12	9	1	0	0	28	10.7	–3	....	....	....	....	....	....	....	....	....	....	....	....	....
1997-98	Boston	NHL	81	33	50	83	60	5	0	8	158	20.9	33	....	....	....	....	....	6	2	6	8	4	1	0	0
1998-99	Boston	NHL	82	23	53	76	68	5	1	3	158	14.6	5	1760	52.2	91	28	22:23	12	2	9	11	6	1	0	0
99-2000	Boston	NHL	37	10	18	28	20	3	0	1	66	15.2	5	100	60.0	61	20	21:33	....	....	....	....	....	....	....	....
	NHL Totals		305	76	152	228	190	17	1	13	513	14.8		1860	52.6	152	48	22:07	18	4	15	19	10	2	0	0

OHL First All-Star Team (1994) • Canadian Major Junior First All-Star Team (1994) • Canadian Major Junior Player of the Year (1994)

Traded to **Boston** by **Washington** with Jim Carey, Anson Carter and Washington's 3rd round choice (Lee Goren) in 1997 Entry Draft for Bill Ranford, Adam Oates and Rick Tocchet, March 1, 1997. • Missed majority of 1999-2000 season recovering from thumb injury suffered in game vs. NY Islanders, January 8, 2000.

AMONTE, Tony

(eh-MAHN-tee, TOH-nee) **CHI.**

Right wing. Shoots left. 6', 200 lbs. Born, Hingham, MA, August 2, 1970. NY Rangers' 3rd choice, 68th overall, in 1988 Entry Draft.

			Regular Season																Playoffs							
Season	Club	League	GP	G	A	Pts	PIM	PP	SH	GW	S	%	+/-	TF	F%	H	SB	Min	GP	G	A	Pts	PIM	PP	SH	GW
1985-86	Thayer Academy	Hi-School	2	0	0	0	0	....	....	....	....	....	....	....	....	....	....	....	....	....	....	....	....	....	....	....
1986-87	Thayer Academy	Hi-School	25	25	32	57	....	....	....	....	....	....	....	....	....	....	....	....	....	....	....	....	....	....	....	....
1987-88	Thayer Academy	Hi-School	28	30	38	68	....	....	....	....	....	....	....	....	....	....	....	....	....	....	....	....	....	....	....	....
1988-89	Thayer Academy	Hi-School	25	35	38	73	....	....	....	....	....	....	....	....	....	....	....	....	....	....	....	....	....	....	....	....
1989-90	Boston University	H-East	41	25	33	58	52	....	....	....	....	....	....	....	....	....	....	....	....	....	....	....	....	....	....	....
1990-91	Boston University	H-East	38	31	37	68	82	....	....	....	....	....	....	....	....	....	....	....	....	....	....	....	....	....	....	....
	NY Rangers	NHL	....	....	....	....	....	....	....	....	....	....	....	....	....	....	....	....	2	0	2	2	2	0	0	0
1991-92	NY Rangers	NHL	79	35	34	69	55	9	0	4	234	15.0	12	....	....	....	....	....	13	3	6	9	2	2	0	0
1992-93	NY Rangers	NHL	83	33	43	76	49	13	0	4	270	12.2	0	....	....	....	....	....	....	....	....	....	....	....	....	....
1993-94	NY Rangers	NHL	72	16	22	38	31	3	0	4	179	8.9	5	....	....	....	....	....	....	....	....	....	....	....	....	....
	Chicago	NHL	7	1	3	4	6	1	0	0	16	6.3	–5	....	....	....	....	....	6	4	2	6	4	1	0	1
1994-95	HC Fassa	Alpenliga	14	22	16	38	10	....	....	....	....	....	....	....	....	....	....	....	....	....	....	....	....	....	....	....
	HC Fassa	EuroHL	2	5	1	6	0	....	....	....	....	....	....	....	....	....	....	....	....	....	....	....	....	....	....	....
	Chicago	NHL	48	15	20	35	41	6	1	3	105	14.3	7	....	....	....	....	....	16	3	3	6	10	0	0	0
1995-96	Chicago	NHL	81	31	32	63	62	5	4	5	216	14.4	10	....	....	....	....	....	7	2	4	6	6	1	0	0
1996-97	Chicago	NHL	81	41	36	77	64	9	2	4	266	15.4	35	....	....	....	....	....	6	4	2	6	8	0	0	0
1997-98	Chicago	NHL	82	31	42	73	66	7	3	5	296	10.5	21	....	....	....	....	....	....	....	....	....	....	....	....	....
	United States	Olympics	4	0	1	1	4	....	....	....	....	....	....	....	....	....	....	....	....	....	....	....	....	....	....	....
1998-99	Chicago	NHL	82	44	31	75	60	14	3	8	256	17.2	0	8	12.5	55	40	22:12	....	....	....	....	....	....	....	....
99-2000	Chicago	NHL	82	43	41	84	48	11	5	2	260	16.5	10	22	22.7	34	44	21:54	....	....	....	....	....	....	....	....
	NHL Totals		697	290	304	594	482	78	18	39	2098	13.8		30	20.0	89	84	22:03	50	16	19	35	32	4	0	1

Hockey East Second All-Star Team (1991) • NCAA Championship All-Tournament Team (1991) • NHL All-Rookie Team (1992) • Played in NHL All-Star Game (1997, 1998, 1999, 2000)

• Missed remainder of 1985-86 season recovering from knee injury, October, 1985. Traded to **Chicago** by **NY Rangers** with the rights to Matt Oates for Stephane Matteau and Brian Noonan, March 21, 1994.

ANDERSSON, Erik

(AN-duhr-suhn, AIR-ihk)

Center. Shoots left. 6'3", 210 lbs. Born, Stockholm, Sweden, August 19, 1971. Calgary's 6th choice, 70th overall, in 1997 Entry Draft.

			Regular Season																Playoffs							
Season	Club	League	GP	G	A	Pts	PIM	PP	SH	GW	S	%	+/-	TF	F%	H	SB	Min	GP	G	A	Pts	PIM	PP	SH	GW
1988-89	Vallentuna BK	Sweden-2	24	2	6	8	4	....	....	....	....	....	....	....	....	....	....	....	....	....	....	....	....	....	....	....
1989-90	Danderyd IK	Sweden-2	30	14	5	19	16	....	....	....	....	....	....	....	....	....	....	....	....	....	....	....	....	....	....	....
1990-91	AIK Solna	Sweden	32	1	1	2	10	....	....	....	....	....	....	....	....	....	....	....	....	....	....	....	....	....	....	....
1991-92	AIK Solna	Sweden	3	0	0	0	0	....	....	....	....	....	....	....	....	....	....	....	....	....	....	....	....	....	....	....
1992-93	U. of Denver	WCHA	DID NOT PLAY – ACADEMICALLY INELIGIBLE																							
1993-94	U. of Denver	WCHA	38	10	20	30	26	....	....	....	....	....	....	....	....	....	....	....	....	....	....	....	....	....	....	....
1994-95	U. of Denver	WCHA	42	12	19	31	42	....	....	....	....	....	....	....	....	....	....	....	....	....	....	....	....	....	....	....
1995-96	U. of Denver	WCHA	39	12	35	47	40	....	....	....	....	....	....	....	....	....	....	....	....	....	....	....	....	....	....	....
1996-97	U. of Denver	WCHA	39	17	17	34	42	....	....	....	....	....	....	....	....	....	....	....	....	....	....	....	....	....	....	....
1997-98	Calgary	NHL	12	2	1	3	8	0	0	0	11	18.2	–4	....	....	....	....	....	....	....	....	....	....	....	....	....
	Saint John Flames	AHL	29	5	9	14	29	....	....	....	....	....	....	....	....	....	....	....	....	....	....	....	....	....	....	....
1998-99	Saint John Flames	AHL	5	0	0	0	4	....	....	....	....	....	....	....	....	....	....	....	....	....	....	....	....	....	....	....
	Indianapolis Ice	IHL	48	5	7	12	24	....	....	....	....	....	....	....	....	....	....	....	4	0	0	0	44	....	....	....
99-2000	AIK Solna	Sweden	50	7	8	15	62	....	....	....	....	....	....	....	....	....	....	....	....	....	....	....	....	....	....	....
	NHL Totals		12	2	1	3	8	0	0	0	11	18.2		....	....	....	....	....	....	....	....	....	....	....	....	....

• Re-entered NHL draft. Originally Los Angeles' 5th choice, 112th overall, in 1990 Entry Draft.

Traded to **Chicago** by **Calgary** with Marty McInnis and Jamie Allison for Jeff Shantz and Steve Dubinsky, October 27, 1998.

ANDERSSON, Mikael

(AN-duhr-suhn, MIH-kaihl)

Left wing. Shoots left. 5'11", 181 lbs. Born, Malmo, Sweden, May 10, 1966. Buffalo's 1st choice, 18th overall, in 1984 Entry Draft.

			Regular Season																Playoffs							
Season	Club	League	GP	G	A	Pts	PIM	PP	SH	GW	S	%	+/-	TF	F%	H	SB	Min	GP	G	A	Pts	PIM	PP	SH	GW
1983-84	Vastra Frolunda	Sweden	18	0	3	3	6	....	....	....	....	....	....	....	....	....	....	....	....	....	....	....	....	....	....	....
1984-85	Vastra Frolunda	Sweden	30	16	11	27	18	....	....	....	....	....	....	....	....	....	....	....	6	3	2	5	2	....	....	....
1985-86	**Buffalo**	**NHL**	**32**	**1**	**9**	**10**	**4**	**0**	**0**	**0**	**13**	**7.7**	**0**	....	....	....	....	....	....	....	....	....	....	....	....	....
	Rochester	AHL	20	10	4	14	6	....	....	....	....	....	....	....	....	....	....	....	....	....	....	....	....	....	....	....
1986-87	**Buffalo**	**NHL**	**16**	**0**	**3**	**3**	**0**	**0**	**0**	**0**	**6**	**0.0**	**-2**	....	....	....	....	....	....	....	....	....	....	....	....	....
	Rochester	AHL	42	6	20	26	14	....	....	....	....	....	....	....	....	....	....	....	9	1	2	3	2	....	....	....
1987-88	**Buffalo**	**NHL**	**37**	**3**	**20**	**23**	**10**	**0**	**1**	**1**	**34**	**8.8**	**7**	....	....	....	....	....	**1**	**1**	**0**	**1**	**0**	**0**	**0**	**0**
	Rochester	AHL	35	12	24	36	16	....	....	....	....	....	....	....	....	....	....	....	....	....	....	....	....	....	....	....
1988-89	**Buffalo**	**NHL**	**14**	**0**	**1**	**1**	**4**	**0**	**0**	**0**	**12**	**0.0**	**-1**	....	....	....	....	....	....	....	....	....	....	....	....	....
	Rochester	AHL	56	18	33	51	12	....	....	....	....	....	....	....	....	....	....	....	....	....	....	....	....	....	....	....
1989-90	**Hartford**	**NHL**	**50**	**13**	**24**	**37**	**6**	**1**	**2**	**2**	**86**	**15.1**	**0**	....	....	....	....	....	**5**	**0**	**3**	**3**	**2**	**0**	**0**	**0**
1990-91	**Hartford**	**NHL**	**41**	**4**	**7**	**11**	**8**	**0**	**0**	**0**	**57**	**7.0**	**0**	....	....	....	....	....	....	....	....	....	....	....	....	....
	Springfield	AHL	26	7	22	29	10	....	....	....	....	....	....	....	....	....	....	....	18	*10	8	18	12	....	....	....
1991-92	**Hartford**	**NHL**	**74**	**18**	**29**	**47**	**14**	**1**	**3**	**1**	**149**	**12.1**	**18**	....	....	....	....	....	**7**	**0**	**2**	**2**	**6**	**0**	**0**	**0**
1992-93	**Tampa Bay**	**NHL**	**77**	**16**	**11**	**27**	**14**	**3**	**2**	**4**	**169**	**9.5**	**-14**	....	....	....	....	....	....	....	....	....	....	....	....	....
1993-94	**Tampa Bay**	**NHL**	**76**	**13**	**12**	**25**	**23**	**1**	**1**	**2**	**136**	**9.6**	**8**	....	....	....	....	....	....	....	....	....	....	....	....	....
1994-95	Vastra Frolunda	Sweden	7	1	0	1	31	....	....	....	....	....	....	....	....	....	....	....	....	....	....	....	....	....	....	....
	Tampa Bay	**NHL**	**36**	**4**	**7**	**11**	**4**	**0**	**0**	**0**	**36**	**11.1**	**-3**	....	....	....	....	....	....	....	....	....	....	....	....	....
1995-96	**Tampa Bay**	**NHL**	**64**	**8**	**11**	**19**	**2**	**0**	**0**	**1**	**104**	**7.7**	**0**	....	....	....	....	....	**6**	**1**	**1**	**2**	**0**	**0**	**0**	**0**
1996-97	**Tampa Bay**	**NHL**	**70**	**5**	**14**	**19**	**8**	**0**	**3**	**1**	**102**	**4.9**	**1**	....	....	....	....	....	....	....	....	....	....	....	....	....
1997-98	**Tampa Bay**	**NHL**	**72**	**6**	**11**	**17**	**29**	**0**	**1**	**1**	**105**	**5.7**	**-4**	....	....	....	....	....	....	....	....	....	....	....	....	....
	Sweden	Olympics	4	1	1	2	0	....	....	....	....	....	....	....	....	....	....	....	....	....	....	....	....	....	....	....
1998-99	**Tampa Bay**	**NHL**	**40**	**2**	**3**	**5**	**4**	**0**	**0**	**0**	**40**	**5.0**	**-8**	**38**	**34.2**	**10**	**13**	**12:39**	....	....	....	....	....	....	....	....
	Philadelphia	**NHL**	**7**	**0**	**1**	**1**	**0**	**0**	**0**	**0**	**11**	**0.0**	**1**	**35**	**28.6**	**5**	**2**	**12:59**	**6**	**0**	**1**	**1**	**2**	**0**	**0**	**0**
99-2000	**Philadelphia**	**NHL**	**36**	**2**	**3**	**5**	**0**	**0**	**1**	**0**	**38**	**5.3**	**-2**	**28**	**39.3**	**14**	**11**	**10:29**	....	....	....	....	....	....	....	....
	NY Islanders	**NHL**	**19**	**0**	**3**	**3**	**4**	**0**	**0**	**0**	**19**	**0.0**	**-1**	**5**	**60.0**	**8**	**2**	**9:33**	....	....	....	....	....	....	....	....
	NHL Totals		**761**	**95**	**169**	**264**	**134**	**6**	**14**	**13**	**1117**	**8.5**		**106**	**34.9**	**37**	**28**	**11:20**	**25**	**2**	**7**	**9**	**10**	**0**	**0**	**0**

Claimed by **Hartford** from **Buffalo** in NHL Waiver Draft, October 2, 1989. Signed as a free agent by **Tampa Bay**, June 29, 1992. Traded to **Philadelphia** by **Tampa Bay** with Sandy McCarthy for Colin Forbes and Philadelphia's 4th round choice (Michal Lanisak) in 1999 Entry Draft, March 20, 1999. Traded to **NY Islanders** by **Philadelphia** with Carolina's 5th round choice (previously acquired, NY Islanders selected Kristofer Ottoson) in 2000 Entry Draft for Gino Odjick, February 15, 2000.

ANDERSSON, Niklas

(AN-duhr-suhn, NIHK-las) **CGY.**

Left wing. Shoots left. 5'9", 180 lbs. Born, Kungalv, Sweden, May 20, 1971. Quebec's 5th choice, 68th overall, in 1989 Entry Draft.

			Regular Season																Playoffs							
Season	Club	League	GP	G	A	Pts	PIM	PP	SH	GW	S	%	+/-	TF	F%	H	SB	Min	GP	G	A	Pts	PIM	PP	SH	GW
1987-88	Vastra Frolunda	Sweden-2	15	5	5	10	6	....	....	....	....	....	....	....	....	....	....	....	8	6	4	10	4	....	....	....
1988-89	Vastra Frolunda	Sweden-2	30	12	24	36	24	....	....	....	....	....	....	....	....	....	....	....	10	4	6	10	4	....	....	....
1989-90	Vastra Frolunda	Sweden	38	10	21	31	14	....	....	....	....	....	....	....	....	....	....	....	....	....	....	....	....	....	....	....
1990-91	Vastra Frolunda	Sweden	22	6	10	16	16	....	....	....	....	....	....	....	....	....	....	....	....	....	....	....	....	....	....	....
1991-92	Halifax Citadels	AHL	57	8	26	34	41	....	....	....	....	....	....	....	....	....	....	....	....	....	....	....	....	....	....	....
1992-93	**Quebec**	**NHL**	**3**	**0**	**1**	**1**	**2**	**0**	**0**	**0**	**4**	**0.0**	**0**	....	....	....	....	....	....	....	....	....	....	....	....	....
	Halifax Citadels	AHL	76	32	50	82	42	....	....	....	....	....	....	....	....	....	....	....	....	....	....	....	....	....	....	....
1993-94	Cornwall Aces	AHL	42	18	34	52	8	....	....	....	....	....	....	....	....	....	....	....	....	....	....	....	....	....	....	....
1994-95	Denver Grizzlies	IHL	66	22	39	61	28	....	....	....	....	....	....	....	....	....	....	....	15	8	13	21	10	....	....	....
1995-96	**NY Islanders**	**NHL**	**47**	**14**	**12**	**26**	**12**	**3**	**2**	**1**	**89**	**15.7**	**-3**	....	....	....	....	....	....	....	....	....	....	....	....	....
	Utah Grizzlies	IHL	30	13	22	35	25	....	....	....	....	....	....	....	....	....	....	....	....	....	....	....	....	....	....	....
1996-97	**NY Islanders**	**NHL**	**74**	**12**	**31**	**43**	**57**	**1**	**1**	**1**	**122**	**9.8**	**4**	....	....	....	....	....	....	....	....	....	....	....	....	....
1997-98	**San Jose**	**NHL**	**5**	**0**	**0**	**0**	**2**	**0**	**0**	**0**	**6**	**0.0**	**-1**	....	....	....	....	....	....	....	....	....	....	....	....	....
	Kentucky	AHL	37	10	28	38	54	....	....	....	....	....	....	....	....	....	....	....	....	....	....	....	....	....	....	....
	Utah Grizzlies	IHL	21	6	20	26	24	....	....	....	....	....	....	....	....	....	....	....	4	3	1	4	4	....	....	....
1998-99	Chicago Wolves	IHL	65	17	47	64	49	....	....	....	....	....	....	....	....	....	....	....	10	2	2	4	10	....	....	....
99-2000	**NY Islanders**	**NHL**	**17**	**3**	**7**	**10**	**8**	**1**	**0**	**0**	**24**	**12.5**	**-3**	**0**	**0.0**	**10**	**4**	**13:19**	....	....	....	....	....	....	....	....
	Chicago Wolves	IHL	52	20	21	41	59	....	....	....	....	....	....	....	....	....	....	....	9	6	1	7	4	....	....	....
	Nashville	**NHL**	**7**	**0**	**1**	**1**	**0**	**0**	**0**	**0**	**7**	**0.0**	**0**	**0**	**0.0**	**1**	**0**	**12:50**	....	....	....	....	....	....	....	....
	NHL Totals		**153**	**29**	**52**	**81**	**81**	**5**	**3**	**2**	**252**	**11.5**		**0**	**0.0**	**11**	**4**	**13:11**	....	....	....	....	....	....	....	....

IHL Second All-Star Team (2000)

Signed as a free agent by **NY Islanders**, July 15, 1994. Signed as a free agent by **San Jose**, September 17, 1997. Signed as a free agent by **Toronto**, September 4, 1998. Traded to **NY Islanders** by **Toronto** for Craig Charron, August 17, 1999. Claimed on waivers by **Nashville** from **NY Islanders**, January 20, 2000. Signed as a free agent by **Calgary**, August 29, 2000.

ANDREYCHUK, Dave

(AN-druh-chuhk, DAYV) **BUF.**

Left wing. Shoots right. 6'4", 220 lbs. Born, Hamilton, Ont., September 29, 1963. Buffalo's 3rd choice, 16th overall, in 1982 Entry Draft.

			Regular Season																Playoffs							
Season	Club	League	GP	G	A	Pts	PIM	PP	SH	GW	S	%	+/-	TF	F%	H	SB	Min	GP	G	A	Pts	PIM	PP	SH	GW
1979-80	Hamilton Hawks	OMHA	21	25	24	49	....	....	....	....	....	....	....	....	....	....	....	....	....	....	....	....	....	....	....	....
1980-81	Oshawa Generals	OMJHL	67	22	22	44	80	....	....	....	....	....	....	....	....	....	....	....	10	3	2	5	20	....	....	....
1981-82	Oshawa Generals	OHL	67	57	43	100	71	....	....	....	....	....	....	....	....	....	....	....	3	1	4	5	16	....	....	....
1982-83	Oshawa Generals	OHL	14	8	24	32	6	....	....	....	....	....	....	....	....	....	....	....	....	....	....	....	....	....	....	....
	Buffalo	**NHL**	**43**	**14**	**23**	**37**	**16**	**3**	**0**	**1**	**66**	**21.2**	**6**	....	....	....	....	....	**4**	**1**	**0**	**1**	**4**	**0**	**0**	**0**
1983-84	**Buffalo**	**NHL**	**78**	**38**	**42**	**80**	**42**	**10**	**0**	**7**	**178**	**21.3**	**20**	....	....	....	....	....	**2**	**0**	**1**	**1**	**2**	**0**	**0**	**0**
1984-85	**Buffalo**	**NHL**	**64**	**31**	**30**	**61**	**54**	**14**	**0**	**2**	**153**	**20.3**	**-4**	....	....	....	....	....	**5**	**4**	**2**	**6**	**4**	**0**	**0**	**2**
1985-86	**Buffalo**	**NHL**	**80**	**36**	**51**	**87**	**61**	**12**	**0**	**3**	**225**	**16.0**	**3**	....	....	....	....	....	....	....	....	....	....	....	....	....
1986-87	**Buffalo**	**NHL**	**77**	**25**	**48**	**73**	**46**	**13**	**0**	**2**	**255**	**9.8**	**2**	....	....	....	....	....	....	....	....	....	....	....	....	....
1987-88	**Buffalo**	**NHL**	**80**	**30**	**48**	**78**	**112**	**15**	**0**	**5**	**253**	**11.9**	**1**	....	....	....	....	....	**6**	**2**	**4**	**6**	**0**	**1**	**0**	**0**
1988-89	**Buffalo**	**NHL**	**56**	**28**	**24**	**52**	**40**	**7**	**0**	**3**	**145**	**19.3**	**0**	....	....	....	....	....	**5**	**0**	**3**	**3**	**0**	**0**	**0**	**0**
1989-90	**Buffalo**	**NHL**	**73**	**40**	**42**	**82**	**42**	**18**	**0**	**3**	**206**	**19.4**	**6**	....	....	....	....	....	**6**	**2**	**5**	**7**	**2**	**1**	**0**	**0**
1990-91	**Buffalo**	**NHL**	**80**	**36**	**33**	**69**	**32**	**13**	**0**	**4**	**234**	**15.4**	**11**	....	....	....	....	....	**6**	**2**	**2**	**4**	**8**	**1**	**0**	**0**
1991-92	**Buffalo**	**NHL**	**80**	**41**	**50**	**91**	**71**	**28**	**0**	**2**	**337**	**12.2**	**-9**	....	....	....	....	....	**7**	**1**	**3**	**4**	**12**	**0**	**0**	**0**
1992-93	**Buffalo**	**NHL**	**52**	**29**	**32**	**61**	**48**	**20**	**0**	**2**	**171**	**17.0**	**-8**	....	....	....	....	....	....	....	....	....	....	....	....	....
	Toronto	**NHL**	**31**	**25**	**13**	**38**	**8**	**12**	**0**	**2**	**139**	**18.0**	**12**	....	....	....	....	....	**21**	**12**	**7**	**19**	**35**	**4**	**0**	**3**
1993-94	**Toronto**	**NHL**	**83**	**53**	**46**	**99**	**98**	**21**	**5**	**8**	**333**	**15.9**	**22**	....	....	....	....	....	**18**	**5**	**5**	**10**	**16**	**3**	**1**	**0**
1994-95	**Toronto**	**NHL**	**48**	**22**	**16**	**38**	**34**	**8**	**0**	**2**	**168**	**13.1**	**-7**	....	....	....	....	....	**7**	**3**	**2**	**5**	**25**	**2**	**0**	**0**
1995-96	**Toronto**	**NHL**	**61**	**20**	**24**	**44**	**54**	**12**	**2**	**3**	**200**	**10.0**	**-11**	....	....	....	....	....	....	....	....	....	....	....	....	....
	New Jersey	**NHL**	**15**	**8**	**5**	**13**	**10**	**2**	**0**	**0**	**41**	**19.5**	**2**	....	....	....	....	....	....	....	....	....	....	....	....	....
1996-97	**New Jersey**	**NHL**	**82**	**27**	**34**	**61**	**48**	**4**	**1**	**2**	**233**	**11.6**	**38**	....	....	....	....	....	**1**	**0**	**0**	**0**	**0**	**0**	**0**	**0**
1997-98	**New Jersey**	**NHL**	**75**	**14**	**34**	**48**	**26**	**4**	**0**	**2**	**180**	**7.8**	**19**	....	....	....	....	....	**6**	**1**	**0**	**1**	**4**	**1**	**0**	**0**
1998-99	**New Jersey**	**NHL**	**52**	**15**	**13**	**28**	**20**	**4**	**0**	**3**	**110**	**13.6**	**1**	**9**	**44.4**	**36**	**17**	**15:32**	**4**	**2**	**0**	**2**	**4**	**0**	**0**	**0**
99-2000	**Boston**	**NHL**	**63**	**19**	**14**	**33**	**28**	**7**	**0**	**2**	**192**	**9.9**	**-11**	**446**	**52.0**	**68**	**66**	**19:50**	....	....	....	....	....	....	....	....
	Colorado	**NHL**	**14**	**1**	**2**	**3**	**2**	**1**	**0**	**1**	**41**	**2.4**	**-9**	**15**	**60.0**	**10**	**9**	**17:16**	**17**	**3**	**2**	**5**	**18**	**2**	**0**	**0**
	NHL Totals		**1287**	**552**	**624**	**1176**	**892**	**228**	**8**	**59**	**3860**	**14.3**		**470**	**52.1**	**114**	**92**	**17:49**	**115**	**38**	**36**	**74**	**134**	**15**	**1**	**5**

Played in NHL All-Star Game (1990, 1994)

Traded to **Toronto** by **Buffalo** with Daren Puppa and Buffalo's 1st round choice (Kenny Jonsson) in 1993 Entry Draft for Grant Fuhr and Toronto's 5th round choice (Kevin Popp) in 1995 Entry Draft, February 2, 1993. Traded to **New Jersey** by **Toronto** for New Jersey's 2nd round choice (Marek Posmyk) in 1996 Entry Draft and New Jersey's 3rd round choice (later traded back to New Jersey - New Jersey selected Andre Lakos) in 1999 Entry Draft, March 13, 1996. Signed as a free agent by Boston, July 29, 1999. Traded to **Colorado** by **Boston** with Ray Bourque for Brian Rolston, Martin Grenier, Sami Pahlsson and New Jersey's 1st round choice (previously acquired, Boston selected Martin Samuelsson) in 200 Entry Draft, March 6, 2000. Signed as a free agent by **Buffalo**, July 13, 2000.

ANDRUSAK, Greg

(AN-druh-sak, GREHG) **S.J.**

Defense. Shoots right. 6'1", 195 lbs. Born, Cranbrook, B.C., November 14, 1969. Pittsburgh's 5th choice, 88th overall, in 1988 Entry Draft.

			Regular Season																Playoffs							
Season	Club	League	GP	G	A	Pts	PIM	PP	SH	GW	S	%	+/-	TF	F%	H	SB	Min	GP	G	A	Pts	PIM	PP	SH	GW
1986-87	Kelowna Packers	BCJHL	45	10	24	34	95	....	....	....	....	....	....	....	....	....	....	....	....	....	....	....	....	....	....	....
1987-88	Minnesota-Duluth	WCHA	37	4	5	9	42	....	....	....	....	....	....	....	....	....	....	....	....	....	....	....	....	....	....	....
1988-89	Minnesota-Duluth	WCHA	35	4	8	12	74	....	....	....	....	....	....	....	....	....	....	....	....	....	....	....	....	....	....	....
	Canada	Nat-Team	2	0	0	0	0	....	....	....	....	....	....	....	....	....	....	....	....	....	....	....	....	....	....	....
1989-90	Minnesota-Duluth	WCHA	35	5	29	34	74	....	....	....	....	....	....	....	....	....	....	....	....	....	....	....	....	....	....	....
1990-91	Canada	Nat-Team	53	4	11	15	34	....	....	....	....	....	....	....	....	....	....	....	....	....	....	....	....	....	....	....
1991-92	Minnesota-Duluth	WCHA	36	7	27	34	125	....	....	....	....	....	....	....	....	....	....	....	....	....	....	....	....	....	....	....

			Regular Season																Playoffs							
Season	Club	League	GP	G	A	Pts	PIM	PP	SH	GW	S	%	+/–	TF	F%	H	SB	Min	GP	G	A	Pts	PIM	PP	SH	GW
1992-93	Cleveland	IHL	55	3	22	25	78	....	....	....	....	....	....	....	....	....	....	....	2	0	0	0	2	....	....	....
	Muskegon Fury	ColHL	2	0	3	3	7	....	....	....	....	....	....	....	....	....	....	....	....	....	....	....	....	....	....	....
1993-94	Pittsburgh	NHL	3	0	0	0	2	0	0	0	4	0.0	–1	....	....	....	....	....	....	....	....	....	....	....	....	....
	Cleveland	IHL	69	13	26	39	109	....	....	....	....	....	....	....	....	....	....	....	....	....	....	....	....	....	....	....
1994-95	Pittsburgh	NHL	7	0	4	4	6	0	0	0	7	0.0	–1	....	....	....	....	....	....	....	....	....	....	....	....	....
	Cleveland	IHL	8	0	8	8	14	....	....	....	....	....	....	....	....	....	....	....	....	....	....	....	....	....	....	....
	Detroit Vipers	IHL	37	5	26	31	50	....	....	....	....	....	....	....	....	....	....	....	....	....	....	....	....	....	....	....
1995-96	Pittsburgh	NHL	2	0	0	0	0	0	0	0	1	0.0	–1	....	....	....	....	....	....	....	....	....	....	....	....	....
	Detroit Vipers	IHL	58	6	30	36	128	....	....	....	....	....	....	....	....	....	....	....	....	....	....	....	....	....	....	....
	Minnesota	IHL	5	0	4	4	8	....	....	....	....	....	....	....	....	....	....	....	....	....	....	....	....	....	....	....
1996-97	Eisbaren Berlin	DEL	45	5	17	22	170	....	....	....	....	....	....	....	....	....	....	....	8	1	1	2	20	....	....	....
1997-98	Eisbaren Berlin	DEL	34	3	7	10	65	....	....	....	....	....	....	....	....	....	....	....	9	0	1	1	8	....	....	....
1998-99	Eisbaren Berlin	DEL	19	2	5	7	12	....	....	....	....	....	....	....	....	....	....	....	....	....	....	....	....	....	....	....
	Eisbaren Berlin	EuroHL	5	0	1	1	18	....	....	....	....	....	....	....	....	....	....	....	....	....	....	....	....	....	....	....
	Geneve-Servette	Switz-2	10	3	13	16	....	....	....	....	....	....	....	....	....	....	....	....	....	....	....	....	....	....	....	....
	Houston Aeros	IHL	3	0	1	1	2	....	....	....	....	....	....	....	....	....	....	....	6	1	4	5	16	....	....	....
	Pittsburgh	NHL	7	0	1	1	4	0	0	0	2	0.0	4	0	0.0	14	3	17:42	12	1	0	1	6	0	0	1
99-2000	Toronto	NHL	9	0	1	1	4	0	0	0	5	0.0	1	0	0.0	14	2	18:25	3	0	0	0	2	0	0	0
	Chicago Wolves	IHL	54	2	23	25	50	....	....	....	....	....	....	....	....	....	....	....	11	1	5	6	20	....	....	....
	NHL Totals		28	0	6	6	16	0	0	0	19	0.0		0	0.0	28	5	18:06	15	1	0	1	8	0	0	1

WCHA First All-Star Team (1992)

Signed as a free agent by **Pittsburgh**, March 19, 1999. Signed as a free agent by **Toronto**, July 19, 1999. Signed as a free agent by **San Jose**, August 14, 2000.

ANTROPOV, Nik

(an-TROH-pahv, NIHK) **TOR.**

Center. Shoots left. 6'5", 203 lbs. Born, Vost, USSR, February 18, 1980. Toronto's 1st choice, 10th overall, in 1998 Entry Draft.

1995-96	Ust-Kamenogorsk	Russia-Jr.	20	18	20	38	30	....	....	....	....	....	....	....	....	....	....	....	....	....	....	....	....	....	....	....
1996-97	Ust-Kamenogorsk	Russia-2	8	2	1	3	6	....	....	....	....	....	....	....	....	....	....	....	....	....	....	....	....	....	....	....
1997-98	Ust-Kamenogorsk	Russia-2	42	15	24	39	62	....	....	....	....	....	....	....	....	....	....	....	....	....	....	....	....	....	....	....
1998-99	Dynamo Moscow	Russia	30	5	9	14	30	....	....	....	....	....	....	....	....	....	....	....	11	0	1	1	4	....	....	....
99-2000	Toronto	NHL	66	12	18	30	41	0	0	2	89	13.5	14	501	46.3	79	22	12:48	3	0	0	0	4	0	0	0
	St. John's Leafs	AHL	2	0	0	0	4	....	....	....	....	....	....	....	....	....	....	....	....	....	....	....	....	....	....	....
	NHL Totals		66	12	18	30	41	0	0	2	89	13.5		501	46.3	79	22	12:48	3	0	0	0	4	0	0	0

ARCHIBALD, Dave

(ahr-CHIH-bohld, DAYV)

Center/Left wing. Shoots left. 6'1", 210 lbs. Born, Chilliwack, B.C., April 14, 1969. Minnesota's 1st choice, 6th overall, in 1987 Entry Draft.

1983-84	Chilliwack	BCAHA	STATISTICS NOT AVAILABLE																							
	Portland	WHL	7	0	1	1	2	....	....	....	....	....	....	....	....	....	....	....	....	....	....	....	....	....	....	....
1984-85	Portland	WHL	47	7	11	18	10	....	....	....	....	....	....	....	....	....	....	....	3	0	2	2	0	....	....	....
1985-86	Portland	WHL	70	29	35	64	56	....	....	....	....	....	....	....	....	....	....	....	15	6	7	13	11	....	....	....
1986-87	Portland	WHL	65	50	57	107	40	....	....	....	....	....	....	....	....	....	....	....	20	10	18	28	11	....	....	....
1987-88	Minnesota	NHL	78	13	20	33	26	3	0	2	96	13.5	–17	....	....	....	....	....	....	....	....	....	....	....	....	....
1988-89	Minnesota	NHL	72	14	19	33	14	7	0	2	105	13.3	–11	....	....	....	....	....	5	0	1	1	0	0	0	0
1989-90	Minnesota	NHL	12	1	5	6	6	1	0	1	26	3.8	1	....	....	....	....	....	....	....	....	....	....	....	....	....
	NY Rangers	NHL	19	2	3	5	6	1	0	0	30	6.7	0	....	....	....	....	....	....	....	....	....	....	....	....	....
	Flint Spirits	IHL	41	14	38	52	16	....	....	....	....	....	....	....	....	....	....	....	4	3	2	5	0	....	....	....
1990-91	Canada	Nat-Team	29	19	12	31	20	....	....	....	....	....	....	....	....	....	....	....	....	....	....	....	....	....	....	....
1991-92	Canada	Nat-Team	58	20	43	63	64	....	....	....	....	....	....	....	....	....	....	....	....	....	....	....	....	....	....	....
	HC Bolzano	Italy	5	4	3	7	16	....	....	....	....	....	....	....	....	....	....	....	7	8	5	13	7	....	....	....
	Canada	Olympics	8	7	1	8	18	....	....	....	....	....	....	....	....	....	....	....	....	....	....	....	....	....	....	....
1992-93	Binghamton	AHL	8	6	3	9	10	....	....	....	....	....	....	....	....	....	....	....	....	....	....	....	....	....	....	....
	Ottawa	NHL	44	9	6	15	32	6	0	0	93	9.7	–16	....	....	....	....	....	....	....	....	....	....	....	....	....
1993-94	Ottawa	NHL	33	10	8	18	14	2	0	1	65	15.4	–7	....	....	....	....	....	....	....	....	....	....	....	....	....
1994-95	Ottawa	NHL	14	2	2	4	19	0	0	1	27	7.4	–7	....	....	....	....	....	....	....	....	....	....	....	....	....
1995-96	Ottawa	NHL	44	6	4	10	18	0	0	1	56	10.7	–14	....	....	....	....	....	....	....	....	....	....	....	....	....
	Utah Grizzlies	IHL	19	1	4	5	10	....	....	....	....	....	....	....	....	....	....	....	....	....	....	....	....	....	....	....
1996-97	NY Islanders	NHL	7	0	0	0	4	0	0	0	4	0.0	–4	....	....	....	....	....	....	....	....	....	....	....	....	....
	Frankfurt Lions	DEL	34	10	19	29	48	....	....	....	....	....	....	....	....	....	....	....	9	4	2	6	16	....	....	....
1997-98	San Antonio	IHL	55	11	21	32	10	....	....	....	....	....	....	....	....	....	....	....	....	....	....	....	....	....	....	....
1998-99	Utah Grizzlies	IHL	76	23	25	48	32	....	....	....	....	....	....	....	....	....	....	....	....	....	....	....	....	....	....	....
99-2000	Linkopings HC	Sweden	21	5	4	9	18	....	....	....	....	....	....	....	....	....	....	....	....	....	....	....	....	....	....	....
	Utah Grizzlies	IHL	27	7	4	11	10	....	....	....	....	....	....	....	....	....	....	....	5	0	0	0	0	....	....	....
	NHL Totals		323	57	67	124	139	20	0	8	502	11.4		....	....	....	....	....	5	0	1	1	0	0	0	0

Traded to **NY Rangers** by **Minnesota** for Jayson More, November 1, 1989. Traded to **Ottawa** by **NY Rangers** for Ottawa's 5th round choice (later traded to LA Kings - LA Kings selected Frederick Beaubien) in 1993 Entry Draft, November 6, 1992. Signed as a free agent by **NY Islanders**, October 10, 1996 Signed as a free agent by **Utah** (IHL) after securing release from **Linkopings HC** (Sweden), February 3, 2000.

ARMSTRONG, Derek

(ahrm-STRAWNG, DEHR-ehk) **NYR**

Center. Shoots right. 5'11", 188 lbs. Born, Ottawa, Ont., April 23, 1973. NY Islanders' 5th choice, 128th overall, in 1992 Entry Draft.

1989-90	Hawkesbury	OJHL	48	8	10	18	30	....	....	....	....	....	....	....	....	....	....	....	....	....	....	....	....	....	....	....
1990-91	Hawkesbury	OJHL	54	27	45	72	49	....	....	....	....	....	....	....	....	....	....	....	....	....	....	....	....	....	....	....
	Sudbury Wolves	OHL	2	0	2	2	0	....	....	....	....	....	....	....	....	....	....	....	....	....	....	....	....	....	....	....
1991-92	Sudbury Wolves	OHL	66	31	54	85	22	....	....	....	....	....	....	....	....	....	....	....	9	2	2	4	2	....	....	....
1992-93	Sudbury Wolves	OHL	66	44	62	106	56	....	....	....	....	....	....	....	....	....	....	....	14	9	10	19	26	....	....	....
1993-94	NY Islanders	NHL	1	0	0	0	0	0	0	0	2	0.0	0	....	....	....	....	....	....	....	....	....	....	....	....	....
	Salt Lake City	IHL	76	23	35	58	61	....	....	....	....	....	....	....	....	....	....	....	....	....	....	....	....	....	....	....
1994-95	Denver Grizzlies	IHL	59	13	18	31	65	....	....	....	....	....	....	....	....	....	....	....	6	0	2	2	0	....	....	....
1995-96	NY Islanders	NHL	19	1	3	4	14	0	0	0	23	4.3	–6	....	....	....	....	....	....	....	....	....	....	....	....	....
	Worcester	AHL	51	11	15	26	33	....	....	....	....	....	....	....	....	....	....	....	4	2	1	3	0	....	....	....
1996-97	NY Islanders	NHL	50	6	7	13	33	0	0	2	36	16.7	–8	....	....	....	....	....	....	....	....	....	....	....	....	....
	Utah Grizzlies	IHL	17	4	8	12	10	....	....	....	....	....	....	....	....	....	....	....	6	0	4	4	4	....	....	....
1997-98	Ottawa	NHL	9	2	0	2	9	0	0	1	8	25.0	1	....	....	....	....	....	....	....	....	....	....	....	....	....
	Detroit Vipers	IHL	10	0	1	1	2	....	....	....	....	....	....	....	....	....	....	....	....	....	....	....	....	....	....	....
	Hartford	AHL	54	16	30	46	40	....	....	....	....	....	....	....	....	....	....	....	15	2	6	8	22	....	....	....
1998-99	NY Rangers	NHL	3	0	0	0	0	0	0	0	1	0.0	0	0	0.0	0	0	2:50	....	....	....	....	....	....	....	....
	Hartford	AHL	59	29	51	80	73	....	....	....	....	....	....	....	....	....	....	....	7	5	4	9	10	....	....	....
99-2000	NY Rangers	NHL	1	0	0	0	0	0	0	0	1	0.0	0	3	33.3	0	0	3:10	....	....	....	....	....	....	....	....
	Hartford	AHL	77	28	54	82	101	....	....	....	....	....	....	....	....	....	....	....	23	7	16	23	24	....	....	....
	NHL Totals		83	9	10	19	56	0	0	3	71	12.7		3	33.3	0	0	2:55	....	....	....	....	....	....	....	....

AHL Second All-Star Team (2000)

Signed as a free agent by **Ottawa**, July 28, 1997. Signed as a free agent by **NY Rangers**, August 10, 1998.

ARNOTT, Jason

(AHR-nawt, JAY-suhn) **N.J.**

Center. Shoots right. 6'4", 225 lbs. Born, Collingwood, Ont., October 11, 1974. Edmonton's 1st choice, 7th overall, in 1993 Entry Draft.

1989-90	Stayner Siskins	OJHL-C	34	21	31	52	12	....	....	....	....	....	....	....	....	....	....	....	....	....	....	....	....	....	....	....
1990-91	Lindsay Bears	OJHL-B	42	17	44	61	10	....	....	....	....	....	....	....	....	....	....	....	8	9	8	17	6	....	....	....
1991-92	Oshawa Generals	OHL	57	9	15	24	12	....	....	....	....	....	....	....	....	....	....	....	....	....	....	....	....	....	....	....
1992-93	Oshawa Generals	OHL	56	41	57	98	74	....	....	....	....	....	....	....	....	....	....	....	13	9	9	18	20	....	....	....
1993-94	Edmonton	NHL	78	33	35	68	104	10	0	4	194	17.0	1	....	....	....	....	....	....	....	....	....	....	....	....	....
1994-95	Edmonton	NHL	42	15	22	37	128	7	0	1	156	9.6	–14	....	....	....	....	....	....	....	....	....	....	....	....	....
1995-96	Edmonton	NHL	64	28	31	59	87	8	0	5	244	11.5	–6	....	....	....	....	....	....	....	....	....	....	....	....	....
1996-97	Edmonton	NHL	67	19	38	57	92	10	1	2	248	7.7	–21	....	....	....	....	....	12	3	6	9	18	1	0	0

			Regular Season																Playoffs							
Season	Club	League	GP	G	A	Pts	PIM	PP	SH	GW	S	%	+/-	TF	F%	H	SB	Min	GP	G	A	Pts	PIM	PP	SH	GW
1997-98	**Edmonton**	**NHL**	**35**	**5**	**13**	**18**	**78**	**1**	**0**	**0**	**100**	**5.0**	**–16**	....	....	....	....	....	....	....	....	....	....	....	....	....
	New Jersey	**NHL**	**35**	**5**	**10**	**15**	**21**	**3**	**0**	**2**	**99**	**5.1**	**–8**	....	....	....	....	....	**5**	**0**	**2**	**2**	**0**	**0**	**0**	**0**
1998-99	**New Jersey**	**NHL**	**74**	**27**	**27**	**54**	**79**	**8**	**0**	**3**	**200**	**13.5**	**10**	**872**	**49.3**	**196**	**16**	**15:24**	**7**	**2**	**2**	**4**	**4**	**1**	**0**	**0**
99-2000♦	**New Jersey**	**NHL**	**76**	**22**	**34**	**56**	**51**	**7**	**0**	**4**	**244**	**9.0**	**22**	**1172**	**46.9**	**194**	**18**	**17:05**	**23**	**8**	**12**	**20**	**18**	**3**	**0**	**1**
	NHL Totals		**471**	**154**	**210**	**364**	**640**	**54**	**1**	**21**	**1485**	**10.4**		**2044**	**47.9**	**390**	**34**	**16:15**	**47**	**13**	**22**	**35**	**40**	**5**	**0**	**1**

NHL All-Rookie Team (1994) • Played in NHL All-Star Game (1997)

Traded to **New Jersey** by **Edmonton** with Bryan Muir for Valeri Zelepukin and Bill Guerin, January 4, 1998.

ARVEDSON, Magnus

(AHR-vehd-suhn, MAGH-nuhs) **OTT.**

Center. Shoots left. 6'2", 198 lbs. Born, Karlstad, Swe., November 25, 1971. Ottawa's 4th choice, 119th overall, in 1997 Entry Draft.

1990-91	Orebro IK	Sweden-2	29	7	11	18	12	....	....	....	....	....	....	....	....	....	....	....	2	0	1	1	2	....	....	....
1991-92	Orebro IK	Sweden-2	32	12	21	33	30	....	....	....	....	....	....	....	....	....	....	....	7	4	4	8	4	....	....	....
1992-93	Orebro IK	Sweden-2	36	11	18	29	34	....	....	....	....	....	....	....	....	....	....	....	6	2	1	3	0	....	....	....
1993-94	Farjestads BK	Sweden	16	1	7	8	10	....	....	....	....	....	....	....	....	....	....	....	....	....	....	....	....	....	....	....
1994-95	Farjestads BK	Swede-Jr.	1	0	0	0	0	....	....	....	....	....	....	....	....	....	....	....	....	....	....	....	....	....	....	....
	Farjestads BK	Sweden	36	1	6	7	45	....	....	....	....	....	....	....	....	....	....	....	4	0	0	0	6	....	....	....
1995-96	Farjestads BK	Sweden	40	10	14	24	40	....	....	....	....	....	....	....	....	....	....	....	8	0	3	3	10	....	....	....
1996-97	Farjestads BK	Sweden	48	13	11	24	36	....	....	....	....	....	....	....	....	....	....	....	14	4	7	11	8	....	....	....
	Farjestads BK	EuroHL	5	1	0	1	2	....	....	....	....	....	....	....	....	....	....	....	2	0	1	1	2	....	....	....
1997-98	**Ottawa**	**NHL**	**61**	**11**	**15**	**26**	**36**	**0**	**1**	**0**	**90**	**12.2**	**2**	....	....	....	....	....	**11**	**0**	**1**	**1**	**6**	**0**	**0**	**0**
1998-99	**Ottawa**	**NHL**	**80**	**21**	**26**	**47**	**50**	**0**	**4**	**6**	**136**	**15.4**	**33**	**25**	**20.0**	**48**	**42**	**17:08**	**3**	**0**	**1**	**1**	**2**	**0**	**0**	**0**
99-2000	**Ottawa**	**NHL**	**47**	**15**	**13**	**28**	**36**	**1**	**1**	**4**	**91**	**16.5**	**4**	**11**	**45.5**	**33**	**43**	**18:04**	**6**	**0**	**0**	**0**	**6**	**0**	**0**	**0**
	NHL Totals		**188**	**47**	**54**	**101**	**122**	**1**	**6**	**10**	**317**	**14.8**		**36**	**27.8**	**81**	**85**	**17:29**	**20**	**0**	**2**	**2**	**14**	**0**	**0**	**0**

ASHAM, Arron

(ASH-uhm, AIR-uhn) **MTL.**

Right wing. Shoots right. 5'11", 191 lbs. Born, Portage La Prairie, Man., April 13, 1978. Montreal's 3rd choice, 71st overall, in 1996 Entry Draft.

1993-94	Portage Terriers	MAHA	21	18	19	37	82	....	....	....	....	....	....	....	....	....	....	....	....	....	....	....	....	....	....	....
1994-95	Red Deer Rebels	WHL	62	11	16	27	126	....	....	....	....	....	....	....	....	....	....	....	....	....	....	....	....	....	....	....
1995-96	Red Deer Rebels	WHL	70	32	45	77	174	....	....	....	....	....	....	....	....	....	....	....	10	6	3	9	20	....	....	....
1996-97	Red Deer Rebels	WHL	67	45	51	96	149	....	....	....	....	....	....	....	....	....	....	....	16	12	14	26	36	....	....	....
1997-98	Red Deer Rebels	WHL	67	43	49	92	153	....	....	....	....	....	....	....	....	....	....	....	5	0	2	2	8	....	....	....
	Fredericton	AHL	2	1	1	2	0	....	....	....	....	....	....	....	....	....	....	....	2	0	1	1	0	....	....	....
1998-99	**Montreal**	**NHL**	**7**	**0**	**0**	**0**	**0**	**0**	**0**	**0**	**5**	**0.0**	**–4**	**0**	**0.0**	**8**	**2**	**7:27**	....	....	....	....	....	....	....	....
	Fredericton	AHL	60	16	18	34	118	....	....	....	....	....	....	....	....	....	....	....	13	8	6	14	11	....	....	....
99-2000	**Montreal**	**NHL**	**33**	**4**	**2**	**6**	**24**	**0**	**1**	**1**	**29**	**13.8**	**–7**	**1**	**0.0**	**47**	**10**	**10:14**	....	....	....	....	....	....	....	....
	Quebec Citadelles	AHL	13	4	5	9	32	....	....	....	....	....	....	....	....	....	....	....	2	0	0	0	2	....	....	....
	NHL Totals		**40**	**4**	**2**	**6**	**24**	**0**	**1**	**1**	**34**	**11.8**		**1**	**0.0**	**55**	**12**	**9:45**	....	....	....	....	....	....	....	....

ASTASHENKO, Kaspars

(ahs-tuh-SHEHN-koh, KAHS-pars) **T.B.**

Defense. Shoots left. 6'2", 183 lbs. Born, Riga, Latvia, February 17, 1975. Tampa Bay's 5th choice, 127th overall, in 1999 Entry Draft.

1993-94	Pardaugava Riga	CIS	4	0	0	0	10	....	....	....	....	....	....	....	....	....	....	....	....	....	....	....	....	....	....	....
1994-95	Pardaugava Riga	CIS	25	0	0	0	24	....	....	....	....	....	....	....	....	....	....	....	....	....	....	....	....	....	....	....
1995-96	CSKA Moscow	CIS	26	0	1	1	10	....	....	....	....	....	....	....	....	....	....	....	....	....	....	....	....	....	....	....
1996-97	CSKA Moscow	Russia	41	0	0	0	48	....	....	....	....	....	....	....	....	....	....	....	2	0	1	1	4	....	....	....
1997-98	CSKA Moscow	Russia	25	1	3	4	6	....	....	....	....	....	....	....	....	....	....	....	....	....	....	....	....	....	....	....
1998-99	Cincinnati	IHL	74	3	11	14	166	....	....	....	....	....	....	....	....	....	....	....	3	0	2	2	6	....	....	....
	Dayton Bombers	ECHL	2	0	1	1	4	....	....	....	....	....	....	....	....	....	....	....	....	....	....	....	....	....	....	....
99-2000	**Tampa Bay**	**NHL**	**8**	**0**	**1**	**1**	**4**	**0**	**0**	**0**	**3**	**0.0**	**–2**	**0**	**0.0**	**11**	**6**	**16:48**	....	....	....	....	....	....	....	....
	Detroit Vipers	IHL	51	1	10	11	86	....	....	....	....	....	....	....	....	....	....	....	....	....	....	....	....	....	....	....
	Long Beach	IHL	14	0	3	3	10	....	....	....	....	....	....	....	....	....	....	....	....	....	....	....	....	....	....	....
	NHL Totals		**8**	**0**	**1**	**1**	**4**	**0**	**0**	**0**	**3**	**0.0**		**0**	**0.0**	**11**	**6**	**16:48**	....	....	....	....	....	....	....	....

ATCHEYNUM, Blair

(ATCH-uh-num, BLAIR) **CHI.**

Right wing. Shoots right. 6'2", 198 lbs. Born, Estevan, Sask., April 20, 1969. Hartford's 2nd choice, 52nd overall, in 1989 Entry Draft.

1984-85	North Battleford	SAHA	26	25	21	46	106	....	....	....	....	....	....	....	....	....	....	....	....	....	....	....	....	....	....	....
1985-86	North Battleford	SJHL	33	16	14	30	41	....	....	....	....	....	....	....	....	....	....	....	6	2	0	2	6	....	....	....
	Saskatoon Blades	WHL	19	1	4	5	22	....	....	....	....	....	....	....	....	....	....	....	....	....	....	....	....	....	....	....
1986-87	Saskatoon Blades	WHL	21	0	4	4	4	....	....	....	....	....	....	....	....	....	....	....	....	....	....	....	....	....	....	....
	Swift Current	WHL	5	2	1	3	0	....	....	....	....	....	....	....	....	....	....	....	....	....	....	....	....	....	....	....
	Moose Jaw	WHL	12	3	0	3	2	....	....	....	....	....	....	....	....	....	....	....	....	....	....	....	....	....	....	....
1987-88	Moose Jaw	WHL	60	32	16	48	52	....	....	....	....	....	....	....	....	....	....	....	....	....	....	....	....	....	....	....
1988-89	Moose Jaw	WHL	71	70	68	138	70	....	....	....	....	....	....	....	....	....	....	....	7	2	5	7	13	....	....	....
1989-90	Binghamton	AHL	78	20	21	41	45	....	....	....	....	....	....	....	....	....	....	....	....	....	....	....	....	....	....	....
1990-91	Springfield	AHL	72	25	27	52	42	....	....	....	....	....	....	....	....	....	....	....	13	0	6	6	6	....	....	....
1991-92	Springfield	AHL	62	16	21	37	64	....	....	....	....	....	....	....	....	....	....	....	6	1	1	2	2	....	....	....
1992-93	**Ottawa**	**NHL**	**4**	**0**	**1**	**1**	**0**	**0**	**0**	**0**	**2**	**0.0**	**–3**	....	....	....	....	....	....	....	....	....	....	....	....	....
	New Haven	AHL	51	16	18	34	47	....	....	....	....	....	....	....	....	....	....	....	....	....	....	....	....	....	....	....
1993-94	Columbus Chill	ECHL	16	15	12	27	10	....	....	....	....	....	....	....	....	....	....	....	....	....	....	....	....	....	....	....
	Portland Pirates	AHL	2	0	0	0	0	....	....	....	....	....	....	....	....	....	....	....	....	....	....	....	....	....	....	....
	Springfield	AHL	40	18	22	40	13	....	....	....	....	....	....	....	....	....	....	....	6	0	2	2	0	....	....	....
1994-95	Minnesota Moose	IHL	17	4	6	10	7	....	....	....	....	....	....	....	....	....	....	....	....	....	....	....	....	....	....	....
	Worcester	AHL	55	17	29	46	26	....	....	....	....	....	....	....	....	....	....	....	....	....	....	....	....	....	....	....
1995-96	Cape Breton	AHL	79	30	42	72	65	....	....	....	....	....	....	....	....	....	....	....	....	....	....	....	....	....	....	....
1996-97	Hershey Bears	AHL	77	42	45	87	57	....	....	....	....	....	....	....	....	....	....	....	13	6	11	17	6	....	....	....
1997-98	**St. Louis**	**NHL**	**61**	**11**	**15**	**26**	**10**	**0**	**1**	**3**	**103**	**10.7**	**5**	....	....	....	....	....	**10**	**0**	**0**	**0**	**2**	**0**	**0**	**0**
1998-99	**Nashville**	**NHL**	**53**	**8**	**6**	**14**	**16**	**2**	**0**	**1**	**70**	**11.4**	**–10**	**5**	**40.0**	**28**	**26**	**14:54**	....	....	....	....	....	....	....	....
	St. Louis	**NHL**	**12**	**2**	**2**	**4**	**2**	**0**	**0**	**1**	**23**	**8.7**	**2**	**2**	**0.0**	**12**	**5**	**15:38**	**13**	**1**	**3**	**4**	**6**	**0**	**0**	**0**
99-2000	**Chicago**	**NHL**	**47**	**5**	**7**	**12**	**6**	**0**	**0**	**0**	**48**	**10.4**	**–8**	**23**	**17.4**	**27**	**17**	**12:15**	....	....	....	....	....	....	....	....
	NHL Totals		**177**	**26**	**31**	**57**	**34**	**2**	**1**	**5**	**246**	**10.6**		**30**	**20.0**	**67**	**48**	**13:52**	**23**	**1**	**3**	**4**	**8**	**0**	**0**	**0**

WHL First All-Star Team (1989) • AHL First All-Star Team (1997)

Claimed by **Ottawa** from **Hartford** in Expansion Draft, June 18, 1992. Signed as a free agent by **St. Louis**, September 15, 1997. Claimed by **Nashville** from **St. Louis** in Expansion Draft, June 26, 1998. Traded to **St. Louis** by **Nashville** for St. Louis' 6th round choice (Zbynek Irgl) in 2000 Entry Draft, March 23, 1999. Signed as a free agent by **Chicago**, September 30, 1999.

AUBIN, Serge

(oh-BEHN, SUHR-je) **CBJ**

Center. Shoots left. 6'1", 194 lbs. Born, Val d'Or, Que., February 15, 1975. Pittsburgh's 9th choice, 161st overall, in 1994 Entry Draft.

1990-91	Temiscamingue	QAAA	27	2	4	6	10	....	....	....	....	....	....	....	....	....	....	....	....	....	....	....	....	....	....	....
1991-92	Temiscamingue	QAAA	42	28	32	60	36	....	....	....	....	....	....	....	....	....	....	....	....	....	....	....	....	....	....	....
1992-93	Drummondville	QMJHL	65	16	34	50	30	....	....	....	....	....	....	....	....	....	....	....	8	0	1	1	16	....	....	....
1993-94	Granby Bisons	QMJHL	63	42	32	74	80	....	....	....	....	....	....	....	....	....	....	....	7	2	3	5	8	....	....	....
1994-95	Granby Bisons	QMJHL	60	37	73	110	55	....	....	....	....	....	....	....	....	....	....	....	11	8	15	23	4	....	....	....
1995-96	Hampton Roads	ECHL	62	24	62	86	74	....	....	....	....	....	....	....	....	....	....	....	3	1	4	5	10	....	....	....
	Cleveland	IHL	2	0	0	0	0	....	....	....	....	....	....	....	....	....	....	....	2	0	0	0	0	....	....	....
1996-97	Cleveland	IHL	57	9	16	25	38	....	....	....	....	....	....	....	....	....	....	....	2	0	0	0	0	....	....	....
1997-98	Syracuse Crunch	AHL	55	6	14	20	57	....	....	....	....	....	....	....	....	....	....	....	....	....	....	....	....	....	....	....
	Hershey Bears	AHL	5	2	1	3	0	....	....	....	....	....	....	....	....	....	....	....	7	1	3	4	6	....	....	....
1998-99	Hershey Bears	AHL	64	30	39	69	58	....	....	....	....	....	....	....	....	....	....	....	3	0	1	1	2	....	....	....
	Colorado	**NHL**	**1**	**0**	**0**	**0**	**0**	**0**	**0**	**0**	**1**	**0.0**	**0**	**1**	**0.0**	**0**	**0**	**4:16**	....	....	....	....	....	....	....	....

			Regular Season																Playoffs							
Season	Club	League	GP	G	A	Pts	PIM	PP	SH	GW	S	%	+/–	TF	F%	H	SB	Min	GP	G	A	Pts	PIM	PP	SH	GW
99-2000	**Colorado**	**NHL**	**15**	**2**	**1**	**3**	**6**	**0**	**0**	**1**	**14**	**14.3**	**1**	**79**	**50.6**	**15**	**3**	**6:37**	**17**	**0**	**1**	**1**	**6**	**0**	**0**	**0**
	Hershey Bears	AHL	58	42	38	80	56	....	....	....	....	....	....	....	....	....	....	....	....	....	....	....	....	....	....	....
	NHL Totals		**16**	**2**	**1**	**3**	**6**	**0**	**0**	**1**	**15**	**13.3**		**80**	**50.0**	**15**	**3**	**6:29**	**17**	**0**	**1**	**1**	**6**	**0**	**0**	**0**

AHL First All-Star Team (2000)
Signed as a free agent by **Hershey** (AHL), July 24, 1998. Signed as a free agent by **Colorado**, December 22, 1998. Signed as a free agent by **Columbus**, July 11, 2000.

AUCOIN, Adrian

(oh-KWEHN, AY-dree-an) **VAN.**

Defense. Shoots right. 6'2", 210 lbs. Born, Ottawa, Ont., July 3, 1973. Vancouver's 7th choice, 117th overall, in 1992 Entry Draft.

Season	Club	League	GP	G	A	Pts	PIM	PP	SH	GW	S	%	+/–	TF	F%	H	SB	Min	GP	G	A	Pts	PIM	PP	SH	GW
1989-90	Nepean Raiders	OJHL	54	2	14	16	95	....	....	....	....	....	....	....	....	....	....	....	4	0	1	1	....	....	....	....
1990-91	Nepean Raiders	OJHL	56	17	33	50	125	....	....	....	....	....	....	....	....	....	....	....	....	....	....	....	....	....	....	....
1991-92	Boston University	H-East	32	2	10	12	60	....	....	....	....	....	....	....	....	....	....	....	....	....	....	....	....	....	....	....
1992-93	Canada	Nat-Team	42	8	10	18	71	....	....	....	....	....	....	....	....	....	....	....	....	....	....	....	....	....	....	....
1993-94	Canada	Nat-Team	59	5	12	17	80	....	....	....	....	....	....	....	....	....	....	....	....	....	....	....	....	....	....	....
	Canada	Olympics	4	0	0	0	2	....	....	....	....	....	....	....	....	....	....	....	....	....	....	....	....	....	....	....
	Hamilton Canucks	AHL	13	1	2	3	19	....	....	....	....	....	....	....	....	....	....	....	4	0	2	2	6	....	....	....
1994-95	**Vancouver**	**NHL**	**1**	**1**	**0**	**1**	**0**	**0**	**0**	**0**	**2**	**50.0**	**1**	....	....	....	....	....	**4**	**1**	**0**	**1**	**0**	**1**	**0**	**0**
	Syracuse Crunch	AHL	71	13	18	31	52	....	....	....	....	....	....	....	....	....	....	....	....	....	....	....	....	....	....	....
1995-96	**Vancouver**	**NHL**	**49**	**4**	**14**	**18**	**34**	**2**	**0**	**0**	**85**	**4.7**	**8**	....	....	....	....	....	**6**	**0**	**0**	**0**	**2**	**0**	**0**	**0**
	Syracuse Crunch	AHL	29	5	13	18	47	....	....	....	....	....	....	....	....	....	....	....	....	....	....	....	....	....	....	....
1996-97	**Vancouver**	**NHL**	**70**	**5**	**16**	**21**	**63**	**1**	**0**	**0**	**116**	**4.3**	**0**	....	....	....	....	....	....	....	....	....	....	....	....	....
1997-98	**Vancouver**	**NHL**	**35**	**3**	**3**	**6**	**21**	**1**	**0**	**1**	**44**	**6.8**	**–4**	....	....	....	....	....	....	....	....	....	....	....	....	....
1998-99	**Vancouver**	**NHL**	**82**	**23**	**11**	**34**	**77**	**18**	**2**	**3**	**174**	**13.2**	**–14**	**1**	**100.0**	**208**	**50**	**23:52**	....	....	....	....	....	....	....	....
99-2000	Canada	Nat-Team	2	0	0	0	2	....	....	....	....	....	....	....	....	....	....	....	....	....	....	....	....	....	....	....
	Vancouver	**NHL**	**57**	**10**	**14**	**24**	**30**	**4**	**0**	**1**	**126**	**7.9**	**7**	**0**	**0.0**	**123**	**36**	**23:06**	....	....	....	....	....	....	....	....
	NHL Totals		**294**	**46**	**58**	**104**	**225**	**26**	**2**	**5**	**547**	**8.4**		**1**	**100.0**	**331**	**86**	**23:33**	**10**	**1**	**0**	**1**	**2**	**1**	**0**	**0**

• Missed majority of 1997-98 season recovering from ankle injury suffered in game vs. Anaheim (October 4, 1997) and groin injury suffered in game vs. Pittsburgh, November 1, 1997.

AUDET, Philippe

(aw-DEHT, fihl-EEP) **PHX.**

Left wing. Shoots left. 6'2", 202 lbs. Born, Ottawa, Ont., June 4, 1977. Detroit's 2nd choice, 52nd overall, in 1995 Entry Draft.

Season	Club	League	GP	G	A	Pts	PIM	PP	SH	GW	S	%	+/–	TF	F%	H	SB	Min	GP	G	A	Pts	PIM	PP	SH	GW
1992-93	Beauce-Amiante	QAAA	28	21	24	45	75	....	....	....	....	....	....	....	....	....	....	....	....	....	....	....	....	....	....	....
1993-94	Trois-Rivieres	QAAA	34	22	21	43	90	....	....	....	....	....	....	....	....	....	....	....	....	....	....	....	....	....	....	....
1994-95	Granby Bisons	QMJHL	62	19	17	36	93	....	....	....	....	....	....	....	....	....	....	....	13	2	5	7	10	....	....	....
1995-96	Granby Bisons	QMJHL	67	40	43	83	162	....	....	....	....	....	....	....	....	....	....	....	21	12	18	30	32	....	....	....
1996-97	Granby Bisons	QMJHL	67	52	56	108	138	....	....	....	....	....	....	....	....	....	....	....	4	4	1	5	35	....	....	....
	Adirondack	AHL	3	1	1	2	0	....	....	....	....	....	....	....	....	....	....	....	1	1	0	1	0	....	....	....
1997-98	Adirondack	AHL	50	7	8	15	43	....	....	....	....	....	....	....	....	....	....	....	1	0	0	0	0	....	....	....
1998-99	**Detroit**	**NHL**	**4**	**0**	**0**	**0**	**0**	**0**	**0**	**0**	**3**	**0.0**	**–2**	**0**	**0.0**	**4**	**1**	**4:19**	....	....	....	....	....	....	....	....
	Adirondack	AHL	70	20	20	40	77	....	....	....	....	....	....	....	....	....	....	....	2	1	0	1	4	....	....	....
99-2000	Cincinnati Ducks	AHL	62	19	22	41	115	....	....	....	....	....	....	....	....	....	....	....	....	....	....	....	....	....	....	....
	Springfield	AHL	14	3	7	10	6	....	....	....	....	....	....	....	....	....	....	....	5	3	1	4	14	....	....	....
	NHL Totals		**4**	**0**	**0**	**0**	**0**	**0**	**0**	**0**	**3**	**0.0**		**0**	**0.0**	**4**	**1**	**4:19**	....	....	....	....	....	....	....	....

Memorial Cup All-Star Team (1996) • QMJHL First All-Star Team (1997)
Traded to **Phoenix** by **Detroit** for Todd Gill, March 13, 2000.

AUDETTE, Donald

(aw-DEHT, DAW-nohld) **ATL.**

Right wing. Shoots right. 5'8", 190 lbs. Born, Laval, Que., September 23, 1969. Buffalo's 8th choice, 183rd overall, in 1989 Entry Draft.

Season	Club	League	GP	G	A	Pts	PIM	PP	SH	GW	S	%	+/–	TF	F%	H	SB	Min	GP	G	A	Pts	PIM	PP	SH	GW
1985-86	Laval-Laurentides	QAAA	41	32	38	70	....	....	....	....	....	....	....	....	....	....	....	....	....	....	....	....	....	....	....	....
1986-87	Laval Titan	QMJHL	66	17	22	39	36	....	....	....	....	....	....	....	....	....	....	....	14	2	6	8	10	....	....	....
1987-88	Laval Titan	QMJHL	63	48	61	109	56	....	....	....	....	....	....	....	....	....	....	....	14	7	12	19	20	....	....	....
1988-89	Laval Titan	QMJHL	70	76	85	161	123	....	....	....	....	....	....	....	....	....	....	....	17	17	12	29	43	....	....	....
1989-90	Rochester	AHL	70	42	46	88	78	....	....	....	....	....	....	....	....	....	....	....	15	9	8	17	29	....	....	....
	Buffalo	**NHL**	....	....	....	....	....	....	....	....	....	....	....	....	....	....	....	....	**2**	**0**	**0**	**0**	**0**	**0**	**0**	**0**
1990-91	**Buffalo**	**NHL**	**8**	**4**	**3**	**7**	**4**	**2**	**0**	**1**	**17**	**23.5**	**–1**	....	....	....	....	....	....	....	....	....	....	....	....	....
	Rochester	AHL	5	4	0	4	2	....	....	....	....	....	....	....	....	....	....	....	....	....	....	....	....	....	....	....
1991-92	**Buffalo**	**NHL**	**63**	**31**	**17**	**48**	**75**	**5**	**0**	**6**	**153**	**20.3**	**–1**	....	....	....	....	....	....	....	....	....	....	....	....	....
1992-93	**Buffalo**	**NHL**	**44**	**12**	**7**	**19**	**51**	**2**	**0**	**0**	**92**	**13.0**	**–8**	....	....	....	....	....	**8**	**2**	**2**	**4**	**6**	**0**	**0**	**0**
	Rochester	AHL	6	8	4	12	10	....	....	....	....	....	....	....	....	....	....	....	....	....	....	....	....	....	....	....
1993-94	**Buffalo**	**NHL**	**77**	**29**	**30**	**59**	**41**	**16**	**1**	**4**	**207**	**14.0**	**2**	....	....	....	....	....	**7**	**0**	**1**	**1**	**6**	**0**	**0**	**0**
1994-95	**Buffalo**	**NHL**	**46**	**24**	**13**	**37**	**27**	**13**	**0**	**7**	**124**	**19.4**	**–3**	....	....	....	....	....	**5**	**1**	**1**	**2**	**4**	**1**	**0**	**0**
1995-96	**Buffalo**	**NHL**	**23**	**12**	**13**	**25**	**18**	**8**	**0**	**1**	**92**	**13.0**	**0**	....	....	....	....	....	....	....	....	....	....	....	....	....
1996-97	**Buffalo**	**NHL**	**73**	**28**	**22**	**50**	**48**	**8**	**0**	**5**	**182**	**15.4**	**–6**	....	....	....	....	....	**11**	**4**	**5**	**9**	**6**	**3**	**0**	**0**
1997-98	**Buffalo**	**NHL**	**75**	**24**	**20**	**44**	**59**	**10**	**0**	**5**	**198**	**12.1**	**10**	....	....	....	....	....	**15**	**5**	**8**	**13**	**10**	**3**	**0**	**2**
1998-99	**Los Angeles**	**NHL**	**49**	**18**	**18**	**36**	**51**	**6**	**0**	**2**	**152**	**11.8**	**7**	**4**	**50.0**	**28**	**9**	**16:50**	....	....	....	....	....	....	....	....
99-2000	**Los Angeles**	**NHL**	**49**	**12**	**20**	**32**	**45**	**1**	**0**	**3**	**112**	**10.7**	**6**	**4**	**50.0**	**12**	**8**	**14:56**	....	....	....	....	....	....	....	....
	Atlanta	**NHL**	**14**	**7**	**4**	**11**	**12**	**0**	**1**	**1**	**50**	**14.0**	**–4**	**0**	**0.0**	**8**	**4**	**21:35**	....	....	....	....	....	....	....	....
	NHL Totals		**521**	**201**	**167**	**368**	**431**	**71**	**2**	**35**	**1379**	**14.6**		**8**	**50.0**	**48**	**21**	**16:36**	**48**	**12**	**17**	**29**	**32**	**7**	**0**	**2**

QMJHL First All-Star Team (1989) • AHL First All-Star Team (1990) • Won Dudley "Red" Garret Memorial Trophy (Top Rookie - AHL) (1990)
Traded to **Los Angeles** by **Buffalo** for Los Angeles' 2nd round choice (Milan Bartovic) in 1999 Entry Draft, December 18, 1998. Traded to **Atlanta** by **Los Angeles** with Frantisek Kaberle for Kelly Buchberger and Nelson Emerson, March 13, 2000.

AUGUSTA, Patrik

(ah-GOOS-tuh, pa-TREEK)

Right wing. Shoots left. 5'10", 170 lbs. Born, Jihlava, Czech., November 13, 1969. Toronto's 8th choice, 149th overall, in 1992 Entry Draft.

Season	Club	League	GP	G	A	Pts	PIM	PP	SH	GW	S	%	+/–	TF	F%	H	SB	Min	GP	G	A	Pts	PIM	PP	SH	GW
1988-89	Dukla Jihlava	Czech.	15	3	1	4	4	....	....	....	....	....	....	....	....	....	....	....	....	....	....	....	....	....	....	....
1989-90	Dukla Jihlava	Czech.	39	9	11	20	....	....	....	....	....	....	....	....	....	....	....	....	7	3	1	4	....	....	....	....
1990-91	Dukla Jihlava	Czech.	51	20	23	43	....	....	....	....	....	....	....	....	....	....	....	....	....	....	....	....	....	....	....	....
1991-92	Dukla Jihlava	Czech.	42	16	16	32	26	....	....	....	....	....	....	....	....	....	....	....	....	....	....	....	....	....	....	....
	Czechoslovakia	Olympics	8	3	2	5	0	....	....	....	....	....	....	....	....	....	....	....	....	....	....	....	....	....	....	....
1992-93	St. John's Leafs	AHL	75	32	45	77	74	....	....	....	....	....	....	....	....	....	....	....	8	3	3	6	23	....	....	....
1993-94	**Toronto**	**NHL**	**2**	**0**	**0**	**0**	**0**	**0**	**0**	**0**	**3**	**0.0**	**0**	....	....	....	....	....	....	....	....	....	....	....	....	....
	St. John's Leafs	AHL	77	*53	43	96	105	....	....	....	....	....	....	....	....	....	....	....	11	4	8	12	4	....	....	....
1994-95	St. John's Leafs	AHL	71	37	32	69	98	....	....	....	....	....	....	....	....	....	....	....	4	2	0	2	7	....	....	....
1995-96	Los Angeles	IHL	79	34	51	85	83	....	....	....	....	....	....	....	....	....	....	....	....	....	....	....	....	....	....	....
1996-97	Long Beach	IHL	82	45	42	87	96	....	....	....	....	....	....	....	....	....	....	....	18	4	4	8	33	....	....	....
1997-98	Long Beach	IHL	82	41	40	81	84	....	....	....	....	....	....	....	....	....	....	....	17	11	7	18	20	....	....	....
1998-99	Long Beach	IHL	68	24	35	59	125	....	....	....	....	....	....	....	....	....	....	....	8	4	6	10	4	....	....	....
	Washington	**NHL**	**2**	**0**	**0**	**0**	**0**	**0**	**0**	**0**	**4**	**0.0**	**0**	**0**	**0.0**	**0**	**1**	**13:38**	....	....	....	....	....	....	....	....
99-2000	Schwenningen	DEL	34	14	15	29	52	....	....	....	....	....	....	....	....	....	....	....	....	....	....	....	....	....	....	....
	NHL Totals		**4**	**0**	**0**	**0**	**0**	**0**	**0**	**0**	**7**	**0.0**		**0**	**0.0**	**0**	**1**	**13:38**	....	....	....	....	....	....	....	....

AHL Second All-Star Team (1994) • IHL Second All-Star Team (1997)
Signed as a free agent by **Washington**, December 11, 1998.

AXELSSON, P.J.

(AHX-ehl-suhn, PAIR, YEW-hahn) **BOS.**

Left wing. Shoots left. 6'1", 176 lbs. Born, Kungalv, Sweden, February 26, 1975. Boston's 7th choice, 177th overall, in 1995 Entry Draft.

Season	Club	League	GP	G	A	Pts	PIM	PP	SH	GW	S	%	+/–	TF	F%	H	SB	Min	GP	G	A	Pts	PIM	PP	SH	GW
1992-93	Vastra Frolunda	Swede-Jr.	16	9	5	14	12	....	....	....	....	....	....	....	....	....	....	....	....	....	....	....	....	....	....	....
1993-94	Vastra Frolunda	Sweden	11	0	0	0	4	....	....	....	....	....	....	....	....	....	....	....	4	0	0	0	0	....	....	....
1994-95	Vastra Frolunda	Swede-Jr.	19	16	9	25	22	....	....	....	....	....	....	....	....	....	....	....	....	....	....	....	....	....	....	....
	Vastra Frolunda	Sweden	8	2	1	3	6	....	....	....	....	....	....	....	....	....	....	....	....	....	....	....	....	....	....	....
1995-96	Vastra Frolunda	Sweden	36	15	5	20	10	....	....	....	....	....	....	....	....	....	....	....	13	3	0	3	10	....	....	....

			Regular Season																Playoffs							
Season	Club	League	GP	G	A	Pts	PIM	PP	SH	GW	S	%	+/-	TF	F%	H	SB	Min	GP	G	A	Pts	PIM	PP	SH	GW
1996-97	Vastra Frolunda	Sweden	50	19	15	34	34												3	0	2	2	0			
	Vastra Frolunda	EuroHL	3	1	1	2	0												3	0	0	0	2			
1997-98	**Boston**	**NHL**	**82**	**8**	**19**	**27**	**38**	**2**	**0**	**1**	**144**	**5.6**	**−14**						**6**	**1**	**0**	**1**	**0**	**0**	**0**	**0**
1998-99	**Boston**	**NHL**	**77**	**7**	**10**	**17**	**18**	**0**	**0**	**2**	**146**	**4.8**	**−14**	**8**	**75.0**	**66**	**22**	**16:38**	**12**	**1**	**1**	**2**	**4**	**0**	**0**	**0**
99-2000	**Boston**	**NHL**	**81**	**10**	**16**	**26**	**24**	**0**	**0**	**4**	**186**	**5.4**	**1**	**22**	**27.3**	**84**	**22**	**16:43**								
	NHL Totals		**240**	**25**	**45**	**70**	**80**	**2**	**0**	**7**	**476**	**5.3**		**30**	**40.0**	**150**	**44**	**16:41**	**18**	**2**	**1**	**3**	**4**	**0**	**0**	**0**

BALMOCHNYKH, Maxim

(bahl-MAWCH-nihky, mahx-EEM) **ANA.**

Left wing. Shoots left. 6'1", 180 lbs. Born, Lipetsk, USSR, March 7, 1979. Anaheim's 2nd choice, 45th overall, in 1997 Entry Draft.

Season	Club	League	GP	G	A	Pts	PIM	PP	SH	GW	S	%	+/-	TF	F%	H	SB	Min	GP	G	A	Pts	PIM	PP	SH	GW
1994-95	HC Lipetsk	CIS-2	3	0	1	1	4																			
1995-96	HC Lipetsk	CIS-2	40	15	5	20	60																			
1996-97	Lada Togliatti	Russia	18	6	1	7	22																			
1997-98	Lada Togliatti	Russia	37	10	4	14	46																			
	HC Chelyabinsk	Russia	2	0	0	0	2																			
1998-99	Quebec Remparts	QMJHL	21	9	22	31	38																			
	Lada Togliatti	Russia	15	2	1	3	10												4	0	1	1	8			
99-2000	**Anaheim**	**NHL**	**6**	**0**	**1**	**1**	**2**	**0**	**0**	**0**	**6**	**0.0**	**2**	**0**	**0.0**	**5**	**0**	**6:44**								
	Cincinnati Ducks	AHL	40	9	12	21	82																			
	NHL Totals		**6**	**0**	**1**	**1**	**2**	**0**	**0**	**0**	**6**	**0.0**		**0**	**0.0**	**5**	**0**	**6:44**								

BANCROFT, Steve

(BAN-crawft, STEEV) **S.J.**

Defense. Shoots left. 6'1", 214 lbs. Born, Toronto, Ont., October 6, 1970. Toronto's 3rd choice, 21st overall, in 1989 Entry Draft.

Season	Club	League	GP	G	A	Pts	PIM	PP	SH	GW	S	%	+/-	TF	F%	H	SB	Min	GP	G	A	Pts	PIM	PP	SH	GW
1985-86	Madoc MTM	OJHL-C	7	1	0	1	21																			
	Trenton Bobcats	OJHL-B	16	1	5	6	16																			
1986-87	Trenton Bobcats	OJHL-B	13	2	3	5	45																			
	St. Catharines	OJHL-B	11	5	8	13	20																			
1987-88	Belleville Bulls	OHL	56	1	8	9	42																			
1988-89	Belleville Bulls	OHL	66	7	30	37	99												5	0	2	2	10			
1989-90	Belleville Bulls	OHL	53	10	33	43	135												11	3	9	12	38			
1990-91	Newmarket	AHL	9	0	3	3	22																			
	Maine Mariners	AHL	53	2	12	14	46												2	0	0	0	2			
1991-92	Maine Mariners	AHL	26	1	3	4	45																			
	Indianapolis Ice	IHL	36	8	23	31	49																			
1992-93	**Chicago**	**NHL**	**1**	**0**	**0**	**0**	**0**	**0**	**0**	**0**	**0**	**0.0**	**0**													
	Indianapolis Ice	IHL	53	10	35	45	138																			
	Moncton Hawks	AHL	21	3	13	16	16												5	0	0	0	16			
1993-94	Cleveland	IHL	33	2	12	14	58																			
1994-95	Detroit Vipers	IHL	6	1	3	4	0																			
	Fort Wayne	IHL	50	7	17	24	100																			
	St. John's Leafs	AHL	4	2	0	2	2												5	0	3	3	8			
1995-96	Los Angeles	IHL	15	3	10	13	22																			
	Chicago Wolves	IHL	64	9	41	50	91												9	1	7	8	22			
1996-97	Chicago Wolves	IHL	39	6	10	16	66																			
	Las Vegas	IHL	36	9	28	37	64												3	0	0	0	2			
1997-98	Las Vegas	IHL	70	15	44	59	148																			
	Saint John Flames	AHL	9	0	4	4	12												19	2	11	13	30			
1998-99	Saint John Flames	AHL	8	1	4	5	22																			
	Providence Bruins	AHL	62	7	34	41	78												15	0	6	6	28			
99-2000	Cincinnati	IHL	39	6	14	20	37																			
	Houston Aeros	IHL	37	2	18	20	47												10	2	6	8	40			
	NHL Totals		**1**	**0**	**0**	**0**	**0**	**0**	**0**	**0**	**0**	**0.0**														

Traded to **Boston** by **Toronto** for Rob Cimetta, November 9, 1990. Traded to **Chicago** by **Boston** with Boston's 11th round choice (later traded to Winnipeg - Winnipeg selected Russel Hewson) in 1993 Entry Draft for Chicago's 11th round choice (Eugene Pavlov) in 1992 Entry Draft, January 8, 1992. Traded to **Winnipeg** by **Chicago** with future considerations for Troy Murray, February 21, 1993. Claimed by **Florida** from **Winnipeg** in Expansion Draft, June 24, 1993. Signed as a free agent by **Pittsburgh**, August 2, 1993. Signed as a free agent by **Carolina**, August 4, 1999. Traded to **Houston** (IHL) by **Cincinnati** (IHL) with Carolina retaining NHL rights for Brian Felsner, January 19, 2000. Signed as a free agent by **San Jose**, August 10, 2000.

BANHAM, Frank

(BAN-ham, FRA-nk)

Right wing. Shoots right. 6', 190 lbs. Born, Calahoo, Alta., April 14, 1975. Washington's 4th choice, 147th overall, in 1993 Entry Draft.

Season	Club	League	GP	G	A	Pts	PIM	PP	SH	GW	S	%	+/-	TF	F%	H	SB	Min	GP	G	A	Pts	PIM	PP	SH	GW
1991-92	Fernie Ghostriders	RMJHL	47	45	45	90	120																			
1992-93	Saskatoon Blades	WHL	71	29	33	62	55												9	2	7	9	8			
1993-94	Saskatoon Blades	WHL	65	28	39	67	99												16	8	11	19	36			
1994-95	Saskatoon Blades	WHL	70	50	39	89	63												8	2	6	8	12			
1995-96	Saskatoon Blades	WHL	72	*83	69	152	116												4	6	0	6	2			
	Baltimore Bandits	AHL	9	1	4	5	0												7	1	1	2	2			
1996-97	**Anaheim**	**NHL**	**3**	**0**	**0**	**0**	**0**	**0**	**0**	**0**	**1**	**0.0**	**−2**													
	Baltimore Bandits	AHL	21	11	13	24	4																			
1997-98	**Anaheim**	**NHL**	**21**	**9**	**2**	**11**	**12**	**1**	**0**	**0**	**43**	**20.9**	**−6**													
	Cincinnati Ducks	AHL	35	7	8	15	39																			
1998-99	Cincinnati Ducks	AHL	66	22	27	49	20												3	0	1	1	0			
99-2000	**Anaheim**	**NHL**	**3**	**0**	**0**	**0**	**2**	**0**	**0**	**0**	**4**	**0.0**	**0**	**5**	**40.0**	**1**	**0**	**6:47**								
	Cincinnati Ducks	AHL	72	19	22	41	58																			
	NHL Totals		**27**	**9**	**2**	**11**	**14**	**1**	**0**	**0**	**48**	**18.8**		**5**	**40.0**	**1**	**0**	**6:47**								

WHL East First All-Star Team (1996)

Signed as a free agent by **Anaheim**, January 27, 1996.

BANNISTER, Drew

(BAN-nihs-stuhr, DREW) **NYR**

Defense. Shoots right. 6'2", 200 lbs. Born, Belleville, Ont., September 4, 1974. Tampa Bay's 2nd choice, 26th overall, in 1992 Entry Draft.

Season	Club	League	GP	G	A	Pts	PIM	PP	SH	GW	S	%	+/-	TF	F%	H	SB	Min	GP	G	A	Pts	PIM	PP	SH	GW
1989-90	Sudbury Legion	NOHA	26	13	14	27	98																			
1990-91	Sault Ste. Marie	OHL	41	2	8	10	51												4	0	0	0	0			
1991-92	Sault Ste. Marie	OHL	64	4	21	25	122												16	3	10	13	36			
1992-93	Sault Ste. Marie	OHL	59	5	28	33	114												18	2	7	9	12			
1993-94	Sault Ste. Marie	OHL	58	7	43	50	108												14	6	9	15	20			
1994-95	Atlanta Knights	IHL	72	5	7	12	74												5	0	2	2	22			
1995-96	**Tampa Bay**	**NHL**	**13**	**0**	**1**	**1**	**4**	**0**	**0**	**0**	**10**	**0.0**	**−1**													
	Atlanta Knights	IHL	61	3	13	16	105												3	0	0	0	4			
1996-97	**Tampa Bay**	**NHL**	**64**	**4**	**13**	**17**	**44**	**1**	**0**	**0**	**57**	**7.0**	**−21**													
	Edmonton	**NHL**	**1**	**0**	**1**	**1**	**0**	**0**	**0**	**0**	**2**	**0.0**	**−2**						**12**	**0**	**0**	**0**	**30**	**0**	**0**	**0**
1997-98	**Edmonton**	**NHL**	**34**	**0**	**2**	**2**	**42**	**0**	**0**	**0**	**27**	**0.0**	**−7**													
	Anaheim	**NHL**	**27**	**0**	**6**	**6**	**47**	**0**	**0**	**0**	**23**	**0.0**	**−2**													
1998-99	Las Vegas	IHL	16	2	1	3	73																			
	Tampa Bay	**NHL**	**21**	**1**	**2**	**3**	**24**	**0**	**0**	**0**	**29**	**3.4**	**−4**	**0**	**0.0**	**25**	**11**	**15:49**								
99-2000	Hartford	AHL	44	6	14	20	121												18	2	9	11	53			
	NHL Totals		**160**	**5**	**25**	**30**	**161**	**1**	**0**	**0**	**148**	**3.4**		**0**	**0.0**	**25**	**11**	**15:49**	**12**	**0**	**0**	**0**	**30**	**0**	**0**	**0**

Memorial Cup All-Star Team (1993) • OHL Second All-Star Team (1994)

Traded to **Edmonton** by **Tampa Bay** with Tampa Bay's 6th round choice (Peter Sarno) in 1997 Entry Draft for Jeff Norton, March 18, 1997. Traded to **Anaheim** by **Edmonton** for Bobby Dollas, January 9, 1998. Traded to **Tampa Bay** by **Anaheim** for Tampa Bay's 5th round choice (Peter Podhradsky) in 2000 Entry Draft, December 10, 1998. Signed as a free agent by **NY Rangers**, October 3, 1999.

BARNABY, Matthew
(BAHR-na-BEE, MAT-thew) **PIT.**

Right wing. Shoots left. 6', 189 lbs. Born, Ottawa, Ont., May 4, 1973. Buffalo's 5th choice, 83rd overall, in 1992 Entry Draft.

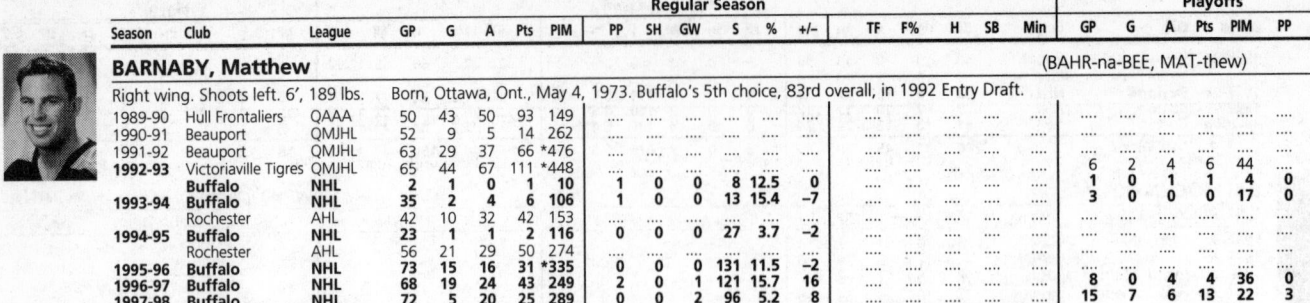

			Regular Season																Playoffs							
Season	Club	League	GP	G	A	Pts	PIM	PP	SH	GW	S	%	+/-	TF	F%	H	SB	Min	GP	G	A	Pts	PIM	PP	SH	GW
1989-90	Hull Frontaliers	QAAA	50	43	50	93	149	....	....	....	....	....	....	....	....	....	....	....	....	....	....	....	....	....	....	....
1990-91	Beauport	QMJHL	52	9	5	14	262	....	....	....	....	....	....	....	....	....	....	....	....	....	....	....	....	....	....	....
1991-92	Beauport	QMJHL	63	29	37	66	*476	....	....	....	....	....	....	....	....	....	....	....	....	....	....	....	....	....	....	....
1992-93	Victoriaville Tigres	QMJHL	65	44	67	111	*448	....	....	....	....	....	....	....	....	....	....	....	6	2	4	6	44	....	....	....
	Buffalo	NHL	2	1	0	1	10	1	0	0	8	12.5	0	....	....	....	....	....	1	0	1	1	4	0	0	0
1993-94	Buffalo	NHL	35	2	4	6	106	1	0	0	13	15.4	–7	....	....	....	....	....	3	0	0	0	17	0	0	0
	Rochester	AHL	42	10	32	42	153	....	....	....	....	....	....	....	....	....	....	....	....	....	....	....	....	....	....	....
1994-95	Buffalo	NHL	23	1	1	2	116	0	0	0	27	3.7	–2	....	....	....	....	....	....	....	....	....	....	....	....	....
	Rochester	AHL	56	21	29	50	274	....	....	....	....	....	....	....	....	....	....	....	....	....	....	....	....	....	....	....
1995-96	Buffalo	NHL	73	15	16	31	*335	0	0	0	131	11.5	–2	....	....	....	....	....	....	....	....	....	....	....	....	....
1996-97	Buffalo	NHL	68	19	24	43	249	2	0	1	121	15.7	16	....	....	....	....	....	8	0	4	4	36	0	0	0
1997-98	Buffalo	NHL	72	5	20	25	289	0	0	2	96	5.2	8	....	....	....	....	....	15	7	6	13	22	3	0	1
1998-99	Buffalo	NHL	44	4	14	18	143	0	0	3	52	7.7	–2	6	16.7	45	8	13:56	....	....	....	....	....	....	....	....
	Pittsburgh	NHL	18	2	2	4	34	1	0	0	27	7.4	–10	3	66.7	40	6	13:33	13	0	0	0	35	0	0	0
99-2000	Pittsburgh	NHL	64	12	12	24	197	0	0	3	80	15.0	3	75	44.0	99	10	12:38	11	0	2	2	29	0	0	0
	NHL Totals		399	61	93	154	1479	5	0	9	555	11.0		84	42.9	184	24	13:13	51	7	13	20	143	3	0	1

Traded to **Pittsburgh** by **Buffalo** for Stu Barnes, March 11, 1999.

BARNES, Stu
(BAHR-nz, STEW) **BUF.**

Center. Shoots right. 5'11", 180 lbs. Born, Spruce Grove, Alta., December 25, 1970. Winnipeg's 1st choice, 4th overall, in 1989 Entry Draft.

Season	Club	League	GP	G	A	Pts	PIM	PP	SH	GW	S	%	+/-	TF	F%	H	SB	Min	GP	G	A	Pts	PIM	PP	SH	GW
1985-86	Spruce Grove	AAHA	STATISTICS NOT AVAILABLE																							
1986-87	St. Albert Saints	AJHL	53	41	34	*75	103	....	....	....	....	....	....	....	....	....	....	....	19	7	15	22	....	....	....	....
1987-88	New Westminster	WHL	71	37	64	101	88	....	....	....	....	....	....	....	....	....	....	....	5	2	3	5	6	....	....	....
1988-89	Tri-City Americans	WHL	70	59	82	141	117	....	....	....	....	....	....	....	....	....	....	....	7	6	5	11	10	....	....	....
1989-90	Tri-City Americans	WHL	63	52	92	144	165	....	....	....	....	....	....	....	....	....	....	....	7	1	5	6	26	....	....	....
1990-91	Canada	Nat-Team	53	22	27	49	68	....	....	....	....	....	....	....	....	....	....	....	....	....	....	....	....	....	....	....
1991-92	Winnipeg	NHL	46	8	9	17	26	4	0	0	75	10.7	–2	....	....	....	....	....	....	....	....	....	....	....	....	....
	Moncton Hawks	AHL	30	13	19	32	10	....	....	....	....	....	....	....	....	....	....	....	11	3	9	12	6	....	....	....
1992-93	Winnipeg	NHL	38	12	10	22	10	3	0	3	73	16.4	–3	....	....	....	....	....	6	1	3	4	2	0	0	0
	Moncton Hawks	AHL	42	23	31	54	58	....	....	....	....	....	....	....	....	....	....	....	....	....	....	....	....	....	....	....
1993-94	Winnipeg	NHL	18	5	4	9	8	2	0	0	24	20.8	–1	....	....	....	....	....	....	....	....	....	....	....	....	....
	Florida	NHL	59	18	20	38	30	6	1	3	148	12.2	5	....	....	....	....	....	....	....	....	....	....	....	....	....
1994-95	Florida	NHL	41	10	19	29	8	1	0	2	93	10.8	7	....	....	....	....	....	....	....	....	....	....	....	....	....
1995-96	Florida	NHL	72	19	25	44	46	8	0	5	158	12.0	–12	....	....	....	....	....	22	6	10	16	4	2	0	2
1996-97	Florida	NHL	19	2	8	10	10	1	0	0	44	4.5	–3	....	....	....	....	....	....	....	....	....	....	....	....	....
	Pittsburgh	NHL	62	17	22	39	16	4	0	3	132	12.9	–20	....	....	....	....	....	5	0	1	1	0	0	0	0
1997-98	Pittsburgh	NHL	78	30	35	65	30	15	1	5	196	15.3	15	....	....	....	....	....	6	3	3	6	2	0	0	1
1998-99	Pittsburgh	NHL	64	20	12	32	20	13	0	3	155	12.9	–12	720	51.9	57	13	17:52	....	....	....	....	....	....	....	....
	Buffalo	NHL	17	0	4	4	10	0	0	0	25	0.0	1	236	51.3	15	4	18:20	21	7	3	10	6	4	0	1
99-2000	Buffalo	NHL	82	20	25	45	16	8	2	2	137	14.6	–3	778	48.5	22	32	17:23	5	3	0	3	2	2	0	1
	NHL Totals		596	161	193	354	230	65	4	26	1260	12.8		1734	50.3	94	49	17:40	65	20	20	40	16	8	0	5

WHL West Second All-Star Team (1988, 1989)

Traded to **Florida** by **Winnipeg** with St. Louis' 6th round choice (previously acquired by Winnipeg - later traded to Edmonton - later traded to Winnipeg - Winnipeg selected Chris Kibermanis) in 1994 Entry Draft for Randy Gilhen, November 25, 1993. Traded to **Pittsburgh** by **Florida** with Jason Woolley for Chris Wells, November 19, 1996. Traded to **Buffalo** by **Pittsburgh** for Matthew Barnaby, March 11, 1999.

BARON, Murray
(BAIR-uhn, MUHR-ray) **VAN.**

Defense. Shoots left. 6'3", 215 lbs. Born, Prince George, B.C., June 1, 1967. Philadelphia's 7th choice, 167th overall, in 1986 Entry Draft.

Season	Club	League	GP	G	A	Pts	PIM	PP	SH	GW	S	%	+/-	TF	F%	H	SB	Min	GP	G	A	Pts	PIM	PP	SH	GW
1984-85	Vernon Lakers	BCJHL	37	5	9	14	93	....	....	....	....	....	....	....	....	....	....	....	13	5	6	11	107	....	....	....
1985-86	Vernon Lakers	BCJHL	46	12	32	44	179	....	....	....	....	....	....	....	....	....	....	....	7	1	2	3	13	....	....	....
1986-87	North Dakota	WCHA	41	4	10	14	62	....	....	....	....	....	....	....	....	....	....	....	....	....	....	....	....	....	....	....
1987-88	North Dakota	WCHA	41	1	10	11	95	....	....	....	....	....	....	....	....	....	....	....	....	....	....	....	....	....	....	....
1988-89	North Dakota	WCHA	40	2	6	8	92	....	....	....	....	....	....	....	....	....	....	....	....	....	....	....	....	....	....	....
	Hershey Bears	AHL	9	0	3	3	8	....	....	....	....	....	....	....	....	....	....	....	....	....	....	....	....	....	....	....
1989-90	Philadelphia	NHL	16	2	2	4	12	0	0	0	18	11.1	–1	....	....	....	....	....	....	....	....	....	....	....	....	....
	Hershey Bears	AHL	50	0	10	10	101	....	....	....	....	....	....	....	....	....	....	....	....	....	....	....	....	....	....	....
1990-91	Philadelphia	NHL	67	8	8	16	74	3	0	1	86	9.3	–3	....	....	....	....	....	....	....	....	....	....	....	....	....
	Hershey Bears	AHL	6	2	3	5	0	....	....	....	....	....	....	....	....	....	....	....	....	....	....	....	....	....	....	....
1991-92	St. Louis	NHL	67	3	8	11	94	0	0	0	55	5.5	–3	....	....	....	....	....	2	0	0	0	2	0	0	0
1992-93	St. Louis	NHL	53	2	2	4	59	0	0	1	42	4.8	–5	....	....	....	....	....	11	0	0	0	12	0	0	0
1993-94	St. Louis	NHL	77	5	9	14	123	0	0	0	73	6.8	–14	....	....	....	....	....	4	0	0	0	10	0	0	0
1994-95	St. Louis	NHL	39	0	5	5	93	0	0	0	28	0.0	9	....	....	....	....	....	7	1	1	2	2	0	0	0
1995-96	St. Louis	NHL	82	2	9	11	190	0	0	0	86	2.3	3	....	....	....	....	....	13	1	0	1	20	0	1	0
1996-97	St. Louis	NHL	11	0	2	2	11	0	0	0	7	0.0	–4	....	....	....	....	....	....	....	....	....	....	....	....	....
	Montreal	NHL	60	1	5	6	107	0	0	0	52	1.9	–16	....	....	....	....	....	....	....	....	....	....	....	....	....
	Phoenix	NHL	8	0	0	0	4	0	0	0	5	0.0	0	....	....	....	....	....	1	0	0	0	0	0	0	0
1997-98	Phoenix	NHL	45	1	5	6	106	0	0	0	23	4.3	–10	....	....	....	....	....	6	0	2	2	6	0	0	0
1998-99	Vancouver	NHL	81	2	6	8	115	0	0	0	53	3.8	–23	0	0.0	192	100	18:14	....	....	....	....	....	....	....	....
99-2000	Vancouver	NHL	81	2	10	12	67	0	0	0	48	4.2	8	2	50.0	187	185	21:36	....	....	....	....	....	....	....	....
	NHL Totals		687	28	71	99	1055	3	0	2	576	4.9		2	50.0	379	285	19:55	44	2	3	5	52	0	1	0

Traded to **St. Louis** by **Philadelphia** with Ron Sutter for Dan Quinn and Rod Brind'Amour, September 22, 1991. Traded to **Montreal** by **St. Louis** with Shayne Corson and St. Louis' 5th round choice (Gennady Razin) in 1997 Entry Draft for Pierre Turgeon, Rory Fitzpatrick and Craig Conroy, October 29, 1996. Traded to **Phoenix** by **Montreal** with Chris Murray for Dave Manson, March 18, 1997. Signed as a free agent by **Vancouver**, July 14, 1998.

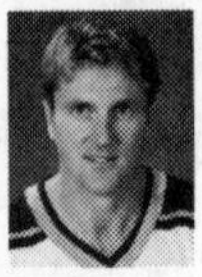

BARRIE, Len
(BAIR-ree, LEHN) **FLA.**

Center. Shoots left. 6', 200 lbs. Born, Kimberley, B.C., June 4, 1969. Edmonton's 7th choice, 124th overall, in 1988 Entry Draft.

Season	Club	League	GP	G	A	Pts	PIM	PP	SH	GW	S	%	+/-	TF	F%	H	SB	Min	GP	G	A	Pts	PIM	PP	SH	GW
1984-85	Kelowna Blazers	BCAHA	20	51	55	106	24	....	....	....	....	....	....	....	....	....	....	....	....	....	....	....	....	....	....	....
1985-86	Calgary Spurs	AJHL	23	7	14	21	86	....	....	....	....	....	....	....	....	....	....	....	....	....	....	....	....	....	....	....
	Calgary Wranglers	WHL	32	3	0	3	18	....	....	....	....	....	....	....	....	....	....	....	....	....	....	....	....	....	....	....
1986-87	Calgary Wranglers	WHL	34	13	13	26	81	....	....	....	....	....	....	....	....	....	....	....	....	....	....	....	....	....	....	....
	Victoria Cougars	WHL	34	7	6	13	92	....	....	....	....	....	....	....	....	....	....	....	5	0	1	1	15	....	....	....
1987-88	Victoria Cougars	WHL	70	37	49	86	192	....	....	....	....	....	....	....	....	....	....	....	8	2	0	2	29	....	....	....
1988-89	Victoria Cougars	WHL	67	39	48	87	157	....	....	....	....	....	....	....	....	....	....	....	7	5	2	7	23	....	....	....
1989-90	Kamloops Blazers	WHL	70	*85	*100	*185	108	....	....	....	....	....	....	....	....	....	....	....	17	*14	23	*37	24	....	....	....
	Philadelphia	NHL	1	0	0	0	0	0	0	0	0	0.0	–2	....	....	....	....	....	....	....	....	....	....	....	....	....
1990-91	Hershey Bears	AHL	63	26	32	58	60	....	....	....	....	....	....	....	....	....	....	....	7	4	0	4	12	....	....	....
1991-92	Hershey Bears	AHL	75	42	43	85	78	....	....	....	....	....	....	....	....	....	....	....	3	0	2	2	32	....	....	....
1992-93	Philadelphia	NHL	8	2	2	4	9	0	0	0	14	14.3	2	....	....	....	....	....	....	....	....	....	....	....	....	....
	Hershey Bears	AHL	61	31	45	76	162	....	....	....	....	....	....	....	....	....	....	....	....	....	....	....	....	....	....	....
1993-94	Florida	NHL	2	0	0	0	0	0	0	0	0	0.0	–2	....	....	....	....	....	....	....	....	....	....	....	....	....
	Cincinnati	IHL	77	45	71	116	246	....	....	....	....	....	....	....	....	....	....	....	11	8	13	21	60	....	....	....
1994-95	Cleveland	IHL	28	13	30	43	137	....	....	....	....	....	....	....	....	....	....	....	....	....	....	....	....	....	....	....
	Pittsburgh	NHL	48	3	11	14	66	0	0	1	37	8.1	–4	....	....	....	....	....	4	1	0	1	8	1	0	0
1995-96	Pittsburgh	NHL	5	0	0	0	18	0	0	0	5	0.0	–1	....	....	....	....	....	....	....	....	....	....	....	....	....
	Cleveland	IHL	55	29	43	72	178	....	....	....	....	....	....	....	....	....	....	....	3	2	3	5	6	....	....	....
1996-97	San Antonio	IHL	57	26	40	66	196	....	....	....	....	....	....	....	....	....	....	....	9	5	5	10	20	....	....	....
1997-98	San Antonio	IHL	32	7	13	20	90	....	....	....	....	....	....	....	....	....	....	....	....	....	....	....	....	....	....	....
	Frankfurt Lions	DEL	25	11	19	30	32	....	....	....	....	....	....	....	....	....	....	....	6	2	3	5	35	....	....	....
1998-99	Frankfurt Lions	DEL	41	24	35	59	105	....	....	....	....	....	....	....	....	....	....	....	8	2	4	6	43	....	....	....

			Regular Season																Playoffs							
Season	Club	League	GP	G	A	Pts	PIM	PP	SH	GW	S	%	+/–	TF	F%	H	SB	Min	GP	G	A	Pts	PIM	PP	SH	GW
99-2000	Los Angeles	NHL	46	5	8	13	56	0	0	0	46	10.9	5	322	52.5	66	5	11:52	....	....	....	....	....	....	....	....
	Long Beach	IHL	17	10	10	20	16	....	....	....	....	....	....	....	....	....	....	....	....	....	....	....	....	....	....	....
	Florida	NHL	14	4	6	10	6	0	0	0	15	26.7	4	98	61.2	18	7	13:57	4	0	0	0	0	0	0	0
	NHL Totals		124	14	27	41	155	0	0	1	117	12.0		420	54.5	84	12	12:21	8	1	0	1	8	1	0	0

WHL West First All-Star Team (1990) • IHL Second All-Star Team (1994)

Signed as a free agent by **Philadelphia**, February 28, 1990. Signed as a free agent by **Florida**, July 20, 1993. Signed as a free agent by **Pittsburgh**, August 15, 1994. Signed as a free agent by **LA Kings**, July 9, 1999. Claimed on waivers by **Florida** from **LA Kings**, March 10, 2000.

BARTECKO, Lubos

(bahr-TEHK-oh, LOO-bohsh) **ST.L.**

Left wing. Shoots left. 6'1", 200 lbs. Born, Kezmarok, Czech., July 14, 1976.

Season	Club	League	GP	G	A	Pts	PIM	PP	SH	GW	S	%	+/–	TF	F%	H	SB	Min	GP	G	A	Pts	PIM	PP	SH	GW
1994-95	SKP Propad	Slovakia	3	1	0	1	0	....	....	....	....	....	....	....	....	....	....	....	....	....	....	....	....	....	....	....
1995-96	Chicoutimi	QMJHL	70	32	41	73	50	....	....	....	....	....	....	....	....	....	....	....	17	8	15	23	10	....	....	....
1996-97	Drummondville	QMJHL	58	40	51	91	49	....	....	....	....	....	....	....	....	....	....	....	8	1	8	9	4	....	....	....
1997-98	Worcester	AHL	34	10	12	22	24	....	....	....	....	....	....	....	....	....	....	....	10	4	2	6	2	....	....	....
1998-99	SKP Poprad	Slovakia	1	1	0	1	0	....	....	....	....	....	....	....	....	....	....	....	....	....	....	....	....	....	....	....
	St. Louis	**NHL**	32	5	11	16	6	0	0	1	37	13.5	4	0	0.0	34	5	13:13	5	0	0	0	2	0	0	0
	Worcester	AHL	49	14	24	38	22	....	....	....	....	....	....	....	....	....	....	....	....	....	....	....	....	....	....	....
99-2000	**St. Louis**	**NHL**	67	16	23	39	51	3	0	3	75	21.3	24	10	50.0	46	12	13:33	7	1	1	2	0	0	0	0
	Worcester	AHL	12	4	7	11	4	....	....	....	....	....	....	....	....	....	....	....	....	....	....	....	....	....	....	....
	NHL Totals		99	21	34	55	57	3	0	4	112	18.8		10	50.0	80	17	13:27	12	1	1	2	2	0	0	0

Signed as a free agent by **St. Louis**, October 3, 1997.

BASHKIROV, Andrei

(bahsh-KIHR-ahf, AWN-dray) **MTL.**

Left wing. Shoots left. 6', 215 lbs. Born, Shelehov, USSR, June 22, 1970. Montreal's 4th choice, 132nd overall, in 1998 Entry Draft.

Season	Club	League	GP	G	A	Pts	PIM	PP	SH	GW	S	%	+/–	TF	F%	H	SB	Min	GP	G	A	Pts	PIM	PP	SH	GW
1991-92	HK Khimik	CIS	11	2	0	2	4	....	....	....	....	....	....	....	....	....	....	....	....	....	....	....	....	....	....	....
1992-93	Yermak Angarsk	CIS-3	STATISTICS NOT AVAILABLE																							
1993-94	Charlotte	ECHL	62	28	42	70	25	....	....	....	....	....	....	....	....	....	....	....	3	1	0	1	0	....	....	....
	Providence Bruins	AHL	1	0	0	0	2	....	....	....	....	....	....	....	....	....	....	....	....	....	....	....	....	....	....	....
1994-95	Charlotte	ECHL	61	19	27	46	20	....	....	....	....	....	....	....	....	....	....	....	3	0	0	0	0	....	....	....
1995-96	Huntington	ECHL	55	19	39	58	35	....	....	....	....	....	....	....	....	....	....	....	....	....	....	....	....	....	....	....
1996-97	Huntington	ECHL	47	29	41	70	12	....	....	....	....	....	....	....	....	....	....	....	....	....	....	....	....	....	....	....
	Detroit Vipers	IHL	2	0	0	0	0	....	....	....	....	....	....	....	....	....	....	....	....	....	....	....	....	....	....	....
	Las Vegas	IHL	27	10	12	22	0	....	....	....	....	....	....	....	....	....	....	....	2	0	0	0	0	....	....	....
1997-98	Las Vegas	IHL	15	2	3	5	5	....	....	....	....	....	....	....	....	....	....	....	....	....	....	....	....	....	....	....
	Port Huron	UHL	3	1	3	4	0	....	....	....	....	....	....	....	....	....	....	....	....	....	....	....	....	....	....	....
	Fort Wayne	IHL	65	28	48	76	16	....	....	....	....	....	....	....	....	....	....	....	4	2	2	4	2	....	....	....
1998-99	**Montreal**	**NHL**	10	0	0	0	0	0	0	0	4	0.0	–3	0	0.0	3	3	6:57	....	....	....	....	....	....	....	....
	Fredericton	AHL	13	7	5	12	4	....	....	....	....	....	....	....	....	....	....	....	....	....	....	....	....	....	....	....
	Fort Wayne	IHL	34	11	25	36	10	....	....	....	....	....	....	....	....	....	....	....	....	....	....	....	....	....	....	....
99-2000	**Montreal**	**NHL**	2	0	0	0	0	0	0	0	0	0.0	0	0	0.0	0	0	5:09	....	....	....	....	....	....	....	....
	Quebec Citadelles	AHL	78	28	33	61	17	....	....	....	....	....	....	....	....	....	....	....	3	0	3	3	0	....	....	....
	NHL Totals		12	0	0	0	0	0	0	0	4	0.0		0	0.0	3	3	6:39	....	....	....	....	....	....	....	....

• Played w/ RHI's Portland Rage in 1994 (17-12-25-37-20) and Sacramento River Rats in 1995 (9-6-18-24-0)

BASSEN, Bob

(BAS-sehn, BAWB)

Center. Shoots left. 5'10", 185 lbs. Born, Calgary, Alta., May 6, 1965.

Season	Club	League	GP	G	A	Pts	PIM	PP	SH	GW	S	%	+/–	TF	F%	H	SB	Min	GP	G	A	Pts	PIM	PP	SH	GW
1982-83	Calgary Spurs	AJHL	STATISTICS NOT AVAILABLE																							
	Medicine Hat	WHL	4	3	2	5	0	....	....	....	....	....	....	....	....	....	....	....	3	0	0	0	4	....	....	....
1983-84	Medicine Hat	WHL	72	29	29	58	93	....	....	....	....	....	....	....	....	....	....	....	14	5	11	16	12	....	....	....
1984-85	Medicine Hat	WHL	65	32	50	82	143	....	....	....	....	....	....	....	....	....	....	....	10	2	8	10	39	....	....	....
1985-86	**NY Islanders**	**NHL**	11	2	1	3	6	0	0	0	5	40.0	0	....	....	....	....	....	3	0	1	1	0	0	0	0
	Springfield	AHL	54	13	21	34	111	....	....	....	....	....	....	....	....	....	....	....	....	....	....	....	....	....	....	....
1986-87	**NY Islanders**	**NHL**	77	7	10	17	89	0	0	1	59	11.9	–17	....	....	....	....	....	14	1	2	3	21	0	0	0
1987-88	**NY Islanders**	**NHL**	77	6	16	22	99	1	0	2	65	9.2	8	....	....	....	....	....	6	0	1	1	23	0	0	0
1988-89	**NY Islanders**	**NHL**	19	1	4	5	21	0	0	0	14	7.1	0	....	....	....	....	....	....	....	....	....	....	....	....	....
	Chicago	**NHL**	49	4	12	16	62	0	0	1	37	10.8	5	....	....	....	....	....	10	1	1	2	34	0	0	0
1989-90	**Chicago**	**NHL**	6	1	1	2	8	0	0	0	7	14.3	1	....	....	....	....	....	1	0	0	0	2	0	0	0
	Indianapolis Ice	IHL	73	22	32	54	179	....	....	....	....	....	....	....	....	....	....	....	12	3	8	11	33	....	....	....
1990-91	**St. Louis**	**NHL**	79	16	18	34	183	0	2	1	117	13.7	17	....	....	....	....	....	13	1	3	4	24	0	0	0
1991-92	**St. Louis**	**NHL**	79	7	25	32	167	0	0	1	101	6.9	12	....	....	....	....	....	6	0	2	2	4	0	0	0
1992-93	**St. Louis**	**NHL**	53	9	10	19	63	0	1	0	61	14.8	0	....	....	....	....	....	11	0	0	0	10	0	0	0
1993-94	**St. Louis**	**NHL**	46	2	7	9	44	0	1	0	73	2.7	–14	....	....	....	....	....	....	....	....	....	....	....	....	....
	Quebec	**NHL**	37	11	8	19	55	1	0	0	56	19.6	–3	....	....	....	....	....	....	....	....	....	....	....	....	....
1994-95	**Quebec**	**NHL**	47	12	15	27	33	0	1	1	66	18.2	14	....	....	....	....	....	5	2	4	6	0	0	0	0
1995-96	**Dallas**	**NHL**	13	0	1	1	15	0	0	0	9	0.0	–6	....	....	....	....	....	....	....	....	....	....	....	....	....
	Michigan K-Wings	IHL	1	0	0	0	4	....	....	....	....	....	....	....	....	....	....	....	....	....	....	....	....	....	....	....
1996-97	**Dallas**	**NHL**	46	5	7	12	41	0	0	2	50	10.0	5	....	....	....	....	....	7	3	1	4	4	0	0	0
1997-98	**Dallas**	**NHL**	58	3	4	7	57	0	0	1	40	7.5	–4	....	....	....	....	....	17	1	0	1	12	0	0	0
1998-99	**Calgary**	**NHL**	41	1	2	3	35	0	0	0	47	2.1	–13	20	40.0	108	17	12:36	....	....	....	....	....	....	....	....
99-2000	Frankfurt Lions	DEL	14	2	9	11	6	....	....	....	....	....	....	....	....	....	....	....	....	....	....	....	....	....	....	....
	St. Louis	**NHL**	27	1	3	4	26	0	0	0	26	3.8	–3	75	46.7	46	6	9:51	....	....	....	....	....	....	....	....
	NHL Totals		765	88	144	232	1004	2	5	10	833	10.6		95	45.3	154	23	11:30	93	9	15	24	134	0	0	0

WHL First All-Star Team (1985) • IHL First All-Star Team (1990)

Signed as a free agent by **NY Islanders**, October 19, 1984. Traded to **Chicago** by **NY Islanders** with Steve Konroyd for Marc Bergevin and Gary Nylund, November 25, 1988. Claimed by **St. Louis** from **Chicago** in NHL Waiver Draft, October 1, 1990. Traded to **Quebec** by **St. Louis** with Garth Butcher and Ron Sutter for Steve Duchesne and Denis Chasse, January 23, 1994. Signed as a free agent by **Dallas**, August 10, 1995. Traded to **Calgary** by **Dallas** for Aaron Gavey, July 14, 1998. Claimed on waivers by **St. Louis** from **Calgary**, December 9, 1999.

BAST, Ryan

(BAST, RIGH-yan)

Defense. Shoots left. 6'2", 190 lbs. Born, Spruce Grove, Alta., August 27, 1975.

Season	Club	League	GP	G	A	Pts	PIM	PP	SH	GW	S	%	+/–	TF	F%	H	SB	Min	GP	G	A	Pts	PIM	PP	SH	GW
1992-93	St. Albert Raiders	AAHA	35	1	18	19	51	....	....	....	....	....	....	....	....	....	....	....	....	....	....	....	....	....	....	....
1993-94	Portland	WHL	6	0	0	0	4	....	....	....	....	....	....	....	....	....	....	....	....	....	....	....	....	....	....	....
	Prince Albert	WHL	47	2	8	10	139	....	....	....	....	....	....	....	....	....	....	....	....	....	....	....	....	....	....	....
1994-95	Prince Albert	WHL	42	1	10	11	149	....	....	....	....	....	....	....	....	....	....	....	14	0	3	3	13	....	....	....
1995-96	Prince Albert	WHL	44	7	15	22	129	....	....	....	....	....	....	....	....	....	....	....	....	....	....	....	....	....	....	....
	Calgary Hitmen	WHL	3	0	0	0	24	....	....	....	....	....	....	....	....	....	....	....	....	....	....	....	....	....	....	....
	Swift Current	WHL	25	2	3	5	50	....	....	....	....	....	....	....	....	....	....	....	6	1	0	1	21	....	....	....
1996-97	Las Vegas	IHL	49	2	3	5	266	....	....	....	....	....	....	....	....	....	....	....	....	....	....	....	....	....	....	....
	Toledo Storm	ECHL	12	2	2	4	75	....	....	....	....	....	....	....	....	....	....	....	....	....	....	....	....	....	....	....
	Saint John Flames	AHL	12	0	0	0	21	....	....	....	....	....	....	....	....	....	....	....	5	0	0	0	4	....	....	....
1997-98	Saint John Flames	AHL	77	3	8	11	187	....	....	....	....	....	....	....	....	....	....	....	21	0	1	1	55	....	....	....
1998-99	Saint John Flames	AHL	2	0	0	0	5	....	....	....	....	....	....	....	....	....	....	....	....	....	....	....	....	....	....	....
	Philadelphia	**NHL**	2	0	1	1	0	0	0	0	1	0.0	0	0	0.0	0	0	13:24	....	....	....	....	....	....	....	....
	Philadelphia	AHL	69	0	11	11	160	....	....	....	....	....	....	....	....	....	....	....	16	0	0	0	30	....	....	....
99-2000	Philadelphia	AHL	71	1	9	10	198	....	....	....	....	....	....	....	....	....	....	....	5	0	0	0	6	....	....	....
	NHL Totals		2	0	1	1	0	0	0	0	1	0.0		0	0.0	0	0	13:24	....	....	....	....	....	....	....	....

AHL Second All-Star Team (1998)

Signed as a free agent by **Las Vegas** (IHL), September 30, 1996. Traded to **Saint John** (AHL) by **Las Vegas** (IHL) for loan of Sasha Lakovic, March 20, 1997. Signed as a free agent by **Philadelphia**, May 18, 1998. • Calgary Flames filed official protest contesting Philadelphia's signing of Bast under the contention that he was property of AHL's Saint John Flames, May 20, 1998. • NHL ruled that Bast was not under contract to Calgary since he was never drafted and had no NHL clause in contract, May 22, 1998. NHL also ruled that Bast was not property of Philadelphia because Flyers' contract offer exceeded NHL rookie salary cap, May 22, 1998. A compromise was reached that traded Bast to **Philadelphia** by **Calgary** with Calgary's 8th round choice (David Nystrom) in 1999 Entry Draft for Philadelphia's 3rd round choice (later traded to NY Rangers - NY Rangers selected Patrik Aufiero) in 1999 Entry Draft, October 13, 1998.

			Regular Season															Playoffs							
Season	Club	League	GP	G	A	Pts	PIM	PP	SH	GW	S	%	+/-	TF	F%	H	SB	Min	GP	G	A	Pts	PIM	PP	SH	GW

BATES, Shawn (BAYTS, SHAWN) BOS.

Center. Shoots right. 5'11", 212 lbs. Born, Melrose, MA, April 3, 1975. Boston's 4th choice, 103rd overall, in 1993 Entry Draft.

Season	Club	League	GP	G	A	Pts	PIM	PP	SH	GW	S	%	+/-	TF	F%	H	SB	Min	GP	G	A	Pts	PIM	PP	SH	GW
1990-91	Medford High	Hi-School	22	18	43	61	6																			
1991-92	Medford High	Hi-School	22	38	41	79	10																			
1992-93	Medford High	Hi-School	25	49	46	95	20																			
1993-94	Boston University	H-East	41	10	19	29	24																			
1994-95	Boston University	H-East	38	18	12	30	48																			
1995-96	Boston University	H-East	40	28	22	50	54																			
1996-97	Boston University	H-East	41	17	18	35	64																			
1997-98	**Boston**	**NHL**	13	2	0	2	2	0	0	0	12	16.7	-3													
	Providence Bruins	AHL	50	15	19	34	22																			
1998-99	**Boston**	**NHL**	33	5	4	9	2	0	0	0	30	16.7	3	178	51.1	47	5	8:35	12	0	0	0	4	0	0	0
	Providence Bruins	AHL	37	25	21	46	39																			
99-2000	**Boston**	**NHL**	44	5	7	12	14	0	0	1	65	7.7	-17	460	47.0	76	8	10:52								
	NHL Totals		90	12	11	23	18	0	0	1	107	11.2		638	48.1	123	13	9:53	12	0	0	0	4	0	0	0

NCAA Championship All-Tournament Team (1995)

BATTAGLIA, Bates (buh-TAG-lee-ah, BAYTS) CAR.

Left wing. Shoots left. 6'2", 205 lbs. Born, Chicago, IL, December 13, 1975. Anaheim's 6th choice, 132nd overall, in 1994 Entry Draft.

Season	Club	League	GP	G	A	Pts	PIM	PP	SH	GW	S	%	+/-	TF	F%	H	SB	Min	GP	G	A	Pts	PIM	PP	SH	GW
1992-93	Team Illinois	MEHL	60	42	42	84	68																			
1993-94	Caledon Canucks	OJHL	44	15	33	48	104																			
1994-95	Lake Superior	CCHA	38	6	14	20	34																			
1995-96	Lake Superior	CCHA	40	13	22	35	48																			
1996-97	Lake Superior	CCHA	38	12	27	39	80																			
1997-98	**Carolina**	**NHL**	33	2	4	6	10	0	0	1	21	9.5	-1													
	New Haven	AHL	48	15	21	36	48												1	0	0	0	0			
1998-99	**Carolina**	**NHL**	60	7	11	18	97	0	0	0	52	13.5	7	144	39.6	67	9	9:53	6	0	3	3	8	0	0	0
99-2000	**Carolina**	**NHL**	77	16	18	34	39	3	0	3	86	18.6	20	23	26.1	128	19	15:12								
	NHL Totals		170	25	33	58	146	3	0	4	159	15.7		167	37.7	195	28	12:52	6	0	3	3	8	0	0	0

Traded to **Hartford** by **Anaheim** with Anaheim's 4th round choice (Josef Vasicek) in 1998 Entry Draft for Mark Janssens, March 18, 1997. Rights transferred to **Carolina** after **Hartford** franchise relocated, June 25, 1997.

BAUMGARTNER, Nolan (BAWM-gahrt-nuhr, NOH-lan) CHI.

Defense. Shoots right. 6'2", 205 lbs. Born, Calgary, Alta., March 23, 1976. Washington's 1st choice, 10th overall, in 1994 Entry Draft.

Season	Club	League	GP	G	A	Pts	PIM	PP	SH	GW	S	%	+/-	TF	F%	H	SB	Min	GP	G	A	Pts	PIM	PP	SH	GW
1991-92	Calgary	AMHL	39	11	29	40	40												11	1	1	2	0			
1992-93	Kamloops Blazers	WHL	43	0	5	5	30												19	3	14	17	33			
1993-94	Kamloops Blazers	WHL	69	13	42	55	109												21	4	13	17	16			
1994-95	Kamloops Blazers	WHL	62	8	36	44	71												16	1	9	10	26			
1995-96	Kamloops Blazers	WHL	28	13	15	28	45																			
	Washington	**NHL**	1	0	0	0	0	0	0	0	0	0.0	-1						1	0	0	0	10	0	0	0
1996-97	Portland Pirates	AHL	8	2	2	4	4																			
1997-98	**Washington**	**NHL**	4	0	1	1	0	0	0	0	4	0.0	0						10	1	4	5	10			
	Portland Pirates	AHL	70	2	24	26	70																			
1998-99	**Washington**	**NHL**	5	0	0	0	0	0	0	0	1	0.0	-3	0	0	1	0	8:41								
	Portland Pirates	AHL	38	5	14	19	62																			
99-2000	**Washington**	**NHL**	8	0	1	1	2	0	0	0	6	0.0	1	0	0.0	8	2	10:31	4	1	2	3	10	0	0	0
	Portland Pirates	AHL	71	5	18	23	56																			
	NHL Totals		18	0	2	2	2	0	0	0	11	0.0		0	0.0	9	2	9:49	1	0	0	0	10	0	0	0

Memorial Cup All-Star Team (1994, 1995) • WHL West First All-Star Team (1995, 1996) • Canadian Major Junior First All-Star Team (1995) • Canadian Major Junior Defenseman of the Year (1995)
Traded to **Chicago** by **Washington** for Remi Royer, July 20, 2000.

BEAUFAIT, Mark (BOH-fayt, MAHRK)

Center. Shoots right. 5'9", 170 lbs. Born, Livonia, MI, May 13, 1970. San Jose's 2nd choice, 7th overall, in 1991 Supplemental Draft.

Season	Club	League	GP	G	A	Pts	PIM	PP	SH	GW	S	%	+/-	TF	F%	H	SB	Min	GP	G	A	Pts	PIM	PP	SH	GW
1988-89	North-Michigan	WCHA	11	2	1	3	2																			
1989-90	North-Michigan	WCHA	34	10	14	24	12																			
1990-91	North-Michigan	WCHA	47	19	30	49	18																			
1991-92	North-Michigan	WCHA	39	31	44	75	43																			
1992-93	**San Jose**	**NHL**	5	1	0	1	0	0	0	0	3	33.3	-1													
	Kansas City	IHL	66	19	40	59	22												9	1	1	2	8			
1993-94	United States	Nat-Team	51	22	29	51	36																			
	United States	Olympics	8	1	4	5	2																			
	Kansas City	IHL	21	12	9	21	18																			
1994-95	San Diego Gulls	IHL	68	24	39	63	22												5	2	2	4	2			
1995-96	Orlando	IHL	77	30	79	109	87												22	9	*19	*28	22			
1996-97	Orlando	IHL	80	26	65	91	63												10	5	8	13	18			
1997-98	Orlando	IHL	76	24	61	85	56												17	6	16	22	10			
1998-99	Orlando	IHL	71	28	43	71	38												15	2	12	14	14			
99-2000	Orlando	IHL	78	28	49	77	87												6	2	0	2	4			
	NHL Totals		5	1	0	1	0	0	0	0	3	33.3														

IHL Second All-Star Team (1997)
Selected by **Orlando** (IHL) from **San Diego** (IHL) in 1995 IHL Expansion Draft, July 13, 1995.

BEDDOES, Clayton (BEHD-dohs, CLAY-tohn)

Center. Shoots left. 5'11", 190 lbs. Born, Bentley, Alta., November 10, 1970.

Season	Club	League	GP	G	A	Pts	PIM	PP	SH	GW	S	%	+/-	TF	F%	H	SB	Min	GP	G	A	Pts	PIM	PP	SH	GW
1989-90	Weyburn Wings	MJHL	63	34	60	94	69												13	7	6	13				
1990-91	Lake Superior	CCHA	45	14	28	42	26																			
1991-92	Lake Superior	CCHA	38	14	26	40	24																			
1992-93	Lake Superior	CCHA	43	18	40	58	30																			
1993-94	Lake Superior	CCHA	44	23	31	54	56																			
1994-95	Providence Bruins	AHL	65	16	20	36	39												13	3	1	4	18			
1995-96	**Boston**	**NHL**	39	1	6	7	44	0	0	0	18	5.6	-5													
	Providence Bruins	AHL	32	10	15	25	24												4	2	3	5	0			
1996-97	**Boston**	**NHL**	21	1	2	3	13	0	0	0	11	9.1	-1						7	2	0	2	4			
	Providence Bruins	AHL	36	11	23	34	60												22	5	10	15	16			
1997-98	Detroit Vipers	IHL	65	22	24	46	63																			
1998-99	Berlin Capitals	DEL	52	17	26	43	12																			
99-2000	Adler Mannheim	DEL	46	13	12	25	41												5	1	0	1	12			
	Adler Mannheim	EuroHL	6	0	1	1	2																			
	NHL Totals		60	2	8	10	57	0	0	0	29	6.9														

CCHA Second All-Star Team (1994) • NCAA West Second All-American Team (1994) • NCAA Championship All-Tournament Team (1994)
Signed as a free agent by **Boston**, June 2, 1994. Signed as a free agent by **Ottawa**, July 28, 1997.

BEGIN, Steve
(bay-ZHIN, STEEV) **CGY.**

Center. Shoots left. 5'11", 190 lbs. Born, Trois-Rivieres, Que., June 14, 1978. Calgary's 3rd choice, 40th overall, in 1996 Entry Draft.

			Regular Season																Playoffs							
Season	Club	League	GP	G	A	Pts	PIM	PP	SH	GW	S	%	+/-	TF	F%	H	SB	Min	GP	G	A	Pts	PIM	PP	SH	GW
1994-95	Cap-d-Madelaine	QAAA	35	9	15	24	48	....	....	....	....	....	....	....	....	....	....	....	....	....	....	....	....	....	....	....
1995-96	Val-d'Or Foreurs	QMJHL	64	13	23	36	218	....	....	....	....	....	....	....	....	....	....	....	13	1	3	4	33	....	....	....
1996-97	Val-d'Or Foreurs	QMJHL	58	13	33	46	229	....	....	....	....	....	....	....	....	....	....	....	10	0	3	3	8	....	....	....
	Saint John Flames	AHL	....	....	....	....	....	....	....	....	....	....	....	....	....	....	....	....	4	0	2	2	6	....	....	....
1997-98	Val-d'Or Foreurs	QMJHL	35	18	17	35	73	....	....	....	....	....	....	....	....	....	....	....	15	2	12	14	34	....	....	....
	Calgary	**NHL**	**5**	**0**	**0**	**0**	**23**	**0**	**0**	**0**	**2**	**0.0**	**0**	....	....	....	....	....	....	....	....	....	....	....	....	....
1998-99	Saint John Flames	AHL	73	11	9	20	156	....	....	....	....	....	....	....	....	....	....	....	7	2	0	2	18	....	....	....
99-2000	**Calgary**	**NHL**	**13**	**1**	**1**	**2**	**18**	**0**	**0**	**0**	**3**	**33.3**	**–3**	**19**	**47.4**	**23**	**2**	**7:13**	....	....	....	....	....	....	....	....
	Saint John Flames	AHL	47	13	12	25	99	....	....	....	....	....	....	....	....	....	....	....	....	....	....	....	....	....	....	....
	NHL Totals		**18**	**1**	**1**	**2**	**41**	**0**	**0**	**0**	**5**	**20.0**		**19**	**47.4**	**23**	**2**	**7:13**	....	....	....	....	....	....	....	....

BEKAR, Derek
(BEH-kahr, DAI-rehk) **ST.L.**

Left wing. Shoots left. 6'3", 194 lbs. Born, Burnaby, B.C., September 15, 1975. St. Louis' 7th choice, 205th overall, in 1995 Entry Draft.

			Regular Season																Playoffs							
Season	Club	League	GP	G	A	Pts	PIM	PP	SH	GW	S	%	+/-	TF	F%	H	SB	Min	GP	G	A	Pts	PIM	PP	SH	GW
1992-93	Notre Dame	AAHA	29	25	24	49	68	....	....	....	....	....	....	....	....	....	....	....	....	....	....	....	....	....	....	....
1993-94	Notre Dame	SJHL	62	20	31	51	77	....	....	....	....	....	....	....	....	....	....	....	....	....	....	....	....	....	....	....
1994-95	Powell River	BCJHL	46	33	29	62	35	....	....	....	....	....	....	....	....	....	....	....	....	....	....	....	....	....	....	....
1995-96	New Hampshire	H-East	34	15	18	33	4	....	....	....	....	....	....	....	....	....	....	....	....	....	....	....	....	....	....	....
1996-97	New Hampshire	H-East	39	18	21	39	34	....	....	....	....	....	....	....	....	....	....	....	....	....	....	....	....	....	....	....
1997-98	New Hampshire	H-East	35	32	28	60	46	....	....	....	....	....	....	....	....	....	....	....	....	....	....	....	....	....	....	....
1998-99	Worcester	AHL	51	16	20	36	6	....	....	....	....	....	....	....	....	....	....	....	4	0	0	0	0	....	....	....
99-2000	**St. Louis**	**NHL**	**1**	**0**	**0**	**0**	**0**	**0**	**0**	**0**	**0**	**0.0**	**0**	**0**	**0.0**	**1**	**0**	**5:14**	....	....	....	....	....	....	....	....
	Worcester	AHL	71	21	19	40	26	....	....	....	....	....	....	....	....	....	....	....	7	0	3	3	2	....	....	....
	NHL Totals		**1**	**0**	**0**	**0**	**0**	**0**	**0**	**0**	**0**	**0.0**		**0**	**0.0**	**1**	**0**	**5:14**	....	....	....	....	....	....	....	....

Hockey East Second All-Star Team (1998)

BELAK, Wade
(BEE-lak, WAYD) **CGY.**

Defense. Shoots right. 6'5", 222 lbs. Born, Saskatoon, Sask., July 3, 1976. Quebec's 1st choice, 12th overall, in 1994 Entry Draft.

			Regular Season																Playoffs							
Season	Club	League	GP	G	A	Pts	PIM	PP	SH	GW	S	%	+/-	TF	F%	H	SB	Min	GP	G	A	Pts	PIM	PP	SH	GW
1991-92	North Battleford	SAHA	57	6	20	26	186	....	....	....	....	....	....	....	....	....	....	....	....	....	....	....	....	....	....	....
1992-93	North Battleford	SJHL	50	5	15	20	146	....	....	....	....	....	....	....	....	....	....	....	....	....	....	....	....	....	....	....
	Saskatoon Blades	WHL	7	0	0	0	23	....	....	....	....	....	....	....	....	....	....	....	7	0	0	0	0	....	....	....
1993-94	Saskatoon Blades	WHL	69	4	13	17	226	....	....	....	....	....	....	....	....	....	....	....	16	2	2	4	43	....	....	....
1994-95	Saskatoon Blades	WHL	72	4	14	18	290	....	....	....	....	....	....	....	....	....	....	....	9	0	0	0	36	....	....	....
	Cornwall Aces	AHL	....	....	....	....	....	....	....	....	....	....	....	....	....	....	....	....	11	1	2	3	40	....	....	....
1995-96	Saskatoon Blades	WHL	63	3	15	18	207	....	....	....	....	....	....	....	....	....	....	....	4	0	0	0	9	....	....	....
	Cornwall Aces	AHL	5	0	0	0	18	....	....	....	....	....	....	....	....	....	....	....	2	0	0	0	2	....	....	....
1996-97	**Colorado**	**NHL**	**5**	**0**	**0**	**0**	**11**	**0**	**0**	**0**	**1**	**0.0**	**–1**	....	....	....	....	....	....	....	....	....	....	....	....	....
	Hershey Bears	AHL	65	1	7	8	320	....	....	....	....	....	....	....	....	....	....	....	16	0	1	1	61	....	....	....
1997-98	**Colorado**	**NHL**	**8**	**1**	**1**	**2**	**27**	**0**	**0**	**1**	**2**	**50.0**	**–3**	....	....	....	....	....	....	....	....	....	....	....	....	....
	Hershey Bears	AHL	11	0	0	0	30	....	....	....	....	....	....	....	....	....	....	....	....	....	....	....	....	....	....	....
1998-99	**Colorado**	**NHL**	**22**	**0**	**0**	**0**	**71**	**0**	**0**	**0**	**5**	**0.0**	**–2**	**0**	**0.0**	**18**	**10**	**6:48**	....	....	....	....	....	....	....	....
	Hershey Bears	AHL	17	0	1	1	49	....	....	....	....	....	....	....	....	....	....	....	....	....	....	....	....	....	....	....
	Calgary	**NHL**	**9**	**0**	**1**	**1**	**23**	**0**	**0**	**0**	**2**	**0.0**	**3**	**0**	**0.0**	**9**	**7**	**10:46**	....	....	....	....	....	....	....	....
	Saint John Flames	AHL	12	0	2	2	43	....	....	....	....	....	....	....	....	....	....	....	6	0	1	1	23	....	....	....
99-2000	**Calgary**	**NHL**	**40**	**0**	**2**	**2**	**122**	**0**	**0**	**0**	**11**	**0.0**	**–4**	**1**	**0.0**	**41**	**23**	**7:33**	....	....	....	....	....	....	....	....
	NHL Totals		**84**	**1**	**4**	**5**	**254**	**0**	**0**	**1**	**21**	**4.8**		**1**	**0.0**	**68**	**40**	**7:44**	....	....	....	....	....	....	....	....

Rights transferred to **Colorado** after **Quebec** franchise relocated, June 21, 1995. Traded to **Calgary** by **Colorado** with Rene Corbet, Robyn Regehr and Colorado's 2nd round compensatory choice (Jarret Stoll) in 2000 Entry Draft for Theoren Fleury and Chris Dingman, February 28, 1999. • Missed majority of 1999-2000 season recovering from shoulder injury suffered in game vs. Colorado, February 10, 2000.

BELANGER, Jesse
(buh-LAWN-zhay, JEH-see) **NYI**

Center. Shoots right. 6'1", 190 lbs. Born, St. Georges de Beauce, Que., June 15, 1969.

			Regular Season																Playoffs							
Season	Club	League	GP	G	A	Pts	PIM	PP	SH	GW	S	%	+/-	TF	F%	H	SB	Min	GP	G	A	Pts	PIM	PP	SH	GW
1987-88	Granby Bisons	QMJHL	69	33	43	76	10	....	....	....	....	....	....	....	....	....	....	....	5	3	3	6	0	....	....	....
1988-89	Granby Bisons	QMJHL	67	40	63	103	26	....	....	....	....	....	....	....	....	....	....	....	4	0	5	5	0	....	....	....
1989-90	Granby Bisons	QMJHL	67	53	54	107	53	....	....	....	....	....	....	....	....	....	....	....	....	....	....	....	....	....	....	....
	Canada	Nat-Team	1	0	0	0	0	....	....	....	....	....	....	....	....	....	....	....	....	....	....	....	....	....	....	....
1990-91	Fredericton	AHL	75	40	58	98	30	....	....	....	....	....	....	....	....	....	....	....	6	2	4	6	0	....	....	....
1991-92	**Montreal**	**NHL**	**4**	**0**	**0**	**0**	**0**	**0**	**0**	**0**	**4**	**0.0**	**–1**	....	....	....	....	....	....	....	....	....	....	....	....	....
	Fredericton	AHL	65	30	41	71	26	....	....	....	....	....	....	....	....	....	....	....	7	3	3	6	2	....	....	....
1992-93♦	**Montreal**	**NHL**	**19**	**4**	**2**	**6**	**4**	**0**	**0**	**0**	**24**	**16.7**	**1**	....	....	....	....	....	**9**	**0**	**1**	**1**	**0**	**0**	**0**	**0**
	Fredericton	AHL	39	19	32	51	24	....	....	....	....	....	....	....	....	....	....	....	....	....	....	....	....	....	....	....
1993-94	**Florida**	**NHL**	**70**	**17**	**33**	**50**	**16**	**11**	**0**	**3**	**104**	**16.3**	**–4**	....	....	....	....	....	....	....	....	....	....	....	....	....
1994-95	**Florida**	**NHL**	**47**	**15**	**14**	**29**	**18**	**6**	**0**	**3**	**89**	**16.9**	**–5**	....	....	....	....	....	....	....	....	....	....	....	....	....
1995-96	**Florida**	**NHL**	**63**	**17**	**21**	**38**	**10**	**7**	**0**	**1**	**140**	**12.1**	**–5**	....	....	....	....	....	....	....	....	....	....	....	....	....
	Vancouver	**NHL**	**9**	**3**	**0**	**3**	**4**	**1**	**0**	**1**	**11**	**27.3**	**0**	....	....	....	....	....	**3**	**0**	**2**	**2**	**2**	**0**	**0**	**0**
1996-97	**Edmonton**	**NHL**	**6**	**0**	**0**	**0**	**0**	**0**	**0**	**0**	**8**	**0.0**	**–3**	....	....	....	....	....	....	....	....	....	....	....	....	....
	Hamilton Bulldogs	AHL	6	4	3	7	0	....	....	....	....	....	....	....	....	....	....	....	....	....	....	....	....	....	....	....
	Quebec Rafales	IHL	47	34	28	62	18	....	....	....	....	....	....	....	....	....	....	....	9	3	5	8	13	....	....	....
1997-98	SC Herisau	Switz.	5	4	3	7	4	....	....	....	....	....	....	....	....	....	....	....	....	....	....	....	....	....	....	....
	Las Vegas	IHL	54	32	36	68	20	....	....	....	....	....	....	....	....	....	....	....	4	0	1	1	0	....	....	....
1998-99	Cleveland	IHL	22	9	13	22	10	....	....	....	....	....	....	....	....	....	....	....	....	....	....	....	....	....	....	....
99-2000	**Montreal**	**NHL**	**16**	**3**	**6**	**9**	**2**	**0**	**0**	**0**	**21**	**14.3**	**2**	**177**	**49.1**	**14**	**4**	**10:41**	....	....	....	....	....	....	....	....
	Quebec Citadelles	AHL	36	15	18	33	20	....	....	....	....	....	....	....	....	....	....	....	3	0	3	3	4	....	....	....
	NHL Totals		**234**	**59**	**76**	**135**	**54**	**25**	**0**	**8**	**401**	**14.7**		**177**	**49.2**	**14**	**4**	**10:41**	**12**	**0**	**3**	**3**	**2**	**0**	**0**	**0**

Signed as a free agent by **Montreal**, October 3, 1990. Claimed by **Florida** from **Montreal** in Expansion Draft, June 24, 1993. Traded to **Vancouver** by **Florida** for Vancouver's 3rd round choice (Oleg Kvasha) in 1996 Entry Draft and future considerations, March 20, 1996. Signed as a free agent by **Edmonton**, September 16, 1996. Signed as a free agent by **Tampa Bay**, August 18, 1998. Signed as a free agent by **Montreal**, July 23, 1999. Signed as a free agent by **NY Islanders**, July 27, 2000.

BELANGER, Ken
(buh-LAWN-zhay, KEHN) **BOS.**

Left wing. Shoots left. 6'4", 225 lbs. Born, Sault Ste. Marie, Ont., May 14, 1974. Hartford's 7th choice, 153rd overall, in 1992 Entry Draft.

			Regular Season																Playoffs							
Season	Club	League	GP	G	A	Pts	PIM	PP	SH	GW	S	%	+/-	TF	F%	H	SB	Min	GP	G	A	Pts	PIM	PP	SH	GW
1990-91	S.S. Marie Legion	NOHA	43	24	29	53	169	....	....	....	....	....	....	....	....	....	....	....	....	....	....	....	....	....	....	....
1991-92	Ottawa 67's	OHL	51	4	4	8	174	....	....	....	....	....	....	....	....	....	....	....	11	0	0	0	24	....	....	....
1992-93	Ottawa 67's	OHL	34	6	12	18	139	....	....	....	....	....	....	....	....	....	....	....	....	....	....	....	....	....	....	....
	Guelph Storm	OHL	29	10	14	24	86	....	....	....	....	....	....	....	....	....	....	....	5	2	1	3	14	....	....	....
1993-94	Guelph Storm	OHL	55	11	22	33	185	....	....	....	....	....	....	....	....	....	....	....	9	2	3	5	30	....	....	....
1994-95	St. John's Leafs	AHL	47	5	5	10	246	....	....	....	....	....	....	....	....	....	....	....	4	0	0	0	30	....	....	....
	Toronto	**NHL**	**3**	**0**	**0**	**0**	**9**	**0**	**0**	**0**	**1**	**0.0**	**0**	....	....	....	....	....	....	....	....	....	....	....	....	....
1995-96	St. John's Leafs	AHL	40	16	14	30	222	....	....	....	....	....	....	....	....	....	....	....	....	....	....	....	....	....	....	....
	NY Islanders	**NHL**	**7**	**0**	**0**	**0**	**27**	**0**	**0**	**0**	**0**	**0.0**	**–2**	....	....	....	....	....	....	....	....	....	....	....	....	....
1996-97	**NY Islanders**	**NHL**	**18**	**0**	**2**	**2**	**102**	**0**	**0**	**0**	**5**	**0.0**	**–1**	....	....	....	....	....	....	....	....	....	....	....	....	....
	Kentucky	AHL	38	10	12	22	164	....	....	....	....	....	....	....	....	....	....	....	4	0	1	1	27	....	....	....
1997-98	**NY Islanders**	**NHL**	**37**	**3**	**1**	**4**	**101**	**0**	**0**	**1**	**10**	**30.0**	**1**	....	....	....	....	....	....	....	....	....	....	....	....	....
1998-99	**NY Islanders**	**NHL**	**9**	**1**	**1**	**2**	**30**	**0**	**0**	**0**	**3**	**33.3**	**1**	**0**	**0.0**	**15**	**1**	**5:05**	....	....	....	....	....	....	....	....
	Boston	**NHL**	**45**	**1**	**4**	**5**	**152**	**0**	**0**	**0**	**16**	**6.3**	**–2**	**1**	**0.0**	**66**	**4**	**4:38**	**12**	**1**	**0**	**1**	**16**	**0**	**0**	**0**
99-2000	**Boston**	**NHL**	**37**	**2**	**2**	**4**	**44**	**0**	**0**	**0**	**20**	**10.0**	**–4**	**1**	**0.0**	**79**	**4**	**5:17**	....	....	....	....	....	....	....	....
	NHL Totals		**156**	**7**	**10**	**17**	**465**	**0**	**0**	**1**	**55**	**12.7**		**2**	**0.0**	**160**	**9**	**4:57**	**12**	**1**	**0**	**1**	**16**	**0**	**0**	**0**

Traded to **Toronto** by **Hartford** for Toronto's 9th round choice (Matt Ball) in 1994 Entry Draft, March 18, 1994. Traded to **NY Islanders** by **Toronto** with Damian Rhodes for future considerations (Kirk Muller and Don Beaupre, January 23, 1996), January 23, 1996. Traded to **Boston** by **NY Islanders** for Ted Donato, November 7, 1998. • Missed majority of 1999-2000 season recovering from head injury suffered in game vs. Toronto, November 11, 1999.

BENDA, Jan (BEHN-duh, YAHN)

Center. Shoots right. 6'2", 208 lbs. Born, Reef, Belgium, March 28, 1972.

			Regular Season																Playoffs							
Season	Club	League	GP	G	A	Pts	PIM	PP	SH	GW	S	%	+/-	TF	F%	H	SB	Min	GP	G	A	Pts	PIM	PP	SH	GW
1988-89	Henry Carr	OJHL-B	18	0	3	3	22	....	....	....	....	....	....	....	....	....	....	....	....	....	....	....	....	....	....	....
1989-90	Oshawa Legion	OJHL-B	44	50	80	130	24	....	....	....	....	....	....	....	....	....	....	....	....	....	....	....	....	....	....	....
	Oshawa Generals	OHL	1	0	1	1	0	....	....	....	....	....	....	....	....	....	....	....	....	....	....	....	....	....	....	....
1990-91	Oshawa Generals	OHL	51	4	11	15	64	....	....	....	....	....	....	....	....	....	....	....	16	2	4	6	19	....	....	....
	Grefrather EC	DEB-3	13	0	0	0	2	....	....	....	....	....	....	....	....	....	....	....	....	....	....	....	....	....	....	....
1991-92	Oshawa Generals	OHL	61	12	23	35	68	....	....	....	....	....	....	....	....	....	....	....	7	1	1	2	12	....	....	....
1992-93	EHC Freiburg	DEL	41	6	11	17	49	....	....	....	....	....	....	....	....	....	....	....	9	3	3	6	12	....	....	....
1993-94	ECH Munich	DEL	43	16	11	27	67	....	....	....	....	....	....	....	....	....	....	....	10	3	2	5	21	....	....	....
	Germany	Olympics	8	0	1	1	6	....	....	....	....	....	....	....	....	....	....	....	....	....	....	....	....	....	....	....
1994-95	Binghamton	AHL	4	0	0	0	0	....	....	....	....	....	....	....	....	....	....	....	....	....	....	....	....	....	....	....
	Richmond	ECHL	62	21	39	60	187	....	....	....	....	....	....	....	....	....	....	....	17	8	5	13	50	....	....	....
1995-96	ESC Essen-West	DEB-2	2	1	0	1	6	....	....	....	....	....	....	....	....	....	....	....	....	....	....	....	....	....	....	....
	Slavia Praha	Cze-Rep	28	8	11	19	....	....	....	....	....	....	....	....	....	....	....	....	7	1	5	6	....	....	....	....
1996-97	Sparta Praha	Cze-Rep	49	7	21	28	61	....	....	....	....	....	....	....	....	....	....	....	10	1	1	2	12	....	....	....
	Sparta Praha	EuroHL	5	1	0	1	4	....	....	....	....	....	....	....	....	....	....	....	4	0	1	1	2	....	....	....
1997-98	Sparta Praha	Cze-Rep	1	0	1	1	4	....	....	....	....	....	....	....	....	....	....	....	....	....	....	....	....	....	....	....
	Washington	**NHL**	**9**	**0**	**3**	**3**	**6**	....	....	....	....	....	....	....	....	....	....	....	....	....	....	....	....	....	....	....
	Portland Pirates	AHL	62	25	29	54	90	....	....	....	....	....	....	....	....	....	....	....	8	0	7	7	6	....	....	....
	Germany	Olympics	4	3	0	3	8	....	....	....	....	....	....	....	....	....	....	....	....	....	....	....	....	....	....	....
1998-99	Assat-Pori	Finland	52	21	22	43	139	....	....	....	....	....	....	....	....	....	....	....	....	....	....	....	....	....	....	....
99-2000	Jokerit Helsinki	Finland	52	19	28	47	99	....	....	....	....	....	....	....	....	....	....	....	11	2	4	6	16	....	....	....
	NHL Totals		**9**	**0**	**3**	**3**	**6**	....	....	....	....	....	....	....	....	....	....	....	....	....	....	....	....	....	....	....

Signed as a free agent by **Washington**, October 1, 1997.

BENYSEK, Ladislav (BEHN-ih-sihk, LAD-ihs-SLAHV) MIN.

Defense. Shoots left. 6'2", 190 lbs. Born, Olomouc, Czech., March 24, 1975. Edmonton's 16th choice, 266th overall, in 1994 Entry Draft.

			Regular Season																Playoffs							
Season	Club	League	GP	G	A	Pts	PIM	PP	SH	GW	S	%	+/-	TF	F%	H	SB	Min	GP	G	A	Pts	PIM	PP	SH	GW
1994-95	Cape Breton	AHL	58	2	7	9	54	....	....	....	....	....	....	....	....	....	....	....	....	....	....	....	....	....	....	....
1995-96	HC Olomouc	Cze-Rep	33	1	4	5	....	....	....	....	....	....	....	....	....	....	....	....	4	0	0	0	....	....	....	....
1996-97	HC Olomouc	Cze-Rep	14	0	1	1	8	....	....	....	....	....	....	....	....	....	....	....	....	....	....	....	....	....	....	....
	Sparta Praha	Cze-Rep	36	5	5	10	28	....	....	....	....	....	....	....	....	....	....	....	5	0	1	1	2	....	....	....
	Sparta Praha	EuroHL	3	0	0	0	4	....	....	....	....	....	....	....	....	....	....	....	4	0	0	0	0	....	....	....
1997-98	Sparta Praha	Cze-Rep	1	0	0	0	0	....	....	....	....	....	....	....	....	....	....	....	....	....	....	....	....	....	....	....
	Edmonton	**NHL**	**2**	**0**	**0**	**0**	**0**	....	....	....	....	....	....	....	....	....	....	....	....	....	....	....	....	....	....	....
	Hamilton Bulldogs	AHL	53	2	14	16	29	....	....	....	....	....	....	....	....	....	....	....	9	1	1	2	2	....	....	....
1998-99	Sparta Praha	Cze-Rep	52	8	11	19	47	....	....	....	....	....	....	....	....	....	....	....	8	0	1	1	....	....	....	....
	Sparta Praha	EuroHL	7	0	0	0	2	....	....	....	....	....	....	....	....	....	....	....	2	0	0	0	0	....	....	....
99-2000	Sparta Praha	Cze-Rep	51	1	5	6	45	....	....	....	....	....	....	....	....	....	....	....	9	0	0	0	4	....	....	....
	Sparta Praha	EuroHL	5	1	1	2	6	....	....	....	....	....	....	....	....	....	....	....	4	0	0	0	4	....	....	....
	NHL Totals		**2**	**0**	**0**	**0**	**0**	....	....	....	....	....	....	....	....	....	....	....	....	....	....	....	....	....	....	....

Claimed by **Anaheim** from **Edmonton** in NHL Waiver Draft, September 30, 1999. Selected by **Minnesota** from **Anaheim** in Expansion Draft, June 23, 2000.

BERANEK, Josef (buh-RAH-nehk, JOH-sehf) PIT.

Left wing/Center. Shoots left. 6'2", 195 lbs. Born, Litvinov, Czech., October 25, 1969. Edmonton's 3rd choice, 78th overall, in 1989 Entry Draft.

			Regular Season																Playoffs							
Season	Club	League	GP	G	A	Pts	PIM	PP	SH	GW	S	%	+/-	TF	F%	H	SB	Min	GP	G	A	Pts	PIM	PP	SH	GW
1987-88	CHZ Litvinov	Czech.	14	7	4	11	12	....	....	....	....	....	....	....	....	....	....	....	....	....	....	....	....	....	....	....
1988-89	CHZ Litvinov	Czech.	32	18	10	28	47	....	....	....	....	....	....	....	....	....	....	....	....	....	....	....	....	....	....	....
1989-90	Dukla Trencin	Czech.	40	16	21	37	....	....	....	....	....	....	....	....	....	....	....	....	9	3	2	5	....	....	....	....
1990-91	CHZ Litvinov	Czech.	58	29	31	60	98	....	....	....	....	....	....	....	....	....	....	....	....	....	....	....	....	....	....	....
1991-92	**Edmonton**	**NHL**	**58**	**12**	**16**	**28**	**18**	**0**	**0**	**1**	**79**	**15.2**	**–2**	....	....	....	....	....	**12**	**2**	**1**	**3**	**0**	**1**	**0**	**1**
1992-93	**Edmonton**	**NHL**	**26**	**2**	**6**	**8**	**28**	**0**	**0**	**0**	**44**	**4.5**	**–7**	....	....	....	....	....	....	....	....	....	....	....	....	....
	Cape Breton	AHL	6	1	2	3	8	....	....	....	....	....	....	....	....	....	....	....	....	....	....	....	....	....	....	....
	Philadelphia	**NHL**	**40**	**13**	**12**	**25**	**50**	**1**	**0**	**0**	**86**	**15.1**	**–1**	....	....	....	....	....	....	....	....	....	....	....	....	....
1993-94	**Philadelphia**	**NHL**	**80**	**28**	**21**	**49**	**85**	**6**	**0**	**2**	**182**	**15.4**	**–2**	....	....	....	....	....	....	....	....	....	....	....	....	....
1994-95	Petra Vsetin	Cze-Rep	16	7	7	14	26	....	....	....	....	....	....	....	....	....	....	....	....	....	....	....	....	....	....	....
	Philadelphia	**NHL**	**14**	**5**	**5**	**10**	**2**	**1**	**0**	**0**	**39**	**12.8**	**3**	....	....	....	....	....	....	....	....	....	....	....	....	....
	Vancouver	**NHL**	**37**	**8**	**13**	**21**	**28**	**2**	**0**	**0**	**95**	**8.4**	**–10**	....	....	....	....	....	**11**	**1**	**1**	**2**	**12**	**0**	**0**	**0**
1995-96	**Vancouver**	**NHL**	**61**	**6**	**14**	**20**	**60**	**0**	**0**	**1**	**131**	**4.6**	**–11**	....	....	....	....	....	**3**	**2**	**1**	**3**	**0**	**0**	**0**	**0**
1996-97	Petra Vsetin	Cze-Rep	39	19	24	43	115	....	....	....	....	....	....	....	....	....	....	....	3	3	2	5	4	....	....	....
	Pittsburgh	**NHL**	**8**	**3**	**1**	**4**	**4**	**1**	**0**	**0**	**15**	**20.0**	**–1**	....	....	....	....	....	**5**	**0**	**0**	**0**	**2**	**0**	**0**	**0**
1997-98	Petra Vsetin	Cze-Rep	45	24	27	51	92	....	....	....	....	....	....	....	....	....	....	....	10	2	8	10	14	....	....	....
	Petra Vsetin	EuroHL	8	5	4	9	10	....	....	....	....	....	....	....	....	....	....	....	....	....	....	....	....	....	....	....
	Czech-Republic	Olympics	6	1	0	1	4	....	....	....	....	....	....	....	....	....	....	....	....	....	....	....	....	....	....	....
1998-99	**Edmonton**	**NHL**	**66**	**19**	**30**	**49**	**23**	**7**	**0**	**2**	**160**	**11.9**	**6**	**1261**	**50.2**	**47**	**21**	**16:25**	**2**	**0**	**0**	**0**	**4**	**0**	**0**	**0**
99-2000	**Edmonton**	**NHL**	**58**	**9**	**8**	**17**	**39**	**3**	**0**	**1**	**107**	**8.4**	**–6**	**558**	**53.4**	**42**	**6**	**13:19**	....	....	....	....	....	....	....	....
	Pittsburgh	**NHL**	**13**	**4**	**4**	**8**	**18**	**1**	**0**	**0**	**32**	**12.5**	**–6**	**73**	**42.5**	**13**	**4**	**19:46**	**11**	**0**	**3**	**3**	**4**	**0**	**0**	**0**
	NHL Totals		**461**	**109**	**130**	**239**	**355**	**22**	**0**	**7**	**970**	**11.2**		**1892**	**50.8**	**102**	**31**	**15:25**	**44**	**5**	**6**	**11**	**22**	**1**	**0**	**1**

Traded to **Philadelphia** by **Edmonton** with Greg Hawgood for Brian Benning, January 16, 1993. Traded to **Vancouver** by **Philadelphia** for Shawn Antoski, February 15, 1995. Traded to **Pittsburgh** by **Vancouver** for future considerations, March 18, 1997. Traded to **Edmonton** by **Pittsburgh** for Bobby Dollas and Tony Hrkac, June 16, 1998. Traded to **Pittsburgh** by **Edmonton** for German Titov, March 14, 2000.

BERARD, Bryan (buh-RAHRD, BRIGH-an) TOR.

Defense. Shoots left. 6'1", 195 lbs. Born, Woonsocket, RI, March 5, 1977. Ottawa's 1st choice, 1st overall, in 1995 Entry Draft.

			Regular Season																Playoffs							
Season	Club	League	GP	G	A	Pts	PIM	PP	SH	GW	S	%	+/-	TF	F%	H	SB	Min	GP	G	A	Pts	PIM	PP	SH	GW
1991-92	Mount St. Charles	Hi-School	15	3	15	18	4	....	....	....	....	....	....	....	....	....	....	....	....	....	....	....	....	....	....	....
1992-93	Mount St. Charles	Hi-School	15	8	12	20	18	....	....	....	....	....	....	....	....	....	....	....	....	....	....	....	....	....	....	....
1993-94	Mount St. Charles	Hi-School	15	11	26	37	4.5	....	....	....	....	....	....	....	....	....	....	....	4	3	3	6	6	....	....	....
1994-95	Detroit Jr. Wings	OHL	58	20	55	75	97	....	....	....	....	....	....	....	....	....	....	....	21	4	20	24	38	....	....	....
1995-96	Detroit Whalers	OHL	56	31	58	89	116	....	....	....	....	....	....	....	....	....	....	....	17	7	18	25	41	....	....	....
1996-97	**NY Islanders**	**NHL**	**82**	**8**	**40**	**48**	**86**	**3**	**0**	**1**	**172**	**4.7**	**1**	....	....	....	....	....	....	....	....	....	....	....	....	....
1997-98	**NY Islanders**	**NHL**	**75**	**14**	**32**	**46**	**59**	**8**	**1**	**2**	**192**	**7.3**	**–32**	....	....	....	....	....	....	....	....	....	....	....	....	....
	United States	Olympics	2	0	0	0	0	....	....	....	....	....	....	....	....	....	....	....	....	....	....	....	....	....	....	....
1998-99	**NY Islanders**	**NHL**	**31**	**4**	**11**	**15**	**26**	**2**	**0**	**3**	**72**	**5.6**	**–6**	**0**	**0.0**	**16**	**32**	**24:45**	....	....	....	....	....	....	....	....
	Toronto	**NHL**	**38**	**5**	**14**	**19**	**22**	**2**	**0**	**2**	**63**	**7.9**	**7**	**0**	**0.0**	**34**	**42**	**22:38**	**17**	**1**	**8**	**9**	**8**	**1**	**0**	**0**
99-2000	**Toronto**	**NHL**	**64**	**3**	**27**	**30**	**42**	**1**	**0**	**0**	**98**	**3.1**	**11**	**0**	**0.0**	**64**	**58**	**19:34**	....	....	....	....	....	....	....	....
	NHL Totals		**290**	**34**	**124**	**158**	**235**	**16**	**1**	**8**	**597**	**5.7**		**0**	**0.0**	**114**	**132**	**21:39**	**17**	**1**	**8**	**9**	**8**	**1**	**0**	**0**

OHL First All-Star Team (1995, 1996) • Canadian Major Junior First All-Star Team (1995, 1996) • Canadian Major Junior Rookie of the Year (1995) • Canadian Major Junior Defenseman of the Year (1996) • NHL All-Rookie Team (1997) • Won Calder Memorial Trophy (1997)

Traded to **NY Islanders** by **Ottawa** with Don Beaupre and Martin Straka for Damian Rhodes and Wade Redden, January 23, 1996. Traded to **Toronto** by **NY Islanders** with NY Islanders' 6th round choice (Jan Socher) in 1999 Entry Draft for Felix Potvin and Toronto's 6th round choice (later traded to Tampa Bay - Tampa Bay selected Fedor Fedorov) in 1999 Entry Draft, January 9, 1999. • Suffered season-ending eye injury in game vs. Ottawa, March 11, 2000.

BEREHOWSKY, Drake (beh-reh-HOW-skee, DRAYK) NSH.

Defense. Shoots right. 6'2", 225 lbs. Born, Toronto, Ont., January 3, 1972. Toronto's 1st choice, 10th overall, in 1990 Entry Draft.

			Regular Season																Playoffs							
Season	Club	League	GP	G	A	Pts	PIM	PP	SH	GW	S	%	+/-	TF	F%	H	SB	Min	GP	G	A	Pts	PIM	PP	SH	GW
1987-88	Barrie Colts	OJHL-B	40	10	36	46	81	....	....	....	....	....	....	....	....	....	....	....	....	....	....	....	....	....	....	....
1988-89	Kingston Raiders	OHL	63	7	39	46	85	....	....	....	....	....	....	....	....	....	....	....	....	....	....	....	....	....	....	....
	Canada	Nat-Team	1	0	0	0	0	....	....	....	....	....	....	....	....	....	....	....	....	....	....	....	....	....	....	....
1989-90	Kingston	OHL	9	3	11	14	28	....	....	....	....	....	....	....	....	....	....	....	....	....	....	....	....	....	....	....
1990-91	Kingston	OHL	13	5	13	18	38	....	....	....	....	....	....	....	....	....	....	....	....	....	....	....	....	....	....	....
	North Bay	OHL	26	7	23	30	51	....	....	....	....	....	....	....	....	....	....	....	10	2	7	9	21	....	....	....
	Toronto	**NHL**	**8**	**0**	**1**	**1**	**25**	**0**	**0**	**0**	**4**	**0.0**	**–6**	....	....	....	....	....	....	....	....	....	....	....	....	....

			Regular Season																Playoffs							
Season	Club	League	GP	G	A	Pts	PIM	PP	SH	GW	S	%	+/-	TF	F%	H	SB	Min	GP	G	A	Pts	PIM	PP	SH	GW
1991-92	North Bay	OHL	62	19	63	82	147	....	....	....	....	....	....	....	....	....	....	....	21	7	24	31	22	....	....	....
	Toronto	**NHL**	**1**	**0**	**0**	**0**	**0**	**0**	**0**	**0**	**0**	**0.0**	**0**	....	....	....	....	....	....	....	....	....	....	....	....	....
	St. John's Leafs	AHL	....	....	....	....	....	....	....	....	....	....	....	....	....	....	....	....	6	0	5	5	21	....	....	....
1992-93	**Toronto**	**NHL**	**41**	**4**	**15**	**19**	**61**	**1**	**0**	**1**	**41**	**9.8**	**1**	....	....	....	....	....	....	....	....	....	....	....	....	....
	St. John's Leafs	AHL	28	10	17	27	38	....	....	....	....	....	....	....	....	....	....	....	....	....	....	....	....	....	....	....
1993-94	**Toronto**	**NHL**	**49**	**2**	**8**	**10**	**63**	**2**	**0**	**2**	**29**	**6.9**	**-3**	....	....	....	....	....	....	....	....	....	....	....	....	....
	St. John's Leafs	AHL	18	3	12	15	40	....	....	....	....	....	....	....	....	....	....	....	....	....	....	....	....	....	....	....
1994-95	**Toronto**	**NHL**	**25**	**0**	**2**	**2**	**15**	**0**	**0**	**0**	**12**	**0.0**	**-10**	....	....	....	....	....	....	....	....	....	....	....	....	....
	Pittsburgh	**NHL**	**4**	**0**	**0**	**0**	**13**	**0**	**0**	**0**	**2**	**0.0**	**1**	....	....	....	....	....	**1**	**0**	**0**	**0**	**0**	**0**	**0**	**0**
1995-96	**Pittsburgh**	**NHL**	**1**	**0**	**0**	**0**	**0**	**0**	**0**	**0**	**0**	**0.0**	**1**	....	....	....	....	....	....	....	....	....	....	....	....	....
	Cleveland	IHL	74	6	28	34	141	....	....	....	....	....	....	....	....	....	....	....	3	0	3	3	6	....	....	....
1996-97	Carolina	AHL	49	2	15	17	55	....	....	....	....	....	....	....	....	....	....	....	....	....	....	....	....	....	....	....
	San Antonio	IHL	16	3	4	7	36	....	....	....	....	....	....	....	....	....	....	....	....	....	....	....	....	....	....	....
1997-98	**Edmonton**	**NHL**	**67**	**1**	**6**	**7**	**169**	**1**	**0**	**1**	**58**	**1.7**	**1**	....	....	....	....	....	**12**	**1**	**2**	**3**	**14**	**0**	**0**	**1**
	Hamilton Bulldogs	AHL	8	2	0	2	21	....	....	....	....	....	....	....	....	....	....	....	....	....	....	....	....	....	....	....
1998-99	**Nashville**	**NHL**	**74**	**2**	**15**	**17**	**140**	**0**	**0**	**0**	**79**	**2.5**	**-9**	**1**	**100.0**	**140**	**109**	**21:43**	....	....	....	....	....	....	....	....
99-2000	**Nashville**	**NHL**	**79**	**12**	**20**	**32**	**87**	**5**	**0**	**1**	**102**	**11.8**	**-4**	**0**	**0.0**	**140**	**110**	**22:39**	....	....	....	....	....	....	....	....
	NHL Totals		**349**	**21**	**67**	**88**	**573**	**9**	**0**	**5**	**327**	**6.4**		**1**	**100.0**	**280**	**219**	**22:12**	**13**	**1**	**2**	**3**	**14**	**0**	**0**	**1**

OHL First All-Star Team (1992) • Canadian Major Junior Defenseman of the Year (1992)

• Missed majority of 1989-90 season recovering from knee injury suffered in game vs. Chicago, October 12, 1989. Traded to **Pittsburgh** by **Toronto** for Grant Jennings, April 7, 1995. Signed as a free agent by **Edmonton**, September 30, 1997. Traded to **Nashville** by **Edmonton** with Eric Fichaud and Greg de Vries for Mikhail Shtalenkov and Jim Dowd, October 1, 1998.

BERENZWEIG, Bubba (BAIR-ehn-zwihg) NSH.

Defense. Shoots left. 6'1", 215 lbs. Born, Arlington Heights, IL, August 8, 1977. NY Islanders' 5th choice, 109th overall, in 1996 Entry Draft.

Season	Club	League	GP	G	A	Pts	PIM	PP	SH	GW	S	%	+/-	TF	F%	H	SB	Min	GP	G	A	Pts	PIM	PP	SH	GW
1992-93	Loomis-Chaffee	Hi-School	22	5	13	18	....	....	....	....	....	....	....	....	....	....	....	....	....	....	....	....	....	....	....	....
1993-94	Loomis-Chaffee	Hi-School	22	12	27	39	....	....	....	....	....	....	....	....	....	....	....	....	....	....	....	....	....	....	....	....
1994-95	Loomis-Chaffee	Hi-School	23	19	23	42	10	....	....	....	....	....	....	....	....	....	....	....	....	....	....	....	....	....	....	....
1995-96	U. of Michigan	CCHA	42	4	8	12	4	....	....	....	....	....	....	....	....	....	....	....	....	....	....	....	....	....	....	....
1996-97	U. of Michigan	CCHA	38	7	12	19	49	....	....	....	....	....	....	....	....	....	....	....	....	....	....	....	....	....	....	....
1997-98	U. of Michigan	CCHA	45	8	11	19	32	....	....	....	....	....	....	....	....	....	....	....	....	....	....	....	....	....	....	....
1998-99	U. of Michigan	CCHA	42	7	24	31	38	....	....	....	....	....	....	....	....	....	....	....	....	....	....	....	....	....	....	....
99-2000	**Nashville**	**NHL**	**2**	**0**	**0**	**0**	**0**	**0**	**0**	**0**	**3**	**0.0**	**-1**	**0**	**0.0**	**5**	**4**	**17:31**	....	....	....	....	....	....	....	....
	Milwaukee	IHL	79	4	23	27	48	....	....	....	....	....	....	....	....	....	....	....	3	1	2	3	0	....	....	....
	NHL Totals		**2**	**0**	**0**	**0**	**0**	**0**	**0**	**0**	**3**	**0.0**		**0**	**0.0**	**5**	**4**	**17:31**	....	....	....	....	....	....	....	....

CCHA Second All-Star Team (1998) • NCAA Championship All-Tournament Team (1998)

Traded to **Nashville** by **NY Islanders** for Nashville's 4th round choice (Johan Halvardsson) in 1999 Entry Draft, April 14, 1999.

BEREZIN, Sergei (BEH-reh-zihn, SAIR-gay) TOR.

Left wing. Shoots right. 5'10", 200 lbs. Born, Voskresensk, USSR, November 5, 1971. Toronto's 8th choice, 256th overall, in 1994 Entry Draft.

Season	Club	League	GP	G	A	Pts	PIM	PP	SH	GW	S	%	+/-	TF	F%	H	SB	Min	GP	G	A	Pts	PIM	PP	SH	GW
1990-91	HK Khimik	USSR	30	6	2	8	4	....	....	....	....	....	....	....	....	....	....	....	....	....	....	....	....	....	....	....
1991-92	HK Khimik	CIS	36	7	5	12	10	....	....	....	....	....	....	....	....	....	....	....	....	....	....	....	....	....	....	....
1992-93	HK Khimik	CIS	38	9	3	12	12	....	....	....	....	....	....	....	....	....	....	....	2	1	0	1	0	....	....	....
1993-94	HK Khimik	CIS	40	31	10	41	16	....	....	....	....	....	....	....	....	....	....	....	3	2	0	2	2	....	....	....
	Russia	Olympics	8	3	2	5	2	....	....	....	....	....	....	....	....	....	....	....	....	....	....	....	....	....	....	....
1994-95	Kolner Haie	DEL	43	*38	19	57	8	....	....	....	....	....	....	....	....	....	....	....	18	*17	8	25	14	....	....	....
1995-96	Kolner Haie	DEL	45	*49	31	80	8	....	....	....	....	....	....	....	....	....	....	....	14	*13	9	22	10	....	....	....
1996-97	**Toronto**	**NHL**	**73**	**25**	**16**	**41**	**2**	**7**	**0**	**2**	**177**	**14.1**	**-3**	....	....	....	....	....	....	....	....	....	....	....	....	....
1997-98	**Toronto**	**NHL**	**68**	**16**	**15**	**31**	**10**	**3**	**0**	**3**	**167**	**9.6**	**-3**	....	....	....	....	....	....	....	....	....	....	....	....	....
1998-99	**Toronto**	**NHL**	**76**	**37**	**22**	**59**	**12**	**9**	**1**	**4**	**263**	**14.1**	**16**	**26**	**57.7**	**24**	**11**	**15:32**	**17**	**6**	**6**	**12**	**4**	**2**	**0**	**2**
99-2000	**Toronto**	**NHL**	**61**	**26**	**13**	**39**	**2**	**5**	**0**	**4**	**241**	**10.8**	**8**	**11**	**45.5**	**18**	**9**	**16:52**	**12**	**4**	**4**	**8**	**0**	**0**	**0**	**1**
	NHL Totals		**278**	**104**	**66**	**170**	**26**	**24**	**1**	**13**	**848**	**12.3**		**37**	**54.1**	**42**	**20**	**16:08**	**29**	**10**	**10**	**20**	**4**	**2**	**0**	**3**

NHL All-Rookie Team (1997)

BERG, Aki (BUHRG, AH-kee) L.A.

Defense. Shoots left. 6'3", 215 lbs. Born, Turku, Finland, July 28, 1977. Los Angeles' 1st choice, 3rd overall, in 1995 Entry Draft.

Season	Club	League	GP	G	A	Pts	PIM	PP	SH	GW	S	%	+/-	TF	F%	H	SB	Min	GP	G	A	Pts	PIM	PP	SH	GW
1992-93	TPS Turku	Finn-Jr.	39	18	24	42	24	....	....	....	....	....	....	....	....	....	....	....	....	....	....	....	....	....	....	....
1993-94	TPS Turku	Finn-Jr.	21	3	11	14	24	....	....	....	....	....	....	....	....	....	....	....	7	0	0	0	10	....	....	....
	Kiekko-67 Turku	Finland-2	12	1	1	2	16	....	....	....	....	....	....	....	....	....	....	....	....	....	....	....	....	....	....	....
	TPS Turku	Finland	6	0	3	3	4	....	....	....	....	....	....	....	....	....	....	....	....	....	....	....	....	....	....	....
1994-95	TPS Turku	Finn-Jr.	8	1	0	1	30	....	....	....	....	....	....	....	....	....	....	....	....	....	....	....	....	....	....	....
	Kiekko-67 Turku	Finland-2	21	3	9	12	24	....	....	....	....	....	....	....	....	....	....	....	7	0	0	0	10	....	....	....
	TPS Turku	Finland	5	0	0	0	4	....	....	....	....	....	....	....	....	....	....	....	....	....	....	....	....	....	....	....
1995-96	**Los Angeles**	**NHL**	**51**	**0**	**7**	**7**	**29**	**0**	**0**	**0**	**56**	**0.0**	**-13**	....	....	....	....	....	....	....	....	....	....	....	....	....
	Phoenix	IHL	20	0	3	3	18	....	....	....	....	....	....	....	....	....	....	....	2	0	0	0	4	....	....	....
1996-97	**Los Angeles**	**NHL**	**41**	**2**	**6**	**8**	**24**	**2**	**0**	**0**	**65**	**3.1**	**-9**	....	....	....	....	....	....	....	....	....	....	....	....	....
	Phoenix	IHL	23	1	3	4	21	....	....	....	....	....	....	....	....	....	....	....	....	....	....	....	....	....	....	....
1997-98	**Los Angeles**	**NHL**	**72**	**0**	**8**	**8**	**61**	**0**	**0**	**0**	**58**	**0.0**	**3**	....	....	....	....	....	**4**	**0**	**3**	**3**	**0**	**0**	**0**	**0**
	Finland	Olympics	6	0	0	0	6	....	....	....	....	....	....	....	....	....	....	....	....	....	....	....	....	....	....	....
1998-99	TPS Turku	Finland	48	8	7	15	137	....	....	....	....	....	....	....	....	....	....	....	9	1	1	2	45	....	....	....
99-2000	**Los Angeles**	**NHL**	**70**	**3**	**13**	**16**	**45**	**0**	**0**	**0**	**70**	**4.3**	**-1**	**0**	**0.0**	**197**	**83**	**16:39**	**2**	**0**	**0**	**0**	**2**	**0**	**0**	**0**
	NHL Totals		**234**	**5**	**34**	**39**	**159**	**2**	**0**	**0**	**249**	**2.0**		**0**	**0.0**	**197**	**83**	**16:39**	**6**	**0**	**3**	**3**	**2**	**0**	**0**	**0**

BERGEVIN, Marc (BUHR-zheh-vihn, MAHRK) ST.L.

Defense. Shoots left. 6'1", 214 lbs. Born, Montreal, Que., August 11, 1965. Chicago's 3rd choice, 60th overall, in 1983 Entry Draft.

Season	Club	League	GP	G	A	Pts	PIM	PP	SH	GW	S	%	+/-	TF	F%	H	SB	Min	GP	G	A	Pts	PIM	PP	SH	GW
1981-82	Mtl-Concordia	QAAA	44	10	20	30	....	....	....	....	....	....	....	....	....	....	....	....	....	....	....	....	....	....	....	....
1982-83	Chicoutimi	QMJHL	64	3	27	30	113	....	....	....	....	....	....	....	....	....	....	....	....	....	....	....	....	....	....	....
1983-84	Chicoutimi	QMJHL	70	10	35	45	125	....	....	....	....	....	....	....	....	....	....	....	....	....	....	....	....	....	....	....
	Springfield	AHL	7	0	1	1	2	....	....	....	....	....	....	....	....	....	....	....	....	....	....	....	....	....	....	....
1984-85	**Chicago**	**NHL**	**60**	**0**	**6**	**6**	**54**	**0**	**0**	**0**	**41**	**0.0**	**-9**	....	....	....	....	....	**6**	**0**	**3**	**3**	**2**	**0**	**0**	**0**
	Springfield	AHL	....	....	....	....	....	....	....	....	....	....	....	....	....	....	....	....	4	0	0	0	0	....	....	....
1985-86	**Chicago**	**NHL**	**71**	**7**	**7**	**14**	**60**	**0**	**0**	**1**	**50**	**14.0**	**0**	....	....	....	....	....	**3**	**0**	**0**	**0**	**0**	**0**	**0**	**0**
1986-87	**Chicago**	**NHL**	**66**	**4**	**10**	**14**	**66**	**0**	**0**	**0**	**56**	**7.1**	**4**	....	....	....	....	....	**3**	**1**	**0**	**1**	**2**	**0**	**0**	**0**
1987-88	**Chicago**	**NHL**	**58**	**1**	**6**	**7**	**85**	**0**	**0**	**0**	**51**	**2.0**	**-19**	....	....	....	....	....	....	....	....	....	....	....	....	....
	Saginaw Hawks	IHL	10	2	7	9	20	....	....	....	....	....	....	....	....	....	....	....	....	....	....	....	....	....	....	....
1988-89	**Chicago**	**NHL**	**11**	**0**	**0**	**0**	**18**	**0**	**0**	**0**	**9**	**0.0**	**-3**	....	....	....	....	....	....	....	....	....	....	....	....	....
	NY Islanders	**NHL**	**58**	**2**	**13**	**15**	**62**	**1**	**0**	**0**	**56**	**3.6**	**2**	....	....	....	....	....	....	....	....	....	....	....	....	....
1989-90	**NY Islanders**	**NHL**	**18**	**0**	**4**	**4**	**30**	**0**	**0**	**0**	**12**	**0.0**	**-8**	....	....	....	....	....	....	....	....	....	....	....	....	....
	Springfield	AHL	47	7	16	23	66	....	....	....	....	....	....	....	....	....	....	....	17	2	11	13	16	....	....	....
1990-91	Capital District	AHL	7	0	5	5	6	....	....	....	....	....	....	....	....	....	....	....	....	....	....	....	....	....	....	....
	Hartford	**NHL**	**4**	**0**	**0**	**0**	**4**	**0**	**0**	**0**	**2**	**0.0**	**-3**	....	....	....	....	....	....	....	....	....	....	....	....	....
	Springfield	AHL	58	4	23	27	85	....	....	....	....	....	....	....	....	....	....	....	18	0	7	7	26	....	....	....
1991-92	**Hartford**	**NHL**	**75**	**7**	**17**	**24**	**64**	**4**	**1**	**1**	**96**	**7.3**	**-13**	....	....	....	....	....	**5**	**0**	**0**	**0**	**2**	**0**	**0**	**0**
1992-93	**Tampa Bay**	**NHL**	**78**	**2**	**12**	**14**	**66**	**0**	**0**	**0**	**69**	**2.9**	**-16**	....	....	....	....	....	....	....	....	....	....	....	....	....
1993-94	**Tampa Bay**	**NHL**	**83**	**1**	**15**	**16**	**87**	**0**	**0**	**1**	**76**	**1.3**	**-5**	....	....	....	....	....	....	....	....	....	....	....	....	....
1994-95	**Tampa Bay**	**NHL**	**44**	**2**	**4**	**6**	**51**	**0**	**1**	**0**	**32**	**6.3**	**-6**	....	....	....	....	....	....	....	....	....	....	....	....	....
1995-96	**Detroit**	**NHL**	**70**	**1**	**9**	**10**	**33**	**0**	**0**	**0**	**26**	**3.8**	**7**	....	....	....	....	....	**17**	**1**	**0**	**1**	**14**	**1**	**0**	**0**
1996-97	**St. Louis**	**NHL**	**82**	**0**	**4**	**4**	**53**	**0**	**0**	**0**	**30**	**0.0**	**-9**	....	....	....	....	....	**6**	**1**	**0**	**1**	**8**	**0**	**0**	**0**
1997-98	**St. Louis**	**NHL**	**81**	**3**	**7**	**10**	**90**	**0**	**0**	**0**	**40**	**7.5**	**-2**	....	....	....	....	....	**10**	**0**	**1**	**1**	**8**	**0**	**0**	**0**

			Regular Season																Playoffs							
Season	Club	League	GP	G	A	Pts	PIM	PP	SH	GW	S	%	+/-	TF	F%	H	SB	Min	GP	G	A	Pts	PIM	PP	SH	GW
1998-99	**St. Louis**	**NHL**	**52**	**1**	**1**	**2**	**99**	**0**	**0**	**0**	**40**	**2.5**	**–14**	**0**	**0.0**	**90**	**40**	**16:09**	....	....	....	....	....	....	....	....
99-2000	**St. Louis**	**NHL**	**81**	**1**	**8**	**9**	**75**	**0**	**0**	**0**	**54**	**1.9**	**27**	**0**	**0.0**	**100**	**98**	**21:16**	**7**	**0**	**1**	**1**	**6**	**0**	**0**	**0**
	NHL Totals		**992**	**32**	**123**	**155**	**997**	**5**	**2**	**3**	**740**	**4.3**		**0**	**0.0**	**190**	**138**	**19:16**	**57**	**3**	**5**	**8**	**42**	**1**	**0**	**0**

Traded to **NY Islanders** by **Chicago** with Gary Nylund for Steve Konroyd and Bob Bassen, November 25, 1988. Traded to **Hartford** by **NY Islanders** for Hartford's 5th round choice (Ryan Duthie) in 1992 Entry Draft, October 30, 1990. Signed as a free agent by **Tampa Bay**, July 9, 1992. Traded to **Detroit** by **Tampa Bay** with Ben Hankinson for Shawn Burr and Detroit's 3rd round choice (later traded to Boston - Boston selected Jason Doyle) in 1996 Entry Draft, August 17, 1995. Signed as a free agent by **St. Louis**, July 31, 1996.

BERTRAND, Eric

(BURH-tran, RIHK) **MTL.**

Left wing. Shoots left. 6'1", 205 lbs. Born, St. Ephrem, Que., April 16, 1975. New Jersey's 9th choice, 207th overall, in 1994 Entry Draft.

Season	Club	League	GP	G	A	Pts	PIM	PP	SH	GW	S	%	+/-	TF	F%	H	SB	Min	GP	G	A	Pts	PIM	PP	SH	GW
1992-93	Granby Bisons	QMJHL	64	10	15	25	82	....	....	....	....	....	....	....	....	....	....	....	....	....	....	....	....	....	....	....
1993-94	Granby Bisons	QMJHL	60	11	15	26	151	....	....	....	....	....	....	....	....	....	....	....	6	1	0	1	18	....	....	....
1994-95	Granby Bisons	QMJHL	56	14	26	40	268	....	....	....	....	....	....	....	....	....	....	....	13	3	8	11	50	....	....	....
1995-96	Albany River Rats	AHL	70	16	13	29	199	....	....	....	....	....	....	....	....	....	....	....	4	0	0	0	6	....	....	....
1996-97	Albany River Rats	AHL	77	16	27	43	204	....	....	....	....	....	....	....	....	....	....	....	8	3	3	6	15	....	....	....
1997-98	Albany River Rats	AHL	76	20	29	49	256	....	....	....	....	....	....	....	....	....	....	....	13	5	5	10	4	....	....	....
1998-99	Albany River Rats	AHL	78	34	31	65	160	....	....	....	....	....	....	....	....	....	....	....	5	4	2	6	0	....	....	....
99-2000	**New Jersey**	**NHL**	**4**	**0**	**0**	**0**	**0**	**0**	**0**	**0**	**1**	**0.0**	**–1**	**0**	**0.0**	**11**	**0**	**7:47**	....	....	....	....	....	....	....	....
	Atlanta	**NHL**	**8**	**0**	**0**	**0**	**4**	**0**	**0**	**0**	**11**	**0.0**	**–5**	**1**	**0.0**	**19**	**1**	**9:56**	....	....	....	....	....	....	....	....
	Philadelphia	AHL	15	3	6	9	67	....	....	....	....	....	....	....	....	....	....	....	....	....	....	....	....	....	....	....
	Milwaukee	IHL	27	7	9	16	56	....	....	....	....	....	....	....	....	....	....	....	3	0	0	0	2	....	....	....
	NHL Totals		**12**	**0**	**0**	**0**	**4**	**0**	**0**	**0**	**12**	**0.0**		**1**	**0.0**	**30**	**1**	**9:13**	....	....	....	....	....	....	....	....

Traded to **Atlanta** by **New Jersey** with Wes Mason for Sylvain Cloutier, Jeff Williams and Atlanta's 7th round choice (Ken Magovan) in 2000 Entry Draft, November 1, 1999. Traded to **Philadelphia** by **Atlanta** for Brian Wesenberg, December 9, 1999. Traded to **Nashville** by **Philadelphia** for future considerations, February 14, 2000. Signed as a free agent by **Montreal**, July 7, 2000.

BERTUZZI, Todd

(buhr-TOO-zee, TAWD) **VAN.**

Center. Shoots left. 6'3", 235 lbs. Born, Sudbury, Ont., February 2, 1975. NY Islanders' 1st choice, 23rd overall, in 1993 Entry Draft.

Season	Club	League	GP	G	A	Pts	PIM	PP	SH	GW	S	%	+/-	TF	F%	H	SB	Min	GP	G	A	Pts	PIM	PP	SH	GW
1990-91	Sudbury Legion	NOHA	48	25	46	71	247	....	....	....	....	....	....	....	....	....	....	....	....	....	....	....	....	....	....	....
	Sudbury Cubs	OJHL	3	3	2	5	10	....	....	....	....	....	....	....	....	....	....	....	....	....	....	....	....	....	....	....
1991-92	Guelph Storm	OHL	47	7	14	21	145	....	....	....	....	....	....	....	....	....	....	....	....	....	....	....	....	....	....	....
1992-93	Guelph Storm	OHL	59	27	32	59	164	....	....	....	....	....	....	....	....	....	....	....	5	2	2	4	6	....	....	....
1993-94	Guelph Storm	OHL	61	28	54	82	165	....	....	....	....	....	....	....	....	....	....	....	9	2	6	8	30	....	....	....
1994-95	Guelph Storm	OHL	62	54	65	119	58	....	....	....	....	....	....	....	....	....	....	....	14	*15	18	33	41	....	....	....
1995-96	**NY Islanders**	**NHL**	**76**	**18**	**21**	**39**	**83**	**4**	**0**	**2**	**127**	**14.2**	**–14**	....	....	....	....	....	....	....	....	....	....	....	....	....
1996-97	**NY Islanders**	**NHL**	**64**	**10**	**13**	**23**	**68**	**3**	**0**	**1**	**79**	**12.7**	**–3**	....	....	....	....	....	....	....	....	....	....	....	....	....
	Utah Grizzlies	IHL	13	5	5	10	16	....	....	....	....	....	....	....	....	....	....	....	....	....	....	....	....	....	....	....
1997-98	**NY Islanders**	**NHL**	**52**	**7**	**11**	**18**	**58**	**1**	**0**	**1**	**63**	**11.1**	**–19**	....	....	....	....	....	....	....	....	....	....	....	....	....
	Vancouver	**NHL**	**22**	**6**	**9**	**15**	**63**	**1**	**1**	**1**	**39**	**15.4**	**2**	....	....	....	....	....	....	....	....	....	....	....	....	....
1998-99	**Vancouver**	**NHL**	**32**	**8**	**8**	**16**	**44**	**1**	**0**	**3**	**72**	**11.1**	**–6**	**191**	**43.5**	**53**	**12**	**18:28**	....	....	....	....	....	....	....	....
99-2000	**Vancouver**	**NHL**	**80**	**25**	**25**	**50**	**126**	**4**	**0**	**2**	**173**	**14.5**	**–2**	**476**	**46.6**	**187**	**16**	**15:24**	....	....	....	....	....	....	....	....
	NHL Totals		**326**	**74**	**87**	**161**	**442**	**14**	**1**	**10**	**553**	**13.4**		**667**	**45.7**	**240**	**28**	**16:16**	....	....	....	....	....	....	....	....

OHL Second All-Star team (1995)

Traded to **Vancouver** by **NY Islanders** with Bryan McCabe and NY Islanders' 3rd round choice (Jarkko Ruutu) in 1998 Entry Draft for Trevor Linden, February 6, 1998. • Missed majority of 1998-99 season recovering from broken leg suffered in game vs. Washington, November 1, 1998.

BERUBE, Craig

(buh-ROO-bee, KRAYG) **WSH.**

Left wing. Shoots left. 6'1", 205 lbs. Born, Calahoo, Alta., December 17, 1965.

Season	Club	League	GP	G	A	Pts	PIM	PP	SH	GW	S	%	+/-	TF	F%	H	SB	Min	GP	G	A	Pts	PIM	PP	SH	GW
1982-83	Williams Lake	PCJHL	33	9	24	33	99	....	....	....	....	....	....	....	....	....	....	....	....	....	....	....	....	....	....	....
	Kamloops Oilers	WHL	4	0	0	0	0	....	....	....	....	....	....	....	....	....	....	....	....	....	....	....	....	....	....	....
1983-84	New Westminster	WHL	70	11	20	31	104	....	....	....	....	....	....	....	....	....	....	....	8	1	2	3	5	....	....	....
1984-85	New Westminster	WHL	70	25	44	69	191	....	....	....	....	....	....	....	....	....	....	....	10	3	2	5	4	....	....	....
1985-86	Kamloops Blazers	WHL	32	17	14	31	119	....	....	....	....	....	....	....	....	....	....	....	....	....	....	....	....	....	....	....
	Medicine Hat	WHL	34	14	16	30	95	....	....	....	....	....	....	....	....	....	....	....	25	7	8	15	102	....	....	....
1986-87	**Philadelphia**	**NHL**	**7**	**0**	**0**	**0**	**57**	**0**	**0**	**0**	**4**	**0.0**	**2**	....	....	....	....	....	**5**	**0**	**0**	**0**	**17**	**0**	**0**	**0**
	Hershey Bears	AHL	63	7	17	24	325	....	....	....	....	....	....	....	....	....	....	....	....	....	....	....	....	....	....	....
1987-88	**Philadelphia**	**NHL**	**27**	**3**	**2**	**5**	**108**	**0**	**0**	**2**	**13**	**23.1**	**1**	....	....	....	....	....	....	....	....	....	....	....	....	....
	Hershey Bears	AHL	31	5	9	14	119	....	....	....	....	....	....	....	....	....	....	....	....	....	....	....	....	....	....	....
1988-89	**Philadelphia**	**NHL**	**53**	**1**	**1**	**2**	**199**	**0**	**0**	**0**	**31**	**3.2**	**–15**	....	....	....	....	....	**16**	**0**	**0**	**0**	**56**	**0**	**0**	**0**
	Hershey Bears	AHL	7	0	2	2	19	....	....	....	....	....	....	....	....	....	....	....	....	....	....	....	....	....	....	....
1989-90	**Philadelphia**	**NHL**	**74**	**4**	**14**	**18**	**291**	**0**	**0**	**0**	**52**	**7.7**	**–7**	....	....	....	....	....	....	....	....	....	....	....	....	....
1990-91	**Philadelphia**	**NHL**	**74**	**8**	**9**	**17**	**293**	**0**	**0**	**0**	**46**	**17.4**	**–6**	....	....	....	....	....	....	....	....	....	....	....	....	....
1991-92	**Toronto**	**NHL**	**40**	**5**	**7**	**12**	**109**	**1**	**0**	**1**	**42**	**11.9**	**–2**	....	....	....	....	....	....	....	....	....	....	....	....	....
	Calgary	**NHL**	**36**	**1**	**4**	**5**	**155**	**0**	**0**	**0**	**27**	**3.7**	**–3**	....	....	....	....	....	....	....	....	....	....	....	....	....
1992-93	**Calgary**	**NHL**	**77**	**4**	**8**	**12**	**209**	**0**	**0**	**2**	**58**	**6.9**	**–6**	....	....	....	....	....	**6**	**0**	**1**	**1**	**21**	**0**	**0**	**0**
1993-94	**Washington**	**NHL**	**84**	**7**	**7**	**14**	**305**	**0**	**0**	**0**	**48**	**14.6**	**–4**	....	....	....	....	....	**8**	**0**	**0**	**0**	**21**	**0**	**0**	**0**
1994-95	**Washington**	**NHL**	**43**	**2**	**4**	**6**	**173**	**0**	**0**	**0**	**22**	**9.1**	**–5**	....	....	....	....	....	**7**	**0**	**0**	**0**	**29**	**0**	**0**	**0**
1995-96	**Washington**	**NHL**	**50**	**2**	**10**	**12**	**151**	**1**	**0**	**1**	**28**	**7.1**	**1**	....	....	....	....	....	**2**	**0**	**0**	**0**	**19**	**0**	**0**	**0**
1996-97	**Washington**	**NHL**	**80**	**4**	**3**	**7**	**218**	**0**	**0**	**1**	**55**	**7.3**	**–11**	....	....	....	....	....	....	....	....	....	....	....	....	....
1997-98	**Washington**	**NHL**	**74**	**6**	**9**	**15**	**189**	**0**	**0**	**0**	**68**	**8.8**	**–3**	....	....	....	....	....	**21**	**1**	**0**	**1**	**21**	**0**	**0**	**1**
1998-99	**Washington**	**NHL**	**66**	**5**	**4**	**9**	**166**	**0**	**0**	**0**	**45**	**11.1**	**–7**	**14**	**42.9**	**85**	**10**	**6:47**	....	....	....	....	....	....	....	....
	Philadelphia	**NHL**	**11**	**0**	**0**	**0**	**28**	**0**	**0**	**0**	**7**	**0.0**	**–3**	**0**	**0.0**	**8**	**1**	**8:15**	**6**	**1**	**0**	**1**	**4**	**0**	**0**	**0**
99-2000	**Philadelphia**	**NHL**	**77**	**4**	**8**	**12**	**162**	**0**	**0**	**0**	**63**	**6.3**	**3**	**4**	**25.0**	**111**	**7**	**8:00**	**18**	**1**	**0**	**1**	**23**	**0**	**0**	**1**
	NHL Totals		**873**	**56**	**90**	**146**	**2813**	**2**	**0**	**7**	**609**	**9.2**		**18**	**38.9**	**204**	**18**	**7:30**	**89**	**3**	**1**	**4**	**211**	**0**	**0**	**2**

Signed as a free agent by **Philadelphia**, March 19, 1986. Traded to **Edmonton** by **Philadelphia** with Craig Fisher and Scott Mellanby for Dave Brown, Corey Foster and Jari Kurri, May 30, 1991. Traded to **Toronto** by **Edmonton** with Grant Fuhr and Glenn Anderson for Vincent Damphousse, Peter Ing, Scott Thornton, Luke Richardson, future considerations and cash, September 19, 1991. Traded to **Calgary** by **Toronto** with Alexander Godynyuk, Gary Leeman, Michel Petit and Jeff Reese for Doug Gilmour, Jamie Macoun, Ric Nattress, Rick Wamsley and Kent Manderville, January 2, 1992. Traded to **Washington** by **Calgary** for Washington's 5th round choice (Darryl Lafrance) in 1993 Entry Draft, June 26, 1993. Traded to **Philadelphia** by **Washington** for cash, March 23, 1999. Signed as a free agent by **Washington**, July 7, 2000.

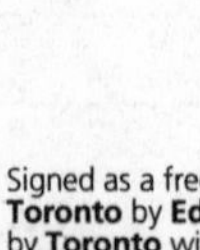

BETIK, Karel

(BEH-tihk, KAHR-ehl)

Defense. Shoots left. 6'2", 208 lbs. Born, Karvina, Czech., October 28, 1978. Tampa Bay's 6th choice, 112th overall, in 1997 Entry Draft.

Season	Club	League	GP	G	A	Pts	PIM	PP	SH	GW	S	%	+/-	TF	F%	H	SB	Min	GP	G	A	Pts	PIM	PP	SH	GW
1995-96	HC Vitkovice-Jr.	Cze-Rep	48	3	12	15	88	....	....	....	....	....	....	....	....	....	....	....	....	....	....	....	....	....	....	....
1996-97	Kelowna Rockets	WHL	56	3	10	13	76	....	....	....	....	....	....	....	....	....	....	....	6	1	1	2	2	....	....	....
1997-98	Kelowna Rockets	WHL	61	5	25	30	121	....	....	....	....	....	....	....	....	....	....	....	7	1	2	3	8	....	....	....
1998-99	**Tampa Bay**	**NHL**	**3**	**0**	**2**	**2**	**2**	**0**	**0**	**0**	**2**	**0.0**	**–3**	**0**	**0.0**	**2**	**2**	**13:28**	....	....	....	....	....	....	....	....
	Cleveland	IHL	74	5	11	16	97	....	....	....	....	....	....	....	....	....	....	....	....	....	....	....	....	....	....	....
99-2000	Detroit Vipers	IHL	17	0	0	0	22	....	....	....	....	....	....	....	....	....	....	....	....	....	....	....	....	....	....	....
	Toledo Storm	ECHL	22	0	7	7	42	....	....	....	....	....	....	....	....	....	....	....	....	....	....	....	....	....	....	....
	NHL Totals		**3**	**0**	**2**	**2**	**2**	**0**	**0**	**0**	**2**	**0.0**		**0**	**0.0**	**2**	**2**	**13:28**								

BIALOWAS, Frank

(bigh-uh-LOH-uhs, FRANK)

Left wing. Shoots left. 5'11", 220 lbs. Born, Winnipeg, Man., September 25, 1969.

Season	Club	League	GP	G	A	Pts	PIM	PP	SH	GW	S	%	+/-	TF	F%	H	SB	Min	GP	G	A	Pts	PIM	PP	SH	GW
1987-88	Estevan Bruins	MJHL	58	8	12	20	161	....	....	....	....	....	....	....	....	....	....	....	....	....	....	....	....	....	....	....
1988/91	Winkler Flyers	MJHL	STATISTICS NOT AVAILABLE																							
1991-92	Roanoke Rebels	ECHL	23	4	2	6	150	....	....	....	....	....	....	....	....	....	....	....	3	0	0	0	4	....	....	....
1992-93	Richmond	ECHL	60	3	18	21	261	....	....	....	....	....	....	....	....	....	....	....	1	0	0	0	2	....	....	....
	St. John's Leafs	AHL	7	1	0	1	28	....	....	....	....	....	....	....	....	....	....	....	1	0	0	0	0	....	....	....
1993-94	**Toronto**	**NHL**	**3**	**0**	**0**	**0**	**12**	**0**	**0**	**0**	**1**	**0.0**	**0**	....	....	....	....	....	....	....	....	....	....	....	....	....
	St. John's Leafs	AHL	69	2	8	10	352	....	....	....	....	....	....	....	....	....	....	....	7	0	3	3	25	....	....	....

			Regular Season																Playoffs							
Season	Club	League	GP	G	A	Pts	PIM	PP	SH	GW	S	%	+/–	TF	F%	H	SB	Min	GP	G	A	Pts	PIM	PP	SH	GW
1994-95	St. John's Leafs	AHL	51	2	3	5	277	....	....	....	....	....	....	....	....	....	....	....	4	0	0	0	12	....	....	....
1995-96	Portland Pirates	AHL	65	4	3	7	211	....	....	....	....	....	....	....	....	....	....	....	7	0	0	0	42	....	....	....
1996-97	Philadelphia	AHL	67	7	6	13	254	....	....	....	....	....	....	....	....	....	....	....	6	0	2	2	41	....	....	....
1997-98	Philadelphia	AHL	65	5	7	12	259	....	....	....	....	....	....	....	....	....	....	....	19	0	0	0	26	....	....	....
1998-99	Philadelphia	AHL	24	0	3	3	42	....	....	....	....	....	....	....	....	....	....	....	....	....	....	....	....	....	....	....
	Portland Pirates	AHL	6	0	0	0	10	....	....	....	....	....	....	....	....	....	....	....	....	....	....	....	....	....	....	....
	Indianapolis Ice	IHL	16	1	0	1	27	....	....	....	....	....	....	....	....	....	....	....	2	0	0	0	6	....	....	....
99-2000	Hershey Bears	AHL	40	4	3	7	65	....	....	....	....	....	....	....	....	....	....	....	8	1	0	1	32	....	....	....
	NHL Totals		**3**	**0**	**0**	**0**	**12**	**0**	**0**	**0**	**1**	**0.0**		....	....	....	....	....	....	....	....	....	....	....	....	....

Signed as a free agent by **Toronto**, March 20, 1994. Signed as a free agent by **Washington**, September 8, 1995. Traded to **Philadelphia** by **Washington** for future considerations, July 18, 1996. Traded to **Chicago** by **Philadelphia** for Dennis Bonvie, January 8, 1999. Signed as a free agent by **Hershey** (AHL), September 9, 1999.

BICANEK, Radim (BEE-chah-nehk, RA-dihm) CBJ

Defense. Shoots left. 6'1", 195 lbs. Born, Uherske Hradiste, Czech., January 18, 1975. Ottawa's 2nd choice, 27th overall, in 1993 Entry Draft.

Season	Club	League	GP	G	A	Pts	PIM	PP	SH	GW	S	%	+/–	TF	F%	H	SB	Min	GP	G	A	Pts	PIM	PP	SH	GW
1992-93	Dukla Jihlava	Czech.	43	2	3	5	....	....	....	....	....	....	....	....	....	....	....	....	....	....	....	....	....	....	....	....
1993-94	Belleville Bulls	OHL	63	16	27	43	49	....	....	....	....	....	....	....	....	....	....	....	12	2	8	10	21	....	....	....
1994-95	Belleville Bulls	OHL	49	13	26	39	61	....	....	....	....	....	....	....	....	....	....	....	16	6	5	11	30	....	....	....
	Ottawa	**NHL**	**6**	**0**	**0**	**0**	**0**	**0**	**0**	**0**	**6**	**0.0**	**3**	....	....	....	....	....	....	....	....	....	....	....	....	....
	P.E.I. Senators	AHL	....	....	....	....	....	....	....	....	....	....	....	....	....	....	....	....	3	0	1	1	0	....	....	....
1995-96	P.E.I. Senators	AHL	74	7	19	26	87	....	....	....	....	....	....	....	....	....	....	....	5	0	2	2	6	....	....	....
1996-97	**Ottawa**	**NHL**	**21**	**0**	**1**	**1**	**8**	**0**	**0**	**0**	**27**	**0.0**	**–4**	....	....	....	....	....	**7**	**0**	**0**	**0**	**8**	**0**	**0**	**0**
	Worcester	AHL	44	1	15	16	22	....	....	....	....	....	....	....	....	....	....	....	....	....	....	....	....	....	....	....
1997-98	**Ottawa**	**NHL**	**1**	**0**	**0**	**0**	**0**	**0**	**0**	**0**	**0**	**0.0**	**0**	....	....	....	....	....	....	....	....	....	....	....	....	....
	Detroit Vipers	IHL	9	1	3	4	16	....	....	....	....	....	....	....	....	....	....	....	....	....	....	....	....	....	....	....
	Manitoba Moose	IHL	42	1	7	8	52	....	....	....	....	....	....	....	....	....	....	....	....	....	....	....	....	....	....	....
1998-99	**Ottawa**	**NHL**	**7**	**0**	**0**	**0**	**4**	**0**	**0**	**0**	**6**	**0.0**	**–1**	**0**	**0.0**	**11**	**4**	**10:51**	....	....	....	....	....	....	....	....
	Grand Rapids	IHL	46	8	17	25	48	....	....	....	....	....	....	....	....	....	....	....	....	....	....	....	....	....	....	....
	Chicago	**NHL**	**7**	**0**	**0**	**0**	**6**	**0**	**0**	**0**	**7**	**0.0**	**–3**	**0**	**0.0**	**7**	**8**	**15:57**	....	....	....	....	....	....	....	....
99-2000	**Chicago**	**NHL**	**11**	**0**	**3**	**3**	**4**	**0**	**0**	**0**	**8**	**0.0**	**7**	**0**	**0.0**	**22**	**7**	**18:27**	....	....	....	....	....	....	....	....
	Cleveland	IHL	70	5	27	32	125	....	....	....	....	....	....	....	....	....	....	....	9	2	2	4	8	....	....	....
	NHL Totals		**53**	**0**	**4**	**4**	**22**	**0**	**0**	**0**	**54**	**0.0**		**0**	**0.0**	**40**	**19**	**15:37**	**7**	**0**	**0**	**0**	**8**	**0**	**0**	**0**

Traded to **Chicago** by **Ottawa** for Los Angeles' 6th round choice (previously acquired, Ottawa selected Martin Prusek) in 1999 Entry Draft, March 12, 1999. Selected by **Columbus** from **Chicago** in Expansion Draft, June 23, 2000.

BIRON, Mathieu (BEE-rawn, mat-yoo) NYI

Defense. Shoots right. 6'6", 212 lbs. Born, Lac St. Charles, Que., April 29, 1980. Los Angeles' 1st choice, 21st overall, in 1998 Entry Draft.

Season	Club	League	GP	G	A	Pts	PIM	PP	SH	GW	S	%	+/–	TF	F%	H	SB	Min	GP	G	A	Pts	PIM	PP	SH	GW
1996-97	Ste-Foy Governors	QAAA	40	4	22	26	49	....	....	....	....	....	....	....	....	....	....	....	....	....	....	....	....	....	....	....
1997-98	Shawinigan	QMJHL	59	8	28	36	60	....	....	....	....	....	....	....	....	....	....	....	6	0	1	1	10	....	....	....
1998-99	Shawinigan	QMJHL	69	13	32	45	116	....	....	....	....	....	....	....	....	....	....	....	6	0	2	2	6	....	....	....
99-2000	**NY Islanders**	**NHL**	**60**	**4**	**4**	**8**	**38**	**2**	**0**	**2**	**70**	**5.7**	**–13**	**2**	**0.0**	**120**	**65**	**15:02**	....	....	....	....	....	....	....	....
	NHL Totals		**60**	**4**	**4**	**8**	**38**	**2**	**0**	**2**	**70**	**5.7**		**2**	**0.0**	**120**	**65**	**15:02**	....	....	....	....	....	....	....	....

Traded to **NY Islanders** by **LA Kings** with Olli Jokinen, Josh Green and LA Kings' 1st round choice (Taylor Pyatt) in 1999 Entry Draft for Zigmund Palffy, Brian Smolinski, Marcel Cousineau and New Jersey's 4th round choice (previously acquired, LA Kings selected Daniel Johanssen) in 1999 Entry Draft, June 20, 1999.

BLACK, James (BLAK, JAYMS) WSH.

Left wing. Shoots left. 6', 202 lbs. Born, Regina, Sask., August 15, 1969. Hartford's 4th choice, 94th overall, in 1989 Entry Draft.

Season	Club	League	GP	G	A	Pts	PIM	PP	SH	GW	S	%	+/–	TF	F%	H	SB	Min	GP	G	A	Pts	PIM	PP	SH	GW
1986-87	Edmonton Mets	AJHL	41	36	48	84	58	....	....	....	....	....	....	....	....	....	....	....	....	....	....	....	....	....	....	....
1987-88	Portland	WHL	72	30	50	80	50	....	....	....	....	....	....	....	....	....	....	....	....	....	....	....	....	....	....	....
1988-89	Portland	WHL	71	45	51	96	57	....	....	....	....	....	....	....	....	....	....	....	19	13	6	19	28	....	....	....
1989-90	**Hartford**	**NHL**	**1**	**0**	**0**	**0**	**0**	**0**	**0**	**0**	**0**	**0.0**	**0**	....	....	....	....	....	....	....	....	....	....	....	....	....
	Binghamton	AHL	80	37	35	72	34	....	....	....	....	....	....	....	....	....	....	....	....	....	....	....	....	....	....	....
1990-91	**Hartford**	**NHL**	**1**	**0**	**0**	**0**	**0**	**0**	**0**	**0**	**0**	**0.0**	**0**	....	....	....	....	....	....	....	....	....	....	....	....	....
	Springfield	AHL	79	35	61	96	34	....	....	....	....	....	....	....	....	....	....	....	18	9	9	18	6	....	....	....
1991-92	**Hartford**	**NHL**	**30**	**4**	**6**	**10**	**10**	**1**	**0**	**1**	**54**	**7.4**	**–4**	....	....	....	....	....	....	....	....	....	....	....	....	....
	Springfield	AHL	47	15	25	40	33	....	....	....	....	....	....	....	....	....	....	....	10	3	2	5	18	....	....	....
1992-93	**Minnesota**	**NHL**	**10**	**2**	**1**	**3**	**4**	**0**	**0**	**0**	**10**	**20.0**	**0**	....	....	....	....	....	....	....	....	....	....	....	....	....
	Kalamazoo	IHL	63	25	45	70	40	....	....	....	....	....	....	....	....	....	....	....	....	....	....	....	....	....	....	....
1993-94	**Dallas**	**NHL**	**13**	**2**	**3**	**5**	**2**	**2**	**0**	**0**	**16**	**12.5**	**–4**	....	....	....	....	....	....	....	....	....	....	....	....	....
	Buffalo	**NHL**	**2**	**0**	**0**	**0**	**0**	**2**	**0**	**0**	**2**	**0.0**	**0**	....	....	....	....	....	....	....	....	....	....	....	....	....
	Rochester	AHL	45	19	32	51	28	....	....	....	....	....	....	....	....	....	....	....	4	2	3	5	0	....	....	....
1994-95	Las Vegas	IHL	78	29	44	73	54	....	....	....	....	....	....	....	....	....	....	....	10	1	6	7	4	....	....	....
1995-96	**Chicago**	**NHL**	**13**	**3**	**3**	**6**	**16**	**0**	**0**	**1**	**23**	**13.0**	**1**	....	....	....	....	....	**8**	**1**	**0**	**1**	**2**	**0**	**0**	**0**
	Indianapolis Ice	IHL	67	32	50	82	56	....	....	....	....	....	....	....	....	....	....	....	....	....	....	....	....	....	....	....
1996-97	**Chicago**	**NHL**	**64**	**12**	**11**	**23**	**20**	**0**	**0**	**3**	**122**	**9.8**	**6**	....	....	....	....	....	**5**	**1**	**1**	**2**	**2**	**0**	**0**	**0**
1997-98	**Chicago**	**NHL**	**52**	**10**	**5**	**15**	**8**	**2**	**1**	**3**	**90**	**11.1**	**–8**	....	....	....	....	....	....	....	....	....	....	....	....	....
1998-99	Chicago Wolves	IHL	5	6	0	6	0	....	....	....	....	....	....	....	....	....	....	....	....	....	....	....	....	....	....	....
	Washington	**NHL**	**75**	**16**	**14**	**30**	**14**	**1**	**1**	**3**	**135**	**11.9**	**5**	**10**	**50.0**	**42**	**30**	**15:04**	....	....	....	....	....	....	....	....
99-2000	**Washington**	**NHL**	**49**	**8**	**9**	**17**	**6**	**1**	**0**	**1**	**71**	**11.3**	**–1**	**18**	**38.9**	**27**	**31**	**12:03**	....	....	....	....	....	....	....	....
	NHL Totals		**310**	**57**	**52**	**109**	**80**	**9**	**2**	**12**	**523**	**10.9**		**28**	**42.9**	**69**	**61**	**13:53**	**13**	**2**	**1**	**3**	**4**	**0**	**0**	**0**

Traded to **Minnesota** by **Hartford** for Mark Janssens, September 3, 1992. Transferred to **Dallas** after **Minnesota** franchise relocated, June 9, 1993. Traded to **Buffalo** by **Dallas** with Dallas' 7th round choice (Steve Webb) in 1994 Entry Draft for Gord Donnelly, December 15, 1993. Signed as a free agent by **Chicago**, September 18, 1995. Traded to **Washington** by **Chicago** for future considerations, October 15, 1998.

BLAKE, Jason (BLAYK, JAY-suhn) L.A.

Center. Shoots left. 5'10", 185 lbs. Born, Moorhead, MN, September 2, 1973.

Season	Club	League	GP	G	A	Pts	PIM	PP	SH	GW	S	%	+/–	TF	F%	H	SB	Min	GP	G	A	Pts	PIM	PP	SH	GW
1993-94	Waterloo Hawks	USHL	47	50	50	100	76	....	....	....	....	....	....	....	....	....	....	....	....	....	....	....	....	....	....	....
1994-95	Ferris State	CCHA	36	16	16	32	46	....	....	....	....	....	....	....	....	....	....	....	....	....	....	....	....	....	....	....
1995-96	North Dakota	CCHA	DID NOT PLAY – TRANSFERRED COLLEGES																							
1996-97	North Dakota	WCHA	43	19	32	51	44	....	....	....	....	....	....	....	....	....	....	....	....	....	....	....	....	....	....	....
1997-98	North Dakota	WCHA	38	24	27	51	62	....	....	....	....	....	....	....	....	....	....	....	....	....	....	....	....	....	....	....
1998-99	North Dakota	WCHA	38	*28	*41	*69	49	....	....	....	....	....	....	....	....	....	....	....	....	....	....	....	....	....	....	....
	Los Angeles	**NHL**	**1**	**1**	**0**	**1**	**0**	**0**	**0**	**0**	**5**	**20.0**	**1**	**14**	**35.7**	**1**	**0**	**17:13**	....	....	....	....	....	....	....	....
	Orlando	IHL	5	3	5	8	6	....	....	....	....	....	....	....	....	....	....	....	13	3	4	7	20	....	....	....
99-2000	**Los Angeles**	**NHL**	**64**	**5**	**18**	**23**	**26**	**0**	**0**	**1**	**131**	**3.8**	**4**	**269**	**43.9**	**68**	**14**	**11:17**	**3**	**0**	**0**	**0**	**0**	**0**	**0**	**0**
	Long Beach	IHL	7	3	6	9	2	....	....	....	....	....	....	....	....	....	....	....	....	....	....	....	....	....	....	....
	NHL Totals		**65**	**6**	**18**	**24**	**26**	**0**	**0**	**1**	**136**	**4.4**		**283**	**43.5**	**69**	**14**	**11:22**	**3**	**0**	**0**	**0**	**0**	**0**	**0**	**0**

WCHA First All-Star Team (1997, 1998, 1999) • NCAA West Second All-American Team (1998) • NCAA West First All-American Team (1999)

Signed as a free agent by **LA Kings**, April 20, 1999.

BLAKE, Rob (BLAYK, RAWB) L.A.

Defense. Shoots right. 6'4", 227 lbs. Born, Simcoe, Ont., December 10, 1969. Los Angeles' 4th choice, 70th overall, in 1988 Entry Draft.

Season	Club	League	GP	G	A	Pts	PIM	PP	SH	GW	S	%	+/–	TF	F%	H	SB	Min	GP	G	A	Pts	PIM	PP	SH	GW
1986-87	Stratford Cullitons	OJHL-B	31	11	20	31	115	....	....	....	....	....	....	....	....	....	....	....	....	....	....	....	....	....	....	....
1987-88	Bowling Green	CCHA	43	5	8	13	88	....	....	....	....	....	....	....	....	....	....	....	....	....	....	....	....	....	....	....
1988-89	Bowling Green	CCHA	46	11	21	32	140	....	....	....	....	....	....	....	....	....	....	....	....	....	....	....	....	....	....	....
1989-90	Bowling Green	CCHA	42	23	36	59	140	....	....	....	....	....	....	....	....	....	....	....	....	....	....	....	....	....	....	....
	Los Angeles	**NHL**	**4**	**0**	**0**	**0**	**4**	**0**	**0**	**0**	**3**	**0.0**	**0**	....	....	....	....	....	**8**	**1**	**3**	**4**	**4**	**1**	**0**	**0**
1990-91	**Los Angeles**	**NHL**	**75**	**12**	**34**	**46**	**125**	**9**	**0**	**2**	**150**	**8.0**	**3**	....	....	....	....	....	**12**	**1**	**4**	**5**	**26**	**1**	**0**	**0**
1991-92	**Los Angeles**	**NHL**	**57**	**7**	**13**	**20**	**102**	**5**	**0**	**0**	**131**	**5.3**	**–5**	....	....	....	....	....	**6**	**2**	**1**	**3**	**12**	**0**	**0**	**0**

Season	Club	League	GP	G	A	Pts	PIM	PP	SH	GW	S	%	+/–	TF	F%	H	SB	Min	GP	G	A	Pts	PIM	PP	SH	GW
			Regular Season																Playoffs							
1992-93	**Los Angeles**	**NHL**	**76**	**16**	**43**	**59**	**152**	**10**	**0**	**4**	**243**	**6.6**	**18**	....	....	....	....	....	**23**	**4**	**6**	**10**	**46**	**1**	**1**	**0**
1993-94	**Los Angeles**	**NHL**	**84**	**20**	**48**	**68**	**137**	**7**	**0**	**6**	**304**	**6.6**	**–7**	....	....	....	....	....	....	....	....	....	....	....	....	....
1994-95	**Los Angeles**	**NHL**	**24**	**4**	**7**	**11**	**38**	**4**	**0**	**1**	**76**	**5.3**	**–16**	....	....	....	....	....	....	....	....	....	....	....	....	....
1995-96	**Los Angeles**	**NHL**	**6**	**1**	**2**	**3**	**8**	**0**	**0**	**0**	**13**	**7.7**	**0**	....	....	....	....	....	....	....	....	....	....	....	....	....
1996-97	**Los Angeles**	**NHL**	**62**	**8**	**23**	**31**	**82**	**4**	**0**	**1**	**169**	**4.7**	**–28**	....	....	....	....	....	....	....	....	....	....	....	....	....
1997-98	**Los Angeles**	**NHL**	**81**	**23**	**27**	**50**	**94**	**11**	**0**	**4**	**261**	**8.8**	**–3**	....	....	....	....	....	**4**	**0**	**0**	**0**	**6**	**0**	**0**	**0**
	Canada	Olympics	6	1	1	2	2	....	....	....	....	....	....	....	....	....	....	....	....	....	....	....	....	....	....	....
1998-99	**Los Angeles**	**NHL**	**62**	**12**	**23**	**35**	**128**	**5**	**1**	**2**	**216**	**5.6**	**–7**	**0**	**0.0**	**132**	**139**	**24:52**	....	....	....	....	....	....	....	....
99-2000	**Los Angeles**	**NHL**	**77**	**18**	**39**	**57**	**112**	**12**	**0**	**5**	**327**	**5.5**	**10**	**0**	**0.0**	**202**	**181**	**28:30**	**4**	**0**	**2**	**2**	**4**	**0**	**0**	**0**
	NHL Totals		**608**	**121**	**259**	**380**	**982**	**67**	**1**	**25**	**1893**	**6.4**		**0**	**0.0**	**334**	**320**	**26:52**	**57**	**8**	**16**	**24**	**98**	**3**	**1**	**0**

CCHA Second All-Star Team (1989) • CCHA First All-Star Team (1990) • NCAA West First All-American Team (1990) • NHL All-Rookie Team (1991) • NHL First All-Star Team (1998) • Won James Norris Memorial Trophy (1998) • NHL Second All-Star Team (2000) • Played in NHL All-Star Game (1994, 1999, 2000)

• Missed remainder of 1995-96 season recovering from knee injury suffered in game vs. Washington, October 20, 1995.

BLOUIN, Sylvain (bluh-WHEN, SIHL-veh) MTL.

Left wing. Shoots left. 6'2", 207 lbs. Born, Montreal, Que., May 21, 1974. NY Rangers' 5th choice, 104th overall, in 1994 Entry Draft.

Season	Club	League	GP	G	A	Pts	PIM	PP	SH	GW	S	%	+/–	TF	F%	H	SB	Min	GP	G	A	Pts	PIM	PP	SH	GW
1991-92	Laval Titan	QMJHL	28	0	0	0	23	....	....	....	....	....	....	....	....	....	....	....	9	0	0	0	35	....	....	....
1992-93	Laval Titan	QMJHL	68	0	10	10	373	....	....	....	....	....	....	....	....	....	....	....	13	1	0	1	*66	....	....	....
1993-94	Laval Titan	QMJHL	62	18	22	40	*492	....	....	....	....	....	....	....	....	....	....	....	21	4	13	17	*177	....	....	....
1994-95	Chicago Wolves	IHL	1	0	0	0	2	....	....	....	....	....	....	....	....	....	....	....	....	....	....	....	....	....	....	....
	Charlotte	ECHL	50	5	7	12	280	....	....	....	....	....	....	....	....	....	....	....	3	0	0	0	6	....	....	....
	Binghamton	AHL	10	1	0	1	46	....	....	....	....	....	....	....	....	....	....	....	2	0	0	0	24	....	....	....
1995-96	Binghamton	AHL	71	5	8	13	*352	....	....	....	....	....	....	....	....	....	....	....	4	0	3	3	4	....	....	....
1996-97	**NY Rangers**	**NHL**	**6**	**0**	**0**	**0**	**18**	**0**	**0**	**0**	**1**	**0.0**	**–1**	....	....	....	....	....	....	....	....	....	....	....	....	....
	Binghamton	AHL	62	13	17	30	301	....	....	....	....	....	....	....	....	....	....	....	4	2	1	3	16	....	....	....
1997-98	**NY Rangers**	**NHL**	**1**	**0**	**0**	**0**	**5**	**0**	**0**	**0**	**0**	**0.0**	**0**	....	....	....	....	....	....	....	....	....	....	....	....	....
	Hartford	AHL	53	8	9	17	286	....	....	....	....	....	....	....	....	....	....	....	9	0	1	1	63	....	....	....
1998-99	**Montreal**	**NHL**	**5**	**0**	**0**	**0**	**19**	**0**	**0**	**0**	**1**	**0.0**	**0**	**0**	**0.0**	**2**	**0**	**3:37**	....	....	....	....	....	....	....	....
	Fredericton	AHL	67	6	10	16	333	....	....	....	....	....	....	....	....	....	....	....	15	2	0	2	*87	....	....	....
99-2000	Worcester	AHL	70	16	18	34	337	....	....	....	....	....	....	....	....	....	....	....	8	3	5	8	30	....	....	....
	NHL Totals		**12**	**0**	**0**	**0**	**42**	**0**	**0**	**0**	**2**	**0.0**		**0**	**0.0**	**2**	**0**	**3:37**	....	....	....	....	....	....	....	....

Traded to **Montreal** by **NY Rangers** with NY Rangers' 6th round choice (later traded to Phoenix - Phoenix selected Erik Leverstrom) in 1999 Entry Draft for Peter Popovic, June 30, 1998. Signed as a free agent by **St. Louis**, August 25, 1999. Signed as a free agent by **Montreal**, July 7, 2000.

BODGER, Doug (BAW-juhr, DUHG)

Defense. Shoots left. 6'2", 210 lbs. Born, Chemainus, B.C., June 18, 1966. Pittsburgh's 2nd choice, 9th overall, in 1984 Entry Draft.

Season	Club	League	GP	G	A	Pts	PIM	PP	SH	GW	S	%	+/–	TF	F%	H	SB	Min	GP	G	A	Pts	PIM	PP	SH	GW
1982-83	Kamloops Oilers	WHL	72	26	66	92	98	....	....	....	....	....	....	....	....	....	....	....	7	0	5	5	2	....	....	....
1983-84	Kamloops Oilers	WHL	70	21	77	98	90	....	....	....	....	....	....	....	....	....	....	....	17	2	15	17	12	....	....	....
1984-85	**Pittsburgh**	**NHL**	**65**	**5**	**26**	**31**	**67**	**3**	**0**	**1**	**119**	**4.2**	**–24**	....	....	....	....	....	....	....	....	....	....	....	....	....
1985-86	**Pittsburgh**	**NHL**	**79**	**4**	**33**	**37**	**63**	**1**	**0**	**1**	**140**	**2.9**	**3**	....	....	....	....	....	....	....	....	....	....	....	....	....
1986-87	**Pittsburgh**	**NHL**	**76**	**11**	**38**	**49**	**52**	**5**	**0**	**1**	**176**	**6.3**	**6**	....	....	....	....	....	....	....	....	....	....	....	....	....
1987-88	**Pittsburgh**	**NHL**	**69**	**14**	**31**	**45**	**103**	**13**	**0**	**1**	**184**	**7.6**	**–4**	....	....	....	....	....	....	....	....	....	....	....	....	....
1988-89	**Pittsburgh**	**NHL**	**10**	**1**	**4**	**5**	**7**	**0**	**0**	**0**	**22**	**4.5**	**6**	....	....	....	....	....	....	....	....	....	....	....	....	....
	Buffalo	**NHL**	**61**	**7**	**40**	**47**	**52**	**6**	**0**	**1**	**134**	**5.2**	**9**	....	....	....	....	....	**5**	**1**	**1**	**2**	**11**	**1**	**0**	**0**
1989-90	**Buffalo**	**NHL**	**71**	**12**	**36**	**48**	**64**	**8**	**0**	**1**	**167**	**7.2**	**0**	....	....	....	....	....	**6**	**1**	**5**	**6**	**6**	**0**	**0**	**0**
1990-91	**Buffalo**	**NHL**	**58**	**5**	**23**	**28**	**54**	**2**	**0**	**0**	**139**	**3.6**	**–8**	....	....	....	....	....	**4**	**0**	**1**	**1**	**0**	**0**	**0**	**0**
1991-92	**Buffalo**	**NHL**	**73**	**11**	**35**	**46**	**108**	**4**	**0**	**1**	**180**	**6.1**	**1**	....	....	....	....	....	**7**	**2**	**1**	**3**	**2**	**2**	**0**	**1**
1992-93	**Buffalo**	**NHL**	**81**	**9**	**45**	**54**	**87**	**6**	**0**	**0**	**154**	**5.8**	**14**	....	....	....	....	....	**8**	**2**	**3**	**5**	**0**	**2**	**0**	**0**
1993-94	**Buffalo**	**NHL**	**75**	**7**	**32**	**39**	**76**	**5**	**1**	**1**	**144**	**4.9**	**8**	....	....	....	....	....	**7**	**0**	**3**	**3**	**6**	**0**	**0**	**0**
1994-95	**Buffalo**	**NHL**	**44**	**3**	**17**	**20**	**47**	**2**	**0**	**0**	**87**	**3.4**	**–3**	....	....	....	....	....	**5**	**0**	**4**	**4**	**0**	**0**	**0**	**0**
1995-96	**Buffalo**	**NHL**	**16**	**0**	**5**	**5**	**18**	**0**	**0**	**0**	**27**	**0.0**	**–6**	....	....	....	....	....	....	....	....	....	....	....	....	....
	San Jose	**NHL**	**57**	**4**	**19**	**23**	**50**	**3**	**0**	**0**	**94**	**4.3**	**–18**	....	....	....	....	....	....	....	....	....	....	....	....	....
1996-97	**San Jose**	**NHL**	**81**	**1**	**15**	**16**	**64**	**0**	**0**	**1**	**96**	**1.0**	**–14**	....	....	....	....	....	....	....	....	....	....	....	....	....
1997-98	**San Jose**	**NHL**	**28**	**4**	**6**	**10**	**32**	**0**	**0**	**1**	**41**	**9.8**	**0**	....	....	....	....	....	....	....	....	....	....	....	....	....
	New Jersey	**NHL**	**49**	**5**	**5**	**10**	**25**	**3**	**0**	**0**	**55**	**9.1**	**–1**	....	....	....	....	....	**5**	**0**	**0**	**0**	**0**	**0**	**0**	**0**
1998-99	**Los Angeles**	**NHL**	**65**	**3**	**11**	**14**	**34**	**0**	**0**	**0**	**67**	**4.5**	**1**	**0**	**0.0**	**75**	**101**	**19:27**	....	....	....	....	....	....	....	....
99-2000	**Vancouver**	**NHL**	**13**	**0**	**1**	**1**	**4**	**0**	**0**	**0**	**11**	**0.0**	**–6**	**0**	**0.0**	**12**	**33**	**16:17**	....	....	....	....	....	....	....	....
	NHL Totals		**1071**	**106**	**422**	**528**	**1007**	**61**	**1**	**10**	**2037**	**5.2**		**0**	**0.0**	**87**	**134**	**18:55**	**47**	**6**	**18**	**24**	**25**	**5**	**0**	**1**

WHL Second All-Star Team (1983) • WHL West First All-Star Team (1984)

Traded to **Buffalo** by **Pittsburgh** wih Darrin Shannon for Tom Barrasso and Buffalo's 3rd round choice (Joe Dziedzic) in 1990 Entry Draft, November 12, 1988. Traded to **San Jose** by **Buffalo** for Vaclav Varada, Martin Spanhel and Philadelphia's 1st (previously acquired by San Jose - later traded to Phoenix - Phoenix selected Daniel Briere) and 4th (previously acquired, Buffalo selected Mike Martone) round choices in 1996 Entry Draft, November 16, 1995. Traded to **New Jersey** by **San Jose** with Dody Wood for John MacLean and Ken Sutton, December 7, 1997. Traded to **LA Kings** by **New Jersey** for Boston's 4th round choice (previously acquired, New Jersey selected Pierre Dagenais) in 1998 Entry Draft, June 18, 1998. Signed as a free agent by **Vancouver**, August 18, 1999. • Officially announced retirement, December 14, 1999.

BOGUNIECKI, Eric (BOH-guhn-ih-kee, ERIHK) FLA.

Center. Shoots right. 5'8", 192 lbs. Born, New Haven, CT, May 6, 1975. St. Louis' 6th choice, 193rd overall, in 1993 Entry Draft.

Season	Club	League	GP	G	A	Pts	PIM	PP	SH	GW	S	%	+/–	TF	F%	H	SB	Min	GP	G	A	Pts	PIM	PP	SH	GW
1992-93	Westminster Prep	Hi-School	24	30	24	54	55	....	....	....	....	....	....	....	....	....	....	....	....	....	....	....	....	....	....	....
1993-94	New Hampshire	H-East	40	17	16	33	66	....	....	....	....	....	....	....	....	....	....	....	....	....	....	....	....	....	....	....
1994-95	New Hampshire	H-East	34	12	16	28	62	....	....	....	....	....	....	....	....	....	....	....	....	....	....	....	....	....	....	....
1995-96	New Hampshire	H-East	32	23	28	51	46	....	....	....	....	....	....	....	....	....	....	....	....	....	....	....	....	....	....	....
1996-97	New Hampshire	H-East	36	26	31	57	58	....	....	....	....	....	....	....	....	....	....	....	....	....	....	....	....	....	....	....
1997-98	Dayton Bombers	ECHL	26	19	18	37	36	....	....	....	....	....	....	....	....	....	....	....	....	....	....	....	....	....	....	....
	Fort Wayne	IHL	35	4	8	12	29	....	....	....	....	....	....	....	....	....	....	....	4	1	2	3	10	....	....	....
1998-99	Fort Wayne	IHL	72	32	34	66	100	....	....	....	....	....	....	....	....	....	....	....	2	0	1	1	2	....	....	....
99-2000	**Florida**	**NHL**	**4**	**0**	**0**	**0**	**2**	**0**	**0**	**0**	**5**	**0.0**	**–1**	**25**	**36.0**	**8**	**0**	**8:35**	....	....	....	....	....	....	....	....
	Louisville	AHL	57	33	42	75	148	....	....	....	....	....	....	....	....	....	....	....	4	3	2	5	20	....	....	....
	NHL Totals		**4**	**0**	**0**	**0**	**2**	**0**	**0**	**0**	**5**	**0.0**		**25**	**36.0**	**8**	**0**	**8:35**	....	....	....	....	....	....	....	....

Hockey East Second All-Star Team (1997)

Signed as a free agent by **Florida**, July 7, 1999.

BOHONOS, Lonny (boh-HOH-nohz, LAW-nee) TOR.

Right wing. Shoots right. 5'11", 190 lbs. Born, Winnipeg, Man., May 20, 1973.

Season	Club	League	GP	G	A	Pts	PIM	PP	SH	GW	S	%	+/–	TF	F%	H	SB	Min	GP	G	A	Pts	PIM	PP	SH	GW
1990-91	Winnipeg Blues	MJHL	46	33	22	55	70	....	....	....	....	....	....	....	....	....	....	....	....	....	....	....	....	....	....	....
1991-92	Winnipeg Blues	MJHL	40	53	36	89	42	....	....	....	....	....	....	....	....	....	....	....	....	....	....	....	....	....	....	....
	Moose Jaw	WHL	8	1	1	2	0	....	....	....	....	....	....	....	....	....	....	....	....	....	....	....	....	....	....	....
1992-93	Seattle T-Birds	WHL	46	13	13	26	27	....	....	....	....	....	....	....	....	....	....	....	....	....	....	....	....	....	....	....
	Portland	WHL	27	20	17	37	16	....	....	....	....	....	....	....	....	....	....	....	15	8	13	21	19	....	....	....
1993-94	Portland	WHL	70	*62	*90	*152	80	....	....	....	....	....	....	....	....	....	....	....	10	8	11	19	13	....	....	....
1994-95	Syracuse Crunch	AHL	67	30	45	75	71	....	....	....	....	....	....	....	....	....	....	....	....	....	....	....	....	....	....	....
1995-96	**Vancouver**	**NHL**	**3**	**0**	**1**	**1**	**0**	**0**	**0**	**0**	**3**	**0.0**	**1**	....	....	....	....	....	....	....	....	....	....	....	....	....
	Syracuse Crunch	AHL	74	40	39	79	82	....	....	....	....	....	....	....	....	....	....	....	16	14	8	22	16	....	....	....
1996-97	**Vancouver**	**NHL**	**36**	**11**	**11**	**22**	**10**	**2**	**0**	**1**	**67**	**16.4**	**–3**	....	....	....	....	....	....	....	....	....	....	....	....	....
	Syracuse Crunch	AHL	41	22	30	52	28	....	....	....	....	....	....	....	....	....	....	....	3	2	2	4	4	....	....	....
1997-98	**Vancouver**	**NHL**	**31**	**2**	**1**	**3**	**4**	**0**	**0**	**0**	**37**	**5.4**	**–9**	....	....	....	....	....	....	....	....	....	....	....	....	....
	Syracuse Crunch	AHL	17	12	12	24	8	....	....	....	....	....	....	....	....	....	....	....	....	....	....	....	....	....	....	....
	Toronto	**NHL**	**6**	**3**	**3**	**6**	**4**	**0**	**0**	**0**	**13**	**23.1**	**1**	....	....	....	....	....	....	....	....	....	....	....	....	....
	St. John's Leafs	AHL	11	7	9	16	10	....	....	....	....	....	....	....	....	....	....	....	2	1	1	2	2	....	....	....

			Regular Season																Playoffs							
Season	Club	League	GP	G	A	Pts	PIM	PP	SH	GW	S	%	+/-	TF	F%	H	SB	Min	GP	G	A	Pts	PIM	PP	SH	GW
1998-99	**Toronto**	**NHL**	**7**	**3**	**0**	**3**	**4**	**0**	**0**	**0**	**13**	**23.1**	**3**	**2**	**50.0**	**3**	**2**	**13:47**	**9**	**3**	**6**	**9**	**2**	**0**	**0**	**0**
	St. John's Leafs	AHL	70	34	48	82	40	....	....	....	....	....	....	....	....	....	....	....	5	2	4	6	2	....	....	....
99-2000	Manitoba Moose	IHL	63	18	33	51	45	....	....	....	....	....	....	....	....	....	....	....	2	0	0	0	2	....	....	....
	NHL Totals		**83**	**19**	**16**	**35**	**22**	**2**	**0**	**1**	**133**	**14.3**		**2**	**50.0**	**3**	**2**	**13:47**	**9**	**3**	**6**	**9**	**2**	**0**	**0**	**0**

WHL West First All-Star Team (1994) • Canadian Major Junior First All-Star Team (1994)

Signed as a free agent by **Vancouver**, May 31, 1994. Traded to **Toronto** by **Vancouver** for Brandon Convery, March 7, 1998. Signed as a free agent by **HC Davos** (Switz.), August 1, 2000.

BOIKOV, Alexandre

(bohy-KAHV, al-ehx-AN-duhr) **NSH.**

Defense. Shoots left. 6', 198 lbs. Born, Chelyabinsk, USSR, February 7, 1975.

1993-94	Victoria Cougars	WHL	70	4	31	35	250	....	....	....	....	....	....	....	....	....	....	....	....	....	....	....	....	....	....	....
1994-95	Prince George	WHL	46	5	23	28	115	....	....	....	....	....	....	....	....	....	....	....	....	....	....	....	....	....	....	....
	Tri-City Americans	WHL	24	3	13	16	63	....	....	....	....	....	....	....	....	....	....	....	17	1	7	8	30	....	....	....
1995-96	Tri-City Americans	WHL	71	3	49	52	230	....	....	....	....	....	....	....	....	....	....	....	11	2	4	6	28	....	....	....
1996-97	Kentucky	AHL	61	1	19	20	182	....	....	....	....	....	....	....	....	....	....	....	4	0	1	1	4	....	....	....
1997-98	Kentucky	AHL	69	5	14	19	153	....	....	....	....	....	....	....	....	....	....	....	3	0	1	1	8	....	....	....
1998-99	Kentucky	AHL	55	5	13	18	116	....	....	....	....	....	....	....	....	....	....	....	....	....	....	....	....	....	....	....
	Rochester	AHL	13	0	1	1	15	....	....	....	....	....	....	....	....	....	....	....	17	1	3	4	24	....	....	....
99-2000	**Nashville**	**NHL**	**2**	**0**	**0**	**0**	**2**	**0**	**0**	**0**	**1**	**0.0**	**0**	**0**	**0.0**	**5**	**0**	**8:31**	....	....	....	....	....	....	....	....
	Milwaukee	IHL	58	1	6	7	120	....	....	....	....	....	....	....	....	....	....	....	....	....	....	....	....	....	....	....
	NHL Totals		**2**	**0**	**0**	**0**	**2**	**0**	**0**	**0**	**1**	**0.0**		**0**	**0.0**	**5**	**0**	**8:31**	....	....	....	....	....	....	....	....

Signed as a free agent by **San Jose**, April 22, 1996. Signed as a free agent by **Nashville**, July 26, 1999.

BOILEAU, Patrick

(BWOI-loh, PA-trihk) **WSH.**

Defense. Shoots right. 6', 202 lbs. Born, Montreal, Que., February 22, 1975. Washington's 3rd choice, 69th overall, in 1993 Entry Draft.

1991-92	Laval Regents	QAAA	42	9	36	45	94	....	....	....	....	....	....	....	....	....	....	....	....	....	....	....	....	....	....	....
1992-93	Laval Titan	QMJHL	69	4	19	23	73	....	....	....	....	....	....	....	....	....	....	....	13	1	2	3	10	....	....	....
1993-94	Laval Titan	QMJHL	64	13	57	70	56	....	....	....	....	....	....	....	....	....	....	....	21	1	7	8	24	....	....	....
1994-95	Laval Titan	QMJHL	38	8	25	33	46	....	....	....	....	....	....	....	....	....	....	....	20	4	16	20	24	....	....	....
1995-96	Portland Pirates	AHL	78	10	28	38	41	....	....	....	....	....	....	....	....	....	....	....	19	1	3	4	12	....	....	....
1996-97	**Washington**	**NHL**	**1**	**0**	**0**	**0**	**0**	**0**	**0**	**0**	**0**	**0.0**	**0**	....	....	....	....	....	....	....	....	....	....	....	....	....
	Portland Pirates	AHL	67	16	28	44	63	....	....	....	....	....	....	....	....	....	....	....	5	1	1	2	4	....	....	....
1997-98	Portland Pirates	AHL	47	6	21	27	53	....	....	....	....	....	....	....	....	....	....	....	10	0	1	1	8	....	....	....
1998-99	**Washington**	**NHL**	**4**	**0**	**1**	**1**	**2**	**0**	**0**	**0**	**7**	**0.0**	**–4**	**0**	**0.0**	**8**	**2**	**15:56**	....	....	....	....	....	....	....	....
	Portland Pirates	AHL	52	6	18	24	52	....	....	....	....	....	....	....	....	....	....	....	....	....	....	....	....	....	....	....
	Indianapolis Ice	IHL	29	8	13	21	27	....	....	....	....	....	....	....	....	....	....	....	4	0	1	1	2	....	....	....
99-2000	Portland Pirates	AHL	63	2	15	17	61	....	....	....	....	....	....	....	....	....	....	....	4	0	0	0	4	....	....	....
	NHL Totals		**5**	**0**	**1**	**1**	**2**	**0**	**0**	**0**	**7**	**0.0**		**0**	**0.0**	**8**	**2**	**15:56**	....	....	....	....	....	....	....	....

Canadian Major Junior Scholastic Player of the Year (1994)

Loaned to **Indianapolis** (IHL) by **Portland** (AHL), February 4, 1999.

BOMBARDIR, Brad

(bawm-bahr-DEER, BRAD) **MIN.**

Defense. Shoots left. 6'1", 205 lbs. Born, Powell River, B.C., May 5, 1972. New Jersey's 5th choice, 56th overall, in 1990 Entry Draft.

1988-89	Powell River	BCJHL	30	6	5	11	24	....	....	....	....	....	....	....	....	....	....	....	6	0	0	0	0	....	....	....
1989-90	Powell River	BCJHL	60	10	35	45	93	....	....	....	....	....	....	....	....	....	....	....	8	2	3	5	4	....	....	....
1990-91	North Dakota	WCHA	33	3	6	9	18	....	....	....	....	....	....	....	....	....	....	....	....	....	....	....	....	....	....	....
1991-92	North Dakota	WCHA	35	3	14	17	54	....	....	....	....	....	....	....	....	....	....	....	....	....	....	....	....	....	....	....
1992-93	North Dakota	WCHA	38	8	15	23	34	....	....	....	....	....	....	....	....	....	....	....	....	....	....	....	....	....	....	....
1993-94	North Dakota	WCHA	38	5	17	22	38	....	....	....	....	....	....	....	....	....	....	....	....	....	....	....	....	....	....	....
1994-95	Albany River Rats	AHL	77	5	22	27	22	....	....	....	....	....	....	....	....	....	....	....	14	0	3	3	6	....	....	....
1995-96	Albany River Rats	AHL	80	6	25	31	63	....	....	....	....	....	....	....	....	....	....	....	3	0	1	1	4	....	....	....
1996-97	Albany River Rats	AHL	32	0	8	8	6	....	....	....	....	....	....	....	....	....	....	....	16	1	3	4	8	....	....	....
1997-98	**New Jersey**	**NHL**	**43**	**1**	**5**	**6**	**8**	**0**	**0**	**0**	**16**	**6.3**	**11**	....	....	....	....	....	....	....	....	....	....	....	....	....
	Albany River Rats	AHL	5	0	0	0	0	....	....	....	....	....	....	....	....	....	....	....	....	....	....	....	....	....	....	....
1998-99	**New Jersey**	**NHL**	**56**	**1**	**7**	**8**	**16**	**0**	**0**	**0**	**47**	**2.1**	**–4**	**1**	**0.0**	**48**	**57**	**15:03**	**5**	**0**	**0**	**0**	**0**	**0**	**0**	**0**
99-2000	**New Jersey**	**NHL**	**32**	**3**	**1**	**4**	**6**	**0**	**0**	**0**	**24**	**12.5**	**–6**	**0**	**0.0**	**31**	**37**	**15:54**	**1**	**0**	**0**	**0**	**0**	**0**	**0**	**0**
	NHL Totals		**131**	**5**	**13**	**18**	**30**	**0**	**0**	**0**	**87**	**5.7**		**1**	**0.0**	**79**	**94**	**15:21**	**6**	**0**	**0**	**0**	**0**	**0**	**0**	**0**

AHL Second All-Star Team (1996)

Traded to **Minnesota** by **New Jersey** for Chris Terreri and Minnesota's 9th round choice (later traded to Tampa Bay - Tampa Bay selected Thomas Ziegler) in 2000 Entry Draft, June 23, 2000.

BONDRA, Peter

(BAWN-druh, PEE-tuhr) **WSH.**

Right wing. Shoots left. 6'1", 205 lbs. Born, Luck, USSR, February 7, 1968. Washington's 9th choice, 156th overall, in 1990 Entry Draft.

1986-87	VSZ Kosice	Czech.	32	4	5	9	24	....	....	....	....	....	....	....	....	....	....	....	....	....	....	....	....	....	....	....
1987-88	VSZ Kosice	Czech.	45	27	11	38	20	....	....	....	....	....	....	....	....	....	....	....	....	....	....	....	....	....	....	....
1988-89	VSZ Kosice	Czech.	40	30	10	40	20	....	....	....	....	....	....	....	....	....	....	....	....	....	....	....	....	....	....	....
1989-90	VSZ Kosice	Czech.	44	29	17	46	....	....	....	....	....	....	....	....	....	....	....	....	5	7	2	9	....	....	....	....
1990-91	**Washington**	**NHL**	**54**	**12**	**16**	**28**	**47**	**4**	**0**	**1**	**95**	**12.6**	**–10**	....	....	....	....	....	**4**	**0**	**1**	**1**	**2**	**0**	**0**	**0**
1991-92	**Washington**	**NHL**	**71**	**28**	**28**	**56**	**42**	**4**	**0**	**3**	**158**	**17.7**	**16**	....	....	....	....	....	**7**	**6**	**2**	**8**	**4**	**1**	**0**	**0**
1992-93	**Washington**	**NHL**	**83**	**37**	**48**	**85**	**70**	**10**	**0**	**7**	**239**	**15.5**	**8**	....	....	....	....	....	**6**	**0**	**6**	**6**	**0**	**0**	**0**	**0**
1993-94	**Washington**	**NHL**	**69**	**24**	**19**	**43**	**40**	**4**	**0**	**2**	**200**	**12.0**	**22**	....	....	....	....	....	**9**	**2**	**4**	**6**	**4**	**0**	**0**	**1**
1994-95	HC Kosice	Slovakia	2	1	0	1	0	....	....	....	....	....	....	....	....	....	....	....	....	....	....	....	....	....	....	....
	Washington	**NHL**	**47**	***34**	**9**	**43**	**24**	**12**	**6**	**3**	**177**	**19.2**	**9**	....	....	....	....	....	**7**	**5**	**3**	**8**	**10**	**2**	**0**	**1**
1995-96	Detroit Vipers	IHL	7	8	1	9	0	....	....	....	....	....	....	....	....	....	....	....	....	....	....	....	....	....	....	....
	Washington	**NHL**	**67**	**52**	**28**	**80**	**40**	**11**	**4**	**7**	**322**	**16.1**	**18**	....	....	....	....	....	**6**	**3**	**2**	**5**	**8**	**2**	**0**	**1**
1996-97	**Washington**	**NHL**	**77**	**46**	**31**	**77**	**72**	**10**	**4**	**3**	**314**	**14.6**	**7**	....	....	....	....	....	....	....	....	....	....	....	....	....
1997-98	**Washington**	**NHL**	**76**	***52**	**26**	**78**	**44**	**11**	**5**	**13**	**284**	**18.3**	**14**	....	....	....	....	....	**17**	**7**	**5**	**12**	**12**	**3**	**0**	**2**
	Slovakia	Olympics	2	1	0	1	25	....	....	....	....	....	....	....	....	....	....	....	....	....	....	....	....	....	....	....
1998-99	**Washington**	**NHL**	**66**	**31**	**24**	**55**	**56**	**6**	**3**	**5**	**284**	**10.9**	**–1**	**1**	**0.0**	**87**	**22**	**20:35**	....	....	....	....	....	....	....	....
99-2000	**Washington**	**NHL**	**62**	**21**	**17**	**38**	**30**	**5**	**3**	**5**	**187**	**11.2**	**5**	**2**	**50.0**	**81**	**22**	**18:48**	**5**	**1**	**1**	**2**	**4**	**1**	**0**	**0**
	NHL Totals		**672**	**337**	**246**	**583**	**465**	**77**	**25**	**49**	**2260**	**14.9**		**3**	**33.3**	**168**	**44**	**19:43**	**61**	**24**	**24**	**48**	**44**	**9**	**0**	**5**

Played in NHL All-Star Game (1993, 1996, 1997, 1998, 1999)

BONIN, Brian

(BAWN-ihn, BRIGH-an) **MIN.**

Center. Shoots left. 5'10", 186 lbs. Born, St. Paul, MN, November 28, 1973. Pittsburgh's 9th choice, 211th overall, in 1992 Entry Draft.

1991-92	White Bear Lake	Hi-School	23	22	35	57	8	....	....	....	....	....	....	....	....	....	....	....	....	....	....	....	....	....	....	....
1992-93	U. of Minnesota	WCHA	38	10	18	28	10	....	....	....	....	....	....	....	....	....	....	....	....	....	....	....	....	....	....	....
1993-94	U. of Minnesota	WCHA	42	24	20	44	14	....	....	....	....	....	....	....	....	....	....	....	....	....	....	....	....	....	....	....
1994-95	U. of Minnesota	WCHA	44	32	31	*63	28	....	....	....	....	....	....	....	....	....	....	....	....	....	....	....	....	....	....	....
1995-96	U. of Minnesota	WCHA	42	34	*47	*81	30	....	....	....	....	....	....	....	....	....	....	....	....	....	....	....	....	....	....	....
1996-97	Cleveland	IHL	60	13	26	39	18	....	....	....	....	....	....	....	....	....	....	....	1	1	0	1	0	....	....	....
1997-98	Syracuse Crunch	AHL	67	31	38	69	46	....	....	....	....	....	....	....	....	....	....	....	5	1	3	4	6	....	....	....
1998-99	**Pittsburgh**	**NHL**	**5**	**0**	**0**	**0**	**0**	**0**	**0**	**0**	**2**	**0.0**	**–2**	**28**	**39.3**	**4**	**2**	**12:19**	**3**	**0**	**0**	**0**	**0**	**0**	**0**	**0**
	Kansas City	IHL	19	2	5	7	10	....	....	....	....	....	....	....	....	....	....	....	....	....	....	....	....	....	....	....
	Adirondack	AHL	54	19	16	35	31	....	....	....	....	....	....	....	....	....	....	....	2	0	0	0	0	....	....	....
99-2000	Syracuse Crunch	AHL	67	19	28	47	20	....	....	....	....	....	....	....	....	....	....	....	4	0	1	1	0	....	....	....
	NHL Totals		**5**	**0**	**0**	**0**	**0**	**0**	**0**	**0**	**2**	**0.0**		**28**	**39.3**	**4**	**2**	**12:19**	**3**	**0**	**0**	**0**	**0**	**0**	**0**	**0**

WCHA First All-Star Team (1995, 1996) • NCAA West First All-American Team (1995, 1996) • Won Hobey Baker Memorial Award (Top U.S. Collegiate Player) (1996)

Signed as a free agent by **Vancouver**, September 9, 1999. Signed as a free agent by **Minnesota**, July 6, 2000.

			Regular Season																Playoffs							
Season	Club	League	GP	G	A	Pts	PIM	PP	SH	GW	S	%	+/-	TF	F%	H	SB	Min	GP	G	A	Pts	PIM	PP	SH	GW

BONK, Radek

(BOHNK, RA-dehk) **OTT.**

Center. Shoots left. 6'3", 210 lbs. Born, Krnov, Czech., January 9, 1976. Ottawa's 1st choice, 3rd overall, in 1994 Entry Draft.

Season	Club	League	GP	G	A	Pts	PIM	PP	SH	GW	S	%	+/-	TF	F%	H	SB	Min	GP	G	A	Pts	PIM	PP	SH	GW
1990-91	HC Opava	Czech-Jr.	35	47	42	89	25	....	....	....	....	....	....	....	....	....	....	....	....	....	....	....	....	....	....	....
1991-92	ZPS Zlin	Czech-Jr.	45	47	36	83	30	....	....	....	....	....	....	....	....	....	....	....	....	....	....	....	....	....	....	....
1992-93	ZPS Zlin	Czech.	30	5	5	10	10	....	....	....	....	....	....	....	....	....	....	....	....	....	....	....	....	....	....	....
1993-94	Las Vegas	IHL	76	42	45	87	208	....	....	....	....	....	....	....	....	....	....	....	5	1	2	3	10	....	....	....
1994-95	Las Vegas	IHL	33	7	13	20	62	....	....	....	....	....	....	....	....	....	....	....	....	....	....	....	....	....	....	....
	Ottawa	**NHL**	**42**	**3**	**8**	**11**	**28**	**1**	**0**	**0**	**40**	**7.5**	**-5**	....	....	....	....	....	....	....	....	....	....	....	....	....
	P.E.I. Senators	AHL	....	....	....	....	....	....	....	....	....	....	....	....	....	....	....	....	1	0	0	0	0	....	....	....
1995-96	**Ottawa**	**NHL**	**76**	**16**	**19**	**35**	**36**	**5**	**0**	**1**	**161**	**9.9**	**-5**	....	....	....	....	....	....	....	....	....	....	....	....	....
1996-97	**Ottawa**	**NHL**	**53**	**5**	**13**	**18**	**14**	**0**	**1**	**0**	**82**	**6.1**	**-4**	....	....	....	....	....	**7**	**0**	**1**	**1**	**4**	**0**	**0**	**0**
1997-98	**Ottawa**	**NHL**	**65**	**7**	**9**	**16**	**16**	**1**	**0**	**0**	**93**	**7.5**	**-13**	....	....	....	....	....	**5**	**0**	**0**	**0**	**2**	**0**	**0**	**0**
1998-99	**Ottawa**	**NHL**	**81**	**16**	**16**	**32**	**48**	**0**	**1**	**6**	**110**	**14.5**	**15**	**1184**	**50.1**	**225**	**30**	**13:44**	**4**	**0**	**0**	**0**	**6**	**0**	**0**	**0**
99-2000	HC Pardubice	Cze-Rep	3	1	0	1	4	....	....	....	....	....	....	....	....	....	....	....	....	....	....	....	....	....	....	....
	Ottawa	**NHL**	**80**	**23**	**37**	**60**	**53**	**10**	**0**	**5**	**167**	**13.8**	**-2**	**1654**	**52.0**	**211**	**45**	**18:14**	**6**	**0**	**0**	**0**	**8**	**0**	**0**	**0**
	NHL Totals		**397**	**70**	**102**	**172**	**195**	**17**	**2**	**12**	**653**	**10.7**		**2838**	**51.2**	**436**	**75**	**15:58**	**22**	**0**	**1**	**1**	**20**	**0**	**0**	**0**

Won Garry F. Longman Memorial Trophy (Top Rookie - IHL) (1994) • Played in NHL All-Star Game (2000)

BONNI, Ryan

(baw-NEE, RIGH-an) **VAN.**

Defense. Shoots left. 6'4", 190 lbs. Born, Winnipeg, Man., February 18, 1979. Vancouver's 2nd choice, 34th overall, in 1997 Entry Draft.

Season	Club	League	GP	G	A	Pts	PIM	PP	SH	GW	S	%	+/-	TF	F%	H	SB	Min	GP	G	A	Pts	PIM	PP	SH	GW
1994-95	Winnipeg Sharks	MAHA	24	3	19	22	59	....	....	....	....	....	....	....	....	....	....	....	....	....	....	....	....	....	....	....
1995-96	Saskatoon Blades	WHL	63	1	7	8	78	....	....	....	....	....	....	....	....	....	....	....	3	0	0	0	0	....	....	....
1996-97	Saskatoon Blades	WHL	69	11	19	30	219	....	....	....	....	....	....	....	....	....	....	....	....	....	....	....	....	....	....	....
1997-98	Saskatoon Blades	WHL	42	5	14	19	100	....	....	....	....	....	....	....	....	....	....	....	0	0	0	0	0	....	....	....
1998-99	Saskatoon Blades	WHL	51	6	26	32	211	....	....	....	....	....	....	....	....	....	....	....	....	....	....	....	....	....	....	....
	Red Deer Rebels	WHL	20	3	10	13	41	....	....	....	....	....	....	....	....	....	....	....	9	0	4	4	25	....	....	....
99-2000	**Vancouver**	**NHL**	**3**	**0**	**0**	**0**	**0**	**0**	**0**	**0**	**1**	**0.0**	**-1**	**0**	**0.0**	**1**	**2**	**9:37**	....	....	....	....	....	....	....	....
	Syracuse Crunch	AHL	71	5	13	18	125	....	....	....	....	....	....	....	....	....	....	....	2	0	1	1	2	....	....	....
	NHL Totals		**3**	**0**	**0**	**0**	**0**	**0**	**0**	**0**	**1**	**0.0**		**0**	**0.0**	**1**	**2**	**9:37**	....	....	....	....	....	....	....	....

BONSIGNORE, Jason

(bohn-SEE-nohr, JAY-suhn)

Center. Shoots right. 6'4", 220 lbs. Born, Rochester, NY, April 15, 1976. Edmonton's 1st choice, 4th overall, in 1994 Entry Draft.

Season	Club	League	GP	G	A	Pts	PIM	PP	SH	GW	S	%	+/-	TF	F%	H	SB	Min	GP	G	A	Pts	PIM	PP	SH	GW
1989-90	Greece High	Hi-School	18	33	33	66	....	....	....	....	....	....	....	....	....	....	....	....	....	....	....	....	....	....	....	....
1990-91	Greece High	Hi-School	18	24	18	42	....	....	....	....	....	....	....	....	....	....	....	....	....	....	....	....	....	....	....	....
1991-92	Rochester	NAJHL	60	31	29	60	42	....	....	....	....	....	....	....	....	....	....	....	....	....	....	....	....	....	....	....
1992-93	Newmarket	OHL	66	22	20	42	6	....	....	....	....	....	....	....	....	....	....	....	7	0	3	3	0	....	....	....
1993-94	Newmarket	OHL	17	7	17	24	22	....	....	....	....	....	....	....	....	....	....	....	....	....	....	....	....	....	....	....
	United States	Nat-Team	5	0	2	2	0	....	....	....	....	....	....	....	....	....	....	....	....	....	....	....	....	....	....	....
	Niagara Falls	OHL	41	15	47	62	41	....	....	....	....	....	....	....	....	....	....	....	....	....	....	....	....	....	....	....
1994-95	Niagara Falls	OHL	26	12	21	33	51	....	....	....	....	....	....	....	....	....	....	....	....	....	....	....	....	....	....	....
	Sudbury Wolves	OHL	23	15	14	29	45	....	....	....	....	....	....	....	....	....	....	....	17	13	10	23	12	....	....	....
	Edmonton	**NHL**	**1**	**1**	**0**	**1**	**0**	**0**	**0**	**0**	**3**	**33.3**	**-1**	....	....	....	....	....	....	....	....	....	....	....	....	....
1995-96	Sudbury Wolves	OHL	18	10	16	26	37	....	....	....	....	....	....	....	....	....	....	....	....	....	....	....	....	....	....	....
	Edmonton	**NHL**	**20**	**0**	**2**	**2**	**4**	**0**	**0**	**0**	**13**	**0.0**	**-6**	....	....	....	....	....	....	....	....	....	....	....	....	....
	Cape Breton	AHL	12	1	4	5	12	....	....	....	....	....	....	....	....	....	....	....	....	....	....	....	....	....	....	....
1996-97	Hamilton Bulldogs	AHL	78	21	33	54	78	....	....	....	....	....	....	....	....	....	....	....	7	0	0	0	4	....	....	....
1997-98	Hamilton Bulldogs	AHL	8	0	2	2	14	....	....	....	....	....	....	....	....	....	....	....	....	....	....	....	....	....	....	....
	San Antonio	IHL	22	3	8	11	34	....	....	....	....	....	....	....	....	....	....	....	....	....	....	....	....	....	....	....
	Tampa Bay	**NHL**	**35**	**2**	**8**	**10**	**22**	**0**	**0**	**0**	**29**	**6.9**	**-11**	....	....	....	....	....	....	....	....	....	....	....	....	....
	Cleveland	IHL	6	4	0	4	32	....	....	....	....	....	....	....	....	....	....	....	8	1	1	2	20	....	....	....
1998-99	**Tampa Bay**	**NHL**	**23**	**0**	**3**	**3**	**8**	**0**	**0**	**0**	**12**	**0.0**	**-4**	**179**	**57.0**	**45**	**2**	**7:25**	....	....	....	....	....	....	....	....
	Cleveland	IHL	48	14	19	33	68	....	....	....	....	....	....	....	....	....	....	....	....	....	....	....	....	....	....	....
99-2000	St. John's Leafs	AHL	29	6	13	19	30	....	....	....	....	....	....	....	....	....	....	....	....	....	....	....	....	....	....	....
	NHL Totals		**79**	**3**	**13**	**16**	**34**	**0**	**0**	**0**	**57**	**5.3**		**179**	**57.0**	**45**	**2**	**7:25**	....	....	....	....	....	....	....	....

Traded to **Tampa Bay** by **Edmonton** with Bryan Marchment and Steve Kelly for Roman Hamrlik and Paul Comrie, December 30, 1997. Signed as a free agent by **Toronto**, July 15, 1999.

BONVIE, Dennis

(BOHN-vee, DEHN-his) **PIT.**

Right wing/Defense. Shoots right. 5'11", 205 lbs. Born, Antigonish, N.S., July 23, 1973.

Season	Club	League	GP	G	A	Pts	PIM	PP	SH	GW	S	%	+/-	TF	F%	H	SB	Min	GP	G	A	Pts	PIM	PP	SH	GW
1989-90	Antigonish	NSAHA	50	15	30	45	52	....	....	....	....	....	....	....	....	....	....	....	....	....	....	....	....	....	....	....
1990-91	Antigonish	MJrHL	40	1	8	9	347	....	....	....	....	....	....	....	....	....	....	....	....	....	....	....	....	....	....	....
1991-92	Kitchener	OHL	7	1	1	2	23	....	....	....	....	....	....	....	....	....	....	....	....	....	....	....	....	....	....	....
	North Bay	OHL	49	0	12	12	261	....	....	....	....	....	....	....	....	....	....	....	21	0	1	1	91	....	....	....
1992-93	North Bay	OHL	64	3	21	24	*316	....	....	....	....	....	....	....	....	....	....	....	5	0	0	0	34	....	....	....
1993-94	Cape Breton	AHL	63	1	10	11	278	....	....	....	....	....	....	....	....	....	....	....	4	0	0	0	11	....	....	....
1994-95	**Edmonton**	**NHL**	**2**	**0**	**0**	**0**	**0**	**0**	**0**	**0**	**0**	**0.0**	**0**	....	....	....	....	....	....	....	....	....	....	....	....	....
	Cape Breton	AHL	74	5	15	20	422	....	....	....	....	....	....	....	....	....	....	....	....	....	....	....	....	....	....	....
1995-96	**Edmonton**	**NHL**	**8**	**0**	**0**	**0**	**47**	**0**	**0**	**0**	**0**	**0.0**	**-3**	....	....	....	....	....	....	....	....	....	....	....	....	....
	Cape Breton	AHL	38	13	14	27	269	....	....	....	....	....	....	....	....	....	....	....	....	....	....	....	....	....	....	....
1996-97	Hamilton Bulldogs	AHL	73	9	20	29	*522	....	....	....	....	....	....	....	....	....	....	....	22	3	11	14	*91	....	....	....
1997-98	**Edmonton**	**NHL**	**4**	**0**	**0**	**0**	**27**	**0**	**0**	**0**	**0**	**0.0**	**0**	....	....	....	....	....	....	....	....	....	....	....	....	....
	Hamilton Bulldogs	AHL	57	11	19	30	295	....	....	....	....	....	....	....	....	....	....	....	9	0	5	5	18	....	....	....
1998-99	**Chicago**	**NHL**	**11**	**0**	**0**	**0**	**44**	**0**	**0**	**0**	**1**	**0.0**	**-4**	**0**	**0.0**	**10**	**0**	**3:59**	....	....	....	....	....	....	....	....
	Portland Pirates	AHL	3	1	0	1	16	....	....	....	....	....	....	....	....	....	....	....	....	....	....	....	....	....	....	....
	Philadelphia	AHL	37	4	10	14	158	....	....	....	....	....	....	....	....	....	....	....	14	3	3	6	26	....	....	....
99-2000	**Pittsburgh**	**NHL**	**28**	**0**	**0**	**0**	**80**	**0**	**0**	**0**	**6**	**0.0**	**-2**	**0**	**0.0**	**28**	**4**	**3:14**	....	....	....	....	....	....	....	....
	Wilkes-Barre	AHL	42	5	26	31	243	....	....	....	....	....	....	....	....	....	....	....	....	....	....	....	....	....	....	....
	NHL Totals		**53**	**0**	**0**	**0**	**198**	**0**	**0**	**0**	**7**	**0.0**		**0**	**0.0**	**38**	**4**	**3:27**	....	....	....	....	....	....	....	....

Signed as a free agent by **Edmonton**, August 25, 1994. Claimed by **Chicago** from **Edmonton** in NHL Waiver Draft, October 5, 1998. Traded to **Philadelphia** by **Chicago** for Frank Bialowas, January 8, 1999. Signed as a free agent by **Pittsburgh**, September 20, 1999.

BORDELEAU, Sebastien

(BOHR-duh-loh, SEH-bas-tehn) **NSH.**

Center. Shoots right. 5'11", 185 lbs. Born, Vancouver, B.C., February 15, 1975. Montreal's 3rd choice, 73rd overall, in 1993 Entry Draft.

Season	Club	League	GP	G	A	Pts	PIM	PP	SH	GW	S	%	+/-	TF	F%	H	SB	Min	GP	G	A	Pts	PIM	PP	SH	GW
1990-91	Laval Regents	QAAA	39	27	36	63	....	....	....	....	....	....	....	....	....	....	....	....	....	....	....	....	....	....	....	....
1991-92	Hull Olympiques	QMJHL	62	26	32	58	91	....	....	....	....	....	....	....	....	....	....	....	5	0	3	3	23	....	....	....
1992-93	Hull Olympiques	QMJHL	60	18	39	57	95	....	....	....	....	....	....	....	....	....	....	....	10	3	8	11	20	....	....	....
1993-94	Hull Olympiques	QMJHL	60	26	57	83	147	....	....	....	....	....	....	....	....	....	....	....	17	6	14	20	26	....	....	....
1994-95	Hull Olympiques	QMJHL	68	52	76	128	142	....	....	....	....	....	....	....	....	....	....	....	18	*13	19	*32	25	....	....	....
	Fredericton	AHL	....	....	....	....	....	....	....	....	....	....	....	....	....	....	....	....	1	0	0	0	0	....	....	....
1995-96	**Montreal**	**NHL**	**4**	**0**	**0**	**0**	**0**	**0**	**0**	**0**	**0**	**0.0**	**-1**	....	....	....	....	....	....	....	....	....	....	....	....	....
	Fredericton	AHL	43	17	29	46	68	....	....	....	....	....	....	....	....	....	....	....	7	0	2	2	8	....	....	....
1996-97	**Montreal**	**NHL**	**28**	**2**	**9**	**11**	**2**	**0**	**0**	**0**	**27**	**7.4**	**-3**	....	....	....	....	....	....	....	....	....	....	....	....	....
	Fredericton	AHL	34	18	22	40	50	....	....	....	....	....	....	....	....	....	....	....	....	....	....	....	....	....	....	....
1997-98	**Montreal**	**NHL**	**53**	**6**	**8**	**14**	**36**	**2**	**1**	**0**	**55**	**10.9**	**5**	....	....	....	....	....	**5**	**0**	**0**	**0**	**2**	**0**	**0**	**0**
1998-99	**Nashville**	**NHL**	**72**	**16**	**24**	**40**	**26**	**1**	**2**	**3**	**168**	**9.5**	**-14**	**1368**	**57.1**	**76**	**22**	**15:18**	....	....	....	....	....	....	....	....
99-2000	**Nashville**	**NHL**	**60**	**10**	**13**	**23**	**30**	**0**	**2**	**1**	**127**	**7.9**	**-12**	**942**	**54.4**	**43**	**22**	**13:56**	....	....	....	....	....	....	....	....
	NHL Totals		**217**	**34**	**54**	**88**	**94**	**3**	**5**	**4**	**377**	**9.0**		**2310**	**56.0**	**119**	**44**	**14:41**	**5**	**0**	**0**	**0**	**2**	**0**	**0**	**0**

QMJHL First All-Star Team (1995)

Traded to **Nashville** by **Montreal** for future considerations, June 26, 1998.

BOTTERILL, Jason
(BOH-tuhr-ihl, JAY-suhn) **CGY.**

Left wing. Shoots left. 6'4", 220 lbs. Born, Edmonton, Alta., May 19, 1976. Dallas' 1st choice, 20th overall, in 1994 Entry Draft.

Season	Club	League	GP	G	A	Pts	PIM	PP	SH	GW	S	%	+/–	TF	F%	H	SB	Min	Playoffs GP	G	A	Pts	PIM	PP	SH	GW
1992-93	St. Paul's Prep	Hi-School	22	22	26	48	....	....	....	....	....	....	....	....	....	....	....	....	....	....	....	....	....	....	....	....
1993-94	U. of Michigan	CCHA	36	20	19	39	94	....	....	....	....	....	....	....	....	....	....	....	....	....	....	....	....	....	....	....
1994-95	U. of Michigan	CCHA	34	14	14	28	117	....	....	....	....	....	....	....	....	....	....	....	....	....	....	....	....	....	....	....
1995-96	U. of Michigan	CCHA	37	*32	25	57	*143	....	....	....	....	....	....	....	....	....	....	....	....	....	....	....	....	....	....	....
1996-97	U. of Michigan	CCHA	42	*37	24	61	129	....	....	....	....	....	....	....	....	....	....	....	....	....	....	....	....	....	....	....
1997-98	**Dallas**	**NHL**	**4**	**0**	**0**	**0**	**19**	**0**	**0**	**0**	**2**	**0.0**	**–1**	....	....	....	....	....	....	....	....	....	....	....	....	....
	Michigan K-Wings	IHL	50	11	11	22	82	....	....	....	....	....	....	....	....	....	....	....	4	0	0	0	5	....	....	....
1998-99	**Dallas**	**NHL**	**17**	**0**	**0**	**0**	**23**	**0**	**0**	**0**	**8**	**0.0**	**–2**	**0**	**0.0**	**27**	**0**	**8:19**	....	....	....	....	....	....	....	....
	Michigan K-Wings	IHL	56	13	25	38	106	....	....	....	....	....	....	....	....	....	....	....	5	2	1	3	4	....	....	....
99-2000	**Atlanta**	**NHL**	**25**	**1**	**4**	**5**	**17**	**0**	**0**	**1**	**17**	**5.9**	**–7**	**2**	**50.0**	**51**	**3**	**11:16**	....	....	....	....	....	....	....	....
	Orlando	IHL	17	7	8	15	27	....	....	....	....	....	....	....	....	....	....	....	....	....	....	....	....	....	....	....
	Calgary	**NHL**	**2**	**0**	**0**	**0**	**0**	**0**	**0**	**0**	**2**	**0.0**	**–4**	**0**	**0.0**	**1**	**0**	**8:00**	....	....	....	....	....	....	....	....
	Saint John Flames	AHL	21	3	4	7	39	....	....	....	....	....	....	....	....	....	....	....	3	0	0	0	19	....	....	....
	NHL Totals		**48**	**1**	**4**	**5**	**59**	**0**	**0**	**1**	**29**	**3.4**		**2**	**50.0**	**79**	**3**	**9:59**	....	....	....	....	....	....	....	....

CCHA Second All-Star Team (1996) • NCAA West Second All-American Team (1997)

Traded to **Atlanta** by **Dallas** for Jamie Pushor, July 15, 1999. Traded to **Calgary** by **Atlanta** with Darryl Shannon for Hnat Domenichelli and Dmitri Vlasenkov, February 11, 2000.

BOUCHARD, Joel
(BOO-shahrd, JOHEL) **PHX.**

Defense. Shoots left. 6', 202 lbs. Born, Montreal, Que., January 23, 1974. Calgary's 7th choice, 129th overall, in 1992 Entry Draft.

Season	Club	League	GP	G	A	Pts	PIM	PP	SH	GW	S	%	+/–	TF	F%	H	SB	Min	Playoffs GP	G	A	Pts	PIM	PP	SH	GW
1989-90	Mtl-Bourassa	QAAA	41	7	17	24	10	....	....	....	....	....	....	....	....	....	....	....	1	1	0	1	0	....	....	....
1990-91	Longueuil	QMJHL	53	3	19	22	34	....	....	....	....	....	....	....	....	....	....	....	8	1	0	1	11	....	....	....
1991-92	Verdun	QMJHL	70	9	20	29	55	....	....	....	....	....	....	....	....	....	....	....	19	1	7	8	20	....	....	....
1992-93	Verdun	QMJHL	60	10	49	59	126	....	....	....	....	....	....	....	....	....	....	....	4	0	2	2	4	....	....	....
1993-94	Verdun	QMJHL	60	15	55	70	62	....	....	....	....	....	....	....	....	....	....	....	4	1	0	1	6	....	....	....
	Saint John Flames	AHL	1	0	0	0	0	....	....	....	....	....	....	....	....	....	....	....	2	0	0	0	0	....	....	....
1994-95	Saint John Flames	AHL	77	6	25	31	63	....	....	....	....	....	....	....	....	....	....	....	5	1	0	1	4	....	....	....
	Calgary	**NHL**	**2**	**0**	**0**	**0**	**0**	**0**	**0**	**0**	**0**	**0.0**	**0**	....	....	....	....	....	....	....	....	....	....	....	....	....
1995-96	**Calgary**	**NHL**	**4**	**0**	**0**	**0**	**4**	**0**	**0**	**0**	**0**	**0.0**	**0**	....	....	....	....	....	....	....	....	....	....	....	....	....
	Saint John Flames	AHL	74	8	25	33	104	....	....	....	....	....	....	....	....	....	....	....	16	1	4	5	10	....	....	....
1996-97	**Calgary**	**NHL**	**76**	**4**	**5**	**9**	**49**	**0**	**1**	**0**	**61**	**6.6**	**–23**	....	....	....	....	....	....	....	....	....	....	....	....	....
1997-98	**Calgary**	**NHL**	**44**	**5**	**7**	**12**	**57**	**0**	**1**	**1**	**51**	**9.8**	**0**	....	....	....	....	....	....	....	....	....	....	....	....	....
	Saint John Flames	AHL	3	2	1	3	6	....	....	....	....	....	....	....	....	....	....	....	....	....	....	....	....	....	....	....
1998-99	**Nashville**	**NHL**	**64**	**4**	**11**	**15**	**60**	**0**	**0**	**0**	**78**	**5.1**	**–10**	**0**	**0.0**	**109**	**67**	**22:34**	....	....	....	....	....	....	....	....
99-2000	**Nashville**	**NHL**	**52**	**1**	**4**	**5**	**23**	**0**	**0**	**0**	**60**	**1.7**	**–11**	**0**	**0.0**	**88**	**48**	**18:41**	....	....	....	....	....	....	....	....
	Dallas	**NHL**	**2**	**0**	**0**	**0**	**2**	**0**	**0**	**0**	**1**	**0.0**	**1**	**0**	**0.0**	**2**	**2**	**9:45**	....	....	....	....	....	....	....	....
	NHL Totals		**244**	**14**	**27**	**41**	**195**	**0**	**2**	**1**	**251**	**5.6**		**0**	**0.0**	**199**	**117**	**20:38**	....	....	....	....	....	....	....	....

QMJHL First All-Star Team (1994)

Claimed by **Nashville** from **Calgary** in Expansion Draft, June 26, 1998. Claimed on waivers by **Dallas** from **Nashville**, March 14, 2000. Signed as a free agent by **Phoenix**, August 31, 2000.

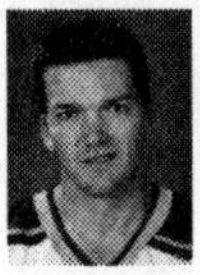

BOUCHER, Philippe
(boo-SHAY, fihl-EEP) **L.A.**

Defense. Shoots right. 6'2", 221 lbs. Born, St. Apollinaire, Que., March 24, 1973. Buffalo's 1st choice, 13th overall, in 1991 Entry Draft.

Season	Club	League	GP	G	A	Pts	PIM	PP	SH	GW	S	%	+/–	TF	F%	H	SB	Min	Playoffs GP	G	A	Pts	PIM	PP	SH	GW
1989-90	Ste-Foy Governors	QAAA	33	18	47	65	64	....	....	....	....	....	....	....	....	....	....	....	9	8	13	21	12	....	....	....
1990-91	Granby Bisons	QMJHL	69	21	46	67	92	....	....	....	....	....	....	....	....	....	....	....	....	....	....	....	....	....	....	....
1991-92	Granby Bisons	QMJHL	49	22	37	59	47	....	....	....	....	....	....	....	....	....	....	....	....	....	....	....	....	....	....	....
	Laval Titans	QMJHL	16	7	11	18	36	....	....	....	....	....	....	....	....	....	....	....	10	5	6	11	8	....	....	....
1992-93	Laval Titans	QMJHL	16	12	15	27	37	....	....	....	....	....	....	....	....	....	....	....	13	6	15	21	12	....	....	....
	Buffalo	**NHL**	**18**	**0**	**4**	**4**	**14**	**0**	**0**	**0**	**28**	**0.0**	**1**	....	....	....	....	....	....	....	....	....	....	....	....	....
	Rochester	AHL	5	4	3	7	8	....	....	....	....	....	....	....	....	....	....	....	3	0	1	1	2	....	....	....
1993-94	**Buffalo**	**NHL**	**38**	**6**	**8**	**14**	**29**	**4**	**0**	**1**	**67**	**9.0**	**–1**	....	....	....	....	....	**7**	**1**	**1**	**2**	**2**	**1**	**0**	**0**
	Rochester	AHL	31	10	22	32	51	....	....	....	....	....	....	....	....	....	....	....	....	....	....	....	....	....	....	....
1994-95	Rochester	AHL	43	14	27	41	26	....	....	....	....	....	....	....	....	....	....	....	....	....	....	....	....	....	....	....
	Buffalo	**NHL**	**9**	**1**	**4**	**5**	**0**	**0**	**0**	**0**	**15**	**6.7**	**6**	....	....	....	....	....	....	....	....	....	....	....	....	....
	Los Angeles	**NHL**	**6**	**1**	**0**	**1**	**4**	**0**	**0**	**0**	**15**	**6.7**	**–3**	....	....	....	....	....	....	....	....	....	....	....	....	....
1995-96	**Los Angeles**	**NHL**	**53**	**7**	**16**	**23**	**31**	**5**	**0**	**1**	**145**	**4.8**	**–26**	....	....	....	....	....	....	....	....	....	....	....	....	....
	Phoenix	IHL	10	4	3	7	4	....	....	....	....	....	....	....	....	....	....	....	....	....	....	....	....	....	....	....
1996-97	**Los Angeles**	**NHL**	**60**	**7**	**18**	**25**	**25**	**2**	**0**	**1**	**159**	**4.4**	**0**	....	....	....	....	....	....	....	....	....	....	....	....	....
1997-98	**Los Angeles**	**NHL**	**45**	**6**	**10**	**16**	**49**	**1**	**0**	**0**	**80**	**7.5**	**6**	....	....	....	....	....	....	....	....	....	....	....	....	....
	Long Beach	IHL	2	0	1	1	4	....	....	....	....	....	....	....	....	....	....	....	....	....	....	....	....	....	....	....
1998-99	**Los Angeles**	**NHL**	**45**	**2**	**6**	**8**	**32**	**1**	**0**	**0**	**87**	**2.3**	**–12**	**0**	**0.0**	**58**	**63**	**17:51**	....	....	....	....	....	....	....	....
99-2000	**Los Angeles**	**NHL**	**1**	**0**	**0**	**0**	**0**	**0**	**0**	**0**	**3**	**0.0**	**0**	**0**	**0.0**	**4**	**3**	**17:04**	....	....	....	....	....	....	....	....
	Long Beach	IHL	14	4	11	15	8	....	....	....	....	....	....	....	....	....	....	....	6	0	9	9	8	....	....	....
	NHL Totals		**275**	**30**	**66**	**96**	**184**	**13**	**0**	**3**	**599**	**5.0**		**0**	**0.0**	**62**	**66**	**17:50**	**7**	**1**	**1**	**2**	**2**	**1**	**0**	**0**

Canadian Major Junior Rookie of the Year (1991) • QMJHL Second All-Star Team (1991, 1992)

Traded to **LA Kings** by **Buffalo** with Denis Tsygurov and Grant Fuhr for Alexei Zhitnik, Robb Stauber, Charlie Huddy and LA Kings' 5th round choice (Marian Menhart) in 1995 Entry Draft, February 14, 1995.
• Missed majority of 1999-2000 season recovering from foot injury that required surgery, September, 1999.

BOUGHNER, Bob
(BOOG-nuhr, BAWB) **PIT.**

Defense. Shoots right. 6', 203 lbs. Born, Windsor, Ont., March 8, 1971. Detroit's 2nd choice, 32nd overall, in 1989 Entry Draft.

Season	Club	League	GP	G	A	Pts	PIM	PP	SH	GW	S	%	+/–	TF	F%	H	SB	Min	Playoffs GP	G	A	Pts	PIM	PP	SH	GW
1986-87	Belle River	OJHL-C	37	3	11	14	88	....	....	....	....	....	....	....	....	....	....	....	....	....	....	....	....	....	....	....
1987-88	St. Mary's	OJHL-B	36	4	18	22	177	....	....	....	....	....	....	....	....	....	....	....	....	....	....	....	....	....	....	....
1988-89	Sault Ste. Marie	OHL	64	6	15	21	182	....	....	....	....	....	....	....	....	....	....	....	....	....	....	....	....	....	....	....
1989-90	Sault Ste. Marie	OHL	49	7	23	30	122	....	....	....	....	....	....	....	....	....	....	....	....	....	....	....	....	....	....	....
1990-91	Sault Ste. Marie	OHL	64	13	33	46	156	....	....	....	....	....	....	....	....	....	....	....	14	2	9	11	35	....	....	....
1991-92	Toledo Storm	ECHL	28	3	10	13	79	....	....	....	....	....	....	....	....	....	....	....	5	2	0	2	15	....	....	....
	Adirondack	AHL	1	0	0	0	7	....	....	....	....	....	....	....	....	....	....	....	....	....	....	....	....	....	....	....
1992-93	Adirondack	AHL	69	1	16	17	190	....	....	....	....	....	....	....	....	....	....	....	....	....	....	....	....	....	....	....
1993-94	Adirondack	AHL	72	8	14	22	292	....	....	....	....	....	....	....	....	....	....	....	10	1	1	2	18	....	....	....
1994-95	Cincinnati	IHL	81	2	14	16	192	....	....	....	....	....	....	....	....	....	....	....	10	0	0	0	18	....	....	....
1995-96	Carolina	AHL	46	2	15	17	127	....	....	....	....	....	....	....	....	....	....	....	....	....	....	....	....	....	....	....
	Buffalo	**NHL**	**31**	**0**	**1**	**1**	**104**	**0**	**0**	**0**	**14**	**0.0**	**3**	....	....	....	....	....	....	....	....	....	....	....	....	....
1996-97	**Buffalo**	**NHL**	**77**	**1**	**7**	**8**	**225**	**0**	**0**	**0**	**34**	**2.9**	**12**	....	....	....	....	....	**11**	**0**	**1**	**1**	**9**	**0**	**0**	**0**
1997-98	**Buffalo**	**NHL**	**69**	**1**	**3**	**4**	**165**	**0**	**0**	**0**	**26**	**3.8**	**5**	....	....	....	....	....	**14**	**0**	**4**	**4**	**15**	**0**	**0**	**0**
1998-99	**Nashville**	**NHL**	**79**	**3**	**10**	**13**	**137**	**0**	**0**	**1**	**59**	**5.1**	**–6**	**0**	**0.0**	**233**	**91**	**18:31**	....	....	....	....	....	....	....	....
99-2000	**Nashville**	**NHL**	**62**	**2**	**4**	**6**	**97**	**0**	**0**	**0**	**32**	**6.3**	**–13**	**0**	**0.0**	**207**	**67**	**17:20**	....	....	....	....	....	....	....	....
	Pittsburgh	**NHL**	**11**	**1**	**0**	**1**	**69**	**1**	**0**	**1**	**8**	**12.5**	**2**	**0**	**0.0**	**26**	**14**	**17:05**	**11**	**0**	**2**	**2**	**15**	**0**	**0**	**0**
	NHL Totals		**329**	**8**	**25**	**33**	**797**	**1**	**0**	**2**	**173**	**4.6**		**0**	**0.0**	**466**	**172**	**17:56**	**36**	**0**	**7**	**7**	**39**	**0**	**0**	**0**

Signed as a free agent by **Florida**, July 25, 1994. Traded to **Buffalo** by **Florida** for Buffalo's 3rd round choice (Chris Allen) in 1996 Entry Draft, February 1, 1996. Claimed by **Nashville** from **Buffalo** in Expansion Draft, June 26, 1998. Traded to **Pittsburgh** by **Buffalo** for Pavel Skrbek, March 13, 2000.

BOUILLON, Francis
(BOO-liawn, FRAN-sihs) **MTL.**

Defense. Shoots left. 5'9", 189 lbs. Born, New York, NY, October 17, 1975.

Season	Club	League	GP	G	A	Pts	PIM	PP	SH	GW	S	%	+/–	TF	F%	H	SB	Min	Playoffs GP	G	A	Pts	PIM	PP	SH	GW
1992-93	Laval Titan	QMJHL	46	0	7	7	45	....	....	....	....	....	....	....	....	....	....	....	....	....	....	....	....	....	....	....
1993-94	Laval Titan	QMJHL	68	3	15	18	129	....	....	....	....	....	....	....	....	....	....	....	19	2	9	11	48	....	....	....
1994-95	Laval Titan	QMJHL	72	8	25	33	115	....	....	....	....	....	....	....	....	....	....	....	20	3	11	14	21	....	....	....
1995-96	Granby	QMJHL	68	11	35	46	156	....	....	....	....	....	....	....	....	....	....	....	21	2	12	14	30	....	....	....
1996-97	Wheeling Nailers	ECHL	69	10	32	42	77	....	....	....	....	....	....	....	....	....	....	....	3	0	2	2	10	....	....	....
1997-98	Quebec Rafales	IHL	71	8	27	35	76	....	....	....	....	....	....	....	....	....	....	....	....	....	....	....	....	....	....	....

Season	Club	League	GP	G	A	Pts	PIM	PP	SH	GW	S	%	+/-	TF	F%	H	SB	Min	GP	G	A	Pts	PIM	PP	SH	GW
			Regular Season																Playoffs							
1998-99	Fredericton	AHL	79	19	36	55	174	....	....	....	....	....	....	....	....	....	....	....	5	2	1	3	0	....	....	....
99-2000	Montreal	NHL	74	3	13	16	38	2	0	1	76	3.9	–7	1	0.0	68	52	15:52	....	....	....	....	....	....	....	....
	NHL Totals		74	3	13	16	38	2	0	1	76	3.9		1	0.0	68	52	15:52	....	....	....	....	....	....	....	....

Signed as a free agent by **Montreal**, August 18, 1998 • Played w/ RHI's Montreal Roadrunners in 1996 (23-4-9-13-63).

BOURQUE, Ray

(BOHRK, RAY) **COL.**

Defense. Shoots left. 5'11", 219 lbs. Born, Montreal, Que., December 28, 1960. Boston's 1st choice, 8th overall, in 1979 Entry Draft.

Season	Club	League	GP	G	A	Pts	PIM	PP	SH	GW	S	%	+/-	TF	F%	H	SB	Min	GP	G	A	Pts	PIM	PP	SH	GW
1976-77	Sorel Eperviers	QMJHL	69	12	36	48	61	....	....	....	....	....	....	....	....	....	....	....	....	....	....	....	....	....	....	....
1977-78	Verdun Eperviers	QMJHL	72	22	57	79	90	....	....	....	....	....	....	....	....	....	....	....	4	2	1	3	0	....	....	....
1978-79	Verdun Eperviers	QMJHL	63	22	71	93	44	....	....	....	....	....	....	....	....	....	....	....	11	3	16	19	18	....	....	....
1979-80	Boston	NHL	80	17	48	65	73	3	2	1	185	9.2	52	....	....	....	....	....	10	2	9	11	27	0	0	0
1980-81	Boston	NHL	67	27	29	56	96	9	1	6	207	13.0	29	....	....	....	....	....	3	0	1	1	2	0	0	0
1981-82	Boston	NHL	65	17	49	66	51	4	0	2	211	8.1	22	....	....	....	....	....	9	1	5	6	16	0	0	1
1982-83	Boston	NHL	65	22	51	73	20	7	0	5	205	10.7	49	....	....	....	....	....	17	8	15	23	10	2	0	1
1983-84	Boston	NHL	78	31	65	96	57	12	1	5	340	9.1	51	....	....	....	....	....	3	0	2	2	0	0	0	0
1984-85	Boston	NHL	73	20	66	86	53	10	1	1	333	6.0	30	....	....	....	....	....	5	0	3	3	4	0	0	0
1985-86	Boston	NHL	74	19	58	77	68	11	0	3	289	6.6	17	....	....	....	....	....	3	0	0	0	0	0	0	0
1986-87	Boston	NHL	78	23	72	95	36	6	1	3	334	6.9	44	....	....	....	....	....	4	1	2	3	0	0	0	0
1987-88	Boston	NHL	78	17	64	81	72	7	1	5	344	4.9	34	....	....	....	....	....	23	3	18	21	26	0	0	1
1988-89	Boston	NHL	60	18	43	61	52	6	0	0	243	7.4	20	....	....	....	....	....	10	0	4	4	6	0	0	0
1989-90	Boston	NHL	76	19	65	84	50	8	0	3	310	6.1	31	....	....	....	....	....	17	5	12	17	16	1	0	0
1990-91	Boston	NHL	76	21	73	94	75	7	0	3	323	6.5	33	....	....	....	....	....	19	7	18	25	12	3	0	0
1991-92	Boston	NHL	80	21	60	81	56	7	1	2	334	6.3	11	....	....	....	....	....	12	3	6	9	12	2	0	0
1992-93	Boston	NHL	78	19	63	82	40	8	0	7	330	5.8	38	....	....	....	....	....	4	1	0	1	2	1	0	0
1993-94	Boston	NHL	72	20	71	91	58	10	3	1	386	5.2	26	....	....	....	....	....	13	2	8	10	0	1	0	0
1994-95	Boston	NHL	46	12	31	43	20	9	0	2	210	5.7	3	....	....	....	....	....	5	0	3	3	0	0	0	0
1995-96	Boston	NHL	82	20	62	82	58	9	2	2	390	5.1	31	....	....	....	....	....	5	1	6	7	2	1	0	0
1996-97	Boston	NHL	62	19	31	50	18	8	1	3	230	8.3	–11	....	....	....	....	....	....	....	....	....	....	....	....	....
1997-98	Boston	NHL	82	13	35	48	80	9	0	3	264	4.9	2	....	....	....	....	....	6	1	4	5	2	1	0	0
	Canada	Olympics	6	1	2	3	4	....	....	....	....	....	....	....	....	....	....	....	....	....	....	....	....	....	....	....
1998-99	Boston	NHL	81	10	47	57	34	8	0	3	262	3.8	–7	2	0.0	173	113	29:31	12	1	9	10	14	0	0	0
99-2000	Boston	NHL	65	10	28	38	20	6	0	0	217	4.6	–11	1	0.0	132	73	27:12	....	....	....	....	....	....	....	....
	Colorado	NHL	14	8	6	14	6	7	0	0	43	18.6	9	0	0.0	32	21	27:08	13	1	8	9	8	0	0	0
	NHL Totals		1532	403	1117	1520	1093	171	14	60	5990	6.7		3	0.0	337	207	28:22	193	37	133	170	159	12	0	3

QMJHL First All-Star Team (1978, 1979) • Won Calder Memorial Trophy (1980) • NHL First All-Star Team (1980, 1982, 1984, 1985, 1987, 1988, 1990, 1991, 1992, 1993, 1994, 1996) • NHL Second All-Star Team (1981, 1983, 1986, 1989, 1995, 1999) • Won James Norris Memorial Trophy (1987, 1988, 1990, 1991, 1994) • Won King Clancy Memorial Trophy (1992) • Played in NHL All-Star Game (1981, 1982, 1983, 1984, 1985, 1986, 1988, 1989, 1990, 1991, 1992, 1993, 1994, 1996, 1997, 1998, 1999, 2000)

Traded to **Colorado** by **Boston** with Dave Andreychuk for Brian Rolston, Martin Grenier, Sami Pahlsson and New Jersey's 1st round choice (previously acquired, Boston selected Martin Samuelsson) in 2000 Entry Draft, March 6, 2000.

BOWEN, Jason

(BOW-ehn, JAY-suhn)

Defense. Shoots left. 6'4", 220 lbs. Born, Port Alice, B.C., November 9, 1973. Philadelphia's 2nd choice, 15th overall, in 1992 Entry Draft.

Season	Club	League	GP	G	A	Pts	PIM	PP	SH	GW	S	%	+/-	TF	F%	H	SB	Min	GP	G	A	Pts	PIM	PP	SH	GW
1988-89	Notre Dame	AAHA	56	10	29	39	40	....	....	....	....	....	....	....	....	....	....	....	....	....	....	....	....	....	....	....
1989-90	Tri-City Americans	WHL	61	8	5	13	129	....	....	....	....	....	....	....	....	....	....	....	7	0	3	3	4	....	....	....
1990-91	Tri-City Americans	WHL	60	7	13	20	252	....	....	....	....	....	....	....	....	....	....	....	6	2	2	4	18	....	....	....
1991-92	Tri-City Americans	WHL	19	5	3	8	135	....	....	....	....	....	....	....	....	....	....	....	5	0	1	1	42	....	....	....
1992-93	Tri-City Americans	WHL	62	10	12	22	219	....	....	....	....	....	....	....	....	....	....	....	3	1	1	2	18	....	....	....
	Philadelphia	NHL	7	1	0	1	2	0	0	0	3	33.3	1	....	....	....	....	....	....	....	....	....	....	....	....	....
1993-94	Philadelphia	NHL	56	1	5	6	87	0	0	1	50	2.0	12	....	....	....	....	....	....	....	....	....	....	....	....	....
1994-95	Philadelphia	NHL	4	0	0	0	0	0	0	0	2	0.0	–2	....	....	....	....	....	....	....	....	....	....	....	....	....
	Hershey Bears	AHL	55	5	5	10	116	....	....	....	....	....	....	....	....	....	....	....	6	0	0	0	46	....	....	....
1995-96	Philadelphia	NHL	2	0	0	0	2	0	0	0	2	0.0	0	....	....	....	....	....	....	....	....	....	....	....	....	....
	Hershey Bears	AHL	72	6	7	13	128	....	....	....	....	....	....	....	....	....	....	....	4	2	0	2	13	....	....	....
1996-97	Philadelphia	NHL	4	0	1	1	8	0	0	0	1	0.0	1	....	....	....	....	....	....	....	....	....	....	....	....	....
	Philadelphia	AHL	61	10	12	22	160	....	....	....	....	....	....	....	....	....	....	....	6	0	1	1	10	....	....	....
1997-98	Philadelphia	AHL	3	0	0	0	19	....	....	....	....	....	....	....	....	....	....	....	....	....	....	....	....	....	....	....
	Edmonton	NHL	4	0	0	0	10	0	0	0	3	0.0	0	....	....	....	....	....	....	....	....	....	....	....	....	....
	Hamilton Bulldogs	AHL	51	5	14	19	108	....	....	....	....	....	....	....	....	....	....	....	7	1	1	2	22	....	....	....
1998-99	Hamilton Bulldogs	AHL	58	3	3	6	178	....	....	....	....	....	....	....	....	....	....	....	11	0	1	1	16	....	....	....
99-2000	Hershey Bears	AHL	54	2	8	10	152	....	....	....	....	....	....	....	....	....	....	....	....	....	....	....	....	....	....	....
	Saint John Flames	AHL	11	0	1	1	28	....	....	....	....	....	....	....	....	....	....	....	2	0	0	0	4	....	....	....
	NHL Totals		77	2	6	8	109	0	0	1	61	3.3		....	....	....	....	....	....	....	....	....	....	....	....	....

Traded to **Edmonton** by **Philadelphia** for Brantt Myhres, October 15, 1997. Signed as a free agent by **Colorado**, August 26, 1999. Loaned to **Saint John** (AHL) by **Colorado**, March 15, 2000.

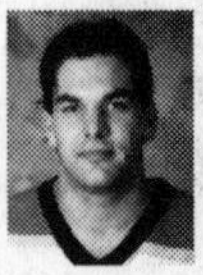

BOYLE, Dan

(BOIL, DAN) **FLA.**

Defense. Shoots right. 5'11", 190 lbs. Born, Ottawa, Ont., July 12, 1976.

Season	Club	League	GP	G	A	Pts	PIM	PP	SH	GW	S	%	+/-	TF	F%	H	SB	Min	GP	G	A	Pts	PIM	PP	SH	GW
1992-93	Gloucester	OJHL	55	22	51	73	60	....	....	....	....	....	....	....	....	....	....	....	....	....	....	....	....	....	....	....
1993-94	Gloucester	OJHL	53	27	54	81	155	....	....	....	....	....	....	....	....	....	....	....	....	....	....	....	....	....	....	....
1994-95	U. of Miami-Ohio	CCHA	35	8	18	26	24	....	....	....	....	....	....	....	....	....	....	....	....	....	....	....	....	....	....	....
1995-96	U. of Miami-Ohio	CCHA	36	7	20	27	70	....	....	....	....	....	....	....	....	....	....	....	....	....	....	....	....	....	....	....
1996-97	U. of Miami-Ohio	CCHA	40	11	43	54	52	....	....	....	....	....	....	....	....	....	....	....	....	....	....	....	....	....	....	....
1997-98	U. of Miami-Ohio	CCHA	37	14	26	40	58	....	....	....	....	....	....	....	....	....	....	....	....	....	....	....	....	....	....	....
1998-99	Florida	NHL	22	3	5	8	6	1	0	1	31	9.7	0	1	100.0	27	14	18:50	....	....	....	....	....	....	....	....
	Kentucky	AHL	53	8	34	42	87	....	....	....	....	....	....	....	....	....	....	....	12	3	5	8	16	....	....	....
99-2000	Florida	NHL	13	0	3	3	4	0	0	0	9	0.0	–2	0	0.0	9	12	16:57	....	....	....	....	....	....	....	....
	Louisville	AHL	58	14	38	52	75	....	....	....	....	....	....	....	....	....	....	....	4	0	2	2	8	....	....	....
	NHL Totals		35	3	8	11	10	1	0	1	40	7.5		1	100.0	36	26	18:08	....	....	....	....	....	....	....	....

CCHA First All-Star Team (1997, 1998) • NCAA West First All-American Team (1997, 1998) • AHL Second All-Star Team (1999, 2000)

Signed as a free agent by **Florida**, March 30, 1998.

BOYNTON, Nick

(BOIN-tuhn, NIHK) **BOS.**

Defense. Shoots right. 6'2", 202 lbs. Born, Nobleton, Ont., January 14, 1979. Boston's 1st choice, 21st overall, in 1999 Entry Draft.

Season	Club	League	GP	G	A	Pts	PIM	PP	SH	GW	S	%	+/-	TF	F%	H	SB	Min	GP	G	A	Pts	PIM	PP	SH	GW
1993-94	Caledon Canucks	OJHL	4	0	1	1	0	....	....	....	....	....	....	....	....	....	....	....	....	....	....	....	....	....	....	....
1994-95	Caledon Canucks	OJHL	44	10	35	45	139	....	....	....	....	....	....	....	....	....	....	....	....	....	....	....	....	....	....	....
1995-96	Ottawa 67's	OHL	64	10	14	24	90	....	....	....	....	....	....	....	....	....	....	....	4	0	3	3	10	....	....	....
1996-97	Ottawa 67's	OHL	63	13	51	64	143	....	....	....	....	....	....	....	....	....	....	....	24	4	*24	28	38	....	....	....
1997-98	Ottawa 67's	OHL	40	7	31	38	94	....	....	....	....	....	....	....	....	....	....	....	13	0	4	4	24	....	....	....
1998-99	Ottawa 67's	OHL	51	11	48	59	83	....	....	....	....	....	....	....	....	....	....	....	9	1	9	10	18	....	....	....
99-2000	Boston	NHL	5	0	0	0	0	0	0	0	6	0.0	–5	0	0.0	6	8	21:21	....	....	....	....	....	....	....	....
	Providence Bruins	AHL	53	5	14	19	66	....	....	....	....	....	....	....	....	....	....	....	12	1	0	1	6	....	....	....
	NHL Totals		5	0	0	0	0	0	0	0	6	0.0		0	0.0	6	8	21:21	....	....	....	....	....	....	....	....

• Re-entered NHL draft. Originally Washington's 1st choice, 9th overall, in 1997 Entry Draft.

Memorial Cup All-Star Team (1999) • Won Stafford Smythe Memorial Trophy (Memorial Cup Tournament MVP) (1999)

			Regular Season																Playoffs							
Season	Club	League	GP	G	A	Pts	PIM	PP	SH	GW	S	%	+/–	TF	F%	H	SB	Min	GP	G	A	Pts	PIM	PP	SH	GW

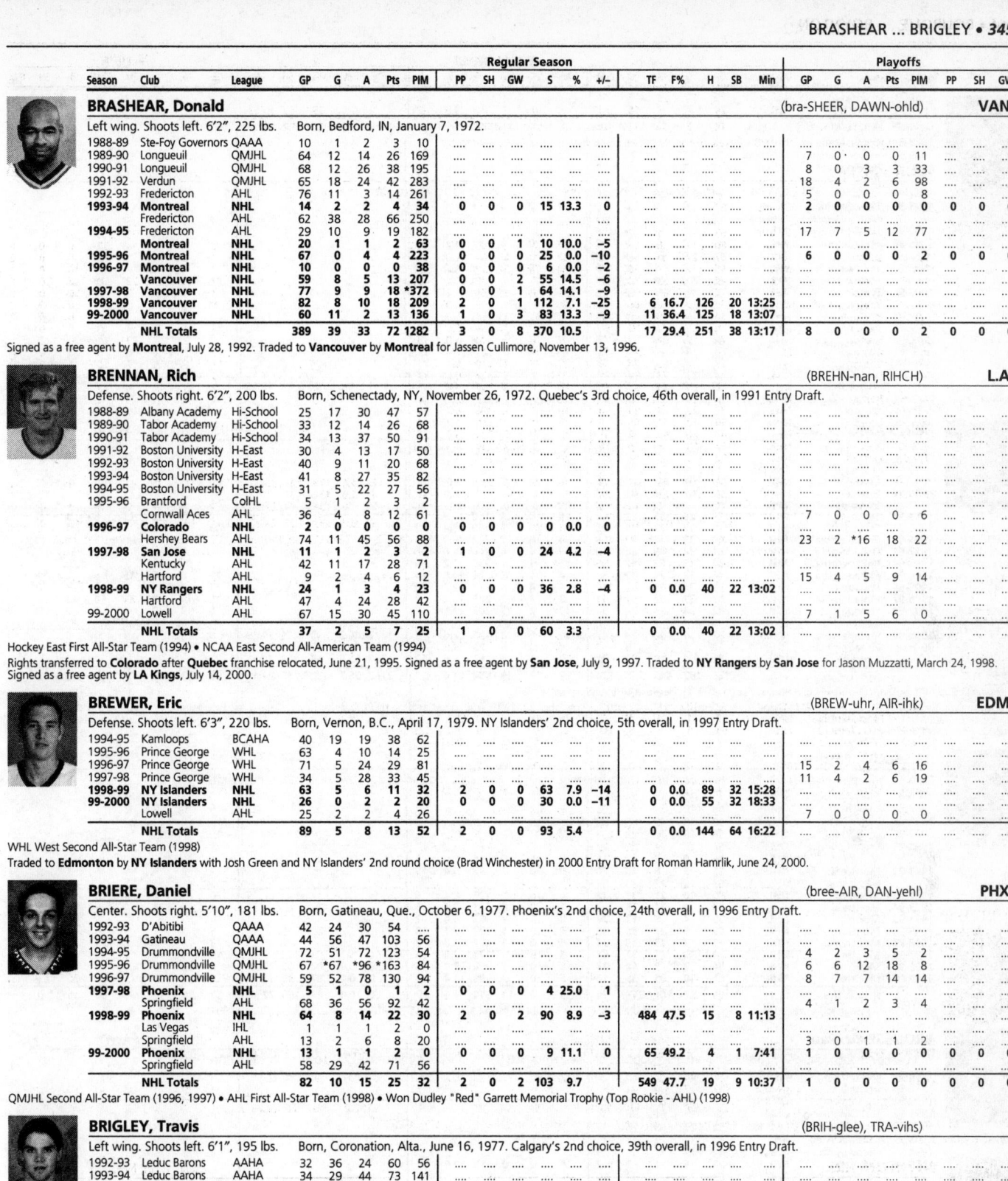

BRASHEAR, Donald
(bra-SHEER, DAWN-ohld) **VAN.**

Left wing. Shoots left. 6'2", 225 lbs. Born, Bedford, IN, January 7, 1972.

Season	Club	League	GP	G	A	Pts	PIM	PP	SH	GW	S	%	+/–	TF	F%	H	SB	Min	GP	G	A	Pts	PIM	PP	SH	GW
1988-89	Ste-Foy Governors	QAAA	10	1	2	3	10	....	....	....	....	....	....	....	....	....	....	....	....	....	....	....	....	....	....	....
1989-90	Longueuil	QMJHL	64	12	14	26	169	....	....	....	....	....	....	....	....	....	....	....	7	0	0	0	11	....	....	....
1990-91	Longueuil	QMJHL	68	12	26	38	195	....	....	....	....	....	....	....	....	....	....	....	8	0	3	3	33	....	....	....
1991-92	Verdun	QMJHL	65	18	24	42	283	....	....	....	....	....	....	....	....	....	....	....	18	4	2	6	98	....	....	....
1992-93	Fredericton	AHL	76	11	3	14	261	....	....	....	....	....	....	....	....	....	....	....	5	0	0	0	8	....	....	....
1993-94	**Montreal**	**NHL**	**14**	**2**	**2**	**4**	**34**	**0**	**0**	**0**	**15**	**13.3**	**0**	....	....	....	....	....	**2**	**0**	**0**	**0**	**0**	**0**	**0**	**0**
	Fredericton	AHL	62	38	28	66	250	....	....	....	....	....	....	....	....	....	....	....	....	....	....	....	....	....	....	....
1994-95	Fredericton	AHL	29	10	9	19	182	....	....	....	....	....	....	....	....	....	....	....	17	7	5	12	77	....	....	....
	Montreal	**NHL**	**20**	**1**	**1**	**2**	**63**	**0**	**0**	**1**	**10**	**10.0**	**–5**	....	....	....	....	....	....	....	....	....	....	....	....	....
1995-96	**Montreal**	**NHL**	**67**	**0**	**4**	**4**	**223**	**0**	**0**	**0**	**25**	**0.0**	**–10**	....	....	....	....	....	**6**	**0**	**0**	**0**	**2**	**0**	**0**	**0**
1996-97	**Montreal**	**NHL**	**10**	**0**	**0**	**0**	**38**	**0**	**0**	**0**	**6**	**0.0**	**–2**	....	....	....	....	....	....	....	....	....	....	....	....	....
	Vancouver	**NHL**	**59**	**8**	**5**	**13**	**207**	**0**	**0**	**2**	**55**	**14.5**	**–6**	....	....	....	....	....	....	....	....	....	....	....	....	....
1997-98	**Vancouver**	**NHL**	**77**	**9**	**9**	**18**	***372**	**0**	**0**	**1**	**64**	**14.1**	**–9**	....	....	....	....	....	....	....	....	....	....	....	....	....
1998-99	**Vancouver**	**NHL**	**82**	**8**	**10**	**18**	**209**	**2**	**0**	**1**	**112**	**7.1**	**–25**	**6**	**16.7**	**126**	**20**	**13:25**	....	....	....	....	....	....	....	....
99-2000	**Vancouver**	**NHL**	**60**	**11**	**2**	**13**	**136**	**1**	**0**	**3**	**83**	**13.3**	**–9**	**11**	**36.4**	**125**	**18**	**13:07**	....	....	....	....	....	....	....	....
	NHL Totals		**389**	**39**	**33**	**72**	**1282**	**3**	**0**	**8**	**370**	**10.5**		**17**	**29.4**	**251**	**38**	**13:17**	**8**	**0**	**0**	**0**	**2**	**0**	**0**	**0**

Signed as a free agent by **Montreal**, July 28, 1992. Traded to **Vancouver** by **Montreal** for Jassen Cullimore, November 13, 1996.

BRENNAN, Rich
(BREHN-nan, RIHCH) **L.A.**

Defense. Shoots right. 6'2", 200 lbs. Born, Schenectady, NY, November 26, 1972. Quebec's 3rd choice, 46th overall, in 1991 Entry Draft.

Season	Club	League	GP	G	A	Pts	PIM	PP	SH	GW	S	%	+/–	TF	F%	H	SB	Min	GP	G	A	Pts	PIM	PP	SH	GW
1988-89	Albany Academy	Hi-School	25	17	30	47	57	....	....	....	....	....	....	....	....	....	....	....	....	....	....	....	....	....	....	....
1989-90	Tabor Academy	Hi-School	33	12	14	26	68	....	....	....	....	....	....	....	....	....	....	....	....	....	....	....	....	....	....	....
1990-91	Tabor Academy	Hi-School	34	13	37	50	91	....	....	....	....	....	....	....	....	....	....	....	....	....	....	....	....	....	....	....
1991-92	Boston University	H-East	30	4	13	17	50	....	....	....	....	....	....	....	....	....	....	....	....	....	....	....	....	....	....	....
1992-93	Boston University	H-East	40	9	11	20	68	....	....	....	....	....	....	....	....	....	....	....	....	....	....	....	....	....	....	....
1993-94	Boston University	H-East	41	8	27	35	82	....	....	....	....	....	....	....	....	....	....	....	....	....	....	....	....	....	....	....
1994-95	Boston University	H-East	31	5	22	27	56	....	....	....	....	....	....	....	....	....	....	....	....	....	....	....	....	....	....	....
1995-96	Brantford	ColHL	5	1	2	3	2	....	....	....	....	....	....	....	....	....	....	....	....	....	....	....	....	....	....	....
	Cornwall Aces	AHL	36	4	8	12	61	....	....	....	....	....	....	....	....	....	....	....	7	0	0	0	6	....	....	....
1996-97	**Colorado**	**NHL**	**2**	**0**	**0**	**0**	**0**	**0**	**0**	**0**	**0**	**0.0**	**0**	....	....	....	....	....	....	....	....	....	....	....	....	....
	Hershey Bears	AHL	74	11	45	56	88	....	....	....	....	....	....	....	....	....	....	....	23	2	*16	18	22	....	....	....
1997-98	**San Jose**	**NHL**	**11**	**1**	**2**	**3**	**2**	**1**	**0**	**0**	**24**	**4.2**	**–4**	....	....	....	....	....	....	....	....	....	....	....	....	....
	Kentucky	AHL	42	11	17	28	71	....	....	....	....	....	....	....	....	....	....	....	....	....	....	....	....	....	....	....
	Hartford	AHL	9	2	4	6	12	....	....	....	....	....	....	....	....	....	....	....	15	4	5	9	14	....	....	....
1998-99	**NY Rangers**	**NHL**	**24**	**1**	**3**	**4**	**23**	**0**	**0**	**0**	**36**	**2.8**	**–4**	**0**	**0.0**	**40**	**22**	**13:02**	....	....	....	....	....	....	....	....
	Hartford	AHL	47	4	24	28	42	....	....	....	....	....	....	....	....	....	....	....	....	....	....	....	....	....	....	....
99-2000	Lowell	AHL	67	15	30	45	110	....	....	....	....	....	....	....	....	....	....	....	7	1	5	6	0	....	....	....
	NHL Totals		**37**	**2**	**5**	**7**	**25**	**1**	**0**	**0**	**60**	**3.3**		**0**	**0.0**	**40**	**22**	**13:02**	....	....	....	....	....	....	....	....

Hockey East First All-Star Team (1994) • NCAA East Second All-American Team (1994)

Rights transferred to **Colorado** after **Quebec** franchise relocated, June 21, 1995. Signed as a free agent by **San Jose**, July 9, 1997. Traded to **NY Rangers** by **San Jose** for Jason Muzzatti, March 24, 1998. Signed as a free agent by **LA Kings**, July 14, 2000.

BREWER, Eric
(BREW-uhr, AIR-ihk) **EDM.**

Defense. Shoots left. 6'3", 220 lbs. Born, Vernon, B.C., April 17, 1979. NY Islanders' 2nd choice, 5th overall, in 1997 Entry Draft.

Season	Club	League	GP	G	A	Pts	PIM	PP	SH	GW	S	%	+/–	TF	F%	H	SB	Min	GP	G	A	Pts	PIM	PP	SH	GW
1994-95	Kamloops	BCAHA	40	19	19	38	62	....	....	....	....	....	....	....	....	....	....	....	....	....	....	....	....	....	....	....
1995-96	Prince George	WHL	63	4	10	14	25	....	....	....	....	....	....	....	....	....	....	....	....	....	....	....	....	....	....	....
1996-97	Prince George	WHL	71	5	24	29	81	....	....	....	....	....	....	....	....	....	....	....	15	2	4	6	16	....	....	....
1997-98	Prince George	WHL	34	5	28	33	45	....	....	....	....	....	....	....	....	....	....	....	11	4	2	6	19	....	....	....
1998-99	**NY Islanders**	**NHL**	**63**	**5**	**6**	**11**	**32**	**2**	**0**	**0**	**63**	**7.9**	**–14**	**0**	**0.0**	**89**	**32**	**15:28**	....	....	....	....	....	....	....	....
99-2000	**NY Islanders**	**NHL**	**26**	**0**	**2**	**2**	**20**	**0**	**0**	**0**	**30**	**0.0**	**–11**	**0**	**0.0**	**55**	**32**	**18:33**	....	....	....	....	....	....	....	....
	Lowell	AHL	25	2	2	4	26	....	....	....	....	....	....	....	....	....	....	....	7	0	0	0	0	....	....	....
	NHL Totals		**89**	**5**	**8**	**13**	**52**	**2**	**0**	**0**	**93**	**5.4**		**0**	**0.0**	**144**	**64**	**16:22**	....	....	....	....	....	....	....	....

WHL West Second All-Star Team (1998)

Traded to **Edmonton** by **NY Islanders** with Josh Green and NY Islanders' 2nd round choice (Brad Winchester) in 2000 Entry Draft for Roman Hamrlik, June 24, 2000.

BRIERE, Daniel
(bree-AIR, DAN-yehl) **PHX.**

Center. Shoots right. 5'10", 181 lbs. Born, Gatineau, Que., October 6, 1977. Phoenix's 2nd choice, 24th overall, in 1996 Entry Draft.

Season	Club	League	GP	G	A	Pts	PIM	PP	SH	GW	S	%	+/–	TF	F%	H	SB	Min	GP	G	A	Pts	PIM	PP	SH	GW
1992-93	D'Abitibi	QAAA	42	24	30	54	....	....	....	....	....	....	....	....	....	....	....	....	....	....	....	....	....	....	....	....
1993-94	Gatineau	QAAA	44	56	47	103	56	....	....	....	....	....	....	....	....	....	....	....	....	....	....	....	....	....	....	....
1994-95	Drummondville	QMJHL	72	51	72	123	54	....	....	....	....	....	....	....	....	....	....	....	4	2	3	5	2	....	....	....
1995-96	Drummondville	QMJHL	67	*67	*96	*163	84	....	....	....	....	....	....	....	....	....	....	....	6	6	12	18	8	....	....	....
1996-97	Drummondville	QMJHL	59	52	78	130	94	....	....	....	....	....	....	....	....	....	....	....	8	7	7	14	14	....	....	....
1997-98	**Phoenix**	**NHL**	**5**	**1**	**0**	**1**	**2**	**0**	**0**	**0**	**4**	**25.0**	**1**	....	....	....	....	....	....	....	....	....	....	....	....	....
	Springfield	AHL	68	36	56	92	42	....	....	....	....	....	....	....	....	....	....	....	4	1	2	3	4	....	....	....
1998-99	**Phoenix**	**NHL**	**64**	**8**	**14**	**22**	**30**	**2**	**0**	**2**	**90**	**8.9**	**–3**	**484**	**47.5**	**15**	**8**	**11:13**	....	....	....	....	....	....	....	....
	Las Vegas	IHL	1	1	1	2	0	....	....	....	....	....	....	....	....	....	....	....	....	....	....	....	....	....	....	....
	Springfield	AHL	13	2	6	8	20	....	....	....	....	....	....	....	....	....	....	....	3	0	1	1	2	....	....	....
99-2000	**Phoenix**	**NHL**	**13**	**1**	**1**	**2**	**0**	**0**	**0**	**0**	**9**	**11.1**	**0**	**65**	**49.2**	**4**	**1**	**7:41**	**1**	**0**	**0**	**0**	**0**	**0**	**0**	**0**
	Springfield	AHL	58	29	42	71	56	....	....	....	....	....	....	....	....	....	....	....	....	....	....	....	....	....	....	....
	NHL Totals		**82**	**10**	**15**	**25**	**32**	**2**	**0**	**2**	**103**	**9.7**		**549**	**47.7**	**19**	**9**	**10:37**	**1**	**0**	**0**	**0**	**0**	**0**	**0**	**0**

QMJHL Second All-Star Team (1996, 1997) • AHL First All-Star Team (1998) • Won Dudley "Red" Garrett Memorial Trophy (Top Rookie - AHL) (1998)

BRIGLEY, Travis
(BRIH-glee), TRA-vihs)

Left wing. Shoots left. 6'1", 195 lbs. Born, Coronation, Alta., June 16, 1977. Calgary's 2nd choice, 39th overall, in 1996 Entry Draft.

Season	Club	League	GP	G	A	Pts	PIM	PP	SH	GW	S	%	+/–	TF	F%	H	SB	Min	GP	G	A	Pts	PIM	PP	SH	GW
1992-93	Leduc Barons	AAHA	32	36	24	60	56	....	....	....	....	....	....	....	....	....	....	....	....	....	....	....	....	....	....	....
1993-94	Leduc Barons	AAHA	34	29	44	73	141	....	....	....	....	....	....	....	....	....	....	....	....	....	....	....	....	....	....	....
	Lethbridge	WHL	1	0	0	0	0	....	....	....	....	....	....	....	....	....	....	....	....	....	....	....	....	....	....	....
1994-95	Lethbridge	WHL	64	14	18	32	14	....	....	....	....	....	....	....	....	....	....	....	....	....	....	....	....	....	....	....
1995-96	Lethbridge	WHL	69	34	43	77	94	....	....	....	....	....	....	....	....	....	....	....	4	2	3	5	8	....	....	....
1996-97	Lethbridge	WHL	71	43	47	90	56	....	....	....	....	....	....	....	....	....	....	....	19	9	9	18	31	....	....	....
1997-98	**Calgary**	**NHL**	**2**	**0**	**0**	**0**	**2**	**0**	**0**	**0**	**1**	**0.0**	**0**	....	....	....	....	....	....	....	....	....	....	....	....	....
	Saint John Flames	AHL	79	17	15	32	28	....	....	....	....	....	....	....	....	....	....	....	8	0	0	0	0	....	....	....
1998-99	Saint John Flames	AHL	74	15	35	50	48	....	....	....	....	....	....	....	....	....	....	....	7	3	1	4	2	....	....	....
99-2000	**Calgary**	**NHL**	**17**	**0**	**2**	**2**	**4**	**0**	**0**	**0**	**17**	**0.0**	**–6**	**2**	**0.0**	**16**	**8**	**14:14**	....	....	....	....	....	....	....	....
	Saint John Flames	AHL	9	3	1	4	4	....	....	....	....	....	....	....	....	....	....	....	....	....	....	....	....	....	....	....
	Detroit Vipers	IHL	29	6	10	16	24	....	....	....	....	....	....	....	....	....	....	....	....	....	....	....	....	....	....	....
	Philadelphia	AHL	15	2	2	4	15	....	....	....	....	....	....	....	....	....	....	....	5	1	0	1	4	....	....	....
	NHL Totals		**19**	**0**	**2**	**2**	**6**	**0**	**0**	**0**	**18**	**0.0**		**2**	**0.0**	**16**	**8**	**14:14**	....	....	....	....	....	....	....	....

Traded to **Philadelphia** by **Calgary** with Calgary's 6th round choice in 2001 Entry Draft for Marc Bureau, March 6, 2000.

BRIMANIS, Aris
(brih-MAN-ihs, AR-ihs) **NYI**

Defense. Shoots right. 6'3", 210 lbs. Born, Cleveland, OH, March 14, 1972. Philadelphia's 3rd choice, 86th overall, in 1991 Entry Draft.

			Regular Season																Playoffs							
Season	Club	League	GP	G	A	Pts	PIM	PP	SH	GW	S	%	+/-	TF	F%	H	SB	Min	GP	G	A	Pts	PIM	PP	SH	GW
1988-89	Culver Academy	Hi-School	38	10	13	23	24	....	....	....	....	....	....	....	....	....	....	....	....	....	....	....	....	....	....	....
1989-90	Culver Academy	Hi-School	37	15	10	25	52	....	....	....	....	....	....	....	....	....	....	....	....	....	....	....	....	....	....	....
1990-91	Bowling Green	CCHA	38	3	6	9	42	....	....	....	....	....	....	....	....	....	....	....	....	....	....	....	....	....	....	....
1991-92	Bowling Green	CCHA	32	2	9	11	38	....	....	....	....	....	....	....	....	....	....	....	....	....	....	....	....	....	....	....
1992-93	Brandon	WHL	71	8	50	58	110	....	....	....	....	....	....	....	....	....	....	....	4	2	1	3	7	....	....	....
1993-94	**Philadelphia**	**NHL**	**1**	**0**	**0**	**0**	**0**	**0**	**0**	**0**	**1**	**0.0**	**–1**	....	....	....	....	....	....	....	....	....	....	....	....	....
	Hershey Bears	AHL	75	8	15	23	65	....	....	....	....	....	....	....	....	....	....	....	11	2	3	5	12	....	....	....
1994-95	Hershey Bears	AHL	76	8	17	25	68	....	....	....	....	....	....	....	....	....	....	....	6	1	1	2	14	....	....	....
1995-96	**Philadelphia**	**NHL**	**17**	**0**	**2**	**2**	**12**	**0**	**0**	**0**	**11**	**0.0**	**–1**	....	....	....	....	....	....	....	....	....	....	....	....	....
	Hershey Bears	AHL	54	9	22	31	64	....	....	....	....	....	....	....	....	....	....	....	5	1	2	3	4	....	....	....
1996-97	**Philadelphia**	**NHL**	**3**	**0**	**1**	**1**	**0**	**0**	**0**	**0**	**1**	**0.0**	**0**	....	....	....	....	....	....	....	....	....	....	....	....	....
	Philadelphia	AHL	65	14	18	32	69	....	....	....	....	....	....	....	....	....	....	....	10	2	2	4	13	....	....	....
1997-98	Philadelphia	AHL	30	1	11	12	26	....	....	....	....	....	....	....	....	....	....	....	....	....	....	....	....	....	....	....
	Michigan K-Wings	IHL	35	3	9	12	24	....	....	....	....	....	....	....	....	....	....	....	4	1	0	1	4	....	....	....
1998-99	Grand Rapids	IHL	66	16	21	37	70	....	....	....	....	....	....	....	....	....	....	....	....	....	....	....	....	....	....	....
	Fredericton	AHL	8	2	4	6	6	....	....	....	....	....	....	....	....	....	....	....	15	3	10	13	18	....	....	....
99-2000	**NY Islanders**	**NHL**	**18**	**2**	**1**	**3**	**6**	**2**	**0**	**0**	**16**	**12.5**	**–5**	**1**	**0.0**	**32**	**28**	**19:60**	....	....	....	....	....	....	....	....
	Kansas City	IHL	46	5	17	22	28	....	....	....	....	....	....	....	....	....	....	....	....	....	....	....	....	....	....	....
	Providence Bruins	AHL	7	0	2	2	2	....	....	....	....	....	....	....	....	....	....	....	14	3	4	7	10	....	....	....
	NHL Totals		**39**	**2**	**4**	**6**	**18**	**2**	**0**	**0**	**29**	**6.9**		**1**	**0.0**	**32**	**28**	**19:60**	....	....	....	....	....	....	....	....

Signed as a free agent by **NY Islanders**, August 16, 1999. Loaned to **Providence** (AHL) by **NY Islanders**, March 14, 2000.

BRIND'AMOUR, Rod
(BRIHND-uh-MOHR, RAWD) **CAR.**

Center. Shoots left. 6'1", 202 lbs. Born, Ottawa, Ont., August 9, 1970. St. Louis' 1st choice, 9th overall, in 1988 Entry Draft.

			Regular Season																Playoffs							
Season	Club	League	GP	G	A	Pts	PIM	PP	SH	GW	S	%	+/-	TF	F%	H	SB	Min	GP	G	A	Pts	PIM	PP	SH	GW
1986-87	Notre Dame	AAHA	33	38	50	88	66	....	....	....	....	....	....	....	....	....	....	....	....	....	....	....	....	....	....	....
1987-88	Notre Dame	SJHL	56	46	61	107	136	....	....	....	....	....	....	....	....	....	....	....	....	....	....	....	....	....	....	....
1988-89	Michigan State	CCHA	42	27	32	59	63	....	....	....	....	....	....	....	....	....	....	....	....	....	....	....	....	....	....	....
	St. Louis	**NHL**	....	....	....	....	....	....	....	....	....	....	....	....	....	....	....	....	**5**	**2**	**0**	**2**	**4**	**0**	**0**	**0**
1989-90	**St. Louis**	**NHL**	**79**	**26**	**35**	**61**	**46**	**10**	**0**	**1**	**160**	**16.3**	**23**	....	....	....	....	....	**12**	**5**	**8**	**13**	**6**	**1**	**0**	**0**
1990-91	**St. Louis**	**NHL**	**78**	**17**	**32**	**49**	**93**	**4**	**0**	**3**	**169**	**10.1**	**2**	....	....	....	....	....	**13**	**2**	**5**	**7**	**10**	**1**	**0**	**0**
1991-92	**Philadelphia**	**NHL**	**80**	**33**	**44**	**77**	**100**	**8**	**4**	**5**	**202**	**16.3**	**–3**	....	....	....	....	....	....	....	....	....	....	....	....	....
1992-93	**Philadelphia**	**NHL**	**81**	**37**	**49**	**86**	**89**	**13**	**4**	**4**	**206**	**18.0**	**–8**	....	....	....	....	....	....	....	....	....	....	....	....	....
1993-94	**Philadelphia**	**NHL**	**84**	**35**	**62**	**97**	**85**	**14**	**1**	**4**	**230**	**15.2**	**–9**	....	....	....	....	....	....	....	....	....	....	....	....	....
1994-95	**Philadelphia**	**NHL**	**48**	**12**	**27**	**39**	**33**	**4**	**1**	**2**	**86**	**14.0**	**–4**	....	....	....	....	....	**15**	**6**	**9**	**15**	**8**	**2**	**1**	**1**
1995-96	**Philadelphia**	**NHL**	**82**	**26**	**61**	**87**	**110**	**4**	**4**	**5**	**213**	**12.2**	**20**	....	....	....	....	....	**12**	**2**	**5**	**7**	**6**	**1**	**0**	**0**
1996-97	**Philadelphia**	**NHL**	**82**	**27**	**32**	**59**	**41**	**8**	**2**	**3**	**205**	**13.2**	**2**	....	....	....	....	....	**19**	***13**	**8**	**21**	**10**	**4**	**2**	**1**
1997-98	**Philadelphia**	**NHL**	**82**	**36**	**38**	**74**	**54**	**10**	**2**	**8**	**205**	**17.6**	**–2**	....	....	....	....	....	**5**	**2**	**2**	**4**	**7**	**0**	**0**	**0**
	Canada	Olympics	6	1	2	3	0	....	....	....	....	....	....	....	....	....	....	....	....	....	....	....	....	....	....	....
1998-99	**Philadelphia**	**NHL**	**82**	**24**	**50**	**74**	**47**	**10**	**0**	**3**	**191**	**12.6**	**3**	**1773**	**56.5**	**90**	**31**	**21:29**	**6**	**1**	**3**	**4**	**0**	**0**	**0**	**0**
99-2000	**Philadelphia**	**NHL**	**12**	**5**	**3**	**8**	**4**	**4**	**0**	**0**	**26**	**19.2**	**–1**	**291**	**60.5**	**17**	**11**	**20:50**	....	....	....	....	....	....	....	....
	Carolina	**NHL**	**33**	**4**	**10**	**14**	**22**	**0**	**1**	**1**	**61**	**6.6**	**–12**	**704**	**55.5**	**62**	**13**	**20:35**	....	....	....	....	....	....	....	....
	NHL Totals		**823**	**282**	**443**	**725**	**724**	**89**	**19**	**39**	**1954**	**14.4**		**2768**	**56.7**	**169**	**55**	**21:11**	**87**	**33**	**40**	**73**	**51**	**9**	**3**	**2**

Centennial Cup All-Star Team (1988) • NHL All-Rookie Team (1990) • Played in NHL All-Star Game (1992)

Traded to **Philadelphia** by **St. Louis** with Dan Quinn for Ron Sutter and Murray Baron, September 22, 1991. Traded to **Carolina** by **Philadelphia** with Jean-Marc Pelletier and Philadelphia's 2nd round choice (later traded to Colorado - Colorado selected Argis Saviels) in 2000 Entry Draft for Keith Primeau and Carolina's 5th round choice (later traded to NY Islanders - NY Islanders selected Kristofer Ottoson) in 2000 Entry Draft, January 23, 2000.

BRISEBOIS, Patrice
(BREES-bwah, pa-TREEZ) **MTL.**

Defense. Shoots right. 6'1", 203 lbs. Born, Montreal, Que., January 27, 1971. Montreal's 2nd choice, 30th overall, in 1989 Entry Draft.

			Regular Season																Playoffs							
Season	Club	League	GP	G	A	Pts	PIM	PP	SH	GW	S	%	+/-	TF	F%	H	SB	Min	GP	G	A	Pts	PIM	PP	SH	GW
1986-87	Mtl-Bourassa	QAAA	39	15	19	34	66	....	....	....	....	....	....	....	....	....	....	....	....	....	....	....	....	....	....	....
1987-88	Laval Titan	QMJHL	48	10	34	44	95	....	....	....	....	....	....	....	....	....	....	....	6	0	2	2	2	....	....	....
1988-89	Laval Titan	QMJHL	50	20	45	65	95	....	....	....	....	....	....	....	....	....	....	....	17	8	14	22	45	....	....	....
1989-90	Laval Titan	QMJHL	56	18	70	88	108	....	....	....	....	....	....	....	....	....	....	....	13	7	9	16	26	....	....	....
1990-91	Drummondville	QMJHL	54	17	44	61	72	....	....	....	....	....	....	....	....	....	....	....	14	6	18	24	49	....	....	....
	Montreal	**NHL**	**10**	**0**	**2**	**2**	**4**	**0**	**0**	**0**	**11**	**0.0**	**1**	....	....	....	....	....	....	....	....	....	....	....	....	....
1991-92	**Montreal**	**NHL**	**26**	**2**	**8**	**10**	**20**	**0**	**0**	**1**	**37**	**5.4**	**9**	....	....	....	....	....	**11**	**2**	**4**	**6**	**6**	**1**	**0**	**1**
	Fredericton	AHL	53	12	27	39	51	....	....	....	....	....	....	....	....	....	....	....	....	....	....	....	....	....	....	....
1992-93♦	**Montreal**	**NHL**	**70**	**10**	**21**	**31**	**79**	**4**	**0**	**2**	**123**	**8.1**	**6**	....	....	....	....	....	**20**	**0**	**4**	**4**	**18**	**0**	**0**	**0**
1993-94	**Montreal**	**NHL**	**53**	**2**	**21**	**23**	**63**	**1**	**0**	**0**	**71**	**2.8**	**5**	....	....	....	....	....	**7**	**0**	**4**	**4**	**6**	**0**	**0**	**0**
1994-95	**Montreal**	**NHL**	**35**	**4**	**8**	**12**	**26**	**0**	**0**	**2**	**67**	**6.0**	**–2**	....	....	....	....	....	....	....	....	....	....	....	....	....
1995-96	**Montreal**	**NHL**	**69**	**9**	**27**	**36**	**65**	**3**	**0**	**1**	**127**	**7.1**	**10**	....	....	....	....	....	**6**	**1**	**2**	**3**	**6**	**0**	**0**	**0**
1996-97	**Montreal**	**NHL**	**49**	**2**	**13**	**15**	**24**	**0**	**0**	**1**	**72**	**2.8**	**–7**	....	....	....	....	....	**3**	**1**	**1**	**2**	**24**	**0**	**0**	**1**
1997-98	**Montreal**	**NHL**	**79**	**10**	**27**	**37**	**67**	**5**	**0**	**1**	**125**	**8.0**	**16**	....	....	....	....	....	**10**	**1**	**0**	**1**	**0**	**0**	**0**	**0**
1998-99	**Montreal**	**NHL**	**54**	**3**	**9**	**12**	**28**	**1**	**0**	**1**	**90**	**3.3**	**–8**	**0**	**0.0**	**62**	**80**	**22:26**	....	....	....	....	....	....	....	....
99-2000	**Montreal**	**NHL**	**54**	**10**	**25**	**35**	**18**	**5**	**0**	**2**	**88**	**11.4**	**–1**	**0**	**0.0**	**82**	**79**	**23:14**	....	....	....	....	....	....	....	....
	NHL Totals		**499**	**52**	**161**	**213**	**394**	**19**	**0**	**11**	**811**	**6.4**		**0**	**0.0**	**144**	**159**	**22:50**	**57**	**5**	**15**	**20**	**60**	**1**	**0**	**2**

QMJHL Second All-Star Team (1990) • Canadian Major Junior Defenseman of the Year (1991) • QMJHL First All-Star Team (1991) • Memorial Cup All-Star Team (1991)

BROUSSEAU, Paul
(BROO-soh, PAWL) **FLA.**

Right wing. Shoots right. 6'2", 203 lbs. Born, Pierrefonds, Que., September 18, 1973. Quebec's 2nd choice, 28th overall, in 1992 Entry Draft.

			Regular Season																Playoffs							
Season	Club	League	GP	G	A	Pts	PIM	PP	SH	GW	S	%	+/-	TF	F%	H	SB	Min	GP	G	A	Pts	PIM	PP	SH	GW
1988-89	Lac St-Louis	QAAA	37	6	17	23	....	....	....	....	....	....	....	....	....	....	....	....	....	....	....	....	....	....	....	....
1989-90	Chicoutimi	QMJHL	57	17	24	41	32	....	....	....	....	....	....	....	....	....	....	....	7	0	3	3	0	....	....	....
1990-91	Trois-Rivieres	QMJHL	67	30	66	96	48	....	....	....	....	....	....	....	....	....	....	....	6	3	2	5	2	....	....	....
1991-92	Hull Olympiques	QMJHL	57	35	61	96	54	....	....	....	....	....	....	....	....	....	....	....	6	3	5	8	10	....	....	....
1992-93	Hull Olympiques	QMJHL	59	27	48	75	49	....	....	....	....	....	....	....	....	....	....	....	10	7	8	15	6	....	....	....
1993-94	Cornwall Aces	AHL	69	18	26	44	35	....	....	....	....	....	....	....	....	....	....	....	1	0	0	0	0	....	....	....
1994-95	Cornwall Aces	AHL	57	19	17	36	29	....	....	....	....	....	....	....	....	....	....	....	7	2	1	3	10	....	....	....
1995-96	**Colorado**	**NHL**	**8**	**1**	**1**	**2**	**2**	**0**	**0**	**0**	**10**	**10.0**	**1**	....	....	....	....	....	....	....	....	....	....	....	....	....
	Cornwall Aces	AHL	63	21	22	43	60	....	....	....	....	....	....	....	....	....	....	....	8	4	0	4	2	....	....	....
1996-97	**Tampa Bay**	**NHL**	**6**	**0**	**0**	**0**	**0**	**0**	**0**	**0**	**3**	**0.0**	**–4**	....	....	....	....	....	....	....	....	....	....	....	....	....
	Adirondack	AHL	66	35	31	66	25	....	....	....	....	....	....	....	....	....	....	....	4	1	2	3	0	....	....	....
1997-98	**Tampa Bay**	**NHL**	**11**	**0**	**2**	**2**	**27**	**0**	**0**	**0**	**6**	**0.0**	**0**	....	....	....	....	....	....	....	....	....	....	....	....	....
	Adirondack	AHL	67	45	20	65	18	....	....	....	....	....	....	....	....	....	....	....	3	1	1	2	0	....	....	....
1998-99	Milwaukee	IHL	5	1	1	2	2	....	....	....	....	....	....	....	....	....	....	....	....	....	....	....	....	....	....	....
	Hershey Bears	AHL	39	11	21	32	15	....	....	....	....	....	....	....	....	....	....	....	5	1	1	2	0	....	....	....
99-2000	Louisville	AHL	36	19	24	43	10	....	....	....	....	....	....	....	....	....	....	....	4	1	1	2	12	....	....	....
	NHL Totals		**25**	**1**	**3**	**4**	**29**	**0**	**0**	**0**	**19**	**5.3**		....	....	....	....	....	....	....	....	....	....	....	....	....

AHL Second All-Star Team (1998)

Rights transferred to **Colorado** after **Quebec** franchise relocated, June 21, 1995. Signed as a free agent by **Tampa Bay**, September 10, 1996. Claimed by **Nashville** from **Tampa Bay** in Expansion Draft, June 26, 1998. Signed as a free agent by **Florida**, September 20, 1999. • Missed majority of the 1999-2000 season recovering from knee injury suffered in game vs. Rochester (AHL), January 8, 2000.

			Regular Season																Playoffs							
Season	Club	League	GP	G	A	Pts	PIM	PP	SH	GW	S	%	+/-	TF	F%	H	SB	Min	GP	G	A	Pts	PIM	PP	SH	GW

BROWN, Brad

(BR-own, BRAD) **CHI.**

Defense. Shoots right. 6'4", 218 lbs. Born, Baie Verte, Nfld., December 27, 1975. Montreal's 1st choice, 18th overall, in 1994 Entry Draft.

1990-91	Toronto Wings	MTHL	80	15	45	60	105	....	....	....	....	....	....	....	....	....	....	....	....	....	....	....	....	....	....	....
	St. Michael's	OJHL-B	2	0	0	0	0	....	....	....	....	....	....	....	....	....	....	....	....	....	....	....	....	....	....	....
1991-92	North Bay	OHL	49	2	9	11	170	....	....	....	....	....	....	....	....	....	....	....	18	0	6	6	43	....	....	....
1992-93	North Bay	OHL	61	4	9	13	228	....	....	....	....	....	....	....	....	....	....	....	2	0	2	2	13	....	....	....
1993-94	North Bay	OHL	66	8	24	32	196	....	....	....	....	....	....	....	....	....	....	....	18	3	12	15	33	....	....	....
1994-95	North Bay	OHL	64	8	38	46	172	....	....	....	....	....	....	....	....	....	....	....	6	1	4	5	8	....	....	....
1995-96	Barrie Colts	OHL	27	3	13	16	82	....	....	....	....	....	....	....	....	....	....	....	....	....	....	....	....	....	....	....
	Fredericton	AHL	38	0	3	3	148	....	....	....	....	....	....	....	....	....	....	....	10	2	1	3	6	....	....	....
1996-97	**Montreal**	**NHL**	8	0	0	0	22	0	0	0	0	0.0	−1	....	....	....	....	....	....	....	....	....	....	....	....	....
	Fredericton	AHL	64	3	7	10	368	....	....	....	....	....	....	....	....	....	....	....	....	....	....	....	....	....	....	....
1997-98	Fredericton	AHL	64	1	8	9	297	....	....	....	....	....	....	....	....	....	....	....	4	0	0	0	29	....	....	....
1998-99	**Montreal**	**NHL**	5	0	0	0	21	0	0	0	0	0.0	0	0	0.0	1	5	6:02	....	....	....	....	....	....	....	....
	Chicago	**NHL**	61	1	7	8	184	0	0	0	26	3.8	−4	0	0.0	145	63	15:08	....	....	....	....	....	....	....	....
99-2000	**Chicago**	**NHL**	57	0	9	9	134	0	0	0	15	0.0	−1	0	0.0	93	64	14:12	....	....	....	....	....	....	....	....
	NHL Totals		131	1	16	17	361	0	0	0	41	2.4		0	0.0	239	132	14:20	....	....	....	....	....	....	....	....

Traded to **Chicago** by **Montreal** with Jocelyn Thibault and Dave Manson for Jeff Hackett, Eric Weinrich, Alain Nasreddine and Tampa Bay's 4th round choice (previously acquired, Montreal selected Chris Dyment) in 1999 Entry Draft, November 16, 1998.

BROWN, Curtis

(BR-own, KUHR-tihs) **BUF.**

Center/Left wing. Shoots left. 6', 196 lbs. Born, Unity, Sask., February 12, 1976. Buffalo's 2nd choice, 43rd overall, in 1994 Entry Draft.

1990-91	Unity Bantams	SAHA	60	93	104	197	55	....	....	....	....	....	....	....	....	....	....	....	....	....	....	....	....	....	....	....
1991-92	Moose Jaw	SAHA	36	35	30	65	44	....	....	....	....	....	....	....	....	....	....	....	....	....	....	....	....	....	....	....
1992-93	Moose Jaw	WHL	71	13	16	29	30	....	....	....	....	....	....	....	....	....	....	....	....	....	....	....	....	....	....	....
1993-94	Moose Jaw	WHL	72	27	38	65	82	....	....	....	....	....	....	....	....	....	....	....	....	....	....	....	....	....	....	....
1994-95	Moose Jaw	WHL	70	51	53	104	63	....	....	....	....	....	....	....	....	....	....	....	10	8	7	15	20	....	....	....
	Buffalo	**NHL**	1	1	1	2	2	0	0	0	4	25.0	2	....	....	....	....	....	....	....	....	....	....	....	....	....
1995-96	Moose Jaw	WHL	25	20	18	38	30	....	....	....	....	....	....	....	....	....	....	....	....	....	....	....	....	....	....	....
	Prince Albert	WHL	19	12	21	33	8	....	....	....	....	....	....	....	....	....	....	....	18	10	15	25	18	....	....	....
	Buffalo	**NHL**	4	0	0	0	0	0	0	0	1	0.0	0	....	....	....	....	....	....	....	....	....	....	....	....	....
	Rochester	AHL	....	....	....	....	....	....	....	....	....	....	....	....	....	....	....	....	12	0	1	1	2	....	....	....
1996-97	**Buffalo**	**NHL**	28	4	3	7	18	0	0	1	31	12.9	4	....	....	....	....	....	....	....	....	....	....	....	....	....
	Rochester	AHL	51	22	21	43	30	....	....	....	....	....	....	....	....	....	....	....	10	4	6	10	4	....	....	....
1997-98	**Buffalo**	**NHL**	63	12	12	24	34	1	1	2	91	13.2	11	....	....	....	....	....	13	1	2	3	10	1	0	0
1998-99	**Buffalo**	**NHL**	78	16	31	47	56	5	1	3	128	12.5	23	1198	45.0	83	64	17:30	21	7	6	13	10	3	0	3
99-2000	**Buffalo**	**NHL**	74	22	29	51	42	5	0	4	149	14.8	19	1318	48.6	48	65	18:11	5	1	3	4	6	1	0	0
	NHL Totals		248	55	76	131	152	11	2	10	404	13.6		2516	46.9	131	129	17:50	39	9	11	20	26	5	0	3

WHL East First All-Star Team (1995) • WHL East Second All-Star Team (1996)

BROWN, Doug

(BR-own, DUHG) **DET.**

Right wing. Shoots right. 5'10", 185 lbs. Born, Southborough, MA, June 12, 1964.

1982-83	Boston College	ECAC	22	9	8	17	0	....	....	....	....	....	....	....	....	....	....	....	....	....	....	....	....	....	....	....
1983-84	Boston College	ECAC	38	11	10	21	6	....	....	....	....	....	....	....	....	....	....	....	....	....	....	....	....	....	....	....
1984-85	Boston College	H-East	45	37	31	68	10	....	....	....	....	....	....	....	....	....	....	....	....	....	....	....	....	....	....	....
1985-86	Boston College	H-East	38	16	40	56	16	....	....	....	....	....	....	....	....	....	....	....	....	....	....	....	....	....	....	....
1986-87	**New Jersey**	**NHL**	4	0	1	1	0	0	0	0	10	0.0	−4	....	....	....	....	....	....	....	....	....	....	....	....	....
	Maine Mariners	AHL	73	24	34	58	15	....	....	....	....	....	....	....	....	....	....	....	....	....	....	....	....	....	....	....
1987-88	**New Jersey**	**NHL**	70	14	11	25	20	1	4	2	112	12.5	7	....	....	....	....	....	19	5	1	6	6	0	1	1
	Utica Devils	AHL	2	0	2	2	2	....	....	....	....	....	....	....	....	....	....	....	....	....	....	....	....	....	....	....
1988-89	**New Jersey**	**NHL**	63	15	10	25	15	4	0	2	110	13.6	−7	....	....	....	....	....	....	....	....	....	....	....	....	....
	Utica Devils	AHL	4	1	4	5	0	....	....	....	....	....	....	....	....	....	....	....	....	....	....	....	....	....	....	....
1989-90	**New Jersey**	**NHL**	69	14	20	34	16	1	3	3	135	10.4	7	....	....	....	....	....	6	0	1	1	2	0	0	0
1990-91	**New Jersey**	**NHL**	58	14	16	30	4	0	2	2	122	11.5	18	....	....	....	....	....	7	2	2	4	2	0	1	0
1991-92	**New Jersey**	**NHL**	71	11	17	28	27	1	2	1	140	7.9	17	....	....	....	....	....	....	....	....	....	....	....	....	....
1992-93	**New Jersey**	**NHL**	15	0	5	5	2	0	0	0	17	0.0	3	....	....	....	....	....	....	....	....	....	....	....	....	....
	Utica Devils	AHL	25	11	17	28	8	....	....	....	....	....	....	....	....	....	....	....	....	....	....	....	....	....	....	....
1993-94	**Pittsburgh**	**NHL**	77	18	37	55	18	2	0	1	152	11.8	19	....	....	....	....	....	6	0	0	0	2	0	0	0
1994-95	**Detroit**	**NHL**	45	9	12	21	16	1	1	2	69	13.0	14	....	....	....	....	....	18	4	8	12	2	0	1	1
1995-96	**Detroit**	**NHL**	62	12	15	27	4	0	1	1	115	10.4	11	....	....	....	....	....	13	3	3	6	4	0	1	0
1996-97♦	**Detroit**	**NHL**	49	6	7	13	8	1	0	0	69	8.7	−3	....	....	....	....	....	14	3	3	6	2	0	0	0
1997-98♦	**Detroit**	**NHL**	80	19	23	42	12	6	1	5	145	13.1	17	....	....	....	....	....	9	4	2	6	0	3	0	1
1998-99	**Detroit**	**NHL**	80	9	19	28	42	3	1	1	180	5.0	5	235	52.8	33	27	13:47	10	2	2	4	4	1	0	1
99-2000	**Detroit**	**NHL**	51	10	8	18	12	0	1	0	67	14.9	8	95	41.1	27	15	12:53	3	0	1	1	0	0	0	0
	NHL Totals		794	151	201	352	196	20	16	20	1443	10.5		330	49.4	60	42	13:26	105	23	23	46	24	4	4	4

Hockey East Second All-Star Team (1985, 1986)

Signed as a free agent by **New Jersey**, August 6, 1986. Signed as a free agent by **Pittsburgh**, September 28, 1993. Claimed by **Detroit** from **Pittsburgh** in NHL Waiver Draft, January 18, 1995. Claimed by **Nashville** from **Detroit** in Expansion Draft, June 26, 1998. Traded to **Detroit** by **Nashville** for Petr Sykora, Detroit's 3rd round choice (later traded to Edmonton - Edmonton selected Mike Comrie) in 1999 Entry Draft and Detroit's compensatory 4th round choice (Alexander Krevsun) in 1999 Entry Draft), July 14, 1998.

BROWN, Kevin

(BR-own, KEH-vihn)

Right wing. Shoots right. 6'1", 212 lbs. Born, Birmingham, England, May 11, 1974. Los Angeles' 3rd choice, 87th overall, in 1992 Entry Draft.

1989-90	Georgetown	OJHL-B	31	3	8	11	59	....	....	....	....	....	....	....	....	....	....	....	....	....	....	....	....	....	....	....
1990-91	Waterloo Hawks	OJHL-B	46	25	33	58	116	....	....	....	....	....	....	....	....	....	....	....	....	....	....	....	....	....	....	....
1991-92	Belleville Bulls	OHL	66	24	24	48	52	....	....	....	....	....	....	....	....	....	....	....	5	1	4	5	8	....	....	....
1992-93	Belleville Bulls	OHL	6	2	5	7	4	....	....	....	....	....	....	....	....	....	....	....	....	....	....	....	....	....	....	....
	Detroit Jr. Wings	OHL	56	48	86	134	76	....	....	....	....	....	....	....	....	....	....	....	15	10	18	28	18	....	....	....
1993-94	Detroit Jr. Wings	OHL	57	54	81	135	85	....	....	....	....	....	....	....	....	....	....	....	17	14	*26	*40	28	....	....	....
1994-95	**Los Angeles**	**NHL**	23	2	3	5	18	0	0	0	25	8.0	−7	....	....	....	....	....	....	....	....	....	....	....	....	....
	Phoenix	IHL	48	19	31	50	64	....	....	....	....	....	....	....	....	....	....	....	....	....	....	....	....	....	....	....
1995-96	**Los Angeles**	**NHL**	7	1	0	1	4	0	0	0	9	11.1	−2	....	....	....	....	....	....	....	....	....	....	....	....	....
	Phoenix	IHL	45	10	16	26	39	....	....	....	....	....	....	....	....	....	....	....	....	....	....	....	....	....	....	....
	P.E.I. Senators	AHL	8	3	6	9	2	....	....	....	....	....	....	....	....	....	....	....	3	1	3	4	0	....	....	....
1996-97	**Hartford**	**NHL**	11	0	4	4	6	0	0	0	12	0.0	−6	....	....	....	....	....	....	....	....	....	....	....	....	....
	Springfield	AHL	48	32	16	48	45	....	....	....	....	....	....	....	....	....	....	....	17	*11	6	17	24	....	....	....
1997-98	**Carolina**	**NHL**	4	0	0	0	0	0	0	0	0	0.0	−2	....	....	....	....	....	....	....	....	....	....	....	....	....
	New Haven	AHL	67	28	44	72	65	....	....	....	....	....	....	....	....	....	....	....	3	0	2	2	0	....	....	....
1998-99	**Edmonton**	**NHL**	12	4	2	6	0	2	0	0	13	30.8	−2	1	0.0	19	3	9:11	....	....	....	....	....	....	....	....
	Hamilton Bulldogs	AHL	32	9	14	23	47	....	....	....	....	....	....	....	....	....	....	....	....	....	....	....	....	....	....	....
	Hartford	AHL	9	3	2	5	14	....	....	....	....	....	....	....	....	....	....	....	5	1	3	4	4	....	....	....
99-2000	Hamilton Bulldogs	AHL	54	21	38	59	53	....	....	....	....	....	....	....	....	....	....	....	4	2	2	4	8	....	....	....
	Louisville	AHL	1	0	0	0	2	....	....	....	....	....	....	....	....	....	....	....	....	....	....	....	....	....	....	....
	Edmonton	**NHL**	7	0	0	0	0	0	0	0	5	0.0	0	1	0.0	6	1	8:21	1	0	0	0	0	0	0	0
	NHL Totals		64	7	9	16	28	2	0	0	64	10.9		2	0.0	25	4	8:53	1	0	0	0	0	0	0	0

OHL Second All-Star Team (1993) • OHL First All-Star Team (1994) • Canadian Major Junior Second All-Star Team (1994)

Traded to **Ottawa** by **LA Kings** for Jaroslav Modry and Ottawa's 8th round choice (Stephen Valiquette) in 1996 Entry Draft, March 20, 1996. Traded to **Anaheim** by **Ottawa** for Mike Maneluk, July 1, 1996. Traded to **Hartford** by **Anaheim** for the rights to Espen Knutsen, October 1, 1996. Transferred to **Carolina** after **Hartford** franchise relocated, June 25, 1997. Signed as a free agent by **Edmonton**, August 14, 1998. Traded to **NY Rangers** by **Edmonton** for Vladimir Vorobiev, March 23, 1999. Signed as a free agent by **Edmonton**, March 7, 2000.

BROWN, Rob

(BR-own, RAWB)

Right wing. Shoots left. 5'10", 177 lbs. Born, Kingston, Ont., April 10, 1968. Pittsburgh's 4th choice, 67th overall, in 1986 Entry Draft.

			Regular Season																Playoffs							
Season	Club	League	GP	G	A	Pts	PIM	PP	SH	GW	S	%	+/-	TF	F%	H	SB	Min	GP	G	A	Pts	PIM	PP	SH	GW
1982-83	St. Albert Royals	AAHA	61	137	122	259	200	....	....	....	....	....	....	....	....	....	....	....	....	....	....	....	....	....	....	....
1983-84	St. Albert Saints	AJHL	1	0	0	0	0	....	....	....	....	....	....	....	....	....	....	....	....	....	....	....	....	....	....	....
	Kamloops Oilers	WHL	50	16	42	58	80	....	....	....	....	....	....	....	....	....	....	....	15	1	2	3	17	....	....	....
1984-85	Kamloops Blazers	WHL	60	29	50	79	95	....	....	....	....	....	....	....	....	....	....	....	15	8	8	26	28	....	....	....
1985-86	Kamloops Blazers	WHL	69	58	*115	*173	171	....	....	....	....	....	....	....	....	....	....	....	16	*18	*28	*46	14	....	....	....
1986-87	Kamloops Blazers	WHL	63	*76	*136	*212	101	....	....	....	....	....	....	....	....	....	....	....	5	6	5	11	6	....	....	....
1987-88	**Pittsburgh**	**NHL**	**51**	**24**	**20**	**44**	**56**	**13**	**0**	**1**	**80**	**30.0**	**8**	....	....	....	....	....	....	....	....	....	....	....	....	....
1988-89	**Pittsburgh**	**NHL**	**68**	**49**	**66**	**115**	**118**	**24**	**0**	**6**	**169**	**29.0**	**27**	....	....	....	....	....	**11**	**5**	**3**	**8**	**22**	**1**	**0**	**3**
1989-90	**Pittsburgh**	**NHL**	**80**	**33**	**47**	**80**	**102**	**12**	**0**	**3**	**157**	**21.0**	**−10**	....	....	....	....	....	....	....	....	....	....	....	....	....
1990-91	**Pittsburgh**	**NHL**	**25**	**6**	**10**	**16**	**31**	**2**	**0**	**0**	**32**	**18.8**	**0**	....	....	....	....	....	....	....	....	....	....	....	....	....
	Hartford	**NHL**	**44**	**18**	**24**	**42**	**101**	**10**	**0**	**2**	**94**	**19.1**	**−7**	....	....	....	....	....	**5**	**1**	**0**	**1**	**7**	**1**	**0**	**1**
1991-92	**Hartford**	**NHL**	**42**	**16**	**15**	**31**	**39**	**13**	**0**	**2**	**65**	**24.6**	**−14**	....	....	....	....	....	....	....	....	....	....	....	....	....
	Chicago	**NHL**	**25**	**5**	**11**	**16**	**34**	**3**	**0**	**1**	**41**	**12.2**	**−1**	....	....	....	....	....	**8**	**2**	**4**	**6**	**4**	**1**	**0**	**0**
1992-93	**Chicago**	**NHL**	**15**	**1**	**6**	**7**	**33**	**0**	**0**	**0**	**16**	**6.3**	**6**	....	....	....	....	....	....	....	....	....	....	....	....	....
	Indianapolis Ice	IHL	19	14	19	33	32	....	....	....	....	....	....	....	....	....	....	....	2	0	1	1	2	....	....	....
1993-94	**Dallas**	**NHL**	**1**	**0**	**0**	**0**	**0**	**0**	**0**	**0**	**1**	**0.0**	**−1**	....	....	....	....	....	....	....	....	....	....	....	....	....
	Kalamazoo Wings	IHL	79	42	*113	*155	188	....	....	....	....	....	....	....	....	....	....	....	5	1	3	4	6	....	....	....
1994-95	Phoenix	IHL	69	34	73	107	135	....	....	....	....	....	....	....	....	....	....	....	9	4	12	16	0	....	....	....
	Los Angeles	**NHL**	**2**	**0**	**0**	**0**	**0**	**0**	**0**	**0**	**1**	**0.0**	**−2**	....	....	....	....	....	....	....	....	....	....	....	....	....
1995-96	Chicago Wolves	IHL	79	52	*91	*143	100	....	....	....	....	....	....	....	....	....	....	....	9	4	11	15	6	....	....	....
1996-97	Chicago Wolves	IHL	76	37	*80	*117	98	....	....	....	....	....	....	....	....	....	....	....	4	2	4	6	16	....	....	....
1997-98	**Pittsburgh**	**NHL**	**82**	**15**	**25**	**40**	**59**	**4**	**0**	**4**	**172**	**8.7**	**−1**	....	....	....	....	....	**6**	**1**	**0**	**1**	**4**	**1**	**0**	**0**
1998-99	**Pittsburgh**	**NHL**	**58**	**13**	**11**	**24**	**16**	**9**	**0**	**1**	**78**	**16.7**	**−15**	**18**	**38.9**	**115**	**18**	**12:35**	**13**	**2**	**5**	**7**	**8**	**2**	**0**	**0**
99-2000	**Pittsburgh**	**NHL**	**50**	**10**	**13**	**23**	**10**	**4**	**0**	**3**	**73**	....	....	**0**	**0.0**	**0**	**0**	**0:00**	**11**	**1**	**2**	**3**	**0**	**0**	**0**	**0**
	NHL Totals		**543**	**190**	**248**	**438**	**599**	**94**	**0**	**23**	**979**	**19.4**		**18**	**38.9**	**115**	**18**	**12:35**	**54**	**12**	**14**	**26**	**45**	**6**	**0**	**4**

WHL West First All-Star Team (1986, 1987) • Canadian Major Junior Player of the Year (1987) • IHL First All-Star Team (1994, 1996, 1997) • Won Leo P. Lamoureux Memorial Trophy (Top Scorer - IHL) (1994, 1996, 1997) • Won James Gatschene Memorial Trophy (MVP - IHL) (1994) • IHL Second All-Star Team (1995) • Played in NHL All-Star Game (1989)

Traded to **Hartford** by **Pittsburgh** for Scott Young, December 21, 1990. Traded to **Chicago** by **Hartford** for Steve Konroyd, January 24, 1992. Signed as a free agent by **Dallas**, August 12, 1993. Signed as a free agent by **LA Kings**, June 14, 1994. Signed as a free agent by **Pittsburgh**, October 1, 1997.

BROWN, Sean

(BR-own, SHAWN) **EDM.**

Defense. Shoots left. 6'3", 205 lbs. Born, Oshawa, Ont., November 5, 1976. Boston's 2nd choice, 21st overall, in 1995 Entry Draft.

Season	Club	League	GP	G	A	Pts	PIM	PP	SH	GW	S	%	+/-	TF	F%	H	SB	Min	GP	G	A	Pts	PIM	PP	SH	GW
1992-93	Oshawa Legion	OMHA	15	0	1	1	9	....	....	....	....	....	....	....	....	....	....	....	....	....	....	....	....	....	....	....
1993-94	Wellington Dukes	OJHL	32	5	14	19	165	....	....	....	....	....	....	....	....	....	....	....	....	....	....	....	....	....	....	....
	Belleville Bulls	OHL	28	1	2	3	53	....	....	....	....	....	....	....	....	....	....	....	8	0	0	0	17	....	....	....
1994-95	Belleville Bulls	OHL	58	2	16	18	200	....	....	....	....	....	....	....	....	....	....	....	16	4	2	6	*67	....	....	....
1995-96	Belleville Bulls	OHL	37	10	23	33	150	....	....	....	....	....	....	....	....	....	....	....	....	....	....	....	....	....	....	....
	Sarnia Sting	OHL	26	8	17	25	112	....	....	....	....	....	....	....	....	....	....	....	10	1	0	1	38	....	....	....
1996-97	**Edmonton**	**NHL**	**5**	**0**	**0**	**0**	**4**	**0**	**0**	**0**	**2**	**0.0**	**−1**	....	....	....	....	....	....	....	....	....	....	....	....	....
	Hamilton Bulldogs	AHL	61	1	7	8	238	....	....	....	....	....	....	....	....	....	....	....	19	1	0	1	47	....	....	....
1997-98	**Edmonton**	**NHL**	**18**	**0**	**1**	**1**	**43**	**0**	**0**	**0**	**9**	**0.0**	**−1**	....	....	....	....	....	....	....	....	....	....	....	....	....
	Hamilton Bulldogs	AHL	43	4	6	10	166	....	....	....	....	....	....	....	....	....	....	....	6	0	2	2	38	....	....	....
1998-99	**Edmonton**	**NHL**	**51**	**0**	**7**	**7**	**188**	**0**	**0**	**0**	**27**	**0.0**	**1**	**0**	**0.0**	**104**	**29**	**12:14**	**1**	**0**	**0**	**0**	**10**	**0**	**0**	**0**
99-2000	**Edmonton**	**NHL**	**72**	**4**	**8**	**12**	**192**	**0**	**0**	**2**	**36**	**11.1**	**1**	**0**	**0.0**	**146**	**46**	**12:41**	**3**	**0**	**0**	**0**	**23**	**0**	**0**	**0**
	NHL Totals		**146**	**4**	**16**	**20**	**427**	**0**	**0**	**2**	**74**	**5.4**		**0**	**0.0**	**250**	**75**	**12:30**	**4**	**0**	**0**	**0**	**33**	**0**	**0**	**0**

OHL Second All-Star Team (1996)

Rights traded to **Edmonton** by **Boston** with Mariusz Czerkawski and Boston's 1st round choice (Matthieu Descoteaux) in 1996 Entry Draft for Bill Ranford, January 11, 1996.

BRULE, Steve

(broo-LAY, STEEV) **N.J.**

Right wing. Shoots right. 6', 200 lbs. Born, Montreal, Que., January 15, 1975. New Jersey's 6th choice, 143rd overall, in 1993 Entry Draft.

Season	Club	League	GP	G	A	Pts	PIM	PP	SH	GW	S	%	+/-	TF	F%	H	SB	Min	GP	G	A	Pts	PIM	PP	SH	GW
1990-91	Montreal L'est	QAAA	32	25	30	55	20	....	....	....	....	....	....	....	....	....	....	....	....	....	....	....	....	....	....	....
1991-92	Mtl-Bourassa	QAAA	38	41	26	67	14	....	....	....	....	....	....	....	....	....	....	....	....	....	....	....	....	....	....	....
1992-93	St-Jean Lynx	QMJHL	70	33	47	80	46	....	....	....	....	....	....	....	....	....	....	....	4	0	0	0	9	....	....	....
1993-94	St-Jean Lynx	QMJHL	66	41	64	105	46	....	....	....	....	....	....	....	....	....	....	....	5	2	1	3	0	....	....	....
1994-95	St-Jean Lynx	QMJHL	69	44	64	108	42	....	....	....	....	....	....	....	....	....	....	....	7	3	4	7	8	....	....	....
	Albany River Rats	AHL	3	1	4	5	0	....	....	....	....	....	....	....	....	....	....	....	14	9	5	14	4	....	....	....
1995-96	Albany River Rats	AHL	80	30	21	51	37	....	....	....	....	....	....	....	....	....	....	....	4	0	0	0	17	....	....	....
1996-97	Albany River Rats	AHL	79	28	48	76	27	....	....	....	....	....	....	....	....	....	....	....	16	7	7	14	12	....	....	....
1997-98	Albany River Rats	AHL	80	34	43	77	34	....	....	....	....	....	....	....	....	....	....	....	13	8	3	11	4	....	....	....
1998-99	Albany River Rats	AHL	78	32	52	84	35	....	....	....	....	....	....	....	....	....	....	....	5	3	1	4	4	....	....	....
99-2000	Albany River Rats	AHL	75	30	46	76	18	....	....	....	....	....	....	....	....	....	....	....	5	1	2	3	0	....	....	....
	New Jersey	**NHL**	....	....	....	....	....	....	....	....	....	....	....	....	....	....	....	....	**1**	**0**	**0**	**0**	**0**	**0**	**0**	**0**
	NHL Totals		....	....	....	....	....	....	....	....	....	....	....	....	....	....	....	....	**1**	**0**	**0**	**0**	**0**	**0**	**0**	**0**

QMJHL Second All-Star Team (1995)

Signed as a free agent by **Detroit**, July 20, 2000.

BRUNET, Benoit

(broo-NAY, BEHN-wah) **MTL.**

Left wing. Shoots left. 5'11", 198 lbs. Born, Ste-Anne-de-Bellevue, Que., August 24, 1968. Montreal's 2nd choice, 27th overall, in 1986 Entry Draft.

Season	Club	League	GP	G	A	Pts	PIM	PP	SH	GW	S	%	+/-	TF	F%	H	SB	Min	GP	G	A	Pts	PIM	PP	SH	GW
1985-86	Hull Olympiques	QMJHL	71	33	37	70	81	....	....	....	....	....	....	....	....	....	....	....	....	....	....	....	....	....	....	....
1986-87	Hull Olympiques	QMJHL	60	43	67	110	105	....	....	....	....	....	....	....	....	....	....	....	6	7	5	12	8	....	....	....
1987-88	Hull Olympiques	QMJHL	62	54	89	143	131	....	....	....	....	....	....	....	....	....	....	....	10	3	10	13	11	....	....	....
1988-89	**Montreal**	**NHL**	**2**	**0**	**1**	**1**	**0**	**0**	**0**	**0**	**1**	**0.0**	**0**	....	....	....	....	....	....	....	....	....	....	....	....	....
	Sherbrooke	AHL	73	41	*76	117	95	....	....	....	....	....	....	....	....	....	....	....	6	2	0	2	4	....	....	....
1989-90	Sherbrooke	AHL	72	32	35	67	82	....	....	....	....	....	....	....	....	....	....	....	12	8	7	15	20	....	....	....
1990-91	**Montreal**	**NHL**	**17**	**1**	**3**	**4**	**0**	**0**	**0**	**0**	**12**	**8.3**	**−1**	....	....	....	....	....	....	....	....	....	....	....	....	....
	Fredericton	AHL	24	13	18	31	16	....	....	....	....	....	....	....	....	....	....	....	6	5	6	11	2	....	....	....
1991-92	**Montreal**	**NHL**	**18**	**4**	**6**	**10**	**14**	**0**	**0**	**0**	**37**	**10.8**	**4**	....	....	....	....	....	....	....	....	....	....	....	....	....
	Fredericton	AHL	6	7	9	16	27	....	....	....	....	....	....	....	....	....	....	....	....	....	....	....	....	....	....	....
1992-93♦	**Montreal**	**NHL**	**47**	**10**	**15**	**25**	**19**	**0**	**0**	**1**	**71**	**14.1**	**13**	....	....	....	....	....	**20**	**2**	**8**	**10**	**8**	**1**	**0**	**1**
1993-94	**Montreal**	**NHL**	**71**	**10**	**20**	**30**	**20**	**0**	**3**	**1**	**92**	**10.9**	**14**	....	....	....	....	....	**7**	**1**	**4**	**5**	**16**	**0**	**0**	**0**
1994-95	**Montreal**	**NHL**	**45**	**7**	**18**	**25**	**16**	**1**	**1**	**2**	**80**	**8.8**	**7**	....	....	....	....	....	....	....	....	....	....	....	....	....
1995-96	**Montreal**	**NHL**	**26**	**7**	**8**	**15**	**17**	**3**	**1**	**4**	**48**	**14.6**	**−4**	....	....	....	....	....	**3**	**0**	**2**	**2**	**0**	**0**	**0**	**0**
	Fredericton	AHL	3	2	1	3	6	....	....	....	....	....	....	....	....	....	....	....	....	....	....	....	....	....	....	....
1996-97	**Montreal**	**NHL**	**39**	**10**	**13**	**23**	**14**	**2**	**0**	**2**	**63**	**15.9**	**6**	....	....	....	....	....	**4**	**1**	**3**	**4**	**4**	**0**	**1**	**0**
1997-98	**Montreal**	**NHL**	**68**	**12**	**20**	**32**	**61**	**1**	**2**	**2**	**87**	**13.8**	**11**	....	....	....	....	....	**8**	**1**	**0**	**1**	**4**	**0**	**0**	**1**
1998-99	**Montreal**	**NHL**	**60**	**14**	**17**	**31**	**31**	**4**	**2**	**0**	**115**	**12.2**	**−1**	**375**	**41.6**	**27**	**37**	**17:47**	....	....	....	....	....	....	....	....
99-2000	**Montreal**	**NHL**	**50**	**14**	**15**	**29**	**13**	**6**	**1**	**2**	**103**	**13.6**	**3**	**293**	**42.7**	**27**	**22**	**17:59**	....	....	....	....	....	....	....	....
	NHL Totals		**443**	**89**	**136**	**225**	**205**	**17**	**10**	**14**	**709**	**12.6**		**668**	**42.1**	**54**	**59**	**17:52**	**42**	**5**	**17**	**22**	**32**	**1**	**1**	**2**

QMJHL Second All-Star Team (1987) • AHL First All-Star Team (1989)

BRUNETTE, Andrew

(broo-NEHT, AN-drew) **ATL.**

Left wing. Shoots left. 6'1", 210 lbs. Born, Sudbury, Ont., August 24, 1973. Washington's 6th choice, 174th overall, in 1993 Entry Draft.

Season	Club	League	GP	G	A	Pts	PIM	PP	SH	GW	S	%	+/-	TF	F%	H	SB	Min	GP	G	A	Pts	PIM	PP	SH	GW
1989-90	Rayside-Balfour	NOHA	32	38	*65	*103	....	....	....	....	....	....	....	....	....	....	....	....	....	....	....	....	....	....	....	....
	Rayside-Balfour	NOJHA	4	1	1	2	0	....	....	....	....	....	....	....	....	....	....	....	....	....	....	....	....	....	....	....
1990-91	Owen Sound	OHL	63	15	20	35	15	....	....	....	....	....	....	....	....	....	....	....	....	....	....	....	....	....	....	....
1991-92	Owen Sound	OHL	66	51	47	98	42	....	....	....	....	....	....	....	....	....	....	....	5	5	0	5	8	....	....	....
1992-93	Owen Sound	OHL	66	*62	*100	*162	91	....	....	....	....	....	....	....	....	....	....	....	8	8	6	14	16	....	....	....

			Regular Season																Playoffs							
Season	Club	League	GP	G	A	Pts	PIM	PP	SH	GW	S	%	+/–	TF	F%	H	SB	Min	GP	G	A	Pts	PIM	PP	SH	GW
1993-94	Portland Pirates	AHL	23	9	11	20	10	....	....	....	....	....	....	....	....	....	....	....	2	0	1	1	0	....	....	....
	Providence Bruins	AHL	3	0	0	0	0	....	....	....	....	....	....	....	....	....	....	....	....	....	....	....	....	....	....	....
	Hampton Roads	ECHL	20	12	18	30	32	....	....	....	....	....	....	....	....	....	....	....	7	7	6	13	18	....	....	....
1994-95	Portland Pirates	AHL	79	30	50	80	53	....	....	....	....	....	....	....	....	....	....	....	7	3	3	6	10	....	....	....
1995-96	**Washington**	**NHL**	**11**	**3**	**3**	**6**	**0**	**0**	**0**	**1**	**16**	**18.8**	**5**	....	....	....	....	....	**6**	**1**	**3**	**4**	**0**	**0**	**0**	**0**
	Portland Pirates	AHL	69	28	66	94	125	....	....	....	....	....	....	....	....	....	....	....	20	11	18	29	15	....	....	....
1996-97	**Washington**	**NHL**	**23**	**4**	**7**	**11**	**12**	**2**	**0**	**0**	**23**	**17.4**	**–3**	....	....	....	....	....	....	....	....	....	....	....	....	....
	Portland Pirates	AHL	50	22	51	73	48	....	....	....	....	....	....	....	....	....	....	....	5	1	2	3	0	....	....	....
1997-98	**Washington**	**NHL**	**28**	**11**	**12**	**23**	**12**	**4**	**0**	**2**	**42**	**26.2**	**2**	....	....	....	....	....	....	....	....	....	....	....	....	....
	Portland Pirates	AHL	43	21	46	67	64	....	....	....	....	....	....	....	....	....	....	....	10	1	11	12	12	....	....	....
1998-99	**Nashville**	**NHL**	**77**	**11**	**20**	**31**	**26**	**7**	**0**	**1**	**65**	**16.9**	**–10**	**8**	**50.0**	**13**	**10**	**13:13**	....	....	....	....	....	....	....	....
99-2000	**Atlanta**	**NHL**	**81**	**23**	**27**	**50**	**30**	**9**	**0**	**2**	**107**	**21.5**	**–32**	**8**	**25.0**	**45**	**17**	**15:42**	....	....	....	....	....	....	....	....
	NHL Totals		**220**	**52**	**69**	**121**	**80**	**22**	**0**	**6**	**253**	**20.6**		**16**	**37.5**	**58**	**27**	**14:30**	**6**	**1**	**3**	**4**	**0**	**0**	**0**	**0**

OHL First All-Star Team (1993) • Canadian Major Junior Second All-Star Team (1993) • AHL Second All-Star Team (1995)

Claimed by **Nashville** from **Washington** in Expansion Draft, June 26, 1998. Traded to **Atlanta** by **Nashville** for Atlanta's 5th round choice (Matt Hendricks) in 2000 Entry Draft, June 21, 1999.

BRYLIN, Sergei

(BRIH-lin, SAIR-gay) **N.J.**

Center. Shoots left. 5'10", 190 lbs. Born, Moscow, USSR, January 13, 1974. New Jersey's 2nd choice, 42nd overall, in 1992 Entry Draft.

1991-92	CSKA Moscow	CIS	44	1	6	7	4	....	....	....	....	....	....	....	....	....	....	....	....	....	....	....	....	....	....	....
1992-93	CSKA Moscow	CIS	42	5	4	9	36	....	....	....	....	....	....	....	....	....	....	....	....	....	....	....	....	....	....	....
1993-94	CSKA Moscow	CIS	39	4	6	10	36	....	....	....	....	....	....	....	....	....	....	....	3	1	0	1	2	....	....	....
	Russian Penguins	IHL	13	4	5	9	18	....	....	....	....	....	....	....	....	....	....	....	....	....	....	....	....	....	....	....
1994-95♦	**New Jersey**	**NHL**	**26**	**6**	**8**	**14**	**8**	**0**	**0**	**0**	**41**	**14.6**	**12**	....	....	....	....	....	**12**	**1**	**2**	**3**	**4**	**0**	**0**	**0**
	Albany River Rats	AHL	63	19	35	54	78	....	....	....	....	....	....	....	....	....	....	....	....	....	....	....	....	....	....	....
1995-96	**New Jersey**	**NHL**	**50**	**4**	**5**	**9**	**26**	**0**	**0**	**1**	**51**	**7.8**	**–2**	....	....	....	....	....	....	....	....	....	....	....	....	....
1996-97	**New Jersey**	**NHL**	**29**	**2**	**2**	**4**	**20**	**0**	**0**	**0**	**34**	**5.9**	**–13**	....	....	....	....	....	....	....	....	....	....	....	....	....
	Albany River Rats	AHL	43	17	24	41	38	....	....	....	....	....	....	....	....	....	....	....	16	4	8	12	12	....	....	....
1997-98	**New Jersey**	**NHL**	**18**	**2**	**3**	**5**	**0**	**0**	**0**	**0**	**20**	**10.0**	**4**	....	....	....	....	....	....	....	....	....	....	....	....	....
	Albany River Rats	AHL	44	21	22	43	60	....	....	....	....	....	....	....	....	....	....	....	....	....	....	....	....	....	....	....
1998-99	**New Jersey**	**NHL**	**47**	**5**	**10**	**15**	**28**	**3**	**0**	**1**	**51**	**9.8**	**8**	**184**	**50.5**	**61**	**7**	**12:55**	**5**	**3**	**1**	**4**	**4**	**1**	**0**	**1**
99-2000♦	**New Jersey**	**NHL**	**64**	**9**	**11**	**20**	**20**	**1**	**0**	**1**	**84**	**10.7**	**0**	**72**	**41.7**	**107**	**21**	**13:23**	**17**	**3**	**5**	**8**	**0**	**0**	**0**	**0**
	NHL Totals		**234**	**28**	**39**	**67**	**102**	**4**	**0**	**3**	**281**	**10.0**		**256**	**48.0**	**168**	**28**	**13:11**	**34**	**7**	**8**	**15**	**8**	**1**	**0**	**1**

BUCHBERGER, Kelly

(BUK-buhr-guhr, KEHL-lee) **L.A.**

Right wing. Shoots left. 6'2", 210 lbs. Born, Langenburg, Sask., December 2, 1966. Edmonton's 8th choice, 188th overall, in 1985 Entry Draft.

1983-84	Melville	SJHL	60	14	11	25	139	....	....	....	....	....	....	....	....	....	....	....	....	....	....	....	....	....	....	....
1984-85	Moose Jaw	WHL	51	12	17	29	114	....	....	....	....	....	....	....	....	....	....	....	....	....	....	....	....	....	....	....
1985-86	Moose Jaw	WHL	72	14	22	36	206	....	....	....	....	....	....	....	....	....	....	....	13	11	4	15	37	....	....	....
1986-87	Nova Scotia	AHL	70	12	20	32	257	....	....	....	....	....	....	....	....	....	....	....	5	0	1	1	23	....	....	....
	♦ Edmonton	**NHL**	....	....	....	....	....	....	....	....	....	....	....	....	....	....	....	....	**3**	**0**	**1**	**1**	**5**	**0**	**0**	**0**
1987-88	**Edmonton**	**NHL**	**19**	**1**	**0**	**1**	**81**	**0**	**0**	**0**	**10**	**10.0**	**–1**	....	....	....	....	....	....	....	....	....	....	....	....	....
	Nova Scotia	AHL	49	21	23	44	206	....	....	....	....	....	....	....	....	....	....	....	2	0	0	0	11	....	....	....
1988-89	**Edmonton**	**NHL**	**66**	**5**	**9**	**14**	**234**	**1**	**0**	**1**	**57**	**8.8**	**–14**	....	....	....	....	....	....	....	....	....	....	....	....	....
1989-90♦	**Edmonton**	**NHL**	**55**	**2**	**6**	**8**	**168**	**0**	**0**	**2**	**35**	**5.7**	**–8**	....	....	....	....	....	**19**	**0**	**5**	**5**	**13**	**0**	**0**	**0**
1990-91	**Edmonton**	**NHL**	**64**	**3**	**1**	**4**	**160**	**0**	**0**	**2**	**54**	**5.6**	**–6**	....	....	....	....	....	**12**	**2**	**1**	**3**	**25**	**0**	**0**	**0**
1991-92	**Edmonton**	**NHL**	**79**	**20**	**24**	**44**	**157**	**0**	**4**	**3**	**90**	**22.2**	**9**	....	....	....	....	....	**16**	**1**	**4**	**5**	**32**	**0**	**0**	**0**
1992-93	**Edmonton**	**NHL**	**83**	**12**	**18**	**30**	**133**	**1**	**2**	**3**	**92**	**13.0**	**–27**	....	....	....	....	....	....	....	....	....	....	....	....	....
1993-94	**Edmonton**	**NHL**	**84**	**3**	**18**	**21**	**199**	**0**	**0**	**0**	**93**	**3.2**	**–20**	....	....	....	....	....	....	....	....	....	....	....	....	....
1994-95	**Edmonton**	**NHL**	**48**	**7**	**17**	**24**	**82**	**2**	**1**	**5**	**73**	**9.6**	**0**	....	....	....	....	....	....	....	....	....	....	....	....	....
1995-96	**Edmonton**	**NHL**	**82**	**11**	**14**	**25**	**184**	**0**	**2**	**3**	**119**	**9.2**	**–20**	....	....	....	....	....	....	....	....	....	....	....	....	....
1996-97	**Edmonton**	**NHL**	**81**	**8**	**30**	**38**	**159**	**0**	**0**	**3**	**78**	**10.3**	**4**	....	....	....	....	....	**12**	**5**	**2**	**7**	**16**	**0**	**0**	**1**
1997-98	**Edmonton**	**NHL**	**82**	**6**	**17**	**23**	**122**	**1**	**1**	**1**	**86**	**7.0**	**–10**	....	....	....	....	....	**12**	**1**	**2**	**3**	**25**	**0**	**0**	**0**
1998-99	**Edmonton**	**NHL**	**52**	**4**	**4**	**8**	**68**	**0**	**2**	**1**	**29**	**13.8**	**–6**	**23**	**26.1**	**41**	**27**	**11:49**	**4**	**0**	**0**	**0**	**0**	**0**	**0**	**0**
99-2000	**Atlanta**	**NHL**	**68**	**5**	**12**	**17**	**139**	**0**	**0**	**0**	**56**	**8.9**	**–34**	**577**	**45.6**	**137**	**47**	**16:21**	....	....	....	....	....	....	....	....
	Los Angeles	**NHL**	**13**	**2**	**1**	**3**	**13**	**0**	**0**	**0**	**20**	**10.0**	**–2**	**6**	**16.7**	**42**	**5**	**14:43**	**4**	**0**	**0**	**0**	**4**	**0**	**0**	**0**
	NHL Totals		**876**	**89**	**171**	**260**	**1899**	**5**	**12**	**24**	**892**	**10.0**		**606**	**44.6**	**220**	**79**	**14:25**	**82**	**9**	**15**	**24**	**120**	**0**	**0**	**1**

Claimed by **Atlanta** from **Edmonton** in Expansion Draft, June 25, 1999. Traded to **Los Angeles** by **Atlanta** with Nelson Emerson for Donald Audette and Frantisek Kaberle, March 13, 2000.

BULIS, Jan

(BOO-lihs, YAHN) **WSH.**

Center. Shoots left. 6'1", 208 lbs. Born, Pardubice, Czech., March 18, 1978. Washington's 3rd choice, 43rd overall, in 1996 Entry Draft.

1993-94	HC Pardubice-Jr.	Cze-Rep	25	16	11	27		....	....	....	....	....	....	....	....	....	....	....	....	....	....	....	....	....	....	....
1994-95	Kelowna Spartans	BCJHL	51	23	25	48	36	....	....	....	....	....	....	....	....	....	....	....	17	7	9	16	0	....	....	....
1995-96	Barrie Colts	OHL	59	29	30	59	22	....	....	....	....	....	....	....	....	....	....	....	7	2	3	5	2	....	....	....
1996-97	Barrie Colts	OHL	64	42	61	103	42	....	....	....	....	....	....	....	....	....	....	....	9	3	7	10	10	....	....	....
1997-98	Kingston	OHL	2	0	1	1	0	....	....	....	....	....	....	....	....	....	....	....	12	8	10	18	12	....	....	....
	Washington	**NHL**	**48**	**5**	**11**	**16**	**18**	**0**	**0**	**0**	**37**	**13.5**	**–5**	....	....	....	....	....	....	....	....	....	....	....	....	....
	Portland Pirates	AHL	3	1	4	5	12	....	....	....	....	....	....	....	....	....	....	....	....	....	....	....	....	....	....	....
1998-99	**Washington**	**NHL**	**38**	**7**	**16**	**23**	**6**	**3**	**0**	**3**	**57**	**12.3**	**3**	**599**	**48.9**	**48**	**3**	**14:27**	....	....	....	....	....	....	....	....
	Cincinnati	IHL	10	2	2	4	14	....	....	....	....	....	....	....	....	....	....	....	....	....	....	....	....	....	....	....
99-2000	**Washington**	**NHL**	**56**	**9**	**22**	**31**	**30**	**0**	**0**	**1**	**92**	**9.8**	**7**	**609**	**45.5**	**66**	**14**	**13:55**	....	....	....	....	....	....	....	....
	NHL Totals		**142**	**21**	**49**	**70**	**54**	**3**	**0**	**4**	**186**	**11.3**		**1208**	**47.2**	**114**	**17**	**14:08**	....	....	....	....	....	....	....	....

BURE, Pavel

(boo-RAY, PA-vehl) **FLA.**

Right wing. Shoots left. 5'10", 189 lbs. Born, Moscow, USSR, March 31, 1971. Vancouver's 4th choice, 113th overall, in 1989 Entry Draft.

1987-88	CSKA Moscow	USSR	5	1	1	2	0	....	....	....	....	....	....	....	....	....	....	....	....	....	....	....	....	....	....	....
1988-89	CSKA Moscow	USSR	32	17	9	26	8	....	....	....	....	....	....	....	....	....	....	....	....	....	....	....	....	....	....	....
1989-90	CSKA Moscow	USSR	46	14	10	24	20	....	....	....	....	....	....	....	....	....	....	....	....	....	....	....	....	....	....	....
1990-91	CSKA Moscow	USSR	44	35	11	46	24	....	....	....	....	....	....	....	....	....	....	....	....	....	....	....	....	....	....	....
1991-92	**Vancouver**	**NHL**	**65**	**34**	**26**	**60**	**30**	**7**	**3**	**6**	**268**	**12.7**	**0**	....	....	....	....	....	**13**	**6**	**4**	**10**	**14**	**0**	**0**	**0**
1992-93	**Vancouver**	**NHL**	**83**	**60**	**50**	**110**	**69**	**13**	**7**	**9**	**407**	**14.7**	**35**	....	....	....	....	....	**12**	**5**	**7**	**12**	**8**	**0**	**0**	**1**
1993-94	**Vancouver**	**NHL**	**76**	***60**	**47**	**107**	**86**	**25**	**4**	**9**	**374**	**16.0**	**1**	....	....	....	....	....	**24**	***16**	**15**	**31**	**40**	**3**	**0**	**2**
1994-95	EV Landshut	DEL	1	3	0	3	2	....	....	....	....	....	....	....	....	....	....	....	....	....	....	....	....	....	....	....
	Spartak Moscow	CIS	1	2	0	2	2	....	....	....	....	....	....	....	....	....	....	....	....	....	....	....	....	....	....	....
	Vancouver	**NHL**	**44**	**20**	**23**	**43**	**47**	**6**	**2**	**2**	**198**	**10.1**	**–8**	....	....	....	....	....	**11**	**7**	**6**	**13**	**10**	**2**	**2**	**0**
1995-96	**Vancouver**	**NHL**	**15**	**6**	**7**	**13**	**8**	**1**	**1**	**0**	**78**	**7.7**	**–2**	....	....	....	....	....	....	....	....	....	....	....	....	....
1996-97	**Vancouver**	**NHL**	**63**	**23**	**32**	**55**	**40**	**4**	**1**	**2**	**265**	**8.7**	**–14**	....	....	....	....	....	....	....	....	....	....	....	....	....
1997-98	**Vancouver**	**NHL**	**82**	**51**	**39**	**90**	**48**	**13**	**6**	**4**	**329**	**15.5**	**5**	....	....	....	....	....	....	....	....	....	....	....	....	....
	Russia	Olympics	6	*9	0	9	2	....	....	....	....	....	....	....	....	....	....	....	....	....	....	....	....	....	....	....
1998-99	**Florida**	**NHL**	**11**	**13**	**3**	**16**	**4**	**5**	**1**	**0**	**44**	**29.5**	**3**	**1**	**0.0**	**2**	**5**	**21:41**	....	....	....	....	....	....	....	....
99-2000	**Florida**	**NHL**	**74**	***58**	**36**	**94**	**16**	**11**	**2**	**14**	**360**	**16.1**	**25**	**1**	**0.0**	**25**	**12**	**24:23**	**4**	**1**	**3**	**4**	**2**	**1**	**0**	**0**
	NHL Totals		**513**	**325**	**263**	**588**	**348**	**85**	**27**	**46**	**2323**	**14.0**		**2**	**0.0**	**27**	**17**	**24:02**	**64**	**35**	**35**	**70**	**74**	**6**	**2**	**3**

• Named Soviet National League Rookie-of-the-Year (1989) • Won Calder Memorial Trophy (1992) • NHL First All-Star Team (1994) • Named Best Forward at Olympic Games (1998) • NHL Second All-Star Team (2000) • Won Maurice Richard Trophy (2000) • Played in NHL All-Star Game (1993, 1994, 1997, 1998, 2000)

Traded to **Florida** by **Vancouver** with Bret Hedican, Brad Ference and Vancouver's 3rd round choice (Robert Fried) in 2000 Entry Draft for Ed Jovanovski, Dave Gagner, Mike Brown, Kevin Weekes and Florida's 1st round choice (Nathan Smith) in 2000 Entry Draft, January 17, 1999. • Missed majority of 1998-99 season after demanding trade (August 10, 1998) and recovering from knee injury suffered in game vs. Pittsburgh, February 5, 1999.

BURE, Valeri (boo-RAY, VAL-uhr-ee) CGY.

Right wing. Shoots right. 5'10", 185 lbs. Born, Moscow, USSR, June 13, 1974. Montreal's 2nd choice, 33rd overall, in 1992 Entry Draft.

			Regular Season																Playoffs							
Season	Club	League	GP	G	A	Pts	PIM	PP	SH	GW	S	%	+/–	TF	F%	H	SB	Min	GP	G	A	Pts	PIM	PP	SH	GW
1990-91	CSKA Moscow	USSR	3	0	0	0	0	....	....	....	....	....	....	....	....	....	....	....	....	....	....	....	....	....	....	....
1991-92	Spokane Chiefs	WHL	53	27	22	49	78	....	....	....	....	....	....	....	....	....	....	....	10	11	6	17	10	....	....	....
1992-93	Spokane Chiefs	WHL	66	68	79	147	49	....	....	....	....	....	....	....	....	....	....	....	9	6	11	17	14	....	....	....
1993-94	Spokane Chiefs	WHL	59	40	62	102	48	....	....	....	....	....	....	....	....	....	....	....	3	5	3	8	2	....	....	....
1994-95	**Montreal**	**NHL**	**24**	**3**	**1**	**4**	**6**	**0**	**0**	**1**	**39**	**7.7**	**–1**	....	....	....	....	....	....	....	....	....	....	....	....	....
	Fredericton	AHL	45	23	25	48	32	....	....	....	....	....	....	....	....	....	....	....	....	....	....	....	....	....	....	....
1995-96	**Montreal**	**NHL**	**77**	**22**	**20**	**42**	**28**	**5**	**0**	**1**	**143**	**15.4**	**10**	....	....	....	....	....	**6**	**0**	**1**	**1**	**6**	**0**	**0**	**0**
1996-97	**Montreal**	**NHL**	**64**	**14**	**21**	**35**	**6**	**4**	**0**	**2**	**131**	**10.7**	**4**	....	....	....	....	....	**5**	**0**	**1**	**1**	**2**	**0**	**0**	**0**
1997-98	**Montreal**	**NHL**	**50**	**7**	**22**	**29**	**33**	**2**	**0**	**1**	**134**	**5.2**	**–5**	....	....	....	....	....	....	....	....	....	....	....	....	....
	Calgary	**NHL**	**16**	**5**	**4**	**9**	**2**	**0**	**0**	**1**	**45**	**11.1**	**0**	....	....	....	....	....	....	....	....	....	....	....	....	....
	Russia	Olympics	6	1	0	1	0	....	....	....	....	....	....	....	....	....	....	....	....	....	....	....	....	....	....	....
1998-99	**Calgary**	**NHL**	**80**	**26**	**27**	**53**	**22**	**7**	**0**	**4**	**260**	**10.0**	**0**	**15**	**40.0**	**25**	**8**	**16:11**	....	....	....	....	....	....	....	....
99-2000	**Calgary**	**NHL**	**82**	**35**	**40**	**75**	**50**	**13**	**0**	**6**	**308**	**11.4**	**–7**	**8**	**25.0**	**28**	**23**	**20:58**	....	....	....	....	....	....	....	....
	NHL Totals		**393**	**112**	**135**	**247**	**147**	**31**	**0**	**16**	**1060**	**10.6**		**23**	**34.8**	**53**	**31**	**18:36**	**11**	**0**	**2**	**2**	**8**	**0**	**0**	**0**

WHL West First All-Star Team (1993) • WHL West Second All-Star Team (1994) • Played in NHL All-Star Game (2000)

Traded to **Calgary** by **Montreal** with Montreal's 4th round choice (Shaun Sutter) in 1998 Entry Draft for Jonas Hoglund and Zarley Zalapski, February 1, 1998.

BUREAU, Marc (BEWR-oh, MAHRK) CGY.

Center. Shoots right. 6'1", 203 lbs. Born, Trois-Rivières, Que., May 19, 1966.

Season	Club	League	GP	G	A	Pts	PIM	PP	SH	GW	S	%	+/–	TF	F%	H	SB	Min	GP	G	A	Pts	PIM	PP	SH	GW
1983-84	Chicoutimi	QMJHL	56	6	16	22	14	....	....	....	....	....	....	....	....	....	....	....	....	....	....	....	....	....	....	....
1984-85	Chicoutimi	QMJHL	41	30	25	55	15	....	....	....	....	....	....	....	....	....	....	....	....	....	....	....	....	....	....	....
	Granby Predateurs	QMJHL	27	20	45	65	14	....	....	....	....	....	....	....	....	....	....	....	....	....	....	....	....	....	....	....
1985-86	Granby Predateurs	QMJHL	19	6	17	23	36	....	....	....	....	....	....	....	....	....	....	....	....	....	....	....	....	....	....	....
	Chicoutimi	QMJHL	44	30	45	75	33	....	....	....	....	....	....	....	....	....	....	....	9	3	7	10	10	....	....	....
1986-87	Longueuil	QMJHL	66	54	58	112	68	....	....	....	....	....	....	....	....	....	....	....	20	17	20	37	12	....	....	....
1987-88	Salt Lake City	IHL	69	7	20	27	86	....	....	....	....	....	....	....	....	....	....	....	7	0	3	3	8	....	....	....
1988-89	Salt Lake City	IHL	76	28	36	64	119	....	....	....	....	....	....	....	....	....	....	....	14	7	5	12	31	....	....	....
1989-90	**Calgary**	**NHL**	**5**	**0**	**0**	**0**	**4**	**0**	**0**	**0**	**3**	**0.0**	**–1**	....	....	....	....	....	....	....	....	....	....	....	....	....
	Salt Lake City	IHL	67	43	48	91	173	....	....	....	....	....	....	....	....	....	....	....	11	4	8	12	0	....	....	....
1990-91	**Calgary**	**NHL**	**5**	**0**	**0**	**0**	**2**	**0**	**0**	**0**	**4**	**0.0**	**–4**	....	....	....	....	....	....	....	....	....	....	....	....	....
	Salt Lake City	IHL	54	40	48	88	101	....	....	....	....	....	....	....	....	....	....	....	....	....	....	....	....	....	....	....
	Minnesota	**NHL**	**9**	**0**	**6**	**6**	**4**	**0**	**0**	**0**	**8**	**0.0**	**–3**	....	....	....	....	....	**23**	**3**	**2**	**5**	**20**	**0**	**1**	**0**
1991-92	**Minnesota**	**NHL**	**46**	**6**	**4**	**10**	**50**	**0**	**0**	**0**	**53**	**11.3**	**–5**	....	....	....	....	....	**5**	**0**	**0**	**0**	**14**	**0**	**0**	**0**
	Kalamazoo Wings	IHL	7	2	8	10	2	....	....	....	....	....	....	....	....	....	....	....	....	....	....	....	....	....	....	....
1992-93	**Tampa Bay**	**NHL**	**63**	**10**	**21**	**31**	**111**	**1**	**2**	**1**	**132**	**7.6**	**–12**	....	....	....	....	....	....	....	....	....	....	....	....	....
1993-94	**Tampa Bay**	**NHL**	**75**	**8**	**7**	**15**	**30**	**0**	**1**	**1**	**110**	**7.3**	**–9**	....	....	....	....	....	....	....	....	....	....	....	....	....
1994-95	**Tampa Bay**	**NHL**	**48**	**2**	**12**	**14**	**30**	**0**	**1**	**0**	**72**	**2.8**	**–8**	....	....	....	....	....	....	....	....	....	....	....	....	....
1995-96	**Montreal**	**NHL**	**65**	**3**	**7**	**10**	**46**	**0**	**0**	**1**	**43**	**7.0**	**–3**	....	....	....	....	....	**6**	**1**	**1**	**2**	**4**	**0**	**0**	**0**
1996-97	**Montreal**	**NHL**	**43**	**6**	**9**	**15**	**16**	**1**	**1**	**2**	**56**	**10.7**	**4**	....	....	....	....	....	....	....	....	....	....	....	....	....
1997-98	**Montreal**	**NHL**	**74**	**13**	**6**	**19**	**12**	**0**	**0**	**2**	**82**	**15.9**	**0**	....	....	....	....	....	**10**	**1**	**2**	**3**	**6**	**0**	**0**	**0**
1998-99	**Philadelphia**	**NHL**	**71**	**4**	**6**	**10**	**10**	**0**	**0**	**0**	**52**	**7.7**	**–2**	**776**	**53.5**	**74**	**28**	**11:02**	**6**	**0**	**2**	**2**	**2**	**0**	**0**	**0**
99-2000	**Philadelphia**	**NHL**	**54**	**2**	**2**	**4**	**10**	**0**	**1**	**0**	**46**	**4.3**	**–1**	**682**	**56.3**	**71**	**25**	**11:02**	....	....	....	....	....	....	....	....
	Calgary	**NHL**	**9**	**1**	**3**	**4**	**2**	**0**	**0**	**0**	**5**	**20.0**	**–3**	**72**	**51.4**	**18**	**5**	**14:13**	....	....	....	....	....	....	....	....
	NHL Totals		**567**	**55**	**83**	**138**	**327**	**2**	**6**	**7**	**666**	**8.3**		**1530**	**54.6**	**163**	**58**	**11:15**	**50**	**5**	**7**	**12**	**46**	**0**	**1**	**0**

IHL Second All-Star Team (1990, 1991)

Signed as a free agent by **Calgary**, May 19, 1987. Traded to **Minnesota** by **Calgary** for Minnesota's 3rd round choice (Sandy McCarthy) in 1991 Entry Draft, March 5, 1991. Claimed on waivers by **Tampa Bay** from **Minnesota**, October 16, 1992. Traded to **Montreal** by **Tampa Bay** for Brian Bellows, June 30, 1995. Signed as a free agent by **Philadelphia**, July 20, 1998. Traded to **Calgary** by **Philadelphia** for Travis Brigley and Calgary's 6th round choice in 2001 Entry Draft, March 6, 2000.

BURT, Adam (BUHRT, A-dam) ATL.

Defense. Shoots left. 6'2", 205 lbs. Born, Detroit, MI, January 15, 1969. Hartford's 2nd choice, 39th overall, in 1987 Entry Draft.

Season	Club	League	GP	G	A	Pts	PIM	PP	SH	GW	S	%	+/–	TF	F%	H	SB	Min	GP	G	A	Pts	PIM	PP	SH	GW
1985-86	North Bay	OHL	49	0	11	11	81	....	....	....	....	....	....	....	....	....	....	....	10	0	0	0	24	....	....	....
1986-87	North Bay	OHL	57	4	27	31	138	....	....	....	....	....	....	....	....	....	....	....	24	1	6	7	68	....	....	....
1987-88	North Bay	OHL	66	17	53	70	176	....	....	....	....	....	....	....	....	....	....	....	2	0	3	3	6	....	....	....
	Binghamton	AHL	....	....	....	....	....	....	....	....	....	....	....	....	....	....	....	....	2	1	1	2	0	....	....	....
1988-89	North Bay	OHL	23	4	11	15	45	....	....	....	....	....	....	....	....	....	....	....	12	2	12	14	12	....	....	....
	Hartford	**NHL**	**5**	**0**	**0**	**0**	**6**	**0**	**0**	**0**	**1**	**0.0**	**–1**	....	....	....	....	....	....	....	....	....	....	....	....	....
	Binghamton	AHL	5	0	2	2	13	....	....	....	....	....	....	....	....	....	....	....	....	....	....	....	....	....	....	....
1989-90	**Hartford**	**NHL**	**63**	**4**	**8**	**12**	**105**	**1**	**0**	**0**	**83**	**4.8**	**3**	....	....	....	....	....	**2**	**0**	**0**	**0**	**0**	**0**	**0**	**0**
1990-91	**Hartford**	**NHL**	**42**	**2**	**7**	**9**	**63**	**1**	**0**	**1**	**43**	**4.7**	**–4**	....	....	....	....	....	....	....	....	....	....	....	....	....
	Springfield	AHL	9	1	3	4	22	....	....	....	....	....	....	....	....	....	....	....	....	....	....	....	....	....	....	....
1991-92	**Hartford**	**NHL**	**66**	**9**	**15**	**24**	**93**	**4**	**0**	**1**	**89**	**10.1**	**–16**	....	....	....	....	....	**2**	**0**	**0**	**0**	**0**	**0**	**0**	**0**
1992-93	**Hartford**	**NHL**	**65**	**6**	**14**	**20**	**116**	**0**	**0**	**0**	**81**	**7.4**	**–11**	....	....	....	....	....	....	....	....	....	....	....	....	....
1993-94	**Hartford**	**NHL**	**63**	**1**	**17**	**18**	**75**	**0**	**0**	**0**	**91**	**1.1**	**–4**	....	....	....	....	....	....	....	....	....	....	....	....	....
1994-95	**Hartford**	**NHL**	**46**	**7**	**11**	**18**	**65**	**3**	**0**	**1**	**73**	**9.6**	**0**	....	....	....	....	....	....	....	....	....	....	....	....	....
1995-96	**Hartford**	**NHL**	**78**	**4**	**9**	**13**	**121**	**0**	**0**	**1**	**90**	**4.4**	**–4**	....	....	....	....	....	....	....	....	....	....	....	....	....
1996-97	**Hartford**	**NHL**	**71**	**2**	**11**	**13**	**79**	**0**	**0**	**0**	**85**	**2.4**	**–13**	....	....	....	....	....	....	....	....	....	....	....	....	....
1997-98	**Carolina**	**NHL**	**76**	**1**	**11**	**12**	**106**	**0**	**1**	**0**	**51**	**2.0**	**–6**	....	....	....	....	....	....	....	....	....	....	....	....	....
1998-99	**Carolina**	**NHL**	**51**	**0**	**3**	**3**	**46**	**0**	**0**	**0**	**37**	**0.0**	**3**	**0**	**0.0**	**78**	**60**	**18:39**	....	....	....	....	....	....	....	....
	Philadelphia	**NHL**	**17**	**0**	**1**	**1**	**14**	**0**	**0**	**0**	**24**	**0.0**	**1**	**0**	**0.0**	**16**	**16**	**17:25**	**6**	**0**	**0**	**0**	**4**	**0**	**0**	**0**
99-2000	**Philadelphia**	**NHL**	**67**	**1**	**6**	**7**	**45**	**0**	**0**	**1**	**49**	**2.0**	**–2**	**0**	**0.0**	**92**	**70**	**16:19**	**11**	**0**	**1**	**1**	**4**	**0**	**0**	**0**
	NHL Totals		**710**	**37**	**113**	**150**	**934**	**9**	**1**	**5**	**797**	**4.6**		**0**	**0.0**	**186**	**146**	**17:20**	**21**	**0**	**1**	**1**	**8**	**0**	**0**	**0**

OHL Second All-Star Team (1988)

Transferred to **Carolina** after **Hartford** franchise relocated, June 25, 1997. Traded to **Philadelphia** by **Carolina** for Andrei Kovalenko, March 6, 1999. Signed as a free agent by **Atlanta**, July 14, 2000.

BUTENSCHON, Sven (BUH-tehn-shohn, SVEHN) PIT.

Defense. Shoots left. 6'4", 215 lbs. Born, Itzehoe, West Germany, March 22, 1976. Pittsburgh's 3rd choice, 57th overall, in 1994 Entry Draft.

Season	Club	League	GP	G	A	Pts	PIM	PP	SH	GW	S	%	+/–	TF	F%	H	SB	Min	GP	G	A	Pts	PIM	PP	SH	GW
1991-92	Eastman Selects	MAHA	36	2	10	12	110	....	....	....	....	....	....	....	....	....	....	....	....	....	....	....	....	....	....	....
1992-93	Eastman Selects	MAHA	35	14	22	36	101	....	....	....	....	....	....	....	....	....	....	....	....	....	....	....	....	....	....	....
1993-94	Brandon	WHL	70	3	19	22	51	....	....	....	....	....	....	....	....	....	....	....	4	0	0	0	6	....	....	....
1994-95	Brandon	WHL	21	1	5	6	44	....	....	....	....	....	....	....	....	....	....	....	18	1	2	3	11	....	....	....
1995-96	Brandon	WHL	70	4	37	41	99	....	....	....	....	....	....	....	....	....	....	....	19	1	12	13	18	....	....	....
1996-97	Cleveland	IHL	75	3	12	15	68	....	....	....	....	....	....	....	....	....	....	....	10	0	1	1	4	....	....	....
1997-98	**Pittsburgh**	**NHL**	**8**	**0**	**0**	**0**	**6**	**0**	**0**	**0**	**4**	**0.0**	**–1**	....	....	....	....	....	....	....	....	....	....	....	....	....
	Syracuse Crunch	AHL	65	14	23	37	66	....	....	....	....	....	....	....	....	....	....	....	5	1	2	3	0	....	....	....
1998-99	**Pittsburgh**	**NHL**	**17**	**0**	**0**	**0**	**6**	**0**	**0**	**0**	**8**	**0.0**	**–7**	**0**	**0.0**	**13**	**12**	**13:08**	....	....	....	....	....	....	....	....
	Houston Aeros	IHL	57	1	4	5	81	....	....	....	....	....	....	....	....	....	....	....	....	....	....	....	....	....	....	....
99-2000	**Pittsburgh**	**NHL**	**3**	**0**	**0**	**0**	**0**	**0**	**0**	**0**	**2**	**0.0**	**3**	**0**	**0.0**	**1**	**2**	**16:25**	....	....	....	....	....	....	....	....
	Wilkes-Barre	AHL	75	19	21	40	101	....	....	....	....	....	....	....	....	....	....	....	....	....	....	....	....	....	....	....
	NHL Totals		**28**	**0**	**0**	**0**	**12**	**0**	**0**	**0**	**14**	**0.0**		**0**	**0.0**	**14**	**14**	**13:38**	....	....	....	....	....	....	....	....

BUTSAYEV, Viacheslav (boot-SIGH-yehf, VYACH-ih-slav) OTT.

Center. Shoots left. 6'2", 228 lbs. Born, Togliatti, USSR, June 13, 1970. Philadelphia's 10th choice, 109th overall, in 1990 Entry Draft.

Season	Club	League	GP	G	A	Pts	PIM	PP	SH	GW	S	%	+/–	TF	F%	H	SB	Min	GP	G	A	Pts	PIM	PP	SH	GW
1987-88	Lada Togliatti	USSR-2	10	1	7	8	....	....	....	....	....	....	....	....	....	....	....	....	....	....	....	....	....	....	....	....
1988-89	Lada Togliatti-2	USSR-3	60	14	7	21	32	....	....	....	....	....	....	....	....	....	....	....	....	....	....	....	....	....	....	....
1989-90	CSKA Moscow	USSR	48	14	4	18	30	....	....	....	....	....	....	....	....	....	....	....	....	....	....	....	....	....	....	....
1990-91	CSKA Moscow	USSR	46	14	9	23	32	....	....	....	....	....	....	....	....	....	....	....	....	....	....	....	....	....	....	....
1991-92	CSKA Moscow	CIS	36	12	13	25	26	....	....	....	....	....	....	....	....	....	....	....	....	....	....	....	....	....	....	....
	Russia	Olympics	8	1	1	2	4	....	....	....	....	....	....	....	....	....	....	....	....	....	....	....	....	....	....	....

			Regular Season																Playoffs							
Season	Club	League	GP	G	A	Pts	PIM	PP	SH	GW	S	%	+/-	TF	F%	H	SB	Min	GP	G	A	Pts	PIM	PP	SH	GW
1992-93	CSKA Moscow	CIS	5	3	4	7	6	....	....	....	....	....	....	....	....	....	....	....	....	....	....	....	....	....	....	....
	Philadelphia	**NHL**	**52**	**2**	**14**	**16**	**61**	**0**	**0**	**0**	**58**	**3.4**	**3**	....	....	....	....	....	....	....	....	....	....	....	....	....
	Hershey Bears	AHL	24	8	10	18	51	....	....	....	....	....	....	....	....	....	....	....	....	....	....	....	....	....	....	....
1993-94	**Philadelphia**	**NHL**	**47**	**12**	**9**	**21**	**58**	**0**	**0**	**3**	**79**	**15.2**	**2**	....	....	....	....	....	....	....	....	....	....	....	....	....
	San Jose	**NHL**	**12**	**0**	**2**	**2**	**10**	**2**	**0**	**0**	**6**	**0.0**	**–2**	....	....	....	....	....	....	....	....	....	....	....	....	....
1994-95	Lada Togliatti	CIS	9	2	6	8	6	....	....	....	....	....	....	....	....	....	....	....	....	....	....	....	....	....	....	....
	San Jose	**NHL**	**6**	**2**	**0**	**2**	**0**	**0**	**0**	**0**	**6**	**33.3**	**–2**	....	....	....	....	....	....	....	....	....	....	....	....	....
	Kansas City	IHL	13	3	4	7	12	....	....	....	....	....	....	....	....	....	....	....	3	0	0	0	2	....	....	....
1995-96	**Anaheim**	**NHL**	**7**	**1**	**0**	**1**	**0**	**0**	**0**	**0**	**9**	**11.1**	**–4**	....	....	....	....	....	....	....	....	....	....	....	....	....
	Baltimore Bandits	AHL	62	23	42	65	70	....	....	....	....	....	....	....	....	....	....	....	12	4	8	12	28	....	....	....
1996-97	Sodertalje SK	Sweden	16	2	4	6	61	....	....	....	....	....	....	....	....	....	....	....	....	....	....	....	....	....	....	....
	Farjestads BK	Sweden	24	4	3	7	47	....	....	....	....	....	....	....	....	....	....	....	8	3	4	7	41	....	....	....
	Farjestads BK	EuroHL	1	0	0	0	0	....	....	....	....	....	....	....	....	....	....	....	....	....	....	....	....	....	....	....
1997-98	Fort Wayne	IHL	76	36	51	87	128	....	....	....	....	....	....	....	....	....	....	....	4	2	2	4	4	....	....	....
1998-99	**Florida**	**NHL**	**1**	**0**	**0**	**0**	**2**	**0**	**0**	**0**	**0**	**0.0**	**–1**	**20**	**60.0**	**0**	**0**	**16:21**	....	....	....	....	....	....	....	....
	Fort Wayne	IHL	71	28	44	72	123	....	....	....	....	....	....	....	....	....	....	....	2	1	0	1	4	....	....	....
	Ottawa	**NHL**	**2**	**0**	**1**	**1**	**2**	**0**	**0**	**0**	**5**	**0.0**	**0**	**6**	**33.3**	**2**	**0**	**11:08**	....	....	....	....	....	....	....	....
99-2000	**Tampa Bay**	**NHL**	**2**	**0**	**0**	**0**	**0**	**0**	**0**	**0**	**1**	**0.0**	**–2**	**13**	**30.8**	**1**	**0**	**8:42**	....	....	....	....	....	....	....	....
	Ottawa	**NHL**	**3**	**0**	**0**	**0**	**0**	**0**	**0**	**0**	**1**	**0.0**	**–2**	**18**	**38.9**	**1**	**0**	**9:19**	....	....	....	....	....	....	....	....
	Grand Rapids	IHL	68	28	35	63	85	....	....	....	....	....	....	....	....	....	....	....	17	4	*12	16	24	....	....	....
	NHL Totals		**132**	**17**	**26**	**43**	**133**	**2**	**0**	**3**	**165**	**10.3**		**57**	**43.9**	**4**	**0**	**10:30**	....	....	....	....	....	....	....	....

IHL Second All-Star Team (1998)

Traded to **San Jose** by **Philadelphia** for Rob Zettler, February 1, 1994. Signed as a free agent by **Anaheim**, October 19, 1995. Signed as a free agent by **Florida**, August 1, 1998. Traded to **Ottawa** by **Florida** for Ottawa's 6th round choice (later traded to Dallas - Dallas selected Justin Cox) in 1999 Entry Draft, March 8, 1999. Claimed by **Tampa Bay** from **Ottawa** in Waiver Draft, September 27, 1999. Claimed on waivers by **Ottawa** from **Tampa Bay**, October 28, 1999.

BUTSAYEV, Yuri

(buht-SIGH-ehv, YOO-ree) **DET.**

Center. Shoots left. 6'1", 183 lbs. Born, Togliatti, USSR, October 11, 1978. Detroit's 1st choice, 49th overall, in 1997 Entry Draft.

Season	Club	League	GP	G	A	Pts	PIM	PP	SH	GW	S	%	+/-	TF	F%	H	SB	Min	GP	G	A	Pts	PIM	PP	SH	GW
1995-96	Lada Togliatti-2	CIS-2	35	19	7	26	....	....	....	....	....	....	....	....	....	....	....	....	....	....	....	....	....	....	....	....
	Lada Togliatti	CIS	1	0	0	0	0	....	....	....	....	....	....	....	....	....	....	....	....	....	....	....	....	....	....	....
1996-97	Lada Togliatti	Russia	42	13	11	24	38	....	....	....	....	....	....	....	....	....	....	....	11	2	2	4	8	....	....	....
1997-98	Lada Togliatti	Russia	44	8	9	17	63	....	....	....	....	....	....	....	....	....	....	....	....	....	....	....	....	....	....	....
	Lada Togliatti	EuroHL	6	2	0	2	8	....	....	....	....	....	....	....	....	....	....	....	....	....	....	....	....	....	....	....
1998-99	Dynamo Moscow	Russia	1	0	1	1	0	....	....	....	....	....	....	....	....	....	....	....	....	....	....	....	....	....	....	....
	Lada Togliatti	Russia	39	10	7	17	55	....	....	....	....	....	....	....	....	....	....	....	7	1	2	3	14	....	....	....
99-2000	**Detroit**	**NHL**	**57**	**5**	**3**	**8**	**12**	**0**	**0**	**0**	**46**	**10.9**	**–6**	**22**	**40.9**	**29**	**11**	**9:36**	....	....	....	....	....	....	....	....
	Cincinnati Ducks	AHL	9	0	1	1	0	....	....	....	....	....	....	....	....	....	....	....	....	....	....	....	....	....	....	....
	NHL Totals		**57**	**5**	**3**	**8**	**12**	**0**	**0**	**0**	**46**	**10.9**		**22**	**40.9**	**29**	**11**	**9:36**	....	....	....	....	....	....	....	....

BUZEK, Petr

(BOO-zehk, PEE-tuhr) **ATL.**

Defense. Shoots left. 6', 205 lbs. Born, Jihlava, Czech., April 26, 1977. Dallas' 3rd choice, 63rd overall, in 1995 Entry Draft.

Season	Club	League	GP	G	A	Pts	PIM	PP	SH	GW	S	%	+/-	TF	F%	H	SB	Min	GP	G	A	Pts	PIM	PP	SH	GW
1993-94	Dukla Jihlava-Jr.	Cze-Rep	3	0	0	0	....	....	....	....	....	....	....	....	....	....	....	....	....	....	....	....	....	....	....	....
1994-95	Dukla Jihlava	Cze-Rep	43	2	5	7	47	....	....	....	....	....	....	....	....	....	....	....	2	0	0	0	2	....	....	....
1995-96	Michigan K-Wings	IHL	Did Not Play – Injured																							
1996-97	Michigan K-Wings	IHL	67	4	6	10	48	....	....	....	....	....	....	....	....	....	....	....	....	....	....	....	....	....	....	....
1997-98	**Dallas**	**NHL**	**2**	**0**	**0**	**0**	**2**	**0**	**0**	**0**	**0**	**0.0**	**1**	....	....	....	....	....	....	....	....	....	....	....	....	....
	Michigan K-Wings	IHL	60	10	15	25	58	....	....	....	....	....	....	....	....	....	....	....	2	0	1	1	17	....	....	....
1998-99	**Dallas**	**NHL**	**2**	**0**	**0**	**0**	**2**	**0**	**0**	**0**	**0**	**0.0**	**0**	**0**	**0.0**	**3**	**0**	**13:50**	....	....	....	....	....	....	....	....
	Michigan K-Wings	IHL	74	5	14	19	68	....	....	....	....	....	....	....	....	....	....	....	5	0	0	0	10	....	....	....
99-2000	**Atlanta**	**NHL**	**63**	**5**	**14**	**19**	**41**	**3**	**0**	**0**	**90**	**5.6**	**–22**	**0**	**0.0**	**139**	**76**	**18:24**	....	....	....	....	....	....	....	....
	NHL Totals		**67**	**5**	**14**	**19**	**45**	**3**	**0**	**0**	**90**	**5.6**		**0**	**0.0**	**142**	**76**	**18:16**	....	....	....	....	....	....	....	....

Played in NHL All-Star Game (2000)

• Missed entire 1995-96 season recovering from injuries suffered in automobile accident, July, 1995. Claimed by **Atlanta** from **Dallas** in Expansion Draft, June 25, 1999.

BYLSMA, Dan

(BEEL-smah, DAN) **ANA.**

Right wing. Shoots left. 6'2", 209 lbs. Born, Grand Haven, MI, September 19, 1970. Winnipeg's 7th choice, 109th overall, in 1989 Entry Draft.

Season	Club	League	GP	G	A	Pts	PIM	PP	SH	GW	S	%	+/-	TF	F%	H	SB	Min	GP	G	A	Pts	PIM	PP	SH	GW
1986-87	Oakville Blades	OJHL-B	10	4	9	13	21	....	....	....	....	....	....	....	....	....	....	....	....	....	....	....	....	....	....	....
	St. Mary's Lincolns	OJHL-B	27	14	28	42	21	....	....	....	....	....	....	....	....	....	....	....	....	....	....	....	....	....	....	....
1987-88	St. Mary's Lincolns	OJHL-B	40	30	39	69	33	....	....	....	....	....	....	....	....	....	....	....	8	8	18	26	....	....	....	....
1988-89	Bowling Green	CCHA	32	3	7	10	10	....	....	....	....	....	....	....	....	....	....	....	....	....	....	....	....	....	....	....
1989-90	Bowling Green	CCHA	44	13	17	30	30	....	....	....	....	....	....	....	....	....	....	....	....	....	....	....	....	....	....	....
1990-91	Bowling Green	CCHA	40	9	12	21	48	....	....	....	....	....	....	....	....	....	....	....	....	....	....	....	....	....	....	....
1991-92	Bowling Green	CCHA	34	11	14	25	24	....	....	....	....	....	....	....	....	....	....	....	....	....	....	....	....	....	....	....
1992-93	Greensboro	ECHL	60	25	35	60	66	....	....	....	....	....	....	....	....	....	....	....	1	0	1	1	10	....	....	....
	Rochester	AHL	2	0	1	1	0	....	....	....	....	....	....	....	....	....	....	....	....	....	....	....	....	....	....	....
1993-94	Greensboro	ECHL	25	14	16	30	52	....	....	....	....	....	....	....	....	....	....	....	....	....	....	....	....	....	....	....
	Albany River Rats	AHL	3	0	1	1	2	....	....	....	....	....	....	....	....	....	....	....	....	....	....	....	....	....	....	....
	Moncton Hawks	AHL	50	12	16	28	25	....	....	....	....	....	....	....	....	....	....	....	21	3	4	7	31	....	....	....
1994-95	Phoenix	IHL	81	19	23	42	41	....	....	....	....	....	....	....	....	....	....	....	9	4	4	8	4	....	....	....
1995-96	**Los Angeles**	**NHL**	**4**	**0**	**0**	**0**	**0**	**0**	**0**	**0**	**6**	**0.0**	**0**	....	....	....	....	....	....	....	....	....	....	....	....	....
	Phoenix	IHL	78	22	20	42	48	....	....	....	....	....	....	....	....	....	....	....	4	1	0	1	2	....	....	....
1996-97	**Los Angeles**	**NHL**	**79**	**3**	**6**	**9**	**32**	**0**	**0**	**0**	**86**	**3.5**	**–15**	....	....	....	....	....	....	....	....	....	....	....	....	....
1997-98	**Los Angeles**	**NHL**	**65**	**3**	**9**	**12**	**33**	**0**	**0**	**0**	**57**	**5.3**	**9**	....	....	....	....	....	**2**	**0**	**0**	**0**	**0**	**0**	**0**	**0**
	Long Beach	IHL	8	2	3	5	0	....	....	....	....	....	....	....	....	....	....	....	....	....	....	....	....	....	....	....
1998-99	**Los Angeles**	**NHL**	**8**	**0**	**0**	**0**	**2**	**0**	**0**	**0**	**3**	**0.0**	**–1**	**0**	**0.0**	**15**	**4**	**9:51**	....	....	....	....	....	....	....	....
	Springfield	AHL	2	0	2	2	2	....	....	....	....	....	....	....	....	....	....	....	....	....	....	....	....	....	....	....
	Long Beach	IHL	58	10	8	18	53	....	....	....	....	....	....	....	....	....	....	....	4	0	0	0	8	....	....	....
99-2000	**Los Angeles**	**NHL**	**64**	**3**	**6**	**9**	**55**	**0**	**1**	**0**	**43**	**7.0**	**–2**	**62**	**43.6**	**168**	**33**	**10:23**	**3**	**0**	**0**	**0**	**0**	**0**	**0**	**0**
	Long Beach	IHL	6	0	3	3	2	....	....	....	....	....	....	....	....	....	....	....	....	....	....	....	....	....	....	....
	Lowell	AHL	2	1	1	2	2	....	....	....	....	....	....	....	....	....	....	....	....	....	....	....	....	....	....	....
	NHL Totals		**220**	**9**	**21**	**30**	**122**	**0**	**1**	**0**	**195**	**4.6**		**62**	**43.5**	**183**	**37**	**10:20**	**5**	**0**	**0**	**0**	**0**	**0**	**0**	**0**

Signed as a free agent by **LA Kings**, July 7, 1994. Signed as a free agent by **Anaheim**, July 13, 2000.

CAIRNS, Eric

(KAIRNZ, AIR-ihk) **NYI**

Defense. Shoots left. 6'6", 230 lbs. Born, Oakville, Ont., June 27, 1974. NY Rangers' 3rd choice, 72nd overall, in 1992 Entry Draft.

Season	Club	League	GP	G	A	Pts	PIM	PP	SH	GW	S	%	+/-	TF	F%	H	SB	Min	GP	G	A	Pts	PIM	PP	SH	GW
1990-91	Burlington	OJHL-B	37	5	16	21	120	....	....	....	....	....	....	....	....	....	....	....	....	....	....	....	....	....	....	....
1991-92	Detroit	OHL	64	1	11	12	237	....	....	....	....	....	....	....	....	....	....	....	7	0	0	0	31	....	....	....
1992-93	Detroit Jr. Wings	OHL	64	3	13	16	194	....	....	....	....	....	....	....	....	....	....	....	15	0	3	3	24	....	....	....
1993-94	Detroit Jr. Wings	OHL	59	7	35	42	204	....	....	....	....	....	....	....	....	....	....	....	17	0	4	4	46	....	....	....
1994-95	Birmingham Bulls	ECHL	11	1	3	4	49	....	....	....	....	....	....	....	....	....	....	....	....	....	....	....	....	....	....	....
	Binghamton	AHL	27	0	3	3	134	....	....	....	....	....	....	....	....	....	....	....	9	1	1	2	28	....	....	....
1995-96	Binghamton	AHL	46	1	13	14	192	....	....	....	....	....	....	....	....	....	....	....	4	0	0	0	37	....	....	....
	Charlotte	ECHL	6	0	1	1	34	....	....	....	....	....	....	....	....	....	....	....	....	....	....	....	....	....	....	....
1996-97	**NY Rangers**	**NHL**	**40**	**0**	**1**	**1**	**147**	**0**	**0**	**0**	**17**	**0.0**	**–7**	....	....	....	....	....	**3**	**0**	**0**	**0**	**0**	**0**	**0**	**0**
	Binghamton	AHL	10	1	1	2	96	....	....	....	....	....	....	....	....	....	....	....	....	....	....	....	....	....	....	....
1997-98	**NY Rangers**	**NHL**	**39**	**0**	**3**	**3**	**92**	**0**	**0**	**0**	**17**	**0.0**	**–3**	....	....	....	....	....	....	....	....	....	....	....	....	....
	Hartford	AHL	7	1	2	3	43	....	....	....	....	....	....	....	....	....	....	....	....	....	....	....	....	....	....	....
1998-99	Hartford	AHL	11	0	2	2	49	....	....	....	....	....	....	....	....	....	....	....	....	....	....	....	....	....	....	....
	NY Islanders	**NHL**	**9**	**0**	**3**	**3**	**23**	**0**	**0**	**0**	**2**	**0.0**	**1**	**0**	**0.0**	**13**	**5**	**10:15**	....	....	....	....	....	....	....	....
	Lowell	AHL	24	0	0	0	91	....	....	....	....	....	....	....	....	....	....	....	3	1	0	1	32	....	....	....

									Regular Season										Playoffs							
Season	Club	League	GP	G	A	Pts	PIM	PP	SH	GW	S	%	+/–	TF	F%	H	SB	Min	GP	G	A	Pts	PIM	PP	SH	GW
99-2000	**NY Islanders**	**NHL**	**67**	**2**	**7**	**9**	**196**	**0**	**0**	**0**	**55**	**3.6**	**–5**	**0**	**0.0**	**182**	**73**	**17:43**	....	....	....	....	....	....	....	....
	Providence Bruins	AHL	4	1	1	2	14	....	....	....	....	....	....	....	....	....	....	....	....	....	....	....	....	....	....	....
	NHL Totals		**155**	**2**	**14**	**16**	**458**	**0**	**0**	**0**	**91**	**2.2**		**0**	**0.0**	**195**	**78**	**16:50**	**3**	**0**	**0**	**0**	**0**	**0**	**0**	**0**

Claimed on waivers by **NY Islanders** from **NY Rangers**, December 22, 1998. Loaned to **Providence** (AHL) by **NY Islanders**, October 6, 1999 and recalled October 13, 1999.

CALDER, Kyle (KAWL-dehr, KIGHLE) CHI.

Center. Shoots left. 5'11", 180 lbs. Born, Mannville, Alta., January 5, 1979. Chicago's 7th choice, 130th overall, in 1997 Entry Draft.

Season	Club	League	GP	G	A	Pts	PIM	PP	SH	GW	S	%	+/–	TF	F%	H	SB	Min	GP	G	A	Pts	PIM	PP	SH	GW
1994-95	Leduc Barons	AAHA	27	25	32	57	22	....	....	....	....	....	....	....	....	....	....	....	....	....	....	....	....	....	....	....
1995-96	Regina Pats	WHL	27	1	7	8	10	....	....	....	....	....	....	....	....	....	....	....	11	0	0	0	0	....	....	....
1996-97	Regina Pats	WHL	62	25	34	59	17	....	....	....	....	....	....	....	....	....	....	....	5	3	0	3	6	....	....	....
1997-98	Regina Pats	WHL	62	27	50	77	58	....	....	....	....	....	....	....	....	....	....	....	2	0	1	1	0	....	....	....
1998-99	Regina Pats	WHL	34	23	28	51	29	....	....	....	....	....	....	....	....	....	....	....	....	....	....	....	....	....	....	....
	Kamloops Blazers	WHL	27	19	18	37	30	....	....	....	....	....	....	....	....	....	....	....	15	6	10	16	6	....	....	....
99-2000	**Chicago**	**NHL**	**8**	**1**	**1**	**2**	**2**	**0**	**0**	**0**	**5**	**20.0**	**–3**	**2**	**0.0**	**5**	**1**	**9:59**	....	....	....	....	....	....	....	....
	Cleveland	IHL	74	14	22	36	43	....	....	....	....	....	....	....	....	....	....	....	9	2	2	4	14	....	....	....
	NHL Totals		**8**	**1**	**1**	**2**	**2**	**0**	**0**	**0**	**5**	**20.0**		**2**	**0.0**	**5**	**1**	**9:59**	....	....	....	....	....	....	....	....

CALLANDER, Jock

Right wing. Shoots right. 6'1", 188 lbs. Born, Regina, Sask., April 23, 1961.

Season	Club	League	GP	G	A	Pts	PIM	PP	SH	GW	S	%	+/–	TF	F%	H	SB	Min	GP	G	A	Pts	PIM	PP	SH	GW
1978-79	Regina Blues	SJHL	42	44	42	86	24	....	....	....	....	....	....	....	....	....	....	....	....	....	....	....	....	....	....	....
	Regina Pats	WHL	19	3	2	5	0	....	....	....	....	....	....	....	....	....	....	....	....	....	....	....	....	....	....	....
1979-80	Regina Pats	WHL	39	9	11	20	25	....	....	....	....	....	....	....	....	....	....	....	18	8	5	13	0	....	....	....
1980-81	Regina Pats	WHL	72	67	86	153	37	....	....	....	....	....	....	....	....	....	....	....	11	6	7	13	14	....	....	....
1981-82	Regina Pats	WHL	71	79	111	*190	59	....	....	....	....	....	....	....	....	....	....	....	20	13	*26	39	37	....	....	....
1982-83	Salt Lake City	CHL	68	20	27	47	26	....	....	....	....	....	....	....	....	....	....	....	6	0	1	1	9	....	....	....
1983-84	Montana Magic	CHL	72	27	32	59	69	....	....	....	....	....	....	....	....	....	....	....	....	....	....	....	....	....	....	....
	Toledo	IHL	2	0	0	0	0	....	....	....	....	....	....	....	....	....	....	....	....	....	....	....	....	....	....	....
1984-85	Muskegon	IHL	82	39	68	107	86	....	....	....	....	....	....	....	....	....	....	....	17	8	*13	*21	33	....	....	....
1985-86	Muskegon	IHL	82	39	72	111	121	....	....	....	....	....	....	....	....	....	....	....	14	*12	11	*23	12	....	....	....
1986-87	Muskegon	IHL	82	54	82	*136	110	....	....	....	....	....	....	....	....	....	....	....	15	13	7	20	23	....	....	....
1987-88	**Pittsburgh**	**NHL**	**41**	**11**	**16**	**27**	**45**	**4**	**0**	**1**	**59**	**18.6**	**–13**	....	....	....	....	....	....	....	....	....	....	....	....	....
	Muskegon	IHL	31	20	36	56	49	....	....	....	....	....	....	....	....	....	....	....	6	2	3	5	25	....	....	....
1988-89	**Pittsburgh**	**NHL**	**30**	**6**	**5**	**11**	**20**	**2**	**0**	**0**	**35**	**17.1**	**–3**	....	....	....	....	....	**10**	**2**	**5**	**7**	**10**	**0**	**0**	**0**
	Muskegon	IHL	48	25	39	64	40	....	....	....	....	....	....	....	....	....	....	....	7	5	5	10	30	....	....	....
1989-90	**Pittsburgh**	**NHL**	**30**	**4**	**7**	**11**	**49**	**0**	**0**	**1**	**22**	**18.2**	**0**	....	....	....	....	....	....	....	....	....	....	....	....	....
	Muskegon	IHL	46	29	49	78	118	....	....	....	....	....	....	....	....	....	....	....	15	6	*14	20	54	....	....	....
1990-91	Muskegon	IHL	30	14	20	34	102	....	....	....	....	....	....	....	....	....	....	....	....	....	....	....	....	....	....	....
1991-92	Muskegon	IHL	81	42	70	112	160	....	....	....	....	....	....	....	....	....	....	....	10	4	10	14	13	....	....	....
	◆ **Pittsburgh**	**NHL**	....	....	....	....	....	....	....	....	....	....	....	....	....	....	....	....	**12**	**1**	**3**	**4**	**2**	**0**	**0**	**0**
1992-93	**Tampa Bay**	**NHL**	**8**	**1**	**1**	**2**	**2**	**0**	**0**	**0**	**12**	**8.3**	**–5**	....	....	....	....	....	....	....	....	....	....	....	....	....
	Atlanta Knights	IHL	69	34	50	84	172	....	....	....	....	....	....	....	....	....	....	....	9	*7	5	12	25	....	....	....
1993-94	Cleveland	IHL	81	31	70	101	126	....	....	....	....	....	....	....	....	....	....	....	....	....	....	....	....	....	....	....
1994-95	Cleveland	IHL	61	24	36	60	90	....	....	....	....	....	....	....	....	....	....	....	4	2	2	4	6	....	....	....
1995-96	Cleveland	IHL	81	42	53	95	150	....	....	....	....	....	....	....	....	....	....	....	3	1	0	1	8	....	....	....
1996-97	Cleveland	IHL	61	20	34	54	56	....	....	....	....	....	....	....	....	....	....	....	14	7	6	13	10	....	....	....
1997-98	Cleveland	IHL	72	20	33	53	105	....	....	....	....	....	....	....	....	....	....	....	10	5	6	11	6	....	....	....
1998-99	Cleveland	IHL	81	28	26	54	121	....	....	....	....	....	....	....	....	....	....	....	....	....	....	....	....	....	....	....
99-2000	Cleveland	IHL	64	16	27	43	83	....	....	....	....	....	....	....	....	....	....	....	9	1	5	6	6	....	....	....
	NHL Totals		**109**	**22**	**29**	**51**	**116**	**6**	**0**	**2**	**128**	**17.2**		....	....	....	....	....	**22**	**3**	**8**	**11**	**12**	**0**	**0**	**0**

IHL First All-Star Team (1987, 1992) • Won Leo P. Lamoureux Memorial Trophy (Top Scorer - IHL) (Tied with Jeff Pyle) (1987) • Won James Gatschene Memorial Trophy (MVP - IHL) (Tied with Jeff Pyle) (1987) • Became IHL's All-Time leading scorer (1383 points) in game vs. Cincinnati (IHL), February 23, 2000.

Signed as a free agent by **St. Louis**, September 28, 1981. Signed as a free agent by **Pittsburgh**, July 31, 1987. Signed as a free agent by **Tampa Bay**, July 29, 1992.

CALOUN, Jan (CHAH-loon, YAHN) CBJ

Right wing. Shoots right. 5'10", 190 lbs. Born, Usti-Nad-Labem, Czech., December 20, 1972. San Jose's 4th choice, 75th overall, in 1992 Entry Draft.

Season	Club	League	GP	G	A	Pts	PIM	PP	SH	GW	S	%	+/–	TF	F%	H	SB	Min	GP	G	A	Pts	PIM	PP	SH	GW
1990-91	CHZ Litvinov	Czech.	50	28	19	47	12	....	....	....	....	....	....	....	....	....	....	....	....	....	....	....	....	....	....	....
1991-92	CHZ Litvinov	Czech.	46	39	13	52	24	....	....	....	....	....	....	....	....	....	....	....	....	....	....	....	....	....	....	....
1992-93	CHZ Litvinov	Czech.	47	45	22	67	....	....	....	....	....	....	....	....	....	....	....	....	....	....	....	....	....	....	....	....
1993-94	CHZ Litvinov	Cze-Rep	38	25	17	42	....	....	....	....	....	....	....	....	....	....	....	....	4	2	2	4	....	....	....	....
1994-95	Kansas City	IHL	76	34	39	73	50	....	....	....	....	....	....	....	....	....	....	....	21	13	10	23	18	....	....	....
1995-96	**San Jose**	**NHL**	**11**	**8**	**3**	**11**	**0**	**2**	**0**	**0**	**20**	**40.0**	**4**	....	....	....	....	....	....	....	....	....	....	....	....	....
	Kansas City	IHL	61	38	30	68	58	....	....	....	....	....	....	....	....	....	....	....	5	0	1	1	6	....	....	....
1996-97	**San Jose**	**NHL**	**2**	**0**	**0**	**0**	**0**	**0**	**0**	**0**	**3**	**0.0**	**–2**	....	....	....	....	....	....	....	....	....	....	....	....	....
	Kentucky	AHL	66	43	43	86	68	....	....	....	....	....	....	....	....	....	....	....	4	0	1	1	4	....	....	....
1997-98	HIFK Helsinki	Finland	41	22	26	48	73	....	....	....	....	....	....	....	....	....	....	....	9	6	*11	*17	6	....	....	....
	Czech-Republic	Olympics	3	0	0	0	6	....	....	....	....	....	....	....	....	....	....	....	....	....	....	....	....	....	....	....
1998-99	HIFK Helsinki	Finland	51	24	*57	*81	95	....	....	....	....	....	....	....	....	....	....	....	8	*8	6	*14	31	....	....	....
	HIFK Helsinki	EuroHL	5	4	2	6	26	....	....	....	....	....	....	....	....	....	....	....	3	1	1	2	30	....	....	....
99-2000	HIFK Helsinki	Finland	44	38	34	72	94	....	....	....	....	....	....	....	....	....	....	....	9	3	6	9	10	....	....	....
	HIFK Helsinki	EuroHL	4	1	3	4	6	....	....	....	....	....	....	....	....	....	....	....	1	0	1	1	0	....	....	....
	NHL Totals		**13**	**8**	**3**	**11**	**0**	**2**	**0**	**0**	**23**	**34.8**		....	....	....	....	....	....	....	....	....	....	....	....	....

AHL Second All-Star Team (1997) • Finnish First All-Star Team (1999, 2000)

Traded to **Columbus** by **San Jose** with San Jose's 9th round choice (Martin Paroulek) in 2000 Entry Draft for future considerations, June 12, 2000.

CAMPBELL, Brian (KAM-behl, BRIGH-an) BUF.

Defense. Shoots left. 6', 190 lbs. Born, Strathroy, Ont., May 23, 1979. Buffalo's 7th choice, 156th overall, in 1997 Entry Draft.

Season	Club	League	GP	G	A	Pts	PIM	PP	SH	GW	S	%	+/–	TF	F%	H	SB	Min	GP	G	A	Pts	PIM	PP	SH	GW
1994-95	Petrolia Barons	OJHL	49	11	27	38	43	....	....	....	....	....	....	....	....	....	....	....	....	....	....	....	....	....	....	....
1995-96	Ottawa 67's	OHL	66	5	22	27	23	....	....	....	....	....	....	....	....	....	....	....	4	0	1	1	2	....	....	....
1996-97	Ottawa 67's	OHL	66	7	36	43	12	....	....	....	....	....	....	....	....	....	....	....	24	2	11	13	8	....	....	....
1997-98	Ottawa 67's	OHL	66	14	39	53	31	....	....	....	....	....	....	....	....	....	....	....	13	1	14	15	0	....	....	....
1998-99	Ottawa 67's	OHL	62	12	75	87	27	....	....	....	....	....	....	....	....	....	....	....	9	2	10	12	6	....	....	....
	Rochester	AHL	....	....	....	....	....	....	....	....	....	....	....	....	....	....	....	....	2	0	0	0	0	....	....	....
99-2000	**Buffalo**	**NHL**	**12**	**1**	**4**	**5**	**4**	**0**	**0**	**0**	**10**	**10.0**	**–2**	**0**	**0.0**	**8**	**3**	**15:48**	....	....	....	....	....	....	....	....
	Rochester	AHL	67	2	24	26	22	....	....	....	....	....	....	....	....	....	....	....	21	0	3	3	0	....	....	....
	NHL Totals		**12**	**1**	**4**	**5**	**4**	**0**	**0**	**0**	**10**	**10.0**		**0**	**0.0**	**8**	**3**	**15:48**	....	....	....	....	....	....	....	....

OHL First All-Star Team (1999) • Canadian Major Junior First All-Star Team (1999) • Won George Parsons Trophy (Memorial Cup Tournament Most Sportsmanlike Player) (1999) • Canadian Major Junior Player of the Year (1999)

CAMPBELL, Jim (KAM-behl, JIHM) MTL.

Right wing. Shoots right. 6'2", 205 lbs. Born, Worcester, MA, April 3, 1973. Montreal's 2nd choice, 28th overall, in 1991 Entry Draft.

Season	Club	League	GP	G	A	Pts	PIM	PP	SH	GW	S	%	+/–	TF	F%	H	SB	Min	GP	G	A	Pts	PIM	PP	SH	GW
1988-89	Northwood Prep	Hi-School	12	12	8	20	6	....	....	....	....	....	....	....	....	....	....	....	....	....	....	....	....	....	....	....
1989-90	Northwood Prep	Hi-School	8	14	7	21	8	....	....	....	....	....	....	....	....	....	....	....	....	....	....	....	....	....	....	....
1990-91	Lawrence Prep	Hi-School	26	36	47	83	26	....	....	....	....	....	....	....	....	....	....	....	....	....	....	....	....	....	....	....
1991-92	Hull Olympiques	QMJHL	64	41	44	85	51	....	....	....	....	....	....	....	....	....	....	....	6	7	3	10	8	....	....	....
1992-93	Hull Olympiques	QMJHL	50	42	29	71	66	....	....	....	....	....	....	....	....	....	....	....	8	11	4	15	43	....	....	....
1993-94	United States	Nat-Team	56	24	33	57	59	....	....	....	....	....	....	....	....	....	....	....	....	....	....	....	....	....	....	....
	United States	Olympics	8	0	0	0	6	....	....	....	....	....	....	....	....	....	....	....	....	....	....	....	....	....	....	....
	Fredericton	AHL	19	6	17	23	6	....	....	....	....	....	....	....	....	....	....	....	....	....	....	....	....	....	....	....

			Regular Season																Playoffs							
Season	Club	League	GP	G	A	Pts	PIM	PP	SH	GW	S	%	+/–	TF	F%	H	SB	Min	GP	G	A	Pts	PIM	PP	SH	GW
1994-95	Fredericton	AHL	77	27	24	51	103	....	....	....	....	....	....	....	....	....	....	....	12	0	7	7	8	....	....	....
1995-96	Fredericton	AHL	44	28	23	51	24	....	....	....	....	....	....	....	....	....	....	....	....	....	....	....	....	....	....	....
	Anaheim	**NHL**	**16**	**2**	**3**	**5**	**36**	**1**	**0**	**0**	**25**	**8.0**	**0**	....	....	....	....	....	....	....	....	....	....	....	....	....
	Baltimore Bandits	AHL	16	13	7	20	8	....	....	....	....	....	....	....	....	....	....	....	12	7	5	12	10	....	....	....
1996-97	**St. Louis**	**NHL**	**68**	**23**	**20**	**43**	**68**	**5**	**0**	**6**	**169**	**13.6**	**3**	....	....	....	....	....	**4**	**1**	**0**	**1**	**6**	**1**	**0**	**0**
1997-98	**St. Louis**	**NHL**	**76**	**22**	**19**	**41**	**55**	**7**	**0**	**6**	**147**	**15.0**	**0**	....	....	....	....	....	**10**	**7**	**3**	**10**	**12**	**4**	**0**	**2**
1998-99	**St. Louis**	**NHL**	**55**	**4**	**21**	**25**	**41**	**1**	**0**	**0**	**99**	**4.0**	**–8**	**7**	**42.9**	**65**	**7**	**13:34**	....	....	....	....	....	....	....	....
99-2000	Manitoba Moose	IHL	10	1	3	4	10	....	....	....	....	....	....	....	....	....	....	....	....	....	....	....	....	....	....	....
	St. Louis	**NHL**	**2**	**0**	**0**	**0**	**9**	**0**	**0**	**0**	**6**	**0.0**	**0**	**0**	**0.0**	**1**	**0**	**15:17**	....	....	....	....	....	....	....	....
	Worcester	AHL	66	31	34	65	88	....	....	....	....	....	....	....	....	....	....	....	9	1	2	3	6	....	....	....
	NHL Totals		**217**	**51**	**63**	**114**	**209**	**14**	**0**	**12**	**446**	**11.4**		**7**	**42.9**	**66**	**7**	**13:38**	**14**	**8**	**3**	**11**	**18**	**5**	**0**	**2**

NHL All-Rookie Team (1997)

Traded to **Anaheim** by **Montreal** for Robert Dirk, January 21, 1996. Signed as a free agent by **St. Louis**, July 11, 1996. Loaned to **Manitoba** (IHL) by **St. Louis**, October 4, 1999 and recalled November 1, 1999. Signed as a free agent by **Montreal**, August 21, 2000.

CARBONNEAU, Guy

(KAR-buhn-oh, GEE)

Center. Shoots right. 5'11", 186 lbs. Born, Sept-Iles, Que., March 18, 1960. Montreal's 4th choice, 44th overall, in 1979 Entry Draft.

Season	Club	League	GP	G	A	Pts	PIM	PP	SH	GW	S	%	+/–	TF	F%	H	SB	Min	GP	G	A	Pts	PIM	PP	SH	GW
1976-77	Chicoutimi	QMJHL	59	9	20	29	8	....	....	....	....	....	....	....	....	....	....	....	4	1	0	1	0	....	....	....
1977-78	Chicoutimi	QMJHL	70	28	55	83	60	....	....	....	....	....	....	....	....	....	....	....	....	....	....	....	....	....	....	....
1978-79	Chicoutimi	QMJHL	72	62	79	141	47	....	....	....	....	....	....	....	....	....	....	....	4	2	1	3	4	....	....	....
1979-80	Chicoutimi	QMJHL	72	72	110	182	66	....	....	....	....	....	....	....	....	....	....	....	12	9	15	24	28	....	....	....
	Nova Scotia	AHL	....	....	....	....	....	....	....	....	....	....	....	....	....	....	....	....	2	1	1	2	2	....	....	....
1980-81	**Montreal**	**NHL**	**2**	**0**	**1**	**1**	**0**	**0**	**0**	**0**	**1**	**0.0**	**0**	....	....	....	....	....	....	....	....	....	....	....	....	....
	Nova Scotia	AHL	78	35	53	88	87	....	....	....	....	....	....	....	....	....	....	....	6	1	3	4	9	....	....	....
1981-82	Nova Scotia	AHL	77	27	67	94	124	....	....	....	....	....	....	....	....	....	....	....	9	2	7	9	8	....	....	....
1982-83	**Montreal**	**NHL**	**77**	**18**	**29**	**47**	**68**	**0**	**5**	**2**	**109**	**16.5**	**18**	....	....	....	....	....	**3**	**0**	**0**	**0**	**2**	**0**	**0**	**0**
1983-84	**Montreal**	**NHL**	**78**	**24**	**30**	**54**	**75**	**3**	**7**	**2**	**166**	**14.5**	**5**	....	....	....	....	....	**15**	**4**	**3**	**7**	**12**	**0**	**0**	**1**
1984-85	**Montreal**	**NHL**	**79**	**23**	**34**	**57**	**43**	**0**	**4**	**2**	**163**	**14.1**	**28**	....	....	....	....	....	**12**	**4**	**3**	**7**	**8**	**0**	**1**	**1**
1985-86♦	**Montreal**	**NHL**	**80**	**20**	**36**	**56**	**57**	**1**	**2**	**3**	**147**	**13.6**	**18**	....	....	....	....	....	**20**	**7**	**5**	**12**	**35**	**0**	**2**	**1**
1986-87	**Montreal**	**NHL**	**79**	**18**	**27**	**45**	**68**	**0**	**0**	**2**	**120**	**15.0**	**9**	....	....	....	....	....	**17**	**3**	**8**	**11**	**20**	**0**	**0**	**0**
1987-88	**Montreal**	**NHL**	**80**	**17**	**21**	**38**	**61**	**0**	**3**	**1**	**109**	**15.6**	**14**	....	....	....	....	....	**11**	**0**	**4**	**4**	**2**	**0**	**0**	**0**
1988-89	**Montreal**	**NHL**	**79**	**26**	**30**	**56**	**44**	**1**	**2**	**10**	**142**	**18.3**	**37**	....	....	....	....	....	**21**	**4**	**5**	**9**	**10**	**0**	**1**	**0**
1989-90	**Montreal**	**NHL**	**68**	**19**	**36**	**55**	**37**	**1**	**1**	**3**	**125**	**15.2**	**21**	....	....	....	....	....	**11**	**2**	**3**	**5**	**6**	**0**	**0**	**0**
1990-91	**Montreal**	**NHL**	**78**	**20**	**24**	**44**	**63**	**4**	**1**	**3**	**131**	**15.3**	**–1**	....	....	....	....	....	**13**	**1**	**5**	**6**	**10**	**0**	**0**	**1**
1991-92	**Montreal**	**NHL**	**72**	**18**	**21**	**39**	**39**	**1**	**1**	**4**	**120**	**15.0**	**2**	....	....	....	....	....	**11**	**1**	**1**	**2**	**6**	**0**	**0**	**0**
1992-93♦	**Montreal**	**NHL**	**61**	**4**	**13**	**17**	**20**	**0**	**1**	**0**	**73**	**5.5**	**–9**	....	....	....	....	....	**20**	**3**	**3**	**6**	**10**	**0**	**1**	**2**
1993-94	**Montreal**	**NHL**	**79**	**14**	**24**	**38**	**48**	**0**	**0**	**1**	**120**	**11.7**	**16**	....	....	....	....	....	**7**	**1**	**3**	**4**	**4**	**0**	**0**	**0**
1994-95	**St. Louis**	**NHL**	**42**	**5**	**11**	**16**	**16**	**1**	**0**	**1**	**33**	**15.2**	**11**	....	....	....	....	....	**7**	**1**	**2**	**3**	**6**	**0**	**0**	**0**
1995-96	**Dallas**	**NHL**	**71**	**8**	**15**	**23**	**38**	**0**	**2**	**1**	**54**	**14.8**	**–2**	....	....	....	....	....	....	....	....	....	....	....	....	....
1996-97	**Dallas**	**NHL**	**73**	**5**	**16**	**21**	**36**	**0**	**1**	**0**	**99**	**5.1**	**9**	....	....	....	....	....	**7**	**0**	**1**	**1**	**6**	**0**	**0**	**0**
1997-98	**Dallas**	**NHL**	**77**	**7**	**17**	**24**	**40**	**0**	**1**	**1**	**81**	**8.6**	**3**	....	....	....	....	....	**16**	**3**	**1**	**4**	**6**	**0**	**0**	**0**
1998-99♦	**Dallas**	**NHL**	**74**	**4**	**12**	**16**	**31**	**0**	**0**	**2**	**60**	**6.7**	**–3**	**1055**	**53.3**	**83**	**57**	**13:21**	**17**	**2**	**4**	**6**	**6**	**0**	**0**	**1**
99-2000	**Dallas**	**NHL**	**69**	**10**	**6**	**16**	**36**	**0**	**1**	**4**	**70**	**14.3**	**10**	**1290**	**53.2**	**135**	**65**	**15:38**	**23**	**2**	**4**	**6**	**12**	**0**	**1**	**1**
	NHL Totals		**1318**	**260**	**403**	**663**	**820**	**12**	**32**	**42**	**1923**	**13.5**		**2345**	**53.2**	**218**	**122**	**14:27**	**231**	**38**	**55**	**93**	**161**	**0**	**6**	**8**

QMJHL Second All-Star Team (1980) • Won Frank J. Selke Trophy (1988, 1989, 1992)

Traded to **St. Louis** by **Montreal** for Jim Montgomery, August 19, 1994. Traded to **Dallas** by **St. Louis** for Paul Broten, October 2, 1995. • Officially announced retirement, June 29, 2000.

CARNEY, Keith

(KAHRN-nee, KEETH) **PHX.**

Defense. Shoots left. 6'2", 211 lbs. Born, Providence, RI, February 3, 1970. Buffalo's 3rd choice, 76th overall, in 1988 Entry Draft.

Season	Club	League	GP	G	A	Pts	PIM	PP	SH	GW	S	%	+/–	TF	F%	H	SB	Min	GP	G	A	Pts	PIM	PP	SH	GW
1987-88	Mount St. Charles	Hi-School	23	12	43	55	....	....	....	....	....	....	....	....	....	....	....	....	....	....	....	....	....	....	....	....
1988-89	U. of Maine	H-East	40	4	22	26	24	....	....	....	....	....	....	....	....	....	....	....	....	....	....	....	....	....	....	....
1989-90	U. of Maine	H-East	41	3	41	44	43	....	....	....	....	....	....	....	....	....	....	....	....	....	....	....	....	....	....	....
1990-91	U. of Maine	H-East	40	7	49	56	38	....	....	....	....	....	....	....	....	....	....	....	....	....	....	....	....	....	....	....
1991-92	United States	Nat-Team	49	2	17	19	16	....	....	....	....	....	....	....	....	....	....	....	....	....	....	....	....	....	....	....
	Buffalo	**NHL**	**14**	**1**	**2**	**3**	**18**	**1**	**0**	**0**	**17**	**5.9**	**–3**	....	....	....	....	....	**7**	**0**	**3**	**3**	**0**	**0**	**0**	**0**
	Rochester	AHL	24	1	10	11	2	....	....	....	....	....	....	....	....	....	....	....	2	0	2	2	0	....	....	....
1992-93	**Buffalo**	**NHL**	**30**	**2**	**4**	**6**	**55**	**0**	**0**	**1**	**26**	**7.7**	**3**	....	....	....	....	....	**8**	**0**	**3**	**3**	**6**	**0**	**0**	**0**
	Rochester	AHL	41	5	21	26	32	....	....	....	....	....	....	....	....	....	....	....	....	....	....	....	....	....	....	....
1993-94	**Buffalo**	**NHL**	**7**	**1**	**3**	**4**	**4**	**0**	**0**	**0**	**6**	**16.7**	**–1**	....	....	....	....	....	....	....	....	....	....	....	....	....
	Chicago	**NHL**	**30**	**3**	**5**	**8**	**35**	**0**	**0**	**0**	**31**	**9.7**	**15**	....	....	....	....	....	**6**	**0**	**1**	**1**	**4**	**0**	**0**	**0**
	Indianapolis Ice	IHL	28	0	14	14	20	....	....	....	....	....	....	....	....	....	....	....	....	....	....	....	....	....	....	....
1994-95	**Chicago**	**NHL**	**18**	**1**	**0**	**1**	**11**	**0**	**0**	**1**	**14**	**7.1**	**–1**	....	....	....	....	....	**4**	**0**	**1**	**1**	**0**	**0**	**0**	**0**
1995-96	**Chicago**	**NHL**	**82**	**5**	**14**	**19**	**94**	**1**	**0**	**1**	**69**	**7.2**	**31**	....	....	....	....	....	**10**	**0**	**3**	**3**	**4**	**0**	**0**	**0**
1996-97	**Chicago**	**NHL**	**81**	**3**	**15**	**18**	**62**	**0**	**0**	**1**	**77**	**3.9**	**26**	....	....	....	....	....	**6**	**1**	**1**	**2**	**2**	**0**	**0**	**0**
1997-98	**Chicago**	**NHL**	**60**	**2**	**13**	**15**	**73**	**0**	**1**	**0**	**53**	**3.8**	**–7**	....	....	....	....	....	....	....	....	....	....	....	....	....
	United States	Olympics	4	0	0	0	2	....	....	....	....	....	....	....	....	....	....	....	....	....	....	....	....	....	....	....
	Phoenix	**NHL**	**20**	**1**	**6**	**7**	**18**	**1**	**0**	**0**	**18**	**5.6**	**5**	....	....	....	....	....	**6**	**0**	**0**	**0**	**4**	**0**	**0**	**0**
1998-99	**Phoenix**	**NHL**	**82**	**2**	**14**	**16**	**62**	**0**	**2**	**0**	**62**	**3.2**	**15**	**0**	**0.0**	**133**	**87**	**22:46**	**7**	**1**	**2**	**3**	**10**	**0**	**0**	**0**
99-2000	**Phoenix**	**NHL**	**82**	**4**	**20**	**24**	**87**	**0**	**0**	**1**	**73**	**5.5**	**11**	**0**	**0.0**	**0**	**0**	**0:00**	**5**	**0**	**0**	**0**	**17**	**0**	**0**	**0**
	NHL Totals		**506**	**25**	**96**	**121**	**519**	**3**	**3**	**5**	**446**	**5.6**		**0**	**0.0**	**133**	**87**	**22:46**	**59**	**2**	**14**	**16**	**47**	**0**	**0**	**0**

Hockey East Second All-Star Team (1990) • NCAA East Second All-American Team (1990) • Hockey East First All-Star Team (1991) • NCAA East First All-American Team (1991)

Traded to **Chicago** by **Buffalo** with Buffalo's 6th round choice (Marc Magliarditi) in 1995 Entry Draft for Craig Muni and Chicago's 5th round choice (Daniel Bienvenue) in 1995 Entry Draft, October 26, 1993. Traded to **Phoenix** by **Chicago** with Jim Cummins for Chad Kilger and Jayson More, March 4, 1998.

CARTER, Anson

(KAHR-tuhr, AN-sohn) **BOS.**

Right wing. Shoots right. 6'1", 200 lbs. Born, Toronto, Ont., June 6, 1974. Quebec's 11th choice, 220th overall, in 1992 Entry Draft.

Season	Club	League	GP	G	A	Pts	PIM	PP	SH	GW	S	%	+/–	TF	F%	H	SB	Min	GP	G	A	Pts	PIM	PP	SH	GW
1989-90	Don Mills Flyers	MTHL	40	15	47	62	105	....	....	....	....	....	....	....	....	....	....	....	....	....	....	....	....	....	....	....
1990-91	Don Mills Flyers	MTHL	67	69	73	142	43	....	....	....	....	....	....	....	....	....	....	....	....	....	....	....	....	....	....	....
1991-92	Wexford Raiders	OJHL	42	18	22	40	24	....	....	....	....	....	....	....	....	....	....	....	....	....	....	....	....	....	....	....
1992-93	Michigan State	CCHA	34	15	7	22	20	....	....	....	....	....	....	....	....	....	....	....	....	....	....	....	....	....	....	....
1993-94	Michigan State	CCHA	39	30	24	54	36	....	....	....	....	....	....	....	....	....	....	....	....	....	....	....	....	....	....	....
1994-95	Michigan State	CCHA	39	34	17	51	40	....	....	....	....	....	....	....	....	....	....	....	....	....	....	....	....	....	....	....
1995-96	Michigan State	CCHA	42	23	20	43	36	....	....	....	....	....	....	....	....	....	....	....	....	....	....	....	....	....	....	....
1996-97	**Washington**	**NHL**	**19**	**3**	**2**	**5**	**7**	**1**	**0**	**1**	**28**	**10.7**	**0**	....	....	....	....	....	....	....	....	....	....	....	....	....
	Portland Pirates	AHL	27	19	19	38	11	....	....	....	....	....	....	....	....	....	....	....	....	....	....	....	....	....	....	....
	Boston	**NHL**	**19**	**8**	**5**	**13**	**2**	**1**	**1**	**1**	**51**	**15.7**	**–7**	....	....	....	....	....	....	....	....	....	....	....	....	....
1997-98	**Boston**	**NHL**	**78**	**16**	**27**	**43**	**31**	**6**	**0**	**4**	**179**	**8.9**	**7**	....	....	....	....	....	**6**	**1**	**1**	**2**	**0**	**0**	**0**	**0**
1998-99	Utah Grizzlies	IHL	6	1	1	2	0	....	....	....	....	....	....	....	....	....	....	....	....	....	....	....	....	....	....	....
	Boston	**NHL**	**55**	**24**	**16**	**40**	**22**	**6**	**0**	**6**	**123**	**19.5**	**7**	**172**	**43.0**	**62**	**5**	**18:44**	**12**	**4**	**3**	**7**	**0**	**1**	**0**	**1**
99-2000	**Boston**	**NHL**	**59**	**22**	**25**	**47**	**14**	**4**	**0**	**1**	**144**	**15.3**	**8**	**793**	**48.2**	**87**	**9**	**20:31**	....	....	....	....	....	....	....	....
	NHL Totals		**230**	**73**	**75**	**148**	**76**	**18**	**1**	**13**	**525**	**13.9**		**965**	**47.3**	**149**	**14**	**19:40**	**18**	**5**	**4**	**9**	**0**	**1**	**0**	**1**

CCHA First All-Star Team (1994, 1995) • NCAA West Second All-American Team (1995) • CCHA Second All-Star Team (1996)

Rights transferred to **Colorado** after **Quebec** franchise relocated, June 21, 1995. Traded to **Washington** by **Colorado** for Washington's 4th round choice (Ben Storey) in 1996 Entry Draft, April 3, 1996. Traded to **Boston** by **Washington** with Jim Carey, Jason Allison and Washington's 3rd round choice (Lee Goren) in 1997 Entry Draft for Bill Ranford, Adam Oates and Rick Tocchet, March 1, 1997.

CASSELS, Andrew

(KAS-uhls, AN-drew) **VAN.**

Center. Shoots left. 6'1", 185 lbs. Born, Bramalea, Ont., July 23, 1969. Montreal's 1st choice, 17th overall, in 1987 Entry Draft.

			Regular Season																Playoffs							
Season	Club	League	GP	G	A	Pts	PIM	PP	SH	GW	S	%	+/–	TF	F%	H	SB	Min	GP	G	A	Pts	PIM	PP	SH	GW
1985-86	Bramalea Blues	OJHL-B	33	18	25	43	26																			
1986-87	Ottawa 67's	OHL	66	26	66	92	28												11	5	9	14	7			
1987-88	Ottawa 67's	OHL	61	48	*103	*151	39												16	8	*24	*32	13			
1988-89	Ottawa 67's	OHL	56	37	97	134	66												12	5	10	15	10			
1989-90	**Montreal**	**NHL**	**6**	**2**	**0**	**2**	**2**	**0**	**0**	**1**	**5**	**40.0**	**1**													
	Sherbrooke	AHL	55	22	45	67	25												12	2	11	13	6			
1990-91	**Montreal**	**NHL**	**54**	**6**	**19**	**25**	**20**	**1**	**0**	**3**	**55**	**10.9**	**2**						**8**	**0**	**2**	**2**	**2**	**0**	**0**	**0**
1991-92	**Hartford**	**NHL**	**67**	**11**	**30**	**41**	**18**	**2**	**2**	**3**	**99**	**11.1**	**3**						**7**	**2**	**4**	**6**	**6**	**1**	**0**	**0**
1992-93	**Hartford**	**NHL**	**84**	**21**	**64**	**85**	**62**	**8**	**3**	**1**	**134**	**15.7**	**–11**													
1993-94	**Hartford**	**NHL**	**79**	**16**	**42**	**58**	**37**	**8**	**1**	**3**	**126**	**12.7**	**–21**													
1994-95	**Hartford**	**NHL**	**46**	**7**	**30**	**37**	**18**	**1**	**0**	**1**	**74**	**9.5**	**–3**													
1995-96	**Hartford**	**NHL**	**81**	**20**	**43**	**63**	**39**	**6**	**0**	**1**	**135**	**14.8**	**8**													
1996-97	**Hartford**	**NHL**	**81**	**22**	**44**	**66**	**46**	**8**	**0**	**2**	**142**	**15.5**	**–16**													
1997-98	**Calgary**	**NHL**	**81**	**17**	**27**	**44**	**32**	**6**	**1**	**2**	**138**	**12.3**	**–7**													
1998-99	**Calgary**	**NHL**	**70**	**12**	**25**	**37**	**18**	**4**	**1**	**3**	**97**	**12.4**	**–12**	**1322**	**51.1**	**25**	**40**	**18:58**								
99-2000	**Vancouver**	**NHL**	**79**	**17**	**45**	**62**	**16**	**6**	**0**	**1**	**109**	**15.6**	**8**	**1127**	**48.3**	**45**	**36**	**19:19**								
	NHL Totals		**728**	**151**	**369**	**520**	**308**	**50**	**8**	**21**	**1114**	**13.6**		**2449**	**49.8**	**70**	**76**	**19:09**	**15**	**2**	**6**	**8**	**8**	**1**	**0**	**0**

OHL First All-Star Team (1988,1989)

Traded to **Hartford** by **Montreal** for Hartford's 2nd round choice (Valeri Bure) in 1992 Entry Draft, September 17, 1991. Transferred to **Carolina** after **Hartford** franchise relocated, June 25, 1997. Traded to **Calgary** by **Carolina** with Jean-Sebastien Giguere for Gary Roberts and Trevor Kidd, August 25, 1997. Signed as a free agent by **Vancouver**, August 19, 1999.

CHAMBERS, Shawn

(CHAYM-buhrs, SHAWN)

Defense. Shoots left. 6'2", 210 lbs. Born, Sterling Hts., MI, October 11, 1966. Minnesota's 1st choice, 4th overall, in 1987 Supplemental Draft.

			Regular Season																Playoffs							
Season	Club	League	GP	G	A	Pts	PIM	PP	SH	GW	S	%	+/–	TF	F%	H	SB	Min	GP	G	A	Pts	PIM	PP	SH	GW
1985-86	Alaska-Fairbanks	G-North	25	15	21	36	34																			
1986-87	Alaska-Fairbanks	G-North	17	11	19	30	84																			
	Seattle T-Birds	WHL	28	8	25	33	58																			
	Fort Wayne	IHL	12	2	6	8	0												10	1	4	5	5			
1987-88	**Minnesota**	**NHL**	**19**	**1**	**7**	**8**	**21**	**1**	**0**	**0**	**28**	**3.6**	**–6**													
	Kalamazoo Wings	IHL	19	1	6	7	22																			
1988-89	**Minnesota**	**NHL**	**72**	**5**	**19**	**24**	**80**	**1**	**2**	**0**	**131**	**3.8**	**–4**						**3**	**0**	**2**	**2**	**0**	**0**	**0**	**0**
1989-90	**Minnesota**	**NHL**	**78**	**8**	**18**	**26**	**81**	**0**	**1**	**2**	**116**	**6.9**	**–2**						**7**	**2**	**1**	**3**	**10**	**1**	**0**	**0**
1990-91	**Minnesota**	**NHL**	**29**	**1**	**3**	**4**	**24**	**0**	**0**	**0**	**55**	**1.8**	**2**						**23**	**0**	**7**	**7**	**16**	**0**	**0**	**0**
	Kalamazoo Wings	IHL	3	1	1	2	0																			
1991-92	**Washington**	**NHL**	**2**	**0**	**0**	**0**	**2**	**0**	**0**	**0**	**1**	**0.0**	**–3**													
	Baltimore	AHL	5	2	3	5	9																			
1992-93	**Tampa Bay**	**NHL**	**55**	**10**	**29**	**39**	**36**	**5**	**0**	**1**	**152**	**6.6**	**–21**													
	Atlanta Knights	IHL	6	0	2	2	18																			
1993-94	**Tampa Bay**	**NHL**	**66**	**11**	**23**	**34**	**23**	**6**	**1**	**1**	**142**	**7.7**	**–6**													
1994-95	**Tampa Bay**	**NHL**	**24**	**2**	**12**	**14**	**6**	**1**	**0**	**0**	**44**	**4.5**	**0**													
♦	**New Jersey**	**NHL**	**21**	**2**	**5**	**7**	**6**	**1**	**0**	**0**	**23**	**8.7**	**2**						**20**	**4**	**5**	**9**	**2**	**2**	**0**	**0**
1995-96	**New Jersey**	**NHL**	**64**	**2**	**21**	**23**	**18**	**2**	**0**	**1**	**112**	**1.8**	**1**													
1996-97	**New Jersey**	**NHL**	**73**	**4**	**17**	**21**	**19**	**1**	**0**	**0**	**114**	**3.5**	**17**						**10**	**1**	**6**	**7**	**6**	**1**	**0**	**0**
1997-98	**Dallas**	**NHL**	**57**	**2**	**22**	**24**	**26**	**1**	**1**	**0**	**73**	**2.7**	**11**						**14**	**0**	**3**	**3**	**20**	**0**	**0**	**0**
1998-99♦	**Dallas**	**NHL**	**61**	**2**	**9**	**11**	**18**	**1**	**0**	**1**	**82**	**2.4**	**6**	**0**	**0.0**	**59**	**76**	**17:23**	**17**	**0**	**2**	**2**	**18**	**0**	**0**	**0**
99-2000	**Dallas**	**NHL**	**4**	**0**	**0**	**0**	**4**	**0**	**0**	**0**	**2**	**0.0**	**–2**	**0**	**0.0**	**3**	**6**	**22:59**								
	NHL Totals		**625**	**50**	**185**	**235**	**364**	**20**	**5**	**6**	**1075**	**4.7**		**0**	**0.0**	**62**	**82**	**17:44**	**94**	**7**	**26**	**33**	**72**	**4**	**0**	**0**

Traded to **Washington** by **Minnesota** for Steve Maltais and Trent Klatt, June 21, 1991. • Missed majority of 1990-91 and 1991-92 seasons recovering from knee injury originally suffered in game vs. Toronto, December 5, 1990. Claimed by **Tampa Bay** from **Washington** in Expansion Draft, June 18, 1992. Traded to **New Jersey** by **Tampa Bay** with Danton Cole for Alexander Semak and Ben Hankinson, March 14, 1995. Signed as a free agent by **Dallas**, July 17, 1997. • Missed remainder of 1999-2000 season recovering from knee injury suffered in game vs. Anaheim, October 8, 1999.

CHARA, Zdeno

(KHAH-rah, ZDEH-noh) **NYI**

Defense. Shoots left. 6'9", 255 lbs. Born, Trencin, Czech., March 18, 1977. NY Islanders' 3rd choice, 56th overall, in 1996 Entry Draft.

			Regular Season																Playoffs							
Season	Club	League	GP	G	A	Pts	PIM	PP	SH	GW	S	%	+/–	TF	F%	H	SB	Min	GP	G	A	Pts	PIM	PP	SH	GW
1994-95	Dukla Trencin	Slovak-Jr.	2	0	0	0	0																			
	Dukla Trencin-B	Slovak-Jr.	30	22	22	44	113																			
1995-96	Dukla Trencin	Slovak-Jr.	22	1	13	14	80																			
	HK Piestany	Slovakia-2	10	1	3	4	10																			
	Sparta Praha-Jr.	Cze-Rep	15	1	2	3	42																			
	Sparta Praha	Cze-Rep	1	0	0	0	0																			
1996-97	Prince George	WHL	49	3	19	22	120												15	1	7	8	45			
1997-98	**NY Islanders**	**NHL**	**25**	**0**	**1**	**1**	**50**	**0**	**0**	**0**	**10**	**0.0**	**1**													
	Kentucky	AHL	48	4	9	13	125												1	0	0	0	4			
1998-99	**NY Islanders**	**NHL**	**59**	**2**	**6**	**8**	**83**	**0**	**1**	**0**	**56**	**3.6**	**–8**	**0**	**0.0**	**214**	**55**	**18:54**								
	Lowell	AHL	23	2	2	4	47																			
99-2000	**NY Islanders**	**NHL**	**65**	**2**	**9**	**11**	**57**	**0**	**0**	**1**	**47**	**4.3**	**–27**	**0**	**0.0**	**309**	**100**	**22:52**								
	NHL Totals		**149**	**4**	**16**	**20**	**190**	**0**	**1**	**1**	**113**	**3.5**		**0**	**0.0**	**523**	**155**	**20:59**								

CHARRON, Eric

(shah-ROHN, AIR-ihk) **MIN.**

Defense. Shoots left. 6'3", 195 lbs. Born, Verdun, Que., January 14, 1970. Montreal's 1st choice, 20th overall, in 1988 Entry Draft.

			Regular Season																Playoffs							
Season	Club	League	GP	G	A	Pts	PIM	PP	SH	GW	S	%	+/–	TF	F%	H	SB	Min	GP	G	A	Pts	PIM	PP	SH	GW
1986-87	Lac St-Louis	QAAA	41	1	8	9	92																			
1987-88	Trois-Rivieres	QMJHL	67	3	13	16	135																			
1988-89	Trois-Rivieres	QMJHL	38	2	16	18	111																			
	Verdun	QMJHL	28	2	15	17	66																			
	Sherbrooke	AHL	1	0	0	0	0																			
1989-90	St-Hyacinthe	QMJHL	68	13	38	51	152												11	3	4	7	67			
	Sherbrooke	AHL																	2	0	0	0	0			
1990-91	Fredericton	AHL	71	1	11	12	108												2	1	0	1	29			
1991-92	Fredericton	AHL	59	2	11	13	98												6	1	0	1	4			
1992-93	**Montreal**	**NHL**	**3**	**0**	**0**	**0**	**2**	**0**	**0**	**0**	**0**	**0.0**	**0**													
	Fredericton	AHL	54	3	13	16	93																			
	Atlanta Knights	IHL	11	0	2	2	12												3	0	1	1	6			
1993-94	**Tampa Bay**	**NHL**	**4**	**0**	**0**	**0**	**2**	**0**	**0**	**0**	**1**	**0.0**	**0**													
	Atlanta Knights	IHL	66	5	18	23	144												14	1	4	5	28			
1994-95	**Tampa Bay**	**NHL**	**45**	**1**	**4**	**5**	**26**	**0**	**0**	**0**	**33**	**3.0**	**1**													
1995-96	**Tampa Bay**	**NHL**	**14**	**0**	**0**	**0**	**18**	**0**	**0**	**0**	**11**	**0.0**	**–6**													
	Washington	**NHL**	**4**	**0**	**1**	**1**	**4**	**0**	**0**	**0**	**2**	**0.0**	**3**						**6**	**0**	**0**	**0**	**8**	**0**	**0**	**0**
	Portland Pirates	AHL	45	0	8	8	88												20	1	1	2	33			
1996-97	**Washington**	**NHL**	**25**	**1**	**1**	**2**	**20**	**0**	**0**	**0**	**11**	**9.1**	**1**													
	Portland Pirates	AHL	29	6	8	14	55												5	0	3	3	0			
1997-98	**Calgary**	**NHL**	**2**	**0**	**0**	**0**	**4**	**0**	**0**	**0**	**1**	**0.0**	**0**													
	Saint John Flames	AHL	56	8	20	28	136												20	1	7	8	55			
1998-99	**Calgary**	**NHL**	**12**	**0**	**1**	**1**	**14**	**0**	**0**	**0**	**9**	**0.0**	**–6**	**0**	**0.0**	**12**	**13**	**13:45**								
	Saint John Flames	AHL	50	10	12	22	148												3	1	0	1	22			
99-2000	**Calgary**	**NHL**	**21**	**0**	**0**	**0**	**37**	**0**	**0**	**0**	**8**	**0.0**	**–3**	**0**	**0.0**	**17**	**20**	**10:29**								
	Saint John Flames	AHL	37	2	15	17	82																			
	NHL Totals		**130**	**2**	**7**	**9**	**127**	**0**	**0**	**0**	**76**	**2.6**		**0**	**0.0**	**29**	**33**	**11:40**	**6**	**0**	**0**	**0**	**8**	**0**	**0**	**0**

Traded to **Tampa Bay** by **Montreal** with Alain Cote and future considerations (Donald Dufresne, June 18, 1993) for Rob Ramage, March 20, 1993. Traded to **Washington** by **Tampa Bay** for Washington's 7th round choice (Eero Somervuori) in 1997 Entry Draft, November 16, 1995. Traded to **Calgary** by **Washington** for Calgary's 7th round choice (Nathan Forster) in 1998 Entry Draft, September 4, 1997. Signed as a free agent by **Minnesota**, August 31, 2000.

CHARTRAND, Brad

(KHAR-trand, BRAD) **L.A.**

Right wing. Shoots left. 5'11", 191 lbs. Born, Winnipeg, Man., December 14, 1974.

			Regular Season																Playoffs							
Season	Club	League	GP	G	A	Pts	PIM	PP	SH	GW	S	%	+/-	TF	F%	H	SB	Min	GP	G	A	Pts	PIM	PP	SH	GW
1988-89	Winnipeg Hawks	MAHA	24	30	50	80	40																			
1989-90	Winnipeg Hawks	MAHA	24	26	55	81	40																			
1990-91	Winnipeg Hawks	MAHA	34	26	45	71	40																			
1991-92	St. James	MJHL	STATISTICS NOT AVAILABLE																							
1992-93	Cornell Big Red	ECAC	26	10	6	16	16																			
1993-94	Cornell Big Red	ECAC	30	4	14	18	48																			
1994-95	Cornell Big Red	ECAC	28	9	9	18	10																			
1995-96	Cornell Big Red	ECAC	34	24	19	43	16																			
1996-97	Canada	Nat-Team	54	10	14	24	42																			
1997-98	Canada	Nat-Team	60	24	30	54	47																			
	HC Rapperswil	Switz.	8	2	3	5	4																			
1998-99	St. John's Leafs	AHL	64	16	14	30	48												5	0	2	2	2			
99-2000	**Los Angeles**	**NHL**	**50**	**6**	**6**	**12**	**17**	**0**	**1**	**3**	**51**	**11.8**	**4**	**62**	**53.2**	**70**	**18**	**11:03**	**4**	**0**	**0**	**0**	**6**	**0**	**0**	**0**
	Lowell	AHL	16	5	10	15	8																			
	Long Beach	IHL	1	0	0	0	0												3	0	0	0	0			
	NHL Totals		**50**	**6**	**6**	**12**	**17**	**0**	**1**	**3**	**51**	**11.8**		**62**	**53.2**	**70**	**18**	**11:03**	**4**	**0**	**0**	**0**	**6**	**0**	**0**	**0**

Signed as a free agent by **LA Kings**, July 15, 1999. Loaned to **Lowell** (AHL) by **LA Kings**, January 26, 2000.

CHASE, Kelly

(CHAYS, KEHL-lee)

Right wing. Shoots right. 5'11", 201 lbs. Born, Porcupine Plain, Sask., October 25, 1967.

			Regular Season																Playoffs							
Season	Club	League	GP	G	A	Pts	PIM	PP	SH	GW	S	%	+/-	TF	F%	H	SB	Min	GP	G	A	Pts	PIM	PP	SH	GW
1985-86	Saskatoon Blades	WHL	57	7	18	25	172												10	3	4	7	37			
1986-87	Saskatoon Blades	WHL	68	17	29	46	285												11	2	8	10	37			
1987-88	Saskatoon Blades	WHL	70	21	34	55	*343												9	3	5	8	32			
1988-89	Peoria Rivermen	IHL	38	14	7	21	278																			
1989-90	**St. Louis**	**NHL**	**43**	**1**	**3**	**4**	**244**	**0**	**0**	**0**	**9**	**11.1**	**–1**						**9**	**1**	**0**	**1**	**46**	**0**	**0**	**0**
	Peoria Rivermen	IHL	10	1	2	3	76																			
1990-91	**St. Louis**	**NHL**	**2**	**1**	**0**	**1**	**15**	**0**	**0**	**1**	**1**	**100.0**	**1**						**6**	**0**	**0**	**0**	**18**	**0**	**0**	**0**
	Peoria Rivermen	IHL	61	20	34	54	406												10	4	3	7	61			
1991-92	**St. Louis**	**NHL**	**46**	**1**	**2**	**3**	**264**	**0**	**0**	**0**	**29**	**3.4**	**–6**						**1**	**0**	**0**	**0**	**7**	**0**	**0**	**0**
1992-93	**St. Louis**	**NHL**	**49**	**2**	**5**	**7**	**204**	**0**	**0**	**0**	**28**	**7.1**	**–9**													
1993-94	**St. Louis**	**NHL**	**68**	**2**	**5**	**7**	**278**	**0**	**0**	**0**	**57**	**3.5**	**–5**						**4**	**0**	**1**	**1**	**6**	**0**	**0**	**0**
1994-95	**Hartford**	**NHL**	**28**	**0**	**4**	**4**	**141**	**0**	**0**	**0**	**15**	**0.0**	**1**													
1995-96	**Hartford**	**NHL**	**55**	**2**	**4**	**6**	**230**	**0**	**0**	**1**	**19**	**10.5**	**–4**													
1996-97	**Hartford**	**NHL**	**28**	**1**	**2**	**3**	**122**	**0**	**0**	**0**	**5**	**20.0**	**2**													
	Toronto	**NHL**	**2**	**0**	**0**	**0**	**27**	**0**	**0**	**0**	**1**	**0.0**	**0**													
1997-98	**St. Louis**	**NHL**	**67**	**4**	**3**	**7**	**231**	**0**	**0**	**1**	**29**	**13.8**	**10**						**7**	**0**	**0**	**0**	**23**	**0**	**0**	**0**
1998-99	**St. Louis**	**NHL**	**45**	**3**	**7**	**10**	**143**	**0**	**0**	**1**	**25**	**12.0**	**2**	**4**	**50.0**	**28**	**1**	**5:56**								
99-2000	**St. Louis**	**NHL**	**25**	**0**	**1**	**1**	**118**	**0**	**0**	**0**	**14**	**0.0**	**–5**	**1**	**0.0**	**8**	**2**	**7:46**								
	NHL Totals		**458**	**17**	**36**	**53**	**2017**	**0**	**0**	**4**	**232**	**7.3**		**5**	**40.0**	**36**	**3**	**6:35**	**27**	**1**	**1**	**2**	**100**	**0**	**0**	**0**

Won King Clancy Memorial Trophy (1998)

Signed as a free agent by **St. Louis**, February 23, 1988. Claimed by **Hartford** from **St. Louis** in NHL Waiver Draft, January 18, 1995. Traded to **Toronto** by **Hartford** for Toronto's 8th round choice (Hartford/Carolina selected Jaroslav Svoboda) in 1998 Entry Draft, March 18, 1997. Traded to **St. Louis** by **Toronto** for future considerations, September 30, 1997. • Missed majority of 1999-2000 season recovering from knee injury suffered in game vs. Dallas, November 8, 1999. • Officially announced retirement and named radio colour analyst on St. Louis Blues' broadcast team, July 28, 2000.

CHEBATURKIN, Vladimir

(cheh-bah-TOOR-kihn) **ST.L.**

Defense. Shoots left. 6'2", 226 lbs. Born, Tyumen, USSR, April 23, 1975. NY Islanders' 3rd choice, 66th overall, in 1993 Entry Draft.

			Regular Season																Playoffs							
Season	Club	League	GP	G	A	Pts	PIM	PP	SH	GW	S	%	+/-	TF	F%	H	SB	Min	GP	G	A	Pts	PIM	PP	SH	GW
1993-94	Kristal Elektrostal	CIS-2	42	4	4	8	38																			
1994-95	Kristal Elektrostal	CIS	52	2	6	8	90																			
1995-96	Kristal Elektrostal	CIS	44	1	6	7	30												1	0	0	0	0			
1996-97	Utah Grizzlies	IHL	68	0	4	4	34																			
1997-98	**NY Islanders**	**NHL**	**2**	**0**	**2**	**2**	**0**	**0**	**0**	**0**	**0**	**0.0**	**–1**													
	Kentucky	AHL	54	6	8	14	52												2	0	0	0	4			
1998-99	**NY Islanders**	**NHL**	**8**	**0**	**0**	**0**	**12**	**0**	**0**	**0**	**4**	**0.0**	**6**	**0**	**0.0**	**27**	**8**	**17:12**								
	Lowell	AHL	69	2	12	14	85												3	0	0	0	0			
99-2000	**NY Islanders**	**NHL**	**17**	**1**	**1**	**2**	**8**	**0**	**0**	**0**	**9**	**11.1**	**–3**	**0**	**0.0**	**58**	**25**	**16:57**								
	Lowell	AHL	63	1	8	9	118												7	0	4	4	11			
	NHL Totals		**27**	**1**	**3**	**4**	**20**	**0**	**0**	**0**	**13**	**7.7**		**0**	**0.0**	**85**	**33**	**17:02**								

Signed as a free agent by **St. Louis**, June 9, 2000.

CHELIOS, Chris

(CHELL-EE-ohs, KRIHS) **DET.**

Defense. Shoots right. 6'1", 190 lbs. Born, Chicago, IL, January 25, 1962. Montreal's 5th choice, 40th overall, in 1981 Entry Draft.

			Regular Season																Playoffs							
Season	Club	League	GP	G	A	Pts	PIM	PP	SH	GW	S	%	+/-	TF	F%	H	SB	Min	GP	G	A	Pts	PIM	PP	SH	GW
1979-80	Moose Jaw	SJHL	53	12	31	43	118																			
1980-81	Moose Jaw	SJHL	54	23	64	87	175																			
1981-82	U. of Wisconsin	WCHA	43	6	43	49	50																			
1982-83	U. of Wisconsin	WCHA	26	9	17	26	50																			
1983-84	United States	Nat-Team	60	14	35	49	58																			
	United States	Olympics	6	0	4	4	8																			
	Montreal	**NHL**	**12**	**0**	**2**	**2**	**12**	**0**	**0**	**0**	**23**	**0.0**	**–5**						**15**	**1**	**9**	**10**	**17**	**1**	**0**	**0**
1984-85	**Montreal**	**NHL**	**74**	**9**	**55**	**64**	**87**	**2**	**1**	**0**	**199**	**4.5**	**11**						**9**	**2**	**8**	**10**	**17**	**2**	**0**	**0**
1985-86♦	**Montreal**	**NHL**	**41**	**8**	**26**	**34**	**67**	**2**	**0**	**0**	**101**	**7.9**	**4**						**20**	**2**	**9**	**11**	**49**	**1**	**0**	**0**
1986-87	**Montreal**	**NHL**	**71**	**11**	**33**	**44**	**124**	**6**	**0**	**2**	**141**	**7.8**	**–5**						**17**	**4**	**9**	**13**	**38**	**2**	**1**	**0**
1987-88	**Montreal**	**NHL**	**71**	**20**	**41**	**61**	**172**	**10**	**1**	**5**	**199**	**10.1**	**14**						**11**	**3**	**1**	**4**	**29**	**1**	**0**	**0**
1988-89	**Montreal**	**NHL**	**80**	**15**	**58**	**73**	**185**	**8**	**0**	**6**	**206**	**7.3**	**35**						**21**	**4**	**15**	**19**	**28**	**1**	**0**	**2**
1989-90	**Montreal**	**NHL**	**53**	**9**	**22**	**31**	**136**	**1**	**2**	**1**	**123**	**7.3**	**20**						**5**	**0**	**1**	**1**	**8**	**0**	**0**	**0**
1990-91	**Chicago**	**NHL**	**77**	**12**	**52**	**64**	**192**	**5**	**2**	**2**	**187**	**6.4**	**23**						**6**	**1**	**7**	**8**	**46**	**1**	**0**	**0**
1991-92	**Chicago**	**NHL**	**80**	**9**	**47**	**56**	**245**	**2**	**2**	**2**	**239**	**3.8**	**24**						**18**	**6**	**15**	**21**	**37**	**3**	**0**	**1**
1992-93	**Chicago**	**NHL**	**84**	**15**	**58**	**73**	**282**	**8**	**0**	**2**	**290**	**5.2**	**14**						**4**	**0**	**2**	**2**	**14**	**0**	**0**	**0**
1993-94	**Chicago**	**NHL**	**76**	**16**	**44**	**60**	**212**	**7**	**1**	**2**	**219**	**7.3**	**12**						**6**	**1**	**1**	**2**	**8**	**1**	**0**	**0**
1994-95	EHC Biel	Switz.	3	0	3	3	4																			
	Chicago	**NHL**	**48**	**5**	**33**	**38**	**72**	**3**	**1**	**0**	**166**	**3.0**	**17**						**16**	**4**	**7**	**11**	**12**	**0**	**1**	**3**
1995-96	**Chicago**	**NHL**	**81**	**14**	**58**	**72**	**140**	**7**	**0**	**3**	**219**	**6.4**	**25**						**9**	**0**	**3**	**3**	**8**	**0**	**0**	**0**
1996-97	**Chicago**	**NHL**	**72**	**10**	**38**	**48**	**112**	**2**	**0**	**2**	**194**	**5.2**	**16**						**6**	**0**	**1**	**1**	**8**	**0**	**0**	**0**
1997-98	**Chicago**	**NHL**	**81**	**3**	**39**	**42**	**151**	**1**	**0**	**0**	**205**	**1.5**	**–7**													
	United States	Olympics	4	2	0	2	2																			
1998-99	**Chicago**	**NHL**	**65**	**8**	**26**	**34**	**89**	**2**	**1**	**0**	**172**	**4.7**	**–4**	**4**	**25.0**	**72**	**109**	**27:19**								
	Detroit	**NHL**	**10**	**1**	**1**	**2**	**4**	**1**	**0**	**1**	**15**	**6.7**	**5**	**0**	**0.0**	**11**	**7**	**22:21**	**10**	**0**	**4**	**4**	**14**	**0**	**0**	**0**
99-2000	**Detroit**	**NHL**	**81**	**3**	**31**	**34**	**103**	**0**	**0**	**0**	**135**	**2.2**	**48**	**0**	**0.0**	**120**	**86**	**25:16**	**9**	**0**	**1**	**1**	**8**	**0**	**0**	**0**
	NHL Totals		**1157**	**168**	**664**	**832**	**2385**	**67**	**11**	**28**	**3033**	**5.5**		**4**	**25.0**	**203**	**202**	**25:56**	**182**	**28**	**93**	**121**	**341**	**13**	**2**	**6**

WCHA Second All-Star Team (1983) • NCAA Championship All-Tournament Team (1983) • NHL All-Rookie Team (1985) • NHL First All-Star Team (1989, 1993, 1995, 1996) • Won James Norris Memorial Trophy (1989, 1993, 1996) • NHL Second All-Star Team (1991, 1997) • Played in NHL All-Star Game (1985, 1990, 1991, 1992, 1993, 1994, 1996, 1997, 1998, 2000)

Traded to **Chicago** by **Montreal** with Montreal's 2nd round choice (Michael Pomichter) in 1991 Entry Draft for Denis Savard, June 29, 1990. Traded to **Detroit** by **Chicago** for Anders Eriksson and Detroit's 1st round choices in 1999 (Steve McCarthy) and 2001 Entry Drafts, March 23, 1999.

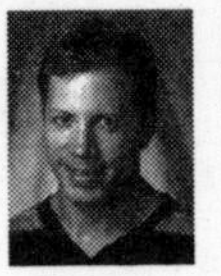

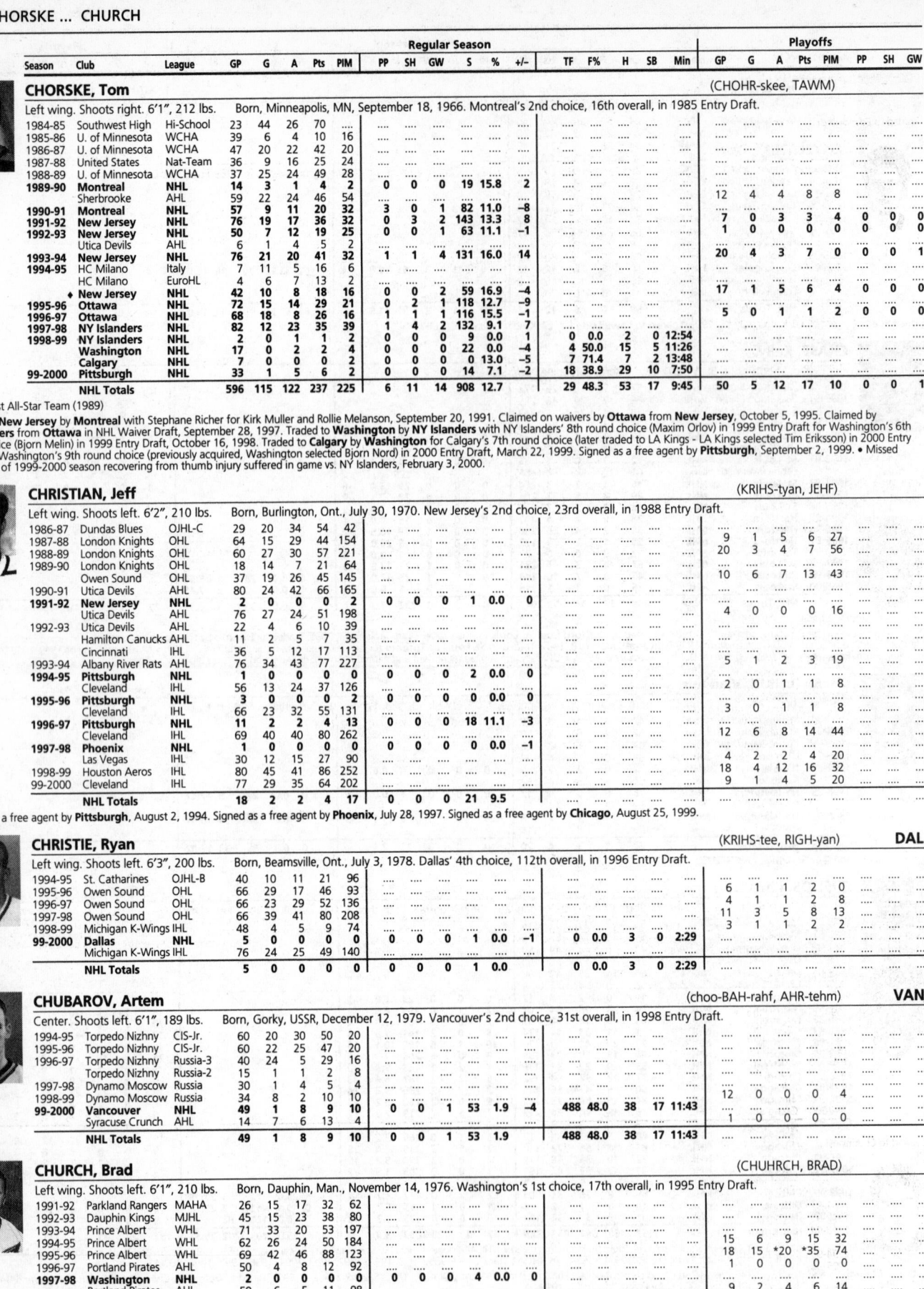

CHORSKE, Tom (CHOHR-skee, TAWM)

Left wing. Shoots right. 6'1", 212 lbs. Born, Minneapolis, MN, September 18, 1966. Montreal's 2nd choice, 16th overall, in 1985 Entry Draft.

			Regular Season																Playoffs							
Season	Club	League	GP	G	A	Pts	PIM	PP	SH	GW	S	%	+/-	TF	F%	H	SB	Min	GP	G	A	Pts	PIM	PP	SH	GW
1984-85	Southwest High	Hi-School	23	44	26	70	....	....	....	....	....	....	....	....	....	....	....	....	....	....	....	....	....	....	....	....
1985-86	U. of Minnesota	WCHA	39	6	4	10	16	....	....	....	....	....	....	....	....	....	....	....	....	....	....	....	....	....	....	....
1986-87	U. of Minnesota	WCHA	47	20	22	42	20	....	....	....	....	....	....	....	....	....	....	....	....	....	....	....	....	....	....	....
1987-88	United States	Nat-Team	36	9	16	25	24	....	....	....	....	....	....	....	....	....	....	....	....	....	....	....	....	....	....	....
1988-89	U. of Minnesota	WCHA	37	25	24	49	28	....	....	....	....	....	....	....	....	....	....	....	....	....	....	....	....	....	....	....
1989-90	**Montreal**	**NHL**	**14**	**3**	**1**	**4**	**2**	**0**	**0**	**0**	**19**	**15.8**	**2**	....	....	....	....	....	....	....	....	....	....	....	....	....
	Sherbrooke	AHL	59	22	24	46	54	....	....	....	....	....	....	....	....	....	....	....	12	4	4	8	8	....	....	....
1990-91	**Montreal**	**NHL**	**57**	**9**	**11**	**20**	**32**	**3**	**0**	**1**	**82**	**11.0**	**–8**	....	....	....	....	....	....	....	....	....	....	....	....	....
1991-92	**New Jersey**	**NHL**	**76**	**19**	**17**	**36**	**32**	**0**	**3**	**2**	**143**	**13.3**	**8**	....	....	....	....	....	**7**	**0**	**3**	**3**	**4**	**0**	**0**	**0**
1992-93	**New Jersey**	**NHL**	**50**	**7**	**12**	**19**	**25**	**0**	**0**	**1**	**63**	**11.1**	**–1**	....	....	....	....	....	**1**	**0**	**0**	**0**	**0**	**0**	**0**	**0**
	Utica Devils	AHL	6	1	4	5	2	....	....	....	....	....	....	....	....	....	....	....	....	....	....	....	....	....	....	....
1993-94	**New Jersey**	**NHL**	**76**	**21**	**20**	**41**	**32**	**1**	**1**	**4**	**131**	**16.0**	**14**	....	....	....	....	....	**20**	**4**	**3**	**7**	**0**	**0**	**0**	**1**
1994-95	HC Milano	Italy	7	11	5	16	6	....	....	....	....	....	....	....	....	....	....	....	....	....	....	....	....	....	....	....
	HC Milano	EuroHL	4	6	7	13	2	....	....	....	....	....	....	....	....	....	....	....	....	....	....	....	....	....	....	....
	♦ **New Jersey**	**NHL**	**42**	**10**	**8**	**18**	**16**	**0**	**0**	**2**	**59**	**16.9**	**–4**	....	....	....	....	....	**17**	**1**	**5**	**6**	**4**	**0**	**0**	**0**
1995-96	**Ottawa**	**NHL**	**72**	**15**	**14**	**29**	**21**	**0**	**2**	**1**	**118**	**12.7**	**–9**	....	....	....	....	....	....	....	....	....	....	....	....	....
1996-97	**Ottawa**	**NHL**	**68**	**18**	**8**	**26**	**16**	**1**	**1**	**1**	**116**	**15.5**	**–1**	....	....	....	....	....	**5**	**0**	**1**	**1**	**2**	**0**	**0**	**0**
1997-98	**NY Islanders**	**NHL**	**82**	**12**	**23**	**35**	**39**	**1**	**4**	**2**	**132**	**9.1**	**7**	....	....	....	....	....	....	....	....	....	....	....	....	....
1998-99	**NY Islanders**	**NHL**	**2**	**0**	**1**	**1**	**2**	**0**	**0**	**0**	**9**	**0.0**	**1**	**0**	**0.0**	**2**	**0**	**12:54**	....	....	....	....	....	....	....	....
	Washington	**NHL**	**17**	**0**	**2**	**2**	**4**	**0**	**0**	**0**	**22**	**0.0**	**–4**	**4**	**50.0**	**15**	**5**	**11:26**	....	....	....	....	....	....	....	....
	Calgary	**NHL**	**7**	**0**	**0**	**0**	**2**	**0**	**0**	**0**	**0**	**13.0**	**–5**	**7**	**71.4**	**7**	**2**	**13:48**	....	....	....	....	....	....	....	....
99-2000	**Pittsburgh**	**NHL**	**33**	**1**	**5**	**6**	**2**	**0**	**0**	**0**	**14**	**7.1**	**–2**	**18**	**38.9**	**29**	**10**	**7:50**	....	....	....	....	....	....	....	....
	NHL Totals		**596**	**115**	**122**	**237**	**225**	**6**	**11**	**14**	**908**	**12.7**		**29**	**48.3**	**53**	**17**	**9:45**	**50**	**5**	**12**	**17**	**10**	**0**	**0**	**1**

WCHA First All-Star Team (1989)

Traded to **New Jersey** by **Montreal** with Stephane Richer for Kirk Muller and Rollie Melanson, September 20, 1991. Claimed on waivers by **Ottawa** from **New Jersey**, October 5, 1995. Claimed by **NY Islanders** from **Ottawa** in NHL Waiver Draft, September 28, 1997. Traded to **Washington** by **NY Islanders** with NY Islanders' 8th round choice (Maxim Orlov) in 1999 Entry Draft for Washington's 6th round choice (Bjorn Melin) in 1999 Entry Draft, October 16, 1998. Traded to **Calgary** by **Washington** for Calgary's 7th round choice (later traded to LA Kings - LA Kings selected Tim Eriksson) in 2000 Entry Draft and Washington's 9th round choice (previously acquired, Washington selected Bjorn Nord) in 2000 Entry Draft, March 22, 1999. Signed as a free agent by **Pittsburgh**, September 2, 1999. • Missed remainder of 1999-2000 season recovering from thumb injury suffered in game vs. NY Islanders, February 3, 2000.

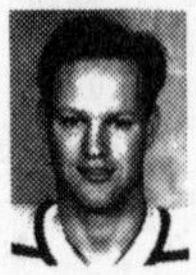

CHRISTIAN, Jeff (KRIHS-tyan, JEHF)

Left wing. Shoots left. 6'2", 210 lbs. Born, Burlington, Ont., July 30, 1970. New Jersey's 2nd choice, 23rd overall, in 1988 Entry Draft.

Season	Club	League	GP	G	A	Pts	PIM	PP	SH	GW	S	%	+/-	TF	F%	H	SB	Min	GP	G	A	Pts	PIM	PP	SH	GW
1986-87	Dundas Blues	OJHL-C	29	20	34	54	42	....	....	....	....	....	....	....	....	....	....	....	....	....	....	....	....	....	....	....
1987-88	London Knights	OHL	64	15	29	44	154	....	....	....	....	....	....	....	....	....	....	....	9	1	5	6	27	....	....	....
1988-89	London Knights	OHL	60	27	30	57	221	....	....	....	....	....	....	....	....	....	....	....	20	3	4	7	56	....	....	....
1989-90	London Knights	OHL	18	14	7	21	64	....	....	....	....	....	....	....	....	....	....	....	....	....	....	....	....	....	....	....
	Owen Sound	OHL	37	19	26	45	145	....	....	....	....	....	....	....	....	....	....	....	10	6	7	13	43	....	....	....
1990-91	Utica Devils	AHL	80	24	42	66	165	....	....	....	....	....	....	....	....	....	....	....	....	....	....	....	....	....	....	....
1991-92	**New Jersey**	**NHL**	**2**	**0**	**0**	**0**	**2**	**0**	**0**	**0**	**1**	**0.0**	**0**	....	....	....	....	....	....	....	....	....	....	....	....	....
	Utica Devils	AHL	76	27	24	51	198	....	....	....	....	....	....	....	....	....	....	....	4	0	0	0	16	....	....	....
1992-93	Utica Devils	AHL	22	4	6	10	39	....	....	....	....	....	....	....	....	....	....	....	....	....	....	....	....	....	....	....
	Hamilton Canucks	AHL	11	2	5	7	35	....	....	....	....	....	....	....	....	....	....	....	....	....	....	....	....	....	....	....
	Cincinnati	IHL	36	5	12	17	113	....	....	....	....	....	....	....	....	....	....	....	....	....	....	....	....	....	....	....
1993-94	Albany River Rats	AHL	76	34	43	77	227	....	....	....	....	....	....	....	....	....	....	....	5	1	2	3	19	....	....	....
1994-95	**Pittsburgh**	**NHL**	**1**	**0**	**0**	**0**	**0**	**0**	**0**	**0**	**2**	**0.0**	**0**	....	....	....	....	....	....	....	....	....	....	....	....	....
	Cleveland	IHL	56	13	24	37	126	....	....	....	....	....	....	....	....	....	....	....	2	0	1	1	8	....	....	....
1995-96	**Pittsburgh**	**NHL**	**3**	**0**	**0**	**0**	**2**	**0**	**0**	**0**	**0**	**0.0**	**0**	....	....	....	....	....	....	....	....	....	....	....	....	....
	Cleveland	IHL	66	23	32	55	131	....	....	....	....	....	....	....	....	....	....	....	3	0	1	1	8	....	....	....
1996-97	**Pittsburgh**	**NHL**	**11**	**2**	**2**	**4**	**13**	**0**	**0**	**0**	**18**	**11.1**	**–3**	....	....	....	....	....	....	....	....	....	....	....	....	....
	Cleveland	IHL	69	40	40	80	262	....	....	....	....	....	....	....	....	....	....	....	12	6	8	14	44	....	....	....
1997-98	**Phoenix**	**NHL**	**1**	**0**	**0**	**0**	**0**	**0**	**0**	**0**	**0**	**0.0**	**–1**	....	....	....	....	....	....	....	....	....	....	....	....	....
	Las Vegas	IHL	30	12	15	27	90	....	....	....	....	....	....	....	....	....	....	....	4	2	2	4	20	....	....	....
1998-99	Houston Aeros	IHL	80	45	41	86	252	....	....	....	....	....	....	....	....	....	....	....	18	4	12	16	32	....	....	....
99-2000	Cleveland	IHL	77	29	35	64	202	....	....	....	....	....	....	....	....	....	....	....	9	1	4	5	20	....	....	....
	NHL Totals		**18**	**2**	**2**	**4**	**17**	**0**	**0**	**0**	**21**	**9.5**		....	....	....	....	....	....	....	....	....	....	....	....	....

Signed as a free agent by **Pittsburgh**, August 2, 1994. Signed as a free agent by **Phoenix**, July 28, 1997. Signed as a free agent by **Chicago**, August 25, 1999.

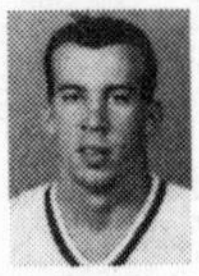

CHRISTIE, Ryan (KRIHS-tee, RIGH-yan) **DAL.**

Left wing. Shoots left. 6'3", 200 lbs. Born, Beamsville, Ont., July 3, 1978. Dallas' 4th choice, 112th overall, in 1996 Entry Draft.

Season	Club	League	GP	G	A	Pts	PIM	PP	SH	GW	S	%	+/-	TF	F%	H	SB	Min	GP	G	A	Pts	PIM	PP	SH	GW
1994-95	St. Catharines	OJHL-B	40	10	11	21	96	....	....	....	....	....	....	....	....	....	....	....	....	....	....	....	....	....	....	....
1995-96	Owen Sound	OHL	66	29	17	46	93	....	....	....	....	....	....	....	....	....	....	....	6	1	1	2	0	....	....	....
1996-97	Owen Sound	OHL	66	23	29	52	136	....	....	....	....	....	....	....	....	....	....	....	4	1	1	2	8	....	....	....
1997-98	Owen Sound	OHL	66	39	41	80	208	....	....	....	....	....	....	....	....	....	....	....	11	3	5	8	13	....	....	....
1998-99	Michigan K-Wings	IHL	48	4	5	9	74	....	....	....	....	....	....	....	....	....	....	....	3	1	1	2	2	....	....	....
99-2000	**Dallas**	**NHL**	**5**	**0**	**0**	**0**	**0**	**0**	**0**	**0**	**1**	**0.0**	**–1**	**0**	**0.0**	**3**	**0**	**2:29**	....	....	....	....	....	....	....	....
	Michigan K-Wings	IHL	76	24	25	49	140	....	....	....	....	....	....	....	....	....	....	....	....	....	....	....	....	....	....	....
	NHL Totals		**5**	**0**	**0**	**0**	**0**	**0**	**0**	**0**	**1**	**0.0**		**0**	**0.0**	**3**	**0**	**2:29**	....	....	....	....	....	....	....	....

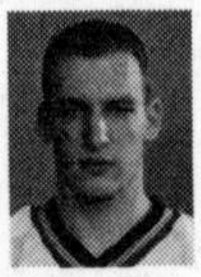

CHUBAROV, Artem (choo-BAH-rahf, AHR-tehm) **VAN.**

Center. Shoots left. 6'1", 189 lbs. Born, Gorky, USSR, December 12, 1979. Vancouver's 2nd choice, 31st overall, in 1998 Entry Draft.

Season	Club	League	GP	G	A	Pts	PIM	PP	SH	GW	S	%	+/-	TF	F%	H	SB	Min	GP	G	A	Pts	PIM	PP	SH	GW
1994-95	Torpedo Nizhny	CIS-Jr.	60	20	30	50	20	....	....	....	....	....	....	....	....	....	....	....	....	....	....	....	....	....	....	....
1995-96	Torpedo Nizhny	CIS-Jr.	60	22	25	47	20	....	....	....	....	....	....	....	....	....	....	....	....	....	....	....	....	....	....	....
1996-97	Torpedo Nizhny	Russia-3	40	24	5	29	16	....	....	....	....	....	....	....	....	....	....	....	....	....	....	....	....	....	....	....
	Torpedo Nizhny	Russia-2	15	1	1	2	8	....	....	....	....	....	....	....	....	....	....	....	....	....	....	....	....	....	....	....
1997-98	Dynamo Moscow	Russia	30	1	4	5	4	....	....	....	....	....	....	....	....	....	....	....	....	....	....	....	....	....	....	....
1998-99	Dynamo Moscow	Russia	34	8	2	10	10	....	....	....	....	....	....	....	....	....	....	....	12	0	0	0	4	....	....	....
99-2000	**Vancouver**	**NHL**	**49**	**1**	**8**	**9**	**10**	**0**	**0**	**1**	**53**	**1.9**	**–4**	**488**	**48.0**	**38**	**17**	**11:43**	....	....	....	....	....	....	....	....
	Syracuse Crunch	AHL	14	7	6	13	4	....	....	....	....	....	....	....	....	....	....	....	1	0	0	0	0	....	....	....
	NHL Totals		**49**	**1**	**8**	**9**	**10**	**0**	**0**	**1**	**53**	**1.9**		**488**	**48.0**	**38**	**17**	**11:43**	....	....	....	....	....	....	....	....

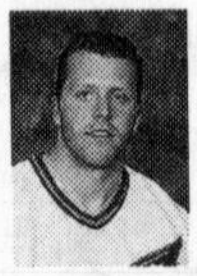

CHURCH, Brad (CHUHRCH, BRAD)

Left wing. Shoots left. 6'1", 210 lbs. Born, Dauphin, Man., November 14, 1976. Washington's 1st choice, 17th overall, in 1995 Entry Draft.

Season	Club	League	GP	G	A	Pts	PIM	PP	SH	GW	S	%	+/-	TF	F%	H	SB	Min	GP	G	A	Pts	PIM	PP	SH	GW
1991-92	Parkland Rangers	MAHA	26	15	17	32	62	....	....	....	....	....	....	....	....	....	....	....	....	....	....	....	....	....	....	....
1992-93	Dauphin Kings	MJHL	45	15	23	38	80	....	....	....	....	....	....	....	....	....	....	....	....	....	....	....	....	....	....	....
1993-94	Prince Albert	WHL	71	33	20	53	197	....	....	....	....	....	....	....	....	....	....	....	....	....	....	....	....	....	....	....
1994-95	Prince Albert	WHL	62	26	24	50	184	....	....	....	....	....	....	....	....	....	....	....	15	6	9	15	32	....	....	....
1995-96	Prince Albert	WHL	69	42	46	88	123	....	....	....	....	....	....	....	....	....	....	....	18	15	*20	*35	74	....	....	....
1996-97	Portland Pirates	AHL	50	4	8	12	92	....	....	....	....	....	....	....	....	....	....	....	1	0	0	0	0	....	....	....
1997-98	**Washington**	**NHL**	**2**	**0**	**0**	**0**	**0**	**0**	**0**	**0**	**4**	**0.0**	**0**	....	....	....	....	....	....	....	....	....	....	....	....	....
	Portland Pirates	AHL	59	6	5	11	98	....	....	....	....	....	....	....	....	....	....	....	9	2	4	6	14	....	....	....
1998-99	Portland Pirates	AHL	10	1	3	4	18	....	....	....	....	....	....	....	....	....	....	....	....	....	....	....	....	....	....	....
	Hampton Roads	ECHL	24	10	9	19	129	....	....	....	....	....	....	....	....	....	....	....	....	....	....	....	....	....	....	....
	Hamilton Bulldogs	AHL	9	0	2	2	4	....	....	....	....	....	....	....	....	....	....	....	....	....	....	....	....	....	....	....
	New Orleans	ECHL	5	3	4	7	4	....	....	....	....	....	....	....	....	....	....	....	11	1	1	2	22	....	....	....

			Regular Season																Playoffs							
Season	Club	League	GP	G	A	Pts	PIM	PP	SH	GW	S	%	+/–	TF	F%	H	SB	Min	GP	G	A	Pts	PIM	PP	SH	GW
99-2000	Hampton Roads	ECHL	11	4	3	7	31	....	....	....	....	....	....	....	....	....	....	....	....	....	....	....	....	....	....	....
	Portland Pirates	AHL	56	9	17	26	52	....	....	....	....	....	....	....	....	....	....	....	4	1	1	2	4	....	....	....
	NHL Totals		**2**	**0**	**0**	**0**	**0**	**0**	**0**	**0**	**4**	**0.0**		....	....	....	....	....	....	....	....	....	....	....	....	....

Traded to **Edmonton** by **Washington** for the rights to Barrie Moore, February 3, 1999.

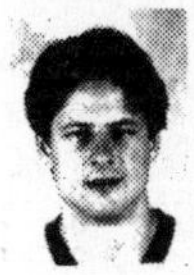

CHYZOWSKI, Dave

(chih-ZOW-skee, DAYV)

Left wing. Shoots left. 6'1", 190 lbs. Born, Edmonton, Alta., July 11, 1971. NY Islanders' 1st choice, 2nd overall, in 1989 Entry Draft.

Season	Club	League	GP	G	A	Pts	PIM	PP	SH	GW	S	%	+/–	TF	F%	H	SB	Min	GP	G	A	Pts	PIM	PP	SH	GW
1986-87	St. Albert Saints	AJHL	49	22	30	52	114	....	....	....	....	....	....	....	....	....	....	....	....	....	....	....	....	....	....	....
1987-88	Kamloops Blazers	WHL	66	16	17	33	117	....	....	....	....	....	....	....	....	....	....	....	18	2	4	6	26	....	....	....
1988-89	Kamloops Blazers	WHL	68	56	48	104	139	....	....	....	....	....	....	....	....	....	....	....	16	15	13	28	32	....	....	....
1989-90	Kamloops Blazers	WHL	4	5	2	7	17	....	....	....	....	....	....	....	....	....	....	....	17	11	6	17	46	....	....	....
	NY Islanders	**NHL**	**34**	**8**	**6**	**14**	**45**	**3**	**0**	**1**	**59**	**13.6**	**–4**	....	....	....	....	....	....	....	....	....	....	....	....	....
	Springfield	AHL	4	0	0	0	7	....	....	....	....	....	....	....	....	....	....	....	....	....	....	....	....	....	....	....
1990-91	**NY Islanders**	**NHL**	**56**	**5**	**9**	**14**	**61**	**0**	**0**	**0**	**66**	**7.6**	**–19**	....	....	....	....	....	....	....	....	....	....	....	....	....
	Capital District	AHL	7	3	6	9	22	....	....	....	....	....	....	....	....	....	....	....	....	....	....	....	....	....	....	....
1991-92	**NY Islanders**	**NHL**	**12**	**1**	**1**	**2**	**17**	**0**	**0**	**0**	**18**	**5.6**	**–4**	....	....	....	....	....	....	....	....	....	....	....	....	....
	Capital District	AHL	55	15	18	33	121	....	....	....	....	....	....	....	....	....	....	....	6	1	1	2	23	....	....	....
1992-93	Capital District	AHL	66	15	21	36	177	....	....	....	....	....	....	....	....	....	....	....	3	2	0	2	0	....	....	....
1993-94	**NY Islanders**	**NHL**	**3**	**1**	**0**	**1**	**4**	**0**	**0**	**0**	**4**	**25.0**	**–1**	....	....	....	....	....	**2**	**0**	**0**	**0**	**0**	**0**	**0**	**0**
	Salt Lake City	IHL	66	27	13	40	151	....	....	....	....	....	....	....	....	....	....	....	....	....	....	....	....	....	....	....
1994-95	**NY Islanders**	**NHL**	**13**	**0**	**0**	**0**	**11**	**0**	**0**	**0**	**11**	**0.0**	**–2**	....	....	....	....	....	....	....	....	....	....	....	....	....
	Kalamazoo Wings	IHL	4	0	4	4	8	....	....	....	....	....	....	....	....	....	....	....	16	9	5	14	27	....	....	....
1995-96	Adirondack	AHL	80	44	39	83	160	....	....	....	....	....	....	....	....	....	....	....	3	0	0	0	6	....	....	....
1996-97	**Chicago**	**NHL**	**8**	**0**	**0**	**0**	**6**	**0**	**0**	**0**	**6**	**0.0**	**1**	....	....	....	....	....	....	....	....	....	....	....	....	....
	Indianapolis Ice	IHL	76	34	40	74	261	....	....	....	....	....	....	....	....	....	....	....	4	0	2	2	38	....	....	....
1997-98	Orlando	IHL	17	9	7	16	32	....	....	....	....	....	....	....	....	....	....	....	....	....	....	....	....	....	....	....
	San Antonio	IHL	10	1	5	6	39	....	....	....	....	....	....	....	....	....	....	....	....	....	....	....	....	....	....	....
	Kansas City	IHL	38	19	14	33	88	....	....	....	....	....	....	....	....	....	....	....	11	5	4	9	11	....	....	....
1998-99	Kansas City	IHL	67	24	15	39	147	....	....	....	....	....	....	....	....	....	....	....	....	....	....	....	....	....	....	....
99-2000	Kansas City	IHL	81	37	33	70	138	....	....	....	....	....	....	....	....	....	....	....	....	....	....	....	....	....	....	....
	NHL Totals		**126**	**15**	**16**	**31**	**144**	**3**	**0**	**1**	**164**	**9.1**		....	....	....	....	....	**2**	**0**	**0**	**0**	**0**	**0**	**0**	**0**

WHL West All-Star Team (1989)

Signed as a free agent by **Detroit**, August 29, 1995. Signed as a free agent by **Chicago**, September 26, 1996.

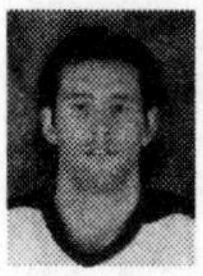

CICCONE, Enrico

(CHIH-koh-nee, EHN-ree-COH **MTL.**

Defense. Shoots left. 6'5", 220 lbs. Born, Montreal, Que., April 10, 1970. Minnesota's 5th choice, 92nd overall, in 1990 Entry Draft.

Season	Club	League	GP	G	A	Pts	PIM	PP	SH	GW	S	%	+/–	TF	F%	H	SB	Min	GP	G	A	Pts	PIM	PP	SH	GW
1986-87	Lac St-Louis	QAAA	38	10	20	30	172	....	....	....	....	....	....	....	....	....	....	....	....	....	....	....	....	....	....	....
1987-88	Shawinigan	QMJHL	61	2	12	14	324	....	....	....	....	....	....	....	....	....	....	....	....	....	....	....	....	....	....	....
1988-89	Shawinigan	QMJHL	34	7	11	18	132	....	....	....	....	....	....	....	....	....	....	....	....	....	....	....	....	....	....	....
	Trois-Rivieres	QMJHL	24	0	7	7	153	....	....	....	....	....	....	....	....	....	....	....	....	....	....	....	....	....	....	....
1989-90	Trois-Rivieres	QMJHL	40	4	24	28	227	....	....	....	....	....	....	....	....	....	....	....	3	0	0	0	15	....	....	....
1990-91	Kalamazoo Wings	IHL	57	4	9	13	384	....	....	....	....	....	....	....	....	....	....	....	4	0	1	1	32	....	....	....
1991-92	**Minnesota**	**NHL**	**11**	**0**	**0**	**0**	**48**	**0**	**0**	**0**	**2**	**0.0**	**–2**	....	....	....	....	....	....	....	....	....	....	....	....	....
	Kalamazoo Wings	IHL	53	4	16	20	406	....	....	....	....	....	....	....	....	....	....	....	10	0	1	1	58	....	....	....
1992-93	**Minnesota**	**NHL**	**31**	**0**	**1**	**1**	**115**	**0**	**0**	**0**	**13**	**0.0**	**2**	....	....	....	....	....	....	....	....	....	....	....	....	....
	Kalamazoo Wings	IHL	13	1	3	4	50	....	....	....	....	....	....	....	....	....	....	....	....	....	....	....	....	....	....	....
	Hamilton Canucks	AHL	6	1	3	4	44	....	....	....	....	....	....	....	....	....	....	....	....	....	....	....	....	....	....	....
1993-94	**Washington**	**NHL**	**46**	**1**	**1**	**2**	**174**	**0**	**0**	**0**	**23**	**4.3**	**–2**	....	....	....	....	....	....	....	....	....	....	....	....	....
	Portland Pirates	AHL	6	0	0	0	27	....	....	....	....	....	....	....	....	....	....	....	....	....	....	....	....	....	....	....
	Tampa Bay	**NHL**	**11**	**0**	**1**	**1**	**52**	**0**	**0**	**0**	**10**	**0.0**	**–2**	....	....	....	....	....	....	....	....	....	....	....	....	....
1994-95	**Tampa Bay**	**NHL**	**41**	**2**	**4**	**6**	***225**	**0**	**0**	**0**	**43**	**4.7**	**3**	....	....	....	....	....	....	....	....	....	....	....	....	....
1995-96	**Tampa Bay**	**NHL**	**55**	**2**	**3**	**5**	**258**	**0**	**0**	**0**	**48**	**4.2**	**–4**	....	....	....	....	....	....	....	....	....	....	....	....	....
	Chicago	**NHL**	**11**	**0**	**1**	**1**	**48**	**0**	**0**	**0**	**12**	**0.0**	**5**	....	....	....	....	....	**9**	**1**	**0**	**1**	**30**	**0**	**0**	**0**
1996-97	**Chicago**	**NHL**	**67**	**2**	**2**	**4**	**233**	**0**	**0**	**1**	**65**	**3.1**	**–1**	....	....	....	....	....	**4**	**0**	**0**	**0**	**18**	**0**	**0**	**0**
1997-98	**Carolina**	**NHL**	**14**	**0**	**3**	**3**	**83**	**0**	**0**	**0**	**8**	**0.0**	**3**	....	....	....	....	....	....	....	....	....	....	....	....	....
	Vancouver	**NHL**	**13**	**0**	**1**	**1**	**47**	**0**	**0**	**0**	**7**	**0.0**	**–2**	....	....	....	....	....	....	....	....	....	....	....	....	....
	Tampa Bay	**NHL**	**12**	**0**	**0**	**0**	**45**	**0**	**0**	**0**	**7**	**0.0**	**–3**	....	....	....	....	....	....	....	....	....	....	....	....	....
1998-99	**Tampa Bay**	**NHL**	**16**	**1**	**1**	**2**	**24**	**0**	**0**	**0**	**9**	**11.1**	**–1**	**0**	**0.0**	**20**	**7**	**10:18**	....	....	....	....	....	....	....	....
	Cleveland	IHL	6	0	0	0	23	....	....	....	....	....	....	....	....	....	....	....	....	....	....	....	....	....	....	....
	Washington	**NHL**	**43**	**2**	**0**	**2**	**103**	**0**	**0**	**0**	**43**	**4.7**	**–6**	**0**	**0.0**	**58**	**21**	**11:29**	....	....	....	....	....	....	....	....
99-2000	Moskitos Essen	DEL	14	0	4	4	101	....	....	....	....	....	....	....	....	....	....	....	....	....	....	....	....	....	....	....
	NHL Totals		**371**	**10**	**18**	**28**	**1455**	**0**	**0**	**1**	**290**	**3.4**		**0**	**0.0**	**78**	**28**	**11:010**	**13**	**1**	**0**	**1**	**48**	**0**	**0**	**0**

Traded to **Washington** by **Dallas** to complete transaction that sent Paul Cavallini to Dallas (June 20, 1993), June 25, 1993. Traded to **Tampa Bay** by **Washington** with Washington's 3rd round choice (later traded to Anaheim - Anaheim selected Craig Reichert) in 1994 Entry Draft and the return of conditional draft choice transferred in the Pat Elynuik trade for Joe Reekie, March 21, 1994. Traded to **Chicago** by **Tampa Bay** with Tampa Bay's 2nd round choice (Jeff Paul) in 1996 Entry Draft for Patrick Poulin, Igor Ulanov and Chicago's 2nd round choice (later traded to New Jersey - New Jersey selected Pierre Dagenais) in 1996 Entry Draft, March 20, 1996. Traded to **Carolina** by **Chicago** for Ryan Risidore and Carolina's 5th round choice (later traded to Toronto - Toronto selected Morgan Warren) in 1998 Entry Draft, July 25, 1997. Traded to **Vancouver** by **Carolina** with Sean Burke and Geoff Sanderson for Kirk McLean and Martin Gelinas, January 3, 1998. Traded to **Tampa Bay** by **Vancouver** for Jamie Huscroft, March 14, 1998. Traded to **Washington** by **Tampa Bay** for cash, December 28, 1998. Signed as a free agent by **Montreal**, July 7, 2000.

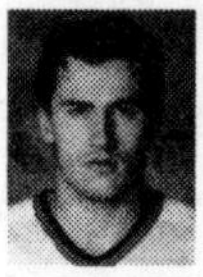

CIERNIK, Ivan

(CHAIR-nihk, ee-VAHN) **OTT.**

Left wing. Shoots left. 6'1", 234 lbs. Born, Levice, Czech., October 30, 1977. Ottawa's 6th choice, 216th overall, in 1996 Entry Draft.

Season	Club	League	GP	G	A	Pts	PIM	PP	SH	GW	S	%	+/–	TF	F%	H	SB	Min	GP	G	A	Pts	PIM	PP	SH	GW
1994-95	MHC Nitra	Slovak-Jr.	30	22	15	37	36	....	....	....	....	....	....	....	....	....	....	....	....	....	....	....	....	....	....	....
	MHC Nitra	Slovakia	7	1	0	1	2	....	....	....	....	....	....	....	....	....	....	....	....	....	....	....	....	....	....	....
1995-96	MHC Nitra	Slovakia	35	9	7	16	36	....	....	....	....	....	....	....	....	....	....	....	8	3	3	6	....	....	....	....
1996-97	MHC Nitra	Slovakia	41	11	19	30	....	....	....	....	....	....	....	....	....	....	....	....	....	....	....	....	....	....	....	....
1997-98	**Ottawa**	**NHL**	**2**	**0**	**0**	**0**	**0**	**0**	**0**	**0**	**0**	**0.0**	**0**	....	....	....	....	....	....	....	....	....	....	....	....	....
	Worcester	AHL	53	9	12	21	38	....	....	....	....	....	....	....	....	....	....	....	1	0	0	0	2	....	....	....
1998-99	Adirondack	AHL	21	1	4	5	4	....	....	....	....	....	....	....	....	....	....	....	....	....	....	....	....	....	....	....
	Cincinnati Ducks	AHL	32	10	3	13	10	....	....	....	....	....	....	....	....	....	....	....	2	0	0	0	2	....	....	....
99-2000	Grand Rapids	IHL	66	13	12	25	64	....	....	....	....	....	....	....	....	....	....	....	6	0	6	6	2	....	....	....
	NHL Totals		**2**	**0**	**0**	**0**	**0**	**0**	**0**	**0**	**0**	**0.0**		....	....	....	....	....	....	....	....	....	....	....	....	....

Loaned to **Cincinnati** (AHL) by **Ottawa** with Ratislav Pavlikovsky and Erich Goldmann, January 12, 1999.

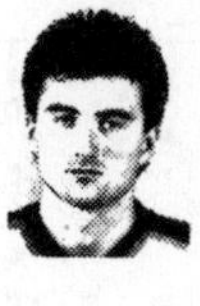

CIERNY, Jozef

(chee-ER-nee, JOH-zehf) **EDM.**

Left wing. Shoots left. 6'2", 185 lbs. Born, Zvolen, Czech., May 13, 1974. Buffalo's 2nd choice, 35th overall, in 1992 Entry Draft.

Season	Club	League	GP	G	A	Pts	PIM	PP	SH	GW	S	%	+/–	TF	F%	H	SB	Min	GP	G	A	Pts	PIM	PP	SH	GW
1991-92	ZTK Zvolen	Czech-2	26	10	3	13	8	....	....	....	....	....	....	....	....	....	....	....	....	....	....	....	....	....	....	....
1992-93	Rochester	AHL	54	27	27	54	36	....	....	....	....	....	....	....	....	....	....	....	....	....	....	....	....	....	....	....
1993-94	**Edmonton**	**NHL**	**1**	**0**	**0**	**0**	**0**	**0**	**0**	**0**	**0**	**0.0**	**–1**	....	....	....	....	....	....	....	....	....	....	....	....	....
	Cape Breton	AHL	73	30	27	57	88	....	....	....	....	....	....	....	....	....	....	....	4	1	1	2	4	....	....	....
1994-95	Cape Breton	AHL	73	28	24	52	58	....	....	....	....	....	....	....	....	....	....	....	....	....	....	....	....	....	....	....
1995-96	Detroit Vipers	IHL	20	2	5	7	16	....	....	....	....	....	....	....	....	....	....	....	....	....	....	....	....	....	....	....
	Los Angeles	IHL	43	23	16	39	36	....	....	....	....	....	....	....	....	....	....	....	....	....	....	....	....	....	....	....
1996-97	Long Beach	IHL	68	27	27	54	106	....	....	....	....	....	....	....	....	....	....	....	16	8	5	13	7	....	....	....
1997-98	EHC Nurnberg	DEL	45	20	22	42	61	....	....	....	....	....	....	....	....	....	....	....	....	....	....	....	....	....	....	....
1998-99	EHC Nurnberg	DEL	47	22	21	43	65	....	....	....	....	....	....	....	....	....	....	....	13	3	2	5	37	....	....	....
99-2000	EHC Nurnberg	DEL	67	19	15	34	68	....	....	....	....	....	....	....	....	....	....	....	....	....	....	....	....	....	....	....
	EHC Nurnberg	EuroHL	5	3	1	4	10	....	....	....	....	....	....	....	....	....	....	....	2	0	0	0	0	....	....	....
	NHL Totals		**1**	**0**	**0**	**0**	**0**	**0**	**0**	**0**	**0**	**0.0**		....	....	....	....	....	....	....	....	....	....	....	....	....

Traded to **Edmonton** by **Buffalo** with Buffalo's 4th round choice (Jussi Tarvainen) in 1994 Entry Draft for Craig Simpson, September 1, 1993.

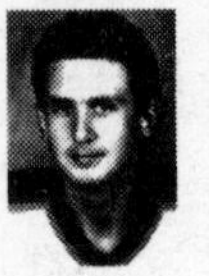

CIGER, Zdeno
(SEE-guhr, ZDEH-noh) **NSH.**

Left wing. Shoots left. 6'1", 190 lbs. Born, Martin, Czech., October 19, 1969. New Jersey's 3rd choice, 54th overall, in 1988 Entry Draft.

			Regular Season																	Playoffs							
Season	Club	League	GP	G	A	Pts	PIM	PP	SH	GW	S	%	+/-	TF	F%	H	SB	Min	GP	G	A	Pts	PIM	PP	SH	GW
1987-88	Dukla Trencin	Czech.	8	3	4	7	2																			
1988-89	Dukla Trencin	Czech.	43	18	13	31	18																			
1989-90	Dukla Trencin	Czech.	44	17	24	41													9	1	4	5				
1990-91	New Jersey	NHL	45	8	17	25	8	2	0	1	82	9.8	3						6	0	2	2	4	0	0	0
	Utica Devils	AHL	8	5	4	9	2																			
1991-92	New Jersey	NHL	20	6	5	11	10	1	0	0	33	18.2	-2						7	2	4	6	0	0	0	1
1992-93	New Jersey	NHL	27	4	8	12	2	2	0	1	39	10.3	-8													
	Edmonton	NHL	37	9	15	24	6	0	0	1	67	13.4	-5													
1993-94	Edmonton	NHL	84	22	35	57	8	8	0	1	158	13.9	-11													
1994-95	Dukla Trencin	Slovakia	34	23	25	48	8												9	2	9	11	2			
	Edmonton	NHL	5	2	2	4	0	1	0	1	10	20.0	-1													
1995-96	Edmonton	NHL	78	31	39	70	41	12	0	3	184	16.8	-15													
1996-97	Slovan Bratislava	Slovakia	44	26	27	53													2	1	3	4				
	Slovan Bratislava	EuroHL	6	4	5	9	2												2	1	1	2	2			
1997-98	Slovan Bratislava	Slovakia	36	14	*31	45	2												11	6	*10	*16	4			
	Slovan Bratislava	EuroHL	8	1	5	6	6																			
	Slovakia	Olympics	4	1	1	2	4																			
1998-99	Slovan Bratislava	Slovakia	40	26	32	*58	8												9	3	*10	13	2			
	Slovan Bratislava	EuroHL	6	4	5	9	8																			
99-2000	Slovan Bratislava	Slovakia	51	23	39	62	48												8	1	*8	*9	0			
	Slovan Bratislava	EuroHL	6	3	4	7	2												2	0	2	2	4			
	NHL Totals		296	82	121	203	75	26	0	8	573	14.3							13	2	6	8	4	0	0	1

Czechoslovakian Rookie of the Year (1989)
Traded to **Edmonton** by **New Jersey** with Kevin Todd for Bernie Nicholls, January 13, 1993. Claimed by **Nashville** from **Edmonton** in NHL Waiver Draft, October 5, 1998.

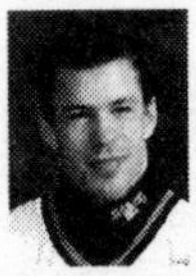

CISAR, Marian
(SIH-sahr, MAIR-eean) **NSH.**

Right wing. Shoots right. 6', 197 lbs. Born, Bratislava, Czech., February 25, 1978. Los Angeles' 2nd choice, 37th overall, in 1996 Entry Draft.

Season	Club	League	GP	G	A	Pts	PIM	PP	SH	GW	S	%	+/-	TF	F%	H	SB	Min	GP	G	A	Pts	PIM	PP	SH	GW
1994-95	Sloven Bratislava	Slovak-Jr.	38	42	28	70	16																			
1995-96	Sloven Bratislava	Slovak-Jr.	16	26	17	43	2																			
	Sloven Bratislava	Slovakia	13	3	3	6	0												6	3	0	3	0			
1996-97	Spokane Chiefs	WHL	70	31	35	66	52												9	6	2	8	4			
1997-98	Spokane Chiefs	WHL	52	33	40	73	34												18	8	5	13	8			
1998-99	Milwaukee	IHL	51	11	17	28	31												2	0	0	0	12			
99-2000	Nashville	NHL	3	0	0	0	4	0	0	0	2	0.0	-2	0	0.0	1	1	8:18								
	Milwaukee	IHL	78	20	32	52	82												1	0	0	0	0			
	NHL Totals		3	0	0	0	4	0	0	0	2	0.0		0	0.0	1	1	8:18								

Traded to **Nashville** by **LA Kings** for future considerations, June 1, 1998.

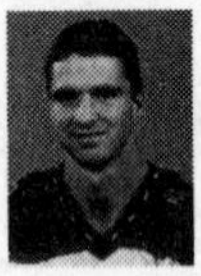

CLARK, Brett
(KLAHRK, BREHT) **ATL.**

Defense. Shoots left. 6'1", 185 lbs. Born, Wapella, Sask., December 23, 1976. Montreal's 7th choice, 154th overall, in 1996 Entry Draft.

Season	Club	League	GP	G	A	Pts	PIM	PP	SH	GW	S	%	+/-	TF	F%	H	SB	Min	GP	G	A	Pts	PIM	PP	SH	GW
1994-95	Melville	SJHL	62	19	32	51	77																			
1995-96	U. of Maine	H-East	39	7	31	38	22																			
1996-97	Canada	Nat-Team	57	6	21	27	52																			
1997-98	Montreal	NHL	41	1	0	1	20	0	0	0	26	3.8	-3													
	Fredericton	AHL	20	0	6	6	6												4	0	1	1	17			
1998-99	Montreal	NHL	61	2	2	4	16	0	0	0	36	5.6	-3	0	0.0	62	43	13:11								
	Fredericton	AHL	3	1	0	1	0																			
99-2000	Atlanta	NHL	14	0	1	1	4	0	0	0	13	0.0	-12	0	0.0	27	19	16:51								
	Orlando	IHL	63	9	17	26	31												6	0	1	1	0			
	NHL Totals		116	3	3	6	40	0	0	0	75	4.0		0	0.0	89	62	13:52								

Claimed by **Atlanta** from **Montreal** in Expansion Draft, June 25, 1999.

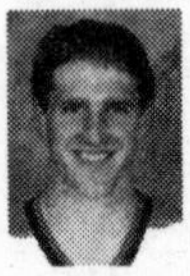

CLARK, Chris
(KLAHRK, KRIHS) **CGY.**

Right wing. Shoots right. 6', 202 lbs. Born, Manchester, CT, March 8, 1976. Calgary's 3rd choice, 77th overall, in 1994 Entry Draft.

Season	Club	League	GP	G	A	Pts	PIM	PP	SH	GW	S	%	+/-	TF	F%	H	SB	Min	GP	G	A	Pts	PIM	PP	SH	GW
1990-91	South Windsor	Hi-School	23	16	15	31	24																			
1991-92	Springfield	EJHL-B	49	21	29	50	56																			
1992-93	Springfield	EJHL-B	43	17	60	77	120																			
1993-94	Springfield	NAJHL	35	31	26	57	185																			
1994-95	Clarkson	ECAC	32	12	11	23	92																			
1995-96	Clarkson	ECAC	38	10	8	18	108																			
1996-97	Clarkson	ECAC	37	23	25	48	*86																			
1997-98	Clarkson	ECAC	35	18	21	39	*106																			
1998-99	Saint John Flames	AHL	73	13	27	40	123												7	2	4	6	15			
99-2000	Calgary	NHL	22	0	1	1	14	0	0	0	17	0.0	-3	0	0.0	22	3	9:02								
	Saint John Flames	AHL	48	16	17	33	134																			
	NHL Totals		22	0	1	1	14	0	0	0	17	0.0		0	0.0	22	3	9:02								

ECAC Second All-Star Team (1998)

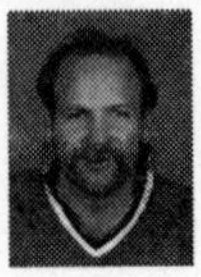

CLARK, Wendel
(KLAHRK, WEHN-dehl)

Left wing/Defense. Shoots left. 5'11", 194 lbs. Born, Kelvington, Sask., October 25, 1966. Toronto's 1st choice, 1st overall, in 1985 Entry Draft.

Season	Club	League	GP	G	A	Pts	PIM	PP	SH	GW	S	%	+/-	TF	F%	H	SB	Min	GP	G	A	Pts	PIM	PP	SH	GW
1982-83	Notre Dame	SAHA	27	21	28	49	83																			
1983-84	Saskatoon	WHL	72	23	45	68	225																			
1984-85	Saskatoon	WHL	64	32	55	87	253												3	3	3	6	7			
1985-86	Toronto	NHL	66	34	11	45	227	4	0	3	164	20.7	-27						10	5	1	6	47	1	0	1
1986-87	Toronto	NHL	80	37	23	60	271	15	0	1	246	15.0	-23						13	6	5	11	38	3	0	1
1987-88	Toronto	NHL	28	12	11	23	80	4	0	1	93	12.9	-13													
1988-89	Toronto	NHL	15	7	4	11	66	3	0	1	30	23.3	-3													
1989-90	Toronto	NHL	38	18	8	26	116	7	0	2	85	21.2	2						5	1	1	2	19	0	0	0
1990-91	Toronto	NHL	63	18	16	34	152	4	0	2	181	9.9	-5													
1991-92	Toronto	NHL	43	19	21	40	123	7	0	4	158	12.0	-14													
1992-93	Toronto	NHL	66	17	22	39	193	2	0	5	146	11.6	2						21	10	10	20	51	2	0	1
1993-94	Toronto	NHL	64	46	30	76	115	21	0	8	275	16.7	10						18	9	7	16	24	2	0	1
1994-95	Quebec	NHL	37	12	18	30	45	5	0	0	95	12.6	-1						6	1	2	3	6	0	0	0
1995-96	NY Islanders	NHL	58	24	19	43	60	6	0	2	192	12.5	-12													
	Toronto	NHL	13	8	7	15	16	2	0	1	45	17.8	7						6	2	2	4	2	1	0	0
1996-97	Toronto	NHL	65	30	19	49	75	6	0	6	212	14.2	-2													
1997-98	Toronto	NHL	47	12	7	19	80	4	0	3	140	8.6	-21													
1998-99	Tampa Bay	NHL	65	28	14	42	35	11	0	2	171	16.4	-25	5	40.0	54	11	15:38								
	Detroit	NHL	12	4	2	6	2	0	0	1	44	9.1	1	2	50.0	11	5	17:01	10	2	3	5	10	1	0	0

			Regular Season																Playoffs							
Season	Club	League	GP	G	A	Pts	PIM	PP	SH	GW	S	%	+/–	TF	F%	H	SB	Min	GP	G	A	Pts	PIM	PP	SH	GW
99-2000	Chicago	NHL	13	2	0	2	13	0	0	0	27	7.4	–2	0	0.0	13	0	12:38	....	....	....	....	....	....	....	....
	Toronto	NHL	20	2	2	4	21	0	0	1	36	5.6	–3	0	0.0	33	4	11:50	6	1	1	2	4	0	0	0
	NHL Totals		793	330	234	564	1690	101	0	43	2340	14.1		7	42.9	111	20	14:44	95	37	32	69	201	10	0	4

WHL East First All-Star Team (1985) • NHL All-Rookie Team (1986) • Played in NHL All-Star Game (1986, 1999)

Traded to **Quebec** by **Toronto** with Sylvain Lefebvre, Landon Wilson and Toronto's 1st round choice (Jeffrey Kealty) in 1994 Entry Draft for Mats Sundin, Garth Butcher, Todd Warriner and Philadelphia's 1st round choice (previously acquired by Quebec - later traded to Washington - Washington selected Nolan Baumgartner) in 1994 Entry Draft, June 28, 1994. Transferred to **Colorado** after **Quebec** franchise relocated, June 21, 1995. Traded to **NY Islanders** by **Colorado** for Claude Lemieux, October 3, 1995. Traded to **Toronto** by **NY Islanders** with Mathieu Schneider and D.J. Smith for Darby Hendrickson, Sean Haggerty, Kenny Jonsson and Toronto's 1st round choice (Roberto Luongo) in 1997 Entry Draft, March 13, 1996. Signed as a free agent by **Tampa Bay**, July 31, 1998. Traded to **Detroit** by **Tampa Bay** with Detroit's 6th round choice (previously acquired, Detroit selected Kent McDonnell) in 1999 Entry Draft for Kevin Hodson and San Jose's 2nd round choice (previously acquired, Tampa Bay selected Sheldon Keefe) in 1999 Entry Draft, March 23, 1999. Signed as a free agent by **Chicago**, August 2, 1999. Signed as a free agent by **Toronto** following release by Chicago, January 14, 2000. • Officially announced retirement, June 29, 2000.

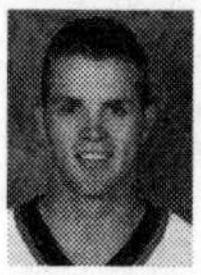

CLEARY, Daniel

(KLIH-ree, DAN-yehl) **EDM.**

Left wing. Shoots left. 6', 203 lbs. Born, Carbonear, Nfld., December 18, 1978. Chicago's 1st choice, 13th overall, in 1997 Entry Draft.

Season	Club	League	GP	G	A	Pts	PIM	PP	SH	GW	S	%	+/–	TF	F%	H	SB	Min	GP	G	A	Pts	PIM	PP	SH	GW
1993-94	Kingston	OJHL	41	18	28	46	33	....	....	....	....	....	....	....	....	....	....	....	2	0	1	1	0	....	....	....
1994-95	Belleville Bulls	OHL	62	26	55	81	62	....	....	....	....	....	....	....	....	....	....	....	16	7	10	17	23	....	....	....
1995-96	Belleville Bulls	OHL	64	53	62	115	74	....	....	....	....	....	....	....	....	....	....	....	14	10	17	27	40	....	....	....
1996-97	Belleville Bulls	OHL	64	32	48	80	88	....	....	....	....	....	....	....	....	....	....	....	6	3	4	7	6	....	....	....
1997-98	Belleville Bulls	OHL	30	16	31	47	14	....	....	....	....	....	....	....	....	....	....	....	10	6	*17	*23	10	....	....	....
	Chicago	NHL	6	0	0	0	0	0	0	0	4	0.0	–2	....	....	....	....	....	....	....	....	....	....	....	....	....
	Indianapolis Ice	IHL	4	2	1	3	6	....	....	....	....	....	....	....	....	....	....	....	....	....	....	....	....	....	....	....
1998-99	Chicago	NHL	35	4	5	9	24	0	0	0	49	8.2	–1	13	46.2	28	9	14:21	....	....	....	....	....	....	....	....
	Portland Pirates	AHL	30	9	17	26	74	....	....	....	....	....	....	....	....	....	....	....	....	....	....	....	....	....	....	....
	Hamilton Bulldogs	AHL	9	0	1	1	7	....	....	....	....	....	....	....	....	....	....	....	3	0	0	0	0	....	....	....
99-2000	Edmonton	NHL	17	3	2	5	8	0	0	1	18	16.7	–1	1	100.0	16	2	9:44	4	0	1	1	2	0	0	0
	Hamilton Bulldogs	AHL	58	22	52	74	108	....	....	....	....	....	....	....	....	....	....	....	5	2	3	5	18	....	....	....
	NHL Totals		58	7	7	14	32	0	0	1	71	9.9		14	50.0	44	11	12:51	4	0	1	1	2	0	0	0

OHL First All-Star Team (1996, 1997) • AHL Second All-Star Team (2000)

Traded to **Edmonton** by **Chicago** with Chad Kilger, Ethan Moreau and Christian Laflamme for Boris Mironov, Dean McAmmond and Jonas Elofsson, March 20, 1999.

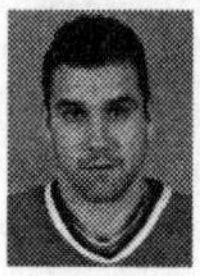

CLOUTIER, Sylvain

(klootz-YAY, SIHL-vehn) **N.J.**

Center. Shoots left. 6', 195 lbs. Born, Mont-Laurier, Que., February 13, 1974. Detroit's 3rd choice, 70th overall, in 1992 Entry Draft.

Season	Club	League	GP	G	A	Pts	PIM	PP	SH	GW	S	%	+/–	TF	F%	H	SB	Min	GP	G	A	Pts	PIM	PP	SH	GW
1990-91	S.S. Marie Legion	NOHA	34	51	40	91	92	....	....	....	....	....	....	....	....	....	....	....	....	....	....	....	....	....	....	....
1991-92	Guelph Storm	OHL	62	35	31	66	74	....	....	....	....	....	....	....	....	....	....	....	....	....	....	....	....	....	....	....
1992-93	Guelph Storm	OHL	44	26	29	55	78	....	....	....	....	....	....	....	....	....	....	....	5	0	5	5	14	....	....	....
1993-94	Guelph Storm	OHL	66	45	71	116	127	....	....	....	....	....	....	....	....	....	....	....	9	7	9	16	32	....	....	....
	Adirondack	AHL	2	0	2	2	2	....	....	....	....	....	....	....	....	....	....	....	....	....	....	....	....	....	....	....
1994-95	Adirondack	AHL	71	7	26	33	144	....	....	....	....	....	....	....	....	....	....	....	....	....	....	....	....	....	....	....
1995-96	Adirondack	AHL	65	11	17	28	118	....	....	....	....	....	....	....	....	....	....	....	3	0	0	0	4	....	....	....
	Toledo Storm	ECHL	6	4	2	6	4	....	....	....	....	....	....	....	....	....	....	....	....	....	....	....	....	....	....	....
1996-97	Adirondack	AHL	77	13	36	49	190	....	....	....	....	....	....	....	....	....	....	....	4	0	2	2	4	....	....	....
1997-98	Adirondack	AHL	72	14	22	36	155	....	....	....	....	....	....	....	....	....	....	....	....	....	....	....	....	....	....	....
	Detroit Vipers	IHL	8	0	1	1	18	....	....	....	....	....	....	....	....	....	....	....	21	7	5	12	31	....	....	....
1998-99	Chicago	NHL	7	0	0	0	0	0	0	0	3	0.0	–1	35	51.4	4	0	5:28	....	....	....	....	....	....	....	....
	Indianapolis Ice	IHL	73	21	33	54	128	....	....	....	....	....	....	....	....	....	....	....	7	3	2	5	12	....	....	....
99-2000	Albany River Rats	AHL	66	15	28	43	127	....	....	....	....	....	....	....	....	....	....	....	5	0	0	0	6	....	....	....
	Orlando	IHL	9	1	1	2	25	....	....	....	....	....	....	....	....	....	....	....	....	....	....	....	....	....	....	....
	NHL Totals		7	0	0	0	0	0	0	0	3	0.0		35	51.4	4	0	5:28	....	....	....	....	....	....	....	....

Signed as a free agent by **Chicago**, August 17, 1998. Claimed by **Atlanta** from **Chicago** in Expansion Draft, June 25, 1999. Traded to **New Jersey** by **Atlanta** with Jeff Williams and Atlanta's 7th round choice (Ken Magovan) in 2000 Entry Draft for Wes Mason and Eric Bertrand, November 1, 1999.

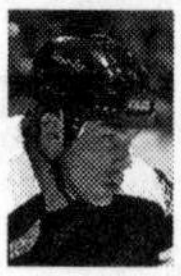

CLYMER, Ben

(KLIH-mehr, BEHN) **T.B.**

Defense. Shoots left. 6'1", 195 lbs. Born, Edina, MN, April 11, 1978. Boston's 3rd choice, 27th overall, in 1997 Entry Draft.

Season	Club	League	GP	G	A	Pts	PIM	PP	SH	GW	S	%	+/–	TF	F%	H	SB	Min	GP	G	A	Pts	PIM	PP	SH	GW
1993-94	Jefferson High	Hi-School	23	3	7	10	20	....	....	....	....	....	....	....	....	....	....	....	....	....	....	....	....	....	....	....
1994-95	Jefferson High	Hi-School	28	11	22	33	36	....	....	....	....	....	....	....	....	....	....	....	....	....	....	....	....	....	....	....
1995-96	Jefferson High	Hi-School	18	12	34	46	34	....	....	....	....	....	....	....	....	....	....	....	5	0	6	6	6	....	....	....
1996-97	U. of Minnesota	WCHA	29	7	13	20	64	....	....	....	....	....	....	....	....	....	....	....	....	....	....	....	....	....	....	....
1997-98	U. of Minnesota	WCHA	1	0	0	0	2	....	....	....	....	....	....	....	....	....	....	....	....	....	....	....	....	....	....	....
1998-99	Seattle T-Birds	WHL	70	12	44	56	93	....	....	....	....	....	....	....	....	....	....	....	11	1	5	6	12	....	....	....
99-2000	Tampa Bay	NHL	60	2	6	8	87	2	0	0	98	2.0	–26	3	66.7	121	41	19:37	....	....	....	....	....	....	....	....
	Detroit Vipers	IHL	19	1	9	10	30	....	....	....	....	....	....	....	....	....	....	....	....	....	....	....	....	....	....	....
	NHL Totals		60	2	6	8	87	2	0	0	98	2.0		3	66.7	121	41	19:37	....	....	....	....	....	....	....	....

• Missed remainder of 1997-98 season recovering from shoulder injury suffered in game vs. U. of Michigan (CCHA), October 10, 1997. Signed as a free agent by **Tampa Bay**, October 2, 1999.

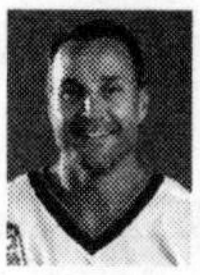

COFFEY, Paul

(CAW-fee, PAWL) **BOS.**

Defense. Shoots left. 6', 205 lbs. Born, Weston, Ont., June 1, 1961. Edmonton's 1st choice, 6th overall, in 1980 Entry Draft.

Season	Club	League	GP	G	A	Pts	PIM	PP	SH	GW	S	%	+/–	TF	F%	H	SB	Min	GP	G	A	Pts	PIM	PP	SH	GW
1977-78	North York	OJHL	50	14	33	47	64	....	....	....	....	....	....	....	....	....	....	....	....	....	....	....	....	....	....	....
	Kingston	OMJHL	8	2	2	4	11	....	....	....	....	....	....	....	....	....	....	....	5	0	0	0	0	....	....	....
1978-79	Sault Ste. Marie	OMJHL	68	17	72	89	103	....	....	....	....	....	....	....	....	....	....	....	....	....	....	....	....	....	....	....
1979-80	Sault Ste. Marie	OMJHL	23	10	21	31	63	....	....	....	....	....	....	....	....	....	....	....	....	....	....	....	....	....	....	....
	Kitchener	OMJHL	52	19	52	71	130	....	....	....	....	....	....	....	....	....	....	....	....	....	....	....	....	....	....	....
1980-81	Edmonton	NHL	74	9	23	32	130	2	0	0	113	8.0	4	....	....	....	....	....	9	4	3	7	22	1	0	0
1981-82	Edmonton	NHL	80	29	60	89	106	13	0	1	234	12.4	35	....	....	....	....	....	5	1	1	2	6	1	0	0
1982-83	Edmonton	NHL	80	29	67	96	87	9	1	2	259	11.2	52	....	....	....	....	....	16	7	7	14	14	2	2	0
1983-84♦	Edmonton	NHL	80	40	86	126	104	14	1	4	258	15.5	52	....	....	....	....	....	19	8	14	22	21	2	0	1
1984-85♦	Edmonton	NHL	80	37	84	121	97	12	2	6	284	13.0	55	....	....	....	....	....	18	12	25	37	44	3	1	4
1985-86	Edmonton	NHL	79	48	90	138	120	9	9	3	307	15.6	61	....	....	....	....	....	10	1	9	10	30	1	0	0
1986-87♦	Edmonton	NHL	59	17	50	67	49	10	2	3	165	10.3	12	....	....	....	....	....	17	3	8	11	30	1	0	1
1987-88	Pittsburgh	NHL	46	15	52	67	93	6	2	2	193	7.8	–1	....	....	....	....	....	....	....	....	....	....	....	....	....
1988-89	Pittsburgh	NHL	75	30	83	113	195	11	0	2	342	8.8	–10	....	....	....	....	....	11	2	13	15	31	2	0	1
1989-90	Pittsburgh	NHL	80	29	74	103	95	10	0	3	324	9.0	–25	....	....	....	....	....	....	....	....	....	....	....	....	....
1990-91♦	Pittsburgh	NHL	76	24	69	93	128	8	0	3	240	10.0	–18	....	....	....	....	....	12	2	9	11	6	0	0	0
1991-92	Pittsburgh	NHL	54	10	54	64	62	5	0	1	207	4.8	4	....	....	....	....	....	....	....	....	....	....	....	....	....
	Los Angeles	NHL	10	1	4	5	25	0	0	0	25	4.0	–3	....	....	....	....	....	6	4	3	7	2	3	0	0
1992-93	Los Angeles	NHL	50	8	49	57	50	2	0	0	182	4.4	9	....	....	....	....	....	....	....	....	....	....	....	....	....
	Detroit	NHL	30	4	26	30	27	3	0	0	72	5.6	7	....	....	....	....	....	7	2	9	11	2	0	0	0
1993-94	Detroit	NHL	80	14	63	77	106	5	0	3	278	5.0	28	....	....	....	....	....	7	1	6	7	8	0	0	0
1994-95	Detroit	NHL	45	14	44	58	72	4	1	2	181	7.7	18	....	....	....	....	....	18	6	12	18	10	2	1	0
1995-96	Detroit	NHL	76	14	60	74	90	3	1	3	234	6.0	19	....	....	....	....	....	17	5	9	14	30	3	2	1
1996-97	Hartford	NHL	20	3	5	8	18	1	0	1	39	7.7	0	....	....	....	....	....	....	....	....	....	....	....	....	....
	Philadelphia	NHL	37	6	20	26	20	0	1	1	71	8.5	11	....	....	....	....	....	17	1	8	9	6	0	0	0
1997-98	Philadelphia	NHL	57	2	27	29	30	1	0	1	107	1.9	3	....	....	....	....	....	....	....	....	....	....	....	....	....

			Regular Season																Playoffs							
Season	Club	League	GP	G	A	Pts	PIM	PP	SH	GW	S	%	+/-	TF	F%	H	SB	Min	GP	G	A	Pts	PIM	PP	SH	GW
1998-99	Chicago	NHL	10	0	4	4	0	0	0	0	8	0.0	–6	0	0.0	1	8	15:22	....	....	....	....	....	....	....	....
	Carolina	NHL	44	2	8	10	28	1	0	0	79	2.5	–1	0	0.0	16	31	19:41	5	0	1	1	2	0	0	0
99-2000	Carolina	NHL	69	11	29	40	40	6	0	3	155	7.1	–6	0	0.0	18	70	22:35	....	....	....	....	....	....	....	....
	NHL Totals		**1391**	**396**	**1131**	**1527**	**1772**	**135**	**20**	**44**	**4357**	**9.1**		**0**	**0.0**	**35**	**109**	**20:58**	**194**	**59**	**137**	**196**	**264**	**21**	**6**	**8**

OMJHL Second All-Star Team (1980) • NHL Second All-Star Team (1982, 1983, 1984, 1990) • Won James Norris Memorial Trophy (1985, 1986, 1995) • NHL First All-Star Team (1985, 1986, 1989, 1995) • Played in NHL All-Star Game (1982, 1983, 1984, 1985, 1986, 1988, 1989, 1990, 1991, 1992, 1993, 1994, 1996, 1997)

Traded to **Pittsburgh** by **Edmonton** with Dave Hunter and Wayne Van Dorp for Craig Simpson, Dave Hannan, Moe Mantha and Chris Joseph, November 24, 1987. Traded to **LA Kings** by **Pittsburgh** for Brian Benning, Jeff Chychrun and LA Kings' 1st round choice (later traded to Philadelphia - Philadelphia selected Jason Bowen) in 1992 Entry Draft, February 19, 1992. Traded to **Detroit** by **LA Kings** with Sylvain Couturier and Jim Hiller for Jimmy Carson, Marc Potvin and Gary Shuchuk, January 29, 1993. Traded to **Hartford** by **Detroit** with Keith Primeau and Detroit's 1st round choice (Nikos Tselios) in 1997 Entry Draft for Brendan Shanahan and Brian Glynn, October 9, 1996. Traded to **Philadelphia** by **Hartford** with Hartford-Carolina's 3rd round choice (Kris Mallette) in 1997 Entry Draft for Kevin Haller, Philadelphia's 1st round choice (later traded to San Jose - San Jose selected Scott Hannan) in 1997 Entry Draft and Hartford's 7th round choice (previously acquired, Carolina selected Andrew Merrick) in 1997 Entry Draft, December 15, 1996. Traded to **Chicago** by **Philadelphia** for NY Islanders' 5th round choice (previously acquired, Philadelphia selected Francis Belanger) in 1998 Entry Draft, June 27, 1998. Traded to **Carolina** by **Chicago** for Nelson Emerson, December 29, 1998. Signed as a free agent by **Boston**, July 13, 2000.

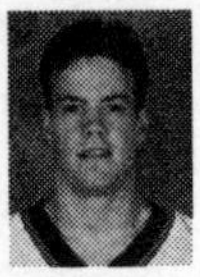

COMRIE, Paul

(KAWM-ree, PAWL) **EDM.**

Center. Shoots left. 5'11", 192 lbs. Born, Edmonton, Alta., February 7, 1977. Tampa Bay's 12th choice, 224th overall, in 1997 Entry Draft.

1993-94	Ft-Saskatchewan	AJHL	55	7	23	30	50	....	....	....	....	....	....	....	....	....	....	....	6	0	1	1	2	....	....	....
1994-95	Ft-Saskatchewan	AJHL	51	30	37	67	121	....	....	....	....	....	....	....	....	....	....	....	....	....	....	....	....	....	....	....
1995-96	U. of Denver	WCHA	38	13	10	23	61	....	....	....	....	....	....	....	....	....	....	....	....	....	....	....	....	....	....	....
1996-97	U. of Denver	WCHA	40	21	28	49	72	....	....	....	....	....	....	....	....	....	....	....	....	....	....	....	....	....	....	....
1997-98	U. of Denver	WCHA	33	17	23	40	72	....	....	....	....	....	....	....	....	....	....	....	....	....	....	....	....	....	....	....
1998-99	U. of Denver	WCHA	40	18	31	49	84	....	....	....	....	....	....	....	....	....	....	....	....	....	....	....	....	....	....	....
	Hamilton Bulldogs	AHL	7	0	1	1	0	....	....	....	....	....	....	....	....	....	....	....	8	1	3	4	2	....	....	....
99-2000	**Edmonton**	**NHL**	**15**	**1**	**2**	**3**	**4**	**0**	**0**	**0**	**11**	**9.1**	**–2**	**4**	**50.0**	**7**	**0**	**10:21**	....	....	....	....	....	....	....	....
	Hamilton Bulldogs	AHL	12	3	3	6	6	....	....	....	....	....	....	....	....	....	....	....	....	....	....	....	....	....	....	....
	NHL Totals		**15**	**1**	**2**	**3**	**4**	**0**	**0**	**0**	**11**	**9.1**		**4**	**50.0**	**7**	**0**	**10:21**	....	....	....	....	....	....	....	....

WCHA First All-Star Team (1999) • NCAA West Second All-American Team (1999)

Traded to **Edmonton** by **Tampa Bay** with Roman Hamrlik for Bryan Marchment, Steve Kelly and Jason Bonsignore, December 30, 1997.

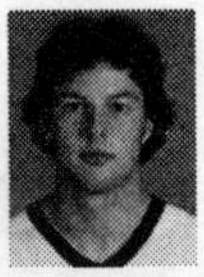

CONNOLLY, Tim

(KAHN-noh-lee, TIHM) **NYI**

Center. Shoots right. 6', 186 lbs. Born, Syracuse, NY, May 7, 1981. NY Islanders' 1st choice, 5th overall, in 1999 Entry Draft.

1996-97	Syracuse	OJHL	50	42	62	104	34	....	....	....	....	....	....	....	....	....	....	....	....	....	....	....	....	....	....	....
1997-98	Erie Otters	OHL	59	30	32	62	32	....	....	....	....	....	....	....	....	....	....	....	7	1	6	7	6	....	....	....
1998-99	Erie Otters	OHL	46	34	34	68	50	....	....	....	....	....	....	....	....	....	....	....	....	....	....	....	....	....	....	....
99-2000	**NY Islanders**	**NHL**	**81**	**14**	**20**	**34**	**44**	**2**	**1**	**1**	**114**	**12.3**	**–25**	**786**	**36.3**	**51**	**29**	**16:18**	....	....	....	....	....	....	....	....
	NHL Totals		**81**	**14**	**20**	**34**	**44**	**2**	**1**	**1**	**114**	**12.3**		**786**	**36.3**	**51**	**29**	**16:18**	....	....	....	....	....	....	....	....

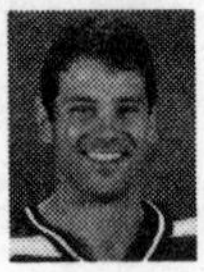

CONROY, Craig

KAHN-roi, KRAYG) **ST.L.**

Center. Shoots right. 6'2", 198 lbs. Born, Potsdam, NY, September 4, 1971. Montreal's 7th choice, 123rd overall, in 1990 Entry Draft.

1989-90	Northwood Prep	Hi-School	31	33	43	76	....	....	....	....	....	....	....	....	....	....	....	....	....	....	....	....	....	....	....	....
1990-91	Clarkson	ECAC	40	8	21	29	24	....	....	....	....	....	....	....	....	....	....	....	....	....	....	....	....	....	....	....
1991-92	Clarkson	ECAC	31	19	17	36	36	....	....	....	....	....	....	....	....	....	....	....	....	....	....	....	....	....	....	....
1992-93	Clarkson	ECAC	35	10	23	33	26	....	....	....	....	....	....	....	....	....	....	....	....	....	....	....	....	....	....	....
1993-94	Clarkson	ECAC	34	26	*40	*66	46	....	....	....	....	....	....	....	....	....	....	....	....	....	....	....	....	....	....	....
1994-95	**Montreal**	**NHL**	**6**	**1**	**0**	**1**	**0**	**0**	**0**	**0**	**4**	**25.0**	**–1**	....	....	....	....	....	....	....	....	....	....	....	....	....
	Fredericton	AHL	55	26	18	44	29	....	....	....	....	....	....	....	....	....	....	....	11	7	3	10	6	....	....	....
1995-96	**Montreal**	**NHL**	**7**	**0**	**0**	**0**	**2**	**0**	**0**	**0**	**1**	**0.0**	**–4**	....	....	....	....	....	....	....	....	....	....	....	....	....
	Fredericton	AHL	67	31	38	69	65	....	....	....	....	....	....	....	....	....	....	....	10	5	7	12	6	....	....	....
1996-97	Fredericton	AHL	9	10	6	16	10	....	....	....	....	....	....	....	....	....	....	....	....	....	....	....	....	....	....	....
	St. Louis	**NHL**	**61**	**6**	**11**	**17**	**43**	**0**	**0**	**1**	**74**	**8.1**	**0**	....	....	....	....	....	**6**	**0**	**0**	**0**	**8**	**0**	**0**	**0**
	Worcester	AHL	5	5	6	11	2	....	....	....	....	....	....	....	....	....	....	....	....	....	....	....	....	....	....	....
1997-98	**St. Louis**	**NHL**	**81**	**14**	**29**	**43**	**46**	**0**	**3**	**1**	**118**	**11.9**	**20**	....	....	....	....	....	**10**	**1**	**2**	**3**	**8**	**0**	**0**	**1**
1998-99	**St. Louis**	**NHL**	**69**	**14**	**25**	**39**	**38**	**0**	**1**	**1**	**134**	**10.4**	**14**	**1190**	**54.6**	**77**	**35**	**16:39**	**13**	**2**	**1**	**3**	**6**	**0**	**0**	**0**
99-2000	**St. Louis**	**NHL**	**79**	**12**	**15**	**27**	**36**	**1**	**2**	**3**	**98**	**12.2**	**5**	**1339**	**53.6**	**105**	**29**	**14:48**	**7**	**0**	**2**	**2**	**2**	**0**	**0**	**0**
	NHL Totals		**303**	**47**	**80**	**127**	**165**	**1**	**6**	**6**	**429**	**11.0**		**2529**	**54.1**	**182**	**64**	**15:40**	**36**	**3**	**5**	**8**	**24**	**0**	**0**	**1**

ECAC First All-Star Team (1994) • NCAA East First All-American Team (1994) • NCAA Final Four All-Tournament Team (1994)

Traded to **St. Louis** by **Montreal** with Pierre Turgeon and Rory Fitzpatrick for Murray Baron, Shayne Corson and St. Louis' 5th round choice (Gennady Razin) in 1997 Entry Draft, October 29, 1996.

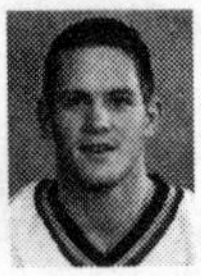

COOKE, Matt

(KOOK, MAT) **VAN.**

Left wing. Shoots left. 5'11", 205 lbs. Born, Belleville, Ont., September 7, 1978. Vancouver's 8th choice, 144th overall, in 1997 Entry Draft.

1994-95	Wellington Dukes	OJHL-B	46	9	23	32	62	....	....	....	....	....	....	....	....	....	....	....	....	....	....	....	....	....	....	....
1995-96	Windsor Spitfires	OHL	61	8	11	19	102	....	....	....	....	....	....	....	....	....	....	....	7	1	3	4	6	....	....	....
1996-97	Windsor Spitfires	OHL	65	45	50	95	146	....	....	....	....	....	....	....	....	....	....	....	5	5	5	10	10	....	....	....
1997-98	Windsor Spitfires	OHL	23	14	19	33	50	....	....	....	....	....	....	....	....	....	....	....	....	....	....	....	....	....	....	....
	Kingston	OHL	25	8	13	21	49	....	....	....	....	....	....	....	....	....	....	....	12	8	8	16	20	....	....	....
1998-99	**Vancouver**	**NHL**	**30**	**0**	**2**	**2**	**27**	**0**	**0**	**0**	**22**	**0.0**	**–12**	**189**	**40.2**	**43**	**7**	**8:07**	....	....	....	....	....	....	....	....
	Syracuse Crunch	AHL	37	15	18	33	119	....	....	....	....	....	....	....	....	....	....	....	....	....	....	....	....	....	....	....
99-2000	**Vancouver**	**NHL**	**51**	**5**	**7**	**12**	**39**	**0**	**1**	**1**	**58**	**8.6**	**3**	**71**	**39.4**	**124**	**14**	**11:48**	....	....	....	....	....	....	....	....
	Syracuse Crunch	AHL	18	5	8	13	27	....	....	....	....	....	....	....	....	....	....	....	....	....	....	....	....	....	....	....
	NHL Totals		**81**	**5**	**9**	**14**	**66**	**0**	**1**	**1**	**80**	**6.3**		**260**	**40.0**	**167**	**21**	**10:26**	....	....	....	....	....	....	....	....

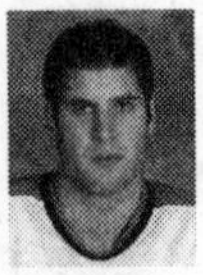

COOPER, David

(KOO-puhr, DAY-vihd)

Defense. Shoots left. 6'2", 204 lbs. Born, Ottawa, Ont., November 2, 1973. Buffalo's 1st choice, 11th overall, in 1992 Entry Draft.

1988-89	Edmonton Mets	AAHA	32	24	22	46	151	....	....	....	....	....	....	....	....	....	....	....	....	....	....	....	....	....	....	....
1989-90	Medicine Hat	WHL	61	4	11	15	65	....	....	....	....	....	....	....	....	....	....	....	3	0	2	2	2	....	....	....
1990-91	Medicine Hat	WHL	64	12	31	43	66	....	....	....	....	....	....	....	....	....	....	....	11	1	3	4	23	....	....	....
1991-92	Medicine Hat	WHL	72	17	47	64	176	....	....	....	....	....	....	....	....	....	....	....	4	1	4	5	8	....	....	....
1992-93	Medicine Hat	WHL	63	15	50	65	88	....	....	....	....	....	....	....	....	....	....	....	10	2	2	4	32	....	....	....
	Rochester	AHL	....	....	....	....	....	....	....	....	....	....	....	....	....	....	....	....	2	0	0	0	2	....	....	....
1993-94	Rochester	AHL	68	10	25	35	82	....	....	....	....	....	....	....	....	....	....	....	4	1	1	2	2	....	....	....
1994-95	Rochester	AHL	21	2	4	6	48	....	....	....	....	....	....	....	....	....	....	....	....	....	....	....	....	....	....	....
	South Carolina	ECHL	39	9	19	28	90	....	....	....	....	....	....	....	....	....	....	....	9	3	8	11	24	....	....	....
1995-96	Rochester	AHL	67	9	18	27	79	....	....	....	....	....	....	....	....	....	....	....	8	0	1	1	12	....	....	....
1996-97	**Toronto**	**NHL**	**19**	**3**	**3**	**6**	**16**	**2**	**0**	**0**	**23**	**13.0**	**–3**	....	....	....	....	....	....	....	....	....	....	....	....	....
	St. John's Leafs	AHL	44	16	19	35	65	....	....	....	....	....	....	....	....	....	....	....	....	....	....	....	....	....	....	....
1997-98	**Toronto**	**NHL**	**9**	**0**	**4**	**4**	**8**	**0**	**0**	**0**	**13**	**0.0**	**2**	....	....	....	....	....	....	....	....	....	....	....	....	....
	St. John's Leafs	AHL	60	19	23	42	117	....	....	....	....	....	....	....	....	....	....	....	4	0	1	1	6	....	....	....
1998-99	Saint John Flames	AHL	65	18	24	42	121	....	....	....	....	....	....	....	....	....	....	....	7	1	4	5	10	....	....	....
99-2000	Kassel Huskies	DEL	55	11	13	24	82	....	....	....	....	....	....	....	....	....	....	....	6	2	1	3	38	....	....	....
	NHL Totals		**28**	**3**	**7**	**10**	**24**	**2**	**0**	**0**	**36**	**8.3**		....	....	....	....	....	....	....	....	....	....	....	....	....

WHL East First All-Star Team (1992) • AHL Second All-Star Team (1998)

Signed as a free agent by **Toronto**, September 26, 1996. Traded to **Calgary** by **Toronto** for Ladislav Kohn, July 2, 1998.

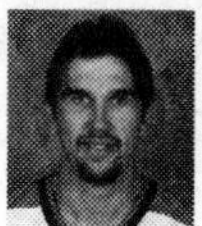

CORBET, Rene
(cohr-BAY, ruh-NAY) **PIT.**

Left wing. Shoots left. 6', 195 lbs. Born, Victoriaville, Que., June 25, 1973. Quebec's 2nd choice, 24th overall, in 1991 Entry Draft.

			Regular Season																Playoffs							
Season	Club	League	GP	G	A	Pts	PIM	PP	SH	GW	S	%	+/–	TF	F%	H	SB	Min	GP	G	A	Pts	PIM	PP	SH	GW
1989-90	Richelieu Regents	QAAA	42	53	63	116	34	....	....	....	....	....	....	....	....	....	....	....	....	....	....	....	....	....	....	....
1990-91	Drummondville	QMJHL	45	25	40	65	34	....	....	....	....	....	....	....	....	....	....	....	14	11	6	17	15	....	....	....
1991-92	Drummondville	QMJHL	56	46	50	96	90	....	....	....	....	....	....	....	....	....	....	....	4	1	2	3	17	....	....	....
1992-93	Drummondville	QMJHL	63	*79	69	*148	143	....	....	....	....	....	....	....	....	....	....	....	10	7	13	20	16	....	....	....
1993-94	**Quebec**	**NHL**	**9**	**1**	**1**	**2**	**0**	**0**	**0**	**0**	**14**	**7.1**	**1**	....	....	....	....	....	....	....	....	....	....	....	....	....
	Cornwall Aces	AHL	68	37	40	77	56	....	....	....	....	....	....	....	....	....	....	....	13	7	2	9	18	....	....	....
1994-95	**Quebec**	**NHL**	**8**	**0**	**3**	**3**	**2**	**0**	**0**	**0**	**4**	**0.0**	**3**	....	....	....	....	....	**2**	**0**	**1**	**1**	**0**	**0**	**0**	**0**
	Cornwall Aces	AHL	65	33	24	57	79	....	....	....	....	....	....	....	....	....	....	....	12	2	8	10	27	....	....	....
1995-96♦	**Colorado**	**NHL**	**33**	**3**	**6**	**9**	**33**	**0**	**0**	**0**	**35**	**8.6**	**10**	....	....	....	....	....	**8**	**3**	**2**	**5**	**2**	**1**	**0**	**1**
	Cornwall Aces	AHL	9	5	6	11	10	....	....	....	....	....	....	....	....	....	....	....	....	....	....	....	....	....	....	....
1996-97	**Colorado**	**NHL**	**76**	**12**	**15**	**27**	**67**	**1**	**0**	**3**	**128**	**9.4**	**14**	....	....	....	....	....	**17**	**2**	**2**	**4**	**27**	**0**	**0**	**0**
1997-98	**Colorado**	**NHL**	**68**	**16**	**12**	**28**	**133**	**4**	**0**	**4**	**117**	**13.7**	**8**	....	....	....	....	....	**2**	**0**	**0**	**0**	**2**	**0**	**0**	**0**
1998-99	**Colorado**	**NHL**	**53**	**8**	**14**	**22**	**58**	**2**	**0**	**1**	**82**	**9.8**	**3**	**211**	**45.0**	**37**	**16**	**11:39**	....	....	....	....	....	....	....	....
	Calgary	**NHL**	**20**	**5**	**4**	**9**	**10**	**1**	**0**	**0**	**45**	**11.1**	**–2**	**4**	**50.0**	**39**	**6**	**18:05**	....	....	....	....	....	....	....	....
99-2000	**Calgary**	**NHL**	**48**	**4**	**10**	**14**	**60**	**0**	**0**	**0**	**100**	**4.0**	**–7**	**20**	**45.0**	**74**	**24**	**11:46**	....	....	....	....	....	....	....	....
	Pittsburgh	**NHL**	**4**	**1**	**0**	**1**	**0**	**1**	**0**	**0**	**9**	**11.1**	**–4**	**0**	**0.0**	**11**	**1**	**9:55**	**7**	**1**	**1**	**2**	**9**	**0**	**0**	**0**
	NHL Totals		**319**	**50**	**65**	**115**	**363**	**9**	**0**	**8**	**534**	**9.4**		**235**	**45.1**	**161**	**47**	**12:40**	**36**	**6**	**6**	**12**	**40**	**1**	**0**	**1**

QMJHL First All-Star Team (1993) • Canadian Major Junior First All-Star Team (1993) • Won Dudley "Red" Garrett Memorial Trophy (Top Rookie - AHL) (1994)

Transferred to **Colorado** after **Quebec** franchise relocated, June 21, 1995. Traded to **Calgary** by **Colorado** with Wade Belak, Robyn Regehr and Colorado's 2nd round compensatory choice (Jarret Stoll) in 2000 Entry Draft for Theoren Fleury and Chris Dingman, February 28, 1999. Traded to **Pittsburgh** by **Calgary** with Tyler Moss for Brad Werenka, March 14, 2000.

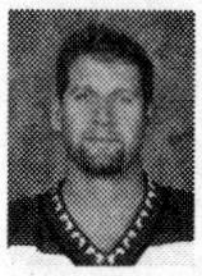

CORKUM, Bob
(KOHR-kuhm, BAWB) **L.A.**

Center. Shoots right. 6', 222 lbs. Born, Salisbury, MA, December 18, 1967. Buffalo's 3rd choice, 47th overall, in 1986 Entry Draft.

1984-85	Triton Regional	Hi-School	18	35	36	71	....	....	....	....	....	....	....	....	....	....	....	....	....	....	....	....	....	....	....	....
1985-86	U. of Maine	H-East	39	7	26	33	53	....	....	....	....	....	....	....	....	....	....	....	....	....	....	....	....	....	....	....
1986-87	U. of Maine	H-East	35	18	11	29	24	....	....	....	....	....	....	....	....	....	....	....	....	....	....	....	....	....	....	....
1987-88	U. of Maine	H-East	40	14	18	32	64	....	....	....	....	....	....	....	....	....	....	....	....	....	....	....	....	....	....	....
1988-89	U. of Maine	H-East	45	17	31	48	64	....	....	....	....	....	....	....	....	....	....	....	....	....	....	....	....	....	....	....
1989-90	**Buffalo**	**NHL**	**8**	**2**	**0**	**2**	**4**	**0**	**0**	**1**	**6**	**33.3**	**2**	....	....	....	....	....	**5**	**1**	**0**	**1**	**4**	**0**	**0**	**0**
	Rochester	AHL	43	8	11	19	45	....	....	....	....	....	....	....	....	....	....	....	12	2	5	7	16	....	....	....
1990-91	Rochester	AHL	69	13	21	34	77	....	....	....	....	....	....	....	....	....	....	....	15	4	4	8	4	....	....	....
1991-92	**Buffalo**	**NHL**	**20**	**2**	**4**	**6**	**21**	**0**	**0**	**0**	**23**	**8.7**	**–9**	....	....	....	....	....	**4**	**1**	**0**	**1**	**0**	**1**	**0**	**0**
	Rochester	AHL	52	16	12	28	47	....	....	....	....	....	....	....	....	....	....	....	8	0	6	6	8	....	....	....
1992-93	**Buffalo**	**NHL**	**68**	**6**	**4**	**10**	**38**	**0**	**1**	**1**	**69**	**8.7**	**–3**	....	....	....	....	....	**5**	**0**	**0**	**0**	**2**	**0**	**0**	**0**
1993-94	**Anaheim**	**NHL**	**76**	**23**	**28**	**51**	**18**	**3**	**3**	**0**	**180**	**12.8**	**4**	....	....	....	....	....	....	....	....	....	....	....	....	....
1994-95	**Anaheim**	**NHL**	**44**	**10**	**9**	**19**	**25**	**0**	**0**	**1**	**100**	**10.0**	**–7**	....	....	....	....	....	....	....	....	....	....	....	....	....
1995-96	**Anaheim**	**NHL**	**48**	**5**	**7**	**12**	**26**	**0**	**0**	**1**	**88**	**5.7**	**0**	....	....	....	....	....	....	....	....	....	....	....	....	....
	Philadelphia	**NHL**	**28**	**4**	**3**	**7**	**8**	**0**	**0**	**2**	**38**	**10.5**	**3**	....	....	....	....	....	**12**	**1**	**2**	**3**	**6**	**0**	**0**	**0**
1996-97	**Phoenix**	**NHL**	**80**	**9**	**11**	**20**	**40**	**0**	**1**	**3**	**119**	**7.6**	**–7**	....	....	....	....	....	**7**	**2**	**2**	**4**	**4**	**0**	**0**	**1**
1997-98	**Phoenix**	**NHL**	**76**	**12**	**9**	**21**	**28**	**0**	**5**	**0**	**105**	**11.4**	**–7**	....	....	....	....	....	**6**	**1**	**0**	**1**	**4**	**0**	**0**	**0**
1998-99	**Phoenix**	**NHL**	**77**	**9**	**10**	**19**	**17**	**0**	**0**	**0**	**146**	**6.2**	**–9**	**1644**	**51.6**	**116**	**28**	**17:15**	**7**	**0**	**1**	**1**	**4**	**0**	**0**	**0**
99-2000	**Los Angeles**	**NHL**	**45**	**5**	**6**	**11**	**14**	**0**	**0**	**0**	**45**	**11.1**	**0**	**910**	**55.3**	**90**	**22**	**14:26**	**4**	**0**	**0**	**0**	**0**	**0**	**0**	**0**
	NHL Totals		**570**	**87**	**91**	**178**	**239**	**3**	**10**	**9**	**919**	**9.5**		**2554**	**52.9**	**206**	**50**	**16:13**	**50**	**6**	**5**	**11**	**24**	**1**	**0**	**1**

Claimed by **Anaheim** from **Buffalo** in Expansion Draft, June 24, 1993. Traded to **Philadelphia** by **Anaheim** for Chris Herperger and Winnipeg's 7th round choice (previously acquired, Anaheim selected Tony Monahan) in 1997 Entry Draft, February 6, 1996. Claimed by **Phoenix** from **Philadelphia** in Waiver Draft, September 30, 1996. Signed as a free agent by **LA Kings**, December 28, 1999.

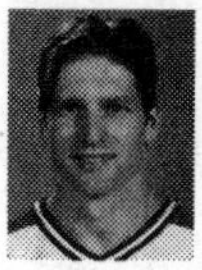

CORSON, Shayne
(KOHR-sohn, SHAYN) **TOR.**

Left wing. Shoots left. 6'1", 202 lbs. Born, Barrie, Ont., August 13, 1966. Montreal's 2nd choice, 8th overall, in 1984 Entry Draft.

1982-83	Barrie Colts	OJHL-B	23	13	29	42	87	....	....	....	....	....	....	....	....	....	....	....	....	....	....	....	....	....	....	....
1983-84	Brantford	OHL	66	25	46	71	165	....	....	....	....	....	....	....	....	....	....	....	6	4	1	5	26	....	....	....
1984-85	Hamilton Hawks	OHL	54	27	63	90	154	....	....	....	....	....	....	....	....	....	....	....	11	3	7	10	19	....	....	....
1985-86	Hamilton Hawks	OHL	47	41	57	98	153	....	....	....	....	....	....	....	....	....	....	....	....	....	....	....	....	....	....	....
	Montreal	**NHL**	**3**	**0**	**0**	**0**	**2**	**0**	**0**	**0**	**1**	**0.0**	**–3**	....	....	....	....	....	....	....	....	....	....	....	....	....
1986-87	**Montreal**	**NHL**	**55**	**12**	**11**	**23**	**144**	**0**	**1**	**3**	**69**	**17.4**	**10**	....	....	....	....	....	**17**	**6**	**5**	**11**	**30**	**1**	**1**	**1**
1987-88	**Montreal**	**NHL**	**71**	**12**	**27**	**39**	**152**	**2**	**0**	**2**	**90**	**13.3**	**22**	....	....	....	....	....	**3**	**1**	**0**	**1**	**12**	**0**	**0**	**0**
1988-89	**Montreal**	**NHL**	**80**	**26**	**24**	**50**	**193**	**10**	**0**	**3**	**133**	**19.5**	**–1**	....	....	....	....	....	**21**	**4**	**5**	**9**	**65**	**2**	**0**	**2**
1989-90	**Montreal**	**NHL**	**76**	**31**	**44**	**75**	**144**	**7**	**0**	**6**	**192**	**16.1**	**33**	....	....	....	....	....	**11**	**2**	**8**	**10**	**20**	**0**	**0**	**0**
1990-91	**Montreal**	**NHL**	**71**	**23**	**24**	**47**	**138**	**7**	**0**	**2**	**164**	**14.0**	**9**	....	....	....	....	....	**13**	**9**	**6**	**15**	**36**	**4**	**1**	**3**
1991-92	**Montreal**	**NHL**	**64**	**17**	**36**	**53**	**118**	**3**	**0**	**2**	**165**	**10.3**	**15**	....	....	....	....	....	**10**	**2**	**5**	**7**	**15**	**0**	**0**	**0**
1992-93	**Edmonton**	**NHL**	**80**	**16**	**31**	**47**	**209**	**9**	**2**	**1**	**164**	**9.8**	**–19**	....	....	....	....	....	....	....	....	....	....	....	....	....
1993-94	**Edmonton**	**NHL**	**64**	**25**	**29**	**54**	**118**	**11**	**0**	**3**	**171**	**14.6**	**–8**	....	....	....	....	....	....	....	....	....	....	....	....	....
1994-95	**Edmonton**	**NHL**	**48**	**12**	**24**	**36**	**86**	**2**	**0**	**1**	**131**	**9.2**	**–17**	....	....	....	....	....	....	....	....	....	....	....	....	....
1995-96	**St. Louis**	**NHL**	**77**	**18**	**28**	**46**	**192**	**13**	**0**	**0**	**150**	**12.0**	**3**	....	....	....	....	....	**13**	**8**	**6**	**14**	**22**	**6**	**1**	**1**
1996-97	**St. Louis**	**NHL**	**11**	**2**	**1**	**3**	**24**	**1**	**0**	**0**	**19**	**10.5**	**–4**	....	....	....	....	....	....	....	....	....	....	....	....	....
	Montreal	**NHL**	**47**	**6**	**15**	**21**	**80**	**2**	**0**	**2**	**96**	**6.3**	**–5**	....	....	....	....	....	**5**	**1**	**0**	**1**	**4**	**0**	**1**	**0**
1997-98	**Montreal**	**NHL**	**62**	**21**	**34**	**55**	**108**	**14**	**1**	**1**	**142**	**14.8**	**2**	....	....	....	....	....	**10**	**3**	**6**	**9**	**26**	**1**	**0**	**1**
	Canada	Olympics	6	1	1	2	2	....	....	....	....	....	....	....	....	....	....	....	....	....	....	....	....	....	....	....
1998-99	**Montreal**	**NHL**	**63**	**12**	**20**	**32**	**147**	**7**	**0**	**4**	**142**	**8.5**	**–10**	**184**	**45.1**	**71**	**38**	**20:42**	....	....	....	....	....	....	....	....
99-2000	**Montreal**	**NHL**	**70**	**8**	**20**	**28**	**115**	**2**	**0**	**1**	**121**	**6.6**	**–2**	**445**	**43.4**	**121**	**48**	**19:05**	....	....	....	....	....	....	....	....
	NHL Totals		**942**	**241**	**368**	**609**	**1970**	**90**	**4**	**31**	**1950**	**12.4**		**629**	**43.9**	**192**	**86**	**19:51**	**103**	**36**	**41**	**77**	**230**	**14**	**4**	**8**

Played in NHL All-Star Game (1990, 1994, 1998)

Traded to **Edmonton** by **Montreal** with Brent Gilchrist and Vladimir Vujtek for Vincent Damphousse and Edmonton's 4th round choice (Adam Wiesel) in 1993 Entry Draft, August 27, 1992. Signed as a free agent by **St. Louis**, July 28, 1995. Traded to **Montreal** by **St. Louis** with Murray Baron and St. Louis' 5th round choice (Gennady Razin) in 1997 Entry Draft for Pierre Turgeon, Rory Fitzpatrick and Craig Conroy, October 29, 1996. Signed as a free agent by **Toronto**, July 4, 2000.

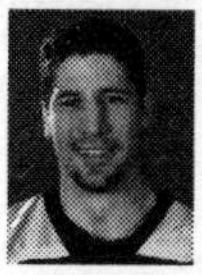

COTE, Patrick
(KOH-tay, PA-trihK) **EDM.**

Left wing. Shoots left. 6'3", 220 lbs. Born, Lasalle, Que., January 24, 1975. Dallas' 2nd choice, 37th overall, in 1995 Entry Draft.

1993-94	Beauport	QMJHL	48	2	4	6	230	....	....	....	....	....	....	....	....	....	....	....	12	1	0	1	61	....	....	....
1994-95	Beauport	QMJHL	56	20	20	40	314	....	....	....	....	....	....	....	....	....	....	....	17	8	8	16	115	....	....	....
1995-96	**Dallas**	**NHL**	**2**	**0**	**0**	**0**	**5**	**0**	**0**	**0**	**0**	**0.0**	**–2**	....	....	....	....	....	....	....	....	....	....	....	....	....
	Michigan K-Wings	IHL	57	4	6	10	239	....	....	....	....	....	....	....	....	....	....	....	3	0	0	0	2	....	....	....
1996-97	**Dallas**	**NHL**	**3**	**0**	**0**	**0**	**27**	**0**	**0**	**0**	**1**	**0.0**	**0**	....	....	....	....	....	....	....	....	....	....	....	....	....
	Michigan K-Wings	IHL	58	14	10	24	237	....	....	....	....	....	....	....	....	....	....	....	4	2	0	2	6	....	....	....
1997-98	**Dallas**	**NHL**	**3**	**0**	**0**	**0**	**15**	**0**	**0**	**0**	**3**	**0.0**	**–1**	....	....	....	....	....	....	....	....	....	....	....	....	....
	Michigan K-Wings	IHL	4	2	0	2	4	....	....	....	....	....	....	....	....	....	....	....	....	....	....	....	....	....	....	....
1998-99	**Nashville**	**NHL**	**70**	**1**	**2**	**3**	**242**	**0**	**0**	**0**	**21**	**4.8**	**–7**	**0**	**0.0**	**47**	**7**	**4:14**	....	....	....	....	....	....	....	....
99-2000	**Nashville**	**NHL**	**21**	**0**	**0**	**0**	**70**	....	....	....	**8**	**0.0**	**–7**	**0**	**0.0**	**0**	**0**	**0:00**	....	....	....	....	....	....	....	....
	NHL Totals		**99**	**1**	**2**	**3**	**359**	**0**	**0**	**0**	**33**	**3.0**		**0**	**0.0**	**47**	**7**	**4:14**	....	....	....	....	....	....	....	....

Claimed by **Nashville** from **Dallas** in Expansion Draft, June 26, 1998. Traded to **Edmonton** by **Nashville** for Phoenix's 5th round choice (previously acquired, Nashville selected Matt Koalska) in 2000 Entry Draft, June 12, 2000.

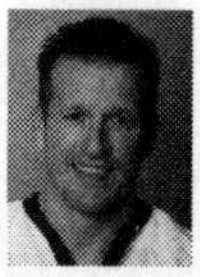

COTE, Sylvain
(KOH-tay, SIHL-vayn) **WSH.**

Defense. Shoots right. 6', 190 lbs. Born, Quebec City, Que., January 19, 1966. Hartford's 1st choice, 11th overall, in 1984 Entry Draft.

1981-82	Ste-Foy Governors	QAAA	37	1	6	7	....	....	....	....	....	....	....	....	....	....	....	....	....	....	....	....	....	....	....	....
1982-83	Quebec Remparts	QMJHL	66	10	24	34	50	....	....	....	....	....	....	....	....	....	....	....	....	....	....	....	....	....	....	....
1983-84	Quebec Remparts	QMJHL	66	15	50	65	89	....	....	....	....	....	....	....	....	....	....	....	5	1	1	2	0	....	....	....
1984-85	**Hartford**	**NHL**	**67**	**3**	**9**	**12**	**17**	**1**	**0**	**1**	**90**	**3.3**	**–30**	....	....	....	....	....	....	....	....	....	....	....	....	....
1985-86	Hull Olympiques	QMJHL	26	10	33	43	14	....	....	....	....	....	....	....	....	....	....	....	13	6	*28	34	22	....	....	....
	Hartford	**NHL**	**2**	**0**	**0**	**0**	**0**	**0**	**0**	**0**	**0**	**0.0**	**1**	....	....	....	....	....	....	....	....	....	....	....	....	....
	Binghamton	AHL	12	2	4	6	0	....	....	....	....	....	....	....	....	....	....	....	....	....	....	....	....	....	....	....

			Regular Season																Playoffs							
Season	Club	League	GP	G	A	Pts	PIM	PP	SH	GW	S	%	+/–	TF	F%	H	SB	Min	GP	G	A	Pts	PIM	PP	SH	GW
1986-87	Hartford	NHL	67	2	8	10	20	0	0	0	100	2.0	11	....	....	....	....	....	2	0	2	2	2	0	0	0
1987-88	Hartford	NHL	67	7	21	28	30	0	1	0	142	4.9	–8	....	....	....	....	....	6	1	1	2	4	1	0	0
1988-89	Hartford	NHL	78	8	9	17	49	1	0	0	130	6.2	–7	....	....	....	....	....	3	0	1	1	4	0	0	0
1989-90	Hartford	NHL	28	4	2	6	14	1	0	1	50	8.0	2	....	....	....	....	....	5	0	0	0	2	0	0	0
1990-91	Hartford	NHL	73	7	12	19	17	1	0	0	154	4.5	–17	....	....	....	....	....	6	0	2	2	2	0	0	0
1991-92	Washington	NHL	78	11	29	40	31	6	0	2	151	7.3	7	....	....	....	....	....	7	1	2	3	4	0	0	0
1992-93	Washington	NHL	77	21	29	50	34	8	2	3	206	10.2	28	....	....	....	....	....	6	1	1	2	4	0	0	0
1993-94	Washington	NHL	84	16	35	51	66	3	2	2	212	7.5	30	....	....	....	....	....	9	1	8	9	6	0	0	0
1994-95	Washington	NHL	47	5	14	19	53	1	0	2	124	4.0	2	....	....	....	....	....	7	1	3	4	2	0	0	0
1995-96	Washington	NHL	81	5	33	38	40	3	0	2	212	2.4	5	....	....	....	....	....	6	2	0	2	12	1	0	0
1996-97	Washington	NHL	57	6	18	24	28	2	0	0	131	4.6	11	....	....	....	....	....	....	....	....	....	....	....	....	....
1997-98	Washington	NHL	59	1	15	16	36	0	0	0	83	1.2	–5	....	....	....	....	....	....	....	....	....	....	....	....	....
	Toronto	NHL	12	3	6	9	6	1	0	1	20	15.0	2	....	....	....	....	....	....	....	....	....	....	....	....	....
1998-99	Toronto	NHL	79	5	24	29	28	0	0	1	119	4.2	22	1	0.0	76	95	21:04	17	2	1	3	10	0	0	0
99-2000	Toronto	NHL	3	0	1	1	0	0	0	0	3	0.0	1	0	0.0	6	3	21:40	....	....	....	....	....	....	....	....
	Chicago	NHL	45	6	18	24	14	5	0	2	78	7.7	–4	1	100.0	49	62	23:22	....	....	....	....	....	....	....	....
	Dallas	NHL	28	2	8	10	14	0	0	0	47	4.3	6	0	0.0	33	23	18:10	23	2	1	3	8	2	0	0
	NHL Totals		1032	112	291	403	497	33	5	17	2052	5.5		2	50.0	164	183	21:13	97	11	22	33	60	4	0	0

QMJHL Second All-Star Team (1984) • QMJHL First All-Star Team (1986)

Traded to **Washington** by **Hartford** for Washington's 2nd round choice (Andrei Nikolishin) in 1992 Entry Draft, September 8, 1991. Traded to **Toronto** by **Washington** for Jeff Brown, March 24, 1998. Traded to **Chicago** by **Toronto** for Chicago's 2nd round choice in 2001 Entry Draft and a conditional choice in 2001 Entry Draft, October 8, 1999. Traded to **Dallas** by **Chicago** with Dave Manson for Kevin Dean, Derek Plante and Dallas' 2nd round choice in 2001 Entry Draft, February 8, 2000. Signed as a free agent by **Washington**, July 7, 2000.

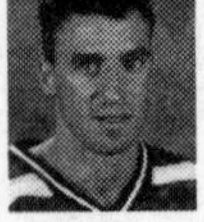

COURTNALL, Geoff

(KOHRT-nahl, JEHF)

Left wing. Shoots left. 6'1", 204 lbs. Born, Duncan, B.C., August 18, 1962.

Season	Club	League	GP	G	A	Pts	PIM	PP	SH	GW	S	%	+/–	TF	F%	H	SB	Min	GP	G	A	Pts	PIM	PP	SH	GW
1980-81	Victoria Cougars	WHL	11	3	4	7	6	....	....	....	....	....	....	....	....	....	....	....	15	2	1	3	7	....	....	....
1981-82	Victoria Cougars	WHL	72	35	57	92	100	....	....	....	....	....	....	....	....	....	....	....	4	1	0	1	2	....	....	....
1982-83	Victoria Cougars	WHL	71	41	73	114	186	....	....	....	....	....	....	....	....	....	....	....	12	6	7	13	42	....	....	....
1983-84	Boston	NHL	4	0	0	0	0	0	0	0	1	0.0	–1	....	....	....	....	....	....	....	....	....	....	....	....	....
	Hershey Bears	AHL	74	14	12	26	51	....	....	....	....	....	....	....	....	....	....	....	....	....	....	....	....	....	....	....
1984-85	Boston	NHL	64	12	16	28	82	0	0	1	91	13.2	–3	....	....	....	....	....	5	0	2	2	7	0	0	0
	Hershey Bears	AHL	9	8	4	12	4	....	....	....	....	....	....	....	....	....	....	....	....	....	....	....	....	....	....	....
1985-86	Boston	NHL	64	21	16	37	61	2	0	4	161	13.0	1	....	....	....	....	....	3	0	0	0	2	0	0	0
	Moncton Flames	AHL	12	8	8	16	6	....	....	....	....	....	....	....	....	....	....	....	....	....	....	....	....	....	....	....
1986-87	Boston	NHL	65	13	23	36	117	2	0	1	178	7.3	–4	....	....	....	....	....	1	0	0	0	0	0	0	0
1987-88	Boston	NHL	62	32	26	58	108	8	0	4	220	14.5	24	....	....	....	....	....	....	....	....	....	....	....	....	....
	♦ Edmonton	NHL	12	4	4	8	15	0	0	1	32	12.5	1	....	....	....	....	....	19	0	3	3	23	0	0	0
1988-89	Washington	NHL	79	42	38	80	112	16	0	6	239	17.6	11	....	....	....	....	....	6	2	5	7	12	1	0	0
1989-90	Washington	NHL	80	35	39	74	104	9	0	2	307	11.4	27	....	....	....	....	....	15	4	9	13	32	1	0	2
1990-91	St. Louis	NHL	66	27	30	57	56	9	0	6	216	12.5	19	....	....	....	....	....	....	....	....	....	....	....	....	....
	Vancouver	NHL	11	6	2	8	8	3	0	2	47	12.8	–3	....	....	....	....	....	6	3	5	8	4	0	0	0
1991-92	Vancouver	NHL	70	23	34	57	116	12	0	3	281	8.2	–6	....	....	....	....	....	12	6	8	14	20	2	0	1
1992-93	Vancouver	NHL	84	31	46	77	167	9	0	11	214	14.5	27	....	....	....	....	....	12	4	10	14	12	1	0	1
1993-94	Vancouver	NHL	82	26	44	70	123	12	1	2	264	9.8	15	....	....	....	....	....	24	9	10	19	51	0	1	3
1994-95	Vancouver	NHL	45	16	18	34	81	7	0	1	144	11.1	2	....	....	....	....	....	11	4	2	6	34	3	1	1
1995-96	St. Louis	NHL	69	24	16	40	101	7	1	1	228	10.5	–9	....	....	....	....	....	13	0	3	3	14	0	0	0
1996-97	St. Louis	NHL	82	17	40	57	86	4	0	2	203	8.4	3	....	....	....	....	....	6	3	1	4	23	1	0	2
1997-98	St. Louis	NHL	79	31	31	62	94	6	0	5	189	16.4	12	....	....	....	....	....	10	2	8	10	18	1	0	0
1998-99	St. Louis	NHL	24	5	7	12	28	1	0	2	60	8.3	2	1	100.0	21	4	14:48	13	2	4	6	10	2	0	0
99-2000	St. Louis	NHL	6	2	2	4	6	0	0	1	15	13.3	3	0	0.0	7	2	14:20	....	....	....	....	....	....	....	....
	NHL Totals		1048	367	432	799	1465	107	2	55	3090	11.9		1	100.0	28	6	14:42	156	39	70	109	262	12	2	10

Signed as a free agent by **Boston**, July 6, 1983. Traded to **Edmonton** by **Boston** with Bill Ranford and Boston's 2nd round choice (Petro Koivunen) in 1988 Entry Draft for Andy Moog, March 8, 1988. Rights traded to **Washington** by **Edmonton** for Greg C. Adams, July 22, 1988. Traded to **St. Louis** by **Washington** for Peter Zezel and Mike Lalor, July 13, 1990. Traded to **Vancouver** by **St. Louis** with Robert Dirk, Sergio Momesso, Cliff Ronning and St. Louis' 5th round choice (Brian Loney) in 1992 Entry Draft for Dan Quinn and Garth Butcher, March 5, 1991. Signed as a free agent by **St. Louis**, July 14, 1995. • Suffered eventual career-ending head injury in game vs. San Jose, November 27, 1998. • Officially announced retirement, November 18, 1999.

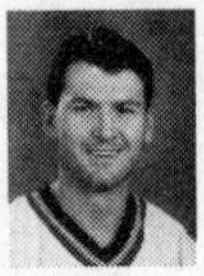

COURVILLE, Larry

(KOOR-vihl, LAIR-ree) **S.J.**

Left wing. Shoots left. 6'1", 180 lbs. Born, Timmins, Ont., April 2, 1975. Vancouver's 2nd choice, 61st overall, in 1995 Entry Draft.

Season	Club	League	GP	G	A	Pts	PIM	PP	SH	GW	S	%	+/–	TF	F%	H	SB	Min	GP	G	A	Pts	PIM	PP	SH	GW
1990-91	Waterloo Siskins	OJHL-B	47	20	18	38	144	....	....	....	....	....	....	....	....	....	....	....	....	....	....	....	....	....	....	....
1991-92	Cornwall Royals	OHL	60	8	12	20	80	....	....	....	....	....	....	....	....	....	....	....	6	0	0	0	8	....	....	....
1992-93	Newmarket	OHL	64	21	18	39	181	....	....	....	....	....	....	....	....	....	....	....	7	0	6	6	14	....	....	....
1993-94	Newmarket	OHL	39	20	19	39	134	....	....	....	....	....	....	....	....	....	....	....	....	....	....	....	....	....	....	....
	Moncton Hawks	AHL	8	2	0	2	37	....	....	....	....	....	....	....	....	....	....	....	10	2	2	4	27	....	....	....
1994-95	Sarnia Sting	OHL	16	9	9	18	58	....	....	....	....	....	....	....	....	....	....	....	....	....	....	....	....	....	....	....
	Oshawa Generals	OHL	28	25	30	55	72	....	....	....	....	....	....	....	....	....	....	....	7	4	10	14	10	....	....	....
1995-96	Vancouver	NHL	3	1	0	1	0	0	0	1	2	50.0	1	....	....	....	....	....	....	....	....	....	....	....	....	....
	Syracuse Crunch	AHL	71	17	32	49	127	....	....	....	....	....	....	....	....	....	....	....	14	5	3	8	10	....	....	....
1996-97	Vancouver	NHL	19	0	2	2	11	0	0	0	11	0.0	–4	....	....	....	....	....	....	....	....	....	....	....	....	....
	Syracuse Crunch	AHL	54	20	24	44	103	....	....	....	....	....	....	....	....	....	....	....	3	0	1	1	20	....	....	....
1997-98	Vancouver	NHL	11	0	0	0	5	0	0	0	3	0.0	–7	....	....	....	....	....	....	....	....	....	....	....	....	....
	Syracuse Crunch	AHL	29	6	12	18	84	....	....	....	....	....	....	....	....	....	....	....	....	....	....	....	....	....	....	....
1998-99	Syracuse Crunch	AHL	71	13	28	41	155	....	....	....	....	....	....	....	....	....	....	....	....	....	....	....	....	....	....	....
99-2000	Kentucky	AHL	61	11	12	23	107	....	....	....	....	....	....	....	....	....	....	....	9	1	5	6	16	....	....	....
	NHL Totals		33	1	2	3	16	0	0	1	16	6.3		....	....	....	....	....	....	....	....	....	....	....	....	....

• Re-entered NHL draft. Originally Winnipeg's 6th choice, 119th overall, in 1993 Entry Draft.

OHL Second All-Star Team (1995)

Signed as a free agent by **Kentucky** (AHL), September 1, 1999. Signed as a free agent by **San Jose**, September 1, 2000.

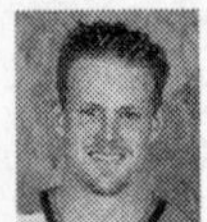

COWAN, Jeff

(KOW-an, JEHF) **CGY.**

Left wing. Shoots left. 6'2", 192 lbs. Born, Scarborough, Ont., September 27, 1976.

Season	Club	League	GP	G	A	Pts	PIM	PP	SH	GW	S	%	+/–	TF	F%	H	SB	Min	GP	G	A	Pts	PIM	PP	SH	GW
1992-93	Guelph Platers	OJHL-B	45	8	8	16	22	....	....	....	....	....	....	....	....	....	....	....	....	....	....	....	....	....	....	....
1993-94	Guelph Platers	OJHL-B	43	30	26	56	96	....	....	....	....	....	....	....	....	....	....	....	....	....	....	....	....	....	....	....
	Guelph Storm	OHL	17	1	0	1	5	....	....	....	....	....	....	....	....	....	....	....	....	....	....	....	....	....	....	....
1994-95	Guelph Storm	OHL	51	10	7	17	14	....	....	....	....	....	....	....	....	....	....	....	14	1	1	2	0	....	....	....
1995-96	Barrie Colts	OHL	66	38	14	52	29	....	....	....	....	....	....	....	....	....	....	....	5	1	2	3	6	....	....	....
1996-97	Saint John Flames	AHL	22	5	5	10	8	....	....	....	....	....	....	....	....	....	....	....	....	....	....	....	....	....	....	....
	Roanoke Express	ECHL	47	21	13	34	42	....	....	....	....	....	....	....	....	....	....	....	....	....	....	....	....	....	....	....
1997-98	Saint John Flames	AHL	69	15	13	28	23	....	....	....	....	....	....	....	....	....	....	....	13	4	1	5	14	....	....	....
1998-99	Saint John Flames	AHL	71	7	12	19	117	....	....	....	....	....	....	....	....	....	....	....	4	0	1	1	10	....	....	....
99-2000	Calgary	NHL	13	4	1	5	16	0	0	0	26	15.4	2	0	0.0	22	5	10:22	....	....	....	....	....	....	....	....
	Saint John Flames	AHL	47	15	10	25	77	....	....	....	....	....	....	....	....	....	....	....	....	....	....	....	....	....	....	....
	NHL Totals		13	4	1	5	16	0	0	0	26	15.4		0	0.0	22	5	10:22	....	....	....	....	....	....	....	....

Signed as a free agent by **Calgary**, October 2, 1995.

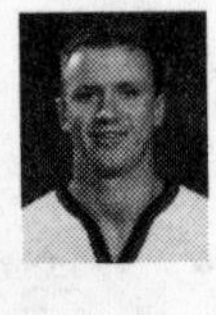

CRAIG, Mike

(KRAYG, MIGHK) **COL.**

Right wing. Shoots right. 6'1", 180 lbs. Born, St. Mary's, Ont., June 6, 1971. Minnesota's 2nd choice, 28th overall, in 1989 Entry Draft.

Season	Club	League	GP	G	A	Pts	PIM	PP	SH	GW	S	%	+/–	TF	F%	H	SB	Min	GP	G	A	Pts	PIM	PP	SH	GW
1986-87	Woodstock Vets	OJHL-C	32	29	19	48	64	....	....	....	....	....	....	....	....	....	....	....	....	....	....	....	....	....	....	....
1987-88	Oshawa Generals	OHL	61	6	10	16	39	....	....	....	....	....	....	....	....	....	....	....	7	7	0	1	11	....	....	....
1988-89	Oshawa Generals	OHL	63	36	36	72	34	....	....	....	....	....	....	....	....	....	....	....	6	3	1	4	6	....	....	....
1989-90	Oshawa Generals	OHL	43	36	40	76	85	....	....	....	....	....	....	....	....	....	....	....	17	10	16	26	46	....	....	....
1990-91	Minnesota	NHL	39	8	4	12	32	1	0	2	59	13.6	–11	....	....	....	....	....	10	1	1	2	20	1	0	1
1991-92	Minnesota	NHL	67	15	16	31	155	4	0	4	136	11.0	–12	....	....	....	....	....	4	1	0	1	7	0	0	0
1992-93	Minnesota	NHL	70	15	23	38	106	7	0	0	131	11.5	–11	....	....	....	....	....	....	....	....	....	....	....	....	....

			Regular Season																Playoffs							
Season	Club	League	GP	G	A	Pts	PIM	PP	SH	GW	S	%	+/-	TF	F%	H	SB	Min	GP	G	A	Pts	PIM	PP	SH	GW
1993-94	**Dallas**	**NHL**	**72**	**13**	**24**	**37**	**139**	**3**	**0**	**2**	**150**	**8.7**	**–14**	....	....	....	....	....	**4**	**0**	**0**	**0**	**2**	**0**	**0**	**0**
1994-95	**Toronto**	**NHL**	**37**	**5**	**5**	**10**	**12**	**1**	**0**	**1**	**61**	**8.2**	**–21**	....	....	....	....	....	**2**	**0**	**1**	**1**	**2**	**0**	**0**	**0**
1995-96	**Toronto**	**NHL**	**70**	**8**	**12**	**20**	**42**	**1**	**0**	**1**	**108**	**7.4**	**–8**	....	....	....	....	....	**6**	**0**	**0**	**0**	**18**	**0**	**0**	**0**
1996-97	**Toronto**	**NHL**	**65**	**7**	**13**	**20**	**62**	**1**	**0**	**0**	**128**	**5.5**	**–20**	....	....	....	....	....	....	....	....	....	....	....	....	....
1997-98	San Antonio	IHL	12	4	1	5	18	....	....	....	....	....	....	....	....	....	....	....	....	....	....	....	....	....	....	....
	Kansas City	IHL	59	14	33	47	68	....	....	....	....	....	....	....	....	....	....	....	11	5	5	10	28	....	....	....
1998-99	**San Jose**	**NHL**	**1**	**0**	**0**	**0**	**0**	**0**	**0**	**0**	**1**	**0.0**	**–1**	**0**	**0.0**	**1**	**1**	**11:25**	....	....	....	....	....	....	....	....
	Kentucky	AHL	52	27	17	44	72	....	....	....	....	....	....	....	....	....	....	....	12	5	4	9	18	....	....	....
99-2000	Kentucky	AHL	76	39	39	78	116	....	....	....	....	....	....	....	....	....	....	....	9	5	5	10	14	....	....	....
	NHL Totals		**421**	**71**	**97**	**168**	**548**	**18**	**0**	**10**	**774**	**9.2**		**0**	**0.0**	**1**	**1**	**11:25**	**26**	**2**	**2**	**4**	**49**	**1**	**0**	**1**

Transferred to **Dallas** after **Minnesota** franchise relocated, June 9, 1993. Signed as a free agent by **Toronto**, July 29, 1994. Signed as a free agent by **San Jose**, July 13, 1998. Signed as a free agent by **Colorado**, August 2, 2000.

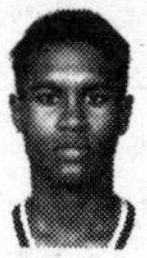

CRAIGWELL, Dale

(KRAYG-wehl, DAYL)

Center. Shoots left. 5'11", 180 lbs. Born, Toronto, Ont., April 24, 1971. San Jose's 11th choice, 199th overall, in 1991 Entry Draft.

Season	Club	League	GP	G	A	Pts	PIM	PP	SH	GW	S	%	+/-	TF	F%	H	SB	Min	GP	G	A	Pts	PIM	PP	SH	GW
1987-88	Oshawa Legion	OMHA	60	49	57	106	42	....	....	....	....	....	....	....	....	....	....	....	....	....	....	....	....	....	....	....
1988-89	Oshawa Generals	OHL	55	9	14	23	15	....	....	....	....	....	....	....	....	....	....	....	....	....	....	....	....	....	....	....
1989-90	Oshawa Generals	OHL	64	22	41	63	39	....	....	....	....	....	....	....	....	....	....	....	17	7	7	14	11	....	....	....
1990-91	Oshawa Generals	OHL	56	27	68	95	34	....	....	....	....	....	....	....	....	....	....	....	16	7	16	23	9	....	....	....
1991-92	**San Jose**	**NHL**	**32**	**5**	**11**	**16**	**8**	**4**	**0**	**2**	**38**	**13.2**	**–3**	....	....	....	....	....	....	....	....	....	....	....	....	....
	Kansas City	IHL	48	6	19	25	29	....	....	....	....	....	....	....	....	....	....	....	12	4	7	11	4	....	....	....
1992-93	**San Jose**	**NHL**	**8**	**3**	**1**	**4**	**4**	**0**	**0**	**0**	**7**	**42.9**	**–4**	....	....	....	....	....	....	....	....	....	....	....	....	....
	Kansas City	IHL	60	15	38	53	24	....	....	....	....	....	....	....	....	....	....	....	12	*7	5	12	2	....	....	....
1993-94	**San Jose**	**NHL**	**58**	**3**	**6**	**9**	**16**	**0**	**1**	**0**	**35**	**8.6**	**–13**	....	....	....	....	....	....	....	....	....	....	....	....	....
	Kansas City	IHL	5	3	1	4	0	....	....	....	....	....	....	....	....	....	....	....	....	....	....	....	....	....	....	....
1994-95	Kansas City	IHL	DID NOT PLAY – INJURED																							
1995-96	San Francisco	IHL	75	11	49	60	38	....	....	....	....	....	....	....	....	....	....	....	4	2	0	2	0	....	....	....
1996-97	Kansas City	IHL	82	17	51	68	34	....	....	....	....	....	....	....	....	....	....	....	3	1	0	1	0	....	....	....
1997-98	Kansas City	IHL	81	13	42	55	12	....	....	....	....	....	....	....	....	....	....	....	11	2	9	11	2	....	....	....
1998-99	Augsburger EV	DEL	16	1	4	5	4	....	....	....	....	....	....	....	....	....	....	....	....	....	....	....	....	....	....	....
	Kansas City	IHL	61	11	28	39	14	....	....	....	....	....	....	....	....	....	....	....	3	0	2	2	2	....	....	....
99-2000	Sheffield Steelers	Britain	24	7	17	24	0	....	....	....	....	....	....	....	....	....	....	....	7	0	6	6	8	....	....	....
	NHL Totals		**98**	**11**	**18**	**29**	**28**	**4**	**1**	**2**	**80**	**13.8**		....	....	....	....	....	....	....	....	....	....	....	....	....

• Missed entire 1994-95 season recovering from ankle injury suffered during training camp, September, 1994.

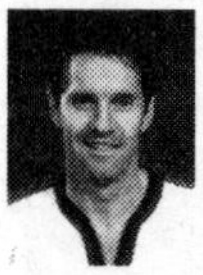

CRAVEN, Murray

(KRAY-vehn, MUHR-ray)

Left wing. Shoots left. 6'3", 195 lbs. Born, Medicine Hat, Alta., July 20, 1964. Detroit's 1st choice, 17th overall, in 1982 Entry Draft.

Season	Club	League	GP	G	A	Pts	PIM	PP	SH	GW	S	%	+/-	TF	F%	H	SB	Min	GP	G	A	Pts	PIM	PP	SH	GW
1980-81	Medicine Hat	WHL	69	5	10	15	18	....	....	....	....	....	....	....	....	....	....	....	5	0	0	0	2	....	....	....
1981-82	Medicine Hat	WHL	72	35	46	81	49	....	....	....	....	....	....	....	....	....	....	....	....	....	....	....	....	....	....	....
1982-83	Medicine Hat	WHL	28	17	29	46	35	....	....	....	....	....	....	....	....	....	....	....	....	....	....	....	....	....	....	....
	Detroit	**NHL**	**31**	**4**	**7**	**11**	**6**	**0**	**0**	**1**	**21**	**19.0**	**4**	....	....	....	....	....	....	....	....	....	....	....	....	....
1983-84	Medicine Hat	WHL	48	38	56	94	53	....	....	....	....	....	....	....	....	....	....	....	4	5	3	8	4	....	....	....
	Detroit	**NHL**	**15**	**0**	**4**	**4**	**6**	**0**	**0**	**0**	**8**	**0.0**	**2**	....	....	....	....	....	....	....	....	....	....	....	....	....
1984-85	**Philadelphia**	**NHL**	**80**	**26**	**35**	**61**	**30**	**2**	**2**	**5**	**142**	**18.3**	**45**	....	....	....	....	....	**19**	**4**	**6**	**10**	**11**	**1**	**1**	**1**
1985-86	**Philadelphia**	**NHL**	**78**	**21**	**33**	**54**	**34**	**2**	**0**	**6**	**182**	**11.5**	**24**	....	....	....	....	....	**5**	**0**	**3**	**3**	**4**	**0**	**0**	**0**
1986-87	**Philadelphia**	**NHL**	**77**	**19**	**30**	**49**	**38**	**5**	**3**	**2**	**98**	**19.4**	**1**	....	....	....	....	....	**12**	**3**	**1**	**4**	**9**	**2**	**0**	**0**
1987-88	**Philadelphia**	**NHL**	**72**	**30**	**46**	**76**	**58**	**6**	**2**	**2**	**184**	**16.3**	**25**	....	....	....	....	....	**7**	**2**	**5**	**7**	**4**	**0**	**0**	**1**
1988-89	**Philadelphia**	**NHL**	**51**	**9**	**28**	**37**	**52**	**0**	**0**	**2**	**89**	**10.1**	**4**	....	....	....	....	....	**1**	**0**	**0**	**0**	**0**	**0**	**0**	**0**
1989-90	**Philadelphia**	**NHL**	**76**	**25**	**50**	**75**	**42**	**7**	**2**	**3**	**175**	**14.3**	**2**	....	....	....	....	....	....	....	....	....	....	....	....	....
1990-91	**Philadelphia**	**NHL**	**77**	**19**	**47**	**66**	**53**	**6**	**0**	**0**	**170**	**11.2**	**–2**	....	....	....	....	....	....	....	....	....	....	....	....	....
1991-92	**Philadelphia**	**NHL**	**12**	**3**	**3**	**6**	**8**	**1**	**0**	**0**	**19**	**15.8**	**2**	....	....	....	....	....	....	....	....	....	....	....	....	....
	Hartford	**NHL**	**61**	**24**	**30**	**54**	**38**	**8**	**4**	**1**	**133**	**18.0**	**–4**	....	....	....	....	....	**7**	**3**	**3**	**6**	**6**	**0**	**1**	**0**
1992-93	**Hartford**	**NHL**	**67**	**25**	**42**	**67**	**20**	**6**	**3**	**2**	**139**	**18.0**	**–4**	....	....	....	....	....	....	....	....	....	....	....	....	....
	Vancouver	**NHL**	**10**	**0**	**10**	**10**	**12**	**0**	**0**	**0**	**12**	**0.0**	**3**	....	....	....	....	....	**12**	**4**	**6**	**10**	**4**	**1**	**0**	**1**
1993-94	**Vancouver**	**NHL**	**78**	**15**	**40**	**55**	**30**	**2**	**1**	**3**	**115**	**13.0**	**5**	....	....	....	....	....	**22**	**4**	**9**	**13**	**18**	**0**	**0**	**1**
1994-95	**Chicago**	**NHL**	**16**	**4**	**3**	**7**	**2**	**1**	**0**	**2**	**29**	**13.8**	**2**	....	....	....	....	....	**16**	**5**	**5**	**10**	**4**	**0**	**0**	**1**
1995-96	**Chicago**	**NHL**	**66**	**18**	**29**	**47**	**36**	**5**	**1**	**7**	**86**	**20.9**	**20**	....	....	....	....	....	**9**	**1**	**4**	**5**	**2**	**1**	**0**	**0**
1996-97	**Chicago**	**NHL**	**75**	**8**	**27**	**35**	**12**	**2**	**0**	**1**	**122**	**6.6**	**0**	....	....	....	....	....	**2**	**0**	**0**	**0**	**2**	**0**	**0**	**0**
1997-98	**San Jose**	**NHL**	**67**	**12**	**17**	**29**	**25**	**2**	**3**	**3**	**107**	**11.2**	**4**	....	....	....	....	....	**6**	**1**	**1**	**2**	**0**	**0**	**0**	**0**
1998-99	**San Jose**	**NHL**	**43**	**4**	**10**	**14**	**18**	**0**	**1**	**1**	**55**	**7.3**	**–3**	**244**	**42.2**	**20**	**21**	**14:26**	....	....	....	....	....	....	....	....
99-2000	**San Jose**	**NHL**	**19**	**0**	**2**	**2**	**4**	**0**	**0**	**0**	**18**	**0.0**	**–2**	**53**	**54.7**	**12**	**7**	**13:06**	....	....	....	....	....	....	....	....
	NHL Totals		**1071**	**266**	**493**	**759**	**524**	**55**	**22**	**41**	**1904**	**14.0**		**297**	**44.4**	**32**	**28**	**14:01**	**118**	**27**	**43**	**70**	**64**	**5**	**2**	**5**

Traded to **Philadelphia** by **Detroit** with Joe Paterson for Darryl Sittler, October 10, 1984. Traded to **Hartford** by **Philadelphia** with Philadelphia's 4th round choice (Kevin Smyth) in 1992 Entry Draft for Kevin Dineen, November 13, 1991. Traded to **Vancouver** by **Hartford** with Vancouver's 5th round choice (previously acquired, Vancouver selected Scott Walker) in 1993 Entry Draft for Robert Kron, Vancouver's 3rd round choice (Marek Malik) in 1993 Entry Draft and future considerations (Jim Sandlak, May 17, 1993), March 22, 1993. Traded to **Chicago** by **Vancouver** for Christian Ruutu, March 10, 1995. Traded to **San Jose** by **Chicago** for the rights to Petri Varis and San Jose's 6th round choice (Jari Viuhkola) in 1998 Entry Draft, July 25, 1997. • Missed remainder of 1999-2000 season recovering from abdominal injury suffered in game vs. New Jersey, November 18, 1999. • Officially released by **San Jose**, December 26, 1999.

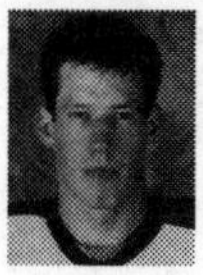

CROSS, Cory

(KRAWS, KOHR-ee) **TOR.**

Defense. Shoots left. 6'5", 220 lbs. Born, Lloydminster, Alta., January 3, 1971. Tampa Bay's 1st choice, 1st overall, in 1992 Supplemental Draft.

Season	Club	League	GP	G	A	Pts	PIM	PP	SH	GW	S	%	+/-	TF	F%	H	SB	Min	GP	G	A	Pts	PIM	PP	SH	GW
1990-91	U. of Alberta	CWUAA	20	2	5	7	16	....	....	....	....	....	....	....	....	....	....	....	....	....	....	....	....	....	....	....
1991-92	U. of Alberta	CWUAA	41	4	11	15	82	....	....	....	....	....	....	....	....	....	....	....	....	....	....	....	....	....	....	....
1992-93	U. of Alberta	CWUAA	43	11	28	39	105	....	....	....	....	....	....	....	....	....	....	....	....	....	....	....	....	....	....	....
	Atlanta Knights	IHL	7	0	1	1	2	....	....	....	....	....	....	....	....	....	....	....	4	0	0	0	6	....	....	....
1993-94	**Tampa Bay**	**NHL**	**5**	**0**	**0**	**0**	**6**	**0**	**0**	**0**	**5**	**0.0**	**–3**	....	....	....	....	....	....	....	....	....	....	....	....	....
	Atlanta Knights	IHL	70	4	14	18	72	....	....	....	....	....	....	....	....	....	....	....	9	1	2	3	14	....	....	....
1994-95	**Tampa Bay**	**NHL**	**43**	**1**	**5**	**6**	**41**	**0**	**0**	**1**	**35**	**2.9**	**–6**	....	....	....	....	....	....	....	....	....	....	....	....	....
	Atlanta Knights	IHL	41	5	10	15	67	....	....	....	....	....	....	....	....	....	....	....	....	....	....	....	....	....	....	....
1995-96	**Tampa Bay**	**NHL**	**75**	**2**	**14**	**16**	**66**	**0**	**0**	**0**	**57**	**3.5**	**4**	....	....	....	....	....	**6**	**0**	**0**	**0**	**22**	**0**	**0**	**0**
1996-97	**Tampa Bay**	**NHL**	**72**	**4**	**5**	**9**	**95**	**0**	**0**	**2**	**75**	**5.3**	**6**	....	....	....	....	....	....	....	....	....	....	....	....	....
1997-98	**Tampa Bay**	**NHL**	**74**	**3**	**6**	**9**	**77**	**0**	**1**	**0**	**72**	**4.2**	**–24**	....	....	....	....	....	....	....	....	....	....	....	....	....
1998-99	**Tampa Bay**	**NHL**	**67**	**2**	**16**	**18**	**92**	**0**	**0**	**0**	**96**	**2.1**	**–25**	**0**	**0.0**	**127**	**82**	**22:38**	....	....	....	....	....	....	....	....
99-2000	**Toronto**	**NHL**	**71**	**4**	**11**	**15**	**64**	**0**	**0**	**1**	**60**	**6.7**	**13**	**0**	**0.0**	**154**	**53**	**15:59**	**12**	**0**	**2**	**2**	**2**	**0**	**0**	**0**
	NHL Totals		**407**	**16**	**57**	**73**	**441**	**0**	**1**	**4**	**400**	**4.0**		**0**	**0.0**	**281**	**135**	**19:13**	**18**	**0**	**2**	**2**	**24**	**0**	**0**	**0**

Traded to **Toronto** by **Tampa Bay** with Tampa Bay's 7th round choice in 2001 Entry Draft for Fredrik Modin, October 1, 1999.

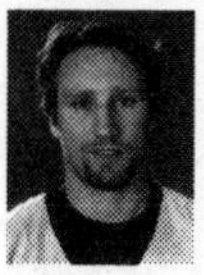

CROWE, Philip

(KROH, fihl-IHP)

Left wing. Shoots right. 6'2", 230 lbs. Born, Nanton, Alta., April 4, 1970.

Season	Club	League	GP	G	A	Pts	PIM	PP	SH	GW	S	%	+/-	TF	F%	H	SB	Min	GP	G	A	Pts	PIM	PP	SH	GW
1989-90	Olds Grizzlys	AJHL	47	8	21	29	248	....	....	....	....	....	....	....	....	....	....	....	....	....	....	....	....	....	....	....
1990-91	Olds Grizzlys	AJHL	50	16	24	40	290	....	....	....	....	....	....	....	....	....	....	....	....	....	....	....	....	....	....	....
1991-92	Adirondack	AHL	6	1	0	1	29	....	....	....	....	....	....	....	....	....	....	....	....	....	....	....	....	....	....	....
	Columbus Chill	ECHL	32	4	7	11	145	....	....	....	....	....	....	....	....	....	....	....	....	....	....	....	....	....	....	....
	Toledo Storm	ECHL	2	0	0	0	0	....	....	....	....	....	....	....	....	....	....	....	....	....	....	....	....	....	....	....
1992-93	Phoenix	IHL	53	3	3	6	190	....	....	....	....	....	....	....	....	....	....	....	5	0	0	0	58	....	....	....
1993-94	Fort Wayne	IHL	5	0	1	1	26	....	....	....	....	....	....	....	....	....	....	....	....	....	....	....	....	....	....	....
	Los Angeles	**NHL**	**31**	**0**	**2**	**2**	**77**	**0**	**0**	**0**	**5**	**0.0**	**4**	....	....	....	....	....	....	....	....	....	....	....	....	....
	Phoenix	IHL	2	0	0	0	0	....	....	....	....	....	....	....	....	....	....	....	....	....	....	....	....	....	....	....
1994-95	Hershey Bears	AHL	46	11	6	17	132	....	....	....	....	....	....	....	....	....	....	....	6	0	1	1	19	....	....	....
1995-96	**Philadelphia**	**NHL**	**16**	**1**	**1**	**2**	**28**	**0**	**0**	**0**	**6**	**16.7**	**0**	....	....	....	....	....	....	....	....	....	....	....	....	....
	Hershey Bears	AHL	39	6	8	14	105	....	....	....	....	....	....	....	....	....	....	....	5	1	2	3	19	....	....	....
1996-97	**Ottawa**	**NHL**	**26**	**0**	**1**	**1**	**30**	**0**	**0**	**0**	**8**	**0.0**	**0**	....	....	....	....	....	**3**	**0**	**0**	**0**	**16**	**0**	**0**	**0**
	Detroit Vipers	IHL	41	7	7	14	83	....	....	....	....	....	....	....	....	....	....	....	....	....	....	....	....	....	....	....

			Regular Season																Playoffs							
Season	Club	League	GP	G	A	Pts	PIM	PP	SH	GW	S	%	+/–	TF	F%	H	SB	Min	GP	G	A	Pts	PIM	PP	SH	GW
1997-98	Ottawa	NHL	9	3	0	3	24	0	0	1	6	50.0	3	....	....	....	....	....	....	....	....	....	....	....	....	....
	Detroit Vipers	IHL	55	6	13	19	160	....	....	....	....	....	....	....	....	....	....	....	20	5	2	7	48	....	....	....
1998-99	Ottawa	NHL	8	0	1	1	4	0	0	0	2	0.0	1	0	0.0	5	1	4:10	....	....	....	....	....	....	....	....
	Cincinnati	IHL	39	2	6	8	62	....	....	....	....	....	....	....	....	....	....	....	....	....	....	....	....	....	....	....
	Detroit Vipers	IHL	2	0	0	0	9	....	....	....	....	....	....	....	....	....	....	....	....	....	....	....	....	....	....	....
	Las Vegas	IHL	14	1	3	4	18	....	....	....	....	....	....	....	....	....	....	....	....	....	....	....	....	....	....	....
99-2000	Nashville	NHL	4	0	0	0	10	0	0	0	1	0.0	0	0	0.0	5	0	4:06	....	....	....	....	....	....	....	....
	Milwaukee	IHL	20	3	1	4	31	....	....	....	....	....	....	....	....	....	....	....	....	....	....	....	....	....	....	....
	NHL Totals		94	4	5	9	173	0	0	1	28	14.3		0	0.0	10	1	4:09	3	0	0	0	16	0	0	0

Signed as a free agent by **LA Kings**, November 8, 1993. Signed as a free agent by **Philadelphia**, July 19, 1994. Signed as a free agent by **Ottawa**, July 29, 1996. Claimed by **Atlanta** from **Ottawa** in Expansion Draft, June 25, 1999. Traded to **Nashville** by **Atlanta** for future considerations, June 26, 1999. • Missed majority of 1999-2000 season recovering from knee injury suffered in game vs. Milwaukee (IHL), January 2, 2000.

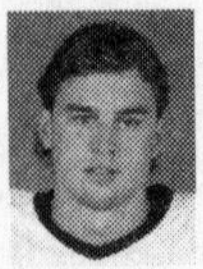

CROWLEY, Mike

(KROH-lee, MIGHK) **ANA.**

Defense. Shoots left. 5'11", 190 lbs. Born, Bloomington, MN, July 4, 1975. Philadelphia's 5th choice, 140th overall, in 1993 Entry Draft.

Season	Club	League	GP	G	A	Pts	PIM	PP	SH	GW	S	%	+/–	TF	F%	H	SB	Min	GP	G	A	Pts	PIM	PP	SH	GW
1990-91	Jefferson High	Hi-School	20	3	9	12	2	....	....	....	....	....	....	....	....	....	....	....	....	....	....	....	....	....	....	....
1991-92	Jefferson High	Hi-School	28	5	18	23	8	....	....	....	....	....	....	....	....	....	....	....	....	....	....	....	....	....	....	....
1992-93	Jefferson High	Hi-School	22	10	32	42	18	....	....	....	....	....	....	....	....	....	....	....	....	....	....	....	....	....	....	....
1993-94	Jefferson High	Hi-School	28	23	54	77	26	....	....	....	....	....	....	....	....	....	....	....	....	....	....	....	....	....	....	....
1994-95	U. of Minnesota	WCHA	41	11	27	38	60	....	....	....	....	....	....	....	....	....	....	....	....	....	....	....	....	....	....	....
1995-96	U. of Minnesota	WCHA	42	17	46	63	28	....	....	....	....	....	....	....	....	....	....	....	....	....	....	....	....	....	....	....
1996-97	U. of Minnesota	WCHA	42	9	*47	*56	24	....	....	....	....	....	....	....	....	....	....	....	....	....	....	....	....	....	....	....
1997-98	Anaheim	NHL	8	2	2	4	8	0	0	1	17	11.8	0	....	....	....	....	....	....	....	....	....	....	....	....	....
	Cincinnati Ducks	AHL	76	12	26	38	91	....	....	....	....	....	....	....	....	....	....	....	....	....	....	....	....	....	....	....
1998-99	Anaheim	NHL	20	2	3	5	16	1	0	1	41	4.9	–10	0	0.0	8	20	16:36	....	....	....	....	....	....	....	....
	Cincinnati Ducks	AHL	44	5	23	28	42	....	....	....	....	....	....	....	....	....	....	....	3	0	3	3	2	....	....	....
99-2000	Long Beach	IHL	67	9	39	48	35	....	....	....	....	....	....	....	....	....	....	....	4	2	1	3	6	....	....	....
	NHL Totals		28	4	5	9	24	1	0	2	58	6.9		0	0.0	8	20	16:36	....	....	....	....	....	....	....	....

WCHA First All-Star Team (1996, 1997) • NCAA West First All-American Team (1996, 1997) • IHL First All-Star Team (2000)

Traded to **Anaheim** by **Philadelphia** with Anatoli Semenov for Brian Wesenberg, March 19, 1996. Signed as a free agent by **Long Beach** (IHL), August 24, 1999.

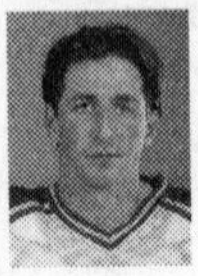

CROWLEY, Ted

(KROH-lee, TEHD)

Defense. Shoots right. 6'2", 188 lbs. Born, Concord, MA, May 3, 1970. Toronto's 4th choice, 69th overall, in 1988 Entry Draft.

Season	Club	League	GP	G	A	Pts	PIM	PP	SH	GW	S	%	+/–	TF	F%	H	SB	Min	GP	G	A	Pts	PIM	PP	SH	GW
1987-88	Lawrence Prep	Hi-School	23	11	23	34		....	....	....	....	....	....	....	....	....	....	....	....	....	....	....	....	....	....	....
1988-89	Lawrence Prep	Hi-School	23	12	24	36	....	....	....	....	....	....	....	....	....	....	....	....	....	....	....	....	....	....	....	....
1989-90	Boston College	H-East	39	7	24	31	34	....	....	....	....	....	....	....	....	....	....	....	....	....	....	....	....	....	....	....
1990-91	Boston College	H-East	39	12	24	36	61	....	....	....	....	....	....	....	....	....	....	....	....	....	....	....	....	....	....	....
1991-92	United States	Nat-Team	42	6	7	13	65	....	....	....	....	....	....	....	....	....	....	....	....	....	....	....	....	....	....	....
	St. John's Leafs	AHL	29	5	4	9	33	....	....	....	....	....	....	....	....	....	....	....	10	3	1	4	11	....	....	....
1992-93	St. John's Leafs	AHL	79	19	38	57	41	....	....	....	....	....	....	....	....	....	....	....	9	2	2	4	4	....	....	....
1993-94	United States	Nat-Team	48	9	13	22	80	....	....	....	....	....	....	....	....	....	....	....	....	....	....	....	....	....	....	....
	United States	Olympics	8	0	2	2	8	....	....	....	....	....	....	....	....	....	....	....	....	....	....	....	....	....	....	....
	Hartford	NHL	21	1	2	3	10	1	0	0	28	3.6	–1	....	....	....	....	....	....	....	....	....	....	....	....	....
1994-95	Chicago Wolves	IHL	53	8	23	31	68	....	....	....	....	....	....	....	....	....	....	....	....	....	....	....	....	....	....	....
	Houston Aeros	IHL	23	4	9	13	35	....	....	....	....	....	....	....	....	....	....	....	3	0	1	1	0	....	....	....
1995-96	Providence Bruins	AHL	72	12	30	42	47	....	....	....	....	....	....	....	....	....	....	....	4	1	2	3	2	....	....	....
1996-97	Cincinnati	IHL	39	9	9	18	24	....	....	....	....	....	....	....	....	....	....	....	....	....	....	....	....	....	....	....
	Phoenix	IHL	30	5	8	13	21	....	....	....	....	....	....	....	....	....	....	....	....	....	....	....	....	....	....	....
1997-98	Springfield	AHL	78	14	35	49	55	....	....	....	....	....	....	....	....	....	....	....	4	1	1	2	2	....	....	....
1998-99	Colorado	NHL	7	0	1	1	2	0	0	0	10	0.0	–1	0	0.0	1	0	7:00	....	....	....	....	....	....	....	....
	Hershey Bears	AHL	18	1	5	6	27	....	....	....	....	....	....	....	....	....	....	....	....	....	....	....	....	....	....	....
	NY Islanders	NHL	6	1	1	2	0	1	0	0	10	10.0	0	0	0.0	3	2	15:11	....	....	....	....	....	....	....	....
	Lowell	AHL	41	3	22	25	51	....	....	....	....	....	....	....	....	....	....	....	3	0	0	0	6	....	....	....
99-2000	Cleveland	IHL	61	9	20	29	94	....	....	....	....	....	....	....	....	....	....	....	....	....	....	....	....	....	....	....
	Utah Grizzlies	IHL	16	3	2	5	16	....	....	....	....	....	....	....	....	....	....	....	5	1	1	2	12	....	....	....
	NHL Totals		34	2	4	6	12	2	0	0	48	4.2		0	0.0	4	2	10:47	....	....	....	....	....	....	....	....

Hockey East First All-Star Team (1991) • NCAA East Second All-American Team (1991)

Traded to **Hartford** by **Toronto** for Mark Greig and Hartford's 6th round choice (Doug Bonner) in 1995 Entry Draft, January 25, 1994. Signed as a free agent by **Boston**, August 9, 1995. Signed as a free agent by **Phoenix**, June 27, 1997. Signed as a free agent by **Colorado**, August 14, 1998. Traded to **NY Islanders** by **Colorado** for Michael Gaul, December 15, 1998. Signed as a free agent by **Chicago**, July 22, 1999. Traded to **Utah** (IHL) by **Cleveland** (IHL) for Ian Gordon, Joe Frederick and Sean Berans, March 16, 2000 with Chicago retaining NHL rights.

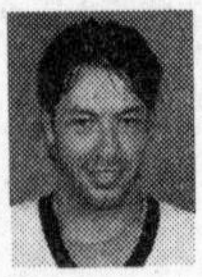

CULLEN, Matt

(KUH-lehn, MAT) **ANA.**

Center. Shoots left. 6'1", 197 lbs. Born, Virginia, MN, November 2, 1976. Anaheim's 2nd choice, 35th overall, in 1996 Entry Draft.

Season	Club	League	GP	G	A	Pts	PIM	PP	SH	GW	S	%	+/–	TF	F%	H	SB	Min	GP	G	A	Pts	PIM	PP	SH	GW
1994-95	Moorehead High	Hi-School	28	47	42	89	78	....	....	....	....	....	....	....	....	....	....	....	....	....	....	....	....	....	....	....
1995-96	St. Cloud State	WCHA	39	12	29	41	28	....	....	....	....	....	....	....	....	....	....	....	....	....	....	....	....	....	....	....
1996-97	St. Cloud State	WCHA	36	15	30	45	70	....	....	....	....	....	....	....	....	....	....	....	....	....	....	....	....	....	....	....
	Baltimore Bandits	AHL	6	3	3	6	7	....	....	....	....	....	....	....	....	....	....	....	3	0	2	2	0	....	....	....
1997-98	Anaheim	NHL	61	6	21	27	23	2	0	0	75	8.0	–4	....	....	....	....	....	....	....	....	....	....	....	....	....
	Cincinnati Ducks	AHL	18	15	12	27	2	....	....	....	....	....	....	....	....	....	....	....	....	....	....	....	....	....	....	....
1998-99	Anaheim	NHL	75	11	14	25	47	5	1	1	112	9.8	–12	1047	47.7	41	22	15:31	4	0	0	0	0	0	0	0
	Cincinnati Ducks	AHL	3	1	2	3	8	....	....	....	....	....	....	....	....	....	....	....	....	....	....	....	....	....	....	....
99-2000	Anaheim	NHL	80	13	26	39	24	1	0	1	137	9.5	5	1247	44.6	74	39	16:54	....	....	....	....	....	....	....	....
	NHL Totals		216	30	61	91	94	8	1	2	324	9.3		2294	46.0	115	61	16:14	4	0	0	0	0	0	0	0

WCHA Second All-Star Team (1997)

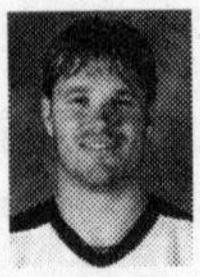

CULLIMORE, Jassen

(KUHL-ih-mohr, JAY-sehn) **T.B.**

Defense. Shoots left. 6'5", 225 lbs. Born, Simcoe, Ont., December 4, 1972. Vancouver's 2nd choice, 29th overall, in 1991 Entry Draft.

Season	Club	League	GP	G	A	Pts	PIM	PP	SH	GW	S	%	+/–	TF	F%	H	SB	Min	GP	G	A	Pts	PIM	PP	SH	GW
1986-87	Caledonia Corvairs	OJHL-C	18	2	0	2	9	....	....	....	....	....	....	....	....	....	....	....	....	....	....	....	....	....	....	....
1987-88	Simcoe Rams	OJHL-C	35	11	14	25	92	....	....	....	....	....	....	....	....	....	....	....	....	....	....	....	....	....	....	....
1988-89	Peterborough	OJHL-B	29	11	17	28	88	....	....	....	....	....	....	....	....	....	....	....	....	....	....	....	....	....	....	....
	Peterborough	OHL	20	2	1	3	6	....	....	....	....	....	....	....	....	....	....	....	....	....	....	....	....	....	....	....
1989-90	Peterborough	OHL	59	2	6	8	61	....	....	....	....	....	....	....	....	....	....	....	11	0	2	2	8	....	....	....
1990-91	Peterborough	OHL	62	8	16	24	74	....	....	....	....	....	....	....	....	....	....	....	4	1	0	1	7	....	....	....
1991-92	Peterborough	OHL	54	9	37	46	65	....	....	....	....	....	....	....	....	....	....	....	10	3	6	9	8	....	....	....
1992-93	Hamilton Canucks	AHL	56	5	7	12	60	....	....	....	....	....	....	....	....	....	....	....	....	....	....	....	....	....	....	....
1993-94	Hamilton Canucks	AHL	71	8	20	28	86	....	....	....	....	....	....	....	....	....	....	....	3	0	1	1	2	....	....	....
1994-95	Vancouver	NHL	34	1	2	3	39	0	0	0	30	3.3	–2	....	....	....	....	....	11	0	0	0	12	0	0	0
	Syracuse Crunch	AHL	33	2	7	9	66	....	....	....	....	....	....	....	....	....	....	....	....	....	....	....	....	....	....	....
1995-96	Vancouver	NHL	27	1	1	2	21	0	0	1	12	8.3	4	....	....	....	....	....	....	....	....	....	....	....	....	....
1996-97	Vancouver	NHL	3	0	0	0	2	0	0	0	2	0.0	–2	....	....	....	....	....	....	....	....	....	....	....	....	....
	Montreal	NHL	49	2	6	8	42	0	1	1	52	3.8	4	....	....	....	....	....	2	0	0	0	2	0	0	0
1997-98	Montreal	NHL	3	0	0	0	4	0	0	0	1	0.0	0	....	....	....	....	....	....	....	....	....	....	....	....	....
	Fredericton	AHL	5	1	0	1	8	....	....	....	....	....	....	....	....	....	....	....	....	....	....	....	....	....	....	....
	Tampa Bay	NHL	25	1	2	3	22	1	0	0	17	5.9	–4	....	....	....	....	....	....	....	....	....	....	....	....	....
1998-99	Tampa Bay	NHL	78	5	12	17	81	1	1	1	73	6.8	–22	0	0.0	161	67	20:14	....	....	....	....	....	....	....	....

			Regular Season																Playoffs							
Season	Club	League	GP	G	A	Pts	PIM	PP	SH	GW	S	%	+/-	TF	F%	H	SB	Min	GP	G	A	Pts	PIM	PP	SH	GW
99-2000	Tampa Bay	NHL	46	1	1	2	66	0	0	0	23	4.3	−12	2	0.0	92	45	15:38	....	....	....	....	....	....	....	....
	Providence Bruins	AHL	16	5	10	15	31	....	....	....	....	....	....	....	....	....	....	....	....	....	....	....	....	....	....	....
	NHL Totals		265	11	24	35	277	2	2	3	210	5.2		2	0.0	253	112	18:31	13	0	0	0	14	0	0	0

OHL Second All-Star Team (1992)

Traded to **Montreal** by **Vancouver** for Donald Brashear, November 13, 1996. Claimed on waivers by **Tampa Bay** from **Montreal**, January 22, 1998. • Loaned to **Providence** (AHL) by **Tampa Bay**, October 1, 1999.

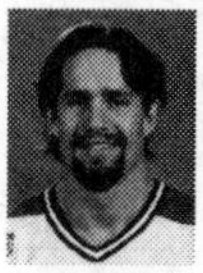

CUMMINS, Jim

(KUH-mihns, JIHM) **ANA.**

Right wing. Shoots right. 6'2", 219 lbs. Born, Dearborn, MI, May 17, 1970. NY Rangers' 5th choice, 67th overall, in 1989 Entry Draft.

1987-88	Detroit	NAJHL	31	11	15	26	146	....	....	....	....	....	....	....	....	....	....	....	....	....	....	....	....	....	....	....
1988-89	Michigan State	CCHA	30	3	8	11	98	....	....	....	....	....	....	....	....	....	....	....	....	....	....	....	....	....	....	....
1989-90	Michigan State	CCHA	41	8	7	15	94	....	....	....	....	....	....	....	....	....	....	....	....	....	....	....	....	....	....	....
1990-91	Michigan State	CCHA	34	9	6	15	110	....	....	....	....	....	....	....	....	....	....	....	....	....	....	....	....	....	....	....
1991-92	Detroit	NHL	1	0	0	0	7	0	0	0	0	0.0	0	....	....	....	....	....	....	....	....	....	....	....	....	....
	Adirondack	AHL	65	7	13	20	338	....	....	....	....	....	....	....	....	....	....	....	5	0	0	0	19	....	....	....
1992-93	Detroit	NHL	7	1	1	2	58	0	0	0	5	20.0	0	....	....	....	....	....	....	....	....	....	....	....	....	....
	Adirondack	AHL	43	16	4	20	179	....	....	....	....	....	....	....	....	....	....	....	9	3	1	4	4	....	....	....
1993-94	Philadelphia	NHL	22	1	2	3	71	0	0	0	17	5.9	0	....	....	....	....	....	....	....	....	....	....	....	....	....
	Hershey Bears	AHL	17	6	6	12	70	....	....	....	....	....	....	....	....	....	....	....	....	....	....	....	....	....	....	....
	Tampa Bay	NHL	4	0	0	0	13	0	0	0	3	0.0	−1	....	....	....	....	....	....	....	....	....	....	....	....	....
	Atlanta Knights	IHL	7	4	5	9	14	....	....	....	....	....	....	....	....	....	....	....	13	1	2	3	90	....	....	....
1994-95	Tampa Bay	NHL	10	1	0	1	41	0	0	1	3	33.3	−3	....	....	....	....	....	....	....	....	....	....	....	....	....
	Chicago	NHL	27	3	1	4	117	0	0	0	20	15.0	−3	....	....	....	....	....	14	1	1	2	4	0	0	1
1995-96	Chicago	NHL	52	2	4	6	180	0	0	2	34	5.9	−1	....	....	....	....	....	10	0	0	0	2	0	0	0
1996-97	Chicago	NHL	65	6	6	12	199	0	0	0	61	9.8	4	....	....	....	....	....	6	0	0	0	24	0	0	0
1997-98	Chicago	NHL	55	0	2	2	178	0	0	0	33	0.0	−9	....	....	....	....	....	....	....	....	....	....	....	....	....
	Phoenix	NHL	20	0	0	0	47	0	0	0	10	0.0	−7	....	....	....	....	....	3	0	0	0	4	0	0	0
1998-99	Phoenix	NHL	55	1	7	8	190	0	0	0	26	3.8	3	0	0.0	74	7	7:07	3	0	1	1	0	0	0	0
99-2000	Montreal	NHL	47	3	5	8	92	0	0	0	33	9.1	−5	4	25.0	59	12	8:58	....	....	....	....	....	....	....	....
	NHL Totals		365	18	28	46	1193	0	0	3	245	7.3		4	25.0	133	19	7:58	36	1	2	3	34	0	0	1

Traded to **Detroit** by **NY Rangers** with Kevin Miller and Dennis Vial for Joey Kocur and Per Djoos, March 5, 1991. Traded to **Philadelphia** by **Detroit** with Philadelphia's 4th round choice (previously acquired by Detroit - later traded to Boston - Boston selected Charles Paquette) in 1993 Entry Draft for Greg Johnson and Philadelphia's 5th round choice (Frederic Deschenes) in 1994 Entry Draft, June 20, 1993. Traded to **Tampa Bay** by **Philadelphia** with Philadelphia's 4th round choice (later traded back to Philadelphia - Philadelphia selected Radovan Somik) in 1995 Entry Draft for Rob DiMaio, March 18, 1994. Traded to **Chicago** by **Tampa Bay** with Tom Tilley and Jeff Buchanan for Paul Ysebaert and Rich Sutter, February 22, 1995. Traded to **Phoenix** by **Chicago** with Keith Carney for Chad Kilger and Jayson More, March 4, 1998. Traded to **Montreal** by **Phoenix** for NY Rangers' 6th round choice (previously acquired, Phoenix selected Erik Leverstrom) in 1999 Entry Draft, June 26, 1999. Signed as a free agent by **Anaheim**, July 5, 2000.

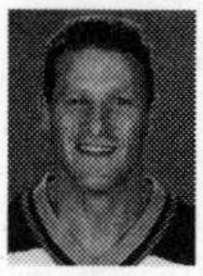

CUNNEYWORTH, Randy

(KUH-nee-wuhrth, RAN-dee) **BUF.**

Left wing. Shoots left. 6', 198 lbs. Born, Etobicoke, Ont., May 10, 1961. Buffalo's 9th choice, 167th overall, in 1980 Entry Draft.

1978-79	Dixie Beehives	OHA-B	44	17	14	31	127	....	....	....	....	....	....	....	....	....	....	....	....	....	....	....	....	....	....	....
1979-80	Ottawa 67's	OMJHL	63	16	25	41	145	....	....	....	....	....	....	....	....	....	....	....	11	0	1	1	13	....	....	....
1980-81	Ottawa 67's	OMJHL	67	54	74	128	240	....	....	....	....	....	....	....	....	....	....	....	15	5	8	13	35	....	....	....
	Buffalo	NHL	1	0	0	0	2	0	0	0	1	0.0	0	....	....	....	....	....	....	....	....	....	....	....	....	....
	Rochester	AHL	1	0	1	1	2	....	....	....	....	....	....	....	....	....	....	....	....	....	....	....	....	....	....	....
1981-82	Buffalo	NHL	20	2	4	6	47	0	0	0	33	6.1	−3	....	....	....	....	....	....	....	....	....	....	....	....	....
	Rochester	AHL	57	12	15	27	86	....	....	....	....	....	....	....	....	....	....	....	9	4	0	4	30	....	....	....
1982-83	Rochester	AHL	78	23	33	56	111	....	....	....	....	....	....	....	....	....	....	....	16	4	4	8	35	....	....	....
1983-84	Rochester	AHL	54	18	17	35	85	....	....	....	....	....	....	....	....	....	....	....	17	5	5	10	55	....	....	....
1984-85	Rochester	AHL	72	30	38	68	148	....	....	....	....	....	....	....	....	....	....	....	5	2	1	3	16	....	....	....
1985-86	Pittsburgh	NHL	75	15	30	45	74	2	2	2	134	11.2	12	....	....	....	....	....	....	....	....	....	....	....	....	....
1986-87	Pittsburgh	NHL	79	26	27	53	142	3	2	5	169	15.4	14	....	....	....	....	....	....	....	....	....	....	....	....	....
1987-88	Pittsburgh	NHL	71	35	39	74	141	14	0	6	229	15.3	13	....	....	....	....	....	....	....	....	....	....	....	....	....
1988-89	Pittsburgh	NHL	70	25	19	44	156	10	0	1	163	15.3	−22	....	....	....	....	....	11	3	5	8	26	1	0	1
1989-90	Winnipeg	NHL	28	5	6	11	34	2	0	1	51	9.8	−7	....	....	....	....	....	....	....	....	....	....	....	....	....
	Hartford	NHL	43	9	9	18	41	2	0	1	70	12.9	−4	....	....	....	....	....	4	0	0	0	2	0	0	0
1990-91	Hartford	NHL	32	9	5	14	49	0	0	1	56	16.1	−6	....	....	....	....	....	1	0	0	0	0	0	0	0
	Springfield	AHL	2	0	0	0	5	....	....	....	....	....	....	....	....	....	....	....	....	....	....	....	....	....	....	....
1991-92	Hartford	NHL	39	7	10	17	71	0	0	1	63	11.1	−5	....	....	....	....	....	7	3	0	3	9	1	1	1
1992-93	Hartford	NHL	39	5	4	9	63	0	0	1	47	10.6	−1	....	....	....	....	....	....	....	....	....	....	....	....	....
1993-94	Hartford	NHL	63	9	8	17	87	0	1	1	121	7.4	−2	....	....	....	....	....	....	....	....	....	....	....	....	....
	Chicago	NHL	16	4	3	7	13	0	0	1	33	12.1	1	....	....	....	....	....	6	0	0	0	8	0	0	0
1994-95	Ottawa	NHL	48	5	5	10	68	2	0	0	71	7.0	−19	....	....	....	....	....	....	....	....	....	....	....	....	....
1995-96	Ottawa	NHL	81	17	19	36	130	4	0	2	142	12.0	−31	....	....	....	....	....	....	....	....	....	....	....	....	....
1996-97	Ottawa	NHL	76	12	24	36	99	6	0	3	115	10.4	−7	....	....	....	....	....	7	1	1	2	10	0	0	0
1997-98	Ottawa	NHL	71	2	11	13	63	1	0	0	81	2.5	−14	....	....	....	....	....	6	0	1	1	6	0	0	0
1998-99	Buffalo	NHL	14	2	2	4	0	0	0	1	12	16.7	1	35	54.3	27	2	8:58	3	0	0	0	0	0	0	0
	Rochester	AHL	52	10	18	28	55	....	....	....	....	....	....	....	....	....	....	....	20	3	14	17	58	....	....	....
99-2000	Rochester	AHL	52	8	16	24	81	....	....	....	....	....	....	....	....	....	....	....	....	....	....	....	....	....	....	....
	NHL Totals		866	189	225	414	1280	46	5	27	1591	11.9		35	54.3	27	2	8:58	45	7	7	14	61	2	1	2

Traded to **Pittsburgh** by **Buffalo** with Mike Moller for Pat Hughes, October 4, 1985. Traded to **Winnipeg** by **Pittsburgh** with Rick Tabaracci and Dave McLlwain for Jim Kyte, Andrew McBain and Randy Gilhen, June 17, 1989. Traded to **Hartford** by **Winnipeg** for Paul MacDermid, December 13, 1989. Traded to **Chicago** by **Hartford** with Gary Suter and Hartford's 3rd round choice (later traded to Vancouver - Vancouver selected Larry Courville) in 1995 Entry Draft for Frantisek Kucera and Jocelyn Lemieux, March 11, 1994. Signed as a free agent by **Ottawa**, July 15, 1994. Signed as a free agent by **Buffalo**, August 27, 1998. • Suffered season-ending knee injury in game vs. Quebec (AHL), February 18, 2000.

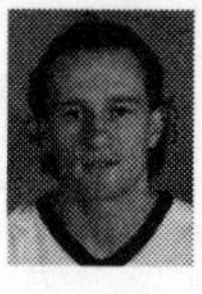

CZERKAWSKI, Mariusz

(chehr-KAWV-skee, MAIR-ee-UHZ) **NYI**

Right wing. Shoots left. 6', 195 lbs. Born, Radomsko, Poland, April 13, 1972. Boston's 5th choice, 106th overall, in 1991 Entry Draft.

1990-91	GKS Tychy	Poland	24	25	15	40	....	....	....	....	....	....	....	....	....	....	....	....	....	....	....	....	....	....	....	....
1991-92	Djurgardens IF	Sweden	39	8	5	13	4	....	....	....	....	....	....	....	....	....	....	....	3	0	0	0	2	....	....	....
	Poland	Olympics	5	0	1	1	4	....	....	....	....	....	....	....	....	....	....	....	....	....	....	....	....	....	....	....
1992-93	SC Hammarby	Sweden-2	32	*39	30	*69	74	....	....	....	....	....	....	....	....	....	....	....	13	*16	7	*23	34	....	....	....
1993-94	Djurgardens IF	Sweden	39	13	21	34	20	....	....	....	....	....	....	....	....	....	....	....	6	3	1	4	2	....	....	....
	Boston	NHL	4	2	1	3	0	1	0	0	11	18.2	−2	....	....	....	....	....	13	3	3	6	4	1	0	0
1994-95	Kiekko Espoo	Finland	7	9	3	12	10	....	....	....	....	....	....	....	....	....	....	....	....	....	....	....	....	....	....	....
	Boston	NHL	47	12	14	26	31	1	0	2	126	9.5	4	....	....	....	....	....	5	1	0	1	0	0	0	0
1995-96	Boston	NHL	33	5	6	11	10	1	0	0	63	7.9	−11	....	....	....	....	....	....	....	....	....	....	....	....	....
	Edmonton	NHL	37	12	17	29	8	2	0	1	79	15.2	7	....	....	....	....	....	....	....	....	....	....	....	....	....
1996-97	Edmonton	NHL	76	26	21	47	16	4	0	3	182	14.3	0	....	....	....	....	....	12	2	1	3	10	0	0	0
1997-98	NY Islanders	NHL	68	12	13	25	23	2	0	1	136	8.8	11	....	....	....	....	....	....	....	....	....	....	....	....	....
1998-99	NY Islanders	NHL	78	21	17	38	14	4	0	1	205	10.2	−10	2	0.0	47	14	14:18	....	....	....	....	....	....	....	....
99-2000	NY Islanders	NHL	79	35	35	70	34	16	0	4	276	12.7	−16	4	25.0	77	25	17:45	....	....	....	....	....	....	....	....
	NHL Totals		422	125	124	249	136	31	0	12	1078	11.6		6	16.7	124	39	16:02	30	6	4	10	14	1	0	0

Played in NHL All-Star Game (2000)

Traded to **Edmonton** by **Boston** with Sean Brown and Boston's 1st round choice (Matthieu Descoteaux) in 1996 Entry Draft for Bill Ranford, January 11, 1996. Traded to **NY Islanders** by **Edmonton** for Dan Lacouture, August 25, 1997.

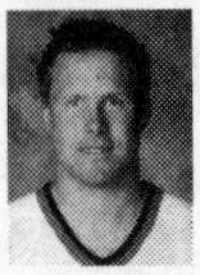

DACKELL, Andreas

(DA-kuhl, an-DRAY-uhs) **OTT.**

Right wing. Shoots right. 5'11", 195 lbs. Born, Gavle, Sweden, December 29, 1972. Ottawa's 3rd choice, 136th overall, in 1996 Entry Draft.

			Regular Season																Playoffs							
Season	Club	League	GP	G	A	Pts	PIM	PP	SH	GW	S	%	+/–	TF	F%	H	SB	Min	GP	G	A	Pts	PIM	PP	SH	GW
1990-91	Stromsbro HC	Sweden-2	29	21	9	30	12																			
	Brynas IF	Sweden	3	0	1	1	2																			
1991-92	Brynas IF	Sweden-2	26	17	24	41	42												2	3	1	4	2			
	Brynas IF	Sweden	4	0	0	0	2												2	0	1	1	4			
1992-93	Brynas IF	Sweden	40	12	15	27	12												10	4	5	9	2			
1993-94	Brynas IF	Sweden	38	12	17	29	47												7	2	2	4	8			
	Sweden	Olympics	4	0	0	0	0																			
1994-95	Brynas IF	Sweden	39	17	16	33	34												14	3	3	6	14			
1995-96	Brynas IF	Sweden	22	6	6	12	8																			
1996-97	**Ottawa**	**NHL**	**79**	**12**	**19**	**31**	**8**	**2**	**0**	**3**	**79**	**15.2**	**–6**						**7**	**1**	**0**	**1**	**0**	**0**	**0**	**0**
1997-98	**Ottawa**	**NHL**	**82**	**15**	**18**	**33**	**24**	**3**	**2**	**2**	**130**	**11.5**	**–11**						**11**	**1**	**1**	**2**	**2**	**1**	**0**	**0**
1998-99	**Ottawa**	**NHL**	**77**	**15**	**35**	**50**	**30**	**6**	**0**	**3**	**107**	**14.0**	**9**	**5**	**40.0**	**34**	**29**	**17:18**	**4**	**0**	**1**	**1**	**0**	**0**	**0**	**0**
99-2000	**Ottawa**	**NHL**	**82**	**10**	**25**	**35**	**18**	**0**	**0**	**1**	**99**	**10.1**	**5**	**1**	**100.0**	**34**	**35**	**16:17**	**6**	**2**	**1**	**3**	**2**	**0**	**0**	**1**
	NHL Totals		**320**	**52**	**97**	**149**	**80**	**11**	**2**	**9**	**415**	**12.5**		**6**	**50.0**	**68**	**64**	**16:46**	**28**	**4**	**3**	**7**	**4**	**1**	**0**	**1**

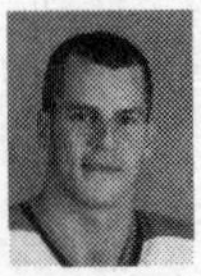

DAHL, Kevin

(DAHL, KEH-vihn) **CBJ**

Defense. Shoots right. 5'11", 190 lbs. Born, Regina, Sask., December 30, 1968. Montreal's 12th choice, 230th overall, in 1988 Entry Draft.

Season	Club	League	GP	G	A	Pts	PIM	PP	SH	GW	S	%	+/–	TF	F%	H	SB	Min	GP	G	A	Pts	PIM	PP	SH	GW
1985-86	Stratford Cullitons	OJHL-B	29	8	15	23	99																			
1986-87	Bowling Green	CCHA	32	2	6	8	54																			
1987-88	Bowling Green	CCHA	44	2	23	25	78																			
1988-89	Bowling Green	CCHA	46	9	26	35	51																			
1989-90	Bowling Green	CCHA	43	8	22	30	74																			
1990-91	Fredericton	AHL	32	1	15	16	45												9	0	1	1	11			
	Winston-Salem	ECHL	36	7	17	24	58																			
1991-92	Canada	Nat-Team	45	2	15	17	44																			
	Canada	Olympics	8	2	0	2	6																			
	Salt Lake City	IHL	13	0	2	2	12												5	0	0	0	13			
1992-93	**Calgary**	**NHL**	**61**	**2**	**9**	**11**	**56**	**1**	**0**	**0**	**40**	**5.0**	**9**						**6**	**0**	**2**	**2**	**8**	**0**	**0**	**0**
1993-94	**Calgary**	**NHL**	**33**	**0**	**3**	**3**	**23**	**0**	**0**	**0**	**20**	**0.0**	**–2**						**6**	**0**	**0**	**0**	**4**	**0**	**0**	**0**
	Saint John Flames	AHL	2	0	0	0	0																			
1994-95	**Calgary**	**NHL**	**34**	**4**	**8**	**12**	**38**	**0**	**0**	**0**	**30**	**13.3**	**8**						**3**	**0**	**0**	**0**	**0**	**0**	**0**	**0**
1995-96	**Calgary**	**NHL**	**32**	**1**	**1**	**2**	**26**	**0**	**0**	**1**	**17**	**5.9**	**–2**						**1**	**0**	**0**	**0**	**0**	**0**	**0**	**0**
	Saint John Flames	AHL	23	4	11	15	37																			
1996-97	**Phoenix**	**NHL**	**2**	**0**	**0**	**0**	**0**	**0**	**0**	**0**	**2**	**0.0**	**0**													
	Las Vegas	IHL	73	10	21	31	101												3	0	0	0	2			
1997-98	**Calgary**	**NHL**	**19**	**0**	**1**	**1**	**6**	**0**	**0**	**0**	**17**	**0.0**	**–3**													
	Chicago Wolves	IHL	45	8	9	17	61												20	1	8	9	32			
1998-99	**Toronto**	**NHL**	**3**	**0**	**0**	**0**	**2**	**0**	**0**	**0**	**0**	**0.0**	**0**	**0**	**0.0**	**6**	**1**	**15:19**								
	Chicago Wolves	IHL	34	3	6	9	61												10	2	3	5	8			
99-2000	Chicago Wolves	IHL	27	1	2	3	44												3	0	1	1	2			
	NHL Totals		**184**	**7**	**22**	**29**	**151**	**1**	**0**	**1**	**126**	**5.6**		**0**	**0.0**	**6**	**1**	**15:19**	**16**	**0**	**2**	**2**	**12**	**0**	**0**	**0**

Signed as a free agent by **Calgary**, July 27, 1991. Signed as a free agent by **Phoenix**, September 4, 1996. Signed as a free agent by **Calgary**, September 8, 1997. Signed as a free agent by **St. Louis**, September 4, 1998. Claimed by **Toronto** from **St. Louis** in NHL Waiver Draft, October 5, 1998. Signed as a free agent by **NY Islanders**, August 12, 1999. Signed as a free agent by **Columbus**, August 24, 2000.

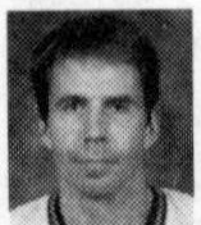

DAHLEN, Ulf

(DAH-lehn, UHLF) **WSH.**

Right wing. Shoots left. 6'3", 195 lbs. Born, Ostersund, Sweden, January 12, 1967. NY Rangers' 1st choice, 7th overall, in 1985 Entry Draft.

Season	Club	League	GP	G	A	Pts	PIM	PP	SH	GW	S	%	+/–	TF	F%	H	SB	Min	GP	G	A	Pts	PIM	PP	SH	GW
1983-84	Ostersunds IK	Sweden-2	36	15	11	26	10																			
1984-85	Ostersunds IK	Sweden-2	31	27	*26	*53	20												5	6	0	6	4			
1985-86	IF Bjorkloven	Sweden	22	4	3	7	8																			
1986-87	IF Bjorkloven	Sweden	31	9	12	21	20												6	6	2	8	4			
1987-88	**NY Rangers**	**NHL**	**70**	**29**	**23**	**52**	**26**	**11**	**0**	**4**	**159**	**18.2**	**5**													
	Colorado Rangers	IHL	2	2	2	4	0																			
1988-89	**NY Rangers**	**NHL**	**56**	**24**	**19**	**43**	**50**	**8**	**0**	**1**	**147**	**16.3**	**–6**						**4**	**0**	**0**	**0**	**0**	**0**	**0**	**0**
1989-90	**NY Rangers**	**NHL**	**63**	**18**	**18**	**36**	**30**	**13**	**0**	**4**	**111**	**16.2**	**–4**													
	Minnesota	**NHL**	**13**	**2**	**4**	**6**	**0**	**0**	**0**	**0**	**24**	**8.3**	**1**						**7**	**1**	**4**	**5**	**2**	**0**	**0**	**0**
1990-91	**Minnesota**	**NHL**	**66**	**21**	**18**	**39**	**6**	**4**	**0**	**3**	**133**	**15.8**	**7**						**15**	**2**	**6**	**8**	**4**	**0**	**0**	**0**
1991-92	**Minnesota**	**NHL**	**79**	**36**	**30**	**66**	**10**	**16**	**1**	**5**	**216**	**16.7**	**–5**						**7**	**0**	**3**	**3**	**2**	**0**	**0**	**0**
1992-93	**Minnesota**	**NHL**	**83**	**35**	**39**	**74**	**6**	**13**	**0**	**6**	**223**	**15.7**	**–20**													
1993-94	**Dallas**	**NHL**	**65**	**19**	**38**	**57**	**10**	**12**	**0**	**3**	**147**	**12.9**	**–1**													
	San Jose	**NHL**	**13**	**6**	**6**	**12**	**0**	**3**	**0**	**2**	**43**	**14.0**	**0**						**14**	**6**	**2**	**8**	**0**	**3**	**0**	**1**
1994-95	**San Jose**	**NHL**	**46**	**11**	**23**	**34**	**11**	**4**	**1**	**4**	**85**	**12.9**	**–2**						**11**	**5**	**4**	**9**	**0**	**3**	**0**	**1**
1995-96	**San Jose**	**NHL**	**59**	**16**	**12**	**28**	**27**	**5**	**0**	**2**	**103**	**15.5**	**–21**													
1996-97	**San Jose**	**NHL**	**43**	**8**	**11**	**19**	**8**	**3**	**0**	**1**	**78**	**10.3**	**–11**													
	Chicago	**NHL**	**30**	**6**	**8**	**14**	**10**	**1**	**0**	**3**	**53**	**11.3**	**9**						**5**	**0**	**1**	**1**	**0**	**0**	**0**	**0**
1997-98	HV Jonkoping	Sweden	29	9	22	31	16												5	1	3	4	12			
	Sweden	Olympics	4	1	0	1	2																			
1998-99	HV Jonkoping	Sweden	25	14	15	29	4																			
99-2000	**Washington**	**NHL**	**75**	**15**	**23**	**38**	**8**	**5**	**0**	**4**	**106**	**14.2**	**11**	**115**	**48.7**	**59**	**11**	**12:40**	**5**	**0**	**1**	**1**	**2**	**0**	**0**	**0**
	NHL Totals		**761**	**246**	**272**	**518**	**202**	**98**	**2**	**42**	**1628**	**15.1**		**115**	**48.7**	**59**	**11**	**12:40**	**68**	**14**	**21**	**35**	**10**	**6**	**0**	**2**

Swedish Junior Player-of-the-Year (1985)

Traded to **Minnesota** by **NY Rangers** with LA Kings' 4th round choice (previously acquired, Minnesota selected Cal McGowan) in 1990 Entry Draft and future considerations for Mike Gartner, March 6, 1990. Transferred to **Dallas** after **Minnesota** franchise relocated, June 9, 1993. Traded to **San Jose** by **Dallas** with Dallas' 7th round choice (Brad Mehalko) in 1995 Entry Draft for Doug Zmolek and Mike Lalor, March 19, 1994. Traded to **Chicago** by **San Jose** with Chris Terreri and Michal Sykora for Ed Belfour, January 25, 1997. Signed as a free agent by **Washington**, August 16, 1999.

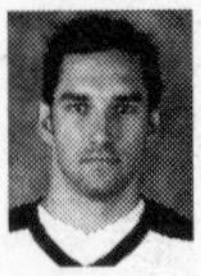

DAIGLE, Alexandre

(DAYG, al-EHX-an-dreh)

Center. Shoots left. 6', 195 lbs. Born, Montreal, Que., February 7, 1975. Ottawa's 1st choice, 1st overall, in 1993 Entry Draft.

Season	Club	League	GP	G	A	Pts	PIM	PP	SH	GW	S	%	+/–	TF	F%	H	SB	Min	GP	G	A	Pts	PIM	PP	SH	GW
1990-91	Laval Regents	QAAA	42	50	60	110	98																			
1991-92	Victoriaville Tigres	QMJHL	66	35	75	110	63																			
1992-93	Victoriaville Tigres	QMJHL	53	45	92	137	85												6	5	6	11	4			
1993-94	**Ottawa**	**NHL**	**84**	**20**	**31**	**51**	**40**	**4**	**0**	**2**	**168**	**11.9**	**–45**													
1994-95	Victoriaville Tigres	QMJHL	18	14	20	34	16																			
	Ottawa	**NHL**	**47**	**16**	**21**	**37**	**14**	**4**	**1**	**2**	**105**	**15.2**	**–22**													
1995-96	**Ottawa**	**NHL**	**50**	**5**	**12**	**17**	**24**	**1**	**0**	**0**	**77**	**6.5**	**–30**													
1996-97	**Ottawa**	**NHL**	**82**	**26**	**25**	**51**	**33**	**4**	**0**	**5**	**203**	**12.8**	**–33**						**7**	**0**	**0**	**0**	**2**	**0**	**0**	**0**
1997-98	**Ottawa**	**NHL**	**38**	**7**	**9**	**16**	**8**	**4**	**0**	**2**	**68**	**10.3**	**–7**													
	Philadelphia	**NHL**	**37**	**9**	**17**	**26**	**6**	**4**	**0**	**3**	**78**	**11.5**	**–1**						**5**	**0**	**2**	**2**	**0**	**0**	**0**	**0**
1998-99	**Philadelphia**	**NHL**	**31**	**3**	**2**	**5**	**2**	**1**	**0**	**1**	**26**	**11.5**	**–1**	**53**	**39.6**	**5**	**3**	**7:59**								
	Tampa Bay	**NHL**	**32**	**6**	**6**	**12**	**2**	**3**	**0**	**0**	**56**	**10.7**	**–12**	**4**	**50.0**	**6**	**8**	**13:59**								
99-2000	**NY Rangers**	**NHL**	**58**	**8**	**18**	**26**	**23**	**1**	**0**	**1**	**52**	**15.4**	**–5**	**339**	**53.1**	**22**	**7**	**10:59**								
	Hartford	AHL	16	6	13	19	4																			
	NHL Totals		**459**	**100**	**141**	**241**	**152**	**26**	**1**	**16**	**833**	**12.0**		**396**	**51.3**	**33**	**18**	**11:00**	**12**	**0**	**2**	**2**	**2**	**0**	**0**	**0**

QMJHL Second All-Star Team (1992) • Canadian Major Junior Rookie of the Year (1992) • QMJHL First All-Star Team (1993)

Traded to **Philadelphia** by **Ottawa** for Vaclav Prospal, Pat Falloon and Dallas' 2nd round choice (previously acquired, Ottawa selected Chris Bala) in 1998 Entry Draft, January 17, 1998. Traded to **Edmonton** by **Philadelphia** for Andrei Kovalenko, January 29, 1999. Traded to **Tampa Bay** by **Edmonton** for Alexander Selivanov, January 29, 1999. Traded to **NY Rangers** by **Tampa Bay** for cash, October 3, 1999.

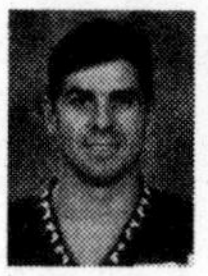

DAIGNEAULT, J.J.

(DAYN-yoh, JAY-JAY) **MIN.**

Defense. Shoots left. 5'10", 192 lbs. Born, Montreal, Que., October 12, 1965. Vancouver's 1st choice, 10th overall, in 1984 Entry Draft.

			Regular Season																Playoffs							
Season	Club	League	GP	G	A	Pts	PIM	PP	SH	GW	S	%	+/-	TF	F%	H	SB	Min	GP	G	A	Pts	PIM	PP	SH	GW
1980-81	Mtl-Concordia	QAAA	48	7	48	55	....	....	....	....	....	....	....	....	....	....	....	....	....	....	....	....	....	....	....	....
1981-82	Laval Voisins	QMJHL	64	4	25	29	41	....	....	....	....	....	....	....	....	....	....	....	18	1	3	4	2	....	....	....
1982-83	Longueuil	QMJHL	70	26	58	84	58	....	....	....	....	....	....	....	....	....	....	....	15	4	11	15	35	....	....	....
1983-84	Longueuil	QMJHL	10	2	11	13	6	....	....	....	....	....	....	....	....	....	....	....	14	3	13	16	30	....	....	....
	Canada	Nat-Team	55	5	14	19	40	....	....	....	....	....	....	....	....	....	....	....	....	....	....	....	....	....	....	....
	Canada	Olympics	7	1	1	2	0	....	....	....	....	....	....	....	....	....	....	....	....	....	....	....	....	....	....	....
1984-85	**Vancouver**	**NHL**	**67**	**4**	**23**	**27**	**69**	**2**	**0**	**0**	**93**	**4.3**	**–14**	....	....	....	....	....	....	....	....	....	....	....	....	....
1985-86	**Vancouver**	**NHL**	**64**	**5**	**23**	**28**	**45**	**4**	**0**	**0**	**114**	**4.4**	**–20**	....	....	....	....	....	**3**	**0**	**2**	**2**	**0**	**0**	**0**	**0**
1986-87	**Philadelphia**	**NHL**	**77**	**6**	**16**	**22**	**56**	**0**	**0**	**1**	**82**	**7.3**	**12**	....	....	....	....	....	**9**	**1**	**0**	**1**	**0**	**0**	**0**	**1**
1987-88	**Philadelphia**	**NHL**	**28**	**2**	**2**	**4**	**12**	**2**	**0**	**0**	**20**	**10.0**	**–8**	....	....	....	....	....	....	....	....	....	....	....	....	....
	Hershey Bears	AHL	10	1	5	6	8	....	....	....	....	....	....	....	....	....	....	....	....	....	....	....	....	....	....	....
1988-89	Hershey Bears	AHL	12	0	10	10	13	....	....	....	....	....	....	....	....	....	....	....	....	....	....	....	....	....	....	....
	Sherbrooke	AHL	63	10	33	43	48	....	....	....	....	....	....	....	....	....	....	....	6	1	3	4	2	....	....	....
1989-90	**Montreal**	**NHL**	**36**	**2**	**10**	**12**	**14**	**0**	**0**	**1**	**40**	**5.0**	**11**	....	....	....	....	....	**9**	**0**	**0**	**0**	**2**	**0**	**0**	**0**
	Sherbrooke	AHL	28	8	19	27	18	....	....	....	....	....	....	....	....	....	....	....	....	....	....	....	....	....	....	....
1990-91	**Montreal**	**NHL**	**51**	**3**	**16**	**19**	**31**	**2**	**0**	**0**	**68**	**4.4**	**–2**	....	....	....	....	....	**5**	**0**	**1**	**1**	**0**	**0**	**0**	**0**
1991-92	**Montreal**	**NHL**	**79**	**4**	**14**	**18**	**36**	**2**	**0**	**0**	**108**	**3.7**	**16**	....	....	....	....	....	**11**	**0**	**3**	**3**	**4**	**0**	**0**	**0**
1992-93 ♦	**Montreal**	**NHL**	**66**	**8**	**10**	**18**	**57**	**0**	**0**	**1**	**68**	**11.8**	**25**	....	....	....	....	....	**20**	**1**	**3**	**4**	**22**	**0**	**0**	**0**
1993-94	**Montreal**	**NHL**	**68**	**2**	**12**	**14**	**73**	**0**	**0**	**1**	**61**	**3.3**	**16**	....	....	....	....	....	**7**	**0**	**1**	**1**	**12**	**0**	**0**	**0**
1994-95	**Montreal**	**NHL**	**45**	**3**	**5**	**8**	**40**	**0**	**0**	**0**	**36**	**8.3**	**2**	....	....	....	....	....	....	....	....	....	....	....	....	....
1995-96	**Montreal**	**NHL**	**7**	**0**	**1**	**1**	**6**	**0**	**0**	**0**	**3**	**0.0**	**0**	....	....	....	....	....	....	....	....	....	....	....	....	....
	St. Louis	**NHL**	**37**	**1**	**3**	**4**	**24**	**0**	**0**	**0**	**45**	**2.2**	**–6**	....	....	....	....	....	....	....	....	....	....	....	....	....
	Worcester	AHL	9	1	10	11	10	....	....	....	....	....	....	....	....	....	....	....	....	....	....	....	....	....	....	....
	Pittsburgh	**NHL**	**13**	**3**	**3**	**6**	**23**	**2**	**0**	**0**	**13**	**23.1**	**0**	....	....	....	....	....	**17**	**1**	**9**	**10**	**36**	**1**	**0**	**1**
1996-97	**Pittsburgh**	**NHL**	**53**	**3**	**14**	**17**	**36**	**0**	**0**	**1**	**49**	**6.1**	**–5**	....	....	....	....	....	....	....	....	....	....	....	....	....
	Anaheim	**NHL**	**13**	**2**	**9**	**11**	**22**	**0**	**0**	**0**	**13**	**15.4**	**5**	....	....	....	....	....	**11**	**2**	**7**	**9**	**16**	**1**	**0**	**1**
1997-98	**Anaheim**	**NHL**	**53**	**2**	**15**	**17**	**28**	**1**	**0**	**1**	**74**	**2.7**	**–10**	....	....	....	....	....	....	....	....	....	....	....	....	....
	NY Islanders	**NHL**	**18**	**0**	**6**	**6**	**21**	**0**	**0**	**0**	**18**	**0.0**	**1**	....	....	....	....	....	....	....	....	....	....	....	....	....
1998-99	**Nashville**	**NHL**	**35**	**2**	**2**	**4**	**38**	**1**	**0**	**1**	**38**	**5.3**	**–4**	**1**	**100.0**	**46**	**29**	**20:47**	....	....	....	....	....	....	....	....
	Phoenix	**NHL**	**35**	**0**	**7**	**7**	**32**	**0**	**0**	**0**	**27**	**0.0**	**–8**	**0**	**0.0**	**58**	**34**	**18:00**	**6**	**0**	**0**	**0**	**8**	**0**	**0**	**0**
99-2000	**Phoenix**	**NHL**	**53**	**1**	**6**	**7**	**22**	**0**	**0**	**0**	**44**	**2.3**	**–16**	**1**	**100.0**	**65**	**65**	**14:12**	**1**	**0**	**0**	**0**	**0**	**0**	**0**	**0**
	NHL Totals		**898**	**53**	**197**	**250**	**685**	**16**	**0**	**7**	**1014**	**5.2**		**2**	**100.0**	**169**	**128**	**16:49**	**99**	**5**	**26**	**31**	**100**	**2**	**0**	**3**

QMJHL First All-Star Team (1983)

Traded to **Philadelphia** by **Vancouver** with Vancouver's 2nd round choice (Kent Hawley) in 1986 Entry Draft and 5th round choice (later traded back to Vancouver - Vancouver selected Sean Fabian) in 1987 Entry Draft for Dave Richter, Rich Sutter and Vancouver's 3rd round choice (previously acquired, Vancouver selected Don Gibson) in 1986 Entry Draft, June 6, 1986. Traded to **Montreal** by **Philadelphia** for Scott Sandelin, November 7, 1988. Traded to **St. Louis** by **Montreal** for Pat Jablonski, November 7, 1995. Traded to **Pittsburgh** by **St. Louis** for Pittsburgh's 6th round choice (Stephen Wagner) in 1996 Entry Draft, March 20, 1996. Traded to **Anaheim** by **Pittsburgh** for Garry Valk, February 21, 1997. Traded to **NY Islanders** by **Anaheim** with Joe Sacco and Mark Janssens for Travis Green, Doug Houda and Tony Tuzzolino, February 6, 1998. Claimed by **Nashville** from **NY Islanders** in Expansion Draft, June 26, 1998. Traded to **Phoenix** by **Nashville** for future considerations, January 13, 1999. Signed as a free agent by **Minnesota**, July 24, 2000.

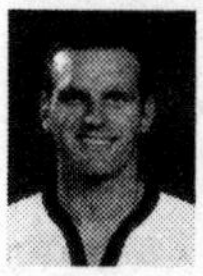

DAMPHOUSSE, Vincent

(DAHM-fooz, VIHN-seht) **S.J.**

Center. Shoots left. 6'1", 200 lbs. Born, Montreal, Que., December 17, 1967. Toronto's 1st choice, 6th overall, in 1986 Entry Draft.

1982-83	Mtl-Bourassa	QAAA	48	33	45	78	....	....	....	....	....	....	....	....	....	....	....	....	....	....	....	....	....	....	....	....
1983-84	Laval Voisins	QMJHL	66	29	36	65	25	....	....	....	....	....	....	....	....	....	....	....	....	....	....	....	....	....	....	....
1984-85	Laval Voisins	QMJHL	68	35	68	103	62	....	....	....	....	....	....	....	....	....	....	....	....	....	....	....	....	....	....	....
1985-86	Laval Voisins	QMJHL	69	45	110	155	70	....	....	....	....	....	....	....	....	....	....	....	14	9	27	36	12	....	....	....
1986-87	**Toronto**	**NHL**	**80**	**21**	**25**	**46**	**26**	**4**	**0**	**1**	**142**	**14.8**	**–6**	....	....	....	....	....	**12**	**1**	**5**	**6**	**8**	**1**	**0**	**0**
1987-88	**Toronto**	**NHL**	**75**	**12**	**36**	**48**	**40**	**1**	**0**	**2**	**111**	**10.8**	**2**	....	....	....	....	....	**6**	**0**	**1**	**1**	**10**	**0**	**0**	**0**
1988-89	**Toronto**	**NHL**	**80**	**26**	**42**	**68**	**75**	**6**	**0**	**4**	**190**	**13.7**	**–8**	....	....	....	....	....	....	....	....	....	....	....	....	....
1989-90	**Toronto**	**NHL**	**80**	**33**	**61**	**94**	**56**	**9**	**0**	**5**	**229**	**14.4**	**2**	....	....	....	....	....	**5**	**0**	**2**	**2**	**2**	**0**	**0**	**0**
1990-91	**Toronto**	**NHL**	**79**	**26**	**47**	**73**	**65**	**10**	**1**	**4**	**247**	**10.5**	**–31**	....	....	....	....	....	....	....	....	....	....	....	....	....
1991-92	**Edmonton**	**NHL**	**80**	**38**	**51**	**89**	**53**	**12**	**1**	**8**	**247**	**15.4**	**10**	....	....	....	....	....	**16**	**6**	**8**	**14**	**8**	**1**	**0**	**0**
1992-93 ♦	**Montreal**	**NHL**	**84**	**39**	**58**	**97**	**98**	**9**	**3**	**8**	**287**	**13.6**	**5**	....	....	....	....	....	**20**	**11**	**12**	**23**	**16**	**5**	**0**	**3**
1993-94	**Montreal**	**NHL**	**84**	**40**	**51**	**91**	**75**	**13**	**0**	**10**	**274**	**14.6**	**0**	....	....	....	....	....	**7**	**1**	**2**	**3**	**8**	**0**	**0**	**0**
1994-95	Ratinger-Lowen	DEL	11	5	7	12	24	....	....	....	....	....	....	....	....	....	....	....	....	....	....	....	....	....	....	....
	Montreal	**NHL**	**48**	**10**	**30**	**40**	**42**	**4**	**0**	**4**	**123**	**8.1**	**15**	....	....	....	....	....	....	....	....	....	....	....	....	....
1995-96	**Montreal**	**NHL**	**80**	**38**	**56**	**94**	**158**	**11**	**4**	**3**	**254**	**15.0**	**5**	....	....	....	....	....	**6**	**4**	**4**	**8**	**0**	**0**	**1**	**2**
1996-97	**Montreal**	**NHL**	**82**	**27**	**54**	**81**	**82**	**7**	**2**	**3**	**244**	**11.1**	**–6**	....	....	....	....	....	**5**	**0**	**0**	**0**	**2**	**0**	**0**	**0**
1997-98	**Montreal**	**NHL**	**76**	**18**	**41**	**59**	**58**	**2**	**1**	**5**	**164**	**11.0**	**14**	....	....	....	....	....	**10**	**3**	**6**	**9**	**22**	**1**	**0**	**0**
1998-99	**Montreal**	**NHL**	**65**	**12**	**24**	**36**	**46**	**3**	**2**	**2**	**147**	**8.2**	**–7**	**1425**	**48.4**	**41**	**37**	**20:27**	....	....	....	....	....	....	....	....
	San Jose	**NHL**	**12**	**7**	**6**	**13**	**4**	**3**	**0**	**1**	**43**	**16.3**	**3**	**230**	**51.3**	**9**	**1**	**19:21**	**6**	**3**	**2**	**5**	**6**	**0**	**2**	**0**
99-2000	**San Jose**	**NHL**	**82**	**21**	**49**	**70**	**58**	**3**	**1**	**1**	**204**	**10.3**	**4**	**1642**	**49.0**	**54**	**38**	**20:26**	**12**	**1**	**7**	**8**	**16**	**1**	**0**	**0**
	NHL Totals		**1087**	**368**	**631**	**999**	**936**	**97**	**15**	**61**	**2906**	**12.7**		**3297**	**48.9**	**104**	**76**	**20:22**	**105**	**30**	**49**	**79**	**98**	**9**	**3**	**5**

QMJHL Second All-Star Team (1986) • Played in NHL All-Star Game (1991, 1992)

Traded to **Edmonton** by **Toronto** with Peter Ing, Scott Thornton, Luke Richardson and cash for Grant Fuhr, Glenn Anderson and Craig Berube, September 19, 1991. Traded to **Montreal** by **Edmonton** with Edmonton's 4th round choice (Adam Wiesel) in 1993 Entry Draft for Shayne Corson, Brent Gilchrist and Vladimir Vujtek, August 27, 1992. Traded to **San Jose** by **Montreal** for Phoenix's 5th round choice (previously acquired, Montreal selected Marc-Andre Thinel) in 1999 Entry Draft, San Jose's 1st round choice (Marcel Hossa) in 2000 Entry Draft and 2nd round choice in 2001 Entry Draft, March 23, 1999.

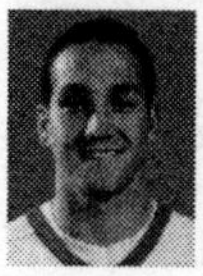

DANDENAULT, Mathieu

(DAHN-deh-noh, MAT-yoo) **DET.**

Right wing/Defense. Shoots right. 6', 200 lbs. Born, Sherbrooke, Que., February 3, 1976. Detroit's 2nd choice, 49th overall, in 1994 Entry Draft.

1990-91	Gloucester	OMHA	44	52	50	102	30	....	....	....	....	....	....	....	....	....	....	....	....	....	....	....	....	....	....	....
1991-92	Vanier Voyageurs	OJHL	33	27	31	58	20	....	....	....	....	....	....	....	....	....	....	....	....	....	....	....	....	....	....	....
	Gloucester	OJHL	6	3	4	7	0	....	....	....	....	....	....	....	....	....	....	....	....	....	....	....	....	....	....	....
1992-93	Gloucester	OJHL	55	11	26	37	64	....	....	....	....	....	....	....	....	....	....	....	....	....	....	....	....	....	....	....
1993-94	Sherbrooke	QMJHL	67	17	36	53	67	....	....	....	....	....	....	....	....	....	....	....	12	4	10	14	12	....	....	....
1994-95	Sherbrooke	QMJHL	67	37	70	107	76	....	....	....	....	....	....	....	....	....	....	....	7	1	7	8	10	....	....	....
1995-96	**Detroit**	**NHL**	**34**	**5**	**7**	**12**	**6**	**1**	**0**	**0**	**32**	**15.6**	**6**	....	....	....	....	....	....	....	....	....	....	....	....	....
	Adirondack	AHL	4	0	0	0	0	....	....	....	....	....	....	....	....	....	....	....	....	....	....	....	....	....	....	....
1996-97 ♦	**Detroit**	**NHL**	**65**	**3**	**9**	**12**	**28**	**0**	**0**	**0**	**81**	**3.7**	**–10**	....	....	....	....	....	....	....	....	....	....	....	....	....
1997-98 ♦	**Detroit**	**NHL**	**68**	**5**	**12**	**17**	**43**	**0**	**0**	**0**	**75**	**6.7**	**5**	....	....	....	....	....	**3**	**1**	**0**	**1**	**0**	**1**	**0**	**0**
1998-99	**Detroit**	**NHL**	**75**	**4**	**10**	**14**	**59**	**0**	**0**	**0**	**94**	**4.3**	**17**	**3**	**0.0**	**109**	**37**	**15:10**	**10**	**0**	**1**	**1**	**0**	**0**	**0**	**0**
99-2000	**Detroit**	**NHL**	**81**	**6**	**12**	**18**	**20**	**0**	**0**	**0**	**98**	**6.1**	**–12**	**1**	**100.0**	**108**	**28**	**12:10**	**6**	**0**	**0**	**0**	**2**	**0**	**0**	**0**
	NHL Totals		**323**	**23**	**50**	**73**	**156**	**1**	**0**	**0**	**380**	**6.1**		**4**	**25.0**	**217**	**65**	**13:37**	**19**	**1**	**1**	**2**	**2**	**1**	**0**	**0**

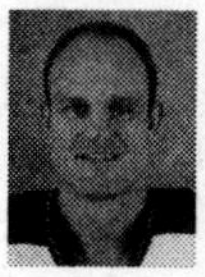

DANEYKO, Ken

(DAN-ee-KOH, KEHN) **N.J.**

Defense. Shoots left. 6'1", 215 lbs. Born, Windsor, Ont., April 17, 1964. New Jersey's 2nd choice, 18th overall, in 1982 Entry Draft.

1980-81	St. Albert Saints	AJHL	1	0	0	0	4	....	....	....	....	....	....	....	....	....	....	....	....	....	....	....	....	....	....	....
	Spokane Flyers	WHL	62	6	13	19	140	....	....	....	....	....	....	....	....	....	....	....	4	0	0	0	6	....	....	....
1981-82	Spokane Flyers	WHL	26	1	11	12	147	....	....	....	....	....	....	....	....	....	....	....	....	....	....	....	....	....	....	....
	Seattle Breakers	WHL	38	1	22	23	151	....	....	....	....	....	....	....	....	....	....	....	14	1	9	10	49	....	....	....
1982-83	Seattle Breakers	WHL	69	17	43	60	150	....	....	....	....	....	....	....	....	....	....	....	4	1	3	4	14	....	....	....
1983-84	Kamloops Oilers	WHL	19	6	28	34	52	....	....	....	....	....	....	....	....	....	....	....	17	4	9	13	28	....	....	....
	New Jersey	**NHL**	**11**	**1**	**4**	**5**	**17**	**0**	**0**	**0**	**17**	**5.9**	**–1**	....	....	....	....	....	....	....	....	....	....	....	....	....
1984-85	**New Jersey**	**NHL**	**1**	**0**	**0**	**0**	**10**	**0**	**0**	**0**	**1**	**0.0**	**–1**	....	....	....	....	....	....	....	....	....	....	....	....	....
	Maine Mariners	AHL	80	4	9	13	206	....	....	....	....	....	....	....	....	....	....	....	11	1	3	4	36	....	....	....
1985-86	**New Jersey**	**NHL**	**44**	**0**	**10**	**10**	**100**	**0**	**0**	**0**	**48**	**0.0**	**0**	....	....	....	....	....	....	....	....	....	....	....	....	....
	Maine Mariners	AHL	21	3	2	5	75	....	....	....	....	....	....	....	....	....	....	....	....	....	....	....	....	....	....	....
1986-87	**New Jersey**	**NHL**	**79**	**2**	**12**	**14**	**183**	**0**	**0**	**0**	**113**	**1.8**	**–13**	....	....	....	....	....	....	....	....	....	....	....	....	....
1987-88	**New Jersey**	**NHL**	**80**	**5**	**7**	**12**	**239**	**1**	**0**	**0**	**82**	**6.1**	**–3**	....	....	....	....	....	**20**	**1**	**6**	**7**	**83**	**0**	**0**	**1**
1988-89	**New Jersey**	**NHL**	**80**	**5**	**5**	**10**	**283**	**1**	**0**	**0**	**108**	**4.6**	**–22**	....	....	....	....	....	....	....	....	....	....	....	....	....
1989-90	**New Jersey**	**NHL**	**74**	**6**	**15**	**21**	**219**	**0**	**1**	**1**	**64**	**9.4**	**15**	....	....	....	....	....	**6**	**2**	**0**	**2**	**21**	**0**	**0**	**0**
1990-91	**New Jersey**	**NHL**	**80**	**4**	**16**	**20**	**249**	**1**	**2**	**1**	**106**	**3.8**	**–10**	....	....	....	....	....	**7**	**0**	**1**	**1**	**10**	**0**	**0**	**0**

Season	Club	League	Regular Season GP	G	A	Pts	PIM	PP	SH	GW	S	%	+/-	TF	F%	H	SB	Min	Playoffs GP	G	A	Pts	PIM	PP	SH	GW
1991-92	New Jersey	NHL	80	1	7	8	170	0	0	0	57	1.8	7	....	....	....	....	....	7	0	3	3	16	0	0	0
1992-93	New Jersey	NHL	84	2	11	13	236	0	0	0	71	2.8	4	....	....	....	....	....	5	0	0	0	8	0	0	0
1993-94	New Jersey	NHL	78	1	9	10	176	0	0	1	60	1.7	27	....	....	....	....	....	20	0	1	1	45	0	0	0
1994-95♦	New Jersey	NHL	25	1	2	3	54	0	0	0	27	3.7	4	....	....	....	....	....	20	1	0	1	22	0	0	0
1995-96	New Jersey	NHL	80	2	4	6	115	0	0	0	67	3.0	–10	....	....	....	....	....	....	....	....	....	....	....	....	....
1996-97	New Jersey	NHL	77	2	7	9	70	0	0	0	63	3.2	24	....	....	....	....	....	10	0	0	0	28	0	0	0
1997-98	New Jersey	NHL	37	0	1	1	57	0	0	0	18	0.0	3	....	....	....	....	....	6	0	1	1	10	0	0	0
1998-99	New Jersey	NHL	82	2	9	11	63	0	0	0	63	3.2	27	1	0.0	182	159	20:03	7	0	0	0	8	0	0	0
99-2000♦	New Jersey	NHL	78	0	6	6	98	0	0	0	74	0.0	13	0	0.0	183	161	18:06	23	1	2	3	14	0	0	0
	NHL Totals		1070	34	125	159	2339	3	3	3	1039	3.3		1	0.0	365	320	19:06	131	5	14	19	265	0	0	1

• Missed majority of 1997-98 season after voluntarily entering NHL/NHLPA substance abuse program, November 6, 1997. • Won Bill Masterton Memorial Trophy (2000)

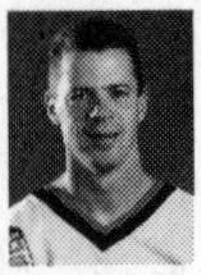

DANIELS, Jeff

(DAN-ehls, JEHF) **CAR.**

Left wing. Shoots left. 6'1", 200 lbs. Born, Oshawa, Ont., June 24, 1968. Pittsburgh's 6th choice, 109th overall, in 1986 Entry Draft.

Season	Club	League	GP	G	A	Pts	PIM	PP	SH	GW	S	%	+/-	TF	F%	H	SB	Min	GP	G	A	Pts	PIM	PP	SH	GW
1983-84	Oshawa Legion	OMHA	57	59	72	131	22	....	....	....	....	....	....	....	....	....	....	....	....	....	....	....	....	....	....	....
1984-85	Oshawa Legion	OJHL-B	7	7	2	9	11	....	....	....	....	....	....	....	....	....	....	....	....	....	....	....	....	....	....	....
	Oshawa Generals	OHL	59	7	11	18	16	....	....	....	....	....	....	....	....	....	....	....	....	....	....	....	....	....	....	....
1985-86	Oshawa Generals	OHL	62	13	19	32	23	....	....	....	....	....	....	....	....	....	....	....	6	0	1	1	0	....	....	....
1986-87	Oshawa Generals	OHL	54	14	9	23	22	....	....	....	....	....	....	....	....	....	....	....	15	3	2	5	5	....	....	....
1987-88	Oshawa Generals	OHL	64	29	39	68	59	....	....	....	....	....	....	....	....	....	....	....	4	2	3	5	0	....	....	....
1988-89	Muskegon	IHL	58	21	21	42	58	....	....	....	....	....	....	....	....	....	....	....	11	3	5	8	11	....	....	....
1989-90	Muskegon	IHL	80	30	47	77	39	....	....	....	....	....	....	....	....	....	....	....	6	1	1	2	7	....	....	....
1990-91	Pittsburgh	NHL	11	0	2	2	2	0	0	0	6	0.0	0	....	....	....	....	....	....	....	....	....	....	....	....	....
	Muskegon	IHL	62	23	29	52	18	....	....	....	....	....	....	....	....	....	....	....	5	1	3	4	2	....	....	....
1991-92	Pittsburgh	NHL	2	0	0	0	0	0	0	0	0	0.0	0	....	....	....	....	....	....	....	....	....	....	....	....	....
	Muskegon	IHL	44	19	16	35	38	....	....	....	....	....	....	....	....	....	....	....	10	5	4	9	9	....	....	....
1992-93	Pittsburgh	NHL	58	5	4	9	14	0	0	1	30	16.7	–5	....	....	....	....	....	12	3	2	5	0	0	0	1
	Cleveland	IHL	3	2	1	3	0	....	....	....	....	....	....	....	....	....	....	....	....	....	....	....	....	....	....	....
1993-94	Pittsburgh	NHL	63	3	5	8	20	0	0	1	46	6.5	–1	....	....	....	....	....	....	....	....	....	....	....	....	....
	Florida	NHL	7	0	0	0	0	0	0	0	6	0.0	0	....	....	....	....	....	....	....	....	....	....	....	....	....
1994-95	Florida	NHL	3	0	0	0	0	0	0	0	0	0.0	0	....	....	....	....	....	....	....	....	....	....	....	....	....
	Detroit Vipers	IHL	25	8	12	20	6	....	....	....	....	....	....	....	....	....	....	....	5	1	0	1	0	....	....	....
1995-96	Springfield	AHL	72	22	20	42	32	....	....	....	....	....	....	....	....	....	....	....	10	3	0	3	2	....	....	....
1996-97	Hartford	NHL	10	0	2	2	0	0	0	0	6	0.0	2	....	....	....	....	....	....	....	....	....	....	....	....	....
	Springfield	AHL	38	18	14	32	19	....	....	....	....	....	....	....	....	....	....	....	16	7	3	10	4	....	....	....
1997-98	Carolina	NHL	2	0	0	0	0	0	0	0	1	0.0	0	....	....	....	....	....	....	....	....	....	....	....	....	....
	New Haven	AHL	71	24	27	51	34	....	....	....	....	....	....	....	....	....	....	....	3	0	1	1	0	....	....	....
1998-99	Nashville	NHL	9	1	3	4	2	0	0	0	8	12.5	–1	1	0.0	9	1	10:56	....	....	....	....	....	....	....	....
	Milwaukee	IHL	62	12	31	43	19	....	....	....	....	....	....	....	....	....	....	....	2	1	1	2	0	....	....	....
99-2000	Carolina	NHL	69	3	4	7	10	0	0	0	28	10.7	–8	47	46.8	54	37	7:42	....	....	....	....	....	....	....	....
	NHL Totals		234	12	20	32	48	0	0	2	131	9.2		48	45.8	63	38	8:04	12	3	2	5	0	0	0	1

Traded to **Florida** by **Pittsburgh** for Greg Hawgood, March 19, 1994. Signed as a free agent by **Hartford**, August 18, 1995. Transferred to **Carolina** after **Hartford** franchise relocated, June 25, 1997. Claimed by **Nashville** from **Carolina** in Expansion Draft, June 26, 1998. Signed as a free agent by **Carolina**, August 31, 1999.

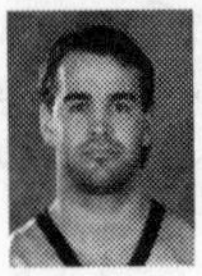

DARBY, Craig

(DAHR-bee, KRAYG) **MTL.**

Center. Shoots right. 6'3", 200 lbs. Born, Oneida, NY, September 26, 1972. Montreal's 3rd choice, 43rd overall, in 1991 Entry Draft.

Season	Club	League	GP	G	A	Pts	PIM	PP	SH	GW	S	%	+/-	TF	F%	H	SB	Min	GP	G	A	Pts	PIM	PP	SH	GW
1989-90	Albany Academy	Hi-School	29	32	53	85	....	....	....	....	....	....	....	....	....	....	....	....	....	....	....	....	....	....	....	....
1990-91	Albany Academy	Hi-School	29	33	61	94	....	....	....	....	....	....	....	....	....	....	....	....	....	....	....	....	....	....	....	....
1991-92	Providence	H-East	35	17	24	41	47	....	....	....	....	....	....	....	....	....	....	....	....	....	....	....	....	....	....	....
1992-93	Providence	H-East	35	11	21	32	62	....	....	....	....	....	....	....	....	....	....	....	....	....	....	....	....	....	....	....
1993-94	Fredericton	AHL	66	23	33	56	51	....	....	....	....	....	....	....	....	....	....	....	....	....	....	....	....	....	....	....
1994-95	Montreal	NHL	10	0	2	2	0	0	0	0	4	0.0	–5	....	....	....	....	....	....	....	....	....	....	....	....	....
	Fredericton	AHL	64	21	47	68	82	....	....	....	....	....	....	....	....	....	....	....	....	....	....	....	....	....	....	....
	NY Islanders	NHL	3	0	0	0	0	0	0	0	1	0.0	–1	....	....	....	....	....	....	....	....	....	....	....	....	....
1995-96	NY Islanders	NHL	10	0	2	2	0	0	0	0	1	0.0	–1	....	....	....	....	....	....	....	....	....	....	....	....	....
	Worcester	AHL	68	22	28	50	47	....	....	....	....	....	....	....	....	....	....	....	4	1	1	2	2	....	....	....
1996-97	Philadelphia	NHL	9	1	4	5	2	0	1	0	13	7.7	2	....	....	....	....	....	....	....	....	....	....	....	....	....
	Philadelphia	AHL	59	26	33	59	24	....	....	....	....	....	....	....	....	....	....	....	10	3	6	9	0	....	....	....
1997-98	Philadelphia	NHL	3	1	0	1	0	0	0	0	3	33.3	0	....	....	....	....	....	....	....	....	....	....	....	....	....
	Philadelphia	AHL	77	*42	45	87	34	....	....	....	....	....	....	....	....	....	....	....	20	5	9	14	4	....	....	....
1998-99	Milwaukee	IHL	81	32	22	54	33	....	....	....	....	....	....	....	....	....	....	....	2	3	0	3	0	....	....	....
99-2000	Montreal	NHL	76	7	10	17	14	0	1	2	90	7.8	–14	1068	48.3	46	18	13:45	....	....	....	....	....	....	....	....
	NHL Totals		111	9	18	27	16	0	2	2	112	8.0		1068	48.3	46	18	13:45	....	....	....	....	....	....	....	....

AHL First All-Star Team (1998)

Traded to **NY Islanders** by **Montreal** with Kirk Muller and Mathieu Schneider for Pierre Turgeon and Vladimir Malakhov, April 5, 1995. Claimed on waivers by **Philadelphia** from **NY Islanders**, June 4, 1996. Claimed by **Nashville** from **Philadelphia** in Expansion Draft, June 26, 1998. Signed as a free agent by **Montreal**, August 4, 1999.

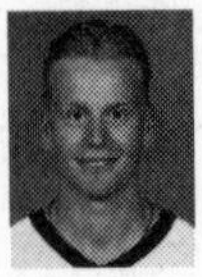

DAVIDSSON, Johan

(DAH-vihd-suhn, YOH-hahn) **NYI**

Center. Shoots right. 6'1", 190 lbs. Born, Jonkoping, Sweden, January 6, 1976. Anaheim's 2nd choice, 28th overall, in 1994 Entry Draft.

Season	Club	League	GP	G	A	Pts	PIM	PP	SH	GW	S	%	+/-	TF	F%	H	SB	Min	GP	G	A	Pts	PIM	PP	SH	GW
1992-93	HV Jonkoping	Sweden	8	1	0	1	0	....	....	....	....	....	....	....	....	....	....	....	....	....	....	....	....	....	....	....
1993-94	HV Jonkoping	Swede-Jr.	5	2	3	5	0	....	....	....	....	....	....	....	....	....	....	....	....	....	....	....	....	....	....	....
	HV Jonkoping	Sweden	38	2	5	7	4	....	....	....	....	....	....	....	....	....	....	....	....	....	....	....	....	....	....	....
1994-95	HV Jonkoping	Swede-Jr.	3	4	1	5	0	....	....	....	....	....	....	....	....	....	....	....	....	....	....	....	....	....	....	....
	HV Jonkoping	Sweden	37	4	7	11	20	....	....	....	....	....	....	....	....	....	....	....	13	3	2	5	0	....	....	....
1995-96	HV Jonkoping	Sweden	39	7	11	18	20	....	....	....	....	....	....	....	....	....	....	....	4	0	2	2	0	....	....	....
1996-97	HV Jonkoping	Sweden	50	18	21	39	18	....	....	....	....	....	....	....	....	....	....	....	5	0	3	3	2	....	....	....
1997-98	HIFK Helsinki	Finland	43	10	30	40	8	....	....	....	....	....	....	....	....	....	....	....	9	3	10	13	0	....	....	....
1998-99	Anaheim	NHL	64	3	5	8	14	1	0	1	48	6.3	–9	516	37.0	34	7	10:37	1	0	0	0	0	0	0	0
	Cincinnati Ducks	AHL	9	1	6	7	2	....	....	....	....	....	....	....	....	....	....	....	....	....	....	....	....	....	....	....
99-2000	Anaheim	NHL	5	1	0	1	2	0	0	1	8	12.5	0	38	42.1	8	0	10:42	....	....	....	....	....	....	....	....
	Cincinnati Ducks	AHL	56	9	31	40	24	....	....	....	....	....	....	....	....	....	....	....	....	....	....	....	....	....	....	....
	NY Islanders	NHL	14	2	4	6	0	0	0	0	21	9.5	0	130	40.0	9	9	11:32	....	....	....	....	....	....	....	....
	NHL Totals		83	6	9	15	16	1	0	2	77	7.8		684	37.9	51	16	10:47	1	0	0	0	0	0	0	0

Traded to **NY Islanders** by **Anaheim** with future considerations for Jorgen Jonsson, March 11, 2000.

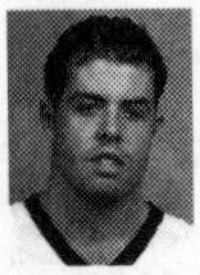

DAWE, Jason

(DAW, JAY-suhn) **NYR**

Right wing. Shoots left. 5'10", 189 lbs. Born, North York, Ont., May 29, 1973. Buffalo's 2nd choice, 35th overall, in 1991 Entry Draft.

Season	Club	League	GP	G	A	Pts	PIM	PP	SH	GW	S	%	+/-	TF	F%	H	SB	Min	GP	G	A	Pts	PIM	PP	SH	GW
1988-89	Don Mills Flyers	MTHL	44	35	28	63	103	....	....	....	....	....	....	....	....	....	....	....	....	....	....	....	....	....	....	....
1989-90	Peterborough	OHL	50	15	18	33	19	....	....	....	....	....	....	....	....	....	....	....	12	4	7	11	4	....	....	....
1990-91	Peterborough	OHL	66	43	27	70	43	....	....	....	....	....	....	....	....	....	....	....	4	3	1	4	0	....	....	....
1991-92	Peterborough	OHL	66	53	55	108	55	....	....	....	....	....	....	....	....	....	....	....	4	5	0	5	0	....	....	....
1992-93	Peterborough	OHL	59	58	68	126	80	....	....	....	....	....	....	....	....	....	....	....	21	18	33	51	18	....	....	....
	Rochester	AHL	....	....	....	....	....	....	....	....	....	....	....	....	....	....	....	....	3	1	0	1	0	....	....	....
1993-94	Buffalo	NHL	32	6	7	13	12	3	0	1	35	17.1	1	....	....	....	....	....	6	0	1	1	6	0	0	0
	Rochester	AHL	48	22	14	36	44	....	....	....	....	....	....	....	....	....	....	....	....	....	....	....	....	....	....	....
1994-95	Rochester	AHL	44	27	19	46	24	....	....	....	....	....	....	....	....	....	....	....	....	....	....	....	....	....	....	....
	Buffalo	NHL	42	7	4	11	19	0	1	2	51	13.7	–6	....	....	....	....	....	5	2	1	3	6	0	0	0
1995-96	Buffalo	NHL	67	25	25	50	33	8	1	0	130	19.2	–8	....	....	....	....	....	....	....	....	....	....	....	....	....
	Rochester	AHL	7	5	4	9	2	....	....	....	....	....	....	....	....	....	....	....	....	....	....	....	....	....	....	....
1996-97	Buffalo	NHL	81	22	26	48	32	4	1	3	136	16.2	14	....	....	....	....	....	11	2	1	3	6	0	0	0
1997-98	Buffalo	NHL	68	19	17	36	36	4	1	3	115	16.5	10	....	....	....	....	....	....	....	....	....	....	....	....	....
	NY Islanders	NHL	13	1	2	3	6	0	0	0	19	5.3	–2	....	....	....	....	....	....	....	....	....	....	....	....	....

Season	Club	League	GP	G	A	Pts	PIM	PP	SH	GW	S	%	+/–	TF	F%	H	SB	Min	GP	G	A	Pts	PIM	PP	SH	GW
			Regular Season																Playoffs							
1998-99	**NY Islanders**	**NHL**	**22**	**2**	**3**	**5**	**8**	**0**	**0**	**0**	**29**	**6.9**	**0**	**4**	**25.0**	**27**	**5**	**11:55**								
	Montreal	**NHL**	**37**	**4**	**5**	**9**	**14**	**1**	**0**	**1**	**52**	**7.7**	**0**	**4**	**0.0**	**44**	**4**	**11:00**								
99-2000	Milwaukee	IHL	41	11	13	24	24																			
	NY Rangers	**NHL**	**3**	**0**	**1**	**1**	**2**	**0**	**0**	**0**	**8**	**0.0**	**0**	**1**	**100.0**	**3**	**0**	**13:35**								
	Hartford	AHL	27	9	9	18	24												21	10	7	17	37			
	NHL Totals		**365**	**86**	**90**	**176**	**162**	**20**	**4**	**10**	**575**	**15.0**		**9**	**22.2**	**74**	**9**	**11:27**	**22**	**4**	**3**	**7**	**18**	**0**	**0**	**0**

OHL First All-Star Team (1993) • Canadian Major Junior Second All-Star Team (1993) • Won George Parsons Trophy (Memorial Cup Tournament Most Sportsmanlike Player) (1993)

Traded to **NY Islanders** by **Buffalo** for Jason Holland and Paul Kruse, March 24, 1998. Claimed on waivers by **Montreal** from **NY Islanders**, December 15, 1998. Signed as a free agent by **Nashville**, October 2, 1999. Traded to **NY Rangers** by **Nashville** for John Namestnikov, February 3, 2000.

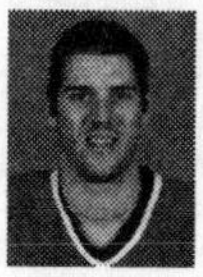

DAZE, Eric

(dah-ZAY, AIR-ihk) **CHI.**

Left wing. Shoots left. 6'6", 234 lbs. Born, Montreal, Que., July 2, 1975. Chicago's 5th choice, 90th overall, in 1993 Entry Draft.

Season	Club	League	GP	G	A	Pts	PIM	PP	SH	GW	S	%	+/–	TF	F%	H	SB	Min	GP	G	A	Pts	PIM	PP	SH	GW
1990-91	Laval Regents	QAAA	30	25	20	45	30																			
1991-92	Laval Regents	QAAA	35	30	29	59	40																			
1992-93	Beauport	QMJHL	68	19	36	55	24																			
1993-94	Beauport	QMJHL	66	59	48	107	31												15	16	8	24	2			
1994-95	Beauport	QMJHL	57	54	45	99	20												16	9	12	21	23			
	Chicago	**NHL**	**4**	**1**	**1**	**2**	**2**	**0**	**0**	**0**	**1**	**100.0**	**2**						**16**	**0**	**1**	**1**	**4**	**0**	**0**	**0**
1995-96	**Chicago**	**NHL**	**80**	**30**	**23**	**53**	**18**	**2**	**0**	**2**	**167**	**18.0**	**16**						**10**	**3**	**5**	**8**	**0**	**0**	**0**	**1**
1996-97	**Chicago**	**NHL**	**71**	**22**	**19**	**41**	**16**	**11**	**0**	**4**	**176**	**12.5**	**–4**						**6**	**2**	**1**	**3**	**2**	**0**	**0**	**0**
1997-98	**Chicago**	**NHL**	**80**	**31**	**11**	**42**	**22**	**10**	**0**	**7**	**216**	**14.4**	**4**													
1998-99	**Chicago**	**NHL**	**72**	**22**	**20**	**42**	**22**	**8**	**0**	**2**	**189**	**11.6**	**–13**	**4**	**0.0**	**92**	**22**	**16:16**								
99-2000	**Chicago**	**NHL**	**59**	**23**	**13**	**36**	**28**	**6**	**0**	**1**	**143**	**16.1**	**–16**	**9**	**22.2**	**91**	**29**	**16:15**								
	NHL Totals		**366**	**129**	**87**	**216**	**108**	**37**	**0**	**16**	**892**	**14.5**		**13**	**15.4**	**183**	**51**	**16:16**	**32**	**5**	**7**	**12**	**6**	**0**	**0**	**1**

QMJHL First All-Star Team (1994, 1995) • Canadian Major Junior Most Sportsmanlike Player of the Year (1995) • NHL All-Rookie Team (1996)

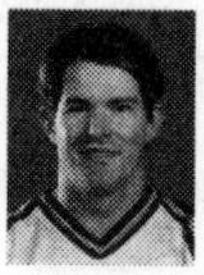

DEADMARSH, Adam

(DEHD-mahrsh, A-dam) **COL.**

Left wing/Center. Shoots right. 6', 195 lbs. Born, Trail, B.C., May 10, 1975. Quebec's 2nd choice, 14th overall, in 1993 Entry Draft.

Season	Club	League	GP	G	A	Pts	PIM	PP	SH	GW	S	%	+/–	TF	F%	H	SB	Min	GP	G	A	Pts	PIM	PP	SH	GW
1990-91	Beaver Valley	KIJHL	35	28	44	72	95																			
1991-92	Portland	WHL	68	30	30	60	81												6	3	3	6	13			
1992-93	Portland	WHL	58	33	36	69	126												16	7	8	15	29			
1993-94	Portland	WHL	65	43	56	99	212												10	9	8	17	33			
1994-95	Portland	WHL	29	28	20	48	129																			
	Quebec	**NHL**	**48**	**9**	**8**	**17**	**56**	**0**	**0**	**0**	**48**	**18.8**	**16**						**6**	**0**	**1**	**1**	**0**	**0**	**0**	**0**
1995-96♦	**Colorado**	**NHL**	**78**	**21**	**27**	**48**	**142**	**3**	**0**	**2**	**151**	**13.9**	**20**						**22**	**5**	**12**	**17**	**25**	**1**	**0**	**0**
1996-97	**Colorado**	**NHL**	**78**	**33**	**27**	**60**	**136**	**10**	**3**	**4**	**198**	**16.7**	**8**						**17**	**3**	**6**	**9**	**24**	**1**	**0**	**1**
1997-98	**Colorado**	**NHL**	**73**	**22**	**21**	**43**	**125**	**10**	**0**	**6**	**187**	**11.8**	**0**						**7**	**2**	**0**	**2**	**4**	**1**	**0**	**0**
	United States	Olympics	4	1	0	1	2																			
1998-99	**Colorado**	**NHL**	**66**	**22**	**27**	**49**	**99**	**10**	**0**	**3**	**152**	**14.5**	**–2**	**621**	**45.9**	**121**	**51**	**20:46**	**19**	**8**	**4**	**12**	**20**	**3**	**0**	**0**
99-2000	**Colorado**	**NHL**	**71**	**18**	**27**	**45**	**106**	**5**	**0**	**4**	**153**	**11.8**	**–10**	**430**	**46.5**	**133**	**45**	**20:27**	**17**	**4**	**11**	**15**	**21**	**1**	**0**	**1**
	NHL Totals		**414**	**125**	**137**	**262**	**664**	**38**	**3**	**19**	**889**	**14.1**		**1051**	**46.1**	**254**	**96**	**20:36**	**88**	**22**	**34**	**56**	**94**	**7**	**0**	**2**

Transferred to **Colorado** after **Quebec** franchise relocated, June 21, 1995.

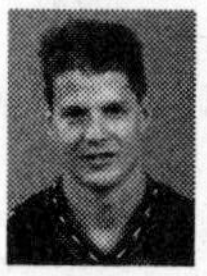

DEAN, Kevin

(DEEN, KEH-vihn) **CHI.**

Defense. Shoots left. 6'3", 210 lbs. Born, Madison, WI, April 1, 1969. New Jersey's 4th choice, 86th overall, in 1987 Entry Draft.

Season	Club	League	GP	G	A	Pts	PIM	PP	SH	GW	S	%	+/–	TF	F%	H	SB	Min	GP	G	A	Pts	PIM	PP	SH	GW
1985-86	Culver Academy	Hi-School	35	28	44	72	48																			
1986-87	Culver Academy	Hi-School	25	19	25	44	30																			
1987-88	New Hampshire	H-East	27	1	6	7	34																			
1988-89	New Hampshire	H-East	34	1	12	13	28																			
1989-90	New Hampshire	H-East	39	2	6	8	42																			
1990-91	New Hampshire	H-East	31	10	12	22	22																			
	Utica Devils	AHL	7	0	1	1	2																			
1991-92	Utica Devils	AHL	23	0	3	3	6																			
	Cincinnati	ECHL	30	3	22	25	43												9	1	6	7	8			
1992-93	Cincinnati	IHL	13	2	1	3	15																			
	Utica Devils	AHL	57	2	16	18	76												5	1	0	1	8			
1993-94	Albany River Rats	AHL	70	9	33	42	92												5	0	2	2	7			
1994-95♦	**New Jersey**	**NHL**	**17**	**0**	**1**	**1**	**4**	**0**	**0**	**0**	**11**	**0.0**	**6**						**3**	**0**	**2**	**2**	**0**	**0**	**0**	**0**
	Albany River Rats	AHL	68	5	37	42	66												8	0	4	4	4			
1995-96	**New Jersey**	**NHL**	**41**	**0**	**6**	**6**	**28**	**0**	**0**	**0**	**29**	**0.0**	**4**													
	Albany River Rats	AHL	1	1	0	1	2																			
1996-97	**New Jersey**	**NHL**	**28**	**2**	**4**	**6**	**6**	**0**	**0**	**0**	**21**	**9.5**	**2**						**1**	**1**	**0**	**1**	**0**	**0**	**0**	**1**
	Albany River Rats	AHL	2	0	1	1	4																			
1997-98	**New Jersey**	**NHL**	**50**	**1**	**8**	**9**	**12**	**1**	**0**	**0**	**28**	**3.6**	**12**						**5**	**1**	**0**	**1**	**2**	**0**	**0**	**0**
	Albany River Rats	AHL	2	0	1	1	2																			
1998-99	**New Jersey**	**NHL**	**62**	**1**	**10**	**11**	**22**	**1**	**0**	**0**	**51**	**2.0**	**4**	**0**	**0.0**	**77**	**59**	**15:42**	**7**	**0**	**0**	**0**	**0**	**0**	**0**	**0**
99-2000	**Atlanta**	**NHL**	**23**	**1**	**0**	**1**	**14**	**0**	**1**	**0**	**9**	**11.1**	**–5**	**1**	**0.0**	**48**	**39**	**16:53**								
	Dallas	**NHL**	**14**	**0**	**0**	**0**	**10**	**0**	**0**	**0**	**6**	**0.0**	**–1**	**0**	**0.0**	**11**	**15**	**11:19**								
	Chicago	**NHL**	**27**	**2**	**8**	**10**	**12**	**0**	**0**	**0**	**32**	**6.3**	**9**	**0**	**0.0**	**34**	**42**	**18:36**								
	NHL Totals		**262**	**7**	**37**	**44**	**108**	**2**	**1**	**0**	**187**	**3.7**		**1**	**0.0**	**170**	**155**	**16:03**	**16**	**2**	**2**	**4**	**2**	**0**	**0**	**1**

AHL First All-Star Team (1995)

Claimed by **Atlanta** from **New Jersey** in Expansion Draft, June 25, 1999. Traded to **Dallas** by **Atlanta** for Dallas' 9th round choice (Mark McRae) in 2000 Entry Draft, December 15, 1999. Traded to **Chicago** by **Dallas** with Derek Plante and Dallas' 2nd round choice in 2001 Entry Draft for Sylvain Cote and Dave Manson, February 8, 2000.

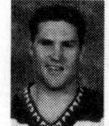

DeBRUSK, Louie

(duh-BRUHSK, LEW-ee) **PHX.**

Left wing. Shoots left. 6'2", 238 lbs. Born, Cambridge, Ont., March 19, 1971. NY Rangers' 4th choice, 49th overall, in 1989 Entry Draft.

Season	Club	League	GP	G	A	Pts	PIM	PP	SH	GW	S	%	+/–	TF	F%	H	SB	Min	GP	G	A	Pts	PIM	PP	SH	GW
1986-87	Port Elgin Huskies	OJHL-C	10	2	1	3	4																			
1987-88	Stratford Cullitons	OJHL-B	45	13	14	27	205																			
1988-89	London Knights	OHL	59	11	11	22	149												19	1	1	2	43			
1989-90	London Knights	OHL	61	21	19	40	198												6	2	2	4	24			
1990-91	London Knights	OHL	61	31	33	64	*223												7	2	2	4	14			
	Binghamton	AHL	2	0	0	0	7												2	0	0	0	9			
1991-92	**Edmonton**	**NHL**	**25**	**2**	**1**	**3**	**124**	**0**	**0**	**1**	**7**	**28.6**	**4**													
	Cape Breton	AHL	28	2	2	4	73																			
1992-93	**Edmonton**	**NHL**	**51**	**8**	**2**	**10**	**205**	**0**	**0**	**1**	**33**	**24.2**	**–16**													
1993-94	**Edmonton**	**NHL**	**48**	**4**	**6**	**10**	**185**	**0**	**0**	**0**	**27**	**14.8**	**–9**													
	Cape Breton	AHL	5	3	1	4	58																			
1994-95	**Edmonton**	**NHL**	**34**	**2**	**0**	**2**	**93**	**0**	**0**	**0**	**14**	**14.3**	**–4**													
1995-96	**Edmonton**	**NHL**	**38**	**1**	**3**	**4**	**96**	**0**	**0**	**0**	**17**	**5.9**	**–7**													
1996-97	**Edmonton**	**NHL**	**32**	**2**	**0**	**2**	**94**	**0**	**0**	**0**	**10**	**20.0**	**–6**						**6**	**0**	**0**	**0**	**4**	**0**	**0**	**0**
1997-98	**Tampa Bay**	**NHL**	**54**	**1**	**2**	**3**	**166**	**0**	**0**	**0**	**14**	**7.1**	**–2**													
	San Antonio	IHL	17	7	4	11	130																			
1998-99	**Phoenix**	**NHL**	**15**	**0**	**0**	**0**	**34**	**0**	**0**	**0**	**6**	**0.0**	**–2**	**0**	**0.0**	**16**	**0**	**5:57**	**6**	**2**	**0**	**2**	**6**	**0**	**0**	**0**
	Las Vegas	IHL	26	3	6	9	160																			
	Springfield	AHL	3	1	0	1	0																			
	Long Beach	IHL	24	5	5	10	134																			
99-2000	**Phoenix**	**NHL**	**61**	**4**	**3**	**7**	**78**	**0**	**0**	**0**	**24**	**16.7**	**1**	**0**	**0.0**	**55**	**4**	**5:21**	**3**	**0**	**0**	**0**	**0**	**0**	**0**	**0**
	NHL Totals		**358**	**24**	**17**	**41**	**1075**	**0**	**0**	**2**	**152**	**15.8**		**0**	**0.0**	**71**	**4**	**5:28**	**15**	**2**	**0**	**2**	**10**	**0**	**0**	**0**

Traded to **Edmonton** by **NY Rangers** with Bernie Nicholls and Steven Rice for Mark Messier and future considerations (Jeff Beukeboom for David Shaw, November 12, 1991), October 4, 1991. Signed as a free agent by **Tampa Bay**, September 23, 1997. Traded to **Phoenix** by **Tampa Bay** with Tampa Bay's 5th round choice (Jay Leach) in 1998 Entry Draft for Craig Janney, June 11, 1998.

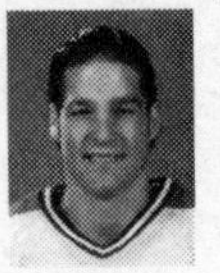

DELISLE, Jonathan
(duh-LIGHL, JOHN-a-THOHN)

Right wing. Shoots right. 5'10", 180 lbs. Born, Ste-Anne-des-Plaines, Que., June 30, 1977. Montreal's 4th choice, 86th overall, in 1995 Entry Draft.

			Regular Season																Playoffs							
Season	Club	League	GP	G	A	Pts	PIM	PP	SH	GW	S	%	+/–	TF	F%	H	SB	Min	GP	G	A	Pts	PIM	PP	SH	GW
1992-93	Laval Regents	QAAA	14	3	3	6	12	....	....	....	....	....	....	....	....	....	....	....	13	2	5	7	24	....	....	....
1993-94	Verdun College	QMJHL	61	16	17	33	130	....	....	....	....	....	....	....	....	....	....	....	4	0	1	1	14	....	....	....
1994-95	Hull Olympiques	QMJHL	60	21	38	59	218	....	....	....	....	....	....	....	....	....	....	....	19	11	8	19	43	....	....	....
1995-96	Hull Olympiques	QMJHL	62	31	57	88	193	....	....	....	....	....	....	....	....	....	....	....	18	6	13	19	64	....	....	....
1996-97	Hull Olympiques	QMJHL	61	35	54	89	228	....	....	....	....	....	....	....	....	....	....	....	14	11	13	24	46	....	....	....
1997-98	Fredericton	AHL	78	15	21	36	138	....	....	....	....	....	....	....	....	....	....	....	4	0	1	1	7	....	....	....
1998-99	Fredericton	AHL	78	7	29	36	118	....	....	....	....	....	....	....	....	....	....	....	15	3	6	9	39	....	....	....
	Montreal	**NHL**	**1**	**0**	**0**	**0**	**0**	**0**	**0**	**0**	**0**	**0.0**	**0**	**0**	**0.0**	**1**	**0**	**4:32**	....	....	....	....	....	....	....	....
99-2000	Quebec Citadelles	AHL	62	7	19	26	142	....	....	....	....	....	....	....	....	....	....	....	3	0	0	0	4	....	....	....
	NHL Totals		**1**	**0**	**0**	**0**	**0**	**0**	**0**	**0**	**0**	**0.0**		**0**	**0.0**	**1**	**0**	**4:32**	....	....	....	....	....	....	....	....

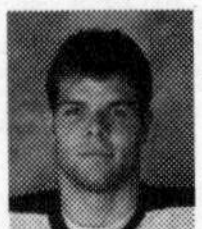

DELISLE, Xavier
(duh-LIGHL, EHX-ay-vuhrz) **MTL.**

Center. Shoots right. 5'11", 182 lbs. Born, Quebec City, Que., May 24, 1977. Tampa Bay's 5th choice, 157th overall, in 1996 Entry Draft.

Season	Club	League	GP	G	A	Pts	PIM	PP	SH	GW	S	%	+/–	TF	F%	H	SB	Min	GP	G	A	Pts	PIM	PP	SH	GW
1992-93	Ste-Foy Governors	QAAA	41	20	23	43	....	....	....	....	....	....	....	....	....	....	....	....	....	....	....	....	....	....	....	....
1993-94	Granby Bisons	QMJHL	46	11	22	33	25	....	....	....	....	....	....	....	....	....	....	....	7	2	0	2	0	....	....	....
1994-95	Granby Bisons	QMJHL	72	18	36	54	48	....	....	....	....	....	....	....	....	....	....	....	13	2	6	8	4	....	....	....
1995-96	Granby Bisons	QMJHL	67	45	75	120	45	....	....	....	....	....	....	....	....	....	....	....	20	13	*27	*40	12	....	....	....
1996-97	Granby Bisons	QMJHL	59	36	56	92	20	....	....	....	....	....	....	....	....	....	....	....	5	1	4	5	6	....	....	....
1997-98	Adirondack	AHL	76	10	19	29	47	....	....	....	....	....	....	....	....	....	....	....	3	0	0	0	0	....	....	....
1998-99	**Tampa Bay**	**NHL**	**2**	**0**	**0**	**0**	**0**	**0**	**0**	**0**	**1**	**0.0**	**0**	**11**	**45.5**	**1**	**0**	**5:51**	....	....	....	....	....	....	....	....
	Cleveland	IHL	77	15	29	44	36	....	....	....	....	....	....	....	....	....	....	....	....	....	....	....	....	....	....	....
99-2000	Detroit Vipers	IHL	20	2	6	8	18	....	....	....	....	....	....	....	....	....	....	....	....	....	....	....	....	....	....	....
	Toledo Storm	ECHL	2	0	1	1	0	....	....	....	....	....	....	....	....	....	....	....	....	....	....	....	....	....	....	....
	Quebec Citadelles	AHL	42	17	28	45	8	....	....	....	....	....	....	....	....	....	....	....	3	1	2	3	0	....	....	....
	NHL Totals		**2**	**0**	**0**	**0**	**0**	**0**	**0**	**0**	**1**	**0.0**		**11**	**45.5**	**1**	**0**	**5:51**	....	....	....	....	....	....	....	....

QMJHL Second All-Star Team (1996) • Memorial Cup All-Star Team (1996)
Signed as a free agent by **Montreal**, August 8, 2000.

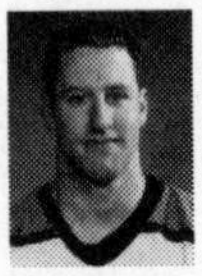

DELMORE, Andy
(DEHL-mohr, AN-dee) **PHI.**

Defense. Shoots right. 6'1", 192 lbs. Born, LaSalle, Ont., December 26, 1976.

Season	Club	League	GP	G	A	Pts	PIM	PP	SH	GW	S	%	+/–	TF	F%	H	SB	Min	GP	G	A	Pts	PIM	PP	SH	GW
1992-93	Chatham Maroons	OJHL-B	47	4	21	25	38	....	....	....	....	....	....	....	....	....	....	....	....	....	....	....	....	....	....	....
1993-94	North Bay	OHL	45	2	7	9	33	....	....	....	....	....	....	....	....	....	....	....	17	0	0	0	2	....	....	....
1994-95	North Bay	OHL	40	2	14	16	21	....	....	....	....	....	....	....	....	....	....	....	....	....	....	....	....	....	....	....
	Sarnia Sting	OHL	27	5	13	18	27	....	....	....	....	....	....	....	....	....	....	....	3	0	0	0	2	....	....	....
1995-96	Sarnia Sting	OHL	64	21	38	59	45	....	....	....	....	....	....	....	....	....	....	....	10	3	7	10	2	....	....	....
1996-97	Sarnia Sting	OHL	64	18	60	78	39	....	....	....	....	....	....	....	....	....	....	....	12	2	10	12	10	....	....	....
	Fredericton	AHL	4	0	1	1	0	....	....	....	....	....	....	....	....	....	....	....	....	....	....	....	....	....	....	....
1997-98	Philadelphia	AHL	73	9	30	39	46	....	....	....	....	....	....	....	....	....	....	....	18	4	4	8	21	....	....	....
1998-99	**Philadelphia**	**NHL**	**2**	**0**	**1**	**1**	**0**	**0**	**0**	**0**	**2**	**0.0**	**–1**	**0**	**0.0**	**1**	**1**	**20:42**	....	....	....	....	....	....	....	....
	Philadelphia	AHL	70	5	18	23	51	....	....	....	....	....	....	....	....	....	....	....	15	1	4	5	6	....	....	....
99-2000	**Philadelphia**	**NHL**	**27**	**2**	**5**	**7**	**8**	**0**	**0**	**1**	**55**	**3.6**	**–1**	**0**	**0.0**	**24**	**31**	**17:17**	**18**	**5**	**2**	**7**	**14**	**1**	**0**	**1**
	Philadelphia	AHL	39	12	14	26	31	....	....	....	....	....	....	....	....	....	....	....	....	....	....	....	....	....	....	....
	NHL Totals		**29**	**2**	**6**	**8**	**8**	**0**	**0**	**1**	**57**	**3.5**		**0**	**0.0**	**25**	**32**	**17:31**	**18**	**5**	**2**	**7**	**14**	**1**	**0**	**1**

OHL First All-Star Team (1997)
Signed as a free agent by **Philadelphia**, June 9, 1997.

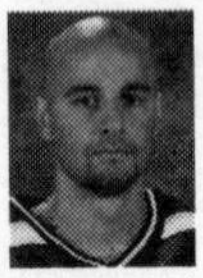

DEMITRA, Pavol
(deh-MIHT-rah, PAH-vohl) **ST.L.**

Left wing. Shoots left. 6', 196 lbs. Born, Dubnica, Czech., November 29, 1974. Ottawa's 9th choice, 227th overall, in 1993 Entry Draft.

Season	Club	League	GP	G	A	Pts	PIM	PP	SH	GW	S	%	+/–	TF	F%	H	SB	Min	GP	G	A	Pts	PIM	PP	SH	GW
1991-92	Spartak Dubnica	Czech-2	28	13	10	23	12	....	....	....	....	....	....	....	....	....	....	....	....	....	....	....	....	....	....	....
1992-93	Spartak Dubnica	Czech-2	4	3	0	3	....	....	....	....	....	....	....	....	....	....	....	....	....	....	....	....	....	....	....	....
	Dukla Trencin	Czech.	46	11	17	28	0	....	....	....	....	....	....	....	....	....	....	....	....	....	....	....	....	....	....	....
1993-94	**Ottawa**	**NHL**	**12**	**1**	**1**	**2**	**4**	**1**	**0**	**0**	**10**	**10.0**	**–7**	....	....	....	....	....	....	....	....	....	....	....	....	....
	P.E.I. Senators	AHL	41	18	23	41	8	....	....	....	....	....	....	....	....	....	....	....	....	....	....	....	....	....	....	....
1994-95	P.E.I. Senators	AHL	61	26	48	74	23	....	....	....	....	....	....	....	....	....	....	....	5	0	7	7	0	....	....	....
	Ottawa	**NHL**	**16**	**4**	**3**	**7**	**0**	**1**	**0**	**0**	**21**	**19.0**	**–4**	....	....	....	....	....	....	....	....	....	....	....	....	....
1995-96	**Ottawa**	**NHL**	**31**	**7**	**10**	**17**	**6**	**2**	**0**	**1**	**66**	**10.6**	**–3**	....	....	....	....	....	....	....	....	....	....	....	....	....
	P.E.I. Senators	AHL	48	28	53	81	44	....	....	....	....	....	....	....	....	....	....	....	....	....	....	....	....	....	....	....
1996-97	Dukla Trencin	Slovakia	1	1	1	2	....	....	....	....	....	....	....	....	....	....	....	....	....	....	....	....	....	....	....	....
	Las Vegas	IHL	22	8	13	21	10	....	....	....	....	....	....	....	....	....	....	....	....	....	....	....	....	....	....	....
	St. Louis	**NHL**	**8**	**3**	**0**	**3**	**2**	**2**	**0**	**1**	**15**	**20.0**	**0**	....	....	....	....	....	**6**	**1**	**3**	**4**	**6**	**0**	**0**	**0**
	Grand Rapids	IHL	42	20	30	50	24	....	....	....	....	....	....	....	....	....	....	....	....	....	....	....	....	....	....	....
1997-98	**St. Louis**	**NHL**	**61**	**22**	**30**	**52**	**22**	**4**	**4**	**6**	**147**	**15.0**	**11**	....	....	....	....	....	**10**	**3**	**3**	**6**	**2**	**0**	**0**	**0**
1998-99	**St. Louis**	**NHL**	**82**	**37**	**52**	**89**	**16**	**14**	**0**	**10**	**259**	**14.3**	**13**	**250**	**44.0**	**31**	**15**	**20:10**	**13**	**5**	**4**	**9**	**4**	**3**	**0**	**1**
99-2000	**St. Louis**	**NHL**	**71**	**28**	**47**	**75**	**8**	**8**	**0**	**4**	**241**	**11.6**	**34**	**41**	**39.0**	**15**	**15**	**19:13**	....	....	....	....	....	....	....	....
	NHL Totals		**281**	**102**	**143**	**245**	**58**	**32**	**4**	**22**	**759**	**13.4**		**291**	**43.3**	**46**	**30**	**19:44**	**29**	**9**	**10**	**19**	**12**	**3**	**0**	**1**

Won Lady Byng Trophy (2000) • Played in NHL All-Star Game (1999, 2000)
Traded to **St. Louis** by **Ottawa** for Christer Olsson, November 27, 1996.

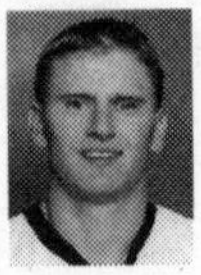

DEMPSEY, Nathan
(DEHMP-see, NAY-than) **TOR.**

Defense. Shoots right. 6', 190 lbs. Born, Spruce Grove, Alta., July 14, 1974. Toronto's 12th choice, 245th overall, in 1992 Entry Draft.

Season	Club	League	GP	G	A	Pts	PIM	PP	SH	GW	S	%	+/–	TF	F%	H	SB	Min	GP	G	A	Pts	PIM	PP	SH	GW
1990-91	St. Albert Saints	AJHL	34	11	20	31	73	....	....	....	....	....	....	....	....	....	....	....	....	....	....	....	....	....	....	....
1991-92	Regina Pats	WHL	70	4	22	26	72	....	....	....	....	....	....	....	....	....	....	....	....	....	....	....	....	....	....	....
1992-93	Regina Pats	WHL	72	12	29	41	95	....	....	....	....	....	....	....	....	....	....	....	13	3	8	11	14	....	....	....
	St. John's Leafs	AHL	....	....	....	....	....	....	....	....	....	....	....	....	....	....	....	....	2	0	0	0	0	....	....	....
1993-94	Regina Pats	WHL	56	14	36	50	100	....	....	....	....	....	....	....	....	....	....	....	4	0	0	0	4	....	....	....
1994-95	St. John's Leafs	AHL	74	7	30	37	91	....	....	....	....	....	....	....	....	....	....	....	5	1	0	1	11	....	....	....
1995-96	St. John's Leafs	AHL	73	5	15	20	103	....	....	....	....	....	....	....	....	....	....	....	4	1	0	1	9	....	....	....
1996-97	**Toronto**	**NHL**	**14**	**1**	**1**	**2**	**2**	**0**	**0**	**0**	**11**	**9.1**	**–2**	....	....	....	....	....	....	....	....	....	....	....	....	....
	St. John's Leafs	AHL	52	8	18	26	108	....	....	....	....	....	....	....	....	....	....	....	6	1	0	1	4	....	....	....
1997-98	St. John's Leafs	AHL	68	12	16	28	85	....	....	....	....	....	....	....	....	....	....	....	4	0	0	0	0	....	....	....
1998-99	St. John's Leafs	AHL	67	2	29	31	70	....	....	....	....	....	....	....	....	....	....	....	5	0	1	1	2	....	....	....
99-2000	**Toronto**	**NHL**	**6**	**0**	**2**	**2**	**2**	**0**	**0**	**0**	**3**	**0.0**	**2**	**1**	**0.0**	**4**	**2**	**13:40**	....	....	....	....	....	....	....	....
	St. John's Leafs	AHL	44	15	12	27	40	....	....	....	....	....	....	....	....	....	....	....	....	....	....	....	....	....	....	....
	NHL Totals		**20**	**1**	**3**	**4**	**4**	**0**	**0**	**0**	**14**	**7.1**		**1**	**0.0**	**4**	**2**	**13:39**	....	....	....	....	....	....	....	....

WHL East Second All-Star Team (1994)

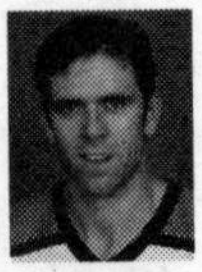

DESJARDINS, Eric
(deh-ZHAHR-dai, AIR-ihk) **PHI.**

Defense. Shoots right. 6'1", 200 lbs. Born, Rouyn, Que., June 14, 1969. Montreal's 3rd choice, 38th overall, in 1987 Entry Draft.

Season	Club	League	GP	G	A	Pts	PIM	PP	SH	GW	S	%	+/–	TF	F%	H	SB	Min	GP	G	A	Pts	PIM	PP	SH	GW
1985-86	Laval Laurentide	QAAA	42	6	30	36	54	....	....	....	....	....	....	....	....	....	....	....	....	....	....	....	....	....	....	....
1986-87	Granby Bisons	QMJHL	66	14	24	38	178	....	....	....	....	....	....	....	....	....	....	....	8	3	2	5	10	....	....	....
1987-88	Granby Bisons	QMJHL	62	18	49	67	138	....	....	....	....	....	....	....	....	....	....	....	5	0	3	3	10	....	....	....
	Sherbrooke	AHL	3	0	0	0	6	....	....	....	....	....	....	....	....	....	....	....	4	0	2	2	2	....	....	....
1988-89	**Montreal**	**NHL**	**36**	**2**	**12**	**14**	**26**	**1**	**0**	**0**	**39**	**5.1**	**9**	....	....	....	....	....	**14**	**1**	**1**	**2**	**6**	**1**	**0**	**0**
1989-90	**Montreal**	**NHL**	**55**	**3**	**13**	**16**	**51**	**1**	**0**	**0**	**48**	**6.3**	**1**	....	....	....	....	....	**6**	**0**	**0**	**0**	**10**	**0**	**0**	**0**
1990-91	**Montreal**	**NHL**	**62**	**7**	**18**	**25**	**27**	**0**	**0**	**1**	**114**	**6.1**	**7**	....	....	....	....	....	**13**	**1**	**4**	**5**	**8**	**1**	**0**	**0**

Season	Club	League	GP	G	A	Pts	PIM	PP	SH	GW	S	%	+/–	TF	F%	H	SB	Min	Playoffs GP	G	A	Pts	PIM	PP	SH	GW
1991-92	Montreal	NHL	77	6	32	38	50	4	0	2	141	4.3	17	....	....	....	....	....	11	3	3	6	4	1	0	0
1992-93♦	Montreal	NHL	82	13	32	45	98	7	0	1	163	8.0	20	....	....	....	....	....	20	4	10	14	23	1	0	1
1993-94	Montreal	NHL	84	12	23	35	97	6	1	3	193	6.2	–1	....	....	....	....	....	7	0	2	2	4	0	0	0
1994-95	Montreal	NHL	9	0	6	6	2	0	0	0	14	0.0	2	....	....	....	....	....	....	....	....	....	....	....	....	....
	Philadelphia	NHL	34	5	18	23	12	1	0	1	79	6.3	10	....	....	....	....	....	15	4	4	8	10	1	0	2
1995-96	Philadelphia	NHL	80	7	40	47	45	5	0	2	184	3.8	19	....	....	....	....	....	12	0	6	6	2	0	0	0
1996-97	Philadelphia	NHL	82	12	34	46	50	5	1	1	183	6.6	25	....	....	....	....	....	19	2	8	10	12	0	0	0
1997-98	Philadelphia	NHL	77	6	27	33	36	2	1	0	150	4.0	11	....	....	....	....	....	5	0	1	1	0	0	0	0
	Canada	Olympics	6	0	0	0	2	....	....	....	....	....	....	....	....	....	....	....	....	....	....	....	....	....	....	....
1998-99	Philadelphia	NHL	68	15	36	51	38	6	0	2	190	7.9	18	0	0.0	36	108	25:48	6	2	2	4	4	1	0	1
99-2000	Philadelphia	NHL	81	14	41	55	32	8	0	4	207	6.8	20	1	0.0	28	141	27:01	18	2	10	12	2	1	0	1
	NHL Totals		827	102	332	434	564	46	3	17	1705	6.0		1	0.0	64	249	26:27	146	19	51	70	85	7	0	5

QMJHL Second All-Star Team (1987) • QMJHL First All-Star Team (1988) • NHL Second All-Star Team (1999, 2000) • Played in NHL All-Star Game (1992, 1996, 2000)
Traded to **Philadelphia** by **Montreal** with Gilbert Dionne and John LeClair for Mark Recchi and Philadelphia's 3rd round choice (Martin Hohenberger) in 1995 Entry Draft, February 9, 1995.

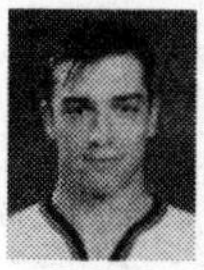

DEULING, Jarrett

(DEW-lihng, JAIR-uht) **S.J.**

Left wing. Shoots left. 6', 205 lbs. Born, Vernon, B.C., March 4, 1974. NY Islanders' 2nd choice, 56th overall, in 1992 Entry Draft.

Season	Club	League	GP	G	A	Pts	PIM	PP	SH	GW	S	%	+/–	TF	F%	H	SB	Min	Playoffs GP	G	A	Pts	PIM	PP	SH	GW
1989-90	Whitehorse Bears	AAHL	28	34	48	72	84	....	....	....	....	....	....	....	....	....	....	....	....	....	....	....	....	....	....	....
1990-91	Kamloops Blazers	WHL	48	4	12	16	43	....	....	....	....	....	....	....	....	....	....	....	12	5	2	7	7	....	....	....
1991-92	Kamloops Blazers	WHL	68	28	26	54	79	....	....	....	....	....	....	....	....	....	....	....	17	10	6	16	18	....	....	....
1992-93	Kamloops Blazers	WHL	68	31	32	63	93	....	....	....	....	....	....	....	....	....	....	....	13	6	7	13	14	....	....	....
1993-94	Kamloops Blazers	WHL	70	44	59	103	171	....	....	....	....	....	....	....	....	....	....	....	18	*13	8	21	43	....	....	....
1994-95	Worcester	AHL	63	11	8	19	37	....	....	....	....	....	....	....	....	....	....	....	....	....	....	....	....	....	....	....
1995-96	NY Islanders	NHL	14	0	1	1	11	0	0	0	11	0.0	–1	....	....	....	....	....	....	....	....	....	....	....	....	....
	Worcester	AHL	57	16	7	23	57	....	....	....	....	....	....	....	....	....	....	....	4	1	2	3	2	....	....	....
1996-97	NY Islanders	NHL	1	0	0	0	0	0	0	0	0	0.0	0	....	....	....	....	....	....	....	....	....	....	....	....	....
	Kentucky	AHL	58	15	31	46	57	....	....	....	....	....	....	....	....	....	....	....	4	3	0	3	8	....	....	....
1997-98	Milwaukee	IHL	64	18	18	36	84	....	....	....	....	....	....	....	....	....	....	....	10	4	3	7	36	....	....	....
1998-99	Kentucky	AHL	60	22	31	53	68	....	....	....	....	....	....	....	....	....	....	....	12	3	6	9	8	....	....	....
99-2000	Kentucky	AHL	75	17	25	42	83	....	....	....	....	....	....	....	....	....	....	....	8	1	1	2	6	....	....	....
	NHL Totals		15	0	1	1	11	0	0	0	11	0.0		....	....	....	....	....	....	....	....	....	....	....	....	....

Signed as a free agent by **San Jose**, August 27, 1998.

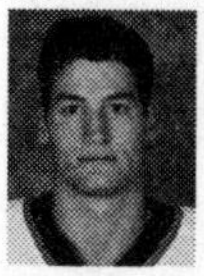

DEVEREAUX, Boyd

(DEH-vuhr-oh, BOID) **DET.**

Center. Shoots left. 6'2", 195 lbs. Born, Seaforth, Ont., April 16, 1978. Edmonton's 1st choice, 6th overall, in 1996 Entry Draft.

Season	Club	League	GP	G	A	Pts	PIM	PP	SH	GW	S	%	+/–	TF	F%	H	SB	Min	Playoffs GP	G	A	Pts	PIM	PP	SH	GW
1992-93	Seaforth Sailors	OJHL-D	34	7	20	27	13	....	....	....	....	....	....	....	....	....	....	....	....	....	....	....	....	....	....	....
1993-94	Stratford Cullitons	OJHL-B	46	12	27	39	8	....	....	....	....	....	....	....	....	....	....	....	....	....	....	....	....	....	....	....
1994-95	Stratford Cullitons	OJHL-B	45	31	74	105	21	....	....	....	....	....	....	....	....	....	....	....	....	....	....	....	....	....	....	....
1995-96	Kitchener	OHL	66	20	38	58	35	....	....	....	....	....	....	....	....	....	....	....	12	3	7	10	4	....	....	....
1996-97	Kitchener	OHL	54	28	41	69	37	....	....	....	....	....	....	....	....	....	....	....	13	4	11	15	8	....	....	....
	Hamilton Bulldogs	AHL	....	....	....	....	....	....	....	....	....	....	....	....	....	....	....	....	1	0	1	1	0	....	....	....
1997-98	Edmonton	NHL	38	1	4	5	6	0	0	0	27	3.7	–5	....	....	....	....	....	....	....	....	....	....	....	....	....
	Hamilton Bulldogs	AHL	14	5	6	11	6	....	....	....	....	....	....	....	....	....	....	....	9	1	1	2	8	....	....	....
1998-99	Edmonton	NHL	61	6	8	14	23	0	1	4	39	15.4	2	409	42.8	32	32	10:09	1	0	0	0	0	0	0	0
	Hamilton Bulldogs	AHL	7	4	6	10	2	....	....	....	....	....	....	....	....	....	....	....	8	0	3	3	4	....	....	....
99-2000	Edmonton	NHL	76	8	19	27	20	0	1	2	108	7.4	7	241	34.9	54	26	12:36	....	....	....	....	....	....	....	....
	NHL Totals		175	15	31	46	49	0	2	6	174	8.6		650	39.8	86	58	11:31	1	0	0	0	0	0	0	0

Canadian Major Junior Scholastic Player of the Year (1996)
Signed as a free agent by **Detroit**, August 23, 2000.

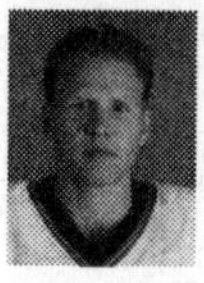

de VRIES, Greg

(deh-VREES, GREHG) **COL.**

Defense. Shoots left. 6'3", 215 lbs. Born, Sundridge, Ont., January 4, 1973.

Season	Club	League	GP	G	A	Pts	PIM	PP	SH	GW	S	%	+/–	TF	F%	H	SB	Min	Playoffs GP	G	A	Pts	PIM	PP	SH	GW
1988-89	Cortina Astros	OMHA	35	28	40	68	....	....	....	....	....	....	....	....	....	....	....	....	....	....	....	....	....	....	....	....
1989-90	Aurora Eagles	OJHL-B	42	1	16	17	32	....	....	....	....	....	....	....	....	....	....	....	....	....	....	....	....	....	....	....
1990-91	Stratford Cullitons	OJHL-B	40	8	32	40	120	....	....	....	....	....	....	....	....	....	....	....	3	2	1	3	20	....	....	....
1991-92	Bowling Green	CCHA	24	0	3	3	20	....	....	....	....	....	....	....	....	....	....	....	....	....	....	....	....	....	....	....
1992-93	Niagara Falls	OHL	62	3	23	26	86	....	....	....	....	....	....	....	....	....	....	....	4	0	1	1	6	....	....	....
1993-94	Niagara Falls	OHL	64	5	40	45	135	....	....	....	....	....	....	....	....	....	....	....	....	....	....	....	....	....	....	....
	Cape Breton	AHL	9	0	0	0	11	....	....	....	....	....	....	....	....	....	....	....	1	0	0	0	0	....	....	....
1994-95	Cape Breton	AHL	77	5	19	24	68	....	....	....	....	....	....	....	....	....	....	....	....	....	....	....	....	....	....	....
1995-96	Edmonton	NHL	13	1	1	2	12	0	0	0	8	12.5	–2	....	....	....	....	....	....	....	....	....	....	....	....	....
	Cape Breton	AHL	58	9	30	39	174	....	....	....	....	....	....	....	....	....	....	....	....	....	....	....	....	....	....	....
1996-97	Edmonton	NHL	37	0	4	4	52	0	0	0	31	0.0	–2	....	....	....	....	....	12	0	1	1	8	0	0	0
	Hamilton Bulldogs	AHL	34	4	14	18	26	....	....	....	....	....	....	....	....	....	....	....	....	....	....	....	....	....	....	....
1997-98	Edmonton	NHL	65	7	4	11	80	1	0	0	53	13.2	–17	....	....	....	....	....	7	0	0	0	21	0	0	0
1998-99	Nashville	NHL	6	0	0	0	4	0	0	0	1	1.0	–4	0	0.0	12	7	18:11	....	....	....	....	....	....	....	....
	Colorado	NHL	67	1	3	4	60	0	0	0	56	56.0	–3	1	100.0	85	69	16:23	19	0	2	2	22	0	0	0
99-2000	Colorado	NHL	69	2	7	9	73	0	0	0	40	5.0	–7	0	0.0	87	61	14:59	5	0	0	0	4	0	0	0
	NHL Totals		257	11	19	30	281	1	0	0	189	5.8		1	100.0	184	137	15:47	43	0	3	3	55	0	0	0

Signed as a free agent by **Edmonton**, March 20, 1994. Traded to **Nashville** by **Edmonton** with Eric Fichaud and Drake Berehowsky for Mikhail Shtalenkov and Jim Dowd, October 1, 1998. Traded to **Colorado** by **Nashville** for Colorado's 2nd round choice (Ed Hill) in 1999 Entry Draft, October 24, 1998.

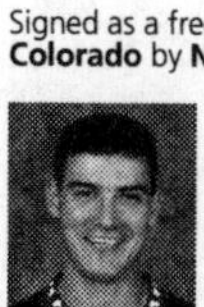

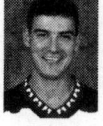

DIDUCK, Gerald

(DIH-duhk, JAIR-ohld) **TOR.**

Defense. Shoots right. 6'1", 216 lbs. Born, Edmonton, Alta., April 6, 1965. NY Islanders' 2nd choice, 16th overall, in 1983 Entry Draft.

Season	Club	League	GP	G	A	Pts	PIM	PP	SH	GW	S	%	+/–	TF	F%	H	SB	Min	Playoffs GP	G	A	Pts	PIM	PP	SH	GW
1981-82	Lethbridge	WHL	71	1	15	16	81	....	....	....	....	....	....	....	....	....	....	....	12	0	3	3	27	....	....	....
1982-83	Lethbridge	WHL	67	8	16	24	151	....	....	....	....	....	....	....	....	....	....	....	20	3	12	15	49	....	....	....
1983-84	Lethbridge	WHL	65	10	24	34	133	....	....	....	....	....	....	....	....	....	....	....	5	1	4	5	27	....	....	....
	Indianapolis	CHL	....	....	....	....	....	....	....	....	....	....	....	....	....	....	....	....	10	1	6	7	19	....	....	....
1984-85	NY Islanders	NHL	65	2	8	10	80	0	0	0	52	3.8	2	....	....	....	....	....	....	....	....	....	....	....	....	....
1985-86	NY Islanders	NHL	10	1	2	3	2	0	0	0	6	16.7	5	....	....	....	....	....	....	....	....	....	....	....	....	....
	Springfield	AHL	61	6	14	20	173	....	....	....	....	....	....	....	....	....	....	....	....	....	....	....	....	....	....	....
1986-87	NY Islanders	NHL	30	2	3	5	67	0	0	0	54	3.7	–3	....	....	....	....	....	14	0	1	1	35	0	0	0
	Springfield	AHL	45	6	8	14	120	....	....	....	....	....	....	....	....	....	....	....	....	....	....	....	....	....	....	....
1987-88	NY Islanders	NHL	68	7	12	19	113	4	0	1	128	5.5	22	....	....	....	....	....	6	1	0	1	42	1	0	0
1988-89	NY Islanders	NHL	65	11	21	32	155	6	0	0	132	8.3	9	....	....	....	....	....	....	....	....	....	....	....	....	....
1989-90	NY Islanders	NHL	76	3	17	20	163	1	0	0	102	2.9	2	....	....	....	....	....	5	0	0	0	12	0	0	0
1990-91	Montreal	NHL	32	1	2	3	39	0	0	0	34	2.9	3	....	....	....	....	....	....	....	....	....	....	....	....	....
	Vancouver	NHL	31	3	7	10	66	0	0	1	66	4.5	–8	....	....	....	....	....	6	1	0	1	11	1	0	0
1991-92	Vancouver	NHL	77	6	21	27	229	2	0	1	128	4.7	–3	....	....	....	....	....	5	0	0	0	10	0	0	0
1992-93	Vancouver	NHL	80	6	14	20	171	0	1	0	92	6.5	32	....	....	....	....	....	12	4	2	6	12	0	0	0
1993-94	Vancouver	NHL	55	1	10	11	72	0	0	0	50	2.0	2	....	....	....	....	....	24	1	7	8	22	0	0	0
1994-95	Vancouver	NHL	22	1	3	4	15	1	0	0	25	4.0	–8	....	....	....	....	....	....	....	....	....	....	....	....	....
	Chicago	NHL	13	1	0	1	48	1	0	0	42	2.4	3	....	....	....	....	....	16	1	3	4	22	0	0	0
1995-96	Hartford	NHL	79	1	9	10	88	0	0	0	93	1.1	7	....	....	....	....	....	....	....	....	....	....	....	....	....
1996-97	Hartford	NHL	56	1	10	11	40	0	0	1	59	1.7	–9	....	....	....	....	....	....	....	....	....	....	....	....	....
	Phoenix	NHL	11	1	2	3	23	1	0	0	21	4.8	2	....	....	....	....	....	7	0	0	0	10	0	0	0
1997-98	Phoenix	NHL	78	8	10	18	118	1	0	4	104	7.7	14	....	....	....	....	....	6	0	2	2	20	0	0	0
1998-99	Phoenix	NHL	44	0	2	2	72	0	0	0	39	0.0	9	0	0.0	127	50	18:32	3	0	0	0	2	0	0	0

			Regular Season																Playoffs							
Season	Club	League	GP	G	A	Pts	PIM	PP	SH	GW	S	%	+/–	TF	F%	H	SB	Min	GP	G	A	Pts	PIM	PP	SH	GW
99-2000	Canada	Nat-Team	12	3	0	3	6																			
	Toronto	**NHL**	**26**	**0**	**3**	**3**	**33**	**0**	**0**	**0**	**18**	**0.0**	**2**	**0**	**0.0**	**84**	**20**	**15:25**	**10**	**0**	**1**	**1**	**14**	**0**	**0**	**0**
	NHL Totals		**918**	**56**	**156**	**212**	**1594**	**17**	**1**	**8**	**1245**	**4.5**		**0**	**0.0**	**211**	**70**	**17:22**	**114**	**8**	**16**	**24**	**212**	**2**	**0**	**0**

Traded to **Montreal** by **NY Islanders** for Craig Ludwig, September 4, 1990. Traded to **Vancouver** by **Montreal** for Vancouver's 4th round choice (Vladimir Vujtek) in 1991 Entry Draft, January 12, 1991. Traded to **Chicago** by **Vancouver** for Bogdan Savenko and Hartford's 3rd round choice (previously acquired, Vancouver selected Larry Courville) in 1995 Entry Draft, April 7, 1995. Signed as a free agent by **Hartford**, August 24, 1995. Traded to **Phoenix** by **Hartford** for Chris Murray, March 18, 1997. Signed as a free agent by **Toronto**, February 3, 2000.

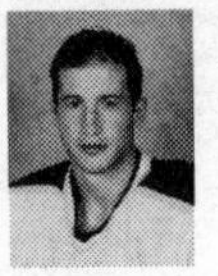

DiMAIO, Rob

(duh-MIGH-oh, RAWB) **CAR.**

Center. Shoots right. 5'10", 190 lbs. Born, Calgary, Alta., February 19, 1968. NY Islanders' 6th choice, 118th overall, in 1987 Entry Draft.

Season	Club	League	GP	G	A	Pts	PIM	PP	SH	GW	S	%	+/–	TF	F%	H	SB	Min	GP	G	A	Pts	PIM	PP	SH	GW
1984-85	Kamloops Blazers	WHL	55	9	18	27	29												7	1	3	4	2			
1985-86	Kamloops Blazers	WHL	6	1	0	1	0																			
	Medicine Hat	WHL	55	20	30	50	82												22	6	6	12	39			
1986-87	Medicine Hat	WHL	70	27	43	70	130												20	7	11	18	46			
1987-88	Medicine Hat	WHL	54	47	43	90	120												14	12	19	*31	59			
1988-89	**NY Islanders**	**NHL**	**16**	**1**	**0**	**1**	**30**	**0**	**0**	**1**	**16**	**6.3**	**–6**													
	Springfield	AHL	40	13	18	31	67																			
1989-90	**NY Islanders**	**NHL**	**7**	**0**	**0**	**0**	**2**	**0**	**0**	**0**	**2**	**0.0**	**0**						**1**	**1**	**0**	**1**	**4**	**0**	**0**	**0**
	Springfield	AHL	54	25	27	52	69												16	4	7	11	45			
1990-91	**NY Islanders**	**NHL**	**1**	**0**	**0**	**0**	**0**	**0**	**0**	**0**	**0**	**0.0**	**0**													
	Capital District	AHL	12	3	4	7	22																			
1991-92	**NY Islanders**	**NHL**	**50**	**5**	**2**	**7**	**43**	**0**	**2**	**0**	**43**	**11.6**	**–23**													
1992-93	**Tampa Bay**	**NHL**	**54**	**9**	**15**	**24**	**62**	**2**	**0**	**0**	**75**	**12.0**	**0**													
1993-94	**Tampa Bay**	**NHL**	**39**	**8**	**7**	**15**	**40**	**2**	**0**	**1**	**51**	**15.7**	**–5**													
	Philadelphia	**NHL**	**14**	**3**	**5**	**8**	**6**	**0**	**0**	**1**	**30**	**10.0**	**1**													
1994-95	**Philadelphia**	**NHL**	**36**	**3**	**1**	**4**	**53**	**0**	**0**	**0**	**34**	**8.8**	**8**						**15**	**2**	**4**	**6**	**4**	**0**	**1**	**1**
1995-96	**Philadelphia**	**NHL**	**59**	**6**	**15**	**21**	**58**	**1**	**1**	**0**	**49**	**12.2**	**0**						**3**	**0**	**0**	**0**	**0**	**0**	**0**	**0**
1996-97	**Boston**	**NHL**	**72**	**13**	**15**	**28**	**82**	**0**	**3**	**2**	**152**	**8.6**	**–21**													
1997-98	**Boston**	**NHL**	**79**	**10**	**17**	**27**	**82**	**0**	**0**	**4**	**112**	**8.9**	**–13**						**6**	**1**	**0**	**1**	**8**	**0**	**0**	**0**
1998-99	**Boston**	**NHL**	**71**	**7**	**14**	**21**	**95**	**1**	**0**	**0**	**121**	**5.8**	**–14**	**83**	**45.8**	**106**	**26**	**16:41**	**12**	**2**	**0**	**2**	**8**	**0**	**0**	**1**
99-2000	**Boston**	**NHL**	**50**	**5**	**16**	**21**	**42**	**0**	**0**	**0**	**93**	**5.4**	**–1**	**278**	**44.2**	**103**	**20**	**16:47**								
	NY Rangers	**NHL**	**12**	**1**	**3**	**4**	**8**	**0**	**0**	**0**	**18**	**5.6**	**–8**	**1**	**0.0**	**16**	**6**	**15:30**								
	NHL Totals		**560**	**71**	**110**	**181**	**603**	**6**	**6**	**9**	**796**	**8.9**		**362**	**44.5**	**225**	**52**	**16:37**	**37**	**6**	**4**	**10**	**24**	**0**	**1**	**2**

Won Stafford Smythe Memorial Trophy (Memorial Cup Tournament MVP) (1988)

Claimed by **Tampa Bay** from **NY Islanders** in Expansion Draft, June 18, 1992. Traded to **Philadelphia** by **Tampa Bay** for Jim Cummins and Philadelphia's 4th round choice (later traded back to Philadelphia - Philadelphia selected Radovan Somik) in 1995 Entry Draft, March 18, 1994. Claimed by **San Jose** from **Philadelphia** in NHL Waiver Draft, September 30, 1996. Traded to **Boston** by **San Jose** for Boston's 5th round choice (Adam Nittel) in 1997 Entry Draft, September 30, 1996. Traded to **NY Rangers** by **Boston** for Mike Knuble, March 10, 2000. Traded to **Carolina** by **NY Rangers** with Darren Langdon for Sandy McCarthy and a 4th round choice in 2001 Entry Draft, August 4, 2000.

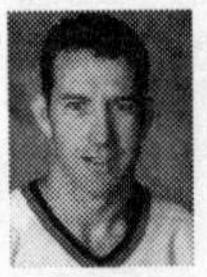

DINEEN, Kevin

(DIH-neen, KEH-vihn) **CBJ**

Right wing. Shoots right. 5'11", 190 lbs. Born, Quebec City, Que., October 28, 1963. Hartford's 3rd choice, 56th overall, in 1982 Entry Draft.

Season	Club	League	GP	G	A	Pts	PIM	PP	SH	GW	S	%	+/–	TF	F%	H	SB	Min	GP	G	A	Pts	PIM	PP	SH	GW
1980-81	St. Michael's	OHA-B	40	15	28	43	167																			
1981-82	U. of Denver	WCHA	26	10	10	20	70																			
1982-83	U. of Denver	WCHA	36	16	13	29	108																			
1983-84	Canada	Nat-Team	52	5	11	16	2																			
	Canada	Olympics	7	0	0	0	8																			
1984-85	**Hartford**	**NHL**	**57**	**25**	**16**	**41**	**120**	**8**	**4**	**2**	**141**	**17.7**	**–6**													
	Binghamton	AHL	25	15	8	23	41																			
1985-86	**Hartford**	**NHL**	**57**	**33**	**35**	**68**	**124**	**6**	**0**	**8**	**167**	**19.8**	**16**						**10**	**6**	**7**	**13**	**18**	**1**	**0**	**2**
1986-87	**Hartford**	**NHL**	**78**	**40**	**39**	**79**	**110**	**11**	**0**	**7**	**234**	**17.1**	**7**						**6**	**2**	**1**	**3**	**31**	**1**	**0**	**0**
1987-88	**Hartford**	**NHL**	**74**	**25**	**25**	**50**	**217**	**5**	**0**	**4**	**223**	**11.2**	**–14**						**6**	**4**	**4**	**8**	**8**	**1**	**0**	**1**
1988-89	**Hartford**	**NHL**	**79**	**45**	**44**	**89**	**167**	**20**	**1**	**4**	**294**	**15.3**	**–6**						**4**	**1**	**0**	**1**	**10**	**0**	**0**	**0**
1989-90	**Hartford**	**NHL**	**67**	**25**	**41**	**66**	**164**	**8**	**2**	**2**	**214**	**11.7**	**7**						**6**	**3**	**2**	**5**	**18**	**0**	**0**	**1**
1990-91	**Hartford**	**NHL**	**61**	**17**	**30**	**47**	**104**	**4**	**0**	**2**	**161**	**10.6**	**–15**						**6**	**1**	**0**	**1**	**16**	**0**	**0**	**0**
1991-92	**Hartford**	**NHL**	**16**	**4**	**2**	**6**	**23**	**1**	**0**	**1**	**28**	**14.3**	**–6**													
	Philadelphia	**NHL**	**64**	**26**	**30**	**56**	**130**	**5**	**3**	**4**	**197**	**13.2**	**1**													
1992-93	**Philadelphia**	**NHL**	**83**	**35**	**28**	**63**	**201**	**6**	**3**	**7**	**241**	**14.5**	**14**													
1993-94	**Philadelphia**	**NHL**	**71**	**19**	**23**	**42**	**113**	**5**	**1**	**2**	**156**	**12.2**	**–9**													
1994-95	Houston Aeros	IHL	17	6	4	10	42																			
	Philadelphia	**NHL**	**40**	**8**	**5**	**13**	**39**	**4**	**0**	**2**	**55**	**14.5**	**–1**						**15**	**6**	**4**	**10**	**18**	**1**	**0**	**1**
1995-96	**Philadelphia**	**NHL**	**26**	**0**	**2**	**2**	**50**	**0**	**0**	**0**	**31**	**0.0**	**–8**													
	Hartford	**NHL**	**20**	**2**	**7**	**9**	**67**	**0**	**0**	**0**	**35**	**5.7**	**7**													
1996-97	**Hartford**	**NHL**	**78**	**19**	**29**	**48**	**141**	**8**	**0**	**5**	**185**	**10.3**	**–6**													
1997-98	**Carolina**	**NHL**	**54**	**7**	**16**	**23**	**105**	**0**	**0**	**1**	**96**	**7.3**	**–7**													
1998-99	**Carolina**	**NHL**	**67**	**8**	**10**	**18**	**97**	**0**	**0**	**1**	**86**	**9.3**	**5**	**6**	**16.7**	**77**	**6**	**9:58**	**6**	**0**	**0**	**0**	**8**	**0**	**0**	**0**
99-2000	**Ottawa**	**NHL**	**67**	**4**	**8**	**12**	**57**	**0**	**0**	**1**	**71**	**5.6**	**2**	**10**	**50.0**	**67**	**14**	**9:31**								
	NHL Totals		**1059**	**342**	**390**	**732**	**2029**	**91**	**14**	**53**	**2615**	**13.1**		**16**	**37.5**	**144**	**20**	**9:44**	**59**	**23**	**18**	**41**	**127**	**4**	**0**	**5**

Won Bud Light/NHL Man of the Year Award (1991) • Played in NHL All-Star Game (1988, 1989)

Traded to **Philadelphia** by **Hartford** for Murray Craven and Philadelphia's 4th round choice (Kevin Smyth) in 1992 Entry Draft, November 13, 1991. Traded to **Hartford** by **Philadelphia** for Hartford/Carolina's 3rd (Kris Mallette) and 7th (later traded back to Hartford/Carolina - Carolina selected Andrew Merrick) round choices in 1997 Entry Draft, December 28, 1995. Transferred to **Carolina** after **Hartford** franchise relocated, June 25, 1997. Signed as a free agent by **Ottawa**, September 1, 1999. Selected by **Columbus** from **Ottawa** in Expansion Draft, June 23, 2000.

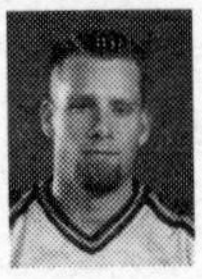

DINGMAN, Chris

(DIHNG-man, KRIHS) **COL.**

Left wing. Shoots left. 6'4", 245 lbs. Born, Edmonton, Alta., July 6, 1976. Calgary's 1st choice, 19th overall, in 1994 Entry Draft.

Season	Club	League	GP	G	A	Pts	PIM	PP	SH	GW	S	%	+/–	TF	F%	H	SB	Min	GP	G	A	Pts	PIM	PP	SH	GW
1991-92	Edmonton Mercs	AAHA	36	23	18	41	72																			
1992-93	Brandon	WHL	50	10	17	27	64												4	0	0	0	0			
1993-94	Brandon	WHL	45	21	20	41	77												13	1	7	8	39			
1994-95	Brandon	WHL	66	40	43	83	201												3	1	0	1	9			
1995-96	Brandon	WHL	40	16	29	45	109												19	12	11	23	60			
	Saint John Flames	AHL																	1	0	0	0	0			
1996-97	Saint John Flames	AHL	71	5	6	11	195																			
1997-98	**Calgary**	**NHL**	**70**	**3**	**3**	**6**	**149**	**1**	**0**	**0**	**47**	**6.4**	**–11**													
1998-99	**Calgary**	**NHL**	**2**	**0**	**0**	**0**	**17**	**0**	**0**	**0**	**1**	**0.0**	**–2**	**0**	**0.0**	**3**	**1**	**8:11**								
	Saint John Flames	AHL	50	5	7	12	140																			
	Colorado	**NHL**	**1**	**0**	**0**	**0**	**7**	**0**	**0**	**0**	**0**	**0.0**	**0**	**0**	**0.0**	**0**	**0**	**0:30**								
	Hershey Bears	AHL	17	1	3	4	102												5	0	2	2	6			
99-2000	**Colorado**	**NHL**	**68**	**8**	**3**	**11**	**132**	**2**	**0**	**1**	**54**	**14.8**	**–2**	**2**	**0.0**	**73**	**18**	**6:29**								
	NHL Totals		**141**	**11**	**6**	**17**	**305**	**3**	**0**	**1**	**102**	**10.8**		**2**	**0.0**	**76**	**19**	**6:27**								

Traded to **Colorado** by **Calgary** with Theoren Fleury for Rene Corbet, Wade Belak, Robyn Regehr and Colorado's 2nd round compensatory choice (Jarret Stoll) in 2000 Entry Draft, February 28, 1999.

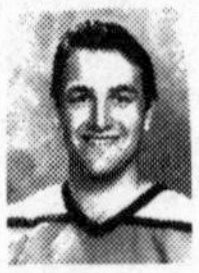

DIONNE, Gilbert

(dee-AHN, ZHIHL-bair) **CAR.**

Left wing. Shoots left. 6', 194 lbs. Born, Drummondville, Que., September 19, 1970. Montreal's 5th choice, 81st overall, in 1990 Entry Draft.

Season	Club	League	GP	G	A	Pts	PIM	PP	SH	GW	S	%	+/–	TF	F%	H	SB	Min	GP	G	A	Pts	PIM	PP	SH	GW
1986-87	Niagara Falls	OJHL-B	17	9	6	15	16																			
1987-88	Niagara Falls	OJHL-B	36	36	48	84	60																			
1988-89	Kitchener	OHL	66	11	33	44	13												5	1	1	2	4			
1989-90	Kitchener	OHL	64	48	57	105	85												17	13	10	23	22			
1990-91	**Montreal**	**NHL**	**2**	**0**	**0**	**0**	**0**	**0**	**0**	**0**	**0**	**0.0**	**–2**													
	Fredericton	AHL	77	40	47	87	62												9	6	5	11	8			
1991-92	**Montreal**	**NHL**	**39**	**21**	**13**	**34**	**10**	**7**	**0**	**2**	**90**	**23.3**	**7**						**11**	**3**	**4**	**7**	**10**	**1**	**0**	**1**
	Fredericton	AHL	29	19	27	46	20																			
1992-93 ♦	**Montreal**	**NHL**	**75**	**20**	**28**	**48**	**63**	**6**	**1**	**2**	**145**	**13.8**	**5**						**20**	**6**	**6**	**12**	**20**	**1**	**0**	**1**
	Fredericton	AHL	3	4	3	7	0																			
1993-94	**Montreal**	**NHL**	**74**	**19**	**26**	**45**	**31**	**3**	**0**	**5**	**162**	**11.7**	**–9**						**5**	**1**	**2**	**3**	**0**	**0**	**0**	**0**

			Regular Season																Playoffs							
Season	Club	League	GP	G	A	Pts	PIM	PP	SH	GW	S	%	+/-	TF	F%	H	SB	Min	GP	G	A	Pts	PIM	PP	SH	GW
1994-95	Montreal	NHL	6	0	3	3	2	0	0	0	4	0.0	−3													
	Philadelphia	NHL	20	0	6	6	2	0	0	0	29	0.0	−1						3	0	0	0	4	0	0	0
1995-96	Philadelphia	NHL	2	0	1	1	0	0	0	0	0	0.0	0													
	Florida	NHL	5	1	2	3	0	0	0	0	12	8.3	0													
	Carolina	AHL	55	43	58	101	29																			
1996-97	Carolina	AHL	72	41	47	88	69																			
1997-98	Cincinnati	IHL	76	42	57	99	54												9	3	4	7	28			
1998-99	Cincinnati	IHL	76	35	53	88	123												3	0	2	2	6			
99-2000	Cincinnati	IHL	81	34	49	83	88												11	4	3	7	8			
	NHL Totals		223	61	79	140	108	16	1	9	442	13.8							39	10	12	22	34	2	0	2

NHL All-Rookie Team (1992) • AHL Second All-Star Team (1996) • IHL First All-Star Team (1998) • IHL Second All-Star Team (2000)

Traded to **Philadelphia** by **Montreal** with Eric Desjardins and John LeClair for Mark Recchi and Philadelphia's 3rd round choice (Martin Hohenberger) in 1995 Entry Draft, February 9, 1995. Signed as a free agent by **Florida**, January 29, 1996. Signed as a free agent by **Cincinnati** (IHL), July 23, 1997. Signed as a free agent by **Carolina**, August 31, 1999.

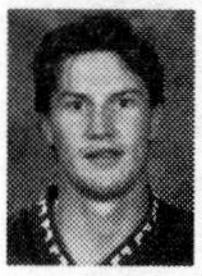

DOAN, Shane

(DOHN, SHAYN) **PHX.**

Right wing. Shoots right. 6'2", 218 lbs. Born, Halkirk, Alta., October 10, 1976. Winnipeg's 1st choice, 7th overall, in 1995 Entry Draft.

			Regular Season																Playoffs							
Season	Club	League	GP	G	A	Pts	PIM	PP	SH	GW	S	%	+/-	TF	F%	H	SB	Min	GP	G	A	Pts	PIM	PP	SH	GW
1991-92	Killam Selects	AAHA	56	80	84	164	74																			
1992-93	Kamloops Blazers	WHL	51	7	12	19	65												13	0	1	1	8			
1993-94	Kamloops Blazers	WHL	52	24	24	48	88																			
1994-95	Kamloops Blazers	WHL	71	37	57	94	106												21	6	10	16	16			
1995-96	Winnipeg	NHL	74	7	10	17	101	1	0	3	106	6.6	−9						6	0	0	0	6	0	0	0
1996-97	Phoenix	NHL	63	4	8	12	49	0	0	0	100	4.0	−3						4	0	0	0	2	0	0	0
1997-98	Phoenix	NHL	33	5	6	11	35	0	0	3	42	11.9	−3						6	1	0	1	6	0	0	0
	Springfield	AHL	39	21	21	42	64																			
1998-99	Phoenix	NHL	79	6	16	22	54	0	0	0	156	3.8	−5	6	16.7	161	15	12:42	7	2	2	4	6	0	0	2
99-2000	Phoenix	NHL	81	26	25	51	66	1	1	4	221	11.8	6	25	36.0	225	11	16:51	4	1	2	3	8	1	0	0
	NHL Totals		330	48	65	113	305	2	1	10	625	7.7		31	32.3	386	26	14:48	27	4	4	8	28	1	0	2

Memorial Cup All-Star Team (1995) • Won Stafford Smythe Memorial Trophy (Memorial Cup Tournament MVP) (1995)

Transferred to **Phoenix** after **Winnipeg** franchise relocated, July 1, 1996.

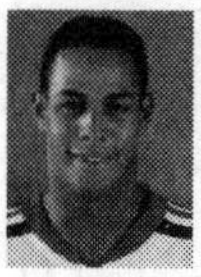

DOIG, Jason

(DOIG, JAY-suhn) **NYR**

Defense. Shoots right. 6'3", 228 lbs. Born, Montreal, Que., January 29, 1977. Winnipeg's 3rd choice, 34th overall, in 1995 Entry Draft.

			Regular Season																Playoffs							
Season	Club	League	GP	G	A	Pts	PIM	PP	SH	GW	S	%	+/-	TF	F%	H	SB	Min	GP	G	A	Pts	PIM	PP	SH	GW
1990-91	North Shore	QAAA	31	30	33	63	53																			
1991-92	North Shore	QAAA	29	11	11	22	20																			
1992-93	Lac St-Louis	QAAA	35	11	16	27	40												7	5	5	10	16			
1993-94	St-Jean Lynx	QMJHL	63	8	17	25	65												5	0	2	2	2			
1994-95	Laval Titan	QMJHL	55	13	42	55	259												20	4	13	17	39			
1995-96	Laval Titan	QMJHL	5	3	6	9	20																			
	Granby	QMJHL	24	4	30	34	91												20	10	22	32	*110			
	Winnipeg	NHL	15	1	1	2	28	0	0	0	7	14.3	−2													
	Springfield	AHL	5	0	0	0	28																			
1996-97	Granby	QMJHL	39	14	33	47	211												5	0	4	4	27			
	Las Vegas	IHL	6	0	1	1	19																			
	Springfield	AHL	5	0	3	3	2												17	1	4	5	37			
1997-98	Phoenix	NHL	4	0	1	1	12	0	0	0	1	0.0	−4													
	Springfield	AHL	46	2	25	27	153												3	0	0	0	2			
1998-99	Phoenix	NHL	9	0	1	1	10	0	0	0	0	0.0	2	0	0.0	1	2	5:08								
	Springfield	AHL	32	3	5	8	67																			
	Hartford	AHL	8	1	4	5	40												7	1	1	2	39			
99-2000	NY Rangers	NHL	7	0	1	1	22	0	0	0	3	0.0	−2	0	0.0	9	6	8:50								
	Hartford	AHL	27	3	11	14	70												21	1	5	6	20			
	NHL Totals		35	1	4	5	72	0	0	0	11	9.1		0	0.0	10	8	6:45								

Memorial Cup All-Star Team (1996)

Transferred to **Phoenix** after **Winnipeg** franchise relocated, July 1, 1996. Traded to **NY Rangers** by **Phoenix** with Phoenix's 6th round choice (Jay Dardis) in 1999 Entry Draft for Stan Neckar, March 23, 1999.

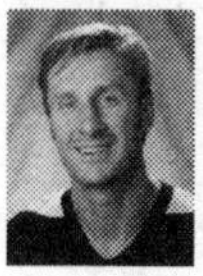

DOLLAS, Bobby

(DAW-luhs, BAW-bee)

Defense. Shoots left. 6'2", 212 lbs. Born, Montreal, Que., January 31, 1965. Winnipeg's 2nd choice, 14th overall, in 1983 Entry Draft.

			Regular Season																Playoffs							
Season	Club	League	GP	G	A	Pts	PIM	PP	SH	GW	S	%	+/-	TF	F%	H	SB	Min	GP	G	A	Pts	PIM	PP	SH	GW
1980-81	Lac-St-Louis	QAAA	46	9	14	23																				
1981-82	Lac St-Louis	QAAA	44	9	31	40	138																			
1982-83	Laval Voisins	QMJHL	63	16	45	61	144												11	5	5	10	23			
1983-84	Laval Voisins	QMJHL	54	12	33	45	80												14	1	8	9	23			
	Winnipeg	NHL	1	0	0	0	0	0	0	0	0	0.0	−2													
1984-85	Winnipeg	NHL	9	0	0	0	0	0	0	0	2	0.0	4													
	Sherbrooke	AHL	8	1	3	4	4												17	3	6	9	17			
1985-86	Winnipeg	NHL	46	0	5	5	66	0	0	0	50	0.0	−3						3	0	0	0	2	0	0	0
	Sherbrooke	AHL	25	4	7	11	29																			
1986-87	Sherbrooke	AHL	75	6	18	24	87												16	2	4	6	13			
1987-88	Quebec	NHL	9	0	0	0	2	0	0	0	5	0.0	−4													
	Moncton Hawks	AHL	26	4	10	14	20																			
	Fredericton	AHL	33	4	8	12	27												15	2	2	4	24			
1988-89	Quebec	NHL	16	0	3	3	16	0	0	0	11	0.0	−11													
	Halifax Citadels	AHL	57	5	19	24	65												4	1	0	1	14			
1989-90	Canada	Nat-Team	68	8	29	37	60																			
1990-91	Detroit	NHL	56	3	5	8	20	0	0	1	59	5.1	6						7	1	0	1	13	0	0	0
1991-92	Detroit	NHL	27	3	1	4	20	0	1	0	26	11.5	4						2	0	1	1	0	0	0	0
	Adirondack	AHL	19	1	6	7	33												18	7	4	11	22			
1992-93	Detroit	NHL	6	0	0	0	2	0	0	0	5	0.0	−1													
	Adirondack	AHL	64	7	36	43	54												11	3	8	11	8			
1993-94	Anaheim	NHL	77	9	11	20	55	1	0	1	121	7.4	20													
1994-95	Anaheim	NHL	45	7	13	20	12	3	1	1	70	10.0	−3													
1995-96	Anaheim	NHL	82	8	22	30	64	0	1	1	117	6.8	9													
1996-97	Anaheim	NHL	79	4	14	18	55	1	0	1	96	4.2	17						11	0	0	0	4	0	0	0
1997-98	Anaheim	NHL	22	0	1	1	27	0	0	0	11	0.0	−12													
	Edmonton	NHL	30	2	5	7	22	0	0	0	27	7.4	6						11	0	0	0	16	0	0	0
1998-99	Pittsburgh	NHL	70	2	8	10	60	0	0	0	34	5.9	−3	0	0.0	47	56	15:35	13	1	0	1	6	0	0	0
99-2000	Long Beach	IHL	13	2	4	6	8																			
	Ottawa	NHL	1	0	0	0	0	0	0	0	0	0.0	2	0	0.0	1	1	16:10								
	Calgary	NHL	49	3	7	10	28	1	0	0	36	8.3	4	0	0.0	52	69	20:09								
	NHL Totals		625	41	95	136	449	6	3	5	670	6.1		0	0.0	100	126	17:27	47	2	1	3	41	0	0	0

QMJHL Second All-Star Team (1983) • AHL First All-Star Team (1993) • Won Eddie Shore Award (AHL's Outstanding Defenseman) (1993)

Traded to **Quebec** by **Winnipeg** for Stu Kulak, December 17, 1987. Signed as a free agent by **Detroit**, October 18, 1990. Claimed by **Anaheim** from **Detroit** in Expansion Draft, June 24, 1993. Traded to **Edmonton** by **Anaheim** for Drew Bannister, January 9, 1998. Traded to **Pittsburgh** by **Edmonton** with Tony Hrkac for Josef Beranek, June 16, 1998. Signed as a free agent by **Long Beach**, October 12, 1999. Signed as a free agent by **Ottawa**, November 9, 1999. Claimed on waivers by **Calgary** from **Ottawa**, November 11, 1999.

DRAKE, Dallas (DRAYK, DAL-lahs) ST.L.

Right wing. Shoots left. 6'1", 190 lbs. Born, Trail, B.C., February 4, 1969. Detroit's 6th choice, 116th overall, in 1989 Entry Draft.

			Regular Season																Playoffs							
Season	Club	League	GP	G	A	Pts	PIM	PP	SH	GW	S	%	+/-	TF	F%	H	SB	Min	GP	G	A	Pts	PIM	PP	SH	GW
1984-85	Rossland	KIJHL	30	13	37	50	....																			
1985-86	Rossland	KIJHL	41	53	73	126	....																			
1986-87	Rossland	KIJHL	40	55	80	135	....																			
1987-88	Vernon Lakers	BCJHL	47	39	85	124	50												11	9	17	26	30			
1988-89	North-Michigan	WCHA	38	17	22	39	22												7	1	2	3	4			
1989-90	North-Michigan	WCHA	36	13	24	37	42																			
1990-91	North-Michigan	WCHA	44	22	36	58	89																			
1991-92	North-Michigan	WCHA	38	*39	41	*80	46																			
1992-93	Detroit	NHL	72	18	26	44	93	3	2	5	89	20.2	15						7	3	3	6	6	1	0	0
1993-94	Detroit	NHL	47	10	22	32	37	0	1	2	78	12.8	5													
	Adirondack	AHL	1	2	0	2	0																			
	Winnipeg	NHL	15	3	5	8	12		1	1	34	8.8	-6													
1994-95	Winnipeg	NHL	43	8	18	26	30	0	0	1	66	12.1	-6													
1995-96	Winnipeg	NHL	69	19	20	39	36	4	4	2	121	15.7	-7						7	0	1	1	2	0	0	0
1996-97	Phoenix	NHL	63	17	19	36	52	5	1	1	113	15.0	-11						7	0	0	0	0	0	0	0
1997-98	Phoenix	NHL	60	11	29	40	71	3	0	2	112	9.8	17						4	0	3	3	4	0	0	1
1998-99	Phoenix	NHL	53	9	22	31	65	0	0	3	105	8.6	17	5	60.0	105	17	15:38	7	4	3	7	4	0	2	1
99-2000	Phoenix	NHL	79	15	30	45	62	0	2	5	127	11.8	17	4	25.0	176	46	15:48	5	0	1	1	4	0	0	1
NHL Totals			501	110	191	301	458	16	11	22	845	13.0		9	44.4	281	63	15:44	33	7	9	16	18	3	0	1

WCHA First All-Star Team (1992) • NCAA West First All-American Team (1992)
Traded to **Winnipeg** by **Detroit** with Tim Cheveldae for Bob Essensa and Sergei Bautin, March 8, 1994. Transferred to **Phoenix** after **Winnipeg** franchise relocated, July 1, 1996. Selected by **Minnesota** from **Phoenix** in Expansion Draft, June 23, 2000. Signed as a free agent by **St. Louis**, July 1, 2000.

DRAPER, Kris (DRAY-puhr, KRIHS) DET.

Center. Shoots left. 5'11", 190 lbs. Born, Toronto, Ont., May 24, 1971. Winnipeg's 4th choice, 62nd overall, in 1989 Entry Draft.

			Regular Season																Playoffs							
Season	Club	League	GP	G	A	Pts	PIM	PP	SH	GW	S	%	+/-	TF	F%	H	SB	Min	GP	G	A	Pts	PIM	PP	SH	GW
1987-88	Don Mills Flyers	MTHL	40	35	32	67	46																			
1988-89	Canada	Nat-Team	60	11	15	26	16																			
1989-90	Canada	Nat-Team	61	12	22	34	44																			
1990-91	Ottawa 67's	OHL	39	19	42	61	35												17	8	11	19	20			
	Winnipeg	NHL	3	1	0	1	5	0	0	0	1	100.0	0													
	Moncton Hawks	AHL	7	2	1	3	2																			
1991-92	Winnipeg	NHL	10	2	0	2	2				19	10.5							2	0	0	0	0			
	Moncton Hawks	AHL	61	11	18	29	113												4	0	1	1	6			
1992-93	Winnipeg	NHL	7	0	0	0	2				5	0.0	-6													
	Moncton Hawks	AHL	67	12	23	35	40												5	2	4	6	18			
1993-94	Detroit	NHL	39	5	8	13	31	0	1	0	55	9.1	11						7	2	2	4	4	0	1	0
	Adirondack	AHL	46	20	23	43	49																			
1994-95	Detroit	NHL	36	2	6	8	22	0	0	0	44	4.5	1						18	4	1	5	12	0	1	1
1995-96	Detroit	NHL	52	7	9	16	32	0	0	1	51	13.7	2						18	4	2	6	18	0	1	0
1996-97	Detroit	NHL	76	8	5	13	73	1	0	1	85	9.4	-11						20	2	4	6	12	0	1	0
1997-98	Detroit	NHL	64	13	10	23	45	1	0	5	96	13.5	5						19	1	3	4	12	0	0	1
1998-99	Detroit	NHL	80	4	14	18	79	0	1	1	78	5.1	2	887	54.6	82	18	12:43	10	0	1	1	6	0	0	0
99-2000	Detroit	NHL	51	5	7	12	28	0	0	0	76	6.6	3	380	57.6	81	34	13:33	9	2	0	2	4	0	0	0
NHL Totals			418	47	59	106	319	2	3	9	510	9.2		1267	55.5	151	31	13:02	103	15	13	28	70	0	4	2

Traded to **Detroit** by **Winnipeg** for future considerations, June 30, 1993.

DROUIN, P.C. (droo-IHN, PEE-CEE)

Left wing. Shoots left. 6'2", 208 lbs. Born, St. Lambert, Que., April 22, 1974.

			Regular Season																Playoffs							
Season	Club	League	GP	G	A	Pts	PIM	PP	SH	GW	S	%	+/-	TF	F%	H	SB	Min	GP	G	A	Pts	PIM	PP	SH	GW
1991-92	Gloucester	OJHL	49	23	51	74	59																			
1992-93	Cornell Big Red	ECAC	23	6	9	15	30																			
1993-94	Cornell Big Red	ECAC	21	6	13	19	32																			
1994-95	Cornell Big Red	ECAC	26	4	16	20	48																			
1995-96	Cornell Big Red	ECAC	31	18	14	32	60																			
1996-97	Boston	NHL	3	0	0	0	0	0	0	0	1	0.0	1													
	Providence Bruins	AHL	42	12	11	23	10																			
1997-98	Providence Bruins	AHL	7	0	2	2	4												7	2	4	6	4			
	Charlotte	ECHL	62	21	46	67	57												7	2	4	6	4			
1998	Bracknell Bees	Britain	42	12	21	33	12												7	4	1	5	0			
99-2000	Bracknell Bees	Britain	35	10	28	38	42												6	2	3	5	4			
NHL Totals			3	0	0	0	0	0	0	0	1	0.0														

Signed as a free agent by **Boston**, October 14, 1996.

DRUKEN, Harold (DROO-kehn, HAIR-ohld) VAN.

Center. Shoots left. 6', 205 lbs. Born, St. John's, Nfld., January 26, 1979. Vancouver's 3rd choice, 36th overall, in 1997 Entry Draft.

			Regular Season																Playoffs							
Season	Club	League	GP	G	A	Pts	PIM	PP	SH	GW	S	%	+/-	TF	F%	H	SB	Min	GP	G	A	Pts	PIM	PP	SH	GW
1995-96	Noble High	Hi-School	30	37	28	65	28																			
1996-97	Detroit Whalers	OHL	63	27	31	58	14												5	3	2	5	0			
1997-98	Plymouth Whalers	OHL	64	38	44	82	12												15	9	11	20	4			
1998-99	Plymouth Whalers	OHL	60	*58	45	103	34												11	9	12	21	14			
99-2000	Vancouver	NHL	33	7	9	16	10	2	0	0	69	10.1	14	307	47.9	13	10	13:01	4	1	2	3	6			
	Syracuse Crunch	AHL	47	20	25	45	32																			
NHL Totals			33	7	9	16	10	2	0	0	69	10.1		307	47.9	13	10	13:01								

OHL Second All-Star Team (1999)

DRULIA, Stan (DROO-lee-ah, STAN) T.B.

Right wing. Shoots right. 5'11", 190 lbs. Born, Elmira, NY, January 5, 1968. Pittsburgh's 11th choice, 214th overall, in 1986 Entry Draft.

			Regular Season																Playoffs							
Season	Club	League	GP	G	A	Pts	PIM	PP	SH	GW	S	%	+/-	TF	F%	H	SB	Min	GP	G	A	Pts	PIM	PP	SH	GW
1983-84	Fort Erie Meteors	OJHL-B	39	24	36	65	104																			
1984-85	Belleville Bulls	OHL	63	24	31	55	33												24	4	11	15	15			
1985-86	Belleville Bulls	OHL	66	43	36	79	73												9	4	4	8	2			
1986-87	Hamilton Hawks	OHL	55	27	51	78	26												4	2	4	6	2			
1987-88	Hamilton Hawks	OHL	65	52	69	121	44												14	10	9	19	16			
1988-89	Niagara Falls	OHL	47	52	93	145	59												17	11	*26	37	18			
	Maine Mariners	AHL	3	1	1	2	0																			
1989-90	Phoenix	IHL	16	6	3	9	2																			
	Cape Breton	AHL	31	5	7	12	2																			
1990-91	Knoxville	ECHL	64	*63	77	*140	49												3	3	2	5	4			
1991-92	New Haven	AHL	77	49	53	102	46												5	2	4	6	4			
1992-93	Tampa Bay	NHL	24	2	1	3	10	0	0	1	22	9.1	1													
	Atlanta Knights	IHL	47	28	26	54	38												3	2	3	5	4			
1993-94	Atlanta Knights	IHL	79	54	60	114	70												14	13	12	25	8			
1994-95	Atlanta Knights	IHL	66	41	49	90	60												5	1	5	6	2			
1995-96	Atlanta Knights	IHL	75	36	58	94	80												3	0	2	2	18			
1996-97	Detroit Vipers	IHL	73	33	38	71	42												21	5	*21	26	14			
1997-98	Detroit Vipers	IHL	58	25	35	60	50												15	2	4	6	16			
1998-99	Detroit Vipers	IHL	82	23	52	75	64		1	2	1	94	11.7	-18	11	18.2	68	41	16:37	11	5	4	9	10			
99-2000	Tampa Bay	NHL	68	11	22	33	24	1	2	2	116	11.2		11	18.2	68	41	16:37								
NHL Totals			92	13	23	36	34	1	2	2	116	11.2		11	18.2	68	41	16:37								

OHL First All-Star Team (1989) • ECHL First All-Star Team (1991) • Named ECHL MVP (1991) • AHL Second All-Star Team (1992) • IHL First All-Star Team (1994, 1995) • Won "Bud" Poile Trophy (Playoff MVP - IHL) (1994)
Signed as a free agent by **Edmonton**, February 24, 1989. Signed as a free agent by **Tampa Bay**, September 1, 1992. Signed as a free agent by **Tampa Bay**, September 29, 1999.

DRURY, Chris (DROO-ree, KRIHS) COL.

Center. Shoots right. 5'10", 180 lbs. Born, Trumbull, CT, August 20, 1976. Quebec's 5th choice, 72nd overall, in 1994 Entry Draft.

			Regular Season																Playoffs							
Season	Club	League	GP	G	A	Pts	PIM	PP	SH	GW	S	%	+/-	TF	F%	H	SB	Min	GP	G	A	Pts	PIM	PP	SH	GW
1991-92	Fairfield Prep	Hi-School	25	22	27	49																				
1992-93	Fairfield Prep	Hi-School	24	25	32	57	15																			
1993-94	Fairfield Prep	Hi-School	24	37	18	55																				
1994-95	Boston University	H-East	39	12	15	27	38																			
1995-96	Boston University	H-East	37	35	33	*68	46																			
1996-97	Boston University	H-East	41	*38	24	62	64																			
1997-98	Boston University	H-East	39	29	57	88																				
1998-99	Colorado	NHL	79	20	24	44	62	6	0	3	138	14.5	9	418	46.9	88	39	13:15	19	6	2	8	4	0	0	4
99-2000	Colorado	NHL	79	20	47	67	42	7	0	2	213	9.4	8	1321	53.1	68	50	18:33	17	4	10	14	4	1	0	2
NHL Totals			161	40	71	111	104	13	0	5	351	11.4		1739	51.6	68	89	15:57	36	10	12	22	8	1	0	6

Hockey East Second All-Star Team (1996, 1997) • NCAA East Second All-American Team (1996) • NCAA East First All-American Team (1997, 1998) • NCAA Championship All-Tournament Team (1997) • Hockey East First All-Star Team (1997) • Won Hobey Baker Memorial Award (Top U.S. Collegiate Player) (1998) • NHL All-Rookie Team (1999) • Won Calder Memorial Trophy (1999)
Rights transferred to **Colorado** after **Quebec** franchise relocated, June 21, 1995.

DRURY, Ted (DROO-ree, TEHD) CBJ

Center. Shoots left. 6', 208 lbs. Born, Boston, MA, September 13, 1971. Calgary's 2nd choice, 42nd overall, in 1989 Entry Draft.

			Regular Season																Playoffs							
Season	Club	League	GP	G	A	Pts	PIM	PP	SH	GW	S	%	+/-	TF	F%	H	SB	Min	GP	G	A	Pts	PIM	PP	SH	GW
1987-88	Fairfield Prep	Hi-School	24	21	28	49																				
1988-89	Fairfield Prep	Hi-School	25	35	31	66																				
1989-90	Harvard University	ECAC	17	9	13	22	10																			
1990-91	Harvard University	ECAC	26	18	18	36	22																			
1991-92	United States	Nat-Team	53	11	23	34	30																			
	United States	Olympics	7	1	1	2	0																			
1992-93	Harvard University	ECAC	31	22	*41	*63	28																			
1993-94	Calgary	NHL	34	5	7	12	26	0	1	1	43	11.6	-5													
	United States	Nat-Team	5	1	5	11																				
	United States	Olympics	7	1	2	3	2																			
	Hartford	NHL	16	1	5	6	10	0	0	0	37	2.7	-10													
1994-95	Hartford	NHL	34	3	6	9	21	0	0	0	31	9.7	-3													
	Springfield	AHL	2	0	1	1	0																			
1995-96	Ottawa	NHL	42	9	7	16	54	1	0	1	80	11.3	-19													
1996-97	Anaheim	NHL	73	9	9	18	54	1	0	2	114	7.9	-19						10	1	4	5	4	0	0	0
1997-98	Anaheim	NHL	73	6	10	16	83	0	0	0	110	5.5	-10													
1998-99	Anaheim	NHL	75	5	6	11	83	0	0	1	99	9.1	-2	449	47.9	77	13	8:15	4	0	0	0	0	0	0	0
99-2000	NY Islanders	NHL	11	1	1	2	3	1	0	0	9	11.1	-2	194	47.9	44	5	7:27								
NHL Totals			413	41	52	93	367	3	2	4	551	7.4		725	47.2	135	30	7:51	14	1	4	5	4	0	0	0

ECAC First All-Star Team (1993) • NCAA East First All-America Team (1993)
Traded to **Hartford** by **Calgary** with Gary Suter and Paul Ranheim for James Patrick, Zarley Zalapski and Michael Nylander, March 10, 1994. Claimed by **Ottawa** from **Hartford** in NHL Waiver Draft, October 2, 1995. Traded to **Anaheim** by **Ottawa** with the rights to Marc Moro for Jason York and Shaun Van Allen, October 1, 1996. Traded to **NY Islanders** by **Anaheim** for Tony Hrkac and Dean Malkoc, October 29, 1999. Selected by **Columbus** from **NY Islanders** in Expansion Draft, June 23, 2000.

DUBE, Christian (doo-BAY, KRIHS-tehn)

Center. Shoots right. 5'11", 170 lbs. Born, Sherbrooke, Que., April 25, 1977. NY Rangers' 1st choice, 39th overall, in 1995 Entry Draft.

			Regular Season																Playoffs							
Season	Club	League	GP	G	A	Pts	PIM	PP	SH	GW	S	%	+/-	TF	F%	H	SB	Min	GP	G	A	Pts	PIM	PP	SH	GW
1992-93	HC Martigny	Switz-2	27	36	40	76	34																			
1993-94	Sherbrooke	QMJHL	72	31	41	72	22												11	3	2	5	8			
1994-95	Sherbrooke	QMJHL	71	36	65	101	43												7	1	7	8	8			
1995-96	Sherbrooke	QMJHL	62	52	93	145	105												7	5	5	10	6			
1996-97	Hull Olympiques	QMJHL	19	15	22	37	37												14	7	16	23	14			
	NY Rangers	NHL	27	1	1	2	4	1	0	0	14	7.1	-4						3	0	0	0	0	0	0	0
1997-98	Hartford	AHL	79	11	46	57	46												9	0	4	4	6			
1998-99	NY Rangers	NHL	6	0	0	0	0	0	0	0	0	0.0		13	38.5	2	1	2:39								
	Hartford	AHL	58	21	30	51	20																			
99-2000	HC Lugano	Switz.	45	*25	26	51	52												14	8	*12	*20	14			
NHL Totals			33	1	1	2	4	1	0	0	14	7.1		13	38.5	2	1	2:39	3	0	0	0	0	0	0	0

QMJHL First All-Star Team (1996) • Canadian Major Junior First All-Star Team (1996) • Canadian Major Junior Player of the Year (1996) • Won Stafford Smythe Memorial Trophy (Memorial Cup Tournament MVP) (1997)

DUBINSKY, Steve (doo-BIHN-skee, STEEV) CHI.

Center. Shoots left. 6', 190 lbs. Born, Montreal, Que., July 9, 1970. Chicago's 9th choice, 226th overall, in 1990 Entry Draft.

			Regular Season																Playoffs							
Season	Club	League	GP	G	A	Pts	PIM	PP	SH	GW	S	%	+/-	TF	F%	H	SB	Min	GP	G	A	Pts	PIM	PP	SH	GW
1989-90	Clarkson	ECAC	35	7	10	17	24																			
1990-91	Clarkson	ECAC	39	13	23	36	26																			
1991-92	Clarkson	ECAC	32	20	31	51	40																			
1992-93	Clarkson	ECAC	35	18	26	44	58																			
1993-94	Chicago	NHL	27	2	6	8	16	0	0	0	20	10.0	1						6	0	0	0	10	0	0	0
	Indianapolis Ice	IHL	54	15	25	40	63																			
1994-95	Chicago	NHL	16	0	0	0	4	0	0	0	16	0.0	-5													
	Indianapolis Ice	IHL	62	16	11	27	29																			
1995-96	Chicago	NHL	43	2	3	5	14	0	0	0	33	6.1	3						1	0	0	0	0			
	Indianapolis Ice	IHL	16	8	8	16	10																			
1996-97	Chicago	NHL	5	0	0	0	0												4	1	1	2	4	0	0	1
	Indianapolis Ice	IHL	77	32	40	72	53												3	1	4	4	0			
1997-98	Chicago	NHL	82	5	13	18	57	0	1	0	112	4.5	-6													
1998-99	Chicago	NHL	1	0	0	0	0							5	60.0	1	0	5:11								
	Calgary	NHL	61	4	10	14	14	0	0	2	69	5.8	-7	223	46.6	161	75	14:38								
99-2000	Calgary	NHL	23	0	1	1	8	0	0	0	34	0.0	-12	207	49.3	58	26	12:05								
NHL Totals			258	13	33	46	113	0	1	2	284	4.6		435	48.0	220	101	13:50	10	1	1	2	14	0	0	1

Traded to **Calgary** by **Chicago** with Jeff Shantz for Marty McInnis, Jamie Allison and Eric Andersson, October 27, 1998. • Missed remainder of 1999-2000 season recovering from knee injury suffered in game vs. Chicago, December 12, 1999. Signed as a free agent by **Chicago**, August 25, 2000.

DUCHESNE, Steve (doo-SHAYN, STEEV) DET.

Defense. Shoots left. 5'11", 195 lbs. Born, Sept-Iles, Que., June 30, 1965.

			Regular Season																Playoffs							
Season	Club	League	GP	G	A	Pts	PIM	PP	SH	GW	S	%	+/-	TF	F%	H	SB	Min	GP	G	A	Pts	PIM	PP	SH	GW
1983-84	Wawa Travellers	NOJHA	10	9	23	32	9																			
	Drummondville	QMJHL	67	1	34	35	79																			
1984-85	Drummondville	QMJHL	65	22	54	76	94																			
1985-86	New Haven	AHL	75	14	35	49	76												5	4	7	11	8			
1986-87	Los Angeles	NHL	75	13	25	38	74	5	0	2	113	11.5	8						5	2	2	4	14	1	0	1
1987-88	Los Angeles	NHL	71	16	39	55	109	8	0	4	190	8.4	0						5	2	4	6	14	1	0	0
1988-89	Los Angeles	NHL	79	25	50	75	92	8	5	2	215	11.6	31						11	4	7	11	6	1	1	1
1989-90	Los Angeles	NHL	79	20	42	62	36	8	0	1	224	8.9	-3						10	3	5	8	6	1	0	0
1990-91	Los Angeles	NHL	78	21	41	62	66	7	0	3	171	12.3	19						12	4	8	12	18	1	0	0
1991-92	Philadelphia	NHL	78	18	38	56	86	7	2	3	229	7.9	-7													

Season	Club	League	GP	G	A	Pts	PIM	PP	SH	GW	S	%	+/-	TF	F%	H	SB	Min	GP	G	A	Pts	PIM	PP	SH	GW
1995-96	San Jose	NHL	74	13	8	21	39	0	1	2	73	17.8	-17													
	Kansas City	IHL	4	0	0	0	8												5	0	0	0	8			
1996-97	San Jose	NHL	73	9	6	15	42	0	1	0	115	7.8	-18													
	Kentucky	AHL	3	1	3	4	18																			
1997-98	San Jose	NHL	20	3	3	6	22	0	0	0	24	12.5	3													
	Colorado	NHL	47	5	7	12	48	0	0	0	57	8.8	3													
1998-99	Colorado	NHL	68	7	12	19	37	1	0	1	81	8.6	4	9	22.2	35	8	8:46	5	0	0	0	2	0	0	0
99-2000	Colorado	NHL	18	1	0	1	8	0	0	0	13	7.7	-4	1	0.0	7	1	5:20								
	Atlanta	NHL	33	4	7	11	18	1	0	0	53	7.5	-13	22	31.8	36	11	14:19								
	NHL Totals		347	42	43	85	220	2	2	4	429	9.8		32	28.1	78	20	9:47	12	0	1	1	8	0	0	0

Traded to **Colorado** by **San Jose** with San Jose's 1st round choice (Alex Tanguay) in 1998 Entry Draft for Mike Ricci and Colorado's 2nd round choice (later traded to Buffalo - Buffalo selected Jaroslav Kristek), in 1998 Entry Draft, November 21, 1997. Traded to **Atlanta** by **Colorado** for Rick Tabaracci, December 8, 1999.

DOURIS, Peter
(DOOR-his, PEE-tuhr)

Right wing. Shoots right. 6'1", 195 lbs.   Born, Toronto, Ont., February 19, 1966. Winnipeg's 1st choice, 30th overall, in 1984 Entry Draft.

Season	Club	League	GP	G	A	Pts	PIM	PP	SH	GW	S	%	+/-	TF	F%	H	SB	Min	GP	G	A	Pts	PIM	PP	SH	GW
1983-84	New Hampshire	ECAC	37	19	15	34	14																			
1984-85	New Hampshire	H-East	42	27	24	51	34																			
1985-86	Canada	Nat-Team	33	16	7	23	18																			
1985-86	Winnipeg	NHL	11	0	0	0	0	0	0	0	0	0.0	-1													
1986-87	Winnipeg	NHL	6	0	0	0	0	0	0	0	3	0.0	-1													
	Sherbrooke	AHL	62	14	28	42	24												17	7	*15	*22	16			
1987-88	Winnipeg	NHL	4	0	2	2	0	0	0	0	2	0.0	-1						1	0	0	0	0	0	0	0
	Moncton Hawks	AHL	73	42	37	79	53																			
1988-89	Peoria Rivermen	IHL	81	28	41	69	32												4	1	2	3	0			
1989-90	Boston	NHL	36	5	6	11	15	1	0	0	63	7.9	8						8	0	1	1	8	0	0	0
	Maine Mariners	AHL	38	17	20	37	14																			
1990-91	Boston	NHL	39	5	2	7	9	1	0	1	46	10.9	-12						7	0	1	1	6	0	0	0
	Maine Mariners	AHL	35	16	15	31	9												2	3	0	3	2			
1991-92	Boston	NHL	54	10	13	23	10	0	0	1	107	9.3	9						7	2	3	5	0	0	0	1
	Maine Mariners	AHL	12	4	3	7	2																			
1992-93	Boston	NHL	19	4	4	8	4	0	1	0	33	12.1	5						4	1	0	1	0	0	0	0
	Providence Bruins	AHL	50	29	26	55	12																			
1993-94	Anaheim	NHL	74	12	22	34	21	1	0	1	142	8.5	-5													
1994-95	Anaheim	NHL	46	10	11	21	12	0	0	4	69	14.5	4													
1995-96	Anaheim	NHL	31	8	7	15	9	2	0	3	45	17.8	-3						3	2	2	4	2			
1996-97	Milwaukee	IHL	80	36	36	72	14																			
1997-98	Dallas	NHL	1	0	0	0	0	0	0	0	3	0.0	-1													
	Michigan K-Wings	IHL	78	26	31	57	29												4	0	5	5	2			
1998-99	EV Landshut	DEL	51	17	26	43	59												3	1	0	1	0			
99-2000	Munich Barons	DEL	56	18	34	52	24												12	3	6	9	2			
	NHL Totals		321	54	67	121	80	5	1	10	513	10.5							27	3	5	8	14	0	0	1

Traded to **St. Louis** by **Winnipeg** for Kent Carlson, St. Louis' 12th round choice (Sergei Kharin) in 1989 Entry Draft and 4th round choice (Scott Levins) in 1990 Entry Draft, September 29, 1988. Signed as a free agent by **Boston**, June 27, 1989. Signed as a free agent by **Anaheim**, July 22, 1993. Signed as a free agent by **Dallas**, July 16, 1997.

DOWD, Jim
(DOWD, JIHM)   **MIN.**

Center. Shoots right. 6'1", 190 lbs.   Born, Brick, NJ, December 25, 1968. New Jersey's 7th choice, 149th overall, in 1987 Entry Draft.

Season	Club	League	GP	G	A	Pts	PIM	PP	SH	GW	S	%	+/-	TF	F%	H	SB	Min	GP	G	A	Pts	PIM	PP	SH	GW
1983-84	Brick High	Hi-School	20	19	30	49																				
1984-85	Brick High	Hi-School	24	58	55	113																				
1985-86	Brick High	Hi-School	24	47	51	98																				
1986-87	Brick High	Hi-School	24	22	33	55																				
1987-88	Lake Superior	CCHA	45	18	27	45	16																			
1988-89	Lake Superior	CCHA	46	24	35	59	40																			
1989-90	Lake Superior	CCHA	46	25	*67	92	30																			
1990-91	Lake Superior	CCHA	44	24	*54	*78	53																			
1991-92	New Jersey	NHL	1	0	0	0	0	0	0	0	0	0.0	0													
	Utica Devils	AHL	78	17	42	59	47												4	2	2	4	4			
1992-93	New Jersey	NHL	1	0	0	0	0	0	0	0	1	0.0	-1													
	Utica Devils	AHL	78	27	45	72	62												5	1	7	8	10			
1993-94	New Jersey	NHL	15	5	10	15	0	2	0	0	26	19.2	8						19	2	6	8	8	0	0	0
	Albany River Rats	AHL	58	26	37	63	76																			
1994-95♦	New Jersey	NHL	10	1	4	5	0	1	0	0	14	7.1	-5						11	2	1	3	8	0	0	1
1995-96	New Jersey	NHL	28	4	9	13	17	0	0	0	41	9.8	-1													
	Vancouver	NHL	38	1	6	7	6	0	0	0	35	2.9	-8						1	0	0	0	0	0	0	0
1996-97	NY Islanders	NHL	3	0	0	0	0	0	0	0	0	0.0	-1													
	Utah Grizzlies	IHL	48	10	21	31	27																			
	Saint John Flames	AHL	24	5	11	16	18												5	1	2	3	0			
1997-98	Calgary	NHL	48	6	8	14	12	0	1	0	58	10.3	10						19	3	13	16	10			
	Saint John Flames	AHL	35	8	30	38	20																			
1998-99	Edmonton	NHL	1	0	0	0	0	0	0	0	1	0.0	0	7	14.3	1	0	9:47	11	3	6	9	8			
	Hamilton Bulldogs	AHL	51	15	29	44	82																			
99-2000	Edmonton	NHL	69	5	18	23	45	2	0	1	103	4.9	10	720	54.0	51	25	13:08	5	2	1	3	4	0	0	0
	NHL Totals		214	22	55	77	80	5	1	1	279	7.9		727	53.6	52	25	13:05	36	6	8	14	20	0	0	1

CCHA Second All-Star Team (1990) • NCAA West Second All-American Team (1990) • CCHA First All-Star Team (1991) • NCAA West First All-American Team (1991)

Traded to **Hartford** by **New Jersey** with New Jersey's 2nd round choice (later traded to Calgary – Calgary selected Dmitri Kokorev) in 1997 Entry Draft for Jocelyn Lemieux and Hartford's 2nd round choice in 1998 Entry Draft, December 19, 1995. Traded to **Vancouver** by **Hartford** with Frantisek Kucera and Hartford's 2nd round choice (Ryan Bonni) in 1997 Entry Draft for Jeff Brown and Vancouver's 3rd round choice in 1998 Entry Draft, December 19, 1995. Claimed by **NY Islanders** from **Vancouver** in NHL Waiver Draft, September 30, 1996. Signed as a free agent by **Calgary**, August, 1997. Traded to **Nashville** by **Calgary** for future considerations, June 26, 1998. Traded to **Edmonton** by **Nashville** with Mikhail Shtalenkov for Eric Fichaud, Drake Berehowsky and Greg de Vries, October 1, 1998. Selected by **Minnesota** from **Edmonton** in Expansion Draft, June 23, 2000.

DOWNEY, Aaron
(DOW-nee, AIR-rohn)   **CHI.**

Right wing. Shoots right. 6', 210 lbs.   Born, Shelburne, Ont., August 27, 1974.

Season	Club	League	GP	G	A	Pts	PIM	PP	SH	GW	S	%	+/-	TF	F%	H	SB	Min	GP	G	A	Pts	PIM	PP	SH	GW
1990-91	Grand Valley	OJHL-C	27	6	8	14	57																			
1991-92	Collingwood Blues	OJHL-B	40	9	8	17	111																			
1992-93	Guelph Storm	OHL	53	3	3	6	88												5	1	0	1	0			
1993-94	Cole Harbour	MJrHL	35	8	20	28	210																			
1994-95	Cole Harbour	MJrHL	40	10	31	41	320																			
1995-96	Hampton Roads	ECHL	65	12	11	23	354																			
1996-97	Manitoba Moose	IHL	2	0	0	0	17																			
	Portland Pirates	AHL	3	0	0	0	19																			
	Hampton Roads	ECHL	64	8	8	16	338												9	0	3	3	26			
1997-98	Providence Bruins	AHL	78	5	10	15	*407																			
1998-99	Providence Bruins	AHL	75	10	12	22	*401												19	1	1	2	46			
99-2000	Boston	NHL	1	0	0	0	0	0	0	0	0	0.0	0	0	0.0	1	0	8:31								
	Providence Bruins	AHL	47	6	4	10	221												14	1	0	1	24			
	NHL Totals		1	0	0	0	0	0	0	0	0	0.0		0	0.0	1	0	8:31								

Signed as a free agent by **Boston**, January 20, 1998. Signed as a free agent by **Chicago**, August 13, 2000.

DRAKE, Dallas
(DRAYK, DAL-lahs) **ST.L.**

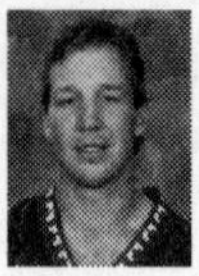

Right wing. Shoots left. 6'1", 190 lbs. Born, Trail, B.C., February 4, 1969. Detroit's 6th choice, 116th overall, in 1989 Entry Draft.

			Regular Season																Playoffs							
Season	Club	League	GP	G	A	Pts	PIM	PP	SH	GW	S	%	+/–	TF	F%	H	SB	Min	GP	G	A	Pts	PIM	PP	SH	GW
1984-85	Rossland	KIJHL	30	13	37	50	....	....	....	....	....	....	....	....	....	....	....	....	....	....	....	....	....	....	....	....
1985-86	Rossland	KIJHL	41	53	73	126	....	....	....	....	....	....	....	....	....	....	....	....	....	....	....	....	....	....	....	....
1986-87	Rossland	KIJHL	40	55	80	135	....	....	....	....	....	....	....	....	....	....	....	....	....	....	....	....	....	....	....	....
1987-88	Vernon Lakers	BCJHL	47	39	85	124	50	....	....	....	....	....	....	....	....	....	....	....	11	9	17	26	30	....	....	....
1988-89	North-Michigan	WCHA	38	17	22	39	22	....	....	....	....	....	....	....	....	....	....	....	7	1	2	3	4	....	....	....
1989-90	North-Michigan	WCHA	36	13	24	37	42	....	....	....	....	....	....	....	....	....	....	....	....	....	....	....	....	....	....	....
1990-91	North-Michigan	WCHA	44	22	36	58	89	....	....	....	....	....	....	....	....	....	....	....	....	....	....	....	....	....	....	....
1991-92	North-Michigan	WCHA	38	*39	41	*80	46	....	....	....	....	....	....	....	....	....	....	....	....	....	....	....	....	....	....	....
1992-93	**Detroit**	**NHL**	**72**	**18**	**26**	**44**	**93**	**3**	**2**	**5**	**89**	**20.2**	**15**	....	....	....	....	....	**7**	**3**	**3**	**6**	**6**	**1**	**0**	**0**
1993-94	**Detroit**	**NHL**	**47**	**10**	**22**	**32**	**37**	**0**	**1**	**2**	**78**	**12.8**	**5**	....	....	....	....	....	....	....	....	....	....	....	....	....
	Adirondack	AHL	1	2	0	2	0	....	....	....	....	....	....	....	....	....	....	....	....	....	....	....	....	....	....	....
	Winnipeg	**NHL**	**15**	**3**	**5**	**8**	**12**	**1**	**1**	**1**	**34**	**8.8**	**–6**	....	....	....	....	....	....	....	....	....	....	....	....	....
1994-95	**Winnipeg**	**NHL**	**43**	**8**	**18**	**26**	**30**	**0**	**0**	**1**	**66**	**12.1**	**–6**	....	....	....	....	....	....	....	....	....	....	....	....	....
1995-96	**Winnipeg**	**NHL**	**69**	**19**	**20**	**39**	**36**	**4**	**4**	**2**	**121**	**15.7**	**–7**	....	....	....	....	....	**3**	**0**	**0**	**0**	**0**	**0**	**0**	**0**
1996-97	**Phoenix**	**NHL**	**63**	**17**	**19**	**36**	**52**	**5**	**1**	**1**	**113**	**15.0**	**–11**	....	....	....	....	....	**7**	**0**	**1**	**1**	**2**	**0**	**0**	**0**
1997-98	**Phoenix**	**NHL**	**60**	**11**	**29**	**40**	**71**	**3**	**0**	**2**	**112**	**9.8**	**17**	....	....	....	....	....	**4**	**0**	**1**	**1**	**2**	**0**	**0**	**0**
1998-99	**Phoenix**	**NHL**	**53**	**9**	**22**	**31**	**65**	**0**	**0**	**3**	**105**	**8.6**	**17**	**5**	**60.0**	**105**	**17**	**15:38**	**7**	**4**	**3**	**7**	**4**	**2**	**0**	**1**
99-2000	**Phoenix**	**NHL**	**79**	**15**	**30**	**45**	**62**	**0**	**2**	**5**	**127**	**11.8**	**11**	**4**	**25.0**	**176**	**46**	**15:48**	**5**	**0**	**1**	**1**	**4**	**0**	**0**	**0**
	NHL Totals		**501**	**110**	**191**	**301**	**458**	**16**	**11**	**22**	**845**	**13.0**		**9**	**44.4**	**281**	**63**	**15:44**	**33**	**7**	**9**	**16**	**18**	**3**	**0**	**1**

WCHA First All-Star Team (1992) • NCAA West First All-American Team (1992)

Traded to **Winnipeg** by **Detroit** with Tim Cheveldae for Bob Essensa and Sergei Bautin, March 8, 1994. Transferred to **Phoenix** after **Winnipeg** franchise relocated, July 1, 1996. Selected by **Minnesota** from **Phoenix** in Expansion Draft, June 23, 2000. Signed as a free agent by **St. Louis**, July 1, 2000.

DRAPER, Kris
(DRAY-puhr, KRIHS) **DET.**

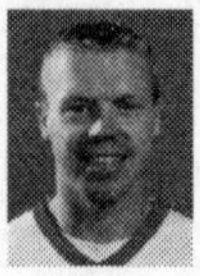

Center. Shoots left. 5'11", 190 lbs. Born, Toronto, Ont., May 24, 1971. Winnipeg's 4th choice, 62nd overall, in 1989 Entry Draft.

Season	Club	League	GP	G	A	Pts	PIM	PP	SH	GW	S	%	+/–	TF	F%	H	SB	Min	GP	G	A	Pts	PIM	PP	SH	GW
1987-88	Don Mills Flyers	MTHL	40	35	32	67	46	....	....	....	....	....	....	....	....	....	....	....	....	....	....	....	....	....	....	....
1988-89	Canada	Nat-Team	60	11	15	26	16	....	....	....	....	....	....	....	....	....	....	....	....	....	....	....	....	....	....	....
1989-90	Canada	Nat-Team	61	12	22	34	44	....	....	....	....	....	....	....	....	....	....	....	....	....	....	....	....	....	....	....
1990-91	Ottawa 67's	OHL	39	19	42	61	35	....	....	....	....	....	....	....	....	....	....	....	17	8	11	19	20	....	....	....
	Winnipeg	**NHL**	**3**	**1**	**0**	**1**	**5**	**0**	**0**	**0**	**1**	**100.0**	**0**	....	....	....	....	....	....	....	....	....	....	....	....	....
	Moncton Hawks	AHL	7	2	1	3	2	....	....	....	....	....	....	....	....	....	....	....	....	....	....	....	....	....	....	....
1991-92	**Winnipeg**	**NHL**	**10**	**2**	**0**	**2**	**2**	**0**	**0**	**0**	**19**	**10.5**	**0**	....	....	....	....	....	**2**	**0**	**0**	**0**	**0**	**0**	**0**	**0**
	Moncton Hawks	AHL	61	11	18	29	113	....	....	....	....	....	....	....	....	....	....	....	4	0	1	1	6	....	....	....
1992-93	**Winnipeg**	**NHL**	**7**	**0**	**0**	**0**	**2**	**0**	**0**	**0**	**5**	**0.0**	**–6**	....	....	....	....	....	....	....	....	....	....	....	....	....
	Moncton Hawks	AHL	67	12	23	35	40	....	....	....	....	....	....	....	....	....	....	....	5	2	2	4	18	....	....	....
1993-94	**Detroit**	**NHL**	**39**	**5**	**8**	**13**	**31**	**0**	**1**	**0**	**55**	**9.1**	**11**	....	....	....	....	....	**7**	**2**	**2**	**4**	**4**	**0**	**1**	**0**
	Adirondack	AHL	46	20	23	43	49	....	....	....	....	....	....	....	....	....	....	....	....	....	....	....	....	....	....	....
1994-95	**Detroit**	**NHL**	**36**	**2**	**6**	**8**	**22**	**0**	**0**	**0**	**44**	**4.5**	**1**	....	....	....	....	....	**18**	**4**	**1**	**5**	**12**	**0**	**1**	**1**
1995-96	**Detroit**	**NHL**	**52**	**7**	**9**	**16**	**32**	**0**	**1**	**0**	**51**	**13.7**	**2**	....	....	....	....	....	**18**	**4**	**2**	**6**	**18**	**0**	**1**	**0**
1996-97♦	**Detroit**	**NHL**	**76**	**8**	**5**	**13**	**73**	**1**	**0**	**1**	**85**	**9.4**	**–11**	....	....	....	....	....	**20**	**2**	**4**	**6**	**12**	**0**	**1**	**0**
1997-98♦	**Detroit**	**NHL**	**64**	**13**	**10**	**23**	**45**	**1**	**0**	**4**	**96**	**13.5**	**5**	....	....	....	....	....	**19**	**1**	**3**	**4**	**12**	**0**	**0**	**1**
1998-99	**Detroit**	**NHL**	**80**	**4**	**14**	**18**	**79**	**0**	**1**	**1**	**78**	**5.1**	**2**	**887**	**54.6**	**82**	**18**	**12:43**	**10**	**0**	**1**	**1**	**6**	**0**	**0**	**0**
99-2000	**Detroit**	**NHL**	**51**	**5**	**7**	**12**	**28**	**0**	**0**	**3**	**76**	**6.6**	**3**	**380**	**57.6**	**69**	**13**	**13:33**	**9**	**2**	**0**	**2**	**6**	**0**	**0**	**0**
	NHL Totals		**418**	**47**	**59**	**106**	**319**	**2**	**3**	**9**	**510**	**9.2**		**1267**	**55.5**	**151**	**31**	**13:02**	**103**	**15**	**13**	**28**	**70**	**0**	**4**	**2**

Traded to **Detroit** by **Winnipeg** for future considerations, June 30, 1993.

DROUIN, P.C.
(droo-IHN, PEE-CEE)

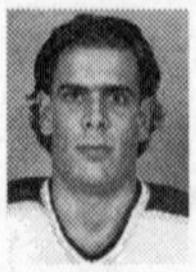

Left wing. Shoots left. 6'2", 208 lbs. Born, St. Lambert, Que., April 22, 1974.

Season	Club	League	GP	G	A	Pts	PIM	PP	SH	GW	S	%	+/–	TF	F%	H	SB	Min	GP	G	A	Pts	PIM	PP	SH	GW
1991-92	Gloucester	OJHL	49	23	51	74	59	....	....	....	....	....	....	....	....	....	....	....	....	....	....	....	....	....	....	....
1992-93	Cornell Big Red	ECAC	23	3	6	9	30	....	....	....	....	....	....	....	....	....	....	....	....	....	....	....	....	....	....	....
1993-94	Cornell Big Red	ECAC	21	6	13	19	32	....	....	....	....	....	....	....	....	....	....	....	....	....	....	....	....	....	....	....
1994-95	Cornell Big Red	ECAC	26	4	16	20	48	....	....	....	....	....	....	....	....	....	....	....	....	....	....	....	....	....	....	....
1995-96	Cornell Big Red	ECAC	31	18	14	32	60	....	....	....	....	....	....	....	....	....	....	....	....	....	....	....	....	....	....	....
1996-97	**Boston**	**NHL**	**3**	**0**	**0**	**0**	**0**	**0**	**0**	**0**	**1**	**0.0**	**1**	....	....	....	....	....	....	....	....	....	....	....	....	....
	Providence Bruins	AHL	42	12	11	23	10	....	....	....	....	....	....	....	....	....	....	....	....	....	....	....	....	....	....	....
1997-98	Providence Bruins	AHL	7	0	2	2	4	....	....	....	....	....	....	....	....	....	....	....	....	....	....	....	....	....	....	....
	Charlotte	ECHL	62	21	46	67	57	....	....	....	....	....	....	....	....	....	....	....	7	2	4	6	4	....	....	....
1998-99	Bracknell Bees	Britain	42	12	21	33	12	....	....	....	....	....	....	....	....	....	....	....	7	4	1	5	0	....	....	....
99-2000	Bracknell Bees	Britain	35	10	28	38	42	....	....	....	....	....	....	....	....	....	....	....	6	2	3	5	4	....	....	....
	NHL Totals		**3**	**0**	**0**	**0**	**0**	**0**	**0**	**0**	**1**	**0.0**		....	....	....	....	....	....	....	....	....	....	....	....	....

Signed as a free agent by **Boston**, October 14, 1996.

DRUKEN, Harold
(DROO-kehn, HAIR-ohld) **VAN.**

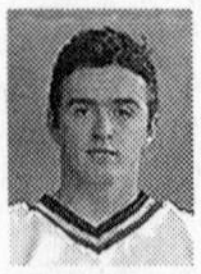

Center. Shoots left. 6', 205 lbs. Born, St. John's, Nfld., January 26, 1979. Vancouver's 3rd choice, 36th overall, in 1997 Entry Draft.

Season	Club	League	GP	G	A	Pts	PIM	PP	SH	GW	S	%	+/–	TF	F%	H	SB	Min	GP	G	A	Pts	PIM	PP	SH	GW
1995-96	Noble High	Hi-School	30	37	28	65	28	....	....	....	....	....	....	....	....	....	....	....	....	....	....	....	....	....	....	....
1996-97	Detroit Whalers	OHL	63	27	31	58	14	....	....	....	....	....	....	....	....	....	....	....	5	3	2	5	0	....	....	....
1997-98	Plymouth Whalers	OHL	64	38	44	82	12	....	....	....	....	....	....	....	....	....	....	....	15	9	11	20	4	....	....	....
1998-99	Plymouth Whalers	OHL	60	*58	45	103	34	....	....	....	....	....	....	....	....	....	....	....	11	9	12	21	14	....	....	....
99-2000	**Vancouver**	**NHL**	**33**	**7**	**9**	**16**	**10**	**2**	**0**	**0**	**69**	**10.1**	**14**	**307**	**47.9**	**13**	**10**	**13:01**	....	....	....	....	....	....	....	....
	Syracuse Crunch	AHL	47	20	25	45	32	....	....	....	....	....	....	....	....	....	....	....	4	1	2	3	6	....	....	....
	NHL Totals		**33**	**7**	**9**	**16**	**10**	**2**	**0**	**0**	**69**	**10.1**		**307**	**47.9**	**13**	**10**	**13:01**	....	....	....	....	....	....	....	....

OHL Second All-Star Team (1999)

DRULIA, Stan
(DROO-lee-ah, STAN) **T.B.**

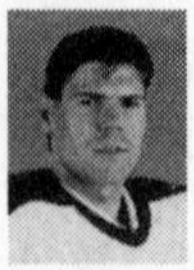

Right wing. Shoots right. 5'11", 190 lbs. Born, Elmira, NY, January 5, 1968. Pittsburgh's 11th choice, 214th overall, in 1986 Entry Draft.

Season	Club	League	GP	G	A	Pts	PIM	PP	SH	GW	S	%	+/–	TF	F%	H	SB	Min	GP	G	A	Pts	PIM	PP	SH	GW
1983-84	Fort Erie Meteors	OJHL-B	39	29	36	65	104	....	....	....	....	....	....	....	....	....	....	....	....	....	....	....	....	....	....	....
1984-85	Belleville Bulls	OHL	63	24	31	55	33	....	....	....	....	....	....	....	....	....	....	....	....	....	....	....	....	....	....	....
1985-86	Belleville Bulls	OHL	66	43	36	79	73	....	....	....	....	....	....	....	....	....	....	....	24	4	11	15	15	....	....	....
1986-87	Hamilton Hawks	OHL	55	27	51	78	26	....	....	....	....	....	....	....	....	....	....	....	9	4	4	8	2	....	....	....
1987-88	Hamilton Hawks	OHL	65	52	69	121	44	....	....	....	....	....	....	....	....	....	....	....	14	8	16	24	12	....	....	....
1988-89	Niagara Falls	OHL	47	52	93	145	59	....	....	....	....	....	....	....	....	....	....	....	17	11	*26	37	18	....	....	....
	Maine Mariners	AHL	3	1	1	2	0	....	....	....	....	....	....	....	....	....	....	....	....	....	....	....	....	....	....	....
1989-90	Phoenix	IHL	16	6	3	9	2	....	....	....	....	....	....	....	....	....	....	....	....	....	....	....	....	....	....	....
	Cape Breton	AHL	31	5	7	12	2	....	....	....	....	....	....	....	....	....	....	....	....	....	....	....	....	....	....	....
1990-91	Knoxville	ECHL	64	*63	77	*140	39	....	....	....	....	....	....	....	....	....	....	....	3	3	2	5	4	....	....	....
1991-92	New Haven	AHL	77	49	53	102	46	....	....	....	....	....	....	....	....	....	....	....	5	2	4	6	4	....	....	....
1992-93	**Tampa Bay**	**NHL**	**24**	**2**	**1**	**3**	**10**	**0**	**0**	**1**	**22**	**9.1**	**1**	....	....	....	....	....	....	....	....	....	....	....	....	....
	Atlanta Knights	IHL	47	28	26	54	38	....	....	....	....	....	....	....	....	....	....	....	3	2	3	5	4	....	....	....
1993-94	Atlanta Knights	IHL	79	54	60	114	70	....	....	....	....	....	....	....	....	....	....	....	14	13	12	25	8	....	....	....
1994-95	Atlanta Knights	IHL	66	41	49	90	60	....	....	....	....	....	....	....	....	....	....	....	5	1	5	6	2	....	....	....
1995-96	Atlanta Knights	IHL	75	38	56	94	80	....	....	....	....	....	....	....	....	....	....	....	3	0	2	2	18	....	....	....
1996-97	Detroit Vipers	IHL	73	33	38	71	42	....	....	....	....	....	....	....	....	....	....	....	21	5	*21	26	14	....	....	....
1997-98	Detroit Vipers	IHL	58	25	35	60	50	....	....	....	....	....	....	....	....	....	....	....	15	2	4	6	16	....	....	....

Season	Club	League	GP	G	A	Pts	PIM	PP	SH	GW	S	%	+/-	TF	F%	H	SB	Min	GP	G	A	Pts	PIM	PP	SH	GW
			Regular Season																Playoffs							
1998-99	Detroit Vipers	IHL	82	23	52	75	64	....	....	....	....	....	....	....	....	....	....	....	11	5	4	9	10	....	....	....
99-2000	**Tampa Bay**	**NHL**	**68**	**11**	**22**	**33**	**24**	**1**	**2**	**1**	**94**	**11.7**	**–18**	**11**	**18.2**	**68**	**41**	**16:37**	....	....	....	....	....	....	....	....
	NHL Totals		**92**	**13**	**23**	**36**	**34**	**1**	**2**	**2**	**116**	**11.2**		**11**	**18.2**	**68**	**41**	**16:37**	....	....	....	....	....	....	....	....

OHL First All-Star Team (1989) • ECHL First All-Star Team (1991) • Named ECHL MVP (1991) • AHL Second All-Star Team (1992) • IHL First All-Star Team (1994, 1995) • Won "Bud" Poile Trophy (Playoff MVP - IHL) (1994)

Signed as a free agent by **Edmonton**, February 24, 1989. Signed as a free agent by **Tampa Bay**, September 1, 1992. Signed as a free agent by **Tampa Bay**, September 29, 1999.

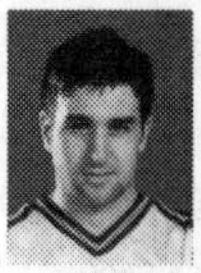

DRURY, Chris
(DROO-ree, KRIHS) **COL.**

Center. Shoots right. 5'10", 180 lbs. Born, Trumbull, CT, August 20, 1976. Quebec's 5th choice, 72nd overall, in 1994 Entry Draft.

Season	Club	League	GP	G	A	Pts	PIM	PP	SH	GW	S	%	+/-	TF	F%	H	SB	Min	GP	G	A	Pts	PIM	PP	SH	GW
1991-92	Fairfield Prep	Hi-School	25	22	27	49	....	....	....	....	....	....	....	....	....	....	....	....	....	....	....	....	....	....	....	....
1992-93	Fairfield Prep	Hi-School	24	25	32	57	15	....	....	....	....	....	....	....	....	....	....	....	....	....	....	....	....	....	....	....
1993-94	Fairfield Prep	Hi-School	24	37	18	55	....	....	....	....	....	....	....	....	....	....	....	....	....	....	....	....	....	....	....	....
1994-95	Boston University	H-East	39	12	15	27	38	....	....	....	....	....	....	....	....	....	....	....	....	....	....	....	....	....	....	....
1995-96	Boston University	H-East	37	35	33	*68	46	....	....	....	....	....	....	....	....	....	....	....	....	....	....	....	....	....	....	....
1996-97	Boston University	H-East	41	*38	24	62	64	....	....	....	....	....	....	....	....	....	....	....	....	....	....	....	....	....	....	....
1997-98	Boston University	H-East	38	28	29	57	88	....	....	....	....	....	....	....	....	....	....	....	....	....	....	....	....	....	....	....
1998-99	**Colorado**	**NHL**	**79**	**20**	**24**	**44**	**62**	**6**	**0**	**3**	**138**	**14.5**	**9**	**418**	**46.9**	**88**	**39**	**13:15**	**19**	**6**	**2**	**8**	**4**	**0**	**0**	**4**
99-2000	**Colorado**	**NHL**	**82**	**20**	**47**	**67**	**42**	**7**	**0**	**2**	**213**	**9.4**	**8**	**1321**	**53.1**	**68**	**50**	**18:33**	**17**	**4**	**10**	**14**	**4**	**1**	**0**	**2**
	NHL Totals		**161**	**40**	**71**	**111**	**104**	**13**	**0**	**5**	**351**	**11.4**		**1739**	**51.6**	**156**	**89**	**15:57**	**36**	**10**	**12**	**22**	**8**	**1**	**0**	**6**

Hockey East Second All-Star Team (1996, 1997) • NCAA East Second All-American Team (1996) • NCAA East First All-American Team (1997, 1998) • NCAA Championship All-Tournament Team (1997) • Hockey East First All-Star Team (1998) • Won Hobey Baker Memorial Award (Top U.S. Collegiate Player) (1998) • NHL All-Rookie Team (1999) • Won Calder Memorial Trophy (1999)

Rights transferred to **Colorado** after **Quebec** franchise relocated, June 21, 1995.

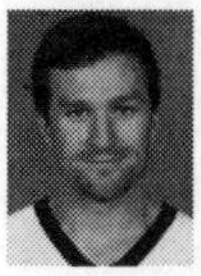

DRURY, Ted
(DROO-ree, TEHD) **CBJ**

Center. Shoots left. 6', 208 lbs. Born, Boston, MA, September 13, 1971. Calgary's 2nd choice, 42nd overall, in 1989 Entry Draft.

Season	Club	League	GP	G	A	Pts	PIM	PP	SH	GW	S	%	+/-	TF	F%	H	SB	Min	GP	G	A	Pts	PIM	PP	SH	GW
1987-88	Fairfield Prep	Hi-School	24	21	28	49	....	....	....	....	....	....	....	....	....	....	....	....	....	....	....	....	....	....	....	....
1988-89	Fairfield Prep	Hi-School	25	35	31	66	....	....	....	....	....	....	....	....	....	....	....	....	....	....	....	....	....	....	....	....
1989-90	Harvard University	ECAC	17	9	13	22	10	....	....	....	....	....	....	....	....	....	....	....	....	....	....	....	....	....	....	....
1990-91	Harvard University	ECAC	25	18	18	36	22	....	....	....	....	....	....	....	....	....	....	....	....	....	....	....	....	....	....	....
1991-92	United States	Nat-Team	53	11	23	34	30	....	....	....	....	....	....	....	....	....	....	....	....	....	....	....	....	....	....	....
	United States	Olympics	7	1	1	2	0	....	....	....	....	....	....	....	....	....	....	....	....	....	....	....	....	....	....	....
1992-93	Harvard University	ECAC	31	22	*41	*63	28	....	....	....	....	....	....	....	....	....	....	....	....	....	....	....	....	....	....	....
1993-94	**Calgary**	**NHL**	**34**	**5**	**7**	**12**	**26**	**0**	**1**	**1**	**43**	**11.6**	**–5**	....	....	....	....	....	....	....	....	....	....	....	....	....
	United States	Nat-Team	11	1	4	5	11	....	....	....	....	....	....	....	....	....	....	....	....	....	....	....	....	....	....	....
	United States	Olympics	7	1	2	3	2	....	....	....	....	....	....	....	....	....	....	....	....	....	....	....	....	....	....	....
	Hartford	**NHL**	**16**	**1**	**5**	**6**	**10**	**0**	**0**	**0**	**37**	**2.7**	**–10**	....	....	....	....	....	....	....	....	....	....	....	....	....
1994-95	**Hartford**	**NHL**	**34**	**3**	**6**	**9**	**21**	**0**	**0**	**0**	**31**	**9.7**	**–3**	....	....	....	....	....	....	....	....	....	....	....	....	....
	Springfield	AHL	2	0	1	1	0	....	....	....	....	....	....	....	....	....	....	....	....	....	....	....	....	....	....	....
1995-96	**Ottawa**	**NHL**	**42**	**9**	**7**	**16**	**54**	**1**	**0**	**1**	**80**	**11.3**	**–19**	....	....	....	....	....	....	....	....	....	....	....	....	....
1996-97	**Anaheim**	**NHL**	**73**	**9**	**9**	**18**	**54**	**1**	**0**	**2**	**114**	**7.9**	**–9**	....	....	....	....	....	**10**	**1**	**0**	**1**	**4**	**0**	**0**	**0**
1997-98	**Anaheim**	**NHL**	**73**	**6**	**10**	**16**	**82**	**0**	**1**	**0**	**110**	**5.5**	**–10**	....	....	....	....	....	....	....	....	....	....	....	....	....
1998-99	**Anaheim**	**NHL**	**75**	**5**	**6**	**11**	**83**	**0**	**0**	**0**	**79**	**6.3**	**2**	**449**	**47.9**	**77**	**13**	**8:15**	**4**	**0**	**0**	**0**	**0**	**0**	**0**	**0**
99-2000	**Anaheim**	**NHL**	**11**	**1**	**1**	**2**	**6**	**0**	**0**	**0**	**9**	**11.1**	**–1**	**82**	**41.5**	**12**	**2**	**7:06**	....	....	....	....	....	....	....	....
	NY Islanders	**NHL**	**55**	**2**	**1**	**3**	**31**	**1**	**0**	**0**	**48**	**4.2**	**–8**	**194**	**47.9**	**46**	**15**	**7:27**	....	....	....	....	....	....	....	....
	NHL Totals		**413**	**41**	**52**	**93**	**367**	**3**	**2**	**4**	**551**	**7.4**		**725**	**47.2**	**135**	**30**	**7:51**	**14**	**1**	**0**	**1**	**4**	**0**	**0**	**0**

ECAC First All-Star Team (1993) • NCAA East First All-America Team (1993)

Traded to **Hartford** by **Calgary** with Gary Suter and Paul Ranheim for James Patrick, Zarley Zalapski and Michael Nylander, March 10, 1994. Claimed by **Ottawa** from **Hartford** in NHL Waiver Draft, October 2, 1995. Traded to **Anaheim** by **Ottawa** with the rights to Marc Moro for Jason York and Shaun Van Allen, October 1, 1996. Traded to **NY Islanders** by **Anaheim** for Tony Hrkac and Dean Malkoc, October 29, 1999. Selected by **Columbus** from **NY Islanders** in Expansion Draft, June 23, 2000.

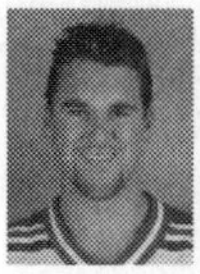

DUBE, Christian
(doo-BAY, KRIHS-tehn)

Center. Shoots right. 5'11", 170 lbs. Born, Sherbrooke, Que., April 25, 1977. NY Rangers' 1st choice, 39th overall, in 1995 Entry Draft.

Season	Club	League	GP	G	A	Pts	PIM	PP	SH	GW	S	%	+/-	TF	F%	H	SB	Min	GP	G	A	Pts	PIM	PP	SH	GW
1992-93	HC Martigny	Switz-2	27	36	40	76	34	....	....	....	....	....	....	....	....	....	....	....	....	....	....	....	....	....	....	....
1993-94	Sherbrooke	QMJHL	72	31	41	72	22	....	....	....	....	....	....	....	....	....	....	....	11	3	2	5	8	....	....	....
1994-95	Sherbrooke	QMJHL	71	36	65	101	43	....	....	....	....	....	....	....	....	....	....	....	7	1	7	8	8	....	....	....
1995-96	Sherbrooke	QMJHL	62	52	93	145	105	....	....	....	....	....	....	....	....	....	....	....	7	5	5	10	6	....	....	....
1996-97	Hull Olympiques	QMJHL	19	15	22	37	37	....	....	....	....	....	....	....	....	....	....	....	14	7	16	23	14	....	....	....
	NY Rangers	**NHL**	**27**	**1**	**1**	**2**	**4**	**1**	**0**	**0**	**14**	**7.1**	**–4**	....	....	....	....	....	**3**	**0**	**0**	**0**	**0**	**0**	**0**	**0**
1997-98	Hartford	AHL	79	11	46	57	46	....	....	....	....	....	....	....	....	....	....	....	9	0	4	4	6	....	....	....
1998-99	**NY Rangers**	**NHL**	**6**	**0**	**0**	**0**	**0**	**0**	**0**	**0**	**0**	**0.0**	**0**	**13**	**38.5**	**2**	**1**	**2:39**	....	....	....	....	....	....	....	....
	Hartford	AHL	58	21	30	51	20	....	....	....	....	....	....	....	....	....	....	....	6	0	3	3	4	....	....	....
99-2000	HC Lugano	Switz.	45	*25	26	51	52	....	....	....	....	....	....	....	....	....	....	....	14	8	*12	*20	14	....	....	....
	NHL Totals		**33**	**1**	**1**	**2**	**4**	**1**	**0**	**0**	**14**	**7.1**		**13**	**38.5**	**2**	**1**	**2:39**	**3**	**0**	**0**	**0**	**0**	**0**	**0**	**0**

QMJHL First All-Star Team (1996) • Canadian Major Junior First All-Star Team (1996) • Canadian Major Junior Player of the Year (1996) • Won Stafford Smythe Memorial Trophy (Memorial Cup Tournament MVP) (1997)

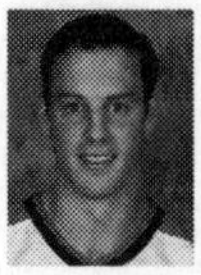

DUBINSKY, Steve
(doo-BIHN-skee, STEEV) **CHI.**

Center. Shoots left. 6', 190 lbs. Born, Montreal, Que., July 9, 1970. Chicago's 9th choice, 226th overall, in 1990 Entry Draft.

Season	Club	League	GP	G	A	Pts	PIM	PP	SH	GW	S	%	+/-	TF	F%	H	SB	Min	GP	G	A	Pts	PIM	PP	SH	GW
1989-90	Clarkson	ECAC	35	7	10	17	24	....	....	....	....	....	....	....	....	....	....	....	....	....	....	....	....	....	....	....
1990-91	Clarkson	ECAC	39	13	23	36	26	....	....	....	....	....	....	....	....	....	....	....	....	....	....	....	....	....	....	....
1991-92	Clarkson	ECAC	32	20	31	51	40	....	....	....	....	....	....	....	....	....	....	....	....	....	....	....	....	....	....	....
1992-93	Clarkson	ECAC	35	18	26	44	58	....	....	....	....	....	....	....	....	....	....	....	....	....	....	....	....	....	....	....
1993-94	**Chicago**	**NHL**	**27**	**2**	**6**	**8**	**16**	**0**	**0**	**0**	**20**	**10.0**	**1**	....	....	....	....	....	**6**	**0**	**0**	**0**	**10**	**0**	**0**	**0**
	Indianapolis Ice	IHL	54	15	25	40	63	....	....	....	....	....	....	....	....	....	....	....	....	....	....	....	....	....	....	....
1994-95	**Chicago**	**NHL**	**16**	**0**	**0**	**0**	**8**	**0**	**0**	**0**	**16**	**0.0**	**–5**	....	....	....	....	....	....	....	....	....	....	....	....	....
	Indianapolis Ice	IHL	62	16	11	27	29	....	....	....	....	....	....	....	....	....	....	....	....	....	....	....	....	....	....	....
1995-96	**Chicago**	**NHL**	**43**	**2**	**3**	**5**	**14**	**0**	**0**	**0**	**33**	**6.1**	**3**	....	....	....	....	....	....	....	....	....	....	....	....	....
	Indianapolis Ice	IHL	16	8	8	16	10	....	....	....	....	....	....	....	....	....	....	....	....	....	....	....	....	....	....	....
1996-97	**Chicago**	**NHL**	**5**	**0**	**0**	**0**	**0**	**0**	**0**	**0**	**4**	**0.0**	**2**	....	....	....	....	....	**4**	**1**	**0**	**1**	**4**	**0**	**0**	**0**
	Indianapolis Ice	IHL	77	32	40	72	53	....	....	....	....	....	....	....	....	....	....	....	1	3	1	4	0	....	....	....
1997-98	**Chicago**	**NHL**	**82**	**5**	**13**	**18**	**57**	**0**	**1**	**0**	**112**	**4.5**	**–6**	....	....	....	....	....	....	....	....	....	....	....	....	....
1998-99	**Chicago**	**NHL**	**1**	**0**	**0**	**0**	**0**	**0**	**0**	**0**	**1**	**0.0**	**0**	**5**	**60.0**	**1**	**0**	**5:11**	....	....	....	....	....	....	....	....
	Calgary	**NHL**	**61**	**4**	**10**	**14**	**14**	**0**	**2**	**0**	**69**	**5.8**	**–7**	**223**	**46.6**	**161**	**75**	**14:38**	....	....	....	....	....	....	....	....
99-2000	**Calgary**	**NHL**	**23**	**0**	**1**	**1**	**4**	**0**	**0**	**0**	**29**	**0.0**	**–12**	**207**	**49.3**	**58**	**26**	**12:05**	....	....	....	....	....	....	....	....
	NHL Totals		**258**	**13**	**33**	**46**	**113**	**0**	**3**	**0**	**284**	**4.6**		**435**	**48.0**	**220**	**101**	**13:50**	**10**	**1**	**0**	**1**	**14**	**0**	**0**	**0**

Traded to **Calgary** by **Chicago** with Jeff Shantz for Marty McInnis, Jamie Allison and Eric Andersson, October 27, 1998. • Missed remainder of 1999-2000 season recovering from knee injury suffered in game vs. Chicago, December 12, 1999. Signed as a free agent by **Chicago**, August 25, 2000.

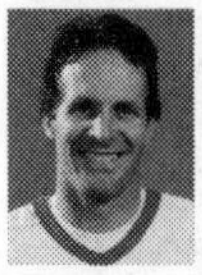

DUCHESNE, Steve
(doo-SHAYN, STEEV) **DET.**

Defense. Shoots left. 5'11", 195 lbs. Born, Sept-Iles, Que., June 30, 1965.

Season	Club	League	GP	G	A	Pts	PIM	PP	SH	GW	S	%	+/-	TF	F%	H	SB	Min	GP	G	A	Pts	PIM	PP	SH	GW
1983-84	Wawa Travellers	NOJHA	10	9	23	32	9	....	....	....	....	....	....	....	....	....	....	....	....	....	....	....	....	....	....	....
	Drummondville	QMJHL	67	1	34	35	79	....	....	....	....	....	....	....	....	....	....	....	....	....	....	....	....	....	....	....
1984-85	Drummondville	QMJHL	65	22	54	76	94	....	....	....	....	....	....	....	....	....	....	....	5	4	7	11	8	....	....	....
1985-86	New Haven	AHL	75	14	35	49	76	....	....	....	....	....	....	....	....	....	....	....	5	0	2	2	9	....	....	....
1986-87	**Los Angeles**	**NHL**	**75**	**13**	**25**	**38**	**74**	**5**	**0**	**2**	**113**	**11.5**	**8**	....	....	....	....	....	**5**	**2**	**2**	**4**	**4**	**1**	**0**	**0**
1987-88	**Los Angeles**	**NHL**	**71**	**16**	**39**	**55**	**109**	**5**	**0**	**4**	**190**	**8.4**	**0**	....	....	....	....	....	**5**	**1**	**3**	**4**	**14**	**1**	**0**	**0**
1988-89	**Los Angeles**	**NHL**	**79**	**25**	**50**	**75**	**92**	**8**	**5**	**2**	**215**	**11.6**	**31**	....	....	....	....	....	**11**	**4**	**4**	**8**	**12**	**2**	**0**	**0**
1989-90	**Los Angeles**	**NHL**	**79**	**20**	**42**	**62**	**36**	**6**	**0**	**1**	**224**	**8.9**	**–3**	....	....	....	....	....	**10**	**2**	**9**	**11**	**6**	**1**	**0**	**0**
1990-91	**Los Angeles**	**NHL**	**78**	**21**	**41**	**62**	**66**	**8**	**0**	**3**	**171**	**12.3**	**19**	....	....	....	....	....	**12**	**4**	**8**	**12**	**8**	**1**	**0**	**0**
1991-92	**Philadelphia**	**NHL**	**78**	**18**	**38**	**56**	**86**	**7**	**2**	**3**	**229**	**7.9**	**–7**	....	....	....	....	....	....	....	....	....	....	....	....	....

			Regular Season																Playoffs							
Season	Club	League	GP	G	A	Pts	PIM	PP	SH	GW	S	%	+/–	TF	F%	H	SB	Min	GP	G	A	Pts	PIM	PP	SH	GW
1992-93	**Quebec**	**NHL**	**82**	**20**	**62**	**82**	**57**	**8**	**0**	**2**	**227**	**8.8**	**15**	....	....	....	....	....	**6**	**0**	**5**	**5**	**6**	**0**	**0**	**0**
1993-94	**St. Louis**	**NHL**	**36**	**12**	**19**	**31**	**14**	**8**	**0**	**1**	**115**	**10.4**	**1**	....	....	....	....	....	**4**	**0**	**2**	**2**	**2**	**0**	**0**	**0**
1994-95	**St. Louis**	**NHL**	**47**	**12**	**26**	**38**	**36**	**1**	**0**	**1**	**116**	**10.3**	**29**	....	....	....	....	....	**7**	**0**	**4**	**4**	**2**	**0**	**0**	**0**
1995-96	**Ottawa**	**NHL**	**62**	**12**	**24**	**36**	**42**	**7**	**0**	**2**	**163**	**7.4**	**–23**	....	....	....	....	....	....	....	....	....	....	....	....	....
1996-97	**Ottawa**	**NHL**	**78**	**19**	**28**	**47**	**38**	**10**	**2**	**3**	**208**	**9.1**	**–9**	....	....	....	....	....	**7**	**1**	**4**	**5**	**0**	**1**	**0**	**1**
1997-98	**St. Louis**	**NHL**	**80**	**14**	**42**	**56**	**32**	**5**	**1**	**1**	**153**	**9.2**	**9**	....	....	....	....	....	**10**	**0**	**4**	**4**	**6**	**0**	**0**	**0**
1998-99	**Los Angeles**	**NHL**	**60**	**4**	**19**	**23**	**22**	**1**	**0**	**1**	**99**	**4.0**	**–6**	**2**	**50.0**	**38**	**95**	**21:11**	....	....	....	....	....	....	....	....
	Philadelphia	**NHL**	**11**	**2**	**5**	**7**	**2**	**1**	**0**	**1**	**19**	**10.5**	**0**	**0**	**0.0**	**5**	**14**	**22:28**	**6**	**0**	**2**	**2**	**2**	**0**	**0**	**0**
99-2000	**Detroit**	**NHL**	**79**	**10**	**31**	**41**	**42**	**1**	**0**	**1**	**154**	**6.5**	**12**	**1**	**0.0**	**41**	**104**	**21:14**	**9**	**0**	**4**	**4**	**10**	**0**	**0**	**0**
	NHL Totals		**995**	**218**	**491**	**709**	**748**	**81**	**10**	**28**	**2396**	**9.1**		**3**	**33.3**	**84**	**213**	**21:18**	**92**	**14**	**51**	**65**	**72**	**7**	**0**	**1**

QMJHL First All-Star Team (1985) • NHL All-Rookie Team (1987) • Played in NHL All-Star Game (1989, 1990, 1993)

Signed as a free agent by **LA Kings**, October 1, 1984. Traded to **Philadelphia** by **LA Kings** with Steve Kasper and LA Kings' 4th round choice (Aris Brimanis) in 1991 Entry Draft for Jari Kurri and Jeff Chychrun, May 30, 1991. Traded to **Quebec** by **Philadelphia** with Peter Forsberg, Kerry Huffman, Mike Ricci, Ron Hextall, Philadelphia's 1st round choice (Jocelyn Thibault) in 1993 Entry Draft, $15,000,000 and future considerations (Chris Simon and Philadelphia's 1st round choice (later traded to Toronto - later traded to Washington - Washington selected Nolan Baumgartner) in 1994 Entry Draft, July 21, 1992) for Eric Lindros, June 30, 1992. Traded to **St. Louis** by **Quebec** with Denis Chasse for Garth Butcher, Ron Sutter and Bob Bassen, January 23, 1994. Traded to **Ottawa** by **St. Louis** for Ottawa's 2nd round choice (later traded to Buffalo - Buffalo selected Cory Sarich) in 1996 Entry Draft, August 4, 1995. Traded to **St. Louis** by **Ottawa** for Igor Kravchuk, August 25, 1997. Signed as a free agent by **LA Kings**, July 2, 1998. Traded to **Philadelphia** by **Los Angeles** for Dave Babych and Philadelphia's 5th round choice (Nathan Marsters) in 2000 Entry Draft, March 23, 1999. Signed as a free agent by **Detroit**, September 3, 1999.

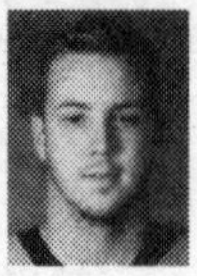

DUERDEN, Dave (DEWER-dehn, DAYV) FLA.

Left wing. Shoots left. 6'2", 201 lbs. Born, Oshawa, Ont., April 11, 1977. Florida's 4th choice, 80th overall, in 1995 Entry Draft.

Season	Club	League	GP	G	A	Pts	PIM	PP	SH	GW	S	%	+/–	TF	F%	H	SB	Min	GP	G	A	Pts	PIM	PP	SH	GW
1991-92	Ajax Knights	OMHA	60	47	48	95	100	....	....	....	....	....	....	....	....	....	....	....	....	....	....	....	....	....	....	....
1992-93	Ajax Knights	OMHA	60	21	48	69	45	....	....	....	....	....	....	....	....	....	....	....	....	....	....	....	....	....	....	....
1993-94	Wexford Raiders	OJHL	47	17	27	44	26	....	....	....	....	....	....	....	....	....	....	....	....	....	....	....	....	....	....	....
1994-95	Peterborough	OHL	66	20	33	53	21	....	....	....	....	....	....	....	....	....	....	....	11	6	2	8	6	....	....	....
1995-96	Peterborough	OHL	66	35	35	70	47	....	....	....	....	....	....	....	....	....	....	....	24	14	13	27	16	....	....	....
1996-97	Peterborough	OHL	66	36	48	84	34	....	....	....	....	....	....	....	....	....	....	....	4	2	4	6	0	....	....	....
1997-98	Port Huron	UHL	7	0	4	4	10	....	....	....	....	....	....	....	....	....	....	....	....	....	....	....	....	....	....	....
	New Haven	AHL	36	6	7	13	10	....	....	....	....	....	....	....	....	....	....	....	....	....	....	....	....	....	....	....
	Fort Wayne	IHL	7	0	1	1	0	....	....	....	....	....	....	....	....	....	....	....	....	....	....	....	....	....	....	....
1998-99	Miami Matadors	ECHL	13	10	7	17	0	....	....	....	....	....	....	....	....	....	....	....	....	....	....	....	....	....	....	....
	Kentucky	AHL	36	8	9	17	9	....	....	....	....	....	....	....	....	....	....	....	6	0	2	2	0	....	....	....
99-2000	**Florida**	**NHL**	**2**	**0**	**0**	**0**	**0**	**0**	**0**	**0**	**1**	**0.0**	**0**	**0**	**0.0**	**0**	**0**	**1:35**	....	....	....	....	....	....	....	....
	Louisville	AHL	74	25	38	63	6	....	....	....	....	....	....	....	....	....	....	....	4	0	1	1	0	....	....	....
	NHL Totals		**2**	**0**	**0**	**0**	**0**	**0**	**0**	**0**	**1**	**0.0**		**0**	**0.0**	**0**	**0**	**1:35**	....	....	....	....	....	....	....	....

OHL Second All-Star Team (1997)

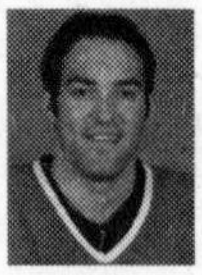

DUMONT, Jean-Pierre (doo-MAWNT, JAHN-PEE-air) BUF.

Right wing. Shoots left. 6'2", 202 lbs. Born, Montreal, Que., April 1, 1978. NY Islanders' 1st choice, 3rd overall, in 1996 Entry Draft.

Season	Club	League	GP	G	A	Pts	PIM	PP	SH	GW	S	%	+/–	TF	F%	H	SB	Min	GP	G	A	Pts	PIM	PP	SH	GW
1993-94	Val-d'Or Foreurs	QMJHL	25	9	11	20	10	....	....	....	....	....	....	....	....	....	....	....	....	....	....	....	....	....	....	....
1994-95	Val-d'Or Foreurs	QMJHL	48	5	14	19	24	....	....	....	....	....	....	....	....	....	....	....	....	....	....	....	....	....	....	....
1995-96	Val-d'Or Foreurs	QMJHL	66	48	57	105	109	....	....	....	....	....	....	....	....	....	....	....	13	12	8	20	22	....	....	....
1996-97	Val-d'Or Foreurs	QMJHL	62	44	64	108	86	....	....	....	....	....	....	....	....	....	....	....	13	9	7	16	12	....	....	....
1997-98	Val-d'Or Foreurs	QMJHL	55	57	42	99	63	....	....	....	....	....	....	....	....	....	....	....	19	31	15	46	18	....	....	....
1998-99	**Chicago**	**NHL**	**25**	**9**	**6**	**15**	**10**	**0**	**0**	**2**	**42**	**21.4**	**7**	**10**	**50.0**	**22**	**8**	**14:14**	....	....	....	....	....	....	....	....
	Portland	AHL	50	32	14	46	39	....	....	....	....	....	....	....	....	....	....	....	....	....	....	....	....	....	....	....
	Chicago Wolves	IHL	....	....	....	....	....	....	....	....	....	....	....	....	....	....	....	....	10	4	1	5	6	....	....	....
99-2000	**Chicago**	**NHL**	**47**	**10**	**8**	**18**	**18**	**0**	**0**	**1**	**86**	**11.6**	**–6**	**12**	**33.3**	**49**	**7**	**12:54**	....	....	....	....	....	....	....	....
	Cleveland	IHL	7	5	2	7	8	....	....	....	....	....	....	....	....	....	....	....	....	....	....	....	....	....	....	....
	Rochester	AHL	13	7	10	17	18	....	....	....	....	....	....	....	....	....	....	....	21	14	7	21	32	....	....	....
	NHL Totals		**72**	**19**	**14**	**33**	**28**	**0**	**0**	**3**	**128**	**14.8**		**22**	**40.9**	**71**	**15**	**13:22**	....	....	....	....	....	....	....	....

QMJHL Second All-Star Team (1997)

Rights traded to **Chicago** by **NY Islanders** with Chicago's 5th round choice (later traded to Philadelphia - Philadelphia selected Francis Belanger) in 1998 Entry Draft for Dmitri Nabokov, May 30, 1998. Traded to **Buffalo** by **Chicago** with Doug Gilmour and future considerations for Michal Grosek, March 10, 2000.

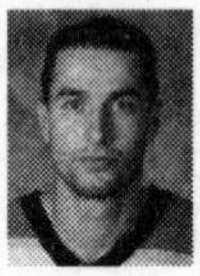

DVORAK, Radek (duh-VOHR-ak, RA-dehk) NYR

Right wing. Shoots right. 6'1", 194 lbs. Born, Tabor, Czech., March 9, 1977. Florida's 1st choice, 10th overall, in 1995 Entry Draft.

Season	Club	League	GP	G	A	Pts	PIM	PP	SH	GW	S	%	+/–	TF	F%	H	SB	Min	GP	G	A	Pts	PIM	PP	SH	GW
1992-93	MC Budejovice	Czech-Jr.	35	44	46	90	....	....	....	....	....	....	....	....	....	....	....	....	....	....	....	....	....	....	....	....
1993-94	MC Budejovice-Jr.	Cze-Rep	20	17	18	35	....	....	....	....	....	....	....	....	....	....	....	....	....	....	....	....	....	....	....	....
	MC Budejovice	Cze-Rep	8	0	0	0	0	....	....	....	....	....	....	....	....	....	....	....	....	....	....	....	....	....	....	....
1994-95	MC Budejovice	Cze-Rep	10	3	5	8	2	....	....	....	....	....	....	....	....	....	....	....	9	5	1	6	....	....	....	....
1995-96	**Florida**	**NHL**	**77**	**13**	**14**	**27**	**20**	**0**	**0**	**4**	**126**	**10.3**	**5**	....	....	....	....	....	**16**	**1**	**3**	**4**	**0**	**0**	**0**	**0**
1996-97	**Florida**	**NHL**	**78**	**18**	**21**	**39**	**30**	**2**	**0**	**1**	**139**	**12.9**	**–2**	....	....	....	....	....	**3**	**0**	**0**	**0**	**0**	**0**	**0**	**0**
1997-98	**Florida**	**NHL**	**64**	**12**	**24**	**36**	**33**	**2**	**3**	**0**	**112**	**10.7**	**–1**	....	....	....	....	....	....	....	....	....	....	....	....	....
1998-99	**Florida**	**NHL**	**82**	**19**	**24**	**43**	**29**	**0**	**4**	**0**	**182**	**10.4**	**7**	**98**	**46.9**	**30**	**33**	**16:13**	....	....	....	....	....	....	....	....
99-2000	**Florida**	**NHL**	**35**	**7**	**10**	**17**	**6**	**0**	**0**	**1**	**67**	**10.4**	**5**	**16**	**37.5**	**5**	**11**	**15:25**	....	....	....	....	....	....	....	....
	NY Rangers	**NHL**	**46**	**11**	**22**	**33**	**10**	**2**	**1**	**0**	**90**	**12.2**	**0**	**34**	**35.3**	**22**	**16**	**18:24**	....	....	....	....	....	....	....	....
	NHL Totals		**382**	**80**	**115**	**195**	**128**	**6**	**8**	**6**	**716**	**11.2**		**148**	**43.2**	**57**	**60**	**16:40**	**19**	**1**	**3**	**4**	**0**	**0**	**0**	**0**

Traded to **San Jose** by **Florida** for Mike Vernon, San Jose's 3rd round choice (Sean O'Connor) in 2000 Entry Draft and future considerations, December 30, 1999. Traded to **NY Rangers** by **San Jose** for Todd Harvey and NY Rangers' 4th round choice in 2001 Entry Draft, December 30, 1999.

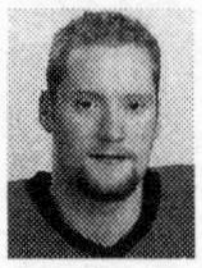

DWYER, Gordie (DWIGHR, GOHR-dee) T.B.

Left wing. Shoots left. 6'2", 216 lbs. Born, Dalhousie, NB, January 25, 1978. Montreal's 5th choice, 152nd overall, in 1998 Entry Draft.

Season	Club	League	GP	G	A	Pts	PIM	PP	SH	GW	S	%	+/–	TF	F%	H	SB	Min	GP	G	A	Pts	PIM	PP	SH	GW
1994-95	Hull Olympiques	QMJHL	57	3	7	10	204	....	....	....	....	....	....	....	....	....	....	....	17	1	3	4	54	....	....	....
1995-96	Hull Olympiques	QMJHL	25	5	9	14	199	....	....	....	....	....	....	....	....	....	....	....	....	....	....	....	....	....	....	....
	Laval Titan	QMJHL	22	5	17	22	72	....	....	....	....	....	....	....	....	....	....	....	....	....	....	....	....	....	....	....
	Beauport	QMJHL	22	4	9	13	87	....	....	....	....	....	....	....	....	....	....	....	20	3	5	8	104	....	....	....
1996-97	Drummondville	QMJHL	66	21	48	69	393	....	....	....	....	....	....	....	....	....	....	....	8	6	1	7	39	....	....	....
1997-98	Quebec Remparts	QMJHL	59	18	27	45	365	....	....	....	....	....	....	....	....	....	....	....	14	4	9	13	67	....	....	....
1998-99	Fredericton	AHL	14	0	0	0	46	....	....	....	....	....	....	....	....	....	....	....	....	....	....	....	....	....	....	....
	New Orleans	ECHL	36	1	3	4	163	....	....	....	....	....	....	....	....	....	....	....	11	0	0	0	27	....	....	....
99-2000	Quebec Citadelles	AHL	7	0	0	0	37	....	....	....	....	....	....	....	....	....	....	....	....	....	....	....	....	....	....	....
	Tampa Bay	**NHL**	**24**	**0**	**1**	**1**	**135**	**0**	**0**	**0**	**7**	**0.0**	**–6**	**0**	**0.0**	**53**	**4**	**4:57**	....	....	....	....	....	....	....	....
	Detroit Vipers	IHL	27	0	2	2	147	....	....	....	....	....	....	....	....	....	....	....	....	....	....	....	....	....	....	....
	NHL Totals		**24**	**0**	**1**	**1**	**135**	**0**	**0**	**0**	**7**	**0.0**		**0**	**0.0**	**53**	**4**	**4:56**	....	....	....	....	....	....	....	....

• Re-entered NHL draft. Originally St. Louis' 2nd choice, 67th overall, in 1996 Entry Draft.

Traded to **Tampa Bay** by **Montreal** for Mike McBain, November 26, 1999.

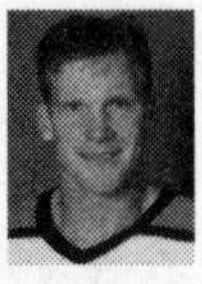

DYKHUIS, Karl (DIGH-kowz, KAHRL) MTL.

Defense. Shoots left. 6'3", 214 lbs. Born, Sept-Iles, Que., July 8, 1972. Chicago's 1st choice, 16th overall, in 1990 Entry Draft.

Season	Club	League	GP	G	A	Pts	PIM	PP	SH	GW	S	%	+/–	TF	F%	H	SB	Min	GP	G	A	Pts	PIM	PP	SH	GW
1987-88	Lac St-Jean	QAAA	37	2	12	14	....	....	....	....	....	....	....	....	....	....	....	....	....	....	....	....	....	....	....	....
1988-89	Hull Olympiques	QMJHL	63	2	29	31	59	....	....	....	....	....	....	....	....	....	....	....	9	1	9	10	6	....	....	....
1989-90	Hull Olympiques	QMJHL	69	10	46	56	119	....	....	....	....	....	....	....	....	....	....	....	11	2	5	7	2	....	....	....
1990-91	Longueuil	QMJHL	3	1	4	5	6	....	....	....	....	....	....	....	....	....	....	....	8	2	5	7	6	....	....	....
	Canada	Nat-Team	37	2	9	11	16	....	....	....	....	....	....	....	....	....	....	....	....	....	....	....	....	....	....	....
1991-92	Verdun College	QMJHL	29	5	19	24	55	....	....	....	....	....	....	....	....	....	....	....	17	0	12	12	14	....	....	....
	Canada	Nat-Team	19	1	2	3	16	....	....	....	....	....	....	....	....	....	....	....	....	....	....	....	....	....	....	....
	Chicago	**NHL**	**6**	**1**	**3**	**4**	**4**	**1**	**0**	**0**	**12**	**8.3**	**–1**	....	....	....	....	....	....	....	....	....	....	....	....	....

			Regular Season																Playoffs							
Season	Club	League	GP	G	A	Pts	PIM	PP	SH	GW	S	%	+/–	TF	F%	H	SB	Min	GP	G	A	Pts	PIM	PP	SH	GW
1992-93	**Chicago**	**NHL**	**12**	**0**	**5**	**5**	**0**	**0**	**0**	**0**	**10**	**0.0**	**2**													
	Indianapolis Ice	IHL	59	5	18	23	76												5	1	1	2	8			
1993-94	Indianapolis Ice	IHL	73	7	25	32	132																			
1994-95	Indianapolis Ice	IHL	52	2	21	23	63																			
	Philadelphia	**NHL**	**33**	**2**	**6**	**8**	**37**	**1**	**0**	**1**	**46**	**4.3**	**7**						**15**	**4**	**4**	**8**	**14**	**2**	**0**	**2**
	Hershey Bears	AHL	1	0	0	0	0																			
1995-96	**Philadelphia**	**NHL**	**82**	**5**	**15**	**20**	**101**	**1**	**0**	**0**	**104**	**4.8**	**12**						**12**	**2**	**2**	**4**	**22**	**1**	**0**	**0**
1996-97	**Philadelphia**	**NHL**	**62**	**4**	**15**	**19**	**35**	**2**	**0**	**1**	**101**	**4.0**	**6**						**18**	**0**	**3**	**3**	**2**	**0**	**0**	**0**
1997-98	**Tampa Bay**	**NHL**	**78**	**5**	**9**	**14**	**110**	**0**	**1**	**0**	**91**	**5.5**	**–8**													
1998-99	**Tampa Bay**	**NHL**	**33**	**2**	**1**	**3**	**18**	**0**	**0**	**0**	**27**	**7.4**	**–21**	**0**	**0.0**	**44**	**39**	**20:14**								
	Philadelphia	**NHL**	**45**	**2**	**4**	**6**	**32**	**1**	**0**	**0**	**61**	**3.3**	**–2**	**0**	**0.0**	**38**	**47**	**18:15**	**5**	**1**	**0**	**1**	**4**	**0**	**0**	**0**
99-2000	**Philadelphia**	**NHL**	**5**	**0**	**1**	**1**	**6**	**0**	**0**	**0**	**5**	**0.0**	**–2**	**0**	**0.0**	**9**	**3**	**14:54**								
	Montreal	**NHL**	**67**	**7**	**12**	**19**	**40**	**3**	**1**	**0**	**64**	**10.9**	**–3**	**0**	**0.0**	**97**	**98**	**19:53**								
	NHL Totals		**423**	**28**	**71**	**99**	**383**	**9**	**2**	**2**	**521**	**5.4**		**0**	**0.0**	**188**	**187**	**19:18**	**50**	**7**	**9**	**16**	**42**	**3**	**0**	**2**

QMJHL First All-Star Team (1990)

Traded to **Philadelphia** by **Chicago** for Bob Wilkie and Philadelphia's 5th round choice (Kyle Calder) in 1995 Entry Draft, February 16, 1995. Traded to **Tampa Bay** by **Philadelphia** with Mikael Renberg for Philadelphia's 1st round choices (previously acquired by Tampa Bay) in 1998 (Simon Gagne), 1999 (Maxime Ouellet), 2000, and 2001 Entry Drafts, August 20, 1997. Traded to **Philadelphia** by **Tampa Bay** for Petr Svoboda, December 28, 1998. Traded to **Montreal** by **Philadelphia** for cash, October 20, 1999.

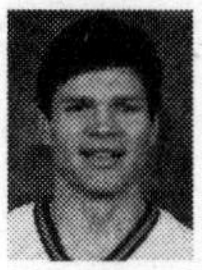

EAGLES, Mike (EE-gehls, MIGHK) WSH.

Center/Left wing. Shoots left. 5'10", 195 lbs. Born, Sussex, N.B., March 7, 1963. Quebec's 5th choice, 116th overall, in 1981 Entry Draft.

Season	Club	League	GP	G	A	Pts	PIM	PP	SH	GW	S	%	+/–	TF	F%	H	SB	Min	GP	G	A	Pts	PIM	PP	SH	GW
1979-80	Melville	SJHL	55	46	30	76	77																			
	Billings Bighorns	WHL	5	0	1	1	0																			
1980-81	Kitchener	OMJHL	56	11	27	38	64												18	4	2	6	36			
1981-82	Kitchener	OHL	62	26	40	66	148												15	3	11	14	27			
1982-83	Kitchener	OHL	58	26	36	62	133												12	5	7	12	27			
	Quebec	**NHL**	**2**	**0**	**0**	**0**	**2**	**0**	**0**	**0**	**1**	**0.0**	**–1**													
1983-84	Fredericton	AHL	68	13	29	42	85												4	0	0	0	5			
1984-85	Fredericton	AHL	36	4	20	24	80												3	0	0	0	2			
1985-86	**Quebec**	**NHL**	**73**	**11**	**12**	**23**	**49**	**1**	**0**	**1**	**68**	**16.2**	**3**						**3**	**0**	**0**	**0**	**2**	**0**	**0**	**0**
1986-87	**Quebec**	**NHL**	**73**	**13**	**19**	**32**	**55**	**0**	**2**	**2**	**95**	**13.7**	**–15**						**4**	**1**	**0**	**1**	**10**	**0**	**0**	**0**
1987-88	**Quebec**	**NHL**	**76**	**10**	**10**	**20**	**74**	**1**	**2**	**2**	**89**	**11.2**	**–18**													
1988-89	**Chicago**	**NHL**	**47**	**5**	**11**	**16**	**44**	**0**	**0**	**0**	**39**	**12.8**	**–8**													
1989-90	**Chicago**	**NHL**	**23**	**1**	**2**	**3**	**34**	**0**	**0**	**0**	**23**	**4.3**	**–4**													
	Indianapolis Ice	IHL	24	11	13	24	47												13	*10	10	20	34			
1990-91	**Winnipeg**	**NHL**	**44**	**0**	**9**	**9**	**79**	**0**	**0**	**0**	**51**	**0.0**	**–10**													
	Indianapolis Ice	IHL	25	15	14	29	47																			
1991-92	**Winnipeg**	**NHL**	**65**	**7**	**10**	**17**	**118**	**0**	**1**	**0**	**60**	**11.7**	**–17**						**7**	**0**	**0**	**0**	**8**	**0**	**0**	**0**
1992-93	**Winnipeg**	**NHL**	**84**	**8**	**18**	**26**	**131**	**1**	**0**	**1**	**67**	**11.9**	**–1**						**5**	**0**	**1**	**1**	**6**	**0**	**0**	**0**
1993-94	**Winnipeg**	**NHL**	**73**	**4**	**8**	**12**	**96**	**0**	**1**	**0**	**53**	**7.5**	**–20**													
1994-95	**Winnipeg**	**NHL**	**27**	**2**	**1**	**3**	**40**	**0**	**0**	**0**	**13**	**15.4**	**–13**													
	Washington	**NHL**	**13**	**1**	**3**	**4**	**8**	**0**	**0**	**0**	**15**	**6.7**	**2**						**7**	**0**	**2**	**2**	**4**	**0**	**0**	**0**
1995-96	**Washington**	**NHL**	**70**	**4**	**7**	**11**	**75**	**0**	**0**	**0**	**70**	**5.7**	**–1**						**6**	**1**	**1**	**2**	**2**	**0**	**0**	**0**
1996-97	**Washington**	**NHL**	**70**	**1**	**7**	**8**	**42**	**0**	**0**	**0**	**38**	**2.6**	**–4**													
1997-98	**Washington**	**NHL**	**36**	**1**	**3**	**4**	**16**	**0**	**0**	**0**	**25**	**4.0**	**–2**						**12**	**0**	**2**	**2**	**2**	**0**	**0**	**0**
1998-99	**Washington**	**NHL**	**52**	**4**	**2**	**6**	**50**	**0**	**0**	**0**	**41**	**9.8**	**–5**	**298**	**53.0**	**94**	**25**	**9:34**								
99-2000	**Washington**	**NHL**	**25**	**2**	**0**	**2**	**15**	**0**	**0**	**1**	**13**	**15.4**	**–7**	**115**	**50.4**	**41**	**14**	**7:37**								
	NHL Totals		**853**	**74**	**122**	**196**	**928**	**3**	**6**	**7**	**761**	**9.7**		**413**	**52.3**	**135**	**39**	**8:56**	**44**	**2**	**6**	**8**	**34**	**0**	**0**	**0**

• Missed majority of 1984-85 season recovering from hand injury suffered in practice, October, 1984. Traded to **Chicago** by **Quebec** for Bob Mason, July 5, 1988. Traded to **Winnipeg** by **Chicago** for Winnipeg's 4th round choice (Igor Kravchuk) in 1991 Entry Draft, December 14, 1990. Traded to **Washington** by **Winnipeg** with Igor Ulanov for Washington's 3rd (later traded to Dallas - Dallas selected Sergei Gusev) and 5th (Brian Elder) round choices in 1995 Entry Draft, April 7, 1995.

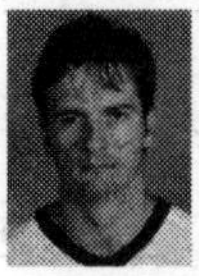

EAKINS, Dallas (EE-kins, DAL-las) CGY.

Defense. Shoots left. 6'2", 200 lbs. Born, Dade City, FL, February 27, 1967. Washington's 11th choice, 208th overall, in 1985 Entry Draft.

Season	Club	League	GP	G	A	Pts	PIM	PP	SH	GW	S	%	+/–	TF	F%	H	SB	Min	GP	G	A	Pts	PIM	PP	SH	GW
1983-84	Peterborough AA	OMHA	29	7	20	27	67																			
	Peterborough B's	OJHL-B	5	0	3	3	4																			
1984-85	Peterborough	OHL	48	0	8	8	96												7	0	0	0	18			
1985-86	Peterborough	OHL	60	6	16	22	134												16	0	1	1	30			
1986-87	Peterborough	OHL	54	3	11	14	145												12	1	4	5	37			
1987-88	Peterborough	OHL	64	11	27	38	129												12	3	12	15	16			
1988-89	Baltimore	AHL	62	0	10	10	139																			
1989-90	Moncton Hawks	AHL	75	2	11	13	189																			
1990-91	Moncton Hawks	AHL	75	1	12	13	132												9	0	1	1	44			
1991-92	Moncton Hawks	AHL	67	3	13	16	136												11	2	1	3	16			
1992-93	**Winnipeg**	**NHL**	**14**	**0**	**2**	**2**	**38**	**0**	**0**	**0**	**9**	**0.0**	**2**													
	Moncton Hawks	AHL	55	4	6	10	132																			
1993-94	**Florida**	**NHL**	**1**	**0**	**0**	**0**	**0**	**0**	**0**	**0**	**2**	**0.0**	**0**													
	Cincinnati	IHL	80	1	18	19	143												8	0	1	1	41			
1994-95	**Florida**	**NHL**	**17**	**0**	**1**	**1**	**35**	**0**	**0**	**0**	**3**	**0.0**	**2**													
	Cincinnati	IHL	59	6	12	18	69																			
1995-96	**St. Louis**	**NHL**	**16**	**0**	**1**	**1**	**34**	**0**	**0**	**0**	**6**	**0.0**	**–2**													
	Worcester	AHL	4	0	0	0	12																			
	Winnipeg	**NHL**	**2**	**0**	**0**	**0**	**0**	**0**	**0**	**0**	**0**	**0.0**	**1**													
1996-97	**Phoenix**	**NHL**	**4**	**0**	**0**	**0**	**10**	**0**	**0**	**0**	**2**	**0.0**	**–3**													
	Springfield	AHL	38	6	7	13	63																			
	NY Rangers	**NHL**	**3**	**0**	**0**	**0**	**6**	**0**	**0**	**0**	**2**	**0.0**	**–1**						**4**	**0**	**0**	**0**	**4**	**0**	**0**	**0**
	Binghamton	AHL	19	1	7	8	15																			
1997-98	**Florida**	**NHL**	**23**	**0**	**1**	**1**	**44**	**0**	**0**	**0**	**16**	**0.0**	**1**													
	New Haven	AHL	4	0	1	1	7																			
1998-99	**Toronto**	**NHL**	**18**	**0**	**2**	**2**	**24**	**0**	**0**	**0**	**11**	**0.0**	**3**	**0**	**0.0**	**20**	**10**	**16:28**	**1**	**0**	**0**	**0**	**0**	**0**	**0**	**0**
	Chicago Wolves	IHL	2	0	0	0	0																			
	St. John's Leafs	AHL	20	3	7	10	16												5	0	1	1	6			
99-2000	**NY Islanders**	**NHL**	**2**	**0**	**1**	**1**	**2**	**0**	**0**	**0**	**4**	**0.0**	**3**	**0**	**0.0**	**2**	**1**	**21:28**								
	Chicago Wolves	IHL	68	5	26	31	99												16	1	4	5	16			
	NHL Totals		**100**	**0**	**8**	**8**	**193**	**0**	**0**	**0**	**55**	**0.0**		**0**	**0.0**	**22**	**11**	**16:58**	**5**	**0**	**0**	**0**	**4**	**0**	**0**	**0**

IHL Second All-Star Team (2000)

Signed as a free agent by **Winnipeg**, October 17, 1989. Signed as a free agent by **Florida**, July 8, 1993. Traded to **St. Louis** by **Florida** for St. Louis' 4th round choice (Ivan Novoseltsev) in 1997 Entry Draft, September 28, 1995. Claimed on waivers by **Winnipeg** from **St. Louis**, March 20, 1996. Transferred to **Phoenix** after **Winnipeg** franchise relocated, July 1, 1996. Traded to **NY Rangers** by **Phoenix** with Mike Eastwood for Jayson More, February 6, 1997. Signed as a free agent by **Florida**, July 30, 1997. Signed as a free agent by **Toronto**, July 28, 1998. Signed as a free agent by **NY Islanders**, August 12, 1999. Traded to **Chicago** by **NY Islanders** for future considerations, March 3, 2000. Signed as a free agent by **Calgary**, July 27, 2000.

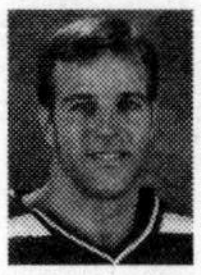

EASTWOOD, Mike (EEST-wuhd, MIGHK) ST.L.

Center. Shoots right. 6'3", 209 lbs. Born, Ottawa, Ont., July 1, 1967. Toronto's 5th choice, 91st overall, in 1987 Entry Draft.

Season	Club	League	GP	G	A	Pts	PIM	PP	SH	GW	S	%	+/–	TF	F%	H	SB	Min	GP	G	A	Pts	PIM	PP	SH	GW
1984-85	Nepean Raiders	OJHL	46	10	13	23	18																			
1985-86	Nepean Raiders	OJHL	7	4	2	6	6																			
1986-87	Pembroke	OJHL	54	58	45	103	62												23	36	11	47	32			
1987-88	Western Michigan	CCHA	42	5	8	13	14																			
1988-89	Western Michigan	CCHA	40	10	13	23	87																			
1989-90	Western Michigan	CCHA	40	25	27	52	36																			
1990-91	Western Michigan	CCHA	42	29	32	61	84																			
1991-92	**Toronto**	**NHL**	**9**	**0**	**2**	**2**	**4**	**0**	**0**	**0**	**6**	**0.0**	**–4**													
	St. John's Leafs	AHL	61	18	25	43	28												16	9	10	19	16			
1992-93	**Toronto**	**NHL**	**12**	**1**	**6**	**7**	**21**	**0**	**0**	**0**	**11**	**9.1**	**–2**						**10**	**1**	**2**	**3**	**8**	**0**	**0**	**0**
	St. John's Leafs	AHL	60	24	35	59	32																			

Season	Club	League	GP	G	A	Pts	PIM	PP	SH	GW	S	%	+/–	TF	F%	H	SB	Min	GP	G	A	Pts	PIM	PP	SH	GW
			Regular Season																Playoffs							
1993-94	Toronto	NHL	54	8	10	18	28	1	0	2	41	19.5	2	....	....	....	....	....	18	3	2	5	12	1	0	1
1994-95	Toronto	NHL	36	5	5	10	32	0	0	0	38	13.2	–12	....	....	....	....	....	....	....	....	....	....	....	....	....
	Winnipeg	NHL	13	3	6	9	4	0	0	0	17	17.6	3	....	....	....	....	....	....	....	....	....	....	....	....	....
1995-96	Winnipeg	NHL	80	14	14	28	20	2	0	3	94	14.9	–14	....	....	....	....	....	6	0	1	1	2	0	0	0
1996-97	Phoenix	NHL	33	1	3	4	4	0	0	0	22	4.5	–3	....	....	....	....	....	....	....	....	....	....	....	....	....
	NY Rangers	NHL	27	1	7	8	10	0	0	0	22	4.5	2	....	....	....	....	....	15	1	2	3	22	0	0	0
1997-98	NY Rangers	NHL	48	5	5	10	16	0	0	0	34	14.7	–2	....	....	....	....	....	....	....	....	....	....	....	....	....
	St. Louis	NHL	10	1	0	1	6	0	0	1	4	25.0	0	....	....	....	....	....	3	1	0	1	0	0	0	1
1998-99	St. Louis	NHL	82	9	21	30	36	0	0	0	76	11.8	6	1235	56.6	40	35	14:59	13	1	1	2	6	0	0	0
99-2000	St. Louis	NHL	79	19	15	34	32	1	3	3	83	22.9	5	872	52.2	43	37	15:08	7	1	1	2	6	0	0	0
	NHL Totals		483	67	94	161	213	4	3	9	448	15.0		2107	54.8	83	72	15:04	72	8	9	17	56	1	0	2

CCHA Second All-Star Team (1991)

Traded to **Winnipeg** by **Toronto** with Toronto's 3rd round choice (Brad Isbister) in 1995 Entry Draft for Tie Domi, April 7, 1995. Transferred to **Phoenix** after **Winnipeg** franchise relocated, July 1, 1996. Traded to **NY Rangers** by **Phoenix** with Dallas Eakins for Jayson More, February 6, 1997. Traded to **St. Louis** by **NY Rangers** for Harry York, March 24, 1998.

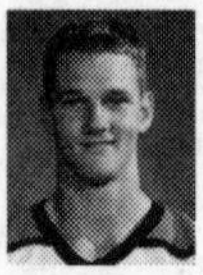

EATON, Mark

(EE-tohn, MAHRK) **PHI.**

Defense. Shoots left. 6'2", 205 lbs. Born, Wilmington, DE, May 6, 1977.

1995-96	Waterloo Hawks	USHL	50	4	21	25	....	....	....	....	....	....	....	....	....	....	....	....	....	....	....	....	....	....	....	....
1996-97	Waterloo Hawks	USHL	50	6	32	38	62	....	....	....	....	....	....	....	....	....	....	....	....	....	....	....	....	....	....	....
1997-98	Notre Dame	CCHA	41	12	17	29	32	....	....	....	....	....	....	....	....	....	....	....	....	....	....	....	....	....	....	....
1998-99	Philadelphia	AHL	74	9	27	36	38	....	....	....	....	....	....	....	....	....	....	....	16	4	8	12	0	....	....	....
99-2000	**Philadelphia**	**NHL**	**27**	**1**	**1**	**2**	**8**	**0**	**0**	**1**	**25**	**4.0**	**1**	**0**	**0.0**	**21**	**35**	**18:17**	**7**	**0**	**0**	**0**	**0**	**0**	**0**	**0**
	Philadelphia	AHL	47	9	17	26	6	....	....	....	....	....	....	....	....	....	....	....	....	....	....	....	....	....	....	....
	NHL Totals		**27**	**1**	**1**	**2**	**8**	**0**	**0**	**1**	**25**	**4.0**		**0**	**0.0**	**21**	**35**	**18:17**	**7**	**0**	**0**	**0**	**0**	**0**	**0**	**0**

Signed as a free agent by **Philadelphia**, August 4, 1998.

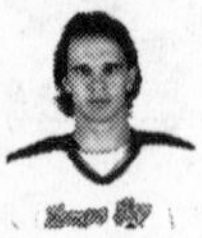

EGELAND, Allan

(eh-GUH-luhnd, AL-lan)

Center. Shoots left. 6', 175 lbs. Born, Lethbridge, Alta., January 31, 1973. Tampa Bay's 3rd choice, 55th overall, in 1993 Entry Draft.

1989-90	Lethbridge Y's	AAHA	36	21	30	51	52	....	....	....	....	....	....	....	....	....	....	....	....	....	....	....	....	....	....	....
1990-91	Lethbridge	WHL	67	2	16	18	57	....	....	....	....	....	....	....	....	....	....	....	9	0	0	0	0	....	....	....
1991-92	Tacoma Rockets	WHL	72	35	39	74	135	....	....	....	....	....	....	....	....	....	....	....	4	0	1	1	18	....	....	....
1992-93	Tacoma Rockets	WHL	71	56	57	113	119	....	....	....	....	....	....	....	....	....	....	....	7	9	7	16	18	....	....	....
1993-94	Tacoma Rockets	WHL	70	47	76	123	204	....	....	....	....	....	....	....	....	....	....	....	8	5	3	8	26	....	....	....
1994-95	Atlanta Knights	IHL	60	8	16	24	112	....	....	....	....	....	....	....	....	....	....	....	5	0	1	1	16	....	....	....
1995-96	**Tampa Bay**	**NHL**	**5**	**0**	**0**	**0**	**2**	**0**	**0**	**0**	**1**	**0.0**	**0**	....	....	....	....	....	....	....	....	....	....	....	....	....
	Atlanta Knights	IHL	68	22	22	44	182	....	....	....	....	....	....	....	....	....	....	....	3	0	1	1	0	....	....	....
1996-97	**Tampa Bay**	**NHL**	**4**	**0**	**0**	**0**	**5**	**0**	**0**	**0**	**1**	**0.0**	**–3**	....	....	....	....	....	....	....	....	....	....	....	....	....
	Adirondack	AHL	52	18	32	50	184	....	....	....	....	....	....	....	....	....	....	....	2	0	1	1	4	....	....	....
1997-98	**Tampa Bay**	**NHL**	**8**	**0**	**0**	**0**	**9**	**0**	**0**	**0**	**4**	**0.0**	**0**	....	....	....	....	....	....	....	....	....	....	....	....	....
	Adirondack	AHL	35	11	22	33	78	....	....	....	....	....	....	....	....	....	....	....	3	0	2	2	10	....	....	....
1998-99	Orlando	IHL	62	7	23	30	182	....	....	....	....	....	....	....	....	....	....	....	....	....	....	....	....	....	....	....
	Saint John Flames	AHL	14	5	5	10	49	....	....	....	....	....	....	....	....	....	....	....	7	1	4	5	21	....	....	....
99-2000	Saint John Flames	AHL	11	1	5	6	42	....	....	....	....	....	....	....	....	....	....	....	....	....	....	....	....	....	....	....
	Long Beach	IHL	47	4	12	16	104	....	....	....	....	....	....	....	....	....	....	....	6	0	0	0	19	....	....	....
	NHL Totals		**17**	**0**	**0**	**0**	**16**	**0**	**0**	**0**	**6**	**0.0**		....	....	....	....	....	....	....	....	....	....	....	....	....

WHL West First All-Star Team (1993) • WHL West Second All-Star Team (1994)

Signed as a free agent by **Calgary**, July 20, 1999. Traded to **Los Angeles** by **Calgary** for future considerations, February 18, 2000.

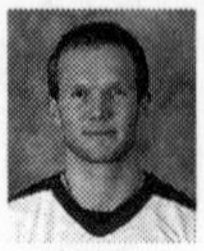

EKMAN, Nils

(EHK-mahn, NIHLS) **T.B.**

Left wing. Shoots left. 5'11", 175 lbs. Born, Stockholm, Sweden, March 11, 1976. Calgary's 6th choice, 107th overall, in 1994 Entry Draft.

1993-94	Hammarby IF	Swede-Jr.	11	4	5	9	14	....	....	....	....	....	....	....	....	....	....	....	....	....	....	....	....	....	....	....
	Hammarby IF	Sweden-2	18	7	2	9	4	....	....	....	....	....	....	....	....	....	....	....	....	....	....	....	....	....	....	....
	Sweden	EJC-A	4	1	1	2	4	....	....	....	....	....	....	....	....	....	....	....	....	....	....	....	....	....	....	....
1994-95	Hammarby IF	Swede-Jr.	2	2	1	3	0	....	....	....	....	....	....	....	....	....	....	....	....	....	....	....	....	....	....	....
	Hammarby IF	Sweden-2	29	10	7	17	18	....	....	....	....	....	....	....	....	....	....	....	....	....	....	....	....	....	....	....
1995-96	Hammarby IF	Sweden-2	26	9	7	16	53	....	....	....	....	....	....	....	....	....	....	....	1	0	0	0	0	....	....	....
1996-97	Kiekko-Espoo	Finland	50	24	19	43	60	....	....	....	....	....	....	....	....	....	....	....	4	2	0	2	4	....	....	....
1997-98	Kiekko-Espoo	Finland	43	14	14	28	86	....	....	....	....	....	....	....	....	....	....	....	7	2	2	4	27	....	....	....
	Saint John Flames	AHL	....	....	....	....	....	....	....	....	....	....	....	....	....	....	....	....	1	0	0	0	2	....	....	....
1998-99	Kiekko-Espoo	Finland	52	20	14	34	96	....	....	....	....	....	....	....	....	....	....	....	3	1	1	2	6	....	....	....
99-2000	Detroit Vipers	IHL	10	7	2	9	8	....	....	....	....	....	....	....	....	....	....	....	....	....	....	....	....	....	....	....
	Tampa Bay	**NHL**	**28**	**2**	**2**	**4**	**36**	**1**	**0**	**0**	**42**	**4.8**	**–8**	**3**	**0.0**	**23**	**8**	**11:12**	....	....	....	....	....	....	....	....
	Long Beach	IHL	27	11	12	23	26	....	....	....	....	....	....	....	....	....	....	....	5	3	3	6	4	....	....	....
	NHL Totals		**28**	**2**	**2**	**4**	**36**	**1**	**0**	**0**	**42**	**4.8**		**3**	**0.0**	**23**	**8**	**11:12**	....	....	....	....	....	....	....	....

• Won Garry F. Longman Memorial Trophy (Top Rookie - IHL) (2000)

Traded to **Tampa Bay** by **Calgary** with Calgary's 4th round choice (later traded to NY Islanders - NY Islanders selected Vladimir Gorbunov) in 2000 Entry Draft for Andreas Johansson, November 20, 1999.

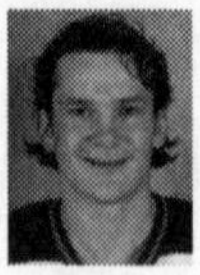

ELIAS, Patrik

(EH-lih-ahsh, PA-trihk) **N.J.**

Left wing. Shoots left. 6'1", 200 lbs. Born, Trebic, Czech., April 13, 1976. New Jersey's 2nd choice, 51st overall, in 1994 Entry Draft.

1992-93	Poldi Kladno	Czech.	2	0	0	0	....	....	....	....	....	....	....	....	....	....	....	....	....	....	....	....	....	....	....	....
1993-94	Poldi Kladno	Cze-Rep	15	1	2	3	....	....	....	....	....	....	....	....	....	....	....	....	11	2	2	4	....	....	....	....
1994-95	Poldi Kladno	Cze-Rep	28	4	3	7	37	....	....	....	....	....	....	....	....	....	....	....	7	1	2	3	12	....	....	....
1995-96	**New Jersey**	**NHL**	**1**	**0**	**0**	**0**	**0**	**0**	**0**	**0**	**2**	**0.0**	**–1**	....	....	....	....	....	....	....	....	....	....	....	....	....
	Albany River Rats	AHL	74	27	36	63	83	....	....	....	....	....	....	....	....	....	....	....	4	1	1	2	2	....	....	....
1996-97	**New Jersey**	**NHL**	**17**	**2**	**3**	**5**	**2**	**0**	**0**	**0**	**23**	**8.7**	**–4**	....	....	....	....	....	**8**	**2**	**3**	**5**	**4**	**1**	**0**	**0**
	Albany River Rats	AHL	57	24	43	67	76	....	....	....	....	....	....	....	....	....	....	....	6	1	2	3	8	....	....	....
1997-98	**New Jersey**	**NHL**	**74**	**18**	**19**	**37**	**28**	**5**	**0**	**6**	**147**	**12.2**	**18**	....	....	....	....	....	**4**	**0**	**1**	**1**	**0**	**0**	**0**	**0**
	Albany River Rats	AHL	3	3	0	3	2	....	....	....	....	....	....	....	....	....	....	....	....	....	....	....	....	....	....	....
1998-99	**New Jersey**	**NHL**	**74**	**17**	**33**	**50**	**34**	**3**	**0**	**2**	**157**	**10.8**	**19**	**99**	**38.4**	**86**	**13**	**15:50**	**7**	**0**	**5**	**5**	**6**	**0**	**0**	**0**
99-2000	SK Trebic-2	Cze-Rep	2	2	1	3	2	....	....	....	....	....	....	....	....	....	....	....	....	....	....	....	....	....	....	....
	HC Pardubice	Cze-Rep	5	1	4	5	31	....	....	....	....	....	....	....	....	....	....	....	....	....	....	....	....	....	....	....
	♦ New Jersey	**NHL**	**72**	**35**	**37**	**72**	**58**	**9**	**0**	**9**	**183**	**19.1**	**16**	**134**	**45.5**	**112**	**12**	**17:28**	**23**	**7**	***13**	**20**	**9**	**2**	**1**	**1**
	NHL Totals		**238**	**72**	**92**	**164**	**122**	**17**	**0**	**17**	**512**	**14.1**		**233**	**42.5**	**198**	**25**	**16:38**	**42**	**9**	**22**	**31**	**19**	**3**	**1**	**1**

NHL All-Rookie Team (1998) • Played in NHL All-Star Game (2000)

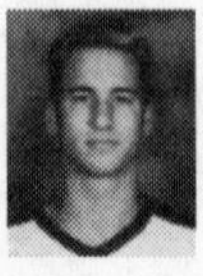

ELICH, Matt

(EHL-ihch, MAT) **T.B.**

Right wing. Shoots right. 6'3", 196 lbs. Born, Detroit, MI, September 22, 1979. Tampa Bay's 3rd choice, 61st overall, in 1997 Entry Draft.

1993-94	Detroit Caesars	MNHL	40	20	20	40	110	....	....	....	....	....	....	....	....	....	....	....	....	....	....	....	....	....	....	....
1994-95	Detroit Caesars	MNHL	45	31	22	53	170	....	....	....	....	....	....	....	....	....	....	....	....	....	....	....	....	....	....	....
1995-96	Windsor Spitfires	OHL	52	10	2	12	17	....	....	....	....	....	....	....	....	....	....	....	5	1	0	1	2	....	....	....
1996-97	Windsor Spitfires	OHL	58	15	13	28	19	....	....	....	....	....	....	....	....	....	....	....	5	0	1	1	6	....	....	....
1997-98	Windsor Spitfires	OHL	20	9	12	21	8	....	....	....	....	....	....	....	....	....	....	....	....	....	....	....	....	....	....	....
	Kingston	OHL	34	14	4	18	2	....	....	....	....	....	....	....	....	....	....	....	12	2	4	6	2	....	....	....
1998-99	Kingston	OHL	67	44	30	74	32	....	....	....	....	....	....	....	....	....	....	....	5	3	5	8	0	....	....	....
99-2000	**Tampa Bay**	**NHL**	**8**	**1**	**1**	**2**	**0**	**0**	**0**	**0**	**5**	**20.0**	**–1**	**0**	**0.0**	**7**	**0**	**6:07**	....	....	....	....	....	....	....	....
	Detroit Vipers	IHL	48	12	4	16	12	....	....	....	....	....	....	....	....	....	....	....	....	....	....	....	....	....	....	....
	NHL Totals		**8**	**1**	**1**	**2**	**0**	**0**	**0**	**0**	**5**	**20.0**		**0**	**0.0**	**7**	**0**	**6:07**	....	....	....	....	....	....	....	....

			Regular Season																Playoffs							
Season	Club	League	GP	G	A	Pts	PIM	PP	SH	GW	S	%	+/-	TF	F%	H	SB	Min	GP	G	A	Pts	PIM	PP	SH	GW

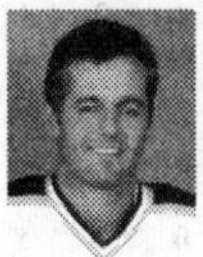

ELLETT, Dave

(EHL-leht, DAYV)

Defense. Shoots left. 6'2", 205 lbs. Born, Cleveland, OH, March 30, 1964. Winnipeg's 3rd choice, 75th overall, in 1982 Entry Draft.

Season	Club	League	GP	G	A	Pts	PIM	PP	SH	GW	S	%	+/-	TF	F%	H	SB	Min	GP	G	A	Pts	PIM	PP	SH	GW
1981-82	Ottawa	OJHL	50	9	35	44	....	....	....	....	....	....	....	....	....	....	....	....	....	....	....	....	....	....	....	....
1982-83	Bowling Green	CCHA	40	4	13	17	34	....	....	....	....	....	....	....	....	....	....	....	....	....	....	....	....	....	....	....
1983-84	Bowling Green	CCHA	43	15	39	54	96	....	....	....	....	....	....	....	....	....	....	....	....	....	....	....	....	....	....	....
1984-85	**Winnipeg**	**NHL**	**80**	**11**	**27**	**38**	**85**	**3**	**0**	**0**	**146**	**7.5**	**20**	....	....	....	....	....	**8**	**1**	**5**	**6**	**4**	**1**	**0**	**0**
1985-86	**Winnipeg**	**NHL**	**80**	**15**	**31**	**46**	**96**	**2**	**0**	**1**	**168**	**8.9**	**–38**	....	....	....	....	....	**3**	**0**	**1**	**1**	**0**	**0**	**0**	**0**
1986-87	**Winnipeg**	**NHL**	**78**	**13**	**31**	**44**	**53**	**5**	**0**	**2**	**159**	**8.2**	**19**	....	....	....	....	....	**10**	**0**	**8**	**8**	**2**	**0**	**0**	**0**
1987-88	**Winnipeg**	**NHL**	**68**	**13**	**45**	**58**	**106**	**5**	**0**	**1**	**198**	**6.6**	**–8**	....	....	....	....	....	**5**	**1**	**2**	**3**	**10**	**1**	**0**	**0**
1988-89	**Winnipeg**	**NHL**	**75**	**22**	**34**	**56**	**62**	**9**	**2**	**5**	**209**	**10.5**	**–18**	....	....	....	....	....	....	....	....	....	....	....	....	....
1989-90	**Winnipeg**	**NHL**	**77**	**17**	**29**	**46**	**96**	**8**	**0**	**1**	**205**	**8.3**	**–15**	....	....	....	....	....	**7**	**2**	**0**	**2**	**6**	**2**	**0**	**1**
1990-91	**Winnipeg**	**NHL**	**17**	**4**	**7**	**11**	**6**	**1**	**1**	**0**	**41**	**9.8**	**–4**	....	....	....	....	....	....	....	....	....	....	....	....	....
	Toronto	**NHL**	**60**	**8**	**30**	**38**	**69**	**5**	**0**	**1**	**154**	**5.2**	**–4**	....	....	....	....	....	....	....	....	....	....	....	....	....
1991-92	**Toronto**	**NHL**	**79**	**18**	**33**	**51**	**95**	**9**	**1**	**4**	**225**	**8.0**	**–13**	....	....	....	....	....	....	....	....	....	....	....	....	....
1992-93	**Toronto**	**NHL**	**70**	**6**	**34**	**40**	**46**	**4**	**0**	**1**	**186**	**3.2**	**19**	....	....	....	....	....	**21**	**4**	**8**	**12**	**8**	**2**	**0**	**0**
1993-94	**Toronto**	**NHL**	**68**	**7**	**36**	**43**	**42**	**5**	**0**	**1**	**146**	**4.8**	**6**	....	....	....	....	....	**18**	**3**	**15**	**18**	**31**	**3**	**0**	**0**
1994-95	**Toronto**	**NHL**	**33**	**5**	**10**	**15**	**26**	**3**	**0**	**1**	**84**	**6.0**	**–6**	....	....	....	....	....	**7**	**0**	**2**	**2**	**0**	**0**	**0**	**0**
1995-96	**Toronto**	**NHL**	**80**	**3**	**19**	**22**	**59**	**1**	**1**	**0**	**153**	**2.0**	**–10**	....	....	....	....	....	**6**	**0**	**0**	**0**	**4**	**0**	**0**	**0**
1996-97	**Toronto**	**NHL**	**56**	**4**	**10**	**14**	**34**	**0**	**0**	**1**	**83**	**4.8**	**–8**	....	....	....	....	....	....	....	....	....	....	....	....	....
	New Jersey	**NHL**	**20**	**2**	**5**	**7**	**6**	**1**	**0**	**1**	**22**	**9.1**	**2**	....	....	....	....	....	**10**	**0**	**3**	**3**	**10**	**0**	**0**	**0**
1997-98	**Boston**	**NHL**	**82**	**3**	**20**	**23**	**67**	**2**	**0**	**1**	**129**	**2.3**	**3**	....	....	....	....	....	**6**	**0**	**1**	**1**	**6**	**0**	**0**	**0**
1998-99	**Boston**	**NHL**	**54**	**0**	**6**	**6**	**25**	**0**	**0**	**0**	**45**	**0.0**	**11**	**0**	**0.0**	**41**	**56**	**14:48**	**8**	**0**	**0**	**0**	**4**	**0**	**0**	**0**
99-2000	**St. Louis**	**NHL**	**52**	**2**	**8**	**10**	**12**	**0**	**0**	**1**	**41**	**4.9**	**–4**	**0**	**0.0**	**22**	**29**	**13:28**	**7**	**0**	**1**	**1**	**2**	**0**	**0**	**0**
	NHL Totals		**1129**	**153**	**415**	**568**	**985**	**63**	**5**	**22**	**2394**	**6.4**		**0**	**0.0**	**63**	**85**	**14:09**	**116**	**11**	**46**	**57**	**87**	**9**	**0**	**1**

CCHA Second All-Star Team (1984) • NCAA Championship All-Tournament Team (1984) • Played in NHL All-Star Game (1989, 1992)

Traded to **Toronto** by **Winnipeg** with Paul Fenton for Ed Olczyk and Mark Osborne, November 10, 1990. Traded to **New Jersey** by **Toronto** with Doug Gilmour and New Jersey's 3rd round choice (previously acquired, New Jersey selected Andre Lakos) in 1999 Entry Draft for Jason Smith, Steve Sullivan and the rights to Alyn McCauley, February 25, 1997. Signed as a free agent by **Boston**, July 29, 1997. Signed as a free agent by **St. Louis**, October 22, 1999.

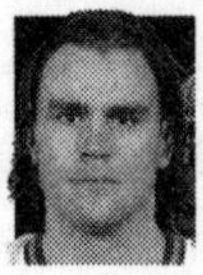

ELOMO, Miika

(eh-LOH-moh, MEE-ka) **CGY.**

Left wing. Shoots left. 6', 200 lbs. Born, Turku, Finland, April 21, 1977. Washington's 2nd choice, 23rd overall, in 1995 Entry Draft.

Season	Club	League	GP	G	A	Pts	PIM	PP	SH	GW	S	%	+/-	TF	F%	H	SB	Min	GP	G	A	Pts	PIM	PP	SH	GW
1993-94	TPS Turku	Finn-Jr.	30	8	5	13	24	....	....	....	....	....	....	....	....	....	....	....	5	1	1	2	2	....	....	....
1994-95	TPS Turku	Finn-Jr.	14	3	8	11	24	....	....	....	....	....	....	....	....	....	....	....	....	....	....	....	....	....	....	....
	Kiekko-67 Turku	Finland-2	14	9	2	11	39	....	....	....	....	....	....	....	....	....	....	....	....	....	....	....	....	....	....	....
1995-96	TPS Turku	Finn-Jr.	6	0	2	2	18	....	....	....	....	....	....	....	....	....	....	....	....	....	....	....	....	....	....	....
	Kiekko-67 Turku	Finland-2	21	9	6	15	100	....	....	....	....	....	....	....	....	....	....	....	....	....	....	....	....	....	....	....
	TPS Turku	Finland	10	1	1	2	8	....	....	....	....	....	....	....	....	....	....	....	3	0	0	0	2	....	....	....
1996-97	Portland	AHL	52	8	9	17	37	....	....	....	....	....	....	....	....	....	....	....	....	....	....	....	....	....	....	....
1997-98	Portland	AHL	33	1	1	2	54	....	....	....	....	....	....	....	....	....	....	....	....	....	....	....	....	....	....	....
	HIFK Helsinki	Finland	16	4	1	5	6	....	....	....	....	....	....	....	....	....	....	....	9	4	3	7	6	....	....	....
1998-99	TPS Turku	Finland	36	5	10	15	76	....	....	....	....	....	....	....	....	....	....	....	10	3	5	8	6	....	....	....
99-2000	**Washington**	**NHL**	**2**	**0**	**1**	**1**	**2**	**0**	**0**	**0**	**3**	**0.0**	**1**	**4**	**100.0**	**5**	**0**	**11:12**	....	....	....	....	....	....	....	....
	Portland	AHL	59	21	14	35	50	....	....	....	....	....	....	....	....	....	....	....	....	....	....	....	....	....	....	....
	NHL Totals		**2**	**0**	**1**	**1**	**2**	**0**	**0**	**0**	**3**	**0.0**		**4**	**100.0**	**5**	**0**	**11:11**	....	....	....	....	....	....	....	....

Traded to **Calgary** by **Washington** with Buffalo's compensatory 4th round choice (previously acquired, Calgary selected Levente Szuper) in 2000 Entry Draft for Anaheim's 2nd round choice (previously acquired, Washington selected Matt Pettinger) in 2000 Entry Draft, June 24, 2000.

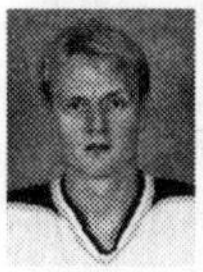

ELORANTA, Mikko

(ehl-oh-RAN-tuh, MEE-koh) **BOS.**

Left wing. Shoots left. 6', 190 lbs. Born, Turku, Finland, August 24, 1972. Boston's 9th choice, 247th overall, in 1999 Entry Draft.

Season	Club	League	GP	G	A	Pts	PIM	PP	SH	GW	S	%	+/-	TF	F%	H	SB	Min	GP	G	A	Pts	PIM	PP	SH	GW
1989-90	TPS Turku	Finn-Jr.	2	0	0	0	0	....	....	....	....	....	....	....	....	....	....	....	....	....	....	....	....	....	....	....
1990-91	TPS Turku	Finn-Jr.	35	8	8	16	18	....	....	....	....	....	....	....	....	....	....	....	....	....	....	....	....	....	....	....
1991-92	TPS Turku	Finn-Jr.	19	3	1	4	8	....	....	....	....	....	....	....	....	....	....	....	8	0	0	0	0	....	....	....
1992-93	TPS Turku	Finn-Jr.	31	11	6	17	20	....	....	....	....	....	....	....	....	....	....	....	6	0	4	4	6	....	....	....
1993-94	Kiekko-67 Turku	Finland-2	45	3	4	7	24	....	....	....	....	....	....	....	....	....	....	....	....	....	....	....	....	....	....	....
1994-95	Kiekko-67 Turku	Finland-2	47	18	14	32	52	....	....	....	....	....	....	....	....	....	....	....	3	3	0	3	4	....	....	....
1995-96	Kiekko-67 Turku	Finland-2	8	6	7	13	2	....	....	....	....	....	....	....	....	....	....	....	....	....	....	....	....	....	....	....
	Ilves Tampere	Finland	43	18	15	33	86	....	....	....	....	....	....	....	....	....	....	....	3	0	2	2	2	....	....	....
1996-97	TPS Turku	EuroHL	6	3	1	4	6	....	....	....	....	....	....	....	....	....	....	....	1	0	0	0	0	....	....	....
	TPS Turku	Finland	31	6	15	21	52	....	....	....	....	....	....	....	....	....	....	....	10	5	2	7	6	....	....	....
1997-98	TPS Turku	EuroHL	3	1	0	1	12	....	....	....	....	....	....	....	....	....	....	....	....	....	....	....	....	....	....	....
	TPS Turku	Finland	46	23	14	37	82	....	....	....	....	....	....	....	....	....	....	....	2	0	0	0	8	....	....	....
1998-99	TPS Turku	Finland	52	19	21	40	103	....	....	....	....	....	....	....	....	....	....	....	10	1	6	7	26	....	....	....
99-2000	**Boston**	**NHL**	**50**	**6**	**12**	**18**	**36**	**1**	**0**	**0**	**59**	**10.2**	**–10**	**77**	**35.1**	**74**	**10**	**12:18**	....	....	....	....	....	....	....	....
	NHL Totals		**50**	**6**	**12**	**18**	**36**	**1**	**0**	**0**	**59**	**10.2**		**77**	**35.1**	**74**	**10**	**12:18**	....	....	....	....	....	....	....	....

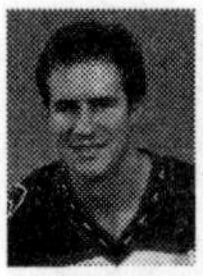

EMERSON, Nelson

(EH-muhr-SOHN, NEHL-sohn) **L.A.**

Right wing. Shoots right. 5'11", 180 lbs. Born, Hamilton, Ont., August 17, 1967. St. Louis''s 2nd choice, 44th overall, in 1985 Entry Draft.

Season	Club	League	GP	G	A	Pts	PIM	PP	SH	GW	S	%	+/-	TF	F%	H	SB	Min	GP	G	A	Pts	PIM	PP	SH	GW
1984-85	Stratford Cullitons	OJHL-B	40	23	38	61	70	....	....	....	....	....	....	....	....	....	....	....	....	....	....	....	....	....	....	....
1985-86	Stratford Cullitons	OJHL-B	39	*54	58	*112	91	....	....	....	....	....	....	....	....	....	....	....	....	....	....	....	....	....	....	....
1986-87	Bowling Green	CCHA	45	26	35	61	28	....	....	....	....	....	....	....	....	....	....	....	....	....	....	....	....	....	....	....
1987-88	Bowling Green	CCHA	45	34	49	83	54	....	....	....	....	....	....	....	....	....	....	....	....	....	....	....	....	....	....	....
1988-89	Bowling Green	CCHA	44	22	46	68	46	....	....	....	....	....	....	....	....	....	....	....	....	....	....	....	....	....	....	....
1989-90	Bowling Green	CCHA	44	30	52	82	42	....	....	....	....	....	....	....	....	....	....	....	....	....	....	....	....	....	....	....
	Peoria Rivermen	IHL	3	1	1	2	0	....	....	....	....	....	....	....	....	....	....	....	....	....	....	....	....	....	....	....
1990-91	**St. Louis**	**NHL**	**4**	**0**	**3**	**3**	**2**	**0**	**0**	**0**	**3**	**0.0**	**–2**	....	....	....	....	....	....	....	....	....	....	....	....	....
	Peoria Rivermen	IHL	73	36	79	115	91	....	....	....	....	....	....	....	....	....	....	....	17	9	12	21	16	....	....	....
1991-92	**St. Louis**	**NHL**	**79**	**23**	**36**	**59**	**66**	**3**	**0**	**2**	**143**	**16.1**	**–5**	....	....	....	....	....	**6**	**3**	**3**	**6**	**21**	**2**	**0**	**0**
1992-93	**St. Louis**	**NHL**	**82**	**22**	**51**	**73**	**62**	**5**	**2**	**4**	**196**	**11.2**	**2**	....	....	....	....	....	**11**	**1**	**6**	**7**	**6**	**0**	**0**	**0**
1993-94	**Winnipeg**	**NHL**	**83**	**33**	**41**	**74**	**80**	**4**	**5**	**6**	**282**	**11.7**	**–38**	....	....	....	....	....	....	....	....	....	....	....	....	....
1994-95	**Winnipeg**	**NHL**	**48**	**14**	**23**	**37**	**26**	**4**	**1**	**1**	**122**	**11.5**	**–12**	....	....	....	....	....	....	....	....	....	....	....	....	....
1995-96	**Hartford**	**NHL**	**81**	**29**	**29**	**58**	**78**	**12**	**2**	**5**	**247**	**11.7**	**–7**	....	....	....	....	....	....	....	....	....	....	....	....	....
1996-97	**Hartford**	**NHL**	**66**	**9**	**29**	**38**	**34**	**2**	**1**	**2**	**194**	**4.6**	**–21**	....	....	....	....	....	....	....	....	....	....	....	....	....
1997-98	**Carolina**	**NHL**	**81**	**21**	**24**	**45**	**50**	**6**	**0**	**4**	**203**	**10.3**	**–17**	....	....	....	....	....	....	....	....	....	....	....	....	....
1998-99	**Carolina**	**NHL**	**35**	**8**	**13**	**21**	**36**	**3**	**0**	**0**	**84**	**9.5**	**1**	**7**	**42.9**	**6**	**7**	**14:30**	....	....	....	....	....	....	....	....
	Chicago	**NHL**	**27**	**4**	**10**	**14**	**13**	**0**	**0**	**1**	**94**	**4.3**	**8**	**169**	**41.4**	**8**	**9**	**19:37**	....	....	....	....	....	....	....	....
	Ottawa	**NHL**	**3**	**1**	**1**	**2**	**2**	**0**	**0**	**0**	**10**	**10.0**	**–1**	**5**	**60.0**	**1**	**0**	**17:05**	**4**	**1**	**3**	**4**	**0**	**0**	**0**	**0**
99-2000	**Atlanta**	**NHL**	**58**	**14**	**19**	**33**	**47**	**4**	**0**	**0**	**183**	**7.7**	**–24**	**124**	**39.5**	**27**	**33**	**19:10**	....	....	....	....	....	....	....	....
	Los Angeles	**NHL**	**5**	**1**	**1**	**2**	**0**	**0**	**0**	**0**	**13**	**7.7**	**1**	**0**	**0.0**	**2**	**0**	**14:39**	**1**	**0**	**0**	**0**	**0**	**0**	**0**	**0**
	NHL Totals		**652**	**179**	**280**	**459**	**496**	**43**	**11**	**25**	**1774**	**10.1**		**305**	**41.0**	**44**	**49**	**17:46**	**22**	**5**	**12**	**17**	**27**	**2**	**0**	**0**

NCAA West Second All-American Team (1988) • CCHA First All-Star Team (1988, 1990) • CCHA Second All-Star Team (1989) • NCAA West First All-American Team (1990) • IHL First All-Star Team (1991) • Won Garry F. Longman Memorial Trophy (Top Rookie - IHL) (1991)

Traded to **Winnipeg** by **St. Louis** with Stephane Quintal for Phil Housley, September 24, 1993. Traded to **Hartford** by **Winnipeg** for Darren Turcotte, October 6, 1995. Transferred to **Carolina** after **Hartford** franchise relocated, June 25, 1997. Traded to **Chicago** by **Carolina** for Paul Coffey, December 29, 1998. Traded to **Ottawa** by **Chicago** for Chris Murray, March 23, 1999. Signed as a free agent by **Atlanta**, August 3, 1999. Traded to **Los Angeles** by **Atlanta** with Kelly Buchberger for Donald Audette and Frantisek Kaberle, March 13, 2000.

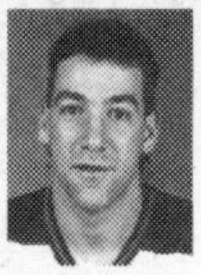

EMMA, David (EH-muh, DAY-vihd) **FLA.**

Center. Shoots left. 5'10", 185 lbs. Born, Cranston, RI, January 14, 1969. New Jersey's 6th choice, 110th overall, in 1989 Entry Draft.

			Regular Season																Playoffs							
Season	Club	League	GP	G	A	Pts	PIM	PP	SH	GW	S	%	+/-	TF	F%	H	SB	Min	GP	G	A	Pts	PIM	PP	SH	GW
1987-88	Boston College	H-East	30	19	16	35	30	....	....	....	....	....	....	....	....	....	....	....	....	....	....	....	....	....	....	....
1988-89	Boston College	H-East	36	20	31	51	36	....	....	....	....	....	....	....	....	....	....	....	....	....	....	....	....	....	....	....
1989-90	Boston College	H-East	42	38	34	*72	46	....	....	....	....	....	....	....	....	....	....	....	....	....	....	....	....	....	....	....
1990-91	Boston College	H-East	39	*35	46	*81	44	....	....	....	....	....	....	....	....	....	....	....	....	....	....	....	....	....	....	....
1991-92	United States	Nat-Team	55	15	16	31	32	....	....	....	....	....	....	....	....	....	....	....	....	....	....	....	....	....	....	....
	United States	Olympics	6	0	1	1	6	....	....	....	....	....	....	....	....	....	....	....	....	....	....	....	....	....	....	....
	Utica Devils	AHL	15	4	7	11	12	....	....	....	....	....	....	....	....	....	....	....	4	1	1	2	2	....	....	....
1992-93	**New Jersey**	**NHL**	**2**	**0**	**0**	**0**	**0**	**0**	**0**	**0**	**2**	**0.0**	**0**	....	....	....	....	....	....	....	....	....	....	....	....	....
	Utica Devils	AHL	61	21	40	61	47	....	....	....	....	....	....	....	....	....	....	....	5	2	1	3	6	....	....	....
1993-94	**New Jersey**	**NHL**	**15**	**5**	**5**	**10**	**2**	**1**	**0**	**2**	**24**	**20.8**	**0**	....	....	....	....	....	....	....	....	....	....	....	....	....
	Albany River Rats	AHL	56	26	29	55	53	....	....	....	....	....	....	....	....	....	....	....	5	1	2	3	8	....	....	....
1994-95	**New Jersey**	**NHL**	**6**	**0**	**1**	**1**	**0**	**0**	**0**	**0**	**4**	**0.0**	**–2**	....	....	....	....	....	....	....	....	....	....	....	....	....
	Albany River Rats	AHL	1	0	0	0	0	....	....	....	....	....	....	....	....	....	....	....	....	....	....	....	....	....	....	....
1995-96	Detroit Vipers	IHL	79	30	32	62	75	....	....	....	....	....	....	....	....	....	....	....	11	5	2	7	2	....	....	....
1996-97	**Boston**	**NHL**	**5**	**0**	**0**	**0**	**0**	**0**	**0**	**0**	**3**	**0.0**	**–1**	....	....	....	....	....	....	....	....	....	....	....	....	....
	Providence Bruins	AHL	53	10	18	28	24	....	....	....	....	....	....	....	....	....	....	....	....	....	....	....	....	....	....	....
	Phoenix	IHL	8	0	4	4	4	....	....	....	....	....	....	....	....	....	....	....	....	....	....	....	....	....	....	....
1997-98	KAC Klagenfurt	Alpenliga	16	6	17	23	....	....	....	....	....	....	....	....	....	....	....	....	....	....	....	....	....	....	....	....
	KAC Klagenfurt	Austria	33	22	22	44	48	....	....	....	....	....	....	....	....	....	....	....	....	....	....	....	....	....	....	....
1998-99	KAC Klagenfurt	Alpenliga	26	15	32	47	49	....	....	....	....	....	....	....	....	....	....	....	....	....	....	....	....	....	....	....
	KAC Klagenfurt	Austria	15	8	7	15	16	....	....	....	....	....	....	....	....	....	....	....	....	....	....	....	....	....	....	....
99-2000	KAC Klagenfurt	IEL	32	26	28	54	28	....	....	....	....	....	....	....	....	....	....	....	....	....	....	....	....	....	....	....
	KAC Klagenfurt	Austria	15	9	6	15	18	....	....	....	....	....	....	....	....	....	....	....	....	....	....	....	....	....	....	....
	NHL Totals		**28**	**5**	**6**	**11**	**2**	**1**	**0**	**2**	**33**	**15.2**		....	....	....	....	....	....	....	....	....	....	....	....	....

Hockey East Second All-Star Team (1989) • Hockey East First All-Star Team (1990, 1991) • NCAA East First All-American Team (1990, 1991) • Won Hobey Baker Memorial Award (Top U.S. Collegiate Player) (1991)

Signed as a free agent by **Boston**, August 27, 1996. Signed as a free agent by **Florida**, August 1, 2000.

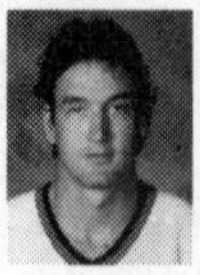

EMMONS, John (eh-mohns, JAWN) **OTT.**

Center. Shoots left. 6'1", 203 lbs. Born, San Jose, CA, August 17, 1974. Calgary's 7th choice, 122nd overall, in 1993 Entry Draft.

Season	Club	League	GP	G	A	Pts	PIM	PP	SH	GW	S	%	+/-	TF	F%	H	SB	Min	GP	G	A	Pts	PIM	PP	SH	GW
1990-91	New Canaan	Hi-School	20	19	37	56	20	....	....	....	....	....	....	....	....	....	....	....	....	....	....	....	....	....	....	....
1991-92	New Canaan Rams	Hi-School	22	24	49	73	24	....	....	....	....	....	....	....	....	....	....	....	....	....	....	....	....	....	....	....
1992-93	Yale University	ECAC	28	3	5	8	66	....	....	....	....	....	....	....	....	....	....	....	....	....	....	....	....	....	....	....
1993-94	Yale University	ECAC	25	5	12	17	66	....	....	....	....	....	....	....	....	....	....	....	....	....	....	....	....	....	....	....
1994-95	Yale University	ECAC	28	4	16	20	57	....	....	....	....	....	....	....	....	....	....	....	....	....	....	....	....	....	....	....
1995-96	Yale University	ECAC	31	8	20	28	124	....	....	....	....	....	....	....	....	....	....	....	....	....	....	....	....	....	....	....
1996-97	Dayton Bombers	ECHL	69	20	37	57	62	....	....	....	....	....	....	....	....	....	....	....	4	0	1	1	2	....	....	....
	Fort Wayne	IHL	1	0	0	0	0	....	....	....	....	....	....	....	....	....	....	....	....	....	....	....	....	....	....	....
1997-98	Michigan K-Wings	IHL	81	9	25	34	85	....	....	....	....	....	....	....	....	....	....	....	4	1	1	2	10	....	....	....
1998-99	Detroit Vipers	IHL	75	13	22	35	172	....	....	....	....	....	....	....	....	....	....	....	11	4	5	9	22	....	....	....
99-2000	**Ottawa**	**NHL**	**10**	**0**	**0**	**0**	**6**	**0**	**0**	**0**	**3**	**0.0**	**–2**	**62**	**58.1**	**11**	**2**	**7:27**	....	....	....	....	....	....	....	....
	Grand Rapids	IHL	64	10	16	26	78	....	....	....	....	....	....	....	....	....	....	....	16	1	4	5	28	....	....	....
	NHL Totals		**10**	**0**	**0**	**0**	**6**	**0**	**0**	**0**	**3**	**0.0**		**62**	**58.1**	**11**	**2**	**7:27**	....	....	....	....	....	....	....	....

Signed as a free agent by **Ottawa**, August 7, 1998.

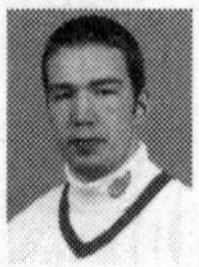

ERIKSSON, Anders (AIR-ihk-suhn, AND-uhrs) **CHI.**

Defense. Shoots left. 6'2", 220 lbs. Born, Bollnas, Sweden, January 9, 1975. Detroit's 1st choice, 22nd overall, in 1993 Entry Draft.

Season	Club	League	GP	G	A	Pts	PIM	PP	SH	GW	S	%	+/-	TF	F%	H	SB	Min	GP	G	A	Pts	PIM	PP	SH	GW
1992-93	MoDo AIK	Swede-Jr.	10	5	3	8	14	....	....	....	....	....	....	....	....	....	....	....	....	....	....	....	....	....	....	....
	MoDo AIK	Sweden	20	0	2	2	2	....	....	....	....	....	....	....	....	....	....	....	1	0	0	0	0	....	....	....
1993-94	MoDo AIK	Swede-Jr.	3	1	2	3	34	....	....	....	....	....	....	....	....	....	....	....	....	....	....	....	....	....	....	....
	MoDo AIK	Sweden	38	2	8	10	42	....	....	....	....	....	....	....	....	....	....	....	11	0	0	0	8	....	....	....
1994-95	MoDo AIK	Sweden	39	3	6	9	54	....	....	....	....	....	....	....	....	....	....	....	....	....	....	....	....	....	....	....
1995-96	**Detroit**	**NHL**	**1**	**0**	**0**	**0**	**2**	**0**	**0**	**0**	**0**	**0.0**	**1**	....	....	....	....	....	**3**	**0**	**0**	**0**	**0**	**0**	**0**	**0**
	Adirondack	AHL	75	6	36	42	64	....	....	....	....	....	....	....	....	....	....	....	3	0	0	0	0	....	....	....
1996-97	**Detroit**	**NHL**	**23**	**0**	**6**	**6**	**10**	**0**	**0**	**0**	**27**	**0.0**	**5**	....	....	....	....	....	....	....	....	....	....	....	....	....
	Adirondack	AHL	44	3	25	28	36	....	....	....	....	....	....	....	....	....	....	....	4	0	1	1	4	....	....	....
1997-98♦	**Detroit**	**NHL**	**66**	**7**	**14**	**21**	**32**	**1**	**0**	**2**	**91**	**7.7**	**21**	....	....	....	....	....	**18**	**0**	**5**	**5**	**16**	**0**	**0**	**0**
1998-99	**Detroit**	**NHL**	**61**	**2**	**10**	**12**	**34**	**0**	**0**	**1**	**67**	**3.0**	**5**	**0**	**0.0**	**72**	**60**	**15:54**	....	....	....	....	....	....	....	....
	Chicago	**NHL**	**11**	**0**	**8**	**8**	**0**	**0**	**0**	**0**	**12**	**0.0**	**6**	**0**	**0.0**	**15**	**20**	**22:51**	....	....	....	....	....	....	....	....
99-2000	**Chicago**	**NHL**	**73**	**3**	**25**	**28**	**20**	**0**	**0**	**1**	**86**	**3.5**	**4**	**1100.0**		**86**	**80**	**21:03**	....	....	....	....	....	....	....	....
	NHL Totals		**235**	**12**	**63**	**75**	**98**	**1**	**0**	**4**	**283**	**4.2**		**1100.0**		**173**	**160**	**19:01**	**21**	**0**	**5**	**5**	**16**	**0**	**0**	**0**

Traded to **Chicago** by **Detroit** with Detroit's 1st round choices in 1999 (Steve McCarthy) and 2001 Entry Drafts for Chris Chelios, March 23, 1999.

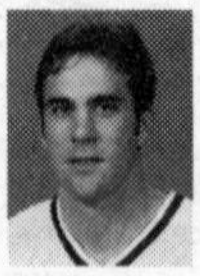

FAIRCHILD, Kelly (FAIR-chighld, KEHL-lee) **COL.**

Center. Shoots left. 5'11", 180 lbs. Born, Hibbing, MN, April 9, 1973. Los Angeles' 6th choice, 152nd overall, in 1991 Entry Draft.

Season	Club	League	GP	G	A	Pts	PIM	PP	SH	GW	S	%	+/-	TF	F%	H	SB	Min	GP	G	A	Pts	PIM	PP	SH	GW
1988-89	Hibbing High	Hi-School	22	9	8	17	24	....	....	....	....	....	....	....	....	....	....	....	....	....	....	....	....	....	....	....
1989-90	Grand Rapids	Hi-School	28	12	17	29	73	....	....	....	....	....	....	....	....	....	....	....	....	....	....	....	....	....	....	....
1990-91	Grand Rapids	Hi-School	28	28	45	73	25	....	....	....	....	....	....	....	....	....	....	....	....	....	....	....	....	....	....	....
1991-92	U. of Wisconsin	WCHA	37	11	10	21	45	....	....	....	....	....	....	....	....	....	....	....	....	....	....	....	....	....	....	....
1992-93	U. of Wisconsin	WCHA	42	25	29	54	54	....	....	....	....	....	....	....	....	....	....	....	....	....	....	....	....	....	....	....
1993-94	U. of Wisconsin	WCHA	42	20	44	*64	81	....	....	....	....	....	....	....	....	....	....	....	....	....	....	....	....	....	....	....
1994-95	St. John's Leafs	AHL	53	27	23	50	51	....	....	....	....	....	....	....	....	....	....	....	4	0	2	2	4	....	....	....
1995-96	**Toronto**	**NHL**	**1**	**0**	**1**	**1**	**2**	**0**	**0**	**0**	**1**	**0.0**	**1**	....	....	....	....	....	....	....	....	....	....	....	....	....
	St. John's Leafs	AHL	78	29	49	78	85	....	....	....	....	....	....	....	....	....	....	....	2	0	1	1	4	....	....	....
1996-97	**Toronto**	**NHL**	**22**	**0**	**2**	**2**	**2**	**0**	**0**	**0**	**14**	**0.0**	**–5**	....	....	....	....	....	....	....	....	....	....	....	....	....
	St. John's Leafs	AHL	29	9	22	31	36	....	....	....	....	....	....	....	....	....	....	....	....	....	....	....	....	....	....	....
	Orlando	IHL	25	9	6	15	20	....	....	....	....	....	....	....	....	....	....	....	9	6	5	11	16	....	....	....
1997-98	St. John's Leafs	AHL	17	5	2	7	24	....	....	....	....	....	....	....	....	....	....	....	....	....	....	....	....	....	....	....
	Orlando	IHL	22	2	6	8	20	....	....	....	....	....	....	....	....	....	....	....	....	....	....	....	....	....	....	....
	Milwaukee	IHL	40	20	24	44	32	....	....	....	....	....	....	....	....	....	....	....	10	5	2	7	4	....	....	....
1998-99	**Dallas**	**NHL**	**1**	**0**	**0**	**0**	**0**	**0**	**0**	**0**	**4**	**0.0**	**0**	**12**	**25.0**	**1**	**1**	**12:37**	....	....	....	....	....	....	....	....
	Michigan K-Wings	IHL	74	17	33	50	88	....	....	....	....	....	....	....	....	....	....	....	5	2	2	4	16	....	....	....
99-2000	Michigan K-Wings	IHL	78	21	41	62	89	....	....	....	....	....	....	....	....	....	....	....	....	....	....	....	....	....	....	....
	NHL Totals		**24**	**0**	**3**	**3**	**4**	**0**	**0**	**0**	**19**	**0.0**		**12**	**25.0**	**1**	**1**	**12:37**	....	....	....	....	....	....	....	....

WCHA First All-Star Team (1994)

Traded to **Toronto** by **LA Kings** with Dixon Ward, Guy Leveque and Shayne Toporowski for Eric Lacroix, Chris Snell and Toronto's 4th round choice (Eric Belanger) in 1996 Entry Draft, October 3, 1994. Traded to **Milwaukee** (IHL) by **Orlando** (IHL) with Dave McIntyre for Sean McCann and Dave Mackey, January 11, 1998. Signed as a free agent by **Dallas**, July 2, 1998. Signed as a free agent by **Colorado**, August, 2000.

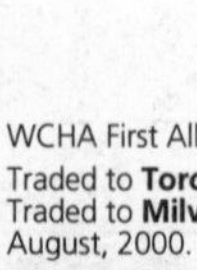

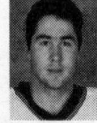

FALLOON, Pat (fah-LOON, PAT)

Right wing. Shoots right. 5'11", 190 lbs. Born, Foxwarren, Man., September 22, 1972. San Jose's 1st choice, 2nd overall, in 1991 Entry Draft.

Season	Club	League	GP	G	A	Pts	PIM	PP	SH	GW	S	%	+/-	TF	F%	H	SB	Min	GP	G	A	Pts	PIM	PP	SH	GW
1987-88	Yellowhead Pass	AAHA	52	74	69	143	50	....	....	....	....	....	....	....	....	....	....	....	....	....	....	....	....	....	....	....
1988-89	Spokane Chiefs	WHL	72	22	56	78	41	....	....	....	....	....	....	....	....	....	....	....	....	....	....	....	....	....	....	....
1989-90	Spokane Chiefs	WHL	71	60	64	124	48	....	....	....	....	....	....	....	....	....	....	....	6	5	8	13	4	....	....	....
1990-91	Spokane Chiefs	WHL	61	64	74	138	33	....	....	....	....	....	....	....	....	....	....	....	15	10	14	24	10	....	....	....
1991-92	**San Jose**	**NHL**	**79**	**25**	**34**	**59**	**16**	**5**	**0**	**1**	**181**	**13.8**	**–32**	....	....	....	....	....	....	....	....	....	....	....	....	....
1992-93	**San Jose**	**NHL**	**41**	**14**	**14**	**28**	**12**	**5**	**1**	**1**	**131**	**10.7**	**–25**	....	....	....	....	....	....	....	....	....	....	....	....	....

			Regular Season																Playoffs							
Season	Club	League	GP	G	A	Pts	PIM	PP	SH	GW	S	%	+/-	TF	F%	H	SB	Min	GP	G	A	Pts	PIM	PP	SH	GW
1993-94	San Jose	NHL	83	22	31	53	18	6	0	1	193	11.4	–3	....	....	....	....	....	14	1	2	3	6	0	0	0
1994-95	San Jose	NHL	46	12	7	19	25	0	0	3	91	13.2	–4	....	....	....	....	....	11	3	1	4	0	0	0	0
1995-96	San Jose	NHL	9	3	0	3	4	0	0	0	18	16.7	–1	....	....	....	....	....	....	....	....	....	....	....	....	....
	Philadelphia	NHL	62	22	26	48	6	9	0	2	152	14.5	15	....	....	....	....	....	12	3	2	5	2	2	0	0
1996-97	Philadelphia	NHL	52	11	12	23	10	2	0	4	124	8.9	–8	....	....	....	....	....	14	3	1	4	2	1	0	0
1997-98	Philadelphia	NHL	30	5	7	12	8	1	0	0	63	7.9	3	....	....	....	....	....	....	....	....	....	....	....	....	....
	Ottawa	NHL	28	3	3	6	8	2	0	0	73	4.1	–11	....	....	....	....	....	1	0	0	0	0	0	0	0
1998-99	Edmonton	NHL	82	17	23	40	20	8	0	2	152	11.2	–4	29	48.3	49	11	14:42	4	0	1	1	4	0	0	0
99-2000	Edmonton	NHL	33	5	13	18	4	1	0	0	51	9.8	6	9	66.7	17	4	13:19	....	....	....	....	....	....	....	....
	Pittsburgh	NHL	30	4	9	13	10	0	0	0	41	9.8	–2	8	62.5	12	2	11:13	10	1	0	1	2	0	0	0
	NHL Totals		575	143	179	322	141	39	1	14	1270	11.3		46	54.3	78	17	13:40	66	11	7	18	16	3	0	0

WHL West Second All-Star Team (1989) • WHL West First All-Star Team (1991) • Canadian Major Junior Most Sportsmanlike Player of the Year (1991) • Memorial Cup All-Star Team (1991) • Won Stafford Smythe Memorial Trophy (Memorial Cup Tournament MVP) (1991)

Traded to **Philadelphia** by **San Jose** for Martin Spanhel, Philadelphia's 1st round choice (later traded to Phoenix - Phoenix selected Daniel Briere) in 1996 Entry Draft and Philadelphia's 4th round choice (later traded to Buffalo - Buffalo selected Mike Martone), in 1996 Entry Draft, November 16, 1995. Traded to **Ottawa** by **Philadelphia** with Vaclav Prospal and Dallas' 2nd round choice (previously acquired, Ottawa selected Chris Bala) in 1998 Entry Draft for Alexandre Daigle, January 17, 1998. Signed as a free agent by **Edmonton**, August 21, 1998. Claimed on waivers by **Pittsburgh** from **Edmonton**, February 4, 2000.

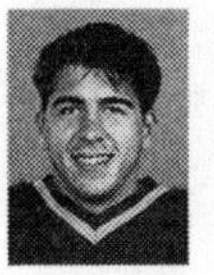

FARKAS, Jeff

(FAHR-kuhs, JEHF) **TOR.**

Center. Shoots left. 6', 185 lbs. Born, Amherst, MA, January 24, 1978. Toronto's 1st choice, 57th overall, in 1997 Entry Draft.

1993-94	Nichols School	Hi-School	28	27	57	99	25	....	....	....	....	....	....	....	....	....	....	....	....	....	....	....	....	....	....	....
1994-95	Niagara Scenics	EJHL-B	47	54	55	99	70	....	....	....	....	....	....	....	....	....	....	....	....	....	....	....	....	....	....	....
1995-96	Niagara Scenics	OJHL	47	42	70	112	75	....	....	....	....	....	....	....	....	....	....	....	....	....	....	....	....	....	....	....
1996-97	Boston College	H-East	35	13	23	36	34	....	....	....	....	....	....	....	....	....	....	....	....	....	....	....	....	....	....	....
1997-98	Boston College	H-East	40	11	28	39	42	....	....	....	....	....	....	....	....	....	....	....	....	....	....	....	....	....	....	....
1998-99	Boston College	H-East	43	32	25	57	56	....	....	....	....	....	....	....	....	....	....	....	....	....	....	....	....	....	....	....
99-2000	Boston College	H-East	41	32	26	*58	61	....	....	....	....	....	....	....	....	....	....	....	....	....	....	....	....	....	....	....
	Toronto	NHL	....	....	....	....	....	....	....	....	....	....	....	....	....	....	....	....	3	1	0	1	0	0	0	0
	NHL Totals		....	....	....	....	....	....	....	....	....	....	....	....	....	....	....	....	3	1	0	1	0	0	0	0

Hockey East First All-Star Team (2000) • NCAA East First All-American Team (2000) • NCAA Championship All-Tournament Team (2000)

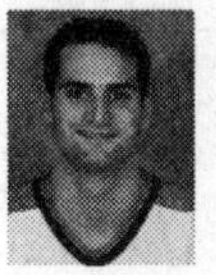

FATA, Rico

(FA-tuh, REE-koh) **CGY.**

Center. Shoots left. 5'11", 197 lbs. Born, Sault Ste. Marie, Ont., February 12, 1980. Calgary's 1st choice, 6th overall, in 1998 Entry Draft.

1995-96	Sault Ste. Marie	OHL	62	11	15	26	52	....	....	....	....	....	....	....	....	....	....	....	4	0	0	0	0	....	....	....
1996-97	London Knights	OHL	59	19	34	53	76	....	....	....	....	....	....	....	....	....	....	....	....	....	....	....	....	....	....	....
1997-98	London Knights	OHL	64	43	33	76	110	....	....	....	....	....	....	....	....	....	....	....	16	9	5	14	*49	....	....	....
1998-99	Calgary	NHL	20	0	1	1	4	0	0	0	13	0.0	0	2	50.0	10	5	7:36	....	....	....	....	....	....	....	....
	London Knights	OHL	23	15	18	33	41	....	....	....	....	....	....	....	....	....	....	....	25	10	12	22	42	....	....	....
99-2000	Calgary	NHL	2	0	0	0	0	0	0	0	0	0.0	–1	0	0.0	3	0	10:06	....	....	....	....	....	....	....	....
	Saint John Flames	AHL	76	29	29	58	65	....	....	....	....	....	....	....	....	....	....	....	3	0	0	0	4	....	....	....
	NHL Totals		22	0	1	1	4	0	0	0	13	0.0		2	50.0	13	5	7:50	....	....	....	....	....	....	....	....

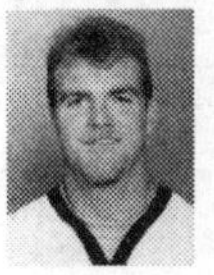

FEATHERSTONE, Glen

(FEH-thuhr-stohn, GLEHN)

Defense. Shoots left. 6'4", 209 lbs. Born, Toronto, Ont., July 8, 1968. St. Louis' 4th choice, 73rd overall, in 1986 Entry Draft.

1984-85	Toronto Nats	MTHL	45	7	24	31	94	....	....	....	....	....	....	....	....	....	....	....	....	....	....	....	....	....	....	....
	North York	OJHL	2	0	0	0	4	....	....	....	....	....	....	....	....	....	....	....	....	....	....	....	....	....	....	....
1985-86	Windsor Spitfires	OHL	49	0	6	6	135	....	....	....	....	....	....	....	....	....	....	....	14	1	1	2	23	....	....	....
1986-87	Windsor Spitfires	OHL	47	6	11	17	154	....	....	....	....	....	....	....	....	....	....	....	14	2	6	8	19	....	....	....
1987-88	Windsor Spitfires	OHL	53	7	27	34	201	....	....	....	....	....	....	....	....	....	....	....	12	6	9	15	47	....	....	....
1988-89	St. Louis	NHL	18	0	2	2	22	0	0	0	9	0.0	–3	....	....	....	....	....	6	0	0	0	25	0	0	0
	Peoria Rivermen	IHL	37	5	19	24	97	....	....	....	....	....	....	....	....	....	....	....	....	....	....	....	....	....	....	....
1989-90	St. Louis	NHL	58	0	12	12	145	0	0	0	34	0.0	–1	....	....	....	....	....	12	0	2	2	47	0	0	0
	Peoria Rivermen	IHL	15	1	4	5	43	....	....	....	....	....	....	....	....	....	....	....	....	....	....	....	....	....	....	....
1990-91	St. Louis	NHL	68	5	15	20	204	1	0	1	59	8.5	19	....	....	....	....	....	9	0	0	0	31	0	0	0
1991-92	Boston	NHL	7	1	0	1	20	0	0	0	8	12.5	–2	....	....	....	....	....	....	....	....	....	....	....	....	....
1992-93	Boston	NHL	34	5	5	10	102	1	0	0	33	15.2	6	....	....	....	....	....	....	....	....	....	....	....	....	....
	Providence Bruins	AHL	8	3	4	7	60	....	....	....	....	....	....	....	....	....	....	....	....	....	....	....	....	....	....	....
1993-94	Boston	NHL	58	1	8	9	152	0	0	1	55	1.8	–5	....	....	....	....	....	1	0	0	0	0	0	0	0
1994-95	NY Rangers	NHL	6	1	0	1	18	0	0	0	6	16.7	0	....	....	....	....	....	....	....	....	....	....	....	....	....
	Hartford	NHL	13	1	1	2	32	0	0	0	16	6.3	–7	....	....	....	....	....	....	....	....	....	....	....	....	....
1995-96	Hartford	NHL	68	2	10	12	138	0	0	1	62	3.2	10	....	....	....	....	....	....	....	....	....	....	....	....	....
1996-97	Hartford	NHL	41	2	5	7	87	0	0	0	40	5.0	0	....	....	....	....	....	....	....	....	....	....	....	....	....
	Calgary	NHL	13	1	3	4	19	0	0	0	27	3.7	–1	....	....	....	....	....	....	....	....	....	....	....	....	....
1997-98	Indianapolis Ice	IHL	73	10	28	38	187	....	....	....	....	....	....	....	....	....	....	....	5	0	3	3	16	....	....	....
1998-99	Chicago Wolves	IHL	62	5	21	26	191	....	....	....	....	....	....	....	....	....	....	....	10	0	3	3	26	....	....	....
99-2000	Chicago Wolves	IHL	62	7	12	19	109	....	....	....	....	....	....	....	....	....	....	....	16	3	5	8	38	....	....	....
	NHL Totals		384	19	61	80	939	2	0	3	349	5.4		....	....	....	....	....	28	0	2	2	103	0	0	0

Signed as a free agent by **Boston**, July 25, 1991. Traded to **NY Rangers** by **Boston** for Daniel Lacroix, August 19, 1994. Traded to **Hartford** by **NY Rangers** with Michael Stewart, NY Rangers' 1st round choice (Jean-Sebastien Giguere) in 1995 Entry Draft and 4th round choice (Steve Wasylko) in 1996 Entry Draft for Pat Verbeek, March 23, 1995. Traded to **Calgary** by **Hartford** with Hnat Domenichelli, New Jersey's 2nd round choice (previously acquired, Calgary selected Dimitri Kokorev) in 1997 Entry Draft and Vancouver's 3rd round choice (previously acquired, Calgary selected Paul Manning) in 1998 Entry Draft for Steve Chiasson and Colorado's 3rd round choice (previously acquired, Carolina selected Francis Lessard) in 1997 Entry Draft, March 5, 1997. Signed as a free agent by **Chicago** (IHL), September 8, 1998.

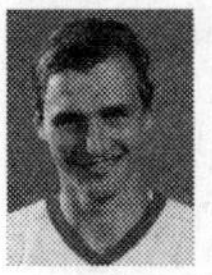

FEDOROV, Sergei

(FEH-duh-rahf, SAIR-gay) **DET.**

Center. Shoots left. 6'1", 200 lbs. Born, Pskov, USSR, December 13, 1969. Detroit's 4th choice, 74th overall, in 1989 Entry Draft.

1985-86	Dynamo Minsk	USSR	15	6	1	7	10	....	....	....	....	....	....	....	....	....	....	....	....	....	....	....	....	....	....	....
1986-87	CSKA Moscow	USSR	29	6	6	12	12	....	....	....	....	....	....	....	....	....	....	....	....	....	....	....	....	....	....	....
1987-88	CSKA Moscow	USSR	48	7	9	16	20	....	....	....	....	....	....	....	....	....	....	....	....	....	....	....	....	....	....	....
1988-89	CSKA Moscow	USSR	44	9	8	17	35	....	....	....	....	....	....	....	....	....	....	....	....	....	....	....	....	....	....	....
1989-90	CSKA Moscow	USSR	48	19	10	29	22	....	....	....	....	....	....	....	....	....	....	....	....	....	....	....	....	....	....	....
1990-91	Detroit	NHL	77	31	48	79	66	11	3	5	259	12.0	11	....	....	....	....	....	7	1	5	6	4	0	0	1
1991-92	Detroit	NHL	80	32	54	86	72	7	2	5	249	12.9	26	....	....	....	....	....	11	5	5	10	8	1	2	1
1992-93	Detroit	NHL	73	34	53	87	72	13	4	3	217	15.7	33	....	....	....	....	....	7	3	6	9	23	1	1	0
1993-94	Detroit	NHL	82	56	64	120	34	13	4	10	337	16.6	48	....	....	....	....	....	7	1	7	8	6	0	0	0
1994-95	Detroit	NHL	42	20	30	50	24	7	3	5	147	13.6	6	....	....	....	....	....	17	7	*17	*24	6	3	0	0
1995-96	Detroit	NHL	78	39	68	107	48	11	3	11	306	12.7	49	....	....	....	....	....	19	2	*18	20	10	0	0	2
1996-97♦	Detroit	NHL	74	30	33	63	30	9	2	4	273	11.0	29	....	....	....	....	....	20	8	12	20	12	3	0	4
1997-98♦	Detroit	NHL	21	6	11	17	25	2	0	2	68	8.8	10	....	....	....	....	....	22	*10	10	20	12	2	1	1
	Russia	Olympics	6	1	5	6	8	....	....	....	....	....	....	....	....	....	....	....	....	....	....	....	....	....	....	....
1998-99	Detroit	NHL	77	26	37	63	66	6	2	3	224	11.6	9	1414	51.7	77	24	19:21	10	1	8	9	8	0	0	0
99-2000	Detroit	NHL	68	27	35	62	22	4	4	7	263	10.3	8	1274	53.8	62	23	20:05	9	4	4	8	4	2	0	1
	NHL Totals		672	301	433	734	459	83	27	55	2343	12.8		2688	52.7	139	47	19:42	129	42	92	134	93	12	4	10

NHL All-Rookie Team (1991) • NHL First All-Star Team (1994) • Won Frank J. Selke Trophy (1994, 1996) • Won Lester B. Pearson Award (1994) • Won Hart Trophy (1994) • Played in NHL All-Star Game (1992, 1994, 1996)

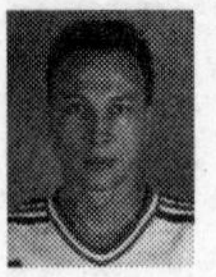

FEDYK, Brent
(FEH-dihk, BREHNT)

Left wing. Shoots right. 6', 194 lbs. Born, Yorkton, Sask., March 8, 1967. Detroit's 1st choice, 8th overall, in 1985 Entry Draft.

			Regular Season																Playoffs							
Season	Club	League	GP	G	A	Pts	PIM	PP	SH	GW	S	%	+/-	TF	F%	H	SB	Min	GP	G	A	Pts	PIM	PP	SH	GW
1982-83	Regina AAA	SAHA	70	78	65	143	20																			
	Regina Pats	WHL	1	0	0	0	0																			
1983-84	Regina Pats	WHL	63	15	28	43	30												23	8	7	15	6			
1984-85	Regina Pats	WHL	66	35	35	70	48												8	5	4	9	0			
1985-86	Regina Pats	WHL	50	43	34	77	47												5	0	1	1	0			
1986-87	Regina Pats	WHL	12	9	6	15	9																			
	Seattle	WHL	13	5	11	16	9																			
	Portland	WHL	11	5	4	9	6												14	5	6	11	0			
1987-88	**Detroit**	**NHL**	**2**	**0**	**1**	**1**	**2**	**0**	**0**	**0**	**2**	**0.0**	**-1**													
	Adirondack	AHL	34	9	11	20	22												5	0	2	2	6			
1988-89	**Detroit**	**NHL**	**5**	**2**	**0**	**2**	**0**	**1**	**0**	**0**	**6**	**33.3**	**-1**													
	Adirondack	AHL	66	40	28	68	33												15	7	8	15	23			
1989-90	**Detroit**	**NHL**	**27**	**1**	**4**	**5**	**6**	**0**	**0**	**0**	**28**	**3.6**	**-1**													
	Adirondack	AHL	33	14	15	29	24												6	2	1	3	4			
1990-91	**Detroit**	**NHL**	**67**	**16**	**19**	**35**	**38**	**0**	**0**	**1**	**74**	**21.6**	**20**						**6**	**1**	**0**	**1**	**2**	**0**	**0**	**1**
1991-92	**Detroit**	**NHL**	**61**	**5**	**8**	**13**	**42**	**0**	**0**	**1**	**60**	**8.3**	**-5**						**1**	**0**	**0**	**0**	**2**	**0**	**0**	**0**
	Adirondack	AHL	1	0	2	2	0																			
1992-93	**Philadelphia**	**NHL**	**74**	**21**	**38**	**59**	**48**	**4**	**1**	**2**	**167**	**12.6**	**14**													
1993-94	**Philadelphia**	**NHL**	**72**	**20**	**18**	**38**	**74**	**5**	**0**	**1**	**104**	**19.2**	**-14**													
1994-95	**Philadelphia**	**NHL**	**30**	**8**	**4**	**12**	**14**	**3**	**0**	**2**	**41**	**19.5**	**-2**						**9**	**2**	**2**	**4**	**8**	**0**	**0**	**0**
1995-96	**Philadelphia**	**NHL**	**24**	**10**	**5**	**15**	**24**	**4**	**0**	**0**	**42**	**23.8**	**1**													
	Dallas	**NHL**	**41**	**10**	**9**	**19**	**30**	**4**	**0**	**0**	**71**	**14.1**	**-17**													
1996-97	Michigan K-Wings	IHL	9	1	2	3	4																			
1997-98	Detroit Vipers	IHL	40	18	23	41	24																			
	Cincinnati	IHL	26	21	13	34	14												9	5	5	10	2			
1998-99	**NY Rangers**	**NHL**	**67**	**4**	**6**	**10**	**30**	**0**	**1**	**0**	**47**	**8.5**	**-11**	**2**	**0.0**	**63**	**21**	**11:06**								
99-2000	Kassel Huskies	Germany	24	5	6	11	8																			
	NHL Totals		**470**	**97**	**112**	**209**	**308**	**21**	**2**	**7**	**642**	**15.1**		**2**	**0.0**	**63**	**21**	**11:06**	**16**	**3**	**2**	**5**	**12**	**0**	**0**	**1**

WHL East Second All-Star Team (1986)

Traded to **Philadelphia** by **Detroit** for Philadelphia's 4th round choice (later traded to Boston — Boston selected Charles Paquette) in 1993 Entry Draft, October 1, 1992. Traded to **Dallas** by **Philadelphia** for Trent Klatt, December 13, 1995. Signed as a free agent by **NY Rangers**, August 13, 1998.

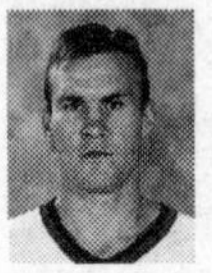

FELSNER, Brian
(FEHLZ-nuhr, BRIGH-an)

Left wing. Shoots left. 5'11", 189 lbs. Born, Mt. Clemens, MI, November 11, 1972.

Season	Club	League	GP	G	A	Pts	PIM	PP	SH	GW	S	%	+/-	TF	F%	H	SB	Min	GP	G	A	Pts	PIM	PP	SH	GW
1992-93	Detroit	NAJHL	50	25	35	60																				
1993-94	Lake Superior	CCHA	6	1	1	2	6																			
1994-95	Lake Superior	CCHA	41	24	28	52	51																			
1995-96	Lake Superior	CCHA	38	16	36	52	40																			
1996-97	Orlando	IHL	75	29	41	70	38												7	2	3	5	6			
1997-98	**Chicago**	**NHL**	**12**	**1**	**3**	**4**	**12**	**0**	**0**	**0**	**14**	**7.1**	**0**													
	Indianapolis Ice	IHL	53	17	36	53	36																			
	Milwaukee	IHL	15	7	8	15	20												10	3	9	12	12			
1998-99	Detroit Vipers	IHL	72	20	35	55	49												11	4	6	10	12			
99-2000	Houston Aeros	IHL	28	7	16	23	20																			
	Cincinnati	IHL	38	15	17	32	18												11	4	5	9	20			
	NHL Totals		**12**	**1**	**3**	**4**	**12**	**0**	**0**	**0**	**14**	**7.1**														

• Played football at Lanse Creuse High School, 1987-1992. • Ruled academically ineligable by NCAA for remainder of 1993-94 season. Signed as a free agent by **Chicago**, September 5, 1997. Traded to **Ottawa** by **Chicago** for Justin Hocking, August 21, 1998. Signed as a free agent by **Houston** (IHL), October 9, 1999. Traded to **Cincinnati** (IHL) by **Houston** (IHL) for Steve Bancroft with Ottawa retaining NHL rights, January 19, 2000.

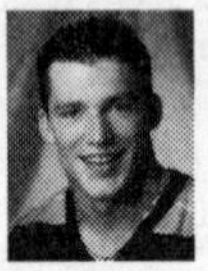

FERENCE, Andrew
(fuhr-EHNS, AN-drew) **PIT.**

Defense. Shoots left. 5'10", 190 lbs. Born, Edmonton, Alta., March 17, 1979. Pittsburgh's 8th choice, 208th overall, in 1997 Entry Draft.

Season	Club	League	GP	G	A	Pts	PIM	PP	SH	GW	S	%	+/-	TF	F%	H	SB	Min	GP	G	A	Pts	PIM	PP	SH	GW
1994-95	Portland	WHL	2	0	0	0	4																			
	Sherwood Park	AMHL	31	4	14	18	74																			
1995-96	Portland	WHL	72	9	31	40	159												7	1	3	4	12			
1996-97	Portland	WHL	72	12	32	44	163												6	1	2	3	12			
1997-98	Portland	WHL	72	11	57	68	142												16	2	18	20	28			
1998-99	Portland	WHL	40	11	21	32	104												4	1	4	5	10			
	Kansas City	IHL	5	1	2	3	4												3	0	0	0	9			
99-2000	**Pittsburgh**	**NHL**	**30**	**2**	**4**	**6**	**20**	**0**	**0**	**1**	**26**	**7.7**	**3**	**0**	**0.0**	**61**	**26**	**16:19**								
	Wilkes-Barre	AHL	44	8	20	28	58																			
	NHL Totals		**30**	**2**	**4**	**6**	**20**	**0**	**0**	**1**	**26**	**7.7**		**0**	**0.0**	**61**	**26**	**16:19**								

WHL West First All-Star Team (1998) • WHL West Second All-Star Team (1999)

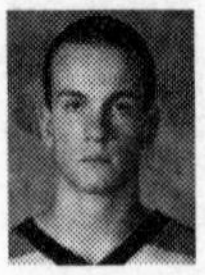

FERENCE, Brad
(FAIR-ehns, BRAD) **FLA.**

Defense. Shoots right. 6'3", 196 lbs. Born, Calgary, Alta., April 2, 1979. Vancouver's 1st choice, 10th overall, in 1997 Entry Draft.

Season	Club	League	GP	G	A	Pts	PIM	PP	SH	GW	S	%	+/-	TF	F%	H	SB	Min	GP	G	A	Pts	PIM	PP	SH	GW
1994-95	Calgary Royals	AAHA	60	19	47	66	220																			
1995-96	Calgary Royals	AAHA	22	7	21	28	140																			
	Spokane Chiefs	WHL	5	0	2	2	18																			
1996-97	Spokane Chiefs	WHL	67	6	20	26	324												9	0	4	4	21			
1997-98	Spokane Chiefs	WHL	54	9	30	39	213												18	0	7	7	59			
1998-99	Spokane Chiefs	WHL	31	3	22	25	125																			
	Tri-City Americans	WHL	20	6	15	21	116												12	1	9	10	63			
99-2000	**Florida**	**NHL**	**13**	**0**	**2**	**2**	**46**	**0**	**0**	**0**	**10**	**0.0**	**2**	**0**	**0.0**	**13**	**17**	**13:40**								
	Louisville	AHL	58	2	7	9	231												2	0	0	0	2			
	NHL Totals		**13**	**0**	**2**	**2**	**46**	**0**	**0**	**0**	**10**	**0.0**		**0**	**0.0**	**13**	**17**	**13:40**								

Memorial Cup All-Star Team (1998)

Traded to **Florida** by **Vancouver** with Pavel Bure, Bret Hedican and Vancouver's 3rd round choice (Robert Fried) in 2000 Entry Draft for Ed Jovanovski, Dave Gagner, Mike Brown, Kevin Weekes and Florida's 1st round choice (Nathan Smith) in 2000 Entry Draft, January 17, 1999.

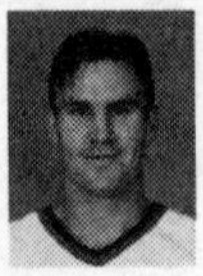

FERGUSON, Craig
(fuhr-GUH-sohn, KRAYG)

Center. Shoots left. 5'11", 190 lbs. Born, Castro Valley, CA, April 8, 1970. Montreal's 7th choice, 146th overall, in 1989 Entry Draft.

Season	Club	League	GP	G	A	Pts	PIM	PP	SH	GW	S	%	+/-	TF	F%	H	SB	Min	GP	G	A	Pts	PIM	PP	SH	GW
1988-89	Yale University	ECAC	24	11	6	17	20																			
1989-90	Yale University	ECAC	28	6	13	19	36																			
1990-91	Yale University	ECAC	29	11	10	21	34																			
1991-92	Yale University	ECAC	27	9	16	25	26																			
1992-93	Fredericton	AHL	55	15	13	28	20												5	0	1	1	2			
	Wheeling	ECHL	9	6	5	11	24																			
1993-94	**Montreal**	**NHL**	**2**	**0**	**1**	**1**	**0**	**0**	**0**	**0**	**0**	**0.0**	**1**													
	Fredericton	AHL	57	29	32	61	60																			
1994-95	Fredericton	AHL	80	27	35	62	62												17	6	2	8	6			
	Montreal	**NHL**	**1**	**0**	**0**	**0**	**0**	**0**	**0**	**0**	**3**	**0.0**	**0**													
1995-96	**Montreal**	**NHL**	**10**	**1**	**0**	**1**	**2**	**0**	**0**	**0**	**9**	**11.1**	**-5**													
	Calgary	**NHL**	**8**	**0**	**0**	**0**	**4**	**0**	**0**	**0**	**11**	**0.0**	**-4**													
	Saint John Flames	AHL	18	5	13	18	8																			
	Phoenix	IHL	31	6	9	15	25												4	0	2	2	6			
1996-97	**Florida**	**NHL**	**3**	**0**	**0**	**0**	**0**	**0**	**0**	**0**	**5**	**0.0**	**-1**													
	Carolina	AHL	74	29	41	70	57																			

			Regular Season																Playoffs							
Season	Club	League	GP	G	A	Pts	PIM	PP	SH	GW	S	%	+/-	TF	F%	H	SB	Min	GP	G	A	Pts	PIM	PP	SH	GW
1997-98	New Haven	AHL	64	24	28	52	41	....	....	....	....	....	....	....	....	....	....	....	3	2	1	3	2	....	....	....
1998-99	New Haven	AHL	61	18	27	45	76	....	....	....	....	....	....	....	....	....	....	....	....	....	....	....	....	....	....	....
99-2000	**Florida**	**NHL**	**3**	**0**	**0**	**0**	**0**	**0**	**0**	**0**	**2**	**0.0**	**–2**	**19**	**47.4**	**0**	**0**	**5:34**	....	....	....	....	....	....	....	....
	Louisville	AHL	61	29	27	56	28	....	....	....	....	....	....	....	....	....	....	....	4	1	3	4	2	....	....	....
	NHL Totals		**27**	**1**	**1**	**2**	**6**	**0**	**0**	**0**	**30**	**3.3**		**19**	**47.4**	**0**	**0**	**5:34**	....	....	....	....	....	....	....	....

Traded to **Calgary** by **Montreal** with Yves Sarault for Calgary's 8th round choice (Petr Kubos) in 1997 Entry Draft, November 26, 1995. Traded to **LA Kings** by **Calgary** for Pat Conacher, February 10, 1996. Signed as a free agent by **Florida**, July 24, 1996.

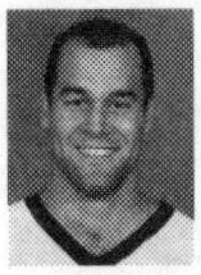

FERGUSON, Scott

(fuhr-GUH-sohn, SKAWT) **EDM.**

Defense. Shoots left. 6'1", 202 lbs. Born, Camrose, Alta., January 6, 1973.

Season	Club	League	GP	G	A	Pts	PIM	PP	SH	GW	S	%	+/-	TF	F%	H	SB	Min	GP	G	A	Pts	PIM	PP	SH	GW
1990-91	Sherwood Park	AJHL	32	2	9	11	91	....	....	....	....	....	....	....	....	....	....	....	....	....	....	....	....	....	....	....
	Kamloops Blazers	WHL	4	0	0	0	0	....	....	....	....	....	....	....	....	....	....	....	....	....	....	....	....	....	....	....
1991-92	Kamloops Blazers	WHL	62	4	10	14	138	....	....	....	....	....	....	....	....	....	....	....	12	0	2	2	21	....	....	....
1992-93	Kamloops Blazers	WHL	71	4	19	23	206	....	....	....	....	....	....	....	....	....	....	....	13	0	2	2	24	....	....	....
1993-94	Kamloops Blazers	WHL	68	5	49	54	180	....	....	....	....	....	....	....	....	....	....	....	19	5	11	16	48	....	....	....
1994-95	Cape Breton	AHL	58	4	6	10	103	....	....	....	....	....	....	....	....	....	....	....	....	....	....	....	....	....	....	....
	Wheeling	ECHL	5	1	5	6	16	....	....	....	....	....	....	....	....	....	....	....	....	....	....	....	....	....	....	....
1995-96	Cape Breton	AHL	80	5	16	21	196	....	....	....	....	....	....	....	....	....	....	....	....	....	....	....	....	....	....	....
1996-97	Hamilton Bulldogs	AHL	74	6	14	20	115	....	....	....	....	....	....	....	....	....	....	....	21	5	7	12	59	....	....	....
1997-98	**Edmonton**	**NHL**	**1**	**0**	**0**	**0**	**0**	**0**	**0**	**0**	**0**	**0.0**	**1**	....	....	....	....	....	....	....	....	....	....	....	....	....
	Hamilton Bulldogs	AHL	77	7	17	24	150	....	....	....	....	....	....	....	....	....	....	....	9	0	3	3	16	....	....	....
1998-99	**Anaheim**	**NHL**	**2**	**0**	**1**	**1**	**0**	**0**	**0**	**0**	**1**	**0.0**	**0**	**0**	**0.0**	**1**	**4**	**15:09**	....	....	....	....	....	....	....	....
	Cincinnati Ducks	AHL	78	4	31	35	59	....	....	....	....	....	....	....	....	....	....	....	3	0	0	0	4	....	....	....
99-2000	Cincinnati Ducks	AHL	77	7	25	32	166	....	....	....	....	....	....	....	....	....	....	....	....	....	....	....	....	....	....	....
	NHL Totals		**3**	**0**	**1**	**1**	**0**	**0**	**0**	**0**	**1**	**0.0**		**0**	**0.0**	**1**	**4**	**15:09**	....	....	....	....	....	....	....	....

WHL West Second All-Star Team (1994)

Signed as a free agent by **Edmonton**, June 2, 1994. Traded to **Ottawa** by **Edmonton** for Frantisek Musil, March 9, 1998. Signed as a free agent by **Anaheim**, July 27, 1998. Signed as a free agent by **Edmonton**, July 5, 2000.

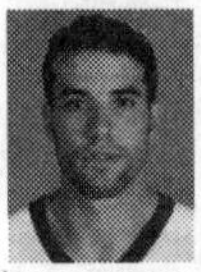

FERRARO, Chris

(fuh-RAHR-oh, KRIHS) **N.J.**

Center. Shoots right. 5'10", 180 lbs. Born, Port Jefferson, NY, January 24, 1973. NY Rangers' 4th choice, 85th overall, in 1992 Entry Draft.

Season	Club	League	GP	G	A	Pts	PIM	PP	SH	GW	S	%	+/-	TF	F%	H	SB	Min	GP	G	A	Pts	PIM	PP	SH	GW
1990-91	Dubuque Saints	USHL	45	53	44	97	84	....	....	....	....	....	....	....	....	....	....	....	8	3	9	12	12	....	....	....
1991-92	Dubuque Saints	USHL	20	30	19	49	52	....	....	....	....	....	....	....	....	....	....	....	....	....	....	....	....	....	....	....
	Waterloo Hawks	USHL	18	19	31	50	54	....	....	....	....	....	....	....	....	....	....	....	4	5	6	11	14	....	....	....
1992-93	U. of Maine	H-East	39	25	26	51	46	....	....	....	....	....	....	....	....	....	....	....	....	....	....	....	....	....	....	....
1993-94	U. of Maine	H-East	4	0	1	1	8	....	....	....	....	....	....	....	....	....	....	....	....	....	....	....	....	....	....	....
	United States	Nat-Team	48	8	34	42	58	....	....	....	....	....	....	....	....	....	....	....	....	....	....	....	....	....	....	....
1994-95	Atlanta Knights	IHL	54	13	14	27	72	....	....	....	....	....	....	....	....	....	....	....	....	....	....	....	....	....	....	....
	Binghamton	AHL	13	6	4	10	38	....	....	....	....	....	....	....	....	....	....	....	10	2	3	5	16	....	....	....
1995-96	**NY Rangers**	**NHL**	**2**	**1**	**0**	**1**	**0**	**1**	**0**	**0**	**4**	**25.0**	**–3**	....	....	....	....	....	....	....	....	....	....	....	....	....
	Binghamton	AHL	77	32	67	99	208	....	....	....	....	....	....	....	....	....	....	....	4	4	2	6	13	....	....	....
1996-97	**NY Rangers**	**NHL**	**12**	**1**	**1**	**2**	**6**	**0**	**0**	**0**	**23**	**4.3**	**1**	....	....	....	....	....	....	....	....	....	....	....	....	....
	Binghamton	AHL	53	29	34	63	94	....	....	....	....	....	....	....	....	....	....	....	....	....	....	....	....	....	....	....
1997-98	**Pittsburgh**	**NHL**	**46**	**3**	**4**	**7**	**43**	**0**	**0**	**0**	**42**	**7.1**	**–2**	....	....	....	....	....	....	....	....	....	....	....	....	....
1998-99	**Edmonton**	**NHL**	**2**	**1**	**0**	**1**	**0**	**0**	**0**	**0**	**1**	**100.0**	**1**	**19**	**52.6**	**0**	**0**	**8:33**	....	....	....	....	....	....	....	....
	Hamilton Bulldogs	AHL	72	35	41	76	104	....	....	....	....	....	....	....	....	....	....	....	11	8	5	13	20	....	....	....
99-2000	**NY Islanders**	**NHL**	**11**	**1**	**3**	**4**	**8**	**0**	**0**	**0**	**15**	**6.7**	**1**	**92**	**50.0**	**8**	**7**	**9:30**	....	....	....	....	....	....	....	....
	Providence Bruins	AHL	21	9	9	18	32	....	....	....	....	....	....	....	....	....	....	....	....	....	....	....	....	....	....	....
	Chicago Wolves	IHL	25	7	18	25	40	....	....	....	....	....	....	....	....	....	....	....	16	5	8	13	14	....	....	....
	NHL Totals		**73**	**7**	**8**	**15**	**57**	**1**	**0**	**0**	**85**	**8.2**		**111**	**50.5**	**8**	**7**	**9:22**	....	....	....	....	....	....	....	....

Claimed on waivers by **Pittsburgh** from **NY Rangers**, October 1, 1997. Signed as a free agent by **Edmonton**, August 13, 1998. Signed as a free agent by **NY Islanders**, July 22, 1999. Signed as a free agent by **New Jersey**, July 20, 2000.

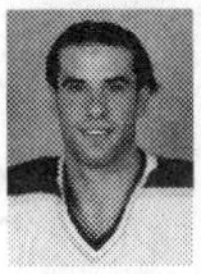

FERRARO, Peter

(fuh-RAHR-oh, PEE-tuhr) **BOS.**

Right wing. Shoots right. 5'10", 180 lbs. Born, Port Jefferson, NY, January 24, 1973. NY Rangers' 1st choice, 24th overall, in 1992 Entry Draft.

Season	Club	League	GP	G	A	Pts	PIM	PP	SH	GW	S	%	+/-	TF	F%	H	SB	Min	GP	G	A	Pts	PIM	PP	SH	GW
1990-91	Dubuque Saints	USHL	29	21	31	52	83	....	....	....	....	....	....	....	....	....	....	....	8	7	5	12	10	....	....	....
1991-92	Dubuque Saints	USHL	21	25	25	50	92	....	....	....	....	....	....	....	....	....	....	....	....	....	....	....	....	....	....	....
	Waterloo Hawks	USHL	21	23	28	51	76	....	....	....	....	....	....	....	....	....	....	....	4	8	5	13	16	....	....	....
1992-93	U. of Maine	H-East	36	18	32	50	106	....	....	....	....	....	....	....	....	....	....	....	....	....	....	....	....	....	....	....
1993-94	U. of Maine	H-East	4	3	6	9	16	....	....	....	....	....	....	....	....	....	....	....	....	....	....	....	....	....	....	....
	United States	Nat-Team	60	30	34	64	87	....	....	....	....	....	....	....	....	....	....	....	....	....	....	....	....	....	....	....
	United States	Olympics	8	6	0	6	6	....	....	....	....	....	....	....	....	....	....	....	....	....	....	....	....	....	....	....
1994-95	Atlanta Knights	IHL	61	15	24	39	118	....	....	....	....	....	....	....	....	....	....	....	....	....	....	....	....	....	....	....
	Binghamton	AHL	12	2	6	8	67	....	....	....	....	....	....	....	....	....	....	....	11	4	3	7	51	....	....	....
1995-96	**NY Rangers**	**NHL**	**5**	**0**	**1**	**1**	**0**	**0**	**0**	**0**	**6**	**0.0**	**–5**	....	....	....	....	....	....	....	....	....	....	....	....	....
	Binghamton	AHL	68	48	53	101	157	....	....	....	....	....	....	....	....	....	....	....	4	1	6	7	22	....	....	....
1996-97	**NY Rangers**	**NHL**	**2**	**0**	**0**	**0**	**0**	**0**	**0**	**0**	**3**	**0.0**	**0**	....	....	....	....	....	**2**	**0**	**0**	**0**	**0**	**0**	**0**	**0**
	Binghamton	AHL	75	38	39	77	171	....	....	....	....	....	....	....	....	....	....	....	4	3	1	4	18	....	....	....
1997-98	**Pittsburgh**	**NHL**	**29**	**3**	**4**	**7**	**12**	**0**	**0**	**0**	**34**	**8.8**	**–2**	....	....	....	....	....	....	....	....	....	....	....	....	....
	NY Rangers	**NHL**	**1**	**0**	**0**	**0**	**2**	**0**	**0**	**0**	**3**	**0.0**	**–2**	....	....	....	....	....	....	....	....	....	....	....	....	....
	Hartford	AHL	36	17	23	40	54	....	....	....	....	....	....	....	....	....	....	....	15	8	6	14	59	....	....	....
1998-99	**Boston**	**NHL**	**46**	**6**	**8**	**14**	**44**	**1**	**0**	**1**	**61**	**9.8**	**10**	**70**	**37.1**	**52**	**21**	**10:12**	....	....	....	....	....	....	....	....
	Providence Bruins	AHL	16	15	10	25	14	....	....	....	....	....	....	....	....	....	....	....	19	9	12	21	38	....	....	....
99-2000	**Boston**	**NHL**	**5**	**0**	**1**	**1**	**0**	**0**	**0**	**0**	**3**	**0.0**	**–1**	**19**	**47.4**	**8**	**1**	**8:11**	....	....	....	....	....	....	....	....
	Providence Bruins	AHL	48	21	25	46	98	....	....	....	....	....	....	....	....	....	....	....	13	5	7	12	14	....	....	....
	NHL Totals		**88**	**9**	**14**	**23**	**58**	**1**	**0**	**1**	**110**	**8.2**		**89**	**39.3**	**60**	**22**	**10:00**	**2**	**0**	**0**	**0**	**0**	**0**	**0**	**0**

AHL First All-Star Team (1996) • Won Jack A. Butterfield Trophy (Playoff MVP - AHL) (1999)

Claimed on waivers by **Pittsburgh** from **NY Rangers**, October 1, 1997. Claimed on waivers by **NY Rangers** from **Pittsburgh**, January 9, 1998. Signed as a free agent by **Boston**, August 5, 1998. Claimed by **Atlanta** from **Boston** in Expansion Draft, June 25, 1999. Traded to **Boston** by **Atlanta** for Randy Robitaille, June 25, 1999.

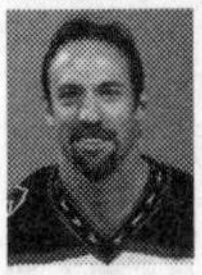

FERRARO, Ray

(fuh-RAHR-oh, RAY) **ATL.**

Center. Shoots left. 5'9", 200 lbs. Born, Trail, B.C., August 23, 1964. Hartford's 5th choice, 88th overall, in 1982 Entry Draft.

Season	Club	League	GP	G	A	Pts	PIM	PP	SH	GW	S	%	+/-	TF	F%	H	SB	Min	GP	G	A	Pts	PIM	PP	SH	GW
1981-82	Penticton	BCJHL	40	65	67	132	90	....	....	....	....	....	....	....	....	....	....	....	....	....	....	....	....	....	....	....
1982-83	Portland	WHL	50	41	49	90	39	....	....	....	....	....	....	....	....	....	....	....	14	14	10	24	13	....	....	....
1983-84	Brandon	WHL	72	*108	84	*192	84	....	....	....	....	....	....	....	....	....	....	....	11	13	15	28	20	....	....	....
1984-85	**Hartford**	**NHL**	**44**	**11**	**17**	**28**	**40**	**6**	**0**	**2**	**59**	**18.6**	**–1**	....	....	....	....	....	....	....	....	....	....	....	....	....
	Binghamton	AHL	37	20	13	33	29	....	....	....	....	....	....	....	....	....	....	....	....	....	....	....	....	....	....	....
1985-86	**Hartford**	**NHL**	**76**	**30**	**47**	**77**	**57**	**14**	**0**	**0**	**132**	**22.7**	**10**	....	....	....	....	....	**10**	**3**	**6**	**9**	**4**	**3**	**0**	**0**
1986-87	**Hartford**	**NHL**	**80**	**27**	**32**	**59**	**42**	**14**	**0**	**2**	**96**	**28.1**	**–9**	....	....	....	....	....	**6**	**1**	**1**	**2**	**8**	**0**	**0**	**0**
1987-88	**Hartford**	**NHL**	**68**	**21**	**29**	**50**	**81**	**6**	**0**	**2**	**105**	**20.0**	**1**	....	....	....	....	....	**6**	**1**	**1**	**2**	**6**	**1**	**0**	**0**
1988-89	**Hartford**	**NHL**	**80**	**41**	**35**	**76**	**86**	**11**	**0**	**7**	**169**	**24.3**	**1**	....	....	....	....	....	**4**	**2**	**0**	**2**	**4**	**0**	**0**	**0**
1989-90	**Hartford**	**NHL**	**79**	**25**	**29**	**54**	**109**	**7**	**0**	**4**	**138**	**18.1**	**–15**	....	....	....	....	....	**7**	**0**	**3**	**3**	**2**	**0**	**0**	**0**
1990-91	**Hartford**	**NHL**	**15**	**2**	**5**	**7**	**18**	**1**	**0**	**0**	**18**	**11.1**	**–1**	....	....	....	....	....	....	....	....	....	....	....	....	....
	NY Islanders	**NHL**	**61**	**19**	**16**	**35**	**52**	**5**	**0**	**1**	**91**	**20.9**	**–11**	....	....	....	....	....	....	....	....	....	....	....	....	....
1991-92	**NY Islanders**	**NHL**	**80**	**40**	**40**	**80**	**92**	**7**	**0**	**4**	**154**	**26.0**	**25**	....	....	....	....	....	....	....	....	....	....	....	....	....
1992-93	**NY Islanders**	**NHL**	**46**	**14**	**13**	**27**	**40**	**3**	**0**	**1**	**72**	**19.4**	**0**	....	....	....	....	....	**18**	**13**	**7**	**20**	**18**	**0**	**0**	**0**
	Capital District	AHL	1	0	2	2	2	....	....	....	....	....	....	....	....	....	....	....	....	....	....	....	....	....	....	....
1993-94	**NY Islanders**	**NHL**	**82**	**21**	**32**	**53**	**83**	**5**	**0**	**3**	**136**	**15.4**	**1**	....	....	....	....	....	**4**	**1**	**0**	**1**	**6**	**0**	**0**	**0**
1994-95	**NY Islanders**	**NHL**	**47**	**22**	**21**	**43**	**30**	**2**	**0**	**1**	**94**	**23.4**	**1**	....	....	....	....	....	....	....	....	....	....	....	....	....
1995-96	**NY Rangers**	**NHL**	**65**	**25**	**29**	**54**	**82**	**8**	**0**	**4**	**160**	**15.6**	**13**	....	....	....	....	....	....	....	....	....	....	....	....	....
	Los Angeles	**NHL**	**11**	**4**	**2**	**6**	**10**	**1**	**0**	**0**	**18**	**22.2**	**–13**	....	....	....	....	....	....	....	....	....	....	....	....	....
1996-97	**Los Angeles**	**NHL**	**81**	**25**	**21**	**46**	**112**	**11**	**0**	**2**	**152**	**16.4**	**–22**	....	....	....	....	....	....	....	....	....	....	....	....	....

			Regular Season																Playoffs							
Season	Club	League	GP	G	A	Pts	PIM	PP	SH	GW	S	%	+/-	TF	F%	H	SB	Min	GP	G	A	Pts	PIM	PP	SH	GW
1997-98	**Los Angeles**	**NHL**	**40**	**6**	**9**	**15**	**42**	**0**	**0**	**2**	**45**	**13.3**	**–10**						**3**	**0**	**1**	**1**	**2**	**0**	**0**	**0**
1998-99	**Los Angeles**	**NHL**	**65**	**13**	**18**	**31**	**59**	**4**	**0**	**4**	**84**	**15.5**	**0**	**979**	**47.8**	**58**	**24**	**14:34**								
99-2000	**Atlanta**	**NHL**	**81**	**19**	**25**	**44**	**88**	**10**	**0**	**3**	**170**	**11.2**	**–33**	**1390**	**51.2**	**111**	**26**	**16:10**								
	NHL Totals		**1101**	**365**	**420**	**785**	**1123**	**115**	**0**	**42**	**1893**	**19.3**		**2369**	**49.8**	**169**	**50**	**15:27**	**58**	**21**	**19**	**40**	**50**	**4**	**0**	**0**

WHL First All-Star Team (1984) • Played in NHL All-Star Game (1992)

Traded to **NY Islanders** by **Hartford** for Doug Crossman, November 13, 1990. Signed as a free agent by **NY Rangers**, August 9, 1995. Traded to **LA Kings** by **NY Rangers** with Ian Laperriere, Mattias Norstrom, Nathan Lafayette and NY Rangers' 4th round choice (Sean Blanchard) in 1997 Entry Draft for Marty McSorley, Jari Kurri and Shane Churla, March 14, 1996. Signed as a free agent by **Atlanta**, August 9, 1999.

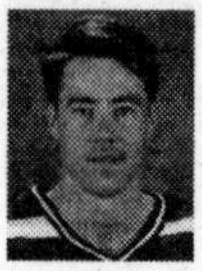

FINLEY, Jeff

(FIHN-lee, JEHF) **ST.L.**

Defense. Shoots left. 6'2", 205 lbs. Born, Edmonton, Alta., April 14, 1967. NY Islanders' 4th choice, 55th overall, in 1985 Entry Draft.

Season	Club	League	GP	G	A	Pts	PIM	PP	SH	GW	S	%	+/-	TF	F%	H	SB	Min	GP	G	A	Pts	PIM	PP	SH	GW
1983-84	Summerland	BCJHL	49	0	21	21	14																			
	Portland	WHL	5	0	0	0	5												5	0	1	1	4			
1984-85	Portland	WHL	69	6	44	50	57												6	1	2	3	2			
1985-86	Portland	WHL	70	11	59	70	83												15	1	7	8	16			
1986-87	Portland	WHL	72	13	53	66	113												20	1	*21	22	27			
1987-88	**NY Islanders**	**NHL**	**10**	**0**	**5**	**5**	**15**	**0**	**0**	**0**	**9**	**0.0**	**5**						**1**	**0**	**0**	**0**	**2**	**0**	**0**	**0**
	Springfield	AHL	52	5	18	23	50																			
1988-89	**NY Islanders**	**NHL**	**4**	**0**	**0**	**0**	**6**	**0**	**0**	**0**	**1**	**0.0**	**1**													
	Springfield	AHL	65	3	16	19	55																			
1989-90	**NY Islanders**	**NHL**	**11**	**0**	**1**	**1**	**0**	**0**	**0**	**0**	**7**	**0.0**	**0**						**5**	**0**	**2**	**2**	**2**	**0**	**0**	**0**
	Springfield	AHL	57	1	15	16	41												13	1	4	5	23			
1990-91	**NY Islanders**	**NHL**	**11**	**0**	**0**	**0**	**4**	**0**	**0**	**0**	**0**	**0.0**	**–1**													
	Capital District	AHL	67	10	34	44	34																			
1991-92	**NY Islanders**	**NHL**	**51**	**1**	**10**	**11**	**26**	**0**	**0**	**0**	**25**	**4.0**	**–6**													
	Capital District	AHL	20	1	9	10	6																			
1992-93	Capital District	AHL	61	6	29	35	34												4	0	1	1	0			
1993-94	**Philadelphia**	**NHL**	**55**	**1**	**8**	**9**	**24**	**0**	**0**	**0**	**43**	**2.3**	**16**													
1994-95	Hershey Bears	AHL	36	2	9	11	33												6	0	1	1	8			
1995-96	**Winnipeg**	**NHL**	**65**	**1**	**5**	**6**	**81**	**0**	**0**	**0**	**27**	**3.7**	**–2**						**6**	**0**	**0**	**0**	**4**	**0**	**0**	**0**
	Springfield	AHL	14	3	12	15	22																			
1996-97	**Phoenix**	**NHL**	**65**	**3**	**7**	**10**	**40**	**1**	**0**	**1**	**38**	**7.9**	**–8**						**1**	**0**	**0**	**0**	**2**	**0**	**0**	**0**
1997-98	**NY Rangers**	**NHL**	**63**	**1**	**6**	**7**	**55**	**0**	**0**	**0**	**32**	**3.1**	**–3**													
1998-99	**NY Rangers**	**NHL**	**2**	**0**	**0**	**0**	**0**	**0**	**0**	**0**	**0**	**0.0**	**–1**	**0**	**0.0**	**2**	**2**	**11:40**								
	Hartford	AHL	42	2	10	12	28																			
	St. Louis	**NHL**	**30**	**1**	**2**	**3**	**20**	**0**	**0**	**0**	**16**	**6.3**	**12**	**0**	**0.0**	**35**	**28**	**17:36**	**13**	**1**	**2**	**3**	**8**	**0**	**0**	**1**
99-2000	**St. Louis**	**NHL**	**74**	**2**	**8**	**10**	**38**	**0**	**0**	**2**	**31**	**6.5**	**26**	**1**	**100.0**	**121**	**67**	**17:49**	**7**	**0**	**2**	**2**	**4**	**0**	**0**	**0**
	NHL Totals		**441**	**10**	**52**	**62**	**309**	**1**	**0**	**3**	**229**	**4.4**		**1**	**100.0**	**158**	**97**	**17:38**	**33**	**1**	**6**	**7**	**22**	**0**	**0**	**1**

Rights traded to **Ottawa** by **NY Islanders** for Chris Luongo, June 30, 1993. Signed as a free agent by **Philadelphia**, July 30, 1993. Traded to **Winnipeg** by **Philadelphia** for Russ Romaniuk, June 27, 1995. Transferred to **Phoenix** after **Winnipeg** franchise relocated, July 1, 1996. Signed as a free agent by **NY Rangers**, August 18, 1997. Traded to **St. Louis** by **NY Rangers** with Geoff Smith for future considerations (Chris Kenady, February 22, 1999), February 13, 1999.

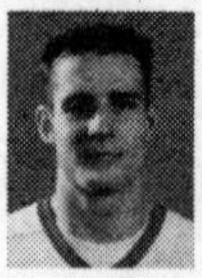

FISCHER, Jiri

(FIHSH-uhr, YIH-ree) **DET.**

Defense. Shoots left. 6'5", 225 lbs. Born, Horovice, Czech., July 31, 1980. Detroit's 1st choice, 25th overall, in 1998 Entry Draft.

Season	Club	League	GP	G	A	Pts	PIM	PP	SH	GW	S	%	+/-	TF	F%	H	SB	Min	GP	G	A	Pts	PIM	PP	SH	GW
1995-96	Poldi Kladno-Jr.	Cze-Rep	39	6	10	16																				
1996-97	Poldi Kladno-Jr.	Cze-Rep	38	7	21	28																				
1997-98	Hull Olympiques	QMJHL	70	3	19	22	112												11	1	4	5	16			
1998-99	Hull Olympiques	QMJHL	65	22	56	78	141												23	6	17	23	44			
99-2000	**Detroit**	**NHL**	**52**	**0**	**8**	**8**	**45**	**0**	**0**	**0**	**41**	**0.0**	**1**	**0**	**0.0**	**68**	**25**	**10:51**								
	Cincinnati Ducks	AHL	7	0	2	2	10																			
	NHL Totals		**52**	**0**	**8**	**8**	**45**	**0**	**0**	**0**	**41**	**0.0**		**0**	**0.0**	**68**	**25**	**10:51**								

QMJHL First All-Star Team (1999)

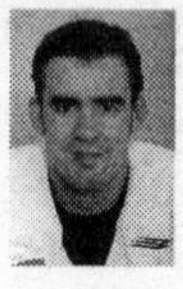

FISHER, Craig

(fih-SHUHR, KRAYG) **BUF.**

Center. Shoots left. 6'3", 180 lbs. Born, Oshawa, Ont., June 30, 1970. Philadelphia's 3rd choice, 56th overall, in 1988 Entry Draft.

Season	Club	League	GP	G	A	Pts	PIM	PP	SH	GW	S	%	+/-	TF	F%	H	SB	Min	GP	G	A	Pts	PIM	PP	SH	GW
1986-87	Oshawa Legion	OJHL-B	34	22	26	48	18																			
1987-88	Oshawa Legion	OJHL-B	36	42	34	76	48																			
1988-89	U. of Miami-Ohio	CCHA	37	22	20	42	37																			
1989-90	U. of Miami-Ohio	CCHA	39	37	29	66	38																			
	Philadelphia	**NHL**	**2**	**0**	**0**	**0**	**0**	**0**	**0**	**0**	**5**	**0.0**	**0**													
1990-91	**Philadelphia**	**NHL**	**2**	**0**	**0**	**0**	**0**	**0**	**0**	**0**	**2**	**0.0**	**0**													
	Hershey Bears	AHL	77	43	36	79	46												7	5	3	8	2			
1991-92	Cape Breton	AHL	60	20	25	45	28												1	0	0	0	0			
1992-93	Cape Breton	AHL	75	32	29	61	74												1	0	0	0	2			
1993-94	Cape Breton	AHL	16	5	5	10	11																			
	Winnipeg	**NHL**	**4**	**0**	**0**	**0**	**2**	**0**	**0**	**0**	**5**	**0.0**	**–1**													
	Moncton Hawks	AHL	46	26	35	61	36												21	11	11	22	28			
1994-95	Indianapolis Ice	IHL	77	53	40	93	65																			
1995-96	Orlando	IHL	82	*74	56	130	81												14	10	7	17	6			
1996-97	Utah Grizzlies	IHL	15	6	7	13	4																			
	Florida	**NHL**	**4**	**0**	**0**	**0**	**0**	**0**	**0**	**0**	**2**	**0.0**	**–2**													
	Carolina	AHL	42	33	29	62	16																			
1997-98	Kolner Haie	DEL	34	9	8	17	34																			
	Kolner Haie	EuroHL	4	0	0	0	4																			
1998-99	Rochester	AHL	70	29	52	81	28												20	9	11	20	10			
99-2000	Rochester	AHL	17	15	8	23	8																			
	NHL Totals		**12**	**0**	**0**	**0**	**2**	**0**	**0**	**0**	**14**	**0.0**														

CCHA First All-Star Team (1990) • IHL First All-Star Team (1996)

Traded to **Edmonton** by **Philadelphia** with Scott Mellanby and Craig Berube for Dave Brown, Corey Foster and Jari Kurri, May 30, 1991. Traded to **Winnipeg** by **Edmonton** for cash, December 9, 1993. Signed as a free agent by **Chicago**, June 9, 1994. Signed as a free agent by **NY Islanders**, July 29, 1996. Traded to **Florida** by **NY Islanders** for cash, December 7, 1996. Signed as a free agent by **Buffalo**, August 31, 1998. • Missed remainder of 1999-2000 season recovering from head injury suffered in game vs. Wilkes-Barre (AHL), November 12, 1999.

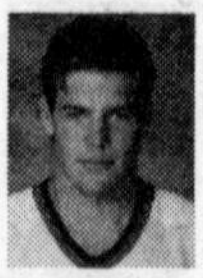

FISHER, Mike

(FIH-suhr, MIGHK) **OTT.**

Center. Shoots right. 6'1", 193 lbs. Born, Peterborough, Ont., June 5, 1980. Ottawa's 2nd choice, 44th overall, in 1998 Entry Draft.

Season	Club	League	GP	G	A	Pts	PIM	PP	SH	GW	S	%	+/-	TF	F%	H	SB	Min	GP	G	A	Pts	PIM	PP	SH	GW
1996-97	Peterborough B's	OJHL	51	26	30	56	35																			
1997-98	Sudbury Wolves	OHL	66	24	25	49	65												9	2	2	4	13			
1998-99	Sudbury Wolves	OHL	68	41	65	106	55												4	2	1	3	4			
99-2000	**Ottawa**	**NHL**	**32**	**4**	**5**	**9**	**15**	**0**	**0**	**1**	**49**	**8.2**	**–6**	**356**	**47.8**	**76**	**13**	**12:57**								
	NHL Totals		**32**	**4**	**5**	**9**	**15**	**0**	**0**	**1**	**49**	**8.2**		**356**	**47.8**	**76**	**13**	**12:57**								

• Missed remainder of 1999-2000 season recovering from knee injury suffered in game vs. Boston, December 30, 1999.

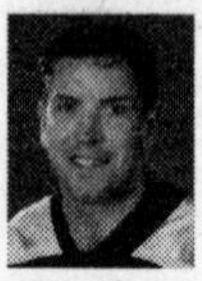

FITZGERALD, Tom

(FIHTZ-jer-awld, TAWM) **NSH.**

Right wing/Center. Shoots right. 6', 195 lbs. Born, Billerica, MA, August 28, 1968. NY Islanders' 1st choice, 17th overall, in 1986 Entry Draft.

Season	Club	League	GP	G	A	Pts	PIM	PP	SH	GW	S	%	+/-	TF	F%	H	SB	Min	GP	G	A	Pts	PIM	PP	SH	GW
1984-85	Austin Prep	Hi-School	18	20	21	41																				
1985-86	Austin Prep	Hi-School	24	35	38	73																				
1986-87	Providence	H-East	27	8	14	22	22																			
1987-88	Providence	H-East	36	19	15	34	50																			
1988-89	**NY Islanders**	**NHL**	**23**	**3**	**5**	**8**	**10**	**0**	**0**	**1**	**24**	**12.5**	**1**													
	Springfield	AHL	61	24	18	42	43																			

											Regular Season											Playoffs				
Season	Club	League	GP	G	A	Pts	PIM	PP	SH	GW	S	%	+/-	TF	F%	H	SB	Min	GP	G	A	Pts	PIM	PP	SH	GW
1989-90	**NY Islanders**	**NHL**	**19**	**2**	**5**	**7**	**4**	**0**	**0**	**1**	**24**	**8.3**	**–3**	....	....	....	....	....	**4**	**1**	**0**	**1**	**4**	**0**	**0**	**0**
	Springfield	AHL	53	30	23	53	32	....	....	....	....	....	....	....	....	....	....	....	14	2	9	11	13	....	....	....
1990-91	**NY Islanders**	**NHL**	**41**	**5**	**5**	**10**	**24**	**0**	**0**	**2**	**60**	**8.3**	**–9**	....	....	....	....	....	....	....	....	....	....	....	....	....
	Capital District	AHL	27	7	7	14	50	....	....	....	....	....	....	....	....	....	....	....	....	....	....	....	....	....	....	....
1991-92	**NY Islanders**	**NHL**	**45**	**6**	**11**	**17**	**28**	**0**	**2**	**2**	**71**	**8.5**	**–3**	....	....	....	....	....	....	....	....	....	....	....	....	....
	Capital District	AHL	4	1	1	2	4	....	....	....	....	....	....	....	....	....	....	....	....	....	....	....	....	....	....	....
1992-93	**NY Islanders**	**NHL**	**77**	**9**	**18**	**27**	**34**	**0**	**3**	**1**	**83**	**10.8**	**–2**	....	....	....	....	....	**18**	**2**	**5**	**7**	**18**	**0**	**0**	**0**
1993-94	**Florida**	**NHL**	**83**	**18**	**14**	**32**	**54**	**0**	**3**	**1**	**144**	**12.5**	**–3**	....	....	....	....	....	....	....	....	....	....	....	....	....
1994-95	**Florida**	**NHL**	**48**	**3**	**13**	**16**	**31**	**0**	**0**	**0**	**78**	**3.8**	**–3**	....	....	....	....	....	....	....	....	....	....	....	....	....
1995-96	**Florida**	**NHL**	**82**	**13**	**21**	**34**	**75**	**1**	**6**	**2**	**141**	**9.2**	**–3**	....	....	....	....	....	**22**	**4**	**4**	**8**	**34**	**0**	**0**	**2**
1996-97	**Florida**	**NHL**	**71**	**10**	**14**	**24**	**64**	**0**	**2**	**1**	**135**	**7.4**	**7**	....	....	....	....	....	**5**	**0**	**1**	**1**	**0**	**0**	**0**	**0**
1997-98	**Florida**	**NHL**	**69**	**10**	**5**	**15**	**57**	**0**	**1**	**1**	**105**	**9.5**	**–4**	....	....	....	....	....	....	....	....	....	....	....	....	....
	Colorado	**NHL**	**11**	**2**	**1**	**3**	**22**	**0**	**1**	**0**	**14**	**14.3**	**0**	....	....	....	....	....	**7**	**0**	**1**	**1**	**20**	**0**	**0**	**0**
1998-99	**Nashville**	**NHL**	**80**	**13**	**19**	**32**	**48**	**0**	**0**	**1**	**180**	**7.2**	**–18**	**155**	**52.3**	**70**	**49**	**17:17**	....	....	....	....	....	....	....	....
99-2000	**Nashville**	**NHL**	**82**	**13**	**9**	**22**	**66**	**0**	**3**	**1**	**119**	**10.9**	**–18**	**264**	**51.9**	**75**	**43**	**13:57**	....	....	....	....	....	....	....	....
	NHL Totals		**731**	**107**	**140**	**247**	**517**	**1**	**21**	**14**	**1178**	**9.1**		**419**	**52.0**	**145**	**92**	**15:36**	**56**	**7**	**11**	**18**	**76**	**0**	**0**	**2**

Claimed by **Florida** from **NY Islanders** in Expansion Draft, June 24, 1993. Traded to **Colorado** by **Florida** for the rights to Mark Parrish and Anaheim's 3rd round choice (previously acquired, Florida selected Lance Ward) in 1998 Entry Draft, March 24, 1998. Signed as a free agent by **Nashville**, July 6, 1998.

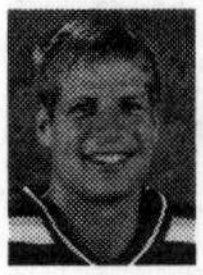

FITZPATRICK, Rory

(FITZ-pa-TRIHK, ROHR-ee) **NSH.**

Defense. Shoots right. 6'2", 208 lbs. Born, Rochester, NY, January 11, 1975. Montreal's 2nd choice, 47th overall, in 1993 Entry Draft.

1990-91	Rochester	USHL-B	40	0	5	5	....	....	....	....	....	....	....	....	....	....	....	....	....	....	....	....	....	....	....	....
1991-92	Rochester	USHL	28	8	28	36	141	....	....	....	....	....	....	....	....	....	....	....	....	....	....	....	....	....	....	....
1992-93	Sudbury Wolves	OHL	58	4	20	24	68	....	....	....	....	....	....	....	....	....	....	....	14	0	0	0	17	....	....	....
1993-94	Sudbury Wolves	OHL	65	12	34	46	112	....	....	....	....	....	....	....	....	....	....	....	10	2	5	7	10	....	....	....
1994-95	Sudbury Wolves	OHL	56	12	36	48	72	....	....	....	....	....	....	....	....	....	....	....	18	3	15	18	21	....	....	....
	Fredericton	AHL	....	....	....	....	....	....	....	....	....	....	....	....	....	....	....	....	10	1	2	3	5	....	....	....
1995-96	**Montreal**	**NHL**	**42**	**0**	**2**	**2**	**18**	**0**	**0**	**0**	**31**	**0.0**	**–7**	....	....	....	....	....	**6**	**1**	**1**	**2**	**0**	**0**	**0**	**0**
	Fredericton	AHL	18	4	6	10	36	....	....	....	....	....	....	....	....	....	....	....	....	....	....	....	....	....	....	....
1996-97	**Montreal**	**NHL**	**6**	**0**	**1**	**1**	**6**	**0**	**0**	**0**	**5**	**0.0**	**–2**	....	....	....	....	....	....	....	....	....	....	....	....	....
	St. Louis	**NHL**	**2**	**0**	**0**	**0**	**2**	**0**	**0**	**0**	**1**	**0.0**	**–2**	....	....	....	....	....	....	....	....	....	....	....	....	....
	Worcester	AHL	49	4	13	17	78	....	....	....	....	....	....	....	....	....	....	....	5	1	2	3	0	....	....	....
1997-98	Worcester	AHL	62	8	22	30	111	....	....	....	....	....	....	....	....	....	....	....	11	0	3	3	26	....	....	....
1998-99	**St. Louis**	**NHL**	**1**	**0**	**0**	**0**	**2**	**0**	**0**	**0**	**0**	**0.0**	**–3**	**0**	**0.0**	**0**	**0**	**4:49**	....	....	....	....	....	....	....	....
	Worcester	AHL	53	5	16	21	82	....	....	....	....	....	....	....	....	....	....	....	4	0	1	1	17	....	....	....
99-2000	Worcester	AHL	28	0	5	5	48	....	....	....	....	....	....	....	....	....	....	....	....	....	....	....	....	....	....	....
	Milwaukee	IHL	27	2	1	3	27	....	....	....	....	....	....	....	....	....	....	....	3	0	2	2	2	....	....	....
	NHL Totals		**51**	**0**	**3**	**3**	**28**	**0**	**0**	**0**	**37**	**0.0**		**0**	**0.0**	**0**	**0**	**4:49**	**6**	**1**	**1**	**2**	**0**	**0**	**0**	**0**

Traded to **St. Louis** by **Montreal** with Pierre Turgeon and Craig Conroy for Murray Baron, Shayne Corson and St. Louis' 5th round choice (Gennady Razin) in 1997 Entry Draft, October 29, 1996. Claimed by **Boston** from **St. Louis** in NHL Waiver Draft, October 5, 1998. Claimed on waivers by **St. Louis** from **Boston**, October 7, 1998. Traded to **Nashville** by **St. Louis** for Dan Keczmer, February 9, 2000.

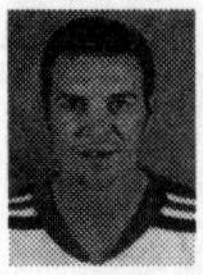

FLEURY, Theoren

(FLUH-ree, THAIR-ihn) **NYR**

Right wing. Shoots right. 5'6", 180 lbs. Born, Oxbow, Sask., June 29, 1968. Calgary's 9th choice, 166th overall, in 1987 Entry Draft.

1983-84	St. James	MAHA	22	33	31	64	88	....	....	....	....	....	....	....	....	....	....	....	....	....	....	....	....	....	....	....
1984-85	Moose Jaw	WHL	71	29	46	75	82	....	....	....	....	....	....	....	....	....	....	....	....	....	....	....	....	....	....	....
1985-86	Moose Jaw	WHL	72	43	65	108	124	....	....	....	....	....	....	....	....	....	....	....	13	7	13	20	16	....	....	....
1986-87	Moose Jaw	WHL	66	61	68	129	110	....	....	....	....	....	....	....	....	....	....	....	9	7	9	16	34	....	....	....
1987-88	Moose Jaw	WHL	65	68	92	*160	235	....	....	....	....	....	....	....	....	....	....	....	....	....	....	....	....	....	....	....
	Salt Lake	IHL	2	3	4	7	7	....	....	....	....	....	....	....	....	....	....	....	8	11	5	16	16	....	....	....
1988-89♦	**Calgary**	**NHL**	**36**	**14**	**20**	**34**	**46**	**5**	**0**	**3**	**89**	**15.7**	**5**	....	....	....	....	....	**22**	**5**	**6**	**11**	**24**	**3**	**0**	**3**
	Salt Lake	IHL	40	37	37	74	81	....	....	....	....	....	....	....	....	....	....	....	....	....	....	....	....	....	....	....
1989-90	**Calgary**	**NHL**	**80**	**31**	**35**	**66**	**157**	**9**	**3**	**6**	**200**	**15.5**	**22**	....	....	....	....	....	**6**	**2**	**3**	**5**	**10**	**0**	**0**	**0**
1990-91	**Calgary**	**NHL**	**79**	**51**	**53**	**104**	**136**	**9**	**7**	**9**	**249**	**20.5**	**48**	....	....	....	....	....	**7**	**2**	**5**	**7**	**14**	**0**	**0**	**1**
1991-92	**Calgary**	**NHL**	**80**	**33**	**40**	**73**	**133**	**11**	**1**	**6**	**225**	**14.7**	**0**	....	....	....	....	....	....	....	....	....	....	....	....	....
1992-93	**Calgary**	**NHL**	**83**	**34**	**66**	**100**	**88**	**12**	**2**	**4**	**250**	**13.6**	**14**	....	....	....	....	....	**6**	**5**	**7**	**12**	**27**	**3**	**1**	**0**
1993-94	**Calgary**	**NHL**	**83**	**40**	**45**	**85**	**186**	**16**	**1**	**6**	**278**	**14.4**	**30**	....	....	....	....	....	**7**	**6**	**4**	**10**	**5**	**1**	**0**	**2**
1994-95	Tappara Tampere	Finland	10	8	9	17	22	....	....	....	....	....	....	....	....	....	....	....	....	....	....	....	....	....	....	....
	Calgary	**NHL**	**47**	**29**	**29**	**58**	**112**	**9**	**2**	**5**	**173**	**16.8**	**6**	....	....	....	....	....	**7**	**7**	**7**	**14**	**2**	**2**	**1**	**0**
1995-96	**Calgary**	**NHL**	**80**	**46**	**50**	**96**	**112**	**17**	**5**	**4**	**353**	**13.0**	**17**	....	....	....	....	....	**4**	**2**	**1**	**3**	**14**	**0**	**0**	**0**
1996-97	**Calgary**	**NHL**	**81**	**29**	**38**	**67**	**104**	**9**	**2**	**3**	**336**	**8.6**	**–12**	....	....	....	....	....	....	....	....	....	....	....	....	....
1997-98	**Calgary**	**NHL**	**82**	**27**	**51**	**78**	**197**	**3**	**2**	**4**	**282**	**9.6**	**0**	....	....	....	....	....	....	....	....	....	....	....	....	....
	Canada	Olympics	6	1	3	4	2	....	....	....	....	....	....	....	....	....	....	....	....	....	....	....	....	....	....	....
1998-99	**Calgary**	**NHL**	**60**	**30**	**39**	**69**	**68**	**7**	**3**	**3**	**250**	**12.0**	**18**	**517**	**59.2**	**51**	**25**	**23:33**	....	....	....	....	....	....	....	....
	Colorado	**NHL**	**15**	**10**	**14**	**24**	**18**	**1**	**0**	**2**	**51**	**19.6**	**8**	**150**	**58.7**	**12**	**3**	**22:33**	**18**	**5**	**12**	**17**	**20**	**2**	**0**	**0**
99-2000	**NY Rangers**	**NHL**	**80**	**15**	**49**	**64**	**68**	**1**	**0**	**1**	**246**	**6.1**	**–4**	**490**	**56.5**	**69**	**31**	**19:41**	....	....	....	....	....	....	....	....
	NHL Totals		**886**	**389**	**529**	**918**	**1425**	**109**	**28**	**56**	**2982**	**13.0**		**1157**	**58.0**	**132**	**59**	**21:27**	**77**	**34**	**45**	**79**	**116**	**11**	**2**	**6**

WHL East Second All-Star Team (1988) • Co-winner of Alka-Seltzer Plus Award with Marty McSorley (1991) • NHL Second All-Star Team (1995) • Played in NHL All-Star Game (1991, 1992, 1996, 1997, 1998, 1999)

Traded to **Colorado** by **Calgary** with Chris Dingman for Rene Corbet, Wade Belak, Robyn Regehr and Colorado's 2nd round compensatory choice (Jarret Stoll) in 2000 Entry Draft, February 28, 1999. Signed as a free agent by **NY Rangers**, July 8, 1999.

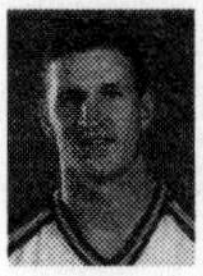

FOOTE, Adam

(FUT, A-dam) **COL.**

Defense. Shoots right. 6'1", 205 lbs. Born, Toronto, Ont., July 10, 1971. Quebec's 2nd choice, 22nd overall, in 1989 Entry Draft.

1987-88	Brooklin Whitby	OMHA	65	25	43	68	108	....	....	....	....	....	....	....	....	....	....	....	....	....	....	....	....	....	....	....
1988-89	Sault Ste. Marie	OHL	66	7	32	39	120	....	....	....	....	....	....	....	....	....	....	....	....	....	....	....	....	....	....	....
1989-90	Sault Ste. Marie	OHL	61	12	43	55	199	....	....	....	....	....	....	....	....	....	....	....	....	....	....	....	....	....	....	....
	Canada	Nat-Team	3	1	0	1	0	....	....	....	....	....	....	....	....	....	....	....	....	....	....	....	....	....	....	....
1990-91	Sault Ste. Marie	OHL	59	18	51	69	93	....	....	....	....	....	....	....	....	....	....	....	14	5	12	17	28	....	....	....
1991-92	**Quebec**	**NHL**	**46**	**2**	**5**	**7**	**44**	**0**	**0**	**0**	**55**	**3.6**	**–4**	....	....	....	....	....	....	....	....	....	....	....	....	....
	Halifax Citadels	AHL	6	0	1	1	2	....	....	....	....	....	....	....	....	....	....	....	....	....	....	....	....	....	....	....
1992-93	**Quebec**	**NHL**	**81**	**4**	**12**	**16**	**168**	**0**	**1**	**0**	**54**	**7.4**	**6**	....	....	....	....	....	**6**	**0**	**1**	**1**	**2**	**0**	**0**	**0**
1993-94	**Quebec**	**NHL**	**45**	**2**	**6**	**8**	**67**	**0**	**0**	**0**	**42**	**4.8**	**3**	....	....	....	....	....	....	....	....	....	....	....	....	....
1994-95	**Quebec**	**NHL**	**35**	**0**	**7**	**7**	**52**	**0**	**0**	**0**	**24**	**0.0**	**17**	....	....	....	....	....	**6**	**0**	**1**	**1**	**14**	**0**	**0**	**0**
1995-96♦	**Colorado**	**NHL**	**73**	**5**	**11**	**16**	**88**	**1**	**0**	**1**	**49**	**10.2**	**27**	....	....	....	....	....	**22**	**1**	**3**	**4**	**36**	**0**	**0**	**0**
1996-97	**Colorado**	**NHL**	**78**	**2**	**19**	**21**	**135**	**0**	**0**	**0**	**60**	**3.3**	**16**	....	....	....	....	....	**17**	**0**	**4**	**4**	**62**	**0**	**0**	**0**
1997-98	**Colorado**	**NHL**	**77**	**3**	**14**	**17**	**124**	**0**	**0**	**1**	**64**	**4.7**	**–3**	....	....	....	....	....	**7**	**0**	**0**	**0**	**23**	**0**	**0**	**0**
	Canada	Olympics	6	0	1	1	4	....	....	....	....	....	....	....	....	....	....	....	....	....	....	....	....	....	....	....
1998-99	**Colorado**	**NHL**	**64**	**5**	**16**	**21**	**92**	**3**	**0**	**0**	**83**	**6.0**	**20**	**0**	**0.0**	**125**	**93**	**24:50**	**19**	**2**	**3**	**5**	**24**	**1**	**0**	**0**
99-2000	**Colorado**	**NHL**	**59**	**5**	**13**	**18**	**98**	**1**	**0**	**2**	**63**	**7.9**	**5**	**0**	**0.0**	**156**	**87**	**25:51**	**16**	**0**	**7**	**7**	**28**	**0**	**0**	**0**
	NHL Totals		**558**	**28**	**103**	**131**	**868**	**5**	**1**	**4**	**494**	**5.7**		**0**	**0.0**	**281**	**180**	**25:19**	**93**	**3**	**19**	**22**	**189**	**1**	**0**	**0**

OHL First All-Star Team (1991)

Transferred to **Colorado** after **Quebec** franchise relocated, June 21, 1995.

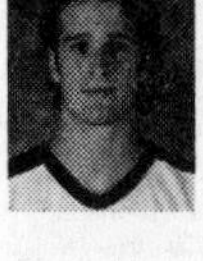

FORBES, Colin

(FOHRBS, COHL-ihn) **OTT.**

Left wing. Shoots left. 6'3", 205 lbs. Born, New Westminster, B.C., February 16, 1976. Philadelphia's 5th choice, 166th overall, in 1994 Entry Draft.

1993-94	Sherwood Park	AJHL	47	18	22	40	76	....	....	....	....	....	....	....	....	....	....	....	....	....	....	....	....	....	....	....
1994-95	Portland	WHL	72	24	31	55	108	....	....	....	....	....	....	....	....	....	....	....	9	1	3	4	10	....	....	....
1995-96	Portland	WHL	72	33	44	77	137	....	....	....	....	....	....	....	....	....	....	....	7	2	5	7	14	....	....	....
	Hershey Bears	AHL	2	1	0	1	2	....	....	....	....	....	....	....	....	....	....	....	4	0	2	2	2	....	....	....
1996-97	**Philadelphia**	**NHL**	**3**	**1**	**0**	**1**	**0**	**0**	**0**	**0**	**3**	**33.3**	**0**	....	....	....	....	....	**3**	**0**	**0**	**0**	**0**	**0**	**0**	**0**
	Philadelphia	AHL	74	21	28	49	108	....	....	....	....	....	....	....	....	....	....	....	10	5	5	10	33	....	....	....

			Regular Season																Playoffs							
Season	Club	League	GP	G	A	Pts	PIM	PP	SH	GW	S	%	+/-	TF	F%	H	SB	Min	GP	G	A	Pts	PIM	PP	SH	GW
1997-98	Philadelphia	NHL	63	12	7	19	59	2	0	2	93	12.9	2	....	....	....	....	....	5	0	0	0	2	0	0	0
	Philadelphia	AHL	13	7	4	11	22	....	....	....	....	....	....	....	....	....	....	....	....	....	....	....	....	....	....	....
1998-99	Philadelphia	NHL	66	9	7	16	51	0	0	4	92	9.8	0	2	50.0	46	10	12:35	....	....	....	....	....	....	....	....
	Tampa Bay	NHL	14	3	1	4	10	0	1	0	25	12.0	–5	0	0.0	21	4	17:30	....	....	....	....	....	....	....	....
99-2000	Tampa Bay	NHL	8	0	0	0	18	0	0	0	3	0.0	–4	1	0.0	9	0	8:53	....	....	....	....	....	....	....	....
	Ottawa	NHL	45	2	5	7	12	0	0	0	54	3.7	–1	82	47.6	70	6	8:34	5	1	0	1	14	0	0	0
	NHL Totals		199	27	20	47	150	2	1	6	270	10.0		85	47.1	146	20	11:31	13	1	0	1	16	0	0	0

Traded to **Tampa Bay** by **Philadelphia** with Philadelphia's 4th round choice (Michal Lanisak) in 1999 Entry Draft for Mikael Andersson and Sandy McCarthy, March 20, 1999. Traded to **Ottawa** by **Tampa Bay** for Bruce Gardiner, November 11, 1999.

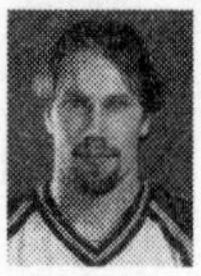

FORSBERG, Peter

(FOHRS-buhrg, PEE-tuhr) **COL.**

Center. Shoots left. 6', 190 lbs. Born, Ornskoldsvik, Sweden, July 20, 1973. Philadelphia's 1st choice, 6th overall, in 1991 Entry Draft.

Season	Club	League	GP	G	A	Pts	PIM	PP	SH	GW	S	%	+/-	TF	F%	H	SB	Min	GP	G	A	Pts	PIM	PP	SH	GW
1989-90	MoDo AIK	Swede-Jr.	30	15	12	27	42	....	....	....	....	....	....	....	....	....	....	....	....	....	....	....	....	....	....	....
	MoDo AIK	Sweden	1	0	1	1	4	....	....	....	....	....	....	....	....	....	....	....	....	....	....	....	....	....	....	....
1990-91	MoDo AIK	Swede-Jr.	39	38	64	102	56	....	....	....	....	....	....	....	....	....	....	....	....	....	....	....	....	....	....	....
	MoDo AIK	Sweden	23	7	10	17	22	....	....	....	....	....	....	....	....	....	....	....	....	....	....	....	....	....	....	....
1991-92	MoDo AIK	Sweden	39	9	18	27	78	....	....	....	....	....	....	....	....	....	....	....	....	....	....	....	....	....	....	....
1992-93	MoDo AIK	Swede-Jr.	2	0	3	3	4	....	....	....	....	....	....	....	....	....	....	....	....	....	....	....	....	....	....	....
	MoDo AIK	Sweden	39	23	24	47	92	....	....	....	....	....	....	....	....	....	....	....	3	4	1	5	0	....	....	....
1993-94	MoDo AIK	Sweden	39	18	26	44	82	....	....	....	....	....	....	....	....	....	....	....	11	9	7	16	14	....	....	....
	Sweden	Olympics	8	2	6	8	6	....	....	....	....	....	....	....	....	....	....	....	....	....	....	....	....	....	....	....
1994-95	MoDo Hockey	Sweden	11	5	9	14	20	....	....	....	....	....	....	....	....	....	....	....	....	....	....	....	....	....	....	....
	Quebec	NHL	47	15	35	50	16	3	0	3	86	17.4	17	....	....	....	....	....	6	2	4	6	4	1	0	0
1995-96♦	Colorado	NHL	82	30	86	116	47	7	3	3	217	13.8	26	....	....	....	....	....	22	10	11	21	18	3	0	1
1996-97	Colorado	NHL	65	28	58	86	73	5	4	4	188	14.9	31	....	....	....	....	....	14	5	12	17	10	3	0	0
1997-98	Colorado	NHL	72	25	66	91	94	7	3	7	202	12.4	6	....	....	....	....	....	7	6	5	11	12	2	0	0
	Sweden	Olympics	4	1	4	5	6	....	....	....	....	....	....	....	....	....	....	....	....	....	....	....	....	....	....	....
1998-99	Colorado	NHL	78	30	67	97	108	9	2	7	217	13.8	27	895	54.4	108	31	23:29	19	8	16	*24	31	1	1	0
99-2000	Colorado	NHL	49	14	37	51	52	3	0	2	105	13.3	9	519	46.6	70	19	20:55	16	7	8	15	12	2	1	4
	NHL Totals		393	142	349	491	390	34	12	26	1015	14.0		1414	51.6	178	50	22:30	84	38	56	94	87	12	2	5

NHL All-Rookie Team (1995) • Won Calder Memorial Trophy (1995) • NHL First All-Star Team (1998, 1999) • Played in NHL All-Star Game (1996, 1998, 1999)

Traded to **Quebec** by **Philadelphia** with Steve Duchesne, Kerry Huffman, Mike Ricci, Ron Hextall, Philadelphia's 1st round choice (Jocelyn Thibault) in 1993 Entry Draft, $15,000,000 and future considerations (Chris Simon and Philadelphia's 1st round choice (later traded to Toronto - later traded to Washington - Washington selected Nolan Baumgartner) in 1994 Entry Draft, July 21, 1992) for Eric Lindros, June 30, 1992. Transferred to **Colorado** after **Quebec** franchise relocated, June 21, 1995.

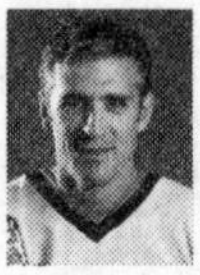

FRANCIS, Ron

(FRAN-sihs, RAWN) **CAR.**

Center. Shoots left. 6'3", 200 lbs. Born, Sault Ste. Marie, Ont., March 1, 1963. Hartford's 1st choice, 4th overall, in 1981 Entry Draft.

Season	Club	League	GP	G	A	Pts	PIM	PP	SH	GW	S	%	+/-	TF	F%	H	SB	Min	GP	G	A	Pts	PIM	PP	SH	GW
1979-80	S.S. Marie Legion	NOHA	45	57	92	149	....	....	....	....	....	....	....	....	....	....	....	....	....	....	....	....	....	....	....	....
1980-81	Sault Ste. Marie	OMJHL	64	26	43	69	33	....	....	....	....	....	....	....	....	....	....	....	19	7	8	15	34	....	....	....
1981-82	Sault Ste. Marie	OHL	25	18	30	48	46	....	....	....	....	....	....	....	....	....	....	....	....	....	....	....	....	....	....	....
	Hartford	NHL	59	25	43	68	51	12	0	1	163	15.3	–13	....	....	....	....	....	....	....	....	....	....	....	....	....
1982-83	Hartford	NHL	79	31	59	90	60	4	2	4	212	14.6	–25	....	....	....	....	....	....	....	....	....	....	....	....	....
1983-84	Hartford	NHL	72	23	60	83	45	5	0	5	202	11.4	–10	....	....	....	....	....	....	....	....	....	....	....	....	....
1984-85	Hartford	NHL	80	24	57	81	66	4	0	1	195	12.3	–23	....	....	....	....	....	....	....	....	....	....	....	....	....
1985-86	Hartford	NHL	53	24	53	77	24	7	1	4	120	20.0	8	....	....	....	....	....	10	1	2	3	4	0	0	0
1986-87	Hartford	NHL	75	30	63	93	45	7	0	7	189	15.9	10	....	....	....	....	....	6	2	2	4	6	1	0	0
1987-88	Hartford	NHL	80	25	50	75	87	11	1	3	172	14.5	–8	....	....	....	....	....	6	2	5	7	2	1	0	0
1988-89	Hartford	NHL	69	29	48	77	36	8	0	4	156	18.6	4	....	....	....	....	....	4	0	2	2	0	0	0	0
1989-90	Hartford	NHL	80	32	69	101	73	15	1	5	170	18.8	13	....	....	....	....	....	7	3	3	6	8	1	0	0
1990-91	Hartford	NHL	67	21	55	76	51	10	1	6	149	14.1	–2	....	....	....	....	....	....	....	....	....	....	....	....	....
♦	Pittsburgh	NHL	14	2	9	11	21	0	0	1	25	8.0	0	....	....	....	....	....	24	7	10	17	24	0	0	4
1991-92♦	Pittsburgh	NHL	70	21	33	54	30	5	1	2	121	17.4	–7	....	....	....	....	....	21	8	*19	27	6	2	0	2
1992-93	Pittsburgh	NHL	84	24	76	100	68	9	2	4	215	11.2	6	....	....	....	....	....	12	6	11	17	19	1	0	1
1993-94	Pittsburgh	NHL	82	27	66	93	62	8	0	2	216	12.5	–3	....	....	....	....	....	6	0	2	2	6	0	0	0
1994-95	Pittsburgh	NHL	44	11	*48	59	18	3	0	1	94	11.7	30	....	....	....	....	....	12	6	13	19	4	2	0	0
1995-96	Pittsburgh	NHL	77	27	*92	119	56	12	1	4	158	17.1	25	....	....	....	....	....	11	3	6	9	4	2	0	1
1996-97	Pittsburgh	NHL	81	27	63	90	20	10	1	2	183	14.8	7	....	....	....	....	....	5	1	2	3	2	1	0	0
1997-98	Pittsburgh	NHL	81	25	62	87	20	7	0	5	189	13.2	12	....	....	....	....	....	6	1	5	6	2	0	0	0
1998-99	Carolina	NHL	82	21	31	52	34	8	0	2	133	15.8	–2	1589	51.5	36	57	21:55	3	0	1	1	0	0	0	0
99-2000	Carolina	NHL	78	23	50	73	18	7	0	4	150	15.3	10	1566	53.3	48	53	21:58	....	....	....	....	....	....	....	....
	NHL Totals		1407	472	1087	1559	885	152	11	67	3212	14.7		3155	52.4	84	110	21:57	133	40	83	123	87	11	0	8

Won Alka-Seltzer Plus Award (1995) • Won Frank J. Selke Trophy (1995) • Won Lady Byng Trophy (1995, 1998) • Played in NHL All-Star Game (1983, 1985, 1990, 1996)

Traded to **Pittsburgh** by **Hartford** with Grant Jennings and Ulf Samuelsson for John Cullen, Jeff Parker and Zarley Zalapski, March 4, 1991. Signed as a free agent by **Carolina**, July 13, 1998.

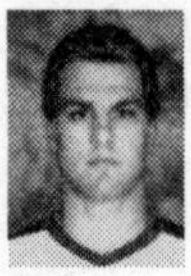

FREADRICH, Kyle

(FREE-drihk, KIGHL) **T.B.**

Left wing. Shoots left. 6'7", 260 lbs. Born, Edmonton, Alta., December 28, 1978. Vancouver's 4th choice, 64th overall, in 1997 Entry Draft.

Season	Club	League	GP	G	A	Pts	PIM	PP	SH	GW	S	%	+/-	TF	F%	H	SB	Min	GP	G	A	Pts	PIM	PP	SH	GW
1995-96	Killam Selects	AAHA	37	11	22	33	176	....	....	....	....	....	....	....	....	....	....	....	....	....	....	....	....	....	....	....
1996-97	Prince George	WHL	12	0	0	0	12	....	....	....	....	....	....	....	....	....	....	....	....	....	....	....	....	....	....	....
	Regina Pats	WHL	50	1	3	4	152	....	....	....	....	....	....	....	....	....	....	....	4	0	0	0	8	....	....	....
1997-98	Regina Pats	WHL	62	6	5	11	259	....	....	....	....	....	....	....	....	....	....	....	9	0	1	1	25	....	....	....
1998-99	Regina Pats	WHL	52	2	2	4	215	....	....	....	....	....	....	....	....	....	....	....	....	....	....	....	....	....	....	....
	Syracuse Crunch	AHL	5	0	0	0	20	....	....	....	....	....	....	....	....	....	....	....	....	....	....	....	....	....	....	....
	Louisiana	ECHL	5	0	0	0	17	....	....	....	....	....	....	....	....	....	....	....	4	0	0	0	2	....	....	....
99-2000	Tampa Bay	NHL	10	0	0	0	39	0	0	0	0	0.0	–1	0	0.0	4	1	2:19	....	....	....	....	....	....	....	....
	Louisiana	ECHL	3	0	0	0	17	....	....	....	....	....	....	....	....	....	....	....	....	....	....	....	....	....	....	....
	Detroit Vipers	IHL	45	0	1	1	203	....	....	....	....	....	....	....	....	....	....	....	....	....	....	....	....	....	....	....
	NHL Totals		10	0	0	0	39	0	0	0	0	0.0		0	0.0	4	1	2:19	....	....	....	....	....	....	....	....

Signed as a free agent by **Tampa Bay**, July 16, 1999.

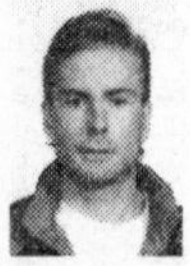

FREER, Mark

(FRIHR, MAHRK)

Center. Shoots left. 5'10", 180 lbs. Born, Peterborough, Ont., July 14, 1968.

Season	Club	League	GP	G	A	Pts	PIM	PP	SH	GW	S	%	+/-	TF	F%	H	SB	Min	GP	G	A	Pts	PIM	PP	SH	GW
1984-85	Peterborough	OMHA	49	53	68	121	63	....	....	....	....	....	....	....	....	....	....	....	....	....	....	....	....	....	....	....
1985-86	Peterborough	OHL	65	16	28	44	24	....	....	....	....	....	....	....	....	....	....	....	14	3	4	7	13	....	....	....
1986-87	Peterborough	OHL	65	39	43	82	44	....	....	....	....	....	....	....	....	....	....	....	12	2	6	8	5	....	....	....
	Philadelphia	NHL	1	0	1	1	0	0	0	0	0	0.0	1	....	....	....	....	....	....	....	....	....	....	....	....	....
1987-88	Peterborough	OHL	63	38	70	108	63	....	....	....	....	....	....	....	....	....	....	....	12	5	12	17	4	....	....	....
	Philadelphia	NHL	1	0	0	0	0	0	0	0	0	0.0	–2	....	....	....	....	....	....	....	....	....	....	....	....	....
1988-89	Philadelphia	NHL	5	0	1	1	0	0	0	0	1	0.0	0	....	....	....	....	....	....	....	....	....	....	....	....	....
	Hershey Bears	AHL	75	30	49	79	77	....	....	....	....	....	....	....	....	....	....	....	12	4	6	10	2	....	....	....
1989-90	Philadelphia	NHL	2	0	0	0	0	0	0	0	2	0.0	0	....	....	....	....	....	....	....	....	....	....	....	....	....
	Hershey Bears	AHL	65	28	36	64	31	....	....	....	....	....	....	....	....	....	....	....	....	....	....	....	....	....	....	....
1990-91	Hershey Bears	AHL	77	18	44	62	45	....	....	....	....	....	....	....	....	....	....	....	7	1	3	4	17	....	....	....
1991-92	Philadelphia	NHL	50	6	7	13	18	0	0	2	41	14.6	–1	....	....	....	....	....	....	....	....	....	....	....	....	....
	Hershey Bears	AHL	31	13	11	24	38	....	....	....	....	....	....	....	....	....	....	....	6	0	3	3	2	....	....	....
1992-93	Ottawa	NHL	63	10	14	24	39	3	3	0	80	12.5	–35	....	....	....	....	....	....	....	....	....	....	....	....	....

			Regular Season																Playoffs							
Season	Club	League	GP	G	A	Pts	PIM	PP	SH	GW	S	%	+/–	TF	F%	H	SB	Min	GP	G	A	Pts	PIM	PP	SH	GW
1993-94	Calgary	NHL	2	0	0	0	4	0	0	0	0	0.0	0	....	....	....	....	....	....	....	....	....	....	....	....	....
	Saint John Flames	AHL	77	33	53	86	45	....	....	....	....	....	....	....	....	....	....	....	7	2	4	6	16	....	....	....
1994-95	Houston Aeros	IHL	80	38	42	80	54	....	....	....	....	....	....	....	....	....	....	....	4	0	1	1	4	....	....	....
1995-96	Houston Aeros	IHL	80	22	31	53	67	....	....	....	....	....	....	....	....	....	....	....	....	....	....	....	....	....	....	....
1996-97	Houston Aeros	IHL	81	21	36	57	43	....	....	....	....	....	....	....	....	....	....	....	12	2	3	5	4	....	....	....
1997-98	Houston Aeros	IHL	74	14	38	52	41	....	....	....	....	....	....	....	....	....	....	....	4	2	2	4	4	....	....	....
1998-99	Houston Aeros	IHL	79	17	28	45	66	....	....	....	....	....	....	....	....	....	....	....	19	*11	11	*22	12	....	....	....
99-2000	Houston Aeros	IHL	75	20	35	55	55	....	....	....	....	....	....	....	....	....	....	....	11	0	4	4	4	....	....	....
	NHL Totals		124	16	23	39	61	3	3	2	124	12.9		....	....	....	....	....	....	....	....	....	....	....	....	....

Won "Bud" Poile Trophy (Playoff MVP - IHL) (1999)

Signed as a free agent by **Philadelphia**, October 7, 1986. Claimed by **Ottawa** from **Philadelphia** in Expansion Draft, June 18, 1992. Signed as a free agent by **Calgary**, August 10, 1993. Signed as a free agent by **Houston** (IHL), July 27, 1994.

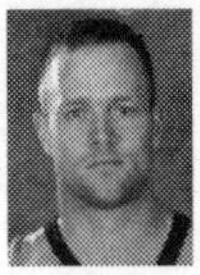

FRIEDMAN, Doug

(FREED-man, DUHG) **S.J.**

Left wing. Shoots left. 6'1", 205 lbs. Born, Cape Elizabeth, ME, September 1, 1971. Quebec's 13th choice, 222nd overall, in 1991 Entry Draft.

Season	Club	League	GP	G	A	Pts	PIM	PP	SH	GW	S	%	+/–	TF	F%	H	SB	Min	GP	G	A	Pts	PIM	PP	SH	GW
1989-90	Lawrence Prep	Hi-School	20	9	26	35	....	....	....	....	....	....	....	....	....	....	....	....	....	....	....	....	....	....	....	....
1990-91	Boston University	H-East	36	6	6	12	37	....	....	....	....	....	....	....	....	....	....	....	....	....	....	....	....	....	....	....
1991-92	Boston University	H-East	34	11	8	19	42	....	....	....	....	....	....	....	....	....	....	....	....	....	....	....	....	....	....	....
1992-93	Boston University	H-East	38	17	24	41	62	....	....	....	....	....	....	....	....	....	....	....	....	....	....	....	....	....	....	....
1993-94	Boston University	H-East	41	9	23	32	110	....	....	....	....	....	....	....	....	....	....	....	....	....	....	....	....	....	....	....
1994-95	Cornwall Aces	AHL	55	6	9	15	56	....	....	....	....	....	....	....	....	....	....	....	3	0	0	0	0	....	....	....
1995-96	Cornwall Aces	AHL	80	12	22	34	178	....	....	....	....	....	....	....	....	....	....	....	8	1	1	2	17	....	....	....
1996-97	Hershey Bears	AHL	61	12	21	33	245	....	....	....	....	....	....	....	....	....	....	....	23	6	9	15	49	....	....	....
1997-98	Edmonton	NHL	16	0	0	0	20	0	0	0	8	0.0	0	....	....	....	....	....	....	....	....	....	....	....	....	....
	Hamilton Bulldogs	AHL	55	19	27	46	235	....	....	....	....	....	....	....	....	....	....	....	9	4	4	8	40	....	....	....
1998-99	Nashville	NHL	2	0	1	1	14	0	0	0	3	0.0	0	0	0.0	2	1	6:60	....	....	....	....	....	....	....	....
	Milwaukee	IHL	69	26	25	51	251	....	....	....	....	....	....	....	....	....	....	....	2	1	2	3	8	....	....	....
99-2000	Kentucky	AHL	73	13	23	36	237	....	....	....	....	....	....	....	....	....	....	....	9	1	3	4	45	....	....	....
	NHL Totals		18	0	1	1	34	0	0	0	11	0.0		0	0.0	2	1	7:00	....	....	....	....	....	....	....	....

Rights transferred to **Colorado** after **Quebec** franchise relocated, June 21, 1995. Signed as a free agent by **Edmonton**, July 14, 1997. Claimed by **Nashville** from **Edmonton** in Expansion Draft, June 26, 1998. Signed as a free agent by **San Jose**, August 26, 1999.

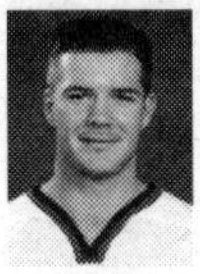

FRIESEN, Jeff

(FREE-zuhn, JEHF) **S.J.**

Center. Shoots left. 6', 205 lbs. Born, Meadow Lake, Sask., August 5, 1976. San Jose's 1st choice, 11th overall, in 1994 Entry Draft.

Season	Club	League	GP	G	A	Pts	PIM	PP	SH	GW	S	%	+/–	TF	F%	H	SB	Min	GP	G	A	Pts	PIM	PP	SH	GW
1991-92	Saskatoon	SAHA	35	37	51	88	75	....	....	....	....	....	....	....	....	....	....	....	....	....	....	....	....	....	....	....
	Regina Pats	WHL	4	3	1	4	2	....	....	....	....	....	....	....	....	....	....	....	....	....	....	....	....	....	....	....
1992-93	Regina Pats	WHL	70	45	38	83	23	....	....	....	....	....	....	....	....	....	....	....	13	7	10	17	8	....	....	....
1993-94	Regina Pats	WHL	66	51	67	118	48	....	....	....	....	....	....	....	....	....	....	....	4	3	2	5	2	....	....	....
1994-95	Regina Pats	WHL	25	21	23	44	22	....	....	....	....	....	....	....	....	....	....	....	....	....	....	....	....	....	....	....
	San Jose	NHL	48	15	10	25	14	5	1	2	86	17.4	–8	....	....	....	....	....	11	1	5	6	4	0	0	0
1995-96	San Jose	NHL	79	15	31	46	42	2	0	0	123	12.2	–19	....	....	....	....	....	....	....	....	....	....	....	....	....
1996-97	San Jose	NHL	82	28	34	62	75	6	2	5	200	14.0	–8	....	....	....	....	....	....	....	....	....	....	....	....	....
1997-98	San Jose	NHL	79	31	32	63	40	7	6	7	186	16.7	8	....	....	....	....	....	6	0	1	1	2	0	0	0
1998-99	San Jose	NHL	78	22	35	57	42	10	1	3	215	10.2	3	24	33.3	99	22	19:25	6	2	2	4	14	1	0	0
99-2000	San Jose	NHL	82	26	35	61	47	11	3	7	191	13.6	–2	3	66.7	110	37	19:48	11	2	2	4	10	0	0	0
	NHL Totals		448	137	177	314	260	41	13	24	1001	13.7		27	37.0	209	59	19:37	34	5	10	15	30	1	0	0

Canadian Major Junior Rookie of the Year (1993) • NHL All-Rookie Team (1995)

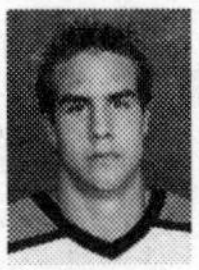

GAGNE, Simon

(GAH-nyay, SIGH-mohn) **PHI.**

Center. Shoots left. 6', 185 lbs. Born, Ste. Foy, Que., February 29, 1980. Philadelphia's 1st choice, 22nd overall, in 1998 Entry Draft.

Season	Club	League	GP	G	A	Pts	PIM	PP	SH	GW	S	%	+/–	TF	F%	H	SB	Min	GP	G	A	Pts	PIM	PP	SH	GW
1995-96	Ste-Foy Governors	QAAA	27	13	9	22	18	....	....	....	....	....	....	....	....	....	....	....	....	....	....	....	....	....	....	....
1996-97	Beauport	QMJHL	51	9	22	31	49	....	....	....	....	....	....	....	....	....	....	....	....	....	....	....	....	....	....	....
1997-98	Quebec Remparts	QMJHL	53	30	39	69	26	....	....	....	....	....	....	....	....	....	....	....	12	11	5	16	23	....	....	....
1998-99	Quebec Remparts	QMJHL	61	50	70	120	42	....	....	....	....	....	....	....	....	....	....	....	13	9	8	17	4	....	....	....
99-2000	Philadelphia	NHL	80	20	28	48	22	8	1	4	159	12.6	11	443	42.2	46	23	14:58	17	5	5	10	2	2	0	1
	NHL Totals		80	20	28	48	22	8	1	4	159	12.6		443	42.2	46	23	14:59	17	5	5	10	2	2	0	1

QMJHL Second All-Star Team (1999) • NHL All-Rookie Team (2000)

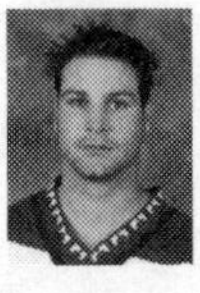

GAGNON, Sean

(gah-NYAWN, SHAWN) **OTT.**

Defense. Shoots left. 6'2", 219 lbs. Born, Sault Ste. Marie, Ont., September 11, 1973.

Season	Club	League	GP	G	A	Pts	PIM	PP	SH	GW	S	%	+/–	TF	F%	H	SB	Min	GP	G	A	Pts	PIM	PP	SH	GW
1989-90	S.S. Marie Elks	NOHA	46	21	26	47	218	....	....	....	....	....	....	....	....	....	....	....	....	....	....	....	....	....	....	....
1990-91	Sudbury Wolves	OHL	4	3	4	7	60	....	....	....	....	....	....	....	....	....	....	....	....	....	....	....	....	....	....	....
1991-92	Sudbury Wolves	OHL	44	3	4	7	60	....	....	....	....	....	....	....	....	....	....	....	5	0	1	1	0	....	....	....
1992-93	Sudbury Wolves	OHL	6	1	1	2	16	....	....	....	....	....	....	....	....	....	....	....	....	....	....	....	....	....	....	....
	Ottawa 67's	OHL	33	2	10	12	68	....	....	....	....	....	....	....	....	....	....	....	....	....	....	....	....	....	....	....
	Sault Ste. Marie	OHL	24	1	5	6	65	....	....	....	....	....	....	....	....	....	....	....	15	2	2	4	25	....	....	....
1993-94	Sault Ste. Marie	OHL	42	4	12	16	147	....	....	....	....	....	....	....	....	....	....	....	14	1	1	2	52	....	....	....
1994-95	Dayton Bombers	ECHL	68	9	23	32	339	....	....	....	....	....	....	....	....	....	....	....	8	0	3	3	69	....	....	....
1995-96	Dayton Bombers	ECHL	68	7	22	29	326	....	....	....	....	....	....	....	....	....	....	....	3	0	1	1	33	....	....	....
1996-97	Fort Wayne	IHL	72	7	7	14	*457	....	....	....	....	....	....	....	....	....	....	....	....	....	....	....	....	....	....	....
1997-98	Phoenix	NHL	5	0	1	1	14	0	0	0	3	0.0	1	....	....	....	....	....	....	....	....	....	....	....	....	....
	Springfield	AHL	54	4	13	17	330	....	....	....	....	....	....	....	....	....	....	....	2	0	1	1	17	....	....	....
1998-99	Phoenix	NHL	2	0	0	0	7	0	0	0	1	0.0	–2	0	0.0	1	2	7:56	....	....	....	....	....	....	....	....
	Springfield	AHL	68	8	14	22	331	....	....	....	....	....	....	....	....	....	....	....	3	0	0	0	14	....	....	....
99-2000	Jokerit Helsinki	Finland	42	3	5	8	183	....	....	....	....	....	....	....	....	....	....	....	11	4	1	5	22	....	....	....
	NHL Totals		7	0	1	1	21	0	0	0	4	0.0		0	0.0	1	2	7:56	....	....	....	....	....	....	....	....

Signed as a free agent by **Phoenix**, May 14, 1997. Signed as a free agent by **Ottawa**, July 7, 2000.

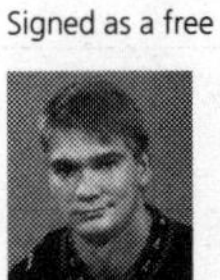

GALANOV, Maxim

(gah-LAH-nahf, mahx-EEM)

Defense. Shoots left. 6'1", 205 lbs. Born, Krasnoyarsk, USSR, March 13, 1974. NY Rangers' 3rd choice, 61st overall, in 1993 Entry Draft.

Season	Club	League	GP	G	A	Pts	PIM	PP	SH	GW	S	%	+/–	TF	F%	H	SB	Min	GP	G	A	Pts	PIM	PP	SH	GW
1992-93	Lada Togliatti	CIS	41	4	2	6	12	....	....	....	....	....	....	....	....	....	....	....	10	1	1	2	12	....	....	....
1993-94	Lada Togliatti	CIS	7	1	0	1	4	....	....	....	....	....	....	....	....	....	....	....	12	1	0	1	8	....	....	....
1994-95	Lada Togliatti	CIS	45	5	6	11	54	....	....	....	....	....	....	....	....	....	....	....	9	0	1	1	12	....	....	....
1995-96	Binghamton	AHL	72	17	36	53	24	....	....	....	....	....	....	....	....	....	....	....	4	1	1	2	0	....	....	....
1996-97	Binghamton	AHL	73	13	30	43	30	....	....	....	....	....	....	....	....	....	....	....	3	0	0	0	2	....	....	....
1997-98	NY Rangers	NHL	6	0	1	1	2	0	0	0	5	0.0	1	....	....	....	....	....	....	....	....	....	....	....	....	....
	Hartford	AHL	61	6	24	30	22	....	....	....	....	....	....	....	....	....	....	....	13	3	6	9	2	....	....	....
1998-99	Pittsburgh	NHL	51	4	3	7	14	2	0	0	44	9.1	–8	1	0.0	32	49	15:13	1	0	0	0	0	0	0	0
99-2000	Atlanta	NHL	40	4	3	7	20	0	0	0	47	8.5	–12	0	0.0	40	56	21:32	....	....	....	....	....	....	....	....
	NHL Totals		97	8	7	15	36	2	0	0	96	8.3		1	0.0	72	105	17:59	1	0	0	0	0	0	0	0

Claimed by **Pittsburgh** from **NY Rangers** in NHL Waiver Draft, October 5, 1998. Claimed by **Atlanta** from **Pittsburgh** in Expansion Draft, June 25, 1999. • Missed majority of 1999-2000 season recovering from hand injury suffered in game vs. NY Rangers, October 17, 1999.

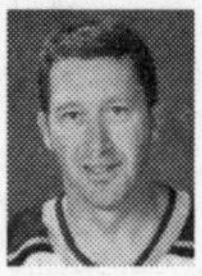

GALLEY, Garry

(GA-lee, GAHR-ee)

Defense. Shoots left. 6', 202 lbs. Born, Montreal, Que., April 16, 1963. Los Angeles' 4th choice, 103rd overall, in 1983 Entry Draft.

			Regular Season																Playoffs							
Season	Club	League	GP	G	A	Pts	PIM	PP	SH	GW	S	%	+/-	TF	F%	H	SB	Min	GP	G	A	Pts	PIM	PP	SH	GW
1980-81	Gloucester	OJHL	49	18	26	44	103	....	....	....	....	....	....	....	....	....	....	....	....	....	....	....	....	....	....	....
1981-82	Bowling Green	CCHA	42	3	36	39	48	....	....	....	....	....	....	....	....	....	....	....	....	....	....	....	....	....	....	....
1982-83	Bowling Green	CCHA	40	17	29	46	40	....	....	....	....	....	....	....	....	....	....	....	....	....	....	....	....	....	....	....
1983-84	Bowling Green	CCHA	44	15	52	67	61	....	....	....	....	....	....	....	....	....	....	....	....	....	....	....	....	....	....	....
1984-85	Los Angeles	NHL	78	8	30	38	82	1	1	2	131	6.1	3	....	....	....	....	....	3	1	0	1	2	0	0	0
1985-86	Los Angeles	NHL	49	9	13	22	46	1	0	1	57	15.8	–9	....	....	....	....	....	....	....	....	....	....	....	....	....
	New Haven	AHL	4	2	6	8	6	....	....	....	....	....	....	....	....	....	....	....	....	....	....	....	....	....	....	....
1986-87	Los Angeles	NHL	30	5	11	16	57	2	0	1	43	11.6	–9	....	....	....	....	....	....	....	....	....	....	....	....	....
	Washington	NHL	18	1	10	11	10	1	0	0	27	3.7	3	....	....	....	....	....	2	0	0	0	0	0	0	0
1987-88	Washington	NHL	58	7	23	30	44	3	0	0	100	7.0	11	....	....	....	....	....	13	2	4	6	13	0	0	0
1988-89	Boston	NHL	78	8	22	30	80	2	1	0	145	5.5	–7	....	....	....	....	....	9	0	1	1	33	0	0	0
1989-90	Boston	NHL	71	8	27	35	75	1	0	0	142	5.6	2	....	....	....	....	....	21	3	3	6	34	1	0	2
1990-91	Boston	NHL	70	6	21	27	84	1	0	0	128	4.7	0	....	....	....	....	....	16	1	5	6	17	0	0	0
1991-92	Boston	NHL	38	2	12	14	83	1	0	0	51	3.9	–3	....	....	....	....	....	....	....	....	....	....	....	....	....
	Philadelphia	NHL	39	3	15	18	34	2	0	1	74	4.1	1	....	....	....	....	....	....	....	....	....	....	....	....	....
1992-93	Philadelphia	NHL	83	13	49	62	115	4	1	3	231	5.6	18	....	....	....	....	....	....	....	....	....	....	....	....	....
1993-94	Philadelphia	NHL	81	10	60	70	91	5	1	0	186	5.4	–11	....	....	....	....	....	....	....	....	....	....	....	....	....
1994-95	Philadelphia	NHL	33	2	20	22	20	1	0	0	66	3.0	0	....	....	....	....	....	....	....	....	....	....	....	....	....
	Buffalo	NHL	14	1	9	10	10	2	0	0	31	3.2	4	....	....	....	....	....	5	0	3	3	4	0	0	0
1995-96	Buffalo	NHL	78	10	44	54	81	7	1	2	175	5.7	–2	....	....	....	....	....	....	....	....	....	....	....	....	....
1996-97	Buffalo	NHL	71	4	34	38	102	1	1	1	84	4.8	10	....	....	....	....	....	12	0	6	6	14	0	0	0
1997-98	Los Angeles	NHL	74	9	28	37	63	7	0	0	128	7.0	–5	....	....	....	....	....	4	0	1	1	2	0	0	0
1998-99	Los Angeles	NHL	60	4	12	16	30	3	0	0	77	5.2	–9	0	0.0	100	59	17:16	....	....	....	....	....	....	....	....
99-2000	Los Angeles	NHL	70	9	21	30	52	2	0	1	96	9.4	9	0	0.0	152	79	20:15	4	0	0	0	0	0	0	0
	NHL Totals		1093	119	461	580	1159	47	6	12	1972	6.0		0	0.0	252	138	18:52	89	7	23	30	119	1	0	2

CCHA First All-Star Team (1983, 1984) • NCAA East First All-American Team (1984) • NCAA Championship All-Tournament Team (1984) • Played in NHL All-Star Game (1991, 1994)

Traded to **Washington** by **LA Kings** for Al Jensen, February 14, 1987. Signed as a free agent by **Boston**, July 8, 1988. Traded to **Philadelphia** by **Boston** with Wes Walz and Boston's 3rd round choice (Milos Holan) in 1993 Entry Draft for Gord Murphy, Brian Dobbin, Philadelphia's 3rd round choice (Sergei Zholtok) in 1992 Entry Draft and 4th round choice (Charles Paquette) in 1993 Entry Draft, January 2, 1992. Traded to **Buffalo** by **Philadelphia** for Petr Svoboda, April 7, 1995. Signed as a free agent by **LA Kings**, July 15, 1997.

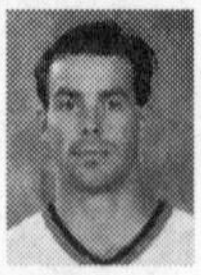

GARDINER, Bruce

(gah-DIHN-uhr, BREWS) **CBJ**

Right wing. Shoots right. 6'1", 193 lbs. Born, Barrie, Ont., February 11, 1972. St. Louis' 6th choice, 131st overall, in 1991 Entry Draft.

Season	Club	League	GP	G	A	Pts	PIM	PP	SH	GW	S	%	+/-	TF	F%	H	SB	Min	GP	G	A	Pts	PIM	PP	SH	GW
1988-89	Barrie Colts	OJHL-B	41	17	28	45	29	....	....	....	....	....	....	....	....	....	....	....	....	....	....	....	....	....	....	....
1989-90	Barrie Colts	OJHL-B	40	19	26	45	89	....	....	....	....	....	....	....	....	....	....	....	13	10	11	21	32	....	....	....
1990-91	Colgate	ECAC	27	4	9	13	72	....	....	....	....	....	....	....	....	....	....	....	....	....	....	....	....	....	....	....
1991-92	Colgate	ECAC	23	7	8	15	77	....	....	....	....	....	....	....	....	....	....	....	....	....	....	....	....	....	....	....
1992-93	Colgate	ECAC	33	17	12	29	64	....	....	....	....	....	....	....	....	....	....	....	....	....	....	....	....	....	....	....
1993-94	Colgate	ECAC	33	23	23	46	68	....	....	....	....	....	....	....	....	....	....	....	....	....	....	....	....	....	....	....
	Peoria	IHL	3	0	0	0	0	....	....	....	....	....	....	....	....	....	....	....	....	....	....	....	....	....	....	....
1994-95	P.E.I. Senators	AHL	72	17	20	37	132	....	....	....	....	....	....	....	....	....	....	....	7	4	1	5	4	....	....	....
1995-96	P.E.I. Senators	AHL	38	11	13	24	87	....	....	....	....	....	....	....	....	....	....	....	5	2	4	6	4	....	....	....
1996-97	Ottawa	NHL	67	11	10	21	49	0	1	2	94	11.7	4	....	....	....	....	....	7	0	1	1	2	0	0	0
1997-98	Ottawa	NHL	55	7	11	18	50	0	0	0	64	10.9	2	....	....	....	....	....	11	1	3	4	2	0	0	1
1998-99	Ottawa	NHL	59	4	8	12	43	0	0	1	70	5.7	6	278	45.7	88	17	12:52	3	0	0	0	4	0	0	0
99-2000	Ottawa	NHL	10	0	3	3	4	0	0	0	18	0.0	1	62	59.7	16	2	13:24	....	....	....	....	....	....	....	....
	Tampa Bay	NHL	41	3	6	9	37	0	0	0	30	10.0	–21	330	56.4	52	28	13:36	....	....	....	....	....	....	....	....
	NHL Totals		232	25	38	63	183	0	1	3	276	9.1		670	52.2	156	47	13:11	21	1	4	5	8	0	0	1

ECAC Second All-Star Team (1994)

Signed as a free agent by **Ottawa**, June 14, 1994. Traded to **Tampa Bay** by **Ottawa** for Colin Forbes, November 11, 1999. Selected by **Columbus** from **Tampa Bay** in Expansion Draft, June 23, 2000.

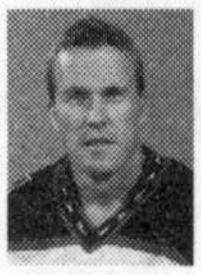

GARPENLOV, Johan

(GAHR-pehn-LAHV, YOH-hahn)

Left wing. Shoots left. 6', 185 lbs. Born, Stockholm, Sweden, March 21, 1968. Detroit's 5th choice, 85th overall, in 1986 Entry Draft.

Season	Club	League	GP	G	A	Pts	PIM	PP	SH	GW	S	%	+/-	TF	F%	H	SB	Min	GP	G	A	Pts	PIM	PP	SH	GW
1984-85	Nacka HK	Sweden-2	4	1	2	3	2	....	....	....	....	....	....	....	....	....	....	....	....	....	....	....	....	....	....	....
1985-86	Nacka HK	Sweden-2	20	8	12	20	22	....	....	....	....	....	....	....	....	....	....	....	....	....	....	....	....	....	....	....
1986-87	Djurgardens IF	Sweden	29	5	8	13	22	....	....	....	....	....	....	....	....	....	....	....	2	0	0	0	0	....	....	....
1987-88	Djurgardens IF	Sweden	30	7	10	17	12	....	....	....	....	....	....	....	....	....	....	....	3	1	3	4	4	....	....	....
1988-89	Djurgardens IF	Sweden	36	12	19	31	20	....	....	....	....	....	....	....	....	....	....	....	8	3	4	7	10	....	....	....
1989-90	Djurgardens IF	Sweden	39	20	13	33	35	....	....	....	....	....	....	....	....	....	....	....	8	2	4	6	4	....	....	....
1990-91	Detroit	NHL	71	18	22	40	18	2	0	3	91	19.8	–4	....	....	....	....	....	6	0	1	1	4	0	0	0
1991-92	Detroit	NHL	16	1	1	2	4	0	0	0	13	7.7	2	....	....	....	....	....	....	....	....	....	....	....	....	....
	Adirondack	AHL	9	3	3	6	6	....	....	....	....	....	....	....	....	....	....	....	....	....	....	....	....	....	....	....
	San Jose	NHL	12	5	6	11	4	1	0	1	21	23.8	–2	....	....	....	....	....	....	....	....	....	....	....	....	....
1992-93	San Jose	NHL	79	22	44	66	56	14	0	1	171	12.9	–26	....	....	....	....	....	....	....	....	....	....	....	....	....
1993-94	San Jose	NHL	80	18	35	53	28	7	0	3	125	14.4	9	....	....	....	....	....	14	4	6	10	6	0	0	2
1994-95	San Jose	NHL	13	1	1	2	2	0	0	0	16	6.3	–3	....	....	....	....	....	....	....	....	....	....	....	....	....
	Florida	NHL	27	3	9	12	0	0	0	0	28	10.7	4	....	....	....	....	....	....	....	....	....	....	....	....	....
1995-96	Florida	NHL	82	23	28	51	36	8	0	7	130	17.7	–10	....	....	....	....	....	20	4	2	6	8	0	0	0
1996-97	Florida	NHL	53	11	25	36	47	1	0	1	83	13.3	10	....	....	....	....	....	4	2	0	2	4	2	0	1
1997-98	Florida	NHL	39	2	3	5	8	0	0	0	43	4.7	–6	....	....	....	....	....	....	....	....	....	....	....	....	....
1998-99	Florida	NHL	64	8	9	17	42	0	1	0	71	11.3	–9	3	0.0	23	13	13:14	....	....	....	....	....	....	....	....
99-2000	Atlanta	NHL	73	2	14	16	31	0	0	0	79	2.5	–30	166	41.6	111	24	15:19	....	....	....	....	....	....	....	....
	NHL Totals		609	114	197	311	276	33	1	16	871	13.1		169	40.8	134	37	14:21	44	10	9	19	22	2	0	3

Traded to **San Jose** by **Detroit** for Bob McGill and Vancouver's 8th round choice (previously acquired, Detroit selected C.J. Denomme) in 1992 Entry Draft, March 9, 1992. Traded to **Florida** by **San Jose** for future considerations, March 3, 1995. Claimed by **Atlanta** from **Florida** in Expansion Draft, June 25, 1999.

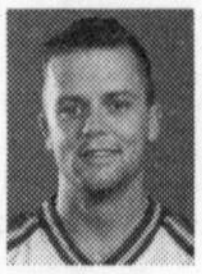

GAUL, Michael

(GAWL, MIGH-kuhl) **CBJ**

Defense. Shoots right. 6'1", 200 lbs. Born, Lachine, Que., April 22, 1973. Los Angeles' 10th choice, 262nd overall, in 1991 Entry Draft.

Season	Club	League	GP	G	A	Pts	PIM	PP	SH	GW	S	%	+/-	TF	F%	H	SB	Min	GP	G	A	Pts	PIM	PP	SH	GW
1989-90	Lac St-Louis	QAAA	39	5	9	14	....	....	....	....	....	....	....	....	....	....	....	....	....	....	....	....	....	....	....	....
1990-91	St. Lawrence	ECAC	31	1	3	4	46	....	....	....	....	....	....	....	....	....	....	....	....	....	....	....	....	....	....	....
1991-92	Laval Titan	QMJHL	50	6	38	44	44	....	....	....	....	....	....	....	....	....	....	....	10	0	2	2	20	....	....	....
1992-93	Laval Titan	QMJHL	57	16	57	73	66	....	....	....	....	....	....	....	....	....	....	....	13	3	10	13	10	....	....	....
1993-94	Laval Titan	QMJHL	22	10	17	27	24	....	....	....	....	....	....	....	....	....	....	....	21	5	15	20	14	....	....	....
1994-95	Phoenix	IHL	4	0	1	1	2	....	....	....	....	....	....	....	....	....	....	....	....	....	....	....	....	....	....	....
	Knoxville	ECHL	68	13	41	54	51	....	....	....	....	....	....	....	....	....	....	....	4	2	1	3	2	....	....	....
1995-96	Knoxville	ECHL	54	13	48	61	44	....	....	....	....	....	....	....	....	....	....	....	....	....	....	....	....	....	....	....
1996-97	ETC Timmendorf	DEB-2	51	40	52	92	100	....	....	....	....	....	....	....	....	....	....	....	....	....	....	....	....	....	....	....
1997-98	Hershey Bears	AHL	60	12	47	59	69	....	....	....	....	....	....	....	....	....	....	....	7	0	7	7	6	....	....	....
	Mobile Mysticks	ECHL	5	0	7	7	0	....	....	....	....	....	....	....	....	....	....	....	....	....	....	....	....	....	....	....
1998-99	Lowell	AHL	18	3	5	8	14	....	....	....	....	....	....	....	....	....	....	....	....	....	....	....	....	....	....	....
	Colorado	NHL	1	0	0	0	0	0	0	0	1	0.0	0	0	0.0	2	0	10:46	....	....	....	....	....	....	....	....
	Hershey Bears	AHL	43	9	31	40	22	....	....	....	....	....	....	....	....	....	....	....	5	1	1	2	6	....	....	....
99-2000	Hershey Bears	AHL	65	12	57	69	52	....	....	....	....	....	....	....	....	....	....	....	12	0	8	8	....	....	....	....
	NHL Totals		1	0	0	0	0	0	0	0	1	0.0		0	0.0	2	0	10:46	....	....	....	....	....	....	....	....

AHL Second All-Star Team (2000)

Signed as a free agent by **NY Islanders**, July 16, 1998. Traded to **Colorado** by **NY Islanders** for Ted Crowley, December 15, 1998. Signed as a free agent by **Columbus**, July 18, 2000.

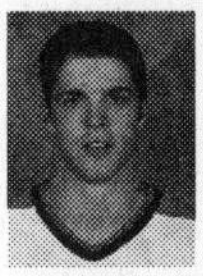

GAUTHIER, Denis

(GOH-tyay, DEH-nihs) **CGY.**

Defense. Shoots left. 6'2", 210 lbs. Born, Montreal, Que., October 1, 1976. Calgary's 1st choice, 20th overall, in 1995 Entry Draft.

Season	Club	League	GP	G	A	Pts	PIM	PP	SH	GW	S	%	+/-	TF	F%	H	SB	Min	Playoffs GP	G	A	Pts	PIM	PP	SH	GW
1992-93	Drummondville	QMJHL	60	1	7	8	136	....	....	....	....	....	....	....	....	....	....	....	10	0	5	5	40	....	....	....
1993-94	Drummondville	QMJHL	60	0	7	7	176	....	....	....	....	....	....	....	....	....	....	....	9	2	0	2	41	....	....	....
1994-95	Drummondville	QMJHL	64	9	31	40	190	....	....	....	....	....	....	....	....	....	....	....	4	0	5	5	12	....	....	....
1995-96	Drummondville	QMJHL	53	25	49	74	140	....	....	....	....	....	....	....	....	....	....	....	6	4	4	8	32	....	....	....
	Saint John Flames	AHL	5	2	0	2	8	....	....	....	....	....	....	....	....	....	....	....	16	1	6	7	20	....	....	....
1996-97	Saint John Flames	AHL	73	3	28	31	74	....	....	....	....	....	....	....	....	....	....	....	5	0	0	0	6	....	....	....
1997-98	**Calgary**	**NHL**	**10**	**0**	**0**	**0**	**16**	**0**	**0**	**0**	**3**	**0.0**	**-5**	....	....	....	....	....	....	....	....	....	....	....	....	....
	Saint John Flames	AHL	68	4	20	24	154	....	....	....	....	....	....	....	....	....	....	....	21	0	4	4	83	....	....	....
1998-99	**Calgary**	**NHL**	**55**	**3**	**4**	**7**	**68**	**0**	**0**	**0**	**40**	**7.5**	**3**	**0**	**0.0**	**162**	**51**	**12:41**	....	....	....	....	....	....	....	....
	Saint John Flames	AHL	16	0	3	3	31	....	....	....	....	....	....	....	....	....	....	....	....	....	....	....	....	....	....	....
99-2000	**Calgary**	**NHL**	**39**	**1**	**1**	**2**	**50**	**0**	**0**	**0**	**29**	**3.4**	**-4**	**0**	**0.0**	**168**	**52**	**19:21**	....	....	....	....	....	....	....	....
	NHL Totals		**104**	**4**	**5**	**9**	**134**	**0**	**0**	**0**	**72**	**5.6**		**0**	**0.0**	**330**	**103**	**15:27**	....	....	....	....	....	....	....	....

QMJHL First All-Star Team (1996) • Canadian Major Junior First All-Star Team (1996) • Missed remainder of 1999-2000 season recovering from hip injury suffered in game vs. St. Louis, February 1, 2000.

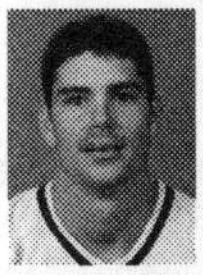

GAVEY, Aaron

(GAY-vee, AIR-ohn) **MIN.**

Center. Shoots left. 6'2", 200 lbs. Born, Sudbury, Ont., February 22, 1974. Tampa Bay's 4th choice, 74th overall, in 1992 Entry Draft.

Season	Club	League	GP	G	A	Pts	PIM	PP	SH	GW	S	%	+/-	TF	F%	H	SB	Min	Playoffs GP	G	A	Pts	PIM	PP	SH	GW
1990-91	Peterborough B's	OJHL-B	42	26	30	56	68	....	....	....	....	....	....	....	....	....	....	....	....	....	....	....	....	....	....	....
1991-92	Sault Ste. Marie	OHL	48	7	11	18	27	....	....	....	....	....	....	....	....	....	....	....	19	5	1	6	10	....	....	....
1992-93	Sault Ste. Marie	OHL	62	45	39	84	116	....	....	....	....	....	....	....	....	....	....	....	18	5	9	14	36	....	....	....
1993-94	Sault Ste. Marie	OHL	60	42	60	102	116	....	....	....	....	....	....	....	....	....	....	....	14	11	10	21	22	....	....	....
1994-95	Atlanta Knights	IHL	66	18	17	35	85	....	....	....	....	....	....	....	....	....	....	....	5	0	1	1	9	....	....	....
1995-96	**Tampa Bay**	**NHL**	**73**	**8**	**4**	**12**	**56**	**1**	**1**	**2**	**65**	**12.3**	**-6**	....	....	....	....	....	**6**	**0**	**0**	**0**	**4**	**0**	**0**	**0**
1996-97	**Tampa Bay**	**NHL**	**16**	**1**	**2**	**3**	**12**	**0**	**0**	**0**	**8**	**12.5**	**-1**	....	....	....	....	....	....	....	....	....	....	....	....	....
	Calgary	**NHL**	**41**	**7**	**9**	**16**	**34**	**3**	**0**	**1**	**54**	**13.0**	**-11**	....	....	....	....	....	....	....	....	....	....	....	....	....
1997-98	**Calgary**	**NHL**	**26**	**2**	**3**	**5**	**24**	**0**	**0**	**1**	**27**	**7.4**	**-5**	....	....	....	....	....	....	....	....	....	....	....	....	....
	Saint John Flames	AHL	8	4	3	7	28	....	....	....	....	....	....	....	....	....	....	....	....	....	....	....	....	....	....	....
1998-99	**Dallas**	**NHL**	**7**	**0**	**0**	**0**	**10**	**0**	**0**	**0**	**4**	**0.0**	**-1**	**43**	**48.8**	**13**	**0**	**8:09**	....	....	....	....	....	....	....	....
	Michigan K-Wings	IHL	67	24	33	57	128	....	....	....	....	....	....	....	....	....	....	....	5	2	3	5	4	....	....	....
99-2000	**Dallas**	**NHL**	**41**	**7**	**6**	**13**	**44**	**1**	**0**	**2**	**39**	**17.9**	**0**	**263**	**51.7**	**88**	**12**	**9:55**	**13**	**1**	**2**	**3**	**10**	**0**	**0**	**1**
	Michigan K-Wings	IHL	28	14	15	29	73	....	....	....	....	....	....	....	....	....	....	....	....	....	....	....	....	....	....	....
	NHL Totals		**204**	**25**	**24**	**49**	**180**	**5**	**1**	**6**	**197**	**12.7**		**306**	**51.3**	**101**	**12**	**9:39**	**19**	**1**	**2**	**3**	**14**	**0**	**0**	**1**

Traded to **Calgary** by **Tampa Bay** for Rick Tabaracci, November 19, 1996. Traded to **Dallas** by **Calgary** for Bob Bassen, July 14, 1998. Traded to **Minnesota** by **Dallas** with Pavel Patera, Dallas' 8th round choice (Eric Johansson) in 2000 Entry Draft and Minnesota's 4th round choice (previously acquired) in 2002 Entry Draft for Brad Lukowich and Minnesota's 3rd and 9th round choices in 2001 Entry Draft, June 25, 2000.

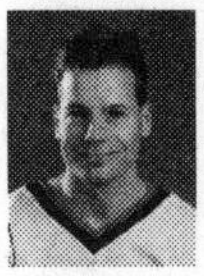

GELINAS, Martin

(ZHEHL-in-nuh, MAHR-tihn) **CAR.**

Left wing. Shoots left. 5'11", 195 lbs. Born, Shawinigan, Que., June 5, 1970. Los Angeles' 1st choice, 7th overall, in 1988 Entry Draft.

Season	Club	League	GP	G	A	Pts	PIM	PP	SH	GW	S	%	+/-	TF	F%	H	SB	Min	Playoffs GP	G	A	Pts	PIM	PP	SH	GW
1985-86	Noranda Aces	NOHA	5	1	1	2	0	....	....	....	....	....	....	....	....	....	....	....	....	....	....	....	....	....	....	....
1986-87	Montreal L'est	QAAA	41	36	42	78	36	....	....	....	....	....	....	....	....	....	....	....	....	....	....	....	....	....	....	....
1987-88	Hull Olympiques	QMJHL	65	63	68	131	74	....	....	....	....	....	....	....	....	....	....	....	17	15	18	33	32	....	....	....
1988-89	Hull Olympiques	QMJHL	41	38	39	77	31	....	....	....	....	....	....	....	....	....	....	....	9	5	4	9	14	....	....	....
	Edmonton	**NHL**	**6**	**1**	**2**	**3**	**0**	**0**	**0**	**0**	**14**	**7.1**	**-1**	....	....	....	....	....	....	....	....	....	....	....	....	....
1989-90♦	**Edmonton**	**NHL**	**46**	**17**	**8**	**25**	**30**	**5**	**0**	**2**	**71**	**23.9**	**0**	....	....	....	....	....	**20**	**2**	**3**	**5**	**6**	**0**	**0**	**0**
1990-91	**Edmonton**	**NHL**	**73**	**20**	**20**	**40**	**34**	**4**	**0**	**2**	**124**	**16.1**	**-7**	....	....	....	....	....	**18**	**3**	**6**	**9**	**25**	**0**	**0**	**1**
1991-92	**Edmonton**	**NHL**	**68**	**11**	**18**	**29**	**62**	**1**	**0**	**0**	**94**	**11.7**	**14**	....	....	....	....	....	**15**	**1**	**3**	**4**	**10**	**0**	**0**	**0**
1992-93	**Edmonton**	**NHL**	**65**	**11**	**12**	**23**	**30**	**0**	**0**	**1**	**93**	**11.8**	**3**	....	....	....	....	....	....	....	....	....	....	....	....	....
1993-94	**Quebec**	**NHL**	**31**	**6**	**6**	**12**	**8**	**0**	**0**	**0**	**53**	**11.3**	**-2**	....	....	....	....	....	....	....	....	....	....	....	....	....
	Vancouver	**NHL**	**33**	**8**	**8**	**16**	**26**	**3**	**0**	**1**	**54**	**14.8**	**-6**	....	....	....	....	....	**24**	**5**	**4**	**9**	**14**	**2**	**0**	**1**
1994-95	**Vancouver**	**NHL**	**46**	**13**	**10**	**23**	**36**	**1**	**0**	**4**	**75**	**17.3**	**8**	....	....	....	....	....	**3**	**0**	**1**	**1**	**0**	**0**	**0**	**0**
1995-96	**Vancouver**	**NHL**	**81**	**30**	**26**	**56**	**59**	**3**	**4**	**5**	**181**	**16.6**	**8**	....	....	....	....	....	**6**	**1**	**1**	**2**	**12**	**1**	**0**	**0**
1996-97	**Vancouver**	**NHL**	**74**	**35**	**33**	**68**	**42**	**6**	**1**	**3**	**177**	**19.8**	**6**	....	....	....	....	....	....	....	....	....	....	....	....	....
1997-98	**Vancouver**	**NHL**	**24**	**4**	**4**	**8**	**10**	**1**	**1**	**1**	**49**	**8.2**	**-6**	....	....	....	....	....	....	....	....	....	....	....	....	....
	Carolina	**NHL**	**40**	**12**	**14**	**26**	**30**	**2**	**1**	**4**	**98**	**12.2**	**1**	....	....	....	....	....	....	....	....	....	....	....	....	....
1998-99	**Carolina**	**NHL**	**76**	**13**	**15**	**28**	**67**	**0**	**0**	**2**	**111**	**11.7**	**3**	**6**	**50.0**	**70**	**13**	**13:13**	**6**	**0**	**3**	**3**	**2**	**0**	**0**	**0**
99-2000	**Carolina**	**NHL**	**72**	**14**	**16**	**30**	**40**	**3**	**0**	**0**	**139**	**10.1**	**-10**	**5**	**40.0**	**85**	**31**	**13:39**	....	....	....	....	....	....	....	....
	NHL Totals		**744**	**195**	**192**	**387**	**474**	**29**	**7**	**25**	**1333**	**14.6**		**11**	**45.5**	**155**	**44**	**13:26**	**92**	**12**	**21**	**33**	**69**	**3**	**0**	**2**

QMJHL First All-Star Team (1988) • Canadian Major Junior Rookie of the Year (1988) • Won George Parsons Trophy (Memorial Cup Tournament Most Sportsmanlike Player) (1988)

Traded to **Edmonton** by **LA Kings** with Jimmy Carson and LA Kings' 1st round choices in 1989 (later traded to New Jersey - New Jersey selected Jason Miller), 1991 (Martin Rucinsky) and 1993 (Nick Stajduhar) Entry Drafts and cash for Wayne Gretzky, Mike Krushelnyski and Marty McSorley, August 9, 1988. Traded to **Quebec** by **Edmonton** with Edmonton's 6th round choice (Nicholas Checco) in 1993 Entry Draft for Scott Pearson, June 20, 1993. Claimed on waivers by **Vancouver** from **Quebec**, January 15, 1994. Traded to **Carolina** by **Vancouver** with Kirk McLean for Sean Burke, Geoff Sanderson and Enrico Ciccone, January 3, 1998.

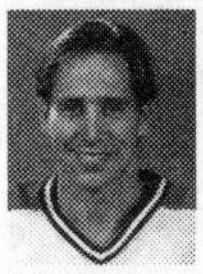

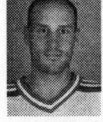

GENDRON, Martin

(ZHEHN-drawn, MAHR-tihn)

Right wing. Shoots right. 5'9", 190 lbs. Born, Valleyfield, Que., February 15, 1974. Washington's 4th choice, 71st overall, in 1992 Entry Draft.

Season	Club	League	GP	G	A	Pts	PIM	PP	SH	GW	S	%	+/-	TF	F%	H	SB	Min	Playoffs GP	G	A	Pts	PIM	PP	SH	GW
1989-90	Lac St-Louis	QAAA	42	42	32	74	26	....	....	....	....	....	....	....	....	....	....	....	2	3	1	4	0	....	....	....
1990-91	St-Hyacinthe	QMJHL	55	34	23	57	33	....	....	....	....	....	....	....	....	....	....	....	4	1	2	3	0	....	....	....
1991-92	St-Hyacinthe	QMJHL	69	*71	66	137	45	....	....	....	....	....	....	....	....	....	....	....	6	7	4	11	14	....	....	....
1992-93	St-Hyacinthe	QMJHL	63	73	61	134	44	....	....	....	....	....	....	....	....	....	....	....	....	....	....	....	....	....	....	....
	Baltimore	AHL	10	1	2	3	2	....	....	....	....	....	....	....	....	....	....	....	3	0	0	0	0	....	....	....
1993-94	Hull Olympiques	QMJHL	37	39	36	75	18	....	....	....	....	....	....	....	....	....	....	....	20	*21	17	38	8	....	....	....
	Canada	Nat-Team	19	4	5	9	2	....	....	....	....	....	....	....	....	....	....	....	....	....	....	....	....	....	....	....
1994-95	**Washington**	**NHL**	**8**	**2**	**1**	**3**	**2**	**0**	**0**	**0**	**11**	**18.2**	**3**	....	....	....	....	....	....	....	....	....	....	....	....	....
	Portland Pirates	AHL	72	36	32	68	54	....	....	....	....	....	....	....	....	....	....	....	4	5	1	6	2	....	....	....
1995-96	**Washington**	**NHL**	**20**	**2**	**1**	**3**	**8**	**0**	**0**	**0**	**22**	**9.1**	**-5**	....	....	....	....	....	....	....	....	....	....	....	....	....
	Portland Pirates	AHL	48	38	29	67	39	....	....	....	....	....	....	....	....	....	....	....	22	*15	18	33	8	....	....	....
1996-97	Las Vegas	IHL	81	51	39	90	20	....	....	....	....	....	....	....	....	....	....	....	3	2	1	3	0	....	....	....
1997-98	**Chicago**	**NHL**	**2**	**0**	**0**	**0**	**0**	**0**	**0**	**0**	**3**	**0.0**	**-1**	....	....	....	....	....	....	....	....	....	....	....	....	....
	Indianapolis Ice	IHL	17	8	6	14	16	....	....	....	....	....	....	....	....	....	....	....	....	....	....	....	....	....	....	....
	Milwaukee	IHL	40	20	19	39	14	....	....	....	....	....	....	....	....	....	....	....	....	....	....	....	....	....	....	....
	Fredericton	AHL	10	5	10	15	4	....	....	....	....	....	....	....	....	....	....	....	2	0	0	0	4	....	....	....
1998-99	Fredericton	AHL	65	33	34	67	26	....	....	....	....	....	....	....	....	....	....	....	15	*12	5	17	2	....	....	....
99-2000	Syracuse Crunch	AHL	64	19	17	36	16	....	....	....	....	....	....	....	....	....	....	....	....	....	....	....	....	....	....	....
	Springfield	AHL	14	6	10	16	6	....	....	....	....	....	....	....	....	....	....	....	4	0	2	2	4	....	....	....
	NHL Totals		**30**	**4**	**2**	**6**	**10**	**0**	**0**	**0**	**36**	**11.1**														

QMJHL First All-Star Team (1992) • Canadian Major Junior Most Sportsmanlike Player of the Year (1992) • QMJHL Second All-Star Team (1993) • Canadian Major Junior First All-Star Team (1993)

Traded to **Chicago** by **Washington** with Washington's 6th round choice (Jonathan Pelletier) in 1998 Entry Draft for Chicago's 5th round choice (Erik Wendell) in 1998 Entry Draft, October 10, 1997. Traded to **Montreal** by **Chicago** for David Ling, March 14, 1998. Signed as a free agent **Vancouver**, August 25, 1999. Loaned to **Springfield** (AHL) by **Syracuse** (AHL) for loan of Sean McCann, March 15, 2000.

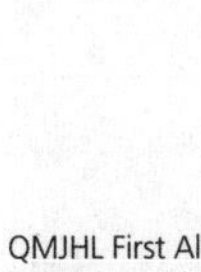

GERNANDER, Ken

(guhr-NAN-duhr, KEHN) **NYR**

Center. Shoots left. 5'10", 175 lbs. Born, Coleraine, MN, June 30, 1969. Winnipeg's 4th choice, 96th overall, in 1987 Entry Draft.

Season	Club	League	GP	G	A	Pts	PIM	PP	SH	GW	S	%	+/-	TF	F%	H	SB	Min	Playoffs GP	G	A	Pts	PIM	PP	SH	GW
1985-86	Greenway High	Hi-School	23	14	23	37	....	....	....	....	....	....	....	....	....	....	....	....	....	....	....	....	....	....	....	....
1986-87	Greenway High	Hi-School	26	35	34	69	....	....	....	....	....	....	....	....	....	....	....	....	....	....	....	....	....	....	....	....
1987-88	U. of Minnesota	WCHA	44	14	14	28	14	....	....	....	....	....	....	....	....	....	....	....	....	....	....	....	....	....	....	....
1988-89	U. of Minnesota	WCHA	44	9	11	20	2	....	....	....	....	....	....	....	....	....	....	....	....	....	....	....	....	....	....	....
1989-90	U. of Minnesota	WCHA	44	32	17	49	24	....	....	....	....	....	....	....	....	....	....	....	....	....	....	....	....	....	....	....
1990-91	U. of Minnesota	WCHA	44	23	20	43	24	....	....	....	....	....	....	....	....	....	....	....	....	....	....	....	....	....	....	....
1991-92	Fort Wayne	IHL	13	7	6	13	2	....	....	....	....	....	....	....	....	....	....	....	....	....	....	....	....	....	....	....
	Moncton Hawks	AHL	43	8	18	26	9	....	....	....	....	....	....	....	....	....	....	....	8	1	1	2	2	....	....	....

			Regular Season																Playoffs							
Season	Club	League	GP	G	A	Pts	PIM	PP	SH	GW	S	%	+/-	TF	F%	H	SB	Min	GP	G	A	Pts	PIM	PP	SH	GW
1992-93	Moncton Hawks	AHL	71	18	29	47	20	....	....	....	....	....	....	....	....	....	....	....	5	1	4	5	0	....	....	....
1993-94	Moncton Hawks	AHL	71	22	25	47	12	....	....	....	....	....	....	....	....	....	....	....	19	6	1	7	0	....	....	....
1994-95	Binghamton	AHL	80	28	25	53	24	....	....	....	....	....	....	....	....	....	....	....	11	2	2	4	6	....	....	....
1995-96	**NY Rangers**	**NHL**	**10**	**2**	**3**	**5**	**4**	**2**	**0**	**0**	**10**	**20.0**	**-3**	....	....	....	....	....	**6**	**0**	**0**	**0**	**0**	**0**	**0**	**0**
	Binghamton	AHL	63	44	29	73	38	....	....	....	....	....	....	....	....	....	....	....	....	....	....	....	....	....	....	....
1996-97	Binghamton	AHL	46	13	18	31	30	....	....	....	....	....	....	....	....	....	....	....	2	0	1	1	0	....	....	....
	NY Rangers	**NHL**	....	....	....	....	....	....	....	....	....	....	....	....	....	....	....	....	**9**	**0**	**0**	**0**	**0**	**0**	**0**	**0**
1997-98	Hartford	AHL	80	35	28	63	26	....	....	....	....	....	....	....	....	....	....	....	12	5	6	11	4	....	....	....
1998-99	Hartford	AHL	70	23	26	49	32	....	....	....	....	....	....	....	....	....	....	....	7	1	2	3	2	....	....	....
99-2000	Hartford	AHL	79	28	29	57	24	....	....	....	....	....	....	....	....	....	....	....	23	5	5	10	0	....	....	....
	NHL Totals		**10**	**2**	**3**	**5**	**4**	**2**	**0**	**0**	**10**	**20.0**		....	....	....	....	....	**15**	**0**	**0**	**0**	**0**	**0**	**0**	**0**

Won Fred Hunt Memorial Trophy (Sportsmanship - AHL) (1996)

Signed as a free agent by **NY Rangers**, July 4, 1994.

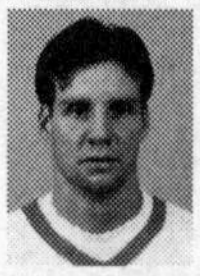

GILCHRIST, Brent
(GIHL-chrihst, BREHNT) **DET.**

Left wing. Shoots left. 5'11", 180 lbs. Born, Moose Jaw, Sask., April 3, 1967. Montreal's 6th choice, 79th overall, in 1985 Entry Draft.

1983-84	Kelowna Wings	WHL	69	16	11	27	16	....	....	....	....	....	....	....	....	....	....	....	....	....	....	....	....	....	....	....
1984-85	Kelowna Wings	WHL	51	35	38	73	58	....	....	....	....	....	....	....	....	....	....	....	6	5	2	7	8	....	....	....
1985-86	Spokane Chiefs	WHL	52	45	45	90	57	....	....	....	....	....	....	....	....	....	....	....	9	6	7	13	19	....	....	....
1986-87	Spokane Chiefs	WHL	46	45	55	100	71	....	....	....	....	....	....	....	....	....	....	....	5	2	7	9	6	....	....	....
	Sherbrooke	AHL	....	....	....	....	....	....	....	....	....	....	....	....	....	....	....	....	10	2	7	9	2	....	....	....
1987-88	Sherbrooke	AHL	77	26	48	74	83	....	....	....	....	....	....	....	....	....	....	....	6	1	3	4	6	....	....	....
1988-89	**Montreal**	**NHL**	**49**	**8**	**16**	**24**	**16**	**0**	**0**	**2**	**68**	**11.8**	**9**	....	....	....	....	....	**9**	**1**	**1**	**2**	**10**	**0**	**0**	**0**
	Sherbrooke	AHL	7	6	5	11	7	....	....	....	....	....	....	....	....	....	....	....	....	....	....	....	....	....	....	....
1989-90	**Montreal**	**NHL**	**57**	**9**	**15**	**24**	**28**	**1**	**0**	**0**	**80**	**11.3**	**3**	....	....	....	....	....	**8**	**2**	**0**	**2**	**2**	**0**	**0**	**0**
1990-91	**Montreal**	**NHL**	**51**	**6**	**9**	**15**	**10**	**1**	**0**	**1**	**81**	**7.4**	**-3**	....	....	....	....	....	**13**	**5**	**3**	**8**	**6**	**0**	**0**	**1**
1991-92	**Montreal**	**NHL**	**79**	**23**	**27**	**50**	**57**	**2**	**0**	**3**	**146**	**15.8**	**29**	....	....	....	....	....	**11**	**2**	**4**	**6**	**6**	**1**	**0**	**0**
1992-93	**Edmonton**	**NHL**	**60**	**10**	**10**	**20**	**47**	**2**	**0**	**0**	**94**	**10.6**	**-10**	....	....	....	....	....	....	....	....	....	....	....	....	....
	Minnesota	**NHL**	**8**	**0**	**1**	**1**	**2**	**0**	**0**	**0**	**12**	**0.0**	**-2**	....	....	....	....	....	....	....	....	....	....	....	....	....
1993-94	**Dallas**	**NHL**	**76**	**17**	**14**	**31**	**31**	**3**	**1**	**5**	**103**	**16.5**	**0**	....	....	....	....	....	**9**	**3**	**1**	**4**	**2**	**1**	**0**	**0**
1994-95	**Dallas**	**NHL**	**32**	**9**	**4**	**13**	**16**	**1**	**3**	**1**	**70**	**12.9**	**-3**	....	....	....	....	....	**5**	**0**	**1**	**1**	**2**	**0**	**0**	**0**
1995-96	**Dallas**	**NHL**	**77**	**20**	**22**	**42**	**36**	**6**	**1**	**2**	**164**	**12.2**	**-11**	....	....	....	....	....	....	....	....	....	....	....	....	....
1996-97	**Dallas**	**NHL**	**67**	**10**	**20**	**30**	**24**	**2**	**0**	**2**	**116**	**8.6**	**6**	....	....	....	....	....	**6**	**2**	**2**	**4**	**2**	**0**	**0**	**0**
1997-98♦	**Detroit**	**NHL**	**61**	**13**	**14**	**27**	**40**	**5**	**0**	**3**	**124**	**10.5**	**4**	....	....	....	....	....	**15**	**2**	**1**	**3**	**12**	**0**	**0**	**0**
1998-99	**Detroit**	**NHL**	**5**	**1**	**0**	**1**	**0**	**0**	**0**	**1**	**4**	**25.0**	**-1**	**28**	**42.9**	**1**	**2**	**11:58**	**3**	**0**	**0**	**0**	**0**	**0**	**0**	**0**
99-2000	**Detroit**	**NHL**	**24**	**4**	**2**	**6**	**24**	**0**	**0**	**0**	**33**	**12.1**	**1**	**180**	**50.0**	**18**	**8**	**11:19**	**6**	**0**	**0**	**0**	**6**	**0**	**0**	**0**
	NHL Totals		**646**	**130**	**154**	**284**	**331**	**23**	**5**	**20**	**1095**	**11.9**		**208**	**49.0**	**19**	**10**	**11:26**	**85**	**17**	**13**	**30**	**48**	**2**	**0**	**1**

Traded to **Edmonton** by **Montreal** with Shayne Corson and Vladimir Vujtek for Vincent Damphousse and Edmonton's 4th round choice (Adam Wiesel) in 1993 Entry Draft, August 27, 1992. Traded to **Minnesota** by **Edmonton** for Todd Elik, March 5, 1993. Transferred to **Dallas** after **Minnesota** franchise relocated, June 9, 1993. Signed as a free agent by **Detroit**, August 1, 1997. Claimed by **Tampa Bay** from **Detroit** in NHL Waiver Draft, October 5, 1998. Traded to **Detroit** by **Tampa Bay** for future considerations, October 5, 1998. • Missed majority of 1998-99 and 1999-2000 seasons recovering from hernia surgery, September 22, 1998.

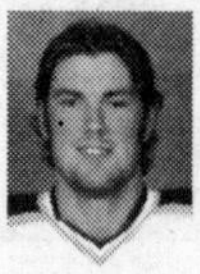

GILL, Hal
(GIHL, HAL) **BOS.**

Defense. Shoots left. 6'7", 235 lbs. Born, Concord, MA, April 6, 1975. Boston's 8th choice, 207th overall, in 1993 Entry Draft.

1992-93	Nashoba High	Hi-School	20	25	25	50	....	....	....	....	....	....	....	....	....	....	....	....	....	....	....	....	....	....	....	....
1993-94	Providence	H-East	31	1	2	3	26	....	....	....	....	....	....	....	....	....	....	....	....	....	....	....	....	....	....	....
1994-95	Providence	H-East	26	1	3	4	22	....	....	....	....	....	....	....	....	....	....	....	....	....	....	....	....	....	....	....
1995-96	Providence	H-East	39	5	12	17	54	....	....	....	....	....	....	....	....	....	....	....	....	....	....	....	....	....	....	....
1996-97	Providence	H-East	35	5	16	21	52	....	....	....	....	....	....	....	....	....	....	....	....	....	....	....	....	....	....	....
1997-98	**Boston**	**NHL**	**68**	**2**	**4**	**6**	**47**	**0**	**0**	**0**	**56**	**3.6**	**4**	....	....	....	....	....	**6**	**0**	**0**	**0**	**4**	**0**	**0**	**0**
	Providence Bruins	AHL	4	1	0	1	23	....	....	....	....	....	....	....	....	....	....	....	....	....	....	....	....	....	....	....
1998-99	**Boston**	**NHL**	**80**	**3**	**7**	**10**	**63**	**0**	**0**	**2**	**102**	**2.9**	**-10**	**1**	**100.0**	**144**	**102**	**20:54**	**12**	**0**	**0**	**0**	**14**	**0**	**0**	**0**
99-2000	**Boston**	**NHL**	**81**	**3**	**9**	**12**	**51**	**0**	**0**	**0**	**120**	**2.5**	**0**	**0**	**0.0**	**245**	**63**	**17:15**	....	....	....	....	....	....	....	....
	NHL Totals		**229**	**8**	**20**	**28**	**161**	**0**	**0**	**2**	**278**	**2.9**		**1**	**100.0**	**389**	**165**	**19:04**	**18**	**0**	**0**	**0**	**18**	**0**	**0**	**0**

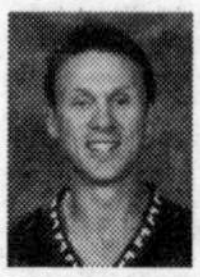

GILL, Todd
(GIHL, TAWD) **DET.**

Defense. Shoots left. 6', 185 lbs. Born, Cardinal, Ont., November 9, 1965. Toronto's 2nd choice, 25th overall, in 1984 Entry Draft.

1980-81	Cardinal Broncos	OHA-B	35	10	14	24	65	....	....	....	....	....	....	....	....	....	....	....	....	....	....	....	....	....	....	....
1981-82	Brockville Braves	OJHL	48	5	16	21	169	....	....	....	....	....	....	....	....	....	....	....	....	....	....	....	....	....	....	....
1982-83	Windsor Spitfires	OHL	70	12	24	36	108	....	....	....	....	....	....	....	....	....	....	....	3	0	0	0	11	....	....	....
1983-84	Windsor Spitfires	OHL	68	9	48	57	184	....	....	....	....	....	....	....	....	....	....	....	3	1	1	2	10	....	....	....
1984-85	Windsor Spitfires	OHL	53	17	40	57	148	....	....	....	....	....	....	....	....	....	....	....	4	0	1	1	14	....	....	....
	Toronto	**NHL**	**10**	**1**	**0**	**1**	**13**	**0**	**0**	**0**	**9**	**11.1**	**-1**	....	....	....	....	....	....	....	....	....	....	....	....	....
1985-86	**Toronto**	**NHL**	**15**	**1**	**2**	**3**	**28**	**0**	**0**	**0**	**9**	**11.1**	**0**	....	....	....	....	....	**1**	**0**	**0**	**0**	**0**	**0**	**0**	**0**
	St. Catharines	AHL	58	8	25	33	90	....	....	....	....	....	....	....	....	....	....	....	10	1	6	7	17	....	....	....
1986-87	**Toronto**	**NHL**	**61**	**4**	**27**	**31**	**92**	**1**	**0**	**0**	**51**	**7.8**	**-3**	....	....	....	....	....	**13**	**2**	**2**	**4**	**42**	**0**	**0**	**0**
	Newmarket Saints	AHL	11	1	8	9	33	....	....	....	....	....	....	....	....	....	....	....	....	....	....	....	....	....	....	....
1987-88	**Toronto**	**NHL**	**65**	**8**	**17**	**25**	**131**	**1**	**0**	**3**	**109**	**7.3**	**-20**	....	....	....	....	....	**6**	**1**	**3**	**4**	**20**	**1**	**0**	**0**
	Newmarket Saints	AHL	2	0	1	1	2	....	....	....	....	....	....	....	....	....	....	....	....	....	....	....	....	....	....	....
1988-89	**Toronto**	**NHL**	**59**	**11**	**14**	**25**	**72**	**0**	**0**	**1**	**92**	**12.0**	**-3**	....	....	....	....	....	....	....	....	....	....	....	....	....
1989-90	**Toronto**	**NHL**	**48**	**1**	**14**	**15**	**92**	**0**	**0**	**0**	**44**	**2.3**	**-8**	....	....	....	....	....	**5**	**0**	**3**	**3**	**16**	**0**	**0**	**0**
1990-91	**Toronto**	**NHL**	**72**	**2**	**22**	**24**	**113**	**0**	**0**	**0**	**90**	**2.2**	**-4**	....	....	....	....	....	....	....	....	....	....	....	....	....
1991-92	**Toronto**	**NHL**	**74**	**2**	**15**	**17**	**91**	**1**	**0**	**0**	**82**	**2.4**	**-22**	....	....	....	....	....	....	....	....	....	....	....	....	....
1992-93	**Toronto**	**NHL**	**69**	**11**	**32**	**43**	**66**	**5**	**0**	**2**	**113**	**9.7**	**4**	....	....	....	....	....	**21**	**1**	**10**	**11**	**26**	**0**	**0**	**0**
1993-94	**Toronto**	**NHL**	**45**	**4**	**24**	**28**	**44**	**2**	**0**	**1**	**74**	**5.4**	**8**	....	....	....	....	....	**18**	**1**	**5**	**6**	**37**	**0**	**0**	**1**
1994-95	**Toronto**	**NHL**	**47**	**7**	**25**	**32**	**64**	**3**	**1**	**2**	**82**	**8.5**	**-8**	....	....	....	....	....	**7**	**0**	**3**	**3**	**6**	**0**	**0**	**0**
1995-96	**Toronto**	**NHL**	**74**	**7**	**18**	**25**	**116**	**1**	**0**	**2**	**109**	**6.4**	**-15**	....	....	....	....	....	**6**	**0**	**0**	**0**	**24**	**0**	**0**	**0**
1996-97	**San Jose**	**NHL**	**79**	**0**	**21**	**21**	**101**	**0**	**0**	**0**	**101**	**0.0**	**-20**	....	....	....	....	....	....	....	....	....	....	....	....	....
1997-98	**San Jose**	**NHL**	**64**	**8**	**13**	**21**	**31**	**4**	**0**	**1**	**100**	**8.0**	**-13**	....	....	....	....	....	....	....	....	....	....	....	....	....
	St. Louis	**NHL**	**11**	**5**	**4**	**9**	**10**	**3**	**0**	**1**	**22**	**22.7**	**2**	....	....	....	....	....	**10**	**2**	**2**	**4**	**10**	**1**	**1**	**0**
1998-99	**St. Louis**	**NHL**	**28**	**2**	**3**	**5**	**16**	**1**	**0**	**0**	**36**	**5.6**	**-6**	**0**	**0.0**	**34**	**16**	**17:36**	....	....	....	....	....	....	....	....
	Detroit	**NHL**	**23**	**2**	**2**	**4**	**11**	**0**	**0**	**1**	**25**	**8.0**	**-4**	**0**	**0.0**	**32**	**13**	**18:45**	**2**	**0**	**1**	**1**	**0**	**0**	**0**	**0**
99-2000	**Phoenix**	**NHL**	**41**	**1**	**6**	**7**	**30**	**0**	**0**	**1**	**41**	**2.4**	**-10**	**0**	**0.0**	**74**	**37**	**16:07**	....	....	....	....	....	....	....	....
	Detroit	**NHL**	**13**	**2**	**0**	**2**	**15**	**0**	**0**	**1**	**20**	**10.0**	**2**	**1**	**100.0**	**12**	**10**	**15:31**	**9**	**0**	**1**	**1**	**4**	**0**	**0**	**0**
	NHL Totals		**898**	**79**	**259**	**338**	**1136**	**22**	**1**	**16**	**1209**	**6.5**		**1**	**100.0**	**152**	**76**	**17:01**	**98**	**7**	**30**	**37**	**185**	**2**	**1**	**1**

Traded to **San Jose** by **Toronto** for Jamie Baker and San Jose's 5th round choice (Peter Cava) in 1996 Entry Draft, June 14, 1996. Traded to **St. Louis** by **San Jose** for Joe Murphy, March 24, 1998. Claimed on waivers by **Detroit** from **St. Louis**, December 30, 1998. Signed as a free agent by **Phoenix**, July 21, 1999. Traded to **Detroit** by **Phoenix** for Philippe Audet, March 13, 2000.

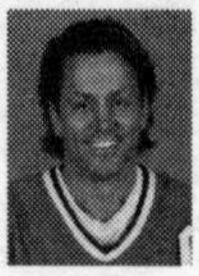

GILMOUR, Doug
(GIHL-mohr, DUHG) **BUF.**

Center/Left wing. Shoots left. 5'11", 180 lbs. Born, Kingston, Ont., June 25, 1963. St. Louis' 4th choice, 134th overall, in 1982 Entry Draft.

1979-80	Kingston	OJHL-B	15	2	5	7	26	....	....	....	....	....	....	....	....	....	....	....	....	....	....	....	....	....	....	....
	Belleville Bulls	OJHL	25	9	14	23	18	....	....	....	....	....	....	....	....	....	....	....	....	....	....	....	....	....	....	....
1980-81	Cornwall Royals	QMJHL	51	12	23	35	35	....	....	....	....	....	....	....	....	....	....	....	....	....	....	....	....	....	....	....
1981-82	Cornwall Royals	OHL	67	46	73	119	42	....	....	....	....	....	....	....	....	....	....	....	5	6	9	15	2	....	....	....
1982-83	Cornwall Royals	OHL	68	70	*107	*177	62	....	....	....	....	....	....	....	....	....	....	....	8	8	10	18	16	....	....	....
1983-84	**St. Louis**	**NHL**	**80**	**25**	**28**	**53**	**57**	**3**	**1**	**1**	**157**	**15.9**	**6**	....	....	....	....	....	**11**	**2**	**9**	**11**	**10**	**1**	**0**	**1**
1984-85	**St. Louis**	**NHL**	**78**	**21**	**36**	**57**	**49**	**3**	**1**	**3**	**162**	**13.0**	**3**	....	....	....	....	....	**3**	**1**	**1**	**2**	**2**	**0**	**0**	**0**
1985-86	**St. Louis**	**NHL**	**74**	**25**	**28**	**53**	**41**	**2**	**1**	**5**	**183**	**13.7**	**-3**	....	....	....	....	....	**19**	**9**	**12**	***21**	**25**	**1**	**2**	**2**
1986-87	**St. Louis**	**NHL**	**80**	**42**	**63**	**105**	**58**	**17**	**1**	**2**	**207**	**20.3**	**-2**	....	....	....	....	....	**6**	**2**	**2**	**4**	**16**	**1**	**0**	**1**
1987-88	**St. Louis**	**NHL**	**72**	**36**	**50**	**86**	**59**	**19**	**2**	**4**	**163**	**22.1**	**-13**	....	....	....	....	....	**10**	**3**	**14**	**17**	**18**	**1**	**0**	**0**
1988-89♦	**Calgary**	**NHL**	**72**	**26**	**59**	**85**	**44**	**11**	**0**	**5**	**161**	**16.1**	**45**	....	....	....	....	....	**22**	**11**	**11**	**22**	**20**	**3**	**0**	**3**
1989-90	**Calgary**	**NHL**	**78**	**24**	**67**	**91**	**54**	**12**	**1**	**3**	**152**	**15.8**	**20**	....	....	....	....	....	**6**	**3**	**1**	**4**	**8**	**0**	**0**	**1**
1990-91	**Calgary**	**NHL**	**78**	**20**	**61**	**81**	**144**	**2**	**2**	**5**	**135**	**14.8**	**27**	....	....	....	....	....	**7**	**1**	**1**	**2**	**0**	**0**	**0**	**1**

Season	Club	League	GP	G	A	Pts	PIM	PP	SH	GW	S	%	+/–	TF	F%	H	SB	Min	GP	G	A	Pts	PIM	PP	SH	GW
			Regular Season																Playoffs							
1991-92	**Calgary**	**NHL**	**38**	**11**	**27**	**38**	**46**	**4**	**1**	**1**	**64**	**17.2**	**12**	....	....	....	....	....	....	....	....	....	....	....	....	....
	Toronto	**NHL**	**40**	**15**	**34**	**49**	**32**	**6**	**0**	**3**	**104**	**14.4**	**13**	....	....	....	....	....	....	....	....	....	....	....	....	....
1992-93	**Toronto**	**NHL**	**83**	**32**	**95**	**127**	**100**	**15**	**3**	**2**	**211**	**15.2**	**32**	....	....	....	....	....	**21**	**10**	***25**	**35**	**30**	**4**	**0**	**1**
1993-94	**Toronto**	**NHL**	**83**	**27**	**84**	**111**	**105**	**10**	**1**	**3**	**167**	**16.2**	**25**	....	....	....	....	....	**18**	**6**	**22**	**28**	**42**	**5**	**0**	**1**
1994-95	HC Rapperswil	Switz.	9	2	13	15	16	....	....	....	....	....	....	....	....	....	....	....	....	....	....	....	....	....	....	....
	Toronto	**NHL**	**44**	**10**	**23**	**33**	**26**	**3**	**0**	**1**	**73**	**13.7**	**–5**	....	....	....	....	....	**7**	**0**	**6**	**6**	**6**	**0**	**0**	**0**
1995-96	**Toronto**	**NHL**	**81**	**32**	**40**	**72**	**77**	**10**	**2**	**3**	**180**	**17.8**	**–5**	....	....	....	....	....	**6**	**1**	**7**	**8**	**12**	**1**	**0**	**0**
1996-97	**Toronto**	**NHL**	**61**	**15**	**45**	**60**	**46**	**2**	**1**	**1**	**103**	**14.6**	**–5**	....	....	....	....	....	....	....	....	....	....	....	....	....
	New Jersey	**NHL**	**20**	**7**	**15**	**22**	**22**	**2**	**0**	**0**	**40**	**17.5**	**7**	....	....	....	....	....	**10**	**0**	**4**	**4**	**14**	**0**	**0**	**0**
1997-98	**New Jersey**	**NHL**	**63**	**13**	**40**	**53**	**68**	**3**	**0**	**5**	**94**	**13.8**	**10**	....	....	....	....	....	**6**	**5**	**2**	**7**	**4**	**1**	**0**	**1**
1998-99	**Chicago**	**NHL**	**72**	**16**	**40**	**56**	**56**	**7**	**1**	**4**	**110**	**14.5**	**–16**	**1619**	**53.6**	**37**	**45**	**22:29**	....	....	....	....	....	....	....	....
99-2000	**Chicago**	**NHL**	**63**	**22**	**34**	**56**	**51**	**8**	**0**	**3**	**100**	**22.0**	**–12**	**941**	**53.7**	**34**	**31**	**19:59**	....	....	....	....	....	....	....	....
	Buffalo	**NHL**	**11**	**3**	**14**	**17**	**12**	**2**	**0**	**0**	**13**	**23.1**	**3**	**35**	**51.4**	**8**	**6**	**18:58**	**5**	**0**	**1**	**1**	**0**	**0**	**0**	**0**
	NHL Totals		**1271**	**422**	**883**	**1305**	**1147**	**141**	**18**	**54**	**2579**	**16.4**		**2595**	**53.6**	**79**	**82**	**21:08**	**157**	**54**	**118**	**172**	**207**	**18**	**2**	**12**

OHL First All-Star Team (1983) • Won Frank J. Selke Trophy (1993) • Played in NHL All-Star Game (1993, 1994)

Traded to **Calgary** by **St. Louis** with Mark Hunter, Steve Bozek and Michael Dark for Mike Bullard, Craig Coxe and Tim Corkery, September 6, 1988. Traded to **Toronto** by **Calgary** with Jamie Macoun, Ric Nattress, Kent Manderville and Rick Wamsley for Gary Leeman, Alexander Godynyuk, Jeff Reese, Michel Petit and Craig Berube, January 2, 1992. Traded to **New Jersey** by **Toronto** with Dave Ellett and New Jersey's 3rd round choice (previously acquired, New Jersey selected Andre Lakos) in 1999 Entry Draft for Jason Smith, Steve Sullivan and the rights to Alyn McCauley, February 25, 1997. Signed as a free agent by **Chicago**, July 28, 1998. Traded to **Buffalo** by **Chicago** with J.P. Dumont and future considerations for Michal Grosek, March 10, 2000.

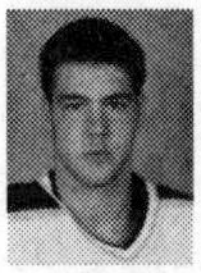

GIRARD, Jonathan

(zhih-RAHR, JOHN-a-THAN) **BOS.**

Defense. Shoots right. 5'11", 196 lbs. Born, Joliette, Que., May 27, 1980. Boston's 1st choice, 48th overall, in 1998 Entry Draft.

1995-96	Laval-Laurentides	QAAA	39	11	22	33	44	....	....	....	....	....	....	....	....	....	....	....	....	....	....	....	....	....	....	....
1996-97	Laval Titan	QMJHL	39	11	23	34	13	....	....	....	....	....	....	....	....	....	....	....	3	0	3	3	0	....	....	....
1997-98	Laval Titan	QMJHL	64	20	47	67	44	....	....	....	....	....	....	....	....	....	....	....	16	2	16	18	13	....	....	....
1998-99	Acadie-Bathurst	QMJHL	50	9	58	67	60	....	....	....	....	....	....	....	....	....	....	....	23	13	18	31	22	....	....	....
	Boston	**NHL**	**3**	**0**	**0**	**0**	**0**	**0**	**0**	**0**	**3**	**0.0**	**1**	**0**	**0.0**	**0**	**0**	**9:28**	....	....	....	....	....	....	....	....
99-2000	Moncton Wildcats	QMJHL	26	10	25	35	36	....	....	....	....	....	....	....	....	....	....	....	16	3	15	18	36	....	....	....
	Boston	**NHL**	**23**	**1**	**2**	**3**	**2**	**0**	**0**	**0**	**17**	**5.9**	**–1**	**0**	**0.0**	**24**	**4**	**9:32**	....	....	....	....	....	....	....	....
	Providence Bruins	AHL	5	0	1	1	0	....	....	....	....	....	....	....	....	....	....	....	....	....	....	....	....	....	....	....
	NHL Totals		**26**	**1**	**2**	**3**	**2**	**0**	**0**	**0**	**20**	**5.0**		**0**	**0.0**	**24**	**4**	**9:32**	....	....	....	....	....	....	....	....

QMJHL Second All-Star Team (1998) • QMJHL First All-Star Team (1999, 2000)

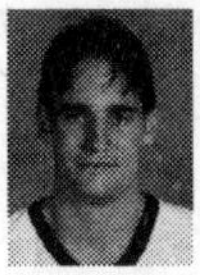

GIROUX, Ray

(zhih-ROO, RAY) **NYI**

Defense. Shoots left. 6', 180 lbs. Born, North Bay, Ont., July 20, 1976. Philadelphia's 7th choice, 202nd overall, in 1994 Entry Draft.

1992-93	Powasson Hawks	NOJHA	45	8	18	26	117	....	....	....	....	....	....	....	....	....	....	....	....	....	....	....	....	....	....	....
1993-94	Powasson	NOJHA	36	10	40	50	42	....	....	....	....	....	....	....	....	....	....	....	....	....	....	....	....	....	....	....
1994-95	Yale University	ECAC	27	1	3	4	8	....	....	....	....	....	....	....	....	....	....	....	....	....	....	....	....	....	....	....
1995-96	Yale University	ECAC	30	3	16	19	36	....	....	....	....	....	....	....	....	....	....	....	....	....	....	....	....	....	....	....
1996-97	Yale University	ECAC	32	9	12	21	38	....	....	....	....	....	....	....	....	....	....	....	....	....	....	....	....	....	....	....
1997-98	Yale University	ECAC	35	9	*30	39	62	....	....	....	....	....	....	....	....	....	....	....	....	....	....	....	....	....	....	....
1998-99	Lowell	AHL	59	13	19	32	92	....	....	....	....	....	....	....	....	....	....	....	3	1	1	2	0	....	....	....
99-2000	**NY Islanders**	**NHL**	**14**	**0**	**9**	**9**	**10**	**0**	**0**	**0**	**24**	**0.0**	**0**	**9**	**22.2**	**34**	**5**	**14:40**	....	....	....	....	....	....	....	....
	Lowell	AHL	49	12	21	33	34	....	....	....	....	....	....	....	....	....	....	....	7	0	0	0	2	....	....	....
	NHL Totals		**14**	**0**	**9**	**9**	**10**	**0**	**0**	**0**	**24**	**0.0**		**9**	**22.2**	**34**	**5**	**14:40**	....	....	....	....	....	....	....	....

ECAC First All-Star Team (1998) • NCAA East First All-American Team (1998)

Rights traded to **NY Islanders** by **Philadelphia** for NY Islanders' 6th round choice (later traded to Montreal - Montreal selected Scott Selig) in 2000 Entry Draft, August 25, 1998.

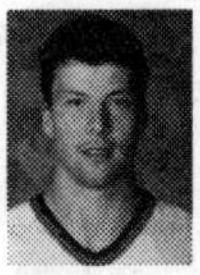

GOLDMANN, Erich

(GOHLD-mahn, AIR-ihk)

Defense. Shoots left. 6'3", 212 lbs. Born, Dingolfing, West Germany, April 7, 1976. Ottawa's 5th choice, 212th overall, in 1996 Entry Draft.

1993-94	EV Landshut	DEL	33	0	0	0	4	....	....	....	....	....	....	....	....	....	....	....	7	0	0	0	0	....	....	....
1994-95	Adler Mannheim	DEL	31	0	0	0	22	....	....	....	....	....	....	....	....	....	....	....	10	1	0	1	2	....	....	....
1995-96	Adler Mannheim	DEL	47	0	3	3	40	....	....	....	....	....	....	....	....	....	....	....	8	0	0	0	4	....	....	....
1996-97	Kaufbeurer Adler	DEL	44	2	4	6	58	....	....	....	....	....	....	....	....	....	....	....	6	1	0	1	2	....	....	....
1997-98	Worcester	AHL	31	0	2	2	40	....	....	....	....	....	....	....	....	....	....	....	....	....	....	....	....	....	....	....
	Germany	Olympics	4	0	1	1	27	....	....	....	....	....	....	....	....	....	....	....	....	....	....	....	....	....	....	....
	Detroit Vipers	IHL	3	0	0	0	2	....	....	....	....	....	....	....	....	....	....	....	....	....	....	....	....	....	....	....
	Dayton Bombers	ECHL	3	0	2	2	5	....	....	....	....	....	....	....	....	....	....	....	5	0	0	0	8	....	....	....
1998-99	Hershey Bears	AHL	21	1	1	2	23	....	....	....	....	....	....	....	....	....	....	....	....	....	....	....	....	....	....	....
	Cincinnati	IHL	5	0	1	1	7	....	....	....	....	....	....	....	....	....	....	....	....	....	....	....	....	....	....	....
	Cincinnati Ducks	AHL	32	0	2	2	18	....	....	....	....	....	....	....	....	....	....	....	3	0	0	0	2	....	....	....
99-2000	**Ottawa**	**NHL**	**1**	**0**	**0**	**0**	**0**	**0**	**0**	**0**	**0**	**0.0**	**0**	**0**	**0.0**	**0**	**1**	**9:44**	....	....	....	....	....	....	....	....
	Grand Rapids	IHL	26	1	1	2	15	....	....	....	....	....	....	....	....	....	....	....	....	....	....	....	....	....	....	....
	Detroit Vipers	IHL	11	1	0	1	13	....	....	....	....	....	....	....	....	....	....	....	....	....	....	....	....	....	....	....
	NHL Totals		**1**	**0**	**0**	**0**	**0**	**0**	**0**	**0**	**0**	**0.0**		**0**	**0.0**	**0**	**1**	**9:44**	....	....	....	....	....	....	....	....

Loaned to **Cincinnati** (AHL) by **Ottawa** with Ratislav Pavlikovsky and Ivan Ciernik, January 12, 1999.

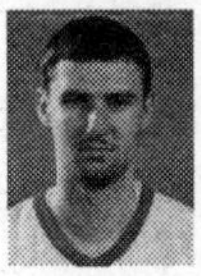

GOLUBOVSKY, Yan

(goh-luh-BOHV-skee, YAN) **DET.**

Defense. Shoots right. 6'3", 183 lbs. Born, Novosibirsk, USSR, March 9, 1976. Detroit's 1st choice, 23rd overall, in 1994 Entry Draft.

1993-94	D'amo Moscow-2	CIS-3	10	0	1	1	....	....	....	....	....	....	....	....	....	....	....	....	....	....	....	....	....	....	....	....
	Russian Penguins	IHL	8	0	0	0	23	....	....	....	....	....	....	....	....	....	....	....	....	....	....	....	....	....	....	....
1994-95	Adirondack	AHL	57	4	2	6	39	....	....	....	....	....	....	....	....	....	....	....	....	....	....	....	....	....	....	....
1995-96	Adirondack	AHL	71	5	16	21	97	....	....	....	....	....	....	....	....	....	....	....	3	0	0	0	2	....	....	....
1996-97	Adirondack	AHL	62	2	11	13	67	....	....	....	....	....	....	....	....	....	....	....	4	0	0	0	0	....	....	....
1997-98	**Detroit**	**NHL**	**12**	**0**	**2**	**2**	**6**	**0**	**0**	**0**	**9**	**0.0**	**1**	....	....	....	....	....	....	....	....	....	....	....	....	....
	Adirondack	AHL	52	1	15	16	57	....	....	....	....	....	....	....	....	....	....	....	3	0	0	0	2	....	....	....
1998-99	**Detroit**	**NHL**	**17**	**0**	**1**	**1**	**16**	**0**	**0**	**0**	**10**	**0.0**	**4**	**0**	**0.0**	**9**	**4**	**9:39**	....	....	....	....	....	....	....	....
	Adirondack	AHL	43	2	2	4	32	....	....	....	....	....	....	....	....	....	....	....	2	0	0	0	4	....	....	....
99-2000	**Detroit**	**NHL**	**21**	**1**	**2**	**3**	**8**	**0**	**0**	**0**	**7**	**14.3**	**3**	**0**	**0.0**	**13**	**23**	**8:54**	....	....	....	....	....	....	....	....
	NHL Totals		**50**	**1**	**5**	**6**	**30**	**0**	**0**	**0**	**26**	**3.8**		**0**	**0.0**	**22**	**27**	**9:14**	....	....	....	....	....	....	....	....

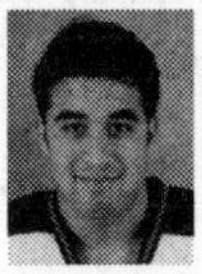

GOMEZ, Scott

(GOH-mehz, SKAWT) **N.J.**

Center. Shoots left. 5'11", 200 lbs. Born, Anchorage, AK, December 23, 1979. New Jersey's 2nd choice, 27th overall, in 1998 Entry Draft.

1994-95	East High T-Birds	Hi-School	28	30	48	78	....	....	....	....	....	....	....	....	....	....	....	....	....	....	....	....	....	....	....	....
1995-96	East High T-Birds	Hi-School	27	*56	49	*101	....	....	....	....	....	....	....	....	....	....	....	....	....	....	....	....	....	....	....	....
	Anchorage Stars	AAHL	40	*70	*67	*137	44	....	....	....	....	....	....	....	....	....	....	....	....	....	....	....	....	....	....	....
1996-97	South Surrey	BCJHL	56	48	76	124	94	....	....	....	....	....	....	....	....	....	....	....	21	18	23	41	57	....	....	....
1997-98	Tri-City Americans	WHL	45	12	37	49	57	....	....	....	....	....	....	....	....	....	....	....	....	....	....	....	....	....	....	....
1998-99	Tri-City Americans	WHL	58	30	*78	108	55	....	....	....	....	....	....	....	....	....	....	....	10	6	13	19	31	....	....	....
99-2000♦	**New Jersey**	**NHL**	**82**	**19**	**51**	**70**	**78**	**7**	**0**	**1**	**204**	**9.3**	**14**	**341**	**44.6**	**49**	**12**	**16:21**	**23**	**4**	**6**	**10**	**4**	**1**	**0**	**2**
	NHL Totals		**82**	**19**	**51**	**70**	**78**	**7**	**0**	**1**	**204**	**9.3**		**341**	**44.6**	**49**	**12**	**16:21**	**23**	**4**	**6**	**10**	**4**	**1**	**0**	**2**

BCJHL All-Rookie Team (1997) • WHL West First All-Star Team (1999) • NHL All-Rookie Team (2000) • Won Calder Memorial Trophy (2000) • Played in NHL All-Star Game (2000)

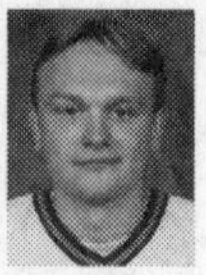

GONCHAR, Sergei
(gohn-CHAR, SAIR-gay) **WSH.**

Defense. Shoots left. 6'2", 212 lbs. Born, Chelyabinsk, USSR, April 13, 1974. Washington's 1st choice, 14th overall, in 1992 Entry Draft.

			Regular Season																Playoffs							
Season	Club	League	GP	G	A	Pts	PIM	PP	SH	GW	S	%	+/-	TF	F%	H	SB	Min	GP	G	A	Pts	PIM	PP	SH	GW
1991-92	SK Chelyabinsk	CIS	31	1	0	1	6	....	....	....	....	....	....	....	....	....	....	....	....	....	....	....	....	....	....	....
1992-93	Dynamo Moscow	CIS	31	1	3	4	70	....	....	....	....	....	....	....	....	....	....	....	10	0	0	0	12	....	....	....
1993-94	Dynamo Moscow	CIS	44	4	5	9	36	....	....	....	....	....	....	....	....	....	....	....	10	0	3	3	14	....	....	....
	Portland Pirates	AHL	....	....	....	....	....	....	....	....	....	....	....	....	....	....	....	....	2	0	0	0	0	....	....	....
1994-95	Portland Pirates	AHL	61	10	32	42	67	....	....	....	....	....	....	....	....	....	....	....	....	....	....	....	....	....	....	....
	Washington	**NHL**	**31**	**2**	**5**	**7**	**22**	**0**	**0**	**0**	**38**	**5.3**	**4**	....	....	....	....	....	**7**	**2**	**2**	**4**	**2**	**0**	**0**	**1**
1995-96	**Washington**	**NHL**	**78**	**15**	**26**	**41**	**60**	**4**	**0**	**4**	**139**	**10.8**	**25**	....	....	....	....	....	**6**	**2**	**4**	**6**	**4**	**1**	**0**	**0**
1996-97	**Washington**	**NHL**	**57**	**13**	**17**	**30**	**36**	**3**	**0**	**3**	**129**	**10.1**	**–11**	....	....	....	....	....	....	....	....	....	....	....	....	....
1997-98	Lada Togliatti	Russia	7	3	2	5	4	....	....	....	....	....	....	....	....	....	....	....	....	....	....	....	....	....	....	....
	Lada Togliatti	EuroHL	1	1	0	1	2	....	....	....	....	....	....	....	....	....	....	....	....	....	....	....	....	....	....	....
	Washington	**NHL**	**72**	**5**	**16**	**21**	**66**	**2**	**0**	**0**	**134**	**3.7**	**2**	....	....	....	....	....	**21**	**7**	**4**	**11**	**30**	**3**	**1**	**2**
	Russia	Olympics	6	0	2	2	0	....	....	....	....	....	....	....	....	....	....	....	....	....	....	....	....	....	....	....
1998-99	**Washington**	**NHL**	**53**	**21**	**10**	**31**	**57**	**13**	**1**	**3**	**180**	**11.7**	**1**	**0**	**0.0**	**72**	**31**	**23:55**	....	....	....	....	....	....	....	....
99-2000	**Washington**	**NHL**	**73**	**18**	**36**	**54**	**52**	**5**	**0**	**3**	**181**	**9.9**	**26**	**0**	**0.0**	**97**	**44**	**21:46**	**5**	**1**	**0**	**1**	**6**	**0**	**0**	**0**
	NHL Totals		**364**	**74**	**110**	**184**	**293**	**27**	**1**	**13**	**801**	**9.2**		**0**	**0.0**	**169**	**75**	**22:40**	**39**	**12**	**10**	**22**	**42**	**4**	**1**	**3**

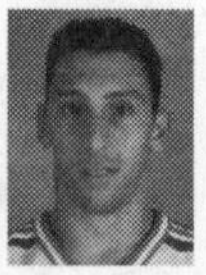

GONEAU, Daniel
(guh-NOH, DAN-yehl) **NYR**

Left wing. Shoots left. 6', 195 lbs. Born, Montreal, Que., January 16, 1976. NY Rangers' 2nd choice, 48th overall, in 1996 Entry Draft.

Season	Club	League	GP	G	A	Pts	PIM	PP	SH	GW	S	%	+/-	TF	F%	H	SB	Min	GP	G	A	Pts	PIM	PP	SH	GW
1990-91	Laval Leafs	QAAA	32	16	18	34	20	....	....	....	....	....	....	....	....	....	....	....	....	....	....	....	....	....	....	....
1991-92	Lac St-Louis	QAAA	42	21	14	35	52	....	....	....	....	....	....	....	....	....	....	....	....	....	....	....	....	....	....	....
1992-93	Laval Titan	QMJHL	62	16	25	41	44	....	....	....	....	....	....	....	....	....	....	....	13	0	4	4	4	....	....	....
1993-94	Laval Titan	QMJHL	68	29	57	86	81	....	....	....	....	....	....	....	....	....	....	....	19	8	21	29	45	....	....	....
1994-95	Laval Titan	QMJHL	56	16	31	47	78	....	....	....	....	....	....	....	....	....	....	....	20	5	10	15	33	....	....	....
1995-96	Granby Bisons	QMJHL	67	54	51	105	115	....	....	....	....	....	....	....	....	....	....	....	21	11	22	33	40	....	....	....
1996-97	**NY Rangers**	**NHL**	**41**	**10**	**3**	**13**	**10**	**3**	**0**	**2**	**44**	**22.7**	**–5**	....	....	....	....	....	....	....	....	....	....	....	....	....
	Binghamton	AHL	39	15	15	30	10	....	....	....	....	....	....	....	....	....	....	....	....	....	....	....	....	....	....	....
1997-98	**NY Rangers**	**NHL**	**11**	**2**	**0**	**2**	**4**	**0**	**0**	**1**	**13**	**15.4**	**–4**	....	....	....	....	....	....	....	....	....	....	....	....	....
	Hartford	AHL	66	21	26	47	44	....	....	....	....	....	....	....	....	....	....	....	13	1	4	5	18	....	....	....
1998-99	Hartford	AHL	72	20	19	39	56	....	....	....	....	....	....	....	....	....	....	....	2	1	0	1	0	....	....	....
99-2000	**NY Rangers**	**NHL**	**1**	**0**	**0**	**0**	**0**	**0**	**0**	**0**	**3**	**0.0**	**–1**	**0**	**0.0**	**0**	**1**	**14:26**	....	....	....	....	....	....	....	....
	Hartford	AHL	51	15	17	32	48	....	....	....	....	....	....	....	....	....	....	....	22	1	2	3	6	....	....	....
	NHL Totals		**53**	**12**	**3**	**15**	**14**	**3**	**0**	**3**	**60**	**20.0**		**0**	**0.0**	**0**	**1**	**14:26**	....	....	....	....	....	....	....	....

• Re-entered NHL draft. Originally Boston's 2nd choice, 47th overall, in 1994 Entry Draft.

QMJHL First All-Star Team (1996)

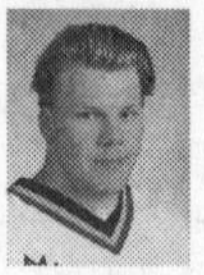

GORDON, Robb
(GOHR-dohn, RAWB)

Center. Shoots right. 5'11", 190 lbs. Born, Murrayville, B.C., January 13, 1976. Vancouver's 2nd choice, 39th overall, in 1994 Entry Draft.

Season	Club	League	GP	G	A	Pts	PIM	PP	SH	GW	S	%	+/-	TF	F%	H	SB	Min	GP	G	A	Pts	PIM	PP	SH	GW
1992-93	Powell River Kings	BCJHL	60	55	38	93	76	....	....	....	....	....	....	....	....	....	....	....	....	....	....	....	....	....	....	....
1993-94	Powell River Kings	BCJHL	60	69	*89	*158	141	....	....	....	....	....	....	....	....	....	....	....	....	....	....	....	....	....	....	....
1994-95	U. of Michigan	CCHA	39	15	26	41	72	....	....	....	....	....	....	....	....	....	....	....	....	....	....	....	....	....	....	....
1995-96	Kelowna Rockets	WHL	58	51	63	114	84	....	....	....	....	....	....	....	....	....	....	....	6	3	6	9	19	....	....	....
1996-97	Syracuse Crunch	AHL	63	11	14	25	72	....	....	....	....	....	....	....	....	....	....	....	3	0	0	0	7	....	....	....
1997-98	Syracuse Crunch	AHL	40	4	6	10	35	....	....	....	....	....	....	....	....	....	....	....	....	....	....	....	....	....	....	....
	Raleigh IceCaps	ECHL	7	3	10	13	28	....	....	....	....	....	....	....	....	....	....	....	....	....	....	....	....	....	....	....
1998-99	**Vancouver**	**NHL**	**4**	**0**	**0**	**0**	**2**	**0**	**0**	**0**	**1**	**0.0**	**0**	**25**	**52.0**	**2**	**0**	**8:50**	....	....	....	....	....	....	....	....
	Syracuse Crunch	AHL	68	16	22	38	98	....	....	....	....	....	....	....	....	....	....	....	....	....	....	....	....	....	....	....
99-2000	Long Beach	IHL	50	7	11	18	54	....	....	....	....	....	....	....	....	....	....	....	1	0	0	0	0	....	....	....
	NHL Totals		**4**	**0**	**0**	**0**	**2**	**0**	**0**	**0**	**1**	**0.0**		**25**	**52.0**	**2**	**0**	**8:50**	....	....	....	....	....	....	....	....

WHL West First All-Star Team (1996) • Signed as a free agent by **Long Beach** (IHL), August 23, 1999.

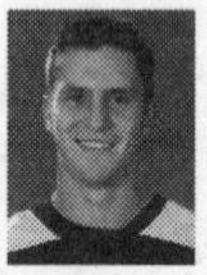

GOSSELIN, David
(GAH-sih-lihn, DAY-vihd) **NSH.**

Right wing. Shoots right. 6'1", 200 lbs. Born, Levis, Que., June 22, 1977. New Jersey's 4th choice, 78th overall, in 1995 Entry Draft.

Season	Club	League	GP	G	A	Pts	PIM	PP	SH	GW	S	%	+/-	TF	F%	H	SB	Min	GP	G	A	Pts	PIM	PP	SH	GW
1992-93	Richelieu	QAAA	40	5	12	17	....	....	....	....	....	....	....	....	....	....	....	....	....	....	....	....	....	....	....	....
1993-94	Richelieu	QAAA	44	26	19	45	62	....	....	....	....	....	....	....	....	....	....	....	....	....	....	....	....	....	....	....
1994-95	Sherbrooke	QMJHL	58	8	8	16	36	....	....	....	....	....	....	....	....	....	....	....	7	0	0	0	2	....	....	....
1995-96	Sherbrooke	QMJHL	55	24	24	48	147	....	....	....	....	....	....	....	....	....	....	....	7	2	2	4	4	....	....	....
1996-97	Sherbrooke	QMJHL	23	11	15	26	52	....	....	....	....	....	....	....	....	....	....	....	....	....	....	....	....	....	....	....
	Chicoutimi	QMJHL	28	16	33	49	65	....	....	....	....	....	....	....	....	....	....	....	12	9	7	16	16	....	....	....
1997-98	Chicoutimi	QMJHL	69	46	64	110	139	....	....	....	....	....	....	....	....	....	....	....	6	1	4	5	8	....	....	....
1998-99	Milwaukee	IHL	74	17	11	28	78	....	....	....	....	....	....	....	....	....	....	....	2	0	2	2	2	....	....	....
99-2000	**Nashville**	**NHL**	**10**	**2**	**1**	**3**	**6**	**0**	**0**	**0**	**14**	**14.3**	**–4**	**0**	**0.0**	**7**	**1**	**9:16**	....	....	....	....	....	....	....	....
	Milwaukee	IHL	70	21	20	41	118	....	....	....	....	....	....	....	....	....	....	....	3	0	0	0	10	....	....	....
	NHL Totals		**10**	**2**	**1**	**3**	**6**	**0**	**0**	**0**	**14**	**14.3**		**0**	**0.0**	**7**	**1**	**9:16**	....	....	....	....	....	....	....	....

Signed as a free agent by **Nashville**, July 1, 1998.

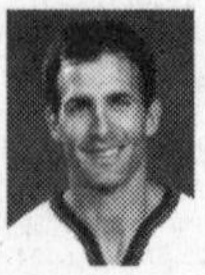

GRANATO, Tony
(gruh-NA-toh, TOH-nee) **S.J.**

Right wing. Shoots right. 5'10", 185 lbs. Born, Downers Grove, IL, July 25, 1964. NY Rangers' 5th choice, 120th overall, in 1982 Entry Draft.

Season	Club	League	GP	G	A	Pts	PIM	PP	SH	GW	S	%	+/-	TF	F%	H	SB	Min	GP	G	A	Pts	PIM	PP	SH	GW
1982-83	Northwood Prep	Hi-School	34	32	60	92	....	....	....	....	....	....	....	....	....	....	....	....	....	....	....	....	....	....	....	....
1983-84	U. of Wisconsin	WCHA	35	14	17	31	48	....	....	....	....	....	....	....	....	....	....	....	....	....	....	....	....	....	....	....
1984-85	U. of Wisconsin	WCHA	42	33	34	67	94	....	....	....	....	....	....	....	....	....	....	....	....	....	....	....	....	....	....	....
1985-86	U. of Wisconsin	WCHA	33	25	24	49	36	....	....	....	....	....	....	....	....	....	....	....	....	....	....	....	....	....	....	....
1986-87	U. of Wisconsin	WCHA	42	28	45	73	64	....	....	....	....	....	....	....	....	....	....	....	....	....	....	....	....	....	....	....
1987-88	United States	Nat-Team	49	40	31	71	55	....	....	....	....	....	....	....	....	....	....	....	....	....	....	....	....	....	....	....
	United States	Olympics	6	1	7	8	4	....	....	....	....	....	....	....	....	....	....	....	....	....	....	....	....	....	....	....
	Colorado Rangers	IHL	22	13	14	27	36	....	....	....	....	....	....	....	....	....	....	....	8	9	4	13	16	....	....	....
1988-89	**NY Rangers**	**NHL**	**78**	**36**	**27**	**63**	**140**	**4**	**4**	**3**	**234**	**15.4**	**17**	....	....	....	....	....	**4**	**1**	**1**	**2**	**21**	**0**	**0**	**0**
1989-90	**NY Rangers**	**NHL**	**37**	**7**	**18**	**25**	**77**	**1**	**0**	**0**	**79**	**8.9**	**1**	....	....	....	....	....	....	....	....	....	....	....	....	....
	Los Angeles	**NHL**	**19**	**5**	**6**	**11**	**45**	**1**	**0**	**0**	**41**	**12.2**	**–2**	....	....	....	....	....	**10**	**5**	**4**	**9**	**12**	**2**	**1**	**2**
1990-91	**Los Angeles**	**NHL**	**68**	**30**	**34**	**64**	**154**	**11**	**1**	**3**	**197**	**15.2**	**22**	....	....	....	....	....	**12**	**1**	**4**	**5**	**28**	**0**	**0**	**0**
1991-92	**Los Angeles**	**NHL**	**80**	**39**	**29**	**68**	**187**	**7**	**2**	**8**	**223**	**17.5**	**4**	....	....	....	....	....	**6**	**1**	**5**	**6**	**10**	**0**	**0**	**0**
1992-93	**Los Angeles**	**NHL**	**81**	**37**	**45**	**82**	**171**	**14**	**2**	**6**	**247**	**15.0**	**–1**	....	....	....	....	....	**24**	**6**	**11**	**17**	**50**	**1**	**0**	**1**
1993-94	**Los Angeles**	**NHL**	**50**	**7**	**14**	**21**	**150**	**2**	**0**	**0**	**117**	**6.0**	**–2**	....	....	....	....	....	....	....	....	....	....	....	....	....
1994-95	**Los Angeles**	**NHL**	**33**	**13**	**11**	**24**	**68**	**2**	**0**	**3**	**106**	**12.3**	**9**	....	....	....	....	....	....	....	....	....	....	....	....	....
1995-96	**Los Angeles**	**NHL**	**49**	**17**	**18**	**35**	**46**	**5**	**0**	**1**	**156**	**10.9**	**–5**	....	....	....	....	....	....	....	....	....	....	....	....	....
1996-97	**San Jose**	**NHL**	**76**	**25**	**15**	**40**	**159**	**5**	**1**	**4**	**231**	**10.8**	**–7**	....	....	....	....	....	....	....	....	....	....	....	....	....
1997-98	**San Jose**	**NHL**	**59**	**16**	**9**	**25**	**70**	**3**	**0**	**2**	**119**	**13.4**	**3**	....	....	....	....	....	**1**	**0**	**0**	**0**	**0**	**0**	**0**	**0**
1998-99	**San Jose**	**NHL**	**35**	**6**	**6**	**12**	**54**	**0**	**1**	**1**	**65**	**9.2**	**4**	**3**	**100.0**	**31**	**4**	**10:29**	**6**	**1**	**1**	**2**	**2**	**0**	**0**	**0**
99-2000	**San Jose**	**NHL**	**48**	**6**	**7**	**13**	**39**	**1**	**0**	**0**	**67**	**9.0**	**2**	**4**	**50.0**	**47**	**6**	**9:05**	**12**	**0**	**1**	**1**	**14**	**0**	**0**	**0**
	NHL Totals		**713**	**244**	**239**	**483**	**1360**	**56**	**11**	**31**	**1882**	**13.0**		**7**	**71.4**	**78**	**10**	**9:40**	**75**	**15**	**27**	**42**	**137**	**3**	**1**	**3**

WCHA Second All-Star Team (1985, 1987) • NCAA West Second All-American Team (1985, 1987) • NHL All-Rookie Team (1989) • Won Bill Masterton Memorial Trophy (1997) • Played in NHL All-Star Game (1997)

Traded to **LA Kings** by **NY Rangers** with Tomas Sandstrom for Bernie Nicholls, January 20, 1990. Signed as a free agent by **San Jose**, August 15, 1996.

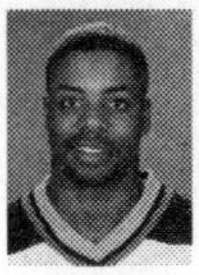

GRAND-PIERRE, Jean-Luc

(GRAHN pee-AIR, ZHAHN-LOOK) **CBJ**

Defense. Shoots right. 6'3", 207 lbs. Born, Montreal, Que., February 2, 1977. St. Louis' 6th choice, 179th overall, in 1995 Entry Draft.

			Regular Season																Playoffs							
Season	Club	League	GP	G	A	Pts	PIM	PP	SH	GW	S	%	+/-	TF	F%	H	SB	Min	GP	G	A	Pts	PIM	PP	SH	GW
1993-94	Beauport	QMJHL	46	1	4	5	27	....	....	....	....	....	....	....	....	....	....	....	1	0	0	0	0	....	....	....
1994-95	Val-d'Or Foreurs	QMJHL	59	10	13	23	126	....	....	....	....	....	....	....	....	....	....	....	....	....	....	....	....	....	....	....
1995-96	Val-d'Or Foreurs	QMJHL	67	13	21	34	209	....	....	....	....	....	....	....	....	....	....	....	13	1	4	5	47	....	....	....
1996-97	Val-d'Or Foreurs	QMJHL	58	9	24	33	186	....	....	....	....	....	....	....	....	....	....	....	13	5	8	13	46	....	....	....
1997-98	Rochester	AHL	75	4	6	10	211	....	....	....	....	....	....	....	....	....	....	....	4	0	0	0	2	....	....	....
1998-99	**Buffalo**	**NHL**	**16**	**0**	**1**	**1**	**17**	**0**	**0**	**0**	**11**	**0.0**	**0**	**0**	**0.0**	**46**	**13**	**13:36**	....	....	....	....	....	....	....	....
	Rochester	AHL	55	5	4	9	90	....	....	....	....	....	....	....	....	....	....	....	....	....	....	....	....	....	....	....
99-2000	**Buffalo**	**NHL**	**11**	**0**	**0**	**0**	**15**	**0**	**0**	**0**	**11**	**0.0**	**−1**	**0**	**0.0**	**29**	**8**	**15:11**	**4**	**0**	**0**	**0**	**4**	**0**	**0**	**0**
	Rochester	AHL	62	5	8	13	124	....	....	....	....	....	....	....	....	....	....	....	17	0	1	1	40	....	....	....
	NHL Totals		**27**	**0**	**1**	**1**	**32**	**0**	**0**	**0**	**22**	**0.0**		**0**	**0.0**	**75**	**21**	**14:15**	**4**	**0**	**0**	**0**	**4**	**0**	**0**	**0**

Traded to **Buffalo** by **St. Louis** with Ottawa's 2nd round choice (previously acquired, Buffalo selected Cory Sarich) in 1996 Entry Draft and St. Louis' 3rd round choice (Maxim Afinogenov) in 1997 Entry Draft for Yuri Khmylev and Buffalo's 8th round choice (Andrei Podkonicky) in 1996 Entry Draft, March 20, 1996. Traded to **Columbus** by **Buffalo** with Matt Davidson, San Jose's 5th round choice (previously acquired, Columbus selected Tyler Kolarik) in 2000 Entry Draft and Buffalo's 5th round choice in 2001 Entry Draft to complete Expansion Draft agreement which had Columbus select Geoff Sanderson and Dwayne Roloson from Buffalo, June 23, 2000.

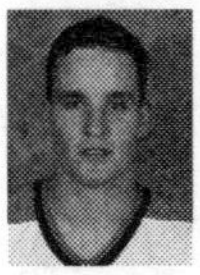

GRATTON, Benoit

(grah-TOHN, BEHN-wah) **CGY.**

Left wing. Shoots left. 5'11", 194 lbs. Born, Montreal, Que., December 28, 1976. Washington's 6th choice, 105th overall, in 1995 Entry Draft.

Season	Club	League	GP	G	A	Pts	PIM	PP	SH	GW	S	%	+/-	TF	F%	H	SB	Min	GP	G	A	Pts	PIM	PP	SH	GW
1992-93	Laval Regents	QAAA	40	19	38	57	74	....	....	....	....	....	....	....	....	....	....	....	13	1	9	10	27	....	....	....
1993-94	Laval Titan	QMJHL	51	9	14	23	70	....	....	....	....	....	....	....	....	....	....	....	20	2	1	3	19	....	....	....
1994-95	Laval Titan	QMJHL	71	30	58	88	199	....	....	....	....	....	....	....	....	....	....	....	20	8	*21	29	42	....	....	....
1995-96	Laval Titan	QMJHL	38	21	39	60	130	....	....	....	....	....	....	....	....	....	....	....	....	....	....	....	....	....	....	....
	Granby Bisons	QMJHL	27	12	46	58	97	....	....	....	....	....	....	....	....	....	....	....	21	13	26	39	68	....	....	....
1996-97	Portland Pirates	AHL	76	6	40	46	140	....	....	....	....	....	....	....	....	....	....	....	5	2	1	3	14	....	....	....
1997-98	**Washington**	**NHL**	**6**	**0**	**1**	**1**	**6**	**0**	**0**	**0**	**5**	**0.0**	**1**						....	....	....	....	....	....	....	....
	Portland Pirates	AHL	58	19	31	50	137	....	....	....	....	....	....	....	....	....	....	....	8	4	2	6	24	....	....	....
1998-99	**Washington**	**NHL**	**16**	**4**	**3**	**7**	**16**	**0**	**0**	**0**	**24**	**16.7**	**−1**	**136**	**54.4**	**26**	**7**	**13:28**	....	....	....	....	....	....	....	....
	Portland Pirates	AHL	64	18	42	60	135	....	....	....	....	....	....	....	....	....	....	....	....	....	....	....	....	....	....	....
99-2000	**Calgary**	**NHL**	**10**	**0**	**2**	**2**	**10**	**0**	**0**	**0**	**4**	**0.0**	**1**	**68**	**63.2**	**8**	**2**	**8:15**	....	....	....	....	....	....	....	....
	Saint John Flames	AHL	65	17	49	66	137	....	....	....	....	....	....	....	....	....	....	....	3	0	1	1	4	....	....	....
	NHL Totals		**32**	**4**	**6**	**10**	**32**	**0**	**0**	**0**	**33**	**12.1**		**204**	**57.4**	**34**	**9**	**11:28**	....	....	....	....	....	....	....	....

Traded to **Calgary** by **Washington** for Steve Shirreffs, August 18, 1999.

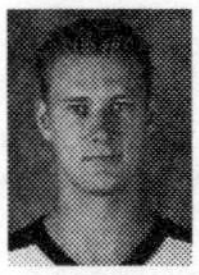

GRATTON, Chris

(GRA-tuhn, KRIHS) **BUF.**

Center. Shoots left. 6'4", 226 lbs. Born, Brantford, Ont., July 5, 1975. Tampa Bay's 1st choice, 3rd overall, in 1993 Entry Draft.

Season	Club	League	GP	G	A	Pts	PIM	PP	SH	GW	S	%	+/-	TF	F%	H	SB	Min	GP	G	A	Pts	PIM	PP	SH	GW
1989-90	Brantford	OJHL-B	1	0	2	2	2	....	....	....	....	....	....	....	....	....	....	....	....	....	....	....	....	....	....	....
1990-91	Brantford	OJHL-B	31	30	30	60	28	....	....	....	....	....	....	....	....	....	....	....	....	....	....	....	....	....	....	....
1991-92	Kingston	OHL	62	27	39	66	37	....	....	....	....	....	....	....	....	....	....	....	....	....	....	....	....	....	....	....
1992-93	Kingston	OHL	58	55	54	109	125	....	....	....	....	....	....	....	....	....	....	....	16	11	18	29	42	....	....	....
1993-94	**Tampa Bay**	**NHL**	**84**	**13**	**29**	**42**	**123**	**5**	**1**	**2**	**161**	**8.1**	**−25**	....	....	....	....	....	....	....	....	....	....	....	....	....
1994-95	**Tampa Bay**	**NHL**	**46**	**7**	**20**	**27**	**89**	**2**	**0**	**0**	**91**	**7.7**	**−2**	....	....	....	....	....	....	....	....	....	....	....	....	....
1995-96	**Tampa Bay**	**NHL**	**82**	**17**	**21**	**38**	**105**	**7**	**0**	**3**	**183**	**9.3**	**−13**	....	....	....	....	....	**6**	**0**	**2**	**2**	**27**	**0**	**0**	**0**
1996-97	**Tampa Bay**	**NHL**	**82**	**30**	**32**	**62**	**201**	**9**	**0**	**4**	**230**	**13.0**	**−28**	....	....	....	....	....	....	....	....	....	....	....	....	....
1997-98	**Philadelphia**	**NHL**	**82**	**22**	**40**	**62**	**159**	**5**	**0**	**2**	**182**	**12.1**	**11**	....	....	....	....	....	**5**	**2**	**0**	**2**	**10**	**0**	**0**	**0**
1998-99	**Philadelphia**	**NHL**	**26**	**1**	**7**	**8**	**41**	**0**	**0**	**0**	**54**	**1.9**	**−8**	**38**	**42.1**	**35**	**0**	**14:25**	....	....	....	....	....	....	....	....
	Tampa Bay	**NHL**	**52**	**7**	**19**	**26**	**102**	**1**	**0**	**1**	**127**	**5.5**	**−20**	**1032**	**53.9**	**74**	**12**	**18:20**	....	....	....	....	....	....	....	....
99-2000	**Tampa Bay**	**NHL**	**58**	**14**	**27**	**41**	**121**	**4**	**0**	**1**	**168**	**8.3**	**−24**	**1341**	**55.9**	**120**	**13**	**20:03**	....	....	....	....	....	....	....	....
	Buffalo	**NHL**	**14**	**1**	**7**	**8**	**15**	**0**	**0**	**0**	**34**	**2.9**	**1**	**256**	**54.3**	**27**	**8**	**16:40**	**5**	**0**	**1**	**1**	**4**	**0**	**0**	**0**
	NHL Totals		**526**	**112**	**202**	**314**	**956**	**33**	**1**	**13**	**1230**	**9.1**		**2667**	**54.7**	**256**	**33**	**18:010**	**16**	**2**	**3**	**5**	**41**	**0**	**0**	**0**

Signed as a free agent by **Philadelphia**, August 14, 1997. Traded to **Tampa Bay** by **Philadelphia** with Mike Sillinger for Mikael Renberg and Daymond Langkow, December 12, 1998. Traded to **Buffalo** by **Tampa Bay** with Tampa Bay's 2nd round choice in 2001 Entry Draft for Cory Sarich, Wayne Primeau, Brian Holzinger and Buffalo's 3rd round choice (Alexandre Kharitonov) in 2000 Entry Draft, March 9, 2000.

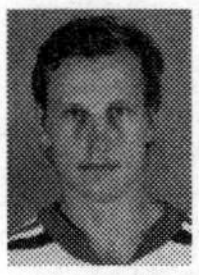

GRAVES, Adam

(GRAYVS, A-dam) **NYR**

Center. Shoots left. 6', 205 lbs. Born, Toronto, Ont., April 12, 1968. Detroit's 2nd choice, 22nd overall, in 1986 Entry Draft.

Season	Club	League	GP	G	A	Pts	PIM	PP	SH	GW	S	%	+/-	TF	F%	H	SB	Min	GP	G	A	Pts	PIM	PP	SH	GW
1984-85	King City Dukes	OJHL-B	25	23	33	56	29	....	....	....	....	....	....	....	....	....	....	....	....	....	....	....	....	....	....	....
1985-86	Windsor Spitfires	OHL	62	27	37	64	35	....	....	....	....	....	....	....	....	....	....	....	16	5	11	16	10	....	....	....
1986-87	Windsor Spitfires	OHL	66	45	55	100	70	....	....	....	....	....	....	....	....	....	....	....	14	9	8	17	32	....	....	....
	Adirondack	AHL	....	....	....	....	....	....	....	....	....	....	....	....	....	....	....	....	5	0	1	1	0	....	....	....
1987-88	Windsor Spitfires	OHL	37	28	32	60	107	....	....	....	....	....	....	....	....	....	....	....	12	14	18	*32	16	....	....	....
	Detroit	**NHL**	**9**	**0**	**1**	**1**	**8**	**0**	**0**	**0**	**9**	**0.0**	**−2**						....	....	....	....	....	....	....	....
1988-89	**Detroit**	**NHL**	**56**	**7**	**5**	**12**	**60**	**0**	**0**	**1**	**60**	**11.7**	**−5**						**5**	**0**	**0**	**0**	**4**	**0**	**0**	**0**
	Adirondack	AHL	14	10	11	21	28	....	....	....	....	....	....	....	....	....	....	....	14	11	7	18	17	....	....	....
1989-90	**Detroit**	**NHL**	**13**	**0**	**1**	**1**	**13**	**0**	**0**	**0**	**10**	**0.0**	**−5**						....	....	....	....	....	....	....	....
	♦ Edmonton	**NHL**	**63**	**9**	**12**	**21**	**123**	**1**	**0**	**1**	**84**	**10.7**	**5**						**22**	**5**	**6**	**11**	**17**	**0**	**0**	**1**
1990-91	**Edmonton**	**NHL**	**76**	**7**	**18**	**25**	**127**	**2**	**0**	**1**	**126**	**5.6**	**−21**						**18**	**2**	**4**	**6**	**22**	**0**	**0**	**0**
1991-92	**NY Rangers**	**NHL**	**80**	**26**	**33**	**59**	**139**	**4**	**4**	**4**	**228**	**11.4**	**19**						**10**	**5**	**3**	**8**	**22**	**1**	**0**	**1**
1992-93	**NY Rangers**	**NHL**	**84**	**36**	**29**	**65**	**148**	**12**	**1**	**6**	**275**	**13.1**	**−4**						....	....	....	....	....	....	....	....
1993-94♦	**NY Rangers**	**NHL**	**84**	**52**	**27**	**79**	**127**	**20**	**4**	**4**	**291**	**17.9**	**27**						**23**	**10**	**7**	**17**	**24**	**3**	**0**	**0**
1994-95	**NY Rangers**	**NHL**	**47**	**17**	**14**	**31**	**51**	**9**	**0**	**3**	**185**	**9.2**	**9**						**10**	**4**	**4**	**8**	**8**	**2**	**0**	**0**
1995-96	**NY Rangers**	**NHL**	**82**	**22**	**36**	**58**	**100**	**9**	**1**	**2**	**266**	**8.3**	**18**						**10**	**7**	**1**	**8**	**4**	**6**	**0**	**2**
1996-97	**NY Rangers**	**NHL**	**82**	**33**	**28**	**61**	**66**	**10**	**4**	**3**	**269**	**12.3**	**10**						**15**	**2**	**1**	**3**	**12**	**1**	**0**	**2**
1997-98	**NY Rangers**	**NHL**	**72**	**23**	**12**	**35**	**41**	**10**	**0**	**2**	**226**	**10.2**	**−30**						....	....	....	....	....	....	....	....
1998-99	**NY Rangers**	**NHL**	**82**	**38**	**15**	**53**	**47**	**14**	**2**	**7**	**239**	**15.9**	**−12**	**347**	**51.3**	**162**	**28**	**20:33**	....	....	....	....	....	....	....	....
99-2000	**NY Rangers**	**NHL**	**77**	**23**	**17**	**40**	**14**	**11**	**0**	**4**	**194**	**11.9**	**−15**	**51**	**49.0**	**166**	**27**	**18:46**	....	....	....	....	....	....	....	....
	NHL Totals		**907**	**293**	**248**	**541**	**1064**	**102**	**16**	**38**	**2462**	**11.9**		**398**	**51.0**	**328**	**55**	**19:41**	**113**	**35**	**26**	**61**	**113**	**13**	**0**	**6**

NHL Second All-Star Team (1994) • Won King Clancy Memorial Trophy (1994) • Played in NHL All-Star Game (1994)

Traded to **Edmonton** by **Detroit** with Petr Klima, Joe Murphy and Jeff Sharples for Jimmy Carson, Kevin McClelland and Edmonton's 5th round choice (later traded to Montreal - Montreal selected Brad Layzell) in 1991 Entry Draft, November 2, 1989. Signed as a free agent by **NY Rangers**, September 3, 1991.

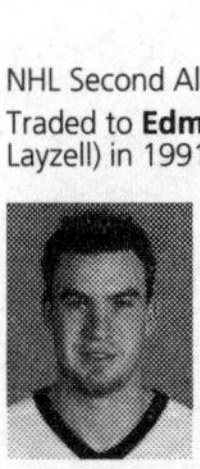

GREEN, Josh

(GREEN, JAWSH) **EDM.**

Left wing. Shoots left. 6'4", 212 lbs. Born, Camrose, Alta., November 16, 1977. Los Angeles' 1st choice, 30th overall, in 1996 Entry Draft.

Season	Club	League	GP	G	A	Pts	PIM	PP	SH	GW	S	%	+/-	TF	F%	H	SB	Min	GP	G	A	Pts	PIM	PP	SH	GW
1992-93	Camrose Kodiaks	AAHA	60	55	45	100	80	....	....	....	....	....	....	....	....	....	....	....	....	....	....	....	....	....	....	....
1993-94	Medicine Hat	WHL	63	22	22	44	43	....	....	....	....	....	....	....	....	....	....	....	3	0	0	0	4	....	....	....
1994-95	Medicine Hat	WHL	68	32	23	55	64	....	....	....	....	....	....	....	....	....	....	....	5	5	1	6	2	....	....	....
1995-96	Medicine Hat	WHL	46	18	25	43	55	....	....	....	....	....	....	....	....	....	....	....	5	2	2	4	4	....	....	....
1996-97	Medicine Hat	WHL	51	25	32	57	61	....	....	....	....	....	....	....	....	....	....	....	....	....	....	....	....	....	....	....
	Swift Current	WHL	23	10	15	25	33	....	....	....	....	....	....	....	....	....	....	....	10	9	7	16	19	....	....	....
1997-98	Swift Current	WHL	5	9	1	10	9	....	....	....	....	....	....	....	....	....	....	....	....	....	....	....	....	....	....	....
	Portland	WHL	26	26	18	44	27	....	....	....	....	....	....	....	....	....	....	....	....	....	....	....	....	....	....	....
	Fredericton	AHL	43	16	15	31	14	....	....	....	....	....	....	....	....	....	....	....	4	1	3	4	6	....	....	....
1998-99	**Los Angeles**	**NHL**	**27**	**1**	**3**	**4**	**8**	**1**	**0**	**0**	**35**	**2.9**	**−5**	**2**	**50.0**	**30**	**1**	**11:44**	....	....	....	....	....	....	....	....
	Springfield	AHL	41	15	15	30	29	....	....	....	....	....	....	....	....	....	....	....	....	....	....	....	....	....	....	....
99-2000	**NY Islanders**	**NHL**	**49**	**12**	**14**	**26**	**41**	**2**	**0**	**3**	**109**	**11.0**	**−7**	**12**	**50.0**	**105**	**8**	**13:36**	....	....	....	....	....	....	....	....
	Lowell	AHL	17	6	2	8	19	....	....	....	....	....	....	....	....	....	....	....	....	....	....	....	....	....	....	....
	NHL Totals		**76**	**13**	**17**	**30**	**49**	**3**	**0**	**3**	**144**	**9.0**		**14**	**50.0**	**135**	**9**	**12:56**	....	....	....	....	....	....	....	....

Traded to **NY Islanders** by **LA Kings** with Olli Jokinen, Mathieu Biron and LA Kings' 1st round choice (Taylor Pyatt) in 1999 Entry Draft for Zigmund Palffy, Brian Smolinski, Marcel Cousineau and New Jersey's 4th round choice (previously acquired, LA Kings selected Daniel Johanssen) in 1999 Entry Draft, June 20, 1999. Traded to **Edmonton** by **NY Islanders** with Eric Brewer and NY Islanders' 2nd round choice (Brad Winchester) in 2000 Entry Draft for Roman Hamrlik, June 24, 2000.

	Regular Season																			Playoffs							
Season	Club	League	GP	G	A	Pts	PIM	PP	SH	GW	S	%	+/-	TF	F%	H	SB	Min	GP	G	A	Pts	PIM	PP	SH	GW

GREEN, Travis

(GREEN, TRA-vihs)   **PHX.**

Center. Shoots right. 6'2", 200 lbs.   Born, Castlegar, B.C., December 20, 1970. NY Islanders' 2nd choice, 23rd overall, in 1989 Entry Draft.

Season	Club	League	GP	G	A	Pts	PIM	PP	SH	GW	S	%	+/-	TF	F%	H	SB	Min	GP	G	A	Pts	PIM	PP	SH	GW
1985-86	Castlegar Rebels	KIJHL	35	30	40	70	41	....	....	....	....	....	....						....	....	....	....	....			
1986-87	Spokane Chiefs	WHL	64	8	17	25	27	....	....	....	....	....	....						3	0	0	0	0			
1987-88	Spokane Chiefs	WHL	72	33	54	87	42	....	....	....	....	....	....						15	10	10	20	13			
1988-89	Spokane Chiefs	WHL	75	51	51	102	79	....	....	....	....	....	....						....	....	....	....	....			
1989-90	Spokane Chiefs	WHL	50	45	44	89	80	....	....	....	....	....	....						....	....	....	....	....			
	Medicine Hat	WHL	25	15	24	39	19	....	....	....	....	....	....						3	0	0	0	2			
1990-91	Capital District	AHL	73	21	34	55	26	....	....	....	....	....	....						....	....	....	....	....			
1991-92	Capital District	AHL	71	23	27	50	10	....	....	....	....	....	....						7	0	4	4	21			
1992-93	**NY Islanders**	**NHL**	61	7	18	25	43	1	0	0	115	6.1	4						12	3	1	4	6	0	0	0
	Capital District	AHL	20	12	11	23	39	....	....	....	....	....	....						....	....	....	....	....			
1993-94	**NY Islanders**	**NHL**	83	18	22	40	44	1	0	2	164	11.0	16						4	0	0	0	2	0	0	0
1994-95	**NY Islanders**	**NHL**	42	5	7	12	25	0	0	0	59	8.5	-10						....	....	....	....	....			
1995-96	**NY Islanders**	**NHL**	69	25	45	70	42	14	1	2	186	13.4	-20						....	....	....	....	....			
1996-97	**NY Islanders**	**NHL**	79	23	41	64	38	10	0	3	177	13.0	-5						....	....	....	....	....			
1997-98	**NY Islanders**	**NHL**	54	14	12	26	66	8	0	2	99	14.1	-19						....	....	....	....	....			
	Anaheim	NHL	22	5	11	16	16	1	0	0	42	11.9	-10						....	....	....	....	....			
1998-99	**Anaheim**	**NHL**	79	13	17	30	81	3	1	2	165	7.9	-7	1325	52.8	97	24	17:17	4	0	1	1	4	0	0	0
99-2000	**Phoenix**	**NHL**	78	25	21	46	45	6	0	2	157	15.9	-4	1322	55.6	120	11	16:36	5	2	1	3	2	0	0	0
	NHL Totals		**567**	**135**	**194**	**329**	**400**	**44**	**2**	**13**	**1164**	**11.6**		**2647**	**54.2**	**217**	**35**	**16:56**	**25**	**5**	**3**	**8**	**14**	**0**	**0**	**0**

Traded to **Anaheim** by NY Islanders with Doug Houda and Tony Tuzzolino for Joe Sacco, J.J. Daigneault and Mark Janssens, February 6, 1998. Traded to **Phoenix** by **Anaheim** with Anaheim's 1st round choice (Scott Kelman) in 1999 Entry Draft for Oleg Tverdovsky, June 26, 1999.

GREIG, Mark

(GREG, MAHRK)   **PHI.**

Right wing. Shoots right. 5'11", 190 lbs.   Born, High River, Alta., January 25, 1970. Hartford's 1st choice, 15th overall, in 1990 Entry Draft.

Season	Club	League	GP	G	A	Pts	PIM	PP	SH	GW	S	%	+/-	TF	F%	H	SB	Min	GP	G	A	Pts	PIM	PP	SH	GW
1985-86	Blackie Bisons	AAHA	31	12	43	55	44	....	....	....	....	....	....						....	....	....	....	....			
1986-87	Calgary Stars	AAHA	18	9	28	37	30	....	....	....	....	....	....						....	....	....	....	....			
	Calgary Wranglers	WHL	5	0	0	0	0	....	....	....	....	....	....						....	....	....	....	....			
1987-88	Lethbridge	WHL	65	9	18	27	38	....	....	....	....	....	....						....	....	....	....	....			
1988-89	Lethbridge	WHL	71	36	72	108	113	....	....	....	....	....	....						8	5	5	10	16			
1989-90	Lethbridge	WHL	65	55	80	135	149	....	....	....	....	....	....						18	11	21	32	35			
1990-91	**Hartford**	**NHL**	4	0	0	0	0	0	0	0	1	0.0	-1						....	....	....	....	....			
	Springfield	AHL	73	32	55	87	73	....	....	....	....	....	....						17	2	6	8	22			
1991-92	**Hartford**	**NHL**	17	0	5	5	6	0	0	0	18	0.0	7						....	....	....	....	....			
	Springfield	AHL	50	20	27	47	38	....	....	....	....	....	....						9	1	1	2	20			
1992-93	**Hartford**	**NHL**	22	1	7	8	27	0	0	0	16	6.3	-11						....	....	....	....	....			
	Springfield	AHL	55	20	38	58	86	....	....	....	....	....	....						....	....	....	....	....			
1993-94	**Hartford**	**NHL**	31	4	5	9	31	0	0	0	41	9.8	-6						....	....	....	....	....			
	Springfield	AHL	4	0	4	4	21	....	....	....	....	....	....						....	....	....	....	....			
	St. John's Leafs	AHL	9	4	6	10	0	....	....	....	....	....	....						11	4	2	6	26			
	Toronto	**NHL**	13	2	2	4	10	0	0	0	14	14.3	1						....	....	....	....	....			
1994-95	**Calgary**	**NHL**	8	1	1	2	2	0	0	0	5	20.0	1						....	....	....	....	....			
	Saint John Flames	AHL	67	31	50	81	82	....	....	....	....	....	....						2	0	1	1	0			
1995-96	Atlanta Knights	IHL	71	25	48	73	104	....	....	....	....	....	....						3	2	1	3	4			
1996-97	Quebec Rafales	IHL	5	1	2	3	0	....	....	....	....	....	....						....	....	....	....	....			
	Houston Aeros	IHL	59	12	30	42	59	....	....	....	....	....	....						13	5	8	13	2			
1997-98	Grand Rapids	IHL	69	26	36	62	103	....	....	....	....	....	....						3	0	4	4	4			
1998-99	**Philadelphia**	**NHL**	7	1	3	4	2	0	0	0	9	11.1	1	0	0.0	5	3	9:55	2	0	1	1	0	0	0	0
	Philadelphia	AHL	67	23	46	69	102	....	....	....	....	....	....						7	1	5	6	14			
99-2000	**Philadelphia**	**NHL**	11	3	2	5	6	0	0	1	14	21.4	0	1	0.0	7	1	11:19	3	0	0	0	0	0	0	0
	Philadelphia	AHL	68	34	48	82	116	....	....	....	....	....	....						5	3	2	5	6			
	NHL Totals		**113**	**12**	**25**	**37**	**84**	**0**	**0**	**1**	**118**	**10.2**		**1**	**0.0**	**12**	**4**	**10:47**	**5**	**0**	**1**	**1**	**0**	**0**	**0**	**0**

WHL East First All-Star Team (1990)

Traded to **Toronto** by **Hartford** with Hartford's 6th round choice (Doug Bonner) in 1995 Entry Draft for Ted Crowley, January 25, 1994. Signed as a free agent by **Calgary**, August 9, 1994. Signed as a free agent by **Philadelphia**, July 28, 1998.

GRIER, Mike

(GREER, MIHK-al)   **EDM.**

Right wing. Shoots right. 6'1", 227 lbs.   Born, Detroit, MI, January 5, 1975. St. Louis' 7th choice, 219th overall, in 1993 Entry Draft.

Season	Club	League	GP	G	A	Pts	PIM	PP	SH	GW	S	%	+/-	TF	F%	H	SB	Min	GP	G	A	Pts	PIM	PP	SH	GW
1992-93	St. Sebastian's	Hi-School	22	16	27	43	32	....	....	....	....	....	....						....	....	....	....	....			
1993-94	Boston University	H-East	39	9	9	18	56	....	....	....	....	....	....						....	....	....	....	....			
1994-95	Boston University	H-East	37	*29	26	55	85	....	....	....	....	....	....						....	....	....	....	....			
1995-96	Boston University	H-East	38	21	25	46	82	....	....	....	....	....	....						....	....	....	....	....			
1996-97	**Edmonton**	**NHL**	79	15	17	32	45	4	0	2	89	16.9	7						12	3	1	4	4	1	0	1
1997-98	**Edmonton**	**NHL**	66	9	6	15	73	1	0	1	90	10.0	-3						12	2	2	4	13	0	0	1
1998-99	**Edmonton**	**NHL**	82	20	24	44	54	3	2	1	143	14.0	5	34	20.6	188	49	15:57	4	1	1	2	6	0	0	0
99-2000	**Edmonton**	**NHL**	65	9	22	31	68	0	3	2	115			0	0.0	0	0	0:00	....	....	....	....	....			
	NHL Totals		**292**	**53**	**69**	**122**	**240**	**8**	**5**	**6**	**437**	**12.1**		**34**	**20.6**	**188**	**49**	**15:57**	**28**	**6**	**4**	**10**	**23**	**1**	**0**	**2**

Hockey East First All-Star Team (1995) • NCAA East First All-American Team (1995)

Rights traded to **Edmonton** by **St. Louis** with Curtis Joseph for St. Louis' 1st round choices (previously acquired) in 1996 (Marty Reasoner) and 1997 (later traded to LA Kings - LA Kings selected Matt Zultek) Entry Drafts, August 4, 1995.

GRIMSON, Stu

(GRIHM-suhn, STOO)   **L.A.**

Left wing. Shoots left. 6'5", 227 lbs.   Born, Kamloops, B.C., May 20, 1965. Calgary's 8th choice, 143rd overall, in 1985 Entry Draft.

Season	Club	League	GP	G	A	Pts	PIM	PP	SH	GW	S	%	+/-	TF	F%	H	SB	Min	GP	G	A	Pts	PIM	PP	SH	GW
1982-83	Regina Pats	WHL	48	0	1	1	105	....	....	....	....	....	....						5	0	0	0	14	....	....	....
1983-84	Regina Pats	WHL	63	8	8	16	131	....	....	....	....	....	....						21	0	1	1	29	....	....	....
1984-85	Regina Pats	WHL	71	24	32	56	248	....	....	....	....	....	....						8	1	2	3	14	....	....	....
1985-86	U. of Manitoba	CWUAA	12	7	4	11	113	....	....	....	....	....	....						8	1	1	2	24	....	....	....
1986-87	U. of Manitoba	CWUAA	29	8	8	16	67	....	....	....	....	....	....						14	4	2	6	28	....	....	....
1987-88	Salt Lake City	IHL	38	9	5	14	268	....	....	....	....	....	....						....	....	....	....	....			
1988-89	**Calgary**	**NHL**	1	0	0	0	5	0	0	0	0	0.0	0						....	....	....	....	....			
	Salt Lake City	IHL	72	9	18	27	397	....	....	....	....	....	....						14	2	3	5	86			
1989-90	**Calgary**	**NHL**	3	0	0	0	17	0	0	0	0	0.0	-1						....	....	....	....	....			
	Salt Lake City	IHL	62	8	8	16	319	....	....	....	....	....	....						4	0	0	0	8			
1990-91	**Chicago**	**NHL**	35	0	1	1	183	0	0	0	14	0.0	-3						5	0	0	0	46	0	0	0
1991-92	**Chicago**	**NHL**	54	2	2	4	234	0	0	0	23	8.7	-2						14	0	1	1	10	0	0	0
	Indianapolis Ice	IHL	5	1	1	2	17	....	....	....	....	....	....						....	....	....	....	....			
1992-93	**Chicago**	**NHL**	78	1	1	2	193	1	0	0	14	7.1	2						2	0	0	0	4	0	0	0
1993-94	**Anaheim**	**NHL**	77	1	5	6	199	0	0	0	34	2.9	-6						....	....	....	....	....			
1994-95	**Anaheim**	**NHL**	31	0	1	1	110	0	0	0	14	0.0	-7						....	....	....	....	....			
	Detroit	**NHL**	11	0	0	0	37	0	0	0	4	0.0	-4						11	1	0	1	26	0	0	0
1995-96	**Detroit**	**NHL**	56	0	1	1	128	0	0	0	19	0.0	-10						2	0	0	0	0	0	0	0
1996-97	**Detroit**	**NHL**	1	0	0	0	0	0	0	0	0	0.0	-1						....	....	....	....	....			
	Hartford	**NHL**	75	2	2	4	218	0	0	0	17	11.8	-7						....	....	....	....	....			
1997-98	**Carolina**	**NHL**	82	3	4	7	204	0	0	1	17	17.6	0						....	....	....	....	....			

			Regular Season																Playoffs							
Season	Club	League	GP	G	A	Pts	PIM	PP	SH	GW	S	%	+/–	TF	F%	H	SB	Min	GP	G	A	Pts	PIM	PP	SH	GW
1998-99	**Anaheim**	**NHL**	**73**	**3**	**0**	**3**	**158**	**0**	**0**	**1**	**10**	**30.0**	**0**	**0**	**0.0**	**25**	**4**	**3:25**	**3**	**0**	**0**	**0**	**30**	**0**	**0**	**0**
99-2000	**Anaheim**	**NHL**	**50**	**1**	**2**	**3**	**116**	**0**	**0**	**0**	**14**	**7.1**	**0**	**0**	**0.0**	**55**	**2**	**5:13**	....	....	....	....	....	....	....	....
	NHL Totals		**627**	**13**	**19**	**32**	**1802**	**1**	**0**	**2**	**180**	**7.2**		**0**	**0.0**	**80**	**6**	**4:09**	**37**	**1**	**1**	**2**	**116**	**0**	**0**	**0**

• Re-entered NHL draft. Originally Detroit's 11th choice, 193rd overall, in 1983 Entry Draft.

Claimed on waivers by **Chicago** from **Calgary**, October 1, 1990. Claimed by **Anaheim** from **Chicago** in Expansion Draft, June 24, 1993. Traded to **Detroit** by **Anaheim** with Mark Ferner and Anaheim's 6th round choice (Magnus Nilsson) in 1996 Entry Draft for Mike Sillinger and Jason York, April 4, 1995. Claimed on waivers by **Hartford** from **Detroit**, October 13, 1996. Transferred to **Carolina** after **Hartford** franchise relocated, June 25, 1997. Traded to **Anaheim** by **Carolina** with Kevin Haller for David Karpa and Anaheim's 4th round choice (later traded to Atlanta - Atlanta selected Blake Robson) in 2000 Entry Draft, August 11, 1998. Signed as a free agent by **LA Kings**, July 6, 2000.

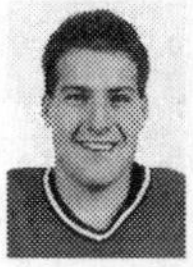

GROLEAU, Francois

(groh-LOH, FRAN-swuh)

Defense. Shoots left. 6', 197 lbs. Born, Longueuil, Que., January 23, 1973. Calgary's 2nd choice, 41st overall, in 1991 Entry Draft.

1988-89	Ste-Foy Governors	QAAA	42	3	24	27	42	....	....	....	....	....	....	....	....	....	....	....	....	....	....	....	....	....	....	....
1989-90	Shawinigan	QMJHL	65	11	54	65	80	....	....	....	....	....	....	....	....	....	....	....	6	0	1	1	12	....	....	....
1990-91	Shawinigan	QMJHL	70	9	60	69	70	....	....	....	....	....	....	....	....	....	....	....	6	0	3	3	2	....	....	....
1991-92	Shawinigan	QMJHL	65	8	70	78	74	....	....	....	....	....	....	....	....	....	....	....	10	5	15	20	8	....	....	....
1992-93	St-Jean Lynx	QMJHL	48	7	38	45	66	....	....	....	....	....	....	....	....	....	....	....	4	0	1	1	14	....	....	....
1993-94	Saint John Flames	AHL	73	8	14	22	49	....	....	....	....	....	....	....	....	....	....	....	7	0	1	1	2	....	....	....
1994-95	Saint John Flames	AHL	65	6	34	40	28	....	....	....	....	....	....	....	....	....	....	....	....	....	....	....	....	....	....	....
	Cornwall Aces	AHL	8	1	2	3	7	....	....	....	....	....	....	....	....	....	....	....	14	2	7	9	16	....	....	....
1995-96	**Montreal**	**NHL**	**2**	**0**	**1**	**1**	**2**	**0**	**0**	**0**	**1**	**0.0**	**2**	....	....	....	....	....	....	....	....	....	....	....	....	....
	San Francisco	IHL	63	6	26	32	60	....	....	....	....	....	....	....	....	....	....	....	....	....	....	....	....	....	....	....
	Fredericton	AHL	12	3	5	8	10	....	....	....	....	....	....	....	....	....	....	....	10	1	6	7	14	....	....	....
1996-97	**Montreal**	**NHL**	**5**	**0**	**0**	**0**	**4**	**0**	**0**	**0**	**3**	**0.0**	**0**	....	....	....	....	....	....	....	....	....	....	....	....	....
	Fredericton	AHL	47	8	24	32	43	....	....	....	....	....	....	....	....	....	....	....	....	....	....	....	....	....	....	....
1997-98	**Montreal**	**NHL**	**1**	**0**	**0**	**0**	**0**	**0**	**0**	**0**	**3**	**0.0**	**1**	....	....	....	....	....	....	....	....	....	....	....	....	....
	Fredericton	AHL	63	14	26	40	70	....	....	....	....	....	....	....	....	....	....	....	4	0	2	2	4	....	....	....
1998-99	Augsburger EV	DEL	52	9	21	30	67	....	....	....	....	....	....	....	....	....	....	....	5	0	4	4	4	....	....	....
99-2000	Quebec Citadelles	AHL	63	7	24	31	48	....	....	....	....	....	....	....	....	....	....	....	3	0	2	2	0	....	....	....
	NHL Totals		**8**	**0**	**1**	**1**	**6**	**0**	**0**	**0**	**7**	**0.0**		....	....	....	....	....	....	....	....	....	....	....	....	....

QMJHL Second All-Star Team (1990) • QMJHL First All-Star Team (1992)

Traded to **Quebec** by **Calgary** for Ed Ward, March 23, 1995. Signed as a free agent by **Montreal**, June 17, 1995.

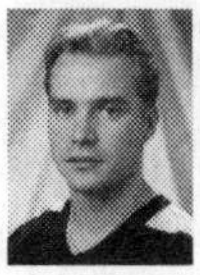

GRONMAN, Tuomas

(GROHN-mahn, TEW-mas)

Defense. Shoots right. 6'3", 219 lbs. Born, Viitasaari, Finland, March 22, 1974. Quebec's 3rd choice, 29th overall, in 1992 Entry Draft.

1990-91	Lukko Rauma	Finn-Jr.	21	8	7	15	14	....	....	....	....	....	....	....	....	....	....	....	14	2	8	10	0	....	....	....
1991-92	Tacoma Rockets	WHL	61	5	18	23	102	....	....	....	....	....	....	....	....	....	....	....	4	0	1	1	2	....	....	....
1992-93	Lukko Rauma	Finn-Jr.	1	0	0	0	0	....	....	....	....	....	....	....	....	....	....	....	....	....	....	....	....	....	....	....
	Lukko Rauma	Finland	45	2	11	13	46	....	....	....	....	....	....	....	....	....	....	....	3	1	0	1	2	....	....	....
1993-94	Lukko Rauma	Finland	44	4	12	16	60	....	....	....	....	....	....	....	....	....	....	....	9	0	1	1	14	....	....	....
1994-95	TPS Turku	Finn-Jr.	1	0	0	0	0	....	....	....	....	....	....	....	....	....	....	....	....	....	....	....	....	....	....	....
	TPS Turku	Finland	47	4	20	24	66	....	....	....	....	....	....	....	....	....	....	....	13	2	2	4	43	....	....	....
1995-96	TPS Turku	Finland	32	5	7	12	85	....	....	....	....	....	....	....	....	....	....	....	11	1	4	5	*16	....	....	....
	Finland	Nat-Team	2	0	0	0	4	....	....	....	....	....	....	....	....	....	....	....	....	....	....	....	....	....	....	....
1996-97	**Chicago**	**NHL**	**16**	**0**	**1**	**1**	**13**	**0**	**0**	**0**	**9**	**0.0**	**–4**	....	....	....	....	....	....	....	....	....	....	....	....	....
	Indianapolis Ice	IHL	51	5	16	21	89	....	....	....	....	....	....	....	....	....	....	....	4	1	1	2	6	....	....	....
1997-98	Indianapolis Ice	IHL	6	0	3	3	6	....	....	....	....	....	....	....	....	....	....	....	....	....	....	....	....	....	....	....
	Pittsburgh	**NHL**	**22**	**1**	**2**	**3**	**25**	**1**	**0**	**1**	**33**	**3.0**	**3**	....	....	....	....	....	**1**	**0**	**0**	**0**	**0**	**0**	**0**	**0**
	Syracuse Crunch	AHL	33	6	14	20	45	....	....	....	....	....	....	....	....	....	....	....	....	....	....	....	....	....	....	....
	Finland	Nat-Team	2	0	0	0	0	....	....	....	....	....	....	....	....	....	....	....	....	....	....	....	....	....	....	....
	Finland	Olympics	4	0	0	0	2	....	....	....	....	....	....	....	....	....	....	....	....	....	....	....	....	....	....	....
1998-99	Kansas City	IHL	4	0	0	0	0	....	....	....	....	....	....	....	....	....	....	....	....	....	....	....	....	....	....	....
99-2000	Jokerit Helsinki	Finland	51	1	9	10	72	....	....	....	....	....	....	....	....	....	....	....	1	0	0	0	0	....	....	....
	NHL Totals		**38**	**1**	**3**	**4**	**38**	**1**	**0**	**1**	**42**	**2.4**		....	....	....	....	....	**1**	**0**	**0**	**0**	**0**	**0**	**0**	**0**

Rights traded to **Chicago** by **Colorado** for Chicago's 2nd round choice (Phillippe Sauve) in 1998 Entry Draft, July 10, 1996. Traded to **Pittsburgh** by **Chicago** for Greg Johnson, October 27, 1997. • Missed majority of 1998-99 season recovering from knee injury suffered in game vs. Houston (IHL), October 16, 1998.

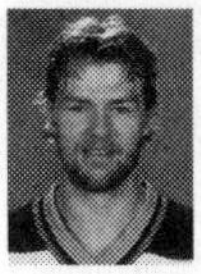

GROSEK, Michal

(GROH-shehk, MIHK-al) **CHI.**

Left wing. Shoots right. 6'2", 207 lbs. Born, Vyskov, Czech., June 1, 1975. Winnipeg's 7th choice, 145th overall, in 1993 Entry Draft.

1992-93	Skoda Zlin	Czech.	17	1	3	4	....	....	....	....	....	....	....	....	....	....	....	....	....	....	....	....	....	....	....	....
1993-94	Tacoma Rockets	WHL	30	25	20	45	106	....	....	....	....	....	....	....	....	....	....	....	7	2	2	4	30	....	....	....
	Winnipeg	**NHL**	**3**	**1**	**0**	**1**	**0**	**0**	**0**	**0**	**4**	**25.0**	**–1**	....	....	....	....	....	....	....	....	....	....	....	....	....
	Moncton Hawks	AHL	20	1	2	3	47	....	....	....	....	....	....	....	....	....	....	....	2	0	0	0	0	....	....	....
1994-95	**Winnipeg**	**NHL**	**24**	**2**	**2**	**4**	**21**	**0**	**0**	**1**	**27**	**7.4**	**–3**	....	....	....	....	....	....	....	....	....	....	....	....	....
	Springfield	AHL	45	10	22	32	98	....	....	....	....	....	....	....	....	....	....	....	....	....	....	....	....	....	....	....
1995-96	**Winnipeg**	**NHL**	**1**	**0**	**0**	**0**	**0**	**0**	**0**	**0**	**1**	**0.0**	**–1**	....	....	....	....	....	....	....	....	....	....	....	....	....
	Springfield	AHL	39	16	19	35	68	....	....	....	....	....	....	....	....	....	....	....	....	....	....	....	....	....	....	....
	Buffalo	**NHL**	**22**	**6**	**4**	**10**	**31**	**2**	**0**	**1**	**33**	**18.2**	**0**	....	....	....	....	....	....	....	....	....	....	....	....	....
1996-97	**Buffalo**	**NHL**	**82**	**15**	**21**	**36**	**71**	**1**	**0**	**2**	**117**	**12.8**	**25**	....	....	....	....	....	**12**	**3**	**3**	**6**	**8**	**0**	**0**	**0**
1997-98	**Buffalo**	**NHL**	**67**	**10**	**20**	**30**	**60**	**2**	**0**	**1**	**114**	**8.8**	**9**	....	....	....	....	....	**15**	**6**	**4**	**10**	**28**	**2**	**0**	**3**
1998-99	**Buffalo**	**NHL**	**76**	**20**	**30**	**50**	**102**	**4**	**0**	**3**	**140**	**14.3**	**21**	**5**	**60.0**	**98**	**20**	**17:14**	**13**	**0**	**4**	**4**	**28**	**0**	**0**	**0**
99-2000	**Buffalo**	**NHL**	**61**	**11**	**23**	**34**	**35**	**2**	**0**	**2**	**96**	**11.5**	**12**	**8**	**25.0**	**58**	**13**	**16:17**	....	....	....	....	....	....	....	....
	Chicago	**NHL**	**14**	**2**	**4**	**6**	**12**	**1**	**0**	**0**	**18**	**11.1**	**–1**	**1**	**0.0**	**28**	**1**	**13:06**	....	....	....	....	....	....	....	....
	NHL Totals		**350**	**67**	**104**	**171**	**332**	**12**	**0**	**10**	**550**	**12.2**		**14**	**35.7**	**184**	**34**	**16:28**	**40**	**9**	**11**	**20**	**64**	**2**	**0**	**3**

Traded to **Buffalo** by **Winnipeg** with Darryl Shannon for Craig Muni, February 15, 1996. Traded to **Chicago** by **Buffalo** for Doug Gilmour, J.P. Dumont and future considerations, March 10, 2000.

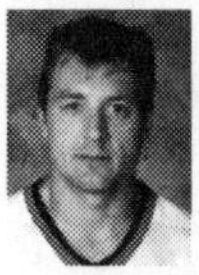

GRUDEN, John

(GROO-duhn, JAWN) **OTT.**

Defense. Shoots left. 6', 203 lbs. Born, Virginia, MN, June 4, 1970. Boston's 7th choice, 168th overall, in 1990 Entry Draft.

1989-90	Waterloo Hawks	USHL	47	7	39	46	35	....	....	....	....	....	....	....	....	....	....	....	....	....	....	....	....	....	....	....
1990-91	Ferris State	CCHA	37	4	11	15	27	....	....	....	....	....	....	....	....	....	....	....	....	....	....	....	....	....	....	....
1991-92	Ferris State	CCHA	37	9	14	23	24	....	....	....	....	....	....	....	....	....	....	....	....	....	....	....	....	....	....	....
1992-93	Ferris State	CCHA	41	16	14	30	58	....	....	....	....	....	....	....	....	....	....	....	....	....	....	....	....	....	....	....
1993-94	Ferris State	CCHA	38	11	25	36	52	....	....	....	....	....	....	....	....	....	....	....	....	....	....	....	....	....	....	....
	Boston	**NHL**	**7**	**0**	**1**	**1**	**2**	**0**	**0**	**0**	**8**	**0.0**	**–3**	....	....	....	....	....	....	....	....	....	....	....	....	....
1994-95	**Boston**	**NHL**	**38**	**0**	**6**	**6**	**22**	**0**	**0**	**0**	**30**	**0.0**	**3**	....	....	....	....	....	....	....	....	....	....	....	....	....
	Providence Bruins	AHL	1	0	1	1	0	....	....	....	....	....	....	....	....	....	....	....	....	....	....	....	....	....	....	....
1995-96	**Boston**	**NHL**	**14**	**0**	**0**	**0**	**4**	**0**	**0**	**0**	**12**	**0.0**	**–3**	....	....	....	....	....	**3**	**0**	**1**	**1**	**0**	**0**	**0**	**0**
	Providence Bruins	AHL	39	5	19	24	29	....	....	....	....	....	....	....	....	....	....	....	....	....	....	....	....	....	....	....
1996-97	Providence Bruins	AHL	78	18	27	45	52	....	....	....	....	....	....	....	....	....	....	....	10	3	6	9	4	....	....	....
1997-98	Detroit Vipers	IHL	76	13	42	55	74	....	....	....	....	....	....	....	....	....	....	....	21	1	8	9	14	....	....	....
1998-99	**Ottawa**	**NHL**	**13**	**0**	**1**	**1**	**8**	**0**	**0**	**0**	**10**	**0.0**	**0**	**0**	**0.0**	**16**	**4**	**13:07**	....	....	....	....	....	....	....	....
	Detroit Vipers	IHL	59	10	28	38	52	....	....	....	....	....	....	....	....	....	....	....	10	0	1	1	6	....	....	....
99-2000	**Ottawa**	**NHL**	**9**	**0**	**0**	**0**	**4**	**0**	**0**	**0**	**3**	**0.0**	**0**	**0**	**0.0**	**6**	**6**	**16:29**	....	....	....	....	....	....	....	....
	Grand Rapids	IHL	50	5	17	22	24	....	....	....	....	....	....	....	....	....	....	....	12	1	4	5	8	....	....	....
	NHL Totals		**81**	**0**	**8**	**8**	**40**	**0**	**0**	**0**	**63**	**0.0**		**0**	**0.0**	**22**	**10**	**14:30**	**3**	**0**	**1**	**1**	**0**	**0**	**0**	**0**

CCHA First All-Star Team (1994) • NCAA West First All-American Team (1994) • IHL Second All-Star Team (1998)

Signed as a free agent by **Ottawa**, August 7, 1998.

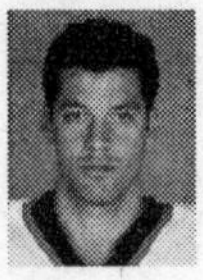

GUERIN, Bill
(GAIR-ihn, BIHL) **EDM.**

Right wing. Shoots right. 6'2", 210 lbs. Born, Wilbraham, MA, November 9, 1970. New Jersey's 1st choice, 5th overall, in 1989 Entry Draft.

			Regular Season																Playoffs							
Season	Club	League	GP	G	A	Pts	PIM	PP	SH	GW	S	%	+/–	TF	F%	H	SB	Min	GP	G	A	Pts	PIM	PP	SH	GW
1985-86	Springfield	NEJHL	48	26	19	45	71	....	....	....	....	....	....	....	....	....	....	....	....	....	....	....	....	....	....	....
1986-87	Springfield	NEJHL	32	34	20	54	40	....	....	....	....	....	....	....	....	....	....	....	....	....	....	....	....	....	....	....
1987-88	Springfield	NEJHL	38	31	44	75	146	....	....	....	....	....	....	....	....	....	....	....	....	....	....	....	....	....	....	....
1988-89	Springfield	NEJHL	31	32	35	67	90	....	....	....	....	....	....	....	....	....	....	....	....	....	....	....	....	....	....	....
1989-90	Boston College	H-East	39	14	11	25	54	....	....	....	....	....	....	....	....	....	....	....	....	....	....	....	....	....	....	....
1990-91	Boston College	H-East	38	26	19	45	102	....	....	....	....	....	....	....	....	....	....	....	....	....	....	....	....	....	....	....
	United States	Nat-Team	46	12	15	27	67	....	....	....	....	....	....	....	....	....	....	....	....	....	....	....	....	....	....	....
1991-92	**New Jersey**	**NHL**	**5**	**0**	**1**	**1**	**9**	**0**	**0**	**0**	**8**	**0.0**	**1**	....	....	....	....	....	**6**	**3**	**0**	**3**	**4**	**0**	**0**	**0**
	Utica Devils	AHL	22	13	10	23	6	....	....	....	....	....	....	....	....	....	....	....	4	1	3	4	14	....	....	....
1992-93	**New Jersey**	**NHL**	**65**	**14**	**20**	**34**	**63**	**0**	**0**	**2**	**123**	**11.4**	**14**	....	....	....	....	....	**5**	**1**	**1**	**2**	**4**	**0**	**0**	**0**
	Utica Devils	AHL	18	10	7	17	47	....	....	....	....	....	....	....	....	....	....	....	....	....	....	....	....	....	....	....
1993-94	**New Jersey**	**NHL**	**81**	**25**	**19**	**44**	**101**	**2**	**0**	**3**	**195**	**12.8**	**14**	....	....	....	....	....	**17**	**2**	**1**	**3**	**35**	**0**	**0**	**1**
1994-95♦	**New Jersey**	**NHL**	**48**	**12**	**13**	**25**	**72**	**4**	**0**	**3**	**96**	**12.5**	**6**	....	....	....	....	....	**20**	**3**	**8**	**11**	**30**	**1**	**0**	**0**
1995-96	**New Jersey**	**NHL**	**80**	**23**	**30**	**53**	**116**	**8**	**0**	**6**	**216**	**10.6**	**7**	....	....	....	....	....	....	....	....	....	....	....	....	....
1996-97	**New Jersey**	**NHL**	**82**	**29**	**18**	**47**	**95**	**7**	**0**	**9**	**177**	**16.4**	**–2**	....	....	....	....	....	**8**	**2**	**1**	**3**	**18**	**1**	**0**	**1**
1997-98	**New Jersey**	**NHL**	**19**	**5**	**5**	**10**	**13**	**1**	**0**	**2**	**48**	**10.4**	**0**	....	....	....	....	....	....	....	....	....	....	....	....	....
	Edmonton	**NHL**	**40**	**13**	**16**	**29**	**80**	**8**	**0**	**2**	**130**	**10.0**	**1**	....	....	....	....	....	**12**	**7**	**1**	**8**	**17**	**4**	**0**	**0**
	United States	Olympics	4	0	3	3	2	....	....	....	....	....	....	....	....	....	....	....	....	....	....	....	....	....	....	....
1998-99	**Edmonton**	**NHL**	**80**	**30**	**34**	**64**	**133**	**13**	**0**	**2**	**261**	**11.5**	**7**	**74**	**40.5**	**131**	**20**	**19:42**	**3**	**0**	**2**	**2**	**2**	**0**	**0**	**0**
99-2000	**Edmonton**	**NHL**	**70**	**24**	**22**	**46**	**123**	**11**	**0**	**2**	**188**	**12.8**	**4**	**13**	**46.1**	**101**	**33**	**18:01**	**5**	**3**	**2**	**5**	**9**	**1**	**0**	**0**
	NHL Totals		**570**	**175**	**178**	**353**	**805**	**54**	**0**	**31**	**1442**	**12.1**		**87**	**41.4**	**232**	**53**	**18:55**	**76**	**21**	**16**	**37**	**119**	**7**	**0**	**2**

Traded to **Edmonton** by **New Jersey** with Valeri Zelepukin for Jason Arnott and Bryan Muir, January 4, 1998.

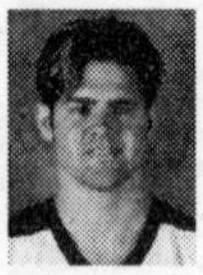

GUOLLA, Stephen
(GUH-wah-lah, STEEV-vuhn) **ATL.**

Left wing. Shoots left. 6', 190 lbs. Born, Scarborough, Ont., March 15, 1973. Ottawa's 1st choice, 3rd overall, in 1994 Supplemental Draft.

Season	Club	League	GP	G	A	Pts	PIM	PP	SH	GW	S	%	+/–	TF	F%	H	SB	Min	GP	G	A	Pts	PIM	PP	SH	GW
1988-89	Toronto Wings	MTHL	25	14	20	34	....	....	....	....	....	....	....	....	....	....	....	....	....	....	....	....	....	....	....	....
1989-90	Toronto Wings	MTHL	40	42	47	89	....	....	....	....	....	....	....	....	....	....	....	....	....	....	....	....	....	....	....	....
1990-91	Wexford Raiders	OJHL-B	44	34	44	78	34	....	....	....	....	....	....	....	....	....	....	....	12	12	16	28	....	....	....	....
1991-92	Michigan State	CCHA	33	4	9	13	8	....	....	....	....	....	....	....	....	....	....	....	....	....	....	....	....	....	....	....
1992-93	Michigan State	CCHA	39	19	35	54	6	....	....	....	....	....	....	....	....	....	....	....	....	....	....	....	....	....	....	....
1993-94	Michigan State	CCHA	41	23	46	69	16	....	....	....	....	....	....	....	....	....	....	....	....	....	....	....	....	....	....	....
1994-95	Michigan State	CCHA	40	16	35	51	16	....	....	....	....	....	....	....	....	....	....	....	....	....	....	....	....	....	....	....
1995-96	P.E.I. Senators	AHL	72	32	48	80	28	....	....	....	....	....	....	....	....	....	....	....	3	0	0	0	0	....	....	....
1996-97	**San Jose**	**NHL**	**43**	**13**	**8**	**21**	**14**	**2**	**0**	**1**	**81**	**16.0**	**–10**	....	....	....	....	....	....	....	....	....	....	....	....	....
	Kentucky	AHL	34	22	22	44	10	....	....	....	....	....	....	....	....	....	....	....	4	2	1	3	0	....	....	....
1997-98	**San Jose**	**NHL**	**7**	**1**	**1**	**2**	**0**	**0**	**0**	**0**	**9**	**11.1**	**–2**	....	....	....	....	....	....	....	....	....	....	....	....	....
	Kentucky	AHL	69	37	63	100	45	....	....	....	....	....	....	....	....	....	....	....	3	0	0	0	0	....	....	....
1998-99	**San Jose**	**NHL**	**14**	**2**	**2**	**4**	**6**	**0**	**0**	**1**	**22**	**9.1**	**3**	**172**	**36.6**	**19**	**6**	**13:54**	....	....	....	....	....	....	....	....
	Kentucky	AHL	53	29	47	76	33	....	....	....	....	....	....	....	....	....	....	....	....	....	....	....	....	....	....	....
99-2000	**Tampa Bay**	**NHL**	**46**	**6**	**10**	**16**	**11**	**2**	**0**	**0**	**52**	**11.5**	**2**	**155**	**45.8**	**33**	**8**	**11:26**	....	....	....	....	....	....	....	....
	Atlanta	**NHL**	**20**	**4**	**9**	**13**	**4**	**2**	**0**	**0**	**34**	**11.8**	**–13**	**345**	**42.6**	**19**	**9**	**17:47**	....	....	....	....	....	....	....	....
	NHL Totals		**130**	**26**	**30**	**56**	**35**	**6**	**0**	**2**	**198**	**13.1**		**672**	**41.8**	**71**	**23**	**13:27**	....	....	....	....	....	....	....	....

CCHA Second All-Star Team (1994) • NCAA West Second All-American Team (1994) • AHL Second All-Star Team (1998, 1999) • Won Les Cunningham Award (MVP - AHL) (1998)

Signed as a free agent by **San Jose**, August 22, 1996. Traded to **Tampa Bay** by **San Jose** with Bill Houlder, Shawn Burr and Andrei Zyuzin for Niklas Sundstrom and NY Rangers' 3rd round choice (previously acquired, later traded to Chicago - Chicago selected Igor Radulov) in 2000 Entry Draft, August 4, 1999. Claimed on waivers by **Atlanta** from **Tampa Bay**, March 1, 2000.

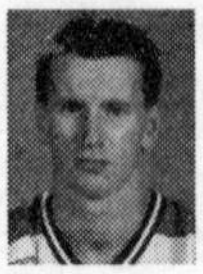

GUREN, Miloslav
(GOO-rihn, MEER-oh-slahf) **MTL.**

Defense. Shoots left. 6'2", 213 lbs. Born, Uherske Hradiste, Czech., September 24, 1976. Montreal's 2nd choice, 60th overall, in 1995 Entry Draft.

Season	Club	League	GP	G	A	Pts	PIM	PP	SH	GW	S	%	+/–	TF	F%	H	SB	Min	GP	G	A	Pts	PIM	PP	SH	GW
1993-94	ZPS Zlin	Cze-Rep	22	1	5	6	....	....	....	....	....	....	....	....	....	....	....	....	3	0	0	0	....	....	....	....
1994-95	ZPS Zlin	Cze-Rep	32	3	7	10	10	....	....	....	....	....	....	....	....	....	....	....	12	1	0	1	6	....	....	....
1995-96	ZPS Zlin	Cze-Rep	28	1	2	3	....	....	....	....	....	....	....	....	....	....	....	....	7	1	0	1	....	....	....	....
1996-97	Fredericton	AHL	79	6	26	32	26	....	....	....	....	....	....	....	....	....	....	....	....	....	....	....	....	....	....	....
1997-98	Fredericton	AHL	78	15	36	51	36	....	....	....	....	....	....	....	....	....	....	....	4	1	2	3	0	....	....	....
1998-99	**Montreal**	**NHL**	**12**	**0**	**1**	**1**	**4**	**0**	**0**	**0**	**11**	**0.0**	**–1**	**0**	**0.0**	**4**	**10**	**12:02**	....	....	....	....	....	....	....	....
	Fredericton	AHL	63	5	16	21	24	....	....	....	....	....	....	....	....	....	....	....	15	4	7	11	10	....	....	....
99-2000	**Montreal**	**NHL**	**24**	**1**	**2**	**3**	**12**	**1**	**0**	**0**	**20**	**5.0**	**–5**	**0**	**0.0**	**20**	**26**	**15:14**	....	....	....	....	....	....	....	....
	Quebec Citadelles	AHL	29	5	12	17	16	....	....	....	....	....	....	....	....	....	....	....	3	0	0	0	2	....	....	....
	NHL Totals		**36**	**1**	**3**	**4**	**16**	**1**	**0**	**0**	**31**	**3.2**		**0**	**0.0**	**24**	**36**	**14:10**	....	....	....	....	....	....	....	....

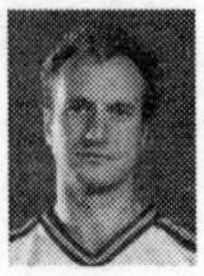

GUSAROV, Alexei
(goo-SAH-rahf) **COL.**

Defense. Shoots left. 6'3", 185 lbs. Born, Leningrad, USSR, July 8, 1964. Quebec's 11th choice, 213th overall, in 1988 Entry Draft.

Season	Club	League	GP	G	A	Pts	PIM	PP	SH	GW	S	%	+/–	TF	F%	H	SB	Min	GP	G	A	Pts	PIM	PP	SH	GW
1981-82	SKA Leningrad	USSR	20	1	2	3	16	....	....	....	....	....	....	....	....	....	....	....	....	....	....	....	....	....	....	....
1982-83	SKA Leningrad	USSR	42	2	1	3	32	....	....	....	....	....	....	....	....	....	....	....	....	....	....	....	....	....	....	....
1983-84	SKA Leningrad	USSR	43	2	3	5	32	....	....	....	....	....	....	....	....	....	....	....	....	....	....	....	....	....	....	....
1984-85	CSKA Moscow	USSR	36	3	2	5	26	....	....	....	....	....	....	....	....	....	....	....	....	....	....	....	....	....	....	....
1985-86	CSKA Moscow	USSR	40	3	5	8	30	....	....	....	....	....	....	....	....	....	....	....	....	....	....	....	....	....	....	....
1986-87	CSKA Moscow	USSR	38	4	7	11	24	....	....	....	....	....	....	....	....	....	....	....	....	....	....	....	....	....	....	....
1987-88	CSKA Moscow	USSR	39	3	2	5	28	....	....	....	....	....	....	....	....	....	....	....	....	....	....	....	....	....	....	....
	Soviet Union	Olympics	8	1	3	4	6	....	....	....	....	....	....	....	....	....	....	....	....	....	....	....	....	....	....	....
1988-89	CSKA Moscow	USSR	42	5	4	9	37	....	....	....	....	....	....	....	....	....	....	....	....	....	....	....	....	....	....	....
1989-90	CSKA Moscow	USSR	42	4	7	11	42	....	....	....	....	....	....	....	....	....	....	....	....	....	....	....	....	....	....	....
1990-91	CSKA Moscow	USSR	15	0	0	0	12	....	....	....	....	....	....	....	....	....	....	....	....	....	....	....	....	....	....	....
	Quebec	**NHL**	**36**	**3**	**9**	**12**	**12**	**1**	**0**	**0**	**36**	**8.3**	**–4**	....	....	....	....	....	....	....	....	....	....	....	....	....
	Halifax Citadels	AHL	2	0	3	3	2	....	....	....	....	....	....	....	....	....	....	....	....	....	....	....	....	....	....	....
1991-92	**Quebec**	**NHL**	**68**	**5**	**18**	**23**	**22**	**3**	**0**	**1**	**66**	**7.6**	**–9**	....	....	....	....	....	....	....	....	....	....	....	....	....
	Halifax Citadels	AHL	3	0	0	0	0	....	....	....	....	....	....	....	....	....	....	....	....	....	....	....	....	....	....	....
1992-93	**Quebec**	**NHL**	**79**	**8**	**22**	**30**	**57**	**0**	**2**	**1**	**60**	**13.3**	**18**	....	....	....	....	....	**5**	**0**	**1**	**1**	**0**	**0**	**0**	**0**
1993-94	**Quebec**	**NHL**	**76**	**5**	**20**	**25**	**38**	**0**	**1**	**0**	**84**	**6.0**	**3**	....	....	....	....	....	....	....	....	....	....	....	....	....
1994-95	**Quebec**	**NHL**	**14**	**1**	**2**	**3**	**6**	**0**	**0**	**1**	**7**	**14.3**	**–1**	....	....	....	....	....	....	....	....	....	....	....	....	....
1995-96♦	**Colorado**	**NHL**	**65**	**5**	**15**	**20**	**56**	**0**	**0**	**0**	**42**	**11.9**	**29**	....	....	....	....	....	**21**	**0**	**9**	**9**	**12**	**0**	**0**	**0**
1996-97	**Colorado**	**NHL**	**58**	**2**	**12**	**14**	**28**	**0**	**0**	**0**	**33**	**6.1**	**4**	....	....	....	....	....	**17**	**0**	**3**	**3**	**14**	**0**	**0**	**0**
1997-98	**Colorado**	**NHL**	**72**	**4**	**10**	**14**	**42**	**0**	**1**	**1**	**47**	**8.5**	**9**	....	....	....	....	....	**7**	**0**	**1**	**1**	**6**	**0**	**0**	**0**
	Russia	Olympics	6	0	1	1	8	....	....	....	....	....	....	....	....	....	....	....	....	....	....	....	....	....	....	....
1998-99	**Colorado**	**NHL**	**54**	**3**	**10**	**13**	**24**	**1**	**0**	**0**	**28**	**10.7**	**12**	**1**	**0.0**	**22**	**65**	**19:57**	**5**	**0**	**0**	**0**	**2**	**0**	**0**	**0**
99-2000	**Colorado**	**NHL**	**34**	**2**	**2**	**4**	**10**	**0**	**0**	**0**	**16**	**12.5**	**–8**	**0**	**0.0**	**13**	**45**	**19:27**	....	....	....	....	....	....	....	....
	NHL Totals		**556**	**38**	**120**	**158**	**295**	**5**	**4**	**4**	**419**	**9.1**		**1**	**0.0**	**35**	**110**	**19:46**	**55**	**0**	**14**	**14**	**34**	**0**	**0**	**0**

• Transferred to **Colorado** after **Quebec** franchise relocated, June 21, 1995. • Missed remainder of 1999-2000 season recovering from leg injury suffered in game vs. Dallas, February 27, 2000.

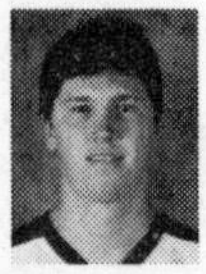

GUSEV, Sergey
(GOO-sehv, SAIR-gay) **T.B.**

Defense. Shoots left. 6'1", 205 lbs. Born, Nizhny Tagil, USSR, July 31, 1975. Dallas' 4th choice, 69th overall, in 1995 Entry Draft.

Season	Club	League	GP	G	A	Pts	PIM	PP	SH	GW	S	%	+/–	TF	F%	H	SB	Min	GP	G	A	Pts	PIM	PP	SH	GW
1994-95	CSK Samara	CIS	50	3	5	8	58	....	....	....	....	....	....	....	....	....	....	....	....	....	....	....	....	....	....	....
1995-96	Michigan K-Wings	IHL	73	11	17	28	76	....	....	....	....	....	....	....	....	....	....	....	....	....	....	....	....	....	....	....
1996-97	Michigan K-Wings	IHL	51	7	8	15	44	....	....	....	....	....	....	....	....	....	....	....	4	0	4	4	6	....	....	....
1997-98	**Dallas**	**NHL**	**9**	**0**	**0**	**0**	**2**	**0**	**0**	**0**	**5**	**0.0**	**–5**	....	....	....	....	....	....	....	....	....	....	....	....	....
	Michigan K-Wings	IHL	36	3	6	9	36	....	....	....	....	....	....	....	....	....	....	....	4	0	2	2	6	....	....	....
1998-99	**Dallas**	**NHL**	**22**	**1**	**4**	**5**	**6**	**0**	**0**	**1**	**30**	**3.3**	**5**	**0**	**0.0**	**12**	**16**	**12:04**	....	....	....	....	....	....	....	....
	Michigan K-Wings	IHL	12	0	6	6	14	....	....	....	....	....	....	....	....	....	....	....	....	....	....	....	....	....	....	....
	Tampa Bay	**NHL**	**14**	**0**	**3**	**3**	**10**	**0**	**0**	**0**	**16**	**0.0**	**–8**	**0**	**0.0**	**13**	**28**	**21:30**	....	....	....	....	....	....	....	....

			Regular Season																Playoffs							
Season	Club	League	GP	G	A	Pts	PIM	PP	SH	GW	S	%	+/-	TF	F%	H	SB	Min	GP	G	A	Pts	PIM	PP	SH	GW
99-2000	**Tampa Bay**	**NHL**	**28**	**2**	**3**	**5**	**6**	**1**	**0**	**0**	**23**	**8.7**	**–9**	**0**	**0.0**	**35**	**46**	**17:34**	....	....	....	....	....	....	....	....
	NHL Totals		**73**	**3**	**10**	**13**	**24**	**1**	**0**	**1**	**74**	**4.1**		**0**	**0.0**	**60**	**90**	**16:32**	....	....	....	....	....	....	....	....

Traded to **Tampa Bay** by **Dallas** for Benoit Hogue and a conditional choice in 2001 Entry Draft, March 21, 1999. • Missed majority of 1999-2000 season recovering from knee injury suffered in game vs. NY Rangers, December 19, 1999.

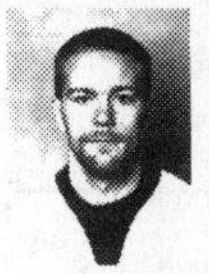

GUSTAFSSON, Per

(GOOS-tahf-suhn, PAIR)

Defense. Shoots left. 6'2", 190 lbs. Born, Osterham, Sweden, June 6, 1970. Florida's 10th choice, 261st overall, in 1994 Entry Draft.

Season	Club	League	GP	G	A	Pts	PIM	PP	SH	GW	S	%	+/-	TF	F%	H	SB	Min	GP	G	A	Pts	PIM	PP	SH	GW
1986-87	IK Oskarshamn	Sweden-3	20	0	2	2	....	....	....	....	....	....	....	....	....	....	....	....	....	....	....	....	....	....	....	....
1987-88	IK Oskarshamn	Sweden-3	36	7	13	20	....	....	....	....	....	....	....	....	....	....	....	....	....	....	....	....	....	....	....	....
1988-89	HV Jonkoping	Sweden	14	1	4	5	8	....	....	....	....	....	....	....	....	....	....	....	3	0	0	0	2	....	....	....
1989-90	HV Jonkoping	Sweden	27	4	3	7	16	....	....	....	....	....	....	....	....	....	....	....	....	....	....	....	....	....	....	....
1990-91	HV Jonkoping	Sweden	31	3	5	8	16	....	....	....	....	....	....	....	....	....	....	....	2	0	0	0	4	....	....	....
1991-92	HV Jonkoping	Sweden	39	9	8	17	22	....	....	....	....	....	....	....	....	....	....	....	3	0	0	0	0	....	....	....
1992-93	HV Jonkoping	Sweden	40	6	3	9	28	....	....	....	....	....	....	....	....	....	....	....	....	....	....	....	....	....	....	....
1993-94	HV Jonkoping	Sweden	34	9	7	16	10	....	....	....	....	....	....	....	....	....	....	....	....	....	....	....	....	....	....	....
1994-95	HV Jonkoping	Sweden	38	10	6	16	14	....	....	....	....	....	....	....	....	....	....	....	13	7	5	12	8	....	....	....
1995-96	HV Jonkoping	Sweden	34	8	13	21	12	....	....	....	....	....	....	....	....	....	....	....	4	3	1	4	2	....	....	....
1996-97	**Florida**	**NHL**	**58**	**7**	**22**	**29**	**22**	**2**	**0**	**1**	**105**	**6.7**	**11**	....	....	....	....	....	....	....	....	....	....	....	....	....
1997-98	**Toronto**	**NHL**	**22**	**1**	**4**	**5**	**10**	**0**	**0**	**0**	**24**	**4.2**	**–5**	....	....	....	....	....	....	....	....	....	....	....	....	....
	St. John's Leafs	AHL	25	7	18	25	10	....	....	....	....	....	....	....	....	....	....	....	....	....	....	....	....	....	....	....
	Ottawa	**NHL**	**9**	**0**	**1**	**1**	**6**	**0**	**0**	**0**	**12**	**0.0**	**3**	....	....	....	....	....	**1**	**0**	**0**	**0**	**0**	**0**	**0**	**0**
1998-99	HV Jonkoping	Sweden	50	12	16	28	52	....	....	....	....	....	....	....	....	....	....	....	....	....	....	....	....	....	....	....
99-2000	HV Jonkoping	Sweden	40	6	15	21	47	....	....	....	....	....	....	....	....	....	....	....	6	1	4	5	10	....	....	....
	NHL Totals		**89**	**8**	**27**	**35**	**38**	**2**	**0**	**1**	**141**	**5.7**		....	....	....	....	....	**1**	**0**	**0**	**0**	**0**	**0**	**0**	**0**

Swedish World All-Star Team (1996)

Traded to **Toronto** by **Florida** for Mike Lankshear, June 13, 1997. Traded to **Ottawa** by **Toronto** for Ottawa's 8th round choice (Dwight Wolfe) in 1998 Entry Draft, March 17, 1998.

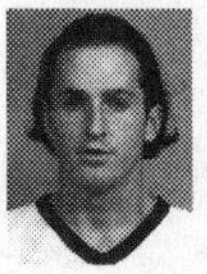

HAGGERTY, Sean

(HA-guhr-tee, SHAWN) **NSH.**

Left wing. Shoots left. 6'1", 186 lbs. Born, Rye, NY, February 11, 1976. Toronto's 2nd choice, 48th overall, in 1994 Entry Draft.

Season	Club	League	GP	G	A	Pts	PIM	PP	SH	GW	S	%	+/-	TF	F%	H	SB	Min	GP	G	A	Pts	PIM	PP	SH	GW
1990-91	Westminster High	Hi-School	25	20	22	42	....	....	....	....	....	....	....	....	....	....	....	....	....	....	....	....	....	....	....	....
1991-92	Westminster High	Hi-School	25	24	36	60	....	....	....	....	....	....	....	....	....	....	....	....	....	....	....	....	....	....	....	....
1992-93	Boston	MBHL	72	70	111	181	80	....	....	....	....	....	....	....	....	....	....	....	....	....	....	....	....	....	....	....
1993-94	Detroit Jr. Wings	OHL	60	31	32	63	21	....	....	....	....	....	....	....	....	....	....	....	17	9	10	19	11	....	....	....
1994-95	Detroit Jr. Wings	OHL	61	40	49	89	37	....	....	....	....	....	....	....	....	....	....	....	21	13	24	37	18	....	....	....
1995-96	Detroit Whalers	OHL	66	*60	51	111	78	....	....	....	....	....	....	....	....	....	....	....	17	15	9	24	30	....	....	....
	Toronto	**NHL**	**1**	**0**	**0**	**0**	**0**	**0**	**0**	**0**	**0**	**0.0**	**0**	....	....	....	....	....	....	....	....	....	....	....	....	....
	Worcester	AHL	....	....	....	....	....	....	....	....	....	....	....	....	....	....	....	....	1	0	0	0	2	....	....	....
1996-97	Kentucky	AHL	77	13	22	35	60	....	....	....	....	....	....	....	....	....	....	....	4	1	0	1	4	....	....	....
1997-98	**NY Islanders**	**NHL**	**5**	**0**	**0**	**0**	**0**	**0**	**0**	**0**	**2**	**0.0**	**–3**	....	....	....	....	....	....	....	....	....	....	....	....	....
	Kentucky	AHL	63	33	20	53	64	....	....	....	....	....	....	....	....	....	....	....	3	0	2	2	4	....	....	....
1998-99	Lowell	AHL	77	19	27	46	40	....	....	....	....	....	....	....	....	....	....	....	3	0	1	1	0	....	....	....
99-2000	**NY Islanders**	**NHL**	**5**	**1**	**1**	**2**	**4**	**0**	**0**	**0**	**2**	**50.0**	**3**	**0**	**0.0**	**6**	**3**	**9:38**	....	....	....	....	....	....	....	....
	Kansas City	IHL	76	27	33	60	94	....	....	....	....	....	....	....	....	....	....	....	....	....	....	....	....	....	....	....
	NHL Totals		**11**	**1**	**1**	**2**	**4**	**0**	**0**	**0**	**4**	**25.0**		**0**	**0.0**	**6**	**3**	**9:38**	....	....	....	....	....	....	....	....

Memorial Cup All-Star Team (1995) • OHL Second All-Star Team (1996) • AHL Second All-Star Team (1998)

Traded to **NY Islanders** by **Toronto** with Darby Hendrickson, Kenny Jonsson and Toronto's 1st round choice (Roberto Luongo) in 1997 Entry Draft for Wendel Clark, Mathieu Schneider and D.J. Smith, March 13, 1996. Claimed on waivers by **Nashville** from **NY Islanders**, May 23, 2000.

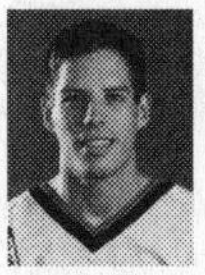

HALKO, Steven

(HAL-koh, STEE-vehn) **CAR.**

Defense. Shoots right. 6'1", 200 lbs. Born, Etobicoke, Ont., March 8, 1974. Hartford's 10th choice, 225th overall, in 1992 Entry Draft.

Season	Club	League	GP	G	A	Pts	PIM	PP	SH	GW	S	%	+/-	TF	F%	H	SB	Min	GP	G	A	Pts	PIM	PP	SH	GW
1989-90	Newmarket 87's	OJHL-B	30	3	5	8	16	....	....	....	....	....	....	....	....	....	....	....	....	....	....	....	....	....	....	....
1990-91	Newmarket 87's	OJHL-B	35	2	13	15	37	....	....	....	....	....	....	....	....	....	....	....	....	....	....	....	....	....	....	....
	Markham	OJHL-B	8	4	3	7	2	....	....	....	....	....	....	....	....	....	....	....	....	....	....	....	....	....	....	....
1991-92	Thornhill Islanders	OJHL	44	15	46	61	43	....	....	....	....	....	....	....	....	....	....	....	....	....	....	....	....	....	....	....
1992-93	U. of Michigan	CCHA	39	1	12	13	12	....	....	....	....	....	....	....	....	....	....	....	....	....	....	....	....	....	....	....
1993-94	U. of Michigan	CCHA	41	2	13	15	32	....	....	....	....	....	....	....	....	....	....	....	....	....	....	....	....	....	....	....
1994-95	U. of Michigan	CCHA	39	2	14	16	20	....	....	....	....	....	....	....	....	....	....	....	....	....	....	....	....	....	....	....
1995-96	U. of Michigan	CCHA	43	4	16	20	32	....	....	....	....	....	....	....	....	....	....	....	....	....	....	....	....	....	....	....
1996-97	Springfield	AHL	70	1	5	6	37	....	....	....	....	....	....	....	....	....	....	....	11	0	2	2	8	....	....	....
1997-98	**Carolina**	**NHL**	**18**	**0**	**2**	**2**	**10**	**0**	**0**	**0**	**7**	**0.0**	**–1**	....	....	....	....	....	....	....	....	....	....	....	....	....
	New Haven	AHL	65	1	19	20	44	....	....	....	....	....	....	....	....	....	....	....	1	0	0	0	0	....	....	....
1998-99	**Carolina**	**NHL**	**20**	**0**	**3**	**3**	**24**	**0**	**0**	**0**	**6**	**0.0**	**5**	**0**	**0.0**	**32**	**11**	**15:57**	**4**	**0**	**0**	**0**	**2**	**0**	**0**	**0**
	New Haven	AHL	42	2	7	9	58	....	....	....	....	....	....	....	....	....	....	....	....	....	....	....	....	....	....	....
99-2000	**Carolina**	**NHL**	**58**	**0**	**8**	**8**	**25**	**0**	**0**	**0**	**54**	**0.0**	**0**	**1**	**100.0**	**85**	**60**	**16:43**	....	....	....	....	....	....	....	....
	NHL Totals		**96**	**0**	**13**	**13**	**59**	**0**	**0**	**0**	**67**	**0.0**		**1**	**100.0**	**117**	**71**	**16:31**	**4**	**0**	**0**	**0**	**2**	**0**	**0**	**0**

CCHA Second All-Star Team (1995, 1996) • NCAA Championship All-Tournament Team (1996)

Transferred to **Carolina** after **Hartford** franchise relocated, June 25, 1997.

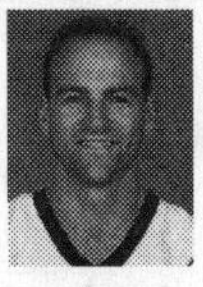

HALLER, Kevin

(HAHL-her, KEH-vihn) **NYI**

Defense. Shoots left. 6'2", 199 lbs. Born, Trochu, Alta., December 5, 1970. Buffalo's 1st choice, 14th overall, in 1989 Entry Draft.

Season	Club	League	GP	G	A	Pts	PIM	PP	SH	GW	S	%	+/-	TF	F%	H	SB	Min	GP	G	A	Pts	PIM	PP	SH	GW
1986-87	Three Hills Braves	AAHA	12	10	11	21	8	....	....	....	....	....	....	....	....	....	....	....	....	....	....	....	....	....	....	....
1987-88	Olds Grizzlys	AJHL	51	13	31	44	58	....	....	....	....	....	....	....	....	....	....	....	....	....	....	....	....	....	....	....
	Regina Pats	WHL	5	0	1	1	2	....	....	....	....	....	....	....	....	....	....	....	4	1	1	2	2	....	....	....
1988-89	Regina Pats	WHL	72	10	31	41	99	....	....	....	....	....	....	....	....	....	....	....	....	....	....	....	....	....	....	....
1989-90	Regina Pats	WHL	58	16	37	53	93	....	....	....	....	....	....	....	....	....	....	....	11	2	9	11	16	....	....	....
	Buffalo	**NHL**	**2**	**0**	**0**	**0**	**0**	**0**	**0**	**0**	**1**	**0.0**	**0**	....	....	....	....	....	....	....	....	....	....	....	....	....
1990-91	**Buffalo**	**NHL**	**21**	**1**	**8**	**9**	**20**	**1**	**0**	**0**	**42**	**2.4**	**9**	....	....	....	....	....	**6**	**1**	**4**	**5**	**10**	**0**	**0**	**0**
	Rochester	AHL	52	2	8	10	53	....	....	....	....	....	....	....	....	....	....	....	10	2	1	3	6	....	....	....
1991-92	**Buffalo**	**NHL**	**58**	**6**	**15**	**21**	**75**	**2**	**0**	**1**	**76**	**7.9**	**–13**	....	....	....	....	....	....	....	....	....	....	....	....	....
	Rochester	AHL	4	0	0	0	18	....	....	....	....	....	....	....	....	....	....	....	....	....	....	....	....	....	....	....
	Montreal	**NHL**	**8**	**2**	**2**	**4**	**17**	**1**	**0**	**0**	**9**	**22.2**	**4**	....	....	....	....	....	**9**	**0**	**0**	**0**	**6**	**0**	**0**	**0**
1992-93♦	**Montreal**	**NHL**	**73**	**11**	**14**	**25**	**117**	**6**	**0**	**1**	**126**	**8.7**	**7**	....	....	....	....	....	**17**	**1**	**6**	**7**	**16**	**1**	**0**	**0**
1993-94	**Montreal**	**NHL**	**68**	**4**	**9**	**13**	**118**	**0**	**0**	**1**	**72**	**5.6**	**3**	....	....	....	....	....	**7**	**1**	**1**	**2**	**19**	**0**	**0**	**0**
1994-95	**Philadelphia**	**NHL**	**36**	**2**	**8**	**10**	**48**	**0**	**0**	**0**	**26**	**7.7**	**16**	....	....	....	....	....	**15**	**4**	**4**	**8**	**10**	**0**	**1**	**1**
1995-96	**Philadelphia**	**NHL**	**69**	**5**	**9**	**14**	**92**	**0**	**2**	**2**	**89**	**5.6**	**18**	....	....	....	....	....	**6**	**0**	**1**	**1**	**8**	**0**	**0**	**0**
1996-97	**Philadelphia**	**NHL**	**27**	**0**	**5**	**5**	**37**	**0**	**0**	**0**	**34**	**0.0**	**–1**	....	....	....	....	....	....	....	....	....	....	....	....	....
	Hartford	**NHL**	**35**	**2**	**6**	**8**	**48**	**0**	**0**	**0**	**43**	**4.7**	**–11**	....	....	....	....	....	....	....	....	....	....	....	....	....
1997-98	**Carolina**	**NHL**	**65**	**3**	**5**	**8**	**94**	**0**	**0**	**0**	**67**	**4.5**	**–5**	....	....	....	....	....	....	....	....	....	....	....	....	....
1998-99	**Anaheim**	**NHL**	**82**	**1**	**6**	**7**	**122**	**0**	**0**	**0**	**64**	**1.6**	**–1**	**0**	**0.0**	**95**	**110**	**20:39**	**4**	**0**	**0**	**0**	**2**	**0**	**0**	**0**
99-2000	**Anaheim**	**NHL**	**67**	**3**	**5**	**8**	**61**	**0**	**0**	**2**	**50**	**6.0**	**–8**	**1**	**100.0**	**107**	**83**	**18:10**	....	....	....	....	....	....	....	....
	NHL Totals		**611**	**40**	**92**	**132**	**849**	**10**	**2**	**7**	**699**	**5.7**		**1**	**100.0**	**202**	**193**	**19:32**	**64**	**7**	**16**	**23**	**71**	**1**	**1**	**1**

WHL East First All-Star Team (1990)

Traded to **Montreal** by **Buffalo** for Petr Svoboda, March 10, 1992. Traded to **Philadelphia** by **Montreal** for Yves Racine, June 29, 1994. Traded to **Hartford** by **Philadelphia** with Philadelphia's 1st round choice (later traded to San Jose - San Jose selected Scott Hannan) in 1997 Entry Draft and Hartford/Carolina's 7th round choice (previously acquired, Carolina selected Andrew Merrick) in 1997 Entry Draft for Paul Coffey and Hartford's 3rd round choice (Kris Mallette) in 1997 Entry Draft, December 15, 1996. Transferred to **Carolina** after **Hartford** franchise relocated, June 25, 1997. Traded to **Anaheim** by **Carolina** with Stu Grimson for David Karpa and Anaheim's 4th round choice (later traded to Atlanta - Atlanta selected Blake Robson) in 2000 Entry Draft, August 11, 1998. Signed as a free agent by **NY Islanders**, July 3, 2000.

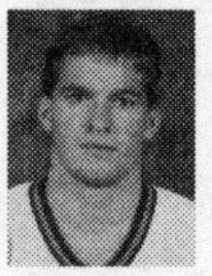

HALPERN, Jeff
(HAL-pehrn, JEHF) **WSH.**

Center. Shoots right. 6', 195 lbs. Born, Potomac, MD, May 3, 1976.

Season	Club	League	GP	G	A	Pts	PIM	PP	SH	GW	S	%	+/-	TF	F%	H	SB	Min	GP	G	A	Pts	PIM	PP	SH	GW
			Regular Season																Playoffs							
1994-95	Stratford Cullitons	OJHL	44	29	54	83	43	....	....	....	....	....	....	....	....	....	....	....	....	....	....	....	....	....	....	....
1995-96	Princeton	ECAC	29	3	11	14	30	....	....	....	....	....	....	....	....	....	....	....	....	....	....	....	....	....	....	....
1996-97	Princeton	ECAC	33	7	24	31	35	....	....	....	....	....	....	....	....	....	....	....	....	....	....	....	....	....	....	....
1997-98	Princeton	ECAC	36	*28	25	*53	46	....	....	....	....	....	....	....	....	....	....	....	....	....	....	....	....	....	....	....
1998-99	Princeton	ECAC	33	*22	22	44	32	....	....	....	....	....	....	....	....	....	....	....	....	....	....	....	....	....	....	....
	Portland Pirates	AHL	6	2	1	3	4	....	....	....	....	....	....	....	....	....	....	....	....	....	....	....	....	....	....	....
99-2000	**Washington**	**NHL**	**79**	**18**	**11**	**29**	**39**	**4**	**4**	**1**	**108**	**16.7**	**21**	**812**	**51.1**	**84**	**44**	**13:14**	**5**	**2**	**1**	**3**	**0**	**1**	**0**	**1**
	NHL Totals		**79**	**18**	**11**	**29**	**39**	**4**	**4**	**1**	**108**	**16.7**		**812**	**51.1**	**84**	**44**	**13:14**	**5**	**2**	**1**	**3**	**0**	**1**	**0**	**1**

ECAC Second All-Star Team (1998, 1999)

Signed as a free agent by **Washington**, March 29, 1999.

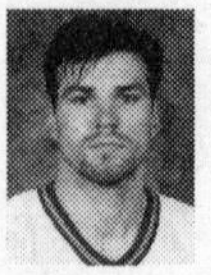

HALVERSON, Trevor
(HAL-vuhr-sohn, TREH-vohr) **WSH.**

Left wing. Shoots left. 6', 200 lbs. Born, White River, Ont., April 6, 1971. Washington's 2nd choice, 21st overall, in 1991 Entry Draft.

Season	Club	League	GP	G	A	Pts	PIM	PP	SH	GW	S	%	+/-	TF	F%	H	SB	Min	GP	G	A	Pts	PIM	PP	SH	GW
1987-88	S.S. Marie Elks	NOHA	33	29	35	64	34	....	....	....	....	....	....	....	....	....	....	....	....	....	....	....	....	....	....	....
	Thessalon Flyers	NOJHA	2	0	0	0	0	....	....	....	....	....	....	....	....	....	....	....	....	....	....	....	....	....	....	....
1988-89	Thessalon Flyers	NOJHA	2	0	0	0	0	....	....	....	....	....	....	....	....	....	....	....	....	....	....	....	....	....	....	....
	North Bay	OHL	52	8	10	18	7	....	....	....	....	....	....	....	....	....	....	....	....	....	....	....	....	....	....	....
1989-90	North Bay	OHL	54	22	20	42	162	....	....	....	....	....	....	....	....	....	....	....	2	2	1	3	2	....	....	....
1990-91	North Bay	OHL	54	22	20	42	172	....	....	....	....	....	....	....	....	....	....	....	2	2	1	3	2	....	....	....
1991-92	North Bay	OHL	64	59	36	95	128	....	....	....	....	....	....	....	....	....	....	....	10	3	6	9	4	....	....	....
1992-93	Hampton Roads	ECHL	9	7	5	12	6	....	....	....	....	....	....	....	....	....	....	....	....	....	....	....	....	....	....	....
	Baltimore	AHL	67	19	21	40	170	....	....	....	....	....	....	....	....	....	....	....	2	1	0	1	0	....	....	....
1993-94	San Diego Gulls	IHL	58	4	9	13	115	....	....	....	....	....	....	....	....	....	....	....	....	....	....	....	....	....	....	....
	Milwaukee	IHL	4	1	0	1	8	....	....	....	....	....	....	....	....	....	....	....	2	0	0	0	17	....	....	....
1994-95	Portland Pirates	AHL	5	0	1	1	9	....	....	....	....	....	....	....	....	....	....	....	....	....	....	....	....	....	....	....
	Hampton Roads	ECHL	42	14	26	40	194	....	....	....	....	....	....	....	....	....	....	....	....	....	....	....	....	....	....	....
1995-96	Las Vegas	IHL	22	6	9	15	86	....	....	....	....	....	....	....	....	....	....	....	....	....	....	....	....	....	....	....
	Utah Grizzlies	IHL	1	0	1	1	0	....	....	....	....	....	....	....	....	....	....	....	....	....	....	....	....	....	....	....
	Hampton Roads	ECHL	38	34	27	61	152	....	....	....	....	....	....	....	....	....	....	....	....	....	....	....	....	....	....	....
	Portland Pirates	AHL	3	0	1	1	0	....	....	....	....	....	....	....	....	....	....	....	....	....	....	....	....	....	....	....
	Indianapolis Ice	IHL	12	0	1	1	18	....	....	....	....	....	....	....	....	....	....	....	5	0	0	0	4	....	....	....
1996-97	Portland Pirates	AHL	50	9	8	17	157	....	....	....	....	....	....	....	....	....	....	....	3	1	1	2	4	....	....	....
1997-98	Fort Wayne	IHL	14	1	4	5	34	....	....	....	....	....	....	....	....	....	....	....	....	....	....	....	....	....	....	....
	Manitoba Moose	IHL	7	0	1	1	20	....	....	....	....	....	....	....	....	....	....	....	....	....	....	....	....	....	....	....
	Portland Pirates	AHL	43	14	13	27	181	....	....	....	....	....	....	....	....	....	....	....	10	2	4	6	20	....	....	....
1998-99	**Washington**	**NHL**	**17**	**0**	**4**	**4**	**28**	**0**	**0**	**0**	**16**	**0.0**	**–5**	**3**	**66.7**	**19**	**8**	**11:57**	....	....	....	....	....	....	....	....
	Portland Pirates	AHL	57	24	25	49	153	....	....	....	....	....	....	....	....	....	....	....	....	....	....	....	....	....	....	....
99-2000	**Washington**	**NHL**	DID NOT PLAY – INJURED																							
	NHL Totals		**17**	**0**	**4**	**4**	**28**	**0**	**0**	**0**	**16**	**0.0**		**3**	**66.7**	**19**	**8**	**11:57**	....	....	....	....	....	....	....	....

Claimed by **Anaheim** from **Washington** in Expansion Draft, June 24, 1993. Signed as a free agent by **Washington**, September, 1998. • Missed entire 1999-2000 season recovering from head injury suffered in training camp, September, 1999.

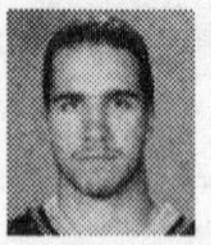

HAMEL, Denis
(ha-MEHL, deh-NEE) **BUF.**

Left wing. Shoots left. 6'2", 200 lbs. Born, Lachute, Que., May 10, 1977. St. Louis' 5th choice, 153rd overall, in 1995 Entry Draft.

Season	Club	League	GP	G	A	Pts	PIM	PP	SH	GW	S	%	+/-	TF	F%	H	SB	Min	GP	G	A	Pts	PIM	PP	SH	GW
1992-93	Lachute Regents	QAAA	32	18	24	42	....	....	....	....	....	....	....	....	....	....	....	....	....	....	....	....	....	....	....	....
1993-94	Abitibi Foresters	QAAA	15	5	7	12	29	....	....	....	....	....	....	....	....	....	....	....	....	....	....	....	....	....	....	....
1994-95	Chicoutimi	QMJHL	66	15	12	27	155	....	....	....	....	....	....	....	....	....	....	....	12	2	0	2	27	....	....	....
1995-96	Chicoutimi	QMJHL	65	40	49	89	199	....	....	....	....	....	....	....	....	....	....	....	17	10	14	24	64	....	....	....
1996-97	Chicoutimi	QMJHL	70	50	50	100	357	....	....	....	....	....	....	....	....	....	....	....	20	15	10	25	58	....	....	....
1997-98	Rochester	AHL	74	10	15	25	98	....	....	....	....	....	....	....	....	....	....	....	4	1	2	3	0	....	....	....
1998-99	Rochester	AHL	74	16	17	33	121	....	....	....	....	....	....	....	....	....	....	....	20	3	4	7	10	....	....	....
99-2000	**Buffalo**	**NHL**	**3**	**1**	**0**	**1**	**0**	**0**	**0**	**0**	**3**	**33.3**	**–1**	**0**	**0.0**	**10**	**0**	**9:45**	....	....	....	....	....	....	....	....
	Rochester	AHL	76	34	24	58	122	....	....	....	....	....	....	....	....	....	....	....	21	6	7	13	49	....	....	....
	NHL Totals		**3**	**1**	**0**	**1**	**0**	**0**	**0**	**0**	**3**	**33.3**		**0**	**0.0**	**10**	**0**	**9:45**	....	....	....	....	....	....	....	....

Traded to **Buffalo** by **St. Louis** for Charlie Huddy and Buffalo's 7th round choice (Daniel Corso) in 1996 Entry Draft, March 19, 1996.

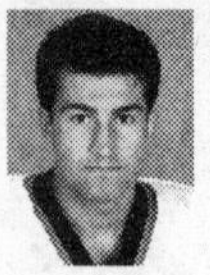

HAMRLIK, Roman
(HAHM-reh-lik, ROH-man) **NYI**

Defense. Shoots left. 6'2", 215 lbs. Born, Gottwaldov, Czech., April 12, 1974. Tampa Bay's 1st choice, 1st overall, in 1992 Entry Draft.

Season	Club	League	GP	G	A	Pts	PIM	PP	SH	GW	S	%	+/-	TF	F%	H	SB	Min	GP	G	A	Pts	PIM	PP	SH	GW
1990-91	ZPS Zlin	Czech.	14	2	2	4	18	....	....	....	....	....	....	....	....	....	....	....	....	....	....	....	....	....	....	....
1991-92	ZPS Zlin	Czech.	34	5	5	10	50	....	....	....	....	....	....	....	....	....	....	....	....	....	....	....	....	....	....	....
1992-93	**Tampa Bay**	**NHL**	**67**	**6**	**15**	**21**	**71**	**1**	**0**	**1**	**113**	**5.3**	**–21**	....	....	....	....	....	....	....	....	....	....	....	....	....
	Atlanta Knights	IHL	2	1	1	2	2	....	....	....	....	....	....	....	....	....	....	....	....	....	....	....	....	....	....	....
1993-94	**Tampa Bay**	**NHL**	**64**	**3**	**18**	**21**	**135**	**0**	**0**	**0**	**158**	**1.9**	**–14**	....	....	....	....	....	....	....	....	....	....	....	....	....
1994-95	ZPS Zlin	Cze-Rep	2	1	0	1	10	....	....	....	....	....	....	....	....	....	....	....	....	....	....	....	....	....	....	....
	Tampa Bay	**NHL**	**48**	**12**	**11**	**23**	**86**	**7**	**1**	**2**	**134**	**9.0**	**–18**	....	....	....	....	....	....	....	....	....	....	....	....	....
1995-96	**Tampa Bay**	**NHL**	**82**	**16**	**49**	**65**	**103**	**12**	**0**	**2**	**281**	**5.7**	**–24**	....	....	....	....	....	**5**	**0**	**1**	**1**	**4**	**0**	**0**	**0**
1996-97	**Tampa Bay**	**NHL**	**79**	**12**	**28**	**40**	**57**	**6**	**0**	**0**	**238**	**5.0**	**–29**	....	....	....	....	....	....	....	....	....	....	....	....	....
1997-98	**Tampa Bay**	**NHL**	**37**	**3**	**12**	**15**	**22**	**1**	**0**	**0**	**86**	**3.5**	**–18**	....	....	....	....	....	....	....	....	....	....	....	....	....
	Edmonton	**NHL**	**41**	**6**	**20**	**26**	**48**	**4**	**1**	**3**	**112**	**5.4**	**3**	....	....	....	....	....	**12**	**0**	**6**	**6**	**12**	**0**	**0**	**0**
	Czech-Republic	Olympics	6	1	0	1	2	....	....	....	....	....	....	....	....	....	....	....	....	....	....	....	....	....	....	....
1998-99	**Edmonton**	**NHL**	**75**	**8**	**24**	**32**	**70**	**3**	**0**	**0**	**172**	**4.7**	**9**	**0**	**0.0**	**144**	**121**	**23:49**	**3**	**0**	**0**	**0**	**2**	**0**	**0**	**0**
99-2000	Barum Zlin	Cze-Rep	6	0	3	3	4	....	....	....	....	....	....	....	....	....	....	....	....	....	....	....	....	....	....	....
	Edmonton	**NHL**	**80**	**8**	**37**	**45**	**68**	**5**	**0**	**0**	**180**	**4.4**	**1**	**0**	**0.0**	**122**	**99**	**25:18**	**5**	**0**	**1**	**1**	**4**	**0**	**0**	**0**
	NHL Totals		**573**	**74**	**214**	**288**	**660**	**39**	**2**	**8**	**1474**	**5.0**		**0**	**0.0**	**266**	**220**	**24:35**	**25**	**0**	**8**	**8**	**22**	**0**	**0**	**0**

Played in NHL All-Star Game (1996, 1999)

Traded to **Edmonton** by **Tampa Bay** with Paul Comrie for Bryan Marchment, Steve Kelly and Jason Bonsignore, December 30, 1997. Traded to **NY Islanders** by **Edmonton** for Eric Brewer, Josh Green and NY Islanders' 2nd round choice (Brad Winchester) in 2000 Entry Draft, June 24, 2000.

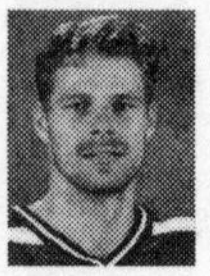

HANDZUS, Michal
(HAHND-zuhs, MEE-chal) **ST.L.**

Center. Shoots left. 6'5", 210 lbs. Born, Banska Bystrica, Czech., March 11, 1977. St. Louis' 3rd choice, 101st overall, in 1995 Entry Draft.

Season	Club	League	GP	G	A	Pts	PIM	PP	SH	GW	S	%	+/-	TF	F%	H	SB	Min	GP	G	A	Pts	PIM	PP	SH	GW
1993-94	Banska Bystrica	Slovak-Jr.	40	23	36	59	....	....	....	....	....	....	....	....	....	....	....	....	....	....	....	....	....	....	....	....
1994-95	Banska Bystrica	Slovak-2	22	15	14	29	10	....	....	....	....	....	....	....	....	....	....	....	....	....	....	....	....	....	....	....
1995-96	Banska Bystrica	Slovakia	19	3	1	4	8	....	....	....	....	....	....	....	....	....	....	....	....	....	....	....	....	....	....	....
1996-97	SKP Poprad	Slovakia	44	15	18	33	....	....	....	....	....	....	....	....	....	....	....	....	....	....	....	....	....	....	....	....
1997-98	Worcester	AHL	69	27	36	63	54	....	....	....	....	....	....	....	....	....	....	....	11	2	6	8	10	....	....	....
1998-99	**St. Louis**	**NHL**	**66**	**4**	**12**	**16**	**30**	**0**	**0**	**0**	**78**	**5.1**	**–9**	**794**	**49.9**	**56**	**38**	**14:48**	**11**	**0**	**2**	**2**	**8**	**0**	**0**	**0**
99-2000	**St. Louis**	**NHL**	**81**	**25**	**28**	**53**	**44**	**3**	**4**	**5**	**166**	**15.1**	**19**	**1243**	**51.5**	**50**	**31**	**17:43**	**7**	**0**	**3**	**3**	**6**	**0**	**0**	**0**
	NHL Totals		**147**	**29**	**40**	**69**	**74**	**3**	**4**	**5**	**244**	**11.9**		**2037**	**50.9**	**106**	**69**	**16:25**	**18**	**0**	**5**	**5**	**14**	**0**	**0**	**0**

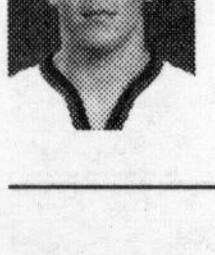

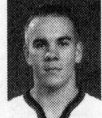

HANNAN, Scott
(HAN-nan, SKAWT) **S.J.**

Defense. Shoots left. 6'2", 220 lbs. Born, Richmond, B.C., January 23, 1979. San Jose's 2nd choice, 23rd overall, in 1997 Entry Draft.

Season	Club	League	GP	G	A	Pts	PIM	PP	SH	GW	S	%	+/-	TF	F%	H	SB	Min	GP	G	A	Pts	PIM	PP	SH	GW
1994-95	Surrey Wolves	BCAHA	70	54	54	108	200	....	....	....	....	....	....	....	....	....	....	....	....	....	....	....	....	....	....	....
	Tacoma Rockets	WHL	2	0	0	0	0	....	....	....	....	....	....	....	....	....	....	....	....	....	....	....	....	....	....	....
1995-96	Kelowna Rockets	WHL	69	4	5	9	76	....	....	....	....	....	....	....	....	....	....	....	6	0	1	1	4	....	....	....
1996-97	Kelowna Rockets	WHL	70	17	26	43	101	....	....	....	....	....	....	....	....	....	....	....	6	0	0	0	8	....	....	....
1997-98	Kelowna Rockets	WHL	47	10	30	40	70	....	....	....	....	....	....	....	....	....	....	....	7	2	7	9	14	....	....	....

			Regular Season																Playoffs							
Season	Club	League	GP	G	A	Pts	PIM	PP	SH	GW	S	%	+/–	TF	F%	H	SB	Min	GP	G	A	Pts	PIM	PP	SH	GW
1998-99	**San Jose**	**NHL**	**5**	**0**	**2**	**2**	**6**	**0**	**0**	**0**	**4**	**0.0**	**0**	**0**	**0.0**	**2**	**0**	**7:15**	....	....	....	....	....	....	....	....
	Kelowna Rockets	WHL	47	15	30	45	92	....	....	....	....	....	....	....	....	....	....	....	6	1	2	3	14	....	....	....
	Kentucky	AHL	2	0	0	0	2	....	....	....	....	....	....	....	....	....	....	....	12	0	2	2	10	....	....	....
99-2000	**San Jose**	**NHL**	**30**	**1**	**2**	**3**	**10**	**0**	**0**	**0**	**28**	**3.6**	**7**	**1**	**0.0**	**27**	**9**	**17:09**	**1**	**0**	**1**	**1**	**0**	**0**	**0**	**0**
	Kentucky	AHL	41	5	12	17	40	....	....	....	....	....	....	....	....	....	....	....	....	....	....	....	....	....	....	....
	NHL Totals		**35**	**1**	**4**	**5**	**16**	**0**	**0**	**0**	**32**	**3.1**		**1**	**0.0**	**29**	**9**	**15:44**	**1**	**0**	**1**	**1**	**0**	**0**	**0**	**0**

WHL West First All-Star Team (1999)

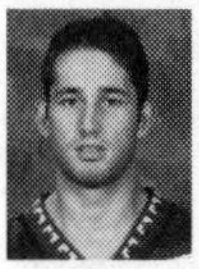

HANSEN, Tavis

(HAN-sehn, TA-vihs) **PHX.**

Center. Shoots right. 6'1", 205 lbs. Born, Prince Albert, Sask., June 17, 1975. Winnipeg's 3rd choice, 58th overall, in 1994 Entry Draft.

Season	Club	League	GP	G	A	Pts	PIM	PP	SH	GW	S	%	+/–	TF	F%	H	SB	Min	GP	G	A	Pts	PIM	PP	SH	GW
1992-93	Shellbrook	SAHA	42	42	63	105	107	....	....	....	....	....	....	....	....	....	....	....	....	....	....	....	....	....	....	....
1993-94	Tacoma Rockets	WHL	71	23	31	54	122	....	....	....	....	....	....	....	....	....	....	....	8	1	3	4	17	....	....	....
1994-95	Tacoma Rockets	WHL	71	32	41	73	142	....	....	....	....	....	....	....	....	....	....	....	4	1	1	2	8	....	....	....
	Winnipeg	**NHL**	**1**	**0**	**0**	**0**	**0**	**0**	**0**	**0**	**0**	**0.0**	**0**	....	....	....	....	....	....	....	....	....	....	....	....	....
1995-96	Springfield	AHL	67	6	16	22	85	....	....	....	....	....	....	....	....	....	....	....	5	1	2	3	2	....	....	....
1996-97	**Phoenix**	**NHL**	**1**	**0**	**0**	**0**	**0**	**0**	**0**	**0**	**0**	**0.0**	**0**	....	....	....	....	....	....	....	....	....	....	....	....	....
	Springfield	AHL	12	3	1	4	23	....	....	....	....	....	....	....	....	....	....	....	....	....	....	....	....	....	....	....
1997-98	Springfield	AHL	73	20	14	34	70	....	....	....	....	....	....	....	....	....	....	....	4	1	2	3	18	....	....	....
1998-99	**Phoenix**	**NHL**	**20**	**2**	**1**	**3**	**12**	**0**	**0**	**0**	**14**	**14.3**	**–4**	**5**	**80.0**	**26**	**3**	**8:07**	**2**	**0**	**0**	**0**	**0**	**0**	**0**	**0**
	Springfield	AHL	63	23	11	34	85	....	....	....	....	....	....	....	....	....	....	....	3	0	1	1	5	....	....	....
99-2000	**Phoenix**	**NHL**	**5**	**0**	**0**	**0**	**0**	**0**	**0**	**0**	**2**	**0.0**	**0**	**0**	**0.0**	**2**	**1**	**4:17**	....	....	....	....	....	....	....	....
	Springfield	AHL	59	21	27	48	164	....	....	....	....	....	....	....	....	....	....	....	5	2	1	3	4	....	....	....
	NHL Totals		**27**	**2**	**1**	**3**	**12**	**0**	**0**	**0**	**16**	**12.5**		**5**	**80.0**	**28**	**4**	**7:21**	**2**	**0**	**0**	**0**	**0**	**0**	**0**	**0**

Transferred to **Phoenix** after **Winnipeg** franchise relocated, July 1, 1996.

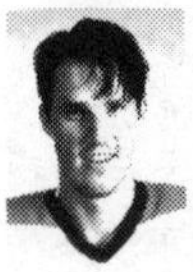

HARKINS, Brett

(HAHR-kihns, BREHT)

Left wing. Shoots left. 6'1", 185 lbs. Born, North Ridgeville, OH, July 2, 1970. NY Islanders' 9th choice, 133rd overall, in 1989 Entry Draft.

Season	Club	League	GP	G	A	Pts	PIM	PP	SH	GW	S	%	+/–	TF	F%	H	SB	Min	GP	G	A	Pts	PIM	PP	SH	GW
1986-87	St. Andrews	Hi-School	30	47	60	107	....	....	....	....	....	....	....	....	....	....	....	....	....	....	....	....	....	....	....	....
1987-88	Brockville Braves	OJHL	55	21	55	76	36	....	....	....	....	....	....	....	....	....	....	....	....	....	....	....	....	....	....	....
1988-89	Detroit	NAJHL	38	23	46	69	94	....	....	....	....	....	....	....	....	....	....	....	....	....	....	....	....	....	....	....
1989-90	Bowling Green	CCHA	41	11	43	54	45	....	....	....	....	....	....	....	....	....	....	....	....	....	....	....	....	....	....	....
1990-91	Bowling Green	CCHA	40	22	38	60	30	....	....	....	....	....	....	....	....	....	....	....	....	....	....	....	....	....	....	....
1991-92	Bowling Green	CCHA	34	8	39	47	32	....	....	....	....	....	....	....	....	....	....	....	....	....	....	....	....	....	....	....
1992-93	Bowling Green	CCHA	35	19	28	47	28	....	....	....	....	....	....	....	....	....	....	....	....	....	....	....	....	....	....	....
1993-94	Adirondack	AHL	80	22	47	69	23	....	....	....	....	....	....	....	....	....	....	....	10	1	5	6	4	....	....	....
1994-95	**Boston**	**NHL**	**1**	**0**	**1**	**1**	**0**	**0**	**0**	**0**	**1**	**0.0**	**0**	....	....	....	....	....	....	....	....	....	....	....	....	....
	Providence Bruins	AHL	80	23	*69	92	32	....	....	....	....	....	....	....	....	....	....	....	13	8	14	22	4	....	....	....
1995-96	**Florida**	**NHL**	**8**	**0**	**3**	**3**	**6**	**0**	**0**	**0**	**4**	**0.0**	**–2**	....	....	....	....	....	....	....	....	....	....	....	....	....
	Carolina	AHL	55	23	*71	94	44	....	....	....	....	....	....	....	....	....	....	....	....	....	....	....	....	....	....	....
1996-97	**Boston**	**NHL**	**44**	**4**	**14**	**18**	**8**	**3**	**0**	**2**	**52**	**7.7**	**–3**	....	....	....	....	....	....	....	....	....	....	....	....	....
	Providence Bruins	AHL	28	9	31	40	32	....	....	....	....	....	....	....	....	....	....	....	10	2	10	12	0	....	....	....
1997-98	Cleveland	IHL	80	32	62	94	82	....	....	....	....	....	....	....	....	....	....	....	10	4	13	17	14	....	....	....
1998-99	Cleveland	IHL	74	20	67	87	84	....	....	....	....	....	....	....	....	....	....	....	....	....	....	....	....	....	....	....
99-2000	Cleveland	IHL	76	20	50	70	79	....	....	....	....	....	....	....	....	....	....	....	9	2	8	10	6	....	....	....
	NHL Totals		**53**	**4**	**18**	**22**	**14**	**3**	**0**	**2**	**57**	**7.0**														

Signed as a free agent by **Boston**, July 1, 1994. Signed as a free agent by **Florida**, July 24, 1995. Signed as a free agent by **Boston**, September 4, 1996. • Played w/ RHI's Utah Rollerbees in 1994 (6-5-10-15-8).

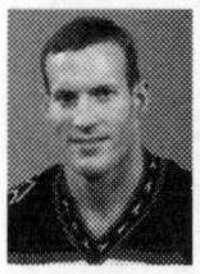

HARLOCK, David

(HAHR-lahk, DAY-vihd) **ATL.**

Defense. Shoots left. 6'2", 220 lbs. Born, Toronto, Ont., March 16, 1971. New Jersey's 2nd choice, 24th overall, in 1990 Entry Draft.

Season	Club	League	GP	G	A	Pts	PIM	PP	SH	GW	S	%	+/–	TF	F%	H	SB	Min	GP	G	A	Pts	PIM	PP	SH	GW
1986-87	Toronto Wings	MTHL	86	17	55	72	60	....	....	....	....	....	....	....	....	....	....	....	....	....	....	....	....	....	....	....
1987-88	Toronto Wings	MTHL	70	16	56	72	100	....	....	....	....	....	....	....	....	....	....	....	....	....	....	....	....	....	....	....
	Henry Carr	OJHL-B	3	0	0	0	4	....	....	....	....	....	....	....	....	....	....	....	....	....	....	....	....	....	....	....
1988-89	St. Michael's	OJHL-B	25	4	16	20	34	....	....	....	....	....	....	....	....	....	....	....	27	3	12	15	14	....	....	....
1989-90	U. of Michigan	CCHA	42	2	13	15	44	....	....	....	....	....	....	....	....	....	....	....	....	....	....	....	....	....	....	....
1990-91	U. of Michigan	CCHA	39	2	8	10	70	....	....	....	....	....	....	....	....	....	....	....	....	....	....	....	....	....	....	....
1991-92	U. of Michigan	CCHA	44	1	6	7	80	....	....	....	....	....	....	....	....	....	....	....	....	....	....	....	....	....	....	....
1992-93	U. of Michigan	CCHA	38	3	9	12	58	....	....	....	....	....	....	....	....	....	....	....	....	....	....	....	....	....	....	....
	Canada	Nat-Team	4	0	0	0	2	....	....	....	....	....	....	....	....	....	....	....	....	....	....	....	....	....	....	....
1993-94	Canada	Nat-Team	41	0	3	3	28	....	....	....	....	....	....	....	....	....	....	....	....	....	....	....	....	....	....	....
	Canada	Olympics	8	0	0	0	8	....	....	....	....	....	....	....	....	....	....	....	....	....	....	....	....	....	....	....
	Toronto	**NHL**	**6**	**0**	**0**	**0**	**0**	**0**	**0**	**0**	**2**	**0.0**	**–2**	....	....	....	....	....	....	....	....	....	....	....	....	....
	St. John's Leafs	AHL	10	0	3	3	2	....	....	....	....	....	....	....	....	....	....	....	9	0	0	0	6	....	....	....
1994-95	**Toronto**	**NHL**	**1**	**0**	**0**	**0**	**0**	**0**	**0**	**0**	**0**	**0.0**	**–1**	....	....	....	....	....	....	....	....	....	....	....	....	....
	St. John's Leafs	AHL	58	0	6	6	44	....	....	....	....	....	....	....	....	....	....	....	5	0	0	0	0	....	....	....
1995-96	**Toronto**	**NHL**	**1**	**0**	**0**	**0**	**0**	**0**	**0**	**0**	**0**	**0.0**	**0**	....	....	....	....	....	....	....	....	....	....	....	....	....
	St. John's Leafs	AHL	77	0	12	12	92	....	....	....	....	....	....	....	....	....	....	....	4	0	1	1	2	....	....	....
1996-97	San Antonio	IHL	69	3	10	13	82	....	....	....	....	....	....	....	....	....	....	....	9	0	0	0	10	....	....	....
1997-98	**Washington**	**NHL**	**6**	**0**	**0**	**0**	**4**	**0**	**0**	**0**	**2**	**0.0**	**2**	....	....	....	....	....	....	....	....	....	....	....	....	....
	Portland Pirates	AHL	71	3	15	18	66	....	....	....	....	....	....	....	....	....	....	....	10	2	2	4	6	....	....	....
1998-99	**NY Islanders**	**NHL**	**70**	**2**	**6**	**8**	**68**	**0**	**0**	**0**	**35**	**5.7**	**–16**	**0**	**0.0**	**172**	**65**	**18:15**	....	....	....	....	....	....	....	....
99-2000	**Atlanta**	**NHL**	**44**	**0**	**6**	**6**	**36**	**0**	**0**	**0**	**29**	**0.0**	**–8**	**0**	**0.0**	**166**	**55**	**19:41**	....	....	....	....	....	....	....	....
	NHL Totals		**128**	**2**	**12**	**14**	**108**	**0**	**0**	**0**	**68**	**2.9**		**0**	**0.0**	**338**	**120**	**18:48**	....	....	....	....	....	....	....	....

Signed as a free agent by **Toronto**, August 20, 1993. Signed as a free agent by **Washington**, August 20, 1997. Signed as a free agent by **NY Islanders**, August 24, 1998. Claimed by **Atlanta** from **NY Islanders** in Expansion Draft, June 25, 1999.

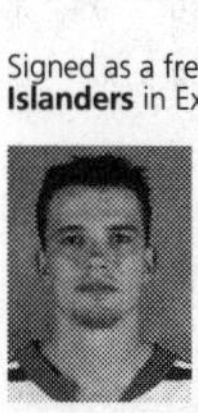

HARVEY, Todd

(HAHR-vee, TAWD) **S.J.**

Center. Shoots right. 6', 205 lbs. Born, Hamilton, Ont., February 17, 1975. Dallas' 1st choice, 9th overall, in 1993 Entry Draft.

Season	Club	League	GP	G	A	Pts	PIM	PP	SH	GW	S	%	+/–	TF	F%	H	SB	Min	GP	G	A	Pts	PIM	PP	SH	GW
1989-90	Cambridge Hawks	OJHL-B	41	35	27	62	213	....	....	....	....	....	....	....	....	....	....	....	....	....	....	....	....	....	....	....
1990-91	Cambridge Hawks	OJHL-B	35	32	39	71	174	....	....	....	....	....	....	....	....	....	....	....	....	....	....	....	....	....	....	....
1991-92	Detroit	OHL	58	21	43	64	141	....	....	....	....	....	....	....	....	....	....	....	7	3	5	8	30	....	....	....
1992-93	Detroit Jr. Wings	OHL	55	50	50	100	83	....	....	....	....	....	....	....	....	....	....	....	15	9	12	21	39	....	....	....
1993-94	Detroit Jr. Wings	OHL	49	34	51	85	75	....	....	....	....	....	....	....	....	....	....	....	17	10	12	22	26	....	....	....
1994-95	Detroit Jr. Wings	OHL	11	8	14	22	12	....	....	....	....	....	....	....	....	....	....	....	....	....	....	....	....	....	....	....
	Dallas	**NHL**	**40**	**11**	**9**	**20**	**67**	**2**	**0**	**1**	**64**	**17.2**	**–3**	....	....	....	....	....	**5**	**0**	**0**	**0**	**8**	**0**	**0**	**0**
1995-96	**Dallas**	**NHL**	**69**	**9**	**20**	**29**	**136**	**3**	**0**	**1**	**101**	**8.9**	**–13**	....	....	....	....	....	....	....	....	....	....	....	....	....
	Michigan K-Wings	IHL	5	1	3	4	8	....	....	....	....	....	....	....	....	....	....	....	....	....	....	....	....	....	....	....
1996-97	**Dallas**	**NHL**	**71**	**9**	**22**	**31**	**142**	**1**	**0**	**2**	**99**	**9.1**	**19**	....	....	....	....	....	**7**	**0**	**1**	**1**	**10**	**0**	**0**	**0**
1997-98	**Dallas**	**NHL**	**59**	**9**	**10**	**19**	**104**	**0**	**0**	**1**	**88**	**10.2**	**5**	....	....	....	....	....	....	....	....	....	....	....	....	....
1998-99	**NY Rangers**	**NHL**	**37**	**11**	**17**	**28**	**72**	**6**	**0**	**2**	**58**	**19.0**	**–1**	**175**	**50.3**	**126**	**22**	**17:19**	....	....	....	....	....	....	....	....
99-2000	**NY Rangers**	**NHL**	**31**	**3**	**3**	**6**	**62**	**0**	**0**	**0**	**31**	**9.7**	**–9**	**173**	**49.1**	**94**	**20**	**12:21**	....	....	....	....	....	....	....	....
	San Jose	**NHL**	**40**	**8**	**4**	**12**	**78**	**2**	**0**	**0**	**59**	**13.6**	**–2**	**44**	**43.2**	**94**	**9**	**12:55**	**12**	**1**	**0**	**1**	**8**	**1**	**0**	**0**
	NHL Totals		**347**	**60**	**85**	**145**	**661**	**14**	**0**	**7**	**500**	**12.0**		**392**	**49.0**	**314**	**51**	**14:16**	**24**	**1**	**1**	**2**	**26**	**1**	**0**	**0**

Traded to **NY Rangers** by **Dallas** with Bob Errey and Dallas' 4th round choice (Boyd Kane) in 1998 Entry Draft for Brian Skrudland, Mike Keane and NY Rangers' 6th round choice (Pavel Patera) in 1998 Entry Draft, March 24, 1998. Traded to **San Jose** by **NY Rangers** with NY Rangers' 4th round choice in 2001 Entry Draft for Radek Dvorak, December 30, 1999.

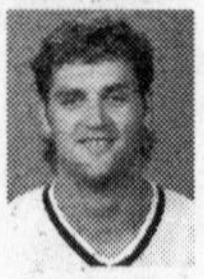

HATCHER, Derian
(HAT-chuhr, DAIR-ee-an_) **DAL.**

Defense. Shoots left. 6'5", 230 lbs. Born, Sterling Heights, MI, June 4, 1972. Minnesota's 1st choice, 8th overall, in 1990 Entry Draft.

			Regular Season																Playoffs							
Season	Club	League	GP	G	A	Pts	PIM	PP	SH	GW	S	%	+/-	TF	F%	H	SB	Min	GP	G	A	Pts	PIM	PP	SH	GW
1987-88	Detroit G.P.D.	MNHL	25	5	13	18	52	....	....	....	....	....	....	....	....	....	....	....	....	....	....	....	....	....	....	....
1988-89	Detroit G.P.D.	MNHL	51	19	35	54	100	....	....	....	....	....	....	....	....	....	....	....	....	....	....	....	....	....	....	....
1989-90	North Bay	OHL	64	14	38	52	81	....	....	....	....	....	....	....	....	....	....	....	5	2	3	5	8	....	....	....
1990-91	North Bay	OHL	64	13	49	62	163	....	....	....	....	....	....	....	....	....	....	....	10	2	10	12	28	....	....	....
1991-92	**Minnesota**	**NHL**	**43**	**8**	**4**	**12**	**88**	**0**	**0**	**2**	**51**	**15.7**	**7**	....	....	....	....	....	**5**	**0**	**2**	**2**	**8**	**0**	**0**	**0**
1992-93	**Minnesota**	**NHL**	**67**	**4**	**15**	**19**	**178**	**0**	**0**	**1**	**73**	**5.5**	**-27**	....	....	....	....	....	....	....	....	....	....	....	....	....
	Kalamazoo	IHL	2	1	2	3	21	....	....	....	....	....	....	....	....	....	....	....	....	....	....	....	....	....	....	....
1993-94	**Dallas**	**NHL**	**83**	**12**	**19**	**31**	**211**	**2**	**1**	**2**	**132**	**9.1**	**19**	....	....	....	....	....	**9**	**0**	**2**	**2**	**14**	**0**	**0**	**0**
1994-95	**Dallas**	**NHL**	**43**	**5**	**11**	**16**	**105**	**2**	**0**	**2**	**74**	**6.8**	**3**	....	....	....	....	....	....	....	....	....	....	....	....	....
1995-96	**Dallas**	**NHL**	**79**	**8**	**23**	**31**	**129**	**2**	**0**	**1**	**125**	**6.4**	**-12**	....	....	....	....	....	....	....	....	....	....	....	....	....
1996-97	**Dallas**	**NHL**	**63**	**3**	**19**	**22**	**97**	**0**	**0**	**0**	**96**	**3.1**	**8**	....	....	....	....	....	**7**	**0**	**2**	**2**	**20**	**0**	**0**	**0**
1997-98	**Dallas**	**NHL**	**70**	**6**	**25**	**31**	**132**	**3**	**0**	**2**	**74**	**8.1**	**9**	....	....	....	....	....	**17**	**3**	**3**	**6**	**39**	**2**	**0**	**0**
	United States	Olympics	4	0	0	0	0	....	....	....	....	....	....	....	....	....	....	....	....	....	....	....	....	....	....	....
1998-99♦	**Dallas**	**NHL**	**80**	**9**	**21**	**30**	**102**	**3**	**0**	**2**	**125**	**7.2**	**21**	**0**	**0.0**	**204**	**97**	**24:44**	**18**	**1**	**6**	**7**	**24**	**0**	**0**	**0**
99-2000	**Dallas**	**NHL**	**57**	**2**	**22**	**24**	**68**	**0**	**0**	**0**	**90**	**2.2**	**6**	**0**	**0.0**	**179**	**82**	**27:33**	**23**	**1**	**3**	**4**	**29**	**0**	**0**	**0**
	NHL Totals		**585**	**57**	**159**	**216**	**1110**	**12**	**1**	**12**	**840**	**6.8**		**0**	**0.0**	**383**	**179**	**25:54**	**79**	**5**	**18**	**23**	**134**	**2**	**0**	**0**

Played in NHL All-Star Game (1997)

Transferred to **Dallas** after **Minnesota** franchise relocated, June 9, 1993.

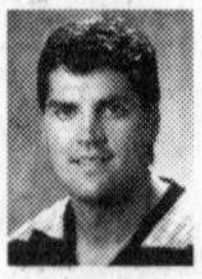

HATCHER, Kevin
(HAT-chuhr, KEH-vihn) **CAR.**

Defense. Shoots right. 6'3", 230 lbs. Born, Detroit, MI, September 9, 1966. Washington's 1st choice, 17th overall, in 1984 Entry Draft.

			Regular Season																Playoffs							
Season	Club	League	GP	G	A	Pts	PIM	PP	SH	GW	S	%	+/-	TF	F%	H	SB	Min	GP	G	A	Pts	PIM	PP	SH	GW
1982-83	Detroit	MNHL	75	30	45	75	120	....	....	....	....	....	....	....	....	....	....	....	....	....	....	....	....	....	....	....
1983-84	North Bay	OHL	67	10	39	49	61	....	....	....	....	....	....	....	....	....	....	....	4	2	2	4	11	....	....	....
1984-85	North Bay	OHL	58	26	37	63	75	....	....	....	....	....	....	....	....	....	....	....	8	3	8	11	9	....	....	....
	Washington	**NHL**	**2**	**1**	**0**	**1**	**0**	**0**	**1**	**0**	**3**	**33.3**	**1**	....	....	....	....	....	**1**	**0**	**0**	**0**	**0**	**0**	**0**	**0**
1985-86	**Washington**	**NHL**	**79**	**9**	**10**	**19**	**119**	**1**	**0**	**1**	**132**	**6.8**	**6**	....	....	....	....	....	**9**	**1**	**1**	**2**	**19**	**0**	**0**	**0**
1986-87	**Washington**	**NHL**	**78**	**8**	**16**	**24**	**144**	**1**	**0**	**2**	**100**	**8.0**	**-29**	....	....	....	....	....	**7**	**1**	**0**	**1**	**20**	**0**	**0**	**0**
1987-88	**Washington**	**NHL**	**71**	**14**	**27**	**41**	**137**	**5**	**0**	**3**	**181**	**7.7**	**1**	....	....	....	....	....	**14**	**5**	**7**	**12**	**55**	**1**	**0**	**1**
1988-89	**Washington**	**NHL**	**62**	**13**	**27**	**40**	**101**	**3**	**0**	**2**	**148**	**8.8**	**19**	....	....	....	....	....	**6**	**1**	**4**	**5**	**20**	**1**	**0**	**0**
1989-90	**Washington**	**NHL**	**80**	**13**	**41**	**54**	**102**	**4**	**0**	**2**	**240**	**5.4**	**4**	....	....	....	....	....	**11**	**0**	**8**	**8**	**32**	**0**	**0**	**0**
1990-91	**Washington**	**NHL**	**79**	**24**	**50**	**74**	**69**	**9**	**2**	**3**	**267**	**9.0**	**-10**	....	....	....	....	....	**11**	**3**	**3**	**6**	**8**	**2**	**0**	**0**
1991-92	**Washington**	**NHL**	**79**	**17**	**37**	**54**	**105**	**8**	**1**	**2**	**246**	**6.9**	**18**	....	....	....	....	....	**7**	**2**	**4**	**6**	**19**	**0**	**1**	**0**
1992-93	**Washington**	**NHL**	**83**	**34**	**45**	**79**	**114**	**13**	**1**	**6**	**329**	**10.3**	**-7**	....	....	....	....	....	**6**	**0**	**1**	**1**	**14**	**0**	**0**	**0**
1993-94	**Washington**	**NHL**	**72**	**16**	**24**	**40**	**108**	**6**	**0**	**3**	**217**	**7.4**	**-13**	....	....	....	....	....	**11**	**3**	**4**	**7**	**37**	**0**	**1**	**0**
1994-95	**Dallas**	**NHL**	**47**	**10**	**19**	**29**	**66**	**3**	**0**	**2**	**138**	**7.2**	**-4**	....	....	....	....	....	**5**	**2**	**1**	**3**	**2**	**1**	**0**	**1**
1995-96	**Dallas**	**NHL**	**74**	**15**	**26**	**41**	**58**	**7**	**0**	**3**	**237**	**6.3**	**-24**	....	....	....	....	....	....	....	....	....	....	....	....	....
1996-97	**Pittsburgh**	**NHL**	**80**	**15**	**39**	**54**	**103**	**9**	**0**	**1**	**199**	**7.5**	**11**	....	....	....	....	....	**5**	**1**	**1**	**2**	**4**	**1**	**0**	**0**
1997-98	**Pittsburgh**	**NHL**	**74**	**19**	**29**	**48**	**66**	**13**	**1**	**3**	**169**	**11.2**	**-3**	....	....	....	....	....	**6**	**1**	**0**	**1**	**12**	**1**	**0**	**0**
	United States	Olympics	3	0	2	2	0	....	....	....	....	....	....	....	....	....	....	....	....	....	....	....	....	....	....	....
1998-99	**Pittsburgh**	**NHL**	**66**	**11**	**27**	**38**	**24**	**4**	**2**	**3**	**131**	**8.4**	**11**	**2**	**50.0**	**87**	**102**	**24:38**	**13**	**2**	**3**	**5**	**4**	**1**	**0**	**0**
99-2000	**NY Rangers**	**NHL**	**74**	**4**	**19**	**23**	**38**	**2**	**0**	**0**	**112**	**3.6**	**-10**	**0**	**0.0**	**135**	**123**	**21:11**	....	....	....	....	....	....	....	....
	NHL Totals		**1100**	**223**	**436**	**659**	**1354**	**88**	**8**	**36**	**2849**	**7.8**		**2**	**50.0**	**222**	**225**	**22:49**	**112**	**22**	**37**	**59**	**246**	**8**	**2**	**2**

OHL Second All-Star Team (1985) • Played in NHL All-Star Game (1990, 1991, 1992, 1996, 1997)

Traded to **Dallas** by **Washington** for Mark Tinordi and Rick Mrozik, January 18, 1995. Traded to **Pittsburgh** by **Dallas** for Sergei Zubov, June 22, 1996. Traded to **NY Rangers** by **Pittsburgh** for Peter Popovic, September 30, 1999. Signed as a free agent by **Carolina**, July 31, 2000.

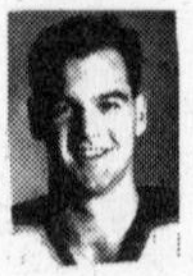

HAUER, Brett
(HOW-uhr, BREHT) **EDM.**

Defense. Shoots right. 6'2", 210 lbs. Born, Richfield, MN, July 11, 1971. Vancouver's 3rd choice, 71st overall, in 1989 Entry Draft.

			Regular Season																Playoffs							
Season	Club	League	GP	G	A	Pts	PIM	PP	SH	GW	S	%	+/-	TF	F%	H	SB	Min	GP	G	A	Pts	PIM	PP	SH	GW
1987-88	Richfield High	Hi-School	24	3	3	6	....	....	....	....	....	....	....	....	....	....	....	....	....	....	....	....	....	....	....	....
1988-89	Richfield High	Hi-School	24	8	15	23	70	....	....	....	....	....	....	....	....	....	....	....	....	....	....	....	....	....	....	....
1989-90	Minnesota-Duluth	WCHA	37	2	6	8	44	....	....	....	....	....	....	....	....	....	....	....	....	....	....	....	....	....	....	....
1990-91	Minnesota-Duluth	WCHA	30	1	7	8	54	....	....	....	....	....	....	....	....	....	....	....	....	....	....	....	....	....	....	....
1991-92	Minnesota-Duluth	WCHA	33	8	14	22	40	....	....	....	....	....	....	....	....	....	....	....	....	....	....	....	....	....	....	....
1992-93	Minnesota-Duluth	WCHA	40	10	46	56	52	....	....	....	....	....	....	....	....	....	....	....	....	....	....	....	....	....	....	....
1993-94	United States	Nat-Team	57	6	14	20	88	....	....	....	....	....	....	....	....	....	....	....	....	....	....	....	....	....	....	....
	United States	Olympics	8	0	0	0	10	....	....	....	....	....	....	....	....	....	....	....	....	....	....	....	....	....	....	....
	Las Vegas	IHL	21	0	7	7	8	....	....	....	....	....	....	....	....	....	....	....	1	0	0	0	0	....	....	....
1994-95	AIK Solna	Sweden	37	1	3	4	38	....	....	....	....	....	....	....	....	....	....	....	....	....	....	....	....	....	....	....
1995-96	**Edmonton**	**NHL**	**29**	**4**	**2**	**6**	**30**	**2**	**0**	**1**	**53**	**7.5**	**-11**	....	....	....	....	....	....	....	....	....	....	....	....	....
	Cape Breton	AHL	17	3	5	8	29	....	....	....	....	....	....	....	....	....	....	....	....	....	....	....	....	....	....	....
1996-97	Chicago Wolves	IHL	81	10	30	40	50	....	....	....	....	....	....	....	....	....	....	....	4	2	0	2	4	....	....	....
1997-98	Manitoba Moose	IHL	82	13	48	61	58	....	....	....	....	....	....	....	....	....	....	....	3	0	0	0	2	....	....	....
1998-99	Manitoba Moose	IHL	81	15	56	71	66	....	....	....	....	....	....	....	....	....	....	....	5	0	5	5	4	....	....	....
99-2000	**Edmonton**	**NHL**	**5**	**0**	**2**	**2**	**2**	**0**	**0**	**0**	**8**	**0.0**	**-2**	**0**	**0.0**	**10**	**2**	**14:48**	....	....	....	....	....	....	....	....
	Manitoba Moose	IHL	77	13	47	60	92	....	....	....	....	....	....	....	....	....	....	....	2	0	1	1	2	....	....	....
	NHL Totals		**34**	**4**	**4**	**8**	**32**	**2**	**0**	**1**	**61**	**6.6**		**0**	**0.0**	**10**	**2**	**14:48**	....	....	....	....	....	....	....	....

WCHA First All-Star Team (1993) • NCAA West First All-American Team (1993) • IHL First All-Star Team (1999, 2000) • Won Larry D. Gordon Trophy (Top Defenseman - IHL) (2000)

Traded to **Edmonton** by **Vancouver** for Edmonton's 7th round choice (Larry Shapley) in 1997 Entry Draft, August 24, 1995. Signed as a free agent by **Manitoba** (IHL), September 15, 1997.

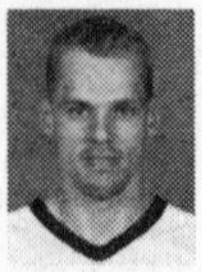

HAVELID, Niclas
(HAHV-lihd, NIHK-lahs) **ANA.**

Defense. Shoots left. 6', 192 lbs. Born, Stockholm, Sweden, April 12, 1973. Anaheim's 2nd choice, 83rd overall, in 1999 Entry Draft.

			Regular Season																Playoffs							
Season	Club	League	GP	G	A	Pts	PIM	PP	SH	GW	S	%	+/-	TF	F%	H	SB	Min	GP	G	A	Pts	PIM	PP	SH	GW
1991-92	AIK Solna	Sweden	10	0	0	0	2	....	....	....	....	....	....	....	....	....	....	....	....	....	....	....	....	....	....	....
1992-93	AIK Solna	Sweden	22	1	0	1	16	....	....	....	....	....	....	....	....	....	....	....	....	....	....	....	....	....	....	....
1993-94	AIK Solna	Sweden-2	40	6	12	18	26	....	....	....	....	....	....	....	....	....	....	....	9	0	1	1	10	....	....	....
1994-95	AIK Solna	Sweden	40	3	7	10	38	....	....	....	....	....	....	....	....	....	....	....	....	....	....	....	....	....	....	....
1995-96	AIK Solna	Sweden	40	5	6	11	30	....	....	....	....	....	....	....	....	....	....	....	....	....	....	....	....	....	....	....
1996-97	AIK Solna	Sweden	49	3	6	9	42	....	....	....	....	....	....	....	....	....	....	....	7	1	2	3	8	....	....	....
1997-98	AIK Solna	Sweden	43	8	4	12	42	....	....	....	....	....	....	....	....	....	....	....	....	....	....	....	....	....	....	....
1998-99	Malmo IF	Sweden	50	10	12	22	42	....	....	....	....	....	....	....	....	....	....	....	8	0	4	4	10	....	....	....
99-2000	**Anaheim**	**NHL**	**50**	**2**	**7**	**9**	**20**	**0**	**0**	**2**	**70**	**2.9**	**0**	**1**	**0.0**	**103**	**66**	**19:10**	....	....	....	....	....	....	....	....
	Cincinnati Ducks	AHL	2	0	0	0	0	....	....	....	....	....	....	....	....	....	....	....	....	....	....	....	....	....	....	....
	NHL Totals		**50**	**2**	**7**	**9**	**20**	**0**	**0**	**2**	**70**	**2.9**		**1**	**0.0**	**103**	**66**	**19:10**								

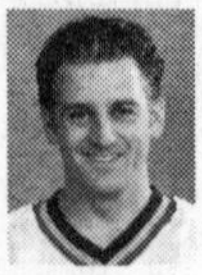

HAWGOOD, Greg
(HAW-guhd, GREHG) **VAN.**

Defense. Shoots left. 5'10", 190 lbs. Born, Edmonton, Alta., August 10, 1968. Boston's 9th choice, 202nd overall, in 1986 Entry Draft.

			Regular Season																Playoffs							
Season	Club	League	GP	G	A	Pts	PIM	PP	SH	GW	S	%	+/-	TF	F%	H	SB	Min	GP	G	A	Pts	PIM	PP	SH	GW
1983-84	Kamloops Blazers	WHL	49	10	23	33	39	....	....	....	....	....	....	....	....	....	....	....	6	0	2	2	2	....	....	....
1984-85	Kamloops Blazers	WHL	66	25	40	65	72	....	....	....	....	....	....	....	....	....	....	....	15	3	15	18	15	....	....	....
1985-86	Kamloops Blazers	WHL	71	34	85	119	86	....	....	....	....	....	....	....	....	....	....	....	16	9	22	31	16	....	....	....
1986-87	Kamloops Blazers	WHL	61	30	93	123	139	....	....	....	....	....	....	....	....	....	....	....	13	7	16	23	18	....	....	....
1987-88	Kamloops Blazers	WHL	63	48	85	133	142	....	....	....	....	....	....	....	....	....	....	....	16	10	16	26	33	....	....	....
	Boston	**NHL**	**1**	**0**	**0**	**0**	**0**	**0**	**0**	**0**	**1**	**0.0**	**-1**	....	....	....	....	....	**3**	**1**	**0**	**1**	**0**	**0**	**0**	**0**
1988-89	**Boston**	**NHL**	**56**	**16**	**24**	**40**	**84**	**5**	**0**	**0**	**132**	**12.1**	**4**	....	....	....	....	....	**10**	**0**	**2**	**2**	**2**	**0**	**0**	**0**
	Maine Mariners	AHL	21	2	9	11	41	....	....	....	....	....	....	....	....	....	....	....	....	....	....	....	....	....	....	....
1989-90	**Boston**	**NHL**	**77**	**11**	**27**	**38**	**76**	**2**	**0**	**1**	**127**	**8.7**	**12**	....	....	....	....	....	**15**	**1**	**3**	**4**	**12**	**1**	**0**	**0**
1990-91	HC Asiago	Italy	2	3	0	3	9	....	....	....	....	....	....	....	....	....	....	....	....	....	....	....	....	....	....	....
	Maine Mariners	AHL	5	0	1	1	13	....	....	....	....	....	....	....	....	....	....	....	....	....	....	....	....	....	....	....
	Edmonton	**NHL**	**6**	**0**	**1**	**1**	**6**	**0**	**0**	**0**	**9**	**0.0**	**-2**	....	....	....	....	....	....	....	....	....	....	....	....	....
	Cape Breton	AHL	55	10	32	42	73	....	....	....	....	....	....	....	....	....	....	....	4	0	3	3	23	....	....	....

			Regular Season																Playoffs							
Season	Club	League	GP	G	A	Pts	PIM	PP	SH	GW	S	%	+/-	TF	F%	H	SB	Min	GP	G	A	Pts	PIM	PP	SH	GW
1991-92	Edmonton	NHL	20	2	11	13	22	0	0	0	24	8.3	19						13	0	3	3	23	0	0	0
	Cape Breton	AHL	56	20	55	75	26												3	2	2	4	0			
1992-93	Edmonton	NHL	29	5	13	18	35	2	0	0	47	10.6	-1													
	Philadelphia	NHL	40	6	22	28	39	5	0	1	91	6.6	-7													
1993-94	Philadelphia	NHL	19	3	12	15	19	3	0	0	37	8.1	2													
	Florida	NHL	33	2	14	16	9	0	0	1	55	3.6	8													
	Pittsburgh	NHL	12	1	2	3	8	1	0	1	20	5.0	-1						1	0	0	0	0	0	0	0
1994-95	Pittsburgh	NHL	21	1	4	5	25	1	0	0	17	5.9	2													
	Cleveland	IHL																	3	1	0	1	4			
1995-96	Las Vegas	IHL	78	20	65	85	101												15	5	11	16	24			
1996-97	San Jose	NHL	63	6	12	18	69	3	0	0	83	7.2	-22													
1997-98	Kolner Haie	DEL	4	0	1	1	16																			
	Kolner Haie	EuroHL	1	0	0	0	2																			
	Houston Aeros	IHL	81	19	52	71	75												4	0	4	4	0			
1998-99	Houston Aeros	IHL	76	17	57	74	90												19	4	8	12	24			
99-2000	Vancouver	NHL	79	5	17	22	26	2	0	0	70	7.1	5	2	50.0	64	57	17:11								
	NHL Totals		456	58	159	217	418	24	0	4	713	8.1		2	50.0	64	57	17:11	42	2	8	10	37	1	0	0

WHL West First All-Star Team (1986, 1987, 1988) • Canadian Major Junior Defenseman of the Year (1988) • AHL First All-Star Team (1992) • Won Eddie Shore Award (Top Defenseman - AHL) (1992) • IHL First All-Star Team (1996, 1998, 1999) • Won Governors' Trophy (Top Defenseman - IHL) (1996, 1999)

Traded to **Edmonton** by **Boston** for Vladimir Ruzicka, October 22, 1990. Traded to **Philadelphia** by **Edmonton** with Josef Beranek for Brian Benning, January 16, 1993. Traded to **Florida** by **Philadelphia** for cash, November 30, 1993. Traded to **Pittsburgh** by **Florida** for Jeff Daniels, March 19, 1994. Signed as a free agent by **San Jose**, September 25, 1996. Signed as a free agent by **Vancouver**, September 30, 1999.

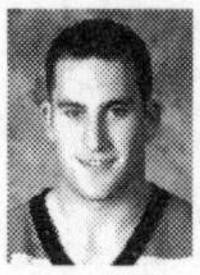

HAY, Dwayne

(HAY, DWAY-neh) **T.B.**

Left wing. Shoots left. 6', 219 lbs. Born, London, Ont., February 11, 1977. Washington's 3rd choice, 43rd overall, in 1995 Entry Draft.

Season	Club	League	GP	G	A	Pts	PIM	PP	SH	GW	S	%	+/-	TF	F%	H	SB	Min	GP	G	A	Pts	PIM	PP	SH	GW
1991-92	London Travellers	OMHA	86	70	56	126	104																			
1992-93	Listowel Cyclones	OJHL-B	50	19	33	52	40																			
1993-94	Listowel Cyclones	OJHL	48	10	24	34	56																			
1994-95	Guelph Storm	OHL	65	26	28	54	37												14	5	7	12	6			
1995-96	Guelph Storm	OHL	60	28	30	58	49												16	4	9	13	18			
1996-97	Guelph Storm	OHL	32	17	17	34	21												11	4	6	10	0			
1997-98	Washington	NHL	2	0	0	0	2	0	0	0	1	0.0	0													
	Portland	AHL	58	6	7	13	35																			
	New Haven	AHL	10	3	2	5	4												2	0	0	0	0			
1998-99	Florida	NHL	9	0	0	0	0	0	0	0	3	0.0	-1	1	0.0	5	0	6:35								
	New Haven	AHL	46	18	17	35	22																			
99-2000	Florida	NHL	6	0	0	0	2	0	0	0	3	0.0	-2	0	0.0	3	1	6:36								
	Louisville	AHL	41	11	20	31	18																			
	Tampa Bay	NHL	13	1	1	2	2	0	0	0	11	9.1	0	1	0.0	15	1	6:04								
	NHL Totals		30	1	1	2	6	0	0	0	18	5.6		2	0.0	23	2	6:21								

Traded to **Florida** by **Washington** with future considerations for Esa Tikkanen, March 9, 1998. Traded to **Tampa Bay** by **Florida** with Ryan Johnson for Mike Sillinger, March 14, 2000.

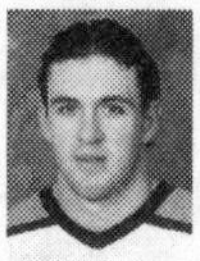

HEALEY, Paul

(HEE-lee, PAWL) **EDM.**

Right wing. Shoots right. 6'2", 185 lbs. Born, Edmonton, Alta., March 20, 1975. Philadelphia's 7th choice, 192nd overall, in 1993 Entry Draft.

Season	Club	League	GP	G	A	Pts	PIM	PP	SH	GW	S	%	+/-	TF	F%	H	SB	Min	GP	G	A	Pts	PIM	PP	SH	GW
1991-92	Ft-Saskatchewan	AJHL	52	11	19	30	40																			
1992-93	Prince Albert	WHL	72	12	20	32	66																			
1993-94	Prince Albert	WHL	63	23	26	49	70																			
1994-95	Prince Albert	WHL	71	43	50	93	67												12	3	4	7	2			
1995-96	Hershey Bears	AHL	60	7	15	22	35																			
1996-97	Philadelphia	NHL	2	0	0	0	0	0	0	0	0	0.0	0													
	Philadelphia	AHL	64	21	19	40	56												10	4	1	5	10			
1997-98	Philadelphia	NHL	4	0	0	0	12	0	0	0	0	0.0	0													
	Philadelphia	AHL	71	34	18	52	48												20	6	2	8	4			
1998-99	Philadelphia	AHL	72	26	20	46	39												15	4	6	10	11			
99-2000	Milwaukee	IHL	76	21	18	39	28												3	1	2	3	0			
	NHL Totals		6	0	0	0	12	0	0	0	0	0.0														

WHL East Second All-Star Team (1995)

Traded to **Nashville** by **Philadelphia** for Matt Henderson, September 27, 1999. Signed as a free agent by **Edmonton**, August 31, 2000.

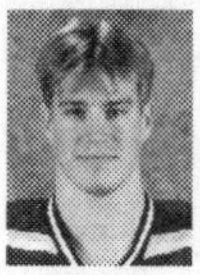

HECHT, Jochen

(HEHKHT, yoh-HEHN) **ST.L.**

Center. Shoots left. 6'3", 196 lbs. Born, Mannheim, West Germany, June 21, 1977. St. Louis' 1st choice, 49th overall, in 1995 Entry Draft.

Season	Club	League	GP	G	A	Pts	PIM	PP	SH	GW	S	%	+/-	TF	F%	H	SB	Min	GP	G	A	Pts	PIM	PP	SH	GW
1994-95	Adler Mannheim	DEL	43	11	12	23	68												10	5	4	9	12			
1995-96	Adler Mannheim	DEL	44	12	16	28	68												8	3	2	5	6			
1996-97	Adler Mannheim	DEL	46	21	21	42	36												9	3	3	6	4			
1997-98	Adler Mannheim	DEL	44	7	19	26	42												10	1	1	2	14			
	Adler Mannheim	EuroHL	5	0	4	4	8																			
	Germany	Olympics	4	1	0	1	6																			
1998-99	St. Louis	NHL	3	0	0	0	0	0	0	0	4	0.0	-2	19	21.1	1	0	13:16	5	2	0	2	0	0	0	0
	Worcester	AHL	74	21	35	56	48												4	1	1	2	2			
99-2000	St. Louis	NHL	63	13	21	34	28	5	0	1	140	9.3	20	75	49.3	36	6	15:25	7	4	6	10	2	1	0	1
	NHL Totals		66	13	21	34	28	5	0	1	144	9.0		94	43.6	37	6	15:19	12	6	6	12	2	1	0	1

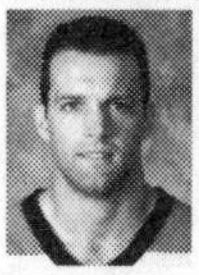

HEDICAN, Bret

(HEH-dih-kan, BREHT) **FLA.**

Defense. Shoots left. 6'2", 205 lbs. Born, St. Paul, MN, August 10, 1970. St. Louis' 10th choice, 198th overall, in 1988 Entry Draft.

Season	Club	League	GP	G	A	Pts	PIM	PP	SH	GW	S	%	+/-	TF	F%	H	SB	Min	GP	G	A	Pts	PIM	PP	SH	GW
1987-88	North St. Paul	Hi-School	23	15	19	34	16																			
1988-89	St. Cloud State	NCAA	28	5	3	8	28																			
1989-90	St. Cloud State	NCAA	36	4	17	21	37																			
1990-91	St. Cloud State	WCHA	41	21	26	47	26																			
1991-92	United States	Nat-Team	54	1	8	9	59																			
	United States	Olympics	8	0	0	0	4																			
	St. Louis	NHL	4	1	0	1	0	0	0	0	1	100.0	1						5	0	0	0	0	0	0	0
1992-93	St. Louis	NHL	42	0	8	8	30	0	0	0	40	0.0	-2						10	0	0	0	14	0	0	0
	Peoria Rivermen	IHL	19	0	8	8	10																			
1993-94	St. Louis	NHL	61	0	11	11	64	0	0	0	78	0.0	-8													
	Vancouver	NHL	8	0	1	1	0	0	0	0	10	0.0	1						24	1	6	7	16	0	0	0
1994-95	Vancouver	NHL	45	2	11	13	34	0	0	0	56	3.6	-3						11	0	2	2	6	0	0	0
1995-96	Vancouver	NHL	77	6	23	29	83	1	0	0	113	5.3	8						6	0	1	1	10	0	0	0
1996-97	Vancouver	NHL	67	4	15	19	51	2	0	1	93	4.3	-3													
1997-98	Vancouver	NHL	71	3	24	27	79	1	0	0	84	3.6	3													
1998-99	Vancouver	NHL	42	2	11	13	34	0	2	0	52	3.8	7	0	0.0	60	32	18:40								
	Florida	NHL	25	3	7	10	17	0	0	1	38	7.9	-2	0	0.0	46	42	22:24								
99-2000	Florida	NHL	76	6	19	25	68	2	0	1	58	10.3	4	0	0.0	128	89	19:36	4	0	0	0	0	0	0	0
	NHL Totals		518	27	130	157	460	6	2	3	623	4.3		0	0.0	234	163	19:49	60	1	9	10	46	0	0	0

WCHA First All-Star Team (1991)

Traded to **Vancouver** by **St. Louis** with Jeff Brown and Nathan Lafayette for Craig Janney, March 21, 1994. Traded to **Florida** by **Vancouver** with Pavel Bure, Brad Ference and Vancouver's 3rd round choice (Robert Fried) in 2000 Entry Draft for Ed Jovanovski, Dave Gagner, Mike Brown, Kevin Weekes and Florida's 1st round choice (Nathan Smith) in 2000 Entry Draft, January 17, 1999.

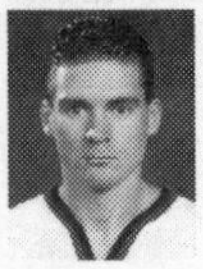

HEINS, Shawn

(HIGHNS, SHAWN) **S.J.**

Defense. Shoots left. 6'4", 210 lbs. Born, Eganville, Ont., December 24, 1973.

Season	Club	League	GP	G	A	Pts	PIM	PP	SH	GW	S	%	+/-	TF	F%	H	SB	Min	GP	G	A	Pts	PIM	PP	SH	GW
			Regular Season																Playoffs							
1991-92	Peterborough	OHL	49	1	1	2	73	....	....	....	....	....	....	....	....	....	....	....	....	....	....	....	....	....	....	....
1992-93	Peterborough	OHL	5	0	0	0	10	....	....	....	....	....	....	....	....	....	....	....	....	....	....	....	....	....	....	....
	Windsor Spitfires	OHL	53	7	10	17	107	....	....	....	....	....	....	....	....	....	....	....	....	....	....	....	....	....	....	....
1993-94	Renfrew T-Wolves	OJHL-B	32	16	34	50	250	....	....	....	....	....	....	....	....	....	....	....	....	....	....	....	....	....	....	....
1994-95	Renfrew T-Wolves	OJHL-B	35	30	49	79	188	....	....	....	....	....	....	....	....	....	....	....	....	....	....	....	....	....	....	....
1995-96	Mobile Mysticks	ECHL	62	7	20	27	152	....	....	....	....	....	....	....	....	....	....	....	....	....	....	....	....	....	....	....
	Cape Breton	AHL	1	0	0	0	0	....	....	....	....	....	....	....	....	....	....	....	....	....	....	....	....	....	....	....
1996-97	Mobile Mysticks	ECHL	56	6	17	23	253	....	....	....	....	....	....	....	....	....	....	....	3	0	2	2	2	....	....	....
	Kansas City	IHL	6	0	0	0	9	....	....	....	....	....	....	....	....	....	....	....	....	....	....	....	....	....	....	....
1997-98	Kansas City	IHL	82	22	28	50	303	....	....	....	....	....	....	....	....	....	....	....	11	1	0	1	49	....	....	....
1998-99	Canada	Nat-Team	36	5	16	21	66	....	....	....	....	....	....	....	....	....	....	....	....	....	....	....	....	....	....	....
	San Jose	**NHL**	**5**	**0**	**0**	**0**	**13**	**0**	**0**	**0**	**4**	**0.0**	**0**	**0**	**0.0**	**4**	**1**	**13:38**	....	....	....	....	....	....	....	....
	Kentucky	AHL	18	2	2	4	108	....	....	....	....	....	....	....	....	....	....	....	12	2	7	9	10	....	....	....
99-2000	**San Jose**	**NHL**	**1**	**0**	**0**	**0**	**2**	**0**	**0**	**0**	**1**	**0.0**	**–1**	**0**	**0.0**	**1**	**2**	**10:57**	....	....	....	....	....	....	....	....
	Kentucky	AHL	69	11	52	63	238	....	....	....	....	....	....	....	....	....	....	....	9	3	3	6	44	....	....	....
	NHL Totals		**6**	**0**	**0**	**0**	**15**	**0**	**0**	**0**	**5**	**0.0**		**0**	**0.0**	**5**	**3**	**13:11**	....	....	....	....	....	....	....	....

AHL First All-Star Team (2000)

Signed as a free agent by **San Jose**, January 5, 1997.

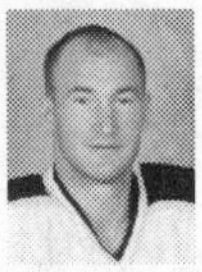

HEINZE, Steve

(HIGHNS, STEEV) **CBJ**

Right wing. Shoots right. 5'11", 202 lbs. Born, Lawrence, MA, January 30, 1970. Boston's 2nd choice, 60th overall, in 1988 Entry Draft.

Season	Club	League	GP	G	A	Pts	PIM	PP	SH	GW	S	%	+/-	TF	F%	H	SB	Min	GP	G	A	Pts	PIM	PP	SH	GW
1986-87	Lawrence Prep	Hi-School	23	26	24	50	....	....	....	....	....	....	....	....	....	....	....	....	....	....	....	....	....	....	....	....
1987-88	Lawrence Prep	Hi-School	23	30	25	55	....	....	....	....	....	....	....	....	....	....	....	....	....	....	....	....	....	....	....	....
1988-89	Boston College	H-East	36	26	23	49	26	....	....	....	....	....	....	....	....	....	....	....	....	....	....	....	....	....	....	....
1989-90	Boston College	H-East	40	27	36	63	41	....	....	....	....	....	....	....	....	....	....	....	....	....	....	....	....	....	....	....
1990-91	Boston College	H-East	35	21	26	47	35	....	....	....	....	....	....	....	....	....	....	....	....	....	....	....	....	....	....	....
1991-92	United States	Nat-Team	49	18	15	33	38	....	....	....	....	....	....	....	....	....	....	....	....	....	....	....	....	....	....	....
	United States	Olympics	8	1	3	4	8	....	....	....	....	....	....	....	....	....	....	....	....	....	....	....	....	....	....	....
	Boston	**NHL**	**14**	**3**	**4**	**7**	**6**	**0**	**0**	**2**	**29**	**10.3**	**–1**	....	....	....	....	....	**7**	**0**	**3**	**3**	**17**	**0**	**0**	**0**
1992-93	**Boston**	**NHL**	**73**	**18**	**13**	**31**	**24**	**0**	**2**	**4**	**146**	**12.3**	**20**	....	....	....	....	....	**4**	**1**	**1**	**2**	**2**	**0**	**0**	**0**
1993-94	**Boston**	**NHL**	**77**	**10**	**11**	**21**	**32**	**0**	**2**	**1**	**183**	**5.5**	**–2**	....	....	....	....	....	**13**	**2**	**3**	**5**	**7**	**0**	**0**	**0**
1994-95	**Boston**	**NHL**	**36**	**7**	**9**	**16**	**23**	**0**	**1**	**0**	**70**	**10.0**	**0**	....	....	....	....	....	**5**	**0**	**0**	**0**	**0**	**0**	**0**	**0**
1995-96	**Boston**	**NHL**	**76**	**16**	**12**	**28**	**43**	**0**	**1**	**3**	**129**	**12.4**	**–3**	....	....	....	....	....	**5**	**1**	**1**	**2**	**4**	**0**	**1**	**0**
1996-97	**Boston**	**NHL**	**30**	**17**	**8**	**25**	**27**	**4**	**2**	**2**	**96**	**17.7**	**–8**	....	....	....	....	....	....	....	....	....	....	....	....	....
1997-98	**Boston**	**NHL**	**61**	**26**	**20**	**46**	**54**	**9**	**0**	**6**	**160**	**16.3**	**8**	....	....	....	....	....	**6**	**0**	**0**	**0**	**6**	**0**	**0**	**0**
1998-99	**Boston**	**NHL**	**73**	**22**	**18**	**40**	**30**	**9**	**0**	**3**	**146**	**15.1**	**7**	**2**	**0.0**	**91**	**13**	**15:48**	**12**	**4**	**3**	**7**	**0**	**2**	**0**	**0**
99-2000	**Boston**	**NHL**	**75**	**12**	**13**	**25**	**36**	**2**	**0**	**2**	**145**	**8.3**	**–8**	**8**	**12.5**	**129**	**10**	**14:57**	....	....	....	....	....	....	....	....
	NHL Totals		**515**	**131**	**108**	**239**	**275**	**24**	**8**	**23**	**1104**	**11.9**		**10**	**10.0**	**220**	**23**	**15:22**	**52**	**8**	**11**	**19**	**36**	**2**	**1**	**0**

Hockey East First All-Star Team (1990) • NCAA East First All-American Team (1990)

Selected by **Columbus** from **Boston** in Expansion Draft, June 23, 2000.

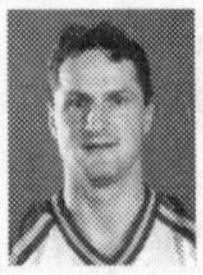

HEJDUK, Milan

(HAY-dook, MEE-lan) **COL.**

Right wing. Shoots right. 5'11", 185 lbs. Born, Usti-nad-Labem, Czech., February 14, 1976. Quebec's 6th choice, 87th overall, in 1994 Entry Draft.

Season	Club	League	GP	G	A	Pts	PIM	PP	SH	GW	S	%	+/-	TF	F%	H	SB	Min	GP	G	A	Pts	PIM	PP	SH	GW
1993-94	HC Pardubice	Cze-Rep	22	6	3	9	....	....	....	....	....	....	....	....	....	....	....	....	10	5	1	6	....	....	....	....
1994-95	HC Pardubice	Cze-Rep	43	11	13	24	6	....	....	....	....	....	....	....	....	....	....	....	6	3	1	4	0	....	....	....
1995-96	HC Pardubice	Cze-Rep	37	13	7	20	....	....	....	....	....	....	....	....	....	....	....	....	....	....	....	....	....	....	....	....
1996-97	HC Pardubice	Cze-Rep	51	27	11	38	10	....	....	....	....	....	....	....	....	....	....	....	10	6	0	6	27	....	....	....
1997-98	HC Pardubice	Cze-Rep	48	26	19	45	20	....	....	....	....	....	....	....	....	....	....	....	3	0	0	0	2	....	....	....
	Czech-Republic	Olympics	4	0	0	0	2	....	....	....	....	....	....	....	....	....	....	....	....	....	....	....	....	....	....	....
1998-99	**Colorado**	**NHL**	**82**	**14**	**34**	**48**	**26**	**4**	**0**	**5**	**178**	**7.9**	**8**	**2**	**50.0**	**50**	**30**	**15:45**	**16**	**6**	**6**	**12**	**4**	**1**	**0**	**3**
99-2000	**Colorado**	**NHL**	**82**	**36**	**36**	**72**	**16**	**13**	**0**	**9**	**228**	**15.8**	**14**	**3**	**100.0**	**46**	**40**	**19:58**	**17**	**5**	**4**	**9**	**6**	**3**	**0**	**1**
	NHL Totals		**164**	**50**	**70**	**120**	**42**	**17**	**0**	**14**	**406**	**12.3**		**5**	**80.0**	**96**	**70**	**17:52**	**33**	**11**	**10**	**21**	**10**	**4**	**0**	**4**

NHL All-Rookie Team (1999) • Played in NHL All-Star Game (2000)

Rights transferred to **Colorado** after **Quebec** franchise relocated, June 21, 1995.

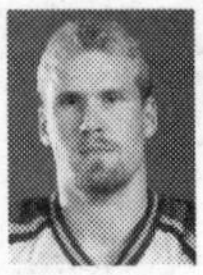

HELENIUS, Sami

(huh-LEHN-ee-uhs, SA-mee) **DAL.**

Defense. Shoots left. 6'5", 225 lbs. Born, Helsinki, Finland, January 22, 1974. Calgary's 5th choice, 102nd overall, in 1992 Entry Draft.

Season	Club	League	GP	G	A	Pts	PIM	PP	SH	GW	S	%	+/-	TF	F%	H	SB	Min	GP	G	A	Pts	PIM	PP	SH	GW
1990-91	Jokerit Helsinki	Finn-Jr.	2	0	0	0	6	....	....	....	....	....	....	....	....	....	....	....	....	....	....	....	....	....	....	....
1991-92	Jokerit Helsinki	Finn-Jr.	14	3	3	6	24	....	....	....	....	....	....	....	....	....	....	....	....	....	....	....	....	....	....	....
	Jokerit Helsinki	Finland-2	13	4	4	8	24	....	....	....	....	....	....	....	....	....	....	....	....	....	....	....	....	....	....	....
1992-93	Jokerit Helsinki	Finn-Jr.	13	2	3	5	18	....	....	....	....	....	....	....	....	....	....	....	....	....	....	....	....	....	....	....
	Vantaa HT	Finland-2	21	3	2	5	50	....	....	....	....	....	....	....	....	....	....	....	....	....	....	....	....	....	....	....
	Jokerit Helsinki	Finland	1	0	0	0	0	....	....	....	....	....	....	....	....	....	....	....	....	....	....	....	....	....	....	....
1993-94	Reipas Lahti	Finn-Jr.	11	3	4	7	48	....	....	....	....	....	....	....	....	....	....	....	....	....	....	....	....	....	....	....
	Reipas Lahti	Finland	37	2	3	5	46	....	....	....	....	....	....	....	....	....	....	....	....	....	....	....	....	....	....	....
1994-95	Saint John Flames	AHL	69	2	5	7	217	....	....	....	....	....	....	....	....	....	....	....	....	....	....	....	....	....	....	....
1995-96	Saint John Flames	AHL	68	0	3	3	231	....	....	....	....	....	....	....	....	....	....	....	10	0	0	0	9	....	....	....
1996-97	**Calgary**	**NHL**	**3**	**0**	**1**	**1**	**0**	**0**	**0**	**0**	**1**	**0.0**	**1**	....	....	....	....	....	....	....	....	....	....	....	....	....
	Saint John Flames	AHL	72	5	10	15	218	....	....	....	....	....	....	....	....	....	....	....	2	0	0	0	0	....	....	....
1997-98	Saint John Flames	AHL	63	1	2	3	185	....	....	....	....	....	....	....	....	....	....	....	....	....	....	....	....	....	....	....
	Las Vegas	IHL	10	0	1	1	19	....	....	....	....	....	....	....	....	....	....	....	4	0	0	0	25	....	....	....
1998-99	**Calgary**	**NHL**	**4**	**0**	**0**	**0**	**8**	**0**	**0**	**0**	**1**	**0.0**	**–2**	**0**	**0.0**	**6**	**6**	**10:16**	....	....	....	....	....	....	....	....
	Las Vegas	IHL	42	2	3	5	193	....	....	....	....	....	....	....	....	....	....	....	....	....	....	....	....	....	....	....
	Tampa Bay	**NHL**	**4**	**1**	**0**	**1**	**15**	**0**	**1**	**0**	**3**	**33.3**	**–3**	**0**	**0.0**	**6**	**3**	**16:53**	....	....	....	....	....	....	....	....
	Chicago Wolves	IHL	4	0	0	0	11	....	....	....	....	....	....	....	....	....	....	....	....	....	....	....	....	....	....	....
	Hershey Bears	AHL	8	0	0	0	29	....	....	....	....	....	....	....	....	....	....	....	5	0	0	0	16	....	....	....
99-2000	**Colorado**	**NHL**	**33**	**0**	**0**	**0**	**46**	**0**	**0**	**0**	**6**	**0.0**	**–5**	**0**	**0.0**	**34**	**19**	**7:04**	....	....	....	....	....	....	....	....
	Hershey Bears	AHL	12	0	1	1	31	....	....	....	....	....	....	....	....	....	....	....	9	0	0	0	40	....	....	....
	NHL Totals		**44**	**1**	**1**	**2**	**69**	**0**	**1**	**0**	**11**	**9.1**		**0**	**0.0**	**46**	**28**	**8:20**	....	....	....	....	....	....	....	....

Traded to **Tampa Bay** by **Calgary** for future considerations, January 29, 1999. Traded to **Colorado** by **Tampa Bay** for future considerations, March 23, 1999. Signed as a free agent by **Dallas**, July 12, 2000.

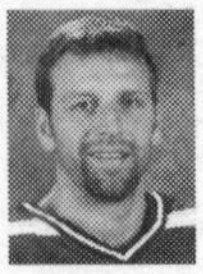

HELMER, Bryan

(HEHL-muhr, BRIGH-an) **VAN.**

Defense. Shoots right. 6'1", 200 lbs. Born, Sault Ste. Marie, Ont., July 15, 1972.

Season	Club	League	GP	G	A	Pts	PIM	PP	SH	GW	S	%	+/-	TF	F%	H	SB	Min	GP	G	A	Pts	PIM	PP	SH	GW
1989-90	Wellington Dukes	OJHL-B	44	4	20	24	204	....	....	....	....	....	....	....	....	....	....	....	....	....	....	....	....	....	....	....
	Belleville Bulls	OHL	6	0	1	1	0	....	....	....	....	....	....	....	....	....	....	....	....	....	....	....	....	....	....	....
1990-91	Wellington Dukes	OJHL	50	11	14	25	109	....	....	....	....	....	....	....	....	....	....	....	....	....	....	....	....	....	....	....
1991-92	Wellington Dukes	OJHL	42	17	31	48	66	....	....	....	....	....	....	....	....	....	....	....	3	2	1	3	0	....	....	....
1992-93	Wellington Dukes	OJHL	48	21	54	75	84	....	....	....	....	....	....	....	....	....	....	....	9	4	8	12	22	....	....	....
1993-94	Albany River Rats	AHL	65	4	19	23	79	....	....	....	....	....	....	....	....	....	....	....	5	0	0	0	9	....	....	....
1994-95	Albany River Rats	AHL	77	7	36	43	101	....	....	....	....	....	....	....	....	....	....	....	7	1	0	1	0	....	....	....
1995-96	Albany River Rats	AHL	80	14	30	44	107	....	....	....	....	....	....	....	....	....	....	....	4	2	0	2	6	....	....	....
1996-97	Albany River Rats	AHL	77	12	27	39	113	....	....	....	....	....	....	....	....	....	....	....	16	1	7	8	10	....	....	....
1997-98	Albany River Rats	AHL	80	14	49	63	101	....	....	....	....	....	....	....	....	....	....	....	13	4	9	13	18	....	....	....
1998-99	**Phoenix**	**NHL**	**11**	**0**	**0**	**0**	**23**	**0**	**0**	**0**	**11**	**0.0**	**2**	**0**	**0.0**	**1**	**2**	**7:43**	....	....	....	....	....	....	....	....
	Las Vegas	IHL	8	1	3	4	28	....	....	....	....	....	....	....	....	....	....	....	....	....	....	....	....	....	....	....
	St. Louis	**NHL**	**29**	**0**	**4**	**4**	**19**	**0**	**0**	**0**	**38**	**0.0**	**3**	**1**	**100.0**	**34**	**28**	**19:08**	....	....	....	....	....	....	....	....
	Worcester	AHL	16	7	8	15	18	....	....	....	....	....	....	....	....	....	....	....	4	0	0	0	12	....	....	....

			Regular Season																Playoffs							
Season	Club	League	GP	G	A	Pts	PIM	PP	SH	GW	S	%	+/-	TF	F%	H	SB	Min	GP	G	A	Pts	PIM	PP	SH	GW
99-2000	**St. Louis**	**NHL**	**15**	**1**	**1**	**2**	**10**	**1**	**0**	**1**	**19**	**5.3**	**–3**	**0**	**0.0**	**16**	**8**	**16:15**	....	....	....	....	....	....	....	....
	Worcester	AHL	54	10	25	35	124	....	....	....	....	....	....	....	....	....	....	....	9	1	4	5	10	....	....	....
	NHL Totals		**55**	**1**	**5**	**6**	**52**	**1**	**0**	**1**	**68**	**1.5**		**1**	**100.0**	**51**	**38**	**16:04**	....	....	....	....	....	....	....	....

AHL First All-Star Team (1998)

Signed as a free agent by **New Jersey**, July 10, 1994. Signed as a free agent by **Phoenix**, July 17, 1998. Claimed on waivers by **St. Louis** from **Phoenix**, December 19, 1998. Signed as a free agent by **Vancouver**, August, 2000.

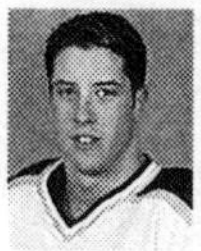

HENDERSON, Jay

(HEHN-duhr-SOHN, JAY) **BOS.**

Left wing. Shoots left. 5'11", 190 lbs. Born, Edmonton, Alta., September 17, 1978. Boston's 12th choice, 246th overall, in 1997 Entry Draft.

1993-94	Sherwood Park	AAHA	31	12	21	33	36	....	....	....	....	....	....	....	....	....	....	....	....	....	....	....	....	....	....	....
1994-95	Red Deer Rebels	WHL	54	3	9	12	80	....	....	....	....	....	....	....	....	....	....	....	....	....	....	....	....	....	....	....
1995-96	Red Deer Rebels	WHL	71	15	13	28	139	....	....	....	....	....	....	....	....	....	....	....	10	1	1	2	11	....	....	....
1996-97	Edmonton Ice	WHL	66	28	32	60	127	....	....	....	....	....	....	....	....	....	....	....	....	....	....	....	....	....	....	....
1997-98	Edmonton Ice	WHL	72	49	45	94	130	....	....	....	....	....	....	....	....	....	....	....	....	....	....	....	....	....	....	....
1998-99	**Boston**	**NHL**	**4**	**0**	**0**	**0**	**2**	**0**	**0**	**0**	**4**	**0.0**	**–1**	**0**	**0.0**	**1**	**1**	**5:39**	....	....	....	....	....	....	....	....
	Providence Bruins	AHL	55	7	9	16	172	....	....	....	....	....	....	....	....	....	....	....	2	0	0	0	2	....	....	....
99-2000	**Boston**	**NHL**	**16**	**1**	**3**	**4**	**9**	**0**	**0**	**0**	**18**	**5.6**	**1**	**2**	**0.0**	**16**	**2**	**5:22**	....	....	....	....	....	....	....	....
	Providence Bruins	AHL	60	18	27	45	200	....	....	....	....	....	....	....	....	....	....	....	14	1	2	3	16	....	....	....
	NHL Totals		**20**	**1**	**3**	**4**	**11**	**0**	**0**	**0**	**22**	**4.5**		**2**	**0.0**	**17**	**3**	**5:26**	....	....	....	....	....	....	....	....

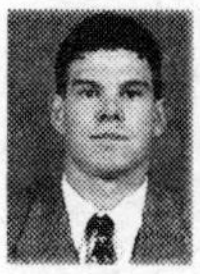

HENDERSON, Matt

(HEHN-duhr-SOHN, MAT) **PHI.**

Right wing. Shoots left. 6'1", 200 lbs. Born, White Bear Lake, MN, June 22, 1974.

1993-94	St. Paul Vulcans	USHL	48	27	24	51	....	....	....	....	....	....	....	....	....	....	....	....	....	....	....	....	....	....	....	....
1994-95	North Dakota	WCHA	19	1	3	4	16	....	....	....	....	....	....	....	....	....	....	....	....	....	....	....	....	....	....	....
1995-96	North Dakota	WCHA	36	9	10	19	34	....	....	....	....	....	....	....	....	....	....	....	2	0	1	1	0	....	....	....
1996-97	North Dakota	WCHA	42	14	17	31	71	....	....	....	....	....	....	....	....	....	....	....	7	5	4	9	10	....	....	....
1997-98	North Dakota	WCHA	38	24	14	38	74	....	....	....	....	....	....	....	....	....	....	....	5	2	2	4	4	....	....	....
1998-99	**Nashville**	**NHL**	**2**	**0**	**0**	**0**	**2**	**0**	**0**	**0**	**0**	**0.0**	**–1**	**0**	**0.0**	**4**	**0**	**6:23**	....	....	....	....	....	....	....	....
	Milwaukee	IHL	77	19	19	38	117	....	....	....	....	....	....	....	....	....	....	....	2	0	0	0	0	....	....	....
99-2000	Philadelphia	AHL	51	4	8	12	37	....	....	....	....	....	....	....	....	....	....	....	5	0	0	0	4	....	....	....
	Trenton Titans	ECHL	16	2	4	6	47	....	....	....	....	....	....	....	....	....	....	....	....	....	....	....	....	....	....	....
	NHL Totals		**2**	**0**	**0**	**0**	**2**	**0**	**0**	**0**	**0**	**0.0**		**0**	**0.0**	**4**	**0**	**6:23**	....	....	....	....	....	....	....	....

NCAA Championship All-Tournament Team (1997) • NCAA Championship Tournament MVP (1997)

Signed as a free agent by **Nashville**, July 14, 1998. Traded to **Philadelphia** by **Nashville** for Paul Healey, September 27, 1999.

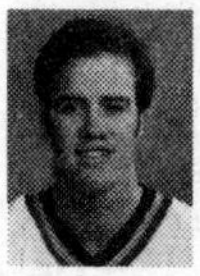

HENDRICKSON, Darby

(HEHN-drihk-SOHN, DAHR-bee) **MIN.**

Center. Shoots left. 6'1", 195 lbs. Born, Richfield, MN, August 28, 1972. Toronto's 3rd choice, 73rd overall, in 1990 Entry Draft.

1987-88	Richfield High	Hi-School	22	12	9	21	10	....	....	....	....	....	....	....	....	....	....	....	....	....	....	....	....	....	....	....
1988-89	Richfield High	Hi-School	22	22	20	42	12	....	....	....	....	....	....	....	....	....	....	....	....	....	....	....	....	....	....	....
1989-90	Richfield High	Hi-School	24	23	27	50	49	....	....	....	....	....	....	....	....	....	....	....	....	....	....	....	....	....	....	....
1990-91	Richfield High	Hi-School	27	32	29	61	....	....	....	....	....	....	....	....	....	....	....	....	....	....	....	....	....	....	....	....
1991-92	U. of Minnesota	WCHA	41	25	28	53	61	....	....	....	....	....	....	....	....	....	....	....	....	....	....	....	....	....	....	....
1992-93	U. of Minnesota	WCHA	31	12	15	27	35	....	....	....	....	....	....	....	....	....	....	....	....	....	....	....	....	....	....	....
1993-94	United States	Nat-Team	59	12	16	28	30	....	....	....	....	....	....	....	....	....	....	....	....	....	....	....	....	....	....	....
	United States	Olympics	8	0	0	0	6	....	....	....	....	....	....	....	....	....	....	....	....	....	....	....	....	....	....	....
	Toronto	**NHL**	....	....	....	....	....	....	....	....	....	....	....	....	....	....	....	....	**2**	**0**	**0**	**0**	**0**	**0**	**0**	**0**
	St. John's Leafs	AHL	6	4	1	5	4	....	....	....	....	....	....	....	....	....	....	....	3	1	1	2	0	....	....	....
1994-95	**Toronto**	**NHL**	**8**	**0**	**1**	**1**	**4**	**0**	**0**	**0**	**4**	**0.0**	**0**	....	....	....	....	....	....	....	....	....	....	....	....	....
	St. John's Leafs	AHL	59	16	20	36	48	....	....	....	....	....	....	....	....	....	....	....	....	....	....	....	....	....	....	....
1995-96	**Toronto**	**NHL**	**46**	**6**	**6**	**12**	**47**	**0**	**0**	**0**	**43**	**14.0**	**–2**	....	....	....	....	....	....	....	....	....	....	....	....	....
	NY Islanders	**NHL**	**16**	**1**	**4**	**5**	**33**	**0**	**0**	**1**	**30**	**3.3**	**–6**	....	....	....	....	....	....	....	....	....	....	....	....	....
1996-97	**Toronto**	**NHL**	**64**	**11**	**6**	**17**	**47**	**0**	**1**	**0**	**105**	**10.5**	**–20**	....	....	....	....	....	....	....	....	....	....	....	....	....
	St. John's Leafs	AHL	12	5	4	9	21	....	....	....	....	....	....	....	....	....	....	....	....	....	....	....	....	....	....	....
1997-98	**Toronto**	**NHL**	**80**	**8**	**4**	**12**	**67**	**0**	**0**	**0**	**115**	**7.0**	**–20**	....	....	....	....	....	....	....	....	....	....	....	....	....
1998-99	**Toronto**	**NHL**	**35**	**2**	**3**	**5**	**30**	**0**	**0**	**0**	**34**	**5.9**	**–4**	**278**	**46.0**	**35**	**8**	**10:16**	....	....	....	....	....	....	....	....
	Vancouver	**NHL**	**27**	**2**	**2**	**4**	**22**	**1**	**0**	**0**	**36**	**5.6**	**–15**	**427**	**46.8**	**24**	**23**	**17:15**	....	....	....	....	....	....	....	....
99-2000	**Vancouver**	**NHL**	**40**	**5**	**4**	**9**	**14**	**0**	**1**	**1**	**39**	**12.8**	**–3**	**407**	**46.2**	**26**	**27**	**11:32**	....	....	....	....	....	....	....	....
	Syracuse Crunch	AHL	20	5	8	13	16	....	....	....	....	....	....	....	....	....	....	....	....	....	....	....	....	....	....	....
	NHL Totals		**316**	**35**	**30**	**65**	**264**	**1**	**2**	**2**	**406**	**8.6**		**1112**	**46.4**	**85**	**58**	**12:37**	**2**	**0**	**0**	**0**	**0**	**0**	**0**	**0**

Traded to **NY Islanders** by **Toronto** with Sean Haggerty, Kenny Jonsson and Toronto's 1st round choice (Roberto Luongo) in 1997 Entry Draft for Wendel Clark, Mathieu Schneider and D.J. Smith, March 13, 1996. Traded to **Toronto** by **NY Islanders** for a conditional choice in 1998 Entry Draft, October 11, 1996. Traded to **Vancouver** by **Toronto** for Chris McAllister, February 16, 1999. Selected by **Minnesota** from **Vancouver** in Expansion Draft, June 23, 2000.

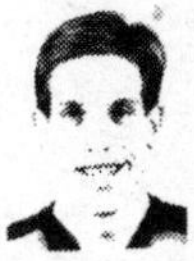

HERBERS, Ian

(HEHR-buhrs, EE-an) **MIN.**

Defense. Shoots left. 6'4", 225 lbs. Born, Jasper, Alta., July 18, 1967. Buffalo's 11th choice, 190th overall, in 1987 Entry Draft.

1984-85	Kelowna Wings	WHL	68	3	14	17	120	....	....	....	....	....	....	....	....	....	....	....	6	0	1	1	9	....	....	....
1985-86	Spokane Chiefs	WHL	29	1	6	7	85	....	....	....	....	....	....	....	....	....	....	....	....	....	....	....	....	....	....	....
	Lethbridge	WHL	32	1	4	5	109	....	....	....	....	....	....	....	....	....	....	....	10	1	0	1	37	....	....	....
1986-87	Swift Current	WHL	72	5	8	13	230	....	....	....	....	....	....	....	....	....	....	....	4	1	1	2	12	....	....	....
1987-88	Swift Current	WHL	56	5	14	19	238	....	....	....	....	....	....	....	....	....	....	....	4	0	2	2	4	....	....	....
1988-89	U. of Alberta	CWUAA	47	4	22	26	137	....	....	....	....	....	....	....	....	....	....	....	....	....	....	....	....	....	....	....
1989-90	U. of Alberta	CWUAA	45	5	31	36	83	....	....	....	....	....	....	....	....	....	....	....	....	....	....	....	....	....	....	....
1990-91	U. of Alberta	CWUAA	45	6	24	30	87	....	....	....	....	....	....	....	....	....	....	....	....	....	....	....	....	....	....	....
1991-92	U. of Alberta	CWUAA	43	14	34	48	86	....	....	....	....	....	....	....	....	....	....	....	....	....	....	....	....	....	....	....
1992-93	Cape Breton	AHL	77	7	15	22	129	....	....	....	....	....	....	....	....	....	....	....	10	0	1	1	16	....	....	....
1993-94	**Edmonton**	**NHL**	**22**	**0**	**2**	**2**	**32**	**0**	**0**	**0**	**16**	**0.0**	**–6**	....	....	....	....	....	....	....	....	....	....	....	....	....
	Cape Breton	AHL	53	7	16	23	122	....	....	....	....	....	....	....	....	....	....	....	5	0	3	3	12	....	....	....
1994-95	Cape Breton	AHL	36	1	11	12	104	....	....	....	....	....	....	....	....	....	....	....	....	....	....	....	....	....	....	....
	Detroit Vipers	IHL	37	1	5	6	46	....	....	....	....	....	....	....	....	....	....	....	5	1	1	2	6	....	....	....
1995-96	Detroit Vipers	IHL	73	3	11	14	140	....	....	....	....	....	....	....	....	....	....	....	12	3	5	8	29	....	....	....
1996-97	Detroit Vipers	IHL	67	3	16	19	129	....	....	....	....	....	....	....	....	....	....	....	21	0	4	4	34	....	....	....
1997-98	Detroit Vipers	IHL	70	6	6	12	100	....	....	....	....	....	....	....	....	....	....	....	23	0	3	3	54	....	....	....
1998-99	Detroit Vipers	IHL	82	8	16	24	142	....	....	....	....	....	....	....	....	....	....	....	11	1	3	4	18	....	....	....
99-2000	**Tampa Bay**	**NHL**	**37**	**0**	**0**	**0**	**45**	**0**	**0**	**0**	**11**	**0.0**	**–12**	**0**	**0.0**	**38**	**46**	**15:06**	....	....	....	....	....	....	....	....
	Detroit Vipers	IHL	13	1	4	5	22	....	....	....	....	....	....	....	....	....	....	....	....	....	....	....	....	....	....	....
	NY Islanders	**NHL**	**6**	**0**	**3**	**3**	**2**	**0**	**0**	**0**	**3**	**0.0**	**6**	**0**	**0.0**	**5**	**10**	**15:29**	....	....	....	....	....	....	....	....
	NHL Totals		**65**	**0**	**5**	**5**	**79**	**0**	**0**	**0**	**30**	**0.0**		**0**	**0.0**	**43**	**56**	**15:09**	....	....	....	....	....	....	....	....

CIAU All-Canadian Team (1991, 1992)

Signed as a free agent by **Edmonton**, September 9, 1992. Signed as a free agent by **Tampa Bay**, September, 1999. Traded to **NY Islanders** by **Tampa Bay** for NY Islanders' 7th round choice (later traded back to NY Islanders - NY Islanders selected Ryan Caldwell) in 2000 Entry Draft, March 9, 2000. Selected by **Minnesota** from **NY Islanders** in Expansion Draft, June 23, 2000.

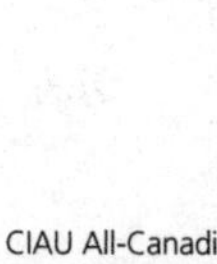

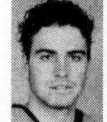

HERPERGER, Chris

(HUHR-puhr-GEHR, KRIHS) **CHI.**

Left wing. Shoots left. 6', 190 lbs. Born, Esterhazy, Sask., February 24, 1974. Philadelphia's 9th choice, 223rd overall, in 1992 Entry Draft.

1990-91	Swift Current	WHL	10	0	1	1	5	....	....	....	....	....	....	....	....	....	....	....	....	....	....	....	....	....	....	....
1991-92	Swift Current	WHL	72	14	19	33	44	....	....	....	....	....	....	....	....	....	....	....	8	0	1	1	9	....	....	....
1992-93	Swift Current	WHL	20	9	7	16	31	....	....	....	....	....	....	....	....	....	....	....	....	....	....	....	....	....	....	....
	Seattle T-Birds	WHL	46	20	11	31	30	....	....	....	....	....	....	....	....	....	....	....	5	1	1	2	6	....	....	....
1993-94	Seattle T-Birds	WHL	71	44	51	95	110	....	....	....	....	....	....	....	....	....	....	....	9	12	10	22	12	....	....	....

			Regular Season																Playoffs							
Season	Club	League	GP	G	A	Pts	PIM	PP	SH	GW	S	%	+/-	TF	F%	H	SB	Min	GP	G	A	Pts	PIM	PP	SH	GW
1994-95	Seattle T-Birds	WHL	59	49	52	101	106	....	....	....	....	....	....	....	....	....	....	....	4	4	0	4	6	....	....	....
	Hershey Bears	AHL	4	0	0	0	0	....	....	....	....	....	....	....	....	....	....	....	....	....	....	....	....	....	....	....
1995-96	Hershey Bears	AHL	46	8	12	20	36	....	....	....	....	....	....	....	....	....	....	....	....	....	....	....	....	....	....	....
	Baltimore Bandits	AHL	21	2	3	5	17	....	....	....	....	....	....	....	....	....	....	....	9	2	3	5	6	....	....	....
1996-97	Baltimore Bandits	AHL	67	19	22	41	88	....	....	....	....	....	....	....	....	....	....	....	3	0	0	0	0	....	....	....
1997-98	Canada	Nat-Team	63	20	30	50	102	....	....	....	....	....	....	....	....	....	....	....	....	....	....	....	....	....	....	....
1998-99	Indianapolis Ice	IHL	79	19	29	48	81	....	....	....	....	....	....	....	....	....	....	....	7	0	4	4	4	....	....	....
99-2000	**Chicago**	**NHL**	**9**	**0**	**0**	**0**	**5**	**0**	**0**	**0**	**2**	**0.0**	**-2**	**52**	**55.8**	**7**	**1**	**7:39**	....	....	....	....	....	....	....	....
	Cleveland	IHL	73	22	26	48	122	....	....	....	....	....	....	....	....	....	....	....	9	3	3	6	8	....	....	....
	NHL Totals		**9**	**0**	**0**	**0**	**5**	**0**	**0**	**0**	**2**	**0.0**		**52**	**55.8**	**7**	**1**	**7:39**	....	....	....	....	....	....	....	....

WHL West Second All-Star Team (1995)

Traded to **Anaheim** by **Philadelphia** with Winnipeg's 7th round choice (previously acquired, Anaheim selected Tony Mohagen) in 1997 Entry Draft for Bob Corkum, February 6, 1996. Signed as a free agent by **Chicago**, September 2, 1998.

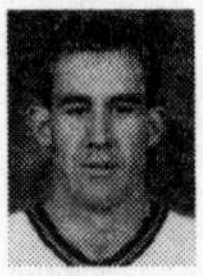

HERR, Matt

(HUHR, MAT) **WSH.**

Center. Shoots left. 6'2", 204 lbs. Born, Hackensack, NJ, May 26, 1976. Washington's 4th choice, 93rd overall, in 1994 Entry Draft.

Season	Club	League	GP	G	A	Pts	PIM	PP	SH	GW	S	%	+/-	TF	F%	H	SB	Min	GP	G	A	Pts	PIM	PP	SH	GW
1990-91	Hotchkiss Prep	Hi-School	26	9	5	14	....	....	....	....	....	....	....	....	....	....	....	....	....	....	....	....	....	....	....	....
1991-92	Hotchkiss Prep	Hi-School	25	17	16	33	....	....	....	....	....	....	....	....	....	....	....	....	....	....	....	....	....	....	....	....
1992-93	Hotchkiss Prep	Hi-School	24	48	30	78	....	....	....	....	....	....	....	....	....	....	....	....	....	....	....	....	....	....	....	....
1993-94	Hotchkiss Prep	Hi-School	24	28	19	47	....	....	....	....	....	....	....	....	....	....	....	....	....	....	....	....	....	....	....	....
1994-95	U. of Michigan	CCHA	37	11	8	19	51	....	....	....	....	....	....	....	....	....	....	....	3	1	0	1	4	....	....	....
1995-96	U. of Michigan	CCHA	40	18	13	31	55	....	....	....	....	....	....	....	....	....	....	....	7	0	4	4	0	....	....	....
1996-97	U. of Michigan	CCHA	43	29	23	52	67	....	....	....	....	....	....	....	....	....	....	....	6	2	2	4	8	....	....	....
1997-98	U. of Michigan	CCHA	31	14	17	31	62	....	....	....	....	....	....	....	....	....	....	....	....	....	....	....	....	....	....	....
1998-99	**Washington**	**NHL**	**30**	**2**	**2**	**4**	**8**	**1**	**0**	**0**	**40**	**5.0**	**-7**	**176**	**52.8**	**42**	**10**	**11:05**	....	....	....	....	....	....	....	....
	Portland	AHL	46	15	14	29	29	....	....	....	....	....	....	....	....	....	....	....	....	....	....	....	....	....	....	....
99-2000	Portland	AHL	77	22	21	43	51	....	....	....	....	....	....	....	....	....	....	....	4	1	1	2	4	....	....	....
	NHL Totals		**30**	**2**	**2**	**4**	**8**	**1**	**0**	**0**	**40**	**5.0**		**176**	**52.8**	**42**	**10**	**11:05**	....	....	....	....	....	....	....	....

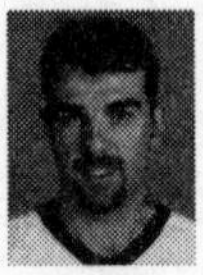

HEWARD, Jamie

(HEW-uhrd, JAY-mee) **CBJ**

Defense. Shoots right. 6'2", 207 lbs. Born, Regina, Sask., March 30, 1971. Pittsburgh's 1st choice, 16th overall, in 1989 Entry Draft.

Season	Club	League	GP	G	A	Pts	PIM	PP	SH	GW	S	%	+/-	TF	F%	H	SB	Min	GP	G	A	Pts	PIM	PP	SH	GW
1987-88	Regina Pats	WHL	68	10	17	27	17	....	....	....	....	....	....	....	....	....	....	....	4	1	1	2	2	....	....	....
1988-89	Regina Pats	WHL	52	31	28	59	29	....	....	....	....	....	....	....	....	....	....	....	....	....	....	....	....	....	....	....
1989-90	Regina Pats	WHL	72	14	44	58	42	....	....	....	....	....	....	....	....	....	....	....	11	2	2	4	10	....	....	....
1990-91	Regina Pats	WHL	71	23	61	84	41	....	....	....	....	....	....	....	....	....	....	....	8	2	9	11	6	....	....	....
1991-92	Muskegon	IHL	54	6	21	27	37	....	....	....	....	....	....	....	....	....	....	....	14	1	4	5	4	....	....	....
1992-93	Cleveland	IHL	58	9	18	27	64	....	....	....	....	....	....	....	....	....	....	....	....	....	....	....	....	....	....	....
1993-94	Cleveland	IHL	73	8	16	24	72	....	....	....	....	....	....	....	....	....	....	....	....	....	....	....	....	....	....	....
1994-95	Canada	Nat-Team	51	11	35	46	32	....	....	....	....	....	....	....	....	....	....	....	....	....	....	....	....	....	....	....
1995-96	**Toronto**	**NHL**	**5**	**0**	**0**	**0**	**0**	**0**	**0**	**0**	**8**	**0.0**	**-1**	....	....	....	....	....	....	....	....	....	....	....	....	....
	St. John's Leafs	AHL	73	22	34	56	33	....	....	....	....	....	....	....	....	....	....	....	3	1	1	2	6	....	....	....
1996-97	**Toronto**	**NHL**	**20**	**1**	**4**	**5**	**6**	**0**	**0**	**0**	**23**	**4.3**	**-6**	....	....	....	....	....	....	....	....	....	....	....	....	....
	St. John's Leafs	AHL	27	8	19	27	26	....	....	....	....	....	....	....	....	....	....	....	9	1	3	4	6	....	....	....
1997-98	Philadelphia	AHL	72	17	48	65	54	....	....	....	....	....	....	....	....	....	....	....	20	3	16	19	10	....	....	....
1998-99	**Nashville**	**NHL**	**63**	**6**	**12**	**18**	**44**	**4**	**0**	**1**	**124**	**4.8**	**-24**	**0**	**0.0**	**80**	**35**	**16:12**	....	....	....	....	....	....	....	....
99-2000	**NY Islanders**	**NHL**	**54**	**6**	**11**	**17**	**26**	**2**	**0**	**1**	**92**	**6.5**	**-9**	**0**	**0.0**	**54**	**74**	**19:58**	....	....	....	....	....	....	....	....
	NHL Totals		**142**	**13**	**27**	**40**	**76**	**6**	**0**	**2**	**247**	**5.3**		**0**	**0.0**	**134**	**109**	**17:56**	....	....	....	....	....	....	....	....

WHL East First All-Star Team (1991) • AHL First All-Star Team (1996, 1998) • Won Eddie Shore Award (Outstanding Defenseman - AHL) (1998)

Signed as a free agent by **Toronto**, May 4, 1995. Signed as a free agent by **Philadelphia**, July 31, 1997. Signed as a free agent by **Nashville**, August 10, 1998. Signed as a free agent by **NY Islanders**, July 27, 1999. Claimed on waivers by **Columbus** from **NY Islanders**, May 26, 2000.

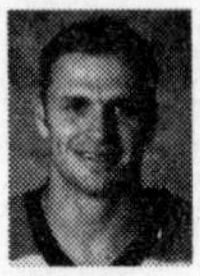

HICKS, Alex

(HIHKS, AL-ehx)

Left wing. Shoots left. 6', 190 lbs. Born, Calgary, Alta., September 4, 1969.

Season	Club	League	GP	G	A	Pts	PIM	PP	SH	GW	S	%	+/-	TF	F%	H	SB	Min	GP	G	A	Pts	PIM	PP	SH	GW
1988-89	Wisc-Eau Claire	NCHA	30	21	26	47	42	....	....	....	....	....	....	....	....	....	....	....	....	....	....	....	....	....	....	....
1989-90	Wisc-Eau Claire	NCHA	34	31	48	79	30	....	....	....	....	....	....	....	....	....	....	....	....	....	....	....	....	....	....	....
1990-91	Wisc-Eau Claire	NCHA	26	22	35	57	43	....	....	....	....	....	....	....	....	....	....	....	....	....	....	....	....	....	....	....
1991-92	Wisc-Eau Claire	NCHA	26	24	42	66	63	....	....	....	....	....	....	....	....	....	....	....	....	....	....	....	....	....	....	....
1992-93	Toledo Storm	ECHL	50	26	34	60	100	....	....	....	....	....	....	....	....	....	....	....	16	5	10	15	79	....	....	....
	Adirondack	AHL	3	0	0	0	0	....	....	....	....	....	....	....	....	....	....	....	....	....	....	....	....	....	....	....
1993-94	Toledo Storm	ECHL	60	31	49	80	240	....	....	....	....	....	....	....	....	....	....	....	14	10	10	20	56	....	....	....
	Adirondack	AHL	8	1	3	4	2	....	....	....	....	....	....	....	....	....	....	....	5	0	2	2	2	....	....	....
1994-95	Las Vegas	IHL	79	24	42	66	212	....	....	....	....	....	....	....	....	....	....	....	9	2	4	6	47	....	....	....
1995-96	**Anaheim**	**NHL**	**64**	**10**	**11**	**21**	**37**	**0**	**0**	**2**	**83**	**12.0**	**11**	....	....	....	....	....	....	....	....	....	....	....	....	....
	Baltimore Bandits	AHL	13	2	10	12	23	....	....	....	....	....	....	....	....	....	....	....	....	....	....	....	....	....	....	....
1996-97	**Anaheim**	**NHL**	**18**	**2**	**6**	**8**	**14**	**0**	**0**	**0**	**21**	**9.5**	**1**	....	....	....	....	....	....	....	....	....	....	....	....	....
	Pittsburgh	**NHL**	**55**	**5**	**15**	**20**	**76**	**0**	**0**	**3**	**57**	**8.8**	**-6**	....	....	....	....	....	**5**	**0**	**1**	**1**	**2**	**0**	**0**	**0**
1997-98	**Pittsburgh**	**NHL**	**58**	**7**	**13**	**20**	**54**	**0**	**0**	**1**	**78**	**9.0**	**4**	....	....	....	....	....	**6**	**0**	**0**	**0**	**2**	**0**	**0**	**0**
1998-99	**San Jose**	**NHL**	**4**	**0**	**1**	**1**	**4**	**0**	**0**	**0**	**4**	**0.0**	**-1**	**0**	**0.0**	**3**	**0**	**4:33**	....	....	....	....	....	....	....	....
	Florida	**NHL**	**51**	**0**	**6**	**6**	**58**	**0**	**0**	**0**	**47**	**0.0**	**-4**	**33**	**42.4**	**89**	**17**	**10:21**	....	....	....	....	....	....	....	....
99-2000	**Florida**	**NHL**	**8**	**1**	**2**	**3**	**4**	**0**	**0**	**0**	**6**	**16.7**	**3**	**1**	**0.0**	**13**	**1**	**8:39**	**4**	**0**	**1**	**1**	**4**	**0**	**0**	**0**
	Louisville	AHL	17	6	5	11	23	....	....	....	....	....	....	....	....	....	....	....	....	....	....	....	....	....	....	....
	NHL Totals		**258**	**25**	**54**	**79**	**247**	**0**	**0**	**6**	**296**	**8.4**		**34**	**41.2**	**105**	**18**	**9:46**	**15**	**0**	**2**	**2**	**8**	**0**	**0**	**0**

NCHA West First All-American Team (1991, 1992)

Signed as a free agent by **Anaheim**, August 17, 1995. Traded to **Pittsburgh** by **Anaheim** with Fredrik Olausson for Shawn Antoski and Dmitri Mironov, November 19, 1996. Signed as a free agent by **San Jose**, October, 1998. Traded to **Florida** by **San Jose** with San Jose's 5th round choice (later traded to NY Islanders - NY Islanders selected Adam Johnson) in 1999 Entry Draft for Jeff Norton, November 11, 1998. • Missed majority of 1999-2000 season recovering from knee injury suffered in training camp after being re-assigned to minors, September 28, 1999. • Played w/ RHI's Buffalo Stampede in 1994 (22-19-32-51-62).

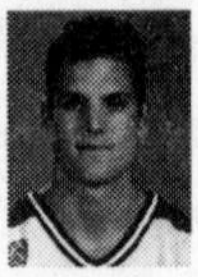

HIGGINS, Matt

(HIH-gihns, MAT) **MTL.**

Center. Shoots left. 6'2", 190 lbs. Born, Calgary, Alta., October 29, 1977. Montreal's 1st choice, 18th overall, in 1996 Entry Draft.

Season	Club	League	GP	G	A	Pts	PIM	PP	SH	GW	S	%	+/-	TF	F%	H	SB	Min	GP	G	A	Pts	PIM	PP	SH	GW
1992-93	Vernon Lakers	BCAHA	70	53	76	129	54	....	....	....	....	....	....	....	....	....	....	....	....	....	....	....	....	....	....	....
1993-94	Moose Jaw	WHL	64	6	10	16	10	....	....	....	....	....	....	....	....	....	....	....	....	....	....	....	....	....	....	....
1994-95	Moose Jaw	WHL	72	36	34	70	26	....	....	....	....	....	....	....	....	....	....	....	10	1	2	3	2	....	....	....
1995-96	Moose Jaw	WHL	67	30	33	63	43	....	....	....	....	....	....	....	....	....	....	....	....	....	....	....	....	....	....	....
1996-97	Moose Jaw	WHL	71	33	57	90	51	....	....	....	....	....	....	....	....	....	....	....	12	3	5	8	2	....	....	....
1997-98	**Montreal**	**NHL**	**1**	**0**	**0**	**0**	**0**	**0**	**0**	**0**	**1**	**0.0**	**-1**	....	....	....	....	....	....	....	....	....	....	....	....	....
	Fredericton	AHL	50	5	22	27	12	....	....	....	....	....	....	....	....	....	....	....	4	1	2	3	2	....	....	....
1998-99	**Montreal**	**NHL**	**25**	**1**	**0**	**1**	**0**	**0**	**0**	**0**	**12**	**8.3**	**-2**	**108**	**45.4**	**9**	**4**	**5:41**	....	....	....	....	....	....	....	....
	Fredericton	AHL	11	3	4	7	6	....	....	....	....	....	....	....	....	....	....	....	5	0	2	2	0	....	....	....
99-2000	**Montreal**	**NHL**	**25**	**0**	**2**	**2**	**4**	**0**	**0**	**0**	**9**	**0.0**	**-6**	**145**	**48.3**	**12**	**13**	**7:57**	....	....	....	....	....	....	....	....
	Quebec Citadelles	AHL	29	1	15	16	21	....	....	....	....	....	....	....	....	....	....	....	....	....	....	....	....	....	....	....
	NHL Totals		**51**	**1**	**2**	**3**	**4**	**0**	**0**	**0**	**22**	**4.5**		**253**	**47.0**	**21**	**17**	**6:49**	....	....	....	....	....	....	....	....

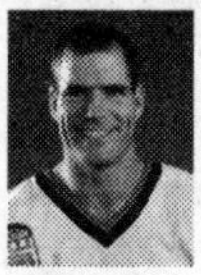

HILL, Sean

(HIHL, SHAWN) **ST.L.**

Defense. Shoots right. 6', 205 lbs. Born, Duluth, MN, February 14, 1970. Montreal's 9th choice, 167th overall, in 1988 Entry Draft.

			Regular Season																Playoffs							
Season	Club	League	GP	G	A	Pts	PIM	PP	SH	GW	S	%	+/-	TF	F%	H	SB	Min	GP	G	A	Pts	PIM	PP	SH	GW
1986-87	Lakefield Chiefs	OJHL-C	3	1	1	2	14	....	....	....	....	....	....	....	....	....	....	....	....	....	....	....	....	....	....	....
1987-88	East Duluth	Hi-School	24	10	17	27	....	....	....	....	....	....	....	....	....	....	....	....	....	....	....	....	....	....	....	....
1988-89	U. of Wisconsin	WCHA	45	2	23	25	69	....	....	....	....	....	....	....	....	....	....	....	....	....	....	....	....	....	....	....
1989-90	U. of Wisconsin	WCHA	42	14	39	53	78	....	....	....	....	....	....	....	....	....	....	....	....	....	....	....	....	....	....	....
1990-91	U. of Wisconsin	WCHA	37	19	32	51	122	....	....	....	....	....	....	....	....	....	....	....	....	....	....	....	....	....	....	....
	Montreal	**NHL**	....	....	....	....	....	....	....	....	....	....	....	....	....	....	....	....	**1**	**0**	**0**	**0**	**0**	**0**	**0**	**0**
	Fredericton	AHL	....	....	....	....	....	....	....	....	....	....	....	....	....	....	....	....	3	0	2	2	2	....	....	....
1991-92	Fredericton	AHL	42	7	20	27	65	....	....	....	....	....	....	....	....	....	....	....	7	1	3	4	6	....	....	....
	United States	Olympics	8	2	0	2	6	....	....	....	....	....	....	....	....	....	....	....	....	....	....	....	....	....	....	....
	United States	Nat-Team	12	4	3	7	16	....	....	....	....	....	....	....	....	....	....	....	....	....	....	....	....	....	....	....
	Montreal	**NHL**	....	....	....	....	....	....	....	....	....	....	....	....	....	....	....	....	**4**	**1**	**0**	**1**	**2**	**0**	**0**	**0**
1992-93♦	**Montreal**	**NHL**	**31**	**2**	**6**	**8**	**54**	**1**	**0**	**1**	**37**	**5.4**	**–5**	....	....	....	....	....	**3**	**0**	**0**	**0**	**4**	**0**	**0**	**0**
	Fredericton	AHL	6	1	3	4	10	....	....	....	....	....	....	....	....	....	....	....	....	....	....	....	....	....	....	....
1993-94	**Anaheim**	**NHL**	**68**	**7**	**20**	**27**	**78**	**2**	**1**	**1**	**165**	**4.2**	**–12**	....	....	....	....	....	....	....	....	....	....	....	....	....
1994-95	**Ottawa**	**NHL**	**45**	**1**	**14**	**15**	**30**	**0**	**0**	**1**	**107**	**0.9**	**–11**	....	....	....	....	....	....	....	....	....	....	....	....	....
1995-96	**Ottawa**	**NHL**	**80**	**7**	**14**	**21**	**94**	**2**	**0**	**2**	**157**	**4.5**	**–26**	....	....	....	....	....	....	....	....	....	....	....	....	....
1996-97	**Ottawa**	**NHL**	**5**	**0**	**0**	**0**	**4**	**0**	**0**	**0**	**9**	**0.0**	**1**	....	....	....	....	....	....	....	....	....	....	....	....	....
1997-98	**Ottawa**	**NHL**	**13**	**1**	**1**	**2**	**6**	**0**	**0**	**0**	**16**	**6.3**	**–3**	....	....	....	....	....	....	....	....	....	....	....	....	....
	Carolina	**NHL**	**42**	**0**	**5**	**5**	**48**	**0**	**0**	**0**	**37**	**0.0**	**–2**	....	....	....	....	....	....	....	....	....	....	....	....	....
1998-99	**Carolina**	**NHL**	**54**	**0**	**10**	**10**	**48**	**0**	**0**	**0**	**44**	**0.0**	**9**	**0**	**0.0**	**194**	**79**	**19:02**	....	....	....	....	....	....	....	....
99-2000	**Carolina**	**NHL**	**62**	**13**	**31**	**44**	**59**	**8**	**0**	**2**	**150**	**8.7**	**3**	**1**	**0.0**	**246**	**94**	**24:31**	....	....	....	....	....	....	....	....
	NHL Totals		**400**	**31**	**101**	**132**	**421**	**13**	**1**	**6**	**722**	**4.3**		**1**	**0.0**	**440**	**173**	**21:58**	**8**	**1**	**0**	**1**	**6**	**0**	**0**	**0**

WCHA Second All-Star Team (1990, 1991) • NCAA West Second All-American Team (1991)

Claimed by **Anaheim** from **Montreal** in Expansion Draft, June 24, 1993. Traded to **Ottawa** by **Anaheim** with Anaheim's 9th round choice (Frederic Cassivi) in 1994 Entry Draft for Ottawa's 3rd round choice (later traded to Tampa Bay - Tampa Bay selected Vadim Epanchintsev) in 1994 Entry Draft, June 29, 1994. Traded to **Carolina** by **Ottawa** for Chris Murray, November 18, 1997. Signed as a free agent by **St. Louis**, July 1, 2000.

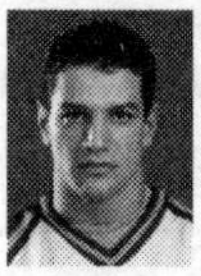

HINOTE, Dan

(HIH-noht, DAN) **COL.**

Right wing. Shoots right. 6', 190 lbs. Born, Leesburg, FL, January 30, 1977. Colorado's 9th choice, 167th overall, in 1996 Entry Draft.

			Regular Season																Playoffs							
Season	Club	League	GP	G	A	Pts	PIM	PP	SH	GW	S	%	+/-	TF	F%	H	SB	Min	GP	G	A	Pts	PIM	PP	SH	GW
1994-95	Army Academy	NCAA	33	20	24	44	20	....	....	....	....	....	....	....	....	....	....	....	....	....	....	....	....	....	....	....
1995-96	Army Academy	NCAA	34	21	24	45	22	....	....	....	....	....	....	....	....	....	....	....	....	....	....	....	....	....	....	....
1996-97	Oshawa Generals	OHL	60	15	13	28	58	....	....	....	....	....	....	....	....	....	....	....	18	4	5	9	8	....	....	....
1997-98	Oshawa Generals	OHL	35	12	15	27	39	....	....	....	....	....	....	....	....	....	....	....	5	2	2	4	7	....	....	....
	Hershey Bears	AHL	24	1	4	5	25	....	....	....	....	....	....	....	....	....	....	....	....	....	....	....	....	....	....	....
1998-99	Hershey Bears	AHL	65	4	16	20	95	....	....	....	....	....	....	....	....	....	....	....	5	3	1	4	6	....	....	....
99-2000	**Colorado**	**NHL**	**27**	**1**	**3**	**4**	**10**	**0**	**0**	**0**	**14**	**7.1**	**0**	**132**	**51.5**	**47**	**8**	**7:51**	....	....	....	....	....	....	....	....
	Hershey Bears	AHL	55	28	31	59	96	....	....	....	....	....	....	....	....	....	....	....	14	4	5	9	19	....	....	....
	NHL Totals		**27**	**1**	**3**	**4**	**10**	**0**	**0**	**0**	**14**	**7.1**		**132**	**51.5**	**47**	**8**	**7:51**	....	....	....	....	....	....	....	....

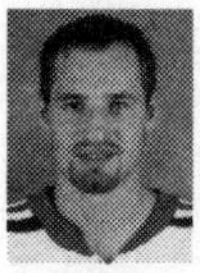

HLAVAC, Jan

(huh-LAH-vahch, YAHN) **NYR**

Left wing. Shoots left. 6', 185 lbs. Born, Prague, Czech., September 20, 1976. NY Islanders' 2nd choice, 28th overall, in 1995 Entry Draft.

			Regular Season																Playoffs							
Season	Club	League	GP	G	A	Pts	PIM	PP	SH	GW	S	%	+/-	TF	F%	H	SB	Min	GP	G	A	Pts	PIM	PP	SH	GW
1993-94	Sparta Praha-Jr.	Cze-Rep.	27	12	15	27	....	....	....	....	....	....	....	....	....	....	....	....	....	....	....	....	....	....	....	....
	Sparta Praha	Cze-Rep	9	1	1	2	....	....	....	....	....	....	....	....	....	....	....	....	....	....	....	....	....	....	....	....
1994-95	Sparta Praha	Cze-Rep	38	7	6	13	18	....	....	....	....	....	....	....	....	....	....	....	5	0	2	2	0	....	....	....
1995-96	Sparta Praha	Cze-Rep	34	8	5	13	....	....	....	....	....	....	....	....	....	....	....	....	12	1	2	3	....	....	....	....
1996-97	Sparta Praha	Cze-Rep	38	8	13	21	24	....	....	....	....	....	....	....	....	....	....	....	10	5	2	7	2	....	....	....
	Sparta Praha	EuroHL	3	4	0	4	6	....	....	....	....	....	....	....	....	....	....	....	....	....	....	....	....	....	....	....
1997-98	Sparta Praha	Cze-Rep	48	17	30	47	40	....	....	....	....	....	....	....	....	....	....	....	5	1	0	1	2	....	....	....
	Sparta Praha	EuroHL	5	0	3	3	4	....	....	....	....	....	....	....	....	....	....	....	....	....	....	....	....	....	....	....
1998-99	Sparta Praha	Cze-Rep	49	*33	20	53	52	....	....	....	....	....	....	....	....	....	....	....	6	1	3	4	....	....	....	....
	Sparta Praha	EuroHL	5	4	2	6	0	....	....	....	....	....	....	....	....	....	....	....	1	1	1	2	0	....	....	....
99-2000	**NY Rangers**	**NHL**	**67**	**19**	**23**	**42**	**16**	**6**	**0**	**2**	**134**	**14.2**	**3**	**6**	**33.3**	**39**	**17**	**15:09**	....	....	....	....	....	....	....	....
	Hartford	AHL	3	1	0	1	0	....	....	....	....	....	....	....	....	....	....	....	....	....	....	....	....	....	....	....
	NHL Totals		**67**	**19**	**23**	**42**	**16**	**6**	**0**	**2**	**134**	**14.2**		**6**	**33.3**	**39**	**17**	**15:09**	....	....	....	....	....	....	....	....

Traded to **Calgary** by **NY Islanders** for Jorgen Jonsson, July 14, 1998. Rights traded to **NY Rangers** by **Calgary** with Calgary's 1st (Jamie Lundmark) and 3rd (later traded back to Calgary - Calgary selected Craig Andersson) round choices in 1999 Entry Draft for Marc Savard and NY Rangers' 1st round choice (Oleg Saprykin) in 1999 Entry Draft, June 26, 1999.

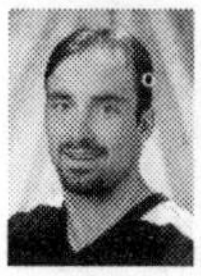

HLUSHKO, Todd

(huh-LUSH-koh, TAWD)

Center. Shoots left. 5'11", 185 lbs. Born, Toronto, Ont., February 7, 1970. Washington's 14th choice, 240th overall, in 1990 Entry Draft.

			Regular Season																Playoffs							
Season	Club	League	GP	G	A	Pts	PIM	PP	SH	GW	S	%	+/-	TF	F%	H	SB	Min	GP	G	A	Pts	PIM	PP	SH	GW
1987-88	Guelph Jr. B's	OJHL-B	44	36	47	83	94	....	....	....	....	....	....	....	....	....	....	....	....	....	....	....	....	....	....	....
1988-89	Guelph Platers	OHL	66	28	18	46	71	....	....	....	....	....	....	....	....	....	....	....	7	5	3	8	18	....	....	....
1989-90	Owen Sound	OHL	25	9	17	26	31	....	....	....	....	....	....	....	....	....	....	....	....	....	....	....	....	....	....	....
	London Knights	OHL	40	27	17	44	39	....	....	....	....	....	....	....	....	....	....	....	6	2	4	6	10	....	....	....
1990-91	Baltimore	AHL	66	9	14	23	55	....	....	....	....	....	....	....	....	....	....	....	....	....	....	....	....	....	....	....
1991-92	Baltimore	AHL	74	16	35	51	113	....	....	....	....	....	....	....	....	....	....	....	....	....	....	....	....	....	....	....
1992-93	Canada	Nat-Team	58	22	26	48	10	....	....	....	....	....	....	....	....	....	....	....	....	....	....	....	....	....	....	....
1993-94	Canada	Nat-Team	55	22	6	28	61	....	....	....	....	....	....	....	....	....	....	....	....	....	....	....	....	....	....	....
	Canada	Olympics	8	5	0	5	6	....	....	....	....	....	....	....	....	....	....	....	....	....	....	....	....	....	....	....
	Philadelphia	**NHL**	**2**	**1**	**0**	**1**	**0**	**0**	**0**	**0**	**2**	**50.0**	**1**	....	....	....	....	....	....	....	....	....	....	....	....	....
	Hershey Bears	AHL	9	6	0	6	4	....	....	....	....	....	....	....	....	....	....	....	6	2	1	3	4	....	....	....
1994-95	**Calgary**	**NHL**	**2**	**0**	**1**	**1**	**2**	**0**	**0**	**0**	**3**	**0.0**	**1**	....	....	....	....	....	**1**	**0**	**0**	**0**	**2**	**0**	**0**	**0**
	Saint John Flames	AHL	46	22	10	32	36	....	....	....	....	....	....	....	....	....	....	....	4	2	2	4	22	....	....	....
1995-96	**Calgary**	**NHL**	**4**	**0**	**0**	**0**	**6**	**0**	**0**	**0**	**6**	**0.0**	**0**	....	....	....	....	....	....	....	....	....	....	....	....	....
	Saint John Flames	AHL	35	14	13	27	70	....	....	....	....	....	....	....	....	....	....	....	16	8	1	9	26	....	....	....
1996-97	**Calgary**	**NHL**	**58**	**7**	**11**	**18**	**49**	**0**	**0**	**0**	**76**	**9.2**	**–2**	....	....	....	....	....	....	....	....	....	....	....	....	....
1997-98	**Calgary**	**NHL**	**13**	**0**	**1**	**1**	**27**	**0**	**0**	**0**	**7**	**0.0**	**0**	....	....	....	....	....	....	....	....	....	....	....	....	....
	Saint John Flames	AHL	33	10	14	24	48	....	....	....	....	....	....	....	....	....	....	....	21	*13	4	17	61	....	....	....
1998-99	Grand Rapids	IHL	82	24	26	50	78	....	....	....	....	....	....	....	....	....	....	....	....	....	....	....	....	....	....	....
	Pittsburgh	**NHL**	....	....	....	....	....	....	....	....	....	....	....	....	....	....	....	....	**2**	**0**	**0**	**0**	**0**	**0**	**0**	**0**
99-2000	Kolner Haie	DEL	55	13	28	41	78	....	....	....	....	....	....	....	....	....	....	....	10	5	2	7	20	....	....	....
	NHL Totals		**79**	**8**	**13**	**21**	**84**	**0**	**0**	**0**	**94**	**8.5**		....	....	....	....	....	**3**	**0**	**0**	**0**	**2**	**0**	**0**	**0**

Signed as a free agent by **Philadelphia**, March 7, 1994. Signed as a free agent by **Calgary**, June 17, 1994. Traded to **Pittsburgh** by **Calgary** with German Titov for Ken Wregget and Dave Roche, June 17, 1998.

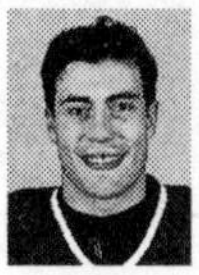

HOCKING, Justin

(HAWK-ihng, JUHS-tihn) **PHX.**

Defense. Shoots right. 6'4", 215 lbs. Born, Stettler, Alta., January 9, 1974. Los Angeles' 1st choice, 39th overall, in 1992 Entry Draft.

			Regular Season																Playoffs							
Season	Club	League	GP	G	A	Pts	PIM	PP	SH	GW	S	%	+/-	TF	F%	H	SB	Min	GP	G	A	Pts	PIM	PP	SH	GW
1990-91	Ft-Saskatchewan	AJHL	38	4	6	10	84	....	....	....	....	....	....	....	....	....	....	....	....	....	....	....	....	....	....	....
1991-92	Spokane Chiefs	WHL	71	4	6	10	309	....	....	....	....	....	....	....	....	....	....	....	10	0	3	3	28	....	....	....
1992-93	Spokane Chiefs	WHL	16	0	1	1	75	....	....	....	....	....	....	....	....	....	....	....	....	....	....	....	....	....	....	....
	Medicine Hat	WHL	54	1	9	10	119	....	....	....	....	....	....	....	....	....	....	....	10	0	1	1	13	....	....	....
1993-94	Medicine Hat	WHL	68	7	26	33	236	....	....	....	....	....	....	....	....	....	....	....	3	0	0	0	6	....	....	....
	Los Angeles	**NHL**	**1**	**0**	**0**	**0**	**0**	**0**	**0**	**0**	**0**	**0.0**	**0**	....	....	....	....	....	....	....	....	....	....	....	....	....
	Phoenix	IHL	3	0	0	0	15	....	....	....	....	....	....	....	....	....	....	....	....	....	....	....	....	....	....	....
1994-95	Syracuse Crunch	AHL	7	0	0	0	24	....	....	....	....	....	....	....	....	....	....	....	....	....	....	....	....	....	....	....
	Portland Pirates	AHL	9	0	1	1	34	....	....	....	....	....	....	....	....	....	....	....	....	....	....	....	....	....	....	....
	Knoxville	ECHL	20	0	6	6	70	....	....	....	....	....	....	....	....	....	....	....	4	0	0	0	26	....	....	....
	Phoenix	IHL	20	1	1	2	50	....	....	....	....	....	....	....	....	....	....	....	1	0	0	0	0	....	....	....
1995-96	P.E.I. Senators	AHL	74	4	8	12	251	....	....	....	....	....	....	....	....	....	....	....	4	0	2	2	5	....	....	....

			Regular Season																Playoffs							
Season	Club	League	GP	G	A	Pts	PIM	PP	SH	GW	S	%	+/–	TF	F%	H	SB	Min	GP	G	A	Pts	PIM	PP	SH	GW
1996-97	Worcester	AHL	68	1	10	11	198	....	....	....	....	....	....	....	....	....	....	....	5	0	3	3	2	....	....	....
1997-98	Worcester	AHL	79	5	12	17	198	....	....	....	....	....	....	....	....	....	....	....	11	1	2	3	19	....	....	....
1998-99	Indianapolis Ice	IHL	34	2	4	6	111	....	....	....	....	....	....	....	....	....	....	....	....	....	....	....	....	....	....	....
	St. John's Leafs	AHL	44	4	6	10	99	....	....	....	....	....	....	....	....	....	....	....	5	0	0	0	2	....	....	....
99-2000	St. John's Leafs	AHL	68	4	9	13	175	....	....	....	....	....	....	....	....	....	....	....	....	....	....	....	....	....	....	....
	NHL Totals		**1**	**0**	**0**	**0**	**0**	**0**	**0**	**0**	**0**	**0.0**		....	....	....	....	....	....	....	....	....	....	....	....	....

WHL East Second All-Star Team (1994)

Claimed by **Ottawa** from **LA Kings** in Waiver Draft, October 2, 1995. Traded to **Chicago** by **Ottawa** for Brian Felsner, August 21, 1998. Signed as a free agent by **Toronto**, July 23, 1999. Signed as a free agent by **Phoenix**, August 1, 2000.

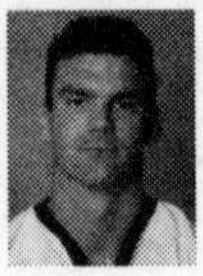

HOGLUND, Jonas

(HOHG-lund, YOH-nuhs) **TOR.**

Right wing. Shoots right. 6'3", 215 lbs. Born, Hammaro, Swe., August 29, 1972. Calgary's 11th choice, 222nd overall, in 1992 Entry Draft.

Season	Club	League	GP	G	A	Pts	PIM	PP	SH	GW	S	%	+/–	TF	F%	H	SB	Min	GP	G	A	Pts	PIM	PP	SH	GW
1988-89	Farjestads BK	Sweden	1	0	0	0	0	....	....	....	....	....	....	....	....	....	....	....	....	....	....	....	....	....	....	....
1989-90	Farjestads BK	Sweden	1	0	0	....	0	....	....	....	....	....	....	....	....	....	....	....	....	....	....	....	....	....	....	....
1990-91	Farjestads BK	Sweden	40	5	5	10	4	....	....	....	....	....	....	....	....	....	....	....	8	1	0	1	0	....	....	....
1991-92	Farjestads BK	Sweden	40	14	11	25	6	....	....	....	....	....	....	....	....	....	....	....	6	2	4	6	2	....	....	....
1992-93	Farjestads BK	Sweden	40	13	13	26	14	....	....	....	....	....	....	....	....	....	....	....	3	1	0	1	0	....	....	....
1993-94	Farjestads BK	Sweden	22	7	2	9	10	....	....	....	....	....	....	....	....	....	....	....	....	....	....	....	....	....	....	....
1994-95	Farjestads BK	Sweden	40	14	12	26	16	....	....	....	....	....	....	....	....	....	....	....	4	3	2	5	0	....	....	....
1995-96	Farjestads BK	Sweden	40	32	11	43	18	....	....	....	....	....	....	....	....	....	....	....	8	2	1	3	6	....	....	....
1996-97	**Calgary**	**NHL**	**68**	**19**	**16**	**35**	**12**	**3**	**0**	**6**	**189**	**10.1**	**–4**	....	....	....	....	....	....	....	....	....	....	....	....	....
1997-98	**Calgary**	**NHL**	**50**	**6**	**8**	**14**	**16**	**0**	**0**	**0**	**124**	**4.8**	**–9**	....	....	....	....	....	....	....	....	....	....	....	....	....
	Montreal	**NHL**	**28**	**6**	**5**	**11**	**6**	**4**	**0**	**0**	**62**	**9.7**	**2**	....	....	....	....	....	**10**	**2**	**0**	**2**	**0**	**0**	**0**	**0**
1998-99	**Montreal**	**NHL**	**74**	**8**	**10**	**18**	**16**	**1**	**0**	**0**	**122**	**6.6**	**–5**	**17**	**29.4**	**41**	**15**	**11:50**	....	....	....	....	....	....	....	....
99-2000	**Toronto**	**NHL**	**82**	**29**	**27**	**56**	**10**	**9**	**1**	**3**	**215**	**13.5**	**–2**	**4**	**50.0**	**55**	**24**	**17:10**	**12**	**2**	**4**	**6**	**2**	**0**	**0**	**0**
	NHL Totals		**302**	**68**	**66**	**134**	**60**	**17**	**1**	**9**	**712**	**9.6**		**21**	**33.3**	**96**	**39**	**14:38**	**22**	**4**	**4**	**8**	**2**	**0**	**0**	**0**

Traded to **Montreal** by **Calgary** with Zarley Zalapski for Valeri Bure and Montreal's 4th round choice (Shaun Sutter) in 1998 Entry Draft, February 1, 1998. Signed as a free agent by **Toronto**, July 13, 1999.

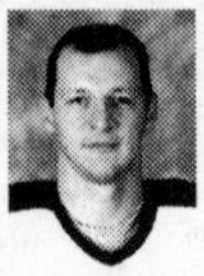

HOGUE, Benoit

(HOHG, BEHN-wah)

Center. Shoots left. 5'10", 194 lbs. Born, Repentigny, Que., October 28, 1966. Buffalo's 2nd choice, 35th overall, in 1985 Entry Draft.

Season	Club	League	GP	G	A	Pts	PIM	PP	SH	GW	S	%	+/–	TF	F%	H	SB	Min	GP	G	A	Pts	PIM	PP	SH	GW
1982-83	Mtl-Bourassa	QAAA	40	20	20	40	....	....	....	....	....	....	....	....	....	....	....	....	....	....	....	....	....	....	....	....
1983-84	St-Jean Castors	QMJHL	59	14	11	25	42	....	....	....	....	....	....	....	....	....	....	....	....	....	....	....	....	....	....	....
1984-85	St-Jean Castors	QMJHL	63	46	44	90	92	....	....	....	....	....	....	....	....	....	....	....	....	....	....	....	....	....	....	....
1985-86	St-Jean Castors	QMJHL	65	54	54	108	115	....	....	....	....	....	....	....	....	....	....	....	9	6	4	10	26	....	....	....
1986-87	Rochester	AHL	52	14	20	34	52	....	....	....	....	....	....	....	....	....	....	....	12	5	4	9	8	....	....	....
1987-88	**Buffalo**	**NHL**	**3**	**1**	**1**	**2**	**0**	**0**	**0**	**1**	**3**	**33.3**	**3**	....	....	....	....	....	....	....	....	....	....	....	....	....
	Rochester	AHL	62	24	31	55	141	....	....	....	....	....	....	....	....	....	....	....	7	6	1	7	46	....	....	....
1988-89	**Buffalo**	**NHL**	**69**	**14**	**30**	**44**	**120**	**1**	**2**	**0**	**114**	**12.3**	**–5**	....	....	....	....	....	**5**	**0**	**0**	**0**	**17**	**0**	**0**	**0**
1989-90	**Buffalo**	**NHL**	**45**	**11**	**7**	**18**	**79**	**1**	**0**	**1**	**73**	**15.1**	**0**	....	....	....	....	....	**3**	**0**	**0**	**0**	**10**	**0**	**0**	**0**
1990-91	**Buffalo**	**NHL**	**76**	**19**	**28**	**47**	**76**	**1**	**0**	**2**	**134**	**14.2**	**–8**	....	....	....	....	....	**5**	**3**	**1**	**4**	**10**	**0**	**0**	**0**
1991-92	**Buffalo**	**NHL**	**3**	**0**	**1**	**1**	**0**	**0**	**0**	**0**	**6**	**0.0**	**0**	....	....	....	....	....	....	....	....	....	....	....	....	....
	NY Islanders	**NHL**	**72**	**30**	**45**	**75**	**67**	**8**	**0**	**5**	**143**	**21.0**	**30**	....	....	....	....	....	....	....	....	....	....	....	....	....
1992-93	**NY Islanders**	**NHL**	**70**	**33**	**42**	**75**	**108**	**5**	**3**	**5**	**147**	**22.4**	**13**	....	....	....	....	....	**18**	**6**	**6**	**12**	**31**	**0**	**0**	**0**
1993-94	**NY Islanders**	**NHL**	**83**	**36**	**33**	**69**	**73**	**9**	**5**	**3**	**218**	**16.5**	**–7**	....	....	....	....	....	**4**	**0**	**1**	**1**	**4**	**0**	**0**	**0**
1994-95	**NY Islanders**	**NHL**	**33**	**6**	**4**	**10**	**34**	**1**	**0**	**1**	**50**	**12.0**	**0**	....	....	....	....	....	....	....	....	....	....	....	....	....
	Toronto	**NHL**	**12**	**3**	**3**	**6**	**0**	**1**	**0**	**1**	**16**	**18.8**	**0**	....	....	....	....	....	**7**	**0**	**0**	**0**	**6**	**0**	**0**	**0**
1995-96	**Toronto**	**NHL**	**44**	**12**	**25**	**37**	**68**	**3**	**0**	**5**	**94**	**12.8**	**6**	....	....	....	....	....	....	....	....	....	....	....	....	....
	Dallas	**NHL**	**34**	**7**	**20**	**27**	**36**	**2**	**0**	**0**	**61**	**11.5**	**4**	....	....	....	....	....	....	....	....	....	....	....	....	....
1996-97	**Dallas**	**NHL**	**73**	**19**	**24**	**43**	**54**	**5**	**0**	**5**	**131**	**14.5**	**8**	....	....	....	....	....	**7**	**2**	**2**	**4**	**6**	**1**	**0**	**0**
1997-98	**Dallas**	**NHL**	**53**	**6**	**16**	**22**	**35**	**3**	**0**	**1**	**55**	**10.9**	**7**	....	....	....	....	....	**17**	**4**	**2**	**6**	**16**	**1**	**0**	**2**
1998-99	**Tampa Bay**	**NHL**	**62**	**11**	**14**	**25**	**50**	**2**	**0**	**3**	**101**	**10.9**	**–12**	**63**	**42.9**	**89**	**24**	**16:23**	....	....	....	....	....	....	....	....
	♦ Dallas	**NHL**	**12**	**1**	**3**	**4**	**4**	**0**	**0**	**0**	**20**	**5.0**	**2**	**52**	**46.2**	**31**	**4**	**15:04**	**14**	**0**	**2**	**2**	**16**	**0**	**0**	**0**
99-2000	**Phoenix**	**NHL**	**27**	**3**	**10**	**13**	**10**	**0**	**0**	**0**	**39**	**7.7**	**–1**	**24**	**37.5**	**56**	**11**	**15:45**	**5**	**1**	**2**	**3**	**2**	**0**	**0**	**0**
	NHL Totals		**771**	**212**	**306**	**518**	**814**	**42**	**10**	**33**	**1405**	**15.1**		**139**	**43.2**	**176**	**39**	**16:03**	**85**	**16**	**16**	**32**	**118**	**2**	**0**	**2**

Traded to **NY Islanders** by **Buffalo** with Pierre Turgeon, Uwe Krupp and Dave McLlwain for Pat LaFontaine, Randy Hillier, Randy Wood and NY Islanders' 4th round choice (Dean Melanson) in 1992 Entry Draft, October 25, 1991. Traded to **Toronto** by **NY Islanders** with NY Islanders' 3rd round choice (Ryan Pepperall) in 1995 Entry Draft and 5th round choice (Brandon Sugden) in 1996 Entry Draft for Eric Fichaud, April 6, 1995. Traded to **Dallas** by **Toronto** with Randy Wood for Dave Gagner and Dallas' 6th round choice (Dmitriy Yakushin) in 1996 Entry Draft, January 29, 1996. Signed as a free agent by **Tampa Bay**, August 19, 1998. Traded to **Dallas** by **Tampa Bay** with a conditional choice in 2001 Entry Draft for Sergey Gusev, March 21, 1999. Signed as a free agent by **Phoenix**, February 3, 2000.

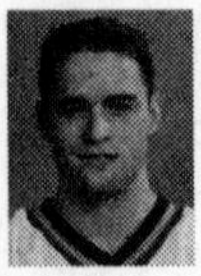

HOLDEN, Josh

(HOHL-dehn, JAWSH) **VAN.**

Center. Shoots left. 6', 190 lbs. Born, Calgary, Alta., January 18, 1978. Vancouver's 1st choice, 12th overall, in 1996 Entry Draft.

Season	Club	League	GP	G	A	Pts	PIM	PP	SH	GW	S	%	+/–	TF	F%	H	SB	Min	GP	G	A	Pts	PIM	PP	SH	GW
1993-94	Calgary Buffaloes	AAHA	34	14	15	29	82	....	....	....	....	....	....	....	....	....	....	....	....	....	....	....	....	....	....	....
1994-95	Regina Pats	WHL	62	20	23	43	45	....	....	....	....	....	....	....	....	....	....	....	4	3	1	4	0	....	....	....
1995-96	Regina Pats	WHL	70	57	55	112	105	....	....	....	....	....	....	....	....	....	....	....	11	4	5	9	23	....	....	....
1996-97	Regina Pats	WHL	58	49	49	98	148	....	....	....	....	....	....	....	....	....	....	....	5	3	2	5	10	....	....	....
1997-98	Regina Pats	WHL	56	41	58	99	134	....	....	....	....	....	....	....	....	....	....	....	2	2	2	4	10	....	....	....
1998-99	**Vancouver**	**NHL**	**30**	**2**	**4**	**6**	**10**	**1**	**0**	**0**	**44**	**4.5**	**–10**	**269**	**39.0**	**38**	**6**	**12:44**	....	....	....	....	....	....	....	....
	Syracuse Crunch	AHL	38	14	15	29	48	....	....	....	....	....	....	....	....	....	....	....	....	....	....	....	....	....	....	....
99-2000	**Vancouver**	**NHL**	**6**	**1**	**5**	**6**	**2**	**0**	**0**	**0**	**5**	**20.0**	**2**	**42**	**42.9**	**14**	**2**	**10:25**	....	....	....	....	....	....	....	....
	Syracuse Crunch	AHL	45	19	32	51	113	....	....	....	....	....	....	....	....	....	....	....	4	1	0	1	10	....	....	....
	NHL Totals		**36**	**3**	**9**	**12**	**12**	**1**	**0**	**0**	**49**	**6.1**		**311**	**39.5**	**52**	**8**	**12:21**	....	....	....	....	....	....	....	....

WHL East Second All-Star Team (1998)

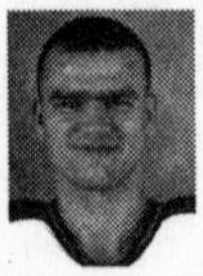

HOLIK, Bobby

(HOH-leek, BAWB-bee) **N.J.**

Center. Shoots right. 6'4", 230 lbs. Born, Jihlava, Czech., January 1, 1971. Hartford's 1st choice, 10th overall, in 1989 Entry Draft.

Season	Club	League	GP	G	A	Pts	PIM	PP	SH	GW	S	%	+/–	TF	F%	H	SB	Min	GP	G	A	Pts	PIM	PP	SH	GW
1987-88	Dukla Jihlava	Czech.	31	5	9	14	16	....	....	....	....	....	....	....	....	....	....	....	....	....	....	....	....	....	....	....
1988-89	Dukla Jihlava	Czech.	24	7	10	17	32	....	....	....	....	....	....	....	....	....	....	....	....	....	....	....	....	....	....	....
1989-90	Dukla Jihlava	Czech.	42	15	26	41	....	....	....	....	....	....	....	....	....	....	....	....	....	....	....	....	....	....	....	....
1990-91	**Hartford**	**NHL**	**78**	**21**	**22**	**43**	**113**	**8**	**0**	**3**	**173**	**12.1**	**–3**	....	....	....	....	....	**6**	**0**	**0**	**0**	**7**	**0**	**0**	**0**
1991-92	**Hartford**	**NHL**	**76**	**21**	**24**	**45**	**44**	**1**	**0**	**2**	**207**	**10.1**	**4**	....	....	....	....	....	**7**	**0**	**1**	**1**	**6**	**0**	**0**	**0**
1992-93	**New Jersey**	**NHL**	**61**	**20**	**19**	**39**	**76**	**7**	**0**	**4**	**180**	**11.1**	**–6**	....	....	....	....	....	**5**	**1**	**1**	**2**	**6**	**0**	**0**	**0**
	Utica Devils	AHL	1	0	0	0	2	....	....	....	....	....	....	....	....	....	....	....	....	....	....	....	....	....	....	....
1993-94	**New Jersey**	**NHL**	**70**	**13**	**20**	**33**	**72**	**2**	**0**	**3**	**130**	**10.0**	**28**	....	....	....	....	....	**20**	**0**	**3**	**3**	**6**	**0**	**0**	**0**
1994-95♦	**New Jersey**	**NHL**	**48**	**10**	**10**	**20**	**18**	**0**	**0**	**2**	**84**	**11.9**	**9**	....	....	....	....	....	**20**	**4**	**4**	**8**	**22**	**2**	**0**	**1**
1995-96	**New Jersey**	**NHL**	**63**	**13**	**17**	**30**	**58**	**1**	**0**	**1**	**157**	**8.3**	**9**	....	....	....	....	....	....	....	....	....	....	....	....	....
1996-97	**New Jersey**	**NHL**	**82**	**23**	**39**	**62**	**54**	**5**	**0**	**6**	**192**	**12.0**	**24**	....	....	....	....	....	**10**	**2**	**3**	**5**	**4**	**1**	**0**	**0**
1997-98	**New Jersey**	**NHL**	**82**	**29**	**36**	**65**	**100**	**8**	**0**	**8**	**238**	**12.2**	**23**	....	....	....	....	....	**5**	**0**	**0**	**0**	**8**	**0**	**0**	**0**
1998-99	**New Jersey**	**NHL**	**78**	**27**	**37**	**64**	**119**	**5**	**0**	**8**	**253**	**10.7**	**16**	**1350**	**53.6**	**217**	**24**	**17:34**	**7**	**0**	**7**	**7**	**6**	**0**	**0**	**0**
99-2000♦	**New Jersey**	**NHL**	**79**	**23**	**23**	**46**	**106**	**7**	**0**	**4**	**257**	**8.9**	**7**	**1390**	**55.6**	**139**	**17**	**16:53**	**23**	**3**	**7**	**10**	**14**	**0**	**0**	**1**
	NHL Totals		**717**	**200**	**247**	**447**	**760**	**44**	**0**	**41**	**1871**	**10.7**		**2740**	**54.6**	**356**	**41**	**17:13**	**103**	**10**	**26**	**36**	**79**	**3**	**0**	**2**

Played in NHL All-Star Game (1998, 1999)

Traded to **New Jersey** by **Hartford** with Hartford's 2nd round choice (Jay Pandolfo) in 1993 Entry Draft for Sean Burke and Eric Weinrich, August 28, 1992.

HOLLAND, Jason
(HAWL-land, JAY-suhn) **BUF.**

Defense. Shoots right. 6'3", 209 lbs.   Born, Morinville, Alta., April 30, 1976. NY Islanders' 2nd choice, 38th overall, in 1994 Entry Draft.

Season	Club	League	GP	G	A	Pts	PIM	PP	SH	GW	S	%	+/-	TF	F%	H	SB	Min	GP	G	A	Pts	PIM	PP	SH	GW
1991-92	St. Albert Eagles	AMHL	38	9	29	38	94																			
1992-93	St. Albert Eagles	AMHL	31	11	25	36	36																			
	Kamloops Blazers	WHL	4	0	0	0	2																			
1993-94	Kamloops Blazers	WHL	59	14	15	29	80												18	2	3	5	4			
1994-95	Kamloops Blazers	WHL	71	9	32	41	65												21	2	7	9	9			
1995-96	Kamloops Blazers	WHL	63	24	33	57	98												16	4	9	13	22			
1996-97	**NY Islanders**	**NHL**	4	1	0	1	0	0	0	0	3	33.3	1													
	Kentucky	AHL	72	14	25	39	46												4	0	2	2	0			
1997-98	**NY Islanders**	**NHL**	8	0	0	0	4	0	0	0	6	0.0	-4													
	Kentucky	AHL	50	10	16	26	29																			
	Rochester	AHL	9	0	4	4	10												4	0	3	3	4			
1998-99	**Buffalo**	**NHL**	3	0	0	0	8	0	0	0	2	0.0	-1	0	0.0		2	10:58								
	Rochester	AHL	74	4	25	29	36												20	2	5	7	8			
99-2000	**Buffalo**	**NHL**	9	0	1	1	0	0	0	0	8	0.0	0	0	0.0	5	3	15:31	1	0	0	0	0	0	0	0
	Rochester	AHL	54	3	15	18	24												12	1	0	1	2			
	NHL Totals		24	1	1	2	12	0	0	0	19	5.3		0	0.0	5	5	14:23	1	0	0	0	0	0	0	0

Won Warwick Trophy (AMHL MVP) (1993) • WHL West First All-Star Team (1996)
Traded to **Buffalo** by **NY Islanders** with Paul Kruse for Jason Dawe, March 24, 1998.

HOLLINGER, Terry
(HAWL-lihn-GUHR, TAIR-ree)

Defense. Shoots left. 6'1", 200 lbs.   Born, Regina, Sask., February 24, 1971. St. Louis' 7th choice, 153rd overall, in 1991 Entry Draft.

Season	Club	League	GP	G	A	Pts	PIM	PP	SH	GW	S	%	+/-	TF	F%	H	SB	Min	GP	G	A	Pts	PIM	PP	SH	GW
1986-87	Regina Cougars	SAHA	31	37	36	73	59																			
1987-88	Regina	SAHA	30	13	36	49	74																			
	Regina Pats	WHL	7	1	1	2	4																			
1988-89	Regina Pats	WHL	65	2	27	29	49																			
1989-90	Regina Pats	WHL	70	14	43	57	40												11	1	3	4	10			
1990-91	Regina Pats	WHL	8	1	6	7	6												16	3	14	17	22			
	Lethbridge	WHL	62	9	32	41	113												5	1	2	3	13			
1991-92	Lethbridge	WHL	65	23	62	85	155												5	0	1	1	0			
	Peoria Rivermen	IHL	1	0	2	2	0																			
1992-93	Peoria Rivermen	IHL	72	2	28	30	67												4	1	1	2	0			
1993-94	**St. Louis**	**NHL**	2	0	0	0	0	0	0	0	0	0.0	1													
	Peoria Rivermen	IHL	78	12	31	43	96												6	0	3	3	31			
1994-95	Peoria Rivermen	IHL	69	7	25	32	137												4	2	4	6	8			
	St. Louis	**NHL**	5	0	0	0	2	0	0	0	1	0.0	-1													
1995-96	Rochester	AHL	62	5	50	55	71												19	3	11	14	12			
1996-97	Rochester	AHL	73	12	51	63	54												10	2	7	9	27			
1997-98	Worcester	AHL	55	8	24	32	34																			
	Houston Aeros	IHL	8	1	1	2	6												4	1	2	3	11			
1998-99	Utah Grizzlies	IHL	58	4	19	23	40																			
	Orlando	IHL	21	9	9	18	18												17	3	5	8	14			
99-2000	Orlando	IHL	20	4	4	8	13																			
	Manitoba Moose	IHL	18	3	10	13	4																			
	Providence Bruins	AHL	4	0	3	3	2												10	1	4	5	6			
	NHL Totals		7	0	0	0	2	0	0	0	1	0.0														

AHL Second All-Star Team (1996) • AHL First All-Star Team (1997)
Signed as a free agent by **Buffalo**, August 23, 1995. Signed as a free agent by **St. Louis**, July 28, 1997. Traded to **Orlando** (IHL) by **Utah** (IHL) for Rob Bonneau and Mike Nicholishen, March 1, 1999. Traded to **Manitoba** (IHL) by **Orlando** (IHL) for Jason McDonald, January 10, 2000. Traded to **Providence** (AHL) by **Manitoba** (IHL) for Sean Pronger and Keith McCambridge, March 16, 2000.

HOLMSTROM, Tomas
(HOHLM-struhm, TAW-mas) **DET.**

Left wing. Shoots left. 6', 200 lbs.   Born, Pitea, Sweden, January 23, 1973. Detroit's 9th choice, 257th overall, in 1994 Entry Draft.

Season	Club	League	GP	G	A	Pts	PIM	PP	SH	GW	S	%	+/-	TF	F%	H	SB	Min	GP	G	A	Pts	PIM	PP	SH	GW
1989-90	Pitea HC	Sweden-2	9	1	0	1	4																			
1990-91	Pitea HC	Sweden-2	26	5	4	9	16																			
1991-92	Pitea HC	Sweden-2	31	15	12	27	44																			
1992-93	Pitea HC	Sweden-2	32	17	15	32	30																			
1993-94	Bodens IK	Sweden-2	34	23	16	39	86												9	3	3	6	24			
1994-95	Lulea HF	Sweden	40	14	14	28	56												8	1	2	3	20			
1995-96	Lulea HF	Sweden	34	12	11	23	78												11	6	2	8	22			
1996-97♦	**Detroit**	**NHL**	47	6	3	9	33	3	0	0	53	11.3	-10						1	0	0	0	0	0	0	0
	Adirondack	AHL	6	3	1	4	7																			
1997-98	**Detroit**	**NHL**	57	5	17	22	44	1	0	1	48	10.4	6						22	7	12	19	16	2	0	0
1998-99	**Detroit**	**NHL**	82	13	21	34	69	5	0	4	100	13.0	-11	0	0.0	94	9	12:22	10	4	3	7	4	2	0	1
99-2000	**Detroit**	**NHL**	72	13	22	35	43	4	0	1	71	18.3	4	0	0.0	68	9	12:06	9	3	1	4	16	1	0	1
	NHL Totals		258	37	63	100	189	13	0	6	272	13.6		0	0.0	162	18	12:15	42	14	16	30	36	5	0	2

HOLZINGER, Brian
(HOHL-zihn-guhr, BRIGH-an) **T.B.**

Center. Shoots right. 5'11", 190 lbs.   Born, Parma, OH, October 10, 1972. Buffalo's 7th choice, 124th overall, in 1991 Entry Draft.

Season	Club	League	GP	G	A	Pts	PIM	PP	SH	GW	S	%	+/-	TF	F%	H	SB	Min	GP	G	A	Pts	PIM	PP	SH	GW
1988-89	Padua High	Hi-School	35	73	65	138																				
1989-90	Detroit	NAJHL	44	36	37	73																				
1990-91	Detroit	NAJHL	37	45	41	86	16																			
1991-92	Bowling Green	CCHA	30	14	8	22	36																			
1992-93	Bowling Green	CCHA	41	31	26	57	44																			
1993-94	Bowling Green	CCHA	38	22	15	37	24																			
1994-95	Bowling Green	CCHA	38	35	33	68	42																			
	Buffalo	**NHL**	4	0	3	3	0	0	0	0	3	0.0	2						4	2	1	3	2	1	0	0
1995-96	**Buffalo**	**NHL**	58	10	10	20	37	5	0	1	71	14.1	-21													
	Rochester	AHL	17	10	11	21	14												19	10	14	24	10			
1996-97	**Buffalo**	**NHL**	81	22	29	51	54	2	2	6	142	15.5	9						12	2	5	7	8	0	1	0
1997-98	**Buffalo**	**NHL**	69	14	21	35	36	4	2	1	116	12.1	-2						15	4	7	11	18	1	1	0
1998-99	**Buffalo**	**NHL**	81	17	17	34	45	5	0	2	143	11.9	2	852	50.4	72	23	16:31	21	3	6	9	33	1	0	0
99-2000	**Buffalo**	**NHL**	59	7	17	24	30	0	1	2	81	8.6	4	839	45.6	60	18	14:38								
	Tampa Bay	**NHL**	14	3	3	6	21	1	1	0	23	13.0	-7	119	46.2	16	3	16:10								
	NHL Totals		366	73	100	173	223	17	6	12	579	12.6		1810	47.9	148	44	15:46	52	11	18	29	61	3	2	0

CCHA Second All-Star Team (1993) • CCHA First All-Star Team (1995) • NCAA West First All-American Team (1995) • Won Hobey Baker Memorial Award (Top U.S. Collegiate Player) (1995)
Traded to **Tampa Bay** by **Buffalo** with Cory Sarich, Wayne Primeau and Buffalo's 3rd round choice (Alexandre Kharitonov) in 2000 Entry Draft for Chris Gratton and Tampa Bay's 2nd round choice in 2001 Entry Draft, March 9, 2000.

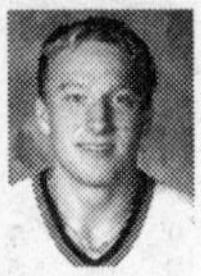

HOSSA, Marian
(HOH-sah, MAIR-ee-an) **OTT.**

Wing. Shoots left. 6'1", 199 lbs. Born, Stara Lubovna, Czech., January 12, 1979. Ottawa's 1st choice, 12th overall, in 1997 Entry Draft.

			Regular Season																Playoffs							
Season	Club	League	GP	G	A	Pts	PIM	PP	SH	GW	S	%	+/-	TF	F%	H	SB	Min	GP	G	A	Pts	PIM	PP	SH	GW
1995-96	Dukla Trencin	Slovak-Jr.	53	42	49	91	26	....	....	....	....	....	....	....	....	....	....	....	....	....	....	....	....	....	....	....
1996-97	Dukla Trencin	Slovakia	46	25	19	44	33	....	....	....	....	....	....	....	....	....	....	....	7	5	5	10	....	....	....	....
1997-98	Portland	WHL	53	45	40	85	50	....	....	....	....	....	....	....	....	....	....	....	16	13	6	19	6	....	....	....
	Ottawa	**NHL**	**7**	**0**	**1**	**1**	**0**	**0**	**0**	**0**	**10**	**0.0**	**–1**	....	....	....	....	....	....	....	....	....	....	....	....	....
1998-99	**Ottawa**	**NHL**	**60**	**15**	**15**	**30**	**37**	**1**	**0**	**2**	**124**	**12.1**	**18**	**4**	**25.0**	**59**	**6**	**13:59**	**4**	**0**	**2**	**2**	**4**	**0**	**0**	**0**
99-2000	**Ottawa**	**NHL**	**78**	**29**	**27**	**56**	**32**	**5**	**0**	**4**	**240**	**12.1**	**5**	**7**	**57.1**	**100**	**18**	**17:12**	**6**	**0**	**0**	**0**	**2**	**0**	**0**	**0**
	NHL Totals		**145**	**44**	**43**	**87**	**69**	**6**	**0**	**6**	**374**	**11.8**		**11**	**45.5**	**159**	**24**	**15:48**	**10**	**0**	**2**	**2**	**6**	**0**	**0**	**0**

WHL West First All-Star Team (1998) • Canadian Major Junior First All-Star Team (1998) • Memorial Cup All-Star Team (1998) • NHL All-Rookie Team (1999)

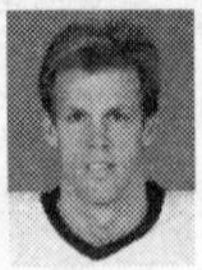

HOUDA, Doug
(HOO-duh, DUHG) **BUF.**

Defense. Shoots right. 6'2", 209 lbs. Born, Blairmore, Alta., June 3, 1966. Detroit's 2nd choice, 28th overall, in 1984 Entry Draft.

			Regular Season																Playoffs							
Season	Club	League	GP	G	A	Pts	PIM	PP	SH	GW	S	%	+/-	TF	F%	H	SB	Min	GP	G	A	Pts	PIM	PP	SH	GW
1982-83	Calgary Wranglers	WHL	71	5	23	28	99	....	....	....	....	....	....	....	....	....	....	....	16	1	3	4	44	....	....	....
1983-84	Calgary Wranglers	WHL	69	6	30	36	195	....	....	....	....	....	....	....	....	....	....	....	4	0	0	0	7	....	....	....
1984-85	Calgary Wranglers	WHL	65	20	54	74	182	....	....	....	....	....	....	....	....	....	....	....	8	3	4	7	29	....	....	....
	Kalamazoo Wings	IHL	....	....	....	....	....	....	....	....	....	....	....	....	....	....	....	....	7	0	2	2	10	....	....	....
1985-86	Calgary Wranglers	WHL	16	4	10	14	60	....	....	....	....	....	....	....	....	....	....	....	....	....	....	....	....	....	....	....
	Medicine Hat	WHL	35	9	23	32	80	....	....	....	....	....	....	....	....	....	....	....	25	4	19	23	64	....	....	....
	Detroit	**NHL**	**6**	**0**	**0**	**0**	**4**	**0**	**0**	**0**	**5**	**0.0**	**–7**	....	....	....	....	....	....	....	....	....	....	....	....	....
1986-87	Adirondack	AHL	77	6	23	29	142	....	....	....	....	....	....	....	....	....	....	....	11	1	8	9	50	....	....	....
1987-88	**Detroit**	**NHL**	**11**	**1**	**1**	**2**	**10**	**0**	**0**	**0**	**10**	**10.0**	**0**	....	....	....	....	....	....	....	....	....	....	....	....	....
	Adirondack	AHL	71	10	32	42	169	....	....	....	....	....	....	....	....	....	....	....	11	0	3	3	44	....	....	....
1988-89	**Detroit**	**NHL**	**57**	**2**	**11**	**13**	**67**	**0**	**0**	**0**	**38**	**5.3**	**17**	....	....	....	....	....	**6**	**0**	**1**	**1**	**0**	**0**	**0**	**0**
	Adirondack	AHL	7	0	3	3	8	....	....	....	....	....	....	....	....	....	....	....	....	....	....	....	....	....	....	....
1989-90	**Detroit**	**NHL**	**73**	**2**	**9**	**11**	**127**	**0**	**0**	**0**	**59**	**3.4**	**–5**	....	....	....	....	....	....	....	....	....	....	....	....	....
1990-91	**Detroit**	**NHL**	**22**	**0**	**4**	**4**	**43**	**0**	**0**	**0**	**21**	**0.0**	**–2**	....	....	....	....	....	....	....	....	....	....	....	....	....
	Adirondack	AHL	38	9	17	26	67	....	....	....	....	....	....	....	....	....	....	....	....	....	....	....	....	....	....	....
	Hartford	**NHL**	**19**	**1**	**2**	**3**	**41**	**0**	**0**	**0**	**21**	**4.8**	**–3**	....	....	....	....	....	**6**	**0**	**0**	**0**	**8**	**0**	**0**	**0**
1991-92	**Hartford**	**NHL**	**56**	**3**	**6**	**9**	**125**	**1**	**0**	**1**	**40**	**7.5**	**–2**	....	....	....	....	....	**6**	**0**	**2**	**2**	**13**	**0**	**0**	**0**
1992-93	**Hartford**	**NHL**	**60**	**2**	**6**	**8**	**167**	**0**	**0**	**0**	**43**	**4.7**	**–19**	....	....	....	....	....	....	....	....	....	....	....	....	....
1993-94	**Hartford**	**NHL**	**7**	**0**	**0**	**0**	**23**	**0**	**0**	**0**	**1**	**0.0**	**–4**	....	....	....	....	....	....	....	....	....	....	....	....	....
	Los Angeles	**NHL**	**54**	**2**	**6**	**8**	**165**	**0**	**0**	**0**	**31**	**6.5**	**–15**	....	....	....	....	....	....	....	....	....	....	....	....	....
1994-95	**Buffalo**	**NHL**	**28**	**1**	**2**	**3**	**68**	**0**	**0**	**0**	**21**	**4.8**	**1**	....	....	....	....	....	....	....	....	....	....	....	....	....
1995-96	**Buffalo**	**NHL**	**38**	**1**	**3**	**4**	**52**	**0**	**0**	**0**	**21**	**4.8**	**3**	....	....	....	....	....	....	....	....	....	....	....	....	....
	Rochester	AHL	21	1	6	7	41	....	....	....	....	....	....	....	....	....	....	....	19	3	5	8	30	....	....	....
1996-97	**NY Islanders**	**NHL**	**70**	**2**	**8**	**10**	**99**	**0**	**0**	**0**	**29**	**6.9**	**1**	....	....	....	....	....	....	....	....	....	....	....	....	....
	Utah Grizzlies	IHL	3	0	0	0	7	....	....	....	....	....	....	....	....	....	....	....	....	....	....	....	....	....	....	....
1997-98	**NY Islanders**	**NHL**	**31**	**1**	**2**	**3**	**47**	**0**	**0**	**0**	**15**	**6.7**	**–6**	....	....	....	....	....	....	....	....	....	....	....	....	....
	Anaheim	**NHL**	**24**	**1**	**2**	**3**	**52**	**0**	**1**	**0**	**9**	**11.1**	**–5**	....	....	....	....	....	....	....	....	....	....	....	....	....
1998-99	**Detroit**	**NHL**	**3**	**0**	**1**	**1**	**0**	**0**	**0**	**0**	**1**	**0.0**	**–2**	**0**	**0.0**	**4**	**1**	**6:51**	....	....	....	....	....	....	....	....
	Adirondack	AHL	73	7	21	28	122	....	....	....	....	....	....	....	....	....	....	....	3	0	1	1	4	....	....	....
99-2000	**Buffalo**	**NHL**	**1**	**0**	**0**	**0**	**12**	**0**	**0**	**0**	**0**	**0.0**	**0**	**0**	**0.0**	**5**	**0**	**9:10**	....	....	....	....	....	....	....	....
	Rochester	AHL	79	7	17	24	175	....	....	....	....	....	....	....	....	....	....	....	21	1	8	9	39	....	....	....
	NHL Totals		**560**	**19**	**63**	**82**	**1102**	**1**	**1**	**1**	**365**	**5.2**		**0**	**0.0**	**9**	**1**	**7:26**	**18**	**0**	**3**	**3**	**21**	**0**	**0**	**0**

WHL East Second All-Star Team (1985) • AHL First All-Star Team (1988)

Traded to **Hartford** by **Detroit** for Doug Crossman, February 20, 1991. Traded to **LA Kings** by **Hartford** for Marc Potvin, November 3, 1993. Traded to **Buffalo** by **LA Kings** for Sean O'Donnell, July 26, 1994. Signed as a free agent by **NY Islanders**, October 26, 1996. Traded to **Anaheim** by **NY Islanders** with Travis Green and Tony Tuzzolino for Joe Sacco, J.J. Daigneault and Mark Janssens, February 6, 1998. Traded to **Detroit** by **Anaheim** for future considerations, October 9, 1998. Signed as a free agent by **Buffalo**, July 13, 1999.

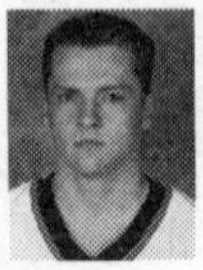

HOUDE, Eric
(OOD, AIR-ihk) **DAL.**

Center. Shoots left. 5'11", 191 lbs. Born, Montreal, Que., December 19, 1976. Montreal's 9th choice, 216th overall, in 1995 Entry Draft.

			Regular Season																Playoffs							
Season	Club	League	GP	G	A	Pts	PIM	PP	SH	GW	S	%	+/-	TF	F%	H	SB	Min	GP	G	A	Pts	PIM	PP	SH	GW
1992-93	St-Hubert	QAAA	35	45	40	85		....	....	....	....	....	....	....	....	....	....	....	....	....	....	....	....	....	....	....
1993-94	St-Jean Lynx	QMJHL	71	16	16	32	14	....	....	....	....	....	....	....	....	....	....	....	5	1	1	2	4	....	....	....
1994-95	St-Jean Lynx	QMJHL	40	10	13	23	23	....	....	....	....	....	....	....	....	....	....	....	....	....	....	....	....	....	....	....
	Halifax	QMJHL	28	13	23	36	8	....	....	....	....	....	....	....	....	....	....	....	3	2	1	3	4	....	....	....
1995-96	Halifax	QMJHL	69	40	48	88	35	....	....	....	....	....	....	....	....	....	....	....	6	3	4	7	2	....	....	....
1996-97	**Montreal**	**NHL**	**13**	**0**	**2**	**2**	**2**	**0**	**0**	**0**	**1**	**0.0**	**1**	....	....	....	....	....	....	....	....	....	....	....	....	....
	Fredericton	AHL	66	30	36	66	20	....	....	....	....	....	....	....	....	....	....	....	....	....	....	....	....	....	....	....
1997-98	**Montreal**	**NHL**	**9**	**1**	**0**	**1**	**0**	**0**	**0**	**1**	**4**	**25.0**	**–3**	....	....	....	....	....	....	....	....	....	....	....	....	....
	Fredericton	AHL	71	28	42	70	24	....	....	....	....	....	....	....	....	....	....	....	4	5	2	7	4	....	....	....
1998-99	**Montreal**	**NHL**	**8**	**1**	**1**	**2**	**2**	**0**	**0**	**1**	**4**	**25.0**	**–2**	**41**	**46.3**	**4**	**0**	**7:11**	....	....	....	....	....	....	....	....
	Fredericton	AHL	69	27	37	64	32	....	....	....	....	....	....	....	....	....	....	....	14	2	7	9	4	....	....	....
99-2000	Hamilton Bulldogs	AHL	18	3	4	7	10	....	....	....	....	....	....	....	....	....	....	....	....	....	....	....	....	....	....	....
	Springfield	AHL	57	28	34	62	43	....	....	....	....	....	....	....	....	....	....	....	5	2	2	4	2	....	....	....
	NHL Totals		**30**	**2**	**3**	**5**	**4**	**0**	**0**	**2**	**9**	**22.2**		**41**	**46.3**	**4**	**0**	**7:11**	....	....	....	....	....	....	....	....

Signed as a free agent by **Edmonton**, August 11, 1999. Traded to **Phoenix** by **Edmonton** for Rob Murray, November 30, 1999. Signed as a free agent by **Dallas**, July 28, 2000.

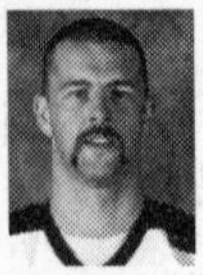

HOULDER, Bill
(HOHL-duhr, BIHL) **NSH.**

Defense. Shoots left. 6'2", 215 lbs. Born, Thunder Bay, Ont., March 11, 1967. Washington's 4th choice, 82nd overall, in 1985 Entry Draft.

			Regular Season																Playoffs							
Season	Club	League	GP	G	A	Pts	PIM	PP	SH	GW	S	%	+/-	TF	F%	H	SB	Min	GP	G	A	Pts	PIM	PP	SH	GW
1983-84	Thunder Bay	TBJHL	23	4	18	22	37	....	....	....	....	....	....	....	....	....	....	....	....	....	....	....	....	....	....	....
1984-85	North Bay	OHL	66	4	20	24	37	....	....	....	....	....	....	....	....	....	....	....	8	0	0	0	2	....	....	....
1985-86	North Bay	OHL	59	5	30	35	97	....	....	....	....	....	....	....	....	....	....	....	10	1	6	7	12	....	....	....
1986-87	North Bay	OHL	62	17	51	68	68	....	....	....	....	....	....	....	....	....	....	....	22	4	19	23	20	....	....	....
1987-88	**Washington**	**NHL**	**30**	**1**	**2**	**3**	**10**	**0**	**0**	**0**	**20**	**5.0**	**–2**	....	....	....	....	....	....	....	....	....	....	....	....	....
	Fort Wayne	IHL	43	10	14	24	32	....	....	....	....	....	....	....	....	....	....	....	....	....	....	....	....	....	....	....
1988-89	**Washington**	**NHL**	**8**	**0**	**3**	**3**	**4**	**0**	**0**	**0**	**5**	**0.0**	**7**	....	....	....	....	....	....	....	....	....	....	....	....	....
	Baltimore	AHL	65	10	36	46	50	....	....	....	....	....	....	....	....	....	....	....	....	....	....	....	....	....	....	....
1989-90	**Washington**	**NHL**	**41**	**1**	**11**	**12**	**28**	**0**	**0**	**0**	**49**	**2.0**	**8**	....	....	....	....	....	....	....	....	....	....	....	....	....
	Baltimore	AHL	26	3	7	10	12	....	....	....	....	....	....	....	....	....	....	....	7	0	2	2	2	....	....	....
1990-91	**Buffalo**	**NHL**	**7**	**0**	**2**	**2**	**4**	**0**	**0**	**0**	**7**	**0.0**	**–2**	....	....	....	....	....	....	....	....	....	....	....	....	....
	Rochester	AHL	69	13	53	66	28	....	....	....	....	....	....	....	....	....	....	....	15	5	13	18	4	....	....	....
1991-92	**Buffalo**	**NHL**	**10**	**1**	**0**	**1**	**8**	**0**	**0**	**0**	**18**	**5.6**	**–2**	....	....	....	....	....	....	....	....	....	....	....	....	....
	Rochester	AHL	42	8	26	34	16	....	....	....	....	....	....	....	....	....	....	....	16	5	6	11	4	....	....	....
1992-93	**Buffalo**	**NHL**	**15**	**3**	**5**	**8**	**6**	**0**	**0**	**0**	**29**	**10.3**	**5**	....	....	....	....	....	**8**	**0**	**2**	**2**	**4**	**0**	**0**	**0**
	San Diego Gulls	IHL	64	24	48	72	39	....	....	....	....	....	....	....	....	....	....	....	....	....	....	....	....	....	....	....
1993-94	**Anaheim**	**NHL**	**80**	**14**	**25**	**39**	**40**	**3**	**0**	**3**	**187**	**7.5**	**–18**	....	....	....	....	....	....	....	....	....	....	....	....	....
1994-95	**St. Louis**	**NHL**	**41**	**5**	**13**	**18**	**20**	**1**	**0**	**0**	**59**	**8.5**	**16**	....	....	....	....	....	**4**	**1**	**1**	**2**	**0**	**0**	**0**	**0**
1995-96	**Tampa Bay**	**NHL**	**61**	**5**	**23**	**28**	**22**	**3**	**0**	**0**	**90**	**5.6**	**1**	....	....	....	....	....	**6**	**0**	**1**	**1**	**4**	**0**	**0**	**0**
1996-97	**Tampa Bay**	**NHL**	**79**	**4**	**21**	**25**	**30**	**0**	**0**	**2**	**116**	**3.4**	**16**	....	....	....	....	....	....	....	....	....	....	....	....	....
1997-98	**San Jose**	**NHL**	**82**	**7**	**25**	**32**	**48**	**4**	**0**	**2**	**102**	**6.9**	**13**	....	....	....	....	....	**6**	**1**	**2**	**3**	**2**	**0**	**0**	**0**
1998-99	**San Jose**	**NHL**	**76**	**9**	**23**	**32**	**40**	**7**	**0**	**5**	**115**	**7.8**	**8**	**0**	**0.0**	**70**	**83**	**22:08**	**6**	**3**	**0**	**3**	**4**	**3**	**0**	**0**
99-2000	**Tampa Bay**	**NHL**	**14**	**1**	**2**	**3**	**2**	**1**	**0**	**0**	**21**	**4.8**	**–3**	**1**	**100.0**	**12**	**26**	**21:29**	....	....	....	....	....	....	....	....
	Nashville	**NHL**	**57**	**2**	**12**	**14**	**24**	**1**	**0**	**1**	**68**	**2.9**	**–6**	**1**	**100.0**	**56**	**71**	**22:36**	....	....	....	....	....	....	....	....
	NHL Totals		**601**	**53**	**167**	**220**	**286**	**20**	**0**	**13**	**886**	**6.0**		**2**	**100.0**	**138**	**180**	**22:15**	**30**	**5**	**6**	**11**	**14**	**3**	**0**	**0**

AHL First All-Star Team (1991) • Won Governor's Trophy (Outstanding Defenseman - IHL) (1993) • IHL First All-Star Team (1993)

Traded to **Buffalo** by **Washington** for Shawn Anderson, September 30, 1990. Claimed by **Anaheim** from **Buffalo** in Expansion Draft, June 24, 1993. Traded to **St. Louis** by **Anaheim** for Jason Marshall, August 29, 1994. Signed as a free agent by **Tampa Bay**, July 26, 1995. Signed as a free agent by **San Jose**, July 16, 1997. Traded to **Tampa Bay** by **San Jose** with Andrei Zyuzin, Shawn Burr and Steve Guolla for Niklas Sundstrom and NY Rangers' 3rd round choice (previously acquired, later traded to Chicago - Chicago selected Igor Radulov) in 2000 Entry Draft, August 4, 1999. Claimed on waivers by **Nashville** from **Tampa Bay**, November 10, 1999.

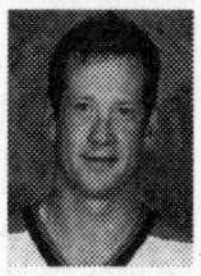

HOUSLEY, Phil

(HOWZ-lee, FIHL) **CGY.**

Defense. Shoots left. 5'10", 185 lbs. Born, St. Paul, MN, March 9, 1964. Buffalo's 1st choice, 6th overall, in 1982 Entry Draft.

			Regular Season																Playoffs							
Season	Club	League	GP	G	A	Pts	PIM	PP	SH	GW	S	%	+/–	TF	F%	H	SB	Min	GP	G	A	Pts	PIM	PP	SH	GW
1980-81	St. Paul Vulcans	USHL	6	7	7	14	6	....	....	....	....	....	....	....	....	....	....	....	10	5	5	10	0	....	....	....
1981-82	South St. Paul	Hi-School	22	31	34	65	18	....	....	....	....	....	....	....	....	....	....	....	....	....	....	....	....	....	....	....
1982-83	**Buffalo**	**NHL**	**77**	**19**	**47**	**66**	**39**	**11**	**0**	**2**	**183**	**10.4**	**–4**	....	....	....	....	....	**10**	**3**	**4**	**7**	**2**	**1**	**0**	**0**
1983-84	**Buffalo**	**NHL**	**75**	**31**	**46**	**77**	**33**	**13**	**2**	**6**	**234**	**13.2**	**3**	....	....	....	....	....	**3**	**0**	**0**	**0**	**6**	**0**	**0**	**0**
1984-85	**Buffalo**	**NHL**	**73**	**16**	**53**	**69**	**28**	**3**	**0**	**4**	**188**	**8.5**	**15**	....	....	....	....	....	**5**	**3**	**2**	**5**	**2**	**0**	**0**	**0**
1985-86	**Buffalo**	**NHL**	**79**	**15**	**47**	**62**	**54**	**7**	**0**	**2**	**180**	**8.3**	**–9**	....	....	....	....	....	....	....	....	....	....	....	....	....
1986-87	**Buffalo**	**NHL**	**78**	**21**	**46**	**67**	**57**	**8**	**1**	**2**	**202**	**10.4**	**–2**	....	....	....	....	....	....	....	....	....	....	....	....	....
1987-88	**Buffalo**	**NHL**	**74**	**29**	**37**	**66**	**96**	**6**	**0**	**1**	**231**	**12.6**	**–17**	....	....	....	....	....	**6**	**2**	**4**	**6**	**6**	**1**	**0**	**0**
1988-89	**Buffalo**	**NHL**	**72**	**26**	**44**	**70**	**47**	**5**	**0**	**3**	**178**	**14.6**	**6**	....	....	....	....	....	**5**	**1**	**3**	**4**	**2**	**0**	**0**	**0**
1989-90	**Buffalo**	**NHL**	**80**	**21**	**60**	**81**	**32**	**8**	**1**	**4**	**201**	**10.4**	**11**	....	....	....	....	....	**6**	**1**	**4**	**5**	**4**	**1**	**0**	**0**
1990-91	**Winnipeg**	**NHL**	**78**	**23**	**53**	**76**	**24**	**12**	**1**	**3**	**206**	**11.2**	**–13**	....	....	....	....	....	....	....	....	....	....	....	....	....
1991-92	**Winnipeg**	**NHL**	**74**	**23**	**63**	**86**	**92**	**11**	**0**	**4**	**234**	**9.8**	**–5**	....	....	....	....	....	**7**	**1**	**4**	**5**	**0**	**1**	**0**	**1**
1992-93	**Winnipeg**	**NHL**	**80**	**18**	**79**	**97**	**52**	**6**	**0**	**2**	**249**	**7.2**	**–14**	....	....	....	....	....	**6**	**0**	**7**	**7**	**2**	**0**	**0**	**0**
1993-94	**St. Louis**	**NHL**	**26**	**7**	**15**	**22**	**12**	**4**	**0**	**1**	**60**	**11.7**	**–5**	....	....	....	....	....	**4**	**2**	**1**	**3**	**4**	**2**	**0**	**0**
1994-95	ZSC Zurich	Switz.	10	6	8	14	34	....	....	....	....	....	....	....	....	....	....	....	....	....	....	....	....	....	....	....
	Calgary	**NHL**	**43**	**8**	**35**	**43**	**18**	**3**	**0**	**0**	**135**	**5.9**	**17**	....	....	....	....	....	**7**	**0**	**9**	**9**	**0**	**0**	**0**	**0**
1995-96	**Calgary**	**NHL**	**59**	**16**	**36**	**52**	**22**	**6**	**0**	**1**	**155**	**10.3**	**–2**	....	....	....	....	....	....	....	....	....	....	....	....	....
	New Jersey	**NHL**	**22**	**1**	**15**	**16**	**8**	**0**	**0**	**0**	**50**	**2.0**	**–4**	....	....	....	....	....	....	....	....	....	....	....	....	....
1996-97	**Washington**	**NHL**	**77**	**11**	**29**	**40**	**24**	**3**	**1**	**2**	**167**	**6.6**	**–10**	....	....	....	....	....	....	....	....	....	....	....	....	....
1997-98	**Washington**	**NHL**	**64**	**6**	**25**	**31**	**24**	**4**	**1**	**0**	**116**	**5.2**	**–10**	....	....	....	....	....	**18**	**0**	**4**	**4**	**4**	**0**	**0**	**0**
1998-99	**Calgary**	**NHL**	**79**	**11**	**43**	**54**	**52**	**4**	**0**	**1**	**193**	**5.7**	**14**	**0**	**0.0**	**21**	**52**	**20:52**	....	....	....	....	....	....	....	....
99-2000	**Calgary**	**NHL**	**78**	**11**	**44**	**55**	**24**	**5**	**0**	**2**	**176**	**6.3**	**–12**	**1**	**0.0**	**23**	**50**	**23:29**	....	....	....	....	....	....	....	....
	NHL Totals		**1288**	**313**	**817**	**1130**	**738**	**119**	**7**	**40**	**3338**	**9.4**		**1**	**0.0**	**44**	**102**	**22:10**	**77**	**13**	**42**	**55**	**32**	**6**	**0**	**1**

NHL All-Rookie Team (1983) • NHL Second All-Star Team (1992) • Played in NHL All-Star Game (1984, 1989, 1990, 1991, 1992, 1993, 2000)

Traded to **Winnipeg** by **Buffalo** with Scott Arniel, Jeff Parker and Buffalo's 1st round choice (Keith Tkachuk) in 1990 Entry Draft for Dale Hawerchuk, Winnipeg's 1st round choice (Brad May) in 1990 Entry Draft and future considerations, June 16, 1990. Traded to **St. Louis** by **Winnipeg** for Nelson Emerson and Stephane Quintal, September 24, 1993. Traded to **Calgary** by **St. Louis** with St. Louis' 2nd round choices in 1996 (Steve Begin) and 1997 (John Tripp) Entry Drafts for Al MacInnis and Calgary's 4th round choice (Didier Tremblay) in 1997 Entry Draft, July 4, 1994. Traded to **New Jersey** by **Calgary** with Dan Keczmer for Tommy Albelin, Cale Hulse and Jocelyn Lemieux, February 26, 1996. Signed as a free agent by **Washington**, July 22, 1996. Claimed on waivers by **Calgary** from **Washington**, July 21, 1998.

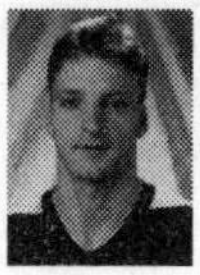

HRDINA, Jan

(hir-DEE-nah, YAN) **PIT.**

Center. Shoots right. 6', 200 lbs. Born, Hradec Kralove, Czech., February 5, 1976. Pittsburgh's 4th choice, 128th overall, in 1995 Entry Draft.

Season	Club	League	GP	G	A	Pts	PIM	PP	SH	GW	S	%	+/–	TF	F%	H	SB	Min	GP	G	A	Pts	PIM	PP	SH	GW
1993-94	HC Stadion-Jr.	Cze-Rep	10	1	6	7	0	....	....	....	....	....	....	....	....	....	....	....	....	....	....	....	....	....	....	....
	HC Stadion	Cze-Rep	23	1	5	6	....	....	....	....	....	....	....	....	....	....	....	....	4	0	1	1	....	....	....	....
1994-95	Seattle T-Birds	WHL	69	41	59	100	79	....	....	....	....	....	....	....	....	....	....	....	4	0	1	1	8	....	....	....
1995-96	Seattle T-Birds	WHL	30	19	28	47	37	....	....	....	....	....	....	....	....	....	....	....	....	....	....	....	....	....	....	....
	Spokane Chiefs	WHL	18	10	16	26	25	....	....	....	....	....	....	....	....	....	....	....	18	5	14	19	49	....	....	....
1996-97	Cleveland	IHL	68	23	31	54	82	....	....	....	....	....	....	....	....	....	....	....	13	1	2	3	8	....	....	....
1997-98	Syracuse Crunch	AHL	72	20	24	44	82	....	....	....	....	....	....	....	....	....	....	....	5	1	3	4	10	....	....	....
1998-99	**Pittsburgh**	**NHL**	**82**	**13**	**29**	**42**	**40**	**3**	**0**	**2**	**94**	**13.8**	**–2**	**1461**	**56.7**	**104**	**26**	**16:26**	**13**	**4**	**1**	**5**	**12**	**1**	**0**	**1**
99-2000	**Pittsburgh**	**NHL**	**70**	**13**	**33**	**46**	**43**	**3**	**0**	**1**	**84**	**15.5**	**13**	**1392**	**53.7**	**57**	**24**	**18:47**	**9**	**4**	**8**	**12**	**2**	**1**	**0**	**0**
	NHL Totals		**152**	**26**	**62**	**88**	**83**	**6**	**0**	**3**	**178**	**14.6**		**2853**	**55.2**	**161**	**50**	**17:31**	**22**	**8**	**9**	**17**	**14**	**2**	**0**	**1**

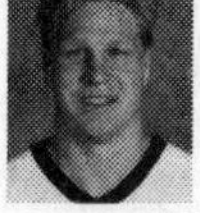

HRKAC, Tony

(HUHR-kuhz, TOH-nee) **ANA.**

Center. Shoots left. 5'11", 170 lbs. Born, Thunder Bay, Ont., July 7, 1966. St. Louis' 2nd choice, 32nd overall, in 1984 Entry Draft.

Season	Club	League	GP	G	A	Pts	PIM	PP	SH	GW	S	%	+/–	TF	F%	H	SB	Min	GP	G	A	Pts	PIM	PP	SH	GW
1983-84	Orillia Travelways	OJHL	42	*52	54	*106	20	....	....	....	....	....	....	....	....	....	....	....	....	....	....	....	....	....	....	....
1984-85	North Dakota	WCHA	36	18	36	54	16	....	....	....	....	....	....	....	....	....	....	....	....	....	....	....	....	....	....	....
1985-86	Canada	Nat-Team	62	19	30	49	36	....	....	....	....	....	....	....	....	....	....	....	....	....	....	....	....	....	....	....
1986-87	North Dakota	WCHA	48	46	70	116	48	....	....	....	....	....	....	....	....	....	....	....	....	....	....	....	....	....	....	....
	St. Louis	**NHL**	....	....	....	....	....	....	....	....	....	....	....	....	....	....	....	....	**3**	**0**	**0**	**0**	**0**	**0**	**0**	**0**
1987-88	**St. Louis**	**NHL**	**67**	**11**	**37**	**48**	**22**	**2**	**1**	**3**	**86**	**12.8**	**5**	....	....	....	....	....	**10**	**6**	**1**	**7**	**4**	**3**	**1**	**1**
1988-89	**St. Louis**	**NHL**	**70**	**17**	**28**	**45**	**8**	**5**	**0**	**1**	**133**	**12.8**	**–10**	....	....	....	....	....	**4**	**1**	**1**	**2**	**0**	**0**	**0**	**1**
1989-90	**St. Louis**	**NHL**	**28**	**5**	**12**	**17**	**8**	**1**	**0**	**0**	**41**	**12.2**	**1**	....	....	....	....	....	....	....	....	....	....	....	....	....
	Quebec	**NHL**	**22**	**4**	**8**	**12**	**2**	**2**	**0**	**0**	**29**	**13.8**	**–5**	....	....	....	....	....	....	....	....	....	....	....	....	....
	Halifax Citadels	AHL	20	12	21	33	4	....	....	....	....	....	....	....	....	....	....	....	6	5	9	14	4	....	....	....
1990-91	**Quebec**	**NHL**	**70**	**16**	**32**	**48**	**16**	**6**	**0**	**0**	**122**	**13.1**	**–22**	....	....	....	....	....	....	....	....	....	....	....	....	....
	Halifax Citadels	AHL	3	4	1	5	2	....	....	....	....	....	....	....	....	....	....	....	....	....	....	....	....	....	....	....
1991-92	**San Jose**	**NHL**	**22**	**2**	**10**	**12**	**4**	**0**	**0**	**0**	**31**	**6.5**	**–2**	....	....	....	....	....	....	....	....	....	....	....	....	....
	Chicago	**NHL**	**18**	**1**	**2**	**3**	**6**	**0**	**0**	**0**	**22**	**4.5**	**4**	....	....	....	....	....	**3**	**0**	**0**	**0**	**2**	**0**	**0**	**0**
1992-93	Indianapolis Ice	IHL	80	45	*87	*132	70	....	....	....	....	....	....	....	....	....	....	....	5	0	2	2	2	....	....	....
1993-94	**St. Louis**	**NHL**	**36**	**6**	**5**	**11**	**8**	**1**	**1**	**1**	**43**	**14.0**	**–11**	....	....	....	....	....	**4**	**0**	**0**	**0**	**0**	**0**	**0**	**0**
	Peoria Rivermen	IHL	45	30	51	81	25	....	....	....	....	....	....	....	....	....	....	....	1	1	2	3	0	....	....	....
1994-95	Milwaukee	IHL	71	24	67	91	26	....	....	....	....	....	....	....	....	....	....	....	15	4	9	13	16	....	....	....
1995-96	Milwaukee	IHL	43	14	28	42	18	....	....	....	....	....	....	....	....	....	....	....	5	1	3	4	4	....	....	....
1996-97	Milwaukee	IHL	81	27	61	88	20	....	....	....	....	....	....	....	....	....	....	....	3	1	1	2	2	....	....	....
1997-98	**Dallas**	**NHL**	**13**	**5**	**3**	**8**	**0**	**3**	**0**	**0**	**14**	**35.7**	**0**	....	....	....	....	....	....	....	....	....	....	....	....	....
	Michigan K-Wings	IHL	20	7	15	22	6	....	....	....	....	....	....	....	....	....	....	....	....	....	....	....	....	....	....	....
	Edmonton	**NHL**	**36**	**8**	**11**	**19**	**10**	**4**	**0**	**1**	**43**	**18.6**	**3**	....	....	....	....	....	**12**	**0**	**3**	**3**	**2**	**0**	**0**	**0**
1998-99♦	**Dallas**	**NHL**	**69**	**13**	**14**	**27**	**26**	**2**	**0**	**2**	**67**	**19.4**	**2**	**666**	**48.0**	**49**	**13**	**12:02**	**5**	**0**	**2**	**2**	**4**	**0**	**0**	**0**
99-2000	**NY Islanders**	**NHL**	**7**	**0**	**2**	**2**	**0**	**0**	**0**	**0**	**2**	**0.0**	**–1**	**34**	**35.3**	**2**	**0**	**11:22**	....	....	....	....	....	....	....	....
	Anaheim	**NHL**	**60**	**4**	**7**	**11**	**8**	**1**	**0**	**0**	**37**	**10.8**	**–2**	**536**	**50.8**	**22**	**11**	**9:04**	....	....	....	....	....	....	....	....
	NHL Totals		**518**	**92**	**171**	**263**	**118**	**27**	**2**	**8**	**670**	**13.7**		**1236**	**48.9**	**73**	**24**	**10:42**	**41**	**7**	**7**	**14**	**12**	**3**	**1**	**2**

WCHA First All-Star Team (1987) • NCAA West First All-American Team (1987) • NCAA Championship All-Tournament Team (1987) • NCAA Championship Tournament MVP (1987) • Won 1987 Hobey Baker Memorial Award (Top U.S. Collegiate Player) (1987) • Won James Gatschene Memorial Trophy (MVP - IHL) (1993) • Won Leo P. Lamoureux Memorial Trophy (Leading Scorer - IHL) (1993) • IHL First All-Star Team (1993)

Traded to **Quebec** by **St. Louis** with Greg Millen for Jeff Brown, December 13, 1989. Traded to **San Jose** by **Quebec** for Greg Paslawski, May 31, 1991. Traded to **Chicago** by **San Jose** for Chicago's 6th round choice (Fredrik Oduya) in 1993 Entry Draft, February 7, 1992. Signed as a free agent by **St. Louis**, July 30, 1993. Signed as a free agent by **Dallas**, August 12, 1997. Claimed on waivers by **Edmonton** from **Dallas**, January 6, 1998. Traded to **Pittsburgh** by **Edmonton** with Bobby Dollas for Josef Beranek, June 16, 1998. Claimed by **Nashville** from **Pittsburgh** in Expansion Draft, June 26, 1998. Traded to **Dallas** by **Nashville** for future considerations, July 9, 1998. Signed as a free agent by **NY Islanders**, July 29, 1999. Traded to **Anaheim** by **NY Islanders** with Dean Malkoc for Ted Drury, October 29, 1999.

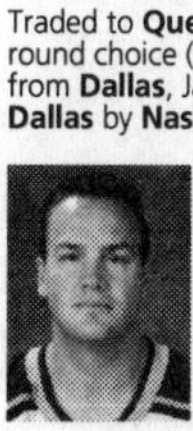

HUARD, Bill

(HEW-ahrd, BIHL)

Left wing. Shoots left. 6'1", 215 lbs. Born, Welland, Ont., June 24, 1967.

Season	Club	League	GP	G	A	Pts	PIM	PP	SH	GW	S	%	+/–	TF	F%	H	SB	Min	GP	G	A	Pts	PIM	PP	SH	GW
1984-85	Fort Erie Meteors	OJHL-B	41	4	9	13	114	....	....	....	....	....	....	....	....	....	....	....	....	....	....	....	....	....	....	....
1985-86	Welland Cougars	OJHL-B	28	8	17	25	123	....	....	....	....	....	....	....	....	....	....	....	....	....	....	....	....	....	....	....
	Peterborough	OHL	7	1	1	2	2	....	....	....	....	....	....	....	....	....	....	....	....	....	....	....	....	....	....	....
1986-87	Peterborough	OHL	61	14	11	25	61	....	....	....	....	....	....	....	....	....	....	....	12	5	2	7	19	....	....	....
1987-88	Peterborough	OHL	66	28	33	61	132	....	....	....	....	....	....	....	....	....	....	....	12	7	8	15	33	....	....	....
1988-89	Carolina	ECHL	40	27	21	48	177	....	....	....	....	....	....	....	....	....	....	....	10	7	2	9	70	....	....	....
1989-90	Utica Devils	AHL	27	1	7	8	67	....	....	....	....	....	....	....	....	....	....	....	5	0	1	1	33	....	....	....
	Nashville Knights	ECHL	34	24	27	51	212	....	....	....	....	....	....	....	....	....	....	....	....	....	....	....	....	....	....	....
1990-91	Utica Devils	AHL	72	11	16	27	359	....	....	....	....	....	....	....	....	....	....	....	....	....	....	....	....	....	....	....
1991-92	Utica Devils	AHL	62	9	11	20	233	....	....	....	....	....	....	....	....	....	....	....	4	1	1	2	4	....	....	....
1992-93	**Boston**	**NHL**	**2**	**0**	**0**	**0**	**0**	**0**	**0**	**0**	**0**	**0.0**	**0**	....	....	....	....	....	....	....	....	....	....	....	....	....
	Providence Bruins	AHL	72	18	19	37	302	....	....	....	....	....	....	....	....	....	....	....	6	3	0	3	9	....	....	....
1993-94	**Ottawa**	**NHL**	**63**	**2**	**2**	**4**	**162**	**0**	**0**	**0**	**24**	**8.3**	**–19**	....	....	....	....	....	....	....	....	....	....	....	....	....
1994-95	**Ottawa**	**NHL**	**26**	**1**	**1**	**2**	**64**	**0**	**0**	**0**	**15**	**6.7**	**–2**	....	....	....	....	....	....	....	....	....	....	....	....	....
	Quebec	**NHL**	**7**	**2**	**2**	**4**	**13**	**0**	**0**	**0**	**6**	**33.3**	**2**	....	....	....	....	....	**1**	**0**	**0**	**0**	**0**	**0**	**0**	**0**
1995-96	**Dallas**	**NHL**	**51**	**6**	**6**	**12**	**176**	**0**	**0**	**0**	**34**	**17.6**	**3**	....	....	....	....	....	....	....	....	....	....	....	....	....
	Michigan K-Wings	IHL	12	1	1	2	74	....	....	....	....	....	....	....	....	....	....	....	....	....	....	....	....	....	....	....

			Regular Season																Playoffs							
Season	Club	League	GP	G	A	Pts	PIM	PP	SH	GW	S	%	+/–	TF	F%	H	SB	Min	GP	G	A	Pts	PIM	PP	SH	GW
1996-97	Dallas	NHL	40	5	6	11	105	0	0	0	34	14.7	5	....	....	....	....	....	....	....	....	....	....	....	....	....
1997-98	Edmonton	NHL	30	0	1	1	72	0	0	0	12	0.0	–5	....	....	....	....	....	4	0	0	0	2	0	0	0
1998-99	Edmonton	NHL	3	0	0	0	0	0	0	0	2	0.0	0	1	100.0	5	0	5:36	....	....	....	....	....	....	....	....
	Houston Aeros	IHL	38	9	5	14	201	....	....	....	....	....	....	....	....	....	....	....	10	0	0	0	8	....	....	....
99-2000	Los Angeles	NHL	1	0	0	0	2	0	0	0	0	0.0	0	0	0.0	1	0	2:14	....	....	....	....	....	....	....	....
	Lowell	AHL	13	2	2	4	65	....	....	....	....	....	....	....	....	....	....	....	....	....	....	....	....	....	....	....
	Orlando	IHL	19	4	2	6	85	....	....	....	....	....	....	....	....	....	....	....	3	0	0	0	10	....	....	....
	NHL Totals		223	16	18	34	594	0	0	0	127	12.6		1	100.0	6	0	4:46	5	0	0	0	2	0	0	0

Signed as a free agent by **New Jersey**, October 1, 1989. Signed as a free agent by **Boston**, December 4, 1992. Signed as a free agent by **Ottawa**, June 30, 1993. Traded to **Quebec** by **Ottawa** for the rights to Mika Stromberg and Quebec's 4th round choice (Kevin Boyd) in 1995 Entry Draft, April 7, 1995. Transferred to **Colorado** after **Quebec** franchise relocated, July 1, 1995. Claimed by **Dallas** from **Colorado** in NHL Waiver Draft, October 2, 1995. Signed as a free agent by **Edmonton**, July 22, 1997. Signed as a free agent by **Houston** (IHL), January 23, 1999. Signed as a free agent by **LA Kings**, July 19, 1999. Traded to **Atlanta** by **LA Kings** for future considerations, January 25, 2000.

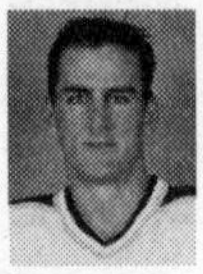

HULBIG, Joe

(HUHL-bihg, JOH) **BOS.**

Left wing. Shoots left. 6'3", 215 lbs. Born, Norwood, MA, September 29, 1973. Edmonton's 1st choice, 13th overall, in 1992 Entry Draft.

1989-90	St. Sebastian's	Hi-School	30	13	12	25	....	....	....	....	....	....	....	....	....	....	....	....	....	....	....	....	....	....	....	....
1990-91	St. Sebastian's	Hi-School	30	23	19	42	....	....	....	....	....	....	....	....	....	....	....	....	....	....	....	....	....	....	....	....
1991-92	St. Sebastian's	Hi-School	17	19	24	43	30	....	....	....	....	....	....	....	....	....	....	....	....	....	....	....	....	....	....	....
1992-93	Providence	H-East	26	3	13	16	22	....	....	....	....	....	....	....	....	....	....	....	....	....	....	....	....	....	....	....
1993-94	Providence	H-East	28	6	4	10	36	....	....	....	....	....	....	....	....	....	....	....	....	....	....	....	....	....	....	....
1994-95	Providence	H-East	37	14	21	35	36	....	....	....	....	....	....	....	....	....	....	....	....	....	....	....	....	....	....	....
1995-96	Providence	H-East	31	14	22	36	56	....	....	....	....	....	....	....	....	....	....	....	....	....	....	....	....	....	....	....
1996-97	Edmonton	NHL	6	0	0	0	0	0	0	0	4	0.0	–1	....	....	....	....	....	6	0	1	1	2	0	0	0
	Hamilton Bulldogs	AHL	73	18	28	46	59	....	....	....	....	....	....	....	....	....	....	....	16	6	10	16	6	....	....	....
1997-98	Edmonton	NHL	17	2	2	4	2	0	0	1	8	25.0	–1	....	....	....	....	....	....	....	....	....	....	....	....	....
	Hamilton Bulldogs	AHL	46	15	16	31	52	....	....	....	....	....	....	....	....	....	....	....	3	0	1	1	2	....	....	....
1998-99	Edmonton	NHL	1	0	0	0	2	0	0	0	2	0.0	1	0	0.0	0	1	8:20	....	....	....	....	....	....	....	....
	Hamilton Bulldogs	AHL	76	22	24	46	68	....	....	....	....	....	....	....	....	....	....	....	11	4	2	6	18	....	....	....
99-2000	Boston	NHL	24	2	2	4	8	0	0	0	15	13.3	–8	2	0.0	52	4	8:18	....	....	....	....	....	....	....	....
	Providence Bruins	AHL	15	4	5	9	17	....	....	....	....	....	....	....	....	....	....	....	....	....	....	....	....	....	....	....
	NHL Totals		48	4	4	8	12	0	0	1	29	13.8		2	0.0	52	5	8:18	6	0	1	1	2	0	0	0

Signed as a free agent by **Boston**, July 23, 1999.

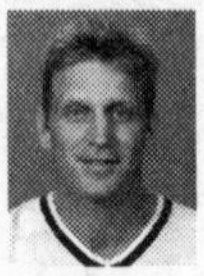

HULL, Brett

(HUHL, BREHT) **DAL.**

Right wing. Shoots right. 5'11", 203 lbs. Born, Belleville, Ont., August 9, 1964. Calgary's 6th choice, 117th overall, in 1984 Entry Draft.

1982-83	Penticton Knights	BCJHL	50	48	56	104	27	....	....	....	....	....	....	....	....	....	....	....	....	....	....	....	....	....	....	....
1983-84	Penticton Knights	BCJHL	56	*105	83	*188	20	....	....	....	....	....	....	....	....	....	....	....	....	....	....	....	....	....	....	....
1984-85	Minnesota-Duluth	WCHA	48	32	28	60	24	....	....	....	....	....	....	....	....	....	....	....	....	....	....	....	....	....	....	....
1985-86	Minnesota-Duluth	WCHA	42	52	32	84	46	....	....	....	....	....	....	....	....	....	....	....	....	....	....	....	....	....	....	....
	Calgary	NHL	....	....	....	....	....	....	....	....	....	....	....	....	....	....	....	....	2	0	0	0	0	0	0	0
1986-87	Calgary	NHL	5	1	0	1	0	0	0	1	5	20.0	–1	....	....	....	....	....	4	2	1	3	0	0	0	0
	Moncton Flames	AHL	67	50	42	92	16	....	....	....	....	....	....	....	....	....	....	....	3	2	2	4	2	....	....	....
1987-88	Calgary	NHL	52	26	24	50	12	4	0	3	153	17.0	10	....	....	....	....	....	....	....	....	....	....	....	....	....
	St. Louis	NHL	13	6	8	14	4	2	0	0	58	10.3	4	....	....	....	....	....	10	7	2	9	4	4	0	3
1988-89	St. Louis	NHL	78	41	43	84	33	16	0	6	305	13.4	–17	....	....	....	....	....	10	5	5	10	6	1	0	2
1989-90	St. Louis	NHL	80	*72	41	113	24	27	0	12	385	18.7	–1	....	....	....	....	....	12	13	8	21	17	7	0	3
1990-91	St. Louis	NHL	78	*86	45	131	22	29	0	11	389	22.1	23	....	....	....	....	....	13	11	8	19	4	3	0	2
1991-92	St. Louis	NHL	73	*70	39	109	48	20	5	9	408	17.2	–2	....	....	....	....	....	6	4	4	8	4	1	1	1
1992-93	St. Louis	NHL	80	54	47	101	41	29	0	2	390	13.8	–27	....	....	....	....	....	11	8	5	13	2	5	0	2
1993-94	St. Louis	NHL	81	57	40	97	38	25	3	6	392	14.5	–3	....	....	....	....	....	4	2	1	3	0	1	0	0
1994-95	St. Louis	NHL	48	29	21	50	10	9	3	6	200	14.5	13	....	....	....	....	....	7	6	2	8	0	2	0	0
1995-96	St. Louis	NHL	70	43	40	83	30	16	5	6	327	13.1	4	....	....	....	....	....	13	6	5	11	10	2	1	1
1996-97	St. Louis	NHL	77	42	40	82	10	12	2	6	302	13.9	–9	....	....	....	....	....	6	2	7	9	2	0	0	0
1997-98	St. Louis	NHL	66	27	45	72	26	10	0	6	211	12.8	–1	....	....	....	....	....	10	3	3	6	2	1	0	1
	United States	Olympics	4	2	1	3	0	....	....	....	....	....	....	....	....	....	....	....	....	....	....	....	....	....	....	....
1998-99♦	Dallas	NHL	60	32	26	58	30	15	0	11	192	16.7	19	12	50.0	9	18	17:24	22	8	7	15	4	3	0	2
99-2000	Dallas	NHL	79	24	35	59	43	11	0	3	223	10.8	–21	10	40.0	27	18	18:37	23	*11	*13	*24	4	3	0	4
	NHL Totals		940	610	494	1104	371	225	18	88	3940	15.5		22	45.5	36	36	18:05	153	88	71	159	59	33	2	21

WCHA First All-Star Team (1986) • AHL First All-Star Team (1987) • Won Dudley "Red" Garrett Memorial Trophy (Top Rookie - AHL) (1987) • NHL First All-Star Team (1990, 1991, 1992) • Won Lady Byng Trophy (1990) • Won Dodge Ram Tough Award (1990, 1991) • Won Hart Memorial Trophy (1991) • Won Lester B. Pearson Award (1991) • Won ProSet/NHL Player of the Year Award (1991) • Played in NHL All-Star Game (1989, 1990, 1992, 1993, 1994, 1996, 1997)

Traded to **St. Louis** by **Calgary** with Steve Bozek for Rob Ramage and Rick Wamsley, March 7, 1988. Signed as a free agent by **Dallas**, July 3, 1998.

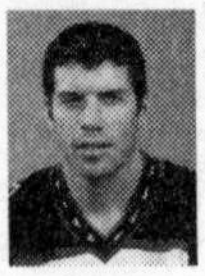

HULL, Jody

(HUHL, JOH-dee) **PHI.**

Right wing. Shoots right. 6'2", 200 lbs. Born, Petrolia, Ont., February 2, 1969. Hartford's 1st choice, 18th overall, in 1987 Entry Draft.

1984-85	Cambridge Hawks	OJHL-B	38	13	17	30	39	....	....	....	....	....	....	....	....	....	....	....	....	....	....	....	....	....	....	....
1985-86	Peterborough	OHL	61	20	22	42	29	....	....	....	....	....	....	....	....	....	....	....	16	1	5	6	4	....	....	....
1986-87	Peterborough	OHL	49	18	34	52	22	....	....	....	....	....	....	....	....	....	....	....	12	4	9	13	14	....	....	....
1987-88	Peterborough	OHL	60	50	44	94	33	....	....	....	....	....	....	....	....	....	....	....	12	10	8	18	8	....	....	....
1988-89	Hartford	NHL	60	16	18	34	10	6	0	2	82	19.5	6	....	....	....	....	....	1	0	0	0	2	0	0	0
1989-90	Hartford	NHL	38	7	10	17	21	2	0	0	46	15.2	–6	....	....	....	....	....	5	0	1	1	2	0	0	0
	Binghamton	AHL	21	7	10	17	6	....	....	....	....	....	....	....	....	....	....	....	....	....	....	....	....	....	....	....
1990-91	NY Rangers	NHL	47	5	8	13	10	0	0	0	57	8.8	2	....	....	....	....	....	....	....	....	....	....	....	....	....
1991-92	NY Rangers	NHL	3	0	0	0	2	0	0	0	4	0.0	–4	....	....	....	....	....	....	....	....	....	....	....	....	....
	Binghamton	AHL	69	34	31	65	28	....	....	....	....	....	....	....	....	....	....	....	11	5	2	7	4	....	....	....
1992-93	Ottawa	NHL	69	13	21	34	14	5	1	0	134	9.7	–24	....	....	....	....	....	....	....	....	....	....	....	....	....
1993-94	Florida	NHL	69	13	13	26	8	0	1	5	100	13.0	6	....	....	....	....	....	....	....	....	....	....	....	....	....
1994-95	Florida	NHL	46	11	8	19	8	0	0	4	63	17.5	–1	....	....	....	....	....	....	....	....	....	....	....	....	....
1995-96	Florida	NHL	78	20	17	37	25	2	0	3	120	16.7	5	....	....	....	....	....	14	3	2	5	0	0	0	0
1996-97	Florida	NHL	67	10	6	16	4	0	1	2	92	10.9	1	....	....	....	....	....	5	0	0	0	0	0	0	0
1997-98	Florida	NHL	21	2	0	2	4	0	1	0	23	8.7	1	....	....	....	....	....	....	....	....	....	....	....	....	....
	Tampa Bay	NHL	28	2	4	6	4	0	0	2	28	7.1	2	....	....	....	....	....	....	....	....	....	....	....	....	....
1998-99	Philadelphia	NHL	72	3	11	14	12	0	0	1	73	4.1	–2	15	53.3	34	28	12:59	6	0	0	0	4	0	0	0
99-2000	Orlando	IHL	1	0	0	0	0	....	....	....	....	....	....	....	....	....	....	....	....	....	....	....	....	....	....	....
	Philadelphia	NHL	67	10	3	13	4	0	2	2	63	15.9	8	36	41.7	28	44	11:58	18	0	1	1	0	0	0	0
	NHL Totals		665	112	119	231	126	15	6	21	885	12.7		51	45.1	62	72	12:30	49	3	4	7	8	0	0	0

OHL Second All-Star Team (1988)

Traded to **NY Rangers** by **Hartford** for Carey Wilson and NY Rangers' 3rd round choice (Michael Nylander) in the 1991 Entry Draft, July 9, 1990. Traded to **Ottawa** by **NY Rangers** for future considerations, July 28, 1992. Signed as a free agent by **Florida**, August 10, 1993. Traded to **Tampa Bay** by **Florida** with Mark Fitzpatrick for Dino Ciccarelli and Jeff Norton, January 15, 1998. Signed as a free agent by **Philadelphia**, October 7, 1998. Claimed by **Atlanta** from **Philadelphia** in Expansion Draft, June 25, 1999. Traded to **Philadelphia** by **Atlanta** for cash, October 15, 1999.

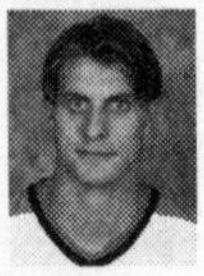

HULSE, Cale

(HUHLS, KAYL) **NSH.**

Defense. Shoots right. 6'3", 220 lbs. Born, Edmonton, Alta., November 10, 1973. New Jersey's 3rd choice, 66th overall, in 1992 Entry Draft.

1990-91	Calgary Royals	AJHL	49	3	23	26	220	....	....	....	....	....	....	....	....	....	....	....	....	....	....	....	....	....	....	....
1991-92	Portland	WHL	70	4	18	22	230	....	....	....	....	....	....	....	....	....	....	....	6	0	2	2	27	....	....	....
1992-93	Portland	WHL	72	10	26	36	284	....	....	....	....	....	....	....	....	....	....	....	16	4	4	8	65	....	....	....
1993-94	Albany River Rats	AHL	79	7	14	21	186	....	....	....	....	....	....	....	....	....	....	....	5	0	3	3	11	....	....	....
1994-95	Albany River Rats	AHL	77	5	13	18	215	....	....	....	....	....	....	....	....	....	....	....	12	1	1	2	17	....	....	....

			Regular Season																Playoffs							
Season	Club	League	GP	G	A	Pts	PIM	PP	SH	GW	S	%	+/-	TF	F%	H	SB	Min	GP	G	A	Pts	PIM	PP	SH	GW
1995-96	**New Jersey**	**NHL**	**8**	**0**	**0**	**0**	**15**	**0**	**0**	**0**	**5**	**0.0**	**–2**	....	....	....	....	....	....	....	....	....	....	....	....	....
	Albany River Rats	AHL	42	4	23	27	107	....	....	....	....	....	....	....	....	....	....	....	....	....	....	....	....	....	....	....
	Calgary	**NHL**	**3**	**0**	**0**	**0**	**5**	**0**	**0**	**0**	**4**	**0.0**	**3**	....	....	....	....	....	**1**	**0**	**0**	**0**	**0**	**0**	**0**	**0**
	Saint John Flames	AHL	13	2	7	9	39	....	....	....	....	....	....	....	....	....	....	....	....	....	....	....	....	....	....	....
1996-97	**Calgary**	**NHL**	**63**	**1**	**6**	**7**	**91**	**0**	**1**	**0**	**58**	**1.7**	**–2**	....	....	....	....	....	....	....	....	....	....	....	....	....
1997-98	**Calgary**	**NHL**	**79**	**5**	**22**	**27**	**169**	**1**	**1**	**0**	**117**	**4.3**	**1**	....	....	....	....	....	....	....	....	....	....	....	....	....
1998-99	**Calgary**	**NHL**	**73**	**3**	**9**	**12**	**117**	**0**	**0**	**0**	**83**	**3.6**	**–8**	**1**	**0.0**	**113**	**74**	**16:38**	....	....	....	....	....	....	....	....
99-2000	**Calgary**	**NHL**	**47**	**1**	**6**	**7**	**47**	**0**	**0**	**0**	**41**	**2.4**	**–11**	**1**	**100.0**	**85**	**37**	**12:38**	....	....	....	....	....	....	....	....
	NHL Totals		**273**	**10**	**43**	**53**	**444**	**1**	**2**	**0**	**308**	**3.2**		**2**	**50.0**	**198**	**111**	**15:04**	**1**	**0**	**0**	**0**	**0**	**0**	**0**	**0**

Traded to **Calgary** by **New Jersey** with Tommy Albelin and Jocelyn Lemieux for Phil Housley and Dan Keczmer, February 26, 1996. Traded to **Nashville** by **Calgary** with Calgary's 3rd round choice in 2001 Entry Draft for Sergei Krivokrasov, March 14, 2000. • Missed remainder of 1999-2000 season recovering from ankle injury suffered in game vs. San Jose, March 12, 2000.

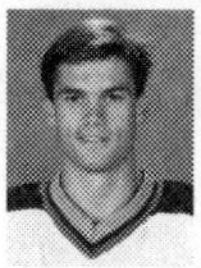

HURLBUT, Mike

(HUHRL-buht, MIGHK)

Defense. Shoots left. 6'2", 206 lbs. Born, Massena, NY, October 7, 1966. NY Rangers' 1st choice, 5th overall, in 1988 Supplemental Draft.

1983-84	Massena High	Hi-School	27	22	31	53	15	....	....	....	....	....	....	....	....	....	....	....	....	....	....	....	....	....	....	....
1984-85	Northwood Prep	Hi-School	34	20	27	47	30	....	....	....	....	....	....	....	....	....	....	....	....	....	....	....	....	....	....	....
1985-86	St. Lawrence	ECAC	25	2	10	12	40	....	....	....	....	....	....	....	....	....	....	....	....	....	....	....	....	....	....	....
1986-87	St. Lawrence	ECAC	35	8	15	23	44	....	....	....	....	....	....	....	....	....	....	....	....	....	....	....	....	....	....	....
1987-88	St. Lawrence	ECAC	38	6	12	18	18	....	....	....	....	....	....	....	....	....	....	....	....	....	....	....	....	....	....	....
1988-89	St. Lawrence	ECAC	36	8	25	33	30	....	....	....	....	....	....	....	....	....	....	....	....	....	....	....	....	....	....	....
	Denver Rangers	IHL	8	0	2	2	13	....	....	....	....	....	....	....	....	....	....	....	4	1	2	3	2	....	....	....
1989-90	Flint Spirits	IHL	74	3	34	37	38	....	....	....	....	....	....	....	....	....	....	....	3	0	1	1	2	....	....	....
1990-91	San Diego Gulls	IHL	2	1	0	1	0	....	....	....	....	....	....	....	....	....	....	....	....	....	....	....	....	....	....	....
	Binghamton	AHL	33	2	11	13	27	....	....	....	....	....	....	....	....	....	....	....	3	0	1	1	0	....	....	....
1991-92	Binghamton	AHL	79	16	39	55	64	....	....	....	....	....	....	....	....	....	....	....	11	2	7	9	8	....	....	....
1992-93	**NY Rangers**	**NHL**	**23**	**1**	**8**	**9**	**16**	**1**	**0**	**0**	**26**	**3.8**	**4**	....	....	....	....	....	....	....	....	....	....	....	....	....
	Binghamton	AHL	45	11	25	36	46	....	....	....	....	....	....	....	....	....	....	....	14	2	5	7	12	....	....	....
1993-94	**Quebec**	**NHL**	**1**	**0**	**0**	**0**	**0**	**0**	**0**	**0**	**1**	**0.0**	**–1**	....	....	....	....	....	....	....	....	....	....	....	....	....
	Cornwall Aces	AHL	77	13	33	46	100	....	....	....	....	....	....	....	....	....	....	....	13	3	7	10	12	....	....	....
1994-95	Cornwall Aces	AHL	74	11	49	60	69	....	....	....	....	....	....	....	....	....	....	....	3	1	0	1	15	....	....	....
1995-96	Minnesota Moose	IHL	22	1	4	5	22	....	....	....	....	....	....	....	....	....	....	....	....	....	....	....	....	....	....	....
	Houston Aeros	IHL	38	3	12	15	33	....	....	....	....	....	....	....	....	....	....	....	....	....	....	....	....	....	....	....
1996-97	Houston Aeros	IHL	70	11	24	35	62	....	....	....	....	....	....	....	....	....	....	....	13	5	8	13	12	....	....	....
1997-98	**Buffalo**	**NHL**	**3**	**0**	**0**	**0**	**2**	**0**	**0**	**0**	**3**	**0.0**	**–1**	....	....	....	....	....	....	....	....	....	....	....	....	....
	Rochester	AHL	45	10	20	30	48	....	....	....	....	....	....	....	....	....	....	....	4	1	1	2	2	....	....	....
1998-99	**Buffalo**	**NHL**	**1**	**0**	**0**	**0**	**0**	**0**	**0**	**0**	**2**	**0.0**	**2**	**0**	**0.0**	**1**	**2**	**17:53**	....	....	....	....	....	....	....	....
	Rochester	AHL	72	15	39	54	46	....	....	....	....	....	....	....	....	....	....	....	20	4	5	9	12	....	....	....
99-2000	**Buffalo**	**NHL**	**1**	**0**	**0**	**0**	**2**	**0**	**0**	**0**	**1**	**0.0**	**1**	**0**	**0.0**	**0**	**1**	**12:25**	....	....	....	....	....	....	....	....
	Rochester	AHL	74	10	29	39	83	....	....	....	....	....	....	....	....	....	....	....	21	5	6	11	14	....	....	....
	NHL Totals		**29**	**1**	**8**	**9**	**20**	**1**	**0**	**0**	**33**	**3.0**		**0**	**0.0**	**1**	**3**	**15:09**	....	....	....	....	....	....	....	....

ECAC First All-Star Team (1989) • NCAA East First All-American Team (1989) • AHL Second All-Star Team (1995)

Traded to **Quebec** by **NY Rangers** for Alexander Karpovtsev, September 7, 1993. Signed as a free agent by **Buffalo**, September 9, 1997.

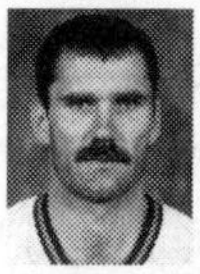

HUSCROFT, Jamie

(HUHS-krawft, JAY-mee) **WSH.**

Defense. Shoots right. 6'3", 210 lbs. Born, Creston, B.C., January 9, 1967. New Jersey's 9th choice, 171st overall, in 1985 Entry Draft.

1983-84	Portland	WHL	18	0	5	5	15	....	....	....	....	....	....	....	....	....	....	....	....	....	....	....	....	....	....	....
	Seattle Breakers	WHL	45	0	7	7	62	....	....	....	....	....	....	....	....	....	....	....	5	0	0	0	15	....	....	....
1984-85	Seattle Breakers	WHL	69	3	13	16	273	....	....	....	....	....	....	....	....	....	....	....	....	....	....	....	....	....	....	....
1985-86	Seattle T-Birds	WHL	66	6	20	26	394	....	....	....	....	....	....	....	....	....	....	....	5	0	1	1	18	....	....	....
1986-87	Seattle T-Birds	WHL	21	1	18	19	99	....	....	....	....	....	....	....	....	....	....	....	....	....	....	....	....	....	....	....
	Medicine Hat	WHL	14	3	3	6	71	....	....	....	....	....	....	....	....	....	....	....	20	0	3	3	*125	....	....	....
1987-88	Utica Devils	AHL	71	5	7	12	316	....	....	....	....	....	....	....	....	....	....	....	....	....	....	....	....	....	....	....
	Flint Spirits	IHL	3	1	0	1	2	....	....	....	....	....	....	....	....	....	....	....	16	0	1	1	110	....	....	....
1988-89	**New Jersey**	**NHL**	**15**	**0**	**2**	**2**	**51**	**0**	**0**	**0**	**9**	**0.0**	**–3**	....	....	....	....	....	....	....	....	....	....	....	....	....
	Utica Devils	AHL	41	2	10	12	215	....	....	....	....	....	....	....	....	....	....	....	5	0	0	0	40	....	....	....
1989-90	**New Jersey**	**NHL**	**42**	**2**	**3**	**5**	**149**	**0**	**0**	**0**	**19**	**10.5**	**–2**	....	....	....	....	....	**5**	**0**	**0**	**0**	**16**	**0**	**0**	**0**
	Utica Devils	AHL	22	3	6	9	122	....	....	....	....	....	....	....	....	....	....	....	....	....	....	....	....	....	....	....
1990-91	**New Jersey**	**NHL**	**8**	**0**	**1**	**1**	**27**	**0**	**0**	**0**	**3**	**0.0**	**1**	....	....	....	....	....	**3**	**0**	**0**	**0**	**6**	**0**	**0**	**0**
	Utica Devils	AHL	59	3	15	18	339	....	....	....	....	....	....	....	....	....	....	....	....	....	....	....	....	....	....	....
1991-92	Utica Devils	AHL	50	4	7	11	224	....	....	....	....	....	....	....	....	....	....	....	....	....	....	....	....	....	....	....
1992-93	Providence Bruins	AHL	69	2	15	17	257	....	....	....	....	....	....	....	....	....	....	....	2	0	1	1	6	....	....	....
1993-94	**Boston**	**NHL**	**36**	**0**	**1**	**1**	**144**	**0**	**0**	**0**	**13**	**0.0**	**–2**	....	....	....	....	....	**4**	**0**	**0**	**0**	**9**	**0**	**0**	**0**
	Providence Bruins	AHL	32	1	10	11	157	....	....	....	....	....	....	....	....	....	....	....	....	....	....	....	....	....	....	....
1994-95	**Boston**	**NHL**	**34**	**0**	**6**	**6**	**103**	**0**	**0**	**0**	**30**	**0.0**	**–3**	....	....	....	....	....	**5**	**0**	**0**	**0**	**11**	**0**	**0**	**0**
	Fresno Falcons	SunHL	3	1	1	2	7	....	....	....	....	....	....	....	....	....	....	....	....	....	....	....	....	....	....	....
1995-96	**Calgary**	**NHL**	**70**	**3**	**9**	**12**	**162**	**0**	**0**	**1**	**57**	**5.3**	**14**	....	....	....	....	....	**4**	**0**	**1**	**1**	**4**	**0**	**0**	**0**
1996-97	**Calgary**	**NHL**	**39**	**0**	**4**	**4**	**117**	**0**	**0**	**0**	**33**	**0.0**	**2**	....	....	....	....	....	....	....	....	....	....	....	....	....
	Tampa Bay	**NHL**	**13**	**0**	**1**	**1**	**34**	**0**	**0**	**0**	**7**	**0.0**	**–4**	....	....	....	....	....	....	....	....	....	....	....	....	....
1997-98	**Tampa Bay**	**NHL**	**44**	**0**	**3**	**3**	**122**	**0**	**0**	**0**	**21**	**0.0**	**–4**	....	....	....	....	....	....	....	....	....	....	....	....	....
	Vancouver	**NHL**	**7**	**0**	**1**	**1**	**55**	**0**	**0**	**0**	**5**	**0.0**	**2**	....	....	....	....	....	....	....	....	....	....	....	....	....
1998-99	**Vancouver**	**NHL**	**26**	**0**	**1**	**1**	**63**	**0**	**0**	**0**	**20**	**0.0**	**–3**	**0**	**0.0**	**36**	**15**	**8:54**	....	....	....	....	....	....	....	....
	Phoenix	**NHL**	**11**	**0**	**1**	**1**	**27**	**0**	**0**	**0**	**7**	**0.0**	**–1**	**0**	**0.0**	**27**	**3**	**11:02**	....	....	....	....	....	....	....	....
99-2000	**Washington**	**NHL**	**7**	**0**	**0**	**0**	**11**	**0**	**0**	**0**	**4**	**0.0**	**–5**	**0**	**0.0**	**15**	**4**	**10:37**	....	....	....	....	....	....	....	....
	Portland Pirates	AHL	56	0	12	12	154	....	....	....	....	....	....	....	....	....	....	....	4	0	0	0	14	....	....	....
	NHL Totals		**352**	**5**	**33**	**38**	**1065**	**0**	**0**	**1**	**228**	**2.2**		**0**	**0.0**	**78**	**22**	**9:42**	**21**	**0**	**1**	**1**	**46**	**0**	**0**	**0**

Signed as a free agent by **Boston**, July 23, 1992. Signed as a free agent by **Calgary**, August 22, 1995. Traded to **Tampa Bay** by **Calgary** for Tyler Moss, March 18, 1997. Traded to **Vancouver** by **Tampa Bay** for Enrico Ciccone, March 14, 1998. Traded to **Phoenix** by **Vancouver** for future considerations, March 8, 1999. Signed as a free agent by **Washington**, August 9, 1999.

HUSKA, Ryan

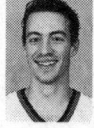

(HUHS-kuh, RIGH-yan)

Left wing. Shoots left. 6'2", 194 lbs. Born, Cranbrook, B.C., July 2, 1975. Chicago's 4th choice, 76th overall, in 1993 Entry Draft.

1990-91	Trail Selects	BCAHA	37	65	70	135	18	....	....	....	....	....	....	....	....	....	....	....	....	....	....	....	....	....	....	....
1991-92	Kamloops Blazers	WHL	44	4	5	9	23	....	....	....	....	....	....	....	....	....	....	....	6	0	1	1	0	....	....	....
1992-93	Kamloops Blazers	WHL	68	17	15	32	50	....	....	....	....	....	....	....	....	....	....	....	13	2	6	8	4	....	....	....
1993-94	Kamloops Blazers	WHL	69	23	31	54	66	....	....	....	....	....	....	....	....	....	....	....	19	9	5	14	23	....	....	....
1994-95	Kamloops Blazers	WHL	66	27	40	67	78	....	....	....	....	....	....	....	....	....	....	....	17	7	8	15	12	....	....	....
1995-96	Indianapolis Ice	IHL	28	2	3	5	15	....	....	....	....	....	....	....	....	....	....	....	5	1	1	2	27	....	....	....
1996-97	Indianapolis Ice	IHL	80	18	12	30	100	....	....	....	....	....	....	....	....	....	....	....	4	0	0	0	4	....	....	....
1997-98	**Chicago**	**NHL**	**1**	**0**	**0**	**0**	**0**	**0**	**0**	**0**	**0**	**0.0**	**0**	....	....	....	....	....	....	....	....	....	....	....	....	....
	Indianapolis Ice	IHL	80	19	16	35	115	....	....	....	....	....	....	....	....	....	....	....	5	0	3	3	10	....	....	....
1998-99	Lowell	AHL	60	5	13	18	70	....	....	....	....	....	....	....	....	....	....	....	2	0	0	0	0	....	....	....
99-2000	Springfield	AHL	61	12	9	21	77	....	....	....	....	....	....	....	....	....	....	....	4	0	1	1	0	....	....	....
	NHL Totals		**1**	**0**	**0**	**0**	**0**	**0**	**0**	**0**	**0**	**0.0**		....	....	....	....	....	....	....	....	....	....	....	....	....

Signed as a free agent by **NY Islanders**, September 9, 1998. Signed as a free agent by **Phoenix**, August 15, 1999.

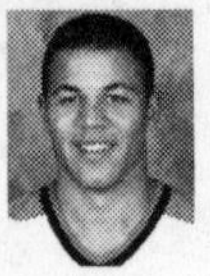

IGINLA, Jarome (ih-GIHN-lah, jah-ROHM) CGY.

Right wing. Shoots right. 6'1", 202 lbs. Born, Edmonton, Alta., July 1, 1977. Dallas' 1st choice, 11th overall, in 1995 Entry Draft.

			Regular Season																Playoffs							
Season	Club	League	GP	G	A	Pts	PIM	PP	SH	GW	S	%	+/–	TF	F%	H	SB	Min	GP	G	A	Pts	PIM	PP	SH	GW
1991-92	St. Albert Raiders	AAHA	36	26	30	56	22	....	....	....	....	....	....	....	....	....	....	....	....	....	....	....	....	....	....	....
1992-93	St. Albert Raiders	AAHA	36	34	53	87	20	....	....	....	....	....	....	....	....	....	....	....	....	....	....	....	....	....	....	....
1993-94	Kamloops Blazers	WHL	48	6	23	29	33	....	....	....	....	....	....	....	....	....	....	....	19	3	6	9	10	....	....	....
1994-95	Kamloops Blazers	WHL	72	33	38	71	111	....	....	....	....	....	....	....	....	....	....	....	21	7	11	18	34	....	....	....
1995-96	Kamloops Blazers	WHL	63	63	73	136	120	....	....	....	....	....	....	....	....	....	....	....	16	16	13	29	44	....	....	....
	Calgary	**NHL**	....	....	....	....	....	....	....	....	....	....	....	....	....	....	....	....	**2**	**1**	**1**	**2**	**0**	**0**	**0**	**0**
1996-97	**Calgary**	**NHL**	**82**	**21**	**29**	**50**	**37**	**8**	**1**	**3**	**169**	**12.4**	**–4**	....	....	....	....	....	....	....	....	....	....	....	....	....
1997-98	**Calgary**	**NHL**	**70**	**13**	**19**	**32**	**29**	**0**	**2**	**1**	**154**	**8.4**	**–10**	....	....	....	....	....	....	....	....	....	....	....	....	....
1998-99	**Calgary**	**NHL**	**82**	**28**	**23**	**51**	**58**	**7**	**0**	**4**	**211**	**13.3**	**1**	**111**	**51.4**	**119**	**25**	**16:30**	....	....	....	....	....	....	....	....
99-2000	**Calgary**	**NHL**	**77**	**29**	**34**	**63**	**26**	**12**	**0**	**4**	**256**	**11.3**	**0**	**278**	**52.9**	**133**	**29**	**18:24**	....	....	....	....	....	....	....	....
	NHL Totals		**311**	**91**	**105**	**196**	**150**	**27**	**3**	**12**	**790**	**11.5**		**389**	**52.4**	**252**	**54**	**17:25**	**2**	**1**	**1**	**2**	**0**	**0**	**0**	**0**

Won George Parsons Trophy (Memorial Cup Tournament Most Sportsmanlike Player) (1995) • WHL West First All-Star Team (1996) • Canadian Major Junior First All-Star Team (1996) • NHL All-Rookie Team (1997)

Traded to **Calgary** by **Dallas** with Corey Millen for Joe Nieuwendyk, December 19, 1995.

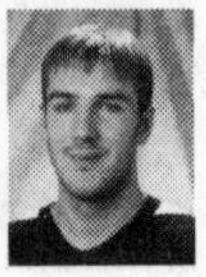

IGNATJEV, Victor (ihg_NYAT-ee-ehv, VIHK-tohr)

Defense. Shoots left. 6'4", 215 lbs. Born, Riga, USSR, April 26, 1970. San Jose's 11th choice, 243rd overall, in 1992 Entry Draft.

Season	Club	League	GP	G	A	Pts	PIM	PP	SH	GW	S	%	+/–	TF	F%	H	SB	Min	GP	G	A	Pts	PIM	PP	SH	GW
1989-90	Dynamo Riga	USSR	40	0	0	0	26	....	....	....	....	....	....	....	....	....	....	....	....	....	....	....	....	....	....	....
1990-91	Dynamo Riga	USSR	10	0	0	0	2	....	....	....	....	....	....	....	....	....	....	....	....	....	....	....	....	....	....	....
1991-92	Dynamo Riga	CIS	22	4	5	9	22	....	....	....	....	....	....	....	....	....	....	....	....	....	....	....	....	....	....	....
1992-93	Kansas City	IHL	64	5	16	21	68	....	....	....	....	....	....	....	....	....	....	....	4	1	2	3	24	....	....	....
1993-94	Kansas City	IHL	67	1	24	25	123	....	....	....	....	....	....	....	....	....	....	....	....	....	....	....	....	....	....	....
1994-95	Oklahoma City	CHL	47	11	35	46	66	....	....	....	....	....	....	....	....	....	....	....	....	....	....	....	....	....	....	....
	Denver Grizzlies	IHL	23	2	11	13	4	....	....	....	....	....	....	....	....	....	....	....	17	3	8	11	8	....	....	....
1995-96	Utah Grizzlies	IHL	73	9	29	38	67	....	....	....	....	....	....	....	....	....	....	....	21	3	8	11	22	....	....	....
1996-97	Long Beach	IHL	82	16	53	69	112	....	....	....	....	....	....	....	....	....	....	....	16	3	4	7	26	....	....	....
1997-98	Long Beach	IHL	71	12	33	45	102	....	....	....	....	....	....	....	....	....	....	....	17	3	11	14	16	....	....	....
1998-99	**Pittsburgh**	**NHL**	**11**	**0**	**1**	**1**	**6**	**0**	**0**	**0**	**15**	**0.0**	**–3**	**0**	**0.0**	**10**	**6**	**12:14**	**1**	**0**	**0**	**0**	**2**	**0**	**0**	**0**
99-2000	EHC Nurnberg	DEL	60	3	15	18	56	....	....	....	....	....	....	....	....	....	....	....	....	....	....	....	....	....	....	....
	EHC Nurnberg	EuroHL	4	0	3	3	22	....	....	....	....	....	....	....	....	....	....	....	2	0	0	0	6	....	....	....
	NHL Totals		**11**	**0**	**1**	**1**	**6**	**0**	**0**	**0**	**15**	**0.0**		**0**	**0.0**	**10**	**6**	**12:14**	**1**	**0**	**0**	**0**	**2**	**0**	**0**	**0**

IHL Second All-Star Team (1997)

Signed as a free agent by **Pittsburgh**, August 11, 1998. • Missed majority of 1998-99 season recovering from shoulder surgery, November, 1998. • Played w/ RHI's Sacramento River Rats in 1996 (21-15-23-38-27).

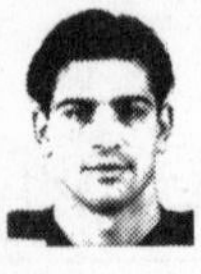

INTRANUOVO, Ralph (ihn-trah-NOO-voh, RALF)

Center. Shoots left. 5'8", 185 lbs. Born, East York, Ont., December 11, 1973. Edmonton's 5th choice, 96th overall, in 1992 Entry Draft.

Season	Club	League	GP	G	A	Pts	PIM	PP	SH	GW	S	%	+/–	TF	F%	H	SB	Min	GP	G	A	Pts	PIM	PP	SH	GW
1989-90	Toronto Nats	MTHL	37	33	26	59	20	....	....	....	....	....	....	....	....	....	....	....	....	....	....	....	....	....	....	....
1990-91	Sault Ste. Marie	OHL	63	25	42	67	22	....	....	....	....	....	....	....	....	....	....	....	14	7	13	20	17	....	....	....
1991-92	Sault Ste. Marie	OHL	65	50	63	113	44	....	....	....	....	....	....	....	....	....	....	....	18	10	14	24	12	....	....	....
1992-93	Sault Ste. Marie	OHL	54	31	47	78	61	....	....	....	....	....	....	....	....	....	....	....	18	10	16	26	30	....	....	....
1993-94	Cape Breton	AHL	66	21	31	52	39	....	....	....	....	....	....	....	....	....	....	....	4	1	2	3	2	....	....	....
1994-95	**Edmonton**	**NHL**	**1**	**0**	**1**	**1**	**0**	**0**	**0**	**0**	**1**	**0.0**	**1**	....	....	....	....	....	....	....	....	....	....	....	....	....
	Cape Breton	AHL	70	46	47	93	62	....	....	....	....	....	....	....	....	....	....	....	....	....	....	....	....	....	....	....
1995-96	**Edmonton**	**NHL**	**13**	**1**	**2**	**3**	**4**	**0**	**0**	**1**	**19**	**5.3**	**–3**	....	....	....	....	....	....	....	....	....	....	....	....	....
	Cape Breton	AHL	52	34	39	73	84	....	....	....	....	....	....	....	....	....	....	....	....	....	....	....	....	....	....	....
1996-97	**Toronto**	**NHL**	**3**	**0**	**1**	**1**	**0**	**0**	**0**	**0**	**4**	**0.0**	**–1**	....	....	....	....	....	....	....	....	....	....	....	....	....
	Edmonton	**NHL**	**5**	**1**	**0**	**1**	**0**	**0**	**0**	**0**	**2**	**50.0**	**0**	....	....	....	....	....	....	....	....	....	....	....	....	....
	Hamilton Bulldogs	AHL	68	36	40	76	88	....	....	....	....	....	....	....	....	....	....	....	22	8	4	12	30	....	....	....
1997-98	Manitoba Moose	IHL	81	26	35	61	68	....	....	....	....	....	....	....	....	....	....	....	3	2	0	2	4	....	....	....
1998-99	Manitoba Moose	IHL	71	29	31	60	70	....	....	....	....	....	....	....	....	....	....	....	5	2	1	3	4	....	....	....
99-2000	Adler Mannheim	DEL	54	14	19	33	20	....	....	....	....	....	....	....	....	....	....	....	5	1	0	1	2	....	....	....
	Adler Mannheim	EuroHL	5	1	4	5	0	....	....	....	....	....	....	....	....	....	....	....	....	....	....	....	....	....	....	....
	NHL Totals		**22**	**2**	**4**	**6**	**4**	**0**	**0**	**1**	**26**	**7.7**		....	....	....	....	....	....	....	....	....	....	....	....	....

Memorial Cup All-Star Team (1993) • Won Stafford Smythe Memorial Trophy (Memorial Cup Tournament MVP) (1993) • AHL Second All-Star Team (1995, 1997)

Claimed by **Toronto** from **Edmonton** in Waiver Draft, September 30, 1996. Claimed on waivers by **Edmonton** from **Toronto**, October 25, 1996.

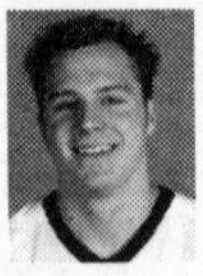

ISBISTER, Brad (IHZ-bihs-tuhr, BRAD) NYI

Left wing. Shoots right. 6'4", 227 lbs. Born, Edmonton, Alta., May 7, 1977. Winnipeg's 4th choice, 67th overall, in 1995 Entry Draft.

Season	Club	League	GP	G	A	Pts	PIM	PP	SH	GW	S	%	+/–	TF	F%	H	SB	Min	GP	G	A	Pts	PIM	PP	SH	GW
1992-93	Calgary Canucks	AAHA	35	24	25	49	74	....	....	....	....	....	....	....	....	....	....	....	....	....	....	....	....	....	....	....
1993-94	Portland	WHL	64	7	10	17	45	....	....	....	....	....	....	....	....	....	....	....	10	0	2	2	0	....	....	....
1994-95	Portland	WHL	67	16	20	36	123	....	....	....	....	....	....	....	....	....	....	....	....	....	....	....	....	....	....	....
1995-96	Portland	WHL	71	45	44	89	184	....	....	....	....	....	....	....	....	....	....	....	7	2	4	6	20	....	....	....
1996-97	Portland	WHL	24	15	18	33	45	....	....	....	....	....	....	....	....	....	....	....	6	2	1	3	16	....	....	....
	Springfield	AHL	7	3	1	4	14	....	....	....	....	....	....	....	....	....	....	....	9	1	2	3	10	....	....	....
1997-98	**Phoenix**	**NHL**	**66**	**9**	**8**	**17**	**102**	**1**	**0**	**1**	**115**	**7.8**	**4**	....	....	....	....	....	**5**	**0**	**0**	**0**	**2**	**0**	**0**	**0**
	Springfield	AHL	9	8	2	10	36	....	....	....	....	....	....	....	....	....	....	....	....	....	....	....	....	....	....	....
1998-99	**Phoenix**	**NHL**	**32**	**4**	**4**	**8**	**46**	**0**	**0**	**2**	**48**	**8.3**	**1**	**3**	**0.0**	**39**	**3**	**11:33**	....	....	....	....	....	....	....	....
	Springfield	AHL	4	1	1	2	12	....	....	....	....	....	....	....	....	....	....	....	....	....	....	....	....	....	....	....
	Las Vegas	IHL	2	0	0	0	9	....	....	....	....	....	....	....	....	....	....	....	....	....	....	....	....	....	....	....
99-2000	**NY Islanders**	**NHL**	**64**	**22**	**20**	**42**	**100**	**9**	**0**	**1**	**135**	**16.3**	**–18**	**55**	**54.6**	**134**	**15**	**16:58**	....	....	....	....	....	....	....	....
	NHL Totals		**162**	**35**	**32**	**67**	**248**	**10**	**0**	**4**	**298**	**11.7**		**58**	**51.7**	**173**	**18**	**15:09**	**5**	**0**	**0**	**0**	**2**	**0**	**0**	**0**

WHL West Second All-Star Team (1997)

Rights transferred to **Phoenix** after **Winnipeg** franchise relocated, July 1, 1996. Traded to **NY Islanders** by **Phoenix** with Phoenix's 3rd round choice (Brian Collins) in 1999 Entry Draft for Robert Reichel, NY Islanders' 3rd round choice (Jason Jaspers) in 1999 Entry Draft and Ottawa's 4th round choice (previously acquired, Phoenix selected Preston Mizzi) in 1999 Entry Draft, March 20, 1999.

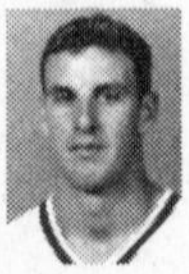

JACKMAN, Richard (JAK-man, RIHCH-urhd) DAL.

Defense. Shoots right. 6'2", 192 lbs. Born, Toronto, Ont., June 28, 1978. Dallas' 1st choice, 5th overall, in 1996 Entry Draft.

Season	Club	League	GP	G	A	Pts	PIM	PP	SH	GW	S	%	+/–	TF	F%	H	SB	Min	GP	G	A	Pts	PIM	PP	SH	GW
1993-94	Mississauga Sens	MTHL	81	35	53	88	156	....	....	....	....	....	....	....	....	....	....	....	....	....	....	....	....	....	....	....
1994-95	Mississauga Sens	MTHL	53	20	37	57	120	....	....	....	....	....	....	....	....	....	....	....	....	....	....	....	....	....	....	....
	Richmond Hill	OJHL	10	2	9	11	16	....	....	....	....	....	....	....	....	....	....	....	....	....	....	....	....	....	....	....
1995-96	Sault Ste. Marie	OHL	66	13	29	42	97	....	....	....	....	....	....	....	....	....	....	....	4	1	0	1	15	....	....	....
1996-97	Sault Ste. Marie	OHL	53	13	34	47	116	....	....	....	....	....	....	....	....	....	....	....	10	2	6	8	24	....	....	....
1997-98	Sault Ste. Marie	OHL	60	33	40	73	111	....	....	....	....	....	....	....	....	....	....	....	....	....	....	....	....	....	....	....
	Michigan K-Wings	IHL	14	1	5	6	10	....	....	....	....	....	....	....	....	....	....	....	4	0	0	0	10	....	....	....
1998-99	Michigan K-Wings	IHL	71	13	17	30	106	....	....	....	....	....	....	....	....	....	....	....	5	0	4	4	6	....	....	....
99-2000	**Dallas**	**NHL**	**22**	**1**	**2**	**3**	**6**	**1**	**0**	**0**	**16**	**6.3**	**–1**	**0**	**0.0**	**18**	**10**	**8:06**	....	....	....	....	....	....	....	....
	Michigan K-Wings	IHL	50	3	16	19	51	....	....	....	....	....	....	....	....	....	....	....	....	....	....	....	....	....	....	....
	NHL Totals		**22**	**1**	**2**	**3**	**6**	**1**	**0**	**0**	**16**	**6.3**		**0**	**0.0**	**18**	**10**	**8:06**	....	....	....	....	....	....	....	....

OHL Second All-Star Team (1998)

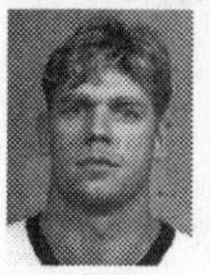

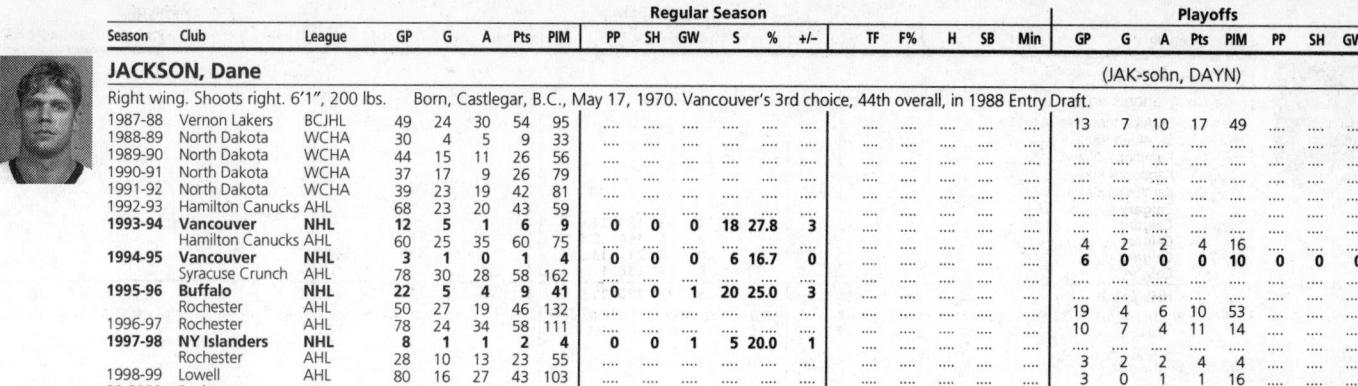

JACKSON, Dane

(JAK-sohn, DAYN)

Right wing. Shoots right. 6'1", 200 lbs. Born, Castlegar, B.C., May 17, 1970. Vancouver's 3rd choice, 44th overall, in 1988 Entry Draft.

			Regular Season																Playoffs							
Season	Club	League	GP	G	A	Pts	PIM	PP	SH	GW	S	%	+/–	TF	F%	H	SB	Min	GP	G	A	Pts	PIM	PP	SH	GW
1987-88	Vernon Lakers	BCJHL	49	24	30	54	95	....	....	....	....	....	....	....	....	....	....	....	13	7	10	17	49	....	....	....
1988-89	North Dakota	WCHA	30	4	5	9	33	....	....	....	....	....	....	....	....	....	....	....	....	....	....	....	....	....	....	....
1989-90	North Dakota	WCHA	44	15	11	26	56	....	....	....	....	....	....	....	....	....	....	....	....	....	....	....	....	....	....	....
1990-91	North Dakota	WCHA	37	17	9	26	79	....	....	....	....	....	....	....	....	....	....	....	....	....	....	....	....	....	....	....
1991-92	North Dakota	WCHA	39	23	19	42	81	....	....	....	....	....	....	....	....	....	....	....	....	....	....	....	....	....	....	....
1992-93	Hamilton Canucks	AHL	68	23	20	43	59	....	....	....	....	....	....	....	....	....	....	....	....	....	....	....	....	....	....	....
1993-94	**Vancouver**	**NHL**	**12**	**5**	**1**	**6**	**9**	**0**	**0**	**0**	**18**	**27.8**	**3**	....	....	....	....	....	....	....	....	....	....	....	....	....
	Hamilton Canucks	AHL	60	25	35	60	75	....	....	....	....	....	....	....	....	....	....	....	4	2	2	4	16	....	....	....
1994-95	**Vancouver**	**NHL**	**3**	**1**	**0**	**1**	**4**	**0**	**0**	**0**	**6**	**16.7**	**0**	....	....	....	....	....	**6**	**0**	**0**	**0**	**10**	**0**	**0**	**0**
	Syracuse Crunch	AHL	78	30	28	58	162	....	....	....	....	....	....	....	....	....	....	....	....	....	....	....	....	....	....	....
1995-96	**Buffalo**	**NHL**	**22**	**5**	**4**	**9**	**41**	**0**	**0**	**1**	**20**	**25.0**	**3**	....	....	....	....	....	....	....	....	....	....	....	....	....
	Rochester	AHL	50	27	19	46	132	....	....	....	....	....	....	....	....	....	....	....	19	4	6	10	53	....	....	....
1996-97	Rochester	AHL	78	24	34	58	111	....	....	....	....	....	....	....	....	....	....	....	10	7	4	11	14	....	....	....
1997-98	**NY Islanders**	**NHL**	**8**	**1**	**1**	**2**	**4**	**0**	**0**	**1**	**5**	**20.0**	**1**	....	....	....	....	....	....	....	....	....	....	....	....	....
	Rochester	AHL	28	10	13	23	55	....	....	....	....	....	....	....	....	....	....	....	3	2	2	4	4	....	....	....
1998-99	Lowell	AHL	80	16	27	43	103	....	....	....	....	....	....	....	....	....	....	....	3	0	1	1	16	....	....	....
99-2000	Rochester	AHL	21	6	9	15	8	....	....	....	....	....	....	....	....	....	....	....	....	....	....	....	....	....	....	....
	NHL Totals		**45**	**12**	**6**	**18**	**58**	**0**	**0**	**2**	**49**	**24.5**		....	....	....	....	....	**6**	**0**	**0**	**0**	**10**	**0**	**0**	**0**

Signed as a free agent by **Buffalo**, September 20, 1995. Signed as a free agent by **NY Islanders**, July 21, 1997. Signed as a free agent by **Rochester** (AHL), August 29, 1999. • Missed remainder of 1999-2000 season recovering from knee injury suffered in game vs. Springfield (AHL), January 21, 2000.

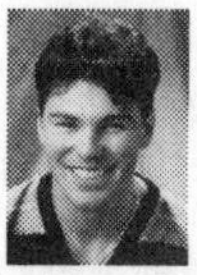

JAGR, Jaromir

(YAH-guhr, YAIR-oh-MEER) **PIT.**

Right wing. Shoots left. 6'2", 234 lbs. Born, Kladno, Czech., February 15, 1972. Pittsburgh's 1st choice, 5th overall, in 1990 Entry Draft.

			Regular Season																Playoffs							
Season	Club	League	GP	G	A	Pts	PIM	PP	SH	GW	S	%	+/–	TF	F%	H	SB	Min	GP	G	A	Pts	PIM	PP	SH	GW
1984-85	Poldi Kladno	Czech-Jr.	34	24	17	41	....	....	....	....	....	....	....	....	....	....	....	....	....	....	....	....	....	....	....	....
1985-86	Poldi Kladno	Czech-Jr.	36	41	29	70	....	....	....	....	....	....	....	....	....	....	....	....	....	....	....	....	....	....	....	....
1986-87	Poldi Kladno	Czech-Jr.	30	35	35	70	....	....	....	....	....	....	....	....	....	....	....	....	....	....	....	....	....	....	....	....
1987-88	Poldi Kladno	Czech-Jr.	35	57	27	84	....	....	....	....	....	....	....	....	....	....	....	....	....	....	....	....	....	....	....	....
1988-89	Poldi Kladno	Czech.	29	3	3	6	4	....	....	....	....	....	....	....	....	....	....	....	10	5	7	12	0	....	....	....
1989-90	Poldi Kladno	Czech.	42	22	28	50	....	....	....	....	....	....	....	....	....	....	....	....	9	*8	2	10	....	....	....	....
1990-91♦	**Pittsburgh**	**NHL**	**80**	**27**	**30**	**57**	**42**	**7**	**0**	**4**	**136**	**19.9**	**–4**	....	....	....	....	....	**24**	**3**	**10**	**13**	**6**	**1**	**0**	**1**
1991-92♦	**Pittsburgh**	**NHL**	**70**	**32**	**37**	**69**	**34**	**4**	**0**	**4**	**194**	**16.5**	**12**	....	....	....	....	....	**21**	**11**	**13**	**24**	**6**	**2**	**0**	**4**
1992-93	**Pittsburgh**	**NHL**	**81**	**34**	**60**	**94**	**61**	**10**	**1**	**9**	**242**	**14.0**	**30**	....	....	....	....	....	**12**	**5**	**4**	**9**	**23**	**1**	**0**	**1**
1993-94	**Pittsburgh**	**NHL**	**80**	**32**	**67**	**99**	**61**	**9**	**0**	**6**	**298**	**10.7**	**15**	....	....	....	....	....	**6**	**2**	**4**	**6**	**16**	**0**	**0**	**1**
1994-95	Poldi Kladno	Cze-Rep	11	8	14	22	10	....	....	....	....	....	....	....	....	....	....	....	....	....	....	....	....	....	....	....
	HC Bolzano	Alpenliga	5	8	8	16	4	....	....	....	....	....	....	....	....	....	....	....	....	....	....	....	....	....	....	....
	HC Bolzano	Italy	1	0	0	0	0	....	....	....	....	....	....	....	....	....	....	....	....	....	....	....	....	....	....	....
	EHC Schalke	DEB-3	1	1	10	11	0	....	....	....	....	....	....	....	....	....	....	....	....	....	....	....	....	....	....	....
	Pittsburgh	**NHL**	**48**	**32**	**38**	***70**	**37**	**8**	**3**	**7**	**192**	**16.7**	**23**	....	....	....	....	....	**12**	**10**	**5**	**15**	**6**	**2**	**1**	**1**
1995-96	**Pittsburgh**	**NHL**	**82**	**62**	**87**	**149**	**96**	**20**	**1**	**12**	**403**	**15.4**	**31**	....	....	....	....	....	**18**	**11**	**12**	**23**	**18**	**5**	**1**	**1**
1996-97	**Pittsburgh**	**NHL**	**63**	**47**	**48**	**95**	**40**	**11**	**2**	**6**	**234**	**20.1**	**22**	....	....	....	....	....	**5**	**4**	**4**	**8**	**4**	**2**	**0**	**0**
1997-98	**Pittsburgh**	**NHL**	**77**	**35**	***67**	***102**	**64**	**7**	**0**	**8**	**262**	**13.4**	**17**	....	....	....	....	....	**6**	**4**	**5**	**9**	**2**	**1**	**0**	**0**
	Czech-Republic	Olympics	6	1	4	5	2	....	....	....	....	....	....	....	....	....	....	....	....	....	....	....	....	....	....	....
1998-99	**Pittsburgh**	**NHL**	**81**	**44**	***83**	***127**	**66**	**10**	**1**	**7**	**343**	**12.8**	**17**	**4**	**50.0**	**27**	**23**	**25:51**	**9**	**5**	**7**	**12**	**16**	**1**	**0**	**1**
99-2000	**Pittsburgh**	**NHL**	**63**	**42**	**54**	***96**	**50**	**10**	**0**	**5**	**290**	**14.5**	**25**	**9**	**22.2**	**19**	**12**	**23:12**	**11**	**8**	**8**	**16**	**6**	**2**	**0**	**4**
	NHL Totals		**725**	**387**	**571**	**958**	**551**	**96**	**8**	**68**	**2594**	**14.9**		**13**	**30.8**	**46**	**35**	**24:41**	**124**	**63**	**72**	**135**	**103**	**17**	**2**	**14**

NHL All-Rookie Team (1991) • NHL First All-Star Team (1995, 1996, 1998, 1999, 2000) • Won Art Ross Trophy (1995, 1998, 1999, 2000) • NHL Second All-Star Team (1997) • Won Lester B. Pearson Award (1999, 2000) • Won Hart Trophy (1999) • Played in NHL All-Star Game (1992, 1993, 1996, 1998, 1999, 2000)

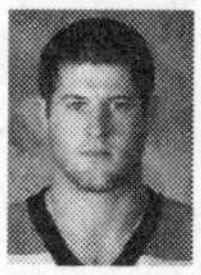

JAKOPIN, John

(JA-koh-pihn, JAWN) **FLA.**

Defense. Shoots right. 6'5", 239 lbs. Born, Toronto, Ont., May 16, 1975. Detroit's 4th choice, 97th overall, in 1993 Entry Draft.

			Regular Season																Playoffs							
Season	Club	League	GP	G	A	Pts	PIM	PP	SH	GW	S	%	+/–	TF	F%	H	SB	Min	GP	G	A	Pts	PIM	PP	SH	GW
1992-93	St. Michael's	OJHL	45	9	21	30	42	....	....	....	....	....	....	....	....	....	....	....	13	3	2	5	4	....	....	....
1993-94	Merrimack College	H-East	36	2	8	10	64	....	....	....	....	....	....	....	....	....	....	....	....	....	....	....	....	....	....	....
1994-95	Merrimack College	H-East	37	4	10	14	42	....	....	....	....	....	....	....	....	....	....	....	....	....	....	....	....	....	....	....
1995-96	Merrimack College	H-East	32	10	15	25	68	....	....	....	....	....	....	....	....	....	....	....	....	....	....	....	....	....	....	....
1996-97	Merrimack College	H-East	31	4	12	16	68	....	....	....	....	....	....	....	....	....	....	....	....	....	....	....	....	....	....	....
	Adirondack	AHL	3	0	0	0	9	....	....	....	....	....	....	....	....	....	....	....	....	....	....	....	....	....	....	....
1997-98	**Florida**	**NHL**	**2**	**0**	**0**	**0**	**4**	**0**	**0**	**0**	**1**	**0.0**	**–3**	....	....	....	....	....	....	....	....	....	....	....	....	....
	New Haven	AHL	60	2	18	20	151	....	....	....	....	....	....	....	....	....	....	....	3	0	0	0	0	....	....	....
1998-99	**Florida**	**NHL**	**3**	**0**	**0**	**0**	**0**	**0**	**0**	**0**	**0**	**0.0**	**–1**	**0**	**0.0**	**8**	**2**	**13:32**	....	....	....	....	....	....	....	....
	New Haven	AHL	60	2	7	9	154	....	....	....	....	....	....	....	....	....	....	....	....	....	....	....	....	....	....	....
99-2000	**Florida**	**NHL**	**17**	**0**	**0**	**0**	**26**	**0**	**0**	**0**	**1**	**0.0**	**–2**	**0**	**0.0**	**37**	**10**	**11:58**	....	....	....	....	....	....	....	....
	Louisville	AHL	23	4	6	10	47	....	....	....	....	....	....	....	....	....	....	....	....	....	....	....	....	....	....	....
	NHL Totals		**22**	**0**	**0**	**0**	**30**	**0**	**0**	**0**	**2**	**0.0**		**0**	**0.0**	**45**	**12**	**12:12**	....	....	....	....	....	....	....	....

Signed as a free agent by **Florida**, May 14, 1997. • Missed remainder of 1999-2000 season recovering from groin injury suffered in game vs. Carolina, February 1, 2000.

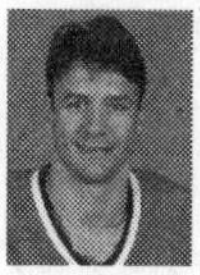

JANSSENS, Mark

(JAN-sehns, MAHRK) **CHI.**

Center. Shoots left. 6'3", 212 lbs. Born, Surrey, B.C., May 19, 1968. NY Rangers' 4th choice, 72nd overall, in 1986 Entry Draft.

			Regular Season																Playoffs							
Season	Club	League	GP	G	A	Pts	PIM	PP	SH	GW	S	%	+/–	TF	F%	H	SB	Min	GP	G	A	Pts	PIM	PP	SH	GW
1983-84	Surrey Eagles	BCAHA	40	40	58	98	64	....	....	....	....	....	....	....	....	....	....	....	....	....	....	....	....	....	....	....
1984-85	Regina Pats	WHL	70	8	22	30	51	....	....	....	....	....	....	....	....	....	....	....	5	1	1	2	0	....	....	....
1985-86	Regina Pats	WHL	71	25	38	63	146	....	....	....	....	....	....	....	....	....	....	....	9	0	2	2	17	....	....	....
1986-87	Regina Pats	WHL	68	24	38	62	209	....	....	....	....	....	....	....	....	....	....	....	3	0	1	1	14	....	....	....
1987-88	Regina Pats	WHL	71	39	51	90	202	....	....	....	....	....	....	....	....	....	....	....	4	3	4	7	6	....	....	....
	NY Rangers	**NHL**	**1**	**0**	**0**	**0**	**0**	**0**	**0**	**0**	**0**	**0.0**	**0**	....	....	....	....	....	....	....	....	....	....	....	....	....
	Colorado Rangers	IHL	6	2	2	4	24	....	....	....	....	....	....	....	....	....	....	....	12	3	2	5	20	....	....	....
1988-89	**NY Rangers**	**NHL**	**5**	**0**	**0**	**0**	**0**	**0**	**0**	**0**	**4**	**0.0**	**–4**	....	....	....	....	....	....	....	....	....	....	....	....	....
	Denver Rangers	IHL	38	19	19	38	104	....	....	....	....	....	....	....	....	....	....	....	4	3	0	3	18	....	....	....
1989-90	**NY Rangers**	**NHL**	**80**	**5**	**8**	**13**	**161**	**0**	**0**	**0**	**61**	**8.2**	**–26**	....	....	....	....	....	**9**	**2**	**1**	**3**	**10**	**0**	**0**	**1**
1990-91	**NY Rangers**	**NHL**	**67**	**9**	**7**	**16**	**172**	**0**	**0**	**1**	**45**	**20.0**	**–1**	....	....	....	....	....	**6**	**3**	**0**	**3**	**6**	**0**	**0**	**0**
1991-92	**NY Rangers**	**NHL**	**4**	**0**	**0**	**0**	**5**	**0**	**0**	**0**	**0**	**0.0**	**–1**	....	....	....	....	....	....	....	....	....	....	....	....	....
	Binghamton	AHL	55	10	23	33	109	....	....	....	....	....	....	....	....	....	....	....	....	....	....	....	....	....	....	....
	Minnesota	**NHL**	**3**	**0**	**0**	**0**	**0**	**0**	**0**	**0**	**1**	**0.0**	**–1**	....	....	....	....	....	....	....	....	....	....	....	....	....
	Kalamazoo Wings	IHL	2	0	0	0	2	....	....	....	....	....	....	....	....	....	....	....	11	1	2	3	22	....	....	....
1992-93	**Hartford**	**NHL**	**76**	**12**	**17**	**29**	**237**	**0**	**0**	**1**	**63**	**19.0**	**–15**	....	....	....	....	....	....	....	....	....	....	....	....	....
1993-94	**Hartford**	**NHL**	**84**	**2**	**10**	**12**	**137**	**0**	**0**	**0**	**52**	**3.8**	**–13**	....	....	....	....	....	....	....	....	....	....	....	....	....
1994-95	**Hartford**	**NHL**	**46**	**2**	**5**	**7**	**93**	**0**	**0**	**0**	**33**	**6.1**	**–8**	....	....	....	....	....	....	....	....	....	....	....	....	....
1995-96	**Hartford**	**NHL**	**81**	**2**	**7**	**9**	**155**	**0**	**0**	**0**	**63**	**3.2**	**–13**	....	....	....	....	....	....	....	....	....	....	....	....	....
1996-97	**Hartford**	**NHL**	**54**	**2**	**4**	**6**	**90**	**0**	**0**	**0**	**30**	**6.7**	**–10**	....	....	....	....	....	....	....	....	....	....	....	....	....
	Anaheim	**NHL**	**12**	**0**	**2**	**2**	**47**	**0**	**0**	**0**	**9**	**0.0**	**–3**	....	....	....	....	....	**11**	**0**	**0**	**0**	**15**	**0**	**0**	**0**
1997-98	**Anaheim**	**NHL**	**55**	**4**	**5**	**9**	**116**	**0**	**0**	**1**	**43**	**9.3**	**–22**	....	....	....	....	....	....	....	....	....	....	....	....	....
	NY Islanders	**NHL**	**12**	**0**	**0**	**0**	**34**	**0**	**0**	**0**	**4**	**0.0**	**–3**	....	....	....	....	....	....	....	....	....	....	....	....	....
	Phoenix	**NHL**	**7**	**1**	**2**	**3**	**4**	**0**	**0**	**0**	**6**	**16.7**	**4**	....	....	....	....	....	**1**	**0**	**0**	**0**	**2**	**0**	**0**	**0**
1998-99	**Chicago**	**NHL**	**60**	**1**	**0**	**1**	**65**	**0**	**0**	**0**	**27**	**3.7**	**–11**	**594**	**57.9**	**34**	**19**	**8:17**	....	....	....	....	....	....	....	....
99-2000	**Chicago**	**NHL**	**36**	**0**	**6**	**6**	**73**	**0**	**0**	**0**	**14**	**0.0**	**–2**	**127**	**51.2**	**15**	**10**	**7:12**	....	....	....	....	....	....	....	....
	NHL Totals		**683**	**40**	**73**	**113**	**1389**	**0**	**0**	**3**	**455**	**8.8**		**721**	**56.7**	**49**	**29**	**7:53**	**27**	**5**	**1**	**6**	**33**	**0**	**0**	**1**

Traded to **Minnesota** by **NY Rangers** for Mario Thyer and Minnesota's 3rd round choice (Maxim Galanov) in 1993 Entry Draft, March 10, 1992. Traded to **Hartford** by **Minnesota** for James Black, September 3, 1992. Traded to **Anaheim** by **Hartford** for Bates Battaglia and Anaheim's 4th round choice (Carolina selected Josef Vasicek) in 1998 Entry Draft, March 18, 1997. Traded to **NY Islanders** by **Anaheim** with Joe Sacco and J.J. Daigneault for Travis Green, Doug Houda and Tony Tuzzolino, February 6, 1998. Traded to **Phoenix** by **NY Islanders** for Phoenix's 9th round choice (Jason Doyle) in 1998 Entry Draft, March 24, 1998. Signed as a free agent by **Chicago**, July 28, 1998. • Missed majority of 1999-2000 season recovering from back injury suffered in game vs. Edmonton, December 3, 1999. Traded to **Philadelphia** by **Chicago** for Philadelphia's 9th round choice (Arne Ramholt) in 2000 Entry Draft, June 12, 2000. Claimed on waivers by **Chicago** from **Philadelphia**, July 6, 2000.

JOHANSSON, Andreas
(yoh-HAHN-suhn, ahn-DRAY-uhs) **CGY.**

Center. Shoots left. 6', 202 lbs. Born, Hofors, Sweden, May 19, 1973. NY Islanders' 7th choice, 136th overall, in 1991 Entry Draft.

			Regular Season																Playoffs							
Season	Club	League	GP	G	A	Pts	PIM	PP	SH	GW	S	%	+/–	TF	F%	H	SB	Min	GP	G	A	Pts	PIM	PP	SH	GW
1987-88	Hofors HC	Sweden-3	1	0	0	0	0	....	....	....	....	....	....	....	....	....	....	....	....	....	....	....	....	....	....	....
1988-89	Hofors HC	Sweden-3	28	19	11	30	....	....	....	....	....	....	....	....	....	....	....	....	....	....	....	....	....	....	....	....
1989-90	Falu IF	Sweden-2	21	3	1	4	14	....	....	....	....	....	....	....	....	....	....	....	....	....	....	....	....	....	....	....
1990-91	Falu IF	Sweden-2	31	12	10	22	38	....	....	....	....	....	....	....	....	....	....	....	....	....	....	....	....	....	....	....
1991-92	Farjestads BK	Sweden	30	3	1	4	10	....	....	....	....	....	....	....	....	....	....	....	6	0	0	0	4	....	....	....
1992-93	Farjestads BK	Sweden	38	4	7	11	38	....	....	....	....	....	....	....	....	....	....	....	2	0	0	0	0	....	....	....
1993-94	Farjestads BK	Sweden	20	3	6	9	6	....	....	....	....	....	....	....	....	....	....	....	....	....	....	....	....	....	....	....
1994-95	Farjestads BK	Sweden	36	9	10	19	42	....	....	....	....	....	....	....	....	....	....	....	4	0	0	0	10	....	....	....
1995-96	**NY Islanders**	**NHL**	**3**	**0**	**1**	**1**	**0**	**0**	**0**	**0**	**6**	**0.0**	**1**	....	....	....	....	....	....	....	....	....	....	....	....	....
	Worcester	AHL	29	5	5	10	32	....	....	....	....	....	....	....	....	....	....	....	....	....	....	....	....	....	....	....
	Utah Grizzlies	IHL	22	4	13	17	28	....	....	....	....	....	....	....	....	....	....	....	12	0	5	5	6	....	....	....
1996-97	**NY Islanders**	**NHL**	**15**	**2**	**2**	**4**	**0**	**1**	**0**	**0**	**21**	**9.5**	**–6**	....	....	....	....	....	....	....	....	....	....	....	....	....
	Pittsburgh	**NHL**	**27**	**2**	**7**	**9**	**20**	**0**	**0**	**0**	**38**	**5.3**	**–6**	....	....	....	....	....	....	....	....	....	....	....	....	....
	Cleveland	IHL	10	2	4	6	42	....	....	....	....	....	....	....	....	....	....	....	11	1	5	6	8	....	....	....
1997-98	**Pittsburgh**	**NHL**	**50**	**5**	**10**	**15**	**20**	**0**	**1**	**0**	**49**	**10.2**	**4**	....	....	....	....	....	**1**	**0**	**0**	**0**	**0**	**0**	**0**	**0**
	Sweden	Olympics	3	0	0	0	2	....	....	....	....	....	....	....	....	....	....	....	....	....	....	....	....	....	....	....
1998-99	**Ottawa**	**NHL**	**69**	**21**	**16**	**37**	**34**	**7**	**0**	**6**	**144**	**14.6**	**1**	**9**	**22.2**	**48**	**8**	**14:39**	**2**	**0**	**0**	**0**	**0**	**0**	**0**	**0**
99-2000	**Tampa Bay**	**NHL**	**12**	**2**	**3**	**5**	**8**	**0**	**0**	**0**	**11**	**18.2**	**1**	**0**	**0.0**	**8**	**2**	**10:50**	....	....	....	....	....	....	....	....
	Calgary	**NHL**	**28**	**3**	**7**	**10**	**14**	**1**	**0**	**0**	**47**	**6.4**	**–3**	**5**	**20.0**	**22**	**8**	**13:33**	....	....	....	....	....	....	....	....
	NHL Totals		**204**	**35**	**46**	**81**	**96**	**9**	**1**	**6**	**316**	**11.1**		**14**	**21.4**	**78**	**18**	**13:57**	**3**	**0**	**0**	**0**	**0**	**0**	**0**	**0**

Swedish World All-Star Team (1995)

Traded to **Pittsburgh** by **NY Islanders** with Darius Kasparaitis for Bryan Smolinski, November 17, 1996. Signed as a free agent by **Ottawa**, September 29, 1998. Traded to **Tampa Bay** by **Ottawa** for Rob Zamuner and future considerations, June 29, 1999. Traded to **Calgary** by **Tampa Bay** for Nils Ekman and Calgary's 4th round choice (later traded to NY Islanders - NY Islanders selected Vladimir Gorbunov) in 2000 Entry Draft, November 13, 1999. • Missed remainder of 1999-2000 season recovering from back injury suffered in game vs. Vancouver, January 2, 2000.

JOHANSSON, Calle
(yoh-HAHN-suhn, KAL-ee) **WSH.**

Defense. Shoots left. 5'11", 200 lbs. Born, Goteborg, Sweden, February 14, 1967. Buffalo's 1st choice, 14th overall, in 1985 Entry Draft.

			Regular Season																Playoffs							
Season	Club	League	GP	G	A	Pts	PIM	PP	SH	GW	S	%	+/–	TF	F%	H	SB	Min	GP	G	A	Pts	PIM	PP	SH	GW
1981-82	KBA-67	Sweden-3	27	3	3	6	....	....	....	....	....	....	....	....	....	....	....	....	....	....	....	....	....	....	....	....
1982-83	KBA-67	Sweden-3	29	12	11	23	....	....	....	....	....	....	....	....	....	....	....	....	....	....	....	....	....	....	....	....
1983-84	Vastra Frolunda	Sweden	28	4	4	8	10	....	....	....	....	....	....	....	....	....	....	....	....	....	....	....	....	....	....	....
1984-85	Vastra Frolunda	Sweden-2	25	8	13	21	16	....	....	....	....	....	....	....	....	....	....	....	6	1	2	3	4	....	....	....
1985-86	Bjorkloven	Sweden	17	1	2	3	4	....	....	....	....	....	....	....	....	....	....	....	....	....	....	....	....	....	....	....
1986-87	Bjorkloven	Sweden	30	2	13	15	20	....	....	....	....	....	....	....	....	....	....	....	6	1	3	4	6	....	....	....
1987-88	**Buffalo**	**NHL**	**71**	**4**	**38**	**42**	**37**	**2**	**0**	**0**	**93**	**4.3**	**12**	....	....	....	....	....	**6**	**0**	**1**	**1**	**0**	**0**	**0**	**0**
1988-89	**Buffalo**	**NHL**	**47**	**2**	**11**	**13**	**33**	**0**	**0**	**1**	**53**	**3.8**	**–7**	....	....	....	....	....	....	....	....	....	....	....	....	....
	Washington	**NHL**	**12**	**1**	**7**	**8**	**4**	**1**	**0**	**0**	**22**	**4.5**	**1**	....	....	....	....	....	**6**	**1**	**2**	**3**	**0**	**1**	**0**	**0**
1989-90	**Washington**	**NHL**	**70**	**8**	**31**	**39**	**25**	**4**	**0**	**2**	**103**	**7.8**	**7**	....	....	....	....	....	**15**	**1**	**6**	**7**	**4**	**0**	**0**	**0**
1990-91	**Washington**	**NHL**	**80**	**11**	**41**	**52**	**23**	**2**	**1**	**2**	**128**	**8.6**	**–2**	....	....	....	....	....	**10**	**2**	**7**	**9**	**8**	**1**	**0**	**0**
1991-92	**Washington**	**NHL**	**80**	**14**	**42**	**56**	**49**	**5**	**2**	**2**	**119**	**11.8**	**2**	....	....	....	....	....	**7**	**0**	**5**	**5**	**4**	**0**	**0**	**0**
1992-93	**Washington**	**NHL**	**77**	**7**	**38**	**45**	**56**	**6**	**0**	**0**	**133**	**5.3**	**3**	....	....	....	....	....	**6**	**0**	**5**	**5**	**4**	**0**	**0**	**0**
1993-94	**Washington**	**NHL**	**84**	**9**	**33**	**42**	**59**	**4**	**0**	**1**	**141**	**6.4**	**3**	....	....	....	....	....	**6**	**1**	**3**	**4**	**4**	**0**	**0**	**1**
1994-95	EHC Kloten	Switz.	5	1	2	3	8	....	....	....	....	....	....	....	....	....	....	....	....	....	....	....	....	....	....	....
	Washington	**NHL**	**46**	**5**	**26**	**31**	**35**	**4**	**0**	**2**	**112**	**4.5**	**–6**	....	....	....	....	....	**7**	**3**	**1**	**4**	**0**	**1**	**0**	**0**
1995-96	**Washington**	**NHL**	**78**	**10**	**25**	**35**	**50**	**4**	**0**	**0**	**182**	**5.5**	**13**	....	....	....	....	....	....	....	....	....	....	....	....	....
1996-97	**Washington**	**NHL**	**65**	**6**	**11**	**17**	**16**	**2**	**0**	**0**	**133**	**4.5**	**–2**	....	....	....	....	....	....	....	....	....	....	....	....	....
1997-98	**Washington**	**NHL**	**73**	**15**	**20**	**35**	**30**	**10**	**1**	**1**	**163**	**9.2**	**–11**	....	....	....	....	....	**21**	**2**	**8**	**10**	**16**	**0**	**0**	**0**
	Sweden	Olympics	4	0	0	0	2	....	....	....	....	....	....	....	....	....	....	....	....	....	....	....	....	....	....	....
1998-99	**Washington**	**NHL**	**67**	**8**	**21**	**29**	**22**	**2**	**0**	**2**	**145**	**5.5**	**10**	**0**	**0.0**	**51**	**140**	**23:58**	....	....	....	....	....	....	....	....
99-2000	**Washington**	**NHL**	**82**	**7**	**25**	**32**	**24**	**1**	**0**	**3**	**138**	**5.1**	**13**	**0**	**0.0**	**67**	**161**	**23:55**	**5**	**1**	**2**	**3**	**0**	**1**	**0**	**0**
	NHL Totals		**932**	**107**	**369**	**476**	**463**	**47**	**4**	**16**	**1665**	**6.4**		**0**	**0.0**	**118**	**301**	**23:56**	**89**	**11**	**40**	**51**	**40**	**4**	**0**	**1**

NHL All-Rookie Team (1988)

Traded to **Washington** by **Buffalo** with Buffalo's 2nd round choice (Byron Dafoe) in 1989 Entry Draft for Clint Malarchuk, Grant Ledyard and Washington's 6th round choice (Brian Holzinger) in 1991 Entry Draft, March 7, 1989.

JOHNSON, Craig
(JAWN-sohn, KRAYG) **L.A.**

Left wing. Shoots left. 6'2", 200 lbs. Born, St. Paul, MN, March 8, 1972. St. Louis' 1st choice, 33rd overall, in 1990 Entry Draft.

			Regular Season																Playoffs							
Season	Club	League	GP	G	A	Pts	PIM	PP	SH	GW	S	%	+/–	TF	F%	H	SB	Min	GP	G	A	Pts	PIM	PP	SH	GW
1987-88	Hill-Murray	Hi-School	28	14	20	34	4	....	....	....	....	....	....	....	....	....	....	....	....	....	....	....	....	....	....	....
1988-89	Hill-Murray	Hi-School	24	22	30	52	10	....	....	....	....	....	....	....	....	....	....	....	....	....	....	....	....	....	....	....
1989-90	Hill-Murray	Hi-School	23	15	36	51	0	....	....	....	....	....	....	....	....	....	....	....	....	....	....	....	....	....	....	....
1990-91	U. of Minnesota	WCHA	33	13	18	31	34	....	....	....	....	....	....	....	....	....	....	....	....	....	....	....	....	....	....	....
1991-92	U. of Minnesota	WCHA	41	17	38	55	66	....	....	....	....	....	....	....	....	....	....	....	....	....	....	....	....	....	....	....
1992-93	U. of Minnesota	WCHA	42	22	24	46	70	....	....	....	....	....	....	....	....	....	....	....	....	....	....	....	....	....	....	....
	Jacksonville	SunHL	23	2	9	11	38	....	....	....	....	....	....	....	....	....	....	....	....	....	....	....	....	....	....	....
1993-94	United States	Nat-Team	54	25	26	51	64	....	....	....	....	....	....	....	....	....	....	....	....	....	....	....	....	....	....	....
	United States	Olympics	8	0	4	4	4	....	....	....	....	....	....	....	....	....	....	....	....	....	....	....	....	....	....	....
1994-95	**St. Louis**	**NHL**	**15**	**3**	**3**	**6**	**6**	**0**	**0**	**0**	**19**	**15.8**	**4**	....	....	....	....	....	**1**	**0**	**0**	**0**	**2**	**0**	**0**	**0**
	Peoria Rivermen	IHL	16	2	6	8	25	....	....	....	....	....	....	....	....	....	....	....	9	0	4	4	10	....	....	....
1995-96	**St. Louis**	**NHL**	**49**	**8**	**7**	**15**	**30**	**1**	**0**	**0**	**69**	**11.6**	**–4**	....	....	....	....	....	....	....	....	....	....	....	....	....
	Worcester	AHL	5	3	0	3	2	....	....	....	....	....	....	....	....	....	....	....	....	....	....	....	....	....	....	....
	Los Angeles	**NHL**	**11**	**5**	**4**	**9**	**6**	**3**	**0**	**0**	**28**	**17.9**	**–4**	....	....	....	....	....	....	....	....	....	....	....	....	....
1996-97	**Los Angeles**	**NHL**	**31**	**4**	**3**	**7**	**26**	**1**	**0**	**0**	**30**	**13.3**	**–7**	....	....	....	....	....	....	....	....	....	....	....	....	....
1997-98	**Los Angeles**	**NHL**	**74**	**17**	**21**	**38**	**42**	**6**	**0**	**2**	**125**	**13.6**	**9**	....	....	....	....	....	**4**	**1**	**0**	**1**	**4**	**0**	**0**	**0**
1998-99	**Los Angeles**	**NHL**	**69**	**7**	**12**	**19**	**32**	**2**	**0**	**2**	**94**	**7.4**	**–12**	**2**	**50.0**	**70**	**11**	**12:02**	....	....	....	....	....	....	....	....
99-2000	**Los Angeles**	**NHL**	**76**	**9**	**14**	**23**	**28**	**1**	**0**	**1**	**106**	**8.5**	**–10**	**9**	**55.6**	**82**	**18**	**13:56**	**4**	**1**	**0**	**1**	**2**	**0**	**0**	**0**
	NHL Totals		**325**	**53**	**64**	**117**	**170**	**14**	**0**	**5**	**471**	**11.3**		**11**	**54.5**	**152**	**29**	**13:02**	**9**	**2**	**0**	**2**	**8**	**0**	**0**	**0**

Traded to **LA Kings** by **St. Louis** with Patrice Tardif, Roman Vopat, St. Louis 5th round choice (Peter Hogan) in 1996 Entry Draft and 1st round choice (Matt Zultek) in 1997 Entry Draft for Wayne Gretzky, February 27, 1996.

JOHNSON, Greg
(JAWN-sohn, GREHG) **NSH.**

Center. Shoots left. 5'11", 202 lbs. Born, Thunder Bay, Ont., March 16, 1971. Philadelphia's 1st choice, 33rd overall, in 1989 Entry Draft.

			Regular Season																Playoffs							
Season	Club	League	GP	G	A	Pts	PIM	PP	SH	GW	S	%	+/–	TF	F%	H	SB	Min	GP	G	A	Pts	PIM	PP	SH	GW
1988-89	Thunder Bay	USHL	47	32	64	96	4	....	....	....	....	....	....	....	....	....	....	....	12	5	13	18	0	....	....	....
1989-90	North Dakota	WCHA	44	17	38	55	11	....	....	....	....	....	....	....	....	....	....	....	....	....	....	....	....	....	....	....
1990-91	North Dakota	WCHA	38	18	*61	79	6	....	....	....	....	....	....	....	....	....	....	....	....	....	....	....	....	....	....	....
1991-92	North Dakota	WCHA	39	20	*54	74	8	....	....	....	....	....	....	....	....	....	....	....	....	....	....	....	....	....	....	....
1992-93	North Dakota	WCHA	34	19	45	64	18	....	....	....	....	....	....	....	....	....	....	....	....	....	....	....	....	....	....	....
	Canada	Nat-Team	23	6	14	20	2	....	....	....	....	....	....	....	....	....	....	....	....	....	....	....	....	....	....	....
1993-94	**Detroit**	**NHL**	**52**	**6**	**11**	**17**	**22**	**1**	**1**	**0**	**48**	**12.5**	**–7**	....	....	....	....	....	**7**	**2**	**2**	**4**	**2**	**1**	**0**	**0**
	Adirondack	AHL	3	2	4	6	0	....	....	....	....	....	....	....	....	....	....	....	4	0	4	4	2	....	....	....
	Canada	Nat-Team	6	2	6	8	4	....	....	....	....	....	....	....	....	....	....	....	....	....	....	....	....	....	....	....
	Canada	Olympics	8	0	3	3	0	....	....	....	....	....	....	....	....	....	....	....	....	....	....	....	....	....	....	....
1994-95	**Detroit**	**NHL**	**22**	**3**	**5**	**8**	**14**	**2**	**0**	**0**	**32**	**9.4**	**1**	....	....	....	....	....	**1**	**0**	**0**	**0**	**0**	**0**	**0**	**0**
1995-96	**Detroit**	**NHL**	**60**	**18**	**22**	**40**	**30**	**5**	**0**	**2**	**87**	**20.7**	**6**	....	....	....	....	....	**13**	**3**	**1**	**4**	**8**	**0**	**0**	**0**
1996-97	**Detroit**	**NHL**	**43**	**6**	**10**	**16**	**12**	**0**	**0**	**0**	**56**	**10.7**	**–5**	....	....	....	....	....	....	....	....	....	....	....	....	....
	Pittsburgh	**NHL**	**32**	**7**	**9**	**16**	**14**	**1**	**0**	**0**	**52**	**13.5**	**–13**	....	....	....	....	....	**5**	**1**	**0**	**1**	**2**	**0**	**0**	**0**
1997-98	**Pittsburgh**	**NHL**	**5**	**1**	**0**	**1**	**2**	**0**	**0**	**0**	**4**	**25.0**	**0**	....	....	....	....	....	....	....	....	....	....	....	....	....
	Chicago	**NHL**	**69**	**11**	**22**	**33**	**38**	**4**	**0**	**3**	**85**	**12.9**	**–2**	....	....	....	....	....	....	....	....	....	....	....	....	....

Season	Club	League	Regular Season GP	G	A	Pts	PIM	PP	SH	GW	S	%	+/-	TF	F%	H	SB	Min	Playoffs GP	G	A	Pts	PIM	PP	SH	GW
1998-99	**Nashville**	**NHL**	**68**	**16**	**34**	**50**	**24**	**2**	**3**	**0**	**120**	**13.3**	**–8**	**1441**	**53.6**	**28**	**36**	**19:26**	....	....	....	....	....	....	....	....
99-2000	**Nashville**	**NHL**	**82**	**11**	**33**	**44**	**40**	**2**	**0**	**1**	**133**	**8.3**	**–15**	**1684**	**50.8**	**17**	**41**	**19:13**	....	....	....	....	....	....	....	....
	NHL Totals		**433**	**79**	**146**	**225**	**196**	**17**	**4**	**6**	**617**	**12.8**		**3125**	**52.1**	**45**	**77**	**19:19**	**26**	**6**	**3**	**9**	**12**	**1**	**0**	**0**

WCHA First All-Star Team (1991, 1992, 1993) • NCAA West First All-American Team (1991, 1993) • NCAA West Second All-American Team (1992)

Traded to **Detroit** by **Philadelphia** with Philadelphia's 5th round choice (Frederic Deschenes) in 1994 Entry Draft for Jim Cummins and Philadelphia's 4th round choice (previously acquired by Detroit - later traded to Boston - Boston selected Charles Paquette) in 1993 Entry Draft, June 20, 1993. Traded to **Pittsburgh** by **Detroit** for Tomas Sandstrom, January 27, 1997. Traded to **Chicago** by **Pittsburgh** for Tuomas Gronman, October 27, 1997. Claimed by **Nashville** from **Chicago** in Expansion Draft, June 26, 1998.

JOHNSON, Matt — ATL.

Left wing. Shoots left. 6'5", 232 lbs. Born, Welland, Ont., November 23, 1975. Los Angeles' 2nd choice, 33rd overall, in 1994 Entry Draft.

Season	Club	League	GP	G	A	Pts	PIM	PP	SH	GW	S	%	+/-	TF	F%	H	SB	Min	GP	G	A	Pts	PIM	PP	SH	GW
1991-92	Welland Aerostars	OJHL-B	38	6	19	25	214	....	....	....	....	....	....	....	....	....	....	....	....	....	....	....	....	....	....	....
	Ajax Axemen	OJHL-B	1	0	0	0	0	....	....	....	....	....	....	....	....	....	....	....	....	....	....	....	....	....	....	....
1992-93	Peterborough	OHL	66	8	17	25	211	....	....	....	....	....	....	....	....	....	....	....	16	1	1	2	56	....	....	....
1993-94	Peterborough	OHL	50	13	24	37	233	....	....	....	....	....	....	....	....	....	....	....	....	....	....	....	....	....	....	....
1994-95	Peterborough	OHL	14	1	2	3	43	....	....	....	....	....	....	....	....	....	....	....	....	....	....	....	....	....	....	....
	Los Angeles	**NHL**	**14**	**1**	**0**	**1**	**102**	**0**	**0**	**0**	**4**	**25.0**	**0**	....	....	....	....	....	....	....	....	....	....	....	....	....
1995-96	**Los Angeles**	**NHL**	**1**	**0**	**0**	**0**	**5**	**0**	**0**	**0**	**1**	**0.0**	**0**	....	....	....	....	....	....	....	....	....	....	....	....	....
	Phoenix	IHL	29	4	4	8	87	....	....	....	....	....	....	....	....	....	....	....	....	....	....	....	....	....	....	....
1996-97	**Los Angeles**	**NHL**	**52**	**1**	**3**	**4**	**194**	**0**	**0**	**0**	**20**	**5.0**	**–4**	....	....	....	....	....	....	....	....	....	....	....	....	....
1997-98	**Los Angeles**	**NHL**	**66**	**2**	**4**	**6**	**249**	**0**	**0**	**0**	**18**	**11.1**	**–8**	....	....	....	....	....	**4**	**0**	**0**	**0**	**6**	**0**	**0**	**0**
1998-99	**Los Angeles**	**NHL**	**49**	**2**	**1**	**3**	**131**	**0**	**0**	**0**	**14**	**14.3**	**–5**	**1**	**0.0**	**62**	**4**	**5:55**	....	....	....	....	....	....	....	....
99-2000	**Atlanta**	**NHL**	**64**	**2**	**5**	**7**	**144**	**0**	**0**	**0**	**54**	**3.7**	**–11**	**1**	**100.0**	**133**	**8**	**8:25**	....	....	....	....	....	....	....	....
	NHL Totals		**246**	**8**	**13**	**21**	**825**	**0**	**0**	**0**	**111**	**7.2**		**2**	**50.0**	**195**	**12**	**7:20**	**4**	**0**	**0**	**0**	**6**	**0**	**0**	**0**

Claimed by **Atlanta** from **Los Angeles** in Expansion Draft, June 25, 1999.

JOHNSON, Mike — (JAWN-sohn, MIHK-al) — T.B.

Right wing. Shoots right. 6'2", 197 lbs. Born, Scarborough, Ont., October 3, 1974.

Season	Club	League	GP	G	A	Pts	PIM	PP	SH	GW	S	%	+/-	TF	F%	H	SB	Min	GP	G	A	Pts	PIM	PP	SH	GW
1991-92	Hillcrest Summits	MTHL	45	43	66	109	....	....	....	....	....	....	....	....	....	....	....	....	20	10	19	29	....	....	....	....
1992-93	Aurora Eagles	OJHL	48	25	40	65	18	....	....	....	....	....	....	....	....	....	....	....	7	7	15	22	....	....	....	....
1993-94	Bowling Green	CCHA	38	6	14	20	18	....	....	....	....	....	....	....	....	....	....	....	....	....	....	....	....	....	....	....
1994-95	Bowling Green	CCHA	37	16	33	49	35	....	....	....	....	....	....	....	....	....	....	....	....	....	....	....	....	....	....	....
1995-96	Bowling Green	CCHA	30	12	19	31	22	....	....	....	....	....	....	....	....	....	....	....	....	....	....	....	....	....	....	....
1996-97	Bowling Green	CCHA	38	30	32	62	46	....	....	....	....	....	....	....	....	....	....	....	....	....	....	....	....	....	....	....
	Toronto	**NHL**	**13**	**2**	**2**	**4**	**4**	**0**	**1**	**1**	**27**	**7.4**	**–2**	....	....	....	....	....	....	....	....	....	....	....	....	....
1997-98	**Toronto**	**NHL**	**82**	**15**	**32**	**47**	**24**	**5**	**0**	**0**	**143**	**10.5**	**–4**	....	....	....	....	....	....	....	....	....	....	....	....	....
1998-99	**Toronto**	**NHL**	**79**	**20**	**24**	**44**	**35**	**5**	**3**	**2**	**149**	**13.4**	**13**	**15**	**53.3**	**70**	**17**	**16:16**	**17**	**3**	**2**	**5**	**4**	**0**	**0**	**1**
99-2000	**Toronto**	**NHL**	**52**	**11**	**14**	**25**	**23**	**2**	**1**	**3**	**89**	**12.4**	**8**	**2**	**50.0**	**58**	**6**	**15:22**	....	....	....	....	....	....	....	....
	Tampa Bay	**NHL**	**28**	**10**	**12**	**22**	**4**	**4**	**0**	**0**	**43**	**23.3**	**–2**	**5**	**60.0**	**26**	**11**	**20:33**	....	....	....	....	....	....	....	....
	NHL Totals		**254**	**58**	**84**	**142**	**90**	**16**	**5**	**6**	**451**	**12.9**		**22**	**54.5**	**154**	**34**	**16:44**	**17**	**3**	**2**	**5**	**4**	**0**	**0**	**1**

NHL All-Rookie Team (1998)

Signed as a free agent by **Toronto**, March 16, 1997. Traded to **Tampa Bay** by **Toronto** with Marek Posmyk, Toronto's 5th (Pavel Sedov) and 6th (Aaron Gionet) round choices in 2000 Entry Draft and future considerations for Darcy Tucker, Tampa Bay's 4th round choice (Miguel Delisle) in 2000 Entry Draft and future considerations, February 9, 2000.

JOHNSON, Ryan — (JAWN-sohn, RIGH-yan) — T.B.

Center. Shoots left. 6'1", 200 lbs. Born, Thunder Bay, Ont., June 14, 1976. Florida's 4th choice, 36th overall, in 1994 Entry Draft.

Season	Club	League	GP	G	A	Pts	PIM	PP	SH	GW	S	%	+/-	TF	F%	H	SB	Min	GP	G	A	Pts	PIM	PP	SH	GW
1992-93	Thunder Bay	TBAHA	60	25	33	58	....	....	....	....	....	....	....	....	....	....	....	....	....	....	....	....	....	....	....	....
1993-94	Thunder Bay	USHL	48	14	36	50	28	....	....	....	....	....	....	....	....	....	....	....	....	....	....	....	....	....	....	....
1994-95	North Dakota	WCHA	38	6	22	28	39	....	....	....	....	....	....	....	....	....	....	....	....	....	....	....	....	....	....	....
1995-96	North Dakota	WCHA	21	2	17	19	14	....	....	....	....	....	....	....	....	....	....	....	....	....	....	....	....	....	....	....
	Canada	Nat-Team	28	5	12	17	14	....	....	....	....	....	....	....	....	....	....	....	....	....	....	....	....	....	....	....
1996-97	Carolina	AHL	79	18	24	42	28	....	....	....	....	....	....	....	....	....	....	....	....	....	....	....	....	....	....	....
1997-98	**Florida**	**NHL**	**10**	**0**	**2**	**2**	**0**	**0**	**0**	**0**	**6**	**0.0**	**–4**	....	....	....	....	....	....	....	....	....	....	....	....	....
	New Haven	AHL	64	19	48	67	12	....	....	....	....	....	....	....	....	....	....	....	3	0	1	1	0	....	....	....
1998-99	**Florida**	**NHL**	**1**	**1**	**0**	**1**	**0**	**0**	**0**	**0**	**1**	**100.0**	**0**	**16**	**37.5**	**1**	**0**	**15:26**	....	....	....	....	....	....	....	....
	New Haven	AHL	37	8	19	27	18	....	....	....	....	....	....	....	....	....	....	....	....	....	....	....	....	....	....	....
99-2000	**Florida**	**NHL**	**66**	**4**	**12**	**16**	**14**	**0**	**0**	**0**	**44**	**9.1**	**1**	**684**	**51.8**	**127**	**29**	**11:47**	....	....	....	....	....	....	....	....
	Tampa Bay	**NHL**	**14**	**0**	**2**	**2**	**2**	**0**	**0**	**0**	**5**	**0.0**	**–9**	**117**	**53.0**	**28**	**6**	**11:02**	....	....	....	....	....	....	....	....
	NHL Totals		**91**	**5**	**16**	**21**	**16**	**0**	**0**	**0**	**56**	**8.9**		**817**	**51.7**	**156**	**35**	**11:42**	....	....	....	....	....	....	....	....

Traded to **Tampa Bay** by **Florida**. with Dwayne Hay for Mike Sillinger, March 14, 2000.

JOHNSSON, Kim — (YAWN-suhn, KIHM) — NYR

Defense. Shoots left. 6'1", 178 lbs. Born, Malmo, Sweden, March 16, 1976. NY Rangers' 15th choice, 286th overall, in 1994 Entry Draft.

Season	Club	League	GP	G	A	Pts	PIM	PP	SH	GW	S	%	+/-	TF	F%	H	SB	Min	GP	G	A	Pts	PIM	PP	SH	GW
1993-94	Malmo IF	Swede-Jr.	14	5	3	8	14	....	....	....	....	....	....	....	....	....	....	....	....	....	....	....	....	....	....	....
	Malmo IF	Sweden	2	0	0	0	0	....	....	....	....	....	....	....	....	....	....	....	....	....	....	....	....	....	....	....
1994-95	Malmo IF	Swede-Jr.	29	6	15	21	40	....	....	....	....	....	....	....	....	....	....	....	....	....	....	....	....	....	....	....
	Malmo IF	Sweden	13	0	0	0	4	....	....	....	....	....	....	....	....	....	....	....	1	0	0	0	0	....	....	....
1995-96	Malmo IF	Sweden	38	2	0	2	30	....	....	....	....	....	....	....	....	....	....	....	4	0	1	1	8	....	....	....
1996-97	Malmo IF	Sweden	49	4	9	13	42	....	....	....	....	....	....	....	....	....	....	....	4	0	0	0	2	....	....	....
1997-98	Malmo IF	Sweden	45	5	9	14	29	....	....	....	....	....	....	....	....	....	....	....	....	....	....	....	....	....	....	....
1998-99	Malmo IF	Sweden	49	9	8	17	76	....	....	....	....	....	....	....	....	....	....	....	8	2	3	5	12	....	....	....
99-2000	**NY Rangers**	**NHL**	**76**	**6**	**15**	**21**	**46**	**1**	**0**	**1**	**101**	**5.9**	**–13**	**0**	**0.0**	**61**	**116**	**18:06**	....	....	....	....	....	....	....	....
	NHL Totals		**76**	**6**	**15**	**21**	**46**	**1**	**0**	**1**	**101**	**5.9**		**0**	**0.0**	**61**	**116**	**18:06**	....	....	....	....	....	....	....	....

JOKINEN, Olli — (YOH-kih-nihn, OH-lee) — FLA.

Center. Shoots left. 6'3", 208 lbs. Born, Kuopio, Finland, December 5, 1978. Los Angeles' 1st choice, 3rd overall, in 1997 Entry Draft.

Season	Club	League	GP	G	A	Pts	PIM	PP	SH	GW	S	%	+/-	TF	F%	H	SB	Min	GP	G	A	Pts	PIM	PP	SH	GW
1992-93	KalPa Kuopio-C	Finn-Jr.	14	8	3	11	12	....	....	....	....	....	....	....	....	....	....	....	....	....	....	....	....	....	....	....
1993-94	KalPa Kuopio-C	Finn-Jr.	31	27	25	52	62	....	....	....	....	....	....	....	....	....	....	....	....	....	....	....	....	....	....	....
1994-95	KalPa Kuopio-B	Finn-Jr.	12	9	14	23	46	....	....	....	....	....	....	....	....	....	....	....	....	....	....	....	....	....	....	....
	KaiPa Kuopio	Finland-2	30	22	28	50	92	....	....	....	....	....	....	....	....	....	....	....	....	....	....	....	....	....	....	....
1995-96	KalPa Kuopio	Finn-Jr.	25	20	14	34	47	....	....	....	....	....	....	....	....	....	....	....	7	4	4	8	20	....	....	....
	KalPa Kuopio	Finland	15	1	1	2	2	....	....	....	....	....	....	....	....	....	....	....	....	....	....	....	....	....	....	....
1996-97	HIFK Helsinki	Finn-Jr.	2	1	0	1	6	....	....	....	....	....	....	....	....	....	....	....	....	....	....	....	....	....	....	....
	HIFK Helsinki	Finland	50	14	27	41	88	....	....	....	....	....	....	....	....	....	....	....	....	....	....	....	....	....	....	....
	Finland	Nat-Team	12	4	3	7	4	....	....	....	....	....	....	....	....	....	....	....	....	....	....	....	....	....	....	....
1997-98	**Los Angeles**	**NHL**	**8**	**0**	**0**	**0**	**6**	**0**	**0**	**0**	**12**	**0.0**	**–5**	....	....	....	....	....	....	....	....	....	....	....	....	....
	HIFK Helsinki	Finland	30	11	28	39	8	....	....	....	....	....	....	....	....	....	....	....	9	*7	2	9	2	....	....	....
	Finland	Nat-Team	5	1	1	2	33	....	....	....	....	....	....	....	....	....	....	....	....	....	....	....	....	....	....	....
1998-99	**Los Angeles**	**NHL**	**66**	**9**	**12**	**21**	**44**	**3**	**1**	**1**	**87**	**10.3**	**–10**	**779**	**43.9**	**109**	**26**	**14:42**	....	....	....	....	....	....	....	....
	Springfield	AHL	9	3	6	9	6	....	....	....	....	....	....	....	....	....	....	....	....	....	....	....	....	....	....	....
99-2000	**NY Islanders**	**NHL**	**82**	**11**	**10**	**21**	**80**	**1**	**2**	**3**	**138**	**8.0**	**0**	**841**	**46.1**	**156**	**27**	**16:15**	....	....	....	....	....	....	....	....
	NHL Totals		**156**	**20**	**22**	**42**	**130**	**4**	**3**	**4**	**237**	**8.4**		**1620**	**45.1**	**265**	**53**	**15:33**	....	....	....	....	....	....	....	....

Finnish Rookie of the Year (1997)

Traded to **NY Islanders** by **LA Kings** with Josh Green, Mathieu Biron and LA Kings' 1st round choice (Taylor Pyatt) in 1999 Entry Draft for Zigmund Palffy, Brian Smolinski, Marcel Cousineau and New Jersey's 4th round choice (previously acquired, LA Kings selected Daniel Johanssen) in 1999 Entry Draft, June 20, 1999. Traded to **Florida** by **NY Islanders** with Roberto Luongo for Mark Parrish and Oleg Kvasha, June 24, 2000.

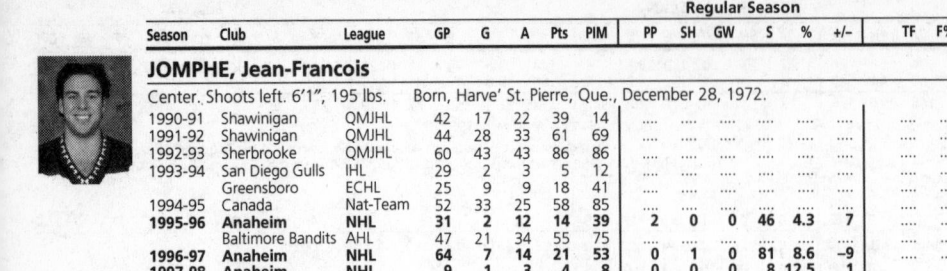

JOMPHE, Jean-Francois (ZHAWMF, ZHAWN-fran-SWUH)

Center. Shoots left. 6'1", 195 lbs. Born, Harve' St. Pierre, Que., December 28, 1972.

			Regular Season																Playoffs							
Season	Club	League	GP	G	A	Pts	PIM	PP	SH	GW	S	%	+/-	TF	F%	H	SB	Min	GP	G	A	Pts	PIM	PP	SH	GW
1990-91	Shawinigan	QMJHL	42	17	22	39	14	....	....	....	....	....	....	....	....	....	....	....	6	2	1	3	2	....	....	....
1991-92	Shawinigan	QMJHL	44	28	33	61	69	....	....	....	....	....	....	....	....	....	....	....	10	6	10	16	10	....	....	....
1992-93	Sherbrooke	QMJHL	60	43	43	86	86	....	....	....	....	....	....	....	....	....	....	....	15	10	13	23	18	....	....	....
1993-94	San Diego Gulls	IHL	29	2	3	5	12	....	....	....	....	....	....	....	....	....	....	....	....	....	....	....	....	....	....	....
	Greensboro	ECHL	25	9	9	18	41	....	....	....	....	....	....	....	....	....	....	....	1	1	0	1	0	....	....	....
1994-95	Canada	Nat-Team	52	33	25	58	85	....	....	....	....	....	....	....	....	....	....	....	....	....	....	....	....	....	....	....
1995-96	**Anaheim**	**NHL**	**31**	**2**	**12**	**14**	**39**	**2**	**0**	**0**	**46**	**4.3**	**7**	....	....	....	....	....	....	....	....	....	....	....	....	....
	Baltimore Bandits	AHL	47	21	34	55	75	....	....	....	....	....	....	....	....	....	....	....	....	....	....	....	....	....	....	....
1996-97	**Anaheim**	**NHL**	**64**	**7**	**14**	**21**	**53**	**0**	**1**	**0**	**81**	**8.6**	**-9**	....	....	....	....	....	....	....	....	....	....	....	....	....
1997-98	**Anaheim**	**NHL**	**9**	**1**	**3**	**4**	**8**	**0**	**0**	**0**	**8**	**12.5**	**1**	....	....	....	....	....	....	....	....	....	....	....	....	....
	Cincinnati Ducks	AHL	38	9	19	28	32	....	....	....	....	....	....	....	....	....	....	....	....	....	....	....	....	....	....	....
	Quebec Rafales	IHL	17	6	4	10	24	....	....	....	....	....	....	....	....	....	....	....	....	....	....	....	....	....	....	....
1998-99	**Phoenix**	**NHL**	**1**	**0**	**0**	**0**	**2**	**0**	**0**	**0**	**0**	**0.0**	**0**	**3**	**66.7**	**3**	**0**	**7:36**	....	....	....	....	....	....	....	....
	Springfield	AHL	29	10	18	28	36	....	....	....	....	....	....	....	....	....	....	....	....	....	....	....	....	....	....	....
	Las Vegas	IHL	32	6	14	20	63	....	....	....	....	....	....	....	....	....	....	....	....	....	....	....	....	....	....	....
	Montreal	**NHL**	**6**	**0**	**0**	**0**	**0**	**0**	**0**	**0**	**4**	**0.0**	**0**	**41**	**48.8**	**10**	**1**	**9:01**	....	....	....	....	....	....	....	....
	Fredericton	AHL	3	1	3	4	6	....	....	....	....	....	....	....	....	....	....	....	15	5	11	16	49	....	....	....
99-2000	Krefeld Pinguine	DEL	47	12	33	45	109	....	....	....	....	....	....	....	....	....	....	....	4	0	1	1	6	....	....	....
	NHL Totals		**111**	**10**	**29**	**39**	**102**	**2**	**1**	**0**	**139**	**7.2**		**44**	**50.0**	**13**	**1**	**8:49**	....	....	....	....	....	....	....	....

Signed as a free agent by **Anaheim**, September 7, 1993. Traded to **Phoenix** by **Anaheim** for Jim McKenzie, June 18, 1998. Traded to **Montreal** by **Phoenix** for cash, March 23, 1999.

JONES, Keith (JOHNS, KEETH) PHI.

Right wing. Shoots left. 6'2", 200 lbs. Born, Brantford, Ont., November 8, 1968. Washington's 7th choice, 141st overall, in 1988 Entry Draft.

			Regular Season																Playoffs							
Season	Club	League	GP	G	A	Pts	PIM	PP	SH	GW	S	%	+/-	TF	F%	H	SB	Min	GP	G	A	Pts	PIM	PP	SH	GW
1985-86	Paris Mounties	OJHL-C	30	26	13	39	61	....	....	....	....	....	....	....	....	....	....	....	....	....	....	....	....	....	....	....
1986-87	Paris Mounties	OJHL-C	30	39	38	77	136	....	....	....	....	....	....	....	....	....	....	....	....	....	....	....	....	....	....	....
1987-88	Niagara Falls	OJHL-B	40	50	80	130	113	....	....	....	....	....	....	....	....	....	....	....	....	....	....	....	....	....	....	....
1988-89	Western Michigan	CCHA	37	9	12	21	51	....	....	....	....	....	....	....	....	....	....	....	....	....	....	....	....	....	....	....
1989-90	Western Michigan	CCHA	40	19	18	37	82	....	....	....	....	....	....	....	....	....	....	....	....	....	....	....	....	....	....	....
1990-91	Western Michigan	CCHA	41	30	19	49	106	....	....	....	....	....	....	....	....	....	....	....	....	....	....	....	....	....	....	....
1991-92	Western Michigan	CCHA	35	25	31	56	77	....	....	....	....	....	....	....	....	....	....	....	....	....	....	....	....	....	....	....
	Baltimore	AHL	6	2	4	6	0	....	....	....	....	....	....	....	....	....	....	....	....	....	....	....	....	....	....	....
1992-93	**Washington**	**NHL**	**71**	**12**	**14**	**26**	**124**	**0**	**0**	**3**	**73**	**16.4**	**18**	....	....	....	....	....	**6**	**0**	**0**	**0**	**10**	**0**	**0**	**0**
	Baltimore	AHL	8	7	3	10	4	....	....	....	....	....	....	....	....	....	....	....	....	....	....	....	....	....	....	....
1993-94	**Washington**	**NHL**	**68**	**16**	**19**	**35**	**149**	**5**	**0**	**1**	**97**	**16.5**	**4**	....	....	....	....	....	**11**	**0**	**1**	**1**	**36**	**0**	**0**	**0**
	Portland Pirates	AHL	6	5	7	12	4	....	....	....	....	....	....	....	....	....	....	....	....	....	....	....	....	....	....	....
1994-95	**Washington**	**NHL**	**40**	**14**	**6**	**20**	**65**	**1**	**0**	**4**	**85**	**16.5**	**-2**	....	....	....	....	....	**7**	**4**	**4**	**8**	**22**	**1**	**0**	**0**
1995-96	**Washington**	**NHL**	**68**	**18**	**23**	**41**	**103**	**5**	**0**	**2**	**155**	**11.6**	**8**	....	....	....	....	....	**2**	**0**	**0**	**0**	**7**	**0**	**0**	**0**
1996-97	**Washington**	**NHL**	**11**	**2**	**3**	**5**	**13**	**1**	**0**	**0**	**12**	**16.7**	**-2**	....	....	....	....	....	....	....	....	....	....	....	....	....
	Colorado	**NHL**	**67**	**23**	**20**	**43**	**105**	**13**	**1**	**7**	**158**	**14.6**	**5**	....	....	....	....	....	**6**	**3**	**3**	**6**	**4**	**1**	**0**	**0**
1997-98	**Colorado**	**NHL**	**23**	**3**	**7**	**10**	**22**	**1**	**0**	**2**	**31**	**9.7**	**-4**	....	....	....	....	....	**7**	**0**	**0**	**0**	**13**	**0**	**0**	**0**
	Hershey Bears	AHL	4	2	1	3	2	....	....	....	....	....	....	....	....	....	....	....	....	....	....	....	....	....	....	....
1998-99	**Colorado**	**NHL**	**12**	**2**	**2**	**4**	**20**	**1**	**0**	**0**	**11**	**18.2**	**-6**	**2**	**100.0**	**16**	**2**	**13:48**	....	....	....	....	....	....	....	....
	Philadelphia	**NHL**	**66**	**18**	**31**	**49**	**78**	**2**	**0**	**3**	**124**	**14.5**	**29**	**78**	**44.9**	**40**	**18**	**16:59**	**6**	**2**	**1**	**3**	**14**	**0**	**0**	**0**
99-2000	**Philadelphia**	**NHL**	**57**	**9**	**16**	**25**	**82**	**1**	**0**	**0**	**92**	**9.8**	**8**	**28**	**32.1**	**28**	**11**	**13:38**	**18**	**3**	**3**	**6**	**14**	**1**	**0**	**0**
	NHL Totals		**483**	**117**	**141**	**258**	**761**	**30**	**1**	**22**	**838**	**14.0**		**108**	**42.6**	**84**	**31**	**15:17**	**63**	**12**	**12**	**24**	**120**	**3**	**0**	**0**

CCHA First All-Star Team (1992)

Traded to **Colorado** by **Washington** with Washington's 1st round choice (Scott Parker) in 1998 Entry Draft and future considerations for Curtis Leschyshyn and Chris Simon, November 2, 1996. Traded to **Philadelphia** by **Colorado** for Shjon Podein, November 12, 1998.

JONES, Ty (JOHNS, TIGH) CHI.

Right wing. Shoots right. 6'3", 218 lbs. Born, Richland, WA, February 22, 1979. Chicago's 2nd choice, 16th overall, in 1997 Entry Draft.

			Regular Season																Playoffs							
Season	Club	League	GP	G	A	Pts	PIM	PP	SH	GW	S	%	+/-	TF	F%	H	SB	Min	GP	G	A	Pts	PIM	PP	SH	GW
1993-94	Alaska All-Stars	AAHL	64	84	104	188	126	....	....	....	....	....	....	....	....	....	....	....	....	....	....	....	....	....	....	....
1994-95	Alaska All-Stars	AAHL	42	33	35	68	98	....	....	....	....	....	....	....	....	....	....	....	....	....	....	....	....	....	....	....
1995-96	Spokane Chiefs	WHL	34	1	0	1	77	....	....	....	....	....	....	....	....	....	....	....	3	0	0	0	6	....	....	....
1996-97	Spokane Chiefs	WHL	67	20	34	54	202	....	....	....	....	....	....	....	....	....	....	....	9	2	4	6	10	....	....	....
1997-98	Spokane Chiefs	WHL	60	36	48	84	161	....	....	....	....	....	....	....	....	....	....	....	18	2	14	16	35	....	....	....
1998-99	Spokane Chiefs	WHL	26	15	12	27	98	....	....	....	....	....	....	....	....	....	....	....	....	....	....	....	....	....	....	....
	Kamloops Blazers	WHL	20	3	16	19	84	....	....	....	....	....	....	....	....	....	....	....	14	5	3	8	22	....	....	....
	Chicago	**NHL**	**8**	**0**	**0**	**0**	**12**	**0**	**0**	**0**	**3**	**0.0**	**-1**	**0**	**0.0**	**5**	**1**	**7:53**	....	....	....	....	....	....	....	....
99-2000	Cleveland	IHL	10	1	1	2	34	....	....	....	....	....	....	....	....	....	....	....	....	....	....	....	....	....	....	....
	Florida Everblades	ECHL	48	11	26	37	81	....	....	....	....	....	....	....	....	....	....	....	5	1	1	2	17	....	....	....
	NHL Totals		**8**	**0**	**0**	**0**	**12**	**0**	**0**	**0**	**3**	**0.0**		**0**	**0.0**	**5**	**1**	**7:53**	....	....	....	....	....	....	....	....

JONSSON, Hans (YAWN-suhn, HANS) PIT.

Defense. Shoots left. 6'1", 202 lbs. Born, Jarved, Sweden, August 2, 1973. Pittsburgh's 11th choice, 286th overall, in 1993 Entry Draft.

			Regular Season																Playoffs							
Season	Club	League	GP	G	A	Pts	PIM	PP	SH	GW	S	%	+/-	TF	F%	H	SB	Min	GP	G	A	Pts	PIM	PP	SH	GW
1991-92	MoDo AIK	Sweden	6	0	1	1	4	....	....	....	....	....	....	....	....	....	....	....	....	....	....	....	....	....	....	....
1992-93	MoDo AIK	Sweden	40	2	2	4	24	....	....	....	....	....	....	....	....	....	....	....	3	0	1	1	2	....	....	....
1993-94	MoDo Hockey	Sweden	23	4	1	5	18	....	....	....	....	....	....	....	....	....	....	....	10	0	1	1	12	....	....	....
1994-95	MoDo Hockey	Sweden	39	4	6	10	30	....	....	....	....	....	....	....	....	....	....	....	....	....	....	....	....	....	....	....
1995-96	MoDo Hockey	Sweden	36	10	6	16	30	....	....	....	....	....	....	....	....	....	....	....	8	2	1	3	24	....	....	....
1996-97	MoDo Hockey	Sweden	27	7	5	12	18	....	....	....	....	....	....	....	....	....	....	....	....	....	....	....	....	....	....	....
1997-98	MoDo Hockey	Sweden	40	8	6	14	40	....	....	....	....	....	....	....	....	....	....	....	8	1	1	2	12	....	....	....
1998-99	MoDo Hockey	Sweden	41	3	4	7	40	....	....	....	....	....	....	....	....	....	....	....	13	2	4	6	22	....	....	....
99-2000	**Pittsburgh**	**NHL**	**68**	**3**	**11**	**14**	**12**	**0**	**1**	**1**	**49**	**6.1**	**-5**	**0**	**0.0**	**79**	**97**	**18:34**	**11**	**0**	**1**	**1**	**6**	**0**	**0**	**0**
	NHL Totals		**68**	**3**	**11**	**14**	**12**	**0**	**1**	**1**	**49**	**6.1**		**0**	**0.0**	**79**	**97**	**18:34**	**11**	**0**	**1**	**1**	**6**	**0**	**0**	**0**

JONSSON, Jorgen (YAWN-suhn, YOHR-gahn)

Left wing. Shoots left. 6', 185 lbs. Born, Angelholm, Sweden, September 29, 1972. Calgary's 11th choice, 227th overall, in 1994 Entry Draft.

			Regular Season																Playoffs							
Season	Club	League	GP	G	A	Pts	PIM	PP	SH	GW	S	%	+/-	TF	F%	H	SB	Min	GP	G	A	Pts	PIM	PP	SH	GW
1989-90	Rogle BK	Sweden-2	1	0	0	0	0	....	....	....	....	....	....	....	....	....	....	....	4	0	0	0	0	....	....	....
1990-91	Rogle BK	Sweden-2	21	4	2	6	2	....	....	....	....	....	....	....	....	....	....	....	12	2	1	3	2	....	....	....
1991-92	Rogle BK	Sweden-2	27	1	8	9	6	....	....	....	....	....	....	....	....	....	....	....	5	0	0	0	0	....	....	....
1992-93	Rogle BK	Sweden	40	17	11	28	28	....	....	....	....	....	....	....	....	....	....	....	....	....	....	....	....	....	....	....
1993-94	Rogle BK	Sweden	40	17	14	31	46	....	....	....	....	....	....	....	....	....	....	....	....	....	....	....	....	....	....	....
	Sweden	Olympics	6	0	0	0	0	....	....	....	....	....	....	....	....	....	....	....	....	....	....	....	....	....	....	....
1994-95	Rogle BK	Sweden	22	4	6	10	18	....	....	....	....	....	....	....	....	....	....	....	....	....	....	....	....	....	....	....
1995-96	Farjestads BK	Sweden	39	11	15	26	36	....	....	....	....	....	....	....	....	....	....	....	8	0	4	4	6	....	....	....
1996-97	Farjestads BK	Sweden	49	12	21	33	58	....	....	....	....	....	....	....	....	....	....	....	14	9	5	14	14	....	....	....
	Farjestads BK	EuroHL	4	2	1	3	2	....	....	....	....	....	....	....	....	....	....	....	....	....	....	....	....	....	....	....
1997-98	Farjestads BK	Sweden	45	22	25	47	53	....	....	....	....	....	....	....	....	....	....	....	12	2	*9	11	12	....	....	....
	Farjestads BK	EuroHL	7	2	4	6	6	....	....	....	....	....	....	....	....	....	....	....	....	....	....	....	....	....	....	....
	Sweden	Olympics	1	0	0	0	0	....	....	....	....	....	....	....	....	....	....	....	....	....	....	....	....	....	....	....
1998-99	Farjestads BK	Sweden	48	17	24	41	44	....	....	....	....	....	....	....	....	....	....	....	4	0	2	2	4	....	....	....
	Farjestads BK	EuroHL	5	2	4	6	4	....	....	....	....	....	....	....	....	....	....	....	2	1	0	1	4	....	....	....
99-2000	**NY Islanders**	**NHL**	**68**	**11**	**17**	**28**	**16**	**1**	**2**	**0**	**95**	**11.6**	**-6**	**642**	**44.2**	**72**	**37**	**16:07**	....	....	....	....	....	....	....	....
	Anaheim	**NHL**	**13**	**1**	**2**	**3**	**0**	**0**	**0**	**1**	**21**	**4.8**	**-2**	**118**	**35.6**	**15**	**8**	**12:51**	....	....	....	....	....	....	....	....
	NHL Totals		**81**	**12**	**19**	**31**	**16**	**1**	**2**	**1**	**116**	**10.3**		**760**	**42.9**	**87**	**45**	**15:35**	....	....	....	....	....	....	....	....

Traded to **NY Islanders** by **Calgary** for Jan Hlavac, July 14, 1998. Traded to **Anaheim** by **NY Islanders** for Johan Davidsson and future considerations, March 11, 2000.

JONSSON, Kenny

(YAWN-suhn, KEHN-nee) **NYI**

Defense. Shoots left. 6'3", 195 lbs. Born, Angelholm, Sweden, October 6, 1974. Toronto's 1st choice, 12th overall, in 1993 Entry Draft.

			Regular Season																Playoffs							
Season	Club	League	GP	G	A	Pts	PIM	PP	SH	GW	S	%	+/-	TF	F%	H	SB	Min	GP	G	A	Pts	PIM	PP	SH	GW
1991-92	Rogle BK	Sweden-2	30	4	11	15	24	....	....	....	....	....	....	....	....	....	....	....	5	0	0	0	0	....	....	....
1992-93	Rogle BK	Swede-Jr.	2	1	2	3	25	....	....	....	....	....	....	....	....	....	....	....	....	....	....	....	....	....	....	....
	Rogle BK	Sweden	39	3	10	13	42	....	....	....	....	....	....	....	....	....	....	....	....	....	....	....	....	....	....	....
1993-94	Rogle BK	Sweden	36	4	13	17	40	....	....	....	....	....	....	....	....	....	....	....	3	1	1	2	2	....	....	....
	Sweden	Olympics	3	1	0	1	0	....	....	....	....	....	....	....	....	....	....	....	....	....	....	....	....	....	....	....
1994-95	Rogle BK	Sweden	8	3	1	4	20	....	....	....	....	....	....	....	....	....	....	....	....	....	....	....	....	....	....	....
	Toronto	**NHL**	**39**	**2**	**7**	**9**	**16**	**0**	**0**	**1**	**50**	**4.0**	**-8**	....	....	....	....	....	**4**	**0**	**0**	**0**	**0**	**0**	**0**	**0**
	St. John's Leafs	AHL	10	2	5	7	2	....	....	....	....	....	....	....	....	....	....	....	....	....	....	....	....	....	....	....
1995-96	**Toronto**	**NHL**	**50**	**4**	**22**	**26**	**22**	**3**	**0**	**1**	**90**	**4.4**	**12**	....	....	....	....	....	....	....	....	....	....	....	....	....
	NY Islanders	**NHL**	**16**	**0**	**4**	**4**	**10**	**0**	**0**	**0**	**40**	**0.0**	**-5**	....	....	....	....	....	....	....	....	....	....	....	....	....
1996-97	**NY Islanders**	**NHL**	**81**	**3**	**18**	**21**	**24**	**1**	**0**	**0**	**92**	**3.3**	**10**	....	....	....	....	....	....	....	....	....	....	....	....	....
1997-98	**NY Islanders**	**NHL**	**81**	**14**	**26**	**40**	**58**	**6**	**0**	**2**	**108**	**13.0**	**-2**	....	....	....	....	....	....	....	....	....	....	....	....	....
1998-99	**NY Islanders**	**NHL**	**63**	**8**	**18**	**26**	**34**	**6**	**0**	**0**	**91**	**8.8**	**-18**	**0**	**0.0**	**57**	**90**	**24:59**	....	....	....	....	....	....	....	....
99-2000	**NY Islanders**	**NHL**	**65**	**1**	**24**	**25**	**32**	**1**	**0**	**0**	**84**	**1.2**	**-15**	**0**	**0.0**	**51**	**113**	**24:29**	....	....	....	....	....	....	....	....
	NHL Totals		**395**	**32**	**119**	**151**	**196**	**17**	**0**	**4**	**555**	**5.8**		**0**	**0.0**	**108**	**203**	**24:44**	**4**	**0**	**0**	**0**	**0**	**0**	**0**	**0**

Swedish Rookie of the Year (1993) • NHL All-Rookie Team (1995)

Traded to **NY Islanders** by **Toronto** with Sean Haggerty, Darby Hendrickson and Toronto's 1st round choice (Roberto Luongo) in 1997 Entry Draft for Wendel Clark, Mathieu Schneider and D.J. Smith, March 13, 1996.

JOSEPH, Chris

(JOH-sehf, KRIHS) **PHX.**

Defense. Shoots right. 6'3", 212 lbs. Born, Burnaby, B.C., September 10, 1969. Pittsburgh's 1st choice, 5th overall, in 1987 Entry Draft.

			Regular Season																Playoffs							
Season	Club	League	GP	G	A	Pts	PIM	PP	SH	GW	S	%	+/-	TF	F%	H	SB	Min	GP	G	A	Pts	PIM	PP	SH	GW
1984-85	Burnaby Beavers	BCAHA	52	18	48	66	52	....	....	....	....	....	....	....	....	....	....	....	....	....	....	....	....	....	....	....
1985-86	Seattle T-Birds	WHL	72	4	8	12	50	....	....	....	....	....	....	....	....	....	....	....	5	0	3	3	12	....	....	....
1986-87	Seattle T-Birds	WHL	67	13	45	58	155	....	....	....	....	....	....	....	....	....	....	....	....	....	....	....	....	....	....	....
1987-88	**Pittsburgh**	**NHL**	**17**	**0**	**4**	**4**	**12**	**0**	**0**	**0**	**13**	**0.0**	**2**	....	....	....	....	....	....	....	....	....	....	....	....	....
	Edmonton	**NHL**	**7**	**0**	**4**	**4**	**6**	**0**	**0**	**0**	**1**	**0.0**	**-3**	....	....	....	....	....	....	....	....	....	....	....	....	....
	Seattle T-Birds	WHL	23	5	14	19	49	....	....	....	....	....	....	....	....	....	....	....	....	....	....	....	....	....	....	....
	Nova Scotia	AHL	8	0	2	2	8	....	....	....	....	....	....	....	....	....	....	....	4	0	0	0	9	....	....	....
1988-89	**Edmonton**	**NHL**	**44**	**4**	**5**	**9**	**54**	**0**	**0**	**0**	**36**	**11.1**	**-9**	....	....	....	....	....	....	....	....	....	....	....	....	....
	Cape Breton	AHL	5	1	1	2	18	....	....	....	....	....	....	....	....	....	....	....	....	....	....	....	....	....	....	....
1989-90	**Edmonton**	**NHL**	**4**	**0**	**2**	**2**	**2**	**0**	**0**	**0**	**5**	**0.0**	**-2**	....	....	....	....	....	....	....	....	....	....	....	....	....
	Cape Breton	AHL	61	10	20	30	69	....	....	....	....	....	....	....	....	....	....	....	6	2	1	3	4	....	....	....
1990-91	**Edmonton**	**NHL**	**49**	**5**	**17**	**22**	**59**	**2**	**0**	**0**	**74**	**6.8**	**3**	....	....	....	....	....	....	....	....	....	....	....	....	....
1991-92	**Edmonton**	**NHL**	**7**	**0**	**0**	**0**	**8**	**0**	**0**	**0**	**5**	**0.0**	**-1**	....	....	....	....	....	**5**	**1**	**3**	**4**	**2**	**0**	**0**	**0**
	Cape Breton	AHL	63	14	29	43	72	....	....	....	....	....	....	....	....	....	....	....	5	0	2	2	8	....	....	....
1992-93	**Edmonton**	**NHL**	**33**	**2**	**10**	**12**	**48**	**1**	**0**	**0**	**49**	**4.1**	**-9**	....	....	....	....	....	....	....	....	....	....	....	....	....
1993-94	**Edmonton**	**NHL**	**10**	**1**	**1**	**2**	**28**	**1**	**0**	**0**	**25**	**4.0**	**-8**	....	....	....	....	....	....	....	....	....	....	....	....	....
	Tampa Bay	**NHL**	**66**	**10**	**19**	**29**	**108**	**7**	**0**	**0**	**154**	**6.5**	**-13**	....	....	....	....	....	....	....	....	....	....	....	....	....
1994-95	**Pittsburgh**	**NHL**	**33**	**5**	**10**	**15**	**46**	**3**	**0**	**0**	**73**	**6.8**	**3**	....	....	....	....	....	**10**	**1**	**1**	**2**	**12**	**0**	**0**	**0**
1995-96	**Pittsburgh**	**NHL**	**70**	**5**	**14**	**19**	**71**	**0**	**0**	**1**	**94**	**5.3**	**6**	....	....	....	....	....	**15**	**1**	**0**	**1**	**8**	**0**	**0**	**0**
1996-97	**Vancouver**	**NHL**	**63**	**3**	**13**	**16**	**62**	**2**	**0**	**1**	**99**	**3.0**	**-21**	....	....	....	....	....	....	....	....	....	....	....	....	....
1997-98	**Philadelphia**	**NHL**	**15**	**1**	**0**	**1**	**19**	**0**	**0**	**1**	**20**	**5.0**	**1**	....	....	....	....	....	**1**	**0**	**0**	**0**	**2**	**0**	**0**	**0**
	Philadelphia	AHL	6	2	3	5	2	....	....	....	....	....	....	....	....	....	....	....	....	....	....	....	....	....	....	....
1998-99	**Philadelphia**	**NHL**	**2**	**0**	**0**	**0**	**2**	**0**	**0**	**0**	**1**	**0.0**	**0**	**0**	**0.0**	**0**	**0**	**9:36**	....	....	....	....	....	....	....	....
	Cincinnati	IHL	27	11	19	30	38	....	....	....	....	....	....	....	....	....	....	....	....	....	....	....	....	....	....	....
	Philadelphia	AHL	51	9	29	38	26	....	....	....	....	....	....	....	....	....	....	....	16	3	10	13	8	....	....	....
99-2000	**Vancouver**	**NHL**	**38**	**2**	**9**	**11**	**6**	**1**	**0**	**0**	**73**	**2.7**	**-4**	**0**	**0.0**	**17**	**24**	**17:14**	....	....	....	....	....	....	....	....
	Phoenix	**NHL**	**9**	**0**	**0**	**0**	**0**	**0**	**0**	**0**	**13**	**0.0**	**-5**	**0**	**0.0**	**8**	**9**	**13:20**	....	....	....	....	....	....	....	....
	NHL Totals		**467**	**38**	**108**	**146**	**531**	**17**	**0**	**3**	**735**	**5.2**		**0**	**0.0**	**25**	**33**	**16:13**	**31**	**3**	**4**	**7**	**24**	**0**	**0**	**0**

WHL West Second All-Star Team (1987) • Won King Clancy Memorial Trophy (2000)

Traded to **Edmonton** by **Pittsburgh** with Craig Simpson, Dave Hannan and Moe Mantha for Paul Coffey, Dave Hunter and Wayne Van Dorp, November 24, 1987. Traded to **Tampa Bay** by **Edmonton** for Bob Beers, November 11, 1993. Claimed by **Pittsburgh** from **Tampa Bay** in NHL Waiver Draft, January 18, 1995. Claimed by **Vancouver** from **Pittsburgh** in NHL Waiver Draft, September 30, 1996. Signed as a free agent by **Philadelphia**, September 11, 1997. Signed as a free agent by **Ottawa**, August 18, 1999. Claimed on waivers by **Vancouver** from **Ottawa**, September 27, 1999. Claimed on waivers by **Phoenix** from **Vancouver**, March 14, 2000.

JOVANOVSKI, Ed

(joh-van-OHV-skee, EHD) **VAN.**

Defense. Shoots left. 6'2", 210 lbs. Born, Windsor, Ont., June 26, 1976. Florida's 1st choice, 1st overall, in 1994 Entry Draft.

			Regular Season																Playoffs							
Season	Club	League	GP	G	A	Pts	PIM	PP	SH	GW	S	%	+/-	TF	F%	H	SB	Min	GP	G	A	Pts	PIM	PP	SH	GW
1991-92	Windsor Bulldogs	OMHA	50	25	40	65	88	....	....	....	....	....	....	....	....	....	....	....	....	....	....	....	....	....	....	....
1992-93	Windsor Bulldogs	OJHL-B	48	7	46	53	88	....	....	....	....	....	....	....	....	....	....	....	....	....	....	....	....	....	....	....
1993-94	Windsor Spitfires	OHL	62	15	36	51	221	....	....	....	....	....	....	....	....	....	....	....	4	0	0	0	15	....	....	....
1994-95	Windsor Spitfires	OHL	50	23	42	65	198	....	....	....	....	....	....	....	....	....	....	....	9	2	7	9	39	....	....	....
1995-96	**Florida**	**NHL**	**70**	**10**	**11**	**21**	**137**	**2**	**0**	**2**	**116**	**8.6**	**-3**	....	....	....	....	....	**22**	**1**	**8**	**9**	**52**	**0**	**0**	**0**
1996-97	**Florida**	**NHL**	**61**	**7**	**16**	**23**	**172**	**3**	**0**	**1**	**80**	**8.8**	**-1**	....	....	....	....	....	**5**	**0**	**0**	**0**	**4**	**0**	**0**	**0**
1997-98	**Florida**	**NHL**	**81**	**9**	**14**	**23**	**158**	**2**	**1**	**3**	**142**	**6.3**	**-12**	....	....	....	....	....	....	....	....	....	....	....	....	....
1998-99	**Florida**	**NHL**	**41**	**3**	**13**	**16**	**82**	**1**	**0**	**1**	**68**	**4.4**	**-4**	**0**	**0.0**	**88**	**36**	**22:35**	....	....	....	....	....	....	....	....
	Vancouver	**NHL**	**31**	**2**	**9**	**11**	**44**	**0**	**0**	**0**	**41**	**4.9**	**-5**	**0**	**0.0**	**68**	**35**	**21:16**	....	....	....	....	....	....	....	....
99-2000	**Vancouver**	**NHL**	**75**	**5**	**21**	**26**	**54**	**1**	**0**	**1**	**109**	**4.6**	**-3**	**0**	**0.0**	**167**	**104**	**24:03**	....	....	....	....	....	....	....	....
	NHL Totals		**359**	**36**	**84**	**120**	**647**	**9**	**1**	**8**	**556**	**6.5**		**0**	**0.0**	**323**	**175**	**23:03**	**27**	**1**	**8**	**9**	**56**	**0**	**0**	**0**

OHL Second All-Star Team (1994) • OHL First All-Star Team (1995) • NHL All-Rookie Team (1996)

Traded to **Vancouver** by **Florida** with Dave Gagner, Mike Brown, Kevin Weekes and Florida's 1st round choice (Nathan Smith) in 2000 Entry Draft for Pavel Bure, Bret Hedican, Brad Ference and Vancouver's 3rd round choice (Robert Fried) in 2000 Entry Draft, January 17, 1999.

JUNEAU, Joe

(ZHOO-noh, ZHOH-ay) **PHX.**

Center. Shoots left. 6', 195 lbs. Born, Pont-Rouge, Que., January 5, 1968. Boston's 3rd choice, 81st overall, in 1988 Entry Draft.

			Regular Season																Playoffs							
Season	Club	League	GP	G	A	Pts	PIM	PP	SH	GW	S	%	+/-	TF	F%	H	SB	Min	GP	G	A	Pts	PIM	PP	SH	GW
1983-84	Ste-Foy Governors	QAAA	30	3	7	10	....	....	....	....	....	....	....	....	....	....	....	....	....	....	....	....	....	....	....	....
1984-85	Ste-Foy Governors	QAAA	41	25	46	71	....	....	....	....	....	....	....	....	....	....	....	....	....	....	....	....	....	....	....	....
1985-86	Levis-Lauzon	CEGEP	STATISTICS NOT AVAILABLE																							
1986-87	Levis-Lauzon	CEGEP	38	27	57	84	....	....	....	....	....	....	....	....	....	....	....	....	....	....	....	....	....	....	....	....
1987-88	RPI Engineers	ECAC	31	16	29	45	18	....	....	....	....	....	....	....	....	....	....	....	....	....	....	....	....	....	....	....
1988-89	RPI Engineers	ECAC	30	12	23	35	40	....	....	....	....	....	....	....	....	....	....	....	....	....	....	....	....	....	....	....
1989-90	RPI Engineers	ECAC	34	18	*52	*70	31	....	....	....	....	....	....	....	....	....	....	....	....	....	....	....	....	....	....	....
	Canada	Nat-Team	3	0	2	2	4	....	....	....	....	....	....	....	....	....	....	....	....	....	....	....	....	....	....	....
1990-91	RPI Engineers	ECAC	29	23	40	63	68	....	....	....	....	....	....	....	....	....	....	....	....	....	....	....	....	....	....	....
	Canada	Nat-Team	7	2	3	5	0	....	....	....	....	....	....	....	....	....	....	....	....	....	....	....	....	....	....	....
1991-92	Canada	Nat-Team	60	20	49	69	35	....	....	....	....	....	....	....	....	....	....	....	....	....	....	....	....	....	....	....
	Canada	Olympics	8	6	*9	*15	4	....	....	....	....	....	....	....	....	....	....	....	....	....	....	....	....	....	....	....
	Boston	**NHL**	**14**	**5**	**14**	**19**	**4**	**2**	**0**	**0**	**38**	**13.2**	**6**	....	....	....	....	....	**15**	**4**	**8**	**12**	**21**	**2**	**0**	**0**
1992-93	**Boston**	**NHL**	**84**	**32**	**70**	**102**	**33**	**9**	**0**	**3**	**229**	**14.0**	**23**	....	....	....	....	....	**4**	**2**	**4**	**6**	**6**	**2**	**0**	**0**
1993-94	**Boston**	**NHL**	**63**	**14**	**58**	**72**	**35**	**4**	**0**	**2**	**142**	**9.9**	**11**	....	....	....	....	....	....	....	....	....	....	....	....	....
	Washington	**NHL**	**11**	**5**	**8**	**13**	**6**	**2**	**0**	**0**	**22**	**22.7**	**0**	....	....	....	....	....	**11**	**4**	**5**	**9**	**6**	**2**	**0**	**1**
1994-95	**Washington**	**NHL**	**44**	**5**	**38**	**43**	**8**	**3**	**0**	**0**	**70**	**7.1**	**-1**	....	....	....	....	....	**7**	**2**	**6**	**8**	**2**	**0**	**0**	**0**
1995-96	**Washington**	**NHL**	**80**	**14**	**50**	**64**	**30**	**7**	**2**	**2**	**176**	**8.0**	**-3**	....	....	....	....	....	**5**	**0**	**7**	**7**	**6**	**0**	**0**	**0**
1996-97	**Washington**	**NHL**	**58**	**15**	**27**	**42**	**8**	**9**	**1**	**3**	**124**	**12.1**	**-11**	....	....	....	....	....	....	....	....	....	....	....	....	....
1997-98	**Washington**	**NHL**	**56**	**9**	**22**	**31**	**26**	**4**	**1**	**1**	**87**	**10.3**	**-8**	....	....	....	....	....	**21**	**7**	**10**	**17**	**8**	**1**	**1**	**4**

			Regular Season																Playoffs							
Season	Club	League	GP	G	A	Pts	PIM	PP	SH	GW	S	%	+/–	TF	F%	H	SB	Min	GP	G	A	Pts	PIM	PP	SH	GW
1998-99	**Washington**	**NHL**	**63**	**14**	**27**	**41**	**20**	**2**	**1**	**3**	**142**	**9.9**	**–3**	**437**	**48.1**	**34**	**26**	**19:28**	....	....	....	....	....	....	....	....
	Buffalo	**NHL**	**9**	**1**	**1**	**2**	**2**	**0**	**0**	**0**	**8**	**12.5**	**–1**	**8**	**12.5**	**3**	**2**	**17:11**	**20**	**3**	**8**	**11**	**10**	**0**	**1**	**0**
99-2000	**Ottawa**	**NHL**	**65**	**13**	**24**	**37**	**22**	**2**	**0**	**2**	**126**	**10.3**	**3**	**830**	**51.6**	**27**	**25**	**18:28**	**6**	**2**	**1**	**3**	**0**	**0**	**0**	**0**
	NHL Totals		**547**	**127**	**339**	**466**	**194**	**44**	**5**	**16**	**1164**	**10.9**		**1275**	**50.1**	**64**	**53**	**18:51**	**89**	**24**	**49**	**73**	**59**	**7**	**2**	**5**

NCAA East First All-American Team (1990) • ECAC Second All-Star Team (1991) • NCAA East Second All-American Team (1991) • NHL All-Rookie Team (1993)

Traded to **Washington** by **Boston** for Al Iafrate, March 21, 1994. Traded to **Buffalo** by **Washington** with Washington's 3rd round choice (Tim Preston) in 1999 Entry Draft for Alexei Tezikov and Buffalo's 4th round compensatory choice (later traded to Calgary - Calgary selected Levente Szuper) in 2000 Entry Draft, March 22, 1999. Signed as a free agent by **Ottawa**, October 25, 1999. Selected by **Minnesota** from **Ottawa** in Expansion Draft, June 23, 2000. Traded to **Phoenix** by **Minnesota** for the rights to Rickard Wallin, June 23, 2000.

KABERLE, Frantisek

(KA-buhr-law, FRAN-tih-sehk) **ATL.**

Defense. Shoots left. 6', 185 lbs. Born, Kladno, Czech., November 8, 1973. Los Angeles' 3rd choice, 76th overall, in 1999 Entry Draft.

Season	Club	League	GP	G	A	Pts	PIM	PP	SH	GW	S	%	+/–	TF	F%	H	SB	Min	GP	G	A	Pts	PIM	PP	SH	GW
1991-92	Poldi Kladno	Czech.	37	1	4	5	8	....	....	....	....	....	....	....	....	....	....	....	8	0	1	1	0	....	....	....
1992-93	Poldi Kladno	Czech.	40	4	5	9	....	....	....	....	....	....	....	....	....	....	....	....	9	2	4	6	....	....	....	....
1993-94	HC Kladno	Cze-Rep	41	4	16	20	....	....	....	....	....	....	....	....	....	....	....	....	11	1	1	2	....	....	....	....
1994-95	HC Kladno	Cze-Rep	40	7	17	24	20	....	....	....	....	....	....	....	....	....	....	....	8	0	3	3	12	....	....	....
1995-96	MoDo Hockey	Sweden	40	5	7	12	34	....	....	....	....	....	....	....	....	....	....	....	8	0	1	1	0	....	....	....
1996-97	MoDo Hockey	Sweden	50	3	11	14	28	....	....	....	....	....	....	....	....	....	....	....	....	....	....	....	....	....	....	....
1997-98	MoDo Hockey	Sweden	46	5	4	9	22	....	....	....	....	....	....	....	....	....	....	....	9	1	1	2	4	....	....	....
1998-99	MoDo Hockey	Sweden	45	15	18	33	4	....	....	....	....	....	....	....	....	....	....	....	13	2	5	7	8	....	....	....
99-2000	**Los Angeles**	**NHL**	**37**	**0**	**9**	**9**	**4**	**0**	**0**	**0**	**41**	**0.0**	**3**	**0**	**0.0**	**29**	**31**	**17:04**	....	....	....	....	....	....	....	....
	Long Beach	IHL	18	2	8	10	8	....	....	....	....	....	....	....	....	....	....	....	....	....	....	....	....	....	....	....
	Atlanta	**NHL**	**14**	**1**	**6**	**7**	**6**	**0**	**1**	**0**	**35**	**2.9**	**–13**	**0**	**0.0**	**25**	**23**	**24:39**	....	....	....	....	....	....	....	....
	Lowell	AHL	4	0	2	2	0	....	....	....	....	....	....	....	....	....	....	....	....	....	....	....	....	....	....	....
	NHL Totals		**51**	**1**	**15**	**16**	**10**	**0**	**1**	**0**	**76**	**1.3**		**0**	**0.0**	**54**	**54**	**19:09**	....	....	....	....	....	....	....	....

Traded to **Atlanta** by **Los Angeles** with Donald Audette for Kelly Buchberger and Nelson Emerson, March 13, 2000.

KABERLE, Tomas

(KA-buhr-law, TAW-mas) **TOR.**

Defense. Shoots left. 6'2", 200 lbs. Born, Rakovnik, Czech., March 2, 1978. Toronto's 13th choice, 204th overall, in 1996 Entry Draft.

Season	Club	League	GP	G	A	Pts	PIM	PP	SH	GW	S	%	+/–	TF	F%	H	SB	Min	GP	G	A	Pts	PIM	PP	SH	GW
1994-95	Poldi Kladno-Jr.	Cze-Rep	37	7	10	17	....	....	....	....	....	....	....	....	....	....	....	....	....	....	....	....	....	....	....	....
	Poldi Kladno	Cze-Rep	4	0	1	1	0	....	....	....	....	....	....	....	....	....	....	....	....	....	....	....	....	....	....	....
1995-96	Poldi Kladno-Jr.	Cze-Rep	23	6	13	19	....	....	....	....	....	....	....	....	....	....	....	....	....	....	....	....	....	....	....	....
	Poldi Kladno	Cze-Rep	23	0	1	1	2	....	....	....	....	....	....	....	....	....	....	....	2	0	0	0	0	....	....	....
1996-97	Poldi Kladno	Cze-Rep	49	0	5	5	26	....	....	....	....	....	....	....	....	....	....	....	3	0	0	0	0	....	....	....
1997-98	Poldi Kladno	Cze-Rep	47	4	19	23	12	....	....	....	....	....	....	....	....	....	....	....	....	....	....	....	....	....	....	....
	St. John's Leafs	AHL	2	0	0	0	0	....	....	....	....	....	....	....	....	....	....	....	....	....	....	....	....	....	....	....
1998-99	**Toronto**	**NHL**	**57**	**4**	**18**	**22**	**12**	**0**	**0**	**2**	**71**	**5.6**	**3**	**0**	**0.0**	**27**	**46**	**18:42**	**14**	**0**	**3**	**3**	**2**	**0**	**0**	**0**
99-2000	**Toronto**	**NHL**	**82**	**7**	**33**	**40**	**24**	**2**	**0**	**0**	**82**	**8.5**	**3**	**0**	**0.0**	**86**	**106**	**22:55**	**12**	**1**	**4**	**5**	**0**	**0**	**0**	**1**
	NHL Totals		**139**	**11**	**51**	**62**	**36**	**2**	**0**	**2**	**153**	**7.2**		**0**	**0.0**	**113**	**152**	**21:11**	**26**	**1**	**7**	**8**	**2**	**0**	**0**	**1**

KALININ, Dmitri

(kah-LIHN-ihn, DIH-mih-TREE) **BUF.**

Defense. Shoots left. 6'2", 206 lbs. Born, Chelyabinsk, USSR, July 22, 1980. Buffalo's 1st choice, 18th overall, in 1998 Entry Draft.

Season	Club	League	GP	G	A	Pts	PIM	PP	SH	GW	S	%	+/–	TF	F%	H	SB	Min	GP	G	A	Pts	PIM	PP	SH	GW
1995-96	HC Chelyabinsk	Russia-Jr.	30	10	10	20	60	....	....	....	....	....	....	....	....	....	....	....	....	....	....	....	....	....	....	....
	HC Chelyabinsk	Russia-2	20	0	3	3	10	....	....	....	....	....	....	....	....	....	....	....	....	....	....	....	....	....	....	....
1996-97	HC Chelyabinsk	Russia	2	0	0	0	0	....	....	....	....	....	....	....	....	....	....	....	2	0	0	0	0	....	....	....
	HC Chelyabinsk-2	Russia-3	20	0	0	0	10	....	....	....	....	....	....	....	....	....	....	....	....	....	....	....	....	....	....	....
1997-98	HC Chelyabinsk	Russia	26	0	2	2	24	....	....	....	....	....	....	....	....	....	....	....	....	....	....	....	....	....	....	....
1998-99	Moncton Wildcats	QMJHL	39	7	18	25	44	....	....	....	....	....	....	....	....	....	....	....	4	1	1	2	0	....	....	....
	Rochester	AHL	3	0	1	1	14	....	....	....	....	....	....	....	....	....	....	....	7	0	0	0	6	....	....	....
99-2000	**Buffalo**	**NHL**	**4**	**0**	**0**	**0**	**4**	**0**	**0**	**0**	**3**	**0.0**	....	**0**	**0.0**	**0**	**0**	**0:00**	....	....	....	....	....	....	....	....
	Rochester	AHL	75	2	19	21	52	....	....	....	....	....	....	....	....	....	....	....	21	2	9	11	8	....	....	....
	NHL Totals		**4**	**0**	**0**	**0**	**4**	**0**	**0**	**0**	**3**	**0.0**		**0**	**0.0**	**0**	**0**	....	....	....	....	....	....	....	....	....

KAMINSKI, Kevin

(kah-MIHN-skee, KEH-vihn)

Center. Shoots left. 5'10", 190 lbs. Born, Churchbridge, Sask., March 13, 1969. Minnesota's 3rd choice, 48th overall, in 1987 Entry Draft.

Season	Club	League	GP	G	A	Pts	PIM	PP	SH	GW	S	%	+/–	TF	F%	H	SB	Min	GP	G	A	Pts	PIM	PP	SH	GW
1985-86	Saskatoon Blaze	SAHA	32	39	64	103	106	....	....	....	....	....	....	....	....	....	....	....	....	....	....	....	....	....	....	....
	Saskatoon Blades	WHL	4	1	1	2	35	....	....	....	....	....	....	....	....	....	....	....	2	0	0	0	5	....	....	....
1986-87	Saskatoon Blades	WHL	67	26	44	70	325	....	....	....	....	....	....	....	....	....	....	....	11	5	6	11	45	....	....	....
1987-88	Saskatoon Blades	WHL	55	38	61	99	247	....	....	....	....	....	....	....	....	....	....	....	10	5	7	12	37	....	....	....
1988-89	Saskatoon Blades	WHL	52	25	43	68	199	....	....	....	....	....	....	....	....	....	....	....	8	4	9	13	25	....	....	....
	Minnesota	**NHL**	**1**	**0**	**0**	**0**	**0**	**0**	**0**	**0**	**0**	**0.0**	**0**	....	....	....	....	....	....	....	....	....	....	....	....	....
1989-90	**Quebec**	**NHL**	**1**	**0**	**0**	**0**	**0**	**0**	**0**	**0**	**0**	**0.0**	**–1**	....	....	....	....	....	....	....	....	....	....	....	....	....
	Halifax Citadels	AHL	19	3	4	7	128	....	....	....	....	....	....	....	....	....	....	....	2	0	0	0	5	....	....	....
1990-91	Halifax Citadels	AHL	7	1	0	1	44	....	....	....	....	....	....	....	....	....	....	....	....	....	....	....	....	....	....	....
	Fort Wayne	IHL	56	9	15	24	*455	....	....	....	....	....	....	....	....	....	....	....	19	4	2	6	*169	....	....	....
1991-92	**Quebec**	**NHL**	**5**	**0**	**0**	**0**	**45**	**0**	**0**	**0**	**6**	**0.0**	**–2**	....	....	....	....	....	....	....	....	....	....	....	....	....
	Halifax Citadels	AHL	63	18	27	45	329	....	....	....	....	....	....	....	....	....	....	....	....	....	....	....	....	....	....	....
1992-93	Halifax Citadels	AHL	79	27	37	64	*345	....	....	....	....	....	....	....	....	....	....	....	....	....	....	....	....	....	....	....
1993-94	**Washington**	**NHL**	**13**	**0**	**5**	**5**	**87**	**0**	**0**	**0**	**9**	**0.0**	**2**	....	....	....	....	....	....	....	....	....	....	....	....	....
	Portland Pirates	AHL	39	10	22	32	263	....	....	....	....	....	....	....	....	....	....	....	16	4	5	9	*91	....	....	....
1994-95	Portland Pirates	AHL	34	15	20	35	292	....	....	....	....	....	....	....	....	....	....	....	....	....	....	....	....	....	....	....
	Washington	**NHL**	**27**	**1**	**1**	**2**	**102**	**0**	**0**	**1**	**12**	**8.3**	**–6**	....	....	....	....	....	**5**	**0**	**0**	**0**	**36**	**0**	**0**	**0**
1995-96	**Washington**	**NHL**	**54**	**1**	**2**	**3**	**164**	**0**	**0**	**0**	**17**	**5.9**	**–1**	....	....	....	....	....	**3**	**0**	**0**	**0**	**16**	**0**	**0**	**0**
1996-97	**Washington**	**NHL**	**38**	**1**	**2**	**3**	**130**	**0**	**0**	**0**	**12**	**8.3**	**0**	....	....	....	....	....	....	....	....	....	....	....	....	....
1997-98	Portland Pirates	AHL	40	8	12	20	242	....	....	....	....	....	....	....	....	....	....	....	8	2	1	3	69	....	....	....
1998-99	Las Vegas	IHL	39	7	10	17	217	....	....	....	....	....	....	....	....	....	....	....	....	....	....	....	....	....	....	....
99-2000	Providence Bruins	AHL	5	0	2	2	17	....	....	....	....	....	....	....	....	....	....	....	....	....	....	....	....	....	....	....
	Orlando	IHL	5	0	0	0	9	....	....	....	....	....	....	....	....	....	....	....	....	....	....	....	....	....	....	....
	NHL Totals		**139**	**3**	**10**	**13**	**528**	**0**	**0**	**1**	**56**	**5.4**		....	....	....	....	....	**8**	**0**	**0**	**0**	**52**	**0**	**0**	**0**

Traded to **Quebec** by **Minnesota** for Gaetan Duchesne, June 19, 1989. Traded to **Washington** by **Quebec** for Mark Matier, June 15, 1993. Signed as a free agent by **Las Vegas** (IHL), September 4, 1998. IHL rights acquired by **Utah** (IHL) from **Las Vegas** (IHL) with Russ Romaniuk, Scott Hollis and Brad Miller after Las Vegas franchise folded, July 6, 1999. Signed as a free agent by **Providence** (AHL), September 9, 1999. Traded to **Orlando** (IHL) by **Providence** (AHL) for cash, November 11, 1999. • Suffered season-ending head injury in game vs. Grand Rapids (IHL), November 20, 1999. • Played w/ RHI's New England Stingers in 1994 (13-16-30-46-30).

KAPANEN, Sami

(KA-pah-nehn, SA-mee) **CAR.**

Left wing. Shoots left. 5'10", 195 lbs. Born, Vantaa, Finland, June 14, 1973. Hartford's 4th choice, 87th overall, in 1995 Entry Draft.

Season	Club	League	GP	G	A	Pts	PIM	PP	SH	GW	S	%	+/–	TF	F%	H	SB	Min	GP	G	A	Pts	PIM	PP	SH	GW
1989-90	KalPa Kuopio	Finn-Jr.	30	14	13	27	4	....	....	....	....	....	....	....	....	....	....	....	....	....	....	....	....	....	....	....
1990-91	KalPa Kuopio	Finn-Jr.	31	9	27	36	10	....	....	....	....	....	....	....	....	....	....	....	....	....	....	....	....	....	....	....
	KalPa Kuopio	Finland	14	1	2	3	2	....	....	....	....	....	....	....	....	....	....	....	8	2	1	3	2	....	....	....
1991-92	KalPa Kuopio	Finn-Jr.	8	1	3	4	12	....	....	....	....	....	....	....	....	....	....	....	....	....	....	....	....	....	....	....
	KalPa Kuopio	Finland	42	15	10	25	8	....	....	....	....	....	....	....	....	....	....	....	....	....	....	....	....	....	....	....
1992-93	KalPa Kuopio	Finn-Jr.	7	11	14	25	2	....	....	....	....	....	....	....	....	....	....	....	....	....	....	....	....	....	....	....
	KalPa Kuopio	Finland	37	4	17	21	12	....	....	....	....	....	....	....	....	....	....	....	....	....	....	....	....	....	....	....
1993-94	KalPa Kuopio	Finland	48	23	32	55	16	....	....	....	....	....	....	....	....	....	....	....	....	....	....	....	....	....	....	....
	Finland	Nat-Team	20	9	3	12	0	....	....	....	....	....	....	....	....	....	....	....	....	....	....	....	....	....	....	....
	Finland	Olympics	8	1	0	1	2	....	....	....	....	....	....	....	....	....	....	....	....	....	....	....	....	....	....	....
1994-95	HIFK Helsinki	Finland	49	14	28	42	42	....	....	....	....	....	....	....	....	....	....	....	3	0	0	0	0	....	....	....
	Finland	Nat-Team	19	3	1	4	8	....	....	....	....	....	....	....	....	....	....	....	....	....	....	....	....	....	....	....

			Regular Season																Playoffs							
Season	Club	League	GP	G	A	Pts	PIM	PP	SH	GW	S	%	+/-	TF	F%	H	SB	Min	GP	G	A	Pts	PIM	PP	SH	GW
1995-96	**Hartford**	**NHL**	**35**	**5**	**4**	**9**	**6**	**0**	**0**	**0**	**46**	**10.9**	**0**													
	Springfield	AHL	28	14	17	31	4												3	1	2	3	0			
	Finland	Nat-Team	2	0	1	1	0																			
1996-97	**Hartford**	**NHL**	**45**	**13**	**12**	**25**	**2**	**3**	**0**	**2**	**82**	**15.9**	**6**													
	Finland	Nat-Team	4	1	0	1	4																			
1997-98	**Carolina**	**NHL**	**81**	**26**	**37**	**63**	**16**	**4**	**0**	**5**	**190**	**13.7**	**9**													
	Finland	Olympics	6	0	1	1	0																			
1998-99	**Carolina**	**NHL**	**81**	**24**	**35**	**59**	**10**	**5**	**0**	**7**	**254**	**9.4**	**–1**	**10**	**50.0**	**123**	**28**	**19:25**	**5**	**1**	**1**	**2**	**0**	**0**	**0**	**0**
99-2000	**Carolina**	**NHL**	**76**	**24**	**24**	**48**	**12**	**7**	**0**	**5**	**229**	**10.5**	**10**	**2**	**50.0**	**91**	**33**	**19:53**								
	NHL Totals		**318**	**92**	**112**	**204**	**46**	**19**	**0**	**19**	**801**	**11.5**		**12**	**50.0**	**214**	**61**	**19:39**	**5**	**1**	**1**	**2**	**0**	**0**	**0**	**0**

Finnish First All-Star Team (1994) • Played in NHL All-Star Game (2000)

Transferred to **Carolina** after **Hartford** franchise relocated, June 25, 1997.

KARALAHTI, Jere

(kar-ah-LAHKH-tee, YEH-reh) **L.A.**

Defense. Shoots right. 6'2", 210 lbs. Born, Helsinki, Finland, March 25, 1975. Los Angeles' 7th choice, 146th overall, in 1993 Entry Draft.

Season	Club	League	GP	G	A	Pts	PIM	PP	SH	GW	S	%	+/-	TF	F%	H	SB	Min	GP	G	A	Pts	PIM	PP	SH	GW
1991-92	HIFK Helsinki	Finn-Jr.	30	12	5	17	36												1	0	0	0	2			
1992-93	HIFK Helsinki	Finn-Jr-B	7	3	1	4	4																			
	HIFK Helsinki	Finn-Jr.	30	2	13	15	49												2	0	0	0	0			
1993-94	HIFK Helsinki	Finn-Jr.	3	0	0	0	0																			
	HIFK Helsinki	Finland	46	1	10	11	36												3	0	0	0	6			
1994-95	HIFK Helsinki	Finn-Jr.	1	0	0	0	8																			
	HIFK Helsinki	Finland	37	1	7	8	42												3	0	0	0	0			
1995-96	HIFK Helsinki	Finn-Jr.	3	1	2	3	2																			
	HIFK Helsinki	Finland	36	4	6	10	102												3	0	0	0	4			
1996-97	HIFK Helsinki	Finland	18	3	5	8	20																			
1997-98	HIFK Helsinki	Finland	43	14	16	30	32												9	2	0	2	8			
1998-99	HIFK Helsinki	Finland	49	11	22	33	65												11	1	1	2	10			
	HIFK Helsinki	EuroHL	6	2	1	3	2												4		2					
99-2000	HIFK Helsinki	Finland	13	2	2	4	55																			
	Los Angeles	**NHL**	**48**	**6**	**10**	**16**	**18**	**4**	**0**	**1**	**69**	**8.7**	**3**	**0**	**0.0**	**108**	**28**	**17:05**	**4**	**0**	**1**	**1**	**2**	**0**	**0**	**0**
	Long Beach	IHL	10	0	3	3	4																			
	NHL Totals		**48**	**6**	**10**	**16**	**18**	**4**	**0**	**1**	**69**	**8.7**		**0**	**0.0**	**108**	**28**	**17:05**	**4**	**0**	**1**	**1**	**2**	**0**	**0**	**0**

KARIYA, Paul

(kah-REE-ah, PAWL) **ANA.**

Left wing. Shoots left. 5'10", 173 lbs. Born, Vancouver, B.C., October 16, 1974. Anaheim's 1st choice, 4th overall, in 1993 Entry Draft.

Season	Club	League	GP	G	A	Pts	PIM	PP	SH	GW	S	%	+/-	TF	F%	H	SB	Min	GP	G	A	Pts	PIM	PP	SH	GW
1990-91	Penticton	BCJHL	54	45	67	112	8																			
1991-92	Penticton	BCJHL	40	46	86	132	18																			
1992-93	U. of Maine	H-East	39	25	*75	*100	12																			
1993-94	U. of Maine	H-East	12	8	16	24	4																			
	Canada	Nat-Team	23	7	34	41	2																			
	Canada	Olympics	8	3	4	7	2																			
1994-95	**Anaheim**	**NHL**	**47**	**18**	**21**	**39**	**4**	**7**	**1**	**3**	**134**	**13.4**	**–17**													
1995-96	**Anaheim**	**NHL**	**82**	**50**	**58**	**108**	**20**	**20**	**3**	**9**	**349**	**14.3**	**9**													
1996-97	**Anaheim**	**NHL**	**69**	**44**	**55**	**99**	**6**	**15**	**3**	**10**	**340**	**12.9**	**36**						**11**	**7**	**6**	**13**	**4**	**4**	**0**	**1**
1997-98	**Anaheim**	**NHL**	**22**	**17**	**14**	**31**	**23**	**3**	**0**	**2**	**103**	**16.5**	**12**													
1998-99	**Anaheim**	**NHL**	**82**	**39**	**62**	**101**	**40**	**11**	**2**	**4**	**429**	**9.1**	**17**	**91**	**48.4**	**35**	**65**	**25:32**	**3**	**1**	**3**	**4**	**0**	**0**	**0**	**0**
99-2000	**Anaheim**	**NHL**	**74**	**42**	**44**	**86**	**24**	**11**	**3**	**3**	**324**	**13.0**	**22**	**99**	**39.4**	**23**	**39**	**24:22**								
	NHL Totals		**376**	**210**	**254**	**464**	**117**	**67**	**12**	**31**	**1679**	**12.5**		**190**	**43.7**	**58**	**104**	**24:59**	**14**	**8**	**9**	**17**	**4**	**4**	**0**	**1**

Hockey East First All-Star Team (1993) • NCAA East First All-American Team (1993) • NCAA Championship All-Tournament Team (1993) • Won Hobey Baker Memorial Award (Top U.S. Collegiate Player) (1993) • NHL All-Rookie Team (1995) • Won Lady Byng Trophy (1996, 1997) • NHL First All-Star Team (1996, 1997, 1999)• NHL Second All-Star Team (2000) • Played in NHL All-Star Game (1996, 1997, 1999, 2000)

KARIYA, Steve

(kah-REE-ah, STEEV) **VAN.**

Left wing. Shoots right. 5'8", 170 lbs. Born, North Vancouver, B.C., December 22, 1977.

Season	Club	League	GP	G	A	Pts	PIM	PP	SH	GW	S	%	+/-	TF	F%	H	SB	Min	GP	G	A	Pts	PIM	PP	SH	GW
1994-95	Nanaimo Clippers	BCJHL	60	36	60	96	4																			
1995-96	U. of Maine	H-East	39	7	16	23	8																			
1996-97	U. of Maine	H-East	35	19	31	50	10																			
1997-98	U. of Maine	H-East	35	25	25	50	22																			
1998-99	U. of Maine	H-East	41	27	38	65	24																			
99-2000	**Vancouver**	**NHL**	**45**	**8**	**11**	**19**	**22**	**0**	**0**	**0**	**41**	**19.5**	**9**	**4**	**50.0**	**29**	**4**	**12:38**								
	Syracuse Crunch	AHL	29	18	23	41	22												4	2	1	3	0			
	NHL Totals		**45**	**8**	**11**	**19**	**22**	**0**	**0**	**0**	**41**	**19.5**		**4**	**50.0**	**29**	**4**	**12:38**								

BCJHL First Team All-Star (1995) • BCJHL Most Sportsmanlike Player (1985) • Hockey East First All-Star Team (1999) • NCAA East First All-American Team (1999)

Signed as a free agent by **Vancouver**, April 21, 1999.

KARLSSON, Andreas

(KARLS-sohn, AN-dree-ahs) **ATL.**

Center. Shoots left. 6'3", 195 lbs. Born, Luvicka, Sweden, August 19, 1975. Calgary's 8th choice, 148th overall, in 1993 Entry Draft.

Season	Club	League	GP	G	A	Pts	PIM	PP	SH	GW	S	%	+/-	TF	F%	H	SB	Min	GP	G	A	Pts	PIM	PP	SH	GW
1992-93	Leksands IF	Sweden	13	0	0	0	6																			
1993-94	Leksands IF	Sweden	21	0	0	0	10												3	0	0	0	0			
1994-95	Leksands IF	Sweden	24	7	8	15	0												4	0	1	1	0			
1995-96	Leksands IF	Sweden	40	10	13	23	10																			
1996-97	Leksands IF	Sweden	49	13	11	24	39												9	2	0	2	2			
1997-98	Leksands IF	Sweden	33	9	14	23	20												4	1	0	1	0			
	Leksands IF	EuroHL	6	2	3	5	2																			
1998-99	Leksands IF	Sweden	49	18	15	33	18												4	1	0	1	6			
	Leksands IF	EuroHL	6	1	3	4	2												2	1	1	2	2			
99-2000	**Atlanta**	**NHL**	**51**	**5**	**9**	**14**	**14**	**1**	**0**	**0**	**74**	**6.8**	**–17**	**552**	**46.7**	**52**	**17**	**12:60**								
	Orlando	IHL	18	5	5	10	6																			
	NHL Totals		**51**	**5**	**9**	**14**	**14**	**1**	**0**	**0**	**74**	**6.8**		**552**	**46.7**	**52**	**17**	**12:60**								

Traded to **Atlanta** by **Calgary** for future considerations, June 25, 1999.

KARPA, Dave

(KAHR-puh, DAYV) **CAR.**

Defense. Shoots right. 6'1", 210 lbs. Born, Regina, Sask., May 7, 1971. Quebec's 4th choice, 68th overall, in 1991 Entry Draft.

Season	Club	League	GP	G	A	Pts	PIM	PP	SH	GW	S	%	+/-	TF	F%	H	SB	Min	GP	G	A	Pts	PIM	PP	SH	GW
1988-89	Notre Dame	SJHL	41	16	37	53	....																			
1989-90	Notre Dame	SJHL	43	9	19	28	271																			
1990-91	Ferris State	CCHA	41	6	19	25	109																			
1991-92	Ferris State	CCHA	34	7	12	19	124																			
	Quebec	**NHL**	**4**	**0**	**0**	**0**	**14**	**0**	**0**	**0**	**2**	**0.0**	**2**													
	Halifax Citadels	AHL	2	0	0	0	4																			
1992-93	**Quebec**	**NHL**	**12**	**0**	**1**	**1**	**13**	**0**	**0**	**0**	**2**	**0.0**	**–6**						**3**	**0**	**0**	**0**	**0**	**0**	**0**	**0**
	Halifax Citadels	AHL	71	4	27	31	167																			
1993-94	**Quebec**	**NHL**	**60**	**5**	**12**	**17**	**148**	**2**	**0**	**0**	**48**	**10.4**	**0**													
	Cornwall Aces	AHL	1	0	0	0	0												12	2	2	4	27			
1994-95	**Quebec**	**NHL**	**2**	**0**	**0**	**0**	**0**	**0**	**0**	**0**	**1**	**0.0**	**–1**													
	Cornwall Aces	AHL	6	0	2	2	19																			
	Anaheim	**NHL**	**26**	**1**	**5**	**6**	**91**	**0**	**0**	**0**	**32**	**3.1**	**0**													
1995-96	**Anaheim**	**NHL**	**72**	**3**	**16**	**19**	**270**	**0**	**1**	**1**	**62**	**4.8**	**–3**													
1996-97	**Anaheim**	**NHL**	**69**	**2**	**11**	**13**	**210**	**0**	**0**	**1**	**90**	**2.2**	**11**						**8**	**1**	**1**	**2**	**20**	**0**	**0**	**1**

			Regular Season																Playoffs							
Season	Club	League	GP	G	A	Pts	PIM	PP	SH	GW	S	%	+/–	TF	F%	H	SB	Min	GP	G	A	Pts	PIM	PP	SH	GW
1997-98	Anaheim	NHL	78	1	11	12	217	0	0	0	64	1.6	–3	....	....	....	....	....	....	....	....	....	....	....	....	....
1998-99	Carolina	NHL	33	0	2	2	55	0	0	0	21	0.0	1	0	0.0	62	45	16:55	2	0	0	0	2	0	0	0
99-2000	Carolina	NHL	27	1	4	5	52	0	0	0	24	4.2	9	0	0.0	68	33	17:21	....	....	....	....	....	....	....	....
	Cincinnati	IHL	39	1	8	9	147	....	....	....	....	....	....	....	....	....	....	....	....	....	....	....	....	....	....	....
	NHL Totals		383	13	62	75	1070	2	1	2	346	3.8		0	0.0	130	78	17:07	13	1	1	2	22	0	0	1

Traded to **Anaheim** by **Quebec** for Anaheim's 4th round choice (later traded to St. Louis - St. Louis selected Jan Horacek) in 1997 Entry Draft, March 9, 1995. Traded to **Carolina** by **Anaheim** with Anaheim's 4th round choice (later traded to Atlanta - Atlanta selected Blake Robson) in 2000 Entry Draft for Stu Grimson and Kevin Haller, August 11, 1998.

KARPOVTSEV, Alexander
(kar-POHV-tzehv, al-ehx-AN-duhr) **TOR.**

Defense. Shoots right. 6'3", 215 lbs. Born, Moscow, USSR, April 7, 1970. Quebec's 7th choice, 158th overall, in 1990 Entry Draft.

Season	Club	League	GP	G	A	Pts	PIM	PP	SH	GW	S	%	+/–	TF	F%	H	SB	Min	GP	G	A	Pts	PIM	PP	SH	GW
1989-90	Dynamo Moscow	USSR	35	1	1	2	27	....	....	....	....	....	....	....	....	....	....	....	....	....	....	....	....	....	....	....
1990-91	Dynamo Moscow	USSR	40	0	5	5	15	....	....	....	....	....	....	....	....	....	....	....	....	....	....	....	....	....	....	....
1991-92	Dynamo Moscow	CIS	35	4	2	6	26	....	....	....	....	....	....	....	....	....	....	....	....	....	....	....	....	....	....	....
1992-93	Dynamo Moscow	CIS	36	3	11	14	100	....	....	....	....	....	....	....	....	....	....	....	7	2	1	3	0	....	....	....
1993-94♦	NY Rangers	NHL	67	3	15	18	58	1	0	1	78	3.8	12	....	....	....	....	....	17	0	4	4	12	0	0	0
1994-95	Dynamo Moscow	CIS	13	0	2	2	10	....	....	....	....	....	....	....	....	....	....	....	....	....	....	....	....	....	....	....
	NY Rangers	NHL	47	4	8	12	30	1	0	1	82	4.9	–4	....	....	....	....	....	8	1	0	1	0	0	0	0
1995-96	NY Rangers	NHL	40	2	16	18	26	1	0	1	71	2.8	12	....	....	....	....	....	6	0	1	1	4	0	0	0
1996-97	NY Rangers	NHL	77	9	29	38	59	6	1	0	84	10.7	1	....	....	....	....	....	13	1	3	4	20	1	0	0
1997-98	NY Rangers	NHL	47	3	7	10	38	1	0	1	46	6.5	–1	....	....	....	....	....	....	....	....	....	....	....	....	....
1998-99	NY Rangers	NHL	2	1	0	1	0	0	0	0	4	25.0	1	0	0.0	2	3	22:38	....	....	....	....	....	....	....	....
	Toronto	NHL	56	2	25	27	52	1	0	1	61	3.3	38	0	0.0	79	103	20:58	14	1	3	4	12	1	0	0
99-2000	Toronto	NHL	69	3	14	17	54	3	0	0	51	5.9	9	2	0.0	88	129	20:14	11	0	3	3	4	0	0	0
	NHL Totals		405	27	114	141	317	14	1	5	477	5.7		2	0.0	169	235	20:36	69	3	14	17	52	2	0	0

Traded to **NY Rangers** by **Quebec** for Mike Hurlbut, September 7, 1993. Traded to **Toronto** by **NY Rangers** with NY Rangers' 4th round choice (Mirko Murovic) in 1999 Entry Draft for Mathieu Schneider, October 14, 1998.

KASPARAITIS, Darius
(KAZ-puhr-IGH-tihz, DAIR-ee-uhs) **PIT.**

Defense. Shoots left. 5'11", 212 lbs. Born, Elektrenai, USSR, October 16, 1972. NY Islanders' 1st choice, 5th overall, in 1992 Entry Draft.

Season	Club	League	GP	G	A	Pts	PIM	PP	SH	GW	S	%	+/–	TF	F%	H	SB	Min	GP	G	A	Pts	PIM	PP	SH	GW
1988-89	Dynamo Moscow	USSR	3	0	0	0	0	....	....	....	....	....	....	....	....	....	....	....	....	....	....	....	....	....	....	....
1989-90	Dynamo Moscow	USSR	1	0	0	0	0	....	....	....	....	....	....	....	....	....	....	....	....	....	....	....	....	....	....	....
1990-91	Dynamo Moscow	USSR	17	0	1	1	10	....	....	....	....	....	....	....	....	....	....	....	....	....	....	....	....	....	....	....
1991-92	Dynamo Moscow	CIS	31	2	10	12	14	....	....	....	....	....	....	....	....	....	....	....	....	....	....	....	....	....	....	....
1992-93	Dynamo Moscow	CIS	7	1	3	4	8	....	....	....	....	....	....	....	....	....	....	....	....	....	....	....	....	....	....	....
	NY Islanders	NHL	79	4	17	21	166	0	0	0	92	4.3	15	....	....	....	....	....	18	0	5	5	31	0	0	0
1993-94	NY Islanders	NHL	76	1	10	11	142	0	0	0	81	1.2	–6	....	....	....	....	....	4	0	0	0	8	0	0	0
1994-95	NY Islanders	NHL	13	0	1	1	22	0	0	0	8	0.0	–11	....	....	....	....	....	....	....	....	....	....	....	....	....
1995-96	NY Islanders	NHL	46	1	7	8	93	0	0	0	34	2.9	–12	....	....	....	....	....	....	....	....	....	....	....	....	....
1996-97	NY Islanders	NHL	18	0	5	5	16	0	0	0	12	0.0	–7	....	....	....	....	....	....	....	....	....	....	....	....	....
	Pittsburgh	NHL	57	2	16	18	84	0	0	0	46	4.3	24	....	....	....	....	....	5	0	0	0	6	0	0	0
1997-98	Pittsburgh	NHL	81	4	8	12	127	0	2	0	71	5.6	3	....	....	....	....	....	5	0	0	0	8	0	0	0
	Russia	Olympics	6	0	2	2	6	....	....	....	....	....	....	....	....	....	....	....	....	....	....	....	....	....	....	....
1998-99	Pittsburgh	NHL	48	1	4	5	70	0	0	0	32	3.1	12	0	0.0	173	48	16:01	....	....	....	....	....	....	....	....
99-2000	Pittsburgh	NHL	73	3	12	15	146	1	0	1	76	3.9	–12	0	0.0	261	119	18:07	11	1	1	2	10	0	0	0
	NHL Totals		491	16	80	96	866	1	2	1	452	3.5		0	0.0	434	167	17:17	43	1	6	7	63	0	0	0

Traded to **Pittsburgh** by **NY Islanders** with Andreas Johansson for Bryan Smolinski, November 17, 1996.

KEANE, Mike
(KEEN, MIGHK) **DAL.**

Right wing. Shoots right. 6', 185 lbs. Born, Winnipeg, Man., May 29, 1967.

Season	Club	League	GP	G	A	Pts	PIM	PP	SH	GW	S	%	+/–	TF	F%	H	SB	Min	GP	G	A	Pts	PIM	PP	SH	GW
1983-84	Winnipeg	MAHA	21	17	19	36	59	....	....	....	....	....	....	....	....	....	....	....	....	....	....	....	....	....	....	....
	Winnipeg	WHL	1	0	0	0	0	....	....	....	....	....	....	....	....	....	....	....	....	....	....	....	....	....	....	....
1984-85	Moose Jaw	WHL	65	17	26	43	141	....	....	....	....	....	....	....	....	....	....	....	....	....	....	....	....	....	....	....
1985-86	Moose Jaw	WHL	67	34	49	83	162	....	....	....	....	....	....	....	....	....	....	....	13	6	8	14	9	....	....	....
1986-87	Moose Jaw	WHL	53	25	45	70	107	....	....	....	....	....	....	....	....	....	....	....	9	3	9	12	11	....	....	....
	Sherbrooke	AHL	....	....	....	....	....	....	....	....	....	....	....	....	....	....	....	....	9	2	2	4	16	....	....	....
1987-88	Sherbrooke	AHL	78	25	43	68	70	....	....	....	....	....	....	....	....	....	....	....	6	1	1	2	18	....	....	....
1988-89	Montreal	NHL	69	16	19	35	69	5	0	1	90	17.8	9	....	....	....	....	....	21	4	3	7	17	2	0	0
1989-90	Montreal	NHL	74	9	15	24	78	1	0	1	92	9.8	0	....	....	....	....	....	11	0	1	1	8	0	0	0
1990-91	Montreal	NHL	73	13	23	36	50	2	1	2	109	11.9	6	....	....	....	....	....	12	3	2	5	6	0	0	0
1991-92	Montreal	NHL	67	11	30	41	64	2	0	2	116	9.5	16	....	....	....	....	....	8	1	1	2	16	0	0	0
1992-93♦	Montreal	NHL	77	15	45	60	95	0	0	1	120	12.5	29	....	....	....	....	....	19	2	13	15	6	0	0	0
1993-94	Montreal	NHL	80	16	30	46	119	6	2	2	129	12.4	6	....	....	....	....	....	6	3	1	4	4	0	0	0
1994-95	Montreal	NHL	48	10	10	20	15	1	0	0	75	13.3	5	....	....	....	....	....	....	....	....	....	....	....	....	....
1995-96	Montreal	NHL	18	0	7	7	6	0	0	0	17	0.0	–6	....	....	....	....	....	....	....	....	....	....	....	....	....
♦	Colorado	NHL	55	10	10	20	40	0	2	2	67	14.9	1	....	....	....	....	....	22	3	2	5	16	0	0	1
1996-97	Colorado	NHL	81	10	17	27	63	0	1	1	91	11.0	2	....	....	....	....	....	17	3	1	4	24	0	0	1
1997-98	NY Rangers	NHL	70	8	10	18	47	2	0	0	113	7.1	–12	....	....	....	....	....	....	....	....	....	....	....	....	....
	Dallas	NHL	13	2	3	5	5	0	0	1	15	13.3	0	....	....	....	....	....	17	4	4	8	0	0	1	1
1998-99♦	Dallas	NHL	81	6	23	29	62	1	1	1	106	5.7	–2	11	27.3	126	36	13:57	23	5	2	7	6	0	1	1
99-2000	Dallas	NHL	81	13	21	34	41	0	4	3	85	15.3	9	10	50.0	163	54	16:10	23	2	4	6	14	0	1	0
	NHL Totals		887	139	263	402	754	20	11	17	1225	11.3		21	38.1	289	90	15:04	179	30	34	64	117	2	2	4

Signed as a free agent by **Montreal**, September 25, 1985. Traded to **Colorado** by **Montreal** with Patrick Roy for Andrei Kovalenko, Martin Rucinsky and Jocelyn Thibault, December 6, 1995. Signed as a free agent by **NY Rangers**, July 30, 1997. Traded to **Dallas** by **NY Rangers** with Brian Skrudland and NY Rangers' 6th round choice (Pavel Patera) in 1998 Entry Draft for Todd Harvey, Bob Errey and Dallas' 4th round choice (Boyd Kane) in 1998 Entry Draft, March 24, 1998.

KECZMER, Dan
(KEHS-muhr, DAN)

Defense. Shoots left. 6'1", 190 lbs. Born, Mt. Clemens, MI, May 25, 1968. Minnesota's 11th choice, 201st overall, in 1986 Entry Draft.

Season	Club	League	GP	G	A	Pts	PIM	PP	SH	GW	S	%	+/–	TF	F%	H	SB	Min	GP	G	A	Pts	PIM	PP	SH	GW
1985-86	Detroit Caesars	NAJHL	65	6	48	54	116	....	....	....	....	....	....	....	....	....	....	....	....	....	....	....	....	....	....	....
1986-87	Lake Superior	CCHA	38	3	5	8	26	....	....	....	....	....	....	....	....	....	....	....	....	....	....	....	....	....	....	....
1987-88	Lake Superior	CCHA	41	2	15	17	34	....	....	....	....	....	....	....	....	....	....	....	....	....	....	....	....	....	....	....
1988-89	Lake Superior	CCHA	46	3	26	29	68	....	....	....	....	....	....	....	....	....	....	....	....	....	....	....	....	....	....	....
1989-90	Lake Superior	CCHA	43	13	23	36	48	....	....	....	....	....	....	....	....	....	....	....	....	....	....	....	....	....	....	....
1990-91	Minnesota	NHL	9	0	1	1	6	0	0	0	6	0.0	0	....	....	....	....	....	....	....	....	....	....	....	....	....
	Kalamazoo Wings	IHL	60	4	20	24	60	....	....	....	....	....	....	....	....	....	....	....	9	1	2	3	10	....	....	....
1991-92	United States	Nat-Team	51	3	11	14	56	....	....	....	....	....	....	....	....	....	....	....	....	....	....	....	....	....	....	....
	Hartford	NHL	1	0	0	0	0	0	0	0	2	0.0	–1	....	....	....	....	....	....	....	....	....	....	....	....	....
	Springfield	AHL	18	3	4	7	10	....	....	....	....	....	....	....	....	....	....	....	4	0	0	0	6	....	....	....
1992-93	Hartford	NHL	23	4	4	8	28	2	0	1	38	10.5	–3	....	....	....	....	....	....	....	....	....	....	....	....	....
	Springfield	AHL	37	1	13	14	38	....	....	....	....	....	....	....	....	....	....	....	12	0	4	4	14	....	....	....
1993-94	Hartford	NHL	12	0	1	1	12	0	0	0	12	0.0	–6	....	....	....	....	....	....	....	....	....	....	....	....	....
	Springfield	AHL	7	0	1	1	4	....	....	....	....	....	....	....	....	....	....	....	....	....	....	....	....	....	....	....
	Calgary	NHL	57	1	20	21	48	0	0	0	104	1.0	–2	....	....	....	....	....	3	0	0	0	4	0	0	0
1994-95	Calgary	NHL	28	2	3	5	10	0	0	0	33	6.1	7	....	....	....	....	....	7	0	1	1	2	0	0	0
1995-96	Calgary	NHL	13	0	0	0	14	0	0	0	13	0.0	–6	....	....	....	....	....	....	....	....	....	....	....	....	....
	Saint John Flames	AHL	22	3	11	14	14	....	....	....	....	....	....	....	....	....	....	....	....	....	....	....	....	....	....	....
	Albany River Rats	AHL	17	0	4	4	4	....	....	....	....	....	....	....	....	....	....	....	1	0	0	0	0	....	....	....
1996-97	Dallas	NHL	13	0	1	1	6	0	0	0	10	0.0	3	....	....	....	....	....	....	....	....	....	....	....	....	....
	Michigan K-Wings	IHL	42	3	17	20	24	....	....	....	....	....	....	....	....	....	....	....	....	....	....	....	....	....	....	....
1997-98	Dallas	NHL	17	1	2	3	26	0	0	0	9	11.1	5	....	....	....	....	....	2	0	0	0	2	0	0	0
	Michigan K-Wings	IHL	44	1	11	12	29	....	....	....	....	....	....	....	....	....	....	....	....	....	....	....	....	....	....	....
1998-99	Dallas	NHL	22	0	1	1	22	0	0	0	12	0.0	–2	1	100.0	28	1	7:08	....	....	....	....	....	....	....	....
	Michigan K-Wings	IHL	5	0	1	1	2	....	....	....	....	....	....	....	....	....	....	....	....	....	....	....	....	....	....	....
	Nashville	NHL	16	0	0	0	12	0	0	0	12	0.0	–3	0	0.0	21	22	16:20	....	....	....	....	....	....	....	....

			Regular Season																Playoffs							
Season	Club	League	GP	G	A	Pts	PIM	PP	SH	GW	S	%	+/–	TF	F%	H	SB	Min	GP	G	A	Pts	PIM	PP	SH	GW
99-2000	**Nashville**	**NHL**	**24**	**0**	**5**	**5**	**28**	**0**	**0**	**0**	**21**	**0.0**	**–2**	**0**	**0.0**	**21**	**26**	**17:56**	....	....	....	....	....	....	....	....
	Milwaukee	IHL	18	1	3	4	10	....	....	....	....	....	....	....	....	....	....	....	....	....	....	....	....	....	....	....
	Worcester	AHL	25	1	9	10	12	....	....	....	....	....	....	....	....	....	....	....	9	0	1	1	10	....	....	....
	NHL Totals		**235**	**8**	**38**	**46**	**212**	**2**	**0**	**1**	**272**	**2.9**		**1**	**100.0**	**70**	**49**	**13:41**	**12**	**0**	**1**	**1**	**8**	**0**	**0**	**0**

CCHA Second All-Star Team (1990)

Claimed by **San Jose** from **Minnesota** in Dispersal Draft, May 30, 1991. Traded to **Hartford** by **San Jose** for Dean Evason, October 2, 1991. Traded to **Calgary** by **Hartford** for Jeff Reese, November 19, 1993. Traded to **New Jersey** by **Calgary** with Phil Housley for Tommy Albelin, Cale Hulse and Jocelyn Lemieux, February 26, 1996. Signed as a free agent by **Dallas**, August 19, 1996. Claimed on waivers by **Nashville** from **Dallas**, March 12, 1999. Traded to **St. Louis** by **Nashville** for Rory Fitzpatrick, February 9, 2000.

KELLY, Steve

(KEHL-lee, STEEV) **N.J.**

Center. Shoots left. 6'2", 210 lbs. Born, Vancouver, B.C., October 26, 1976. Edmonton's 1st choice, 6th overall, in 1995 Entry Draft.

Season	Club	League	GP	G	A	Pts	PIM	PP	SH	GW	S	%	+/–	TF	F%	H	SB	Min	GP	G	A	Pts	PIM	PP	SH	GW
1991-92	Westbank West	BCAHA	30	25	60	85	75	....	....	....	....	....	....	....	....	....	....	....	....	....	....	....	....	....	....	....
1992-93	Prince Albert	WHL	65	11	9	20	75	....	....	....	....	....	....	....	....	....	....	....	....	....	....	....	....	....	....	....
1993-94	Prince Albert	WHL	65	19	42	61	106	....	....	....	....	....	....	....	....	....	....	....	....	....	....	....	....	....	....	....
1994-95	Prince Albert	WHL	68	31	41	72	153	....	....	....	....	....	....	....	....	....	....	....	15	7	9	16	35	....	....	....
1995-96	Prince Albert	WHL	70	27	74	101	203	....	....	....	....	....	....	....	....	....	....	....	18	13	18	31	47	....	....	....
1996-97	**Edmonton**	**NHL**	**8**	**1**	**0**	**1**	**6**	**0**	**0**	**1**	**6**	**16.7**	**–1**	....	....	....	....	....	**6**	**0**	**0**	**0**	**2**	**0**	**0**	**0**
	Hamilton Bulldogs	AHL	48	9	29	38	111	....	....	....	....	....	....	....	....	....	....	....	11	3	3	6	24	....	....	....
1997-98	**Edmonton**	**NHL**	**19**	**0**	**2**	**2**	**8**	**0**	**0**	**0**	**5**	**0.0**	**–4**	....	....	....	....	....	....	....	....	....	....	....	....	....
	Hamilton Bulldogs	AHL	11	2	8	10	18	....	....	....	....	....	....	....	....	....	....	....	....	....	....	....	....	....	....	....
	Tampa Bay	**NHL**	**24**	**2**	**1**	**3**	**15**	**1**	**0**	**0**	**17**	**11.8**	**–9**	....	....	....	....	....	....	....	....	....	....	....	....	....
	Milwaukee	IHL	5	0	1	1	19	....	....	....	....	....	....	....	....	....	....	....	....	....	....	....	....	....	....	....
	Cleveland	IHL	5	1	1	2	29	....	....	....	....	....	....	....	....	....	....	....	1	0	1	1	0	....	....	....
1998-99	**Tampa Bay**	**NHL**	**34**	**1**	**3**	**4**	**27**	**0**	**0**	**1**	**15**	**6.7**	**–15**	**11**	**54.5**	**12**	**13**	**10:51**	....	....	....	....	....	....	....	....
	Cleveland	IHL	18	6	7	13	36	....	....	....	....	....	....	....	....	....	....	....	....	....	....	....	....	....	....	....
99-2000	Detroit Vipers	IHL	1	0	0	0	4	....	....	....	....	....	....	....	....	....	....	....	....	....	....	....	....	....	....	....
	New Jersey	**NHL**	**1**	**0**	**0**	**0**	**0**	**0**	**0**	**0**	**0**	**0.0**	**0**	**0**	**0.0**	**0**	**0**	**4:28**	**10**	**0**	**0**	**0**	**4**	**0**	**0**	**0**
	Albany River Rats	AHL	76	21	36	57	131	....	....	....	....	....	....	....	....	....	....	....	3	1	1	2	2	....	....	....
	NHL Totals		**86**	**4**	**6**	**10**	**56**	**1**	**0**	**2**	**43**	**9.3**		**11**	**54.5**	**12**	**13**	**10:40**	**16**	**0**	**0**	**0**	**6**	**0**	**0**	**0**

Traded to **Tampa Bay** by **Edmonton** with Bryan Marchment and Jason Bonsignore for Roman Hamrlik and Paul Comrie, December 30, 1997. Traded to **New Jersey** by **Tampa Bay** for New Jersey's 7th round choice (Brian Eklund) in 2000 Entry Draft, October 7, 1999.

KENADY, Chris

(KEHN-a-dee, KRIHS)

Right wing. Shoots right. 6'2", 195 lbs. Born, Mound, MN, April 10, 1973. St. Louis' 8th choice, 175th overall, in 1991 Entry Draft.

Season	Club	League	GP	G	A	Pts	PIM	PP	SH	GW	S	%	+/–	TF	F%	H	SB	Min	GP	G	A	Pts	PIM	PP	SH	GW
1990-91	St. Paul Vulcans	USHL	45	16	20	36	57	....	....	....	....	....	....	....	....	....	....	....	....	....	....	....	....	....	....	....
1991-92	U. of Denver	WCHA	36	8	5	13	56	....	....	....	....	....	....	....	....	....	....	....	....	....	....	....	....	....	....	....
1992-93	U. of Denver	WCHA	38	8	16	24	95	....	....	....	....	....	....	....	....	....	....	....	....	....	....	....	....	....	....	....
1993-94	U. of Denver	WCHA	37	14	11	25	125	....	....	....	....	....	....	....	....	....	....	....	....	....	....	....	....	....	....	....
1994-95	U. of Denver	WCHA	39	21	17	38	113	....	....	....	....	....	....	....	....	....	....	....	....	....	....	....	....	....	....	....
1995-96	Worcester	AHL	43	9	10	19	58	....	....	....	....	....	....	....	....	....	....	....	2	0	0	0	0	....	....	....
1996-97	Worcester	AHL	73	23	26	49	131	....	....	....	....	....	....	....	....	....	....	....	5	0	1	1	2	....	....	....
1997-98	**St. Louis**	**NHL**	**5**	**0**	**2**	**2**	**0**	**0**	**0**	**0**	**3**	**0.0**	**1**	....	....	....	....	....	....	....	....	....	....	....	....	....
	Worcester	AHL	63	23	22	45	84	....	....	....	....	....	....	....	....	....	....	....	11	1	5	6	26	....	....	....
1998-99	Utah Grizzlies	IHL	35	7	6	13	68	....	....	....	....	....	....	....	....	....	....	....	....	....	....	....	....	....	....	....
	Long Beach	IHL	19	1	6	7	47	....	....	....	....	....	....	....	....	....	....	....	....	....	....	....	....	....	....	....
	Hartford	AHL	22	2	6	8	52	....	....	....	....	....	....	....	....	....	....	....	2	0	1	1	6	....	....	....
99-2000	**NY Rangers**	**NHL**	**2**	**0**	**0**	**0**	**0**	**0**	**0**	**0**	**1**	**0.0**	**–1**	**0**	**0.0**	**6**	**0**	**7:27**	....	....	....	....	....	....	....	....
	Hartford	AHL	71	15	16	31	196	....	....	....	....	....	....	....	....	....	....	....	21	8	3	11	40	....	....	....
	NHL Totals		**7**	**0**	**2**	**2**	**0**	**0**	**0**	**0**	**4**	**0.0**		**0**	**0.0**	**6**	**0**	**7:27**	....	....	....	....	....	....	....	....

Traded to **NY Rangers** by **St. Louis** to complete transaction that sent sent Jeff Finley and Geoff Smith to St. Louis (February 13, 1999), February 22, 1999.

KENNEDY, Mike

(KEHN-a-dee, MIGHK)

Center. Shoots right. 6'1", 195 lbs. Born, Vancouver, B.C., April 13, 1972. Minnesota's 3rd choice, 97th overall, in 1991 Entry Draft.

Season	Club	League	GP	G	A	Pts	PIM	PP	SH	GW	S	%	+/–	TF	F%	H	SB	Min	GP	G	A	Pts	PIM	PP	SH	GW
1989-90	U.B.C. T-Birds	CWUAA	9	5	7	12	0	....	....	....	....	....	....	....	....	....	....	....	....	....	....	....	....	....	....	....
1990-91	U.B.C. T-Birds	CWUAA	28	17	17	34	18	....	....	....	....	....	....	....	....	....	....	....	....	....	....	....	....	....	....	....
1991-92	Seattle T-Birds	WHL	71	42	47	89	134	....	....	....	....	....	....	....	....	....	....	....	15	11	6	17	20	....	....	....
1992-93	Kalamazoo Wings	IHL	77	21	30	51	39	....	....	....	....	....	....	....	....	....	....	....	....	....	....	....	....	....	....	....
1993-94	Kalamazoo Wings	IHL	63	20	18	38	42	....	....	....	....	....	....	....	....	....	....	....	3	1	2	3	2	....	....	....
1994-95	**Dallas**	**NHL**	**44**	**6**	**12**	**18**	**33**	**2**	**0**	**0**	**76**	**7.9**	**4**	....	....	....	....	....	**5**	**0**	**0**	**0**	**9**	**0**	**0**	**0**
	Kalamazoo Wings	IHL	42	20	28	48	29	....	....	....	....	....	....	....	....	....	....	....	....	....	....	....	....	....	....	....
1995-96	**Dallas**	**NHL**	**61**	**9**	**17**	**26**	**48**	**4**	**0**	**1**	**111**	**8.1**	**–7**	....	....	....	....	....	....	....	....	....	....	....	....	....
1996-97	**Dallas**	**NHL**	**24**	**1**	**6**	**7**	**13**	**0**	**0**	**1**	**26**	**3.8**	**3**	....	....	....	....	....	....	....	....	....	....	....	....	....
	Michigan K-Wings	IHL	2	0	1	1	2	....	....	....	....	....	....	....	....	....	....	....	....	....	....	....	....	....	....	....
1997-98	**Toronto**	**NHL**	**13**	**0**	**1**	**1**	**14**	**0**	**0**	**0**	**12**	**0.0**	**–2**	....	....	....	....	....	....	....	....	....	....	....	....	....
	St. John's Leafs	AHL	49	11	17	28	86	....	....	....	....	....	....	....	....	....	....	....	....	....	....	....	....	....	....	....
	Dallas	**NHL**	**2**	**0**	**0**	**0**	**2**	**0**	**0**	**0**	**0**	**0.0**	**1**	....	....	....	....	....	....	....	....	....	....	....	....	....
1998-99	**NY Islanders**	**NHL**	**1**	**0**	**0**	**0**	**2**	**0**	**0**	**0**	**0**	**0.0**	**0**	**0**	**0.0**	**4**	**0**	**10:50**	....	....	....	....	....	....	....	....
	Lowell	AHL	62	14	26	40	52	....	....	....	....	....	....	....	....	....	....	....	3	1	0	1	0	....	....	....
99-2000	Munich Barons	DEL	13	2	5	7	6	....	....	....	....	....	....	....	....	....	....	....	12	4	4	8	28	....	....	....
	NHL Totals		**145**	**16**	**36**	**52**	**112**	**6**	**0**	**2**	**225**	**7.1**		**0**	**0.0**	**4**	**0**	**10:50**	**5**	**0**	**0**	**0**	**9**	**0**	**0**	**0**

WHL West Second All-Star Team (1992)

Rights transferred to **Dallas** after **Minnesota** franchise relocated, June 9, 1993. Signed as a free agent by **Toronto**, July 2, 1997. Traded to **Dallas** by **Toronto** for Dallas' 8th round choice (Mikhail Travnicek) in 1998 Entry Draft, March 24, 1998. Signed as a free agent by **NY Islanders**, July 1, 1998. • Missed majority of 1999-2000 season recovering from ankle injury suffered in game vs. Moskitos Essen (DEL), September 17, 1999. • Played w/ RHI's Vancouver Voodoo in 1993 (11-10-16-26-14) and 1994 (17-22-36-58-4); Oklahoma Coyotes in 1995 (1-0-0-0-0).

KESA, Dan

(KEH-suh, DAN) **T.B.**

Right wing. Shoots right. 6', 198 lbs. Born, Vancouver, B.C., November 23, 1971. Vancouver's 4th choice, 95th overall, in 1991 Entry Draft.

Season	Club	League	GP	G	A	Pts	PIM	PP	SH	GW	S	%	+/–	TF	F%	H	SB	Min	GP	G	A	Pts	PIM	PP	SH	GW
1988-89	Richmond	BCJHL	44	21	21	42	71	....	....	....	....	....	....	....	....	....	....	....	....	....	....	....	....	....	....	....
1989-90	Richmond	BCJHL	54	39	38	77	103	....	....	....	....	....	....	....	....	....	....	....	....	....	....	....	....	....	....	....
1990-91	Prince Albert	WHL	69	30	23	53	116	....	....	....	....	....	....	....	....	....	....	....	3	1	1	2	0	....	....	....
1991-92	Prince Albert	WHL	62	46	51	97	201	....	....	....	....	....	....	....	....	....	....	....	10	9	10	19	27	....	....	....
1992-93	Hamilton Canucks	AHL	62	16	24	40	76	....	....	....	....	....	....	....	....	....	....	....	....	....	....	....	....	....	....	....
1993-94	**Vancouver**	**NHL**	**19**	**2**	**4**	**6**	**18**	**1**	**0**	**1**	**18**	**11.1**	**–3**	....	....	....	....	....	....	....	....	....	....	....	....	....
	Hamilton Canucks	AHL	53	37	33	70	33	....	....	....	....	....	....	....	....	....	....	....	4	1	4	5	4	....	....	....
1994-95	Syracuse Crunch	AHL	70	34	44	78	81	....	....	....	....	....	....	....	....	....	....	....	....	....	....	....	....	....	....	....
1995-96	**Dallas**	**NHL**	**3**	**0**	**0**	**0**	**0**	**0**	**0**	**0**	**0**	**0.0**	**–1**	....	....	....	....	....	....	....	....	....	....	....	....	....
	Michigan K-Wings	IHL	15	4	11	15	33	....	....	....	....	....	....	....	....	....	....	....	....	....	....	....	....	....	....	....
	Springfield	AHL	22	10	5	15	13	....	....	....	....	....	....	....	....	....	....	....	....	....	....	....	....	....	....	....
	Detroit Vipers	IHL	27	9	6	15	22	....	....	....	....	....	....	....	....	....	....	....	12	6	4	10	4	....	....	....
1996-97	Detroit Vipers	IHL	60	22	21	43	19	....	....	....	....	....	....	....	....	....	....	....	20	7	5	12	20	....	....	....
1997-98	Detroit Vipers	IHL	76	40	37	77	40	....	....	....	....	....	....	....	....	....	....	....	20	*13	5	18	14	....	....	....
1998-99	**Pittsburgh**	**NHL**	**67**	**2**	**8**	**10**	**27**	**0**	**0**	**0**	**33**	**6.1**	**–9**	**392**	**48.2**	**91**	**46**	**10:07**	**13**	**1**	**0**	**1**	**0**	**1**	**0**	**1**
	Detroit Vipers	IHL	8	3	5	8	12	....	....	....	....	....	....	....	....	....	....	....	....	....	....	....	....	....	....	....
99-2000	**Tampa Bay**	**NHL**	**50**	**4**	**10**	**14**	**21**	**0**	**1**	**1**	**55**	**7.3**	**–11**	**234**	**43.6**	**112**	**22**	**13:34**	....	....	....	....	....	....	....	....
	Manitoba Moose	IHL	1	0	0	0	0	....	....	....	....	....	....	....	....	....	....	....	....	....	....	....	....	....	....	....
	Detroit Vipers	IHL	5	3	0	3	2	....	....	....	....	....	....	....	....	....	....	....	....	....	....	....	....	....	....	....
	NHL Totals		**139**	**8**	**22**	**30**	**66**	**1**	**1**	**2**	**106**	**7.5**		**626**	**46.5**	**203**	**68**	**11:36**	**13**	**1**	**0**	**1**	**0**	**1**	**0**	**1**

Traded to **Dallas** by **Vancouver** with Greg Adams and Vancouver's 5th round choice (later traded to LA Kings - LA Kings selected Jason Morgan) in 1995 Entry Draft for Russ Courtnall, April 7, 1995. Traded to **Hartford** by **Dallas** for Robert Petrovicky, November 29, 1995. Signed as a free agent by **Pittsburgh**, August 20, 1998. Signed as a free agent by **Tampa Bay**, September 6, 1999.

KHRISTICH, Dmitri
(KRIH-stihch, dih-MEE-tree) **TOR.**

Left wing/Center. Shoots right. 6'2", 195 lbs. Born, Kiev, USSR, July 23, 1969. Washington's 6th choice, 120th overall, in 1988 Entry Draft.

			Regular Season																Playoffs							
Season	Club	League	GP	G	A	Pts	PIM	PP	SH	GW	S	%	+/-	TF	F%	H	SB	Min	GP	G	A	Pts	PIM	PP	SH	GW
1985-86	Sokol Kiev	USSR	4	0	0	0	0	....	....	....	....	....	....	....	....	....	....	....	....	....	....	....	....	....	....	....
1986-87	Sokol Kiev	USSR	20	3	0	3	4	....	....	....	....	....	....	....	....	....	....	....	....	....	....	....	....	....	....	....
1987-88	Sokol Kiev	USSR	37	9	1	10	18	....	....	....	....	....	....	....	....	....	....	....	....	....	....	....	....	....	....	....
1988-89	Sokol Kiev	USSR	42	17	10	27	15	....	....	....	....	....	....	....	....	....	....	....	....	....	....	....	....	....	....	....
1989-90	Sokol Kiev	USSR	47	14	22	36	32	....	....	....	....	....	....	....	....	....	....	....	....	....	....	....	....	....	....	....
1990-91	Sokol Kiev	USSR	28	10	12	22	20	....	....	....	....	....	....	....	....	....	....	....	....	....	....	....	....	....	....	....
	Washington	**NHL**	**40**	**13**	**14**	**27**	**21**	**1**	**0**	**0**	**77**	**16.9**	**-1**	....	....	....	....	....	**11**	**1**	**3**	**4**	**6**	**0**	**0**	**0**
	Baltimore	AHL	3	0	0	0	0	....	....	....	....	....	....	....	....	....	....	....	....	....	....	....	....	....	....	....
1991-92	**Washington**	**NHL**	**80**	**36**	**37**	**73**	**35**	**14**	**1**	**7**	**188**	**19.1**	**24**	....	....	....	....	....	**7**	**3**	**2**	**5**	**15**	**3**	**0**	**1**
1992-93	**Washington**	**NHL**	**64**	**31**	**35**	**66**	**28**	**9**	**1**	**1**	**127**	**24.4**	**29**	....	....	....	....	....	**6**	**2**	**5**	**7**	**2**	**1**	**0**	**0**
1993-94	**Washington**	**NHL**	**83**	**29**	**29**	**58**	**73**	**10**	**0**	**4**	**195**	**14.9**	**-2**	....	....	....	....	....	**11**	**2**	**3**	**5**	**10**	**0**	**0**	**0**
1994-95	**Washington**	**NHL**	**48**	**12**	**14**	**26**	**41**	**8**	**0**	**2**	**92**	**13.0**	**0**	....	....	....	....	....	**7**	**1**	**4**	**5**	**0**	**0**	**0**	**0**
1995-96	**Los Angeles**	**NHL**	**76**	**27**	**37**	**64**	**44**	**12**	**0**	**3**	**204**	**13.2**	**0**	....	....	....	....	....	....	....	....	....	....	....	....	....
1996-97	**Los Angeles**	**NHL**	**75**	**19**	**37**	**56**	**38**	**3**	**0**	**2**	**135**	**14.1**	**8**	....	....	....	....	....	....	....	....	....	....	....	....	....
1997-98	**Boston**	**NHL**	**82**	**29**	**37**	**66**	**42**	**13**	**2**	**1**	**144**	**20.1**	**25**	....	....	....	....	....	**6**	**2**	**2**	**4**	**2**	**2**	**0**	**0**
1998-99	**Boston**	**NHL**	**79**	**29**	**42**	**71**	**48**	**13**	**1**	**6**	**144**	**20.1**	**11**	**76**	**44.7**	**80**	**39**	**19:46**	**12**	**3**	**4**	**7**	**6**	**0**	**0**	**1**
99-2000	**Toronto**	**NHL**	**53**	**12**	**18**	**30**	**24**	**3**	**0**	**0**	**79**	**15.2**	**8**	**84**	**45.2**	**52**	**19**	**16:10**	**12**	**1**	**2**	**3**	**0**	**1**	**0**	**0**
	NHL Totals		**680**	**237**	**300**	**537**	**394**	**86**	**5**	**26**	**1385**	**17.1**		**160**	**45.0**	**132**	**58**	**18:19**	**72**	**15**	**25**	**40**	**41**	**7**	**0**	**2**

Played in NHL All-Star Game (1997, 1999)

Traded to **LA Kings** by **Washington** with Byron Dafoe for LA Kings' 1st round choice (Alexander Volchkov) and Dallas' 4th round choice (previously acquired, Washington selected Justin Davis) in 1996 Entry Draft, July 8, 1995. Traded to **Boston** by **LA Kings** with Byron Dafoe for Jozef Stumpel, Sandy Moger and Boston's 4th round choice (later traded to New Jersey - New Jersey selected Pierre Dagenais) in 1998 Entry Draft, August 29, 1997. Traded to **Toronto** by **Boston** for Toronto's 2nd round choice (Ivan Huml) in 2000 Entry Draft, October 20, 1999.

KILGER, Chad
(KIHL-guhr, CHAD) **EDM.**

Center. Shoots left. 6'3", 215 lbs. Born, Cornwall, Ont., November 27, 1976. Anaheim's 1st choice, 4th overall, in 1995 Entry Draft.

			Regular Season																Playoffs							
Season	Club	League	GP	G	A	Pts	PIM	PP	SH	GW	S	%	+/-	TF	F%	H	SB	Min	GP	G	A	Pts	PIM	PP	SH	GW
1992-93	Cornwall Colts	OJHL	55	30	36	66	26	....	....	....	....	....	....	....	....	....	....	....	6	0	0	0	0	....	....	....
1993-94	Kingston	OHL	66	17	35	52	23	....	....	....	....	....	....	....	....	....	....	....	6	7	2	9	8	....	....	....
1994-95	Kingston	OHL	65	42	53	95	95	....	....	....	....	....	....	....	....	....	....	....	6	5	2	7	10	....	....	....
1995-96	**Anaheim**	**NHL**	**45**	**5**	**7**	**12**	**22**	**0**	**0**	**1**	**38**	**13.2**	**-2**	....	....	....	....	....	....	....	....	....	....	....	....	....
	Winnipeg	**NHL**	**29**	**2**	**3**	**5**	**12**	**0**	**0**	**0**	**19**	**10.5**	**-2**	....	....	....	....	....	**4**	**1**	**0**	**1**	**0**	**0**	**0**	**1**
1996-97	**Phoenix**	**NHL**	**24**	**4**	**3**	**7**	**13**	**1**	**0**	**0**	**30**	**13.3**	**-5**	....	....	....	....	....	....	....	....	....	....	....	....	....
	Springfield	AHL	52	17	28	45	36	....	....	....	....	....	....	....	....	....	....	....	16	5	7	12	56	....	....	....
1997-98	**Phoenix**	**NHL**	**10**	**0**	**1**	**1**	**4**	**0**	**0**	**0**	**9**	**0.0**	**-2**	....	....	....	....	....	....	....	....	....	....	....	....	....
	Springfield	AHL	35	14	14	28	33	....	....	....	....	....	....	....	....	....	....	....	....	....	....	....	....	....	....	....
	Chicago	**NHL**	**22**	**3**	**8**	**11**	**6**	**2**	**0**	**1**	**23**	**13.0**	**2**	....	....	....	....	....	....	....	....	....	....	....	....	....
1998-99	**Chicago**	**NHL**	**64**	**14**	**11**	**25**	**30**	**2**	**1**	**1**	**68**	**20.6**	**-1**	**488**	**56.6**	**124**	**27**	**14:03**	....	....	....	....	....	....	....	....
	Edmonton	**NHL**	**13**	**1**	**1**	**2**	**4**	**0**	**0**	**0**	**13**	**7.7**	**-3**	**82**	**53.7**	**33**	**3**	**11:22**	**4**	**0**	**0**	**0**	**4**	**0**	**0**	**0**
99-2000	**Edmonton**	**NHL**	**40**	**3**	**2**	**5**	**18**	**0**	**0**	**0**	**32**	**9.4**	**-6**	**269**	**48.0**	**60**	**7**	**8:33**	**3**	**0**	**0**	**0**	**0**	**0**	**0**	**0**
	Hamilton Bulldogs	AHL	7	4	2	6	4	....	....	....	....	....	....	....	....	....	....	....	....	....	....	....	....	....	....	....
	NHL Totals		**247**	**32**	**36**	**68**	**109**	**5**	**1**	**3**	**232**	**13.8**		**839**	**53.5**	**217**	**37**	**11:52**	**11**	**1**	**0**	**1**	**4**	**0**	**0**	**1**

Traded to **Winnipeg** by **Anaheim** with Oleg Tverdovsky and Anaheim's 3rd round choice (Per-Anton Lundstrom) in 1996 Entry Draft for Teemu Selanne, Marc Chouinard and Winnipeg's 4th round choice (later traded to Toronto - later traded to Montreal - Montreal selected Kim Staal) in 1996 Entry Draft, February 7, 1996. Transferred to **Phoenix** after **Winnipeg** franchise relocated, July 1, 1996. Traded to **Chicago** by **Phoenix** with Jayson More for Keith Carney and Jim Cummins, March 4, 1998. Traded to **Edmonton** by **Chicago** with Daniel Cleary, Ethan Moreau and Christian Laflamme for Boris Mironov, Dean McAmmond and Jonas Elofsson, March 20, 1999.

KING, Derek
(KIHNG, DAIR-ehk) **OTT.**

Left wing. Shoots left. 6'1", 203 lbs. Born, Hamilton, Ont., February 11, 1967. NY Islanders' 2nd choice, 13th overall, in 1985 Entry Draft.

			Regular Season																Playoffs							
Season	Club	League	GP	G	A	Pts	PIM	PP	SH	GW	S	%	+/-	TF	F%	H	SB	Min	GP	G	A	Pts	PIM	PP	SH	GW
1982-83	Hamilton A's	OJHL	8	1	2	3	0	....	....	....	....	....	....	....	....	....	....	....	....	....	....	....	....	....	....	....
1983-84	Hamilton A's	OJHL	37	10	14	24	142	....	....	....	....	....	....	....	....	....	....	....	....	....	....	....	....	....	....	....
1984-85	Sault Ste. Marie	OHL	63	35	38	73	106	....	....	....	....	....	....	....	....	....	....	....	16	3	13	16	11	....	....	....
1985-86	Sault Ste. Marie	OHL	25	12	17	29	33	....	....	....	....	....	....	....	....	....	....	....	....	....	....	....	....	....	....	....
	Oshawa Generals	OHL	19	8	13	21	15	....	....	....	....	....	....	....	....	....	....	....	6	3	2	5	13	....	....	....
1986-87	Oshawa Generals	OHL	57	53	53	106	74	....	....	....	....	....	....	....	....	....	....	....	17	14	10	24	40	....	....	....
	NY Islanders	**NHL**	**2**	**0**	**0**	**0**	**0**	**0**	**0**	**0**	**5**	**0.0**	**0**	....	....	....	....	....	....	....	....	....	....	....	....	....
1987-88	**NY Islanders**	**NHL**	**55**	**12**	**24**	**36**	**30**	**1**	**0**	**4**	**94**	**12.8**	**7**	....	....	....	....	....	**5**	**0**	**2**	**2**	**2**	**0**	**0**	**0**
	Springfield	AHL	10	7	6	13	6	....	....	....	....	....	....	....	....	....	....	....	....	....	....	....	....	....	....	....
1988-89	**NY Islanders**	**NHL**	**60**	**14**	**29**	**43**	**14**	**4**	**0**	**0**	**103**	**13.6**	**10**	....	....	....	....	....	....	....	....	....	....	....	....	....
	Springfield	AHL	4	4	0	4	0	....	....	....	....	....	....	....	....	....	....	....	....	....	....	....	....	....	....	....
1989-90	**NY Islanders**	**NHL**	**46**	**13**	**27**	**40**	**20**	**5**	**0**	**1**	**91**	**14.3**	**2**	....	....	....	....	....	**4**	**0**	**0**	**0**	**4**	**0**	**0**	**0**
	Springfield	AHL	21	11	12	23	33	....	....	....	....	....	....	....	....	....	....	....	....	....	....	....	....	....	....	....
1990-91	**NY Islanders**	**NHL**	**66**	**19**	**26**	**45**	**44**	**2**	**0**	**2**	**130**	**14.6**	**1**	....	....	....	....	....	....	....	....	....	....	....	....	....
1991-92	**NY Islanders**	**NHL**	**80**	**40**	**38**	**78**	**46**	**21**	**0**	**6**	**189**	**21.2**	**-10**	....	....	....	....	....	....	....	....	....	....	....	....	....
1992-93	**NY Islanders**	**NHL**	**77**	**38**	**38**	**76**	**47**	**21**	**0**	**7**	**201**	**18.9**	**-4**	....	....	....	....	....	**18**	**3**	**11**	**14**	**14**	**0**	**0**	**0**
1993-94	**NY Islanders**	**NHL**	**78**	**30**	**40**	**70**	**59**	**10**	**0**	**7**	**171**	**17.5**	**18**	....	....	....	....	....	**4**	**0**	**1**	**1**	**0**	**0**	**0**	**0**
1994-95	**NY Islanders**	**NHL**	**43**	**10**	**16**	**26**	**41**	**7**	**0**	**0**	**118**	**8.5**	**-5**	....	....	....	....	....	....	....	....	....	....	....	....	....
1995-96	**NY Islanders**	**NHL**	**61**	**12**	**20**	**32**	**23**	**5**	**1**	**0**	**154**	**7.8**	**-10**	....	....	....	....	....	....	....	....	....	....	....	....	....
1996-97	**NY Islanders**	**NHL**	**70**	**23**	**30**	**53**	**20**	**5**	**0**	**3**	**153**	**15.0**	**-6**	....	....	....	....	....	....	....	....	....	....	....	....	....
	Hartford	**NHL**	**12**	**3**	**3**	**6**	**2**	**1**	**0**	**0**	**28**	**10.7**	**0**	....	....	....	....	....	....	....	....	....	....	....	....	....
1997-98	**Toronto**	**NHL**	**77**	**21**	**25**	**46**	**43**	**4**	**0**	**3**	**166**	**12.7**	**-7**	....	....	....	....	....	....	....	....	....	....	....	....	....
1998-99	**Toronto**	**NHL**	**81**	**24**	**28**	**52**	**20**	**8**	**0**	**4**	**150**	**16.0**	**15**	**1**	**0.0**	**36**	**20**	**14:02**	**16**	**1**	**3**	**4**	**4**	**0**	**0**	**0**
99-2000	**Toronto**	**NHL**	**3**	**0**	**0**	**0**	**2**	**0**	**0**	**0**	**4**	**0.0**	**-2**	**0**	**0.0**	**3**	**0**	**11:29**	....	....	....	....	....	....	....	....
	St. Louis	**NHL**	**19**	**2**	**7**	**9**	**6**	**1**	**0**	**0**	**29**	**6.9**	**0**	**0**	**0.0**	**5**	**11**	**12:44**	....	....	....	....	....	....	....	....
	Grand Rapids	IHL	52	19	30	49	25	....	....	....	....	....	....	....	....	....	....	....	17	7	8	15	8	....	....	....
	NHL Totals		**830**	**261**	**351**	**612**	**417**	**95**	**1**	**37**	**1786**	**14.6**		**1**	**0.0**	**44**	**31**	**13:43**	**47**	**4**	**17**	**21**	**24**	**0**	**0**	**0**

OHL First All-Star Team (1987)

Traded to **Hartford** by **NY Islanders** for Hartford's 5th round choice (Adam Edinger) in 1997 Entry Draft, March 18, 1997. Signed as a free agent by **Toronto**, July 4, 1997. Traded to **St. Louis** by **Toronto** with a conditional choice in 2001 Entry Draft for Tyler Harlton and a conditional choice in 2001 Entry Draft, October 20, 1999. Signed as a free agent by **Ottawa**, August 10, 2000.

KING, Kris
(KIHNG, KRIHS)

Left wing. Shoots left. 5'11", 208 lbs. Born, Bracebridge, Ont., February 18, 1966. Washington's 4th choice, 80th overall, in 1984 Entry Draft.

			Regular Season																Playoffs							
Season	Club	League	GP	G	A	Pts	PIM	PP	SH	GW	S	%	+/-	TF	F%	H	SB	Min	GP	G	A	Pts	PIM	PP	SH	GW
1982-83	Gravenhurst	OJHL-C	32	*72	53	*125	115	....	....	....	....	....	....	....	....	....	....	....	....	....	....	....	....	....	....	....
1983-84	Peterborough	OHL	62	13	18	31	168	....	....	....	....	....	....	....	....	....	....	....	8	3	3	6	14	....	....	....
1984-85	Peterborough	OHL	61	18	35	53	222	....	....	....	....	....	....	....	....	....	....	....	16	2	8	10	28	....	....	....
1985-86	Peterborough	OHL	58	19	40	59	254	....	....	....	....	....	....	....	....	....	....	....	8	4	0	4	21	....	....	....
1986-87	Peterborough	OHL	46	23	33	56	160	....	....	....	....	....	....	....	....	....	....	....	12	5	8	13	41	....	....	....
	Binghamton	AHL	7	0	0	0	18	....	....	....	....	....	....	....	....	....	....	....	....	....	....	....	....	....	....	....
1987-88	**Detroit**	**NHL**	**3**	**1**	**0**	**1**	**2**	**0**	**0**	**0**	**3**	**33.3**	**1**	....	....	....	....	....	....	....	....	....	....	....	....	....
	Adirondack	AHL	76	21	32	53	337	....	....	....	....	....	....	....	....	....	....	....	10	4	4	8	53	....	....	....
1988-89	**Detroit**	**NHL**	**55**	**2**	**3**	**5**	**168**	**0**	**0**	**0**	**34**	**5.9**	**-7**	....	....	....	....	....	**2**	**0**	**0**	**0**	**2**	**0**	**0**	**0**
1989-90	**NY Rangers**	**NHL**	**68**	**6**	**7**	**13**	**286**	**0**	**0**	**0**	**49**	**12.2**	**2**	....	....	....	....	....	**10**	**0**	**1**	**1**	**38**	**0**	**0**	**0**
1990-91	**NY Rangers**	**NHL**	**72**	**11**	**14**	**25**	**154**	**0**	**0**	**0**	**107**	**10.3**	**-1**	....	....	....	....	....	**6**	**2**	**0**	**2**	**36**	**0**	**0**	**1**
1991-92	**NY Rangers**	**NHL**	**79**	**10**	**9**	**19**	**224**	**0**	**0**	**2**	**97**	**10.3**	**13**	....	....	....	....	....	**13**	**4**	**1**	**5**	**14**	**0**	**0**	**3**
1992-93	**NY Rangers**	**NHL**	**30**	**0**	**3**	**3**	**67**	**0**	**0**	**0**	**23**	**0.0**	**-1**	....	....	....	....	....	....	....	....	....	....	....	....	....
	Winnipeg	**NHL**	**48**	**8**	**8**	**16**	**136**	**0**	**0**	**1**	**51**	**15.7**	**5**	....	....	....	....	....	**6**	**1**	**1**	**2**	**4**	**0**	**0**	**0**
1993-94	**Winnipeg**	**NHL**	**83**	**4**	**8**	**12**	**205**	**0**	**0**	**1**	**86**	**4.7**	**-22**	....	....	....	....	....	....	....	....	....	....	....	....	....
1994-95	**Winnipeg**	**NHL**	**48**	**4**	**2**	**6**	**85**	**0**	**0**	**0**	**58**	**6.9**	**0**	....	....	....	....	....	....	....	....	....	....	....	....	....
1995-96	**Winnipeg**	**NHL**	**81**	**9**	**11**	**20**	**151**	**0**	**1**	**2**	**89**	**10.1**	**-7**	....	....	....	....	....	**5**	**0**	**1**	**1**	**4**	**0**	**0**	**0**
1996-97	**Phoenix**	**NHL**	**81**	**3**	**11**	**14**	**185**	**0**	**0**	**0**	**57**	**5.3**	**-7**	....	....	....	....	....	**7**	**0**	**0**	**0**	**17**	**0**	**0**	**0**
1997-98	**Toronto**	**NHL**	**82**	**3**	**3**	**6**	**199**	**0**	**0**	**2**	**53**	**5.7**	**-13**	....	....	....	....	....	....	....	....	....	....	....	....	....
1998-99	**Toronto**	**NHL**	**67**	**2**	**2**	**4**	**105**	**0**	**1**	**1**	**34**	**5.9**	**-16**	**6**	**50.0**	**116**	**14**	**9:22**	**17**	**1**	**1**	**2**	**25**	**0**	**0**	**0**

Season	Club	League	Regular Season																Playoffs							
			GP	G	A	Pts	PIM	PP	SH	GW	S	%	+/-	TF	F%	H	SB	Min	GP	G	A	Pts	PIM	PP	SH	GW
99-2000	Toronto	NHL	39	2	4	6	55	0	0	0	24	8.3	4	0	0.0	60	7	8:31	1	0	0	0	2	0	0	0
	Chicago Wolves	IHL	15	2	4	6	19																			
	NHL Totals		836	65	85	150	2022	0	2	9	765	8.5		6	50.0	176	21	9:03	67	8	5	13	142	0	0	4

Won King Clancy Memorial Trophy (1996)

Signed as a free agent by **Detroit**, March 23, 1987. Traded to **NY Rangers** by **Detroit** for Chris McRae and Detroit's 5th round choice (previously acquired, Detroit selected Tony Burns) in 1990 Entry Draft, September 7, 1989. Traded to **Winnipeg** by **NY Rangers** with Tie Domi for Ed Olczyk, December 28, 1992. Transferred to **Phoenix** after **Winnipeg** franchise relocated, July 1, 1996. Signed as a free agent by **Toronto**, July 23, 1997.

KING, Steven

(KIHNG, STEEV)

Right wing. Shoots right. 6', 195 lbs. Born, Greenwich, RI, July 22, 1969. NY Rangers' 1st choice, 21st overall, in 1991 Supplemental Draft.

Season	Club	League	GP	G	A	Pts	PIM	PP	SH	GW	S	%	+/-	TF	F%	H	SB	Min	GP	G	A	Pts	PIM	PP	SH	GW
1987-88	Brown University	ECAC	24	10	5	15	30																			
1988-89	Brown University	ECAC	26	8	5	13	73																			
1989-90	Brown University	ECAC	27	19	8	27	53																			
1990-91	Brown University	ECAC	27	19	15	34	76																			
1991-92	Binghamton	AHL	66	27	15	42	56												10	2	0	2	14			
1992-93	NY Rangers	NHL	24	7	5	12	16	5	0	2	42	16.7	4													
	Binghamton	AHL	53	35	33	68	100												14	7	9	16	26			
1993-94	Anaheim	NHL	36	8	3	11	44	3	0	1	50	16.0	–7													
1994-95	Anaheim	NHL	DID NOT PLAY – INJURED																							
1995-96	Anaheim	NHL	7	2	0	2	15	1	0	1	5	40.0	–1													
	Baltimore Bandits	AHL	68	40	21	61	95												12	7	5	12	20			
1996-97	Philadelphia	AHL	39	17	10	27	47																			
	Michigan K-Wings	IHL	39	15	11	26	39												4	1	2	3	12			
1997-98	Cincinnati	IHL	41	17	9	26	22																			
	Rochester	AHL	28	15	15	30	28												4	1	1	2	4			
1998-99	Providence Bruins	AHL	3	1	0	1	0												13	7	4	11	12			
99-2000	Springfield	AHL	23	10	6	16	20																			
	NHL Totals		67	17	8	25	75	9	0	4	97	17.5														

Claimed by **Anaheim** from **NY Rangers** in Expansion Draft, June 24, 1993. • Missed majority of 1993-94 and entire 1994-95 seasons recovering from shoulder surgery, January 5, 1994. Signed as a free agent by **Philadelphia**, July 31, 1996. • Missed remainder of 1998-99 and majority of 1999-2000 seasons recovering from shoulder surgery, August, 1998. Signed as a free agent by **Phoenix**, July 28, 1999.

KINNEAR, Geordie

(kih-NEER, JOHR-dee) **ATL.**

Defense. Shoots left. 6'1", 195 lbs. Born, Simcoe, Ont., July 9, 1973. New Jersey's 8th choice, 162nd overall, in 1992 Entry Draft.

Season	Club	League	GP	G	A	Pts	PIM	PP	SH	GW	S	%	+/-	TF	F%	H	SB	Min	GP	G	A	Pts	PIM	PP	SH	GW
1989-90	Norwich	OJHL-C	1	0	0	0	19																			
	Tillsonburg Titans	OJHL-B	34	2	5	7	153																			
1990-91	Peterborough B's	OJHL-B	6	0	6	6	51																			
	Peterborough	OHL	37	1	0	1	76												2	0	0	0	10			
1991-92	Peterborough	OHL	63	5	16	21	195												10	0	2	2	36			
1992-93	Peterborough	OHL	58	6	22	28	161												19	1	5	6	43			
1993-94	Albany River Rats	AHL	59	3	12	15	197												5	0	0	0	21			
1994-95	Albany River Rats	AHL	68	5	11	16	136												9	1	1	2	7			
1995-96	Albany River Rats	AHL	73	4	7	11	170												4	0	1	1	2			
1996-97	Albany River Rats	AHL	59	2	9	11	175												10	0	1	1	15			
1997-98	Albany River Rats	AHL	78	1	15	16	206												13	1	1	2	68			
1998-99	Albany River Rats	AHL	55	1	13	14	162												5	0	1	1	0			
99-2000	Atlanta	NHL	4	0	0	0	13	0	0	0	2	0.0	–1	0	0.0	8	13	18:27								
	Orlando	IHL	69	1	5	6	231												6	0	0	0	9			
	NHL Totals		4	0	0	0	13	0	0	0	2	0.0		0	0.0	8	13	18:27								

Signed as a free agent by **Atlanta**, August 12, 1999.

KJELLBERG, Patric

(CHEHL-buhrg, PA-trihk) **NSH.**

Left wing. Shoots left. 6'3", 210 lbs. Born, Trelleborg, Sweden, June 7, 1969. Montreal's 4th choice, 83rd overall, in 1988 Entry Draft.

Season	Club	League	GP	G	A	Pts	PIM	PP	SH	GW	S	%	+/-	TF	F%	H	SB	Min	GP	G	A	Pts	PIM	PP	SH	GW
1985-86	Falun IF	Sweden-2	5	0	2	2	0																			
1986-87	Falun IF	Sweden-2	32	11	13	24	16																			
1987-88	Falun IF	Sweden-2	29	15	10	25	6																			
1988-89	AIK Solna	Sweden	25	7	9	16	8																			
1989-90	AIK Solna	Sweden	33	8	16	24	6												3	1	0	1	0			
1990-91	AIK Solna	Sweden	38	4	11	15	18																			
1991-92	AIK Solna	Sweden	40	20	13	33	14												3	1	0	1	2			
	Sweden	Olympics	8	1	3	4	0																			
1992-93	Montreal	NHL	7	0	0	0	2	0	0	0	7	0.0	–3													
	Fredericton	AHL	41	10	27	37	14												5	2	2	4	0			
1993-94	HV Jonkoping	Sweden	40	11	17	28	18																			
	Sweden	Olympics	8	0	1	1	2																			
1994-95	HV Jonkoping	Sweden	29	5	15	20	12																			
1995-96	Djurgardens IF	Sweden	40	9	7	16	10												4	0	2	2	2			
1996-97	Djurgardens IF	Sweden	49	29	11	40	18												4	2	3	5	4			
1997-98	Djurgardens IF	Sweden	46	*30	18	48	16												15	7	3	10	12			
1998-99	Nashville	NHL	71	11	20	31	24	2	0	2	103	10.7	–13	83	37.3	44	18	17:41								
99-2000	Nashville	NHL	82	23	23	46	14	9	0	3	129	17.8	–11	22	31.8	44	24	18:12								
	NHL Totals		160	34	43	77	40	11	0	5	239	14.2		105	36.2	88	42	17:58								

Signed as a free agent by **Nashville**, June 27, 1998.

KLATT, Trent

(KLAT, TREHNT) **VAN.**

Right wing. Shoots right. 6'1", 210 lbs. Born, Robbinsdale, MN, January 30, 1971. Washington's 5th choice, 82nd overall, in 1989 Entry Draft.

Season	Club	League	GP	G	A	Pts	PIM	PP	SH	GW	S	%	+/-	TF	F%	H	SB	Min	GP	G	A	Pts	PIM	PP	SH	GW
1986-87	Osseo High	Hi-School	22	9	27	36																				
1987-88	Osseo High	Hi-School	22	19	17	36																				
1988-89	Osseo High	Hi-School	22	24	39	63																				
1989-90	U. of Minnesota	WCHA	38	22	14	36	16																			
1990-91	U. of Minnesota	WCHA	39	16	28	44	58																			
1991-92	U. of Minnesota	WCHA	41	27	36	63	76																			
	Minnesota	NHL	1	0	0	0	0	0	0	0	1	0.0	0						6	0	0	0	2	0	0	0
1992-93	Minnesota	NHL	47	4	19	23	38	1	0	0	69	5.8	2													
	Kalamazoo Wings	IHL	31	8	11	19	18																			
1993-94	Dallas	NHL	61	14	24	38	30	3	0	2	86	16.3	13						9	2	1	3	4	1	0	0
	Kalamazoo Wings	IHL	6	3	2	5	4																			
1994-95	Dallas	NHL	47	12	10	22	26	5	0	3	91	13.2	–2						5	1	0	1	0	1	0	0
1995-96	Dallas	NHL	22	4	4	8	23	0	0	1	37	10.8	0													
	Michigan K-Wings	IHL	2	1	2	3	5																			
	Philadelphia	NHL	49	3	8	11	21	0	0	1	64	4.7	2						12	4	1	5	0	0	0	0
1996-97	Philadelphia	NHL	76	24	21	45	20	5	5	5	131	18.3	9						19	4	3	7	12	0	0	2
1997-98	Philadelphia	NHL	82	14	28	42	16	5	0	3	143	9.8	2						5	0	0	0	0	0	0	0
1998-99	Philadelphia	NHL	2	0	0	0	0	0	0	0	2	0.0	0	0	0.0	3	2	11:11								
	Vancouver	NHL	73	4	10	14	12	0	0	0	58	6.9	–3	37	32.4	73	29	11:21								
99-2000	Vancouver	NHL	47	10	10	20	26	8	0	0	100	10.0	–8	19	63.2	129	14	16:04								
	Syracuse Crunch	AHL	24	13	10	23	6																			
	NHL Totals		507	89	134	223	212	27	5	15	782	11.4		56	42.9	205	4513:010		56	11	5	16	18	2	0	2

Traded to **Minnesota** by **Washington** with Steve Maltais for Shawn Chambers, June 21, 1991. Transferred to **Dallas** after **Minnesota** franchise relocated, June 9, 1993. Traded to **Philadelphia** by **Dallas** for Brent Fedyk, December 13, 1995. Traded to **Vancouver** by **Philadelphia** for Vancouver's 6th round choice (later traded to Atlanta - Atlanta selected Jeff Dwyer) in 2000 Entry Draft, October 19, 1998.

KLEE, Ken (KLEE, KEHN) WSH.

Defense. Shoots right. 6'1", 212 lbs. Born, Indianapolis, IN, April 24, 1971. Washington's 11th choice, 177th overall, in 1990 Entry Draft.

Season	Club	League	Regular Season GP	G	A	Pts	PIM	PP	SH	GW	S	%	+/-	TF	F%	H	SB	Min	Playoffs GP	G	A	Pts	PIM	PP	SH	GW
1988-89	St. Michael's	OJHL-B	40	9	23	32	64	....	....	....	....	....	....	....	....	....	....	....	27	5	12	17	54	....	....	....
1989-90	Bowling Green	CCHA	39	0	5	5	52	....	....	....	....	....	....	....	....	....	....	....	....	....	....	....	....	....	....	....
1990-91	Bowling Green	CCHA	37	7	28	35	50	....	....	....	....	....	....	....	....	....	....	....	....	....	....	....	....	....	....	....
1991-92	Bowling Green	CCHA	10	0	1	1	14	....	....	....	....	....	....	....	....	....	....	....	....	....	....	....	....	....	....	....
1992-93	Baltimore	AHL	77	4	14	18	93	....	....	....	....	....	....	....	....	....	....	....	7	0	1	1	15	....	....	....
1993-94	Portland Pirates	AHL	65	2	9	11	87	....	....	....	....	....	....	....	....	....	....	....	17	1	2	3	14	....	....	....
1994-95	**Washington**	**NHL**	23	3	1	4	41	0	0	0	18	16.7	2	....	....	....	....	....	7	0	0	0	4	0	0	0
	Portland Pirates	AHL	49	5	7	12	89	....	....	....	....	....	....	....	....	....	....	....	....	....	....	....	....	....	....	....
1995-96	**Washington**	**NHL**	66	8	3	11	60	0	1	2	76	10.5	–1	....	....	....	....	....	1	0	0	0	0	0	0	0
1996-97	**Washington**	**NHL**	80	3	8	11	115	0	0	2	108	2.8	–5	....	....	....	....	....	....	....	....	....	....	....	....	....
1997-98	**Washington**	**NHL**	51	4	2	6	46	0	0	1	44	9.1	–3	....	....	....	....	....	9	1	0	1	10	0	0	0
1998-99	**Washington**	**NHL**	78	7	13	20	80	0	0	1	132	5.3	–9	0	0.0	248	71	19:07	....	....	....	....	....	....	....	....
99-2000	**Washington**	**NHL**	80	7	13	20	79	0	0	2	113	6.2	8	0	0.0	307	134	20:29	5	0	1	1	10	0	0	0
	NHL Totals		378	32	40	72	421	0	1	8	491	6.5		0	0.0	555	205	19:48	22	1	1	2	24	0	0	0

KLEMM, Jon (KLEHM, JAWN) COL.

Defense. Shoots right. 6'3", 200 lbs. Born, Cranbrook, B.C., January 8, 1970.

Season	Club	League	GP	G	A	Pts	PIM	PP	SH	GW	S	%	+/-	TF	F%	H	SB	Min	GP	G	A	Pts	PIM	PP	SH	GW
1986-87	Cranbrook Colts	KIJHL	59	20	51	71	54	....	....	....	....	....	....	....	....	....	....	....	....	....	....	....	....	....	....	....
1987-88	Seattle T-Birds	WHL	68	6	7	13	24	....	....	....	....	....	....	....	....	....	....	....	....	....	....	....	....	....	....	....
1988-89	Seattle T-Birds	WHL	2	1	1	2	0	....	....	....	....	....	....	....	....	....	....	....	....	....	....	....	....	....	....	....
	Spokane Chiefs	WHL	66	6	34	40	42	....	....	....	....	....	....	....	....	....	....	....	....	....	....	....	....	....	....	....
1989-90	Spokane Chiefs	WHL	66	3	28	31	100	....	....	....	....	....	....	....	....	....	....	....	6	1	1	2	5	....	....	....
1990-91	Spokane Chiefs	WHL	72	7	58	65	65	....	....	....	....	....	....	....	....	....	....	....	15	3	6	9	8	....	....	....
1991-92	**Quebec**	**NHL**	4	0	1	1	0	0	0	0	2	0.0	2	....	....	....	....	....	....	....	....	....	....	....	....	....
	Halifax Citadels	AHL	70	6	13	19	40	....	....	....	....	....	....	....	....	....	....	....	....	....	....	....	....	....	....	....
1992-93	Halifax Citadels	AHL	80	3	20	23	32	....	....	....	....	....	....	....	....	....	....	....	....	....	....	....	....	....	....	....
1993-94	**Quebec**	**NHL**	7	0	0	0	4	0	0	0	11	0.0	–1	....	....	....	....	....	....	....	....	....	....	....	....	....
	Cornwall Aces	AHL	66	4	26	30	78	....	....	....	....	....	....	....	....	....	....	....	13	1	2	3	6	....	....	....
1994-95	Cornwall Aces	AHL	65	6	13	19	84	....	....	....	....	....	....	....	....	....	....	....	....	....	....	....	....	....	....	....
	Quebec	**NHL**	4	1	0	1	2	0	0	0	5	20.0	3	....	....	....	....	....	....	....	....	....	....	....	....	....
1995-96♦	**Colorado**	**NHL**	56	3	12	15	20	0	1	1	61	4.9	12	....	....	....	....	....	15	2	1	3	0	1	0	0
1996-97	**Colorado**	**NHL**	80	9	15	24	37	1	2	1	103	8.7	12	....	....	....	....	....	17	1	1	2	6	0	0	0
1997-98	**Colorado**	**NHL**	67	6	8	14	30	0	0	0	60	10.0	–3	....	....	....	....	....	4	0	0	0	0	0	0	0
1998-99	**Colorado**	**NHL**	39	1	2	3	31	0	0	0	28	3.6	4	14	35.7	38	21	13:43	19	0	1	1	10	0	0	0
99-2000	**Colorado**	**NHL**	73	5	7	12	34	0	0	0	64	7.8	26	17	47.1	129	80	17:22	17	2	1	3	9	0	0	0
	NHL Totals		330	25	45	70	158	1	3	2	334	7.5		31	41.9	167	101	16:06	72	5	4	9	25	1	0	0

WHL West Second All-Star Team (1991)

Signed as a free agent by **Quebec**, May 14, 1991. Transferred to **Colorado** after **Quebec** franchise relocated, June 21, 1995. • Missed majority of 1998-99 season recovering from knee injury suffered in game vs. Phoenix, November 10, 1998.

KNIPSCHEER, Fred (kuh-NIHP-sheer, FREHD)

Center. Shoots left. 5'11", 185 lbs. Born, Ft. Wayne, IN, September 3, 1969.

Season	Club	League	GP	G	A	Pts	PIM	PP	SH	GW	S	%	+/-	TF	F%	H	SB	Min	GP	G	A	Pts	PIM	PP	SH	GW
1988-89	Omaha Lancers	USHL	47	32	33	65	123	....	....	....	....	....	....	....	....	....	....	....	....	....	....	....	....	....	....	....
1989-90	Omaha Lancers	USHL	48	38	46	84	66	....	....	....	....	....	....	....	....	....	....	....	....	....	....	....	....	....	....	....
1990-91	St. Cloud State	WCHA	40	9	10	19	57	....	....	....	....	....	....	....	....	....	....	....	....	....	....	....	....	....	....	....
1991-92	St. Cloud State	WCHA	33	15	17	32	48	....	....	....	....	....	....	....	....	....	....	....	....	....	....	....	....	....	....	....
1992-93	St. Cloud State	WCHA	36	34	26	60	68	....	....	....	....	....	....	....	....	....	....	....	....	....	....	....	....	....	....	....
1993-94	**Boston**	**NHL**	11	3	2	5	14	0	0	1	15	20.0	3	....	....	....	....	....	12	2	1	3	6	0	0	1
	Providence Bruins	AHL	62	26	13	39	50	....	....	....	....	....	....	....	....	....	....	....	....	....	....	....	....	....	....	....
1994-95	Providence Bruins	AHL	71	29	34	63	81	....	....	....	....	....	....	....	....	....	....	....	....	....	....	....	....	....	....	....
	Boston	**NHL**	16	3	1	4	2	0	0	1	20	15.0	1	....	....	....	....	....	4	0	0	0	0	0	0	0
1995-96	**St. Louis**	**NHL**	1	0	0	0	2	0	0	0	2	0.0	0	....	....	....	....	....	....	....	....	....	....	....	....	....
	Worcester	AHL	68	36	37	73	93	....	....	....	....	....	....	....	....	....	....	....	3	0	0	0	2	....	....	....
1996-97	Phoenix	IHL	24	5	11	16	19	....	....	....	....	....	....	....	....	....	....	....	....	....	....	....	....	....	....	....
	Indianapolis Ice	IHL	41	10	9	19	46	....	....	....	....	....	....	....	....	....	....	....	4	0	2	2	10	....	....	....
1997-98	Kentucky	AHL	17	0	7	7	8	....	....	....	....	....	....	....	....	....	....	....	3	0	1	1	7	....	....	....
	Utah Grizzlies	IHL	58	21	32	53	69	....	....	....	....	....	....	....	....	....	....	....	2	0	0	0	4	....	....	....
1998-99	Utah Grizzlies	IHL	21	4	9	13	20	....	....	....	....	....	....	....	....	....	....	....	....	....	....	....	....	....	....	....
	Cincinnati	IHL	43	14	15	29	44	....	....	....	....	....	....	....	....	....	....	....	3	2	1	3	4	....	....	....
99-2000	Cincinnati	IHL	8	1	0	1	2	....	....	....	....	....	....	....	....	....	....	....	....	....	....	....	....	....	....	....
	Milwaukee	IHL	40	8	23	31	26	....	....	....	....	....	....	....	....	....	....	....	3	2	2	4	0	....	....	....
	NHL Totals		28	6	3	9	18	0	0	2	37	16.2		....	....	....	....	....	16	2	1	3	6	0	0	1

WCHA First All-Star Team (1993) • NCAA West Second All-American Team (1993)

Signed as a free agent by **Boston**, April 30, 1993. Traded to **St. Louis** by **Boston** for Rick Zombo, October 2, 1995. Signed as a free agent by **Chicago**, August 16, 1996. Traded to **Cincinnati** (IHL) by **Utah** (IHL) for Don Biggs, December 3, 1998. Signed as a free agent by **Milwaukee** (IHL), December 10, 1999.

KNUBLE, Mike (KUH-noo-buhl, MIGHK) BOS.

Right wing. Shoots right. 6'3", 208 lbs. Born, Toronto, Ont., July 4, 1972. Detroit's 4th choice, 76th overall, in 1991 Entry Draft.

Season	Club	League	GP	G	A	Pts	PIM	PP	SH	GW	S	%	+/-	TF	F%	H	SB	Min	GP	G	A	Pts	PIM	PP	SH	GW
1988-89	East Kentwood	Hi-School	28	52	37	89	60	....	....	....	....	....	....	....	....	....	....	....	....	....	....	....	....	....	....	....
1989-90	East Kentwood	Hi-School	29	63	40	103	40	....	....	....	....	....	....	....	....	....	....	....	....	....	....	....	....	....	....	....
1990-91	Kalamazoo	NAJHL	36	18	24	42	30	....	....	....	....	....	....	....	....	....	....	....	....	....	....	....	....	....	....	....
1991-92	U. of Michigan	CCHA	43	7	8	15	48	....	....	....	....	....	....	....	....	....	....	....	....	....	....	....	....	....	....	....
1992-93	U. of Michigan	CCHA	39	26	16	42	57	....	....	....	....	....	....	....	....	....	....	....	....	....	....	....	....	....	....	....
1993-94	U. of Michigan	CCHA	41	32	26	58	71	....	....	....	....	....	....	....	....	....	....	....	....	....	....	....	....	....	....	....
1994-95	U. of Michigan	CCHA	34	*38	22	60	62	....	....	....	....	....	....	....	....	....	....	....	....	....	....	....	....	....	....	....
	Adirondack	AHL	....	....	....	....	....	....	....	....	....	....	....	....	....	....	....	....	3	0	0	0	0	....	....	....
1995-96	Adirondack	AHL	80	22	23	45	59	....	....	....	....	....	....	....	....	....	....	....	3	1	0	1	0	....	....	....
1996-97	**Detroit**	**NHL**	9	1	0	1	0	0	0	0	10	10.0	–1	....	....	....	....	....	....	....	....	....	....	....	....	....
	Adirondack	AHL	68	28	35	63	54	....	....	....	....	....	....	....	....	....	....	....	....	....	....	....	....	....	....	....
1997-98♦	**Detroit**	**NHL**	53	7	6	13	16	0	0	0	54	13.0	2	....	....	....	....	....	3	0	1	1	0	0	0	0
1998-99	**NY Rangers**	**NHL**	82	15	20	35	26	3	0	1	113	13.3	–7	1	100.0	180	32	14:52	....	....	....	....	....	....	....	....
99-2000	**NY Rangers**	**NHL**	59	9	5	14	18	1	0	1	50	18.0	–5	9	55.6	101	18	10:39	....	....	....	....	....	....	....	....
	Boston	**NHL**	14	3	3	6	8	1	0	1	28	10.7	–2	3	0.0	25	8	19:29	....	....	....	....	....	....	....	....
	NHL Totals		217	35	34	69	68	5	0	3	255	13.7		13	46.2	306	58	13:41	3	0	1	1	0	0	0	0

CCHA Second All-Star Team (1994, 1995) • NCAA West Second All-American Team (1995)

Traded to **NY Rangers** by **Detroit** for NY Rangers' 3rd round choice in 2000 Entry Draft, October 1, 1998. Traded to **Boston** by **NY Rangers** for Rob DiMaio, March 10, 2000.

KNUTSEN, Espen (kuh-NOOT-suhn, EHS-pehn) CBJ

Center. Shoots left. 5'11", 180 lbs. Born, Oslo, Norway, January 12, 1972. Hartford's 9th choice, 204th overall, in 1990 Entry Draft.

Season	Club	League	GP	G	A	Pts	PIM	PP	SH	GW	S	%	+/-	TF	F%	H	SB	Min	GP	G	A	Pts	PIM	PP	SH	GW
1988-89	Valerengen IF	Norge-Jr.	36	14	7	21	18	....	....	....	....	....	....	....	....	....	....	....	....	....	....	....	....	....	....	....
1989-90	Valerengen IF	Norway	40	25	28	53	44	....	....	....	....	....	....	....	....	....	....	....	....	....	....	....	....	....	....	....
1990-91	Valerengen IF	Norway	31	30	24	54	42	....	....	....	....	....	....	....	....	....	....	....	5	3	4	7	....	....	....	....
1991-92	Valerengen IF	Norway	30	28	26	54	37	....	....	....	....	....	....	....	....	....	....	....	8	7	8	15	....	....	....	....
1992-93	Valerengen IF	Norway	13	11	13	24	4	....	....	....	....	....	....	....	....	....	....	....	....	....	....	....	....	....	....	....
1993-94	Valerengen IF	Norway	38	32	26	58	20	....	....	....	....	....	....	....	....	....	....	....	....	....	....	....	....	....	....	....
	Norway	Olympics	7	1	3	4	2	....	....	....	....	....	....	....	....	....	....	....	....	....	....	....	....	....	....	....
1994-95	Djurgardens IF	Sweden	30	6	14	20	18	....	....	....	....	....	....	....	....	....	....	....	3	0	1	1	0	....	....	....

			Regular Season																Playoffs							
Season	Club	League	GP	G	A	Pts	PIM	PP	SH	GW	S	%	+/-	TF	F%	H	SB	Min	GP	G	A	Pts	PIM	PP	SH	GW
1995-96	Djurgardens IF	Sweden	32	10	23	33	50												4	1	0	1	2			
1996-97	Djurgardens IF	Sweden	39	16	33	49	20												4	2	4	6	6			
1997-98	**Anaheim**	**NHL**	**19**	**3**	**0**	**3**	**6**	**1**	**0**	**0**	**21**	**14.3**	**–10**													
	Cincinnati Ducks	AHL	41	4	13	17	18																			
1998-99	Djurgardens IF	Sweden	39	18	24	42	32												4	0	1	1	2			
	Djurgardens IF	EuroHL	4	2	2	4	2																			
99-2000	Djurgardens IF	Sweden	48	18	35	53	65												13	5	*16	*21	2			
	NHL Totals		**19**	**3**	**0**	**3**	**6**	**1**	**0**	**0**	**21**	**14.3**														

Norwegian Player of the Year (1994)
Rights traded to **Anaheim** by **Hartford** for Kevin Brown, October 1, 1996. Traded to **Columbus** by **Anaheim** for Columbus' 4th round choice in 2001 Entry Draft, May 25, 2000.

KOCUR, Joe

(KOH-suhr, JOH)

Right wing. Shoots right. 6', 205 lbs. Born, Calgary, Alta., December 21, 1964. Detroit's 6th choice, 91st overall, in 1983 Entry Draft.

Season	Club	League	GP	G	A	Pts	PIM	PP	SH	GW	S	%	+/-	TF	F%	H	SB	Min	GP	G	A	Pts	PIM	PP	SH	GW
1980-81	Yorkton Terriers	SJHL	48	6	9	15	307																			
1981-82	Yorkton Terriers	SJHL	47	20	21	41	199																			
1982-83	Saskatoon Blades	WHL	62	23	17	40	289												6	2	3	5	25			
1983-84	Saskatoon Blades	WHL	69	40	41	81	258																			
	Adirondack	AHL																	5	0	0	0	20			
1984-85	**Detroit**	**NHL**	**17**	**1**	**0**	**1**	**64**	**0**	**0**	**0**	**7**	**14.3**	**–4**						**3**	**1**	**0**	**1**	**5**	**0**	**0**	**0**
	Adirondack	AHL	47	12	7	19	171																			
1985-86	**Detroit**	**NHL**	**59**	**9**	**6**	**15**	***377**	**2**	**0**	**0**	**65**	**13.8**	**–24**													
	Adirondack	AHL	9	6	2	8	34																			
1986-87	**Detroit**	**NHL**	**77**	**9**	**9**	**18**	**276**	**2**	**0**	**2**	**81**	**11.1**	**–10**						**16**	**2**	**3**	**5**	**71**	**1**	**0**	**2**
1987-88	**Detroit**	**NHL**	**63**	**7**	**7**	**14**	**263**	**0**	**0**	**1**	**41**	**17.1**	**–11**						**10**	**0**	**1**	**1**	**13**	**0**	**0**	**0**
1988-89	**Detroit**	**NHL**	**60**	**9**	**9**	**18**	**213**	**1**	**0**	**1**	**76**	**11.8**	**–4**						**3**	**0**	**1**	**1**	**6**	**0**	**0**	**0**
1989-90	**Detroit**	**NHL**	**71**	**16**	**20**	**36**	**268**	**1**	**0**	**5**	**128**	**12.5**	**–4**													
1990-91	**Detroit**	**NHL**	**52**	**5**	**4**	**9**	**253**	**0**	**0**	**0**	**67**	**7.5**	**–6**													
	NY Rangers	**NHL**	**5**	**0**	**0**	**0**	**36**	**0**	**0**	**0**	**6**	**0.0**	**–1**						**6**	**0**	**2**	**2**	**21**	**0**	**0**	**0**
1991-92	**NY Rangers**	**NHL**	**51**	**7**	**4**	**11**	**121**	**0**	**0**	**2**	**72**	**9.7**	**–4**						**12**	**1**	**1**	**2**	**38**	**0**	**0**	**0**
1992-93	**NY Rangers**	**NHL**	**65**	**3**	**6**	**9**	**131**	**2**	**0**	**0**	**43**	**7.0**	**–9**													
1993-94♦	**NY Rangers**	**NHL**	**71**	**2**	**1**	**3**	**129**	**0**	**0**	**0**	**43**	**4.7**	**–9**						**20**	**1**	**1**	**2**	**17**	**0**	**0**	**0**
1994-95	**NY Rangers**	**NHL**	**48**	**1**	**2**	**3**	**71**	**0**	**0**	**0**	**25**	**4.0**	**–4**						**10**	**0**	**0**	**0**	**8**	**0**	**0**	**0**
1995-96	**NY Rangers**	**NHL**	**38**	**1**	**2**	**3**	**49**	**0**	**0**	**0**	**19**	**5.3**	**–4**													
	Vancouver	**NHL**	**7**	**0**	**1**	**1**	**19**	**0**	**0**	**0**	**1**	**0.0**	**–3**						**1**	**0**	**0**	**0**	**0**	**0**	**0**	**0**
1996-97	San Antonio	IHL	5	1	1	2	24																			
	♦ **Detroit**	**NHL**	**34**	**2**	**1**	**3**	**70**	**0**	**0**	**1**	**38**	**5.3**	**–7**						**19**	**1**	**3**	**4**	**22**	**0**	**0**	**0**
1997-98♦	**Detroit**	**NHL**	**63**	**6**	**5**	**11**	**92**	**0**	**0**	**2**	**53**	**11.3**	**7**						**18**	**4**	**0**	**4**	**30**	**0**	**0**	**0**
1998-99	**Detroit**	**NHL**	**39**	**2**	**5**	**7**	**87**	**0**	**0**	**0**	**20**	**10.0**	**0**	**7**	**14.3**	**41**	**7**	**6:44**								
99-2000	**Detroit**	**NHL**	DID NOT PLAY – INJURED																							
	NHL Totals		**820**	**80**	**82**	**162**	**2519**	**8**	**0**	**14**	**785**	**10.2**		**7**	**14.3**	**41**	**7**	**6:44**	**118**	**10**	**12**	**22**	**231**	**1**	**0**	**2**

Traded to **NY Rangers** by **Detroit** with Per Djoos for Kevin Miller, Jim Cummins and Dennis Vial, March 5, 1991. Traded to **Vancouver** by **NY Rangers** for Kay Whitmore, March 20, 1996. Signed as a free agent by **Detroit**, December 27, 1996. • Missed remainder of 1998-99 and entire 1999-2000 seasons recovering from hernia injury and surgery, May, 1999.

KOHN, Ladislav

(KOHN, LA-dih-slahf) **ANA.**

Right wing. Shoots left. 5'11", 194 lbs. Born, Uherske Hradiste, Czech., March 4, 1975. Calgary's 9th choice, 175th overall, in 1994 Entry Draft.

Season	Club	League	GP	G	A	Pts	PIM	PP	SH	GW	S	%	+/-	TF	F%	H	SB	Min	GP	G	A	Pts	PIM	PP	SH	GW
1993-94	Brandon	WHL	2	0	0	0	0																			
	Swift Current	WHL	69	33	35	68	68												7	5	4	9	8			
1994-95	Swift Current	WHL	65	32	60	92	122												6	2	6	8	14			
	Saint John Flames	AHL	1	0	0	0	0																			
1995-96	**Calgary**	**NHL**	**5**	**1**	**0**	**1**	**2**	**0**	**0**	**0**	**8**	**12.5**	**–1**													
	Saint John Flames	AHL	73	28	45	73	97												16	6	5	11	12			
1996-97	Saint John Flames	AHL	76	28	29	57	81												5	0	0	0	0			
1997-98	**Calgary**	**NHL**	**4**	**0**	**1**	**1**	**0**	**0**	**0**	**0**	**2**	**0.0**	**2**													
	Saint John Flames	AHL	65	25	31	56	90												21	14	6	20	20			
1998-99	**Toronto**	**NHL**	**16**	**1**	**3**	**4**	**4**	**0**	**0**	**0**	**23**	**4.3**	**1**	**16**	**18.8**	**15**	**3**	**12:34**	**2**	**0**	**0**	**0**	**5**	**0**	**0**	**0**
	St. John's Leafs	AHL	61	27	42	69	90																			
99-2000	**Anaheim**	**NHL**	**77**	**5**	**16**	**21**	**27**	**1**	**0**	**1**	**123**	**4.1**	**–17**	**15**	**33.3**	**121**	**16**	**12:06**								
	NHL Totals		**102**	**7**	**20**	**27**	**33**	**1**	**0**	**1**	**156**	**4.5**		**31**	**25.8**	**136**	**19**	**12:11**	**2**	**0**	**0**	**0**	**5**	**0**	**0**	**0**

Traded to **Toronto** by **Calgary** for David Cooper, July 2, 1998. Claimed by **Atlanta** from **Toronto** in Waiver Draft, September 27, 1999. Traded to **Anaheim** by **Atlanta** for Anaheim's 8th round choice (Evan Nielsen) in 2000 Entry Draft, September 27, 1999.

KOIVU, Saku

(KOY-voo, SA-koo) **MTL.**

Center. Shoots left. 5'10", 181 lbs. Born, Turku, Finland, November 23, 1974. Montreal's 1st choice, 21st overall, in 1993 Entry Draft.

Season	Club	League	GP	G	A	Pts	PIM	PP	SH	GW	S	%	+/-	TF	F%	H	SB	Min	GP	G	A	Pts	PIM	PP	SH	GW
1990-91	TPS Turku-B	Finn-Jr.	24	20	28	48	26																			
1991-92	TPS Turku-B	Finn-Jr.	12	3	7	10	6																			
	TPS Turku	Finn-Jr.	34	25	28	53	57												8	5	*9	*14	6			
1992-93	TPS Turku	Finland	46	3	7	10	28												11	3	2	5	2			
	Finland	Nat-Team	4	2	2	4	2																			
1993-94	TPS Turku	Finland	47	23	30	53	42												11	4	8	12	16			
	Finland	Nat-Team	7	2	3	5	12																			
	Finland	Olympics	8	4	3	7	12																			
1994-95	TPS Turku	Finland	45	27	*47	*74	73												13	*7	10	17	16			
	Finland	Nat-Team	7	1	5	6	8																			
1995-96	**Montreal**	**NHL**	**82**	**20**	**25**	**45**	**40**	**8**	**3**	**2**	**136**	**14.7**	**–7**						**6**	**3**	**1**	**4**	**8**	**0**	**0**	**0**
1996-97	**Montreal**	**NHL**	**50**	**17**	**39**	**56**	**38**	**5**	**0**	**3**	**135**	**12.6**	**7**						**5**	**1**	**3**	**4**	**10**	**0**	**0**	**0**
	Finland	Nat-Team	7	1	5	6	8																			
1997-98	**Montreal**	**NHL**	**69**	**14**	**43**	**57**	**48**	**2**	**2**	**3**	**145**	**9.7**	**8**						**6**	**2**	**3**	**5**	**2**	**1**	**0**	**0**
	Finland	Olympics	6	2	*8	*10	4																			
1998-99	**Montreal**	**NHL**	**65**	**14**	**30**	**44**	**38**	**4**	**2**	**0**	**145**	**9.7**	**–7**	**1427**	**52.6**	**53**	**12**	**20:02**								
99-2000	**Montreal**	**NHL**	**24**	**3**	**18**	**21**	**14**	**1**	**0**	**0**	**53**	**5.7**	**7**	**495**	**52.9**	**21**	**3**	**19:13**								
	NHL Totals		**290**	**68**	**155**	**223**	**178**	**20**	**7**	**8**	**614**	**11.1**		**1922**	**52.7**	**74**	**15**	**19:49**	**17**	**6**	**7**	**13**	**20**	**1**	**0**	**0**

Finnish First All-Star Team (1995) • Finnish Player of the Year (1995) • Played in NHL All-Star Game (1998)
• Missed majority of 1999-2000 season recovering from shoulder injury suffered in game vs. NY Rangers, October 30, 1999.

KOMARNISKI, Zenith

(KOH-mahr-NIHS-kee, ZEE-nihth) **VAN.**

Defense. Shoots left. 6', 200 lbs. Born, Edmonton, Alta., August 13, 1978. Vancouver's 2nd choice, 75th overall, in 1996 Entry Draft.

Season	Club	League	GP	G	A	Pts	PIM	PP	SH	GW	S	%	+/-	TF	F%	H	SB	Min	GP	G	A	Pts	PIM	PP	SH	GW
1993-94	Ft-Saskatchewan	AAHA	32	14	32	46	42																			
1994-95	Tri-City Americans	WHL	66	5	19	24	110												17	1	2	3	47			
1995-96	Tri-City Americans	WHL	42	5	21	26	85																			
1996-97	Tri-City Americans	WHL	58	12	44	56	112																			
1997-98	Tri-City Americans	WHL	3	0	4	4	18																			
	Spokane Chiefs	WHL	43	7	20	27	90												18	4	6	10	49			
1998-99	Syracuse Crunch	AHL	58	9	19	28	89																			
99-2000	**Vancouver**	**NHL**	**18**	**1**	**1**	**2**	**8**	**0**	**0**	**0**	**21**	**4.8**	**–1**	**0**	**0.0**	**40**	**29**	**16:11**								
	Syracuse Crunch	AHL	42	4	12	16	130												4	2	0	2	6			
	NHL Totals		**18**	**1**	**1**	**2**	**8**	**0**	**0**	**0**	**21**	**4.8**		**0**	**0.0**	**40**	**29**	**16:11**								

WHL West First All-Star Team (1997)

Regular Season / Playoffs

KONOWALCHUK, Steve

(kahn-uh-WAHL-chuhk, STEEV) **WSH.**

Center. Shoots left. 6'2", 207 lbs. Born, Salt Lake City, UT, November 11, 1972. Washington's 5th choice, 58th overall, in 1991 Entry Draft.

Season	Club	League	GP	G	A	Pts	PIM	PP	SH	GW	S	%	+/-	TF	F%	H	SB	Min	GP	G	A	Pts	PIM	PP	SH	GW
1989-90	Prince Albert	SAHA	36	30	28	58	22																			
1990-91	Portland	WHL	72	43	49	92	78																			
1991-92	Portland	WHL	64	51	53	104	95												6	3	6	9	12			
	Washington	**NHL**	**1**	**0**	**0**	**0**	**0**	**0**	**0**	**0**	**1**	**0.0**	**0**													
	Baltimore	AHL	3	1	1	2	0																			
1992-93	**Washington**	**NHL**	**36**	**4**	**7**	**11**	**16**	**1**	**0**	**1**	**34**	**11.8**	**4**						**2**	**0**	**1**	**1**	**0**	**0**	**0**	**0**
	Baltimore	AHL	37	18	28	46	74																			
1993-94	**Washington**	**NHL**	**62**	**12**	**14**	**26**	**33**	**0**	**0**	**0**	**63**	**19.0**	**9**						**11**	**0**	**1**	**1**	**10**	**0**	**0**	**0**
	Portland Pirates	AHL	8	11	4	15	4																			
1994-95	**Washington**	**NHL**	**46**	**11**	**14**	**25**	**44**	**3**	**3**	**3**	**88**	**12.5**	**7**						**7**	**2**	**5**	**7**	**12**	**0**	**1**	**0**
1995-96	**Washington**	**NHL**	**70**	**23**	**22**	**45**	**92**	**7**	**1**	**3**	**197**	**11.7**	**13**						**2**	**0**	**2**	**2**	**0**	**0**	**0**	**0**
1996-97	**Washington**	**NHL**	**78**	**17**	**25**	**42**	**67**	**2**	**1**	**3**	**155**	**11.0**	**−3**													
1997-98	**Washington**	**NHL**	**80**	**10**	**24**	**34**	**80**	**2**	**0**	**2**	**131**	**7.6**	**9**													
1998-99	**Washington**	**NHL**	**45**	**12**	**12**	**24**	**26**	**4**	**1**	**2**	**98**	**12.2**	**0**	**124**	**51.6**	**125**	**13**	**17:50**								
99-2000	**Washington**	**NHL**	**82**	**16**	**27**	**43**	**80**	**3**	**0**	**1**	**146**	**11.0**	**19**	**147**	**49.7**	**245**	**39**	**17:36**	**5**	**1**	**0**	**1**	**2**	**0**	**1**	**0**
	NHL Totals		**500**	**105**	**145**	**250**	**438**	**22**	**6**	**15**	**913**	**11.5**		**271**	**50.6**	**370**	**52**	**17:41**	**27**	**3**	**9**	**12**	**24**	**0**	**2**	**0**

WHL First All-Star Team (1992)

KOROLEV, Evgeny

(KOH-roh-lehv, ehv-GEHN-ee) **NYI**

Defense. Shoots left. 6'1", 186 lbs. Born, Moscow, USSR, July 24, 1978. NY Islanders' 6th choice, 182nd overall, in 1998 Entry Draft.

Season	Club	League	GP	G	A	Pts	PIM	PP	SH	GW	S	%	+/-	TF	F%	H	SB	Min	GP	G	A	Pts	PIM	PP	SH	GW
1995-96	Peterborough	OHL	60	2	12	14	60												6	0	0	0	2			
1996-97	Peterborough	OHL	64	5	17	22	60												11	1	1	2	8			
1997-98	Peterborough	OHL	37	5	21	26	39																			
	London Knights	OHL	27	4	10	14	36												15	2	7	9	29			
1998-99	Roanoke	ECHL	2	0	1	1	0																			
	Lowell	AHL	54	2	6	8	48												2	0	1	1	0			
99-2000	**NY Islanders**	**NHL**	**17**	**1**	**2**	**3**	**8**	**0**	**0**	**0**	**7**	**14.3**	**−10**	**0**	**0.0**	**34**	**19**	**16:12**								
	Lowell	AHL	57	1	10	11	61												6	0	0	0	4			
	NHL Totals		**17**	**1**	**2**	**3**	**8**	**0**	**0**	**0**	**7**	**14.3**		**0**	**0.0**	**34**	**19**	**16:12**								

• Re-entered NHL draft. Originally NY Islanders' 9th choice, 192nd overall, in 1996 Entry Draft.

KOROLEV, Igor

(KOH-roh-lehv, EE-gohr) **TOR.**

Center/Left wing. Shoots left. 6'1", 190 lbs. Born, Moscow, USSR, September 6, 1970. St. Louis' 1st choice, 38th overall, in 1992 Entry Draft.

Season	Club	League	GP	G	A	Pts	PIM	PP	SH	GW	S	%	+/-	TF	F%	H	SB	Min	GP	G	A	Pts	PIM	PP	SH	GW
1988-89	Dynamo Moscow	USSR	1	0	0	0	2																			
1989-90	Dynamo Moscow	USSR	17	3	2	5	2																			
1990-91	Dynamo Moscow	USSR	38	12	4	16	12																			
1991-92	Dynamo Moscow	CIS	39	15	12	27	16																			
1992-93	Dynamo Moscow	CIS	5	1	2	3	4																			
	St. Louis	**NHL**	**74**	**4**	**23**	**27**	**20**	**2**	**0**	**0**	**76**	**5.3**	**−1**						**3**	**0**	**0**	**0**	**0**	**0**	**0**	**0**
1993-94	**St. Louis**	**NHL**	**73**	**6**	**10**	**16**	**40**	**0**	**0**	**1**	**93**	**6.5**	**−12**						**2**	**0**	**0**	**0**	**0**	**0**	**0**	**0**
1994-95	Dynamo Moscow	CIS	13	4	6	10	18																			
	Winnipeg	**NHL**	**45**	**8**	**22**	**30**	**10**	**1**	**0**	**1**	**85**	**9.4**	**1**													
1995-96	**Winnipeg**	**NHL**	**73**	**22**	**29**	**51**	**42**	**8**	**0**	**5**	**165**	**13.3**	**1**						**6**	**0**	**3**	**3**	**0**	**0**	**0**	**0**
1996-97	**Phoenix**	**NHL**	**41**	**3**	**7**	**10**	**28**	**2**	**0**	**0**	**41**	**7.3**	**−5**						**1**	**0**	**0**	**0**	**0**	**0**	**0**	**0**
	Michigan K-Wings	IHL	4	2	2	4	0																			
	Phoenix	IHL	4	2	6	8	4																			
1997-98	**Toronto**	**NHL**	**78**	**17**	**22**	**39**	**22**	**6**	**3**	**5**	**97**	**17.5**	**−18**													
1998-99	**Toronto**	**NHL**	**66**	**13**	**34**	**47**	**46**	**1**	**0**	**2**	**99**	**13.1**	**11**	**973**	**42.0**	**23**	**13**	**18:06**	**1**	**0**	**0**	**0**	**0**	**0**	**0**	**0**
99-2000	**Toronto**	**NHL**	**80**	**20**	**26**	**46**	**22**	**5**	**3**	**4**	**101**	**19.8**	**12**	**964**	**41.3**	**42**	**26**	**17:56**	**12**	**0**	**4**	**4**	**6**	**0**	**0**	**0**
	NHL Totals		**530**	**93**	**173**	**266**	**230**	**25**	**6**	**18**	**757**	**12.3**		**1937**	**41.7**	**65**	**39**	**18:01**	**25**	**0**	**7**	**7**	**6**	**0**	**0**	**0**

Claimed by **Winnipeg** from **St. Louis** in NHL Waiver Draft, January 18, 1995. Transferred to **Phoenix** after **Winnipeg** franchise relocated, July 1, 1996. Signed as a free agent by **Toronto**, September 29, 1997.

KOROLYUK, Alexander

(koh-roh-LYUHK, al-ehx-AN-duhr) **S.J.**

Right wing. Shoots left. 5'9", 195 lbs. Born, Moscow, USSR, January 15, 1976. San Jose's 6th choice, 141st overall, in 1994 Entry Draft.

Season	Club	League	GP	G	A	Pts	PIM	PP	SH	GW	S	%	+/-	TF	F%	H	SB	Min	GP	G	A	Pts	PIM	PP	SH	GW
1993-94	Krylja Sovetov	CIS	22	4	4	8	20												3	1	0	1	4			
1994-95	Krylja Sovetov	CIS	52	16	13	29	62												4	1	2	3	4			
1995-96	Krylja Sovetov	CIS	50	30	19	49	77																			
1996-97	Krylja Sovetov	Russia	17	8	5	13	46																			
	Manitoba Moose	IHL	42	20	16	36	71																			
1997-98	**San Jose**	**NHL**	**19**	**2**	**3**	**5**	**6**	**1**	**0**	**0**	**23**	**8.7**	**−5**													
	Kentucky	AHL	44	16	23	39	96												3	0	0	0	0			
1998-99	**San Jose**	**NHL**	**55**	**12**	**18**	**30**	**26**	**2**	**0**	**0**	**96**	**12.5**	**3**	**4**	**50.0**	**66**	**7**	**13:53**	**6**	**1**	**3**	**4**	**2**	**0**	**0**	**1**
	Kentucky	AHL	23	9	13	22	16																			
99-2000	**San Jose**	**NHL**	**57**	**14**	**21**	**35**	**35**	**3**	**0**	**1**	**124**	**11.3**	**4**	**1**	**100.0**	**47**	**12**	**13:36**	**9**	**0**	**3**	**3**	**6**	**0**	**0**	**0**
	NHL Totals		**131**	**28**	**42**	**70**	**67**	**6**	**0**	**1**	**243**	**11.5**		**5**	**60.0**	**113**	**19**	**13:45**	**15**	**1**	**6**	**7**	**8**	**0**	**0**	**1**

KOVALENKO, Andrei

(koh-vah-LEHN-koh, AWN-dray) **BOS.**

Right wing. Shoots left. 5'10", 200 lbs. Born, Balakovo, USSR, June 7, 1970. Quebec's 6th choice, 148th overall, in 1990 Entry Draft.

Season	Club	League	GP	G	A	Pts	PIM	PP	SH	GW	S	%	+/-	TF	F%	H	SB	Min	GP	G	A	Pts	PIM	PP	SH	GW
1987-88	Torpedo Gorky	USSR	2	1	0	1	0																			
1988-89	SKA Kalinin	USSR-2	30	8	7	15	29																			
	CSKA Moscow	USSR	10	1	0	1	0																			
1989-90	CSKA Moscow	USSR	48	8	5	13	20																			
1990-91	CSKA Moscow	USSR	45	13	8	21	26																			
1991-92	CSKA Moscow	CIS	44	19	13	32	32																			
	Russia	Olympics	8	1	1	2	2																			
1992-93	CSKA Moscow	CIS	3	3	1	4	4																			
	Quebec	**NHL**	**81**	**27**	**41**	**68**	**57**	**8**	**1**	**4**	**153**	**17.6**	**13**						**4**	**1**	**0**	**1**	**2**	**0**	**0**	**0**
1993-94	**Quebec**	**NHL**	**58**	**16**	**17**	**33**	**46**	**5**	**0**	**4**	**92**	**17.4**	**−5**													
1994-95	Lada Togliatti	CIS	11	9	2	11	14																			
	Quebec	**NHL**	**45**	**14**	**10**	**24**	**31**	**1**	**0**	**3**	**63**	**22.2**	**−4**						**6**	**0**	**1**	**1**	**2**	**0**	**0**	**0**
1995-96	**Colorado**	**NHL**	**26**	**11**	**11**	**22**	**16**	**3**	**0**	**3**	**46**	**23.9**	**11**													
	Montreal	**NHL**	**51**	**17**	**17**	**34**	**33**	**3**	**0**	**3**	**85**	**20.0**	**9**						**6**	**0**	**0**	**0**	**6**	**0**	**0**	**0**
1996-97	**Edmonton**	**NHL**	**74**	**32**	**27**	**59**	**81**	**14**	**0**	**2**	**163**	**19.6**	**−5**						**12**	**4**	**3**	**7**	**6**	**3**	**0**	**0**
1997-98	**Edmonton**	**NHL**	**59**	**6**	**17**	**23**	**28**	**1**	**0**	**2**	**89**	**6.7**	**−14**						**1**	**0**	**0**	**0**	**2**	**0**	**0**	**0**
	Russia	Olympics	6	4	1	5	14																			
1998-99	**Edmonton**	**NHL**	**43**	**13**	**14**	**27**	**30**	**2**	**0**	**3**	**75**	**17.3**	**−4**	**0**	**0.0**	**40**	**7**	**16:19**								
	Philadelphia	**NHL**	**13**	**0**	**1**	**1**	**2**	**0**	**0**	**0**	**8**	**0.0**	**−5**	**0**	**0.0**	**12**	**1**	**8:02**								
	Carolina	**NHL**	**18**	**6**	**6**	**12**	**0**	**1**	**0**	**1**	**21**	**28.6**	**3**	**1**	**0.0**	**40**	**2**	**13:53**	**4**	**0**	**2**	**2**	**2**	**0**	**0**	**0**
99-2000	**Carolina**	**NHL**	**76**	**15**	**24**	**39**	**38**	**2**	**0**	**3**	**114**	**13.2**	**−13**	**4**	**75.0**	**143**	**21**	**14:59**								
	NHL Totals		**544**	**157**	**185**	**342**	**362**	**40**	**1**	**28**	**909**	**17.3**		**5**	**60.0**	**235**	**31**	**14:38**	**33**	**5**	**6**	**11**	**20**	**3**	**0**	**0**

Transferred to **Colorado** after **Quebec** franchise relocated, June 21, 1995. Traded to **Montreal** by **Colorado** with Martin Rucinsky and Jocelyn Thibault for Patrick Roy and Mike Keane, December 6, 1995. Traded to **Edmonton** by **Montreal** for Scott Thornton, September 6, 1996. Traded to **Philadelphia** by **Edmonton** for Alexandre Daigle, January 29, 1999. Traded to **Carolina** by **Philadelphia** for Adam Burt, March 6, 1999. Signed as a free agent by **Boston**, July 25, 2000.

KOVALEV, Alexei

(koh-VAH-lehv, al-EHX-ay) **PIT.**

Right wing. Shoots left. 6'1", 215 lbs. Born, Togliatti, USSR, February 24, 1973. NY Rangers' 1st choice, 15th overall, in 1991 Entry Draft.

			Regular Season																Playoffs							
Season	Club	League	GP	G	A	Pts	PIM	PP	SH	GW	S	%	+/-	TF	F%	H	SB	Min	GP	G	A	Pts	PIM	PP	SH	GW
1989-90	Dynamo Moscow	USSR	1	0	0	0	0	....	....	....	....	....	....	....	....	....	....	....	....	....	....	....	....	....	....	....
1990-91	Dynamo Moscow	USSR	18	1	2	3	4	....	....	....	....	....	....	....	....	....	....	....	....	....	....	....	....	....	....	....
1991-92	Dynamo Moscow	CIS	33	16	9	25	20	....	....	....	....	....	....	....	....	....	....	....	....	....	....	....	....	....	....	....
	Russia	Olympics	8	1	2	3	14	....	....	....	....	....	....	....	....	....	....	....	....	....	....	....	....	....	....	....
1992-93	**NY Rangers**	**NHL**	**65**	**20**	**18**	**38**	**79**	**3**	**0**	**3**	**134**	**14.9**	**-10**	....	....	....	....	....	....	....	....	....	....	....	....	....
	Binghamton	AHL	13	13	11	24	35	....	....	....	....	....	....	....	....	....	....	....	9	3	5	8	14	....	....	....
1993-94♦	**NY Rangers**	**NHL**	**76**	**23**	**33**	**56**	**154**	**7**	**0**	**3**	**184**	**12.5**	**18**	....	....	....	....	....	**23**	**9**	**12**	**21**	**18**	**5**	**0**	**2**
1994-95	Lada Togliatti	CIS	12	8	8	16	49	....	....	....	....	....	....	....	....	....	....	....	....	....	....	....	....	....	....	....
	NY Rangers	**NHL**	**48**	**13**	**15**	**28**	**30**	**1**	**1**	**1**	**103**	**12.6**	**-6**	....	....	....	....	....	**10**	**4**	**7**	**11**	**10**	**0**	**0**	**0**
1995-96	**NY Rangers**	**NHL**	**81**	**24**	**34**	**58**	**98**	**8**	**1**	**7**	**206**	**11.7**	**5**	....	....	....	....	....	**11**	**3**	**4**	**7**	**14**	**0**	**0**	**1**
1996-97	**NY Rangers**	**NHL**	**45**	**13**	**22**	**35**	**42**	**1**	**0**	**0**	**110**	**11.8**	**11**	....	....	....	....	....	....	....	....	....	....	....	....	....
1997-98	**NY Rangers**	**NHL**	**73**	**23**	**30**	**53**	**44**	**8**	**0**	**3**	**173**	**13.3**	**-22**	....	....	....	....	....	....	....	....	....	....	....	....	....
1998-99	**NY Rangers**	**NHL**	**14**	**3**	**4**	**7**	**12**	**1**	**0**	**1**	**35**	**8.6**	**-6**	**18**	**44.4**	**13**	**5**	**19:53**	....	....	....	....	....	....	....	....
	Pittsburgh	**NHL**	**63**	**20**	**26**	**46**	**37**	**5**	**1**	**4**	**156**	**12.8**	**8**	**226**	**43.4**	**82**	**40**	**20:30**	**10**	**5**	**7**	**12**	**14**	**0**	**0**	**1**
99-2000	**Pittsburgh**	**NHL**	**82**	**26**	**40**	**66**	**94**	**9**	**2**	**4**	**254**	**10.2**	**-3**	**306**	**47.4**	**90**	**25**	**22:53**	**11**	**1**	**5**	**6**	**10**	**0**	**0**	**0**
	NHL Totals		**547**	**165**	**222**	**387**	**590**	**43**	**5**	**26**	**1355**	**12.2**		**550**	**45.6**	**185**	**70**	**21:40**	**65**	**22**	**35**	**57**	**66**	**5**	**0**	**4**

Traded to **Pittsburgh** by **NY Rangers** with Harry York for Petr Nedved, Chris Tamer and Sean Pronger, November 25, 1998.

KOZLOV, Viktor

(KAHS-lahf, VIHK-tohr) **FLA.**

Center. Shoots right. 6'5", 232 lbs. Born, Togliatti, USSR, February 14, 1975. San Jose's 1st choice, 6th overall, in 1993 Entry Draft.

			Regular Season																Playoffs							
Season	Club	League	GP	G	A	Pts	PIM	PP	SH	GW	S	%	+/-	TF	F%	H	SB	Min	GP	G	A	Pts	PIM	PP	SH	GW
1990-91	Lada Togliatti	USSR-2	2	2	0	2	0	....	....	....	....	....	....	....	....	....	....	....	....	....	....	....	....	....	....	....
1991-92	Lada Togliatti	CIS	3	0	0	0	0	....	....	....	....	....	....	....	....	....	....	....	....	....	....	....	....	....	....	....
1992-93	Dynamo Moscow	CIS	30	6	5	11	4	....	....	....	....	....	....	....	....	....	....	....	10	3	0	3	0	....	....	....
1993-94	Dynamo Moscow	CIS	42	16	9	25	14	....	....	....	....	....	....	....	....	....	....	....	7	3	2	5	0	....	....	....
1994-95	Dynamo Moscow	CIS	3	1	1	2	2	....	....	....	....	....	....	....	....	....	....	....	....	....	....	....	....	....	....	....
	San Jose	**NHL**	**16**	**2**	**0**	**2**	**2**	**0**	**0**	**0**	**23**	**8.7**	**-5**	....	....	....	....	....	....	....	....	....	....	....	....	....
	Kansas City	IHL	4	1	1	2	0	....	....	....	....	....	....	....	....	....	....	....	13	4	5	9	12	....	....	....
1995-96	**San Jose**	**NHL**	**62**	**6**	**13**	**19**	**6**	**1**	**0**	**0**	**107**	**5.6**	**-15**	....	....	....	....	....	....	....	....	....	....	....	....	....
	Kansas City	IHL	15	4	7	11	12	....	....	....	....	....	....	....	....	....	....	....	....	....	....	....	....	....	....	....
1996-97	**San Jose**	**NHL**	**78**	**16**	**25**	**41**	**40**	**4**	**0**	**4**	**184**	**8.7**	**-16**	....	....	....	....	....	....	....	....	....	....	....	....	....
1997-98	**San Jose**	**NHL**	**18**	**5**	**2**	**7**	**2**	**2**	**0**	**0**	**51**	**9.8**	**-2**	....	....	....	....	....	....	....	....	....	....	....	....	....
	Florida	**NHL**	**46**	**12**	**11**	**23**	**14**	**3**	**2**	**0**	**114**	**10.5**	**-1**	....	....	....	....	....	....	....	....	....	....	....	....	....
1998-99	**Florida**	**NHL**	**65**	**16**	**35**	**51**	**24**	**5**	**1**	**1**	**209**	**7.7**	**13**	**985**	**41.2**	**32**	**30**	**19:03**	....	....	....	....	....	....	....	....
99-2000	**Florida**	**NHL**	**80**	**17**	**53**	**70**	**16**	**6**	**0**	**2**	**223**	**7.6**	**24**	**1616**	**42.9**	**62**	**33**	**19:27**	**4**	**0**	**1**	**1**	**0**	**0**	**0**	**0**
	NHL Totals		**365**	**74**	**139**	**213**	**104**	**21**	**3**	**7**	**911**	**8.1**		**2601**	**42.3**	**94**	**63**	**19:16**	**4**	**0**	**1**	**1**	**0**	**0**	**0**	**0**

Played in NHL All-Star Game (2000)

Traded to **Florida** by **San Jose** with Florida's 5th round choice (previously acquired, Florida selected Jaroslav Spacek) in 1998 Entry Draft for Dave Lowry and Florida's 1st round choice (later traded to Tampa Bay - Tampa Bay selected Vincent Lecavalier) in 1998 Entry Draft, November 13, 1997.

KOZLOV, Vyacheslav

(KAHS-lahf, VYACH-ih-slav) **DET.**

Center. Shoots left. 5'10", 180 lbs. Born, Voskresensk, USSR, May 3, 1972. Detroit's 2nd choice, 45th overall, in 1990 Entry Draft.

			Regular Season																Playoffs							
Season	Club	League	GP	G	A	Pts	PIM	PP	SH	GW	S	%	+/-	TF	F%	H	SB	Min	GP	G	A	Pts	PIM	PP	SH	GW
1987-88	HK Khimik	USSR	2	0	0	0	0	....	....	....	....	....	....	....	....	....	....	....	....	....	....	....	....	....	....	....
1988-89	HK Khimik	USSR	14	0	1	1	2	....	....	....	....	....	....	....	....	....	....	....	....	....	....	....	....	....	....	....
1989-90	HK Khimik	USSR	45	14	12	26	38	....	....	....	....	....	....	....	....	....	....	....	....	....	....	....	....	....	....	....
1990-91	HK Khimik	USSR	45	11	13	24	46	....	....	....	....	....	....	....	....	....	....	....	....	....	....	....	....	....	....	....
1991-92	CSKA Moscow	CIS	11	6	5	11	12	....	....	....	....	....	....	....	....	....	....	....	....	....	....	....	....	....	....	....
	Detroit	**NHL**	**7**	**0**	**2**	**2**	**2**	**0**	**0**	**0**	**9**	**0.0**	**-2**	....	....	....	....	....	....	....	....	....	....	....	....	....
1992-93	**Detroit**	**NHL**	**17**	**4**	**1**	**5**	**14**	**0**	**0**	**0**	**26**	**15.4**	**-1**	....	....	....	....	....	**4**	**0**	**2**	**2**	**2**	**0**	**0**	**0**
	Adirondack	AHL	45	23	36	59	54	....	....	....	....	....	....	....	....	....	....	....	4	1	1	2	4	....	....	....
1993-94	**Detroit**	**NHL**	**77**	**34**	**39**	**73**	**50**	**8**	**2**	**6**	**202**	**16.8**	**27**	....	....	....	....	....	**7**	**2**	**5**	**7**	**12**	**0**	**0**	**0**
	Adirondack	AHL	3	0	1	1	15	....	....	....	....	....	....	....	....	....	....	....	....	....	....	....	....	....	....	....
1994-95	CSKA Moscow	CIS	10	3	4	7	14	....	....	....	....	....	....	....	....	....	....	....	....	....	....	....	....	....	....	....
	Detroit	**NHL**	**46**	**13**	**20**	**33**	**45**	**5**	**0**	**3**	**97**	**13.4**	**12**	....	....	....	....	....	**18**	**9**	**7**	**16**	**10**	**1**	**0**	**4**
1995-96	**Detroit**	**NHL**	**82**	**36**	**37**	**73**	**70**	**9**	**0**	**7**	**237**	**15.2**	**33**	....	....	....	....	....	**19**	**5**	**7**	**12**	**10**	**2**	**0**	**1**
1996-97♦	**Detroit**	**NHL**	**75**	**23**	**22**	**45**	**46**	**3**	**0**	**6**	**211**	**10.9**	**21**	....	....	....	....	....	**20**	**8**	**5**	**13**	**14**	**4**	**0**	**2**
1997-98♦	**Detroit**	**NHL**	**80**	**25**	**27**	**52**	**46**	**6**	**0**	**1**	**221**	**11.3**	**14**	....	....	....	....	....	**22**	**6**	**8**	**14**	**10**	**1**	**0**	**4**
1998-99	**Detroit**	**NHL**	**79**	**29**	**29**	**58**	**45**	**6**	**1**	**4**	**209**	**13.9**	**10**	**38**	**36.8**	**41**	**20**	**16:02**	**10**	**6**	**1**	**7**	**4**	**3**	**0**	**0**
99-2000	**Detroit**	**NHL**	**72**	**18**	**18**	**36**	**28**	**4**	**0**	**3**	**165**	**10.9**	**11**	**28**	**35.7**	**35**	**20**	**15:30**	**8**	**2**	**1**	**3**	**12**	**1**	**0**	**1**
	NHL Totals		**535**	**182**	**195**	**377**	**346**	**41**	**3**	**30**	**1377**	**13.2**		**66**	**36.4**	**76**	**40**	**15:47**	**108**	**38**	**36**	**74**	**74**	**12**	**0**	**12**

USSR Rookie of the Year (1990)

KRAVCHUK, Igor

(krahv-CHOOK, EE-gohr) **OTT.**

Defense. Shoots left. 6'1", 218 lbs. Born, Ufa, USSR, September 13, 1966. Chicago's 5th choice, 71st overall, in 1991 Entry Draft.

			Regular Season																Playoffs							
Season	Club	League	GP	G	A	Pts	PIM	PP	SH	GW	S	%	+/-	TF	F%	H	SB	Min	GP	G	A	Pts	PIM	PP	SH	GW
1984-85	Salavat Yulayev	USSR-2	50	3	2	5	22	....	....	....	....	....	....	....	....	....	....	....	....	....	....	....	....	....	....	....
1985-86	Salavat Yulayev	USSR	21	2	2	4	6	....	....	....	....	....	....	....	....	....	....	....	....	....	....	....	....	....	....	....
1986-87	Salavat Yulayev	USSR	22	0	1	1	8	....	....	....	....	....	....	....	....	....	....	....	....	....	....	....	....	....	....	....
1987-88	CSKA Moscow	USSR	48	1	8	9	12	....	....	....	....	....	....	....	....	....	....	....	....	....	....	....	....	....	....	....
	Soviet Union	Olympics	6	1	0	1	0	....	....	....	....	....	....	....	....	....	....	....	....	....	....	....	....	....	....	....
1988-89	CSKA Moscow	USSR	22	3	3	6	2	....	....	....	....	....	....	....	....	....	....	....	....	....	....	....	....	....	....	....
1989-90	CSKA Moscow	USSR	48	1	3	4	16	....	....	....	....	....	....	....	....	....	....	....	....	....	....	....	....	....	....	....
1990-91	CSKA Moscow	USSR	41	6	5	11	16	....	....	....	....	....	....	....	....	....	....	....	....	....	....	....	....	....	....	....
1991-92	CSKA Moscow	CIS	30	3	8	11	6	....	....	....	....	....	....	....	....	....	....	....	....	....	....	....	....	....	....	....
	Russia	Olympics	8	3	2	5	6	....	....	....	....	....	....	....	....	....	....	....	....	....	....	....	....	....	....	....
	Chicago	**NHL**	**18**	**1**	**8**	**9**	**4**	**0**	**0**	**1**	**40**	**2.5**	**-3**	....	....	....	....	....	**18**	**2**	**6**	**8**	**8**	**1**	**0**	**0**
1992-93	**Chicago**	**NHL**	**38**	**6**	**9**	**15**	**30**	**3**	**0**	**0**	**101**	**5.9**	**11**	....	....	....	....	....	....	....	....	....	....	....	....	....
	Edmonton	**NHL**	**17**	**4**	**8**	**12**	**2**	**1**	**0**	**0**	**42**	**9.5**	**-8**	....	....	....	....	....	....	....	....	....	....	....	....	....
1993-94	**Edmonton**	**NHL**	**81**	**12**	**38**	**50**	**16**	**5**	**0**	**2**	**197**	**6.1**	**-12**	....	....	....	....	....	....	....	....	....	....	....	....	....
1994-95	**Edmonton**	**NHL**	**36**	**7**	**11**	**18**	**29**	**3**	**1**	**0**	**93**	**7.5**	**-15**	....	....	....	....	....	....	....	....	....	....	....	....	....
1995-96	**Edmonton**	**NHL**	**26**	**4**	**4**	**8**	**10**	**3**	**0**	**0**	**59**	**6.8**	**-13**	....	....	....	....	....	....	....	....	....	....	....	....	....
	St. Louis	**NHL**	**40**	**3**	**12**	**15**	**24**	**0**	**0**	**1**	**114**	**2.6**	**-6**	....	....	....	....	....	**10**	**1**	**5**	**6**	**4**	**0**	**0**	**1**
1996-97	**St. Louis**	**NHL**	**82**	**4**	**24**	**28**	**35**	**1**	**0**	**0**	**142**	**2.8**	**7**	....	....	....	....	....	**2**	**0**	**0**	**0**	**2**	**0**	**0**	**0**
1997-98	**Ottawa**	**NHL**	**81**	**8**	**27**	**35**	**8**	**3**	**1**	**1**	**191**	**4.2**	**-19**	....	....	....	....	....	**11**	**2**	**3**	**5**	**4**	**0**	**0**	**0**
	Russia	Olympics	6	0	2	2	2	....	....	....	....	....	....	....	....	....	....	....	....	....	....	....	....	....	....	....
1998-99	**Ottawa**	**NHL**	**79**	**4**	**21**	**25**	**32**	**3**	**0**	**0**	**171**	**2.3**	**14**	**0**	**0.0**	**89**	**115**	**23:51**	**4**	**0**	**0**	**0**	**0**	**0**	**0**	**0**
99-2000	**Ottawa**	**NHL**	**64**	**6**	**12**	**18**	**20**	**5**	**0**	**1**	**126**	**4.8**	**-5**	**0**	**0.0**	**57**	**78**	**20:41**	**6**	**1**	**1**	**2**	**0**	**0**	**0**	**0**
	NHL Totals		**562**	**59**	**174**	**233**	**210**	**27**	**2**	**6**	**1276**	**4.6**		**0**	**0.0**	**146**	**193**	**22:26**	**51**	**6**	**15**	**21**	**18**	**1**	**0**	**1**

Played in NHL All-Star Game (1999)

Traded to **Edmonton** by **Chicago** with Dean McAmmond for Joe Murphy, February 24, 1993. Traded to **St. Louis** by **Edmonton** with Ken Sutton for Jeff Norton and Donald Dufresne, January 4, 1996. Traded to **Ottawa** by **St. Louis** for Steve Duchesne, August 25, 1997.

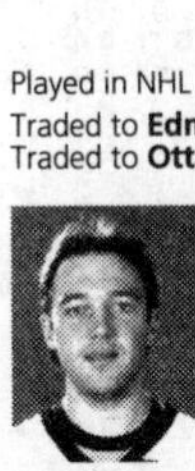

KRIVOKRASOV, Sergei

(krih-vuh-KRA-sahf, SAIR-gay) **MIN.**

Right wing. Shoots left. 5'11", 185 lbs. Born, Angarsk, USSR, April 15, 1974. Chicago's 1st choice, 12th overall, in 1992 Entry Draft.

			Regular Season																Playoffs							
Season	Club	League	GP	G	A	Pts	PIM	PP	SH	GW	S	%	+/-	TF	F%	H	SB	Min	GP	G	A	Pts	PIM	PP	SH	GW
1990-91	CSKA Moscow	USSR	41	4	0	4	8	....	....	....	....	....	....	....	....	....	....	....	....	....	....	....	....	....	....	....
1991-92	CSKA Moscow	CIS	42	10	8	18	35	....	....	....	....	....	....	....	....	....	....	....	....	....	....	....	....	....	....	....
1992-93	**Chicago**	**NHL**	**4**	**0**	**0**	**0**	**2**	**0**	**0**	**0**	**0**	**0.0**	**-2**	....	....	....	....	....	....	....	....	....	....	....	....	....
	Indianapolis Ice	IHL	78	36	33	69	157	....	....	....	....	....	....	....	....	....	....	....	5	3	1	4	2	....	....	....
1993-94	**Chicago**	**NHL**	**9**	**1**	**0**	**1**	**4**	**0**	**0**	**0**	**7**	**14.3**	**-2**	....	....	....	....	....	....	....	....	....	....	....	....	....
	Indianapolis Ice	IHL	53	19	26	45	145	....	....	....	....	....	....	....	....	....	....	....	....	....	....	....	....	....	....	....

			Regular Season																Playoffs							
Season	Club	League	GP	G	A	Pts	PIM	PP	SH	GW	S	%	+/–	TF	F%	H	SB	Min	GP	G	A	Pts	PIM	PP	SH	GW
1994-95	Indianapolis Ice	IHL	29	12	15	27	41	....	....	....	....	....	....	....	....	....	....	....	....	....	....	....	....	....	....	....
	Chicago	**NHL**	**41**	**12**	**7**	**19**	**33**	**6**	**0**	**2**	**72**	**16.7**	**9**	....	....	....	....	....	**10**	**0**	**0**	**0**	**8**	**0**	**0**	**0**
1995-96	**Chicago**	**NHL**	**46**	**6**	**10**	**16**	**32**	**0**	**0**	**1**	**52**	**11.5**	**10**	....	....	....	....	....	**5**	**1**	**0**	**1**	**2**	**0**	**0**	**1**
	Indianapolis Ice	IHL	9	4	5	9	28	....	....	....	....	....	....	....	....	....	....	....	....	....	....	....	....	....	....	....
1996-97	**Chicago**	**NHL**	**67**	**13**	**11**	**24**	**42**	**2**	**0**	**3**	**104**	**12.5**	**–1**	....	....	....	....	....	**6**	**1**	**0**	**1**	**4**	**0**	**0**	**0**
1997-98	**Chicago**	**NHL**	**58**	**10**	**13**	**23**	**33**	**1**	**0**	**2**	**127**	**7.9**	**–1**	....	....	....	....	....	....	....	....	....	....	....	....	....
	Russia	Olympics	6	0	0	0	4	....	....	....	....	....	....	....	....	....	....	....	....	....	....	....	....	....	....	....
1998-99	**Nashville**	**NHL**	**70**	**25**	**23**	**48**	**42**	**10**	**0**	**6**	**208**	**12.0**	**–5**	**0**	**0.0**	**19**	**7**	**16:08**	....	....	....	....	....	....	....	....
99-2000	**Nashville**	**NHL**	**63**	**9**	**17**	**26**	**40**	**3**	**0**	**2**	**132**	**6.8**	**–7**	**1**	**0.0**	**24**	**5**	**13:08**	....	....	....	....	....	....	....	....
	Calgary	**NHL**	**12**	**1**	**10**	**11**	**4**	**0**	**0**	**0**	**27**	**3.7**	**2**	**0**	**0.0**	**3**	**2**	**13:22**	....	....	....	....	....	....	....	....
	NHL Totals		**370**	**77**	**91**	**168**	**232**	**22**	**0**	**16**	**729**	**10.6**		**1**	**0.0**	**46**	**14**	**14:36**	**21**	**2**	**0**	**2**	**14**	**0**	**0**	**1**

Played in NHL All-Star Game (1999)

Traded to **Nashville** by **Chicago** for future considerations, June 26, 1998. Traded to **Calgary** by **Nashville** for Cale Hulse and Calgary's 3rd round choice in 2001 Entry Draft, March 14, 2000. Selected by **Minnesota** from **Calgary** in Expansion Draft, June 23, 2000.

KROG, Jason

(KRAWG, JAY-suhn) **NYI**

Center. Shoots right. 5'11", 191 lbs. Born, Fernie, B.C., October 9, 1975.

Season	Club	League	GP	G	A	Pts	PIM	PP	SH	GW	S	%	+/–	TF	F%	H	SB	Min	GP	G	A	Pts	PIM	PP	SH	GW
1992-93	Chilliwack Chiefs	BCJHL	52	30	27	57	52	....	....	....	....	....	....	....	....	....	....	....	....	....	....	....	....	....	....	....
1993-94	Chilliwack Chiefs	BCJHL	42	19	36	55	20	....	....	....	....	....	....	....	....	....	....	....	....	....	....	....	....	....	....	....
1994-95	Chilliwack Chiefs	BCJHL	60	47	81	128	36	....	....	....	....	....	....	....	....	....	....	....	....	....	....	....	....	....	....	....
1995-96	New Hampshire	H-East	34	4	16	20	20	....	....	....	....	....	....	....	....	....	....	....	....	....	....	....	....	....	....	....
1996-97	New Hampshire	H-East	39	23	*44	*67	28	....	....	....	....	....	....	....	....	....	....	....	....	....	....	....	....	....	....	....
1997-98	New Hampshire	H-East	38	*33	33	66	44	....	....	....	....	....	....	....	....	....	....	....	....	....	....	....	....	....	....	....
1998-99	New Hampshire	H-East	41	*34	*51	*85	38	....	....	....	....	....	....	....	....	....	....	....	....	....	....	....	....	....	....	....
99-2000	**NY Islanders**	**NHL**	**17**	**2**	**4**	**6**	**6**	**1**	**0**	**0**	**22**	**9.1**	**–1**	**81**	**53.1**	**15**	**6**	**10:03**	....	....	....	....	....	....	....	....
	Lowell	AHL	45	6	21	27	22	....	....	....	....	....	....	....	....	....	....	....	....	....	....	....	....	....	....	....
	Providence Bruins	AHL	11	9	8	17	4	....	....	....	....	....	....	....	....	....	....	....	6	2	2	4	0	....	....	....
	NHL Totals		**17**	**2**	**4**	**6**	**6**	**1**	**0**	**0**	**22**	**9.1**		**81**	**53.1**	**15**	**6**	**10:03**	....	....	....	....	....	....	....	....

Hockey East All-Star Team (1997) • NCAA East Second All-American Team (1997) • Hockey East First All-Star Team (1998, 1999) • NCAA East First All-American Team (1999) • NCAA Championship All-Tournament Team (1999) • Won Hobey Baker Memorial Award (Top U.S. Collegiate Player) (1999)

Signed as a free agent by **NY Islanders**, May 14, 1999. Loaned to **Providence** (AHL) by **NY Islanders**, March 1, 2000.

KRON, Robert

(KROHN, RAW-buhrt) **CBJ**

Left wing. Shoots left. 5'11", 185 lbs. Born, Brno, Czech., February 27, 1967. Vancouver's 5th choice, 88th overall, in 1985 Entry Draft.

Season	Club	League	GP	G	A	Pts	PIM	PP	SH	GW	S	%	+/–	TF	F%	H	SB	Min	GP	G	A	Pts	PIM	PP	SH	GW
1983-84	Ingstav Brno	Czech-2	3	0	1	1	0	....	....	....	....	....	....	....	....	....	....	....	....	....	....	....	....	....	....	....
1984-85	Zetor Brno	Czech.	40	6	8	14	6	....	....	....	....	....	....	....	....	....	....	....	....	....	....	....	....	....	....	....
1985-86	Zetor Brno	Czech.	44	5	6	11	....	....	....	....	....	....	....	....	....	....	....	....	....	....	....	....	....	....	....	....
1986-87	Zetor Brno	Czech.	34	18	11	29	10	....	....	....	....	....	....	....	....	....	....	....	....	....	....	....	....	....	....	....
1987-88	Zetor Brno	Czech.	44	14	7	21	30	....	....	....	....	....	....	....	....	....	....	....	....	....	....	....	....	....	....	....
1988-89	Dukla Trencin	Czech.	43	28	19	47	26	....	....	....	....	....	....	....	....	....	....	....	....	....	....	....	....	....	....	....
1989-90	Dukla Trencin	Czech.	39	22	22	44	....	....	....	....	....	....	....	....	....	....	....	....	....	....	....	....	....	....	....	....
1990-91	**Vancouver**	**NHL**	**76**	**12**	**20**	**32**	**21**	**2**	**3**	**0**	**124**	**9.7**	**–11**	....	....	....	....	....	....	....	....	....	....	....	....	....
1991-92	**Vancouver**	**NHL**	**36**	**2**	**2**	**4**	**2**	**0**	**0**	**0**	**49**	**4.1**	**–9**	....	....	....	....	....	**11**	**1**	**2**	**3**	**2**	**0**	**1**	**0**
1992-93	**Vancouver**	**NHL**	**32**	**10**	**11**	**21**	**14**	**2**	**2**	**2**	**60**	**16.7**	**10**	....	....	....	....	....	....	....	....	....	....	....	....	....
	Hartford	**NHL**	**13**	**4**	**2**	**6**	**4**	**2**	**0**	**0**	**37**	**10.8**	**–5**	....	....	....	....	....	....	....	....	....	....	....	....	....
1993-94	**Hartford**	**NHL**	**77**	**24**	**26**	**50**	**8**	**2**	**1**	**3**	**194**	**12.4**	**0**	....	....	....	....	....	....	....	....	....	....	....	....	....
1994-95	**Hartford**	**NHL**	**37**	**10**	**8**	**18**	**10**	**3**	**1**	**1**	**88**	**11.4**	**–3**	....	....	....	....	....	....	....	....	....	....	....	....	....
1995-96	**Hartford**	**NHL**	**77**	**22**	**28**	**50**	**6**	**8**	**1**	**3**	**203**	**10.8**	**–1**	....	....	....	....	....	....	....	....	....	....	....	....	....
1996-97	**Hartford**	**NHL**	**68**	**10**	**12**	**22**	**10**	**2**	**0**	**4**	**182**	**5.5**	**–18**	....	....	....	....	....	....	....	....	....	....	....	....	....
1997-98	**Carolina**	**NHL**	**81**	**16**	**20**	**36**	**12**	**4**	**0**	**2**	**175**	**9.1**	**–8**	....	....	....	....	....	....	....	....	....	....	....	....	....
1998-99	**Carolina**	**NHL**	**75**	**9**	**16**	**25**	**10**	**3**	**1**	**2**	**134**	**6.7**	**–13**	**244**	**38.9**	**88**	**27**	**16:14**	**5**	**2**	**0**	**2**	**0**	**0**	**0**	**1**
99-2000	**Carolina**	**NHL**	**81**	**13**	**27**	**40**	**8**	**2**	**1**	**3**	**134**	**9.7**	**–4**	**717**	**43.0**	**48**	**21**	**15:14**	....	....	....	....	....	....	....	....
	NHL Totals		**653**	**132**	**172**	**304**	**105**	**30**	**10**	**20**	**1380**	**9.6**		**961**	**41.9**	**136**	**48**	**15:43**	**16**	**3**	**2**	**5**	**2**	**0**	**1**	**1**

Traded to **Hartford** by **Vancouver** with Vancouver's 3rd round choice (Marek Malik) in 1993 Entry Draft and future considerations (Jim Sandlak, May 17, 1993) for Murray Craven and Vancouver's 5th round choice (previously acquired, Vancouver selected Scott Walker) in 1993 Entry Draft, March 22, 1993. Transferred to **Carolina** after **Hartford** franchise relocated, June 25, 1997. Selected by **Columbus** from **Carolina** in Expansion Draft, June 23, 2000.

KROUPA, Vlastimil

(KROO-pah, VLAS-tuh-meel)

Defense. Shoots left. 6'3", 215 lbs. Born, Most, Czech., April 27, 1975. San Jose's 3rd choice, 45th overall, in 1993 Entry Draft.

Season	Club	League	GP	G	A	Pts	PIM	PP	SH	GW	S	%	+/–	TF	F%	H	SB	Min	GP	G	A	Pts	PIM	PP	SH	GW
1991-92	CHZ Litvinov	Czech-Jr.	37	9	16	25	....	....	....	....	....	....	....	....	....	....	....	....	....	....	....	....	....	....	....	....
1992-93	CHZ Litvinov	Czech.	9	0	1	1	....	....	....	....	....	....	....	....	....	....	....	....	....	....	....	....	....	....	....	....
1993-94	**San Jose**	**NHL**	**27**	**1**	**3**	**4**	**20**	**0**	**0**	**0**	**16**	**6.3**	**–6**	....	....	....	....	....	**14**	**1**	**2**	**3**	**21**	**0**	**0**	**1**
	Kansas City	IHL	39	3	12	15	12	....	....	....	....	....	....	....	....	....	....	....	....	....	....	....	....	....	....	....
1994-95	**San Jose**	**NHL**	**14**	**0**	**2**	**2**	**16**	**0**	**0**	**0**	**4**	**0.0**	**–7**	....	....	....	....	....	**6**	**0**	**0**	**0**	**4**	**0**	**0**	**0**
	Kansas City	IHL	51	4	8	12	49	....	....	....	....	....	....	....	....	....	....	....	12	2	4	6	22	....	....	....
1995-96	**San Jose**	**NHL**	**27**	**1**	**7**	**8**	**18**	**0**	**0**	**0**	**11**	**9.1**	**–17**	....	....	....	....	....	....	....	....	....	....	....	....	....
	Kansas City	IHL	39	5	22	27	44	....	....	....	....	....	....	....	....	....	....	....	5	0	1	1	6	....	....	....
1996-97	**San Jose**	**NHL**	**35**	**2**	**6**	**8**	**12**	**2**	**0**	**1**	**24**	**8.3**	**–17**	....	....	....	....	....	....	....	....	....	....	....	....	....
	Kentucky	AHL	5	0	3	3	0	....	....	....	....	....	....	....	....	....	....	....	....	....	....	....	....	....	....	....
1997-98	**New Jersey**	**NHL**	**2**	**0**	**1**	**1**	**0**	**0**	**0**	**0**	**1**	**0.0**	**1**	....	....	....	....	....	....	....	....	....	....	....	....	....
	Albany River Rats	AHL	71	5	29	34	48	....	....	....	....	....	....	....	....	....	....	....	12	0	3	3	6	....	....	....
1998-99	Albany River Rats	AHL	2	0	1	1	4	....	....	....	....	....	....	....	....	....	....	....	....	....	....	....	....	....	....	....
	Kansas City	IHL	77	6	32	38	52	....	....	....	....	....	....	....	....	....	....	....	3	0	1	1	0	....	....	....
99-2000	Albany River Rats	AHL	1	1	0	1	0	....	....	....	....	....	....	....	....	....	....	....	....	....	....	....	....	....	....	....
	Moskitos Essen	Germany	56	6	13	19	56	....	....	....	....	....	....	....	....	....	....	....	....	....	....	....	....	....	....	....
	NHL Totals		**105**	**4**	**19**	**23**	**66**	**2**	**0**	**1**	**56**	**7.1**		....	....	....	....	....	**20**	**1**	**2**	**3**	**25**	**0**	**0**	**1**

Traded to **New Jersey** by **San Jose** for New Jersey's 3rd round choice (later traded to Nashville — Nashville selected Geoff Koch) in 1998 Entry Draft, August 22, 1997.

KRUPP, Uwe

(KROOP, OO-VAY)

Defense. Shoots right. 6'6", 235 lbs. Born, Cologne, West Germany, June 24, 1965. Buffalo's 13th choice, 223rd overall, in 1983 Entry Draft.

Season	Club	League	GP	G	A	Pts	PIM	PP	SH	GW	S	%	+/–	TF	F%	H	SB	Min	GP	G	A	Pts	PIM	PP	SH	GW
1982-83	Kolner EC	Germany	11	0	0	0	0	....	....	....	....	....	....	....	....	....	....	....	....	....	....	....	....	....	....	....
1983-84	Kolner EC	Germany	26	0	4	4	22	....	....	....	....	....	....	....	....	....	....	....	....	....	....	....	....	....	....	....
1984-85	Kolner EC	Germany	31	7	7	14	....	....	....	....	....	....	....	....	....	....	....	....	9	4	1	5	....	....	....	....
1985-86	Kolner EC	Germany	35	6	18	24	83	....	....	....	....	....	....	....	....	....	....	....	10	4	3	7	....	....	....	....
1986-87	**Buffalo**	**NHL**	**26**	**1**	**4**	**5**	**23**	**0**	**0**	**0**	**34**	**2.9**	**–9**	....	....	....	....	....	....	....	....	....	....	....	....	....
	Rochester	AHL	42	3	19	22	50	....	....	....	....	....	....	....	....	....	....	....	17	1	11	12	16	....	....	....
1987-88	**Buffalo**	**NHL**	**75**	**2**	**9**	**11**	**151**	**0**	**0**	**0**	**84**	**2.4**	**–1**	....	....	....	....	....	**6**	**0**	**0**	**0**	**15**	**0**	**0**	**0**
1988-89	**Buffalo**	**NHL**	**70**	**5**	**13**	**18**	**55**	**0**	**1**	**0**	**51**	**9.8**	**0**	....	....	....	....	....	**5**	**0**	**1**	**1**	**4**	**0**	**0**	**0**
1989-90	**Buffalo**	**NHL**	**74**	**3**	**20**	**23**	**85**	**0**	**1**	**1**	**69**	**4.3**	**15**	....	....	....	....	....	**6**	**0**	**0**	**0**	**4**	**0**	**0**	**0**
1990-91	**Buffalo**	**NHL**	**74**	**12**	**32**	**44**	**66**	**6**	**0**	**0**	**138**	**8.7**	**14**	....	....	....	....	....	**6**	**1**	**1**	**2**	**6**	**1**	**0**	**0**
1991-92	**Buffalo**	**NHL**	**8**	**2**	**0**	**2**	**6**	**0**	**0**	**0**	**13**	**15.4**	**0**	....	....	....	....	....	....	....	....	....	....	....	....	....
	NY Islanders	**NHL**	**59**	**6**	**29**	**35**	**43**	**2**	**0**	**0**	**115**	**5.2**	**13**	....	....	....	....	....	....	....	....	....	....	....	....	....
1992-93	**NY Islanders**	**NHL**	**80**	**9**	**29**	**38**	**67**	**2**	**0**	**2**	**116**	**7.8**	**6**	....	....	....	....	....	**18**	**1**	**5**	**6**	**12**	**0**	**0**	**0**
1993-94	**NY Islanders**	**NHL**	**41**	**7**	**14**	**21**	**30**	**3**	**0**	**0**	**82**	**8.5**	**11**	....	....	....	....	....	**4**	**0**	**1**	**1**	**4**	**0**	**0**	**0**
1994-95	EV Landshut	Germany	5	1	2	3	6	....	....	....	....	....	....	....	....	....	....	....	....	....	....	....	....	....	....	....
	Quebec	**NHL**	**44**	**6**	**17**	**23**	**20**	**3**	**0**	**1**	**102**	**5.9**	**14**	....	....	....	....	....	**5**	**0**	**2**	**2**	**2**	**0**	**0**	**0**
1995-96♦	**Colorado**	**NHL**	**6**	**0**	**3**	**3**	**4**	**0**	**0**	**0**	**9**	**0.0**	**4**	....	....	....	....	....	**22**	**4**	**12**	**16**	**33**	**1**	**0**	**2**
1996-97	**Colorado**	**NHL**	**60**	**4**	**17**	**21**	**48**	**2**	**0**	**1**	**107**	**3.7**	**12**	....	....	....	....	....	....	....	....	....	....	....	....	....
1997-98	**Colorado**	**NHL**	**78**	**9**	**22**	**31**	**38**	**5**	**0**	**2**	**149**	**6.0**	**21**	....	....	....	....	....	**7**	**0**	**1**	**1**	**4**	**0**	**0**	**0**
	Germany	Olympics	2	0	2	2	4	....	....	....	....	....	....	....	....	....	....	....	....	....	....	....	....	....	....	....

			Regular Season																Playoffs							
Season	Club	League	GP	G	A	Pts	PIM	PP	SH	GW	S	%	+/–	TF	F%	H	SB	Min	GP	G	A	Pts	PIM	PP	SH	GW
1998-99	Detroit	NHL	22	3	2	5	6	0	0	0	32	9.4	0	0	0.0	41	37	21:23	....	....	....	....	....	....	....	....
99-2000	Detroit	NHL	DID NOT PLAY – INJURED																							
	NHL Totals		717	69	211	280	642	23	2	7	1101	6.3		0	0.0	41	37	21:23	79	6	23	29	84	2	0	2

Played in NHL All-Star Game (1991)

Traded to **NY Islanders** by **Buffalo** with Pierre Turgeon, Benoit Hogue and Dave McLlwain for Pat LaFontaine, Randy Hillier, Randy Wood and NY Islanders' 4th round choice (Dean Melanson) in 1992 Entry Draft, October 25, 1991. Traded to **Quebec** by **NY Islanders** with NY Islanders' 1st round choice (Wade Belak) in 1994 Entry Draft for Ron Sutter and Quebec's 1st round choice (Brett Lindros) in 1994 Entry Draft, June 28, 1994. Transferred to **Colorado** after **Quebec** franchise relocated, June 21, 1995. Claimed by **Nashville** from **Colorado** in Expansion Draft, June 26, 1998. Signed as a free agent by **Detroit**, July 7, 1998. • Missed remainder of 1998-99 and entire 1999-2000 seasons recovering from back injury suffered prior to game vs. Phoenix, December 19, 1998.

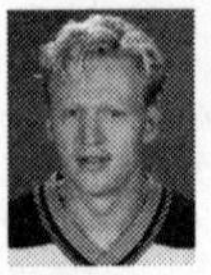

KRUSE, Paul

(KROOZ, PAWL) **BUF.**

Left wing. Shoots left. 6', 202 lbs. Born, Merritt, B.C., March 15, 1970. Calgary's 6th choice, 83rd overall, in 1990 Entry Draft.

Season	Club	League	GP	G	A	Pts	PIM	PP	SH	GW	S	%	+/–	TF	F%	H	SB	Min	GP	G	A	Pts	PIM	PP	SH	GW
1986-87	Merritt	BCJHL	35	8	15	23	120	....	....	....	....	....	....	....	....	....	....	....	....	....	....	....	....	....	....	....
1987-88	Merritt	BCJHL	44	12	32	44	223	....	....	....	....	....	....	....	....	....	....	....	4	1	4	5	18	....	....	....
	Moose Jaw	WHL	1	0	0	0	0	....	....	....	....	....	....	....	....	....	....	....	....	....	....	....	....	....	....	....
1988-89	Kamloops Blazers	WHL	68	8	15	23	209	....	....	....	....	....	....	....	....	....	....	....	16	0	0	0	36	....	....	....
1989-90	Kamloops Blazers	WHL	67	22	23	45	291	....	....	....	....	....	....	....	....	....	....	....	17	3	5	8	79	....	....	....
1990-91	**Calgary**	**NHL**	**1**	**0**	**0**	**0**	**7**	**0**	**0**	**0**	**0**	**0.0**	**–1**	....	....	....	....	....	....	....	....	....	....	....	....	....
	Salt Lake City	IHL	83	24	20	44	313	....	....	....	....	....	....	....	....	....	....	....	4	1	1	2	4	....	....	....
1991-92	**Calgary**	**NHL**	**16**	**3**	**1**	**4**	**65**	**0**	**0**	**0**	**12**	**25.0**	**1**	....	....	....	....	....	....	....	....	....	....	....	....	....
	Salt Lake City	IHL	57	14	15	29	267	....	....	....	....	....	....	....	....	....	....	....	5	1	2	3	19	....	....	....
1992-93	**Calgary**	**NHL**	**27**	**2**	**3**	**5**	**41**	**0**	**0**	**0**	**17**	**11.8**	**2**	....	....	....	....	....	....	....	....	....	....	....	....	....
	Salt Lake City	IHL	35	1	4	5	206	....	....	....	....	....	....	....	....	....	....	....	....	....	....	....	....	....	....	....
1993-94	**Calgary**	**NHL**	**68**	**3**	**8**	**11**	**185**	**0**	**0**	**0**	**52**	**5.8**	**–6**	....	....	....	....	....	**7**	**0**	**0**	**0**	**14**	**0**	**0**	**0**
1994-95	**Calgary**	**NHL**	**45**	**11**	**5**	**16**	**141**	**0**	**0**	**2**	**52**	**21.2**	**13**	....	....	....	....	....	**7**	**4**	**2**	**6**	**10**	**0**	**1**	**0**
1995-96	**Calgary**	**NHL**	**75**	**3**	**12**	**15**	**145**	**0**	**0**	**0**	**83**	**3.6**	**–5**	....	....	....	....	....	**3**	**0**	**0**	**0**	**4**	**0**	**0**	**0**
1996-97	**Calgary**	**NHL**	**14**	**2**	**0**	**2**	**30**	**0**	**0**	**1**	**10**	**20.0**	**–4**	....	....	....	....	....	....	....	....	....	....	....	....	....
	NY Islanders	**NHL**	**48**	**4**	**2**	**6**	**111**	**0**	**0**	**0**	**39**	**10.3**	**–5**	....	....	....	....	....	....	....	....	....	....	....	....	....
1997-98	**NY Islanders**	**NHL**	**62**	**6**	**1**	**7**	**138**	**0**	**0**	**2**	**44**	**13.6**	**–12**	....	....	....	....	....	....	....	....	....	....	....	....	....
	Buffalo	**NHL**	**12**	**1**	**1**	**2**	**49**	**0**	**0**	**0**	**8**	**12.5**	**1**	....	....	....	....	....	**1**	**1**	**0**	**1**	**4**	**0**	**0**	**0**
1998-99	**Buffalo**	**NHL**	**43**	**3**	**0**	**3**	**114**	**0**	**0**	**0**	**33**	**9.1**	**0**	**3**	**33.3**	**56**	**8**	**6:24**	**10**	**0**	**0**	**0**	**4**	**0**	**0**	**0**
99-2000	**Buffalo**	**NHL**	**11**	**0**	**0**	**0**	**43**	**0**	**0**	**0**	**7**	**0.0**	**–2**	**0**	**0.0**	**13**	**2**	**6:15**	....	....	....	....	....	....	....	....
	Utah Grizzlies	IHL	44	10	13	23	71	....	....	....	....	....	....	....	....	....	....	....	5	0	3	3	28	....	....	....
	NHL Totals		**422**	**38**	**33**	**71**	**1069**	**0**	**0**	**5**	**357**	**10.6**		**3**	**33.3**	**69**	**10**	**6:22**	**28**	**5**	**2**	**7**	**36**	**0**	**1**	**0**

Traded to **NY Islanders** by **Calgary** for Colorado's 3rd round choice (previously acquired by NY Islanders — later traded to Hartford — Hartford selected Francis Lessard) in 1997 Entry Draft, November 27, 1996. Traded to **Buffalo** by **NY Islanders** with Jason Holland for Jason Dawe, March 24, 1998. Loaned to **Utah** (IHL) by **Buffalo** after clearing NHL waivers, January 11, 2000.

KRYGIER, Todd

(KREE-guhr, TAWD)

Left wing. Shoots left. 6', 185 lbs. Born, Chicago Heights, IL, October 12, 1965. Hartford's 1st choice, 16th overall, in 1988 Supplemental Draft.

Season	Club	League	GP	G	A	Pts	PIM	PP	SH	GW	S	%	+/–	TF	F%	H	SB	Min	GP	G	A	Pts	PIM	PP	SH	GW
1984-85	U. of Connecticut	ECAC-2	14	14	11	25	12	....	....	....	....	....	....	....	....	....	....	....	....	....	....	....	....	....	....	....
1985-86	U. of Connecticut	ECAC-2	32	29	27	56	46	....	....	....	....	....	....	....	....	....	....	....	....	....	....	....	....	....	....	....
1986-87	U. of Connecticut	ECAC-2	28	24	24	48	44	....	....	....	....	....	....	....	....	....	....	....	....	....	....	....	....	....	....	....
1987-88	U. of Connecticut	ECAC-2	27	32	39	71	28	....	....	....	....	....	....	....	....	....	....	....	....	....	....	....	....	....	....	....
	New Haven	AHL	13	1	5	6	34	....	....	....	....	....	....	....	....	....	....	....	....	....	....	....	....	....	....	....
1988-89	Binghamton	AHL	76	26	42	68	77	....	....	....	....	....	....	....	....	....	....	....	....	....	....	....	....	....	....	....
1989-90	**Hartford**	**NHL**	**58**	**18**	**12**	**30**	**52**	**5**	**1**	**3**	**103**	**17.5**	**4**	....	....	....	....	....	**7**	**2**	**1**	**3**	**4**	**0**	**0**	**0**
	Binghamton	AHL	12	1	9	10	16	....	....	....	....	....	....	....	....	....	....	....	....	....	....	....	....	....	....	....
1990-91	**Hartford**	**NHL**	**72**	**13**	**17**	**30**	**95**	**3**	**0**	**2**	**113**	**11.5**	**1**	....	....	....	....	....	**6**	**0**	**2**	**2**	**0**	**0**	**0**	**0**
1991-92	**Washington**	**NHL**	**67**	**13**	**17**	**30**	**107**	**1**	**0**	**1**	**127**	**10.2**	**–1**	....	....	....	....	....	**5**	**2**	**1**	**3**	**4**	**0**	**0**	**0**
1992-93	**Washington**	**NHL**	**77**	**11**	**12**	**23**	**60**	**0**	**2**	**0**	**133**	**8.3**	**–13**	....	....	....	....	....	**6**	**1**	**1**	**2**	**4**	**0**	**1**	**0**
1993-94	**Washington**	**NHL**	**66**	**12**	**18**	**30**	**60**	**0**	**1**	**3**	**146**	**8.2**	**–4**	....	....	....	....	....	**5**	**2**	**0**	**2**	**10**	**0**	**0**	**0**
1994-95	**Anaheim**	**NHL**	**35**	**11**	**11**	**22**	**10**	**1**	**0**	**1**	**90**	**12.2**	**1**	....	....	....	....	....	....	....	....	....	....	....	....	....
1995-96	**Anaheim**	**NHL**	**60**	**9**	**28**	**37**	**70**	**2**	**1**	**0**	**153**	**5.9**	**–9**	....	....	....	....	....	....	....	....	....	....	....	....	....
	Washington	**NHL**	**16**	**6**	**5**	**11**	**12**	**1**	**0**	**0**	**28**	**21.4**	**8**	....	....	....	....	....	**6**	**2**	**0**	**2**	**12**	**0**	**0**	**1**
1996-97	**Washington**	**NHL**	**47**	**5**	**11**	**16**	**37**	**1**	**0**	**1**	**121**	**4.1**	**–10**	....	....	....	....	....	....	....	....	....	....	....	....	....
1997-98	**Washington**	**NHL**	**45**	**2**	**12**	**14**	**30**	**0**	**0**	**1**	**71**	**2.8**	**–3**	....	....	....	....	....	**13**	**1**	**2**	**3**	**6**	**0**	**0**	**1**
	Portland Pirates	AHL	6	3	4	7	6	....	....	....	....	....	....	....	....	....	....	....	....	....	....	....	....	....	....	....
1998-99	Orlando	IHL	65	19	40	59	82	....	....	....	....	....	....	....	....	....	....	....	17	9	10	19	16	....	....	....
99-2000	Orlando	IHL	28	7	13	20	12	....	....	....	....	....	....	....	....	....	....	....	6	2	1	3	2	....	....	....
	NHL Totals		**543**	**100**	**143**	**243**	**533**	**14**	**5**	**12**	**1085**	**9.2**		....	....	....	....	....	**48**	**10**	**7**	**17**	**40**	**0**	**1**	**2**

NCAA (College Div.) East Second All-American Team (1987)

Traded to **Washington** by **Hartford** for Washington's 4th round choice (later traded to Calgary - Calgary selected Jason Smith) in 1993 Entry Draft, October 3, 1991. Traded to **Anaheim** by **Washington** for Anaheim's 4th round choice (later traded to Dallas - Dallas selected Mike Hurley) in 1996 Entry Draft, February 2, 1995. Traded to **Washington** by **Anaheim** for Mike Torchia, March 8, 1996. Signed as a free agent by **Orlando** (IHL), November 11, 1999.

KUBA, Filip

(KOO-bah, FIHL-ihp) **MIN.**

Defense. Shoots left. 6'3", 205 lbs. Born, Ostrava, Czech., December 29, 1976. Florida's 8th choice, 192nd overall, in 1995 Entry Draft.

Season	Club	League	GP	G	A	Pts	PIM	PP	SH	GW	S	%	+/–	TF	F%	H	SB	Min	GP	G	A	Pts	PIM	PP	SH	GW
1994-95	HC Vitkovice-Jr.	Cze-Rep	35	10	15	25	....	....	....	....	....	....	....	....	....	....	....	....	....	....	....	....	....	....	....	....
	HC Vitkovice	Cze-Rep	....	....	....	....	....	....	....	....	....	....	....	....	....	....	....	....	4	0	0	0	2	....	....	....
1995-96	HC Vitkovice	Cze-Rep	19	0	1	1	....	....	....	....	....	....	....	....	....	....	....	....	....	....	....	....	....	....	....	....
1996-97	Carolina	AHL	51	0	12	12	38	....	....	....	....	....	....	....	....	....	....	....	....	....	....	....	....	....	....	....
1997-98	New Haven	AHL	77	4	13	17	58	....	....	....	....	....	....	....	....	....	....	....	3	1	1	2	0	....	....	....
1998-99	**Florida**	**NHL**	**5**	**0**	**1**	**1**	**0**	**0**	**0**	**0**	**5**	**0.0**	**2**	**0**	**0.0**	**7**	**6**	**22:29**	....	....	....	....	....	....	....	....
	Kentucky	AHL	45	2	8	10	33	....	....	....	....	....	....	....	....	....	....	....	10	0	1	1	4	....	....	....
99-2000	**Florida**	**NHL**	**13**	**1**	**5**	**6**	**2**	**1**	**0**	**1**	**16**	**6.3**	**–3**	**0**	**0.0**	**10**	**13**	**13:52**	....	....	....	....	....	....	....	....
	Houston Aeros	IHL	27	3	6	9	13	....	....	....	....	....	....	....	....	....	....	....	11	1	2	3	4	....	....	....
	NHL Totals		**18**	**1**	**6**	**7**	**2**	**1**	**0**	**1**	**21**	**4.8**		**0**	**0.0**	**17**	**19**	**16:15**	....	....	....	....	....	....	....	....

Traded to **Calgary** by **Florida** for Rocky Thompson, March 16, 2000. Selected by **Minnesota** from **Calgary** in Expansion Draft, June 23, 2000.

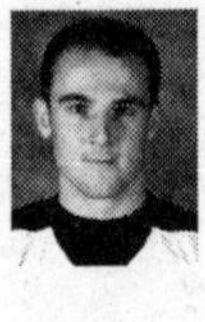

KUBINA, Pavel

(koo-BEE-nuh, PAH-vehl) **T.B.**

Defense. Shoots right. 6'3", 213 lbs. Born, Celadna, Czech., April 15, 1977. Tampa Bay's 6th choice, 179th overall, in 1996 Entry Draft.

Season	Club	League	GP	G	A	Pts	PIM	PP	SH	GW	S	%	+/–	TF	F%	H	SB	Min	GP	G	A	Pts	PIM	PP	SH	GW
1993-94	HC Vitkovice-Jr.	Cze-Rep	35	4	3	7	....	....	....	....	....	....	....	....	....	....	....	....	....	....	....	....	....	....	....	....
	HC Vitkovice	Cze-Rep	1	0	0	0	....	....	....	....	....	....	....	....	....	....	....	....	....	....	....	....	....	....	....	....
1994-95	HC Vitkovice-Jr.	Cze-Rep	20	6	10	16	....	....	....	....	....	....	....	....	....	....	....	....	....	....	....	....	....	....	....	....
	HC Vitkovice	Cze-Rep	8	2	0	2	10	....	....	....	....	....	....	....	....	....	....	....	4	0	0	0	0	....	....	....
1995-96	HC Vitkovice-Jr.	Cze-Rep	16	5	10	15	....	....	....	....	....	....	....	....	....	....	....	....	....	....	....	....	....	....	....	....
	HC Vitkovice	Cze-Rep	33	3	4	7	32	....	....	....	....	....	....	....	....	....	....	....	4	0	0	0	0	....	....	....
1996-97	HC Vitkovice	Cze-Rep	1	0	0	0	0	....	....	....	....	....	....	....	....	....	....	....	....	....	....	....	....	....	....	....
	Moose Jaw	WHL	61	12	32	44	116	....	....	....	....	....	....	....	....	....	....	....	11	2	5	7	27	....	....	....
1997-98	**Tampa Bay**	**NHL**	**10**	**1**	**2**	**3**	**22**	**0**	**0**	**0**	**8**	**12.5**	**–1**	....	....	....	....	....	....	....	....	....	....	....	....	....
	Adirondack	AHL	55	4	8	12	86	....	....	....	....	....	....	....	....	....	....	....	1	1	0	1	14	....	....	....
1998-99	**Tampa Bay**	**NHL**	**68**	**9**	**12**	**21**	**80**	**3**	**1**	**1**	**119**	**7.6**	**–33**	**2**	**0.0**	**156**	**82**	**22:47**	....	....	....	....	....	....	....	....
	Cleveland	IHL	6	2	2	4	16	....	....	....	....	....	....	....	....	....	....	....	....	....	....	....	....	....	....	....
99-2000	**Tampa Bay**	**NHL**	**69**	**8**	**18**	**26**	**93**	**6**	**0**	**3**	**128**	**6.3**	**–19**	**0**	**0.0**	**121**	**78**	**22:32**	....	....	....	....	....	....	....	....
	NHL Totals		**147**	**18**	**32**	**50**	**195**	**9**	**1**	**4**	**255**	**7.1**		**2**	**0.0**	**277**	**160**	**22:39**	....	....	....	....	....	....	....	....

KUCERA, Frantisek
(koo-CHAIR-uh, FRAN-tih-sehk) **CBJ**

Defense. Shoots right. 6'2", 205 lbs. Born, Prague, Czech., February 3, 1968. Chicago's 3rd choice, 77th overall, in 1986 Entry Draft.

Season	Club	League	GP	G	A	Pts	PIM	PP	SH	GW	S	%	+/-	TF	F%	H	SB	Min	GP	G	A	Pts	PIM	PP	SH	GW
			Regular Season																Playoffs							
1985-86	Sparta Praha	Czech.	15	0	0	0																				
1986-87	Sparta Praha	Czech.	40	5	2	7	14																			
1987-88	Sparta Praha	Czech.	46	7	2	9	30																			
1988-89	Dukla Jihlava	Czech.	45	10	9	19	28																			
1989-90	Dukla Jihlava	Czech.	42	8	10	18													1	1	0	1				
1990-91	**Chicago**	**NHL**	**40**	**2**	**12**	**14**	**32**	**1**	**0**	**0**	**65**	**3.1**	**3**													
	Indianapolis Ice	IHL	35	8	19	27	23												7	0	1	1	15			
1991-92	**Chicago**	**NHL**	**61**	**3**	**10**	**13**	**36**	**1**	**0**	**1**	**82**	**3.7**	**3**						**6**	**0**	**0**	**0**	**0**	**0**	**0**	**0**
	Indianapolis Ice	IHL	7	1	2	3	4																			
1992-93	**Chicago**	**NHL**	**71**	**5**	**14**	**19**	**59**	**1**	**0**	**1**	**117**	**4.3**	**7**													
1993-94	**Chicago**	**NHL**	**60**	**4**	**13**	**17**	**34**	**2**	**0**	**0**	**90**	**4.4**	**9**													
	Hartford	**NHL**	**16**	**1**	**3**	**4**	**14**	**1**	**0**	**0**	**32**	**3.1**	**-12**													
1994-95	Sparta Praha	Cze-Rep	16	1	2	3	14																			
	Hartford	**NHL**	**48**	**3**	**17**	**20**	**30**	**0**	**0**	**1**	**73**	**4.1**	**3**													
1995-96	**Hartford**	**NHL**	**30**	**2**	**6**	**8**	**10**	**0**	**0**	**1**	**43**	**4.7**	**-3**													
	Vancouver	**NHL**	**24**	**1**	**0**	**1**	**10**	**0**	**0**	**0**	**34**	**2.9**	**5**						**6**	**0**	**1**	**1**	**0**	**0**	**0**	**0**
1996-97	**Vancouver**	**NHL**	**2**	**0**	**0**	**0**	**0**	**0**	**0**	**0**	**3**	**0.0**	**0**													
	Syracuse Crunch	AHL	42	6	29	35	36																			
	Houston Aeros	IHL	12	0	3	3	20																			
	Philadelphia	**NHL**	**2**	**0**	**0**	**0**	**2**	**0**	**0**	**0**	**2**	**0.0**	**-2**													
	Philadelphia	AHL	9	1	5	6	2												10	1	6	7	20			
1997-98	Sparta Praha	Cze-Rep	43	8	12	20	49												9	3	1	4	*53			
	Sparta Praha	EuroHL	4	0	1	1	2																			
	Czech-Republic	Olympics	6	0	0	0	0																			
1998-99	Sparta Praha	Cze-Rep	42	3	12	15	92												8	0	2	2				
	Sparta Praha	EuroHL	6	0	2	2	10												2	0	0	0	2			
99-2000	Sparta Praha	Cze-Rep	51	7	26	33	40												9	1	9	10	4			
	Sparta Praha	EuroHL	6	0	2	2	4												4	0	1	1	2			
	NHL Totals		**354**	**21**	**75**	**96**	**227**	**6**	**0**	**4**	**541**	**3.9**							**12**	**0**	**1**	**1**	**0**	**0**	**0**	**0**

Traded to **Hartford** by **Chicago** with Jocelyn Lemieux for Gary Suter, Randy Cunneyworth and Hartford's 3rd round choice (later traded to Vancouver - Vancouver selected Larry Courville) in 1995 Entry Draft, March 11, 1994. Traded to **Vancouver** by **Hartford** with Jim Dowd and Hartford's 2nd round choice (Ryan Bonni) in 1997 Entry Draft for Jeff Brown and Vancouver's 3rd round choice (later traded to Calgary - Calgary selected Paul Manning) in 1998 Entry Draft, December 19, 1995. Traded to **Philadelphia** by **Vancouver** for future considerations, March 18, 1997. Signed as a free agent by **Columbus**, July 7, 2000.

KVASHA, Oleg
(kuh-VAH-shah, OH-lehg) **NYI**

Center/Left wing. Shoots right. 6'5", 215 lbs. Born, Moscow, USSR, July 26, 1978. Florida's 3rd choice, 65th overall, in 1996 Entry Draft.

Season	Club	League	GP	G	A	Pts	PIM	PP	SH	GW	S	%	+/-	TF	F%	H	SB	Min	GP	G	A	Pts	PIM	PP	SH	GW
1995-96	CSKA Moscow	CIS	38	2	3	5	14												2	0	0	0	0			
1996-97	CSKA Moscow	Russia	44	20	22	42	115																			
1997-98	New Haven	AHL	57	13	16	29	46												3	2	1	3	0			
1998-99	**Florida**	**NHL**	**68**	**12**	**13**	**25**	**45**	**4**	**0**	**2**	**138**	**8.7**	**5**	**373**	**28.4**	**21**	**13**	**12:48**								
99-2000	**Florida**	**NHL**	**78**	**5**	**20**	**25**	**34**	**2**	**0**	**0**	**110**	**4.5**	**3**	**553**	**34.9**	**22**	**22**	**11:24**	**4**	**0**	**0**	**0**	**0**	**0**	**0**	**0**
	NHL Totals		**146**	**17**	**33**	**50**	**79**	**6**	**0**	**2**	**248**	**6.9**		**926**	**32.3**	**43**	**35**	**12:03**	**4**	**0**	**0**	**0**	**0**	**0**	**0**	**0**

Traded to **NY Islanders** by **Florida** with Mark Parrish for Roberto Luongo and Olli Jokinen, June 24, 2000.

LAAKSONEN, Antti
(lah-AHK-soh-nehn, AHN-tee) **MIN.**

Left wing. Shoots left. 6', 180 lbs. Born, Tammela, Finland, October 3, 1973. Boston's 10th choice, 191st overall, in 1997 Entry Draft.

Season	Club	League	GP	G	A	Pts	PIM	PP	SH	GW	S	%	+/-	TF	F%	H	SB	Min	GP	G	A	Pts	PIM	PP	SH	GW
1991-92	FoPS Forssa	Finn-Jr.	24	19	23	42	22																			
	FoPS Forssa	Finland-2	41	16	15	31	8																			
1992-93	FoPS Forssa	Finn-Jr.	9	5	3	8	10																			
	HPK Hameenlinna	Finn-Jr.	1	1	1	2	0																			
	FoPS Forssa	Finland-2	34	11	19	30	36																			
	HPK Hameenlinna	Finland	2	0	0	0	0																			
1993-94	U. of Denver	WCHA	36	12	9	21	38																			
1994-95	U. of Denver	WCHA	40	17	18	35	42																			
1995-96	U. of Denver	WCHA	39	25	28	53	71																			
1996-97	U. of Denver	WCHA	39	21	17	38	63																			
1997-98	Providence Bruins	AHL	38	3	2	5	14																			
	Charlotte	ECHL	15	4	3	7	12												6	0	3	3	0			
1998-99	**Boston**	**NHL**	**11**	**1**	**2**	**3**	**2**	**0**	**0**	**0**	**8**	**12.5**	**-1**	**0**	**0.0**	**5**	**3**	**9:20**								
	Providence Bruins	AHL	66	25	33	58	52												19	7	2	9	28			
99-2000	**Boston**	**NHL**	**27**	**6**	**3**	**9**	**2**	**0**	**0**	**1**	**23**	**26.1**	**3**	**3**	**66.7**	**22**	**2**	**7:50**								
	Providence Bruins	AHL	40	10	12	22	57												14	5	4	9	4			
	NHL Totals		**38**	**7**	**5**	**12**	**4**	**0**	**0**	**1**	**31**	**22.6**		**3**	**66.7**	**27**	**5**	**8:16**								

WCHA Second All-Star Team (1996)

Signed as a free agent by **Minnesota**, July 14, 2000.

LACHANCE, Scott
(lah-CHANTS, SKAWT) **VAN.**

Defense. Shoots left. 6'1", 209 lbs. Born, Charlottesville, VA, October 22, 1972. NY Islanders' 1st choice, 4th overall, in 1991 Entry Draft.

Season	Club	League	GP	G	A	Pts	PIM	PP	SH	GW	S	%	+/-	TF	F%	H	SB	Min	GP	G	A	Pts	PIM	PP	SH	GW
1988-89	Springfield Blues	NEJHL	36	8	28	36	20																			
1989-90	Springfield Blues	NEJHL	34	25	41	66	62																			
1990-91	Boston University	H-East	31	5	19	24	48																			
1991-92	United States	Nat-Team	36	1	10	11	34																			
	United States	Olympics	8	0	1	1	6																			
	NY Islanders	**NHL**	**17**	**1**	**4**	**5**	**9**	**0**	**0**	**0**	**20**	**5.0**	**13**													
1992-93	**NY Islanders**	**NHL**	**75**	**7**	**17**	**24**	**67**	**0**	**1**	**2**	**62**	**11.3**	**-1**													
1993-94	**NY Islanders**	**NHL**	**74**	**3**	**11**	**14**	**70**	**0**	**0**	**1**	**59**	**5.1**	**-5**						**3**	**0**	**0**	**0**	**0**	**0**	**0**	**0**
1994-95	**NY Islanders**	**NHL**	**26**	**6**	**7**	**13**	**26**	**3**	**0**	**0**	**56**	**10.7**	**2**													
1995-96	**NY Islanders**	**NHL**	**55**	**3**	**10**	**13**	**54**	**1**	**0**	**0**	**81**	**3.7**	**-19**													
1996-97	**NY Islanders**	**NHL**	**81**	**3**	**11**	**14**	**47**	**1**	**0**	**0**	**97**	**3.1**	**-7**													
1997-98	**NY Islanders**	**NHL**	**63**	**2**	**11**	**13**	**45**	**1**	**0**	**0**	**62**	**3.2**	**-11**													
1998-99	**NY Islanders**	**NHL**	**59**	**1**	**8**	**9**	**30**	**1**	**0**	**0**	**37**	**2.7**	**-19**	**0**	**0.0**	**67**	**92**	**21:34**								
	Montreal	**NHL**	**17**	**1**	**1**	**2**	**11**	**0**	**0**	**0**	**22**	**4.5**	**-2**	**0**	**0.0**	**19**	**47**	**22:29**								
99-2000	**Montreal**	**NHL**	**57**	**0**	**6**	**6**	**22**	**0**	**0**	**0**	**41**	**0.0**	**-4**	**0**	**0.0**	**95**	**86**	**17:47**								
	NHL Totals		**524**	**27**	**86**	**113**	**381**	**7**	**1**	**3**	**537**	**5.0**		**0**	**0.0**	**181**	**225**	**20:04**	**3**	**0**	**0**	**0**	**0**	**0**	**0**	**0**

Played in NHL All-Star Game (1997)

Traded to **Montreal** by **NY Islanders** for Montreal's 3rd round choice (Mattias Weinhandl) in 1999 Entry Draft, March 9, 1999. Signed as a free agent by **Vancouver**, August 13, 2000.

LaCOUTURE, Dan
(la-koo-TUHR, DAN) **EDM.**

Left wing. Shoots left. 6'3", 210 lbs. Born, Hyannis, MA, April 18, 1977. NY Islanders' 2nd choice, 29th overall, in 1996 Entry Draft.

Season	Club	League	GP	G	A	Pts	PIM	PP	SH	GW	S	%	+/-	TF	F%	H	SB	Min	GP	G	A	Pts	PIM	PP	SH	GW
1992-93	Natick Academy	Hi-School	20	38	34	72	46																			
1993-94	Natick Academy	Hi-School	21	52	49	101	58																			
1994-95	Springfield Pics	IJHL	52	44	56	100	98																			
1995-96	Springfield	NAJHL	41	36	41	77	87												13	12	13	25	23			
1996-97	Boston University	H-East	31	13	12	25	18																			
1997-98	Hamilton Bulldogs	AHL	77	15	10	25	31												5	1	0	1	0			

			Regular Season																Playoffs							
Season	Club	League	GP	G	A	Pts	PIM	PP	SH	GW	S	%	+/–	TF	F%	H	SB	Min	GP	G	A	Pts	PIM	PP	SH	GW
1998-99	**Edmonton**	**NHL**	**3**	**0**	**0**	**0**	**0**	**0**	**0**	**0**	**0**	**0.0**	**1**	**0**	**0.0**	**3**	**0**	**6:30**	....	....	....	....	....	....	....	....
	Hamilton Bulldogs	AHL	72	17	14	31	73	....	....	....	....	....	....	....	....	....	....	....	9	2	1	3	2	....	....	....
99-2000	**Edmonton**	**NHL**	**5**	**0**	**0**	**0**	**10**	**0**	**0**	**0**	**2**	**0.0**	**0**	**0**	**0.0**	**7**	**1**	**7:02**	**1**	**0**	**0**	**0**	**0**	**0**	**0**	**0**
	Hamilton Bulldogs	AHL	70	23	17	40	85	....	....	....	....	....	....	....	....	....	....	....	6	2	1	3	0	....	....	....
	NHL Totals		**8**	**0**	**0**	**0**	**10**	**0**	**0**	**0**	**2**	**0.0**		**0**	**0.0**	**10**	**1**	**6:50**	**1**	**0**	**0**	**0**	**0**	**0**	**0**	**0**

Traded to **Edmonton** by **NY Islanders** for Mariusz Czerkawski, August 25, 1997.

LACROIX, Daniel

(luh-KWAH, DAN-yehl)

Left wing. Shoots left. 6'2", 205 lbs. Born, Montreal, Que., March 11, 1969. NY Rangers' 2nd choice, 31st overall, in 1987 Entry Draft.

Season	Club	League	GP	G	A	Pts	PIM	PP	SH	GW	S	%	+/–	TF	F%	H	SB	Min	GP	G	A	Pts	PIM	PP	SH	GW
1985-86	Hull Frontaliers	QAAA	37	10	13	23	46	....	....	....	....	....	....	....	....	....	....	....	....	....	....	....	....	....	....	....
1986-87	Granby Bisons	QMJHL	54	9	16	25	311	....	....	....	....	....	....	....	....	....	....	....	8	1	2	3	22	....	....	....
1987-88	Granby Bisons	QMJHL	58	24	50	74	468	....	....	....	....	....	....	....	....	....	....	....	5	0	4	4	12	....	....	....
1988-89	Granby Bisons	QMJHL	70	45	49	94	320	....	....	....	....	....	....	....	....	....	....	....	4	1	1	2	57	....	....	....
	Denver Rangers	IHL	2	0	1	1	0	....	....	....	....	....	....	....	....	....	....	....	2	0	1	1	0	....	....	....
1989-90	Flint Spirits	IHL	61	12	16	28	128	....	....	....	....	....	....	....	....	....	....	....	4	2	0	2	24	....	....	....
1990-91	Binghamton	AHL	54	7	12	19	237	....	....	....	....	....	....	....	....	....	....	....	5	1	0	1	24	....	....	....
1991-92	Binghamton	AHL	52	12	20	32	149	....	....	....	....	....	....	....	....	....	....	....	11	2	4	6	28	....	....	....
1992-93	Binghamton	AHL	73	21	22	43	255	....	....	....	....	....	....	....	....	....	....	....	....	....	....	....	....	....	....	....
1993-94	**NY Rangers**	**NHL**	**4**	**0**	**0**	**0**	**0**	**0**	**0**	**0**	**0**	**0.0**	**0**	....	....	....	....	....	....	....	....	....	....	....	....	....
	Binghamton	AHL	59	20	23	43	278	....	....	....	....	....	....	....	....	....	....	....	....	....	....	....	....	....	....	....
1994-95	Providence Bruins	AHL	40	15	11	26	266	....	....	....	....	....	....	....	....	....	....	....	....	....	....	....	....	....	....	....
	Boston	**NHL**	**23**	**1**	**0**	**1**	**38**	**0**	**0**	**0**	**14**	**7.1**	**–2**	....	....	....	....	....	....	....	....	....	....	....	....	....
	NY Rangers	**NHL**	**1**	**0**	**0**	**0**	**0**	**0**	**0**	**0**	**0**	**0.0**	**0**	....	....	....	....	....	....	....	....	....	....	....	....	....
1995-96	**NY Rangers**	**NHL**	**25**	**2**	**2**	**4**	**30**	**0**	**0**	**0**	**14**	**14.3**	**–1**	....	....	....	....	....	....	....	....	....	....	....	....	....
	Binghamton	AHL	26	12	15	27	155	....	....	....	....	....	....	....	....	....	....	....	....	....	....	....	....	....	....	....
1996-97	**Philadelphia**	**NHL**	**74**	**7**	**1**	**8**	**163**	**1**	**0**	**0**	**54**	**13.0**	**–1**	....	....	....	....	....	**12**	**0**	**1**	**1**	**22**	**0**	**0**	**0**
1997-98	**Philadelphia**	**NHL**	**56**	**1**	**4**	**5**	**135**	**0**	**0**	**0**	**28**	**3.6**	**0**	....	....	....	....	....	**4**	**0**	**0**	**0**	**4**	**0**	**0**	**0**
1998-99	**Edmonton**	**NHL**	**4**	**0**	**0**	**0**	**13**	**0**	**0**	**0**	**5**	**0.0**	**0**	**10**	**40.0**	**5**	**0**	**6:22**	....	....	....	....	....	....	....	....
	Hamilton Bulldogs	AHL	46	13	9	22	260	....	....	....	....	....	....	....	....	....	....	....	11	3	1	4	65	....	....	....
99-2000	**NY Islanders**	**NHL**	**1**	**0**	**0**	**0**	**0**	**0**	**0**	**0**	**0**	**0.0**	**–1**	**0**	**0.0**	**3**	**0**	**10:40**	....	....	....	....	....	....	....	....
	Chicago Wolves	IHL	61	3	10	13	194	....	....	....	....	....	....	....	....	....	....	....	7	0	0	0	28	....	....	....
	NHL Totals		**188**	**11**	**7**	**18**	**379**	**1**	**0**	**0**	**115**	**9.6**		**10**	**40.0**	**8**	**0**	**7:14**	**16**	**0**	**1**	**1**	**26**	**0**	**0**	**0**

Traded to **Boston** by **NY Rangers** for Glen Featherstone, August 19, 1994. Claimed on waivers by **NY Rangers** from **Boston**, March 23, 1995. Signed as a free agent by **Philadelphia**, July 18, 1996. Traded to **Edmonton** by **Philadelphia** for Valeri Zelepukin, October 5, 1998. Signed as a free agent by **NY Islanders**, August 11, 1999.

LACROIX, Eric

(luh-KWAH, AIR-ihk) **NYR**

Left wing. Shoots left. 6'1", 210 lbs. Born, Montreal, Que., July 15, 1971. Toronto's 6th choice, 136th overall, in 1990 Entry Draft.

Season	Club	League	GP	G	A	Pts	PIM	PP	SH	GW	S	%	+/–	TF	F%	H	SB	Min	GP	G	A	Pts	PIM	PP	SH	GW
1989-90	Dummer Academy	Hi-School	25	23	18	41	....	....	....	....	....	....	....	....	....	....	....	....	....	....	....	....	....	....	....	....
1990-91	St. Lawrence	ECAC	35	13	11	24	35	....	....	....	....	....	....	....	....	....	....	....	....	....	....	....	....	....	....	....
1991-92	St. Lawrence	ECAC	34	11	20	31	40	....	....	....	....	....	....	....	....	....	....	....	....	....	....	....	....	....	....	....
1992-93	St. John's Leafs	AHL	76	15	19	34	59	....	....	....	....	....	....	....	....	....	....	....	9	5	3	8	4	....	....	....
1993-94	**Toronto**	**NHL**	**3**	**0**	**0**	**0**	**2**	**0**	**0**	**0**	**3**	**0.0**	**0**	....	....	....	....	....	**2**	**0**	**0**	**0**	**0**	**0**	**0**	**0**
	St. John's Leafs	AHL	59	17	22	39	69	....	....	....	....	....	....	....	....	....	....	....	11	5	3	8	6	....	....	....
1994-95	St. John's Leafs	AHL	1	0	0	0	2	....	....	....	....	....	....	....	....	....	....	....	....	....	....	....	....	....	....	....
	Phoenix	IHL	25	7	1	8	31	....	....	....	....	....	....	....	....	....	....	....	....	....	....	....	....	....	....	....
	Los Angeles	**NHL**	**45**	**9**	**7**	**16**	**54**	**2**	**1**	**1**	**64**	**14.1**	**2**	....	....	....	....	....	....	....	....	....	....	....	....	....
1995-96	**Los Angeles**	**NHL**	**72**	**16**	**16**	**32**	**110**	**3**	**0**	**1**	**107**	**15.0**	**–11**	....	....	....	....	....	....	....	....	....	....	....	....	....
1996-97	**Colorado**	**NHL**	**81**	**18**	**18**	**36**	**26**	**2**	**0**	**4**	**141**	**12.8**	**16**	....	....	....	....	....	**17**	**1**	**4**	**5**	**19**	**0**	**0**	**0**
1997-98	**Colorado**	**NHL**	**82**	**16**	**15**	**31**	**84**	**5**	**0**	**6**	**126**	**12.7**	**0**	....	....	....	....	....	**7**	**0**	**0**	**0**	**6**	**0**	**0**	**0**
1998-99	**Colorado**	**NHL**	**7**	**0**	**0**	**0**	**2**	**0**	**0**	**0**	**4**	**0.0**	**–2**	**1**	**0.0**	**14**	**5**	**11:58**	....	....	....	....	....	....	....	....
	Los Angeles	**NHL**	**27**	**0**	**1**	**1**	**12**	**0**	**0**	**0**	**17**	**0.0**	**–5**	**2**	**50.0**	**82**	**10**	**8:37**	....	....	....	....	....	....	....	....
	NY Rangers	**NHL**	**30**	**2**	**1**	**3**	**4**	**0**	**0**	**1**	**17**	**11.8**	**–5**	**14**	**100.0**	**49**	**12**	**4:05**	....	....	....	....	....	....	....	....
99-2000	**NY Rangers**	**NHL**	**70**	**4**	**8**	**12**	**24**	**0**	**0**	**1**	**46**	**8.7**	**–12**	**4**	**25.0**	**142**	**48**	**10:02**	....	....	....	....	....	....	....	....
	NHL Totals		**417**	**65**	**66**	**131**	**318**	**12**	**1**	**14**	**525**	**12.4**		**21**	**76.2**	**287**	**75**	**8:31**	**26**	**1**	**4**	**5**	**25**	**0**	**0**	**0**

Traded to **LA Kings** by **Toronto** with Chris Snell and Toronto's 4th round choice (Eric Belanger) in 1996 Entry Draft for Dixon Ward, Guy Leveque, Kelly Fairchild and Shayne Toporowski, October 3, 1994. Traded to **Colorado** by **LA Kings** with LA Kings' 1st round choice (Martin Skoula) in 1998 Entry Draft for Stephane Fiset and Colorado's 1st round choice (Mathieu Biron) in 1998 Entry Draft, June 20, 1996. Traded to **Los Angeles** by **Colorado** for Roman Vopat and Los Angeles' 6th round choice (later traded to Ottawa - Ottawa selected Martin Brusek) in 1999 Entry Draft, October 29, 1998. Traded to **NY Rangers** by **Los Angeles** for Sean Pronger, February 12, 1999.

LaFAYETTE, Nathan

(LAH-fay-eht, NAY-than)

Center. Shoots right. 6'1", 205 lbs. Born, New Westminster, B.C., February 17, 1973. St. Louis' 3rd choice, 65th overall, in 1991 Entry Draft.

Season	Club	League	GP	G	A	Pts	PIM	PP	SH	GW	S	%	+/–	TF	F%	H	SB	Min	GP	G	A	Pts	PIM	PP	SH	GW
1988-89	Toronto Marlies	MTHL	69	38	68	106	24	....	....	....	....	....	....	....	....	....	....	....	....	....	....	....	....	....	....	....
	Pickering Panthers	OJHL-B	1	0	0	0	0	....	....	....	....	....	....	....	....	....	....	....	....	....	....	....	....	....	....	....
1989-90	Kingston	OHL	53	6	8	14	14	....	....	....	....	....	....	....	....	....	....	....	7	0	1	1	0	....	....	....
1990-91	Kingston	OHL	35	13	13	26	10	....	....	....	....	....	....	....	....	....	....	....	....	....	....	....	....	....	....	....
	Cornwall Royals	OHL	28	16	22	38	25	....	....	....	....	....	....	....	....	....	....	....	....	....	....	....	....	....	....	....
1991-92	Cornwall Royals	OHL	66	28	45	73	26	....	....	....	....	....	....	....	....	....	....	....	6	2	5	7	15	....	....	....
1992-93	Newmarket	OHL	58	49	38	87	26	....	....	....	....	....	....	....	....	....	....	....	7	4	5	9	19	....	....	....
1993-94	**St. Louis**	**NHL**	**38**	**2**	**3**	**5**	**14**	**0**	**0**	**0**	**23**	**8.7**	**–9**	....	....	....	....	....	....	....	....	....	....	....	....	....
	Peoria Rivermen	IHL	27	13	11	24	20	....	....	....	....	....	....	....	....	....	....	....	....	....	....	....	....	....	....	....
	Vancouver	**NHL**	**11**	**1**	**1**	**2**	**4**	**0**	**0**	**0**	**11**	**9.1**	**2**	....	....	....	....	....	**20**	**2**	**7**	**9**	**4**	**0**	**0**	**0**
1994-95	Syracuse Crunch	AHL	27	9	9	18	10	....	....	....	....	....	....	....	....	....	....	....	....	....	....	....	....	....	....	....
	Vancouver	**NHL**	**27**	**4**	**4**	**8**	**2**	**0**	**1**	**0**	**30**	**13.3**	**2**	....	....	....	....	....	....	....	....	....	....	....	....	....
	NY Rangers	**NHL**	**12**	**0**	**0**	**0**	**0**	**0**	**0**	**0**	**5**	**0.0**	**1**	....	....	....	....	....	**8**	**0**	**0**	**0**	**2**	**0**	**0**	**0**
1995-96	**NY Rangers**	**NHL**	**5**	**0**	**0**	**0**	**2**	**0**	**0**	**0**	**5**	**0.0**	**–1**	....	....	....	....	....	....	....	....	....	....	....	....	....
	Binghamton	AHL	57	21	27	48	32	....	....	....	....	....	....	....	....	....	....	....	....	....	....	....	....	....	....	....
	Los Angeles	**NHL**	**12**	**2**	**4**	**6**	**6**	**1**	**0**	**0**	**23**	**8.7**	**–3**	....	....	....	....	....	....	....	....	....	....	....	....	....
1996-97	**Los Angeles**	**NHL**	**15**	**1**	**3**	**4**	**8**	**0**	**1**	**1**	**26**	**3.8**	**–8**	....	....	....	....	....	....	....	....	....	....	....	....	....
	Phoenix	IHL	31	2	5	7	16	....	....	....	....	....	....	....	....	....	....	....	....	....	....	....	....	....	....	....
	Syracuse Crunch	AHL	26	14	11	25	18	....	....	....	....	....	....	....	....	....	....	....	3	1	0	1	2	....	....	....
1997-98	**Los Angeles**	**NHL**	**34**	**5**	**3**	**8**	**32**	**1**	**0**	**1**	**60**	**8.3**	**2**	....	....	....	....	....	**4**	**0**	**0**	**0**	**2**	**0**	**0**	**0**
	Fredericton	AHL	28	7	8	15	36	....	....	....	....	....	....	....	....	....	....	....	....	....	....	....	....	....	....	....
1998-99	**Los Angeles**	**NHL**	**33**	**2**	**2**	**4**	**35**	**0**	**1**	**1**	**42**	**4.8**	**0**	**276**	**45.7**	**49**	**14**	**11:50**	....	....	....	....	....	....	....	....
	Long Beach	IHL	41	9	13	22	24	....	....	....	....	....	....	....	....	....	....	....	7	1	0	1	8	....	....	....
99-2000	Lowell	AHL	42	7	15	22	33	....	....	....	....	....	....	....	....	....	....	....	....	....	....	....	....	....	....	....
	NHL Totals		**187**	**17**	**20**	**37**	**103**	**2**	**3**	**3**	**225**	**7.6**		**276**	**45.7**	**49**	**14**	**11:50**	**32**	**2**	**7**	**9**	**8**	**0**	**0**	**0**

Canadian Major Junior Scholastic Player of the Year (1992)

Traded to **Vancouver** by **St. Louis** with Jeff Brown and Bret Hedican for Craig Janney, March 21, 1994. Traded to **NY Rangers** by **Vancouver** for Corey Hirsch, April 7, 1995. Traded to **LA Kings** by **NY Rangers** with Ray Ferraro, Mattias Norstrom, Ian Laperriere and NY Rangers' 4th round choice (Sean Blanchard) in 1997 Entry Draft for Marty McSorley, Jari Kurri and Shane Churla, March 14, 1996.

LAFLAMME, Christian

(lah-FLAM, KRIHS-tan) **MTL.**

Defense. Shoots right. 6'1", 210 lbs. Born, St. Charles, Que., November 24, 1976. Chicago's 2nd choice, 45th overall, in 1995 Entry Draft.

Season	Club	League	GP	G	A	Pts	PIM	PP	SH	GW	S	%	+/–	TF	F%	H	SB	Min	GP	G	A	Pts	PIM	PP	SH	GW
1991-92	Ste-Foy Governors	QAAA	42	5	27	32	100	....	....	....	....	....	....	....	....	....	....	....	....	....	....	....	....	....	....	....
1992-93	Verdun	QMJHL	69	2	17	19	85	....	....	....	....	....	....	....	....	....	....	....	3	0	2	2	6	....	....	....
1993-94	Verdun	QMJHL	72	4	34	38	85	....	....	....	....	....	....	....	....	....	....	....	4	0	3	3	4	....	....	....
1994-95	Beauport	QMJHL	67	6	41	47	82	....	....	....	....	....	....	....	....	....	....	....	8	1	4	5	6	....	....	....
1995-96	Beauport	QMJHL	41	13	23	36	63	....	....	....	....	....	....	....	....	....	....	....	20	7	17	24	32	....	....	....
1996-97	**Chicago**	**NHL**	**4**	**0**	**1**	**1**	**2**	**0**	**0**	**0**	**3**	**0.0**	**3**	....	....	....	....	....	....	....	....	....	....	....	....	....
	Indianapolis Ice	IHL	62	5	15	20	60	....	....	....	....	....	....	....	....	....	....	....	4	1	1	2	16	....	....	....
1997-98	**Chicago**	**NHL**	**72**	**0**	**11**	**11**	**59**	**0**	**0**	**0**	**75**	**0.0**	**14**	....	....	....	....	....	....	....	....	....	....	....	....	....

			Regular Season																Playoffs							
Season	Club	League	GP	G	A	Pts	PIM	PP	SH	GW	S	%	+/–	TF	F%	H	SB	Min	GP	G	A	Pts	PIM	PP	SH	GW
1998-99	Chicago	NHL	62	2	11	13	70	0	0	0	53	3.8	0	0	0.0	154	58	18:51	....	....	....	....	....	....	....	....
	Portland	AHL	2	0	1	1	2	....	....	....	....	....	....	....	....	....	....	....	....	....	....	....	....	....	....	....
	Edmonton	NHL	11	0	1	1	0	0	0	0	15	0.0	–3	0	0.0	22	14	16:33	4	0	1	1	2	0	0	0
99-2000	Edmonton	NHL	50	0	5	5	32	0	0	0	18	0.0	–4	5	40.0	113	33	13:40	....	....	....	....	....	....	....	....
	Montreal	NHL	15	0	2	2	8	0	0	0	6	0.0	–5	0	0.0	28	11	14:32	....	....	....	....	....	....	....	....
	NHL Totals		214	2	31	33	171	0	0	0	170	1.2		5	40.0	317	116	16:19	4	0	1	1	2	0	0	0

QMJHL Second All-Star Team (1995)

Traded to **Edmonton** by **Chicago** with Daniel Cleary, Ethan Moreau and Chad Kilger for Boris Mironov, Dean McAmmond and Jonas Elofsson, March 20, 1999. Traded to **Montreal** by **Edmonton** with Matthieu Descoteaux for Igor Ulanov and Alain Nasreddine, March 9, 2000.

LAKOVIC, Sasha

(LA-koh-vik, SA-shuh)

Right wing. Shoots left. 6', 220 lbs. Born, Vancouver, B.C., September 7, 1971.

Season	Club	League	GP	G	A	Pts	PIM	PP	SH	GW	S	%	+/–	TF	F%	H	SB	Min	GP	G	A	Pts	PIM	PP	SH	GW
1991-92	Kelowna Spartans	BCJHL	4	1	0	1	14	....	....	....	....	....	....	....	....	....	....	....	....	....	....	....	....	....	....	....
	Bellingham Hawks	BCJHL	24	8	3	11	67	....	....	....	....	....	....	....	....	....	....	....	....	....	....	....	....	....	....	....
1992-93	Brantford Wheels	ColHL	28	7	5	12	235	....	....	....	....	....	....	....	....	....	....	....	....	....	....	....	....	....	....	....
	Columbus Chill	ECHL	27	7	9	16	162	....	....	....	....	....	....	....	....	....	....	....	....	....	....	....	....	....	....	....
	Binghamton	AHL	3	0	0	0	0	....	....	....	....	....	....	....	....	....	....	....	....	....	....	....	....	....	....	....
	Brantford Smoke	ColHL	....	....	....	....	....	....	....	....	....	....	....	....	....	....	....	....	5	2	1	3	66	....	....	....
1993-94	Toledo Storm	ECHL	24	5	10	15	198	....	....	....	....	....	....	....	....	....	....	....	....	....	....	....	....	....	....	....
	Chatham Wheels	ColHL	13	11	7	18	61	....	....	....	....	....	....	....	....	....	....	....	....	....	....	....	....	....	....	....
1994-95	Tulsa Oilers	CHL	40	20	24	44	214	....	....	....	....	....	....	....	....	....	....	....	5	1	3	4	88	....	....	....
1995-96	Las Vegas	IHL	49	1	2	3	416	....	....	....	....	....	....	....	....	....	....	....	13	1	1	2	*57	....	....	....
1996-97	Calgary	NHL	19	0	1	1	54	0	0	0	10	0.0	–1	....	....	....	....	....	....	....	....	....	....	....	....	....
	Saint John Flames	AHL	18	1	8	9	182	....	....	....	....	....	....	....	....	....	....	....	....	....	....	....	....	....	....	....
	Las Vegas	IHL	10	0	0	0	81	....	....	....	....	....	....	....	....	....	....	....	2	0	0	0	14	....	....	....
1997-98	New Jersey	NHL	2	0	0	0	5	0	0	0	2	0.0	0	....	....	....	....	....	....	....	....	....	....	....	....	....
	Albany River Rats	AHL	30	7	6	13	158	....	....	....	....	....	....	....	....	....	....	....	13	3	4	7	*84	....	....	....
1998-99	New Jersey	NHL	16	0	3	3	59	0	0	0	10	0.0	0	0	0.0	41	1	6:20	....	....	....	....	....	....	....	....
	Albany River Rats	AHL	10	1	1	2	93	....	....	....	....	....	....	....	....	....	....	....	....	....	....	....	....	....	....	....
99-2000	Albany River Rats	AHL	51	10	16	26	144	....	....	....	....	....	....	....	....	....	....	....	5	0	0	0	14	....	....	....
	NHL Totals		37	0	4	4	118	0	0	0	22	0.0		0	0.0	41	1	6:20	....	....	....	....	....	....	....	....

Signed as a free agent by **Calgary**, October 10, 1996. Signed as a free agent by **New Jersey**, September 24, 1997. • Played w/ RHI's Vancouver Voodoo in 1993 (11-14-10-24-83) and 1994 (3-2-5-7-0); Oakland Skates in 1994 (4-4-3-7-40) and 1995 (17-17-14-31-80); San Jose Sting in 1997 (21-18-13-31-108) and MLRH's Philadelphia Sting in 1998 (3-5-5-10-23).

LAMBERT, Denny

(lahm-BAIR, DEH-nee) **ATL.**

Left wing. Shoots left. 5'10", 215 lbs. Born, Wawa, Ont., January 7, 1970.

Season	Club	League	GP	G	A	Pts	PIM	PP	SH	GW	S	%	+/–	TF	F%	H	SB	Min	GP	G	A	Pts	PIM	PP	SH	GW
1986-87	S.S. Marie Legion	NOHA	22	8	13	21	129	....	....	....	....	....	....	....	....	....	....	....	....	....	....	....	....	....	....	....
1987-88	S.S. Marie T-Birds	NOJHA	32	25	27	52	184	....	....	....	....	....	....	....	....	....	....	....	....	....	....	....	....	....	....	....
1988-89	Sault Ste. Marie	OHL	61	14	15	29	203	....	....	....	....	....	....	....	....	....	....	....	....	....	....	....	....	....	....	....
1989-90	Sault Ste. Marie	OHL	61	23	29	52	276	....	....	....	....	....	....	....	....	....	....	....	....	....	....	....	....	....	....	....
1990-91	Sault Ste. Marie	OHL	59	28	39	67	169	....	....	....	....	....	....	....	....	....	....	....	14	7	9	16	48	....	....	....
1991-92	San Diego Gulls	IHL	71	17	14	31	229	....	....	....	....	....	....	....	....	....	....	....	3	0	0	0	10	....	....	....
	St. Thomas	ColHL	5	2	6	8	9	....	....	....	....	....	....	....	....	....	....	....	....	....	....	....	....	....	....	....
1992-93	San Diego Gulls	IHL	56	18	12	30	277	....	....	....	....	....	....	....	....	....	....	....	14	1	1	2	44	....	....	....
1993-94	San Diego Gulls	IHL	79	13	14	27	314	....	....	....	....	....	....	....	....	....	....	....	6	1	0	1	55	....	....	....
1994-95	San Diego Gulls	IHL	75	25	35	60	222	....	....	....	....	....	....	....	....	....	....	....	....	....	....	....	....	....	....	....
	Anaheim	NHL	13	1	3	4	4	0	0	0	14	7.1	3	....	....	....	....	....	....	....	....	....	....	....	....	....
1995-96	Anaheim	NHL	33	0	8	8	55	0	0	0	28	0.0	–2	....	....	....	....	....	....	....	....	....	....	....	....	....
	Baltimore Bandits	AHL	44	14	28	42	126	....	....	....	....	....	....	....	....	....	....	....	12	3	9	12	39	....	....	....
1996-97	Ottawa	NHL	80	4	16	20	217	0	0	1	58	6.9	–4	....	....	....	....	....	6	0	1	1	9	0	0	0
1997-98	Ottawa	NHL	72	9	10	19	250	0	0	1	76	11.8	4	....	....	....	....	....	11	0	0	0	19	0	0	0
1998-99	Nashville	NHL	76	5	11	16	218	1	0	0	66	7.6	–3	1	100.0	57	17	10:20	....	....	....	....	....	....	....	....
99-2000	Atlanta	NHL	73	5	6	11	*219	2	0	0	83	6.0	–17	5	0.0	127	22	11:39	....	....	....	....	....	....	....	....
	NHL Totals		347	24	54	78	963	3	0	2	325	7.4		6	16.7	184	39	10:59	17	0	1	1	28	0	0	0

Signed as a free agent by **Anaheim**, August 16, 1993. Signed as a free agent by **Ottawa**, July 29, 1996. Claimed by **Nashville** from **Ottawa** in Expansion Draft, June 26, 1998. Traded to **Atlanta** by **Nashville** for the rights to Randy Robitaille, August 16, 1999.

LANDRY, Eric

(LAN-dree, AIR-ihk) **MTL.**

Center. Shoots left. 5'11", 190 lbs. Born, Gatineau, Que., January 20, 1975.

Season	Club	League	GP	G	A	Pts	PIM	PP	SH	GW	S	%	+/–	TF	F%	H	SB	Min	GP	G	A	Pts	PIM	PP	SH	GW
1993-94	St-Hyacinthe	QMJHL	69	42	34	76	128	....	....	....	....	....	....	....	....	....	....	....	7	4	2	6	13	....	....	....
1994-95	St-Hyacinthe	QMJHL	68	38	36	74	249	....	....	....	....	....	....	....	....	....	....	....	5	2	1	3	10	....	....	....
1995-96	Cape Breton	AHL	74	19	33	52	187	....	....	....	....	....	....	....	....	....	....	....	....	....	....	....	....	....	....	....
1996-97	Hamilton Bulldogs	AHL	74	15	17	32	139	....	....	....	....	....	....	....	....	....	....	....	22	6	7	13	43	....	....	....
1997-98	Calgary	NHL	12	1	0	1	4	0	0	0	7	14.3	–2	....	....	....	....	....	....	....	....	....	....	....	....	....
	Saint John Flames	AHL	61	17	21	38	194	....	....	....	....	....	....	....	....	....	....	....	20	4	6	10	58	....	....	....
1998-99	Calgary	NHL	3	0	1	1	0	0	0	0	1	0.0	1	15	46.7	8	0	9:54	....	....	....	....	....	....	....	....
	Saint John Flames	AHL	56	19	22	41	158	....	....	....	....	....	....	....	....	....	....	....	7	2	5	7	12	....	....	....
99-2000	Kentucky	AHL	79	35	31	66	170	....	....	....	....	....	....	....	....	....	....	....	9	3	6	9	2	....	....	....
	NHL Totals		15	1	1	2	4	0	0	0	8	12.5		15	46.7	8	0	9:54	....	....	....	....	....	....	....	....

Signed as a free agent by **Calgary**, August 20, 1997. Traded to **San Jose** by **Calgary** for Fredrik Oduya, July 12, 1999. Signed as a free agent by **Montreal**, July 7, 2000.

LANG, Robert

(LANG, RAW-buhrt) **PIT.**

Center. Shoots right. 6'2", 216 lbs. Born, Teplice, Czech., December 19, 1970. Los Angeles' 6th choice, 133rd overall, in 1990 Entry Draft.

Season	Club	League	GP	G	A	Pts	PIM	PP	SH	GW	S	%	+/–	TF	F%	H	SB	Min	GP	G	A	Pts	PIM	PP	SH	GW
1988-89	CHZ Litvinov	Czech.	7	3	2	5	0	....	....	....	....	....	....	....	....	....	....	....	....	....	....	....	....	....	....	....
1989-90	CHZ Litvinov	Czech.	32	8	7	15	....	....	....	....	....	....	....	....	....	....	....	....	8	3	3	6	....	....	....	....
1990-91	CHZ Litvinov	Czech.	56	26	26	52	38	....	....	....	....	....	....	....	....	....	....	....	....	....	....	....	....	....	....	....
1991-92	CHZ Litvinov	Czech.	43	12	31	43	34	....	....	....	....	....	....	....	....	....	....	....	....	....	....	....	....	....	....	....
	Czechoslovakia	Olympics	8	5	8	13	8	....	....	....	....	....	....	....	....	....	....	....	....	....	....	....	....	....	....	....
1992-93	Los Angeles	NHL	11	0	5	5	2	0	0	0	3	0.0	–3	....	....	....	....	....	....	....	....	....	....	....	....	....
	Phoenix	IHL	38	9	21	30	20	....	....	....	....	....	....	....	....	....	....	....	....	....	....	....	....	....	....	....
1993-94	Los Angeles	NHL	32	9	10	19	10	0	0	0	41	22.0	7	....	....	....	....	....	....	....	....	....	....	....	....	....
	Phoenix	IHL	44	11	24	35	34	....	....	....	....	....	....	....	....	....	....	....	....	....	....	....	....	....	....	....
1994-95	CHZ Litvinov	Cze-Rep	16	4	19	23	28	....	....	....	....	....	....	....	....	....	....	....	....	....	....	....	....	....	....	....
	Los Angeles	NHL	36	4	8	12	4	0	0	0	38	10.5	–7	....	....	....	....	....	....	....	....	....	....	....	....	....
1995-96	Los Angeles	NHL	68	6	16	22	10	0	2	0	71	8.5	–15	....	....	....	....	....	....	....	....	....	....	....	....	....
1996-97	Sparta Praha	Cze-Rep	38	14	27	41	30	....	....	....	....	....	....	....	....	....	....	....	5	1	2	3	4	....	....	....
	Sparta Praha	EuroHL	4	2	2	4	0	....	....	....	....	....	....	....	....	....	....	....	4	2	1	3	2	....	....	....
1997-98	Boston	NHL	3	0	0	0	2	0	0	0	2	0.0	1	....	....	....	....	....	....	....	....	....	....	....	....	....
	Czech-Republic	Olympics	6	0	3	3	0	....	....	....	....	....	....	....	....	....	....	....	....	....	....	....	....	....	....	....
	Pittsburgh	NHL	51	9	13	22	14	1	1	2	64	14.1	6	....	....	....	....	....	6	0	3	3	2	0	0	0
	Houston Aeros	IHL	9	1	7	8	4	....	....	....	....	....	....	....	....	....	....	....	....	....	....	....	....	....	....	....
1998-99	Pittsburgh	NHL	72	21	23	44	24	7	0	3	137	15.3	–10	964	44.8	84	22	16:24	12	0	2	2	0	0	0	0
99-2000	Pittsburgh	NHL	78	23	42	65	14	13	0	5	142	16.2	–9	1433	50.7	60	51	19:22	11	3	3	6	0	2	0	0
	NHL Totals		351	72	117	189	80	21	3	10	498	14.5		2397	48.3	144	73	17:56	29	3	8	11	2	2	0	0

Signed as a free agent by **Pittsburgh**, September 2, 1997. Claimed by **Boston** from **Pittsburgh** in NHL Waiver Draft, September 28, 1997. Claimed on waivers by **Pittsburgh** from **Boston**, October 25, 1997.

LANGDON, Darren

(LAIG-duhn, DAIR-uhn) **CAR.**

Left wing. Shoots left. 6'1", 205 lbs. Born, Deer Lake, Nfld., January 8, 1971.

			Regular Season																Playoffs							
Season	Club	League	GP	G	A	Pts	PIM	PP	SH	GW	S	%	+/–	TF	F%	H	SB	Min	GP	G	A	Pts	PIM	PP	SH	GW
1991-92	Summerside	MJrHL	44	34	49	83	441																			
1992-93	Binghamton	AHL	18	3	4	7	115												8	0	1	1	14			
	Dayton Bombers	ECHL	54	23	22	45	429												3	0	1	1	40			
1993-94	Binghamton	AHL	54	2	7	9	327																			
1994-95	Binghamton	AHL	55	6	14	20	296												11	1	3	4	*84			
	NY Rangers	**NHL**	**18**	**1**	**1**	**2**	**62**	**0**	**0**	**0**	**6**	**16.7**	**0**													
1995-96	**NY Rangers**	**NHL**	**64**	**7**	**4**	**11**	**175**	**0**	**0**	**1**	**29**	**24.1**	**2**						**2**	**0**	**0**	**0**	**0**	**0**	**0**	**0**
	Binghamton	AHL	1	0	0	0	12																			
1996-97	**NY Rangers**	**NHL**	**60**	**3**	**6**	**9**	**195**	**0**	**0**	**1**	**24**	**12.5**	**–1**						**10**	**0**	**0**	**0**	**2**	**0**	**0**	**0**
1997-98	**NY Rangers**	**NHL**	**70**	**3**	**3**	**6**	**197**	**0**	**0**	**0**	**15**	**20.0**	**0**													
1998-99	**NY Rangers**	**NHL**	**44**	**0**	**0**	**0**	**80**	**0**	**0**	**0**	**8**	**0.0**	**–3**	**0**	**0.0**	**37**	**5**	**3:33**								
99-2000	**NY Rangers**	**NHL**	**21**	**0**	**1**	**1**	**26**	**0**	**0**	**0**	**13**	**0.0**	**–2**	**0**	**0.0**	**22**	**2**	**5:36**								
	NHL Totals		**277**	**14**	**15**	**29**	**735**	**0**	**0**	**2**	**95**	**14.7**		**0**	**0.0**	**59**	**7**	**4:13**	**12**	**0**	**0**	**0**	**2**	**0**	**0**	**0**

Signed as a free agent by **NY Rangers**, August 16, 1993. • Missed remainder of 1999-2000 season recovering from hernia injury suffered in game vs. New Jersey, December 1, 1999. Traded to **Carolina** by **NY Rangers** with Rob DiMaio for Sandy McCarthy and a 4th round choice in 2001 Entry Draft, August 4, 2000. • Played w/ RHI's Anaheim Bullfrogs in 1994 (21-3-23-26-119).

LANGENBRUNNER, Jamie

(lan-gehn-BRUH-nuhr, JAY-mee) **DAL.**

Center. Shoots right. 6'1", 200 lbs. Born, Duluth, MN, July 24, 1975. Dallas' 2nd choice, 35th overall, in 1993 Entry Draft.

			Regular Season																Playoffs							
Season	Club	League	GP	G	A	Pts	PIM	PP	SH	GW	S	%	+/–	TF	F%	H	SB	Min	GP	G	A	Pts	PIM	PP	SH	GW
1990-91	Cloquet High	Hi-School	20	6	16	22	8																			
1991-92	Cloquet High	Hi-School	23	16	23	39	24																			
1992-93	Cloquet High	Hi-School	27	27	62	89	18																			
1993-94	Peterborough	OHL	62	33	58	91	53												7	4	6	10	2			
1994-95	Peterborough	OHL	62	42	57	99	84												11	8	14	22	12			
	Dallas	**NHL**	**2**	**0**	**0**	**0**	**2**	**0**	**0**	**0**	**1**	**0.0**	**0**													
	Kalamazoo Wings	IHL																	11	1	3	4	2			
1995-96	**Dallas**	**NHL**	**12**	**2**	**2**	**4**	**6**	**1**	**0**	**0**	**15**	**13.3**	**–2**													
	Michigan K-Wings	IHL	59	25	40	65	129												10	3	10	13	8			
1996-97	**Dallas**	**NHL**	**76**	**13**	**26**	**39**	**51**	**3**	**0**	**3**	**112**	**11.6**	**–2**						**5**	**1**	**1**	**2**	**14**	**0**	**0**	**1**
1997-98	**Dallas**	**NHL**	**81**	**23**	**29**	**52**	**61**	**8**	**0**	**6**	**159**	**14.5**	**9**						**16**	**1**	**4**	**5**	**14**	**0**	**0**	**1**
	United States	Olympics	3	0	0	0	4																			
1998-99♦	**Dallas**	**NHL**	**75**	**12**	**33**	**45**	**62**	**4**	**0**	**1**	**145**	**8.3**	**10**	**217**	**46.1**	**129**	**21**	**15:51**	**23**	**10**	**7**	**17**	**16**	**4**	**0**	**3**
99-2000	**Dallas**	**NHL**	**65**	**18**	**21**	**39**	**68**	**4**	**2**	**6**	**153**	**11.8**	**16**	**40**	**50.0**	**117**	**10**	**17:33**	**15**	**1**	**7**	**8**	**18**	**1**	**0**	**0**
	NHL Totals		**311**	**68**	**111**	**179**	**250**	**20**	**2**	**16**	**585**	**11.6**		**257**	**46.7**	**246**	**31**	**16:38**	**59**	**13**	**19**	**32**	**62**	**5**	**0**	**5**

LANGKOW, Daymond

(LAING-kow, DAY-muhn) **PHI.**

Center. Shoots left. 5'11", 175 lbs. Born, Edmonton, Alta, September 27, 1976. Tampa Bay's 1st choice, 5th overall, in 1995 Entry Draft.

			Regular Season																Playoffs							
Season	Club	League	GP	G	A	Pts	PIM	PP	SH	GW	S	%	+/–	TF	F%	H	SB	Min	GP	G	A	Pts	PIM	PP	SH	GW
1991-92	Edmonton Pats	AMHL	35	36	45	81	100																			
	Tri-City Americans	WHL	1	0	0	0	0																			
1992-93	Tri-City Americans	WHL	64	22	42	64	100												4	1	0	1	4			
1993-94	Tri-City Americans	WHL	61	40	43	83	174												4	2	2	4	15			
1994-95	Tri-City Americans	WHL	72	*67	73	*140	142												17	12	15	27	52			
1995-96	Tri-City Americans	WHL	48	30	61	91	103												11	14	13	27	20			
	Tampa Bay	**NHL**	**4**	**0**	**1**	**1**	**0**	**0**	**0**	**0**	**4**	**0.0**	**–1**													
1996-97	**Tampa Bay**	**NHL**	**79**	**15**	**13**	**28**	**35**	**3**	**1**	**1**	**170**	**8.8**	**1**													
	Adirondack	AHL	2	1	1	2	0																			
1997-98	**Tampa Bay**	**NHL**	**68**	**8**	**14**	**22**	**62**	**2**	**0**	**1**	**156**	**5.1**	**–9**													
1998-99	**Tampa Bay**	**NHL**	**22**	**4**	**6**	**10**	**15**	**1**	**0**	**1**	**40**	**10.0**	**0**	**399**	**48.4**	**20**	**8**	**17:10**								
	Cleveland	IHL	4	1	1	2	18																			
	Philadelphia	**NHL**	**56**	**10**	**13**	**23**	**24**	**3**	**1**	**1**	**109**	**9.2**	**–8**	**738**	**48.0**	**35**	**12**	**15:12**	**6**	**0**	**2**	**2**	**2**	**0**	**0**	**0**
99-2000	**Philadelphia**	**NHL**	**82**	**18**	**32**	**50**	**56**	**5**	**0**	**7**	**222**	**8.1**	**1**	**1263**	**45.1**	**78**	**41**	**16:57**	**16**	**5**	**5**	**10**	**23**	**1**	**1**	**2**
	NHL Totals		**311**	**55**	**79**	**134**	**192**	**14**	**2**	**11**	**701**	**7.8**		**2400**	**46.5**	**133**	**61**	**16:22**	**22**	**5**	**7**	**12**	**25**	**1**	**1**	**2**

WHL West First All-Star Team (1995) • Canadian Major Junior First All-Star Team (1995) • WHL West Second All-Star Team (1996)
Traded to **Philadelphia** by **Tampa Bay** with Mikael Renberg for Chris Gratton and Mike Sillinger, December 12, 1998.

LANK, Jeff

(LANK, JEHF)

Defense. Shoots left. 6'3", 205 lbs. Born, Indian Head, Sask., March 1, 1975. Philadelphia's 9th choice, 230th overall, in 1995 Entry Draft.

			Regular Season																Playoffs							
Season	Club	League	GP	G	A	Pts	PIM	PP	SH	GW	S	%	+/–	TF	F%	H	SB	Min	GP	G	A	Pts	PIM	PP	SH	GW
1990-91	Columbia Valley	KIJHL	54	6	28	34	33																			
1991-92	Prince Albert	WHL	56	2	8	10	26												9	0	0	0	2			
1992-93	Prince Albert	WHL	63	1	11	12	60																			
1993-94	Prince Albert	WHL	72	9	38	47	62																			
1994-95	Prince Albert	WHL	68	12	25	37	60												13	2	10	12	8			
1995-96	Hershey Bears	AHL	72	7	13	20	70												5	0	0	0	8			
1996-97	Philadelphia	AHL	44	2	12	14	49												7	2	1	3	4			
1997-98	Philadelphia	AHL	69	7	9	16	59												20	1	4	5	22			
1998-99	Philadelphia	AHL	51	5	10	15	36												2	0	0	0	2			
99-2000	**Philadelphia**	**NHL**	**2**	**0**	**0**	**0**	**2**	**0**	**0**	**0**	**0**	**0.0**	**0**	**0**	**0.0**	**1**	**2**	**13:06**								
	Philadelphia	AHL	26	1	4	5	16												3	0	0	0	2			
	NHL Totals		**2**	**0**	**0**	**0**	**2**	**0**	**0**	**0**	**0**	**0.0**		**0**	**0.0**	**1**	**2**	**13:06**								

• Re-entered NHL draft. Originally Montreal's 6th choice, 113th overall, in 1993 Entry Draft.

LAPERRIERE, Ian

(luh-PAIR-ee-YAIR, EE-ihn) **L.A.**

Center. Shoots right. 6'1", 201 lbs. Born, Montreal, Que., January 19, 1974. St. Louis' 6th choice, 158th overall, in 1992 Entry Draft.

			Regular Season																Playoffs							
Season	Club	League	GP	G	A	Pts	PIM	PP	SH	GW	S	%	+/–	TF	F%	H	SB	Min	GP	G	A	Pts	PIM	PP	SH	GW
1989-90	Mtl-Bourassa	QAAA	22	4	10	14	10												3	0	1	1	0			
1990-91	Drummondville	QMJHL	65	19	29	48	117												14	2	9	11	48			
1991-92	Drummondville	QMJHL	70	28	49	77	160												4	2	2	4	9			
1992-93	Drummondville	QMJHL	60	44	*96	140	188												10	6	13	19	20			
1993-94	Drummondville	QMJHL	62	41	72	113	150												9	4	6	10	35			
	St. Louis	**NHL**	**1**	**0**	**0**	**0**	**0**	**0**	**0**	**0**	**1**	**0.0**	**0**													
	Peoria Rivermen	IHL																	5	1	3	4	2			
1994-95	Peoria Rivermen	IHL	51	16	32	48	111																			
	St. Louis	**NHL**	**37**	**13**	**14**	**27**	**85**	**1**	**0**	**1**	**53**	**24.5**	**12**						**7**	**0**	**4**	**4**	**21**	**0**	**0**	**0**
1995-96	**St. Louis**	**NHL**	**33**	**3**	**6**	**9**	**87**	**1**	**0**	**1**	**31**	**9.7**	**–4**													
	Worcester	AHL	3	2	1	3	22																			
	NY Rangers	**NHL**	**28**	**1**	**2**	**3**	**53**	**0**	**0**	**0**	**21**	**4.8**	**–5**													
	Los Angeles	**NHL**	**10**	**2**	**3**	**5**	**15**	**0**	**0**	**0**	**18**	**11.1**	**–2**													
1996-97	**Los Angeles**	**NHL**	**62**	**8**	**15**	**23**	**102**	**0**	**1**	**2**	**84**	**9.5**	**–25**													
1997-98	**Los Angeles**	**NHL**	**77**	**6**	**15**	**21**	**131**	**0**	**1**	**1**	**74**	**8.1**	**0**						**4**	**1**	**0**	**1**	**6**	**0**	**0**	**0**
1998-99	**Los Angeles**	**NHL**	**72**	**3**	**10**	**13**	**138**	**0**	**0**	**1**	**62**	**4.8**	**–5**	**643**	**47.3**	**149**	**60**	**11:47**								
99-2000	**Los Angeles**	**NHL**	**79**	**9**	**13**	**22**	**185**	**0**	**0**	**1**	**87**	**10.3**	**–14**	**1111**	**53.6**	**181**	**60**	**13:15**	**4**	**0**	**0**	**0**	**2**	**0**	**0**	**0**
	NHL Totals		**399**	**45**	**78**	**123**	**796**	**2**	**2**	**7**	**431**	**10.4**		**1754**	**51.3**	**330**	**120**	**12:33**	**15**	**1**	**4**	**5**	**29**	**0**	**0**	**0**

QMJHL Second All-Star Team (1993)
Traded to **NY Rangers** by **St. Louis** for Stephane Matteau, December 28, 1995. Traded to **LA Kings** by **NY Rangers** with Ray Ferraro, Mattias Norstrom, Nathan Lafayette and NY Rangers' 4th round choice (Sean Blanchard) in 1997 Entry Draft for Marty McSorley, Jari Kurri and Shane Churla, March 14, 1996.

LAPLANTE, Darryl

(LA-plawnt, DAIR-ihl) **MIN.**

Center. Shoots left. 6', 198 lbs. Born, Calgary, Alta., March 28, 1977. Detroit's 3rd choice, 58th overall, in 1995 Entry Draft.

			Regular Season																Playoffs							
Season	Club	League	GP	G	A	Pts	PIM	PP	SH	GW	S	%	+/–	TF	F%	H	SB	Min	GP	G	A	Pts	PIM	PP	SH	GW
1992-93	Calgary Royals	AAHA	32	20	26	46	60	....	....	....	....	....	....	....	....	....	....	....	....	....	....	....	....	....	....	....
1993-94	Calgary Royals	AAHA	35	24	27	51	50	....	....	....	....	....	....	....	....	....	....	....	....	....	....	....	....	....	....	....
1994-95	Moose Jaw	WHL	71	22	24	46	66	....	....	....	....	....	....	....	....	....	....	....	10	2	2	4	7	....	....	....
1995-96	Moose Jaw	WHL	72	42	40	82	76	....	....	....	....	....	....	....	....	....	....	....	....	....	....	....	....	....	....	....
1996-97	Moose Jaw	WHL	69	38	42	80	79	....	....	....	....	....	....	....	....	....	....	....	12	2	4	6	15	....	....	....
1997-98	**Detroit**	**NHL**	**2**	**0**	**0**	**0**	**0**	**0**	**0**	**0**	**2**	**0.0**	**0**	....	....	....	....	....	....	....	....	....	....	....	....	....
	Adirondack	AHL	77	15	10	25	51	....	....	....	....	....	....	....	....	....	....	....	3	0	1	1	4	....	....	....
1998-99	**Detroit**	**NHL**	**3**	**0**	**0**	**0**	**0**	**0**	**0**	**0**	**0**	**0.0**	**0**	**0**	**0.0**	**0**	**1**	**1:59**	....	....	....	....	....	....	....	....
	Adirondack	AHL	71	17	15	32	96	....	....	....	....	....	....	....	....	....	....	....	3	0	1	1	0	....	....	....
99-2000	**Detroit**	**NHL**	**30**	**0**	**6**	**6**	**10**	**0**	**0**	**0**	**19**	**0.0**	**–2**	**58**	**53.5**	**44**	**9**	**9:35**	....	....	....	....	....	....	....	....
	Cincinnati Ducks	AHL	35	13	9	22	47	....	....	....	....	....	....	....	....	....	....	....	....	....	....	....	....	....	....	....
	NHL Totals		**35**	**0**	**6**	**6**	**10**	**0**	**0**	**0**	**21**	**0.0**		**58**	**53.4**	**44**	**10**	**8:53**	....	....	....	....	....	....	....	....

Selected by **Minnesota** from **Detroit** in Expansion Draft, June 23, 2000.

LAPOINTE, Claude

(luh-PWAH, KLOHD) **NYI**

Center. Shoots left. 5'9", 181 lbs. Born, Lachine, Que., October 11, 1968. Quebec's 12th choice, 234th overall, in 1988 Entry Draft.

			Regular Season																Playoffs							
Season	Club	League	GP	G	A	Pts	PIM	PP	SH	GW	S	%	+/–	TF	F%	H	SB	Min	GP	G	A	Pts	PIM	PP	SH	GW
1983-84	Lac St-Louis	QAAA	42	28	29	57	....	....	....	....	....	....	....	....	....	....	....	....	....	....	....	....	....	....	....	....
1984-85	Lac St-Louis	QAAA	42	20	32	52	....	....	....	....	....	....	....	....	....	....	....	....	....	....	....	....	....	....	....	....
1985-86	Trois-Rivieres	QMJHL	63	14	32	46	70	....	....	....	....	....	....	....	....	....	....	....	9	5	6	11	4	....	....	....
1986-87	Trois-Rivieres	QMJHL	70	47	57	104	123	....	....	....	....	....	....	....	....	....	....	....	....	....	....	....	....	....	....	....
1987-88	Laval Titan	QMJHL	69	37	83	120	143	....	....	....	....	....	....	....	....	....	....	....	13	2	17	19	53	....	....	....
1988-89	Laval Titan	QMJHL	63	32	72	104	158	....	....	....	....	....	....	....	....	....	....	....	17	5	14	19	66	....	....	....
1989-90	Halifax Citadels	AHL	63	18	19	37	51	....	....	....	....	....	....	....	....	....	....	....	6	1	1	2	34	....	....	....
1990-91	**Quebec**	**NHL**	**13**	**2**	**2**	**4**	**4**	**0**	**0**	**0**	**7**	**28.6**	**3**	....	....	....	....	....	....	....	....	....	....	....	....	....
	Halifax Citadels	AHL	43	17	17	34	46	....	....	....	....	....	....	....	....	....	....	....	....	....	....	....	....	....	....	....
1991-92	**Quebec**	**NHL**	**78**	**13**	**20**	**33**	**86**	**0**	**2**	**2**	**95**	**13.7**	**–8**	....	....	....	....	....	....	....	....	....	....	....	....	....
1992-93	**Quebec**	**NHL**	**74**	**10**	**26**	**36**	**98**	**0**	**0**	**1**	**91**	**11.0**	**5**	....	....	....	....	....	**6**	**2**	**4**	**6**	**8**	**0**	**0**	**0**
1993-94	**Quebec**	**NHL**	**59**	**11**	**17**	**28**	**70**	**1**	**1**	**1**	**73**	**15.1**	**2**	....	....	....	....	....	....	....	....	....	....	....	....	....
1994-95	**Quebec**	**NHL**	**29**	**4**	**8**	**12**	**41**	**0**	**0**	**0**	**40**	**10.0**	**5**	....	....	....	....	....	**5**	**0**	**0**	**0**	**8**	**0**	**0**	**0**
1995-96	**Colorado**	**NHL**	**3**	**0**	**0**	**0**	**0**	**0**	**0**	**0**	**0**	**0.0**	**–1**	....	....	....	....	....	....	....	....	....	....	....	....	....
	Calgary	**NHL**	**32**	**4**	**5**	**9**	**20**	**0**	**2**	**1**	**44**	**9.1**	**2**	....	....	....	....	....	**2**	**0**	**0**	**0**	**0**	**0**	**0**	**0**
	Saint John Flames	AHL	12	5	3	8	10	....	....	....	....	....	....	....	....	....	....	....	....	....	....	....	....	....	....	....
1996-97	**NY Islanders**	**NHL**	**73**	**13**	**5**	**18**	**49**	**0**	**3**	**3**	**80**	**16.3**	**–12**	....	....	....	....	....	....	....	....	....	....	....	....	....
	Utah Grizzlies	IHL	9	7	6	13	14	....	....	....	....	....	....	....	....	....	....	....	....	....	....	....	....	....	....	....
1997-98	**NY Islanders**	**NHL**	**78**	**10**	**10**	**20**	**47**	**0**	**1**	**3**	**82**	**12.2**	**–9**	....	....	....	....	....	....	....	....	....	....	....	....	....
1998-99	**NY Islanders**	**NHL**	**82**	**14**	**23**	**37**	**62**	**2**	**2**	**1**	**134**	**10.4**	**–19**	**1218**	**56.6**	**168**	**60**	**19:21**	....	....	....	....	....	....	....	....
99-2000	**NY Islanders**	**NHL**	**76**	**15**	**16**	**31**	**60**	**2**	**1**	**3**	**129**	**11.6**	**–22**	**1284**	**54.0**	**147**	**71**	**19:39**	....	....	....	....	....	....	....	....
	NHL Totals		**597**	**96**	**132**	**228**	**537**	**5**	**12**	**15**	**775**	**12.4**		**2502**	**55.2**	**315**	**131**	**19:29**	**13**	**2**	**4**	**6**	**16**	**0**	**0**	**0**

Transferred to **Colorado** after **Quebec** franchise relocated, June 21, 1995. Traded to **Calgary** by **Colorado** for Calgary's 7th round choice (Samuel Pahlsson) in 1996 Entry Draft, November 1, 1995. Signed as a free agent by **NY Islanders**, August 14, 1996.

LAPOINTE, Martin

(luh-POYNT, MAHR-tihn) **DET.**

Right wing. Shoots right. 5'11", 200 lbs. Born, Ville Ste. Pierre, Que., September 12, 1973. Detroit's 1st choice, 10th overall, in 1991 Entry Draft.

			Regular Season																Playoffs							
Season	Club	League	GP	G	A	Pts	PIM	PP	SH	GW	S	%	+/–	TF	F%	H	SB	Min	GP	G	A	Pts	PIM	PP	SH	GW
1988-89	Lac St-Louis	QAAA	42	39	45	84	....	....	....	....	....	....	....	....	....	....	....	....	....	....	....	....	....	....	....	....
1989-90	Laval Titan	QMJHL	65	42	54	96	77	....	....	....	....	....	....	....	....	....	....	....	14	8	17	25	54	....	....	....
1990-91	Laval Titan	QMJHL	64	44	54	98	66	....	....	....	....	....	....	....	....	....	....	....	13	7	14	21	26	....	....	....
1991-92	Laval Titan	QMJHL	31	25	30	55	84	....	....	....	....	....	....	....	....	....	....	....	10	4	10	14	32	....	....	....
	Detroit	**NHL**	**4**	**0**	**1**	**1**	**5**	**0**	**0**	**0**	**2**	**0.0**	**2**	....	....	....	....	....	**3**	**0**	**1**	**1**	**4**	**0**	**0**	**0**
	Adirondack	AHL	....	....	....	....	....	....	....	....	....	....	....	....	....	....	....	....	8	2	2	4	4	....	....	....
1992-93	Laval Titan	QMJHL	35	38	51	89	41	....	....	....	....	....	....	....	....	....	....	....	13	*13	*17	*30	22	....	....	....
	Detroit	**NHL**	**3**	**0**	**0**	**0**	**0**	**0**	**0**	**0**	**2**	**0.0**	**–2**	....	....	....	....	....	....	....	....	....	....	....	....	....
	Adirondack	AHL	8	1	2	3	9	....	....	....	....	....	....	....	....	....	....	....	....	....	....	....	....	....	....	....
1993-94	**Detroit**	**NHL**	**50**	**8**	**8**	**16**	**55**	**2**	**0**	**0**	**45**	**17.8**	**7**	....	....	....	....	....	**4**	**0**	**0**	**0**	**6**	**0**	**0**	**0**
	Adirondack	AHL	28	25	21	46	47	....	....	....	....	....	....	....	....	....	....	....	4	1	1	2	8	....	....	....
1994-95	Adirondack	AHL	39	29	16	45	80	....	....	....	....	....	....	....	....	....	....	....	....	....	....	....	....	....	....	....
	Detroit	**NHL**	**39**	**4**	**6**	**10**	**73**	**0**	**0**	**1**	**46**	**8.7**	**1**	....	....	....	....	....	**2**	**0**	**1**	**1**	**8**	**0**	**0**	**0**
1995-96	**Detroit**	**NHL**	**58**	**6**	**3**	**9**	**93**	**1**	**0**	**0**	**76**	**7.9**	**0**	....	....	....	....	....	**11**	**1**	**2**	**3**	**12**	**0**	**0**	**0**
1996-97♦	**Detroit**	**NHL**	**78**	**16**	**17**	**33**	**167**	**5**	**1**	**1**	**149**	**10.7**	**–14**	....	....	....	....	....	**20**	**4**	**8**	**12**	**60**	**1**	**0**	**1**
1997-98♦	**Detroit**	**NHL**	**79**	**15**	**19**	**34**	**106**	**4**	**0**	**3**	**154**	**9.7**	**0**	....	....	....	....	....	**21**	**9**	**6**	**15**	**20**	**2**	**1**	**1**
1998-99	**Detroit**	**NHL**	**77**	**16**	**13**	**29**	**141**	**7**	**1**	**4**	**153**	**10.5**	**7**	**217**	**47.9**	**167**	**16**	**15:06**	**10**	**0**	**2**	**2**	**20**	**0**	**0**	**0**
99-2000	**Detroit**	**NHL**	**82**	**16**	**25**	**41**	**121**	**1**	**1**	**2**	**127**	**12.6**	**17**	**287**	**54.4**	**207**	**19**	**14:43**	**9**	**3**	**1**	**4**	**20**	**2**	**0**	**1**
	NHL Totals		**470**	**81**	**92**	**173**	**761**	**20**	**3**	**11**	**754**	**10.7**		**504**	**51.6**	**374**	**35**	**14:54**	**80**	**17**	**21**	**38**	**150**	**5**	**1**	**3**

QMJHL First All-Star Team (1990, 1993) • QMJHL Second All-Star Team (1991) • Memorial Cup All-Star Team (1993)

LARAQUE, Georges

(luh-RAK, zhawrzh) **EDM.**

Right wing. Shoots right. 6'3", 240 lbs. Born, Montreal, Que., December 7, 1976. Edmonton's 2nd choice, 31st overall, in 1995 Entry Draft.

			Regular Season																Playoffs							
Season	Club	League	GP	G	A	Pts	PIM	PP	SH	GW	S	%	+/–	TF	F%	H	SB	Min	GP	G	A	Pts	PIM	PP	SH	GW
1991-92	Mtl-Bourassa	QAAA	28	20	20	40	30	....	....	....	....	....	....	....	....	....	....	....	....	....	....	....	....	....	....	....
1992-93	Mtl-Bourassa	QAAA	37	8	20	28	50	....	....	....	....	....	....	....	....	....	....	....	3	1	2	3	2	....	....	....
1993-94	St-Jean Lynx	QMJHL	70	11	11	22	142	....	....	....	....	....	....	....	....	....	....	....	4	0	0	0	7	....	....	....
1994-95	St-Jean Lynx	QMJHL	62	19	22	41	259	....	....	....	....	....	....	....	....	....	....	....	7	1	1	2	42	....	....	....
1995-96	Laval Titan	QMJHL	11	8	13	21	76	....	....	....	....	....	....	....	....	....	....	....	....	....	....	....	....	....	....	....
	St-Hyacinthe	QMJHL	8	3	4	7	59	....	....	....	....	....	....	....	....	....	....	....	....	....	....	....	....	....	....	....
	Granby Bisons	QMJHL	22	9	7	16	125	....	....	....	....	....	....	....	....	....	....	....	18	7	6	13	104	....	....	....
1996-97	Hamilton Bulldogs	AHL	73	14	20	34	179	....	....	....	....	....	....	....	....	....	....	....	15	1	3	4	12	....	....	....
1997-98	**Edmonton**	**NHL**	**11**	**0**	**0**	**0**	**59**	**0**	**0**	**0**	**4**	**0.0**	**–4**	....	....	....	....	....	....	....	....	....	....	....	....	....
	Hamilton Bulldogs	AHL	46	10	20	30	154	....	....	....	....	....	....	....	....	....	....	....	3	0	0	0	11	....	....	....
1998-99	**Edmonton**	**NHL**	**39**	**3**	**2**	**5**	**57**	**0**	**0**	**0**	**17**	**17.6**	**–1**	**0**	**0.0**	**32**	**4**	**5:31**	**4**	**0**	**0**	**0**	**2**	**0**	**0**	**0**
	Hamilton Bulldogs	AHL	25	6	8	14	93	....	....	....	....	....	....	....	....	....	....	....	....	....	....	....	....	....	....	....
99-2000	**Edmonton**	**NHL**	**76**	**8**	**8**	**16**	**123**	**0**	**0**	**0**	**56**	**14.3**	**5**	**0**	**0.0**	**84**	**21**	**8:28**	**5**	**0**	**1**	**1**	**6**	**0**	**0**	**0**
	NHL Totals		**126**	**11**	**10**	**21**	**239**	**0**	**0**	**0**	**77**	**14.3**		**0**	**0.0**	**116**	**25**	**7:28**	**9**	**0**	**1**	**1**	**8**	**0**	**0**	**0**

LARIONOV, Igor

(LAIR-ee-AH-nohv, EE-gohr) **FLA.**

Center. Shoots left. 5'9", 170 lbs. Born, Voskresensk, USSR, December 3, 1960. Vancouver's 11th choice, 214th overall, in 1985 Entry Draft.

			Regular Season																Playoffs							
Season	Club	League	GP	G	A	Pts	PIM	PP	SH	GW	S	%	+/–	TF	F%	H	SB	Min	GP	G	A	Pts	PIM	PP	SH	GW
1977-78	HK Khimik	USSR	6	3	0	3	4	....	....	....	....	....	....	....	....	....	....	....	....	....	....	....	....	....	....	....
1978-79	HK Khimik	USSR	32	3	4	7	12	....	....	....	....	....	....	....	....	....	....	....	....	....	....	....	....	....	....	....
1979-80	HK Khimik	USSR	42	11	7	18	24	....	....	....	....	....	....	....	....	....	....	....	....	....	....	....	....	....	....	....
1980-81	HK Khimik	USSR	43	22	23	45	36	....	....	....	....	....	....	....	....	....	....	....	....	....	....	....	....	....	....	....
1981-82	CSKA Moscow	USSR	46	31	22	53	6	....	....	....	....	....	....	....	....	....	....	....	....	....	....	....	....	....	....	....
1982-83	CSKA Moscow	USSR	44	20	19	39	20	....	....	....	....	....	....	....	....	....	....	....	....	....	....	....	....	....	....	....
1983-84	CSKA Moscow	USSR	43	15	26	41	30	....	....	....	....	....	....	....	....	....	....	....	....	....	....	....	....	....	....	....
	Soviet Union	Olympics	6	1	4	5	6	....	....	....	....	....	....	....	....	....	....	....	....	....	....	....	....	....	....	....
1984-85	CSKA Moscow	USSR	40	18	28	46	20	....	....	....	....	....	....	....	....	....	....	....	....	....	....	....	....	....	....	....
1985-86	CSKA Moscow	USSR	40	21	31	52	33	....	....	....	....	....	....	....	....	....	....	....	....	....	....	....	....	....	....	....
1986-87	CSKA Moscow	USSR	39	20	26	46	34	....	....	....	....	....	....	....	....	....	....	....	....	....	....	....	....	....	....	....
1987-88	CSKA Moscow	USSR	51	25	32	57	54	....	....	....	....	....	....	....	....	....	....	....	....	....	....	....	....	....	....	....
	Soviet Union	Olympics	8	4	*9	13	4	....	....	....	....	....	....	....	....	....	....	....	....	....	....	....	....	....	....	....
1988-89	CSKA Moscow	USSR	31	15	12	27	22	....	....	....	....	....	....	....	....	....	....	....	....	....	....	....	....	....	....	....
1989-90	**Vancouver**	**NHL**	**74**	**17**	**27**	**44**	**20**	**8**	**0**	**2**	**118**	**14.4**	**–5**	....	....	....	....	....	....	....	....	....	....	....	....	....

Season	Club	League	Regular Season GP	G	A	Pts	PIM	PP	SH	GW	S	%	+/-	TF	F%	H	SB	Min	Playoffs GP	G	A	Pts	PIM	PP	SH	GW
1990-91	**Vancouver**	**NHL**	**64**	**13**	**21**	**34**	**14**	**1**	**1**	**0**	**66**	**19.7**	**–3**	....	....	....	....	....	**6**	**1**	**0**	**1**	**6**	**0**	**0**	**0**
1991-92	**Vancouver**	**NHL**	**72**	**21**	**44**	**65**	**54**	**10**	**3**	**4**	**97**	**21.6**	**7**	....	....	....	....	....	**13**	**3**	**7**	**10**	**4**	**1**	**0**	**0**
1992-93	HC Lugano	Switz.	24	10	19	29	44	....	....	....	....	....	....	....	....	....	....	....	8	3	15	18	0	....	....	....
1993-94	**San Jose**	**NHL**	**60**	**18**	**38**	**56**	**40**	**3**	**2**	**2**	**72**	**25.0**	**20**	....	....	....	....	....	**14**	**5**	**13**	**18**	**10**	**0**	**0**	**0**
1994-95	**San Jose**	**NHL**	**33**	**4**	**20**	**24**	**14**	**0**	**0**	**1**	**69**	**5.8**	**–3**	....	....	....	....	....	**11**	**1**	**8**	**9**	**2**	**0**	**0**	**0**
1995-96	**San Jose**	**NHL**	**4**	**1**	**1**	**2**	**0**	**1**	**0**	**0**	**5**	**20.0**	**–6**	....	....	....	....	....	....	....	....	....	....	....	....	....
	Detroit	**NHL**	**69**	**21**	**50**	**71**	**34**	**9**	**1**	**5**	**108**	**19.4**	**37**	....	....	....	....	....	**19**	**6**	**7**	**13**	**6**	**3**	**0**	**2**
1996-97♦	**Detroit**	**NHL**	**64**	**12**	**42**	**54**	**26**	**2**	**1**	**4**	**95**	**12.6**	**31**	....	....	....	....	....	**20**	**4**	**8**	**12**	**8**	**3**	**0**	**1**
1997-98♦	**Detroit**	**NHL**	**69**	**8**	**39**	**47**	**40**	**3**	**0**	**2**	**93**	**8.6**	**14**	....	....	....	....	....	**22**	**3**	**10**	**13**	**12**	**0**	**0**	**0**
1998-99	**Detroit**	**NHL**	**75**	**14**	**49**	**63**	**48**	**4**	**2**	**2**	**83**	**16.9**	**13**	**867**	**49.8**	**13**	**16**	**17:20**	**7**	**0**	**2**	**2**	**0**	**0**	**0**	**0**
99-2000	**Detroit**	**NHL**	**79**	**9**	**38**	**47**	**28**	**3**	**0**	**4**	**69**	**13.0**	**13**	**729**	**43.6**	**22**	**18**	**16:05**	**9**	**1**	**2**	**3**	**6**	**1**	**0**	**0**
	NHL Totals		**663**	**138**	**369**	**507**	**318**	**44**	**10**	**26**	**875**	**15.8**		**1596**	**47.0**	**35**	**34**	**16:41**	**121**	**24**	**57**	**81**	**54**	**8**	**0**	**3**

USSR First All-Star (1983, 1986, 1987, 1988) • USSR Player of the Year (1988) • Played in NHL All-Star Game (1998)

Claimed by **San Jose** from **Vancouver** in NHL Waiver Draft, October 4, 1992. Traded to **Detroit** by **San Jose** with future considerations for Ray Sheppard, October 24, 1995. Signed as a free agent by **Florida**, July 1, 2000.

LAROCQUE, Mario

(luh-RAWK, MAIR-ee-oh) **T.B.**

Defense. Shoots left. 6'2", 182 lbs. Born, Montreal, Que., April 24, 1978. Tampa Bay's 1st choice, 16th overall, in 1996 Entry Draft.

Season	Club	League	GP	G	A	Pts	PIM	PP	SH	GW	S	%	+/-	TF	F%	H	SB	Min	GP	G	A	Pts	PIM	PP	SH	GW
1994-95	Mtl-Bourassa	QAAA	43	0	6	6	153	....	....	....	....	....	....	....	....	....	....	....	....	....	....	....	....	....	....	....
1995-96	Hull Olympiques	QMJHL	68	7	19	26	196	....	....	....	....	....	....	....	....	....	....	....	14	2	5	7	16	....	....	....
1996-97	Hull Olympiques	QMJHL	64	14	36	50	155	....	....	....	....	....	....	....	....	....	....	....	14	2	6	8	36	....	....	....
1997-98	Sherbrooke	QMJHL	28	6	10	16	125	....	....	....	....	....	....	....	....	....	....	....	....	....	....	....	....	....	....	....
1998-99	**Tampa Bay**	**NHL**	**5**	**0**	**0**	**0**	**16**	**0**	**0**	**0**	**3**	**0.0**	**–4**	**0**	**0.0**	**8**	**1**	**12:33**	....	....	....	....	....	....	....	....
	Cleveland	IHL	59	5	7	12	202	....	....	....	....	....	....	....	....	....	....	....	....	....	....	....	....	....	....	....
99-2000	Detroit Vipers	IHL	60	0	5	5	234	....	....	....	....	....	....	....	....	....	....	....	....	....	....	....	....	....	....	....
	NHL Totals		**5**	**0**	**0**	**0**	**16**	**0**	**0**	**0**	**3**	**0.0**		**0**	**0.0**	**8**	**1**	**12:33**	....	....	....	....	....	....	....	....

LAROUCHE, Steve

(luh-ROOSH, STEEV)

Center. Shoots right. 6', 180 lbs. Born, Rouyn, Que., April 14, 1971. Montreal's 3rd choice, 41st overall, in 1989 Entry Draft.

Season	Club	League	GP	G	A	Pts	PIM	PP	SH	GW	S	%	+/-	TF	F%	H	SB	Min	GP	G	A	Pts	PIM	PP	SH	GW
1986-87	Richelieu Regents	QAAA	42	25	35	60	....	....	....	....	....	....	....	....	....	....	....	....	....	....	....	....	....	....	....	....
1987-88	Trois-Rivieres	QMJHL	66	11	29	40	25	....	....	....	....	....	....	....	....	....	....	....	....	....	....	....	....	....	....	....
1988-89	Trois-Rivieres	QMJHL	70	51	102	153	53	....	....	....	....	....	....	....	....	....	....	....	4	4	2	6	6	....	....	....
1989-90	Trois-Rivieres	QMJHL	60	55	90	145	40	....	....	....	....	....	....	....	....	....	....	....	7	3	5	8	8	....	....	....
	Canada	Nat-Team	1	1	0	1	0	....	....	....	....	....	....	....	....	....	....	....	....	....	....	....	....	....	....	....
1990-91	Chicoutimi	QMJHL	45	35	41	76	64	....	....	....	....	....	....	....	....	....	....	....	17	*13	*20	*33	20	....	....	....
1991-92	Fredericton	AHL	74	21	35	56	41	....	....	....	....	....	....	....	....	....	....	....	7	1	0	1	0	....	....	....
1992-93	Fredericton	AHL	77	27	65	92	52	....	....	....	....	....	....	....	....	....	....	....	5	2	5	7	6	....	....	....
1993-94	Atlanta Knights	IHL	80	43	53	96	73	....	....	....	....	....	....	....	....	....	....	....	14	*16	10	*26	16	....	....	....
1994-95	P.E.I. Senators	AHL	70	*53	48	101	54	....	....	....	....	....	....	....	....	....	....	....	2	1	0	1	0	....	....	....
	Ottawa	**NHL**	**18**	**8**	**7**	**15**	**6**	**2**	**0**	**2**	**38**	**21.1**	**–5**	....	....	....	....	....	....	....	....	....	....	....	....	....
1995-96	**NY Rangers**	**NHL**	**1**	**0**	**0**	**0**	**0**	**0**	**0**	**0**	**1**	**0.0**	**0**	....	....	....	....	....	....	....	....	....	....	....	....	....
	Binghamton	AHL	39	20	46	66	47	....	....	....	....	....	....	....	....	....	....	....	....	....	....	....	....	....	....	....
	Los Angeles	**NHL**	**7**	**1**	**2**	**3**	**4**	**1**	**0**	**0**	**13**	**7.7**	**0**	....	....	....	....	....	....	....	....	....	....	....	....	....
	Phoenix	IHL	33	19	17	36	14	....	....	....	....	....	....	....	....	....	....	....	4	0	1	1	8	....	....	....
1996-97	Quebec Rafales	IHL	79	49	53	102	78	....	....	....	....	....	....	....	....	....	....	....	9	3	10	13	18	....	....	....
1997-98	Quebec Rafales	IHL	68	23	44	67	40	....	....	....	....	....	....	....	....	....	....	....	....	....	....	....	....	....	....	....
	Chicago Wolves	IHL	13	9	10	19	20	....	....	....	....	....	....	....	....	....	....	....	22	9	11	20	14	....	....	....
1998-99	Chicago Wolves	IHL	33	13	25	38	18	....	....	....	....	....	....	....	....	....	....	....	....	....	....	....	....	....	....	....
99-2000	Chicago Wolves	IHL	82	31	*57	88	52	....	....	....	....	....	....	....	....	....	....	....	16	6	8	14	22	....	....	....
	NHL Totals		**26**	**9**	**9**	**18**	**10**	**3**	**0**	**2**	**52**	**17.3**		....	....	....	....	....	....	....	....	....	....	....	....	....

QMJHL Second All-Star Team (1990) • AHL First All-Star Team (1995) • Won Fred Hunt Memorial Trophy (Sportsmanship - AHL) (1995) • Won Les Cunningham Award (MVP - AHL) (1995) • IHL First All-Star Team (1997, 2000)

Signed as a free agent by **Ottawa**, September 11, 1994. Traded to **NY Rangers** by **Ottawa** for Jean-Yves Roy, October 5, 1995. Traded to **LA Kings** by **NY Rangers** for Chris Snell, January 14, 1996. Traded to **Chicago Wolves** (IHL) by **Quebec** (IHL) for cash, March 19, 1998. • Missed remainder of 1999-2000 season recovering from knee injury suffered in game vs. Detroit (IHL), December 29, 1998.

LARSEN, Brad

(LARH-sehn, BRAD) **COL.**

Left wing. Shoots left. 5'11", 212 lbs. Born, Nakusp, B.C., January 28, 1977. Colorado's 5th choice, 87th overall, in 1997 Entry Draft.

Season	Club	League	GP	G	A	Pts	PIM	PP	SH	GW	S	%	+/-	TF	F%	H	SB	Min	GP	G	A	Pts	PIM	PP	SH	GW
1992-93	Nelson Leafs	RMJHL	42	31	37	68	164	....	....	....	....	....	....	....	....	....	....	....	....	....	....	....	....	....	....	....
1993-94	Swift Current	WHL	64	15	18	33	32	....	....	....	....	....	....	....	....	....	....	....	7	1	2	3	4	....	....	....
1994-95	Swift Current	WHL	62	24	33	57	73	....	....	....	....	....	....	....	....	....	....	....	6	0	1	1	2	....	....	....
1995-96	Swift Current	WHL	51	30	47	77	67	....	....	....	....	....	....	....	....	....	....	....	6	3	2	5	13	....	....	....
1996-97	Swift Current	WHL	61	36	46	82	61	....	....	....	....	....	....	....	....	....	....	....	....	....	....	....	....	....	....	....
1997-98	**Colorado**	**NHL**	**1**	**0**	**0**	**0**	**0**	**0**	**0**	**0**	**0**	**0.0**	**0**	....	....	....	....	....	....	....	....	....	....	....	....	....
	Hershey Bears	AHL	65	12	10	22	80	....	....	....	....	....	....	....	....	....	....	....	7	3	2	5	2	....	....	....
1998-99	Hershey Bears	AHL	18	3	4	7	11	....	....	....	....	....	....	....	....	....	....	....	5	0	1	1	6	....	....	....
99-2000	Hershey Bears	AHL	52	13	26	39	66	....	....	....	....	....	....	....	....	....	....	....	14	5	2	7	29	....	....	....
	NHL Totals		**1**	**0**	**0**	**0**	**0**	**0**	**0**	**0**	**0**	**0.0**		....	....	....	....	....	....	....	....	....	....	....	....	....

• Re-entered NHL draft. Originally Ottawa's 3rd choice, 53rd overall, in 1995 Entry Draft.

WHL East Second All-Star Team (1997)

Rights traded to **Colorado** by **Ottawa** for Janne Laukkanen, January 26, 1996. • Missed majority of 1998-99 season recovering from abdominal injury suffered in game vs. Albany (AHL), November 20, 1998.

LAUER, Brad

(LAU-er, BRAD)

Left wing. Shoots left. 6', 195 lbs. Born, Humboldt, Sask., October 27, 1966. NY Islanders' 3rd choice, 34th overall, in 1985 Entry Draft.

Season	Club	League	GP	G	A	Pts	PIM	PP	SH	GW	S	%	+/-	TF	F%	H	SB	Min	GP	G	A	Pts	PIM	PP	SH	GW
1983-84	Regina Pats	WHL	60	5	7	12	51	....	....	....	....	....	....	....	....	....	....	....	16	0	1	1	24	....	....	....
1984-85	Regina Pats	WHL	72	33	46	79	57	....	....	....	....	....	....	....	....	....	....	....	8	6	6	12	9	....	....	....
1985-86	Regina Pats	WHL	57	36	38	74	69	....	....	....	....	....	....	....	....	....	....	....	10	4	5	9	2	....	....	....
1986-87	**NY Islanders**	**NHL**	**61**	**7**	**14**	**21**	**65**	**1**	**0**	**1**	**75**	**9.3**	**0**	....	....	....	....	....	**6**	**2**	**0**	**2**	**4**	**0**	**0**	**0**
1987-88	**NY Islanders**	**NHL**	**69**	**17**	**18**	**35**	**67**	**3**	**0**	**4**	**94**	**18.1**	**13**	....	....	....	....	....	**5**	**3**	**1**	**4**	**4**	**0**	**0**	**0**
1988-89	**NY Islanders**	**NHL**	**14**	**3**	**2**	**5**	**2**	**0**	**0**	**0**	**21**	**14.3**	**–2**	....	....	....	....	....	....	....	....	....	....	....	....	....
	Springfield	AHL	8	1	5	6	0	....	....	....	....	....	....	....	....	....	....	....	....	....	....	....	....	....	....	....
1989-90	**NY Islanders**	**NHL**	**63**	**6**	**18**	**24**	**19**	**0**	**0**	**2**	**86**	**7.0**	**5**	....	....	....	....	....	**4**	**0**	**2**	**2**	**10**	**0**	**0**	**0**
	Springfield	AHL	7	4	2	6	0	....	....	....	....	....	....	....	....	....	....	....	....	....	....	....	....	....	....	....
1990-91	**NY Islanders**	**NHL**	**44**	**4**	**8**	**12**	**45**	**0**	**1**	**0**	**70**	**5.7**	**–6**	....	....	....	....	....	....	....	....	....	....	....	....	....
	Capital District	AHL	11	5	11	16	14	....	....	....	....	....	....	....	....	....	....	....	....	....	....	....	....	....	....	....
1991-92	**NY Islanders**	**NHL**	**8**	**1**	**0**	**1**	**2**	**0**	**1**	**0**	**12**	**8.3**	**–2**	....	....	....	....	....	....	....	....	....	....	....	....	....
	Chicago	**NHL**	**6**	**0**	**0**	**0**	**4**	**0**	**0**	**0**	**6**	**0.0**	**–3**	....	....	....	....	....	**7**	**1**	**1**	**2**	**2**	**0**	**0**	**0**
	Indianapolis Ice	IHL	57	24	30	54	46	....	....	....	....	....	....	....	....	....	....	....	....	....	....	....	....	....	....	....
1992-93	**Chicago**	**NHL**	**7**	**0**	**1**	**1**	**2**	**0**	**0**	**0**	**8**	**0.0**	**–1**	....	....	....	....	....	....	....	....	....	....	....	....	....
	Indianapolis Ice	IHL	62	*50	41	91	80	....	....	....	....	....	....	....	....	....	....	....	5	3	1	4	6	....	....	....
1993-94	**Ottawa**	**NHL**	**30**	**2**	**5**	**7**	**6**	**0**	**1**	**0**	**45**	**4.4**	**–15**	....	....	....	....	....	....	....	....	....	....	....	....	....
	Las Vegas	IHL	32	21	21	42	30	....	....	....	....	....	....	....	....	....	....	....	4	1	0	1	2	....	....	....
1994-95	Cleveland	IHL	51	32	27	59	48	....	....	....	....	....	....	....	....	....	....	....	4	4	2	6	6	....	....	....
1995-96	**Pittsburgh**	**NHL**	**21**	**4**	**1**	**5**	**6**	**1**	**0**	**1**	**29**	**13.8**	**–5**	....	....	....	....	....	**12**	**1**	**1**	**2**	**4**	**0**	**0**	**0**
	Cleveland	IHL	53	25	27	52	44	....	....	....	....	....	....	....	....	....	....	....	....	....	....	....	....	....	....	....
1996-97	Cleveland	IHL	64	27	21	48	61	....	....	....	....	....	....	....	....	....	....	....	14	4	6	10	8	....	....	....
1997-98	Cleveland	IHL	68	22	33	55	74	....	....	....	....	....	....	....	....	....	....	....	10	0	3	3	12	....	....	....

Season	Club	League	GP	G	A	Pts	PIM	PP	SH	GW	S	%	+/–	TF	F%	H	SB	Min	GP	G	A	Pts	PIM	PP	SH	GW
			Regular Season																Playoffs							
1998-99	Utah Grizzlies	IHL	78	31	30	61	68	....	....	....	....	....	....	....	....	....	....	....	....	....	....	....	....	....	....	....
99-2000	Utah Grizzlies	IHL	71	26	22	48	73	....	....	....	....	....	....	....	....	....	....	....	5	0	1	1	2	....	....	....
	NHL Totals		**323**	**44**	**67**	**111**	**218**	**5**	**3**	**8**	**446**	**9.9**		....	....	....	....	....	**34**	**7**	**5**	**12**	**24**	**0**	**0**	**0**

IHL First All-Star Team (1993)

• Missed majority of 1988-89 season recovering from knee injury suffered in training camp, October, 1988. Traded to **Chicago** by **NY Islanders** with Brent Sutter for Adam Creighton and Steve Thomas, October 25, 1991. Signed as a free agent by **Ottawa**, January 3, 1994. Signed as a free agent by **Pittsburgh**, August 10, 1995.

LAUKKANEN, Janne

(LOW-kah-nehn, JAN-nee) **PIT.**

Defense. Shoots left. 6'1", 194 lbs. Born, Lahti, Finland, March 19, 1970. Quebec's 8th choice, 156th overall, in 1991 Entry Draft.

Season	Club	League	GP	G	A	Pts	PIM	PP	SH	GW	S	%	+/–	TF	F%	H	SB	Min	GP	G	A	Pts	PIM	PP	SH	GW
1986-87	Kiekko Lahti	Finn-Jr.	1	0	0	0	0	....	....	....	....	....	....	....	....	....	....	....	....	....	....	....	....	....	....	....
1987-88	Kiekko Lahti-2	Finn-Jr.	20	5	5	10	48	....	....	....	....	....	....	....	....	....	....	....	....	....	....	....	....	....	....	....
1988-89	Sport Academy	Finn-Jr.	6	0	1	1	6	....	....	....	....	....	....	....	....	....	....	....	....	....	....	....	....	....	....	....
	Kiekko Lahti-2	Finland-2	33	1	7	8	24	....	....	....	....	....	....	....	....	....	....	....	....	....	....	....	....	....	....	....
1989-90	Reipas Lahti	Finn-Jr.	2	2	2	4	2	....	....	....	....	....	....	....	....	....	....	....	....	....	....	....	....	....	....	....
	Reipas Lahti	Finland-2	44	8	22	30	60	....	....	....	....	....	....	....	....	....	....	....	....	....	....	....	....	....	....	....
1990-91	Reipas Lahti	Finland	44	8	14	22	56	....	....	....	....	....	....	....	....	....	....	....	....	....	....	....	....	....	....	....
1991-92	HPK Hameenlinna	Finland	43	5	14	19	62	....	....	....	....	....	....	....	....	....	....	....	....	....	....	....	....	....	....	....
	Finland	Olympics	8	0	1	1	6	....	....	....	....	....	....	....	....	....	....	....	....	....	....	....	....	....	....	....
1992-93	HPK Hameenlinna	Finland	47	8	21	29	76	....	....	....	....	....	....	....	....	....	....	....	12	1	4	5	10	....	....	....
1993-94	HPK Hameenlinna	Finland	48	5	24	29	46	....	....	....	....	....	....	....	....	....	....	....	....	....	....	....	....	....	....	....
	Finland	Olympics	8	0	2	2	12	....	....	....	....	....	....	....	....	....	....	....	....	....	....	....	....	....	....	....
	MC Budejovice	Cze-Rep	....	....	....	....	....	....	....	....	....	....	....	....	....	....	....	....	3	0	1	1	0	....	....	....
1994-95	Cornwall Aces	AHL	55	8	26	34	41	....	....	....	....	....	....	....	....	....	....	....	....	....	....	....	....	....	....	....
	Quebec	**NHL**	**11**	**0**	**3**	**3**	**4**	**0**	**0**	**0**	**12**	**0.0**	**3**	....	....	....	....	....	**6**	**1**	**0**	**1**	**2**	**0**	**0**	**0**
1995-96	**Colorado**	**NHL**	**3**	**1**	**0**	**1**	**0**	**1**	**0**	**0**	**4**	**25.0**	**–1**	....	....	....	....	....	....	....	....	....	....	....	....	....
	Cornwall Aces	AHL	35	7	20	27	60	....	....	....	....	....	....	....	....	....	....	....	....	....	....	....	....	....	....	....
	Ottawa	**NHL**	**20**	**0**	**2**	**2**	**14**	**0**	**0**	**0**	**31**	**0.0**	**0**	....	....	....	....	....	....	....	....	....	....	....	....	....
1996-97	**Ottawa**	**NHL**	**76**	**3**	**18**	**21**	**76**	**2**	**0**	**0**	**109**	**2.8**	**–14**	....	....	....	....	....	**7**	**0**	**1**	**1**	**6**	**0**	**0**	**0**
1997-98	**Ottawa**	**NHL**	**60**	**4**	**17**	**21**	**64**	**2**	**0**	**2**	**69**	**5.8**	**–15**	....	....	....	....	....	**11**	**2**	**2**	**4**	**8**	**1**	**0**	**1**
	Finland	Olympics	6	0	0	0	4	....	....	....	....	....	....	....	....	....	....	....	....	....	....	....	....	....	....	....
1998-99	**Ottawa**	**NHL**	**50**	**1**	**11**	**12**	**40**	**0**	**0**	**0**	**46**	**2.2**	**18**	**0**	**0.0**	**87**	**80**	**18:37**	**4**	**0**	**0**	**0**	**4**	**0**	**0**	**0**
99-2000	**Ottawa**	**NHL**	**60**	**1**	**11**	**12**	**55**	**0**	**0**	**0**	**62**	**1.6**	**14**	**0**	**0.0**	**108**	**108**	**19:47**	....	....	....	....	....	....	....	....
	Pittsburgh	**NHL**	**11**	**1**	**7**	**8**	**12**	**1**	**0**	**0**	**19**	**5.3**	**3**	**0**	**0.0**	**20**	**9**	**16:55**	**11**	**2**	**4**	**6**	**10**	**1**	**0**	**1**
	NHL Totals		**291**	**11**	**69**	**80**	**265**	**6**	**0**	**2**	**352**	**3.1**		**0**	**0.0**	**215**	**197**	**19:02**	**39**	**5**	**7**	**12**	**30**	**2**	**0**	**2**

Finnish First All-Star Team (1993)

Transferred to **Colorado** after **Quebec** franchise relocated, June 21, 1995. Traded to **Ottawa** by **Colorado** for the rights to Brad Larsen, January 26, 1996. Traded to **Pittsburgh** by **Ottawa** with Ron Tugnutt for Tom Barrasso, March 14, 2000.

LAUS, Paul

(LOWZ, PAWL) **FLA.**

Right wing. Shoots right. 6'1", 212 lbs. Born, Beamsville, Ont., September 26, 1970. Pittsburgh's 2nd choice, 37th overall, in 1989 Entry Draft.

Season	Club	League	GP	G	A	Pts	PIM	PP	SH	GW	S	%	+/–	TF	F%	H	SB	Min	GP	G	A	Pts	PIM	PP	SH	GW
1986-87	St. Catharines	OJHL-B	40	1	8	9	56	....	....	....	....	....	....	....	....	....	....	....	....	....	....	....	....	....	....	....
1987-88	Hamilton Hawks	OHL	56	1	9	10	171	....	....	....	....	....	....	....	....	....	....	....	14	0	0	0	28	....	....	....
1988-89	Niagara Falls	OHL	49	1	10	11	225	....	....	....	....	....	....	....	....	....	....	....	15	0	5	5	56	....	....	....
1989-90	Niagara Falls	OHL	60	13	35	48	231	....	....	....	....	....	....	....	....	....	....	....	16	6	16	22	71	....	....	....
1990-91	Albany Choppers	IHL	7	0	0	0	7	....	....	....	....	....	....	....	....	....	....	....	....	....	....	....	....	....	....	....
	Knoxville	ECHL	20	6	12	18	83	....	....	....	....	....	....	....	....	....	....	....	....	....	....	....	....	....	....	....
	Muskegon	IHL	35	3	4	7	103	....	....	....	....	....	....	....	....	....	....	....	4	0	0	0	13	....	....	....
1991-92	Muskegon	IHL	75	0	21	21	248	....	....	....	....	....	....	....	....	....	....	....	14	2	5	7	70	....	....	....
1992-93	Cleveland	IHL	76	8	18	26	427	....	....	....	....	....	....	....	....	....	....	....	4	1	0	1	27	....	....	....
1993-94	**Florida**	**NHL**	**39**	**2**	**0**	**2**	**109**	**0**	**0**	**1**	**15**	**13.3**	**9**	....	....	....	....	....	....	....	....	....	....	....	....	....
1994-95	**Florida**	**NHL**	**37**	**0**	**7**	**7**	**138**	**0**	**0**	**0**	**18**	**0.0**	**12**	....	....	....	....	....	....	....	....	....	....	....	....	....
1995-96	**Florida**	**NHL**	**78**	**3**	**6**	**9**	**236**	**0**	**0**	**0**	**45**	**6.7**	**–2**	....	....	....	....	....	**21**	**2**	**6**	**8**	***62**	**0**	**0**	**0**
1996-97	**Florida**	**NHL**	**77**	**0**	**12**	**12**	**313**	**0**	**0**	**0**	**63**	**0.0**	**13**	....	....	....	....	....	**5**	**0**	**1**	**1**	**4**	**0**	**0**	**0**
1997-98	**Florida**	**NHL**	**77**	**0**	**11**	**11**	**293**	**0**	**0**	**0**	**64**	**0.0**	**–5**	....	....	....	....	....	....	....	....	....	....	....	....	....
1998-99	**Florida**	**NHL**	**75**	**1**	**9**	**10**	**218**	**0**	**0**	**0**	**54**	**1.9**	**–1**	**0**	**0.0**	**93**	**20**	**11:09**	....	....	....	....	....	....	....	....
99-2000	**Florida**	**NHL**	**77**	**3**	**8**	**11**	**172**	**0**	**0**	**0**	**44**	**6.8**	**–1**	**1**	**0.0**	**106**	**15**	**7:37**	**4**	**0**	**0**	**0**	**8**	**0**	**0**	**0**
	NHL Totals		**460**	**9**	**53**	**62**	**1479**	**0**	**0**	**1**	**303**	**3.0**		**1**	**0.0**	**199**	**35**	**9:22**	**30**	**2**	**7**	**9**	**74**	**0**	**0**	**0**

Claimed by **Florida** from **Pittsburgh** in Expansion Draft, June 24, 1993.

LAWRENCE, Mark

(LAW-rehns, MAHRK) **NYI**

Right wing. Shoots right. 6'4", 215 lbs. Born, Burlington, Ont., January 27, 1972. Minnesota's 4th choice, 118th overall, in 1991 Entry Draft.

Season	Club	League	GP	G	A	Pts	PIM	PP	SH	GW	S	%	+/–	TF	F%	H	SB	Min	GP	G	A	Pts	PIM	PP	SH	GW
1987-88	Burlington	OJHL-B	40	11	12	23	90	....	....	....	....	....	....	....	....	....	....	....	....	....	....	....	....	....	....	....
1988-89	Niagara Falls	OHL	63	9	27	36	142	....	....	....	....	....	....	....	....	....	....	....	....	....	....	....	....	....	....	....
1989-90	Niagara Falls	OHL	54	15	18	33	123	....	....	....	....	....	....	....	....	....	....	....	16	2	5	7	42	....	....	....
1990-91	Detroit	OHL	66	27	38	65	53	....	....	....	....	....	....	....	....	....	....	....	....	....	....	....	....	....	....	....
1991-92	Detroit	OHL	28	19	26	45	54	....	....	....	....	....	....	....	....	....	....	....	....	....	....	....	....	....	....	....
	North Bay	OHL	24	13	14	27	21	....	....	....	....	....	....	....	....	....	....	....	21	*23	12	35	36	....	....	....
1992-93	Dayton Bombers	ECHL	20	8	14	22	46	....	....	....	....	....	....	....	....	....	....	....	....	....	....	....	....	....	....	....
	Kalamazoo Wings	IHL	57	22	13	35	47	....	....	....	....	....	....	....	....	....	....	....	....	....	....	....	....	....	....	....
1993-94	Kalamazoo Wings	IHL	64	17	20	37	90	....	....	....	....	....	....	....	....	....	....	....	....	....	....	....	....	....	....	....
1994-95	Kalamazoo Wings	IHL	77	21	29	50	92	....	....	....	....	....	....	....	....	....	....	....	16	3	7	10	28	....	....	....
	Dallas	**NHL**	**2**	**0**	**0**	**0**	**0**	**0**	**0**	**0**	**3**	**0.0**	**0**	....	....	....	....	....	....	....	....	....	....	....	....	....
1995-96	**Dallas**	**NHL**	**13**	**0**	**1**	**1**	**17**	**0**	**0**	**0**	**13**	**0.0**	**0**	....	....	....	....	....	....	....	....	....	....	....	....	....
	Michigan K-Wings	IHL	55	15	14	29	92	....	....	....	....	....	....	....	....	....	....	....	10	3	4	7	30	....	....	....
1996-97	Michigan K-Wings	IHL	68	15	21	36	141	....	....	....	....	....	....	....	....	....	....	....	4	0	0	0	18	....	....	....
1997-98	**NY Islanders**	**NHL**	**2**	**0**	**0**	**0**	**2**	**0**	**0**	**0**	**4**	**0.0**	**0**	....	....	....	....	....	....	....	....	....	....	....	....	....
	Utah Grizzlies	IHL	80	36	28	64	102	....	....	....	....	....	....	....	....	....	....	....	4	1	1	2	4	....	....	....
1998-99	**NY Islanders**	**NHL**	**60**	**14**	**16**	**30**	**38**	**4**	**0**	**2**	**88**	**15.9**	**–8**	**0**	**0.0**	**99**	**10**	**14:08**	....	....	....	....	....	....	....	....
	Lowell	AHL	21	10	6	16	28	....	....	....	....	....	....	....	....	....	....	....	....	....	....	....	....	....	....	....
99-2000	**NY Islanders**	**NHL**	**29**	**1**	**5**	**6**	**26**	**0**	**0**	**0**	**33**	**3.0**	**–13**	**0**	**0.0**	**55**	**6**	**13:57**	....	....	....	....	....	....	....	....
	Chicago Wolves	IHL	16	4	6	10	32	....	....	....	....	....	....	....	....	....	....	....	....	....	....	....	....	....	....	....
	Lowell	AHL	18	4	4	8	8	....	....	....	....	....	....	....	....	....	....	....	7	2	2	4	10	....	....	....
	NHL Totals		**106**	**15**	**22**	**37**	**83**	**4**	**0**	**2**	**141**	**10.6**		**0**	**0.0**	**154**	**16**	**14:04**	....	....	....	....	....	....	....	....

Rights transferred to **Dallas** after **Minnesota** franchise relocated, June 9, 1993. Signed as a free agent by **NY Islanders**, August 25, 1997.

LEACH, Stephen

(LEECH, STEE-fen)

Right wing. Shoots right. 5'11", 197 lbs. Born, Cambridge, MA, January 16, 1966. Washington's 2nd choice, 34th overall, in 1984 Entry Draft.

Season	Club	League	GP	G	A	Pts	PIM	PP	SH	GW	S	%	+/–	TF	F%	H	SB	Min	GP	G	A	Pts	PIM	PP	SH	GW
1982-83	Matignon High	Hi-School	23	17	21	38	....	....	....	....	....	....	....	....	....	....	....	....	....	....	....	....	....	....	....	....
1983-84	Matignon High	Hi-School	21	27	22	49	49	....	....	....	....	....	....	....	....	....	....	....	....	....	....	....	....	....	....	....
1984-85	New Hampshire	H-East	41	12	25	37	53	....	....	....	....	....	....	....	....	....	....	....	....	....	....	....	....	....	....	....
1985-86	New Hampshire	H-East	25	22	6	28	30	....	....	....	....	....	....	....	....	....	....	....	....	....	....	....	....	....	....	....
	Washington	**NHL**	**11**	**1**	**1**	**2**	**2**	**0**	**0**	**0**	**4**	**25.0**	**0**	....	....	....	....	....	**6**	**0**	**1**	**1**	**0**	**0**	**0**	**0**
1986-87	**Washington**	**NHL**	**15**	**1**	**0**	**1**	**6**	**0**	**0**	**0**	**17**	**5.9**	**–4**	....	....	....	....	....	....	....	....	....	....	....	....	....
	Binghamton	AHL	54	18	21	39	39	....	....	....	....	....	....	....	....	....	....	....	13	3	1	4	6	....	....	....
1987-88	United States	Nat-Team	49	26	20	46	30	....	....	....	....	....	....	....	....	....	....	....	....	....	....	....	....	....	....	....
	United States	Olympics	6	1	2	3	0	....	....	....	....	....	....	....	....	....	....	....	....	....	....	....	....	....	....	....
	Washington	**NHL**	**8**	**1**	**1**	**2**	**17**	**0**	**0**	**1**	**5**	**20.0**	**2**	....	....	....	....	....	**9**	**2**	**1**	**3**	**0**	**0**	**0**	**1**
1988-89	**Washington**	**NHL**	**74**	**11**	**19**	**30**	**94**	**4**	**0**	**0**	**145**	**7.6**	**–4**	....	....	....	....	....	**6**	**1**	**0**	**1**	**12**	**1**	**0**	**0**
1989-90	**Washington**	**NHL**	**70**	**18**	**14**	**32**	**104**	**0**	**0**	**2**	**122**	**14.8**	**10**	....	....	....	....	....	**14**	**2**	**2**	**4**	**8**	**0**	**0**	**0**
1990-91	**Washington**	**NHL**	**68**	**11**	**19**	**30**	**99**	**4**	**0**	**1**	**134**	**8.2**	**–9**	....	....	....	....	....	**9**	**1**	**2**	**3**	**8**	**0**	**0**	**0**
1991-92	**Boston**	**NHL**	**78**	**31**	**29**	**60**	**147**	**12**	**0**	**4**	**243**	**12.8**	**–8**	....	....	....	....	....	**15**	**4**	**0**	**4**	**10**	**0**	**0**	**1**

Season	Club	League	GP	G	A	Pts	PIM	PP	SH	GW	S	%	+/-	TF	F%	H	SB	Min	GP	G	A	Pts	PIM	PP	SH	GW
			Regular Season																Playoffs							
1992-93	Boston	NHL	79	26	25	51	126	9	0	4	256	10.2	-6	....	....	....	....	....	4	1	1	2	2	0	0	0
1993-94	Boston	NHL	42	5	10	15	74	1	0	1	89	5.6	-10	....	....	....	....	....	5	0	1	1	2	0	0	0
1994-95	Boston	NHL	35	5	6	11	68	1	0	1	82	6.1	-3	....	....	....	....	....	....	....	....	....	....	....	....	....
1995-96	Boston	NHL	59	9	13	22	86	1	0	2	124	7.3	-4	....	....	....	....	....	....	....	....	....	....	....	....	....
	St. Louis	NHL	14	2	4	6	22	0	0	0	33	6.1	-3	....	....	....	....	....	11	3	2	5	10	1	0	1
1996-97	St. Louis	NHL	17	2	1	3	24	0	0	0	33	6.1	-2	....	....	....	....	....	6	0	0	0	33	0	0	0
1997-98	Carolina	NHL	45	4	5	9	42	1	1	2	60	6.7	-19	....	....	....	....	....	....	....	....	....	....	....	....	....
1998-99	Ottawa	NHL	9	0	2	2	6	0	0	0	4	0.0	-1	2	50.0	10	0	11:00	....	....	....	....	....	....	....	....
	Detroit Vipers	IHL	4	0	0	0	2	....	....	....	....	....	....	....	....	....	....	....	....	....	....	....	....	....	....	....
	Phoenix	NHL	22	1	1	2	37	0	0	0	23	4.3	-6	0	0.0	17	4	7:18	7	1	1	2	2	0	0	0
	Springfield	AHL	13	5	3	8	10	....	....	....	....	....	....	....	....	....	....	....	....	....	....	....	....	....	....	....
99-2000	Pittsburgh	NHL	56	2	3	5	24	0	0	1	41	4.9	-11	15	20.0	45	9	6:39	....	....	....	....	....	....	....	....
	Wilkes-Barre	AHL	4	2	3	5	4	....	....	....	....	....	....	....	....	....	....	....	....	....	....	....	....	....	....	....
	NHL Totals		702	130	153	283	978	33	1	19	1415	9.2		17	23.5	72	13	7:16	92	15	11	26	87	2	0	3

Traded to **Boston** by **Washington** for Randy Burridge, June 21, 1991. Traded to **St. Louis** by **Boston** for Kevin Sawyer and Steve Staios, March 8, 1996. Traded to **Carolina** by **St. Louis** for Alexander Godynyuk and Carolina's 6th round choice in 1998 Entry Draft, June 27, 1997. Signed as a free agent by **Ottawa**, October 4, 1998. Signed as a free agent by **Phoenix**, December 3, 1998. Signed as a free agent by **Pittsburgh**, October 19, 1999.

LEBEAU, Patrick

(leh-BOH, PA-trihk)

Left wing. Shoots left. 5'10", 172 lbs. Born, St. Jerome, Que., March 17, 1970. Montreal's 9th choice, 167th overall, in 1989 Entry Draft.

1984-85	Montreal L'est	QAAA	38	16	19	35	....	....	....	....	....	....	....	....	....	....	....	....	....	....	....	....	....	....	....	....
1985-86	Montreal L'est	QAAA	42	43	47	90	....	....	....	....	....	....	....	....	....	....	....	....	....	....	....	....	....	....	....	....
1986-87	Shawinigan	QMJHL	66	26	52	78	90	....	....	....	....	....	....	....	....	....	....	....	13	2	6	8	17	....	....	....
1987-88	Shawinigan	QMJHL	53	43	56	99	116	....	....	....	....	....	....	....	....	....	....	....	11	3	9	12	16	....	....	....
1988-89	Shawinigan	QMJHL	17	19	17	36	18	....	....	....	....	....	....	....	....	....	....	....	....	....	....	....	....	....	....	....
	St-Jean	QMJHL	49	43	70	113	71	....	....	....	....	....	....	....	....	....	....	....	4	4	3	7	6	....	....	....
1989-90	Victoriaville	QMJHL	72	68	*106	*174	109	....	....	....	....	....	....	....	....	....	....	....	16	7	15	22	12	....	....	....
1990-91	Montreal	NHL	2	1	1	2	0	0	0	0	3	33.3	0	....	....	....	....	....	....	....	....	....	....	....	....	....
	Fredericton	AHL	69	50	51	101	32	....	....	....	....	....	....	....	....	....	....	....	9	4	7	11	8	....	....	....
1991-92	Fredericton	AHL	55	33	38	71	48	....	....	....	....	....	....	....	....	....	....	....	7	4	5	9	10	....	....	....
	Canada	Nat-Team	7	4	2	6	6	....	....	....	....	....	....	....	....	....	....	....	....	....	....	....	....	....	....	....
	Canada	Olympics	8	1	3	4	4	....	....	....	....	....	....	....	....	....	....	....	....	....	....	....	....	....	....	....
1992-93	Calgary	NHL	1	0	0	0	0	0	0	0	0	0.0	0	....	....	....	....	....	....	....	....	....	....	....	....	....
	Salt Lake	IHL	75	40	60	100	65	....	....	....	....	....	....	....	....	....	....	....	....	....	....	....	....	....	....	....
1993-94	Florida	NHL	4	1	1	2	4	1	0	0	4	25.0	0	....	....	....	....	....	....	....	....	....	....	....	....	....
	Cincinnati	IHL	74	47	42	89	90	....	....	....	....	....	....	....	....	....	....	....	11	4	8	12	14	....	....	....
1994-95	ZSC Zurich	Switz.	36	27	25	52	22	....	....	....	....	....	....	....	....	....	....	....	5	4	6	10	6	....	....	....
1995-96	ZSC Zurich	Switz.	11	6	8	14	0	....	....	....	....	....	....	....	....	....	....	....	....	....	....	....	....	....	....	....
	Dusseldorfer EG	Germany	17	13	8	21	18	....	....	....	....	....	....	....	....	....	....	....	13	11	5	16	14	....	....	....
1996-97	ZSC Zurich	Switz.	38	27	19	46	26	....	....	....	....	....	....	....	....	....	....	....	4	1	0	1	25	....	....	....
1997-98	Chaux-de-Fonds	Switz.	40	17	45	62	32	....	....	....	....	....	....	....	....	....	....	....	....	....	....	....	....	....	....	....
1998-99	Pittsburgh	NHL	8	1	0	1	2	0	0	0	4	25.0	-2	0	0.0	11	3	9:32	....	....	....	....	....	....	....	....
99-2000	Ambri-Piotta	Switz.	44	*25	38	63	32	....	....	....	....	....	....	....	....	....	....	....	9	5	5	10	8	....	....	....
	NHL Totals		15	3	2	5	6	1	0	0	11	27.3		0	0.0	11	3	9:32	....	....	....	....	....	....	....	....

• Brother of Stephan • QMJHL First All-Star Team (1990) • AHL Second All-Star Team (1991) • Won Dudley "Red" Garrett Memorial Award (Top Rookie - AHL) (1991)

Traded to **Calgary** by **Montreal** for future considerations, September 27, 1986. Signed as a free agent by **Florida**, July 26, 1993. Signed as a free agent by **Pittsburgh**, October 18, 1998.

LeBOUTILLIER, Peter

(lih-BOO-tihl-eer, PEE-tuhr) **L.A.**

Right wing. Shoots right. 6'1", 190 lbs. Born, Minnedosa, Man., January 11, 1975. Anaheim's 5th choice, 133rd overall, in 1995 Entry Draft.

1989-90	Souris South	MAHA	55	91	109	200	64	....	....	....	....	....	....	....	....	....	....	....	....	....	....	....	....	....	....	....
1990-91	Souris South	MAHA	10	7	12	19	6	....	....	....	....	....	....	....	....	....	....	....	....	....	....	....	....	....	....	....
1991-92	Neepawa Natives	MJHL	35	11	14	25	99	....	....	....	....	....	....	....	....	....	....	....	....	....	....	....	....	....	....	....
	Brandon	WHL	2	0	0	0	5	....	....	....	....	....	....	....	....	....	....	....	....	....	....	....	....	....	....	....
1992-93	Red Deer Rebels	WHL	67	8	26	34	284	....	....	....	....	....	....	....	....	....	....	....	2	0	1	1	5	....	....	....
1993-94	Red Deer Rebels	WHL	66	19	20	39	300	....	....	....	....	....	....	....	....	....	....	....	2	0	1	1	4	....	....	....
1994-95	Red Deer Rebels	WHL	59	27	16	43	159	....	....	....	....	....	....	....	....	....	....	....	....	....	....	....	....	....	....	....
1995-96	Baltimore Bandits	AHL	68	7	9	16	228	....	....	....	....	....	....	....	....	....	....	....	11	0	0	0	33	....	....	....
1996-97	Anaheim	NHL	23	1	0	1	121	0	0	0	5	20.0	0	....	....	....	....	....	....	....	....	....	....	....	....	....
	Baltimore Bandits	AHL	47	6	12	18	175	....	....	....	....	....	....	....	....	....	....	....	....	....	....	....	....	....	....	....
1997-98	Anaheim	NHL	12	1	1	2	55	0	0	0	6	16.7	-1	....	....	....	....	....	....	....	....	....	....	....	....	....
	Cincinnati Ducks	AHL	51	9	11	20	143	....	....	....	....	....	....	....	....	....	....	....	....	....	....	....	....	....	....	....
1998-99	Cincinnati Ducks	AHL	63	12	12	24	189	....	....	....	....	....	....	....	....	....	....	....	3	0	0	0	2	....	....	....
99-2000	Cincinnati Ducks	AHL	19	2	1	3	69	....	....	....	....	....	....	....	....	....	....	....	....	....	....	....	....	....	....	....
	NHL Totals		35	2	1	3	176	0	0	0	11	18.2		....	....	....	....	....	....	....	....	....	....	....	....	....

• Re-entered NHL draft. Originally NY Islanders' 6th choice, 144th overall, in 1993 Entry Draft.

Signed as a free agent by **LA Kings**, August 11, 2000.

LECAVALIER, Vincent

(luh-KAV-uhl-YAY, VIHH-sehnt) **T.B.**

Center. Shoots left. 6'4", 180 lbs. Born, Ile Bizard, Que., April 21, 1980. Tampa Bay's 1st choice, 1st overall, in 1998 Entry Draft.

1995-96	Notre Dame	SAHA	22	52	52	104	....	....	....	....	....	....	....	....	....	....	....	....	....	....	....	....	....	....	....	....
1996-97	Rimouski Oceanic	QMJHL	64	42	61	103	38	....	....	....	....	....	....	....	....	....	....	....	4	4	3	7	2	....	....	....
1997-98	Rimouski Oceanic	QMJHL	58	44	71	115	117	....	....	....	....	....	....	....	....	....	....	....	18	*15	*26	*41	46	....	....	....
1998-99	Tampa Bay	NHL	82	13	15	28	23	2	0	2	125	10.4	-19	953	40.3	52	15	13:40	....	....	....	....	....	....	....	....
99-2000	Tampa Bay	NHL	80	25	42	67	43	6	0	3	166	15.1	-25	1288	44.4	116	19	19:18	....	....	....	....	....	....	....	....
	NHL Totals		162	38	57	95	66	8	0	5	291	13.1		2241	42.7	168	34	16:27	....	....	....	....	....	....	....	....

QMJHL First All-Star Team (1998) • Canadian Major Junior First All-Star Team (1998) • Canadian Major Junior Rookie of the Year (1997)

LeCLAIR, John

(luh-KLAIR, JAWN) **PHI.**

Left wing. Shoots left. 6'3", 226 lbs. Born, St. Albans, VT, July 5, 1969. Montreal's 2nd choice, 33rd overall, in 1987 Entry Draft.

1985-86	Bellows Academy	Hi-School	22	41	28	69	14	....	....	....	....	....	....	....	....	....	....	....	....	....	....	....	....	....	....	....
1986-87	Bellows Academy	Hi-School	23	44	40	84	14	....	....	....	....	....	....	....	....	....	....	....	....	....	....	....	....	....	....	....
1987-88	U. of Vermont	ECAC	31	12	22	34	62	....	....	....	....	....	....	....	....	....	....	....	....	....	....	....	....	....	....	....
1988-89	U. of Vermont	ECAC	18	9	12	21	40	....	....	....	....	....	....	....	....	....	....	....	....	....	....	....	....	....	....	....
1989-90	U. of Vermont	ECAC	10	10	6	16	38	....	....	....	....	....	....	....	....	....	....	....	....	....	....	....	....	....	....	....
1990-91	U. of Vermont	ECAC	33	25	20	45	58	....	....	....	....	....	....	....	....	....	....	....	....	....	....	....	....	....	....	....
	Montreal	NHL	10	2	5	7	2	0	0	1	12	16.7	1	....	....	....	....	....	3	0	0	0	0	0	0	0
1991-92	Montreal	NHL	59	8	11	19	14	3	0	0	73	11.0	5	....	....	....	....	....	8	1	1	2	4	0	0	0
	Fredericton	AHL	8	7	7	14	10	....	....	....	....	....	....	....	....	....	....	....	2	0	0	0	4	....	....	....
1992-93♦	Montreal	NHL	72	19	25	44	33	2	0	2	139	13.7	11	....	....	....	....	....	20	4	6	10	14	0	0	3
1993-94	Montreal	NHL	74	19	24	43	32	1	0	1	153	12.4	17	....	....	....	....	....	7	2	1	3	8	1	0	0
1994-95	Montreal	NHL	9	1	4	5	10	1	0	0	18	5.6	-1	....	....	....	....	....	....	....	....	....	....	....	....	....
	Philadelphia	NHL	37	25	24	49	20	5	0	7	113	22.1	21	....	....	....	....	....	15	5	7	12	4	1	0	1
1995-96	Philadelphia	NHL	82	51	46	97	64	19	0	10	270	18.9	21	....	....	....	....	....	11	6	5	11	6	4	0	1
1996-97	Philadelphia	NHL	82	50	47	97	58	10	0	5	324	15.4	44	....	....	....	....	....	19	9	12	21	10	4	0	3
1997-98	Philadelphia	NHL	82	51	36	87	32	16	0	9	303	16.8	30	....	....	....	....	....	5	1	1	2	8	1	0	1
	United States	Olympics	4	0	1	1	0	....	....	....	....	....	....	....	....	....	....	....	....	....	....	....	....	....	....	....

								Regular Season											Playoffs							
Season	Club	League	GP	G	A	Pts	PIM	PP	SH	GW	S	%	+/–	TF	F%	H	SB	Min	GP	G	A	Pts	PIM	PP	SH	GW
1998-99	**Philadelphia**	**NHL**	**76**	**43**	**47**	**90**	**30**	**16**	**0**	**7**	**246**	**17.5**	**36**	**7**	**14.3**	**86**	**10**	**21:03**	**6**	**3**	**0**	**3**	**12**	**2**	**0**	**0**
99-2000	**Philadelphia**	**NHL**	**82**	**40**	**37**	**77**	**36**	**13**	**0**	**7**	**249**	**16.1**	**8**	**7**	**28.6**	**106**	**26**	**20:18**	**18**	**6**	**7**	**13**	**6**	**4**	**0**	**2**
	NHL Totals		**665**	**309**	**306**	**615**	**331**	**86**	**0**	**49**	**1900**	**16.3**		**14**	**21.4**	**192**	**36**	**20:39**	**112**	**37**	**40**	**77**	**72**	**17**	**0**	**11**

ECAC Second All-Star Team (1991) • NHL First All-Star Team (1995, 1998) • NHL Second All-Star Team (1996, 1997, 1999) • Won Bud Light Plus/Minus Award (1997) • Won Bud Ice Plus/Minus Award (1999) • Played in NHL All-Star Game (1996, 1997, 1998, 1999, 2000)

• Missed majority of 1989-90 and 1990-91 seasons recovering from knee surgery, January 20, 1990. Traded to **Philadelphia** by **Montreal** with Eric Desjardins and Gilbert Dionne for Mark Recchi and Philadelphia's 3rd round choice (Martin Hohenberger) in 1995 Entry Draft, February 9, 1995.

LECLERC, Mike

(luh-KLUHRK, MIGHK) **ANA.**

Left wing. Shoots left. 6'1", 206 lbs. Born, Winnipeg, Man., November 10, 1976. Anaheim's 3rd choice, 55th overall, in 1995 Entry Draft.

Season	Club	League	GP	G	A	Pts	PIM	PP	SH	GW	S	%	+/–	TF	F%	H	SB	Min	GP	G	A	Pts	PIM	PP	SH	GW
1991-92	St. Boniface	MJHL	43	16	12	28	25	....	....	....	....	....	....	....	....	....	....	....	....	....	....	....	....	....	....	....
	Victoria Cougars	WHL	2	0	0	0	0	....	....	....	....	....	....	....	....	....	....	....	....	....	....	....	....	....	....	....
1992-93	Victoria Cougars	WHL	70	4	11	15	118	....	....	....	....	....	....	....	....	....	....	....	....	....	....	....	....	....	....	....
1993-94	Victoria Cougars	WHL	68	29	11	40	112	....	....	....	....	....	....	....	....	....	....	....	....	....	....	....	....	....	....	....
1994-95	Prince George	WHL	43	20	36	56	78	....	....	....	....	....	....	....	....	....	....	....	....	....	....	....	....	....	....	....
	Brandon	WHL	23	5	8	13	50	....	....	....	....	....	....	....	....	....	....	....	18	10	6	16	33	....	....	....
1995-96	Brandon	WHL	71	58	53	111	161	....	....	....	....	....	....	....	....	....	....	....	19	6	19	25	25	....	....	....
1996-97	**Anaheim**	**NHL**	**5**	**1**	**1**	**2**	**0**	**0**	**0**	**1**	**3**	**33.3**	**2**	....	....	....	....	....	**1**	**0**	**0**	**0**	**0**	**0**	**0**	**0**
	Baltimore Bandits	AHL	71	29	27	56	134	....	....	....	....	....	....	....	....	....	....	....	....	....	....	....	....	....	....	....
1997-98	**Anaheim**	**NHL**	**7**	**0**	**0**	**0**	**6**	**0**	**0**	**0**	**11**	**0.0**	**–6**	....	....	....	....	....	....	....	....	....	....	....	....	....
	Cincinnati Ducks	AHL	48	18	22	40	83	....	....	....	....	....	....	....	....	....	....	....	....	....	....	....	....	....	....	....
1998-99	**Anaheim**	**NHL**	**7**	**0**	**0**	**0**	**4**	**0**	**0**	**0**	**1**	**0.0**	**–2**	**0**	**0.0**	**9**	**2**	**5:52**	**1**	**0**	**0**	**0**	**0**	**0**	**0**	**0**
	Cincinnati Ducks	AHL	65	25	28	53	153	....	....	....	....	....	....	....	....	....	....	....	3	0	1	1	19	....	....	....
99-2000	**Anaheim**	**NHL**	**69**	**8**	**11**	**19**	**70**	**0**	**0**	**2**	**105**	**7.6**	**–15**	**1**	**0.0**	**145**	**11**	**12:08**	....	....	....	....	....	....	....	....
	NHL Totals		**88**	**9**	**12**	**21**	**80**	**0**	**0**	**3**	**120**	**7.5**		**1**	**0.0**	**154**	**13**	**11:33**	**2**	**0**	**0**	**0**	**0**	**0**	**0**	**0**

WHL East Second All-Star Team (1996)

LEDYARD, Grant

(LEHD-yahrd, GRANT)

Defense. Shoots left. 6'2", 195 lbs. Born, Winnipeg, Man., November 19, 1961.

Season	Club	League	GP	G	A	Pts	PIM	PP	SH	GW	S	%	+/–	TF	F%	H	SB	Min	GP	G	A	Pts	PIM	PP	SH	GW
1979-80	Fort Garry Blues	MJHL	49	13	24	37	90	....	....	....	....	....	....	....	....	....	....	....	....	....	....	....	....	....	....	....
1980-81	Saskatoon Blades	WHL	71	9	28	37	148	....	....	....	....	....	....	....	....	....	....	....	....	....	....	....	....	....	....	....
1981-82	Fort Garry Blues	MJHL	63	25	45	70	150	....	....	....	....	....	....	....	....	....	....	....	....	....	....	....	....	....	....	....
1982-83	Tulsa Oilers	CHL	80	13	29	42	115	....	....	....	....	....	....	....	....	....	....	....	....	....	....	....	....	....	....	....
1983-84	Tulsa Oilers	CHL	58	9	17	26	71	....	....	....	....	....	....	....	....	....	....	....	9	5	4	9	10	....	....	....
1984-85	**NY Rangers**	**NHL**	**42**	**8**	**12**	**20**	**53**	**1**	**0**	**1**	**91**	**8.8**	**8**	....	....	....	....	....	**3**	**0**	**2**	**2**	**4**	**0**	**0**	**0**
	New Haven	AHL	36	6	20	26	18	....	....	....	....	....	....	....	....	....	....	....	....	....	....	....	....	....	....	....
1985-86	**NY Rangers**	**NHL**	**27**	**2**	**9**	**11**	**20**	**0**	**0**	**0**	**57**	**3.5**	**–7**	....	....	....	....	....	....	....	....	....	....	....	....	....
	Los Angeles	**NHL**	**52**	**7**	**18**	**25**	**78**	**4**	**0**	**2**	**113**	**6.2**	**–22**	....	....	....	....	....	....	....	....	....	....	....	....	....
1986-87	**Los Angeles**	**NHL**	**67**	**14**	**23**	**37**	**93**	**5**	**0**	**1**	**144**	**9.7**	**–40**	....	....	....	....	....	**5**	**0**	**0**	**0**	**10**	**0**	**0**	**0**
1987-88	**Los Angeles**	**NHL**	**23**	**1**	**7**	**8**	**52**	**1**	**0**	**0**	**40**	**2.5**	**–7**	....	....	....	....	....	....	....	....	....	....	....	....	....
	New Haven	AHL	3	2	1	3	4	....	....	....	....	....	....	....	....	....	....	....	....	....	....	....	....	....	....	....
	Washington	**NHL**	**21**	**4**	**3**	**7**	**14**	**1**	**0**	**1**	**41**	**9.8**	**–4**	....	....	....	....	....	**14**	**1**	**0**	**1**	**30**	**0**	**0**	**0**
1988-89	**Washington**	**NHL**	**61**	**3**	**11**	**14**	**43**	**1**	**0**	**1**	**81**	**3.7**	**1**	....	....	....	....	....	....	....	....	....	....	....	....	....
	Buffalo	**NHL**	**13**	**1**	**5**	**6**	**8**	**0**	**0**	**1**	**25**	**4.0**	**1**	....	....	....	....	....	**5**	**1**	**2**	**3**	**2**	**0**	**0**	**0**
1989-90	**Buffalo**	**NHL**	**67**	**2**	**13**	**15**	**37**	**0**	**0**	**1**	**91**	**2.2**	**2**	....	....	....	....	....	....	....	....	....	....	....	....	....
1990-91	**Buffalo**	**NHL**	**60**	**8**	**23**	**31**	**46**	**2**	**1**	**1**	**118**	**6.8**	**13**	....	....	....	....	....	**6**	**3**	**3**	**6**	**10**	**0**	**0**	**0**
1991-92	**Buffalo**	**NHL**	**50**	**5**	**16**	**21**	**45**	**0**	**0**	**0**	**87**	**5.7**	**–4**	....	....	....	....	....	....	....	....	....	....	....	....	....
1992-93	**Buffalo**	**NHL**	**50**	**2**	**14**	**16**	**45**	**1**	**0**	**0**	**79**	**2.5**	**–2**	....	....	....	....	....	**8**	**0**	**0**	**0**	**8**	**0**	**0**	**0**
	Rochester	AHL	5	0	2	2	8	....	....	....	....	....	....	....	....	....	....	....	....	....	....	....	....	....	....	....
1993-94	**Dallas**	**NHL**	**84**	**9**	**37**	**46**	**42**	**6**	**0**	**1**	**177**	**5.1**	**7**	....	....	....	....	....	**9**	**1**	**2**	**3**	**6**	**0**	**0**	**1**
1994-95	**Dallas**	**NHL**	**38**	**5**	**13**	**18**	**20**	**4**	**0**	**0**	**79**	**6.3**	**6**	....	....	....	....	....	**3**	**0**	**0**	**0**	**2**	**0**	**0**	**0**
1995-96	**Dallas**	**NHL**	**73**	**5**	**19**	**24**	**20**	**2**	**0**	**1**	**123**	**4.1**	**–15**	....	....	....	....	....	....	....	....	....	....	....	....	....
1996-97	**Dallas**	**NHL**	**67**	**1**	**15**	**16**	**61**	**0**	**0**	**0**	**99**	**1.0**	**31**	....	....	....	....	....	**7**	**0**	**2**	**2**	**0**	**0**	**0**	**0**
1997-98	**Vancouver**	**NHL**	**49**	**2**	**13**	**15**	**14**	**1**	**0**	**0**	**57**	**3.5**	**–2**	....	....	....	....	....	....	....	....	....	....	....	....	....
	Boston	**NHL**	**22**	**2**	**7**	**9**	**6**	**1**	**0**	**0**	**33**	**6.1**	**–2**	....	....	....	....	....	**6**	**0**	**0**	**0**	**2**	**0**	**0**	**0**
1998-99	**Boston**	**NHL**	**47**	**4**	**8**	**12**	**33**	**1**	**0**	**2**	**47**	**8.5**	**–8**	**1**	**0.0**	**65**	**49**	**17:31**	**2**	**0**	**0**	**0**	**2**	**0**	**0**	**0**
99-2000	**Ottawa**	**NHL**	**40**	**2**	**4**	**6**	**8**	**0**	**0**	**1**	**42**	**4.8**	**–3**	**0**	**0.0**	**58**	**31**	**14:45**	**6**	**0**	**0**	**0**	**16**	**0**	**0**	**0**
	NHL Totals		**953**	**87**	**270**	**357**	**738**	**31**	**1**	**14**	**1624**	**5.4**		**1**	**0.0**	**123**	**80**	**16:15**	**74**	**6**	**11**	**17**	**92**	**0**	**0**	**1**

Won Bob Gassoff Trophy (CHL's Most Improved Defenseman) (1984)

Signed as a free agent by **NY Rangers**, July 7, 1982. Traded to **LA Kings** by **NY Rangers** with Rollie Melanson for LA Kings' 4th round choice (Mike Sullivan) in 1987 Entry Draft and Brian MacLellan, December 9, 1985. Traded to **Washington** by **LA Kings** for Craig Laughlin, February 9, 1988. Traded to **Buffalo** by **Washington** with Clint Malarchuk and Washington's 6th round choice (Brian Holzinger) in 1991 Entry Draft for Calle Johansson and Buffalo's 2nd round choice (Byron Dafoe) in 1989 Entry Draft, March 7, 1989. Signed as a free agent by **Dallas**, August 12, 1993. Signed as a free agent by **Vancouver**, July 17, 1997. Traded to **Boston** by **Vancouver** for Boston's 8th round choice (Curtis Valentine) in 1998 Entry Draft, March 3, 1998. Signed as a free agent by **Ottawa**, November 16, 1999.

LEEB, Brad

(LEEB, BRAD) **VAN.**

Right wing. Shoots right. 5'11", 180 lbs. Born, Red Deer, Alta., August 27, 1979.

Season	Club	League	GP	G	A	Pts	PIM	PP	SH	GW	S	%	+/–	TF	F%	H	SB	Min	GP	G	A	Pts	PIM	PP	SH	GW
1994-95	Red Deer Chiefs	AMHL	36	31	14	45	93	....	....	....	....	....	....	....	....	....	....	....	....	....	....	....	....	....	....	....
	Red Deer Rebels	WHL	3	0	0	0	4	....	....	....	....	....	....	....	....	....	....	....	....	....	....	....	....	....	....	....
1995-96	Red Deer Rebels	WHL	38	3	6	9	30	....	....	....	....	....	....	....	....	....	....	....	10	2	0	2	11	....	....	....
1996-97	Red Deer Rebels	WHL	70	15	20	35	76	....	....	....	....	....	....	....	....	....	....	....	16	3	3	6	6	....	....	....
1997-98	Red Deer Rebels	WHL	63	23	23	46	88	....	....	....	....	....	....	....	....	....	....	....	3	2	0	2	2	....	....	....
1998-99	Red Deer Rebels	WHL	64	32	47	79	84	....	....	....	....	....	....	....	....	....	....	....	9	5	9	14	10	....	....	....
99-2000	**Vancouver**	**NHL**	**2**	**0**	**0**	**0**	**2**	**0**	**0**	**0**	**3**	**0.0**	....	**0**	**0.0**	**0**	**0**	**0:00**	....	....	....	....	....	....	....	....
	Syracuse Crunch	AHL	61	19	18	37	50	....	....	....	....	....	....	....	....	....	....	....	4	0	0	0	6	....	....	....
	NHL Totals		**2**	**0**	**0**	**0**	**2**	**0**	**0**	**0**	**3**	**0.0**	....	**0**	**0.0**	**0**	**0**	....	....	....	....	....	....	....	....	....

WHL East Second All-Star Team (1999)

Signed as a free agent by **Vancouver**, October 8, 1999.

LEETCH, Brian

(LEECH, BRIGH-uhn) **NYR**

Defense. Shoots left. 6'1", 190 lbs. Born, Corpus Christi, TX, March 3, 1968. NY Rangers' 1st choice, 9th overall, in 1986 Entry Draft.

Season	Club	League	GP	G	A	Pts	PIM	PP	SH	GW	S	%	+/–	TF	F%	H	SB	Min	GP	G	A	Pts	PIM	PP	SH	GW
1983-84	Avon Old Farms	Hi-School	28	52	49	101	24	....	....	....	....	....	....	....	....	....	....	....	....	....	....	....	....	....	....	....
1984-85	Avon Old Farms	Hi-School	26	30	46	76	15	....	....	....	....	....	....	....	....	....	....	....	....	....	....	....	....	....	....	....
1985-86	Avon Old Farms	Hi-School	28	40	44	84	18	....	....	....	....	....	....	....	....	....	....	....	....	....	....	....	....	....	....	....
1986-87	Boston College	H-East	37	9	38	47	10	....	....	....	....	....	....	....	....	....	....	....	....	....	....	....	....	....	....	....
1987-88	United States	Nat-Team	50	13	61	74	38	....	....	....	....	....	....	....	....	....	....	....	....	....	....	....	....	....	....	....
	United States	Olympics	6	1	5	6	4	....	....	....	....	....	....	....	....	....	....	....	....	....	....	....	....	....	....	....
	NY Rangers	**NHL**	**17**	**2**	**12**	**14**	**0**	**1**	**0**	**1**	**40**	**5.0**	**5**	....	....	....	....	....	....	....	....	....	....	....	....	....
1988-89	**NY Rangers**	**NHL**	**68**	**23**	**48**	**71**	**50**	**8**	**3**	**1**	**268**	**8.6**	**8**	....	....	....	....	....	**4**	**3**	**2**	**5**	**2**	**2**	**0**	**0**
1989-90	**NY Rangers**	**NHL**	**72**	**11**	**45**	**56**	**26**	**5**	**0**	**2**	**222**	**5.0**	**–18**	....	....	....	....	....	....	....	....	....	....	....	....	....
1990-91	**NY Rangers**	**NHL**	**80**	**16**	**72**	**88**	**42**	**6**	**0**	**4**	**206**	**7.8**	**2**	....	....	....	....	....	**6**	**1**	**3**	**4**	**0**	**0**	**0**	**0**
1991-92	**NY Rangers**	**NHL**	**80**	**22**	**80**	**102**	**26**	**10**	**1**	**3**	**245**	**9.0**	**25**	....	....	....	....	....	**13**	**4**	**11**	**15**	**4**	**1**	**1**	**0**
1992-93	**NY Rangers**	**NHL**	**36**	**6**	**30**	**36**	**26**	**2**	**1**	**1**	**150**	**4.0**	**2**	....	....	....	....	....	....	....	....	....	....	....	....	....
1993-94♦	**NY Rangers**	**NHL**	**84**	**23**	**56**	**79**	**67**	**17**	**1**	**4**	**328**	**7.0**	**28**	....	....	....	....	....	**23**	**11**	***23**	***34**	**6**	**4**	**0**	**4**
1994-95	**NY Rangers**	**NHL**	**48**	**9**	**32**	**41**	**18**	**3**	**0**	**2**	**182**	**4.9**	**0**	....	....	....	....	....	**10**	**6**	**8**	**14**	**8**	**3**	**0**	**1**
1995-96	**NY Rangers**	**NHL**	**82**	**15**	**70**	**85**	**30**	**7**	**0**	**3**	**276**	**5.4**	**12**	....	....	....	....	....	**11**	**1**	**6**	**7**	**4**	**1**	**0**	**0**
1996-97	**NY Rangers**	**NHL**	**82**	**20**	**58**	**78**	**40**	**9**	**0**	**2**	**256**	**7.8**	**31**	....	....	....	....	....	**15**	**2**	**8**	**10**	**6**	**1**	**0**	**1**
1997-98	**NY Rangers**	**NHL**	**76**	**17**	**33**	**50**	**32**	**11**	**0**	**2**	**230**	**7.4**	**–36**	....	....	....	....	....	....	....	....	....	....	....	....	....
	United States	Olympics	4	1	1	2	0	....	....	....	....	....	....	....	....	....	....	....	....	....	....	....	....	....	....	....

			Regular Season																Playoffs							
Season	Club	League	GP	G	A	Pts	PIM	PP	SH	GW	S	%	+/-	TF	F%	H	SB	Min	GP	G	A	Pts	PIM	PP	SH	GW
1998-99	NY Rangers	NHL	82	13	42	55	42	4	0	1	184	7.1	–7	0	0.0	173	212	29:52	....	....	....	....	....	....	....	....
99-2000	NY Rangers	NHL	50	7	19	26	20	3	0	2	124	5.6	–16	0	0.0	82	94	26:57	....	....	....	....	....	....	....	....
	NHL Totals		857	184	597	781	419	86	6	28	2711	6.8		0	0.0	255	306	28:46	82	28	61	89	30	12	1	6

Hockey East First All-Star Team (1987) • NCAA East First All-American Team (1987) • NHL All-Rookie Team (1989) • Won Calder Memorial Trophy (1989) • NHL Second All-Star Team (1991, 1994, 1996) • Won James Norris Memorial Trophy (1992, 1997) • NHL First All-Star Team (1992, 1997) • Won Conn Smythe Trophy (1994) • Played in NHL All-Star Game (1990, 1991, 1992, 1994, 1996, 1997, 1998)

LEFEBVRE, Patrice

(luh-FAYV, puh-TREES)

Right wing. Shoots left. 5'6", 160 lbs. Born, Montreal, Que., June 28, 1967.

Season	Club	League	GP	G	A	Pts	PIM	PP	SH	GW	S	%	+/-	TF	F%	H	SB	Min	GP	G	A	Pts	PIM	PP	SH	GW
1983-84	Mtl-Concordia	QAAA	42	36	45	81	....	....	....	....	....	....	....	....	....	....	....	....	....	....	....	....	....	....	....	....
1984-85	Shawinigan	QMJHL	68	28	52	80	63	....	....	....	....	....	....	....	....	....	....	....	....	....	....	....	....	....	....	....
1985-86	Shawinigan	QMJHL	69	38	98	136	119	....	....	....	....	....	....	....	....	....	....	....	....	....	....	....	....	....	....	....
1986-87	Shawinigan	QMJHL	69	57	122	179	144	....	....	....	....	....	....	....	....	....	....	....	12	9	16	25	19	....	....	....
1987-88	Shawinigan	QMJHL	70	64	136	200	142	....	....	....	....	....	....	....	....	....	....	....	....	....	....	....	....	....	....	....
1988-89	Paris Volants	France	38	32	36	68	46	....	....	....	....	....	....	....	....	....	....	....	....	....	....	....	....	....	....	....
1989-90	HC Ajoie	Switz	32	23	23	46	....	....	....	....	....	....	....	....	....	....	....	....	....	....	....	....	....	....	....	....
1990-91	HC Langnau	Switz-2	3	1	8	9	....	....	....	....	....	....	....	....	....	....	....	....	....	....	....	....	....	....	....	....
	Louisville	ECHL	26	17	26	43	32	....	....	....	....	....	....	....	....	....	....	....	7	2	5	7	8	....	....	....
	Milwaukee	IHL	16	6	4	10	13	....	....	....	....	....	....	....	....	....	....	....	....	....	....	....	....	....	....	....
	Springfield	AHL	1	0	0	0	2	....	....	....	....	....	....	....	....	....	....	....	....	....	....	....	....	....	....	....
1991-92	HC Kloten	Switz	10	4	12	16	....	....	....	....	....	....	....	....	....	....	....	....	....	....	....	....	....	....	....	....
	HC Sierre	Switz-2	3	3	2	5	....	....	....	....	....	....	....	....	....	....	....	....	....	....	....	....	....	....	....	....
1992-93	Billingham	Britain	36	56	109	165	75	....	....	....	....	....	....	....	....	....	....	....	6	5	13	18	26	....	....	....
1993-94	Las Vegas	IHL	76	31	67	98	71	....	....	....	....	....	....	....	....	....	....	....	5	3	4	7	4	....	....	....
1994-95	Las Vegas	IHL	75	32	62	94	74	....	....	....	....	....	....	....	....	....	....	....	10	2	3	5	2	....	....	....
1995-96	Las Vegas	IHL	77	36	78	114	85	....	....	....	....	....	....	....	....	....	....	....	15	9	11	20	12	....	....	....
1996-97	Las Vegas	IHL	82	21	73	94	94	....	....	....	....	....	....	....	....	....	....	....	3	0	2	2	2	....	....	....
1997-98	Las Vegas	IHL	77	27	*89	*116	113	....	....	....	....	....	....	....	....	....	....	....	4	2	0	2	2	....	....	....
1998-99	Las Vegas	IHL	42	11	26	37	40	....	....	....	....	....	....	....	....	....	....	....	....	....	....	....	....	....	....	....
	Washington	**NHL**	**3**	**0**	**0**	**0**	**2**	**0**	**0**	**0**	**2**	**0.0**	**–2**	**0**	**0.0**	**0**	**1**	**11:11**	....	....	....	....	....	....	....	....
	Long Beach	IHL	14	1	12	13	8	....	....	....	....	....	....	....	....	....	....	....	8	0	3	3	2	....	....	....
99-2000	Adler Mannheim	DEL	54	20	31	51	148	....	....	....	....	....	....	....	....	....	....	....	5	1	2	3	4	....	....	....
	NHL Totals		**3**	**0**	**0**	**0**	**2**	**0**	**0**	**0**	**2**	**0.0**		**0**	**0.0**	**0**	**1**	**11:11**	....	....	....	....	....	....	....	....

QMJHL Second All-Star Team (1986) • QMJHL First All-Star Team (1987, 1988) • IHL First All-Star Team (1998) • Won Leo P. Lamoureux Memorial Trophy (Top Scorer - IHL) (1998) • Won James Gatschene Memorial Trophy (MVP - IHL) (1998)

Signed as a free agent by **Washington**, December 18, 1998. • Played w/ RHI's Montreal Roadrunners in 1994 (8-10-18-28-10) and 1997 (4-5-10-15-13).

LEFEBVRE, Sylvain

(luh-FAYV, SIHL-veh) **NYR**

Defense. Shoots left. 6'2", 205 lbs. Born, Richmond, Que., October 14, 1967.

Season	Club	League	GP	G	A	Pts	PIM	PP	SH	GW	S	%	+/-	TF	F%	H	SB	Min	GP	G	A	Pts	PIM	PP	SH	GW
1984-85	Laval Titan	QMJHL	66	7	5	12	31	....	....	....	....	....	....	....	....	....	....	....	....	....	....	....	....	....	....	....
1985-86	Laval Titan	QMJHL	71	8	17	25	48	....	....	....	....	....	....	....	....	....	....	....	14	1	0	1	25	....	....	....
1986-87	Laval Titan	QMJHL	70	10	36	46	44	....	....	....	....	....	....	....	....	....	....	....	15	1	6	7	12	....	....	....
1987-88	Sherbrooke	AHL	79	3	24	27	73	....	....	....	....	....	....	....	....	....	....	....	6	2	3	5	4	....	....	....
1988-89	Sherbrooke	AHL	77	15	32	47	119	....	....	....	....	....	....	....	....	....	....	....	6	1	3	4	4	....	....	....
1989-90	**Montreal**	**NHL**	**68**	**3**	**10**	**13**	**61**	**0**	**0**	**0**	**89**	**3.4**	**18**	....	....	....	....	....	**6**	**0**	**0**	**0**	**2**	**0**	**0**	**0**
1990-91	**Montreal**	**NHL**	**63**	**5**	**18**	**23**	**30**	**1**	**0**	**1**	**76**	**6.6**	**–11**	....	....	....	....	....	**11**	**1**	**0**	**1**	**6**	**0**	**0**	**0**
1991-92	**Montreal**	**NHL**	**69**	**3**	**14**	**17**	**91**	**0**	**0**	**0**	**85**	**3.5**	**9**	....	....	....	....	....	**2**	**0**	**0**	**0**	**2**	**0**	**0**	**0**
1992-93	**Toronto**	**NHL**	**81**	**2**	**12**	**14**	**90**	**0**	**0**	**0**	**81**	**2.5**	**8**	....	....	....	....	....	**21**	**3**	**3**	**6**	**20**	**0**	**0**	**0**
1993-94	**Toronto**	**NHL**	**84**	**2**	**9**	**11**	**79**	**0**	**0**	**0**	**96**	**2.1**	**33**	....	....	....	....	....	**18**	**0**	**3**	**3**	**16**	**0**	**0**	**0**
1994-95	**Quebec**	**NHL**	**48**	**2**	**11**	**13**	**17**	**0**	**0**	**0**	**81**	**2.5**	**13**	....	....	....	....	....	**6**	**0**	**2**	**2**	**2**	**0**	**0**	**0**
1995-96♦	**Colorado**	**NHL**	**75**	**5**	**11**	**16**	**49**	**2**	**0**	**0**	**115**	**4.3**	**26**	....	....	....	....	....	**22**	**0**	**5**	**5**	**12**	**0**	**0**	**0**
1996-97	**Colorado**	**NHL**	**71**	**2**	**11**	**13**	**30**	**1**	**0**	**0**	**77**	**2.6**	**12**	....	....	....	....	....	**17**	**0**	**0**	**0**	**25**	**0**	**0**	**0**
1997-98	**Colorado**	**NHL**	**81**	**0**	**10**	**10**	**48**	**0**	**0**	**0**	**66**	**0.0**	**2**	....	....	....	....	....	**7**	**0**	**0**	**0**	**4**	**0**	**0**	**0**
1998-99	**Colorado**	**NHL**	**76**	**2**	**18**	**20**	**48**	**0**	**0**	**0**	**64**	**3.1**	**18**	**0**	**0.0**	**120**	**79**	**20:56**	**19**	**0**	**1**	**1**	**12**	**0**	**0**	**0**
99-2000	**NY Rangers**	**NHL**	**82**	**2**	**10**	**12**	**43**	**0**	**0**	**0**	**67**	**3.0**	**–13**	**0**	**0.0**	**181**	**142**	**18:36**	....	....	....	....	....	....	....	....
	NHL Totals		**798**	**28**	**134**	**162**	**586**	**4**	**0**	**1**	**897**	**3.1**		**0**	**0.0**	**301**	**221**	**19:43**	**129**	**4**	**14**	**18**	**101**	**0**	**0**	**0**

AHL Second All-Star Team (1989)

Signed as a free agent by **Montreal**, September 24, 1986. Traded to **Toronto** by **Montreal** for Toronto's 3rd round choice (Martin Belanger) in 1994 Entry Draft, August 20, 1992. Traded to **Quebec** by **Toronto** with Wendel Clark, Landon Wilson and Toronto's 1st round choice (Jeffrey Kealty) in 1994 Entry Draft for Mats Sundin, Garth Butcher, Todd Warriner and Philadelphia's 1st round choice (previously acquired by Quebec - later traded to Washington - Washington selected Nolan Baumgartner) in 1994 Entry Draft, June 28, 1994. Transferred to **Colorado** after **Quebec** franchise relocated, June 21, 1995. Signed as a free agent by **NY Rangers**, July 22, 1999.

LEGWAND, David

(LEHG-wuhnd, DAY-vihd) **NSH.**

Center. Shoots left. 6'2", 190 lbs. Born, Detroit, MI, August 17, 1980. Nashville's 1st choice, 2nd overall, in 1998 Entry Draft.

Season	Club	League	GP	G	A	Pts	PIM	PP	SH	GW	S	%	+/-	TF	F%	H	SB	Min	GP	G	A	Pts	PIM	PP	SH	GW
1996-97	Detroit	MNHL	44	21	41	62	58	....	....	....	....	....	....	....	....	....	....	....	....	....	....	....	....	....	....	....
1997-98	Plymouth Whalers	OHL	59	54	51	105	56	....	....	....	....	....	....	....	....	....	....	....	15	8	12	20	24	....	....	....
1998-99	Plymouth Whalers	OHL	55	31	49	80	65	....	....	....	....	....	....	....	....	....	....	....	11	3	8	11	8	....	....	....
	Nashville	**NHL**	**1**	**0**	**0**	**0**	**0**	**0**	**0**	**0**	**2**	**0.0**	**0**	**9**	**55.6**	**0**	**1**	**12:50**	....	....	....	....	....	....	....	....
99-2000	**Nashville**	**NHL**	**71**	**13**	**15**	**28**	**30**	**4**	**0**	**2**	**111**	**11.7**	**–6**	**637**	**41.6**	**48**	**27**	**14:43**	....	....	....	....	....	....	....	....
	NHL Totals		**72**	**13**	**15**	**28**	**30**	**4**	**0**	**2**	**113**	**11.5**		**646**	**41.8**	**48**	**28**	**14:42**	....	....	....	....	....	....	....	....

OHL First All-Star Team (1998) • Canadian Major Junior Rookie of the Year (1998)

LEHTINEN, Jere

(lehkh-TIH-nehn, YUH-ree) **DAL.**

Right wing. Shoots right. 6', 200 lbs. Born, Espoo, Finland, June 24, 1973. Minnesota's 3rd choice, 88th overall, in 1992 Entry Draft.

Season	Club	League	GP	G	A	Pts	PIM	PP	SH	GW	S	%	+/-	TF	F%	H	SB	Min	GP	G	A	Pts	PIM	PP	SH	GW
1989-90	Kiekoo-67 Turku	Finn-Jr.	32	23	23	46	6	....	....	....	....	....	....	....	....	....	....	....	5	0	3	3	0	....	....	....
1990-91	Kiekko-Espoo	Finn-Jr.	3	3	1	4	0	....	....	....	....	....	....	....	....	....	....	....	....	....	....	....	....	....	....	....
	Kiekko-Espoo	Finland-2	32	15	9	24	12	....	....	....	....	....	....	....	....	....	....	....	....	....	....	....	....	....	....	....
1991-92	Kiekoo-67 Turku	Finn-Jr.	8	5	4	9	2	....	....	....	....	....	....	....	....	....	....	....	....	....	....	....	....	....	....	....
	Kiekko-Espoo	Finland-2	43	32	17	49	6	....	....	....	....	....	....	....	....	....	....	....	....	....	....	....	....	....	....	....
1992-93	Kiekoo-67 Turku	Finn-Jr.	4	5	3	8	8	....	....	....	....	....	....	....	....	....	....	....	....	....	....	....	....	....	....	....
	Kiekko-Espoo	Finland	45	13	14	27	6	....	....	....	....	....	....	....	....	....	....	....	....	....	....	....	....	....	....	....
1993-94	TPS Turku	Finland	42	19	20	39	6	....	....	....	....	....	....	....	....	....	....	....	11	*11	2	13	*2	....	....	....
	Finland	Olympics	8	3	0	3	0	....	....	....	....	....	....	....	....	....	....	....	....	....	....	....	....	....	....	....
1994-95	TPS Turku	Finland	39	19	23	42	33	....	....	....	....	....	....	....	....	....	....	....	13	*8	6	14	4	....	....	....
1995-96	**Dallas**	**NHL**	**57**	**6**	**22**	**28**	**16**	**0**	**0**	**1**	**109**	**5.5**	**5**	....	....	....	....	....	....	....	....	....	....	....	....	....
	Michigan K-Wings	IHL	1	1	0	1	0	....	....	....	....	....	....	....	....	....	....	....	....	....	....	....	....	....	....	....
1996-97	**Dallas**	**NHL**	**63**	**16**	**27**	**43**	**2**	**3**	**1**	**2**	**134**	**11.9**	**26**	....	....	....	....	....	**7**	**2**	**2**	**4**	**0**	**0**	**0**	**0**
1997-98	**Dallas**	**NHL**	**72**	**23**	**19**	**42**	**20**	**7**	**2**	**6**	**201**	**11.4**	**19**	....	....	....	....	....	**12**	**3**	**5**	**8**	**2**	**1**	**0**	**0**
	Finland	Olympics	6	4	2	6	2	....	....	....	....	....	....	....	....	....	....	....	....	....	....	....	....	....	....	....
1998-99♦	**Dallas**	**NHL**	**74**	**20**	**32**	**52**	**18**	**7**	**1**	**2**	**173**	**11.6**	**29**	**9**	**33.3**	**72**	**47**	**19:36**	**23**	**10**	**3**	**13**	**2**	**1**	**1**	**0**
99-2000	**Dallas**	**NHL**	**17**	**3**	**5**	**8**	**0**	**0**	**0**	**1**	**29**	**10.3**	**1**	**0**	**0.0**	**17**	**6**	**17:31**	**13**	**1**	**5**	**6**	**2**	**0**	**0**	**0**
	NHL Totals		**283**	**68**	**105**	**173**	**56**	**17**	**4**	**12**	**646**	**10.5**		**9**	**33.3**	**89**	**53**	**19:13**	**55**	**16**	**15**	**31**	**6**	**2**	**1**	**0**

Finnish First All-Star Team (1995) • Won Frank J. Selke Trophy (1998, 1999) • Played in NHL All-Star Game (1998)

Rights transferred to **Dallas** after **Minnesota** franchise relocated, June 9, 1993. • Missed majority of 1999-2000 season recovering from broken leg suffered in game vs. Nashville, October 16, 1999.

LEMIEUX, Claude

(lehm-YOO, KLOHD)

Right wing. Shoots right. 6'1", 215 lbs. Born, Buckingham, Que., July 16, 1965. Montreal's 2nd choice, 26th overall, in 1983 Entry Draft.

			Regular Season																Playoffs							
Season	Club	League	GP	G	A	Pts	PIM	PP	SH	GW	S	%	+/-	TF	F%	H	SB	Min	GP	G	A	Pts	PIM	PP	SH	GW
1981-82	Richelieu Regents	QAAA	48	24	48	72	96	....	....	....	....	....	....	....	....	....	....	....	....	....	....	....	....	....	....	....
1982-83	Trois-Rivieres	QMJHL	62	28	38	66	187	....	....	....	....	....	....	....	....	....	....	....	4	1	0	1	30	....	....	....
1983-84	Verdun Juniors	QMJHL	51	41	45	86	225	....	....	....	....	....	....	....	....	....	....	....	9	8	12	20	63	....	....	....
	Montreal	NHL	8	1	1	2	12	0	0	0	7	14.3	-2	....	....	....	....	....	....	....	....	....	....	....	....	....
	Nova Scotia	AHL	....	....	....	....	....	....	....	....	....	....	....	....	....	....	....	....	2	1	0	1	0	....	....	....
1984-85	Verdun	QMJHL	52	58	66	124	152	....	....	....	....	....	....	....	....	....	....	....	14	23	17	40	38	....	....	....
	Montreal	NHL	1	0	1	1	7	0	0	0	0	0.0	1	....	....	....	....	....	....	....	....	....	....	....	....	....
1985-86♦	Montreal	NHL	10	1	2	3	22	1	0	0	16	6.3	-6	....	....	....	....	....	20	10	6	16	68	4	0	4
	Sherbrooke	AHL	58	21	32	53	145	....	....	....	....	....	....	....	....	....	....	....	....	....	....	....	....	....	....	....
1986-87	Montreal	NHL	76	27	26	53	156	5	0	1	184	14.7	0	....	....	....	....	....	17	4	9	13	41	2	0	0
1987-88	Montreal	NHL	78	31	30	61	137	6	0	3	241	12.9	16	....	....	....	....	....	11	3	2	5	20	0	0	2
1988-89	Montreal	NHL	69	29	22	51	136	7	0	3	220	13.2	14	....	....	....	....	....	18	4	3	7	58	0	0	0
1989-90	Montreal	NHL	39	8	10	18	106	3	0	1	104	7.7	-8	....	....	....	....	....	11	1	3	4	38	0	0	1
1990-91	New Jersey	NHL	78	30	17	47	105	10	0	2	271	11.1	-8	....	....	....	....	....	7	4	0	4	34	2	0	1
1991-92	New Jersey	NHL	74	41	27	68	109	13	1	8	296	13.9	9	....	....	....	....	....	7	4	3	7	26	1	0	0
1992-93	New Jersey	NHL	77	30	51	81	155	13	0	3	311	9.6	3	....	....	....	....	....	5	2	0	2	19	1	0	0
1993-94	New Jersey	NHL	79	18	26	44	86	5	0	5	181	9.9	13	....	....	....	....	....	20	7	11	18	44	0	0	2
1994-95♦	New Jersey	NHL	45	6	13	19	86	1	0	1	117	5.1	2	....	....	....	....	....	20	*13	3	16	20	0	0	3
1995-96♦	Colorado	NHL	79	39	32	71	117	9	2	10	315	12.4	14	....	....	....	....	....	19	5	7	12	55	3	0	0
1996-97	Colorado	NHL	45	11	17	28	43	5	0	4	168	6.5	-4	....	....	....	....	....	17	*13	10	23	32	4	0	4
1997-98	Colorado	NHL	78	26	27	53	115	11	1	1	261	10.0	-7	....	....	....	....	....	7	3	3	6	8	1	0	1
1998-99	Colorado	NHL	82	27	24	51	102	11	0	8	292	9.2	0	43	41.9	110	26	21:14	19	3	11	14	26	1	0	0
99-2000	Colorado	NHL	13	3	6	9	4	1	0	0	36	8.3	0	2	50.0	20	2	18:40	....	....	....	....	....	....	....	....
	♦ New Jersey	NHL	70	17	21	38	86	7	0	3	221	7.7	-3	49	28.6	116	15	17:55	23	4	6	10	28	1	0	0
	NHL Totals		1001	345	353	698	1584	107	4	53	3241	10.6		94	35.1	246	43	19:37	221	80	77	157	517	20	0	18

QMJHL Second All-Star Team (1984) • QMJHL First All-Star Team (1985) • Won Conn Smythe Trophy (1995)

• Missed majority of 1989-90 season recovering from abdominal injury suffered in game vs. Boston, October 9, 1989. Traded to **New Jersey** by **Montreal** for Sylvain Turgeon, September 4, 1990. Traded to **NY Islanders** by **New Jersey** for Steve Thomas, October 3, 1995. Traded to **Colorado** by **NY Islanders** for Wendel Clark, October 3, 1995. Traded to **New Jersey** by **Colorado** with Colorado's 1st (David Hale) and 2nd (Matt DeMarchi) round choices in 2000 Entry Draft for Brian Rolston, New Jersey's 1st round choice (later traded to Boston - Boston selected Martin Samuelsson) in 2000 Entry Draft and future considerations, November 3, 1999.

LEROUX, Francois

(leh-ROO, FRAN-swuh) **PHX.**

Defense. Shoots left. 6'6", 247 lbs. Born, Ste.-Adele, Que., April 18, 1970. Edmonton's 1st choice, 19th overall, in 1988 Entry Draft.

			Regular Season																Playoffs							
Season	Club	League	GP	G	A	Pts	PIM	PP	SH	GW	S	%	+/-	TF	F%	H	SB	Min	GP	G	A	Pts	PIM	PP	SH	GW
1986-87	Laval Laurentide	QAAA	42	5	11	16	76	....	....	....	....	....	....	....	....	....	....	....	....	....	....	....	....	....	....	....
1987-88	St-Jean Lynx	QMJHL	58	3	8	11	143	....	....	....	....	....	....	....	....	....	....	....	7	2	0	2	21	....	....	....
1988-89	St-Jean Lynx	QMJHL	57	8	34	42	185	....	....	....	....	....	....	....	....	....	....	....	....	....	....	....	....	....	....	....
	Edmonton	NHL	2	0	0	0	0	0	0	0	0	0.0	1	....	....	....	....	....	....	....	....	....	....	....	....	....
1989-90	Victoriaville Tigres	QMJHL	54	4	33	37	169	....	....	....	....	....	....	....	....	....	....	....	....	....	....	....	....	....	....	....
	Edmonton	NHL	3	0	1	1	0	0	0	0	0	0.0	-2	....	....	....	....	....	....	....	....	....	....	....	....	....
1990-91	Edmonton	NHL	1	0	2	2	0	0	0	0	1	0.0	1	....	....	....	....	....	....	....	....	....	....	....	....	....
	Cape Breton	AHL	71	2	7	9	124	....	....	....	....	....	....	....	....	....	....	....	4	0	1	1	19	....	....	....
1991-92	Edmonton	NHL	4	0	0	0	7	0	0	0	0	0.0	-1	....	....	....	....	....	....	....	....	....	....	....	....	....
	Cape Breton	AHL	61	7	22	29	114	....	....	....	....	....	....	....	....	....	....	....	5	0	0	0	8	....	....	....
1992-93	Edmonton	NHL	1	0	0	0	4	0	0	0	0	0.0	0	....	....	....	....	....	....	....	....	....	....	....	....	....
	Cape Breton	AHL	55	10	24	34	139	....	....	....	....	....	....	....	....	....	....	....	16	0	5	5	29	....	....	....
1993-94	Ottawa	NHL	23	0	1	1	70	0	0	0	8	0.0	-4	....	....	....	....	....	....	....	....	....	....	....	....	....
	P.E.I. Senators	AHL	25	4	6	10	52	....	....	....	....	....	....	....	....	....	....	....	....	....	....	....	....	....	....	....
1994-95	P.E.I. Senators	AHL	45	4	14	18	137	....	....	....	....	....	....	....	....	....	....	....	....	....	....	....	....	....	....	....
	Pittsburgh	NHL	40	0	2	2	114	0	0	0	19	0.0	7	....	....	....	....	....	12	0	2	2	14	0	0	0
1995-96	Pittsburgh	NHL	66	2	9	11	161	0	0	0	43	4.7	2	....	....	....	....	....	18	1	1	2	20	0	0	1
1996-97	Pittsburgh	NHL	59	0	3	3	81	0	0	0	5	0.0	-3	....	....	....	....	....	3	0	0	0	0	0	0	0
1997-98	Colorado	NHL	50	1	2	3	140	0	0	0	14	7.1	-3	....	....	....	....	....	....	....	....	....	....	....	....	....
1998-99	Grand Rapids	IHL	13	1	1	2	22	....	....	....	....	....	....	....	....	....	....	....	....	....	....	....	....	....	....	....
99-2000	Springfield	AHL	64	3	6	9	162	....	....	....	....	....	....	....	....	....	....	....	5	0	0	0	2	....	....	....
	NHL Totals		249	3	20	23	577	0	0	0	90	3.3		....	....	....	....	....	33	1	3	4	34	0	0	1

Claimed on waivers by **Ottawa** from **Edmonton**, October 6, 1993. Claimed by **Pittsburgh** from **Ottawa** in Waiver Draft, January 18, 1995. Traded to **Colorado** by **Pittsburgh** for Colorado's 3rd round choice (David Cameron) in 1998 Entry Draft, September 28, 1997. Signed as a free agent by **Grand Rapids** (IHL), February 18, 1999. Signed as a free agent by **Phoenix**, July 20, 1999.

LEROUX, Jean-Yves

(leh-ROO, JOH-EE-vehs) **CHI.**

Left wing. Shoots left. 6'2", 211 lbs. Born, Montreal, Que., June 24, 1976. Chicago's 2nd choice, 40th overall, in 1994 Entry Draft.

			Regular Season																Playoffs							
Season	Club	League	GP	G	A	Pts	PIM	PP	SH	GW	S	%	+/-	TF	F%	H	SB	Min	GP	G	A	Pts	PIM	PP	SH	GW
1991-92	Mtl-Bourassa	QAAA	35	14	31	45	29	....	....	....	....	....	....	....	....	....	....	....	....	....	....	....	....	....	....	....
1992-93	Beauport	QMJHL	62	20	25	45	33	....	....	....	....	....	....	....	....	....	....	....	....	....	....	....	....	....	....	....
1993-94	Beauport	QMJHL	45	14	25	39	43	....	....	....	....	....	....	....	....	....	....	....	15	7	6	13	33	....	....	....
1994-95	Beauport	QMJHL	59	19	33	52	125	....	....	....	....	....	....	....	....	....	....	....	17	4	6	10	39	....	....	....
1995-96	Beauport	QMJHL	54	41	41	82	176	....	....	....	....	....	....	....	....	....	....	....	20	5	18	23	20	....	....	....
1996-97	Chicago	NHL	1	0	1	1	5	0	0	0	0	0.0	1	....	....	....	....	....	....	....	....	....	....	....	....	....
	Indianapolis Ice	IHL	69	14	17	31	112	....	....	....	....	....	....	....	....	....	....	....	4	1	0	1	2	....	....	....
1997-98	Chicago	NHL	66	6	7	13	55	0	0	0	57	10.5	-2	....	....	....	....	....	....	....	....	....	....	....	....	....
1998-99	Chicago	NHL	40	3	5	8	21	0	0	0	47	6.4	-7	10	50.0	98	8	12:43	....	....	....	....	....	....	....	....
	Chicago Wolves	IHL	....	....	....	....	....	....	....	....	....	....	....	....	....	....	....	....	10	1	1	2	18	....	....	....
99-2000	Chicago	NHL	54	3	5	8	43	0	0	1	36	8.3	-10	7	0.0	96	9	10:44	....	....	....	....	....	....	....	....
	NHL Totals		161	12	18	30	124	0	0	1	140	8.6		17	29.4	194	17	11:35	....	....	....	....	....	....	....	....

QMJHL Second All-Star Team (1994)

LESCHYSHYN, Curtis

(luh-SIH-shuhn, KUHR-tihs) **MIN.**

Defense. Shoots left. 6'1", 205 lbs. Born, Thompson, Man., September 21, 1969. Quebec's 1st choice, 3rd overall, in 1988 Entry Draft.

			Regular Season																Playoffs							
Season	Club	League	GP	G	A	Pts	PIM	PP	SH	GW	S	%	+/-	TF	F%	H	SB	Min	GP	G	A	Pts	PIM	PP	SH	GW
1985-86	Saskatoon Blaze	SAHA	34	9	34	43	52	....	....	....	....	....	....	....	....	....	....	....	....	....	....	....	....	....	....	....
	Saskatoon Blades	WHL	1	0	0	0	0	....	....	....	....	....	....	....	....	....	....	....	....	....	....	....	....	....	....	....
1986-87	Saskatoon Blades	WHL	70	14	26	40	107	....	....	....	....	....	....	....	....	....	....	....	11	1	5	6	14	....	....	....
1987-88	Saskatoon Blades	WHL	56	14	41	55	86	....	....	....	....	....	....	....	....	....	....	....	10	2	5	7	16	....	....	....
1988-89	Quebec	NHL	71	4	9	13	71	1	1	0	58	6.9	-32	....	....	....	....	....	....	....	....	....	....	....	....	....
1989-90	Quebec	NHL	68	2	6	8	44	1	0	0	42	4.8	-41	....	....	....	....	....	....	....	....	....	....	....	....	....
1990-91	Quebec	NHL	55	3	7	10	49	2	0	1	57	5.3	-19	....	....	....	....	....	....	....	....	....	....	....	....	....
1991-92	Quebec	NHL	42	5	12	17	42	3	0	1	61	8.2	-28	....	....	....	....	....	....	....	....	....	....	....	....	....
	Halifax Citadels	AHL	6	0	2	2	4	....	....	....	....	....	....	....	....	....	....	....	....	....	....	....	....	....	....	....
1992-93	Quebec	NHL	82	9	23	32	61	4	0	2	73	12.3	25	....	....	....	....	....	6	1	1	2	6	1	0	0
1993-94	Quebec	NHL	72	5	17	22	65	3	0	2	97	5.2	-2	....	....	....	....	....	....	....	....	....	....	....	....	....
1994-95	Quebec	NHL	44	2	13	15	20	0	0	0	43	4.7	29	....	....	....	....	....	3	0	1	1	4	0	0	0
1995-96♦	Colorado	NHL	77	4	15	19	73	0	0	1	76	5.3	32	....	....	....	....	....	17	1	2	3	8	0	0	0
1996-97	Colorado	NHL	11	0	5	5	6	0	0	0	8	0.0	1	....	....	....	....	....	....	....	....	....	....	....	....	....
	Washington	NHL	2	0	0	0	2	0	0	0	0	0.0	0	....	....	....	....	....	....	....	....	....	....	....	....	....
	Hartford	NHL	64	4	13	17	30	1	1	1	94	4.3	-19	....	....	....	....	....	....	....	....	....	....	....	....	....
1997-98	Carolina	NHL	73	2	10	12	45	1	0	1	53	3.8	-2	....	....	....	....	....	....	....	....	....	....	....	....	....
1998-99	Carolina	NHL	65	2	7	9	50	1	0	0	35	5.7	-1	0	0.0	208	103	19:18	6	0	0	0	6	0	0	0
99-2000	Carolina	NHL	53	0	2	2	14	0	0	0	31	0.0	-19	0	0.0	164	85	17:47	....	....	....	....	....	....	....	....
	NHL Totals		779	42	139	181	572	16	2	9	728	5.8		0	0.0	372	188	18:37	32	2	4	6	24	1	0	0

Transferred to **Colorado** after **Quebec** franchise relcoated, June 21, 1995. Traded to **Washington** by **Colorado** with Chris Simon for Keith Jones, Washington's 1st (Mathieu Biron) and 4th (Chris Corrinet) round choices in 1998 Entry Draft, November 2, 1996. Traded to **Hartford** by **Washington** for Andrei Nikolishin, November 9, 1996. Transferred to **Carolina** after **Hartford** franchise relocated, June 25, 1997. Selected by **Minnesota** from **Carolina** in Expansion Draft, June 23, 2000.

LETANG, Alan
(leh-TANG, A-luhn) **DAL.**

Defense. Shoots left. 6', 205 lbs. Born, Renfrew, Ont., September 4, 1975. Montreal's 10th choice, 203rd overall, in 1993 Entry Draft.

Season	Club	League	GP	G	A	Pts	PIM	PP	SH	GW	S	%	+/-	TF	F%	H	SB	Min	GP	G	A	Pts	PIM	PP	SH	GW
			Regular Season																Playoffs							
1990-91	Ottawa Valley	OMHA	32	3	26	29	16	....	....	....	....	....	....	....	....	....	....	....	....	....	....	....	....	....	....	....
1991-92	Cornwall Royals	OHL	47	1	4	5	16	....	....	....	....	....	....	....	....	....	....	....	6	0	0	0	2	....	....	....
1992-93	Newmarket	OHL	66	1	25	26	14	....	....	....	....	....	....	....	....	....	....	....	6	0	3	3	2	....	....	....
1993-94	Newmarket	OHL	58	3	21	24	30	....	....	....	....	....	....	....	....	....	....	....	....	....	....	....	....	....	....	....
1994-95	Sarnia Sting	OHL	62	5	36	41	35	....	....	....	....	....	....	....	....	....	....	....	4	2	2	4	6	....	....	....
1995-96	Fredericton	AHL	71	0	26	26	40	....	....	....	....	....	....	....	....	....	....	....	10	0	3	3	4	....	....	....
1996-97	Fredericton	AHL	60	2	9	11	8	....	....	....	....	....	....	....	....	....	....	....	....	....	....	....	....	....	....	....
1997-98	EV Kaufenbeuren	DEL	15	1	5	6	8	....	....	....	....	....	....	....	....	....	....	....	....	....	....	....	....	....	....	....
	SC Langnau	Switz-2	11	4	3	7	6	....	....	....	....	....	....	....	....	....	....	....	....	....	....	....	....	....	....	....
	Augsburger EV	DEL	17	0	1	1	4	....	....	....	....	....	....	....	....	....	....	....	....	....	....	....	....	....	....	....
1998-99	Canada	Nat-Team	41	3	9	12	20	....	....	....	....	....	....	....	....	....	....	....	....	....	....	....	....	....	....	....
	EV Zug	Switz.	....	....	....	....	....	....	....	....	....	....	....	....	....	....	....	....	9	0	4	4	4	....	....	....
	Michigan K-Wings	IHL	12	3	3	6	0	....	....	....	....	....	....	....	....	....	....	....	5	0	2	2	0	....	....	....
99-2000	**Dallas**	**NHL**	**8**	**0**	**0**	**0**	**2**	**0**	**0**	**0**	**1**	**0.0**	**-5**	**0**	**0.0**	**2**	**4**	**9:57**	....	....	....	....	....	....	....	....
	Michigan K-Wings	IHL	51	1	12	13	30	....	....	....	....	....	....	....	....	....	....	....	....	....	....	....	....	....	....	....
	NHL Totals		**8**	**0**	**0**	**0**	**2**	**0**	**0**	**0**	**1**	**0.0**		**0**	**0.0**	**2**	**4**	**9:57**	....	....	....	....	....	....	....	....

Signed as a free agent by **Dallas**, March 22, 1999.

LETOWSKI, Trevor
(leh-TOW-skee, TREH-vuhr) **PHX.**

Center. Shoots right. 5'10", 176 lbs. Born, Thunder Bay, Ont., April 5, 1977. Phoenix's 6th choice, 174th overall, in 1996 Entry Draft.

Season	Club	League	GP	G	A	Pts	PIM	PP	SH	GW	S	%	+/-	TF	F%	H	SB	Min	GP	G	A	Pts	PIM	PP	SH	GW
1993-94	Thunder Bay	TBAHA	64	41	60	101	48	....	....	....	....	....	....	....	....	....	....	....	....	....	....	....	....	....	....	....
1994-95	Sarnia Sting	OHL	66	22	19	41	33	....	....	....	....	....	....	....	....	....	....	....	4	0	1	1	9	....	....	....
1995-96	Sarnia Sting	OHL	66	36	63	99	66	....	....	....	....	....	....	....	....	....	....	....	10	9	5	14	10	....	....	....
1996-97	Sarnia Sting	OHL	55	35	73	108	51	....	....	....	....	....	....	....	....	....	....	....	12	9	12	21	20	....	....	....
1997-98	Springfield	AHL	75	11	20	31	26	....	....	....	....	....	....	....	....	....	....	....	4	1	0	1	2	....	....	....
1998-99	**Phoenix**	**NHL**	**14**	**2**	**2**	**4**	**2**	**0**	**0**	**0**	**8**	**25.0**	**1**	**49**	**55.1**	**4**	**3**	**6:01**	....	....	....	....	....	....	....	....
	Springfield	AHL	67	32	35	67	46	....	....	....	....	....	....	....	....	....	....	....	3	1	0	1	2	....	....	....
99-2000	**Phoenix**	**NHL**	**82**	**19**	**20**	**39**	**20**	**3**	**4**	**3**	**125**	**15.2**	**2**	**692**	**47.7**	**24**	**33**	**16:03**	**5**	**1**	**1**	**2**	**4**	**0**	**0**	**0**
	NHL Totals		**96**	**21**	**22**	**43**	**22**	**3**	**4**	**3**	**133**	**15.8**		**741**	**48.2**	**28**	**36**	**14:35**	**5**	**1**	**1**	**2**	**4**	**0**	**0**	**0**

LEVINS, Scott
(LEH-vihns, SKAWT)

Center/Right wing. Shoots right. 6'4", 210 lbs. Born, Spokane, WA, January 30, 1970. Winnipeg's 4th choice, 75th overall, in 1990 Entry Draft.

Season	Club	League	GP	G	A	Pts	PIM	PP	SH	GW	S	%	+/-	TF	F%	H	SB	Min	GP	G	A	Pts	PIM	PP	SH	GW
1987-88	Spokane Braves	KIJHL	42	49	59	108	180	....	....	....	....	....	....	....	....	....	....	....	....	....	....	....	....	....	....	....
1988-89	Penticton Knights	BCJHL	50	27	58	85	154	....	....	....	....	....	....	....	....	....	....	....	....	....	....	....	....	....	....	....
1989-90	Tri-City Americans	WHL	71	25	37	62	132	....	....	....	....	....	....	....	....	....	....	....	6	2	3	5	18	....	....	....
1990-91	Moncton Hawks	AHL	74	12	26	38	133	....	....	....	....	....	....	....	....	....	....	....	4	0	0	0	4	....	....	....
1991-92	Moncton Hawks	AHL	69	15	18	33	271	....	....	....	....	....	....	....	....	....	....	....	11	3	4	7	30	....	....	....
1992-93	**Winnipeg**	**NHL**	**9**	**0**	**1**	**1**	**18**	**0**	**0**	**0**	**8**	**0.0**	**-2**	....	....	....	....	....	....	....	....	....	....	....	....	....
	Moncton Hawks	AHL	54	22	26	48	158	....	....	....	....	....	....	....	....	....	....	....	5	1	3	4	14	....	....	....
1993-94	**Florida**	**NHL**	**29**	**5**	**6**	**11**	**69**	**2**	**0**	**1**	**38**	**13.2**	**0**	....	....	....	....	....	....	....	....	....	....	....	....	....
	Ottawa	**NHL**	**33**	**3**	**5**	**8**	**93**	**2**	**0**	**0**	**39**	**7.7**	**-26**	....	....	....	....	....	....	....	....	....	....	....	....	....
1994-95	**Ottawa**	**NHL**	**24**	**5**	**6**	**11**	**51**	**0**	**0**	**0**	**34**	**14.7**	**4**	....	....	....	....	....	....	....	....	....	....	....	....	....
	P.E.I. Senators	AHL	6	0	4	4	14	....	....	....	....	....	....	....	....	....	....	....	....	....	....	....	....	....	....	....
1995-96	**Ottawa**	**NHL**	**27**	**0**	**2**	**2**	**80**	**0**	**0**	**0**	**6**	**0.0**	**-3**	....	....	....	....	....	....	....	....	....	....	....	....	....
	Detroit Vipers	IHL	9	0	0	0	9	....	....	....	....	....	....	....	....	....	....	....	....	....	....	....	....	....	....	....
1996-97	Springfield	AHL	68	24	23	47	267	....	....	....	....	....	....	....	....	....	....	....	11	5	4	9	37	....	....	....
1997-98	**Phoenix**	**NHL**	**2**	**0**	**0**	**0**	**5**	**0**	**0**	**0**	**2**	**0.0**	**-1**	....	....	....	....	....	....	....	....	....	....	....	....	....
	Springfield	AHL	79	28	39	67	177	....	....	....	....	....	....	....	....	....	....	....	4	2	0	2	24	....	....	....
1998-99	New Haven	AHL	80	32	26	58	189	....	....	....	....	....	....	....	....	....	....	....	....	....	....	....	....	....	....	....
99-2000	Revier Lowen	DEL	48	14	12	26	124	....	....	....	....	....	....	....	....	....	....	....	....	....	....	....	....	....	....	....
	Quad City	UHL	11	4	4	8	46	....	....	....	....	....	....	....	....	....	....	....	....	....	....	....	....	....	....	....
	NHL Totals		**124**	**13**	**20**	**33**	**316**	**4**	**0**	**1**	**127**	**10.2**		....	....	....	....	....	....	....	....	....	....	....	....	....

WHL West Second All-Star Team (1990)

Claimed by **Florida** from **Winnipeg** in Expansion Draft, June 24, 1993. Traded to **Ottawa** by **Florida** with Evgeny Davydov, Florida's 6th round choice (Mike Gaffney) in 1994 Entry Draft and Dallas' 4th round choice (previously acquired, Ottawa selected Kevin Bolibruck) in 1995 Entry Draft for Bob Kudelski, January 6, 1994. Signed as a free agent by **Phoenix**, October 3, 1996. Signed as a free agent by **Carolina**, August 18, 1998.

LIDSTROM, Nicklas
(LID-struhm, NIHK-las) **DET.**

Defense. Shoots left. 6'2", 185 lbs. Born, Vasteras, Sweden, April 28, 1970. Detroit's 3rd choice, 53rd overall, in 1989 Entry Draft.

Season	Club	League	GP	G	A	Pts	PIM	PP	SH	GW	S	%	+/-	TF	F%	H	SB	Min	GP	G	A	Pts	PIM	PP	SH	GW
1987-88	Vasteras IK	Sweden-2	3	0	0	0	0	....	....	....	....	....	....	....	....	....	....	....	5	0	0	0	6	....	....	....
1991-92	**Detroit**	**NHL**	**80**	**11**	**49**	**60**	**22**	**5**	**0**	**1**	**168**	**6.5**	**36**	....	....	....	....	....	**11**	**1**	**2**	**3**	**0**	**1**	**0**	**0**
1992-93	**Detroit**	**NHL**	**84**	**7**	**34**	**41**	**28**	**3**	**0**	**2**	**156**	**4.5**	**7**	....	....	....	....	....	**7**	**1**	**0**	**1**	**0**	**1**	**0**	**0**
1993-94	**Detroit**	**NHL**	**84**	**10**	**46**	**56**	**26**	**4**	**0**	**3**	**200**	**5.0**	**43**	....	....	....	....	....	**7**	**3**	**2**	**5**	**0**	**1**	**1**	**0**
1994-95	**Detroit**	**NHL**	**43**	**10**	**16**	**26**	**6**	**7**	**0**	**0**	**90**	**11.1**	**15**	....	....	....	....	....	**18**	**4**	**12**	**16**	**8**	**3**	**0**	**2**
1995-96	**Detroit**	**NHL**	**81**	**17**	**50**	**67**	**20**	**8**	**1**	**1**	**211**	**8.1**	**29**	....	....	....	....	....	**19**	**5**	**9**	**14**	**10**	**1**	**0**	**0**
1996-97♦	**Detroit**	**NHL**	**79**	**15**	**42**	**57**	**30**	**8**	**0**	**1**	**214**	**7.0**	**11**	....	....	....	....	....	**20**	**2**	**6**	**8**	**2**	**0**	**0**	**0**
1997-98♦	**Detroit**	**NHL**	**80**	**17**	**42**	**59**	**18**	**7**	**1**	**1**	**205**	**8.3**	**22**	....	....	....	....	....	**22**	**6**	**13**	**19**	**8**	**2**	**0**	**2**
1998-99	**Detroit**	**NHL**	**81**	**14**	**43**	**57**	**14**	**6**	**2**	**3**	**205**	**6.8**	**14**	**0**	**0.0**	**53**	**88**	**26:31**	**10**	**2**	**9**	**11**	**4**	**2**	**0**	**0**
99-2000	**Detroit**	**NHL**	**81**	**20**	**53**	**73**	**18**	**9**	**4**	**3**	**218**	**9.2**	**19**	**0**	**0.0**	**59**	**95**	**28:45**	**9**	**2**	**4**	**6**	**4**	**1**	**0**	**0**
	NHL Totals		**693**	**121**	**375**	**496**	**182**	**57**	**8**	**15**	**1667**	**7.3**		**0**	**0.0**	**112**	**183**	**27:38**	**123**	**26**	**57**	**83**	**36**	**12**	**1**	**4**

NHL All-Rookie Team (1992) • NHL First All-Star Team (1998, 1999, 2000) • Played in NHL All-Star Game (1996, 1998, 1999, 2000)

LIND, Juha
(LIHND, YOO-huh) **MTL.**

Center. Shoots left. 5'11", 185 lbs. Born, Helsinki, Finland, January 2, 1974. Minnesota's 6th choice, 178th overall, in 1992 Entry Draft.

Season	Club	League	GP	G	A	Pts	PIM	PP	SH	GW	S	%	+/-	TF	F%	H	SB	Min	GP	G	A	Pts	PIM	PP	SH	GW
1990-91	Jokerit Helsinki	Finn-Jr.	8	1	1	2	0	....	....	....	....	....	....	....	....	....	....	....	....	....	....	....	....	....	....	....
1991-92	Jokerit Helsinki-2	Finn-Jr.	14	9	16	25	2	....	....	....	....	....	....	....	....	....	....	....	14	7	8	15	8	....	....	....
1992-93	Vantaa HT	Finland-2	25	8	12	20	8	....	....	....	....	....	....	....	....	....	....	....	....	....	....	....	....	....	....	....
	Jokerit Helsinki	Finland-2	3	2	4	6	2	....	....	....	....	....	....	....	....	....	....	....	....	....	....	....	....	....	....	....
	Jokerit Helsinki	Finland	6	0	0	0	2	....	....	....	....	....	....	....	....	....	....	....	1	0	0	0	0	....	....	....
1993-94	Jokerit Helsinki	Finland-2	11	6	7	13	4	....	....	....	....	....	....	....	....	....	....	....	....	....	....	....	....	....	....	....
	Jokerit Helsinki	Finland	47	17	11	28	37	....	....	....	....	....	....	....	....	....	....	....	11	2	5	7	4	....	....	....
1994-95	Jokerit Helsinki	Finn-Jr.	3	2	1	3	2	....	....	....	....	....	....	....	....	....	....	....	....	....	....	....	....	....	....	....
	Jokerit Helsinki	Finland	50	10	8	18	12	....	....	....	....	....	....	....	....	....	....	....	11	1	2	3	6	....	....	....
1995-96	Jokerit Helsinki	Finland	50	15	22	37	32	....	....	....	....	....	....	....	....	....	....	....	11	4	5	9	4	....	....	....
1996-97	Jokerit Helsinki	Finland	50	16	22	38	28	....	....	....	....	....	....	....	....	....	....	....	9	5	3	8	0	....	....	....
	Jokerit Helsinki	EuroHL	6	4	1	5	6	....	....	....	....	....	....	....	....	....	....	....	2	1	0	1	0	....	....	....
1997-98	**Dallas**	**NHL**	**39**	**2**	**3**	**5**	**6**	**0**	**0**	**0**	**27**	**7.4**	**4**	....	....	....	....	....	**15**	**2**	**2**	**4**	**8**	**0**	**0**	**1**
	Michigan K-Wings	IHL	8	2	2	4	2	....	....	....	....	....	....	....	....	....	....	....	....	....	....	....	....	....	....	....
	Finland	Olympics	6	0	1	1	6	....	....	....	....	....	....	....	....	....	....	....	....	....	....	....	....	....	....	....
1998-99	Jokerit Helsinki	Finland	50	20	19	39	22	....	....	....	....	....	....	....	....	....	....	....	3	3	1	4	2	....	....	....
	Jokerit Helsinki	EuroHL	6	6	2	8	14	....	....	....	....	....	....	....	....	....	....	....	2	0	2	2	0	....	....	....
99-2000	**Dallas**	**NHL**	**34**	**3**	**4**	**7**	**6**	**0**	**0**	**0**	**36**	**8.3**	**-1**	**8**	**50.0**	**52**	**4**	**10:49**	....	....	....	....	....	....	....	....
	Montreal	**NHL**	**13**	**1**	**2**	**3**	**4**	**0**	**0**	**0**	**6**	**16.7**	**-2**	**0**	**0.0**	**18**	**3**	**9:37**	....	....	....	....	....	....	....	....
	NHL Totals		**86**	**6**	**9**	**15**	**16**	**0**	**0**	**0**	**69**	**8.7**		**8**	**50.0**	**70**	**7**	**10:29**	**15**	**2**	**2**	**4**	**8**	**0**	**0**	**1**

Rights transferred to **Dallas** after **Minnesota** franchise relocated, June 9, 1993. Traded to **Montreal** by **Dallas** for Scott Thornton, January 22, 2000.

LINDEN, Trevor

(LIHND-dehn, TREH-vohr) **MTL.**

Center/Right wing. Shoots right. 6'5", 211 lbs. Born, Medicine Hat, Alta., April 11, 1970. Vancouver's 1st choice, 2nd overall, in 1988 Entry Draft.

			Regular Season																Playoffs							
Season	Club	League	GP	G	A	Pts	PIM	PP	SH	GW	S	%	+/–	TF	F%	H	SB	Min	GP	G	A	Pts	PIM	PP	SH	GW
1985-86	Medicine Hat	AAHA	40	14	22	36	14	....	....	....	....	....	....	....	....	....	....	....	....	....	....	....	....	....	....	....
	Medicine Hat	WHL	5	2	0	2	0	....	....	....	....	....	....	....	....	....	....	....	....	....	....	....	....	....	....	....
1986-87	Medicine Hat	WHL	72	14	22	36	59	....	....	....	....	....	....	....	....	....	....	....	20	5	4	9	17	....	....	....
1987-88	Medicine Hat	WHL	67	46	64	110	76	....	....	....	....	....	....	....	....	....	....	....	16	*13	12	25	19	....	....	....
1988-89	**Vancouver**	**NHL**	80	30	29	59	41	10	1	2	186	16.1	–10	....	....	....	....	....	7	3	4	7	8	2	1	0
1989-90	**Vancouver**	**NHL**	73	21	30	51	43	6	2	3	171	12.3	–17	....	....	....	....	....	....	....	....	....	....	....	....	....
1990-91	**Vancouver**	**NHL**	80	33	37	70	65	16	2	4	229	14.4	–25	....	....	....	....	....	6	0	7	7	2	0	0	0
1991-92	**Vancouver**	**NHL**	80	31	44	75	101	6	1	6	201	15.4	3	....	....	....	....	....	13	4	8	12	6	2	0	1
1992-93	**Vancouver**	**NHL**	84	33	39	72	64	8	0	3	209	15.8	19	....	....	....	....	....	12	5	8	13	16	2	0	1
1993-94	**Vancouver**	**NHL**	84	32	29	61	73	10	2	3	234	13.7	6	....	....	....	....	....	24	12	13	25	18	5	1	1
1994-95	**Vancouver**	**NHL**	48	18	22	40	40	9	0	1	129	14.0	–5	....	....	....	....	....	11	2	6	8	12	1	0	0
1995-96	**Vancouver**	**NHL**	82	33	47	80	42	12	1	2	202	16.3	6	....	....	....	....	....	6	4	4	8	6	2	0	0
1996-97	**Vancouver**	**NHL**	49	9	31	40	27	2	2	2	84	10.7	5	....	....	....	....	....	....	....	....	....	....	....	....	....
1997-98	**Vancouver**	**NHL**	42	7	14	21	49	2	0	1	74	9.5	–13	....	....	....	....	....	....	....	....	....	....	....	....	....
	NY Islanders	**NHL**	25	10	7	17	33	3	2	1	59	16.9	–1	....	....	....	....	....	....	....	....	....	....	....	....	....
	Canada	Olympics	6	1	0	1	10	....	....	....	....	....	....	....	....	....	....	....	....	....	....	....	....	....	....	....
1998-99	**NY Islanders**	**NHL**	82	18	29	47	32	8	1	1	167	10.8	–14	261	50.2	144	47	21:29	....	....	....	....	....	....	....	....
99-2000	**Montreal**	**NHL**	50	13	17	30	34	4	0	3	87	14.9	–3	860	56.3	88	29	17:51	....	....	....	....	....	....	....	....
	NHL Totals		859	288	375	663	644	96	14	32	2032	14.2		1121	54.9	232	76	20:06	79	30	50	80	68	14	2	3

WHL East Second All-Star Team (1988) • NHL All-Rookie Team (1989) • Won King Clancy Memorial Trophy (1997) • Played in NHL All-Star Game (1991, 1992)

Traded to **NY Islanders** by **Vancouver** for Todd Bertuzzi, Bryan McCabe and NY Islanders' 3rd round choice (Jarkko Ruutu) in 1998 Entry Draft, February 6, 1998. Traded to **Montreal** by **NY Islanders** for Montreal's 1st round choice (Branislav Mezel) in 1999 Entry Draft, May 29, 1999.

LINDGREN, Mats

(LIHND-gruhn, MAHTS) **NYI**

Center/Left Wing. Shoots left. 6'2", 202 lbs. Born, Skelleftea, Sweden, October 1, 1974. Winnipeg's 1st choice, 15th overall, in 1993 Entry Draft.

Season	Club	League	GP	G	A	Pts	PIM	PP	SH	GW	S	%	+/–	TF	F%	H	SB	Min	GP	G	A	Pts	PIM	PP	SH	GW
1990-91	Skelleftea AIK	Sweden-2	10	0	1	1	0	....	....	....	....	....	....	....	....	....	....	....	....	....	....	....	....	....	....	....
1991-92	Skelleftea AIK	Sweden-2	29	14	18	32	12	....	....	....	....	....	....	....	....	....	....	....	3	3	2	5	2	....	....	....
1992-93	Skelleftea AIK	Sweden-2	32	20	18	38	18	....	....	....	....	....	....	....	....	....	....	....	3	0	0	0	2	....	....	....
1993-94	Farjestads BK	Sweden	22	11	6	17	26	....	....	....	....	....	....	....	....	....	....	....	....	....	....	....	....	....	....	....
1994-95	Farjestads BK	Sweden	37	17	15	32	20	....	....	....	....	....	....	....	....	....	....	....	3	0	0	0	4	....	....	....
1995-96	Cape Breton	AHL	13	7	5	12	6	....	....	....	....	....	....	....	....	....	....	....	....	....	....	....	....	....	....	....
1996-97	**Edmonton**	**NHL**	69	11	14	25	12	2	3	1	71	15.5	–7	....	....	....	....	....	12	0	4	4	0	0	0	0
	Hamilton Bulldogs	AHL	9	6	7	13	6	....	....	....	....	....	....	....	....	....	....	....	....	....	....	....	....	....	....	....
1997-98	**Edmonton**	**NHL**	82	13	13	26	42	1	3	3	131	9.9	0	....	....	....	....	....	12	1	1	2	10	0	0	0
	Sweden	Olympics	4	0	0	0	2	....	....	....	....	....	....	....	....	....	....	....	....	....	....	....	....	....	....	....
1998-99	**Edmonton**	**NHL**	48	5	12	17	22	0	1	0	53	9.4	4	363	47.9	44	16	11:31	....	....	....	....	....	....	....	....
	NY Islanders	**NHL**	12	5	3	8	2	3	0	1	30	16.7	2	180	48.9	18	4	20:08	....	....	....	....	....	....	....	....
99-2000	**NY Islanders**	**NHL**	43	9	7	16	24	1	0	1	68	13.2	0	551	49.2	54	25	19:17	....	....	....	....	....	....	....	....
	NHL Totals		254	43	49	92	102	7	7	6	353	12.2		1094	48.7	116	45	15:46	24	1	5	6	10	0	0	0

Swedish Rookie of the Year (1994)

Traded to **Edmonton** by **Winnipeg** with Boris Mironov, Winnipeg's 1st round choice (Jason Bonsignore) in 1994 Entry Draft and Florida's 4th round choice (previously acquired, Edmonton selected Adam Copeland) in 1994 Entry Draft for Dave Manson and St. Louis' 6th round choice (previously acquired, Winnipeg selected Chris Kibermanis) in 1994 Entry Draft, March 15, 1994. Traded to **NY Islanders** by **Edmonton** with Edmonton's 8th round choice (Radek Martinek) in 1999 Entry Draft for Tommy Salo, March 20, 1999.

LINDQUIST, Fredrik

(LIHND-kvihst, FREHD-rihk) **EDM.**

Center. Shoots left. 6', 190 lbs. Born, Stockholm, Sweden, June 21, 1973. New Jersey's 4th choice, 55th overall, in 1991 Entry Draft.

Season	Club	League	GP	G	A	Pts	PIM	PP	SH	GW	S	%	+/–	TF	F%	H	SB	Min	GP	G	A	Pts	PIM	PP	SH	GW
1989-90	Huddinge IF	Swede-2	2	0	0	0	0	....	....	....	....	....	....	....	....	....	....	....	....	....	....	....	....	....	....	....
1990-91	Djurgardens IF	Sweden	28	6	4	10	0	....	....	....	....	....	....	....	....	....	....	....	7	1	0	1	2	....	....	....
1991-92	Djurgardens IF	Sweden	39	9	6	15	14	....	....	....	....	....	....	....	....	....	....	....	10	1	1	2	2	....	....	....
1992-93	Djurgardens IF	Sweden	39	9	11	20	8	....	....	....	....	....	....	....	....	....	....	....	4	1	2	3	2	....	....	....
1993-94	Djurgardens IF	Swede-Jr.	1	0	1	1	0	....	....	....	....	....	....	....	....	....	....	....	....	....	....	....	....	....	....	....
	Djurgardens IF	Sweden	25	5	8	13	8	....	....	....	....	....	....	....	....	....	....	....	6	2	1	3	2	....	....	....
1994-95	Djurgardens IF	Sweden	40	11	16	27	14	....	....	....	....	....	....	....	....	....	....	....	3	0	0	0	2	....	....	....
1995-96	Djurgardens IF	Sweden	33	12	19	31	16	....	....	....	....	....	....	....	....	....	....	....	1	0	0	0	0	....	....	....
1996-97	Djurgardens IF	Sweden	44	19	28	47	20	....	....	....	....	....	....	....	....	....	....	....	4	0	3	3	2	....	....	....
1997-98	Djurgardens IF	Sweden	42	10	*32	42	30	....	....	....	....	....	....	....	....	....	....	....	13	3	6	9	4	....	....	....
1998-99	**Edmonton**	**NHL**	8	0	0	0	2	0	0	0	6	0.0	–2	0	0.0	1	1	12:18	....	....	....	....	....	....	....	....
	Hamilton Bulldogs	AHL	57	18	36	54	20	....	....	....	....	....	....	....	....	....	....	....	11	2	2	4	2	....	....	....
99-2000	HC Davos	Switz.	44	14	27	41	20	....	....	....	....	....	....	....	....	....	....	....	5	2	3	5	4	....	....	....
	NHL Totals		8	0	0	0	2	0	0	0	6	0.0		0	0.0	1	1	12:18	....	....	....	....	....	....	....	....

Traded to **Edmonton** by **New Jersey** with New Jersey's 4th (Kristian Antila) and 5th (Oleg Smirnov) round choices in 1998 Entry Draft for Pittsburgh's 3rd round choice (previously acquired, New Jersey selected Brian Gionta) in 1998 Entry Draft, June 27, 1998.

LINDROS, Eric

(LIHND-rahz, AIR-ihk)

Center. Shoots right. 6'4", 236 lbs. Born, London, Ont., February 28, 1973. Quebec's 1st choice, 1st overall, in 1991 Entry Draft.

Season	Club	League	GP	G	A	Pts	PIM	PP	SH	GW	S	%	+/–	TF	F%	H	SB	Min	GP	G	A	Pts	PIM	PP	SH	GW
1988-89	St. Michael's	OJHL-B	37	24	43	67	193	....	....	....	....	....	....	....	....	....	....	....	27	23	25	48	155	....	....	....
	Canada	Nat-Team	2	1	0	1	0	....	....	....	....	....	....	....	....	....	....	....	....	....	....	....	....	....	....	....
1989-90	Detroit	NAJHL	14	23	29	52	123	....	....	....	....	....	....	....	....	....	....	....	....	....	....	....	....	....	....	....
	Canada	Nat-Team	3	1	0	1	4	....	....	....	....	....	....	....	....	....	....	....	....	....	....	....	....	....	....	....
	Oshawa Generals	OHL	25	17	19	36	61	....	....	....	....	....	....	....	....	....	....	....	17	18	18	36	76	....	....	....
1990-91	Oshawa Generals	OHL	57	*71	78	*149	189	....	....	....	....	....	....	....	....	....	....	....	16	*18	20	*38	*93	....	....	....
1991-92	Oshawa Generals	OHL	13	9	22	31	54	....	....	....	....	....	....	....	....	....	....	....	....	....	....	....	....	....	....	....
	Canada	Nat-Team	24	19	16	35	34	....	....	....	....	....	....	....	....	....	....	....	....	....	....	....	....	....	....	....
	Canada	Olympics	8	5	6	11	5	....	....	....	....	....	....	....	....	....	....	....	....	....	....	....	....	....	....	....
1992-93	**Philadelphia**	**NHL**	61	41	34	75	147	8	1	5	180	22.8	28	....	....	....	....	....	....	....	....	....	....	....	....	....
1993-94	**Philadelphia**	**NHL**	65	44	53	97	103	13	2	9	197	22.3	16	....	....	....	....	....	....	....	....	....	....	....	....	....
1994-95	**Philadelphia**	**NHL**	46	29	41	*70	60	7	0	4	144	20.1	27	....	....	....	....	....	12	4	11	15	18	0	0	1
1995-96	**Philadelphia**	**NHL**	73	47	68	115	163	15	0	4	294	16.0	26	....	....	....	....	....	12	6	6	12	43	3	0	2
1996-97	**Philadelphia**	**NHL**	52	32	47	79	136	9	0	7	198	16.2	31	....	....	....	....	....	19	12	14	*26	40	4	0	1
1997-98	**Philadelphia**	**NHL**	63	30	41	71	134	10	1	4	202	14.9	14	....	....	....	....	....	5	1	2	3	17	0	0	0
	Canada	Olympics	6	2	3	5	2	....	....	....	....	....	....	....	....	....	....	....	....	....	....	....	....	....	....	....
1998-99	**Philadelphia**	**NHL**	71	40	53	93	120	10	1	2	242	16.5	35	1529	60.0	117	17	22:56	....	....	....	....	....	....	....	....
99-2000	**Philadelphia**	**NHL**	55	27	32	59	83	10	1	2	187	14.4	11	1318	57.8	130	29	22:02	2	1	0	1	0	0	0	0
	NHL Totals		486	290	369	659	946	82	6	37	1644	17.6		2847	59.0	247	46	22:32	50	24	33	57	118	7	0	4

Memorial Cup All-Star Team (1990) • OHL First All-Star Team (1991) • Canadian Major Junior Player of the Year (1991) • NHL All-Rookie Team (1993) • NHL First All-Star Team (1995) • Won Lester B. Pearson Award (1995) • Won Hart Trophy (1995) • NHL Second All-Star Team (1996) • Played in NHL All-Star Game (1994, 1996, 1997, 1998, 1999, 2000)

Rights traded to **Oshawa** (OHL) by **Sault Ste. Marie** (OHL) for Mike DeCoff, Jason Denomme, Mike Lenarduzzi and Oshawa's 2nd round choice in 1991 and 4th round choice (Joe Vanvolsen) in 1992 OHL Priority Draft, December 17, 1989. Traded to **Philadelphia** by **Quebec** for Peter Forsberg, Steve Duchesne, Kerry Huffman, Mike Ricci, Ron Hextall, Philadelphia's 1st round choice (Jocelyn Thibault) in 1993 Entry Draft, $15,000,000 and future considerations (Chris Simon and Philadelphia's 1st round choice (later traded to Toronto - later traded to Washington - Washington selected Nolan Baumgartner) in 1994 Entry Draft, July 21, 1992), June 30, 1992.

LINDSAY, Bill

(LIHND-see, BIHL) **CGY.**

Left wing. Shoots left. 6', 195 lbs. Born, Big Fork, MT, May 17, 1971. Quebec's 6th choice, 103rd overall, in 1991 Entry Draft.

Season	Club	League	GP	G	A	Pts	PIM	PP	SH	GW	S	%	+/–	TF	F%	H	SB	Min	GP	G	A	Pts	PIM	PP	SH	GW
1988-89	Vernon Lakers	BCJHL	56	24	29	53	166	....	....	....	....	....	....	....	....	....	....	....	....	....	....	....	....	....	....	....
1989-90	Tri-City Americans	WHL	72	40	45	85	84	....	....	....	....	....	....	....	....	....	....	....	7	3	0	3	17	....	....	....
1990-91	Tri-City Americans	WHL	63	46	47	93	151	....	....	....	....	....	....	....	....	....	....	....	5	3	6	9	10	....	....	....
1991-92	Tri-City Americans	WHL	42	34	59	93	81	....	....	....	....	....	....	....	....	....	....	....	3	2	3	5	16	....	....	....
	Quebec	**NHL**	23	2	4	6	14	0	0	1	35	5.7	–6	....	....	....	....	....	....	....	....	....	....	....	....	....

			Regular Season																	Playoffs							
Season	**Club**	**League**	**GP**	**G**	**A**	**Pts**	**PIM**	**PP**	**SH**	**GW**	**S**	**%**	**+/-**	**TF**	**F%**	**H**	**SB**	**Min**	**GP**	**G**	**A**	**Pts**	**PIM**	**PP**	**SH**	**GW**
1992-93	**Quebec**	**NHL**	**44**	**4**	**9**	**13**	**16**	**0**	**0**	**0**	**58**	**6.9**	**0**	....	....	....	....	....	....	....	....	....	....	....	....	....
	Halifax Citadels	AHL	20	11	13	24	18	....	....	....	....	....	....	....	....	....	....	....	....	....	....	....	....	....	....	....
1993-94	**Florida**	**NHL**	**84**	**6**	**6**	**12**	**97**	**0**	**0**	**0**	**90**	**6.7**	**–2**	....	....	....	....	....	....	....	....	....	....	....	....	....
1994-95	**Florida**	**NHL**	**48**	**10**	**9**	**19**	**46**	**0**	**1**	**0**	**63**	**15.9**	**1**	....	....	....	....	....	....	....	....	....	....	....	....	....
1995-96	**Florida**	**NHL**	**73**	**12**	**22**	**34**	**57**	**0**	**3**	**2**	**118**	**10.2**	**13**	....	....	....	....	....	**22**	**5**	**5**	**10**	**18**	**0**	**1**	**1**
1996-97	**Florida**	**NHL**	**81**	**11**	**23**	**34**	**120**	**0**	**1**	**3**	**168**	**6.5**	**1**	....	....	....	....	....	**3**	**0**	**1**	**1**	**8**	**0**	**0**	**0**
1997-98	**Florida**	**NHL**	**82**	**12**	**16**	**28**	**80**	**0**	**2**	**5**	**150**	**8.0**	**–2**	....	....	....	....	....	....	....	....	....	....	....	....	....
1998-99	**Florida**	**NHL**	**75**	**12**	**15**	**27**	**92**	**0**	**1**	**2**	**135**	**8.9**	**–1**	**57**	**40.4**	**149**	**20**	**13:37**	....	....	....	....	....	....	....	....
99-2000	**Calgary**	**NHL**	**80**	**8**	**12**	**20**	**86**	**0**	**0**	**2**	**147**	**5.4**	**–7**	**28**	**39.3**	**122**	**50**	**12:55**	....	....	....	....	....	....	....	....
	NHL Totals		**590**	**77**	**116**	**193**	**608**	**0**	**8**	**15**	**964**	**8.0**		**85**	**40.0**	**271**	**70**	**13:15**	**25**	**5**	**6**	**11**	**26**	**0**	**1**	**1**

WHL West Second All-Star Team (1992)

Claimed by **Florida** from **Quebec** in Expansion Draft, June 24, 1993. Traded to **Calgary** by **Florida** for Todd Simpson, September 30, 1999.

LING, David

(LIHNG, DAY-vihd) **DAL.**

Right wing. Shoots right. 5'9", 185 lbs. Born, Halifax, N.S., January 9, 1975. Quebec's 9th choice, 179th overall, in 1993 Entry Draft.

Season	Club	League	GP	G	A	Pts	PIM	PP	SH	GW	S	%	+/-	TF	F%	H	SB	Min	GP	G	A	Pts	PIM	PP	SH	GW
1991-92	Charlottetown	MJrHL	30	33	42	75	270	....	....	....	....	....	....	....	....	....	....	....	....	....	....	....	....	....	....	....
	St. Michael's	OJHL	8	5	14	19	25	....	....	....	....	....	....	....	....	....	....	....	....	....	....	....	....	....	....	....
1992-93	Kingston	OHL	64	17	46	63	275	....	....	....	....	....	....	....	....	....	....	....	16	3	12	15	*72	....	....	....
1993-94	Kingston	OHL	61	37	40	77	*254	....	....	....	....	....	....	....	....	....	....	....	6	4	2	6	16	....	....	....
1994-95	Kingston	OHL	62	*61	74	135	136	....	....	....	....	....	....	....	....	....	....	....	6	7	8	15	12	....	....	....
1995-96	Saint John Flames	AHL	75	24	32	56	179	....	....	....	....	....	....	....	....	....	....	....	9	0	5	5	12	....	....	....
1996-97	Saint John Flames	AHL	5	0	2	2	19	....	....	....	....	....	....	....	....	....	....	....	....	....	....	....	....	....	....	....
	Montreal	**NHL**	**2**	**0**	**0**	**0**	**0**	**0**	**0**	**0**	**0**	**0.0**	**0**	....	....	....	....	....	....	....	....	....	....	....	....	....
	Fredericton	AHL	48	22	36	58	229	....	....	....	....	....	....	....	....	....	....	....	....	....	....	....	....	....	....	....
1997-98	**Montreal**	**NHL**	**1**	**0**	**0**	**0**	**0**	**0**	**0**	**0**	**1**	**0.0**	**–1**	....	....	....	....	....	....	....	....	....	....	....	....	....
	Fredericton	AHL	67	25	41	66	148	....	....	....	....	....	....	....	....	....	....	....	....	....	....	....	....	....	....	....
	Indianapolis Ice	IHL	12	8	6	14	30	....	....	....	....	....	....	....	....	....	....	....	5	4	1	5	31	....	....	....
1998-99	Kansas City	IHL	82	30	42	72	112	....	....	....	....	....	....	....	....	....	....	....	3	1	0	1	20	....	....	....
99-2000	Kansas City	IHL	82	35	48	83	210	....	....	....	....	....	....	....	....	....	....	....	....	....	....	....	....	....	....	....
	NHL Totals		**3**	**0**	**0**	**0**	**0**	**0**	**0**	**0**	**1**	**0.0**		....	....	....	....	....	....	....	....	....	....	....	....	....

OHL First All-Star Team (1995) • Canadian Major Junior First All-Star Team (1995) • Canadian Junior Player of the Year (1995) • IHL First All-Star Team (2000)

Rights transferred to **Colorado** after **Quebec** franchise relocated, June 21, 1995. Traded to **Calgary** by **Colorado** with Colorado's 9th round choice (Steve Shirreffs) in 1995 Entry Draft for Calgary's 9th round choice (Chris George) in 1995 Entry Draft, July 7, 1995. Traded to **Montreal** by **Calgary** with Calgary's 6th round choice (Gordie Dwyer) in 1998 Entry Draft for Scott Fraser, October 24, 1996. Traded to **Chicago** by **Montreal** for Martin Gendron, March 14, 1998. Signed as a free agent by **Kansas City** (IHL) with Chicago retaining NHL rights, September 3, 1998. Traded to **Dallas** by **Chicago** for future considerations, August 11, 2000.

LINTNER, Richard

(LIHNT-nuhr, RIH-chahrd) **NSH.**

Defense. Shoots right. 6'3", 214 lbs. Born, Trencin, Czech., November 15, 1977. Phoenix's 4th choice, 119th overall, in 1996 Entry Draft.

Season	Club	League	GP	G	A	Pts	PIM	PP	SH	GW	S	%	+/-	TF	F%	H	SB	Min	GP	G	A	Pts	PIM	PP	SH	GW
1994-95	Dukla Trencin	Slovak-Jr.	42	12	13	25	20	....	....	....	....	....	....	....	....	....	....	....	....	....	....	....	....	....	....	....
1995-96	Dukla Trencin	Slovak-Jr.	30	15	17	32	210	....	....	....	....	....	....	....	....	....	....	....	....	....	....	....	....	....	....	....
	Dukla Trencin	Slovakia	2	0	0	0	0	....	....	....	....	....	....	....	....	....	....	....	....	....	....	....	....	....	....	....
1996-97	Spisska Nova	Slovakia	35	2	1	3	....	....	....	....	....	....	....	....	....	....	....	....	....	....	....	....	....	....	....	....
1997-98	Springfield	AHL	71	6	9	15	61	....	....	....	....	....	....	....	....	....	....	....	3	1	1	2	4	....	....	....
1998-99	Springfield	AHL	8	0	1	1	16	....	....	....	....	....	....	....	....	....	....	....	....	....	....	....	....	....	....	....
	Milwaukee	IHL	66	9	16	25	75	....	....	....	....	....	....	....	....	....	....	....	....	....	....	....	....	....	....	....
99-2000	Milwaukee	IHL	31	13	8	21	37	....	....	....	....	....	....	....	....	....	....	....	....	....	....	....	....	....	....	....
	Nashville	**NHL**	**33**	**1**	**5**	**6**	**22**	**0**	**0**	**0**	**58**	**1.7**	**–6**	**0**	**0.0**	**44**	**15**	**14:51**	....	....	....	....	....	....	....	....
	NHL Totals		**33**	**1**	**5**	**6**	**22**	**0**	**0**	**0**	**58**	**1.7**		**0**	**0.0**	**44**	**15**	**14:51**	....	....	....	....	....	....	....	....

Traded to **Nashville** by **Phoenix** with Cliff Ronning for future considerations, October 31, 1998.

LIPUMA, Chris

(lih-POO-muh, KRIHS)

Defense. Shoots left. 6', 183 lbs. Born, Bridgeview, IL, March 23, 1971.

Season	Club	League	GP	G	A	Pts	PIM	PP	SH	GW	S	%	+/-	TF	F%	H	SB	Min	GP	G	A	Pts	PIM	PP	SH	GW
1987-88	Chicago Amerks	MEHL	19	6	16	22	31	....	....	....	....	....	....	....	....	....	....	....	....	....	....	....	....	....	....	....
1988-89	Kitchener	OJHL	2	0	0	0	17	....	....	....	....	....	....	....	....	....	....	....	....	....	....	....	....	....	....	....
	Kitchener	OHL	59	7	13	20	101	....	....	....	....	....	....	....	....	....	....	....	....	....	....	....	....	....	....	....
1989-90	Kitchener	OHL	63	11	26	37	125	....	....	....	....	....	....	....	....	....	....	....	17	1	4	5	6	....	....	....
1990-91	Kitchener	OHL	61	6	30	36	145	....	....	....	....	....	....	....	....	....	....	....	4	0	1	1	4	....	....	....
1991-92	Kitchener	OHL	61	13	59	72	115	....	....	....	....	....	....	....	....	....	....	....	14	4	9	13	34	....	....	....
1992-93	**Tampa Bay**	**NHL**	**15**	**0**	**5**	**5**	**34**	**0**	**0**	**0**	**17**	**0.0**	**1**	....	....	....	....	....	....	....	....	....	....	....	....	....
	Atlanta Knights	IHL	66	4	14	18	379	....	....	....	....	....	....	....	....	....	....	....	9	1	1	2	35	....	....	....
1993-94	**Tampa Bay**	**NHL**	**27**	**0**	**4**	**4**	**77**	**0**	**0**	**0**	**20**	**0.0**	**1**	....	....	....	....	....	....	....	....	....	....	....	....	....
	Atlanta Knights	IHL	42	2	10	12	254	....	....	....	....	....	....	....	....	....	....	....	11	1	1	2	28	....	....	....
1994-95	Atlanta Knights	IHL	41	5	12	17	191	....	....	....	....	....	....	....	....	....	....	....	....	....	....	....	....	....	....	....
	Tampa Bay	**NHL**	**1**	**0**	**0**	**0**	**0**	**0**	**0**	**0**	**1**	**0.0**	**2**	....	....	....	....	....	....	....	....	....	....	....	....	....
	Nashville Knights	ECHL	1	0	0	0	0	....	....	....	....	....	....	....	....	....	....	....	....	....	....	....	....	....	....	....
1995-96	**Tampa Bay**	**NHL**	**21**	**0**	**0**	**0**	**13**	**0**	**0**	**0**	**8**	**0.0**	**–7**	....	....	....	....	....	....	....	....	....	....	....	....	....
	Atlanta Knights	IHL	48	5	11	16	146	....	....	....	....	....	....	....	....	....	....	....	....	....	....	....	....	....	....	....
1996-97	**San Jose**	**NHL**	**8**	**0**	**0**	**0**	**22**	**0**	**0**	**0**	**4**	**0.0**	**–2**	....	....	....	....	....	....	....	....	....	....	....	....	....
	Kentucky	AHL	48	6	17	23	93	....	....	....	....	....	....	....	....	....	....	....	4	0	3	3	6	....	....	....
1997-98	Orlando	IHL	13	1	4	5	63	....	....	....	....	....	....	....	....	....	....	....	....	....	....	....	....	....	....	....
	San Antonio	IHL	60	1	10	11	116	....	....	....	....	....	....	....	....	....	....	....	....	....	....	....	....	....	....	....
1998-99	Chicago Wolves	IHL	34	0	10	10	186	....	....	....	....	....	....	....	....	....	....	....	....	....	....	....	....	....	....	....
99-2000	Chicago Wolves	IHL	42	0	4	4	98	....	....	....	....	....	....	....	....	....	....	....	5	0	0	0	8	....	....	....
	NHL Totals		**72**	**0**	**9**	**9**	**146**	**0**	**0**	**0**	**50**	**0.0**		....	....	....	....	....	....	....	....	....	....	....	....	....

Signed as a free agent by **Tampa Bay**, June 29, 1992. Signed as a free agent by **San Jose**, August 23, 1996. Claimed on waivers by **New Jersey** from **San Jose**, March 18, 1997. Signed as a free agent by **Chicago** (IHL), September 8, 1998.

LOWRY, Dave

(LOW-ree, DAYV) **CGY.**

Left wing. Shoots left. 6'1", 200 lbs. Born, Sudbury, Ont., February 14, 1965. Vancouver's 6th choice, 114th overall, in 1983 Entry Draft.

Season	Club	League	GP	G	A	Pts	PIM	PP	SH	GW	S	%	+/-	TF	F%	H	SB	Min	GP	G	A	Pts	PIM	PP	SH	GW
1981-82	Nepean Raiders	OMHA	60	50	64	114	46	....	....	....	....	....	....	....	....	....	....	....	....	....	....	....	....	....	....	....
1982-83	London Knights	OHL	42	11	16	27	48	....	....	....	....	....	....	....	....	....	....	....	3	0	0	0	14	....	....	....
1983-84	London Knights	OHL	66	29	47	76	125	....	....	....	....	....	....	....	....	....	....	....	8	6	6	12	41	....	....	....
1984-85	London Knights	OHL	61	60	60	120	94	....	....	....	....	....	....	....	....	....	....	....	8	6	5	11	10	....	....	....
1985-86	**Vancouver**	**NHL**	**73**	**10**	**8**	**18**	**143**	**1**	**0**	**1**	**66**	**15.2**	**–21**	....	....	....	....	....	**3**	**0**	**0**	**0**	**0**	**0**	**0**	**0**
1986-87	**Vancouver**	**NHL**	**70**	**8**	**10**	**18**	**176**	**0**	**0**	**1**	**74**	**10.8**	**–23**	....	....	....	....	....	....	....	....	....	....	....	....	....
1987-88	**Vancouver**	**NHL**	**22**	**1**	**3**	**4**	**38**	**0**	**0**	**0**	**14**	**7.1**	**–2**	....	....	....	....	....	....	....	....	....	....	....	....	....
	Fredericton	AHL	46	18	27	45	59	....	....	....	....	....	....	....	....	....	....	....	14	7	3	10	72	....	....	....
1988-89	**St. Louis**	**NHL**	**21**	**3**	**3**	**6**	**11**	**0**	**1**	**0**	**22**	**13.6**	**1**	....	....	....	....	....	**10**	**0**	**5**	**5**	**4**	**0**	**0**	**0**
	Peoria Rivermen	IHL	58	31	35	66	45	....	....	....	....	....	....	....	....	....	....	....	....	....	....	....	....	....	....	....
1989-90	**St. Louis**	**NHL**	**78**	**19**	**6**	**25**	**75**	**0**	**2**	**1**	**98**	**19.4**	**1**	....	....	....	....	....	**12**	**2**	**1**	**3**	**39**	**0**	**0**	**0**
1990-91	**St. Louis**	**NHL**	**79**	**19**	**21**	**40**	**168**	**0**	**2**	**5**	**123**	**15.4**	**19**	....	....	....	....	....	**13**	**1**	**4**	**5**	**35**	**0**	**0**	**0**
1991-92	**St. Louis**	**NHL**	**75**	**7**	**13**	**20**	**77**	**0**	**0**	**1**	**85**	**8.2**	**–11**	....	....	....	....	....	**6**	**0**	**1**	**1**	**20**	**0**	**0**	**0**
1992-93	**St. Louis**	**NHL**	**58**	**5**	**8**	**13**	**101**	**0**	**0**	**0**	**59**	**8.5**	**–18**	....	....	....	....	....	**11**	**2**	**0**	**2**	**14**	**0**	**1**	**0**
1993-94	**Florida**	**NHL**	**80**	**15**	**22**	**37**	**64**	**3**	**0**	**3**	**122**	**12.3**	**–4**	....	....	....	....	....	....	....	....	....	....	....	....	....
1994-95	**Florida**	**NHL**	**45**	**10**	**10**	**20**	**25**	**2**	**0**	**3**	**70**	**14.3**	**–3**	....	....	....	....	....	....	....	....	....	....	....	....	....
1995-96	**Florida**	**NHL**	**63**	**10**	**14**	**24**	**36**	**0**	**0**	**1**	**83**	**12.0**	**–2**	....	....	....	....	....	**22**	**10**	**7**	**17**	**39**	**4**	**0**	**2**
1996-97	**Florida**	**NHL**	**77**	**15**	**14**	**29**	**51**	**2**	**0**	**2**	**96**	**15.6**	**2**	....	....	....	....	....	**5**	**0**	**0**	**0**	**0**	**0**	**0**	**0**
1997-98	**Florida**	**NHL**	**7**	**0**	**0**	**0**	**2**	**0**	**0**	**0**	**4**	**0.0**	**–1**	....	....	....	....	....	....	....	....	....	....	....	....	....
	San Jose	**NHL**	**50**	**4**	**4**	**8**	**51**	**0**	**0**	**1**	**47**	**8.5**	**0**	....	....	....	....	....	**6**	**0**	**0**	**0**	**18**	**0**	**0**	**0**

			Regular Season																Playoffs							
Season	Club	League	GP	G	A	Pts	PIM	PP	SH	GW	S	%	+/–	TF	F%	H	SB	Min	GP	G	A	Pts	PIM	PP	SH	GW
1998-99	**San Jose**	**NHL**	**61**	**6**	**9**	**15**	**24**	**2**	**0**	**0**	**58**	**10.3**	**–5**	**6**	**50.0**	**70**	**7**	**9:14**	**1**	**0**	**0**	**0**	**0**	**0**	**0**	**0**
99-2000	**San Jose**	**NHL**	**32**	**1**	**4**	**5**	**18**	**0**	**0**	**0**	**25**	**4.0**	**1**	**1**	**100.0**	**81**	**3**	**9:11**	**12**	**1**	**2**	**3**	**6**	**0**	**0**	**0**
	NHL Totals		**891**	**133**	**149**	**282**	**1060**	**10**	**5**	**19**	**1046**	**12.7**		**7**	**57.1**	**151**	**10**	**9:13**	**101**	**16**	**20**	**36**	**175**	**4**	**1**	**2**

OHL First All-Star Team (1985)

Traded to **St. Louis** by **Vancouver** for Ernie Vargas, September 29, 1988. Claimed by **Florida** from **St. Louis** in Expansion Draft, June 24, 1993. Traded to **San Jose** by **Florida** with Florida's 1st round choice (later traded to Tampa Bay - Tampa Bay selected Vincent Lecavalier) for Viktor Kozlov and Florida's 5th round choice (previously acquired, Florida selected Jaroslav Spacek) in 1998 Entry Draft, November 13, 1997. • Missed majority of 1999-2000 season recovering from shoulder injury suffered in game vs. Montreal, November 23, 1999. Signed as a free agent by **Calgary**, July 24, 2000.

LUHNING, Warren

(LOO-nihng, WOH-rehn)

Right wing. Shoots right. 6'2", 185 lbs. Born, Edmonton, Alta., July 3, 1975. NY Islanders' 4th choice, 92nd overall, in 1993 Entry Draft.

1992-93	Calgary Royals	AJHL	46	18	25	43	287	....	....	....	....	....	....	....	....	....	....	....	....	....	....	....	....	....	....	....
1993-94	U. of Michigan	CCHA	38	13	6	19	83	....	....	....	....	....	....	....	....	....	....	....	....	....	....	....	....	....	....	....
1994-95	U. of Michigan	CCHA	36	17	23	40	80	....	....	....	....	....	....	....	....	....	....	....	....	....	....	....	....	....	....	....
1995-96	U. of Michigan	CCHA	40	20	32	52	123	....	....	....	....	....	....	....	....	....	....	....	....	....	....	....	....	....	....	....
1996-97	U. of Michigan	CCHA	43	22	23	45	106	....	....	....	....	....	....	....	....	....	....	....	....	....	....	....	....	....	....	....
1997-98	**NY Islanders**	**NHL**	**8**	**0**	**0**	**0**	**0**	**0**	**0**	**0**	**6**	**0.0**	**–4**	....	....	....	....	....	....	....	....	....	....	....	....	....
	Kentucky	AHL	51	6	7	13	82	....	....	....	....	....	....	....	....	....	....	....	....	....	....	....	....	....	....	....
1998-99	**NY Islanders**	**NHL**	**11**	**0**	**0**	**0**	**8**	**0**	**0**	**0**	**11**	**0.0**	**–4**	**0**	**0.0**	**11**	**2**	**9:17**	....	....	....	....	....	....	....	....
	Lowell	AHL	56	20	20	40	67	....	....	....	....	....	....	....	....	....	....	....	3	0	3	3	16	....	....	....
99-2000	**Dallas**	**NHL**	**10**	**0**	**1**	**1**	**13**	**0**	**0**	**0**	**7**	**0.0**	**–2**	**0**	**0.0**	**26**	**2**	**10:21**	....	....	....	....	....	....	....	....
	Michigan K-Wings	IHL	3	1	1	2	4	....	....	....	....	....	....	....	....	....	....	....	....	....	....	....	....	....	....	....
	NHL Totals		**29**	**0**	**1**	**1**	**21**	**0**	**0**	**0**	**24**	**0.0**		**0**	**0.0**	**37**	**4**	**9:47**	....	....	....	....	....	....	....	....

Traded to **Dallas** by **NY Islanders** for Dallas' 3rd round choice (previously acquired, Dallas selected Mathias Tjarnqvist) in 1999 Entry Draft, June 25, 1999.

LUKOWICH, Brad

(loo-KUH-which, BRAD) **DAL.**

Defense. Shoots left. 6'1", 200 lbs. Born, Cranbrook, B.C., August 12, 1976. NY Islanders' 4th choice, 90th overall, in 1994 Entry Draft.

1992-93	Cranbrook Colts	KIJHL	54	21	41	62	162	....	....	....	....	....	....	....	....	....	....	....	....	....	....	....	....	....	....	....
	Kamloops Blazers	WHL	1	0	0	0	0	....	....	....	....	....	....	....	....	....	....	....	....	....	....	....	....	....	....	....
1993-94	Kamloops Blazers	WHL	42	5	11	16	166	....	....	....	....	....	....	....	....	....	....	....	16	0	1	1	35	....	....	....
1994-95	Kamloops Blazers	WHL	63	10	35	45	125	....	....	....	....	....	....	....	....	....	....	....	18	0	7	7	21	....	....	....
1995-96	Kamloops Blazers	WHL	65	14	55	69	114	....	....	....	....	....	....	....	....	....	....	....	13	2	10	12	29	....	....	....
1996-97	Michigan K-Wings	IHL	69	2	6	8	77	....	....	....	....	....	....	....	....	....	....	....	4	0	1	1	2	....	....	....
1997-98	**Dallas**	**NHL**	**4**	**0**	**1**	**1**	**2**	**0**	**0**	**0**	**2**	**0.0**	**–2**	....	....	....	....	....	....	....	....	....	....	....	....	....
	Michigan K-Wings	IHL	60	6	27	33	104	....	....	....	....	....	....	....	....	....	....	....	4	0	4	4	14	....	....	....
1998-99♦	**Dallas**	**NHL**	**14**	**1**	**2**	**3**	**19**	**0**	**0**	**0**	**8**	**12.5**	**3**	**0**	**0.0**	**32**	**12**	**16:18**	**8**	**0**	**1**	**1**	**4**	**0**	**0**	**0**
	Michigan K-Wings	IHL	67	8	21	29	95	....	....	....	....	....	....	....	....	....	....	....	....	....	....	....	....	....	....	....
99-2000	**Dallas**	**NHL**	**60**	**3**	**1**	**4**	**50**	**0**	**0**	**1**	**33**	**9.1**	**–14**	**1**	**0.0**	**96**	**42**	**11:44**	....	....	....	....	....	....	....	....
	NHL Totals		**78**	**4**	**4**	**8**	**71**	**0**	**0**	**1**	**43**	**9.3**		**1**	**0.0**	**128**	**54**	**12:36**	**8**	**0**	**1**	**1**	**4**	**0**	**0**	**0**

Traded to **Dallas** by **NY Islanders** for Dallas' 3rd round choice (Robert Schnabel) in 1997 Entry Draft, June 1, 1996. Traded to **Minnesota** by **Dallas** with Manny Fernandez for Minnesota's 3rd round choice (Joel Lundqvist) in 2000 Entry Draft and 4th round choice in 2001 Entry Draft, June 12, 2000. Traded to **Dallas** by **Minnesota** with Minnesota's 3rd and 9th round choices in 2001 Entry Draft for Aaron Gavey, Pavel Patera, Dallas' 8th round choice (Eric Johansson) in 2000 Entry Draft and Minnesota's 4th round choice (previously acquired) in 2002 Entry Draft, June 25, 2000.

LUMME, Jyrki

(LOO-mee, YUHR-kee) **PHX.**

Defense. Shoots left. 6'1", 209 lbs. Born, Tampere, Finland, July 16, 1966. Montreal's 3rd choice, 57th overall, in 1986 Entry Draft.

1983-84	KooVee Tampere	Finn-Jr.	28	5	4	9	61	....	....	....	....	....	....	....	....	....	....	....	....	....	....	....	....	....	....	....
1984-85	KooVee Tampere	Finland-3	30	6	4	10	44	....	....	....	....	....	....	....	....	....	....	....	....	....	....	....	....	....	....	....
1985-86	Ilves Tampere	Finn-Jr.	6	3	3	6	6	....	....	....	....	....	....	....	....	....	....	....	4	0	0	0	8	....	....	....
	Ilves Tampere	Finland	31	1	4	5	4	....	....	....	....	....	....	....	....	....	....	....	....	....	....	....	....	....	....	....
1986-87	Ilves Tampere	Finn-Jr.	1	0	1	1	6	....	....	....	....	....	....	....	....	....	....	....	1	1	0	1	6	....	....	....
	Ilves Tampere	Finland	43	12	12	24	52	....	....	....	....	....	....	....	....	....	....	....	4	0	1	1	2	....	....	....
1987-88	Ilves Tampere	Finland	43	8	22	30	75	....	....	....	....	....	....	....	....	....	....	....	....	....	....	....	....	....	....	....
	Finland	Olympics	6	0	1	1	2	....	....	....	....	....	....	....	....	....	....	....	....	....	....	....	....	....	....	....
1988-89	**Montreal**	**NHL**	**21**	**1**	**3**	**4**	**10**	**1**	**0**	**0**	**18**	**5.6**	**3**	....	....	....	....	....	....	....	....	....	....	....	....	....
	Sherbrooke	AHL	26	4	11	15	10	....	....	....	....	....	....	....	....	....	....	....	6	1	3	4	4	....	....	....
1989-90	**Montreal**	**NHL**	**54**	**1**	**19**	**20**	**41**	**0**	**0**	**0**	**79**	**1.3**	**17**	....	....	....	....	....	....	....	....	....	....	....	....	....
	Vancouver	**NHL**	**11**	**3**	**7**	**10**	**8**	**0**	**0**	**1**	**30**	**10.0**	**0**	....	....	....	....	....	....	....	....	....	....	....	....	....
1990-91	**Vancouver**	**NHL**	**80**	**5**	**27**	**32**	**59**	**1**	**0**	**0**	**157**	**3.2**	**–15**	....	....	....	....	....	**6**	**2**	**3**	**5**	**0**	**1**	**1**	**0**
1991-92	**Vancouver**	**NHL**	**75**	**12**	**32**	**44**	**65**	**3**	**1**	**1**	**106**	**11.3**	**25**	....	....	....	....	....	**13**	**2**	**3**	**5**	**4**	**1**	**0**	**1**
1992-93	**Vancouver**	**NHL**	**74**	**8**	**36**	**44**	**55**	**3**	**2**	**1**	**123**	**6.5**	**30**	....	....	....	....	....	**12**	**0**	**5**	**5**	**6**	**0**	**0**	**0**
1993-94	**Vancouver**	**NHL**	**83**	**13**	**42**	**55**	**50**	**1**	**3**	**3**	**161**	**8.1**	**3**	....	....	....	....	....	**24**	**2**	**11**	**13**	**16**	**2**	**0**	**1**
1994-95	Ilves Tampere	Finland	12	4	4	8	24	....	....	....	....	....	....	....	....	....	....	....	....	....	....	....	....	....	....	....
	Vancouver	**NHL**	**36**	**5**	**12**	**17**	**26**	**3**	**0**	**1**	**78**	**6.4**	**4**	....	....	....	....	....	**11**	**2**	**6**	**8**	**8**	**1**	**0**	**0**
1995-96	**Vancouver**	**NHL**	**80**	**17**	**37**	**54**	**50**	**8**	**0**	**2**	**192**	**8.9**	**–9**	....	....	....	....	....	**6**	**1**	**3**	**4**	**2**	**1**	**0**	**0**
1996-97	**Vancouver**	**NHL**	**66**	**11**	**24**	**35**	**32**	**5**	**0**	**2**	**107**	**10.3**	**8**	....	....	....	....	....	....	....	....	....	....	....	....	....
1997-98	**Vancouver**	**NHL**	**74**	**9**	**21**	**30**	**34**	**4**	**0**	**1**	**117**	**7.7**	**–25**	....	....	....	....	....	....	....	....	....	....	....	....	....
	Finland	Olympics	6	1	0	1	16	....	....	....	....	....	....	....	....	....	....	....	....	....	....	....	....	....	....	....
1998-99	**Phoenix**	**NHL**	**60**	**7**	**21**	**28**	**34**	**1**	**0**	**4**	**121**	**5.8**	**5**	**0**	**0.0**	**26**	**71**	**23:20**	**7**	**0**	**1**	**1**	**6**	**0**	**0**	**0**
99-2000	**Phoenix**	**NHL**	**74**	**8**	**32**	**40**	**44**	**4**	**0**	**3**	**142**	**5.6**	**9**	**0**	**0.0**	**51**	**105**	**23:36**	**5**	**0**	**1**	**1**	**2**	**0**	**0**	**0**
	NHL Totals		**788**	**100**	**313**	**413**	**508**	**34**	**6**	**19**	**1431**	**7.0**		**0**	**0.0**	**77**	**176**	**23:29**	**84**	**9**	**33**	**42**	**44**	**6**	**1**	**2**

Traded to **Vancouver** by **Montreal** for St. Louis' 2nd round choice (previously acquired, Montreal selected Craig Darby) in 1991 Entry Draft, March 6, 1990. Signed as a free agent by **Phoenix**, July 3, 1998.

LYASHENKO, Roman

(LIGH-a-SHEHN-koh, ROH-man) **DAL.**

Center. Shoots right. 6', 189 lbs. Born, Murmansk, Russia, May 2, 1979. Dallas' 2nd choice, 52nd overall, in 1997 Entry Draft.

1995-96	Torpedo Yaroslavl	CIS-2	60	7	10	17	12	....	....	....	....	....	....	....	....	....	....	....	....	....	....	....	....	....	....	....
1996-97	Torpedo Yaroslavl	Russia-3	2	1	1	2	8	....	....	....	....	....	....	....	....	....	....	....	....	....	....	....	....	....	....	....
	Torpedo Yaroslavl	Russia	42	5	7	12	16	....	....	....	....	....	....	....	....	....	....	....	9	3	0	3	6	....	....	....
1997-98	Torpedo Yaroslavl	Russia	46	7	6	13	28	....	....	....	....	....	....	....	....	....	....	....	....	....	....	....	....	....	....	....
	Torpedo Yaroslavl	EuroHL	10	1	1	2	2	....	....	....	....	....	....	....	....	....	....	....	....	....	....	....	....	....	....	....
1998-99	Torpedo Yaroslavl	Russia	42	10	9	19	51	....	....	....	....	....	....	....	....	....	....	....	9	0	4	4	8	....	....	....
99-2000	**Dallas**	**NHL**	**58**	**6**	**6**	**12**	**10**	**0**	**0**	**1**	**51**	**11.8**	**–2**	**339**	**45.7**	**46**	**15**	**10:56**	**16**	**2**	**1**	**3**	**0**	**0**	**0**	**2**
	Michigan K-Wings	IHL	9	3	2	5	8	....	....	....	....	....	....	....	....	....	....	....	....	....	....	....	....	....	....	....
	NHL Totals		**58**	**6**	**6**	**12**	**10**	**0**	**0**	**1**	**51**	**11.8**		**339**	**45.7**	**46**	**15**	**10:56**	**16**	**2**	**1**	**3**	**0**	**0**	**0**	**2**

MacDONALD, Craig

(MAC-DAWN-ohld, KRAYG) **CAR.**

Center. Shoots left. 6'2", 195 lbs. Born, Antigonish, N.S., April 7, 1977. Hartford's 3rd choice, 88th overall, in 1996 Entry Draft.

1994-95	Lawrence Prep	Hi-School	30	25	52	77	10	....	....	....	....	....	....	....	....	....	....	....	....	....	....	....	....	....	....	....
1995-96	Harvard University	ECAC	34	7	10	17	10	....	....	....	....	....	....	....	....	....	....	....	....	....	....	....	....	....	....	....
1996-97	Harvard University	ECAC	32	6	10	16	20	....	....	....	....	....	....	....	....	....	....	....	....	....	....	....	....	....	....	....
1997-98	Canada	Nat-Team	58	18	29	47	38	....	....	....	....	....	....	....	....	....	....	....	....	....	....	....	....	....	....	....
1998-99	**Carolina**	**NHL**	**11**	**0**	**0**	**0**	**0**	**0**	**0**	**0**	**5**	**0.0**	**0**	**2**	**100.0**	**6**	**1**	**2:29**	**1**	**0**	**0**	**0**	**0**	**0**	**0**	**0**
	New Haven	AHL	62	17	31	48	77	....	....	....	....	....	....	....	....	....	....	....	....	....	....	....	....	....	....	....
99-2000	Cincinnati	IHL	78	12	24	36	76	....	....	....	....	....	....	....	....	....	....	....	11	4	1	5	8	....	....	....
	NHL Totals		**11**	**0**	**0**	**0**	**0**	**0**	**0**	**0**	**5**	**0.0**		**2**	**100.0**	**6**	**1**	**2:29**	**1**	**0**	**0**	**0**	**0**	**0**	**0**	**0**

Rights transferred to **Carolina** after **Hartford** franchise relocated, June 25, 1997

MacINNIS, Al

(MAC-IHN-his, AL) **ST.L.**

Defense. Shoots right. 6'2", 209 lbs. Born, Inverness, N.S., July 11, 1963. Calgary's 1st choice, 15th overall, in 1981 Entry Draft.

			Regular Season																Playoffs							
Season	Club	League	GP	G	A	Pts	PIM	PP	SH	GW	S	%	+/-	TF	F%	H	SB	Min	GP	G	A	Pts	PIM	PP	SH	GW
1979-80	Regina Blues	SJHL	59	20	28	48	110	....	....	....	....	....	....	....	....	....	....	....	....	....	....	....	....	....	....	....
1980-81	Kitchener	OMJHL	47	11	28	39	59	....	....	....	....	....	....	....	....	....	....	....	18	4	12	16	20	....	....	....
1981-82	Kitchener	OHL	59	25	50	75	145	....	....	....	....	....	....	....	....	....	....	....	15	5	10	15	44	....	....	....
	Calgary	**NHL**	**2**	**0**	**0**	**0**	**0**	**0**	**0**	**0**	**2**	**0.0**	**0**	....	....	....	....	....	....	....	....	....	....	....	....	....
1982-83	Kitchener	OHL	51	38	46	84	67	....	....	....	....	....	....	....	....	....	....	....	8	3	8	11	9	....	....	....
	Calgary	**NHL**	**14**	**1**	**3**	**4**	**9**	**0**	**0**	**0**	**7**	**14.3**	**0**	....	....	....	....	....	....	....	....	....	....	....	....	....
1983-84	**Calgary**	**NHL**	**51**	**11**	**34**	**45**	**42**	**7**	**0**	**2**	**160**	**6.9**	**0**	....	....	....	....	....	**11**	**2**	**12**	**14**	**13**	**2**	**0**	**1**
	Colorado Flames	CHL	19	5	14	19	22	....	....	....	....	....	....	....	....	....	....	....	....	....	....	....	....	....	....	....
1984-85	**Calgary**	**NHL**	**67**	**14**	**52**	**66**	**75**	**8**	**0**	**0**	**259**	**5.4**	**7**	....	....	....	....	....	**4**	**1**	**2**	**3**	**8**	**1**	**0**	**0**
1985-86	**Calgary**	**NHL**	**77**	**11**	**57**	**68**	**76**	**4**	**0**	**0**	**241**	**4.6**	**38**	....	....	....	....	....	**21**	**4**	***15**	**19**	**30**	**2**	**0**	**0**
1986-87	**Calgary**	**NHL**	**79**	**20**	**56**	**76**	**97**	**7**	**0**	**2**	**262**	**7.6**	**20**	....	....	....	....	....	**4**	**1**	**0**	**1**	**0**	**1**	**0**	**0**
1987-88	**Calgary**	**NHL**	**80**	**25**	**58**	**83**	**114**	**7**	**2**	**2**	**245**	**10.2**	**13**	....	....	....	....	....	**7**	**3**	**6**	**9**	**18**	**2**	**0**	**0**
1988-89♦	**Calgary**	**NHL**	**79**	**16**	**58**	**74**	**126**	**8**	**0**	**3**	**277**	**5.8**	**38**	....	....	....	....	....	**22**	**7**	***24**	***31**	**46**	**5**	**0**	**4**
1989-90	**Calgary**	**NHL**	**79**	**28**	**62**	**90**	**82**	**14**	**1**	**3**	**304**	**9.2**	**20**	....	....	....	....	....	**6**	**2**	**3**	**5**	**8**	**1**	**0**	**0**
1990-91	**Calgary**	**NHL**	**78**	**28**	**75**	**103**	**90**	**17**	**0**	**1**	**305**	**9.2**	**42**	....	....	....	....	....	**7**	**2**	**3**	**5**	**8**	**2**	**0**	**0**
1991-92	**Calgary**	**NHL**	**72**	**20**	**57**	**77**	**83**	**11**	**0**	**0**	**304**	**6.6**	**13**	....	....	....	....	....	....	....	....	....	....	....	....	....
1992-93	**Calgary**	**NHL**	**50**	**11**	**43**	**54**	**61**	**7**	**0**	**4**	**201**	**5.5**	**15**	....	....	....	....	....	**6**	**1**	**6**	**7**	**10**	**1**	**0**	**0**
1993-94	**Calgary**	**NHL**	**75**	**28**	**54**	**82**	**95**	**12**	**1**	**5**	**324**	**8.6**	**35**	....	....	....	....	....	**7**	**2**	**6**	**8**	**12**	**1**	**0**	**0**
1994-95	**St. Louis**	**NHL**	**32**	**8**	**20**	**28**	**43**	**2**	**0**	**0**	**110**	**7.3**	**19**	....	....	....	....	....	**7**	**1**	**5**	**6**	**10**	**0**	**0**	**0**
1995-96	**St. Louis**	**NHL**	**82**	**17**	**44**	**61**	**88**	**9**	**1**	**1**	**317**	**5.4**	**5**	....	....	....	....	....	**13**	**3**	**4**	**7**	**20**	**1**	**0**	**0**
1996-97	**St. Louis**	**NHL**	**72**	**13**	**30**	**43**	**65**	**6**	**1**	**1**	**296**	**4.4**	**2**	....	....	....	....	....	**6**	**1**	**2**	**3**	**4**	**1**	**0**	**0**
1997-98	**St. Louis**	**NHL**	**71**	**19**	**30**	**49**	**80**	**9**	**1**	**2**	**227**	**8.4**	**6**	....	....	....	....	....	**8**	**2**	**6**	**8**	**12**	**1**	**0**	**0**
	Canada	Olympics	6	2	0	2	2	....	....	....	....	....	....	....	....	....	....	....	....	....	....	....	....	....	....	....
1998-99	**St. Louis**	**NHL**	**82**	**20**	**42**	**62**	**70**	**11**	**1**	**2**	**314**	**6.4**	**33**	**0**	**0.0**	**56**	**128**	**29:07**	**13**	**4**	**8**	**12**	**20**	**2**	**0**	**0**
99-2000	**St. Louis**	**NHL**	**61**	**11**	**28**	**39**	**34**	**6**	**0**	**7**	**245**	**4.5**	**20**	**0**	**0.0**	**44**	**72**	**26:07**	**7**	**1**	**3**	**4**	**14**	**1**	**0**	**0**
	NHL Totals		**1203**	**301**	**803**	**1104**	**1330**	**145**	**8**	**35**	**4400**	**6.8**		**0**	**0.0**	**100**	**200**	**27:50**	**149**	**37**	**105**	**142**	**233**	**24**	**0**	**5**

OHL First All-Star Team (1982, 1983) • NHL Second All-Star Team (1987, 1989, 1994) • Won Conn Smythe Trophy (1989) • NHL First All-Star Team (1990, 1991, 1999) • Won James Norris Memorial Trophy (1999) • Played in NHL All-Star Game (1985, 1988, 1990, 1991, 1992, 1994, 1996, 1997, 1998, 1999, 2000)

Traded to **St. Louis** by **Calgary** with Calgary's 4th round choice (Didier Tremblay) in 1997 Entry Draft for Phil Housley and St. Louis' 2nd round choices in 1996 (Steve Begin) and 1997 (John Tripp) Entry Drafts, July 4, 1994.

MacLEAN, Don

(MAC-layn, DAW-nohld) **TOR.**

Center. Shoots left. 6'2", 199 lbs. Born, Sydney, N.S., January 14, 1977. Los Angeles' 2nd choice, 33rd overall, in 1995 Entry Draft.

			Regular Season																Playoffs							
Season	Club	League	GP	G	A	Pts	PIM	PP	SH	GW	S	%	+/-	TF	F%	H	SB	Min	GP	G	A	Pts	PIM	PP	SH	GW
1992-93	Halifax Hawks	NSAHA	27	15	25	40	34	....	....	....	....	....	....	....	....	....	....	....	....	....	....	....	....	....	....	....
1993-94	Halifax Hawks	NSAHA	25	35	35	70	151	....	....	....	....	....	....	....	....	....	....	....	....	....	....	....	....	....	....	....
1994-95	Beauport	QMJHL	64	15	27	42	37	....	....	....	....	....	....	....	....	....	....	....	17	4	4	8	6	....	....	....
1995-96	Beauport	QMJHL	1	0	1	1	0	....	....	....	....	....	....	....	....	....	....	....	....	....	....	....	....	....	....	....
	Laval Titan	QMJHL	21	17	11	28	29	....	....	....	....	....	....	....	....	....	....	....	....	....	....	....	....	....	....	....
	Hull Olympiques	QMJHL	39	26	34	60	44	....	....	....	....	....	....	....	....	....	....	....	17	6	7	13	14	....	....	....
1996-97	Hull Olympiques	QMJHL	69	34	47	81	67	....	....	....	....	....	....	....	....	....	....	....	14	11	10	21	39	....	....	....
1997-98	**Los Angeles**	**NHL**	**22**	**5**	**2**	**7**	**4**	**2**	**0**	**0**	**25**	**20.0**	**–1**	....	....	....	....	....	....	....	....	....	....	....	....	....
	Fredericton	AHL	39	9	5	14	32	....	....	....	....	....	....	....	....	....	....	....	4	1	3	4	2	....	....	....
1998-99	Springfield	AHL	41	5	14	19	31	....	....	....	....	....	....	....	....	....	....	....	....	....	....	....	....	....	....	....
	Grand Rapids	IHL	28	6	13	19	8	....	....	....	....	....	....	....	....	....	....	....	....	....	....	....	....	....	....	....
99-2000	Lowell	AHL	40	11	17	28	18	....	....	....	....	....	....	....	....	....	....	....	....	....	....	....	....	....	....	....
	St. John's Leafs	AHL	21	14	12	26	8	....	....	....	....	....	....	....	....	....	....	....	....	....	....	....	....	....	....	....
	NHL Totals		**22**	**5**	**2**	**7**	**4**	**2**	**0**	**0**	**25**	**20.0**		....	....	....	....	....	....	....	....	....	....	....	....	....

Traded to **Toronto** by **Los Angeles** for Craig Charron, February 23, 2000.

MacLEAN, John

(MAC-layn, JAWN) **NYR**

Right wing. Shoots right. 6', 200 lbs. Born, Oshawa, Ont., November 20, 1964. New Jersey's 1st choice, 6th overall, in 1983 Entry Draft.

			Regular Season																Playoffs							
Season	Club	League	GP	G	A	Pts	PIM	PP	SH	GW	S	%	+/-	TF	F%	H	SB	Min	GP	G	A	Pts	PIM	PP	SH	GW
1980-81	Oshawa Legion	OJHL	41	35	35	70	151	....	....	....	....	....	....	....	....	....	....	....	....	....	....	....	....	....	....	....
1981-82	Oshawa Generals	OHL	67	17	22	39	197	....	....	....	....	....	....	....	....	....	....	....	12	3	6	9	63	....	....	....
1982-83	Oshawa Generals	OHL	66	47	51	98	138	....	....	....	....	....	....	....	....	....	....	....	17	*18	20	*38	35	....	....	....
1983-84	Oshawa Generals	OHL	30	23	36	59	58	....	....	....	....	....	....	....	....	....	....	....	7	2	5	7	18	....	....	....
	New Jersey	**NHL**	**23**	**1**	**0**	**1**	**10**	**0**	**0**	**0**	**22**	**4.5**	**–7**	....	....	....	....	....	....	....	....	....	....	....	....	....
1984-85	**New Jersey**	**NHL**	**61**	**13**	**20**	**33**	**44**	**1**	**0**	**4**	**92**	**14.1**	**–11**	....	....	....	....	....	....	....	....	....	....	....	....	....
1985-86	**New Jersey**	**NHL**	**74**	**21**	**36**	**57**	**112**	**1**	**0**	**4**	**139**	**15.1**	**–3**	....	....	....	....	....	....	....	....	....	....	....	....	....
1986-87	**New Jersey**	**NHL**	**80**	**31**	**36**	**67**	**120**	**9**	**0**	**4**	**197**	**15.7**	**–23**	....	....	....	....	....	....	....	....	....	....	....	....	....
1987-88	**New Jersey**	**NHL**	**76**	**23**	**16**	**39**	**147**	**12**	**0**	**4**	**204**	**11.3**	**–10**	....	....	....	....	....	**20**	**7**	**11**	**18**	**60**	**2**	**0**	**2**
1988-89	**New Jersey**	**NHL**	**74**	**42**	**45**	**87**	**122**	**14**	**0**	**4**	**266**	**15.8**	**26**	....	....	....	....	....	....	....	....	....	....	....	....	....
1989-90	**New Jersey**	**NHL**	**80**	**41**	**38**	**79**	**80**	**10**	**3**	**11**	**322**	**12.7**	**17**	....	....	....	....	....	**6**	**4**	**1**	**5**	**12**	**2**	**1**	**0**
1990-91	**New Jersey**	**NHL**	**78**	**45**	**33**	**78**	**150**	**19**	**2**	**7**	**292**	**15.4**	**8**	....	....	....	....	....	**7**	**5**	**3**	**8**	**20**	**1**	**0**	**0**
1991-92	**New Jersey**	**NHL**	DID NOT PLAY – INJURED																							
1992-93	**New Jersey**	**NHL**	**80**	**24**	**24**	**48**	**102**	**7**	**1**	**3**	**195**	**12.3**	**–6**	....	....	....	....	....	**5**	**0**	**1**	**1**	**10**	**0**	**0**	**0**
1993-94	**New Jersey**	**NHL**	**80**	**37**	**33**	**70**	**95**	**8**	**0**	**4**	**277**	**13.4**	**30**	....	....	....	....	....	**20**	**6**	**10**	**16**	**22**	**2**	**0**	**1**
1994-95♦	**New Jersey**	**NHL**	**46**	**17**	**12**	**29**	**32**	**2**	**1**	**0**	**139**	**12.2**	**13**	....	....	....	....	....	**20**	**5**	**13**	**18**	**14**	**2**	**0**	**0**
1995-96	**New Jersey**	**NHL**	**76**	**20**	**28**	**48**	**91**	**3**	**3**	**3**	**237**	**8.4**	**3**	....	....	....	....	....	....	....	....	....	....	....	....	....
1996-97	**New Jersey**	**NHL**	**80**	**29**	**25**	**54**	**49**	**5**	**0**	**6**	**254**	**11.4**	**11**	....	....	....	....	....	**10**	**4**	**5**	**9**	**4**	**2**	**1**	**1**
1997-98	**New Jersey**	**NHL**	**26**	**3**	**8**	**11**	**14**	**1**	**0**	**1**	**74**	**4.1**	**–6**	....	....	....	....	....	....	....	....	....	....	....	....	....
	San Jose	**NHL**	**51**	**13**	**19**	**32**	**28**	**5**	**0**	**2**	**139**	**9.4**	**0**	....	....	....	....	....	**6**	**2**	**3**	**5**	**4**	**1**	**0**	**0**
1998-99	**NY Rangers**	**NHL**	**82**	**28**	**27**	**55**	**46**	**11**	**1**	**2**	**231**	**12.1**	**5**	**20**	**35.0**	**120**	**30**	**20:43**	....	....	....	....	....	....	....	....
99-2000	**NY Rangers**	**NHL**	**77**	**18**	**24**	**42**	**52**	**6**	**2**	**3**	**158**	**11.4**	**–2**	**40**	**55.0**	**48**	**43**	**14:44**	....	....	....	....	....	....	....	....
	NHL Totals		**1144**	**406**	**424**	**830**	**1294**	**114**	**13**	**62**	**3238**	**12.5**		**60**	**48.3**	**168**	**73**	**17:49**	**94**	**33**	**47**	**80**	**146**	**12**	**2**	**4**

Memorial Cup All-Star Team (1983) • Played in NHL All-Star Game (1989, 1991)

• Missed entire 1991-92 season recovering from knee surgery, June, 1991. Traded to **San Jose** by **New Jersey** with Ken Sutton for Doug Bodger and Dody Wood, December 7, 1997. Signed as a free agent by **NY Rangers**, July 22, 1998.

MADDEN, John

(MA-dehn, JAWN) **N.J.**

Left wing. Shoots left. 5'11", 195 lbs. Born, Barrie, Ont., May 4, 1975.

			Regular Season																Playoffs							
Season	Club	League	GP	G	A	Pts	PIM	PP	SH	GW	S	%	+/-	TF	F%	H	SB	Min	GP	G	A	Pts	PIM	PP	SH	GW
1989-90	Alliston Hornets	OJHL-C	31	24	25	49	26	....	....	....	....	....	....	....	....	....	....	....	....	....	....	....	....	....	....	....
1990-91	Alliston Hornets	OJHL-C	14	15	21	36	10	....	....	....	....	....	....	....	....	....	....	....	....	....	....	....	....	....	....	....
	Barrie Colts	OJHL-B	1	0	0	0	0	....	....	....	....	....	....	....	....	....	....	....	....	....	....	....	....	....	....	....
1991-92	Barrie Colts	OJHL-B	42	50	54	104	46	....	....	....	....	....	....	....	....	....	....	....	13	10	9	19	14	....	....	....
1992-93	Barrie Colts	OJHL	43	49	75	124	62	....	....	....	....	....	....	....	....	....	....	....	....	....	....	....	....	....	....	....
1993-94	U. of Michigan	CCHA	36	6	11	17	14	....	....	....	....	....	....	....	....	....	....	....	....	....	....	....	....	....	....	....
1994-95	U. of Michigan	CCHA	39	21	22	43	8	....	....	....	....	....	....	....	....	....	....	....	....	....	....	....	....	....	....	....
1995-96	U. of Michigan	CCHA	43	27	30	57	45	....	....	....	....	....	....	....	....	....	....	....	....	....	....	....	....	....	....	....
1996-97	U. of Michigan	CCHA	42	26	37	63	56	....	....	....	....	....	....	....	....	....	....	....	....	....	....	....	....	....	....	....
1997-98	Albany River Rats	AHL	74	20	36	56	40	....	....	....	....	....	....	....	....	....	....	....	13	3	13	16	14	....	....	....
1998-99	**New Jersey**	**NHL**	**4**	**0**	**1**	**1**	**0**	**0**	**0**	**0**	**4**	**0.0**	**–2**	**0**	**0.0**	**3**	**1**	**9:13**	....	....	....	....	....	....	....	....
	Albany River Rats	AHL	75	38	60	98	44	....	....	....	....	....	....	....	....	....	....	....	5	2	2	4	6	....	....	....
99-2000♦	**New Jersey**	**NHL**	**74**	**16**	**9**	**25**	**6**	**0**	**6**	**3**	**115**	**13.9**	**7**	**770**	**47.5**	**92**	**25**	**11:40**	**20**	**3**	**4**	**7**	**0**	**0**	**1**	**2**
	NHL Totals		**78**	**16**	**10**	**26**	**6**	**0**	**6**	**3**	**119**	**13.4**		**770**	**47.5**	**95**	**26**	**11:32**	**20**	**3**	**4**	**7**	**0**	**0**	**1**	**2**

CCHA First All-Star Team (1997) • NCAA West First All-American Team (1997)

Signed as a free agent by **New Jersey**, June 26, 1997.

MAIR, Adam
(MAIR, A-dam) **TOR.**

Center. Shoots right. 6'2", 195 lbs. Born, Hamilton, Ont., February 15, 1979. Toronto's 2nd choice, 84th overall, in 1997 Entry Draft.

			Regular Season																Playoffs							
Season	Club	League	GP	G	A	Pts	PIM	PP	SH	GW	S	%	+/–	TF	F%	H	SB	Min	GP	G	A	Pts	PIM	PP	SH	GW
1994-95	Ohsweken Eagles	OJHL-B	39	21	23	44	91																			
1995-96	Owen Sound	OHL	62	12	15	27	63												6	0	0	0	2			
1996-97	Owen Sound	OHL	65	16	35	51	113												4	1	0	1	2			
1997-98	Owen Sound	OHL	56	25	27	52	179												11	6	3	9	31			
1998-99	Owen Sound	OHL	43	23	41	64	109												16	10	10	20	*47			
	St. John's Leafs	AHL																	3	1	0	1	6			
	Toronto	**NHL**																	**5**	**1**	**0**	**1**	**14**	**0**	**0**	**0**
99-2000	**Toronto**	**NHL**	**8**	**1**	**0**	**1**	**6**	**0**	**0**	**0**	**7**	**14.3**	**–1**	**9**	**33.3**	**14**	**1**	**11:33**	**5**	**0**	**0**	**0**	**8**	**0**	**0**	**0**
	St. John's Leafs	AHL	66	22	27	49	124																			
	NHL Totals		**8**	**1**	**0**	**1**	**6**	**0**	**0**	**0**	**7**	**14.3**		**9**	**33.3**	**14**	**1**	**11:33**	**10**	**1**	**0**	**1**	**22**	**0**	**0**	**0**

MAJOR, Mark
(MAY-johr, MAHRK)

Left wing. Shoots left. 6'3", 223 lbs. Born, Toronto, Ont., March 20, 1970. Pittsburgh's 2nd choice, 25th overall, in 1988 Entry Draft.

			Regular Season																Playoffs							
Season	Club	League	GP	G	A	Pts	PIM	PP	SH	GW	S	%	+/–	TF	F%	H	SB	Min	GP	G	A	Pts	PIM	PP	SH	GW
1986-87	Don Mills Flyers	MTHL	36	12	14	26	81																			
1987-88	North Bay	OHL	57	16	17	33	272												4	0	2	2	8			
1988-89	North Bay	OHL	11	3	2	5	58																			
	Kingston Raiders	OHL	53	22	29	51	193																			
1989-90	Kingston	OHL	62	29	32	61	168												6	3	3	6	12			
1990-91	Muskegon	IHL	60	8	10	18	160												5	0	0	0	0			
1991-92	Muskegon	IHL	80	13	18	31	302												12	1	3	4	29			
1992-93	Cleveland	IHL	82	13	15	28	155												3	0	0	0	0			
1993-94	Providence Bruins	AHL	61	17	9	26	176																			
1994-95	Detroit Vipers	IHL	78	17	19	36	229												5	0	1	1	23			
1995-96	Adirondack	AHL	78	10	19	29	234												3	0	0	0	21			
1996-97	**Detroit**	**NHL**	**2**	**0**	**0**	**0**	**5**	**0**	**0**	**0**	**0**	**0.0**	**0**													
	Adirondack	AHL	78	17	18	35	213												4	0	0	0	13			
1997-98	Portland Pirates	AHL	79	13	2	15	355												10	2	1	3	52			
1998-99	Portland Pirates	AHL	66	5	4	9	250																			
99-2000	Houston Aeros	IHL	20	1	0	1	81																			
	Flint Generals	UHL	36	23	18	41	135												15	8	3	11	67			
	NHL Totals		**2**	**0**	**0**	**0**	**5**	**0**	**0**	**0**	**0**	**0.0**														

Signed as a free agent by **Boston**, July 22, 1993. Signed as a free agent by **Detroit**, June 26, 1995. Signed as a free agent by **Washington**, August 20, 1997. Signed as a free agent by **Flint** (UHL), August 17, 2000. • Played w/ RHI's Buffalo Stampede in 1994 (21-18-14-32-63) and 1995 (23-17-20-37-97); Empire State Cobras in 1996 (23-11-19-30-98); New Jersey R&R in 1997 (10-8-8-16-73); Buffalo Wings in 1998 (13-21-10-31-85) and 1999 (23-24-34-58-111).

MALAKHOV, Vladimir
(mah-LAH-kahf, VLA-dih-meer) **NYR**

Defense. Shoots left. 6'4", 230 lbs. Born, Ekaterinburg, USSR, August 30, 1968. NY Islanders' 12th choice, 191st overall, in 1989 Entry Draft.

			Regular Season																Playoffs							
Season	Club	League	GP	G	A	Pts	PIM	PP	SH	GW	S	%	+/–	TF	F%	H	SB	Min	GP	G	A	Pts	PIM	PP	SH	GW
1986-87	SKA Spartak	USSR	22	0	1	1	12																			
1987-88	SKA Spartak	USSR	28	2	2	4	26																			
1988-89	CSKA Moscow	USSR	34	6	2	8	16																			
1989-90	CSKA Moscow	USSR	48	2	10	12	34																			
1990-91	CSKA Moscow	USSR	46	5	13	18	22																			
1991-92	CSKA Moscow	CIS	40	1	9	10	12																			
	Russia	Olympics	8	3	0	3	4																			
1992-93	**NY Islanders**	**NHL**	**64**	**14**	**38**	**52**	**59**	**7**	**0**	**0**	**178**	**7.9**	**14**						**17**	**3**	**6**	**9**	**12**	**0**	**0**	**0**
	Capital District	AHL	3	2	1	3	11																			
1993-94	**NY Islanders**	**NHL**	**76**	**10**	**47**	**57**	**80**	**4**	**0**	**2**	**235**	**4.3**	**29**						**4**	**0**	**0**	**0**	**6**	**0**	**0**	**0**
1994-95	**NY Islanders**	**NHL**	**26**	**3**	**13**	**16**	**32**	**1**	**0**	**0**	**61**	**4.9**	**–1**													
	Montreal	**NHL**	**14**	**1**	**4**	**5**	**14**	**0**	**0**	**0**	**30**	**3.3**	**–2**													
1995-96	**Montreal**	**NHL**	**61**	**5**	**23**	**28**	**79**	**2**	**0**	**0**	**122**	**4.1**	**7**													
1996-97	**Montreal**	**NHL**	**65**	**10**	**20**	**30**	**43**	**5**	**0**	**1**	**177**	**5.6**	**3**						**5**	**0**	**0**	**0**	**6**	**0**	**0**	**0**
1997-98	**Montreal**	**NHL**	**74**	**13**	**31**	**44**	**70**	**8**	**0**	**2**	**166**	**7.8**	**16**						**9**	**3**	**4**	**7**	**10**	**2**	**0**	**0**
1998-99	**Montreal**	**NHL**	**62**	**13**	**21**	**34**	**77**	**8**	**0**	**3**	**143**	**9.1**	**–7**	**0**	**0.0**	**74**	**88**	**23:29**								
99-2000	**Montreal**	**NHL**	**7**	**0**	**0**	**0**	**4**	**0**	**0**	**0**	**7**	**0.0**	**0**	**0**	**0.0**	**6**	**9**	**21:20**								
	♦ New Jersey	**NHL**	**17**	**1**	**4**	**5**	**19**	**1**	**0**	**1**	**11**	**9.1**	**1**	**0**	**0.0**	**20**	**13**	**20:18**	**23**	**1**	**4**	**5**	**18**	**1**	**0**	**0**
	NHL Totals		**466**	**70**	**201**	**271**	**477**	**36**	**0**	**9**	**1130**	**6.2**		**0**	**0.0**	**100**	**110**	**22:41**	**58**	**7**	**14**	**21**	**52**	**3**	**0**	**0**

NHL All-Rookie Team (1993)

Traded to **Montreal** by **NY Islanders** with Pierre Turgeon for Kirk Muller, Mathieu Schneider and Craig Darby, April 5, 1995. • Missed majority of 1999-2000 season recovering from knee injury suffered in exhibition game vs. Boston, September 27, 1999. Traded to **New Jersey** by **Montreal** for Sheldon Souray, Josh DeWolf and New Jersey's 2nd round choice in 2001 Entry Draft, March 1, 2000. Signed as a free agent by **NY Rangers**, July 10, 2000.

MALGUNAS, Stewart
(mal-GOO-nuhs, STEW-ahrt) **COL.**

Defense. Shoots left. 6', 200 lbs. Born, Prince George, B.C., April 21, 1970. Detroit's 3rd choice, 66th overall, in 1990 Entry Draft.

			Regular Season																Playoffs							
Season	Club	League	GP	G	A	Pts	PIM	PP	SH	GW	S	%	+/–	TF	F%	H	SB	Min	GP	G	A	Pts	PIM	PP	SH	GW
1985-86	Prince George	BCAHA	49	10	25	35	85																			
1986-87	Prince George	BCAHA	50	11	31	42	102																			
1987-88	Prince George	BCJHL	48	12	34	46	99																			
	New Westminster	WHL	6	0	0	0	0																			
1988-89	Seattle T-Birds	WHL	72	11	41	52	51																			
1989-90	Seattle T-Birds	WHL	63	15	48	63	116												13	2	9	11	32			
1990-91	Adirondack	AHL	78	5	19	24	70												2	0	0	0	4			
1991-92	Adirondack	AHL	69	4	28	32	82												18	2	6	8	28			
1992-93	Adirondack	AHL	45	3	12	15	39												11	3	3	6	8			
1993-94	**Philadelphia**	**NHL**	**67**	**1**	**3**	**4**	**86**	**0**	**0**	**0**	**54**	**1.9**	**2**													
1994-95	**Philadelphia**	**NHL**	**4**	**0**	**0**	**0**	**4**	**0**	**0**	**0**	**1**	**0.0**	**–1**													
	Hershey Bears	AHL	32	3	5	8	28												6	2	1	3	31			
1995-96	**Winnipeg**	**NHL**	**29**	**0**	**1**	**1**	**32**	**0**	**0**	**0**	**13**	**0.0**	**–10**													
	Washington	**NHL**	**1**	**0**	**0**	**0**	**0**	**0**	**0**	**0**	**0**	**0.0**	**0**													
	Portland Pirates	AHL	16	2	5	7	18												13	1	3	4	19			
1996-97	**Washington**	**NHL**	**6**	**0**	**0**	**0**	**2**	**0**	**0**	**0**	**3**	**0.0**	**2**													
	Portland Pirates	AHL	68	6	12	18	59												5	0	0	0	8			
1997-98	**Washington**	**NHL**	**8**	**0**	**0**	**0**	**12**	**0**	**0**	**0**	**5**	**0.0**	**1**													
	Portland Pirates	AHL	69	14	25	39	73												9	1	1	2	19			
1998-99	**Washington**	**NHL**	**10**	**0**	**0**	**0**	**6**	**0**	**0**	**0**	**2**	**0.0**	**–5**	**0**	**0.0**	**12**	**9**	**9:02**								
	Portland Pirates	AHL	33	2	10	12	49																			
	Detroit Vipers	IHL	9	0	2	2	10												11	0	1	1	21			
99-2000	Utah Grizzlies	IHL	34	4	9	13	55																			
	Calgary	**NHL**	**4**	**0**	**1**	**1**	**2**	**0**	**0**	**0**	**0**	**0.0**	**1**	**0**	**0.0**	**7**	**4**	**12:57**								
	NHL Totals		**129**	**1**	**5**	**6**	**144**	**0**	**0**	**0**	**78**	**1.3**		**0**	**0.0**	**19**	**13**	**10:09**								

WHL West First All-Star Team (1990)

Traded to **Philadelphia** by **Detroit** for Philadelphia's 5th round choice (David Arsenault) in 1995 Entry Draft, September 9, 1993. Signed as a free agent by **Winnipeg**, August 9, 1995. Traded to **Washington** by **Winnipeg** for Denis Chasse, February 15, 1996. Traded to **Nashville** by **Washington** for future considerations, February 2, 2000. Claimed on waivers by **Calgary** from **Nashville**, February 3, 2000. • Missed remainder of 1999-2000 season recovering from head injury suffered in game vs. Los Angeles, February 14, 2000. Signed as a free agent by **Colorado**, August, 2000.

MALHOTRA, Manny

(mal-HOH-truh, MAHN-ee) **NYR**

Center. Shoots left. 6'2", 210 lbs. Born, Mississauga, Ont., May 18, 1980. NY Rangers' 1st choice, 7th overall, in 1998 Entry Draft.

			Regular Season																Playoffs							
Season	Club	League	GP	G	A	Pts	PIM	PP	SH	GW	S	%	+/–	TF	F%	H	SB	Min	GP	G	A	Pts	PIM	PP	SH	GW
1995-96	Mississauga Reps	MTHL	54	27	44	71	62	....	....	....	....	....	....	....	....	....	....	....	....	....	....	....	....	....	....	....
1996-97	Guelph Storm	OHL	61	16	28	44	26	....	....	....	....	....	....	....	....	....	....	....	18	7	7	14	11	....	....	....
1997-98	Guelph Storm	OHL	57	16	35	51	29	....	....	....	....	....	....	....	....	....	....	....	12	7	6	13	8	....	....	....
1998-99	**NY Rangers**	**NHL**	**73**	**8**	**8**	**16**	**13**	**1**	**0**	**2**	**61**	**13.1**	**–2**	**588**	**43.9**	**115**	**17**	**8:36**	....	....	....	....	....	....	....	....
99-2000	**NY Rangers**	**NHL**	**27**	**0**	**0**	**0**	**4**	**0**	**0**	**0**	**18**	**0.0**	**–6**	**132**	**44.7**	**37**	**7**	**6:42**	....	....	....	....	....	....	....	....
	Guelph Storm	OHL	5	2	2	4	4	....	....	....	....	....	....	....	....	....	....	....	6	0	2	2	4	....	....	....
	Hartford	AHL	12	1	5	6	2	....	....	....	....	....	....	....	....	....	....	....	23	1	2	3	10	....	....	....
	NHL Totals		**100**	**8**	**8**	**16**	**17**	**1**	**0**	**2**	**79**	**10.1**		**720**	**44.0**	**152**	**24**	**8:05**	....	....	....	....	....	....	....	....

Memorial Cup All-Star Team (1998) • Won George Parsons Trophy (Memorial Cup Tournament Most Sportsmanlike Player) (1998)

MALIK, Marek

(MAW-leck, MAIR-ehk) **CAR.**

Defense. Shoots left. 6'5", 215 lbs. Born, Ostrava, Czech., June 24, 1975. Hartford's 2nd choice, 72nd overall, in 1993 Entry Draft.

Season	Club	League	GP	G	A	Pts	PIM	PP	SH	GW	S	%	+/–	TF	F%	H	SB	Min	GP	G	A	Pts	PIM	PP	SH	GW
1992-93	TJ Vitkovice	Czech-Jr.	20	5	10	15	16	....	....	....	....	....	....	....	....	....	....	....	....	....	....	....	....	....	....	....
1993-94	HC Vitkovice	Cze-Rep	38	3	3	6	0	....	....	....	....	....	....	....	....	....	....	....	3	0	1	1	0	....	....	....
1994-95	Springfield	AHL	58	11	30	41	91	....	....	....	....	....	....	....	....	....	....	....	....	....	....	....	....	....	....	....
	Hartford	**NHL**	**1**	**0**	**1**	**1**	**0**	**0**	**0**	**0**	**0**	**0.0**	**1**	....	....	....	....	....	....	....	....	....	....	....	....	....
1995-96	**Hartford**	**NHL**	**7**	**0**	**0**	**0**	**4**	**0**	**0**	**0**	**2**	**0.0**	**–3**	....	....	....	....	....	....	....	....	....	....	....	....	....
	Springfield	AHL	68	8	14	22	135	....	....	....	....	....	....	....	....	....	....	....	8	1	3	4	20	....	....	....
1996-97	**Hartford**	**NHL**	**47**	**1**	**5**	**6**	**50**	**0**	**0**	**1**	**33**	**3.0**	**5**	....	....	....	....	....	....	....	....	....	....	....	....	....
	Springfield	AHL	3	0	3	3	4	....	....	....	....	....	....	....	....	....	....	....	....	....	....	....	....	....	....	....
1997-98	Malmo IF	Sweden	37	1	5	6	21	....	....	....	....	....	....	....	....	....	....	....	....	....	....	....	....	....	....	....
1998-99	HC Vitkovice	Cze-Rep	1	1	0	1	6	....	....	....	....	....	....	....	....	....	....	....	....	....	....	....	....	....	....	....
	Carolina	**NHL**	**52**	**2**	**9**	**11**	**36**	**1**	**0**	**0**	**36**	**5.6**	**–6**	**0**	**0.0**	**101**	**76**	**21:14**	**4**	**0**	**0**	**0**	**4**	**0**	**0**	**0**
	New Haven	AHL	21	2	8	10	28	....	....	....	....	....	....	....	....	....	....	....	....	....	....	....	....	....	....	....
99-2000	**Carolina**	**NHL**	**57**	**4**	**10**	**14**	**63**	**0**	**0**	**1**	**57**	**7.0**	**13**	**0**	**0.0**	**44**	**64**	**18:00**	....	....	....	....	....	....	....	....
	NHL Totals		**164**	**7**	**25**	**32**	**153**	**1**	**0**	**2**	**128**	**5.5**		**0**	**0.0**	**145**	**140**	**19:33**	**4**	**0**	**0**	**0**	**4**	**0**	**0**	**0**

Transferred to **Carolina** after **Hartford** franchise relocated, June 25, 1997.

MALKOC, Dean

(mal-KAWK, DEEN) **ANA.**

Defense. Shoots left. 6'3", 215 lbs. Born, Vancouver, B.C., January 26, 1970. New Jersey's 7th choice, 95th overall, in 1990 Entry Draft.

Season	Club	League	GP	G	A	Pts	PIM	PP	SH	GW	S	%	+/–	TF	F%	H	SB	Min	GP	G	A	Pts	PIM	PP	SH	GW
1987-88	Williams Lake	PCJHL	55	6	32	38	215	....	....	....	....	....	....	....	....	....	....	....	....	....	....	....	....	....	....	....
1988-89	Powell River	BCJHL	55	10	32	42	370	....	....	....	....	....	....	....	....	....	....	....	....	....	....	....	....	....	....	....
1989-90	Kamloops Blazers	WHL	48	3	18	21	209	....	....	....	....	....	....	....	....	....	....	....	17	0	3	3	56	....	....	....
1990-91	Kamloops Blazers	WHL	8	1	4	5	47	....	....	....	....	....	....	....	....	....	....	....	....	....	....	....	....	....	....	....
	Swift Current	WHL	56	10	23	33	248	....	....	....	....	....	....	....	....	....	....	....	3	0	2	2	5	....	....	....
	Utica Devils	AHL	1	0	0	0	0	....	....	....	....	....	....	....	....	....	....	....	....	....	....	....	....	....	....	....
1991-92	Utica Devils	AHL	66	1	11	12	274	....	....	....	....	....	....	....	....	....	....	....	4	0	2	2	6	....	....	....
1992-93	Utica Devils	AHL	73	5	19	24	255	....	....	....	....	....	....	....	....	....	....	....	5	0	1	1	8	....	....	....
1993-94	Albany River Rats	AHL	79	0	9	9	296	....	....	....	....	....	....	....	....	....	....	....	5	0	0	0	21	....	....	....
1994-95	Albany River Rats	AHL	9	0	1	1	52	....	....	....	....	....	....	....	....	....	....	....	....	....	....	....	....	....	....	....
	Indianapolis Ice	IHL	62	1	3	4	193	....	....	....	....	....	....	....	....	....	....	....	....	....	....	....	....	....	....	....
1995-96	**Vancouver**	**NHL**	**41**	**0**	**2**	**2**	**136**	**0**	**0**	**0**	**8**	**0.0**	**–10**	....	....	....	....	....	....	....	....	....	....	....	....	....
1996-97	**Boston**	**NHL**	**33**	**0**	**0**	**0**	**70**	**0**	**0**	**0**	**7**	**0.0**	**–14**	....	....	....	....	....	....	....	....	....	....	....	....	....
	Providence Bruins	AHL	4	0	2	2	28	....	....	....	....	....	....	....	....	....	....	....	....	....	....	....	....	....	....	....
1997-98	**Boston**	**NHL**	**40**	**1**	**0**	**1**	**86**	**0**	**0**	**0**	**15**	**6.7**	**–12**	....	....	....	....	....	....	....	....	....	....	....	....	....
1998-99	**NY Islanders**	**NHL**	**2**	**0**	**1**	**1**	**7**	**0**	**0**	**0**	**1**	**0.0**	**3**	**0**	**0.0**	**2**	**6**	**15:22**	....	....	....	....	....	....	....	....
	Lowell	AHL	61	2	8	10	193	....	....	....	....	....	....	....	....	....	....	....	3	0	0	0	8	....	....	....
99-2000	Chicago Wolves	IHL	62	2	8	10	130	....	....	....	....	....	....	....	....	....	....	....	1	0	0	0	0	....	....	....
	NHL Totals		**116**	**1**	**3**	**4**	**299**	**0**	**0**	**0**	**31**	**3.2**		**0**	**0.0**	**2**	**6**	**15:22**	....	....	....	....	....	....	....	....

Traded to **Chicago** by **New Jersey** for Rob Conn, January 30, 1995. Signed as a free agent by **Vancouver**, September 8, 1995. Claimed by **Boston** from **Vancouver** in NHL Waiver Draft, September 30, 1996. Signed as a free agent by **NY Islanders**, August 19, 1998. Traded to **Anaheim** by **NY Islanders** with Tony Hrkac for Ted Drury, October 29, 1999.

MALTAIS, Steve

(MAHL-tay, STEEV)

Left wing. Shoots left. 6'2", 205 lbs. Born, Arvida, Que., January 25, 1969. Washington's 2nd choice, 57th overall, in 1987 Entry Draft.

Season	Club	League	GP	G	A	Pts	PIM	PP	SH	GW	S	%	+/–	TF	F%	H	SB	Min	GP	G	A	Pts	PIM	PP	SH	GW
1985-86	Wexford Hawks	MTHL	33	35	19	54	38	....	....	....	....	....	....	....	....	....	....	....	....	....	....	....	....	....	....	....
	Wexford Raiders	OJHL-B	1	1	0	1	0	....	....	....	....	....	....	....	....	....	....	....	....	....	....	....	....	....	....	....
1986-87	Cornwall Royals	OHL	65	32	12	44	29	....	....	....	....	....	....	....	....	....	....	....	5	0	0	0	2	....	....	....
1987-88	Cornwall Royals	OHL	59	39	46	85	30	....	....	....	....	....	....	....	....	....	....	....	11	9	6	15	33	....	....	....
1988-89	Cornwall Royals	OHL	58	53	70	123	67	....	....	....	....	....	....	....	....	....	....	....	18	14	16	30	16	....	....	....
	Fort Wayne	IHL	....	....	....	....	....	....	....	....	....	....	....	....	....	....	....	....	4	2	1	3	0	....	....	....
1989-90	**Washington**	**NHL**	**8**	**0**	**0**	**0**	**2**	**0**	**0**	**0**	**11**	**0.0**	**–2**	....	....	....	....	....	**1**	**0**	**0**	**0**	**0**	**0**	**0**	**0**
	Baltimore	AHL	67	29	37	66	54	....	....	....	....	....	....	....	....	....	....	....	12	6	10	16	6	....	....	....
1990-91	**Washington**	**NHL**	**7**	**0**	**0**	**0**	**2**	**0**	**0**	**0**	**3**	**0.0**	**–1**	....	....	....	....	....	....	....	....	....	....	....	....	....
	Baltimore	AHL	73	36	43	79	97	....	....	....	....	....	....	....	....	....	....	....	6	1	4	5	10	....	....	....
1991-92	**Minnesota**	**NHL**	**12**	**2**	**1**	**3**	**2**	**0**	**0**	**0**	**6**	**33.3**	**–1**	....	....	....	....	....	....	....	....	....	....	....	....	....
	Kalamazoo Wings	IHL	48	25	31	56	51	....	....	....	....	....	....	....	....	....	....	....	....	....	....	....	....	....	....	....
	Halifax Citadels	AHL	10	3	3	6	0	....	....	....	....	....	....	....	....	....	....	....	....	....	....	....	....	....	....	....
1992-93	**Tampa Bay**	**NHL**	**63**	**7**	**13**	**20**	**35**	**4**	**0**	**1**	**96**	**7.3**	**–20**	....	....	....	....	....	....	....	....	....	....	....	....	....
	Atlanta Knights	IHL	16	14	10	24	22	....	....	....	....	....	....	....	....	....	....	....	....	....	....	....	....	....	....	....
1993-94	**Detroit**	**NHL**	**4**	**0**	**1**	**1**	**0**	**0**	**0**	**0**	**2**	**0.0**	**–1**	....	....	....	....	....	....	....	....	....	....	....	....	....
	Adirondack	AHL	73	35	49	84	79	....	....	....	....	....	....	....	....	....	....	....	12	5	11	16	14	....	....	....
1994-95	Chicago Wolves	IHL	79	*57	40	97	145	....	....	....	....	....	....	....	....	....	....	....	3	1	1	2	0	....	....	....
1995-96	Chicago Wolves	IHL	81	56	66	122	161	....	....	....	....	....	....	....	....	....	....	....	9	7	7	14	20	....	....	....
1996-97	Chicago Wolves	IHL	81	*60	54	114	62	....	....	....	....	....	....	....	....	....	....	....	4	2	0	2	4	....	....	....
1997-98	Chicago Wolves	IHL	82	*46	57	103	120	....	....	....	....	....	....	....	....	....	....	....	22	8	11	19	28	....	....	....
1998-99	Chicago Wolves	IHL	82	*56	44	100	164	....	....	....	....	....	....	....	....	....	....	....	10	4	6	10	2	....	....	....
99-2000	Chicago Wolves	IHL	82	*44	46	*90	78	....	....	....	....	....	....	....	....	....	....	....	16	9	4	13	14	....	....	....
	NHL Totals		**94**	**9**	**15**	**24**	**41**	**4**	**0**	**1**	**118**	**7.6**		....	....	....	....	....	**1**	**0**	**0**	**0**	**0**	**0**	**0**	**0**

OHL Second All-Star Team (1989) • IHL First All-Star Team (1995, 1999, 2000) • IHL Second All-Star Team (1996, 1997) • Won Leo P. Lamoureux Memorial Trophy (Top Scorer - IHL) (2000)

Traded to **Minnesota** by **Washington** with Trent Klatt for Shawn Chambers, June 21, 1991. Traded to **Quebec** by **Minnesota** for Kip Miller, March 8, 1992. Claimed by **Tampa Bay** from **Quebec** in Expansion Draft, June 18, 1992. Traded to **Detroit** by **Tampa Bay** for Dennis Vial, June 8, 1993. Signed as a free agent by **Chicago Wolves** (IHL), August 25, 1998.

MALTBY, Kirk

(MAHLT-bee, KUHRK) **DET.**

Right wing. Shoots right. 6', 180 lbs. Born, Guelph, Ont., December 22, 1972. Edmonton's 4th choice, 65th overall, in 1992 Entry Draft.

Season	Club	League	GP	G	A	Pts	PIM	PP	SH	GW	S	%	+/–	TF	F%	H	SB	Min	GP	G	A	Pts	PIM	PP	SH	GW
1988-89	Cambridge Hawks	OJHL-B	48	28	18	46	138	....	....	....	....	....	....	....	....	....	....	....	....	....	....	....	....	....	....	....
1989-90	Owen Sound	OHL	61	12	15	27	90	....	....	....	....	....	....	....	....	....	....	....	12	1	6	7	15	....	....	....
1990-91	Owen Sound	OHL	66	34	32	66	100	....	....	....	....	....	....	....	....	....	....	....	....	....	....	....	....	....	....	....
1991-92	Owen Sound	OHL	66	50	41	91	99	....	....	....	....	....	....	....	....	....	....	....	5	3	3	6	18	....	....	....
1992-93	Cape Breton	AHL	73	22	23	45	130	....	....	....	....	....	....	....	....	....	....	....	16	3	3	6	45	....	....	....
1993-94	**Edmonton**	**NHL**	**68**	**11**	**8**	**19**	**74**	**0**	**1**	**1**	**89**	**12.4**	**–2**	....	....	....	....	....	....	....	....	....	....	....	....	....
1994-95	**Edmonton**	**NHL**	**47**	**8**	**3**	**11**	**49**	**0**	**2**	**1**	**73**	**11.0**	**–11**	....	....	....	....	....	....	....	....	....	....	....	....	....
1995-96	**Edmonton**	**NHL**	**49**	**2**	**6**	**8**	**61**	**0**	**0**	**1**	**51**	**3.9**	**–16**	....	....	....	....	....	....	....	....	....	....	....	....	....
	Cape Breton	AHL	4	1	2	3	6	....	....	....	....	....	....	....	....	....	....	....	....	....	....	....	....	....	....	....
	Detroit	**NHL**	**6**	**1**	**0**	**1**	**6**	**0**	**0**	**0**	**4**	**25.0**	**0**	....	....	....	....	....	**8**	**0**	**1**	**1**	**4**	**0**	**0**	**0**
1996-97♦	**Detroit**	**NHL**	**66**	**3**	**5**	**8**	**75**	**0**	**0**	**0**	**62**	**4.8**	**3**	....	....	....	....	....	**20**	**5**	**2**	**7**	**24**	**0**	**1**	**1**
1997-98♦	**Detroit**	**NHL**	**65**	**14**	**9**	**23**	**89**	**2**	**1**	**3**	**106**	**13.2**	**11**	....	....	....	....	....	**22**	**3**	**1**	**4**	**30**	**0**	**1**	**0**

Season	Club	League	GP	G	A	Pts	PIM	PP	SH	GW	S	%	+/–	TF	F%	H	SB	Min	GP	G	A	Pts	PIM	PP	SH	GW
			Regular Season																Playoffs							
1998-99	Detroit	NHL	53	8	6	14	34	0	1	2	76	10.5	–6	10	40.0	129	33	13:13	10	1	0	1	8	0	0	1
99-2000	Detroit	NHL	41	6	8	14	24	0	2	1	71	8.5	1	2	50.0	90	34	13:30	8	0	1	1	4	0	0	0
	NHL Totals		395	53	45	98	412	2	7	9	532	10.0		12	41.7	219	67	13:21	68	9	5	14	70	0	2	2

Traded to **Detroit** by **Edmonton** for Dan McGillis, March 20, 1996. • Missed majority of 1999-2000 season recovering from hernia injury suffered in game vs. Dallas, October 5, 1999.

MANDERVILLE, Kent

(MAN-duhr-VIHL, KEHNT) **PHI.**

Left wing. Shoots left. 6'3", 210 lbs. Born, Edmonton, Alta., April 12, 1971. Calgary's 1st choice, 24th overall, in 1989 Entry Draft.

Season	Club	League	GP	G	A	Pts	PIM	PP	SH	GW	S	%	+/–	TF	F%	H	SB	Min	GP	G	A	Pts	PIM	PP	SH	GW
1987-88	Notre Dame	SAHA	32	22	18	40	42	....	....	....	....	....	....	....	....	....	....	....	....	....	....	....	....	....	....	....
1988-89	Notre Dame	SJHL	58	39	36	75	165	....	....	....	....	....	....	....	....	....	....	....	....	....	....	....	....	....	....	....
1989-90	Cornell Big Red	ECAC	26	11	15	26	28	....	....	....	....	....	....	....	....	....	....	....	....	....	....	....	....	....	....	....
1990-91	Cornell Big Red	ECAC	28	17	14	31	60	....	....	....	....	....	....	....	....	....	....	....	....	....	....	....	....	....	....	....
	Canada	Nat-Team	3	1	2	3	0	....	....	....	....	....	....	....	....	....	....	....	....	....	....	....	....	....	....	....
1991-92	Canada	Nat-Team	63	16	24	40	78	....	....	....	....	....	....	....	....	....	....	....	....	....	....	....	....	....	....	....
	Canada	Olympics	8	1	2	3	0	....	....	....	....	....	....	....	....	....	....	....	....	....	....	....	....	....	....	....
	Toronto	NHL	15	0	4	4	0	0	0	0	14	0.0	1	....	....	....	....	....	....	....	....	....	....	....	....	....
	St. John's Leafs	AHL	....	....	....	....	....	....	....	....	....	....	....	....	....	....	....	....	12	5	9	14	14	....	....	....
1992-93	Toronto	NHL	18	1	1	2	17	0	0	1	15	6.7	–9	....	....	....	....	....	18	1	0	1	8	0	0	0
	St. John's Leafs	AHL	56	19	28	47	86	....	....	....	....	....	....	....	....	....	....	....	2	0	2	2	0	....	....	....
1993-94	Toronto	NHL	67	7	9	16	63	0	0	1	81	8.6	5	....	....	....	....	....	12	1	0	1	4	0	1	0
1994-95	Toronto	NHL	36	0	1	1	22	0	0	0	43	0.0	–2	....	....	....	....	....	7	0	0	0	6	0	0	0
1995-96	Edmonton	NHL	37	3	5	8	38	0	2	0	63	4.8	–5	....	....	....	....	....	....	....	....	....	....	....	....	....
	St. John's Leafs	AHL	27	16	12	28	26	....	....	....	....	....	....	....	....	....	....	....	....	....	....	....	....	....	....	....
1996-97	Hartford	NHL	44	6	5	11	18	0	0	1	51	11.8	3	....	....	....	....	....	....	....	....	....	....	....	....	....
	Springfield	AHL	23	5	20	25	18	....	....	....	....	....	....	....	....	....	....	....	....	....	....	....	....	....	....	....
1997-98	Carolina	NHL	77	4	4	8	31	0	0	0	80	5.0	–6	....	....	....	....	....	....	....	....	....	....	....	....	....
1998-99	Carolina	NHL	81	5	11	16	38	0	0	0	71	7.0	9	609	46.3	140	28	8:07	6	0	0	0	2	0	0	0
99-2000	Carolina	NHL	56	1	4	5	12	0	0	1	45	2.2	–8	399	47.1	96	26	8:15	....	....	....	....	....	....	....	....
	Philadelphia	NHL	13	0	3	3	4	0	0	0	17	0.0	2	148	54.1	21	2	11:56	18	0	1	1	22	0	0	0
	NHL Totals		444	27	47	74	243	0	2	4	480	5.6		1156	47.6	257	56	8:30	61	2	1	3	42	0	1	0

Traded to **Toronto** by **Calgary** with Doug Gilmour, Jamie Macoun, Rick Wamsley and Ric Nattress for Gary Leeman, Alexander Godynyuk, Jeff Reese, Michel Petit and Craig Berube, January 2, 1992. Traded to **Edmonton** by **Toronto** for Peter White and Edmonton's 4th round choice (Jason Sessa) in 1996 Entry Draft, December 4, 1995. Signed as a free agent by **Hartford**, October 2, 1996. Transferred to **Carolina** after **Hartford** franchise relocated, June 25, 1997. Traded to **Philadelphia** by **Carolina** for Sandy McCarthy, March 14, 2000.

MANELUK, Mike

(MAN-uh-luhk, MIGHK) **CBJ**

Left wing. Shoots right. 5'11", 190 lbs. Born, Winnipeg, Man., October 1, 1973.

Season	Club	League	GP	G	A	Pts	PIM	PP	SH	GW	S	%	+/–	TF	F%	H	SB	Min	GP	G	A	Pts	PIM	PP	SH	GW
1989-90	Winnipeg Hawks	MAHA	40	49	38	87	92	....	....	....	....	....	....	....	....	....	....	....	....	....	....	....	....	....	....	....
1990-91	St. Boniface	MJHL	45	29	41	70	199	....	....	....	....	....	....	....	....	....	....	....	....	....	....	....	....	....	....	....
1991-92	Brandon	WHL	68	23	30	53	102	....	....	....	....	....	....	....	....	....	....	....	....	....	....	....	....	....	....	....
1992-93	Brandon	WHL	72	36	51	87	75	....	....	....	....	....	....	....	....	....	....	....	4	2	1	3	2	....	....	....
1993-94	Brandon	WHL	63	50	47	97	112	....	....	....	....	....	....	....	....	....	....	....	13	11	3	14	23	....	....	....
	San Diego Gulls	IHL	....	....	....	....	....	....	....	....	....	....	....	....	....	....	....	....	1	0	0	0	0	....	....	....
1994-95	Canada	Nat-Team	44	36	24	60	34	....	....	....	....	....	....	....	....	....	....	....	....	....	....	....	....	....	....	....
	San Diego Gulls	IHL	10	0	1	1	4	....	....	....	....	....	....	....	....	....	....	....	....	....	....	....	....	....	....	....
1995-96	Baltimore Bandits	AHL	74	33	38	71	73	....	....	....	....	....	....	....	....	....	....	....	6	4	3	7	14	....	....	....
1996-97	Worcester	AHL	70	27	27	54	89	....	....	....	....	....	....	....	....	....	....	....	5	1	2	3	14	....	....	....
1997-98	Worcester	AHL	5	3	3	6	4	....	....	....	....	....	....	....	....	....	....	....	....	....	....	....	....	....	....	....
	Philadelphia	AHL	66	27	35	62	62	....	....	....	....	....	....	....	....	....	....	....	20	*13	*21	*34	30	....	....	....
1998-99	Philadelphia	NHL	13	2	6	8	8	0	0	0	23	8.7	4	0	0.0	8	1	14:02	....	....	....	....	....	....	....	....
	Chicago	NHL	28	4	3	7	8	1	0	0	3	13.8	2	0	0.0	19	7	11:28	....	....	....	....	....	....	....	....
	NY Rangers	NHL	4	0	0	0	4	0	0	0	3	0.0	–1	0	0.0	3	0	7:18	....	....	....	....	....	....	....	....
99-2000	Philadelphia	NHL	1	0	0	0	4	0	0	0	2	0.0	0	0	0.0	0	0	7:34	....	....	....	....	....	....	....	....
	Philadelphia	AHL	73	*47	40	87	158	....	....	....	....	....	....	....	....	....	....	....	4	1	2	3	4	....	....	....
	NHL Totals		46	6	9	15	24	1	0	0	31	19.4		0	0.0	30	8	9:39	....	....	....	....	....	....	....	....

Won Jack A. Butterfield Trophy (Playoff MVP - AHL) (1998) • AHL First All-Star Team (2000)

Signed as a free agent by **Anaheim**, January 28, 1994. Traded to **Ottawa** by **Anaheim** for Kevin Brown, July 1, 1996. Traded to **Philadelphia** by **Ottawa** for future considerations, October 21, 1997. Traded to **Chicago** by **Philadelphia** for Roman Vopat, November 17, 1998. Claimed on waivers by **NY Rangers** from **Chicago**, March 4, 1999. Signed as a free agent by **Philadelphia**, August 2, 1999. Signed as a free agent by **Columbus**, August 24, 2000.

MANN, Cameron

(MAN, CAM-uhr-ROHN) **BOS.**

Right wing. Shoots right. 6', 195 lbs. Born, Thompson, Man., April 20, 1977. Boston's 5th choice, 99th overall, in 1995 Entry Draft.

Season	Club	League	GP	G	A	Pts	PIM	PP	SH	GW	S	%	+/–	TF	F%	H	SB	Min	GP	G	A	Pts	PIM	PP	SH	GW
1992-93	Kenora Thistles	NOJHA	35	23	24	47	49	....	....	....	....	....	....	....	....	....	....	....	....	....	....	....	....	....	....	....
1993-94	Peterborough	OJHL	16	3	14	17	23	....	....	....	....	....	....	....	....	....	....	....	....	....	....	....	....	....	....	....
	Peterborough	OHL	49	8	17	25	18	....	....	....	....	....	....	....	....	....	....	....	7	1	1	2	2	....	....	....
1994-95	Peterborough	OHL	64	19	24	43	40	....	....	....	....	....	....	....	....	....	....	....	11	3	8	11	4	....	....	....
1995-96	Peterborough	OHL	66	42	60	102	108	....	....	....	....	....	....	....	....	....	....	....	24	*27	16	*43	33	....	....	....
1996-97	Peterborough	OHL	51	33	50	83	91	....	....	....	....	....	....	....	....	....	....	....	11	10	18	28	16	....	....	....
1997-98	Boston	NHL	9	0	1	1	4	0	0	0	6	0.0	1	....	....	....	....	....	....	....	....	....	....	....	....	....
	Providence Bruins	AHL	71	21	26	47	99	....	....	....	....	....	....	....	....	....	....	....	....	....	....	....	....	....	....	....
1998-99	Boston	NHL	33	5	2	7	17	1	0	1	42	11.9	0	22	36.4	28	4	10:40	1	0	0	0	0	0	0	0
	Providence Bruins	AHL	43	21	25	46	65	....	....	....	....	....	....	....	....	....	....	....	11	7	7	14	4	....	....	....
99-2000	Boston	NHL	32	8	4	12	13	1	0	0	48	16.7	–6	16	25.0	28	2	12:50	....	....	....	....	....	....	....	....
	Providence Bruins	AHL	29	7	12	19	45	....	....	....	....	....	....	....	....	....	....	....	11	6	7	13	0	....	....	....
	NHL Totals		74	13	7	20	34	2	0	1	96	13.5		38	31.6	56	6	11:44	1	0	0	0	0	0	0	0

OHL First All-Star Team (1996, 1997) • Memorial Cup All-Star Team (1996) • Won Stafford Smythe Memorial Trophy (Memorial Cup Tournament MVP) (1996)

MANSON, Dave

(MAN-suhn, DAIV) **TOR.**

Defense. Shoots left. 6'2", 200 lbs. Born, Prince Albert, Sask., January 27, 1967. Chicago's 1st choice, 11th overall, in 1985 Entry Draft.

Season	Club	League	GP	G	A	Pts	PIM	PP	SH	GW	S	%	+/–	TF	F%	H	SB	Min	GP	G	A	Pts	PIM	PP	SH	GW
1982-83	Prince Albert	SAHA	28	11	11	22	170	....	....	....	....	....	....	....	....	....	....	....	....	....	....	....	....	....	....	....
	Prince Albert	WHL	6	0	1	1	9	....	....	....	....	....	....	....	....	....	....	....	....	....	....	....	....	....	....	....
1983-84	Prince Albert	WHL	70	2	7	9	233	....	....	....	....	....	....	....	....	....	....	....	5	0	0	0	4	....	....	....
1984-85	Prince Albert	WHL	72	8	30	38	247	....	....	....	....	....	....	....	....	....	....	....	13	1	0	1	34	....	....	....
1985-86	Prince Albert	WHL	70	14	34	48	177	....	....	....	....	....	....	....	....	....	....	....	20	1	8	9	63	....	....	....
1986-87	Chicago	NHL	63	1	8	9	146	0	0	0	42	2.4	–2	....	....	....	....	....	3	0	0	0	10	0	0	0
1987-88	Chicago	NHL	54	1	6	7	185	0	0	0	47	2.1	–12	....	....	....	....	....	5	0	0	0	27	0	0	0
	Saginaw Hawks	IHL	6	0	3	3	37	....	....	....	....	....	....	....	....	....	....	....	....	....	....	....	....	....	....	....
1988-89	Chicago	NHL	79	18	36	54	352	8	1	0	224	8.0	5	....	....	....	....	....	16	0	8	8	84	0	0	0
1989-90	Chicago	NHL	59	5	23	28	301	1	0	1	126	4.0	4	....	....	....	....	....	20	2	4	6	46	1	0	0
1990-91	Chicago	NHL	75	14	15	29	191	6	1	2	154	9.1	20	....	....	....	....	....	6	0	1	1	36	0	0	0
1991-92	Edmonton	NHL	79	15	32	47	220	7	0	2	206	7.3	9	....	....	....	....	....	16	3	9	12	44	1	0	0
1992-93	Edmonton	NHL	83	15	30	45	210	9	1	1	244	6.1	–28	....	....	....	....	....	....	....	....	....	....	....	....	....
1993-94	Edmonton	NHL	57	3	13	16	140	1	0	0	144	2.1	–4	....	....	....	....	....	....	....	....	....	....	....	....	....
	Winnipeg	NHL	13	1	4	5	51	1	0	0	36	2.8	–10	....	....	....	....	....	....	....	....	....	....	....	....	....
1994-95	Winnipeg	NHL	44	3	15	18	139	2	0	1	104	2.9	–20	....	....	....	....	....	....	....	....	....	....	....	....	....
1995-96	Winnipeg	NHL	82	7	23	30	205	3	0	0	189	3.7	8	....	....	....	....	....	6	2	1	3	30	0	0	1
1996-97	Phoenix	NHL	66	3	17	20	164	2	0	0	153	2.0	–25	....	....	....	....	....	....	....	....	....	....	....	....	....
	Montreal	NHL	9	1	1	2	23	0	0	0	22	4.5	–1	....	....	....	....	....	5	0	0	0	17	0	0	0
1997-98	Montreal	NHL	81	4	30	34	122	2	0	0	148	2.7	22	....	....	....	....	....	10	0	1	1	14	0	0	0
1998-99	Montreal	NHL	11	0	2	2	48	0	0	0	11	0.0	–3	0	0.0	14	8	17:19	....	....	....	....	....	....	....	....
	Chicago	NHL	64	6	15	21	107	2	0	0	134	4.5	4	0	0.0	127	51	22:37	....	....	....	....	....	....	....	....

								Regular Season											Playoffs							
Season	**Club**	**League**	**GP**	**G**	**A**	**Pts**	**PIM**	**PP**	**SH**	**GW**	**S**	**%**	**+/-**	**TF**	**F%**	**H**	**SB**	**Min**	**GP**	**G**	**A**	**Pts**	**PIM**	**PP**	**SH**	**GW**
99-2000	**Chicago**	**NHL**	**37**	**0**	**7**	**7**	**40**	**0**	**0**	**0**	**45**	**0.0**	**2**	**0**	**0.0**	**46**	**27**	**17:29**	....	....	....	....	....	....	....	....
	Dallas	**NHL**	**26**	**1**	**2**	**3**	**22**	**0**	**0**	**0**	**21**	**4.8**	**10**	**0**	**0.0**	**34**	**6**	**13:16**	**23**	**0**	**0**	**0**	**33**	**0**	**0**	**0**
	NHL Totals		**982**	**98**	**279**	**377**	**2666**	**43**	**3**	**7**	**2050**	**4.8**		**0**	**0.0**	**221**	**92**	**19:03**	**110**	**7**	**24**	**31**	**341**	**2**	**0**	**1**

WHL East Second All-Star Team (1986) • Played in NHL All-Star Game (1989, 1993)

Traded to **Edmonton** by **Chicago** with Chicago's 3rd round choice (Kirk Maltby) in 1992 Entry Draft for Steve Smith, October 2, 1991. Traded to **Winnipeg** by **Edmonton** with St. Louis' 6th round choice (previously acquired, Winnipeg selected Chris Kibermanis) in 1994 Entry Draft for Boris Mironov, Mats Lindgren, Winnipeg's 1st round choice (Jason Bonsignore) in 1994 Entry Draft and Florida's 4th round choice (previously acquired, Edmonton selected Adam Copeland) in 1994 Entry Draft, March 15, 1994. Transferred to **Phoenix** after **Winnipeg** franchise relocated, July 1, 1996. Traded to **Montreal** by **Phoenix** for Murray Baron and Chris Murray, March 18, 1997. Traded to **Chicago** by **Montreal** with Jocelyn Thibault and Brad Brown for Jeff Hackett, Eric Weinrich, Alain Nasreddine and Tampa Bay's 4th round choice (previously acquired, Montreal selected Chris Dyment) in 1999 Entry Draft, November 16, 1998. Traded to **Dallas** by **Chicago** with Sylvain Cote for Kevin Dean, Derek Plante and Dallas' 2nd round choice in 2001 Entry Draft, February 8, 2000. Signed as a free agent by **Toronto**, August 16, 2000.

MARA, Paul (MAIR-uh, PAWL) T.B.

Defense. Shoots left. 6'4", 202 lbs. Born, Ridgewood, NJ, September 7, 1979. Tampa Bay's 1st choice, 7th overall, in 1997 Entry Draft.

Season	Club	League	GP	G	A	Pts	PIM	PP	SH	GW	S	%	+/-	TF	F%	H	SB	Min	GP	G	A	Pts	PIM	PP	SH	GW
1994-95	Belmont Hill	Hi-School	28	5	17	22	28	....	....	....	....	....	....	....	....	....	....	....	....	....	....	....	....	....	....	....
1995-96	Belmont Hill	Hi-School	28	18	20	38	40	....	....	....	....	....	....	....	....	....	....	....	....	....	....	....	....	....	....	....
1996-97	Sudbury Wolves	OHL	44	9	34	43	61	....	....	....	....	....	....	....	....	....	....	....	....	....	....	....	....	....	....	....
1997-98	Sudbury Wolves	OHL	25	8	18	26	79	....	....	....	....	....	....	....	....	....	....	....	....	....	....	....	....	....	....	....
	Plymouth Whalers	OHL	25	8	15	23	30	....	....	....	....	....	....	....	....	....	....	....	15	3	14	17	30	....	....	....
1998-99	Plymouth Whalers	OHL	52	13	41	54	95	....	....	....	....	....	....	....	....	....	....	....	11	5	7	12	28	....	....	....
	Tampa Bay	**NHL**	**1**	**1**	**1**	**2**	**0**	**1**	**0**	**0**	**1**	**100.0**	**–3**	**0**	**0.0**	**1**	**3**	**19:34**	....	....	....	....	....	....	....	....
99-2000	**Tampa Bay**	**NHL**	**54**	**7**	**11**	**18**	**73**	**4**	**0**	**1**	**78**	**9.0**	**–27**	**0**	**0.0**	**62**	**49**	**22:13**	....	....	....	....	....	....	....	....
	Detroit Vipers	IHL	15	3	5	8	22	....	....	....	....	....	....	....	....	....	....	....	....	....	....	....	....	....	....	....
	NHL Totals		**55**	**8**	**12**	**20**	**73**	**5**	**0**	**1**	**79**	**10.1**		**0**	**0.0**	**63**	**52**	**22:11**	....	....	....	....	....	....	....	....

MARCHANT, Todd (mahr-SHAHNT, TAWD) EDM.

Center. Shoots left. 5'10", 178 lbs. Born, Buffalo, NY, August 12, 1973. NY Rangers' 8th choice, 164th overall, in 1993 Entry Draft.

Season	Club	League	GP	G	A	Pts	PIM	PP	SH	GW	S	%	+/-	TF	F%	H	SB	Min	GP	G	A	Pts	PIM	PP	SH	GW
1990-91	Niagara Scenics	NAJHL	37	31	47	78	....	....	....	....	....	....	....	....	....	....	....	....	....	....	....	....	....	....	....	....
1991-92	Clarkson	ECAC	32	20	12	32	32	....	....	....	....	....	....	....	....	....	....	....	....	....	....	....	....	....	....	....
1992-93	Clarkson	ECAC	33	18	28	46	38	....	....	....	....	....	....	....	....	....	....	....	....	....	....	....	....	....	....	....
1993-94	United States	Nat-Team	59	28	39	67	48	....	....	....	....	....	....	....	....	....	....	....	....	....	....	....	....	....	....	....
	United States	Olympics	8	1	1	2	6	....	....	....	....	....	....	....	....	....	....	....	....	....	....	....	....	....	....	....
	NY Rangers	**NHL**	**1**	**0**	**0**	**0**	**0**	**0**	**0**	**0**	**1**	**0.0**	**–1**	....	....	....	....	....	....	....	....	....	....	....	....	....
	Binghamton	AHL	8	2	7	9	6	....	....	....	....	....	....	....	....	....	....	....	....	....	....	....	....	....	....	....
	Edmonton	**NHL**	**3**	**0**	**1**	**1**	**2**	**0**	**0**	**0**	**5**	**0.0**	**–1**	....	....	....	....	....	....	....	....	....	....	....	....	....
	Cape Breton	AHL	3	1	4	5	2	....	....	....	....	....	....	....	....	....	....	....	5	1	1	2	0	....	....	....
1994-95	Cape Breton	AHL	38	22	25	47	25	....	....	....	....	....	....	....	....	....	....	....	....	....	....	....	....	....	....	....
	Edmonton	**NHL**	**45**	**13**	**14**	**27**	**32**	**3**	**2**	**2**	**95**	**13.7**	**–3**	....	....	....	....	....	....	....	....	....	....	....	....	....
1995-96	**Edmonton**	**NHL**	**81**	**19**	**19**	**38**	**66**	**2**	**3**	**2**	**221**	**8.6**	**–19**	....	....	....	....	....	....	....	....	....	....	....	....	....
1996-97	**Edmonton**	**NHL**	**79**	**14**	**19**	**33**	**44**	**0**	**4**	**3**	**202**	**6.9**	**11**	....	....	....	....	....	**12**	**4**	**2**	**6**	**12**	**0**	**3**	**1**
1997-98	**Edmonton**	**NHL**	**76**	**14**	**21**	**35**	**71**	**2**	**1**	**3**	**194**	**7.2**	**9**	....	....	....	....	....	**12**	**1**	**1**	**2**	**10**	**0**	**0**	**0**
1998-99	**Edmonton**	**NHL**	**82**	**14**	**22**	**36**	**65**	**3**	**1**	**2**	**183**	**7.7**	**3**	**1449**	**50.0**	**133**	**57**	**16:47**	**4**	**1**	**1**	**2**	**12**	**0**	**0**	**0**
99-2000	**Edmonton**	**NHL**	**82**	**17**	**23**	**40**	**70**	**0**	**1**	**0**	**170**	**10.0**	**7**	**1593**	**52.9**	**92**	**58**	**17:08**	**3**	**1**	**0**	**1**	**2**	**0**	**0**	**0**
	NHL Totals		**449**	**91**	**119**	**210**	**350**	**10**	**12**	**12**	**1071**	**8.5**		**3042**	**51.5**	**225**	**115**	**16:58**	**31**	**7**	**4**	**11**	**36**	**0**	**3**	**1**

ECAC Second All-Star Team (1993)

Traded to **Edmonton** by **NY Rangers** for Craig MacTavish, March 21, 1994.

MARCHMENT, Bryan (MAHRCH-mehnt, BRIGH-an) S.J.

Defense. Shoots left. 6'1", 195 lbs. Born, Scarborough, Ont., May 1, 1969. Winnipeg's 1st choice, 16th overall, in 1987 Entry Draft.

Season	Club	League	GP	G	A	Pts	PIM	PP	SH	GW	S	%	+/-	TF	F%	H	SB	Min	GP	G	A	Pts	PIM	PP	SH	GW
1984-85	Toronto Nats	MTHL	69	14	35	49	229	....	....	....	....	....	....	....	....	....	....	....	....	....	....	....	....	....	....	....
1985-86	Belleville Bulls	OHL	57	5	15	20	225	....	....	....	....	....	....	....	....	....	....	....	21	0	7	7	83	....	....	....
1986-87	Belleville Bulls	OHL	52	6	38	44	238	....	....	....	....	....	....	....	....	....	....	....	6	0	4	4	17	....	....	....
1987-88	Belleville Bulls	OHL	56	7	51	58	200	....	....	....	....	....	....	....	....	....	....	....	6	1	3	4	19	....	....	....
1988-89	Belleville Bulls	OHL	43	14	36	50	118	....	....	....	....	....	....	....	....	....	....	....	5	0	1	1	12	....	....	....
	Winnipeg	**NHL**	**2**	**0**	**0**	**0**	**2**	**0**	**0**	**0**	**1**	**0.0**	**0**	....	....	....	....	....	....	....	....	....	....	....	....	....
1989-90	**Winnipeg**	**NHL**	**7**	**0**	**2**	**2**	**28**	**0**	**0**	**0**	**5**	**0.0**	**0**	....	....	....	....	....	....	....	....	....	....	....	....	....
	Moncton Hawks	AHL	56	4	19	23	217	....	....	....	....	....	....	....	....	....	....	....	....	....	....	....	....	....	....	....
1990-91	**Winnipeg**	**NHL**	**28**	**2**	**2**	**4**	**91**	**0**	**0**	**0**	**24**	**8.3**	**–5**	....	....	....	....	....	....	....	....	....	....	....	....	....
	Moncton Hawks	AHL	33	2	11	13	101	....	....	....	....	....	....	....	....	....	....	....	....	....	....	....	....	....	....	....
1991-92	**Chicago**	**NHL**	**58**	**5**	**10**	**15**	**168**	**2**	**0**	**0**	**55**	**9.1**	**–4**	....	....	....	....	....	**16**	**1**	**0**	**1**	**36**	**0**	**0**	**0**
1992-93	**Chicago**	**NHL**	**78**	**5**	**15**	**20**	**313**	**1**	**0**	**1**	**75**	**6.7**	**15**	....	....	....	....	....	**4**	**0**	**0**	**0**	**12**	**0**	**0**	**0**
1993-94	**Chicago**	**NHL**	**13**	**1**	**4**	**5**	**42**	**0**	**0**	**0**	**18**	**5.6**	**–2**	....	....	....	....	....	....	....	....	....	....	....	....	....
	Hartford	**NHL**	**42**	**3**	**7**	**10**	**124**	**0**	**1**	**1**	**74**	**4.1**	**–12**	....	....	....	....	....	....	....	....	....	....	....	....	....
1994-95	**Edmonton**	**NHL**	**40**	**1**	**5**	**6**	**184**	**0**	**0**	**0**	**57**	**1.8**	**–11**	....	....	....	....	....	....	....	....	....	....	....	....	....
1995-96	**Edmonton**	**NHL**	**78**	**3**	**15**	**18**	**202**	**0**	**0**	**0**	**96**	**3.1**	**–7**	....	....	....	....	....	....	....	....	....	....	....	....	....
1996-97	**Edmonton**	**NHL**	**71**	**3**	**13**	**16**	**132**	**1**	**0**	**0**	**89**	**3.4**	**13**	....	....	....	....	....	**3**	**0**	**0**	**0**	**4**	**0**	**0**	**0**
1997-98	**Edmonton**	**NHL**	**27**	**0**	**4**	**4**	**58**	**0**	**0**	**0**	**23**	**0.0**	**–2**	....	....	....	....	....	....	....	....	....	....	....	....	....
	Tampa Bay	**NHL**	**22**	**2**	**4**	**6**	**43**	**0**	**0**	**0**	**20**	**10.0**	**–3**	....	....	....	....	....	....	....	....	....	....	....	....	....
	San Jose	**NHL**	**12**	**0**	**3**	**3**	**43**	**0**	**0**	**0**	**13**	**0.0**	**2**	....	....	....	....	....	**6**	**0**	**0**	**0**	**10**	**0**	**0**	**0**
1998-99	**San Jose**	**NHL**	**59**	**2**	**6**	**8**	**101**	**0**	**0**	**0**	**49**	**4.1**	**–7**	**0**	**0.0**	**108**	**64**	**17:43**	**6**	**0**	**0**	**0**	**4**	**0**	**0**	**0**
99-2000	**San Jose**	**NHL**	**49**	**0**	**4**	**4**	**72**	**0**	**0**	**0**	**51**	**0.0**	**3**	**0**	**0.0**	**127**	**51**	**18:55**	**11**	**2**	**1**	**3**	**12**	**0**	**0**	**0**
	NHL Totals		**586**	**27**	**94**	**121**	**1603**	**4**	**1**	**2**	**650**	**4.2**		**0**	**0.0**	**235**	**115**	**18:16**	**46**	**3**	**1**	**4**	**78**	**0**	**0**	**0**

OHL Second All-Star Team (1989)

Traded to **Chicago** by **Winnipeg** with Chris Norton for Troy Murray and Warren Rychel, July 22, 1991. Traded to **Hartford** by **Chicago** with Steve Larmer for Eric Weinrich and Patrick Poulin, November 2, 1993. Transferred to **Edmonton** from **Hartford** as compensation for Hartford's signing of free agent Steven Rice, August 30, 1994. Traded to **Tampa Bay** by **Edmonton** with Steve Kelly and Jason Bonsignore for Roman Hamrlik and Paul Comrie, December 30, 1997. Traded to **San Jose** by **Tampa Bay** with David Shaw and Tampa Bay's 1st round choice (later traded to Nashville - Nashville selected David Legwand) in 1998 Entry Draft for Andrei Nazarov and Florida's 1st round choice (previously acquired, Tampa Bay selected Vincent Lecavallier) in 1998 Entry Draft, March 24, 1998.

MARHA, Josef (MAHR-hah, JOH-sehf) CHI.

Center. Shoots left. 6', 176 lbs. Born, Havlickuv, Czech., June 2, 1976. Quebec's 3rd choice, 35th overall, in 1994 Entry Draft.

Season	Club	League	GP	G	A	Pts	PIM	PP	SH	GW	S	%	+/-	TF	F%	H	SB	Min	GP	G	A	Pts	PIM	PP	SH	GW
1991-92	Dukla Jihlava	Czech-Jr.	25	12	13	25	0	....	....	....	....	....	....	....	....	....	....	....	....	....	....	....	....	....	....	....
1992-93	Dukla Jihlava	Czech.	7	2	2	4	....	....	....	....	....	....	....	....	....	....	....	....	....	....	....	....	....	....	....	....
1993-94	Dukla Jihlava	Cze-Rep	41	7	2	9	....	....	....	....	....	....	....	....	....	....	....	....	3	0	1	1	....	....	....	....
1994-95	Dukla Jihlava	Cze-Rep	35	3	7	10	6	....	....	....	....	....	....	....	....	....	....	....	....	....	....	....	....	....	....	....
1995-96	**Colorado**	**NHL**	**2**	**0**	**1**	**1**	**0**	**0**	**0**	**0**	**2**	**0.0**	**1**	....	....	....	....	....	....	....	....	....	....	....	....	....
	Cornwall Aces	AHL	74	18	30	48	30	....	....	....	....	....	....	....	....	....	....	....	8	1	2	3	10	....	....	....
1996-97	**Colorado**	**NHL**	**6**	**0**	**1**	**1**	**0**	**0**	**0**	**0**	**6**	**0.0**	**0**	....	....	....	....	....	....	....	....	....	....	....	....	....
	Hershey Bears	AHL	67	23	49	72	44	....	....	....	....	....	....	....	....	....	....	....	19	6	*16	*22	10	....	....	....
1997-98	**Colorado**	**NHL**	**11**	**2**	**5**	**7**	**4**	**0**	**0**	**0**	**10**	**20.0**	**0**	....	....	....	....	....	....	....	....	....	....	....	....	....
	Hershey Bears	AHL	55	6	46	52	30	....	....	....	....	....	....	....	....	....	....	....	....	....	....	....	....	....	....	....
	Anaheim	**NHL**	**12**	**7**	**4**	**11**	**0**	**3**	**0**	**0**	**21**	**33.3**	**4**	....	....	....	....	....	....	....	....	....	....	....	....	....
1998-99	**Anaheim**	**NHL**	**10**	**0**	**1**	**1**	**0**	**0**	**0**	**0**	**13**	**0.0**	**–4**	**107**	**40.2**	**3**	**1**	**12:02**	....	....	....	....	....	....	....	....
	Cincinnati Ducks	AHL	3	1	0	1	4	....	....	....	....	....	....	....	....	....	....	....	....	....	....	....	....	....	....	....
	Chicago	**NHL**	**22**	**2**	**5**	**7**	**4**	**1**	**0**	**1**	**32**	**6.3**	**5**	**275**	**50.9**	**6**	**10**	**14:37**	....	....	....	....	....	....	....	....
	Portland Pirates	AHL	8	0	8	8	2	....	....	....	....	....	....	....	....	....	....	....	....	....	....	....	....	....	....	....
99-2000	**Chicago**	**NHL**	**81**	**10**	**12**	**22**	**18**	**2**	**1**	**3**	**91**	**11.0**	**–10**	**1110**	**46.3**	**26**	**31**	**13:20**	....	....	....	....	....	....	....	....
	NHL Totals		**144**	**21**	**29**	**50**	**26**	**6**	**1**	**4**	**175**	**12.0**		**1492**	**46.7**	**35**	**42**	**13:28**	....	....	....	....	....	....	....	....

Rights transferred to **Colorado** after **Quebec** franchise relocated, June 21, 1995. Traded to **Anaheim** by **Colorado** for Warren Rychel and Anaheim's 4th round choice (Sanny Lindstrom) in 1999 Entry Draft, March 24, 1998. Traded to **Chicago** by **Anaheim** for Chicago's 4th round choice (Alexandr Chagodayev) in 1999 Entry Draft, January 28, 1999.

Season	Club	League	GP	G	A	Pts	PIM	PP	SH	GW	S	%	+/-	TF	F%	H	SB	Min	GP	G	A	Pts	PIM	PP	SH	GW
			Regular Season																Playoffs							

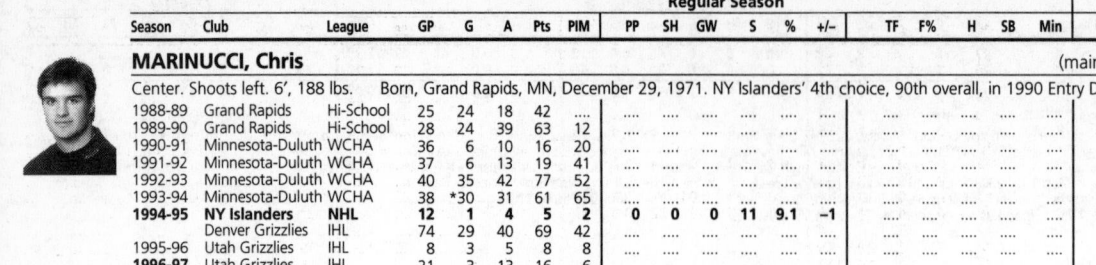

MARINUCCI, Chris

(mair-ihn-OO-chee, KRIHS)

Center. Shoots left. 6', 188 lbs. Born, Grand Rapids, MN, December 29, 1971. NY Islanders' 4th choice, 90th overall, in 1990 Entry Draft.

Season	Club	League	GP	G	A	Pts	PIM	PP	SH	GW	S	%	+/-	TF	F%	H	SB	Min	GP	G	A	Pts	PIM	PP	SH	GW
1988-89	Grand Rapids	Hi-School	25	24	18	42																				
1989-90	Grand Rapids	Hi-School	28	24	39	63	12																			
1990-91	Minnesota-Duluth	WCHA	36	6	10	16	20																			
1991-92	Minnesota-Duluth	WCHA	37	6	13	19	41																			
1992-93	Minnesota-Duluth	WCHA	40	35	42	77	52																			
1993-94	Minnesota-Duluth	WCHA	38	*30	31	61	65																			
1994-95	**NY Islanders**	**NHL**	**12**	**1**	**4**	**5**	**2**	**0**	**0**	**0**	**11**	**9.1**	**–1**													
	Denver Grizzlies	IHL	74	29	40	69	42												14	3	4	7	12			
1995-96	Utah Grizzlies	IHL	8	3	5	8	8																			
1996-97	Utah Grizzlies	IHL	21	3	13	16	6																			
	Los Angeles	**NHL**	**1**	**0**	**0**	**0**	**0**	**0**	**0**	**0**	**1**	**0.0**	**–2**													
	Phoenix	IHL	62	23	29	52	26																			
1997-98	Chicago Wolves	IHL	78	27	48	75	35												22	7	6	13	12			
1998-99	Chicago Wolves	IHL	82	41	40	81	24												10	3	5	8	10			
99-2000	Chicago Wolves	IHL	80	31	33	64	18												16	5	4	9	10			
	NHL Totals		**13**	**1**	**4**	**5**	**2**	**0**	**0**	**0**	**12**	**8.3**														

WCHA Second All-Star Team (1993) • WCHA First All-Star Team (1994) • NCAA West First All-American Team (1994) • Won Hobey Baker Memorial Award (Top U.S. Collegiate Player) (1994) • IHL Second All-Star Team (1999)

Traded to **LA Kings** by **NY Islanders** for Nick Vachon, November 19, 1996.

MARKOV, Danny

(MAHR-kahf, DA-nee) **TOR.**

Defense. Shoots left. 6'1", 190 lbs. Born, Moscow, USSR, July 11, 1976. Toronto's 7th choice, 223rd overall, in 1995 Entry Draft.

Season	Club	League	GP	G	A	Pts	PIM	PP	SH	GW	S	%	+/-	TF	F%	H	SB	Min	GP	G	A	Pts	PIM	PP	SH	GW
1993-94	Spartak Moscow	CIS	13	1	0	1	6												1	0	0	0	0			
1994-95	Spartak Moscow	CIS	39	0	1	1	36																			
1995-96	Spartak Moscow	CIS	38	2	0	2	12												2	0	0	0	2			
1996-97	Spartak Moscow	Russia	39	3	6	9	41																			
	St. John's Leafs	AHL	10	2	4	6	18												11	2	6	8	14			
1997-98	**Toronto**	**NHL**	**25**	**2**	**5**	**7**	**28**	**1**	**0**	**0**	**15**	**13.3**	**0**													
	St. John's Leafs	AHL	52	3	23	26	124												2	0	1	1	0			
1998-99	**Toronto**	**NHL**	**57**	**4**	**8**	**12**	**47**	**0**	**0**	**0**	**34**	**11.8**	**5**	**0**	**0.0**	**92**	**66**	**18:41**	**17**	**0**	**6**	**6**	**18**	**0**	**0**	**0**
99-2000	**Toronto**	**NHL**	**59**	**0**	**10**	**10**	**28**	**0**	**0**	**0**	**38**	**0.0**	**13**	**1**	**0.0**	**97**	**100**	**20:08**	**12**	**0**	**3**	**3**	**10**	**0**	**0**	**0**
	NHL Totals		**141**	**6**	**23**	**29**	**103**	**1**	**0**	**0**	**87**	**6.9**		**1**	**0.0**	**189**	**166**	**19:25**	**29**	**0**	**9**	**9**	**28**	**0**	**0**	**0**

MARLEAU, Patrick

(mahr-LOH, PAT-rihk) **S.J.**

Center. Shoots left. 6'2", 210 lbs. Born, Aneroid, Sask., September 15, 1979. San Jose's 1st choice, 2nd overall, in 1997 Entry Draft.

Season	Club	League	GP	G	A	Pts	PIM	PP	SH	GW	S	%	+/-	TF	F%	H	SB	Min	GP	G	A	Pts	PIM	PP	SH	GW
1993-94	Swift Current A's	SAHA	53	72	95	167																				
1994-95	Swift Current	SAHA	31	30	22	52	18																			
1995-96	Seattle T-Birds	WHL	72	32	42	74	22												5	3	4	7	4			
1996-97	Seattle T-Birds	WHL	71	51	74	125	37												15	7	16	23	12			
1997-98	**San Jose**	**NHL**	**74**	**13**	**19**	**32**	**14**	**1**	**0**	**2**	**90**	**14.4**	**5**						**5**	**0**	**1**	**1**	**0**	**0**	**0**	**0**
1998-99	**San Jose**	**NHL**	**81**	**21**	**24**	**45**	**24**	**4**	**0**	**4**	**134**	**15.7**	**10**	**1121**	**43.4**	**59**	**15**	**15:11**	**6**	**2**	**1**	**3**	**4**	**2**	**0**	**0**
99-2000	**San Jose**	**NHL**	**81**	**17**	**23**	**40**	**36**	**3**	**0**	**3**	**161**	**10.6**	**–9**	**851**	**42.0**	**74**	**13**	**14:11**	**5**	**1**	**1**	**2**	**2**	**1**	**0**	**0**
	NHL Totals		**236**	**51**	**66**	**117**	**74**	**8**	**0**	**9**	**385**	**13.2**		**1972**	**42.8**	**133**	**28**	**14:41**	**16**	**3**	**3**	**6**	**6**	**3**	**0**	**0**

WHL West First All-Star Team (1997)

MARSHALL, Grant

(MAHR-shahl, GRANT) **DAL.**

Right wing. Shoots right. 6'1", 200 lbs. Born, Mississauga, Ont., June 9, 1973. Toronto's 2nd choice, 23rd overall, in 1992 Entry Draft.

Season	Club	League	GP	G	A	Pts	PIM	PP	SH	GW	S	%	+/-	TF	F%	H	SB	Min	GP	G	A	Pts	PIM	PP	SH	GW
1989-90	Toronto Nats	MTHL	39	15	28	43	56																			
1990-91	Ottawa 67's	OHL	26	6	11	17	25												1	0	0	0	0			
1991-92	Ottawa 67's	OHL	61	32	51	83	132												11	6	11	17	11			
1992-93	Ottawa 67's	OHL	30	14	29	43	83																			
	Newmarket	OHL	31	11	25	36	89												7	4	7	11	20			
	St. John's Leafs	AHL	2	0	0	0	0												2	0	0	0	2			
1993-94	St. John's Leafs	AHL	67	11	29	40	155												11	1	5	6	17			
1994-95	**Dallas**	**NHL**	**2**	**0**	**1**	**1**	**0**	**0**	**0**	**0**	**0**	**0.0**	**1**													
	Kalamazoo Wings	IHL	61	17	29	46	96												16	9	3	12	27			
1995-96	**Dallas**	**NHL**	**70**	**9**	**19**	**28**	**111**	**0**	**0**	**0**	**62**	**14.5**	**0**													
1996-97	**Dallas**	**NHL**	**56**	**6**	**4**	**10**	**98**	**0**	**0**	**0**	**0**	**0.0**	**5**						**5**	**0**	**2**	**2**	**8**	**0**	**0**	**0**
1997-98	**Dallas**	**NHL**	**72**	**9**	**10**	**19**	**96**	**3**	**0**	**1**	**91**	**9.9**	**–2**						**17**	**0**	**2**	**2**	***47**	**0**	**0**	**0**
1998-99♦	**Dallas**	**NHL**	**82**	**13**	**18**	**31**	**85**	**2**	**0**	**4**	**112**	**11.6**	**1**	**2**	**50.0**	**172**	**12**	**12:39**	**14**	**0**	**3**	**3**	**20**	**0**	**0**	**0**
99-2000	**Dallas**	**NHL**	**45**	**2**	**6**	**8**	**38**	**1**	**0**	**0**	**43**	**4.7**	**–5**	**3**	**0.0**	**111**	**6**	**11:19**	**14**	**0**	**1**	**1**	**4**	**0**	**0**	**0**
	NHL Totals		**327**	**39**	**58**	**97**	**428**	**6**	**0**	**5**	**308**	**12.7**		**5**	**20.0**	**283**	**18**	**12:10**	**50**	**0**	**8**	**8**	**79**	**0**	**0**	**0**

• Missed majority of 1990-91 season recovering from neck injury suffered in game vs. Sudbury (OHL), December 4, 1990. Transferred to **Dallas** from **Toronto** with Peter Zezel as compensation for Toronto's signing of free agent Mike Craig, August 10, 1994.

MARSHALL, Jason

(MAHR-shahl, JAY-suhn) **ANA.**

Defense. Shoots right. 6'2", 200 lbs. Born, Cranbrook, B.C., February 22, 1971. St. Louis' 1st choice, 9th overall, in 1989 Entry Draft.

Season	Club	League	GP	G	A	Pts	PIM	PP	SH	GW	S	%	+/-	TF	F%	H	SB	Min	GP	G	A	Pts	PIM	PP	SH	GW
1987-88	Columbia Valley	RMJHL	40	4	28	32	150																			
1988-89	Vernon Lakers	BCJHL	48	10	30	40	197												31	6	6	12	14			
	Canada	Nat-Team	2	0	1	1	0																			
1989-90	Canada	Nat-Team	73	1	11	12	57																			
1990-91	Tri-City Americans	WHL	59	10	34	44	236												7	1	2	3	20			
	Peoria Rivermen	IHL																	18	0	1	1	48			
1991-92	**St. Louis**	**NHL**	**2**	**1**	**0**	**1**	**4**	**0**	**0**	**0**	**2**	**50.0**	**0**													
	Peoria Rivermen	IHL	78	4	18	22	178												10	0	1	1	16			
1992-93	Peoria Rivermen	IHL	77	4	16	20	229												4	0	0	0	20			
1993-94	Canada	Nat-Team	41	3	10	13	60																			
	Peoria Rivermen	IHL	20	1	1	2	72												3	2	0	2	2			
1994-95	**Anaheim**	**NHL**	**1**	**0**	**0**	**0**	**0**	**0**	**0**	**0**	**1**	**0.0**	**–2**													
	San Diego Gulls	IHL	80	7	18	25	218												5	0	1	1	8			
1995-96	**Anaheim**	**NHL**	**24**	**0**	**1**	**1**	**42**	**0**	**0**	**0**	**9**	**0.0**	**3**													
	Baltimore Bandits	AHL	57	1	13	14	150																			
1996-97	**Anaheim**	**NHL**	**73**	**1**	**9**	**10**	**140**	**0**	**0**	**0**	**34**	**2.9**	**6**						**7**	**0**	**1**	**1**	**4**	**0**	**0**	**0**
1997-98	**Anaheim**	**NHL**	**72**	**3**	**6**	**9**	**189**	**1**	**0**	**0**	**68**	**4.4**	**–8**													
1998-99	**Anaheim**	**NHL**	**72**	**1**	**7**	**8**	**142**	**0**	**0**	**0**	**63**	**1.6**	**–5**	**0**	**0.0**	**150**	**95**	**19:06**	**4**	**1**	**0**	**1**	**10**	**1**	**0**	**0**
99-2000	**Anaheim**	**NHL**	**55**	**0**	**3**	**3**	**88**	**0**	**0**	**0**	**41**	**0.0**	**–10**	**2**	**50.0**	**143**	**57**	**16:33**								
	NHL Totals		**299**	**6**	**26**	**32**	**605**	**1**	**0**	**0**	**218**	**2.8**		**2**	**50.0**	**293**	**152**	**17:60**	**11**	**1**	**1**	**2**	**14**	**1**	**0**	**0**

Traded to **Anaheim** by **St. Louis** for Bill Houlder, August 29, 1994.

MARTIN, Matt

(MAHR-tihn, MAT)

Defense. Shoots left. 6'3", 230 lbs. Born, Hamden, CT, April 30, 1971. Toronto's 4th choice, 66th overall, in 1989 Entry Draft.

Season	Club	League	GP	G	A	Pts	PIM	PP	SH	GW	S	%	+/-	TF	F%	H	SB	Min	GP	G	A	Pts	PIM	PP	SH	GW
1987-88	Connecticut	MBHL	23	3	7	10																				
1988-89	Avon Old Farms	Hi-School	25	9	23	32																				
1989-90	Avon Old Farms	Hi-School	STATISTICS NOT AVAILABLE																							
1990-91	U. of Maine	H-East	35	3	12	15	48																			
1991-92	U. of Maine	H-East	30	4	14	18	46																			

			Regular Season																Playoffs							
Season	Club	League	GP	G	A	Pts	PIM	PP	SH	GW	S	%	+/-	TF	F%	H	SB	Min	GP	G	A	Pts	PIM	PP	SH	GW
1992-93	U. of Maine	H-East	44	6	26	32	88	....	....	....	....	....	....	....	....	....	....	....	....	....	....	....	....	....	....	....
	St. John's Leafs	AHL	2	0	0	0	2	....	....	....	....	....	....	....	....	....	....	....	9	1	5	6	4	....	....	....
1993-94	United States	Nat-Team	39	7	8	15	127	....	....	....	....	....	....	....	....	....	....	....	....	....	....	....	....	....	....	....
	United States	Olympics	8	0	2	2	8	....	....	....	....	....	....	....	....	....	....	....	....	....	....	....	....	....	....	....
	Toronto	**NHL**	**12**	**0**	**1**	**1**	**6**	**0**	**0**	**0**	**6**	**0.0**	**0**	....	....	....	....	....	....	....	....	....	....	....	....	....
	St. John's Leafs	AHL	12	1	5	6	9	....	....	....	....	....	....	....	....	....	....	....	11	1	5	6	33	....	....	....
1994-95	**Toronto**	**NHL**	**15**	**0**	**0**	**0**	**13**	**0**	**0**	**0**	**14**	**0.0**	**2**	....	....	....	....	....	....	....	....	....	....	....	....	....
	St. John's Leafs	AHL	49	2	16	18	54	....	....	....	....	....	....	....	....	....	....	....	....	....	....	....	....	....	....	....
1995-96	**Toronto**	**NHL**	**13**	**0**	**0**	**0**	**14**	**0**	**0**	**0**	**3**	**0.0**	**–1**	....	....	....	....	....	....	....	....	....	....	....	....	....
1996-97	**Toronto**	**NHL**	**36**	**0**	**4**	**4**	**38**	**0**	**0**	**0**	**30**	**0.0**	**–12**	....	....	....	....	....	....	....	....	....	....	....	....	....
	St. John's Leafs	AHL	12	1	3	4	4	....	....	....	....	....	....	....	....	....	....	....	....	....	....	....	....	....	....	....
1997-98	Chicago Wolves	IHL	78	7	22	29	95	....	....	....	....	....	....	....	....	....	....	....	19	0	5	5	24	....	....	....
1998-99	Michigan K-Wings	IHL	76	3	12	15	114	....	....	....	....	....	....	....	....	....	....	....	5	0	0	0	10	....	....	....
99-2000	Michigan K-Wings	IHL	76	0	11	11	66	....	....	....	....	....	....	....	....	....	....	....	....	....	....	....	....	....	....	....
	NHL Totals		**76**	**0**	**5**	**5**	**71**	**0**	**0**	**0**	**53**	**0.0**		....	....	....	....	....	....	....	....	....	....	....	....	....

Signed as a free agent by **Dallas**, July 24, 1998.

MARTINS, Steve

(MAHR-tihns, STEEV) **T.B.**

Center. Shoots left. 5'9", 175 lbs. Born, Gatineau, Que., April 13, 1972. Hartford's 1st choice, 5th overall, in 1994 Supplemental Draft.

Season	Club	League	GP	G	A	Pts	PIM	PP	SH	GW	S	%	+/-	TF	F%	H	SB	Min	GP	G	A	Pts	PIM	PP	SH	GW
1991-92	Harvard University	ECAC	20	13	14	27	26	....	....	....	....	....	....	....	....	....	....	....	....	....	....	....	....	....	....	....
1992-93	Harvard University	ECAC	18	6	8	14	40	....	....	....	....	....	....	....	....	....	....	....	....	....	....	....	....	....	....	....
1993-94	Harvard University	ECAC	32	25	35	60	*93	....	....	....	....	....	....	....	....	....	....	....	....	....	....	....	....	....	....	....
1994-95	Harvard University	ECAC	28	15	23	38	93	....	....	....	....	....	....	....	....	....	....	....	....	....	....	....	....	....	....	....
1995-96	**Hartford**	**NHL**	**23**	**1**	**3**	**4**	**8**	**0**	**0**	**0**	**27**	**3.7**	**–3**	....	....	....	....	....	....	....	....	....	....	....	....	....
	Springfield	AHL	30	9	20	29	10	....	....	....	....	....	....	....	....	....	....	....	....	....	....	....	....	....	....	....
1996-97	**Hartford**	**NHL**	**2**	**0**	**1**	**1**	**0**	**0**	**0**	**0**	**2**	**0.0**	**0**	....	....	....	....	....	....	....	....	....	....	....	....	....
	Springfield	AHL	63	12	31	43	78	....	....	....	....	....	....	....	....	....	....	....	17	1	3	4	26	....	....	....
1997-98	**Carolina**	**NHL**	**3**	**0**	**0**	**0**	**0**	**0**	**0**	**0**	**0**	**0.0**	**0**	....	....	....	....	....	....	....	....	....	....	....	....	....
	Chicago Wolves	IHL	78	20	41	61	122	....	....	....	....	....	....	....	....	....	....	....	21	6	14	20	28	....	....	....
1998-99	**Ottawa**	**NHL**	**36**	**4**	**3**	**7**	**10**	**1**	**0**	**1**	**27**	**14.8**	**4**	**191**	**56.0**	**23**	**2**	**8:28**	....	....	....	....	....	....	....	....
	Detroit Vipers	IHL	4	1	6	7	16	....	....	....	....	....	....	....	....	....	....	....	....	....	....	....	....	....	....	....
99-2000	**Ottawa**	**NHL**	**2**	**1**	**0**	**1**	**0**	**0**	**0**	**0**	**3**	**33.3**	**–1**	**3**	**0.0**	**2**	**2**	**11:10**	....	....	....	....	....	....	....	....
	Tampa Bay	**NHL**	**57**	**5**	**7**	**12**	**37**	**0**	**1**	**1**	**62**	**8.1**	**–11**	**806**	**50.9**	**56**	**36**	**13:27**	....	....	....	....	....	....	....	....
	NHL Totals		**123**	**11**	**14**	**25**	**55**	**1**	**1**	**2**	**121**	**9.1**		**1000**	**51.7**	**81**	**40**	**11:31**	....	....	....	....	....	....	....	....

ECAC First All-Star Team (1994) • NCAA East First All-American Team (1994) • NCAA Final Four All-Tournament Team (1994)

Transferred to **Carolina** after **Hartford** franchise relocated, June 25, 1997. Signed as a free agent by **Ottawa**, July 20, 1998. Claimed on waivers by **Tampa Bay** from **Ottawa**, October 29, 1999.

MATHIEU, Marquis

(MA-thew, MAHR-kwihs)

Center. Shoots right. 5'11", 190 lbs. Born, Hartford, CT, May 31, 1973.

Season	Club	League	GP	G	A	Pts	PIM	PP	SH	GW	S	%	+/-	TF	F%	H	SB	Min	GP	G	A	Pts	PIM	PP	SH	GW
1990-91	Hawkesbury	OJHL	20	6	8	14	62	....	....	....	....	....	....	....	....	....	....	....	....	....	....	....	....	....	....	....
	Beauport	QMJHL	26	4	13	17	73	....	....	....	....	....	....	....	....	....	....	....	....	....	....	....	....	....	....	....
1991-92	St-Jean Lynx	QMJHL	70	20	36	56	166	....	....	....	....	....	....	....	....	....	....	....	....	....	....	....	....	....	....	....
1992-93	St-Jean Lynx	QMJHL	61	31	36	67	115	....	....	....	....	....	....	....	....	....	....	....	2	1	0	1	33	....	....	....
1993-94	Wheeling	ECHL	42	12	11	23	75	....	....	....	....	....	....	....	....	....	....	....	9	1	3	4	23	....	....	....
	Fredericton	AHL	22	4	6	10	28	....	....	....	....	....	....	....	....	....	....	....	....	....	....	....	....	....	....	....
1994-95	Toledo Storm	ECHL	33	13	22	35	168	....	....	....	....	....	....	....	....	....	....	....	....	....	....	....	....	....	....	....
	Raleigh Icecaps	ECHL	33	15	17	32	181	....	....	....	....	....	....	....	....	....	....	....	....	....	....	....	....	....	....	....
	Worcester	AHL	2	0	0	0	0	....	....	....	....	....	....	....	....	....	....	....	....	....	....	....	....	....	....	....
1995-96	Johnstown Chiefs	ECHL	25	4	17	21	89	....	....	....	....	....	....	....	....	....	....	....	....	....	....	....	....	....	....	....
	Worcester	AHL	17	3	10	13	26	....	....	....	....	....	....	....	....	....	....	....	....	....	....	....	....	....	....	....
	Houston Aeros	IHL	2	1	0	1	9	....	....	....	....	....	....	....	....	....	....	....	....	....	....	....	....	....	....	....
	Birmingham Bulls	ECHL	18	5	7	12	87	....	....	....	....	....	....	....	....	....	....	....	....	....	....	....	....	....	....	....
1996-97	Worcester	AHL	30	8	16	24	88	....	....	....	....	....	....	....	....	....	....	....	1	0	0	0	0	....	....	....
1997-98	Wheeling Nailers	ECHL	58	26	29	55	276	....	....	....	....	....	....	....	....	....	....	....	15	1	10	11	38	....	....	....
1998-99	**Boston**	**NHL**	**9**	**0**	**0**	**0**	**8**	**0**	**0**	**0**	**4**	**0.0**	**–1**	**84**	**63.1**	**9**	**1**	**7:20**	....	....	....	....	....	....	....	....
	Providence Bruins	AHL	64	15	15	30	166	....	....	....	....	....	....	....	....	....	....	....	19	4	7	11	30	....	....	....
99-2000	**Boston**	**NHL**	**6**	**0**	**2**	**2**	**4**	**0**	**0**	**0**	**3**	**0.0**	**–2**	**48**	**60.4**	**12**	**2**	**6:04**	....	....	....	....	....	....	....	....
	Providence Bruins	AHL	18	3	3	6	45	....	....	....	....	....	....	....	....	....	....	....	....	....	....	....	....	....	....	....
	NHL Totals		**15**	**0**	**2**	**2**	**12**	**0**	**0**	**0**	**7**	**0.0**		**132**	**62.1**	**21**	**3**	**6:49**	....	....	....	....	....	....	....	....

Signed as a free agent by **Boston**, October 26, 1998. • Missed majority of 1999-2000 season recovering from hip surgery, June 1999.

MATTE, Christian

(MA-the, KRIH-stan) **MIN.**

Right wing. Shoots right. 6', 190 lbs. Born, Hull, Que., January 20, 1975. Quebec's 8th choice, 153rd overall, in 1993 Entry Draft.

Season	Club	League	GP	G	A	Pts	PIM	PP	SH	GW	S	%	+/-	TF	F%	H	SB	Min	GP	G	A	Pts	PIM	PP	SH	GW
1991-92	Timiscaminque	QAAA	42	18	27	45	30	....	....	....	....	....	....	....	....	....	....	....	....	....	....	....	....	....	....	....
1992-93	Granby Bisons	QMJHL	68	17	36	53	59	....	....	....	....	....	....	....	....	....	....	....	....	....	....	....	....	....	....	....
1993-94	Granby Bisons	QMJHL	59	50	47	97	103	....	....	....	....	....	....	....	....	....	....	....	7	5	5	10	12	....	....	....
	Cornwall Aces	AHL	1	0	0	0	0	....	....	....	....	....	....	....	....	....	....	....	....	....	....	....	....	....	....	....
1994-95	Granby Bisons	QMJHL	66	50	66	116	86	....	....	....	....	....	....	....	....	....	....	....	13	11	7	18	12	....	....	....
	Cornwall Aces	AHL	....	....	....	....	....	....	....	....	....	....	....	....	....	....	....	....	3	0	1	1	2	....	....	....
1995-96	Cornwall Aces	AHL	64	20	32	52	51	....	....	....	....	....	....	....	....	....	....	....	7	1	1	2	6	....	....	....
1996-97	**Colorado**	**NHL**	**5**	**1**	**1**	**2**	**0**	**0**	**0**	**0**	**6**	**16.7**	**1**	....	....	....	....	....	....	....	....	....	....	....	....	....
	Hershey Bears	AHL	49	18	18	36	78	....	....	....	....	....	....	....	....	....	....	....	22	8	3	11	25	....	....	....
1997-98	**Colorado**	**NHL**	**5**	**0**	**0**	**0**	**6**	**0**	**0**	**0**	**5**	**0.0**	**0**	....	....	....	....	....	....	....	....	....	....	....	....	....
	Hershey Bears	AHL	71	33	40	73	109	....	....	....	....	....	....	....	....	....	....	....	7	3	2	5	4	....	....	....
1998-99	**Colorado**	**NHL**	**7**	**1**	**1**	**2**	**0**	**0**	**0**	**0**	**9**	**11.1**	**–2**	**13**	**30.8**	**4**	**1**	**7:45**	....	....	....	....	....	....	....	....
	Hershey Bears	AHL	60	31	47	78	48	....	....	....	....	....	....	....	....	....	....	....	5	2	1	3	8	....	....	....
99-2000	**Colorado**	**NHL**	**5**	**0**	**1**	**1**	**4**	**0**	**0**	**0**	**1**	**0.0**	**–2**	**2**	**0.0**	**6**	**1**	**8:37**	....	....	....	....	....	....	....	....
	Hershey Bears	AHL	73	43	*61	*104	85	....	....	....	....	....	....	....	....	....	....	....	14	8	6	14	10	....	....	....
	NHL Totals		**22**	**2**	**3**	**5**	**10**	**0**	**0**	**0**	**21**	**9.5**		**15**	**26.7**	**10**	**2**	**8:06**	....	....	....	....	....	....	....	....

QMJHL Second All-Star Team (1994) • AHL First All-Star Team (2000) • Won John P. Sollenberger Trophy (Top Scorer - AHL) (2000)

Rights transferred to **Colorado** after **Quebec** franchise relocated, June 21, 1995. Signed as a free agent by **Minnesota**, July 11, 2000.

MATTEAU, Stephane

(mah-TOH, STEH-fan) **S.J.**

Left wing. Shoots left. 6'4", 220 lbs. Born, Rouyn-Noranda, Que., September 2, 1969. Calgary's 2nd choice, 25th overall, in 1987 Entry Draft.

Season	Club	League	GP	G	A	Pts	PIM	PP	SH	GW	S	%	+/-	TF	F%	H	SB	Min	GP	G	A	Pts	PIM	PP	SH	GW
1985-86	Hull Olympiques	QMJHL	60	6	8	14	19	....	....	....	....	....	....	....	....	....	....	....	4	0	0	0	0	....	....	....
1986-87	Hull Olympiques	QMJHL	69	27	48	75	113	....	....	....	....	....	....	....	....	....	....	....	8	3	7	10	8	....	....	....
1987-88	Hull Olympiques	QMJHL	57	17	40	57	179	....	....	....	....	....	....	....	....	....	....	....	18	5	14	19	94	....	....	....
1988-89	Hull Olympiques	QMJHL	59	44	45	89	202	....	....	....	....	....	....	....	....	....	....	....	9	8	6	14	30	....	....	....
	Salt Lake City	IHL	....	....	....	....	....	....	....	....	....	....	....	....	....	....	....	....	9	0	4	4	13	....	....	....
1989-90	Salt Lake City	IHL	81	23	35	58	130	....	....	....	....	....	....	....	....	....	....	....	10	6	3	9	38	....	....	....
1990-91	**Calgary**	**NHL**	**78**	**15**	**19**	**34**	**93**	**0**	**1**	**1**	**114**	**13.2**	**17**	....	....	....	....	....	**5**	**0**	**1**	**1**	**0**	**0**	**0**	**0**
1991-92	**Calgary**	**NHL**	**4**	**1**	**0**	**1**	**19**	**0**	**0**	**0**	**7**	**14.3**	**2**	....	....	....	....	....	....	....	....	....	....	....	....	....
	Chicago	**NHL**	**20**	**5**	**8**	**13**	**45**	**1**	**0**	**0**	**31**	**16.1**	**3**	....	....	....	....	....	**18**	**4**	**6**	**10**	**24**	**1**	**1**	**0**
1992-93	**Chicago**	**NHL**	**79**	**15**	**18**	**33**	**98**	**2**	**0**	**4**	**95**	**15.8**	**6**	....	....	....	....	....	**3**	**0**	**1**	**1**	**2**	**0**	**0**	**0**
1993-94	**Chicago**	**NHL**	**65**	**15**	**16**	**31**	**55**	**2**	**0**	**2**	**113**	**13.3**	**10**	....	....	....	....	....	....	....	....	....	....	....	....	....
	♦ NY Rangers	**NHL**	**12**	**4**	**3**	**7**	**2**	**1**	**0**	**0**	**22**	**18.2**	**5**	....	....	....	....	....	**23**	**6**	**3**	**9**	**20**	**1**	**0**	**2**
1994-95	**NY Rangers**	**NHL**	**41**	**3**	**5**	**8**	**25**	**0**	**0**	**0**	**37**	**8.1**	**–8**	....	....	....	....	....	**9**	**0**	**1**	**1**	**10**	**0**	**0**	**0**
1995-96	**NY Rangers**	**NHL**	**32**	**4**	**2**	**6**	**22**	**1**	**0**	**0**	**39**	**10.3**	**–4**	....	....	....	....	....	....	....	....	....	....	....	....	....
	St. Louis	**NHL**	**46**	**7**	**13**	**20**	**65**	**3**	**0**	**2**	**70**	**10.0**	**–4**	....	....	....	....	....	**11**	**0**	**2**	**2**	**8**	**0**	**0**	**0**
1996-97	**St. Louis**	**NHL**	**74**	**16**	**20**	**36**	**50**	**1**	**2**	**2**	**98**	**16.3**	**11**	....	....	....	....	....	**5**	**0**	**0**	**0**	**0**	**0**	**0**	**0**
1997-98	**San Jose**	**NHL**	**73**	**15**	**14**	**29**	**60**	**1**	**0**	**2**	**79**	**19.0**	**4**	....	....	....	....	....	**4**	**0**	**1**	**1**	**0**	**0**	**0**	**0**

			Regular Season																Playoffs							
Season	Club	League	GP	G	A	Pts	PIM	PP	SH	GW	S	%	+/-	TF	F%	H	SB	Min	GP	G	A	Pts	PIM	PP	SH	GW
1998-99	San Jose	NHL	68	8	15	23	73	0	0	0	72	11.1	2	13	38.5	58	20	13:34	5	0	0	0	6	0	0	0
99-2000	San Jose	NHL	69	12	12	24	61	0	0	3	73	16.4	-3	8	50.0	83	14	11:52	10	0	2	2	8	0	0	0
	NHL Totals		661	120	145	265	668	12	3	16	850	14.1		21	42.9	141	34	12:42	93	10	17	27	78	2	1	2

• Missed majority of 1991-92 season recovering from thigh injury suffered in game vs. LA Kings, October 10, 1991. Traded to **Chicago** by **Calgary** for Trent Yawney, December 16, 1991. Traded to **NY Rangers** by **Chicago** with Brian Noonan for Tony Amonte and the rights to Matt Oates, March 21, 1994. Traded to **St. Louis** by **NY Rangers** for Ian Laperriere, December 28, 1995. Traded to **San Jose** by **St. Louis** for Darren Turcotte, July 24, 1997.

MATVICHUK, Richard
(MAT-vih-chuhk, RIH-chahrd) **DAL.**

Defense. Shoots left. 6'2", 215 lbs. Born, Edmonton, Alta., February 5, 1973. Minnesota's 1st choice, 8th overall, in 1991 Entry Draft.

Season	Club	League	GP	G	A	Pts	PIM	PP	SH	GW	S	%	+/-	TF	F%	H	SB	Min	GP	G	A	Pts	PIM	PP	SH	GW
1988-89	Ft-Saskatchewan	AJHL	58	7	36	43	147	....	....	....	....	....	....	....	....	....	....	....	....	....	....	....	....	....	....	....
1989-90	Saskatoon Blades	WHL	56	8	24	32	126	....	....	....	....	....	....	....	....	....	....	....	10	2	8	10	16	....	....	....
1990-91	Saskatoon Blades	WHL	68	13	36	49	117	....	....	....	....	....	....	....	....	....	....	....	....	....	....	....	....	....	....	....
1991-92	Saskatoon Blades	WHL	58	14	40	54	126	....	....	....	....	....	....	....	....	....	....	....	22	1	9	10	61	....	....	....
1992-93	**Minnesota**	**NHL**	53	2	3	5	26	1	0	0	51	3.9	-8	....	....	....	....	....	....	....	....	....	....	....	....	....
	Kalamazoo Wings	IHL	3	0	1	1	6	....	....	....	....	....	....	....	....	....	....	....	....	....	....	....	....	....	....	....
1993-94	**Dallas**	**NHL**	25	0	3	3	22	0	0	0	18	0.0	1	....	....	....	....	....	7	1	1	2	12	1	0	0
	Kalamazoo Wings	IHL	43	8	17	25	84	....	....	....	....	....	....	....	....	....	....	....	....	....	....	....	....	....	....	....
1994-95	**Dallas**	**NHL**	14	0	2	2	14	0	0	0	21	0.0	-7	....	....	....	....	....	5	0	2	2	4	0	0	0
	Kalamazoo Wings	IHL	17	0	6	6	16	....	....	....	....	....	....	....	....	....	....	....	....	....	....	....	....	....	....	....
1995-96	**Dallas**	**NHL**	73	6	16	22	71	0	0	1	81	7.4	4	....	....	....	....	....	....	....	....	....	....	....	....	....
1996-97	**Dallas**	**NHL**	57	5	7	12	87	0	2	0	83	6.0	1	....	....	....	....	....	7	0	1	1	20	0	0	0
1997-98	**Dallas**	**NHL**	74	3	15	18	63	0	0	0	71	4.2	7	....	....	....	....	....	16	1	1	2	14	0	0	0
1998-99♦	**Dallas**	**NHL**	64	3	9	12	51	1	0	0	54	5.6	23	0	0.0	186	153	21:19	22	1	5	6	20	0	0	0
99-2000	**Dallas**	**NHL**	70	4	21	25	42	0	0	1	73	5.5	7	0	0.0	208	150	24:27	23	2	5	7	14	0	0	0
	NHL Totals		430	23	76	99	376	2	2	2	452	5.1		0	0.0	394	303	22:57	80	5	15	20	84	1	0	0

WHL East First All-Star Team (1992)

Transferred to **Dallas** after **Minnesota** franchise relocated, June 9, 1993.

MAY, Brad
(MAY, BRAD) **PHX.**

Left wing. Shoots left. 6'1", 210 lbs. Born, Toronto, Ont., November 29, 1971. Buffalo's 1st choice, 14th overall, in 1990 Entry Draft.

Season	Club	League	GP	G	A	Pts	PIM	PP	SH	GW	S	%	+/-	TF	F%	H	SB	Min	GP	G	A	Pts	PIM	PP	SH	GW
1987-88	Markham Selects	OMHA	31	22	37	59	58	....	....	....	....	....	....	....	....	....	....	....	....	....	....	....	....	....	....	....
	Markham	OJHL	6	1	1	2	21	....	....	....	....	....	....	....	....	....	....	....	....	....	....	....	....	....	....	....
1988-89	Niagara Falls	OHL	65	8	14	22	304	....	....	....	....	....	....	....	....	....	....	....	17	0	1	1	55	....	....	....
1989-90	Niagara Falls	OHL	61	32	58	90	223	....	....	....	....	....	....	....	....	....	....	....	16	9	13	22	64	....	....	....
1990-91	Niagara Falls	OHL	34	37	32	69	93	....	....	....	....	....	....	....	....	....	....	....	14	11	14	25	53	....	....	....
1991-92	**Buffalo**	**NHL**	69	11	6	17	309	1	0	3	82	13.4	-12	....	....	....	....	....	7	1	4	5	2	0	0	1
1992-93	**Buffalo**	**NHL**	82	13	13	26	242	0	0	1	114	11.4	3	....	....	....	....	....	8	1	1	2	14	0	0	1
1993-94	**Buffalo**	**NHL**	84	18	27	45	171	3	0	3	166	10.8	-6	....	....	....	....	....	7	0	2	2	9	0	0	0
1994-95	**Buffalo**	**NHL**	33	3	3	6	87	1	0	0	42	7.1	5	....	....	....	....	....	4	0	0	0	2	0	0	0
1995-96	**Buffalo**	**NHL**	79	15	29	44	295	3	0	4	168	8.9	6	....	....	....	....	....	....	....	....	....	....	....	....	....
1996-97	**Buffalo**	**NHL**	42	3	4	7	106	1	0	1	75	4.0	-8	....	....	....	....	....	10	1	1	2	32	0	0	0
1997-98	**Buffalo**	**NHL**	36	4	7	11	113	0	0	0	41	9.8	2	....	....	....	....	....	....	....	....	....	....	....	....	....
	Vancouver	**NHL**	27	9	3	12	41	4	0	2	56	16.1	0	....	....	....	....	....	....	....	....	....	....	....	....	....
1998-99	**Vancouver**	**NHL**	66	6	11	17	102	1	0	1	91	6.6	-14	8	12.5	109	14	13:04	....	....	....	....	....	....	....	....
99-2000	**Vancouver**	**NHL**	59	9	7	16	90	0	0	3	66	13.6	-2	3	0.0	117	10	10:24	....	....	....	....	....	....	....	....
	NHL Totals		577	91	110	201	1556	14	0	18	901	10.1		11	9.1	226	24	11:48	36	3	8	11	59	0	0	2

OHL Second All-Star Team (1990, 1991)

• Missed majority of 1990-91 season recovering from knee injury suffered at Team Canada Juniors evaluation camp, August 21, 1990. Traded to **Vancouver** by **Buffalo** with Buffalo's 3rd round choice (later traded to Tampa Bay - Tampa Bay selected Jimmie Olvestad) in 1999 Entry Draft for Geoff Sanderson, February 4, 1998. Traded to **Phoenix** by **Vancouver** for future considerations, June 24, 2000.

MAYERS, Jamal
(MAI-uhz, JUH-MAHL) **ST.L.**

Center. Shoots right. 6'1", 212 lbs. Born, Toronto, Ont., October 24, 1974. St. Louis' 3rd choice, 89th overall, in 1993 Entry Draft.

Season	Club	League	GP	G	A	Pts	PIM	PP	SH	GW	S	%	+/-	TF	F%	H	SB	Min	GP	G	A	Pts	PIM	PP	SH	GW
1990-91	Thornhill Rattlers	OJHL	44	12	24	36	78	....	....	....	....	....	....	....	....	....	....	....	....	....	....	....	....	....	....	....
1991-92	Thornhill Rattlers	OJHL	56	38	69	107	36	....	....	....	....	....	....	....	....	....	....	....	....	....	....	....	....	....	....	....
1992-93	Western Michigan	CCHA	38	8	17	25	26	....	....	....	....	....	....	....	....	....	....	....	....	....	....	....	....	....	....	....
1993-94	Western Michigan	CCHA	40	17	32	49	40	....	....	....	....	....	....	....	....	....	....	....	....	....	....	....	....	....	....	....
1994-95	Western Michigan	CCHA	39	13	32	45	40	....	....	....	....	....	....	....	....	....	....	....	....	....	....	....	....	....	....	....
1995-96	Western Michigan	CCHA	38	17	22	39	75	....	....	....	....	....	....	....	....	....	....	....	....	....	....	....	....	....	....	....
1996-97	**St. Louis**	**NHL**	6	0	1	1	2	0	0	0	7	0.0	-3	....	....	....	....	....	....	....	....	....	....	....	....	....
	Worcester	AHL	62	12	14	26	104	....	....	....	....	....	....	....	....	....	....	....	5	4	5	9	4	....	....	....
1997-98	Worcester	AHL	61	19	24	43	117	....	....	....	....	....	....	....	....	....	....	....	11	3	4	7	10	....	....	....
1998-99	**St. Louis**	**NHL**	34	4	5	9	40	0	0	0	48	8.3	-3	2	50.0	56	3	8:08	11	0	1	1	8	0	0	0
	Worcester	AHL	20	9	7	16	34	....	....	....	....	....	....	....	....	....	....	....	....	....	....	....	....	....	....	....
99-2000	**St. Louis**	**NHL**	79	7	10	17	90	0	0	0	99	7.1	0	77	52.0	150	11	9:46	7	0	4	4	2	0	0	0
	NHL Totals		119	11	16	27	132	0	0	0	154	7.1		79	51.9	206	14	9:16	18	0	5	5	10	0	0	0

McALLISTER, Chris
(MIHK-kal-his-tuhr, KRIHS) **TOR.**

Defense. Shoots left. 6'8", 225 lbs. Born, Saskatoon, Sask., June 16, 1975. Vancouver's 1st choice, 40th overall, in 1995 Entry Draft.

Season	Club	League	GP	G	A	Pts	PIM	PP	SH	GW	S	%	+/-	TF	F%	H	SB	Min	GP	G	A	Pts	PIM	PP	SH	GW
1992-93	Saskatoon Royals	SJHL-B	40	14	14	28	224	....	....	....	....	....	....	....	....	....	....	....	....	....	....	....	....	....	....	....
	Saskatoon Blades	WHL	4	0	0	0	2	....	....	....	....	....	....	....	....	....	....	....	....	....	....	....	....	....	....	....
1993-94	Humboldt Broncos	SJHL	50	3	5	8	150	....	....	....	....	....	....	....	....	....	....	....	....	....	....	....	....	....	....	....
	Saskatoon Blades	WHL	2	0	0	0	5	....	....	....	....	....	....	....	....	....	....	....	....	....	....	....	....	....	....	....
1994-95	Saskatoon Blades	WHL	65	2	8	10	134	....	....	....	....	....	....	....	....	....	....	....	10	0	0	0	28	....	....	....
1995-96	Syracuse Crunch	AHL	68	0	2	2	142	....	....	....	....	....	....	....	....	....	....	....	16	0	0	0	34	....	....	....
1996-97	Syracuse Crunch	AHL	43	3	1	4	108	....	....	....	....	....	....	....	....	....	....	....	3	0	0	0	6	....	....	....
1997-98	**Vancouver**	**NHL**	36	1	2	3	106	0	0	0	15	6.7	-12	....	....	....	....	....	....	....	....	....	....	....	....	....
	Syracuse Crunch	AHL	23	0	1	1	71	....	....	....	....	....	....	....	....	....	....	....	5	0	0	0	21	....	....	....
1998-99	**Vancouver**	**NHL**	28	1	1	2	63	0	0	0	6	16.7	-7	0	0.0	19	5	5:53	....	....	....	....	....	....	....	....
	Syracuse Crunch	AHL	5	0	0	0	24	....	....	....	....	....	....	....	....	....	....	....	....	....	....	....	....	....	....	....
	Toronto	**NHL**	20	0	2	2	39	0	0	0	12	0.0	4	0	0.0	37	17	13:59	6	0	1	1	4	0	0	0
99-2000	**Toronto**	**NHL**	36	0	3	3	68	0	0	0	12	0.0	-4	0	0.0	65	26	12:02	....	....	....	....	....	....	....	....
	NHL Totals		120	2	8	10	276	0	0	0	45	4.4		0	0.0	121	48	10:27	6	0	1	1	4	0	0	0

Traded to **Toronto** by **Vancouver** for Darby Hendrickson, February 16, 1999.

McALPINE, Chris
(MIHK-AL-pighn, KRIHS) **CHI.**

Defense. Shoots right. 6', 210 lbs. Born, Roseville, MN, December 1, 1971. New Jersey's 10th choice, 137th overall, in 1990 Entry Draft.

Season	Club	League	GP	G	A	Pts	PIM	PP	SH	GW	S	%	+/-	TF	F%	H	SB	Min	GP	G	A	Pts	PIM	PP	SH	GW
1989-90	Roseville High	Hi-School	25	15	13	28	....	....	....	....	....	....	....	....	....	....	....	....	....	....	....	....	....	....	....	....
1990-91	U. of Minnesota	WCHA	38	7	9	16	112	....	....	....	....	....	....	....	....	....	....	....	....	....	....	....	....	....	....	....
1991-92	U. of Minnesota	WCHA	39	3	9	12	126	....	....	....	....	....	....	....	....	....	....	....	....	....	....	....	....	....	....	....
1992-93	U. of Minnesota	WCHA	41	14	9	23	82	....	....	....	....	....	....	....	....	....	....	....	....	....	....	....	....	....	....	....
1993-94	U. of Minnesota	WCHA	36	12	18	30	121	....	....	....	....	....	....	....	....	....	....	....	....	....	....	....	....	....	....	....
1994-95	Albany River Rats	AHL	48	4	18	22	49	....	....	....	....	....	....	....	....	....	....	....	....	....	....	....	....	....	....	....
	♦ New Jersey	**NHL**	24	0	3	3	17	0	0	0	19	0.0	4	....	....	....	....	....	....	....	....	....	....	....	....	....
1995-96	Albany River Rats	AHL	57	5	14	19	72	....	....	....	....	....	....	....	....	....	....	....	4	0	0	0	13	....	....	....
1996-97	Albany River Rats	AHL	44	1	9	10	48	....	....	....	....	....	....	....	....	....	....	....	....	....	....	....	....	....	....	....
	St. Louis	**NHL**	15	0	0	0	24	0	0	0	3	0.0	-2	....	....	....	....	....	4	0	1	1	0	0	0	0
1997-98	**St. Louis**	**NHL**	54	3	7	10	36	0	0	0	35	8.6	14	....	....	....	....	....	10	0	0	0	16	0	0	0
1998-99	**St. Louis**	**NHL**	51	1	1	2	50	0	0	0	56	1.8	-10	0	0.0	75	42	12:51	13	0	0	0	2	0	0	0

			Regular Season																Playoffs							
Season	Club	League	GP	G	A	Pts	PIM	PP	SH	GW	S	%	+/–	TF	F%	H	SB	Min	GP	G	A	Pts	PIM	PP	SH	GW
99-2000	St. Louis	NHL	21	1	1	2	14	0	0	0	25	4.0	1	0	0.0	28	14	11:41	....	....	....	....	....	....	....	....
	Worcester	AHL	10	1	4	5	4	....	....	....	....	....	....	....	....	....	....	....	....	....	....	....	....	....	....	....
	Tampa Bay	NHL	10	1	1	2	10	0	0	0	5	20.0	–5	0	0.0	15	12	18:23	....	....	....	....	....	....	....	....
	Atlanta	NHL	3	0	0	0	2	0	0	0	4	0.0	–4	0	0.0	7	4	19:40	....	....	....	....	....	....	....	....
	Detroit Vipers	IHL	8	0	0	0	6	....	....	....	....	....	....	....	....	....	....	....	....	....	....	....	....	....	....	....
	NHL Totals		178	6	13	19	153	0	0	0	147	4.1		0	0.0	125	72	13:27	27	0	1	1	18	0	0	0

WCHA First All-Star Team (1994) • NCAA West Second All-American Team (1994)

Traded to **St. Louis** by **New Jersey** with New Jersey's 9th round choice (James Desmarais) in 1999 Entry Draft for Peter Zezel, February 11, 1997. Traded to **Tampa Bay** by **St. Louis** with Rich Parent for Stephane Richer, January 13, 2000. Traded to **Atlanta** by **Tampa Bay** for Mikko Kuparinen, March 11, 2000. Signed as a free agent by **Chicago**, July 27, 2000.

McAMMOND, Dean

(MIHK-AM-uhnd, DEEN) **CHI.**

Center. Shoots left. 5'11", 200 lbs. Born, Grand Cache, Alta., June 15, 1973. Chicago's 1st choice, 22nd overall, in 1991 Entry Draft.

Season	Club	League	GP	G	A	Pts	PIM	PP	SH	GW	S	%	+/–	TF	F%	H	SB	Min	GP	G	A	Pts	PIM	PP	SH	GW
1988-89	St. Albert Raiders	AAHA	36	33	44	77	132	....	....	....	....	....	....	....	....	....	....	....	....	....	....	....	....	....	....	....
1989-90	Prince Albert	WHL	53	11	11	22	49	....	....	....	....	....	....	....	....	....	....	....	14	2	3	5	18	....	....	....
1990-91	Prince Albert	WHL	71	33	35	68	108	....	....	....	....	....	....	....	....	....	....	....	2	0	1	1	6	....	....	....
1991-92	Prince Albert	WHL	63	37	54	91	189	....	....	....	....	....	....	....	....	....	....	....	10	12	11	23	26	....	....	....
	Chicago	NHL	5	0	2	2	0	0	0	0	4	0.0	–2	....	....	....	....	....	3	0	0	0	2	0	0	0
1992-93	Prince Albert	WHL	30	19	29	48	44	....	....	....	....	....	....	....	....	....	....	....	....	....	....	....	....	....	....	....
	Swift Current	WHL	18	10	13	23	24	....	....	....	....	....	....	....	....	....	....	....	17	*16	19	35	20	....	....	....
1993-94	Edmonton	NHL	45	6	21	27	16	2	0	0	52	11.5	12	....	....	....	....	....	....	....	....	....	....	....	....	....
	Cape Breton	AHL	28	9	12	21	38	....	....	....	....	....	....	....	....	....	....	....	....	....	....	....	....	....	....	....
1994-95	Edmonton	NHL	6	0	0	0	0	0	0	0	3	0.0	–1	....	....	....	....	....	....	....	....	....	....	....	....	....
1995-96	Edmonton	NHL	53	15	15	30	23	4	0	0	79	19.0	6	....	....	....	....	....	....	....	....	....	....	....	....	....
	Cape Breton	AHL	22	9	15	24	55	....	....	....	....	....	....	....	....	....	....	....	....	....	....	....	....	....	....	....
1996-97	Edmonton	NHL	57	12	17	29	28	4	0	6	106	11.3	–15	....	....	....	....	....	....	....	....	....	....	....	....	....
1997-98	Edmonton	NHL	77	19	31	50	46	8	0	3	128	14.8	9	....	....	....	....	....	12	1	4	5	12	0	0	0
1998-99	Edmonton	NHL	65	9	16	25	36	1	0	0	122	7.4	5	26	38.5	116	21	14:15	....	....	....	....	....	....	....	....
	Chicago	NHL	12	1	4	5	2	0	0	1	16	6.3	3	37	48.6	22	4	15:43	....	....	....	....	....	....	....	....
99-2000	Chicago	NHL	76	14	18	32	72	1	0	1	118	11.9	11	257	39.7	121	35	16:25	....	....	....	....	....	....	....	....
	NHL Totals		396	76	124	200	223	20	0	11	628	12.1		320	40.6	259	60	15:27	15	1	4	5	14	0	0	0

Traded to **Edmonton** by **Chicago** with Igor Kravchuk for Joe Murphy, February 24, 1993. Traded to **Chicago** by **Edmonton** with Boris Mironov and Jonas Elofsson for Chad Kilger, Daniel Cleary, Ethan Moreau and Christian Laflamme, March 20, 1999.

McBAIN, Jason

(MIHK-BAYN, JAY-suhn)

Defense. Shoots left. 6'2", 180 lbs. Born, Ilion, NY, April 12, 1974. Hartford's 5th choice, 81st overall, in 1992 Entry Draft.

Season	Club	League	GP	G	A	Pts	PIM	PP	SH	GW	S	%	+/–	TF	F%	H	SB	Min	GP	G	A	Pts	PIM	PP	SH	GW
1989-90	Kimberley	BCAHA	37	20	38	58	77	....	....	....	....	....	....	....	....	....	....	....	....	....	....	....	....	....	....	....
1990-91	Lethbridge	WHL	52	2	7	9	39	....	....	....	....	....	....	....	....	....	....	....	1	0	0	0	0	....	....	....
1991-92	Lethbridge	WHL	13	0	1	1	12	....	....	....	....	....	....	....	....	....	....	....	....	....	....	....	....	....	....	....
	Portland	WHL	54	9	23	32	95	....	....	....	....	....	....	....	....	....	....	....	6	1	0	1	13	....	....	....
1992-93	Portland	WHL	71	9	35	44	76	....	....	....	....	....	....	....	....	....	....	....	16	2	12	14	14	....	....	....
1993-94	Portland	WHL	63	15	51	66	86	....	....	....	....	....	....	....	....	....	....	....	10	2	7	9	14	....	....	....
1994-95	Springfield	AHL	77	16	28	44	92	....	....	....	....	....	....	....	....	....	....	....	....	....	....	....	....	....	....	....
1995-96	Hartford	NHL	3	0	0	0	0	0	0	0	0	0.0	–1	....	....	....	....	....	....	....	....	....	....	....	....	....
	Springfield	AHL	73	11	33	44	43	....	....	....	....	....	....	....	....	....	....	....	8	1	1	2	2	....	....	....
1996-97	Hartford	NHL	6	0	0	0	0	0	0	0	1	0.0	–4	....	....	....	....	....	....	....	....	....	....	....	....	....
	Springfield	AHL	58	8	26	34	40	....	....	....	....	....	....	....	....	....	....	....	16	0	8	8	12	....	....	....
1997-98	Cleveland	IHL	65	8	22	30	62	....	....	....	....	....	....	....	....	....	....	....	3	0	2	2	2	....	....	....
1998-99	Las Vegas	IHL	65	9	37	46	54	....	....	....	....	....	....	....	....	....	....	....	....	....	....	....	....	....	....	....
	Providence Bruins	AHL	9	1	7	8	10	....	....	....	....	....	....	....	....	....	....	....	19	1	8	9	16	....	....	....
99-2000	Quebec Citadelles	AHL	51	8	16	24	29	....	....	....	....	....	....	....	....	....	....	....	....	....	....	....	....	....	....	....
	Grand Rapids	IHL	16	1	6	7	23	....	....	....	....	....	....	....	....	....	....	....	15	2	5	7	12	....	....	....
	NHL Totals		9	0	0	0	0	0	0	0	1	0.0		....	....	....	....	....	....	....	....	....	....	....	....	....

Transferred to **Carolina** after **Hartford** franchise relocated, June 25, 1997. Signed as a free agent by **Montreal**, August 23, 1999. Loaned to **Grand Rapids** (IHL) by **Montreal**, March 16, 2000.

McBAIN, Mike

(MIHK-BAYN, MIGHK) **MTL.**

Defense. Shoots left. 6'2", 195 lbs. Born, Kimberley, B.C., January 12, 1977. Tampa Bay's 2nd choice, 30th overall, in 1995 Entry Draft.

Season	Club	League	GP	G	A	Pts	PIM	PP	SH	GW	S	%	+/–	TF	F%	H	SB	Min	GP	G	A	Pts	PIM	PP	SH	GW
1991-92	Kimberley	BCAHA	35	25	62	87	39	....	....	....	....	....	....	....	....	....	....	....	....	....	....	....	....	....	....	....
1992-93	Kimberley	RMJHL	35	0	4	4	48	....	....	....	....	....	....	....	....	....	....	....	....	....	....	....	....	....	....	....
1993-94	Red Deer Rebels	WHL	58	4	13	17	41	....	....	....	....	....	....	....	....	....	....	....	4	0	0	0	0	....	....	....
1994-95	Red Deer Rebels	WHL	68	6	28	34	55	....	....	....	....	....	....	....	....	....	....	....	....	....	....	....	....	....	....	....
1995-96	Red Deer Rebels	WHL	68	7	34	41	68	....	....	....	....	....	....	....	....	....	....	....	10	1	7	8	10	....	....	....
1996-97	Red Deer Rebels	WHL	59	14	35	49	55	....	....	....	....	....	....	....	....	....	....	....	15	1	6	7	9	....	....	....
1997-98	Tampa Bay	NHL	27	0	1	1	8	0	0	0	17	0.0	–10	....	....	....	....	....	....	....	....	....	....	....	....	....
	Adirondack	AHL	42	2	13	15	28	....	....	....	....	....	....	....	....	....	....	....	....	....	....	....	....	....	....	....
1998-99	Tampa Bay	NHL	37	0	6	6	14	0	0	0	22	0.0	–11	0	0.0	22	30	14:49	....	....	....	....	....	....	....	....
	Cleveland	IHL	28	2	4	6	15	....	....	....	....	....	....	....	....	....	....	....	....	....	....	....	....	....	....	....
99-2000	Detroit Vipers	IHL	16	0	3	3	4	....	....	....	....	....	....	....	....	....	....	....	....	....	....	....	....	....	....	....
	Quebec Citadelles	AHL	53	5	7	12	34	....	....	....	....	....	....	....	....	....	....	....	3	0	0	0	2	....	....	....
	NHL Totals		64	0	7	7	22	0	0	0	39	0.0		0	0.0	22	30	14:49	....	....	....	....	....	....	....	....

Traded to **Montreal** by **Tampa Bay** for Gordie Dwyer, November 26, 1999.

McCABE, Bryan

MIHK-kayb, BRIGH-an) **CHI.**

Defense. Shoots left. 6'1", 210 lbs. Born, St. Catharines, Ont., June 8, 1975. NY Islanders' 2nd choice, 40th overall, in 1993 Entry Draft.

Season	Club	League	GP	G	A	Pts	PIM	PP	SH	GW	S	%	+/–	TF	F%	H	SB	Min	GP	G	A	Pts	PIM	PP	SH	GW
1990-91	Calgary Canucks	AAHA	33	14	34	48	55	....	....	....	....	....	....	....	....	....	....	....	....	....	....	....	....	....	....	....
1991-92	Medicine Hat	WHL	68	6	24	30	157	....	....	....	....	....	....	....	....	....	....	....	4	0	0	0	6	....	....	....
1992-93	Medicine Hat	WHL	14	0	13	13	83	....	....	....	....	....	....	....	....	....	....	....	....	....	....	....	....	....	....	....
	Spokane Chiefs	WHL	46	3	44	47	134	....	....	....	....	....	....	....	....	....	....	....	6	1	5	6	28	....	....	....
1993-94	Spokane Chiefs	WHL	64	22	62	84	218	....	....	....	....	....	....	....	....	....	....	....	3	0	4	4	4	....	....	....
1994-95	Spokane Chiefs	WHL	42	14	39	53	115	....	....	....	....	....	....	....	....	....	....	....	....	....	....	....	....	....	....	....
	Brandon	WHL	20	6	10	16	38	....	....	....	....	....	....	....	....	....	....	....	18	4	13	17	59	....	....	....
1995-96	NY Islanders	NHL	82	7	16	23	156	3	0	1	130	5.4	–24	....	....	....	....	....	....	....	....	....	....	....	....	....
1996-97	NY Islanders	NHL	82	8	20	28	165	2	1	2	117	6.8	–2	....	....	....	....	....	....	....	....	....	....	....	....	....
1997-98	NY Islanders	NHL	56	3	9	12	145	1	0	0	81	3.7	9	....	....	....	....	....	....	....	....	....	....	....	....	....
	Vancouver	NHL	26	1	11	12	64	0	1	0	42	2.4	10	....	....	....	....	....	....	....	....	....	....	....	....	....
1998-99	Vancouver	NHL	69	7	14	21	120	1	2	0	98	7.1	–11	1	0.0	107	117	24:13	....	....	....	....	....	....	....	....
99-2000	Chicago	NHL	79	6	19	25	139	2	0	2	119	5.0	–8	1	0.0	196	109	23:23	....	....	....	....	....	....	....	....
	NHL Totals		394	32	89	121	789	9	4	5	587	5.5		2	0.0	303	226	23:46	....	....	....	....	....	....	....	....

WHL West Second All-Star Team (1993) • WHL West First All-Star Team (1994) • WHL East First All-Star Team (1995) • Memorial Cup All-Star Team (1995)

Traded to **Vancouver** by **NY Islanders** with Todd Bertuzzi and NY Islanders' 3rd round choice (Jarkko Ruutu) in 1998 Entry Draft for Trevor Linden, February 6, 1998. Traded to **Chicago** by **Vancouver** with Vancouver's 1st round choice (Pavel Vorobiev) in 2000 Entry Draft for Chicago's 1st round choice (later traded to Tampa Bay - later traded to NY Rangers - NY Rangers selected Pavel Brendl) in 1999 Entry Draft, June 25, 1999.

McCARTHY, Sandy

(MIHK-KAHR-thee, SAN-dee) **NYR**

Right wing. Shoots right. 6'3", 225 lbs. Born, Toronto, Ont., June 15, 1972. Calgary's 3rd choice, 52nd overall, in 1991 Entry Draft.

Season	Club	League	GP	G	A	Pts	PIM	PP	SH	GW	S	%	+/–	TF	F%	H	SB	Min	GP	G	A	Pts	PIM	PP	SH	GW
1987-88	Midland	OJHL-C	18	2	1	3	70	....	....	....	....	....	....	....	....	....	....	....	....	....	....	....	....	....	....	....
1988-89	Hawkesbury	OJHL	42	4	11	15	139	....	....	....	....	....	....	....	....	....	....	....	....	....	....	....	....	....	....	....
1989-90	Laval Titan	QMJHL	65	10	11	21	269	....	....	....	....	....	....	....	....	....	....	....	14	3	3	6	60	....	....	....
1990-91	Laval Titan	QMJHL	68	21	19	40	297	....	....	....	....	....	....	....	....	....	....	....	13	6	5	11	67	....	....	....
1991-92	Laval Titan	QMJHL	62	39	51	90	326	....	....	....	....	....	....	....	....	....	....	....	8	4	5	9	81	....	....	....

			Regular Season																Playoffs							
Season	Club	League	GP	G	A	Pts	PIM	PP	SH	GW	S	%	+/-	TF	F%	H	SB	Min	GP	G	A	Pts	PIM	PP	SH	GW
1992-93	Salt Lake City	IHL	77	18	20	38	220																			
1993-94	**Calgary**	**NHL**	**79**	**5**	**5**	**10**	**173**	**0**	**0**	**0**	**39**	**12.8**	**-3**						**7**	**0**	**0**	**0**	**34**	**0**	**0**	**0**
1994-95	**Calgary**	**NHL**	**37**	**5**	**3**	**8**	**101**	**0**	**0**	**2**	**29**	**17.2**	**1**						**6**	**0**	**1**	**1**	**17**	**0**	**0**	**0**
1995-96	**Calgary**	**NHL**	**75**	**9**	**7**	**16**	**173**	**3**	**0**	**1**	**98**	**9.2**	**-8**						**4**	**0**	**0**	**0**	**10**	**0**	**0**	**0**
1996-97	**Calgary**	**NHL**	**33**	**3**	**5**	**8**	**113**	**1**	**0**	**1**	**38**	**7.9**	**-8**													
1997-98	**Calgary**	**NHL**	**52**	**8**	**5**	**13**	**170**	**1**	**0**	**1**	**68**	**11.8**	**-18**													
	Tampa Bay	**NHL**	**14**	**0**	**5**	**5**	**71**	**0**	**0**	**0**	**26**	**0.0**	**-1**													
1998-99	**Tampa Bay**	**NHL**	**67**	**5**	**7**	**12**	**135**	**1**	**0**	**0**	**89**	**5.6**	**-22**	**0**	**0.0**	**118**	**13**	**11:02**								
	Philadelphia	**NHL**	**13**	**0**	**1**	**1**	**25**	**0**	**0**	**0**	**18**	**0.0**	**-2**	**2**	**50.0**	**26**	**2**	**11:09**	**6**	**0**	**1**	**1**	**0**	**0**	**0**	**0**
99-2000	**Philadelphia**	**NHL**	**58**	**6**	**5**	**11**	**111**	**1**	**0**	**0**	**68**	**8.8**	**-5**	**4**	**0.0**	**121**	**5**	**10:27**								
	Carolina	**NHL**	**13**	**0**	**0**	**0**	**9**	**0**	**0**	**0**	**12**	**0.0**	**2**	**0**	**0.0**	**20**	**1**	**7:24**								
	NHL Totals		**441**	**41**	**43**	**84**	**1081**	**7**	**0**	**5**	**485**	**8.5**		**6**	**16.7**	**285**	**21**	**10:30**	**23**	**0**	**2**	**2**	**61**	**0**	**0**	**0**

Traded to **Tampa Bay** by **Calgary** with Calgary's 3rd (Brad Richards) and 5th (Curtis Rich) round choices in 1998 Entry Draft for Jason Wiemer, March 24, 1998. Traded to **Philadelphia** by **Tampa Bay** with Mikael Andersson for Colin Forbes and Philadelphia's 4th round choice (Michal Lanisak) in 1999 Entry Draft, March 20, 1999. Traded to **Carolina** by **Philadelphia** for Kent Manderville, March 14, 2000. Traded to **NY Rangers** by **Carolina** with a 4th round choice in 2001 Entry Draft for Darren Langdon and Rob DiMaio, August 4, 2000.

McCARTHY, Steve

(MIHK-ahr-thee, STEEV) **CHI.**

Defense. Shoots left. 6', 197 lbs. Born, Trail, B.C., February 3, 1981. Chicago's 1st choice, 23rd overall, in 1999 Entry Draft.

Season	Club	League	GP	G	A	Pts	PIM	PP	SH	GW	S	%	+/-	TF	F%	H	SB	Min	GP	G	A	Pts	PIM	PP	SH	GW
1996-97	B.C. River Rats	BCAHA	57	25	52	77	81																			
	Edmonton Ice	WHL	2	0	0	0	0																			
1997-98	Edmonton Ice	WHL	58	11	29	40	59																			
1998-99	Kootenay Ice	WHL	57	19	33	52	79												6	0	5	5	8			
99-2000	**Chicago**	**NHL**	**5**	**1**	**1**	**2**	**4**	**1**	**0**	**0**	**4**	**25.0**	**0**	**0**	**0.0**	**4**	**2**	**15:09**								
	Kootenay Ice	WHL	37	13	23	36	36																			
	NHL Totals		**5**	**1**	**1**	**2**	**4**	**1**	**0**	**0**	**4**	**25.0**		**0**	**0.0**	**4**	**2**	**15:09**								

Returned to **Kootenay** (WHL) by **Chicago**, October 22, 1999. • Suffered season-ending shoulder injury in game vs. Swift Current (WHL), March 3, 2000.

McCARTY, Darren

(MIHK-KAHR-tee, DAIR-rehn) **DET.**

Right wing. Shoots right. 6'1", 210 lbs. Born, Burnaby, B.C., April 1, 1972. Detroit's 2nd choice, 46th overall, in 1992 Entry Draft.

Season	Club	League	GP	G	A	Pts	PIM	PP	SH	GW	S	%	+/-	TF	F%	H	SB	Min	GP	G	A	Pts	PIM	PP	SH	GW
1988-89	Peterborough B's	OJHL-B	34	18	17	35	135																			
1989-90	Belleville Bulls	OHL	63	12	15	27	142												11	1	1	2	21			
1990-91	Belleville Bulls	OHL	60	30	37	67	151												6	2	2	4	13			
1991-92	Belleville Bulls	OHL	65	*55	72	127	177												5	1	4	5	13			
1992-93	Adirondack	AHL	73	17	19	36	278												11	0	1	1	33			
1993-94	**Detroit**	**NHL**	**67**	**9**	**17**	**26**	**181**	**0**	**0**	**2**	**81**	**11.1**	**12**						**7**	**2**	**2**	**4**	**8**	**0**	**0**	**0**
1994-95	**Detroit**	**NHL**	**31**	**5**	**8**	**13**	**88**	**1**	**0**	**2**	**27**	**18.5**	**5**						**18**	**3**	**2**	**5**	**14**	**0**	**0**	**0**
1995-96	**Detroit**	**NHL**	**63**	**15**	**14**	**29**	**158**	**8**	**0**	**1**	**102**	**14.7**	**14**						**19**	**3**	**2**	**5**	**20**	**0**	**0**	**1**
1996-97♦	**Detroit**	**NHL**	**68**	**19**	**30**	**49**	**126**	**5**	**0**	**6**	**171**	**11.1**	**14**						**20**	**3**	**4**	**7**	**34**	**0**	**0**	**2**
1997-98♦	**Detroit**	**NHL**	**71**	**15**	**22**	**37**	**157**	**5**	**1**	**2**	**166**	**9.0**	**0**						**22**	**3**	**8**	**11**	**34**	**0**	**0**	**1**
1998-99	**Detroit**	**NHL**	**69**	**14**	**26**	**40**	**108**	**6**	**0**	**1**	**140**	**10.0**	**10**	**15**	**33.3**	**217**	**34**	**17:04**	**10**	**1**	**1**	**2**	**23**	**0**	**0**	**0**
99-2000	**Detroit**	**NHL**	**24**	**6**	**6**	**12**	**48**	**0**	**0**	**1**	**40**	**15.0**	**1**	**1**	**0.0**	**129**	**7**	**13:40**	**9**	**0**	**1**	**1**	**12**	**0**	**0**	**0**
	NHL Totals		**393**	**83**	**123**	**206**	**866**	**25**	**1**	**15**	**727**	**11.4**		**16**	**31.3**	**346**	**41**	**16:11**	**105**	**15**	**20**	**35**	**145**	**0**	**0**	**4**

OHL First All-Star Team (1992)
• Missed majority of 1999-2000 season recovering from hernia injury suffered in game vs. Dallas, November 10, 1999.

McCAULEY, Alyn

(MIHK-KAW-lee, AL-ihn) **TOR.**

Center. Shoots left. 5'11", 190 lbs. Born, Brockville, Ont., May 29, 1977. New Jersey's 5th choice, 79th overall, in 1995 Entry Draft.

Season	Club	League	GP	G	A	Pts	PIM	PP	SH	GW	S	%	+/-	TF	F%	H	SB	Min	GP	G	A	Pts	PIM	PP	SH	GW
1991-92	Kingston	OJHL	37	5	17	22	6																			
1992-93	Kingston	OJHL	38	31	29	60	18																			
1993-94	Ottawa 67's	OHL	38	13	23	36	10												13	5	14	19	4			
1994-95	Ottawa 67's	OHL	65	16	38	54	20																			
1995-96	Ottawa 67's	OHL	55	34	48	82	24												2	0	0	0	0			
1996-97	Ottawa 67's	OHL	50	*56	56	112	16												22	14	22	36	14			
	St. John's Leafs	AHL																	3	0	1	1	0			
1997-98	**Toronto**	**NHL**	**60**	**6**	**10**	**16**	**6**	**0**	**0**	**1**	**77**	**7.8**	**-7**													
1998-99	**Toronto**	**NHL**	**39**	**9**	**15**	**24**	**2**	**1**	**0**	**1**	**76**	**11.8**	**7**	**591**	**46.4**	**10**	**4**	**15:10**								
99-2000	**Toronto**	**NHL**	**45**	**5**	**5**	**10**	**10**	**1**	**0**	**0**	**41**	**12.2**	**-6**	**450**	**47.8**	**22**	**11**	**10:46**	**5**	**0**	**0**	**0**	**6**	**0**	**0**	**0**
	St. John's Leafs	AHL	5	1	1	2	0																			
	NHL Totals		**144**	**20**	**30**	**50**	**18**	**2**	**0**	**2**	**194**	**10.3**		**1041**	**47.0**	**32**	**15**	**12:49**	**5**	**0**	**0**	**0**	**6**	**0**	**0**	**0**

OHL First All-Star Team (1996, 1997) • Canadian Major Junior First All-Star Team (1997) • Canadian Major Junior Player of the Year (1997)

Rights traded to **Toronto** by **New Jersey** with Jason Smith and Steve Sullivan for Doug Gilmour, Dave Ellett and New Jersey's 3rd round choice (previously acquired, New Jersey selected Andre Lakos) in 1999 Entry Draft, February 25, 1997.

McCLEARY, Trent

(MIHK-LEER-ee, TREHNT) **MTL.**

Right wing. Shoots right. 6', 182 lbs. Born, Swift Current, Sask., September 8, 1972.

Season	Club	League	GP	G	A	Pts	PIM	PP	SH	GW	S	%	+/-	TF	F%	H	SB	Min	GP	G	A	Pts	PIM	PP	SH	GW
1988-89	Swift Current	SAHA	34	12	12	24	85																			
	Swift Current	WHL	3	0	0	0	0																			
1989-90	Swift Current	WHL	70	3	15	18	43												4	1	0	1	0			
1990-91	Swift Current	WHL	70	16	24	40	53												3	0	0	0	2			
1991-92	Swift Current	WHL	72	23	22	45	190												8	1	2	3	16			
1992-93	Swift Current	WHL	63	17	33	50	138												17	5	4	9	16			
	New Haven	AHL	2	1	0	1	6																			
1993-94	P.E.I. Senators	AHL	4	0	0	0	6																			
	Thunder Bay	ColHL	51	23	17	40	123												9	2	11	13	15			
1994-95	P.E.I. Senators	AHL	51	9	20	29	60												9	2	3	5	26			
1995-96	**Ottawa**	**NHL**	**75**	**4**	**10**	**14**	**68**	**0**	**1**	**0**	**58**	**6.9**	**-15**													
1996-97	**Boston**	**NHL**	**59**	**3**	**5**	**8**	**33**	**0**	**0**	**1**	**41**	**7.3**	**-16**													
1997-98	Detroit Vipers	IHL	21	1	1	2	45																			
	Las Vegas	IHL	54	7	6	13	120												3	1	0	1	2			
1998-99	**Montreal**	**NHL**	**46**	**0**	**0**	**0**	**29**	**0**	**0**	**0**	**18**	**0.0**	**-1**	**113**	**45.1**	**81**	**15**	**5:50**								
99-2000	**Montreal**	**NHL**	**12**	**1**	**0**	**1**	**4**	**0**	**0**	**0**	**4**	**25.0**	**2**	**42**	**54.8**	**26**	**4**	**6:14**								
	NHL Totals		**192**	**8**	**15**	**23**	**134**	**0**	**1**	**1**	**121**	**6.6**		**155**	**47.7**	**107**	**19**	**5:55**								

Signed as a free agent by **Ottawa**, October 9, 1992. Traded to **Boston** by **Ottawa** with Ottawa's 3rd round choice (Eric Naud) in 1996 Entry Draft for Shawn McEachern, June 22, 1996. Signed as a free agent by **Montreal**, October 9, 1998. • Missed remainder of 1999-2000 season recovering from throat injury suffered in game vs. Philadelphia, January 29, 2000.

McEACHERN, Shawn

(muh-GEH-kruhn, SHAWN) **OTT.**

Left wing. Shoots left. 5'11", 193 lbs. Born, Waltham, MA, February 28, 1969. Pittsburgh's 6th choice, 110th overall, in 1987 Entry Draft.

Season	Club	League	GP	G	A	Pts	PIM	PP	SH	GW	S	%	+/-	TF	F%	H	SB	Min	GP	G	A	Pts	PIM	PP	SH	GW
1985-86	Matignon High	Hi-School	20	32	20	52																				
1986-87	Matignon High	Hi-School	16	29	28	57																				
1987-88	Matignon High	Hi-School	22	52	40	92																				
1988-89	Boston University	H-East	36	20	28	48	32																			
1989-90	Boston University	H-East	43	25	31	56	78																			
1990-91	Boston University	H-East	41	34	48	82	43																			
1991-92	United States	Nat-Team	57	26	23	49	38																			
	United States	Olympics	8	1	0	1	10																			
	♦ **Pittsburgh**	**NHL**	**15**	**0**	**4**	**4**	**0**	**0**	**0**	**0**	**14**	**0.0**	**1**						**19**	**2**	**7**	**9**	**4**	**0**	**0**	**0**
1992-93	**Pittsburgh**	**NHL**	**84**	**28**	**33**	**61**	**46**	**7**	**0**	**6**	**196**	**14.3**	**21**						**12**	**3**	**2**	**5**	**10**	**0**	**0**	**1**
1993-94	**Los Angeles**	**NHL**	**49**	**8**	**13**	**21**	**24**	**0**	**3**	**0**	**81**	**9.9**	**1**													
	Pittsburgh	**NHL**	**27**	**12**	**9**	**21**	**10**	**0**	**2**	**1**	**78**	**15.4**	**13**						**6**	**1**	**0**	**1**	**2**	**0**	**0**	**0**

			Regular Season																Playoffs							
Season	Club	League	GP	G	A	Pts	PIM	PP	SH	GW	S	%	+/–	TF	F%	H	SB	Min	GP	G	A	Pts	PIM	PP	SH	GW
1994-95	Kiekko-Espoo	Finland	8	1	3	4	6	....	....	....	....	....	....	....	....	....	....	....	....	....	....	....	....	....	....	....
	Pittsburgh	**NHL**	**44**	**13**	**13**	**26**	**22**	**1**	**2**	**1**	**97**	**13.4**	**4**	....	....	....	....	....	**11**	**0**	**2**	**2**	**8**	**0**	**0**	**0**
1995-96	**Boston**	**NHL**	**82**	**24**	**29**	**53**	**34**	**3**	**2**	**3**	**238**	**10.1**	**–5**	....	....	....	....	....	**5**	**2**	**1**	**3**	**8**	**0**	**0**	**0**
1996-97	**Ottawa**	**NHL**	**65**	**11**	**20**	**31**	**18**	**0**	**1**	**2**	**150**	**7.3**	**–5**	....	....	....	....	....	**7**	**2**	**0**	**2**	**8**	**1**	**0**	**0**
1997-98	**Ottawa**	**NHL**	**81**	**24**	**24**	**48**	**42**	**8**	**2**	**4**	**229**	**10.5**	**1**	....	....	....	....	....	**11**	**0**	**4**	**4**	**8**	**0**	**0**	**0**
1998-99	**Ottawa**	**NHL**	**77**	**31**	**25**	**56**	**46**	**7**	**0**	**4**	**223**	**13.9**	**8**	**441**	**48.5**	**37**	**23**	**18:45**	**4**	**2**	**0**	**2**	**6**	**1**	**0**	**0**
99-2000	**Ottawa**	**NHL**	**69**	**29**	**22**	**51**	**24**	**10**	**0**	**4**	**219**	**13.2**	**2**	**54**	**50.0**	**45**	**13**	**17:50**	**6**	**0**	**3**	**3**	**4**	**0**	**0**	**0**
	NHL Totals		**593**	**180**	**192**	**372**	**266**	**36**	**12**	**25**	**1525**	**11.8**		**495**	**48.7**	**82**	**36**	**18:19**	**81**	**12**	**19**	**31**	**58**	**2**	**0**	**1**

Hockey East Second All-Star Team (1990) • Hockey East First All-Star Team (1991) • NCAA East First All-American Team (1991)

Traded to **LA Kings** by **Pittsburgh** for Marty McSorley, August 27, 1993. Traded to **Pittsburgh** by **LA Kings** with Tomas Sandstrom for Marty McSorley and Jim Paek, February 16, 1994. Traded to **Boston** by **Pittsburgh** with Kevin Stevens for Glen Murray, Bryan Smolinski and Boston's 3rd round choice (Boyd Kane) in 1996 Entry Draft, August 2, 1995. Traded to **Ottawa** by **Boston** for Trent McCleary and Ottawa's 3rd round choice (Eric Naud) in 1996 Entry Draft, June 22, 1996.

McGILLIS, Dan

(MIHK-gihl-his, DAN) **PHI.**

Defense. Shoots left. 6'2", 225 lbs. Born, Hawkesbury, Ont., July 1, 1972. Detroit's 10th choice, 238th overall, in 1992 Entry Draft.

Season	Club	League	GP	G	A	Pts	PIM	PP	SH	GW	S	%	+/–	TF	F%	H	SB	Min	GP	G	A	Pts	PIM	PP	SH	GW
1989-90	Hawkesbury	OJHL	55	2	1	3	52	....	....	....	....	....	....	....	....	....	....	....	....	....	....	....	....	....	....	....
1990-91	Hawkesbury	OJHL	56	8	22	30	92	....	....	....	....	....	....	....	....	....	....	....	....	....	....	....	....	....	....	....
1991-92	Hawkesbury	OJHL	36	5	19	24	106	....	....	....	....	....	....	....	....	....	....	....	....	....	....	....	....	....	....	....
1992-93	Northeastern	H-East	35	5	12	17	42	....	....	....	....	....	....	....	....	....	....	....	....	....	....	....	....	....	....	....
1993-94	Northeastern	H-East	38	4	25	29	82	....	....	....	....	....	....	....	....	....	....	....	....	....	....	....	....	....	....	....
1994-95	Northeastern	H-East	34	9	22	31	70	....	....	....	....	....	....	....	....	....	....	....	....	....	....	....	....	....	....	....
1995-96	Northeastern	H-East	34	12	24	36	50	....	....	....	....	....	....	....	....	....	....	....	....	....	....	....	....	....	....	....
1996-97	**Edmonton**	**NHL**	**73**	**6**	**16**	**22**	**52**	**2**	**1**	**2**	**139**	**4.3**	**2**	....	....	....	....	....	**12**	**0**	**5**	**5**	**24**	**0**	**0**	**0**
1997-98	**Edmonton**	**NHL**	**67**	**10**	**15**	**25**	**74**	**5**	**0**	**3**	**119**	**8.4**	**–17**	....	....	....	....	....	....	....	....	....	....	....	....	....
	Philadelphia	**NHL**	**13**	**1**	**5**	**6**	**35**	**1**	**0**	**0**	**18**	**5.6**	**–4**	....	....	....	....	....	**5**	**1**	**2**	**3**	**10**	**1**	**0**	**0**
1998-99	**Philadelphia**	**NHL**	**78**	**8**	**37**	**45**	**61**	**6**	**0**	**4**	**164**	**4.9**	**16**	**0**	**0.0**	**220**	**71**	**21:41**	**6**	**0**	**1**	**1**	**12**	**0**	**0**	**0**
99-2000	**Philadelphia**	**NHL**	**68**	**4**	**14**	**18**	**55**	**3**	**0**	**1**	**128**	**3.1**	**16**	**0**	**0.0**	**264**	**63**	**20:04**	**18**	**2**	**6**	**8**	**12**	**0**	**0**	**0**
	NHL Totals		**299**	**29**	**87**	**116**	**277**	**17**	**1**	**10**	**568**	**5.1**		**0**	**0.0**	**484**	**134**	**20:56**	**41**	**3**	**14**	**17**	**58**	**1**	**0**	**0**

Hockey East First All-Star Team (1995, 1996) • NCAA East First All-American Team (1996)

Traded to **Edmonton** by **Detroit** for Kirk Maltby, March 20, 1996. Traded to **Philadelphia** by **Edmonton** with Edmonton's 2nd round choice (Jason Beckett) in 1998 Entry Draft for Janne Niinimaa, March 24, 1998.

McINNIS, Marty

(MAK-ih-nihs, MAHR-tee) **ANA.**

Left wing. Shoots right. 6', 192 lbs. Born, Weymouth, MA., June 2, 1970. NY Islanders' 10th choice, 163rd overall, in 1988 Entry Draft.

Season	Club	League	GP	G	A	Pts	PIM	PP	SH	GW	S	%	+/–	TF	F%	H	SB	Min	GP	G	A	Pts	PIM	PP	SH	GW
1986-87	Milton Academy	Hi-School	25	21	19	40	....	....	....	....	....	....	....	....	....	....	....	....	....	....	....	....	....	....	....	....
1987-88	Milton Academy	Hi-School	25	26	25	51	....	....	....	....	....	....	....	....	....	....	....	....	....	....	....	....	....	....	....	....
1988-89	Boston College	H-East	39	13	19	32	8	....	....	....	....	....	....	....	....	....	....	....	....	....	....	....	....	....	....	....
1989-90	Boston College	H-East	41	24	29	53	43	....	....	....	....	....	....	....	....	....	....	....	....	....	....	....	....	....	....	....
1990-91	Boston College	H-East	38	21	36	57	40	....	....	....	....	....	....	....	....	....	....	....	....	....	....	....	....	....	....	....
1991-92	United States	Nat-Team	54	15	19	34	20	....	....	....	....	....	....	....	....	....	....	....	....	....	....	....	....	....	....	....
	United States	Olympics	8	5	2	7	4	....	....	....	....	....	....	....	....	....	....	....	....	....	....	....	....	....	....	....
	NY Islanders	**NHL**	**15**	**3**	**5**	**8**	**0**	**0**	**0**	**0**	**24**	**12.5**	**6**	....	....	....	....	....	....	....	....	....	....	....	....	....
1992-93	**NY Islanders**	**NHL**	**56**	**10**	**20**	**30**	**24**	**0**	**1**	**0**	**60**	**16.7**	**7**	....	....	....	....	....	**3**	**0**	**1**	**1**	**0**	**0**	**0**	**0**
	Capital District	AHL	10	4	12	16	2	....	....	....	....	....	....	....	....	....	....	....	....	....	....	....	....	....	....	....
1993-94	**NY Islanders**	**NHL**	**81**	**25**	**31**	**56**	**24**	**3**	**5**	**3**	**136**	**18.4**	**31**	....	....	....	....	....	**4**	**0**	**0**	**0**	**0**	**0**	**0**	**0**
1994-95	**NY Islanders**	**NHL**	**41**	**9**	**7**	**16**	**8**	**0**	**0**	**1**	**68**	**13.2**	**–1**	....	....	....	....	....	....	....	....	....	....	....	....	....
1995-96	**NY Islanders**	**NHL**	**74**	**12**	**34**	**46**	**39**	**2**	**0**	**1**	**167**	**7.2**	**–11**	....	....	....	....	....	....	....	....	....	....	....	....	....
1996-97	**NY Islanders**	**NHL**	**70**	**20**	**22**	**42**	**20**	**4**	**1**	**4**	**163**	**12.3**	**–7**	....	....	....	....	....	....	....	....	....	....	....	....	....
	Calgary	**NHL**	**10**	**3**	**4**	**7**	**2**	**1**	**0**	**0**	**19**	**15.8**	**–1**	....	....	....	....	....	....	....	....	....	....	....	....	....
1997-98	**Calgary**	**NHL**	**75**	**19**	**25**	**44**	**34**	**5**	**4**	**0**	**128**	**14.8**	**1**	....	....	....	....	....	....	....	....	....	....	....	....	....
1998-99	**Calgary**	**NHL**	**6**	**1**	**1**	**2**	**6**	**0**	**0**	**0**	**7**	**14.3**	**–1**	**28**	**32.1**	**5**	**0**	**13:51**	....	....	....	....	....	....	....	....
	Anaheim	**NHL**	**75**	**18**	**34**	**52**	**36**	**11**	**1**	**5**	**139**	**12.9**	**–14**	**390**	**46.9**	**52**	**15**	**18:59**	**4**	**2**	**0**	**2**	**2**	**2**	**0**	**0**
99-2000	**Anaheim**	**NHL**	**62**	**10**	**18**	**28**	**26**	**2**	**1**	**2**	**129**	**7.8**	**–4**	**355**	**50.1**	**60**	**9**	**19:04**	....	....	....	....	....	....	....	....
	NHL Totals		**565**	**130**	**201**	**331**	**219**	**28**	**13**	**16**	**1040**	**12.5**		**773**	**47.9**	**117**	**24**	**18:48**	**11**	**2**	**1**	**3**	**2**	**2**	**0**	**0**

Traded to **Calgary** by **NY Islanders** with Tyrone Garner and Calgary's 6th round choice (previously acquired, Calgary selected Ilja Demidov) in 1997 Entry Draft for Robert Reichel, March 18, 1997. Traded to **Chicago** by **Calgary** with Eric Andersson and Jamie Allison for Jeff Shantz and Steve Dubinsky, October 27, 1998. Traded to **Anaheim** by **Chicago** for Toronto's 4th round choice (previously acquired, later traded to Washington - Washington selected Ryan Vanbuskirk) in 2000 Entry Draft, October 27, 1998.

McKAY, Randy

(MIHK-ay, RAN-dee) **N.J.**

Right wing. Shoots right. 6'2", 210 lbs. Born, Montreal, Que., January 25, 1967. Detroit's 6th choice, 113th overall, in 1985 Entry Draft.

Season	Club	League	GP	G	A	Pts	PIM	PP	SH	GW	S	%	+/–	TF	F%	H	SB	Min	GP	G	A	Pts	PIM	PP	SH	GW
1983-84	Lac St-Louis	QAAA	38	18	28	46	62	....	....	....	....	....	....	....	....	....	....	....	....	....	....	....	....	....	....	....
1984-85	Michigan Tech	WCHA	25	4	5	9	32	....	....	....	....	....	....	....	....	....	....	....	....	....	....	....	....	....	....	....
1985-86	Michigan Tech	WCHA	40	12	22	34	46	....	....	....	....	....	....	....	....	....	....	....	....	....	....	....	....	....	....	....
1986-87	Michigan Tech	WCHA	39	5	11	16	46	....	....	....	....	....	....	....	....	....	....	....	....	....	....	....	....	....	....	....
1987-88	Michigan Tech	WCHA	41	17	24	41	70	....	....	....	....	....	....	....	....	....	....	....	....	....	....	....	....	....	....	....
	Adirondack	AHL	10	0	3	3	12	....	....	....	....	....	....	....	....	....	....	....	6	0	4	4	0	....	....	....
1988-89	**Detroit**	**NHL**	**3**	**0**	**0**	**0**	**0**	**0**	**0**	**0**	**2**	**0.0**	**–1**	....	....	....	....	....	**2**	**0**	**0**	**0**	**2**	**0**	**0**	**0**
	Adirondack	AHL	58	29	34	63	170	....	....	....	....	....	....	....	....	....	....	....	14	4	7	11	60	....	....	....
1989-90	**Detroit**	**NHL**	**33**	**3**	**6**	**9**	**51**	**0**	**0**	**0**	**33**	**9.1**	**1**	....	....	....	....	....	....	....	....	....	....	....	....	....
	Adirondack	AHL	36	16	23	39	99	....	....	....	....	....	....	....	....	....	....	....	6	3	0	3	35	....	....	....
1990-91	**Detroit**	**NHL**	**47**	**1**	**7**	**8**	**183**	**0**	**0**	**0**	**22**	**4.5**	**–15**	....	....	....	....	....	**5**	**0**	**1**	**1**	**41**	....	....	....
1991-92	**New Jersey**	**NHL**	**80**	**17**	**16**	**33**	**246**	**2**	**0**	**1**	**111**	**15.3**	**6**	....	....	....	....	....	**7**	**1**	**3**	**4**	**10**	**0**	**0**	**0**
1992-93	**New Jersey**	**NHL**	**73**	**11**	**11**	**22**	**206**	**1**	**0**	**2**	**94**	**11.7**	**0**	....	....	....	....	....	**5**	**0**	**0**	**0**	**16**	**1**	**0**	**0**
1993-94	**New Jersey**	**NHL**	**78**	**12**	**15**	**27**	**244**	**0**	**0**	**1**	**77**	**15.6**	**24**	....	....	....	....	....	**20**	**1**	**2**	**3**	**24**	**0**	**0**	**0**
1994-95♦	**New Jersey**	**NHL**	**33**	**5**	**7**	**12**	**44**	**0**	**0**	**0**	**44**	**11.4**	**10**	....	....	....	....	....	**19**	**8**	**4**	**12**	**11**	**2**	**0**	**2**
1995-96	**New Jersey**	**NHL**	**76**	**11**	**10**	**21**	**145**	**3**	**0**	**3**	**97**	**11.3**	**7**	....	....	....	....	....	....	....	....	....	....	....	....	....
1996-97	**New Jersey**	**NHL**	**77**	**9**	**18**	**27**	**109**	**0**	**0**	**2**	**92**	**9.8**	**15**	....	....	....	....	....	**10**	**1**	**1**	**2**	**0**	**0**	**0**	**0**
1997-98	**New Jersey**	**NHL**	**74**	**24**	**24**	**48**	**86**	**8**	**0**	**5**	**141**	**17.0**	**30**	....	....	....	....	....	**6**	**0**	**1**	**1**	**0**	**0**	**0**	**0**
1998-99	**New Jersey**	**NHL**	**70**	**17**	**20**	**37**	**143**	**3**	**0**	**5**	**136**	**12.5**	**10**	**1**	**0.0**	**124**	**11**	**16:06**	**7**	**3**	**2**	**5**	**2**	**0**	**0**	**1**
99-2000♦	**New Jersey**	**NHL**	**67**	**16**	**23**	**39**	**80**	**3**	**0**	**4**	**116**	**13.8**	**8**	**2**	**0.0**	**144**	**16**	**15:39**	**23**	**0**	**6**	**6**	**9**	**0**	**0**	**0**
	NHL Totals		**711**	**126**	**157**	**283**	**1537**	**20**	**0**	**23**	**965**	**13.1**		**3**	**0.0**	**268**	**27**	**15:53**	**104**	**14**	**20**	**34**	**115**	**3**	**0**	**3**

Transferred to **New Jersey** by **Detroit** with Dave Barr as compensation for Detroit's signing of free agent Troy Crowder, September 9, 1991.

McKEE, Jay

(MIHK-ee, JAY) **BUF.**

Defense. Shoots left. 6'4", 201 lbs. Born, Kingston, Ont., September 8, 1977. Buffalo's 1st choice, 14th overall, in 1995 Entry Draft.

Season	Club	League	GP	G	A	Pts	PIM	PP	SH	GW	S	%	+/–	TF	F%	H	SB	Min	GP	G	A	Pts	PIM	PP	SH	GW
1991-92	Kingston	OJHL	1	0	0	0	0	....	....	....	....	....	....	....	....	....	....	....	....	....	....	....	....	....	....	....
	Mimico Monarchs	OJHL	39	7	9	16	67	....	....	....	....	....	....	....	....	....	....	....	....	....	....	....	....	....	....	....
1992-93	Ernestown Jets	OJHL-C	36	0	17	17	37	....	....	....	....	....	....	....	....	....	....	....	....	....	....	....	....	....	....	....
	Kingston	OJHL	2	0	0	0	0	....	....	....	....	....	....	....	....	....	....	....	....	....	....	....	....	....	....	....
1993-94	Sudbury Wolves	OHL	51	0	1	1	51	....	....	....	....	....	....	....	....	....	....	....	3	0	0	0	0	....	....	....
1994-95	Sudbury Wolves	OHL	39	6	6	12	91	....	....	....	....	....	....	....	....	....	....	....	....	....	....	....	....	....	....	....
	Niagara Falls	OHL	26	3	13	16	60	....	....	....	....	....	....	....	....	....	....	....	6	2	3	5	10	....	....	....
1995-96	Niagara Falls	OHL	64	5	41	46	129	....	....	....	....	....	....	....	....	....	....	....	10	1	5	6	16	....	....	....
	Buffalo	**NHL**	**1**	**0**	**1**	**1**	**2**	**0**	**0**	**0**	**2**	**0.0**	**1**	....	....	....	....	....	....	....	....	....	....	....	....	....
	Rochester	AHL	4	0	1	1	15	....	....	....	....	....	....	....	....	....	....	....	....	....	....	....	....	....	....	....
1996-97	**Buffalo**	**NHL**	**43**	**1**	**9**	**10**	**35**	**0**	**0**	**0**	**29**	**3.4**	**3**	....	....	....	....	....	**3**	**0**	**0**	**0**	**0**	**0**	**0**	**0**
	Rochester	AHL	7	2	5	7	4	....	....	....	....	....	....	....	....	....	....	....	....	....	....	....	....	....	....	....
1997-98	**Buffalo**	**NHL**	**56**	**1**	**13**	**14**	**42**	**0**	**0**	**0**	**55**	**1.8**	**–1**	....	....	....	....	....	**1**	**0**	**0**	**0**	**0**	**0**	**0**	**0**
	Rochester	AHL	13	1	7	8	11	....	....	....	....	....	....	....	....	....	....	....	....	....	....	....	....	....	....	....

			Regular Season																Playoffs							
Season	Club	League	GP	G	A	Pts	PIM	PP	SH	GW	S	%	+/-	TF	F%	H	SB	Min	GP	G	A	Pts	PIM	PP	SH	GW
1998-99	**Buffalo**	**NHL**	**72**	**0**	**6**	**6**	**75**	**0**	**0**	**0**	**57**	**0.0**	**20**	**0**	**0.0**	**204**	**129**	**20:28**	**21**	**0**	**3**	**3**	**24**	**0**	**0**	**0**
99-2000	**Buffalo**	**NHL**	**78**	**5**	**12**	**17**	**50**	**1**	**0**	**1**	**84**	**6.0**	**5**	**0**	**0.0**	**153**	**170**	**20:58**	**1**	**0**	**0**	**0**	**0**	**0**	**0**	**0**
	NHL Totals		**250**	**7**	**41**	**48**	**204**	**1**	**0**	**1**	**227**	**3.1**		**0**	**0.0**	**357**	**299**	**20:44**	**26**	**0**	**3**	**3**	**24**	**0**	**0**	**0**

OHL Second All-Star Team (1996)

McKENNA, Steve

(MIHK-ehn-aw, STEEV) **MIN.**

Left wing. Shoots left. 6'8", 255 lbs. Born, Toronto, Ont., August 21, 1973.

1991-92	Cambridge Hawks	OJHL-B	48	21	23	44	173	....	....	....	....	....	....	....	....	....	....	....	....	....	....	....	....	....	....	....
1992-93	Notre Dame	SJHL	STATISTICS NOT AVAILABLE																							
1993-94	Merrimack	H-East	37	1	2	3	74	....	....	....	....	....	....	....	....	....	....	....	....	....	....	....	....	....	....	....
1994-95	Merrimack	H-East	37	1	9	10	74	....	....	....	....	....	....	....	....	....	....	....	....	....	....	....	....	....	....	....
1995-96	Merrimack	H-East	33	3	11	14	67	....	....	....	....	....	....	....	....	....	....	....	....	....	....	....	....	....	....	....
1996-97	**Los Angeles**	**NHL**	**9**	**0**	**0**	**0**	**37**	**0**	**0**	**0**	**6**	**0.0**	**1**	....	....	....	....	....	....	....	....	....	....	....	....	....
	Phoenix	IHL	66	6	5	11	187	....	....	....	....	....	....	....	....	....	....	....	....	....	....	....	....	....	....	....
1997-98	**Los Angeles**	**NHL**	**62**	**4**	**4**	**8**	**150**	**1**	**0**	**0**	**42**	**9.5**	**-9**	....	....	....	....	....	**3**	**0**	**1**	**1**	**8**	**0**	**0**	**0**
	Fredericton	AHL	6	2	1	3	48	....	....	....	....	....	....	....	....	....	....	....	....	....	....	....	....	....	....	....
1998-99	**Los Angeles**	**NHL**	**20**	**1**	**0**	**1**	**36**	**0**	**0**	**0**	**12**	**8.3**	**-3**	**0**	**0.0**	**35**	**4**	**8:24**	....	....	....	....	....	....	....	....
99-2000	**Los Angeles**	**NHL**	**46**	**0**	**5**	**5**	**125**	**0**	**0**	**0**	**14**	**0.0**	**3**	**1**	**0.0**	**39**	**5**	**4:53**	....	....	....	....	....	....	....	....
	NHL Totals		**137**	**5**	**9**	**14**	**348**	**1**	**0**	**0**	**74**	**6.8**		**1**	**0.0**	**74**	**9**	**5:57**	**3**	**0**	**1**	**1**	**8**	**0**	**0**	**0**

Signed as a free agent by **LA Kings**, May 23, 1996. Selected by **Minnesota** from **LA Kings** in Expansion Draft, June 23, 2000.

McKENZIE, Jim

(MIHK-ehn-zee, JIHM) **N.J.**

Left wing. Shoots left. 6'4", 220 lbs. Born, Gull Lake, Sask., November 3, 1969. Hartford's 3rd choice, 73rd overall, in 1989 Entry Draft.

1985-86	Moose Jaw	SAHA	36	18	26	44	89	....	....	....	....	....	....	....	....	....	....	....	....	....	....	....	....	....	....	....
	Moose Jaw	WHL	3	0	2	2	0	....	....	....	....	....	....	....	....	....	....	....	....	....	....	....	....	....	....	....
1986-87	Moose Jaw	WHL	65	5	3	8	125	....	....	....	....	....	....	....	....	....	....	....	9	0	0	0	7	....	....	....
1987-88	Moose Jaw	WHL	62	1	17	18	134	....	....	....	....	....	....	....	....	....	....	....	....	....	....	....	....	....	....	....
1988-89	Victoria Cougars	WHL	67	15	27	42	176	....	....	....	....	....	....	....	....	....	....	....	8	1	4	5	30	....	....	....
1989-90	**Hartford**	**NHL**	**5**	**0**	**0**	**0**	**4**	**0**	**0**	**0**	**0**	**0.0**	**0**	....	....	....	....	....	....	....	....	....	....	....	....	....
	Binghamton	AHL	56	4	12	16	149	....	....	....	....	....	....	....	....	....	....	....	....	....	....	....	....	....	....	....
1990-91	**Hartford**	**NHL**	**41**	**4**	**3**	**7**	**108**	**0**	**0**	**0**	**16**	**25.0**	**-7**	....	....	....	....	....	**6**	**0**	**0**	**0**	**8**	**0**	**0**	**0**
	Springfield	AHL	24	3	4	7	102	....	....	....	....	....	....	....	....	....	....	....	....	....	....	....	....	....	....	....
1991-92	**Hartford**	**NHL**	**67**	**5**	**1**	**6**	**87**	**0**	**0**	**0**	**34**	**14.7**	**-6**	....	....	....	....	....	....	....	....	....	....	....	....	....
1992-93	**Hartford**	**NHL**	**64**	**3**	**6**	**9**	**202**	**0**	**0**	**0**	**36**	**8.3**	**-10**	....	....	....	....	....	....	....	....	....	....	....	....	....
1993-94	**Hartford**	**NHL**	**26**	**1**	**2**	**3**	**67**	**0**	**0**	**0**	**9**	**11.1**	**-6**	....	....	....	....	....	....	....	....	....	....	....	....	....
	Dallas	**NHL**	**34**	**2**	**3**	**5**	**63**	**0**	**0**	**1**	**18**	**11.1**	**4**	....	....	....	....	....	....	....	....	....	....	....	....	....
	Pittsburgh	**NHL**	**11**	**0**	**0**	**0**	**16**	**0**	**0**	**0**	**6**	**0.0**	**-5**	....	....	....	....	....	**3**	**0**	**0**	**0**	**0**	**0**	**0**	**0**
1994-95	**Pittsburgh**	**NHL**	**39**	**2**	**1**	**3**	**63**	**0**	**0**	**1**	**16**	**12.5**	**-7**	....	....	....	....	....	**5**	**0**	**0**	**0**	**4**	**0**	**0**	**0**
1995-96	**Winnipeg**	**NHL**	**73**	**4**	**2**	**6**	**202**	**0**	**0**	**0**	**28**	**14.3**	**-4**	....	....	....	....	....	**1**	**0**	**0**	**0**	**2**	**0**	**0**	**0**
1996-97	**Phoenix**	**NHL**	**65**	**5**	**3**	**8**	**200**	**0**	**0**	**1**	**38**	**13.2**	**-5**	....	....	....	....	....	**7**	**0**	**0**	**0**	**2**	**0**	**0**	**0**
1997-98	**Phoenix**	**NHL**	**64**	**3**	**4**	**7**	**146**	**0**	**0**	**0**	**35**	**8.6**	**-7**	....	....	....	....	....	**1**	**0**	**0**	**0**	**0**	**0**	**0**	**0**
1998-99	**Anaheim**	**NHL**	**73**	**5**	**4**	**9**	**99**	**1**	**0**	**1**	**59**	**8.5**	**-18**	**8**	**50.0**	**85**	**8**	**10:22**	**4**	**0**	**0**	**0**	**4**	**0**	**0**	**0**
99-2000	**Anaheim**	**NHL**	**31**	**3**	**3**	**6**	**48**	**0**	**0**	**0**	**22**	**13.6**	**-5**	**2**	**0.0**	**50**	**2**	**10:26**	....	....	....	....	....	....	....	....
	Washington	**NHL**	**30**	**1**	**2**	**3**	**16**	**0**	**0**	**0**	**10**	**10.0**	**0**	**0**	**0.0**	**27**	**5**	**6:22**	**1**	**0**	**0**	**0**	**0**	**0**	**0**	**0**
	NHL Totals		**623**	**38**	**34**	**72**	**1321**	**1**	**0**	**4**	**327**	**11.6**		**10**	**40.0**	**162**	**15**	**9:29**	**28**	**0**	**0**	**0**	**20**	**0**	**0**	**0**

Traded to **Florida** by **Hartford** for Alexander Godynyuk, December 16, 1993. Traded to **Dallas** by **Florida** for Dallas' 4th round choice (later traded to Ottawa - Ottawa selected Kevin Bolibruck) in 1995 Entry Draft, December 16, 1993. Traded to **Pittsburgh** by **Dallas** for Mike Needham, March 21, 1994. Signed as a free agent by **NY Islanders**, August 2, 1995. Claimed by **Winnipeg** from **NY Islanders** in NHL Waiver Draft, October 2, 1995. Transferred to **Phoenix** after **Winnipeg** franchise relocated, July 1, 1996. Traded to **Anaheim** by **Phoenix** for J.F. Jomphe, June 18, 1998. Claimed on waivers by **Washington** from **Anaheim**, January 20, 2000. Signed as a free agent by **New Jersey**, July 3, 2000.

McLAREN, Kyle

(MIHK-LAH-rehn, KIGHL) **BOS.**

Defense. Shoots left. 6'4", 230 lbs. Born, Humboldt, Sask., June 18, 1977. Boston's 1st choice, 9th overall, in 1995 Entry Draft.

1992-93	Lethbridge	AAHA	60	28	28	56	84	....	....	....	....	....	....	....	....	....	....	....	....	....	....	....	....	....	....	....
1993-94	Tacoma Rockets	WHL	62	1	9	10	53	....	....	....	....	....	....	....	....	....	....	....	6	1	4	5	6	....	....	....
1994-95	Tacoma Rockets	WHL	47	13	19	32	68	....	....	....	....	....	....	....	....	....	....	....	4	1	1	2	4	....	....	....
1995-96	**Boston**	**NHL**	**74**	**5**	**12**	**17**	**73**	**0**	**0**	**0**	**74**	**6.8**	**16**	....	....	....	....	....	**5**	**0**	**0**	**0**	**14**	**0**	**0**	**0**
1996-97	**Boston**	**NHL**	**58**	**5**	**9**	**14**	**54**	**0**	**0**	**1**	**68**	**7.4**	**-9**	....	....	....	....	....	....	....	....	....	....	....	....	....
1997-98	**Boston**	**NHL**	**66**	**5**	**20**	**25**	**56**	**2**	**0**	**0**	**101**	**5.0**	**13**	....	....	....	....	....	**6**	**1**	**0**	**1**	**4**	**1**	**0**	**0**
1998-99	**Boston**	**NHL**	**52**	**6**	**18**	**24**	**48**	**3**	**0**	**0**	**97**	**6.2**	**1**	**0**	**0.0**	**205**	**69**	**23:25**	**12**	**0**	**3**	**3**	**10**	**0**	**0**	**0**
99-2000	**Boston**	**NHL**	**71**	**8**	**11**	**19**	**67**	**2**	**0**	**3**	**142**	**5.6**	**-4**	**5**	**40.0**	**282**	**155**	**23:18**	....	....	....	....	....	....	....	....
	NHL Totals		**321**	**29**	**70**	**99**	**298**	**7**	**0**	**4**	**482**	**6.0**		**5**	**40.0**	**487**	**224**	**23:21**	**23**	**1**	**3**	**4**	**28**	**1**	**0**	**0**

NHL All-Rookie Team (1996)

McSORLEY, Marty

(MIHK-SOHR-lee, MAHR-tee)

Defense. Shoots right. 6'1", 235 lbs. Born, Hamilton, Ont., May 18, 1963.

1979-80	Cayuga Wings	OHA-D	27	8	18	26	92	....	....	....	....	....	....	....	....	....	....	....	....	....	....	....	....	....	....	....
1980-81	Hamilton Kilty B's	OHA-B	40	16	17	33	72	....	....	....	....	....	....	....	....	....	....	....	....	....	....	....	....	....	....	....
1981-82	Belleville Bulls	OHL	58	6	13	19	234	....	....	....	....	....	....	....	....	....	....	....	....	....	....	....	....	....	....	....
1982-83	Belleville Bulls	OHL	70	10	41	51	183	....	....	....	....	....	....	....	....	....	....	....	4	0	0	0	7	....	....	....
	Baltimore	AHL	2	0	0	0	22	....	....	....	....	....	....	....	....	....	....	....	....	....	....	....	....	....	....	....
1983-84	**Pittsburgh**	**NHL**	**72**	**2**	**7**	**9**	**224**	**0**	**0**	**0**	**75**	**2.7**	**-39**	....	....	....	....	....	....	....	....	....	....	....	....	....
1984-85	**Pittsburgh**	**NHL**	**15**	**0**	**0**	**0**	**15**	**0**	**0**	**0**	**11**	**0.0**	**-3**	....	....	....	....	....	....	....	....	....	....	....	....	....
	Baltimore	AHL	58	6	24	30	154	....	....	....	....	....	....	....	....	....	....	....	14	0	7	7	47	....	....	....
1985-86	**Edmonton**	**NHL**	**59**	**11**	**12**	**23**	**265**	**0**	**0**	**2**	**72**	**15.3**	**9**	....	....	....	....	....	**8**	**0**	**2**	**2**	**50**	**0**	**0**	**0**
	Nova Scotia	AHL	9	2	4	6	34	....	....	....	....	....	....	....	....	....	....	....	....	....	....	....	....	....	....	....
1986-87♦	**Edmonton**	**NHL**	**41**	**2**	**4**	**6**	**159**	**0**	**0**	**0**	**32**	**6.3**	**-4**	....	....	....	....	....	**21**	**4**	**3**	**7**	**65**	**0**	**0**	**1**
	Nova Scotia	AHL	7	2	2	4	48	....	....	....	....	....	....	....	....	....	....	....	....	....	....	....	....	....	....	....
1987-88♦	**Edmonton**	**NHL**	**60**	**9**	**17**	**26**	**223**	**0**	**0**	**1**	**66**	**13.6**	**23**	....	....	....	....	....	**16**	**0**	**3**	**3**	**67**	**0**	**0**	**0**
1988-89	**Los Angeles**	**NHL**	**66**	**10**	**17**	**27**	**350**	**2**	**0**	**1**	**87**	**11.5**	**3**	....	....	....	....	....	**11**	**0**	**2**	**2**	**33**	**0**	**0**	**0**
1989-90	**Los Angeles**	**NHL**	**75**	**15**	**21**	**36**	**322**	**2**	**1**	**0**	**127**	**11.8**	**2**	....	....	....	....	....	**10**	**1**	**3**	**4**	**18**	**1**	**0**	**0**
1990-91	**Los Angeles**	**NHL**	**61**	**7**	**32**	**39**	**221**	**1**	**1**	**1**	**100**	**7.0**	**48**	....	....	....	....	....	**12**	**0**	**0**	**0**	**58**	**0**	**0**	**0**
1991-92	**Los Angeles**	**NHL**	**71**	**7**	**22**	**29**	**268**	**2**	**1**	**0**	**119**	**5.9**	**-13**	....	....	....	....	....	**6**	**1**	**0**	**1**	**21**	**0**	**0**	**0**
1992-93	**Los Angeles**	**NHL**	**81**	**15**	**26**	**41**	***399**	**3**	**3**	**0**	**197**	**7.6**	**1**	....	....	....	....	....	**24**	**4**	**6**	**10**	***60**	**2**	**0**	**1**
1993-94	**Pittsburgh**	**NHL**	**47**	**3**	**18**	**21**	**139**	**0**	**0**	**0**	**122**	**2.5**	**-9**	....	....	....	....	....	....	....	....	....	....	....	....	....
	Los Angeles	**NHL**	**18**	**4**	**6**	**10**	**55**	**1**	**0**	**1**	**38**	**10.5**	**-3**	....	....	....	....	....	....	....	....	....	....	....	....	....
1994-95	**Los Angeles**	**NHL**	**41**	**3**	**18**	**21**	**83**	**1**	**0**	**0**	**75**	**4.0**	**-14**	....	....	....	....	....	....	....	....	....	....	....	....	....
1995-96	**Los Angeles**	**NHL**	**59**	**10**	**21**	**31**	**148**	**1**	**1**	**1**	**118**	**8.5**	**-14**	....	....	....	....	....	....	....	....	....	....	....	....	....
	NY Rangers	**NHL**	**9**	**0**	**2**	**2**	**21**	**0**	**0**	**0**	**12**	**0.0**	**-6**	....	....	....	....	....	**4**	**0**	**0**	**0**	**0**	**0**	**0**	**0**
1996-97	**San Jose**	**NHL**	**57**	**4**	**12**	**16**	**186**	**0**	**1**	**1**	**74**	**5.4**	**-6**	....	....	....	....	....	....	....	....	....	....	....	....	....
1997-98	**San Jose**	**NHL**	**56**	**2**	**10**	**12**	**140**	**0**	**0**	**0**	**46**	**4.3**	**10**	....	....	....	....	....	....	....	....	....	....	....	....	....
1998-99	**Edmonton**	**NHL**	**46**	**2**	**3**	**5**	**101**	**0**	**0**	**0**	**29**	**6.9**	**-5**	**0**	**0.0**	**47**	**55**	**16:58**	**3**	**0**	**0**	**0**	**2**	**0**	**0**	**0**
99-2000	**Boston**	**NHL**	**27**	**2**	**3**	**5**	**62**	**0**	**0**	**0**	**24**	**8.3**	**2**	**0**	**0.0**	**35**	**11**	**14:01**	....	....	....	....	....	....	....	....
	NHL Totals		**961**	**108**	**251**	**359**	**3381**	**13**	**8**	**8**	**1424**	**7.6**		**0**	**0.0**	**82**	**66**	**15:53**	**115**	**10**	**19**	**29**	**374**	**3**	**0**	**2**

Co-winner of Alka-Seltzer Plus Award with Theoren Fleury (1991)

Signed as a free agent by **Pittsburgh**, July 30, 1982. Traded to **Edmonton** by **Pittsburgh** with Tim Hrynewich and future considerations (Craig Muni, October 6, 1986) for Gilles Meloche, September 11, 1985. Traded to **LA Kings** by **Edmonton** with Wayne Gretzky and Mike Krushelnyski for Jimmy Carson, Martin Gelinas, LA Kings' 1st round choices in 1989 (later traded to New Jersey - New Jersey selected Jason Miller), 1991 (Martin Rucinsky) and 1993 (Nick Stajduhar) Entry Drafts and cash, August 9, 1988. Traded to **Pittsburgh** by **LA Kings**, for Shawn McEachern, August 27, 1993. Traded to **LA Kings** by **Pittsburgh** with Jim Paek for Tomas Sandstrom and Shawn McEachern, February 16, 1994. Traded to **NY Rangers** by **LA Kings** with Jari Kurri and Shane Churla for Ray Ferraro, Ian Laperriere, Mattias Norstrom, Nathan Lafayette and NY Rangers' 4th round choice (Sean Blanchard) in 1997 Entry Draft, March 14, 1996. Traded to **San Jose** by **NY Rangers** for Jayson More, Brian Swanson and San Jose's 4th round choice (later traded back to San Jose - San Jose selected Adam Colagiacomo) in 1997 Entry Draft, August 20, 1996. Signed as a free agent by **Edmonton**, October 1, 1998. Signed as a free agent by **Boston**, December 9, 1999. • Suspended by NHL for remainder of 1999-2000 season for stick assault on Donald Brashear in game vs. Vancouver, February 21, 2000.

McTAVISH, Dale

(MIHK-TA-vihsh, DAYL) **CGY.**

Center. Shoots left. 6'1", 200 lbs. Born, Eganville, Ont., February 28, 1972.

			Regular Season																Playoffs							
Season	Club	League	GP	G	A	Pts	PIM	PP	SH	GW	S	%	+/–	TF	F%	H	SB	Min	GP	G	A	Pts	PIM	PP	SH	GW
1988-89	Pembroke	OJHL	56	26	24	50	58	....	....	....	....	....	....	....	....	....	....	....	....	....	....	....	....	....	....	....
1989-90	Peterborough	OHL	66	26	35	61	34	....	....	....	....	....	....	....	....	....	....	....	12	1	5	6	2	....	....	....
1990-91	Peterborough	OHL	66	21	27	48	44	....	....	....	....	....	....	....	....	....	....	....	4	1	0	1	0	....	....	....
1991-92	Peterborough	OHL	60	25	31	56	59	....	....	....	....	....	....	....	....	....	....	....	10	2	5	7	11	....	....	....
1992-93	Peterborough	OHL	66	31	50	81	98	....	....	....	....	....	....	....	....	....	....	....	21	9	8	17	22	....	....	....
1993-94	St. FX University	AUAA	27	30	24	54	71	....	....	....	....	....	....	....	....	....	....	....	....	....	....	....	....	....	....	....
1994-95	St. FX University	AUAA	27	25	27	52	59	....	....	....	....	....	....	....	....	....	....	....	....	....	....	....	....	....	....	....
1995-96	Canada	Nat-Team	53	24	32	56	91	....	....	....	....	....	....	....	....	....	....	....	....	....	....	....	....	....	....	....
	Saint John Flames	AHL	4	2	3	5	5	....	....	....	....	....	....	....	....	....	....	....	15	5	4	9	15	....	....	....
1996-97	**Calgary**	**NHL**	**9**	**1**	**2**	**3**	**2**	**0**	**0**	**0**	**14**	**7.1**	**–4**	....	....	....	....	....	....	....	....	....	....	....	....	....
	Saint John Flames	AHL	53	16	21	37	65	....	....	....	....	....	....	....	....	....	....	....	3	0	1	1	0	....	....	....
1997-98	SaiPa	Finland	47	*25	18	43	73	....	....	....	....	....	....	....	....	....	....	....	3	0	3	3	4	....	....	....
1998-99	SaiPa	Finland	44	22	17	39	117	....	....	....	....	....	....	....	....	....	....	....	7	4	5	9	2	....	....	....
	Canada	Nat-Team	4	1	1	2	2	....	....	....	....	....	....	....	....	....	....	....	....	....	....	....	....	....	....	....
99-2000	Blues Espoo	Finland	53	32	19	51	87	....	....	....	....	....	....	....	....	....	....	....	4	1	0	1	12	....	....	....
	Canada	Nat-Team	4	0	3	3	2	....	....	....	....	....	....	....	....	....	....	....	....	....	....	....	....	....	....	....
	NHL Totals		**9**	**1**	**2**	**3**	**2**	**0**	**0**	**0**	**14**	**7.1**		....	....	....	....	....	....	....	....	....	....	....	....	....

Signed as a free agent by **Calgary**, August 1, 1996. • Played w/ RHI's New Jersey R&R in 1995 (6-2-3-5-20).

MELANSON, Dean

(meh-LAHN-suhn, DEEN) **PHI.**

Defense. Shoots right. 5'11", 190 lbs. Born, Antigonish, N.S., November 19, 1973. Buffalo's 4th choice, 80th overall, in 1992 Entry Draft.

			Regular Season																Playoffs							
Season	Club	League	GP	G	A	Pts	PIM	PP	SH	GW	S	%	+/–	TF	F%	H	SB	Min	GP	G	A	Pts	PIM	PP	SH	GW
1990-91	St-Hyacinthe	QMJHL	69	10	17	27	110	....	....	....	....	....	....	....	....	....	....	....	4	0	1	1	2	....	....	....
1991-92	St-Hyacinthe	QMJHL	42	8	19	27	158	....	....	....	....	....	....	....	....	....	....	....	6	1	2	3	25	....	....	....
1992-93	St-Hyacinthe	QMJHL	57	13	29	42	253	....	....	....	....	....	....	....	....	....	....	....	....	....	....	....	....	....	....	....
	Rochester	AHL	8	0	1	1	6	....	....	....	....	....	....	....	....	....	....	....	14	1	6	7	18	....	....	....
1993-94	Rochester	AHL	80	1	21	22	138	....	....	....	....	....	....	....	....	....	....	....	4	0	1	1	2	....	....	....
1994-95	**Buffalo**	**NHL**	**5**	**0**	**0**	**0**	**4**	**0**	**0**	**0**	**1**	**0.0**	**–1**	....	....	....	....	....	....	....	....	....	....	....	....	....
	Rochester	AHL	43	4	7	11	84	....	....	....	....	....	....	....	....	....	....	....	....	....	....	....	....	....	....	....
1995-96	Rochester	AHL	70	3	13	16	204	....	....	....	....	....	....	....	....	....	....	....	14	3	3	6	22	....	....	....
1996-97	Quebec Rafales	IHL	72	3	21	24	95	....	....	....	....	....	....	....	....	....	....	....	7	0	2	2	12	....	....	....
1997-98	Rochester	AHL	73	7	9	16	228	....	....	....	....	....	....	....	....	....	....	....	4	0	2	2	0	....	....	....
1998-99	Rochester	AHL	79	7	27	34	192	....	....	....	....	....	....	....	....	....	....	....	17	3	2	5	32	....	....	....
99-2000	Philadelphia	AHL	58	11	25	36	178	....	....	....	....	....	....	....	....	....	....	....	4	2	3	5	10	....	....	....
	NHL Totals		**5**	**0**	**0**	**0**	**4**	**0**	**0**	**0**	**1**	**0.0**		....	....	....	....	....	....	....	....	....	....	....	....	....

Signed as a free agent by **Philadelphia**, July 22, 1999.

MELLANBY, Scott

(MEH-lihn-bee, SKAWT) **FLA.**

Right wing. Shoots right. 6'1", 205 lbs. Born, Montreal, Que., June 11, 1966. Philadelphia's 2nd choice, 27th overall, in 1984 Entry Draft.

			Regular Season																Playoffs							
Season	Club	League	GP	G	A	Pts	PIM	PP	SH	GW	S	%	+/–	TF	F%	H	SB	Min	GP	G	A	Pts	PIM	PP	SH	GW
1982-83	Don Mills Flyers	MTHL	72	66	52	118	38	....	....	....	....	....	....	....	....	....	....	....	....	....	....	....	....	....	....	....
1983-84	Henry Carr	OJHL-B	39	37	37	74	97	....	....	....	....	....	....	....	....	....	....	....	....	....	....	....	....	....	....	....
1984-85	U. of Wisconsin	WCHA	40	14	24	38	60	....	....	....	....	....	....	....	....	....	....	....	....	....	....	....	....	....	....	....
1985-86	U. of Wisconsin	WCHA	32	21	23	44	89	....	....	....	....	....	....	....	....	....	....	....	....	....	....	....	....	....	....	....
	Philadelphia	**NHL**	**2**	**0**	**0**	**0**	**0**	**0**	**0**	**0**	**0**	**0.0**	**–1**	....	....	....	....	....	....	....	....	....	....	....	....	....
1986-87	**Philadelphia**	**NHL**	**71**	**11**	**21**	**32**	**94**	**1**	**0**	**0**	**118**	**9.3**	**8**	....	....	....	....	....	**24**	**5**	**5**	**10**	**46**	**0**	**0**	**1**
1987-88	**Philadelphia**	**NHL**	**75**	**25**	**26**	**51**	**185**	**7**	**0**	**2**	**190**	**13.2**	**–7**	....	....	....	....	....	**7**	**0**	**1**	**1**	**16**	**0**	**0**	**0**
1988-89	**Philadelphia**	**NHL**	**76**	**21**	**29**	**50**	**183**	**11**	**0**	**3**	**202**	**10.4**	**–13**	....	....	....	....	....	**19**	**4**	**5**	**9**	**28**	**0**	**0**	**0**
1989-90	**Philadelphia**	**NHL**	**57**	**6**	**17**	**23**	**77**	**0**	**0**	**1**	**104**	**5.8**	**–4**	....	....	....	....	....	....	....	....	....	....	....	....	....
1990-91	**Philadelphia**	**NHL**	**74**	**20**	**21**	**41**	**155**	**5**	**0**	**6**	**165**	**12.1**	**8**	....	....	....	....	....	....	....	....	....	....	....	....	....
1991-92	**Edmonton**	**NHL**	**80**	**23**	**27**	**50**	**197**	**7**	**0**	**5**	**159**	**14.5**	**5**	....	....	....	....	....	**16**	**2**	**1**	**3**	**29**	**1**	**0**	**1**
1992-93	**Edmonton**	**NHL**	**69**	**15**	**17**	**32**	**147**	**6**	**0**	**3**	**114**	**13.2**	**–4**	....	....	....	....	....	....	....	....	....	....	....	....	....
1993-94	**Florida**	**NHL**	**80**	**30**	**30**	**60**	**149**	**17**	**0**	**4**	**204**	**14.7**	**0**	....	....	....	....	....	....	....	....	....	....	....	....	....
1994-95	**Florida**	**NHL**	**48**	**13**	**12**	**25**	**90**	**4**	**0**	**5**	**130**	**10.0**	**–16**	....	....	....	....	....	....	....	....	....	....	....	....	....
1995-96	**Florida**	**NHL**	**79**	**32**	**38**	**70**	**160**	**19**	**0**	**3**	**225**	**14.2**	**4**	....	....	....	....	....	**22**	**3**	**6**	**9**	**44**	**2**	**0**	**0**
1996-97	**Florida**	**NHL**	**82**	**27**	**29**	**56**	**170**	**9**	**1**	**4**	**221**	**12.2**	**7**	....	....	....	....	....	**5**	**0**	**2**	**2**	**4**	**0**	**0**	**0**
1997-98	**Florida**	**NHL**	**79**	**15**	**24**	**39**	**127**	**6**	**0**	**1**	**188**	**8.0**	**–14**	....	....	....	....	....	....	....	....	....	....	....	....	....
1998-99	**Florida**	**NHL**	**67**	**18**	**27**	**45**	**85**	**4**	**0**	**3**	**136**	**13.2**	**5**	**11**	**27.3**	**64**	**15**	**16:14**	....	....	....	....	....	....	....	....
99-2000	**Florida**	**NHL**	**77**	**18**	**28**	**46**	**126**	**6**	**0**	**2**	**134**	**13.4**	**14**	**20**	**60.0**	**80**	**25**	**14:51**	**4**	**0**	**1**	**1**	**2**	**0**	**0**	**0**
	NHL Totals		**1016**	**274**	**346**	**620**	**1945**	**102**	**1**	**42**	**2290**	**12.0**		**31**	**48.4**	**144**	**40**	**15:30**	**97**	**14**	**21**	**35**	**169**	**3**	**0**	**2**

Played in NHL All-Star Game (1996)

Traded to **Edmonton** by **Philadelphia** with Craig Fisher and Craig Berube for Dave Brown, Corey Foster and Jari Kurri, May 30, 1991. Claimed by **Florida** from **Edmonton** in Expansion Draft, June 24, 1993.

MERTZIG, Jan

(MUHR-tzihg, YAN)

Defense. Shoots left. 6'4", 218 lbs. Born, Huddinge, Sweden, July 18, 1970. NY Rangers' 9th choice, 235th overall, in 1998 Entry Draft.

			Regular Season																Playoffs							
Season	Club	League	GP	G	A	Pts	PIM	PP	SH	GW	S	%	+/–	TF	F%	H	SB	Min	GP	G	A	Pts	PIM	PP	SH	GW
1989-90	Huddinge IF	Sweden-2	11	0	1	1	6	....	....	....	....	....	....	....	....	....	....	....	2	0	0	0	0	....	....	....
1990-91	Huddinge IF	Sweden-2	33	5	9	14	14	....	....	....	....	....	....	....	....	....	....	....	....	....	....	....	....	....	....	....
1991-92	Huddinge IF	Sweden-2	28	1	6	7	10	....	....	....	....	....	....	....	....	....	....	....	4	2	0	2	4	....	....	....
1992-93	Huddinge IF	Sweden-2	35	3	7	10	18	....	....	....	....	....	....	....	....	....	....	....	9	1	0	1	10	....	....	....
1993-94	Huddinge IF	Sweden-2	35	5	7	12	26	....	....	....	....	....	....	....	....	....	....	....	2	1	0	1	4	....	....	....
1994-95	Huddinge IF	Sweden-2	34	10	8	18	16	....	....	....	....	....	....	....	....	....	....	....	2	0	1	1	0	....	....	....
1995-96	Lulea HF	Sweden	38	8	9	17	14	....	....	....	....	....	....	....	....	....	....	....	13	3	3	6	6	....	....	....
1996-97	Lulea HF	Sweden	47	15	10	25	30	....	....	....	....	....	....	....	....	....	....	....	9	0	2	2	4	....	....	....
1997-98	Lulea HF	Sweden	45	7	8	15	27	....	....	....	....	....	....	....	....	....	....	....	3	1	0	1	4	....	....	....
1998-99	**NY Rangers**	**NHL**	**23**	**0**	**2**	**2**	**8**	**0**	**0**	**0**	**10**	**0.0**	**–5**	**0**	**0.0**	**16**	**17**	**12:02**	....	....	....	....	....	....	....	....
	Hartford	AHL	35	3	2	5	14	....	....	....	....	....	....	....	....	....	....	....	....	....	....	....	....	....	....	....
	Utah Grizzlies	IHL	5	0	1	1	6	....	....	....	....	....	....	....	....	....	....	....	....	....	....	....	....	....	....	....
99-2000	KAC Klagenfurt	IEL	34	8	21	29	38	....	....	....	....	....	....	....	....	....	....	....	....	....	....	....	....	....	....	....
	KAC Klagenfurt	Austria	16	8	5	13	14	....	....	....	....	....	....	....	....	....	....	....	....	....	....	....	....	....	....	....
	NHL Totals		**23**	**0**	**2**	**2**	**8**	**0**	**0**	**0**	**10**	**0.0**		**0**	**0.0**	**16**	**17**	**12:02**	....	....	....	....	....	....	....	....

MESSIER, Eric

(MEHS-see-ay, AIR-ihk) **COL.**

Defense. Shoots left. 6'2", 200 lbs. Born, Drummondville, Que., October 29, 1973.

			Regular Season																Playoffs							
Season	Club	League	GP	G	A	Pts	PIM	PP	SH	GW	S	%	+/–	TF	F%	H	SB	Min	GP	G	A	Pts	PIM	PP	SH	GW
1991-92	Trois-Rivieres	QMJHL	58	2	10	12	28	....	....	....	....	....	....	....	....	....	....	....	15	2	2	4	13	....	....	....
1992-93	Sherbrooke	QMJHL	51	4	17	21	82	....	....	....	....	....	....	....	....	....	....	....	15	0	4	4	18	....	....	....
1993-94	Sherbrooke	QMJHL	67	4	24	28	69	....	....	....	....	....	....	....	....	....	....	....	12	1	7	8	14	....	....	....
1994-95	U. of Quebec	OUAA	13	8	5	13	20	....	....	....	....	....	....	....	....	....	....	....	4	0	3	3	8	....	....	....
1995-96	Cornwall Aces	AHL	72	5	9	14	111	....	....	....	....	....	....	....	....	....	....	....	8	1	1	2	20	....	....	....
1996-97	**Colorado**	**NHL**	**21**	**0**	**0**	**0**	**4**	**0**	**0**	**0**	**11**	**0.0**	**7**	....	....	....	....	....	**6**	**0**	**0**	**0**	**4**	**0**	**0**	**0**
	Hershey Bears	AHL	55	16	26	42	69	....	....	....	....	....	....	....	....	....	....	....	9	3	8	11	14	....	....	....
1997-98	**Colorado**	**NHL**	**62**	**4**	**12**	**16**	**20**	**0**	**0**	**0**	**66**	**6.1**	**4**	....	....	....	....	....	....	....	....	....	....	....	....	....
1998-99	**Colorado**	**NHL**	**31**	**4**	**2**	**6**	**14**	**1**	**0**	**1**	**30**	**13.3**	**0**	**0**	**0.0**	**29**	**22**	**13:43**	**3**	**0**	**0**	**0**	**0**	**0**	**0**	**0**
	Hershey Bears	AHL	6	1	3	4	4	....	....	....	....	....	....	....	....	....	....	....	....	....	....	....	....	....	....	....
99-2000	**Colorado**	**NHL**	**61**	**3**	**6**	**9**	**24**	**1**	**0**	**0**	**28**	**10.7**	**0**	**4**	**25.0**	**52**	**26**	**10:27**	**14**	**0**	**1**	**1**	**4**	**0**	**0**	**0**
	NHL Totals		**175**	**11**	**20**	**31**	**62**	**2**	**0**	**1**	**135**	**8.1**		**4**	**25.0**	**81**	**48**	**11:33**	**23**	**0**	**1**	**1**	**8**	**0**	**0**	**0**

QMJHL Second All-Star Team (1994)

Signed as a free agent by **Colorado**, June 14, 1995. • Missed majority of 1998-99 season recovering from elbow injury suffered in game vs. Ottawa, October 10, 1998. • Played w/ RHI's Montreal Roadrunners in 1995 (22-0-11-11-46).

MESSIER, Mark

(MEHS-see-ay, MAHRK) **NYR**

Center. Shoots left. 6'1", 210 lbs. Born, Edmonton, Alta., January 18, 1961. Edmonton's 2nd choice, 48th overall, in 1979 Entry Draft.

			Regular Season																Playoffs							
Season	Club	League	GP	G	A	Pts	PIM	PP	SH	GW	S	%	+/–	TF	F%	H	SB	Min	GP	G	A	Pts	PIM	PP	SH	GW
1976-77	Spruce Grove	AJHL	57	27	39	66	91																			
1977-78	St. Albert Saints	AJHL	54	25	49	74	194																			
	Portland	WHL																	7	4	1	5	2			
1978-79	St. Albert Saints	AJHL	17	15	18	33	64																			
	Indianapolis	WHA	5	0	0	0	0																			
	Cincinnati Stingers	WHA	47	1	10	11	58																			
1979-80	Edmonton	NHL	75	12	21	33	120	1	1	1	113	10.6	–10						3	1	2	3	2	0	1	0
	Houston Apollos	CHL	4	0	3	3	4																			
1980-81	Edmonton	NHL	72	23	40	63	102	4	0	1	179	12.8	–12						9	2	5	7	13	0	0	0
1981-82	Edmonton	NHL	78	50	38	88	119	10	0	3	235	21.3	21						5	1	2	3	8	0	0	0
1982-83	Edmonton	NHL	77	48	58	106	72	12	1	2	237	20.3	19						15	15	6	21	14	4	2	0
1983-84♦	Edmonton	NHL	73	37	64	101	165	7	4	7	219	16.9	40						19	8	18	26	19	1	1	2
1984-85♦	Edmonton	NHL	55	23	31	54	57	4	5	1	136	16.9	8						18	12	13	25	12	1	1	1
1985-86	Edmonton	NHL	63	35	49	84	68	10	5	7	201	17.4	36						10	4	6	10	18	0	2	0
1986-87♦	Edmonton	NHL	77	37	70	107	73	7	4	5	208	17.8	21						21	12	16	28	16	1	2	1
1987-88♦	Edmonton	NHL	77	37	74	111	103	12	3	7	182	20.3	21						19	11	23	34	29	7	1	0
1988-89	Edmonton	NHL	72	33	61	94	130	6	6	4	164	20.1	–5						7	1	11	12	8	0	0	0
1989-90♦	Edmonton	NHL	79	45	84	129	79	13	6	3	211	21.3	19						22	9	*22	*31	20	1	1	1
1990-91	Edmonton	NHL	53	12	52	64	34	3	1	2	109	11.0	15						18	4	11	15	16	1	0	0
1991-92	NY Rangers	NHL	79	35	72	107	76	12	4	6	212	16.5	31						11	7	7	14	6	2	2	0
1992-93	NY Rangers	NHL	75	25	66	91	72	7	2	2	215	11.6	–6													
1993-94♦	NY Rangers	NHL	76	26	58	84	76	6	2	5	216	12.0	25						23	12	18	30	33	2	1	4
1994-95	NY Rangers	NHL	46	14	39	53	40	3	3	2	126	11.1	8						10	3	10	13	8	2	0	1
1995-96	NY Rangers	NHL	74	47	52	99	122	14	1	5	241	19.5	29						11	4	7	11	16	2	0	1
1996-97	NY Rangers	NHL	71	36	48	84	88	7	5	9	227	15.9	12						15	3	9	12	6	0	0	1
1997-98	Vancouver	NHL	82	22	38	60	58	8	2	2	139	15.8	–10													
1998-99	Vancouver	NHL	59	13	35	48	33	4	2	2	97	13.4	–12	1536	53.9	29	35	22:36								
99-2000	Vancouver	NHL	66	17	37	54	30	6	0	4	131	13.0	–15	1684	56.8	50	26	21:12								
	NHL Totals		1479	627	1087	1714	1717	156	57	80	3798	16.5		3220	55.4	79	61	21:52	236	109	186	295	244	24	14	12

NHL First All-Star Team (1982, 1983, 1990, 1992) • NHL Second All-Star Team (1984) • Won Conn Smythe Trophy (1984) • Won Lester B. Pearson Award (1990, 1992) • Won Hart Trophy (1990, 1992) • Played in NHL All-Star Game (1982, 1983, 1984, 1986, 1988, 1989, 1990, 1991, 1992, 1994, 1996, 1997, 1998, 2000)

Signed as an underage free agent by **Indianapolis** (WHA) to a 10-game tryout contract, November 5, 1978. Signed as a free agent by **Cincinnati** (WHA) after **Indianapolis** (WHA) franchise folded, December, 1978. Traded to **NY Rangers** by **Edmonton** with future considerations (Jeff Beukeboom for David Shaw, November 12, 1991) for Bernie Nicholls, Steven Rice and Louie DeBrusk, October 4, 1991. Signed as a free agent by **Vancouver**, July 30, 1997. Signed as a free agent by **NY Rangers**, July 13, 2000.

METROPOLIT, Glen

(MEH-troh-poh-LIHT, GLEHN) **WSH.**

Right wing. Shoots right. 5'11", 185 lbs. Born, Toronto, Ont., June 25, 1974.

			Regular Season																Playoffs							
Season	Club	League	GP	G	A	Pts	PIM	PP	SH	GW	S	%	+/–	TF	F%	H	SB	Min	GP	G	A	Pts	PIM	PP	SH	GW
1992-93	Richmond Hill	OJHL	43	27	36	63	36																			
1993-94	Richmond Hill	OJHL	49	38	62	100	83																			
1994-95	Vernon Lakers	BCJHL	60	43	74	117	92																			
1995-96	Nashville Knights	ECHL	58	30	31	61	62												5	3	8	11	2			
	Atlanta Knights	IHL	1	0	0	0	0																			
1996-97	Pensacola	ECHL	54	35	47	82	45												12	9	16	25	28			
	Quebec Rafales	IHL	22	5	4	9	14												5	0	0	0	2			
1997-98	Grand Rapids	IHL	79	20	35	55	90												3	1	1	2	0			
1998-99	Grand Rapids	IHL	77	28	53	81	92																			
99-2000	Washington	NHL	30	6	13	19	4	1	0	1	57	10.5	5	37	46.0	48	7	13:17	2	0	0	0	2	0	0	0
	Portland Pirates	AHL	48	18	42	60	73												1	1	0	1	0			
	NHL Totals		30	6	13	19	4	1	0	1	57	10.5		37	45.9	48	7	13:17	2	0	0	0	2	0	0	0

Signed as a free agent by **Washington**, July 19, 1999. • Played w/ RHI's Long Island Jawz in 1996 (28-32-39-71-29), Anaheim Bulldogs (4-5-2-7-4) and New Jersey (2-1-1-2-0) in 1997.

MIKA, Petr

(MEE-kah, PEE-tuhr) **NYI**

Left wing. Shoots right. 6'4", 194 lbs. Born, Prague, Czech., February 12, 1979. NY Islanders' 6th choice, 85th overall, in 1997 Entry Draft.

			Regular Season																Playoffs							
Season	Club	League	GP	G	A	Pts	PIM	PP	SH	GW	S	%	+/–	TF	F%	H	SB	Min	GP	G	A	Pts	PIM	PP	SH	GW
1995-96	Slavia Praha-Jr.	Cze-Rep	26	5	12	17																				
	Slavia Praha	Cze-Rep	1	0	0	0	0																			
1996-97	HC Beroun-2	Cze-Rep	9	1	0	1																				
	Slavia Praha-2	Cze-Rep	20	1	2	3	6																			
	Slavia Praha	Cze-Rep	15	8	0	8																				
1997-98	Ottawa 67's	OHL	41	10	8	18	28																			
1998-99	Slavia Praha	Cze-Rep	49	6	5	11	57																			
99-2000	NY Islanders	NHL	3	0	0	0	0	0	0	0	1	0.0	–1	0	0.0	3	2	4:30								
	Lowell	AHL	50	8	9	17	20												6	0	0	0	0			
	NHL Totals		3	0	0	0	0	0	0	0	1	0.0		0	0.0	3	2	4:30								

MILLAR, Craig

(MIHL-uhr, KRAYG) **NSH.**

Defense. Shoots left. 6'2", 212 lbs. Born, Winnipeg, Man., July 12, 1976. Buffalo's 10th choice, 225th overall, in 1994 Entry Draft.

			Regular Season																Playoffs							
Season	Club	League	GP	G	A	Pts	PIM	PP	SH	GW	S	%	+/–	TF	F%	H	SB	Min	GP	G	A	Pts	PIM	PP	SH	GW
1992-93	Swift Current	WHL	43	2	1	3	8																			
1993-94	Swift Current	WHL	66	2	9	11	53												7	0	3	3	4			
1994-95	Swift Current	WHL	72	8	42	50	80												6	1	1	2	10			
1995-96	Swift Current	WHL	72	31	46	77	151												6	1	0	1	22			
1996-97	Rochester	AHL	64	7	18	25	65																			
	Edmonton	NHL	1	0	0	0	2	0	0	0	1	0.0	0													
	Hamilton Bulldogs	AHL	10	1	3	4	10												22	4	4	8	21			
1997-98	Edmonton	NHL	11	4	0	4	8	1	0	0	10	40.0	–3													
	Hamilton Bulldogs	AHL	60	10	22	32	113												9	3	1	4	22			
1998-99	Edmonton	NHL	24	0	2	2	19	0	0	0	18	0.0	–6	0	0.0	23	24	15:09								
	Hamilton Bulldogs	AHL	43	3	17	20	38												11	1	5	6	18			
99-2000	Nashville	NHL	57	3	11	14	28	0	0	1	50	6.0	–6	1	0.0	56	38	16:53								
	Milwaukee	IHL	8	1	5	6	6																			
	NHL Totals		93	7	13	20	57	1	0	1	79	8.9		1	0.0	79	62	16:22								

WHL East First All-Star Team (1996)

Traded to **Edmonton** by **Buffalo** with Barrie Moore for Miroslav Satan, March 18, 1997. Traded to **Nashville** by **Edmonton** for Detroit's 3rd round choice (previously acquired, Edmonton selected Mike Comrie) in 1999 Entry Draft, June 26, 1999.

MILLER, Aaron

(MIHL-luhr, AIR-ohn) **COL.**

Defense. Shoots right. 6'3", 200 lbs. Born, Buffalo, NY, August 11, 1971. NY Rangers' 6th choice, 88th overall, in 1989 Entry Draft.

			Regular Season																Playoffs							
Season	Club	League	GP	G	A	Pts	PIM	PP	SH	GW	S	%	+/–	TF	F%	H	SB	Min	GP	G	A	Pts	PIM	PP	SH	GW
1987-88	Niagara Scenics	NAJHL	30	4	9	13	2																			
1988-89	Niagara Scenics	NAJHL	59	24	38	62	60																			
1989-90	U. of Vermont	ECAC	31	1	15	16	24																			
1990-91	U. of Vermont	ECAC	30	3	7	10	22																			
1991-92	U. of Vermont	ECAC	31	3	16	19	28																			
1992-93	U. of Vermont	ECAC	30	4	13	17	16																			
1993-94	Quebec	NHL	1	0	0	0	0	0	0	0	0	0.0	–1													
	Cornwall Aces	AHL	64	4	10	14	49												13	0	2	2	10			
1994-95	Quebec	NHL	9	0	3	3	6	0	0	0	12	0.0	2													
	Cornwall Aces	AHL	76	4	18	22	69																			
1995-96	Colorado	NHL	5	0	0	0	0	0	0	0	2	0.0	0													
	Cornwall Aces	AHL	62	4	23	27	77												8	0	1	1	6			
1996-97	Colorado	NHL	56	5	12	17	15	0	0	3	47	10.6	15						17	1	2	3	10	0	0	0

Season	Club	League	Regular Season																Playoffs							
			GP	G	A	Pts	PIM	PP	SH	GW	S	%	+/-	TF	F%	H	SB	Min	GP	G	A	Pts	PIM	PP	SH	GW
1997-98	Colorado	NHL	55	2	2	4	51	0	0	0	29	6.9	0	....	....	....	....	....	7	0	0	0	8	0	0	0
1998-99	Colorado	NHL	76	5	13	18	42	1	0	2	87	5.7	3	0	0.0	115	128	21:49	19	1	5	6	10	0	0	0
99-2000	Colorado	NHL	53	1	7	8	36	0	0	0	44	2.3	3	0	0.0	64	76	19:05	17	1	1	2	6	0	0	0
	NHL Totals		255	13	37	50	150	1	0	5	221	5.9		0	0.0	179	204	20:42	60	3	8	11	34	0	0	0

ECAC First All-Star Team (1993) • NCAA East Second All-American Team (1993)

Traded to **Quebec** by **NY Rangers** with NY Rangers' 5th round choice (Bill Lindsay) in 1991 Entry Draft for Joe Cirella, January 17, 1991. Transferred to **Colorado** after **Quebec** franchise relocated, June 21, 1995.

MILLER, Kevin

(MIHL-luhr, KEH-vihn)

Center. Shoots right. 5'11", 184 lbs. Born, Lansing, MI, September 2, 1965. NY Rangers' 10th choice, 202nd overall, in 1984 Entry Draft.

Season	Club	League	GP	G	A	Pts	PIM	PP	SH	GW	S	%	+/-	TF	F%	H	SB	Min	GP	G	A	Pts	PIM	PP	SH	GW
1983-84	Redford Royals	GLJHL	44	28	57	85	....	....	....	....	....	....	....	....	....	....	....	....	....	....	....	....	....	....	....	....
1984-85	Michigan State	CCHA	44	11	29	40	84	....	....	....	....	....	....	....	....	....	....	....	....	....	....	....	....	....	....	....
1985-86	Michigan State	CCHA	45	19	52	71	112	....	....	....	....	....	....	....	....	....	....	....	....	....	....	....	....	....	....	....
1986-87	Michigan State	CCHA	42	25	56	81	63	....	....	....	....	....	....	....	....	....	....	....	....	....	....	....	....	....	....	....
1987-88	Michigan State	CCHA	9	6	3	9	18	....	....	....	....	....	....	....	....	....	....	....	....	....	....	....	....	....	....	....
	United States	Nat-Team	48	31	32	63	33	....	....	....	....	....	....	....	....	....	....	....	....	....	....	....	....	....	....	....
	United States	Olympics	5	1	3	4	4	....	....	....	....	....	....	....	....	....	....	....	....	....	....	....	....	....	....	....
1988-89	NY Rangers	NHL	24	3	5	8	2	0	0	1	40	7.5	–1	....	....	....	....	....	....	....	....	....	....	....	....	....
	Denver Rangers	IHL	55	29	47	76	19	....	....	....	....	....	....	....	....	....	....	....	4	2	1	3	2	....	....	....
1989-90	NY Rangers	NHL	16	0	5	5	2	0	0	0	9	0.0	–1	....	....	....	....	....	1	0	0	0	0	0	0	0
	Flint Spirits	IHL	48	19	23	42	41	....	....	....	....	....	....	....	....	....	....	....	....	....	....	....	....	....	....	....
1990-91	NY Rangers	NHL	63	17	27	44	63	1	2	3	113	15.0	1	....	....	....	....	....	....	....	....	....	....	....	....	....
	Detroit	NHL	11	5	2	7	4	0	1	0	23	21.7	–4	....	....	....	....	....	7	3	2	5	20	0	1	0
1991-92	Detroit	NHL	80	20	26	46	53	3	1	4	130	15.4	6	....	....	....	....	....	9	0	2	2	4	0	0	0
1992-93	Washington	NHL	10	0	3	3	35	0	0	0	10	0.0	–4	....	....	....	....	....	....	....	....	....	....	....	....	....
	St. Louis	NHL	72	24	22	46	65	8	3	4	153	15.7	6	....	....	....	....	....	10	0	3	3	11	0	0	0
1993-94	St. Louis	NHL	75	23	25	48	83	6	3	5	154	14.9	6	....	....	....	....	....	3	1	0	1	4	0	1	0
1994-95	St. Louis	NHL	15	2	5	7	0	0	0	0	19	10.5	4	....	....	....	....	....	....	....	....	....	....	....	....	....
	San Jose	NHL	21	6	7	13	13	1	1	2	41	14.6	0	....	....	....	....	....	6	0	0	0	2	0	0	0
1995-96	San Jose	NHL	68	22	20	42	41	2	2	2	146	15.1	–8	....	....	....	....	....	....	....	....	....	....	....	....	....
	Pittsburgh	NHL	13	6	5	11	4	1	0	0	33	18.2	4	....	....	....	....	....	18	3	2	5	8	0	0	0
1996-97	Chicago	NHL	69	14	17	31	41	5	1	2	139	10.1	–10	....	....	....	....	....	6	0	1	1	0	0	0	0
1997-98	Chicago	NHL	37	4	7	11	8	0	0	1	37	10.8	–4	....	....	....	....	....	....	....	....	....	....	....	....	....
	Indianapolis Ice	IHL	26	11	11	22	41	....	....	....	....	....	....	....	....	....	....	....	2	1	1	2	0	....	....	....
1998-99	NY Islanders	NHL	33	1	5	6	13	0	0	0	37	2.7	–5	114	49.1	42	11	10:19	....	....	....	....	....	....	....	....
	Chicago Wolves	IHL	30	11	20	31	8	....	....	....	....	....	....	....	....	....	....	....	10	2	7	9	22	....	....	....
99-2000	Ottawa	NHL	9	3	2	5	2	1	0	2	11	27.3	1	34	41.2	9	2	8:10	1	0	0	0	0	0	0	0
	Grand Rapids	IHL	63	20	34	54	51	....	....	....	....	....	....	....	....	....	....	....	17	*11	7	*18	30	....	....	....
	NHL Totals		616	150	183	333	429	28	14	26	1095	13.7		148	47.3	51	13	9:51	61	7	10	17	49	0	2	0

Traded to **Detroit** by **NY Rangers** with Jim Cummins and Dennis Vial for Joey Kocur and Per Djoos, March 5, 1991. Traded to **Washington** by **Detroit** for Dino Ciccarelli, June 20, 1992. Traded to **St. Louis** by **Washington** for Paul Cavallini, November 2, 1992. Traded to **San Jose** by **St. Louis** for Todd Elik, March 23, 1995. Traded to **Pittsburgh** by **San Jose** for Pittsburgh's 5th round choice (later traded to Boston - Boston selected Elias Abrahamsson) in 1996 Entry Draft , March 20, 1996. Signed as a free agent by **Chicago**, July 18, 1996. Signed as a free agent by **NY Islanders**, October 9, 1998. Signed as a free agent by **Ottawa**, August 24, 1999.

MILLER, Kip

(MIHL-luhr, KIHP)

Center. Shoots left. 5'10", 190 lbs. Born, Lansing, MI, June 11, 1969. Quebec's 4th choice, 72nd overall, in 1987 Entry Draft.

Season	Club	League	GP	G	A	Pts	PIM	PP	SH	GW	S	%	+/-	TF	F%	H	SB	Min	GP	G	A	Pts	PIM	PP	SH	GW
1984-85	Detroit	MNHL	65	69	63	132	....	....	....	....	....	....	....	....	....	....	....	....	....	....	....	....	....	....	....	....
1985-86	Detroit	GLJHL	30	25	28	53	....	....	....	....	....	....	....	....	....	....	....	....	....	....	....	....	....	....	....	....
1986-87	Michigan State	CCHA	41	20	19	39	92	....	....	....	....	....	....	....	....	....	....	....	....	....	....	....	....	....	....	....
1987-88	Michigan State	CCHA	39	16	25	41	51	....	....	....	....	....	....	....	....	....	....	....	....	....	....	....	....	....	....	....
1988-89	Michigan State	CCHA	47	32	45	77	94	....	....	....	....	....	....	....	....	....	....	....	....	....	....	....	....	....	....	....
1989-90	Michigan State	CCHA	45	*48	53	*101	60	....	....	....	....	....	....	....	....	....	....	....	....	....	....	....	....	....	....	....
1990-91	Quebec	NHL	13	4	3	7	7	0	0	0	16	25.0	–1	....	....	....	....	....	....	....	....	....	....	....	....	....
	Halifax Citadels	AHL	66	36	33	69	40	....	....	....	....	....	....	....	....	....	....	....	....	....	....	....	....	....	....	....
1991-92	Quebec	NHL	36	5	10	15	12	1	0	2	46	10.9	–21	....	....	....	....	....	....	....	....	....	....	....	....	....
	Halifax Citadels	AHL	24	9	17	26	8	....	....	....	....	....	....	....	....	....	....	....	....	....	....	....	....	....	....	....
	Minnesota	NHL	3	1	2	3	2	1	0	0	3	33.3	–1	....	....	....	....	....	....	....	....	....	....	....	....	....
	Kalamazoo	IHL	6	1	8	9	4	....	....	....	....	....	....	....	....	....	....	....	12	3	9	12	12	....	....	....
1992-93	Kalamazoo	IHL	61	17	39	56	59	....	....	....	....	....	....	....	....	....	....	....	....	....	....	....	....	....	....	....
1993-94	San Jose	NHL	11	2	2	4	6	0	0	0	21	9.5	–1	....	....	....	....	....	....	....	....	....	....	....	....	....
	Kansas City	IHL	71	38	54	92	51	....	....	....	....	....	....	....	....	....	....	....	....	....	....	....	....	....	....	....
1994-95	Denver Grizzlies	IHL	71	46	60	106	54	....	....	....	....	....	....	....	....	....	....	....	17	*15	14	29	8	....	....	....
	NY Islanders	NHL	8	0	1	1	0	0	0	0	11	0.0	1	....	....	....	....	....	....	....	....	....	....	....	....	....
1995-96	Chicago	NHL	10	1	4	5	2	0	0	0	12	8.3	1	....	....	....	....	....	....	....	....	....	....	....	....	....
	Indianapolis Ice	IHL	73	32	59	91	46	....	....	....	....	....	....	....	....	....	....	....	5	2	6	8	2	....	....	....
1996-97	Chicago Wolves	IHL	43	11	41	52	32	....	....	....	....	....	....	....	....	....	....	....	....	....	....	....	....	....	....	....
	Indianapolis Ice	IHL	37	17	24	41	18	....	....	....	....	....	....	....	....	....	....	....	4	2	2	4	2	....	....	....
1997-98	Utah Grizzlies	IHL	72	38	59	97	30	....	....	....	....	....	....	....	....	....	....	....	4	3	2	5	10	....	....	....
	NY Islanders	NHL	9	1	3	4	2	0	0	0	11	9.1	–2	....	....	....	....	....	....	....	....	....	....	....	....	....
1998-99	Pittsburgh	NHL	77	19	23	42	22	1	0	4	125	15.2	1	150	44.7	67	25	16:55	13	2	7	9	19	1	0	0
99-2000	Pittsburgh	NHL	44	4	15	19	10	0	0	1	50	8.0	–1	132	40.1	23	13	14:18	....	....	....	....	....	....	....	....
	Anaheim	NHL	30	6	17	23	4	2	0	1	32	18.8	1	7	42.9	28	1	13:44	....	....	....	....	....	....	....	....
	NHL Totals		241	43	80	123	67	5	0	8	327	13.1		289	42.6	118	39	15:31	13	2	7	9	19	1	0	0

CCHA First All-Star Team (1989, 1990) • NCAA West First All-American Team (1989, 1990) • Won Hobey Baker Memorial Award (Top U.S. Collegiate Player) (1990)

Traded to **Minnesota** by **Quebec** for Steve Maltais, March 8, 1992. Signed as a free agent by **San Jose**, August 10, 1993. Signed as a free agent by **NY Islanders**, July 7, 1994. Signed as a free agent by **Chicago**, July 21, 1995. Signed as a free agent by **NY Islanders**, November 26, 1997. Claimed by **Pittsburgh** from **NY Islanders** in NHL Waiver Draft, October 5, 1998. Traded to **Anaheim** by **Pittsburgh** for Anaheim's 9th round choice (Roman Simicek) in 2000 Entry Draft, January 29, 2000.

MILLS, Craig

(MIHLS, KRAYG) **PHX.**

Right wing. Shoots right. 6', 190 lbs. Born, Toronto, Ont., August 27, 1976. Winnipeg's 5th choice, 108th overall, in 1994 Entry Draft.

Season	Club	League	GP	G	A	Pts	PIM	PP	SH	GW	S	%	+/-	TF	F%	H	SB	Min	GP	G	A	Pts	PIM	PP	SH	GW
1992-93	St. Michael's	OJHL-B	44	9	21	30	42	....	....	....	....	....	....	....	....	....	....	....	15	1	6	7	8	....	....	....
1993-94	Belleville Bulls	OHL	63	15	18	33	88	....	....	....	....	....	....	....	....	....	....	....	12	2	1	3	11	....	....	....
1994-95	Belleville Bulls	OHL	62	39	41	80	104	....	....	....	....	....	....	....	....	....	....	....	13	7	9	16	8	....	....	....
1995-96	Belleville Bulls	OHL	48	10	19	29	113	....	....	....	....	....	....	....	....	....	....	....	14	4	5	9	32	....	....	....
	Winnipeg	NHL	4	0	2	2	0	0	0	0	0	0.0	0	....	....	....	....	....	1	0	0	0	0	0	0	0
	Springfield	AHL	....	....	....	....	....	....	....	....	....	....	....	....	....	....	....	....	2	0	0	0	0	....	....	....
1996-97	Indianapolis Ice	IHL	80	12	7	19	199	....	....	....	....	....	....	....	....	....	....	....	4	0	0	0	4	....	....	....
1997-98	Chicago	NHL	20	0	3	3	34	0	0	0	5	0.0	1	....	....	....	....	....	....	....	....	....	....	....	....	....
	Indianapolis Ice	IHL	42	8	11	19	119	....	....	....	....	....	....	....	....	....	....	....	5	0	0	0	27	....	....	....
1998-99	Chicago	NHL	7	0	0	0	2	0	0	0	1	0.0	–2	0	0.0	4	0	5:48	....	....	....	....	....	....	....	....
	Chicago Wolves	IHL	5	0	0	0	14	....	....	....	....	....	....	....	....	....	....	....	....	....	....	....	....	....	....	....
	Portland Pirates	AHL	48	7	11	18	59	....	....	....	....	....	....	....	....	....	....	....	....	....	....	....	....	....	....	....
	Indianapolis Ice	IHL	12	2	3	5	14	....	....	....	....	....	....	....	....	....	....	....	6	1	0	1	5	....	....	....
99-2000	Springfield	AHL	78	10	13	23	151	....	....	....	....	....	....	....	....	....	....	....	5	2	1	3	6	....	....	....
	NHL Totals		31	0	5	5	36	0	0	0	6	0.0		0	0.0	4	0	5:48	1	0	0	0	0	0	0	0

Canadian Major Junior Humanitarian Player of the Year (1996)

Rights transferred to **Phoenix** after **Winnipeg** franchise relocated, July 1, 1996. Traded to **Chicago** by **Phoenix** with Alexei Zhamnov and Phoenix's 1st round choice (Ty Jones) in 1997 Entry Draft for Jeremy Roenick, August 16, 1996. Traded to **Phoenix** by **Chicago** for cash, September 11, 1999.

MIRONOV, Boris (mih-RAWN-ohv, BOHR-ihs) CHI.

Defense. Shoots right. 6'3", 223 lbs. Born, Moscow, USSR, March 21, 1972. Winnipeg's 2nd choice, 27th overall, in 1992 Entry Draft.

			Regular Season																Playoffs							
Season	Club	League	GP	G	A	Pts	PIM	PP	SH	GW	S	%	+/-	TF	F%	H	SB	Min	GP	G	A	Pts	PIM	PP	SH	GW
1988-89	CSKA Moscow	USSR	1	0	0	0	0	....	....	....	....	....	....	....	....	....	....	....	....	....	....	....	....	....	....	....
1989-90	CSKA Moscow	USSR	7	0	0	0	0	....	....	....	....	....	....	....	....	....	....	....	....	....	....	....	....	....	....	....
1990-91	CSKA Moscow	USSR	36	1	5	6	16	....	....	....	....	....	....	....	....	....	....	....	....	....	....	....	....	....	....	....
1991-92	CSKA Moscow	CIS	36	2	1	3	22	....	....	....	....	....	....	....	....	....	....	....	....	....	....	....	....	....	....	....
1992-93	CSKA Moscow	CIS	19	0	5	5	20	....	....	....	....	....	....	....	....	....	....	....	....	....	....	....	....	....	....	....
1993-94	**Winnipeg**	**NHL**	**65**	**7**	**22**	**29**	**96**	**5**	**0**	**0**	**122**	**5.7**	**-29**	....	....	....	....	....	....	....	....	....	....	....	....	....
	Edmonton	**NHL**	**14**	**0**	**2**	**2**	**14**	**0**	**0**	**0**	**23**	**0.0**	**-4**	....	....	....	....	....	....	....	....	....	....	....	....	....
1994-95	**Edmonton**	**NHL**	**29**	**1**	**7**	**8**	**40**	**0**	**0**	**0**	**48**	**2.1**	**-9**	....	....	....	....	....	....	....	....	....	....	....	....	....
	Cape Breton	AHL	4	2	5	7	23	....	....	....	....	....	....	....	....	....	....	....	....	....	....	....	....	....	....	....
1995-96	**Edmonton**	**NHL**	**78**	**8**	**24**	**32**	**101**	**7**	**0**	**1**	**158**	**5.1**	**-23**	....	....	....	....	....	....	....	....	....	....	....	....	....
1996-97	**Edmonton**	**NHL**	**55**	**6**	**26**	**32**	**85**	**2**	**0**	**1**	**147**	**4.1**	**2**	....	....	....	....	....	**12**	**2**	**8**	**10**	**16**	**2**	**0**	**0**
1997-98	**Edmonton**	**NHL**	**81**	**16**	**30**	**46**	**100**	**10**	**1**	**1**	**203**	**7.9**	**-8**	....	....	....	....	....	**12**	**3**	**3**	**6**	**27**	**1**	**0**	**1**
	Russia	Olympics	6	0	2	2	2	....	....	....	....	....	....	....	....	....	....	....	....	....	....	....	....	....	....	....
1998-99	**Edmonton**	**NHL**	**63**	**11**	**29**	**40**	**104**	**5**	**0**	**4**	**138**	**8.0**	**6**	**0**	**0.0**	**142**	**103**	**25:55**	....	....	....	....	....	....	....	....
	Chicago	**NHL**	**12**	**0**	**9**	**9**	**27**	**0**	**0**	**0**	**35**	**0.0**	**7**	**0**	**0.0**	**32**	**17**	**24:17**	....	....	....	....	....	....	....	....
99-2000	**Chicago**	**NHL**	**58**	**9**	**28**	**37**	**72**	**4**	**2**	**1**	**144**	**6.3**	**-3**	**1**	**100.0**	**121**	**60**	**24:53**	....	....	....	....	....	....	....	....
	NHL Totals		**455**	**58**	**177**	**235**	**639**	**33**	**3**	**8**	**1018**	**5.7**		**1**	**100.0**	**295**	**180**	**25:19**	**24**	**5**	**11**	**16**	**43**	**3**	**0**	**1**

NHL All-Rookie Team (1994)

Traded to **Edmonton** by **Winnipeg** with Mats Lindgren, Winnipeg's 1st round choice (Jason Bonsignore) in 1994 Entry Draft and Florida's 4th round choice (previously acquired, Edmonton selected Adam Copeland) in 1994 Entry Draft for Dave Manson and St. Louis' 6th round choice (previously acquired, Winnipeg selected Chris Kibermanis) in 1994 Entry Draft, March 15, 1994. Traded to **Chicago** by **Edmonton** with Dean McAmmond and Jonas Elofsson for Chad Kilger, Daniel Cleary, Ethan Moreau and Christian Laflamme, March 20, 1999.

MIRONOV, Dmitri (mih-RAWN-ohv, dih-MEE-tree) WSH.

Defense. Shoots right. 6'4", 224 lbs. Born, Moscow, USSR, December 25, 1965. Toronto's 7th choice, 160th overall, in 1991 Entry Draft.

Season	Club	League	GP	G	A	Pts	PIM	PP	SH	GW	S	%	+/-	TF	F%	H	SB	Min	GP	G	A	Pts	PIM	PP	SH	GW
1985-86	CSKA Moscow	USSR	9	0	1	1	8	....	....	....	....	....	....	....	....	....	....	....	....	....	....	....	....	....	....	....
1986-87	CSKA Moscow	USSR	20	1	3	4	10	....	....	....	....	....	....	....	....	....	....	....	....	....	....	....	....	....	....	....
1987-88	Krylja Sovetov	USSR	44	12	6	18	30	....	....	....	....	....	....	....	....	....	....	....	....	....	....	....	....	....	....	....
1988-89	Krylja Sovetov	USSR	44	5	6	11	44	....	....	....	....	....	....	....	....	....	....	....	....	....	....	....	....	....	....	....
1989-90	Krylja Sovetov	USSR	45	4	11	15	34	....	....	....	....	....	....	....	....	....	....	....	....	....	....	....	....	....	....	....
1990-91	Krylja Sovetov	USSR	45	16	12	28	22	....	....	....	....	....	....	....	....	....	....	....	....	....	....	....	....	....	....	....
1991-92	Krylja Sovetov	CIS	35	15	16	31	62	....	....	....	....	....	....	....	....	....	....	....	....	....	....	....	....	....	....	....
	Toronto	**NHL**	**7**	**1**	**0**	**1**	**0**	**0**	**0**	**1**	**7**	**14.3**	**-4**	....	....	....	....	....	....	....	....	....	....	....	....	....
	Russia	Olympics	8	3	1	4	6	....	....	....	....	....	....	....	....	....	....	....	....	....	....	....	....	....	....	....
1992-93	**Toronto**	**NHL**	**59**	**7**	**24**	**31**	**40**	**4**	**0**	**1**	**105**	**6.7**	**-1**	....	....	....	....	....	**14**	**1**	**2**	**3**	**2**	**1**	**0**	**0**
1993-94	**Toronto**	**NHL**	**76**	**9**	**27**	**36**	**78**	**3**	**0**	**0**	**147**	**6.1**	**5**	....	....	....	....	....	**18**	**6**	**9**	**15**	**6**	**6**	**0**	**0**
1994-95	**Toronto**	**NHL**	**33**	**5**	**12**	**17**	**28**	**2**	**0**	**0**	**68**	**7.4**	**6**	....	....	....	....	....	**6**	**2**	**1**	**3**	**2**	**1**	**0**	**0**
1995-96	**Pittsburgh**	**NHL**	**72**	**3**	**31**	**34**	**88**	**1**	**0**	**1**	**86**	**3.5**	**19**	....	....	....	....	....	**15**	**0**	**1**	**1**	**10**	**0**	**0**	**0**
1996-97	**Pittsburgh**	**NHL**	**15**	**1**	**5**	**6**	**24**	**0**	**0**	**1**	**19**	**5.3**	**-4**	....	....	....	....	....	....	....	....	....	....	....	....	....
	Anaheim	**NHL**	**62**	**12**	**34**	**46**	**77**	**3**	**1**	**1**	**158**	**7.6**	**20**	....	....	....	....	....	**11**	**1**	**10**	**11**	**10**	**1**	**0**	**0**
1997-98	**Anaheim**	**NHL**	**66**	**6**	**30**	**36**	**115**	**2**	**0**	**1**	**142**	**4.2**	**-7**	....	....	....	....	....	....	....	....	....	....	....	....	....
	Russia	Olympics	6	0	3	3	0	....	....	....	....	....	....	....	....	....	....	....	....	....	....	....	....	....	....	....
	♦ **Detroit**	**NHL**	**11**	**2**	**5**	**7**	**4**	**1**	**0**	**0**	**28**	**7.1**	**0**	....	....	....	....	....	**7**	**0**	**3**	**3**	**14**	**0**	**0**	**0**
1998-99	**Washington**	**NHL**	**46**	**2**	**14**	**16**	**80**	**2**	**0**	**0**	**86**	**2.3**	**-5**	**0**	**0.0**	**47**	**37**	**19:51**	....	....	....	....	....	....	....	....
99-2000	**Washington**	**NHL**	**73**	**3**	**19**	**22**	**28**	**1**	**0**	**0**	**99**	**3.0**	**7**	**1**	**0.0**	**93**	**52**	**20:22**	**4**	**0**	**0**	**0**	**4**	**0**	**0**	**0**
	NHL Totals		**520**	**51**	**201**	**252**	**562**	**19**	**1**	**6**	**945**	**5.4**		**1**	**0.0**	**140**	**89**	**20:010**	**75**	**10**	**26**	**36**	**48**	**9**	**0**	**0**

Played in NHL All-Star Game (1998)

Traded to **Pittsburgh** by **Toronto** with Toronto's 2nd round choice (later traded to New Jersey - New Jersey selected Joshua Dewolf) in 1996 Entry Draft for Larry Murphy, July 8, 1995. Traded to **Anaheim** by **Pittsburgh** with Shawn Antoski for Alex Hicks and Fredrik Olausson, November 19, 1996. Traded to **Detroit** by **Anaheim** for Jamie Pushor and Detroit's 4th round choice (Viktor Wallin) in 1998 Entry Draft, March 24, 1998. Signed as a free agent by **Washington**, July 29, 1998.

MITCHELL, Jeff (MIHT-chehl, JEHF)

Center/Right wing. Shoots right. 6'1", 190 lbs. Born, Wayne, MI, May 16, 1975. Los Angeles' 2nd choice, 68th overall, in 1993 Entry Draft.

Season	Club	League	GP	G	A	Pts	PIM	PP	SH	GW	S	%	+/-	TF	F%	H	SB	Min	GP	G	A	Pts	PIM	PP	SH	GW
1990-91	Fruehauf Flyers	MNHL	62	52	63	115	196	....	....	....	....	....	....	....	....	....	....	....	....	....	....	....	....	....	....	....
1991-92	Fraser Falcons	MNHL	65	65	52	117	114	....	....	....	....	....	....	....	....	....	....	....	....	....	....	....	....	....	....	....
1992-93	Detroit Jr. Wings	OHL	62	10	15	25	100	....	....	....	....	....	....	....	....	....	....	....	15	3	3	6	16	....	....	....
1993-94	Detroit Jr. Wings	OHL	59	25	18	43	99	....	....	....	....	....	....	....	....	....	....	....	17	3	5	8	22	....	....	....
1994-95	Detroit Jr. Wings	OHL	61	30	30	60	121	....	....	....	....	....	....	....	....	....	....	....	21	9	12	21	48	....	....	....
1995-96	Michigan K-Wings	IHL	50	5	4	9	119	....	....	....	....	....	....	....	....	....	....	....	....	....	....	....	....	....	....	....
1996-97	Michigan K-Wings	IHL	24	0	3	3	40	....	....	....	....	....	....	....	....	....	....	....	....	....	....	....	....	....	....	....
	Philadelphia	AHL	31	7	5	12	103	....	....	....	....	....	....	....	....	....	....	....	10	1	1	2	20	....	....	....
1997-98	**Dallas**	**NHL**	**7**	**0**	**0**	**0**	**7**	**0**	**0**	**0**	**3**	**0.0**	**0**	....	....	....	....	....	....	....	....	....	....	....	....	....
	Michigan K-Wings	IHL	62	9	8	17	206	....	....	....	....	....	....	....	....	....	....	....	4	0	0	0	30	....	....	....
1998-99	Michigan K-Wings	IHL	50	4	4	8	122	....	....	....	....	....	....	....	....	....	....	....	2	0	0	0	0	....	....	....
99-2000	Cincinnati Ducks	AHL	20	0	3	3	16	....	....	....	....	....	....	....	....	....	....	....	....	....	....	....	....	....	....	....
	Cincinnati	IHL	1	0	0	0	0	....	....	....	....	....	....	....	....	....	....	....	....	....	....	....	....	....	....	....
	Dayton Bombers	ECHL	36	23	17	40	186	....	....	....	....	....	....	....	....	....	....	....	....	....	....	....	....	....	....	....
	NHL Totals		**7**	**0**	**0**	**0**	**7**	**0**	**0**	**0**	**3**	**0.0**							....	....	....	....	....	....	....	....

Rights traded to **Dallas** by **LA Kings** for Vancouver's 5th round choice (previously acquired, LA Kings selected Jason Morgan) in 1995 Entry Draft, June 7, 1995.

MITCHELL, Willie (MIHT-chehl, WIHL-lee) N.J.

Defense. Shoots left. 6'3", 205 lbs. Born, Port McNeill, B.C., April 23, 1977. New Jersey's 12th choice, 199th overall, in 1996 Entry Draft.

Season	Club	League	GP	G	A	Pts	PIM	PP	SH	GW	S	%	+/-	TF	F%	H	SB	Min	GP	G	A	Pts	PIM	PP	SH	GW
1995-96	Melfort Mustangs	SJHL	19	2	6	8	....	....	....	....	....	....	....	....	....	....	....	....	14	0	2	2	12	....	....	....
1996-97	Melfort Mustangs	SJHL	64	14	42	56	227	....	....	....	....	....	....	....	....	....	....	....	4	0	1	1	23	....	....	....
1997-98	Clarkson	ECAC	34	9	17	26	105	....	....	....	....	....	....	....	....	....	....	....	....	....	....	....	....	....	....	....
1998-99	Clarkson	ECAC	34	10	19	29	40	....	....	....	....	....	....	....	....	....	....	....	....	....	....	....	....	....	....	....
	Albany River Rats	AHL	6	1	3	4	29	....	....	....	....	....	....	....	....	....	....	....	....	....	....	....	....	....	....	....
99-2000	**New Jersey**	**NHL**	**2**	**0**	**0**	**0**	**0**	**0**	**0**	**0**	**2**	**0.0**	**1**	**0**	**0.0**	**1**	**3**	**16:04**	....	....	....	....	....	....	....	....
	Albany River Rats	AHL	63	5	14	19	71	....	....	....	....	....	....	....	....	....	....	....	5	1	2	3	4	....	....	....
	NHL Totals		**2**	**0**	**0**	**0**	**0**	**0**	**0**	**0**	**2**	**0.0**		**0**	**0.0**	**1**	**3**	**16:04**	....	....	....	....	....	....	....	....

ECAC Second All-Star Team (1998) • ECAC First All-Star Team (1999) • NCAA East Second All-American Team (1999)

MODANO, Mike (moh-DA-noh, MIGHK) DAL.

Center. Shoots left. 6'3", 205 lbs. Born, Livonia, MI, June 7, 1970. Minnesota's 1st choice, 1st overall, in 1988 Entry Draft.

Season	Club	League	GP	G	A	Pts	PIM	PP	SH	GW	S	%	+/-	TF	F%	H	SB	Min	GP	G	A	Pts	PIM	PP	SH	GW
1985-86	Detroit	MNHL	69	66	65	131	32	....	....	....	....	....	....	....	....	....	....	....	....	....	....	....	....	....	....	....
1986-87	Prince Albert	WHL	70	32	30	62	96	....	....	....	....	....	....	....	....	....	....	....	8	1	4	5	4	....	....	....
1987-88	Prince Albert	WHL	65	47	80	127	80	....	....	....	....	....	....	....	....	....	....	....	9	7	11	18	18	....	....	....
1988-89	Prince Albert	WHL	41	39	66	105	74	....	....	....	....	....	....	....	....	....	....	....	....	....	....	....	....	....	....	....
	Minnesota	**NHL**	....	....	....	....	....	....	....	....	....	....	....	....	....	....	....	....	**2**	**0**	**0**	**0**	**0**	**0**	**0**	**0**
1989-90	**Minnesota**	**NHL**	**80**	**29**	**46**	**75**	**63**	**12**	**0**	**2**	**172**	**16.9**	**-7**	....	....	....	....	....	**7**	**1**	**1**	**2**	**12**	**0**	**0**	**0**
1990-91	**Minnesota**	**NHL**	**79**	**28**	**36**	**64**	**65**	**9**	**0**	**2**	**232**	**12.1**	**2**	....	....	....	....	....	**23**	**8**	**12**	**20**	**16**	**3**	**0**	**1**
1991-92	**Minnesota**	**NHL**	**76**	**33**	**44**	**77**	**46**	**5**	**0**	**8**	**256**	**12.9**	**-9**	....	....	....	....	....	**7**	**3**	**2**	**5**	**4**	**1**	**0**	**0**
1992-93	**Minnesota**	**NHL**	**82**	**33**	**60**	**93**	**83**	**9**	**0**	**7**	**307**	**10.7**	**-7**	....	....	....	....	....	....	....	....	....	....	....	....	....
1993-94	**Dallas**	**NHL**	**76**	**50**	**43**	**93**	**54**	**18**	**0**	**4**	**281**	**17.8**	**-8**	....	....	....	....	....	**9**	**7**	**3**	**10**	**16**	**2**	**0**	**2**
1994-95	**Dallas**	**NHL**	**30**	**12**	**17**	**29**	**8**	**4**	**1**	**0**	**100**	**12.0**	**7**	....	....	....	....	....	....	....	....	....	....	....	....	....
1995-96	**Dallas**	**NHL**	**78**	**36**	**45**	**81**	**63**	**8**	**4**	**4**	**320**	**11.3**	**-12**	....	....	....	....	....	....	....	....	....	....	....	....	....
1996-97	**Dallas**	**NHL**	**80**	**35**	**48**	**83**	**42**	**9**	**5**	**9**	**291**	**12.0**	**43**	....	....	....	....	....	**7**	**4**	**1**	**5**	**0**	**1**	**1**	**2**
1997-98	**Dallas**	**NHL**	**52**	**21**	**38**	**59**	**32**	**7**	**5**	**2**	**191**	**11.0**	**25**	....	....	....	....	....	**17**	**4**	**10**	**14**	**12**	**1**	**0**	**1**
	United States	Olympics	4	2	0	2	0	....	....	....	....	....	....	....	....	....	....	....	....	....	....	....	....	....	....	....

			Regular Season																Playoffs							
Season	Club	League	GP	G	A	Pts	PIM	PP	SH	GW	S	%	+/-	TF	F%	H	SB	Min	GP	G	A	Pts	PIM	PP	SH	GW
1998-99♦	**Dallas**	**NHL**	**77**	**34**	**47**	**81**	**44**	**6**	**4**	**7**	**224**	**15.2**	**29**	**1572**	**51.1**	**15**	**33**	**20:50**	**23**	**5**	***18**	**23**	**16**	**1**	**1**	**1**
99-2000	**Dallas**	**NHL**	**77**	**38**	**43**	**81**	**48**	**11**	**1**	**8**	**188**	**20.2**	**0**	**1763**	**51.4**	**16**	**43**	**22:55**	**23**	**10**	***13**	**23**	**10**	**4**	**0**	**2**
	NHL Totals		**787**	**349**	**467**	**816**	**548**	**98**	**20**	**53**	**2562**	**13.6**		**3335**	**51.2**	**31**	**76**	**21:52**	**118**	**42**	**60**	**102**	**86**	**13**	**2**	**9**

WHL East All-Star Team (1989) • NHL All-Rookie Team (1990) • NHL Second All-Star Team (2000) • Played in NHL All-Star Game (1993, 1998, 1999, 2000)

Transferred to **Dallas** after **Minnesota** franchise relocated, June 9, 1993.

MODIN, Fredrik

(muh-DEEN, FREHD-rihk) **T.B.**

Left wing. Shoots left. 6'4", 220 lbs. Born, Sundsvall, Sweden, October 8, 1974. Toronto's 3rd choice, 64th overall, in 1994 Entry Draft.

Season	Club	League	GP	G	A	Pts	PIM	PP	SH	GW	S	%	+/-	TF	F%	H	SB	Min	GP	G	A	Pts	PIM	PP	SH	GW
1991-92	Timra IF	Sweden-2	11	1	0	1	0	....	....	....	....	....	....	....	....	....	....	....	....	....	....	....	....	....	....	....
1992-93	Timra IF	Sweden-2	30	5	7	12	12	....	....	....	....	....	....	....	....	....	....	....	5	1	0	1	0	....	....	....
1993-94	Timra IF	Sweden-2	30	16	15	31	36	....	....	....	....	....	....	....	....	....	....	....	2	0	1	1	6	....	....	....
1994-95	Brynas IF	Sweden	38	9	10	19	33	....	....	....	....	....	....	....	....	....	....	....	14	4	4	8	6	....	....	....
1995-96	Brynas IF	Sweden	22	4	8	12	22	....	....	....	....	....	....	....	....	....	....	....	....	....	....	....	....	....	....	....
1996-97	**Toronto**	**NHL**	**76**	**6**	**7**	**13**	**24**	**0**	**0**	**0**	**85**	**7.1**	**–14**	....	....	....	....	....	....	....	....	....	....	....	....	....
1997-98	**Toronto**	**NHL**	**74**	**16**	**16**	**32**	**32**	**1**	**0**	**4**	**137**	**11.7**	**–5**	....	....	....	....	....	....	....	....	....	....	....	....	....
1998-99	**Toronto**	**NHL**	**67**	**16**	**15**	**31**	**35**	**1**	**0**	**3**	**108**	**14.8**	**14**	**2**	**50.0**	**77**	**12**	**13:34**	**8**	**0**	**0**	**0**	**6**	**0**	**0**	**0**
99-2000	**Tampa Bay**	**NHL**	**80**	**22**	**26**	**48**	**18**	**3**	**0**	**5**	**167**	**13.2**	**–26**	**6**	**50.0**	**123**	**25**	**15:32**	....	....	....	....	....	....	....	....
	NHL Totals		**297**	**60**	**64**	**124**	**109**	**5**	**0**	**12**	**497**	**12.1**		**8**	**50.0**	**200**	**37**	**14:38**	**8**	**0**	**0**	**0**	**6**	**0**	**0**	**0**

Traded to **Tampa Bay** by **Toronto** for Cory Cross and Tampa Bay's 7th round choice in 2001 Entry Draft, October 1, 1999.

MODRY, Jaroslav

(MOHD-ree, YAHRO-slahv) **L.A.**

Defense. Shoots left. 6'2", 215 lbs. Born, Ceske-Budejovice, Czech., February 27, 1971. New Jersey's 11th choice, 179th overall, in 1990 Entry Draft.

Season	Club	League	GP	G	A	Pts	PIM	PP	SH	GW	S	%	+/-	TF	F%	H	SB	Min	GP	G	A	Pts	PIM	PP	SH	GW
1987-88	MC Budejovice	Czech.	3	0	0	0	0	....	....	....	....	....	....	....	....	....	....	....	....	....	....	....	....	....	....	....
1988-89	MC Budejovice	Czech.	28	0	1	1	8	....	....	....	....	....	....	....	....	....	....	....	....	....	....	....	....	....	....	....
1989-90	MC Budejovice	Czech.	41	2	2	4	....	....	....	....	....	....	....	....	....	....	....	....	....	....	....	....	....	....	....	....
1990-91	Dukla Trencin	Czech.	33	1	9	10	6	....	....	....	....	....	....	....	....	....	....	....	....	....	....	....	....	....	....	....
1991-92	MC Budejovice	Czech-2	14	4	10	14	....	....	....	....	....	....	....	....	....	....	....	....	....	....	....	....	....	....	....	....
	Dukla Trencin	Czech.	18	0	4	4	6	....	....	....	....	....	....	....	....	....	....	....	....	....	....	....	....	....	....	....
1992-93	Utica Devils	AHL	80	7	35	42	62	....	....	....	....	....	....	....	....	....	....	....	5	0	2	2	2	....	....	....
1993-94	**New Jersey**	**NHL**	**41**	**2**	**15**	**17**	**18**	**2**	**0**	**0**	**35**	**5.7**	**10**	....	....	....	....	....	....	....	....	....	....	....	....	....
	Albany River Rats	AHL	19	1	5	6	25	....	....	....	....	....	....	....	....	....	....	....	....	....	....	....	....	....	....	....
1994-95	HC Budejovice	Cze-Rep	19	1	3	4	30	....	....	....	....	....	....	....	....	....	....	....	....	....	....	....	....	....	....	....
	New Jersey	**NHL**	**11**	**0**	**0**	**0**	**0**	**0**	**0**	**0**	**10**	**0.0**	**–1**	....	....	....	....	....	....	....	....	....	....	....	....	....
	Albany River Rats	AHL	18	5	6	11	14	....	....	....	....	....	....	....	....	....	....	....	14	3	3	6	4	....	....	....
1995-96	**Ottawa**	**NHL**	**64**	**4**	**14**	**18**	**38**	**1**	**0**	**1**	**89**	**4.5**	**–17**	....	....	....	....	....	....	....	....	....	....	....	....	....
	Los Angeles	**NHL**	**9**	**0**	**3**	**3**	**6**	**0**	**0**	**0**	**17**	**0.0**	**–4**	....	....	....	....	....	....	....	....	....	....	....	....	....
1996-97	**Los Angeles**	**NHL**	**30**	**3**	**3**	**6**	**25**	**1**	**1**	**0**	**32**	**9.4**	**–13**	....	....	....	....	....	....	....	....	....	....	....	....	....
	Phoenix	IHL	23	3	12	15	17	....	....	....	....	....	....	....	....	....	....	....	....	....	....	....	....	....	....	....
	Utah Grizzlies	IHL	11	1	4	5	20	....	....	....	....	....	....	....	....	....	....	....	7	0	1	1	6	....	....	....
1997-98	Utah Grizzlies	IHL	74	12	21	33	72	....	....	....	....	....	....	....	....	....	....	....	4	0	2	2	6	....	....	....
1998-99	**Los Angeles**	**NHL**	**5**	**0**	**1**	**1**	**0**	**0**	**0**	**0**	**11**	**0.0**	**1**	**0**	**0.0**	**6**	**7**	**26:00**	....	....	....	....	....	....	....	....
	Long Beach	IHL	64	6	29	35	44	....	....	....	....	....	....	....	....	....	....	....	8	4	2	6	4	....	....	....
99-2000	**Los Angeles**	**NHL**	**26**	**5**	**4**	**9**	**18**	**5**	**0**	**1**	**32**	**15.6**	**–2**	**0**	**0.0**	**20**	**24**	**19:13**	**2**	**0**	**0**	**0**	**2**	**0**	**0**	**0**
	Long Beach	IHL	11	2	4	6	8	....	....	....	....	....	....	....	....	....	....	....	....	....	....	....	....	....	....	....
	NHL Totals		**186**	**14**	**40**	**54**	**105**	**9**	**1**	**2**	**226**	**6.2**		**0**	**0.0**	**26**	**31**	**20:19**	**2**	**0**	**0**	**0**	**2**	**0**	**0**	**0**

Traded to **Ottawa** by **New Jersey** for Ottawa's 4th round choice (Alyn McCauley) in 1995 Entry Draft, July 8, 1995. Traded to **LA Kings** by **Ottawa** with Ottawa's 8th round choice (Stephen Valiquette) in 1996 Entry Draft for Kevin Brown, March 20, 1996.

MOGER, Sandy

(MOH-guhr, SAN-dee)

Center. Shoots right. 6'4", 220 lbs. Born, 100 Mile House, B.C., March 21, 1969. Vancouver's 7th choice, 176th overall, in 1989 Entry Draft.

Season	Club	League	GP	G	A	Pts	PIM	PP	SH	GW	S	%	+/-	TF	F%	H	SB	Min	GP	G	A	Pts	PIM	PP	SH	GW
1986-87	Vernon Lakers	BCJHL	13	5	4	9	10	....	....	....	....	....	....	....	....	....	....	....	....	....	....	....	....	....	....	....
1987-88	Yorkton Terriers	SJHL	60	39	41	80	144	....	....	....	....	....	....	....	....	....	....	....	16	7	6	13	....	....	....	....
1988-89	Lake Superior	CCHA	21	3	5	8	26	....	....	....	....	....	....	....	....	....	....	....	....	....	....	....	....	....	....	....
1989-90	Lake Superior	CCHA	46	17	15	32	76	....	....	....	....	....	....	....	....	....	....	....	....	....	....	....	....	....	....	....
1990-91	Lake Superior	CCHA	45	27	21	48	*172	....	....	....	....	....	....	....	....	....	....	....	....	....	....	....	....	....	....	....
1991-92	Lake Superior	CCHA	38	24	24	48	93	....	....	....	....	....	....	....	....	....	....	....	....	....	....	....	....	....	....	....
1992-93	Hamilton Canucks	AHL	78	23	26	49	57	....	....	....	....	....	....	....	....	....	....	....	....	....	....	....	....	....	....	....
1993-94	Hamilton Canucks	AHL	29	9	8	17	41	....	....	....	....	....	....	....	....	....	....	....	....	....	....	....	....	....	....	....
1994-95	**Boston**	**NHL**	**18**	**2**	**6**	**8**	**6**	**2**	**0**	**0**	**32**	**6.3**	**–1**	....	....	....	....	....	....	....	....	....	....	....	....	....
	Providence Bruins	AHL	63	32	29	61	105	....	....	....	....	....	....	....	....	....	....	....	....	....	....	....	....	....	....	....
1995-96	**Boston**	**NHL**	**80**	**15**	**14**	**29**	**65**	**4**	**0**	**6**	**103**	**14.6**	**–9**	....	....	....	....	....	**5**	**2**	**2**	**4**	**12**	**1**	**0**	**0**
1996-97	**Boston**	**NHL**	**34**	**10**	**3**	**13**	**45**	**3**	**0**	**0**	**54**	**18.5**	**–12**	....	....	....	....	....	....	....	....	....	....	....	....	....
	Providence Bruins	AHL	3	0	2	2	19	....	....	....	....	....	....	....	....	....	....	....	....	....	....	....	....	....	....	....
1997-98	**Los Angeles**	**NHL**	**62**	**11**	**13**	**24**	**70**	**1**	**0**	**2**	**89**	**12.4**	**4**	....	....	....	....	....	....	....	....	....	....	....	....	....
1998-99	**Los Angeles**	**NHL**	**42**	**3**	**2**	**5**	**26**	**0**	**0**	**2**	**28**	**10.7**	**–9**	**2**	**50.0**	**80**	**5**	**10:19**	....	....	....	....	....	....	....	....
99-2000	Houston Aeros	IHL	45	13	10	23	43	....	....	....	....	....	....	....	....	....	....	....	2	1	1	2	4	....	....	....
	NHL Totals		**236**	**41**	**38**	**79**	**212**	**10**	**0**	**10**	**306**	**13.4**		**2**	**50.0**	**80**	**5**	**10:19**	**5**	**2**	**2**	**4**	**12**	**1**	**0**	**0**

CCHA Second All-Star Team (1992)

Signed as a free agent by **Boston**, June 22, 1994. • Missed majority of 1996-97 season recovering from elbow injury suffered in game vs. Buffalo, December 14, 1996. Traded to **LA Kings** by **Boston** with Jozef Stumpel and Boston's 4th round choice (later traded to New Jersey - New Jersey selected Pierre Dagenais) in 1998 Entry Draft for Dimitri Khristich and Byron Dafoe, August 29, 1997. Signed as a free agent by **Houston** (IHL), September 6, 1999.

MOGILNY, Alexander

(moh-GIHL-nee, al-ehx-AN-duhr) **N.J.**

Right wing. Shoots left. 5'11", 200 lbs. Born, Khabarovsk, USSR, February 18, 1969. Buffalo's 4th choice, 89th overall, in 1988 Entry Draft.

Season	Club	League	GP	G	A	Pts	PIM	PP	SH	GW	S	%	+/-	TF	F%	H	SB	Min	GP	G	A	Pts	PIM	PP	SH	GW
1986-87	CSKA Moscow	USSR	28	15	1	16	4	....	....	....	....	....	....	....	....	....	....	....	....	....	....	....	....	....	....	....
1987-88	CSKA Moscow	USSR	39	12	8	20	14	....	....	....	....	....	....	....	....	....	....	....	....	....	....	....	....	....	....	....
	Soviet Union	Olympics	6	3	2	5	2	....	....	....	....	....	....	....	....	....	....	....	....	....	....	....	....	....	....	....
1988-89	CSKA Moscow	USSR	31	11	11	22	24	....	....	....	....	....	....	....	....	....	....	....	....	....	....	....	....	....	....	....
1989-90	**Buffalo**	**NHL**	**65**	**15**	**28**	**43**	**16**	**4**	**0**	**2**	**130**	**11.5**	**8**	....	....	....	....	....	**4**	**0**	**1**	**1**	**2**	**0**	**0**	**0**
1990-91	**Buffalo**	**NHL**	**62**	**30**	**34**	**64**	**16**	**3**	**3**	**5**	**201**	**14.9**	**14**	....	....	....	....	....	**6**	**0**	**6**	**6**	**2**	**0**	**0**	**0**
1991-92	**Buffalo**	**NHL**	**67**	**39**	**45**	**84**	**73**	**15**	**0**	**2**	**236**	**16.5**	**7**	....	....	....	....	....	**2**	**0**	**2**	**2**	**0**	**0**	**0**	**0**
1992-93	**Buffalo**	**NHL**	**77**	***76**	**51**	**127**	**40**	**27**	**0**	**11**	**360**	**21.1**	**7**	....	....	....	....	....	**7**	**7**	**3**	**10**	**6**	**2**	**0**	**0**
1993-94	**Buffalo**	**NHL**	**66**	**32**	**47**	**79**	**22**	**17**	**0**	**7**	**258**	**12.4**	**8**	....	....	....	....	....	**7**	**4**	**2**	**6**	**6**	**1**	**0**	**0**
1994-95	Spartak Moscow	CIS	1	0	1	1	0	....	....	....	....	....	....	....	....	....	....	....	....	....	....	....	....	....	....	....
	Buffalo	**NHL**	**44**	**19**	**28**	**47**	**36**	**12**	**0**	**2**	**148**	**12.8**	**0**	....	....	....	....	....	**5**	**3**	**2**	**5**	**2**	**0**	**0**	**0**
1995-96	**Vancouver**	**NHL**	**79**	**55**	**52**	**107**	**16**	**10**	**5**	**6**	**292**	**18.8**	**14**	....	....	....	....	....	**6**	**1**	**8**	**9**	**8**	**0**	**0**	**0**
1996-97	**Vancouver**	**NHL**	**76**	**31**	**42**	**73**	**18**	**7**	**1**	**4**	**174**	**17.8**	**9**	....	....	....	....	....	....	....	....	....	....	....	....	....
1997-98	**Vancouver**	**NHL**	**51**	**18**	**27**	**45**	**36**	**5**	**4**	**1**	**118**	**15.3**	**–6**	....	....	....	....	....	....	....	....	....	....	....	....	....
1998-99	**Vancouver**	**NHL**	**59**	**14**	**31**	**45**	**58**	**3**	**2**	**1**	**110**	**12.7**	**0**	**47**	**23.4**	**34**	**10**	**20:35**	....	....	....	....	....	....	....	....
99-2000	**Vancouver**	**NHL**	**47**	**21**	**17**	**38**	**16**	**3**	**1**	**1**	**126**	**16.7**	**7**	**9**	**11.1**	**37**	**12**	**19:34**	....	....	....	....	....	....	....	....
	♦ New Jersey	**NHL**	**12**	**3**	**3**	**6**	**4**	**2**	**0**	**0**	**35**	**8.6**	**–4**	**0**	**0.0**	**4**	**3**	**17:04**	**23**	**4**	**3**	**7**	**4**	**2**	**0**	**1**
	NHL Totals		**705**	**353**	**405**	**758**	**351**	**108**	**16**	**42**	**2188**	**16.1**		**56**	**21.4**	**75**	**25**	**19:49**	**60**	**19**	**27**	**46**	**30**	**5**	**0**	**1**

NHL Second All-Star Team (1993, 1996) • Played in NHL All-Star Game (1992, 1993, 1994, 1996)

Traded to **Vancouver** by **Buffalo** with Buffalo's 5th round choice (Todd Norman) in 1995 Entry Draft for Mike Peca, Mike Wilson and Vancouver's 1st round choice (Jay McKee) in 1995 Entry Draft, July 8, 1995. Traded to **New Jersey** by **Vancouver** for Brendan Morrison and Denis Pederson, March 14, 2000.

MONTGOMERY, Jim

(MOHNT-GUHM-ree, JIHM) **S.J.**

Center. Shoots right. 5'10", 180 lbs. Born, Montreal, Que., June 30, 1969.

Season	Club	League	GP	G	A	Pts	PIM	PP	SH	GW	S	%	+/-	TF	F%	H	SB	Min	Playoffs GP	G	A	Pts	PIM	PP	SH	GW
1988-89	Pembroke	OJHL	50	53	*101	154	112																			
1989-90	U. of Maine	H-East	45	26	34	60	35																			
1990-91	U. of Maine	H-East	43	24	*57	81	44																			
1991-92	U. of Maine	H-East	37	21	44	65	46																			
1992-93	U. of Maine	H-East	45	32	63	95	40																			
1993-94	**St. Louis**	**NHL**	**67**	**6**	**14**	**20**	**44**	**0**	**0**	**1**	**67**	**9.0**	**–1**													
	Peoria Rivermen	IHL	12	7	8	15	10																			
1994-95	**Montreal**	**NHL**	**5**	**0**	**0**	**0**	**2**	**0**	**0**	**0**	**3**	**0.0**	**–2**													
	Philadelphia	**NHL**	**8**	**1**	**1**	**2**	**6**	**0**	**0**	**0**	**10**	**10.0**	**–2**						**7**	**1**	**0**	**1**	**2**	**0**	**0**	**0**
	Hershey Bears	AHL	16	8	6	14	14												6	3	2	5	25			
1995-96	**Philadelphia**	**NHL**	**5**	**1**	**2**	**3**	**9**	**0**	**0**	**0**	**4**	**25.0**	**1**						**1**	**0**	**0**	**0**	**0**	**0**	**0**	**0**
	Hershey Bears	AHL	78	34	*71	105	95												4	3	2	5	6			
1996-97	Kolner Haie	DEL	50	12	35	47	111												4	0	1	1	6			
	Kolner Haie	EuroHL	6	0	1	1	16																			
1997-98	Philadelphia	AHL	68	19	43	62	75												20	*13	16	29	55			
1998-99	Philadelphia	AHL	78	29	58	87	89												16	4	11	15	20			
99-2000	Philadelphia	AHL	13	3	9	12	22																			
	Manitoba Moose	IHL	67	18	28	46	111																			
	NHL Totals		**85**	**8**	**17**	**25**	**61**	**0**	**0**	**1**	**84**	**9.5**							**8**	**1**	**0**	**1**	**2**	**0**	**0**	**0**

Hockey East Second All-Star Team (1991, 1992) • Hockey East First All-Star Team (1993) • NCAA East Second All-American Team (1993) • NCAA Championship All-Tournament Team (1993) • NCAA Championship Tournament MVP (1993) • AHL Second All-Star Team (1996)

Signed as a free agent by **St. Louis**, June 2, 1993. Traded to **Montreal** by **St. Louis** for Guy Carbonneau, August 19, 1994. Claimed on waivers by **Philadelphia** from **Montreal**, February 10, 1995. Signed as a free agent by **San Jose**, August 15, 2000.

MOORE, Barrie

(MEW-uhr, BAIR-ee)

Left wing. Shoots left. 5'11", 198 lbs. Born, London, Ont., May 22, 1975. Buffalo's 7th choice, 220th overall, in 1993 Entry Draft.

Season	Club	League	GP	G	A	Pts	PIM	PP	SH	GW	S	%	+/-	TF	F%	H	SB	Min	Playoffs GP	G	A	Pts	PIM	PP	SH	GW
1990-91	Strathroy Rockets	OJHL-B	24	9	10	19	14																			
1991-92	Sudbury Wolves	OHL	62	15	38	53	57												11	0	7	7	12			
1992-93	Sudbury Wolves	OHL	57	13	26	39	71												14	4	3	7	19			
1993-94	Sudbury Wolves	OHL	65	36	49	85	69												10	3	5	8	14			
1994-95	Sudbury Wolves	OHL	60	47	42	89	67												18	*15	14	29	24			
1995-96	**Buffalo**	**NHL**	**3**	**0**	**0**	**0**	**0**	**0**	**0**	**0**	**3**	**0.0**	**0**													
	Rochester	AHL	64	26	30	56	40												18	3	6	9	18			
1996-97	**Buffalo**	**NHL**	**31**	**2**	**6**	**8**	**18**	**1**	**0**	**0**	**42**	**4.8**	**1**													
	Rochester	AHL	32	14	15	29	14																			
	Edmonton	**NHL**	**4**	**0**	**0**	**0**	**0**	**0**	**0**	**0**	**1**	**0.0**	**0**													
	Hamilton Bulldogs	AHL	9	5	2	7	0												22	2	6	8	15			
1997-98	Hamilton Bulldogs	AHL	70	22	29	51	64												8	0	1	1	4			
1998-99	Indianapolis Ice	IHL	43	9	10	19	18																			
	Portland Pirates	AHL	23	3	7	10	4																			
99-2000	**Washington**	**NHL**	**1**	**0**	**0**	**0**	**0**	**0**	**0**	**0**	**2**	**0.0**	**0**	**0**	**0.0**	**0**	**0**	**9:50**								
	Portland Pirates	AHL	80	18	33	51	50												4	0	0	0	6			
	NHL Totals		**39**	**2**	**6**	**8**	**18**	**1**	**0**	**0**	**48**	**4.2**		**0**	**0.0**	**0**	**0**	**9:50**								

Traded to **Edmonton** by **Buffalo** with Craig Millar for Miroslav Satan, March 18, 1997. Rights traded to **Washington** by **Edmonton** for Brad Church, February 3, 1999. Selected by **Columbus** from **Washington** in Expansion Draft, June 23, 2000.

MORAN, Ian

(moh-RAN, EE-an) **PIT.**

Right wing. Shoots right. 6', 206 lbs. Born, Cleveland, OH, August 24, 1972. Pittsburgh's 5th choice, 107th overall, in 1990 Entry Draft.

Season	Club	League	GP	G	A	Pts	PIM	PP	SH	GW	S	%	+/-	TF	F%	H	SB	Min	Playoffs GP	G	A	Pts	PIM	PP	SH	GW
1987-88	Belmont Hill	Hi-School	25	3	13	16	15																			
1988-89	Belmont Hill	Hi-School	23	7	25	32	8																			
1989-90	Belmont Hill	Hi-School	23	10	36	46																				
1990-91	Belmont Hill	Hi-School	23	7	44	51	12																			
1991-92	Boston College	H-East	30	2	16	18	44																			
1992-93	Boston College	H-East	31	8	12	20	32																			
1993-94	United States	Nat-Team	50	8	15	23	69																			
	Cleveland	IHL	33	5	13	18	39																			
1994-95	Cleveland	IHL	64	7	31	38	94												4	0	1	1	2			
	Pittsburgh	**NHL**																	**8**	**0**	**0**	**0**	**0**	**0**	**0**	**0**
1995-96	**Pittsburgh**	**NHL**	**51**	**1**	**1**	**2**	**47**	**0**	**0**	**0**	**44**	**2.3**	**–1**													
1996-97	**Pittsburgh**	**NHL**	**36**	**4**	**5**	**9**	**22**	**0**	**0**	**0**	**50**	**8.0**	**–11**						**5**	**1**	**2**	**3**	**4**	**0**	**0**	**0**
	Cleveland	IHL	36	6	23	29	26																			
1997-98	**Pittsburgh**	**NHL**	**37**	**1**	**6**	**7**	**19**	**0**	**0**	**1**	**33**	**3.0**	**0**						**6**	**0**	**0**	**0**	**2**	**0**	**0**	**0**
1998-99	**Pittsburgh**	**NHL**	**62**	**4**	**5**	**9**	**37**	**0**	**1**	**0**	**65**	**6.2**	**1**	**32**	**34.4**	**48**	**98**	**16:34**	**13**	**0**	**2**	**2**	**8**	**0**	**0**	**0**
99-2000	**Pittsburgh**	**NHL**	**73**	**4**	**8**	**12**	**28**	**0**	**0**	**0**	**58**	**6.9**	**–10**	**210**	**33.8**	**48**	**62**	**11:21**	**11**	**0**	**1**	**1**	**2**	**0**	**0**	**0**
	NHL Totals		**259**	**14**	**25**	**39**	**153**	**0**	**1**	**1**	**250**	**5.6**		**242**	**33.9**	**96**	**160**	**13:45**	**43**	**1**	**5**	**6**	**16**	**0**	**0**	**0**

• Missed majority of 1997-98 season recovering from kneecap injury suffered in training camp, September 30, 1997.

MORAVEC, David

(muh-RAHV-ehts, DAY-vihd) **BUF.**

Right wing. Shoots left. 6', 180 lbs. Born, Vitkovice, Czech., March 24, 1973. Buffalo's 9th choice, 218th overall, in 1998 Entry Draft.

Season	Club	League	GP	G	A	Pts	PIM	PP	SH	GW	S	%	+/-	TF	F%	H	SB	Min	Playoffs GP	G	A	Pts	PIM	PP	SH	GW
1994-95	HC Vitkovice	Cze-Rep	38	4	13	17	12												6	1	7	8	0			
1995-96	HC Vitkovice	Cze-Rep	37	6	5	11	14												4	0	0	0	4			
1996-97	HC Vitkovice	Cze-Rep	52	18	22	40	30												9	6	3	9	0			
1997-98	HC Vitkovice	Cze-Rep	51	*38	26	64	28												11	6	9	15	8			
1998-99	HC Vitkovice	Cze-Rep	50	21	22	43	44												4	1	1	2				
99-2000	HC Vitkovice	Cze-Rep	38	11	18	29	34																			
	Buffalo	**NHL**	**1**	**0**	**0**	**0**	**0**	**0**	**0**	**0**	**2**	**0.0**	**–1**	**2**	**50.0**	**0**	**0**	**15:15**								
	NHL Totals		**1**	**0**	**0**	**0**	**0**	**0**	**0**	**0**	**2**	**0.0**		**2**	**50.0**	**0**	**0**	**15:15**								

MORE, Jay

(MOHR, JAY)

Defense. Shoots right. 6'1", 210 lbs. Born, Souris, Man., January 12, 1969. NY Rangers' 1st choice, 10th overall, in 1987 Entry Draft.

Season	Club	League	GP	G	A	Pts	PIM	PP	SH	GW	S	%	+/-	TF	F%	H	SB	Min	Playoffs GP	G	A	Pts	PIM	PP	SH	GW
1984-85	Lethbridge	WHL	71	3	9	12	101												4	1	0	1	7			
1985-86	Lethbridge	WHL	61	7	18	25	155												9	0	2	2	36			
1986-87	Brandon	WHL	21	4	6	10	62																			
	New Westminster	WHL	43	4	23	27	155																			
1987-88	New Westminster	WHL	70	13	47	60	270												5	0	2	2	26			
1988-89	**NY Rangers**	**NHL**	**1**	**0**	**0**	**0**	**0**	**0**	**0**	**0**	**0**	**0.0**	**–1**													
	Denver Rangers	IHL	62	7	15	22	138												3	0	1	1	26			
1989-90	Flint Spirits	IHL	9	1	5	6	41																			
	Minnesota	**NHL**	**5**	**0**	**0**	**0**	**16**	**0**	**0**	**0**	**4**	**0.0**	**1**													
	Kalamazoo Wings	IHL	64	9	25	34	316												10	0	3	3	13			
1990-91	Kalamazoo Wings	IHL	10	0	5	5	46																			
	Fredericton	AHL	57	7	17	24	152												9	1	1	2	34			
1991-92	**San Jose**	**NHL**	**46**	**4**	**13**	**17**	**85**	**1**	**0**	**1**	**60**	**6.7**	**–32**													
	Kansas City	IHL	2	0	2	2	4																			
1992-93	**San Jose**	**NHL**	**73**	**5**	**6**	**11**	**179**	**0**	**1**	**0**	**107**	**4.7**	**–35**													
1993-94	**San Jose**	**NHL**	**49**	**1**	**6**	**7**	**63**	**0**	**0**	**0**	**38**	**2.6**	**–5**						**13**	**0**	**2**	**2**	**32**	**0**	**0**	**0**
	Kansas City	IHL	2	1	0	1	25																			
1994-95	**San Jose**	**NHL**	**45**	**0**	**6**	**6**	**71**	**0**	**0**	**0**	**25**	**0.0**	**7**						**11**	**0**	**4**	**4**	**6**	**0**	**0**	**0**

			Regular Season																Playoffs							
Season	Club	League	GP	G	A	Pts	PIM	PP	SH	GW	S	%	+/–	TF	F%	H	SB	Min	GP	G	A	Pts	PIM	PP	SH	GW
1995-96	**San Jose**	**NHL**	**74**	**2**	**7**	**9**	**147**	**0**	**0**	**0**	**67**	**3.0**	**–32**	....	....	....	....	....	....	....	....	....	....	....	....	....
1996-97	**NY Rangers**	**NHL**	**14**	**0**	**1**	**1**	**25**	**0**	**0**	**0**	**10**	**0.0**	**0**	....	....	....	....	....	....	....	....	....	....	....	....	....
	Phoenix	**NHL**	**23**	**1**	**6**	**7**	**37**	**0**	**0**	**1**	**18**	**5.6**	**10**	....	....	....	....	....	**7**	**0**	**0**	**0**	**7**	**0**	**0**	**0**
1997-98	**Phoenix**	**NHL**	**41**	**5**	**5**	**10**	**53**	**0**	**1**	**0**	**40**	**12.5**	**0**	....	....	....	....	....	....	....	....	....	....	....	....	....
	Chicago	**NHL**	**17**	**0**	**2**	**2**	**8**	**0**	**0**	**0**	**17**	**0.0**	**7**	....	....	....	....	....	....	....	....	....	....	....	....	....
1998-99	**Nashville**	**NHL**	**18**	**0**	**2**	**2**	**18**	**0**	**0**	**0**	**24**	**0.0**	**2**	**0**	**0.0**	**34**	**9**	**16:30**	....	....	....	....	....	....	....	....
99-2000	**Nashville**	**NHL**	DID NOT PLAY – INJURED																							
	NHL Totals		**406**	**18**	**54**	**72**	**702**	**1**	**2**	**2**	**410**	**4.4**		**0**	**0.0**	**34**	**9**	**16:30**	**31**	**0**	**6**	**6**	**45**	**0**	**0**	**0**

WHL All-Star Team (1988)

Traded to **Minnesota** by **NY Rangers** for Dave Archibald, November 1, 1989. Traded to **Montreal** by **Minnesota** for Brian Hayward, November 7, 1990. Claimed by **San Jose** from **Montreal** in Expansion Draft, May 30, 1991. Traded to **NY Rangers** by **San Jose** with Brian Swanson and San Jose's 4th round choice (later traded back to San Jose - San Jose selected Adam Colagiacomo) in 1997 Entry Draft for Marty McSorley, August 20, 1996. Traded to **Phoenix** by **NY Rangers** for Mike Eastwood and Dallas Eakins, February 6, 1997. Traded to **Chicago** by **Phoenix** with Chad Kilger for Keith Carney and Jim Cummins, March 4, 1998. Signed as a free agent by **Nashville**, June 4, 1998. • Missed majority of 1998-99 season and entire 1999-2000 season recovering from head injury suffered in game vs. Florida, December 10, 1998.

MOREAU, Ethan

(moh-ROH, EE-than) **EDM.**

Left wing. Shoots left. 6'2", 211 lbs. Born, Huntsville, Ont., September 22, 1975. Chicago's 1st choice, 14th overall, in 1994 Entry Draft.

Season	Club	League	GP	G	A	Pts	PIM	PP	SH	GW	S	%	+/–	TF	F%	H	SB	Min	GP	G	A	Pts	PIM	PP	SH	GW
1990-91	Orillia Terriers	OJHL-B	42	17	22	39	26	....	....	....	....	....	....	....	....	....	....	....	12	6	6	12	18	....	....	....
1991-92	Niagara Falls	OHL	62	20	35	55	39	....	....	....	....	....	....	....	....	....	....	....	17	4	6	10	4	....	....	....
1992-93	Niagara Falls	OHL	65	32	41	73	69	....	....	....	....	....	....	....	....	....	....	....	4	0	3	3	4	....	....	....
1993-94	Niagara Falls	OHL	59	44	54	98	100	....	....	....	....	....	....	....	....	....	....	....	....	....	....	....	....	....	....	....
1994-95	Niagara Falls	OHL	39	25	41	66	69	....	....	....	....	....	....	....	....	....	....	....	....	....	....	....	....	....	....	....
	Sudbury Wolves	OHL	23	13	17	30	22	....	....	....	....	....	....	....	....	....	....	....	18	6	12	18	26	....	....	....
1995-96	**Chicago**	**NHL**	**8**	**0**	**1**	**1**	**4**	**0**	**0**	**0**	**1**	**0.0**	**1**	....	....	....	....	....	....	....	....	....	....	....	....	....
	Indianapolis Ice	IHL	71	21	20	41	126	....	....	....	....	....	....	....	....	....	....	....	5	4	0	4	8	....	....	....
1996-97	**Chicago**	**NHL**	**82**	**15**	**16**	**31**	**123**	**0**	**0**	**1**	**114**	**13.2**	**13**	....	....	....	....	....	**6**	**1**	**0**	**1**	**9**	**0**	**0**	**0**
1997-98	**Chicago**	**NHL**	**54**	**9**	**9**	**18**	**73**	**2**	**0**	**0**	**87**	**10.3**	**0**	....	....	....	....	....	....	....	....	....	....	....	....	....
1998-99	**Chicago**	**NHL**	**66**	**9**	**6**	**15**	**84**	**0**	**0**	**1**	**80**	**11.3**	**–5**	**3**	**33.3**	**113**	**15**	**12:30**	....	....	....	....	....	....	....	....
	Edmonton	**NHL**	**14**	**1**	**5**	**6**	**8**	**0**	**0**	**1**	**16**	**6.3**	**2**	**1**	**0.0**	**26**	**9**	**11:47**	**4**	**0**	**3**	**3**	**6**	**0**	**0**	**0**
99-2000	**Edmonton**	**NHL**	**73**	**17**	**10**	**27**	**62**	**1**	**0**	**3**	**106**	**16.0**	**8**	**8**	**62.5**	**158**	**35**	**15:07**	**5**	**0**	**1**	**1**	**0**	**0**	**0**	**0**
	NHL Totals		**297**	**51**	**47**	**98**	**354**	**3**	**0**	**6**	**404**	**12.6**		**12**	**50.0**	**297**	**59**	**13:41**	**15**	**1**	**4**	**5**	**15**	**0**	**0**	**0**

Traded to **Edmonton** by **Chicago** with Daniel Cleary, Chad Kilger and Christian Laflamme for Boris Mironov, Dean McAmmond and Jonas Elofsson, March 20, 1999.

MORGAN, Jason

(MOHR-gan, JAY-son)

Center. Shoots left. 6'1", 200 lbs. Born, St. John's, Nfld., October 9, 1976. Los Angeles' 5th choice, 118th overall, in 1995 Entry Draft.

Season	Club	League	GP	G	A	Pts	PIM	PP	SH	GW	S	%	+/–	TF	F%	H	SB	Min	GP	G	A	Pts	PIM	PP	SH	GW
1992-93	Kitchener	OMHA	69	44	40	84	85	....	....	....	....	....	....	....	....	....	....	....	....	....	....	....	....	....	....	....
1993-94	Kitchener	OHL	65	6	15	21	16	....	....	....	....	....	....	....	....	....	....	....	5	1	0	1	0	....	....	....
1994-95	Kitchener	OHL	35	3	15	18	25	....	....	....	....	....	....	....	....	....	....	....	....	....	....	....	....	....	....	....
	Kingston	OHL	20	0	3	3	14	....	....	....	....	....	....	....	....	....	....	....	6	0	2	2	0	....	....	....
1995-96	Kingston	OHL	66	16	38	54	50	....	....	....	....	....	....	....	....	....	....	....	6	1	2	3	0	....	....	....
1996-97	**Los Angeles**	**NHL**	**3**	**0**	**0**	**0**	**0**	**0**	**0**	**0**	**4**	**0.0**	**–3**	....	....	....	....	....	....	....	....	....	....	....	....	....
	Phoenix	IHL	57	3	6	9	29	....	....	....	....	....	....	....	....	....	....	....	....	....	....	....	....	....	....	....
	Mississippi	ECHL	6	3	0	3	0	....	....	....	....	....	....	....	....	....	....	....	3	1	1	2	6	....	....	....
1997-98	**Los Angeles**	**NHL**	**11**	**1**	**0**	**1**	**4**	**0**	**0**	**0**	**5**	**20.0**	**–7**	....	....	....	....	....	....	....	....	....	....	....	....	....
	Springfield	AHL	58	13	22	35	66	....	....	....	....	....	....	....	....	....	....	....	3	1	0	1	18	....	....	....
1998-99	Long Beach	IHL	13	4	6	10	18	....	....	....	....	....	....	....	....	....	....	....	....	....	....	....	....	....	....	....
	Springfield	AHL	46	6	16	22	51	....	....	....	....	....	....	....	....	....	....	....	3	0	0	0	6	....	....	....
99-2000	Cincinnati	IHL	15	1	3	4	14	....	....	....	....	....	....	....	....	....	....	....	....	....	....	....	....	....	....	....
	Florida Everblades	ECHL	48	14	25	39	79	....	....	....	....	....	....	....	....	....	....	....	5	2	2	4	16	....	....	....
	NHL Totals		**14**	**1**	**0**	**1**	**4**	**0**	**0**	**0**	**9**	**11.1**		....	....	....	....	....	....	....	....	....	....	....	....	....

MORISSETTE, Dave

(MOH-rih-seht, DAYV)

Left wing. Shoots left. 6'1", 224 lbs. Born, Baie Comeau, Que., December 24, 1971. Washington's 7th choice, 146th overall, in 1991 Entry Draft.

Season	Club	League	GP	G	A	Pts	PIM	PP	SH	GW	S	%	+/–	TF	F%	H	SB	Min	GP	G	A	Pts	PIM	PP	SH	GW
1987-88	Lac St-Jean	QAAA	41	11	25	36	....	....	....	....	....	....	....	....	....	....	....	....	....	....	....	....	....	....	....	....
1988-89	Shawinigan	QMJHL	66	4	11	15	298	....	....	....	....	....	....	....	....	....	....	....	....	....	....	....	....	....	....	....
1989-90	Shawinigan	QMJHL	66	2	9	11	269	....	....	....	....	....	....	....	....	....	....	....	....	....	....	....	....	....	....	....
1990-91	Shawinigan	QMJHL	64	20	26	46	224	....	....	....	....	....	....	....	....	....	....	....	6	1	1	2	17	....	....	....
1991-92	Hampton Roads	ECHL	47	6	10	16	293	....	....	....	....	....	....	....	....	....	....	....	13	1	3	4	74	....	....	....
	Baltimore	AHL	2	0	0	0	6	....	....	....	....	....	....	....	....	....	....	....	....	....	....	....	....	....	....	....
1992-93	Hampton Roads	ECHL	54	9	13	22	226	....	....	....	....	....	....	....	....	....	....	....	2	0	0	0	2	....	....	....
1993-94	Roanoke Express	ECHL	45	8	10	18	278	....	....	....	....	....	....	....	....	....	....	....	2	0	1	1	4	....	....	....
1994-95	Minnesota Moose	IHL	50	1	4	5	174	....	....	....	....	....	....	....	....	....	....	....	....	....	....	....	....	....	....	....
1995-96	Minnesota Moose	IHL	33	3	2	5	104	....	....	....	....	....	....	....	....	....	....	....	....	....	....	....	....	....	....	....
1996-97	Houston Aeros	IHL	59	2	1	3	214	....	....	....	....	....	....	....	....	....	....	....	2	0	0	0	0	....	....	....
	Austin Ice Bats	WPHL	5	2	3	5	10	....	....	....	....	....	....	....	....	....	....	....	....	....	....	....	....	....	....	....
1997-98	Houston Aeros	IHL	67	4	4	8	254	....	....	....	....	....	....	....	....	....	....	....	2	0	0	0	2	....	....	....
1998-99	**Montreal**	**NHL**	**10**	**0**	**0**	**0**	**52**	**0**	**0**	**0**	**2**	**0.0**	**1**	**0**	**0.0**	**5**	**2**	**2:13**	....	....	....	....	....	....	....	....
	Fredericton	AHL	39	4	4	8	152	....	....	....	....	....	....	....	....	....	....	....	12	0	1	1	31	....	....	....
99-2000	**Montreal**	**NHL**	**1**	**0**	**0**	**0**	**5**	**0**	**0**	**0**	**0**	**0.0**	**0**	**0**	**0.0**	**2**	**1**	**3:50**	....	....	....	....	....	....	....	....
	Quebec Citadelles	AHL	47	2	4	6	231	....	....	....	....	....	....	....	....	....	....	....	2	0	0	0	0	....	....	....
	NHL Totals		**11**	**0**	**0**	**0**	**57**	**0**	**0**	**0**	**2**	**0.0**		**0**	**0.0**	**7**	**3**	**2:22**	....	....	....	....	....	....	....	....

Signed as a free agent by **Montreal**, June 10, 1998.

MORO, Marc

(MOH-roh, MAHRK) **NSH.**

Defense. Shoots left. 6'1", 220 lbs. Born, Toronto, Ont., July 17, 1977. Ottawa's 2nd choice, 27th overall, in 1995 Entry Draft.

Season	Club	League	GP	G	A	Pts	PIM	PP	SH	GW	S	%	+/–	TF	F%	H	SB	Min	GP	G	A	Pts	PIM	PP	SH	GW
1992-93	Mississauga Reps	MTHL	42	9	18	27	56	....	....	....	....	....	....	....	....	....	....	....	....	....	....	....	....	....	....	....
	Mississauga	OJHL	2	0	0	0	0	....	....	....	....	....	....	....	....	....	....	....	....	....	....	....	....	....	....	....
1993-94	Kingston	OJHL	12	0	2	2	10	....	....	....	....	....	....	....	....	....	....	....	....	....	....	....	....	....	....	....
	Kingston	OHL	43	0	3	3	81	....	....	....	....	....	....	....	....	....	....	....	....	....	....	....	....	....	....	....
1994-95	Kingston	OHL	64	4	12	16	255	....	....	....	....	....	....	....	....	....	....	....	6	0	0	0	23	....	....	....
1995-96	Kingston	OHL	66	4	17	21	261	....	....	....	....	....	....	....	....	....	....	....	6	0	0	0	12	....	....	....
	P.E.I. Senators	AHL	2	0	0	0	7	....	....	....	....	....	....	....	....	....	....	....	2	0	0	0	4	....	....	....
1996-97	Kingston	OHL	37	4	8	12	97	....	....	....	....	....	....	....	....	....	....	....	....	....	....	....	....	....	....	....
	Sault Ste. Marie	OHL	26	0	5	5	74	....	....	....	....	....	....	....	....	....	....	....	11	1	6	7	38	....	....	....
1997-98	**Anaheim**	**NHL**	**1**	**0**	**0**	**0**	**0**	**0**	**0**	**0**	**0**	**0.0**	**0**	....	....	....	....	....	....	....	....	....	....	....	....	....
	Cincinnati Ducks	AHL	74	1	6	7	181	....	....	....	....	....	....	....	....	....	....	....	....	....	....	....	....	....	....	....
1998-99	Milwaukee	IHL	80	0	5	5	264	....	....	....	....	....	....	....	....	....	....	....	2	0	0	0	4	....	....	....
99-2000	**Nashville**	**NHL**	**8**	**0**	**0**	**0**	**40**	**0**	**0**	**0**	**3**	**0.0**	**–3**	**0**	**0.0**	**19**	**2**	**10:55**	....	....	....	....	....	....	....	....
	Milwaukee	IHL	64	5	5	10	203	....	....	....	....	....	....	....	....	....	....	....	....	....	....	....	....	....	....	....
	NHL Totals		**9**	**0**	**0**	**0**	**40**	**0**	**0**	**0**	**3**	**0.0**		**0**	**0.0**	**19**	**2**	**10:55**	....	....	....	....	....	....	....	....

Rights traded to **Anaheim** by **Ottawa** with Ted Drury for Jason York and Shaun Van Allen, October 1, 1996. Traded to **Nashville** by **Anaheim** with Chris Mason for Dominic Roussel, October 5, 1998.

MOROZOV, Aleksey (moh-ROH-zohv, ah-LEHK-see) PIT.

Right wing. Shoots left. 6'1", 196 lbs. Born, Moscow, USSR, February 16, 1977. Pittsburgh's 1st choice, 24th overall, in 1995 Entry Draft.

			Regular Season																Playoffs							
Season	Club	League	GP	G	A	Pts	PIM	PP	SH	GW	S	%	+/-	TF	F%	H	SB	Min	GP	G	A	Pts	PIM	PP	SH	GW
1993-94	Krylja Sovetov	CIS	7	0	0	0	0	....	....	....	....	....	....	....	....	....	....	....	3	0	0	0	2	....	....	....
1994-95	Krylja Sovetov	CIS	48	15	12	27	53	....	....	....	....	....	....	....	....	....	....	....	4	0	3	3	0	....	....	....
1995-96	Krylja Sovetov	CIS	47	13	9	22	26	....	....	....	....	....	....	....	....	....	....	....	....	....	....	....	....	....	....	....
1996-97	Krylja Sovetov	Russia	44	21	11	32	32	....	....	....	....	....	....	....	....	....	....	....	2	0	1	1	2	....	....	....
1997-98	Krylja Sovetov	Russia	6	2	1	3	4	....	....	....	....	....	....	....	....	....	....	....	....	....	....	....	....	....	....	....
	Pittsburgh	**NHL**	**76**	**13**	**13**	**26**	**8**	**2**	**0**	**3**	**80**	**16.3**	**-4**	....	....	....	....	....	**6**	**0**	**1**	**1**	**2**	**0**	**0**	**0**
	Russia	Olympics	6	2	2	4	0	....	....	....	....	....	....	....	....	....	....	....	....	....	....	....	....	....	....	....
1998-99	**Pittsburgh**	**NHL**	**67**	**9**	**10**	**19**	**14**	**0**	**0**	**0**	**75**	**12.0**	**5**	**7**	**42.9**	**44**	**33**	**11:50**	**10**	**1**	**1**	**2**	**0**	**0**	**0**	**0**
99-2000	**Pittsburgh**	**NHL**	**68**	**12**	**19**	**31**	**14**	**0**	**1**	**0**	**101**	**11.9**	**12**	**27**	**33.3**	**33**	**20**	**13:51**	**5**	**0**	**0**	**0**	**0**	**0**	**0**	**0**
	NHL Totals		**211**	**34**	**42**	**76**	**36**	**2**	**1**	**3**	**256**	**13.3**		**34**	**35.3**	**77**	**53**	**12:51**	**21**	**1**	**2**	**3**	**2**	**0**	**0**	**0**

CIS Rookie of the Year (1995)

MORRIS, Derek (MOH-rihs, DAIR-ihk) CGY.

Defense. Shoots right. 5'11", 200 lbs. Born, Edmonton, Alta., August 24, 1978. Calgary's 1st choice, 13th overall, in 1996 Entry Draft.

Season	Club	League	GP	G	A	Pts	PIM	PP	SH	GW	S	%	+/-	TF	F%	H	SB	Min	GP	G	A	Pts	PIM	PP	SH	GW
1994-95	Red Deer Chiefs	AAHA	31	6	35	41	74	....	....	....	....	....	....	....	....	....	....	....	....	....	....	....	....	....	....	....
1995-96	Regina Pats	WHL	67	8	44	52	70	....	....	....	....	....	....	....	....	....	....	....	11	1	7	8	26	....	....	....
1996-97	Regina Pats	WHL	67	18	57	75	180	....	....	....	....	....	....	....	....	....	....	....	5	0	3	3	9	....	....	....
	Saint John Flames	AHL	7	0	3	3	7	....	....	....	....	....	....	....	....	....	....	....	5	0	3	3	7	....	....	....
1997-98	**Calgary**	**NHL**	**82**	**9**	**20**	**29**	**88**	**5**	**1**	**1**	**120**	**7.5**	**1**	....	....	....	....	....	....	....	....	....	....	....	....	....
1998-99	**Calgary**	**NHL**	**71**	**7**	**27**	**34**	**73**	**3**	**0**	**2**	**150**	**4.7**	**4**	**0**	**0.0**	**93**	**78**	**20:44**	....	....	....	....	....	....	....	....
99-2000	**Calgary**	**NHL**	**78**	**9**	**29**	**38**	**80**	**3**	**0**	**2**	**193**	**4.7**	**2**	**0**	**0.0**	**127**	**119**	**24:51**	....	....	....	....	....	....	....	....
	NHL Totals		**231**	**25**	**76**	**101**	**241**	**11**	**1**	**5**	**463**	**5.4**		**0**	**0.0**	**220**	**197**	**22:53**	....	....	....	....	....	....	....	....

WHL East First All-Star Team (1997) • NHL All-Rookie Team (1998)

MORRISON, Brendan (MOHR-rihs-OHN, BREHN-dan) VAN.

Center. Shoots left. 5'11", 190 lbs. Born, Pitt Meadows, B.C., August 15, 1975. New Jersey's 3rd choice, 39th overall, in 1993 Entry Draft.

Season	Club	League	GP	G	A	Pts	PIM	PP	SH	GW	S	%	+/-	TF	F%	H	SB	Min	GP	G	A	Pts	PIM	PP	SH	GW
1990-91	Ridge Meadows	BCAHA	77	126	127	253	88	....	....	....	....	....	....	....	....	....	....	....	....	....	....	....	....	....	....	....
1991-92	Ridge Meadows	BCAHA	55	56	111	167	56	....	....	....	....	....	....	....	....	....	....	....	....	....	....	....	....	....	....	....
1992-93	Penticton	BCJHL	56	35	59	94	45	....	....	....	....	....	....	....	....	....	....	....	....	....	....	....	....	....	....	....
1993-94	U. of Michigan	CCHA	38	20	28	48	24	....	....	....	....	....	....	....	....	....	....	....	5	2	7	9	2	....	....	....
1994-95	U. of Michigan	CCHA	39	23	*53	*76	42	....	....	....	....	....	....	....	....	....	....	....	5	1	11	12	6	....	....	....
1995-96	U. of Michigan	CCHA	35	28	44	*72	41	....	....	....	....	....	....	....	....	....	....	....	7	6	9	15	4	....	....	....
1996-97	U. of Michigan	CCHA	43	31	*57	*88	52	....	....	....	....	....	....	....	....	....	....	....	6	6	8	14	8	....	....	....
1997-98	**New Jersey**	**NHL**	**11**	**5**	**4**	**9**	**0**	**0**	**0**	**1**	**19**	**26.3**	**3**	....	....	....	....	....	**3**	**0**	**1**	**1**	**0**	**0**	**0**	**0**
	Albany River Rats	AHL	72	35	49	84	44	....	....	....	....	....	....	....	....	....	....	....	8	3	4	7	19	....	....	....
1998-99	**New Jersey**	**NHL**	**76**	**13**	**33**	**46**	**18**	**5**	**0**	**2**	**111**	**11.7**	**-4**	**920**	**51.1**	**63**	**19**	**13:55**	**7**	**0**	**2**	**2**	**0**	**0**	**0**	**0**
99-2000	SK Trebic-2	Cze-Rep	2	0	0	0	0	....	....	....	....	....	....	....	....	....	....	....	....	....	....	....	....	....	....	....
	HC Pardubice	Cze-Rep	6	5	2	7	2	....	....	....	....	....	....	....	....	....	....	....	....	....	....	....	....	....	....	....
	New Jersey	**NHL**	**44**	**5**	**21**	**26**	**8**	**2**	**0**	**1**	**79**	**6.3**	**8**	**572**	**51.1**	**53**	**18**	**16:09**	....	....	....	....	....	....	....	....
	Vancouver	**NHL**	**12**	**2**	**7**	**9**	**10**	**0**	**0**	**0**	**17**	**11.8**	**4**	**48**	**54.2**	**11**	**3**	**14:41**	....	....	....	....	....	....	....	....
	NHL Totals		**143**	**25**	**65**	**90**	**36**	**7**	**0**	**4**	**226**	**11.1**		**1540**	**51.2**	**127**	**40**	**14:44**	**10**	**0**	**3**	**3**	**0**	**0**	**0**	**0**

CCHA First All-Star Team (1995, 1996, 1997) • NCAA West First All-American Team (1995, 1996, 1997) • NCAA Championship All-Tournament Team (1996) • NCAA Championship Tournament MVP (1996) • Won Hobey Baker Memorial Award (Top U.S. Collegiate Player) (1997)

Traded to **Vancouver** by **New Jersey** with Denis Pederson for Alexander Mogilny, March 14, 2000.

MORROW, Brenden (MOHR-rohw, BREHN-dehn) DAL.

Left wing. Shoots left. 5'11", 200 lbs. Born, Carlyle, Sask., January 16, 1979. Dallas' 1st choice, 25th overall, in 1997 Entry Draft.

Season	Club	League	GP	G	A	Pts	PIM	PP	SH	GW	S	%	+/-	TF	F%	H	SB	Min	GP	G	A	Pts	PIM	PP	SH	GW
1994-95	Estevan Bruins	SAHA	60	117	72	189	45	....	....	....	....	....	....	....	....	....	....	....	....	....	....	....	....	....	....	....
1995-96	Portland	WHL	65	13	12	25	61	....	....	....	....	....	....	....	....	....	....	....	7	0	0	0	8	....	....	....
1996-97	Portland	WHL	71	39	49	88	178	....	....	....	....	....	....	....	....	....	....	....	6	2	1	3	4	....	....	....
1997-98	Portland	WHL	68	34	52	86	184	....	....	....	....	....	....	....	....	....	....	....	16	10	8	18	65	....	....	....
1998-99	Portland	WHL	61	41	44	85	248	....	....	....	....	....	....	....	....	....	....	....	4	0	4	4	18	....	....	....
99-2000	**Dallas**	**NHL**	**64**	**14**	**19**	**33**	**81**	**3**	**0**	**3**	**113**	**12.4**	**8**	**25**	**48.0**	**170**	**24**	**15:51**	**21**	**2**	**4**	**6**	**22**	**1**	**0**	**0**
	Michigan K-Wings	IHL	9	2	0	2	18	....	....	....	....	....	....	....	....	....	....	....	....	....	....	....	....	....	....	....
	NHL Totals		**64**	**14**	**19**	**33**	**81**	**3**	**0**	**3**	**113**	**12.4**		**25**	**48.0**	**170**	**24**	**15:51**	**21**	**2**	**4**	**6**	**22**	**1**	**0**	**0**

WHL West First All-Star Team (1999)

MOWERS, Mark (MAHW-uhrs, MAHRK) NSH.

Right wing. Shoots right. 5'11", 187 lbs. Born, Whitesboro, NY, February 16, 1974.

Season	Club	League	GP	G	A	Pts	PIM	PP	SH	GW	S	%	+/-	TF	F%	H	SB	Min	GP	G	A	Pts	PIM	PP	SH	GW
1992-93	Saginaw Gears	NAJHL	39	31	39	70	....	....	....	....	....	....	....	....	....	....	....	....	....	....	....	....	....	....	....	....
1993-94	Dubuque Saints	USHL	47	51	31	82	80	....	....	....	....	....	....	....	....	....	....	....	....	....	....	....	....	....	....	....
1994-95	New Hampshire	H-East	36	13	23	36	16	....	....	....	....	....	....	....	....	....	....	....	....	....	....	....	....	....	....	....
1995-96	New Hampshire	H-East	34	21	26	47	18	....	....	....	....	....	....	....	....	....	....	....	....	....	....	....	....	....	....	....
1996-97	New Hampshire	H-East	39	26	32	58	52	....	....	....	....	....	....	....	....	....	....	....	....	....	....	....	....	....	....	....
1997-98	New Hampshire	H-East	35	25	31	56	32	....	....	....	....	....	....	....	....	....	....	....	....	....	....	....	....	....	....	....
1998-99	**Nashville**	**NHL**	**30**	**0**	**6**	**6**	**4**	**0**	**0**	**0**	**24**	**0.0**	**-4**	**241**	**49.0**	**19**	**2**	**9:22**	....	....	....	....	....	....	....	....
	Milwaukee	IHL	51	14	22	36	24	....	....	....	....	....	....	....	....	....	....	....	1	0	0	0	0	....	....	....
99-2000	**Nashville**	**NHL**	**41**	**4**	**5**	**9**	**10**	**0**	**0**	**0**	**50**	**8.0**	**0**	**312**	**45.2**	**30**	**11**	**10:58**	....	....	....	....	....	....	....	....
	Milwaukee	IHL	23	11	15	26	34	....	....	....	....	....	....	....	....	....	....	....	....	....	....	....	....	....	....	....
	NHL Totals		**71**	**4**	**11**	**15**	**14**	**0**	**0**	**0**	**74**	**5.4**		**553**	**46.8**	**49**	**13**	**10:17**	....	....	....	....	....	....	....	....

Hockey East Second All-Star Team (1998) • NCAA East First All-American Team (1998)

Signed as a free agent by **Nashville**, June 8, 1998.

MUCKALT, Bill (MUH-kawlt, BIHL) NYI

Right wing. Shoots right. 6'1", 200 lbs. Born, Surrey, B.C., July 15, 1974. Vancouver's 9th choice, 221st overall, in 1994 Entry Draft.

Season	Club	League	GP	G	A	Pts	PIM	PP	SH	GW	S	%	+/-	TF	F%	H	SB	Min	GP	G	A	Pts	PIM	PP	SH	GW
1991-92	Merritt	BCJHL	55	14	11	25	75	....	....	....	....	....	....	....	....	....	....	....	....	....	....	....	....	....	....	....
1992-93	Merritt	BCJHL	59	31	43	74	80	....	....	....	....	....	....	....	....	....	....	....	....	....	....	....	....	....	....	....
1993-94	Merritt	BCJHL	43	58	51	109	99	....	....	....	....	....	....	....	....	....	....	....	....	....	....	....	....	....	....	....
	Kelowna Spartans	BCJHL	15	12	10	22	20	....	....	....	....	....	....	....	....	....	....	....	....	....	....	....	....	....	....	....
1994-95	U. of Michigan	CCHA	39	19	18	37	42	....	....	....	....	....	....	....	....	....	....	....	5	1	1	2	6	....	....	....
1995-96	U. of Michigan	CCHA	41	28	30	58	34	....	....	....	....	....	....	....	....	....	....	....	7	5	6	11	6	....	....	....
1996-97	U. of Michigan	CCHA	36	26	38	64	69	....	....	....	....	....	....	....	....	....	....	....	6	5	9	14	2	....	....	....
1997-98	U. of Michigan	CCHA	46	32	*35	*67	94	....	....	....	....	....	....	....	....	....	....	....	....	....	....	....	....	....	....	....
1998-99	**Vancouver**	**NHL**	**73**	**16**	**20**	**36**	**98**	**4**	**2**	**1**	**119**	**13.4**	**-9**	**68**	**55.9**	**66**	**23**	**15:24**	....	....	....	....	....	....	....	....
99-2000	**Vancouver**	**NHL**	**33**	**4**	**8**	**12**	**17**	**1**	**0**	**1**	**53**	**7.5**	**6**	**6**	**50.0**	**38**	**6**	**14:34**	....	....	....	....	....	....	....	....
	NY Islanders	**NHL**	**12**	**4**	**3**	**7**	**4**	**0**	**0**	**0**	**26**	**15.4**	**5**	**8**	**50.0**	**20**	**1**	**12:23**	....	....	....	....	....	....	....	....
	NHL Totals		**118**	**24**	**31**	**55**	**119**	**5**	**2**	**2**	**198**	**12.1**		**82**	**54.9**	**124**	**30**	**14:51**	....	....	....	....	....	....	....	....

CCHA First All-Star Team (1998) • NCAA West First All-American Team (1998)

Traded to **NY Islanders** by **Vancouver** with Kevin Weekes and Dave Scatchard for Felix Potvin and NY Islanders' compensatory 2nd (later traded to New Jersey - New Jersey selected Teemu Laine) and 3rd (Thatcher Bell) round choices in 2000 Entry Draft, December 19, 1999. • Missed remainder of 1999-2000 season recovering from shoulder injury suffered in game vs. Tampa Bay, January 13, 2000.

MUIR, Bryan

(MEWR, BRIGH-an) **T.B.**

Defense. Shoots left. 6'4", 220 lbs. Born, Winnipeg, Man., June 8, 1973.

			Regular Season																Playoffs							
Season	Club	League	GP	G	A	Pts	PIM	PP	SH	GW	S	%	+/-	TF	F%	H	SB	Min	GP	G	A	Pts	PIM	PP	SH	GW
1991-92	Wexford Raiders	OJHL	44	3	19	22	35																			
1992-93	New Hampshire	H-East	26	1	2	3	24																			
1993-94	New Hampshire	H-East	40	0	4	4	48																			
1994-95	New Hampshire	H-East	28	9	9	18	46																			
1995-96	Canada	Nat-Team	42	6	12	18	38																			
	Edmonton	**NHL**	**5**	**0**	**0**	**0**	**6**	**0**	**0**	**0**	**4**	**0.0**	**-4**													
1996-97	Hamilton Bulldogs	AHL	75	8	16	24	80												14	0	5	5	12			
	Edmonton	**NHL**																	**5**	**0**	**0**	**0**	**4**	**0**	**0**	**0**
1997-98	**Edmonton**	**NHL**	**7**	**0**	**0**	**0**	**17**	**0**	**0**	**0**	**6**	**0.0**	**0**													
	Hamilton Bulldogs	AHL	28	3	10	13	62																			
	Albany River Rats	AHL	41	3	10	13	67												13	3	0	3	12			
1998-99	**New Jersey**	**NHL**	**1**	**0**	**0**	**0**	**0**	**0**	**0**	**0**	**4**	**0.0**	**0**	**0**	**0.0**	**0**	**0**	**9:54**								
	Albany River Rats	AHL	10	0	0	0	29																			
	Chicago	**NHL**	**53**	**1**	**4**	**5**	**50**	**0**	**0**	**0**	**78**	**1.3**	**1**	**0**	**0.0**	**82**	**59**	**18:49**								
	Portland Pirates	AHL	2	1	1	2	2																			
99-2000	**Chicago**	**NHL**	**11**	**2**	**3**	**5**	**13**	**0**	**1**	**0**	**19**	**10.5**	**-1**	**0**	**0.0**	**17**	**18**	**17:54**								
	Tampa Bay	**NHL**	**30**	**1**	**1**	**2**	**32**	**0**	**0**	**0**	**32**	**3.1**	**-8**	**1**	**100.0**	**41**	**28**	**19:29**								
	NHL Totals		**107**	**4**	**8**	**12**	**118**	**0**	**1**	**0**	**143**	**2.8**		**1**	**100.0**	**140**	**105**	**18:50**	**5**	**0**	**0**	**0**	**4**	**0**	**0**	**0**

Signed to five-game Amateur try-out contract by **Edmonton**, February 29, 1996. Signed as a free agent by **Edmonton**, April 30, 1996. Traded to **New Jersey** by **Edmonton** with Jason Arnott for Valeri Zelepukin and Bill Guerin, January 4, 1998. Traded to **Chicago** by **New Jersey** for Chicago's 3rd round choice (Michael Rupp) in the 2000 Entry Draft, November 13, 1998. Traded to **Tampa Bay** by **Chicago** with Reid Simpson for Michael Nylander, November 12, 1999. • Missed majority of 1999-2000 season recovering from leg injury suffered in game vs. Atlanta, November 17, 1999.

MULHERN, Ryan

(muhl-HUHRN, RIGH-yan) **WSH.**

Center. Shoots right. 6'1", 202 lbs. Born, Philadelphia, PA, January 11, 1973. Calgary's 9th choice, 174th overall, in 1992 Entry Draft.

Season	Club	League	GP	G	A	Pts	PIM	PP	SH	GW	S	%	+/-	TF	F%	H	SB	Min	GP	G	A	Pts	PIM	PP	SH	GW
1991-92	Canterbury High	Hi-School	37	51	27	78	50																			
1992-93	Brown University	ECAC	31	15	9	24	46																			
1993-94	Brown University	ECAC	27	18	17	35	48																			
1994-95	Brown University	ECAC	30	18	16	34	*108																			
1995-96	Brown University	ECAC	32	10	16	26	78																			
1996-97	Hampton Roads	ECHL	40	22	16	38	52																			
	Portland Pirates	AHL	38	19	15	34	16												5	1	1	2	2			
1997-98	**Washington**	**NHL**	**3**	**0**	**0**	**0**	**0**	**0**	**0**	**0**	**1**	**0.0**	**0**													
	Portland Pirates	AHL	71	25	40	65	85												6	1	0	1	12			
1998-99	Kansas City	IHL	59	7	11	18	82																			
	Las Vegas	IHL	23	9	6	15	8																			
99-2000	Portland Pirates	AHL	73	20	16	36	61												3	0	0	0	6			
	NHL Totals		**3**	**0**	**0**	**0**	**0**	**0**	**0**	**0**	**1**	**0.0**														

AHL First All-Star Team (1998)

Signed as a free agent by **Washington**, March 17, 1997. • Played w/ RHI's New Jersey in 1997 (22-21-9-30-29) and Philadelphia Sting 1998 (1-1-1-2-1).

MULLER, Kirk

(MUHL-luhr, KUHRK) **DAL.**

Left wing. Shoots left. 6', 205 lbs. Born, Kingston, Ont., February 8, 1966. New Jersey's 1st choice, 2nd overall, in 1984 Entry Draft.

Season	Club	League	GP	G	A	Pts	PIM	PP	SH	GW	S	%	+/-	TF	F%	H	SB	Min	GP	G	A	Pts	PIM	PP	SH	GW
1980-81	Kingston	OHA-B	42	17	37	54	5																			
	Kingston	OMJHL	2	0	0	0	0																			
1981-82	Kingston	OHL	67	12	39	51	27												4	5	1	6	4			
1982-83	Guelph Platers	OHL	66	52	60	112	41																			
1983-84	Guelph Platers	OHL	49	31	63	94	27																			
	Canada	Nat-Team	15	2	2	4	16																			
	Canada	Olympics	6	2	1	3	0																			
1984-85	**New Jersey**	**NHL**	**80**	**17**	**37**	**54**	**69**	**9**	**1**	**0**	**157**	**10.8**	**-31**													
1985-86	**New Jersey**	**NHL**	**77**	**25**	**41**	**66**	**45**	**5**	**1**	**1**	**168**	**14.9**	**-20**													
1986-87	**New Jersey**	**NHL**	**79**	**26**	**50**	**76**	**75**	**10**	**1**	**4**	**193**	**13.5**	**-7**													
1987-88	**New Jersey**	**NHL**	**80**	**37**	**57**	**94**	**114**	**17**	**2**	**1**	**215**	**17.2**	**19**						**20**	**4**	**8**	**12**	**37**	**0**	**0**	**0**
1988-89	**New Jersey**	**NHL**	**80**	**31**	**43**	**74**	**119**	**12**	**1**	**4**	**182**	**17.0**	**-23**													
1989-90	**New Jersey**	**NHL**	**80**	**30**	**56**	**86**	**74**	**9**	**0**	**6**	**200**	**15.0**	**-1**						**6**	**1**	**3**	**4**	**11**	**0**	**0**	**0**
1990-91	**New Jersey**	**NHL**	**80**	**19**	**51**	**70**	**76**	**7**	**0**	**3**	**221**	**8.6**	**1**						**7**	**0**	**2**	**2**	**10**	**0**	**0**	**0**
1991-92	**Montreal**	**NHL**	**78**	**36**	**41**	**77**	**86**	**15**	**1**	**7**	**191**	**18.8**	**15**						**11**	**4**	**3**	**7**	**31**	**2**	**1**	**1**
1992-93♦	**Montreal**	**NHL**	**80**	**37**	**57**	**94**	**77**	**12**	**0**	**4**	**231**	**16.0**	**8**						**20**	**10**	**7**	**17**	**18**	**3**	**0**	**3**
1993-94	**Montreal**	**NHL**	**76**	**23**	**34**	**57**	**96**	**9**	**2**	**3**	**168**	**13.7**	**-1**						**7**	**6**	**2**	**8**	**4**	**3**	**0**	**2**
1994-95	**Montreal**	**NHL**	**33**	**8**	**11**	**19**	**33**	**3**	**0**	**1**	**81**	**9.9**	**-21**													
	NY Islanders	**NHL**	**12**	**3**	**5**	**8**	**14**	**1**	**1**	**1**	**16**	**18.8**	**3**													
1995-96	**NY Islanders**	**NHL**	**15**	**4**	**3**	**7**	**15**	**0**	**0**	**0**	**23**	**17.4**	**-10**													
	Toronto	**NHL**	**36**	**9**	**16**	**25**	**42**	**7**	**0**	**1**	**79**	**11.4**	**-3**						**6**	**3**	**2**	**5**	**0**	**2**	**0**	**0**
1996-97	**Toronto**	**NHL**	**66**	**20**	**17**	**37**	**85**	**9**	**1**	**3**	**153**	**13.1**	**-23**													
	Florida	**NHL**	**10**	**1**	**2**	**3**	**4**	**1**	**0**	**1**	**21**	**4.8**	**-2**						**5**	**1**	**2**	**3**	**4**	**1**	**0**	**0**
1997-98	**Florida**	**NHL**	**70**	**8**	**21**	**29**	**54**	**1**	**0**	**3**	**115**	**7.0**	**-14**													
1998-99	**Florida**	**NHL**	**82**	**4**	**11**	**15**	**49**	**0**	**0**	**1**	**107**	**3.7**	**-11**	**1157**	**49.1**	**68**	**39**	**14:28**								
99-2000	**Dallas**	**NHL**	**47**	**7**	**15**	**22**	**24**	**3**	**0**	**2**	**57**	**12.3**	**-3**	**443**	**48.5**	**77**	**19**	**16:24**	**23**	**2**	**3**	**5**	**18**	**0**	**0**	**1**
	NHL Totals		**1161**	**345**	**568**	**913**	**1151**	**130**	**11**	**46**	**2578**	**13.4**		**1600**	**48.9**	**145**	**58**	**15:10**	**105**	**31**	**32**	**63**	**133**	**11**	**1**	**7**

Played in NHL All-Star Game (1985, 1986, 1988, 1990, 1992, 1993)

Traded to **Montreal** by **New Jersey** with Rollie Melanson for Stephane Richer and Tom Chorske, September 20, 1991. Traded to **NY Islanders** by **Montreal** with Mathieu Schneider and Craig Darby for Pierre Turgeon and Vladimir Malakhov, April 5, 1995. Traded to **Toronto** by **NY Islanders** with Don Beaupre to complete transaction that sent Damian Rhodes and Ken Belanger to NY Islanders (January 23, 1996), January 23, 1996. Traded to **Florida** by **Toronto** for Jason Podollan, March 18, 1997. Signed as a free agent by **Dallas**, December 15, 1999.

MURPHY, Gord

(MUHR-fee, GOHRD) **ATL.**

Defense. Shoots right. 6'2", 195 lbs. Born, Willowdale, Ont., March 23, 1967. Philadelphia's 10th choice, 189th overall, in 1985 Entry Draft.

Season	Club	League	GP	G	A	Pts	PIM	PP	SH	GW	S	%	+/-	TF	F%	H	SB	Min	GP	G	A	Pts	PIM	PP	SH	GW
1983-84	Don Mills Flyers	MTHL	65	24	42	66	130																			
1984-85	Oshawa Generals	OHL	59	3	12	15	25																			
1985-86	Oshawa Generals	OHL	64	7	15	22	56												6	1	1	2	6			
1986-87	Oshawa Generals	OHL	56	7	30	37	95												24	6	16	22	22			
1987-88	Hershey Bears	AHL	62	8	20	28	44												12	0	8	8	12			
1988-89	**Philadelphia**	**NHL**	**75**	**4**	**31**	**35**	**68**	**3**	**0**	**1**	**116**	**3.4**	**-3**						**19**	**2**	**7**	**9**	**13**	**1**	**0**	**1**
1989-90	**Philadelphia**	**NHL**	**75**	**14**	**27**	**41**	**95**	**4**	**0**	**1**	**160**	**8.8**	**-7**													
1990-91	**Philadelphia**	**NHL**	**80**	**11**	**31**	**42**	**58**	**6**	**0**	**2**	**203**	**5.4**	**-7**													
1991-92	**Philadelphia**	**NHL**	**31**	**2**	**8**	**10**	**33**	**0**	**0**	**0**	**50**	**4.0**	**-4**													
	Boston	**NHL**	**42**	**3**	**6**	**9**	**51**	**0**	**0**	**0**	**82**	**3.7**	**2**						**15**	**1**	**0**	**1**	**12**	**0**	**0**	**0**
1992-93	**Boston**	**NHL**	**49**	**5**	**12**	**17**	**62**	**3**	**0**	**2**	**68**	**7.4**	**-13**													
	Providence Bruins	AHL	2	1	3	4	2																			
1993-94	**Florida**	**NHL**	**84**	**14**	**29**	**43**	**71**	**9**	**0**	**2**	**172**	**8.1**	**-11**													
1994-95	**Florida**	**NHL**	**46**	**6**	**16**	**22**	**24**	**5**	**0**	**0**	**94**	**6.4**	**-14**													
1995-96	**Florida**	**NHL**	**70**	**8**	**22**	**30**	**30**	**4**	**0**	**0**	**125**	**6.4**	**5**						**14**	**0**	**4**	**4**	**6**	**0**	**0**	**0**
1996-97	**Florida**	**NHL**	**80**	**8**	**15**	**23**	**51**	**2**	**0**	**0**	**137**	**5.8**	**3**						**5**	**0**	**5**	**5**	**4**	**0**	**0**	**0**
1997-98	**Florida**	**NHL**	**79**	**6**	**11**	**17**	**46**	**3**	**0**	**0**	**123**	**4.9**	**-3**													
1998-99	**Florida**	**NHL**	**51**	**0**	**7**	**7**	**16**	**0**	**0**	**0**	**56**	**0.0**	**4**	**1**	**0.0**	**44**	**58**	**19:57**								
99-2000	**Atlanta**	**NHL**	**58**	**1**	**10**	**11**	**38**	**0**	**0**	**0**	**74**	**1.4**	**-26**	**0**	**0.0**	**96**	**132**	**22:41**								
	NHL Totals		**820**	**82**	**225**	**307**	**643**	**39**	**0**	**8**	**1460**	**5.6**		**1**	**0.0**	**140**	**190**	**21:24**	**53**	**3**	**16**	**19**	**35**	**1**	**0**	**1**

Traded to **Boston** by **Philadelphia** with Brian Dobbin, Philadelphia's 3rd round choice (Sergei Zholtok) in 1992 Entry Draft and 4th round choice (Charles Paquette) in 1993 Entry Draft, for Garry Galley, Wes Walz and Boston's 3rd round choice (Milos Holan) in 1993 Entry Draft, January 2, 1992. Traded to **Dallas** by **Boston** for future considerations (Jon Casey to Boston for Andy Moog, June 25, 1993), June 20, 1993. Claimed by **Florida** from **Dallas** in Expansion Draft, June 24, 1993. Traded to **Atlanta** by **Florida** with Herbert Vasiljevs, Daniel Tjarnqvist and Ottawa's 6th round choice (previously acquired, later traded to Dallas - Dallas selected Justin Cox) in 1999 Entry Draft for Trevor Kidd, June 25, 1999.

			Regular Season																Playoffs							
Season	Club	League	GP	G	A	Pts	PIM	PP	SH	GW	S	%	+/-	TF	F%	H	SB	Min	GP	G	A	Pts	PIM	PP	SH	GW

MURPHY, Joe

(MUHR-fee, JOH) **WSH.**

Right wing. Shoots left. 6', 190 lbs. Born, London, Ont., October 16, 1967. Detroit's 1st choice, 1st overall, in 1986 Entry Draft.

Season	Club	League	GP	G	A	Pts	PIM	PP	SH	GW	S	%	+/-	TF	F%	H	SB	Min	GP	G	A	Pts	PIM	PP	SH	GW
1984-85	Penticton	BCJHL	51	68	84	*152	92	....	....	....	....	....	....	....	....	....	....	....	....	....	....	....	....	....	....	....
1985-86	Michigan State	CCHA	35	24	37	61	50	....	....	....	....	....	....	....	....	....	....	....	....	....	....	....	....	....	....	....
	Canada	Nat-Team	8	3	3	6	2	....	....	....	....	....	....	....	....	....	....	....	....	....	....	....	....	....	....	....
1986-87	**Detroit**	**NHL**	**5**	**0**	**1**	**1**	**2**	**0**	**0**	**0**	**3**	**0.0**	**0**	....	....	....	....	....	....	....	....	....	....	....	....	....
	Adirondack	AHL	71	21	38	59	61	....	....	....	....	....	....	....	....	....	....	....	10	2	1	3	33	....	....	....
1987-88	**Detroit**	**NHL**	**50**	**10**	**9**	**19**	**37**	**1**	**0**	**2**	**82**	**12.2**	**–4**	....	....	....	....	....	**8**	**0**	**1**	**1**	**6**	**0**	**0**	**0**
	Adirondack	AHL	6	5	6	11	4	....	....	....	....	....	....	....	....	....	....	....	....	....	....	....	....	....	....	....
1988-89	**Detroit**	**NHL**	**26**	**1**	**7**	**8**	**28**	**0**	**0**	**0**	**29**	**3.4**	**–7**	....	....	....	....	....	....	....	....	....	....	....	....	....
	Adirondack	AHL	47	31	35	66	66	....	....	....	....	....	....	....	....	....	....	....	16	6	11	17	17	....	....	....
1989-90	**Detroit**	**NHL**	**9**	**3**	**1**	**4**	**4**	**0**	**0**	**1**	**16**	**18.8**	**4**	....	....	....	....	....	....	....	....	....	....	....	....	....
	♦ Edmonton	**NHL**	**62**	**7**	**18**	**25**	**56**	**2**	**0**	**0**	**101**	**6.9**	**1**	....	....	....	....	....	**22**	**6**	**8**	**14**	**16**	**0**	**0**	**2**
1990-91	**Edmonton**	**NHL**	**80**	**27**	**35**	**62**	**35**	**4**	**1**	**4**	**141**	**19.1**	**2**	....	....	....	....	....	**15**	**2**	**5**	**7**	**14**	**1**	**0**	**1**
1991-92	**Edmonton**	**NHL**	**80**	**35**	**47**	**82**	**52**	**10**	**2**	**2**	**193**	**18.1**	**17**	....	....	....	....	....	**16**	**8**	**16**	**24**	**12**	**4**	**0**	**2**
1992-93	**Chicago**	**NHL**	**19**	**7**	**10**	**17**	**18**	**5**	**0**	**1**	**43**	**16.3**	**–3**	....	....	....	....	....	**4**	**0**	**0**	**0**	**8**	**0**	**0**	**0**
1993-94	**Chicago**	**NHL**	**81**	**31**	**39**	**70**	**111**	**7**	**4**	**4**	**222**	**14.0**	**1**	....	....	....	....	....	**6**	**1**	**3**	**4**	**25**	**0**	**0**	**0**
1994-95	**Chicago**	**NHL**	**40**	**23**	**18**	**41**	**89**	**7**	**0**	**3**	**120**	**19.2**	**7**	....	....	....	....	....	**16**	**9**	**3**	**12**	**29**	**3**	**0**	**3**
1995-96	**Chicago**	**NHL**	**70**	**22**	**29**	**51**	**86**	**8**	**0**	**3**	**212**	**10.4**	**–3**	....	....	....	....	....	**10**	**6**	**2**	**8**	**33**	**0**	**0**	**2**
1996-97	**St. Louis**	**NHL**	**75**	**20**	**25**	**45**	**69**	**4**	**1**	**2**	**151**	**13.2**	**–1**	....	....	....	....	....	**6**	**1**	**1**	**2**	**10**	**1**	**0**	**0**
1997-98	**St. Louis**	**NHL**	**27**	**4**	**9**	**13**	**22**	**2**	**0**	**0**	**52**	**7.7**	**8**	....	....	....	....	....	....	....	....	....	....	....	....	....
	San Jose	**NHL**	**10**	**5**	**4**	**9**	**14**	**2**	**0**	**0**	**29**	**17.2**	**1**	....	....	....	....	....	**6**	**1**	**1**	**2**	**20**	**1**	**0**	**0**
1998-99	**San Jose**	**NHL**	**76**	**25**	**23**	**48**	**73**	**7**	**0**	**2**	**176**	**14.2**	**10**	**15**	**40.0**	**29**	**9**	**14:45**	**6**	**0**	**3**	**3**	**4**	**0**	**0**	**0**
99-2000	**Boston**	**NHL**	**26**	**7**	**7**	**14**	**41**	**3**	**0**	**0**	**68**	**10.3**	**–7**	**2**	**50.0**	**39**	**5**	**15:13**	....	....	....	....	....	....	....	....
	Washington	**NHL**	**29**	**5**	**8**	**13**	**53**	**1**	**0**	**2**	**50**	**10.0**	**8**	**3**	**0.0**	**29**	**9**	**14:27**	**5**	**0**	**0**	**0**	**8**	**0**	**0**	**0**
	NHL Totals		**765**	**232**	**290**	**522**	**790**	**63**	**8**	**26**	**1688**	**13.7**		**20**	**35.0**	**97**	**23**	**14:47**	**120**	**34**	**43**	**77**	**185**	**10**	**0**	**10**

Traded to **Edmonton** by **Detroit** with Petr Klima, Adam Graves and Jeff Sharples for Jimmy Carson, Kevin McClelland and Edmonton's 5th round choice (later traded to Montreal - Montreal selected Brad Layzell) in 1991 Entry Draft, November 2, 1989. • Missed majority of 1992-93 season after failing to come to contract terms with Edmonton Oilers. Traded to **Chicago** by **Edmonton** for Igor Kravchuk and Dean McAmmond, February 24, 1993. Signed as a free agent by **St. Louis**, July 8, 1996. Traded to **San Jose** by **St. Louis** for Todd Gill, March 24, 1998. Signed as a free agent by **Boston**, November 12, 1999. Claimed on waivers by **Washington** from **Boston**, February 10, 2000.

MURPHY, Larry

(MUHR-fee, LAIR-ree) **DET.**

Defense. Shoots right. 6'2", 210 lbs. Born, Scarborough, Ont., March 8, 1961. Los Angeles' 1st choice, 4th overall, in 1980 Entry Draft.

Season	Club	League	GP	G	A	Pts	PIM	PP	SH	GW	S	%	+/-	TF	F%	H	SB	Min	GP	G	A	Pts	PIM	PP	SH	GW
1977-78	Toronto Nats	OHA-B	36	10	20	30	25	....	....	....	....	....	....	....	....	....	....	....	....	....	....	....	....	....	....	....
1978-79	Peterborough	OMJHL	66	6	21	27	82	....	....	....	....	....	....	....	....	....	....	....	19	1	9	10	42	....	....	....
1979-80	Peterborough	OMJHL	68	21	68	89	88	....	....	....	....	....	....	....	....	....	....	....	14	4	13	17	20	....	....	....
1980-81	**Los Angeles**	**NHL**	**80**	**16**	**60**	**76**	**79**	**5**	**1**	**1**	**153**	**10.5**	**17**	....	....	....	....	....	**4**	**3**	**0**	**3**	**2**	**1**	**0**	**0**
1981-82	**Los Angeles**	**NHL**	**79**	**22**	**44**	**66**	**95**	**8**	**1**	**2**	**191**	**11.5**	**–13**	....	....	....	....	....	**10**	**2**	**8**	**10**	**12**	**1**	**0**	**0**
1982-83	**Los Angeles**	**NHL**	**77**	**14**	**48**	**62**	**81**	**9**	**0**	**2**	**172**	**8.1**	**2**	....	....	....	....	....	....	....	....	....	....	....	....	....
1983-84	**Los Angeles**	**NHL**	**6**	**0**	**3**	**3**	**0**	**0**	**0**	**0**	**11**	**0.0**	**–4**	....	....	....	....	....	....	....	....	....	....	....	....	....
	Washington	**NHL**	**72**	**13**	**33**	**46**	**50**	**2**	**0**	**2**	**138**	**9.4**	**12**	....	....	....	....	....	**8**	**0**	**3**	**3**	**6**	**0**	**0**	**0**
1984-85	**Washington**	**NHL**	**79**	**13**	**42**	**55**	**51**	**3**	**0**	**0**	**153**	**8.5**	**21**	....	....	....	....	....	**5**	**2**	**3**	**5**	**0**	**2**	**0**	**0**
1985-86	**Washington**	**NHL**	**78**	**21**	**44**	**65**	**50**	**8**	**1**	**2**	**180**	**11.7**	**2**	....	....	....	....	....	**9**	**1**	**5**	**6**	**6**	**1**	**0**	**0**
1986-87	**Washington**	**NHL**	**80**	**23**	**58**	**81**	**39**	**8**	**0**	**4**	**226**	**10.2**	**25**	....	....	....	....	....	**7**	**2**	**2**	**4**	**6**	**0**	**0**	**1**
1987-88	**Washington**	**NHL**	**79**	**8**	**53**	**61**	**72**	**7**	**0**	**1**	**201**	**4.0**	**2**	....	....	....	....	....	**13**	**4**	**4**	**8**	**33**	**2**	**0**	**1**
1988-89	**Washington**	**NHL**	**65**	**7**	**29**	**36**	**70**	**3**	**0**	**0**	**129**	**5.4**	**–5**	....	....	....	....	....	....	....	....	....	....	....	....	....
	Minnesota	**NHL**	**13**	**4**	**6**	**10**	**12**	**3**	**0**	**1**	**31**	**12.9**	**5**	....	....	....	....	....	**5**	**0**	**2**	**2**	**8**	**0**	**0**	**0**
1989-90	**Minnesota**	**NHL**	**77**	**10**	**58**	**68**	**44**	**4**	**0**	**1**	**173**	**5.8**	**–13**	....	....	....	....	....	**7**	**1**	**2**	**3**	**31**	**0**	**0**	**1**
1990-91	**Minnesota**	**NHL**	**31**	**4**	**11**	**15**	**38**	**1**	**0**	**2**	**103**	**3.9**	**–8**	....	....	....	....	....	....	....	....	....	....	....	....	....
	♦ Pittsburgh	**NHL**	**44**	**5**	**23**	**28**	**30**	**2**	**0**	**0**	**85**	**5.9**	**2**	....	....	....	....	....	**23**	**5**	**18**	**23**	**44**	**4**	**0**	**0**
1991-92♦	**Pittsburgh**	**NHL**	**77**	**21**	**56**	**77**	**48**	**7**	**2**	**3**	**206**	**10.2**	**33**	....	....	....	....	....	**21**	**6**	**10**	**16**	**19**	**3**	**0**	**1**
1992-93	**Pittsburgh**	**NHL**	**83**	**22**	**63**	**85**	**73**	**6**	**2**	**2**	**230**	**9.6**	**45**	....	....	....	....	....	**12**	**2**	**11**	**13**	**10**	**2**	**0**	**1**
1993-94	**Pittsburgh**	**NHL**	**84**	**17**	**56**	**73**	**44**	**7**	**0**	**4**	**236**	**7.2**	**10**	....	....	....	....	....	**6**	**0**	**5**	**5**	**0**	**0**	**0**	**0**
1994-95	**Pittsburgh**	**NHL**	**48**	**13**	**25**	**38**	**18**	**4**	**0**	**3**	**124**	**10.5**	**12**	....	....	....	....	....	**12**	**2**	**13**	**15**	**0**	**1**	**0**	**0**
1995-96	**Toronto**	**NHL**	**82**	**12**	**49**	**61**	**34**	**8**	**0**	**1**	**182**	**6.6**	**–2**	....	....	....	....	....	**6**	**0**	**2**	**2**	**4**	**0**	**0**	**0**
1996-97	**Toronto**	**NHL**	**69**	**7**	**32**	**39**	**20**	**4**	**0**	**0**	**137**	**5.1**	**1**	....	....	....	....	....	....	....	....	....	....	....	....	....
	♦ Detroit	**NHL**	**12**	**2**	**4**	**6**	**0**	**1**	**0**	**1**	**21**	**9.5**	**2**	....	....	....	....	....	**20**	**2**	**9**	**11**	**8**	**1**	**0**	**1**
1997-98♦	**Detroit**	**NHL**	**82**	**11**	**41**	**52**	**37**	**2**	**1**	**2**	**129**	**8.5**	**35**	....	....	....	....	....	**22**	**3**	**12**	**15**	**2**	**1**	**2**	**1**
1998-99	**Detroit**	**NHL**	**80**	**10**	**42**	**52**	**42**	**5**	**1**	**2**	**168**	**6.0**	**21**	**0**	**0.0**	**36**	**100**	**24:15**	**10**	**0**	**2**	**2**	**8**	**0**	**0**	**0**
99-2000	**Detroit**	**NHL**	**81**	**10**	**30**	**40**	**45**	**7**	**0**	**0**	**146**	**6.8**	**4**	**1**	**100.0**	**38**	**92**	**21:50**	**9**	**2**	**3**	**5**	**2**	**1**	**1**	**0**
	NHL Totals		**1558**	**285**	**910**	**1195**	**1072**	**114**	**9**	**36**	**3525**	**8.1**		**1**	**100.0**	**74**	**192**	**23:02**	**209**	**37**	**114**	**151**	**201**	**20**	**3**	**7**

OMJHL First All-Star Team (1980) • NHL Second All-Star Team (1987, 1993, 1995) • Played in NHL All-Star Game (1994, 1996, 1999)

Traded to **Washington** by **LA Kings** for Ken Houston and Brian Engblom, October 18, 1983. Traded to **Minnesota** by **Washington** with Mike Gartner for Dino Ciccarelli and Bob Rouse, March 7, 1989. Traded to **Pittsburgh** by **Minnesota** with Peter Taglianetti for Chris Dahlquist and Jim Johnson, December 11, 1990. Traded to **Toronto** by **Pittsburgh** for Dmitri Mironov and Toronto's 2nd round choice (later traded to New Jersey - New Jersey selected Joshua Dewolf) in 1996 Entry Draft, July 8, 1995. Traded to **Detroit** by **Toronto** for future considerations, March 18, 1997.

MURRAY, Chris

(MUHR-ray, KRIHS) **ST.L.**

Right wing. Shoots right. 6'2", 209 lbs. Born, Port Hardy, B.C., October 25, 1974. Montreal's 3rd choice, 54th overall, in 1994 Entry Draft.

Season	Club	League	GP	G	A	Pts	PIM	PP	SH	GW	S	%	+/-	TF	F%	H	SB	Min	GP	G	A	Pts	PIM	PP	SH	GW
1990-91	Bellingham	BCJHL	54	5	8	13	150	....	....	....	....	....	....	....	....	....	....	....	....	....	....	....	....	....	....	....
1991-92	Kamloops Blazers	WHL	33	1	1	2	218	....	....	....	....	....	....	....	....	....	....	....	5	0	0	0	10	....	....	....
1992-93	Kamloops Blazers	WHL	62	6	10	16	217	....	....	....	....	....	....	....	....	....	....	....	13	0	4	4	34	....	....	....
1993-94	Kamloops Blazers	WHL	59	14	16	30	260	....	....	....	....	....	....	....	....	....	....	....	15	4	2	6	*107	....	....	....
1994-95	**Montreal**	**NHL**	**3**	**0**	**0**	**0**	**4**	**0**	**0**	**0**	**0**	**0.0**	**0**	....	....	....	....	....	....	....	....	....	....	....	....	....
	Fredericton	AHL	55	6	12	18	234	....	....	....	....	....	....	....	....	....	....	....	12	1	1	2	50	....	....	....
1995-96	**Montreal**	**NHL**	**48**	**3**	**4**	**7**	**163**	**0**	**0**	**1**	**32**	**9.4**	**5**	....	....	....	....	....	**4**	**0**	**0**	**0**	**4**	**0**	**0**	**0**
	Fredericton	AHL	30	13	13	26	217	....	....	....	....	....	....	....	....	....	....	....	....	....	....	....	....	....	....	....
1996-97	**Montreal**	**NHL**	**56**	**4**	**2**	**6**	**114**	**0**	**0**	**0**	**32**	**12.5**	**–8**	....	....	....	....	....	....	....	....	....	....	....	....	....
	Hartford	**NHL**	**8**	**1**	**1**	**2**	**10**	**0**	**0**	**0**	**9**	**11.1**	**1**	....	....	....	....	....	....	....	....	....	....	....	....	....
1997-98	**Carolina**	**NHL**	**7**	**0**	**1**	**1**	**22**	**0**	**0**	**0**	**3**	**0.0**	**2**	....	....	....	....	....	....	....	....	....	....	....	....	....
	Ottawa	**NHL**	**46**	**5**	**3**	**8**	**96**	**0**	**0**	**2**	**48**	**10.4**	**1**	....	....	....	....	....	**11**	**1**	**0**	**1**	**8**	**0**	**0**	**0**
1998-99	**Ottawa**	**NHL**	**38**	**1**	**6**	**7**	**65**	**0**	**0**	**0**	**33**	**3.0**	**–2**	**1**	**100.0**	**30**	**5**	**7:06**	....	....	....	....	....	....	....	....
	Chicago	**NHL**	**4**	**0**	**0**	**0**	**14**	**0**	**0**	**0**	**4**	**0.0**	**0**	**1**	**100.0**	**3**	**0**	**7:20**	....	....	....	....	....	....	....	....
99-2000	**Dallas**	**NHL**	**32**	**2**	**1**	**3**	**62**	**0**	**0**	**0**	**25**	**8.0**	**–7**	**0**	**0.0**	**25**	**2**	**5:19**	....	....	....	....	....	....	....	....
	Michigan K-Wings	IHL	31	5	2	7	78	....	....	....	....	....	....	....	....	....	....	....	....	....	....	....	....	....	....	....
	NHL Totals		**242**	**16**	**18**	**34**	**550**	**0**	**0**	**3**	**186**	**8.6**		**2**	**100.0**	**58**	**7**	**6:20**	**15**	**1**	**0**	**1**	**12**	**0**	**0**	**0**

Traded to **Phoenix** by **Montreal** with Murray Baron for Dave Manson, March 18, 1997. Traded to **Hartford** by **Phoenix** for Gerald Diduck, March 18, 1997. Transferred to **Carolina** after **Hartford** franchise relocated, June 25, 1997. Traded to **Ottawa** by **Carolina** for Sean Hill, November 18, 1997. Traded to **Chicago** by **Ottawa** for Nelson Emerson, March 23, 1999. Claimed by **Dallas** from **Chicago** in Waiver Draft, September 30, 1999. Signed as a free agent by **St. Louis**, July 27, 2000.

MURRAY, Glen

(MUHR-ray, GLEHN) **L.A.**

Right wing. Shoots right. 6'3", 225 lbs. Born, Halifax, N.S., November 1, 1972. Boston's 1st choice, 18th overall, in 1991 Entry Draft.

Season	Club	League	GP	G	A	Pts	PIM	PP	SH	GW	S	%	+/-	TF	F%	H	SB	Min	GP	G	A	Pts	PIM	PP	SH	GW
1988-89	Bridgewater	NSAHA	45	50	56	106	62	....	....	....	....	....	....	....	....	....	....	....	....	....	....	....	....	....	....	....
1989-90	Sudbury Wolves	OHL	62	8	28	36	17	....	....	....	....	....	....	....	....	....	....	....	7	0	0	0	4	....	....	....
1990-91	Sudbury Wolves	OHL	66	27	38	65	82	....	....	....	....	....	....	....	....	....	....	....	5	8	4	12	10	....	....	....
1991-92	Sudbury Wolves	OHL	54	37	47	84	93	....	....	....	....	....	....	....	....	....	....	....	11	7	4	11	18	....	....	....
	Boston	**NHL**	**5**	**3**	**1**	**4**	**0**	**1**	**0**	**0**	**20**	**15.0**	**2**	....	....	....	....	....	**15**	**4**	**2**	**6**	**10**	**1**	**0**	**0**
1992-93	**Boston**	**NHL**	**27**	**3**	**4**	**7**	**8**	**2**	**0**	**1**	**28**	**10.7**	**–6**	....	....	....	....	....	....	....	....	....	....	....	....	....
	Providence Bruins	AHL	48	30	26	56	42	....	....	....	....	....	....	....	....	....	....	....	6	1	4	5	4	....	....	....
1993-94	**Boston**	**NHL**	**81**	**18**	**13**	**31**	**48**	**0**	**0**	**4**	**114**	**15.8**	**–1**	....	....	....	....	....	**13**	**4**	**5**	**9**	**14**	**0**	**0**	**0**
1994-95	**Boston**	**NHL**	**35**	**5**	**2**	**7**	**46**	**0**	**0**	**2**	**64**	**7.8**	**–11**	....	....	....	....	....	**2**	**0**	**0**	**0**	**2**	**0**	**0**	**0**
1995-96	**Pittsburgh**	**NHL**	**69**	**14**	**15**	**29**	**57**	**0**	**0**	**2**	**100**	**14.0**	**4**	....	....	....	....	....	**18**	**2**	**6**	**8**	**10**	**0**	**0**	**1**
1996-97	**Pittsburgh**	**NHL**	**66**	**11**	**11**	**22**	**24**	**3**	**0**	**1**	**127**	**8.7**	**–19**	....	....	....	....	....	....	....	....	....	....	....	....	....
	Los Angeles	**NHL**	**11**	**5**	**3**	**8**	**8**	**0**	**0**	**0**	**26**	**19.2**	**–2**	....	....	....	....	....	....	....	....	....	....	....	....	....
1997-98	**Los Angeles**	**NHL**	**81**	**29**	**31**	**60**	**54**	**7**	**3**	**7**	**193**	**15.0**	**6**	....	....	....	....	....	**4**	**2**	**0**	**2**	**6**	**0**	**0**	**0**

			Regular Season																Playoffs							
Season	Club	League	GP	G	A	Pts	PIM	PP	SH	GW	S	%	+/–	TF	F%	H	SB	Min	GP	G	A	Pts	PIM	PP	SH	GW
1998-99	**Los Angeles**	**NHL**	**61**	**16**	**15**	**31**	**36**	**3**	**3**	**3**	**173**	**9.2**	**–14**	**12**	**25.0**	**63**	**15**	**20:33**	....	....	....	....	....	....	....	....
99-2000	**Los Angeles**	**NHL**	**78**	**29**	**33**	**62**	**60**	**10**	**1**	**2**	**202**	**14.4**	**13**	**15**	**80.0**	**85**	**24**	**18:30**	**4**	**0**	**0**	**0**	**2**	**0**	**0**	**0**
	NHL Totals		**514**	**133**	**128**	**261**	**341**	**26**	**7**	**22**	**1047**	**12.7**		**27**	**55.6**	**148**	**39**	**19:24**	**56**	**12**	**13**	**25**	**44**	**1**	**0**	**1**

Traded to **Pittsburgh** by **Boston** with Bryan Smolinski and Boston's 3rd round choice (Boyd Kane) in 1996 Entry Draft for Kevin Stevens and Shawn McEachern, August 2, 1995. Traded to **LA Kings** by **Pittsburgh** for Ed Olczyk, March 18, 1997.

MURRAY, Marty

(MUHR-ray, MAHR-tee) **CGY.**

Center. Shoots left. 5'9", 178 lbs. Born, Deloraine, Man., February 16, 1975. Calgary's 5th choice, 96th overall, in 1993 Entry Draft.

Season	Club	League	GP	G	A	Pts	PIM	PP	SH	GW	S	%	+/–	TF	F%	H	SB	Min	GP	G	A	Pts	PIM	PP	SH	GW
1990-91	S-W Cougars	MAHA	36	46	47	93	50	....	....	....	....	....	....	....	....	....	....	....	....	....	....	....	....	....	....	....
1991-92	Brandon	WHL	68	20	36	56	22	....	....	....	....	....	....	....	....	....	....	....	....	....	....	....	....	....	....	....
1992-93	Brandon	WHL	67	29	65	94	50	....	....	....	....	....	....	....	....	....	....	....	4	1	3	4	0	....	....	....
1993-94	Brandon	WHL	64	43	71	114	33	....	....	....	....	....	....	....	....	....	....	....	14	6	14	20	14	....	....	....
1994-95	Brandon	WHL	65	40	*88	128	53	....	....	....	....	....	....	....	....	....	....	....	18	9	*20	29	16	....	....	....
1995-96	**Calgary**	**NHL**	**15**	**3**	**3**	**6**	**0**	**2**	**0**	**0**	**22**	**13.6**	**–4**	....	....	....	....	....	....	....	....	....	....	....	....	....
	Saint John Flames	AHL	58	25	31	56	20	....	....	....	....	....	....	....	....	....	....	....	14	2	4	6	4	....	....	....
1996-97	**Calgary**	**NHL**	**2**	**0**	**0**	**0**	**4**	**0**	**0**	**0**	**2**	**0.0**	**0**	....	....	....	....	....	....	....	....	....	....	....	....	....
	Saint John Flames	AHL	67	19	39	58	40	....	....	....	....	....	....	....	....	....	....	....	5	2	3	5	4	....	....	....
1997-98	**Calgary**	**NHL**	**2**	**0**	**0**	**0**	**2**	**0**	**0**	**0**	**2**	**0.0**	**1**	....	....	....	....	....	....	....	....	....	....	....	....	....
	Saint John Flames	AHL	41	10	30	40	16	....	....	....	....	....	....	....	....	....	....	....	21	10	10	20	12	....	....	....
1998-99	VSV Villach	Alpenliga	33	26	41	67	12	....	....	....	....	....	....	....	....	....	....	....	....	....	....	....	....	....	....	....
	VSV Villach	Austria	17	13	17	30	6	....	....	....	....	....	....	....	....	....	....	....	6	1	4	5	0	....	....	....
	Canada	Nat-Team	5	1	3	4	2	....	....	....	....	....	....	....	....	....	....	....	....	....	....	....	....	....	....	....
99-2000	Kolner Haie	DEL	56	12	47	59	28	....	....	....	....	....	....	....	....	....	....	....	10	4	3	7	2	....	....	....
	NHL Totals		**19**	**3**	**3**	**6**	**6**	**2**	**0**	**0**	**26**	**11.5**		....	....	....	....	....	....	....	....	....	....	....	....	....

WHL East First All-Star Team (1994, 1995) • Canadian Major Junior Second All-Star Team (1994)

MURRAY, Rem

(MUHR-ray, REHM) **EDM.**

Center/Left wing. Shoots left. 6'2", 195 lbs. Born, Stratford, Ont., October 9, 1972. Los Angeles' 5th choice, 135th overall, in 1992 Entry Draft.

Season	Club	League	GP	G	A	Pts	PIM	PP	SH	GW	S	%	+/–	TF	F%	H	SB	Min	GP	G	A	Pts	PIM	PP	SH	GW
1989-90	Stratford Cullitons	OJHL-B	46	19	32	51	48	....	....	....	....	....	....	....	....	....	....	....	....	....	....	....	....	....	....	....
1990-91	Stratford Cullitons	OJHL-B	48	39	59	98	39	....	....	....	....	....	....	....	....	....	....	....	....	....	....	....	....	....	....	....
1991-92	Michigan State	CCHA	41	12	36	48	16	....	....	....	....	....	....	....	....	....	....	....	....	....	....	....	....	....	....	....
1992-93	Michigan State	CCHA	40	22	35	57	24	....	....	....	....	....	....	....	....	....	....	....	....	....	....	....	....	....	....	....
1993-94	Michigan State	CCHA	41	16	38	54	18	....	....	....	....	....	....	....	....	....	....	....	....	....	....	....	....	....	....	....
1994-95	Michigan State	CCHA	40	20	36	56	21	....	....	....	....	....	....	....	....	....	....	....	....	....	....	....	....	....	....	....
1995-96	Cape Breton	AHL	79	31	59	90	40	....	....	....	....	....	....	....	....	....	....	....	....	....	....	....	....	....	....	....
1996-97	**Edmonton**	**NHL**	**82**	**11**	**20**	**31**	**16**	**1**	**0**	**2**	**85**	**12.9**	**9**	....	....	....	....	....	**12**	**1**	**2**	**3**	**4**	**0**	**0**	**0**
1997-98	**Edmonton**	**NHL**	**61**	**9**	**9**	**18**	**39**	**2**	**2**	**0**	**59**	**15.3**	**–9**	....	....	....	....	....	**11**	**1**	**4**	**5**	**2**	**0**	**0**	**0**
1998-99	**Edmonton**	**NHL**	**78**	**21**	**18**	**39**	**20**	**4**	**1**	**4**	**116**	**18.1**	**4**	**1013**	**48.1**	**68**	**30**	**15:50**	**4**	**1**	**1**	**2**	**2**	**0**	**0**	**0**
99-2000	**Edmonton**	**NHL**	**44**	**9**	**5**	**14**	**8**	**2**	**0**	**3**	**65**	**13.8**	**–2**	**303**	**50.5**	**22**	**14**	**14:16**	**5**	**0**	**1**	**1**	**2**	**0**	**0**	**0**
	NHL Totals		**265**	**50**	**52**	**102**	**83**	**9**	**3**	**9**	**325**	**15.4**		**1316**	**48.6**	**90**	**44**	**15:16**	**32**	**3**	**8**	**11**	**10**	**0**	**0**	**0**

CCHA Second All-Star Team (1995)

Signed as a free agent by **Edmonton**, September 19, 1995.

MURRAY, Rob

(MUHR-ray, RAWB) **PHI.**

Center. Shoots right. 6'1", 180 lbs. Born, Toronto, Ont., April 4, 1967. Washington's 3rd choice, 61st overall, in 1985 Entry Draft.

Season	Club	League	GP	G	A	Pts	PIM	PP	SH	GW	S	%	+/–	TF	F%	H	SB	Min	GP	G	A	Pts	PIM	PP	SH	GW
1983-84	Mississauga Reps	MTHL	35	18	36	54	32	....	....	....	....	....	....	....	....	....	....	....	....	....	....	....	....	....	....	....
1984-85	Peterborough	OHL	63	12	9	21	155	....	....	....	....	....	....	....	....	....	....	....	17	2	7	9	45	....	....	....
1985-86	Peterborough	OHL	52	14	18	32	125	....	....	....	....	....	....	....	....	....	....	....	16	1	2	3	50	....	....	....
1986-87	Peterborough	OHL	62	17	37	54	204	....	....	....	....	....	....	....	....	....	....	....	3	1	4	5	8	....	....	....
1987-88	Fort Wayne	IHL	80	12	21	33	139	....	....	....	....	....	....	....	....	....	....	....	6	0	2	2	16	....	....	....
1988-89	Baltimore	AHL	80	11	23	34	235	....	....	....	....	....	....	....	....	....	....	....	....	....	....	....	....	....	....	....
1989-90	**Washington**	**NHL**	**41**	**2**	**7**	**9**	**58**	**0**	**0**	**0**	**29**	**6.9**	**–10**	....	....	....	....	....	**9**	**0**	**0**	**0**	**18**	**0**	**0**	**0**
	Baltimore	AHL	23	5	4	9	63	....	....	....	....	....	....	....	....	....	....	....	....	....	....	....	....	....	....	....
1990-91	**Washington**	**NHL**	**17**	**0**	**3**	**3**	**19**	**0**	**0**	**0**	**8**	**0.0**	**0**	....	....	....	....	....	....	....	....	....	....	....	....	....
	Baltimore	AHL	48	6	20	26	177	....	....	....	....	....	....	....	....	....	....	....	4	0	0	0	12	....	....	....
1991-92	**Winnipeg**	**NHL**	**9**	**0**	**1**	**1**	**18**	**0**	**0**	**0**	**2**	**0.0**	**–2**	....	....	....	....	....	....	....	....	....	....	....	....	....
	Moncton Hawks	AHL	60	16	15	31	247	....	....	....	....	....	....	....	....	....	....	....	8	0	1	1	56	....	....	....
1992-93	**Winnipeg**	**NHL**	**10**	**1**	**0**	**1**	**6**	**0**	**0**	**1**	**4**	**25.0**	**0**	....	....	....	....	....	....	....	....	....	....	....	....	....
	Moncton Hawks	AHL	56	16	21	37	147	....	....	....	....	....	....	....	....	....	....	....	3	0	0	0	6	....	....	....
1993-94	**Winnipeg**	**NHL**	**6**	**0**	**0**	**0**	**2**	**0**	**0**	**0**	**1**	**0.0**	**0**	....	....	....	....	....	....	....	....	....	....	....	....	....
	Moncton Hawks	AHL	69	25	32	57	280	....	....	....	....	....	....	....	....	....	....	....	21	2	3	5	60	....	....	....
1994-95	Springfield	AHL	78	16	38	54	373	....	....	....	....	....	....	....	....	....	....	....	....	....	....	....	....	....	....	....
	Winnipeg	**NHL**	**10**	**0**	**2**	**2**	**2**	**0**	**0**	**0**	**5**	**0.0**	**1**	....	....	....	....	....	....	....	....	....	....	....	....	....
1995-96	**Winnipeg**	**NHL**	**1**	**0**	**0**	**0**	**2**	**0**	**0**	**0**	**1**	**0.0**	**–1**	....	....	....	....	....	....	....	....	....	....	....	....	....
	Springfield	AHL	74	10	28	38	263	....	....	....	....	....	....	....	....	....	....	....	10	1	6	7	32	....	....	....
1996-97	Springfield	AHL	78	16	27	43	234	....	....	....	....	....	....	....	....	....	....	....	17	2	3	5	66	....	....	....
1997-98	Springfield	AHL	80	7	30	37	255	....	....	....	....	....	....	....	....	....	....	....	4	0	2	2	2	....	....	....
1998-99	**Phoenix**	**NHL**	**13**	**1**	**2**	**3**	**4**	**0**	**0**	**0**	**11**	**9.1**	**2**	**28**	**46.4**	**11**	**9**	**8:18**	....	....	....	....	....	....	....	....
	Springfield	AHL	68	6	19	25	197	....	....	....	....	....	....	....	....	....	....	....	3	0	0	0	4	....	....	....
99-2000	Springfield	AHL	22	1	3	4	70	....	....	....	....	....	....	....	....	....	....	....	....	....	....	....	....	....	....	....
	Hamilton Bulldogs	AHL	55	11	20	31	100	....	....	....	....	....	....	....	....	....	....	....	10	2	3	5	4	....	....	....
	NHL Totals		**107**	**4**	**15**	**19**	**111**	**0**	**0**	**1**	**61**	**6.6**		**28**	**46.4**	**11**	**9**	**8:18**	**9**	**0**	**0**	**0**	**18**	**0**	**0**	**0**

Claimed by **Minnesota** from **Washington** in Expansion Draft, May 30, 1991. Traded to **Winnipeg** by **Minnesota** with future considerations for Winnipeg's 7th round choice (Geoff Finch) in 1991 Entry Draft and future considerations, May 31, 1991. Transferred to **Phoenix** after **Winnipeg** franchise relocated, July 1, 1996. Traded to **Edmonton** by **Phoenix** for Eric Houde, November 30, 1999. Signed as a free agent by **Philadelphia**, July 24, 2000.

MUSIL, Frantisek

(moo-SIHL, FRAN-tih-sehk) **EDM.**

Defense. Shoots left. 6'3", 215 lbs. Born, Pardubice, Czech., December 17, 1964. Minnesota's 3rd choice, 38th overall, in 1983 Entry Draft.

Season	Club	League	GP	G	A	Pts	PIM	PP	SH	GW	S	%	+/–	TF	F%	H	SB	Min	GP	G	A	Pts	PIM	PP	SH	GW
1980-81	HC Pardubice	Czech.	2	0	0	0	0	....	....	....	....	....	....	....	....	....	....	....	....	....	....	....	....	....	....	....
1981-82	HC Pardubice	Czech.	35	1	3	4	34	....	....	....	....	....	....	....	....	....	....	....	....	....	....	....	....	....	....	....
1982-83	HC Pardubice	Czech.	33	1	2	3	44	....	....	....	....	....	....	....	....	....	....	....	....	....	....	....	....	....	....	....
1983-84	HC Pardubice	Czech.	37	4	8	12	72	....	....	....	....	....	....	....	....	....	....	....	....	....	....	....	....	....	....	....
1984-85	Dukla Jihlava	Czech.	44	4	6	10	76	....	....	....	....	....	....	....	....	....	....	....	....	....	....	....	....	....	....	....
1985-86	Dukla Jihlava	Czech.	34	4	7	11	42	....	....	....	....	....	....	....	....	....	....	....	....	....	....	....	....	....	....	....
1986-87	**Minnesota**	**NHL**	**72**	**2**	**9**	**11**	**148**	**0**	**0**	**0**	**83**	**2.4**	**0**	....	....	....	....	....	....	....	....	....	....	....	....	....
1987-88	**Minnesota**	**NHL**	**80**	**9**	**8**	**17**	**213**	**1**	**1**	**0**	**78**	**11.5**	**–2**	....	....	....	....	....	....	....	....	....	....	....	....	....
1988-89	**Minnesota**	**NHL**	**55**	**1**	**19**	**20**	**54**	**0**	**0**	**1**	**78**	**1.3**	**4**	....	....	....	....	....	**5**	**1**	**1**	**2**	**4**	**0**	**0**	**0**
1989-90	**Minnesota**	**NHL**	**56**	**2**	**8**	**10**	**109**	**0**	**0**	**1**	**78**	**2.6**	**0**	....	....	....	....	....	**4**	**0**	**0**	**0**	**14**	**0**	**0**	**0**
1990-91	**Minnesota**	**NHL**	**8**	**0**	**2**	**2**	**23**	**0**	**0**	**0**	**5**	**0.0**	**0**	....	....	....	....	....	....	....	....	....	....	....	....	....
	Calgary	**NHL**	**67**	**7**	**14**	**21**	**160**	**2**	**0**	**1**	**68**	**10.3**	**12**	....	....	....	....	....	**7**	**0**	**0**	**0**	**10**	**0**	**0**	**0**
1991-92	**Calgary**	**NHL**	**78**	**4**	**8**	**12**	**103**	**1**	**1**	**0**	**71**	**5.6**	**12**	....	....	....	....	....	....	....	....	....	....	....	....	....
1992-93	**Calgary**	**NHL**	**80**	**6**	**10**	**16**	**131**	**0**	**0**	**1**	**87**	**6.9**	**28**	....	....	....	....	....	**6**	**1**	**1**	**2**	**7**	**0**	**0**	**0**
1993-94	**Calgary**	**NHL**	**75**	**1**	**8**	**9**	**50**	**0**	**0**	**0**	**65**	**1.5**	**38**	....	....	....	....	....	**7**	**0**	**1**	**1**	**4**	**0**	**0**	**0**
1994-95	Sparta Praha	Cze-Rep	19	1	4	5	50	....	....	....	....	....	....	....	....	....	....	....	....	....	....	....	....	....	....	....
	HC Saxonia	DEL	1	0	0	0	2	....	....	....	....	....	....	....	....	....	....	....	....	....	....	....	....	....	....	....
	Calgary	**NHL**	**35**	**0**	**5**	**5**	**61**	**0**	**0**	**0**	**18**	**0.0**	**6**	....	....	....	....	....	**5**	**0**	**1**	**1**	**0**	**0**	**0**	**0**
1995-96	Karlovy Vary-2	Cze-Rep	16	7	4	11	16	....	....	....	....	....	....	....	....	....	....	....	....	....	....	....	....	....	....	....
	Ottawa	**NHL**	**65**	**1**	**3**	**4**	**85**	**0**	**0**	**0**	**37**	**2.7**	**–10**	....	....	....	....	....	....	....	....	....	....	....	....	....
1996-97	**Ottawa**	**NHL**	**57**	**0**	**5**	**5**	**58**	**0**	**0**	**0**	**24**	**0.0**	**6**	....	....	....	....	....	....	....	....	....	....	....	....	....
1997-98	Indianapolis Ice	IHL	52	5	8	13	122	....	....	....	....	....	....	....	....	....	....	....	....	....	....	....	....	....	....	....
	Detroit Vipers	IHL	9	0	0	0	6	....	....	....	....	....	....	....	....	....	....	....	....	....	....	....	....	....	....	....
	Edmonton	**NHL**	**17**	**1**	**2**	**3**	**8**	**0**	**1**	**1**	**8**	**12.5**	**1**	....	....	....	....	....	**7**	**0**	**0**	**0**	**6**	**0**	**0**	**0**

			Regular Season																Playoffs							
Season	Club	League	GP	G	A	Pts	PIM	PP	SH	GW	S	%	+/-	TF	F%	H	SB	Min	GP	G	A	Pts	PIM	PP	SH	GW
1998-99	Edmonton	NHL	39	0	3	3	34	0	0	0	9	0.0	0	0	0.0	60	56	14:21	1	0	0	0	2	0	0	0
99-2000	Edmonton	NHL	DID NOT PLAY – INJURED																							
	NHL Totals		784	34	104	138	1237	4	3	5	709	4.8		0	0.0	60	56	14:21	42	2	4	6	47	0	0	0

Traded to **Calgary** by **Minnesota** for Brian Glynn, October 26, 1990. Traded to **Ottawa** by **Calgary** for Ottawa's 4th round choice (Chris St. Croix) in 1997 Entry Draft, October 7, 1995. Traded to **Edmonton** by **Ottawa** for Scott Ferguson, March 9, 1998. • Missed entire 1999-2000 season recovering from spinal cord injury suffered in training camp, October 2, 1999.

MYHRES, Brantt (MIGH-uhrs, BRANT) NSH.

Right wing. Shoots right. 6'3", 220 lbs. Born, Edmonton, Alta., March 18, 1974. Tampa Bay's 5th choice, 97th overall, in 1992 Entry Draft.

Season	Club	League	GP	G	A	Pts	PIM	PP	SH	GW	S	%	+/-	TF	F%	H	SB	Min	GP	G	A	Pts	PIM	PP	SH	GW
1989-90	Bonneyville	AAHA	60	40	62	102	195	....	....	....	....	....	....	....	....	....	....	....	....	....	....	....	....	....	....	....
1990-91	Portland	WHL	59	2	7	9	125	....	....	....	....	....	....	....	....	....	....	....	....	....	....	....	....	....	....	....
1991-92	Portland	WHL	4	0	2	2	22	....	....	....	....	....	....	....	....	....	....	....	....	....	....	....	....	....	....	....
	Lethbridge	WHL	53	4	11	15	359	....	....	....	....	....	....	....	....	....	....	....	5	0	0	0	36	....	....	....
1992-93	Lethbridge	WHL	64	13	35	48	277	....	....	....	....	....	....	....	....	....	....	....	3	0	0	0	11	....	....	....
1993-94	Lethbridge	WHL	34	10	21	31	103	....	....	....	....	....	....	....	....	....	....	....	....	....	....	....	....	....	....	....
	Spokane Chiefs	WHL	27	10	22	32	139	....	....	....	....	....	....	....	....	....	....	....	3	1	4	5	7	....	....	....
	Atlanta Knights	IHL	2	0	0	0	17	....	....	....	....	....	....	....	....	....	....	....	....	....	....	....	....	....	....	....
1994-95	Atlanta Knights	IHL	40	5	5	10	213	....	....	....	....	....	....	....	....	....	....	....	....	....	....	....	....	....	....	....
	Tampa Bay	**NHL**	**15**	**2**	**0**	**2**	**81**	**0**	**0**	**1**	**4**	**50.0**	**–2**	....	....	....	....	....	....	....	....	....	....	....	....	....
1995-96	Atlanta Knights	IHL	12	0	2	2	58	....	....	....	....	....	....	....	....	....	....	....	....	....	....	....	....	....	....	....
1996-97	**Tampa Bay**	**NHL**	**47**	**3**	**1**	**4**	**136**	**0**	**0**	**1**	**13**	**23.1**	**1**	....	....	....	....	....	....	....	....	....	....	....	....	....
	San Antonio	IHL	12	0	0	0	98	....	....	....	....	....	....	....	....	....	....	....	....	....	....	....	....	....	....	....
1997-98	**Philadelphia**	**NHL**	**23**	**0**	**0**	**0**	**169**	**0**	**0**	**0**	**0**	**0.0**	**–1**	....	....	....	....	....	....	....	....	....	....	....	....	....
	Philadelphia	AHL	18	4	4	8	67	....	....	....	....	....	....	....	....	....	....	....	....	....	....	....	....	....	....	....
1998-99	**San Jose**	**NHL**	**30**	**1**	**0**	**1**	**116**	**0**	**0**	**0**	**7**	**14.3**	**–2**	**1**	**0.0**	**15**	**2**	**4:47**	....	....	....	....	....	....	....	....
	Kentucky	AHL	4	0	0	0	16	....	....	....	....	....	....	....	....	....	....	....	....	....	....	....	....	....	....	....
99-2000	**San Jose**	**NHL**	**13**	**0**	**1**	**1**	**97**	**0**	**0**	**0**	**2**	**0.0**	**0**	**1**	**0.0**	**9**	**1**	**3:03**	....	....	....	....	....	....	....	....
	Kentucky	AHL	10	1	5	6	18	....	....	....	....	....	....	....	....	....	....	....	7	0	1	1	21	....	....	....
	NHL Totals		**128**	**6**	**2**	**8**	**599**	**0**	**0**	**2**	**26**	**23.1**		**2**	**0.0**	**24**	**3**	**4:16**	....	....	....	....	....	....	....	....

Traded to **Edmonton** by **Tampa Bay** with Toronto's 3rd round choice (previously acquired, Edmonton selected Alex Henry) in 1998 Entry Draft for Vladimir Vujtek and Edmonton's 3rd round choice (Dimitri Afanasenkov) in 1998 Entry Draft, July 16, 1997. Traded to **Philadelphia** by **Edmonton** for Jason Bowen, October 15, 1997. Signed as a free agent by **San Jose**, September 11, 1998. Signed as a free agent by **Nashville**, August 15, 2000.

MYRVOLD, Anders (MYOOR-vohld, AN-duhrs) NYI

Defense. Shoots left. 6'2", 200 lbs. Born, Lorenskog, Norway, August 12, 1975. Quebec's 6th choice, 127th overall, in 1993 Entry Draft.

Season	Club	League	GP	G	A	Pts	PIM	PP	SH	GW	S	%	+/-	TF	F%	H	SB	Min	GP	G	A	Pts	PIM	PP	SH	GW
1991-92	Storhamr IL	Norway	1	0	0	0	4	....	....	....	....	....	....	....	....	....	....	....	....	....	....	....	....	....	....	....
1992-93	Farjestads BK	Sweden	2	0	0	0	0	....	....	....	....	....	....	....	....	....	....	....	....	....	....	....	....	....	....	....
1993-94	Grums HC	Sweden-2	24	1	0	1	59	....	....	....	....	....	....	....	....	....	....	....	....	....	....	....	....	....	....	....
1994-95	Laval Titan	QMJHL	64	14	50	64	173	....	....	....	....	....	....	....	....	....	....	....	20	4	10	14	68	....	....	....
	Cornwall Aces	AHL	....	....	....	....	....	....	....	....	....	....	....	....	....	....	....	....	3	0	1	1	2	....	....	....
1995-96	**Colorado**	**NHL**	**4**	**0**	**1**	**1**	**6**	**0**	**0**	**0**	**4**	**0.0**	**–2**	....	....	....	....	....	....	....	....	....	....	....	....	....
	Cornwall Aces	AHL	70	5	24	29	125	....	....	....	....	....	....	....	....	....	....	....	5	1	0	1	19	....	....	....
1996-97	Hershey Bears	AHL	20	0	3	3	16	....	....	....	....	....	....	....	....	....	....	....	....	....	....	....	....	....	....	....
	Boston	**NHL**	**9**	**0**	**2**	**2**	**4**	**0**	**0**	**0**	**8**	**0.0**	**–1**	....	....	....	....	....	....	....	....	....	....	....	....	....
	Providence Bruins	AHL	53	6	15	21	107	....	....	....	....	....	....	....	....	....	....	....	10	0	1	1	6	....	....	....
1997-98	Providence Bruins	AHL	75	4	21	25	91	....	....	....	....	....	....	....	....	....	....	....	....	....	....	....	....	....	....	....
1998-99	Djurgardens IF	Sweden	29	3	4	7	52	....	....	....	....	....	....	....	....	....	....	....	....	....	....	....	....	....	....	....
	Djurgardens IF	EuroHL	3	0	1	1	4	....	....	....	....	....	....	....	....	....	....	....	....	....	....	....	....	....	....	....
	AIK Solna	Sweden	19	1	3	4	24	....	....	....	....	....	....	....	....	....	....	....	....	....	....	....	....	....	....	....
99-2000	AIK Solna	Sweden	49	1	3	4	87	....	....	....	....	....	....	....	....	....	....	....	....	....	....	....	....	....	....	....
	NHL Totals		**13**	**0**	**3**	**3**	**10**	**0**	**0**	**0**	**12**	**0.0**		....	....	....	....	....	....	....	....	....	....	....	....	....

Rights transferred to **Colorado** after **Quebec** franchise relocated, June 21, 1995. Traded to **Boston** by **Colorado** with Landon Wilson for Boston's 1st round choice (Robyn Regehr) in 1998 Entry Draft, November 22, 1996. Signed as a free agent by **NY Islanders**, August 28, 2000.

NABOKOV, Dmitri (nuh-BAW-kahv, dih-MEE-tree) NYI

Center/Left Wing. Shoots right. 6'2", 209 lbs. Born, Novosibirsk, USSR, January 4, 1977. Chicago's 1st choice, 19th overall, in 1995 Entry Draft.

Season	Club	League	GP	G	A	Pts	PIM	PP	SH	GW	S	%	+/-	TF	F%	H	SB	Min	GP	G	A	Pts	PIM	PP	SH	GW
1993-94	Krylja Sovetov	CIS	17	0	2	2	6	....	....	....	....	....	....	....	....	....	....	....	3	0	0	0	0	....	....	....
1994-95	Krylja Sovetov	CIS	49	15	12	27	32	....	....	....	....	....	....	....	....	....	....	....	4	5	0	5	6	....	....	....
1995-96	Krylja Sovetov	CIS	50	12	14	26	51	....	....	....	....	....	....	....	....	....	....	....	....	....	....	....	....	....	....	....
1996-97	Krylja Sovetov	Russia	1	0	0	0	0	....	....	....	....	....	....	....	....	....	....	....	....	....	....	....	....	....	....	....
	Regina Pats	WHL	50	39	56	95	61	....	....	....	....	....	....	....	....	....	....	....	5	2	3	5	2	....	....	....
	Indianapolis Ice	IHL	2	0	0	0	0	....	....	....	....	....	....	....	....	....	....	....	....	....	....	....	....	....	....	....
1997-98	**Chicago**	**NHL**	**25**	**7**	**4**	**11**	**10**	**3**	**0**	**2**	**34**	**20.6**	**–1**	....	....	....	....	....	....	....	....	....	....	....	....	....
	Indianapolis Ice	IHL	46	6	15	21	16	....	....	....	....	....	....	....	....	....	....	....	5	2	1	3	0	....	....	....
1998-99	**NY Islanders**	**NHL**	**4**	**0**	**2**	**2**	**2**	**0**	**0**	**0**	**4**	**0.0**	**4**	**0**	**0.0**	**3**	**0**	**11:38**	....	....	....	....	....	....	....	....
	Lowell	AHL	73	17	25	42	46	....	....	....	....	....	....	....	....	....	....	....	3	0	1	1	0	....	....	....
99-2000	**NY Islanders**	**NHL**	**26**	**4**	**7**	**11**	**16**	**0**	**0**	**0**	**40**	**10.0**	**–8**	**12**	**25.0**	**36**	**10**	**13:33**	....	....	....	....	....	....	....	....
	Lowell	AHL	51	8	26	34	42	....	....	....	....	....	....	....	....	....	....	....	6	1	2	3	2	....	....	....
	NHL Totals		**55**	**11**	**13**	**24**	**28**	**3**	**0**	**2**	**78**	**14.1**		**12**	**25.0**	**39**	**10**	**13:18**	....	....	....	....	....	....	....	....

WHL East Second All-Star Team (1997)

Traded to **NY Islanders** by **Chicago** for Jean-Pierre Dumont and Chicago's 5th round choice (later traded to Philadelphia - Philadelphia selected Francis Belanger) in 1998 Entry Draft, June 1, 1998.

NAGY, Ladislav (NA-gee, LA-dih-slahv) ST.L.

Center. Shoots left. 5'11", 183 lbs. Born, Saca, Czech., June 1, 1979. St. Louis' 6th choice, 177th overall, in 1997 Entry Draft.

Season	Club	League	GP	G	A	Pts	PIM	PP	SH	GW	S	%	+/-	TF	F%	H	SB	Min	GP	G	A	Pts	PIM	PP	SH	GW
1996-97	HC Kosice	Slovak-Jr.	45	29	30	59	105	....	....	....	....	....	....	....	....	....	....	....	....	....	....	....	....	....	....	....
	Dragon Presov	Slovak-2	11	6	5	11	....	....	....	....	....	....	....	....	....	....	....	....	....	....	....	....	....	....	....	....
1997-98	HC Kosice	Slovakia	29	19	15	34	41	....	....	....	....	....	....	....	....	....	....	....	11	2	4	6	6	....	....	....
1998-99	Halifax	QMJHL	63	71	55	126	148	....	....	....	....	....	....	....	....	....	....	....	5	3	3	6	18	....	....	....
	Worcester	AHL	....	....	....	....	....	....	....	....	....	....	....	....	....	....	....	....	3	2	2	4	0	....	....	....
99-2000	**St. Louis**	**NHL**	**11**	**2**	**4**	**6**	**2**	**1**	**0**	**0**	**15**	**13.3**	**2**	**6**	**33.3**	**6**	**3**	**12:19**	**6**	**1**	**1**	**2**	**0**	**0**	**0**	**0**
	Worcester	AHL	69	23	28	51	67	....	....	....	....	....	....	....	....	....	....	....	2	1	0	1	0	....	....	....
	NHL Totals		**11**	**2**	**4**	**6**	**2**	**1**	**0**	**0**	**15**	**13.3**		**6**	**33.3**	**6**	**3**	**12:19**	**6**	**1**	**1**	**2**	**0**	**0**	**0**	**0**

NAMESTNIKOV, John (nah-MEST-nih-kov, JAWN) NSH.

Defense. Shoots right. 5'11", 190 lbs. Born, Arzamis-Ig, USSR, October 9, 1971. Vancouver's 5th choice, 117th overall, in 1991 Entry Draft.

Season	Club	League	GP	G	A	Pts	PIM	PP	SH	GW	S	%	+/-	TF	F%	H	SB	Min	GP	G	A	Pts	PIM	PP	SH	GW
1988-89	Torpedo Gorky	USSR	2	0	0	0	2	....	....	....	....	....	....	....	....	....	....	....	....	....	....	....	....	....	....	....
1989-90	Torpedo Gorky	USSR	23	0	0	0	25	....	....	....	....	....	....	....	....	....	....	....	....	....	....	....	....	....	....	....
1990-91	Torpedo Nizhny	USSR	42	1	2	3	49	....	....	....	....	....	....	....	....	....	....	....	....	....	....	....	....	....	....	....
1991-92	CSKA Moscow	CIS	42	1	1	2	47	....	....	....	....	....	....	....	....	....	....	....	....	....	....	....	....	....	....	....
1992-93	CSKA Moscow	CIS	42	5	5	10	68	....	....	....	....	....	....	....	....	....	....	....	....	....	....	....	....	....	....	....
1993-94	**Vancouver**	**NHL**	**17**	**0**	**5**	**5**	**10**	**0**	**0**	**0**	**11**	**0.0**	**–2**	....	....	....	....	....	....	....	....	....	....	....	....	....
	Hamilton Canucks	AHL	59	7	27	34	97	....	....	....	....	....	....	....	....	....	....	....	4	0	2	2	19	....	....	....
1994-95	Syracuse Crunch	AHL	59	11	22	33	59	....	....	....	....	....	....	....	....	....	....	....	....	....	....	....	....	....	....	....
	Vancouver	**NHL**	**16**	**0**	**3**	**3**	**4**	**0**	**0**	**0**	**18**	**0.0**	**2**	....	....	....	....	....	**1**	**0**	**0**	**0**	**2**	**0**	**0**	**0**
1995-96	Syracuse Crunch	AHL	59	13	34	47	85	....	....	....	....	....	....	....	....	....	....	....	15	1	8	9	16	....	....	....
	Vancouver	**NHL**	....	....	....	....	....	....	....	....	....	....	....	....	....	....	....	....	**1**	**0**	**0**	**0**	**0**	**0**	**0**	**0**
1996-97	**Vancouver**	**NHL**	**2**	**0**	**0**	**0**	**4**	**0**	**0**	**0**	**1**	**0.0**	**–1**	....	....	....	....	....	....	....	....	....	....	....	....	....
	Syracuse Crunch	AHL	55	9	37	46	73	....	....	....	....	....	....	....	....	....	....	....	3	2	0	2	0	....	....	....
1997-98	**NY Islanders**	**NHL**	**6**	**0**	**1**	**1**	**4**	**0**	**0**	**0**	**2**	**0.0**	**–1**	....	....	....	....	....	....	....	....	....	....	....	....	....
	Utah Grizzlies	IHL	62	6	19	25	48	....	....	....	....	....	....	....	....	....	....	....	4	1	0	1	2	....	....	....

			Regular Season																	Playoffs							
Season	Club	League	GP	G	A	Pts	PIM	PP	SH	GW	S	%	+/–	TF	F%	H	SB	Min	GP	G	A	Pts	PIM	PP	SH	GW
1998-99	Lowell	AHL	42	12	14	26	42	....	....	....	....	....	....	....	....	....	....	....	....	....	....	....	....	....	....	....
99-2000	Hartford	AHL	33	1	9	10	14	....	....	....	....	....	....	....	....	....	....	....	....	....	....	....	....	....	....	....
	Nashville	**NHL**	**2**	**0**	**0**	**0**	**2**	**0**	**0**	**0**	**3**	**0.0**	....	**0**	**0.0**	**0**	**0**	**0:00**	....	....	....	....	....	....	....	....
	Milwaukee	IHL	12	2	3	5	17	....	....	....	....	....	....	....	....	....	....	....	3	0	0	0	0	....	....	....
	NHL Totals		**43**	**0**	**9**	**9**	**24**	**0**	**0**	**0**	**35**	**0.0**		**0**	**0.0**	**0**	**0**	....	**2**	**0**	**0**	**0**	**2**	**0**	**0**	**0**

Signed as a free agent by **NY Islanders**, July 21, 1997. Signed as a free agent by **NY Rangers**, August 9, 1999. Traded to **Nashville** by **NY Rangers** for Jason Dawe, February 3, 2000.

NASH, Tyson
(NASH, TIGH-sohn) **ST.L.**

Left wing. Shoots left. 6', 185 lbs. Born, Edmonton, Alta., March 11, 1975. Vancouver's 10th choice, 247th overall, in 1994 Entry Draft.

1990-91	Sherwood Park	AMHL	40	17	28	43	63	....	....	....	....	....	....	....	....	....	....	....	....	....	....	....	....	....	....	....
1991-92	Kamloops Blazers	WHL	33	1	6	7	62	....	....	....	....	....	....	....	....	....	....	....	4	0	0	0	0	....	....	....
1992-93	Kamloops Blazers	WHL	61	10	16	26	78	....	....	....	....	....	....	....	....	....	....	....	13	3	2	5	32	....	....	....
1993-94	Kamloops Blazers	WHL	65	20	36	56	135	....	....	....	....	....	....	....	....	....	....	....	16	3	4	7	12	....	....	....
1994-95	Kamloops Blazers	WHL	63	34	41	75	70	....	....	....	....	....	....	....	....	....	....	....	21	10	7	17	30	....	....	....
1995-96	Syracuse Crunch	AHL	50	4	7	11	58	....	....	....	....	....	....	....	....	....	....	....	4	0	0	0	11	....	....	....
	Raleigh IceCaps	ECHL	6	1	1	2	8	....	....	....	....	....	....	....	....	....	....	....	....	....	....	....	....	....	....	....
1996-97	Syracuse Crunch	AHL	77	17	17	34	105	....	....	....	....	....	....	....	....	....	....	....	3	0	2	2	0	....	....	....
1997-98	Syracuse Crunch	AHL	74	20	20	40	184	....	....	....	....	....	....	....	....	....	....	....	5	0	2	2	28	....	....	....
1998-99	**St. Louis**	**NHL**	**2**	**0**	**0**	**0**	**5**	**0**	**0**	**0**	**1**	**0.0**	**–1**	**0**	**0.0**	**8**	**0**	**7:44**	**1**	**0**	**0**	**0**	**2**	**0**	**0**	**0**
	Worcester	AHL	55	14	22	36	143	....	....	....	....	....	....	....	....	....	....	....	4	4	1	5	27	....	....	....
99-2000	**St. Louis**	**NHL**	**66**	**4**	**9**	**13**	**150**	**0**	**1**	**1**	**68**	**5.9**	**6**	**0**	**0.0**	**193**	**7**	**8:35**	**6**	**1**	**0**	**1**	**24**	**0**	**0**	**0**
	NHL Totals		**68**	**4**	**9**	**13**	**155**	**0**	**1**	**1**	**69**	**5.8**		**0**	**0.0**	**201**	**7**	**8:34**	**7**	**1**	**0**	**1**	**26**	**0**	**0**	**0**

Signed as a free agent by **St. Louis**, July 14, 1998.

NASLUND, Markus
(NAZ-luhnd, MAHR-kuhs) **VAN.**

Right wing. Shoots left. 5'11", 195 lbs. Born, Ornskoldsvik, Sweden, July 30, 1973. Pittsburgh's 1st choice, 16th overall, in 1991 Entry Draft.

1988-89	Ornskoldsviks IF	Sweden-3	14	7	6	13	....	....	....	....	....	....	....	....	....	....	....	....	....	....	....	....	....	....	....	....
1989-90	MoDo AIK	Swede-Jr.	33	43	35	78	20	....	....	....	....	....	....	....	....	....	....	....	....	....	....	....	....	....	....	....
1990-91	MoDo AIK	Sweden	32	10	9	19	14	....	....	....	....	....	....	....	....	....	....	....	....	....	....	....	....	....	....	....
1991-92	MoDo AIK	Sweden	39	22	18	40	54	....	....	....	....	....	....	....	....	....	....	....	....	....	....	....	....	....	....	....
1992-93	MoDo AIK	Swede-Jr.	2	4	1	5	2	....	....	....	....	....	....	....	....	....	....	....	....	....	....	....	....	....	....	....
	MoDo AIK	Sweden	39	22	17	39	67	....	....	....	....	....	....	....	....	....	....	....	3	3	2	5	0	....	....	....
1993-94	**Pittsburgh**	**NHL**	**71**	**4**	**7**	**11**	**27**	**1**	**0**	**0**	**80**	**5.0**	**–3**	....	....	....	....	....	....	....	....	....	....	....	....	....
	Cleveland	IHL	5	1	6	7	4	....	....	....	....	....	....	....	....	....	....	....	....	....	....	....	....	....	....	....
1994-95	**Pittsburgh**	**NHL**	**14**	**2**	**2**	**4**	**2**	**0**	**0**	**0**	**13**	**15.4**	**0**	....	....	....	....	....	....	....	....	....	....	....	....	....
	Cleveland	IHL	7	3	4	7	6	....	....	....	....	....	....	....	....	....	....	....	4	1	3	4	8	....	....	....
1995-96	**Pittsburgh**	**NHL**	**66**	**19**	**33**	**52**	**36**	**3**	**0**	**4**	**125**	**15.2**	**17**	....	....	....	....	....	....	....	....	....	....	....	....	....
	Vancouver	**NHL**	**10**	**3**	**0**	**3**	**6**	**1**	**0**	**1**	**19**	**15.8**	**3**	....	....	....	....	....	**6**	**1**	**2**	**3**	**8**	**1**	**0**	**0**
1996-97	**Vancouver**	**NHL**	**78**	**21**	**20**	**41**	**30**	**4**	**0**	**4**	**120**	**17.5**	**–15**	....	....	....	....	....	....	....	....	....	....	....	....	....
1997-98	**Vancouver**	**NHL**	**76**	**14**	**20**	**34**	**56**	**2**	**1**	**0**	**106**	**13.2**	**5**	....	....	....	....	....	....	....	....	....	....	....	....	....
1998-99	**Vancouver**	**NHL**	**80**	**36**	**30**	**66**	**74**	**15**	**2**	**3**	**205**	**17.6**	**–13**	**14**	**57.1**	**40**	**20**	**19:57**	....	....	....	....	....	....	....	....
99-2000	**Vancouver**	**NHL**	**82**	**27**	**38**	**65**	**64**	**6**	**2**	**3**	**271**	**10.0**	**–5**	**13**	**46.1**	**50**	**28**	**20:13**	....	....	....	....	....	....	....	....
	NHL Totals		**477**	**126**	**150**	**276**	**295**	**32**	**5**	**15**	**939**	**13.4**		**27**	**51.9**	**90**	**48**	**20:05**	**6**	**1**	**2**	**3**	**8**	**1**	**0**	**0**

Played in NHL All-Star Game (1999)

Traded to **Vancouver** by **Pittsburgh** for Alek Stojanov, March 20, 1996.

NASREDDINE, Alain
(NAS-ruh-deen, AL-eh) **EDM.**

Defense. Shoots left. 6'1", 201 lbs. Born, Montreal, Que., July 10, 1975. Florida's 8th choice, 135th overall, in 1993 Entry Draft.

1990-91	Mtl-Bourassa	QAAA	35	10	25	35	50	....	....	....	....	....	....	....	....	....	....	....	....	....	....	....	....	....	....	....
1991-92	Drummondville	QMJHL	61	1	9	10	78	....	....	....	....	....	....	....	....	....	....	....	4	0	0	0	17	....	....	....
1992-93	Drummondville	QMJHL	64	0	14	14	137	....	....	....	....	....	....	....	....	....	....	....	10	0	1	1	36	....	....	....
1993-94	Chicoutimi	QMJHL	60	3	24	27	218	....	....	....	....	....	....	....	....	....	....	....	26	2	10	12	118	....	....	....
1994-95	Chicoutimi	QMJHL	67	8	31	39	342	....	....	....	....	....	....	....	....	....	....	....	13	3	5	8	40	....	....	....
1995-96	Carolina	AHL	63	0	5	5	245	....	....	....	....	....	....	....	....	....	....	....	....	....	....	....	....	....	....	....
1996-97	Carolina	AHL	26	0	4	4	109	....	....	....	....	....	....	....	....	....	....	....	....	....	....	....	....	....	....	....
	Indianapolis Ice	IHL	49	0	2	2	248	....	....	....	....	....	....	....	....	....	....	....	4	1	1	2	27	....	....	....
1997-98	Indianapolis Ice	IHL	75	1	12	13	258	....	....	....	....	....	....	....	....	....	....	....	5	0	2	2	12	....	....	....
1998-99	**Chicago**	**NHL**	**7**	**0**	**0**	**0**	**19**	**0**	**0**	**0**	**2**	**0.0**	**–2**	**0**	**0.0**	**5**	**1**	**12:11**	....	....	....	....	....	....	....	....
	Portland Pirates	AHL	7	0	1	1	36	....	....	....	....	....	....	....	....	....	....	....	....	....	....	....	....	....	....	....
	Montreal	**NHL**	**8**	**0**	**0**	**0**	**33**	**0**	**0**	**0**	**1**	**0.0**	**1**	**0**	**0.0**	**7**	**1**	**8:12**	....	....	....	....	....	....	....	....
	Fredericton	AHL	38	0	10	10	108	....	....	....	....	....	....	....	....	....	....	....	15	0	3	3	39	....	....	....
99-2000	Quebec Citadelles	AHL	59	1	6	7	178	....	....	....	....	....	....	....	....	....	....	....	....	....	....	....	....	....	....	....
	Hamilton Bulldogs	AHL	11	0	0	0	12	....	....	....	....	....	....	....	....	....	....	....	10	1	1	2	14	....	....	....
	NHL Totals		**15**	**0**	**0**	**0**	**52**	**0**	**0**	**0**	**3**	**0.0**		**0**	**0.0**	**12**	**2**	**10:04**	....	....	....	....	....	....	....	....

QMJHL Second All-Star Team (1995)

Traded to **Chicago** by **Florida** with a conditional choice in 1999 Entry Draft for Ivan Droppa, December 18, 1996. Traded to **Montreal** by **Chicago** with Jeff Hackett, Eric Weinrich and Tampa Bay's 4th round choice (previously acquired, Montreal selected Chris Dyment) in 1999 Entry Draft for Jocelyn Thibault, Dave Manson and Brad Brown, November 16, 1998. Traded to **Edmonton** by **Montreal** with Igor Ulanov for Christian Laflamme and Matthieu Descoteaux, March 9, 2000.

NAZAROV, Andrei
(nah-ZAH-rohv, AWN-dray) **CGY.**

Left wing. Shoots right. 6'5", 234 lbs. Born, Chelyabinsk, USSR, May 22, 1974. San Jose's 2nd choice, 10th overall, in 1992 Entry Draft.

1991-92	Dynamo Moscow	CIS	2	1	0	1	2	....	....	....	....	....	....	....	....	....	....	....	....	....	....	....	....	....	....	....
1992-93	Dynamo Moscow	CIS	42	8	2	10	79	....	....	....	....	....	....	....	....	....	....	....	10	1	1	2	8	....	....	....
1993-94	Dynamo Moscow	CIS	6	2	2	4	0	....	....	....	....	....	....	....	....	....	....	....	....	....	....	....	....	....	....	....
	San Jose	**NHL**	**1**	**0**	**0**	**0**	**0**	**0**	**0**	**0**	**0**	**0.0**	**0**	....	....	....	....	....	....	....	....	....	....	....	....	....
	Kansas City	IHL	71	15	18	33	64	....	....	....	....	....	....	....	....	....	....	....	....	....	....	....	....	....	....	....
1994-95	Kansas City	IHL	43	15	10	25	55	....	....	....	....	....	....	....	....	....	....	....	....	....	....	....	....	....	....	....
	San Jose	**NHL**	**26**	**3**	**5**	**8**	**94**	**0**	**0**	**0**	**19**	**15.8**	**–1**	....	....	....	....	....	**6**	**0**	**0**	**0**	**9**	**0**	**0**	**0**
1995-96	**San Jose**	**NHL**	**42**	**7**	**7**	**14**	**62**	**2**	**0**	**1**	**55**	**12.7**	**–15**	....	....	....	....	....	....	....	....	....	....	....	....	....
	Kansas City	IHL	27	4	6	10	118	....	....	....	....	....	....	....	....	....	....	....	2	0	0	0	2	....	....	....
1996-97	**San Jose**	**NHL**	**60**	**12**	**15**	**27**	**222**	**1**	**0**	**1**	**116**	**10.3**	**–4**	....	....	....	....	....	....	....	....	....	....	....	....	....
	Kentucky	AHL	3	1	2	3	4	....	....	....	....	....	....	....	....	....	....	....	....	....	....	....	....	....	....	....
1997-98	**San Jose**	**NHL**	**40**	**1**	**1**	**2**	**112**	**0**	**0**	**0**	**31**	**3.2**	**–4**	....	....	....	....	....	....	....	....	....	....	....	....	....
	Tampa Bay	**NHL**	**14**	**1**	**1**	**2**	**58**	**0**	**0**	**0**	**19**	**5.3**	**–9**	....	....	....	....	....	....	....	....	....	....	....	....	....
1998-99	**Tampa Bay**	**NHL**	**26**	**2**	**0**	**2**	**43**	**0**	**0**	**0**	**18**	**11.1**	**–5**	**4**	**50.0**	**26**	**2**	**8:13**	....	....	....	....	....	....	....	....
	Calgary	**NHL**	**36**	**5**	**9**	**14**	**30**	**0**	**0**	**2**	**53**	**9.4**	**1**	**0**	**0.0**	**38**	**10**	**14:31**	....	....	....	....	....	....	....	....
99-2000	**Calgary**	**NHL**	**76**	**10**	**22**	**32**	**78**	**1**	**0**	**1**	**110**	**9.1**	**3**	**2**	**100.0**	**79**	**16**	**11:44**	....	....	....	....	....	....	....	....
	NHL Totals		**321**	**41**	**60**	**101**	**699**	**4**	**0**	**5**	**421**	**9.7**		**6**	**66.7**	**143**	**28**	**11:48**	**6**	**0**	**0**	**0**	**9**	**0**	**0**	**0**

Traded to **Tampa Bay** by **San Jose** with Florida's 1st round choice (previously acquired, Tampa Bay selected Vincent Lecavalier) for Bryan Marchment, David Shaw and Tampa Bay's 1st round choice (later traded to Nashville - Nashville selected David Legwand) in 1998 Entry Draft, March 24, 1998. Traded to **Calgary** by **Tampa Bay** for Michael Nylander, January 19, 1999.

NDUR, Rumun
(nih-DOOR, ROO-muhn) **ATL.**

Defense. Shoots left. 6'2", 222 lbs. Born, Zaria, Nigeria, July 7, 1975. Buffalo's 3rd choice, 69th overall, in 1994 Entry Draft.

1990-91	Belmont Bombers	OJHL-D	36	3	11	14	70	....	....	....	....	....	....	....	....	....	....	....	....	....	....	....	....	....	....	....
1991-92	Sarnia Bees	OJHL-B	30	2	5	7	46	....	....	....	....	....	....	....	....	....	....	....	....	....	....	....	....	....	....	....
	Clearwater	OJHL-C	4	0	4	4	4	....	....	....	....	....	....	....	....	....	....	....	....	....	....	....	....	....	....	....
1992-93	Guelph Platers	OJHL-B	24	7	8	15	202	....	....	....	....	....	....	....	....	....	....	....	....	....	....	....	....	....	....	....
	Guelph Storm	OHL	22	1	3	4	30	....	....	....	....	....	....	....	....	....	....	....	4	0	1	1	4	....	....	....
1993-94	Guelph Storm	OHL	61	6	33	39	176	....	....	....	....	....	....	....	....	....	....	....	9	4	1	5	24	....	....	....

			Regular Season																Playoffs							
Season	Club	League	GP	G	A	Pts	PIM	PP	SH	GW	S	%	+/–	TF	F%	H	SB	Min	GP	G	A	Pts	PIM	PP	SH	GW
1994-95	Guelph Storm	OHL	63	10	21	31	187	....	....	....	....	....	....	....	....	....	....	....	14	0	4	4	28	....	....	....
1995-96	Rochester	AHL	73	2	12	14	306	....	....	....	....	....	....	....	....	....	....	....	17	1	2	3	33	....	....	....
1996-97	**Buffalo**	**NHL**	**2**	**0**	**0**	**0**	**2**	**0**	**0**	**0**	**0**	**0.0**	**1**	....	....	....	....	....	....	....	....	....	....	....	....	....
	Rochester	AHL	68	5	11	16	282	....	....	....	....	....	....	....	....	....	....	....	10	3	1	4	21	....	....	....
1997-98	**Buffalo**	**NHL**	**1**	**0**	**0**	**0**	**2**	**0**	**0**	**0**	**0**	**0.0**	**–1**	....	....	....	....	....	....	....	....	....	....	....	....	....
	Rochester	AHL	50	1	12	13	207	....	....	....	....	....	....	....	....	....	....	....	4	0	2	2	16	....	....	....
1998-99	**Buffalo**	**NHL**	**8**	**0**	**0**	**0**	**16**	**0**	**0**	**0**	**1**	**0.0**	**1**	**0**	**0.0**	**11**	**2**	**10:58**	....	....	....	....	....	....	....	....
	NY Rangers	**NHL**	**31**	**1**	**3**	**4**	**46**	**0**	**0**	**0**	**21**	**4.8**	**–2**	**0**	**0.0**	**58**	**11**	**11:58**	....	....	....	....	....	....	....	....
	Hartford	AHL	6	0	1	1	4	....	....	....	....	....	....	....	....	....	....	....	....	....	....	....	....	....	....	....
99-2000	Hartford	AHL	2	0	0	0	0	....	....	....	....	....	....	....	....	....	....	....	....	....	....	....	....	....	....	....
	Atlanta	**NHL**	**27**	**1**	**0**	**1**	**71**	**0**	**0**	**0**	**6**	**16.7**	**–17**	**0**	**0.0**	**64**	**18**	**13:12**	....	....	....	....	....	....	....	....
	NHL Totals		**69**	**2**	**3**	**5**	**137**	**0**	**0**	**0**	**28**	**7.1**		**0**	**0.0**	**133**	**31**	**12:21**	....	....	....	....	....	....	....	....

Claimed on waivers by **NY Rangers** from **Buffalo**, December 18, 1998. Claimed on waivers by **Atlanta** from **NY Rangers**, December 11, 1999.

NECKAR, Stanislav

(NEHTS-kahrzh, STAN-ihs-lahv) **PHX.**

Defense. Shoots left. 6'1", 207 lbs. Born, Ceske Budejovice, Czech., December 22, 1975. Ottawa's 2nd choice, 29th overall, in 1994 Entry Draft.

Season	Club	League	GP	G	A	Pts	PIM	PP	SH	GW	S	%	+/–	TF	F%	H	SB	Min	GP	G	A	Pts	PIM	PP	SH	GW
1991-92	MC Budejovice	Czech-Jr.	18	1	3	4	....	....	....	....	....	....	....	....	....	....	....	....	....	....	....	....	....	....	....	....
1992-93	MC Budejovice	Czech.	42	2	9	11	12	....	....	....	....	....	....	....	....	....	....	....	....	....	....	....	....	....	....	....
1993-94	HC Budejovice	Cze-Rep	12	3	2	5	2	....	....	....	....	....	....	....	....	....	....	....	3	0	0	0	....	....	....	....
1994-95	Detroit Vipers	IHL	15	2	2	4	15	....	....	....	....	....	....	....	....	....	....	....	....	....	....	....	....	....	....	....
	Ottawa	**NHL**	**48**	**1**	**3**	**4**	**37**	**0**	**0**	**0**	**34**	**2.9**	**–20**	....	....	....	....	....	....	....	....	....	....	....	....	....
1995-96	**Ottawa**	**NHL**	**82**	**3**	**9**	**12**	**54**	**1**	**0**	**0**	**57**	**5.3**	**–16**	....	....	....	....	....	....	....	....	....	....	....	....	....
1996-97	**Ottawa**	**NHL**	**5**	**0**	**0**	**0**	**2**	**0**	**0**	**0**	**3**	**0.0**	**2**	....	....	....	....	....	....	....	....	....	....	....	....	....
1997-98	**Ottawa**	**NHL**	**60**	**2**	**2**	**4**	**31**	**0**	**0**	**0**	**43**	**4.7**	**–14**	....	....	....	....	....	**9**	**0**	**0**	**0**	**2**	**0**	**0**	**0**
1998-99	**Ottawa**	**NHL**	**3**	**0**	**2**	**2**	**0**	**0**	**0**	**0**	**2**	**0.0**	**–1**	**0**	**0.0**	**6**	**3**	**15:53**	....	....	....	....	....	....	....	....
	NY Rangers	**NHL**	**18**	**0**	**0**	**0**	**8**	**0**	**0**	**0**	**8**	**0.0**	**–1**	**0**	**0.0**	**30**	**27**	**13:46**	....	....	....	....	....	....	....	....
	Phoenix	**NHL**	**11**	**0**	**1**	**1**	**10**	**0**	**0**	**0**	**6**	**0.0**	**3**	**0**	**0.0**	**26**	**10**	**15:08**	**6**	**0**	**1**	**1**	**4**	**0**	**0**	**0**
99-2000	**Phoenix**	**NHL**	**66**	**2**	**8**	**10**	**36**	**0**	**0**	**0**	**34**	**5.9**	**1**	**0**	**0.0**	**119**	**54**	**14:27**	**5**	**0**	**0**	**0**	**0**	**0**	**0**	**0**
	NHL Totals		**293**	**8**	**25**	**33**	**178**	**1**	**0**	**0**	**187**	**4.3**		**0**	**0.0**	**181**	**94**	**14:27**	**20**	**0**	**1**	**1**	**6**	**0**	**0**	**0**

Traded to **NY Rangers** by **Ottawa** for Bill Berg and NY Rangers' 2nd round choice (later traded to Anaheim, Anaheim selected Jordan Leopold) in 1999 Entry Draft, November 27, 1998. Traded to **Phoenix** by **NY Rangers** for Jason Doig and Phoenix's 6th round choice (Jay Dardis) in 1999 Entry Draft, March 23, 1999.

NEDVED, Petr

(NEHD-VEHD, PEE-tuhr) **NYR**

Center. Shoots left. 6'3", 195 lbs. Born, Liberec, Czech., December 9, 1971. Vancouver's 1st choice, 2nd overall, in 1990 Entry Draft.

Season	Club	League	GP	G	A	Pts	PIM	PP	SH	GW	S	%	+/–	TF	F%	H	SB	Min	GP	G	A	Pts	PIM	PP	SH	GW
1988-89	CHZ Litvinov	Czech-Jr.	20	32	19	51	12	....	....	....	....	....	....	....	....	....	....	....	....	....	....	....	....	....	....	....
1989-90	Seattle T-Birds	WHL	71	65	80	145	80	....	....	....	....	....	....	....	....	....	....	....	11	4	9	13	2	....	....	....
1990-91	**Vancouver**	**NHL**	**61**	**10**	**6**	**16**	**20**	**1**	**0**	**0**	**97**	**10.3**	**–21**	....	....	....	....	....	**6**	**0**	**1**	**1**	**0**	**0**	**0**	**0**
1991-92	**Vancouver**	**NHL**	**77**	**15**	**22**	**37**	**36**	**5**	**0**	**1**	**99**	**15.2**	**–3**	....	....	....	....	....	**10**	**1**	**4**	**5**	**16**	**0**	**0**	**0**
1992-93	**Vancouver**	**NHL**	**84**	**38**	**33**	**71**	**96**	**2**	**1**	**3**	**149**	**25.5**	**20**	....	....	....	....	....	**12**	**2**	**3**	**5**	**2**	**0**	**0**	**0**
1993-94	Canada	Nat-Team	17	19	12	31	16	....	....	....	....	....	....	....	....	....	....	....	....	....	....	....	....	....	....	....
	Canada	Olympics	8	5	1	6	6	....	....	....	....	....	....	....	....	....	....	....	....	....	....	....	....	....	....	....
	St. Louis	**NHL**	**19**	**6**	**14**	**20**	**8**	**2**	**0**	**0**	**63**	**9.5**	**2**	....	....	....	....	....	**4**	**0**	**1**	**1**	**4**	**0**	**0**	**0**
1994-95	**NY Rangers**	**NHL**	**46**	**11**	**12**	**23**	**26**	**1**	**0**	**3**	**123**	**8.9**	**–1**	....	....	....	....	....	**10**	**3**	**2**	**5**	**6**	**2**	**0**	**0**
1995-96	**Pittsburgh**	**NHL**	**80**	**45**	**54**	**99**	**68**	**8**	**1**	**5**	**204**	**22.1**	**37**	....	....	....	....	....	**18**	**10**	**10**	**20**	**16**	**4**	**0**	**2**
1996-97	**Pittsburgh**	**NHL**	**74**	**33**	**38**	**71**	**66**	**12**	**3**	**4**	**189**	**17.5**	**–2**	....	....	....	....	....	**5**	**1**	**2**	**3**	**12**	**0**	**1**	**0**
1997-98	HC Liberec-2	Cze-Rep	2	0	3	3	....	....	....	....	....	....	....	....	....	....	....	....	....	....	....	....	....	....	....	....
	Novy Jicin-3	Cze-Rep	7	9	16	25	....	....	....	....	....	....	....	....	....	....	....	....	....	....	....	....	....	....	....	....
	Sparta Praha	Cze-Rep	5	2	3	5	8	....	....	....	....	....	....	....	....	....	....	....	6	0	2	2	52	....	....	....
	Las Vegas	IHL	3	3	3	6	4	....	....	....	....	....	....	....	....	....	....	....	....	....	....	....	....	....	....	....
1998-99	Las Vegas	IHL	13	8	10	18	32	....	....	....	....	....	....	....	....	....	....	....	....	....	....	....	....	....	....	....
	NY Rangers	**NHL**	**56**	**20**	**27**	**47**	**50**	**9**	**1**	**3**	**153**	**13.1**	**–6**	**1069**	**52.5**	**58**	**34**	**20:31**	....	....	....	....	....	....	....	....
99-2000	**NY Rangers**	**NHL**	**76**	**24**	**44**	**68**	**40**	**6**	**2**	**4**	**201**	**11.9**	**2**	**1354**	**54.0**	**55**	**33**	**19:54**	....	....	....	....	....	....	....	....
	NHL Totals		**573**	**202**	**250**	**452**	**410**	**46**	**8**	**23**	**1278**	**15.8**		**2423**	**53.3**	**113**	**67**	**20:010**	**65**	**17**	**23**	**40**	**56**	**6**	**1**	**2**

Canadian Major Junior Rookie of the Year (1990)

Signed as a free agent by **St. Louis**, March 5, 1994. Traded to **NY Rangers** by **St. Louis** for Esa Tikkanen and Doug Lidster, July 24, 1994. Traded to **Pittsburgh** by **NY Rangers** with Sergei Zubov for Luc Robitaille and Ulf Samuelsson, August 31, 1995. Traded to **NY Rangers** by **Pittsburgh** with Chris Tamer and Sean Pronger for Alexei Kovalev and Harry York, November 25, 1998.

NEDVED, Zdenek

(NEHD-VEHD, ZEH-dehn-EHK)

Right wing. Shoots left. 6', 180 lbs. Born, Lany, Czech., March 3, 1975. Toronto's 3rd choice, 123rd overall, in 1993 Entry Draft.

Season	Club	League	GP	G	A	Pts	PIM	PP	SH	GW	S	%	+/–	TF	F%	H	SB	Min	GP	G	A	Pts	PIM	PP	SH	GW
1991-92	Poldi Kladno	Czech-Jr.	19	15	12	27	22	....	....	....	....	....	....	....	....	....	....	....	....	....	....	....	....	....	....	....
1992-93	Sudbury Wolves	OHL	18	3	9	12	6	....	....	....	....	....	....	....	....	....	....	....	....	....	....	....	....	....	....	....
1993-94	Sudbury Wolves	OHL	60	50	50	100	42	....	....	....	....	....	....	....	....	....	....	....	10	7	8	15	10	....	....	....
1994-95	Sudbury Wolves	OHL	59	47	51	98	36	....	....	....	....	....	....	....	....	....	....	....	18	12	16	28	16	....	....	....
	Toronto	**NHL**	**1**	**0**	**0**	**0**	**2**	**0**	**0**	**0**	**0**	**0.0**	**0**	....	....	....	....	....	....	....	....	....	....	....	....	....
1995-96	**Toronto**	**NHL**	**7**	**1**	**1**	**2**	**6**	**0**	**0**	**0**	**7**	**14.3**	**–1**	....	....	....	....	....	....	....	....	....	....	....	....	....
	St. John's Leafs	AHL	41	13	14	27	22	....	....	....	....	....	....	....	....	....	....	....	4	2	0	2	0	....	....	....
1996-97	**Toronto**	**NHL**	**23**	**3**	**5**	**8**	**6**	**1**	**0**	**0**	**22**	**13.6**	**4**	....	....	....	....	....	....	....	....	....	....	....	....	....
	St. John's Leafs	AHL	51	9	25	34	34	....	....	....	....	....	....	....	....	....	....	....	7	2	2	4	6	....	....	....
1997-98	Long Beach	IHL	19	3	8	11	18	....	....	....	....	....	....	....	....	....	....	....	....	....	....	....	....	....	....	....
	St. John's Leafs	AHL	45	7	8	15	24	....	....	....	....	....	....	....	....	....	....	....	3	1	0	1	2	....	....	....
1998-99	Sparta Praha	Cze-Rep	10	0	2	2	8	....	....	....	....	....	....	....	....	....	....	....	....	....	....	....	....	....	....	....
	Sparta Praha	EuroHL	3	0	0	0	0	....	....	....	....	....	....	....	....	....	....	....	....	....	....	....	....	....	....	....
	Lukko Rauma	Finland	30	4	7	11	22	....	....	....	....	....	....	....	....	....	....	....	....	....	....	....	....	....	....	....
99-2000	Lukko Rauma	Finland	54	28	18	46	50	....	....	....	....	....	....	....	....	....	....	....	4	0	0	0	2	....	....	....
	NHL Totals		**31**	**4**	**6**	**10**	**14**	**1**	**0**	**0**	**29**	**13.8**		....	....	....	....	....	....	....	....	....	....	....	....	....

NELSON, Jeff

(NEHL-sohn, JEHF) **WSH.**

Center. Shoots left. 5'11", 190 lbs. Born, Prince Albert, Sask., December 18, 1972. Washington's 4th choice, 36th overall, in 1991 Entry Draft.

Season	Club	League	GP	G	A	Pts	PIM	PP	SH	GW	S	%	+/–	TF	F%	H	SB	Min	GP	G	A	Pts	PIM	PP	SH	GW
1987-88	Prince Albert	AAHA	31	24	32	56	32	....	....	....	....	....	....	....	....	....	....	....	....	....	....	....	....	....	....	....
1988-89	Prince Albert	WHL	71	30	57	87	74	....	....	....	....	....	....	....	....	....	....	....	4	0	3	3	4	....	....	....
1989-90	Prince Albert	WHL	72	28	69	97	79	....	....	....	....	....	....	....	....	....	....	....	14	2	11	13	10	....	....	....
1990-91	Prince Albert	WHL	72	46	74	120	58	....	....	....	....	....	....	....	....	....	....	....	3	1	1	2	4	....	....	....
1991-92	Prince Albert	WHL	64	48	65	113	84	....	....	....	....	....	....	....	....	....	....	....	9	7	14	21	18	....	....	....
1992-93	Baltimore	AHL	72	14	38	52	12	....	....	....	....	....	....	....	....	....	....	....	7	1	3	4	2	....	....	....
1993-94	Portland Pirates	AHL	80	34	73	107	92	....	....	....	....	....	....	....	....	....	....	....	17	10	5	15	20	....	....	....
1994-95	Portland Pirates	AHL	64	33	50	83	57	....	....	....	....	....	....	....	....	....	....	....	7	1	4	5	8	....	....	....
	Washington	**NHL**	**10**	**1**	**0**	**1**	**2**	**0**	**0**	**0**	**4**	**25.0**	**–2**	....	....	....	....	....	....	....	....	....	....	....	....	....
1995-96	**Washington**	**NHL**	**33**	**0**	**7**	**7**	**16**	**0**	**0**	**0**	**21**	**0.0**	**3**	....	....	....	....	....	**3**	**0**	**0**	**0**	**4**	**0**	**0**	**0**
	Portland Pirates	AHL	39	15	32	47	62	....	....	....	....	....	....	....	....	....	....	....	....	....	....	....	....	....	....	....
1996-97	Grand Rapids	IHL	82	34	55	89	85	....	....	....	....	....	....	....	....	....	....	....	5	0	4	4	4	....	....	....
1997-98	Milwaukee	IHL	52	20	34	54	30	....	....	....	....	....	....	....	....	....	....	....	10	2	7	9	15	....	....	....
1998-99	**Nashville**	**NHL**	**9**	**2**	**1**	**3**	**2**	**0**	**0**	**0**	**8**	**25.0**	**–1**	**138**	**55.1**	**4**	**8**	**16:09**	....	....	....	....	....	....	....	....
	Milwaukee	IHL	70	20	31	51	66	....	....	....	....	....	....	....	....	....	....	....	2	0	0	0	0	....	....	....
99-2000	Portland Pirates	AHL	73	24	30	54	38	....	....	....	....	....	....	....	....	....	....	....	1	0	0	0	0	....	....	....
	NHL Totals		**52**	**3**	**8**	**11**	**20**	**0**	**0**	**0**	**33**	**9.1**		**138**	**55.1**	**4**	**8**	**16:09**	**3**	**0**	**0**	**0**	**4**	**0**	**0**	**0**

Canadian Major Junior Scholastic Player of the Year (1989, 1990) • WHL East Second All-Star Team (1991, 1992)

Traded to **Nashville** by **Washington** for future considerations, August 19, 1998. Traded to **Washington** by **Nashville** for cash, June 21, 1999.

			Regular Season																Playoffs							
Season	Club	League	GP	G	A	Pts	PIM	PP	SH	GW	S	%	+/-	TF	F%	H	SB	Min	GP	G	A	Pts	PIM	PP	SH	GW

NEMCHINOV, Sergei

(nehm-CHEE-nahf, SAIR-gay) **N.J.**

Left wing. Shoots left. 6', 205 lbs. Born, Moscow, USSR, January 14, 1964. NY Rangers' 14th choice, 244th overall, in 1990 Entry Draft.

Season	Club	League	GP	G	A	Pts	PIM	PP	SH	GW	S	%	+/-	TF	F%	H	SB	Min	GP	G	A	Pts	PIM	PP	SH	GW
1981-82	Krylja Sovetov	USSR	15	1	0	1	0	....	....	....	....	....	....	....	....	....	....	....	....	....	....	....	....	....	....	....
1982-83	CSKA Moscow	USSR	11	0	0	0	2	....	....	....	....	....	....	....	....	....	....	....	....	....	....	....	....	....	....	....
1983-84	CSKA Moscow	USSR	20	6	5	11	4	....	....	....	....	....	....	....	....	....	....	....	....	....	....	....	....	....	....	....
1984-85	CSKA Moscow	USSR	31	2	4	6	4	....	....	....	....	....	....	....	....	....	....	....	....	....	....	....	....	....	....	....
1985-86	Krylja Sovetov	USSR	39	7	12	19	28	....	....	....	....	....	....	....	....	....	....	....	....	....	....	....	....	....	....	....
1986-87	Krylja Sovetov	USSR	40	13	9	22	24	....	....	....	....	....	....	....	....	....	....	....	....	....	....	....	....	....	....	....
1987-88	Krylja Sovetov	USSR	48	17	11	28	26	....	....	....	....	....	....	....	....	....	....	....	....	....	....	....	....	....	....	....
1988-89	Krylja Sovetov	USSR	43	15	14	29	28	....	....	....	....	....	....	....	....	....	....	....	....	....	....	....	....	....	....	....
1989-90	Krylja Sovetov	USSR	48	17	16	33	34	....	....	....	....	....	....	....	....	....	....	....	....	....	....	....	....	....	....	....
1990-91	Krylja Sovetov	USSR	46	21	24	45	30	....	....	....	....	....	....	....	....	....	....	....	....	....	....	....	....	....	....	....
1991-92	**NY Rangers**	**NHL**	**73**	**30**	**28**	**58**	**15**	**2**	**0**	**5**	**124**	**24.2**	**19**	....	....	....	....	....	**13**	**1**	**4**	**5**	**8**	**0**	**0**	**0**
1992-93	**NY Rangers**	**NHL**	**81**	**23**	**31**	**54**	**34**	**0**	**1**	**3**	**144**	**16.0**	**15**	....	....	....	....	....	....	....	....	....	....	....	....	....
1993-94♦	**NY Rangers**	**NHL**	**76**	**22**	**27**	**49**	**36**	**4**	**0**	**6**	**144**	**15.3**	**13**	....	....	....	....	....	**23**	**2**	**5**	**7**	**6**	**0**	**0**	**0**
1994-95	**NY Rangers**	**NHL**	**47**	**7**	**6**	**13**	**16**	**0**	**0**	**3**	**67**	**10.4**	**–6**	....	....	....	....	....	**10**	**4**	**5**	**9**	**2**	**0**	**0**	**1**
1995-96	**NY Rangers**	**NHL**	**78**	**17**	**15**	**32**	**38**	**0**	**0**	**2**	**118**	**14.4**	**9**	....	....	....	....	....	**6**	**0**	**1**	**1**	**2**	**0**	**0**	**0**
1996-97	**NY Rangers**	**NHL**	**63**	**6**	**13**	**19**	**12**	**1**	**0**	**1**	**90**	**6.7**	**5**	....	....	....	....	....	....	....	....	....	....	....	....	....
	Vancouver	**NHL**	**6**	**2**	**3**	**5**	**4**	**0**	**0**	**1**	**7**	**28.6**	**4**	....	....	....	....	....	....	....	....	....	....	....	....	....
1997-98	**NY Islanders**	**NHL**	**74**	**10**	**19**	**29**	**24**	**2**	**1**	**1**	**94**	**10.6**	**3**	....	....	....	....	....	....	....	....	....	....	....	....	....
	Russia	Olympics	6	1	0	1	0	....	....	....	....	....	....	....	....	....	....	....	....	....	....	....	....	....	....	....
1998-99	**NY Islanders**	**NHL**	**67**	**8**	**8**	**16**	**22**	**1**	**0**	**0**	**61**	**13.1**	**–17**	**606**	**42.4**	**52**	**44**	**14:21**	....	....	....	....	....	....	....	....
	New Jersey	**NHL**	**10**	**4**	**0**	**4**	**6**	**1**	**0**	**1**	**13**	**30.8**	**4**	**38**	**52.6**	**13**	**0**	**15:36**	**4**	**0**	**0**	**0**	**0**	**0**	**0**	**0**
99-2000♦	**New Jersey**	**NHL**	**53**	**10**	**16**	**26**	**18**	**0**	**1**	**1**	**55**	**18.2**	**1**	**453**	**45.7**	**47**	**19**	**13:42**	**21**	**3**	**2**	**5**	**2**	**1**	**0**	**0**
	NHL Totals		**628**	**139**	**166**	**305**	**225**	**11**	**3**	**24**	**917**	**15.2**		**1097**	**44.1**	**112**	**63**	**14:11**	**77**	**10**	**17**	**27**	**20**	**1**	**0**	**1**

Traded to **Vancouver** by **NY Rangers** with Brian Noonan for Esa Tikkanen and Russ Courtnall, March 8, 1997. Signed as a free agent by **NY Islanders**, July 10, 1997. Traded to **New Jersey** by **NY Islanders** for New Jersey's 4th round choice (later traded to Los Angeles - Los Angeles selected Daniel Johansson) in 1999 Entry Draft, March 22, 1999.

NEMECEK, Jan

(NEHM-eh-chehk, YAHN) **L.A.**

Defense. Shoots right. 6'1", 220 lbs. Born, Pisek, Czech., February 14, 1976. Los Angeles' 7th choice, 215th overall, in 1994 Entry Draft.

Season	Club	League	GP	G	A	Pts	PIM	PP	SH	GW	S	%	+/-	TF	F%	H	SB	Min	GP	G	A	Pts	PIM	PP	SH	GW
1992-93	MC Budejovice	Czech.	15	0	0	0	....	....	....	....	....	....	....	....	....	....	....	....	....	....	....	....	....	....	....	....
1993-94	MC Budejovice	Cze-Rep	16	0	1	1	16	....	....	....	....	....	....	....	....	....	....	....	....	....	....	....	....	....	....	....
1994-95	Hull Olympiques	QMJHL	49	10	16	26	48	....	....	....	....	....	....	....	....	....	....	....	21	5	9	14	10	....	....	....
1995-96	Hull Olympiques	QMJHL	57	17	49	66	58	....	....	....	....	....	....	....	....	....	....	....	17	2	13	15	10	....	....	....
1996-97	Mississippi	ECHL	20	3	9	12	16	....	....	....	....	....	....	....	....	....	....	....	3	0	0	0	4	....	....	....
	Phoenix	IHL	24	1	1	2	2	....	....	....	....	....	....	....	....	....	....	....	....	....	....	....	....	....	....	....
1997-98	Fredericton	AHL	65	7	24	31	43	....	....	....	....	....	....	....	....	....	....	....	2	0	0	0	0	....	....	....
1998-99	**Los Angeles**	**NHL**	**6**	**1**	**0**	**1**	**4**	**0**	**0**	**1**	**8**	**12.5**	**–1**	**0**	**0.0**	**2**	**4**	**16:42**	....	....	....	....	....	....	....	....
	Long Beach	IHL	66	5	16	21	42	....	....	....	....	....	....	....	....	....	....	....	....	....	....	....	....	....	....	....
99-2000	**Los Angeles**	**NHL**	**1**	**0**	**0**	**0**	**0**	**0**	**0**	**0**	**0**	**0.0**	**0**	**0**	**0.0**	**0**	**0**	**9:36**	....	....	....	....	....	....	....	....
	Long Beach	IHL	71	9	15	24	22	....	....	....	....	....	....	....	....	....	....	....	6	1	0	1	4	....	....	....
	NHL Totals		**7**	**1**	**0**	**1**	**4**	**0**	**0**	**1**	**8**	**12.5**		**0**	**0.0**	**2**	**4**	**15:41**	....	....	....	....	....	....	....	....

QMJHL Second All-Star Team (1996)

NEMIROVSKY, David

(neh-mih-ROHV-skee, DAY-vihd) **TOR.**

Right wing. Shoots right. 6'2", 205 lbs. Born, Toronto, Ont., August 1, 1976. Florida's 5th choice, 84th overall, in 1994 Entry Draft.

Season	Club	League	GP	G	A	Pts	PIM	PP	SH	GW	S	%	+/-	TF	F%	H	SB	Min	GP	G	A	Pts	PIM	PP	SH	GW
1991-92	Pickering	OJHL	14	3	10	13	5	....	....	....	....	....	....	....	....	....	....	....	....	....	....	....	....	....	....	....
	Weston Dukes	OJHL	23	6	13	19	2	....	....	....	....	....	....	....	....	....	....	....	....	....	....	....	....	....	....	....
1992-93	Weston Dukes	OJHL	2	0	3	3	0	....	....	....	....	....	....	....	....	....	....	....	....	....	....	....	....	....	....	....
	North York	OJHL	40	19	23	42	27	....	....	....	....	....	....	....	....	....	....	....	....	....	....	....	....	....	....	....
1993-94	Ottawa 67's	OHL	64	21	31	52	18	....	....	....	....	....	....	....	....	....	....	....	17	10	10	20	2	....	....	....
1994-95	Ottawa 67's	OHL	59	27	29	56	25	....	....	....	....	....	....	....	....	....	....	....	....	....	....	....	....	....	....	....
1995-96	Sarnia Sting	OHL	26	18	27	45	14	....	....	....	....	....	....	....	....	....	....	....	10	8	8	16	6	....	....	....
	Florida	**NHL**	**9**	**0**	**2**	**2**	**2**	**0**	**0**	**0**	**6**	**0.0**	**–1**	....	....	....	....	....	....	....	....	....	....	....	....	....
	Carolina	AHL	5	1	2	3	0	....	....	....	....	....	....	....	....	....	....	....	....	....	....	....	....	....	....	....
1996-97	**Florida**	**NHL**	**39**	**7**	**7**	**14**	**32**	**1**	**0**	**0**	**53**	**13.2**	**1**	....	....	....	....	....	**3**	**1**	**0**	**1**	**0**	**0**	**0**	**0**
	Carolina	AHL	34	21	21	42	18	....	....	....	....	....	....	....	....	....	....	....	....	....	....	....	....	....	....	....
1997-98	**Florida**	**NHL**	**41**	**9**	**12**	**21**	**8**	**2**	**0**	**1**	**62**	**14.5**	**–3**	....	....	....	....	....	....	....	....	....	....	....	....	....
	New Haven	AHL	29	10	15	25	10	....	....	....	....	....	....	....	....	....	....	....	1	1	0	1	0	....	....	....
1998-99	**Florida**	**NHL**	**2**	**0**	**1**	**1**	**0**	**0**	**0**	**0**	**2**	**0.0**	**1**	**0**	**0.0**	**0**	**0**	**8:58**	....	....	....	....	....	....	....	....
	Fort Wayne	IHL	44	22	13	35	24	....	....	....	....	....	....	....	....	....	....	....	....	....	....	....	....	....	....	....
	St. John's Leafs	AHL	22	3	9	12	18	....	....	....	....	....	....	....	....	....	....	....	5	4	1	5	0	....	....	....
99-2000	St. John's Leafs	AHL	57	18	25	43	69	....	....	....	....	....	....	....	....	....	....	....	....	....	....	....	....	....	....	....
	NHL Totals		**91**	**16**	**22**	**38**	**42**	**3**	**0**	**1**	**123**	**13.0**		**0**	**0.0**	**0**	**0**	**8:58**	**3**	**1**	**0**	**1**	**0**	**0**	**0**	**0**

Traded to **Toronto** by **Florida** for Jeff Ware, February 17, 1999.

NICHOL, Scott

(NIH-KOHL, SKAWT) **BUF.**

Center. Shoots right. 5'8", 160 lbs. Born, Edmonton, Alta., December 31, 1974. Buffalo's 9th choice, 272nd overall, in 1993 Entry Draft.

Season	Club	League	GP	G	A	Pts	PIM	PP	SH	GW	S	%	+/-	TF	F%	H	SB	Min	GP	G	A	Pts	PIM	PP	SH	GW
1991-92	Calgary	AAHA	23	26	16	42	132	....	....	....	....	....	....	....	....	....	....	....	....	....	....	....	....	....	....	....
1992-93	Portland	WHL	67	31	33	64	146	....	....	....	....	....	....	....	....	....	....	....	16	8	8	16	41	....	....	....
1993-94	Portland	WHL	65	40	53	93	144	....	....	....	....	....	....	....	....	....	....	....	10	3	8	11	16	....	....	....
1994-95	Rochester	AHL	71	11	16	27	136	....	....	....	....	....	....	....	....	....	....	....	5	0	3	3	14	....	....	....
1995-96	**Buffalo**	**NHL**	**2**	**0**	**0**	**0**	**10**	**0**	**0**	**0**	**4**	**0.0**	**0**	....	....	....	....	....	....	....	....	....	....	....	....	....
	Rochester	AHL	62	14	18	32	170	....	....	....	....	....	....	....	....	....	....	....	19	7	6	13	36	....	....	....
1996-97	Rochester	AHL	68	22	21	43	133	....	....	....	....	....	....	....	....	....	....	....	10	2	1	3	26	....	....	....
1997-98	**Buffalo**	**NHL**	**3**	**0**	**0**	**0**	**4**	**0**	**0**	**0**	**5**	**0.0**	**0**	....	....	....	....	....	....	....	....	....	....	....	....	....
	Rochester	AHL	35	13	7	20	113	....	....	....	....	....	....	....	....	....	....	....	....	....	....	....	....	....	....	....
1998-99	Rochester	AHL	52	13	20	33	120	....	....	....	....	....	....	....	....	....	....	....	....	....	....	....	....	....	....	....
99-2000	Rochester	AHL	37	7	11	18	141	....	....	....	....	....	....	....	....	....	....	....	....	....	....	....	....	....	....	....
	NHL Totals		**5**	**0**	**0**	**0**	**14**	**0**	**0**	**0**	**9**	**0.0**		....	....	....	....	....	....	....	....	....	....	....	....	....

• Missed remainder of 1999-2000 season recovering from knee injury suffered in game vs. Saint John (AHL), February 16, 2000.

NICKULAS, Eric

(NICK-luhs, AIR-ihk) **BOS.**

Center. Shoots right. 5'11", 200 lbs. Born, Hyannis, MA, March 25, 1975. Boston's 3rd choice, 99th overall, in 1994 Entry Draft.

Season	Club	League	GP	G	A	Pts	PIM	PP	SH	GW	S	%	+/-	TF	F%	H	SB	Min	GP	G	A	Pts	PIM	PP	SH	GW
1991-92	Barnstable High	Hi-School	24	30	25	55	....	....	....	....	....	....	....	....	....	....	....	....	....	....	....	....	....	....	....	....
1992-93	Tabor Academy	Hi-School	28	25	25	50	....	....	....	....	....	....	....	....	....	....	....	....	....	....	....	....	....	....	....	....
1993-94	Cushing Academy	Hi-School	25	46	36	82	....	....	....	....	....	....	....	....	....	....	....	....	....	....	....	....	....	....	....	....
1994-95	New Hampshire	H-East	33	15	9	24	32	....	....	....	....	....	....	....	....	....	....	....	....	....	....	....	....	....	....	....
1995-96	New Hampshire	H-East	34	26	12	38	66	....	....	....	....	....	....	....	....	....	....	....	....	....	....	....	....	....	....	....
1996-97	New Hampshire	H-East	39	29	22	51	80	....	....	....	....	....	....	....	....	....	....	....	....	....	....	....	....	....	....	....
1997-98	Orlando	IHL	76	22	9	31	77	....	....	....	....	....	....	....	....	....	....	....	6	0	0	0	10	....	....	....
1998-99	**Boston**	**NHL**	**2**	**0**	**0**	**0**	**0**	**0**	**0**	**0**	**0**	**0.0**	**0**	**0**	**0.0**	**0**	**0**	**3:27**	**1**	**0**	**0**	**0**	**2**	**0**	**0**	**0**
	Providence Bruins	AHL	75	31	27	58	83	....	....	....	....	....	....	....	....	....	....	....	18	8	12	20	33	....	....	....
99-2000	**Boston**	**NHL**	**20**	**5**	**6**	**11**	**12**	**1**	**0**	**0**	**28**	**17.9**	**–1**	**4**	**50.0**	**31**	**3**	**11:13**	....	....	....	....	....	....	....	....
	Providence Bruins	AHL	40	6	6	12	37	....	....	....	....	....	....	....	....	....	....	....	12	2	3	5	20	....	....	....
	NHL Totals		**22**	**5**	**6**	**11**	**12**	**1**	**0**	**0**	**28**	**17.9**		**4**	**50.0**	**31**	**3**	**10:30**	**1**	**0**	**0**	**0**	**2**	**0**	**0**	**0**

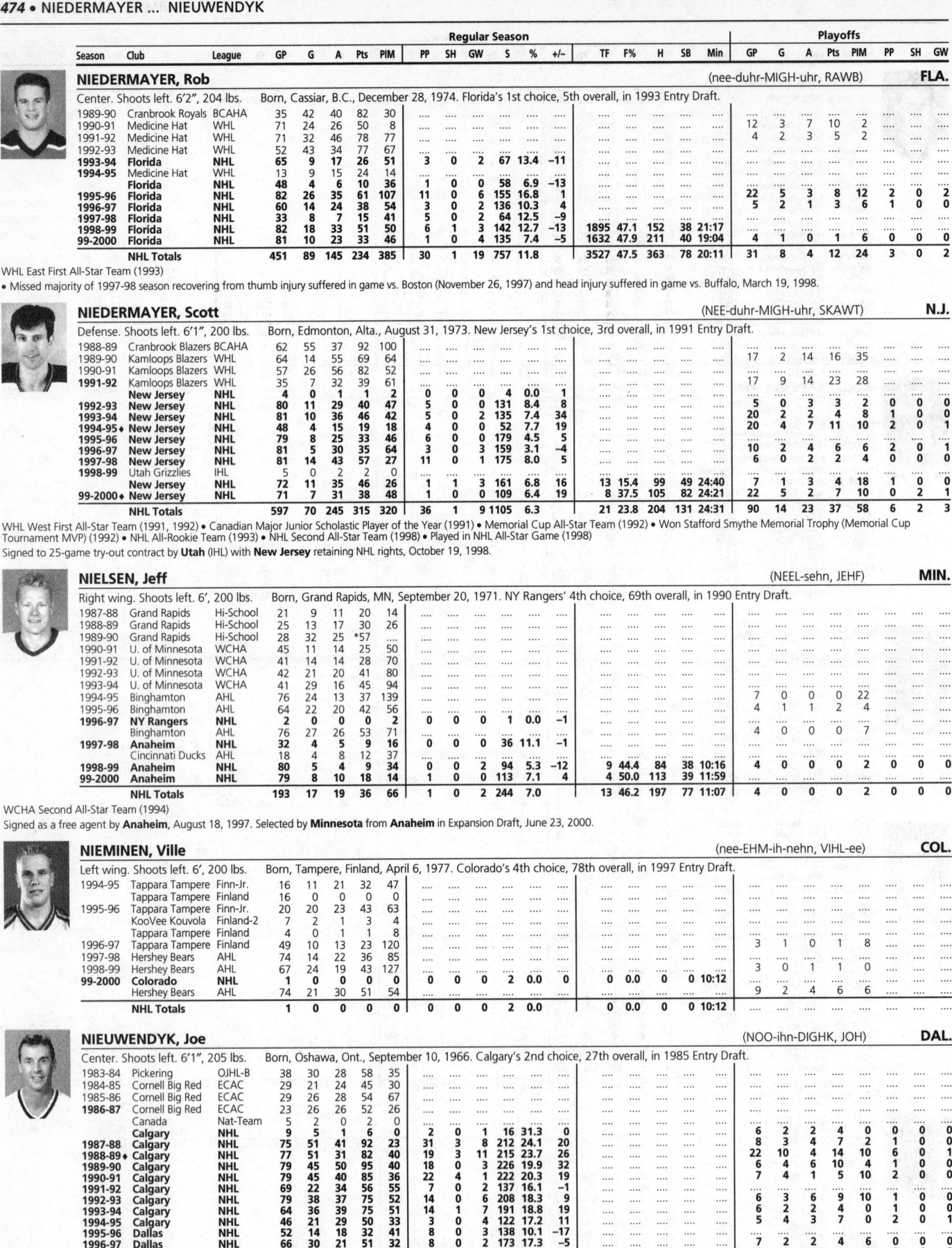

NIEDERMAYER, Rob

(nee-duhr-MIGH-uhr, RAWB) **FLA.**

Center. Shoots left. 6'2", 204 lbs. Born, Cassiar, B.C., December 28, 1974. Florida's 1st choice, 5th overall, in 1993 Entry Draft.

Season	Club	League	GP	G	A	Pts	PIM	PP	SH	GW	S	%	+/-	TF	F%	H	SB	Min	Playoffs GP	G	A	Pts	PIM	PP	SH	GW
1989-90	Cranbrook Royals	BCAHA	35	42	40	82	30	....	....	....	....	....	....	....	....	....	....	....	....	....	....	....	....	....	....	....
1990-91	Medicine Hat	WHL	71	24	26	50	8	....	....	....	....	....	....	....	....	....	....	....	12	3	7	10	2	....	....	....
1991-92	Medicine Hat	WHL	71	32	46	78	77	....	....	....	....	....	....	....	....	....	....	....	4	2	3	5	2	....	....	....
1992-93	Medicine Hat	WHL	52	43	34	77	67	....	....	....	....	....	....	....	....	....	....	....	....	....	....	....	....	....	....	....
1993-94	**Florida**	**NHL**	**65**	**9**	**17**	**26**	**51**	**3**	**0**	**2**	**67**	**13.4**	**-11**	....	....	....	....	....	....	....	....	....	....	....	....	....
1994-95	Medicine Hat	WHL	13	9	15	24	14	....	....	....	....	....	....	....	....	....	....	....	....	....	....	....	....	....	....	....
	Florida	**NHL**	**48**	**4**	**6**	**10**	**36**	**1**	**0**	**0**	**58**	**6.9**	**-13**	....	....	....	....	....	....	....	....	....	....	....	....	....
1995-96	**Florida**	**NHL**	**82**	**26**	**35**	**61**	**107**	**11**	**0**	**6**	**155**	**16.8**	**1**	....	....	....	....	....	**22**	**5**	**3**	**8**	**12**	**2**	**0**	**2**
1996-97	**Florida**	**NHL**	**60**	**14**	**24**	**38**	**54**	**3**	**0**	**2**	**136**	**10.3**	**4**	....	....	....	....	....	**5**	**2**	**1**	**3**	**6**	**1**	**0**	**0**
1997-98	**Florida**	**NHL**	**33**	**8**	**7**	**15**	**41**	**5**	**0**	**2**	**64**	**12.5**	**-9**	....	....	....	....	....	....	....	....	....	....	....	....	....
1998-99	**Florida**	**NHL**	**82**	**18**	**33**	**51**	**50**	**6**	**1**	**3**	**142**	**12.7**	**-13**	**1895**	**47.1**	**152**	**38**	**21:17**	....	....	....	....	....	....	....	....
99-2000	**Florida**	**NHL**	**81**	**10**	**23**	**33**	**46**	**1**	**0**	**4**	**135**	**7.4**	**-5**	**1632**	**47.9**	**211**	**40**	**19:04**	**4**	**1**	**0**	**1**	**6**	**0**	**0**	**0**
	NHL Totals		**451**	**89**	**145**	**234**	**385**	**30**	**1**	**19**	**757**	**11.8**		**3527**	**47.5**	**363**	**78**	**20:11**	**31**	**8**	**4**	**12**	**24**	**3**	**0**	**2**

WHL East First All-Star Team (1993)

• Missed majority of 1997-98 season recovering from thumb injury suffered in game vs. Boston (November 26, 1997) and head injury suffered in game vs. Buffalo, March 19, 1998.

NIEDERMAYER, Scott

(NEE-duhr-MIGH-uhr, SKAWT) **N.J.**

Defense. Shoots left. 6'1", 200 lbs. Born, Edmonton, Alta., August 31, 1973. New Jersey's 1st choice, 3rd overall, in 1991 Entry Draft.

Season	Club	League	GP	G	A	Pts	PIM	PP	SH	GW	S	%	+/-	TF	F%	H	SB	Min	Playoffs GP	G	A	Pts	PIM	PP	SH	GW
1988-89	Cranbrook Blazers	BCAHA	62	55	37	92	100	....	....	....	....	....	....	....	....	....	....	....	....	....	....	....	....	....	....	....
1989-90	Kamloops Blazers	WHL	64	14	55	69	64	....	....	....	....	....	....	....	....	....	....	....	17	2	14	16	35	....	....	....
1990-91	Kamloops Blazers	WHL	57	26	56	82	52	....	....	....	....	....	....	....	....	....	....	....	....	....	....	....	....	....	....	....
1991-92	Kamloops Blazers	WHL	35	7	32	39	61	....	....	....	....	....	....	....	....	....	....	....	17	9	14	23	28	....	....	....
	New Jersey	**NHL**	**4**	**0**	**1**	**1**	**2**	**0**	**0**	**0**	**4**	**0.0**	**1**	....	....	....	....	....	....	....	....	....	....	....	....	....
1992-93	**New Jersey**	**NHL**	**80**	**11**	**29**	**40**	**47**	**5**	**0**	**0**	**131**	**8.4**	**8**	....	....	....	....	....	**5**	**0**	**3**	**3**	**2**	**0**	**0**	**0**
1993-94	**New Jersey**	**NHL**	**81**	**10**	**36**	**46**	**42**	**5**	**0**	**2**	**135**	**7.4**	**34**	....	....	....	....	....	**20**	**2**	**2**	**4**	**8**	**1**	**0**	**0**
1994-95♦	**New Jersey**	**NHL**	**48**	**4**	**15**	**19**	**18**	**4**	**0**	**0**	**52**	**7.7**	**19**	....	....	....	....	....	**20**	**4**	**7**	**11**	**10**	**2**	**0**	**1**
1995-96	**New Jersey**	**NHL**	**79**	**8**	**25**	**33**	**46**	**6**	**0**	**0**	**179**	**4.5**	**5**	....	....	....	....	....	....	....	....	....	....	....	....	....
1996-97	**New Jersey**	**NHL**	**81**	**5**	**30**	**35**	**64**	**3**	**0**	**3**	**159**	**3.1**	**-4**	....	....	....	....	....	**10**	**2**	**4**	**6**	**6**	**2**	**0**	**1**
1997-98	**New Jersey**	**NHL**	**81**	**14**	**43**	**57**	**27**	**11**	**0**	**1**	**175**	**8.0**	**5**	....	....	....	....	....	**6**	**0**	**2**	**2**	**4**	**0**	**0**	**0**
1998-99	Utah Grizzlies	IHL	5	0	2	2	0	....	....	....	....	....	....	....	....	....	....	....	....	....	....	....	....	....	....	....
	New Jersey	**NHL**	**72**	**11**	**35**	**46**	**26**	**1**	**1**	**3**	**161**	**6.8**	**16**	**13**	**15.4**	**99**	**49**	**24:40**	**7**	**1**	**3**	**4**	**18**	**1**	**0**	**0**
99-2000♦	**New Jersey**	**NHL**	**71**	**7**	**31**	**38**	**48**	**1**	**0**	**0**	**109**	**6.4**	**19**	**8**	**37.5**	**105**	**82**	**24:21**	**22**	**5**	**2**	**7**	**10**	**0**	**2**	**1**
	NHL Totals		**597**	**70**	**245**	**315**	**320**	**36**	**1**	**9**	**1105**	**6.3**		**21**	**23.8**	**204**	**131**	**24:31**	**90**	**14**	**23**	**37**	**58**	**6**	**2**	**3**

WHL West First All-Star Team (1991, 1992) • Canadian Major Junior Scholastic Player of the Year (1991) • Memorial Cup All-Star Team (1992) • Won Stafford Smythe Memorial Trophy (Memorial Cup Tournament MVP) (1992) • NHL All-Rookie Team (1993) • NHL Second All-Star Team (1998) • Played in NHL All-Star Game (1998)

Signed to 25-game try-out contract by **Utah** (IHL) with **New Jersey** retaining NHL rights, October 19, 1998.

NIELSEN, Jeff

(NEEL-sehn, JEHF) **MIN.**

Right wing. Shoots left. 6', 200 lbs. Born, Grand Rapids, MN, September 20, 1971. NY Rangers' 4th choice, 69th overall, in 1990 Entry Draft.

Season	Club	League	GP	G	A	Pts	PIM	PP	SH	GW	S	%	+/-	TF	F%	H	SB	Min	Playoffs GP	G	A	Pts	PIM	PP	SH	GW
1987-88	Grand Rapids	Hi-School	21	9	11	20	14	....	....	....	....	....	....	....	....	....	....	....	....	....	....	....	....	....	....	....
1988-89	Grand Rapids	Hi-School	25	13	17	30	26	....	....	....	....	....	....	....	....	....	....	....	....	....	....	....	....	....	....	....
1989-90	Grand Rapids	Hi-School	28	32	25	*57	....	....	....	....	....	....	....	....	....	....	....	....	....	....	....	....	....	....	....	....
1990-91	U. of Minnesota	WCHA	45	11	14	25	50	....	....	....	....	....	....	....	....	....	....	....	....	....	....	....	....	....	....	....
1991-92	U. of Minnesota	WCHA	41	14	14	28	70	....	....	....	....	....	....	....	....	....	....	....	....	....	....	....	....	....	....	....
1992-93	U. of Minnesota	WCHA	42	21	20	41	80	....	....	....	....	....	....	....	....	....	....	....	....	....	....	....	....	....	....	....
1993-94	U. of Minnesota	WCHA	41	29	16	45	94	....	....	....	....	....	....	....	....	....	....	....	....	....	....	....	....	....	....	....
1994-95	Binghamton	AHL	76	24	13	37	139	....	....	....	....	....	....	....	....	....	....	....	7	0	0	0	22	....	....	....
1995-96	Binghamton	AHL	64	22	20	42	56	....	....	....	....	....	....	....	....	....	....	....	4	1	1	2	4	....	....	....
1996-97	**NY Rangers**	**NHL**	**2**	**0**	**0**	**0**	**2**	**0**	**0**	**0**	**1**	**0.0**	**-1**	....	....	....	....	....	....	....	....	....	....	....	....	....
	Binghamton	AHL	76	27	26	53	71	....	....	....	....	....	....	....	....	....	....	....	4	0	0	0	7	....	....	....
1997-98	**Anaheim**	**NHL**	**32**	**4**	**5**	**9**	**16**	**0**	**0**	**0**	**36**	**11.1**	**-1**	....	....	....	....	....	....	....	....	....	....	....	....	....
	Cincinnati Ducks	AHL	18	4	8	12	37	....	....	....	....	....	....	....	....	....	....	....	....	....	....	....	....	....	....	....
1998-99	**Anaheim**	**NHL**	**80**	**5**	**4**	**9**	**34**	**0**	**0**	**2**	**94**	**5.3**	**-12**	**9**	**44.4**	**84**	**38**	**10:16**	**4**	**0**	**0**	**0**	**2**	**0**	**0**	**0**
99-2000	**Anaheim**	**NHL**	**79**	**8**	**10**	**18**	**14**	**1**	**0**	**0**	**113**	**7.1**	**4**	**4**	**50.0**	**113**	**39**	**11:59**	....	....	....	....	....	....	....	....
	NHL Totals		**193**	**17**	**19**	**36**	**66**	**1**	**0**	**2**	**244**	**7.0**		**13**	**46.2**	**197**	**77**	**11:07**	**4**	**0**	**0**	**0**	**2**	**0**	**0**	**0**

WCHA Second All-Star Team (1994)

Signed as a free agent by **Anaheim**, August 18, 1997. Selected by **Minnesota** from **Anaheim** in Expansion Draft, June 23, 2000.

NIEMINEN, Ville

(nee-EHM-ih-nehn, VIHL-ee) **COL.**

Left wing. Shoots left. 6', 200 lbs. Born, Tampere, Finland, April 6, 1977. Colorado's 4th choice, 78th overall, in 1997 Entry Draft.

Season	Club	League	GP	G	A	Pts	PIM	PP	SH	GW	S	%	+/-	TF	F%	H	SB	Min	Playoffs GP	G	A	Pts	PIM	PP	SH	GW
1994-95	Tappara Tampere	Finn-Jr.	16	11	21	32	47	....	....	....	....	....	....	....	....	....	....	....	....	....	....	....	....	....	....	....
	Tappara Tampere	Finland	16	0	0	0	0	....	....	....	....	....	....	....	....	....	....	....	....	....	....	....	....	....	....	....
1995-96	Tappara Tampere	Finn-Jr.	20	20	23	43	63	....	....	....	....	....	....	....	....	....	....	....	....	....	....	....	....	....	....	....
	KooVee Kouvola	Finland-2	7	2	1	3	4	....	....	....	....	....	....	....	....	....	....	....	....	....	....	....	....	....	....	....
	Tappara Tampere	Finland	4	0	1	1	8	....	....	....	....	....	....	....	....	....	....	....	....	....	....	....	....	....	....	....
1996-97	Tappara Tampere	Finland	49	10	13	23	120	....	....	....	....	....	....	....	....	....	....	....	3	1	0	1	8	....	....	....
1997-98	Hershey Bears	AHL	74	14	22	36	85	....	....	....	....	....	....	....	....	....	....	....	....	....	....	....	....	....	....	....
1998-99	Hershey Bears	AHL	67	24	19	43	127	....	....	....	....	....	....	....	....	....	....	....	3	0	1	1	0	....	....	....
99-2000	**Colorado**	**NHL**	**1**	**0**	**0**	**0**	**0**	**0**	**0**	**0**	**2**	**0.0**	**0**	**0**	**0.0**	**0**	**0**	**10:12**	....	....	....	....	....	....	....	....
	Hershey Bears	AHL	74	21	30	51	54	....	....	....	....	....	....	....	....	....	....	....	9	2	4	6	6	....	....	....
	NHL Totals		**1**	**0**	**0**	**0**	**0**	**0**	**0**	**0**	**2**	**0.0**		**0**	**0.0**	**0**	**0**	**10:12**	....	....	....	....	....	....	....	....

NIEUWENDYK, Joe

(NOO-ihn-DIGHK, JOH) **DAL.**

Center. Shoots left. 6'1", 205 lbs. Born, Oshawa, Ont., September 10, 1966. Calgary's 2nd choice, 27th overall, in 1985 Entry Draft.

Season	Club	League	GP	G	A	Pts	PIM	PP	SH	GW	S	%	+/-	TF	F%	H	SB	Min	Playoffs GP	G	A	Pts	PIM	PP	SH	GW
1983-84	Pickering	OJHL-B	38	30	28	58	35	....	....	....	....	....	....	....	....	....	....	....	....	....	....	....	....	....	....	....
1984-85	Cornell Big Red	ECAC	29	21	24	45	30	....	....	....	....	....	....	....	....	....	....	....	....	....	....	....	....	....	....	....
1985-86	Cornell Big Red	ECAC	29	26	28	54	67	....	....	....	....	....	....	....	....	....	....	....	....	....	....	....	....	....	....	....
1986-87	Cornell Big Red	ECAC	23	26	26	52	26	....	....	....	....	....	....	....	....	....	....	....	....	....	....	....	....	....	....	....
	Canada	Nat-Team	5	2	0	2	0	....	....	....	....	....	....	....	....	....	....	....	....	....	....	....	....	....	....	....
	Calgary	**NHL**	**9**	**5**	**1**	**6**	**0**	**2**	**0**	**1**	**16**	**31.3**	**0**	....	....	....	....	....	**6**	**2**	**2**	**4**	**0**	**0**	**0**	**0**
1987-88	**Calgary**	**NHL**	**75**	**51**	**41**	**92**	**23**	**31**	**3**	**8**	**212**	**24.1**	**20**	....	....	....	....	....	**8**	**3**	**4**	**7**	**2**	**1**	**0**	**0**
1988-89♦	**Calgary**	**NHL**	**77**	**51**	**31**	**82**	**40**	**19**	**3**	**11**	**215**	**23.7**	**26**	....	....	....	....	....	**22**	**10**	**4**	**14**	**10**	**6**	**0**	**1**
1989-90	**Calgary**	**NHL**	**79**	**45**	**50**	**95**	**40**	**18**	**0**	**3**	**226**	**19.9**	**32**	....	....	....	....	....	**6**	**4**	**6**	**10**	**4**	**1**	**0**	**0**
1990-91	**Calgary**	**NHL**	**79**	**45**	**40**	**85**	**36**	**22**	**4**	**1**	**222**	**20.3**	**19**	....	....	....	....	....	**7**	**4**	**1**	**5**	**10**	**2**	**0**	**0**
1991-92	**Calgary**	**NHL**	**69**	**22**	**34**	**56**	**55**	**7**	**0**	**2**	**137**	**16.1**	**-1**	....	....	....	....	....	....	....	....	....	....	....	....	....
1992-93	**Calgary**	**NHL**	**79**	**38**	**37**	**75**	**52**	**14**	**0**	**6**	**208**	**18.3**	**9**	....	....	....	....	....	**6**	**3**	**6**	**9**	**10**	**1**	**0**	**0**
1993-94	**Calgary**	**NHL**	**64**	**36**	**39**	**75**	**51**	**14**	**1**	**7**	**191**	**18.8**	**19**	....	....	....	....	....	**6**	**2**	**2**	**4**	**0**	**1**	**0**	**0**
1994-95	**Calgary**	**NHL**	**46**	**21**	**29**	**50**	**33**	**3**	**0**	**4**	**122**	**17.2**	**11**	....	....	....	....	....	**5**	**4**	**3**	**7**	**0**	**2**	**0**	**1**
1995-96	**Dallas**	**NHL**	**52**	**14**	**18**	**32**	**41**	**8**	**0**	**3**	**138**	**10.1**	**-17**	....	....	....	....	....	....	....	....	....	....	....	....	....
1996-97	**Dallas**	**NHL**	**66**	**30**	**21**	**51**	**32**	**8**	**0**	**2**	**173**	**17.3**	**-5**	....	....	....	....	....	**7**	**2**	**2**	**4**	**6**	**0**	**0**	**0**
1997-98	**Dallas**	**NHL**	**73**	**39**	**30**	**69**	**30**	**14**	**0**	**11**	**203**	**19.2**	**16**	....	....	....	....	....	**1**	**1**	**0**	**1**	**0**	**0**	**0**	**0**
	Canada	Olympics	6	2	3	5	2	....	....	....	....	....	....	....	....	....	....	....	....	....	....	....	....	....	....	....
1998-99♦	**Dallas**	**NHL**	**67**	**28**	**27**	**55**	**34**	**8**	**0**	**8**	**157**	**17.8**	**11**	**1170**	**63.2**	**42**	**9**	**15:33**	**23**	***11**	**10**	**21**	**19**	**3**	**0**	**6**
99-2000	**Dallas**	**NHL**	**48**	**15**	**19**	**34**	**26**	**7**	**0**	**2**	**110**	**13.6**	**-1**	**924**	**59.1**	**17**	**8**	**16:15**	**23**	**7**	**3**	**10**	**18**	**3**	**0**	**2**
	NHL Totals		**883**	**440**	**417**	**857**	**493**	**175**	**11**	**69**	**2330**	**18.9**		**2094**	**61.4**	**59**	**17**	**15:51**	**120**	**53**	**43**	**96**	**79**	**20**	**0**	**10**

ECAC First All-Star Team (1986, 1987) • NCAA East First All-American Team (1986, 1987) • NHL All-Rookie Team (1988) • Won Calder Memorial Trophy (1988) • Won Dodge Ram Tough Award (1988) • Won King Clancy Memorial Trophy (1995) • Won Conn Smythe Trophy (1999) • Played in NHL All-Star Game (1988, 1989, 1990, 1994)

Traded to **Dallas** by **Calgary** for Corey Millen and Jarome Iginla, December 19, 1995.

NIINIMAA, Janne

(nihn-EE-mah, YAH-nee)   **EDM.**

Defense. Shoots left. 6'1", 220 lbs.   Born, Raahe, Finland, May 22, 1975. Philadelphia's 1st choice, 36th overall, in 1993 Entry Draft.

Season	Club	League	GP	G	A	Pts	PIM	PP	SH	GW	S	%	+/-	TF	F%	H	SB	Min	GP	G	A	Pts	PIM	PP	SH	GW
1990-91	Karput Oulu	Finn-Jr.	3	1	0	1	2																			
1991-92	Karput Oulu	Finn-Jr.	3	0	0	0	4																			
	Karput Oulu	Finland-2	41	2	11	13	49																			
1992-93	Karput Oulu	Finn-Jr.	10	3	9	12	16																			
	KKP Kiiminki	Finland-3	1	0	2	2	4																			
	Karput Oulu	Finland-2	29	2	3	5	14																			
1993-94	Jokerit Helsinki	Finn-Jr.	10	2	6	8	41																			
	Jokerit Helsinki	Finland	45	3	8	11	24												12	1	1	2	4			
1994-95	Jokerit Helsinki	Finn-Jr.	3	1	2	3	4																			
	Jokerit Helsinki	Finland	42	7	10	17	36												10	1	4	5	35			
1995-96	Jokerit Helsinki	Finland	49	5	15	20	79												11	0	2	2	12			
	Jokerit Helsinki	Finn-Jr.																	2	3	4	7	6			
1996-97	**Philadelphia**	**NHL**	77	4	40	44	58	1	0	2	141	2.8	12						19	1	12	13	16	1	0	1
1997-98	**Philadelphia**	**NHL**	66	3	31	34	56	2	0	1	115	2.6	6													
	Finland	Olympics	6	0	3	3	8																			
	Edmonton	**NHL**	11	1	8	9	6	1	0	0	19	5.3	7						11	1	1	2	12	0	0	1
1998-99	**Edmonton**	**NHL**	81	4	24	28	88	2	0	1	142	2.8	7	1	0.0	144	122	23:54	4	0	0	0	2	0	0	0
99-2000	**Edmonton**	**NHL**	81	8	25	33	89	2	2	0	133	6.0	14	0	0.0	124	107	24:28	5	0	2	2	2	0	0	0
	NHL Totals		316	20	128	148	297	8	2	4	550	3.6		1	0.0	268	229	24:11	39	2	15	17	32	1	0	2

NHL All-Rookie Team (1997)
Traded to **Edmonton** by **Philadelphia** for Dan McGillis and Edmonton's 2nd round choice (Jason Beckett) in 1998 Entry Draft, March 24, 1998.

NIKOLISHIN, Andrei

(nee-koh-LEE-shin, AWN-dray)   **WSH.**

Left wing. Shoots left. 5'11", 214 lbs.   Born, Vorkuta, USSR, March 25, 1973. Hartford's 2nd choice, 47th overall, in 1992 Entry Draft.

Season	Club	League	GP	G	A	Pts	PIM	PP	SH	GW	S	%	+/-	TF	F%	H	SB	Min	GP	G	A	Pts	PIM	PP	SH	GW
1990-91	Dynamo Moscow	USSR	2	0	0	0	0																			
1991-92	Dynamo Moscow	CIS	18	1	0	1	4																			
1992-93	Dynamo Moscow	CIS	42	5	7	12	30												10	2	1	3	8			
1993-94	Dynamo Moscow	CIS	41	8	12	20	30												9	1	3	4	4			
	Russia	Olympics	8	2	5	7	6																			
1994-95	Dynamo Moscow	CIS	12	7	2	9	6																			
	Hartford	**NHL**	39	8	10	18	10	1	1	0	57	14.0	7													
1995-96	**Hartford**	**NHL**	61	14	37	51	34	4	1	3	83	16.9	-2													
1996-97	**Hartford**	**NHL**	12	2	5	7	2	0	0	0	25	8.0	-2													
	Washington	**NHL**	59	7	14	21	30	1	0	0	73	9.6	5													
1997-98	**Washington**	**NHL**	38	6	10	16	14	1	0	1	40	15.0	1						21	1	13	14	12	1	0	0
	Portland Pirates	AHL	2	0	0	0	2																			
1998-99	Dynamo Moscow	Russia	4	0	0	0	0																			
	Washington	**NHL**	73	8	27	35	28	0	1	1	121	6.6	0	1354	52.5	70	31	17:34								
99-2000	**Washington**	**NHL**	76	11	14	25	28	0	2	2	98	11.2	6	1190	54.7	61	39	15:44	5	0	2	2	4	0	0	0
	NHL Totals		358	56	117	173	146	7	5	7	497	11.3		2544	53.5	131	70	16:38	26	1	15	16	16	1	0	0

CIS First All-Star Team (1994) • CIS Player of the Year (1994)
Traded to **Washington** by **Hartford** for Curtis Leschyshyn, November 9, 1996.

NILSON, Marcus

(NIHL-suhn, MAHR-kuhs)   **FLA.**

Right wing. Shoots right. 6'2", 193 lbs.   Born, Balsta, Sweden, March 1, 1978. Florida's 1st choice, 20th overall, in 1996 Entry Draft.

Season	Club	League	GP	G	A	Pts	PIM	PP	SH	GW	S	%	+/-	TF	F%	H	SB	Min	GP	G	A	Pts	PIM	PP	SH	GW
1994-95	Djurgardens IF	Swede-Jr.	24	7	8	15	22																			
1995-96	Djurgardens IF	Swede-Jr.	25	19	17	36	46												2	1	1	2	12			
	Djurgardens IF	Sweden	12	0	0	0	0												1	0	0	0	0			
1996-97	Djurgardens IF	Sweden	37	0	3	3	33												4	0	0	0	0			
1997-98	Djurgardens IF	Sweden	41	4	7	11	18												15	2	1	3	16			
1998-99	**Florida**	**NHL**	8	1	1	2	5	0	0	1	7	14.3	2	6	50.0	6	3	12:24								
	New Haven	AHL	69	8	25	33	10																			
99-2000	**Florida**	**NHL**	9	0	2	2	2	0	0	0	6	0.0	2	14	64.3	5	3	7:56								
	Louisville	AHL	64	9	23	32	52												4	0	0	0	2			
	NHL Totals		17	1	3	4	7	0	0	1	13	7.7		20	60.0	11	6	10:02								

NOLAN, Owen

(NOH-lan, OH-wehn)   **S.J.**

Right wing. Shoots right. 6'1", 210 lbs.   Born, Belfast, Ireland, February 12, 1972. Quebec's 1st choice, 1st overall, in 1990 Entry Draft.

Season	Club	League	GP	G	A	Pts	PIM	PP	SH	GW	S	%	+/-	TF	F%	H	SB	Min	GP	G	A	Pts	PIM	PP	SH	GW
1987-88	Thorold Hawks	OMHA	28	53	32	85	24																			
	Thorold Hawks	OJHL-B	3	1	0	1	2																			
1988-89	Cornwall Royals	OHL	62	34	25	59	213												18	5	11	16	41			
1989-90	Cornwall Royals	OHL	58	51	59	110	240												6	7	5	12	26			
1990-91	**Quebec**	**NHL**	59	3	10	13	109	0	0	0	54	5.6	-19													
	Halifax Citadels	AHL	6	4	4	8	11																			
1991-92	**Quebec**	**NHL**	75	42	31	73	183	17	0	0	190	22.1	-9													
1992-93	**Quebec**	**NHL**	73	36	41	77	185	15	0	4	241	14.9	-1						5	1	0	1	2	0	0	0
1993-94	**Quebec**	**NHL**	6	2	2	4	8	0	0	0	15	13.3	2													
1994-95	**Quebec**	**NHL**	46	30	19	49	46	13	2	8	137	21.9	21						6	2	3	5	6	0	0	0
1995-96	**Colorado**	**NHL**	9	4	4	8	9	4	0	0	23	17.4	-3													
	San Jose	**NHL**	72	29	32	61	137	12	1	2	184	15.8	-30													
1996-97	**San Jose**	**NHL**	72	31	32	63	155	10	0	3	225	13.8	-19													
1997-98	**San Jose**	**NHL**	75	14	27	41	144	3	1	1	192	7.3	-2						6	2	2	4	26	2	0	1
1998-99	**San Jose**	**NHL**	78	19	26	45	129	6	2	3	207	9.2	-16	657	49.3	174	15	19:09	6	1	1	2	6	0	0	0
99-2000	**San Jose**	**NHL**	78	44	40	84	110	18	4	6	261	16.9	-1	357	50.7	209	29	21:07	10	8	2	10	6	2	2	3
	NHL Totals		643	254	264	518	1215	98	10	27	1729	14.7		1014	49.8	383	44	20:08	33	14	8	22	46	4	2	4

OHL First All-Star Team (1990) • Played in NHL All-Star Game (1992, 1996, 1997, 2000)
• Missed remainder of 1993-94 season recovering from shoulder injury suffered in game vs. Tampa Bay, November 13, 1983. Transferred to **Colorado** after **Quebec** franchise relocated, June 21, 1995.
Traded to **San Jose** by **Colorado** for Sandis Ozolinsh, October 26, 1995.

NOONAN, Brian

(NOON-an, BRIGH-an)

Right wing. Shoots right. 6'1", 200 lbs.   Born, Boston, MA, May 29, 1965. Chicago's 10th choice, 186th overall, in 1983 Entry Draft.

Season	Club	League	GP	G	A	Pts	PIM	PP	SH	GW	S	%	+/-	TF	F%	H	SB	Min	GP	G	A	Pts	PIM	PP	SH	GW
1982-83	Bishop Williams	Hi-School	21	26	17	43	....																			
1983-84	Bishop Williams	Hi-School	17	14	23	37	....																			
1984-85	New Westminster	WHL	72	50	66	116	76												11	8	7	15	4			
1985-86	Nova Scotia	AHL	2	0	0	0	0																			
	Saginaw Generals	IHL	76	39	39	78	69												11	6	3	9	6			
1986-87	Nova Scotia	AHL	70	25	26	51	30												5	3	1	4	4			
1987-88	**Chicago**	**NHL**	77	10	20	30	44	3	0	2	87	11.5	-27						3	0	0	0	4	0	0	0
1988-89	**Chicago**	**NHL**	45	4	12	16	28	2	0	0	84	4.8	-2						1	0	0	0	0	0	0	0
	Saginaw Hawks	IHL	19	18	13	31	36												1	0	0	0	0			
1989-90	**Chicago**	**NHL**	8	0	2	2	6	0	0	0	13	0.0														
	Indianapolis Ice	IHL	56	40	36	76	85												14	6	9	15	20			
1990-91	**Chicago**	**NHL**	7	0	4	4	2	0	0	0	12	0.0	-1													
	Indianapolis Ice	IHL	59	38	53	91	67												7	4	10	14	....			
1991-92	**Chicago**	**NHL**	65	19	12	31	81	4	0	0	154	12.3	9						18	6	9	15	30	3	0	1
1992-93	**Chicago**	**NHL**	63	16	14	30	82	5	0	3	129	12.4	3						4	3	0	3	4	1	0	0
1993-94	**Chicago**	**NHL**	64	14	21	35	57	8	0	3	134	10.4	2													
	♦ **NY Rangers**	**NHL**	12	4	2	6	12	2	0	3	26	15.4	5						22	4	7	11	17	2	0	1

			Regular Season																Playoffs							
Season	Club	League	GP	G	A	Pts	PIM	PP	SH	GW	S	%	+/–	TF	F%	H	SB	Min	GP	G	A	Pts	PIM	PP	SH	GW
1994-95	NY Rangers	NHL	45	14	13	27	26	7	0	1	95	14.7	–3	....	....	....	....	....	5	0	0	0	8	0	0	0
1995-96	St. Louis	NHL	81	13	22	35	84	3	1	6	131	9.9	2	....	....	....	....	....	13	4	1	5	10	0	0	0
1996-97	St. Louis	NHL	13	2	5	7	0	0	0	0	13	15.4	2	....	....	....	....	....	....	....	....	....	....	....	....	....
	NY Rangers	NHL	44	6	9	15	28	3	0	1	62	9.7	–7	....	....	....	....	....	....	....	....	....	....	....	....	....
	Vancouver	NHL	16	4	8	12	6	0	1	0	25	16.0	2	....	....	....	....	....	....	....	....	....	....	....	....	....
1997-98	Vancouver	NHL	82	10	15	25	62	1	0	2	87	11.5	–19	....	....	....	....	....	....	....	....	....	....	....	....	....
1998-99	Phoenix	NHL	7	0	0	0	0	0	0	0	1	0.0	–3	1	0.0	7	1	8:16	5	0	2	2	4	0	0	0
	Indianapolis Ice	IHL	65	19	44	63	128	....	....	....	....	....	....	....	....	....	....	....	....	....	....	....	....	....	....	....
99-2000	Chicago Wolves	IHL	80	30	32	62	80	....	....	....	....	....	....	....	....	....	....	....	16	4	7	11	10	....	....	....
	NHL Totals		629	116	159	275	518	38	2	21	1053	11.0		1	0.0	7	1	8:16	71	17	19	36	77	6	0	2

IHL Second All-Star Team (1990) • IHL First All-Star Team (1991)

Traded to **NY Rangers** by **Chicago** with Stephane Matteau for Tony Amonte and the rights to Matt Oates, March 21, 1994. Signed as a free agent by **St. Louis**, July 24, 1995. Traded to **NY Rangers** by **St. Louis** for Sergio Momesso, November 13, 1996. Traded to **Vancouver** by **NY Rangers** with Sergei Nemchinov for Esa Tikkanen and Russ Courtnall, March 8, 1997. Signed as a free agent by **Phoenix**, March 17, 1999. Signed as a free agent by **Chicago Wolves** (IHL), September 14, 1999.

NORDSTROM, Peter

(NOHRD-struhm, PEE-tuhr) **BOS.**

Center. Shoots left. 6'1", 200 lbs. Born, Munkfors, Sweden, July 26, 1974. Boston's 3rd choice, 78th overall, in 1998 Entry Draft.

1989-90	IFK Munkfors	Sweden-3	21	2	1	3	8	....	....	....	....	....	....	....	....	....	....	....	....	....	....	....	....	....	....	....
1990-91	IFK Munkfors	Sweden-3	32	10	18	28	20	....	....	....	....	....	....	....	....	....	....	....	....	....	....	....	....	....	....	....
1991-92	IFK Munkfors	Sweden-3	31	12	20	32	42	....	....	....	....	....	....	....	....	....	....	....	....	....	....	....	....	....	....	....
1992-93	IFK Munkfors	Sweden-3	35	19	11	30	44	....	....	....	....	....	....	....	....	....	....	....	....	....	....	....	....	....	....	....
1993-94	IFK Munkfors	Sweden-3	31	17	26	43	87	....	....	....	....	....	....	....	....	....	....	....	....	....	....	....	....	....	....	....
1994-95	IFK Munkfors	Sweden-2	21	8	17	25	30	....	....	....	....	....	....	....	....	....	....	....	....	....	....	....	....	....	....	....
	Leksands IF	Sweden	13	1	0	1	0	....	....	....	....	....	....	....	....	....	....	....	....	....	....	....	....	....	....	....
1995-96	Farjestads BK	Sweden	40	6	5	11	36	....	....	....	....	....	....	....	....	....	....	....	8	0	3	3	12	....	....	....
1996-97	Farjestads BK	Sweden	44	9	5	14	32	....	....	....	....	....	....	....	....	....	....	....	14	1	2	3	6	....	....	....
1997-98	Farjestads BK	Sweden	45	6	19	25	46	....	....	....	....	....	....	....	....	....	....	....	12	5	7	*12	8	....	....	....
1998-99	Farjestads BK	Sweden	21	4	4	8	14	....	....	....	....	....	....	....	....	....	....	....	4	1	1	2	2	....	....	....
	Farjestads BK	EuroHL	2	1	0	1	2	....	....	....	....	....	....	....	....	....	....	....	....	....	....	....	....	....	....	....
	Boston	NHL	2	0	0	0	0	0	0	0	0	0.0	–1	0	0.0	1	0	8:04	....	....	....	....	....	....	....	....
	Providence Bruins	AHL	13	2	1	3	2	....	....	....	....	....	....	....	....	....	....	....	....	....	....	....	....	....	....	....
99-2000	Farjestads BK	Sweden	45	8	14	22	48	....	....	....	....	....	....	....	....	....	....	....	7	0	3	3	2	....	....	....
	NHL Totals		2	0	0	0	0	0	0	0	0	0.0		0	0.0	1	0	8:04	....	....	....	....	....	....	....	....

NORSTROM, Mattias

(NOHR-struhm, MAT-tee-ahs) **L.A.**

Defense. Shoots left. 6'2", 201 lbs. Born, Stockholm, Sweden, January 2, 1972. NY Rangers' 2nd choice, 48th overall, in 1992 Entry Draft.

1990-91	Mora IK	Sweden-2	9	1	1	2	6	....	....	....	....	....	....	....	....	....	....	....	1	0	0	0	2	....	....	....
1991-92	AIK Solna	Sweden	39	4	3	7	28	....	....	....	....	....	....	....	....	....	....	....	3	0	2	2	2	....	....	....
1992-93	AIK Solna	Sweden	22	0	1	1	16	....	....	....	....	....	....	....	....	....	....	....	....	....	....	....	....	....	....	....
1993-94	NY Rangers	NHL	9	0	2	2	6	0	0	0	3	0.0	0	....	....	....	....	....	....	....	....	....	....	....	....	....
	Binghamton	AHL	55	1	9	10	70	....	....	....	....	....	....	....	....	....	....	....	....	....	....	....	....	....	....	....
1994-95	Binghamton	AHL	63	9	10	19	91	....	....	....	....	....	....	....	....	....	....	....	....	....	....	....	....	....	....	....
	NY Rangers	NHL	9	0	3	3	2	0	0	0	4	0.0	2	....	....	....	....	....	3	0	0	0	0	0	0	0
1995-96	NY Rangers	NHL	25	2	1	3	22	0	0	0	17	11.8	5	....	....	....	....	....	....	....	....	....	....	....	....	....
	Los Angeles	NHL	11	0	1	1	18	0	0	0	17	0.0	–8	....	....	....	....	....	....	....	....	....	....	....	....	....
1996-97	Los Angeles	NHL	80	1	21	22	84	0	0	0	106	0.9	–4	....	....	....	....	....	....	....	....	....	....	....	....	....
1997-98	Los Angeles	NHL	73	1	12	13	90	0	0	0	61	1.6	14	....	....	....	....	....	4	0	0	0	2	0	0	0
	Sweden	Olympics	4	0	1	1	2	....	....	....	....	....	....	....	....	....	....	....	....	....	....	....	....	....	....	....
1998-99	Los Angeles	NHL	78	2	5	7	36	0	1	0	61	3.3	–10	1	0.0	236	157	20:20	....	....	....	....	....	....	....	....
99-2000	Los Angeles	NHL	82	1	13	14	66	0	0	0	62	1.6	22	0	0.0	261	127	21:49	4	0	0	0	6	0	0	0
	NHL Totals		367	7	58	65	324	0	1	0	331	2.1		1	0.0	497	284	21:06	11	0	0	0	8	0	0	0

Played in NHL All-Star Game (1999)

Traded to **LA Kings** by **NY Rangers** with Ray Ferraro, Ian Laperriere, Nathan Lafayette and NY Rangers' 4th round choice (Sean Blanchard) in 1997 Entry Draft for Marty McSorley, Jari Kurri and Shane Churla, March 14, 1996.

NORTON, Jeff

(NOHR-tohn, JEHF)

Defense. Shoots left. 6'2", 200 lbs. Born, Acton, MA, November 25, 1965. NY Islanders' 3rd choice, 62nd overall, in 1984 Entry Draft.

1983-84	Cushing Academy	Hi-School	21	22	33	55	....	....	....	....	....	....	....	....	....	....	....	....	....	....	....	....	....	....	....	....
1984-85	U. of Michigan	CCHA	37	8	16	24	103	....	....	....	....	....	....	....	....	....	....	....	....	....	....	....	....	....	....	....
1985-86	U. of Michigan	CCHA	37	15	30	45	99	....	....	....	....	....	....	....	....	....	....	....	....	....	....	....	....	....	....	....
1986-87	U. of Michigan	CCHA	39	12	36	48	92	....	....	....	....	....	....	....	....	....	....	....	....	....	....	....	....	....	....	....
1987-88	United States	Nat-Team	54	7	22	29	52	....	....	....	....	....	....	....	....	....	....	....	....	....	....	....	....	....	....	....
	United States	Olympics	6	0	4	4	4	....	....	....	....	....	....	....	....	....	....	....	....	....	....	....	....	....	....	....
	NY Islanders	NHL	15	1	6	7	14	1	0	1	18	5.6	3	....	....	....	....	....	3	0	2	2	13	0	0	0
1988-89	NY Islanders	NHL	69	1	30	31	74	1	0	0	126	0.8	–24	....	....	....	....	....	....	....	....	....	....	....	....	....
1989-90	NY Islanders	NHL	60	4	49	53	65	4	0	0	104	3.8	–9	....	....	....	....	....	4	1	3	4	17	0	0	0
1990-91	NY Islanders	NHL	44	3	25	28	16	2	1	0	87	3.4	–13	....	....	....	....	....	....	....	....	....	....	....	....	....
1991-92	NY Islanders	NHL	28	1	18	19	18	0	1	0	34	2.9	2	....	....	....	....	....	....	....	....	....	....	....	....	....
1992-93	NY Islanders	NHL	66	12	38	50	45	5	0	0	127	9.4	–3	....	....	....	....	....	10	1	1	2	4	0	0	0
1993-94	San Jose	NHL	64	7	33	40	36	1	0	0	92	7.6	16	....	....	....	....	....	14	1	5	6	20	0	0	0
1994-95	San Jose	NHL	20	1	9	10	39	0	0	0	21	4.8	1	....	....	....	....	....	....	....	....	....	....	....	....	....
	St. Louis	NHL	28	2	18	20	33	0	0	1	27	7.4	21	....	....	....	....	....	7	1	1	2	11	0	0	0
1995-96	St. Louis	NHL	36	4	7	11	26	0	0	1	33	12.1	4	....	....	....	....	....	....	....	....	....	....	....	....	....
	Edmonton	NHL	30	4	16	20	16	1	0	1	52	7.7	5	....	....	....	....	....	....	....	....	....	....	....	....	....
1996-97	Edmonton	NHL	62	2	11	13	42	0	0	0	68	2.9	–7	....	....	....	....	....	....	....	....	....	....	....	....	....
	Tampa Bay	NHL	13	0	5	5	16	0	0	0	13	0.0	0	....	....	....	....	....	....	....	....	....	....	....	....	....
1997-98	Tampa Bay	NHL	37	4	6	10	26	4	0	0	41	9.8	–25	....	....	....	....	....	....	....	....	....	....	....	....	....
	Florida	NHL	19	0	7	7	18	0	0	0	20	0.0	–7	....	....	....	....	....	....	....	....	....	....	....	....	....
1998-99	Florida	NHL	3	0	0	0	2	0	0	0	2	0.0	0	0	0.0	1	3	17:26	....	....	....	....	....	....	....	....
	San Jose	NHL	69	4	18	22	42	2	0	1	68	5.9	2	0	0.0	37	86	20:55	6	0	7	7	10	0	0	0
99-2000	San Jose	NHL	62	0	20	20	49	0	0	0	45	0.0	–2	0	0.0	29	74	19:32	12	0	1	1	7	0	0	0
	NHL Totals		725	50	316	366	577	21	2	5	978	5.1		0	0.0	67	163	20:12	56	4	20	24	82	0	0	0

CCHA Second All-Star Team (1987)

• Missed remainder of 1991-92 season recovering from wrist injury suffered in game vs. Buffalo, January 3, 1992. Traded to **San Jose** by **NY Islanders** for San Jose's 3rd round choice (Jason Strudwick) in 1994 Entry Draft, June 20, 1993. Traded to **St. Louis** by **San Jose** with San Jose's 3rd round choice (later traded to Colorado - Colorado selected Rick Berry) in 1997 Entry Draft for Craig Janney and cash, March 6, 1995. Traded to **Edmonton** by **St. Louis** with Donald Dufresne for Igor Kravchuk and Ken Sutton, January 4, 1996. Traded to **Tampa Bay** by **Edmonton** for Drew Bannister and Tampa Bay's 6th round choice (Peter Sarno) in 1997 Entry Draft, March 18, 1997. Traded to **Florida** by **Tampa Bay** with Dino Ciccarelli for Mark Fitzpatrick and Jody Hull, January 15, 1998. Traded to **San Jose** by **Florida** for Alex Hicks and San Jose's 5th round choice (later traded to NY Islanders - NY Islanders selected Adam Johnson) in 1999 Entry Draft, November 11, 1998.

NOVOSELTSEV, Ivan

(noh-voh-SEHLT-sehv, ee-VAHN) **FLA.**

Left wing. Shoots left. 6'1", 183 lbs. Born, Golitsino, USSR, January 23, 1979. Florida's 5th choice, 95th overall, in 1997 Entry Draft.

1995-96	Krylja Sovetov	CIS	1	0	0	0	2	....	....	....	....	....	....	....	....	....	....	....	....	....	....	....	....	....	....	....
1996-97	Krylja Sovetov	Russia	30	0	3	3	18	....	....	....	....	....	....	....	....	....	....	....	2	0	0	0	4	....	....	....
	Krylja Sovetov	Russia-3	19	5	3	8	39	....	....	....	....	....	....	....	....	....	....	....	....	....	....	....	....	....	....	....
1997-98	Sarnia Sting	OHL	53	26	22	48	41	....	....	....	....	....	....	....	....	....	....	....	5	1	1	2	8	....	....	....
1998-99	Sarnia Sting	OHL	68	57	39	96	45	....	....	....	....	....	....	....	....	....	....	....	5	2	4	6	6	....	....	....
99-2000	Florida	NHL	14	2	1	3	8	2	0	0	8	25.0	–3	1	100.0	3	3	10:29	....	....	....	....	....	....	....	....
	Louisville	AHL	47	14	21	35	22	....	....	....	....	....	....	....	....	....	....	....	4	1	0	1	6	....	....	....
	NHL Totals		14	2	1	3	8	2	0	0	8	25.0		1	100.0	3	3	10:29	....	....	....	....	....	....	....	....

OHL First All-Star Team (1999)

NUMMINEN, Teppo

(NOO-mih-nehn, TEH-poh) **PHX.**

Defense. Shoots right. 6'2", 199 lbs. Born, Tampere, Finland, July 3, 1968. Winnipeg's 2nd choice, 29th overall, in 1986 Entry Draft.

			Regular Season																Playoffs							
Season	Club	League	GP	G	A	Pts	PIM	PP	SH	GW	S	%	+/-	TF	F%	H	SB	Min	GP	G	A	Pts	PIM	PP	SH	GW
1984-85	Tappara Tampere	Finn-Jr.	30	14	17	31	10																			
	Whitby Lawmen	OJHL	16	3	9	12	0																			
1985-86	Tappara Tampere	Finn-Jr.	2	0	0	0	0												3	0	1	1	2			
	Tappara Tampere	Finland	31	2	4	6	6												8	0	0	0	0			
1986-87	Tappara Tampere	Finland	44	9	9	18	16												9	4	1	5	4			
1987-88	Tappara Tampere	Finland	40	10	10	20	29												10	6	6	12	6			
	Finland	Olympics	6	1	4	5	0																			
1988-89	Winnipeg	NHL	69	1	14	15	36	0	1	0	85	1.2	–11													
1989-90	Winnipeg	NHL	79	11	32	43	20	1	0	1	105	10.5	–4						7	1	2	3	10	0	0	0
1990-91	Winnipeg	NHL	80	8	25	33	28	3	0	0	151	5.3	–15													
1991-92	Winnipeg	NHL	80	5	34	39	32	4	0	1	143	3.5	15						7	0	0	0	0	0	0	0
1992-93	Winnipeg	NHL	66	7	30	37	33	3	1	0	103	6.8	4						6	1	1	2	2	1	0	0
1993-94	Winnipeg	NHL	57	5	18	23	28	4	0	1	89	5.6	–23													
1994-95	TuTo Turku	Finland	12	3	8	11	4																			
	Winnipeg	NHL	42	5	16	21	16	2	0	0	86	5.8	12													
1995-96	Winnipeg	NHL	74	11	43	54	22	6	0	3	165	6.7	–4						6	0	0	0	2	0	0	0
1996-97	Phoenix	NHL	82	2	25	27	28	0	0	0	135	1.5	–3						7	3	3	6	0	1	0	1
1997-98	Phoenix	NHL	82	11	40	51	30	6	0	2	126	8.7	25						1	0	0	0	0	0	0	0
	Finland	Olympics	6	1	1	2	2																			
1998-99	Phoenix	NHL	82	10	30	40	30	1	0	0	156	6.4	3	2	0.0	73	99	24:26	7	2	1	3	4	2	0	0
99-2000	Phoenix	NHL	79	8	34	42	16	2	0	2	126	6.3	21	1	0.0	75	96	23:37	5	1	1	2	0	0	0	0
	NHL Totals		872	84	341	425	319	32	2	10	1470	5.7		3	0.0	148	195	24:02	46	8	8	16	18	4	0	1

Played in NHL All-Star Game (1999, 2000)

Transferred to **Phoenix** after **Winnipeg** franchise relocated, July 1, 1996.

NURMINEN, Kai

(NUHR-mih-nehn, KIGH) **MIN.**

Left wing. Shoots left. 6'1", 198 lbs. Born, Turku, Finland, March 29, 1969. Los Angeles' 9th choice, 193rd overall, in 1996 Entry Draft.

1986-87	TPS Turku	Finn-Jr.	2	0	1	1	0																			
1987-88	TPS Turku	Finn-Jr.	32	9	7	16	16																			
1988-89	TPS Turku	Finn-Jr.	22	13	10	23	14																			
1989-90	TPS Turku	Finn-Jr.	22	13	10	23	14																			
1990-91	TuTo Turku	Finland-2	33	26	20	46	14																			
1991-92	Kiekko-67 Turku	Finland-2	44	44	19	63	34																			
1992-93	Kiekko-67 Turku	Finland-2	8	6	4	10	2																			
	TPS Turku	Finland	31	4	6	10	13												7	1	2	3	0			
1993-94	TPS Turku	Finland	45	23	12	35	20												11	0	3	3	4			
1994-95	HPK Hameenlinna	Finland	49	*30	25	55	40																			
1995-96	HV Jonkoping	Sweden	40	31	24	55	30												4	3	1	4	8			
1996-97	Los Angeles	NHL	67	16	11	27	22	4	0	1	112	14.3	–3													
1997-98	Vasteras IK	Sweden	23	9	7	16	24																			
	Jokerit Helsinki	Finland	20	7	9	16	30												8	5	3	8	4			
1998-99	HC Davos	Switz.	42	26	14	40	26																			
99-2000	TPS Turku	Finland	54	*41	37	*78	40												10	5	*9	*14	0			
	NHL Totals		67	16	11	27	22	4	0	1	112	14.3														

Finnish First All-Star Team (1995)

Signed as a free agent by **Minnesota**, May 24, 2000.

NYLANDER, Michael

(NEE-lan-duhr, MIHK-ayl) **CHI.**

Center. Shoots left. 5'11", 195 lbs. Born, Stockholm, Sweden, October 3, 1972. Hartford's 4th choice, 59th overall, in 1991 Entry Draft.

1989-90	Huddinge IK	Sweden-2	31	7	15	22	4												5	3	0	3	0			
1990-91	Huddinge IK	Sweden-2	33	14	20	34	10												2	0	0	0	0			
1991-92	AIK Solna	Sweden	40	11	17	28	30												3	1	4	5	4			
1992-93	Hartford	NHL	59	11	22	33	36	3	0	1	85	12.9	–7													
	Springfield	AHL																	3	3	3	6	2			
1993-94	Hartford	NHL	58	11	33	44	24	4	0	1	74	14.9	–2													
	Springfield	AHL	4	0	9	9	0																			
	Calgary	NHL	15	2	9	11	6	0	0	0	21	9.5	10						3	0	0	0	0	0	0	0
1994-95	JyP Jyvaskyla	Finland	16	11	19	30	63																			
	Calgary	NHL	6	0	1	1	2	0	0	0	2	0.0	1						6	0	6	6	2	0	0	0
1995-96	Calgary	NHL	73	17	38	55	20	4	0	6	163	10.4	0						4	0	0	0	0	0	0	0
1996-97	HC Lugano	Switz.	36	12	43	55	28												8	3	8	11	8			
1997-98	Calgary	NHL	65	13	23	36	24	0	0	2	117	11.1	10													
	Sweden	Olympics	4	0	0	0	6																			
1998-99	Calgary	NHL	9	2	3	5	2	1	0	0	7	28.6	1	25	60.0	1	0	11:10								
	Tampa Bay	NHL	24	2	7	9	6	0	0	0	26	7.7	–10	75	44.0	4	6	13:29								
99-2000	Tampa Bay	NHL	11	1	2	3	4	1	0	0	10	10.0	–3	35	57.1	0	0	10:32								
	Chicago	NHL	66	23	28	51	26	4	0	2	112	20.5	9	561	46.9	9	11	16:39								
	NHL Totals		386	82	166	248	150	17	0	12	617	13.3		696	47.6	14	17	14:54	13	0	6	6	2	0	0	0

Swedish Rookie of the Year (1992) • Swedish World All-Star Team (1996, 1997)

Traded to **Calgary** by **Hartford** with James Patrick and Zarley Zalapski for Gary Suter, Paul Ranheim and Ted Drury, March 10, 1994. • Missed majority of 1994-95 season recovering from wrist injury suffered in game vs. Detroit, January 26, 1995. Traded to **Tampa Bay** by **Calgary** for Andrei Nazarov, January 19, 1999. Traded to **Chicago** by **Tampa Bay** for Bryan Muir and Reid Simpson, November 12, 1999.

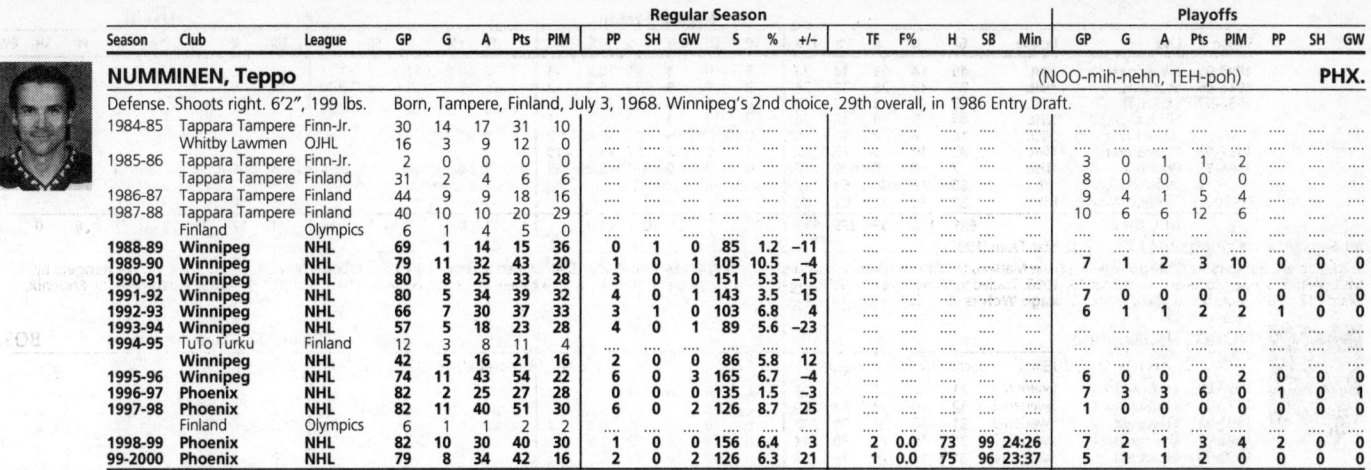

OATES, Adam

(OHTS, A-dam) **WSH.**

Center. Shoots right. 5'11", 180 lbs. Born, Weston, Ont., August 27, 1962.

1979-80	Port Credit Titans	OJHL-B	34	30	36	66	41																			
	Markham Waxers	OJHL-B	9	1	6	7	2																			
1980-81	Markham Waxers	OJHL-B	43	36	53	89	89																			
1981-82	Markham Waxers	OJHL-B	40	59	110	169																				
1982-83	RPI Engineers	ECAC	22	9	33	42	8																			
1983-84	RPI Engineers	ECAC	38	26	57	83	15																			
1984-85	RPI Engineers	ECAC	38	31	60	91	29																			
1985-86	Detroit	NHL	38	9	11	20	10	1	0	1	49	18.4	–24													
	Adirondack	AHL	34	18	28	46	4												17	7	14	21	4			
1986-87	Detroit	NHL	76	15	32	47	21	4	0	1	138	10.9	0						16	4	7	11	6	0	0	1
1987-88	Detroit	NHL	63	14	40	54	20	3	0	3	111	12.6	16						16	8	12	20	6	4	0	1
1988-89	Detroit	NHL	69	16	62	78	14	2	0	1	127	12.6	–1						6	0	8	8	2	0	0	0
1989-90	St. Louis	NHL	80	23	79	102	30	6	2	3	168	13.7	9						12	2	12	14	4	1	0	0
1990-91	St. Louis	NHL	61	25	90	115	29	3	1	3	139	18.0	15						13	7	13	20	10	2	0	1
1991-92	St. Louis	NHL	54	10	59	69	12	3	0	3	118	8.5	–4													
	Boston	NHL	26	10	20	30	10	3	0	1	73	13.7	–5						15	5	14	19	4	3	0	2
1992-93	Boston	NHL	84	45	*97	142	32	24	1	11	254	17.7	15						4	0	9	9	4	0	0	0
1993-94	Boston	NHL	77	32	80	112	45	16	2	3	197	16.2	10						13	3	9	12	8	2	0	0
1994-95	Boston	NHL	48	12	41	53	8	4	1	2	109	11.0	–11						5	1	0	1	2	1	0	0
1995-96	Boston	NHL	70	25	67	92	18	7	1	2	183	13.7	16						5	2	5	7	2	0	1	0
1996-97	Boston	NHL	63	18	52	70	10	2	2	4	138	13.0	–3													
	Washington	NHL	17	4	8	12	4	1	0	1	22	18.2	–2													
1997-98	Washington	NHL	82	18	58	76	36	3	2	3	121	14.9	6						21	6	11	17	8	1	1	1

			Regular Season																Playoffs							
Season	Club	League	GP	G	A	Pts	PIM	PP	SH	GW	S	%	+/-	TF	F%	H	SB	Min	GP	G	A	Pts	PIM	PP	SH	GW
1998-99	Washington	NHL	59	12	42	54	22	3	0	0	79	15.2	–1	1330	59.2	17	22	20:34	....	....	....	....	....	....	....	....
99-2000	Washington	NHL	82	15	56	71	14	5	0	6	93	16.1	13	2176	56.8	19	45	22:20	5	0	3	3	4	0	0	0
	NHL Totals		1049	303	894	1197	335	90	12	48	2119	14.3		3506	57.7	36	67	21:36	131	38	103	141	60	14	2	6

ECAC Second All-Star Team (1984) • NCAA East First All-American Team (1984, 1985) • ECAC First All-Star Team (1985) • NCAA Championship All-Tournament Team (1985) • NHL Second All-Star Team (1991) • Played in NHL All-Star Game (1991, 1992, 1993, 1994, 1997)

Signed as a free agent by **Detroit**, June 28, 1985. Traded to **St. Louis** by **Detroit** with Paul MacLean for Bernie Federko and Tony McKegney, June 15, 1989. Traded to **Boston** by **St. Louis** for Craig Janney and Stephane Quintal, February 7, 1992. Traded to **Washington** by **Boston** with Bill Ranford and Rick Tocchet for Jim Carey, Anson Carter, Jason Allison and Washington's 3rd round choice (Lee Goren) in 1997 Entry Draft, March 1, 1997.

ODELEIN, Lyle
(OH-duh-LIGHN, LIGHL) **CBJ**

Defense. Shoots right. 5'11", 210 lbs. Born, Quill Lake, Sask., July 21, 1968. Montreal's 8th choice, 141st overall, in 1986 Entry Draft.

Season	Club	League	GP	G	A	Pts	PIM	PP	SH	GW	S	%	+/-	TF	F%	H	SB	Min	GP	G	A	Pts	PIM	PP	SH	GW
1984-85	Regina	AAHA	26	12	13	25	30	....	....	....	....	....	....	....	....	....	....	....	....	....	....	....	....	....	....	....
1985-86	Moose Jaw	WHL	67	9	37	46	117	....	....	....	....	....	....	....	....	....	....	....	13	1	6	7	34	....	....	....
1986-87	Moose Jaw	WHL	59	9	50	59	70	....	....	....	....	....	....	....	....	....	....	....	9	2	5	7	26	....	....	....
1987-88	Moose Jaw	WHL	63	15	43	58	166	....	....	....	....	....	....	....	....	....	....	....	....	....	....	....	....	....	....	....
1988-89	Sherbrooke	AHL	33	3	4	7	120	....	....	....	....	....	....	....	....	....	....	....	3	0	2	2	5	....	....	....
	Peoria Rivermen	IHL	36	2	8	10	116	....	....	....	....	....	....	....	....	....	....	....	....	....	....	....	....	....	....	....
1989-90	**Montreal**	**NHL**	**8**	**0**	**2**	**2**	**33**	**0**	**0**	**0**	**1**	**0.0**	**–1**	....	....	....	....	....	....	....	....	....	....	....	....	....
	Sherbrooke	AHL	68	7	24	31	265	....	....	....	....	....	....	....	....	....	....	....	12	6	5	11	79	....	....	....
1990-91	**Montreal**	**NHL**	**52**	**0**	**2**	**2**	**259**	**0**	**0**	**0**	**25**	**0.0**	**7**	....	....	....	....	....	**12**	**0**	**0**	**0**	**54**	**0**	**0**	**0**
1991-92	**Montreal**	**NHL**	**71**	**1**	**7**	**8**	**212**	**0**	**0**	**0**	**43**	**2.3**	**15**	....	....	....	....	....	**7**	**0**	**0**	**0**	**11**	**0**	**0**	**0**
1992-93♦	**Montreal**	**NHL**	**83**	**2**	**14**	**16**	**205**	**0**	**0**	**0**	**79**	**2.5**	**35**	....	....	....	....	....	**20**	**1**	**5**	**6**	**30**	**0**	**0**	**0**
1993-94	**Montreal**	**NHL**	**79**	**11**	**29**	**40**	**276**	**6**	**0**	**2**	**116**	**9.5**	**8**	....	....	....	....	....	**7**	**0**	**0**	**0**	**17**	**0**	**0**	**0**
1994-95	**Montreal**	**NHL**	**48**	**3**	**7**	**10**	**152**	**0**	**0**	**0**	**74**	**4.1**	**–13**	....	....	....	....	....	....	....	....	....	....	....	....	....
1995-96	**Montreal**	**NHL**	**79**	**3**	**14**	**17**	**230**	**0**	**1**	**0**	**74**	**4.1**	**8**	....	....	....	....	....	**6**	**1**	**1**	**2**	**6**	**0**	**1**	**0**
1996-97	**New Jersey**	**NHL**	**79**	**3**	**13**	**16**	**110**	**1**	**0**	**2**	**93**	**3.2**	**16**	....	....	....	....	....	**10**	**2**	**2**	**4**	**19**	**1**	**0**	**0**
1997-98	**New Jersey**	**NHL**	**79**	**4**	**19**	**23**	**171**	**1**	**0**	**0**	**76**	**5.3**	**11**	....	....	....	....	....	**6**	**1**	**1**	**2**	**21**	**1**	**0**	**1**
1998-99	**New Jersey**	**NHL**	**70**	**5**	**26**	**31**	**114**	**1**	**0**	**0**	**101**	**5.0**	**6**	**0**	**0.0**	**51**	**71**	**19:53**	**7**	**0**	**3**	**3**	**10**	**0**	**0**	**0**
99-2000	**New Jersey**	**NHL**	**57**	**1**	**15**	**16**	**104**	**0**	**0**	**1**	**59**	**1.7**	**–10**	**0**	**0.0**	**44**	**63**	**16:42**	....	....	....	....	....	....	....	....
	Phoenix	**NHL**	**16**	**1**	**7**	**8**	**19**	**1**	**0**	**0**	**30**	**3.3**	**1**	**0**	**0.0**	**13**	**28**	**21:45**	**5**	**0**	**0**	**0**	**16**	**0**	**0**	**0**
	NHL Totals		**721**	**34**	**155**	**189**	**1885**	**10**	**1**	**5**	**771**	**4.4**		**0**	**0.0**	**108**	**162**	**18:49**	**80**	**5**	**12**	**17**	**184**	**2**	**1**	**1**

Traded to **New Jersey** by **Montreal** for Stephane Richer, August 22, 1996. Traded to **Phoenix** by **New Jersey** for Deron Quint and a conditional choice in 2001 Entry Draft, March 7, 2000. Selected by **Columbus** from **Phoenix** in Expansion Draft, June 23, 2000.

ODGERS, Jeff
(AWD-juhrs, JEHF) **MIN.**

Right wing. Shoots right. 6', 200 lbs. Born, Spy Hill, Sask., May 31, 1969.

Season	Club	League	GP	G	A	Pts	PIM	PP	SH	GW	S	%	+/-	TF	F%	H	SB	Min	GP	G	A	Pts	PIM	PP	SH	GW
1985-86	Saskatoon Blaze	AAHA	36	27	29	56	74	....	....	....	....	....	....	....	....	....	....	....	....	....	....	....	....	....	....	....
1986-87	Brandon	WHL	70	7	14	21	150	....	....	....	....	....	....	....	....	....	....	....	....	....	....	....	....	....	....	....
1987-88	Brandon	WHL	70	17	18	35	202	....	....	....	....	....	....	....	....	....	....	....	4	1	1	2	14	....	....	....
1988-89	Brandon	WHL	71	31	29	60	277	....	....	....	....	....	....	....	....	....	....	....	....	....	....	....	....	....	....	....
1989-90	Brandon	WHL	64	37	28	65	209	....	....	....	....	....	....	....	....	....	....	....	....	....	....	....	....	....	....	....
1990-91	Kansas City	IHL	77	12	19	31	318	....	....	....	....	....	....	....	....	....	....	....	....	....	....	....	....	....	....	....
1991-92	**San Jose**	**NHL**	**61**	**7**	**4**	**11**	**217**	**0**	**0**	**0**	**64**	**10.9**	**–21**	....	....	....	....	....	....	....	....	....	....	....	....	....
	Kansas City	IHL	12	2	2	4	56	....	....	....	....	....	....	....	....	....	....	....	4	2	1	3	0	....	....	....
1992-93	**San Jose**	**NHL**	**66**	**12**	**15**	**27**	**253**	**6**	**0**	**0**	**100**	**12.0**	**–26**	....	....	....	....	....	....	....	....	....	....	....	....	....
1993-94	**San Jose**	**NHL**	**81**	**13**	**8**	**21**	**222**	**7**	**0**	**0**	**73**	**17.8**	**–13**	....	....	....	....	....	**11**	**0**	**0**	**0**	**11**	**0**	**0**	**0**
1994-95	**San Jose**	**NHL**	**48**	**4**	**3**	**7**	**117**	**0**	**0**	**1**	**47**	**8.5**	**–8**	....	....	....	....	....	**11**	**1**	**1**	**2**	**23**	**0**	**0**	**0**
1995-96	**San Jose**	**NHL**	**78**	**12**	**4**	**16**	**192**	**0**	**0**	**1**	**84**	**14.3**	**–4**	....	....	....	....	....	....	....	....	....	....	....	....	....
1996-97	**Boston**	**NHL**	**80**	**7**	**8**	**15**	**197**	**1**	**0**	**1**	**84**	**8.3**	**–15**	....	....	....	....	....	....	....	....	....	....	....	....	....
1997-98	Providence Bruins	AHL	4	0	0	0	31	....	....	....	....	....	....	....	....	....	....	....	....	....	....	....	....	....	....	....
	Colorado	**NHL**	**68**	**5**	**8**	**13**	**213**	**0**	**0**	**0**	**47**	**10.6**	**5**	....	....	....	....	....	**6**	**0**	**0**	**0**	**25**	**0**	**0**	**0**
1998-99	**Colorado**	**NHL**	**75**	**2**	**3**	**5**	**259**	**1**	**0**	**0**	**39**	**5.1**	**–3**	**8**	**37.5**	**56**	**6**	**5:07**	**15**	**1**	**0**	**1**	**14**	**0**	**0**	**1**
99-2000	**Colorado**	**NHL**	**62**	**1**	**2**	**3**	**162**	**0**	**0**	**1**	**29**	**3.4**	**–7**	**2**	**50.0**	**64**	**8**	**5:23**	**4**	**0**	**0**	**0**	**0**	**0**	**0**	**0**
	NHL Totals		**619**	**63**	**55**	**118**	**1832**	**15**	**0**	**4**	**567**	**11.1**		**10**	**40.0**	**120**	**14**	**5:14**	**47**	**2**	**1**	**3**	**73**	**0**	**0**	**1**

Signed as a free agent by **San Jose**, September 3, 1991. Traded to **Boston** by **San Jose** with Pittsburgh's 5th round choice (previously acquired, Boston selected Elias Abrahamsson) in 1996 Entry Draft for Al Iafrate, June 21, 1996. Signed as a free agent by **Colorado**, October 24, 1997. Selected by **Minnesota** from **Colorado** in Expansion Draft, June 23, 2000.

ODJICK, Gino
(OH-jihk, GEE-noh) **PHI.**

Left wing. Shoots left. 6'3", 210 lbs. Born, Maniwaki, Que., September 7, 1970. Vancouver's 5th choice, 86th overall, in 1990 Entry Draft.

Season	Club	League	GP	G	A	Pts	PIM	PP	SH	GW	S	%	+/-	TF	F%	H	SB	Min	GP	G	A	Pts	PIM	PP	SH	GW
1987-88	Hawkesbury	OJHL	40	2	4	6	167	....	....	....	....	....	....	....	....	....	....	....	....	....	....	....	....	....	....	....
1988-89	Laval Titan	QMJHL	50	9	15	24	278	....	....	....	....	....	....	....	....	....	....	....	16	0	9	9	129	....	....	....
1989-90	Laval Titan	QMJHL	51	12	26	38	280	....	....	....	....	....	....	....	....	....	....	....	13	6	5	11	110	....	....	....
1990-91	**Vancouver**	**NHL**	**45**	**7**	**1**	**8**	**296**	**0**	**0**	**0**	**39**	**17.9**	**–6**	....	....	....	....	....	**6**	**0**	**0**	**0**	**18**	**0**	**0**	**0**
	Milwaukee	IHL	17	7	3	10	102	....	....	....	....	....	....	....	....	....	....	....	....	....	....	....	....	....	....	....
1991-92	**Vancouver**	**NHL**	**65**	**4**	**6**	**10**	**348**	**0**	**0**	**0**	**68**	**5.9**	**–1**	....	....	....	....	....	**4**	**0**	**0**	**0**	**6**	**0**	**0**	**0**
1992-93	**Vancouver**	**NHL**	**75**	**4**	**13**	**17**	**370**	**0**	**0**	**1**	**79**	**5.1**	**3**	....	....	....	....	....	**1**	**0**	**0**	**0**	**0**	**0**	**0**	**0**
1993-94	**Vancouver**	**NHL**	**76**	**16**	**13**	**29**	**271**	**4**	**0**	**5**	**121**	**13.2**	**13**	....	....	....	....	....	**10**	**0**	**0**	**0**	**18**	**0**	**0**	**0**
1994-95	**Vancouver**	**NHL**	**23**	**4**	**5**	**9**	**109**	**0**	**0**	**0**	**35**	**11.4**	**–3**	....	....	....	....	....	**5**	**0**	**0**	**0**	**47**	**0**	**0**	**0**
1995-96	**Vancouver**	**NHL**	**55**	**3**	**4**	**7**	**181**	**0**	**0**	**0**	**59**	**5.1**	**–16**	....	....	....	....	....	**6**	**3**	**1**	**4**	**6**	**0**	**0**	**2**
1996-97	**Vancouver**	**NHL**	**70**	**5**	**8**	**13**	***371**	**1**	**0**	**0**	**85**	**5.9**	**–5**	....	....	....	....	....	....	....	....	....	....	....	....	....
1997-98	**Vancouver**	**NHL**	**35**	**3**	**2**	**5**	**181**	**0**	**0**	**1**	**36**	**8.3**	**–3**	....	....	....	....	....	....	....	....	....	....	....	....	....
	NY Islanders	**NHL**	**13**	**0**	**0**	**0**	**31**	**0**	**0**	**0**	**16**	**0.0**	**1**	....	....	....	....	....	....	....	....	....	....	....	....	....
1998-99	**NY Islanders**	**NHL**	**23**	**4**	**3**	**7**	**133**	**1**	**0**	**2**	**28**	**14.3**	**–2**	**2**	**0.0**	**20**	**2**	**9:51**	....	....	....	....	....	....	....	....
99-2000	**NY Islanders**	**NHL**	**46**	**5**	**10**	**15**	**90**	**0**	**0**	**3**	**91**	**5.5**	**–7**	**3**	**33.3**	**56**	**8**	**12:10**	....	....	....	....	....	....	....	....
	Philadelphia	**NHL**	**13**	**3**	**1**	**4**	**10**	**0**	**0**	**1**	**24**	**12.5**	**2**	**0**	**0.0**	**11**	**2**	**9:03**	....	....	....	....	....	....	....	....
	NHL Totals		**539**	**58**	**66**	**124**	**2391**	**6**	**0**	**13**	**681**	**8.5**		**5**	**20.0**	**87**	**12**	**11:02**	**32**	**3**	**1**	**4**	**95**	**0**	**0**	**2**

Traded to **NY Islanders** by **Vancouver** for Jason Strudwick, March 23, 1998. Traded to **Philadelphia** by **NY Islanders** for Mikael Andersson and Carolina's 5th round choice (previously acquired, NY Islanders selected Kristofer Ottoson) in 2000 Entry Draft, February 15, 2000.

O'DONNELL, Sean
(OH-DOHN-ehl, SHAWN) **MIN.**

Defense. Shoots left. 6'3", 230 lbs. Born, Ottawa, Ont., October 13, 1971. Buffalo's 6th choice, 123rd overall, in 1991 Entry Draft.

Season	Club	League	GP	G	A	Pts	PIM	PP	SH	GW	S	%	+/-	TF	F%	H	SB	Min	GP	G	A	Pts	PIM	PP	SH	GW
1987-88	Kanata Valley	OJHL	54	4	25	29	96	....	....	....	....	....	....	....	....	....	....	....	....	....	....	....	....	....	....	....
1988-89	Sudbury Wolves	OHL	56	1	9	10	49	....	....	....	....	....	....	....	....	....	....	....	....	....	....	....	....	....	....	....
1989-90	Sudbury Wolves	OHL	64	7	19	26	84	....	....	....	....	....	....	....	....	....	....	....	7	1	2	3	8	....	....	....
1990-91	Sudbury Wolves	OHL	66	8	23	31	114	....	....	....	....	....	....	....	....	....	....	....	5	1	4	5	10	....	....	....
1991-92	Rochester	AHL	73	4	9	13	193	....	....	....	....	....	....	....	....	....	....	....	16	1	2	3	21	....	....	....
1992-93	Rochester	AHL	74	3	18	21	203	....	....	....	....	....	....	....	....	....	....	....	17	1	6	7	38	....	....	....
1993-94	Rochester	AHL	64	2	10	12	242	....	....	....	....	....	....	....	....	....	....	....	4	0	1	1	21	....	....	....
1994-95	Phoenix	IHL	61	2	18	20	132	....	....	....	....	....	....	....	....	....	....	....	9	0	1	1	21	....	....	....
	Los Angeles	**NHL**	**15**	**0**	**2**	**2**	**49**	**0**	**0**	**0**	**12**	**0.0**	**–2**	....	....	....	....	....	....	....	....	....	....	....	....	....
1995-96	**Los Angeles**	**NHL**	**71**	**2**	**5**	**7**	**127**	**0**	**0**	**0**	**65**	**3.1**	**3**	....	....	....	....	....	....	....	....	....	....	....	....	....
1996-97	**Los Angeles**	**NHL**	**55**	**5**	**12**	**17**	**144**	**2**	**0**	**0**	**68**	**7.4**	**–13**	....	....	....	....	....	....	....	....	....	....	....	....	....
1997-98	**Los Angeles**	**NHL**	**80**	**2**	**15**	**17**	**179**	**0**	**0**	**1**	**71**	**2.8**	**7**	....	....	....	....	....	**4**	**1**	**0**	**1**	**36**	**0**	**0**	**0**
1998-99	**Los Angeles**	**NHL**	**80**	**1**	**13**	**14**	**186**	**0**	**0**	**0**	**64**	**1.6**	**1**	**0**	**0.0**	**133**	**71**	**19:10**	....	....	....	....	....	....	....	....
99-2000	**Los Angeles**	**NHL**	**80**	**2**	**12**	**14**	**198**	**0**	**0**	**1**	**51**	**3.9**	**4**	**0**	**0.0**	**154**	**80**	**17:41**	**4**	**1**	**0**	**1**	**4**	**0**	**0**	**0**
	NHL Totals		**381**	**12**	**59**	**71**	**719**	**2**	**0**	**2**	**331**	**3.6**		**0**	**0.0**	**287**	**151**	**18:25**	**8**	**2**	**0**	**2**	**40**	**0**	**0**	**0**

Traded to **LA Kings** by **Buffalo** for Doug Houda, July 26, 1994. Selected by **Minnesota** from **LA Kings** in Expansion Draft, June 23, 2000.

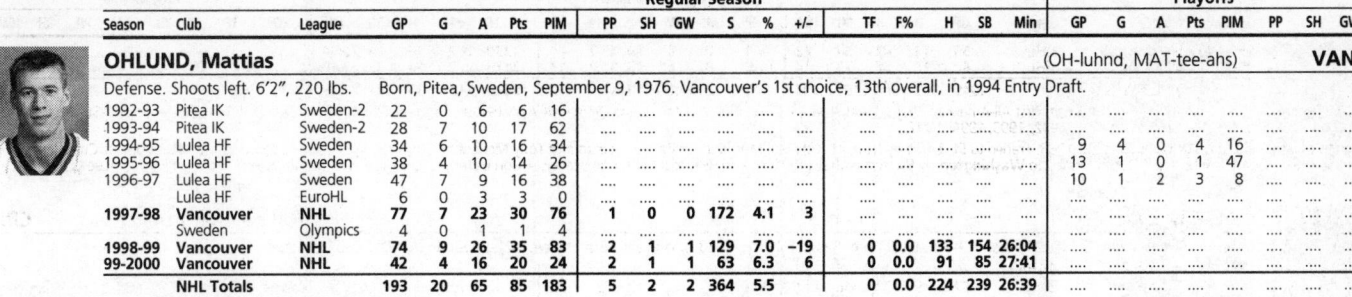

			Regular Season																Playoffs							
Season	Club	League	GP	G	A	Pts	PIM	PP	SH	GW	S	%	+/–	TF	F%	H	SB	Min	GP	G	A	Pts	PIM	PP	SH	GW

OHLUND, Mattias

(OH-luhnd, MAT-tee-ahs) **VAN.**

Defense. Shoots left. 6'2", 220 lbs. Born, Pitea, Sweden, September 9, 1976. Vancouver's 1st choice, 13th overall, in 1994 Entry Draft.

1992-93	Pitea IK	Sweden-2	22	0	6	6	16	....	....	....	....	....	....	....	....	....	....	....	....	....	....	....	....	....	....	....
1993-94	Pitea IK	Sweden-2	28	7	10	17	62	....	....	....	....	....	....	....	....	....	....	....	....	....	....	....	....	....	....	....
1994-95	Lulea HF	Sweden	34	6	10	16	34	....	....	....	....	....	....	....	....	....	....	....	9	4	0	4	16	....	....	....
1995-96	Lulea HF	Sweden	38	4	10	14	26	....	....	....	....	....	....	....	....	....	....	....	13	1	0	1	47	....	....	....
1996-97	Lulea HF	Sweden	47	7	9	16	38	....	....	....	....	....	....	....	....	....	....	....	10	1	2	3	8	....	....	....
	Lulea HF	EuroHL	6	0	3	3	0	....	....	....	....	....	....	....	....	....	....	....	....	....	....	....	....	....	....	....
1997-98	**Vancouver**	**NHL**	**77**	**7**	**23**	**30**	**76**	**1**	**0**	**0**	**172**	**4.1**	**3**	....	....	....	....	....	....	....	....	....	....	....	....	....
	Sweden	Olympics	4	0	1	1	4	....	....	....	....	....	....	....	....	....	....	....	....	....	....	....	....	....	....	....
1998-99	**Vancouver**	**NHL**	**74**	**9**	**26**	**35**	**83**	**2**	**1**	**1**	**129**	**7.0**	**–19**	**0**	**0.0**	**133**	**154**	**26:04**	....	....	....	....	....	....	....	....
99-2000	**Vancouver**	**NHL**	**42**	**4**	**16**	**20**	**24**	**2**	**1**	**1**	**63**	**6.3**	**6**	**0**	**0.0**	**91**	**85**	**27:41**	....	....	....	....	....	....	....	....
	NHL Totals		**193**	**20**	**65**	**85**	**183**	**5**	**2**	**2**	**364**	**5.5**		**0**	**0.0**	**224**	**239**	**26:39**	....	....	....	....	....	....	....	....

NHL All-Rookie Team (1998) • Played in NHL All-Star Game (1999)

OLAUSSON, Fredrik

(OHL-ah-suhn, FREHD-rihk)

Defense. Shoots right. 6'2", 198 lbs. Born, Dadesjo, Sweden, October 5, 1966. Winnipeg's 4th choice, 81st overall, in 1985 Entry Draft.

1982-83	Nybro SK	Sweden-2	31	4	4	8	12	....	....	....	....	....	....	....	....	....	....	....	....	....	....	....	....	....	....	....
1983-84	Nybro SK	Sweden-2	28	8	14	22	32	....	....	....	....	....	....	....	....	....	....	....	....	....	....	....	....	....	....	....
1984-85	Farjestads BK	Sweden	29	5	12	17	22	....	....	....	....	....	....	....	....	....	....	....	3	1	0	1	0	....	....	....
1985-86	Farjestads BK	Sweden	33	4	12	16	22	....	....	....	....	....	....	....	....	....	....	....	8	3	2	5	6	....	....	....
1986-87	**Winnipeg**	**NHL**	**72**	**7**	**29**	**36**	**24**	**1**	**0**	**2**	**119**	**5.9**	**–3**	....	....	....	....	....	**10**	**2**	**3**	**5**	**4**	**1**	**0**	**0**
1987-88	**Winnipeg**	**NHL**	**38**	**5**	**10**	**15**	**18**	**2**	**0**	**2**	**65**	**7.7**	**3**	....	....	....	....	....	**5**	**1**	**1**	**2**	**0**	**0**	**0**	**0**
1988-89	**Winnipeg**	**NHL**	**75**	**15**	**47**	**62**	**32**	**4**	**0**	**1**	**178**	**8.4**	**6**	....	....	....	....	....	....	....	....	....	....	....	....	....
1989-90	**Winnipeg**	**NHL**	**77**	**9**	**46**	**55**	**32**	**3**	**0**	**0**	**147**	**6.1**	**–1**	....	....	....	....	....	**7**	**0**	**2**	**2**	**2**	**0**	**0**	**0**
1990-91	**Winnipeg**	**NHL**	**71**	**12**	**29**	**41**	**24**	**5**	**0**	**0**	**168**	**7.1**	**–22**	....	....	....	....	....	....	....	....	....	....	....	....	....
1991-92	**Winnipeg**	**NHL**	**77**	**20**	**42**	**62**	**34**	**13**	**1**	**2**	**227**	**8.8**	**–31**	....	....	....	....	....	**7**	**1**	**5**	**6**	**4**	**1**	**0**	**0**
1992-93	**Winnipeg**	**NHL**	**68**	**16**	**41**	**57**	**22**	**11**	**0**	**3**	**165**	**9.7**	**–4**	....	....	....	....	....	**6**	**0**	**2**	**2**	**2**	**0**	**0**	**0**
1993-94	**Winnipeg**	**NHL**	**18**	**2**	**5**	**7**	**10**	**1**	**0**	**0**	**41**	**4.9**	**–3**	....	....	....	....	....	....	....	....	....	....	....	....	....
	Edmonton	**NHL**	**55**	**9**	**19**	**28**	**20**	**6**	**0**	**1**	**85**	**10.6**	**–4**	....	....	....	....	....	....	....	....	....	....	....	....	....
1994-95	EV Ehrwald	Austria-2	10	4	3	7	8	....	....	....	....	....	....	....	....	....	....	....	....	....	....	....	....	....	....	....
	Edmonton	**NHL**	**33**	**0**	**10**	**10**	**20**	**0**	**0**	**0**	**52**	**0.0**	**–4**	....	....	....	....	....	....	....	....	....	....	....	....	....
1995-96	**Edmonton**	**NHL**	**20**	**0**	**6**	**6**	**14**	**0**	**0**	**0**	**20**	**0.0**	**–14**	....	....	....	....	....	....	....	....	....	....	....	....	....
	Anaheim	**NHL**	**36**	**2**	**16**	**18**	**24**	**1**	**0**	**0**	**63**	**3.2**	**7**	....	....	....	....	....	....	....	....	....	....	....	....	....
1996-97	**Anaheim**	**NHL**	**20**	**2**	**9**	**11**	**8**	**1**	**0**	**0**	**35**	**5.7**	**–5**	....	....	....	....	....	....	....	....	....	....	....	....	....
	Pittsburgh	**NHL**	**51**	**7**	**20**	**27**	**24**	**2**	**0**	**3**	**75**	**9.3**	**21**	....	....	....	....	....	**4**	**0**	**1**	**1**	**0**	**0**	**0**	**0**
1997-98	**Pittsburgh**	**NHL**	**76**	**6**	**27**	**33**	**42**	**2**	**0**	**1**	**89**	**6.7**	**13**	....	....	....	....	....	**6**	**0**	**3**	**3**	**2**	**0**	**0**	**0**
1998-99	**Anaheim**	**NHL**	**74**	**16**	**40**	**56**	**30**	**10**	**0**	**2**	**121**	**13.2**	**17**	**0**	**0.0**	**41**	**56**	**19:47**	**4**	**0**	**2**	**2**	**4**	**0**	**0**	**0**
99-2000	**Anaheim**	**NHL**	**70**	**15**	**19**	**34**	**28**	**8**	**0**	**1**	**120**	**12.5**	**–13**	**0**	**0.0**	**62**	**45**	**20:01**	....	....	....	....	....	....	....	....
	NHL Totals		**931**	**143**	**415**	**558**	**406**	**70**	**1**	**18**	**1770**	**8.1**		**0**	**0.0**	**103**	**101**	**19:54**	**49**	**4**	**19**	**23**	**18**	**2**	**0**	**0**

Swedish World All-Star Team (1986)

Traded to **Edmonton** by **Winnipeg** with Winnipeg's 7th round choice (Curtis Sheptak) in 1994 Entry Draft for Edmonton's 3rd round choice (Tavis Hansen) in 1994 Entry Draft, December 6, 1993. Claimed on waivers by **Anaheim** from **Edmonton**, January 16, 1996. Traded to **Pittsburgh** by **Anaheim** with Alex Hicks for Shawn Antoski and Dmitri Mironov, November 19, 1996. Signed as a free agent by **Anaheim**, August 28, 1998.

OLCZYK, Ed

(OHL-chehk, EHD)

Center. Shoots left. 6'1", 207 lbs. Born, Chicago, IL, August 16, 1966. Chicago's 1st choice, 3rd overall, in 1984 Entry Draft.

1981-82	Team Illinois	MEHL	56	74	95	169	63	....	....	....	....	....	....	....	....	....	....	....	....	....	....	....	....	....	....	....
1982-83	Stratford Cullitons	OJHL-B	42	*50	*92	*142	54	....	....	....	....	....	....	....	....	....	....	....	....	....	....	....	....	....	....	....
1983-84	United States	Nat-Team	62	21	47	68	36	....	....	....	....	....	....	....	....	....	....	....	....	....	....	....	....	....	....	....
	United States	Olympics	6	2	5	7	0	....	....	....	....	....	....	....	....	....	....	....	....	....	....	....	....	....	....	....
1984-85	**Chicago**	**NHL**	**70**	**20**	**30**	**50**	**67**	**1**	**1**	**2**	**136**	**14.7**	**11**	....	....	....	....	....	**15**	**6**	**5**	**11**	**11**	**1**	**1**	**0**
1985-86	**Chicago**	**NHL**	**79**	**29**	**50**	**79**	**47**	**8**	**1**	**2**	**218**	**13.3**	**2**	....	....	....	....	....	**3**	**0**	**0**	**0**	**0**	**0**	**0**	**0**
1986-87	**Chicago**	**NHL**	**79**	**16**	**35**	**51**	**119**	**2**	**1**	**2**	**181**	**8.8**	**–4**	....	....	....	....	....	**4**	**1**	**1**	**2**	**4**	**0**	**0**	**0**
1987-88	**Toronto**	**NHL**	**80**	**42**	**33**	**75**	**55**	**14**	**4**	**3**	**243**	**17.3**	**–22**	....	....	....	....	....	**6**	**5**	**4**	**9**	**2**	**1**	**1**	**1**
1988-89	**Toronto**	**NHL**	**80**	**38**	**52**	**90**	**75**	**11**	**2**	**4**	**249**	**15.3**	**0**	....	....	....	....	....	....	....	....	....	....	....	....	....
1989-90	**Toronto**	**NHL**	**79**	**32**	**56**	**88**	**78**	**6**	**0**	**4**	**208**	**15.4**	**0**	....	....	....	....	....	**5**	**1**	**2**	**3**	**14**	**0**	**0**	**0**
1990-91	**Toronto**	**NHL**	**18**	**4**	**10**	**14**	**13**	**0**	**0**	**0**	**45**	**8.9**	**–7**	....	....	....	....	....	....	....	....	....	....	....	....	....
	Winnipeg	**NHL**	**61**	**26**	**31**	**57**	**69**	**14**	**0**	**2**	**181**	**14.4**	**–20**	....	....	....	....	....	....	....	....	....	....	....	....	....
1991-92	**Winnipeg**	**NHL**	**64**	**32**	**33**	**65**	**67**	**12**	**0**	**7**	**245**	**13.1**	**11**	....	....	....	....	....	**6**	**2**	**1**	**3**	**4**	**0**	**0**	**1**
1992-93	**Winnipeg**	**NHL**	**25**	**8**	**12**	**20**	**26**	**2**	**0**	**0**	**81**	**9.9**	**–11**	....	....	....	....	....	....	....	....	....	....	....	....	....
	NY Rangers	**NHL**	**46**	**13**	**16**	**29**	**26**	**0**	**0**	**1**	**109**	**11.9**	**9**	....	....	....	....	....	....	....	....	....	....	....	....	....
1993-94♦	**NY Rangers**	**NHL**	**37**	**3**	**5**	**8**	**28**	**0**	**0**	**1**	**40**	**7.5**	**–1**	....	....	....	....	....	**1**	**0**	**0**	**0**	**0**	**0**	**0**	**0**
1994-95	**NY Rangers**	**NHL**	**20**	**2**	**1**	**3**	**4**	**1**	**0**	**0**	**29**	**6.9**	**–2**	....	....	....	....	....	....	....	....	....	....	....	....	....
	Winnipeg	**NHL**	**13**	**2**	**8**	**10**	**8**	**1**	**0**	**0**	**27**	**7.4**	**1**	....	....	....	....	....	....	....	....	....	....	....	....	....
1995-96	**Winnipeg**	**NHL**	**51**	**27**	**22**	**49**	**65**	**16**	**0**	**1**	**147**	**18.4**	**0**	....	....	....	....	....	**6**	**1**	**2**	**3**	**6**	**0**	**0**	**0**
1996-97	**Los Angeles**	**NHL**	**67**	**21**	**23**	**44**	**45**	**0**	**0**	**5**	**166**	**12.7**	**–22**	....	....	....	....	....	....	....	....	....	....	....	....	....
	Pittsburgh	**NHL**	**12**	**4**	**7**	**11**	**6**	**5**	**1**	**1**	**29**	**13.8**	**8**	....	....	....	....	....	**5**	**1**	**0**	**1**	**12**	**0**	**1**	**1**
1997-98	**Pittsburgh**	**NHL**	**56**	**11**	**11**	**22**	**35**	**5**	**1**	**1**	**123**	**8.9**	**–9**	....	....	....	....	....	**6**	**2**	**0**	**2**	**4**	**1**	**1**	**1**
1998-99	**Chicago**	**NHL**	**61**	**10**	**15**	**25**	**29**	**2**	**1**	**2**	**88**	**11.4**	**–3**	**441**	**51.9**	**54**	**12**	**14:44**	....	....	....	....	....	....	....	....
	Chicago Wolves	IHL	7	2	2	4	6	....	....	....	....	....	....	....	....	....	....	....	....	....	....	....	....	....	....	....
99-2000	**Chicago**	**NHL**	**33**	**2**	**2**	**4**	**12**	**0**	**0**	**0**	**33**	**6.1**	**–8**	**147**	**59.9**	**16**	**11**	**9:18**	....	....	....	....	....	....	....	....
	NHL Totals		**1031**	**342**	**452**	**794**	**874**	**100**	**12**	**38**	**2578**	**13.3**		**588**	**53.9**	**70**	**23**	**12:50**	**57**	**19**	**15**	**34**	**57**	**3**	**4**	**4**

Traded to **Toronto** by **Chicago** with Al Secord for Rick Vaive, Steve Thomas and Bob McGill, September 3, 1987. Traded to **Winnipeg** by **Toronto** with Mark Osborne for Dave Ellett and Paul Fenton, November 10, 1990. Traded to **NY Rangers** by **Winnipeg** for Kris King and Tie Domi, December 28, 1992. • Missed majority of 1993-94 season recovering from thumb injury suffered in game vs. Florida, January 3, 1994. Traded to **Winnipeg** by **NY Rangers** for Winnipeg's 5th round choice (Alexei Vasiliev) in 1995 Entry Draft, April 7, 1995. Signed as a free agent by **LA Kings**, July 8, 1996. Traded to **Pittsburgh** by **LA Kings** for Glen Murray, March 18, 1997. Signed as a free agent by **Chicago**, August 26, 1998. • Missed majority of 1999-2000 season recovering from hernia injury suffered in game vs. Pittsburgh, Oct. 16, 1999.

OLIVER, David

(AWL-ih-vuhr, DAY-vihd) **OTT.**

Right wing. Shoots right. 6', 190 lbs. Born, Sechelt, B.C., April 17, 1971. Edmonton's 7th choice, 144th overall, in 1991 Entry Draft.

1988-89	Vernon Lakers	BCJHL	58	41	38	79	38	....	....	....	....	....	....	....	....	....	....	....	....	....	....	....	....	....	....	....
1989-90	Vernon Lakers	BCJHL	58	51	48	99	22	....	....	....	....	....	....	....	....	....	....	....	....	....	....	....	....	....	....	....
1990-91	U. of Michigan	CCHA	27	13	11	24	34	....	....	....	....	....	....	....	....	....	....	....	....	....	....	....	....	....	....	....
1991-92	U. of Michigan	CCHA	44	31	27	58	32	....	....	....	....	....	....	....	....	....	....	....	....	....	....	....	....	....	....	....
1992-93	U. of Michigan	CCHA	40	35	20	55	18	....	....	....	....	....	....	....	....	....	....	....	....	....	....	....	....	....	....	....
1993-94	U. of Michigan	CCHA	41	28	40	68	16	....	....	....	....	....	....	....	....	....	....	....	....	....	....	....	....	....	....	....
1994-95	Cape Breton	AHL	32	11	18	29	8	....	....	....	....	....	....	....	....	....	....	....	....	....	....	....	....	....	....	....
	Edmonton	**NHL**	**44**	**16**	**14**	**30**	**20**	**10**	**0**	**0**	**79**	**20.3**	**–11**	....	....	....	....	....	....	....	....	....	....	....	....	....
1995-96	**Edmonton**	**NHL**	**80**	**20**	**19**	**39**	**34**	**14**	**0**	**0**	**131**	**15.3**	**–22**	....	....	....	....	....	....	....	....	....	....	....	....	....
1996-97	**Edmonton**	**NHL**	**17**	**1**	**2**	**3**	**4**	**0**	**0**	**0**	**22**	**4.5**	**–8**	....	....	....	....	....	....	....	....	....	....	....	....	....
	NY Rangers	**NHL**	**14**	**2**	**1**	**3**	**4**	**0**	**0**	**0**	**13**	**15.4**	**3**	....	....	....	....	....	**3**	**0**	**0**	**0**	**0**	**0**	**0**	**0**
1997-98	Houston Aeros	IHL	78	38	27	65	60	....	....	....	....	....	....	....	....	....	....	....	4	3	0	3	4	....	....	....
1998-99	**Ottawa**	**NHL**	**17**	**2**	**5**	**7**	**4**	**0**	**0**	**0**	**18**	**11.1**	**1**	**3**	**33.3**	**8**	**2**	**10:34**	....	....	....	....	....	....	....	....
	Houston Aeros	IHL	37	18	17	35	30	....	....	....	....	....	....	....	....	....	....	....	19	10	6	16	22	....	....	....
99-2000	**Phoenix**	**NHL**	**9**	**1**	**0**	**1**	**2**	**1**	**0**	**0**	**6**	**16.7**	**0**	**0**	**0.0**	**11**	**1**	**7:38**	....	....	....	....	....	....	....	....
	Houston Aeros	IHL	45	16	11	27	40	....	....	....	....	....	....	....	....	....	....	....	11	3	4	7	8	....	....	....
	NHL Totals		**181**	**42**	**41**	**83**	**68**	**25**	**0**	**0**	**269**	**15.6**		**3**	**33.3**	**19**	**3**	**9:33**	**3**	**0**	**0**	**0**	**0**	**0**	**0**	**0**

CCHA Second All-Star Team (1993) • CCHA First All-Star Team (1994) • NCAA West First All-American Team (1994)

Claimed on waivers by **NY Rangers** from **Edmonton**, February 21, 1997. Signed as a free agent by **Ottawa**, July 2, 1998. Signed as a free agent by **Phoenix**, July 20, 1999. Signed as a free agent by **Ottawa**, August 2, 2000.

			Regular Season																Playoffs							
Season	Club	League	GP	G	A	Pts	PIM	PP	SH	GW	S	%	+/-	TF	F%	H	SB	Min	GP	G	A	Pts	PIM	PP	SH	GW

OLIWA, Krzysztof

(oh-LEE-vuh, KHRIH-stahf) — CBJ

Left wing. Shoots left. 6'5", 235 lbs.   Born, Tychy, Poland, April 12, 1973. New Jersey's 4th choice, 65th overall, in 1993 Entry Draft.

Season	Club	League	GP	G	A	Pts	PIM	PP	SH	GW	S	%	+/-	TF	F%	H	SB	Min	GP	G	A	Pts	PIM	PP	SH	GW
1990-91	GKS Katowski	Poland-Jr.	5	4	4	8	10	....	....	....	....	....	....						....	....	....	....	....			
1991-92	GKS Tychy	Poland	10	3	7	10	6	....	....	....	....	....	....						....	....	....	....	....			
1992-93	Welland Cougars	OJHL-B	30	13	21	34	127	....	....	....	....	....	....						....	....	....	....	....			
1993-94	Albany River Rats	AHL	33	2	4	6	151	....	....	....	....	....	....						....	....	....	....	....			
	Raleigh IceCaps	ECHL	15	0	2	2	65	....	....	....	....	....	....						9	0	0	0	35			
1994-95	Albany River Rats	AHL	20	1	1	2	77	....	....	....	....	....	....						....	....	....	....	....			
	Saint John Flames	AHL	14	1	4	5	79	....	....	....	....	....	....						....	....	....	....	....			
	Raleigh IceCaps	ECHL	5	0	2	2	32	....	....	....	....	....	....						....	....	....	....	....			
	Detroit Vipers	IHL	4	0	1	1	24	....	....	....	....	....	....						....	....	....	....	....			
1995-96	Albany River Rats	AHL	51	5	11	16	217	....	....	....	....	....	....						....	....	....	....	....			
	Raleigh IceCaps	ECHL	9	1	0	1	53	....	....	....	....	....	....						....	....	....	....	....			
1996-97	**New Jersey**	**NHL**	1	0	0	0	5	0	0	0	0	0.0	-1						....	....	....	....	....			
	Albany River Rats	AHL	60	13	14	27	322	....	....	....	....	....	....						15	7	1	8	49			
1997-98	**New Jersey**	**NHL**	73	2	3	5	295	0	0	2	53	3.8	3						6	0	0	0	23	0	0	0
1998-99	**New Jersey**	**NHL**	64	5	7	12	240	0	0	1	59	8.5	4	1	0.0	117	9	7:02	1	0	0	0	2	0	0	0
99-2000	**New Jersey**	**NHL**	69	6	10	16	184	1	0	2	61	9.8	-2	3	66.7	84	4	6:45								
	NHL Totals		207	13	20	33	724	1	0	5	173	7.5		4	50.0	201	13	6:53	7	0	0	0	25	0	0	0

Traded to **Columbus** by **New Jersey** with future considerations (Deron Quint, June 23, 2000) for Columbus' 3rd round choice in 2001 Entry Draft and future considerations (Turner Stevenson, June 23, 2000), June 12, 2000.

O'NEILL, Jeff

(OH-NEEL, JEHF) — CAR.

Center. Shoots right. 6'1", 190 lbs.   Born, Richmond Hill, Ont., February 23, 1976. Hartford's 1st choice, 5th overall, in 1994 Entry Draft.

Season	Club	League	GP	G	A	Pts	PIM	PP	SH	GW	S	%	+/-	TF	F%	H	SB	Min	GP	G	A	Pts	PIM	PP	SH	GW
1990-91	Richmond Hill	OMHA	78	56	134	190	....	....	....	....	....	....	....						....	....	....	....	....			
1991-92	Thornhill	OJHL	43	27	53	80	48	....	....	....	....	....	....						....	....	....	....	....			
1992-93	Guelph Storm	OHL	65	32	47	79	88	....	....	....	....	....	....						5	2	2	4	6			
1993-94	Guelph Storm	OHL	66	45	81	126	95	....	....	....	....	....	....						9	2	11	13	31			
1994-95	Guelph Storm	OHL	57	43	81	124	56	....	....	....	....	....	....						14	8	18	26	34			
1995-96	**Hartford**	**NHL**	65	8	19	27	40	1	0	1	65	12.3	-3						....	....	....	....	....			
1996-97	**Hartford**	**NHL**	72	14	16	30	40	2	1	2	101	13.9	-24						....	....	....	....	....			
	Springfield	AHL	1	0	0	0	0	....	....	....	....	....	....						....	....	....	....	....			
1997-98	**Carolina**	**NHL**	74	19	20	39	67	7	1	4	114	16.7	-8						....	....	....	....	....			
1998-99	**Carolina**	**NHL**	75	16	15	31	66	4	0	2	121	13.2	3	941	45.6	207	19	16:44	6	0	1	1	0	0	0	0
99-2000	**Carolina**	**NHL**	80	25	38	63	72	4	0	7	189	13.2	-9	1337	49.5	165	33	19:20								
	NHL Totals		366	82	108	190	285	18	2	16	590	13.9		2278	47.9	372	52	18:04	6	0	1	1	0	0	0	0

OHL First All-Star Team (1995)
Transferred to **Carolina** after **Hartford** franchise relocated, June 25, 1997.

ORSZAGH, Vladimir

(OHR-sahk, VLAD-ih-meer)

Right wing. Shoots left. 5'11", 173 lbs.   Born, Banska Bystrica, Czech., May 24, 1977. NY Islanders' 4th choice, 106th overall, in 1995 Entry Draft.

Season	Club	League	GP	G	A	Pts	PIM	PP	SH	GW	S	%	+/-	TF	F%	H	SB	Min	GP	G	A	Pts	PIM	PP	SH	GW
1993-94	Banska Bystrica	Slovak-Jr.	38	38	27	65	....	....	....	....	....	....	....						....	....	....	....	....			
1994-95	Banska Bystrica	Slovak-2	38	18	12	30	....	....	....	....	....	....	....						....	....	....	....	....			
1995-96	Banska Bystrica	Slovakia	31	9	5	14	22	....	....	....	....	....	....						....	....	....	....	....			
1996-97	Utah Grizzlies	IHL	68	12	15	27	30	....	....	....	....	....	....						3	0	1	1	4			
1997-98	**NY Islanders**	**NHL**	11	0	1	1	2	0	0	0	9	0.0	-3						....	....	....	....	....			
	Utah Grizzlies	IHL	62	13	10	23	60	....	....	....	....	....	....						4	2	0	2	0			
1998-99	**NY Islanders**	**NHL**	12	1	0	1	6	0	0	0	4	0.0	2	0	0.0	0	0	0:00								
	Lowell	AHL	68	18	23	41	57	....	....	....	....	....	....						3	2	2	4	2			
99-2000	**NY Islanders**	**NHL**	11	2	1	3	4	0	0	0	16	12.5	1	2	0.0	16	6	11:55								
	Lowell	AHL	55	8	12	20	22	....	....	....	....	....	....						7	3	3	6	2			
	NHL Totals		34	3	2	5	12	0	0	0	29	10.3		2	0.0	16	6	11:55	....	....	....	....	....			

O'SULLIVAN, Chris

(OH-SUHL-lih-van, KRIHS) — ANA.

Defense. Shoots left. 6'2", 205 lbs.   Born, Dorchester, MA, May 15, 1974. Calgary's 2nd choice, 30th overall, in 1992 Entry Draft.

Season	Club	League	GP	G	A	Pts	PIM	PP	SH	GW	S	%	+/-	TF	F%	H	SB	Min	GP	G	A	Pts	PIM	PP	SH	GW
1991-92	Catholic Memorial	Hi-School	26	26	23	49	65	....	....	....	....	....	....						....	....	....	....	....			
1992-93	Boston University	H-East	5	0	2	2	4	....	....	....	....	....	....						....	....	....	....	....			
1993-94	Boston University	H-East	32	5	18	23	25	....	....	....	....	....	....						....	....	....	....	....			
1994-95	Boston University	H-East	40	23	33	56	48	....	....	....	....	....	....						....	....	....	....	....			
1995-96	Boston University	H-East	37	12	35	47	50	....	....	....	....	....	....						....	....	....	....	....			
1996-97	**Calgary**	**NHL**	27	2	8	10	2	1	0	1	41	4.9	0						....	....	....	....	....			
	Saint John Flames	AHL	29	3	8	11	17	....	....	....	....	....	....						5	0	4	4	0			
1997-98	**Calgary**	**NHL**	12	0	2	2	10	0	0	0	12	0.0	4						....	....	....	....	....			
	Saint John Flames	AHL	32	4	10	14	2	....	....	....	....	....	....						21	2	17	19	18			
1998-99	**Calgary**	**NHL**	10	0	1	1	2	0	0	0	10	0.0	-1	1	0.0	4	1	9:07								
	Saint John Flames	AHL	41	7	29	36	24	....	....	....	....	....	....						....	....	....	....	....			
	Hartford	AHL	10	1	4	5	0	....	....	....	....	....	....						7	1	3	4	11			
99-2000	**Vancouver**	**NHL**	11	0	5	5	2	0	0	0	16	0.0	2	0	0.0	4	2	17:47								
	Syracuse Crunch	AHL	59	18	47	65	24	....	....	....	....	....	....						4	0	1	1	0			
	NHL Totals		60	2	16	18	16	1	0	1	79	2.5		1	0.0	8	3	13:39	....	....	....	....	....			

Hockey East First All-Star Team (1995) • NCAA East Second All-American Team (1995) • NCAA Championship All-Tournament Team (1995) • NCAA Championship Tournament MVP (1995)

• Missed majority of 1992-93 season recovering from neck injury suffered in game vs. Boston College, November 11, 1992. Traded to **NY Rangers** by **Calgary** for Lee Sorochan, March 23, 1999. Signed as a free agent by **Vancouver**, August 20, 1999. Signed as a free agent by **Anaheim**, July 20, 2000.

OZOLINSH, Sandis

(OH-zoh-LIHNCH, SAN-dihz) — CAR.

Defense. Shoots left. 6'3", 205 lbs.   Born, Riga, Latvia, August 3, 1972. San Jose's 3rd choice, 30th overall, in 1991 Entry Draft.

Season	Club	League	GP	G	A	Pts	PIM	PP	SH	GW	S	%	+/-	TF	F%	H	SB	Min	GP	G	A	Pts	PIM	PP	SH	GW
1990-91	Dynamo Riga	USSR	44	0	3	3	51	....	....	....	....	....	....						....	....	....	....	....			
1991-92	Dynamo Riga	CIS	30	6	0	6	42	....	....	....	....	....	....						....	....	....	....	....			
	Kansas City	IHL	34	6	9	15	20	....	....	....	....	....	....						15	2	5	7	22			
1992-93	**San Jose**	**NHL**	37	7	16	23	40	2	0	0	83	8.4	-9						....	....	....	....	....			
1993-94	**San Jose**	**NHL**	81	26	38	64	24	4	0	3	157	16.6	16						14	0	10	10	8	0	0	0
1994-95	**San Jose**	**NHL**	48	9	16	25	30	3	1	2	83	10.8	-6						11	3	2	5	6	1	0	0
1995-96	San Francisco	IHL	2	1	0	1	0	....	....	....	....	....	....						....	....	....	....	....			
	San Jose	**NHL**	7	1	3	4	4	1	0	0	21	4.8	2						....	....	....	....	....			
	♦ **Colorado**	**NHL**	66	13	37	50	50	7	1	1	145	9.0	0						22	5	14	19	16	2	0	1
1996-97	**Colorado**	**NHL**	80	23	45	68	88	13	0	4	232	9.9	4						17	4	13	17	24	2	0	1
1997-98	**Colorado**	**NHL**	66	13	38	51	65	9	0	2	135	9.6	-12						7	0	7	7	14	0	0	0
1998-99	**Colorado**	**NHL**	39	7	25	32	22	4	0	3	81	8.6	10	0	0.0	34	23	22:06	19	4	8	12	22	3	0	1
99-2000	**Colorado**	**NHL**	82	16	36	52	46	6	0	1	210	7.6	17	0	0.0	71	47	22:41	17	5	5	10	20	3	0	1
	NHL Totals		506	115	254	369	369	49	2	16	1147	10.0		0	0.0	105	70	22:30	107	21	59	80	110	11	0	4

NHL First All-Star Team (1997) • Played in NHL All-Star Game (1994, 1997, 1998, 2000)

• Missed remainder of 1992-93 season recovering from knee injury suffered in game vs. Philadelphia, December 30, 1992. Traded to **Colorado** by **San Jose** for Owen Nolan, October 26, 1995. Traded to **Carolina** by **Colorado** with Columbus' 2nd round choice (previously acquired, Carolina selected Tomas Kurka) in 2000 Entry Draft for Nolan Pratt, Carolina's 1st (Vaclav Nedorost) and 2nd (Jared Aulin) round choices in 2000 Entry Draft and Philadelphia's 2nd round choice (previously acquired, Colorado selected Argis Saviels) in 2000 Entry Draft, June 24, 2000.

PALFFY, Ziggy

(PAHL-fee, ZIHG-gee) **L.A.**

Right wing. Shoots left. 5'10", 183 lbs. Born, Skalica, Czech., May 5, 1972. NY Islanders' 2nd choice, 26th overall, in 1991 Entry Draft.

			Regular Season																Playoffs							
Season	Club	League	GP	G	A	Pts	PIM	PP	SH	GW	S	%	+/–	TF	F%	H	SB	Min	GP	G	A	Pts	PIM	PP	SH	GW
1990-91	AC Nitra	Czech.	50	34	16	50	18	....	....	....	....	....	....	....	....	....	....	....	....	....	....	....	....	....	....	....
1991-92	Dukla Trencin	Czech.	45	41	33	74	36	....	....	....	....	....	....	....	....	....	....	....	....	....	....	....	....	....	....	....
1992-93	Dukla Trencin	Czech.	43	38	41	79	....	....	....	....	....	....	....	....	....	....	....	....	....	....	....	....	....	....	....	....
1993-94	**NY Islanders**	**NHL**	**5**	**0**	**0**	**0**	**0**	**0**	**0**	**0**	**5**	**0.0**	**–6**	....	....	....	....	....	....	....	....	....	....	....	....	....
	Salt Lake City	IHL	57	25	32	57	83	....	....	....	....	....	....	....	....	....	....	....	....	....	....	....	....	....	....	....
	Slovakia	Olympics	8	3	*7	*10	8	....	....	....	....	....	....	....	....	....	....	....	....	....	....	....	....	....	....	....
1994-95	Denver Grizzlies	IHL	33	20	23	43	40	....	....	....	....	....	....	....	....	....	....	....	....	....	....	....	....	....	....	....
	NY Islanders	**NHL**	**33**	**10**	**7**	**17**	**6**	**1**	**0**	**1**	**75**	**13.3**	**3**	....	....	....	....	....	....	....	....	....	....	....	....	....
1995-96	**NY Islanders**	**NHL**	**81**	**43**	**44**	**87**	**56**	**17**	**1**	**6**	**257**	**16.7**	**–17**	....	....	....	....	....	....	....	....	....	....	....	....	....
1996-97	Dukla Trencin	Slovakia	1	0	0	0	....	....	....	....	....	....	....	....	....	....	....	....	....	....	....	....	....	....	....	....
	NY Islanders	**NHL**	**80**	**48**	**42**	**90**	**43**	**6**	**4**	**6**	**292**	**16.4**	**21**	....	....	....	....	....	....	....	....	....	....	....	....	....
1997-98	**NY Islanders**	**NHL**	**82**	**45**	**42**	**87**	**34**	**17**	**2**	**5**	**277**	**16.2**	**–2**	....	....	....	....	....	....	....	....	....	....	....	....	....
1998-99	HK-36 Skalica	Slovakia	9	11	8	19	6	....	....	....	....	....	....	....	....	....	....	....	....	....	....	....	....	....	....	....
	NY Islanders	**NHL**	**50**	**22**	**28**	**50**	**34**	**5**	**2**	**1**	**168**	**13.1**	**–6**	**1**	**100.0**	**28**	**34**	**22:04**	....	....	....	....	....	....	....	....
99-2000	**Los Angeles**	**NHL**	**64**	**27**	**39**	**66**	**32**	**4**	**0**	**3**	**186**	**14.5**	**18**	**7**	**42.9**	**63**	**19**	**19:39**	**4**	**2**	**0**	**2**	**0**	**0**	**0**	**0**
	NHL Totals		**395**	**195**	**202**	**397**	**205**	**50**	**9**	**22**	**1260**	**15.5**		**8**	**50.0**	**91**	**53**	**20:43**	**4**	**2**	**0**	**2**	**0**	**0**	**0**	**0**

Czechoslovakian Rookie of the Year (1991) • Czechoslovakian First All-Star Team (1992) • Played in NHL All-Star Game (1998)

Traded to **LA Kings** by **NY Islanders** with Brian Smolinski, Marcel Cousineau and New Jersey's 4th round choice (previously acquired, LA Kings selected Daniel Johanssen) in 1999 Entry Draft for Olli Jokinen, Josh Green, Mathieu Biron and LA Kings' 1st round choice (Taylor Pyatt) in 1999 Entry Draft, June 20, 1999.

PANDOLFO, Jay

(pan-DAHL-foh, JAY) **N.J.**

Left wing. Shoots left. 6'1", 190 lbs. Born, Winchester, MA, December 27, 1974. New Jersey's 2nd choice, 32nd overall, in 1993 Entry Draft.

Season	Club	League	GP	G	A	Pts	PIM	PP	SH	GW	S	%	+/–	TF	F%	H	SB	Min	GP	G	A	Pts	PIM	PP	SH	GW
1989-90	Burlington Prep	Hi-School	23	33	30	63	18	....	....	....	....	....	....	....	....	....	....	....	....	....	....	....	....	....	....	....
1990-91	Burlington Prep	Hi-School	20	19	27	46	10	....	....	....	....	....	....	....	....	....	....	....	....	....	....	....	....	....	....	....
1991-92	Burlington Prep	Hi-School	20	35	34	69	14	....	....	....	....	....	....	....	....	....	....	....	....	....	....	....	....	....	....	....
1992-93	Boston University	H-East	37	16	22	38	16	....	....	....	....	....	....	....	....	....	....	....	....	....	....	....	....	....	....	....
1993-94	Boston University	H-East	37	17	25	42	27	....	....	....	....	....	....	....	....	....	....	....	....	....	....	....	....	....	....	....
1994-95	Boston University	H-East	20	7	13	20	6	....	....	....	....	....	....	....	....	....	....	....	....	....	....	....	....	....	....	....
1995-96	Boston University	H-East	39	*38	29	67	6	....	....	....	....	....	....	....	....	....	....	....	....	....	....	....	....	....	....	....
	Albany River Rats	AHL	5	3	1	4	0	....	....	....	....	....	....	....	....	....	....	....	3	0	0	0	0	....	....	....
1996-97	**New Jersey**	**NHL**	**46**	**6**	**8**	**14**	**6**	**0**	**0**	**1**	**61**	**9.8**	**–1**	....	....	....	....	....	**6**	**0**	**1**	**1**	**0**	**0**	**0**	**0**
	Albany River Rats	AHL	12	3	9	12	0	....	....	....	....	....	....	....	....	....	....	....	....	....	....	....	....	....	....	....
1997-98	**New Jersey**	**NHL**	**23**	**1**	**3**	**4**	**4**	**0**	**0**	**0**	**23**	**4.3**	**–4**	....	....	....	....	....	**3**	**0**	**2**	**2**	**0**	**0**	**0**	**0**
	Albany River Rats	AHL	51	18	19	37	24	....	....	....	....	....	....	....	....	....	....	....	....	....	....	....	....	....	....	....
1998-99	**New Jersey**	**NHL**	**70**	**14**	**13**	**27**	**10**	**1**	**1**	**4**	**100**	**14.0**	**3**	**10**	**40.0**	**103**	**39**	**15:13**	**7**	**1**	**0**	**1**	**0**	**0**	**0**	**0**
99-2000♦	**New Jersey**	**NHL**	**71**	**7**	**8**	**15**	**4**	**0**	**0**	**0**	**86**	**8.1**	**0**	**19**	**47.4**	**91**	**22**	**13:25**	**23**	**0**	**5**	**5**	**0**	**0**	**0**	**0**
	NHL Totals		**210**	**28**	**32**	**60**	**24**	**1**	**1**	**5**	**270**	**10.4**		**29**	**44.8**	**194**	**61**	**14:19**	**39**	**1**	**8**	**9**	**0**	**0**	**0**	**0**

Hockey East First All-Star Team (1996) • NCAA East First All-American Team (1996)

PANKEWICZ, Greg

(PAN-kuh-wihts, GREHG)

Right wing. Shoots right. 6', 185 lbs. Born, Drayton Valley, Alta., November 6, 1970.

Season	Club	League	GP	G	A	Pts	PIM	PP	SH	GW	S	%	+/–	TF	F%	H	SB	Min	GP	G	A	Pts	PIM	PP	SH	GW
1988-89	Sherwood Park	AJHL	53	26	18	44	307	....	....	....	....	....	....	....	....	....	....	....	....	....	....	....	....	....	....	....
1989-90	Regina Pats	WHL	63	14	24	38	136	....	....	....	....	....	....	....	....	....	....	....	10	1	3	4	19	....	....	....
1990-91	Regina Pats	WHL	72	39	41	80	134	....	....	....	....	....	....	....	....	....	....	....	8	4	7	11	12	....	....	....
1991-92	Knoxville	ECHL	59	41	39	80	214	....	....	....	....	....	....	....	....	....	....	....	....	....	....	....	....	....	....	....
1992-93	New Haven	AHL	62	23	20	43	163	....	....	....	....	....	....	....	....	....	....	....	....	....	....	....	....	....	....	....
1993-94	**Ottawa**	**NHL**	**3**	**0**	**0**	**0**	**2**	**0**	**0**	**0**	**3**	**0.0**	**–1**	....	....	....	....	....	....	....	....	....	....	....	....	....
	P.E.I. Senators	AHL	69	33	29	62	241	....	....	....	....	....	....	....	....	....	....	....	....	....	....	....	....	....	....	....
1994-95	P.E.I. Senators	AHL	75	37	30	67	161	....	....	....	....	....	....	....	....	....	....	....	6	1	1	2	24	....	....	....
1995-96	Portland Pirates	AHL	28	9	12	21	99	....	....	....	....	....	....	....	....	....	....	....	....	....	....	....	....	....	....	....
	Chicago Wolves	IHL	45	9	16	25	164	....	....	....	....	....	....	....	....	....	....	....	5	4	0	4	8	....	....	....
1996-97	Manitoba Moose	IHL	79	32	34	66	222	....	....	....	....	....	....	....	....	....	....	....	....	....	....	....	....	....	....	....
1997-98	Manitoba Moose	IHL	76	42	34	76	246	....	....	....	....	....	....	....	....	....	....	....	3	0	0	0	6	....	....	....
1998-99	**Calgary**	**NHL**	**18**	**0**	**3**	**3**	**20**	**0**	**0**	**0**	**10**	**0.0**	**0**	**3**	**66.7**	**17**	**2**	**7:26**	....	....	....	....	....	....	....	....
	Saint John Flames	AHL	30	10	14	24	84	....	....	....	....	....	....	....	....	....	....	....	....	....	....	....	....	....	....	....
	Kentucky	AHL	10	2	3	5	7	....	....	....	....	....	....	....	....	....	....	....	11	4	1	5	10	....	....	....
99-2000	Houston Aeros	IHL	62	22	19	41	134	....	....	....	....	....	....	....	....	....	....	....	5	2	1	3	18	....	....	....
	NHL Totals		**21**	**0**	**3**	**3**	**22**	**0**	**0**	**0**	**13**	**0.0**		**3**	**66.7**	**17**	**2**	**7:26**	....	....	....	....	....	....	....	....

Signed as a free agent by **Ottawa**, May 27, 1993. Signed as a free agent by **Calgary**, September 1, 1998. Traded to **San Jose** by **Calgary** for cash, March 23, 1999.

PARK, Richard

(PAHRK, RIH-chahrd) **MIN.**

Center. Shoots right. 5'11", 190 lbs. Born, Seoul, S. Korea, May 27, 1976. Pittsburgh's 2nd choice, 50th overall, in 1994 Entry Draft.

Season	Club	League	GP	G	A	Pts	PIM	PP	SH	GW	S	%	+/–	TF	F%	H	SB	Min	GP	G	A	Pts	PIM	PP	SH	GW
1991-92	Toronto Nats	MTHL	76	49	58	107	91	....	....	....	....	....	....	....	....	....	....	....	....	....	....	....	....	....	....	....
1992-93	Belleville Bulls	OHL	66	23	38	61	38	....	....	....	....	....	....	....	....	....	....	....	5	0	0	0	14	....	....	....
1993-94	Belleville Bulls	OHL	59	27	49	76	70	....	....	....	....	....	....	....	....	....	....	....	12	3	5	8	18	....	....	....
1994-95	Belleville Bulls	OHL	45	28	51	79	35	....	....	....	....	....	....	....	....	....	....	....	16	9	18	27	12	....	....	....
	Pittsburgh	**NHL**	**1**	**0**	**1**	**1**	**2**	**0**	**0**	**0**	**4**	**0.0**	**1**	....	....	....	....	....	**3**	**0**	**0**	**0**	**2**	**0**	**0**	**0**
1995-96	Belleville Bulls	OHL	6	7	6	13	2	....	....	....	....	....	....	....	....	....	....	....	14	18	12	30	10	....	....	....
	Pittsburgh	**NHL**	**56**	**4**	**6**	**10**	**36**	**0**	**1**	**1**	**62**	**6.5**	**3**	....	....	....	....	....	**1**	**0**	**0**	**0**	**0**	**0**	**0**	**0**
1996-97	**Pittsburgh**	**NHL**	**1**	**0**	**0**	**0**	**0**	**0**	**0**	**0**	**1**	**0.0**	**–1**	....	....	....	....	....	....	....	....	....	....	....	....	....
	Cleveland	IHL	50	12	15	27	30	....	....	....	....	....	....	....	....	....	....	....	....	....	....	....	....	....	....	....
	Anaheim	**NHL**	**11**	**1**	**1**	**2**	**10**	**0**	**0**	**0**	**9**	**11.1**	**0**	....	....	....	....	....	**11**	**0**	**1**	**1**	**2**	**0**	**0**	**0**
1997-98	**Anaheim**	**NHL**	**15**	**0**	**2**	**2**	**8**	**0**	**0**	**0**	**14**	**0.0**	**–3**	....	....	....	....	....	....	....	....	....	....	....	....	....
	Cincinnati Ducks	AHL	56	17	26	43	36	....	....	....	....	....	....	....	....	....	....	....	....	....	....	....	....	....	....	....
1998-99	**Philadelphia**	**NHL**	**7**	**0**	**0**	**0**	**0**	**0**	**0**	**0**	**5**	**0.0**	**–1**	**15**	**53.3**	**2**	**0**	**9:21**	....	....	....	....	....	....	....	....
	Philadelphia	AHL	75	41	42	83	33	....	....	....	....	....	....	....	....	....	....	....	16	9	6	15	4	....	....	....
99-2000	Utah Grizzlies	IHL	82	28	32	60	36	....	....	....	....	....	....	....	....	....	....	....	5	1	0	1	0	....	....	....
	NHL Totals		**91**	**5**	**10**	**15**	**56**	**0**	**1**	**1**	**95**	**5.3**		**15**	**53.3**	**2**	**0**	**9:21**	**15**	**0**	**1**	**1**	**4**	**0**	**0**	**0**

AHL Second All-Star Team (1999)

Traded to **Anaheim** by **Pittsburgh** for Roman Oksiuta, March 18, 1997. Signed as a free agent by **Philadelphia**, August 24, 1998. Signed as a free agent by **Utah** (IHL), September 22, 1999. Signed as a free agent by **Minnesota**, September, 2000.

PARKER, Scott

(PAR-kuhr, SKAWT) **COL.**

Right wing. Shoots right. 6'5", 230 lbs. Born, Hanford, CA, January 29, 1978. Colorado's 4th choice, 20th overall, in 1998 Entry Draft.

Season	Club	League	GP	G	A	Pts	PIM	PP	SH	GW	S	%	+/–	TF	F%	H	SB	Min	GP	G	A	Pts	PIM	PP	SH	GW
1993-94	Alaska Artic Ice	AAHL	34	8	12	20	86	....	....	....	....	....	....	....	....	....	....	....	....	....	....	....	....	....	....	....
1994-95	Spokane Braves	KIJHL	43	7	21	28	128	....	....	....	....	....	....	....	....	....	....	....	....	....	....	....	....	....	....	....
1995-96	Kelowna Rockets	WHL	64	3	4	7	159	....	....	....	....	....	....	....	....	....	....	....	6	0	0	0	12	....	....	....
1996-97	Kelowna Rockets	WHL	68	18	8	26	*330	....	....	....	....	....	....	....	....	....	....	....	6	0	2	2	4	....	....	....
1997-98	Kelowna Rockets	WHL	71	30	22	52	243	....	....	....	....	....	....	....	....	....	....	....	7	6	0	6	23	....	....	....
1998-99	**Colorado**	**NHL**	**27**	**0**	**0**	**0**	**71**	**0**	**0**	**0**	**3**	**0.0**	**–3**	**1**	**0.0**	**10**	**0**	**1:37**	....	....	....	....	....	....	....	....
	Hershey Bears	AHL	32	4	3	7	143	....	....	....	....	....	....	....	....	....	....	....	4	0	0	0	6	....	....	....
99-2000	Hershey Bears	AHL	68	12	7	19	206	....	....	....	....	....	....	....	....	....	....	....	11	1	1	2	56	....	....	....
	NHL Totals		**27**	**0**	**0**	**0**	**71**	**0**	**0**	**0**	**3**	**0.0**		**1**	**0.0**	**10**	**0**	**1:37**	....	....	....	....	....	....	....	....

• Re-entered NHL draft. Originally New Jersey's 6th choice, 63rd overall, in 1996 Entry Draft.

			Regular Season																Playoffs							
Season	Club	League	GP	G	A	Pts	PIM	PP	SH	GW	S	%	+/–	TF	F%	H	SB	Min	GP	G	A	Pts	PIM	PP	SH	GW

PARRISH, Mark

(PAIR-ihsh, MAHRK) **NYI**

Right wing. Shoots right. 5'11", 191 lbs. Born, Edina, MN, February 2, 1977. Colorado's 3rd choice, 79th overall, in 1996 Entry Draft.

1994-95	Jefferson High	Hi-School	27	40	20	60	42	....	....	....	....	....	....	....	....	....	....	....	....	....	....	....	....	....	....	....
1995-96	St. Cloud State	WCHA	39	15	13	28	30	....	....	....	....	....	....	....	....	....	....	....	....	....	....	....	....	....	....	....
1996-97	St. Cloud State	WCHA	35	*27	15	42	60	....	....	....	....	....	....	....	....	....	....	....	....	....	....	....	....	....	....	....
1997-98	Seattle T-Birds	WHL	54	54	38	92	29	....	....	....	....	....	....	....	....	....	....	....	5	2	3	5	2	....	....	....
	New Haven	AHL	1	1	0	1	2	....	....	....	....	....	....	....	....	....	....	....	....	....	....	....	....	....	....	....
1998-99	**Florida**	**NHL**	**73**	**24**	**13**	**37**	**25**	**5**	**0**	**5**	**129**	**18.6**	**–6**	**1**	**0.0**	**56**	**5**	**13:59**	....	....	....	....	....	....	....	....
	New Haven	AHL	2	1	0	1	0	....	....	....	....	....	....	....	....	....	....	....	....	....	....	....	....	....	....	....
99-2000	**Florida**	**NHL**	**81**	**26**	**18**	**44**	**39**	**6**	**0**	**3**	**152**	**17.1**	**1**	**8**	**75.0**	**113**	**8**	**14:04**	**4**	**0**	**1**	**1**	**0**	**0**	**0**	**0**
	NHL Totals		**154**	**50**	**31**	**81**	**64**	**11**	**0**	**8**	**281**	**17.8**		**9**	**66.7**	**169**	**13**	**14:02**	**4**	**0**	**1**	**1**	**0**	**0**	**0**	**0**

NCAA West Second All-American Team (1997) • WHL West First All-Star Team (1998)

Rights traded to **Florida** by **Colorado** with Anaheim's 3rd round choice (previously acquired, Florida selected Lance Ward) in 1998 Entry Draft for Tom Fitzgerald, March 24, 1998. Traded to **NY Islanders** by **Florida** with Oleg Kvasha for Roberto Luongo and Olli Jokinen, June 24, 2000.

PATERA, Pavel

(puh-TEHR-uh, PAH-vehl) **MIN.**

Center. Shoots left. 6'1", 181 lbs. Born, Kladno, Czech., September 6, 1971. Dallas' 4th choice, 153rd overall, in 1998 Entry Draft.

1990-91	Poldi Kladno	Czech.	3	0	0	0	....	....	....	....	....	....	....	....	....	....	....	....	....	....	....	....	....	....	....	....
1991-92	Poldi Kladno	Czech.	38	12	13	25	26	....	....	....	....	....	....	....	....	....	....	....	8	8	4	12	0	....	....	....
1992-93	Poldi Kladno	Czech.	42	9	23	32	....	....	....	....	....	....	....	....	....	....	....	....	....	....	....	....	....	....	....	....
1993-94	Poldi Kladno	Cze-Rep	43	21	39	60	....	....	....	....	....	....	....	....	....	....	....	....	11	5	10	15	....	....	....	....
1994-95	Poldi Kladno	Cze-Rep	43	26	49	75	24	....	....	....	....	....	....	....	....	....	....	....	11	5	7	12	6	....	....	....
1995-96	Poldi Kladno	Cze-Rep	40	24	31	55	38	....	....	....	....	....	....	....	....	....	....	....	8	3	1	4	34	....	....	....
1996-97	AIK Solna	Sweden	50	19	24	43	44	....	....	....	....	....	....	....	....	....	....	....	7	2	3	5	6	....	....	....
1997-98	AIK Solna	Sweden	46	8	17	25	50	....	....	....	....	....	....	....	....	....	....	....	....	....	....	....	....	....	....	....
1998-99	HC Vsetin	Cze-Rep	52	16	37	53	58	....	....	....	....	....	....	....	....	....	....	....	12	5	*10	15	....	....	....	....
99-2000	**Dallas**	**NHL**	**12**	**1**	**4**	**5**	**4**	**0**	**0**	**0**	**18**	**5.6**	**–1**	**61**	**49.2**	**2**	**1**	**14:04**	....	....	....	....	....	....	....	....
	Slovnaft Vsetin	Cze-Rep	29	8	14	22	36	....	....	....	....	....	....	....	....	....	....	....	9	3	4	7	8	....	....	....
	NHL Totals		**12**	**1**	**4**	**5**	**4**	**0**	**0**	**0**	**18**	**5.6**		**61**	**49.2**	**2**	**1**	**14:04**	....	....	....	....	....	....	....	....

Traded to **Minnesota** by **Dallas** with Aaron Gavey, Dallas' 8th round choice (Eric Johansson) in 2000 Entry Draft and Minnesota's 4th round choice (previously acquired) in 2002 Entry Draft for Brad Lukowich and Minnesota's 3rd and 9th round choices in 2001 Entry Draft, June 25, 2000.

PATRICK, James

(PAT-rihk, JAYMS) **BUF.**

Defense. Shoots right. 6'3", 201 lbs. Born, Winnipeg, Man., June 14, 1963. NY Rangers' 1st choice, 9th overall, in 1981 Entry Draft.

1980-81	Prince Albert	SJHL	59	21	61	82	162	....	....	....	....	....	....	....	....	....	....	....	....	....	....	....	....	....	....	....
1981-82	North Dakota	WCHA	42	5	24	29	26	....	....	....	....	....	....	....	....	....	....	....	....	....	....	....	....	....	....	....
1982-83	North Dakota	WCHA	36	12	36	48	29	....	....	....	....	....	....	....	....	....	....	....	....	....	....	....	....	....	....	....
1983-84	Canada	Nat-Team	63	7	24	31	52	....	....	....	....	....	....	....	....	....	....	....	....	....	....	....	....	....	....	....
	Canada	Olympics	7	0	3	3	4	....	....	....	....	....	....	....	....	....	....	....	....	....	....	....	....	....	....	....
	NY Rangers	**NHL**	**12**	**1**	**7**	**8**	**2**	**0**	**0**	**0**	**15**	**6.7**	**6**	....	....	....	....	....	**5**	**0**	**3**	**3**	**2**	**0**	**0**	**0**
1984-85	**NY Rangers**	**NHL**	**75**	**8**	**28**	**36**	**71**	**4**	**1**	**1**	**101**	**7.9**	**–17**	....	....	....	....	....	**3**	**0**	**0**	**0**	**4**	**0**	**0**	**0**
1985-86	**NY Rangers**	**NHL**	**75**	**14**	**29**	**43**	**88**	**2**	**1**	**1**	**131**	**10.7**	**14**	....	....	....	....	....	**16**	**1**	**5**	**6**	**34**	**0**	**0**	**0**
1986-87	**NY Rangers**	**NHL**	**78**	**10**	**45**	**55**	**62**	**5**	**0**	**0**	**143**	**7.0**	**13**	....	....	....	....	....	**6**	**1**	**2**	**3**	**2**	**2**	**0**	**1**
1987-88	**NY Rangers**	**NHL**	**70**	**17**	**45**	**62**	**52**	**9**	**0**	**1**	**187**	**9.1**	**16**	....	....	....	....	....	....	....	....	....	....	....	....	....
1988-89	**NY Rangers**	**NHL**	**68**	**11**	**36**	**47**	**41**	**6**	**0**	**2**	**147**	**7.5**	**3**	....	....	....	....	....	**4**	**0**	**1**	**1**	**2**	**0**	**0**	**0**
1989-90	**NY Rangers**	**NHL**	**73**	**14**	**43**	**57**	**50**	**9**	**0**	**0**	**136**	**10.3**	**4**	....	....	....	....	....	**10**	**3**	**8**	**11**	**0**	**2**	**0**	**1**
1990-91	**NY Rangers**	**NHL**	**74**	**10**	**49**	**59**	**58**	**6**	**0**	**2**	**138**	**7.2**	**–5**	....	....	....	....	....	**6**	**0**	**0**	**0**	**6**	**0**	**0**	**0**
1991-92	**NY Rangers**	**NHL**	**80**	**14**	**57**	**71**	**54**	**6**	**0**	**1**	**148**	**9.5**	**34**	....	....	....	....	....	**13**	**0**	**7**	**7**	**12**	**0**	**0**	**0**
1992-93	**NY Rangers**	**NHL**	**60**	**5**	**21**	**26**	**61**	**3**	**0**	**0**	**99**	**5.1**	**1**	....	....	....	....	....	....	....	....	....	....	....	....	....
1993-94	**NY Rangers**	**NHL**	**6**	**0**	**3**	**3**	**2**	**0**	**0**	**0**	**6**	**0.0**	**1**	....	....	....	....	....	....	....	....	....	....	....	....	....
	Hartford	**NHL**	**47**	**8**	**20**	**28**	**32**	**4**	**1**	**2**	**65**	**12.3**	**–12**	....	....	....	....	....	....	....	....	....	....	....	....	....
	Calgary	**NHL**	**15**	**2**	**2**	**4**	**6**	**1**	**0**	**0**	**20**	**10.0**	**6**	....	....	....	....	....	**7**	**0**	**1**	**1**	**6**	**0**	**0**	**0**
1994-95	**Calgary**	**NHL**	**43**	**0**	**10**	**10**	**14**	**0**	**0**	**0**	**43**	**0.0**	**–3**	....	....	....	....	....	**5**	**0**	**1**	**1**	**0**	**0**	**0**	**0**
1995-96	**Calgary**	**NHL**	**80**	**3**	**32**	**35**	**30**	**1**	**0**	**0**	**116**	**2.6**	**3**	....	....	....	....	....	**4**	**0**	**0**	**0**	**2**	**0**	**0**	**0**
1996-97	**Calgary**	**NHL**	**19**	**3**	**1**	**4**	**6**	**1**	**0**	**0**	**22**	**13.6**	**2**	....	....	....	....	....	....	....	....	....	....	....	....	....
1997-98	**Calgary**	**NHL**	**60**	**6**	**11**	**17**	**26**	**1**	**0**	**1**	**57**	**10.5**	**–2**	....	....	....	....	....	....	....	....	....	....	....	....	....
1998-99	**Buffalo**	**NHL**	**45**	**1**	**7**	**8**	**16**	**0**	**0**	**0**	**31**	**3.2**	**12**	**0**	**0.0**	**23**	**38**	**14:45**	**20**	**0**	**1**	**1**	**12**	**0**	**0**	**0**
99-2000	**Buffalo**	**NHL**	**66**	**5**	**8**	**13**	**22**	**0**	**0**	**3**	**40**	**12.5**	**8**	**0**	**0.0**	**44**	**61**	**15:59**	**5**	**0**	**1**	**1**	**2**	**0**	**0**	**0**
	NHL Totals		**1046**	**132**	**454**	**586**	**693**	**58**	**3**	**14**	**1645**	**8.0**		**0**	**0.0**	**67**	**99**	**15:29**	**104**	**5**	**30**	**35**	**84**	**4**	**0**	**2**

WCHA Second All-Star Team (1982) • NCAA Chamionship All-Tournament Team (1982) • WCHA First All-Star Team (1983) • NCAA West All American Team (1983)

Traded to **Hartford** by **NY Rangers** with Darren Turcotte for Steve Larmer, Nick Kypreos, Barry Richter and Hartford's 6th round choice (Yuri Litvinov) in 1994 Entry Draft, November 2, 1993. Traded to **Calgary** by **Hartford** with Zarley Zalapski and Michael Nylander for Gary Suter, Paul Ranheim and Ted Drury, March 10, 1994. • Missed remainder of 1996-97 season recovering from knee injury originally suffered in game vs. Pittsburgh, October 24, 1996. Signed as a free agent by **Buffalo**, October 7, 1998.

PATTERSON, Ed

(PAT-uhr-SOHN, EHD)

Right wing. Shoots right. 6'2", 213 lbs. Born, Delta, B.C., November 14, 1972. Pittsburgh's 7th choice, 148th overall, in 1991 Entry Draft.

1987-88	South Delta	BCAHA	50	40	70	110	60	....	....	....	....	....	....	....	....	....	....	....	....	....	....	....	....	....	....	....
1988-89	Seattle T-Birds	WHL	46	4	6	10	55	....	....	....	....	....	....	....	....	....	....	....	....	....	....	....	....	....	....	....
1989-90	Seattle T-Birds	WHL	18	9	2	11	19	....	....	....	....	....	....	....	....	....	....	....	....	....	....	....	....	....	....	....
	Swift Current	WHL	15	1	3	4	0	....	....	....	....	....	....	....	....	....	....	....	4	0	0	0	2	....	....	....
1990-91	Swift Current	WHL	7	2	7	9	0	....	....	....	....	....	....	....	....	....	....	....	....	....	....	....	....	....	....	....
	Kamloops Blazers	WHL	55	14	33	47	134	....	....	....	....	....	....	....	....	....	....	....	5	0	0	0	7	....	....	....
1991-92	Kamloops Blazers	WHL	38	19	25	44	100	....	....	....	....	....	....	....	....	....	....	....	1	0	0	0	0	....	....	....
1992-93	Cleveland	IHL	63	4	16	20	131	....	....	....	....	....	....	....	....	....	....	....	3	1	1	2	2	....	....	....
1993-94	**Pittsburgh**	**NHL**	**27**	**3**	**1**	**4**	**10**	**0**	**0**	**0**	**15**	**20.0**	**–5**	....	....	....	....	....	....	....	....	....	....	....	....	....
	Cleveland	IHL	55	21	32	53	73	....	....	....	....	....	....	....	....	....	....	....	....	....	....	....	....	....	....	....
1994-95	Cleveland	IHL	58	13	17	30	93	....	....	....	....	....	....	....	....	....	....	....	4	1	2	3	6	....	....	....
1995-96	**Pittsburgh**	**NHL**	**35**	**0**	**2**	**2**	**38**	**0**	**0**	**0**	**17**	**0.0**	**–5**	....	....	....	....	....	....	....	....	....	....	....	....	....
1996-97	**Pittsburgh**	**NHL**	**6**	**0**	**0**	**0**	**8**	**0**	**0**	**0**	**2**	**0.0**	**0**	....	....	....	....	....	....	....	....	....	....	....	....	....
	Cleveland	IHL	40	6	12	18	75	....	....	....	....	....	....	....	....	....	....	....	13	2	4	6	61	....	....	....
1997-98	Grand Rapids	IHL	81	12	31	43	226	....	....	....	....	....	....	....	....	....	....	....	3	2	1	3	8	....	....	....
1998-99	Cincinnati	IHL	73	8	25	33	227	....	....	....	....	....	....	....	....	....	....	....	3	1	0	1	4	....	....	....
99-2000	Grand Rapids	IHL	74	20	21	41	141	....	....	....	....	....	....	....	....	....	....	....	5	4	0	4	2	....	....	....
	NHL Totals		**68**	**3**	**3**	**6**	**56**	**0**	**0**	**0**	**34**	**8.8**		....	....	....	....	....	....	....	....	....	....	....	....	....

Signed as a free agent by **Grand Rapids** (IHL), September 14, 1999.

PEARSON, Rob

(PEER-sohn, RAWB)

Right wing. Shoots right. 6'3", 198 lbs. Born, Oshawa, Ont., March 8, 1971. Toronto's 2nd choice, 12th overall, in 1989 Entry Draft.

1987-88	Oshawa Legion	OMHA	72	68	65	133	188	....	....	....	....	....	....	....	....	....	....	....	....	....	....	....	....	....	....	....
1988-89	Belleville Bulls	OHL	26	8	12	20	51	....	....	....	....	....	....	....	....	....	....	....	....	....	....	....	....	....	....	....
1989-90	Belleville Bulls	OHL	58	48	40	88	174	....	....	....	....	....	....	....	....	....	....	....	11	5	5	10	26	....	....	....
1990-91	Belleville Bulls	OHL	10	6	3	9	27	....	....	....	....	....	....	....	....	....	....	....	....	....	....	....	....	....	....	....
	Oshawa Generals	OHL	41	57	52	109	76	....	....	....	....	....	....	....	....	....	....	....	16	16	17	33	39	....	....	....
	Newmarket	AHL	3	0	0	0	29	....	....	....	....	....	....	....	....	....	....	....	....	....	....	....	....	....	....	....
1991-92	**Toronto**	**NHL**	**47**	**14**	**10**	**24**	**58**	**6**	**0**	**0**	**79**	**17.7**	**–16**	....	....	....	....	....	....	....	....	....	....	....	....	....
	St. John's Leafs	AHL	27	15	14	29	107	....	....	....	....	....	....	....	....	....	....	....	13	5	4	9	40	....	....	....
1992-93	**Toronto**	**NHL**	**78**	**23**	**14**	**37**	**211**	**8**	**0**	**3**	**164**	**14.0**	**–2**	....	....	....	....	....	**14**	**2**	**2**	**4**	**31**	**0**	**0**	**0**
1993-94	**Toronto**	**NHL**	**67**	**12**	**18**	**30**	**189**	**1**	**0**	**4**	**119**	**10.1**	**–6**	....	....	....	....	....	**14**	**1**	**0**	**1**	**32**	**0**	**0**	**0**
1994-95	**Washington**	**NHL**	**32**	**0**	**6**	**6**	**96**	**0**	**0**	**0**	**34**	**0.0**	**–6**	....	....	....	....	....	**3**	**1**	**0**	**1**	**17**	**0**	**0**	**1**
1995-96	Portland Pirates	AHL	44	18	24	42	143	....	....	....	....	....	....	....	....	....	....	....	....	....	....	....	....	....	....	....
	St. Louis	**NHL**	**27**	**6**	**4**	**10**	**54**	**1**	**0**	**1**	**51**	**11.8**	**4**	....	....	....	....	....	**2**	**0**	**0**	**0**	**14**	**0**	**0**	**0**

Season	Club	League	GP	G	A	Pts	PIM	PP	SH	GW	S	%	+/-	TF	F%	H	SB	Min	GP	G	A	Pts	PIM	PP	SH	GW
			Regular Season																Playoffs							
1996-97	**St. Louis**	**NHL**	**18**	**1**	**2**	**3**	**37**	**0**	**0**	**0**	**14**	**7.1**	**-5**	....	....	....	....	....	....	....	....	....	....	....	....	....
	Worcester	AHL	46	11	16	27	199	....	....	....	....	....	....	....	....	....	....	....	5	3	0	3	16	....	....	....
1997-98	Cleveland	IHL	46	17	14	31	118	....	....	....	....	....	....	....	....	....	....	....	10	6	4	10	43	....	....	....
1998-99	Cleveland	IHL	20	3	10	13	27	....	....	....	....	....	....	....	....	....	....	....	....	....	....	....	....	....	....	....
	Orlando	IHL	11	6	2	8	41	....	....	....	....	....	....	....	....	....	....	....	17	8	6	14	24	....	....	....
99-2000	Long Beach	IHL	60	17	23	40	145	....	....	....	....	....	....	....	....	....	....	....	4	0	0	0	8	....	....	....
	NHL Totals		**269**	**56**	**54**	**110**	**645**	**16**	**0**	**8**	**461**	**12.1**		....	....	....	....	....	**33**	**4**	**2**	**6**	**94**	**0**	**0**	**1**

OHL First All-Star Team (1991)

Traded to **Washington** by **Toronto** with Philadelphia's 1st round choice (previously acquired, Washington selected Nolan Baumgartner) in 1994 Entry Draft for Mike Ridley and St. Louis' 1st round choice (previously acquired, Toronto selected Eric Fichaud) in 1994 Entry Draft, June 28, 1994. Traded to **St. Louis** by **Washington** for Denis Chasse, January 29, 1996. Signed as a free agent by **Long Beach** (IHL), August 5, 1999.

PEARSON, Scott

(PEER-sohn, SKAWT)

Left wing. Shoots left. 6'1", 205 lbs. Born, Cornwall, Ont., December 19, 1969. Toronto's 1st choice, 6th overall, in 1988 Entry Draft.

Season	Club	League	GP	G	A	Pts	PIM	PP	SH	GW	S	%	+/-	TF	F%	H	SB	Min	GP	G	A	Pts	PIM	PP	SH	GW
1984-85	Cornwall Royals	OMHA	60	40	40	80	60	....	....	....	....	....	....	....	....	....	....	....	....	....	....	....	....	....	....	....
1985-86	Kingston	OHL	63	16	23	39	56	....	....	....	....	....	....	....	....	....	....	....	....	....	....	....	....	....	....	....
1986-87	Kingston	OHL	62	30	24	54	101	....	....	....	....	....	....	....	....	....	....	....	9	3	3	6	42	....	....	....
1987-88	Kingston	OHL	46	26	32	58	117	....	....	....	....	....	....	....	....	....	....	....	....	....	....	....	....	....	....	....
1988-89	Kingston Raiders	OHL	13	9	8	17	34	....	....	....	....	....	....	....	....	....	....	....	....	....	....	....	....	....	....	....
	Niagara Falls	OHL	32	26	34	60	90	....	....	....	....	....	....	....	....	....	....	....	17	14	10	24	53	....	....	....
	Toronto	**NHL**	**9**	**0**	**1**	**1**	**2**	**0**	**0**	**0**	**6**	**0.0**	**0**	....	....	....	....	....	....	....	....	....	....	....	....	....
1989-90	**Toronto**	**NHL**	**41**	**5**	**10**	**15**	**90**	**0**	**0**	**1**	**66**	**7.6**	**-7**	....	....	....	....	....	**2**	**2**	**0**	**2**	**10**	**0**	**0**	**0**
	Newmarket	AHL	18	12	11	23	64	....	....	....	....	....	....	....	....	....	....	....	....	....	....	....	....	....	....	....
1990-91	**Toronto**	**NHL**	**12**	**0**	**0**	**0**	**20**	**0**	**0**	**0**	**13**	**0.0**	**-5**	....	....	....	....	....	....	....	....	....	....	....	....	....
	Quebec	**NHL**	**35**	**11**	**4**	**15**	**86**	**0**	**0**	**0**	**61**	**18.0**	**-4**	....	....	....	....	....	....	....	....	....	....	....	....	....
	Halifax Citadels	AHL	24	12	15	27	44	....	....	....	....	....	....	....	....	....	....	....	....	....	....	....	....	....	....	....
1991-92	**Quebec**	**NHL**	**10**	**1**	**2**	**3**	**14**	**0**	**0**	**0**	**14**	**7.1**	**-5**	....	....	....	....	....	....	....	....	....	....	....	....	....
	Halifax Citadels	AHL	5	2	1	3	4	....	....	....	....	....	....	....	....	....	....	....	....	....	....	....	....	....	....	....
1992-93	**Quebec**	**NHL**	**41**	**13**	**1**	**14**	**95**	**0**	**0**	**1**	**45**	**28.9**	**3**	....	....	....	....	....	**3**	**0**	**0**	**0**	**0**	**0**	**0**	**0**
	Halifax Citadels	AHL	5	3	1	4	25	....	....	....	....	....	....	....	....	....	....	....	....	....	....	....	....	....	....	....
1993-94	**Edmonton**	**NHL**	**72**	**19**	**18**	**37**	**165**	**3**	**0**	**7**	**160**	**11.9**	**-4**	....	....	....	....	....	....	....	....	....	....	....	....	....
1994-95	**Edmonton**	**NHL**	**28**	**1**	**4**	**5**	**54**	**0**	**0**	**0**	**21**	**4.8**	**-11**	....	....	....	....	....	....	....	....	....	....	....	....	....
	Buffalo	**NHL**	**14**	**2**	**1**	**3**	**20**	**0**	**0**	**0**	**19**	**10.5**	**-3**	....	....	....	....	....	**5**	**0**	**0**	**0**	**4**	**0**	**0**	**0**
1995-96	**Buffalo**	**NHL**	**27**	**4**	**0**	**4**	**67**	**0**	**0**	**1**	**26**	**15.4**	**-4**	....	....	....	....	....	....	....	....	....	....	....	....	....
	Rochester	AHL	26	8	8	16	113	....	....	....	....	....	....	....	....	....	....	....	....	....	....	....	....	....	....	....
1996-97	**Toronto**	**NHL**	**1**	**0**	**0**	**0**	**2**	**0**	**0**	**0**	**0**	**0.0**	**0**	....	....	....	....	....	....	....	....	....	....	....	....	....
	St. John's Leafs	AHL	14	5	2	7	26	....	....	....	....	....	....	....	....	....	....	....	9	5	2	7	14	....	....	....
1997-98	Chicago Wolves	IHL	78	34	17	51	225	....	....	....	....	....	....	....	....	....	....	....	22	12	6	18	50	....	....	....
1998-99	Chicago Wolves	IHL	62	23	13	36	154	....	....	....	....	....	....	....	....	....	....	....	8	4	1	5	*50	....	....	....
99-2000	**NY Islanders**	**NHL**	**2**	**0**	**1**	**1**	**0**	**0**	**0**	**0**	**5**	**0.0**	**1**	**0**	**0.0**	**6**	**0**	**13:15**	....	....	....	....	....	....	....	....
	Chicago Wolves	IHL	77	19	14	33	124	....	....	....	....	....	....	....	....	....	....	....	16	5	5	10	28	....	....	....
	NHL Totals		**292**	**56**	**42**	**98**	**615**	**3**	**0**	**10**	**436**	**12.8**		**0**	**0.0**	**6**	**0**	**13:15**	**10**	**2**	**0**	**2**	**14**	**0**	**0**	**0**

Traded to **Quebec** by **Toronto** with Toronto's 2nd round choices in 1991 (later traded to Washington - Washington selected Eric Lavigne) and 1992 (Tuomas Gronman) Entry Drafts for Aaron Broten, Lucien Deblois and Michel Petit, November 17, 1990. Traded to **Edmonton** by **Quebec** for Martin Gelinas and Edmonton's 6th round choice (Nicholas Checco) in 1993 Entry Draft, June 20, 1993. Traded to **Buffalo** by **Edmonton** for Ken Sutton, April 7, 1995. Signed as a free agent by **Toronto**, July 24, 1996. • Missed majority of 1996-97 season recovering from abdominal surgery, November, 1996. Signed as a free agent by **NY Islanders**, August 9, 1999.

PECA, Michael

(PEH-kuh,MIHK-awl) **BUF.**

Center. Shoots right. 5'11", 190 lbs. Born, Toronto, Ont., March 26, 1974. Vancouver's 2nd choice, 40th overall, in 1992 Entry Draft.

Season	Club	League	GP	G	A	Pts	PIM	PP	SH	GW	S	%	+/-	TF	F%	H	SB	Min	GP	G	A	Pts	PIM	PP	SH	GW
1989-90	Toronto Nats	MTHL	39	42	53	95	40	....	....	....	....	....	....	....	....	....	....	....	....	....	....	....	....	....	....	....
1990-91	Sudbury Wolves	OHL	62	14	27	41	24	....	....	....	....	....	....	....	....	....	....	....	5	1	0	1	7	....	....	....
1991-92	Sudbury Wolves	OHL	39	16	34	50	61	....	....	....	....	....	....	....	....	....	....	....	....	....	....	....	....	....	....	....
	Ottawa 67's	OHL	27	8	17	25	32	....	....	....	....	....	....	....	....	....	....	....	11	6	10	16	6	....	....	....
1992-93	Ottawa 67's	OHL	55	38	64	102	80	....	....	....	....	....	....	....	....	....	....	....	....	....	....	....	....	....	....	....
	Hamilton Canucks	AHL	9	6	3	9	11	....	....	....	....	....	....	....	....	....	....	....	....	....	....	....	....	....	....	....
1993-94	Ottawa 67's	OHL	55	50	63	113	101	....	....	....	....	....	....	....	....	....	....	....	17	7	22	29	30	....	....	....
	Vancouver	**NHL**	**4**	**0**	**0**	**0**	**2**	**0**	**0**	**0**	**5**	**0.0**	**-1**	....	....	....	....	....	....	....	....	....	....	....	....	....
1994-95	Syracuse Crunch	AHL	35	10	24	34	75	....	....	....	....	....	....	....	....	....	....	....	....	....	....	....	....	....	....	....
	Vancouver	**NHL**	**33**	**6**	**6**	**12**	**30**	**2**	**0**	**1**	**46**	**13.0**	**-6**	....	....	....	....	....	**5**	**0**	**1**	**1**	**8**	**0**	**0**	**0**
1995-96	**Buffalo**	**NHL**	**68**	**11**	**20**	**31**	**67**	**4**	**3**	**1**	**109**	**10.1**	**-1**	....	....	....	....	....	....	....	....	....	....	....	....	....
1996-97	**Buffalo**	**NHL**	**79**	**20**	**29**	**49**	**80**	**5**	**6**	**4**	**137**	**14.6**	**26**	....	....	....	....	....	**10**	**0**	**2**	**2**	**8**	**0**	**0**	**0**
1997-98	**Buffalo**	**NHL**	**61**	**18**	**22**	**40**	**57**	**6**	**5**	**1**	**132**	**13.6**	**12**	....	....	....	....	....	**13**	**3**	**2**	**5**	**8**	**0**	**0**	**1**
1998-99	**Buffalo**	**NHL**	**82**	**27**	**29**	**56**	**81**	**10**	**0**	**8**	**199**	**13.6**	**7**	**1855**	**49.4**	**181**	**64**	**20:44**	**21**	**5**	**8**	**13**	**18**	**2**	**1**	**0**
99-2000	**Buffalo**	**NHL**	**73**	**20**	**21**	**41**	**67**	**2**	**0**	**3**	**144**	**13.9**	**6**	**1604**	**48.6**	**132**	**76**	**19:57**	**5**	**0**	**1**	**1**	**4**	**0**	**0**	**0**
	NHL Totals		**400**	**102**	**127**	**229**	**384**	**29**	**14**	**18**	**772**	**13.2**		**3459**	**49.0**	**313**	**140**	**20:22**	**54**	**8**	**14**	**22**	**46**	**2**	**1**	**1**

Won Frank J. Selke Trophy (1997)

Traded to **Buffalo** by **Vancouver** with Mike Wilson and Vancouver's 1st round choice (Jay McKee) in 1995 Entry Draft for Alexander Mogilny and Buffalo's 5th round choice (Todd Norman) in 1995 Entry Draft, July 8, 1995.

PEDERSON, Denis

(PEE-duhr-suhn, DEH-nihs) **VAN.**

Center. Shoots right. 6'2", 205 lbs. Born, Prince Albert, Sask., September 10, 1975. New Jersey's 1st choice, 13th overall, in 1993 Entry Draft.

Season	Club	League	GP	G	A	Pts	PIM	PP	SH	GW	S	%	+/-	TF	F%	H	SB	Min	GP	G	A	Pts	PIM	PP	SH	GW
1990-91	Prince Albert	AAHA	30	25	17	42	84	....	....	....	....	....	....	....	....	....	....	....	....	....	....	....	....	....	....	....
1991-92	Prince Albert	AAHA	21	33	25	58	40	....	....	....	....	....	....	....	....	....	....	....	....	....	....	....	....	....	....	....
	Prince Albert	WHL	10	0	0	0	6	....	....	....	....	....	....	....	....	....	....	....	7	0	1	1	13	....	....	....
1992-93	Prince Albert	WHL	72	33	40	73	134	....	....	....	....	....	....	....	....	....	....	....	....	....	....	....	....	....	....	....
1993-94	Prince Albert	WHL	71	53	45	98	157	....	....	....	....	....	....	....	....	....	....	....	....	....	....	....	....	....	....	....
1994-95	Prince Albert	WHL	63	30	38	68	122	....	....	....	....	....	....	....	....	....	....	....	15	11	14	25	14	....	....	....
	Albany River Rats	AHL	....	....	....	....	....	....	....	....	....	....	....	....	....	....	....	....	3	0	0	0	2	....	....	....
1995-96	**New Jersey**	**NHL**	**10**	**3**	**1**	**4**	**0**	**1**	**0**	**2**	**6**	**50.0**	**-1**	....	....	....	....	....	....	....	....	....	....	....	....	....
	Albany River Rats	AHL	68	28	43	71	104	....	....	....	....	....	....	....	....	....	....	....	4	1	2	3	0	....	....	....
1996-97	**New Jersey**	**NHL**	**70**	**12**	**20**	**32**	**62**	**3**	**0**	**3**	**106**	**11.3**	**7**	....	....	....	....	....	**9**	**0**	**0**	**0**	**2**	**0**	**0**	**0**
	Albany River Rats	AHL	3	1	3	4	7	....	....	....	....	....	....	....	....	....	....	....	....	....	....	....	....	....	....	....
1997-98	**New Jersey**	**NHL**	**80**	**15**	**13**	**28**	**97**	**7**	**0**	**1**	**135**	**11.1**	**-6**	....	....	....	....	....	**6**	**1**	**1**	**2**	**2**	**0**	**1**	**0**
1998-99	**New Jersey**	**NHL**	**76**	**11**	**12**	**23**	**66**	**3**	**0**	**1**	**145**	**7.6**	**-10**	**540**	**42.8**	**105**	**39**	**15:19**	**3**	**0**	**1**	**1**	**0**	**0**	**0**	**0**
99-2000	**New Jersey**	**NHL**	**35**	**3**	**3**	**6**	**16**	**0**	**0**	**0**	**41**	**7.3**	**-7**	**125**	**48.8**	**41**	**9**	**10:42**	....	....	....	....	....	....	....	....
	Vancouver	**NHL**	**12**	**3**	**2**	**5**	**2**	**0**	**0**	**1**	**15**	**20.0**	**1**	**70**	**45.7**	**15**	**3**	**12:41**	....	....	....	....	....	....	....	....
	NHL Totals		**283**	**47**	**51**	**98**	**243**	**14**	**0**	**8**	**448**	**10.5**		**735**	**44.1**	**161**	**51**	**13:45**	**18**	**1**	**2**	**3**	**4**	**0**	**1**	**0**

WHL East Second All-Star Team (1994)

Traded to **Vancouver** by **New Jersey** with Brendan Morrison for Alexander Mogilny, March 14, 2000.

PELLERIN, Scott

(PEHL-ih-rihn, SKAWT) **MIN.**

Left wing. Shoots left. 5'11", 172 lbs. Born, Shediac, N.B., January 9, 1970. New Jersey's 4th choice, 47th overall, in 1989 Entry Draft.

Season	Club	League	GP	G	A	Pts	PIM	PP	SH	GW	S	%	+/-	TF	F%	H	SB	Min	GP	G	A	Pts	PIM	PP	SH	GW
1986-87	Notre Dame	SAHA	72	62	68	130	98	....	....	....	....	....	....	....	....	....	....	....	....	....	....	....	....	....	....	....
1987-88	Notre Dame	•SJHL	57	37	49	86	139	....	....	....	....	....	....	....	....	....	....	....	....	....	....	....	....	....	....	....
1988-89	U. of Maine	H-East	45	29	33	62	92	....	....	....	....	....	....	....	....	....	....	....	....	....	....	....	....	....	....	....
1989-90	U. of Maine	H-East	42	22	34	56	68	....	....	....	....	....	....	....	....	....	....	....	....	....	....	....	....	....	....	....
1990-91	U. of Maine	H-East	43	23	25	48	60	....	....	....	....	....	....	....	....	....	....	....	....	....	....	....	....	....	....	....
1991-92	U. of Maine	H-East	37	*32	25	57	54	....	....	....	....	....	....	....	....	....	....	....	....	....	....	....	....	....	....	....
	Utica Devils	AHL	....	....	....	....	....	....	....	....	....	....	....	....	....	....	....	....	3	1	0	1	0	....	....	....
1992-93	**New Jersey**	**NHL**	**45**	**10**	**11**	**21**	**41**	**1**	**2**	**0**	**60**	**16.7**	**-1**	....	....	....	....	....	....	....	....	....	....	....	....	....
	Utica Devils	AHL	27	15	18	33	33	....	....	....	....	....	....	....	....	....	....	....	2	0	1	1	0	....	....	....

			Regular Season																Playoffs							
Season	Club	League	GP	G	A	Pts	PIM	PP	SH	GW	S	%	+/-	TF	F%	H	SB	Min	GP	G	A	Pts	PIM	PP	SH	GW
1993-94	**New Jersey**	**NHL**	**1**	**0**	**0**	**0**	**2**	**0**	**0**	**0**	**0**	**0.0**	**0**	....	....	....	....	....	....	....	....	....	....	....	....	....
	Albany River Rats	AHL	73	28	46	74	84	....	....	....	....	....	....	....	....	....	....	....	5	2	1	3	11	....	....	....
1994-95	Albany River Rats	AHL	74	23	33	56	95	....	....	....	....	....	....	....	....	....	....	....	14	6	4	10	8	....	....	....
1995-96	**New Jersey**	**NHL**	**6**	**2**	**1**	**3**	**0**	**0**	**0**	**0**	**9**	**22.2**	**1**	....	....	....	....	....	....	....	....	....	....	....	....	....
	Albany River Rats	AHL	75	35	47	82	142	....	....	....	....	....	....	....	....	....	....	....	4	0	3	3	10	....	....	....
1996-97	**St. Louis**	**NHL**	**54**	**8**	**10**	**18**	**35**	**0**	**2**	**2**	**76**	**10.5**	**12**	....	....	....	....	....	**6**	**0**	**0**	**0**	**6**	**0**	**0**	**0**
	Worcester	AHL	24	10	16	26	37	....	....	....	....	....	....	....	....	....	....	....	....	....	....	....	....	....	....	....
1997-98	**St. Louis**	**NHL**	**80**	**8**	**21**	**29**	**62**	**1**	**1**	**0**	**96**	**8.3**	**14**	....	....	....	....	....	**10**	**0**	**2**	**2**	**10**	**0**	**0**	**0**
1998-99	**St. Louis**	**NHL**	**80**	**20**	**21**	**41**	**42**	**0**	**5**	**4**	**138**	**14.5**	**1**	**6**	**66.7**	**90**	**50**	**17:18**	**8**	**1**	**0**	**1**	**4**	**0**	**0**	**0**
99-2000	**St. Louis**	**NHL**	**80**	**8**	**15**	**23**	**48**	**0**	**2**	**2**	**120**	**6.7**	**9**	**6**	**16.7**	**132**	**33**	**14:47**	**7**	**0**	**0**	**0**	**2**	**0**	**0**	**0**
	NHL Totals		**346**	**56**	**79**	**135**	**230**	**2**	**12**	**8**	**499**	**11.2**		**12**	**41.7**	**222**	**83**	**16:03**	**31**	**1**	**2**	**3**	**22**	**0**	**0**	**0**

Hockey East First All-Star Team (1992) • NCAA East First All-American Team (1992) • Won Hobey Baker Memorial Award (Top U.S. Collegiate Player) (1992)

Signed as a free agent by **St. Louis**, July 10, 1996. Selected by **Minnesota** from **St. Louis** in Expansion Draft, June 23, 2000.

PELTONEN, Ville

(PEHL-TOH-nen, VIHL) **NSH.**

Left wing. Shoots left. 5'11", 188 lbs. Born, Vantaa, Finland, May 24, 1973. San Jose's 4th choice, 58th overall, in 1993 Entry Draft.

Season	Club	League	GP	G	A	Pts	PIM	PP	SH	GW	S	%	+/-	TF	F%	H	SB	Min	GP	G	A	Pts	PIM	PP	SH	GW
1990-91	HIFK Helsinki	Finn-Jr.	36	21	16	37	16	....	....	....	....	....	....	....	....	....	....	....	7	2	3	5	10	....	....	....
1991-92	HIFK Helsinki	Finn-Jr.	37	28	23	51	28	....	....	....	....	....	....	....	....	....	....	....	4	0	2	2	0	....	....	....
	HIFK Helsinki	Finland	6	0	0	0	0	....	....	....	....	....	....	....	....	....	....	....	....	....	....	....	....	....	....	....
1992-93	HIFK Helsinki	Finn-Jr.	2	4	2	6	4	....	....	....	....	....	....	....	....	....	....	....	....	....	....	....	....	....	....	....
	HIFK Helsinki	Finland	46	13	24	37	16	....	....	....	....	....	....	....	....	....	....	....	4	0	2	2	2	....	....	....
1993-94	HIFK Helsinki	Finland	43	16	22	38	14	....	....	....	....	....	....	....	....	....	....	....	3	0	0	0	2	....	....	....
	Finland	Nat-Team	19	6	4	10	6	....	....	....	....	....	....	....	....	....	....	....	....	....	....	....	....	....	....	....
	Finland	Olympics	8	4	3	7	0	....	....	....	....	....	....	....	....	....	....	....	....	....	....	....	....	....	....	....
1994-95	HIFK Helsinki	Finland	45	20	16	36	16	....	....	....	....	....	....	....	....	....	....	....	3	0	0	0	0	....	....	....
	Finland	Nat-Team	16	3	3	6	4	....	....	....	....	....	....	....	....	....	....	....	....	....	....	....	....	....	....	....
1995-96	**San Jose**	**NHL**	**31**	**2**	**11**	**13**	**14**	**0**	**0**	**0**	**58**	**3.4**	**–7**	....	....	....	....	....	....	....	....	....	....	....	....	....
	Kansas City	IHL	29	5	13	18	8	....	....	....	....	....	....	....	....	....	....	....	....	....	....	....	....	....	....	....
	Finland	Nat-Team	1	0	0	0	0	....	....	....	....	....	....	....	....	....	....	....	....	....	....	....	....	....	....	....
1996-97	**San Jose**	**NHL**	**28**	**2**	**3**	**5**	**0**	**1**	**0**	**0**	**35**	**5.7**	**–8**	....	....	....	....	....	....	....	....	....	....	....	....	....
	Kentucky	AHL	40	22	30	52	21	....	....	....	....	....	....	....	....	....	....	....	....	....	....	....	....	....	....	....
	Finland	Nat-Team	3	0	1	1	2	....	....	....	....	....	....	....	....	....	....	....	....	....	....	....	....	....	....	....
1997-98	Vastra Frolunda	Sweden	45	22	29	*51	44	....	....	....	....	....	....	....	....	....	....	....	7	4	2	6	0	....	....	....
	Finland	Nat-Team	16	4	8	12	10	....	....	....	....	....	....	....	....	....	....	....	....	....	....	....	....	....	....	....
	Finland	Olympics	6	2	1	3	6	....	....	....	....	....	....	....	....	....	....	....	....	....	....	....	....	....	....	....
1998-99	**Nashville**	**NHL**	**14**	**5**	**5**	**10**	**2**	**1**	**0**	**0**	**31**	**16.1**	**1**	**0**	**0.0**	**4**	**4**	**15:54**	....	....	....	....	....	....	....	....
99-2000	**Nashville**	**NHL**	**79**	**6**	**22**	**28**	**22**	**2**	**0**	**2**	**125**	**4.8**	**–1**	**1**	**100.0**	**41**	**14**	**14:41**	....	....	....	....	....	....	....	....
	NHL Totals		**152**	**15**	**41**	**56**	**38**	**4**	**0**	**2**	**249**	**6.0**		**1**	**100.0**	**45**	**18**	**14:52**	....	....	....	....	....	....	....	....

Finnish Rookie of the Year (1993)

Traded to **Nashville** by **San Jose** for Nashville's 5th round choice (later traded to Phoenix - Phoenix selected Josh Blackburn) in 1998 Entry Draft, June 26, 1998. • Missed majority of 1998-99 season recovering from shoulder surgery, December 10, 1998.

PERREAULT, Yanic

(puh-ROH, YAH-nihk) **TOR.**

Center. Shoots left. 5'10", 185 lbs. Born, Sherbrooke, Que., April 4, 1971. Toronto's 1st choice, 47th overall, in 1991 Entry Draft.

Season	Club	League	GP	G	A	Pts	PIM	PP	SH	GW	S	%	+/-	TF	F%	H	SB	Min	GP	G	A	Pts	PIM	PP	SH	GW
1987-88	Montreal L'est	QAAA	42	70	57	127	....	....	....	....	....	....	....	....	....	....	....	....	....	....	....	....	....	....	....	....
1988-89	Trois-Rivieres	QMJHL	70	53	55	108	48	....	....	....	....	....	....	....	....	....	....	....	....	....	....	....	....	....	....	....
1989-90	Trois-Rivieres	QMJHL	63	51	63	114	75	....	....	....	....	....	....	....	....	....	....	....	7	6	5	11	19	....	....	....
1990-91	Trois-Rivieres	QMJHL	67	*87	98	*185	103	....	....	....	....	....	....	....	....	....	....	....	6	4	7	11	6	....	....	....
1991-92	St. John's Leafs	AHL	62	38	38	76	19	....	....	....	....	....	....	....	....	....	....	....	16	7	8	15	4	....	....	....
1992-93	St. John's Leafs	AHL	79	49	46	95	56	....	....	....	....	....	....	....	....	....	....	....	9	4	5	9	2	....	....	....
1993-94	**Toronto**	**NHL**	**13**	**3**	**3**	**6**	**0**	**2**	**0**	**0**	**24**	**12.5**	**1**	....	....	....	....	....	....	....	....	....	....	....	....	....
	St. John's Leafs	AHL	62	45	60	105	38	....	....	....	....	....	....	....	....	....	....	....	11	*12	6	18	14	....	....	....
1994-95	Phoenix	IHL	68	51	48	99	52	....	....	....	....	....	....	....	....	....	....	....	....	....	....	....	....	....	....	....
	Los Angeles	**NHL**	**26**	**2**	**5**	**7**	**20**	**0**	**0**	**1**	**43**	**4.7**	**3**	....	....	....	....	....	....	....	....	....	....	....	....	....
1995-96	**Los Angeles**	**NHL**	**78**	**25**	**24**	**49**	**16**	**8**	**3**	**7**	**175**	**14.3**	**–11**	....	....	....	....	....	....	....	....	....	....	....	....	....
1996-97	**Los Angeles**	**NHL**	**41**	**11**	**14**	**25**	**20**	**1**	**1**	**0**	**98**	**11.2**	**0**	....	....	....	....	....	....	....	....	....	....	....	....	....
1997-98	**Los Angeles**	**NHL**	**79**	**28**	**20**	**48**	**32**	**3**	**2**	**3**	**206**	**13.6**	**6**	....	....	....	....	....	**4**	**1**	**2**	**3**	**6**	**1**	**0**	**0**
1998-99	**Los Angeles**	**NHL**	**64**	**10**	**17**	**27**	**30**	**2**	**2**	**1**	**113**	**8.8**	**–3**	**1024**	**56.5**	**35**	**33**	**15:24**	....	....	....	....	....	....	....	....
	Toronto	**NHL**	**12**	**7**	**8**	**15**	**12**	**2**	**1**	**2**	**28**	**25.0**	**10**	**164**	**62.8**	**9**	**1**	**13:20**	**17**	**3**	**6**	**9**	**6**	**0**	**0**	**2**
99-2000	**Toronto**	**NHL**	**58**	**18**	**27**	**45**	**22**	**5**	**0**	**4**	**114**	**15.8**	**3**	**987**	**61.8**	**23**	**10**	**15:18**	**1**	**0**	**1**	**1**	**0**	**0**	**0**	**0**
	NHL Totals		**371**	**104**	**118**	**222**	**152**	**23**	**9**	**18**	**801**	**13.0**		**2175**	**59.4**	**67**	**44**	**15:10**	**22**	**4**	**9**	**13**	**12**	**1**	**0**	**2**

Canadian Major Junior Rookie of the Year (1989) • QMJHL First All-Star Team (1991)

Traded to **LA Kings** by **Toronto** for LA Kings' 4th round choice (later traded to Philadelphia - later traded to LA Kings - LA Kings selected Mikael Simons) in 1996 Entry Draft, July 11, 1994. Traded to **Toronto** by **Los Angeles** for Jason Podollan and Toronto's 3rd round choice (Cory Campbell) in 1999 Entry Draft, March 23, 1999.

PERSSON, Ricard

(PAIR-suhn, RIH-kahrd) **OTT.**

Defense. Shoots left. 6'1", 201 lbs. Born, Ostersund, Sweden, August 24, 1969. New Jersey's 2nd choice, 23rd overall, in 1987 Entry Draft.

Season	Club	League	GP	G	A	Pts	PIM	PP	SH	GW	S	%	+/-	TF	F%	H	SB	Min	GP	G	A	Pts	PIM	PP	SH	GW
1984-85	Ostersunds IK	Sweden-2	13	0	3	3	6	....	....	....	....	....	....	....	....	....	....	....	....	....	....	....	....	....	....	....
1985-86	Ostersunds IK	Sweden-2	24	2	2	4	16	....	....	....	....	....	....	....	....	....	....	....	....	....	....	....	....	....	....	....
1986-87	Ostersunds IK	Sweden-2	31	10	11	21	28	....	....	....	....	....	....	....	....	....	....	....	....	....	....	....	....	....	....	....
1987-88	Leksands IF	Sweden	31	2	0	2	8	....	....	....	....	....	....	....	....	....	....	....	2	0	1	1	2	....	....	....
1988-89	Leksands IF	Sweden	33	2	4	6	28	....	....	....	....	....	....	....	....	....	....	....	9	0	1	1	6	....	....	....
1989-90	Leksands IF	Sweden	43	9	10	19	62	....	....	....	....	....	....	....	....	....	....	....	3	0	0	0	6	....	....	....
1990-91	Leksands IF	Sweden	37	6	9	15	42	....	....	....	....	....	....	....	....	....	....	....	....	....	....	....	....	....	....	....
1991-92	Leksands IF	Sweden	21	0	7	7	28	....	....	....	....	....	....	....	....	....	....	....	....	....	....	....	....	....	....	....
1992-93	Leksands IF	Sweden	36	7	15	22	63	....	....	....	....	....	....	....	....	....	....	....	2	0	2	2	0	....	....	....
1993-94	Malmo IF	Sweden	40	11	9	20	38	....	....	....	....	....	....	....	....	....	....	....	11	2	0	2	12	....	....	....
1994-95	Malmo IF	Sweden	31	3	13	16	38	....	....	....	....	....	....	....	....	....	....	....	9	0	2	2	8	....	....	....
	Albany River Rats	AHL	3	0	0	0	0	....	....	....	....	....	....	....	....	....	....	....	9	3	5	8	7	....	....	....
1995-96	**New Jersey**	**NHL**	**12**	**2**	**1**	**3**	**8**	**1**	**0**	**0**	**41**	**4.9**	**5**	....	....	....	....	....	....	....	....	....	....	....	....	....
	Albany River Rats	AHL	67	15	31	46	59	....	....	....	....	....	....	....	....	....	....	....	4	0	0	0	7	....	....	....
1996-97	**New Jersey**	**NHL**	**1**	**0**	**0**	**0**	**0**	**0**	**0**	**0**	**2**	**0.0**	**0**	....	....	....	....	....	....	....	....	....	....	....	....	....
	Albany River Rats	AHL	13	1	4	5	8	....	....	....	....	....	....	....	....	....	....	....	....	....	....	....	....	....	....	....
	St. Louis	**NHL**	**53**	**4**	**8**	**12**	**45**	**1**	**0**	**0**	**68**	**5.9**	**–2**	....	....	....	....	....	**6**	**0**	**0**	**0**	**27**	**0**	**0**	**0**
1997-98	**St. Louis**	**NHL**	**1**	**0**	**0**	**0**	**0**	**0**	**0**	**0**	**0**	**0.0**	**0**	....	....	....	....	....	....	....	....	....	....	....	....	....
	Worcester	AHL	32	2	16	18	58	....	....	....	....	....	....	....	....	....	....	....	10	3	7	10	24	....	....	....
1998-99	**St. Louis**	**NHL**	**54**	**1**	**12**	**13**	**94**	**0**	**0**	**0**	**52**	**1.9**	**4**	**1**	**100.0**	**33**	**81**	**19:58**	**13**	**0**	**3**	**3**	**17**	**0**	**0**	**0**
	Worcester	AHL	19	6	4	10	42	....	....	....	....	....	....	....	....	....	....	....	....	....	....	....	....	....	....	....
99-2000	**St. Louis**	**NHL**	**41**	**0**	**8**	**8**	**38**	**0**	**0**	**0**	**30**	**0.0**	**–2**	**0**	**0.0**	**17**	**32**	**12:24**	**3**	**1**	**0**	**1**	**0**	**0**	**0**	**0**
	Worcester	AHL	2	0	1	1	0	....	....	....	....	....	....	....	....	....	....	....	....	....	....	....	....	....	....	....
	NHL Totals		**162**	**7**	**29**	**36**	**185**	**2**	**0**	**0**	**193**	**3.6**		**1**	**100.0**	**50**	**113**	**16:42**	**22**	**1**	**3**	**4**	**44**	**0**	**0**	**0**

Traded to **St. Louis** by **New Jersey** with Mike Peluso for Ken Sutton and St. Louis' 2nd round choice (Brett Clouthier) in 1999 Entry Draft, November 26, 1996. Signed as a free agent by **Ottawa**, July 12, 2000.

PETERSON, Brent

(PEE-tuhr-sohn, BREHNT)

Left wing. Shoots left. 6'3", 200 lbs. Born, Calgary, Alta., July 20, 1972. Tampa Bay's 1st choice, 3rd overall, in 1993 Supplemental Draft.

Season	Club	League	GP	G	A	Pts	PIM	PP	SH	GW	S	%	+/-	TF	F%	H	SB	Min	GP	G	A	Pts	PIM	PP	SH	GW
1990-91	Thunder Bay	USHL	48	27	40	67	10	....	....	....	....	....	....	....	....	....	....	....	10	8	9	17	4	....	....	....
1991-92	Michigan Tech	WCHA	39	11	9	20	18	....	....	....	....	....	....	....	....	....	....	....	....	....	....	....	....	....	....	....
1992-93	Michigan Tech	WCHA	37	24	18	42	32	....	....	....	....	....	....	....	....	....	....	....	....	....	....	....	....	....	....	....
1993-94	Michigan Tech	WCHA	43	25	21	46	30	....	....	....	....	....	....	....	....	....	....	....	....	....	....	....	....	....	....	....
1994-95	Michigan Tech	WCHA	39	20	16	36	27	....	....	....	....	....	....	....	....	....	....	....	....	....	....	....	....	....	....	....

			Regular Season																Playoffs							
Season	**Club**	**League**	**GP**	**G**	**A**	**Pts**	**PIM**	**PP**	**SH**	**GW**	**S**	**%**	**+/-**	**TF**	**F%**	**H**	**SB**	**Min**	**GP**	**G**	**A**	**Pts**	**PIM**	**PP**	**SH**	**GW**
1995-96	Atlanta Knights	IHL	69	9	19	28	33	....	....	....	....	....	....	....	....	....	....	....	3	0	0	0	0	....	....	....
1996-97	**Tampa Bay**	**NHL**	**17**	**2**	**0**	**2**	**4**	**0**	**0**	**0**	**11**	**18.2**	**–4**	....	....	....	....	....	....	....	....	....	....	....	....	....
	Adirondack	AHL	52	22	23	45	56	....	....	....	....	....	....	....	....	....	....	....	4	3	1	4	2	....	....	....
1997-98	**Tampa Bay**	**NHL**	**19**	**5**	**0**	**5**	**2**	**0**	**0**	**0**	**15**	**33.3**	**–2**	....	....	....	....	....	....	....	....	....	....	....	....	....
	Milwaukee	IHL	63	20	39	59	48	....	....	....	....	....	....	....	....	....	....	....	8	5	3	8	22	....	....	....
1998-99	**Tampa Bay**	**NHL**	**20**	**2**	**1**	**3**	**0**	**0**	**0**	**0**	**16**	**12.5**	**–2**	**1**	**100.0**	**14**	**3**	**8:58**	....	....	....	....	....	....	....	....
	Cleveland	IHL	18	6	7	13	31	....	....	....	....	....	....	....	....	....	....	....	....	....	....	....	....	....	....	....
	Grand Rapids	IHL	17	7	5	12	14	....	....	....	....	....	....	....	....	....	....	....	....	....	....	....	....	....	....	....
99-2000	Milwaukee	IHL	66	8	24	32	62	....	....	....	....	....	....	....	....	....	....	....	3	3	2	5	4	....	....	....
	NHL Totals		**56**	**9**	**1**	**10**	**6**	**0**	**0**	**0**	**42**	**21.4**		**1**	**100.0**	**14**	**3**	**8:58**	....	....	....	....	....	....	....	....

Traded to **Pittsburgh** by **Tampa Bay** for cash, March 18, 1999. Signed as a free agent by **Nashville**, July 24, 1999.

PETROV, Oleg

(PEH-trahf, OH-lehg) **MTL.**

Right wing. Shoots left. 5'9", 175 lbs. Born, Moscow, USSR, April 18, 1971. Montreal's 9th choice, 127th overall, in 1991 Entry Draft.

1989-90	CSKA Moscow	USSR	30	4	7	11	4	....	....	....	....	....	....	....	....	....	....	....	....	....	....	....	....	....	....	....
1990-91	CSKA Moscow	USSR	43	7	4	11	8	....	....	....	....	....	....	....	....	....	....	....	....	....	....	....	....	....	....	....
1991-92	CSKA Moscow	CIS	42	10	16	26	8	....	....	....	....	....	....	....	....	....	....	....	....	....	....	....	....	....	....	....
1992-93♦	**Montreal**	**NHL**	**9**	**2**	**1**	**3**	**10**	**0**	**0**	**1**	**20**	**10.0**	**2**	....	....	....	....	....	**1**	**0**	**0**	**0**	**0**	**0**	**0**	**0**
	Fredericton	AHL	55	26	29	55	36	....	....	....	....	....	....	....	....	....	....	....	5	4	1	5	0	....	....	....
1993-94	**Montreal**	**NHL**	**55**	**12**	**15**	**27**	**2**	**1**	**0**	**1**	**107**	**11.2**	**7**	....	....	....	....	....	**2**	**0**	**0**	**0**	**0**	**0**	**0**	**0**
	Fredericton	AHL	23	8	20	28	18	....	....	....	....	....	....	....	....	....	....	....	....	....	....	....	....	....	....	....
1994-95	**Montreal**	**NHL**	**12**	**2**	**3**	**5**	**4**	**0**	**0**	**0**	**26**	**7.7**	**–7**	....	....	....	....	....	....	....	....	....	....	....	....	....
	Fredericton	AHL	17	7	11	18	12	....	....	....	....	....	....	....	....	....	....	....	17	5	6	11	10	....	....	....
1995-96	**Montreal**	**NHL**	**36**	**4**	**7**	**11**	**23**	**0**	**0**	**2**	**44**	**9.1**	**–9**	....	....	....	....	....	**5**	**0**	**1**	**1**	**0**	**0**	**0**	**0**
	Fredericton	AHL	22	12	18	30	71	....	....	....	....	....	....	....	....	....	....	....	6	2	6	8	0	....	....	....
1996-97	Ambri-Piotta	Switz.	45	24	28	52	44	....	....	....	....	....	....	....	....	....	....	....	....	....	....	....	....	....	....	....
	HC Meran	Italy	12	5	12	17	4	....	....	....	....	....	....	....	....	....	....	....	....	....	....	....	....	....	....	....
1997-98	Ambri-Piotta	Switz.	40	30	*63	*93	60	....	....	....	....	....	....	....	....	....	....	....	14	11	11	22	40	....	....	....
1998-99	Ambri-Piotta	Switz.	45	35	*52	*87	52	....	....	....	....	....	....	....	....	....	....	....	15	9	11	*20	32	....	....	....
99-2000	**Montreal**	**NHL**	**44**	**2**	**24**	**26**	**8**	**1**	**0**	**0**	**96**	**2.1**	**10**	**9**	**33.3**	**36**	**10**	**15:51**	....	....	....	....	....	....	....	....
	Quebec Citadelles	AHL	16	7	7	14	4	....	....	....	....	....	....	....	....	....	....	....	....	....	....	....	....	....	....	....
	NHL Totals		**156**	**22**	**50**	**72**	**47**	**2**	**0**	**4**	**293**	**7.5**		**9**	**33.3**	**36**	**10**	**15:51**	**8**	**0**	**1**	**1**	**0**	**0**	**0**	**0**

NHL All-Rookie Team (1994)

Signed as a free agent by **Montreal**, July 15, 1999.

PETROVICKY, Robert

(PEHT-roh-vih-kee, RAW-buhrt) **NYI**

Center. Shoots left. 5'11", 172 lbs. Born, Kosice, Czech., October 26, 1973. Hartford's 1st choice, 9th overall, in 1992 Entry Draft.

1990-91	Dukla Trencin	Czech.	33	9	14	23	12	....	....	....	....	....	....	....	....	....	....	....	....	....	....	....	....	....	....	....
1991-92	Dukla Trencin	Czech.	46	25	36	61	28	....	....	....	....	....	....	....	....	....	....	....	....	....	....	....	....	....	....	....
1992-93	**Hartford**	**NHL**	**42**	**3**	**6**	**9**	**45**	**0**	**0**	**0**	**41**	**7.3**	**–10**	....	....	....	....	....	....	....	....	....	....	....	....	....
	Springfield	AHL	16	5	3	8	39	....	....	....	....	....	....	....	....	....	....	....	15	5	6	11	14	....	....	....
1993-94	Dukla Trencin	Slovakia	1	0	0	0	0	....	....	....	....	....	....	....	....	....	....	....	....	....	....	....	....	....	....	....
	Hartford	**NHL**	**33**	**6**	**5**	**11**	**39**	**1**	**0**	**0**	**33**	**18.2**	**–1**	....	....	....	....	....	....	....	....	....	....	....	....	....
	Springfield	AHL	30	16	8	24	39	....	....	....	....	....	....	....	....	....	....	....	4	0	2	2	4	....	....	....
	Slovakia	Olympics	8	1	6	7	18	....	....	....	....	....	....	....	....	....	....	....	....	....	....	....	....	....	....	....
1994-95	Springfield	AHL	74	30	52	82	121	....	....	....	....	....	....	....	....	....	....	....	....	....	....	....	....	....	....	....
	Hartford	**NHL**	**2**	**0**	**0**	**0**	**0**	**0**	**0**	**0**	**1**	**0.0**	**0**	....	....	....	....	....	....	....	....	....	....	....	....	....
1995-96	Springfield	AHL	9	4	8	12	18	....	....	....	....	....	....	....	....	....	....	....	....	....	....	....	....	....	....	....
	Detroit Vipers	IHL	12	5	3	8	16	....	....	....	....	....	....	....	....	....	....	....	....	....	....	....	....	....	....	....
	Dallas	**NHL**	**5**	**1**	**1**	**2**	**0**	**1**	**0**	**1**	**3**	**33.3**	**1**	....	....	....	....	....	....	....	....	....	....	....	....	....
	Michigan	IHL	50	23	23	46	63	....	....	....	....	....	....	....	....	....	....	....	7	3	1	4	16	....	....	....
1996-97	**St. Louis**	**NHL**	**44**	**7**	**12**	**19**	**10**	**0**	**0**	**1**	**54**	**13.0**	**2**	....	....	....	....	....	**2**	**0**	**0**	**0**	**0**	**0**	**0**	**0**
	Worcester	AHL	12	5	4	9	19	....	....	....	....	....	....	....	....	....	....	....	....	....	....	....	....	....	....	....
1997-98	Worcester	AHL	65	27	34	61	97	....	....	....	....	....	....	....	....	....	....	....	10	3	4	7	12	....	....	....
	Slovakia	Olympics	4	2	1	3	0	....	....	....	....	....	....	....	....	....	....	....	....	....	....	....	....	....	....	....
1998-99	Grand Rapids	IHL	49	26	32	58	87	....	....	....	....	....	....	....	....	....	....	....	....	....	....	....	....	....	....	....
	Tampa Bay	**NHL**	**28**	**3**	**4**	**7**	**6**	**0**	**0**	**0**	**32**	**9.4**	**–8**	**35**	**34.3**	**21**	**8**	**10:33**	....	....	....	....	....	....	....	....
99-2000	**Tampa Bay**	**NHL**	**43**	**7**	**10**	**17**	**14**	**1**	**0**	**0**	**50**	**14.0**	**2**	**38**	**47.4**	**32**	**5**	**10:05**	....	....	....	....	....	....	....	....
	Grand Rapids	IHL	7	5	3	8	4	....	....	....	....	....	....	....	....	....	....	....	....	....	....	....	....	....	....	....
	NHL Totals		**197**	**27**	**38**	**65**	**114**	**3**	**0**	**2**	**214**	**12.6**		**73**	**41.1**	**53**	**13**	**10:16**	**2**	**0**	**0**	**0**	**0**	**0**	**0**	**0**

Czechoslovakian First All-Star Team (1992)

Traded to **Dallas** by **Hartford** for Dan Kesa, November 29, 1995. Signed as a free agent by **St. Louis**, September 6, 1996. Signed as a free agent by **Tampa Bay**, February 15, 1999. Signed as a free agent by **NY Islanders**, July 28, 2000.

PHILLIPS, Chris

(FIHL-ihps, KRIHS) **OTT.**

Defense. Shoots left. 6'3", 215 lbs. Born, Fort McMurray, Alta., March 9, 1978. Ottawa's 1st choice, 1st overall, in 1996 Entry Draft.

1993-94	Fort McMurray	AJHL	56	6	16	22	72	....	....	....	....	....	....	....	....	....	....	....	10	0	3	3	16	....	....	....
1994-95	Fort McMurray	AJHL	48	16	32	48	127	....	....	....	....	....	....	....	....	....	....	....	11	4	2	6	10	....	....	....
1995-96	Prince Albert	WHL	61	10	30	40	97	....	....	....	....	....	....	....	....	....	....	....	18	2	12	14	30	....	....	....
1996-97	Prince Albert	WHL	32	3	23	26	58	....	....	....	....	....	....	....	....	....	....	....	....	....	....	....	....	....	....	....
	Lethbridge	WHL	26	4	18	22	28	....	....	....	....	....	....	....	....	....	....	....	19	4	*21	25	20	....	....	....
1997-98	**Ottawa**	**NHL**	**72**	**5**	**11**	**16**	**38**	**2**	**0**	**2**	**107**	**4.7**	**2**	....	....	....	....	....	**11**	**0**	**2**	**2**	**2**	**0**	**0**	**0**
1998-99	**Ottawa**	**NHL**	**34**	**3**	**3**	**6**	**32**	**2**	**0**	**0**	**51**	**5.9**	**–5**	**0**	**0.0**	**53**	**28**	**18:06**	**3**	**0**	**0**	**0**	**0**	**0**	**0**	**0**
99-2000	**Ottawa**	**NHL**	**65**	**5**	**14**	**19**	**39**	**0**	**0**	**1**	**96**	**5.2**	**12**	**0**	**0.0**	**143**	**50**	**16:50**	**6**	**0**	**1**	**1**	**4**	**0**	**0**	**0**
	NHL Totals		**171**	**13**	**28**	**41**	**109**	**4**	**0**	**3**	**254**	**5.1**		**0**	**0.0**	**196**	**78**	**17:16**	**20**	**0**	**3**	**3**	**6**	**0**	**0**	**0**

WHL East First All-Star Team (1997) • Canadian Major Junior First All-Star Team (1997)

• Missed majority of 1998-99 season recovering from ankle injury suffered in game vs. Buffalo, December 30, 1998.

PICARD, Michel

(PEE-cahr, mih-SHEHL) **PHI.**

Left wing. Shoots left. 5'11", 190 lbs. Born, Beauport, Que., November 7, 1969. Hartford's 8th choice, 178th overall, in 1989 Entry Draft.

1985-86	Ste-Foy Governors	QAAA	42	53	34	87	....	....	....	....	....	....	....	....	....	....	....	....	....	....	....	....	....	....	....	....
1986-87	Trois-Rivieres	QMJHL	66	33	35	68	53	....	....	....	....	....	....	....	....	....	....	....	....	....	....	....	....	....	....	....
1987-88	Trois-Rivieres	QMJHL	69	40	55	95	71	....	....	....	....	....	....	....	....	....	....	....	....	....	....	....	....	....	....	....
1988-89	Trois-Rivieres	QMJHL	66	59	81	140	170	....	....	....	....	....	....	....	....	....	....	....	4	1	3	4	2	....	....	....
1989-90	Binghamton	AHL	67	16	24	40	98	....	....	....	....	....	....	....	....	....	....	....	....	....	....	....	....	....	....	....
1990-91	**Hartford**	**NHL**	**5**	**1**	**0**	**1**	**2**	**0**	**0**	**0**	**7**	**14.3**	**–2**	....	....	....	....	....	....	....	....	....	....	....	....	....
	Springfield	AHL	77	*56	40	96	61	....	....	....	....	....	....	....	....	....	....	....	18	8	13	21	18	....	....	....
1991-92	**Hartford**	**NHL**	**25**	**3**	**5**	**8**	**6**	**1**	**0**	**0**	**41**	**7.3**	**–2**	....	....	....	....	....	....	....	....	....	....	....	....	....
	Springfield	AHL	40	21	17	38	44	....	....	....	....	....	....	....	....	....	....	....	11	2	0	2	34	....	....	....
1992-93	**San Jose**	**NHL**	**25**	**4**	**0**	**4**	**24**	**2**	**0**	**0**	**32**	**12.5**	**–17**	....	....	....	....	....	....	....	....	....	....	....	....	....
	Kansas City	IHL	33	7	10	17	51	....	....	....	....	....	....	....	....	....	....	....	12	3	2	5	20	....	....	....
1993-94	Portland Pirates	AHL	61	41	44	85	99	....	....	....	....	....	....	....	....	....	....	....	17	11	10	21	22	....	....	....
1994-95	P.E.I. Senators	AHL	57	32	57	89	58	....	....	....	....	....	....	....	....	....	....	....	8	4	4	8	6	....	....	....
	Ottawa	**NHL**	**24**	**5**	**8**	**13**	**14**	**1**	**0**	**0**	**33**	**15.2**	**–1**	....	....	....	....	....	....	....	....	....	....	....	....	....
1995-96	**Ottawa**	**NHL**	**17**	**2**	**6**	**8**	**10**	**0**	**0**	**1**	**21**	**9.5**	**–1**	....	....	....	....	....	....	....	....	....	....	....	....	....
	P.E.I. Senators	AHL	55	37	45	82	79	....	....	....	....	....	....	....	....	....	....	....	5	5	1	6	2	....	....	....
1996-97	Vastra Frolunda	Sweden	3	0	1	1	0	....	....	....	....	....	....	....	....	....	....	....	....	....	....	....	....	....	....	....
	Grand Rapids	IHL	82	46	55	101	58	....	....	....	....	....	....	....	....	....	....	....	5	2	0	2	10	....	....	....
1997-98	Grand Rapids	IHL	58	28	41	69	42	....	....	....	....	....	....	....	....	....	....	....	....	....	....	....	....	....	....	....
	St. Louis	**NHL**	**16**	**1**	**8**	**9**	**29**	**0**	**0**	**0**	**19**	**5.3**	**3**	....	....	....	....	....	....	....	....	....	....	....	....	....

Season	Club	League	Regular Season GP	G	A	Pts	PIM	PP	SH	GW	S	%	+/-	TF	F%	H	SB	Min	Playoffs GP	G	A	Pts	PIM	PP	SH	GW
1998-99	**St. Louis**	**NHL**	**45**	**11**	**11**	**22**	**16**	**0**	**0**	**2**	**69**	**15.9**	**5**	**1**	**100.0**	**9**	**6**	**14:20**	**5**	**0**	**0**	**0**	**2**	**0**	**0**	**0**
	Grand Rapids	IHL	6	2	2	4	2	....	....	....	....	....	....	....	....	....	....	....	....	....	....	....	....	....	....	....
99-2000	Grand Rapids	IHL	65	33	35	68	50	....	....	....	....	....	....	....	....	....	....	....	17	8	10	*18	4	....	....	....
	Edmonton	**NHL**	**2**	**0**	**0**	**0**	**2**	**0**	**0**	**0**	**2**	**0.0**	**0**	**0**	**0.0**	**4**	**0**	**9:56**	....	....	....	....	....	....	....	....
	NHL Totals		**159**	**27**	**38**	**65**	**103**	**4**	**0**	**3**	**224**	**12.1**		**1**	**100.0**	**13**	**6**	**14:09**	**5**	**0**	**0**	**0**	**2**	**0**	**0**	**0**

QMJHL Second All-Star Team (1989) • AHL First All-Star Team (1991, 1995) • AHL Second All-Star Team (1994) • IHL First All-Star Team (1997)

Traded to **San Jose** by **Hartford** for future considerations (Yvon Corriveau, January 21, 1993), October 9, 1992. Signed as a free agent by **Ottawa**, June 16, 1994. Traded to **Washington** by **Ottawa** for cash, May 21, 1996. Signed as a free agent by **St. Louis**, January 5, 1998. Signed as a free agent by **Edmonton**, December 2, 1999. Signed as a free agent by **Philadelphia**, August 14, 2000.

PILON, Richard

(PEE-lahn, RIH-chahrd) **NYR**

Defense. Shoots left. 6'2", 220 lbs. Born, Saskatoon, Sask., April 30, 1968. NY Islanders' 9th choice, 143rd overall, in 1986 Entry Draft.

Season	Club	League	GP	G	A	Pts	PIM	PP	SH	GW	S	%	+/-	TF	F%	H	SB	Min	GP	G	A	Pts	PIM	PP	SH	GW
1984-85	Prince Albert	SAHA	26	3	11	14	41	....	....	....	....	....	....	....	....	....	....	....	....	....	....	....	....	....	....	....
1985-86	Prince Albert	SAHA	35	3	28	31	142	....	....	....	....	....	....	....	....	....	....	....	....	....	....	....	....	....	....	....
	Prince Albert	WHL	6	0	0	0	0	....	....	....	....	....	....	....	....	....	....	....	....	....	....	....	....	....	....	....
1986-87	Prince Albert	WHL	68	4	21	25	192	....	....	....	....	....	....	....	....	....	....	....	7	1	6	7	17	....	....	....
1987-88	Prince Albert	WHL	65	13	34	47	177	....	....	....	....	....	....	....	....	....	....	....	9	0	6	6	38	....	....	....
1988-89	**NY Islanders**	**NHL**	**62**	**0**	**14**	**14**	**242**	**0**	**0**	**0**	**47**	**0.0**	**-9**	....	....	....	....	....	....	....	....	....	....	....	....	....
1989-90	**NY Islanders**	**NHL**	**14**	**0**	**2**	**2**	**31**	**0**	**0**	**0**	**5**	**0.0**	**2**	....	....	....	....	....	....	....	....	....	....	....	....	....
1990-91	**NY Islanders**	**NHL**	**60**	**1**	**4**	**5**	**126**	**0**	**0**	**0**	**33**	**3.0**	**-12**	....	....	....	....	....	....	....	....	....	....	....	....	....
1991-92	**NY Islanders**	**NHL**	**65**	**1**	**6**	**7**	**183**	**0**	**0**	**0**	**27**	**3.7**	**-1**	....	....	....	....	....	....	....	....	....	....	....	....	....
1992-93	**NY Islanders**	**NHL**	**44**	**1**	**3**	**4**	**164**	**0**	**0**	**0**	**20**	**5.0**	**-4**	....	....	....	....	....	**15**	**0**	**0**	**0**	**50**	**0**	**0**	**0**
	Capital District	AHL	6	0	1	1	8	....	....	....	....	....	....	....	....	....	....	....	....	....	....	....	....	....	....	....
1993-94	**NY Islanders**	**NHL**	**28**	**1**	**4**	**5**	**75**	**0**	**0**	**0**	**20**	**5.0**	**-4**	....	....	....	....	....	....	....	....	....	....	....	....	....
	Salt Lake City	IHL	2	0	0	0	8	....	....	....	....	....	....	....	....	....	....	....	....	....	....	....	....	....	....	....
1994-95	**NY Islanders**	**NHL**	**20**	**1**	**1**	**2**	**40**	**0**	**0**	**0**	**11**	**9.1**	**-3**	....	....	....	....	....	....	....	....	....	....	....	....	....
1995-96	**NY Islanders**	**NHL**	**27**	**0**	**3**	**3**	**72**	**0**	**0**	**0**	**7**	**0.0**	**-9**	....	....	....	....	....	....	....	....	....	....	....	....	....
1996-97	**NY Islanders**	**NHL**	**52**	**1**	**4**	**5**	**179**	**0**	**0**	**0**	**17**	**5.9**	**4**	....	....	....	....	....	....	....	....	....	....	....	....	....
1997-98	**NY Islanders**	**NHL**	**76**	**0**	**7**	**7**	**291**	**0**	**0**	**0**	**37**	**0.0**	**1**	....	....	....	....	....	....	....	....	....	....	....	....	....
1998-99	**NY Islanders**	**NHL**	**52**	**0**	**4**	**4**	**88**	**0**	**0**	**0**	**27**	**0.0**	**-8**	**0**	**0.0**	**155**	**49**	**16:35**	....	....	....	....	....	....	....	....
99-2000	**NY Islanders**	**NHL**	**9**	**0**	**2**	**2**	**34**	**0**	**0**	**0**	**0**	**0.0**	**-2**	**0**	**0.0**	**22**	**17**	**16:21**	....	....	....	....	....	....	....	....
	NY Rangers	**NHL**	**45**	**0**	**4**	**4**	**36**	**0**	**0**	**0**	**16**	**0.0**	**0**	**0**	**0.0**	**135**	**67**	**16:29**	....	....	....	....	....	....	....	....
	NHL Totals		**554**	**6**	**58**	**64**	**1561**	**0**	**0**	**0**	**267**	**2.2**		**0**	**0.0**	**312**	**133**	**16:31**	**15**	**0**	**0**	**0**	**50**	**0**	**0**	**0**

WHL East Second All-Star Team (1988)

• Missed remainder of 1989-90 season recovering from eye injury suffered in game vs. Detroit, November 4, 1989. • Missed majority of 1993-94 season recovering from shoulder injury originally suffered in game vs. Boston, November 13, 1993. • Missed remainder of 1994-95 and majority of 1995-96 seasons recovering from wrist injury suffered in game vs. Quebec, April 18, 1995. Claimed by **NY Rangers** from **NY Islanders** on waivers, December 1, 1999.

PITLICK, Lance

(PIHT-lihk, LANS) **FLA.**

Defense. Shoots right. 6', 205 lbs. Born, Minneapolis, MN, November 5, 1967. Minnesota's 10th choice, 180th overall, in 1986 Entry Draft.

Season	Club	League	GP	G	A	Pts	PIM	PP	SH	GW	S	%	+/-	TF	F%	H	SB	Min	GP	G	A	Pts	PIM	PP	SH	GW
1984-85	Cooper High	Hi-School	23	8	4	12	....	....	....	....	....	....	....	....	....	....	....	....	....	....	....	....	....	....	....	....
1985-86	Cooper High	Hi-School	21	17	8	25	247	....	....	....	....	....	....	....	....	....	....	....	....	....	....	....	....	....	....	....
1986-87	U. of Minnesota	WCHA	45	0	9	9	88	....	....	....	....	....	....	....	....	....	....	....	....	....	....	....	....	....	....	....
1987-88	U. of Minnesota	WCHA	38	3	9	12	76	....	....	....	....	....	....	....	....	....	....	....	....	....	....	....	....	....	....	....
1988-89	U. of Minnesota	WCHA	47	4	9	13	95	....	....	....	....	....	....	....	....	....	....	....	....	....	....	....	....	....	....	....
1989-90	U. of Minnesota	WCHA	14	3	2	5	26	....	....	....	....	....	....	....	....	....	....	....	....	....	....	....	....	....	....	....
1990-91	Hershey Bears	AHL	64	6	15	21	75	....	....	....	....	....	....	....	....	....	....	....	3	0	0	0	9	....	....	....
1991-92	United States	Nat-Team	19	0	1	1	38	....	....	....	....	....	....	....	....	....	....	....	....	....	....	....	....	....	....	....
	Hershey Bears	AHL	4	0	0	0	6	....	....	....	....	....	....	....	....	....	....	....	3	0	0	0	4	....	....	....
1992-93	Hershey Bears	AHL	53	5	10	15	77	....	....	....	....	....	....	....	....	....	....	....	....	....	....	....	....	....	....	....
1993-94	Hershey Bears	AHL	58	4	13	17	93	....	....	....	....	....	....	....	....	....	....	....	11	1	0	1	11	....	....	....
1994-95	P.E.I. Senators	AHL	61	8	19	27	55	....	....	....	....	....	....	....	....	....	....	....	11	1	4	5	10	....	....	....
	Ottawa	**NHL**	**15**	**0**	**1**	**1**	**6**	**0**	**0**	**0**	**11**	**0.0**	**-5**	....	....	....	....	....	....	....	....	....	....	....	....	....
1995-96	**Ottawa**	**NHL**	**28**	**1**	**6**	**7**	**20**	**0**	**0**	**0**	**13**	**7.7**	**-8**	....	....	....	....	....	....	....	....	....	....	....	....	....
	P.E.I. Senators	AHL	29	4	10	14	39	....	....	....	....	....	....	....	....	....	....	....	5	0	0	0	0	....	....	....
1996-97	**Ottawa**	**NHL**	**66**	**5**	**5**	**10**	**91**	**0**	**0**	**1**	**54**	**9.3**	**2**	....	....	....	....	....	**7**	**0**	**0**	**0**	**4**	**0**	**0**	**0**
1997-98	**Ottawa**	**NHL**	**69**	**2**	**7**	**9**	**50**	**0**	**0**	**0**	**66**	**3.0**	**8**	....	....	....	....	....	**11**	**0**	**1**	**1**	**17**	**0**	**0**	**0**
1998-99	**Ottawa**	**NHL**	**50**	**3**	**6**	**9**	**33**	**0**	**0**	**0**	**34**	**8.8**	**7**	**0**	**0.0**	**120**	**64**	**16:39**	**2**	**0**	**0**	**0**	**0**	**0**	**0**	**0**
99-2000	**Florida**	**NHL**	**62**	**3**	**5**	**8**	**44**	**0**	**0**	**1**	**26**	**11.5**	**7**	**0**	**0.0**	**142**	**91**	**16:33**	**4**	**0**	**1**	**1**	**0**	**0**	**0**	**0**
	NHL Totals		**290**	**14**	**30**	**44**	**244**	**0**	**0**	**2**	**204**	**6.9**		**0**	**0.0**	**262**	**155**	**16:36**	**24**	**0**	**2**	**2**	**21**	**0**	**0**	**0**

Signed as a free agent by **Philadelphia**, September 5, 1990. Signed as a free agent by **Ottawa**, June 22, 1994. Signed as a free agent by **Florida**, July 21, 1999.

PITTIS, Domenic

(PIH-THIS, DOHM-eh-nihk) **EDM.**

Center. Shoots left. 5'11", 190 lbs. Born, Calgary, Alta., October 1, 1974. Pittsburgh's 2nd choice, 52nd overall, in 1993 Entry Draft.

Season	Club	League	GP	G	A	Pts	PIM	PP	SH	GW	S	%	+/-	TF	F%	H	SB	Min	GP	G	A	Pts	PIM	PP	SH	GW
1990-91	Calgary Buffaloes	AAHA	35	23	54	77	43	....	....	....	....	....	....	....	....	....	....	....	....	....	....	....	....	....	....	....
1991-92	Lethbridge	WHL	65	6	17	23	18	....	....	....	....	....	....	....	....	....	....	....	5	0	2	2	4	....	....	....
1992-93	Lethbridge	WHL	66	46	73	119	69	....	....	....	....	....	....	....	....	....	....	....	4	3	3	6	8	....	....	....
1993-94	Lethbridge	WHL	72	58	69	127	93	....	....	....	....	....	....	....	....	....	....	....	8	4	11	15	16	....	....	....
1994-95	Cleveland	IHL	62	18	32	50	66	....	....	....	....	....	....	....	....	....	....	....	3	0	2	2	2	....	....	....
1995-96	Cleveland	IHL	74	10	28	38	100	....	....	....	....	....	....	....	....	....	....	....	3	0	0	0	2	....	....	....
1996-97	**Pittsburgh**	**NHL**	**1**	**0**	**0**	**0**	**0**	**0**	**0**	**0**	**0**	**0.0**	**-1**	....	....	....	....	....	....	....	....	....	....	....	....	....
	Long Beach	IHL	65	23	43	66	91	....	....	....	....	....	....	....	....	....	....	....	18	5	9	14	26	....	....	....
1997-98	Syracuse Crunch	AHL	75	23	41	64	90	....	....	....	....	....	....	....	....	....	....	....	5	1	3	4	4	....	....	....
1998-99	**Buffalo**	**NHL**	**3**	**0**	**0**	**0**	**2**	**0**	**0**	**0**	**1**	**0.0**	**0**	**19**	**42.1**	**4**	**1**	**8:35**	....	....	....	....	....	....	....	....
	Rochester	AHL	76	38	66	*104	108	....	....	....	....	....	....	....	....	....	....	....	20	7	*14	*21	40	....	....	....
99-2000	**Buffalo**	**NHL**	**7**	**1**	**0**	**1**	**6**	**0**	**0**	**0**	**6**	**16.7**	**1**	**65**	**44.6**	**7**	**0**	**11:27**	....	....	....	....	....	....	....	....
	Rochester	AHL	53	17	48	65	85	....	....	....	....	....	....	....	....	....	....	....	21	4	*26	*30	28	....	....	....
	NHL Totals		**11**	**1**	**0**	**1**	**8**	**0**	**0**	**0**	**7**	**14.3**		**84**	**44.0**	**11**	**1**	**10:35**	....	....	....	....	....	....	....	....

WHL East Second All-Star Team (1994) • Won John P. Sollenberger Trophy (Top Scorer - AHL) (1999)

Signed as a free agent by **Buffalo**, August 10, 1998. Signed as a free agent by **Edmonton**, July 25, 2000.

PIVONKA, Michal

(pih-VAHN-kuh, MIHK-al)

Center. Shoots left. 6'2", 200 lbs. Born, Kladno, Czech., January 28, 1966. Washington's 3rd choice, 59th overall, in 1984 Entry Draft.

Season	Club	League	GP	G	A	Pts	PIM	PP	SH	GW	S	%	+/-	TF	F%	H	SB	Min	GP	G	A	Pts	PIM	PP	SH	GW
1984-85	Dukla Jihlava	Czech.	33	8	11	19	18	....	....	....	....	....	....	....	....	....	....	....	....	....	....	....	....	....	....	....
1985-86	Dukla Jihlava	Czech.	42	5	13	18	18	....	....	....	....	....	....	....	....	....	....	....	....	....	....	....	....	....	....	....
1986-87	**Washington**	**NHL**	**73**	**18**	**25**	**43**	**41**	**4**	**0**	**2**	**117**	**15.4**	**-19**	....	....	....	....	....	**7**	**1**	**1**	**2**	**2**	**0**	**0**	**0**
1987-88	**Washington**	**NHL**	**71**	**11**	**23**	**34**	**28**	**3**	**0**	**0**	**96**	**11.5**	**1**	....	....	....	....	....	**14**	**4**	**9**	**13**	**4**	**2**	**0**	**0**
1988-89	**Washington**	**NHL**	**52**	**8**	**19**	**27**	**30**	**1**	**0**	**1**	**73**	**11.0**	**9**	....	....	....	....	....	**6**	**3**	**1**	**4**	**10**	**0**	**1**	**0**
	Baltimore	AHL	31	12	24	36	19	....	....	....	....	....	....	....	....	....	....	....	....	....	....	....	....	....	....	....
1989-90	**Washington**	**NHL**	**77**	**25**	**39**	**64**	**54**	**10**	**3**	**0**	**149**	**16.8**	**-7**	....	....	....	....	....	**11**	**0**	**2**	**2**	**6**	**0**	**0**	**0**
1990-91	**Washington**	**NHL**	**79**	**20**	**50**	**70**	**34**	**6**	**0**	**4**	**172**	**11.6**	**3**	....	....	....	....	....	**11**	**2**	**3**	**5**	**8**	**0**	**0**	**0**
1991-92	**Washington**	**NHL**	**80**	**23**	**57**	**80**	**47**	**7**	**4**	**2**	**177**	**13.0**	**10**	....	....	....	....	....	**7**	**1**	**5**	**6**	**13**	**1**	**0**	**1**
1992-93	**Washington**	**NHL**	**69**	**21**	**53**	**74**	**66**	**6**	**1**	**5**	**147**	**14.3**	**14**	....	....	....	....	....	**6**	**0**	**2**	**2**	**0**	**0**	**0**	**0**
1993-94	**Washington**	**NHL**	**82**	**14**	**36**	**50**	**38**	**5**	**0**	**4**	**138**	**10.1**	**2**	....	....	....	....	....	**7**	**4**	**4**	**8**	**4**	**1**	**0**	**0**
1994-95	KAC Klagenfurt	Austria	7	2	4	6	4	....	....	....	....	....	....	....	....	....	....	....	....	....	....	....	....	....	....	....
	Washington	**NHL**	**46**	**10**	**23**	**33**	**50**	**4**	**2**	**2**	**80**	**12.5**	**3**	....	....	....	....	....	**7**	**1**	**4**	**5**	**21**	**0**	**0**	**0**
1995-96	Detroit Vipers	IHL	7	1	9	10	19	....	....	....	....	....	....	....	....	....	....	....	....	....	....	....	....	....	....	....
	Washington	**NHL**	**73**	**16**	**65**	**81**	**36**	**6**	**2**	**5**	**168**	**9.5**	**18**	....	....	....	....	....	**6**	**3**	**2**	**5**	**18**	**1**	**0**	**0**
1996-97	**Washington**	**NHL**	**54**	**7**	**16**	**23**	**22**	**2**	**0**	**1**	**83**	**8.4**	**-15**	....	....	....	....	....	....	....	....	....	....	....	....	....
1997-98	**Washington**	**NHL**	**33**	**3**	**6**	**9**	**20**	**0**	**0**	**1**	**38**	**7.9**	**5**	....	....	....	....	....	**13**	**0**	**3**	**3**	**0**	**0**	**0**	**0**

Season	Club	League	GP	G	A	Pts	PIM	PP	SH	GW	S	%	+/-	TF	F%	H	SB	Min	GP	G	A	Pts	PIM	PP	SH	GW
			Regular Season																Playoffs							
1998-99	Washington	NHL	36	5	6	11	12	2	0	0	30	16.7	-6	420	49.0	29	13	13:12	....	....	....	....	....	....	....	....
99-2000	Kansas City	IHL	52	16	34	50	38	....	....	....	....	....	....	....	....	....	....	....	....	....	....	....	....	....	....	....
	NHL Totals		825	181	418	599	478	56	12	27	1468	12.3		420	49.0	29	13	13:12	95	19	36	55	86	5	1	1

• Missed majority of 1997-98 season recovering from wrist injury suffered in game vs. Pittsburgh, November 12, 1997. • Missed majority of 1998-99 season recovering from groin injury suffered in game vs. Buffalo, February 7, 1998. Signed as a free agent by **Kansas City** (IHL), September 27, 1999.

PLANTE, Dan

(PLAHNT, DAN)

Right wing. Shoots right. 5'11", 202 lbs. Born, Hayward, WI, October 5, 1971. NY Islanders' 3rd choice, 48th overall, in 1990 Entry Draft.

Season	Club	League	GP	G	A	Pts	PIM	PP	SH	GW	S	%	+/-	TF	F%	H	SB	Min	GP	G	A	Pts	PIM	PP	SH	GW
1988-89	Edina High	Hi-School	27	10	26	36	23	....	....	....	....	....	....	....	....	....	....	....	....	....	....	....	....	....	....	....
1989-90	Edina High	Hi-School	24	8	18	26	12	....	....	....	....	....	....	....	....	....	....	....	....	....	....	....	....	....	....	....
1990-91	U. of Wisconsin	WCHA	33	1	2	3	54	....	....	....	....	....	....	....	....	....	....	....	....	....	....	....	....	....	....	....
1991-92	U. of Wisconsin	WCHA	36	13	13	26	107	....	....	....	....	....	....	....	....	....	....	....	....	....	....	....	....	....	....	....
1992-93	U. of Wisconsin	WCHA	42	26	31	57	142	....	....	....	....	....	....	....	....	....	....	....	....	....	....	....	....	....	....	....
1993-94	NY Islanders	NHL	12	0	1	1	4	0	0	0	9	0.0	-2	....	....	....	....	....	1	1	0	1	2	0	0	0
	Salt Lake City	IHL	66	7	17	24	148	....	....	....	....	....	....	....	....	....	....	....	....	....	....	....	....	....	....	....
1994-95	Denver Grizzlies	IHL	2	0	0	0	4	....	....	....	....	....	....	....	....	....	....	....	....	....	....	....	....	....	....	....
1995-96	NY Islanders	NHL	73	5	3	8	50	0	2	0	103	4.9	-22	....	....	....	....	....	....	....	....	....	....	....	....	....
1996-97	NY Islanders	NHL	67	4	9	13	75	0	2	0	61	6.6	-6	....	....	....	....	....	....	....	....	....	....	....	....	....
1997-98	NY Islanders	NHL	7	0	1	1	6	0	0	0	7	0.0	-1	....	....	....	....	....	....	....	....	....	....	....	....	....
	Utah Grizzlies	IHL	73	22	27	49	125	....	....	....	....	....	....	....	....	....	....	....	4	0	2	2	14	....	....	....
1998-99	Chicago Wolves	IHL	81	21	12	33	119	....	....	....	....	....	....	....	....	....	....	....	10	1	5	6	10	....	....	....
99-2000	Chicago Wolves	IHL	79	11	11	22	71	....	....	....	....	....	....	....	....	....	....	....	16	3	5	8	14	....	....	....
	NHL Totals		159	9	14	23	135	0	4	0	180	5.0		....	....	....	....	....	1	1	0	1	2	0	0	0

• Missed remainder of 1994-95 season recovering from knee injury suffered in game vs. Houston (IHL), October 2, 1994. Signed as a free agent by **Chicago** (IHL), July 21, 1999.

PLANTE, Derek

(PLAHNT, DAIR-ehk) **PHI.**

Center. Shoots left. 5'11", 181 lbs. Born, Cloquet, MN, January 17, 1971. Buffalo's 7th choice, 161st overall, in 1989 Entry Draft.

Season	Club	League	GP	G	A	Pts	PIM	PP	SH	GW	S	%	+/-	TF	F%	H	SB	Min	GP	G	A	Pts	PIM	PP	SH	GW
1987-88	Cloquet High	Hi-School	23	16	25	41	....	....	....	....	....	....	....	....	....	....	....	....	....	....	....	....	....	....	....	....
1988-89	Cloquet High	Hi-School	24	30	33	63	....	....	....	....	....	....	....	....	....	....	....	....	....	....	....	....	....	....	....	....
1989-90	Minnesota-Duluth	WCHA	28	10	11	21	12	....	....	....	....	....	....	....	....	....	....	....	....	....	....	....	....	....	....	....
1990-91	Minnesota-Duluth	WCHA	36	23	20	43	6	....	....	....	....	....	....	....	....	....	....	....	....	....	....	....	....	....	....	....
1991-92	Minnesota-Duluth	WCHA	37	27	36	63	28	....	....	....	....	....	....	....	....	....	....	....	....	....	....	....	....	....	....	....
1992-93	Minnesota-Duluth	WCHA	37	*36	*56	*92	30	....	....	....	....	....	....	....	....	....	....	....	....	....	....	....	....	....	....	....
1993-94	Buffalo	NHL	77	21	35	56	24	8	1	2	147	14.3	4	....	....	....	....	....	7	1	0	1	0	0	0	0
	United States	Nat-Team	2	0	1	1	0	....	....	....	....	....	....	....	....	....	....	....	....	....	....	....	....	....	....	....
1994-95	Buffalo	NHL	47	3	19	22	12	2	0	0	94	3.2	-4	....	....	....	....	....	....	....	....	....	....	....	....	....
1995-96	Buffalo	NHL	76	23	33	56	28	4	0	5	203	11.3	-4	....	....	....	....	....	....	....	....	....	....	....	....	....
1996-97	Buffalo	NHL	82	27	26	53	24	5	0	6	191	14.1	14	....	....	....	....	....	12	4	6	10	4	1	0	2
1997-98	Buffalo	NHL	72	13	21	34	26	5	0	1	150	8.7	8	....	....	....	....	....	11	0	3	3	10	0	0	0
1998-99	Buffalo	NHL	41	4	11	15	12	0	0	0	66	6.1	3	598	46.2	10	24	15:31	....	....	....	....	....	....	....	....
	♦ Dallas	NHL	10	2	3	5	4	1	0	0	24	8.3	1	113	58.4	9	4	13:42	6	1	0	1	4	0	0	0
99-2000	Dallas	NHL	16	1	1	2	2	1	0	0	17	5.9	-4	119	51.3	5	7	10:05	....	....	....	....	....	....	....	....
	Michigan K-Wings	IHL	13	0	4	4	2	....	....	....	....	....	....	....	....	....	....	....	....	....	....	....	....	....	....	....
	Chicago	NHL	17	1	1	2	2	0	0	0	14	7.1	-1	98	38.8	6	3	7:48	....	....	....	....	....	....	....	....
	Chicago Wolves	IHL	4	2	1	3	2	....	....	....	....	....	....	....	....	....	....	....	8	3	1	4	6	....	....	....
	NHL Totals		438	95	150	245	134	26	1	14	906	10.5		928	47.5	30	38	12:42	36	6	9	15	18	1	0	2

WCHA Second All-Star Team (1992) • WCHA First All-Star Team (1993) • NCAA West First All-American Team (1993)

Traded to **Dallas** by **Buffalo** for Dallas' 2nd round choice (Michael Zigomanis) in 1999 Entry Draft, March 23, 1999. Traded to **Chicago** by **Dallas** with Kevin Dean and Dallas' 2nd round choice in 2001 Entry Draft for Sylvain Cote and Dave Manson, February 8, 2000. Signed as a free agent by **Philadelphia**, July 26, 2000.

POAPST, Steve

(POHPST, STEEV) **CHI.**

Defense. Shoots left. 6', 200 lbs. Born, Cornwall, Ont., January 3, 1969.

Season	Club	League	GP	G	A	Pts	PIM	PP	SH	GW	S	%	+/-	TF	F%	H	SB	Min	GP	G	A	Pts	PIM	PP	SH	GW
1986-87	Smith Falls Bears	OJHL	54	10	27	37	94	....	....	....	....	....	....	....	....	....	....	....	....	....	....	....	....	....	....	....
1987-88	Colgate University	ECAC	32	3	13	16	22	....	....	....	....	....	....	....	....	....	....	....	....	....	....	....	....	....	....	....
1988-89	Colgate University	ECAC	30	0	5	5	38	....	....	....	....	....	....	....	....	....	....	....	....	....	....	....	....	....	....	....
1989-90	Colgate University	ECAC	38	4	15	19	54	....	....	....	....	....	....	....	....	....	....	....	....	....	....	....	....	....	....	....
1990-91	Colgate University	ECAC	32	6	15	21	43	....	....	....	....	....	....	....	....	....	....	....	....	....	....	....	....	....	....	....
1991-92	Hampton Roads	ECHL	55	8	20	28	29	....	....	....	....	....	....	....	....	....	....	....	14	1	4	5	12	....	....	....
1992-93	Hampton Roads	ECHL	63	10	35	45	57	....	....	....	....	....	....	....	....	....	....	....	4	0	1	1	4	....	....	....
	Baltimore	AHL	7	0	1	1	4	....	....	....	....	....	....	....	....	....	....	....	7	0	3	3	6	....	....	....
1993-94	Portland Pirates	AHL	78	14	21	35	47	....	....	....	....	....	....	....	....	....	....	....	12	0	3	3	8	....	....	....
1994-95	Portland Pirates	AHL	71	8	22	30	60	....	....	....	....	....	....	....	....	....	....	....	7	0	1	1	16	....	....	....
1995-96	Washington	NHL	3	1	0	1	0	0	0	1	2	50.0	-1	....	....	....	....	....	6	0	0	0	0	0	0	0
	Portland Pirates	AHL	70	10	24	34	79	....	....	....	....	....	....	....	....	....	....	....	20	2	6	8	16	....	....	....
1996-97	Portland Pirates	AHL	47	1	20	21	34	....	....	....	....	....	....	....	....	....	....	....	5	0	1	1	6	....	....	....
1997-98	Portland Pirates	AHL	76	8	29	37	46	....	....	....	....	....	....	....	....	....	....	....	10	2	3	5	8	....	....	....
1998-99	Washington	NHL	22	0	0	0	8	0	0	0	11	0.0	-8	0	0.0	48	6	12:26	....	....	....	....	....	....	....	....
	Portland Pirates	AHL	54	3	21	24	36	....	....	....	....	....	....	....	....	....	....	....	....	....	....	....	....	....	....	....
99-2000	Portland Pirates	AHL	58	0	14	14	20	....	....	....	....	....	....	....	....	....	....	....	3	1	0	1	2	....	....	....
	NHL Totals		25	1	0	1	8	0	0	1	13	7.7		0	0.0	48	6	12:26	6	0	0	0	0	0	0	0

ECHL First All-Star Team (1993)

Signed as a free agent by **Washington**, February 4, 1995. Signed as a free agent by **Chicago**, July 27, 2000.• Played w/ RHI's New England Stingers in 1994 (20-6-23-29-47).

PODEIN, Shjon

(poh-DEEN, SHAWN) **COL.**

Left wing. Shoots left. 6'2", 200 lbs. Born, Rochester, MN, March 5, 1968. Edmonton's 9th choice, 166th overall, in 1988 Entry Draft.

Season	Club	League	GP	G	A	Pts	PIM	PP	SH	GW	S	%	+/-	TF	F%	H	SB	Min	GP	G	A	Pts	PIM	PP	SH	GW
1985-86	John Marshall	Hi-School	25	34	30	64	....	....	....	....	....	....	....	....	....	....	....	....	....	....	....	....	....	....	....	....
1986-87	U.S. International	NCAA-2	6	0	1	1	0	....	....	....	....	....	....	....	....	....	....	....	....	....	....	....	....	....	....	....
1987-88	Minnesota-Duluth	WCHA	30	4	4	8	48	....	....	....	....	....	....	....	....	....	....	....	....	....	....	....	....	....	....	....
1988-89	Minnesota-Duluth	WCHA	36	7	5	12	46	....	....	....	....	....	....	....	....	....	....	....	....	....	....	....	....	....	....	....
1989-90	Minnesota-Duluth	WCHA	35	21	18	39	36	....	....	....	....	....	....	....	....	....	....	....	....	....	....	....	....	....	....	....
1990-91	Cape Breton	AHL	63	14	15	29	65	....	....	....	....	....	....	....	....	....	....	....	4	0	0	0	5	....	....	....
1991-92	Cape Breton	AHL	80	30	24	54	46	....	....	....	....	....	....	....	....	....	....	....	5	3	1	4	2	....	....	....
1992-93	Edmonton	NHL	40	13	6	19	25	2	1	1	64	20.3	-2	....	....	....	....	....	....	....	....	....	....	....	....	....
	Cape Breton	AHL	38	18	21	39	32	....	....	....	....	....	....	....	....	....	....	....	9	2	2	4	29	....	....	....
1993-94	Edmonton	NHL	28	3	5	8	8	0	0	0	26	11.5	3	....	....	....	....	....	....	....	....	....	....	....	....	....
	Cape Breton	AHL	5	4	4	8	4	....	....	....	....	....	....	....	....	....	....	....	....	....	....	....	....	....	....	....
1994-95	Philadelphia	NHL	44	3	7	10	33	0	0	1	48	6.3	-2	....	....	....	....	....	15	1	3	4	10	0	0	0
1995-96	Philadelphia	NHL	79	15	10	25	89	0	4	4	115	13.0	25	....	....	....	....	....	12	1	2	3	50	0	0	1
1996-97	Philadelphia	NHL	82	14	18	32	41	0	0	4	153	9.2	7	....	....	....	....	....	19	4	3	7	16	0	0	1
1997-98	Philadelphia	NHL	82	11	13	24	53	1	1	2	126	8.7	8	....	....	....	....	....	5	0	0	0	10	0	0	0
1998-99	Philadelphia	NHL	14	1	0	1	0	0	0	0	26	3.8	-2	2	50.0	13	4	11:52	....	....	....	....	....	....	....	....
	Colorado	NHL	41	2	6	8	24	0	0	0	49	4.1	-3	21	42.9	41	24	11:49	19	1	1	2	12	0	0	0
99-2000	Colorado	NHL	75	11	8	19	29	0	1	3	104	10.6	12	17	64.7	84	60	13:31	17	5	0	5	8	0	0	1
	NHL Totals		485	73	73	146	302	3	7	15	711	10.3		40	52.5	138	88	12:48	87	12	9	21	106	0	0	3

Signed as a free agent by **Philadelphia**, July 27, 1994. Traded to **Colorado** by **Philadelphia** for Keith Jones, November 12, 1998.

			Regular Season																Playoffs						
Season	Club	League	GP	G	A	Pts	PIM	PP	SH	GW	S	%	+/-	TF	F%	H	SB	Min	GP	G	A	Pts	PIM	PP	SH	GW

PODOLLAN, Jason — Right wing. Shoots right. 6'1", 198 lbs. Born, Vernon, B.C., February 18, 1976. Florida's 3rd choice, 31st overall, in 1994 Entry Draft. (poh-DOH-luhn, JAY-suhn) **L.A.**

Season	Club	League	GP	G	A	Pts	PIM	PP	SH	GW	S	%	+/-	TF	F%	H	SB	Min	GP	G	A	Pts	PIM
1990-91	Sherwood Park	AAHA	61	105	111	216	133																
1991-92	Penticton	BCJHL	59	20	26	46	66																
	Spokane Chiefs	WHL	2	0	0	0	2												10	3	1	4	16
1992-93	Spokane Chiefs	WHL	72	36	33	69	108												10	4	4	8	14
1993-94	Spokane Chiefs	WHL	69	29	37	66	108												3	3	0	3	2
1994-95	Spokane Chiefs	WHL	72	43	41	84	102												11	5	7	12	18
	Cincinnati	IHL																	3	0	0	0	2
1995-96	Spokane Chiefs	WHL	56	37	25	62	103												18	*21	12	33	28
1996-97	**Florida**	**NHL**	19	1	1	2	4	1	0	0	20	5.0	–3										
	Carolina	AHL	39	21	25	46	36																
	Toronto	**NHL**	10	0	3	3	6	0	0	0	10	0.0	–2										
	St. John's Leafs	AHL																	11	2	3	5	6
1997-98	St. John's Leafs	AHL	70	30	31	61	116												4	1	0	1	10
1998-99	**Toronto**	**NHL**	4	0	0	0	0	0	0	0	2	0.0	0	0	0.0	5	0	6:29					
	St. John's Leafs	AHL	68	42	26	68	65																
	Los Angeles	**NHL**	6	0	0	0	5	0	0	0	7	0.0	–3	0	0.0	13	1	10:15					
	Long Beach	IHL	8	5	3	8	2												6	1	2	3	4
99-2000	**Los Angeles**	**NHL**	1	0	1	1	2	0	0	0	2	0.0	0	0	0.0	3	0	16:13					
	Lowell	AHL	71	29	26	55	91												4	0	0	0	0
	NHL Totals		40	1	5	6	17	1	0	0	41	2.4		0	0.0	21	1	9:25					

WHL West Second All-Star Team (1996)
Traded to **Toronto** by **Florida** for Kirk Muller, March 18, 1997. Traded to **Los Angeles** by **Toronto** with Toronto's 3rd round choice (Cory Campbell) in 1999 Entry Draft for Yanic Perreault, March 23, 1999.

POESCHEK, Rudy — Right wing/Defense. Shoots right. 6'2", 218 lbs. Born, Kamloops, B.C., September 29, 1966. NY Rangers' 12th choice, 238th overall, in 1985 Entry Draft. (POH-shehk, REW-dee)

Season	Club	League	GP	G	A	Pts	PIM	PP	SH	GW	S	%	+/-	TF	F%	H	SB	Min	GP	G	A	Pts	PIM	PP	SH	GW
1982-83	Vernon Lakers	BCJHL	54	4	10	14	100																			
1983-84	Revelstoke	BCJHL	22	5	21	26	107																			
	Kamloops Blazers	WHL	47	3	9	12	93												8	0	2	2	7			
1984-85	Kamloops Blazers	WHL	34	6	7	13	100												15	0	3	3	56			
1985-86	Kamloops Blazers	WHL	32	3	13	16	92												16	3	7	10	40			
1986-87	Kamloops Blazers	WHL	54	13	18	31	153												15	2	4	6	37			
1987-88	**NY Rangers**	**NHL**	1	0	0	0	2	0	0	0	1	0.0	0													
	Colorado	IHL	82	7	31	38	210												12	2	2	4	31			
1988-89	**NY Rangers**	**NHL**	52	0	2	2	199	0	0	0	17	0.0	–8													
	Colorado	IHL	2	0	0	0	6																			
1989-90	**NY Rangers**	**NHL**	15	0	0	0	55	0	0	0	1	0.0	–1													
	Flint Spirits	IHL	38	8	13	21	109												4	0	0	0	16			
1990-91	Binghamton	AHL	38	1	3	4	162																			
	Winnipeg	**NHL**	1	0	0	0	5	0	0	0	0	0.0	0													
	Moncton Hawks	AHL	23	2	4	6	67												9	1	1	2	41			
1991-92	**Winnipeg**	**NHL**	4	0	0	0	17	0	0	0	1	0.0	–5													
	Moncton Hawks	AHL	63	4	18	22	170												11	0	2	2	48			
1992-93	St. John's Leafs	AHL	78	7	24	31	189												9	0	4	4	13			
1993-94	**Tampa Bay**	**NHL**	71	3	6	9	118	0	0	1	46	6.5	3													
1994-95	**Tampa Bay**	**NHL**	25	1	1	2	92	0	0	0	14	7.1	0													
1995-96	**Tampa Bay**	**NHL**	57	1	3	4	88	0	0	0	36	2.8	–2						3	0	0	0	12	0	0	0
1996-97	**Tampa Bay**	**NHL**	60	0	6	6	120	0	0	0	30	0.0	–3													
1997-98	**St. Louis**	**NHL**	50	1	7	8	64	0	0	0	29	3.4	–5						2	0	0	0	6	0	0	0
1998-99	**St. Louis**	**NHL**	16	0	0	0	33	0	0	0	8	0.0	–3	0	0.0	8	5	10:14								
99-2000	**St. Louis**	**NHL**	12	0	0	0	24	0	0	0	8	0.0	–3	0	0.0	13	11	11:15								
	Worcester	AHL	5	0	0	0	4																			
	Houston Aeros	IHL	32	2	6	8	51																			
	NHL Totals		364	6	25	31	817	0	0	1	191	3.1		0	0.0	21	16	10:40	5	0	0	0	18	0	0	0

Traded to **Winnipeg** by **NY Rangers** for Guy Larose, January 22, 1991. Signed as a free agent by **Toronto**, July 8, 1992. Signed as a free agent by **Tampa Bay**, August 10, 1993. Signed as a free agent by **St. Louis**, July 31, 1997. Loaned to **Houston** (IHL) by **St. Louis**, November 11, 1999.

POPOVIC, Peter — Defense. Shoots left. 6'6", 243 lbs. Born, Koping, Sweden, February 10, 1968. Montreal's 5th choice, 93rd overall, in 1988 Entry Draft. (puh-PUH-vihch, PEE-tuhr) **BOS.**

Season	Club	League	GP	G	A	Pts	PIM	PP	SH	GW	S	%	+/-	TF	F%	H	SB	Min	GP	G	A	Pts	PIM	PP	SH	GW
1986-87	Vasteras IK	Sweden-2	24	1	2	3	10												12	2	8	10	6			
1987-88	Vasteras IK	Sweden-2	28	3	17	20	16												15	1	4	5	20			
1988-89	Vasteras IK	Sweden	22	1	4	5	32																			
1989-90	Vasteras IK	Sweden	30	2	10	12	24												2	0	1	1	2			
1990-91	Vasteras IK	Sweden	40	3	2	5	62												4	0	0	0	4			
1991-92	Vasteras IK	Sweden	34	7	10	17	30																			
1992-93	Vasteras IK	Sweden	39	6	12	18	46												3	0	1	1	2			
1993-94	**Montreal**	**NHL**	47	2	12	14	26	1	0	0	58	3.4	10						6	0	1	1	0	0	0	0
1994-95	Vasteras IK	Sweden	11	0	3	3	10																			
	Montreal	**NHL**	33	0	5	5	8	0	0	0	23	0.0	–10													
1995-96	**Montreal**	**NHL**	76	2	12	14	69	0	0	0	59	3.4	21						6	0	2	2	4	0	0	0
1996-97	**Montreal**	**NHL**	78	1	13	14	32	0	0	0	82	1.2	9						3	0	0	0	2	0	0	0
1997-98	**Montreal**	**NHL**	69	2	6	8	38	0	0	0	40	5.0	–6						10	1	1	2	2	0	0	0
1998-99	**NY Rangers**	**NHL**	68	1	4	5	40	0	0	0	64	1.6	–12	2	0.0	112	178	20:41								
99-2000	**Pittsburgh**	**NHL**	54	1	5	6	30	0	0	0	23	4.3	–8	2	0.0	59	85	16:12	10	0	0	0	10	0	0	0
	NHL Totals		425	9	57	66	243	1	0	0	349	2.6		4	0.0	171	263	18:42	35	1	4	5	18	0	0	0

Traded to **NY Rangers** by **Montreal** for Sylvain Blouin and NY Rangers' 6th round choice (later traded to Phoenix - Phoenix selected Erik Leverstrom) in 1999 Entry Draft, June 30, 1998. Traded to **Pittsburgh** by **NY Rangers** for Kevin Hatcher, September 30, 1999. Signed as a free agent by **Boston**, July 2, 2000.

POSMYK, Marek — Defense. Shoots right. 6'5", 228 lbs. Born, Jihlava, Czech., September 15, 1978. Toronto's 1st choice, 36th overall, in 1996 Entry Draft. (PAWZ-mihk, MAHR-ehk) **T.B.**

Season	Club	League	GP	G	A	Pts	PIM	PP	SH	GW	S	%	+/-	TF	F%	H	SB	Min	GP	G	A	Pts	PIM
1994-95	Dukla Jihlava-Jr.	Cze-Rep	16	1	3	4																	
1995-96	Dukla Jihlava-Jr.	Cze-Rep	16	6	5	11																	
	Dukla Jihlava	Cze-Rep	18	1	2	3													1	0	0	0	0
1996-97	Dukla Jihlava	Cze-Rep	24	1	7	8	44																
	St. John's Leafs	AHL	2	0	0	0	2																
1997-98	Sarnia Sting	OHL	48	8	16	24	94												5	0	2	2	6
	St. John's Leafs	AHL	3	0	0	0	4																
1998-99	St. John's Leafs	AHL	41	1	0	1	36																
99-2000	**Tampa Bay**	**NHL**	18	1	2	3	20	0	0	0	22	4.5	1	1100.0	21	13	13:12						
	Detroit Vipers	IHL	1	0	1	1	0																
	NHL Totals		18	1	2	3	20	0	0	0	22	4.5		1100.0	21	13	13:12						

Traded to **Tampa Bay** by **Toronto** with Mike Johnson, Toronto's 5th (Pavel Sedov) and 6th (Aaron Gionet) round choices in 2000 Entry Draft and future considerations for Darcy Tucker, Tampa Bay's 4th round choice (Miguel Delisle) in 2000 Entry Draft and future considerations, February 9, 2000.

			Regular Season																Playoffs							
Season	Club	League	GP	G	A	Pts	PIM	PP	SH	GW	S	%	+/-	TF	F%	H	SB	Min	GP	G	A	Pts	PIM	PP	SH	GW

POTI, Tom
(POH-tee, TAWM) **EDM.**

Defense. Shoots left. 6'3", 215 lbs. Born, Worcester, MA, March 22, 1977. Edmonton's 4th choice, 59th overall, in 1996 Entry Draft.

Season	Club	League	GP	G	A	Pts	PIM	PP	SH	GW	S	%	+/-	TF	F%	H	SB	Min	GP	G	A	Pts	PIM	PP	SH	GW
1992-93	St. Peter's	Hi-School	55	25	46	71																				
1993-94	Cushing Academy	Hi-School	30	10	35	45																				
1994-95	Cushing Academy	Hi-School	36	17	54	71	35																			
	Central-Mass	MBHL	8	8	10	18																				
1995-96	Cushing Academy	Hi-School	29	14	59	73	18																			
1996-97	Boston University	H-East	38	4	17	21	54																			
1997-98	Boston University	H-East	38	13	29	42	60																			
1998-99	**Edmonton**	**NHL**	**73**	**5**	**16**	**21**	**42**	**2**	**0**	**3**	**94**	**5.3**	**10**	**0**	**0.0**	**35**	**82**	**19:33**	**4**	**0**	**1**	**1**	**2**	**0**	**0**	**0**
99-2000	**Edmonton**	**NHL**	**76**	**9**	**26**	**35**	**65**	**2**	**1**	**1**	**125**	**7.2**	**8**	**0**	**0.0**	**38**	**119**	**24:10**	**5**	**0**	**1**	**1**	**0**	**0**	**0**	**0**
	NHL Totals		**149**	**14**	**42**	**56**	**107**	**4**	**1**	**4**	**219**	**6.4**		**0**	**0.0**	**73**	**201**	**21:54**	**9**	**0**	**2**	**2**	**2**	**0**	**0**	**0**

NCAA Championship All-Tournament Team (1997) • Hockey East First All-Star Team (1998) • NCAA East First All-American Team (1998) • NHL All-Rookie Team (1999)

POTOMSKI, Barry
(poh-TAWM-skee, BAIR-ree)

Left wing. Shoots left. 6'2", 215 lbs. Born, Windsor, Ont., November 24, 1972.

Season	Club	League	GP	G	A	Pts	PIM	PP	SH	GW	S	%	+/-	TF	F%	H	SB	Min	GP	G	A	Pts	PIM	PP	SH	GW
1988-89	Windsor	OMHA	56	24	22	46																				
1989-90	Tillsonburg Titans	OJHL-B	32	11	17	28	158																			
	London Knights	OHL	9	0	2	2	18																			
1990-91	London Knights	OHL	65	14	17	31	202												7	0	2	2	10			
1991-92	London Knights	OHL	61	19	32	51	224												10	5	1	6	22			
1992-93	Erie Panthers	ECHL	5	1	1	2	31																			
	Toledo Storm	ECHL	43	5	18	23	184												14	5	2	7	73			
1993-94	Toledo Storm	ECHL	13	9	4	13	81																			
	Adirondack	AHL	50	9	5	14	224												11	1	1	2	44			
1994-95	Phoenix	IHL	42	5	6	11	171																			
1995-96	**Los Angeles**	**NHL**	**33**	**3**	**2**	**5**	**104**	**1**	**0**	**0**	**23**	**13.0**	**–7**													
	Phoenix	IHL	24	5	2	7	74												3	1	0	1	8			
1996-97	**Los Angeles**	**NHL**	**26**	**3**	**2**	**5**	**93**	**0**	**0**	**1**	**18**	**16.7**	**–8**													
	Phoenix	IHL	28	2	11	13	58																			
1997-98	**San Jose**	**NHL**	**9**	**0**	**1**	**1**	**30**	**0**	**0**	**0**	**4**	**0.0**	**1**													
	Las Vegas	IHL	31	3	2	5	143												4	1	0	1	13			
1998-99	Adirondack	AHL	75	9	7	16	220												1	0	0	0	2			
99-2000	Long Beach	IHL	1	0	0	0	0																			
	San Diego Gulls	WCHL	51	13	30	43	211												9	4	4	8	12			
	NHL Totals		**68**	**6**	**5**	**11**	**227**	**1**	**0**	**1**	**45**	**13.3**														

Signed as a free agent by **LA Kings**, July 7, 1994. Signed as a free agent by **San Jose**, August 15, 1997. Signed as a free agent by **Detroit**, August 13, 1998. • Played w/ RHI's Anaheim Bullfrogs in 1993 (13-5-14-19-56).

POULIN, Patrick
(poo-LIHN, PAT-rihk) **MTL.**

Center. Shoots left. 6'1", 216 lbs. Born, Vanier, Que., April 23, 1973. Hartford's 1st choice, 9th overall, in 1991 Entry Draft.

Season	Club	League	GP	G	A	Pts	PIM	PP	SH	GW	S	%	+/-	TF	F%	H	SB	Min	GP	G	A	Pts	PIM	PP	SH	GW
1988-89	Ste-Foy Governors	QAAA	42	28	42	70	44												13	13	23	36	24			
1989-90	St-Hyacinthe	QMJHL	60	25	26	51	55												12	1	9	10	5			
1990-91	St-Hyacinthe	QMJHL	56	32	38	70	82												4	0	2	2	23			
1991-92	St-Hyacinthe	QMJHL	56	52	86	*138	58												5	2	2	4	4			
	Hartford	**NHL**	**1**	**0**	**0**	**0**	**2**	**0**	**0**	**0**	**0**	**0.0**	**–1**						**7**	**2**	**1**	**3**	**0**	**1**	**0**	**0**
	Springfield	AHL																	1	0	0	0	0			
1992-93	**Hartford**	**NHL**	**81**	**20**	**31**	**51**	**37**	**4**	**0**	**2**	**160**	**12.5**	**–19**													
1993-94	**Hartford**	**NHL**	**9**	**2**	**1**	**3**	**11**	**1**	**0**	**0**	**13**	**15.4**	**–8**													
	Chicago	**NHL**	**58**	**12**	**13**	**25**	**40**	**1**	**0**	**3**	**83**	**14.5**	**0**						**4**	**0**	**0**	**0**	**0**	**0**	**0**	**0**
1994-95	**Chicago**	**NHL**	**45**	**15**	**15**	**30**	**53**	**4**	**0**	**2**	**77**	**19.5**	**13**						**16**	**4**	**1**	**5**	**8**	**1**	**0**	**0**
1995-96	**Chicago**	**NHL**	**38**	**7**	**8**	**15**	**16**	**1**	**0**	**0**	**40**	**17.5**	**7**													
	Indianapolis Ice	IHL	1	0	1	1	0																			
	Tampa Bay	**NHL**	**8**	**0**	**1**	**1**	**0**	**0**	**0**	**0**	**11**	**0.0**	**0**						**2**	**0**	**0**	**0**	**0**	**0**	**0**	**0**
1996-97	**Tampa Bay**	**NHL**	**73**	**12**	**14**	**26**	**56**	**2**	**3**	**1**	**124**	**9.7**	**–16**													
1997-98	**Tampa Bay**	**NHL**	**44**	**2**	**7**	**9**	**19**	**0**	**0**	**0**	**49**	**4.1**	**–3**													
	Montreal	**NHL**	**34**	**4**	**6**	**10**	**8**	**0**	**1**	**1**	**39**	**10.3**	**–1**						**3**	**0**	**0**	**0**	**0**	**0**	**0**	**0**
1998-99	**Montreal**	**NHL**	**81**	**8**	**17**	**25**	**21**	**0**	**1**	**1**	**87**	**9.2**	**6**	**112**	**30.4**	**92**	**29**	**13:30**								
99-2000	**Montreal**	**NHL**	**82**	**10**	**5**	**15**	**17**	**0**	**1**	**2**	**82**	**12.2**	**–15**	**35**	**34.3**	**79**	**38**	**12:34**								
	NHL Totals		**554**	**92**	**118**	**210**	**280**	**13**	**6**	**12**	**765**	**12.0**		**147**	**31.3**	**171**	**67**	**13:02**	**32**	**6**	**2**	**8**	**8**	**2**	**0**	**0**

QMJHL First All-Star Team (1992) • Canadian Major Junior Player of the Year (1992)

Traded to **Chicago** by **Hartford** with Eric Weinrich for Steve Larmer and Bryan Marchment, November 2, 1993. Traded to **Tampa Bay** by **Chicago** with Igor Ulanov and Chicago's 2nd round choice (later traded to New Jersey - New Jersey selected Pierre Dagenais) in 1996 Entry Draft for Enrico Ciccone and Tampa Bay's 2nd round choice (Jeff Paul) in 1996 Entry Draft, March 20, 1996. Traded to **Montreal** by **Tampa Bay** with Mick Vukota and Igor Ulanov for Stephane Richer, Darcy Tucker and David Wilkie, January 15, 1998.

PRATT, Nolan
PRAT, NOH-lan) **COL.**

Defense. Shoots left. 6'2", 200 lbs. Born, Fort McMurray, Alta., August 14, 1975. Hartford's 4th choice, 115th overall, in 1993 Entry Draft.

Season	Club	League	GP	G	A	Pts	PIM	PP	SH	GW	S	%	+/-	TF	F%	H	SB	Min	GP	G	A	Pts	PIM	PP	SH	GW
1991-92	Portland	WHL	22	2	9	11	13												6	1	3	4	12			
1992-93	Portland	WHL	70	4	19	23	97												16	2	7	9	31			
1993-94	Portland	WHL	72	4	32	36	105												10	1	2	3	14			
1994-95	Portland	WHL	72	6	37	43	196												9	1	6	7	10			
1995-96	Springfield	AHL	62	2	6	8	72												2	0	0	0	0			
	Richmond	ECHL	4	1	0	1	2																			
1996-97	**Hartford**	**NHL**	**9**	**0**	**2**	**2**	**6**	**0**	**0**	**0**	**4**	**0.0**	**0**													
	Springfield	AHL	66	1	18	19	127												17	0	3	3	18			
1997-98	**Carolina**	**NHL**	**23**	**0**	**2**	**2**	**44**	**0**	**0**	**0**	**11**	**0.0**	**–2**													
	New Haven	AHL	54	3	15	18	135																			
1998-99	**Carolina**	**NHL**	**61**	**1**	**14**	**15**	**95**	**0**	**0**	**1**	**46**	**2.2**	**15**	**0**	**0.0**	**121**	**59**	**16:45**	**3**	**0**	**0**	**0**	**2**	**0**	**0**	**0**
99-2000	**Carolina**	**NHL**	**64**	**3**	**1**	**4**	**90**	**0**	**0**	**1**	**47**	**6.4**	**–22**	**0**	**0.0**	**155**	**74**	**19:10**								
	NHL Totals		**157**	**4**	**19**	**23**	**235**	**0**	**0**	**2**	**108**	**3.7**		**0**	**0.0**	**276**	**133**	**17:59**	**3**	**0**	**0**	**0**	**2**	**0**	**0**	**0**

Transferred to **Carolina** after **Hartford** franchise relocated, June 25, 1997. Traded to **Colorado** by **Carolina** with Carolina's 1st (Vaclav Nedorost) and 2nd (Jared Aulin) round choices in 2000 Entry Draft and Philadelphia's 2nd round choice (previously acquired, Colorado selected Argis Saviels) in 2000 Entry Draft for Sandis Ozolinsh and Columbus' 2nd round choice (previously acquired, Carolina selected Tomas Kurka) in 2000 Entry Draft, June 24, 2000.

PRIMEAU, Keith
(PREE-moh, KEETH) **PHI.**

Center. Shoots left. 6'4", 210 lbs. Born, Toronto, Ont., November 24, 1971. Detroit's 1st choice, 3rd overall, in 1990 Entry Draft.

Season	Club	League	GP	G	A	Pts	PIM	PP	SH	GW	S	%	+/-	TF	F%	H	SB	Min	GP	G	A	Pts	PIM	PP	SH	GW
1986-87	Whitby Flyers	OMHA	65	69	80	149	116																			
1987-88	Hamilton Kilty B's	OJHL-B	19	19	17	36	16																			
	Hamilton Hawks	OHL	47	6	6	12	69												11	0	2	2	2			
1988-89	Niagara Falls	OHL	48	20	35	55	56												17	9	16	25	12			
1989-90	Niagara Falls	OHL	65	*57	70	*127	97												16	*16	17	*33	49			
1990-91	**Detroit**	**NHL**	**58**	**3**	**12**	**15**	**106**	**0**	**0**	**1**	**33**	**9.1**	**–12**						**5**	**1**	**1**	**2**	**25**	**0**	**0**	**0**
	Adirondack	AHL	6	3	5	8	8																			
1991-92	**Detroit**	**NHL**	**35**	**6**	**10**	**16**	**83**	**0**	**0**	**0**	**27**	**22.2**	**9**						**11**	**0**	**0**	**0**	**14**	**0**	**0**	**0**
	Adirondack	AHL	42	21	24	45	89												9	1	7	8	27			
1992-93	**Detroit**	**NHL**	**73**	**15**	**17**	**32**	**152**	**4**	**1**	**2**	**75**	**20.0**	**–6**						**7**	**0**	**2**	**2**	**26**	**0**	**0**	**0**
1993-94	**Detroit**	**NHL**	**78**	**31**	**42**	**73**	**173**	**7**	**3**	**4**	**155**	**20.0**	**34**						**7**	**0**	**2**	**2**	**6**	**0**	**0**	**0**
1994-95	**Detroit**	**NHL**	**45**	**15**	**27**	**42**	**99**	**1**	**0**	**3**	**96**	**15.6**	**17**						**17**	**4**	**5**	**9**	**45**	**2**	**0**	**0**
1995-96	**Detroit**	**NHL**	**74**	**27**	**25**	**52**	**168**	**6**	**2**	**7**	**150**	**18.0**	**19**						**17**	**1**	**4**	**5**	**28**	**0**	**0**	**0**
1996-97	**Hartford**	**NHL**	**75**	**26**	**25**	**51**	**161**	**6**	**3**	**2**	**169**	**15.4**	**–3**													

			Regular Season																Playoffs							
Season	Club	League	GP	G	A	Pts	PIM	PP	SH	GW	S	%	+/–	TF	F%	H	SB	Min	GP	G	A	Pts	PIM	PP	SH	GW
1997-98	Carolina	NHL	81	26	37	63	110	7	3	2	180	14.4	19	....	....	....	....	....	....	....	....	....	....	....	....	....
	Canada	Olympics	6	2	1	3	4	....	....	....	....	....	....	....	....	....	....	....	....	....	....	....	....	....	....	....
1998-99	Carolina	NHL	78	30	32	62	75	9	1	5	178	16.9	8	1823	53.5	231	62	21:21	6	0	3	3	6	0	0	0
99-2000	Philadelphia	NHL	23	7	10	17	31	1	0	1	51	13.7	10	478	54.2	37	18	17:38	18	2	11	13	13	0	0	1
	NHL Totals		620	186	237	423	1158	41	13	27	1114	16.7		2301	53.6	268	80	20:30	88	8	28	36	163	2	0	1

OHL Second All-Star Team (1990) • Played in NHL All-Star Game (1999)

Traded to **Hartford** by **Detroit** with Paul Coffey and Detroit's 1st round choice (Nikos Tselios) in 1997 Entry Draft for Brendan Shanahan and Brian Glynn, October 9, 1996. Transferred to **Carolina** after **Hartford** franchise relocated, June 25, 1997. • Sat out majority of 1999-2000 season in contract dispute with Carolina management. Traded to **Philadelphia** by **Carolina** with Carolina's 5th round choice (later traded to NY Islanders - NY Islanders selected Kristofer Ottoston) in 2000 Entry Draft for Rod Brind'Amour, Jean-Marc Pelletier and Philadelphia's 2nd round choice (later traded to Colorado - Colorado selected Argis Saviels) in 2000 Entry Draft, January 23, 2000.

PRIMEAU, Wayne

(PREE-moh, WAYN) **T.B.**

Center. Shoots left. 6'3", 220 lbs. Born, Scarborough, Ont., June 4, 1976. Buffalo's 1st choice, 17th overall, in 1994 Entry Draft.

Season	Club	League	GP	G	A	Pts	PIM	PP	SH	GW	S	%	+/–	TF	F%	H	SB	Min	GP	G	A	Pts	PIM	PP	SH	GW
1991-92	Whitby Flyers	OMHA	63	36	50	86	96	....	....	....	....	....	....	....	....	....	....	....	....	....	....	....	....	....	....	....
1992-93	Owen Sound	OHL	66	10	27	37	108	....	....	....	....	....	....	....	....	....	....	....	8	1	4	5	0	....	....	....
1993-94	Owen Sound	OHL	65	25	50	75	75	....	....	....	....	....	....	....	....	....	....	....	9	1	6	7	8	....	....	....
1994-95	Owen Sound	OHL	66	34	62	96	84	....	....	....	....	....	....	....	....	....	....	....	10	4	9	13	15	....	....	....
	Buffalo	NHL	1	1	0	1	0	0	0	1	2	50.0	–2	....	....	....	....	....	....	....	....	....	....	....	....	....
1995-96	Owen Sound	OHL	28	15	29	44	52	....	....	....	....	....	....	....	....	....	....	....	....	....	....	....	....	....	....	....
	Oshawa Generals	OHL	24	12	13	25	33	....	....	....	....	....	....	....	....	....	....	....	3	2	3	5	2	....	....	....
	Buffalo	NHL	2	0	0	0	0	0	0	0	0	0.0	0	....	....	....	....	....	....	....	....	....	....	....	....	....
	Rochester	AHL	8	2	3	5	6	....	....	....	....	....	....	....	....	....	....	....	17	3	1	4	11	....	....	....
1996-97	Buffalo	NHL	45	2	4	6	64	1	0	0	25	8.0	–2	....	....	....	....	....	9	0	0	0	6	0	0	0
	Rochester	AHL	24	9	5	14	27	....	....	....	....	....	....	....	....	....	....	....	1	0	0	0	0	....	....	....
1997-98	Buffalo	NHL	69	6	6	12	87	2	0	1	51	11.8	9	....	....	....	....	....	14	1	3	4	6	0	0	0
1998-99	Buffalo	NHL	67	5	8	13	38	0	0	0	55	9.1	–6	529	48.6	74	15	10:19	19	3	4	7	6	1	0	0
99-2000	Buffalo	NHL	41	5	7	12	38	2	0	1	40	12.5	–8	430	45.6	47	8	11:03	....	....	....	....	....	....	....	....
	Tampa Bay	NHL	17	2	3	5	25	0	0	0	35	5.7	–4	290	45.5	26	9	14:21	....	....	....	....	....	....	....	....
	NHL Totals		242	21	28	49	252	5	0	3	208	10.1		1249	46.8	147	32	11:06	42	4	7	11	18	1	0	0

Traded to **Tampa Bay** by **Buffalo** with Cory Sarich, Brian Holzinger and Buffalo's 3rd round choice (Alexandre Kharitonov) in 2000 Entry Draft for Chris Gratton and Tampa Bay's 2nd round choice in 2001 Entry Draft, March 9, 2000.

PROBERT, Bob

(PROH-buhrt, BAWB) **CHI.**

Left wing. Shoots left. 6'3", 225 lbs. Born, Windsor, Ont., June 5, 1965. Detroit's 3rd choice, 46th overall, in 1983 Entry Draft.

Season	Club	League	GP	G	A	Pts	PIM	PP	SH	GW	S	%	+/–	TF	F%	H	SB	Min	GP	G	A	Pts	PIM	PP	SH	GW
1981-82	Windsor 240	OMHA	55	60	40	100	40	....	....	....	....	....	....	....	....	....	....	....	....	....	....	....	....	....	....	....
1982-83	Brantford	OHL	51	12	16	28	133	....	....	....	....	....	....	....	....	....	....	....	8	2	2	4	23	....	....	....
1983-84	Brantford	OHL	65	35	28	63	189	....	....	....	....	....	....	....	....	....	....	....	6	0	3	3	16	....	....	....
1984-85	Hamilton Hawks	OHL	4	0	1	1	21	....	....	....	....	....	....	....	....	....	....	....	....	....	....	....	....	....	....	....
	Sault Ste. Marie	OHL	44	20	52	72	172	....	....	....	....	....	....	....	....	....	....	....	15	6	11	17	60	....	....	....
1985-86	Detroit	NHL	44	8	13	21	186	3	0	0	46	17.4	–14	....	....	....	....	....	....	....	....	....	....	....	....	....
	Adirondack	AHL	32	12	15	27	152	....	....	....	....	....	....	....	....	....	....	....	10	2	3	5	68	....	....	....
1986-87	Detroit	NHL	63	13	11	24	221	2	0	0	56	23.2	–6	....	....	....	....	....	16	3	4	7	63	1	0	1
	Adirondack	AHL	7	1	4	5	15	....	....	....	....	....	....	....	....	....	....	....	....	....	....	....	....	....	....	....
1987-88	Detroit	NHL	74	29	33	62	*398	15	0	5	126	23.0	16	....	....	....	....	....	16	8	13	21	51	5	0	1
1988-89	Detroit	NHL	25	4	2	6	106	1	0	0	23	17.4	–11	....	....	....	....	....	....	....	....	....	....	....	....	....
1989-90	Detroit	NHL	4	3	0	3	21	0	0	1	12	25.0	0	....	....	....	....	....	....	....	....	....	....	....	....	....
1990-91	Detroit	NHL	55	16	23	39	315	4	0	3	88	18.2	–3	....	....	....	....	....	6	1	2	3	50	0	0	0
1991-92	Detroit	NHL	63	20	24	44	276	8	0	1	96	20.8	16	....	....	....	....	....	11	1	6	7	28	0	0	0
1992-93	Detroit	NHL	80	14	29	43	292	6	0	3	128	10.9	–9	....	....	....	....	....	7	0	3	3	10	0	0	0
1993-94	Detroit	NHL	66	7	10	17	275	1	0	0	105	6.7	–1	....	....	....	....	....	7	1	1	2	8	0	0	0
1994-95	Chicago	NHL	DID NOT PLAY – SUSPENDED																							
1995-96	Chicago	NHL	78	19	21	40	237	1	0	3	97	19.6	15	....	....	....	....	....	10	0	2	2	23	0	0	0
1996-97	Chicago	NHL	82	9	14	23	326	1	0	3	111	8.1	–3	....	....	....	....	....	6	2	1	3	41	0	0	0
1997-98	Chicago	NHL	14	2	1	3	48	2	0	0	18	11.1	–7	....	....	....	....	....	....	....	....	....	....	....	....	....
1998-99	Chicago	NHL	78	7	14	21	206	0	0	3	87	8.0	–11	45	51.1	105	12	10:38	....	....	....	....	....	....	....	....
99-2000	Chicago	NHL	69	4	11	15	114	0	0	0	38	10.5	10	32	40.6	87	15	10:28	....	....	....	....	....	....	....	....
	NHL Totals		795	155	206	361	3021	44	0	22	1031	15.0		77	46.8	192	27	10:33	79	16	32	48	274	6	0	2

Played in NHL All-Star Game (1988)

Signed as a free agent by **Chicago**, July 23, 1994. • Suspended for entire 1994-95 season for violating NHL substance abuse policy, September 2, 1994. • Missed majority of 1997-98 season recovering from rotator cuff injury suffered in game vs. Detroit, November 16, 1997.

PROCHAZKA, Martin

(pro-HAHS-kah, MAHR-tihn)

Right wing. Shoots right. 5'11", 180 lbs. Born, Slany, Czech., March 3, 1972. Toronto's 6th choice, 135th overall, in 1991 Entry Draft.

Season	Club	League	GP	G	A	Pts	PIM	PP	SH	GW	S	%	+/–	TF	F%	H	SB	Min	GP	G	A	Pts	PIM	PP	SH	GW
1989-90	Poldi Kladno	Czech.	49	18	12	30	....	....	....	....	....	....	....	....	....	....	....	....	....	....	....	....	....	....	....	....
1990-91	Poldi Kladno	Czech.	50	19	10	29	21	....	....	....	....	....	....	....	....	....	....	....	....	....	....	....	....	....	....	....
1991-92	Dukla Jihlava	Czech.	44	18	11	29	2	....	....	....	....	....	....	....	....	....	....	....	....	....	....	....	....	....	....	....
1992-93	Poldi Kladno	Czech.	46	26	12	38	....	....	....	....	....	....	....	....	....	....	....	....	....	....	....	....	....	....	....	....
1993-94	Poldi Kladno	Cze-Rep	43	24	16	40	0	....	....	....	....	....	....	....	....	....	....	....	2	2	0	2	....	....	....	....
1994-95	Poldi Kladno	Cze-Rep	41	25	33	58	18	....	....	....	....	....	....	....	....	....	....	....	11	8	4	12	4	....	....	....
1995-96	Poldi Kladno	Cze-Rep	37	15	27	42	....	....	....	....	....	....	....	....	....	....	....	....	8	2	4	6	....	....	....	....
1996-97	AIK Solna	Sweden	49	16	23	39	38	....	....	....	....	....	....	....	....	....	....	....	7	2	3	5	8	....	....	....
1997-98	Toronto	NHL	29	2	4	6	8	0	0	0	40	5.0	–1	....	....	....	....	....	....	....	....	....	....	....	....	....
	Czech-Republic	Olympics	6	1	1	2	0	....	....	....	....	....	....	....	....	....	....	....	....	....	....	....	....	....	....	....
1998-99	Petra Vsetin	Cze-Rep	47	20	29	49	12	....	....	....	....	....	....	....	....	....	....	....	12	*10	9	*19	....	....	....	....
99-2000	Atlanta	NHL	3	0	1	1	0	0	0	0	5	0.0	–1	0	0.0	2	2	16:37	....	....	....	....	....	....	....	....
	Slovnaft Vsetin	Cze-Rep	31	10	10	20	16	....	....	....	....	....	....	....	....	....	....	....	9	2	0	2	0	....	....	....
	NHL Totals		32	2	5	7	8	0	0	0	45	4.4		0	0.0	2	2	16:37	....	....	....	....	....	....	....	....

Traded to **Atlanta** by **Toronto** for Atlanta's 6th round choice in 2001 Entry Draft, July 15, 1999.

PROKOPEC, Mike

(PROH-koh-pehk, MIGHK)

Right wing. Shoots right. 6'2", 190 lbs. Born, Toronto, Ont., May 17, 1974. Chicago's 7th choice, 161st overall, in 1992 Entry Draft.

Season	Club	League	GP	G	A	Pts	PIM	PP	SH	GW	S	%	+/–	TF	F%	H	SB	Min	GP	G	A	Pts	PIM	PP	SH	GW
1990-91	Barrie Colts	OJHL-B	39	17	20	37	63	....	....	....	....	....	....	....	....	....	....	....	....	....	....	....	....	....	....	....
1991-92	Cornwall Royals	OHL	59	12	15	27	75	....	....	....	....	....	....	....	....	....	....	....	6	0	0	0	0	....	....	....
1992-93	Newmarket	OHL	40	6	14	20	70	....	....	....	....	....	....	....	....	....	....	....	....	....	....	....	....	....	....	....
	Guelph Storm	OHL	28	10	14	24	27	....	....	....	....	....	....	....	....	....	....	....	5	1	0	1	14	....	....	....
1993-94	Guelph Storm	OHL	66	52	58	110	93	....	....	....	....	....	....	....	....	....	....	....	9	12	4	16	17	....	....	....
1994-95	Indianapolis Ice	IHL	70	21	12	33	80	....	....	....	....	....	....	....	....	....	....	....	....	....	....	....	....	....	....	....
1995-96	Chicago	NHL	9	0	0	0	5	0	0	0	5	0.0	–4	....	....	....	....	....	....	....	....	....	....	....	....	....
	Indianapolis Ice	IHL	67	18	22	40	131	....	....	....	....	....	....	....	....	....	....	....	5	2	0	2	4	....	....	....
1996-97	Chicago	NHL	6	0	0	0	6	0	0	0	2	0.0	–1	....	....	....	....	....	....	....	....	....	....	....	....	....
	Indianapolis Ice	IHL	57	13	18	31	143	....	....	....	....	....	....	....	....	....	....	....	....	....	....	....	....	....	....	....
	Detroit Vipers	IHL	3	2	0	2	4	....	....	....	....	....	....	....	....	....	....	....	8	2	1	3	14	....	....	....
1997-98	Worcester	AHL	62	21	25	46	112	....	....	....	....	....	....	....	....	....	....	....	11	1	2	3	10	....	....	....
1998-99	Detroit Vipers	IHL	75	25	28	53	125	....	....	....	....	....	....	....	....	....	....	....	10	3	6	9	26	....	....	....
99-2000	Manitoba Moose	IHL	68	23	21	44	100	....	....	....	....	....	....	....	....	....	....	....	....	....	....	....	....	....	....	....
	NHL Totals		15	0	0	0	11	0	0	0	7	0.0		....	....	....	....	....	....	....	....	....	....	....	....	....

Traded to **Ottawa** by **Chicago** for Denis Chasse, the rights to Kevin Bolibruck and future considerations, March 18, 1997. Signed as a free agent by **Manitoba** (IHL), August 24, 1999.

PRONGER, Chris
(PRAHN-guhr, KRIHS) **ST.L.**

Defense. Shoots left. 6'6", 220 lbs. Born, Dryden, Ont., October 10, 1974. Hartford's 1st choice, 2nd overall, in 1993 Entry Draft.

			Regular Season																Playoffs							
Season	Club	League	GP	G	A	Pts	PIM	PP	SH	GW	S	%	+/-	TF	F%	H	SB	Min	GP	G	A	Pts	PIM	PP	SH	GW
1990-91	Stratford Cullitons	OJHL-B	48	15	37	52	132																			
1991-92	Peterborough	OHL	63	17	45	62	90												10	1	8	9	28			
1992-93	Peterborough	OHL	61	15	62	77	108												21	15	25	40	51			
1993-94	**Hartford**	**NHL**	**81**	**5**	**25**	**30**	**113**	**2**	**0**	**0**	**174**	**2.9**	**-3**													
1994-95	**Hartford**	**NHL**	**43**	**5**	**9**	**14**	**54**	**3**	**0**	**1**	**94**	**5.3**	**-12**													
1995-96	**St. Louis**	**NHL**	**78**	**7**	**18**	**25**	**110**	**3**	**1**	**1**	**138**	**5.1**	**-18**						**13**	**1**	**5**	**6**	**16**	**0**	**0**	**0**
1996-97	**St. Louis**	**NHL**	**79**	**11**	**24**	**35**	**143**	**4**	**0**	**0**	**147**	**7.5**	**15**						**6**	**1**	**1**	**2**	**22**	**0**	**0**	**0**
1997-98	**St. Louis**	**NHL**	**81**	**9**	**27**	**36**	**180**	**1**	**0**	**2**	**145**	**6.2**	**47**						**10**	**1**	**9**	**10**	**26**	**0**	**0**	**0**
	Canada	Olympics	6	0	0	0	4																			
1998-99	**St. Louis**	**NHL**	**67**	**13**	**33**	**46**	**113**	**8**	**0**	**0**	**172**	**7.6**	**3**	**0**	**0.0**	**132**	**119**	**30:36**	**13**	**1**	**4**	**5**	**28**	**1**	**0**	**0**
99-2000	**St. Louis**	**NHL**	**79**	**14**	**48**	**62**	**92**	**8**	**0**	**3**	**192**	**7.3**	**52**	**1**	**0.0**	**106**	**185**	**30:14**	**7**	**3**	**4**	**7**	**32**	**2**	**0**	**2**
	NHL Totals		**508**	**64**	**184**	**248**	**805**	**29**	**1**	**7**	**1062**	**6.0**		**1**	**0.0**	**238**	**304**	**30:24**	**49**	**7**	**23**	**30**	**124**	**3**	**0**	**2**

OHL First All-Star Team (1993) • Canadian Major Junior First All-Star Team (1993) • Canadian Major Junior Defenseman of the Year (1993) • NHL All-Rookie Team (1994) • NHL Second All-Star Team (1998) • Won Bud Ice Plus/Minus Award (1998) • NHL First All-Star Team (2000) • Won James Norris Trophy (2000) • Won Hart Trophy (2000) • Played in NHL All-Star Game (1999, 2000)

Traded to **St. Louis** by **Hartford** for Brendan Shanahan, July 27, 1995.

PRONGER, Sean
(PRAHN-guhr, SHAWN) **BOS.**

Center. Shoots left. 6'2", 205 lbs. Born, Dryden, Ont., November 30, 1972. Vancouver's 3rd choice, 51st overall, in 1991 Entry Draft.

Season	Club	League	GP	G	A	Pts	PIM	PP	SH	GW	S	%	+/-	TF	F%	H	SB	Min	GP	G	A	Pts	PIM	PP	SH	GW
1988-89	Kenora Boise	NOJHA	33	38	30	68																				
1989-90	Thunder Bay	USHL	48	18	34	52	61																			
1990-91	Bowling Green	CCHA	40	3	7	10	30																			
1991-92	Bowling Green	CCHA	34	9	7	16	28																			
1992-93	Bowling Green	CCHA	39	23	23	46	35																			
1993-94	Bowling Green	CCHA	38	17	17	34	38																			
1994-95	Knoxville	ECHL	34	18	23	41	55																			
	Greensboro	ECHL	2	0	2	2	0																			
	San Diego Gulls	IHL	8	0	0	0	2																			
1995-96	**Anaheim**	**NHL**	**7**	**0**	**1**	**1**	**6**	**0**	**0**	**0**	**3**	**0.0**	**0**													
	Baltimore Bandits	AHL	72	16	17	33	61												12	3	7	10	16			
1996-97	**Anaheim**	**NHL**	**39**	**7**	**7**	**14**	**20**	**1**	**0**	**1**	**43**	**16.3**	**6**						**9**	**0**	**2**	**2**	**4**	**0**	**0**	**0**
	Baltimore Bandits	AHL	41	26	17	43	17																			
1997-98	**Anaheim**	**NHL**	**62**	**5**	**15**	**20**	**30**	**1**	**0**	**2**	**68**	**7.4**	**-9**													
	Pittsburgh	**NHL**	**5**	**1**	**0**	**1**	**2**	**0**	**0**	**1**	**5**	**20.0**	**-1**						**5**	**0**	**0**	**0**	**4**	**0**	**0**	**0**
1998-99	**Pittsburgh**	**NHL**	**2**	**0**	**0**	**0**	**0**	**0**	**0**	**0**	**3**	**0.0**	**0**	**4**	**75.0**	**2**	**0**	**8:48**								
	Houston Aeros	IHL	16	11	7	18	32																			
	NY Rangers	**NHL**	**14**	**0**	**3**	**3**	**4**	**0**	**0**	**0**	**3**	**0.0**	**-3**	**15**	**20.0**	**12**	**1**	**6:28**								
	Los Angeles	**NHL**	**13**	**0**	**1**	**1**	**4**	**0**	**0**	**0**	**8**	**0.0**	**2**	**20**	**35.0**	**13**	**5**	**11:00**								
99-2000	**Boston**	**NHL**	**11**	**0**	**1**	**1**	**13**	**0**	**0**	**0**	**7**	**0.0**	**-4**	**116**	**46.6**	**28**	**3**	**10:47**								
	Providence Bruins	AHL	51	11	18	29	26																			
	Manitoba Moose	IHL	14	3	5	8	21												2	0	1	1	2			
	NHL Totals		**153**	**13**	**28**	**41**	**79**	**2**	**0**	**4**	**140**	**9.3**		**155**	**43.2**	**55**	**9**	**9:15**	**14**	**0**	**2**	**2**	**8**	**0**	**0**	**0**

Signed as a free agent by **Anaheim**, February 14, 1995. Traded to **Pittsburgh** by **Anaheim** for the rights to Patrick Lalime, March 24, 1998. Traded to **NY Rangers** by **Pittsburgh** with Chris Tamer and Petr Nedved for Alexei Kovalev and Harry York, November 25, 1998. Traded to **Los Angeles** by **NY Rangers** for Eric Lacroix, February 12, 1999. Signed as a free agent by **Boston**, August 25, 1999. Traded to **Manitoba** (IHL) by **Providence** (AHL) with Keith McCambridge for Terry Hollinger, March 16, 2000 with Boston retaining Pronger's NHL rights.

PROSPAL, Vaclav
(PRAWS-pahl, VAHT-slahv) **OTT.**

Center. Shoots left. 6'2", 195 lbs. Born, Ceske-Budejovice, Czech., February 17, 1975. Philadelphia's 2nd choice, 71st overall, in 1993 Entry Draft.

Season	Club	League	GP	G	A	Pts	PIM	PP	SH	GW	S	%	+/-	TF	F%	H	SB	Min	GP	G	A	Pts	PIM	PP	SH	GW
1991-92	MC Budjevoice	Czech-Jr.	36	16	16	32	12																			
1992-93	MC Budejovice	Czech-Jr.	32	26	31	57	24																			
1993-94	Hershey Bears	AHL	55	14	21	35	38												2	0	0	0	2			
1994-95	Hershey Bears	AHL	69	13	32	45	36												2	1	0	1	4			
1995-96	Hershey Bears	AHL	68	15	36	51	59												5	2	4	6	2			
1996-97	**Philadelphia**	**NHL**	**18**	**5**	**10**	**15**	**4**	**0**	**0**	**0**	**35**	**14.3**	**3**						**5**	**1**	**3**	**4**	**4**	**0**	**0**	**0**
	Philadelphia	AHL	63	32	63	95	70																			
1997-98	**Philadelphia**	**NHL**	**41**	**5**	**13**	**18**	**17**	**4**	**0**	**0**	**60**	**8.3**	**-10**													
	Ottawa	**NHL**	**15**	**1**	**6**	**7**	**4**	**0**	**0**	**0**	**28**	**3.6**	**-1**						**6**	**0**	**0**	**0**	**0**	**0**	**0**	**0**
1998-99	**Ottawa**	**NHL**	**79**	**10**	**26**	**36**	**58**	**2**	**0**	**3**	**114**	**8.8**	**8**	**997**	**56.2**	**202**	**20**	**13:03**	**4**	**0**	**0**	**0**	**0**	**0**	**0**	**0**
99-2000	**Ottawa**	**NHL**	**79**	**22**	**33**	**55**	**40**	**5**	**0**	**4**	**204**	**10.8**	**-2**	**1331**	**49.6**	**92**	**26**	**16:26**	**6**	**0**	**4**	**4**	**4**	**0**	**0**	**0**
	NHL Totals		**232**	**43**	**88**	**131**	**123**	**11**	**0**	**7**	**441**	**9.8**		**2328**	**52.4**	**294**	**46**	**14:45**	**21**	**1**	**7**	**8**	**8**	**0**	**0**	**0**

AHL First All-Star Team (1997)

Traded to **Ottawa** by **Philadelphia** with Pat Falloon and Dallas' 2nd round choice (previously acquired, Ottawa selected Chris Bala) in 1998 Entry Draft for Alexandre Daigle, January 17, 1998.

PRPIC, Joel
(puhr-PIHCH, JOHL) **COL.**

Center. Shoots left. 6'7", 225 lbs. Born, Sudbury, Ont., September 25, 1974. Boston's 9th choice, 233rd overall, in 1993 Entry Draft.

Season	Club	League	GP	G	A	Pts	PIM	PP	SH	GW	S	%	+/-	TF	F%	H	SB	Min	GP	G	A	Pts	PIM	PP	SH	GW
1992-93	Waterloo Siskins	OJHL-B	45	17	43	60	160																			
1993-94	St. Lawrence	ECAC	31	2	4	6	90																			
1994-95	St. Lawrence	ECAC	32	7	10	17	62																			
1995-96	St. Lawrence	ECAC	32	3	10	13	77																			
1996-97	St. Lawrence	ECAC	34	10	8	18	57																			
1997-98	**Boston**	**NHL**	**1**	**0**	**0**	**0**	**2**	**0**	**0**	**0**	**0**	**0.0**	**0**													
	Providence Bruins	AHL	73	17	18	35	53																			
1998-99	Providence Bruins	AHL	75	14	16	30	163												18	4	6	10	48			
99-2000	**Boston**	**NHL**	**14**	**0**	**3**	**3**	**0**	**0**	**0**	**0**	**13**	**0.0**	**-6**	**117**	**52.1**	**10**	**2**	**6:47**								
	Providence Bruins	AHL	70	9	20	29	143												14	3	4	7	58			
	NHL Totals		**15**	**0**	**3**	**3**	**2**	**0**	**0**	**0**	**13**	**0.0**		**117**	**52.1**	**10**	**2**	**6:47**								

Signed as a free agent by **Colorado**, August, 2000.

PURINTON, Dale
(PUHR-ihn-TOHN, DAYL) **NYR**

Defense. Shoots left. 6'3", 214 lbs. Born, Fort Wayne, IN, October 11, 1976. NY Rangers' 5th choice, 117th overall, in 1995 Entry Draft.

Season	Club	League	GP	G	A	Pts	PIM	PP	SH	GW	S	%	+/-	TF	F%	H	SB	Min	GP	G	A	Pts	PIM	PP	SH	GW
1992-93	Moose Jaw	SAHA	34	1	16	17	107																			
	Moose Jaw	WHL	2	0	0	0	2																			
1993-94	Vernon Lakers	BCJHL	42	1	6	7	194																			
1994-95	Tacoma Rockets	WHL	65	0	8	8	291												3	0	0	0	13			
1995-96	Kelowna Rockets	WHL	22	1	4	5	88																			
	Lethbridge	WHL	37	3	6	9	144												4	1	1	2	25			
1996-97	Lethbridge	WHL	51	6	26	32	254												18	3	5	8	*88			
1997-98	Hartford	AHL	17	0	0	0	95																			
	Charlotte	ECHL	34	3	5	8	186																			
1998-99	Hartford	AHL	45	1	3	4	306												7	0	2	2	24			
99-2000	**NY Rangers**	**NHL**	**1**	**0**	**0**	**0**	**7**	**0**	**0**	**0**	**1**	**0.0**	**-1**	**0**	**0.0**	**1**	**1**	**12:45**								
	Hartford	AHL	62	4	4	8	415												23	0	3	3	*87			
	NHL Totals		**1**	**0**	**0**	**0**	**7**	**0**	**0**	**0**	**1**	**0.0**		**0**	**0.0**	**1**	**1**	**12:45**								

PUSHOR, Jamie

(PUH-shohr, JAY-mee) **CBJ**

Defense. Shoots right. 6'3", 218 lbs. Born, Lethbridge, Alta., February 11, 1973. Detroit's 2nd choice, 32nd overall, in 1991 Entry Draft.

			Regular Season																Playoffs							
Season	Club	League	GP	G	A	Pts	PIM	PP	SH	GW	S	%	+/-	TF	F%	H	SB	Min	GP	G	A	Pts	PIM	PP	SH	GW
1988-89	Lethbridge	AAHA	37	1	8	9	20	....	....	....	....	....	....	....	....	....	....	....	....	....	....	....	....	....	....	....
	Lethbridge	WHL	2	0	0	0	0	....	....	....	....	....	....	....	....	....	....	....	....	....	....	....	....	....	....	....
1989-90	Lethbridge	AAHA	35	6	27	33	92	....	....	....	....	....	....	....	....	....	....	....	....	....	....	....	....	....	....	....
	Lethbridge	WHL	10	0	2	2	2	....	....	....	....	....	....	....	....	....	....	....	16	0	0	0	63	....	....	....
1990-91	Lethbridge	WHL	71	1	13	14	202	....	....	....	....	....	....	....	....	....	....	....	....	....	....	....	....	....	....	....
1991-92	Lethbridge	WHL	49	2	15	17	232	....	....	....	....	....	....	....	....	....	....	....	5	0	0	0	33	....	....	....
1992-93	Lethbridge	WHL	72	6	22	28	200	....	....	....	....	....	....	....	....	....	....	....	4	0	1	1	9	....	....	....
1993-94	Adirondack	AHL	73	1	17	18	124	....	....	....	....	....	....	....	....	....	....	....	12	0	0	0	22	....	....	....
1994-95	Adirondack	AHL	58	2	11	13	129	....	....	....	....	....	....	....	....	....	....	....	4	0	1	1	0	....	....	....
1995-96	**Detroit**	**NHL**	**5**	**0**	**1**	**1**	**17**	**0**	**0**	**0**	**6**	**0.0**	**2**	....	....	....	....	....	....	....	....	....	....	....	....	....
	Adirondack	AHL	65	2	16	18	126	....	....	....	....	....	....	....	....	....	....	....	3	0	0	0	5	....	....	....
1996-97♦	**Detroit**	**NHL**	**75**	**4**	**7**	**11**	**129**	**0**	**0**	**0**	**63**	**6.3**	**1**	....	....	....	....	....	**5**	**0**	**1**	**1**	**5**	**0**	**0**	**0**
1997-98	**Detroit**	**NHL**	**54**	**2**	**5**	**7**	**71**	**0**	**0**	**0**	**43**	**4.7**	**2**	....	....	....	....	....	....	....	....	....	....	....	....	....
	Anaheim	**NHL**	**10**	**0**	**2**	**2**	**10**	**0**	**0**	**0**	**8**	**0.0**	**1**	....	....	....	....	....	....	....	....	....	....	....	....	....
1998-99	**Anaheim**	**NHL**	**70**	**1**	**2**	**3**	**112**	**0**	**0**	**0**	**75**	**1.3**	**-20**	**0**	**0.0**	**110**	**153**	**19:16**	**4**	**0**	**0**	**0**	**6**	**0**	**0**	**0**
99-2000	**Dallas**	**NHL**	**62**	**0**	**8**	**8**	**53**	**0**	**0**	**0**	**27**	**0.0**	**0**	**0**	**0.0**	**99**	**43**	**11:36**	**5**	**0**	**0**	**0**	**5**	**0**	**0**	**0**
	NHL Totals		**276**	**7**	**25**	**32**	**392**	**0**	**0**	**0**	**222**	**3.2**		**0**	**0.0**	**209**	**196**	**15:40**	**14**	**0**	**1**	**1**	**16**	**0**	**0**	**0**

Traded to **Anaheim** by **Detroit** with Detroit's 4th round choice (Viktor Wallin) in 1998 Entry Draft for Dmitri Mironov, March 24, 1998. Claimed by **Atlanta** from **Anaheim** in Expansion Draft, June 25, 1999. Traded to **Dallas** by **Atlanta** for Jason Botterill, July 15, 1999. Selected by **Columbus** from **Dallas** in Expansion Draft, June 23, 2000.

QUINT, Deron

(KWIHNT, DAIR-ohn) **CBJ**

Defense. Shoots left. 6'2", 219 lbs. Born, Durham, NH, March 12, 1976. Winnipeg's 1st choice, 30th overall, in 1994 Entry Draft.

			Regular Season																Playoffs							
Season	Club	League	GP	G	A	Pts	PIM	PP	SH	GW	S	%	+/-	TF	F%	H	SB	Min	GP	G	A	Pts	PIM	PP	SH	GW
1990-91	Cardigan High	Hi-School	31	67	54	121	....	....	....	....	....	....	....	....	....	....	....	....	....	....	....	....	....	....	....	....
1991-92	Cardigan High	Hi-School	21	111	58	169	....	....	....	....	....	....	....	....	....	....	....	....	....	....	....	....	....	....	....	....
1992-93	Tabor Academy	Hi-School	28	15	26	41	30	....	....	....	....	....	....	....	....	....	....	....	1	0	2	2	0	....	....	....
1993-94	Seattle T-Birds	WHL	63	15	29	44	47	....	....	....	....	....	....	....	....	....	....	....	9	4	12	16	8	....	....	....
1994-95	Seattle T-Birds	WHL	65	29	60	89	82	....	....	....	....	....	....	....	....	....	....	....	3	1	2	3	6	....	....	....
1995-96	**Winnipeg**	**NHL**	**51**	**5**	**13**	**18**	**22**	**2**	**0**	**0**	**97**	**5.2**	**-2**	....	....	....	....	....	....	....	....	....	....	....	....	....
	Springfield	AHL	11	2	3	5	4	....	....	....	....	....	....	....	....	....	....	....	10	2	3	5	6	....	....	....
	Seattle T-Birds	WHL	....	....	....	....	....	....	....	....	....	....	....	....	....	....	....	....	5	4	1	5	6	....	....	....
1996-97	**Phoenix**	**NHL**	**27**	**3**	**11**	**14**	**4**	**1**	**0**	**0**	**63**	**4.8**	**-4**	....	....	....	....	....	**7**	**0**	**2**	**2**	**0**	**0**	**0**	**0**
	Springfield	AHL	43	6	18	24	20	....	....	....	....	....	....	....	....	....	....	....	12	2	7	9	4	....	....	....
1997-98	**Phoenix**	**NHL**	**32**	**4**	**7**	**11**	**16**	**1**	**0**	**1**	**61**	**6.6**	**-6**	....	....	....	....	....	....	....	....	....	....	....	....	....
	Springfield	AHL	8	1	7	8	10	....	....	....	....	....	....	....	....	....	....	....	1	0	0	0	0	....	....	....
1998-99	**Phoenix**	**NHL**	**60**	**5**	**8**	**13**	**20**	**2**	**0**	**0**	**94**	**5.3**	**-10**	**0**	**0.0**	**53**	**32**	**16:12**	....	....	....	....	....	....	....	....
99-2000	**Phoenix**	**NHL**	**50**	**3**	**7**	**10**	**22**	**0**	**0**	**1**	**88**	**3.4**	**0**	**0**	**0.0**	**61**	**31**	**16:39**	....	....	....	....	....	....	....	....
	New Jersey	**NHL**	**4**	**1**	**0**	**1**	**2**	**0**	**0**	**0**	**6**	**16.7**	**-2**	**0**	**0.0**	**6**	**3**	**16:26**	....	....	....	....	....	....	....	....
	NHL Totals		**224**	**21**	**46**	**67**	**86**	**6**	**0**	**2**	**409**	**5.1**		**0**	**0.0**	**120**	**66**	**16:24**	**7**	**0**	**2**	**2**	**0**	**0**	**0**	**0**

WHL West First All-Star Team (1995)

Transferred to **Phoenix** after **Winnipeg** franchise relocated, July 1, 1996. Traded to **New Jersey** by **Phoenix** with a conditional choice in 2001 Entry Draft for Lyle Odelein, March 7, 2000. Traded to **Columbus** by **New Jersey** to complete transaction that sent Krzyszof Oliwa to Columbus (June 12, 2000) and Turner Stevenson to New Jersey (June 23, 2000), June 23, 2000.

QUINTAL, Stephane

(KAYN-tahl, STEH-fan) **NYR**

Defense. Shoots right. 6'3", 228 lbs. Born, Boucherville, Que., October 22, 1968. Boston's 2nd choice, 14th overall, in 1987 Entry Draft.

			Regular Season																Playoffs							
Season	Club	League	GP	G	A	Pts	PIM	PP	SH	GW	S	%	+/-	TF	F%	H	SB	Min	GP	G	A	Pts	PIM	PP	SH	GW
1984-85	Richelieu Regents	QAAA	41	1	10	11	....	....	....	....	....	....	....	....	....	....	....	....	....	....	....	....	....	....	....	....
1985-86	Granby Bisons	QMJHL	67	2	17	19	144	....	....	....	....	....	....	....	....	....	....	....	....	....	....	....	....	....	....	....
1986-87	Granby Bisons	QMJHL	67	13	41	54	178	....	....	....	....	....	....	....	....	....	....	....	8	0	9	9	10	....	....	....
1987-88	Hull Olympiques	QMJHL	38	13	23	36	138	....	....	....	....	....	....	....	....	....	....	....	19	7	12	19	30	....	....	....
1988-89	**Boston**	**NHL**	**26**	**0**	**1**	**1**	**29**	**0**	**0**	**0**	**23**	**0.0**	**-5**	....	....	....	....	....	....	....	....	....	....	....	....	....
	Maine Mariners	AHL	16	4	10	14	28	....	....	....	....	....	....	....	....	....	....	....	....	....	....	....	....	....	....	....
1989-90	**Boston**	**NHL**	**38**	**2**	**2**	**4**	**22**	**0**	**0**	**0**	**43**	**4.7**	**-11**	....	....	....	....	....	....	....	....	....	....	....	....	....
	Maine Mariners	AHL	37	4	16	20	27	....	....	....	....	....	....	....	....	....	....	....	....	....	....	....	....	....	....	....
1990-91	**Boston**	**NHL**	**45**	**2**	**6**	**8**	**89**	**1**	**0**	**0**	**54**	**3.7**	**2**	....	....	....	....	....	**3**	**0**	**1**	**1**	**7**	**0**	**0**	**0**
	Maine Mariners	AHL	23	1	5	6	30	....	....	....	....	....	....	....	....	....	....	....	....	....	....	....	....	....	....	....
1991-92	**Boston**	**NHL**	**49**	**4**	**10**	**14**	**77**	**0**	**0**	**0**	**52**	**7.7**	**-8**	....	....	....	....	....	....	....	....	....	....	....	....	....
	St. Louis	**NHL**	**26**	**0**	**6**	**6**	**32**	**0**	**0**	**0**	**19**	**0.0**	**-3**	....	....	....	....	....	**4**	**1**	**2**	**3**	**6**	**1**	**0**	**0**
1992-93	**St. Louis**	**NHL**	**75**	**1**	**10**	**11**	**100**	**0**	**1**	**0**	**81**	**1.2**	**-6**	....	....	....	....	....	**9**	**0**	**0**	**0**	**8**	**0**	**0**	**0**
1993-94	**Winnipeg**	**NHL**	**81**	**8**	**18**	**26**	**119**	**1**	**1**	**1**	**154**	**5.2**	**-25**	....	....	....	....	....	....	....	....	....	....	....	....	....
1994-95	**Winnipeg**	**NHL**	**43**	**6**	**17**	**23**	**78**	**3**	**0**	**2**	**107**	**5.6**	**0**	....	....	....	....	....	....	....	....	....	....	....	....	....
1995-96	**Montreal**	**NHL**	**68**	**2**	**14**	**16**	**117**	**0**	**1**	**1**	**104**	**1.9**	**-4**	....	....	....	....	....	**6**	**0**	**1**	**1**	**6**	**0**	**0**	**0**
1996-97	**Montreal**	**NHL**	**71**	**7**	**15**	**22**	**100**	**1**	**0**	**0**	**139**	**5.0**	**1**	....	....	....	....	....	**5**	**0**	**1**	**1**	**6**	**0**	**0**	**0**
1997-98	**Montreal**	**NHL**	**71**	**6**	**10**	**16**	**97**	**0**	**0**	**0**	**88**	**6.8**	**13**	....	....	....	....	....	**9**	**0**	**2**	**2**	**4**	**0**	**0**	**0**
1998-99	**Montreal**	**NHL**	**82**	**8**	**19**	**27**	**84**	**1**	**1**	**4**	**159**	**5.0**	**-23**	**0**	**0.0**	**98**	**125**	**22:06**	....	....	....	....	....	....	....	....
99-2000	**NY Rangers**	**NHL**	**75**	**2**	**14**	**16**	**77**	**0**	**0**	**1**	**102**	**2.0**	**-10**	**0**	**0.0**	**133**	**125**	**19:04**	....	....	....	....	....	....	....	....
	NHL Totals		**750**	**48**	**142**	**190**	**1021**	**7**	**4**	**9**	**1125**	**4.3**		**0**	**0.0**	**231**	**250**	**20:39**	**36**	**1**	**7**	**8**	**37**	**1**	**0**	**0**

QMJHL First All-Star Team (1987)

Traded to **St. Louis** by **Boston** with Craig Janney for Adam Oates, February 7, 1992. Traded to **Winnipeg** by **St. Louis** with Nelson Emerson for Phil Housley, September 24, 1993. Traded to **Montreal** by **Winnipeg** for Montreal's 2nd round choice (Jason Doig) in 1995 Entry Draft, July 8, 1995. Signed as a free agent by **NY Rangers**, July 13, 1999.

RACHUNEK, Karel

(ra-KHOO-nehk, KAH-rehl) **OTT.**

Defense. Shoots right. 6'2", 202 lbs. Born, Gottwaldov, Czech., August 27, 1979. Ottawa's 8th choice, 229th overall, in 1997 Entry Draft.

			Regular Season																Playoffs							
Season	Club	League	GP	G	A	Pts	PIM	PP	SH	GW	S	%	+/-	TF	F%	H	SB	Min	GP	G	A	Pts	PIM	PP	SH	GW
1995-96	ZPS Zlin-Jr.	Cze-Rep	38	8	11	19	....	....	....	....	....	....	....	....	....	....	....	....	....	....	....	....	....	....	....	....
1996-97	ZPS Zlin-Jr.	Cze-Rep	27	2	11	13	....	....	....	....	....	....	....	....	....	....	....	....	....	....	....	....	....	....	....	....
1997-98	ZPS Zlin	Cze-Rep	27	1	2	3	16	....	....	....	....	....	....	....	....	....	....	....	....	....	....	....	....	....	....	....
1998-99	ZPS Zlin	Cze-Rep	39	3	9	12	88	....	....	....	....	....	....	....	....	....	....	....	6	0	0	0	....	....	....	....
99-2000	**Ottawa**	**NHL**	**6**	**0**	**0**	**0**	**2**	**0**	**0**	**0**	**3**	**0.0**	**0**	**0**	**0.0**	**10**	**5**	**8:03**	....	....	....	....	....	....	....	....
	Grand Rapids	IHL	62	6	20	26	64	....	....	....	....	....	....	....	....	....	....	....	9	0	5	5	6	....	....	....
	NHL Totals		**6**	**0**	**0**	**0**	**2**	**0**	**0**	**0**	**3**	**0.0**		**0**	**0.0**	**10**	**5**	**8:03**	....	....	....	....	....	....	....	....

RAFALSKI, Brian

(ra-FAWL-skee, BRIGH-an) **N.J.**

Defense. Shoots right. 5'9", 200 lbs. Born, Dearborn, MI, September 28, 1973.

			Regular Season																Playoffs							
Season	Club	League	GP	G	A	Pts	PIM	PP	SH	GW	S	%	+/-	TF	F%	H	SB	Min	GP	G	A	Pts	PIM	PP	SH	GW
1990-91	Madison Capitals	USHL	47	12	11	23	28	....	....	....	....	....	....	....	....	....	....	....	....	....	....	....	....	....	....	....
1991-92	U. of Wisconsin	WCHA	34	3	14	17	34	....	....	....	....	....	....	....	....	....	....	....	....	....	....	....	....	....	....	....
1992-93	U. of Wisconsin	WCHA	32	0	13	13	10	....	....	....	....	....	....	....	....	....	....	....	....	....	....	....	....	....	....	....
1993-94	U. of Wisconsin	WCHA	37	6	17	23	26	....	....	....	....	....	....	....	....	....	....	....	....	....	....	....	....	....	....	....
1994-95	U. of Wisconsin	WCHA	43	11	34	45	48	....	....	....	....	....	....	....	....	....	....	....	....	....	....	....	....	....	....	....
1995-96	Brynas IF	Sweden	22	1	8	9	14	....	....	....	....	....	....	....	....	....	....	....	....	....	....	....	....	....	....	....
	Brynas IF	Swede-Q	18	3	6	9	12	....	....	....	....	....	....	....	....	....	....	....	9	0	1	1	2	....	....	....
1996-97	HK Hameenlinna	Finland	49	11	24	35	26	....	....	....	....	....	....	....	....	....	....	....	10	6	5	11	4	....	....	....
1997-98	HIFK Helsinki	Finland	40	13	10	23	20	....	....	....	....	....	....	....	....	....	....	....	9	5	6	11	0	....	....	....
1998-99	HIFK Helsinki	Finland	53	19	34	53	18	....	....	....	....	....	....	....	....	....	....	....	11	5	*9	*14	4	....	....	....
	HIFK Helsinki	EuroHL	6	4	6	10	10	....	....	....	....	....	....	....	....	....	....	....	4	1	0	1	2	....	....	....
99-2000♦	**New Jersey**	**NHL**	**75**	**5**	**27**	**32**	**28**	**1**	**0**	**1**	**128**	**3.9**	**21**	**1**	**0.0**	**102**	**68**	**18:51**	**23**	**2**	**6**	**8**	**8**	**0**	**0**	**1**
	NHL Totals		**75**	**5**	**27**	**32**	**28**	**1**	**0**	**1**	**128**	**3.9**		**1**	**0.0**	**102**	**68**	**18:51**	**23**	**2**	**6**	**8**	**8**	**0**	**0**	**1**

WCHA First All-Star Team (1995) • NCAA West First All-American Team (1995) • Finnish Elite League First All-Star Team (1998, 1999) • Named Best Defender in Finnish Elite League (1998, 1999) • NHL All-Rookie Team (2000)

Signed as a free agent by **New Jersey**, May 7, 1999.

RAGNARSSON, Marcus
(RAG-nahr-suhn, MAHR-kuhs) **S.J.**

Defense. Shoots left. 6'1", 215 lbs. Born, Ostervala, Sweden, August 13, 1971. San Jose's 5th choice, 99th overall, in 1992 Entry Draft.

			Regular Season																Playoffs							
Season	Club	League	GP	G	A	Pts	PIM	PP	SH	GW	S	%	+/-	TF	F%	H	SB	Min	GP	G	A	Pts	PIM	PP	SH	GW
1986-87	Ostervala IF	Sweden-3	28	1	6	7	....	....	....	....	....	....	....	....	....	....	....	....	....	....	....	....	....	....	....	....
1987-88	Ostervala IF	Sweden-3	25	3	12	15	....	....	....	....	....	....	....	....	....	....	....	....	....	....	....	....	....	....	....	....
1988-89	Ostervala IF	Sweden-3	30	15	14	29	....	....	....	....	....	....	....	....	....	....	....	....	....	....	....	....	....	....	....	....
1989-90	Nacka HK	Sweden-2	9	2	3	5	4	....	....	....	....	....	....	....	....	....	....	....	....	....	....	....	....	....	....	....
	Djurgardens IF	Sweden	13	0	2	2	0	....	....	....	....	....	....	....	....	....	....	....	1	0	0	0	0	....	....	....
1990-91	Djurgardens IF	Sweden	35	4	1	5	12	....	....	....	....	....	....	....	....	....	....	....	7	0	0	0	6	....	....	....
1991-92	Djurgardens IF	Sweden	40	8	5	13	14	....	....	....	....	....	....	....	....	....	....	....	10	0	1	1	4	....	....	....
1992-93	Djurgardens IF	Sweden	35	3	3	6	53	....	....	....	....	....	....	....	....	....	....	....	6	0	3	3	8	....	....	....
1993-94	Djurgardens IF	Sweden	19	0	4	4	24	....	....	....	....	....	....	....	....	....	....	....	....	....	....	....	....	....	....	....
1994-95	Djurgardens IF	Sweden	38	7	9	16	20	....	....	....	....	....	....	....	....	....	....	....	3	0	0	0	4	....	....	....
1995-96	**San Jose**	**NHL**	**71**	**8**	**31**	**39**	**42**	**4**	**0**	**0**	**94**	**8.5**	**–24**	....	....	....	....	....	....	....	....	....	....	....	....	....
1996-97	**San Jose**	**NHL**	**69**	**3**	**14**	**17**	**63**	**2**	**0**	**0**	**57**	**5.3**	**–18**	....	....	....	....	....	....	....	....	....	....	....	....	....
1997-98	**San Jose**	**NHL**	**79**	**5**	**20**	**25**	**65**	**3**	**0**	**2**	**91**	**5.5**	**–11**	....	....	....	....	....	**6**	**0**	**0**	**0**	**4**	**0**	**0**	**0**
	Sweden	Olympics	3	0	1	1	0	....	....	....	....	....	....	....	....	....	....	....	....	....	....	....	....	....	....	....
1998-99	**San Jose**	**NHL**	**74**	**0**	**13**	**13**	**66**	**0**	**0**	**0**	**87**	**0.0**	**7**	**3**	**66.7**	**99**	**66**	**21:55**	**6**	**0**	**1**	**1**	**6**	**0**	**0**	**0**
99-2000	**San Jose**	**NHL**	**63**	**3**	**13**	**16**	**38**	**0**	**0**	**0**	**60**	**5.0**	**13**	**0**	**0.0**	**92**	**76**	**22:52**	**12**	**0**	**3**	**3**	**10**	**0**	**0**	**0**
	NHL Totals		**356**	**19**	**91**	**110**	**274**	**9**	**0**	**2**	**389**	**4.9**		**3**	**66.7**	**191**	**142**	**22:21**	**24**	**0**	**4**	**4**	**20**	**0**	**0**	**0**

RANHEIM, Paul
(RAN-highm, PAWL) **PHI.**

Left wing. Shoots right. 6'1", 210 lbs. Born, St. Louis, MO, January 25, 1966. Calgary's 3rd choice, 38th overall, in 1984 Entry Draft.

Season	Club	League	GP	G	A	Pts	PIM	PP	SH	GW	S	%	+/-	TF	F%	H	SB	Min	GP	G	A	Pts	PIM	PP	SH	GW
1982-83	Edina High	Hi-School	26	12	25	37	4	....	....	....	....	....	....	....	....	....	....	....	....	....	....	....	....	....	....	....
1983-84	Edina High	Hi-School	26	16	24	40	6	....	....	....	....	....	....	....	....	....	....	....	....	....	....	....	....	....	....	....
1984-85	U. of Wisconsin	WCHA	42	11	11	22	40	....	....	....	....	....	....	....	....	....	....	....	....	....	....	....	....	....	....	....
1985-86	U. of Wisconsin	WCHA	33	17	17	34	34	....	....	....	....	....	....	....	....	....	....	....	....	....	....	....	....	....	....	....
1986-87	U. of Wisconsin	WCHA	42	24	35	59	54	....	....	....	....	....	....	....	....	....	....	....	....	....	....	....	....	....	....	....
1987-88	U. of Wisconsin	WCHA	44	36	26	62	63	....	....	....	....	....	....	....	....	....	....	....	....	....	....	....	....	....	....	....
1988-89	**Calgary**	**NHL**	**5**	**0**	**0**	**0**	**0**	**0**	**0**	**0**	**4**	**0.0**	**–3**	....	....	....	....	....	....	....	....	....	....	....	....	....
	Salt Lake City	IHL	75	*68	29	97	16	....	....	....	....	....	....	....	....	....	....	....	14	5	5	10	8	....	....	....
1989-90	**Calgary**	**NHL**	**80**	**26**	**28**	**54**	**23**	**1**	**3**	**4**	**197**	**13.2**	**27**	....	....	....	....	....	**6**	**1**	**3**	**4**	**2**	**0**	**0**	**0**
1990-91	**Calgary**	**NHL**	**39**	**14**	**16**	**30**	**4**	**2**	**0**	**2**	**108**	**13.0**	**20**	....	....	....	....	....	**7**	**2**	**2**	**4**	**0**	**0**	**0**	**0**
1991-92	**Calgary**	**NHL**	**80**	**23**	**20**	**43**	**32**	**1**	**3**	**3**	**159**	**14.5**	**16**	....	....	....	....	....	....	....	....	....	....	....	....	....
1992-93	**Calgary**	**NHL**	**83**	**21**	**22**	**43**	**26**	**3**	**4**	**1**	**179**	**11.7**	**–4**	....	....	....	....	....	**6**	**0**	**1**	**1**	**0**	**0**	**0**	**0**
1993-94	**Calgary**	**NHL**	**67**	**10**	**14**	**24**	**20**	**0**	**2**	**2**	**110**	**9.1**	**–7**	....	....	....	....	....	....	....	....	....	....	....	....	....
	Hartford	**NHL**	**15**	**0**	**3**	**3**	**2**	**0**	**0**	**0**	**21**	**0.0**	**–11**	....	....	....	....	....	....	....	....	....	....	....	....	....
1994-95	**Hartford**	**NHL**	**47**	**6**	**14**	**20**	**10**	**0**	**0**	**1**	**73**	**8.2**	**–3**	....	....	....	....	....	....	....	....	....	....	....	....	....
1995-96	**Hartford**	**NHL**	**73**	**10**	**20**	**30**	**14**	**0**	**1**	**1**	**126**	**7.9**	**–2**	....	....	....	....	....	....	....	....	....	....	....	....	....
1996-97	**Hartford**	**NHL**	**67**	**10**	**11**	**21**	**18**	**0**	**3**	**1**	**96**	**10.4**	**–13**	....	....	....	....	....	....	....	....	....	....	....	....	....
1997-98	**Carolina**	**NHL**	**73**	**5**	**9**	**14**	**28**	**0**	**1**	**2**	**77**	**6.5**	**–11**	....	....	....	....	....	....	....	....	....	....	....	....	....
1998-99	**Carolina**	**NHL**	**78**	**9**	**10**	**19**	**39**	**0**	**2**	**1**	**67**	**13.4**	**4**	**10**	**50.0**	**72**	**32**	**9:02**	**6**	**0**	**0**	**0**	**2**	**0**	**0**	**0**
99-2000	**Carolina**	**NHL**	**79**	**9**	**13**	**22**	**6**	**0**	**0**	**2**	**98**	**9.2**	**–14**	**78**	**46.1**	**107**	**31**	**11:19**	....	....	....	....	....	....	....	....
	NHL Totals		**786**	**143**	**180**	**323**	**222**	**7**	**19**	**20**	**1315**	**10.9**		**88**	**46.6**	**179**	**63**	**10:11**	**25**	**3**	**6**	**9**	**4**	**0**	**0**	**0**

WCHA Second All-Star Team (1987) • NCAA West First All-American Team (1988) • WCHA First All-Star Team (1988) • IHL Second All-Star Team (1989) • Won Garry F. Longman Memorial Trophy (Top Rookie - IHL) (1989)

• Missed majority of 1989-90 season recovering from ankle injury suffered in game vs. Minnesota, December 11, 1990. Traded to **Hartford** by **Calgary** with Gary Suter and Ted Drury for James Patrick, Zarley Zalapski and Michael Nylander, March 10, 1994. Transferred to **Carolina** after **Hartford** franchise relocated, June 25, 1997. Traded to **Philadelphia** by **Carolina** for Philadelphia's 8th round choice in 2002 Entry Draft, May 31, 2000.

RASMUSSEN, Erik
(RAS-moo-suhn, AIR-ihk) **BUF.**

Center/Left wing. Shoots left. 6'3", 208 lbs. Born, Minneapolis, MN, March 28, 1977. Buffalo's 1st choice, 7th overall, in 1996 Entry Draft.

Season	Club	League	GP	G	A	Pts	PIM	PP	SH	GW	S	%	+/-	TF	F%	H	SB	Min	GP	G	A	Pts	PIM	PP	SH	GW
1992-93	St. Louis High	Hi-School	23	16	24	40	50	....	....	....	....	....	....	....	....	....	....	....	....	....	....	....	....	....	....	....
1993-94	St. Louis High	Hi-School	18	25	18	43	80	....	....	....	....	....	....	....	....	....	....	....	....	....	....	....	....	....	....	....
1994-95	St. Louis High	Hi-School	23	19	33	52	80	....	....	....	....	....	....	....	....	....	....	....	....	....	....	....	....	....	....	....
1995-96	U. of Minnesota	WCHA	40	16	32	48	55	....	....	....	....	....	....	....	....	....	....	....	....	....	....	....	....	....	....	....
1996-97	U. of Minnesota	WCHA	34	15	12	27	*123	....	....	....	....	....	....	....	....	....	....	....	....	....	....	....	....	....	....	....
1997-98	**Buffalo**	**NHL**	**21**	**2**	**3**	**5**	**14**	**0**	**0**	**0**	**28**	**7.1**	**2**	....	....	....	....	....	....	....	....	....	....	....	....	....
	Rochester	AHL	53	9	14	23	83	....	....	....	....	....	....	....	....	....	....	....	1	0	0	0	5	....	....	....
1998-99	**Buffalo**	**NHL**	**42**	**3**	**7**	**10**	**37**	**0**	**0**	**0**	**40**	**7.5**	**6**	**67**	**40.3**	**104**	**18**	**12:22**	**21**	**2**	**4**	**6**	**18**	**0**	**0**	**1**
	Rochester	AHL	37	12	14	26	47	....	....	....	....	....	....	....	....	....	....	....	....	....	....	....	....	....	....	....
99-2000	**Buffalo**	**NHL**	**67**	**8**	**6**	**14**	**43**	**0**	**0**	**2**	**76**	**10.5**	**1**	**130**	**44.6**	**175**	**12**	**11:27**	**3**	**0**	**0**	**0**	**4**	**0**	**0**	**0**
	NHL Totals		**130**	**13**	**16**	**29**	**94**	**0**	**0**	**2**	**144**	**9.0**		**197**	**43.1**	**279**	**30**	**11:48**	**24**	**2**	**4**	**6**	**22**	**0**	**0**	**1**

RATCHUK, Peter
(RAT-chuhk, PEE-tuhr) **FLA.**

Defense. Shoots left. 6'1", 185 lbs. Born, Buffalo, NY, September 10, 1977. Colorado's 1st choice, 25th overall, in 1996 Entry Draft.

Season	Club	League	GP	G	A	Pts	PIM	PP	SH	GW	S	%	+/-	TF	F%	H	SB	Min	GP	G	A	Pts	PIM	PP	SH	GW
1994-95	Lawrence Prep	Hi-School	31	8	15	23	18	....	....	....	....	....	....	....	....	....	....	....	....	....	....	....	....	....	....	....
1995-96	Shattuck School	Hi-School	35	22	28	50	24	....	....	....	....	....	....	....	....	....	....	....	....	....	....	....	....	....	....	....
1996-97	Bowling Green	CCHA	35	9	12	21	14	....	....	....	....	....	....	....	....	....	....	....	....	....	....	....	....	....	....	....
1997-98	Hull Olympiques	QMJHL	60	23	31	54	34	....	....	....	....	....	....	....	....	....	....	....	11	3	6	9	8	....	....	....
1998-99	**Florida**	**NHL**	**24**	**1**	**1**	**2**	**10**	**0**	**0**	**0**	**34**	**2.9**	**–1**	**0**	**0.0**	**16**	**14**	**13:55**	....	....	....	....	....	....	....	....
	New Haven	AHL	53	7	20	27	44	....	....	....	....	....	....	....	....	....	....	....	....	....	....	....	....	....	....	....
99-2000	Louisville	AHL	76	9	17	26	64	....	....	....	....	....	....	....	....	....	....	....	4	1	2	3	0	....	....	....
	NHL Totals		**24**	**1**	**1**	**2**	**10**	**0**	**0**	**0**	**34**	**2.9**		**0**	**0.0**	**16**	**14**	**13:55**	....	....	....	....	....	....	....	....

Signed as a free agent by **Florida**, June 15, 1998.

RATHJE, Mike
(RATH-jee, MIGHK) **S.J.**

Defense. Shoots left. 6'5", 235 lbs. Born, Mannville, Alta., May 11, 1974. San Jose's 1st choice, 3rd overall, in 1992 Entry Draft.

Season	Club	League	GP	G	A	Pts	PIM	PP	SH	GW	S	%	+/-	TF	F%	H	SB	Min	GP	G	A	Pts	PIM	PP	SH	GW
1989-90	Sherwood Park	AAHA	33	6	11	17	30	....	....	....	....	....	....	....	....	....	....	....	....	....	....	....	....	....	....	....
1990-91	Medicine Hat	WHL	64	1	16	17	28	....	....	....	....	....	....	....	....	....	....	....	12	0	4	4	2	....	....	....
1991-92	Medicine Hat	WHL	67	11	23	34	99	....	....	....	....	....	....	....	....	....	....	....	4	0	1	1	2	....	....	....
1992-93	Medicine Hat	WHL	57	12	37	49	103	....	....	....	....	....	....	....	....	....	....	....	10	3	3	6	12	....	....	....
	Kansas City	IHL	....	....	....	....	....	....	....	....	....	....	....	....	....	....	....	....	5	0	0	0	12	....	....	....
1993-94	**San Jose**	**NHL**	**47**	**1**	**9**	**10**	**59**	**1**	**0**	**0**	**30**	**3.3**	**–9**	....	....	....	....	....	**1**	**0**	**0**	**0**	**0**	**0**	**0**	**0**
	Kansas City	IHL	6	0	2	2	0	....	....	....	....	....	....	....	....	....	....	....	....	....	....	....	....	....	....	....
1994-95	**San Jose**	**NHL**	**42**	**2**	**7**	**9**	**29**	**0**	**0**	**0**	**38**	**5.3**	**–1**	....	....	....	....	....	**11**	**5**	**2**	**7**	**4**	**5**	**0**	**0**
	Kansas City	IHL	6	0	1	1	7	....	....	....	....	....	....	....	....	....	....	....	....	....	....	....	....	....	....	....
1995-96	**San Jose**	**NHL**	**27**	**0**	**7**	**7**	**14**	**0**	**0**	**0**	**26**	**0.0**	**–16**	....	....	....	....	....	....	....	....	....	....	....	....	....
	Kansas City	IHL	36	6	11	17	34	....	....	....	....	....	....	....	....	....	....	....	....	....	....	....	....	....	....	....
1996-97	**San Jose**	**NHL**	**31**	**0**	**8**	**8**	**21**	**0**	**0**	**0**	**22**	**0.0**	**–1**	....	....	....	....	....	....	....	....	....	....	....	....	....
1997-98	**San Jose**	**NHL**	**81**	**3**	**12**	**15**	**59**	**1**	**0**	**0**	**61**	**4.9**	**–4**	....	....	....	....	....	**6**	**1**	**0**	**1**	**6**	**1**	**0**	**0**
1998-99	**San Jose**	**NHL**	**82**	**5**	**9**	**14**	**36**	**2**	**0**	**1**	**67**	**7.5**	**15**	**0**	**0.0**	**100**	**64**	**20:07**	**6**	**0**	**0**	**0**	**4**	**0**	**0**	**0**
99-2000	**San Jose**	**NHL**	**66**	**2**	**14**	**16**	**31**	**0**	**0**	**0**	**46**	**4.3**	**–2**	**0**	**0.0**	**82**	**54**	**22:11**	**12**	**1**	**3**	**4**	**8**	**0**	**0**	**0**
	NHL Totals		**376**	**13**	**66**	**79**	**249**	**4**	**0**	**1**	**290**	**4.5**		**0**	**0.0**	**182**	**118**	**21:02**	**36**	**7**	**5**	**12**	**22**	**6**	**0**	**0**

WHL East Second All-Star Team (1992, 1993)

• Missed majority of 1996-97 season recovering from groin injury suffered in game vs. Dallas, November 8, 1996.

RAY, Rob

(RAY, RAWB) **BUF.**

Right wing. Shoots left. 6', 216 lbs. Born, Stirling, Ont., June 8, 1968. Buffalo's 5th choice, 97th overall, in 1988 Entry Draft.

			Regular Season																Playoffs							
Season	Club	League	GP	G	A	Pts	PIM	PP	SH	GW	S	%	+/-	TF	F%	H	SB	Min	GP	G	A	Pts	PIM	PP	SH	GW
1983-84	Trenton Bobcats	OJHL-B	40	11	10	21	57	....	....	....	....	....	....	....	....	....	....	....	....	....	....	....	....	....	....	....
1984-85	Whitby Lawmen	OJHL	35	5	10	15	318	....	....	....	....	....	....	....	....	....	....	....	....	....	....	....	....	....	....	....
1985-86	Cornwall Royals	OHL	53	6	13	19	253	....	....	....	....	....	....	....	....	....	....	....	6	0	0	0	26	....	....	....
1986-87	Cornwall Royals	OHL	46	17	20	37	158	....	....	....	....	....	....	....	....	....	....	....	5	1	1	2	16	....	....	....
1987-88	Cornwall Royals	OHL	61	11	41	52	179	....	....	....	....	....	....	....	....	....	....	....	11	2	3	5	33	....	....	....
1988-89	Rochester	AHL	74	11	18	29	*446	....	....	....	....	....	....	....	....	....	....	....	....	....	....	....	....	....	....	....
1989-90	**Buffalo**	**NHL**	**27**	**2**	**1**	**3**	**99**	**0**	**0**	**0**	**20**	**10.0**	**–2**	....	....	....	....	....	....	....	....	....	....	....	....	....
	Rochester	AHL	43	2	13	15	335	....	....	....	....	....	....	....	....	....	....	....	17	1	3	4	115	....	....	....
1990-91	**Buffalo**	**NHL**	**66**	**8**	**8**	**16**	***350**	**0**	**0**	**1**	**54**	**14.8**	**–11**	....	....	....	....	....	**6**	**1**	**1**	**2**	**56**	**0**	**0**	**1**
	Rochester	AHL	8	1	1	2	15	....	....	....	....	....	....	....	....	....	....	....	....	....	....	....	....	....	....	....
1991-92	**Buffalo**	**NHL**	**63**	**5**	**3**	**8**	**354**	**0**	**0**	**0**	**29**	**17.2**	**–9**	....	....	....	....	....	**7**	**0**	**0**	**0**	**2**	**0**	**0**	**0**
1992-93	**Buffalo**	**NHL**	**68**	**3**	**2**	**5**	**211**	**1**	**0**	**0**	**28**	**10.7**	**–3**	....	....	....	....	....	....	....	....	....	....	....	....	....
1993-94	**Buffalo**	**NHL**	**82**	**3**	**4**	**7**	**274**	**0**	**0**	**0**	**34**	**8.8**	**2**	....	....	....	....	....	**7**	**1**	**0**	**1**	**43**	**0**	**0**	**0**
1994-95	**Buffalo**	**NHL**	**47**	**0**	**3**	**3**	**173**	**0**	**0**	**0**	**7**	**0.0**	**–4**	....	....	....	....	....	**5**	**0**	**0**	**0**	**14**	**0**	**0**	**0**
1995-96	**Buffalo**	**NHL**	**71**	**3**	**6**	**9**	**287**	**0**	**0**	**0**	**21**	**14.3**	**–8**	....	....	....	....	....	....	....	....	....	....	....	....	....
1996-97	**Buffalo**	**NHL**	**82**	**7**	**3**	**10**	**286**	**0**	**0**	**1**	**45**	**15.6**	**3**	....	....	....	....	....	**12**	**0**	**1**	**1**	**28**	**0**	**0**	**0**
1997-98	**Buffalo**	**NHL**	**63**	**2**	**4**	**6**	**234**	**1**	**0**	**1**	**19**	**10.5**	**2**	....	....	....	....	....	**10**	**0**	**0**	**0**	**24**	**0**	**0**	**0**
1998-99	**Buffalo**	**NHL**	**76**	**0**	**4**	**4**	***261**	**0**	**0**	**0**	**23**	**0.0**	**–2**	**0**	**0.0**	**60**	**4**	**5:11**	**5**	**1**	**0**	**1**	**0**	**0**	**0**	**1**
99-2000	**Buffalo**	**NHL**	**69**	**1**	**3**	**4**	**158**	**0**	**0**	**0**	**17**	**5.9**	**0**	**0**	**0.0**	**55**	**4**	**4:13**	....	....	....	....	....	....	....	....
	NHL Totals		**714**	**34**	**41**	**75**	**2687**	**2**	**0**	**3**	**297**	**11.4**		**0**	**0.0**	**115**	**8**	**4:43**	**52**	**3**	**2**	**5**	**167**	**0**	**0**	**2**

Won King Clancy Memorial Trophy (1999)

REASONER, Marty

(REE-sohn-uhr, MAHR-tee) **ST.L.**

Center. Shoots left. 6'1", 203 lbs. Born, Rochester, NY, February 26, 1977. St. Louis' 1st choice, 14th overall, in 1996 Entry Draft.

			Regular Season																Playoffs							
Season	Club	League	GP	G	A	Pts	PIM	PP	SH	GW	S	%	+/-	TF	F%	H	SB	Min	GP	G	A	Pts	PIM	PP	SH	GW
1993-94	Deerfield Academy	Hi-School	22	27	25	52	....	....	....	....	....	....	....	....	....	....	....	....	....	....	....	....	....	....	....	....
1994-95	Deerfield Academy	Hi-School	26	25	32	57	14	....	....	....	....	....	....	....	....	....	....	....	....	....	....	....	....	....	....	....
1995-96	Boston College	H-East	34	16	29	45	32	....	....	....	....	....	....	....	....	....	....	....	....	....	....	....	....	....	....	....
1996-97	Boston College	H-East	35	20	24	44	31	....	....	....	....	....	....	....	....	....	....	....	....	....	....	....	....	....	....	....
1997-98	Boston College	H-East	42	*33	40	*73	56	....	....	....	....	....	....	....	....	....	....	....	....	....	....	....	....	....	....	....
1998-99	**St. Louis**	**NHL**	**22**	**3**	**7**	**10**	**8**	**1**	**0**	**0**	**33**	**9.1**	**2**	**224**	**53.6**	**19**	**1**	**13:55**	....	....	....	....	....	....	....	....
	Worcester	AHL	44	17	22	39	24	....	....	....	....	....	....	....	....	....	....	....	4	2	1	3	6	....	....	....
99-2000	**St. Louis**	**NHL**	**32**	**10**	**14**	**24**	**20**	**3**	**0**	**0**	**51**	**19.6**	**9**	**379**	**49.6**	**26**	**5**	**15:20**	**7**	**2**	**1**	**3**	**4**	**1**	**0**	**0**
	Worcester	AHL	44	23	28	51	39	....	....	....	....	....	....	....	....	....	....	....	....	....	....	....	....	....	....	....
	NHL Totals		**54**	**13**	**21**	**34**	**28**	**4**	**0**	**0**	**84**	**15.5**		**603**	**51.1**	**45**	**6**	**14:45**	**7**	**2**	**1**	**3**	**4**	**1**	**0**	**0**

Hockey East First All-Star Team (1997, 1998) • NCAA East First All-American Team (1998) • NCAA Championship All-Tournament Team (1998)

RECCHI, Mark

(REH-kee, MAHRK) **PHI.**

Right wing. Shoots left. 5'10", 185 lbs. Born, Kamloops, B.C., February 1, 1968. Pittsburgh's 4th choice, 67th overall, in 1988 Entry Draft.

			Regular Season																Playoffs							
Season	Club	League	GP	G	A	Pts	PIM	PP	SH	GW	S	%	+/-	TF	F%	H	SB	Min	GP	G	A	Pts	PIM	PP	SH	GW
1984-85	Langley Eagles	BCJHL	51	26	39	65	39	....	....	....	....	....	....	....	....	....	....	....	....	....	....	....	....	....	....	....
	New Westminster	WHL	4	1	0	1	0	....	....	....	....	....	....	....	....	....	....	....	....	....	....	....	....	....	....	....
1985-86	New Westminster	WHL	72	21	40	61	55	....	....	....	....	....	....	....	....	....	....	....	....	....	....	....	....	....	....	....
1986-87	Kamloops Blazers	WHL	40	26	50	76	63	....	....	....	....	....	....	....	....	....	....	....	13	3	16	19	17	....	....	....
1987-88	Kamloops Blazers	WHL	62	61	*93	154	75	....	....	....	....	....	....	....	....	....	....	....	17	10	*21	*31	18	....	....	....
1988-89	**Pittsburgh**	**NHL**	**15**	**1**	**1**	**2**	**0**	**0**	**0**	**0**	**11**	**9.1**	**–2**	....	....	....	....	....	....	....	....	....	....	....	....	....
	Muskegon	IHL	63	50	49	99	86	....	....	....	....	....	....	....	....	....	....	....	14	7	*14	*21	28	....	....	....
1989-90	**Pittsburgh**	**NHL**	**74**	**30**	**37**	**67**	**44**	**6**	**2**	**4**	**143**	**21.0**	**6**	....	....	....	....	....	....	....	....	....	....	....	....	....
	Muskegon	IHL	4	7	4	11	2	....	....	....	....	....	....	....	....	....	....	....	....	....	....	....	....	....	....	....
1990-91♦	**Pittsburgh**	**NHL**	**78**	**40**	**73**	**113**	**48**	**12**	**0**	**9**	**184**	**21.7**	**0**	....	....	....	....	....	**24**	**10**	**24**	**34**	**33**	**5**	**0**	**2**
1991-92	**Pittsburgh**	**NHL**	**58**	**33**	**37**	**70**	**78**	**16**	**1**	**4**	**156**	**21.2**	**–16**	....	....	....	....	....	....	....	....	....	....	....	....	....
	Philadelphia	**NHL**	**22**	**10**	**17**	**27**	**18**	**4**	**0**	**1**	**54**	**18.5**	**–5**	....	....	....	....	....	....	....	....	....	....	....	....	....
1992-93	**Philadelphia**	**NHL**	**84**	**53**	**70**	**123**	**95**	**15**	**4**	**6**	**274**	**19.3**	**1**	....	....	....	....	....	....	....	....	....	....	....	....	....
1993-94	**Philadelphia**	**NHL**	**84**	**40**	**67**	**107**	**46**	**11**	**0**	**5**	**217**	**18.4**	**–2**	....	....	....	....	....	....	....	....	....	....	....	....	....
1994-95	**Philadelphia**	**NHL**	**10**	**2**	**3**	**5**	**12**	**1**	**0**	**2**	**17**	**11.8**	**–6**	....	....	....	....	....	....	....	....	....	....	....	....	....
	Montreal	**NHL**	**39**	**14**	**29**	**43**	**16**	**8**	**0**	**1**	**104**	**13.5**	**–3**	....	....	....	....	....	....	....	....	....	....	....	....	....
1995-96	**Montreal**	**NHL**	**82**	**28**	**50**	**78**	**69**	**11**	**2**	**6**	**191**	**14.7**	**20**	....	....	....	....	....	**6**	**3**	**3**	**6**	**0**	**3**	**0**	**0**
1996-97	**Montreal**	**NHL**	**82**	**34**	**46**	**80**	**58**	**7**	**2**	**3**	**202**	**16.8**	**–1**	....	....	....	....	....	**5**	**4**	**2**	**6**	**2**	**0**	**0**	**0**
1997-98	**Montreal**	**NHL**	**82**	**32**	**42**	**74**	**51**	**9**	**1**	**6**	**216**	**14.8**	**11**	....	....	....	....	....	**10**	**4**	**8**	**12**	**6**	**0**	**0**	**2**
	Canada	Olympics	5	0	2	2	0	....	....	....	....	....	....	....	....	....	....	....	....	....	....	....	....	....	....	....
1998-99	**Montreal**	**NHL**	**61**	**12**	**35**	**47**	**28**	**3**	**0**	**2**	**152**	**7.9**	**–4**	**239**	**44.8**	**76**	**23**	**20:37**	....	....	....	....	....	....	....	....
	Philadelphia	**NHL**	**10**	**4**	**2**	**6**	**6**	**0**	**0**	**0**	**19**	**21.1**	**–3**	**4**	**25.0**	**21**	**1**	**19:30**	**6**	**0**	**1**	**1**	**2**	**0**	**0**	**0**
99-2000	**Philadelphia**	**NHL**	**82**	**28**	***63**	**91**	**50**	**7**	**1**	**5**	**223**	**12.6**	**20**	**353**	**49.6**	**95**	**39**	**21:43**	**18**	**6**	**12**	**18**	**6**	**2**	**0**	**1**
	NHL Totals		**863**	**361**	**572**	**933**	**619**	**110**	**13**	**54**	**2163**	**16.7**		**596**	**47.5**	**192**	**63**	**21:08**	**69**	**27**	**50**	**77**	**49**	**10**	**0**	**5**

WHL West All-Star Team (1988) • IHL Second All-Star Team (1989) • NHL Second All-Star Team (1992) • Played in NHL All-Star Game (1991, 1993, 1994, 1997, 1998, 1999, 2000)

Traded to **Philadelphia** by **Pittsburgh** with Brian Benning and LA Kings' 1st round choice (previously acquired, Philadelphia selected Jason Bowen) in 1992 Entry Draft for Rick Tocchet, Kjell Samuelsson, Ken Wregget and Philadelphia's 3rd round choice (Dave Roche) in 1993 Entry Draft, February 19, 1992. Traded to **Montreal** by **Philadelphia** with Philadelphia's 3rd round choice (Martin Hohenberger) in 1995 Entry Draft for Eric Desjardins, Gilbert Dionne and John LeClair, February 9, 1995. Traded to **Philadelphia** by **Montreal** for Danius Zubrus, Philadelphia's 2nd round choice (Matt Carkner) in 1999 Entry Draft and NY Islanders' 6th round choice (previously acquired, Montreal selected Scott Selig) in 2000 Entry Draft, March 10, 1999.

REDDEN, Wade

(REHD-dehn, WAYD) **OTT.**

Defense. Shoots left. 6'2", 205 lbs. Born, Lloydminster, Sask., June 12, 1977. NY Islanders' 1st choice, 2nd overall, in 1995 Entry Draft.

			Regular Season																Playoffs							
Season	Club	League	GP	G	A	Pts	PIM	PP	SH	GW	S	%	+/-	TF	F%	H	SB	Min	GP	G	A	Pts	PIM	PP	SH	GW
1992-93	Lloydminster	SJHL	34	4	11	15	64	....	....	....	....	....	....	....	....	....	....	....	....	....	....	....	....	....	....	....
1993-94	Brandon	WHL	63	4	35	39	98	....	....	....	....	....	....	....	....	....	....	....	14	2	4	6	10	....	....	....
1994-95	Brandon	WHL	64	14	46	60	83	....	....	....	....	....	....	....	....	....	....	....	18	5	10	15	8	....	....	....
1995-96	Brandon	WHL	51	9	45	54	55	....	....	....	....	....	....	....	....	....	....	....	19	5	10	15	19	....	....	....
1996-97	**Ottawa**	**NHL**	**82**	**6**	**24**	**30**	**41**	**2**	**0**	**1**	**102**	**5.9**	**1**	....	....	....	....	....	**7**	**1**	**3**	**4**	**2**	**0**	**0**	**0**
1997-98	**Ottawa**	**NHL**	**80**	**8**	**14**	**22**	**27**	**3**	**0**	**2**	**103**	**7.8**	**17**	....	....	....	....	....	**9**	**0**	**2**	**2**	**2**	**0**	**0**	**0**
1998-99	**Ottawa**	**NHL**	**72**	**8**	**21**	**29**	**54**	**3**	**0**	**1**	**127**	**6.3**	**7**	**0**	**0.0**	**83**	**73**	**23:27**	**4**	**1**	**2**	**3**	**2**	**1**	**0**	**0**
99-2000	**Ottawa**	**NHL**	**81**	**10**	**26**	**36**	**49**	**3**	**0**	**2**	**163**	**6.1**	**–1**	**0**	**0.0**	**119**	**103**	**23:43**	....	....	....	....	....	....	....	....
	NHL Totals		**315**	**32**	**85**	**117**	**171**	**11**	**0**	**6**	**495**	**6.5**		**0**	**0.0**	**202**	**176**	**23:35**	**20**	**2**	**7**	**9**	**6**	**1**	**0**	**0**

WHL East Second All-Star Team (1995) • WHL East First All-Star Team (1996) • Memorial Cup All-Star Team (1996)

Traded to **Ottawa** by **NY Islanders** with Damian Rhodes for Don Beaupre, Martin Straka and Bryan Berard, January 23, 1996.

REEKIE, Joe

(REE-kee, JOH) **WSH.**

Defense. Shoots left. 6'3", 220 lbs. Born, Victoria, B.C., February 22, 1965. Buffalo's 6th choice, 119th overall, in 1985 Entry Draft.

			Regular Season																Playoffs							
Season	Club	League	GP	G	A	Pts	PIM	PP	SH	GW	S	%	+/-	TF	F%	H	SB	Min	GP	G	A	Pts	PIM	PP	SH	GW
1981-82	Nepean Raiders	OJHL	16	2	5	7	4	....	....	....	....	....	....	....	....	....	....	....	....	....	....	....	....	....	....	....
1982-83	Pembroke	OJHL	7	2	1	3	16	....	....	....	....	....	....	....	....	....	....	....	....	....	....	....	....	....	....	....
	North Bay	OHL	59	2	9	11	49	....	....	....	....	....	....	....	....	....	....	....	8	0	1	1	11	....	....	....
1983-84	North Bay	OHL	9	1	0	1	18	....	....	....	....	....	....	....	....	....	....	....	....	....	....	....	....	....	....	....
	Cornwall Royals	OHL	53	6	27	33	166	....	....	....	....	....	....	....	....	....	....	....	3	0	0	0	4	....	....	....
1984-85	Cornwall Royals	OHL	65	19	63	82	134	....	....	....	....	....	....	....	....	....	....	....	9	4	13	17	18	....	....	....
1985-86	**Buffalo**	**NHL**	**3**	**0**	**0**	**0**	**14**	**0**	**0**	**0**	**1**	**0.0**	**–2**	....	....	....	....	....	....	....	....	....	....	....	....	....
	Rochester	AHL	77	3	25	28	178	....	....	....	....	....	....	....	....	....	....	....	....	....	....	....	....	....	....	....
1986-87	**Buffalo**	**NHL**	**56**	**1**	**8**	**9**	**82**	**0**	**0**	**0**	**56**	**1.8**	**6**	....	....	....	....	....	....	....	....	....	....	....	....	....
	Rochester	AHL	22	0	6	6	52	....	....	....	....	....	....	....	....	....	....	....	....	....	....	....	....	....	....	....
1987-88	**Buffalo**	**NHL**	**30**	**1**	**4**	**5**	**68**	**0**	**0**	**0**	**23**	**4.3**	**–3**	....	....	....	....	....	**2**	**0**	**0**	**0**	**4**	**0**	**0**	**0**
1988-89	**Buffalo**	**NHL**	**15**	**1**	**3**	**4**	**26**	**1**	**0**	**0**	**14**	**7.1**	**6**	....	....	....	....	....	....	....	....	....	....	....	....	....
	Rochester	AHL	21	1	2	3	56	....	....	....	....	....	....	....	....	....	....	....	....	....	....	....	....	....	....	....
1989-90	**NY Islanders**	**NHL**	**31**	**1**	**8**	**9**	**43**	**0**	**0**	**1**	**22**	**4.5**	**13**	....	....	....	....	....	....	....	....	....	....	....	....	....
	Springfield	AHL	15	1	4	5	24	....	....	....	....	....	....	....	....	....	....	....	....	....	....	....	....	....	....	....

			Regular Season																Playoffs							
Season	Club	League	GP	G	A	Pts	PIM	PP	SH	GW	S	%	+/-	TF	F%	H	SB	Min	GP	G	A	Pts	PIM	PP	SH	GW
1990-91	NY Islanders	NHL	66	3	16	19	96	0	0	2	70	4.3	17													
	Capital District	AHL	2	1	0	1	0																			
1991-92	NY Islanders	NHL	54	4	12	16	85	0	0	0	59	6.8	15													
	Capital District	AHL	3	2	2	4	2																			
1992-93	Tampa Bay	NHL	42	2	11	13	69	0	0	0	53	3.8	2													
1993-94	Tampa Bay	NHL	73	1	11	12	127	0	0	0	88	1.1	8													
	Washington	NHL	12	0	5	5	29	0	0	0	10	0.0	7						11	2	1	3	29	0	1	1
1994-95	Washington	NHL	48	1	6	7	97	0	0	0	52	1.9	10						7	0	0	0	2	0	0	0
1995-96	Washington	NHL	78	3	7	10	149	0	0	0	52	5.8	7													
1996-97	Washington	NHL	65	1	8	9	107	0	0	0	65	1.5	8													
1997-98	Washington	NHL	68	2	8	10	70	0	0	1	59	3.4	15						21	1	2	3	20	0	0	0
1998-99	Washington	NHL	73	0	10	10	68	0	0	0	81	0.0	11	0	0.0	182	101	21:53								
99-2000	Washington	NHL	59	0	7	7	50	0	0	0	32	0.0	21	0	0.0	99	77	17:32	5	0	1	1	2	0	0	0
	NHL Totals		773	21	124	145	1180	1	0	4	737	2.8		0	0.0	281	178	19:56	46	3	4	7	57	0	1	1

• Re-entered NHL draft. Originally Hartford's 8th choice, 128th overall, in 1983 Entry Draft.

• Missed majority of 1987-88 and 1988-89 seasons recovering from knee injury originally suffered in game vs. Toronto, November 11, 1987. Traded to **NY Islanders** by **Buffalo** for NY Islanders' 6th round choice (Bill Pye) in 1989 Entry Draft, June 17, 1989. Claimed by **Tampa Bay** from **NY Islanders** in Expansion Draft, June 18, 1992. Traded to **Washington** by **Tampa Bay** for Enrico Ciccone, Washington's 3rd round choice (later traded to Anaheim - Anaheim selected Craig Reichert) in 1994 Entry Draft and the return of conditional draft choice transferred in the Pat Elynuik trade, March 21, 1994.

REGEHR, Robyn (reh-GUHR, RAW-bihn) CGY.

Defense. Shoots left. 6'2", 225 lbs. Born, Recife, Brazil, April 19, 1980. Colorado's 3rd choice, 19th overall, in 1998 Entry Draft.

			Regular Season																Playoffs							
Season	Club	League	GP	G	A	Pts	PIM	PP	SH	GW	S	%	+/-	TF	F%	H	SB	Min	GP	G	A	Pts	PIM	PP	SH	GW
1995-96	Prince Albert	SAHA	59	8	24	32	157																			
1996-97	Kamloops Blazers	WHL	64	4	19	23	96												5	0	1	1	18			
1997-98	Kamloops Blazers	WHL	65	4	10	14	120												5	0	3	3	8			
1998-99	Kamloops Blazers	WHL	54	12	20	32	130												12	1	4	5	21			
99-2000	Calgary	NHL	57	5	7	12	46	2	0	0	64	7.8	-2	0	0.0	135	62	18:24								
	Saint John Flames	AHL	5	0	0	0	0																			
	NHL Totals		57	5	7	12	46	2	0	0	64	7.8		0	0.0	135	62	18:24								

WHL West First All-Star Team (1999)

Traded to **Calgary** by **Colorado** with Rene Corbet, Wade Belak and Colorado's 2nd round compensatory choice (Jarret Stoll) in 2000 Entry Draft for Theoren Fleury and Chris Dingman, February 28, 1999.

REICHEL, Robert (RIGH-khul, RAW-buhrt) PHX.

Center. Shoots left. 5'10", 185 lbs. Born, Litvinov, Czech., June 25, 1971. Calgary's 5th choice, 70th overall, in 1989 Entry Draft.

			Regular Season																Playoffs							
Season	Club	League	GP	G	A	Pts	PIM	PP	SH	GW	S	%	+/-	TF	F%	H	SB	Min	GP	G	A	Pts	PIM	PP	SH	GW
1987-88	CHZ Litvinov	Czech.	36	17	10	27	8																			
1988-89	CHZ Litvinov	Czech.	44	23	25	48	32																			
1989-90	CHZ Litvinov	Czech.	44	*43	28	*71													8	6	6	12				
1990-91	Calgary	NHL	66	19	22	41	22	3	0	3	131	14.5	17						6	1	1	2	0	1	0	0
1991-92	Calgary	NHL	77	20	34	54	32	8	0	3	181	11.0	1													
1992-93	Calgary	NHL	80	40	48	88	54	12	0	5	238	16.8	25						6	2	4	6	2	2	0	0
1993-94	Calgary	NHL	84	40	53	93	58	14	0	6	249	16.1	20						7	0	5	5	0	0	0	0
1994-95	Frankfurt Lions	DEL	21	19	24	43	41																			
	Calgary	NHL	48	18	17	35	28	5	0	2	160	11.3	-2						7	2	4	6	4	0	0	1
1995-96	Frankfurt Lions	DEL	46	47	54	101	84												3	1	3	4	0			
1996-97	Calgary	NHL	70	16	27	43	22	6	0	3	181	8.8	-2													
	NY Islanders	NHL	12	5	14	19	4	0	1	0	33	15.2	7													
1997-98	NY Islanders	NHL	82	25	40	65	32	8	0	2	201	12.4	-11													
	Czech-Republic	Olympics	6	3	0	3	0																			
1998-99	NY Islanders	NHL	70	19	37	56	50	5	1	1	186	10.2	-15	1241	51.7	52	19	19:36								
	Phoenix	NHL	13	7	6	13	4	3	0	3	50	14.0	2	241	48.5	10	4	20:03	7	1	3	4	2	0	0	0
99-2000	CHZ Litvinov	Cze-Rep	45	25	32	57	24												7	3	4	7	2			
	NHL Totals		602	209	298	507	306	64	2	28	1610	13.0		1482	51.2	62	23	19:40	33	6	17	23	8	3	0	1

Czechoslovakian First All-Star Team (1990)

Traded to **NY Islanders** by **Calgary** for Marty McInnis, Tyrone Garner and Calgary's 6th round choice (previously acquired, Calgary selected Ilja Demidov) in 1997 Entry Draft, March 18, 1997. Traded to **Phoenix** by **NY Islanders** with NY Islanders' 3rd round choice (Jason Jaspers) in 1999 Entry Draft and Ottawa's 4th round choice (previously acquired, Phoenix selected Preston Mizzi) in 1999 Entry Draft for Brad Isbister and Phoenix's 3rd round choice (Brian Collins) in 1999 Entry Draft, March 20, 1999.

REICHERT, Craig (RIGH-kuhrt, KRAYG)

Right wing. Shoots right. 6'1", 200 lbs. Born, Winnipeg, Man., May 11, 1974. Anaheim's 3rd choice, 67th overall, in 1994 Entry Draft.

			Regular Season																Playoffs							
Season	Club	League	GP	G	A	Pts	PIM	PP	SH	GW	S	%	+/-	TF	F%	H	SB	Min	GP	G	A	Pts	PIM	PP	SH	GW
1990-91	Calgary Buffaloes	AAHA	47	32	36	68	54												13	13	28	41	27			
1991-92	Spokane Chiefs	WHL	68	13	20	33	56												4	1	0	1	4			
1992-93	Red Deer Rebels	WHL	66	32	33	65	62												4	3	1	4	2			
1993-94	Red Deer Rebels	WHL	72	52	67	119	153												4	2	2	4	8			
1994-95	San Diego Gulls	IHL	49	4	12	16	28																			
1995-96	Baltimore Bandits	AHL	68	10	17	27	50												1	0	0	0	0			
1996-97	Anaheim	NHL	3	0	0	0	0	0	0	0	3	0.0	-2													
	Baltimore Bandits	AHL	77	22	53	75	54												3	0	2	2	0			
1997-98	Cincinnati Ducks	AHL	78	28	59	87	28																			
1998-99	Cincinnati Ducks	AHL	72	28	41	69	56												3	2	0	2	0			
99-2000	Louisville	AHL	72	16	42	58	41												4	1	1	2	2			
	NHL Totals		3	0	0	0	0	0	0	0	3	0.0														

Signed as a free agent by **Florida**, July 21, 1999.

REID, Dave (REED, DAYV) COL.

Left wing. Shoots left. 6'1", 217 lbs. Born, Toronto, Ont., May 15, 1964. Boston's 4th choice, 60th overall, in 1982 Entry Draft.

			Regular Season																Playoffs							
Season	Club	League	GP	G	A	Pts	PIM	PP	SH	GW	S	%	+/-	TF	F%	H	SB	Min	GP	G	A	Pts	PIM	PP	SH	GW
1979-80	Royal York Royals	OJHL	41	4	7	11	93																			
1980-81	Mississauga Reps	MTHL	39	21	28	49																				
	Dixie Beehives	OHA-B	4	2	3	5	0																			
1981-82	Peterborough	OHL	68	10	32	42	41												9	2	3	5	11			
1982-83	Peterborough	OHL	70	23	34	57	33												4	3	1	4	0			
1983-84	Peterborough	OHL	60	33	64	97	12																			
	Boston	NHL	8	1	0	1	2	0	0	0	4	25.0	1													
1984-85	Boston	NHL	35	14	13	27	27	2	0	5	52	26.9	-1						5	1	0	1	0	0	0	0
	Hershey Bears	AHL	43	10	14	24	6																			
1985-86	Boston	NHL	37	10	10	20	10	4	0	1	53	18.9	2													
	Moncton Flames	AHL	26	14	18	32	4																			
1986-87	Boston	NHL	12	3	3	6	0	0	0	0	19	15.8	-1						2	0	0	0	0	0	0	0
	Moncton Flames	AHL	40	12	22	34	23												5	0	1	1	0			
1987-88	Boston	NHL	3	0	0	0	0	0	0	0	2	0.0	0													
	Maine Mariners	AHL	63	21	37	58	40												10	6	7	13	0			
1988-89	Toronto	NHL	77	9	21	30	22	1	1	0	87	10.3	12													
1989-90	Toronto	NHL	70	9	19	28	9	0	4	1	97	9.3	-8						3	0	0	0	0	0	0	0
1990-91	Toronto	NHL	69	15	13	28	18	1	8	0	110	13.6	-10													
1991-92	Boston	NHL	43	7	7	14	27	2	1	0	70	10.0	5						15	2	5	7	4	0	0	1
	Maine Mariners	AHL	12	1	5	6	4																			
1992-93	Boston	NHL	65	20	16	36	10	1	5	2	116	17.2	12													
1993-94	Boston	NHL	83	6	17	23	25	0	2	1	145	4.1	10						13	2	1	3	2	0	1	0
1994-95	Boston	NHL	38	5	5	10	10	0	0	0	47	10.6	8						5	0	0	0	0	0	0	0
	Providence Bruins	AHL	7	3	0	3	0																			
1995-96	Boston	NHL	63	23	21	44	4	1	6	3	160	14.4	14						5	0	2	2	2	0	0	0
1996-97	Dallas	NHL	82	19	20	39	10	1	1	4	135	14.1	12						7	1	0	1	4	0	0	0
1997-98	Dallas	NHL	65	6	12	18	14	3	0	1	90	6.7	-15						5	0	3	3	2	0	0	0

			Regular Season																Playoffs							
Season	Club	League	GP	G	A	Pts	PIM	PP	SH	GW	S	%	+/-	TF	F%	H	SB	Min	GP	G	A	Pts	PIM	PP	SH	GW
1998-99♦	**Dallas**	**NHL**	73	6	11	17	16	1	0	1	81	7.4	0	39	41.0	45	34	11:34	23	2	8	10	14	0	0	0
99-2000	**Colorado**	**NHL**	65	11	7	18	28	0	0	3	86	12.8	12	46	34.8	30	41	14:57	17	1	3	4	0	0	0	0
	NHL Totals		888	164	195	359	232	17	28	22	1354	12.1		85	37.6	75	75	13:09	100	9	22	31	28	0	1	1

Signed as a free agent by **Toronto**, June 23, 1988. Signed as a free agent by **Boston**, December 1, 1991. Signed as a free agent by **Dallas**, July 11, 1996. Signed as a free agent by **Colorado**, October 6, 1999.

REINPRECHT, Steve

L.A.

Center. Shoots left. 6', 190 lbs. Born, Edmonton, AB, May 7, 1976.

			Regular Season																Playoffs							
Season	Club	League	GP	G	A	Pts	PIM	PP	SH	GW	S	%	+/-	TF	F%	H	SB	Min	GP	G	A	Pts	PIM	PP	SH	GW
1995-96	St. Albert Saints	AJHL	32	24	36	60	....	....	....	....	....	....	....	....	....	....	....	....	....	....	....	....	....	....	....	....
1996-97	U. of Wisconsin	WCHA	38	11	9	20	12	....	....	....	....	....	....	....	....	....	....	....	....	....	....	....	....	....	....	....
1997-98	U. of Wisconsin	WCHA	41	19	24	43	18	....	....	....	....	....	....	....	....	....	....	....	....	....	....	....	....	....	....	....
1998-99	U. of Wisconsin	WCHA	38	16	17	33	14	....	....	....	....	....	....	....	....	....	....	....	....	....	....	....	....	....	....	....
99-2000	U. of Wisconsin	WCHA	37	26	40	*66	14	....	....	....	....	....	....	....	....	....	....	....	....	....	....	....	....	....	....	....
	Los Angeles	**NHL**	1	0	0	0	2	0	0	0	0	0.0	0	6	50.0	0	0	6:01	....	....	....	....	....	....	....	....
	NHL Totals		1	0	0	0	2	0	0	0	0	0.0		6	50.0	0	0	6:01	....	....	....	....	....	....	....	....

WCHA Second All-Star Team (1998) • WCHA First All-Star Team (2000) • NCAA West First All-American Team (2000)

Signed as a free agent by **LA Kings**, March 31, 2000.

REIRDEN, Todd

(REER-dehn, TAWD) **ST.L.**

Defense. Shoots left. 6'5", 220 lbs. Born, Deerfield, IL, June 25, 1971. New Jersey's 14th choice, 242nd overall, in 1990 Entry Draft.

			Regular Season																Playoffs							
Season	Club	League	GP	G	A	Pts	PIM	PP	SH	GW	S	%	+/-	TF	F%	H	SB	Min	GP	G	A	Pts	PIM	PP	SH	GW
1987-88	Deerfield High	Hi-School	22	19	32	51	....	....	....	....	....	....	....	....	....	....	....	....	....	....	....	....	....	....	....	....
1988-89	Tabor Academy	Hi-School	22	6	16	22	....	....	....	....	....	....	....	....	....	....	....	....	....	....	....	....	....	....	....	....
1989-90	Tabor Academy	Hi-School	22	10	28	38	....	....	....	....	....	....	....	....	....	....	....	....	....	....	....	....	....	....	....	....
1990-91	Bowling Green	CCHA	28	1	5	6	22	....	....	....	....	....	....	....	....	....	....	....	....	....	....	....	....	....	....	....
1991-92	Bowling Green	CCHA	33	8	7	15	34	....	....	....	....	....	....	....	....	....	....	....	....	....	....	....	....	....	....	....
1992-93	Bowling Green	CCHA	41	8	17	25	48	....	....	....	....	....	....	....	....	....	....	....	....	....	....	....	....	....	....	....
1993-94	Bowling Green	CCHA	38	7	23	30	56	....	....	....	....	....	....	....	....	....	....	....	....	....	....	....	....	....	....	....
1994-95	Albany River Rats	AHL	2	0	1	1	2	....	....	....	....	....	....	....	....	....	....	....	....	....	....	....	....	....	....	....
	Raleigh Icecaps	ECHL	26	2	13	15	33	....	....	....	....	....	....	....	....	....	....	....	....	....	....	....	....	....	....	....
	Tallahassee	ECHL	43	5	25	30	61	....	....	....	....	....	....	....	....	....	....	....	13	2	5	7	40	....	....	....
1995-96	Tallahassee	ECHL	7	1	3	4	10	....	....	....	....	....	....	....	....	....	....	....	....	....	....	....	....	....	....	....
	Jacksonville	ECHL	15	1	10	11	41	....	....	....	....	....	....	....	....	....	....	....	1	0	2	2	4	....	....	....
	Chicago Wolves	IHL	31	0	2	2	39	....	....	....	....	....	....	....	....	....	....	....	9	0	2	2	16	....	....	....
1996-97	Chicago Wolves	IHL	57	3	10	13	108	....	....	....	....	....	....	....	....	....	....	....	....	....	....	....	....	....	....	....
	San Antonio	IHL	23	2	5	7	51	....	....	....	....	....	....	....	....	....	....	....	9	0	1	1	17	....	....	....
1997-98	San Antonio	IHL	70	5	14	19	132	....	....	....	....	....	....	....	....	....	....	....	....	....	....	....	....	....	....	....
	Fort Wayne	IHL	11	2	2	4	16	....	....	....	....	....	....	....	....	....	....	....	4	0	2	2	4	....	....	....
1998-99	**Edmonton**	**NHL**	17	2	3	5	20	0	0	0	26	7.7	–1	0	0.0	18	18	17:17	....	....	....	....	....	....	....	....
	Hamilton Bulldogs	AHL	58	9	25	34	84	....	....	....	....	....	....	....	....	....	....	....	11	0	5	5	6	....	....	....
99-2000	**St. Louis**	**NHL**	56	4	21	25	32	0	0	1	77	5.2	18	1	0.0	59	49	18:18	4	0	1	1	0	0	0	0
	NHL Totals		73	6	24	30	52	0	0	1	103	5.8		1	0.0	77	67	18:04	4	0	1	1	0	0	0	0

Signed as a free agent by **Edmonton**, September 17, 1998. Claimed on waivers by **St. Louis** from **Edmonton**, September 30, 1999.

RENBERG, Mikael

(REHN-buhrg, MIHK-al) **PHX.**

Right wing. Shoots left. 6'2", 218 lbs. Born, Pitea, Sweden, May 5, 1972. Philadelphia's 3rd choice, 40th overall, in 1990 Entry Draft.

			Regular Season																Playoffs							
Season	Club	League	GP	G	A	Pts	PIM	PP	SH	GW	S	%	+/-	TF	F%	H	SB	Min	GP	G	A	Pts	PIM	PP	SH	GW
1988-89	Pitea HC	Sweden-2	12	6	3	9	....	....	....	....	....	....	....	....	....	....	....	....	....	....	....	....	....	....	....	....
1989-90	Pitea HC	Sweden-2	29	15	19	34	....	....	....	....	....	....	....	....	....	....	....	....	....	....	....	....	....	....	....	....
1990-91	Lulea HF	Sweden	29	11	6	17	12	....	....	....	....	....	....	....	....	....	....	....	5	1	1	2	4	....	....	....
1991-92	Lulea HF	Sweden	38	8	15	23	20	....	....	....	....	....	....	....	....	....	....	....	2	0	0	0	0	....	....	....
1992-93	Lulea HF	Sweden	39	19	13	32	61	....	....	....	....	....	....	....	....	....	....	....	11	4	4	8	4	....	....	....
1993-94	**Philadelphia**	**NHL**	83	38	44	82	36	9	0	1	195	19.5	8	....	....	....	....	....	....	....	....	....	....	....	....	....
1994-95	Lulea HF	Sweden	10	9	4	13	16	....	....	....	....	....	....	....	....	....	....	....	....	....	....	....	....	....	....	....
	Philadelphia	**NHL**	47	26	31	57	20	8	0	4	143	18.2	20	....	....	....	....	....	15	6	7	13	6	2	0	0
1995-96	**Philadelphia**	**NHL**	51	23	20	43	45	9	0	4	198	11.6	8	....	....	....	....	....	11	3	6	9	14	1	0	0
1996-97	**Philadelphia**	**NHL**	77	22	37	59	65	1	0	4	249	8.8	36	....	....	....	....	....	18	5	6	11	4	2	0	0
1997-98	**Tampa Bay**	**NHL**	68	16	22	38	34	6	3	0	175	9.1	–37	....	....	....	....	....	....	....	....	....	....	....	....	....
	Sweden	Olympics	4	1	2	3	4	....	....	....	....	....	....	....	....	....	....	....	....	....	....	....	....	....	....	....
1998-99	**Tampa Bay**	**NHL**	20	4	8	12	4	2	0	0	42	9.5	–2	2	100.0	1	4	15:32	....	....	....	....	....	....	....	....
	Philadelphia	**NHL**	46	11	15	26	14	4	0	2	112	9.8	7	1	0.0	8	5	16:00	6	0	1	1	0	0	0	0
99-2000	**Philadelphia**	**NHL**	62	8	21	29	30	3	0	1	106	7.5	–1	3	33.3	23	10	13:27	....	....	....	....	....	....	....	....
	Phoenix	**NHL**	10	2	4	6	2	0	0	0	16	12.5	0	0	0.0	2	1	15:31	5	1	2	3	4	0	0	1
	NHL Totals		464	150	202	352	250	42	3	16	1236	12.1		6	50.0	34	20	14:45	55	15	22	37	28	5	0	1

NHL All-Rookie Team (1994)

Traded to **Tampa Bay** by **Philadelphia** with Karl Dykhuis for Philadelphia's 1st round choices (previously acquired by Tampa Bay) in 1998 (Simon Gagne), 1999 (Maxime Ouellet), 2000 and 2001 Entry Drafts, August 20, 1997. Traded to **Philadelphia** by **Tampa Bay** with Daymond Langkow for Chris Gratton and Mike Sillinger, December 12, 1998. Traded to **Phoenix** by **Philadelphia** for Rick Tocchet, March 8, 2000.

RHEAUME, Pascal

(RAY-awm, PAS-kal) **ST.L.**

Left wing. Shoots left. 6'1", 209 lbs. Born, Quebec, Que., June 21, 1973.

			Regular Season																Playoffs							
Season	Club	League	GP	G	A	Pts	PIM	PP	SH	GW	S	%	+/-	TF	F%	H	SB	Min	GP	G	A	Pts	PIM	PP	SH	GW
1990-91	Ste-Foy Governors	QAAA	37	20	38	58	25	....	....	....	....	....	....	....	....	....	....	....	....	....	....	....	....	....	....	....
1991-92	Trois-Rivieres	QMJHL	65	17	20	37	84	....	....	....	....	....	....	....	....	....	....	....	14	5	4	9	23	....	....	....
1992-93	Sherbrooke	QMJHL	65	28	34	62	88	....	....	....	....	....	....	....	....	....	....	....	14	6	5	11	31	....	....	....
1993-94	Albany River Rats	AHL	55	17	18	35	43	....	....	....	....	....	....	....	....	....	....	....	5	0	1	1	0	....	....	....
1994-95	Albany River Rats	AHL	78	19	25	44	46	....	....	....	....	....	....	....	....	....	....	....	14	3	6	9	19	....	....	....
1995-96	Albany River Rats	AHL	68	26	42	68	50	....	....	....	....	....	....	....	....	....	....	....	4	1	2	3	2	....	....	....
1996-97	**New Jersey**	**NHL**	2	1	0	1	0	0	0	0	5	20.0	1	....	....	....	....	....	....	....	....	....	....	....	....	....
	Albany River Rats	AHL	51	22	23	45	40	....	....	....	....	....	....	....	....	....	....	....	16	2	8	10	16	....	....	....
1997-98	**St. Louis**	**NHL**	48	6	9	15	35	1	0	0	45	13.3	4	....	....	....	....	....	10	1	3	4	8	1	0	0
1998-99	**St. Louis**	**NHL**	60	9	18	27	24	2	0	0	85	10.6	10	21	71.4	105	14	13:19	5	1	0	1	4	0	0	0
99-2000	**St. Louis**	**NHL**	7	1	1	2	6	0	0	0	5	20.0	–2	2	0.0	9	1	10:08	....	....	....	....	....	....	....	....
	Worcester	AHL	7	1	1	2	4	....	....	....	....	....	....	....	....	....	....	....	....	....	....	....	....	....	....	....
	NHL Totals		117	17	28	45	65	3	0	0	140	12.1		23	65.2	114	15	12:59	15	2	3	5	12	1	0	0

Signed as a free agent by **New Jersey**, October 1, 1993. Claimed by **St. Louis** from **New Jersey** in NHL Waiver Draft, September 28, 1997. • Missed majority of 1999-2000 season recovering from shoulder surgery, August, 1999.

RIBEIRO, Mike

(rih-bee-AIR-roh, MIGHK) **MTL.**

Center. Shoots left. 5'11", 164 lbs. Born, Montreal, Que., February 10, 1980. Montreal's 2nd choice, 45th overall, in 1998 Entry Draft.

			Regular Season																Playoffs							
Season	Club	League	GP	G	A	Pts	PIM	PP	SH	GW	S	%	+/-	TF	F%	H	SB	Min	GP	G	A	Pts	PIM	PP	SH	GW
1996-97	Montreal L'est	QAAA	43	32	57	89	48	....	....	....	....	....	....	....	....	....	....	....	....	....	....	....	....	....	....	....
1997-98	Rouyn Noranda	QMJHL	67	40	*85	125	55	....	....	....	....	....	....	....	....	....	....	....	6	3	1	4	0	....	....	....
1998-99	Rouyn-Noranda	QMJHL	69	*67	*100	*167	137	....	....	....	....	....	....	....	....	....	....	....	11	5	11	16	12	....	....	....
	Fredericton	AHL	....	....	....	....	....	....	....	....	....	....	....	....	....	....	....	....	5	0	1	1	2	....	....	....
99-2000	**Montreal**	**NHL**	19	1	1	2	2	1	0	0	18	5.6	–6	95	34.7	15	5	10:40	....	....	....	....	....	....	....	....
	Quebec Citadelles	AHL	3	0	0	0	2	....	....	....	....	....	....	....	....	....	....	....	....	....	....	....	....	....	....	....
	Rouyn-Noranda	QMJHL	2	1	3	4	0	....	....	....	....	....	....	....	....	....	....	....	....	....	....	....	....	....	....	....
	Quebec Remparts	QMJHL	21	17	28	45	30	....	....	....	....	....	....	....	....	....	....	....	11	3	20	23	38	....	....	....
	NHL Totals		19	1	1	2	2	1	0	0	18	5.6		95	34.7	15	5	10:40	....	....	....	....	....	....	....	....

QMJHL Second All-Star Team (1998) • QMJHL First All-Star Team (1999) • Canadian Major Junior First All-Star Team (1999)

Assigned to **Rouyn-Noranda** QMJHL) by **Montreal**, January 5, 2000.

RICCI, Mike
(REE-CHEE, MIGHK) **S.J.**

Center. Shoots left. 6', 190 lbs. Born, Scarborough, Ont., October 27, 1971. Philadelphia's 1st choice, 4th overall, in 1990 Entry Draft.

			Regular Season																Playoffs							
Season	Club	League	GP	G	A	Pts	PIM	PP	SH	GW	S	%	+/-	TF	F%	H	SB	Min	GP	G	A	Pts	PIM	PP	SH	GW
1986-87	Toronto Marlies	MTHL	38	39	42	81	27	....	....	....	....	....	....	....	....	....	....	....	....	....	....	....	....	....	....	....
1987-88	Peterborough	OHL	41	24	37	61	20	....	....	....	....	....	....	....	....	....	....	....	8	5	5	10	4	....	....	....
1988-89	Peterborough	OHL	60	54	52	106	43	....	....	....	....	....	....	....	....	....	....	....	17	19	16	35	18	....	....	....
1989-90	Peterborough	OHL	60	52	64	116	39	....	....	....	....	....	....	....	....	....	....	....	12	5	7	12	26	....	....	....
1990-91	**Philadelphia**	**NHL**	68	21	20	41	64	9	0	4	121	17.4	–8	....	....	....	....	....	....	....	....	....	....	....	....	....
1991-92	**Philadelphia**	**NHL**	78	20	36	56	93	11	2	0	149	13.4	–10	....	....	....	....	....	....	....	....	....	....	....	....	....
1992-93	**Quebec**	**NHL**	77	27	51	78	123	12	1	10	142	19.0	8	....	....	....	....	....	6	0	6	6	8	0	0	0
1993-94	**Quebec**	**NHL**	83	30	21	51	113	13	3	6	138	21.7	–9	....	....	....	....	....	....	....	....	....	....	....	....	....
1994-95	**Quebec**	**NHL**	48	15	21	36	40	9	0	1	73	20.5	5	....	....	....	....	....	6	1	3	4	8	0	0	0
1995-96♦	**Colorado**	**NHL**	62	6	21	27	52	3	0	1	73	8.2	1	....	....	....	....	....	22	6	11	17	18	3	0	1
1996-97	**Colorado**	**NHL**	63	13	19	32	59	5	0	3	74	17.6	–3	....	....	....	....	....	17	2	4	6	17	0	0	1
1997-98	**Colorado**	**NHL**	6	0	4	4	2	0	0	0	5	0.0	0	....	....	....	....	....	....	....	....	....	....	....	....	....
	San Jose	**NHL**	59	9	14	23	30	5	0	2	86	10.5	–4	....	....	....	....	....	6	1	3	4	6	0	0	0
1998-99	**San Jose**	**NHL**	82	13	26	39	68	2	1	2	98	13.3	1	1465	49.6	73	41	15:23	6	2	3	5	10	1	0	0
99-2000	**San Jose**	**NHL**	82	20	24	44	60	10	0	5	134	14.9	14	1522	50.7	94	52	16:52	12	5	1	6	2	3	0	1
	NHL Totals		**708**	**174**	**257**	**431**	**704**	**79**	**7**	**34**	**1093**	**15.9**		**2987**	**50.2**	**167**	**93**	**16:08**	**75**	**17**	**31**	**48**	**69**	**7**	**0**	**3**

OHL Second All-Star Team (1989) • Canadian Major Junior Player of the Year (1990) • OHL First All-Star Team (1990)

Traded to **Quebec** by **Philadelphia** with Steve Duchesne, Peter Forsberg, Kerry Huffman, Ron Hextall, Philadelphia's 1st round choice (Jocelyn Thibault) in 1993 Entry Draft, $15,000,000 and future considerations (Chris Simon and Philadelphia's 1st round choice (later traded to Toronto - later traded to Washington - Washington selected Nolan Baumgartner) in 1994 Entry Draft, July 21, 1992) for Eric Lindros, June 30, 1992. Transferred to **Colorado** after **Quebec** franchise relocated, June 21, 1995. Traded to **San Jose** by **Colorado** with Colorado's 2nd round choice (later traded to Buffalo - Buffalo selected Jaroslav Kristek) in 1998 Entry Draft for Shean Donovan and San Jose's 1st round choice (Alex Tanguay) in 1998 Entry Draft, November 21, 1997.

RICHARDSON, Luke
(RIH-chahrd-sohn, LEWK) **PHI.**

Defense. Shoots left. 6'3", 210 lbs. Born, Ottawa, Ont., March 26, 1969. Toronto's 1st choice, 7th overall, in 1987 Entry Draft.

			Regular Season																Playoffs							
Season	Club	League	GP	G	A	Pts	PIM	PP	SH	GW	S	%	+/-	TF	F%	H	SB	Min	GP	G	A	Pts	PIM	PP	SH	GW
1984-85	Ottawa	OJHL	35	5	26	31	72	....	....	....	....	....	....	....	....	....	....	....	....	....	....	....	....	....	....	....
1985-86	Peterborough	OHL	63	6	18	24	57	....	....	....	....	....	....	....	....	....	....	....	16	2	1	3	50	....	....	....
1986-87	Peterborough	OHL	59	13	32	45	70	....	....	....	....	....	....	....	....	....	....	....	12	0	5	5	24	....	....	....
1987-88	**Toronto**	**NHL**	78	4	6	10	90	0	0	0	49	8.2	–25	....	....	....	....	....	2	0	0	0	0	0	0	0
1988-89	**Toronto**	**NHL**	55	2	7	9	106	0	0	0	59	3.4	–15	....	....	....	....	....	....	....	....	....	....	....	....	....
1989-90	**Toronto**	**NHL**	67	4	14	18	122	0	0	0	80	5.0	–1	....	....	....	....	....	5	0	0	0	22	0	0	0
1990-91	**Toronto**	**NHL**	78	1	9	10	238	0	0	0	68	1.5	–28	....	....	....	....	....	....	....	....	....	....	....	....	....
1991-92	**Edmonton**	**NHL**	75	2	19	21	118	0	0	0	85	2.4	–9	....	....	....	....	....	16	0	5	5	45	0	0	0
1992-93	**Edmonton**	**NHL**	82	3	10	13	142	0	2	0	78	3.8	–18	....	....	....	....	....	....	....	....	....	....	....	....	....
1993-94	**Edmonton**	**NHL**	69	2	6	8	131	0	0	0	92	2.2	–13	....	....	....	....	....	....	....	....	....	....	....	....	....
1994-95	**Edmonton**	**NHL**	46	3	10	13	40	1	1	1	51	5.9	–6	....	....	....	....	....	....	....	....	....	....	....	....	....
1995-96	**Edmonton**	**NHL**	82	2	9	11	108	0	0	0	61	3.3	–27	....	....	....	....	....	....	....	....	....	....	....	....	....
1996-97	**Edmonton**	**NHL**	82	1	11	12	91	0	0	0	67	1.5	9	....	....	....	....	....	12	0	2	2	14	0	0	0
1997-98	**Philadelphia**	**NHL**	81	2	3	5	139	2	0	0	57	3.5	7	....	....	....	....	....	5	0	0	0	0	0	0	0
1998-99	**Philadelphia**	**NHL**	78	0	6	6	106	0	0	0	49	0.0	–3	0	0.0	116	94	16:33	....	....	....	....	....	....	....	....
99-2000	**Philadelphia**	**NHL**	74	2	5	7	140	0	0	1	50	4.0	14	0	0.0	125	109	16:11	18	0	1	1	41	0	0	0
	NHL Totals		**947**	**28**	**115**	**143**	**1571**	**3**	**3**	**2**	**846**	**3.3**		**0**	**0.0**	**241**	**203**	**16:22**	**58**	**0**	**8**	**8**	**122**	**0**	**0**	**0**

Traded to **Edmonton** by **Toronto** with Vincent Damphousse, Peter Ing, Scott Thornton, future considerations and cash for Grant Fuhr, Glenn Anderson and Craig Berube, September 19, 1991. Signed as a free agent by **Philadelphia**, July 23, 1997.

RICHER, Stephane
(REE-shay, STEH-fan) **WSH.**

Right wing. Shoots right. 6'2", 215 lbs. Born, Ripon, Que., June 7, 1966. Montreal's 3rd choice, 29th overall, in 1984 Entry Draft.

			Regular Season																Playoffs							
Season	Club	League	GP	G	A	Pts	PIM	PP	SH	GW	S	%	+/-	TF	F%	H	SB	Min	GP	G	A	Pts	PIM	PP	SH	GW
1982-83	Laval Insulaires	QAAA	48	47	54	101	86	....	....	....	....	....	....	....	....	....	....	....	....	....	....	....	....	....	....	....
1983-84	Granby Bisons	QMJHL	67	39	37	76	58	....	....	....	....	....	....	....	....	....	....	....	3	1	1	2	4	....	....	....
1984-85	Granby Bisons	QMJHL	30	30	27	57	31	....	....	....	....	....	....	....	....	....	....	....	....	....	....	....	....	....	....	....
	Chicoutimi	QMJHL	27	31	32	63	40	....	....	....	....	....	....	....	....	....	....	....	12	13	13	26	25	....	....	....
	Montreal	**NHL**	1	0	0	0	0	0	0	0	0	0.0	0	....	....	....	....	....	....	....	....	....	....	....	....	....
	Sherbrooke	AHL	....	....	....	....	....	....	....	....	....	....	....	....	....	....	....	....	9	6	3	9	10	....	....	....
1985-86♦	**Montreal**	**NHL**	65	21	16	37	50	5	0	2	112	18.8	1	....	....	....	....	....	16	4	1	5	23	3	0	1
1986-87	**Montreal**	**NHL**	57	20	19	39	80	4	0	3	109	18.3	11	....	....	....	....	....	5	3	2	5	0	0	0	1
	Sherbrooke	AHL	12	10	4	14	11	....	....	....	....	....	....	....	....	....	....	....	....	....	....	....	....	....	....	....
1987-88	**Montreal**	**NHL**	72	50	28	78	72	16	0	11	263	19.0	12	....	....	....	....	....	8	7	5	12	6	1	0	2
1988-89	**Montreal**	**NHL**	68	25	35	60	61	11	0	6	214	11.7	4	....	....	....	....	....	21	6	5	11	14	2	0	3
1989-90	**Montreal**	**NHL**	75	51	40	91	46	9	0	8	269	19.0	35	....	....	....	....	....	9	7	3	10	2	1	0	1
1990-91	**Montreal**	**NHL**	75	31	30	61	53	9	0	4	221	14.0	0	....	....	....	....	....	13	9	5	14	6	1	0	1
1991-92	**New Jersey**	**NHL**	74	29	35	64	25	5	1	6	240	12.1	–1	....	....	....	....	....	7	1	2	3	0	0	0	0
1992-93	**New Jersey**	**NHL**	78	38	35	73	44	7	1	7	286	13.3	–1	....	....	....	....	....	5	2	2	4	2	1	0	0
1993-94	**New Jersey**	**NHL**	80	36	36	72	16	7	3	9	217	16.6	31	....	....	....	....	....	20	7	5	12	6	3	0	2
1994-95♦	**New Jersey**	**NHL**	45	23	16	39	10	1	2	5	133	17.3	8	....	....	....	....	....	19	6	15	21	2	3	1	2
1995-96	**New Jersey**	**NHL**	73	20	12	32	30	3	4	3	192	10.4	–8	....	....	....	....	....	....	....	....	....	....	....	....	....
1996-97	**Montreal**	**NHL**	63	22	24	46	32	2	0	2	126	17.5	0	....	....	....	....	....	5	0	0	0	0	0	0	0
1997-98	**Montreal**	**NHL**	14	5	4	9	5	2	0	0	24	20.8	1	....	....	....	....	....	....	....	....	....	....	....	....	....
	Tampa Bay	**NHL**	26	9	11	20	36	3	0	2	71	12.7	–7	....	....	....	....	....	....	....	....	....	....	....	....	....
1998-99	**Tampa Bay**	**NHL**	64	12	21	33	22	3	2	1	139	8.6	–10	67	31.3	32	11	16:47	....	....	....	....	....	....	....	....
99-2000	**Tampa Bay**	**NHL**	20	7	5	12	4	1	0	0	47	14.9	2	7	57.1	14	6	14:31	....	....	....	....	....	....	....	....
	Detroit Vipers	IHL	2	0	0	0	0	....	....	....	....	....	....	....	....	....	....	....	....	....	....	....	....	....	....	....
	St. Louis	**NHL**	36	8	17	25	14	4	0	1	63	12.7	7	0	0.0	21	3	13:27	3	1	0	1	0	0	0	0
	NHL Totals		**986**	**407**	**384**	**791**	**600**	**92**	**13**	**70**	**2726**	**14.9**		**74**	**33.8**	**67**	**20**	**15:24**	**131**	**53**	**45**	**98**	**61**	**15**	**1**	**13**

QMJHL Rookie of the Year (1984) • QMJHL Second All-Star Team (1985) • Played in NHL All-Star Game (1990)

Traded to **New Jersey** by **Montreal** with Tom Chorske for Kirk Muller and Rollie Melanson, September 20, 1991. Traded to **Montreal** by **New Jersey** for Lyle Odelein, August 22, 1996. Traded to **Tampa Bay** by **Montreal** with Darcy Tucker and David Wilkie for Patrick Poulin, Mick Vukota and Igor Ulanov, January 15, 1998. Traded to **St. Louis** by **Tampa Bay** for Rich Parent and Chris McAlpine, January 13, 2000. Signed as a free agent by **Washington** August 25, 2000.

RICHTER, Barry
(RIHK-tuhr, BAIR-ree) **MTL.**

Defense. Shoots left. 6'2", 200 lbs. Born, Madison, WI, September 11, 1970. Hartford's 2nd choice, 32nd overall, in 1988 Entry Draft.

			Regular Season																Playoffs							
Season	Club	League	GP	G	A	Pts	PIM	PP	SH	GW	S	%	+/-	TF	F%	H	SB	Min	GP	G	A	Pts	PIM	PP	SH	GW
1986-87	Culver Academy	Hi-School	39	15	30	45		....	....	....	....	....	....	....	....	....	....	....	....	....	....	....	....	....	....	....
1987-88	Culver Academy	Hi-School	35	24	29	53	18	....	....	....	....	....	....	....	....	....	....	....	....	....	....	....	....	....	....	....
1988-89	Culver Academy	Hi-School	19	21	29	50	16	....	....	....	....	....	....	....	....	....	....	....	....	....	....	....	....	....	....	....
1989-90	U. of Wisconsin	WCHA	42	13	23	36	36	....	....	....	....	....	....	....	....	....	....	....	....	....	....	....	....	....	....	....
1990-91	U. of Wisconsin	WCHA	43	15	20	35	42	....	....	....	....	....	....	....	....	....	....	....	....	....	....	....	....	....	....	....
1991-92	U. of Wisconsin	WCHA	39	10	25	35	62	....	....	....	....	....	....	....	....	....	....	....	....	....	....	....	....	....	....	....
1992-93	U. of Wisconsin	WCHA	42	14	32	46	74	....	....	....	....	....	....	....	....	....	....	....	....	....	....	....	....	....	....	....
1993-94	United States	Nat-Team	56	7	16	23	50	....	....	....	....	....	....	....	....	....	....	....	....	....	....	....	....	....	....	....
	United States	Olympics	8	0	3	3	4	....	....	....	....	....	....	....	....	....	....	....	....	....	....	....	....	....	....	....
	Binghamton	AHL	21	0	9	9	12	....	....	....	....	....	....	....	....	....	....	....	....	....	....	....	....	....	....	....
1994-95	Binghamton	AHL	73	15	41	56	54	....	....	....	....	....	....	....	....	....	....	....	11	4	5	9	12	....	....	....
1995-96	**NY Rangers**	**NHL**	4	0	1	1	0	0	0	0	3	0.0	2	....	....	....	....	....	....	....	....	....	....	....	....	....
	Binghamton	AHL	69	20	61	81	64	....	....	....	....	....	....	....	....	....	....	....	3	0	3	3	0	....	....	....
1996-97	**Boston**	**NHL**	50	5	13	18	32	1	0	0	79	6.3	–7	....	....	....	....	....	....	....	....	....	....	....	....	....
	Providence Bruins	AHL	19	2	6	8	4	....	....	....	....	....	....	....	....	....	....	....	10	4	4	8	4	....	....	....
1997-98	Providence Bruins	AHL	75	16	29	45	47	....	....	....	....	....	....	....	....	....	....	....	....	....	....	....	....	....	....	....
1998-99	**NY Islanders**	**NHL**	72	6	18	24	34	0	0	2	111	5.4	–4	0	0.0	52	49	21:08	....	....	....	....	....	....	....	....

			Regular Season																Playoffs							
Season	Club	League	GP	G	A	Pts	PIM	PP	SH	GW	S	%	+/–	TF	F%	H	SB	Min	GP	G	A	Pts	PIM	PP	SH	GW
99-2000	**Montreal**	**NHL**	**23**	**0**	**2**	**2**	**8**	**0**	**0**	**0**	**13**	**0.0**	**–5**	**1**	**100.0**	**20**	**13**	**12:15**	....	....	....	....	....	....	....	....
	Quebec Citadelles	AHL	2	0	0	0	0	....	....	....	....	....	....	....	....	....	....	....	....	....	....	....	....	....	....	....
	Manitoba Moose	IHL	19	5	4	9	6	....	....	....	....	....	....	....	....	....	....	....	2	1	1	2	0	....	....	....
	NHL Totals		**149**	**11**	**34**	**45**	**74**	**1**	**0**	**2**	**206**	**5.3**		**1**	**100.0**	**72**	**62**	**18:59**	....	....	....	....	....	....	....	....

NCAA Championship All-Tournament Team (1992) • WCHA First All-Star Team (1993) • NCAA West First All-American Team (1993) • AHL First All-Star Team (1996) • Won Eddie Shore Award (Outstanding Defenseman - AHL) (1996)

Traded to **NY Rangers** by **Hartford** with Steve Larmer, Nick Kypreos and Hartford's 6th round choice (Yuri Litvinov) in 1994 Entry Draft for Darren Turcotte and James Patrick, November 2, 1993. Signed as a free agent by **Boston**, July 19, 1996. Signed as a free agent by **NY Islanders**, August 17, 1998. Signed as a free agent by **Montreal**, August 20, 1999. Loaned to **Manitoba** (IHL) by **Montreal** for loan of Patrice Tardif to **Quebec** (AHL), March 3, 2000.

RITCHIE, Byron

(RIHT-chee, BIGH-rohn) **CAR.**

Center. Shoots left. 5'10", 185 lbs. Born, Burnaby, B.C., April 24, 1977. Hartford's 6th choice, 165th overall, in 1995 Entry Draft.

Season	Club	League	GP	G	A	Pts	PIM	PP	SH	GW	S	%	+/–	TF	F%	H	SB	Min	GP	G	A	Pts	PIM	PP	SH	GW
1992-93	North Delta	BCAHA	60	102	151	253	147	....	....	....	....	....	....	....	....	....	....	....	....	....	....	....	....	....	....	....
1993-94	Lethbridge	WHL	44	4	11	15	44	....	....	....	....	....	....	....	....	....	....	....	6	0	0	0	14	....	....	....
1994-95	Lethbridge	WHL	58	22	28	50	132	....	....	....	....	....	....	....	....	....	....	....	....	....	....	....	....	....	....	....
1995-96	Lethbridge	WHL	66	55	51	106	163	....	....	....	....	....	....	....	....	....	....	....	4	0	2	2	4	....	....	....
	Springfield	AHL	6	2	1	3	4	....	....	....	....	....	....	....	....	....	....	....	8	0	3	3	0	....	....	....
1996-97	Lethbridge	WHL	63	50	76	126	115	....	....	....	....	....	....	....	....	....	....	....	18	*16	12	*28	28	....	....	....
1997-98	New Haven	AHL	65	13	18	31	97	....	....	....	....	....	....	....	....	....	....	....	....	....	....	....	....	....	....	....
1998-99	**Carolina**	**NHL**	**3**	**0**	**0**	**0**	**0**	**0**	**0**	**0**	**0**	**0.0**	**0**	**5**	**20.0**	**1**	**0**	**3:25**	....	....	....	....	....	....	....	....
	New Haven	AHL	66	24	33	57	139	....	....	....	....	....	....	....	....	....	....	....	....	....	....	....	....	....	....	....
99-2000	**Carolina**	**NHL**	**26**	**0**	**2**	**2**	**17**	**0**	**0**	**0**	**13**	**0.0**	**–10**	**155**	**49.7**	**33**	**7**	**7:24**	....	....	....	....	....	....	....	....
	Cincinnati	IHL	34	8	13	21	81	....	....	....	....	....	....	....	....	....	....	....	10	1	6	7	32	....	....	....
	NHL Totals		**29**	**0**	**2**	**2**	**17**	**0**	**0**	**0**	**13**	**0.0**		**160**	**48.8**	**34**	**7**	**6:60**	....	....	....	....	....	....	....	....

WHL East Second All-Star Team (1996, 1997)

Rights transferred to **Carolina** after **Hartford** franchise relocated, June 25, 1997.

RIVERS, Jamie

(RIH-vuhrs, JAY-mee)

Defense. Shoots left. 6', 197 lbs. Born, Ottawa, Ont., March 16, 1975. St. Louis' 2nd choice, 63rd overall, in 1993 Entry Draft.

Season	Club	League	GP	G	A	Pts	PIM	PP	SH	GW	S	%	+/–	TF	F%	H	SB	Min	GP	G	A	Pts	PIM	PP	SH	GW
1989-90	Ottawa South	OMHA	50	26	46	72	46	....	....	....	....	....	....	....	....	....	....	....	....	....	....	....	....	....	....	....
1990-91	Ottawa	OJHL	55	4	30	34	74	....	....	....	....	....	....	....	....	....	....	....	....	....	....	....	....	....	....	....
1991-92	Sudbury Wolves	OHL	55	3	13	16	20	....	....	....	....	....	....	....	....	....	....	....	8	0	0	0	0	....	....	....
1992-93	Sudbury Wolves	OHL	62	12	43	55	20	....	....	....	....	....	....	....	....	....	....	....	14	7	19	26	4	....	....	....
1993-94	Sudbury Wolves	OHL	65	32	*89	121	58	....	....	....	....	....	....	....	....	....	....	....	10	1	9	10	14	....	....	....
1994-95	Sudbury Wolves	OHL	46	9	56	65	30	....	....	....	....	....	....	....	....	....	....	....	18	7	26	33	22	....	....	....
1995-96	**St. Louis**	**NHL**	**3**	**0**	**0**	**0**	**2**	**0**	**0**	**0**	**5**	**0.0**	**–1**	....	....	....	....	....	....	....	....	....	....	....	....	....
	Worcester	AHL	75	7	45	52	130	....	....	....	....	....	....	....	....	....	....	....	4	0	1	1	4	....	....	....
1996-97	**St. Louis**	**NHL**	**15**	**2**	**5**	**7**	**6**	**1**	**0**	**0**	**9**	**22.2**	**–4**	....	....	....	....	....	....	....	....	....	....	....	....	....
	Worcester	AHL	63	8	35	43	83	....	....	....	....	....	....	....	....	....	....	....	5	1	2	3	14	....	....	....
1997-98	**St. Louis**	**NHL**	**59**	**2**	**4**	**6**	**36**	**1**	**0**	**1**	**53**	**3.8**	**5**	....	....	....	....	....	....	....	....	....	....	....	....	....
1998-99	**St. Louis**	**NHL**	**76**	**2**	**5**	**7**	**47**	**1**	**0**	**0**	**78**	**2.6**	**–3**	**0**	**0.0**	**131**	**63**	**14:10**	**9**	**1**	**1**	**2**	**2**	**1**	**0**	**1**
99-2000	**NY Islanders**	**NHL**	**75**	**1**	**16**	**17**	**84**	**1**	**0**	**0**	**95**	**1.1**	**–4**	**0**	**0.0**	**219**	**112**	**19:39**	....	....	....	....	....	....	....	....
	NHL Totals		**228**	**7**	**30**	**37**	**175**	**4**	**0**	**1**	**240**	**2.9**		**0**	**0.0**	**350**	**175**	**16:53**	**9**	**1**	**1**	**2**	**2**	**1**	**0**	**1**

OHL First All-Star Team (1994) • Canadian Major Junior Second All-Star Team (1994) • OHL Second All-Star Team (1995) • AHL Second All-Star Team (1997)

Claimed by **NY Islanders** from **St. Louis** in NHL Waiver Draft, September 27, 1999.

RIVET, Craig

(rih-VAY, KRAYG) **MTL.**

Defense. Shoots right. 6'2", 197 lbs. Born, North Bay, Ont., September 13, 1974. Montreal's 4th choice, 68th overall, in 1992 Entry Draft.

Season	Club	League	GP	G	A	Pts	PIM	PP	SH	GW	S	%	+/–	TF	F%	H	SB	Min	GP	G	A	Pts	PIM	PP	SH	GW
1990-91	Barrie Colts	OJHL-B	42	9	17	26	55	....	....	....	....	....	....	....	....	....	....	....	....	....	....	....	....	....	....	....
1991-92	Kingston	OHL	66	5	21	26	97	....	....	....	....	....	....	....	....	....	....	....	....	....	....	....	....	....	....	....
1992-93	Kingston	OHL	64	19	55	74	117	....	....	....	....	....	....	....	....	....	....	....	16	5	7	12	39	....	....	....
1993-94	Kingston	OHL	61	12	52	64	100	....	....	....	....	....	....	....	....	....	....	....	6	0	3	3	6	....	....	....
	Fredericton	AHL	4	0	2	2	2	....	....	....	....	....	....	....	....	....	....	....	....	....	....	....	....	....	....	....
1994-95	Fredericton	AHL	78	5	27	32	126	....	....	....	....	....	....	....	....	....	....	....	12	0	4	4	17	....	....	....
	Montreal	**NHL**	**5**	**0**	**1**	**1**	**5**	**0**	**0**	**0**	**2**	**0.0**	**2**	....	....	....	....	....	....	....	....	....	....	....	....	....
1995-96	**Montreal**	**NHL**	**19**	**1**	**4**	**5**	**54**	**0**	**0**	**0**	**9**	**11.1**	**4**	....	....	....	....	....	....	....	....	....	....	....	....	....
	Fredericton	AHL	49	5	18	23	189	....	....	....	....	....	....	....	....	....	....	....	6	0	0	0	12	....	....	....
1996-97	**Montreal**	**NHL**	**35**	**0**	**4**	**4**	**54**	**0**	**0**	**0**	**24**	**0.0**	**7**	....	....	....	....	....	**5**	**0**	**1**	**1**	**14**	**0**	**0**	**0**
	Fredericton	AHL	23	3	12	15	99	....	....	....	....	....	....	....	....	....	....	....	....	....	....	....	....	....	....	....
1997-98	**Montreal**	**NHL**	**61**	**0**	**2**	**2**	**93**	**0**	**0**	**0**	**26**	**0.0**	**–3**	....	....	....	....	....	**5**	**0**	**0**	**0**	**2**	**0**	**0**	**0**
1998-99	**Montreal**	**NHL**	**66**	**2**	**8**	**10**	**66**	**0**	**0**	**0**	**39**	**5.1**	**–3**	**0**	**0.0**	**78**	**40**	**14:20**	....	....	....	....	....	....	....	....
99-2000	**Montreal**	**NHL**	**61**	**3**	**14**	**17**	**76**	**0**	**0**	**1**	**71**	**4.2**	**11**	**0**	**0.0**	**80**	**59**	**19:03**	....	....	....	....	....	....	....	....
	NHL Totals		**247**	**6**	**33**	**39**	**348**	**0**	**0**	**1**	**171**	**3.5**		**0**	**0.0**	**158**	**99**	**16:36**	**10**	**0**	**1**	**1**	**16**	**0**	**0**	**0**

ROBERTS, Gary

(RAW-buhrts, GAIR-ree) **TOR.**

Left wing. Shoots left. 6'1", 190 lbs. Born, North York, Ont., May 23, 1966. Calgary's 1st choice, 12th overall, in 1984 Entry Draft.

Season	Club	League	GP	G	A	Pts	PIM	PP	SH	GW	S	%	+/–	TF	F%	H	SB	Min	GP	G	A	Pts	PIM	PP	SH	GW
1980-81	Hamilton Kilty B's	OHA-B	3	0	1	1	0	....	....	....	....	....	....	....	....	....	....	....	....	....	....	....	....	....	....	....
1981-82	Whitby Selects	OMHA	44	55	31	86	133	....	....	....	....	....	....	....	....	....	....	....	....	....	....	....	....	....	....	....
1982-83	Ottawa 67's	OHL	53	12	8	20	83	....	....	....	....	....	....	....	....	....	....	....	5	1	0	1	19	....	....	....
1983-84	Ottawa 67's	OHL	48	27	30	57	144	....	....	....	....	....	....	....	....	....	....	....	13	10	7	17	62	....	....	....
1984-85	Ottawa 67's	OHL	59	44	62	106	186	....	....	....	....	....	....	....	....	....	....	....	5	2	8	10	10	....	....	....
	Moncton Flames	AHL	7	4	2	6	7	....	....	....	....	....	....	....	....	....	....	....	....	....	....	....	....	....	....	....
1985-86	Ottawa 67's	OHL	24	26	25	51	83	....	....	....	....	....	....	....	....	....	....	....	....	....	....	....	....	....	....	....
	Guelph Platers	OHL	23	18	15	33	65	....	....	....	....	....	....	....	....	....	....	....	20	18	13	31	43	....	....	....
1986-87	**Calgary**	**NHL**	**32**	**5**	**10**	**15**	**85**	**0**	**0**	**0**	**38**	**13.2**	**6**	....	....	....	....	....	**2**	**0**	**0**	**0**	**4**	**0**	**0**	**0**
	Moncton Flames	AHL	38	20	18	38	72	....	....	....	....	....	....	....	....	....	....	....	....	....	....	....	....	....	....	....
1987-88	**Calgary**	**NHL**	**74**	**13**	**15**	**28**	**282**	**0**	**0**	**1**	**118**	**11.0**	**24**	....	....	....	....	....	**9**	**2**	**3**	**5**	**29**	**0**	**0**	**0**
1988-89 ♦	**Calgary**	**NHL**	**71**	**22**	**16**	**38**	**250**	**0**	**1**	**2**	**123**	**17.9**	**32**	....	....	....	....	....	**22**	**5**	**7**	**12**	**57**	**0**	**0**	**0**
1989-90	**Calgary**	**NHL**	**78**	**39**	**33**	**72**	**222**	**5**	**0**	**5**	**175**	**22.3**	**31**	....	....	....	....	....	**6**	**2**	**5**	**7**	**41**	**0**	**0**	**0**
1990-91	**Calgary**	**NHL**	**80**	**22**	**31**	**53**	**252**	**0**	**0**	**3**	**132**	**16.7**	**15**	....	....	....	....	....	**7**	**1**	**3**	**4**	**18**	**0**	**0**	**0**
1991-92	**Calgary**	**NHL**	**76**	**53**	**37**	**90**	**207**	**15**	**0**	**2**	**196**	**27.0**	**32**	....	....	....	....	....	....	....	....	....	....	....	....	....
1992-93	**Calgary**	**NHL**	**58**	**38**	**41**	**79**	**172**	**8**	**3**	**4**	**166**	**22.9**	**32**	....	....	....	....	....	**5**	**1**	**6**	**7**	**43**	**1**	**0**	**0**
1993-94	**Calgary**	**NHL**	**73**	**41**	**43**	**84**	**145**	**12**	**3**	**5**	**202**	**20.3**	**37**	....	....	....	....	....	**7**	**2**	**6**	**8**	**24**	**1**	**0**	**1**
1994-95	**Calgary**	**NHL**	**8**	**2**	**2**	**4**	**43**	**2**	**0**	**0**	**20**	**10.0**	**1**	....	....	....	....	....	....	....	....	....	....	....	....	....
1995-96	**Calgary**	**NHL**	**35**	**22**	**20**	**42**	**78**	**9**	**0**	**5**	**84**	**26.2**	**15**	....	....	....	....	....	....	....	....	....	....	....	....	....
1996-97	**Calgary**	**NHL**	DID NOT PLAY – INJURED																							
1997-98	**Carolina**	**NHL**	**61**	**20**	**29**	**49**	**103**	**4**	**0**	**2**	**106**	**18.9**	**3**													
1998-99	**Carolina**	**NHL**	**77**	**14**	**28**	**42**	**178**	**1**	**1**	**4**	**138**	**10.1**	**2**	**15**	**46.7**	**260**	**16**	**19:36**	**6**	**1**	**1**	**2**	**8**	**0**	**0**	**0**
99-2000	**Carolina**	**NHL**	**69**	**23**	**30**	**53**	**62**	**12**	**0**	**1**	**150**	**15.3**	**–10**	**7**	**28.6**	**212**	**27**	**18:31**	....	....	....	....	....	....	....	....
	NHL Totals		**792**	**314**	**335**	**649**	**2079**	**68**	**8**	**34**	**1648**	**19.1**		**22**	**40.9**	**472**	**43**	**19:06**	**64**	**14**	**31**	**45**	**224**	**2**	**0**	**1**

OHL Second All-Star Team (1985, 1986) • Won Bill Masterton Memorial Trophy (1996) • Played in NHL All-Star Game (1992, 1993)

• Missed remainder of 1994-95 and majority of 1995-96 seasons recovering from neck injury suffered in game vs. Toronto, February 4, 1995. • Missed remainder of 1995-96 and entire 1996-97 seasons recovering from neck injury suffered in game vs. Vancouver, April 3, 1996. Traded to **Carolina** by **Calgary** with Trevor Kidd for Andrew Cassels and Jean-Sebastien Giguere, August 25, 1997. Signed as a free agent by **Toronto**, July 4, 2000.

ROBERTSSON, Bert

(ROH-behrt-suhn, BUHRT) **CBJ**

Defense. Shoots left. 6'3", 205 lbs. Born, Sodertalje, Sweden, June 30, 1974. Vancouver's 8th choice, 254th overall, in 1993 Entry Draft.

			Regular Season																Playoffs							
Season	Club	League	GP	G	A	Pts	PIM	PP	SH	GW	S	%	+/-	TF	F%	H	SB	Min	GP	G	A	Pts	PIM	PP	SH	GW
1992-93	Sodertalje SK	Swede-Jr.	12	1	5	6	20	....	....	....	....	....	....	....	....	....	....	....	....	....	....	....	....	....	....	....
	Sodertalje SK	Sweden-2	23	2	1	3	24	....	....	....	....	....	....	....	....	....	....	....	2	0	0	0	0	....	....	....
1993-94	Sodertalje SK	Sweden-2	28	0	1	1	12	....	....	....	....	....	....	....	....	....	....	....	1	0	0	0	0	....	....	....
1994-95	Sodertalje SK	Swede-Jr.	11	2	3	5	4	....	....	....	....	....	....	....	....	....	....	....	....	....	....	....	....	....	....	....
	Sodertalje SK	Sweden-2	23	1	2	3	24	....	....	....	....	....	....	....	....	....	....	....	3	0	1	1	2	....	....	....
1995-96	Syracuse Crunch	AHL	65	1	7	8	109	....	....	....	....	....	....	....	....	....	....	....	16	0	1	1	26	....	....	....
1996-97	Syracuse Crunch	AHL	80	4	9	13	132	....	....	....	....	....	....	....	....	....	....	....	3	1	0	1	4	....	....	....
1997-98	**Vancouver**	**NHL**	**30**	**2**	**4**	**6**	**24**	**0**	**0**	**0**	**19**	**10.5**	**2**	....	....	....	....	....	....	....	....	....	....	....	....	....
	Syracuse Crunch	AHL	42	5	9	14	87	....	....	....	....	....	....	....	....	....	....	....	3	0	0	0	6	....	....	....
1998-99	**Vancouver**	**NHL**	**39**	**2**	**2**	**4**	**13**	**0**	**0**	**0**	**13**	**15.4**	**–7**	**0**	**0.0**	**28**	**6**	**7:26**	....	....	....	....	....	....	....	....
	Syracuse Crunch	AHL	8	1	0	1	21	....	....	....	....	....	....	....	....	....	....	....	....	....	....	....	....	....	....	....
99-2000	**Edmonton**	**NHL**	**52**	**0**	**4**	**4**	**34**	**0**	**0**	**0**	**31**	**0.0**	**–3**	**3**	**0.0**	**62**	**28**	**10:49**	**5**	**0**	**0**	**0**	**0**	**0**	**0**	**0**
	Hamilton Bulldogs	AHL	6	0	3	3	12	....	....	....	....	....	....	....	....	....	....	....	....	....	....	....	....	....	....	....
	NHL Totals		**121**	**4**	**10**	**14**	**71**	**0**	**0**	**0**	**63**	**6.3**		**3**	**0.0**	**90**	**34**	**9:22**	**5**	**0**	**0**	**0**	**0**	**0**	**0**	**0**

Signed as a free agent by **Edmonton**, August 19, 1999. Selected by **Columbus** from **Edmonton** in Expansion Draft, June 23, 2000.

ROBIDAS, Stephane

(ROH-bih-dah, STEH-fan) **MTL.**

Defense. Shoots right. 5'11", 180 lbs. Born, Sherbrooke, Que., March 3, 1977. Montreal's 7th choice, 164th overall, in 1995 Entry Draft.

			Regular Season																Playoffs							
Season	Club	League	GP	G	A	Pts	PIM	PP	SH	GW	S	%	+/-	TF	F%	H	SB	Min	GP	G	A	Pts	PIM	PP	SH	GW
1992-93	Magog Selectes	QAAA	41	3	12	15	....	....	....	....	....	....	....	....	....	....	....	....	....	....	....	....	....	....	....	....
1993-94	Shawinigan	QMJHL	67	3	18	21	33	....	....	....	....	....	....	....	....	....	....	....	1	0	0	0	0	....	....	....
1994-95	Shawinigan	QMJHL	71	13	56	69	44	....	....	....	....	....	....	....	....	....	....	....	15	7	12	19	4	....	....	....
1995-96	Shawinigan	QMJHL	67	23	56	79	53	....	....	....	....	....	....	....	....	....	....	....	6	1	5	6	10	....	....	....
1996-97	Shawinigan	QMJHL	67	24	51	75	59	....	....	....	....	....	....	....	....	....	....	....	7	4	6	10	14	....	....	....
1997-98	Fredericton	AHL	79	10	21	31	50	....	....	....	....	....	....	....	....	....	....	....	4	0	2	2	0	....	....	....
1998-99	Fredericton	AHL	79	8	33	41	59	....	....	....	....	....	....	....	....	....	....	....	15	1	5	6	10	....	....	....
99-2000	**Montreal**	**NHL**	**1**	**0**	**0**	**0**	**0**	**0**	**0**	**0**	**0**	**0.0**	**0**	**0**	**0.0**	**1**	**1**	**15:54**	....	....	....	....	....	....	....	....
	Quebec Citadelles	AHL	76	14	31	45	36	....	....	....	....	....	....	....	....	....	....	....	3	0	1	1	0	....	....	....
	NHL Totals		**1**	**0**	**0**	**0**	**0**	**0**	**0**	**0**	**0**	**0.0**		**0**	**0.0**	**1**	**1**	**15:54**	....	....	....	....	....	....	....	....

QMJHL First All-Star Team (1996, 1997)

ROBITAILLE, Luc

(ROH-buh-tigh, LEWK) **L.A.**

Left wing. Shoots left. 6'1", 215 lbs. Born, Montreal, Que., February 17, 1966. Los Angeles' 9th choice, 171st overall, in 1984 Entry Draft.

			Regular Season																Playoffs							
Season	Club	League	GP	G	A	Pts	PIM	PP	SH	GW	S	%	+/-	TF	F%	H	SB	Min	GP	G	A	Pts	PIM	PP	SH	GW
1982-83	Mtl-Bourassa	QAAA	48	36	57	93	....	....	....	....	....	....	....	....	....	....	....	....	....	....	....	....	....	....	....	....
1983-84	Hull Olympiques	QMJHL	70	32	53	85	48	....	....	....	....	....	....	....	....	....	....	....	....	....	....	....	....	....	....	....
1984-85	Hull Olympiques	QMJHL	64	55	94	149	115	....	....	....	....	....	....	....	....	....	....	....	5	4	2	6	27	....	....	....
1985-86	Hull Olympiques	QMJHL	63	68	123	191	91	....	....	....	....	....	....	....	....	....	....	....	15	17	27	44	28	....	....	....
1986-87	**Los Angeles**	**NHL**	**79**	**45**	**39**	**84**	**28**	**18**	**0**	**3**	**199**	**22.6**	**–18**	....	....	....	....	....	**5**	**1**	**4**	**5**	**2**	**0**	**0**	**0**
1987-88	**Los Angeles**	**NHL**	**80**	**53**	**58**	**111**	**82**	**17**	**0**	**6**	**220**	**24.1**	**–9**	....	....	....	....	....	**5**	**2**	**5**	**7**	**18**	**2**	**0**	**1**
1988-89	**Los Angeles**	**NHL**	**78**	**46**	**52**	**98**	**65**	**10**	**0**	**4**	**237**	**19.4**	**5**	....	....	....	....	....	**11**	**2**	**6**	**8**	**10**	**0**	**0**	**1**
1989-90	**Los Angeles**	**NHL**	**80**	**52**	**49**	**101**	**38**	**20**	**0**	**7**	**210**	**24.8**	**8**	....	....	....	....	....	**10**	**5**	**5**	**10**	**10**	**1**	**0**	**1**
1990-91	**Los Angeles**	**NHL**	**76**	**45**	**46**	**91**	**68**	**11**	**0**	**5**	**229**	**19.7**	**28**	....	....	....	....	....	**12**	**12**	**4**	**16**	**22**	**5**	**0**	**2**
1991-92	**Los Angeles**	**NHL**	**80**	**44**	**63**	**107**	**95**	**26**	**0**	**6**	**240**	**18.3**	**–4**	....	....	....	....	....	**6**	**3**	**4**	**7**	**12**	**1**	**0**	**1**
1992-93	**Los Angeles**	**NHL**	**84**	**63**	**62**	**125**	**100**	**24**	**2**	**8**	**265**	**23.8**	**18**	....	....	....	....	....	**24**	**9**	**13**	**22**	**28**	**4**	**0**	**2**
1993-94	**Los Angeles**	**NHL**	**83**	**44**	**42**	**86**	**86**	**24**	**0**	**3**	**267**	**16.5**	**–20**	....	....	....	....	....	....	....	....	....	....	....	....	....
1994-95	**Pittsburgh**	**NHL**	**46**	**23**	**19**	**42**	**37**	**5**	**0**	**3**	**109**	**21.1**	**10**	....	....	....	....	....	**12**	**7**	**4**	**11**	**26**	**0**	**0**	**2**
1995-96	**NY Rangers**	**NHL**	**77**	**23**	**46**	**69**	**80**	**11**	**0**	**4**	**223**	**10.3**	**13**	....	....	....	....	....	**11**	**1**	**5**	**6**	**8**	**0**	**0**	**0**
1996-97	**NY Rangers**	**NHL**	**69**	**24**	**24**	**48**	**48**	**5**	**0**	**4**	**200**	**12.0**	**16**	....	....	....	....	....	**15**	**4**	**7**	**11**	**4**	**0**	**0**	**0**
1997-98	**Los Angeles**	**NHL**	**57**	**16**	**24**	**40**	**66**	**5**	**0**	**7**	**130**	**12.3**	**5**	....	....	....	....	....	**4**	**1**	**2**	**3**	**6**	**0**	**0**	**0**
1998-99	**Los Angeles**	**NHL**	**82**	**39**	**35**	**74**	**54**	**11**	**0**	**7**	**292**	**13.4**	**–1**	**7**	**57.1**	**40**	**22**	**19:11**	....	....	....	....	....	....	....	....
99-2000	**Los Angeles**	**NHL**	**71**	**36**	**38**	**74**	**68**	**13**	**0**	**7**	**221**	**16.3**	**11**	**10**	**30.0**	**29**	**12**	**18:34**	**4**	**2**	**2**	**4**	**6**	**0**	**0**	**0**
	NHL Totals		**1042**	**553**	**597**	**1150**	**915**	**200**	**2**	**74**	**3042**	**18.2**		**17**	**41.2**	**69**	**34**	**18:54**	**119**	**49**	**61**	**110**	**152**	**13**	**0**	**10**

QMJHL Second All-Star Team (1985) • QMJHL First All-Star Team (1986) • Canadian Major Junior Player of the Year (1986) • NHL All-Rookie Team (1987) • Won Calder Memorial Trophy (1987) • NHL Second All-Star Team (1987, 1992) • NHL First All-Star Team (1988, 1989, 1990, 1991, 1993) • Played in NHL All-Star Game (1988, 1989, 1990, 1991, 1992, 1993, 1999)

Traded to **Pittsburgh** by **LA Kings** for Rick Tocchet and Pittsburgh's 2nd round choice (Pavel Rosa) in 1995 Entry Draft, July 29, 1994. Traded to **NY Rangers** by **Pittsburgh** with Ulf Samuelsson for Petr Nedved and Sergei Zubov, August 31, 1995. Traded to **LA Kings** by **NY Rangers** for Kevin Stevens, August 28, 1997.

ROBITAILLE, Randy

(ROH-buh-tigh, RAN-dee) **NSH.**

Center. Shoots left. 5'11", 196 lbs. Born, Ottawa, Ont., October 12, 1975.

			Regular Season																Playoffs							
Season	Club	League	GP	G	A	Pts	PIM	PP	SH	GW	S	%	+/-	TF	F%	H	SB	Min	GP	G	A	Pts	PIM	PP	SH	GW
1993-94	Ottawa	OJHL	57	33	55	88	31	....	....	....	....	....	....	....	....	....	....	....	....	....	....	....	....	....	....	....
1994-95	Ottawa	OJHL	54	48	77	125	111	....	....	....	....	....	....	....	....	....	....	....	....	....	....	....	....	....	....	....
1995-96	U. of Miami-Ohio	CCHA	36	14	31	45	26	....	....	....	....	....	....	....	....	....	....	....	....	....	....	....	....	....	....	....
1996-97	U. of Miami-Ohio	CCHA	39	27	34	61	44	....	....	....	....	....	....	....	....	....	....	....	....	....	....	....	....	....	....	....
	Boston	**NHL**	**1**	**0**	**0**	**0**	**0**	**0**	**0**	**0**	**0**	**0.0**	**0**	....	....	....	....	....	....	....	....	....	....	....	....	....
1997-98	**Boston**	**NHL**	**4**	**0**	**0**	**0**	**0**	**0**	**0**	**0**	**5**	**0.0**	**–2**	....	....	....	....	....	....	....	....	....	....	....	....	....
	Providence Bruins	AHL	48	15	29	44	16	....	....	....	....	....	....	....	....	....	....	....	....	....	....	....	....	....	....	....
1998-99	**Boston**	**NHL**	**4**	**0**	**2**	**2**	**0**	**0**	**0**	**0**	**5**	**0.0**	**–1**	**24**	**25.0**	**0**	**0**	**10:11**	**1**	**0**	**0**	**0**	**0**	**0**	**0**	**0**
	Providence Bruins	AHL	74	28	*74	102	34	....	....	....	....	....	....	....	....	....	....	....	19	6	*14	20	20	....	....	....
99-2000	**Nashville**	**NHL**	**69**	**11**	**14**	**25**	**10**	**2**	**0**	**1**	**113**	**9.7**	**–13**	**528**	**51.5**	**30**	**14**	**12:52**	....	....	....	....	....	....	....	....
	NHL Totals		**78**	**11**	**16**	**27**	**10**	**2**	**0**	**1**	**123**	**8.9**		**552**	**50.4**	**30**	**14**	**12:43**	**1**	**0**	**0**	**0**	**0**	**0**	**0**	**0**

CCHA First All-Star Team (1997) • NCAA West First All-American Team (1997) • AHL First All-Star Team (1999) • Won Les Cunningham Award (MVP - AHL) (1999)

Signed as a free agent by **Boston**, March 27, 1997. Traded to **Atlanta** by **Boston** for Peter Ferraro, June 25, 1999. Traded to **Nashville** by **Atlanta** for Denny Lambert, August 16, 1999.

ROCHE, Dave

(ROHSH, DAYV) **CGY.**

Center. Shoots left. 6'4", 230 lbs. Born, Lindsay, Ont., June 13, 1975. Pittsburgh's 3rd choice, 62nd overall, in 1993 Entry Draft.

			Regular Season																Playoffs							
Season	Club	League	GP	G	A	Pts	PIM	PP	SH	GW	S	%	+/-	TF	F%	H	SB	Min	GP	G	A	Pts	PIM	PP	SH	GW
1990-91	Peterborough	OJHL-B	40	22	17	39	86	....	....	....	....	....	....	....	....	....	....	....	....	....	....	....	....	....	....	....
1991-92	Peterborough	OHL	62	10	17	27	134	....	....	....	....	....	....	....	....	....	....	....	10	0	0	0	34	....	....	....
1992-93	Peterborough	OHL	56	40	60	100	105	....	....	....	....	....	....	....	....	....	....	....	21	14	15	29	42	....	....	....
1993-94	Peterborough	OHL	34	15	22	37	127	....	....	....	....	....	....	....	....	....	....	....	....	....	....	....	....	....	....	....
	Windsor Spitfires	OHL	29	14	20	34	73	....	....	....	....	....	....	....	....	....	....	....	4	1	1	2	15	....	....	....
1994-95	Windsor Spitfires	OHL	66	55	59	114	180	....	....	....	....	....	....	....	....	....	....	....	10	9	6	15	16	....	....	....
1995-96	**Pittsburgh**	**NHL**	**71**	**7**	**7**	**14**	**130**	**0**	**0**	**1**	**65**	**10.8**	**–5**	....	....	....	....	....	**16**	**2**	**7**	**9**	**26**	**0**	**0**	**0**
1996-97	**Pittsburgh**	**NHL**	**61**	**5**	**5**	**10**	**155**	**2**	**0**	**0**	**53**	**9.4**	**–13**	....	....	....	....	....	....	....	....	....	....	....	....	....
	Cleveland	IHL	18	5	5	10	25	....	....	....	....	....	....	....	....	....	....	....	13	6	3	9	*87	....	....	....
1997-98	Syracuse Crunch	AHL	73	12	20	32	307	....	....	....	....	....	....	....	....	....	....	....	5	2	0	2	10	....	....	....
1998-99	**Calgary**	**NHL**	**36**	**3**	**3**	**6**	**44**	**1**	**0**	**2**	**30**	**10.0**	**–1**	**0**	**0.0**	**35**	**9**	**7:15**	....	....	....	....	....	....	....	....
	Saint John Flames	AHL	7	0	3	3	6	....	....	....	....	....	....	....	....	....	....	....	....	....	....	....	....	....	....	....
99-2000	**Calgary**	**NHL**	**2**	**0**	**0**	**0**	**5**	**0**	**0**	**0**	**3**	**0.0**	**–1**	**0**	**0.0**	**5**	**0**	**8:33**	....	....	....	....	....	....	....	....
	Saint John Flames	AHL	67	22	21	43	130	....	....	....	....	....	....	....	....	....	....	....	3	0	1	1	8	....	....	....
	NHL Totals		**170**	**15**	**15**	**30**	**334**	**3**	**0**	**3**	**151**	**9.9**		**0**	**0.0**	**40**	**9**	**7:19**	**16**	**2**	**7**	**9**	**26**	**0**	**0**	**0**

OHL First All-Star Team (1995)

Traded to **Calgary** by **Pittsburgh** with Ken Wregget for German Titov and Todd Hlushko, June 17, 1998.

			Regular Season																Playoffs							
Season	Club	League	GP	G	A	Pts	PIM	PP	SH	GW	S	%	+/–	TF	F%	H	SB	Min	GP	G	A	Pts	PIM	PP	SH	GW

RODGERS, Marc

(RAWD-juhrs, MAHRK) **DET.**

Right wing. Shoots right. 5'9", 185 lbs. Born, Shawville, Que., March 16, 1972.

Season	Club	League	GP	G	A	Pts	PIM	PP	SH	GW	S	%	+/–	TF	F%	H	SB	Min	GP	G	A	Pts	PIM	PP	SH	GW
1986-87	L'Outaouaus	QAAA	42	16	18	34	....	....	....	....	....	....	....	....	....	....	....	....	....	....	....	....	....	....	....	....
1987-88	L'Outaouaus	QAAA	38	30	37	67	....	....	....	....	....	....	....	....	....	....	....	....	....	....	....	....	....	....	....	....
1988-89	Granby Bisons	QMJHL	65	11	21	32	70	....	....	....	....	....	....	....	....	....	....	....	4	0	2	2	44	....	....	....
1989-90	Granby Bisons	QMJHL	61	24	31	55	155	....	....	....	....	....	....	....	....	....	....	....	....	....	....	....	....	....	....	....
1990-91	Granby Bisons	QMJHL	64	28	49	77	41	....	....	....	....	....	....	....	....	....	....	....	....	....	....	....	....	....	....	....
1991-92	Granby Bisons	QMJHL	36	30	57	87	49	....	....	....	....	....	....	....	....	....	....	....	....	....	....	....	....	....	....	....
	Verdun College	QMJHL	29	14	19	33	0	....	....	....	....	....	....	....	....	....	....	....	18	3	13	16	26	....	....	....
1992-93	Wheeling	ECHL	64	23	40	63	91	....	....	....	....	....	....	....	....	....	....	....	6	1	1	2	8	....	....	....
1993-94	Knoxville	ECHL	27	12	18	30	83	....	....	....	....	....	....	....	....	....	....	....	....	....	....	....	....	....	....	....
	Las Vegas	IHL	40	7	7	14	110	....	....	....	....	....	....	....	....	....	....	....	4	0	2	2	17	....	....	....
1994-95	Las Vegas	IHL	58	17	19	36	131	....	....	....	....	....	....	....	....	....	....	....	10	2	6	8	25	....	....	....
1995-96	Utah Grizzlies	IHL	31	6	14	20	51	....	....	....	....	....	....	....	....	....	....	....	21	4	4	8	16	....	....	....
	Las Vegas	IHL	51	13	16	29	65	....	....	....	....	....	....	....	....	....	....	....	....	....	....	....	....	....	....	....
1996-97	Utah Grizzlies	IHL	5	2	2	4	10	....	....	....	....	....	....	....	....	....	....	....	....	....	....	....	....	....	....	....
	Quebec Rafales	IHL	70	25	42	67	115	....	....	....	....	....	....	....	....	....	....	....	9	1	9	10	14	....	....	....
1997-98	Quebec Rafales	IHL	61	20	22	42	61	....	....	....	....	....	....	....	....	....	....	....	....	....	....	....	....	....	....	....
	Chicago Wolves	IHL	11	5	5	10	22	....	....	....	....	....	....	....	....	....	....	....	22	9	9	18	10	....	....	....
1998-99	Adirondack	AHL	80	19	38	57	66	....	....	....	....	....	....	....	....	....	....	....	3	0	0	0	10	....	....	....
99-2000	**Detroit**	**NHL**	**21**	**1**	**1**	**2**	**10**	**0**	**0**	**0**	**17**	**5.9**	**–3**	**2**	**100.0**	**48**	**3**	**7:55**	....	....	....	....	....	....	....	....
	Manitoba Moose	IHL	34	8	10	18	77	....	....	....	....	....	....	....	....	....	....	....	2	1	0	1	6	....	....	....
	NHL Totals		**21**	**1**	**1**	**2**	**10**	**0**	**0**	**0**	**17**	**5.9**		**2**	**100.0**	**48**	**3**	**7:55**	....	....	....	....	....	....	....	....

Signed as a free agent by **Detroit**, August 3, 1998.

ROENICK, Jeremy

(ROH-nihk, JAIR-eh-mee) **PHX.**

Center. Shoots right. 6', 207 lbs. Born, Boston, MA, January 17, 1970. Chicago's 1st choice, 8th overall, in 1988 Entry Draft.

Season	Club	League	GP	G	A	Pts	PIM	PP	SH	GW	S	%	+/–	TF	F%	H	SB	Min	GP	G	A	Pts	PIM	PP	SH	GW
1986-87	Thayer Academy	Hi-School	24	31	34	65	....	....	....	....	....	....	....	....	....	....	....	....	....	....	....	....	....	....	....	....
1987-88	Thayer Academy	Hi-School	24	34	50	84	....	....	....	....	....	....	....	....	....	....	....	....	....	....	....	....	....	....	....	....
1988-89	Hull Olympiques	QMJHL	28	34	36	70	14	....	....	....	....	....	....	....	....	....	....	....	....	....	....	....	....	....	....	....
	Chicago	**NHL**	**20**	**9**	**9**	**18**	**4**	**2**	**0**	**0**	**52**	**17.3**	**4**	....	....	....	....	....	**10**	**1**	**3**	**4**	**7**	**1**	**0**	**1**
1989-90	**Chicago**	**NHL**	**78**	**26**	**40**	**66**	**54**	**6**	**0**	**4**	**173**	**15.0**	**2**	....	....	....	....	....	**20**	**11**	**7**	**18**	**8**	**4**	**0**	**1**
1990-91	**Chicago**	**NHL**	**79**	**41**	**53**	**94**	**80**	**15**	**4**	**10**	**194**	**21.1**	**38**	....	....	....	....	....	**6**	**3**	**5**	**8**	**4**	**1**	**0**	**1**
1991-92	**Chicago**	**NHL**	**80**	**53**	**50**	**103**	**98**	**22**	**3**	**13**	**234**	**22.6**	**23**	....	....	....	....	....	**18**	**12**	**10**	**22**	**12**	**4**	**0**	**3**
1992-93	**Chicago**	**NHL**	**84**	**50**	**57**	**107**	**86**	**22**	**3**	**3**	**255**	**19.6**	**15**	....	....	....	....	....	**4**	**1**	**2**	**3**	**2**	**0**	**0**	**0**
1993-94	**Chicago**	**NHL**	**84**	**46**	**61**	**107**	**125**	**24**	**5**	**5**	**281**	**16.4**	**21**	....	....	....	....	....	**6**	**1**	**6**	**7**	**2**	**0**	**0**	**1**
1994-95	Kolner Haie	DEL	3	3	1	4	2	....	....	....	....	....	....	....	....	....	....	....	....	....	....	....	....	....	....	....
	Chicago	**NHL**	**33**	**10**	**24**	**34**	**14**	**5**	**0**	**1**	**93**	**10.8**	**5**	....	....	....	....	....	**8**	**1**	**2**	**3**	**16**	**0**	**0**	**0**
1995-96	**Chicago**	**NHL**	**66**	**32**	**35**	**67**	**109**	**12**	**4**	**2**	**171**	**18.7**	**9**	....	....	....	....	....	**10**	**5**	**7**	**12**	**2**	**1**	**0**	**1**
1996-97	**Phoenix**	**NHL**	**72**	**29**	**40**	**69**	**115**	**10**	**3**	**7**	**228**	**12.7**	**–7**	....	....	....	....	....	**6**	**2**	**4**	**6**	**4**	**0**	**0**	**0**
1997-98	**Phoenix**	**NHL**	**79**	**24**	**32**	**56**	**103**	**6**	**1**	**3**	**182**	**13.2**	**5**	....	....	....	....	....	**6**	**5**	**3**	**8**	**4**	**2**	**2**	**2**
	United States	Olympics	4	0	1	1	6	....	....	....	....	....	....	....	....	....	....	....	....	....	....	....	....	....	....	....
1998-99	**Phoenix**	**NHL**	**78**	**24**	**48**	**72**	**130**	**4**	**0**	**3**	**203**	**11.8**	**7**	**956**	**47.6**	**154**	**30**	**20:10**	**1**	**0**	**0**	**0**	**0**	**0**	**0**	**0**
99-2000	**Phoenix**	**NHL**	**75**	**34**	**44**	**78**	**102**	**6**	**3**	**12**	**192**	**17.7**	**11**	**925**	**50.1**	**125**	**28**	**20:51**	**5**	**2**	**2**	**4**	**10**	**1**	**0**	**0**
	NHL Totals		**828**	**378**	**493**	**871**	**1020**	**134**	**26**	**63**	**2258**	**16.7**		**1881**	**48.8**	**279**	**58**	**20:30**	**100**	**44**	**51**	**95**	**71**	**14**	**2**	**10**

QMJHL Second All-Star Team (1989) • Played in NHL All-Star Game (1991, 1992, 1993, 1994, 1999, 2000)

Traded to **Phoenix** by **Chicago** for Alexei Zhamnov, Craig Mills and Phoenix's 1st round choice (Ty Jones) in 1997 Entry Draft, August 16, 1996.

ROEST, Stacy

(ROHST, STAY-see) **MIN.**

Center. Shoots right. 5'9", 185 lbs. Born, Lethbridge, Alta., March 15, 1974.

Season	Club	League	GP	G	A	Pts	PIM	PP	SH	GW	S	%	+/–	TF	F%	H	SB	Min	GP	G	A	Pts	PIM	PP	SH	GW
1990-91	Lethbridge	AMHL	34	22	50	72	38	....	....	....	....	....	....	....	....	....	....	....	....	....	....	....	....	....	....	....
	Medicine Hat	WHL	5	1	2	3	0	....	....	....	....	....	....	....	....	....	....	....	12	5	5	10	4	....	....	....
1991-92	Medicine Hat	WHL	72	22	43	65	20	....	....	....	....	....	....	....	....	....	....	....	4	2	1	3	0	....	....	....
1992-93	Medicine Hat	WHL	72	33	73	106	30	....	....	....	....	....	....	....	....	....	....	....	10	3	10	13	6	....	....	....
1993-94	Medicine Hat	WHL	72	48	72	120	48	....	....	....	....	....	....	....	....	....	....	....	3	1	0	1	4	....	....	....
1994-95	Medicine Hat	WHL	69	37	78	115	32	....	....	....	....	....	....	....	....	....	....	....	5	2	7	9	2	....	....	....
	Adirondack	AHL	3	0	0	0	0	....	....	....	....	....	....	....	....	....	....	....	....	....	....	....	....	....	....	....
1995-96	Adirondack	AHL	76	16	39	55	40	....	....	....	....	....	....	....	....	....	....	....	3	0	0	0	0	....	....	....
1996-97	Adirondack	AHL	78	25	41	66	30	....	....	....	....	....	....	....	....	....	....	....	4	1	1	2	0	....	....	....
1997-98	Adirondack	AHL	80	34	58	92	30	....	....	....	....	....	....	....	....	....	....	....	3	2	1	3	6	....	....	....
1998-99	**Detroit**	**NHL**	**59**	**4**	**8**	**12**	**14**	**0**	**0**	**1**	**50**	**8.0**	**–7**	**234**	**57.3**	**72**	**7**	**8:04**	....	....	....	....	....	....	....	....
	Adirondack	AHL	2	0	1	1	0	....	....	....	....	....	....	....	....	....	....	....	....	....	....	....	....	....	....	....
99-2000	**Detroit**	**NHL**	**49**	**7**	**9**	**16**	**12**	**1**	**0**	**1**	**56**	**12.5**	**–1**	**397**	**55.4**	**54**	**12**	**9:56**	**3**	**0**	**0**	**0**	**0**	**0**	**0**	**0**
	NHL Totals		**108**	**11**	**17**	**28**	**26**	**1**	**0**	**2**	**106**	**10.4**		**631**	**56.1**	**126**	**19**	**8:55**	**3**	**0**	**0**	**0**	**0**	**0**	**0**	**0**

WHL East First All-Star Team (1994) • WHL East Second All-Star Team (1995)

Signed as a free agent by **Detroit**, June 9, 1997. Selected by **Minnesota** from **Detroit** in Expansion Draft, June 23, 2000.

ROHLOFF, Jon

(ROH-lawf, JAWN) **CAR.**

Defense. Shoots right. 5'11", 220 lbs. Born, Mankato, MN, October 3, 1969. Boston's 7th choice, 186th overall, in 1988 Entry Draft.

Season	Club	League	GP	G	A	Pts	PIM	PP	SH	GW	S	%	+/–	TF	F%	H	SB	Min	GP	G	A	Pts	PIM	PP	SH	GW
1986-87	Grand Rapids	Hi-School	21	12	23	35	16	....	....	....	....	....	....	....	....	....	....	....	....	....	....	....	....	....	....	....
1987-88	Grand Rapids	Hi-School	28	10	13	23	....	....	....	....	....	....	....	....	....	....	....	....	....	....	....	....	....	....	....	....
1988-89	Minnesota-Duluth	WCHA	39	1	2	3	44	....	....	....	....	....	....	....	....	....	....	....	....	....	....	....	....	....	....	....
1989-90	Minnesota-Duluth	WCHA	5	0	1	1	6	....	....	....	....	....	....	....	....	....	....	....	....	....	....	....	....	....	....	....
1990-91	Minnesota-Duluth	WCHA	32	6	11	17	38	....	....	....	....	....	....	....	....	....	....	....	....	....	....	....	....	....	....	....
1991-92	Minnesota-Duluth	WCHA	27	9	9	18	48	....	....	....	....	....	....	....	....	....	....	....	....	....	....	....	....	....	....	....
1992-93	Minnesota-Duluth	WCHA	36	15	20	35	87	....	....	....	....	....	....	....	....	....	....	....	....	....	....	....	....	....	....	....
1993-94	Providence Bruins	AHL	55	12	23	35	59	....	....	....	....	....	....	....	....	....	....	....	....	....	....	....	....	....	....	....
1994-95	Providence Bruins	AHL	4	2	1	3	6	....	....	....	....	....	....	....	....	....	....	....	....	....	....	....	....	....	....	....
	Boston	**NHL**	**34**	**3**	**8**	**11**	**39**	**0**	**0**	**1**	**51**	**5.9**	**1**	....	....	....	....	....	**5**	**0**	**0**	**0**	**6**	**0**	**0**	**0**
1995-96	**Boston**	**NHL**	**79**	**1**	**12**	**13**	**59**	**1**	**0**	**0**	**106**	**0.9**	**–8**	....	....	....	....	....	**5**	**1**	**2**	**3**	**2**	**1**	**0**	**0**
1996-97	**Boston**	**NHL**	**37**	**3**	**5**	**8**	**31**	**1**	**0**	**0**	**69**	**4.3**	**–14**	....	....	....	....	....	....	....	....	....	....	....	....	....
	Providence Bruins	AHL	3	1	1	2	0	....	....	....	....	....	....	....	....	....	....	....	....	....	....	....	....	....	....	....
1997-98	Providence Bruins	AHL	58	6	17	23	46	....	....	....	....	....	....	....	....	....	....	....	....	....	....	....	....	....	....	....
1998-99	Kentucky	AHL	12	0	1	1	8	....	....	....	....	....	....	....	....	....	....	....	....	....	....	....	....	....	....	....
	Kansas City	IHL	41	5	13	18	42	....	....	....	....	....	....	....	....	....	....	....	3	0	0	0	18	....	....	....
99-2000	Kansas City	IHL	44	5	18	23	38	....	....	....	....	....	....	....	....	....	....	....	....	....	....	....	....	....	....	....
	NHL Totals		**150**	**7**	**25**	**32**	**129**	**2**	**0**	**1**	**226**	**3.1**		....	....	....	....	....	**10**	**1**	**2**	**3**	**8**	**1**	**0**	**0**

WCHA Second All-Star Team (1993)

Signed as a free agent by **San Jose**, July 23, 1998. Signed as a free agent by **Carolina**, August 1, 2000.

ROLSTON, Brian

(ROHL-stuhn, BRIGH-an) **BOS.**

Center. Shoots left. 6'2", 205 lbs. Born, Flint, MI, February 21, 1973. New Jersey's 2nd choice, 11th overall, in 1991 Entry Draft.

Season	Club	League	GP	G	A	Pts	PIM	PP	SH	GW	S	%	+/–	TF	F%	H	SB	Min	GP	G	A	Pts	PIM	PP	SH	GW
1989-90	Detroit	NAJHL	40	36	37	73	57	....	....	....	....	....	....	....	....	....	....	....	....	....	....	....	....	....	....	....
1990-91	Detroit	NAJHL	36	49	46	95	14	....	....	....	....	....	....	....	....	....	....	....	....	....	....	....	....	....	....	....
1991-92	Lake Superior	CCHA	37	14	23	37	14	....	....	....	....	....	....	....	....	....	....	....	....	....	....	....	....	....	....	....
1992-93	Lake Superior	CCHA	39	33	31	64	20	....	....	....	....	....	....	....	....	....	....	....	....	....	....	....	....	....	....	....
1993-94	United States	Nat-Team	41	20	28	48	36	....	....	....	....	....	....	....	....	....	....	....	....	....	....	....	....	....	....	....
	United States	Olympics	8	7	0	7	8	....	....	....	....	....	....	....	....	....	....	....	....	....	....	....	....	....	....	....
	Albany River Rats	AHL	17	5	5	10	8	....	....	....	....	....	....	....	....	....	....	....	5	1	2	3	0	....	....	....

			Regular Season																Playoffs							
Season	Club	League	GP	G	A	Pts	PIM	PP	SH	GW	S	%	+/-	TF	F%	H	SB	Min	GP	G	A	Pts	PIM	PP	SH	GW
1994-95	Albany River Rats	AHL	18	9	11	20	10	....	....	....	....	....	....	....	....	....	....	....	....	....	....	....	....	....	....	....
	♦ **New Jersey**	**NHL**	**40**	**7**	**11**	**18**	**17**	**2**	**0**	**3**	**92**	**7.6**	**5**	....	....	....	....	....	**6**	**2**	**1**	**3**	**4**	**1**	**0**	**0**
1995-96	**New Jersey**	**NHL**	**58**	**13**	**11**	**24**	**8**	**3**	**1**	**4**	**139**	**9.4**	**9**	....	....	....	....	....	....	....	....	....	....	....	....	....
1996-97	**New Jersey**	**NHL**	**81**	**18**	**27**	**45**	**20**	**2**	**2**	**3**	**237**	**7.6**	**6**	....	....	....	....	....	**10**	**4**	**1**	**5**	**6**	**1**	**2**	**0**
1997-98	**New Jersey**	**NHL**	**76**	**16**	**14**	**30**	**16**	**0**	**2**	**1**	**185**	**8.6**	**7**	....	....	....	....	....	**6**	**1**	**0**	**1**	**2**	**0**	**1**	**0**
1998-99	**New Jersey**	**NHL**	**82**	**24**	**33**	**57**	**14**	**5**	**5**	**3**	**210**	**11.4**	**11**	**51**	**45.1**	**70**	**20**	**18:49**	**7**	**1**	**0**	**1**	**2**	**0**	**1**	**0**
99-2000	**New Jersey**	**NHL**	**11**	**3**	**1**	**4**	**0**	**1**	**0**	**2**	**33**	**9.1**	**–2**	**37**	**37.8**	**13**	**2**	**19:09**	....	....	....	....	....	....	....	....
	Colorado	**NHL**	**50**	**8**	**10**	**18**	**12**	**1**	**0**	**3**	**107**	**7.5**	**–6**	**65**	**41.5**	**28**	**19**	**16:18**	....	....	....	....	....	....	....	....
	Boston	**NHL**	**16**	**5**	**4**	**9**	**6**	**3**	**0**	**1**	**66**	**7.6**	**–4**	**265**	**41.1**	**22**	**11**	**22:13**	....	....	....	....	....	....	....	....
	NHL Totals		**414**	**94**	**111**	**205**	**93**	**17**	**10**	**20**	**1069**	**8.8**		**418**	**41.4**	**133**	**52**	**18:23**	**29**	**8**	**2**	**10**	**14**	**2**	**4**	**0**

NCAA Championship All-Tournament Team (1992, 1993) • CCHA First All-Star Team (1993) • NCAA West Second All-American Team (1993)

Traded to **Colorado** by **New Jersey** with New Jersey's 1st round choice (later traded to Boston - Boston selected Martin Samuelsson) and future considerations for Claude Lemieux and Colorado's 1st (David Hale) and 2nd (Matt DeMarchi) round choices in 2000 Entry Draft, November 3, 1999. Traded to **Boston** by **Colorado** with Martin Grenier, Sami Pahlsson and New Jersey's 1st round choice (previously acquired, Boston selected Martin Samuelsson) in 2000 Entry Draft for Ray Bourque and Dave Andreychuk, March 6, 2000.

ROMINSKI, Dale

(ROH-mihn-SKEE, DAYL) **T.B.**

Right wing. Shoots right. 6'2", 200 lbs. Born, Farmington Hills, MI, October 1, 1975.

Season	Club	League	GP	G	A	Pts	PIM	PP	SH	GW	S	%	+/-	TF	F%	H	SB	Min	GP	G	A	Pts	PIM	PP	SH	GW
1993-94	Brother Rice	Hi-School	25	25	20	45	....	....	....	....	....	....	....	....	....	....	....	....	....	....	....	....	....	....	....	....
1994-95	Detroit	NAJHL	40	21	21	42	30	....	....	....	....	....	....	....	....	....	....	....	....	....	....	....	....	....	....	....
1995-96	U. of Michigan	CCHA	35	8	7	15	37	....	....	....	....	....	....	....	....	....	....	....	....	....	....	....	....	....	....	....
1996-97	U. of Michigan	CCHA	38	6	7	13	58	....	....	....	....	....	....	....	....	....	....	....	....	....	....	....	....	....	....	....
1997-98	U. of Michigan	CCHA	46	10	14	24	102	....	....	....	....	....	....	....	....	....	....	....	....	....	....	....	....	....	....	....
1998-99	U. of Michigan	CCHA	41	15	8	23	80	....	....	....	....	....	....	....	....	....	....	....	....	....	....	....	....	....	....	....
99-2000	**Tampa Bay**	**NHL**	**3**	**0**	**1**	**1**	**2**	**0**	**0**	**0**	**0**	**0.0**	**1**	**0**	**0.0**	**5**	**0**	**8:23**	....	....	....	....	....	....	....	....
	Detroit Vipers	IHL	78	14	15	29	68	....	....	....	....	....	....	....	....	....	....	....	....	....	....	....	....	....	....	....
	NHL Totals		**3**	**0**	**1**	**1**	**2**	**0**	**0**	**0**	**0**	**0.0**		**0**	**0.0**	**5**	**0**	**8:23**	....	....	....	....	....	....	....	....

Signed as a free agent by **Tampa Bay**, August 31, 1999.

RONNING, Cliff

(ROHN-nihng, KLIHF) **NSH.**

Center. Shoots left. 5'8", 165 lbs. Born, Burnaby, B.C., October 1, 1965. St. Louis' 9th choice, 134th overall, in 1984 Entry Draft.

Season	Club	League	GP	G	A	Pts	PIM	PP	SH	GW	S	%	+/-	TF	F%	H	SB	Min	GP	G	A	Pts	PIM	PP	SH	GW
1982-83	New Westminster	BCJHL	52	83	68	151	22	....	....	....	....	....	....	....	....	....	....	....	....	....	....	....	....	....	....	....
1983-84	New Westminster	WHL	71	69	67	136	10	....	....	....	....	....	....	....	....	....	....	....	9	8	13	21	10	....	....	....
1984-85	New Westminster	WHL	70	*89	108	*197	20	....	....	....	....	....	....	....	....	....	....	....	11	10	14	24	4	....	....	....
1985-86	Canada	Nat-Team	71	55	63	118	....	....	....	....	....	....	....	....	....	....	....	....	....	....	....	....	....	....	....	....
	St. Louis	**NHL**	....	....	....	....	....	....	....	....	....	....	....	....	....	....	....	....	**5**	**1**	**1**	**2**	**2**	**1**	**0**	**0**
1986-87	Canada	Nat-Team	26	17	16	33	12	....	....	....	....	....	....	....	....	....	....	....	....	....	....	....	....	....	....	....
	St. Louis	**NHL**	**42**	**11**	**14**	**25**	**6**	**2**	**0**	**2**	**68**	**16.2**	**–1**	....	....	....	....	....	**4**	**0**	**1**	**1**	**0**	**0**	**0**	**0**
1987-88	**St. Louis**	**NHL**	**26**	**5**	**8**	**13**	**12**	**1**	**0**	**1**	**38**	**13.2**	**6**	....	....	....	....	....	....	....	....	....	....	....	....	....
1988-89	**St. Louis**	**NHL**	**64**	**24**	**31**	**55**	**18**	**16**	**0**	**1**	**150**	**16.0**	**3**	....	....	....	....	....	**7**	**1**	**3**	**4**	**0**	**1**	**0**	**0**
	Peoria Rivermen	IHL	12	11	20	31	8	....	....	....	....	....	....	....	....	....	....	....	....	....	....	....	....	....	....	....
1989-90	HC Asiago	Italy	36	67	49	116	25	....	....	....	....	....	....	....	....	....	....	....	6	7	12	19	4	....	....	....
1990-91	**St. Louis**	**NHL**	**48**	**14**	**18**	**32**	**10**	**5**	**0**	**2**	**81**	**17.3**	**2**	....	....	....	....	....	....	....	....	....	....	....	....	....
	Vancouver	**NHL**	**11**	**6**	**6**	**12**	**0**	**2**	**0**	**0**	**32**	**18.8**	**–2**	....	....	....	....	....	**6**	**6**	**3**	**9**	**12**	**2**	**0**	**2**
1991-92	**Vancouver**	**NHL**	**80**	**24**	**47**	**71**	**42**	**6**	**0**	**2**	**216**	**11.1**	**18**	....	....	....	....	....	**13**	**8**	**5**	**13**	**6**	**1**	**0**	**1**
1992-93	**Vancouver**	**NHL**	**79**	**29**	**56**	**85**	**30**	**10**	**0**	**2**	**209**	**13.9**	**19**	....	....	....	....	....	**12**	**2**	**9**	**11**	**6**	**0**	**0**	**0**
1993-94	**Vancouver**	**NHL**	**76**	**25**	**43**	**68**	**42**	**10**	**0**	**4**	**197**	**12.7**	**7**	....	....	....	....	....	**24**	**5**	**10**	**15**	**16**	**2**	**0**	**2**
1994-95	**Vancouver**	**NHL**	**41**	**6**	**19**	**25**	**27**	**3**	**0**	**2**	**93**	**6.5**	**–4**	....	....	....	....	....	**11**	**3**	**5**	**8**	**2**	**1**	**0**	**2**
1995-96	**Vancouver**	**NHL**	**79**	**22**	**45**	**67**	**42**	**5**	**0**	**1**	**187**	**11.8**	**16**	....	....	....	....	....	**6**	**0**	**2**	**2**	**6**	**0**	**0**	**0**
1996-97	**Phoenix**	**NHL**	**69**	**19**	**32**	**51**	**26**	**8**	**0**	**2**	**171**	**11.1**	**–9**	....	....	....	....	....	**7**	**0**	**7**	**7**	**12**	**0**	**0**	**0**
1997-98	**Phoenix**	**NHL**	**80**	**11**	**44**	**55**	**36**	**3**	**0**	**0**	**197**	**5.6**	**5**	....	....	....	....	....	**6**	**1**	**3**	**4**	**4**	**0**	**0**	**0**
1998-99	**Phoenix**	**NHL**	**7**	**2**	**5**	**7**	**2**	**2**	**0**	**1**	**18**	**11.1**	**3**	**81**	**51.9**	**0**	**1**	**15:22**	....	....	....	....	....	....	....	....
	Nashville	**NHL**	**72**	**18**	**35**	**53**	**40**	**8**	**0**	**3**	**239**	**7.5**	**–6**	**1129**	**47.7**	**11**	**35**	**19:42**	....	....	....	....	....	....	....	....
99-2000	**Nashville**	**NHL**	**82**	**26**	**36**	**62**	**34**	**7**	**0**	**2**	**248**	**10.5**	**–13**	**611**	**45.7**	**8**	**20**	**18:11**	....	....	....	....	....	....	....	....
	NHL Totals		**856**	**242**	**439**	**681**	**367**	**88**	**0**	**25**	**2144**	**11.3**		**1821**	**47.2**	**19**	**56**	**18:44**	**101**	**27**	**49**	**76**	**66**	**8**	**0**	**7**

WHL First All-Star Team (1985)

Traded to **Vancouver** by **St. Louis** with Geoff Courtnall, Robert Dirk, Sergio Momesso and St. Louis' 5th round choice (Brian Loney) in 1992 Entry Draft for Dan Quinn and Garth Butcher, March 5, 1991. Signed as a free agent by **Phoenix**, July 1, 1996. Traded to **Nashville** by **Phoenix** with Richard Lintner for future considerations, October 31, 1998.

ROSA, Pavel

(ROHZA, PAH-vehl) **L.A.**

Right wing. Shoots right. 6', 195 lbs. Born, Most, Czech., June 7, 1977. Los Angeles' 3rd choice, 50th overall, in 1995 Entry Draft.

Season	Club	League	GP	G	A	Pts	PIM	PP	SH	GW	S	%	+/-	TF	F%	H	SB	Min	GP	G	A	Pts	PIM	PP	SH	GW
1994-95	HC Litvinov-Jr.	Cze-Rep	40	56	42	98	....	....	....	....	....	....	....	....	....	....	....	....	....	....	....	....	....	....	....	....
	HC Litvinov	Cze-Rep	2	0	0	0	0	....	....	....	....	....	....	....	....	....	....	....	1	0	0	0	0	....	....	....
1995-96	Hull Olympiques	QMJHL	61	46	70	116	39	....	....	....	....	....	....	....	....	....	....	....	18	14	22	36	25	....	....	....
1996-97	Hull Olympiques	QMJHL	68	*63	*90	*153	66	....	....	....	....	....	....	....	....	....	....	....	14	18	13	31	16	....	....	....
1997-98	Fredericton	AHL	1	0	0	0	0	....	....	....	....	....	....	....	....	....	....	....	....	....	....	....	....	....	....	....
	Long Beach	IHL	2	0	1	1	0	....	....	....	....	....	....	....	....	....	....	....	1	1	1	2	0	....	....	....
1998-99	**Los Angeles**	**NHL**	**29**	**4**	**12**	**16**	**6**	**0**	**0**	**0**	**61**	**6.6**	**0**	**0**	**0.0**	**24**	**6**	**13:34**	....	....	....	....	....	....	....	....
	Long Beach	IHL	31	17	13	30	28	....	....	....	....	....	....	....	....	....	....	....	6	1	2	3	0	....	....	....
99-2000	**Los Angeles**	**NHL**	**3**	**0**	**0**	**0**	**0**	**0**	**0**	**0**	**1**	**0.0**	**–1**	**0**	**0.0**	**6**	**1**	**11:21**	....	....	....	....	....	....	....	....
	Long Beach	IHL	74	22	31	53	76	....	....	....	....	....	....	....	....	....	....	....	6	2	2	4	4	....	....	....
	NHL Totals		**32**	**4**	**12**	**16**	**6**	**0**	**0**	**0**	**62**	**6.5**		**0**	**0.0**	**30**	**7**	**13:21**	....	....	....	....	....	....	....	....

QMJHL First All-Star Team (1997) • Canadian Major Junior First All-Star Team (1997)

• Missed majority of 1997-98 season recovering from head injury originally suffered in training camp, September, 1997.

ROUSE, Bob

(ROWS, BAWB)

Defense. Shoots right. 6'2", 215 lbs. Born, Surrey, B.C., June 18, 1964. Minnesota's 3rd choice, 80th overall, in 1982 Entry Draft.

Season	Club	League	GP	G	A	Pts	PIM	PP	SH	GW	S	%	+/-	TF	F%	H	SB	Min	GP	G	A	Pts	PIM	PP	SH	GW
1980-81	Billings Bighorns	WHL	70	0	13	13	116	....	....	....	....	....	....	....	....	....	....	....	5	0	0	0	2	....	....	....
1981-82	Billings Bighorns	WHL	71	7	22	29	209	....	....	....	....	....	....	....	....	....	....	....	5	0	2	2	10	....	....	....
1982-83	Nanaimo Islanders	WHL	29	7	20	27	86	....	....	....	....	....	....	....	....	....	....	....	....	....	....	....	....	....	....	....
	Lethbridge	WHL	42	8	30	38	82	....	....	....	....	....	....	....	....	....	....	....	20	2	13	15	55	....	....	....
1983-84	Lethbridge	WHL	71	18	42	60	101	....	....	....	....	....	....	....	....	....	....	....	5	0	1	1	28	....	....	....
	Minnesota	**NHL**	**1**	**0**	**0**	**0**	**0**	**0**	**0**	**0**	**0**	**0.0**	**0**	....	....	....	....	....	....	....	....	....	....	....	....	....
1984-85	**Minnesota**	**NHL**	**63**	**2**	**9**	**11**	**113**	**0**	**0**	**0**	**80**	**2.5**	**–14**	....	....	....	....	....	....	....	....	....	....	....	....	....
	Springfield	AHL	8	0	3	3	6	....	....	....	....	....	....	....	....	....	....	....	....	....	....	....	....	....	....	....
1985-86	**Minnesota**	**NHL**	**75**	**1**	**14**	**15**	**151**	**0**	**0**	**1**	**91**	**1.1**	**15**	....	....	....	....	....	**3**	**0**	**0**	**0**	**0**	**0**	**0**	**0**
1986-87	**Minnesota**	**NHL**	**72**	**2**	**10**	**12**	**179**	**0**	**0**	**0**	**71**	**2.8**	**6**	....	....	....	....	....	....	....	....	....	....	....	....	....
1987-88	**Minnesota**	**NHL**	**74**	**0**	**12**	**12**	**168**	**0**	**0**	**0**	**62**	**0.0**	**–30**	....	....	....	....	....	....	....	....	....	....	....	....	....
1988-89	**Minnesota**	**NHL**	**66**	**4**	**13**	**17**	**124**	**0**	**0**	**1**	**66**	**6.1**	**–5**	....	....	....	....	....	....	....	....	....	....	....	....	....
	Washington	**NHL**	**13**	**0**	**2**	**2**	**36**	**0**	**0**	**0**	**19**	**0.0**	**2**	....	....	....	....	....	**6**	**2**	**0**	**2**	**4**	**0**	**0**	**0**
1989-90	**Washington**	**NHL**	**70**	**4**	**16**	**20**	**123**	**0**	**0**	**2**	**72**	**5.6**	**–2**	....	....	....	....	....	**15**	**2**	**3**	**5**	**47**	**1**	**0**	**0**
1990-91	**Washington**	**NHL**	**47**	**5**	**15**	**20**	**65**	**1**	**0**	**0**	**50**	**10.0**	**–7**	....	....	....	....	....	....	....	....	....	....	....	....	....
	Toronto	**NHL**	**13**	**2**	**4**	**6**	**10**	**1**	**0**	**0**	**15**	**13.3**	**–11**	....	....	....	....	....	....	....	....	....	....	....	....	....
1991-92	**Toronto**	**NHL**	**79**	**3**	**19**	**22**	**97**	**1**	**0**	**0**	**115**	**2.6**	**–20**	....	....	....	....	....	....	....	....	....	....	....	....	....
1992-93	**Toronto**	**NHL**	**82**	**3**	**11**	**14**	**130**	**0**	**1**	**1**	**78**	**3.8**	**7**	....	....	....	....	....	**21**	**3**	**8**	**11**	**29**	**1**	**0**	**1**
1993-94	**Toronto**	**NHL**	**63**	**5**	**11**	**16**	**101**	**1**	**1**	**0**	**77**	**6.5**	**8**	....	....	....	....	....	**18**	**0**	**3**	**3**	**29**	**0**	**0**	**0**
1994-95	**Detroit**	**NHL**	**48**	**1**	**7**	**8**	**36**	**0**	**0**	**1**	**51**	**2.0**	**14**	....	....	....	....	....	**18**	**0**	**3**	**3**	**8**	**0**	**0**	**0**
1995-96	**Detroit**	**NHL**	**58**	**0**	**6**	**6**	**48**	**0**	**0**	**0**	**49**	**0.0**	**5**	....	....	....	....	....	**7**	**0**	**1**	**1**	**4**	**0**	**0**	**0**
1996-97 ♦	**Detroit**	**NHL**	**70**	**4**	**9**	**13**	**58**	**0**	**2**	**0**	**70**	**5.7**	**8**	....	....	....	....	....	**20**	**0**	**0**	**0**	**55**	**0**	**0**	**0**
1997-98 ♦	**Detroit**	**NHL**	**71**	**1**	**11**	**12**	**57**	**0**	**0**	**0**	**54**	**1.9**	**–9**	....	....	....	....	....	**22**	**0**	**3**	**3**	**16**	**0**	**0**	**0**

			Regular Season																Playoffs							
Season	Club	League	GP	G	A	Pts	PIM	PP	SH	GW	S	%	+/-	TF	F%	H	SB	Min	GP	G	A	Pts	PIM	PP	SH	GW
1998-99	**San Jose**	**NHL**	**70**	**0**	**11**	**11**	**44**	**0**	**0**	**0**	**75**	**0.0**	**0**	**0**	**0.0**	**73**	**68**	**16:57**	**6**	**0**	**0**	**0**	**6**	**0**	**0**	**0**
99-2000	**San Jose**	**NHL**	**26**	**0**	**1**	**1**	**19**	**0**	**0**	**0**	**20**	**0.0**	**–3**	**0**	**0.0**	**22**	**17**	**14:56**	....	....	....	....	....	....	....	....
	NHL Totals		**1061**	**37**	**181**	**218**	**1559**	**4**	**4**	**6**	**1115**	**3.3**		**0**	**0.0**	**95**	**85**	**16:24**	**136**	**7**	**21**	**28**	**198**	**2**	**0**	**1**

WHL East First All-Star Team (1984)

Traded to **Washington** by **Minnesota** with Dino Ciccarelli for Mike Gartner and Larry Murphy, March 7, 1989. Traded to **Toronto** by **Washington** with Peter Zezel for Al Iafrate, January 16, 1991. Signed as a free agent by **Detroit**, August 5, 1994. Signed as a free agent by **San Jose**, July 13, 1998. • Officially released by **San Jose**, December 26, 1999.

ROY, Andre

(WAH, AHN-dray) **OTT.**

Left wing. Shoots left. 6'4", 213 lbs. Born, Port Chester, NY, February 8, 1975. Boston's 5th choice, 151st overall, in 1994 Entry Draft.

Season	Club	League	GP	G	A	Pts	PIM	PP	SH	GW	S	%	+/-	TF	F%	H	SB	Min	GP	G	A	Pts	PIM	PP	SH	GW
1992-93	Carleton Place	OJHL-B	40	16	15	31	80	....	....	....	....	....	....	....	....	....	....	....	....	....	....	....	....	....	....	....
1993-94	Beauport	QMJHL	33	6	7	13	125	....	....	....	....	....	....	....	....	....	....	....	....	....	....	....	....	....	....	....
	Chicoutimi	QMJHL	32	4	14	18	152	....	....	....	....	....	....	....	....	....	....	....	25	3	6	9	94	....	....	....
1994-95	Chicoutimi	QMJHL	20	15	8	23	90	....	....	....	....	....	....	....	....	....	....	....	....	....	....	....	....	....	....	....
	Drummondville	QMJHL	34	18	13	31	233	....	....	....	....	....	....	....	....	....	....	....	4	2	0	2	34	....	....	....
1995-96	**Boston**	**NHL**	**3**	**0**	**0**	**0**	**0**	**0**	**0**	**0**	**0**	**0.0**	**0**	....	....	....	....	....	....	....	....	....	....	....	....	....
	Providence Bruins	AHL	58	7	8	15	167	....	....	....	....	....	....	....	....	....	....	....	1	0	0	0	10	....	....	....
1996-97	**Boston**	**NHL**	**10**	**0**	**2**	**2**	**12**	**0**	**0**	**0**	**12**	**0.0**	**–5**	....	....	....	....	....	....	....	....	....	....	....	....	....
	Providence Bruins	AHL	50	17	11	28	234	....	....	....	....	....	....	....	....	....	....	....	....	....	....	....	....	....	....	....
1997-98	Providence Bruins	AHL	36	3	11	14	154	....	....	....	....	....	....	....	....	....	....	....	....	....	....	....	....	....	....	....
	Charlotte	ECHL	27	10	8	18	132	....	....	....	....	....	....	....	....	....	....	....	7	2	3	5	34	....	....	....
1998-99	Fort Wayne	IHL	65	15	6	21	*395	....	....	....	....	....	....	....	....	....	....	....	2	0	0	0	11	....	....	....
99-2000	**Ottawa**	**NHL**	**73**	**4**	**3**	**7**	**145**	**0**	**0**	**1**	**39**	**10.3**	**3**	**3**	**33.3**	**109**	**5**	**6:29**	**5**	**0**	**0**	**0**	**2**	**0**	**0**	**0**
	NHL Totals		**86**	**4**	**5**	**9**	**157**	**0**	**0**	**1**	**51**	**7.8**		**3**	**33.3**	**109**	**5**	**6:29**	**5**	**0**	**0**	**0**	**2**	**0**	**0**	**0**

Signed as a free agent by **Ottawa**, April 28, 1999.

ROYER, Remi

(ROHY-uhr, REH-mee) **WSH.**

Defense. Shoots right. 6'2", 200 lbs. Born, Donnacona, Que., February 12, 1978. Chicago's 1st choice, 31st overall, in 1996 Entry Draft.

Season	Club	League	GP	G	A	Pts	PIM	PP	SH	GW	S	%	+/-	TF	F%	H	SB	Min	GP	G	A	Pts	PIM	PP	SH	GW
1993-94	Ste-Foy Governors	QAAA	44	8	24	32	....	....	....	....	....	....	....	....	....	....	....	....	....	....	....	....	....	....	....	....
1994-95	Victoriaville Tigres	QMJHL	57	3	17	20	144	....	....	....	....	....	....	....	....	....	....	....	4	0	1	1	7	....	....	....
1995-96	Victoriaville Tigres	QMJHL	43	12	14	26	209	....	....	....	....	....	....	....	....	....	....	....	....	....	....	....	....	....	....	....
	St-Hyacinthe	QMJHL	19	10	9	19	80	....	....	....	....	....	....	....	....	....	....	....	12	1	4	5	29	....	....	....
1996-97	Rouyn-Noranda	QMJHL	29	3	12	15	85	....	....	....	....	....	....	....	....	....	....	....	....	....	....	....	....	....	....	....
	Indianapolis Ice	IHL	10	0	1	1	17	....	....	....	....	....	....	....	....	....	....	....	....	....	....	....	....	....	....	....
1997-98	Rouyn-Noranda	QMJHL	66	20	48	68	205	....	....	....	....	....	....	....	....	....	....	....	6	1	3	4	8	....	....	....
	Indianapolis Ice	IHL	5	0	2	2	4	....	....	....	....	....	....	....	....	....	....	....	5	1	2	3	12	....	....	....
1998-99	**Chicago**	**NHL**	**18**	**0**	**0**	**0**	**67**	**0**	**0**	**0**	**24**	**0.0**	**–10**	**0**	**0.0**	**25**	**11**	**13:37**	....	....	....	....	....	....	....	....
	Indianapolis Ice	IHL	54	4	15	19	164	....	....	....	....	....	....	....	....	....	....	....	7	0	0	0	44	....	....	....
	Portland Pirates	AHL	2	0	1	1	2	....	....	....	....	....	....	....	....	....	....	....	....	....	....	....	....	....	....	....
99-2000	Cleveland	IHL	57	3	13	16	204	....	....	....	....	....	....	....	....	....	....	....	8	1	1	2	12	....	....	....
	NHL Totals		**18**	**0**	**0**	**0**	**67**	**0**	**0**	**0**	**24**	**0.0**		**0**	**0.0**	**25**	**11**	**13:37**	....	....	....	....	....	....	....	....

QMJHL First All-Star Team (1998)

Traded to **Washington** by **Chicago** for Nolan Baumgartner, July 20, 2000.

ROZSIVAL, Michal

(roh-ZIH-vahl, mee-KHUHL) **PIT.**

Defense. Shoots right. 6'1", 208 lbs. Born, Vlasim, Czech., September 3, 1978. Pittsburgh's 5th choice, 105th overall, in 1996 Entry Draft.

Season	Club	League	GP	G	A	Pts	PIM	PP	SH	GW	S	%	+/-	TF	F%	H	SB	Min	GP	G	A	Pts	PIM	PP	SH	GW
1994-95	Dukla Jihlava-Jr.	Cze-Rep	31	8	13	21	....	....	....	....	....	....	....	....	....	....	....	....	....	....	....	....	....	....	....	....
1995-96	Dukla Jihlava	Cze-Rep	36	3	4	7	....	....	....	....	....	....	....	....	....	....	....	....	....	....	....	....	....	....	....	....
1996-97	Swift Current	WHL	63	8	31	39	80	....	....	....	....	....	....	....	....	....	....	....	10	0	6	6	15	....	....	....
1997-98	Swift Current	WHL	71	14	55	69	122	....	....	....	....	....	....	....	....	....	....	....	12	0	5	5	33	....	....	....
1998-99	Syracuse Crunch	AHL	49	3	22	25	72	....	....	....	....	....	....	....	....	....	....	....	....	....	....	....	....	....	....	....
99-2000	**Pittsburgh**	**NHL**	**75**	**4**	**17**	**21**	**48**	**1**	**0**	**1**	**73**	**5.5**	**11**	**1**	**0.0**	**124**	**72**	**19:01**	**2**	**0**	**0**	**0**	**4**	**0**	**0**	**0**
	NHL Totals		**75**	**4**	**17**	**21**	**48**	**1**	**0**	**1**	**73**	**5.5**		**1**	**0.0**	**124**	**72**	**19:01**	**2**	**0**	**0**	**0**	**4**	**0**	**0**	**0**

WHL East First All-Star Team (1998)

RUCCHIN, Steve

(ROO-chihn, STEEV) **ANA.**

Center. Shoots left. 6'3", 212 lbs. Born, Thunder Bay, Ont., July 4, 1971. Anaheim's 1st choice, 2nd overall, in 1994 Supplemental Draft.

Season	Club	League	GP	G	A	Pts	PIM	PP	SH	GW	S	%	+/-	TF	F%	H	SB	Min	GP	G	A	Pts	PIM	PP	SH	GW
1989-90	Banting High	Hi-School	STATISTICS NOT AVAILABLE																							
	Thamesford	OJHL-D	2	1	2	3	0	....	....	....	....	....	....	....	....	....	....	....	....	....	....	....	....	....	....	....
1990-91	Western Ontario	OUAA	34	13	16	29	14	....	....	....	....	....	....	....	....	....	....	....	....	....	....	....	....	....	....	....
1991-92	Western Ontario	OUAA	37	28	34	62	36	....	....	....	....	....	....	....	....	....	....	....	....	....	....	....	....	....	....	....
1992-93	Western Ontario	OUAA	34	22	26	48	16	....	....	....	....	....	....	....	....	....	....	....	....	....	....	....	....	....	....	....
1993-94	Western Ontario	OUAA	35	30	23	53	30	....	....	....	....	....	....	....	....	....	....	....	....	....	....	....	....	....	....	....
1994-95	San Diego Gulls	IHL	41	11	15	26	14	....	....	....	....	....	....	....	....	....	....	....	....	....	....	....	....	....	....	....
	Anaheim	**NHL**	**43**	**6**	**11**	**17**	**23**	**0**	**0**	**1**	**59**	**10.2**	**7**	....	....	....	....	....	....	....	....	....	....	....	....	....
1995-96	**Anaheim**	**NHL**	**64**	**19**	**25**	**44**	**12**	**8**	**1**	**4**	**113**	**16.8**	**3**	....	....	....	....	....	....	....	....	....	....	....	....	....
1996-97	**Anaheim**	**NHL**	**79**	**19**	**48**	**67**	**24**	**6**	**1**	**2**	**153**	**12.4**	**26**	....	....	....	....	....	**8**	**1**	**2**	**3**	**10**	**0**	**0**	**0**
1997-98	**Anaheim**	**NHL**	**72**	**17**	**36**	**53**	**13**	**8**	**1**	**3**	**131**	**13.0**	**8**	....	....	....	....	....	....	....	....	....	....	....	....	....
1998-99	**Anaheim**	**NHL**	**69**	**23**	**39**	**62**	**22**	**5**	**1**	**5**	**145**	**15.9**	**11**	**1845**	**52.3**	**43**	**72**	**22:33**	**4**	**0**	**3**	**3**	**0**	**0**	**0**	**0**
99-2000	**Anaheim**	**NHL**	**71**	**19**	**38**	**57**	**16**	**10**	**0**	**2**	**131**	**14.5**	**9**	**1996**	**53.4**	**69**	**69**	**22:12**	....	....	....	....	....	....	....	....
	NHL Totals		**398**	**103**	**197**	**300**	**110**	**37**	**4**	**17**	**732**	**14.1**		**3841**	**52.9**	**112**	**141**	**22:22**	**12**	**1**	**5**	**6**	**10**	**0**	**0**	**0**

RUCINSKI, Mike

(roo-SIHN-skee, MIGHK) **CAR.**

Defense. Shoots left. 5'11", 179 lbs. Born, Trenton, MI, March 30, 1975. Hartford's 8th choice, 217th overall, in 1995 Entry Draft.

Season	Club	League	GP	G	A	Pts	PIM	PP	SH	GW	S	%	+/-	TF	F%	H	SB	Min	GP	G	A	Pts	PIM	PP	SH	GW
1991-92	Detroit Caesars	MNHL	29	4	15	19	38	....	....	....	....	....	....	....	....	....	....	....	....	....	....	....	....	....	....	....
1992-93	Detroit Jr. Wings	OHL	66	6	13	19	59	....	....	....	....	....	....	....	....	....	....	....	15	0	4	4	12	....	....	....
1993-94	Detroit Jr. Wings	OHL	66	2	26	28	58	....	....	....	....	....	....	....	....	....	....	....	17	0	7	7	15	....	....	....
1994-95	Detroit Jr. Wings	OHL	64	9	18	27	61	....	....	....	....	....	....	....	....	....	....	....	21	3	3	6	8	....	....	....
1995-96	Detroit Whalers	OHL	51	10	26	36	65	....	....	....	....	....	....	....	....	....	....	....	11	2	4	6	14	....	....	....
1996-97	Richmond	ECHL	61	20	23	43	85	....	....	....	....	....	....	....	....	....	....	....	8	2	6	8	18	....	....	....
	Springfield	AHL	6	0	1	1	0	....	....	....	....	....	....	....	....	....	....	....	....	....	....	....	....	....	....	....
1997-98	**Carolina**	**NHL**	**9**	**0**	**1**	**1**	**2**	**0**	**0**	**0**	**3**	**0.0**	**0**	....	....	....	....	....	....	....	....	....	....	....	....	....
	New Haven	AHL	65	5	17	22	50	....	....	....	....	....	....	....	....	....	....	....	1	0	0	0	0	....	....	....
	Cleveland	IHL	2	0	0	0	4	....	....	....	....	....	....	....	....	....	....	....	....	....	....	....	....	....	....	....
1998-99	**Carolina**	**NHL**	**15**	**0**	**1**	**1**	**8**	**0**	**0**	**0**	**8**	**0.0**	**1**	**0**	**0.0**	**8**	**4**	**10:29**	....	....	....	....	....	....	....	....
	New Haven	AHL	23	2	6	8	27	....	....	....	....	....	....	....	....	....	....	....	....	....	....	....	....	....	....	....
	Florida Everblades	ECHL	16	2	5	7	13	....	....	....	....	....	....	....	....	....	....	....	....	....	....	....	....	....	....	....
	Charlotte	ECHL	16	6	10	16	4	....	....	....	....	....	....	....	....	....	....	....	....	....	....	....	....	....	....	....
99-2000	Cincinnati	IHL	66	3	10	13	34	....	....	....	....	....	....	....	....	....	....	....	11	0	0	0	28	....	....	....
	NHL Totals		**24**	**0**	**2**	**2**	**10**	**0**	**0**	**0**	**11**	**0.0**		**0**	**0.0**	**8**	**4**	**10:29**	....	....	....	....	....	....	....	....

Rights transferred to **Carolina** after **Hartford** franchise relocated, June 25, 1997.

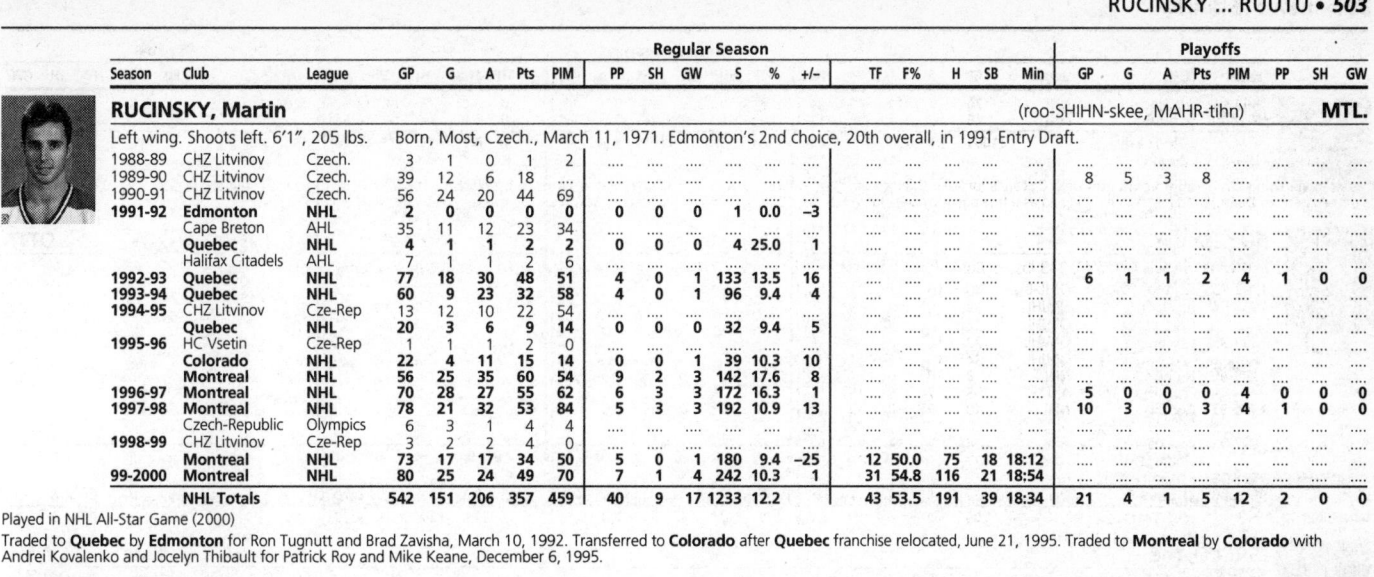

RUCINSKY, Martin (roo-SHIHN-skee, MAHR-tihn) MTL.

Left wing. Shoots left. 6'1", 205 lbs. Born, Most, Czech., March 11, 1971. Edmonton's 2nd choice, 20th overall, in 1991 Entry Draft.

			Regular Season															Playoffs							
Season	Club	League	GP	G	A	Pts	PIM	PP	SH	GW	S	%	+/-	TF	F%	H	SB	Min	GP	G	A	Pts	PIM	PP	SH	GW
1988-89	CHZ Litvinov	Czech.	3	1	0	1	2	....	....	....	....	....	....	....	....	....	....	....	....	....	....	....	....	....	....	....
1989-90	CHZ Litvinov	Czech.	39	12	6	18	....	....	....	....	....	....	....	....	....	....	....	....	8	5	3	8	....	....	....	....
1990-91	CHZ Litvinov	Czech.	56	24	20	44	69	....	....	....	....	....	....	....	....	....	....	....	....	....	....	....	....	....	....	....
1991-92	**Edmonton**	**NHL**	**2**	**0**	**0**	**0**	**0**	0	0	0	1	0.0	–3	....	....	....	....	....	....	....	....	....	....	....	....	....
	Cape Breton	AHL	35	11	12	23	34	....	....	....	....	....	....	....	....	....	....	....	....	....	....	....	....	....	....	....
	Quebec	**NHL**	**4**	**1**	**1**	**2**	**2**	0	0	0	4	25.0	1	....	....	....	....	....	....	....	....	....	....	....	....	....
	Halifax Citadels	AHL	7	1	1	2	6	....	....	....	....	....	....	....	....	....	....	....	....	....	....	....	....	....	....	....
1992-93	**Quebec**	**NHL**	**77**	**18**	**30**	**48**	**51**	4	0	1	133	13.5	16	....	....	....	....	....	**6**	**1**	**1**	**2**	**4**	**1**	**0**	**0**
1993-94	**Quebec**	**NHL**	**60**	**9**	**23**	**32**	**58**	4	0	1	96	9.4	4	....	....	....	....	....	....	....	....	....	....	....	....	....
1994-95	CHZ Litvinov	Cze-Rep	13	12	10	22	54	....	....	....	....	....	....	....	....	....	....	....	....	....	....	....	....	....	....	....
	Quebec	**NHL**	**20**	**3**	**6**	**9**	**14**	0	0	0	32	9.4	5	....	....	....	....	....	....	....	....	....	....	....	....	....
1995-96	HC Vsetin	Cze-Rep	1	1	1	2	0	....	....	....	....	....	....	....	....	....	....	....	....	....	....	....	....	....	....	....
	Colorado	**NHL**	**22**	**4**	**11**	**15**	**14**	0	0	1	39	10.3	10	....	....	....	....	....	....	....	....	....	....	....	....	....
	Montreal	**NHL**	**56**	**25**	**35**	**60**	**54**	9	2	3	142	17.6	8	....	....	....	....	....	....	....	....	....	....	....	....	....
1996-97	**Montreal**	**NHL**	**70**	**28**	**27**	**55**	**62**	6	3	3	172	16.3	1	....	....	....	....	....	**5**	**0**	**0**	**0**	**4**	**0**	**0**	**0**
1997-98	**Montreal**	**NHL**	**78**	**21**	**32**	**53**	**84**	5	3	3	192	10.9	13	....	....	....	....	....	**10**	**3**	**0**	**3**	**4**	**1**	**0**	**0**
	Czech-Republic	Olympics	6	3	1	4	4	....	....	....	....	....	....	....	....	....	....	....	....	....	....	....	....	....	....	....
1998-99	CHZ Litvinov	Cze-Rep	3	2	2	4	0	....	....	....	....	....	....	....	....	....	....	....	....	....	....	....	....	....	....	....
	Montreal	**NHL**	**73**	**17**	**17**	**34**	**50**	5	0	1	180	9.4	–25	12	50.0	75	18	18:12	....	....	....	....	....	....	....	....
99-2000	**Montreal**	**NHL**	**80**	**25**	**24**	**49**	**70**	7	1	4	242	10.3	1	31	54.8	116	21	18:54	....	....	....	....	....	....	....	....
	NHL Totals		**542**	**151**	**206**	**357**	**459**	40	9	17	1233	12.2		43	53.5	191	39	18:34	21	4	1	5	12	2	0	0

Played in NHL All-Star Game (2000)

Traded to **Quebec** by **Edmonton** for Ron Tugnutt and Brad Zavisha, March 10, 1992. Transferred to **Colorado** after **Quebec** franchise relocated, June 21, 1995. Traded to **Montreal** by **Colorado** with Andrei Kovalenko and Jocelyn Thibault for Patrick Roy and Mike Keane, December 6, 1995.

RUMBLE, Darren (RUHM-buhl, DAIR-rehn) ST.L.

Defense. Shoots left. 6'1", 200 lbs. Born, Barrie, Ont., January 23, 1969. Philadelphia's 1st choice, 20th overall, in 1987 Entry Draft.

			Regular Season															Playoffs							
Season	Club	League	GP	G	A	Pts	PIM	PP	SH	GW	S	%	+/-	TF	F%	H	SB	Min	GP	G	A	Pts	PIM	PP	SH	GW
1985-86	Barrie Colts	OJHL-B	46	14	32	46	91	....	....	....	....	....	....	....	....	....	....	....	....	....	....	....	....	....	....	....
1986-87	Kitchener	OHL	64	11	32	43	44	....	....	....	....	....	....	....	....	....	....	....	4	0	1	1	9	....	....	....
1987-88	Kitchener	OHL	55	15	50	65	64	....	....	....	....	....	....	....	....	....	....	....	....	....	....	....	....	....	....	....
1988-89	Kitchener	OHL	46	11	28	39	25	....	....	....	....	....	....	....	....	....	....	....	5	1	0	1	2	....	....	....
1989-90	Hershey Bears	AHL	57	2	13	15	31	....	....	....	....	....	....	....	....	....	....	....	....	....	....	....	....	....	....	....
1990-91	**Philadelphia**	**NHL**	**3**	**1**	**0**	**1**	**0**	0	0	0	2	50.0	1	....	....	....	....	....	....	....	....	....	....	....	....	....
	Hershey Bears	AHL	73	6	35	41	48	....	....	....	....	....	....	....	....	....	....	....	3	0	5	5	2	....	....	....
1991-92	Hershey Bears	AHL	79	12	54	66	118	....	....	....	....	....	....	....	....	....	....	....	6	0	3	3	2	....	....	....
1992-93	**Ottawa**	**NHL**	**69**	**3**	**13**	**16**	**61**	0	0	0	92	3.3	–24	....	....	....	....	....	....	....	....	....	....	....	....	....
	New Haven	AHL	2	1	0	1	0	....	....	....	....	....	....	....	....	....	....	....	....	....	....	....	....	....	....	....
1993-94	**Ottawa**	**NHL**	**70**	**6**	**9**	**15**	**116**	0	0	0	95	6.3	–50	....	....	....	....	....	....	....	....	....	....	....	....	....
	P.E.I. Senators	AHL	3	2	0	2	0	....	....	....	....	....	....	....	....	....	....	....	....	....	....	....	....	....	....	....
1994-95	P.E.I. Senators	AHL	70	7	46	53	77	....	....	....	....	....	....	....	....	....	....	....	11	0	6	6	4	....	....	....
1995-96	**Philadelphia**	**NHL**	**5**	**0**	**0**	**0**	**4**	0	0	0	7	0.0	0	....	....	....	....	....	....	....	....	....	....	....	....	....
	Hershey Bears	AHL	58	13	37	50	83	....	....	....	....	....	....	....	....	....	....	....	5	0	0	0	6	....	....	....
1996-97	**Philadelphia**	**NHL**	**10**	**0**	**0**	**0**	**0**	0	0	0	9	0.0	–2	....	....	....	....	....	....	....	....	....	....	....	....	....
	Philadelphia	AHL	72	18	44	62	83	....	....	....	....	....	....	....	....	....	....	....	7	0	3	3	19	....	....	....
1997-98	Adler Mannheim	DEL	21	2	7	9	18	....	....	....	....	....	....	....	....	....	....	....	....	....	....	....	....	....	....	....
	Adler Mannheim	EuroHL	4	0	1	1	4	....	....	....	....	....	....	....	....	....	....	....	....	....	....	....	....	....	....	....
	San Antonio	IHL	46	7	22	29	47	....	....	....	....	....	....	....	....	....	....	....	....	....	....	....	....	....	....	....
1998-99	Utah Grizzlies	IHL	10	1	4	5	10	....	....	....	....	....	....	....	....	....	....	....	....	....	....	....	....	....	....	....
	Grand Rapids	IHL	53	6	22	28	44	....	....	....	....	....	....	....	....	....	....	....	....	....	....	....	....	....	....	....
99-2000	Grand Rapids	IHL	29	3	10	13	20	....	....	....	....	....	....	....	....	....	....	....	....	....	....	....	....	....	....	....
	Worcester	AHL	39	0	17	17	31	....	....	....	....	....	....	....	....	....	....	....	9	0	2	2	6	....	....	....
	NHL Totals		**157**	**10**	**22**	**32**	**181**	0	0	0	205	4.9														

AHL Second All-Star Team (1995) • AHL First All-Star Team (1997) • Won Eddie Shore Award (Outstanding Defenseman - AHL) (1997)

Claimed by **Ottawa** from **Philadelphia** in Expansion Draft, June 18, 1992. Signed as a free agent by **Philadelphia**, July 31, 1995. Signed as a free agent by **St. Louis**, February 1, 2000.

RUSSELL, Cam (RUH-sehl, KAM)

Defense. Shoots left. 6'4", 200 lbs. Born, Halifax, N.S., January 12, 1969. Chicago's 3rd choice, 50th overall, in 1987 Entry Draft.

			Regular Season															Playoffs							
Season	Club	League	GP	G	A	Pts	PIM	PP	SH	GW	S	%	+/-	TF	F%	H	SB	Min	GP	G	A	Pts	PIM	PP	SH	GW
1985-86	Hull Olympiques	QMJHL	56	3	4	7	24	....	....	....	....	....	....	....	....	....	....	....	15	0	2	2	4	....	....	....
1986-87	Hull Olympiques	QMJHL	66	3	16	19	119	....	....	....	....	....	....	....	....	....	....	....	8	0	1	1	16	....	....	....
1987-88	Hull Olympiques	QMJHL	53	9	18	27	141	....	....	....	....	....	....	....	....	....	....	....	19	2	5	7	39	....	....	....
1988-89	Hull Olympiques	QMJHL	66	8	32	40	109	....	....	....	....	....	....	....	....	....	....	....	9	2	6	8	6	....	....	....
1989-90	**Chicago**	**NHL**	**19**	**0**	**1**	**1**	**27**	0	0	0	10	0.0	–3	....	....	....	....	....	**1**	**0**	**0**	**0**	**0**	**0**	**0**	**0**
	Indianapolis Ice	IHL	46	3	15	18	114	....	....	....	....	....	....	....	....	....	....	....	9	0	1	1	24	....	....	....
1990-91	**Chicago**	**NHL**	**3**	**0**	**0**	**0**	**5**	0	0	0	0	0.0	1	....	....	....	....	....	**1**	**0**	**0**	**0**	**0**	**0**	**0**	**0**
	Indianapolis Ice	IHL	53	5	9	14	125	....	....	....	....	....	....	....	....	....	....	....	6	0	2	2	30	....	....	....
1991-92	**Chicago**	**NHL**	**19**	**0**	**0**	**0**	**34**	0	0	0	9	0.0	–8	....	....	....	....	....	**12**	**0**	**2**	**2**	**2**	**0**	**0**	**0**
	Indianapolis Ice	IHL	41	4	9	13	78	....	....	....	....	....	....	....	....	....	....	....	....	....	....	....	....	....	....	....
1992-93	**Chicago**	**NHL**	**67**	**2**	**4**	**6**	**151**	0	0	0	49	4.1	5	....	....	....	....	....	**4**	**0**	**0**	**0**	**0**	**0**	**0**	**0**
1993-94	**Chicago**	**NHL**	**67**	**1**	**7**	**8**	**200**	0	0	0	41	2.4	10	....	....	....	....	....	....	....	....	....	....	....	....	....
1994-95	**Chicago**	**NHL**	**33**	**1**	**3**	**4**	**88**	0	0	0	18	5.6	4	....	....	....	....	....	**16**	**0**	**3**	**3**	**8**	**0**	**0**	**0**
1995-96	**Chicago**	**NHL**	**61**	**2**	**2**	**4**	**129**	0	0	0	22	9.1	8	....	....	....	....	....	**6**	**0**	**0**	**0**	**2**	**0**	**0**	**0**
1996-97	**Chicago**	**NHL**	**44**	**1**	**1**	**2**	**65**	0	0	0	19	5.3	–8	....	....	....	....	....	**4**	**0**	**0**	**0**	**4**	**0**	**0**	**0**
1997-98	**Chicago**	**NHL**	**41**	**1**	**1**	**2**	**79**	0	0	1	18	5.6	3	....	....	....	....	....	....	....	....	....	....	....	....	....
1998-99	**Chicago**	**NHL**	**7**	**0**	**0**	**0**	**10**	0	0	0	1	0.0	1	0	0.0	7	0	5:58	....	....	....	....	....	....	....	....
	Colorado	**NHL**	**35**	**1**	**2**	**3**	**84**	0	0	0	14	7.1	–5	0	0.0	44	32	12:30	....	....	....	....	....	....	....	....
99-2000	**Colorado**	**NHL**	DID NOT PLAY – INJURED																							
	NHL Totals		**396**	**9**	**21**	**30**	**872**	0	0	1	201	4.5		0	0.0	51	32	11:25	44	0	5	5	16	0	0	0

Traded to **Colorado** by **Chicago** for Roman Vopat and Los Angeles' 6th round choice (previously acquired, later traded to Ottawa, Ottawa selected Martin Brusek) in 1999 Entry Draft, November 10, 1998. • Missed remainder of 1998-99 and entire 1999-2000 seasons recovering from torn rotator cuff injury suffered in game vs. Philadelphia, February 14, 1999.

RUUTU, Jarkko (ROO-too, YAHR-koh) VAN.

Left wing. Shoots left. 6'2", 194 lbs. Born, Vantaa, Finland, August 23, 1975. Vancouver's 3rd choice, 68th overall, in 1998 Entry Draft.

			Regular Season															Playoffs							
Season	Club	League	GP	G	A	Pts	PIM	PP	SH	GW	S	%	+/-	TF	F%	H	SB	Min	GP	G	A	Pts	PIM	PP	SH	GW
1991-92	HIFK Helsinki	Finn-Jr.	1	0	0	0	0	....	....	....	....	....	....	....	....	....	....	....	....	....	....	....	....	....	....	....
1992-93	HIFK Helsinki-B	Finn-Jr.	33	26	21	47	53	....	....	....	....	....	....	....	....	....	....	....	....	....	....	....	....	....	....	....
	HIFK Helsinki	Finn-Jr.	1	0	0	0	0	....	....	....	....	....	....	....	....	....	....	....	....	....	....	....	....	....	....	....
1993-94	HIFK Helsinki	Finn-Jr.	19	9	12	21	44	....	....	....	....	....	....	....	....	....	....	....	....	....	....	....	....	....	....	....
1994-95	HIFK Helsinki	Finn-Jr.	35	26	22	48	117	....	....	....	....	....	....	....	....	....	....	....	....	....	....	....	....	....	....	....
1995-96	Michigan Tech	WCHA	39	12	10	22	96	....	....	....	....	....	....	....	....	....	....	....	....	....	....	....	....	....	....	....
1996-97	HIFK Helsinki	Finland	48	11	10	21	*155	....	....	....	....	....	....	....	....	....	....	....	....	....	....	....	....	....	....	....
1997-98	HIFK Helsinki	Finland	37	10	10	20	87	....	....	....	....	....	....	....	....	....	....	....	8	*7	4	11	10	....	....	....
1998-99	HIFK Helsinki	Finland	25	10	4	14	136	....	....	....	....	....	....	....	....	....	....	....	9	0	2	2	43	....	....	....
	HIFK Helsinki	EuroHL	5	1	2	3	8	....	....	....	....	....	....	....	....	....	....	....	....	....	....	....	....	....	....	....
99-2000	**Vancouver**	**NHL**	**8**	**0**	**1**	**1**	**6**	0	0	0	4	0.0	–1	0	0.0	14	0	8:47	....	....	....	....	....	....	....	....
	Syracuse Crunch	AHL	65	26	32	58	164	....	....	....	....	....	....	....	....	....	....	....	4	3	1	4	8	....	....	....
	NHL Totals		**8**	**0**	**1**	**1**	**6**	0	0	0	4	0.0		0	0.0	14	0	8:47	....	....	....	....	....	....	....	....

RYAN, Terry

(RIGH-yan, TAIR-ree)

Left wing. Shoots left. 6'1", 202 lbs. Born, St. John's, Nfld., January 14, 1977. Montreal's 1st choice, 8th overall, in 1995 Entry Draft.

			Regular Season																Playoffs							
Season	Club	League	GP	G	A	Pts	PIM	PP	SH	GW	S	%	+/–	TF	F%	H	SB	Min	GP	G	A	Pts	PIM	PP	SH	GW
1991-92	Quesnel	RMJHL	49	26	41	67	217	....	....	....	....	....	....	....	....	....	....	....	....	....	....	....	....	....	....	....
1992-93	Quesnel	RMJHL	29	31	25	56	222	....	....	....	....	....	....	....	....	....	....	....	....	....	....	....	....	....	....	....
	Vernon Lakers	BCJHL	9	5	6	11	15	....	....	....	....	....	....	....	....	....	....	....	....	....	....	....	....	....	....	....
	Tri-City Americans	WHL	1	0	0	0	0	....	....	....	....	....	....	....	....	....	....	....	1	0	1	1	5	....	....	....
1993-94	Tri-City Americans	WHL	61	16	17	33	176	....	....	....	....	....	....	....	....	....	....	....	4	0	1	1	25	....	....	....
1994-95	Tri-City Americans	WHL	70	50	60	110	207	....	....	....	....	....	....	....	....	....	....	....	17	12	15	27	36	....	....	....
1995-96	Tri-City Americans	WHL	59	32	37	69	133	....	....	....	....	....	....	....	....	....	....	....	5	0	0	0	4	....	....	....
	Fredericton	AHL	....	....	....	....	....	....	....	....	....	....	....	....	....	....	....	....	3	0	0	0	2	....	....	....
1996-97	Red Deer Rebels	WHL	16	13	22	35	10	....	....	....	....	....	....	....	....	....	....	....	16	18	6	24	32	....	....	....
	Montreal	NHL	3	0	0	0	0	0	0	0	0	0.0	0	....	....	....	....	....	....	....	....	....	....	....	....	....
1997-98	Montreal	NHL	4	0	0	0	31	0	0	0	0	0.0	0	....	....	....	....	....	....	....	....	....	....	....	....	....
	Fredericton	AHL	71	21	18	39	256	....	....	....	....	....	....	....	....	....	....	....	3	1	1	2	0	....	....	....
1998-99	Montreal	NHL	1	0	0	0	5	0	0	0	0	0.0	0	0	0.0	0	0	3:09	....	....	....	....	....	....	....	....
	Fredericton	AHL	55	16	27	43	189	....	....	....	....	....	....	....	....	....	....	....	11	1	3	4	10	....	....	....
99-2000	Utah Grizzlies	IHL	6	0	3	3	24	....	....	....	....	....	....	....	....	....	....	....	....	....	....	....	....	....	....	....
	Long Beach	IHL	1	0	0	0	4	....	....	....	....	....	....	....	....	....	....	....	....	....	....	....	....	....	....	....
	St. John's Leafs	AHL	50	7	17	24	176	....	....	....	....	....	....	....	....	....	....	....	....	....	....	....	....	....	....	....
	NHL Totals		8	0	0	0	36	0	0	0	0	0.0		0	0.0	0	0	3:09	....	....	....	....	....	....	....	....

WHL West Second All-Star Team (1995)

Signed as a free agent by **Utah** (IHL) with **Montreal** retaining NHL rights, October 15, 1999. Signed as a free agent by **St. John's** (AHL) following release by **Utah** (IHL) with **Montreal** retaining NHL rights, November 12, 1999.

SACCO, Joe

(SAK-oh, JOH) **WSH.**

Right wing. Shoots left. 6'1", 190 lbs. Born, Medford, MA, February 4, 1969. Toronto's 4th choice, 71st overall, in 1987 Entry Draft.

Season	Club	League	GP	G	A	Pts	PIM	PP	SH	GW	S	%	+/–	TF	F%	H	SB	Min	GP	G	A	Pts	PIM	PP	SH	GW
1985-86	Medford Prep	Hi-School	20	30	30	60	....	....	....	....	....	....	....	....	....	....	....	....	....	....	....	....	....	....	....	....
1986-87	Medford Prep	Hi-School	21	22	32	54	....	....	....	....	....	....	....	....	....	....	....	....	....	....	....	....	....	....	....	....
1987-88	Boston University	H-East	34	16	20	36	40	....	....	....	....	....	....	....	....	....	....	....	....	....	....	....	....	....	....	....
1988-89	Boston University	H-East	33	21	19	40	66	....	....	....	....	....	....	....	....	....	....	....	....	....	....	....	....	....	....	....
1989-90	Boston University	H-East	44	28	24	52	70	....	....	....	....	....	....	....	....	....	....	....	....	....	....	....	....	....	....	....
1990-91	Toronto	NHL	20	0	5	5	2	0	0	0	20	0.0	–5	....	....	....	....	....	....	....	....	....	....	....	....	....
	Newmarket	AHL	49	18	17	35	24	....	....	....	....	....	....	....	....	....	....	....	....	....	....	....	....	....	....	....
1991-92	United States	Nat-Team	50	11	26	37	61	....	....	....	....	....	....	....	....	....	....	....	....	....	....	....	....	....	....	....
	United States	Olympics	8	0	2	2	0	....	....	....	....	....	....	....	....	....	....	....	....	....	....	....	....	....	....	....
	Toronto	NHL	17	7	4	11	4	0	0	1	40	17.5	8	....	....	....	....	....	....	....	....	....	....	....	....	....
	St. John's Leafs	AHL	....	....	....	....	....	....	....	....	....	....	....	....	....	....	....	....	1	1	1	2	0	....	....	....
1992-93	Toronto	NHL	23	4	4	8	8	0	0	0	38	10.5	–4	....	....	....	....	....	....	....	....	....	....	....	....	....
	St. John's Leafs	AHL	37	14	16	30	45	....	....	....	....	....	....	....	....	....	....	....	7	6	4	10	2	....	....	....
1993-94	Anaheim	NHL	84	19	18	37	61	3	1	2	206	9.2	–11	....	....	....	....	....	....	....	....	....	....	....	....	....
1994-95	Anaheim	NHL	41	10	8	18	23	2	0	0	77	13.0	–8	....	....	....	....	....	....	....	....	....	....	....	....	....
1995-96	Anaheim	NHL	76	13	14	27	40	....	....	....	....	....	....	....	....	....	....	....	....	....	....	....	....	....	....	....
1996-97	Anaheim	NHL	77	12	17	29	35	1	1	2	131	9.2	1	....	....	....	....	....	11	2	0	2	2	0	0	0
1997-98	Anaheim	NHL	55	8	11	19	24	0	2	2	90	8.9	–1	....	....	....	....	....	....	....	....	....	....	....	....	....
	NY Islanders	NHL	25	3	3	6	10	0	0	0	32	9.4	1	....	....	....	....	....	....	....	....	....	....	....	....	....
1998-99	NY Islanders	NHL	73	3	0	3	45	0	1	2	84	3.6	–24	32	56.3	58	27	9:59	....	....	....	....	....	....	....	....
99-2000	Washington	NHL	79	7	16	23	50	0	0	1	117	6.0	7	9	33.3	146	40	11:51	5	0	0	0	4	0	0	0
	NHL Totals		570	86	100	186	302	6	5	10	835	10.3		41	51.2	204	67	10:57	16	2	0	2	6	0	0	0

Claimed by **Anaheim** from **Toronto** in Expansion Draft, June 24, 1993. Traded to **NY Islanders** by **Anaheim** with J.J. Daigneault and Mark Janssens for Travis Green, Doug Houda and Tony Tuzzolino, February 6, 1998. Signed as a free agent by **Washington**, August 9, 1999.

SAKIC, Joe

(SAK-ihk, JOH) **COL.**

Center. Shoots left. 5'11", 185 lbs. Born, Burnaby, B.C., July 7, 1969. Quebec's 2nd choice, 15th overall, in 1987 Entry Draft.

Season	Club	League	GP	G	A	Pts	PIM	PP	SH	GW	S	%	+/–	TF	F%	H	SB	Min	GP	G	A	Pts	PIM	PP	SH	GW
1985-86	Burnaby	BCAHA	80	83	73	156	96	....	....	....	....	....	....	....	....	....	....	....	....	....	....	....	....	....	....	....
	Lethbridge	WHL	3	0	0	0	0	....	....	....	....	....	....	....	....	....	....	....	....	....	....	....	....	....	....	....
1986-87	Swift Current	WHL	72	60	73	133	31	....	....	....	....	....	....	....	....	....	....	....	4	0	1	1	0	....	....	....
	Canada	Nat-Team	1	0	0	0	0	....	....	....	....	....	....	....	....	....	....	....	....	....	....	....	....	....	....	....
1987-88	Swift Current	WHL	64	*78	82	*160	64	....	....	....	....	....	....	....	....	....	....	....	10	11	13	24	12	....	....	....
1988-89	Quebec	NHL	70	23	39	62	24	10	0	2	148	15.5	–36	....	....	....	....	....	....	....	....	....	....	....	....	....
1989-90	Quebec	NHL	80	39	63	102	27	8	1	2	234	16.7	–40	....	....	....	....	....	....	....	....	....	....	....	....	....
1990-91	Quebec	NHL	80	48	61	109	24	12	3	7	245	19.6	–26	....	....	....	....	....	....	....	....	....	....	....	....	....
1991-92	Quebec	NHL	69	29	65	94	20	6	3	1	217	13.4	5	....	....	....	....	....	....	....	....	....	....	....	....	....
1992-93	Quebec	NHL	78	48	57	105	40	20	2	4	264	18.2	–3	....	....	....	....	....	6	3	3	6	2	1	0	0
1993-94	Quebec	NHL	84	28	64	92	18	10	1	9	279	10.0	–8	....	....	....	....	....	....	....	....	....	....	....	....	....
1994-95	Quebec	NHL	47	19	43	62	30	3	2	5	157	12.1	7	....	....	....	....	....	6	4	1	5	0	1	1	1
1995-96♦	Colorado	NHL	82	51	69	120	44	17	6	7	339	15.0	14	....	....	....	....	....	22	*18	16	*34	14	6	0	6
1996-97	Colorado	NHL	65	22	52	74	34	10	2	5	261	8.4	–10	....	....	....	....	....	17	8	*17	25	14	3	0	0
1997-98	Colorado	NHL	64	27	36	63	50	12	1	2	254	10.6	0	....	....	....	....	....	6	2	3	5	6	0	1	2
	Canada	Olympics	4	1	2	3	4	....	....	....	....	....	....	....	....	....	....	....	....	....	....	....	....	....	....	....
1998-99	Colorado	NHL	73	41	55	96	29	12	5	6	255	16.1	23	1723	51.4	31	47	25:35	19	6	13	19	8	1	1	1
99-2000	Colorado	NHL	60	28	53	81	28	5	1	5	242	11.6	30	1392	53.8	19	26	23:16	17	2	7	9	8	2	0	0
	NHL Totals		852	403	657	1060	368	125	27	55	2895	13.9		3115	52.5	50	73	24:32	93	43	60	103	52	14	3	10

WHL East Second All-Star Team (1987) • Canadian Major Junior Player of the Year (1988) • WHL East First All-Star Team (1988) • Won Conn Smythe Trophy (1996) • Played in NHL All-Star Game (1990, 1991, 1992, 1993, 1994, 1996, 1998, 2000)

Transferred to **Colorado** after **Quebec** franchise relocated, June 21, 1995.

SALEI, Ruslan

(sah-LEE, ROOS-luhn) **ANA.**

Defense. Shoots left. 6'1", 212 lbs. Born, Minsk, USSR, November 2, 1974. Anaheim's 1st choice, 9th overall, in 1996 Entry Draft.

Season	Club	League	GP	G	A	Pts	PIM	PP	SH	GW	S	%	+/–	TF	F%	H	SB	Min	GP	G	A	Pts	PIM	PP	SH	GW
1992-93	Dynamo Minsk	CIS	9	1	0	1	10	....	....	....	....	....	....	....	....	....	....	....	....	....	....	....	....	....	....	....
1993-94	Tivali Minsk	CIS	39	2	3	5	50	....	....	....	....	....	....	....	....	....	....	....	....	....	....	....	....	....	....	....
1994-95	Tivali Minsk	CIS	51	4	2	6	44	....	....	....	....	....	....	....	....	....	....	....	....	....	....	....	....	....	....	....
1995-96	Las Vegas	IHL	76	7	23	30	123	....	....	....	....	....	....	....	....	....	....	....	15	3	7	10	18	....	....	....
1996-97	Anaheim	NHL	30	0	1	1	37	0	0	0	14	0.0	–8	....	....	....	....	....	....	....	....	....	....	....	....	....
	Baltimore Bandits	AHL	12	1	4	5	12	....	....	....	....	....	....	....	....	....	....	....	....	....	....	....	....	....	....	....
	Las Vegas	IHL	8	0	2	2	24	....	....	....	....	....	....	....	....	....	....	....	3	2	1	3	6	....	....	....
1997-98	Anaheim	NHL	66	5	10	15	70	1	0	0	104	4.8	7	....	....	....	....	....	....	....	....	....	....	....	....	....
	Cincinnati Ducks	AHL	6	3	6	9	14	....	....	....	....	....	....	....	....	....	....	....	....	....	....	....	....	....	....	....
	Belarus	Olympics	7	1	0	1	4	....	....	....	....	....	....	....	....	....	....	....	....	....	....	....	....	....	....	....
1998-99	Anaheim	NHL	74	2	14	16	65	1	0	0	123	1.6	1	0	0.0	154	105	22:03	3	0	0	0	4	0	0	0
99-2000	Anaheim	NHL	71	5	5	10	94	1	0	0	116	4.3	3	0	0.0	205	107	20:21	....	....	....	....	....	....	....	....
	NHL Totals		241	12	30	42	266	3	0	0	357	3.4		0	0.0	359	212	21:13	3	0	0	0	4	0	0	0

			Regular Season																	Playoffs							
Season	Club	League	GP	G	A	Pts	PIM	PP	SH	GW	S	%	+/-	TF	F%	H	SB	Min	GP	G	A	Pts	PIM	PP	SH	GW

SALO, Sami (SA-loh, SA-mee) **OTT.**
Defense. Shoots right. 6'3", 192 lbs. Born, Turku, Finland, September 2, 1974. Ottawa's 7th choice, 239th overall, in 1996 Entry Draft.

Season	Club	League	GP	G	A	Pts	PIM	PP	SH	GW	S	%	+/-	TF	F%	H	SB	Min	GP	G	A	Pts	PIM	PP	SH	GW
1991-92	Kiekko-67 Turku	Finn-Jr.	23	4	5	9	26	....	....	....	....	....	....	....	....	....	....	....	....	....	....	....	....	....	....	....
1992-93	Kiekko Turku-2	Finn-Jr.	21	9	4	13	4	....	....	....	....	....	....	....	....	....	....	....	....	....	....	....	....	....	....	....
	Kiekko-67 Turku	Finn-Jr.	13	6	2	8	2	....	....	....	....	....	....	....	....	....	....	....	....	....	....	....	....	....	....	....
1993-94	TPS Turku	Finn-Jr.	36	7	13	20	16	....	....	....	....	....	....	....	....	....	....	....	7	0	1	1	10	....	....	....
1994-95	TPS Turku	Finn-Jr.	14	1	3	4	6	....	....	....	....	....	....	....	....	....	....	....	....	....	....	....	....	....	....	....
	Kiekko-67 Turku	Finland-2	19	4	2	6	4	....	....	....	....	....	....	....	....	....	....	....	1	0	0	0	0	....	....	....
	TPS Turku	Finland	7	1	2	3	8	....	....	....	....	....	....	....	....	....	....	....	....	....	....	....	....	....	....	....
1995-96	TPS Turku	Finland	47	7	14	21	32	....	....	....	....	....	....	....	....	....	....	....	11	1	3	4	8	....	....	....
1996-97	TPS Turku	Finland	48	9	6	15	10	....	....	....	....	....	....	....	....	....	....	....	10	2	3	5	4	....	....	....
1997-98	Jokerit Helsinki	Finland	35	3	5	8	10	....	....	....	....	....	....	....	....	....	....	....	8	0	1	1	2	....	....	....
1998-99	**Ottawa**	**NHL**	61	7	12	19	24	2	0	1	106	6.6	20	0	0.0	90	58	19:42	4	0	0	0	0	0	0	0
	Detroit Vipers	IHL	5	0	2	2	0	....	....	....	....	....	....	....	....	....	....	....	....	....	....	....	....	....	....	....
99-2000	**Ottawa**	**NHL**	37	6	8	14	2	3	0	1	85	7.1	6	0	0.0	52	29	20:18	6	1	1	2	0	1	0	0
	NHL Totals		98	13	20	33	26	5	0	2	191	6.8		0	0.0	142	87	19:56	10	1	1	2	0	1	0	0

NHL All-Rookie Team (1999) • Missed majority of 1999-2000 season recovering from wrist injury originally suffered in game vs. Philadelphia, November 28, 1999.

SAMSONOV, Sergei (sam-SAWN-nahf, SAIR-gay) **BOS.**
Left wing. Shoots right. 5'8", 180 lbs. Born, Moscow, USSR, October 27, 1978. Boston's 2nd choice, 8th overall, in 1997 Entry Draft.

Season	Club	League	GP	G	A	Pts	PIM	PP	SH	GW	S	%	+/-	TF	F%	H	SB	Min	GP	G	A	Pts	PIM	PP	SH	GW
1994-95	CSKA Moscow	CIS-Jr.	50	110	72	182	....	....	....	....	....	....	....	....	....	....	....	2	0	0	0	0	....	....	....
	CSKA Moscow	CIS	13	2	2	4	14	....	....	....	....	....	....	....	....	....	....	....	....	....	....	....	....	....	....	....
1995-96	CSKA Moscow	CIS	51	21	17	38	12	....	....	....	....	....	....	....	....	....	....	....	3	1	1	2	4	....	....	....
1996-97	Detroit Vipers	IHL	73	29	35	64	18	....	....	....	....	....	....	....	....	....	....	....	19	8	4	12	12	....	....	....
1997-98	**Boston**	**NHL**	81	22	25	47	8	7	0	3	159	13.8	9	....	....	....	....	....	6	2	5	7	0	0	0	1
1998-99	**Boston**	**NHL**	79	25	26	51	18	6	0	8	160	15.6	-6	0	0.0	39	10	16:23	11	3	1	4	0	0	0	0
99-2000	**Boston**	**NHL**	77	19	26	45	4	6	0	3	145	13.1	-6	3	0.0	29	9	16:32	....	....	....	....	....	....	....	....
	NHL Totals		237	66	77	143	30	19	0	14	464	14.2		3	0.0	68	19	16:27	17	5	6	11	0	0	0	1

Won Garry F. Longman Memorial Trophy (Top Rookie - IHL) (1997) • NHL All-Rookie Team (1998) • Won Calder Memorial Trophy (1998)

SAMUELSSON, Ulf (SAM-yuhl-suhn, UHLF)
Defense. Shoots left. 6'1", 205 lbs. Born, Fagersta, Sweden, March 26, 1964. Hartford's 4th choice, 67th overall, in 1982 Entry Draft.

Season	Club	League	GP	G	A	Pts	PIM	PP	SH	GW	S	%	+/-	TF	F%	H	SB	Min	GP	G	A	Pts	PIM	PP	SH	GW
1980-81	Fagersta AIK	Sweden-3	22	11	5	16	....	....	....	....	....	....	....	....	....	....	....	....	....	....	....	....	....	....	....	....
1981-82	Leksands IF	Sweden	31	3	1	4	40	....	....	....	....	....	....	....	....	....	....	....	....	....	....	....	....	....	....	....
1982-83	Leksands IF	Sweden	33	9	6	15	72	....	....	....	....	....	....	....	....	....	....	....	....	....	....	....	....	....	....	....
1983-84	Leksands IF	Sweden	36	5	11	16	53	....	....	....	....	....	....	....	....	....	....	....	....	....	....	....	....	....	....	....
1984-85	**Hartford**	**NHL**	41	2	6	8	83	0	0	0	32	6.3	-6	....	....	....	....	....	....	....	....	....	....	....	....	....
	Binghamton	AHL	36	5	11	16	92	....	....	....	....	....	....	....	....	....	....	....	....	....	....	....	....	....	....	....
1985-86	Hartford	NHL	80	5	19	24	174	0	1	1	72	6.9	7	....	....	....	....	....	10	1	2	3	38	0	0	1
1986-87	Hartford	NHL	78	2	31	33	162	0	0	0	104	1.9	28	....	....	....	....	....	5	0	1	1	41	-2	0	0
1987-88	Hartford	NHL	76	8	33	41	159	3	0	0	156	5.1	-10	....	....	....	....	....	5	0	0	0	8	0	0	0
1988-89	Hartford	NHL	71	9	26	35	181	3	0	2	122	7.4	23	....	....	....	....	....	4	0	2	2	4	0	0	0
1989-90	Hartford	NHL	55	2	11	13	177	0	0	0	57	3.5	15	....	....	....	....	....	7	1	0	1	2	0	0	0
1990-91	Hartford	NHL	62	3	18	21	174	0	0	0	110	2.7	13	....	....	....	....	....	....	....	....	....	....	....	....	....
◆	Pittsburgh	NHL	14	1	4	5	37	0	0	0	15	6.7	4	....	....	....	....	....	20	3	2	5	34	1	0	1
1991-92 ◆	Pittsburgh	NHL	62	1	14	15	206	1	0	1	75	1.3	2	....	....	....	....	....	21	0	2	2	39	0	0	0
1992-93	Pittsburgh	NHL	77	3	26	29	249	0	0	1	96	3.1	36	....	....	....	....	....	12	1	5	6	24	0	0	0
1993-94	Pittsburgh	NHL	80	5	24	29	199	1	0	0	106	4.7	23	....	....	....	....	....	6	0	1	1	14	0	0	0
1994-95	Leksands IF	Sweden	2	0	0	0	8	....	....	....	....	....	....	....	....	....	....	....	....	....	....	....	....	....	....	....
	Pittsburgh	NHL	44	1	15	16	113	0	0	0	47	2.1	11	....	....	....	....	....	7	0	1	1	2	0	0	0
1995-96	NY Rangers	NHL	74	1	18	19	122	0	0	0	66	1.5	9	....	....	....	....	....	11	1	5	6	16	0	0	0
1996-97	NY Rangers	NHL	73	6	11	17	138	1	0	1	77	7.8	3	....	....	....	....	....	15	0	2	2	30	0	0	0
1997-98	NY Rangers	NHL	73	3	9	12	122	0	0	2	59	5.1	1	....	....	....	....	....	....	....	....	....	....	....	....	....
	Sweden	Olympics	3	0	1	1	4	....	....	....	....	....	....	....	....	....	....	....	....	....	....	....	....	....	....	....
1998-99	**NY Rangers**	**NHL**	67	4	8	12	93	0	0	0	37	10.8	6	0	0.0	172	176	20:29	....	....	....	....	....	....	....	....
	Detroit	**NHL**	4	0	0	0	6	0	0	0	2	0.0	-1	0	0.0	4	3	17:32	9	0	3	3	10	0	0	0
99-2000	**Philadelphia**	**NHL**	49	1	2	3	58	0	0	1	17	5.9	8	0	0.0	69	81	15:40	....	....	....	....	....	....	....	....
	NHL Totals		1080	57	275	332	2453	9	1	9	1250	4.6		0	0.0	245	260	18:25	132	7	27	34	272	-1	0	2

Traded to **Pittsburgh** by **Hartford** with Ron Francis and Grant Jennings for John Cullen, Jeff Parker and Zarley Zalapski, March 4, 1991. Traded to **NY Rangers** by **Pittsburgh** with Luc Robitaille for Petr Nedved and Sergei Zubov, August 31, 1995. Traded to **Detroit** by **NY Rangers** for Detroit's 2nd round choice (David Inman) in 1999 Entry Draft and NY Rangers' 3rd round choice (previously acquired, NY Rangers' selected Johan Asplund) in 2000 Entry Draft, March 23, 1999. Traded to **Atlanta** by **Detroit** for future considerations, June 25, 1999. Signed as a free agent by **Philadelphia**, October 19, 1999.

SANDERSON, Geoff (SAN-duhr-sohn, JEHF) **CBJ**
Left wing. Shoots left. 6', 190 lbs. Born, Hay River, N.W.T., February 1, 1972. Hartford's 2nd choice, 36th overall, in 1990 Entry Draft.

Season	Club	League	GP	G	A	Pts	PIM	PP	SH	GW	S	%	+/-	TF	F%	H	SB	Min	GP	G	A	Pts	PIM	PP	SH	GW
1987-88	St. Albert Royals	AAHA	45	65	55	120	175	....	....	....	....	....	....	....	....	....	....	....	....	....	....	....	....	....	....	....
1988-89	Swift Current	WHL	58	17	11	28	16	....	....	....	....	....	....	....	....	....	....	....	12	3	5	8	6	....	....	....
1989-90	Swift Current	WHL	70	32	62	94	56	....	....	....	....	....	....	....	....	....	....	....	4	1	4	5	8	....	....	....
1990-91	Swift Current	WHL	70	62	50	112	57	....	....	....	....	....	....	....	....	....	....	....	3	1	2	3	4	....	....	....
	Hartford	**NHL**	2	1	0	1	0	0	0	0	2	50.0	-2	....	....	....	....	....	3	0	0	0	0	0	0	0
	Springfield	AHL	....	....	....	....	....	....	....	....	....	....	....	....	....	....	....	....	1	0	0	0	2	....	....	....
1991-92	Hartford	NHL	64	13	18	31	18	2	0	1	98	13.3	5	....	....	....	....	....	7	1	0	1	2	0	0	0
1992-93	Hartford	NHL	82	46	43	89	28	21	2	4	271	17.0	-21	....	....	....	....	....	....	....	....	....	....	....	....	....
1993-94	Hartford	NHL	82	41	26	67	42	15	1	6	266	15.4	-13	....	....	....	....	....	....	....	....	....	....	....	....	....
1994-95	HPK Hameenlinna	Finland	12	6	4	10	24	....	....	....	....	....	....	....	....	....	....	....	....	....	....	....	....	....	....	....
	Hartford	NHL	46	18	14	32	24	4	0	4	170	10.6	-10	....	....	....	....	....	....	....	....	....	....	....	....	....
1995-96	Hartford	NHL	81	34	31	65	40	6	0	7	314	10.8	0	....	....	....	....	....	....	....	....	....	....	....	....	....
1996-97	Hartford	NHL	82	36	31	67	29	12	1	4	297	12.1	-9	....	....	....	....	....	....	....	....	....	....	....	....	....
1997-98	Carolina	NHL	40	7	10	17	14	2	0	0	96	7.3	-4	....	....	....	....	....	....	....	....	....	....	....	....	....
	Vancouver	NHL	9	0	3	3	4	0	0	0	29	0.0	-1	....	....	....	....	....	....	....	....	....	....	....	....	....
	Buffalo	NHL	26	4	5	9	20	0	0	2	72	5.6	6	....	....	....	....	....	14	3	1	4	4	1	0	1
1998-99	**Buffalo**	**NHL**	75	12	18	30	22	1	0	1	155	7.7	8	4	50.0	43	9	12:55	19	4	6	10	14	0	0	1
99-2000	**Buffalo**	**NHL**	67	13	13	26	22	4	0	3	136	9.6	4	3	100.0	38	17	12:54	5	0	2	2	8	0	0	0
	NHL Totals		656	225	212	437	263	67	4	32	1906	11.8		7	71.4	81	26	12:55	48	8	9	17	28	1	0	2

Played in NHL All-Star Game (1994, 1997)

Transferred to **Carolina** after **Hartford** franchise relocated, June 25, 1997. Traded to **Vancouver** by **Carolina** with Sean Burke and Enrico Ciccone for Kirk McLean and Martin Gelinas, January 3, 1998. Traded to **Buffalo** by **Vancouver** for Brad May and Buffalo's 3rd round choice (later traded to Tampa Bay - Tampa Bay selected Jimmie Olvestad) in 1999 Entry Draft, February 4, 1998. Selected by **Columbus** from **Buffalo** in Expansion Draft, June 23, 2000.

SANDSTROM, Tomas (SAND-struhm, TOH-mas)
Right wing. Shoots left. 6'2", 205 lbs. Born, Jakobstad, Finland, September 4, 1964. NY Rangers' 2nd choice, 36th overall, in 1982 Entry Draft.

Season	Club	League	GP	G	A	Pts	PIM	PP	SH	GW	S	%	+/-	TF	F%	H	SB	Min	GP	G	A	Pts	PIM	PP	SH	GW
1979-80	Fagersta HK	Sweden-2	6	1	1	2	0	....	....	....	....	....	....	....	....	....	....	....	....	....	....	....	....	....	....	....
1980-81	Fagersta HK	Sweden-2	20	23	5	28	....	....	....	....	....	....	....	....	....	....	....	....	....	....	....	....	....	....	....	....
1981-82	Fagersta HK	Sweden-2	32	28	11	39	74	....	....	....	....	....	....	....	....	....	....	....	....	....	....	....	....	....	....	....
1982-83	Brynas IF	Sweden	36	23	14	37	50	....	....	....	....	....	....	....	....	....	....	....	....	....	....	....	....	....	....	....
1983-84	Brynas IF	Sweden	34	19	10	29	81	....	....	....	....	....	....	....	....	....	....	....	....	....	....	....	....	....	....	....
	Sweden	Olympics	7	2	1	3	6	....	....	....	....	....	....	....	....	....	....	....	....	....	....	....	....	....	....	....
1984-85	**NY Rangers**	**NHL**	74	29	29	58	51	5	0	3	190	15.3	3	....	....	....	....	....	3	0	2	2	4	0	0	0
1985-86	**NY Rangers**	**NHL**	73	25	29	54	109	8	2	1	238	10.5	-4	....	....	....	....	....	16	4	6	10	20	0	0	1
1986-87	**NY Rangers**	**NHL**	64	40	34	74	60	13	0	5	240	16.7	8	....	....	....	....	....	6	1	2	3	20	0	0	0
1987-88	**NY Rangers**	**NHL**	69	28	40	68	95	11	0	3	204	13.7	-6	....	....	....	....	....	....	....	....	....	....	....	....	....
1988-89	**NY Rangers**	**NHL**	79	32	56	88	148	11	2	4	240	13.3	5	....	....	....	....	....	4	3	2	5	12	2	0	0

			Regular Season																Playoffs							
Season	Club	League	GP	G	A	Pts	PIM	PP	SH	GW	S	%	+/-	TF	F%	H	SB	Min	GP	G	A	Pts	PIM	PP	SH	GW
1989-90	**NY Rangers**	**NHL**	**48**	**19**	**19**	**38**	**100**	**6**	**0**	**3**	**166**	**11.4**	**–10**	....	....	....	....	....	....	....	....	....	....	....	....	....
	Los Angeles	**NHL**	**28**	**13**	**20**	**33**	**28**	**1**	**1**	**0**	**83**	**15.7**	**–1**	....	....	....	....	....	**10**	**5**	**4**	**9**	**19**	**0**	**0**	**0**
1990-91	**Los Angeles**	**NHL**	**68**	**45**	**44**	**89**	**106**	**16**	**0**	**6**	**221**	**20.4**	**27**	....	....	....	....	....	**10**	**4**	**4**	**8**	**14**	**3**	**0**	**0**
1991-92	**Los Angeles**	**NHL**	**49**	**17**	**22**	**39**	**70**	**5**	**0**	**4**	**147**	**11.6**	**–2**	....	....	....	....	....	**6**	**0**	**3**	**3**	**8**	**0**	**0**	**0**
1992-93	**Los Angeles**	**NHL**	**39**	**25**	**27**	**52**	**57**	**8**	**0**	**3**	**134**	**18.7**	**12**	....	....	....	....	....	**24**	**8**	**17**	**25**	**12**	**2**	**0**	**2**
1993-94	**Los Angeles**	**NHL**	**51**	**17**	**24**	**41**	**59**	**4**	**0**	**2**	**121**	**14.0**	**–12**	....	....	....	....	....	....	....	....	....	....	....	....	....
	Pittsburgh	**NHL**	**27**	**6**	**11**	**17**	**24**	**0**	**0**	**1**	**72**	**8.3**	**5**	....	....	....	....	....	**6**	**0**	**0**	**0**	**4**	**0**	**0**	**0**
1994-95	Malmo IF	Sweden	12	10	5	15	14	....	....	....	....	....	....	....	....	....	....	....	....	....	....	....	....	....	....	....
	Pittsburgh	**NHL**	**47**	**21**	**23**	**44**	**42**	**4**	**1**	**3**	**116**	**18.1**	**1**	....	....	....	....	....	**12**	**3**	**3**	**6**	**16**	**2**	**0**	**0**
1995-96	**Pittsburgh**	**NHL**	**58**	**35**	**35**	**70**	**69**	**17**	**1**	**2**	**187**	**18.7**	**4**	....	....	....	....	....	**18**	**4**	**2**	**6**	**30**	**0**	**0**	**1**
1996-97	**Pittsburgh**	**NHL**	**40**	**9**	**15**	**24**	**33**	**1**	**1**	**0**	**73**	**12.3**	**4**	....	....	....	....	....	....	....	....	....	....	....	....	....
	♦ Detroit	**NHL**	**34**	**9**	**9**	**18**	**36**	**0**	**1**	**2**	**66**	**13.6**	**2**	....	....	....	....	....	**20**	**0**	**4**	**4**	**24**	**0**	**0**	**0**
1997-98	**Anaheim**	**NHL**	**77**	**9**	**8**	**17**	**64**	**2**	**1**	**0**	**136**	**6.6**	**–25**	....	....	....	....	....	....	....	....	....	....	....	....	....
	Sweden	Olympics	4	0	1	1	0	....	....	....	....	....	....	....	....	....	....	....	....	....	....	....	....	....	....	....
1998-99	**Anaheim**	**NHL**	**58**	**15**	**17**	**32**	**42**	**7**	**0**	**2**	**107**	**14.0**	**–5**	**8**	**25.0**	**47**	**11**	**17:22**	**4**	**0**	**0**	**0**	**4**	**0**	**0**	**0**
99-2000	Malmo IF	Sweden	42	16	13	29	28	....	....	....	....	....	....	....	....	....	....	....	6	3	2	5	10	....	....	....
	NHL Totals		**983**	**394**	**462**	**856**	**1193**	**119**	**10**	**44**	**2741**	**14.4**		**8**	**25.0**	**47**	**11**	**17:22**	**139**	**32**	**49**	**81**	**183**	**9**	**0**	**4**

NHL All-Rookie Team (1985) • Played in NHL All-Star Game (1988, 1991)

Traded to **LA Kings** by **NY Rangers** with Tony Granato for Bernie Nicholls, January 20, 1990. Traded to **Pittsburgh** by **LA Kings** with Shawn McEachern for Marty McSorley and Jim Paek, February 16, 1994. Traded to **Detroit** by **Pittsburgh** for Greg Johnson, January 27, 1997. Signed as a free agent by **Anaheim**, October 20, 1997.

SANDWITH, Terran

(SAND-wihth, TAIR-ran) **EDM.**

Defense. Shoots left. 6'4", 210 lbs. Born, Edmonton, Alta., April 17, 1972. Philadelphia's 4th choice, 42nd overall, in 1990 NHL Entry Draft.

1987-88	Hobbema Hawks	AJHL	58	5	8	13	106	....	....	....	....	....	....	....	....	....	....	....	....	....	....	....	....	....	....	....
1988-89	Tri-City Americans	WHL	31	0	0	0	29	....	....	....	....	....	....	....	....	....	....	....	6	0	0	0	4	....	....	....
1989-90	Tri-City Americans	WHL	70	4	14	18	92	....	....	....	....	....	....	....	....	....	....	....	7	0	2	2	14	....	....	....
1990-91	Tri-City Americans	WHL	46	5	17	22	132	....	....	....	....	....	....	....	....	....	....	....	7	1	0	1	14	....	....	....
1991-92	Brandon	WHL	41	6	14	20	115	....	....	....	....	....	....	....	....	....	....	....	....	....	....	....	....	....	....	....
	Saskatoon Blades	WHL	18	2	5	7	53	....	....	....	....	....	....	....	....	....	....	....	18	2	1	3	28	....	....	....
1992-93	Hershey Bears	AHL	61	1	12	13	140	....	....	....	....	....	....	....	....	....	....	....	....	....	....	....	....	....	....	....
1993-94	Hershey Bears	AHL	62	3	5	8	169	....	....	....	....	....	....	....	....	....	....	....	2	0	1	1	4	....	....	....
1994-95	Hershey Bears	AHL	11	1	1	2	32	....	....	....	....	....	....	....	....	....	....	....	....	....	....	....	....	....	....	....
	Kansas City	IHL	25	0	3	3	73	....	....	....	....	....	....	....	....	....	....	....	....	....	....	....	....	....	....	....
1995-96	Canada	Nat-Team	47	3	12	15	63	....	....	....	....	....	....	....	....	....	....	....	....	....	....	....	....	....	....	....
	Cape Breton	AHL	5	0	2	2	4	....	....	....	....	....	....	....	....	....	....	....	....	....	....	....	....	....	....	....
1996-97	Hamilton Bulldogs	AHL	78	3	6	9	213	....	....	....	....	....	....	....	....	....	....	....	22	0	2	2	27	....	....	....
1997-98	**Edmonton**	**NHL**	**8**	**0**	**0**	**0**	**6**	**0**	**0**	**0**	**4**	**0.0**	**–4**	....	....	....	....	....	....	....	....	....	....	....	....	....
	Hamilton Bulldogs	AHL	54	4	8	12	131	....	....	....	....	....	....	....	....	....	....	....	9	0	0	0	10	....	....	....
1998-99	Cincinnati Ducks	AHL	40	0	6	6	77	....	....	....	....	....	....	....	....	....	....	....	....	....	....	....	....	....	....	....
99-2000	St. John's Leafs	AHL	78	1	10	11	155	....	....	....	....	....	....	....	....	....	....	....	....	....	....	....	....	....	....	....
	NHL Totals		**8**	**0**	**0**	**0**	**6**	**0**	**0**	**0**	**4**	**0.0**		....	....	....	....	....	....	....	....	....	....	....	....	....

Signed as a free agent by **Edmonton**, April 10, 1996. Signed as a free agent by **Anaheim**, July 13, 1998. Signed as a free agent by **Toronto**, July 2, 1999. Signed as a free agent by **Edmonton**, July 19, 2000. • Played w/ RHI's LA Blades in 1995 (11-4-7-11-35).

SAPRYKIN, Oleg

(sah-PRIH-kihn, OH-lehg) **CGY.**

Center. Shoots left. 6', 195 lbs. Born, Moscow, USSR, February 12, 1981. Calgary's 1st choice, 11th overall, in 1999 Entry Draft.

1997-98	CSKA Moscow	Russia-2	15	0	3	3	6	....	....	....	....	....	....	....	....	....	....	....	....	....	....	....	....	....	....	....
	CSKA Moscow	Russia	20	0	2	2	8	....	....	....	....	....	....	....	....	....	....	....	....	....	....	....	....	....	....	....
1998-99	Seattle T-Birds	WHL	66	47	46	93	107	....	....	....	....	....	....	....	....	....	....	....	11	5	11	16	36	....	....	....
99-2000	Seattle T-Birds	WHL	48	30	36	66	91	....	....	....	....	....	....	....	....	....	....	....	6	3	3	6	37	....	....	....
	Calgary	**NHL**	**4**	**0**	**1**	**1**	**2**	**0**	**0**	**0**	**2**	**0.0**	**–4**	**0**	**0.0**	**7**	**2**	**12:35**	....	....	....	....	....	....	....	....
	NHL Totals		**4**	**0**	**1**	**1**	**2**	**0**	**0**	**0**	**2**	**0.0**		**0**	**0.0**	**7**	**2**	**12:35**	....	....	....	....	....	....	....	....

WHL West Second All-Star Team (1999, 2000)

SARAULT, Yves

(sah-ROH, EEV) **ATL.**

Left wing. Shoots left. 6', 200 lbs. Born, Valleyfield, Que., December 23, 1972. Montreal's 4th choice, 61st overall, in 1991 Entry Draft.

1988-89	Lac St-Louis	QAAA	42	23	30	53	64	....	....	....	....	....	....	....	....	....	....	....	....	....	....	....	....	....	....	....
1989-90	Victoriaville Tigres	QMJHL	70	12	28	40	140	....	....	....	....	....	....	....	....	....	....	....	16	0	3	3	26	....	....	....
1990-91	St-Jean Lynx	QMJHL	56	22	24	46	113	....	....	....	....	....	....	....	....	....	....	....	....	....	....	....	....	....	....	....
1991-92	St-Jean Lynx	QMJHL	50	28	38	66	96	....	....	....	....	....	....	....	....	....	....	....	....	....	....	....	....	....	....	....
	Trois-Rivieres	QMJHL	18	15	14	29	12	....	....	....	....	....	....	....	....	....	....	....	15	10	10	20	18	....	....	....
1992-93	Fredericton	AHL	59	14	17	31	41	....	....	....	....	....	....	....	....	....	....	....	3	0	1	1	2	....	....	....
	Wheeling	ECHL	2	1	3	4	0	....	....	....	....	....	....	....	....	....	....	....	....	....	....	....	....	....	....	....
1993-94	Fredericton	AHL	60	13	14	27	72	....	....	....	....	....	....	....	....	....	....	....	....	....	....	....	....	....	....	....
1994-95	Fredericton	AHL	69	24	21	45	96	....	....	....	....	....	....	....	....	....	....	....	13	2	1	3	33	....	....	....
	Montreal	**NHL**	**8**	**0**	**1**	**1**	**0**	**0**	**0**	**0**	**9**	**0.0**	**–1**	....	....	....	....	....	....	....	....	....	....	....	....	....
1995-96	**Montreal**	**NHL**	**14**	**0**	**0**	**0**	**4**	**0**	**0**	**0**	**14**	**0.0**	**–7**	....	....	....	....	....	....	....	....	....	....	....	....	....
	Calgary	**NHL**	**11**	**2**	**1**	**3**	**4**	**0**	**0**	**1**	**12**	**16.7**	**–2**	....	....	....	....	....	....	....	....	....	....	....	....	....
	Saint John Flames	AHL	26	10	12	22	34	....	....	....	....	....	....	....	....	....	....	....	16	6	2	8	33	....	....	....
1996-97	**Colorado**	**NHL**	**28**	**2**	**1**	**3**	**6**	**0**	**0**	**0**	**41**	**4.9**	**0**	....	....	....	....	....	**5**	**0**	**0**	**0**	**2**	**0**	**0**	**0**
	Hershey Bears	AHL	6	2	3	5	8	....	....	....	....	....	....	....	....	....	....	....	....	....	....	....	....	....	....	....
1997-98	**Colorado**	**NHL**	**2**	**1**	**0**	**1**	**0**	**0**	**0**	**0**	**1**	**100.0**	**1**	....	....	....	....	....	....	....	....	....	....	....	....	....
	Hershey Bears	AHL	63	23	36	59	43	....	....	....	....	....	....	....	....	....	....	....	7	1	2	3	14	....	....	....
1998-99	**Ottawa**	**NHL**	**11**	**0**	**1**	**1**	**4**	**0**	**0**	**0**	**7**	**0.0**	**1**	**0**	**0.0**	**15**	**1**	**7:15**	....	....	....	....	....	....	....	....
	Detroit Vipers	IHL	36	11	12	23	52	....	....	....	....	....	....	....	....	....	....	....	11	7	2	9	40	....	....	....
99-2000	**Ottawa**	**NHL**	**11**	**0**	**2**	**2**	**7**	**0**	**0**	**0**	**13**	**0.0**	**–3**	**1**	**0.0**	**5**	**1**	**9:03**	....	....	....	....	....	....	....	....
	Grand Rapids	IHL	62	17	26	43	77	....	....	....	....	....	....	....	....	....	....	....	17	7	4	11	32	....	....	....
	NHL Totals		**85**	**5**	**6**	**11**	**25**	**0**	**0**	**1**	**97**	**5.2**		**1**	**0.0**	**20**	**2**	**8:09**	**5**	**0**	**0**	**0**	**2**	**0**	**0**	**0**

QMJHL Second All-Star Team (1992)

Traded to **Calgary** by **Montreal** with Craig Ferguson for Calgary's 8th round choice (Petr Kubos) in 1997 Entry Draft, November 26, 1995. Signed as a free agent by **Colorado**, September 13, 1996. Signed as a free agent by **Ottawa**, August 7, 1998. Signed as a free agent by **Atlanta**, July 20, 2000.

SARICH, Cory

(SAHR-ihch, KOH-ree) **T.B.**

Defense. Shoots right. 6'3", 193 lbs. Born, Saskatoon, Sask., August 16, 1978. Buffalo's 2nd choice, 27th overall, in 1996 Entry Draft.

1994-95	Saskatoon	SAHA	31	5	22	27	99	....	....	....	....	....	....	....	....	....	....	....	....	....	....	....	....	....	....	....
	Saskatoon Blades	WHL	6	0	0	0	4	....	....	....	....	....	....	....	....	....	....	....	3	0	1	1	0	....	....	....
1995-96	Saskatoon Blades	WHL	59	5	18	23	54	....	....	....	....	....	....	....	....	....	....	....	3	0	0	0	4	....	....	....
1996-97	Saskatoon Blades	WHL	58	6	27	33	158	....	....	....	....	....	....	....	....	....	....	....	....	....	....	....	....	....	....	....
1997-98	Saskatoon Blades	WHL	33	5	24	29	90	....	....	....	....	....	....	....	....	....	....	....	....	....	....	....	....	....	....	....
	Seattle T-Birds	WHL	13	3	16	19	47	....	....	....	....	....	....	....	....	....	....	....	0	0	0	0	0	....	....	....
1998-99	**Buffalo**	**NHL**	**4**	**0**	**0**	**0**	**0**	**0**	**0**	**0**	**2**	**0.0**	**3**	**0**	**0.0**	**7**	**0**	**13:11**	....	....	....	....	....	....	....	....
	Rochester	AHL	77	3	26	29	82	....	....	....	....	....	....	....	....	....	....	....	20	2	4	6	14	....	....	....
99-2000	**Buffalo**	**NHL**	**42**	**0**	**4**	**4**	**35**	**0**	**0**	**0**	**49**	**0.0**	**2**	**0**	**0.0**	**108**	**31**	**17:42**	....	....	....	....	....	....	....	....
	Rochester	AHL	15	0	6	6	44	....	....	....	....	....	....	....	....	....	....	....	....	....	....	....	....	....	....	....
	Tampa Bay	**NHL**	**17**	**0**	**2**	**2**	**42**	**0**	**0**	**0**	**20**	**0.0**	**–8**	**0**	**0.0**	**44**	**12**	**20:42**	....	....	....	....	....	....	....	....
	NHL Totals		**63**	**0**	**6**	**6**	**77**	**0**	**0**	**0**	**71**	**0.0**		**0**	**0.0**	**159**	**43**	**18:13**	....	....	....	....	....	....	....	....

WHL West Second All-Star Team (1998)

Traded to **Tampa Bay** by **Buffalo** with Wayne Primeau, Brian Holzinger and Buffalo's 3rd round choice (Alexandre Kharitonov) in 2000 Entry Draft for Chris Gratton and Tampa Bay's 2nd round choice in 2001 Entry Draft, March 9, 2000.

Season	Club	League	GP	G	A	Pts	PIM	PP	SH	GW	S	%	+/-	TF	F%	H	SB	Min	Playoffs GP	G	A	Pts	PIM	PP	SH	GW
			Regular Season																Playoffs							

SATAN, Miroslav

(SHA-tuhn, MEER-oh-slahv) **BUF.**

Left/Right wing. Shoots left. 6'3", 192 lbs. Born, Topolcany, Czech., October 22, 1974. Edmonton's 6th choice, 111th overall, in 1993 Entry Draft.

Season	Club	League	GP	G	A	Pts	PIM	PP	SH	GW	S	%	+/-	TF	F%	H	SB	Min	GP	G	A	Pts	PIM	PP	SH	GW
1991-92	HC Topocalny	Czech-Jr.	31	30	22	52	....																			
	HC Topocalny	Czech-2	9	2	1	3	6																			
1992-93	Dukla Trencin	Czech.	38	11	6	17	....																			
1993-94	Dukla Trencin	Slovakia	30	32	16	48	16																			
	Slovakia	Olympics	8	*9	0	9	0																			
1994-95	Cape Breton	AHL	25	24	16	40	15																			
	Detroit Vipers	IHL	8	1	3	4	4																			
	San Diego Gulls	IHL	6	0	2	2	6																			
1995-96	**Edmonton**	**NHL**	**62**	**18**	**17**	**35**	**22**	**6**	**0**	**4**	**113**	**15.9**	**0**													
1996-97	**Edmonton**	**NHL**	**64**	**17**	**11**	**28**	**22**	**5**	**0**	**2**	**90**	**18.9**	**-4**													
	Buffalo	**NHL**	**12**	**8**	**2**	**10**	**4**	**2**	**0**	**1**	**29**	**27.6**	**1**						**7**	**0**	**0**	**0**	**0**	**0**	**0**	**0**
1997-98	**Buffalo**	**NHL**	**79**	**22**	**24**	**46**	**34**	**9**	**0**	**4**	**139**	**15.8**	**2**						**14**	**5**	**4**	**9**	**4**	**4**	**0**	**1**
1998-99	**Buffalo**	**NHL**	**81**	**40**	**26**	**66**	**44**	**13**	**3**	**6**	**208**	**19.2**	**24**	**9**	**55.6**	**42**	**24**	**20:49**	**12**	**3**	**5**	**8**	**2**	**1**	**0**	**1**
99-2000	Dukla Trencin	Slovakia	3	2	8	10	2																			
	Buffalo	**NHL**	**81**	**33**	**34**	**67**	**32**	**5**	**3**	**5**	**265**	**12.5**	**16**	**7**	**14.3**	**45**	**28**	**20:35**	**5**	**3**	**2**	**5**	**0**	**0**	**0**	**0**
	NHL Totals		**379**	**138**	**114**	**252**	**158**	**40**	**6**	**22**	**844**	**16.4**		**16**	**37.5**	**87**	**52**	**20:42**	**38**	**11**	**11**	**22**	**6**	**5**	**0**	**2**

Played in NHL All-Star Game (2000)

Traded to **Buffalo** by **Edmonton** for Barrie Moore and Craig Millar, March 18, 1997.

SAVAGE, Andre

(SA-vahj, AWN-dray) **BOS.**

Center. Shoots right. 6', 195 lbs. Born, Ottawa, Ont., May 27, 1975.

Season	Club	League	GP	G	A	Pts	PIM	PP	SH	GW	S	%	+/-	TF	F%	H	SB	Min	GP	G	A	Pts	PIM	PP	SH	GW
1992-93	Gloucester	OJHL	54	34	34	68	38																			
1993-94	Gloucester	OJHL	57	43	74	117	44																			
1994-95	Michigan Tech	WCHA	39	7	17	24	56																			
1995-96	Michigan Tech	WCHA	38	13	27	40	42																			
1996-97	Michigan Tech	WCHA	37	18	20	38	34																			
1997-98	Michigan Tech	WCHA	33	14	27	41	34																			
1998-99	**Boston**	**NHL**	**6**	**1**	**0**	**1**	**0**	**0**	**0**	**0**	**8**	**12.5**	**2**	**32**	**65.6**	**3**	**1**	**9:31**								
	Providence Bruins	AHL	63	27	42	69	54												5	0	1	1	0			
99-2000	**Boston**	**NHL**	**43**	**7**	**13**	**20**	**10**	**2**	**0**	**1**	**70**	**10.0**	**-8**	**619**	**55.1**	**50**	**10**	**14:40**								
	Providence Bruins	AHL	30	15	17	32	22												14	6	7	13	22			
	NHL Totals		**49**	**8**	**13**	**21**	**10**	**2**	**0**	**1**	**78**	**10.3**		**651**	**55.6**	**53**	**11**	**14:02**								

WCHA First All-Star Team (1998)

Signed as a free agent by **Boston**, June 18, 1998.

SAVAGE, Brian

(SA-vuhj, BRIGH-an) **MTL.**

Right wing. Shoots left. 6'2", 193 lbs. Born, Sudbury, Ont., February 24, 1971. Montreal's 11th choice, 171st overall, in 1991 Entry Draft.

Season	Club	League	GP	G	A	Pts	PIM	PP	SH	GW	S	%	+/-	TF	F%	H	SB	Min	GP	G	A	Pts	PIM	PP	SH	GW
1989-90	Sudbury Cubs	NOJHA	32	45	40	85	61																			
1990-91	U. of Miami-Ohio	CCHA	28	5	6	11	26																			
1991-92	U. of Miami-Ohio	CCHA	40	24	16	40	43																			
1992-93	U. of Miami-Ohio	CCHA	38	*37	21	58	44																			
	Canada	Nat-Team	9	3	0	3	12																			
1993-94	Canada	Nat-Team	51	20	26	46	38																			
	Canada	Olympics	8	2	2	4	6																			
	Montreal	**NHL**	**3**	**1**	**0**	**1**	**0**	**0**	**0**	**0**	**3**	**33.3**	**0**						**3**	**0**	**2**	**2**	**0**	**0**	**0**	**0**
	Fredericton	AHL	17	12	15	27	4																			
1994-95	**Montreal**	**NHL**	**37**	**12**	**7**	**19**	**27**	**0**	**0**	**0**	**64**	**18.8**	**5**													
1995-96	**Montreal**	**NHL**	**75**	**25**	**8**	**33**	**28**	**4**	**0**	**4**	**150**	**16.7**	**-8**						**6**	**0**	**2**	**2**	**2**	**0**	**0**	**0**
1996-97	**Montreal**	**NHL**	**81**	**23**	**37**	**60**	**39**	**5**	**0**	**2**	**219**	**10.5**	**-14**						**5**	**1**	**1**	**2**	**0**	**0**	**0**	**0**
1997-98	**Montreal**	**NHL**	**64**	**26**	**17**	**43**	**36**	**8**	**0**	**7**	**152**	**17.1**	**11**						**9**	**0**	**2**	**2**	**6**	**0**	**0**	**0**
1998-99	**Montreal**	**NHL**	**54**	**16**	**10**	**26**	**20**	**5**	**0**	**4**	**124**	**12.9**	**-14**	**70**	**44.3**	**57**	**14**	**16:30**								
99-2000	**Montreal**	**NHL**	**38**	**17**	**12**	**29**	**19**	**6**	**1**	**5**	**107**	**15.9**	**-4**	**67**	**47.8**	**27**	**12**	**17:56**								
	NHL Totals		**352**	**120**	**91**	**211**	**169**	**28**	**1**	**22**	**819**	**14.7**		**137**	**46.0**	**84**	**26**	**17:06**	**23**	**1**	**7**	**8**	**8**	**0**	**0**	**0**

CCHA First All-Star Team (1993) • NCAA West Second All-American Team (1993)

• Missed majority of 1999-2000 season recovering from neck injury suffered in game vs. LA Kings, November 20, 1999.

SAVAGE, Reggie

(SA-vuhj, REH-jee) **CBJ**

Center. Shoots left. 5'10", 197 lbs. Born, Montreal, Que., May 1, 1970. Washington's 1st choice, 15th overall, in 1988 Entry Draft.

Season	Club	League	GP	G	A	Pts	PIM	PP	SH	GW	S	%	+/-	TF	F%	H	SB	Min	GP	G	A	Pts	PIM	PP	SH	GW
1985-86	Richelieu Regents	QAAA	40	38	26	64	....																			
1986-87	Richelieu Regents	QAAA	42	82	57	139	44																			
1987-88	Victoriaville Tigres	QMJHL	68	68	54	122	77												5	2	3	5	8			
1988-89	Victoriaville Tigres	QMJHL	54	58	55	113	178												16	15	13	28	52			
1989-90	Victoriaville Tigres	QMJHL	63	51	43	94	79												16	13	10	23	40			
1990-91	**Washington**	**NHL**	**1**	**0**	**0**	**0**	**0**	**0**	**0**	**0**	**2**	**0.0**	**-1**													
	Baltimore	AHL	62	32	29	61	10												6	1	1	2	6			
1991-92	Baltimore	AHL	77	42	28	70	51																			
1992-93	**Washington**	**NHL**	**16**	**2**	**3**	**5**	**12**	**2**	**0**	**0**	**20**	**10.0**	**-4**													
	Baltimore	AHL	40	37	18	55	28																			
1993-94	**Quebec**	**NHL**	**17**	**3**	**4**	**7**	**16**	**1**	**0**	**0**	**25**	**12.0**	**3**													
	Cornwall Aces	AHL	33	21	13	34	56																			
1994-95	Cornwall Aces	AHL	34	13	7	20	56												14	5	6	11	40			
1995-96	Atlanta Knights	IHL	66	22	14	36	118																			
	Syracuse Crunch	AHL	10	9	5	14	28												16	9	6	15	54			
1996-97	Springfield	AHL	68	32	25	57	103												17	6	7	13	24			
1997-98	Kansas City	IHL	51	6	10	16	60																			
	San Antonio	IHL	22	6	12	18	24																			
	Orlando	IHL	10	5	5	10	18												17	2	9	11	60			
1998-99	HC Asiago	Alpenliga	27	25	27	52	69																			
	HC Asiago	Italy	16	18	15	33	8												2	1	0	1	22			
99-2000	Syracuse Crunch	AHL	78	36	34	70	135												4	0	0	0	8			
	NHL Totals		**34**	**5**	**7**	**12**	**28**	**3**	**0**	**0**	**47**	**10.6**														

Traded to **Quebec** by **Washington** with Paul MacDermid for Mike Hough, June 20, 1993. Signed as a free agent by **Phoenix**, August 28, 1996. Signed as a free agent by **Vancouver**, June 17, 1999. Signed as a free agent by **Columbus**, June 2, 2000.

SAVARD, Marc

(sa-VAHR, MAHRK) **CGY.**

Center. Shoots left. 5'10", 184 lbs. Born, Ottawa, Ont., July 17, 1977. NY Rangers' 3rd choice, 91st overall, in 1995 Entry Draft.

Season	Club	League	GP	G	A	Pts	PIM	PP	SH	GW	S	%	+/-	TF	F%	H	SB	Min	GP	G	A	Pts	PIM	PP	SH	GW
1992-93	Metcalfe Jets	OJHL-B	36	*44	55	*99	38																			
1993-94	Oshawa Generals	OHL	61	18	39	57	20												5	4	3	7	8			
1994-95	Oshawa Generals	OHL	66	43	96	*139	78												7	5	6	11	8			
1995-96	Oshawa Generals	OHL	48	28	59	87	77												5	4	5	9	6			
1996-97	Oshawa Generals	OHL	64	43	*87	*130	94												18	13	*24	*37	20			
1997-98	**NY Rangers**	**NHL**	**28**	**1**	**5**	**6**	**4**	**0**	**0**	**0**	**32**	**3.1**	**-4**													
	Hartford	AHL	58	21	53	74	66												15	8	19	27	24			

			Regular Season																Playoffs							
Season	Club	League	GP	G	A	Pts	PIM	PP	SH	GW	S	%	+/–	TF	F%	H	SB	Min	GP	G	A	Pts	PIM	PP	SH	GW
1998-99	**NY Rangers**	**NHL**	**70**	**9**	**36**	**45**	**38**	**4**	**0**	**1**	**116**	**7.8**	**–7**	**956**	**48.4**	**30**	**18**	**14:35**	....	....	....	....	....	....	....	....
	Hartford	AHL	9	3	10	13	16	....	....	....	....	....	....	....	....	....	....	....	7	1	12	13	16	....	....	....
99-2000	**Calgary**	**NHL**	**78**	**22**	**31**	**53**	**56**	**4**	**0**	**3**	**184**	**12.0**	**–2**	**1021**	**49.6**	**44**	**33**	**16:36**	....	....	....	....	....	....	....	....
	NHL Totals		**176**	**32**	**72**	**104**	**98**	**8**	**0**	**4**	**332**	**9.6**		**1977**	**49.0**	**74**	**51**	**15:39**	....	....	....	....	....	....	....	....

OHL Second All-Star Team (1995)

Traded to **Calgary** by **NY Rangers** with NY Rangers 1st round choice (Oleg Saprykin) in 1999 Entry Draft for the rights to Jan Hlavac and Calgary's 1st (Jamie Lundmark) and 3rd (later traded back to Calgary - Calgary selected Craig Andersson) round choices in 1999 Entry Draft, June 26, 1999.

SAVOIA, Ryan

(sa-VOI-ah, RIGH-yan)

Center. Shoots right. 6'1", 204 lbs. Born, Thorold, Ont., May 6, 1973.

Season	Club	League	GP	G	A	Pts	PIM	PP	SH	GW	S	%	+/–	TF	F%	H	SB	Min	GP	G	A	Pts	PIM	PP	SH	GW
1989-90	Thorold Eagles	OJHL-B	40	13	16	29	14	....	....	....	....	....	....	....	....	....	....	....	....	....	....	....	....	....	....	....
1990-91	Thorold Eagles	OJHL-B	35	13	20	33	28	....	....	....	....	....	....	....	....	....	....	....	....	....	....	....	....	....	....	....
1991-92	Thorold Eagles	OJHL-B	41	26	24	50	46	....	....	....	....	....	....	....	....	....	....	....	....	....	....	....	....	....	....	....
1992-93	Thorold Eagles	OJHL-B	39	27	41	68	74	....	....	....	....	....	....	....	....	....	....	....	....	....	....	....	....	....	....	....
1993-94	Thorold Eagles	OJHL-B	39	51	51	102	48	....	....	....	....	....	....	....	....	....	....	....	....	....	....	....	....	....	....	....
1994-95	Brock University	OUAA	38	35	48	83	24	....	....	....	....	....	....	....	....	....	....	....	....	....	....	....	....	....	....	....
	Cleveland	IHL	1	0	0	0	0	....	....	....	....	....	....	....	....	....	....	....	....	....	....	....	....	....	....	....
1995-96	Cleveland	IHL	49	6	7	13	31	....	....	....	....	....	....	....	....	....	....	....	....	....	....	....	....	....	....	....
1996-97	Johnstown Chiefs	ECHL	60	35	44	79	100	....	....	....	....	....	....	....	....	....	....	....	....	....	....	....	....	....	....	....
	Cleveland	IHL	4	1	0	1	2	....	....	....	....	....	....	....	....	....	....	....	....	....	....	....	....	....	....	....
	Fort Wayne	IHL	8	0	2	2	2	....	....	....	....	....	....	....	....	....	....	....	....	....	....	....	....	....	....	....
1997-98	HIFK Helsinki	Finland	1	0	0	0	0	....	....	....	....	....	....	....	....	....	....	....	....	....	....	....	....	....	....	....
	Syracuse Crunch	AHL	7	0	4	4	2	....	....	....	....	....	....	....	....	....	....	....	....	....	....	....	....	....	....	....
	Johnstown Chiefs	ECHL	6	1	5	6	0	....	....	....	....	....	....	....	....	....	....	....	....	....	....	....	....	....	....	....
1998-99	**Pittsburgh**	**NHL**	**3**	**0**	**0**	**0**	**0**	**0**	**0**	**0**	**0**	**0.0**	**–1**	**0**	**0.0**	**1**	**0**	**2:27**	....	....	....	....	....	....	....	....
	Syracuse Crunch	AHL	54	9	22	31	40	....	....	....	....	....	....	....	....	....	....	....	....	....	....	....	....	....	....	....
99-2000	Canada	Nat-Team	56	21	30	51	91	....	....	....	....	....	....	....	....	....	....	....	....	....	....	....	....	....	....	....
	NHL Totals		**3**	**0**	**0**	**0**	**0**	**0**	**0**	**0**	**0**	**0.0**		**0**	**0.0**	**1**	**0**	**2:27**	....	....	....	....	....	....	....	....

Signed as a free agent by **Pittsburgh**, April 7, 1995.

SAWYER, Kevin

(SAW-yuhr, KEH-vihn) **ANA.**

Left wing. Shoots left. 6'2", 205 lbs. Born, Christina Lake, B.C., February 21, 1974.

Season	Club	League	GP	G	A	Pts	PIM	PP	SH	GW	S	%	+/–	TF	F%	H	SB	Min	GP	G	A	Pts	PIM	PP	SH	GW
1991-92	Grand Forks	KIJHL	24	9	11	20	200	....	....	....	....	....	....	....	....	....	....	....	....	....	....	....	....	....	....	....
	Kelowna Spartans	BCJHL	3	0	0	0	9	....	....	....	....	....	....	....	....	....	....	....	....	....	....	....	....	....	....	....
	Vernon Lakers	BCJHL	12	0	1	1	18	....	....	....	....	....	....	....	....	....	....	....	....	....	....	....	....	....	....	....
	Penticton	BCJHL	3	0	0	0	13	....	....	....	....	....	....	....	....	....	....	....	....	....	....	....	....	....	....	....
1992-93	Spokane Chiefs	WHL	62	4	3	7	274	....	....	....	....	....	....	....	....	....	....	....	8	1	1	2	13	....	....	....
1993-94	Spokane Chiefs	WHL	60	10	15	25	350	....	....	....	....	....	....	....	....	....	....	....	3	0	1	1	6	....	....	....
1994-95	Spokane Chiefs	WHL	54	7	9	16	365	....	....	....	....	....	....	....	....	....	....	....	11	2	0	2	58	....	....	....
	Peoria Rivermen	IHL	....	....	....	....	....	....	....	....	....	....	....	....	....	....	....	....	2	0	0	0	12	....	....	....
1995-96	**St. Louis**	**NHL**	**6**	**0**	**0**	**0**	**23**	**0**	**0**	**0**	**1**	**0.0**	**–2**	....	....	....	....	....	....	....	....	....	....	....	....	....
	Worcester	AHL	41	3	4	7	268	....	....	....	....	....	....	....	....	....	....	....	....	....	....	....	....	....	....	....
	Boston	**NHL**	**2**	**0**	**0**	**0**	**5**	**0**	**0**	**0**	**0**	**0.0**	**1**	....	....	....	....	....	....	....	....	....	....	....	....	....
	Providence Bruins	AHL	4	0	0	0	29	....	....	....	....	....	....	....	....	....	....	....	4	0	1	1	9	....	....	....
1996-97	**Boston**	**NHL**	**2**	**0**	**0**	**0**	**0**	**0**	**0**	**0**	**0**	**0.0**	**0**	....	....	....	....	....	....	....	....	....	....	....	....	....
	Providence Bruins	AHL	60	8	9	17	367	....	....	....	....	....	....	....	....	....	....	....	6	0	0	0	32	....	....	....
1997-98	Michigan K-Wings	IHL	60	2	5	7	*398	....	....	....	....	....	....	....	....	....	....	....	3	0	0	0	23	....	....	....
1998-99	Worcester	AHL	70	8	14	22	299	....	....	....	....	....	....	....	....	....	....	....	4	0	1	1	4	....	....	....
99-2000	**Phoenix**	**NHL**	**3**	**0**	**0**	**0**	**12**	**0**	**0**	**0**	**0**	**0.0**	**1**	**0**	**0.0**	**4**	**0**	**2:20**	....	....	....	....	....	....	....	....
	Springfield	AHL	56	4	8	12	321	....	....	....	....	....	....	....	....	....	....	....	4	0	0	0	6	....	....	....
	NHL Totals		**13**	**0**	**0**	**0**	**40**	**0**	**0**	**0**	**1**	**0.0**		**0**	**0.0**	**4**	**0**	**2:20**	....	....	....	....	....	....	....	....

Signed as a free agent by **St. Louis**, February 28, 1995. Traded to **Boston** by **St. Louis** with Steve Staios for Steve Leach, March 8, 1996. Signed as a free agent by **Dallas**, August 19, 1997. Signed as a free agent by **St. Louis**, September 4, 1998. Signed as a free agent by **Phoenix**, August 15, 1999. Signed as a free agent by **Anaheim**, July 13, 2000.

SCATCHARD, Dave

(SKAT-chuhrd, DAYV) **NYI**

Center. Shoots right. 6'2", 220 lbs. Born, Hinton, Alta., February 20, 1976. Vancouver's 3rd choice, 42nd overall, in 1994 Entry Draft.

Season	Club	League	GP	G	A	Pts	PIM	PP	SH	GW	S	%	+/–	TF	F%	H	SB	Min	GP	G	A	Pts	PIM	PP	SH	GW
1991-92	Salmon Arm	BCAHA	65	98	100	198	167	....	....	....	....	....	....	....	....	....	....	....	....	....	....	....	....	....	....	....
1992-93	Kimberley	RMJHL	51	20	23	43	61	....	....	....	....	....	....	....	....	....	....	....	....	....	....	....	....	....	....	....
1993-94	Portland	WHL	47	9	11	20	46	....	....	....	....	....	....	....	....	....	....	....	10	2	1	3	4	....	....	....
1994-95	Portland	WHL	71	20	30	50	148	....	....	....	....	....	....	....	....	....	....	....	8	0	3	3	21	....	....	....
1995-96	Portland	WHL	59	19	28	47	146	....	....	....	....	....	....	....	....	....	....	....	7	1	8	9	14	....	....	....
	Syracuse Crunch	AHL	1	0	0	0	0	....	....	....	....	....	....	....	....	....	....	....	15	2	5	7	29	....	....	....
1996-97	Syracuse Crunch	AHL	26	8	7	15	65	....	....	....	....	....	....	....	....	....	....	....	....	....	....	....	....	....	....	....
1997-98	**Vancouver**	**NHL**	**76**	**13**	**11**	**24**	**165**	**0**	**0**	**1**	**85**	**15.3**	**–4**	....	....	....	....	....	....	....	....	....	....	....	....	....
1998-99	**Vancouver**	**NHL**	**82**	**13**	**13**	**26**	**140**	**0**	**2**	**2**	**130**	**10.0**	**–12**	**1007**	**56.3**	**147**	**33**	**13:46**	....	....	....	....	....	....	....	....
99-2000	**Vancouver**	**NHL**	**21**	**0**	**4**	**4**	**24**	**0**	**0**	**0**	**25**	**0.0**	**–3**	**190**	**59.5**	**40**	**6**	**10:12**	....	....	....	....	....	....	....	....
	NY Islanders	**NHL**	**44**	**12**	**14**	**26**	**93**	**0**	**1**	**1**	**103**	**11.7**	**0**	**710**	**55.8**	**123**	**21**	**13:42**	....	....	....	....	....	....	....	....
	NHL Totals		**223**	**38**	**42**	**80**	**422**	**0**	**3**	**4**	**343**	**11.1**		**1907**	**56.4**	**310**	**60**	**13:14**	....	....	....	....	....	....	....	....

Traded to **NY Islanders** by **Vancouver** with Kevin Weekes and Bill Muckalt for Felix Potvin and NY Islanders' compensatory 2nd (later traded to New Jersey - New Jersey selected Teemu Laine) and 3rd (Thatcher Bell) round choices in 2000 Entry Draft, December 19, 1999.

SCHAEFER, Peter

(SHAY-fuhr, PEE-tuhr) **VAN.**

Left wing. Shoots left. 5'11", 195 lbs. Born, Yellow Grass, Sask., July 12, 1977. Vancouver's 3rd choice, 66th overall, in 1995 Entry Draft.

Season	Club	League	GP	G	A	Pts	PIM	PP	SH	GW	S	%	+/–	TF	F%	H	SB	Min	GP	G	A	Pts	PIM	PP	SH	GW
1993-94	Yorkton Mallers	AAHA	32	27	14	41	133	....	....	....	....	....	....	....	....	....	....	....	....	....	....	....	....	....	....	....
	Brandon	WHL	2	1	0	1	0	....	....	....	....	....	....	....	....	....	....	....	....	....	....	....	....	....	....	....
1994-95	Brandon	WHL	68	27	32	59	34	....	....	....	....	....	....	....	....	....	....	....	18	5	3	8	18	....	....	....
1995-96	Brandon	WHL	69	47	61	108	53	....	....	....	....	....	....	....	....	....	....	....	19	10	13	23	5	....	....	....
1996-97	Brandon	WHL	61	49	74	123	85	....	....	....	....	....	....	....	....	....	....	....	6	1	4	5	4	....	....	....
	Syracuse Crunch	AHL	5	0	3	3	0	....	....	....	....	....	....	....	....	....	....	....	3	1	3	4	14	....	....	....
1997-98	Syracuse Crunch	AHL	73	19	44	63	41	....	....	....	....	....	....	....	....	....	....	....	5	2	1	3	2	....	....	....
1998-99	**Vancouver**	**NHL**	**25**	**4**	**4**	**8**	**8**	**1**	**0**	**1**	**24**	**16.7**	**–1**	**6**	**0.0**	**27**	**6**	**13:21**	....	....	....	....	....	....	....	....
	Syracuse Crunch	AHL	41	10	19	29	66	....	....	....	....	....	....	....	....	....	....	....	....	....	....	....	....	....	....	....
99-2000	**Vancouver**	**NHL**	**71**	**16**	**15**	**31**	**20**	**2**	**2**	**4**	**101**	**15.8**	**0**	**21**	**19.1**	**56**	**32**	**15:28**	....	....	....	....	....	....	....	....
	Syracuse Crunch	AHL	2	0	0	0	2	....	....	....	....	....	....	....	....	....	....	....	....	....	....	....	....	....	....	....
	NHL Totals		**96**	**20**	**19**	**39**	**28**	**3**	**2**	**5**	**125**	**16.0**		**27**	**14.8**	**83**	**38**	**14:55**	....	....	....	....	....	....	....	....

WHL East First All-Star Team (1996, 1997) • Canadian Major Junior First All-Star Team (1997)

SCHASTLIVY, Petr

(schust-LEE-vee, PEH-tuhr) **OTT.**

Left wing. Shoots left. 6'1", 204 lbs. Born, Angarsk, USSR, April 18, 1979. Ottawa's 5th choice, 101st overall, in 1998 Entry Draft.

Season	Club	League	GP	G	A	Pts	PIM	PP	SH	GW	S	%	+/–	TF	F%	H	SB	Min	GP	G	A	Pts	PIM	PP	SH	GW
1997-98	Torpedo Yaroslavl	Russia-3	47	15	9	24	34	....	....	....	....	....	....	....	....	....	....	....	....	....	....	....	....	....	....	....
	Torpedo Yaroslavl	Russia	4	0	0	0	0	....	....	....	....	....	....	....	....	....	....	....	....	....	....	....	....	....	....	....
1998-99	Torpedo Yaroslavl	Russia	40	6	1	7	28	....	....	....	....	....	....	....	....	....	....	....	6	0	0	0	2	....	....	....
99-2000	**Ottawa**	**NHL**	**13**	**2**	**5**	**7**	**2**	**1**	**0**	**1**	**22**	**9.1**	**4**	**0**	**0.0**	**2**	**2**	**12:18**	**1**	**0**	**0**	**0**	**0**	**0**	**0**	**0**
	Grand Rapids	IHL	46	16	12	28	10	....	....	....	....	....	....	....	....	....	....	....	17	8	7	15	6	....	....	....
	NHL Totals		**13**	**2**	**5**	**7**	**2**	**1**	**0**	**1**	**22**	**9.1**		**0**	**0.0**	**2**	**2**	**12:18**	**1**	**0**	**0**	**0**	**0**	**0**	**0**	**0**

SCHNEIDER, Mathieu

(SHNIGH-duhr, MAT-yoo) **L.A.**

Defense. Shoots left. 5'10", 192 lbs. Born, New York, NY, June 12, 1969. Montreal's 4th choice, 44th overall, in 1987 Entry Draft.

			Regular Season																Playoffs							
Season	Club	League	GP	G	A	Pts	PIM	PP	SH	GW	S	%	+/-	TF	F%	H	SB	Min	GP	G	A	Pts	PIM	PP	SH	GW
1985-86	Mount St. Charles	Hi-School	19	3	27	30																				
1986-87	Cornwall Royals	OHL	63	7	29	36	75												5	0	0	0	22			
1987-88	Cornwall Royals	OHL	48	21	40	61	83												11	2	6	8	14			
	Montreal	**NHL**	**4**	**0**	**0**	**0**	**2**	**0**	**0**	**0**	**2**	**0.0**	**−1**													
	Sherbrooke	AHL																	3	0	3	3	12			
1988-89	Cornwall Royals	OHL	59	16	57	73	96												18	7	20	27	30			
1989-90	**Montreal**	**NHL**	**44**	**7**	**14**	**21**	**25**	**5**	**0**	**1**	**84**	**8.3**	**2**						**9**	**1**	**3**	**4**	**31**	**1**	**0**	**0**
	Sherbrooke	AHL	28	6	13	19	20																			
1990-91	**Montreal**	**NHL**	**69**	**10**	**20**	**30**	**63**	**5**	**0**	**3**	**164**	**6.1**	**7**						**13**	**2**	**7**	**9**	**18**	**1**	**0**	**0**
1991-92	**Montreal**	**NHL**	**78**	**8**	**24**	**32**	**72**	**2**	**0**	**1**	**194**	**4.1**	**10**						**10**	**1**	**4**	**5**	**6**	**1**	**0**	**0**
1992-93♦	**Montreal**	**NHL**	**60**	**13**	**31**	**44**	**91**	**3**	**0**	**2**	**169**	**7.7**	**8**						**11**	**1**	**2**	**3**	**16**	**0**	**0**	**0**
1993-94	**Montreal**	**NHL**	**75**	**20**	**32**	**52**	**62**	**11**	**0**	**4**	**193**	**10.4**	**15**						**1**	**0**	**0**	**0**	**0**	**0**	**0**	**0**
1994-95	**Montreal**	**NHL**	**30**	**5**	**15**	**20**	**49**	**2**	**0**	**0**	**82**	**6.1**	**−3**													
	NY Islanders	**NHL**	**13**	**3**	**6**	**9**	**30**	**1**	**0**	**2**	**36**	**8.3**	**−5**													
1995-96	**NY Islanders**	**NHL**	**65**	**11**	**36**	**47**	**93**	**7**	**0**	**1**	**155**	**7.1**	**−18**													
	Toronto	**NHL**	**13**	**2**	**5**	**7**	**10**	**0**	**0**	**0**	**36**	**5.6**	**−2**						**6**	**0**	**4**	**4**	**8**	**0**	**0**	**0**
1996-97	**Toronto**	**NHL**	**26**	**5**	**7**	**12**	**20**	**1**	**0**	**1**	**63**	**7.9**	**3**													
1997-98	**Toronto**	**NHL**	**76**	**11**	**26**	**37**	**44**	**4**	**1**	**1**	**181**	**6.1**	**−12**													
	United States	Olympics	4	0	0	0	6																			
1998-99	**NY Rangers**	**NHL**	**75**	**10**	**24**	**34**	**71**	**5**	**0**	**2**	**159**	**6.3**	**−19**	**0**	**0.0**	**182**	**149**	**24:35**								
99-2000	**NY Rangers**	**NHL**	**80**	**10**	**20**	**30**	**78**	**3**	**0**	**1**	**228**	**4.4**	**−6**	**0**	**0.0**	**178**	**183**	**22:31**								
	NHL Totals		**708**	**115**	**260**	**375**	**710**	**49**	**1**	**19**	**1746**	**6.6**		**0**	**0.0**	**360**	**332**	**23:31**	**50**	**5**	**20**	**25**	**79**	**3**	**0**	**0**

OHL First All-Star Team (1988, 1989 • Played in NHL All-Star Game (1996)

Traded to **NY Islanders** by **Montreal** with Kirk Muller and Craig Darby for Pierre Turgeon and Vladimir Malakhov, April 5, 1995. Traded to **Toronto** by **NY Islanders** with Wendel Clark and D.J. Smith for Darby Hendrickson, Sean Haggerty, Kenny Jonsson and Toronto's 1st round choice (Roberto Luongo) in 1997 Entry Draft, March 13, 1996. • Missed majority of 1996-97 season recovering from groin injury suffered in game vs. St. Louis, December 27, 1996. Rights traded to **NY Rangers** by **Toronto** for Alexander Karpovtsev and NY Rangers' 4th round choice (Mirko Murovic) in 1999 Entry Draft, October 14, 1998. Selected by **Columbus** from **NY Rangers** in Expansion Draft, June 23, 2000. Signed as a free agent by **LA Kings**, August 14, 2000.

SCHULTZ, Ray

(SHUHLTZ, RAY) **NYI**

Defense. Shoots left. 6'2", 200 lbs. Born, Red Deer, Alta., November 14, 1976. Ottawa's 8th choice, 184th overall, in 1995 Entry Draft.

Season	Club	League	GP	G	A	Pts	PIM	PP	SH	GW	S	%	+/-	TF	F%	H	SB	Min	GP	G	A	Pts	PIM	PP	SH	GW
1993-94	Edmonton SSA	AAHA	31	3	24	27	94																			
	Tri-City Americans	WHL	3	0	0	0	11																			
1994-95	Tri-City Americans	WHL	63	1	8	9	209												11	0	0	0	16			
1995-96	Calgary Hitmen	WHL	66	3	17	20	282																			
1996-97	Calgary Hitmen	WHL	32	3	17	20	141																			
	Kelowna Rockets	WHL	23	3	11	14	63												6	0	2	2	12			
1997-98	**NY Islanders**	**NHL**	**13**	**0**	**1**	**1**	**45**	**0**	**0**	**0**	**4**	**0.0**	**3**													
	Kentucky	AHL	51	2	4	6	179												1	0	0	0	25			
1998-99	**NY Islanders**	**NHL**	**4**	**0**	**0**	**0**	**7**	**0**	**0**	**0**	**2**	**0.0**	**−2**	**1**	**0.0**	**5**	**1**	**15:21**								
	Lowell	AHL	54	0	3	3	184												1	0	0	0	4			
99-2000	**NY Islanders**	**NHL**	**9**	**0**	**1**	**1**	**30**	**0**	**0**	**0**	**2**	**0.0**	**1**	**0**	**0.0**	**21**	**5**	**14:18**								
	Kansas City	IHL	65	5	5	10	208																			
	NHL Totals		**26**	**0**	**2**	**2**	**82**	**0**	**0**	**0**	**8**	**0.0**		**1**	**0.0**	**26**	**6**	**14:37**								

Signed as a free agent by **NY Islanders**, June 9, 1997.

SCOVILLE, Darryl

(SKO-vihl, DAIR-uhl) **CGY.**

Defense. Shoots left. 6'3", 214 lbs. Born, Swift Current, SK, October 13, 1975.

Season	Club	League	GP	G	A	Pts	PIM	PP	SH	GW	S	%	+/-	TF	F%	H	SB	Min	GP	G	A	Pts	PIM	PP	SH	GW
1995-96	Merrimack	H-East	34	6	20	26	54																			
1996-97	Merrimack	H-East	35	7	16	23	71																			
1997-98	Merrimack	H-East	38	4	26	30	84																			
1998-99	Saint John Flames	AHL	61	1	7	8	66												7	1	2	3	13			
99-2000	**Calgary**	**NHL**	**6**	**0**	**0**	**0**	**2**	**0**	**0**	**0**	**1**	**0.0**	**1**	**0**	**0.0**	**11**	**1**	**9:18**								
	Saint John Flames	AHL	64	11	25	36	99												3	1	2	3	0			
	NHL Totals		**6**	**0**	**0**	**0**	**2**	**0**	**0**	**0**	**1**	**0.0**		**0**	**0.0**	**11**	**1**	**9:18**								

Signed as a free agent by **Calgary**, June 12, 1998.

SELANNE, Teemu

(SEH-lahn-nay, TEE-moo) **ANA.**

Right wing. Shoots right. 6', 204 lbs. Born, Helsinki, Finland, July 3, 1970. Winnipeg's 1st choice, 10th overall, in 1988 Entry Draft.

Season	Club	League	GP	G	A	Pts	PIM	PP	SH	GW	S	%	+/-	TF	F%	H	SB	Min	GP	G	A	Pts	PIM	PP	SH	GW
1986-87	Jokerit Helsinki	Finn-Jr.	33	10	12	22	8																			
1987-88	Jokerit Helsinki	Finn-Jr.	33	*43	23	*66	18												5	4	3	7	2			
	Jokerit Helsinki	Finland-2	5	1	1	2	0																			
1988-89	Army Sports	Finn-Jr.	3	3	1	4	2																			
	Jokerit Helsinki	Finn-Jr.	3	8	8	16	4																			
	Jokerit Helsinki	Finland-2	34	35	33	68	12												5	7	3	10	4			
1989-90	Jokerit Helsinki	Finland	11	4	8	12	0																			
1990-91	Jokerit Helsinki	Finn-Jr.	1	0	0	0	0																			
	Jokerit Helsinki	Finland	42	33	25	58	12																			
1991-92	Jokerit Helsinki	Finland	44	*39	23	62	20												10	*10	7	*17	18			
	Finland	Olympics	8	7	4	11	6																			
1992-93	**Winnipeg**	**NHL**	**84**	***76**	**56**	**132**	**45**	**24**	**0**	**7**	**387**	**19.6**	**8**						**6**	**4**	**2**	**6**	**2**	**2**	**0**	**2**
1993-94	**Winnipeg**	**NHL**	**51**	**25**	**29**	**54**	**22**	**11**	**0**	**2**	**191**	**13.1**	**−23**													
1994-95	Jokerit Helsinki	Finland	20	7	12	19	6																			
	Winnipeg	**NHL**	**45**	**22**	**26**	**48**	**2**	**8**	**2**	**1**	**167**	**13.2**	**1**													
1995-96	**Winnipeg**	**NHL**	**51**	**24**	**48**	**72**	**18**	**6**	**1**	**4**	**163**	**14.7**	**3**													
	Anaheim	**NHL**	**28**	**16**	**20**	**36**	**4**	**3**	**0**	**1**	**104**	**15.4**	**2**													
1996-97	**Anaheim**	**NHL**	**78**	**51**	**58**	**109**	**34**	**11**	**1**	**8**	**273**	**18.7**	**28**						**11**	**7**	**3**	**10**	**4**	**3**	**0**	**1**
1997-98	**Anaheim**	**NHL**	**73**	***52**	**34**	**86**	**30**	**10**	**1**	**10**	**268**	**19.4**	**12**													
	Finland	Olympics	5	4	6	*10	8																			
1998-99	**Anaheim**	**NHL**	**75**	***47**	**60**	**107**	**30**	**25**	**0**	**7**	**281**	**16.7**	**18**	**5**	**20.0**	**27**	**16**	**22:47**	**4**	**2**	**2**	**4**	**2**	**1**	**0**	**0**
99-2000	**Anaheim**	**NHL**	**79**	**33**	**52**	**85**	**12**	**8**	**0**	**6**	**236**	**14.0**	**6**	**13**	**23.1**	**43**	**19**	**22:44**								
	NHL Totals		**564**	**346**	**383**	**729**	**197**	**106**	**5**	**46**	**2070**	**16.7**		**18**	**22.2**	**70**	**35**	**22:45**	**21**	**13**	**7**	**20**	**8**	**6**	**0**	**3**

Won Calder Memorial Trophy (1993) • NHL First All-Star Team (1993, 1997) • NHL All-Rookie Team (1993) • NHL Second All-Star Team (1998, 1999) • Won Maurice "Rocket" Richard Trophy (1999) • Played in NHL All-Star Game (1993, 1994, 1996, 1997, 1998, 1999, 2000)

• Missed majority of 1989-90 season recovering from leg injury suffered in game vs. HIFK Helsinki, October 19, 1989. Traded to **Anaheim** by **Winnipeg** with Marc Chouinard and Winnipeg's 4th round choice (later traded to Toronto - later traded to Montreal - Montreal selected Kim Staal) in 1996 Entry Draft for Chad Kilger, Oleg Tverdovsky and Anaheim's 3rd round choice (Per-Anton Lundstrom) in 1996 Entry Draft, February 7, 1996.

SELIVANOV, Alex

(seh-lih-VAH-nohv, AL-ehx)

Right wing. Shoots left. 6', 208 lbs. Born, Moscow, USSR, March 23, 1971. Philadelphia's 4th choice, 140th overall, in 1994 Entry Draft.

Season	Club	League	GP	G	A	Pts	PIM	PP	SH	GW	S	%	+/-	TF	F%	H	SB	Min	GP	G	A	Pts	PIM	PP	SH	GW
1988-89	SKA Spartak	USSR	1	0	0	0	0																			
1989-90	SKA Spartak	USSR	4	0	0	0	0																			
1990-91	SKA Spartak	USSR	21	3	1	4	6																			
1991-92	SKA Spartak	CIS	31	6	7	13	16																			
1992-93	SKA Spartak	CIS	42	12	19	31	66												3	2	0	2	2			
1993-94	SKA Spartak	CIS	45	30	11	41	50												6	5	1	6	2			
1994-95	Atlanta Knights	IHL	4	0	3	3	2																			
	Chicago Wolves	IHL	14	4	1	5	8																			
	Tampa Bay	**NHL**	**43**	**10**	**6**	**16**	**14**	**4**	**0**	**3**	**94**	**10.6**	**−2**													
1995-96	**Tampa Bay**	**NHL**	**79**	**31**	**21**	**52**	**93**	**13**	**0**	**5**	**215**	**14.4**	**3**						**6**	**2**	**2**	**4**	**6**	**0**	**0**	**1**

Season	Club	League	GP	G	A	Pts	PIM	PP	SH	GW	S	%	+/-	TF	F%	H	SB	Min	GP	G	A	Pts	PIM	PP	SH	GW
			Regular Season																Playoffs							
1996-97	**Tampa Bay**	**NHL**	**69**	**15**	**18**	**33**	**61**	**3**	**0**	**4**	**187**	**8.0**	**-3**	....	....	....	....	....	....	....	....	....	....	....	....	....
1997-98	**Tampa Bay**	**NHL**	**70**	**16**	**19**	**35**	**85**	**4**	**0**	**3**	**206**	**7.8**	**-38**	....	....	....	....	....	....	....	....	....	....	....	....	....
1998-99	**Tampa Bay**	**NHL**	**43**	**6**	**13**	**19**	**18**	**1**	**0**	**0**	**120**	**5.0**	**-8**	**0**	**0.0**	**40**	**5**	**15:44**	....	....	....	....	....	....	....	....
	Cleveland	IHL	2	0	1	1	4	....	....	....	....	....	....	....	....	....	....	....	....	....	....	....	....	....	....	....
	Edmonton	**NHL**	**29**	**8**	**6**	**14**	**24**	**1**	**0**	**1**	**57**	**14.0**	**0**	**5**	**60.0**	**20**	**5**	**13:28**	**2**	**0**	**1**	**1**	**2**	**0**	**0**	**0**
99-2000	**Edmonton**	**NHL**	**67**	**27**	**20**	**47**	**46**	**10**	**0**	**5**	**122**	**22.1**	**2**	**5**	**0.0**	**29**	**6**	**14:28**	**5**	**0**	**0**	**0**	**8**	**0**	**0**	**0**
	NHL Totals		**400**	**113**	**103**	**216**	**341**	**36**	**0**	**21**	**1001**	**11.3**		**10**	**30.0**	**89**	**16**	**14:39**	**13**	**2**	**3**	**5**	**16**	**0**	**0**	**1**

Traded to **Tampa Bay** by **Philadelphia** for Philadelphia's 4th round choice (previously acquired, Philadelphia selected Radovan Somik) in 1995 Entry Draft, September 6, 1994. Traded to **Edmonton** by **Tampa Bay** for Alexandre Daigle, January 29, 1999.

SEVERYN, Brent

(SEH-vuh-rihn, BREHNT)

Left wing. Shoots left. 6'2", 211 lbs. Born, Vegreville, Alta., February 22, 1966. Winnipeg's 5th choice, 99th overall, in 1984 Entry Draft.

Season	Club	League	GP	G	A	Pts	PIM	PP	SH	GW	S	%	+/-	TF	F%	H	SB	Min	GP	G	A	Pts	PIM	PP	SH	GW
1982-83	Vegreville Rangers	AJHL	21	20	22	42	10	....	....	....	....	....	....	....	....	....	....	....	....	....	....	....	....	....	....	....
1983-84	Seattle T-Birds	WHL	72	14	22	36	49	....	....	....	....	....	....	....	....	....	....	....	5	2	1	3	2	....	....	....
1984-85	Seattle T-Birds	WHL	26	7	16	23	57	....	....	....	....	....	....	....	....	....	....	....	....	....	....	....	....	....	....	....
	Brandon	WHL	41	8	32	40	54	....	....	....	....	....	....	....	....	....	....	....	....	....	....	....	....	....	....	....
1985-86	Saskatoon Blades	WHL	9	1	4	5	38	....	....	....	....	....	....	....	....	....	....	....	....	....	....	....	....	....	....	....
	Seattle T-Birds	WHL	33	11	20	31	164	....	....	....	....	....	....	....	....	....	....	....	5	0	4	4	4	....	....	....
1986-87	U. of Alberta	CWUAA	43	7	19	26	171	....	....	....	....	....	....	....	....	....	....	....	....	....	....	....	....	....	....	....
1987-88	U. of Alberta	CWUAA	46	21	29	50	178	....	....	....	....	....	....	....	....	....	....	....	....	....	....	....	....	....	....	....
1988-89	Halifax Citadels	AHL	47	2	12	14	141	....	....	....	....	....	....	....	....	....	....	....	....	....	....	....	....	....	....	....
1989-90	**Quebec**	**NHL**	**35**	**0**	**2**	**2**	**42**	**0**	**0**	**0**	**28**	**0.0**	**-19**	....	....	....	....	....	....	....	....	....	....	....	....	....
	Halifax Citadels	AHL	43	6	9	15	105	....	....	....	....	....	....	....	....	....	....	....	6	1	2	3	49	....	....	....
1990-91	Halifax Citadels	AHL	50	7	26	33	202	....	....	....	....	....	....	....	....	....	....	....	....	....	....	....	....	....	....	....
1991-92	Utica Devils	AHL	80	11	33	44	211	....	....	....	....	....	....	....	....	....	....	....	4	0	1	1	4	....	....	....
1992-93	Utica Devils	AHL	77	20	32	52	240	....	....	....	....	....	....	....	....	....	....	....	5	0	0	0	35	....	....	....
1993-94	**Florida**	**NHL**	**67**	**4**	**7**	**11**	**156**	**1**	**0**	**1**	**93**	**4.3**	**-1**	....	....	....	....	....	....	....	....	....	....	....	....	....
1994-95	**Florida**	**NHL**	**9**	**1**	**1**	**2**	**37**	**1**	**0**	**0**	**10**	**10.0**	**-3**	....	....	....	....	....	....	....	....	....	....	....	....	....
	NY Islanders	**NHL**	**19**	**1**	**3**	**4**	**34**	**0**	**0**	**0**	**22**	**4.5**	**1**	....	....	....	....	....	....	....	....	....	....	....	....	....
1995-96	**NY Islanders**	**NHL**	**65**	**1**	**8**	**9**	**180**	**0**	**0**	**0**	**40**	**2.5**	**3**	....	....	....	....	....	....	....	....	....	....	....	....	....
1996-97	**Colorado**	**NHL**	**66**	**1**	**4**	**5**	**193**	**0**	**0**	**0**	**55**	**1.8**	**-6**	....	....	....	....	....	**8**	**0**	**0**	**0**	**12**	**0**	**0**	**0**
1997-98	**Anaheim**	**NHL**	**37**	**1**	**3**	**4**	**133**	**0**	**0**	**0**	**27**	**3.7**	**-3**	....	....	....	....	....	....	....	....	....	....	....	....	....
1998-99	**Dallas**	**NHL**	**30**	**1**	**2**	**3**	**50**	**0**	**0**	**0**	**22**	**4.5**	**-2**	**0**	**0.0**	**20**	**0**	**5:07**	....	....	....	....	....	....	....	....
	Michigan K-Wings	IHL	3	0	0	0	0	....	....	....	....	....	....	....	....	....	....	....	....	....	....	....	....	....	....	....
99-2000	Munich Barons	DEL	18	2	6	8	42	....	....	....	....	....	....	....	....	....	....	....	12	0	3	3	14	....	....	....
	NHL Totals		**328**	**10**	**30**	**40**	**825**	**2**	**0**	**1**	**297**	**3.4**		**0**	**0.0**	**20**	**0**	**5:07**	**8**	**0**	**0**	**0**	**12**	**0**	**0**	**0**

AHL First All-Star Team (1993)

Signed as a free agent by **Quebec**, July 15, 1988. Traded to **New Jersey** by **Quebec** for Dave Marcinyshyn, June 3, 1991. Traded to **Winnipeg** by **New Jersey** for Winnipeg's 6th round choice (Ryan Smart) in 1994 Entry Draft, September 30, 1993. Traded to **Florida** by **Winnipeg** for Milan Tichy, October 3, 1993. Traded to **NY Islanders** by **Florida** for NY Islanders' 4th round choice (Dave Duerden) in 1995 Entry Draft, March 3, 1995. Traded to **Colorado** by **NY Islanders** for Colorado's 3rd round choice (later traded to Calgary - later traded to Hartford/Carolina - Carolina selected Francis Lessard) in 1997 Entry Draft, September 4, 1996. Claimed by **Anaheim** from **Colorado** in NHL Waiver Draft, September 28, 1997. • Missed majority of 1997-98 season recovering from back injury suffered in game vs. Detroit, October 22, 1997. Signed as a free agent by **Dallas**, August 26, 1998.

SEVIGNY, Pierre

(seh-VIH-nee, PEE-air)

Left wing. Shoots left. 6', 195 lbs. Born, Trois-Rivières, Que., September 8, 1971. Montreal's 4th choice, 51st overall, in 1989 Entry Draft.

Season	Club	League	GP	G	A	Pts	PIM	PP	SH	GW	S	%	+/-	TF	F%	H	SB	Min	GP	G	A	Pts	PIM	PP	SH	GW
1987-88	Montreal L'est	QAAA	40	43	78	121	72	....	....	....	....	....	....	....	....	....	....	....	....	....	....	....	....	....	....	....
1988-89	Verdun Canucks	QMJHL	67	27	43	70	88	....	....	....	....	....	....	....	....	....	....	....	....	....	....	....	....	....	....	....
1989-90	St-Hyacinthe	QMJHL	67	47	72	119	205	....	....	....	....	....	....	....	....	....	....	....	12	8	8	16	42	....	....	....
1990-91	St-Hyacinthe	QMJHL	60	36	46	82	203	....	....	....	....	....	....	....	....	....	....	....	....	....	....	....	....	....	....	....
1991-92	Fredericton	AHL	74	22	37	59	145	....	....	....	....	....	....	....	....	....	....	....	7	1	1	2	26	....	....	....
1992-93	Fredericton	AHL	80	36	40	76	113	....	....	....	....	....	....	....	....	....	....	....	5	1	1	2	2	....	....	....
1993-94	**Montreal**	**NHL**	**43**	**4**	**5**	**9**	**42**	**1**	**0**	**1**	**19**	**21.1**	**6**	....	....	....	....	....	**3**	**0**	**1**	**1**	**0**	**0**	**0**	**0**
1994-95	**Montreal**	**NHL**	**19**	**0**	**0**	**0**	**15**	**0**	**0**	**0**	**6**	**0.0**	**-5**	....	....	....	....	....	....	....	....	....	....	....	....	....
1995-96	Fredericton	AHL	76	39	42	81	188	....	....	....	....	....	....	....	....	....	....	....	10	5	9	14	20	....	....	....
1996-97	**Montreal**	**NHL**	**13**	**0**	**0**	**0**	**5**	**0**	**0**	**0**	**1**	**0.0**	**0**	....	....	....	....	....	....	....	....	....	....	....	....	....
	Fredericton	AHL	32	9	17	26	58	....	....	....	....	....	....	....	....	....	....	....	....	....	....	....	....	....	....	....
1997-98	**NY Rangers**	**NHL**	**3**	**0**	**0**	**0**	**2**	**0**	**0**	**0**	**1**	**0.0**	**0**	....	....	....	....	....	....	....	....	....	....	....	....	....
	Hartford	AHL	40	18	13	31	94	....	....	....	....	....	....	....	....	....	....	....	12	3	5	8	14	....	....	....
1998-99	Long Beach	IHL	6	1	3	4	7	....	....	....	....	....	....	....	....	....	....	....	....	....	....	....	....	....	....	....
	Orlando	IHL	43	11	21	32	44	....	....	....	....	....	....	....	....	....	....	....	15	4	5	9	32	....	....	....
99-2000	Quebec Citadelles	AHL	78	24	43	67	154	....	....	....	....	....	....	....	....	....	....	....	3	3	0	3	17	....	....	....
	NHL Totals		**78**	**4**	**5**	**9**	**64**	**1**	**0**	**1**	**27**	**14.8**		....	....	....	....	....	**3**	**0**	**1**	**1**	**0**	**0**	**0**	**0**

QMJHL First All-Star Team (1981) • QMJHL Second All-Star Team (1990, 1991)

Signed as a free agent by **NY Rangers**, August 26, 1997

SHALDYBIN, Yevgeny

(shahl-DAY-bihn, yehv-GEH-nee)

Defense. Shoots left. 6'2", 198 lbs. Born, Novosibirsk, USSR, July 29, 1975. Boston's 6th choice, 151st overall, in 1995 Entry Draft.

Season	Club	League	GP	G	A	Pts	PIM	PP	SH	GW	S	%	+/-	TF	F%	H	SB	Min	GP	G	A	Pts	PIM	PP	SH	GW
1993-94	Torpedo Yaroslavl	CIS	14	0	0	0	0	....	....	....	....	....	....	....	....	....	....	....	....	....	....	....	....	....	....	....
1994-95	Torpedo Yaroslavl	CIS	42	2	5	7	10	....	....	....	....	....	....	....	....	....	....	....	4	0	1	1	0	....	....	....
1995-96	Torpedo Yaroslavl	CIS	41	0	2	2	10	....	....	....	....	....	....	....	....	....	....	....	3	0	1	1	2	....	....	....
1996-97	**Boston**	**NHL**	**3**	**1**	**0**	**1**	**0**	**0**	**0**	**0**	**5**	**20.0**	**-2**	....	....	....	....	....	....	....	....	....	....	....	....	....
	Providence Bruins	AHL	65	4	13	17	28	....	....	....	....	....	....	....	....	....	....	....	3	0	0	0	2	....	....	....
1997-98	Providence Bruins	AHL	63	5	7	12	54	....	....	....	....	....	....	....	....	....	....	....	....	....	....	....	....	....	....	....
1998-99	Providence Bruins	AHL	1	0	0	0	0	....	....	....	....	....	....	....	....	....	....	....	....	....	....	....	....	....	....	....
	Las Vegas	IHL	13	1	3	4	6	....	....	....	....	....	....	....	....	....	....	....	....	....	....	....	....	....	....	....
	B.C. Icemen	UHL	61	14	38	52	38	....	....	....	....	....	....	....	....	....	....	....	....	....	....	....	....	....	....	....
99-2000	Nizhny Novgorod	Russia	4	0	0	0	2	....	....	....	....	....	....	....	....	....	....	....	....	....	....	....	....	....	....	....
	B.C. Icemen	UHL	71	16	52	68	36	....	....	....	....	....	....	....	....	....	....	....	6	1	4	5	8	....	....	....
	NHL Totals		**3**	**1**	**0**	**1**	**0**	**0**	**0**	**0**	**5**	**20.0**														

SHANAHAN, Brendan

(SHAN-na-HAN, BREHN-dan) **DET.**

Left wing. Shoots right. 6'3", 218 lbs. Born, Mimico, Ont., January 23, 1969. New Jersey's 1st choice, 2nd overall, in 1987 Entry Draft.

Season	Club	League	GP	G	A	Pts	PIM	PP	SH	GW	S	%	+/-	TF	F%	H	SB	Min	GP	G	A	Pts	PIM	PP	SH	GW
1984-85	Mississauga Reps	MTHL	36	20	21	41	26	....	....	....	....	....	....	....	....	....	....	....	....	....	....	....	....	....	....	....
	Dixie Beehives	OJHL	1	0	0	0	0	....	....	....	....	....	....	....	....	....	....	....	....	....	....	....	....	....	....	....
1985-86	London Knights	OHL	59	28	34	62	70	....	....	....	....	....	....	....	....	....	....	....	5	5	5	10	5	....	....	....
1986-87	London Knights	OHL	56	39	53	92	92	....	....	....	....	....	....	....	....	....	....	....	....	....	....	....	....	....	....	....
1987-88	**New Jersey**	**NHL**	**65**	**7**	**19**	**26**	**131**	**2**	**0**	**2**	**72**	**9.7**	**-20**	....	....	....	....	....	**12**	**2**	**1**	**3**	**44**	**1**	**0**	**0**
1988-89	**New Jersey**	**NHL**	**68**	**22**	**28**	**50**	**115**	**9**	**0**	**0**	**152**	**14.5**	**2**	....	....	....	....	....	....	....	....	....	....	....	....	....
1989-90	**New Jersey**	**NHL**	**73**	**30**	**42**	**72**	**137**	**8**	**0**	**5**	**196**	**15.3**	**15**	....	....	....	....	....	**6**	**3**	**3**	**6**	**20**	**1**	**0**	**1**
1990-91	**New Jersey**	**NHL**	**75**	**29**	**37**	**66**	**141**	**7**	**0**	**2**	**195**	**14.9**	**4**	....	....	....	....	....	**7**	**3**	**5**	**8**	**12**	**2**	**0**	**0**
1991-92	**St. Louis**	**NHL**	**80**	**33**	**36**	**69**	**171**	**13**	**0**	**2**	**215**	**15.3**	**-3**	....	....	....	....	....	**6**	**2**	**3**	**5**	**14**	**1**	**0**	**0**
1992-93	**St. Louis**	**NHL**	**71**	**51**	**43**	**94**	**174**	**18**	**0**	**8**	**232**	**22.0**	**10**	....	....	....	....	....	**11**	**4**	**3**	**7**	**18**	**2**	**0**	**0**
1993-94	**St. Louis**	**NHL**	**81**	**52**	**50**	**102**	**211**	**15**	**7**	**8**	**397**	**13.1**	**-9**	....	....	....	....	....	**4**	**2**	**5**	**7**	**4**	**0**	**0**	**0**
1994-95	Dusseldorfer EG	DEL	3	5	3	8	4	....	....	....	....	....	....	....	....	....	....	....	....	....	....	....	....	....	....	....
	St. Louis	**NHL**	**45**	**20**	**21**	**41**	**136**	**6**	**2**	**6**	**153**	**13.1**	**7**	....	....	....	....	....	**5**	**4**	**5**	**9**	**14**	**1**	**0**	**1**
1995-96	**Hartford**	**NHL**	**74**	**44**	**34**	**78**	**125**	**17**	**2**	**6**	**280**	**15.7**	**2**	....	....	....	....	....	....	....	....	....	....	....	....	....
1996-97	**Hartford**	**NHL**	**2**	**1**	**0**	**1**	**0**	**0**	**1**	**0**	**13**	**7.7**	**1**	....	....	....	....	....	....	....	....	....	....	....	....	....
	♦ Detroit	**NHL**	**79**	**46**	**41**	**87**	**131**	**20**	**2**	**7**	**323**	**14.2**	**31**	....	....	....	....	....	**20**	**9**	**8**	**17**	**43**	**2**	**0**	**2**
1997-98♦	**Detroit**	**NHL**	**75**	**28**	**29**	**57**	**154**	**15**	**1**	**9**	**266**	**10.5**	**6**	....	....	....	....	....	**20**	**5**	**4**	**9**	**22**	**3**	**0**	**2**
	Canada	Olympics	6	2	0	2	0	....	....	....	....	....	....	....	....	....	....	....	....	....	....	....	....	....	....	....
1998-99	**Detroit**	**NHL**	**81**	**31**	**27**	**58**	**123**	**5**	**0**	**5**	**288**	**10.8**	**2**	**18**	**44.4**	**119**	**35**	**17:31**	**10**	**3**	**7**	**10**	**6**	**1**	**0**	**1**

			Regular Season																Playoffs							
Season	Club	League	GP	G	A	Pts	PIM	PP	SH	GW	S	%	+/-	TF	F%	H	SB	Min	GP	G	A	Pts	PIM	PP	SH	GW
99-2000	Detroit	NHL	78	41	37	78	105	13	1	9	283	14.5	24	24	50.0	104	34	18:35	9	3	2	5	10	0	0	0
	NHL Totals		947	435	444	879	1854	148	16	69	3065	14.2		42	47.6	223	69	18:02	110	40	46	86	207	14	0	7

NHL First All-Star Team (1994, 2000) • Played in NHL All-Star Game (1994, 1996, 1997, 1998, 1999, 2000)

Signed as a free agent by **St. Louis**, July 25, 1991. Traded to **Hartford** by **St. Louis** for Chris Pronger, July 27, 1995. Traded to **Detroit** by **Hartford** with Brian Glynn for Paul Coffey, Keith Primeau and Detroit's 1st round choice (Nikos Tselios) in 1997 Entry Draft, October 9, 1996.

SHANNON, Darrin

(SHA-nohn, DAIR-ihn)

Left wing. Shoots left. 6'2", 210 lbs. Born, Barrie, Ont., December 8, 1969. Pittsburgh's 1st choice, 4th overall, in 1988 Entry Draft.

Season	Club	League	GP	G	A	Pts	PIM	PP	SH	GW	S	%	+/-	TF	F%	H	SB	Min	GP	G	A	Pts	PIM	PP	SH	GW
1984-85	Alliston Hornets	OJHL-C	36	28	33	61	2																			
1985-86	Barrie Colts	OJHL-B	40	13	22	35	21																			
1986-87	Windsor Spitfires	OHL	60	16	67	83	116												14	4	6	10	8			
1987-88	Windsor Spitfires	OHL	43	33	41	74	49												12	6	12	18	9			
1988-89	Windsor Spitfires	OHL	54	33	48	81	47												4	1	6	7	2			
	Buffalo	NHL	3	0	0	0	0	0	0	0	0	0.0	–2						2	0	0	0	0	0	0	0
1989-90	Buffalo	NHL	17	2	7	9	4	0	0	0	20	10.0	6						6	0	1	1	4	0	0	0
	Rochester	AHL	50	20	23	43	25												9	4	1	5	2			
1990-91	Buffalo	NHL	34	8	6	14	12	1	0	0	56	14.3	–11						6	1	2	3	4	0	0	0
	Rochester	AHL	49	26	34	60	56												10	3	5	8	22			
1991-92	Buffalo	NHL	1	0	1	1	0	0	0	0	2	0.0	1													
	Winnipeg	NHL	68	13	26	39	41	3	0	3	91	14.3	5						7	0	1	1	10	0	0	0
1992-93	Winnipeg	NHL	84	20	40	60	91	12	0	2	116	17.2	–4						6	2	4	6	6	1	0	0
1993-94	Winnipeg	NHL	77	21	37	58	87	9	0	2	124	16.9	–18													
1994-95	Winnipeg	NHL	19	5	3	8	14	3	0	1	26	19.2	–6													
1995-96	Winnipeg	NHL	63	5	18	23	28	0	0	1	74	6.8	–5						6	1	0	1	6	0	0	0
1996-97	Phoenix	NHL	82	11	13	24	41	1	0	2	104	10.6	4						7	3	1	4	4	0	0	1
1997-98	Phoenix	NHL	58	2	12	14	26	0	0	0	57	3.5	4						5	0	1	1	4	0	0	0
1998-99	Grand Rapids	IHL	10	1	5	6	12																			
99-2000	St. John's Leafs	AHL	8	2	0	2	2																			
	Chicago Wolves	IHL	9	1	3	4	6																			
	NHL Totals		506	87	163	250	344	29	0	11	670	13.0							45	7	10	17	38	1	0	1

Canadian Major Junior Scholastic Player of the Year (1988)

Traded to **Buffalo** by **Pittsburgh** with Doug Bodger for Tom Barrasso and Buffalo's 3rd round choice (Joe Dziedzic) in 1990 Entry Draft, November 12, 1988. Traded to **Winnipeg** by **Buffalo** with Mike Hartman and Dean Kennedy for Dave McLlwain, Gord Donnelly, Winnipeg's 5th round choice (Yuri Khmylev) in 1992 Entry Draft and future considerations, October 11, 1991. Transferred to **Phoenix** after **Winnipeg** franchise relocated, July 1, 1996. • Missed majority of 1998-99 and 1999-2000 seasons recovering from knee surgery, June 1998. Signed as a free agent by **Grand Rapids** (IHL), February 18, 1999. Signed as a free agent by **Toronto**, August 25, 1999.

SHANNON, Darryl

(SHA-nohn, DAIR-ihl)

Defense. Shoots left. 6'2", 208 lbs. Born, Barrie, Ont., June 21, 1968. Toronto's 2nd choice, 36th overall, in 1986 Entry Draft.

Season	Club	League	GP	G	A	Pts	PIM	PP	SH	GW	S	%	+/-	TF	F%	H	SB	Min	GP	G	A	Pts	PIM	PP	SH	GW
1983-84	Alliston Hornets	OJHL-C	30	18	22	40	70																			
1984-85	Richmond Hill	OJHL	1	0	0	0	0																			
	Barrie Colts	OJHL-B	39	5	23	28	50																			
1985-86	Windsor Spitfires	OHL	57	6	21	27	52												16	5	6	11	22			
1986-87	Windsor Spitfires	OHL	64	23	27	50	83												14	4	8	12	18			
1987-88	Windsor Spitfires	OHL	60	16	67	83	116												12	3	8	11	17			
1988-89	Toronto	NHL	14	1	3	4	6	0	0	0	16	6.3	5													
	Newmarket	AHL	61	5	24	29	37												5	0	3	3	10			
1989-90	Toronto	NHL	10	0	1	1	12	0	0	0	16	0.0	–10													
	Newmarket	AHL	47	4	15	19	58																			
1990-91	Toronto	NHL	10	0	1	1	0	0	0	0	3	0.0	1													
	Newmarket	AHL	47	2	14	16	51																			
1991-92	Toronto	NHL	48	2	8	10	23	1	0	0	50	4.0	–17													
1992-93	Toronto	NHL	16	0	0	0	11	0	0	0	10	0.0	–5													
	St. John's Leafs	AHL	7	1	1	2	4																			
1993-94	Winnipeg	NHL	20	0	4	4	18	0	0	0	14	0.0	–6													
	Moncton Hawks	AHL	37	1	10	11	62												20	1	7	8	32			
1994-95	Winnipeg	NHL	40	5	9	14	48	0	1	0	42	11.9	1													
1995-96	Winnipeg	NHL	48	2	7	9	72	0	0	0	34	5.9	5													
	Buffalo	NHL	26	2	6	8	20	0	0	0	25	8.0	10													
1996-97	Buffalo	NHL	82	4	19	23	112	1	0	1	94	4.3	23						12	2	3	5	8	1	0	0
1997-98	Buffalo	NHL	76	3	19	22	56	1	0	1	85	3.5	26						15	2	4	6	8	0	1	0
1998-99	Buffalo	NHL	71	3	12	15	52	1	0	0	80	3.8	28	1	0.0	103	111	20:10	2	0	0	0	0	0	0	0
99-2000	Atlanta	NHL	49	5	13	18	65	1	0	1	66	7.6	–14	1	0.0	86	84	21:21								
	Calgary	NHL	27	1	8	9	22	0	0	0	46	2.2	–13	0	0.0	32	44	23:33								
	NHL Totals		537	28	110	138	517	5	1	3	581	4.8		2	0.0	221	239	21:11	29	4	7	11	16	1	1	0

OHL Second All-Star Team (1987) • OHL First All-Star Team (1988)

Signed as a free agent by **Winnipeg**, June 30, 1993. Traded to **Buffalo** by **Winnipeg** with Michal Grosek for Craig Muni, February 15, 1996. Claimed by **Atlanta** from **Buffalo** in Expansion Draft, June 25, 1999. Traded to **Calgary** by **Atlanta** with Jason Botterill for Hnat Domenichelli and Dmitri Vlasenkov, February 11, 2000.

SHANTZ, Jeff

(SHAWNTS, JEHF) **CGY.**

Center. Shoots right. 6', 195 lbs. Born, Duchess, Alta., October 10, 1973. Chicago's 2nd choice, 36th overall, in 1992 Entry Draft.

Season	Club	League	GP	G	A	Pts	PIM	PP	SH	GW	S	%	+/-	TF	F%	H	SB	Min	GP	G	A	Pts	PIM	PP	SH	GW
1989-90	Medicine Hat	AAHA	36	18	31	49	30																			
	Regina Pats	WHL	1	0	0	0	0																			
1990-91	Regina Pats	WHL	69	16	21	37	22												8	2	2	4	2			
1991-92	Regina Pats	WHL	72	39	50	89	35																			
1992-93	Regina Pats	WHL	64	29	54	83	75												13	2	12	14	14			
1993-94	Chicago	NHL	52	3	13	16	30	0	0	0	56	5.4	–14						6	0	0	0	6	0	0	0
	Indianapolis Ice	IHL	19	5	9	14	20																			
1994-95	Indianapolis Ice	IHL	32	9	15	24	20																			
	Chicago	NHL	45	6	12	18	33	0	2	0	58	10.3	11						16	3	1	4	2	0	0	0
1995-96	Chicago	NHL	78	6	14	20	24	1	2	0	72	8.3	12						10	2	3	5	6	0	0	0
1996-97	Chicago	NHL	69	9	21	30	28	0	1	1	86	10.5	11						6	0	4	4	6	0	0	0
1997-98	Chicago	NHL	61	11	20	31	36	1	2	2	69	15.9	0													
1998-99	Chicago	NHL	7	1	0	1	4	0	0	0	5	20.0	–1	72	38.9	16	1	15:14								
	Calgary	NHL	69	12	17	29	40	1	1	3	77	15.6	15	1112	48.4	83	35	16:47								
99-2000	Calgary	NHL	74	13	18	31	30	6	0	1	112	11.6	–13	1576	51.1	43	71	18:15								
	NHL Totals		455	61	115	176	225	9	8	7	535	11.4		2760	49.7	142	107	17:26	38	5	8	13	20	0	0	0

WHL East First All-Star Team (1993)

Traded to **Calgary** by **Chicago** with Steve Dubinsky for Marty McInnis, Jamie Allison and Eric Andersson, October 27, 1998.

SHARIFIJANOV, Vadim

(shah-rih-FYAH-nohv, VA-dihm) **VAN.**

Right wing. Shoots left. 6', 205 lbs. Born, Ufa, USSR, December 23, 1975. New Jersey's 1st choice, 25th overall, in 1994 Entry Draft.

Season	Club	League	GP	G	A	Pts	PIM	PP	SH	GW	S	%	+/-	TF	F%	H	SB	Min	GP	G	A	Pts	PIM	PP	SH	GW
1992-93	Ufa Salavat	CIS	37	6	4	10	16												2	1	0	1	0			
1993-94	Ufa Salavat	CIS	46	10	6	16	36												5	3	0	3	4			
1994-95	CSKA Moscow	CIS	34	7	3	10	26												2	0	0	0	0			
	Albany River Rats	AHL	1	1	1	2	0												9	3	3	6	10			
1995-96	Albany River Rats	AHL	69	14	28	42	28																			
1996-97	New Jersey	NHL	2	0	0	0	0	0	0	0	4	0.0	0													
	Albany River Rats	AHL	70	14	27	41	89												10	3	3	6	6			
1997-98	Albany River Rats	AHL	72	23	27	50	69												12	4	9	13	6			
1998-99	New Jersey	NHL	53	11	16	27	28	1	0	2	71	15.5	11	2	50.0	43	10	13:39	4	0	0	0	0	0	0	0
	Albany River Rats	AHL	2	1	1	2	0																			
99-2000	New Jersey	NHL	20	3	4	7	8	0	0	0	20	15.0	–6	0	0.0	19	0	10:58								

Season	Club	League	Regular Season																Playoffs							
			GP	G	A	Pts	PIM	PP	SH	GW	S	%	+/-	TF	F%	H	SB	Min	GP	G	A	Pts	PIM	PP	SH	GW
	Vancouver	**NHL**	**17**	**2**	**1**	**3**	**14**	**1**	**0**	**0**	**26**	**7.7**	**–7**	**3**	**33.3**	**13**	**0**	**13:11**								
	NHL Totals		**92**	**16**	**21**	**37**	**50**	**2**	**0**	**2**	**121**	**13.2**		**5**	**40.0**	**75**	**10**	**12:58**	**4**	**0**	**0**	**0**	**0**	**0**	**0**	**0**

Traded to **Vancouver** by **New Jersey** with New Jersey's 3rd round choice (Tim Branham) in 2000 Entry Draft for NY Islanders' compensatory 2nd round choice (previously acquired, New Jersey selected Teemu Laine) in 2000 Entry Draft and Atlanta's third round choice (previously acquired, New Jersey selected Max Birbraer) in 2000 Entry Draft, January 14, 2000.

SHEPPARD, Ray

(SHEH-pahrd, RAY)

Right wing. Shoots right. 6'1", 195 lbs. Born, Pembroke, Ont., May 27, 1966. Buffalo's 3rd choice, 60th overall, in 1984 Entry Draft.

1982-83	Brockville Braves	OJHL	48	27	36	63	81																			
1983-84	Cornwall Royals	OHL	68	44	36	80	69																			
1984-85	Cornwall Royals	OHL	49	25	33	58	51												9	2	12	14	4			
1985-86	Cornwall Royals	OHL	63	*81	61	*142	25												6	7	4	11	0			
1986-87	Rochester	AHL	55	18	13	31	11												15	12	3	15	2			
1987-88	**Buffalo**	**NHL**	**74**	**38**	**27**	**65**	**14**	**15**	**0**	**5**	**173**	**22.0**	**–6**						**6**	**1**	**1**	**2**	**2**	**1**	**0**	**0**
1988-89	**Buffalo**	**NHL**	**67**	**22**	**21**	**43**	**15**	**7**	**0**	**4**	**147**	**15.0**	**–7**						**1**	**0**	**1**	**1**	**0**	**0**	**0**	**0**
1989-90	**Buffalo**	**NHL**	**18**	**4**	**2**	**6**	**0**	**1**	**0**	**1**	**31**	**12.9**	**3**													
	Rochester	AHL	5	3	5	8	2												17	8	7	15	9			
1990-91	**NY Rangers**	**NHL**	**59**	**24**	**23**	**47**	**21**	**7**	**0**	**5**	**129**	**18.6**	**8**													
1991-92	**Detroit**	**NHL**	**74**	**36**	**26**	**62**	**27**	**11**	**1**	**4**	**178**	**20.2**	**7**						**11**	**6**	**2**	**8**	**4**	**3**	**0**	**0**
1992-93	**Detroit**	**NHL**	**70**	**32**	**34**	**66**	**29**	**10**	**0**	**1**	**183**	**17.5**	**7**						**7**	**2**	**3**	**5**	**0**	**2**	**0**	**0**
1993-94	**Detroit**	**NHL**	**82**	**52**	**41**	**93**	**26**	**19**	**0**	**5**	**260**	**20.0**	**13**						**7**	**2**	**1**	**3**	**4**	**0**	**0**	**0**
1994-95	**Detroit**	**NHL**	**43**	**30**	**10**	**40**	**17**	**11**	**0**	**5**	**125**	**24.0**	**11**						**17**	**4**	**3**	**7**	**5**	**2**	**0**	**0**
1995-96	**Detroit**	**NHL**	**5**	**2**	**2**	**4**	**2**	**0**	**0**	**1**	**9**	**22.2**	**0**													
	San Jose	**NHL**	**51**	**27**	**19**	**46**	**10**	**12**	**0**	**4**	**170**	**15.9**	**–19**													
	Florida	**NHL**	**14**	**8**	**2**	**10**	**4**	**2**	**0**	**2**	**52**	**15.4**	**0**						**21**	**8**	**8**	**16**	**4**	**3**	**0**	**0**
1996-97	**Florida**	**NHL**	**68**	**29**	**31**	**60**	**4**	**13**	**0**	**7**	**226**	**12.8**	**4**						**5**	**2**	**0**	**2**	**0**	**1**	**0**	**0**
1997-98	**Florida**	**NHL**	**61**	**14**	**17**	**31**	**21**	**5**	**0**	**1**	**136**	**10.3**	**–13**													
	Carolina	**NHL**	**10**	**4**	**2**	**6**	**2**	**2**	**0**	**1**	**33**	**12.1**	**2**													
1998-99	**Carolina**	**NHL**	**74**	**25**	**33**	**58**	**16**	**5**	**0**	**4**	**188**	**13.3**	**4**	**7**	**71.4**	**20**	**6**	**18:12**	**6**	**5**	**1**	**6**	**2**	**1**	**0**	**1**
99-2000	**Florida**	**NHL**	**47**	**10**	**10**	**20**	**4**	**5**	**0**	**2**	**74**	**13.5**	**–4**	**4**	**0.0**	**7**	**5**	**13:38**								
	NHL Totals		**817**	**357**	**300**	**657**	**212**	**125**	**1**	**52**	**2114**	**16.9**		**11**	**45.5**	**27**	**11**	**16:25**	**81**	**30**	**20**	**50**	**21**	**13**	**0**	**1**

OHL First All-Star Team (1986) • NHL All-Rookie Team (1988)

• Missed majority of 1989-90 season recovering from ankle injury suffered in game vs. Quebec, January 31, 1990. Traded to **NY Rangers** by **Buffalo** for cash and future considerations, July 9, 1990. Signed as a free agent by **Detroit**, August 5, 1991. Traded to **San Jose** by **Detroit** for Igor Larionov and future considerations, October 24, 1995. Traded to **Florida** by **San Jose** with San Jose's 4th round choice (Joey Tetarenko) in 1996 Entry Draft for Florida's 2nd (later traded to Chicago - Chicago selected Geoff Peters) and 4th (Matt Bradley) round choices in 1996 Entry Draft, March 16, 1996. Traded to **Carolina** by **Florida** for Kirk McLean, March 24, 1998.

SHEVALIER, Jeff

(sheh-VAL-ee-ay, JEHF)

Left wing. Shoots left. 5'11", 180 lbs. Born, Mississauga, Ont., March 14, 1974. Los Angeles' 4th choice, 111th overall, in 1992 Entry Draft.

1989-90	Acton Sabres	OJHL-C	33	30	34	64	59																			
1990-91	Acton Sabres	OJHL-C	28	29	31	60	62																			
	Georgetown	OJHL-B	12	11	11	22	8																			
	Oakville Blades	OJHL-B	5	1	4	5	0																			
1991-92	North Bay	OHL	64	28	29	57	26												21	5	11	16	25			
1992-93	North Bay	OHL	62	59	54	113	46												2	1	2	3	4			
1993-94	North Bay	OHL	64	52	49	101	52												17	8	14	22	18			
1994-95	Phoenix	IHL	68	31	39	70	•44												9	5	4	9	0			
	Los Angeles	**NHL**	**1**	**1**	**0**	**1**	**0**	**0**	**0**	**0**	**1**	**100.0**	**1**													
1995-96	Phoenix	IHL	79	29	38	67	72												4	2	2	4	2			
1996-97	**Los Angeles**	**NHL**	**26**	**4**	**9**	**13**	**6**	**1**	**0**	**0**	**42**	**9.5**	**–6**													
	Phoenix	IHL	46	16	21	37	26																			
1997-98	Springfield	AHL	66	23	30	53	38												4	1	1	2	0			
1998-99	Cincinnati	IHL	76	29	34	63	57												3	1	1	2	0			
99-2000	**Tampa Bay**	**NHL**	**5**	**0**	**0**	**0**	**2**	**0**	**0**	**0**	**2**	**0.0**	**–1**	**2**	**0.0**	**1**	**0**	**2:14**								
	Detroit Vipers	IHL	46	11	25	36	42																			
	Quebec Citadelles	AHL	5	0	2	2	2																			
	Grand Rapids	IHL	2	0	0	0	0																			
	NHL Totals		**32**	**5**	**9**	**14**	**8**	**1**	**0**	**0**	**45**	**11.1**		**2**	**0.0**	**1**	**0**	**2:14**								

OHL First All-Star Team (1994)

Signed as a free agent by **Tampa Bay**, July 8, 1999. Traded to **Ottawa** by **Tampa Bay** for future considerations, March 8, 2000.

SILLINGER, Mike

(sih-LIHN-juhr, MIGHK) **FLA.**

Center. Shoots right. 5'10", 190 lbs. Born, Regina, Sask., June 29, 1971. Detroit's 1st choice, 11th overall, in 1989 Entry Draft.

1986-87	Regina Kings	SAHA	31	83	51	134																				
1987-88	Regina Pats	WHL	67	18	25	43	17												4	2	2	4	0			
1988-89	Regina Pats	WHL	72	53	78	131	52																			
1989-90	Regina Pats	WHL	70	57	72	129	41												11	12	10	22	2			
	Adirondack	AHL																	1	0	0	0	0			
1990-91	Regina Pats	WHL	57	50	66	116	42												8	6	9	15	4			
	Detroit	**NHL**	**3**	**0**	**1**	**1**	**0**	**0**	**0**	**0**	**6**	**0.0**	**–2**						**3**	**0**	**1**	**1**	**0**	**0**	**0**	**0**
1991-92	Adirondack	AHL	64	25	41	66	26												15	9	*19	*28	12			
	Detroit	**NHL**																	**8**	**2**	**2**	**4**	**2**	**0**	**0**	**0**
1992-93	**Detroit**	**NHL**	**51**	**4**	**17**	**21**	**16**	**0**	**0**	**0**	**47**	**8.5**	**0**													
	Adirondack	AHL	15	10	20	30	31												11	5	13	18	10			
1993-94	**Detroit**	**NHL**	**62**	**8**	**21**	**29**	**10**	**0**	**1**	**1**	**91**	**8.8**	**2**													
1994-95	WEV Wien	Austria	13	13	14	27	10																			
	Detroit	**NHL**	**13**	**2**	**6**	**8**	**2**	**0**	**0**	**0**	**11**	**18.2**	**3**													
	Anaheim	**NHL**	**15**	**2**	**5**	**7**	**6**	**2**	**0**	**0**	**28**	**7.1**	**1**													
1995-96	**Anaheim**	**NHL**	**62**	**13**	**21**	**34**	**32**	**7**	**0**	**2**	**143**	**9.1**	**–20**													
	Vancouver	**NHL**	**12**	**1**	**3**	**4**	**6**	**0**	**1**	**0**	**16**	**6.3**	**2**						**6**	**0**	**0**	**0**	**2**	**0**	**0**	**0**
1996-97	**Vancouver**	**NHL**	**78**	**17**	**20**	**37**	**25**	**3**	**3**	**2**	**112**	**15.2**	**–3**													
1997-98	**Vancouver**	**NHL**	**48**	**10**	**9**	**19**	**34**	**1**	**2**	**1**	**56**	**17.9**	**–14**													
	Philadelphia	**NHL**	**27**	**11**	**11**	**22**	**16**	**1**	**2**	**0**	**40**	**27.5**	**3**						**3**	**1**	**0**	**1**	**0**	**0**	**0**	**0**
1998-99	**Philadelphia**	**NHL**	**25**	**0**	**3**	**3**	**8**	**0**	**0**	**0**	**23**	**0.0**	**–9**	**229**	**62.9**	**12**	**5**	**10:42**								
	Tampa Bay	**NHL**	**54**	**8**	**2**	**10**	**28**	**0**	**2**	**0**	**69**	**11.6**	**–20**	**320**	**57.8**	**70**	**35**	**13:57**								
99-2000	**Tampa Bay**	**NHL**	**67**	**19**	**25**	**44**	**86**	**6**	**3**	**1**	**126**	**15.1**	**–29**	**493**	**56.0**	**69**	**39**	**19:42**								
	Florida	**NHL**	**13**	**4**	**4**	**8**	**16**	**2**	**0**	**1**	**20**	**20.0**	**–1**	**248**	**61.3**	**15**	**14**	**19:33**	**4**	**2**	**1**	**3**	**2**	**0**	**0**	**0**
	NHL Totals		**530**	**99**	**148**	**247**	**285**	**22**	**14**	**8**	**788**	**12.6**		**1290**	**58.7**	**166**	**93**	**16:19**	**24**	**5**	**4**	**9**	**6**	**0**	**0**	**0**

WHL East Second All-Star Team (1990) • WHL East First All-Star Team (1991)

Traded to **Anaheim** by **Detroit** with Jason York for Stu Grimson, Mark Ferner and Anaheim's 6th round choice (Magnus Nilsson) in 1996 Entry Draft, April 4, 1995. Traded to **Vancouver** by **Anaheim** for Roman Oksiuta, March 15, 1996. Traded to **Philadelphia** by **Vancouver** for Philadelphia's 5th round choice (traded back to Philadelphia - Philadelphia selected Garrett Prosofsky) in 1998 Entry Draft, February 5, 1998. Traded to **Tampa Bay** by **Philadelphia** with Chris Gratton for Mikael Renberg and Daymond Langkow, December 12, 1998. Traded to **Florida** by **Tampa Bay** for Ryan Johnson and Dwayne Hay, March 14, 2000.

SIM, Jonathan

SIHM, JAW-nuh-thun) **DAL.**

Center. Shoots left. 5'10", 184 lbs. Born, New Glasgow, N.S., September 29, 1977. Dallas' 2nd choice, 70th overall, in 1996 Entry Draft.

1994-95	Laval Titan	QMJHL	9	0	1	1	6																			
	Sarnia Sting	OHL	25	9	12	21	19												4	3	2	5	2			
1995-96	Sarnia Sting	OHL	63	56	46	102	130												10	8	7	15	26			
1996-97	Sarnia Sting	OHL	64	*56	39	95	109												12	9	5	14	32			
1997-98	Sarnia Sting	OHL	59	44	50	94	95												5	1	4	5	14			
1998-99♦	**Dallas**	**NHL**	**7**	**1**	**0**	**1**	**12**	**0**	**0**	**0**	**8**	**12.5**	**1**	**6**	**50.0**	**15**	**0**	**11:26**	**4**	**0**	**0**	**0**	**0**	**0**	**0**	**0**

Season	Club	League	GP	G	A	Pts	PIM	PP	SH	GW	S	%	+/-	TF	F%	H	SB	Min	Playoffs GP	G	A	Pts	PIM	PP	SH	GW
	Michigan K-Wings	IHL	68	24	27	51	91												5	3	1	4	18			
99-2000	Michigan K-Wings	IHL	35	14	16	30	65																			
	Dallas	NHL	25	5	3	8	10	2	0	1	44	11.4	4	4	75.0	29	2	10:51	7	1	0	1	6	0	0	0
	NHL Totals		32	6	3	9	22	2	0	1	52	11.5		10	60.0	44	2	10:58	11	1	0	1	6	0	0	0

OHL Second All-Star Team (1998)

SIMON, Chris

(SIGH-mohn, KRIHS) **WSH.**

Left wing. Shoots left. 6'4", 235 lbs. Born, Wawa, Ont., January 30, 1972. Philadelphia's 2nd choice, 25th overall, in 1990 Entry Draft.

Season	Club	League	GP	G	A	Pts	PIM	PP	SH	GW	S	%	+/-	TF	F%	H	SB	Min	Playoffs GP	G	A	Pts	PIM	PP	SH	GW
1986-87	Wawa Flyers	OMHA	36	12	20	32	108																			
1987-88	S.S. Marie T-Birds	OMHA	55	42	36	78	172																			
1988-89	Ottawa 67's	OHL	36	4	2	6	31																			
1989-90	Ottawa 67's	OHL	57	36	38	74	146												3	2	1	3	4			
1990-91	Ottawa 67's	OHL	20	16	6	22	69												17	5	9	14	59			
1991-92	Ottawa 67's	OHL	2	1	1	2	24																			
	Sault Ste. Marie	OHL	31	19	25	44	143												11	5	8	13	49			
1992-93	Quebec	NHL	16	1	1	2	67	0	0	1	15	6.7	-2						5	0	0	0	26	0	0	0
	Halifax Citadels	AHL	36	12	6	18	131																			
1993-94	Quebec	NHL	37	4	4	8	132	0	0	1	39	10.3	-2													
1994-95	Quebec	NHL	29	3	9	12	106	0	0	0	33	9.1	14						6	1	1	2	19	0	0	1
1995-96♦	Colorado	NHL	64	16	18	34	250	4	0	1	105	15.2	10						12	1	2	3	11	0	0	0
1996-97	Washington	NHL	42	9	13	22	165	3	0	1	89	10.1	-1													
1997-98	Washington	NHL	28	7	10	17	38	4	0	1	71	9.9	-1						18	1	0	1	26	0	0	0
1998-99	Washington	NHL	23	3	7	10	48	0	0	0	29	10.3	-4	2	50.0	53	5	12:08								
99-2000	Washington	NHL	75	29	20	49	146	7	0	5	201	14.4	11	7	28.6	141	19	15:32	4	2	0	2	24	0	0	0
	NHL Totals		314	72	82	154	952	18	0	10	582	12.4		9	33.3	194	24	14:44	45	5	3	8	106	0	0	1

• Missed majority of 1990-91 season recovering from shoulder surgery, October, 1990. Traded to **Quebec** by **Philadelphia** with Philadelphia's 1st round choice (later traded to Toronto - later traded to Washington - Washington selected Nolan Baumgartner) in 1994 Entry Draft to complete transaction that sent Eric Lindros to Philadelphia (June 30, 1992), July 21, 1992. Transferred to **Colorado** after **Quebec** franchise relocated, June 21, 1995. Traded to **Washington** by **Colorado** with Curtis Leschyshyn for Keith Jones and Washington's 1st (Scott Parker) and 4th (later traded back to Washington - Washington selected Krys Barch) round choices in 1998 Entry Draft, November 2, 1996.

SIMON, Jason

(SIGH-mohn, JAY-suhn)

Left wing. Shoots left. 6'1", 210 lbs. Born, Sarnia, Ont., March 21, 1969. New Jersey's 9th choice, 215th overall, in 1989 Entry Draft.

Season	Club	League	GP	G	A	Pts	PIM	PP	SH	GW	S	%	+/-	TF	F%	H	SB	Min	Playoffs GP	G	A	Pts	PIM	PP	SH	GW
1985-86	Chatham	OJHL-B	32	5	19	24	118																			
1986-87	London Knights	OHL	33	1	2	3	33																			
	Sudbury Wolves	OHL	26	2	3	5	50																			
1987-88	Sudbury Wolves	OHL	26	5	7	12	35																			
	Hamilton Hawks	OHL	29	5	13	18	124												11	0	2	2	15			
1988-89	Kingston Raiders	OHL	17	7	12	19	58																			
	Windsor Spitfires	OHL	45	16	27	43	135												4	1	4	5	13			
1989-90	Utica Devils	AHL	16	3	4	7	28												2	0	0	0	12			
	Nashville Knights	ECHL	13	4	3	7	81												5	1	3	4	17			
1990-91	Utica Devils	AHL	50	2	12	14	189																			
	Johnstown Chiefs	ECHL	22	11	9	20	55																			
1991-92	Utica Devils	AHL	1	0	0	0	12																			
	San Diego Gulls	IHL	13	1	4	5	45												3	0	1	1	9			
1992-93	Detroit Falcons	ColHL	11	7	13	20	38																			
	Flint Generals	ColHL	44	17	32	49	202																			
1993-94	Salt Lake City	IHL	50	7	7	14	*323																			
	NY Islanders	NHL	4	0	0	0	34	0	0	0	0	0.0	0													
	Detroit Falcons	ColHL	13	9	16	25	87																			
1994-95	Denver Grizzlies	IHL	61	3	6	9	300												1	0	0	0	12			
1995-96	Springfield	AHL	18	2	2	4	90												7	1	0	1	26			
1996-97	Phoenix	NHL	1	0	0	0	0	0	0	0	0	0.0	-1													
	Las Vegas	IHL	64	4	3	7	402												3	0	0	0	0			
1997-98	Hershey Bears	AHL	26	0	1	1	170																			
	Quebec Rafales	IHL	30	6	3	9	127																			
1998-99	Colorado Kings	WCHL	60	16	23	39	419												3	1	1	2	17			
99-2000	Port Huron	UHL	45	21	22	43	118																			
	Louisville	AHL	11	1	0	1	28																			
	NHL Totals		5	0	0	0	34	0	0	0	0	0.0														

Signed as a free agent by **NY Islanders**, January 6, 1994. Signed as a free agent by **Winnipeg**, August 9, 1995. Transferred to **Phoenix** after **Winnipeg** franchise relocated, July 1, 1996. Signed as a free agent by **Colorado**, August 22, 1997.

SIMPSON, Reid

(SIHMP-sohn, REED) **ST.L.**

Left wing. Shoots left. 6'2", 220 lbs. Born, Flin Flon, Man., May 21, 1969. Philadelphia's 3rd choice, 72nd overall, in 1989 Entry Draft.

Season	Club	League	GP	G	A	Pts	PIM	PP	SH	GW	S	%	+/-	TF	F%	H	SB	Min	Playoffs GP	G	A	Pts	PIM	PP	SH	GW
1984-85	Flin Flon Selects	MAHA	50	60	70	130	100																			
1985-86	Flin Flon Bombers	MJHL	40	20	21	41	200																			
	New Westminster	WHL	2	0	0	0	0																			
1986-87	Prince Albert	WHL	47	3	8	11	105												8	2	3	5	13			
1987-88	Prince Albert	WHL	72	13	14	27	164												10	1	0	1	43			
1988-89	Prince Albert	WHL	59	26	29	55	264												4	2	1	3	30			
1989-90	Prince Albert	WHL	29	15	17	32	121												14	4	7	11	34			
	Hershey Bears	AHL	28	2	2	4	175																			
1990-91	Hershey Bears	AHL	54	9	15	24	183												1	0	0	0	0			
1991-92	Philadelphia	NHL	1	0	0	0	0	0	0	0	0	0.0	0													
	Hershey Bears	AHL	60	11	7	18	145																			
1992-93	Minnesota	NHL	1	0	0	0	5	0	0	0	0	0.0	0													
	Kalamazoo Wings	IHL	45	5	5	10	193																			
1993-94	Kalamazoo Wings	IHL	5	0	0	0	16																			
	Albany River Rats	AHL	37	9	5	14	135												5	1	1	2	18			
1994-95	Albany River Rats	AHL	70	18	25	43	268												14	1	8	9	13			
	New Jersey	NHL	9	0	0	0	27	0	0	0	5	0.0	-1													
1995-96	New Jersey	NHL	23	1	5	6	79	0	0	0	8	12.5	2													
	Albany River Rats	AHL	6	1	3	4	17																			
1996-97	New Jersey	NHL	27	0	4	4	60	0	0	0	17	0.0	0						5	0	0	0	29	0	0	0
	Albany River Rats	AHL	3	0	0	0	10																			
1997-98	New Jersey	NHL	6	0	0	0	16	0	0	0	5	0.0	-2													
	Chicago	NHL	38	3	2	5	102	1	0	0	19	15.8	-1													
1998-99	Chicago	NHL	53	5	4	9	145	1	0	0	23	21.7	2	5	40.0	37	1	5:56								
99-2000	Cleveland	IHL	12	2	2	4	56																			
	Tampa Bay	NHL	26	1	0	1	103	0	0	0	13	7.7	-3	1	100.0	30	5	4:33								
	NHL Totals		184	10	15	25	537	2	0	0	90	11.1		6	50.0	67	6	5:29	5	0	0	0	29	0	0	0

Signed as a free agent by **Minnesota**, December 14, 1992. Transferred to **Dallas** after **Minnesota** franchise relocated, June 9, 1993. Traded to **New Jersey** by **Dallas** with Roy Mitchell for future considerations, March 21, 1994. Traded to **Chicago** by **New Jersey** for Chicago's 4th round choice (Mikko Jokela) in 1998 Entry Draft and future considerations, January 8, 1998. Traded to **Tampa Bay** by **Chicago** with Bryan Muir for Michael Nylander, November 12, 1999. • Missed remainder of 1999-2000 season recovering from jaw injury suffered in game vs. NY Islanders, January 13, 2000. Signed as a free agent by **St. Louis**, August 24, 2000.

SIMPSON, Todd

(SIHMP-sohn, TAWD) **FLA.**

Defense. Shoots left. 6'3", 215 lbs. Born, North Vancouver, B.C., May 28, 1973.

			Regular Season																Playoffs							
Season	Club	League	GP	G	A	Pts	PIM	PP	SH	GW	S	%	+/-	TF	F%	H	SB	Min	GP	G	A	Pts	PIM	PP	SH	GW
1989-90	Don Mills Flyers	MTHL	42	36	48	84	36																			
1990-91	Port Colborne	OJHL-B	45	40	43	83	120																			
1991-92	Brown University	ECAC	18	1	4	5	38																			
1992-93	Tri-City Americans	WHL	69	5	18	23	196												4	0	0	0	13			
1993-94	Tri-City Americans	WHL	12	2	3	5	32																			
	Saskatoon Blades	WHL	51	7	19	26	175												16	1	5	6	42			
1994-95	Saint John Flames	AHL	80	3	10	13	321												5	0	0	0	4			
1995-96	**Calgary**	**NHL**	**6**	**0**	**0**	**0**	**32**	0	0	0	3	0.0	0													
	Saint John Flames	AHL	66	4	13	17	277												16	2	3	5	32			
1996-97	**Calgary**	**NHL**	**82**	**1**	**13**	**14**	**208**	0	0	0	85	1.2	–14													
1997-98	**Calgary**	**NHL**	**53**	**1**	**5**	**6**	**109**	0	0	1	51	2.0	–10													
1998-99	**Calgary**	**NHL**	**73**	**2**	**8**	**10**	**151**	0	0	0	52	3.8	18	1	100.0	91	62	17:19								
99-2000	**Florida**	**NHL**	**82**	**1**	**6**	**7**	**202**	0	0	0	50	2.0	5	0	0.0	112	77	16:35	4	0	0	0	4	0	0	0
	NHL Totals		**296**	**5**	**32**	**37**	**702**	0	0	1	241	2.1		1	100.0	203	139	16:56	4	0	0	0	4	0	0	0

Signed as free agent by **Calgary**, July 6, 1994. Traded to **Florida** by **Calgary** for Bill Lindsay, September 30, 1999.

SKALDE, Jarrod

(SKAHL-dee, JAIR-ruhd) **ATL.**

Center. Shoots left. 6', 185 lbs. Born, Niagara Falls, Ont., February 26, 1971. New Jersey's 3rd choice, 26th overall, in 1989 Entry Draft.

			Regular Season																Playoffs							
Season	Club	League	GP	G	A	Pts	PIM	PP	SH	GW	S	%	+/-	TF	F%	H	SB	Min	GP	G	A	Pts	PIM	PP	SH	GW
1986-87	Fort Erie Meteors	OJHL-B	41	27	34	61	36																			
1987-88	Oshawa Generals	OHL	60	12	16	28	24												7	2	1	3	2			
1988-89	Oshawa Generals	OHL	65	38	38	76	36												6	1	5	6	2			
1989-90	Oshawa Generals	OHL	62	40	52	92	66												17	10	7	17	6			
1990-91	Oshawa Generals	OHL	15	8	14	22	14																			
	Belleville Bulls	OHL	40	30	52	82	21												6	9	6	15	10			
	New Jersey	**NHL**	**1**	**0**	**1**	**1**	**0**	0	0	0	2	0.0	0													
	Utica Devils	AHL	3	3	2	5	0																			
1991-92	**New Jersey**	**NHL**	**15**	**2**	**4**	**6**	**4**	0	0	2	25	8.0	–1													
	Utica Devils	AHL	62	20	20	40	56												4	3	1	4	8			
1992-93	**New Jersey**	**NHL**	**11**	**0**	**2**	**2**	**4**	0	0	0	11	0.0	–3													
	Utica Devils	AHL	59	21	39	60	76												5	0	2	2	19			
	Cincinnati	IHL	4	1	2	3	4																			
1993-94	**Anaheim**	**NHL**	**20**	**5**	**4**	**9**	**10**	2	0	2	25	20.0	–3													
	San Diego Gulls	IHL	57	25	38	63	79												9	3	12	15	10			
1994-95	Las Vegas	IHL	74	34	41	75	103												9	2	4	6	8			
1995-96	Baltimore Bandits	AHL	11	2	6	8	55																			
	Calgary	**NHL**	**1**	**0**	**0**	**0**	**0**	0	0	0	0	0.0	0													
	Saint John Flames	AHL	68	27	40	67	98												16	4	9	13	6			
1996-97	Saint John Flames	AHL	65	32	36	68	94												3	0	0	0	14			
1997-98	**San Jose**	**NHL**	**22**	**4**	**6**	**10**	**14**	0	0	0	30	13.3	–2													
	Kentucky	AHL	6	2	6	8	10																			
	Chicago	**NHL**	**4**	**0**	**1**	**1**	**2**	0	0	0	4	0.0	0													
	Indianapolis Ice	IHL	2	0	2	2	0																			
	Dallas	**NHL**	**1**	**0**	**0**	**0**	**0**	0	0	0	0	0.0	0													
	Chicago	**NHL**	**3**	**0**	**0**	**0**	**2**	0	0	0	0	0.0	0													
	Kentucky	AHL	17	3	9	12	38												3	3	0	3	6			
1998-99	**San Jose**	**NHL**	**17**	**1**	**1**	**2**	**4**	0	0	0	17	5.9	–6	191	52.4	17	1	10:07								
	Kentucky	AHL	54	17	40	57	75												12	4	5	9	16			
99-2000	Utah Grizzlies	IHL	77	25	54	79	98												5	0	1	1	10			
	NHL Totals		**95**	**12**	**19**	**31**	**40**	2	0	4	114	10.5		191	52.4	17	1	10:07								

OHL Second All-Star Team (1991) • IHL First All-Star Team (2000)

Claimed by **Anaheim** from **New Jersey** in Expansion Draft, June 24, 1993. Traded to **Calgary** by **Anaheim** for Bobby Marshall, October 30, 1995. Signed as a free agent by **San Jose**, August 14, 1997. Claimed on waivers by **Chicago** from **San Jose**, January 8, 1998. Claimed on waivers by **San Jose** from **Chicago**, January 23, 1998. Claimed on waivers by **Dallas** from **San Jose**, January 27, 1998. Claimed on waivers by **Chicago** from **Dallas**, February 10, 1998. Claimed on waivers by **San Jose** from **Chicago**, March 6, 1998. Signed as a free agent by **Atlanta**, July 21, 2000.

SKOPINTSEV, Andrei

(skuh-PIHN-sehf, AWN-dray)

Defense. Shoots right. 6', 185 lbs. Born, Elekrostal, USSR, September 28, 1971. Tampa Bay's 7th choice, 153rd overall, in 1997 Entry Draft.

			Regular Season																Playoffs							
Season	Club	League	GP	G	A	Pts	PIM	PP	SH	GW	S	%	+/-	TF	F%	H	SB	Min	GP	G	A	Pts	PIM	PP	SH	GW
1989-90	Krylja Sovetov	USSR	20	0	0	0	10																			
1990-91	Krylja Sovetov	USSR	16	0	1	1	2																			
1991-92	Krylja Sovetov	CIS	36	1	1	2	14																			
1992-93	Krylja Sovetov	CIS	12	1	0	1	4												7	1	0	1	2			
1993-94	Krylja Sovetov	CIS	43	4	8	12	14												3	1	0	1	0			
1994-95	Krylja Sovetov	CIS	52	8	12	20	55												4	1	1	2	0			
1995-96	Augsburger EV	DEL	46	10	20	30	32												7	3	2	5	22			
1996-97	TPS Turku	Finland	46	3	6	9	80												10	1	1	2	4			
	TPS Turku	EuroHL	5	0	1	1	4																			
1997-98	TPS Turku	Finland	48	2	9	11	8												4	0	1	1	4			
	TPS Turku	EuroHL	5	0	1	1	4																			
1998-99	**Tampa Bay**	**NHL**	**19**	**1**	**1**	**2**	**10**	0	0	0	17	5.9	1	0	0.0	13	15	16:05								
	Cleveland	IHL	19	3	2	5	8																			
99-2000	**Tampa Bay**	**NHL**	**4**	**0**	**0**	**0**	**6**	0	0	0	0	0.0	–4	0	0.0	8	7	14:07								
	Detroit Vipers	IHL	51	4	15	19	44																			
	NHL Totals		**23**	**1**	**1**	**2**	**16**	0	0	0	17	5.9		0	0.0	21	22	15:44								

SKOULA, Martin

(SHKOH-la, MAHR-tihn) **COL.**

Defense. Shoots left. 6'2", 195 lbs. Born, Litomerice, Czech., October 28, 1979. Colorado's 2nd choice, 17th overall, in 1998 Entry Draft.

			Regular Season																Playoffs							
Season	Club	League	GP	G	A	Pts	PIM	PP	SH	GW	S	%	+/-	TF	F%	H	SB	Min	GP	G	A	Pts	PIM	PP	SH	GW
1995-96	CHZ Litvinov-Jr.	Cze-Rep	38	0	4	4																				
	CHZ Litvinov	Cze-Rep																	1	0	0	0	0			
1996-97	CHZ Litvinov-Jr.	Cze-Rep	38	2	9	11																				
	CHZ Litvinov	Cze-Rep	1	0	0	0	0																			
1997-98	Barrie Colts	OHL	66	8	36	44	36												6	1	3	4	4			
1998-99	Barrie Colts	OHL	67	13	46	59	46												12	3	10	13	13			
	Hershey Bears	AHL																	1	0	0	0	0			
99-2000	**Colorado**	**NHL**	**80**	**3**	**13**	**16**	**20**	2	0	0	66	4.5	5	0	0.0	100	45	18:15	17	0	2	2	4	0	0	0
	NHL Totals		**80**	**3**	**13**	**16**	**20**	2	0	0	66	4.5		0	0.0	100	45	18:15	17	0	2	2	4	0	0	0

OHL Second All-Star Team (1999)

SKRASTINS, Karlis

(SKRAS-tinsh, kar-LIHS) **NSH.**

Defense. Shoots left. 6'1", 208 lbs. Born, Riga, USSR, July 9, 1974. Nashville's 8th choice, 230th overall, in 1998 Entry Draft.

			Regular Season																Playoffs							
Season	Club	League	GP	G	A	Pts	PIM	PP	SH	GW	S	%	+/-	TF	F%	H	SB	Min	GP	G	A	Pts	PIM	PP	SH	GW
1992-93	Pardaugava Riga	CIS	40	3	5	8	16												2	0	0	0	0			
1993-94	Pardaugava Riga	CIS	42	7	5	12	18												2	1	0	1	4			
1994-95	Pardaugava Riga	CIS	52	4	14	18	69																			
1995-96	TPS Turku	Finland	50	4	11	15	32												11	2	2	4	10			
1996-97	TPS Turku	Finland	50	2	8	10	20												12	0	4	4	2			
	TPS Turku	EuroHL	6	0	1	1	4												4	0	0	0	14			
1997-98	TPS Turku	Finland	48	4	15	19	67												4	0	0	0	0			
	TPS Turku	EuroHL	6	0	1	1	6																			
1998-99	**Nashville**	**NHL**	**2**	**0**	**1**	**1**	**0**	0	0	0	0	0.0	0	0	0.0	1	1	11:47								
	Milwaukee	IHL	75	8	36	44	47												2	0	1	1	2			

			Regular Season																Playoffs							
Season	Club	League	GP	G	A	Pts	PIM	PP	SH	GW	S	%	+/-	TF	F%	H	SB	Min	GP	G	A	Pts	PIM	PP	SH	GW
99-2000	Nashville	NHL	59	5	6	11	20	1	0	2	51	9.8	–7	0	0.0	104	110	20:51	....	....	....	....	....	....	....	....
	Milwaukee	IHL	19	3	8	11	10	....	....	....	....	....	....	....	....	....	....	....	....	....	....	....	....	....	....	....
	NHL Totals		61	5	7	12	20	1	0	2	51	9.8		0	0.0	105	111	20:33	....	....	....	....	....	....	....	....

SKRBEK, Pavel

(skuhr-BEHK, PAH-vehl) **NSH.**

Defense. Shoots left. 6'3", 215 lbs. Born, Kladno, Czech., August 9, 1978. Pittsburgh's 2nd choice, 28th overall, in 1996 Entry Draft.

			Regular Season																Playoffs							
Season	Club	League	GP	G	A	Pts	PIM	PP	SH	GW	S	%	+/-	TF	F%	H	SB	Min	GP	G	A	Pts	PIM	PP	SH	GW
1994-95	Poldi Kladno-Jr.	Cze-Rep	29	7	6	13	....	....	....	....	....	....	....	....	....	....	....	....	....	....	....	....	....	....	....	....
1995-96	Poldi Kladno-Jr.	Cze-Rep	29	10	12	22	....	....	....	....	....	....	....	....	....	....	....	....	....	....	....	....	....	....	....	....
	Poldi Kladno	Cze-Rep	13	0	1	1	....	....	....	....	....	....	....	....	....	....	....	....	5	0	0	0	....	....	....	....
1996-97	Poldi Kladno	Cze-Rep	35	1	5	6	26	....	....	....	....	....	....	....	....	....	....	....	3	0	0	0	4	....	....	....
1997-98	Poldi Kladno	Cze-Rep	47	4	10	14	126	....	....	....	....	....	....	....	....	....	....	....	....	....	....	....	....	....	....	....
1998-99	Pittsburgh	NHL	4	0	0	0	2	0	0	0	1	0.0	2	0	0.0	6	3	14:21	....	....	....	....	....	....	....	....
	Syracuse Crunch	AHL	64	6	16	22	38	....	....	....	....	....	....	....	....	....	....	....	....	....	....	....	....	....	....	....
99-2000	Wilkes-Barre	AHL	51	7	16	23	50	....	....	....	....	....	....	....	....	....	....	....	....	....	....	....	....	....	....	....
	Milwaukee	IHL	6	0	0	0	0	....	....	....	....	....	....	....	....	....	....	....	....	....	....	....	....	....	....	....
	NHL Totals		4	0	0	0	2	0	0	0	1	0.0		0	0.0	6	3	14:21	....	....	....	....	....	....	....	....

Traded to **Nashville** by **Pittsburgh** for Bob Boughner, March 13, 2000.

SKRUDLAND, Brian

(SKROOD-luhnd, BRIGH-an)

Center. Shoots left. 6', 195 lbs. Born, Peace River, Alta., July 31, 1963.

			Regular Season																Playoffs							
Season	Club	League	GP	G	A	Pts	PIM	PP	SH	GW	S	%	+/-	TF	F%	H	SB	Min	GP	G	A	Pts	PIM	PP	SH	GW
1980-81	Saskatoon Blades	WHL	66	15	27	42	97	....	....	....	....	....	....	....	....	....	....	....	....	....	....	....	....	....	....	....
1981-82	Saskatoon Blades	WHL	71	27	29	56	135	....	....	....	....	....	....	....	....	....	....	....	5	0	1	1	2	....	....	....
1982-83	Saskatoon Blades	WHL	71	35	59	94	42	....	....	....	....	....	....	....	....	....	....	....	6	1	3	4	19	....	....	....
1983-84	Nova Scotia	AHL	56	13	12	25	55	....	....	....	....	....	....	....	....	....	....	....	12	2	8	10	14	....	....	....
1984-85	Sherbrooke	AHL	70	22	28	50	109	....	....	....	....	....	....	....	....	....	....	....	17	9	8	17	23	....	....	....
1985-86♦	Montreal	NHL	65	9	13	22	57	0	2	0	62	14.5	3	....	....	....	....	....	20	2	4	6	76	0	0	1
1986-87	Montreal	NHL	79	11	17	28	107	0	1	0	72	15.3	18	....	....	....	....	....	14	1	5	6	29	0	0	0
1987-88	Montreal	NHL	79	12	24	36	112	0	1	3	96	12.5	14	....	....	....	....	....	11	1	5	6	24	0	0	0
1988-89	Montreal	NHL	71	12	29	41	84	1	1	5	98	12.2	22	....	....	....	....	....	21	3	7	10	40	0	0	0
1989-90	Montreal	NHL	59	11	31	42	56	4	0	1	70	15.7	21	....	....	....	....	....	11	3	5	8	30	0	0	1
1990-91	Montreal	NHL	57	15	19	34	85	1	1	2	71	21.1	12	....	....	....	....	....	13	3	10	13	42	1	0	0
1991-92	Montreal	NHL	42	3	3	6	36	0	0	1	51	5.9	–4	....	....	....	....	....	11	1	1	2	20	0	0	0
1992-93	Montreal	NHL	23	5	3	8	55	0	2	1	29	17.2	1	....	....	....	....	....	....	....	....	....	....	....	....	....
	Calgary	NHL	16	2	4	6	10	0	0	0	22	9.1	3	....	....	....	....	....	6	0	3	3	12	0	0	0
1993-94	Florida	NHL	79	15	25	40	136	0	2	1	110	13.6	13	....	....	....	....	....	....	....	....	....	....	....	....	....
1994-95	Florida	NHL	47	5	9	14	88	1	0	0	44	11.4	0	....	....	....	....	....	....	....	....	....	....	....	....	....
1995-96	Florida	NHL	79	7	20	27	129	0	1	1	90	7.8	6	....	....	....	....	....	21	1	3	4	18	0	0	0
1996-97	Florida	NHL	51	5	13	18	48	0	0	2	57	8.8	4	....	....	....	....	....	....	....	....	....	....	....	....	....
1997-98	NY Rangers	NHL	59	5	6	11	39	0	0	1	42	11.9	–4	....	....	....	....	....	....	....	....	....	....	....	....	....
	Dallas	NHL	13	2	0	2	10	0	0	0	13	15.4	–2	....	....	....	....	....	17	0	1	1	16	0	0	0
1998-99♦	Dallas	NHL	40	4	1	5	33	0	0	1	33	12.1	2	274	44.5	37	12	9:25	19	0	2	2	16	0	0	0
99-2000	Dallas	NHL	22	1	2	3	22	0	0	0	16	6.3	0	195	58.0	20	8	8:24	....	....	....	....	....	....	....	....
	NHL Totals		881	124	219	343	1107	7	11	19	976	12.7		469	50.1	57	20	9:04	164	15	46	61	323	1	0	2

Won Jack A. Butterfield Trophy (Playoff MVP - AHL) (1985)

Signed as a free agent by **Montreal**, September 13, 1983. Traded to **Calgary** by **Montreal** for Gary Leeman, January 28, 1993. Claimed by **Florida** from **Calgary** in Expansion Draft, June 24, 1993. Signed as a free agent by **NY Rangers**, August 21, 1997. Traded to **Dallas** by **NY Rangers** with Mike Keane and NY Rangers' 6th round choice (Pavel Patera) in 1998 Entry Draft for Todd Harvey, Bob Errey and Dallas' 4th round choice (Boyd Kane) in 1998 Entry Draft, March 24, 1998. • Missed majority of 1999-2000 season recovering from rib injury originally suffered in game vs. Anaheim, October 8, 1999.

SLANEY, John

(SLAY-nee, JAWN) **PIT.**

Defense. Shoots left. 6', 189 lbs. Born, St. John's, Nfld., February 2, 1972. Washington's 1st choice, 9th overall, in 1990 Entry Draft.

			Regular Season																Playoffs							
Season	Club	League	GP	G	A	Pts	PIM	PP	SH	GW	S	%	+/-	TF	F%	H	SB	Min	GP	G	A	Pts	PIM	PP	SH	GW
1987-88	St. John's Caps	NFAHA	65	41	69	110	70	....	....	....	....	....	....	....	....	....	....	....	....	....	....	....	....	....	....	....
1988-89	Cornwall Royals	OHL	66	16	43	59	23	....	....	....	....	....	....	....	....	....	....	....	18	8	16	24	10	....	....	....
1989-90	Cornwall Royals	OHL	64	38	59	97	68	....	....	....	....	....	....	....	....	....	....	....	6	0	8	8	11	....	....	....
1990-91	Cornwall Royals	OHL	34	21	25	46	28	....	....	....	....	....	....	....	....	....	....	....	....	....	....	....	....	....	....	....
1991-92	Cornwall Royals	OHL	34	19	41	60	43	....	....	....	....	....	....	....	....	....	....	....	6	3	8	11	0	....	....	....
	Baltimore	AHL	6	2	4	6	0	....	....	....	....	....	....	....	....	....	....	....	....	....	....	....	....	....	....	....
1992-93	Baltimore	AHL	79	20	46	66	60	....	....	....	....	....	....	....	....	....	....	....	7	0	7	7	8	....	....	....
1993-94	Washington	NHL	47	7	9	16	27	3	0	1	70	10.0	3	....	....	....	....	....	11	1	1	2	2	1	0	0
	Portland Pirates	AHL	29	14	13	27	17	....	....	....	....	....	....	....	....	....	....	....	....	....	....	....	....	....	....	....
1994-95	Washington	NHL	16	0	3	3	6	0	0	0	21	0.0	–3	....	....	....	....	....	....	....	....	....	....	....	....	....
	Portland Pirates	AHL	8	3	10	13	4	....	....	....	....	....	....	....	....	....	....	....	7	1	3	4	4	....	....	....
1995-96	Colorado	NHL	7	0	3	3	4	0	0	0	12	0.0	2	....	....	....	....	....	....	....	....	....	....	....	....	....
	Cornwall Aces	AHL	5	0	4	4	2	....	....	....	....	....	....	....	....	....	....	....	....	....	....	....	....	....	....	....
	Los Angeles	NHL	31	6	11	17	10	3	1	0	63	9.5	5	....	....	....	....	....	....	....	....	....	....	....	....	....
1996-97	Los Angeles	NHL	32	3	11	14	4	1	0	1	60	5.0	–10	....	....	....	....	....	....	....	....	....	....	....	....	....
	Phoenix	IHL	35	9	25	34	8	....	....	....	....	....	....	....	....	....	....	....	....	....	....	....	....	....	....	....
1997-98	Phoenix	NHL	55	3	14	17	24	1	0	1	74	4.1	–3	....	....	....	....	....	....	....	....	....	....	....	....	....
	Las Vegas	IHL	5	2	2	4	10	....	....	....	....	....	....	....	....	....	....	....	....	....	....	....	....	....	....	....
1998-99	Nashville	NHL	46	2	12	14	14	0	0	1	84	2.4	–12	0	0.0	54	49	20:39	....	....	....	....	....	....	....	....
	Milwaukee	IHL	7	0	1	1	0	....	....	....	....	....	....	....	....	....	....	....	....	....	....	....	....	....	....	....
99-2000	Pittsburgh	NHL	29	1	4	5	10	1	0	0	27	3.7	–10	35	40.0	22	8	12:13	2	1	0	1	2	1	0	0
	Wilkes-Barre	AHL	49	30	30	60	25	....	....	....	....	....	....	....	....	....	....	....	....	....	....	....	....	....	....	....
	NHL Totals		263	22	67	89	99	9	1	4	411	5.4		35	40.0	76	57	17:23	13	2	1	3	4	2	0	0

OHL First All-Star Team (1990) • Canadian Major Junior Defenseman of the Year (1990) • OHL Second All-Star Team (1991)

Traded to **Colorado** by **Washington** for Philadelphia's 3rd round choice (previously acquired, Washington selected Shawn McNeil) in 1996 Entry Draft, July 12, 1995. Traded to **LA Kings** by **Colorado** for Winnipeg's 6th round choice (previously acquired, Colorado selected Brian Willsie) in 1996 Entry Draft, December 28, 1995. Signed as a free agent by **Phoenix**, August 19, 1997. Claimed by **Nashville** from **Phoenix** in Expansion Draft, June 26, 1998. Signed as a free agent by **Pittsburgh**, September 30, 1999.

SLEGR, Jiri

(SLAY-guhr, YOO-ree) **PIT.**

Defense. Shoots left. 6', 216 lbs. Born, Jihlava, Czech., May 30, 1971. Vancouver's 3rd choice, 23rd overall, in 1990 Entry Draft.

			Regular Season																Playoffs							
Season	Club	League	GP	G	A	Pts	PIM	PP	SH	GW	S	%	+/-	TF	F%	H	SB	Min	GP	G	A	Pts	PIM	PP	SH	GW
1987-88	CHZ Litvinov	Czech.	4	1	1	2	0	....	....	....	....	....	....	....	....	....	....	....	....	....	....	....	....	....	....	....
1988-89	CHZ Litvinov	Czech.	8	0	0	0	4	....	....	....	....	....	....	....	....	....	....	....	....	....	....	....	....	....	....	....
1989-90	CHZ Litvinov	Czech.	51	4	15	19	....	....	....	....	....	....	....	....	....	....	....	....	....	....	....	....	....	....	....	....
1990-91	CHZ Litvinov	Czech.	47	11	36	47	26	....	....	....	....	....	....	....	....	....	....	....	....	....	....	....	....	....	....	....
1991-92	CHZ Litvinov	Czech.	42	9	23	32	38	....	....	....	....	....	....	....	....	....	....	....	....	....	....	....	....	....	....	....
	Czechoslovakia	Olympics	8	1	1	2	14	....	....	....	....	....	....	....	....	....	....	....	....	....	....	....	....	....	....	....
1992-93	Vancouver	NHL	41	4	22	26	109	2	0	0	89	4.5	16	....	....	....	....	....	5	0	3	3	4	0	0	0
	Hamilton Canucks	AHL	21	4	14	18	42	....	....	....	....	....	....	....	....	....	....	....	....	....	....	....	....	....	....	....
1993-94	Vancouver	NHL	78	5	33	38	86	1	0	0	160	3.1	0	....	....	....	....	....	....	....	....	....	....	....	....	....
1994-95	CHZ Litvinov	Cze-Rep	11	3	10	13	80	....	....	....	....	....	....	....	....	....	....	....	....	....	....	....	....	....	....	....
	Vancouver	NHL	19	1	5	6	32	0	0	1	42	2.4	0	....	....	....	....	....	....	....	....	....	....	....	....	....
	Edmonton	NHL	12	1	5	6	14	1	0	0	27	3.7	–5	....	....	....	....	....	....	....	....	....	....	....	....	....
1995-96	Edmonton	NHL	57	4	13	17	74	0	1	1	91	4.4	–1	....	....	....	....	....	....	....	....	....	....	....	....	....
	Cape Breton	AHL	4	1	2	3	4	....	....	....	....	....	....	....	....	....	....	....	....	....	....	....	....	....	....	....
1996-97	CHZ Litvinov	Cze-Rep	1	0	0	0	0	....	....	....	....	....	....	....	....	....	....	....	....	....	....	....	....	....	....	....
	Sodertalje SK	Sweden	30	4	14	18	62	....	....	....	....	....	....	....	....	....	....	....	....	....	....	....	....	....	....	....
	Sodertalje SK	Swede-Q	10	4	2	6	32	....	....	....	....	....	....	....	....	....	....	....	....	....	....	....	....	....	....	....
1997-98	Pittsburgh	NHL	73	5	12	17	109	1	1	0	131	3.8	10	....	....	....	....	....	6	0	4	4	2	0	0	0
	Czech-Republic	Olympics	6	1	0	1	8	....	....	....	....	....	....	....	....	....	....	....	....	....	....	....	....	....	....	....

Season	Club	League	GP	G	A	Pts	PIM	PP	SH	GW	S	%	+/-	TF	F%	H	SB	Min	GP	G	A	Pts	PIM	PP	SH	GW
																	Regular Season						Playoffs			
1998-99	Pittsburgh	NHL	63	3	20	23	86	1	0	0	91	3.3	13	2	0.0	78	59	18:42	13	1	3	4	12	0	0	1
99-2000	Pittsburgh	NHL	74	11	20	31	82	0	0	2	144	7.6	20	3	66.7	106	66	21:22	10	2	3	5	19	0	0	1
	NHL Totals		417	34	130	164	592	6	2	4	775	4.4		5	40.0	184	125	20:08	34	3	13	16	37	0	0	2

Czechoslovakian First All-Star Team (1991)
Traded to **Edmonton** by **Vancouver** for Roman Oksiuta, April 7, 1995. Traded to **Pittsburgh** by **Edmonton** for Pittsburgh's 3rd round choice (later traded to New Jersey — New Jersey selected Brian Gionta) in 1998 Entry Draft, August 12, 1997.

SLOAN, Blake

(SLOHN, BLAYK)   **DAL.**

Right wing. Shoots right. 5'10", 196 lbs.   Born, Park Ridge, IL, July 27, 1975.

Season	Club	League	GP	G	A	Pts	PIM	PP	SH	GW	S	%	+/-	TF	F%	H	SB	Min	GP	G	A	Pts	PIM	PP	SH	GW
1992-93	Tabor Academy	Hi-School	33	7	15	22	....																			
1993-94	U. of Michigan	CCHA	38	2	4	6	48																			
1994-95	U. of Michigan	CCHA	39	2	15	17	60																			
1995-96	U. of Michigan	CCHA	41	6	24	30	55																			
1996-97	U. of Michigan	CCHA	41	2	15	17	52																			
1997-98	Houston Aeros	IHL	70	2	13	15	86												2	0	0	0	0			
1998-99 ◆	Dallas	NHL	14	0	0	0	10	0	0	0	7	0.0	–1	0	0.0	27	3	9:01	19	0	2	2	8	0	0	0
	Houston Aeros	IHL	62	8	10	18	76																			
99-2000	Dallas	NHL	67	4	13	17	50	0	0	1	78	5.1	11	2	50.0	165	25	13:30	16	0	0	0	12	0	0	0
	NHL Totals		81	4	13	17	60	0	0	1	85	4.7		2	50.0	192	28	12:43	35	0	2	2	20	0	0	0

Signed as a free agent by **Dallas**, March 10, 1998.

SMEHLIK, Richard

(SHMEH-lihk, RIH-chahrd)   **BUF.**

Defense. Shoots left. 6'4", 222 lbs.   Born, Ostrava, Czech., January 23, 1970. Buffalo's 3rd choice, 97th overall, in 1990 Entry Draft.

Season	Club	League	GP	G	A	Pts	PIM	PP	SH	GW	S	%	+/-	TF	F%	H	SB	Min	GP	G	A	Pts	PIM	PP	SH	GW
1988-89	TJ Vitkovice	Czech.	38	2	5	7	12												7	1	1	2	4			
1989-90	TJ Vitkovice	Czech.	44	4	3	7	....																			
1990-91	Dukla Jihlava	Czech.	58	4	3	7	22																			
1991-92	TJ Vitkovice	Czech.	47	9	10	19	42																			
	Czechoslovakia	Olympics	8	0	1	1	2																			
1992-93	Buffalo	NHL	80	4	27	31	59	0	0	0	82	4.9	9						8	0	4	4	2	0	0	0
1993-94	Buffalo	NHL	84	14	27	41	69	3	3	1	106	13.2	22						7	0	2	2	10	0	0	0
1994-95	HC Vitkovice	Cze-Rep	13	5	2	7	12																			
	Buffalo	NHL	39	4	7	11	46	0	1	1	49	8.2	5						5	0	0	0	2	0	0	0
1995-96	Buffalo	NHL	DID NOT PLAY – INJURED																							
1996-97	Buffalo	NHL	62	11	19	30	43	2	0	1	100	11.0	19						12	0	2	2	4	0	0	0
1997-98	Buffalo	NHL	72	3	17	20	62	0	1	0	90	3.3	11						15	0	2	2	6	0	0	0
	Czech-Republic	Olympics	6	0	1	1	4																			
1998-99	Buffalo	NHL	72	3	11	14	44	0	0	0	61	4.9	–9	0	0.0	107	87	21:50	21	0	3	3	10	0	0	0
99-2000	Buffalo	NHL	64	2	9	11	50	0	0	0	67	3.0	13	0	0.0	65	52	21:04	5	1	0	1	0	0	0	0
	NHL Totals		473	41	117	158	373	5	5	3	555	7.4		0	0.0	172	139	21:29	73	1	13	14	34	0	0	0

• Missed entire 1995-96 season recovering from knee surgery, August 11, 1995.

SMITH, Brandon

(SMIHTH, BRAN-dohn)   **BOS.**

Defense. Shoots left. 6'1", 198 lbs.   Born, Hazelton, B.C., February 25, 1973.

Season	Club	League	GP	G	A	Pts	PIM	PP	SH	GW	S	%	+/-	TF	F%	H	SB	Min	GP	G	A	Pts	PIM	PP	SH	GW
1989-90	Portland	WHL	59	2	17	19	16																			
1990-91	Portland	WHL	17	8	5	13	8																			
1991-92	Portland	WHL	70	12	32	44	63												16	4	9	13	6			
1992-93	Portland	WHL	72	20	54	74	38												10	2	10	12	8			
1993-94	Portland	WHL	72	19	63	82	47												4	2	3	5	0			
1994-95	Dayton Bombers	ECHL	60	16	49	65	57																			
	Minnesota Moose	IHL	1	0	0	0	0												3	0	0	0	0			
	Adirondack	AHL	14	1	2	3	7												3	0	1	1	2			
1995-96	Adirondack	AHL	48	4	13	17	22												4	0	0	0	0			
1996-97	Adirondack	AHL	80	8	26	34	30												1	0	1	1	0			
1997-98	Adirondack	AHL	64	9	27	36	26																			
1998-99	Boston	NHL	5	0	0	0	0	0	0	0	2	0.0	2	0	0.0	9	2	9:38								
	Providence Bruins	AHL	72	16	46	62	32												19	1	9	10	12			
99-2000	Boston	NHL	22	2	4	6	10	0	0	0	24	8.3	–4	0	0.0	28	25	19:29								
	Providence Bruins	AHL	55	8	30	38	20												14	1	11	12	2			
	NHL Totals		27	2	4	6	10	0	0	0	26	7.7		0	0.0	37	27	17:39								

WHL West Second All-Star Team (1993, 1994) • ECHL First All-Star Team (1995) • Top Defenseman - ECHL (1995) • AHL First All-Star Team (1999)
Signed as a free agent by **Detroit**, July 22, 1997. Signed as a free agent by **Boston**, August 5, 1998.

SMITH, D.J.

(SMIHTH, DEE-JAY)   **TOR.**

Defense. Shoots left. 6'2", 205 lbs.   Born, Windsor, Ont., May 13, 1977. NY Islanders' 3rd choice, 41st overall, in 1995 Entry Draft.

Season	Club	League	GP	G	A	Pts	PIM	PP	SH	GW	S	%	+/-	TF	F%	H	SB	Min	GP	G	A	Pts	PIM	PP	SH	GW
1992-93	Belle River	OJHL-C	40	5	18	23	39																			
	Windsor Bulldogs	OJHL-B	1	0	0	0	0																			
1993-94	Windsor Bulldogs	OJHL-B	51	8	34	42	267												10	1	3	4	41			
1994-95	Windsor Spitfires	OHL	61	4	13	17	201												7	1	7	8	23			
1995-96	Windsor Spitfires	OHL	64	14	45	59	260																			
	St. John's Leafs	AHL	1	0	0	0	0												5	1	7	8	11			
1996-97	Windsor Spitfires	OHL	63	15	52	67	190																			
	Toronto	NHL	8	0	1	1	7	0	0	0	4	0.0	–5						1	0	0	0	0			
1997-98	St. John's Leafs	AHL	65	4	11	15	237												4	0	0	0	4			
1998-99	St. John's Leafs	AHL	79	7	28	35	216												5	0	1	1	0			
99-2000	Toronto	NHL	3	0	0	0	5	0	0	0	2	0.0	–1	0	0.0	7	1	12:37								
	St. John's Leafs	AHL	74	6	22	28	197																			
	NHL Totals		11	0	1	1	12	0	0	0	6	0.0		0	0.0	7	1	12:37								

OHL Second All-Star Team (1997)
Traded to **Toronto** by **NY Islanders** with Wendel Clark and Mathieu Schneider for Darby Hendrickson, Sean Haggerty, Kenny Jonsson and Toronto's 1st round choice (Roberto Luongo) in 1997 Entry Draft, March 13, 1996.

SMITH, Dan

(SMIHTH, DAN)   **COL.**

Defense. Shoots left. 6'2", 200 lbs.   Born, Fernie, B.C., October 19, 1976. Colorado's 7th choice, 181st overall, in 1995 Entry Draft.

Season	Club	League	GP	G	A	Pts	PIM	PP	SH	GW	S	%	+/-	TF	F%	H	SB	Min	GP	G	A	Pts	PIM	PP	SH	GW
1994-95	U.B.C. T-Birds	CWUAA	28	1	3	4	26												11	1	3	4	14			
1995-96	Tri-City Americans	WHL	58	1	21	22	70												15	0	1	1	25			
1996-97	Tri-City Americans	WHL	72	5	19	24	174												6	0	0	0	4			
	Hershey Bears	AHL	8	0	1	1	6																			
1997-98	Hershey Bears	AHL	50	1	2	3	71																			
1998-99	Colorado	NHL	12	0	0	0	9	0	0	0	6	0.0	5	0	0.0	3	11	12:14	5	0	1	1	0			
	Hershey Bears	AHL	54	5	7	12	72																			
99-2000	Colorado	NHL	3	0	0	0	0	0	0	0	0	0.0	2	0	0.0	1	1	11:03								
	Hershey Bears	AHL	49	7	15	22	56																			
	NHL Totals		15	0	0	0	9	0	0	0	6	0.0		0	0.0	4	12	11:60								

SMITH, Jason (SMIHTH, JAY-suhn) EDM.

Defense. Shoots right. 6'3", 210 lbs. Born, Calgary, Alta., November 2, 1973. New Jersey's 1st choice, 18th overall, in 1992 Entry Draft.

			Regular Season																Playoffs							
Season	Club	League	GP	G	A	Pts	PIM	PP	SH	GW	S	%	+/-	TF	F%	H	SB	Min	GP	G	A	Pts	PIM	PP	SH	GW
1990-91	Calgary Canucks	AJHL	45	3	15	18	69	....	....	....	....	....	....	....	....	....	....	....	....	....	....	....	....	....	....	....
	Regina Pats	WHL	2	0	0	0	7	....	....	....	....	....	....	....	....	....	....	....	4	0	0	0	2	....	....	....
1991-92	Regina Pats	WHL	62	9	29	38	138	....	....	....	....	....	....	....	....	....	....	....	....	....	....	....	....	....	....	....
1992-93	Regina Pats	WHL	64	14	52	66	175	....	....	....	....	....	....	....	....	....	....	....	13	4	8	12	39	....	....	....
	Utica Devils	AHL	....	....	....	....	....	....	....	....	....	....	....	....	....	....	....	....	1	0	0	0	2	....	....	....
1993-94	New Jersey	NHL	41	0	5	5	43	0	0	0	47	0.0	7	....	....	....	....	....	6	0	0	0	7	0	0	0
	Albany River Rats	AHL	20	6	3	9	31	....	....	....	....	....	....	....	....	....	....	....	....	....	....	....	....	....	....	....
1994-95	New Jersey	NHL	2	0	0	0	0	0	0	0	5	0.0	–3	....	....	....	....	....	....	....	....	....	....	....	....	....
	Albany River Rats	AHL	7	0	2	2	15	....	....	....	....	....	....	....	....	....	....	....	11	2	2	4	19	....	....	....
1995-96	New Jersey	NHL	64	2	1	3	86	0	0	0	52	3.8	5	....	....	....	....	....	....	....	....	....	....	....	....	....
1996-97	New Jersey	NHL	57	1	2	3	38	0	0	0	48	2.1	–8	....	....	....	....	....	....	....	....	....	....	....	....	....
	Toronto	NHL	21	0	5	5	16	0	0	0	26	0.0	–4	....	....	....	....	....	....	....	....	....	....	....	....	....
1997-98	Toronto	NHL	81	3	13	16	100	0	0	0	97	3.1	–5	....	....	....	....	....	....	....	....	....	....	....	....	....
1998-99	Toronto	NHL	60	2	11	13	40	0	0	0	53	3.8	–9	0	0.0	113	67	17:31	....	....	....	....	....	....	....	....
	Edmonton	NHL	12	1	1	2	11	0	0	0	15	6.7	0	0	0.0	35	26	20:26	4	0	1	1	4	0	0	0
99-2000	Edmonton	NHL	80	3	11	14	60	0	0	1	96	3.1	16	1	100.0	260	167	21:15	5	0	1	1	4	0	0	0
	NHL Totals		418	12	49	61	394	0	0	1	439	2.7		1	100.0	408	260	19:43	15	0	2	2	15	0	0	0

WHL East First All-Star Team (1993) • Canadian Major Junior First All-Star Team (1993)

Traded to **Toronto** by **New Jersey** with Steve Sullivan and the rights to Alyn McCauley for Doug Gilmour, Dave Ellett and New Jersey's 4th round choice (previously acquired, New Jersey selected Andre Lakps) in 1999 Entry Draft, February 25, 1997. Traded to **Edmonton** by **Toronto** for Edmonton's 4th round choice (Jonathon Zion) in 1999 Entry Draft and 2nd round choice (Kris Vernarsky) in 2000 Entry Draft, March 23, 1999.

SMITH, Steve (SMIHTH, STEEV) CGY.

Defense. Shoots left. 6'4", 215 lbs. Born, Glasgow, Scotland, April 30, 1963. Edmonton's 5th choice, 111th overall, in 1981 Entry Draft.

			Regular Season																Playoffs							
Season	Club	League	GP	G	A	Pts	PIM	PP	SH	GW	S	%	+/-	TF	F%	H	SB	Min	GP	G	A	Pts	PIM	PP	SH	GW
1979-80	Fergus Green	OHA-D	23	10	14	24	40	....	....	....	....	....	....	....	....	....	....	....	....	....	....	....	....	....	....	....
1980-81	London Knights	OMJHL	62	4	12	16	141	....	....	....	....	....	....	....	....	....	....	....	....	....	....	....	....	....	....	....
1981-82	London Knights	OHL	58	10	36	46	207	....	....	....	....	....	....	....	....	....	....	....	4	1	2	3	13	....	....	....
1982-83	London Knights	OHL	50	6	35	41	133	....	....	....	....	....	....	....	....	....	....	....	3	1	0	1	10	....	....	....
	Moncton Alpines	AHL	2	0	0	0	0	....	....	....	....	....	....	....	....	....	....	....	....	....	....	....	....	....	....	....
1983-84	Brantford	OHL	7	1	1	2	0	....	....	....	....	....	....	....	....	....	....	....	....	....	....	....	....	....	....	....
	Moncton Alpines	AHL	64	1	8	9	176	....	....	....	....	....	....	....	....	....	....	....	....	....	....	....	....	....	....	....
1984-85	Edmonton	NHL	2	0	0	0	2	0	0	0	3	0.0	–2	....	....	....	....	....	....	....	....	....	....	....	....	....
	Nova Scotia	AHL	68	2	28	30	161	....	....	....	....	....	....	....	....	....	....	....	5	0	3	3	40	....	....	....
1985-86	Edmonton	NHL	55	4	20	24	166	1	0	1	74	5.4	30	....	....	....	....	....	6	0	1	1	14	0	0	0
	Nova Scotia	AHL	4	0	2	2	11	....	....	....	....	....	....	....	....	....	....	....	....	....	....	....	....	....	....	....
1986-87♦	Edmonton	NHL	62	7	15	22	165	2	0	1	71	9.9	11	....	....	....	....	....	15	1	3	4	45	0	0	0
1987-88♦	Edmonton	NHL	79	12	43	55	286	5	0	1	116	10.3	40	....	....	....	....	....	19	1	11	12	55	1	0	0
1988-89	Edmonton	NHL	35	3	19	22	97	0	0	0	47	6.4	5	....	....	....	....	....	7	2	2	4	20	0	0	1
1989-90♦	Edmonton	NHL	75	7	34	41	171	3	0	1	125	5.6	6	....	....	....	....	....	22	5	10	15	37	0	1	1
1990-91	Edmonton	NHL	77	13	41	54	193	4	0	2	114	11.4	14	....	....	....	....	....	18	1	2	3	45	1	0	0
1991-92	Chicago	NHL	76	9	21	30	304	3	0	1	153	5.9	23	....	....	....	....	....	18	1	11	12	16	1	0	0
1992-93	Chicago	NHL	78	10	47	57	214	7	1	2	212	4.7	12	....	....	....	....	....	4	0	0	0	10	0	0	0
1993-94	Chicago	NHL	57	5	22	27	174	1	0	1	89	5.6	–5	....	....	....	....	....	....	....	....	....	....	....	....	....
1994-95	Chicago	NHL	48	1	12	13	128	0	0	0	43	2.3	6	....	....	....	....	....	16	0	1	1	26	0	0	0
1995-96	Chicago	NHL	37	0	9	9	71	0	0	0	17	0.0	12	....	....	....	....	....	6	0	0	0	16	0	0	0
1996-97	Chicago	NHL	21	0	0	0	29	0	0	0	7	0.0	4	....	....	....	....	....	3	0	0	0	4	0	0	0
1998-99	Calgary	NHL	69	1	14	15	80	0	0	0	42	2.4	3	0	0.0	93	98	22:33	....	....	....	....	....	....	....	....
99-2000	Calgary	NHL	20	0	4	4	42	0	0	0	10	0.0	–13	0	0.0	39	33	21:07	....	....	....	....	....	....	....	....
	NHL Totals		791	72	301	373	2122	26	1	10	1123	6.4		0	0.0	132	131	22:14	134	11	41	52	288	3	1	2

Played in NHL All-Star Game (1991)

Traded to **Chicago** by **Edmonton** for Dave Manson and Chicago's 3rd round choice (Kirk Maltby) in 1992 Entry Draft, October 2, 1991. Signed as a free agent by **Calgary**, August 17, 1998. • Missed remainder of 1999-2000 season recovering from neck injury suffered in game vs. Los Angeles, January 12, 2000.

SMITH, Wyatt (SMIHTH, WIGH-at) PHX.

Center. Shoots left. 5'11", 208 lbs. Born, Thief River Falls, MN, February 13, 1977. Phoenix's 6th choice, 233rd overall, in 1997 Entry Draft.

			Regular Season																Playoffs							
Season	Club	League	GP	G	A	Pts	PIM	PP	SH	GW	S	%	+/-	TF	F%	H	SB	Min	GP	G	A	Pts	PIM	PP	SH	GW
1994-95	Warroad High	Hi-School	28	29	31	60	28	....	....	....	....	....	....	....	....	....	....	....	....	....	....	....	....	....	....	....
1995-96	U. of Minnesota	WCHA	32	4	5	9	32	....	....	....	....	....	....	....	....	....	....	....	....	....	....	....	....	....	....	....
1996-97	U. of Minnesota	WCHA	38	16	14	30	44	....	....	....	....	....	....	....	....	....	....	....	....	....	....	....	....	....	....	....
1997-98	U. of Minnesota	WCHA	39	24	23	47	62	....	....	....	....	....	....	....	....	....	....	....	....	....	....	....	....	....	....	....
1998-99	U. of Minnesota	WCHA	43	23	20	43	37	....	....	....	....	....	....	....	....	....	....	....	....	....	....	....	....	....	....	....
99-2000	Phoenix	NHL	2	0	0	0	0	0	0	0	0	0.0	–2	20	30.0	1	1	11:39	....	....	....	....	....	....	....	....
	Springfield	AHL	60	14	26	40	26	....	....	....	....	....	....	....	....	....	....	....	5	2	3	5	13	....	....	....
	NHL Totals		2	0	0	0	0	0	0	0	0	0.0		20	30.0	1	1	11:39	....	....	....	....	....	....	....	....

SMOLINSKI, Bryan (smoh-LIHN-skee, BRIGH-an) L.A.

Center/Right wing. Shoots right. 6'1", 208 lbs. Born, Toledo, OH, December 27, 1971. Boston's 1st choice, 21st overall, in 1990 Entry Draft.

			Regular Season																Playoffs							
Season	Club	League	GP	G	A	Pts	PIM	PP	SH	GW	S	%	+/-	TF	F%	H	SB	Min	GP	G	A	Pts	PIM	PP	SH	GW
1987-88	Detroit Caesars	MNHL	80	43	77	120	....	....	....	....	....	....	....	....	....	....	....	....	....	....	....	....	....	....	....	....
1988-89	Stratford Cullitons	OJHL-B	46	32	62	94	132	....	....	....	....	....	....	....	....	....	....	....	....	....	....	....	....	....	....	....
1989-90	Michigan State	CCHA	35	9	13	22	34	....	....	....	....	....	....	....	....	....	....	....	....	....	....	....	....	....	....	....
1990-91	Michigan State	CCHA	35	9	12	21	24	....	....	....	....	....	....	....	....	....	....	....	....	....	....	....	....	....	....	....
1991-92	Michigan State	CCHA	41	28	33	61	55	....	....	....	....	....	....	....	....	....	....	....	....	....	....	....	....	....	....	....
1992-93	Michigan State	CCHA	40	31	37	*68	93	....	....	....	....	....	....	....	....	....	....	....	....	....	....	....	....	....	....	....
	Boston	NHL	9	1	3	4	0	0	0	0	10	10.0	3	....	....	....	....	....	4	1	0	1	2	0	0	0
1993-94	Boston	NHL	83	31	20	51	82	4	3	5	179	17.3	4	....	....	....	....	....	13	5	4	9	4	2	0	0
1994-95	Boston	NHL	44	18	13	31	31	6	0	5	121	14.9	–3	....	....	....	....	....	5	0	1	1	4	0	0	0
1995-96	Pittsburgh	NHL	81	24	40	64	69	8	2	1	229	10.5	6	....	....	....	....	....	18	5	4	9	10	0	0	1
1996-97	Detroit Vipers	IHL	6	5	7	12	10	....	....	....	....	....	....	....	....	....	....	....	....	....	....	....	....	....	....	....
	NY Islanders	NHL	64	28	28	56	25	9	0	1	183	15.3	9	....	....	....	....	....	....	....	....	....	....	....	....	....
1997-98	NY Islanders	NHL	81	13	30	43	34	3	0	4	203	6.4	–16	....	....	....	....	....	....	....	....	....	....	....	....	....
1998-99	NY Islanders	NHL	82	16	24	40	49	7	0	3	223	7.2	–7	1011	48.3	105	50	19:19	....	....	....	....	....	....	....	....
99-2000	Los Angeles	NHL	79	20	36	56	48	2	0	0	160	12.5	2	1545	50.9	129	58	18:35	4	0	0	0	2	0	0	0
	NHL Totals		523	151	194	345	338	39	5	19	1308	11.5		2556	49.8	234	108	18:58	44	11	9	20	22	2	0	1

CCHA First All-Star Team (1993) • NCAA West First All-American Team (1993)

Traded to **Pittsburgh** by **Boston** with Glen Murray and Boston's 3rd round choice (Boyd Kane) in 1996 Entry Draft for Kevin Stevens and Shawn McEachern, August 2, 1995. Traded to **NY Islanders** by **Pittsburgh** for Darius Kasparaitis and Andreas Johansson, November 17, 1996. Traded to **LA Kings** by **NY Islanders** with Zigmund Palffy, Marcel Cousineau and New Jersey's 4th round choice (previously acquired, LA Kings selected Daniel Johanssen) in 1999 Entry Draft for Olli Jokinen, Josh Green, Mathieu Biron and LA Kings' 1st round choice (Taylor Pyatt) in 1999 Entry Draft, June 20, 1999.

SMYTH, Brad (SMIHTH, BRAD) NYR

Right wing. Shoots right. 6', 195 lbs. Born, Ottawa, Ont., March 13, 1973.

			Regular Season																Playoffs							
Season	Club	League	GP	G	A	Pts	PIM	PP	SH	GW	S	%	+/-	TF	F%	H	SB	Min	GP	G	A	Pts	PIM	PP	SH	GW
1989-90	Nepean Raiders	OMHA	55	53	36	89	105	....	....	....	....	....	....	....	....	....	....	....	....	....	....	....	....	....	....	....
1990-91	London Knights	OHL	29	2	6	8	22	....	....	....	....	....	....	....	....	....	....	....	....	....	....	....	....	....	....	....
1991-92	London Knights	OHL	58	17	18	35	93	....	....	....	....	....	....	....	....	....	....	....	10	2	0	2	8	....	....	....
1992-93	London Knights	OHL	66	54	55	109	118	....	....	....	....	....	....	....	....	....	....	....	12	7	8	15	25	....	....	....
1993-94	Cincinnati	IHL	30	7	3	10	54	....	....	....	....	....	....	....	....	....	....	....	....	....	....	....	....	....	....	....
	Birmingham Bulls	ECHL	29	26	30	56	38	....	....	....	....	....	....	....	....	....	....	....	10	8	8	16	19	....	....	....
1994-95	Springfield	AHL	3	0	0	0	7	....	....	....	....	....	....	....	....	....	....	....	....	....	....	....	....	....	....	....
	Birmingham Bulls	ECHL	36	33	35	68	52	....	....	....	....	....	....	....	....	....	....	....	3	5	2	7	0	....	....	....
	Cincinnati	IHL	26	2	11	13	34	....	....	....	....	....	....	....	....	....	....	....	1	0	0	0	2	....	....	....

			Regular Season																Playoffs							
Season	Club	League	GP	G	A	Pts	PIM	PP	SH	GW	S	%	+/-	TF	F%	H	SB	Min	GP	G	A	Pts	PIM	PP	SH	GW
1995-96	**Florida**	**NHL**	**7**	**1**	**1**	**2**	**4**	**1**	**0**	**0**	**12**	**8.3**	**-3**	....	....	....	....	....	....	....	....	....	....	....	....	....
	Carolina	AHL	68	*68	58	*126	80	....	....	....	....	....	....	....	....	....	....	....	....	....	....	....	....	....	....	....
1996-97	**Florida**	**NHL**	**8**	**1**	**0**	**1**	**2**	**0**	**0**	**0**	**10**	**10.0**	**-3**	....	....	....	....	....	....	....	....	....	....	....	....	....
	Los Angeles	**NHL**	**44**	**8**	**8**	**16**	**74**	**0**	**0**	**1**	**74**	**10.8**	**-7**	....	....	....	....	....	....	....	....	....	....	....	....	....
	Phoenix	IHL	3	5	2	7	0	....	....	....	....	....	....	....	....	....	....	....	....	....	....	....	....	....	....	....
1997-98	**Los Angeles**	**NHL**	**9**	**1**	**3**	**4**	**4**	**0**	**0**	**0**	**12**	**8.3**	**-1**	....	....	....	....	....	....	....	....	....	....	....	....	....
	NY Rangers	**NHL**	**1**	**0**	**0**	**0**	**0**	**0**	**0**	**0**	**1**	**0.0**	**0**	....	....	....	....	....	....	....	....	....	....	....	....	....
	Hartford	AHL	57	29	33	62	79	....	....	....	....	....	....	....	....	....	....	....	15	12	8	20	11	....	....	....
1998-99	**Nashville**	**NHL**	**3**	**0**	**0**	**0**	**6**	**0**	**0**	**0**	**5**	**0.0**	**-1**	**0**	**0.0**	**1**	**0**	**9:54**	....	....	....	....	....	....	....	....
	Milwaukee	IHL	34	11	16	27	21	....	....	....	....	....	....	....	....	....	....	....	....	....	....	....	....	....	....	....
	Hartford	AHL	36	25	19	44	48	....	....	....	....	....	....	....	....	....	....	....	7	6	0	6	14	....	....	....
99-2000	Hartford	AHL	80	39	37	76	62	....	....	....	....	....	....	....	....	....	....	....	23	*13	10	23	8	....	....	....
	NHL Totals		**72**	**11**	**12**	**23**	**90**	**1**	**0**	**1**	**114**	**9.6**		**0**	**0.0**	**1**	**0**	**9:54**	....	....	....	....	....	....	....	....

AHL First All-Star Team (1996) • Won John B. Sollenberger Trophy (Top Scorer - AHL) (1996) • Won Les Cunningham Award (MVP - AHL) (1996)

Signed as a free agent by **Florida**, October 4, 1993. Traded to **LA Kings** by **Florida** for LA Kings' 3rd round choice (Vratislav Czech) in 1997 Entry Draft, November 28, 1996. Traded to **NY Rangers** by **LA Kings** for future considerations, November 14, 1997. Signed as a free agent by **Nashville**, July 16, 1998. Traded to **NY Rangers** by **Nashville** for future considerations, May 3, 1999. • Played w/ RHI's Ottawa Loggers 1996 (21-20-23-43-24).

SMYTH, Ryan (SMIHTH, RIGH-yan) EDM.

Left wing. Shoots left. 6'1", 195 lbs. Born, Banff, Alta., February 21, 1976. Edmonton's 2nd choice, 6th overall, in 1994 Entry Draft.

Season	Club	League	GP	G	A	Pts	PIM	PP	SH	GW	S	%	+/-	TF	F%	H	SB	Min	GP	G	A	Pts	PIM	PP	SH	GW
1990-91	Banff Blazers	AAHA	25	100	50	150	....	....	....	....	....	....	....	....	....	....	....	....	....	....	....	....	....	....	....	....
	Lethbridge Y's	AMHL	34	8	21	29	....	....	....	....	....	....	....	....	....	....	....	....	....	....	....	....	....	....	....	....
1991-92	Caronport	SAHA	35	55	61	116	98	....	....	....	....	....	....	....	....	....	....	....	....	....	....	....	....	....	....	....
	Moose Jaw	WHL	2	0	0	0	0	....	....	....	....	....	....	....	....	....	....	....	....	....	....	....	....	....	....	....
1992-93	Moose Jaw	WHL	64	19	14	33	59	....	....	....	....	....	....	....	....	....	....	....	....	....	....	....	....	....	....	....
1993-94	Moose Jaw	WHL	72	50	55	105	88	....	....	....	....	....	....	....	....	....	....	....	....	....	....	....	....	....	....	....
1994-95	Moose Jaw	WHL	50	41	45	86	66	....	....	....	....	....	....	....	....	....	....	....	10	6	9	15	22	....	....	....
	Edmonton	**NHL**	**3**	**0**	**0**	**0**	**0**	**0**	**0**	**0**	**2**	**0.0**	**-1**	....	....	....	....	....	....	....	....	....	....	....	....	....
1995-96	**Edmonton**	**NHL**	**48**	**2**	**9**	**11**	**28**	**1**	**0**	**0**	**65**	**3.1**	**-10**	....	....	....	....	....	....	....	....	....	....	....	....	....
	Cape Breton	AHL	9	6	5	11	4	....	....	....	....	....	....	....	....	....	....	....	....	....	....	....	....	....	....	....
1996-97	**Edmonton**	**NHL**	**82**	**39**	**22**	**61**	**76**	**20**	**0**	**4**	**265**	**14.7**	**-7**	....	....	....	....	....	**12**	**5**	**5**	**10**	**12**	**1**	**0**	**2**
1997-98	**Edmonton**	**NHL**	**65**	**20**	**13**	**33**	**44**	**10**	**0**	**2**	**205**	**9.8**	**-24**	....	....	....	....	....	**12**	**1**	**3**	**4**	**16**	**1**	**0**	**0**
1998-99	**Edmonton**	**NHL**	**71**	**13**	**18**	**31**	**62**	**6**	**0**	**2**	**161**	**8.1**	**0**	**5**	**20.0**	**84**	**20**	**14:26**	**3**	**3**	**0**	**3**	**0**	**2**	**0**	**0**
99-2000	**Edmonton**	**NHL**	**82**	**28**	**26**	**54**	**58**	**11**	**0**	**4**	**238**	**11.8**	**-2**	**24**	**54.2**	**84**	**34**	**19:12**	**5**	**1**	**0**	**1**	**6**	**0**	**1**	**0**
	NHL Totals		**351**	**102**	**88**	**190**	**268**	**48**	**0**	**12**	**936**	**10.9**		**29**	**48.3**	**168**	**54**	**16:59**	**32**	**10**	**8**	**18**	**34**	**4**	**1**	**2**

WHL East Second All-Star Team (1995)

SONNENBERG, Martin (SOHN-nehn-BUHRG, MAHR-tihn) PIT.

Left wing. Shoots left. 6', 184 lbs. Born, Wetaskiwin, Alta., January 23, 1978.

Season	Club	League	GP	G	A	Pts	PIM	PP	SH	GW	S	%	+/-	TF	F%	H	SB	Min	GP	G	A	Pts	PIM	PP	SH	GW
1994-95	Leduc Oil Kings	AMHL	35	28	40	68	34	....	....	....	....	....	....	....	....	....	....	....	....	....	....	....	....	....	....	....
1995-96	Saskatoon Blades	WHL	58	8	7	15	24	....	....	....	....	....	....	....	....	....	....	....	3	0	0	0	2	....	....	....
1996-97	Saskatoon Blades	WHL	72	38	26	64	79	....	....	....	....	....	....	....	....	....	....	....	....	....	....	....	....	....	....	....
1997-98	Saskatoon Blades	WHL	72	40	52	92	87	....	....	....	....	....	....	....	....	....	....	....	6	1	3	4	9	....	....	....
1998-99	**Pittsburgh**	**NHL**	**44**	**1**	**1**	**2**	**19**	**0**	**0**	**0**	**12**	**8.3**	**-2**	**2**	**0.0**	**33**	**5**	**4:00**	**7**	**0**	**0**	**0**	**0**	**0**	**0**	**0**
	Syracuse Crunch	AHL	36	15	9	24	31	....	....	....	....	....	....	....	....	....	....	....	....	....	....	....	....	....	....	....
99-2000	**Pittsburgh**	**NHL**	**14**	**1**	**2**	**3**	**0**	**1**	**0**	**0**	**19**	**5.3**	**0**	**7**	**28.6**	**10**	**7**	**7:26**	....	....	....	....	....	....	....	....
	Wilkes-Barre	AHL	62	20	33	53	109	....	....	....	....	....	....	....	....	....	....	....	....	....	....	....	....	....	....	....
	NHL Totals		**58**	**2**	**3**	**5**	**19**	**1**	**0**	**0**	**31**	**6.5**		**9**	**22.2**	**43**	**12**	**4:50**	**7**	**0**	**0**	**0**	**0**	**0**	**0**	**0**

Signed as a free agent by **Pittsburgh**, October 9, 1998.

SOPEL, Brent (SOH-puhl, BREHT) VAN.

Defense. Shoots right. 6'1", 205 lbs. Born, Calgary, Alta., January 7, 1977. Vancouver's 6th choice, 144th overall, in 1995 Entry Draft.

Season	Club	League	GP	G	A	Pts	PIM	PP	SH	GW	S	%	+/-	TF	F%	H	SB	Min	GP	G	A	Pts	PIM	PP	SH	GW
1992-93	Saskatoon Legion	SAHA	36	7	17	24	95	....	....	....	....	....	....	....	....	....	....	....	....	....	....	....	....	....	....	....
1993-94	Saskatoon Legion	SAHA	34	9	30	39	180	....	....	....	....	....	....	....	....	....	....	....	....	....	....	....	....	....	....	....
	Saskatoon Blades	WHL	11	2	2	4	2	....	....	....	....	....	....	....	....	....	....	....	....	....	....	....	....	....	....	....
1994-95	Saskatoon Blades	WHL	22	1	10	11	31	....	....	....	....	....	....	....	....	....	....	....	....	....	....	....	....	....	....	....
	Swift Current	WHL	41	4	19	23	50	....	....	....	....	....	....	....	....	....	....	....	3	0	3	3	0	....	....	....
1995-96	Swift Current	WHL	71	13	48	61	87	....	....	....	....	....	....	....	....	....	....	....	6	1	2	3	4	....	....	....
	Syracuse Crunch	AHL	1	0	0	0	0	....	....	....	....	....	....	....	....	....	....	....	....	....	....	....	....	....	....	....
1996-97	Swift Current	WHL	62	15	41	56	109	....	....	....	....	....	....	....	....	....	....	....	10	5	11	16	32	....	....	....
	Syracuse Crunch	AHL	2	0	0	0	0	....	....	....	....	....	....	....	....	....	....	....	3	0	0	0	0	....	....	....
1997-98	Syracuse Crunch	AHL	76	10	33	43	70	....	....	....	....	....	....	....	....	....	....	....	5	0	7	7	12	....	....	....
1998-99	**Vancouver**	**NHL**	**5**	**1**	**0**	**1**	**4**	**1**	**0**	**0**	**5**	**20.0**	**-1**	**0**	**0.0**	**4**	**1**	**11:58**	....	....	....	....	....	....	....	....
	Syracuse Crunch	AHL	53	10	21	31	59	....	....	....	....	....	....	....	....	....	....	....	....	....	....	....	....	....	....	....
99-2000	**Vancouver**	**NHL**	**18**	**2**	**4**	**6**	**12**	**0**	**0**	**1**	**11**	**18.2**	**9**	**0**	**0.0**	**29**	**13**	**10:31**	....	....	....	....	....	....	....	....
	Syracuse Crunch	AHL	50	6	25	31	67	....	....	....	....	....	....	....	....	....	....	....	4	0	2	2	8	....	....	....
	NHL Totals		**23**	**3**	**4**	**7**	**16**	**1**	**0**	**1**	**16**	**18.8**		**0**	**0.0**	**33**	**14**	**10:50**	....	....	....	....	....	....	....	....

SOROCHAN, Lee (soh-RAW-kihn, LEE)

Defense. Shoots left. 5'11", 210 lbs. Born, Edmonton, Alta., September 9, 1975. NY Rangers' 2nd choice, 34th overall, in 1993 Entry Draft.

Season	Club	League	GP	G	A	Pts	PIM	PP	SH	GW	S	%	+/-	TF	F%	H	SB	Min	GP	G	A	Pts	PIM	PP	SH	GW
1990-91	Sherwood Park	AAHA	34	10	17	27	46	....	....	....	....	....	....	....	....	....	....	....	....	....	....	....	....	....	....	....
1991-92	Lethbridge	WHL	67	2	9	11	105	....	....	....	....	....	....	....	....	....	....	....	5	0	2	2	6	....	....	....
1992-93	Lethbridge	WHL	69	8	32	40	208	....	....	....	....	....	....	....	....	....	....	....	4	0	1	1	12	....	....	....
1993-94	Lethbridge	WHL	46	5	27	32	123	....	....	....	....	....	....	....	....	....	....	....	9	4	3	7	16	....	....	....
1994-95	Lethbridge	WHL	29	4	15	19	93	....	....	....	....	....	....	....	....	....	....	....	....	....	....	....	....	....	....	....
	Saskatoon Blades	WHL	24	5	13	18	63	....	....	....	....	....	....	....	....	....	....	....	10	3	6	9	34	....	....	....
	Binghamton	AHL	....	....	....	....	....	....	....	....	....	....	....	....	....	....	....	....	8	0	0	0	11	....	....	....
1995-96	Binghamton	AHL	45	2	8	10	26	....	....	....	....	....	....	....	....	....	....	....	1	0	0	0	0	....	....	....
1996-97	Binghamton	AHL	77	4	27	31	160	....	....	....	....	....	....	....	....	....	....	....	4	0	2	2	18	....	....	....
1997-98	Hartford	AHL	73	7	11	18	197	....	....	....	....	....	....	....	....	....	....	....	13	0	2	2	51	....	....	....
1998-99	Fort Wayne	IHL	45	0	10	10	204	....	....	....	....	....	....	....	....	....	....	....	....	....	....	....	....	....	....	....
	Hartford	AHL	16	0	2	2	33	....	....	....	....	....	....	....	....	....	....	....	....	....	....	....	....	....	....	....
	Calgary	**NHL**	**2**	**0**	**0**	**0**	**0**	**0**	**0**	**0**	**5**	**0.0**	**-3**	**0**	**0.0**	**3**	**3**	**15:43**	....	....	....	....	....	....	....	....
	Saint John Flames	AHL	3	1	3	4	4	....	....	....	....	....	....	....	....	....	....	....	7	3	3	6	29	....	....	....
99-2000	**Calgary**	**NHL**	**1**	**0**	**0**	**0**	**0**	**0**	**0**	**0**	**0**	**0.0**	**0**	**0**	**0.0**	**2**	**0**	**3:40**	....	....	....	....	....	....	....	....
	Saint John Flames	AHL	60	4	37	41	124	....	....	....	....	....	....	....	....	....	....	....	3	2	1	3	12	....	....	....
	NHL Totals		**3**	**0**	**0**	**0**	**0**	**0**	**0**	**0**	**5**	**0.0**		**0**	**0.0**	**5**	**3**	**11:42**	....	....	....	....	....	....	....	....

Traded to **Calgary** by **NY Rangers** for Chris O'Sullivan, March 23, 1999.

SOURAY, Sheldon (SUHR-ee, SHEHL-dohn) MTL.

Defense. Shoots left. 6'4", 230 lbs. Born, Elk Point, Alta., July 13, 1976. New Jersey's 3rd choice, 71st overall, in 1994 Entry Draft.

Season	Club	League	GP	G	A	Pts	PIM	PP	SH	GW	S	%	+/-	TF	F%	H	SB	Min	GP	G	A	Pts	PIM	PP	SH	GW
1990-91	Bonneyville Sabres	AAHA	30	15	20	35	100	....	....	....	....	....	....	....	....	....	....	....	....	....	....	....	....	....	....	....
1991-92	Quesnel	BCAHA	20	5	15	20	200	....	....	....	....	....	....	....	....	....	....	....	....	....	....	....	....	....	....	....
	Alberta Cycle	AAHA	11	0	5	5	87	....	....	....	....	....	....	....	....	....	....	....	....	....	....	....	....	....	....	....
1992-93	Ft-Saskatchewan	AJHL	35	0	12	12	125	....	....	....	....	....	....	....	....	....	....	....	....	....	....	....	....	....	....	....
	Tri-City Americans	WHL	2	0	0	0	0	....	....	....	....	....	....	....	....	....	....	....	....	....	....	....	....	....	....	....
1993-94	Tri-City Americans	WHL	42	3	6	9	122	....	....	....	....	....	....	....	....	....	....	....	....	....	....	....	....	....	....	....

			Regular Season																Playoffs							
Season	Club	League	GP	G	A	Pts	PIM	PP	SH	GW	S	%	+/–	TF	F%	H	SB	Min	GP	G	A	Pts	PIM	PP	SH	GW
1994-95	Tri-City Americans	WHL	40	2	24	26	140	....	....	....	....	....	....	....	....	....	....	....	....	....	....	....	....	....	....	....
	Prince George	WHL	11	2	3	5	23	....	....	....	....	....	....	....	....	....	....	....	....	....	....	....	....	....	....	....
	Albany River Rats	AHL	7	0	2	2	8	....	....	....	....	....	....	....	....	....	....	....	....	....	....	....	....	....	....	....
1995-96	Prince George	WHL	32	9	18	27	91	....	....	....	....	....	....	....	....	....	....	....	....	....	....	....	....	....	....	....
	Kelowna Rockets	WHL	27	7	20	27	94	....	....	....	....	....	....	....	....	....	....	....	6	0	5	5	2	....	....	....
	Albany River Rats	AHL	6	0	2	2	12	....	....	....	....	....	....	....	....	....	....	....	4	0	1	1	4	....	....	....
1996-97	Albany River Rats	AHL	70	2	11	13	160	....	....	....	....	....	....	....	....	....	....	....	16	2	3	5	47	....	....	....
1997-98	**New Jersey**	**NHL**	**60**	**3**	**7**	**10**	**85**	**0**	**0**	**1**	**74**	**4.1**	**18**	....	....	....	....	....	**3**	**0**	**1**	**1**	**2**	**0**	**0**	**0**
	Albany River Rats	AHL	6	0	0	0	8	....	....	....	....	....	....	....	....	....	....	....	....	....	....	....	....	....	....	....
1998-99	**New Jersey**	**NHL**	**70**	**1**	**7**	**8**	**110**	**0**	**0**	**0**	**101**	**1.0**	**5**	**0**	**0.0**	**109**	**57**	**14:56**	**2**	**0**	**1**	**1**	**0**	**0**	**0**	**0**
99-2000	**New Jersey**	**NHL**	**52**	**0**	**8**	**8**	**70**	**0**	**0**	**0**	**74**	**0.0**	**–6**	**0**	**0.0**	**97**	**51**	**17:12**	....	....	....	....	....	....	....	....
	Montreal	**NHL**	**19**	**3**	**0**	**3**	**44**	**0**	**0**	**0**	**39**	**7.7**	**7**	**0**	**0.0**	**23**	**34**	**19:18**	....	....	....	....	....	....	....	....
	NHL Totals		**201**	**7**	**22**	**29**	**309**	**0**	**0**	**1**	**288**	**2.4**		**0**	**0.0**	**229**	**142**	**16:21**	**5**	**0**	**2**	**2**	**2**	**0**	**0**	**0**

WHL West Second All-Star Team (1996)

Traded to **Montreal** by **New Jersey** with Josh DeWolf and New Jersey's 2nd round choice in 2001 Entry Draft for Vladimir Malakhov, March 1, 2000.

SPACEK, Jaroslav

(SPAH-chehk, YA-roh-slahv) **FLA.**

Defense. Shoots left. 5'11", 198 lbs. Born, Rokycany, Czech., February 11, 1974. Florida's 5th choice, 117th overall, in 1998 Entry Draft.

Season	Club	League	GP	G	A	Pts	PIM	PP	SH	GW	S	%	+/–	TF	F%	H	SB	Min	GP	G	A	Pts	PIM	PP	SH	GW
1992-93	Skoda Plzen	Czech.	16	1	3	4	....	....	....	....	....	....	....	....	....	....	....	....	....	....	....	....	....	....	....	....
1993-94	ZKZ Plzen	Cze-Rep	34	2	6	8	....	....	....	....	....	....	....	....	....	....	....	....	....	....	....	....	....	....	....	....
1994-95	ZKZ Plzen	Cze-Rep	38	4	8	12	14	....	....	....	....	....	....	....	....	....	....	....	3	1	0	1	2	....	....	....
1995-96	ZKZ Plzen	Cze-Rep	40	3	10	13	42	....	....	....	....	....	....	....	....	....	....	....	3	0	1	1	4	....	....	....
1996-97	ZKZ Plzen	Cze-Rep	52	9	29	38	44	....	....	....	....	....	....	....	....	....	....	....	....	....	....	....	....	....	....	....
1997-98	Farjestads BK	Sweden	45	10	16	26	63	....	....	....	....	....	....	....	....	....	....	....	12	2	5	7	14	....	....	....
	Farjestads BK	EuroHL	6	2	3	5	2	....	....	....	....	....	....	....	....	....	....	....	....	....	....	....	....	....	....	....
1998-99	**Florida**	**NHL**	**63**	**3**	**12**	**15**	**28**	**2**	**1**	**0**	**92**	**3.3**	**15**	**1**	**100.0**	**78**	**41**	**19:27**	....	....	....	....	....	....	....	....
	New Haven	AHL	14	4	8	12	15	....	....	....	....	....	....	....	....	....	....	....	....	....	....	....	....	....	....	....
99-2000	**Florida**	**NHL**	**82**	**10**	**26**	**36**	**53**	**4**	**0**	**1**	**111**	**9.0**	**7**	**1**	**0.0**	**122**	**98**	**22:40**	**4**	**0**	**0**	**0**	**0**	**0**	**0**	**0**
	NHL Totals		**145**	**13**	**38**	**51**	**81**	**6**	**1**	**1**	**203**	**6.4**		**2**	**50.0**	**200**	**139**	**21:16**	**4**	**0**	**0**	**0**	**0**	**0**	**0**	**0**

SPRING, Corey

(SPRIHNG, KOHR-ee)

Right wing. Shoots right. 6'4", 214 lbs. Born, Cranbrook, B.C., May 31, 1971.

Season	Club	League	GP	G	A	Pts	PIM	PP	SH	GW	S	%	+/–	TF	F%	H	SB	Min	GP	G	A	Pts	PIM	PP	SH	GW
1990-91	Vernon Lakers	BCJHL	60	43	43	86	104	....	....	....	....	....	....	....	....	....	....	....	....	....	....	....	....	....	....	....
1991-92	Alaska-Fairbanks	NCAA	35	3	8	11	30	....	....	....	....	....	....	....	....	....	....	....	....	....	....	....	....	....	....	....
1992-93	Alaska-Fairbanks	CCHA	28	5	5	10	20	....	....	....	....	....	....	....	....	....	....	....	....	....	....	....	....	....	....	....
1993-94	Alaska-Fairbanks	CCHA	38	19	18	37	34	....	....	....	....	....	....	....	....	....	....	....	....	....	....	....	....	....	....	....
1994-95	Alaska-Fairbanks	CCHA	33	18	14	32	56	....	....	....	....	....	....	....	....	....	....	....	....	....	....	....	....	....	....	....
1995-96	Atlanta Knights	IHL	73	14	14	28	104	....	....	....	....	....	....	....	....	....	....	....	2	0	0	0	0	....	....	....
1996-97	Adirondack	AHL	69	20	26	46	118	....	....	....	....	....	....	....	....	....	....	....	4	0	0	0	14	....	....	....
1997-98	**Tampa Bay**	**NHL**	**8**	**1**	**0**	**1**	**10**	**0**	**0**	**0**	**12**	**8.3**	**–1**	....	....	....	....	....	....	....	....	....	....	....	....	....
	Adirondack	AHL	57	19	25	44	120	....	....	....	....	....	....	....	....	....	....	....	3	0	0	0	6	....	....	....
1998-99	**Tampa Bay**	**NHL**	**8**	**0**	**1**	**1**	**2**	**0**	**0**	**0**	**6**	**0.0**	**0**	**0**	**0.0**	**9**	**0**	**5:32**	....	....	....	....	....	....	....	....
	Cleveland	IHL	48	18	10	28	98	....	....	....	....	....	....	....	....	....	....	....	....	....	....	....	....	....	....	....
99-2000	Detroit Vipers	IHL	22	5	4	9	48	....	....	....	....	....	....	....	....	....	....	....	....	....	....	....	....	....	....	....
	Manitoba Moose	IHL	8	2	2	4	8	....	....	....	....	....	....	....	....	....	....	....	....	....	....	....	....	....	....	....
	Augsburger EV	DEL	7	2	0	2	10	....	....	....	....	....	....	....	....	....	....	....	....	....	....	....	....	....	....	....
	NHL Totals		**16**	**1**	**1**	**2**	**12**	**0**	**0**	**0**	**18**	**5.6**		**0**	**0.0**	**9**	**0**	**5:32**	....	....	....	....	....	....	....	....

Signed as a free agent by **Tampa Bay**, July 24, 1995.

ST-LOUIS, Martin

(san-LOO-ee, mah-THE) **T.B.**

Right wing. Shoots left. 5'9", 185 lbs. Born, Laval, Que., June 18, 1975.

Season	Club	League	GP	G	A	Pts	PIM	PP	SH	GW	S	%	+/–	TF	F%	H	SB	Min	GP	G	A	Pts	PIM	PP	SH	GW
1991-92	Laval-Laurentides	QAAA	42	29	74	103	....	....	....	....	....	....	....	....	....	....	....	....	....	....	....	....	....	....	....	....
1992-93	Hawkesbury	OJHL	31	37	50	87	70	....	....	....	....	....	....	....	....	....	....	....	....	....	....	....	....	....	....	....
1993-94	U. of Vermont	ECAC	33	15	36	51	24	....	....	....	....	....	....	....	....	....	....	....	....	....	....	....	....	....	....	....
1994-95	U. of Vermont	ECAC	35	23	48	71	36	....	....	....	....	....	....	....	....	....	....	....	....	....	....	....	....	....	....	....
1995-96	U. of Vermont	ECAC	35	29	56	85	38	....	....	....	....	....	....	....	....	....	....	....	....	....	....	....	....	....	....	....
1996-97	U. of Vermont	ECAC	36	24	*36	60	65	....	....	....	....	....	....	....	....	....	....	....	....	....	....	....	....	....	....	....
1997-98	Cleveland	IHL	56	16	34	50	24	....	....	....	....	....	....	....	....	....	....	....	....	....	....	....	....	....	....	....
	Saint John Flames	AHL	25	15	11	26	20	....	....	....	....	....	....	....	....	....	....	....	20	5	15	20	16	....	....	....
1998-99	**Calgary**	**NHL**	**13**	**1**	**1**	**2**	**10**	**0**	**0**	**0**	**14**	**7.1**	**–2**	**0**	**0.0**	**8**	**4**	**8:15**	....	....	....	....	....	....	....	....
	Saint John Flames	AHL	53	28	34	62	30	....	....	....	....	....	....	....	....	....	....	....	7	4	4	8	2	....	....	....
99-2000	**Calgary**	**NHL**	**56**	**3**	**15**	**18**	**22**	**0**	**0**	**1**	**73**	**4.1**	**–5**	**3**	**0.0**	**47**	**45**	**14:41**	....	....	....	....	....	....	....	....
	Saint John Flames	AHL	17	15	11	26	14	....	....	....	....	....	....	....	....	....	....	....	....	....	....	....	....	....	....	....
	NHL Totals		**69**	**4**	**16**	**20**	**32**	**0**	**0**	**1**	**87**	**4.6**		**3**	**0.0**	**55**	**49**	**13:28**	....	....	....	....	....	....	....	....

ECAC First All-Star Team (1995, 1996, 1997) • NCAA East First All-American Team (1995, 1996, 1997) • NCAA Championship All-Tournament Team (1996)

Signed as a free agent by **Calgary**, February 19, 1998. Signed as a free agent by **Tampa Bay**, July 31, 2000.

STAIOS, Steve

(STAY-uhs, STEEV) **ATL.**

Defense/Right wing. Shoots right. 6'1", 200 lbs. Born, Hamilton, Ont., July 28, 1973. St. Louis' 1st choice, 27th overall, in 1991 Entry Draft.

Season	Club	League	GP	G	A	Pts	PIM	PP	SH	GW	S	%	+/–	TF	F%	H	SB	Min	GP	G	A	Pts	PIM	PP	SH	GW
1988-89	Hamilton Huskies	OMHA	58	13	39	52	78	....	....	....	....	....	....	....	....	....	....	....	....	....	....	....	....	....	....	....
1989-90	Hamilton Kilty B's	OJHL-B	40	9	27	36	66	....	....	....	....	....	....	....	....	....	....	....	....	....	....	....	....	....	....	....
1990-91	Niagara Falls	OHL	66	17	29	46	115	....	....	....	....	....	....	....	....	....	....	....	12	2	3	5	10	....	....	....
1991-92	Niagara Falls	OHL	65	11	42	53	122	....	....	....	....	....	....	....	....	....	....	....	17	7	8	15	27	....	....	....
1992-93	Niagara Falls	OHL	12	4	14	18	30	....	....	....	....	....	....	....	....	....	....	....	....	....	....	....	....	....	....	....
	Sudbury Wolves	OHL	53	13	44	57	67	....	....	....	....	....	....	....	....	....	....	....	11	5	6	11	22	....	....	....
1993-94	Peoria Rivermen	IHL	38	3	9	12	42	....	....	....	....	....	....	....	....	....	....	....	....	....	....	....	....	....	....	....
1994-95	Peoria Rivermen	IHL	60	3	13	16	64	....	....	....	....	....	....	....	....	....	....	....	6	0	0	0	10	....	....	....
1995-96	Peoria Rivermen	IHL	6	0	1	1	14	....	....	....	....	....	....	....	....	....	....	....	....	....	....	....	....	....	....	....
	Worcester	AHL	57	1	11	12	114	....	....	....	....	....	....	....	....	....	....	....	....	....	....	....	....	....	....	....
	Boston	**NHL**	**12**	**0**	**0**	**0**	**4**	**0**	**0**	**0**	**4**	**0.0**	**–5**	....	....	....	....	....	**3**	**0**	**0**	**0**	**0**	**0**	**0**	**0**
	Providence Bruins	AHL	7	1	4	5	8	....	....	....	....	....	....	....	....	....	....	....	....	....	....	....	....	....	....	....
1996-97	**Boston**	**NHL**	**54**	**3**	**8**	**11**	**71**	**0**	**0**	**0**	**56**	**5.4**	**–26**	....	....	....	....	....	....	....	....	....	....	....	....	....
	Vancouver	**NHL**	**9**	**0**	**6**	**6**	**20**	**0**	**0**	**0**	**10**	**0.0**	**2**	....	....	....	....	....	....	....	....	....	....	....	....	....
1997-98	**Vancouver**	**NHL**	**77**	**3**	**4**	**7**	**134**	**0**	**0**	**1**	**45**	**6.7**	**–3**	....	....	....	....	....	....	....	....	....	....	....	....	....
1998-99	**Vancouver**	**NHL**	**57**	**0**	**2**	**2**	**54**	**0**	**0**	**0**	**33**	**0.0**	**–12**	**4**	**25.0**	**58**	**8**	**6:53**	....	....	....	....	....	....	....	....
99-2000	**Atlanta**	**NHL**	**27**	**2**	**3**	**5**	**66**	**0**	**0**	**0**	**38**	**5.3**	**–5**	**2**	**50.0**	**60**	**14**	**13:01**	....	....	....	....	....	....	....	....
	NHL Totals		**236**	**8**	**23**	**31**	**349**	**0**	**0**	**1**	**186**	**4.3**		**6**	**33.3**	**118**	**22**	**8:51**	**3**	**0**	**0**	**0**	**0**	**0**	**0**	**0**

Traded to **Boston** by **St. Louis** with Kevin Sawyer for Steve Leach, March 8, 1996. Claimed on waivers by **Vancouver** from **Boston**, March 18, 1997. Claimed by **Atlanta** from **Vancouver** in Expansion Draft, June 25, 1999. • Missed majority of 1999-2000 season recovering from knee injury originally suffered in game vs. Colorado, October 23, 1999. Traded to **New Jersey** by **Atlanta** for New Jersey's 9th round choice (Simon Gamache) in 2000 Entry Draft, June 12, 2000. Traded to **Atlanta** by **New Jersey** for future considerations, July 10, 2000.

STAPLETON, Mike

(STAY-puhl-TOHN, MIGHK) **NYI**

Center. Shoots right. 5'10", 183 lbs. Born, Sarnia, Ont., May 5, 1966. Chicago's 7th choice, 132nd overall, in 1984 Entry Draft.

Season	Club	League	GP	G	A	Pts	PIM	PP	SH	GW	S	%	+/–	TF	F%	H	SB	Min	GP	G	A	Pts	PIM	PP	SH	GW
1982-83	Strathroy Rockets	OJHL-B	40	39	38	77	99	....	....	....	....	....	....	....	....	....	....	....	....	....	....	....	....	....	....	....
1983-84	Cornwall Royals	OHL	70	24	45	69	94	....	....	....	....	....	....	....	....	....	....	....	3	1	2	3	4	....	....	....
1984-85	Cornwall Royals	OHL	56	41	44	85	68	....	....	....	....	....	....	....	....	....	....	....	9	2	4	6	23	....	....	....
1985-86	Cornwall Royals	OHL	56	39	64	103	74	....	....	....	....	....	....	....	....	....	....	....	6	2	3	5	2	....	....	....
1986-87	Canada	Nat-Team	21	2	4	6	4	....	....	....	....	....	....	....	....	....	....	....	....	....	....	....	....	....	....	....
	Chicago	**NHL**	**39**	**3**	**6**	**9**	**6**	**0**	**0**	**0**	**54**	**5.6**	**–9**	....	....	....	....	....	**4**	**0**	**0**	**0**	**2**	**0**	**0**	**0**

Season	Club	League	GP	G	A	Pts	PIM	PP	SH	GW	S	%	+/-	TF	F%	H	SB	Min	GP	G	A	Pts	PIM	PP	SH	GW
			Regular Season																Playoffs							
1987-88	**Chicago**	**NHL**	**53**	**2**	**9**	**11**	**59**	**0**	**0**	**1**	**50**	**4.0**	**–10**	....	....	....	....	....	....	....	....	....	....	....	....	....
	Saginaw Hawks	IHL	31	11	19	30	52	....	....	....	....	....	....	....	....	....	....	....	10	5	6	11	10	....	....	....
1988-89	**Chicago**	**NHL**	**7**	**0**	**1**	**1**	**7**	**0**	**0**	**0**	**6**	**0.0**	**–1**	....	....	....	....	....	....	....	....	....	....	....	....	....
	Saginaw Hawks	IHL	69	21	47	68	162	....	....	....	....	....	....	....	....	....	....	....	6	1	3	4	4	....	....	....
1989-90	Arvika IF	Sweden-3	30	15	18	33	....	....	....	....	....	....	....	....	....	....	....	....	....	....	....	....	....	....	....	....
	Indianapolis Ice	IHL	16	5	10	15	6	....	....	....	....	....	....	....	....	....	....	....	13	9	10	19	38	....	....	....
1990-91	**Chicago**	**NHL**	**7**	**0**	**1**	**1**	**2**	**0**	**0**	**0**	**6**	**0.0**	**0**	....	....	....	....	....	....	....	....	....	....	....	....	....
	Indianapolis Ice	IHL	75	29	52	81	76	....	....	....	....	....	....	....	....	....	....	....	7	1	4	5	0	....	....	....
1991-92	**Chicago**	**NHL**	**19**	**4**	**4**	**8**	**8**	**1**	**0**	**0**	**32**	**12.5**	**0**	....	....	....	....	....	....	....	....	....	....	....	....	....
	Indianapolis Ice	IHL	59	18	40	58	65	....	....	....	....	....	....	....	....	....	....	....	....	....	....	....	....	....	....	....
1992-93	**Pittsburgh**	**NHL**	**78**	**4**	**9**	**13**	**10**	**0**	**1**	**1**	**78**	**5.1**	**–8**	....	....	....	....	....	**4**	**0**	**0**	**0**	**0**	**0**	**0**	**0**
1993-94	**Pittsburgh**	**NHL**	**58**	**7**	**4**	**11**	**18**	**3**	**0**	**0**	**59**	**11.9**	**–4**	....	....	....	....	....	....	....	....	....	....	....	....	....
	Edmonton	**NHL**	**23**	**5**	**9**	**14**	**28**	**1**	**0**	**0**	**43**	**11.6**	**–1**	....	....	....	....	....	....	....	....	....	....	....	....	....
1994-95	**Edmonton**	**NHL**	**46**	**6**	**11**	**17**	**21**	**3**	**0**	**2**	**59**	**10.2**	**–12**	....	....	....	....	....	....	....	....	....	....	....	....	....
1995-96	**Winnipeg**	**NHL**	**58**	**10**	**14**	**24**	**37**	**3**	**1**	**0**	**91**	**11.0**	**–4**	....	....	....	....	....	**6**	**0**	**0**	**0**	**21**	**0**	**0**	**0**
1996-97	**Phoenix**	**NHL**	**55**	**4**	**11**	**15**	**36**	**2**	**0**	**1**	**74**	**5.4**	**–4**	....	....	....	....	....	**7**	**0**	**0**	**0**	**14**	**0**	**0**	**0**
1997-98	**Phoenix**	**NHL**	**64**	**5**	**5**	**10**	**36**	**1**	**1**	**1**	**69**	**7.2**	**–4**	....	....	....	....	....	**6**	**0**	**0**	**0**	**2**	**0**	**0**	**0**
1998-99	**Phoenix**	**NHL**	**76**	**9**	**9**	**18**	**34**	**0**	**2**	**2**	**106**	**8.5**	**–6**	**345**	**46.1**	**67**	**40**	**13:40**	**7**	**1**	**0**	**1**	**0**	**0**	**0**	**0**
99-2000	**Atlanta**	**NHL**	**62**	**10**	**12**	**22**	**30**	**4**	**0**	**1**	**146**	**6.8**	**–29**	**717**	**48.0**	**72**	**44**	**17:18**	....	....	....	....	....	....	....	....
	NHL Totals		**645**	**69**	**105**	**174**	**332**	**18**	**5**	**9**	**873**	**7.9**		**1062**	**47.4**	**139**	**84**	**15:18**	**34**	**1**	**0**	**1**	**39**	**0**	**0**	**0**

Signed as a free agent by **Pittsburgh**, September 30, 1992. Claimed on waivers by **Edmonton** from **Pittsburgh**, February 19, 1994. Signed as a free agent by **Winnipeg**, August 18, 1995. Transferred to **Phoenix** after **Winnipeg** franchise relocated, July 1, 1996. Claimed by **Atlanta** from **Phoenix** in Expansion Draft, June 25, 1999. Signed as a free agent by **NY Islanders**, July 3, 2000.

STEFAN, Patrik (SHTEH-fan, PAT-rihk) ATL.

Center. Shoots left. 6'3", 205 lbs. Born, Pribram, Czech., September 16, 1980. Atlanta's 1st choice, 1st overall, in 1999 Entry Draft.

Season	Club	League	GP	G	A	Pts	PIM	PP	SH	GW	S	%	+/-	TF	F%	H	SB	Min	GP	G	A	Pts	PIM	PP	SH	GW
1996-97	Sparta Praha	Cze-Rep	5	0	1	1	2	....	....	....	....	....	....	....	....	....	....	....	7	1	0	1	0	....	....	....
1997-98	Sparta Praha	Cze-Rep	27	2	6	8	16	....	....	....	....	....	....	....	....	....	....	....	....	....	....	....	....	....	....	....
	Long Beach	IHL	25	5	10	15	10	....	....	....	....	....	....	....	....	....	....	....	10	1	1	2	2	....	....	....
1998-99	Long Beach	IHL	33	11	24	35	26	....	....	....	....	....	....	....	....	....	....	....	....	....	....	....	....	....	....	....
99-2000	**Atlanta**	**NHL**	**72**	**5**	**20**	**25**	**30**	**1**	**0**	**0**	**117**	**4.3**	**–20**	**988**	**41.4**	**58**	**22**	**14:49**	....	....	....	....	....	....	....	....
	NHL Totals		**72**	**5**	**20**	**25**	**30**	**1**	**0**	**0**	**117**	**4.3**		**988**	**41.4**	**58**	**22**	**14:49**	....	....	....	....	....	....	....	....

STERN, Ron (STUHRN, RAWN)

Right wing. Shoots right. 6', 200 lbs. Born, Ste. Agathe, Que., January 11, 1967. Vancouver's 3rd choice, 70th overall, in 1986 Entry Draft.

Season	Club	League	GP	G	A	Pts	PIM	PP	SH	GW	S	%	+/-	TF	F%	H	SB	Min	GP	G	A	Pts	PIM	PP	SH	GW
1983-84	Laval Laurentides	QAAA	39	6	6	12	....	....	....	....	....	....	....	....	....	....	....	....	....	....	....	....	....	....	....	....
1984-85	Longueuil	QMJHL	67	6	14	20	176	....	....	....	....	....	....	....	....	....	....	....	....	....	....	....	....	....	....	....
1985-86	Longueuil	QMJHL	70	39	33	72	317	....	....	....	....	....	....	....	....	....	....	....	....	....	....	....	....	....	....	....
1986-87	Longueuil	QMJHL	56	32	39	71	266	....	....	....	....	....	....	....	....	....	....	....	19	11	9	20	55	....	....	....
1987-88	**Vancouver**	**NHL**	**15**	**0**	**0**	**0**	**52**	**0**	**0**	**0**	**7**	**0.0**	**–7**	....	....	....	....	....	....	....	....	....	....	....	....	....
	Fredericton	AHL	2	1	0	1	4	....	....	....	....	....	....	....	....	....	....	....	....	....	....	....	....	....	....	....
	Flint Spirits	IHL	55	14	19	33	294	....	....	....	....	....	....	....	....	....	....	....	16	8	8	16	94	....	....	....
1988-89	**Vancouver**	**NHL**	**17**	**1**	**0**	**1**	**49**	**0**	**0**	**0**	**13**	**7.7**	**–6**	....	....	....	....	....	**3**	**0**	**1**	**1**	**17**	**0**	**0**	**0**
	Milwaukee	IHL	45	19	23	42	280	....	....	....	....	....	....	....	....	....	....	....	5	1	0	1	11	....	....	....
1989-90	**Vancouver**	**NHL**	**34**	**2**	**3**	**5**	**208**	**0**	**0**	**0**	**27**	**7.4**	**–17**	....	....	....	....	....	....	....	....	....	....	....	....	....
	Milwaukee	IHL	26	8	9	17	165	....	....	....	....	....	....	....	....	....	....	....	....	....	....	....	....	....	....	....
1990-91	**Vancouver**	**NHL**	**31**	**2**	**3**	**5**	**171**	**0**	**0**	**0**	**30**	**6.7**	**–14**	....	....	....	....	....	....	....	....	....	....	....	....	....
	Milwaukee	IHL	7	2	2	4	81	....	....	....	....	....	....	....	....	....	....	....	....	....	....	....	....	....	....	....
	Calgary	**NHL**	**13**	**1**	**3**	**4**	**69**	**0**	**0**	**0**	**15**	**6.7**	**0**	....	....	....	....	....	**7**	**1**	**3**	**4**	**14**	**0**	**0**	**0**
1991-92	**Calgary**	**NHL**	**72**	**13**	**9**	**22**	**338**	**0**	**1**	**1**	**96**	**13.5**	**0**	....	....	....	....	....	....	....	....	....	....	....	....	....
1992-93	**Calgary**	**NHL**	**70**	**10**	**15**	**25**	**207**	**0**	**0**	**1**	**82**	**12.2**	**4**	....	....	....	....	....	**6**	**0**	**0**	**0**	**43**	**0**	**0**	**0**
1993-94	**Calgary**	**NHL**	**71**	**9**	**20**	**29**	**243**	**0**	**1**	**3**	**105**	**8.6**	**6**	....	....	....	....	....	**7**	**2**	**0**	**2**	**12**	**0**	**0**	**0**
1994-95	**Calgary**	**NHL**	**39**	**9**	**4**	**13**	**163**	**1**	**0**	**0**	**69**	**13.0**	**4**	....	....	....	....	....	**7**	**3**	**1**	**4**	**8**	**1**	**1**	**0**
1995-96	**Calgary**	**NHL**	**52**	**10**	**5**	**15**	**111**	**0**	**0**	**1**	**64**	**15.6**	**2**	....	....	....	....	....	**4**	**0**	**2**	**2**	**8**	**0**	**0**	**0**
1996-97	**Calgary**	**NHL**	**79**	**7**	**10**	**17**	**157**	**0**	**1**	**1**	**98**	**7.1**	**–4**	....	....	....	....	....	....	....	....	....	....	....	....	....
1997-98	**Calgary**	**NHL**	DID NOT PLAY – INJURED																							
1998-99	**San Jose**	**NHL**	**78**	**7**	**9**	**16**	**158**	**1**	**0**	**2**	**94**	**7.4**	**–3**	**1**	**0.0**	**153**	**18**	**11:37**	**6**	**0**	**0**	**0**	**6**	**0**	**0**	**0**
99-2000	**San Jose**	**NHL**	**67**	**4**	**5**	**9**	**151**	**0**	**0**	**0**	**63**	**6.3**	**–9**	**3**	**33.3**	**142**	**14**	**9:07**	**3**	**1**	**0**	**1**	**11**	**0**	**0**	**0**
	NHL Totals		**638**	**75**	**86**	**161**	**2077**	**2**	**3**	**9**	**763**	**9.8**		**4**	**25.0**	**295**	**32**	**10:28**	**43**	**7**	**7**	**14**	**119**	**1**	**1**	**0**

Traded to **Calgary** by **Vancouver** with Kevan Guy for Dana Murzyn, March 5, 1991. • Missed entire 1997-98 season recovering from knee surgery, October, 1997. Signed as a free agent by **San Jose**, August 25, 1998.

STEVENS, Kevin (STEE-vehns, KEH-vihn) PHI.

Left wing. Shoots left. 6'3", 230 lbs. Born, Brockton, MA, April 15, 1965. Los Angeles' 6th choice, 112th overall, in 1983 Entry Draft.

Season	Club	League	GP	G	A	Pts	PIM	PP	SH	GW	S	%	+/-	TF	F%	H	SB	Min	GP	G	A	Pts	PIM	PP	SH	GW
1982-83	Silver Lake	Hi-School	18	24	27	51	....	....	....	....	....	....	....	....	....	....	....	....	....	....	....	....	....	....	....	....
1983-84	Boston College	ECAC	37	6	14	20	36	....	....	....	....	....	....	....	....	....	....	....	....	....	....	....	....	....	....	....
1984-85	Boston College	H-East	40	13	23	36	36	....	....	....	....	....	....	....	....	....	....	....	....	....	....	....	....	....	....	....
1985-86	Boston College	H-East	42	17	27	44	56	....	....	....	....	....	....	....	....	....	....	....	....	....	....	....	....	....	....	....
1986-87	Boston College	H-East	39	35	35	70	54	....	....	....	....	....	....	....	....	....	....	....	....	....	....	....	....	....	....	....
1987-88	United States	Nat-Team	44	22	23	45	52	....	....	....	....	....	....	....	....	....	....	....	....	....	....	....	....	....	....	....
	United States	Olympics	5	1	3	4	2	....	....	....	....	....	....	....	....	....	....	....	....	....	....	....	....	....	....	....
	Pittsburgh	**NHL**	**16**	**5**	**2**	**7**	**8**	**2**	**0**	**0**	**22**	**22.7**	**–6**	....	....	....	....	....	....	....	....	....	....	....	....	....
1988-89	**Pittsburgh**	**NHL**	**24**	**12**	**3**	**15**	**19**	**4**	**0**	**3**	**52**	**23.1**	**–8**	....	....	....	....	....	**11**	**3**	**7**	**10**	**16**	**0**	**0**	**0**
	Muskegon	IHL	45	24	41	65	113	....	....	....	....	....	....	....	....	....	....	....	....	....	....	....	....	....	....	....
1989-90	**Pittsburgh**	**NHL**	**76**	**29**	**41**	**70**	**171**	**12**	**0**	**1**	**179**	**16.2**	**–13**	....	....	....	....	....	....	....	....	....	....	....	....	....
1990-91♦	**Pittsburgh**	**NHL**	**80**	**40**	**46**	**86**	**133**	**18**	**0**	**6**	**253**	**15.8**	**–1**	....	....	....	....	....	**24**	***17**	**16**	**33**	**53**	**7**	**0**	**4**
1991-92♦	**Pittsburgh**	**NHL**	**80**	**54**	**69**	**123**	**254**	**19**	**0**	**4**	**325**	**16.6**	**8**	....	....	....	....	....	**21**	**13**	**15**	**28**	**28**	**4**	**0**	**3**
1992-93	**Pittsburgh**	**NHL**	**72**	**55**	**56**	**111**	**177**	**26**	**0**	**5**	**326**	**16.9**	**17**	....	....	....	....	....	**12**	**5**	**11**	**16**	**22**	**4**	**0**	**0**
1993-94	**Pittsburgh**	**NHL**	**83**	**41**	**47**	**88**	**155**	**21**	**0**	**4**	**284**	**14.4**	**–24**	....	....	....	....	....	**6**	**1**	**1**	**2**	**10**	**0**	**0**	**0**
1994-95	**Pittsburgh**	**NHL**	**27**	**15**	**12**	**27**	**51**	**6**	**0**	**4**	**80**	**18.8**	**0**	....	....	....	....	....	**12**	**4**	**7**	**11**	**21**	**3**	**0**	**1**
1995-96	**Boston**	**NHL**	**41**	**10**	**13**	**23**	**49**	**3**	**0**	**1**	**101**	**9.9**	**1**	....	....	....	....	....	....	....	....	....	....	....	....	....
	Los Angeles	**NHL**	**20**	**3**	**10**	**13**	**22**	**3**	**0**	**0**	**69**	**4.3**	**–11**	....	....	....	....	....	....	....	....	....	....	....	....	....
1996-97	**Los Angeles**	**NHL**	**69**	**14**	**20**	**34**	**96**	**4**	**0**	**1**	**175**	**8.0**	**–27**	....	....	....	....	....	....	....	....	....	....	....	....	....
1997-98	**NY Rangers**	**NHL**	**80**	**14**	**27**	**41**	**130**	**5**	**0**	**3**	**144**	**9.7**	**–7**	....	....	....	....	....	....	....	....	....	....	....	....	....
1998-99	**NY Rangers**	**NHL**	**81**	**23**	**20**	**43**	**64**	**8**	**0**	**3**	**136**	**16.9**	**–10**	**11**	**45.5**	**176**	**27**	**15:12**	....	....	....	....	....	....	....	....
99-2000	**NY Rangers**	**NHL**	**38**	**3**	**5**	**8**	**43**	**1**	**0**	**0**	**44**	**6.8**	**–7**	**11**	**54.6**	**78**	**20**	**12:29**	....	....	....	....	....	....	....	....
	NHL Totals		**787**	**318**	**371**	**689**	**1372**	**132**	**0**	**35**	**2190**	**14.5**		**22**	**50.0**	**254**	**47**	**14:20**	**86**	**43**	**57**	**100**	**150**	**18**	**0**	**8**

Hockey East First All-Star Team (1987) • NCAA East Second All-American Team (1987) • NHL Second All-Star Team (1991, 1993) • NHL First All-Star Team (1992) • Played in NHL All-Star Game (1991, 1992, 1993)

Rights traded to **Pittsburgh** by **LA Kings** for Anders Hakansson, September 9, 1983. Traded to **Boston** by **Pittsburgh** with Shawn McEachern for Glen Murray, Bryan Smolinski and Boston's 3rd round choice (Boyd Kane) in 1996 Entry Draft, August 2, 1995. Traded to **LA Kings** by **Boston** for Rick Tocchet, January 25, 1996. Traded to **NY Rangers** by **LA Kings** for Luc Robitaille, August 28, 1997. • Missed majority of 1999-2000 season after entering NHL/NHLPA substance abuse program, January 23, 2000. Signed as a free agent by **Philadelphia**, July 7, 2000.

STEVENS, Scott (STEE-vehns, SKAWT) N.J.

Defense. Shoots left. 6'1", 215 lbs. Born, Kitchener, Ont., April 1, 1964. Washington's 1st choice, 5th overall, in 1982 Entry Draft.

Season	Club	League	GP	G	A	Pts	PIM	PP	SH	GW	S	%	+/-	TF	F%	H	SB	Min	GP	G	A	Pts	PIM	PP	SH	GW
1980-81	Kitchener B's	OHA-B	39	7	33	40	82	....	....	....	....	....	....	....	....	....	....	....	....	....	....	....	....	....	....	....
	Kitchener	OMJHL	1	0	0	0	0	....	....	....	....	....	....	....	....	....	....	....	....	....	....	....	....	....	....	....
1981-82	Kitchener	OHL	68	6	36	42	158	....	....	....	....	....	....	....	....	....	....	....	15	1	10	11	71	....	....	....
1982-83	**Washington**	**NHL**	**77**	**9**	**16**	**25**	**195**	**0**	**0**	**0**	**121**	**7.4**	**14**	....	....	....	....	....	**4**	**1**	**0**	**1**	**26**	**0**	**0**	**0**
1983-84	**Washington**	**NHL**	**78**	**13**	**32**	**45**	**201**	**7**	**0**	**2**	**155**	**8.4**	**26**	....	....	....	....	....	**8**	**1**	**8**	**9**	**21**	**1**	**0**	**0**
1984-85	**Washington**	**NHL**	**80**	**21**	**44**	**65**	**221**	**16**	**0**	**5**	**170**	**12.4**	**19**	....	....	....	....	....	**5**	**0**	**1**	**1**	**20**	**0**	**0**	**0**
1985-86	**Washington**	**NHL**	**73**	**15**	**38**	**53**	**165**	**3**	**0**	**2**	**121**	**12.4**	**0**	....	....	....	....	....	**9**	**3**	**8**	**11**	**12**	**2**	**0**	**2**
1986-87	**Washington**	**NHL**	**77**	**10**	**51**	**61**	**283**	**2**	**0**	**0**	**165**	**6.1**	**13**	....	....	....	....	....	**7**	**0**	**5**	**5**	**19**	**0**	**0**	**0**
1987-88	**Washington**	**NHL**	**80**	**12**	**60**	**72**	**184**	**5**	**1**	**2**	**231**	**5.2**	**14**	....	....	....	....	....	**13**	**1**	**11**	**12**	**46**	**0**	**0**	**0**

			Regular Season																Playoffs							
Season	Club	League	GP	G	A	Pts	PIM	PP	SH	GW	S	%	+/-	TF	F%	H	SB	Min	GP	G	A	Pts	PIM	PP	SH	GW
1988-89	Washington	NHL	80	7	61	68	225	6	0	3	195	3.6	1	....	....	....	....	....	6	1	4	5	11	0	0	0
1989-90	Washington	NHL	56	11	29	40	154	7	0	0	143	7.7	1	....	....	....	....	....	15	2	7	9	25	1	0	0
1990-91	St. Louis	NHL	78	5	44	49	150	1	0	1	160	3.1	23	....	....	....	....	....	13	0	3	3	36	0	0	0
1991-92	New Jersey	NHL	68	17	42	59	124	7	1	2	156	10.9	24	....	....	....	....	....	7	2	1	3	29	2	0	1
1992-93	New Jersey	NHL	81	12	45	57	120	8	0	1	146	8.2	14	....	....	....	....	....	5	2	2	4	10	1	0	0
1993-94	New Jersey	NHL	83	18	60	78	112	5	1	4	215	8.4	53	....	....	....	....	....	20	2	9	11	42	2	0	1
1994-95♦	New Jersey	NHL	48	2	20	22	56	1	0	1	111	1.8	4	....	....	....	....	....	20	1	7	8	24	0	0	1
1995-96	New Jersey	NHL	82	5	23	28	100	2	1	1	174	2.9	7	....	....	....	....	....	....	....	....	....	....	....	....	....
1996-97	New Jersey	NHL	79	5	19	24	70	0	0	1	166	3.0	26	....	....	....	....	....	10	0	4	4	2	0	0	0
1997-98	New Jersey	NHL	80	4	22	26	80	1	0	1	94	4.3	19	....	....	....	....	....	6	1	0	1	8	0	0	0
	Canada	Olympics	6	0	0	0	2	....	....	....	....	....	....	....	....	....	....	....	....	....	....	....	....	....	....	....
1998-99	New Jersey	NHL	75	5	22	27	64	0	0	1	111	4.5	29	1	0.0	187	149	24:11	7	2	1	3	10	2	0	0
99-2000♦	New Jersey	NHL	78	8	21	29	103	0	1	1	133	6.0	30	0	0.0	169	130	23:23	23	3	8	11	6	0	0	2
	NHL Totals		1353	179	649	828	2607	71	5	28	2767	6.5		1	0.0	356	279	23:46	178	22	79	101	347	11	0	7

NHL All-Rookie Team (1983) • NHL First All-Star Team (1988, 1994) • NHL Second All-Star Team (1992, 1997) • Won Alka-Seltzer Plus Award (1994) • Played in NHL All-Star Game (1985, 1989, 1991, 1992, 1993, 1994, 1996, 1997, 1998, 1999, 2000)

Signed as a free agent by **St. Louis**, July 16, 1990. Transferred to **New Jersey** from **St. Louis** as compensation for St. Louis' signing of free agent Brendan Shanahan, September 3, 1991.

STEVENSON, Jeremy
(STEE-vehn-sohn, JAIR-eh-mee)

Left wing. Shoots left. 6'2", 220 lbs. Born, San Bernadino, CA, July 28, 1974. Anaheim's 10th choice, 262nd overall, in 1994 Entry Draft.

1989-90	Elliot Lake Vikings	NOHA	61	39	26	65	203	....	....	....	....	....	....	....	....	....	....	....	....	....	....	....	....	....	....	....
1990-91	Cornwall Royals	OHL	58	13	20	33	124	....	....	....	....	....	....	....	....	....	....	....	....	....	....	....	....	....	....	....
1991-92	Cornwall Royals	OHL	63	15	23	38	176	....	....	....	....	....	....	....	....	....	....	....	6	3	1	4	4	....	....	....
1992-93	Newmarket Royals	OHL	54	28	28	56	144	....	....	....	....	....	....	....	....	....	....	....	5	5	1	6	28	....	....	....
1993-94	Newmarket Royals	OHL	9	2	4	6	27	....	....	....	....	....	....	....	....	....	....	....	....	....	....	....	....	....	....	....
	Sault Ste. Marie	OHL	48	18	19	37	183	....	....	....	....	....	....	....	....	....	....	....	14	1	1	2	23	....	....	....
1994-95	Greensboro	ECHL	43	14	13	27	231	....	....	....	....	....	....	....	....	....	....	....	17	6	11	17	64	....	....	....
1995-96	Anaheim	NHL	3	0	1	1	12	0	0	0	1	0.0	1	....	....	....	....	....	....	....	....	....	....	....	....	....
	Baltimore Bandits	AHL	60	11	10	21	295	....	....	....	....	....	....	....	....	....	....	....	12	4	2	6	23	....	....	....
1996-97	Anaheim	NHL	5	0	0	0	14	0	0	0	1	0.0	–1	....	....	....	....	....	....	....	....	....	....	....	....	....
	Baltimore Bandits	AHL	25	8	8	16	125	....	....	....	....	....	....	....	....	....	....	....	3	0	0	0	8	....	....	....
1997-98	Anaheim	NHL	45	3	5	8	101	0	0	1	43	7.0	–4	....	....	....	....	....	....	....	....	....	....	....	....	....
	Cincinnati Ducks	AHL	10	5	0	5	34	....	....	....	....	....	....	....	....	....	....	....	....	....	....	....	....	....	....	....
1998-99	Cincinnati Ducks	AHL	22	4	4	8	83	....	....	....	....	....	....	....	....	....	....	....	3	1	0	1	2	....	....	....
99-2000	Anaheim	NHL	3	0	0	0	7	0	0	0	2	0.0	–1	0	0.0	4	1	6:50	....	....	....	....	....	....	....	....
	Cincinnati Ducks	AHL	41	11	14	25	100	....	....	....	....	....	....	....	....	....	....	....	....	....	....	....	....	....	....	....
	NHL Totals		56	3	6	9	134	0	0	1	47	6.4		0	0.0	4	1	6:50	....	....	....	....	....	....	....	....

• Re-entered NHL draft. Originally Winnipeg's 3rd choice, 60th overall, in 1992 Entry Draft.

STEVENSON, Turner
(STEE-vehn-sohn, TUHR-nuhr) **N.J.**

Right wing. Shoots right. 6'3", 225 lbs. Born, Prince George, B.C., May 18, 1972. Montreal's 1st choice, 12th overall, in 1990 Entry Draft.

1987-88	Prince George	BCAHA	53	45	46	91	127	....	....	....	....	....	....	....	....	....	....	....	....	....	....	....	....	....	....	....
1988-89	Seattle T-Birds	WHL	69	15	12	27	84	....	....	....	....	....	....	....	....	....	....	....	....	....	....	....	....	....	....	....
1989-90	Seattle T-Birds	WHL	62	29	32	61	276	....	....	....	....	....	....	....	....	....	....	....	13	3	2	5	35	....	....	....
1990-91	Seattle T-Birds	WHL	57	36	27	63	222	....	....	....	....	....	....	....	....	....	....	....	6	1	5	6	15	....	....	....
	Fredericton	AHL	....	....	....	....	....	....	....	....	....	....	....	....	....	....	....	....	4	0	0	0	5	....	....	....
1991-92	Seattle T-Birds	WHL	58	20	32	52	264	....	....	....	....	....	....	....	....	....	....	....	15	9	3	12	55	....	....	....
1992-93	Montreal	NHL	1	0	0	0	0	0	0	0	1	0.0	–1	....	....	....	....	....	....	....	....	....	....	....	....	....
	Fredericton	AHL	79	25	34	59	102	....	....	....	....	....	....	....	....	....	....	....	5	2	3	5	11	....	....	....
1993-94	Montreal	NHL	2	0	0	0	2	0	0	0	0	0.0	–2	....	....	....	....	....	3	0	2	2	0	0	0	0
	Fredericton	AHL	66	19	28	47	155	....	....	....	....	....	....	....	....	....	....	....	....	....	....	....	....	....	....	....
1994-95	Fredericton	AHL	37	12	12	24	109	....	....	....	....	....	....	....	....	....	....	....	....	....	....	....	....	....	....	....
	Montreal	NHL	41	6	1	7	86	0	0	1	35	17.1	0	....	....	....	....	....	....	....	....	....	....	....	....	....
1995-96	Montreal	NHL	80	9	16	25	167	0	0	2	101	8.9	–2	....	....	....	....	....	6	0	1	1	2	0	0	0
1996-97	Montreal	NHL	65	8	13	21	97	1	0	0	76	10.5	–14	....	....	....	....	....	5	1	1	2	2	0	0	0
1997-98	Montreal	NHL	63	4	6	10	110	1	0	0	43	9.3	–8	....	....	....	....	....	10	3	4	7	12	0	0	0
1998-99	Montreal	NHL	69	10	17	27	88	0	0	2	102	9.8	6	29	37.9	142	20	12:57	....	....	....	....	....	....	....	....
99-2000	Montreal	NHL	64	8	13	21	61	0	0	2	94	8.5	–1	5	20.0	160	18	13:10	....	....	....	....	....	....	....	....
	NHL Totals		385	45	66	111	611	2	0	7	452	10.0		34	35.3	302	38	13:03	24	4	8	12	16	0	0	0

WHL West First All-Star Team (1992) • Memorial Cup All-Star Team (1992).

Selected by **Columbus** from **Montreal** in Expansion Draft, June 23, 2000. Traded to **New Jersey** by **Columbus** to complete transaction that sent Krzysztof Oliwa (June 12, 2000) and Deron Quint (June 23, 2000) to **Columbus**, June 23, 2000.

STEWART, Cam
(STEW-ahrt, KAM) **MIN.**

Left wing. Shoots left. 5'11", 196 lbs. Born, Kitchener, Ont., September 18, 1971. Boston's 2nd choice, 63rd overall, in 1990 Entry Draft.

1987-88	Woolrich Regents	OMHA	21	25	32	57	65	....	....	....	....	....	....	....	....	....	....	....	....	....	....	....	....	....	....	....
1988-89	Elmira Kings	OJHL-B	43	38	50	88	138	....	....	....	....	....	....	....	....	....	....	....	....	....	....	....	....	....	....	....
1989-90	Elmira Kings	OJHL-B	46	43	95	138	174	....	....	....	....	....	....	....	....	....	....	....	....	....	....	....	....	....	....	....
1990-91	U. of Michigan	CCHA	44	8	24	32	122	....	....	....	....	....	....	....	....	....	....	....	....	....	....	....	....	....	....	....
1991-92	U. of Michigan	CCHA	44	13	15	28	106	....	....	....	....	....	....	....	....	....	....	....	....	....	....	....	....	....	....	....
1992-93	U. of Michigan	CCHA	39	20	39	59	69	....	....	....	....	....	....	....	....	....	....	....	....	....	....	....	....	....	....	....
1993-94	Boston	NHL	57	3	6	9	66	0	0	1	55	5.5	–6	....	....	....	....	....	8	0	3	3	7	0	0	0
	Providence Bruins	AHL	14	3	2	5	5	....	....	....	....	....	....	....	....	....	....	....	....	....	....	....	....	....	....	....
1994-95	Boston	NHL	5	0	0	0	2	0	0	0	2	0.0	0	....	....	....	....	....	....	....	....	....	....	....	....	....
	Providence Bruins	AHL	31	13	11	24	38	....	....	....	....	....	....	....	....	....	....	....	9	2	5	7	0	....	....	....
1995-96	Boston	NHL	6	0	0	0	0	0	0	0	2	0.0	–2	....	....	....	....	....	5	1	0	1	2	0	0	0
	Providence Bruins	AHL	54	17	25	42	39	....	....	....	....	....	....	....	....	....	....	....	....	....	....	....	....	....	....	....
1996-97	Boston	NHL	15	0	1	1	4	0	0	0	21	0.0	–2	....	....	....	....	....	....	....	....	....	....	....	....	....
	Providence Bruins	AHL	18	4	3	7	37	....	....	....	....	....	....	....	....	....	....	....	....	....	....	....	....	....	....	....
	Cincinnati	IHL	7	3	2	5	8	....	....	....	....	....	....	....	....	....	....	....	1	0	0	0	0	....	....	....
1997-98	Houston Aeros	IHL	63	18	27	45	51	....	....	....	....	....	....	....	....	....	....	....	4	0	1	1	18	....	....	....
1998-99	Houston Aeros	IHL	61	36	26	62	75	....	....	....	....	....	....	....	....	....	....	....	19	10	5	15	26	....	....	....
99-2000	Florida	NHL	65	9	7	16	30	0	0	3	52	17.3	–2	13	7.7	78	11	9:04	....	....	....	....	....	....	....	....
	NHL Totals		148	12	14	26	102	0	0	4	132	9.1		13	7.7	78	11	9:04	13	1	3	4	9	0	0	0

Signed as a free agent by **Florida**, July 21, 1999. Selected by **Minnesota** from **Florida** in Expansion Draft, June 23, 2000.

STILLMAN, Cory
(STIHL-mahn, KOHR-ee) **CGY.**

Center. Shoots left. 6', 194 lbs. Born, Peterborough, Ont., December 20, 1973. Calgary's 1st choice, 6th overall, in 1992 Entry Draft.

1989-90	Peterborough B's	OJHL-B	41	30	*54	84	76	....	....	....	....	....	....	....	....	....	....	....	....	....	....	....	....	....	....	....
1990-91	Windsor Spitfires	OHL	64	31	70	101	31	....	....	....	....	....	....	....	....	....	....	....	11	3	6	9	8	....	....	....
1991-92	Windsor Spitfires	OHL	53	29	61	90	59	....	....	....	....	....	....	....	....	....	....	....	7	2	4	6	8	....	....	....
1992-93	Peterborough	OHL	61	25	55	80	55	....	....	....	....	....	....	....	....	....	....	....	18	3	8	11	18	....	....	....
	Canada	Nat-Team	1	0	0	0	0	....	....	....	....	....	....	....	....	....	....	....	....	....	....	....	....	....	....	....
1993-94	Saint John Flames	AHL	79	35	48	83	52	....	....	....	....	....	....	....	....	....	....	....	7	2	4	6	16	....	....	....
1994-95	Saint John Flames	AHL	63	28	53	81	70	....	....	....	....	....	....	....	....	....	....	....	5	0	2	2	2	....	....	....
	Calgary	NHL	10	0	2	2	2	0	0	0	7	0.0	1	....	....	....	....	....	....	....	....	....	....	....	....	....
1995-96	Calgary	NHL	74	16	19	35	41	4	1	3	132	12.1	–5	....	....	....	....	....	2	1	1	2	0	0	0	0
1996-97	Calgary	NHL	58	6	20	26	14	2	0	0	112	5.4	–6	....	....	....	....	....	....	....	....	....	....	....	....	....
1997-98	Calgary	NHL	72	27	22	49	40	9	4	1	178	15.2	–9	....	....	....	....	....	....	....	....	....	....	....	....	....

			Regular Season																Playoffs							
Season	Club	League	GP	G	A	Pts	PIM	PP	SH	GW	S	%	+/-	TF	F%	H	SB	Min	GP	G	A	Pts	PIM	PP	SH	GW
1998-99	**Calgary**	**NHL**	**76**	**27**	**30**	**57**	**38**	**9**	**3**	**5**	**175**	**15.4**	**7**	**535**	**46.5**	**128**	**33**	**16:19**	....	....	....	....	....	....	....	....
99-2000	**Calgary**	**NHL**	**37**	**12**	**9**	**21**	**12**	**6**	**0**	**3**	**59**	**20.3**	**-9**	**283**	**54.4**	**39**	**27**	**17:45**	....	....	....	....	....	....	....	....
	NHL Totals		**327**	**88**	**102**	**190**	**147**	**30**	**8**	**12**	**663**	**13.3**		**818**	**49.3**	**167**	**60**	**16:47**	**2**	**1**	**1**	**2**	**0**	**0**	**0**	**0**

• Missed remainder of 1999-2000 season recovering from shoulder injury suffered in game vs. Philadelphia, December 27, 1999.

STOCK, P.J. (STAWK, PEE-JAY) MTL.

Left wing. Shoots left. 5'10", 190 lbs. Born, Victoriaville, Que., May 26, 1975.

1994-95	Victoriaville Tigres	QMJHL	70	9	46	55	386	....	....	....	....	....	....	....	....	....	....	....	4	0	0	0	60	....	....	....
1995-96	Victoriaville Tigres	QMJHL	67	19	43	62	432	....	....	....	....	....	....	....	....	....	....	....	12	5	4	9	79	....	....	....
1996-97	St. FX University	AUAA	27	11	20	31	110	....	....	....	....	....	....	....	....	....	....	....	3	0	4	4	14	....	....	....
1997-98	Hartford	AHL	41	8	8	16	202	....	....	....	....	....	....	....	....	....	....	....	11	1	3	4	79	....	....	....
	NY Rangers	**NHL**	**38**	**2**	**3**	**5**	**114**	**0**	**0**	**1**	**9**	**22.2**	**4**	....	....	....	....	....	....	....	....	....	....	....	....	....
1998-99	**NY Rangers**	**NHL**	**5**	**0**	**0**	**0**	**6**	**0**	**0**	**0**	**0**	**0.0**	**-1**	**8**	**50.0**	**8**	**0**	**2:42**	....	....	....	....	....	....	....	....
	Hartford	AHL	55	4	14	18	250	....	....	....	....	....	....	....	....	....	....	....	6	0	1	1	35	....	....	....
99-2000	**NY Rangers**	**NHL**	**11**	**0**	**1**	**1**	**11**	**0**	**0**	**0**	**2**	**0.0**	**1**	**63**	**31.8**	**14**	**1**	**6:13**	....	....	....	....	....	....	....	....
	Hartford	AHL	64	13	23	36	290	....	....	....	....	....	....	....	....	....	....	....	23	1	11	12	69	....	....	....
	NHL Totals		**54**	**2**	**4**	**6**	**131**	**0**	**0**	**1**	**11**	**18.2**		**71**	**33.8**	**22**	**1**	**5:07**	....	....	....	....	....	....	....	....

Signed as a free agent by **NY Rangers**, November 18, 1997. Signed as a free agent by **Montreal**, July 7, 2000.

STOJANOV, Alek (STOY-uh-nahf, A-lehk)

Right wing. Shoots left. 6'4", 225 lbs. Born, Windsor, Ont., April 25, 1973. Vancouver's 1st choice, 7th overall, in 1991 Entry Draft.

1988-89	Windsor Riversides	OMHA	26	19	15	34	53	....	....	....	....	....	....	....	....	....	....	....	....	....	....	....	....	....	....	....
	Belle River	OJHL-C	7	3	2	5	42	....	....	....	....	....	....	....	....	....	....	....	....	....	....	....	....	....	....	....
	Amherstburg	OJHL-C	1	0	0	0	2	....	....	....	....	....	....	....	....	....	....	....	....	....	....	....	....	....	....	....
1989-90	Hamilton Dukes	OHL	37	4	4	8	91	....	....	....	....	....	....	....	....	....	....	....	....	....	....	....	....	....	....	....
1990-91	Hamilton Dukes	OHL	62	25	20	45	181	....	....	....	....	....	....	....	....	....	....	....	4	1	1	2	14	....	....	....
1991-92	Guelph Storm	OHL	33	12	15	27	91	....	....	....	....	....	....	....	....	....	....	....	....	....	....	....	....	....	....	....
1992-93	Guelph Storm	OHL	36	27	28	55	62	....	....	....	....	....	....	....	....	....	....	....	....	....	....	....	....	....	....	....
	Newmarket	OHL	14	9	7	16	26	....	....	....	....	....	....	....	....	....	....	....	7	1	3	4	26	....	....	....
	Hamilton Canucks	AHL	4	4	0	4	0	....	....	....	....	....	....	....	....	....	....	....	....	....	....	....	....	....	....	....
1993-94	Hamilton Canucks	AHL	4	0	1	1	5	....	....	....	....	....	....	....	....	....	....	....	....	....	....	....	....	....	....	....
1994-95	Syracuse Crunch	AHL	73	18	12	30	270	....	....	....	....	....	....	....	....	....	....	....	....	....	....	....	....	....	....	....
	Vancouver	**NHL**	**4**	**0**	**0**	**0**	**13**	**0**	**0**	**0**	**1**	**0.0**	**-2**	....	....	....	....	....	**5**	**0**	**0**	**0**	**2**	**0**	**0**	**0**
1995-96	**Vancouver**	**NHL**	**58**	**0**	**1**	**1**	**123**	**0**	**0**	**0**	**16**	**0.0**	**-12**	....	....	....	....	....	....	....	....	....	....	....	....	....
	Pittsburgh	**NHL**	**10**	**1**	**0**	**1**	**7**	**0**	**0**	**0**	**4**	**25.0**	**-1**	....	....	....	....	....	**9**	**0**	**0**	**0**	**19**	**0**	**0**	**0**
1996-97	**Pittsburgh**	**NHL**	**35**	**1**	**4**	**5**	**79**	**0**	**0**	**0**	**11**	**9.1**	**3**	....	....	....	....	....	....	....	....	....	....	....	....	....
1997-98	Syracuse Crunch	AHL	41	5	4	9	215	....	....	....	....	....	....	....	....	....	....	....	3	1	0	1	4	....	....	....
1998-99	Hamilton Bulldogs	AHL	12	0	1	1	35	....	....	....	....	....	....	....	....	....	....	....	....	....	....	....	....	....	....	....
	Milwaukee	IHL	13	0	1	1	58	....	....	....	....	....	....	....	....	....	....	....	....	....	....	....	....	....	....	....
	Detroit Vipers	IHL	27	1	3	4	91	....	....	....	....	....	....	....	....	....	....	....	....	....	....	....	....	....	....	....
99-2000	Detroit Vipers	IHL	43	4	10	14	135	....	....	....	....	....	....	....	....	....	....	....	....	....	....	....	....	....	....	....
	NHL Totals		**107**	**2**	**5**	**7**	**222**	**0**	**0**	**0**	**32**	**6.3**		....	....	....	....	....	**14**	**0**	**0**	**0**	**21**	**0**	**0**	**0**

Traded to **Pittsburgh** by **Vancouver** for Markus Naslund, March 20, 1996.

STRAKA, Martin (STRAH-kuh, MAHR-tihn) PIT.

Center. Shoots left. 5'9", 176 lbs. Born, Plzen, Czech., September 3, 1972. Pittsburgh's 1st choice, 19th overall, in 1992 Entry Draft.

1989-90	Skoda Plzen	Czech.	1	0	3	3	....	....	....	....	....	....	....	....	....	....	....	....	....	....	....	....	....	....	....	....
1990-91	Skoda Plzen	Czech.	47	7	24	31	6	....	....	....	....	....	....	....	....	....	....	....	....	....	....	....	....	....	....	....
1991-92	Skoda Plzen	Czech.	50	27	28	55	20	....	....	....	....	....	....	....	....	....	....	....	....	....	....	....	....	....	....	....
1992-93	**Pittsburgh**	**NHL**	**42**	**3**	**13**	**16**	**29**	**0**	**0**	**1**	**28**	**10.7**	**2**	....	....	....	....	....	**11**	**2**	**1**	**3**	**2**	**0**	**0**	**0**
	Cleveland	IHL	4	4	3	7	0	....	....	....	....	....	....	....	....	....	....	....	....	....	....	....	....	....	....	....
1993-94	**Pittsburgh**	**NHL**	**84**	**30**	**34**	**64**	**24**	**2**	**0**	**6**	**130**	**23.1**	**24**	....	....	....	....	....	**6**	**1**	**0**	**1**	**2**	**0**	**0**	**0**
1994-95	ZKZ Plzen	Cze-Rep	19	10	11	21	18	....	....	....	....	....	....	....	....	....	....	....	....	....	....	....	....	....	....	....
	Pittsburgh	**NHL**	**31**	**4**	**12**	**16**	**16**	**0**	**0**	**0**	**36**	**11.1**	**0**	....	....	....	....	....	....	....	....	....	....	....	....	....
	Ottawa	**NHL**	**6**	**1**	**1**	**2**	**0**	**0**	**0**	**0**	**13**	**7.7**	**-1**	....	....	....	....	....	....	....	....	....	....	....	....	....
1995-96	**Ottawa**	**NHL**	**43**	**9**	**16**	**25**	**29**	**5**	**0**	**1**	**63**	**14.3**	**-14**	....	....	....	....	....	....	....	....	....	....	....	....	....
	NY Islanders	**NHL**	**22**	**2**	**10**	**12**	**6**	**0**	**0**	**0**	**18**	**11.1**	**-6**	....	....	....	....	....	....	....	....	....	....	....	....	....
	Florida	**NHL**	**12**	**2**	**4**	**6**	**6**	**1**	**0**	**0**	**17**	**11.8**	**1**	....	....	....	....	....	**13**	**2**	**2**	**4**	**2**	**0**	**0**	**0**
1996-97	**Florida**	**NHL**	**55**	**7**	**22**	**29**	**12**	**2**	**0**	**1**	**94**	**7.4**	**9**	....	....	....	....	....	**4**	**0**	**0**	**0**	**0**	**0**	**0**	**0**
1997-98	**Pittsburgh**	**NHL**	**75**	**19**	**23**	**42**	**28**	**4**	**3**	**4**	**117**	**16.2**	**-1**	....	....	....	....	....	**6**	**2**	**0**	**2**	**2**	**0**	**1**	**0**
	Czech-Republic	Olympics	6	1	2	3	0	....	....	....	....	....	....	....	....	....	....	....	....	....	....	....	....	....	....	....
1998-99	**Pittsburgh**	**NHL**	**80**	**35**	**48**	**83**	**26**	**5**	**4**	**4**	**177**	**19.8**	**12**	**845**	**43.6**	**75**	**59**	**23:35**	**13**	**6**	**9**	**15**	**6**	**1**	**0**	**0**
99-2000	**Pittsburgh**	**NHL**	**71**	**20**	**39**	**59**	**26**	**3**	**1**	**2**	**146**	**13.7**	**24**	**651**	**42.9**	**62**	**35**	**23:58**	**11**	**3**	**9**	**12**	**10**	**1**	**0**	**0**
	NHL Totals		**521**	**132**	**222**	**354**	**202**	**22**	**8**	**19**	**839**	**15.7**		**1496**	**43.2**	**137**	**94**	**23:46**	**64**	**16**	**21**	**37**	**24**	**2**	**1**	**0**

Czechoslovakian First All-Star Team (1992) • Played in NHL All-Star Game (1999)

Traded to **Ottawa** by **Pittsburgh** for Troy Murray and Norm Maciver, April 7, 1995. Traded to **NY Islanders** by **Ottawa** with Don Beaupre and Bryan Berard for Damian Rhodes and Wade Redden, January 23, 1996. Claimed on waivers by **Florida** from **NY Islanders**, March 15, 1996. Signed as a free agent by **Pittsburgh**, August 6, 1997.

STRUDWICK, Jason (STRUHD-wihk, JAY-suhn)

Defense. Shoots left. 6'3", 215 lbs. Born, Edmonton, Alta., July 17, 1975. NY Islanders' 3rd choice, 63rd overall, in 1994 Entry Draft.

1991-92	Edmonton Pats	AAHA	35	3	8	11	67	....	....	....	....	....	....	....	....	....	....	....	....	....	....	....	....	....	....	....
1992-93	Edmonton Legion	AAHA	33	8	20	28	135	....	....	....	....	....	....	....	....	....	....	....	....	....	....	....	....	....	....	....
1993-94	Kamloops Blazers	WHL	61	6	8	14	118	....	....	....	....	....	....	....	....	....	....	....	19	0	4	4	24	....	....	....
1994-95	Kamloops Blazers	WHL	72	3	11	14	183	....	....	....	....	....	....	....	....	....	....	....	21	1	1	2	39	....	....	....
1995-96	**NY Islanders**	**NHL**	**1**	**0**	**0**	**0**	**7**	**0**	**0**	**0**	**0**	**0.0**	**0**	....	....	....	....	....	....	....	....	....	....	....	....	....
	Worcester	AHL	60	2	7	9	119	....	....	....	....	....	....	....	....	....	....	....	4	0	1	1	0	....	....	....
1996-97	Kentucky	AHL	80	1	9	10	198	....	....	....	....	....	....	....	....	....	....	....	4	0	0	0	0	....	....	....
1997-98	**NY Islanders**	**NHL**	**17**	**0**	**1**	**1**	**36**	**0**	**0**	**0**	**3**	**0.0**	**1**	....	....	....	....	....	....	....	....	....	....	....	....	....
	Kentucky	AHL	39	3	1	4	87	....	....	....	....	....	....	....	....	....	....	....	....	....	....	....	....	....	....	....
	Vancouver	**NHL**	**11**	**0**	**1**	**1**	**29**	**0**	**0**	**0**	**5**	**0.0**	**-3**	....	....	....	....	....	....	....	....	....	....	....	....	....
	Syracuse Crunch	AHL	....	....	....	....	....	....	....	....	....	....	....	....	....	....	....	....	3	0	0	0	6	....	....	....
1998-99	**Vancouver**	**NHL**	**65**	**0**	**3**	**3**	**114**	**0**	**0**	**0**	**25**	**0.0**	**-19**	**0**	**0.0**	**62**	**52**	**12:49**	....	....	....	....	....	....	....	....
99-2000	**Vancouver**	**NHL**	**63**	**1**	**3**	**4**	**64**	**0**	**0**	**0**	**18**	**5.6**	**-13**	**0**	**0.0**	**105**	**87**	**15:12**	....	....	....	....	....	....	....	....
	NHL Totals		**157**	**1**	**8**	**9**	**250**	**0**	**0**	**0**	**51**	**2.0**		**0**	**0.0**	**167**	**139**	**13:59**	....	....	....	....	....	....	....	....

Traded to **Vancouver** by **NY Islanders** for Gino Odjick, March 23, 1998.

STUART, Brad (STEW-ahrt, BRAD) S.J.

Defense. Shoots left. 6'2", 210 lbs. Born, Rocky Mountain House, Alta., November 6, 1979. San Jose's 1st choice, 3rd overall, in 1998 Entry Draft.

1995-96	Red Deer Chiefs	AAHA	35	12	25	37	83	....	....	....	....	....	....	....	....	....	....	....	....	....	....	....	....	....	....	....
	Regina Pats	WHL	3	0	0	0	0	....	....	....	....	....	....	....	....	....	....	....	....	....	....	....	....	....	....	....
1996-97	Regina Pats	WHL	57	7	36	43	58	....	....	....	....	....	....	....	....	....	....	....	5	0	4	4	14	....	....	....
1997-98	Regina Pats	WHL	72	20	45	65	82	....	....	....	....	....	....	....	....	....	....	....	9	3	4	7	10	....	....	....
1998-99	Regina Pats	WHL	29	10	19	29	43	....	....	....	....	....	....	....	....	....	....	....	....	....	....	....	....	....	....	....
	Calgary Hitmen	WHL	30	11	22	33	26	....	....	....	....	....	....	....	....	....	....	....	21	8	15	23	59	....	....	....
99-2000	**San Jose**	**NHL**	**82**	**10**	**26**	**36**	**32**	**5**	**1**	**3**	**133**	**7.5**	**3**	**0**	**0.0**	**123**	**57**	**20:24**	**12**	**1**	**0**	**1**	**6**	**1**	**0**	**0**
	NHL Totals		**82**	**10**	**26**	**36**	**32**	**5**	**1**	**3**	**133**	**7.5**		**0**	**0.0**	**123**	**57**	**20:24**	**12**	**1**	**0**	**1**	**6**	**1**	**0**	**0**

WHL East Second All-Star Team (1998) • WHL East First All-Star Team (1999) • Canadian Major Junior First All-Star Team (1999) • Canadian Major Junior Defenseman of the Year (1999) • NHL All-Rookie Team (2000)

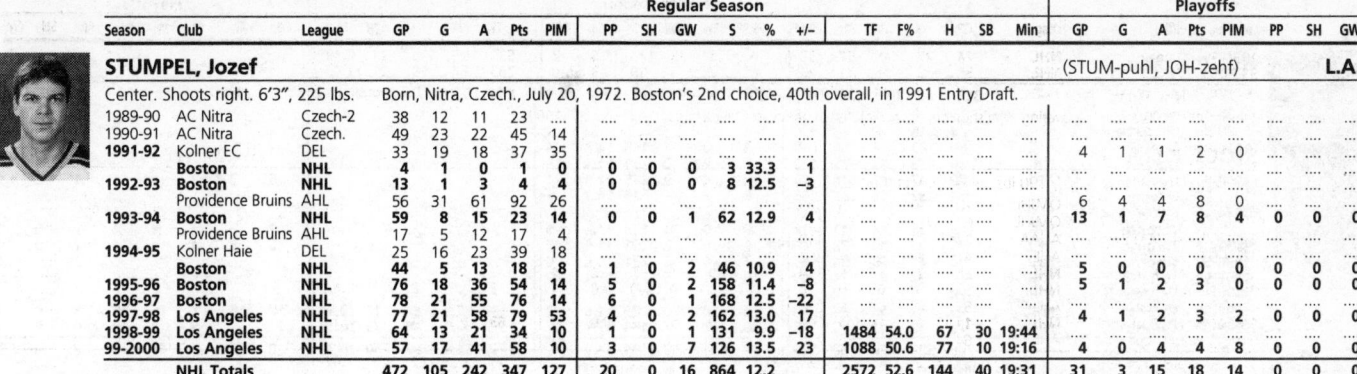

STUMPEL, Jozef

(STUM-puhl, JOH-zehf) **L.A.**

Center. Shoots right. 6'3", 225 lbs. Born, Nitra, Czech., July 20, 1972. Boston's 2nd choice, 40th overall, in 1991 Entry Draft.

			Regular Season																Playoffs							
Season	Club	League	GP	G	A	Pts	PIM	PP	SH	GW	S	%	+/-	TF	F%	H	SB	Min	GP	G	A	Pts	PIM	PP	SH	GW
1989-90	AC Nitra	Czech-2	38	12	11	23		....	....	....	....	....	....	....	....	....	....	....	....	....	....	....	....	....	....	....
1990-91	AC Nitra	Czech.	49	23	22	45	14	....	....	....	....	....	....	....	....	....	....	....	....	....	....	....	....	....	....	....
1991-92	Kolner EC	DEL	33	19	18	37	35	....	....	....	....	....	....	....	....	....	....	....	4	1	1	2	0	....	....	....
	Boston	**NHL**	**4**	**1**	**0**	**1**	**0**	**0**	**0**	**0**	**3**	**33.3**	**1**	....	....	....	....	....	....	....	....	....	....	....	....	....
1992-93	**Boston**	**NHL**	**13**	**1**	**3**	**4**	**4**	**0**	**0**	**0**	**8**	**12.5**	**-3**	....	....	....	....	....	....	....	....	....	....	....	....	....
	Providence Bruins	AHL	56	31	61	92	26	....	....	....	....	....	....	....	....	....	....	....	6	4	4	8	0	....	....	....
1993-94	**Boston**	**NHL**	**59**	**8**	**15**	**23**	**14**	**0**	**0**	**1**	**62**	**12.9**	**4**	....	....	....	....	....	**13**	**1**	**7**	**8**	**4**	**0**	**0**	**0**
	Providence Bruins	AHL	17	5	12	17	4	....	....	....	....	....	....	....	....	....	....	....	....	....	....	....	....	....	....	....
1994-95	Kolner Haie	DEL	25	16	23	39	18	....	....	....	....	....	....	....	....	....	....	....	....	....	....	....	....	....	....	....
	Boston	**NHL**	**44**	**5**	**13**	**18**	**8**	**1**	**0**	**2**	**46**	**10.9**	**4**	....	....	....	....	....	**5**	**0**	**0**	**0**	**0**	**0**	**0**	**0**
1995-96	**Boston**	**NHL**	**76**	**18**	**36**	**54**	**14**	**5**	**0**	**2**	**158**	**11.4**	**-8**	....	....	....	....	....	**5**	**1**	**2**	**3**	**0**	**0**	**0**	**0**
1996-97	**Boston**	**NHL**	**78**	**21**	**55**	**76**	**14**	**6**	**0**	**1**	**168**	**12.5**	**-22**	....	....	....	....	....	....	....	....	....	....	....	....	....
1997-98	**Los Angeles**	**NHL**	**77**	**21**	**58**	**79**	**53**	**4**	**0**	**2**	**162**	**13.0**	**17**	....	....	....	....	....	**4**	**1**	**2**	**3**	**2**	**0**	**0**	**0**
1998-99	**Los Angeles**	**NHL**	**64**	**13**	**21**	**34**	**10**	**1**	**0**	**1**	**131**	**9.9**	**-18**	**1484**	**54.0**	**67**	**30**	**19:44**	....	....	....	....	....	....	....	....
99-2000	**Los Angeles**	**NHL**	**57**	**17**	**41**	**58**	**10**	**3**	**0**	**7**	**126**	**13.5**	**23**	**1088**	**50.6**	**77**	**10**	**19:16**	**4**	**0**	**4**	**4**	**8**	**0**	**0**	**0**
	NHL Totals		**472**	**105**	**242**	**347**	**127**	**20**	**0**	**16**	**864**	**12.2**		**2572**	**52.6**	**144**	**40**	**19:31**	**31**	**3**	**15**	**18**	**14**	**0**	**0**	**0**

Traded to **LA Kings** by **Boston** with Sandy Moger and Boston's 4th round choice (later traded to New Jersey - New Jersey selected Pierre Dagenais) in 1998 Entry Draft for Dimitri Kristich and Byron Dafoe, August 29, 1997.

STURM, Marco

(STURHM, MAHR-koh) **S.J.**

Center. Shoots left. 6', 195 lbs. Born, Dingolfing, Germany, September 8, 1978. San Jose's 2nd choice, 21st overall, in 1996 Entry Draft.

Season	Club	League	GP	G	A	Pts	PIM	PP	SH	GW	S	%	+/-	TF	F%	H	SB	Min	GP	G	A	Pts	PIM	PP	SH	GW
1995-96	EV Landshut	DEL	47	12	20	32	50	....	....	....	....	....	....	....	....	....	....	....	11	1	3	4	18	....	....	....
1996-97	EV Landshut	DEL	46	16	27	43	40	....	....	....	....	....	....	....	....	....	....	....	7	1	4	5	6	....	....	....
1997-98	**San Jose**	**NHL**	**74**	**10**	**20**	**30**	**40**	**2**	**0**	**3**	**118**	**8.5**	**-2**	....	....	....	....	....	**2**	**0**	**0**	**0**	**0**	**0**	**0**	**0**
	Germany	Olympics	2	0	0	0	0	....	....	....	....	....	....	....	....	....	....	....	....	....	....	....	....	....	....	....
1998-99	**San Jose**	**NHL**	**78**	**16**	**22**	**38**	**52**	**3**	**2**	**3**	**140**	**11.4**	**7**	**576**	**45.0**	**98**	**37**	**15:23**	**6**	**2**	**2**	**4**	**4**	**0**	**0**	**1**
99-2000	**San Jose**	**NHL**	**74**	**12**	**15**	**27**	**22**	**2**	**4**	**3**	**120**	**10.0**	**4**	**183**	**45.4**	**102**	**28**	**14:07**	**12**	**1**	**3**	**4**	**6**	**0**	**0**	**0**
	NHL Totals		**226**	**38**	**57**	**95**	**114**	**7**	**6**	**9**	**378**	**10.1**		**759**	**45.1**	**200**	**65**	**14:46**	**20**	**3**	**5**	**8**	**10**	**0**	**0**	**1**

Played in NHL All-Star Game (1999)

SUCHY, Radoslav

(soo-KHEE, RAD-oh-slav) **PHX.**

Defense. Shoots left. 6'1", 185 lbs. Born, Kezmarok, Czech., April 7, 1976.

Season	Club	League	GP	G	A	Pts	PIM	PP	SH	GW	S	%	+/-	TF	F%	H	SB	Min	GP	G	A	Pts	PIM	PP	SH	GW
1993-94	SKP Poprad	Slovak-Jr.	30	11	12	23	16	....	....	....	....	....	....	....	....	....	....	....	....	....	....	....	....	....	....	....
	SKP Poprad	Slovakia	3	0	0	0	0	....	....	....	....	....	....	....	....	....	....	....	....	....	....	....	....	....	....	....
1994-95	Sherbrooke	QMJHL	69	12	32	44	30	....	....	....	....	....	....	....	....	....	....	....	7	0	3	3	2	....	....	....
1995-96	Sherbrooke	QMJHL	68	15	53	68	68	....	....	....	....	....	....	....	....	....	....	....	7	0	3	3	2	....	....	....
1996-97	Sherbrooke	QMJHL	32	6	34	40	14	....	....	....	....	....	....	....	....	....	....	....	....	....	....	....	....	....	....	....
	Chicoutimi	QMJHL	28	5	24	29	26	....	....	....	....	....	....	....	....	....	....	....	19	6	15	21	12	....	....	....
1997-98	Las Vegas	IHL	26	1	4	5	10	....	....	....	....	....	....	....	....	....	....	....	....	....	....	....	....	....	....	....
	Springfield	AHL	41	6	15	21	16	....	....	....	....	....	....	....	....	....	....	....	4	0	1	1	2	....	....	....
1998-99	Springfield	AHL	69	4	32	36	10	....	....	....	....	....	....	....	....	....	....	....	3	0	1	1	0	....	....	....
99-2000	**Phoenix**	**NHL**	**60**	**0**	**6**	**6**	**16**	**0**	**0**	**0**	**36**	**0.0**	**2**	**0**	**0.0**	**57**	**55**	**15:09**	**5**	**0**	**1**	**1**	**0**	**0**	**0**	**0**
	Springfield	AHL	2	0	1	1	0	....	....	....	....	....	....	....	....	....	....	....	....	....	....	....	....	....	....	....
	NHL Totals		**60**	**0**	**6**	**6**	**16**	**0**	**0**	**0**	**36**	**0.0**		**0**	**0.0**	**57**	**55**	**15:09**	**5**	**0**	**1**	**1**	**0**	**0**	**0**	**0**

QMJHL Second All-Star Team (1997) • Won George Parsons Trophy (Memorial Cup Tournament Most Sportsmanlike Player) (1997)

Signed as a free agent by **Phoenix**, September 26, 1997.

SULLIVAN, Mike

(SUH-lih-van, MIGHK) **PHX.**

Center. Shoots left. 6'2", 201 lbs. Born, Marshfield, MA, February 27, 1968. NY Rangers' 4th choice, 69th overall, in 1987 Entry Draft.

Season	Club	League	GP	G	A	Pts	PIM	PP	SH	GW	S	%	+/-	TF	F%	H	SB	Min	GP	G	A	Pts	PIM	PP	SH	GW
1985-86	Boston Prep	Hi-School	22	26	33	59	....	....	....	....	....	....	....	....	....	....	....	....	....	....	....	....	....	....	....	....
1986-87	Boston University	H-East	37	13	18	31	18	....	....	....	....	....	....	....	....	....	....	....	....	....	....	....	....	....	....	....
1987-88	Boston University	H-East	30	18	22	40	30	....	....	....	....	....	....	....	....	....	....	....	....	....	....	....	....	....	....	....
1988-89	Boston University	H-East	36	19	17	36	30	....	....	....	....	....	....	....	....	....	....	....	....	....	....	....	....	....	....	....
1989-90	Boston University	H-East	38	11	20	31	26	....	....	....	....	....	....	....	....	....	....	....	....	....	....	....	....	....	....	....
1990-91	San Diego Gulls	IHL	74	12	23	35	27	....	....	....	....	....	....	....	....	....	....	....	....	....	....	....	....	....	....	....
1991-92	**San Jose**	**NHL**	**64**	**8**	**11**	**19**	**15**	**1**	**0**	**1**	**72**	**11.1**	**-18**	....	....	....	....	....	....	....	....	....	....	....	....	....
	Kansas City	IHL	10	2	8	10	8	....	....	....	....	....	....	....	....	....	....	....	....	....	....	....	....	....	....	....
1992-93	**San Jose**	**NHL**	**81**	**6**	**8**	**14**	**30**	**0**	**2**	**0**	**95**	**6.3**	**-42**	....	....	....	....	....	....	....	....	....	....	....	....	....
1993-94	**San Jose**	**NHL**	**26**	**2**	**2**	**4**	**4**	**0**	**2**	**1**	**21**	**9.5**	**-3**	....	....	....	....	....	....	....	....	....	....	....	....	....
	Kansas City	IHL	6	3	3	6	0	....	....	....	....	....	....	....	....	....	....	....	....	....	....	....	....	....	....	....
	Calgary	**NHL**	**19**	**2**	**3**	**5**	**6**	**0**	**2**	**0**	**27**	**7.4**	**2**	....	....	....	....	....	**7**	**1**	**1**	**2**	**8**	**0**	**1**	**0**
	Saint John Flames	AHL	5	2	0	2	4	....	....	....	....	....	....	....	....	....	....	....	....	....	....	....	....	....	....	....
1994-95	**Calgary**	**NHL**	**38**	**4**	**7**	**11**	**14**	**0**	**0**	**2**	**31**	**12.9**	**-2**	....	....	....	....	....	**7**	**3**	**5**	**8**	**2**	**0**	**1**	**1**
1995-96	**Calgary**	**NHL**	**81**	**9**	**12**	**21**	**24**	**0**	**1**	**1**	**106**	**8.5**	**-6**	....	....	....	....	....	**4**	**0**	**0**	**0**	**0**	**0**	**0**	**0**
1996-97	**Calgary**	**NHL**	**67**	**5**	**6**	**11**	**10**	**0**	**3**	**2**	**64**	**7.8**	**-11**	....	....	....	....	....	....	....	....	....	....	....	....	....
1997-98	**Boston**	**NHL**	**77**	**5**	**13**	**18**	**34**	**0**	**0**	**2**	**83**	**6.0**	**-1**	....	....	....	....	....	**6**	**0**	**1**	**1**	**2**	**0**	**0**	**0**
1998-99	**Phoenix**	**NHL**	**63**	**2**	**4**	**6**	**24**	**0**	**1**	**1**	**66**	**3.0**	**-11**	**74**	**50.0**	**52**	**40**	**12:09**	**5**	**0**	**0**	**0**	**2**	**0**	**0**	**0**
99-2000	**Phoenix**	**NHL**	**79**	**5**	**10**	**15**	**10**	**0**	**2**	**1**	**59**	**8.5**	**-4**	**820**	**51.5**	**77**	**37**	**11:36**	**5**	**0**	**1**	**1**	**0**	**0**	**0**	**0**
	NHL Totals		**595**	**48**	**76**	**124**	**171**	**1**	**13**	**11**	**624**	**7.7**		**894**	**51.3**	**129**	**77**	**11:51**	**34**	**4**	**8**	**12**	**14**	**0**	**2**	**1**

Rights traded to **Minnesota** by **NY Rangers** with Mark Tinordi, Paul Jerrard, the rights to Bret Barnett and LA Kings' 3rd round choice (previously acquired, Minnesota selected Murray Garbutt) in 1989 Entry Draft for Brian Lawton, Igor Liba and the rights to Eric Bennett, October 11, 1988. Signed as a free agent by **San Jose**, August 9, 1991. Claimed on waivers by **Calgary** from **San Jose**, January 6, 1994. Traded to **Boston** by **Calgary** for Boston's 7th round choice (Radek Duda) in 1998 Entry Draft, June 21, 1997. Claimed by **Nashville** from **Boston** in Expansion Draft, June 26, 1998. Traded to **Phoenix** by **Nashville** for Phoenix's 7th round choice in 1999 Entry Draft, June 30, 1998.

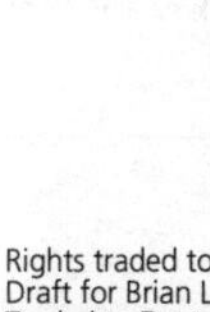

SULLIVAN, Steve

(SUH-lih-van, STEEV) **CHI.**

Center. Shoots right. 5'9", 160 lbs. Born, Timmins, Ont., July 6, 1974. New Jersey's 10th choice, 233rd overall, in 1994 Entry Draft.

Season	Club	League	GP	G	A	Pts	PIM	PP	SH	GW	S	%	+/-	TF	F%	H	SB	Min	GP	G	A	Pts	PIM	PP	SH	GW
1991-92	Timmins Bears	NOJHL	47	66	55	121	141	....	....	....	....	....	....	....	....	....	....	....	....	....	....	....	....	....	....	....
1992-93	Sault Ste. Marie	OHL	62	36	27	63	44	....	....	....	....	....	....	....	....	....	....	....	16	3	8	11	18	....	....	....
1993-94	Sault Ste. Marie	OHL	63	51	62	113	82	....	....	....	....	....	....	....	....	....	....	....	14	9	16	25	22	....	....	....
1994-95	Albany River Rats	AHL	75	31	50	81	124	....	....	....	....	....	....	....	....	....	....	....	14	4	7	11	10	....	....	....
1995-96	**New Jersey**	**NHL**	**16**	**5**	**4**	**9**	**8**	**2**	**0**	**1**	**23**	**21.7**	**3**	....	....	....	....	....	....	....	....	....	....	....	....	....
	Albany River Rats	AHL	53	33	42	75	127	....	....	....	....	....	....	....	....	....	....	....	4	3	0	3	6	....	....	....
1996-97	**New Jersey**	**NHL**	**33**	**8**	**14**	**22**	**14**	**2**	**0**	**2**	**63**	**12.7**	**9**	....	....	....	....	....	....	....	....	....	....	....	....	....
	Albany River Rats	AHL	15	8	7	15	16	....	....	....	....	....	....	....	....	....	....	....	....	....	....	....	....	....	....	....
	Toronto	**NHL**	**21**	**5**	**11**	**16**	**23**	**1**	**0**	**1**	**45**	**11.1**	**5**	....	....	....	....	....	....	....	....	....	....	....	....	....
1997-98	**Toronto**	**NHL**	**63**	**10**	**18**	**28**	**40**	**1**	**0**	**1**	**112**	**8.9**	**-8**	....	....	....	....	....	....	....	....	....	....	....	....	....
1998-99	**Toronto**	**NHL**	**63**	**20**	**20**	**40**	**28**	**4**	**0**	**5**	**110**	**18.2**	**12**	**685**	**44.4**	**26**	**11**	**14:12**	**13**	**3**	**3**	**6**	**14**	**2**	**0**	**0**
99-2000	**Toronto**	**NHL**	**7**	**0**	**1**	**1**	**4**	**0**	**0**	**0**	**11**	**0.0**	**-1**	**47**	**48.9**	**1**	**0**	**11:52**	....	....	....	....	....	....	....	....
	Chicago	**NHL**	**73**	**22**	**42**	**64**	**52**	**2**	**1**	**6**	**169**	**13.0**	**20**	**692**	**48.0**	**39**	**15**	**18:05**	....	....	....	....	....	....	....	....
	NHL Totals		**276**	**70**	**110**	**180**	**169**	**12**	**1**	**16**	**533**	**13.1**		**1424**	**46.3**	**66**	**26**	**16:04**	**13**	**3**	**3**	**6**	**14**	**2**	**0**	**0**

AHL First All-Star Team (1996)

Traded to **Toronto** by **New Jersey** with Jason Smith and the rights to Alyn McCauley for Doug Gilmour, Dave Ellett and New Jersey's 3rd round choice (previously acquired, New Jersey selected Andre Lakos) in 1999 Entry Draft, February 25, 1997. Claimed on waivers by **Chicago** from **Toronto**, October 23, 1999.

			Regular Season																Playoffs							
Season	Club	League	GP	G	A	Pts	PIM	PP	SH	GW	S	%	+/–	TF	F%	H	SB	Min	GP	G	A	Pts	PIM	PP	SH	GW

SUNDIN, Mats

(SUHN-deen, MATS) **TOR.**

Center/Right wing. Shoots right. 6'4", 220 lbs. Born, Bromma, Sweden, February 13, 1971. Quebec's 1st choice, 1st overall, in 1989 Entry Draft.

1988-89	Nacka IK	Sweden-2	25	10	8	18	18	....	....	....	....	....	....	....	....	....	....	....	....	....	....	....	....	....	....	....
1989-90	Djurgardens IF	Sweden	34	10	8	18	16	....	....	....	....	....	....	....	....	....	....	....	8	7	0	7	4	....	....	....
1990-91	Quebec	NHL	80	23	36	59	58	4	0	0	155	14.8	–24	....	....	....	....	....	....	....	....	....	....	....	....	....
1991-92	Quebec	NHL	80	33	43	76	103	8	2	2	231	14.3	–19	....	....	....	....	....	....	....	....	....	....	....	....	....
1992-93	Quebec	NHL	80	47	67	114	96	13	4	9	215	21.9	21	....	....	....	....	....	6	3	1	4	6	1	0	0
1993-94	Quebec	NHL	84	32	53	85	60	6	2	4	226	14.2	1	....	....	....	....	....	....	....	....	....	....	....	....	....
1994-95	Djurgardens IF	Sweden	12	7	2	9	14	....	....	....	....	....	....	....	....	....	....	....	....	....	....	....	....	....	....	....
	Toronto	NHL	47	23	24	47	14	9	0	4	173	13.3	–5	....	....	....	....	....	7	5	4	9	4	2	0	1
1995-96	Toronto	NHL	76	33	50	83	46	7	6	7	301	11.0	8	....	....	....	....	....	6	3	1	4	4	2	0	1
1996-97	Toronto	NHL	82	41	53	94	59	7	4	8	281	14.6	6	....	....	....	....	....	....	....	....	....	....	....	....	....
1997-98	Toronto	NHL	82	33	41	74	49	9	1	5	219	15.1	–3	....	....	....	....	....	....	....	....	....	....	....	....	....
	Sweden	Olympics	4	3	0	3	4	....	....	....	....	....	....	....	....	....	....	....	....	....	....	....	....	....	....	....
1998-99	Toronto	NHL	82	31	52	83	58	4	0	6	209	14.8	22	1993	57.3	54	17	20:41	17	8	8	16	16	3	0	2
99-2000	Toronto	NHL	73	32	41	73	46	10	2	7	184	17.4	16	1619	50.8	48	33	20:11	12	3	5	8	10	0	0	1
	NHL Totals		766	328	460	788	589	77	21	52	2194	14.9		3612	54.4	102	50	20:27	48	22	19	41	40	8	0	5

Swedish World All-Star Team (1991, 1992, 1994, 1997) • Played in NHL All-Star Game (1996, 1997, 1998, 1999, 2000)

Traded to **Toronto** by **Quebec** with Garth Butcher, Todd Warriner and Philadelphia's 1st round choice (previously acquired by Quebec - later traded to Washington - Washington selected Nolan Baumgartner) in 1994 Entry Draft for Wendel Clark, Sylvain Lefebvre, Landon Wilson and Toronto's 1st round choice (Jeffrey Kealty) in 1994 Entry Draft, June 28, 1994.

SUNDSTROM, Niklas

(SUHN-struhm, NIHK-las) **S.J.**

Left wing. Shoots left. 6', 200 lbs. Born, Ornskoldsvik, Sweden, June 6, 1975. NY Rangers' 1st choice, 8th overall, in 1993 Entry Draft.

1991-92	MoDo AIK	Sweden	9	1	3	4	0	....	....	....	....	....	....	....	....	....	....	....	....	....	....	....	....	....	....	....
1992-93	MoDo AIK	Swede-Jr.	2	3	1	4	0	....	....	....	....	....	....	....	....	....	....	....	....	....	....	....	....	....	....	....
	MoDo AIK	Sweden	40	7	11	18	18	....	....	....	....	....	....	....	....	....	....	....	3	0	0	0	0	....	....	....
1993-94	MoDo AIK	Swede-Jr.	3	3	4	7	2	....	....	....	....	....	....	....	....	....	....	....	....	....	....	....	....	....	....	....
	MoDo AIK	Sweden	37	7	12	19	28	....	....	....	....	....	....	....	....	....	....	....	11	4	3	7	2	....	....	....
1994-95	MoDo Hockey	Sweden	33	8	13	21	30	....	....	....	....	....	....	....	....	....	....	....	....	....	....	....	....	....	....	....
1995-96	NY Rangers	NHL	82	9	12	21	14	1	1	2	90	10.0	2	....	....	....	....	....	11	4	3	7	4	1	0	0
1996-97	NY Rangers	NHL	82	24	28	52	20	5	1	4	132	18.2	23	....	....	....	....	....	9	0	5	5	2	0	0	0
1997-98	NY Rangers	NHL	70	19	28	47	24	4	0	1	115	16.5	0	....	....	....	....	....	....	....	....	....	....	....	....	....
	Sweden	Olympics	4	1	1	2	2	....	....	....	....	....	....	....	....	....	....	....	....	....	....	....	....	....	....	....
1998-99	NY Rangers	NHL	81	13	30	43	20	1	2	3	89	14.6	–2	376	40.4	118	55	19:11	....	....	....	....	....	....	....	....
99-2000	San Jose	NHL	79	12	25	37	22	2	1	2	90	13.3	9	10	50.0	44	12	15:10	12	0	2	2	2	0	0	0
	NHL Totals		394	77	123	200	100	13	5	12	516	14.9		386	40.7	162	67	17:12	32	4	10	14	8	1	0	0

Traded to **Tampa Bay** by **NY Rangers** with Dan Cloutier and NY Rangers' 1st (Nikita Alexeev) and 3rd (later traded to San Jose - later traded to Chicago - Chicago selected Igor Radulov) round choices in 2000 Entry Draft for Chicago's 1st round choice (previously acquired, NY Rangers selected Pavel Brendl) in 1999 Entry Draft, June 26, 1999. Traded to **San Jose** by **Tampa Bay** with NY Rangers' 3rd round choice (previously acquired, later traded to Chicago - Chicago selected Igor Radulov) in 2000 Entry Draft for Bill Houlder, Andrei Zyuzin, Shawn Burr and Steve Guolla, August 4, 1999.

SUTER, Gary

(SOO-tuhr, GAIR-ee) **S.J.**

Defense. Shoots left. 6', 215 lbs. Born, Madison, WI, June 24, 1964. Calgary's 9th choice, 180th overall, in 1984 Entry Draft.

1981-82	Dubuque Saints	USHL	18	3	4	7	32	....	....	....	....	....	....	....	....	....	....	....	....	....	....	....	....	....	....	....
1982-83	Dubuque Saints	USHL	41	9	30	39	112	....	....	....	....	....	....	....	....	....	....	....	....	....	....	....	....	....	....	....
1983-84	U. of Wisconsin	WCHA	35	4	18	22	32	....	....	....	....	....	....	....	....	....	....	....	....	....	....	....	....	....	....	....
1984-85	U. of Wisconsin	WCHA	39	12	39	51	110	....	....	....	....	....	....	....	....	....	....	....	....	....	....	....	....	....	....	....
1985-86	Calgary	NHL	80	18	50	68	141	9	0	4	195	9.2	11	....	....	....	....	....	10	2	8	10	8	0	0	1
1986-87	Calgary	NHL	68	9	40	49	70	4	0	0	152	5.9	–10	....	....	....	....	....	6	0	3	3	10	0	0	0
1987-88	Calgary	NHL	75	21	70	91	124	6	1	3	204	10.3	39	....	....	....	....	....	9	1	9	10	6	0	1	0
1988-89♦	Calgary	NHL	63	13	49	62	78	8	0	1	216	6.0	26	....	....	....	....	....	5	0	3	3	10	0	0	0
1989-90	Calgary	NHL	76	16	60	76	97	5	0	1	211	7.6	4	....	....	....	....	....	6	0	1	1	14	0	0	0
1990-91	Calgary	NHL	79	12	58	70	102	6	0	1	258	4.7	26	....	....	....	....	....	7	1	6	7	12	1	0	0
1991-92	Calgary	NHL	70	12	43	55	128	4	0	0	189	6.3	1	....	....	....	....	....	....	....	....	....	....	....	....	....
1992-93	Calgary	NHL	81	23	58	81	112	10	1	2	263	8.7	–1	....	....	....	....	....	6	2	3	5	8	0	1	0
1993-94	Calgary	NHL	25	4	9	13	20	2	1	0	51	7.8	–3	....	....	....	....	....	....	....	....	....	....	....	....	....
	Chicago	NHL	16	2	3	5	18	2	0	0	35	5.7	–9	....	....	....	....	....	6	3	2	5	6	2	0	0
1994-95	Chicago	NHL	48	10	27	37	42	5	0	0	144	6.9	14	....	....	....	....	....	12	2	5	7	10	1	0	0
1995-96	Chicago	NHL	82	20	47	67	80	12	2	4	242	8.3	3	....	....	....	....	....	10	3	3	6	8	2	0	1
1996-97	Chicago	NHL	82	7	21	28	70	3	0	0	225	3.1	–4	....	....	....	....	....	6	1	4	5	8	0	0	0
1997-98	Chicago	NHL	73	14	28	42	74	5	2	0	199	7.0	1	....	....	....	....	....	....	....	....	....	....	....	....	....
	United States	Olympics	4	0	0	0	2	....	....	....	....	....	....	....	....	....	....	....	....	....	....	....	....	....	....	....
1998-99	San Jose	NHL	1	0	0	0	0	0	0	0	1	0.0	0	0	0.0	0	0	12:56	....	....	....	....	....	....	....	....
99-2000	San Jose	NHL	76	6	28	34	52	2	1	0	175	3.4	7	0	0.0	118	102	23:30	12	2	5	7	12	1	0	1
	NHL Totals		995	187	591	778	1208	83	8	16	2760	6.8		0	0.0	118	102	23:21	95	17	52	69	112	7	2	3

Won Calder Memorial Trophy (1986) • NHL All-Rookie Team (1986) • NHL Second All-Star Team (1988) • Played in NHL All-Star Game (1986, 1988, 1989, 1991)

Traded to **Hartford** by **Calgary** with Paul Ranheim and Ted Drury for James Patrick, Zarley Zalapski and Michael Nylander, March 10, 1994. Traded to **Chicago** by **Hartford** with Randy Cunneyworth and Hartford's 3rd round choice (later traded to Vancouver - Vancouver selected Larry Courville) in 1995 Entry Draft for Frantisek Kucera and Jocelyn Lemieux, March 11, 1994. Signed as a free agent by **San Jose**, July 1, 1998. • Missed remainder of 1998-99 season recovering from tricep muscle injury suffered in game vs. Dallas, October 24, 1998.

SUTTER, Ron

(SUH-tuhr, RAWN)

Center. Shoots right. 6', 180 lbs. Born, Viking, Alta., December 2, 1963. Philadelphia's 1st choice, 4th overall, in 1982 Entry Draft.

1979-80	Red Deer Rustlers	AJHL	60	12	33	45	44	....	....	....	....	....	....	....	....	....	....	....	....	....	....	....	....	....	....	....
1980-81	Lethbridge	WHL	72	13	32	45	152	....	....	....	....	....	....	....	....	....	....	....	9	2	5	7	29	....	....	....
1981-82	Lethbridge	WHL	59	38	54	92	207	....	....	....	....	....	....	....	....	....	....	....	12	6	5	11	28	....	....	....
1982-83	Lethbridge	WHL	58	35	48	83	98	....	....	....	....	....	....	....	....	....	....	....	20	*22	*19	*41	45	....	....	....
	Philadelphia	NHL	10	1	1	2	9	0	0	1	4	25.0	0	....	....	....	....	....	....	....	....	....	....	....	....	....
1983-84	Philadelphia	NHL	79	19	32	51	101	5	3	3	145	13.1	4	....	....	....	....	....	3	0	0	0	22	0	0	0
1984-85	Philadelphia	NHL	73	16	29	45	94	2	0	5	140	11.4	13	....	....	....	....	....	19	4	8	12	28	0	0	1
1985-86	Philadelphia	NHL	75	18	42	60	159	0	0	4	145	12.4	26	....	....	....	....	....	5	0	2	2	10	0	0	0
1986-87	Philadelphia	NHL	39	10	17	27	69	0	0	0	68	14.7	10	....	....	....	....	....	16	1	7	8	12	0	0	0
1987-88	Philadelphia	NHL	69	8	25	33	146	1	0	0	107	7.5	–9	....	....	....	....	....	7	0	1	1	26	0	0	0
1988-89	Philadelphia	NHL	55	26	22	48	80	4	1	2	106	24.5	25	....	....	....	....	....	19	1	9	10	51	0	0	0
1989-90	Philadelphia	NHL	75	22	26	48	104	0	2	6	157	14.0	2	....	....	....	....	....	....	....	....	....	....	....	....	....
1990-91	Philadelphia	NHL	80	17	28	45	92	2	0	1	149	11.4	2	....	....	....	....	....	....	....	....	....	....	....	....	....
1991-92	St. Louis	NHL	68	19	27	46	91	5	4	1	106	17.9	9	....	....	....	....	....	6	1	3	4	8	1	0	0
1992-93	St. Louis	NHL	59	12	15	27	99	4	0	3	90	13.3	–11	....	....	....	....	....	....	....	....	....	....	....	....	....
1993-94	St. Louis	NHL	36	6	12	18	46	2	0	2	42	14.3	–1	....	....	....	....	....	....	....	....	....	....	....	....	....
	Quebec	NHL	37	9	13	22	44	4	0	0	66	13.6	3	....	....	....	....	....	....	....	....	....	....	....	....	....
1994-95	NY Islanders	NHL	27	1	4	5	21	0	0	1	29	3.4	–8	....	....	....	....	....	....	....	....	....	....	....	....	....
1995-96	Phoenix	IHL	25	6	13	19	28	....	....	....	....	....	....	....	....	....	....	....	....	....	....	....	....	....	....	....
	Boston	NHL	18	5	7	12	24	0	1	0	34	14.7	10	....	....	....	....	....	5	0	0	0	8	0	0	0
1996-97	San Jose	NHL	78	5	7	12	65	1	2	1	78	6.4	–8	....	....	....	....	....	....	....	....	....	....	....	....	....
1997-98	San Jose	NHL	57	2	7	9	22	0	0	1	57	3.5	–2	....	....	....	....	....	6	1	0	1	14	0	0	0
1998-99	San Jose	NHL	59	3	6	9	40	0	0	1	67	4.5	–8	636	49.1	83	18	9:54	6	0	0	0	4	0	0	0
99-2000	San Jose	NHL	78	5	6	11	34	0	1	1	68	7.4	–3	825	54.8	94	31	9:34	12	0	2	2	10	0	0	0
	NHL Totals		1072	204	326	530	1340	29	14	33	1658	12.3		1461	52.3	177	49	9:42	104	8	32	40	193	1	0	1

Traded to **St. Louis** by **Philadelphia** with Murray Baron for Dan Quinn and Rod Brind'Amour, September 22, 1991. Traded to **Quebec** by **St. Louis** with Garth Butcher and Bob Bassen for Steve Duchesne and Denis Chasse, January 23, 1994. Traded to **NY Islanders** by **Quebec** with Quebec's 1st round choice (Brett Lindros) in 1994 Entry Draft for Uwe Krupp and NY Islanders' 1st round choice (Wade Belak) in 1994 Entry Draft, June 28, 1994. Signed as a free agent by **Boston**, March 9, 1996. Signed as a free agent by **San Jose**, October 12, 1996.

SUTTON, Andy
(SUH-tohn, AN-dee) **MIN.**

Defense. Shoots left. 6'6", 245 lbs. Born, Edmonton, Alta., March 10, 1975.

Season	Club	League	GP	G	A	Pts	PIM	PP	SH	GW	S	%	+/-	TF	F%	H	SB	Min	Playoffs GP	G	A	Pts	PIM	PP	SH	GW
1991-92	Gananoque	OJHL-B	50	20	30	50	....	....	....	....	....	....	....	....	....	....	....	....	....	....	....	....	....	....	....	....
1992-93	Gananoque	OJHL-B	50	25	27	52	....	....	....	....	....	....	....	....	....	....	....	....	....	....	....	....	....	....	....	....
1993-94	St. Michael's	OJHL	48	17	23	40	161	....	....	....	....	....	....	....	....	....	....	....	3	0	0	0	20	....	....	....
1994-95	Michigan Tech	WCHA	19	2	1	3	42	....	....	....	....	....	....	....	....	....	....	....	....	....	....	....	....	....	....	....
1995-96	Michigan Tech	WCHA	33	2	2	4	58	....	....	....	....	....	....	....	....	....	....	....	....	....	....	....	....	....	....	....
1996-97	Michigan Tech	WCHA	32	2	7	9	73	....	....	....	....	....	....	....	....	....	....	....	....	....	....	....	....	....	....	....
1997-98	Michigan Tech	WCHA	38	16	24	40	97	....	....	....	....	....	....	....	....	....	....	....	....	....	....	....	....	....	....	....
	Kentucky	AHL	7	0	0	0	33	....	....	....	....	....	....	....	....	....	....	....	....	....	....	....	....	....	....	....
1998-99	**San Jose**	**NHL**	**31**	**0**	**3**	**3**	**65**	**0**	**0**	**0**	**24**	**0.0**	**-4**	**0**	**0.0**	**50**	**14**	**12:58**	....	....	....	....	....	....	....	....
	Kentucky	AHL	21	5	10	15	53	....	....	....	....	....	....	....	....	....	....	....	5	0	0	0	23	....	....	....
99-2000	**San Jose**	**NHL**	**40**	**1**	**1**	**2**	**80**	**0**	**0**	**0**	**29**	**3.4**	**-5**	**0**	**0.0**	**93**	**22**	**12:57**	....	....	....	....	....	....	....	....
	Kentucky	AHL	3	0	1	1	0	....	....	....	....	....	....	....	....	....	....	....	....	....	....	....	....	....	....	....
	NHL Totals		**71**	**1**	**4**	**5**	**145**	**0**	**0**	**0**	**53**	**1.9**		**0**	**0.0**	**143**	**36**	**12:58**	....	....	....	....	....	....	....	....

WCHA Second All-Star Team (1998)

Signed as a free agent by **San Jose**, March 20, 1998. Traded to **Minnesota** by **San Jose** with San Jose's 7th round choice (Peter Bartos) in 2000 Entry Draft and 3rd round choice in 2001 Entry Draft for Minnesota's 8th round choice in 2001 Entry Draft and future considerations, June 12, 2000.

SUTTON, Ken
(SUH-tohn, KEHN) **N.J.**

Defense. Shoots left. 6'1", 205 lbs. Born, Edmonton, Alta., November 5, 1969. Buffalo's 4th choice, 98th overall, in 1989 Entry Draft.

Season	Club	League	GP	G	A	Pts	PIM	PP	SH	GW	S	%	+/-	TF	F%	H	SB	Min	Playoffs GP	G	A	Pts	PIM	PP	SH	GW
1987-88	Calgary Canucks	AJHL	53	13	43	56	228	....	....	....	....	....	....	....	....	....	....	....	....	....	....	....	....	....	....	....
1988-89	Saskatoon Blades	WHL	71	22	31	53	104	....	....	....	....	....	....	....	....	....	....	....	8	2	5	7	12	....	....	....
1989-90	Rochester	AHL	57	5	14	19	83	....	....	....	....	....	....	....	....	....	....	....	11	1	6	7	15	....	....	....
1990-91	**Buffalo**	**NHL**	**15**	**3**	**6**	**9**	**13**	**2**	**0**	**0**	**26**	**11.5**	**2**	....	....	....	....	....	**6**	**0**	**1**	**1**	**2**	**0**	**0**	**0**
	Rochester	AHL	62	7	24	31	65	....	....	....	....	....	....	....	....	....	....	....	3	1	1	2	14	....	....	....
1991-92	**Buffalo**	**NHL**	**64**	**2**	**18**	**20**	**71**	**0**	**0**	**0**	**81**	**2.5**	**5**	....	....	....	....	....	**7**	**0**	**2**	**2**	**4**	**0**	**0**	**0**
1992-93	**Buffalo**	**NHL**	**63**	**8**	**14**	**22**	**30**	**1**	**0**	**2**	**77**	**10.4**	**-3**	....	....	....	....	....	**8**	**3**	**1**	**4**	**8**	**0**	**0**	**0**
1993-94	**Buffalo**	**NHL**	**78**	**4**	**20**	**24**	**71**	**1**	**0**	**0**	**95**	**4.2**	**-6**	....	....	....	....	....	**4**	**0**	**0**	**0**	**2**	**0**	**0**	**0**
1994-95	**Buffalo**	**NHL**	**12**	**1**	**2**	**3**	**30**	**0**	**0**	**1**	**12**	**8.3**	**-2**	....	....	....	....	....	....	....	....	....	....	....	....	....
	Edmonton	**NHL**	**12**	**3**	**1**	**4**	**12**	**0**	**0**	**0**	**28**	**10.7**	**-1**	....	....	....	....	....	....	....	....	....	....	....	....	....
1995-96	**Edmonton**	**NHL**	**32**	**0**	**8**	**8**	**39**	**0**	**0**	**0**	**38**	**0.0**	**-12**	....	....	....	....	....	....	....	....	....	....	....	....	....
	St. Louis	**NHL**	**6**	**0**	**0**	**0**	**4**	**0**	**0**	**0**	**3**	**0.0**	**-1**	....	....	....	....	....	**1**	**0**	**0**	**0**	**0**	**0**	**0**	**0**
	Worcester	AHL	32	4	16	20	60	....	....	....	....	....	....	....	....	....	....	....	4	0	2	2	21	....	....	....
1996-97	Manitoba Moose	IHL	20	3	10	13	48	....	....	....	....	....	....	....	....	....	....	....	....	....	....	....	....	....	....	....
	Albany River Rats	AHL	61	6	13	19	79	....	....	....	....	....	....	....	....	....	....	....	16	4	8	12	55	....	....	....
1997-98	**New Jersey**	**NHL**	**13**	**0**	**0**	**0**	**6**	**0**	**0**	**0**	**5**	**0.0**	**1**	....	....	....	....	....	....	....	....	....	....	....	....	....
	Albany River Rats	AHL	10	0	7	7	15	....	....	....	....	....	....	....	....	....	....	....	....	....	....	....	....	....	....	....
	San Jose	**NHL**	**8**	**0**	**0**	**0**	**15**	**0**	**0**	**0**	**7**	**0.0**	**-4**	....	....	....	....	....	....	....	....	....	....	....	....	....
1998-99	**New Jersey**	**NHL**	**5**	**1**	**0**	**1**	**0**	**0**	**0**	**0**	**5**	**20.0**	**1**	**0**	**0.0**	**3**	**1**	**13:02**	....	....	....	....	....	....	....	....
	Albany River Rats	AHL	75	13	42	55	118	....	....	....	....	....	....	....	....	....	....	....	5	0	2	2	12	....	....	....
99-2000	**New Jersey**	**NHL**	**6**	**0**	**2**	**2**	**2**	**0**	**0**	**0**	**10**	**0.0**	**2**	**0**	**0.0**	**4**	**5**	**17:20**	....	....	....	....	....	....	....	....
	Albany River Rats	AHL	57	5	16	21	129	....	....	....	....	....	....	....	....	....	....	....	....	....	....	....	....	....	....	....
	NHL Totals		**314**	**22**	**71**	**93**	**293**	**4**	**0**	**3**	**387**	**5.7**		**0**	**0.0**	**7**	**6**	**15:23**	**26**	**3**	**4**	**7**	**16**	**0**	**0**	**0**

Memorial Cup All-Star Team (1989) • AHL First All-Star Team (1999) • Won Eddie Shore Award (Outstanding Defenseman - AHL) (1999)

Traded to **Edmonton** by **Buffalo** for Scott Pearson, April 7, 1995. Traded to **St. Louis** by **Edmonton** with Igor Kravchuk for Jeff Norton and Donald Dufresne, January 4, 1996. Traded to **New Jersey** by **St. Louis** with St. Louis' 2nd round choice (Brett Clouthier) in 1999 Entry Draft for Mike Peluso and Ricard Persson, November 26, 1996. Traded to **San Jose** by **New Jersey** with John MacLean for Doug Bodger and Dody Wood, December 7, 1997. Traded to **New Jersey** by **San Jose** for future considerations, August 26, 1998. Claimed by **Washington** from **New Jersey** in Waiver Draft, September 27, 1999. Traded to **New Jersey** by **Washington** for future considerations, October 5, 1999.

SVARTVADET, Per
(svahrt-VAH-deht, PAIR) **ATL.**

Center. Shoots left. 6'1", 190 lbs. Born, Solleftea, Sweden, May 17, 1975. Dallas' 5th choice, 139th overall, in 1993 Entry Draft.

Season	Club	League	GP	G	A	Pts	PIM	PP	SH	GW	S	%	+/-	TF	F%	H	SB	Min	Playoffs GP	G	A	Pts	PIM	PP	SH	GW
1992-93	MoDo AIK	Swede-Jr.	14	5	10	15	18	....	....	....	....	....	....	....	....	....	....	....	....	....	....	....	....	....	....	....
	MoDo AIK	Sweden	2	0	0	0	0	....	....	....	....	....	....	....	....	....	....	....	....	....	....	....	....	....	....	....
1993-94	MoDo AIK	Swede-Jr.	12	7	12	19	6	....	....	....	....	....	....	....	....	....	....	....	....	....	....	....	....	....	....	....
	MoDo AIK	Sweden	36	2	1	3	4	....	....	....	....	....	....	....	....	....	....	....	11	0	0	0	6	....	....	....
1994-95	MoDo Hockey	Sweden	40	6	9	15	31	....	....	....	....	....	....	....	....	....	....	....	....	....	....	....	....	....	....	....
1995-96	MoDo Hockey	Sweden	40	9	14	23	26	....	....	....	....	....	....	....	....	....	....	....	8	2	3	5	0	....	....	....
1996-97	MoDo Hockey	Sweden	50	7	18	25	38	....	....	....	....	....	....	....	....	....	....	....	....	....	....	....	....	....	....	....
1997-98	MoDo Hockey	Sweden	46	6	12	18	28	....	....	....	....	....	....	....	....	....	....	....	7	3	2	5	2	....	....	....
1998-99	MoDo Hockey	Sweden	50	9	23	32	30	....	....	....	....	....	....	....	....	....	....	....	13	3	6	9	6	....	....	....
99-2000	**Atlanta**	**NHL**	**38**	**3**	**4**	**7**	**6**	**0**	**0**	**0**	**36**	**8.3**	**-8**	**452**	**45.6**	**29**	**16**	**13:24**	....	....	....	....	....	....	....	....
	Orlando	IHL	27	4	6	10	10	....	....	....	....	....	....	....	....	....	....	....	5	0	1	1	0	....	....	....
	NHL Totals		**38**	**3**	**4**	**7**	**6**	**0**	**0**	**0**	**36**	**8.3**		**452**	**45.6**	**29**	**16**	**13:24**	....	....	....	....	....	....	....	....

Traded to **Atlanta** by **Dallas** for Ottawa's 6th round choice (previously acquired, Dallas selected Justin Cox) in 1999 Entry Draft, June 26, 1999.

SVEHLA, Robert
(SHVEH-lah, RAW-buhrt) **FLA.**

Defense. Shoots right. 6'1", 210 lbs. Born, Martin, Czech., January 2, 1969. Calgary's 4th choice, 78th overall, in 1992 Entry Draft.

Season	Club	League	GP	G	A	Pts	PIM	PP	SH	GW	S	%	+/-	TF	F%	H	SB	Min	Playoffs GP	G	A	Pts	PIM	PP	SH	GW
1989-90	Dukla Trencin	Czech.	29	4	3	7	....	....	....	....	....	....	....	....	....	....	....	....	....	....	....	....	....	....	....	....
1990-91	Dukla Trencin	Czech.	52	16	9	25	62	....	....	....	....	....	....	....	....	....	....	....	....	....	....	....	....	....	....	....
1991-92	Dukla Trencin	Czech.	51	23	28	51	74	....	....	....	....	....	....	....	....	....	....	....	....	....	....	....	....	....	....	....
	Czechoslovakia	Olympics	8	2	1	3	8	....	....	....	....	....	....	....	....	....	....	....	....	....	....	....	....	....	....	....
1992-93	Malmo IF	Sweden	40	19	10	29	86	....	....	....	....	....	....	....	....	....	....	....	6	0	1	1	14	....	....	....
1993-94	Malmo IF	Sweden	37	14	25	39	*127	....	....	....	....	....	....	....	....	....	....	....	10	5	1	6	23	....	....	....
	Slovakia	Olympics	8	2	4	6	26	....	....	....	....	....	....	....	....	....	....	....	....	....	....	....	....	....	....	....
1994-95	Malmo IF	Sweden	32	11	13	24	83	....	....	....	....	....	....	....	....	....	....	....	9	2	3	5	6	....	....	....
	Florida	**NHL**	**5**	**1**	**1**	**2**	**0**	**1**	**0**	**0**	**6**	**16.7**	**3**	....	....	....	....	....	....	....	....	....	....	....	....	....
1995-96	**Florida**	**NHL**	**81**	**8**	**49**	**57**	**94**	**7**	**0**	**0**	**146**	**5.5**	**-3**	....	....	....	....	....	**22**	**0**	**6**	**6**	**32**	**0**	**0**	**0**
1996-97	**Florida**	**NHL**	**82**	**13**	**32**	**45**	**86**	**5**	**0**	**3**	**159**	**8.2**	**2**	....	....	....	....	....	**5**	**1**	**4**	**5**	**4**	**1**	**0**	**0**
1997-98	**Florida**	**NHL**	**79**	**9**	**34**	**43**	**113**	**3**	**0**	**0**	**144**	**6.3**	**-3**	....	....	....	....	....	....	....	....	....	....	....	....	....
	Slovakia	Olympics	2	0	1	1	0	....	....	....	....	....	....	....	....	....	....	....	....	....	....	....	....	....	....	....
1998-99	**Florida**	**NHL**	**80**	**8**	**29**	**37**	**83**	**4**	**0**	**0**	**157**	**5.1**	**-13**	**2**	**0.0**	**101**	**92**	**24:45**	....	....	....	....	....	....	....	....
99-2000	**Florida**	**NHL**	**82**	**9**	**40**	**49**	**64**	**3**	**0**	**1**	**143**	**6.3**	**23**	**1**	**0.0**	**97**	**169**	**24:33**	**4**	**0**	**1**	**1**	**4**	**0**	**0**	**0**
	NHL Totals		**409**	**48**	**185**	**233**	**440**	**23**	**0**	**4**	**755**	**6.4**		**3**	**0.0**	**198**	**261**	**24:39**	**31**	**1**	**11**	**12**	**40**	**1**	**0**	**0**

Czechoslovakian First All-Star Team (1992) • Played in NHL All-Star Game (1997)

Traded to **Florida** by **Calgary** with Magnus Svensson for Florida's 3rd round choice (Dmitri Vlasenkov) in 1996 Entry Draft and 4th round choice (Ryan Ready) in 1997 Entry Draft, September 29, 1994.

SVEJKOVSKY, Jaroslav
(svehzh-KOHV-skee, YAHR-oh-slav) **T.B.**

Right wing. Shoots right. 6'1", 193 lbs. Born, Plzen, Czech., October 1, 1976. Washington's 2nd choice, 17th overall, in 1996 Entry Draft.

Season	Club	League	GP	G	A	Pts	PIM	PP	SH	GW	S	%	+/-	TF	F%	H	SB	Min	Playoffs GP	G	A	Pts	PIM	PP	SH	GW
1993-94	ZKZ Plzen	Cze-Rep	8	0	0	0	8	....	....	....	....	....	....	....	....	....	....	....	....	....	....	....	....	....	....	....
1994-95	ZKZ Plzen-Jr.	Cze-Rep	25	18	19	37	30	....	....	....	....	....	....	....	....	....	....	....	....	....	....	....	....	....	....	....
	SK Tabor	Cze-Rep	11	6	7	13	....	....	....	....	....	....	....	....	....	....	....	....	....	....	....	....	....	....	....	....
1995-96	Tri-City Americans	WHL	70	58	43	101	118	....	....	....	....	....	....	....	....	....	....	....	11	10	9	19	8	....	....	....
1996-97	**Washington**	**NHL**	**19**	**7**	**3**	**10**	**4**	**2**	**0**	**1**	**30**	**23.3**	**-1**	....	....	....	....	....	....	....	....	....	....	....	....	....
	Portland Pirates	AHL	54	38	28	66	56	....	....	....	....	....	....	....	....	....	....	....	5	2	0	2	6	....	....	....
1997-98	**Washington**	**NHL**	**17**	**4**	**1**	**5**	**10**	**2**	**0**	**1**	**29**	**13.8**	**-5**	....	....	....	....	....	**1**	**0**	**0**	**0**	**2**	**0**	**0**	**0**
	Portland Pirates	AHL	16	12	7	19	16	....	....	....	....	....	....	....	....	....	....	....	7	1	2	3	2	....	....	....
1998-99	**Washington**	**NHL**	**25**	**6**	**8**	**14**	**12**	**4**	**0**	**2**	**50**	**12.0**	**-2**	**0**	**0.0**	**40**	**6**	**13:36**	....	....	....	....	....	....	....	....

			Regular Season																Playoffs							
Season	Club	League	GP	G	A	Pts	PIM	PP	SH	GW	S	%	+/-	TF	F%	H	SB	Min	GP	G	A	Pts	PIM	PP	SH	GW
99-2000	Washington	NHL	23	1	2	3	2	1	0	0	18	5.6	-7	1	0.0	26	3	8:60	....	....	....	....	....	....	....	....
	Tampa Bay	NHL	29	5	5	10	28	0	0	0	42	11.9	-7	5	80.0	27	9	12:22	....	....	....	....	....	....	....	....
	NHL Totals		113	23	19	42	56	9	0	4	169	13.6		6	66.7	93	18	11:46	1	0	0	0	2	0	0	0

WHL West Second All-Star Team (1996) • Won Dudley "Red" Garrett Memorial Trophy (Top Rookie - AHL) (1997)

Traded to **Tampa Bay** by **Washington** for Tampa Bay's 7th round choice (later traded to LA Kings - LA Kings selected Evgeny Federov) in 2000 Entry Draft and 3rd round choice in 2001 Entry Draft, January 17, 2000.

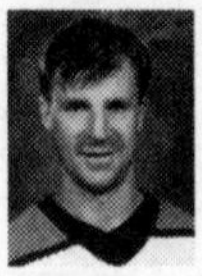

SVOBODA, Petr (svah-BOH-duh, PEE-tuhr) T.B.

Defense. Shoots left. 6'1", 198 lbs. Born, Most, Czech., February 14, 1966. Montreal's 1st choice, 5th overall, in 1984 Entry Draft.

Season	Club	League	GP	G	A	Pts	PIM	PP	SH	GW	S	%	+/-	TF	F%	H	SB	Min	GP	G	A	Pts	PIM	PP	SH	GW
1982-83	CHZ Litvinov	Czech.	4	0	0	0	2	....	....	....	....	....	....	....	....	....	....	....	....	....	....	....	....	....	....	....
1983-84	CHZ Litvinov	Czech.	18	3	1	4	20	....	....	....	....	....	....	....	....	....	....	....	....	....	....	....	....	....	....	....
1984-85	Montreal	NHL	73	4	27	31	65	0	0	1	80	5.0	16	....	....	....	....	....	7	1	1	2	12	0	0	0
1985-86♦	Montreal	NHL	73	1	18	19	93	0	0	0	63	1.6	24	....	....	....	....	....	8	0	0	0	21	0	0	0
1986-87	Montreal	NHL	70	5	17	22	63	1	0	1	80	6.3	14	....	....	....	....	....	14	0	5	5	10	0	0	0
1987-88	Montreal	NHL	69	7	22	29	149	2	0	1	138	5.1	46	....	....	....	....	....	10	0	5	5	12	0	0	0
1988-89	Montreal	NHL	71	8	37	45	147	4	0	1	131	6.1	28	....	....	....	....	....	21	1	11	12	16	0	0	0
1989-90	Montreal	NHL	60	5	31	36	98	2	0	2	90	5.6	20	....	....	....	....	....	10	0	5	5	7	0	0	0
1990-91	Montreal	NHL	60	4	22	26	52	3	0	1	67	6.0	5	....	....	....	....	....	2	0	1	1	2	0	0	0
1991-92	Montreal	NHL	58	5	16	21	94	1	0	3	88	5.7	9	....	....	....	....	....	....	....	....	....	....	....	....	....
	Buffalo	NHL	13	1	6	7	52	0	0	0	23	4.3	-8	....	....	....	....	....	7	1	4	5	6	0	1	0
1992-93	Buffalo	NHL	40	2	24	26	59	1	0	1	61	3.3	3	....	....	....	....	....	....	....	....	....	....	....	....	....
1993-94	Buffalo	NHL	60	2	14	16	89	1	0	0	80	2.5	11	....	....	....	....	....	3	0	0	0	4	0	0	0
1994-95	CHZ Litvinov	Cze-Rep	8	2	0	2	50	....	....	....	....	....	....	....	....	....	....	....	....	....	....	....	....	....	....	....
	Buffalo	NHL	26	0	5	5	60	0	0	0	22	0.0	-5	....	....	....	....	....	....	....	....	....	....	....	....	....
	Philadelphia	NHL	11	0	3	3	10	0	0	0	17	0.0	0	....	....	....	....	....	14	0	4	4	8	0	0	0
1995-96	Philadelphia	NHL	73	1	28	29	105	0	0	0	91	1.1	28	....	....	....	....	....	12	0	6	6	22	0	0	0
1996-97	Philadelphia	NHL	67	2	12	14	94	1	0	0	36	5.6	10	....	....	....	....	....	16	1	2	3	16	0	0	0
1997-98	Philadelphia	NHL	56	3	15	18	83	2	0	0	44	6.8	19	....	....	....	....	....	3	0	1	1	4	0	0	0
	Czech-Republic	Olympics	6	1	1	2	*39	....	....	....	....	....	....	....	....	....	....	....	....	....	....	....	....	....	....	....
1998-99	Philadelphia	NHL	25	4	2	6	28	1	1	1	37	10.8	5	0	0.0	13	24	20:15	....	....	....	....	....	....	....	....
	Tampa Bay	NHL	34	1	16	17	53	0	0	0	46	2.2	-4	0	0.0	47	61	25:33	....	....	....	....	....	....	....	....
99-2000	Tampa Bay	NHL	70	2	23	25	170	2	0	0	93	2.2	-11	0	0.0	0	0	0:00	....	....	....	....	....	....	....	....
	NHL Totals		1009	57	338	395	1564	21	1	12	1287	4.4		0	0.0	60	85	23:18	127	4	45	49	140	0	1	0

Played in NHL All-Star Game (2000)

Traded to **Buffalo** by **Montreal** for Kevin Haller, March 10, 1992. Traded to **Philadelphia** by **Buffalo** for Garry Galley, April 7, 1995. Traded to **Tampa Bay** by **Philadelphia** for Karl Dykhuis, December 28, 1998.

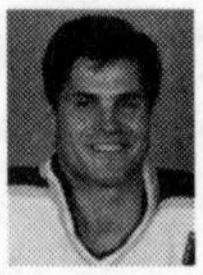

SWEENEY, Don (SWEE-nee, DAWN) BOS.

Defense. Shoots left. 5'10", 186 lbs. Born, St. Stephen, N.B., August 17, 1966. Boston's 8th choice, 166th overall, in 1984 Entry Draft.

Season	Club	League	GP	G	A	Pts	PIM	PP	SH	GW	S	%	+/-	TF	F%	H	SB	Min	GP	G	A	Pts	PIM	PP	SH	GW
1983-84	South St. Paul	Hi-School	22	33	26	59	....	....	....	....	....	....	....	....	....	....	....	....	....	....	....	....	....	....	....	....
1984-85	Harvard University	ECAC	29	3	7	10	30	....	....	....	....	....	....	....	....	....	....	....	....	....	....	....	....	....	....	....
1985-86	Harvard University	ECAC	31	4	5	9	12	....	....	....	....	....	....	....	....	....	....	....	....	....	....	....	....	....	....	....
1986-87	Harvard University	ECAC	34	7	4	11	*22	....	....	....	....	....	....	....	....	....	....	....	....	....	....	....	....	....	....	....
1987-88	Harvard University	ECAC	30	6	23	29	37	....	....	....	....	....	....	....	....	....	....	....	....	....	....	....	....	....	....	....
	Maine Mariners	AHL	....	....	....	....	....	....	....	....	....	....	....	....	....	....	....	....	6	1	3	4	0			
1988-89	Boston	NHL	36	3	5	8	20	0	0	0	35	8.6	-6	....	....	....	....	....	....	....	....	....	....	....	....	....
	Maine Mariners	AHL	42	8	17	25	24	....	....	....	....	....	....	....	....	....	....	....	....	....	....	....	....	....	....	....
1989-90	Boston	NHL	58	3	5	8	58	0	0	0	49	6.1	11	....	....	....	....	....	21	1	5	6	18	1	0	0
	Maine Mariners	AHL	11	0	8	8	8	....	....	....	....	....	....	....	....	....	....	....	....	....	....	....	....	....	....	....
1990-91	Boston	NHL	77	8	13	21	67	0	1	3	102	7.8	2	....	....	....	....	....	19	3	0	3	25	0	0	0
1991-92	Boston	NHL	75	3	11	14	74	0	0	1	92	3.3	-9	....	....	....	....	....	15	0	0	0	10	0	0	0
1992-93	Boston	NHL	84	7	27	34	68	0	1	0	107	6.5	34	....	....	....	....	....	4	0	0	0	4	0	0	0
1993-94	Boston	NHL	75	6	15	21	50	1	2	2	136	4.4	29	....	....	....	....	....	12	2	1	3	4	0	0	1
1994-95	Boston	NHL	47	3	19	22	24	1	0	2	102	2.9	6	....	....	....	....	....	5	0	0	0	4	0	0	0
1995-96	Boston	NHL	77	4	24	28	42	2	0	3	142	2.8	-4	....	....	....	....	....	5	0	2	2	6	0	0	0
1996-97	Boston	NHL	82	3	23	26	39	0	0	0	113	2.7	-5	....	....	....	....	....	....	....	....	....	....	....	....	....
1997-98	Boston	NHL	59	1	15	16	24	0	0	0	55	1.8	12	....	....	....	....	....	....	....	....	....	....	....	....	....
1998-99	Boston	NHL	81	2	10	12	64	0	0	0	79	2.5	14	0	0.0	205	85	19:31	11	3	0	3	6	1	0	0
99-2000	Boston	NHL	81	1	13	14	48	0	0	0	82	1.2	-14	1	0.0	301	84	21:08	....	....	....	....	....	....	....	....
	NHL Totals		832	44	180	224	578	4	4	11	1094	4.0		1	0.0	506	169	20:20	92	9	8	17	77	2	0	1

NCAA East All-American Team (1988) • ECAC First All-Star Team (1988)

SYDOR, Darryl (sih-DOHR, DAIR-ihl) DAL.

Defense. Shoots left. 6'1", 205 lbs. Born, Edmonton, Alta., May 13, 1972. Los Angeles' 1st choice, 7th overall, in 1990 Entry Draft.

Season	Club	League	GP	G	A	Pts	PIM	PP	SH	GW	S	%	+/-	TF	F%	H	SB	Min	GP	G	A	Pts	PIM	PP	SH	GW
1985-86	Genstar Cement	AMHL	34	20	17	37	60	....	....	....	....	....	....	....	....	....	....	....	....	....	....	....	....	....	....	....
1986-87	Genstar Cement	AMHL	36	15	20	35	60	....	....	....	....	....	....	....	....	....	....	....	....	....	....	....	....	....	....	....
1987-88	Edmonton Mets	AMHL	38	10	11	21	54	....	....	....	....	....	....	....	....	....	....	....	....	....	....	....	....	....	....	....
1988-89	Kamloops Blazers	WHL	65	12	14	26	86	....	....	....	....	....	....	....	....	....	....	....	15	1	4	5	19	....	....	....
1989-90	Kamloops Blazers	WHL	67	29	66	95	129	....	....	....	....	....	....	....	....	....	....	....	17	2	9	11	28	....	....	....
1990-91	Kamloops Blazers	WHL	66	27	78	105	88	....	....	....	....	....	....	....	....	....	....	....	12	3	*22	25	10	....	....	....
1991-92	Kamloops Blazers	WHL	29	9	39	48	33	....	....	....	....	....	....	....	....	....	....	....	17	3	15	18	18	....	....	....
	Los Angeles	NHL	18	1	5	6	22	0	0	0	18	5.6	-3	....	....	....	....	....	....	....	....	....	....	....	....	....
1992-93	Los Angeles	NHL	80	6	23	29	63	0	0	1	112	5.4	-2	....	....	....	....	....	24	3	8	11	16	2	0	0
1993-94	Los Angeles	NHL	84	8	27	35	94	1	0	0	146	5.5	-9	....	....	....	....	....	....	....	....	....	....	....	....	....
1994-95	Los Angeles	NHL	48	4	19	23	36	3	0	0	96	4.2	-2	....	....	....	....	....	....	....	....	....	....	....	....	....
1995-96	Los Angeles	NHL	58	1	11	12	34	1	0	0	84	1.2	-11	....	....	....	....	....	....	....	....	....	....	....	....	....
	Dallas	NHL	26	2	6	8	41	1	0	0	33	6.1	-1	....	....	....	....	....	....	....	....	....	....	....	....	....
1996-97	Dallas	NHL	82	8	40	48	51	2	0	2	142	5.6	37	....	....	....	....	....	7	0	2	2	0	0	0	0
1997-98	Dallas	NHL	79	11	35	46	51	4	1	1	166	6.6	17	....	....	....	....	....	17	0	5	5	14	0	0	0
1998-99♦	Dallas	NHL	74	14	34	48	50	9	0	2	163	8.6	-1	1	100.0	83	83	21:16	23	3	9	12	16	1	0	1
99-2000	Dallas	NHL	74	8	26	34	32	5	0	1	132	6.1	6	1	0.0	85	76	23:09	23	1	6	7	6	0	0	0
	NHL Totals		623	63	226	289	474	26	1	7	1092	5.8		2	50.0	168	159	22:12	94	7	30	37	52	3	0	1

WHL West First All-Star Team (1990, 1991, 1992) • Played in NHL All-Star Game (1998, 1999)

Traded to **Dallas** by **LA Kings** with LA Kings' 5th round choice (Ryan Christie) in 1996 Entry Draft for Shane Churla and Doug Zmolek, February 17, 1996.

SYKORA, Michal (SEE-koh-ra, MIHK-al) PHI.

Defense. Shoots left. 6'5", 225 lbs. Born, Pardubice, Czech., July 5, 1973. San Jose's 6th choice, 123rd overall, in 1992 Entry Draft.

Season	Club	League	GP	G	A	Pts	PIM	PP	SH	GW	S	%	+/-	TF	F%	H	SB	Min	GP	G	A	Pts	PIM	PP	SH	GW
1990-91	HC Tesla	Czech-Jr.	40	17	26	43	45	....	....	....	....	....	....	....	....	....	....	....	....	....	....	....	....	....	....	....
	HC Pardubice	Czech.	2	0	0	0	....	....	....	....	....	....	....	....	....	....	....	....	....	....	....	....	....	....	....	....
1991-92	Tacoma Rockets	WHL	61	13	23	36	46	....	....	....	....	....	....	....	....	....	....	....	4	0	2	2	2	....	....	....
1992-93	Tacoma Rockets	WHL	70	23	50	73	73	....	....	....	....	....	....	....	....	....	....	....	7	4	8	12	2	....	....	....
1993-94	San Jose	NHL	22	1	4	5	14	0	0	0	22	4.5	-4	....	....	....	....	....	....	....	....	....	....	....	....	....
	Kansas City	IHL	47	5	11	16	30	....	....	....	....	....	....	....	....	....	....	....	....	....	....	....	....	....	....	....
1994-95	Kansas City	IHL	36	1	10	11	30	....	....	....	....	....	....	....	....	....	....	....	....	....	....	....	....	....	....	....
	San Jose	NHL	16	0	4	4	10	0	0	0	6	0.0	6	....	....	....	....	....	....	....	....	....	....	....	....	....
1995-96	San Jose	NHL	79	4	16	20	54	1	0	0	80	5.0	-14	....	....	....	....	....	....	....	....	....	....	....	....	....
1996-97	San Jose	NHL	35	2	5	7	59	1	0	0	39	5.1	0	....	....	....	....	....	....	....	....	....	....	....	....	....
	Chicago	NHL	28	1	9	10	10	0	0	0	38	2.6	4	....	....	....	....	....	1	0	0	0	0	0	0	0
1997-98	Chicago	NHL	28	1	3	4	12	0	0	0	35	2.9	-10	....	....	....	....	....	....	....	....	....	....	....	....	....
	Indianapolis Ice	IHL	6	0	0	0	4	....	....	....	....	....	....	....	....	....	....	....	....	....	....	....	....	....	....	....
	HC Pardubice	Cze-Rep	1	1	0	1	2	....	....	....	....	....	....	....	....	....	....	....	....	....	....	....	....	....	....	....

Season	Club	League	GP	G	A	Pts	PIM	PP	SH	GW	S	%	+/–	TF	F%	H	SB	Min	GP	G	A	Pts	PIM	PP	SH	GW
			Regular Season																Playoffs							
1998-99	Sparta Praha	Cze-Rep	26	4	9	13	38	....	....	....	....	....	....	....	....	....	....	....	8	2	0	2	....	....	....	....
	Sparta Praha	EuroHL	2	2	2	4	4	....	....	....	....	....	....	....	....	....	....	....	2	2	2	4	0	....	....	....
	Tampa Bay	**NHL**	**10**	**1**	**2**	**3**	**0**	**0**	**0**	**1**	**24**	**4.2**	**–7**	**0**	**0.0**	**10**	**8**	**16:20**	....	....	....	....	....	....	....	....
99-2000	Sparta Praha	Cze-Rep	48	11	14	25	89	....	....	....	....	....	....	....	....	....	....	....	9	5	3	8	8	....	....	....
	NHL Totals		**218**	**10**	**43**	**53**	**159**	**2**	**0**	**1**	**244**	**4.1**		**0**	**0.0**	**10**	**8**	**16:20**	**1**	**0**	**0**	**0**	**0**	**0**	**0**	**0**

WHL West First All-Star Team (1993)

Traded to **Chicago** by **San Jose** with Chris Terreri and Ulf Dahlen for Ed Belfour, January 25, 1997. Traded to **Tampa Bay** by **Chicago** for Mark Fitzpatrick and Tampa Bay's 4th round choice (later traded to Montreal - Montreal selected Chris Dyment) in 1999 Entry Draft, July 17, 1998. Signed as a free agent by **Philadelphia**, July 6, 2000.

SYKORA, Petr

(SEE-koh-ra, PEE-tuhr) **N.J.**

Right wing. Shoots left. 6', 190 lbs. Born, Plzen, Czech., November 19, 1976. New Jersey's 1st choice, 18th overall, in 1995 Entry Draft.

Season	Club	League	GP	G	A	Pts	PIM	PP	SH	GW	S	%	+/–	TF	F%	H	SB	Min	GP	G	A	Pts	PIM	PP	SH	GW
1991-92	Skoda Plzen	Czech-Jr.	30	50	50	100	....	....	....	....	....	....	....	....	....	....	....	....	....	....	....	....	....	....	....	....
1992-93	Skoda Plzen	Czech.	19	12	5	17	....	....	....	....	....	....	....	....	....	....	....	....	....	....	....	....	....	....	....	....
1993-94	Skoda Plzen	Cze-Rep	37	10	16	26	....	....	....	....	....	....	....	....	....	....	....	....	4	0	1	1	....	....	....	....
	Cleveland	IHL	13	4	5	9	8	....	....	....	....	....	....	....	....	....	....	....	....	....	....	....	....	....	....	....
1994-95	Detroit Vipers	IHL	29	12	17	29	16	....	....	....	....	....	....	....	....	....	....	....	....	....	....	....	....	....	....	....
1995-96	**New Jersey**	**NHL**	**63**	**18**	**24**	**42**	**32**	**8**	**0**	**3**	**128**	**14.1**	**7**	....	....	....	....	....	....	....	....	....	....	....	....	....
	Albany River Rats	AHL	5	4	1	5	0	....	....	....	....	....	....	....	....	....	....	....	....	....	....	....	....	....	....	....
1996-97	**New Jersey**	**NHL**	**19**	**1**	**2**	**3**	**4**	**0**	**0**	**0**	**26**	**3.8**	**–8**	....	....	....	....	....	**2**	**0**	**0**	**0**	**2**	**0**	**0**	**0**
	Albany River Rats	AHL	43	20	25	45	48	....	....	....	....	....	....	....	....	....	....	....	4	1	4	5	2	....	....	....
1997-98	**New Jersey**	**NHL**	**58**	**16**	**20**	**36**	**22**	**3**	**1**	**4**	**130**	**12.3**	**0**	....	....	....	....	....	**2**	**0**	**0**	**0**	**0**	**0**	**0**	**0**
	Albany River Rats	AHL	2	4	1	5	0	....	....	....	....	....	....	....	....	....	....	....	....	....	....	....	....	....	....	....
1998-99	**New Jersey**	**NHL**	**80**	**29**	**43**	**72**	**22**	**15**	**0**	**7**	**222**	**13.1**	**16**	**33**	**33.3**	**65**	**16**	**16:14**	**7**	**3**	**3**	**6**	**4**	**0**	**0**	**1**
99-2000♦	**New Jersey**	**NHL**	**79**	**25**	**43**	**68**	**26**	**5**	**1**	**4**	**222**	**11.3**	**24**	**0**	**0.0**	**0**	**0**	**0:00**	**23**	**9**	**8**	**17**	**10**	**1**	**0**	**3**
	NHL Totals		**299**	**89**	**132**	**221**	**106**	**31**	**2**	**18**	**728**	**12.2**		**33**	**33.3**	**65**	**16**	**16:14**	**34**	**12**	**11**	**23**	**16**	**1**	**0**	**4**

NHL All-Rookie Team (1996)

SYKORA, Petr

(SEE-koh-ra, PEE-tuhr) **NSH.**

Center. Shoots right. 6'3", 206 lbs. Born, Pardubice, Czech., December 21, 1978. Detroit's 2nd choice, 76th overall, in 1997 Entry Draft.

Season	Club	League	GP	G	A	Pts	PIM	PP	SH	GW	S	%	+/–	TF	F%	H	SB	Min	GP	G	A	Pts	PIM	PP	SH	GW
1994-95	HC Pardubice-Jr.	Cze-Rep	38	35	33	68	....	....	....	....	....	....	....	....	....	....	....	....	....	....	....	....	....	....	....	....
1995-96	HC Pardubice-Jr.	Cze-Rep	16	26	17	43	....	....	....	....	....	....	....	....	....	....	....	....	....	....	....	....	....	....	....	....
1996-97	HC Pardubice-Jr.	Cze-Rep	12	14	4	18	....	....	....	....	....	....	....	....	....	....	....	....	....	....	....	....	....	....	....	....
	HC Pardubice	Cze-Rep	29	1	3	4	4	....	....	....	....	....	....	....	....	....	....	....	....	....	....	....	....	....	....	....
1997-98	HC Pardubice	Cze-Rep	39	4	5	9	8	....	....	....	....	....	....	....	....	....	....	....	3	0	0	0	....	....	....	....
1998-99	**Nashville**	**NHL**	**2**	**0**	**0**	**0**	**0**	**0**	**0**	**0**	**2**	**0.0**	**–1**	**11**	**45.5**	**0**	**0**	**8:19**	....	....	....	....	....	....	....	....
	Milwaukee	IHL	73	14	15	29	50	....	....	....	....	....	....	....	....	....	....	....	2	1	1	2	0	....	....	....
99-2000	Milwaukee	IHL	3	0	1	*1	2	....	....	....	....	....	....	....	....	....	....	....	....	....	....	....	....	....	....	....
	HC Pardubice	Cze-Rep	36	7	13	20	49	....	....	....	....	....	....	....	....	....	....	....	3	0	0	0	2	....	....	....
	NHL Totals		**2**	**0**	**0**	**0**	**0**	**0**	**0**	**0**	**2**	**0.0**		**11**	**45.5**	**0**	**0**	**8:19**	....	....	....	....	....	....	....	....

Traded to **Nashville** by **Detroit** with Detroit's 3rd round choice (later traded to Edmonton - Edmonton selected Mike Comrie) in 1999 Entry Draft and future considerations (Detroit's compensatory 4th round choice (Alexander Krevsun) in 1999 Entry Draft) for Doug Brown, July 14, 1998.

SYLVESTER, Dean

(sihl-VEHS-tuhr, DEEN) **ATL.**

Right wing. Shoots right. 6'2", 210 lbs. Born, Hanson, MA, December 30, 1972.

Season	Club	League	GP	G	A	Pts	PIM	PP	SH	GW	S	%	+/–	TF	F%	H	SB	Min	GP	G	A	Pts	PIM	PP	SH	GW
1990-91	Boston Prep	Hi-School	18	19	13	32		....	....	....	....	....	....	....	....	....	....	....	....	....	....	....	....	....	....	....
1991-92	Kent State	NCAA	31	7	21	28	10	....	....	....	....	....	....	....	....	....	....	....	....	....	....	....	....	....	....	....
1992-93	Kent State	NCAA	38	33	20	53	28	....	....	....	....	....	....	....	....	....	....	....	....	....	....	....	....	....	....	....
1993-94	Kent State	NCAA	39	22	24	46	28	....	....	....	....	....	....	....	....	....	....	....	....	....	....	....	....	....	....	....
1994-95	Michigan State	CCHA	40	15	15	30	38	....	....	....	....	....	....	....	....	....	....	....	....	....	....	....	....	....	....	....
1995-96	Mobile Mysticks	ECHL	44	24	27	51	35	....	....	....	....	....	....	....	....	....	....	....	....	....	....	....	....	....	....	....
	Kansas City	IHL	36	11	10	21	15	....	....	....	....	....	....	....	....	....	....	....	4	0	0	0	2	....	....	....
1996-97	Kansas City	IHL	77	23	22	45	47	....	....	....	....	....	....	....	....	....	....	....	3	1	1	2	0	....	....	....
1997-98	Kansas City	IHL	77	33	20	53	63	....	....	....	....	....	....	....	....	....	....	....	11	5	2	7	4	....	....	....
1998-99	**Buffalo**	**NHL**	**1**	**0**	**0**	**0**	**0**	**0**	**0**	**0**	**1**	**0.0**	**–1**	**0**	**0.0**	**1**	**0**	**14:31**	**4**	**0**	**0**	**0**	**0**	**0**	**0**	**0**
	Rochester	AHL	76	35	30	65	46	....	....	....	....	....	....	....	....	....	....	....	18	*12	5	17	8	....	....	....
99-2000	**Atlanta**	**NHL**	**52**	**16**	**10**	**26**	**24**	**1**	**0**	**2**	**98**	**16.3**	**–14**	**14**	**35.7**	**108**	**17**	**13:44**	....	....	....	....	....	....	....	....
	Orlando	IHL	16	4	3	7	43	....	....	....	....	....	....	....	....	....	....	....	....	....	....	....	....	....	....	....
	NHL Totals		**53**	**16**	**10**	**26**	**24**	**1**	**0**	**2**	**99**	**16.2**		**14**	**35.7**	**109**	**17**	**13:45**	**4**	**0**	**0**	**0**	**0**	**0**	**0**	**0**

Signed as a free agent by **Buffalo**, October 1, 1998. Traded to **Atlanta** by **Buffalo** for future considerations, June 25, 1999.

TAMER, Chris

(TAY-muhr, KRIHS) **ATL.**

Defense. Shoots left. 6'2", 215 lbs. Born, Dearborn, MI, November 17, 1970. Pittsburgh's 3rd choice, 68th overall, in 1990 Entry Draft.

Season	Club	League	GP	G	A	Pts	PIM	PP	SH	GW	S	%	+/–	TF	F%	H	SB	Min	GP	G	A	Pts	PIM	PP	SH	GW
1987-88	Redford Royals	NAJHL	40	10	20	30	217	....	....	....	....	....	....	....	....	....	....	....	....	....	....	....	....	....	....	....
1988-89	Redford Royals	NAJHL	31	6	13	19	79	....	....	....	....	....	....	....	....	....	....	....	....	....	....	....	....	....	....	....
1989-90	U. of Michigan	CCHA	42	2	7	9	147	....	....	....	....	....	....	....	....	....	....	....	....	....	....	....	....	....	....	....
1990-91	U. of Michigan	CCHA	45	8	19	27	130	....	....	....	....	....	....	....	....	....	....	....	....	....	....	....	....	....	....	....
1991-92	U. of Michigan	CCHA	43	4	15	19	125	....	....	....	....	....	....	....	....	....	....	....	....	....	....	....	....	....	....	....
1992-93	U. of Michigan	CCHA	39	5	18	23	113	....	....	....	....	....	....	....	....	....	....	....	....	....	....	....	....	....	....	....
1993-94	**Pittsburgh**	**NHL**	**12**	**0**	**0**	**0**	**9**	**0**	**0**	**0**	**10**	**0.0**	**3**	....	....	....	....	....	**5**	**0**	**0**	**0**	**2**	**0**	**0**	**0**
	Cleveland	IHL	53	1	2	3	160	....	....	....	....	....	....	....	....	....	....	....	....	....	....	....	....	....	....	....
1994-95	Cleveland	IHL	48	4	10	14	204	....	....	....	....	....	....	....	....	....	....	....	....	....	....	....	....	....	....	....
	Pittsburgh	**NHL**	**36**	**2**	**0**	**2**	**82**	**0**	**0**	**0**	**26**	**7.7**	**0**	....	....	....	....	....	**4**	**0**	**0**	**0**	**18**	**0**	**0**	**0**
1995-96	**Pittsburgh**	**NHL**	**70**	**4**	**10**	**14**	**153**	**0**	**0**	**1**	**75**	**5.3**	**20**	....	....	....	....	....	**18**	**0**	**7**	**7**	**24**	**0**	**0**	**0**
1996-97	**Pittsburgh**	**NHL**	**45**	**2**	**4**	**6**	**131**	**0**	**1**	**0**	**56**	**3.6**	**–25**	....	....	....	....	....	**4**	**0**	**0**	**0**	**4**	**0**	**0**	**0**
1997-98	**Pittsburgh**	**NHL**	**79**	**0**	**7**	**7**	**181**	**0**	**0**	**0**	**55**	**0.0**	**4**	....	....	....	....	....	**6**	**0**	**1**	**1**	**4**	**0**	**0**	**0**
1998-99	**Pittsburgh**	**NHL**	**11**	**0**	**0**	**0**	**32**	**0**	**0**	**0**	**2**	**0.0**	**–2**	**0**	**0.0**	**6**	**8**	**5:59**	....	....	....	....	....	....	....	....
99-2000	**Atlanta**	**NHL**	**69**	**2**	**8**	**10**	**91**	**0**	**0**	**0**	**61**	**3.3**	**–32**	**5**	**40.0**	**129**	**102**	**18:29**	....	....	....	....	....	....	....	....
	NHL Totals		**322**	**10**	**29**	**39**	**679**	**0**	**1**	**1**	**285**	**3.5**		**5**	**40.0**	**135**	**110**	**16:46**	**37**	**0**	**8**	**8**	**52**	**0**	**0**	**0**

Traded to **NY Rangers** by **Pittsburgh** with Petr Nedved and Sean Pronger for Alexei Kovalev and Harry York, November 25, 1998. Claimed by **Atlanta** from **NY Rangers** in Expansion Draft, June 25, 1999.

TANABE, David

(TA-nayb, DAY-vihd) **CAR.**

Defense. Shoots right. 6'1", 190 lbs. Born, Minneapolis, MN, July 19, 1980. Carolina's 1st choice, 16th overall, in 1999 Entry Draft.

Season	Club	League	GP	G	A	Pts	PIM	PP	SH	GW	S	%	+/–	TF	F%	H	SB	Min	GP	G	A	Pts	PIM	PP	SH	GW
1996-97	Hill-Murray	Hi-School	28	12	14	26	....	....	....	....	....	....	....	....	....	....	....	....	....	....	....	....	....	....	....	....
1997-98	Team USA	Under-18	73	8	21	29	96	....	....	....	....	....	....	....	....	....	....	....	....	....	....	....	....	....	....	....
1998-99	U. of Wisconsin	WCHA	35	10	12	22	44	....	....	....	....	....	....	....	....	....	....	....	....	....	....	....	....	....	....	....
99-2000	**Carolina**	**NHL**	**31**	**4**	**0**	**4**	**14**	**3**	**0**	**0**	**28**	**14.3**	**–4**	**0**	**0.0**	**11**	**10**	**12:53**	....	....	....	....	....	....	....	....
	Cincinnati	IHL	32	0	13	13	14	....	....	....	....	....	....	....	....	....	....	....	11	1	4	5	6	....	....	....
	NHL Totals		**31**	**4**	**0**	**4**	**14**	**3**	**0**	**0**	**28**	**14.3**		**0**	**0.0**	**11**	**10**	**12:53**	....	....	....	....	....	....	....	....

TANCILL, Chris

(TAN-sihl, KRIHS)

Center. Shoots left. 5'10", 185 lbs. Born, Livonia, MI, February 7, 1968. Hartford's 1st choice, 15th overall, in 1989 Supplemental Draft.

Season	Club	League	GP	G	A	Pts	PIM	PP	SH	GW	S	%	+/–	TF	F%	H	SB	Min	GP	G	A	Pts	PIM	PP	SH	GW
1984-85	St. Clair Shores	NAJHL	45	51	99	150	....	....	....	....	....	....	....	....	....	....	....	....	....	....	....	....	....	....	....	....
1986-87	U. of Wisconsin	WCHA	40	9	23	32	26	....	....	....	....	....	....	....	....	....	....	....	....	....	....	....	....	....	....	....
1987-88	U. of Wisconsin	WCHA	44	13	14	27	48	....	....	....	....	....	....	....	....	....	....	....	....	....	....	....	....	....	....	....
1988-89	U. of Wisconsin	WCHA	44	20	23	43	50	....	....	....	....	....	....	....	....	....	....	....	....	....	....	....	....	....	....	....
1989-90	U. of Wisconsin	WCHA	45	39	32	71	44	....	....	....	....	....	....	....	....	....	....	....	....	....	....	....	....	....	....	....

Season	Club	League	GP	G	A	Pts	PIM	PP	SH	GW	S	%	+/–	TF	F%	H	SB	Min	Playoffs GP	G	A	Pts	PIM	PP	SH	GW
			Regular Season																Playoffs							
1990-91	**Hartford**	**NHL**	**9**	**1**	**1**	**2**	**4**	**0**	**1**	**0**	**6**	**16.7**	**2**													
	Springfield	AHL	72	37	35	72	46												17	8	4	12	32			
1991-92	**Hartford**	**NHL**	**10**	**0**	**0**	**0**	**2**	**0**	**0**	**0**	**13**	**0.0**	**–6**													
	Springfield	AHL	17	12	7	19	20																			
	Detroit	**NHL**	**1**	**0**	**0**	**0**	**0**	**0**	**0**	**0**	**0**	**0.0**	**0**													
	Adirondack	AHL	50	36	34	70	42												19	7	9	16	31			
1992-93	**Detroit**	**NHL**	**4**	**1**	**0**	**1**	**2**	**0**	**0**	**0**	**3**	**33.3**	**–2**													
	Adirondack	AHL	68	*59	43	102	62												10	7	7	14	10			
1993-94	**Dallas**	**NHL**	**12**	**1**	**3**	**4**	**8**	**0**	**0**	**0**	**18**	**5.6**	**–7**													
	Kalamazoo Wings	IHL	60	41	54	95	55												5	0	2	2	8			
1994-95	Kansas City	IHL	64	31	28	59	40																			
	San Jose	**NHL**	**26**	**3**	**11**	**14**	**10**	**0**	**1**	**0**	**39**	**7.7**	**1**						**11**	**1**	**1**	**2**	**8**	**0**	**0**	**0**
1995-96	**San Jose**	**NHL**	**45**	**7**	**16**	**23**	**20**	**0**	**1**	**0**	**93**	**7.5**	**–12**													
	Kansas City	IHL	27	12	16	28	18																			
1996-97	**San Jose**	**NHL**	**25**	**4**	**0**	**4**	**8**	**1**	**0**	**0**	**20**	**20.0**	**–5**													
	Kentucky	AHL	42	19	26	45	31												4	2	0	2	2			
1997-98	**Dallas**	**NHL**	**2**	**0**	**1**	**1**	**0**	**0**	**0**	**0**	**1**	**0.0**	**–1**													
	Michigan K-Wings	IHL	70	30	39	69	86												4	3	0	3	14			
1998-99	EHC Kloten	Switz.	42	19	30	49	46												12	4	2	6	16			
99-2000	EV Zug	Switz.	45	*25	26	51	56												11	6	4	10	10			
	NHL Totals		**134**	**17**	**32**	**49**	**54**	**1**	**3**	**0**	**193**	**8.8**							**11**	**1**	**1**	**2**	**8**	**0**	**0**	**0**

NCAA Championship All-Tournament Team (1990) • NCAA Championship Tournament MVP (1990) • AHL First All-Star Team (1992, 1993)

Traded to **Detroit** by **Hartford** for Daniel Shank, December 18, 1991. Signed as a free agent by **Dallas**, August 28, 1993. Signed as a free agent by **San Jose**, August 24, 1994. Signed as a free agent by **Dallas**, August 6, 1997.

TANGUAY, Alex
(TAN-guay, AL-ehx) **COL.**

Center. Shoots left. 6', 180 lbs. Born, Ste-Justine, Que., November 21, 1979. Colorado's 1st choice, 12th overall, in 1998 Entry Draft.

Season	Club	League	GP	G	A	Pts	PIM	PP	SH	GW	S	%	+/–	TF	F%	H	SB	Min	Playoffs GP	G	A	Pts	PIM	PP	SH	GW
1995-96	Cap-d-Madelaine	QAAA	44	29	34	63	64																			
1996-97	Halifax	QMJHL	70	27	41	68	60												12	5	8	13	8			
1997-98	Halifax	QMJHL	51	47	38	85	32												5	7	6	13	4			
1998-99	Halifax	QMJHL	31	27	34	61	30												5	1	2	3	2			
	Hershey Bears	AHL	5	1	2	3	2												5	0	2	2	0			
99-2000	**Colorado**	**NHL**	**76**	**17**	**34**	**51**	**22**	**5**	**0**	**3**	**74**	**23.0**	**6**	**11**	**45.5**	**72**	**23**	**15:38**	**17**	**2**	**1**	**3**	**2**	**1**	**0**	**1**
	NHL Totals		**76**	**17**	**34**	**51**	**22**	**5**	**0**	**3**	**74**	**23.0**		**11**	**45.5**	**72**	**23**	**15:38**	**17**	**2**	**1**	**3**	**2**	**1**	**0**	**1**

TARDIF, Patrice
(tahr-DIHF, PA-trees)

Center. Shoots left. 6'2", 202 lbs. Born, Thetford Mines, Que., October 30, 1970. St. Louis' 2nd choice, 54th overall, in 1990 Entry Draft.

Season	Club	League	GP	G	A	Pts	PIM	PP	SH	GW	S	%	+/–	TF	F%	H	SB	Min	Playoffs GP	G	A	Pts	PIM	PP	SH	GW
1988-89	Black Lake Miners	QJHL-B	32	37	33	70																				
1989-90	Lennoxville	QCAA	27	58	36	94	36																			
1990-91	U. of Maine	H-East	36	13	12	25	18																			
1991-92	U. of Maine	H-East	31	18	20	38	14																			
1992-93	U. of Maine	H-East	45	23	25	48	22																			
1993-94	U. of Maine	H-East	34	18	15	33	42																			
	Peoria Rivermen	IHL	11	4	4	8	21												4	2	0	2	4			
1994-95	Peoria Rivermen	IHL	53	27	18	45	83																			
	St. Louis	**NHL**	**27**	**3**	**10**	**13**	**29**	**1**	**0**	**0**	**46**	**6.5**	**4**													
1995-96	**St. Louis**	**NHL**	**23**	**3**	**0**	**3**	**12**	**0**	**0**	**1**	**21**	**14.3**	**–2**													
	Worcester	AHL	30	13	13	26	69																			
	Los Angeles	**NHL**	**15**	**1**	**1**	**2**	**37**	**1**	**0**	**0**	**29**	**3.4**	**–9**													
1996-97	Phoenix	IHL	9	0	3	3	13																			
	Detroit Vipers	IHL	66	24	23	47	70												11	0	1	1	8			
1997-98	Rochester	AHL	41	13	13	26	68																			
	Detroit Vipers	IHL	28	10	9	19	24												15	3	7	10	14			
1998-99	Manitoba Moose	IHL	63	21	35	56	88												5	1	2	3	0			
99-2000	Manitoba Moose	IHL	50	12	18	30	70																			
	Quebec Citadelles	AHL	18	9	10	19	23												3	1	1	2	8			
	NHL Totals		**65**	**7**	**11**	**18**	**78**	**2**	**0**	**1**	**96**	**7.3**														

Traded to **LA Kings** by **St. Louis** with Craig Johnson, Roman Vopat, St. Louis' 5th round choice (Peter Hogan) in 1996 Entry Draft and 1st round choice (Matt Zultek) in 1997 Entry Draft for Wayne Gretzky, February 27, 1996. Signed as a free agent by **Buffalo**, September 9, 1997. Signed as a free agent by **Manitoba** (IHL), August 31, 1998. Loaned to **Quebec** (AHL) by **Manitoba** (IHL) for loan of Barry Richter, March 3, 2000.

TAYLOR, Chris
(TAY-lohr, KRIHS)

Center. Shoots left. 6'2", 195 lbs. Born, Stratford, Ont., March 6, 1972. NY Islanders' 2nd choice, 27th overall, in 1990 Entry Draft.

Season	Club	League	GP	G	A	Pts	PIM	PP	SH	GW	S	%	+/–	TF	F%	H	SB	Min	Playoffs GP	G	A	Pts	PIM	PP	SH	GW
1987-88	Stratford Cullitons	OJHL-B	52	28	37	65	112																			
1988-89	London Knights	OHL	62	7	16	23	52												15	0	2	2	15			
1989-90	London Knights	OHL	66	45	60	105	60												6	3	2	5	6			
1990-91	London Knights	OHL	65	50	78	128	50												7	4	8	12	6			
1991-92	London Knights	OHL	66	48	74	122	57												10	8	16	24	9			
1992-93	Capital District	AHL	77	19	43	62	32												4	0	1	1	2			
1993-94	Salt Lake City	IHL	79	21	20	41	38																			
1994-95	Denver Grizzlies	IHL	78	38	48	86	47												14	7	6	13	10			
	NY Islanders	**NHL**	**10**	**0**	**3**	**3**	**2**	**0**	**0**	**0**	**13**	**0.0**	**1**													
1995-96	**NY Islanders**	**NHL**	**11**	**0**	**1**	**1**	**2**	**0**	**0**	**0**	**4**	**0.0**	**1**													
	Utah Grizzlies	IHL	50	18	23	41	60												22	5	11	16	26			
1996-97	**NY Islanders**	**NHL**	**1**	**0**	**0**	**0**	**0**	**0**	**0**	**0**	**1**	**0.0**	**0**													
	Utah Grizzlies	IHL	71	27	40	67	24												7	1	2	3	0			
1997-98	Utah Grizzlies	IHL	79	28	56	84	66												4	0	2	2	6			
1998-99	**Boston**	**NHL**	**37**	**3**	**5**	**8**	**12**	**0**	**1**	**0**	**60**	**5.0**	**–3**	**512**	**53.7**	**52**	**16**	**14:24**								
	Providence Bruins	AHL	21	6	11	17	6																			
	Las Vegas	IHL	14	3	12	15	2																			
99-2000	**Buffalo**	**NHL**	**11**	**1**	**1**	**2**	**2**	**0**	**0**	**0**	**15**	**6.7**	**–2**	**125**	**45.6**	**15**	**3**	**10:54**	**2**	**0**	**0**	**0**	**2**	**0**	**0**	**0**
	Rochester	AHL	49	21	28	49	21																			
	NHL Totals		**70**	**4**	**10**	**14**	**18**	**0**	**1**	**0**	**93**	**4.3**		**637**	**52.1**	**67**	**19**	**13:36**	**2**	**0**	**0**	**0**	**2**	**0**	**0**	**0**

Signed as a free agent by **LA Kings**, July 25, 1997. Signed as a free agent by **Boston**, August 5, 1998. Signed as a free agent by **Buffalo**, August 13, 1999.

TAYLOR, Tim
(TAY-lohr, TIHM) **NYR**

Center. Shoots left. 6'1", 185 lbs. Born, Stratford, Ont., February 6, 1969. Washington's 2nd choice, 36th overall, in 1988 Entry Draft.

Season	Club	League	GP	G	A	Pts	PIM	PP	SH	GW	S	%	+/–	TF	F%	H	SB	Min	Playoffs GP	G	A	Pts	PIM	PP	SH	GW
1985-86	Stratford Cullitons	OJHL-B	1	0	0	0	0																			
1986-87	Stratford Cullitons	OJHL-B	31	25	26	51	51																			
	London Knights	OHL	34	7	9	16	11																			
1987-88	London Knights	OHL	64	46	50	96	66												12	9	9	18	26			
1988-89	London Knights	OHL	61	34	80	114	93												21	*21	25	*46	58			
1989-90	Baltimore	AHL	79	31	36	67	124												9	2	2	4	13			
1990-91	Baltimore	AHL	79	25	42	67	75												5	0	1	1	4			
1991-92	Baltimore	AHL	65	9	18	27	131																			
1992-93	Baltimore	AHL	41	15	16	31	49																			
	Hamilton Canucks	AHL	36	15	22	37	37																			
1993-94	**Detroit**	**NHL**	**1**	**1**	**0**	**1**	**0**	**0**	**0**	**0**	**4**	**25.0**	**–1**													
	Adirondack	AHL	79	36	*81	*117	86												12	2	10	12	12			
1994-95	**Detroit**	**NHL**	**22**	**0**	**4**	**4**	**16**	**0**	**0**	**0**	**21**	**0.0**	**3**						**6**	**0**	**1**	**1**	**12**	**0**	**0**	**0**
1995-96	**Detroit**	**NHL**	**72**	**11**	**14**	**25**	**39**	**1**	**1**	**4**	**81**	**13.6**	**11**						**18**	**0**	**4**	**4**	**4**	**0**	**0**	**0**

			Regular Season																Playoffs							
Season	Club	League	GP	G	A	Pts	PIM	PP	SH	GW	S	%	+/–	TF	F%	H	SB	Min	GP	G	A	Pts	PIM	PP	SH	GW
1996-97♦	**Detroit**	**NHL**	**44**	**3**	**4**	**7**	**52**	**0**	**1**	**0**	**44**	**6.8**	**–6**	....	....	....	....	....	**2**	**0**	**0**	**0**	**0**	**0**	**0**	**0**
1997-98	**Boston**	**NHL**	**79**	**20**	**11**	**31**	**57**	**1**	**3**	**0**	**127**	**15.7**	**–16**	....	....	....	....	....	**6**	**0**	**0**	**0**	**10**	**0**	**0**	**0**
1998-99	**Boston**	**NHL**	**49**	**4**	**7**	**11**	**55**	**0**	**0**	**1**	**76**	**5.3**	**–10**	**834**	**58.3**	**93**	**16**	**15:56**	**12**	**0**	**3**	**3**	**8**	**0**	**0**	**0**
99-2000	**NY Rangers**	**NHL**	**76**	**9**	**11**	**20**	**72**	**0**	**0**	**2**	**79**	**11.4**	**–4**	**1276**	**58.9**	**94**	**41**	**14:09**	....	....	....	....	....	....	....	....
	NHL Totals		**343**	**48**	**51**	**99**	**291**	**2**	**5**	**7**	**432**	**11.1**		**2110**	**58.6**	**187**	**57**	**14:51**	**44**	**0**	**8**	**8**	**34**	**0**	**0**	**0**

AHL First All-Star Team (1994) • Won John B. Sollenberger Trophy (Top Scorer - AHL) (1994)

Traded to **Vancouver** by **Washington** for Eric Murano, January 29, 1993. Signed as a free agent by **Detroit**, July 28, 1993. Claimed by **Boston** from **Detroit** in NHL Waiver Draft, September 28, 1998. Signed as a free agent by **NY Rangers**, July 30, 1999.

TEZIKOV, Alexei

(TEH-zih-kahf, al-EHX-ay) **WSH.**

Defense. Shoots left. 6'1", 208 lbs. Born, Togliatti, USSR, June 22, 1978. Buffalo's 7th choice, 115th overall, in 1996 Entry Draft.

1995-96	Lada Togliatti	CIS	14	0	0	0	8	....	....	....	....	....	....	....	....	....	....	....	....	....	....	....	....	....	....	....
1996-97	Lada Togliatti	Russia	7	0	0	0	4	....	....	....	....	....	....	....	....	....	....	....	....	....	....	....	....	....	....	....
	Torpedo Nizhny	Russia	5	0	2	2	2	....	....	....	....	....	....	....	....	....	....	....	....	....	....	....	....	....	....	....
1997-98	Moncton Wildcats	QMJHL	60	15	33	48	144	....	....	....	....	....	....	....	....	....	....	....	10	3	8	11	20	....	....	....
1998-99	Moncton Wildcats	QMJHL	25	9	21	30	52	....	....	....	....	....	....	....	....	....	....	....	....	....	....	....	....	....	....	....
	Rochester	AHL	31	3	7	10	41	....	....	....	....	....	....	....	....	....	....	....	....	....	....	....	....	....	....	....
	Washington	**NHL**	**5**	**0**	**0**	**0**	**0**	**0**	**0**	**0**	**4**	**0.0**	**–1**	**0**	**0.0**	**9**	**3**	**18:11**	....	....	....	....	....	....	....	....
	Cincinnati	IHL	5	0	0	0	2	....	....	....	....	....	....	....	....	....	....	....	3	0	0	0	10	....	....	....
99-2000	**Washington**	**NHL**	**23**	**1**	**1**	**2**	**2**	**1**	**0**	**1**	**18**	**5.6**	**–2**	**0**	**0.0**	**17**	**9**	**10:30**	....	....	....	....	....	....	....	....
	Portland Pirates	AHL	53	6	9	15	70	....	....	....	....	....	....	....	....	....	....	....	....	....	....	....	....	....	....	....
	NHL Totals		**28**	**1**	**1**	**2**	**2**	**1**	**0**	**1**	**22**	**4.5**		**0**	**0.0**	**26**	**12**	**11:52**	....	....	....	....	....	....	....	....

QMJHL Second All-Star Team (1998)

Traded to **Washington** by **Buffalo** with Buffalo's 4th round compensatory choice (later traded to Calgary - Calgary selected Levente Szuper) in 2000 Entry Draft for Joe Juneau and Washington's 3rd round choice (Tim Preston) in 1999 Entry Draft, March 22, 1999.

THERIEN, Chris

(TEH-ree-ehn, KRIHS) **PHI.**

Defense. Shoots left. 6'4", 230 lbs. Born, Ottawa, Ont., December 14, 1971. Philadelphia's 7th choice, 47th overall, in 1990 Entry Draft.

1988-89	Ottawa	OJHL	8	3	1	4	22	....	....	....	....	....	....	....	....	....	....	....	....	....	....	....	....	....	....	....
1989-90	Ottawa	OJHL	3	0	2	2	2	....	....	....	....	....	....	....	....	....	....	....	....	....	....	....	....	....	....	....
	Northwood Prep	Hi-School	31	35	37	72	54	....	....	....	....	....	....	....	....	....	....	....	....	....	....	....	....	....	....	....
1990-91	Providence	H-East	36	4	18	22	36	....	....	....	....	....	....	....	....	....	....	....	....	....	....	....	....	....	....	....
1991-92	Providence	H-East	36	16	25	41	38	....	....	....	....	....	....	....	....	....	....	....	....	....	....	....	....	....	....	....
1992-93	Providence	H-East	33	8	11	19	52	....	....	....	....	....	....	....	....	....	....	....	....	....	....	....	....	....	....	....
	Canada	Nat-Team	8	1	4	5	8	....	....	....	....	....	....	....	....	....	....	....	....	....	....	....	....	....	....	....
1993-94	Canada	Nat-Team	59	7	15	22	46	....	....	....	....	....	....	....	....	....	....	....	....	....	....	....	....	....	....	....
	Canada	Olympics	4	0	0	0	4	....	....	....	....	....	....	....	....	....	....	....	....	....	....	....	....	....	....	....
	Hershey Bears	AHL	6	0	0	0	2	....	....	....	....	....	....	....	....	....	....	....	....	....	....	....	....	....	....	....
1994-95	Hershey Bears	AHL	34	3	13	16	27	....	....	....	....	....	....	....	....	....	....	....	....	....	....	....	....	....	....	....
	Philadelphia	**NHL**	**48**	**3**	**10**	**13**	**38**	**1**	**0**	**0**	**53**	**5.7**	**8**	....	....	....	....	....	**15**	**0**	**0**	**0**	**10**	**0**	**0**	**0**
1995-96	**Philadelphia**	**NHL**	**82**	**6**	**17**	**23**	**89**	**3**	**0**	**1**	**123**	**4.9**	**16**	....	....	....	....	....	**12**	**0**	**0**	**0**	**18**	**0**	**0**	**0**
1996-97	**Philadelphia**	**NHL**	**71**	**2**	**22**	**24**	**64**	**0**	**0**	**0**	**107**	**1.9**	**27**	....	....	....	....	....	**19**	**1**	**6**	**7**	**6**	**0**	**0**	**1**
1997-98	**Philadelphia**	**NHL**	**78**	**3**	**16**	**19**	**80**	**1**	**0**	**1**	**102**	**2.9**	**5**	....	....	....	....	....	**5**	**0**	**1**	**1**	**4**	**0**	**0**	**0**
1998-99	**Philadelphia**	**NHL**	**74**	**3**	**15**	**18**	**48**	**1**	**0**	**0**	**115**	**2.6**	**16**	**0**	**0.0**	**167**	**103**	**20:45**	**6**	**0**	**0**	**0**	**6**	**0**	**0**	**0**
99-2000	**Philadelphia**	**NHL**	**80**	**4**	**9**	**13**	**66**	**1**	**0**	**1**	**126**	**3.2**	**11**	**0**	**0.0**	**171**	**137**	**20:12**	**18**	**0**	**1**	**1**	**12**	**0**	**0**	**0**
	NHL Totals		**433**	**21**	**89**	**110**	**385**	**7**	**0**	**3**	**626**	**3.4**		**0**	**0.0**	**338**	**240**	**20:28**	**75**	**1**	**8**	**9**	**56**	**0**	**0**	**1**

Hockey East Second All-Star Team (1993) • NHL All-Rookie Team (1995)

THOMAS, Scott

(TAW-mas, SKAWT) **L.A.**

Right wing. Shoots right. 6'2", 200 lbs. Born, Buffalo, NY, January 18, 1970. Buffalo's 2nd choice, 56th overall, in 1989 Entry Draft.

1987-88	Nichols High	Hi-School	16	23	39	62	62	....	....	....	....	....	....	....	....	....	....	....	....	....	....	....	....	....	....	....
1988-89	Nichols High	Hi-School	17	38	52	90	....	....	....	....	....	....	....	....	....	....	....	....	....	....	....	....	....	....	....	....
1989-90	Clarkson	ECAC	34	19	13	32	95	....	....	....	....	....	....	....	....	....	....	....	....	....	....	....	....	....	....	....
1990-91	Clarkson	ECAC	40	28	14	42	89	....	....	....	....	....	....	....	....	....	....	....	....	....	....	....	....	....	....	....
1991-92	Clarkson	ECAC	29	22	20	42	57	....	....	....	....	....	....	....	....	....	....	....	....	....	....	....	....	....	....	....
	Rochester	AHL	....	....	....	....	....	....	....	....	....	....	....	....	....	....	....	....	9	0	1	1	17	....	....	....
1992-93	**Buffalo**	**NHL**	**7**	**1**	**1**	**2**	**15**	**0**	**0**	**0**	**4**	**25.0**	**2**	....	....	....	....	....	....	....	....	....	....	....	....	....
	Rochester	AHL	65	32	27	59	38	....	....	....	....	....	....	....	....	....	....	....	17	8	5	13	6	....	....	....
1993-94	**Buffalo**	**NHL**	**32**	**2**	**2**	**4**	**8**	**1**	**0**	**0**	**26**	**7.7**	**–6**	....	....	....	....	....	....	....	....	....	....	....	....	....
	Rochester	AHL	11	4	5	9	0	....	....	....	....	....	....	....	....	....	....	....	....	....	....	....	....	....	....	....
1994-95	Rochester	AHL	55	21	25	46	115	....	....	....	....	....	....	....	....	....	....	....	5	4	0	4	4	....	....	....
1995-96	Cincinnati	IHL	78	32	28	60	54	....	....	....	....	....	....	....	....	....	....	....	17	*13	2	15	4	....	....	....
1996-97	Cincinnati	IHL	71	32	29	61	46	....	....	....	....	....	....	....	....	....	....	....	3	0	0	0	0	....	....	....
1997-98	Detroit Vipers	IHL	44	11	16	27	18	....	....	....	....	....	....	....	....	....	....	....	....	....	....	....	....	....	....	....
	Manitoba Moose	IHL	26	12	4	16	8	....	....	....	....	....	....	....	....	....	....	....	3	0	1	1	2	....	....	....
1998-99	Manitoba Moose	IHL	78	45	25	70	32	....	....	....	....	....	....	....	....	....	....	....	5	3	4	7	4	....	....	....
99-2000	Long Beach	IHL	52	15	16	31	18	....	....	....	....	....	....	....	....	....	....	....	6	2	1	3	6	....	....	....
	NHL Totals		**39**	**3**	**3**	**6**	**23**	**1**	**0**	**0**	**30**	**10.0**		....	....	....	....	....	....	....	....	....	....	....	....	....

Signed as a free agent by **LA Kings**, July 30, 1999.

THOMAS, Steve

(TAW-mas, STEEV) **TOR.**

Right wing. Shoots left. 5'10", 185 lbs. Born, Stockport, England, July 15, 1963.

1980-81	Markham Waxers	OJHL	42	22	25	47	76	....	....	....	....	....	....	....	....	....	....	....	....	....	....	....	....	....	....	....
	Toronto Marlies	OMJHL	1	0	0	0	0	....	....	....	....	....	....	....	....	....	....	....	....	....	....	....	....	....	....	....
1981-82	Markham Waxers	OJHL	48	68	57	125	113	....	....	....	....	....	....	....	....	....	....	....	....	....	....	....	....	....	....	....
	Toronto Marlies	OHL	1	0	0	0	0	....	....	....	....	....	....	....	....	....	....	....	....	....	....	....	....	....	....	....
1982-83	Toronto Marlies	OHL	61	18	20	38	42	....	....	....	....	....	....	....	....	....	....	....	....	....	....	....	....	....	....	....
1983-84	Toronto Marlies	OHL	70	51	54	105	77	....	....	....	....	....	....	....	....	....	....	....	....	....	....	....	....	....	....	....
1984-85	**Toronto**	**NHL**	**18**	**1**	**1**	**2**	**2**	**0**	**0**	**0**	**26**	**3.8**	**–13**	....	....	....	....	....	....	....	....	....	....	....	....	....
	St. Catharines	AHL	64	42	48	90	56	....	....	....	....	....	....	....	....	....	....	....	....	....	....	....	....	....	....	....
1985-86	**Toronto**	**NHL**	**65**	**20**	**37**	**57**	**36**	**5**	**0**	**5**	**197**	**10.2**	**–15**	....	....	....	....	....	**10**	**6**	**8**	**14**	**9**	**3**	**0**	**0**
	St. Catharines	AHL	19	18	14	32	35	....	....	....	....	....	....	....	....	....	....	....	....	....	....	....	....	....	....	....
1986-87	**Toronto**	**NHL**	**78**	**35**	**27**	**62**	**114**	**3**	**0**	**7**	**245**	**14.3**	**–3**	....	....	....	....	....	**13**	**2**	**3**	**5**	**13**	**0**	**0**	**0**
1987-88	**Chicago**	**NHL**	**30**	**13**	**13**	**26**	**40**	**5**	**0**	**3**	**69**	**18.8**	**1**	....	....	....	....	....	**3**	**1**	**2**	**3**	**6**	**0**	**0**	**0**
1988-89	**Chicago**	**NHL**	**45**	**21**	**19**	**40**	**69**	**8**	**0**	**0**	**124**	**16.9**	**–2**	....	....	....	....	....	**12**	**3**	**5**	**8**	**10**	**1**	**0**	**2**
1989-90	**Chicago**	**NHL**	**76**	**40**	**30**	**70**	**91**	**13**	**0**	**7**	**235**	**17.0**	**–3**	....	....	....	....	....	**20**	**7**	**6**	**13**	**33**	**1**	**0**	**3**
1990-91	**Chicago**	**NHL**	**69**	**19**	**35**	**54**	**129**	**2**	**0**	**3**	**192**	**9.9**	**8**	....	....	....	....	....	**6**	**1**	**2**	**3**	**15**	**0**	**0**	**0**
1991-92	**Chicago**	**NHL**	**11**	**2**	**6**	**8**	**26**	**0**	**0**	**1**	**35**	**5.7**	**–3**	....	....	....	....	....	....	....	....	....	....	....	....	....
	NY Islanders	**NHL**	**71**	**28**	**42**	**70**	**71**	**3**	**0**	**2**	**210**	**13.3**	**11**	....	....	....	....	....	....	....	....	....	....	....	....	....
1992-93	**NY Islanders**	**NHL**	**79**	**37**	**50**	**87**	**111**	**12**	**0**	**7**	**264**	**14.0**	**3**	....	....	....	....	....	**18**	**9**	**8**	**17**	**37**	**0**	**0**	**0**
1993-94	**NY Islanders**	**NHL**	**78**	**42**	**33**	**75**	**139**	**17**	**0**	**5**	**249**	**16.9**	**–9**	....	....	....	....	....	**4**	**1**	**0**	**1**	**8**	**1**	**0**	**0**
1994-95	**NY Islanders**	**NHL**	**47**	**11**	**15**	**26**	**60**	**3**	**0**	**2**	**133**	**8.3**	**–14**	....	....	....	....	....	....	....	....	....	....	....	....	....
1995-96	**New Jersey**	**NHL**	**81**	**26**	**35**	**61**	**98**	**6**	**0**	**6**	**192**	**13.5**	**–2**	....	....	....	....	....	....	....	....	....	....	....	....	....
1996-97	**New Jersey**	**NHL**	**57**	**15**	**19**	**34**	**46**	**1**	**0**	**2**	**124**	**12.1**	**9**	....	....	....	....	....	**10**	**1**	**1**	**2**	**18**	**0**	**0**	**0**
1997-98	**New Jersey**	**NHL**	**55**	**14**	**10**	**24**	**32**	**3**	**0**	**4**	**111**	**12.6**	**4**	....	....	....	....	....	**6**	**0**	**3**	**3**	**2**	**0**	**0**	**0**
1998-99	**Toronto**	**NHL**	**78**	**28**	**45**	**73**	**33**	**11**	**0**	**7**	**209**	**13.4**	**26**	**4**	**25.0**	**65**	**25**	**18:23**	**17**	**6**	**3**	**9**	**12**	**2**	**0**	**1**
99-2000	**Toronto**	**NHL**	**81**	**26**	**37**	**63**	**68**	**9**	**0**	**9**	**151**	**17.2**	**1**	**8**	**50.0**	**62**	**20**	**16:19**	**12**	**6**	**3**	**9**	**10**	**0**	**0**	**1**
	NHL Totals		**1019**	**378**	**454**	**832**	**1165**	**101**	**0**	**70**	**2766**	**13.7**		**12**	**41.7**	**127**	**45**	**17:20**	**131**	**43**	**44**	**87**	**173**	**8**	**0**	**7**

Won Dudley "Red" Garrett Memorial Trophy (Top Rookie - AHL) (1985) • AHL First All-Star Team (1985)

Signed as a free agent by **Toronto,** May 12, 1984. Traded to **Chicago** by **Toronto** with Rick Vaive and Bob McGill for Al Secord and Ed Olczyk, September 3, 1987. Traded to **NY Islanders** by **Chicago** with Adam Creighton for Brent Sutter and Brad Lauer, October 25, 1991. Traded to **New Jersey** by **NY Islanders** for Claude Lemieux, October 3, 1995. Signed as a free agent by **Toronto**, July 30, 1998.

						Regular Season													Playoffs						
Season	Club	League	GP	G	A	Pts	PIM	PP	SH	GW	S	%	+/-	TF	F%	H	SB	Min	GP	G	A	Pts	PIM	PP	SH	GW

THOMPSON, Brent

(THOHMP-sohn, BREHNT) **FLA.**

Defense. Shoots left. 6'2", 205 lbs.   Born, Calgary, Alta., January 9, 1971. Los Angeles' 1st choice, 39th overall, in 1989 Entry Draft.

Season	Club	League	GP	G	A	Pts	PIM	PP	SH	GW	S	%	+/-	TF	F%	H	SB	Min	GP	G	A	Pts	PIM	PP	SH	GW
1987-88	Calgary Stars	AAHA	25	0	13	13	33	....	....	....	....	....	....	....	....											
1988-89	Medicine Hat	WHL	72	3	10	13	160	....	....	....	....	....	....	....	....											
1989-90	Medicine Hat	WHL	68	10	35	45	167	....	....	....	....	....	....	....	....				3	0	0	0	2			
1990-91	Medicine Hat	WHL	51	5	40	45	87	....	....	....	....	....	....	....	....				3	0	1	1	14			
	Phoenix	IHL	....	....	....	....	....	....	....	....	....	....	....						12	1	7	8	16			
1991-92	**Los Angeles**	**NHL**	27	0	5	5	89	0	0	0	18	0.0	-7						4	0	1	1	6			
	Phoenix	IHL	42	4	13	17	139	....	....	....	....	....	....						4	0	0	0	4	0	0	0
1992-93	**Los Angeles**	**NHL**	30	0	4	4	76	0	0	0	18	0.0	-4						....	....	....	....	....			
	Phoenix	IHL	22	0	5	5	112	....	....	....	....	....	....						....	....	....	....	....			
1993-94	**Los Angeles**	**NHL**	24	1	0	1	81	0	0	0	9	11.1	-1						....	....	....	....	....			
	Phoenix	IHL	26	1	11	12	118	....	....	....	....	....	....						....	....	....	....	....			
1994-95	**Winnipeg**	**NHL**	29	0	0	0	78	0	0	0	16	0.0	-17						....	....	....	....	....			
1995-96	**Winnipeg**	**NHL**	10	0	1	1	21	0	0	0	7	0.0	-2						....	....	....	....	....			
	Springfield	AHL	58	2	10	12	203	....	....	....	....	....	....						10	1	4	5	*55			
1996-97	**Phoenix**	**NHL**	1	0	0	0	7	0	0	0	0	0.0	-1						....	....	....	....	....			
	Springfield	AHL	64	2	15	17	215	....	....	....	....	....	....						17	0	2	2	31			
	Phoenix	IHL	12	0	1	1	67	....	....	....	....	....	....						....	....	....	....	....			
1997-98	Hartford	AHL	77	4	15	19	308	....	....	....	....	....	....						15	0	4	4	25			
1998-99	Hartford	AHL	76	3	15	18	265	....	....	....	....	....	....						7	0	0	0	23			
99-2000	Louisville	AHL	67	4	22	26	311	....	....	....	....	....	....						3	0	0	0	11			
	NHL Totals		121	1	10	11	352	0	0	0	68	1.5		....	....	....			4	0	0	0	4	0	0	0

WHL East Second All-Star Team (1991)

Traded to **Winnipeg** by **LA Kings** with cash for the rights to Ruslan Batyrshin and Winnipeg's 2nd round choice (Marian Cisar) in 1996 Entry Draft, August 8, 1994. Transferred to **Phoenix** after **Winnipeg** franchise relocated, July 1, 1996. Signed as a free agent by **NY Rangers**, August 26, 1997. Signed as a free agent by **Florida**, July 27, 1999.

THOMPSON, Rocky

(THOHMP-sohn, RAW-kee) **FLA.**

Right wing. Shoots right. 6'2", 205 lbs.   Born, Calgary, Alta., August 8, 1977. Calgary's 3rd choice, 72nd overall, in 1995 Entry Draft.

Season	Club	League	GP	G	A	Pts	PIM	PP	SH	GW	S	%	+/-	TF	F%	H	SB	Min	GP	G	A	Pts	PIM	PP	SH	GW
1992-93	Spruce Grove	AAHA	65	13	50	63	295	....	....	....	....	....	....						....	....	....	....	....			
1993-94	Medicine Hat	WHL	68	1	4	5	166	....	....	....	....	....	....						3	0	0	0	2			
1994-95	Medicine Hat	WHL	63	1	6	7	220	....	....	....	....	....	....						5	0	0	0	17			
1995-96	Medicine Hat	WHL	71	9	20	29	260	....	....	....	....	....	....						5	2	3	5	26			
	Saint John Flames	AHL	4	0	0	0	33	....	....	....	....	....	....						....	....	....	....	....			
1996-97	Medicine Hat	WHL	47	6	9	15	170	....	....	....	....	....	....						....	....	....	....	....			
	Swift Current	WHL	22	3	5	8	90	....	....	....	....	....	....						10	1	2	3	22			
1997-98	**Calgary**	**NHL**	12	0	0	0	61	0	0	0	3	0.0	0						....	....	....	....	....			
	Saint John Flames	AHL	51	3	0	3	187	....	....	....	....	....	....						18	1	1	2	47			
1998-99	**Calgary**	**NHL**	3	0	0	0	25	0	0	0	0	0.0	0	0	0	0	0	2:01	....	....	....	....	....			
99-2000	Saint John Flames	AHL	27	2	2	4	108	....	....	....	....	....	....						....	....	....	....	....			
	Louisville	AHL	53	2	8	10	125	....	....	....	....	....	....						4	0	0	0	4			
	Louisville	AHL	3	0	1	1	54	....	....	....	....	....	....						....	....	....	....	....			
	NHL Totals		15	0	0	0	86	0	0	0	3	0.0		0	0.0	0	0	2:01	....	....	....	....	....			

Traded to **Florida** by **Calgary** for Filip Kuba, March 16, 2000.

THORNTON, Joe

(THOHRN-tuhn, JOH) **BOS.**

Center. Shoots left. 6'4", 215 lbs.   Born, London, Ont., July 2, 1979. Boston's 1st choice, 1st overall, in 1997 Entry Draft.

Season	Club	League	GP	G	A	Pts	PIM	PP	SH	GW	S	%	+/-	TF	F%	H	SB	Min	GP	G	A	Pts	PIM	PP	SH	GW
1993-94	Elgin Elks	OMHA	67	83	85	168	45	....	....	....	....	....	....						....	....	....	....	....			
	St. Thomas Stars	OJHL-B	6	2	6	8	2	....	....	....	....	....	....						....	....	....	....	....			
1994-95	St. Thomas Stars	OJHL-B	50	40	64	104	53	....	....	....	....	....	....						....	....	....	....	....			
1995-96	Sault Ste. Marie	OHL	66	30	46	76	53	....	....	....	....	....	....						4	1	1	2	11			
1996-97	Sault Ste. Marie	OHL	59	41	81	122	123	....	....	....	....	....	....						11	11	8	19	24			
1997-98	**Boston**	**NHL**	55	3	4	7	19	0	0	1	33	9.1	-6						6	0	0	0	9	0	0	0
1998-99	**Boston**	**NHL**	81	16	25	41	69	7	0	1	128	12.5	3	1073	48.7	124	11	15:21	11	3	6	9	4	0	0	2
99-2000	**Boston**	**NHL**	81	23	37	60	82	5	0	3	171	13.5	-5	1861	49.5	134	14	21:18	....	....	....	....	....			
	NHL Totals		217	42	66	108	170	12	0	5	332	12.7		2934	49.2	258	25	18:20	17	3	6	9	13	2	0	2

Canadian Major Junior Rookie of the Year (1996) • OHL Second All-Star Team (1997)

THORNTON, Scott

(THOHRN-tuhn, SKAWT) **S.J.**

Center. Shoots left. 6'3", 216 lbs.   Born, London, Ont., January 9, 1971. Toronto's 1st choice, 3rd overall, in 1989 Entry Draft.

Season	Club	League	GP	G	A	Pts	PIM	PP	SH	GW	S	%	+/-	TF	F%	H	SB	Min	GP	G	A	Pts	PIM	PP	SH	GW
1986-87	London Diamonds	OJHL-B	31	10	7	17	10	....	....	....	....	....	....						....	....	....	....	....			
1987-88	Belleville Bulls	OHL	62	11	19	30	54	....	....	....	....	....	....						6	0	1	1	2			
1988-89	Belleville Bulls	OHL	59	28	34	62	103	....	....	....	....	....	....						5	1	1	2	6			
1989-90	Belleville Bulls	OHL	47	21	28	49	91	....	....	....	....	....	....						11	2	10	12	15			
1990-91	Belleville Bulls	OHL	3	2	1	3	2	....	....	....	....	....	....						6	0	7	7	14			
	Toronto	**NHL**	33	1	3	4	30	0	0	0	31	3.2	-15						....	....	....	....	....			
	Newmarket	AHL	5	1	0	1	4	....	....	....	....	....	....						....	....	....	....	....			
1991-92	**Edmonton**	**NHL**	15	0	1	1	43	0	0	0	11	0.0	-6						1	0	0	0	0	0	0	0
	Cape Breton	AHL	49	9	14	23	40	....	....	....	....	....	....						5	1	0	1	8			
1992-93	**Edmonton**	**NHL**	9	0	1	1	0	0	0	0	7	0.0	-4						....	....	....	....	....			
	Cape Breton	AHL	58	23	27	50	102	....	....	....	....	....	....						16	1	2	3	35			
1993-94	**Edmonton**	**NHL**	61	4	7	11	104	0	0	0	65	6.2	-15						....	....	....	....	....			
	Cape Breton	AHL	2	1	1	2	31	....	....	....	....	....	....						....	....	....	....	....			
1994-95	**Edmonton**	**NHL**	47	10	12	22	89	0	1	0	69	14.5	-4						....	....	....	....	....			
1995-96	**Edmonton**	**NHL**	77	9	9	18	149	0	2	3	95	9.5	-25						....	....	....	....	....			
1996-97	**Montreal**	**NHL**	73	10	10	20	128	1	1	1	110	9.1	-19						5	1	0	1	2	0	0	0
1997-98	**Montreal**	**NHL**	67	6	9	15	158	1	0	1	51	11.8	0						9	0	2	2	10	0	0	0
1998-99	**Montreal**	**NHL**	47	7	4	11	87	1	0	1	56	12.5	-2	466	52.8	74	13	12:24	....	....	....	....	....			
99-2000	**Montreal**	**NHL**	35	2	3	5	70	0	0	0	36	5.6	-7	253	51.8	43	13	12:40	....	....	....	....	....			
	Dallas	**NHL**	30	6	3	9	38	1	0	0	47	12.8	-5	14	14.3	66	7	13:03	23	2	7	9	28	0	0	1
	NHL Totals		494	55	62	117	896	4	4	8	578	9.5		733	51.7	183	33	12:39	38	3	9	12	40	0	0	1

Traded to **Edmonton** by **Toronto** with Vincent Damphousse, Peter Ing, Luke Richardson and cash for Grant Fuhr, Glenn Anderson and Craig Berube, September 19, 1991. Traded to **Montreal** by **Edmonton** for Andrei Kovalenko, September 6, 1996. Traded to **Dallas** by **Montreal** for Juha Lind, January 22, 2000. Signed as a free agent by **San Jose**, July 1, 2000.

TIKKANEN, Esa

(TEE-kuh-nehn, EHS-uh)

Left wing. Shoots left. 6'1", 190 lbs.   Born, Helsinki, Finland, January 25, 1965. Edmonton's 4th choice, 82nd overall, in 1983 Entry Draft.

Season	Club	League	GP	G	A	Pts	PIM	PP	SH	GW	S	%	+/-	TF	F%	H	SB	Min	GP	G	A	Pts	PIM	PP	SH	GW
1981-82	Regina Blues	SJHL	59	38	37	75	216	....	....	....	....	....	....						....	....	....	....	....			
	Regina Pats	WHL	2	0	0	0	0	....	....	....	....	....	....						....	....	....	....	....			
1982-83	HIFK Helsinki	Finn-Jr.	30	34	31	65	*104	....	....	....	....	....	....						4	4	3	7	10			
	HIFK Helsinki	Finland	....	....	....	....	....	....	....	....	....	....	....						1	0	0	0	2			
1983-84	HIFK Helsinki	Finn-Jr.	6	5	9	14	13	....	....	....	....	....	....						4	4	3	7	2			
	HIFK Helsinki	Finland	36	19	11	30	30	....	....	....	....	....	....						2	0	0	0	0			
1984-85	HIFK Helsinki	Finland	36	21	33	54	42	....	....	....	....	....	....						....	....	....	....	....			
	♦ **Edmonton**	**NHL**	....	....	....	....	....	....	....	....	....	....	....						3	0	0	0	2	0	0	0
1985-86	**Edmonton**	**NHL**	35	4	7	6	13	28	0	0	2	44	15.9	5					8	3	2	5	7	0	0	0
	Nova Scotia	AHL	15	4	8	12	17	....	....	....	....	....	....						....	....	....	....	....			
1986-87	**Edmonton**	**NHL**	76	34	44	78	120	7	0	6	156	27.0	44						21	7	2	9	22	1	0	1
1987-88 ♦	**Edmonton**	**NHL**	80	23	51	74	153	6	1	2	142	16.2	21						19	10	17	27	72	5	0	1
1988-89	**Edmonton**	**NHL**	67	31	47	78	92	6	8	4	151	20.5	10						7	1	3	4	12	0	0	0
1989-90 ♦	**Edmonton**	**NHL**	79	30	33	63	161	6	3	6	199	15.1	17						22	13	11	24	26	2	2	0
1990-91	**Edmonton**	**NHL**	79	27	42	69	85	3	4	6	235	11.5	22						18	8	20	24	24	3	0	3

			Regular Season																Playoffs							
Season	Club	League	GP	G	A	Pts	PIM	PP	SH	GW	S	%	+/-	TF	F%	H	SB	Min	GP	G	A	Pts	PIM	PP	SH	GW
1991-92	Edmonton	NHL	40	12	16	28	44	6	2	1	117	10.3	–8	....	....	....	....	....	16	5	3	8	8	1	0	1
1992-93	Edmonton	NHL	66	14	19	33	76	2	4	3	162	8.6	–11	....	....	....	....	....	....	....	....	....	....	....	....	....
	NY Rangers	NHL	15	2	5	7	18	0	0	0	40	5.0	–13	....	....	....	....	....	....	....	....	....	....	....	....	....
1993-94♦	NY Rangers	NHL	83	22	32	54	114	5	3	4	257	8.6	5	....	....	....	....	....	23	4	4	8	34	0	0	1
1994-95	HIFK Helsinki	Finland	19	2	11	13	16	....	....	....	....	....	....	....	....	....	....	....	....	....	....	....	....	....	....	....
	St. Louis	NHL	43	12	23	35	22	5	2	1	107	11.2	13	....	....	....	....	....	7	2	2	4	20	1	0	1
1995-96	St. Louis	NHL	11	1	4	5	18	0	1	0	19	5.3	1	....	....	....	....	....	....	....	....	....	....	....	....	....
	New Jersey	NHL	9	0	2	2	4	0	0	0	15	0.0	–6	....	....	....	....	....	....	....	....	....	....	....	....	....
	Vancouver	NHL	38	13	24	37	14	8	0	2	61	21.3	6	....	....	....	....	....	6	3	2	5	2	2	0	0
1996-97	Vancouver	NHL	62	12	15	27	66	4	1	2	103	11.7	–9	....	....	....	....	....	....	....	....	....	....	....	....	....
	NY Rangers	NHL	14	1	2	3	6	0	1	0	30	3.3	0	....	....	....	....	....	15	9	3	12	26	3	1	3
1997-98	Florida	NHL	28	1	8	9	16	0	0	0	34	2.9	–7	....	....	....	....	....	....	....	....	....	....	....	....	....
	Finland	Olympics	6	1	1	2	0	....	....	....	....	....	....	....	....	....	....	....	....	....	....	....	....	....	....	....
	Washington	NHL	20	2	10	12	2	1	0	2	33	6.1	–4	....	....	....	....	....	21	3	3	6	20	1	0	0
1998-99	NY Rangers	NHL	32	0	3	3	38	0	0	0	25	0.0	–5	312	47.4	30	14	13:38	....	....	....	....	....	....	....	....
99-2000	Jokerit Helsinki	Finland	43	10	13	23	85	....	....	....	....	....	....	....	....	....	....	....	11	1	6	7	10	....	....	....
	NHL Totals		877	244	386	630	1077	59	29	41	1900	12.8		312	47.4	30	14	13:38	186	72	60	132	275	19	3	11

Traded to **NY Rangers** by **Edmonton** for Doug Weight, March 17, 1993. Traded to **St. Louis** by **NY Rangers** with Doug Lidster for Petr Nedved, July 24, 1994. Traded to **New Jersey** by **St. Louis** for New Jersey's 3rd round choice (later traded to Colorado - Colorado selected Ville Nielnen) in 1997 Entry Draft, November 1, 1995. Traded to **Vancouver** by **New Jersey** for Vancouver's 2nd round choice (Wesley Mason) in 1996 Entry Draft, November 23, 1995. Traded to **NY Rangers** by **Vancouver** with Russ Courtnall for Sergei Nemchinov and Brian Noonan, March 8, 1997. Signed as a free agent by **Florida**, September 17, 1997. Traded to **Washington** by **Florida** for Dwayne Hay and future considerations, March 9, 1998. Signed as a free agent by **NY Rangers**, October 9, 1998.

TILEY, Brad

(TIHL-ee, BRAD) **PHI.**

Defense. Shoots left. 6'1", 204 lbs. Born, Markdale, Ont., July 5, 1971. Boston's 4th choice, 84th overall, in 1991 Entry Draft.

Season	Club	League	GP	G	A	Pts	PIM	PP	SH	GW	S	%	+/-	TF	F%	H	SB	Min	GP	G	A	Pts	PIM	PP	SH	GW
1987-88	Owen Sound	OJHL-B	45	18	25	43	69	....	....	....	....	....	....	....	....	....	....	....	....	....	....	....	....	....	....	....
1988-89	Sault Ste. Marie	OHL	50	4	11	15	31	....	....	....	....	....	....	....	....	....	....	....	....	....	....	....	....	....	....	....
1989-90	Sault Ste. Marie	OHL	66	9	32	41	47	....	....	....	....	....	....	....	....	....	....	....	....	....	....	....	....	....	....	....
1990-91	Sault Ste. Marie	OHL	66	11	55	66	29	....	....	....	....	....	....	....	....	....	....	....	14	4	15	19	12	....	....	....
1991-92	Maine Mariners	AHL	62	7	22	29	36	....	....	....	....	....	....	....	....	....	....	....	....	....	....	....	....	....	....	....
1992-93	Phoenix	IHL	46	11	27	38	35	....	....	....	....	....	....	....	....	....	....	....	....	....	....	....	....	....	....	....
	Binghamton	AHL	26	6	10	16	19	....	....	....	....	....	....	....	....	....	....	....	8	0	1	1	2	....	....	....
1993-94	Binghamton	AHL	29	6	10	16	6	....	....	....	....	....	....	....	....	....	....	....	....	....	....	....	....	....	....	....
	Phoenix	IHL	35	8	15	23	21	....	....	....	....	....	....	....	....	....	....	....	....	....	....	....	....	....	....	....
1994-95	Detroit Vipers	IHL	56	7	19	26	32	....	....	....	....	....	....	....	....	....	....	....	....	....	....	....	....	....	....	....
	Fort Wayne	IHL	14	1	6	7	2	....	....	....	....	....	....	....	....	....	....	....	3	1	2	3	0	....	....	....
1995-96	Orlando	IHL	69	11	23	34	82	....	....	....	....	....	....	....	....	....	....	....	23	2	4	6	16	....	....	....
1996-97	Phoenix	IHL	66	8	28	36	34	....	....	....	....	....	....	....	....	....	....	....	....	....	....	....	....	....	....	....
	Long Beach	IHL	3	1	0	1	2	....	....	....	....	....	....	....	....	....	....	....	....	....	....	....	....	....	....	....
1997-98	Phoenix	NHL	1	0	0	0	0	....	....	....	....	....	....	....	....	....	....	....	....	....	....	....	....	....	....	....
	Springfield	AHL	60	10	31	41	36	....	....	....	....	....	....	....	....	....	....	....	4	0	4	4	2	....	....	....
1998-99	Phoenix	NHL	8	0	0	0	0	0	0	0	1	0.0	–1	0	0.0	5	3	11:29	1	0	0	0	0	0	0	0
	Springfield	AHL	69	9	35	44	14	....	....	....	....	....	....	....	....	....	....	....	1	0	0	0	0	....	....	....
99-2000	Springfield	AHL	80	14	54	68	51	....	....	....	....	....	....	....	....	....	....	....	5	0	4	4	2	....	....	....
	NHL Totals		9	0	0	0	0	0	0	0	1	0.0		0	0.0	5	3	11:29	1	0	0	0	0	0	0	0

Memorial Cup All-Star Team (1991) • AHL First All-Star Team (2000) • Won Eddie Shore Award (Top Defenseman - AHL) (2000)

Signed as a free agent by **NY Rangers**, September 4, 1992. Traded to **LA Kings** by **NY Rangers** for LA Kings' 11th round choice (Jamie Butt) in 1994 Entry Draft, January 28, 1994. Signed as a free agent by **Phoenix**, September 4, 1997. Signed as a free agent by **Philadelphia**, July 14, 2000. • Played w/ RHI's Anaheim Bullfrogs in 1995 (17-3-11-14-19).

TIMANDER, Mattias

(tih-MAHN-duhr, MA-tee-uhs) **CBJ**

Defense. Shoots left. 6'2", 210 lbs. Born, Sollefteа, Sweden, April 16, 1974. Boston's 7th choice, 208th overall, in 1992 Entry Draft.

Season	Club	League	GP	G	A	Pts	PIM	PP	SH	GW	S	%	+/-	TF	F%	H	SB	Min	GP	G	A	Pts	PIM	PP	SH	GW
1992-93	MoDo AIK	Swede-Jr.	4	0	0	0	0	....	....	....	....	....	....	....	....	....	....	....	....	....	....	....	....	....	....	....
	Husums IF	Sweden-2	27	4	9	13	22	....	....	....	....	....	....	....	....	....	....	....	....	....	....	....	....	....	....	....
	MoDo AIK	Sweden	1	0	0	0	0	....	....	....	....	....	....	....	....	....	....	....	....	....	....	....	....	....	....	....
1993-94	MoDo AIK	Swede-Jr.	3	2	2	4	10	....	....	....	....	....	....	....	....	....	....	....	....	....	....	....	....	....	....	....
	MoDo AIK	Sweden	23	2	2	4	6	....	....	....	....	....	....	....	....	....	....	....	11	2	0	2	10	....	....	....
1994-95	MoDo Hockey	Sweden	39	8	9	17	24	....	....	....	....	....	....	....	....	....	....	....	....	....	....	....	....	....	....	....
1995-96	MoDo Hockey	Sweden	37	4	10	14	34	....	....	....	....	....	....	....	....	....	....	....	7	1	1	2	8	....	....	....
1996-97	Boston	NHL	41	1	8	9	14	0	0	0	62	1.6	–9	....	....	....	....	....	....	....	....	....	....	....	....	....
	Providence Bruins	AHL	32	3	11	14	20	....	....	....	....	....	....	....	....	....	....	....	10	1	1	2	12	....	....	....
1997-98	Boston	NHL	23	1	1	2	6	0	0	0	17	5.9	–9	....	....	....	....	....	....	....	....	....	....	....	....	....
	Providence Bruins	AHL	31	3	7	10	25	....	....	....	....	....	....	....	....	....	....	....	....	....	....	....	....	....	....	....
1998-99	Boston	NHL	22	0	6	6	10	0	0	0	22	0.0	4	0	0.0	14	13	12:54	4	1	1	2	2	0	0	0
	Providence Bruins	AHL	43	2	22	24	24	....	....	....	....	....	....	....	....	....	....	....	....	....	....	....	....	....	....	....
99-2000	Boston	NHL	60	0	8	8	22	0	0	0	39	0.0	–11	0	0.0	50	63	12:29	....	....	....	....	....	....	....	....
	Hershey Bears	AHL	1	0	0	0	2	....	....	....	....	....	....	....	....	....	....	....	....	....	....	....	....	....	....	....
	NHL Totals		146	2	23	25	52	0	0	0	140	1.4		0	0.0	64	76	12:36	4	1	1	2	2	0	0	0

Selected by **Columbus** from **Boston** in Expansion Draft, June 23, 2000.

TIMONEN, Kimmo

(TEEM-oh-nehn, KEE-moh) **NSH.**

Defense. Shoots left. 5'10", 196 lbs. Born, Kuopio, Finland, March 18, 1975. Los Angeles' 11th choice, 250th overall, in 1993 Entry Draft.

Season	Club	League	GP	G	A	Pts	PIM	PP	SH	GW	S	%	+/-	TF	F%	H	SB	Min	GP	G	A	Pts	PIM	PP	SH	GW
1990-91	KalPa Kuopio	Finn-Jr.	4	0	1	1	2	....	....	....	....	....	....	....	....	....	....	....	....	....	....	....	....	....	....	....
1991-92	KalPa Kuopio	Finn-Jr.	32	7	10	17	4	....	....	....	....	....	....	....	....	....	....	....	....	....	....	....	....	....	....	....
	KalPa Kuopio	Finland	5	0	0	0	0	....	....	....	....	....	....	....	....	....	....	....	....	....	....	....	....	....	....	....
1992-93	KalPa Kuopio	Finn-Jr.	16	9	15	24	10	....	....	....	....	....	....	....	....	....	....	....	....	....	....	....	....	....	....	....
	KalPa Kuopio	Finland	33	0	2	2	4	....	....	....	....	....	....	....	....	....	....	....	....	....	....	....	....	....	....	....
1993-94	KalPa Kuopio	Finn-Jr.	5	4	7	11	0	....	....	....	....	....	....	....	....	....	....	....	....	....	....	....	....	....	....	....
	KalPa Kuopio	Finland	46	6	7	13	55	....	....	....	....	....	....	....	....	....	....	....	....	....	....	....	....	....	....	....
1994-95	TPS Turku	Finn-Jr.	1	0	0	0	0	....	....	....	....	....	....	....	....	....	....	....	....	....	....	....	....	....	....	....
	TPS Turku	Finland	45	3	4	7	10	....	....	....	....	....	....	....	....	....	....	....	13	0	1	1	6	....	....	....
1995-96	TPS Turku	Finland	48	3	21	24	22	....	....	....	....	....	....	....	....	....	....	....	9	1	2	3	12	....	....	....
1996-97	TPS Turku	Finland	50	10	14	24	18	....	....	....	....	....	....	....	....	....	....	....	12	2	7	9	8	....	....	....
1997-98	HIFK Helsinki	Finland	45	10	15	25	59	....	....	....	....	....	....	....	....	....	....	....	9	3	4	7	8	....	....	....
	Finland	Olympics	6	0	1	1	2	....	....	....	....	....	....	....	....	....	....	....	....	....	....	....	....	....	....	....
1998-99	Nashville	NHL	50	4	8	12	30	1	0	0	75	5.3	–4	0	0.0	68	34	19:04	....	....	....	....	....	....	....	....
	Milwaukee	IHL	29	2	13	15	22	....	....	....	....	....	....	....	....	....	....	....	....	....	....	....	....	....	....	....
99-2000	Nashville	NHL	51	8	25	33	26	2	1	2	97	8.2	–5	0	0.0	48	34	21:06	....	....	....	....	....	....	....	....
	NHL Totals		101	12	33	45	56	3	1	2	172	7.0		0	0.0	116	68	20:05	....	....	....	....	....	....	....	....

Traded to **Nashville** by **LA Kings** with Jan Vopat for future considerations, June 26, 1998.

TINORDI, Mark

(tih-NOHR-dee, MAHRK)

Defense. Shoots left. 6'4", 213 lbs. Born, Red Deer, Alta., May 9, 1966.

Season	Club	League	GP	G	A	Pts	PIM	PP	SH	GW	S	%	+/-	TF	F%	H	SB	Min	GP	G	A	Pts	PIM	PP	SH	GW
1982-83	Lethbridge	WHL	64	0	4	4	50	....	....	....	....	....	....	....	....	....	....	....	20	1	1	2	6	....	....	....
1983-84	Lethbridge	WHL	72	5	14	19	53	....	....	....	....	....	....	....	....	....	....	....	5	0	1	1	7	....	....	....
1984-85	Lethbridge	WHL	58	10	15	25	134	....	....	....	....	....	....	....	....	....	....	....	4	0	2	2	12	....	....	....
1985-86	Lethbridge	WHL	58	8	30	38	139	....	....	....	....	....	....	....	....	....	....	....	8	1	3	4	15	....	....	....
1986-87	Calgary Wranglers	WHL	61	29	37	66	148	....	....	....	....	....	....	....	....	....	....	....	....	....	....	....	....	....	....	....
	New Haven	AHL	2	0	0	0	2	....	....	....	....	....	....	....	....	....	....	....	2	0	0	0	0	....	....	....
1987-88	NY Rangers	NHL	24	1	2	3	50	0	0	0	13	7.7	–5	....	....	....	....	....	....	....	....	....	....	....	....	....
	Colorado Rangers	IHL	41	8	19	27	150	....	....	....	....	....	....	....	....	....	....	....	11	1	5	6	31	....	....	....
1988-89	Minnesota	NHL	47	2	3	5	107	0	0	0	39	5.1	–9	....	....	....	....	....	5	0	0	0	0	0	0	0
	Kalamazoo Wings	IHL	10	0	0	0	35	....	....	....	....	....	....	....	....	....	....	....	....	....	....	....	....	....	....	....

			Regular Season																Playoffs							
Season	Club	League	GP	G	A	Pts	PIM	PP	SH	GW	S	%	+/–	TF	F%	H	SB	Min	GP	G	A	Pts	PIM	PP	SH	GW
1989-90	**Minnesota**	**NHL**	**66**	**3**	**7**	**10**	**240**	**1**	**0**	**0**	**50**	**6.0**	**0**	....	....	....	....	....	**7**	**0**	**1**	**1**	**16**	**0**	**0**	**0**
1990-91	**Minnesota**	**NHL**	**69**	**5**	**27**	**32**	**189**	**1**	**0**	**2**	**92**	**5.4**	**1**	....	....	....	....	....	**23**	**5**	**6**	**11**	**78**	**4**	**0**	**0**
1991-92	**Minnesota**	**NHL**	**63**	**4**	**24**	**28**	**179**	**4**	**0**	**0**	**93**	**4.3**	**–13**	....	....	....	....	....	**7**	**1**	**2**	**3**	**11**	**0**	**0**	**0**
1992-93	**Minnesota**	**NHL**	**69**	**15**	**27**	**42**	**157**	**7**	**0**	**2**	**122**	**12.3**	**–1**	....	....	....	....	....	....	....	....	....	....	....	....	....
1993-94	**Dallas**	**NHL**	**61**	**6**	**18**	**24**	**143**	**1**	**0**	**0**	**112**	**5.4**	**6**	....	....	....	....	....	....	....	....	....	....	....	....	....
1994-95	**Washington**	**NHL**	**42**	**3**	**9**	**12**	**71**	**2**	**0**	**1**	**71**	**4.2**	**–5**	....	....	....	....	....	**1**	**0**	**0**	**0**	**2**	**0**	**0**	**0**
1995-96	**Washington**	**NHL**	**71**	**3**	**10**	**13**	**113**	**2**	**0**	**0**	**82**	**3.7**	**26**	....	....	....	....	....	**6**	**0**	**0**	**0**	**16**	**0**	**0**	**0**
1996-97	**Washington**	**NHL**	**56**	**2**	**6**	**8**	**118**	**0**	**0**	**0**	**53**	**3.8**	**3**	....	....	....	....	....	....	....	....	....	....	....	....	....
1997-98	**Washington**	**NHL**	**47**	**8**	**9**	**17**	**39**	**0**	**1**	**0**	**57**	**14.0**	**9**	....	....	....	....	....	**21**	**1**	**2**	**3**	**42**	**0**	**0**	**0**
1998-99	**Washington**	**NHL**	**48**	**0**	**6**	**6**	**108**	**0**	**0**	**0**	**32**	**0.0**	**–6**	**0**	**0.0**	**133**	**49**	**20:25**	....	....	....	....	....	....	....	....
99-2000			DID NOT PLAY – INJURED																....	....	....	....	....	....	....	....
	NHL Totals		**663**	**52**	**148**	**200**	**1514**	**18**	**1**	**5**	**816**	**6.4**		**0**	**0.0**	**133**	**49**	**20:25**	**70**	**7**	**11**	**18**	**165**	**4**	**0**	**0**

Played in NHL All-Star Game (1992)

Signed as a free agent by **NY Rangers**, January 4, 1987. Traded to **Minnesota** by **NY Rangers** with Paul Jerrard, the rights to Bret Barnett and Mike Sullivan and LA Kings' 3rd round choice (previously acquired, Minnesota selected Murray Garbutt) in 1989 Entry Draft for Brian Lawton, Igor Liba and the rights to Eric Bennett, October 11, 1988. Transferred to **Dallas** after **Minnesota** franchise relocated, June 9, 1993. Traded to **Washington** by **Dallas** with Rich Mrozik for Kevin Hatcher, January 18, 1995. Claimed by **Atlanta** from **Washington** in Expansion Draft, June 25, 1999. • Missed entire 1999-2000 season recovering from knee surgery, August, 1999.

TITOV, German

(TEE-tahf, GUHR-mihn) **ANA.**

Center. Shoots left. 6'1", 201 lbs. Born, Moscow, USSR, October 16, 1965. Calgary's 10th choice, 252nd overall, in 1993 Entry Draft.

Season	Club	League	GP	G	A	Pts	PIM	PP	SH	GW	S	%	+/–	TF	F%	H	SB	Min	GP	G	A	Pts	PIM	PP	SH	GW
1986-87	HK Khimik	USSR	23	1	0	1	10	....	....	....	....	....	....	....	....	....	....	....	....	....	....	....	....	....	....	....
1987-88	HK Khimik	USSR	39	6	5	11	10	....	....	....	....	....	....	....	....	....	....	....	....	....	....	....	....	....	....	....
1988-89	HK Khimik	USSR	44	10	3	13	24	....	....	....	....	....	....	....	....	....	....	....	....	....	....	....	....	....	....	....
1989-90	HK Khimik	USSR	44	6	14	20	19	....	....	....	....	....	....	....	....	....	....	....	....	....	....	....	....	....	....	....
1990-91	HK Khimik	USSR	45	13	11	24	28	....	....	....	....	....	....	....	....	....	....	....	....	....	....	....	....	....	....	....
1991-92	HK Khimik	CIS	42	18	13	31	35	....	....	....	....	....	....	....	....	....	....	....	....	....	....	....	....	....	....	....
1992-93	TPS Turku	Finland	47	25	19	44	49	....	....	....	....	....	....	....	....	....	....	....	12	5	12	17	10	....	....	....
1993-94	**Calgary**	**NHL**	**76**	**27**	**18**	**45**	**28**	**8**	**3**	**2**	**153**	**17.6**	**20**	....	....	....	....	....	**7**	**2**	**1**	**3**	**4**	**1**	**0**	**0**
1994-95	TPS Turku	Finland	14	6	6	12	20	....	....	....	....	....	....	....	....	....	....	....	....	....	....	....	....	....	....	....
	Calgary	**NHL**	**40**	**12**	**12**	**24**	**16**	**3**	**2**	**3**	**88**	**13.6**	**6**	....	....	....	....	....	**7**	**5**	**3**	**8**	**10**	**0**	**1**	**0**
1995-96	**Calgary**	**NHL**	**82**	**28**	**39**	**67**	**24**	**13**	**2**	**2**	**214**	**13.1**	**9**	....	....	....	....	....	**4**	**0**	**2**	**2**	**0**	**0**	**0**	**0**
1996-97	**Calgary**	**NHL**	**79**	**22**	**30**	**52**	**36**	**12**	**0**	**4**	**192**	**11.5**	**–12**	....	....	....	....	....	....	....	....	....	....	....	....	....
1997-98	**Calgary**	**NHL**	**68**	**18**	**22**	**40**	**38**	**6**	**1**	**2**	**133**	**13.5**	**–1**	....	....	....	....	....	....	....	....	....	....	....	....	....
	Russia	Olympics	6	1	0	1	6	....	....	....	....	....	....	....	....	....	....	....	....	....	....	....	....	....	....	....
1998-99	**Pittsburgh**	**NHL**	**72**	**11**	**45**	**56**	**34**	**3**	**1**	**3**	**113**	**9.7**	**18**	**41**	**39.0**	**67**	**50**	**19:31**	**11**	**3**	**5**	**8**	**4**	**0**	**0**	**0**
99-2000	**Pittsburgh**	**NHL**	**63**	**17**	**25**	**42**	**34**	**4**	**2**	**3**	**111**	**15.3**	**–3**	**102**	**37.3**	**58**	**26**	**20:20**	....	....	....	....	....	....	....	....
	Edmonton	**NHL**	**7**	**0**	**4**	**4**	**4**	**0**	**0**	**0**	**11**	**0.0**	**2**	**0**	**0.0**	**5**	**4**	**13:33**	**5**	**1**	**1**	**2**	**0**	**0**	**0**	**0**
	NHL Totals		**487**	**135**	**195**	**330**	**214**	**49**	**11**	**19**	**1015**	**13.3**		**143**	**37.8**	**130**	**80**	**19:35**	**34**	**11**	**12**	**23**	**18**	**1**	**1**	**0**

Traded to **Pittsburgh** by **Calgary** with Todd Hlushko for Ken Wregget and Dave Roche, June 17, 1998. Traded to **Edmonton** by **Pittsburgh** for Josef Beranek, March 14, 2000. Signed as a free agent by **Anaheim**, July 1, 2000.

TKACHUK, Keith

(kuh-CHUK, KEETH) **PHX.**

Left wing. Shoots left. 6'2", 225 lbs. Born, Melrose, MA, March 28, 1972. Winnipeg's 1st choice, 19th overall, in 1990 Entry Draft.

Season	Club	League	GP	G	A	Pts	PIM	PP	SH	GW	S	%	+/–	TF	F%	H	SB	Min	GP	G	A	Pts	PIM	PP	SH	GW
1988-89	Malden High	Hi-School	21	30	16	46	....	....	....	....	....	....	....	....	....	....	....	....	....	....	....	....	....	....	....	....
1989-90	Malden High	Hi-School	6	12	14	26	....	....	....	....	....	....	....	....	....	....	....	....	....	....	....	....	....	....	....	....
1990-91	Boston University	H-East	36	17	23	40	70	....	....	....	....	....	....	....	....	....	....	....	....	....	....	....	....	....	....	....
1991-92	United States	Nat-Team	45	10	10	20	141	....	....	....	....	....	....	....	....	....	....	....	....	....	....	....	....	....	....	....
	United States	Olympics	8	1	1	2	12	....	....	....	....	....	....	....	....	....	....	....	....	....	....	....	....	....	....	....
	Winnipeg	**NHL**	**17**	**3**	**5**	**8**	**28**	**2**	**0**	**0**	**22**	**13.6**	**0**	....	....	....	....	....	**7**	**3**	**0**	**3**	**30**	**0**	**0**	**0**
1992-93	**Winnipeg**	**NHL**	**83**	**28**	**23**	**51**	**201**	**12**	**0**	**2**	**199**	**14.1**	**–13**	....	....	....	....	....	**6**	**4**	**0**	**4**	**14**	**1**	**0**	**0**
1993-94	**Winnipeg**	**NHL**	**84**	**41**	**40**	**81**	**255**	**22**	**3**	**3**	**218**	**18.8**	**–12**	....	....	....	....	....	....	....	....	....	....	....	....	....
1994-95	**Winnipeg**	**NHL**	**48**	**22**	**29**	**51**	**152**	**7**	**2**	**2**	**129**	**17.1**	**–4**	....	....	....	....	....	....	....	....	....	....	....	....	....
1995-96	**Winnipeg**	**NHL**	**76**	**50**	**48**	**98**	**156**	**20**	**2**	**6**	**249**	**20.1**	**11**	....	....	....	....	....	**6**	**1**	**2**	**3**	**22**	**0**	**0**	**0**
1996-97	**Phoenix**	**NHL**	**81**	***52**	**34**	**86**	**228**	**9**	**2**	**7**	**296**	**17.6**	**–1**	....	....	....	....	....	**7**	**6**	**0**	**6**	**7**	**2**	**0**	**0**
1997-98	**Phoenix**	**NHL**	**69**	**40**	**26**	**66**	**147**	**11**	**0**	**8**	**232**	**17.2**	**9**	....	....	....	....	....	**6**	**3**	**3**	**6**	**10**	**0**	**0**	**0**
	United States	Olympics	4	0	2	2	6	....	....	....	....	....	....	....	....	....	....	....	....	....	....	....	....	....	....	....
1998-99	**Phoenix**	**NHL**	**68**	**36**	**32**	**68**	**151**	**11**	**2**	**7**	**258**	**14.0**	**22**	**770**	**47.7**	**102**	**20**	**20:59**	**7**	**1**	**3**	**4**	**13**	**1**	**0**	**0**
99-2000	**Phoenix**	**NHL**	**50**	**22**	**21**	**43**	**82**	**5**	**1**	**1**	**183**	**12.0**	**7**	**500**	**50.4**	**100**	**9**	**19:21**	**5**	**1**	**1**	**2**	**4**	**1**	**0**	**0**
	NHL Totals		**576**	**294**	**258**	**552**	**1400**	**99**	**12**	**36**	**1786**	**16.5**		**1270**	**48.7**	**202**	**29**	**20:17**	**44**	**19**	**9**	**28**	**100**	**5**	**0**	**0**

NHL Second All-Star Team (1995, 1998) • Played in NHL All-Star Game (1997, 1998, 1999)

Transferred to **Phoenix** after **Winnipeg** franchise relocated, July 1, 1996.

TOCCHET, Rick

(TAH-keht, RIHK) **PHI.**

Right wing. Shoots right. 6', 210 lbs. Born, Scarborough, Ont., April 9, 1964. Philadelphia's 5th choice, 125th overall, in 1983 Entry Draft.

Season	Club	League	GP	G	A	Pts	PIM	PP	SH	GW	S	%	+/–	TF	F%	H	SB	Min	GP	G	A	Pts	PIM	PP	SH	GW
1980-81	St. Mike's Midgets	MTHL	41	28	46	74	....	....	....	....	....	....	....	....	....	....	....	....	....	....	....	....	....	....	....	....
	St. Michael's	OHA-B	5	1	1	2	2	....	....	....	....	....	....	....	....	....	....	....	....	....	....	....	....	....	....	....
1981-82	Sault Ste. Marie	OHL	59	7	15	22	184	....	....	....	....	....	....	....	....	....	....	....	11	1	1	2	28	....	....	....
1982-83	Sault Ste. Marie	OHL	66	32	34	66	146	....	....	....	....	....	....	....	....	....	....	....	16	4	13	17	67	....	....	....
1983-84	Sault Ste. Marie	OHL	64	44	64	108	209	....	....	....	....	....	....	....	....	....	....	....	16	*22	14	*36	41	....	....	....
1984-85	**Philadelphia**	**NHL**	**75**	**14**	**25**	**39**	**181**	**0**	**0**	**0**	**112**	**12.5**	**6**	....	....	....	....	....	**19**	**3**	**4**	**7**	**72**	**0**	**0**	**2**
1985-86	**Philadelphia**	**NHL**	**69**	**14**	**21**	**35**	**284**	**3**	**0**	**1**	**107**	**13.1**	**12**	....	....	....	....	....	**5**	**1**	**2**	**3**	**26**	**0**	**0**	**0**
1986-87	**Philadelphia**	**NHL**	**69**	**21**	**28**	**49**	**288**	**1**	**1**	**5**	**147**	**14.3**	**16**	....	....	....	....	....	**26**	**11**	**10**	**21**	**72**	**0**	**1**	**2**
1987-88	**Philadelphia**	**NHL**	**65**	**31**	**33**	**64**	**299**	**10**	**2**	**3**	**182**	**17.0**	**3**	....	....	....	....	....	**5**	**1**	**4**	**5**	**55**	**2**	**1**	**0**
1988-89	**Philadelphia**	**NHL**	**66**	**45**	**36**	**81**	**183**	**16**	**1**	**5**	**220**	**20.5**	**–1**	....	....	....	....	....	**16**	**6**	**6**	**12**	**69**	**2**	**0**	**1**
1989-90	**Philadelphia**	**NHL**	**75**	**37**	**59**	**96**	**196**	**15**	**1**	**0**	**269**	**13.8**	**4**	....	....	....	....	....	....	....	....	....	....	....	....	....
1990-91	**Philadelphia**	**NHL**	**70**	**40**	**31**	**71**	**150**	**8**	**0**	**5**	**217**	**18.4**	**2**	....	....	....	....	....	....	....	....	....	....	....	....	....
1991-92	**Philadelphia**	**NHL**	**42**	**13**	**16**	**29**	**102**	**4**	**0**	**1**	**107**	**12.1**	**3**	....	....	....	....	....	....	....	....	....	....	....	....	....
	♦ Pittsburgh	**NHL**	**19**	**14**	**16**	**30**	**49**	**4**	**1**	**1**	**59**	**23.7**	**12**	....	....	....	....	....	**14**	**6**	**13**	**19**	**24**	**3**	**0**	**1**
1992-93	**Pittsburgh**	**NHL**	**80**	**48**	**61**	**109**	**252**	**20**	**4**	**5**	**240**	**20.0**	**28**	....	....	....	....	....	**12**	**7**	**6**	**13**	**24**	**1**	**0**	**0**
1993-94	**Pittsburgh**	**NHL**	**51**	**14**	**26**	**40**	**134**	**5**	**1**	**2**	**150**	**9.3**	**–15**	....	....	....	....	....	**6**	**2**	**3**	**5**	**20**	**1**	**0**	**1**
1994-95	**Los Angeles**	**NHL**	**36**	**18**	**17**	**35**	**70**	**7**	**1**	**3**	**95**	**18.9**	**–8**	....	....	....	....	....	....	....	....	....	....	....	....	....
1995-96	**Los Angeles**	**NHL**	**44**	**13**	**23**	**36**	**117**	**4**	**0**	**0**	**100**	**13.0**	**3**	....	....	....	....	....	....	....	....	....	....	....	....	....
	Boston	**NHL**	**27**	**16**	**8**	**24**	**64**	**6**	**0**	**3**	**85**	**18.8**	**7**	....	....	....	....	....	**5**	**4**	**0**	**4**	**21**	**3**	**0**	**1**
1996-97	**Boston**	**NHL**	**40**	**16**	**14**	**30**	**67**	**3**	**0**	**1**	**120**	**13.3**	**–3**	....	....	....	....	....	....	....	....	....	....	....	....	....
	Washington	**NHL**	**13**	**5**	**5**	**10**	**31**	**1**	**0**	**1**	**37**	**13.5**	**0**	....	....	....	....	....	....	....	....	....	....	....	....	....
1997-98	**Phoenix**	**NHL**	**68**	**26**	**19**	**45**	**157**	**8**	**0**	**6**	**161**	**16.1**	**1**	....	....	....	....	....	**6**	**6**	**2**	**8**	**25**	**3**	**0**	**0**
1998-99	**Phoenix**	**NHL**	**81**	**26**	**30**	**56**	**147**	**6**	**1**	**5**	**178**	**14.6**	**5**	**4**	**25.0**	**115**	**13**	**18:34**	**7**	**0**	**3**	**3**	**8**	**0**	**0**	**0**
99-2000	**Phoenix**	**NHL**	**64**	**12**	**17**	**29**	**67**	**2**	**0**	**1**	**107**	**11.2**	**–5**	**1**	**0.0**	**103**	**17**	**15:54**	....	....	....	....	....	....	....	....
	Philadelphia	**NHL**	**16**	**3**	**3**	**6**	**23**	**2**	**0**	**0**	**23**	**13.0**	**4**	**0**	**0.0**	**26**	**3**	**14:47**	**18**	**5**	**6**	**11**	***49**	**2**	**0**	**1**
	NHL Totals		**1070**	**426**	**488**	**914**	**2861**	**125**	**13**	**48**	**2716**	**15.7**		**5**	**20.0**	**244**	**33**	**17:08**	**139**	**52**	**59**	**111**	**465**	**17**	**2**	**9**

Played in NHL All-Star Game (1989, 1990, 1991, 1993)

Traded to **Pittsburgh** by **Philadelphia** with Kjell Samuelsson, Ken Wregget and Philadelphia's 3rd round choice (Dave Roche) in 1993 Entry Draft for Mark Recchi, Brian Benning and LA Kings' 1st round choice (previously acquired, Philadelphia selected Jason Bowen) in 1992 Entry Draft, February 19, 1992 Traded to **LA Kings** by **Pittsburgh** with Pittsburgh's 2nd round choice (Pavel Rosa) in 1995 Entry Draft for Luc Robitaille, July 29, 1994. Traded to **Boston** by **LA Kings** for Kevin Stevens, January 25, 1996. Traded to **Washington** by **Boston** with Bill Ranford and Adam Oates for Jim Carey, Anson Carter, Jason Allison and Washington's 3rd round choice (Lee Goren) in 1997 Entry Draft, March 1, 1997. Signed as a free agent by **Phoenix**, July 23, 1997. Traded to **Philadelphia** by **Phoenix** for Mikael Renberg, March 8, 2000.

TOMS, Jeff
(TAWMs, JEHF) **NYI**

Left wing. Shoots left. 6'5", 200 lbs. Born, Swift Current, Sask., June 4, 1974. New Jersey's 10th choice, 210th overall, in 1992 Entry Draft.

			Regular Season																Playoffs							
Season	Club	League	GP	G	A	Pts	PIM	PP	SH	GW	S	%	+/-	TF	F%	H	SB	Min	GP	G	A	Pts	PIM	PP	SH	GW
1990-91	Oakville	OMHA	58	34	47	81	72	....	....	....	....	....	....	....	....	....	....	....	....	....	....	....	....	....	....	....
1991-92	Sault Ste. Marie	OHL	36	9	5	14	0	....	....	....	....	....	....	....	....	....	....	....	16	0	1	1	2	....	....	....
1992-93	Sault Ste. Marie	OHL	59	16	23	39	20	....	....	....	....	....	....	....	....	....	....	....	16	4	4	8	7	....	....	....
1993-94	Sault Ste. Marie	OHL	64	52	45	97	19	....	....	....	....	....	....	....	....	....	....	....	14	11	4	15	2	....	....	....
1994-95	Atlanta Knights	IHL	40	7	8	15	10	....	....	....	....	....	....	....	....	....	....	....	4	0	0	0	4	....	....	....
1995-96	**Tampa Bay**	**NHL**	**1**	**0**	**0**	**0**	**0**	**0**	**0**	**0**	**1**	**0.0**	**0**	....	....	....	....	....	....	....	....	....	....	....	....	....
	Atlanta Knights	IHL	68	16	18	34	18	....	....	....	....	....	....	....	....	....	....	....	1	0	0	0	0	....	....	....
1996-97	**Tampa Bay**	**NHL**	**34**	**2**	**8**	**10**	**10**	**0**	**0**	**1**	**53**	**3.8**	**2**	....	....	....	....	....	....	....	....	....	....	....	....	....
	Adirondack	AHL	37	11	16	27	8	....	....	....	....	....	....	....	....	....	....	....	4	1	2	3	0	....	....	....
1997-98	**Tampa Bay**	**NHL**	**13**	**1**	**2**	**3**	**7**	**0**	**0**	**0**	**14**	**7.1**	**–6**	....	....	....	....	....	....	....	....	....	....	....	....	....
	Washington	**NHL**	**33**	**3**	**4**	**7**	**8**	**0**	**0**	**1**	**55**	**5.5**	**–11**	....	....	....	....	....	**1**	**0**	**0**	**0**	**0**	**0**	**0**	**0**
1998-99	**Washington**	**NHL**	**21**	**1**	**5**	**6**	**2**	**0**	**0**	**0**	**30**	**3.3**	**0**	**92**	**54.3**	**9**	**1**	**13:35**	....	....	....	....	....	....	....	....
	Portland Pirates	AHL	20	3	7	10	8	....	....	....	....	....	....	....	....	....	....	....	....	....	....	....	....	....	....	....
99-2000	**Washington**	**NHL**	**20**	**1**	**2**	**3**	**4**	**0**	**0**	**1**	**18**	**5.6**	**–1**	**17**	**52.9**	**8**	**2**	**8:26**	....	....	....	....	....	....	....	....
	Portland Pirates	AHL	33	16	21	37	16	....	....	....	....	....	....	....	....	....	....	....	4	1	1	2	2	....	....	....
	NHL Totals		**122**	**8**	**21**	**29**	**31**	**0**	**0**	**3**	**171**	**4.7**		**109**	**54.1**	**17**	**3**	**11:04**	**1**	**0**	**0**	**0**	**0**	**0**	**0**	**0**

Traded to **Tampa Bay** by **New Jersey** for Vancouver's 4th round choice (previously acquired by Tampa Bay - later traded to New Jersey - later traded to Calgary - Calgary selected Ryan Duthie) in 1994 Entry Draft, May 31, 1994. Claimed by on waivers by **Washington** from **Tampa Bay**, November 19, 1997. Signed as a free agent by **NY Islanders**, July 27, 2000.

TOPOROWSKI, Shayne
(toh-poh-ROW-skee, SHAYN)

Right wing. Shoots right. 6'2", 216 lbs. Born, Paddockwood, Sask., August 6, 1975. Los Angeles' 1st choice, 42nd overall, in 1993 Entry Draft.

			Regular Season																Playoffs							
Season	Club	League	GP	G	A	Pts	PIM	PP	SH	GW	S	%	+/-	TF	F%	H	SB	Min	GP	G	A	Pts	PIM	PP	SH	GW
1990-91	Prince Albert	SAHA	30	19	13	32	91	....	....	....	....	....	....	....	....	....	....	....	....	....	....	....	....	....	....	....
1991-92	Prince Albert	SAHA	27	23	29	52	91	....	....	....	....	....	....	....	....	....	....	....	....	....	....	....	....	....	....	....
	Prince Albert	WHL	6	2	0	2	2	....	....	....	....	....	....	....	....	....	....	....	7	2	1	3	6	....	....	....
1992-93	Prince Albert	WHL	72	25	32	57	235	....	....	....	....	....	....	....	....	....	....	....	....	....	....	....	....	....	....	....
1993-94	Prince Albert	WHL	68	37	45	82	183	....	....	....	....	....	....	....	....	....	....	....	....	....	....	....	....	....	....	....
1994-95	Prince Albert	WHL	72	36	38	74	151	....	....	....	....	....	....	....	....	....	....	....	15	10	8	18	25	....	....	....
1995-96	St. John's Leafs	AHL	72	11	26	37	216	....	....	....	....	....	....	....	....	....	....	....	4	1	1	2	4	....	....	....
1996-97	**Toronto**	**NHL**	**3**	**0**	**0**	**0**	**7**	**0**	**0**	**0**	**3**	**0.0**	**0**	....	....	....	....	....	....	....	....	....	....	....	....	....
	St. John's Leafs	AHL	72	20	17	37	210	....	....	....	....	....	....	....	....	....	....	....	11	3	2	5	16	....	....	....
1997-98	Worcester	AHL	73	9	21	30	128	....	....	....	....	....	....	....	....	....	....	....	11	5	3	8	44	....	....	....
1998-99	Worcester	AHL	75	18	29	47	124	....	....	....	....	....	....	....	....	....	....	....	4	1	0	1	6	....	....	....
99-2000	Springfield	AHL	80	27	28	55	191	....	....	....	....	....	....	....	....	....	....	....	5	0	1	1	10	....	....	....
	NHL Totals		**3**	**0**	**0**	**0**	**7**	**0**	**0**	**0**	**3**	**0.0**		....	....	....	....	....	....	....	....	....	....	....	....	....

Traded to **Toronto** by **LA Kings** with Dixon Ward, Guy Leveque and Kelly Fairchild for Eric Lacroix, Chris Snell and Toronto's 4th round choice (Eric Belanger) in 1996 Entry Draft, October 3, 1994. Signed as a free agent by **St. Louis**, September 9, 1997. Signed as a free agent by **Phoenix**, August 17, 1999.

TRAVERSE, Patrick
(tra-VAIRZ, PAT-rihk) **ANA.**

Defense. Shoots left. 6'3", 190 lbs. Born, Montreal, Que., March 14, 1974. Ottawa's 3rd choice, 50th overall, in 1992 Entry Draft.

			Regular Season																Playoffs							
Season	Club	League	GP	G	A	Pts	PIM	PP	SH	GW	S	%	+/-	TF	F%	H	SB	Min	GP	G	A	Pts	PIM	PP	SH	GW
1990-91	Mtl-Bourassa	QAAA	42	4	19	23	10	....	....	....	....	....	....	....	....	....	....	....	5	0	3	3	2	....	....	....
1991-92	Shawinigan	QMJHL	59	3	11	14	12	....	....	....	....	....	....	....	....	....	....	....	10	0	0	0	4	....	....	....
1992-93	Shawinigan	QMJHL	53	5	24	29	24	....	....	....	....	....	....	....	....	....	....	....	....	....	....	....	....	....	....	....
	St-Jean Lynx	QMJHL	15	1	6	7	0	....	....	....	....	....	....	....	....	....	....	....	4	0	1	1	2	....	....	....
	New Haven	AHL	2	0	0	0	2	....	....	....	....	....	....	....	....	....	....	....	....	....	....	....	....	....	....	....
1993-94	St-Jean Lynx	QMJHL	66	15	37	52	30	....	....	....	....	....	....	....	....	....	....	....	5	0	4	4	4	....	....	....
	P.E.I. Senators	AHL	3	0	1	1	2	....	....	....	....	....	....	....	....	....	....	....	....	....	....	....	....	....	....	....
1994-95	P.E.I. Senators	AHL	70	5	13	18	19	....	....	....	....	....	....	....	....	....	....	....	7	0	2	2	0	....	....	....
1995-96	**Ottawa**	**NHL**	**5**	**0**	**0**	**0**	**2**	**0**	**0**	**0**	**2**	**0.0**	**–1**	....	....	....	....	....	....	....	....	....	....	....	....	....
	P.E.I. Senators	AHL	55	4	21	25	32	....	....	....	....	....	....	....	....	....	....	....	5	1	2	3	2	....	....	....
1996-97	Worcester	AHL	24	0	4	4	23	....	....	....	....	....	....	....	....	....	....	....	....	....	....	....	....	....	....	....
	Grand Rapids	IHL	10	2	1	3	10	....	....	....	....	....	....	....	....	....	....	....	2	0	1	1	2	....	....	....
1997-98	Hershey Bears	AHL	71	14	15	29	67	....	....	....	....	....	....	....	....	....	....	....	7	1	3	4	4	....	....	....
1998-99	**Ottawa**	**NHL**	**46**	**1**	**9**	**10**	**22**	**0**	**0**	**0**	**35**	**2.9**	**12**	**0**	**0.0**	**41**	**42**	**14:56**	....	....	....	....	....	....	....	....
99-2000	**Ottawa**	**NHL**	**66**	**6**	**17**	**23**	**21**	**1**	**0**	**0**	**73**	**8.2**	**17**	**0**	**0.0**	**51**	**78**	**18:43**	**6**	**0**	**0**	**0**	**2**	**0**	**0**	**0**
	NHL Totals		**117**	**7**	**26**	**33**	**45**	**1**	**0**	**0**	**110**	**6.4**		**0**	**0.0**	**92**	**120**	**17:010**	**6**	**0**	**0**	**0**	**2**	**0**	**0**	**0**

Traded to **Anaheim** by **Ottawa** for Joel Kwiatkowski, June 12, 2000.

TREBIL, Daniel
(TREH-bihl, DAN-yehl) **NYI**

Defense. Shoots right. 6'3", 210 lbs. Born, Bloomington, MN, April 10, 1974. New Jersey's 7th choice, 138th overall, in 1992 Entry Draft.

			Regular Season																Playoffs							
Season	Club	League	GP	G	A	Pts	PIM	PP	SH	GW	S	%	+/-	TF	F%	H	SB	Min	GP	G	A	Pts	PIM	PP	SH	GW
1989-90	Jefferson High	Hi-School	22	3	6	9	10	....	....	....	....	....	....	....	....	....	....	....	....	....	....	....	....	....	....	....
1990-91	Jefferson High	Hi-School	23	4	12	16	8	....	....	....	....	....	....	....	....	....	....	....	....	....	....	....	....	....	....	....
1991-92	Jefferson High	Hi-School	28	7	26	33	6	....	....	....	....	....	....	....	....	....	....	....	....	....	....	....	....	....	....	....
1992-93	U. of Minnesota	WCHA	36	2	11	13	16	....	....	....	....	....	....	....	....	....	....	....	....	....	....	....	....	....	....	....
1993-94	U. of Minnesota	WCHA	42	1	21	22	24	....	....	....	....	....	....	....	....	....	....	....	....	....	....	....	....	....	....	....
1994-95	U. of Minnesota	WCHA	44	10	33	43	10	....	....	....	....	....	....	....	....	....	....	....	....	....	....	....	....	....	....	....
1995-96	U. of Minnesota	WCHA	42	11	35	46	36	....	....	....	....	....	....	....	....	....	....	....	....	....	....	....	....	....	....	....
1996-97	**Anaheim**	**NHL**	**29**	**3**	**3**	**6**	**23**	**0**	**0**	**0**	**30**	**10.0**	**5**	....	....	....	....	....	**9**	**0**	**1**	**1**	**6**	**0**	**0**	**0**
	Baltimore Bandits	AHL	49	4	20	24	38	....	....	....	....	....	....	....	....	....	....	....	....	....	....	....	....	....	....	....
1997-98	**Anaheim**	**NHL**	**21**	**0**	**1**	**1**	**2**	**0**	**0**	**0**	**11**	**0.0**	**–8**	....	....	....	....	....	....	....	....	....	....	....	....	....
	Cincinnati Ducks	AHL	32	5	15	20	21	....	....	....	....	....	....	....	....	....	....	....	....	....	....	....	....	....	....	....
1998-99	**Anaheim**	**NHL**	**6**	**0**	**0**	**0**	**0**	**0**	**0**	**0**	**1**	**0.0**	**–2**	**1**	**0.0**	**7**	**7**	**15:02**	**1**	**0**	**0**	**0**	**2**	**0**	**0**	**0**
	Cincinnati Ducks	AHL	52	6	15	21	31	....	....	....	....	....	....	....	....	....	....	....	....	....	....	....	....	....	....	....
99-2000	Cincinnati Ducks	AHL	52	7	21	28	48	....	....	....	....	....	....	....	....	....	....	....	....	....	....	....	....	....	....	....
	Pittsburgh	**NHL**	**3**	**1**	**0**	**1**	**0**	**0**	**0**	**0**	**2**	**50.0**	**2**	**0**	**0.0**	**3**	**1**	**12:33**	....	....	....	....	....	....	....	....
	NHL Totals		**59**	**4**	**4**	**8**	**25**	**0**	**0**	**0**	**44**	**9.1**		**1**	**0.0**	**10**	**8**	**14:12**	**10**	**0**	**1**	**1**	**8**	**0**	**0**	**0**

WCHA Second All-Star Team (1996) • NCAA West Second All-American Team (1996)

Signed as a free agent by **Anaheim**, May 30, 1996. Traded to **Pittsburgh** by **Anaheim** for Pittsburgh's 5th round choice (Bill Cass) in 2000 Entry Draft, March 14, 2000. Signed as a free agent by **NY Islanders**, July 31, 2000.

TREMBLAY, Yannick
(TRAHM-blay, YA-nihk) **ATL.**

Defense. Shoots right. 6'2", 185 lbs. Born, Pointe-aux-Trembles, Que., November 15, 1975. Toronto's 4th choice, 145th overall, in 1995 Entry Draft.

			Regular Season																Playoffs							
Season	Club	League	GP	G	A	Pts	PIM	PP	SH	GW	S	%	+/-	TF	F%	H	SB	Min	GP	G	A	Pts	PIM	PP	SH	GW
1991-92	Mtl-Bourassa	QAAA	35	2	5	7	55	....	....	....	....	....	....	....	....	....	....	....	....	....	....	....	....	....	....	....
1992-93	Mtl-Bourassa	CEGEP	21	2	5	7	10	....	....	....	....	....	....	....	....	....	....	....	3	0	0	0	2	....	....	....
1993-94	St. Thomas U.	AUAA	25	2	3	5	10	....	....	....	....	....	....	....	....	....	....	....	....	....	....	....	....	....	....	....
1994-95	Beauport	QMJHL	70	10	32	42	22	....	....	....	....	....	....	....	....	....	....	....	17	6	8	14	6	....	....	....
1995-96	Beauport	QMJHL	61	12	33	45	42	....	....	....	....	....	....	....	....	....	....	....	20	3	16	19	18	....	....	....
	St. John's Leafs	AHL	3	0	1	1	0	....	....	....	....	....	....	....	....	....	....	....	....	....	....	....	....	....	....	....
1996-97	**St. John's Leafs**	**NHL**	**5**	**0**	**0**	**0**	**0**	**0**	**0**	**0**	**2**	**0.0**	**–4**	....	....	....	....	....	....	....	....	....	....	....	....	....
	St. John's Leafs	AHL	67	7	25	32	34	....	....	....	....	....	....	....	....	....	....	....	11	2	9	11	0	....	....	....
1997-98	**Toronto**	**NHL**	**38**	**2**	**4**	**6**	**6**	**1**	**0**	**0**	**45**	**4.4**	**–6**	....	....	....	....	....	....	....	....	....	....	....	....	....
	St. John's Leafs	AHL	17	3	7	10	4	....	....	....	....	....	....	....	....	....	....	....	4	0	1	1	5	....	....	....
1998-99	**Toronto**	**NHL**	**35**	**2**	**7**	**9**	**16**	**0**	**0**	**0**	**37**	**5.4**	**0**	**0**	**0.0**	**20**	**28**	**17:39**	....	....	....	....	....	....	....	....
99-2000	**Atlanta**	**NHL**	**75**	**10**	**21**	**31**	**22**	**4**	**1**	**2**	**139**	**7.2**	**–42**	**3**	**0.0**	**117**	**91**	**19:27**	....	....	....	....	....	....	....	....
	NHL Totals		**153**	**14**	**32**	**46**	**44**	**5**	**1**	**2**	**223**	**6.3**		**3**	**0.0**	**137**	**119**	**18:53**	....	....	....	....	....	....	....	....

Claimed by **Atlanta** from **Toronto** in Expansion Draft, June 25, 1999.

TREPANIER, Pascal

(truh-PAN-yai, PAS-kal) **ANA.**

Defense. Shoots right. 6', 210 lbs. Born, Gaspe, Que., September 4, 1973.

			Regular Season																Playoffs							
Season	Club	League	GP	G	A	Pts	PIM	PP	SH	GW	S	%	+/-	TF	F%	H	SB	Min	GP	G	A	Pts	PIM	PP	SH	GW
1990-91	Hull Olympiques	QMJHL	46	3	3	6	56	....	....	....	....	....	....	....	....	....	....	....	4	0	2	2	7	....	....	....
1991-92	Trois-Rivieres	QMJHL	53	4	18	22	125	....	....	....	....	....	....	....	....	....	....	....	15	3	5	8	21	....	....	....
1992-93	Sherbrooke	QMJHL	59	15	33	48	130	....	....	....	....	....	....	....	....	....	....	....	15	5	7	12	36	....	....	....
1993-94	Sherbrooke	QMJHL	48	16	41	57	67	....	....	....	....	....	....	....	....	....	....	....	12	1	8	9	14	....	....	....
1994-95	Dayton Bombers	ECHL	36	16	28	44	113	....	....	....	....	....	....	....	....	....	....	....	9	2	4	6	20	....	....	....
	Kalamazoo Wings	IHL	14	1	2	3	47	....	....	....	....	....	....	....	....	....	....	....	....	....	....	....	....	....	....	....
	Cornwall Aces	AHL	4	0	0	0	9	....	....	....	....	....	....	....	....	....	....	....	14	2	7	9	32	....	....	....
1995-96	Cornwall Aces	AHL	70	13	20	33	142	....	....	....	....	....	....	....	....	....	....	....	8	1	2	3	24	....	....	....
1996-97	Hershey Bears	AHL	73	14	39	53	151	....	....	....	....	....	....	....	....	....	....	....	23	6	13	19	59	....	....	....
1997-98	**Colorado**	**NHL**	**15**	**0**	**1**	**1**	**18**	**0**	**0**	**0**	**9**	**0.0**	**-2**	....	....	....	....	....	....	....	....	....	....	....	....	....
	Hershey Bears	AHL	43	13	18	31	105	....	....	....	....	....	....	....	....	....	....	....	7	4	2	6	8	....	....	....
1998-99	**Anaheim**	**NHL**	**45**	**2**	**4**	**6**	**48**	**0**	**0**	**1**	**49**	**4.1**	**0**	**1**	**0.0**	**65**	**52**	**12:42**	....	....	....	....	....	....	....	....
99-2000	**Anaheim**	**NHL**	**37**	**0**	**4**	**4**	**54**	**0**	**0**	**0**	**33**	**0.0**	**2**	**1**	**0.0**	**61**	**30**	**11:18**	....	....	....	....	....	....	....	....
	NHL Totals		**97**	**2**	**9**	**11**	**120**	**0**	**0**	**1**	**91**	**2.2**		**2**	**0.0**	**126**	**82**	**12:04**	....	....	....	....	....	....	....	....

AHL Second All-Star Team (1997)

Signed as a free agent by **Colorado**, August 30, 1995. Claimed by **Anaheim** from **Colorado** in NHL Waiver Draft, October 5, 1998.

TRNKA, Pavel

(truhn-KAH, PAH-vehl) **ANA.**

Defense. Shoots left. 6'3", 200 lbs. Born, Plzen, Czech., July 27, 1976. Anaheim's 5th choice, 106th overall, in 1994 Entry Draft.

			Regular Season																Playoffs							
Season	Club	League	GP	G	A	Pts	PIM	PP	SH	GW	S	%	+/-	TF	F%	H	SB	Min	GP	G	A	Pts	PIM	PP	SH	GW
1993-94	ZKZ Plzen	Cze-Rep	12	0	1	1	....	....	....	....	....	....	....	....	....	....	....	....	....	....	....	....	....	....	....	....
1994-95	Poldi Kladno	Cze-Rep	28	0	5	5	24	....	....	....	....	....	....	....	....	....	....	....	....	....	....	....	....	....	....	....
	ZKZ Plzen	Cze-Rep	6	0	0	0	0	....	....	....	....	....	....	....	....	....	....	....	....	....	....	....	....	....	....	....
1995-96	Baltimore Bandits	AHL	69	2	6	8	44	....	....	....	....	....	....	....	....	....	....	....	6	0	0	0	2	....	....	....
1996-97	Baltimore Bandits	AHL	69	6	14	20	86	....	....	....	....	....	....	....	....	....	....	....	3	0	0	0	2	....	....	....
1997-98	**Anaheim**	**NHL**	**48**	**3**	**4**	**7**	**40**	**1**	**0**	**0**	**46**	**6.5**	**-4**	....	....	....	....	....	....	....	....	....	....	....	....	....
	Cincinnati Ducks	AHL	23	3	5	8	28	....	....	....	....	....	....	....	....	....	....	....	....	....	....	....	....	....	....	....
1998-99	**Anaheim**	**NHL**	**63**	**0**	**4**	**4**	**60**	**0**	**0**	**0**	**50**	**0.0**	**-6**	**0**	**0.0**	**115**	**41**	**16:06**	**4**	**0**	**1**	**1**	**2**	**0**	**0**	**0**
99-2000	**Anaheim**	**NHL**	**57**	**2**	**15**	**17**	**34**	**0**	**0**	**0**	**54**	**3.7**	**12**	**0**	**0.0**	**152**	**48**	**19:21**	....	....	....	....	....	....	....	....
	NHL Totals		**168**	**5**	**23**	**28**	**134**	**1**	**0**	**0**	**150**	**3.3**		**0**	**0.0**	**267**	**89**	**17:39**	**4**	**0**	**1**	**1**	**2**	**0**	**0**	**0**

TRUDEL, Jean-Guy

(TROO-dehl, zhawn-gee) **PHX.**

Left wing. Shoots left. 5'11", 202 lbs. Born, Sudbury, Ont., October 18, 1975.

			Regular Season																Playoffs							
Season	Club	League	GP	G	A	Pts	PIM	PP	SH	GW	S	%	+/-	TF	F%	H	SB	Min	GP	G	A	Pts	PIM	PP	SH	GW
1991-92	Beauport	QMJHL	35	5	7	12	20	....	....	....	....	....	....	....	....	....	....	....	....	....	....	....	....	....	....	....
1992-93	Beauport	QMJHL	56	1	4	5	20	....	....	....	....	....	....	....	....	....	....	....	....	....	....	....	....	....	....	....
	Verdun College	QMJHL	10	1	0	1	0	....	....	....	....	....	....	....	....	....	....	....	2	0	0	0	5	....	....	....
1993-94			DID NOT PLAY																							
1994-95	Hull Olympiques	QMJHL	54	29	42	71	76	....	....	....	....	....	....	....	....	....	....	....	19	4	13	17	25	....	....	....
1995-96	Hull Olympiques	QMJHL	70	50	71	121	96	....	....	....	....	....	....	....	....	....	....	....	17	11	18	29	8	....	....	....
1996-97	Quad City	ColHL	5	8	7	15	4	....	....	....	....	....	....	....	....	....	....	....	....	....	....	....	....	....	....	....
	Chicago Wolves	IHL	6	1	2	3	2	....	....	....	....	....	....	....	....	....	....	....	....	....	....	....	....	....	....	....
	San Antonio	IHL	12	1	5	6	4	....	....	....	....	....	....	....	....	....	....	....	....	....	....	....	....	....	....	....
	Peoria Rivermen	ECHL	37	25	29	54	47	....	....	....	....	....	....	....	....	....	....	....	9	9	10	19	22	....	....	....
1997-98	Peoria Rivermen	ECHL	62	39	74	113	147	....	....	....	....	....	....	....	....	....	....	....	3	0	0	0	2	....	....	....
1998-99	Kansas City	IHL	76	24	25	49	66	....	....	....	....	....	....	....	....	....	....	....	3	1	0	1	0	....	....	....
99-2000	**Phoenix**	**NHL**	**1**	**0**	**0**	**0**	**0**	**0**	**0**	**0**	**0**	**0.0**	**-1**	**0**	**0.0**	**4**	**0**	**4:33**	....	....	....	....	....	....	....	....
	Springfield	AHL	72	34	39	73	80	....	....	....	....	....	....	....	....	....	....	....	3	0	1	1	4	....	....	....
	NHL Totals		**1**	**0**	**0**	**0**	**0**	**0**	**0**	**0**	**0**	**0.0**		**0**	**0.0**	**4**	**0**	**4:33**	....	....	....	....	....	....	....	....

AHL Second All-Star Team (2000)

• Sat out entire 1993-94 season to regain eligibility for U.S. College scholarship. Signed as a free agent by **Phoenix**, July 17, 1999.

TSYPLAKOV, Vladimir

(tsih-plah-KAHF, VLA-dih-meer) **BUF.**

Left wing. Shoots left. 6'1", 197 lbs. Born, Inta, USSR, April 18, 1969. Los Angeles' 4th choice, 59th overall, in 1995 Entry Draft.

			Regular Season																Playoffs							
Season	Club	League	GP	G	A	Pts	PIM	PP	SH	GW	S	%	+/-	TF	F%	H	SB	Min	GP	G	A	Pts	PIM	PP	SH	GW
1988-89	Dynamo Minsk	USSR	19	6	1	7	4	....	....	....	....	....	....	....	....	....	....	....	....	....	....	....	....	....	....	....
1989-90	Dynamo Minsk	USSR	47	11	6	17	20	....	....	....	....	....	....	....	....	....	....	....	....	....	....	....	....	....	....	....
1990-91	Dynamo Minsk	USSR	28	6	5	11	14	....	....	....	....	....	....	....	....	....	....	....	....	....	....	....	....	....	....	....
1991-92	Dynamo Minsk	CIS	29	10	9	19	16	....	....	....	....	....	....	....	....	....	....	....	....	....	....	....	....	....	....	....
1992-93	Detroit Falcons	ColHL	44	33	43	76	20	....	....	....	....	....	....	....	....	....	....	....	6	5	4	9	6	....	....	....
	Indianapolis Ice	IHL	11	6	7	13	4	....	....	....	....	....	....	....	....	....	....	....	5	1	1	2	2	....	....	....
1993-94	Fort Wayne	IHL	63	31	32	63	51	....	....	....	....	....	....	....	....	....	....	....	14	6	8	14	16	....	....	....
1994-95	Fort Wayne	IHL	79	38	40	78	39	....	....	....	....	....	....	....	....	....	....	....	4	2	4	6	2	....	....	....
1995-96	**Los Angeles**	**NHL**	**23**	**5**	**5**	**10**	**4**	**0**	**0**	**0**	**40**	**12.5**	**1**	....	....	....	....	....	....	....	....	....	....	....	....	....
	Las Vegas	IHL	9	5	6	11	4	....	....	....	....	....	....	....	....	....	....	....	....	....	....	....	....	....	....	....
1996-97	**Los Angeles**	**NHL**	**67**	**16**	**23**	**39**	**12**	**1**	**0**	**2**	**118**	**13.6**	**8**	....	....	....	....	....	....	....	....	....	....	....	....	....
1997-98	**Los Angeles**	**NHL**	**73**	**18**	**34**	**52**	**18**	**2**	**0**	**1**	**113**	**15.9**	**15**	....	....	....	....	....	**4**	**0**	**1**	**1**	**8**	**0**	**0**	**0**
	Belarus	Olympics	5	1	1	2	2	....	....	....	....	....	....	....	....	....	....	....	....	....	....	....	....	....	....	....
1998-99	**Los Angeles**	**NHL**	**69**	**11**	**12**	**23**	**32**	**0**	**2**	**2**	**111**	**9.9**	**-7**	**1**	**100.0**	**72**	**14**	**16:23**	....	....	....	....	....	....	....	....
99-2000	**Los Angeles**	**NHL**	**29**	**6**	**7**	**13**	**4**	**1**	**0**	**1**	**30**	**20.0**	**6**	**3**	**0.0**	**32**	**5**	**10:39**	....	....	....	....	....	....	....	....
	Buffalo	**NHL**	**34**	**6**	**13**	**19**	**10**	**0**	**0**	**1**	**46**	**13.0**	**17**	**0**	**0.0**	**44**	**4**	**13:41**	**5**	**0**	**1**	**1**	**4**	**0**	**0**	**0**
	NHL Totals		**295**	**62**	**94**	**156**	**80**	**4**	**2**	**7**	**458**	**13.5**		**4**	**25.0**	**148**	**23**	**14:26**	**9**	**0**	**2**	**2**	**12**	**0**	**0**	**0**

ColHL First All-Star Team (1993)

Traded to **Buffalo** by **LA Kings** for Buffalo's 8th round choice (Dan Welch) in 2000 Entry Draft and future considerations, January 24, 2000.

TUCKER, Darcy

TUH-kuhr, DAHR-see) **TOR.**

Center. Shoots left. 5'11", 185 lbs. Born, Castor, Alta., March 15, 1975. Montreal's 8th choice, 151st overall, in 1993 Entry Draft.

			Regular Season																Playoffs							
Season	Club	League	GP	G	A	Pts	PIM	PP	SH	GW	S	%	+/-	TF	F%	H	SB	Min	GP	G	A	Pts	PIM	PP	SH	GW
1990-91	Red Deer Chiefs	AAHA	47	70	90	160	48	....	....	....	....	....	....	....	....	....	....	....	....	....	....	....	....	....	....	....
1991-92	Kamloops Blazers	WHL	26	3	10	13	32	....	....	....	....	....	....	....	....	....	....	....	9	0	1	1	16	....	....	....
1992-93	Kamloops Blazers	WHL	67	31	58	89	155	....	....	....	....	....	....	....	....	....	....	....	13	7	6	13	34	....	....	....
1993-94	Kamloops Blazers	WHL	66	52	88	140	143	....	....	....	....	....	....	....	....	....	....	....	19	9	*18	*27	43	....	....	....
1994-95	Kamloops Blazers	WHL	64	64	73	137	94	....	....	....	....	....	....	....	....	....	....	....	21	*16	15	*31	19	....	....	....
1995-96	**Montreal**	**NHL**	**3**	**0**	**0**	**0**	**0**	**0**	**0**	**0**	**1**	**0.0**	**-1**	....	....	....	....	....	....	....	....	....	....	....	....	....
	Fredericton	AHL	74	29	64	93	174	....	....	....	....	....	....	....	....	....	....	....	7	7	3	10	14	....	....	....
1996-97	**Montreal**	**NHL**	**73**	**7**	**13**	**20**	**110**	**1**	**0**	**3**	**62**	**11.3**	**-5**	....	....	....	....	....	**4**	**0**	**0**	**0**	**0**	**0**	**0**	**0**
1997-98	**Montreal**	**NHL**	**39**	**1**	**5**	**6**	**57**	**0**	**0**	**0**	**19**	**5.3**	**-6**	....	....	....	....	....	....	....	....	....	....	....	....	....
	Tampa Bay	**NHL**	**35**	**6**	**8**	**14**	**89**	**1**	**1**	**0**	**44**	**13.6**	**-8**	....	....	....	....	....	....	....	....	....	....	....	....	....
1998-99	**Tampa Bay**	**NHL**	**82**	**21**	**22**	**43**	**176**	**8**	**2**	**3**	**178**	**11.8**	**-34**	**1470**	**45.6**	**120**	**49**	**19:24**	....	....	....	....	....	....	....	....
99-2000	**Tampa Bay**	**NHL**	**50**	**14**	**20**	**34**	**108**	**1**	**0**	**2**	**98**	**14.3**	**-15**	**152**	**48.7**	**106**	**19**	**19:58**	....	....	....	....	....	....	....	....
	Toronto	**NHL**	**27**	**7**	**10**	**17**	**55**	**0**	**2**	**3**	**40**	**17.5**	**3**	**11**	**54.6**	**62**	**19**	**16:41**	**12**	**4**	**2**	**6**	**15**	**1**	**0**	**2**
	NHL Totals		**309**	**56**	**78**	**134**	**595**	**11**	**5**	**11**	**442**	**12.7**		**1633**	**45.9**	**288**	**87**	**19:07**	**16**	**4**	**2**	**6**	**15**	**1**	**0**	**2**

WHL West First All-Star Team (1994, 1995) • Canadian Major Junior First All-Star Team (1994) • Memorial Cup All-Star Team (1994, 1995) • Won Stafford Smythe Memorial Trophy (Memorial Cup Tournament MVP) (1994) • Won Dudley "Red" Garrett Memorial Trophy (Top Rookie - AHL) (1996)

Traded to **Tampa Bay** by **Montreal** with Stephane Richer and David Wilkie for Patrick Poulin, Mick Vukota and Igor Ulanov, January 15, 1998. Traded to **Toronto** by **Tampa Bay** with Tampa Bay's 4th round choice (Miguel Delisle) in 2000 Entry Draft and future considerations for Mike Johnson, Marek Posmyk, Toronto's 5th (Pavel Sedov) and 6th (Aaron Gionet) round choices in 2000 Entry Draft and future considerations, February 9, 2000.

TUOMAINEN, Marko

(TOO-oh-migh-nehn, MAHR-koh)

Right wing. Shoots right. 6'3", 218 lbs. Born, Kuopio, Finland, April 25, 1972. Edmonton's 10th choice, 205th overall, in 1992 Entry Draft.

			Regular Season																Playoffs							
Season	Club	League	GP	G	A	Pts	PIM	PP	SH	GW	S	%	+/-	TF	F%	H	SB	Min	GP	G	A	Pts	PIM	PP	SH	GW
1988-89	KalPa Kuopio	Finn-Jr.	7	6	6	12	4	....	....	....	....	....	....	....	....	....	....	....	....	....	....	....	....	....	....	....
1989-90	KalPa Kuopio	Finn-Jr.	36	13	24	37	30	....	....	....	....	....	....	....	....	....	....	....	....	....	....	....	....	....	....	....
	KalPa Kuopio	Finland	5	0	0	0	0	....	....	....	....	....	....	....	....	....	....	....	....	....	....	....	....	....	....	....
1990-91	KalPa Kuopio	Finn-Jr.	35	36	17	53	61	....	....	....	....	....	....	....	....	....	....	....	....	....	....	....	....	....	....	....
	KalPa Kuopio	Finland	30	2	1	3	2	....	....	....	....	....	....	....	....	....	....	....	8	0	0	0	6	....	....	....
1991-92	Clarkson	ECAC	28	11	12	23	32	....	....	....	....	....	....	....	....	....	....	....	....	....	....	....	....	....	....	....
1992-93	Clarkson	ECAC	35	25	30	55	26	....	....	....	....	....	....	....	....	....	....	....	....	....	....	....	....	....	....	....
1993-94	Clarkson	ECAC	34	23	29	52	60	....	....	....	....	....	....	....	....	....	....	....	....	....	....	....	....	....	....	....
1994-95	Clarkson	ECAC	37	23	38	61	34	....	....	....	....	....	....	....	....	....	....	....	....	....	....	....	....	....	....	....
	Edmonton	**NHL**	**4**	**0**	**0**	**0**	**0**	**0**	**0**	**0**	**5**	**0.0**	**0**	....	....	....	....	....	....	....	....	....	....	....	....	....
1995-96	Cape Breton	AHL	58	25	35	60	71	....	....	....	....	....	....	....	....	....	....	....	....	....	....	....	....	....	....	....
1996-97	Hamilton Bulldogs	AHL	79	31	21	52	130	....	....	....	....	....	....	....	....	....	....	....	22	7	5	12	4	....	....	....
1997-98	HIFK Helsinki	Finland	46	13	9	22	20	....	....	....	....	....	....	....	....	....	....	....	9	0	3	3	0	....	....	....
1998-99	HIFK Helsinki	Finland	48	11	17	28	*173	....	....	....	....	....	....	....	....	....	....	....	11	1	3	4	12	....	....	....
	HIFK Helsinki	EuroHL	6	0	1	1	8	....	....	....	....	....	....	....	....	....	....	....	4	3	0	3	4	....	....	....
99-2000	**Los Angeles**	**NHL**	**63**	**9**	**8**	**17**	**80**	**2**	**1**	**1**	**74**	**12.2**	**–12**	**8**	**25.0**	**69**	**9**	**11:30**	**1**	**0**	**0**	**0**	**0**	**0**	**0**	**0**
	NHL Totals		**67**	**9**	**8**	**17**	**80**	**2**	**1**	**1**	**79**	**11.4**		**8**	**25.0**	**69**	**9**	**11:30**	**1**	**0**	**0**	**0**	**0**	**0**	**0**	**0**

ECAC First All-Star Team (1993, 1995) • NCAA East Second All-American Team (1995)

Signed as a free agent by **Los Angeles**, June 20, 1999.

TURCOTTE, Darren

(TUHR-koht, DAIR-ehn)

Center. Shoots left. 6', 182 lbs. Born, Boston, MA, May 2, 1968. NY Rangers' 6th choice, 114th overall, in 1986 Entry Draft.

			Regular Season																Playoffs							
Season	Club	League	GP	G	A	Pts	PIM	PP	SH	GW	S	%	+/-	TF	F%	H	SB	Min	GP	G	A	Pts	PIM	PP	SH	GW
1983-84	North Bay	NOHA	70	61	40	101	28	....	....	....	....	....	....	....	....	....	....	....	....	....	....	....	....	....	....	....
1984-85	North Bay	OHL	62	33	32	65	28	....	....	....	....	....	....	....	....	....	....	....	8	0	2	2	0	....	....	....
1985-86	North Bay	OHL	62	35	37	72	35	....	....	....	....	....	....	....	....	....	....	....	10	3	4	7	8	....	....	....
1986-87	North Bay	OHL	55	30	48	78	20	....	....	....	....	....	....	....	....	....	....	....	18	12	8	20	6	....	....	....
1987-88	North Bay	OHL	32	30	33	63	16	....	....	....	....	....	....	....	....	....	....	....	4	3	0	3	4	....	....	....
	Colorado Rangers	IHL	8	4	3	7	9	....	....	....	....	....	....	....	....	....	....	....	6	2	6	8	8	....	....	....
1988-89	**NY Rangers**	**NHL**	**20**	**7**	**3**	**10**	**4**	**2**	**0**	**2**	**49**	**14.3**	**0**	....	....	....	....	....	**1**	**0**	**0**	**0**	**0**	**0**	**0**	**0**
	Denver Rangers	IHL	40	21	28	49	32	....	....	....	....	....	....	....	....	....	....	....	....	....	....	....	....	....	....	....
1989-90	**NY Rangers**	**NHL**	**76**	**32**	**34**	**66**	**32**	**10**	**1**	**4**	**205**	**15.6**	**3**	....	....	....	....	....	**10**	**1**	**6**	**7**	**4**	**0**	**0**	**1**
1990-91	**NY Rangers**	**NHL**	**74**	**26**	**41**	**67**	**37**	**15**	**2**	**3**	**212**	**12.3**	**–5**	....	....	....	....	....	**6**	**1**	**2**	**3**	**0**	**1**	**0**	**0**
1991-92	**NY Rangers**	**NHL**	**71**	**30**	**23**	**53**	**57**	**13**	**1**	**4**	**216**	**13.9**	**11**	....	....	....	....	....	**8**	**4**	**0**	**4**	**6**	**2**	**1**	**0**
1992-93	**NY Rangers**	**NHL**	**71**	**25**	**28**	**53**	**40**	**7**	**3**	**3**	**213**	**11.7**	**–3**	....	....	....	....	....	....	....	....	....	....	....	....	....
1993-94	**NY Rangers**	**NHL**	**13**	**2**	**4**	**6**	**13**	**0**	**0**	**0**	**17**	**11.8**	**–2**	....	....	....	....	....	....	....	....	....	....	....	....	....
	Hartford	**NHL**	**19**	**2**	**11**	**13**	**4**	**0**	**0**	**0**	**43**	**4.7**	**–11**	....	....	....	....	....	....	....	....	....	....	....	....	....
1994-95	**Hartford**	**NHL**	**47**	**17**	**18**	**35**	**22**	**3**	**1**	**3**	**121**	**14.0**	**1**	....	....	....	....	....	....	....	....	....	....	....	....	....
1995-96	**Winnipeg**	**NHL**	**59**	**16**	**16**	**32**	**26**	**2**	**0**	**2**	**134**	**11.9**	**–3**	....	....	....	....	....	....	....	....	....	....	....	....	....
	San Jose	**NHL**	**9**	**6**	**5**	**11**	**4**	**0**	**1**	**2**	**33**	**18.2**	**8**	....	....	....	....	....	....	....	....	....	....	....	....	....
1996-97	**San Jose**	**NHL**	**65**	**16**	**21**	**37**	**16**	**3**	**1**	**4**	**126**	**12.7**	**–8**	....	....	....	....	....	....	....	....	....	....	....	....	....
1997-98	**St. Louis**	**NHL**	**62**	**12**	**6**	**18**	**26**	**3**	**0**	**1**	**75**	**16.0**	**6**	....	....	....	....	....	**10**	**0**	**0**	**0**	**2**	**0**	**0**	**0**
1998-99	**Nashville**	**NHL**	**40**	**4**	**5**	**9**	**16**	**0**	**0**	**1**	**73**	**5.5**	**–11**	**701**	**44.5**	**8**	**15**	**15:51**	....	....	....	....	....	....	....	....
99-2000	**Nashville**	**NHL**	**9**	**0**	**1**	**1**	**4**	**0**	**0**	**0**	**13**	**0.0**	**0**	**30**	**30.0**	**1**	**1**	**9:13**	....	....	....	....	....	....	....	....
	NHL Totals		**635**	**195**	**216**	**411**	**301**	**58**	**10**	**29**	**1530**	**12.7**		**731**	**43.9**	**9**	**16**	**14:38**	**35**	**6**	**8**	**14**	**12**	**3**	**1**	**1**

Played in NHL All-Star Game (1991)

Traded to **Hartford** by **NY Rangers** with James Patrick for Steve Larmer, Nick Kypreos, Barry Richter and Hartford's 6th round choice (Yuri Litvinov) in 1994 Entry Draft, November 2, 1993. Traded to **Winnipeg** by **Hartford** for Nelson Emerson, October 6, 1995. Traded to **San Jose** by **Winnipeg** with Dallas' 2nd round choice (previously acquired and later traded to Chicago - Chicago selected Remi Royer) in 1996 Entry Draft for Craig Janney, March 18, 1996. Traded to **St. Louis** by **San Jose** for Stephane Matteau, July 24, 1997. Traded to **Nashville** by **St. Louis** for future considerations, June 26, 1998. • Missed remainder of 1999-2000 season recovering from knee injury suffered in game vs. Montreal, November 18, 1999.

TURGEON, Pierre

(TUHR-zhaw, PEE-air) **ST.L.**

Center. Shoots left. 6'1", 199 lbs. Born, Rouyn, Que., August 28, 1969. Buffalo's 1st choice, 1st overall, in 1987 Entry Draft.

			Regular Season																Playoffs							
Season	Club	League	GP	G	A	Pts	PIM	PP	SH	GW	S	%	+/-	TF	F%	H	SB	Min	GP	G	A	Pts	PIM	PP	SH	GW
1984-85	Mtl-Bourassa	QAAA	41	49	52	101	....	....	....	....	....	....	....	....	....	....	....	....	....	....	....	....	....	....	....	....
1985-86	Granby Bisons	QMJHL	69	47	67	114	31	....	....	....	....	....	....	....	....	....	....	....	....	....	....	....	....	....	....	....
	Canada	Nat-Team	11	2	4	6	2	....	....	....	....	....	....	....	....	....	....	....	....	....	....	....	....	....	....	....
1986-87	Granby Bisons	QMJHL	58	69	85	154	8	....	....	....	....	....	....	....	....	....	....	....	7	9	6	15	15	....	....	....
1987-88	**Buffalo**	**NHL**	**76**	**14**	**28**	**42**	**34**	**8**	**0**	**3**	**101**	**13.9**	**–8**	....	....	....	....	....	**6**	**4**	**3**	**7**	**4**	**3**	**0**	**0**
1988-89	**Buffalo**	**NHL**	**80**	**34**	**54**	**88**	**26**	**19**	**0**	**5**	**182**	**18.7**	**–2**	....	....	....	....	....	**5**	**3**	**5**	**8**	**2**	**1**	**0**	**0**
1989-90	**Buffalo**	**NHL**	**80**	**40**	**66**	**106**	**29**	**17**	**1**	**10**	**193**	**20.7**	**10**	....	....	....	....	....	**6**	**2**	**4**	**6**	**2**	**0**	**0**	**1**
1990-91	**Buffalo**	**NHL**	**78**	**32**	**47**	**79**	**26**	**13**	**2**	**3**	**174**	**18.4**	**14**	....	....	....	....	....	**6**	**3**	**1**	**4**	**6**	**1**	**0**	**0**
1991-92	**Buffalo**	**NHL**	**8**	**2**	**6**	**8**	**4**	**0**	**0**	**0**	**14**	**14.3**	**–1**	....	....	....	....	....	....	....	....	....	....	....	....	....
	NY Islanders	**NHL**	**69**	**38**	**49**	**87**	**16**	**13**	**0**	**6**	**193**	**19.7**	**8**	....	....	....	....	....	....	....	....	....	....	....	....	....
1992-93	**NY Islanders**	**NHL**	**83**	**58**	**74**	**132**	**26**	**24**	**0**	**10**	**301**	**19.3**	**–1**	....	....	....	....	....	**11**	**6**	**7**	**13**	**0**	**0**	**0**	**0**
1993-94	**NY Islanders**	**NHL**	**69**	**38**	**56**	**94**	**18**	**10**	**4**	**6**	**254**	**15.0**	**14**	....	....	....	....	....	**4**	**0**	**1**	**1**	**0**	**0**	**0**	**0**
1994-95	**NY Islanders**	**NHL**	**34**	**13**	**14**	**27**	**10**	**3**	**2**	**2**	**93**	**14.0**	**–12**	....	....	....	....	....	....	....	....	....	....	....	....	....
	Montreal	**NHL**	**15**	**11**	**9**	**20**	**4**	**2**	**0**	**2**	**67**	**16.4**	**12**	....	....	....	....	....	....	....	....	....	....	....	....	....
1995-96	**Montreal**	**NHL**	**80**	**38**	**58**	**96**	**44**	**17**	**1**	**6**	**297**	**12.8**	**19**	....	....	....	....	....	**6**	**2**	**4**	**6**	**2**	**0**	**0**	**0**
1996-97	**Montreal**	**NHL**	**9**	**1**	**10**	**11**	**2**	**0**	**0**	**0**	**22**	**4.5**	**4**	....	....	....	....	....	....	....	....	....	....	....	....	....
	St. Louis	**NHL**	**69**	**25**	**49**	**74**	**12**	**5**	**0**	**7**	**194**	**12.9**	**4**	....	....	....	....	....	**5**	**1**	**1**	**2**	**2**	**1**	**0**	**0**
1997-98	**St. Louis**	**NHL**	**60**	**22**	**46**	**68**	**24**	**6**	**0**	**4**	**140**	**15.7**	**13**	....	....	....	....	....	**10**	**4**	**4**	**8**	**2**	**2**	**0**	**0**
1998-99	**St. Louis**	**NHL**	**67**	**31**	**34**	**65**	**36**	**10**	**0**	**5**	**193**	**16.1**	**4**	**1285**	**50.0**	**16**	**24**	**19:07**	**13**	**4**	**9**	**13**	**6**	**0**	**0**	**2**
99-2000	**St. Louis**	**NHL**	**52**	**26**	**40**	**66**	**8**	**8**	**0**	**3**	**139**	**18.7**	**30**	**1016**	**53.1**	**5**	**19**	**19:13**	**7**	**0**	**7**	**7**	**0**	**0**	**0**	**0**
	NHL Totals		**929**	**423**	**640**	**1063**	**319**	**155**	**10**	**72**	**2557**	**16.5**		**2301**	**51.4**	**21**	**43**	**19:010**	**79**	**29**	**46**	**75**	**26**	**8**	**0**	**3**

Won Lady Byng Memorial Trophy (1993) • Played in NHL All-Star Game (1990, 1993, 1994, 1996)

Traded to **NY Islanders** by **Buffalo** with Uwe Krupp, Benoit Hogue and Dave McLlwain for Pat LaFontaine, Randy Hillier, Randy Wood and NY Islanders' 4th round choice (Dean Melanson) in 1992 Entry Draft, October 25, 1991. Traded to **Montreal** by **NY Islanders** with Vladimir Malakhov for Kirk Muller, Mathieu Schneider and Craig Darby, April 5, 1995. Traded to **St. Louis** by **Montreal** with Rory Fitzpatrick and Craig Conroy for Murray Baron, Shayne Corson and St. Louis' 5th round choice (Gennady Razin) in 1997 Entry Draft, October 29, 1996.

TUZZOLINO, Tony

(too-zuh-LEE-noh, TOH-nee)

Right wing. Shoots right. 6'2", 208 lbs. Born, Buffalo, NY, October 9, 1975. Quebec's 7th choice, 113th overall, in 1994 Entry Draft.

			Regular Season																Playoffs							
Season	Club	League	GP	G	A	Pts	PIM	PP	SH	GW	S	%	+/-	TF	F%	H	SB	Min	GP	G	A	Pts	PIM	PP	SH	GW
1989-90	Amherst Knights	NYAHA	29	50	95	145	....	....	....	....	....	....	....	....	....	....	....	....	....	....	....	....	....	....	....	....
1990-91	Buffalo Regals	NAJHL	55	39	47	86	....	....	....	....	....	....	....	....	....	....	....	....	....	....	....	....	....	....	....	....
1991-92	Niagara Scenics	NAJHL	45	19	27	46	82	....	....	....	....	....	....	....	....	....	....	....	....	....	....	....	....	....	....	....
1992-93	Niagara Scenics	NAJHL	50	36	41	77	134	....	....	....	....	....	....	....	....	....	....	....	....	....	....	....	....	....	....	....
1993-94	Michigan State	CCHA	35	4	3	7	46	....	....	....	....	....	....	....	....	....	....	....	....	....	....	....	....	....	....	....
1994-95	Michigan State	CCHA	39	9	18	27	81	....	....	....	....	....	....	....	....	....	....	....	....	....	....	....	....	....	....	....
1995-96	Michigan State	CCHA	41	12	17	29	120	....	....	....	....	....	....	....	....	....	....	....	....	....	....	....	....	....	....	....
1996-97	Michigan State	CCHA	39	14	18	32	120	....	....	....	....	....	....	....	....	....	....	....	....	....	....	....	....	....	....	....
1997-98	Kentucky	AHL	35	9	14	23	83	....	....	....	....	....	....	....	....	....	....	....	....	....	....	....	....	....	....	....
	Anaheim	**NHL**	**1**	**0**	**0**	**0**	**2**	**0**	**0**	**0**	**0**	**0.0**	**–2**	....	....	....	....	....	....	....	....	....	....	....	....	....
	Cincinnati Ducks	AHL	13	3	3	6	6	....	....	....	....	....	....	....	....	....	....	....	....	....	....	....	....	....	....	....
1998-99	Cincinnati Ducks	AHL	50	4	10	14	55	....	....	....	....	....	....	....	....	....	....	....	....	....	....	....	....	....	....	....
	Cleveland	IHL	15	2	4	6	22	....	....	....	....	....	....	....	....	....	....	....	....	....	....	....	....	....	....	....
99-2000	Cincinnati Ducks	AHL	15	0	3	3	8	....	....	....	....	....	....	....	....	....	....	....	....	....	....	....	....	....	....	....
	Huntington	ECHL	20	6	13	19	43	....	....	....	....	....	....	....	....	....	....	....	....	....	....	....	....	....	....	....
	Hartford	AHL	32	3	8	11	41	....	....	....	....	....	....	....	....	....	....	....	19	2	2	4	16	....	....	....
	NHL Totals		**1**	**0**	**0**	**0**	**2**	**0**	**0**	**0**	**0**	**0.0**		....	....	....	....	....	....	....	....	....	....	....	....	....

Rights transferred to **Colorado** after **Quebec** franchise relocated, June 21, 1995. Signed as a free agent by **NY Islanders**, April 26, 1997. Traded to **Anaheim** by **NY Islanders** with Travis Green and Doug Houda for Joe Sacco, J.J. Daigneault and Mark Janssens, February 6, 1998.

TVERDOVSKY, Oleg

(tvehr-DOHV-skee) **ANA.**

Defense. Shoots left. 6', 200 lbs. Born, Donetsk, USSR, May 18, 1976. Anaheim's 1st choice, 2nd overall, in 1994 Entry Draft.

Season	Club	League	GP	G	A	Pts	PIM	PP	SH	GW	S	%	+/–	TF	F%	H	SB	Min	Playoffs GP	G	A	Pts	PIM	PP	SH	GW
1992-93	Krylja Sovetov	CIS	21	0	1	1	6	....	....	....	....	....	....	....	....	....	....	....	6	0	0	0	0	....	....	....
1993-94	Krylja Sovetov	CIS	46	4	10	14	22	....	....	....	....	....	....	....	....	....	....	....	3	1	0	1	2	....	....	....
1994-95	Brandon	WHL	7	1	4	5	4	....	....	....	....	....	....	....	....	....	....	....	....	....	....	....	....	....	....	....
	Anaheim	NHL	36	3	9	12	14	1	1	0	26	11.5	–6	....	....	....	....	....	....	....	....	....	....	....	....	....
1995-96	Anaheim	NHL	51	7	15	22	35	2	0	0	84	8.3	0	....	....	....	....	....	....	....	....	....	....	....	....	....
	Winnipeg	NHL	31	0	8	8	6	0	0	0	35	0.0	–7	....	....	....	....	....	6	0	1	1	0	0	0	0
1996-97	Phoenix	NHL	82	10	45	55	30	3	1	2	144	6.9	–5	....	....	....	....	....	7	0	1	1	0	0	0	0
1997-98	Hamilton Bulldogs	AHL	9	8	6	14	2	....	....	....	....	....	....	....	....	....	....	....	....	....	....	....	....	....	....	....
	Phoenix	NHL	46	7	12	19	12	4	0	1	83	8.4	1	....	....	....	....	....	6	0	7	7	0	0	0	0
1998-99	Phoenix	NHL	82	7	18	25	32	2	0	2	117	6.0	11	1	0.0	50	53	20:48	6	0	2	2	6	0	0	0
99-2000	Anaheim	NHL	82	15	36	51	30	5	0	5	153	9.8	5	1	0.0	79	89	22:46	....	....	....	....	....	....	....	....
	NHL Totals		410	49	143	192	159	17	2	10	642	7.6		2	0.0	129	142	21:47	25	0	11	11	6	0	0	0

Played in NHL All-Star Game (1997)

Traded to **Winnipeg** by **Anaheim** with Chad Kilger and Anaheim's 3rd round choice (Per-Anton Lundstrom) in 1996 Entry Draft for Teemu Selanne, Marc Chouinard and Winnipeg's 4th round choice (later traded to Toronto - later traded to Montreal - Montreal selected Kim Staal) in 1996 Entry Draft, February 7, 1996. Transferred to **Phoenix** after **Winnipeg** franchise relocated, July 1, 1996. Traded to **Anaheim** by **Phoenix** for Travis Green and Anaheim's 1st round choice (Scott Kelman) in 1999 Entry Draft, June 26, 1999.

TWIST, Tony

(TWIHST, TOH-nee)

Left wing. Shoots left. 6'1", 220 lbs. Born, Sherwood Park, Alta., May 9, 1968. St. Louis' 9th choice, 177th overall, in 1988 Entry Draft.

Season	Club	League	GP	G	A	Pts	PIM	PP	SH	GW	S	%	+/–	TF	F%	H	SB	Min	Playoffs GP	G	A	Pts	PIM	PP	SH	GW
1985-86	Prince George	BCJHL	42	32	20	52	162	....	....	....	....	....	....	....	....	....	....	....	....	....	....	....	....	....	....	....
1986-87	Saskatoon Blades	WHL	64	0	8	8	181	....	....	....	....	....	....	....	....	....	....	....	....	....	....	....	....	....	....	....
1987-88	Saskatoon Blades	WHL	55	1	8	9	226	....	....	....	....	....	....	....	....	....	....	....	10	1	1	2	6	....	....	....
1988-89	Peoria Rivermen	IHL	67	3	8	11	312	....	....	....	....	....	....	....	....	....	....	....	....	....	....	....	....	....	....	....
1989-90	St. Louis	NHL	28	0	0	0	124	0	0	0	2	0.0	–2	....	....	....	....	....	....	....	....	....	....	....	....	....
	Peoria Rivermen	IHL	36	1	5	6	200	....	....	....	....	....	....	....	....	....	....	....	5	0	1	1	8	....	....	....
1990-91	Peoria Rivermen	IHL	38	2	10	12	244	....	....	....	....	....	....	....	....	....	....	....	....	....	....	....	....	....	....	....
	Quebec	NHL	24	0	0	0	104	0	0	0	2	0.0	–4	....	....	....	....	....	....	....	....	....	....	....	....	....
1991-92	Quebec	NHL	44	0	1	1	164	0	0	0	9	0.0	–3	....	....	....	....	....	....	....	....	....	....	....	....	....
1992-93	Quebec	NHL	34	0	2	2	64	0	0	0	14	0.0	0	....	....	....	....	....	....	....	....	....	....	....	....	....
1993-94	Quebec	NHL	49	0	4	4	101	0	0	0	15	0.0	–1	....	....	....	....	....	....	....	....	....	....	....	....	....
1994-95	St. Louis	NHL	28	3	0	3	89	0	0	1	8	37.5	0	....	....	....	....	....	1	0	0	0	6	0	0	0
1995-96	St. Louis	NHL	51	3	2	5	100	0	0	1	12	25.0	–1	....	....	....	....	....	10	1	1	2	16	0	0	0
1996-97	St. Louis	NHL	64	1	2	3	121	0	0	0	21	4.8	–8	....	....	....	....	....	6	0	0	0	0	0	0	0
1997-98	St. Louis	NHL	60	1	1	2	105	0	0	0	17	5.9	–4	....	....	....	....	....	....	....	....	....	....	....	....	....
1998-99	St. Louis	NHL	63	2	6	8	149	0	0	0	23	8.7	0	1	0.0	47	5	5:10	1	0	0	0	0	0	0	0
99-2000	St. Louis	NHL	DID NOT PLAY – INJURED																							
	NHL Totals		445	10	18	28	1121	0	0	2	123	8.1		1	0.0	47	5	5:10	18	1	1	2	22	0	0	0

Traded to **Quebec** by **St. Louis** with Herb Raglan and Andy Rymsha for Darin Kimble, February 4, 1991. Signed as a free agent by **St. Louis**, August 16, 1994. • Missed entire 1999-2000 season recovering from injuries suffered in motorcycle accident, July, 1999.

ULANOV, Igor

(yoo-LAH-nahf, EE-gohr) **EDM.**

Defense. Shoots left. 6'3", 211 lbs. Born, Krasnokamsk, USSR, October 1, 1969. Winnipeg's 8th choice, 203rd overall, in 1991 Entry Draft.

Season	Club	League	GP	G	A	Pts	PIM	PP	SH	GW	S	%	+/–	TF	F%	H	SB	Min	Playoffs GP	G	A	Pts	PIM	PP	SH	GW
1990-91	HK Khimik	USSR	41	2	2	4	52	....	....	....	....	....	....	....	....	....	....	....	....	....	....	....	....	....	....	....
1991-92	HK Khimik	CIS	27	1	4	5	24	....	....	....	....	....	....	....	....	....	....	....	....	....	....	....	....	....	....	....
	Winnipeg	NHL	27	2	9	11	67	0	0	0	23	8.7	5	....	....	....	....	....	7	0	0	0	39	0	0	0
	Moncton Hawks	AHL	3	0	1	1	16	....	....	....	....	....	....	....	....	....	....	....	....	....	....	....	....	....	....	....
1992-93	Winnipeg	NHL	56	2	14	16	124	0	0	0	26	7.7	6	....	....	....	....	....	4	0	0	0	4	0	0	0
	Moncton Hawks	AHL	9	1	3	4	26	....	....	....	....	....	....	....	....	....	....	....	....	....	....	....	....	....	....	....
	Fort Wayne	IHL	3	0	1	1	29	....	....	....	....	....	....	....	....	....	....	....	....	....	....	....	....	....	....	....
1993-94	Winnipeg	NHL	74	0	17	17	165	0	0	0	46	0.0	–11	....	....	....	....	....	....	....	....	....	....	....	....	....
1994-95	Winnipeg	NHL	19	1	3	4	27	0	0	0	13	7.7	–2	....	....	....	....	....	....	....	....	....	....	....	....	....
	Washington	NHL	3	0	1	1	2	0	0	0	0	0.0	3	....	....	....	....	....	2	0	0	0	4	0	0	0
1995-96	Chicago	NHL	53	1	8	9	92	0	0	0	24	4.2	12	....	....	....	....	....	....	....	....	....	....	....	....	....
	Indianapolis Ice	IHL	1	0	0	0	0	....	....	....	....	....	....	....	....	....	....	....	....	....	....	....	....	....	....	....
	Tampa Bay	NHL	11	2	1	3	24	0	0	1	13	15.4	–1	....	....	....	....	....	5	0	0	0	15	0	0	0
1996-97	Tampa Bay	NHL	59	1	7	8	108	0	0	0	56	1.8	2	....	....	....	....	....	....	....	....	....	....	....	....	....
1997-98	Tampa Bay	NHL	45	2	7	9	85	1	0	0	32	6.3	–5	....	....	....	....	....	....	....	....	....	....	....	....	....
	Montreal	NHL	4	0	1	1	12	0	0	0	4	0.0	–2	....	....	....	....	....	10	1	4	5	12	0	0	0
1998-99	Montreal	NHL	76	3	9	12	109	0	0	0	55	5.5	–3	0	0.0	136	163	17:35	....	....	....	....	....	....	....	....
99-2000	Montreal	NHL	43	1	5	6	76	0	0	0	33	3.0	–11	0	0.0	79	86	16:33	....	....	....	....	....	....	....	....
	Edmonton	NHL	14	0	3	3	10	0	0	0	6	0.0	–3	0	0.0	20	21	16:23	5	0	0	0	6	0	0	0
	NHL Totals		484	15	85	100	901	1	0	1	331	4.5		0	0.0	235	270	17:08	33	1	4	5	80	0	0	0

Traded to **Washington** by **Winnipeg** with Mike Eagles for Washington's 3rd (later traded to Dallas - Dallas selected Sergei Gusev) and 5th (Brian Elder) round choices in 1995 Entry Draft, April 7, 1995. Traded to **Chicago** by **Washington** for Chicago's 3rd round choice (Dave Weninger) in 1996 Entry Draft, October 17, 1995. Traded to **Tampa Bay** by **Chicago** with Patrick Poulin and Chicago's 2nd round choice (later traded to New Jersey - New Jersey selected Pierre Dagenais) in 1996 Entry Draft for Enrico Ciccone and Tampa Bay's 2nd round choice (Jeff Paul) in 1996 Entry Draft, March 20, 1996. Traded to **Montreal** by **Tampa Bay** with Patrick Poulin and Mick Vukota for Stephane Richer, Darcy Tucker and David Wilkie, January 15, 1998. Traded to **Edmonton** by **Montreal** with Alain Nasreddine for Christian Laflamme and Matthieu Descoteaux, March 9, 2000.

USTORF, Stefan

(OOSH-tohrf, SHTEH-fuhn) **WSH.**

Center. Shoots left. 6', 195 lbs. Born, Kaufbeuren, Germany, January 3, 1974. Washington's 3rd choice, 53rd overall, in 1992 Entry Draft.

Season	Club	League	GP	G	A	Pts	PIM	PP	SH	GW	S	%	+/–	TF	F%	H	SB	Min	Playoffs GP	G	A	Pts	PIM	PP	SH	GW
1989-90	ESV Kaufbeuren	DEL-Jr.	8	10	11	21	8	....	....	....	....	....	....	....	....	....	....	....	....	....	....	....	....	....	....	....
1990-91	ESV Kaufbeuren	DEL-Jr.	37	33	34	67	78	....	....	....	....	....	....	....	....	....	....	....	....	....	....	....	....	....	....	....
1991-92	ESV Kaufbeuren	DEL	41	2	22	24	46	....	....	....	....	....	....	....	....	....	....	....	5	2	7	9	6	....	....	....
1992-93	ESV Kaufbeuren	DEL	37	14	18	32	32	....	....	....	....	....	....	....	....	....	....	....	3	1	0	1	10	....	....	....
1993-94	ESV Kaufbeuren	DEL	38	10	20	30	21	....	....	....	....	....	....	....	....	....	....	....	3	0	0	0	4	....	....	....
	Germany	Olympics	8	1	2	3	2	....	....	....	....	....	....	....	....	....	....	....	....	....	....	....	....	....	....	....
1994-95	Portland Pirates	AHL	63	21	38	59	51	....	....	....	....	....	....	....	....	....	....	....	7	1	6	7	7	....	....	....
1995-96	Washington	NHL	48	7	10	17	14	0	0	1	39	17.9	8	....	....	....	....	....	5	0	0	0	0	0	0	0
	Portland Pirates	AHL	8	1	4	5	6	....	....	....	....	....	....	....	....	....	....	....	....	....	....	....	....	....	....	....
1996-97	Washington	NHL	6	0	0	0	2	0	0	0	7	0.0	–3	....	....	....	....	....	....	....	....	....	....	....	....	....
	Portland Pirates	AHL	36	7	17	24	27	....	....	....	....	....	....	....	....	....	....	....	....	....	....	....	....	....	....	....
1997-98	Berlin Capitals	DEL	45	17	23	40	54	....	....	....	....	....	....	....	....	....	....	....	....	....	....	....	....	....	....	....
	Germany	Olympics	4	0	0	0	0	....	....	....	....	....	....	....	....	....	....	....	....	....	....	....	....	....	....	....
1998-99	Las Vegas	IHL	40	11	17	28	40	....	....	....	....	....	....	....	....	....	....	....	....	....	....	....	....	....	....	....
	Detroit Vipers	IHL	14	3	7	10	11	....	....	....	....	....	....	....	....	....	....	....	11	4	7	11	2	....	....	....
99-2000	Cincinnati	IHL	79	20	34	54	53	....	....	....	....	....	....	....	....	....	....	....	11	1	4	5	10	....	....	....
	NHL Totals		54	7	10	17	16	0	0	1	46	15.2		....	....	....	....	....	5	0	0	0	0	0	0	0

Signed as a free agent by **Cincinnati** (IHL), September 29, 1999. Signed as a free agent by **Washington**, July 13, 2000.

VAIC, Lubomir

(VIGHTZ, LEW-boh-MEER) **VAN.**

Center. Shoots left. 5'9", 178 lbs. Born, Spisska Nova Ves, Czech., March 6, 1977. Vancouver's 8th choice, 227th overall, in 1996 Entry Draft.

Season	Club	League	GP	G	A	Pts	PIM	PP	SH	GW	S	%	+/–	TF	F%	H	SB	Min	Playoffs GP	G	A	Pts	PIM	PP	SH	GW
1993-94	SKP Poprad	Slovakia	28	10	6	16	10	....	....	....	....	....	....	....	....	....	....	....	....	....	....	....	....	....	....	....
1994-95	VTJ Spisska	Slovakia	19	5	4	9	2	....	....	....	....	....	....	....	....	....	....	....	....	....	....	....	....	....	....	....
1995-96	VSV Kosice	Slovakia	36	7	19	26	10	....	....	....	....	....	....	....	....	....	....	....	13	0	7	7		....	....	....
1996-97	VSV Kosice	Slovakia	36	13	12	25		....	....	....	....	....	....	....	....	....	....	....	7	2	0	2		....	....	....
1997-98	Vancouver	NHL	5	1	1	2	2	0	0	0	8	12.5	–2	....	....	....	....	....	....	....	....	....	....	....	....	....
	Syracuse Crunch	AHL	50	12	15	27	22	....	....	....	....	....	....	....	....	....	....	....	3	0	0	0	4	....	....	....
1998-99	VTJ Spisska	Slovakia	35	20	22	42	42	....	....	....	....	....	....	....	....	....	....	....	....	....	....	....	....	....	....	....
	VSV Kosice	Slovakia	....	....	....	....	....	....	....	....	....	....	....	....	....	....	....	....	11	2	3	5	8	....	....	....

			Regular Season																Playoffs							
Season	Club	League	GP	G	A	Pts	PIM	PP	SH	GW	S	%	+/–	TF	F%	H	SB	Min	GP	G	A	Pts	PIM	PP	SH	GW
99-2000	Vancouver	NHL	4	0	0	0	0	0	0	0	2	0.0	0	30	46.7	4	0	7:28	....	....	....	....	....	....	....	....
	Syracuse Crunch	AHL	63	13	29	42	42	....	....	....	....	....	....	....	....	....	....	....	4	0	3	3	8	....	....	....
	NHL Totals		9	1	1	2	2	0	0	0	10	10.0		30	46.7	4	0	7:28	....	....	....	....	....	....	....	....

VALICEVIC, Robert

(val-IH-seh-VIK, RAW-buhrt) **NSH.**

Right wing. Shoots right. 6'1", 198 lbs. Born, Detroit, MI, January 6, 1971. NY Islanders' 6th choice, 114th overall, in 1991 Entry Draft.

Season	Club	League	GP	G	A	Pts	PIM	PP	SH	GW	S	%	+/–	TF	F%	H	SB	Min	GP	G	A	Pts	PIM	PP	SH	GW
1990-91	Detroit	NAJHL	39	31	44	75	54	....	....	....	....	....	....	....	....	....	....	....	....	....	....	....	....	....	....	....
1991-92	Lake Superior	CCHA	32	8	4	12	12	....	....	....	....	....	....	....	....	....	....	....	....	....	....	....	....	....	....	....
1992-93	Lake Superior	CCHA	43	21	20	41	28	....	....	....	....	....	....	....	....	....	....	....	....	....	....	....	....	....	....	....
1993-94	Lake Superior	CCHA	45	18	20	38	46	....	....	....	....	....	....	....	....	....	....	....	....	....	....	....	....	....	....	....
1994-95	Lake Superior	CCHA	37	10	21	31	40	....	....	....	....	....	....	....	....	....	....	....	....	....	....	....	....	....	....	....
1995-96	Louisiana Gators	ECHL	60	42	20	62	85	....	....	....	....	....	....	....	....	....	....	....	5	2	3	5	8	....	....	....
	Springfield	AHL	2	0	0	0	2	....	....	....	....	....	....	....	....	....	....	....	....	....	....	....	....	....	....	....
1996-97	Louisiana Gators	ECHL	8	7	2	9	21	....	....	....	....	....	....	....	....	....	....	....	....	....	....	....	....	....	....	....
	Houston Aeros	IHL	58	11	12	23	42	....	....	....	....	....	....	....	....	....	....	....	12	1	3	4	11	....	....	....
1997-98	Houston Aeros	IHL	72	29	28	57	47	....	....	....	....	....	....	....	....	....	....	....	4	2	0	2	2	....	....	....
1998-99	**Nashville**	**NHL**	**19**	**4**	**2**	**6**	**2**	**0**	**0**	**2**	**23**	**17.4**	**4**	**17**	**29.4**	**8**	**8**	**11:01**	....	....	....	....	....	....	....	....
	Houston Aeros	IHL	57	16	33	49	62	....	....	....	....	....	....	....	....	....	....	....	19	7	10	17	8	....	....	....
99-2000	**Nashville**	**NHL**	**80**	**14**	**11**	**25**	**21**	**2**	**1**	**3**	**113**	**12.4**	**–11**	**50**	**44.0**	**100**	**38**	**14:31**	....	....	....	....	....	....	....	....
	NHL Totals		**99**	**18**	**13**	**31**	**23**	**2**	**1**	**5**	**136**	**13.2**		**67**	**40.3**	**108**	**46**	**13:50**	....	....	....	....	....	....	....	....

Signed as a free agent by **Nashville**, May 28, 1998.

VALK, Garry

(VAHLK, GAIR-ee) **TOR.**

Right wing. Shoots left. 6'1", 200 lbs. Born, Edmonton, Alta., November 27, 1967. Vancouver's 5th choice, 108th overall, in 1987 Entry Draft.

Season	Club	League	GP	G	A	Pts	PIM	PP	SH	GW	S	%	+/–	TF	F%	H	SB	Min	GP	G	A	Pts	PIM	PP	SH	GW
1984-85	Sherwood Park	AJHL	55	20	22	42	46	....	....	....	....	....	....	....	....	....	....	....	....	....	....	....	....	....	....	....
1985-86	Sherwood Park	AJHL	40	20	26	46	116	....	....	....	....	....	....	....	....	....	....	....	....	....	....	....	....	....	....	....
1986-87	Sherwood Park	AJHL	59	42	44	86	204	....	....	....	....	....	....	....	....	....	....	....	....	....	....	....	....	....	....	....
1987-88	North Dakota	WCHA	38	23	12	35	64	....	....	....	....	....	....	....	....	....	....	....	....	....	....	....	....	....	....	....
1988-89	North Dakota	WCHA	40	14	17	31	71	....	....	....	....	....	....	....	....	....	....	....	....	....	....	....	....	....	....	....
1989-90	North Dakota	WCHA	43	22	17	39	92	....	....	....	....	....	....	....	....	....	....	....	....	....	....	....	....	....	....	....
1990-91	**Vancouver**	**NHL**	**59**	**10**	**11**	**21**	**67**	**1**	**0**	**1**	**90**	**11.1**	**–23**	....	....	....	....	....	**5**	**0**	**0**	**0**	**20**	**0**	**0**	**0**
	Milwaukee	IHL	10	12	4	16	13	....	....	....	....	....	....	....	....	....	....	....	3	0	0	0	2	....	....	....
1991-92	**Vancouver**	**NHL**	**65**	**8**	**17**	**25**	**56**	**2**	**1**	**2**	**93**	**8.6**	**3**	....	....	....	....	....	**4**	**0**	**0**	**0**	**5**	**0**	**0**	**0**
1992-93	**Vancouver**	**NHL**	**48**	**6**	**7**	**13**	**77**	**0**	**0**	**2**	**46**	**13.0**	**6**	....	....	....	....	....	**7**	**0**	**1**	**1**	**12**	**0**	**0**	**0**
	Hamilton Canucks	AHL	7	3	6	9	6	....	....	....	....	....	....	....	....	....	....	....	....	....	....	....	....	....	....	....
1993-94	**Anaheim**	**NHL**	**78**	**18**	**27**	**45**	**100**	**4**	**1**	**5**	**165**	**10.9**	**8**	....	....	....	....	....	....	....	....	....	....	....	....	....
1994-95	**Anaheim**	**NHL**	**36**	**3**	**6**	**9**	**34**	**0**	**0**	**0**	**53**	**5.7**	**–4**	....	....	....	....	....	....	....	....	....	....	....	....	....
1995-96	**Anaheim**	**NHL**	**79**	**12**	**12**	**24**	**125**	**1**	**1**	**2**	**108**	**11.1**	**8**	....	....	....	....	....	....	....	....	....	....	....	....	....
1996-97	**Anaheim**	**NHL**	**53**	**7**	**7**	**14**	**53**	**0**	**0**	**1**	**68**	**10.3**	**–2**	....	....	....	....	....	....	....	....	....	....	....	....	....
	Pittsburgh	**NHL**	**17**	**3**	**4**	**7**	**25**	**0**	**0**	**0**	**32**	**9.4**	**–6**	....	....	....	....	....	....	....	....	....	....	....	....	....
1997-98	**Pittsburgh**	**NHL**	**39**	**2**	**1**	**3**	**33**	**0**	**0**	**0**	**32**	**6.3**	**–3**	....	....	....	....	....	....	....	....	....	....	....	....	....
1998-99	**Toronto**	**NHL**	**77**	**8**	**21**	**29**	**53**	**1**	**0**	**0**	**93**	**8.6**	**8**	**19**	**36.8**	**99**	**20**	**13:53**	**17**	**3**	**4**	**7**	**22**	**0**	**0**	**1**
99-2000	**Toronto**	**NHL**	**73**	**10**	**14**	**24**	**44**	**0**	**1**	**1**	**91**	**11.0**	**–2**	**10**	**30.0**	**109**	**14**	**12:51**	**12**	**1**	**2**	**3**	**14**	**0**	**0**	**0**
	NHL Totals		**624**	**87**	**127**	**214**	**667**	**9**	**4**	**14**	**871**	**10.0**		**29**	**34.5**	**208**	**34**	**13:23**	**45**	**4**	**7**	**11**	**73**	**0**	**0**	**1**

Claimed by **Anaheim** from **Vancouver** in NHL Waiver Draft, October 3, 1993. Traded to **Pittsburgh** by **Anaheim** for Jean-Jacques Daigneault, February 21, 1997. Signed as a free agent by **Toronto**, October 8, 1998.

VAN ALLEN, Shaun

(VAN-AL-ehn, SHAWN) **DAL.**

Center. Shoots left. 6'1", 204 lbs. Born, Calgary, Alta., August 29, 1967. Edmonton's 5th choice, 105th overall, in 1987 Entry Draft.

Season	Club	League	GP	G	A	Pts	PIM	PP	SH	GW	S	%	+/–	TF	F%	H	SB	Min	GP	G	A	Pts	PIM	PP	SH	GW
1984-85	Swift Current	SJHL	61	12	20	32	136	....	....	....	....	....	....	....	....	....	....	....	....	....	....	....	....	....	....	....
1985-86	Saskatoon Blades	WHL	55	12	11	23	43	....	....	....	....	....	....	....	....	....	....	....	13	4	8	12	28	....	....	....
1986-87	Saskatoon Blades	WHL	72	38	59	97	116	....	....	....	....	....	....	....	....	....	....	....	11	4	6	10	24	....	....	....
1987-88	Milwaukee	IHL	40	14	28	42	34	....	....	....	....	....	....	....	....	....	....	....	....	....	....	....	....	....	....	....
	Nova Scotia	AHL	19	4	10	14	17	....	....	....	....	....	....	....	....	....	....	....	4	1	1	2	4	....	....	....
1988-89	Cape Breton	AHL	76	32	42	74	81	....	....	....	....	....	....	....	....	....	....	....	....	....	....	....	....	....	....	....
1989-90	Cape Breton	AHL	61	25	44	69	83	....	....	....	....	....	....	....	....	....	....	....	4	0	2	2	8	....	....	....
1990-91	**Edmonton**	**NHL**	**2**	**0**	**0**	**0**	**0**	**0**	**0**	**0**	**0**	**0.0**	**0**	....	....	....	....	....	....	....	....	....	....	....	....	....
	Cape Breton	AHL	76	25	75	100	182	....	....	....	....	....	....	....	....	....	....	....	4	0	1	1	8	....	....	....
1991-92	Cape Breton	AHL	77	29	*84	*113	80	....	....	....	....	....	....	....	....	....	....	....	5	3	7	10	14	....	....	....
1992-93	**Edmonton**	**NHL**	**21**	**1**	**4**	**5**	**6**	**0**	**0**	**0**	**19**	**5.3**	**–2**	....	....	....	....	....	....	....	....	....	....	....	....	....
	Cape Breton	AHL	43	14	62	76	68	....	....	....	....	....	....	....	....	....	....	....	15	8	9	17	18	....	....	....
1993-94	**Anaheim**	**NHL**	**80**	**8**	**25**	**33**	**64**	**2**	**2**	**1**	**104**	**7.7**	**0**	....	....	....	....	....	....	....	....	....	....	....	....	....
1994-95	**Anaheim**	**NHL**	**45**	**8**	**21**	**29**	**32**	**1**	**1**	**1**	**68**	**11.8**	**–4**	....	....	....	....	....	....	....	....	....	....	....	....	....
1995-96	**Anaheim**	**NHL**	**49**	**8**	**17**	**25**	**41**	**0**	**0**	**2**	**78**	**10.3**	**13**	....	....	....	....	....	....	....	....	....	....	....	....	....
1996-97	**Ottawa**	**NHL**	**80**	**11**	**14**	**25**	**35**	**1**	**1**	**2**	**123**	**8.9**	**–8**	....	....	....	....	....	**7**	**0**	**1**	**1**	**4**	**0**	**0**	**0**
1997-98	**Ottawa**	**NHL**	**80**	**4**	**15**	**19**	**48**	**0**	**0**	**0**	**104**	**3.8**	**4**	....	....	....	....	....	**11**	**0**	**1**	**1**	**10**	**0**	**0**	**0**
1998-99	**Ottawa**	**NHL**	**79**	**6**	**11**	**17**	**30**	**0**	**1**	**0**	**47**	**12.8**	**3**	**656**	**47.4**	**84**	**23**	**11:07**	**4**	**0**	**0**	**0**	**0**	**0**	**0**	**0**
99-2000	**Ottawa**	**NHL**	**75**	**9**	**19**	**28**	**37**	**0**	**2**	**4**	**75**	**12.0**	**20**	**911**	**48.6**	**119**	**35**	**11:49**	**6**	**0**	**1**	**1**	**9**	**0**	**0**	**0**
	NHL Totals		**511**	**55**	**126**	**181**	**293**	**4**	**7**	**10**	**618**	**8.9**		**1567**	**48.1**	**203**	**58**	**11:27**	**28**	**0**	**3**	**3**	**23**	**0**	**0**	**0**

AHL Second All-Star Team (1991) • AHL First All-Star Team (1992) • Won John B. Sollenberger Trophy (Top Scorer - AHL) (1992)

Signed as a free agent by **Anaheim**, July 22, 1993. Traded to **Ottawa** by **Anaheim** with Jason York for Ted Drury and the rights to Marc Moro, October 1, 1996. Signed as a free agent by **Dallas**, July 12, 2000.

VANDENBUSSCHE, Ryan

(van-dehn-BUHSH, RIGH-yan) **CHI.**

Right wing. Shoots right. 6', 200 lbs. Born, Simcoe, Ont., February 28, 1973. Toronto's 9th choice, 173rd overall, in 1992 Entry Draft.

Season	Club	League	GP	G	A	Pts	PIM	PP	SH	GW	S	%	+/–	TF	F%	H	SB	Min	GP	G	A	Pts	PIM	PP	SH	GW
1988-89	Delhi Flames	OJHL-D	3	1	1	2	2	....	....	....	....	....	....	....	....	....	....	....	....	....	....	....	....	....	....	....
1989-90	Norwich	OJHL-C	21	12	10	22	146	....	....	....	....	....	....	....	....	....	....	....	....	....	....	....	....	....	....	....
	Tillsonburg Titans	OJHL-B	24	0	5	5	113	....	....	....	....	....	....	....	....	....	....	....	....	....	....	....	....	....	....	....
1990-91	Massena	OJHL	10	2	3	5	46	....	....	....	....	....	....	....	....	....	....	....	....	....	....	....	....	....	....	....
	Cornwall Royals	OHL	49	3	8	11	139	....	....	....	....	....	....	....	....	....	....	....	....	....	....	....	....	....	....	....
1991-92	Cornwall Royals	OHL	61	13	15	28	232	....	....	....	....	....	....	....	....	....	....	....	6	0	2	2	9	....	....	....
1992-93	Newmarket	OHL	30	15	12	27	161	....	....	....	....	....	....	....	....	....	....	....	....	....	....	....	....	....	....	....
	Guelph Storm	OHL	29	3	14	17	99	....	....	....	....	....	....	....	....	....	....	....	5	1	3	4	13	....	....	....
	St. John's Leafs	AHL	1	0	0	0	0	....	....	....	....	....	....	....	....	....	....	....	....	....	....	....	....	....	....	....
1993-94	St. John's Leafs	AHL	44	4	10	14	124	....	....	....	....	....	....	....	....	....	....	....	....	....	....	....	....	....	....	....
	Springfield	AHL	9	1	2	3	29	....	....	....	....	....	....	....	....	....	....	....	5	0	0	0	16	....	....	....
1994-95	St. John's Leafs	AHL	53	2	13	15	239	....	....	....	....	....	....	....	....	....	....	....	3	0	0	0	17	....	....	....
1995-96	Binghamton	AHL	68	3	17	20	240	....	....	....	....	....	....	....	....	....	....	....	4	0	0	0	9	....	....	....
1996-97	**NY Rangers**	**NHL**	**11**	**1**	**0**	**1**	**30**	**0**	**0**	**0**	**4**	**25.0**	**–2**	....	....	....	....	....	....	....	....	....	....	....	....	....
	Binghamton	AHL	38	8	11	19	133	....	....	....	....	....	....	....	....	....	....	....	....	....	....	....	....	....	....	....
1997-98	**NY Rangers**	**NHL**	**16**	**1**	**0**	**1**	**38**	**0**	**0**	**0**	**2**	**50.0**	**–2**	....	....	....	....	....	....	....	....	....	....	....	....	....
	Hartford	AHL	15	2	0	2	45	....	....	....	....	....	....	....	....	....	....	....	....	....	....	....	....	....	....	....
	Chicago	**NHL**	**4**	**0**	**1**	**1**	**5**	**0**	**0**	**0**	**0**	**0.0**	**0**	....	....	....	....	....	....	....	....	....	....	....	....	....
	Indianapolis Ice	IHL	3	1	1	2	4	....	....	....	....	....	....	....	....	....	....	....	....	....	....	....	....	....	....	....
1998-99	**Chicago**	**NHL**	**6**	**0**	**0**	**0**	**17**	**0**	**0**	**0**	**3**	**0.0**	**0**	**0**	**0.0**	**13**	**2**	**9:29**	....	....	....	....	....	....	....	....
	Indianapolis Ice	IHL	34	3	10	13	130	....	....	....	....	....	....	....	....	....	....	....	....	....	....	....	....	....	....	....
	Portland Pirates	AHL	37	4	1	5	119	....	....	....	....	....	....	....	....	....	....	....	....	....	....	....	....	....	....	....
99-2000	**Chicago**	**NHL**	**52**	**0**	**1**	**1**	**143**	**0**	**0**	**0**	**19**	**0.0**	**–3**	**3**	**0.0**	**68**	**3**	**5:37**	....	....	....	....	....	....	....	....
	NHL Totals		**89**	**2**	**2**	**4**	**233**	**0**	**0**	**0**	**28**	**7.1**		**3**	**0.0**	**81**	**5**	**6:01**	....	....	....	....	....	....	....	....

Signed as a free agent by **NY Rangers**, August 22, 1995. Traded to **Chicago** by **NY Rangers** for Ryan Risidore, March 24, 1998.

VAN DRUNEN, David

van-DREW-ehn, DAY-vihd)

Defense. Shoots right. 6', 204 lbs. Born, Sherwood Park, Alta., January 31, 1976.

Season	Club	League	Regular Season GP	G	A	Pts	PIM	PP	SH	GW	S	%	+/-	TF	F%	H	SB	Min	Playoffs GP	G	A	Pts	PIM	PP	SH	GW
1992-93	Sherwood Park	AAHA	32	3	16	19	114	....	....	....	....	....	....	....	....	....	....	....	....	....	....	....	....	....	....	....
1993-94	Prince Albert	WHL	63	3	10	13	95	....	....	....	....	....	....	....	....	....	....	....	....	....	....	....	....	....	....	....
1994-95	Prince Albert	WHL	71	2	14	16	132	....	....	....	....	....	....	....	....	....	....	....	15	3	4	7	36	....	....	....
1995-96	Prince Albert	WHL	70	10	23	33	172	....	....	....	....	....	....	....	....	....	....	....	18	1	5	6	37	....	....	....
1996-97	Prince Albert	WHL	72	18	47	65	218	....	....	....	....	....	....	....	....	....	....	....	4	0	4	4	24	....	....	....
1997-98	Hershey Bears	AHL	5	0	0	0	2	....	....	....	....	....	....	....	....	....	....	....	....	....	....	....	....	....	....	....
	Portland Pirates	AHL	4	0	0	0	2	....	....	....	....	....	....	....	....	....	....	....	....	....	....	....	....	....	....	....
	Baton Rouge	ECHL	59	8	22	30	107	....	....	....	....	....	....	....	....	....	....	....	....	....	....	....	....	....	....	....
	Detroit Vipers	IHL	1	0	0	0	2	....	....	....	....	....	....	....	....	....	....	....	....	....	....	....	....	....	....	....
1998-99	Saginaw Gears	UHL	63	5	17	22	107	....	....	....	....	....	....	....	....	....	....	....	....	....	....	....	....	....	....	....
	Cincinnati	IHL	1	0	0	0	0	....	....	....	....	....	....	....	....	....	....	....	....	....	....	....	....	....	....	....
	Dayton Bombers	ECHL	9	2	4	6	12	....	....	....	....	....	....	....	....	....	....	....	4	0	0	0	12	....	....	....
99-2000	**Ottawa**	**NHL**	**1**	**0**	**0**	**0**	**0**	**0**	**0**	**0**	**0**	**0.0**	**0**	**0**	**0.0**	**2**	**0**	**4:38**	....	....	....	....	....	....	....	....
	Grand Rapids	IHL	36	0	6	6	76	....	....	....	....	....	....	....	....	....	....	....	1	0	0	0	2	....	....	....
	Mobile Mysticks	ECHL	29	1	9	10	78	....	....	....	....	....	....	....	....	....	....	....	5	1	1	2	14	....	....	....
	NHL Totals		**1**	**0**	**0**	**0**	**0**	**0**	**0**	**0**	**0**	**0.0**		**0**	**0.0**	**2**	**0**	**4:38**	....	....	....	....	....	....	....	....

WHL East Second All-Star Team (1997)

Signed as a free agent by **Ottawa**, May 2, 1997.

VAN IMPE, Darren

(van-IHMP, DAIR-ehn) **BOS.**

Defense. Shoots left. 6'1", 205 lbs. Born, Saskatoon, Sask., May 18, 1973. NY Islanders' 7th choice, 170th overall, in 1993 Entry Draft.

Season	Club	League	GP	G	A	Pts	PIM	PP	SH	GW	S	%	+/-	TF	F%	H	SB	Min	GP	G	A	Pts	PIM	PP	SH	GW
1989-90	Prince Albert	AAHA	32	16	31	47	100	....	....	....	....	....	....	....	....	....	....	....	....	....	....	....	....	....	....	....
	Prince Albert	WHL	1	0	1	1	0	....	....	....	....	....	....	....	....	....	....	....	....	....	....	....	....	....	....	....
1990-91	Prince Albert	WHL	70	15	45	60	57	....	....	....	....	....	....	....	....	....	....	....	3	1	1	2	2	....	....	....
1991-92	Prince Albert	WHL	69	9	37	46	89	....	....	....	....	....	....	....	....	....	....	....	8	1	5	6	10	....	....	....
1992-93	Red Deer Rebels	WHL	54	23	47	70	118	....	....	....	....	....	....	....	....	....	....	....	4	2	5	7	16	....	....	....
1993-94	Red Deer Rebels	WHL	58	20	64	84	125	....	....	....	....	....	....	....	....	....	....	....	4	2	4	6	6	....	....	....
1994-95	San Diego Gulls	IHL	76	6	17	23	74	....	....	....	....	....	....	....	....	....	....	....	5	0	0	0	0	....	....	....
	Anaheim	**NHL**	**1**	**0**	**1**	**1**	**4**	**0**	**0**	**0**	**0**	**0.0**	**0**	....	....	....	....	....	....	....	....	....	....	....	....	....
1995-96	**Anaheim**	**NHL**	**16**	**1**	**2**	**3**	**14**	**0**	**0**	**1**	**13**	**7.7**	**8**	....	....	....	....	....	....	....	....	....	....	....	....	....
	Baltimore Bandits	AHL	63	11	47	58	79	....	....	....	....	....	....	....	....	....	....	....	....	....	....	....	....	....	....	....
1996-97	**Anaheim**	**NHL**	**74**	**4**	**19**	**23**	**90**	**2**	**0**	**0**	**107**	**3.7**	**3**	....	....	....	....	....	**9**	**0**	**2**	**2**	**16**	**0**	**0**	**0**
1997-98	**Anaheim**	**NHL**	**19**	**1**	**3**	**4**	**4**	**0**	**0**	**0**	**21**	**4.8**	**−10**	....	....	....	....	....	....	....	....	....	....	....	....	....
	Boston	**NHL**	**50**	**2**	**8**	**10**	**36**	**2**	**0**	**0**	**50**	**4.0**	**4**	....	....	....	....	....	**6**	**2**	**1**	**3**	**0**	**1**	**0**	**1**
1998-99	**Boston**	**NHL**	**60**	**5**	**15**	**20**	**66**	**4**	**0**	**0**	**92**	**5.4**	**−5**	**0**	**0.0**	**45**	**60**	**17:54**	**11**	**1**	**2**	**3**	**4**	**1**	**0**	**0**
99-2000	**Boston**	**NHL**	**79**	**5**	**23**	**28**	**73**	**4**	**0**	**0**	**97**	**5.2**	**−19**	**0**	**0.0**	**93**	**87**	**19:31**	....	....	....	....	....	....	....	....
	NHL Totals		**299**	**18**	**71**	**89**	**287**	**12**	**0**	**1**	**380**	**4.7**		**0**	**0.0**	**138**	**147**	**18:49**	**26**	**3**	**5**	**8**	**20**	**2**	**0**	**1**

WHL East First All-Star Team (1993, 1994)

Traded to **Anaheim** by **NY Islanders** for Anaheim's 8th round choice (Mike Broda) in 1995 Entry Draft, August 31, 1994. Claimed on waivers by **Boston** from **Anaheim**, November 26, 1997.

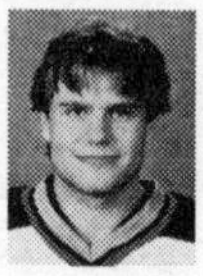

VARADA, Vaclav

(VAH-rah-dah, vah-KLAHV) **BUF.**

Right wing. Shoots left. 6', 214 lbs. Born, Vsetin, Czech., April 26, 1976. San Jose's 4th choice, 89th overall, in 1994 Entry Draft.

Season	Club	League	GP	G	A	Pts	PIM	PP	SH	GW	S	%	+/-	TF	F%	H	SB	Min	GP	G	A	Pts	PIM	PP	SH	GW
1993-94	HC Vitkovice	Cze-Rep	24	6	7	13	....	....	....	....	....	....	....	....	....	....	....	....	5	1	1	2	....	....	....	....
1994-95	Tacoma Rockets	WHL	68	50	38	88	108	....	....	....	....	....	....	....	....	....	....	....	4	4	3	7	11	....	....	....
1995-96	Kelowna Rockets	WHL	59	39	46	85	100	....	....	....	....	....	....	....	....	....	....	....	6	3	3	6	16	....	....	....
	Buffalo	**NHL**	**1**	**0**	**0**	**0**	**0**	**0**	**0**	**0**	**2**	**0.0**	**0**	....	....	....	....	....	....	....	....	....	....	....	....	....
	Rochester	AHL	5	3	0	3	4	....	....	....	....	....	....	....	....	....	....	....	....	....	....	....	....	....	....	....
1996-97	**Buffalo**	**NHL**	**5**	**0**	**0**	**0**	**2**	**0**	**0**	**0**	**2**	**0.0**	**0**	....	....	....	....	....	....	....	....	....	....	....	....	....
	Rochester	AHL	53	23	25	48	81	....	....	....	....	....	....	....	....	....	....	....	10	1	6	7	27	....	....	....
1997-98	**Buffalo**	**NHL**	**27**	**5**	**6**	**11**	**15**	**0**	**0**	**1**	**27**	**18.5**	**0**	....	....	....	....	....	**15**	**3**	**4**	**7**	**18**	**0**	**0**	**0**
	Rochester	AHL	45	30	26	56	74	....	....	....	....	....	....	....	....	....	....	....	....	....	....	....	....	....	....	....
1998-99	**Buffalo**	**NHL**	**72**	**7**	**24**	**31**	**61**	**1**	**0**	**1**	**123**	**5.7**	**11**	**1**	**0.0**	**185**	**12**	**14:30**	**21**	**5**	**4**	**9**	**14**	**1**	**0**	**0**
99-2000	HC Vitkovice	Cze-Rep	5	2	3	5	12	....	....	....	....	....	....	....	....	....	....	....	....	....	....	....	....	....	....	....
	Buffalo	**NHL**	**76**	**10**	**27**	**37**	**62**	**0**	**0**	**0**	**140**	**7.1**	**12**	**1**	**0.0**	**150**	**16**	**14:58**	**5**	**0**	**0**	**0**	**8**	**0**	**0**	**0**
	NHL Totals		**181**	**22**	**57**	**79**	**140**	**1**	**0**	**2**	**294**	**7.5**		**2**	**0.0**	**335**	**28**	**14:44**	**41**	**8**	**8**	**16**	**40**	**1**	**0**	**0**

Traded to **Buffalo** by **San Jose** with Martin Spahnel and Philadelphia's 1st (previously acquired by San Jose - later traded to Phoenix - Phoenix selected Daniel Briere) and 4th (previously acquired, Buffalo selected Mike Martone) round choices in 1996 Entry Draft for Doug Bodger, November 16, 1995.

VARIS, Petri

(VAH-rihs, PEE-tree)

Left wing. Shoots left. 6'1", 200 lbs. Born, Varkaus, Finland, May 13, 1969. San Jose's 7th choice, 132nd overall, in 1993 Entry Draft.

Season	Club	League	GP	G	A	Pts	PIM	PP	SH	GW	S	%	+/-	TF	F%	H	SB	Min	GP	G	A	Pts	PIM	PP	SH	GW
1986-87	Karhu Kissat	Finn-Jr.	2	0	1	1	0	....	....	....	....	....	....	....	....	....	....	....	....	....	....	....	....	....	....	....
1987-88	Karhu Kissat	Finland-2	42	9	15	24	21	....	....	....	....	....	....	....	....	....	....	....	....	....	....	....	....	....	....	....
1988-89	Karhu Kissat	Finn-Jr.	7	4	5	9	10	....	....	....	....	....	....	....	....	....	....	....	....	....	....	....	....	....	....	....
	Karhu Kissat	Finland-2	44	18	19	37	26	....	....	....	....	....	....	....	....	....	....	....	....	....	....	....	....	....	....	....
1989-90	Karhu Kissat	Finland-2	42	30	24	54	44	....	....	....	....	....	....	....	....	....	....	....	....	....	....	....	....	....	....	....
1990-91	KooKoo Kouvola	Finland-2	44	20	31	51	42	....	....	....	....	....	....	....	....	....	....	....	....	....	....	....	....	....	....	....
1991-92	Assat-Pori	Finland	36	13	23	36	24	....	....	....	....	....	....	....	....	....	....	....	....	....	....	....	....	....	....	....
1992-93	Assat-Pori	Finland	46	14	35	49	42	....	....	....	....	....	....	....	....	....	....	....	8	2	2	4	12	....	....	....
1993-94	Jokerit Helsinki	Finland	31	14	15	29	16	....	....	....	....	....	....	....	....	....	....	....	11	3	4	7	6	....	....	....
	Finland	Olympics	5	1	1	2	2	....	....	....	....	....	....	....	....	....	....	....	....	....	....	....	....	....	....	....
1994-95	HJK Jarvanpaa	Finland-2	1	0	1	1	2	....	....	....	....	....	....	....	....	....	....	....	....	....	....	....	....	....	....	....
	Jokerit Helsinki	Finland	47	21	20	41	53	....	....	....	....	....	....	....	....	....	....	....	11	7	2	9	10	....	....	....
1995-96	Jokerit Helsinki	Finland	50	*28	28	56	22	....	....	....	....	....	....	....	....	....	....	....	11	*12	7	19	6	....	....	....
1996-97	Jokerit Helsinki	Finland	50	*36	23	*59	38	....	....	....	....	....	....	....	....	....	....	....	9	*7	4	11	14	....	....	....
	Jokerit Helsinki	EuroHL	6	2	8	10	2	....	....	....	....	....	....	....	....	....	....	....	....	....	....	....	....	....	....	....
1997-98	**Chicago**	**NHL**	**1**	**0**	**0**	**0**	**0**	**0**	**0**	**0**	**0**	**0.0**	**0**	....	....	....	....	....	....	....	....	....	....	....	....	....
	Indianapolis Ice	IHL	77	18	54	72	32	....	....	....	....	....	....	....	....	....	....	....	5	3	4	7	4	....	....	....
1998-99	Kolner Haie	DEL	52	10	25	35	22	....	....	....	....	....	....	....	....	....	....	....	5	3	0	5	4	....	....	....
99-2000	Jokerit Helsinki	Finland	53	21	25	46	42	....	....	....	....	....	....	....	....	....	....	....	10	0	6	6	14	....	....	....
	NHL Totals		**1**	**0**	**0**	**0**	**0**	**0**	**0**	**0**	**0**	**0.0**		....	....	....	....	....	....	....	....	....	....	....	....	....

Finnish Rookie of the Year (1992)

Rights traded to **Chicago** by **San Jose** with San Jose's 6th round choice (Jari Viuhkola) in 1998 Entry Draft for Murray Craven, July 25, 1997.

VARLAMOV, Sergei

(vahr-LAHM-uhf, SAIR-gay) **CGY.**

Left wing. Shoots left. 5'11", 195 lbs. Born, Kiev, USSR, July 21, 1978.

Season	Club	League	GP	G	A	Pts	PIM	PP	SH	GW	S	%	+/-	TF	F%	H	SB	Min	GP	G	A	Pts	PIM	PP	SH	GW
1994-95	Nelson Leafs	RMJHL	26	11	15	26	56	....	....	....	....	....	....	....	....	....	....	....	....	....	....	....	....	....	....	....
1995-96	Swift Current	WHL	55	23	21	44	65	....	....	....	....	....	....	....	....	....	....	....	....	....	....	....	....	....	....	....
1996-97	Swift Current	WHL	72	46	39	85	94	....	....	....	....	....	....	....	....	....	....	....	10	3	8	11	10	....	....	....
	Saint John Flames	AHL	1	0	0	0	0	....	....	....	....	....	....	....	....	....	....	....	....	....	....	....	....	....	....	....
1997-98	Swift Current	WHL	72	*66	53	*119	132	....	....	....	....	....	....	....	....	....	....	....	12	10	5	15	28	....	....	....
	Calgary	**NHL**	**1**	**0**	**0**	**0**	**0**	**0**	**0**	**0**	**0**	**0.0**	**0**	....	....	....	....	....	....	....	....	....	....	....	....	....
	Saint John Flames	AHL	....	....	....	....	....	....	....	....	....	....	....	....	....	....	....	....	3	0	0	0	0	....	....	....
1998-99	Saint John Flames	AHL	76	24	33	57	66	....	....	....	....	....	....	....	....	....	....	....	7	0	4	4	8	....	....	....

			Regular Season																Playoffs							
Season	Club	League	GP	G	A	Pts	PIM	PP	SH	GW	S	%	+/–	TF	F%	H	SB	Min	GP	G	A	Pts	PIM	PP	SH	GW
99-2000	**Calgary**	**NHL**	**7**	**3**	**0**	**3**	**0**	**0**	**0**	**1**	**11**	**27.3**	**0**	**1**	**0.0**	**4**	**1**	**10:22**	....	....	....	....	....	....	....	....
	Saint John Flames	AHL	68	20	21	41	88	....	....	....	....	....	....	....	....	....	....	....	3	0	0	0	24	....	....	....
	NHL Totals		**8**	**3**	**0**	**3**	**0**	**0**	**0**	**1**	**11**	**27.3**		**1**	**0.0**	**4**	**1**	**10:22**	....	....	....	....	....	....	....	....

WHL East First All-Star Team (1998) • Canadian Major Junior First All-Star Team (1998) • Canadian Major Junior Player of the Year (1998)

Signed as a free agent by **Calgary**, September 18, 1996.

VASILEVSKI, Alexander

(vah-sih-LEHV-skee, al-ehx-AN-duhr)

Right wing. Shoots left. 5'11", 190 lbs. Born, Kiev, USSR, January 8, 1975. St. Louis' 9th choice, 271st overall, in 1993 Entry Draft.

Season	Club	League	GP	G	A	Pts	PIM	PP	SH	GW	S	%	+/–	TF	F%	H	SB	Min	GP	G	A	Pts	PIM	PP	SH	GW
1992-93	Victoria Cougars	WHL	71	27	25	52	52	....	....	....	....	....	....	....	....	....	....	....	....	....	....	....	....	....	....	....
1993-94	Victoria Cougars	WHL	69	34	51	85	78	....	....	....	....	....	....	....	....	....	....	....	....	....	....	....	....	....	....	....
1994-95	Prince George	WHL	48	32	34	66	52	....	....	....	....	....	....	....	....	....	....	....	....	....	....	....	....	....	....	....
	Brandon	WHL	23	6	11	17	39	....	....	....	....	....	....	....	....	....	....	....	18	3	6	9	34	....	....	....
1995-96	**St. Louis**	**NHL**	**1**	**0**	**0**	**0**	**0**	**0**	**0**	**0**	**0**	**0.0**	**–1**	....	....	....	....	....	....	....	....	....	....	....	....	....
	Worcester	AHL	69	18	21	39	112	....	....	....	....	....	....	....	....	....	....	....	4	2	1	3	10	....	....	....
1996-97	**St. Louis**	**NHL**	**3**	**0**	**0**	**0**	**2**	**0**	**0**	**0**	**3**	**0.0**	**–1**	....	....	....	....	....	....	....	....	....	....	....	....	....
	Worcester	AHL	61	9	23	32	100	....	....	....	....	....	....	....	....	....	....	....	....	....	....	....	....	....	....	....
	Grand Rapids	IHL	10	1	5	6	43	....	....	....	....	....	....	....	....	....	....	....	5	0	1	1	19	....	....	....
1997-98	Hamilton Bulldogs	AHL	41	3	14	17	60	....	....	....	....	....	....	....	....	....	....	....	....	....	....	....	....	....	....	....
	Detroit Vipers	IHL	9	1	1	2	7	....	....	....	....	....	....	....	....	....	....	....	....	....	....	....	....	....	....	....
1998-99	SK Severstal	Russia	2	0	0	0	0	....	....	....	....	....	....	....	....	....	....	....	....	....	....	....	....	....	....	....
	Krylja Sovetov	Russia	7	2	1	3	4	....	....	....	....	....	....	....	....	....	....	....	....	....	....	....	....	....	....	....
99-2000	Muskegon Fury	UHL	19	10	8	18	22	....	....	....	....	....	....	....	....	....	....	....	....	....	....	....	....	....	....	....
	Long Beach	IHL	51	8	25	33	109	....	....	....	....	....	....	....	....	....	....	....	5	0	3	3	4	....	....	....
	NHL Totals		**4**	**0**	**0**	**0**	**2**	**0**	**0**	**0**	**3**	**0.0**		....	....	....	....	....	....	....	....	....	....	....	....	....

VASILIEV, Alexei

(vah-SEE-lee-ehf, al-EHX-ay) **NYR**

Defense. Shoots left. 6'1", 192 lbs. Born, Yaroslavl, USSR, September 1, 1977. NY Rangers' 4th choice, 110th overall, in 1995 Entry Draft.

Season	Club	League	GP	G	A	Pts	PIM	PP	SH	GW	S	%	+/–	TF	F%	H	SB	Min	GP	G	A	Pts	PIM	PP	SH	GW
1995-96	Torpedo Yaroslavl	CIS	40	4	7	11	4	....	....	....	....	....	....	....	....	....	....	....	....	....	....	....	....	....	....	....
1996-97	Torpedo Yaroslavl	Russia	44	2	8	10	10	....	....	....	....	....	....	....	....	....	....	....	9	1	1	2	8	....	....	....
1997-98	Hartford	AHL	DID NOT PLAY – INJURED																							
1998-99	Hartford	AHL	75	8	19	27	24	....	....	....	....	....	....	....	....	....	....	....	6	0	1	1	2	....	....	....
99-2000	**NY Rangers**	**NHL**	**1**	**0**	**0**	**0**	**2**	**0**	**0**	**0**	**0**	**0.0**	....	**0**	**0.0**	**0**	**0**	**0:00**	....	....	....	....	....	....	....	....
	Hartford	AHL	75	10	28	38	20	....	....	....	....	....	....	....	....	....	....	....	15	3	1	4	2	....	....	....
	NHL Totals		**1**	**0**	**0**	**0**	**2**	**0**	**0**	**0**	**0**	**0.0**	....	**0**	**0.0**	**0**	**0**	....	....	....	....	....	....	....	....	....

• Missed entire 1997-98 season recovering from knee injury suffered in training camp, October, 1997.

VASILJEVS, Herbert

(vah-SEE-lee-ehf, HUHR-buhrt) **ATL.**

Center. Shoots right. 5'11", 180 lbs. Born, Riga, Latvia, May 27, 1976.

Season	Club	League	GP	G	A	Pts	PIM	PP	SH	GW	S	%	+/–	TF	F%	H	SB	Min	GP	G	A	Pts	PIM	PP	SH	GW
1994-95	Krefelder EV	DEL	42	4	5	9	24	....	....	....	....	....	....	....	....	....	....	....	15	1	4	5	10	....	....	....
1995-96	Guelph Storm	OHL	65	34	33	67	63	....	....	....	....	....	....	....	....	....	....	....	16	6	13	19	6	....	....	....
1996-97	Carolina	AHL	54	13	18	31	30	....	....	....	....	....	....	....	....	....	....	....	....	....	....	....	....	....	....	....
	Port Huron	ColHL	3	3	2	5	4	....	....	....	....	....	....	....	....	....	....	....	....	....	....	....	....	....	....	....
1997-98	New Haven	AHL	76	36	30	66	60	....	....	....	....	....	....	....	....	....	....	....	3	1	0	1	2	....	....	....
1998-99	**Florida**	**NHL**	**5**	**0**	**0**	**0**	**2**	**0**	**0**	**0**	**6**	**0.0**	**–1**	**3**	**66.7**	**0**	**0**	**11:06**	....	....	....	....	....	....	....	....
	Kentucky	AHL	76	28	48	76	66	....	....	....	....	....	....	....	....	....	....	....	12	2	1	3	4	....	....	....
99-2000	**Atlanta**	**NHL**	**7**	**1**	**0**	**1**	**4**	**0**	**0**	**0**	**2**	**50.0**	**–3**	**27**	**48.1**	**10**	**3**	**9:18**	....	....	....	....	....	....	....	....
	Orlando	IHL	73	25	35	60	60	....	....	....	....	....	....	....	....	....	....	....	6	2	2	4	6	....	....	....
	NHL Totals		**12**	**1**	**0**	**1**	**6**	**0**	**0**	**0**	**8**	**12.5**		**30**	**50.0**	**10**	**3**	**10:03**	....	....	....	....	....	....	....	....

Signed as a free agent by **Florida**, October 3, 1996. Traded to **Atlanta** by **Florida** with Gord Murphy, Daniel Tjarnqvist and Ottawa's 6th round choice (previously acquired, later traded to Dallas - Dallas selected Justin Cox) in 1999 Entry Draft for Trevor Kidd, June 25, 1999.

VASILYEV, Andrei

(vah-SEE-lee-ehf, AWN-dray)

Left wing. Shoots right. 5'9", 180 lbs. Born, Voskresensk, USSR, March 30, 1972. NY Islanders' 11th choice, 248th overall, in 1992 Entry Draft.

Season	Club	League	GP	G	A	Pts	PIM	PP	SH	GW	S	%	+/–	TF	F%	H	SB	Min	GP	G	A	Pts	PIM	PP	SH	GW
1991-92	CSKA Moscow	CIS	28	7	2	9	2	....	....	....	....	....	....	....	....	....	....	....	....	....	....	....	....	....	....	....
1992-93	HK Khimik	CIS	34	4	8	12	20	....	....	....	....	....	....	....	....	....	....	....	....	....	....	....	....	....	....	....
1993-94	CSKA Moscow	CIS	46	17	6	23	8	....	....	....	....	....	....	....	....	....	....	....	3	1	0	1	0	....	....	....
1994-95	**NY Islanders**	**NHL**	**2**	**0**	**0**	**0**	**2**	**0**	**0**	**0**	**2**	**0.0**	**0**	....	....	....	....	....	....	....	....	....	....	....	....	....
	Denver Grizzlies	IHL	74	28	37	65	48	....	....	....	....	....	....	....	....	....	....	....	13	9	4	13	22	....	....	....
1995-96	**NY Islanders**	**NHL**	**10**	**2**	**5**	**7**	**2**	**0**	**0**	**1**	**12**	**16.7**	**4**	....	....	....	....	....	....	....	....	....	....	....	....	....
	Utah Grizzlies	IHL	43	26	20	46	34	....	....	....	....	....	....	....	....	....	....	....	22	12	4	16	18	....	....	....
1996-97	**NY Islanders**	**NHL**	**3**	**0**	**0**	**0**	**2**	**0**	**0**	**0**	**1**	**0.0**	**–3**	....	....	....	....	....	....	....	....	....	....	....	....	....
	Utah Grizzlies	IHL	56	16	18	34	42	....	....	....	....	....	....	....	....	....	....	....	7	4	1	5	0	....	....	....
1997-98	Long Beach	IHL	62	33	34	67	60	....	....	....	....	....	....	....	....	....	....	....	17	9	4	13	14	....	....	....
1998-99	**Phoenix**	**NHL**	**1**	**0**	**0**	**0**	**0**	**0**	**0**	**0**	**0**	**0.0**	**–2**	**0**	**0.0**	**0**	**0**	**1:19**	....	....	....	....	....	....	....	....
	Las Vegas	IHL	15	3	6	9	6	....	....	....	....	....	....	....	....	....	....	....	....	....	....	....	....	....	....	....
	Grand Rapids	IHL	59	21	27	48	24	....	....	....	....	....	....	....	....	....	....	....	....	....	....	....	....	....	....	....
99-2000	Frankfurt Lions	DEL	54	26	21	47	18	....	....	....	....	....	....	....	....	....	....	....	5	2	1	3	30	....	....	....
	NHL Totals		**16**	**2**	**5**	**7**	**6**	**0**	**0**	**1**	**15**	**13.3**		**0**	**0.0**	**0**	**0**	**1:19**	....	....	....	....	....	....	....	....

Signed as a free agent by **Phoenix**, August 26, 1998.

VERBEEK, Pat

(vuhr-BEEK, PAT) **DET.**

Right/Left wing. Shoots right. 5'9", 192 lbs. Born, Sarnia, Ont., May 24, 1964. New Jersey's 3rd choice, 43rd overall, in 1982 Entry Draft.

Season	Club	League	GP	G	A	Pts	PIM	PP	SH	GW	S	%	+/–	TF	F%	H	SB	Min	GP	G	A	Pts	PIM	PP	SH	GW
1979-80	Petrolia Jets	OHA-B	41	17	24	41	85	....	....	....	....	....	....	....	....	....	....	....	....	....	....	....	....	....	....	....
1980-81	Petrolia Jets	OHA-B	42	44	44	88	155	....	....	....	....	....	....	....	....	....	....	....	....	....	....	....	....	....	....	....
1981-82	Sudbury Wolves	OHL	66	37	51	88	180	....	....	....	....	....	....	....	....	....	....	....	....	....	....	....	....	....	....	....
1982-83	Sudbury Wolves	OHL	61	40	67	107	184	....	....	....	....	....	....	....	....	....	....	....	....	....	....	....	....	....	....	....
	New Jersey	**NHL**	**6**	**3**	**2**	**5**	**8**	**0**	**0**	**0**	**12**	**25.0**	**–2**	....	....	....	....	....	....	....	....	....	....	....	....	....
1983-84	**New Jersey**	**NHL**	**79**	**20**	**27**	**47**	**158**	**5**	**1**	**2**	**167**	**12.0**	**–19**	....	....	....	....	....	....	....	....	....	....	....	....	....
1984-85	**New Jersey**	**NHL**	**78**	**15**	**18**	**33**	**162**	**5**	**1**	**1**	**147**	**10.2**	**–24**	....	....	....	....	....	....	....	....	....	....	....	....	....
1985-86	**New Jersey**	**NHL**	**76**	**25**	**28**	**53**	**79**	**4**	**1**	**0**	**159**	**15.7**	**–24**	....	....	....	....	....	....	....	....	....	....	....	....	....
1986-87	**New Jersey**	**NHL**	**74**	**35**	**24**	**59**	**120**	**17**	**0**	**5**	**143**	**24.5**	**–23**	....	....	....	....	....	....	....	....	....	....	....	....	....
1987-88	**New Jersey**	**NHL**	**73**	**46**	**31**	**77**	**227**	**13**	**0**	**8**	**179**	**25.7**	**29**	....	....	....	....	....	**20**	**4**	**8**	**12**	**51**	**2**	**0**	**1**
1988-89	**New Jersey**	**NHL**	**77**	**26**	**21**	**47**	**189**	**9**	**0**	**1**	**175**	**14.9**	**–18**	....	....	....	....	....	....	....	....	....	....	....	....	....
1989-90	**Hartford**	**NHL**	**80**	**44**	**45**	**89**	**228**	**14**	**0**	**5**	**219**	**20.1**	**1**	....	....	....	....	....	**7**	**2**	**2**	**4**	**26**	**1**	**0**	**1**
1990-91	**Hartford**	**NHL**	**80**	**43**	**39**	**82**	**246**	**15**	**0**	**5**	**247**	**17.4**	**0**	....	....	....	....	....	**6**	**3**	**2**	**5**	**40**	**2**	**0**	**0**
1991-92	**Hartford**	**NHL**	**76**	**22**	**35**	**57**	**243**	**10**	**0**	**3**	**163**	**13.5**	**–16**	....	....	....	....	....	**7**	**0**	**2**	**2**	**12**	**0**	**0**	**0**
1992-93	**Hartford**	**NHL**	**84**	**39**	**43**	**82**	**197**	**16**	**0**	**6**	**235**	**16.6**	**–7**	....	....	....	....	....	....	....	....	....	....	....	....	....
1993-94	**Hartford**	**NHL**	**84**	**37**	**38**	**75**	**177**	**15**	**1**	**3**	**226**	**16.4**	**–15**	....	....	....	....	....	....	....	....	....	....	....	....	....
1994-95	**Hartford**	**NHL**	**29**	**7**	**11**	**18**	**53**	**3**	**0**	**0**	**75**	**9.3**	**0**	....	....	....	....	....	....	....	....	....	....	....	....	....
	NY Rangers	**NHL**	**19**	**10**	**5**	**15**	**18**	**4**	**0**	**2**	**56**	**17.9**	**–2**	....	....	....	....	....	**10**	**4**	**6**	**10**	**20**	**3**	**0**	**0**
1995-96	**NY Rangers**	**NHL**	**69**	**41**	**41**	**82**	**129**	**17**	**0**	**6**	**252**	**16.3**	**29**	....	....	....	....	....	**11**	**3**	**6**	**9**	**12**	**1**	**0**	**0**
1996-97	**Dallas**	**NHL**	**81**	**17**	**36**	**53**	**128**	**5**	**0**	**4**	**172**	**9.9**	**3**	....	....	....	....	....	**7**	**1**	**3**	**4**	**16**	**1**	**0**	**0**
1997-98	**Dallas**	**NHL**	**82**	**31**	**26**	**57**	**170**	**9**	**0**	**8**	**190**	**16.3**	**15**	....	....	....	....	....	**17**	**3**	**2**	**5**	**26**	**2**	**0**	**1**
1998-99 ♦	**Dallas**	**NHL**	**78**	**17**	**17**	**34**	**133**	**8**	**0**	**2**	**134**	**12.7**	**11**	**1**	**100.0**	**130**	**15**	**14:34**	**18**	**3**	**4**	**7**	**14**	**0**	**0**	**1**
99-2000	**Detroit**	**NHL**	**68**	**22**	**26**	**48**	**95**	**7**	**0**	**5**	**138**	**15.9**	**22**	**1**	**0.0**	**148**	**8**	**16:04**	**9**	**1**	**1**	**2**	**2**	**1**	**0**	**1**
	NHL Totals		**1293**	**500**	**513**	**1013**	**2760**	**176**	**4**	**66**	**3089**	**16.2**		**2**	**50.0**	**278**	**23**	**15:16**	**112**	**24**	**36**	**60**	**219**	**13**	**0**	**5**

Played in NHL All-Star Game (1991, 1996)

Traded to **Hartford** by **New Jersey** for Sylvain Turgeon, June 17, 1989. Traded to **NY Rangers** by **Hartford** for Glen Featherstone, Michael Stewart, NY Rangers' 1st round choice (Jean-Sebastien Giguere) in 1995 Entry Draft and 4th round choice (Steve Wasylko) in 1996 Entry Draft, March 23, 1995. Signed as a free agent by **Dallas**, August 21, 1996. Signed as a free agent by **Detroit**, November 11, 1999.

			Regular Season																Playoffs							
Season	Club	League	GP	G	A	Pts	PIM	PP	SH	GW	S	%	+/-	TF	F%	H	SB	Min	GP	G	A	Pts	PIM	PP	SH	GW

VIAL, Dennis   (vee-AL, DEH-nihs)

Defense/Left wing. Shoots left. 6'1", 220 lbs.   Born, Sault Ste. Marie, Ont., April 10, 1969. NY Rangers' 5th choice, 110th overall, in 1988 Entry Draft.

Season	Club	League	GP	G	A	Pts	PIM	PP	SH	GW	S	%	+/-	TF	F%	H	SB	Min	GP	G	A	Pts	PIM	PP	SH	GW
1984-85	S.S. Marie Legion	OMHA	31	4	19	23	40	....	....	....	....	....	....	....	....	....	....	....	....	....	....	....	....	....	....	....
1985-86	Hamilton Kilty B's	OJHL-B	27	11	7	18	215	....	....	....	....	....	....	....	....	....	....	....	....	....	....	....	....	....	....	....
	Hamilton Hawks	OHL	31	1	1	2	66	....	....	....	....	....	....	....	....	....	....	....	....	....	....	....	....	....	....	....
1986-87	Hamilton Hawks	OHL	53	1	8	9	194	....	....	....	....	....	....	....	....	....	....	....	8	0	0	0	8	....	....	....
1987-88	Hamilton Hawks	OHL	52	3	17	20	229	....	....	....	....	....	....	....	....	....	....	....	13	2	2	4	49	....	....	....
1988-89	Niagara Falls	OHL	50	10	27	37	227	....	....	....	....	....	....	....	....	....	....	....	15	1	7	8	44	....	....	....
1989-90	Flint Spirits	IHL	79	6	29	35	351	....	....	....	....	....	....	....	....	....	....	....	4	0	0	0	10	....	....	....
1990-91	**NY Rangers**	**NHL**	21	0	0	0	61	0	0	0	5	0.0	-4													
	Binghamton	AHL	40	2	7	9	250	....	....	....	....	....	....	....	....	....	....	....	....	....	....	....	....	....	....
	Detroit	**NHL**	9	0	0	0	16	0	0	0	3	0.0	-3													
1991-92	**Detroit**	**NHL**	27	1	0	1	72	0	0	0	6	16.7	1													
	Adirondack	AHL	20	2	4	6	107	....	....	....	....	....	....	....	....	....	....	....	17	1	3	4	43	....	....	....
1992-93	**Detroit**	**NHL**	9	0	1	1	20	0	0	0	5	0.0	1													
	Adirondack	AHL	30	2	11	13	177	....	....	....	....	....	....	....	....	....	....	....	11	1	1	2	14	....	....	....
1993-94	**Ottawa**	**NHL**	55	2	5	7	214	0	0	0	37	5.4	-9													
1994-95	**Ottawa**	**NHL**	27	0	4	4	65	0	0	0	9	0.0	0													
1995-96	**Ottawa**	**NHL**	64	1	4	5	276	0	0	0	33	3.0	-13													
1996-97	**Ottawa**	**NHL**	11	0	1	1	25	0	0	0	4	0.0	0													
1997-98	**Ottawa**	**NHL**	19	0	0	0	45	0	0	0	9	0.0	0													
	Chicago Wolves	IHL	24	1	3	4	86	....	....	....	....	....	....	....	....	....	....	....	1	0	0	0	2	....	....	....
1998-99	Chicago Wolves	IHL	55	1	4	5	213	....	....	....	....	....	....	....	....	....	....	....	....	....	....	....	....	....	....
99-2000	Sheffield Steelers	Britain	24	2	3	5	78	....	....	....	....	....	....	....	....	....	....	....	7	0	1	1	10	....	....	....
	NHL Totals		242	4	15	19	794	0	0	0	111	3.6														

Traded to **Detroit** by **NY Rangers** with Kevin Miller and Jim Cummins for Joey Kocur and Per Djoos, March 5, 1991. Traded to **Quebec** by **Detroit** with Doug Crossman for cash, June 15, 1992. Traded to **Detroit** by **Quebec** for cash, September 9, 1992. Traded to **Tampa Bay** by **Detroit** for Steve Maltais, June 8, 1993. Claimed by **Anaheim** from **Tampa Bay** in Expansion Draft, June 24, 1993. Claimed by **Ottawa** from **Anaheim** in Phase II of Expansion Draft, June 25, 1993.

VIRTUE, Terry   (VIR-too, TAIR-ee)   **NYR**

Defense. Shoots right. 6', 207 lbs.   Born, Scarborough, Ont., August 12, 1970.

Season	Club	League	GP	G	A	Pts	PIM	PP	SH	GW	S	%	+/-	TF	F%	H	SB	Min	GP	G	A	Pts	PIM	PP	SH	GW
1988-89	Hobbema Hawks	AJHL	56	6	31	37	339	....	....	....	....	....	....	....	....	....	....	....	....	....	....	....	....	....	....
	Victoria Cougars	WHL	8	1	1	2	13	....	....	....	....	....	....	....	....	....	....	....	....	....	....	....	....	....	....
1989-90	Victoria Cougars	WHL	24	1	9	10	85	....	....	....	....	....	....	....	....	....	....	....	....	....	....	....	....	....	....
	Tri-City Americans	WHL	34	1	10	11	82	....	....	....	....	....	....	....	....	....	....	....	6	0	0	0	30	....	....	....
1990-91	Tri-City Americans	WHL	11	1	8	9	24	....	....	....	....	....	....	....	....	....	....	....	....	....	....	....	....	....	....
	Portland	WHL	59	9	44	53	127	....	....	....	....	....	....	....	....	....	....	....	....	....	....	....	....	....	....
1991-92	Roanoke Valley	ECHL	38	4	22	26	165	....	....	....	....	....	....	....	....	....	....	....	....	....	....	....	....	....	....
	Louisville	ECHL	23	1	15	16	58	....	....	....	....	....	....	....	....	....	....	....	13	0	8	8	49	....	....	....
1992-93	Louisville	ECHL	28	0	17	17	84	....	....	....	....	....	....	....	....	....	....	....	16	3	5	8	18	....	....	....
	Wheeling	ECHL	31	3	15	18	86	....	....	....	....	....	....	....	....	....	....	....	....	....	....	....	....	....	....
1993-94	Wheeling	ECHL	34	5	28	33	61	....	....	....	....	....	....	....	....	....	....	....	6	2	2	4	4	....	....	....
	Cape Breton	AHL	26	4	6	10	10	....	....	....	....	....	....	....	....	....	....	....	5	0	0	0	17	....	....	....
1994-95	Worcester	AHL	73	14	25	39	183	....	....	....	....	....	....	....	....	....	....	....	....	....	....	....	....	....	....
	Atlanta Knights	IHL	1	0	0	0	2	....	....	....	....	....	....	....	....	....	....	....	....	....	....	....	....	....	....
1995-96	Worcester	AHL	76	7	31	38	234	....	....	....	....	....	....	....	....	....	....	....	4	0	0	0	4	....	....	....
1996-97	Worcester	AHL	80	16	26	42	220	....	....	....	....	....	....	....	....	....	....	....	5	0	4	4	8	....	....	....
1997-98	Worcester	AHL	74	8	26	34	233	....	....	....	....	....	....	....	....	....	....	....	11	1	4	5	41	....	....	....
1998-99	**Boston**	**NHL**	4	0	0	0	0	0		0	2	0.0	2	0	0.0	4	2	9:41								
	Providence Bruins	AHL	76	8	48	56	117	....	....	....	....	....	....	....	....	....	....	....	17	2	12	14	29	....	....	....
99-2000	**NY Rangers**	**NHL**	1	0	0	0	0	0		0	2	0.0	-2	0	0.0	3	1	12:32								
	Hartford	AHL	67	5	22	27	166	....	....	....	....	....	....	....	....	....	....	....	23	3	7	10	51	....	....	....
	NHL Totals		5	0	0	0	0	0	0	0	4	0.0		0	0.0	7	3	10:15								

AHL Second All-Star Team (1999)

Signed as a free agent by **St. Louis**, January 29, 1996. Signed as a free agent by **Boston**, August 28, 1998. Signed as a free agent by **NY Rangers**, July 29, 1999. • Played w/ RHI's Atlanta Fire Ants in 1994 (22-10-26-54).

VISHNEVSKI, Vitaly   (vihsh-NEHV-skee, vih-TAL-ee)   **ANA.**

Defense. Shoots left. 6'2", 200 lbs.   Born, Kharkov, USSR, March 18, 1980. Anaheim's 1st choice, 5th overall, in 1998 Entry Draft.

Season	Club	League	GP	G	A	Pts	PIM	PP	SH	GW	S	%	+/-	TF	F%	H	SB	Min	GP	G	A	Pts	PIM	PP	SH	GW
1995-96	Torpedo Yaroslavl	Russia-2	40	4	4	8	20	....	....	....	....	....	....	....	....	....	....	....	....	....	....	....	....	....	....
1996-97	Torpedo Yaroslavl	Russia-3	45	0	2	2	30	....	....	....	....	....	....	....	....	....	....	....	....	....	....	....	....	....	....
1997-98	Torpedo Yaroslavl	Russia-2	47	8	9	17	164	....	....	....	....	....	....	....	....	....	....	....	....	....	....	....	....	....	....
1998-99	Torpedo Yaroslavl	Russia	34	3	4	7	38	....	....	....	....	....	....	....	....	....	....	....	10	0	0	0	4	....	....	....
99-2000	**Anaheim**	**NHL**	31	1	1	2	26	1	0	0	17	5.9		0	0.0	0	0	0:00								
	Cincinnati Ducks	AHL	35	1	3	4	45	....	....	....	....	....	....	....	....	....	....	....	....	....	....	....	....	....	....
	NHL Totals		31	1	1	2	26	1	0	0	17	5.9		0	0.0	0	0	....								

VOLCHKOV, Alexandre   (VOHLCH-kahf, al-ehx-AN-duhr)   **EDM.**

Center. Shoots left. 6'2", 204 lbs.   Born, Moscow, USSR, September 25, 1977. Washington's 1st choice, 4th overall, in 1996 Entry Draft.

Season	Club	League	GP	G	A	Pts	PIM	PP	SH	GW	S	%	+/-	TF	F%	H	SB	Min	GP	G	A	Pts	PIM	PP	SH	GW
1994-95	CSKA Moscow	CIS	1	0	0	0	0	....	....	....	....	....	....	....	....	....	....	....	....	....	....	....	....	....	....
1995-96	Barrie Colts	OHL	47	37	27	64	36	....	....	....	....	....	....	....	....	....	....	....	7	2	3	5	12	....	....	....
1996-97	Barrie Colts	OHL	56	29	53	82	76	....	....	....	....	....	....	....	....	....	....	....	9	6	9	15	12	....	....	....
	Portland Pirates	AHL	....	....	....	....	....	....	....	....	....	....	....	....	....	....	....	....	4	0	0	0	0	....	....	....
1997-98	Portland Pirates	AHL	34	2	5	7	20	....	....	....	....	....	....	....	....	....	....	....	1	0	0	0	0	....	....	....
1998-99	Portland Pirates	AHL	27	3	8	11	24	....	....	....	....	....	....	....	....	....	....	....	....	....	....	....	....	....	....
	Cincinnati	IHL	25	1	3	4	8	....	....	....	....	....	....	....	....	....	....	....	....	....	....	....	....	....	....
99-2000	**Washington**	**NHL**	3	0	0	0	0	0	0	0	1	0.0	-2	0	0.0	2	0	10:07								
	Portland Pirates	AHL	35	11	15	26	47	....	....	....	....	....	....	....	....	....	....	....	....	....	....	....	....	....	....
	Hamilton Bulldogs	AHL	25	2	6	8	11	....	....	....	....	....	....	....	....	....	....	....	....	....	....	....	....	....	....
	NHL Totals		3	0	0	0	0	0	0	0	1	0.0		0	0.0	2	0	10:07								

OHL Second All-Star Team (1997)

Traded to **Edmonton** by **Washington** for a conditional choice in 2001 Entry Draft, February 4, 2000.

VON STEFENELLI, Phil   (VAWN-STEH-fan-ehl-EE, FIHL)

Defense. Shoots left. 6'1", 200 lbs.   Born, Vancouver, B.C., April 10, 1969. Vancouver's 5th choice, 122nd overall, in 1988 Entry Draft.

Season	Club	League	GP	G	A	Pts	PIM	PP	SH	GW	S	%	+/-	TF	F%	H	SB	Min	GP	G	A	Pts	PIM	PP	SH	GW
1985-86	Richmond	BCJHL	41	6	11	17	28	....	....	....	....	....	....	....	....	....	....	....	....	....	....	....	....	....	....
1986-87	Richmond	BCJHL	35	5	19	24	39	....	....	....	....	....	....	....	....	....	....	....	....	....	....	....	....	....	....
	Langley Eagles	BCJHL	17	0	13	13	12	....	....	....	....	....	....	....	....	....	....	....	....	....	....	....	....	....	....
1987-88	Boston University	H-East	34	3	13	16	38	....	....	....	....	....	....	....	....	....	....	....	....	....	....	....	....	....	....
1988-89	Boston University	H-East	33	2	6	8	34	....	....	....	....	....	....	....	....	....	....	....	....	....	....	....	....	....	....
1989-90	Boston University	H-East	44	8	20	28	40	....	....	....	....	....	....	....	....	....	....	....	....	....	....	....	....	....	....
1990-91	Boston University	H-East	41	7	23	30	32	....	....	....	....	....	....	....	....	....	....	....	....	....	....	....	....	....	....
1991-92	Milwaukee	IHL	80	2	34	36	40	....	....	....	....	....	....	....	....	....	....	....	5	1	2	3	2	....	....	....
1992-93	Hamilton Canucks	AHL	78	11	20	31	75	....	....	....	....	....	....	....	....	....	....	....	....	....	....	....	....	....	....
1993-94	Hamilton Canucks	AHL	80	10	31	41	89	....	....	....	....	....	....	....	....	....	....	....	4	1	0	1	2	....	....	....
1994-95	Providence Bruins	AHL	75	6	13	19	93	....	....	....	....	....	....	....	....	....	....	....	13	2	4	6	6	....	....	....
1995-96	**Boston**	**NHL**	27	0	4	4	16	0	0	0	20	0.0	2													
	Providence Bruins	AHL	42	9	21	30	52	....	....	....	....	....	....	....	....	....	....	....	....	....	....	....	....	....	....

			Regular Season																Playoffs							
Season	Club	League	GP	G	A	Pts	PIM	PP	SH	GW	S	%	+/-	TF	F%	H	SB	Min	GP	G	A	Pts	PIM	PP	SH	GW
1996-97	Ottawa	NHL	6	0	1	1	7	0	0	0	2	0.0	–3	....	....	....	....	....	....	....	....	....	....	....	....	....
	Detroit Vipers	IHL	67	14	26	40	86	....	....	....	....	....	....	....	....	....	....	....	21	2	4	6	20	....	....	....
1997-98	EHC Chur	Switz-2	40	10	26	36	75	....	....	....	....	....	....	....	....	....	....	....	9	1	3	4	30	....	....	....
	HC Fassa	Italy	....	....	....	....	....	....	....	....	....	....	....	....	....	....	....	....	7	2	3	5	2	....	....	....
1998-99	Frankfurt Lions	DEL	51	4	12	16	75	....	....	....	....	....	....	....	....	....	....	....	8	0	0	0	6	....	....	....
	Frankfurt Lions	EuroHL	6	2	1	3	32	....	....	....	....	....	....	....	....	....	....	....	....	....	....	....	....	....	....	....
99-2000	Krefelder EV	DEL	50	4	7	11	82	....	....	....	....	....	....	....	....	....	....	....	4	1	2	3	4	....	....	....
	NHL Totals		33	0	5	5	23	0	0	0	22	0.0		....	....	....	....	....	....	....	....	....	....	....	....	....

Signed as a free agent by **Boston**, September 10, 1994. Signed as a free agent by **Ottawa**, July 17, 1996. Signed as a free agent by **Tampa Bay**, July 22, 1999.

VOPAT, Jan

(VOH-paht, YAN)

Defense. Shoots left. 6', 205 lbs. Born, Most, Czech., March 22, 1973. Hartford's 3rd choice, 57th overall, in 1992 Entry Draft.

Season	Club	League	GP	G	A	Pts	PIM	PP	SH	GW	S	%	+/-	TF	F%	H	SB	Min	GP	G	A	Pts	PIM	PP	SH	GW
1990-91	CHZ Litvinov	Czech.	25	1	4	5	4	....	....	....	....	....	....	....	....	....	....	....	....	....	....	....	....	....	....	....
1991-92	CHZ Litvinov	Czech.	46	4	2	6	16	....	....	....	....	....	....	....	....	....	....	....	....	....	....	....	....	....	....	....
1992-93	CHZ Litvinov	Czech.	45	12	10	22	....	....	....	....	....	....	....	....	....	....	....	....	....	....	....	....	....	....	....	....
1993-94	CHZ Litvinov	Cze-Rep	41	9	19	28	0	....	....	....	....	....	....	....	....	....	....	....	4	1	1	2		....	....	....
	Czech-Republic	Olympics	8	0	1	1	8	....	....	....	....	....	....	....	....	....	....	....	....	....	....	....	....	....	....	....
1994-95	CHZ Litvinov	Cze-Rep	42	7	18	25	49	....	....	....	....	....	....	....	....	....	....	....	4	0	2	2	2	....	....	....
1995-96	Los Angeles	NHL	11	1	4	5	4	0	0	0	13	7.7	3	....	....	....	....	....	....	....	....	....	....	....	....	....
	Phoenix	IHL	47	0	9	9	34	....	....	....	....	....	....	....	....	....	....	....	4	0	2	2	4	....	....	....
1996-97	Los Angeles	NHL	33	4	5	9	22	0	0	1	44	9.1	3	....	....	....	....	....	....	....	....	....	....	....	....	....
	Phoenix	IHL	4	0	6	6	6	....	....	....	....	....	....	....	....	....	....	....	....	....	....	....	....	....	....	....
1997-98	Los Angeles	NHL	21	1	5	6	10	0	0	1	13	7.7	8	....	....	....	....	....	2	0	1	1	2	0	0	0
	Utah Grizzlies	IHL	38	8	13	21	24	....	....	....	....	....	....	....	....	....	....	....	....	....	....	....	....	....	....	....
1998-99	Nashville	NHL	55	5	6	11	28	0	0	0	46	10.9	0	0	0.0	98	70	18:05	....	....	....	....	....	....	....	....
99-2000	Nashville	NHL	6	0	0	0	6	0	0	0	3	0.0	1	0	0.0	8	6	17:55	....	....	....	....	....	....	....	....
	Milwaukee	IHL	2	1	0	1	2	....	....	....	....	....	....	....	....	....	....	....	....	....	....	....	....	....	....	....
	NHL Totals		126	11	20	31	70	0	0	2	119	9.2		0	0.0	106	76	18:04	2	0	1	1	2	0	0	0

Rights traded to **LA Kings** by **Hartford** for LA Kings' 4th round choice (Ian MacNeil) in 1995 Entry Draft, May 31, 1995. Traded to **Nashville** by **LA Kings** with Kimmo Timonen for future considerations, June 26, 1998. • Missed remainder of 1999-2000 season recovering from rare skin allergy, December 10, 1999.

VOPAT, Roman

(VOH-paht, ROH-man)

Center. Shoots left. 6'3", 223 lbs. Born, Litvinov, Czech., April 21, 1976. St. Louis' 4th choice, 172nd overall, in 1994 Entry Draft.

Season	Club	League	GP	G	A	Pts	PIM	PP	SH	GW	S	%	+/-	TF	F%	H	SB	Min	GP	G	A	Pts	PIM	PP	SH	GW
1993-94	CHZ Litvinov	Cze-Rep	7	0	0	0	0	....	....	....	....	....	....	....	....	....	....	....	....	....	....	....	....	....	....	....
1994-95	Moose Jaw	WHL	72	23	20	43	141	....	....	....	....	....	....	....	....	....	....	....	10	4	1	5	28	....	....	....
	Peoria Rivermen	IHL	....	....	....	....	....	....	....	....	....	....	....	....	....	....	....	....	6	0	2	2	2	....	....	....
1995-96	Moose Jaw	WHL	7	0	4	4	34	....	....	....	....	....	....	....	....	....	....	....	....	....	....	....	....	....	....	....
	Prince Albert	WHL	22	15	5	20	81	....	....	....	....	....	....	....	....	....	....	....	18	9	8	17	57	....	....	....
	St. Louis	NHL	25	2	3	5	48	1	0	1	33	6.1	–8	....	....	....	....	....	....	....	....	....	....	....	....	....
	Worcester	AHL	5	2	0	2	14	....	....	....	....	....	....	....	....	....	....	....	....	....	....	....	....	....	....	....
1996-97	Los Angeles	NHL	29	4	5	9	60	1	0	2	54	7.4	–7	....	....	....	....	....	....	....	....	....	....	....	....	....
	Phoenix	IHL	50	8	8	16	139	....	....	....	....	....	....	....	....	....	....	....	....	....	....	....	....	....	....	....
1997-98	Los Angeles	NHL	25	0	3	3	55	0	0	0	36	0.0	–7	....	....	....	....	....	....	....	....	....	....	....	....	....
	Fredericton	AHL	29	10	10	20	93	....	....	....	....	....	....	....	....	....	....	....	....	....	....	....	....	....	....	....
1998-99	Los Angeles	NHL	3	0	0	0	6	0	0	0	2	0.0	0	10	50.0	3	0	4:13	....	....	....	....	....	....	....	....
	Chicago	NHL	3	0	0	0	4	0	0	0	0	0.0	–4	14	35.7	4	0	6:35	....	....	....	....	....	....	....	....
	Philadelphia	NHL	48	0	3	3	80	0	0	0	25	0.0	–3	26	53.8	41	6	5:36	....	....	....	....	....	....	....	....
99-2000	Philadelphia	AHL	12	1	0	1	12	....	....	....	....	....	....	....	....	....	....	....	....	....	....	....	....	....	....	....
	Moskitos Essen	DEL	44	8	15	23	171	....	....	....	....	....	....	....	....	....	....	....	....	....	....	....	....	....	....	....
	NHL Totals		133	6	14	20	253	2	0	3	150	4.0		50	48.0	48	6	5:35	....	....	....	....	....	....	....	....

Traded to **LA Kings** by **St. Louis** with Craig Johnson, Patrice Tardif, St. Louis 5th round choice (Peter Hogan) in 1996 Entry Draft and 1st round choice (Matt Zultek) in 1997 Entry Draft for Wayne Gretzky, February 27, 1996. Traded to **Colorado** by **Los Angeles** with Los Angeles' 6th round choice (later traded to Chicago, later traded to Ottawa, Ottawa selected Martin Brusek) in 1999 Entry Draft for Eric Lacroix, October 29, 1998. Traded to **Chicago** by **Colorado** with Los Angeles' 6th round choice (previously acquired, later traded to Ottawa, Ottawa selected Martin Brusek) in 1999 Entry Draft for Cam Russell, November 10, 1998. Traded to **Philadelphia** by **Chicago** for Mike Maneluk, November 17, 1998. Signed as a free agent by **Moskitos Essen** (Germany) following release by **Philadelphia**, December 19, 1999.

VOROBIEV, Vladimir

(vah-roh-BEE-ehf, VLA-dih-MEER)

Left wing. Shoots right. 6', 185 lbs. Born, Cherepovets, USSR, October 2, 1972. NY Rangers' 10th choice, 240th overall, in 1992 Entry Draft.

Season	Club	League	GP	G	A	Pts	PIM	PP	SH	GW	S	%	+/-	TF	F%	H	SB	Min	GP	G	A	Pts	PIM	PP	SH	GW
1992-93	HC Cherepovets	CIS	42	18	5	23	18	....	....	....	....	....	....	....	....	....	....	....	....	....	....	....	....	....	....	....
1993-94	Dynamo Moscow	CIS	11	3	1	4	2	....	....	....	....	....	....	....	....	....	....	....	....	....	....	....	....	....	....	....
1994-95	Dynamo Moscow	CIS	48	9	20	29	28	....	....	....	....	....	....	....	....	....	....	....	14	1	7	8	2	....	....	....
1995-96	Dynamo Moscow	CIS	42	19	9	28	49	....	....	....	....	....	....	....	....	....	....	....	9	2	8	10	2	....	....	....
1996-97	NY Rangers	NHL	16	5	5	10	6	2	0	0	42	11.9	4	....	....	....	....	....	....	....	....	....	....	....	....	....
	Binghamton	AHL	61	22	27	49	6	....	....	....	....	....	....	....	....	....	....	....	4	1	1	2	2	....	....	....
1997-98	NY Rangers	NHL	15	2	2	4	6	0	0	1	27	7.4	–10	....	....	....	....	....	....	....	....	....	....	....	....	....
	Hartford	AHL	56	20	28	48	18	....	....	....	....	....	....	....	....	....	....	....	15	11	8	19	4	....	....	....
1998-99	Hartford	AHL	65	24	41	65	22	....	....	....	....	....	....	....	....	....	....	....	....	....	....	....	....	....	....	....
	Edmonton	NHL	2	2	0	2	2	0	0	0	5	40.0	1	0	0.0	0	1	11:35	1	0	0	0	0	0	0	0
	Hamilton Bulldogs	AHL	8	3	6	9	2	....	....	....	....	....	....	....	....	....	....	....	6	0	1	1	2	....	....	....
99-2000	Hamilton Bulldogs	AHL	37	9	9	18	16	....	....	....	....	....	....	....	....	....	....	....	....	....	....	....	....	....	....	....
	Long Beach	IHL	23	6	7	13	0	....	....	....	....	....	....	....	....	....	....	....	1	0	0	0	2	....	....	....
	NHL Totals		33	9	7	16	14	2	0	1	74	12.2		0	0.0	0	1	11:35	1	0	0	0	0	0	0	0

Traded to **Edmonton** by **NY Rangers** for Kevin Brown, March 23, 1999.

VUJTEK, Vladimir

(VYOO-tehk, VLAD-dih-MEER)

Left wing. Shoots left. 6'1", 190 lbs. Born, Ostrava, Czech., February 17, 1972. Montreal's 5th choice, 73rd overall, in 1991 Entry Draft.

Season	Club	League	GP	G	A	Pts	PIM	PP	SH	GW	S	%	+/-	TF	F%	H	SB	Min	GP	G	A	Pts	PIM	PP	SH	GW
1988-89	TJ Vitkovice	Czech.	3	0	1	1	0	....	....	....	....	....	....	....	....	....	....	....	....	....	....	....	....	....	....	....
1989-90	TJ Vitkovice	Czech.	22	3	4	7	....	....	....	....	....	....	....	....	....	....	....	....	7	4	3	7		....	....	....
1990-91	TJ Vitkovice	Czech.	26	7	4	11	....	....	....	....	....	....	....	....	....	....	....	....	....	....	....	....	....	....	....	....
	Tri-City Americans	WHL	37	26	18	44	74	....	....	....	....	....	....	....	....	....	....	....	7	2	3	5	4	....	....	....
1991-92	Tri-City Americans	WHL	53	41	61	102	114	....	....	....	....	....	....	....	....	....	....	....	....	....	....	....	....	....	....	....
	Montreal	NHL	2	0	0	0	0	0	0	0	1	0.0	–1	....	....	....	....	....	....	....	....	....	....	....	....	....
1992-93	Edmonton	NHL	30	1	10	11	8	0	0	0	49	2.0	–1	....	....	....	....	....	....	....	....	....	....	....	....	....
	Cape Breton	AHL	20	10	9	19	14	....	....	....	....	....	....	....	....	....	....	....	1	0	0	0	0	....	....	....
1993-94	Edmonton	NHL	40	4	15	19	14	1	0	0	66	6.1	–7	....	....	....	....	....	....	....	....	....	....	....	....	....
1994-95	HC Vitkovice	Cze-Rep	18	5	7	12	51	....	....	....	....	....	....	....	....	....	....	....	....	....	....	....	....	....	....	....
	Cape Breton	AHL	30	10	11	21	30	....	....	....	....	....	....	....	....	....	....	....	....	....	....	....	....	....	....	....
	Las Vegas	IHL	1	0	0	0	0	....	....	....	....	....	....	....	....	....	....	....	....	....	....	....	....	....	....	....
1995-96	HC Vitkovice	Cze-Rep	26	6	7	13	....	....	....	....	....	....	....	....	....	....	....	....	4	1	1	2		....	....	....
1996-97	Assat-Pori	Finland	50	27	31	58	48	....	....	....	....	....	....	....	....	....	....	....	4	1	2	3	2	....	....	....
1997-98	Tampa Bay	NHL	30	2	4	6	16	0	0	1	44	4.5	–2	....	....	....	....	....	....	....	....	....	....	....	....	....
	Adirondack	AHL	2	1	2	3	0	....	....	....	....	....	....	....	....	....	....	....	....	....	....	....	....	....	....	....
1998-99	HC Vitkovice	Cze-Rep	47	20	35	55	75	....	....	....	....	....	....	....	....	....	....	....	....	....	....	....	....	....	....	....
99-2000	Atlanta	NHL	3	0	0	0	0	0	0	0	2	0.0	0	0	0.0	1	0	10:52	....	....	....	....	....	....	....	....
	Sparta Praha	Cze-Rep	21	12	19	31	10	....	....	....	....	....	....	....	....	....	....	....	8	2	3	5	10	....	....	....
	NHL Totals		105	7	29	36	38	1	0	1	162	4.3		0	0.0	1	0	10:52	....	....	....	....	....	....	....	....

WHL West First All-Star Team (1992)

Traded to **Edmonton** by **Montreal** with Shayne Corson and Brent Gilchrist for Vincent Damphousse and Edmonton's 4th round choice (Adam Wiesel) in 1993 Entry Draft, August 27, 1992. Traded to **Tampa Bay** by **Edmonton** with Edmonton's 3rd round choice (Dmitri Afanasenkov) in 1998 Entry Draft for Brantt Myhres and Toronto's 3rd round choice (previously acquired, Edmonton selected Alex Henry) in 1998 Entry Draft, July 16, 1997. • Missed majority of 1997-98 season recovering from Epstein-Barr Virus, December, 1997. Signed as a free agent by **Atlanta**, July 29, 1999. • Missed majority of 1999-2000 season recovering from facial injuries suffered in exhibition game vs. NY Rangers, September 18, 1999.

			Regular Season																Playoffs							
Season	Club	League	GP	G	A	Pts	PIM	PP	SH	GW	S	%	+/-	TF	F%	H	SB	Min	GP	G	A	Pts	PIM	PP	SH	GW

VUKOTA, Mick

(vuh-KOH-tuh, MIHK)

Right wing. Shoots right. 6'1", 225 lbs. Born, Saskatoon, Sask., September 14, 1966.

Season	Club	League	GP	G	A	Pts	PIM	PP	SH	GW	S	%	+/-	TF	F%	H	SB	Min	GP	G	A	Pts	PIM	PP	SH	GW
1983-84	Winnipeg	WHL	3	1	1	2	10	....	....	....	....	....	....	....	....	....	....	....	....	....	....	....	....	....	....	....
1984-85	Kelowna Wings	WHL	66	10	6	16	247	....	....	....	....	....	....	....	....	....	....	....	6	0	0	0	56	....	....	....
1985-86	Spokane Chiefs	WHL	64	19	14	33	369	....	....	....	....	....	....	....	....	....	....	....	9	6	4	10	68	....	....	....
1986-87	Spokane Chiefs	WHL	61	25	28	53	*337	....	....	....	....	....	....	....	....	....	....	....	4	0	0	0	40	....	....	....
1987-88	**NY Islanders**	**NHL**	**17**	**1**	**0**	**1**	**82**	**0**	**0**	**0**	**7**	**14.3**	**1**	....	....	....	....	....	**2**	**0**	**0**	**0**	**23**	**0**	**0**	**0**
	Springfield	AHL	52	7	9	16	375	....	....	....	....	....	....	....	....	....	....	....	....	....	....	....	....	....	....	....
1988-89	**NY Islanders**	**NHL**	**48**	**2**	**2**	**4**	**237**	**0**	**0**	**0**	**19**	**10.5**	**–17**	....	....	....	....	....	....	....	....	....	....	....	....	....
	Springfield	AHL	3	1	0	1	33	....	....	....	....	....	....	....	....	....	....	....	....	....	....	....	....	....	....	....
1989-90	**NY Islanders**	**NHL**	**76**	**4**	**8**	**12**	**290**	**0**	**0**	**0**	**55**	**7.3**	**10**	....	....	....	....	....	**1**	**0**	**0**	**0**	**17**	**0**	**0**	**0**
1990-91	**NY Islanders**	**NHL**	**60**	**2**	**4**	**6**	**238**	**0**	**0**	**0**	**39**	**5.1**	**–13**	....	....	....	....	....	....	....	....	....	....	....	....	....
	Capital District	AHL	2	0	0	0	9	....	....	....	....	....	....	....	....	....	....	....	....	....	....	....	....	....	....	....
1991-92	**NY Islanders**	**NHL**	**74**	**0**	**6**	**6**	**293**	**0**	**0**	**0**	**34**	**0.0**	**–6**	....	....	....	....	....	....	....	....	....	....	....	....	....
1992-93	**NY Islanders**	**NHL**	**74**	**2**	**5**	**7**	**216**	**0**	**0**	**0**	**37**	**5.4**	**3**	....	....	....	....	....	**15**	**0**	**0**	**0**	**16**	**0**	**0**	**0**
1993-94	**NY Islanders**	**NHL**	**72**	**3**	**1**	**4**	**237**	**0**	**0**	**0**	**26**	**11.5**	**–5**	....	....	....	....	....	**4**	**0**	**0**	**0**	**17**	**0**	**0**	**0**
1994-95	**NY Islanders**	**NHL**	**40**	**0**	**2**	**2**	**109**	**0**	**0**	**0**	**11**	**0.0**	**1**	....	....	....	....	....	....	....	....	....	....	....	....	....
1995-96	**NY Islanders**	**NHL**	**32**	**1**	**1**	**2**	**106**	**0**	**0**	**0**	**11**	**9.1**	**–3**	....	....	....	....	....	....	....	....	....	....	....	....	....
1996-97	**NY Islanders**	**NHL**	**17**	**1**	**0**	**1**	**71**	**0**	**0**	**0**	**7**	**14.3**	**–2**	....	....	....	....	....	....	....	....	....	....	....	....	....
	Utah Grizzlies	IHL	43	11	11	22	185	....	....	....	....	....	....	....	....	....	....	....	7	1	2	3	20	....	....	....
1997-98	**Tampa Bay**	**NHL**	**42**	**1**	**0**	**1**	**116**	**0**	**0**	**0**	**15**	**6.7**	**0**	....	....	....	....	....	....	....	....	....	....	....	....	....
	Montreal	**NHL**	**22**	**0**	**0**	**0**	**76**	**0**	**0**	**0**	**8**	**0.0**	**–4**	....	....	....	....	....	**1**	**0**	**0**	**0**	**0**	**0**	**0**	**0**
1998-99	Utah Grizzlies	IHL	48	8	7	15	226	....	....	....	....	....	....	....	....	....	....	....	....	....	....	....	....	....	....	....
99-2000	Utah Grizzlies	IHL	71	6	15	21	249	....	....	....	....	....	....	....	....	....	....	....	4	0	0	0	2	....	....	....
	NHL Totals		**574**	**17**	**29**	**46**	**2071**	**0**	**0**	**0**	**269**	**6.3**		....	....	....	....	....	**23**	**0**	**0**	**0**	**73**	**0**	**0**	**0**

Signed as a free agent by **NY Islanders**, March 2, 1987. Claimed by **Tampa Bay** from **NY Islanders** in NHL Waiver Draft, September 28, 1997. Traded to **Montreal** by **Tampa Bay** with Patrick Poulin and Igor Ulanov for Stephane Richer, Darcy Tucker and David Wilkie, January 15, 1998.

VYSHEDKEVICH, Sergei

(vee-shehd-KAY-vihch, SAIR-gay) **ATL.**

Defense. Shoots left. 6', 195 lbs. Born, Dedovsk, USSR, January 3, 1975. New Jersey's 3rd choice, 70th overall, in 1995 Entry Draft.

Season	Club	League	GP	G	A	Pts	PIM	PP	SH	GW	S	%	+/-	TF	F%	H	SB	Min	GP	G	A	Pts	PIM	PP	SH	GW
1994-95	Dynamo Moscow	CIS	49	6	7	13	67	....	....	....	....	....	....	....	....	....	....	....	14	2	0	2	12	....	....	....
1995-96	Dynamo Moscow	CIS	49	5	4	9	12	....	....	....	....	....	....	....	....	....	....	....	13	1	1	2	6	....	....	....
1996-97	Albany River Rats	AHL	65	8	27	35	16	....	....	....	....	....	....	....	....	....	....	....	12	0	6	6	0	....	....	....
1997-98	Albany River Rats	AHL	54	12	16	28	12	....	....	....	....	....	....	....	....	....	....	....	13	0	10	10	4	....	....	....
1998-99	Albany River Rats	AHL	79	11	38	49	28	....	....	....	....	....	....	....	....	....	....	....	5	0	3	3	0	....	....	....
99-2000	**Atlanta**	**NHL**	**7**	**1**	**3**	**4**	**2**	**1**	**0**	**0**	**5**	**20.0**	**–3**	**0**	**0.0**	**14**	**8**	**23:18**	....	....	....	....	....	....	....	....
	Orlando	IHL	69	11	24	35	32	....	....	....	....	....	....	....	....	....	....	....	6	3	3	6	8	....	....	....
	NHL Totals		**7**	**1**	**3**	**4**	**2**	**1**	**0**	**0**	**5**	**20.0**		**0**	**0.0**	**14**	**8**	**23:18**	....	....	....	....	....	....	....	....

Traded to **Atlanta** by **New Jersey** for future considerations, June 25, 1999.

WALKER, Scott

(WAH-kuhr, SKAWT) **NSH.**

Center. Shoots right. 5'10", 195 lbs. Born, Cambridge, Ont., July 19, 1973. Vancouver's 4th choice, 124th overall, in 1993 Entry Draft.

Season	Club	League	GP	G	A	Pts	PIM	PP	SH	GW	S	%	+/-	TF	F%	H	SB	Min	GP	G	A	Pts	PIM	PP	SH	GW
1989-90	Kitchener B's	OJHL-B	6	0	5	5	4	....	....	....	....	....	....	....	....	....	....	....	....	....	....	....	....	....	....	....
	Cambridge Hawks	OJHL-B	27	7	22	29	87	....	....	....	....	....	....	....	....	....	....	....	....	....	....	....	....	....	....	....
1990-91	Cambridge Hawks	OJHL-B	45	10	27	37	241	....	....	....	....	....	....	....	....	....	....	....	....	....	....	....	....	....	....	....
1991-92	Owen Sound	OHL	53	7	31	38	128	....	....	....	....	....	....	....	....	....	....	....	5	0	7	7	8	....	....	....
1992-93	Owen Sound	OHL	57	23	68	91	110	....	....	....	....	....	....	....	....	....	....	....	8	1	5	6	16	....	....	....
	Canada	Nat-Team	2	3	0	3	0	....	....	....	....	....	....	....	....	....	....	....	....	....	....	....	....	....	....	....
1993-94	Hamilton Canucks	AHL	77	10	29	39	272	....	....	....	....	....	....	....	....	....	....	....	4	0	1	1	25	....	....	....
1994-95	Syracuse Crunch	AHL	74	14	38	52	334	....	....	....	....	....	....	....	....	....	....	....	....	....	....	....	....	....	....	....
	Vancouver	**NHL**	**11**	**0**	**1**	**1**	**33**	**0**	**0**	**0**	**8**	**0.0**	**0**	....	....	....	....	....	....	....	....	....	....	....	....	....
1995-96	**Vancouver**	**NHL**	**63**	**4**	**8**	**12**	**137**	**0**	**1**	**1**	**45**	**8.9**	**–7**	....	....	....	....	....	....	....	....	....	....	....	....	....
	Syracuse Crunch	AHL	15	3	12	15	52	....	....	....	....	....	....	....	....	....	....	....	16	9	8	17	39	....	....	....
1996-97	**Vancouver**	**NHL**	**64**	**3**	**15**	**18**	**132**	**0**	**0**	**0**	**55**	**5.5**	**2**	....	....	....	....	....	....	....	....	....	....	....	....	....
1997-98	**Vancouver**	**NHL**	**59**	**3**	**10**	**13**	**164**	**0**	**1**	**1**	**40**	**7.5**	**–8**	....	....	....	....	....	....	....	....	....	....	....	....	....
1998-99	**Nashville**	**NHL**	**71**	**15**	**25**	**40**	**103**	**0**	**1**	**2**	**96**	**15.6**	**0**	**265**	**48.3**	**82**	**41**	**16:21**	....	....	....	....	....	....	....	....
99-2000	**Nashville**	**NHL**	**69**	**7**	**21**	**28**	**90**	**0**	**1**	**0**	**98**	**7.1**	**–16**	**30**	**36.7**	**121**	**36**	**15:49**	....	....	....	....	....	....	....	....
	NHL Totals		**337**	**32**	**80**	**112**	**659**	**0**	**4**	**4**	**342**	**9.4**		**295**	**47.1**	**203**	**77**	**16:05**	....	....	....	....	....	....	....	....

OHL Second All-Star Team (1993)

Claimed by **Nashville** from **Vancouver** in Expansion Draft, June 26, 1998.

WALLIN, Jesse

(WAHL-ihn, JEH-see) **DET.**

Defense. Shoots left. 6'2", 190 lbs. Born, Saskatoon, Sask., March 10, 1978. Detroit's 1st choice, 26th overall, in 1996 Entry Draft.

Season	Club	League	GP	G	A	Pts	PIM	PP	SH	GW	S	%	+/-	TF	F%	H	SB	Min	GP	G	A	Pts	PIM	PP	SH	GW
1993-94	North Battleford	SAHA	32	1	7	8	41	....	....	....	....	....	....	....	....	....	....	....	....	....	....	....	....	....	....	....
1994-95	Red Deer Rebels	WHL	72	4	20	24	72	....	....	....	....	....	....	....	....	....	....	....	....	....	....	....	....	....	....	....
1995-96	Red Deer Rebels	WHL	70	5	19	24	61	....	....	....	....	....	....	....	....	....	....	....	9	0	3	3	4	....	....	....
1996-97	Red Deer Rebels	WHL	59	6	33	39	70	....	....	....	....	....	....	....	....	....	....	....	16	1	4	5	10	....	....	....
1997-98	Red Deer Rebels	WHL	14	1	6	7	17	....	....	....	....	....	....	....	....	....	....	....	5	0	1	1	2	....	....	....
1998-99	Adirondack	AHL	76	4	12	16	34	....	....	....	....	....	....	....	....	....	....	....	3	0	2	2	2	....	....	....
99-2000	**Detroit**	**NHL**	**1**	**0**	**0**	**0**	**0**	**0**	**0**	**0**	**0**	**0.0**	**–2**	**0**	**0.0**	**2**	**1**	**19:22**	....	....	....	....	....	....	....	....
	Cincinnati Ducks	AHL	75	3	14	17	61	....	....	....	....	....	....	....	....	....	....	....	....	....	....	....	....	....	....	....
	NHL Totals		**1**	**0**	**0**	**0**	**0**	**0**	**0**	**0**	**0**	**0.0**		**0**	**0.0**	**2**	**1**	**19:22**	....	....	....	....	....	....	....	....

Canadian Major Junior Humanitarian Player of the Year (1997)

WALZ, Wes

(WAHLZ, WEHS) **MIN.**

Center. Shoots right. 5'10", 180 lbs. Born, Calgary, Alta., May 15, 1970. Boston's 3rd choice, 57th overall, in 1989 Entry Draft.

Season	Club	League	GP	G	A	Pts	PIM	PP	SH	GW	S	%	+/-	TF	F%	H	SB	Min	GP	G	A	Pts	PIM	PP	SH	GW
1987-88	Calgary Stars	AAHA	35	47	52	99	72	....	....	....	....	....	....	....	....	....	....	....	....	....	....	....	....	....	....	....
	Prince Albert	WHL	1	1	1	2	0	....	....	....	....	....	....	....	....	....	....	....	....	....	....	....	....	....	....	....
1988-89	Lethbridge	WHL	63	29	75	104	32	....	....	....	....	....	....	....	....	....	....	....	8	1	5	6	6	....	....	....
1989-90	Lethbridge	WHL	56	54	86	140	69	....	....	....	....	....	....	....	....	....	....	....	19	13	*24	*37	33	....	....	....
	Boston	**NHL**	**2**	**1**	**1**	**2**	**0**	**1**	**0**	**0**	**1**	**100.0**	**–1**	....	....	....	....	....	....	....	....	....	....	....	....	....
1990-91	**Boston**	**NHL**	**56**	**8**	**8**	**16**	**32**	**1**	**0**	**1**	**57**	**14.0**	**–14**	....	....	....	....	....	**2**	**0**	**0**	**0**	**0**	**0**	**0**	**0**
	Maine Mariners	AHL	20	8	12	20	19	....	....	....	....	....	....	....	....	....	....	....	2	0	0	0	21	....	....	....
1991-92	**Boston**	**NHL**	**15**	**0**	**3**	**3**	**12**	**0**	**0**	**0**	**17**	**0.0**	**–3**	....	....	....	....	....	....	....	....	....	....	....	....	....
	Maine Mariners	AHL	21	13	11	24	38	....	....	....	....	....	....	....	....	....	....	....	....	....	....	....	....	....	....	....
	Philadelphia	**NHL**	**2**	**1**	**0**	**1**	**0**	**0**	**0**	**1**	**2**	**50.0**	**1**	....	....	....	....	....	....	....	....	....	....	....	....	....
	Hershey Bears	AHL	41	13	28	41	37	....	....	....	....	....	....	....	....	....	....	....	6	1	2	3	0	....	....	....
1992-93	Hershey Bears	AHL	78	35	45	80	106	....	....	....	....	....	....	....	....	....	....	....	....	....	....	....	....	....	....	....
1993-94	**Calgary**	**NHL**	**53**	**11**	**27**	**38**	**16**	**1**	**0**	**0**	**79**	**13.9**	**20**	....	....	....	....	....	**6**	**3**	**0**	**3**	**2**	**0**	**0**	**0**
	Saint John Flames	AHL	15	6	6	12	14	....	....	....	....	....	....	....	....	....	....	....	....	....	....	....	....	....	....	....
1994-95	**Calgary**	**NHL**	**39**	**6**	**12**	**18**	**11**	**4**	**0**	**1**	**73**	**8.2**	**7**	....	....	....	....	....	**1**	**0**	**0**	**0**	**0**	**0**	**0**	**0**
1995-96	**Detroit**	**NHL**	**2**	**0**	**0**	**0**	**0**	**0**	**0**	**0**	**2**	**0.0**	**0**	....	....	....	....	....	....	....	....	....	....	....	....	....
	Adirondack	AHL	38	20	35	55	58	....	....	....	....	....	....	....	....	....	....	....	....	....	....	....	....	....	....	....
1996-97	EV Zug	Switz.	41	24	22	46	67	....	....	....	....	....	....	....	....	....	....	....	9	5	1	6	39	....	....	....
1997-98	EV Zug	Switz.	38	18	34	52	32	....	....	....	....	....	....	....	....	....	....	....	20	*16	*12	*28	18	....	....	....
	EV Zug	EuroHL	5	1	3	4	10	....	....	....	....	....	....	....	....	....	....	....	....	....	....	....	....	....	....	....
1998-99	EV Zug	Switz.	42	22	27	49	75	....	....	....	....	....	....	....	....	....	....	....	10	3	9	12	2	....	....	....
	EV Zug	EuroHL	6	7	5	12	4	....	....	....	....	....	....	....	....	....	....	....	2	0	0	0	12	....	....	....

			Regular Season																Playoffs							
Season	Club	League	GP	G	A	Pts	PIM	PP	SH	GW	S	%	+/-	TF	F%	H	SB	Min	GP	G	A	Pts	PIM	PP	SH	GW
99-2000	Long Beach	IHL	6	4	3	7	8	....	....	....	....	....	....	....	....	....	....	....	....	....	....	....	....	....	....	....
	HC Lugano	Switz.	13	7	11	18	14	....	....	....	....	....	....	....	....	....	....	....	5	3	4	7	4	....	....	....
	NHL Totals		**169**	**27**	**51**	**78**	**71**	**7**	**0**	**3**	**231**	**11.7**		....	....	....	....	....	**9**	**3**	**0**	**3**	**2**	**0**	**0**	**0**

WHL East First All-Star Team (1990)

Traded to **Philadelphia** by **Boston** with Garry Galley and Boston's 3rd round choice (Milos Holan) in 1993 Entry Draft for Gord Murphy, Brian Dobbin, Philadelphia's 3rd round choice (Sergei Zholtok) in 1992 Entry Draft and 4th round choice (Charles Paquette) in 1993 Entry Draft, January 2, 1992. Signed as a free agent by **Calgary**, August 26, 1993. Signed as a free agent by **Detroit**, September 6, 1995. Signed as a free agent by **Long Beach** (IHL), October 12, 1999. Signed as a free agent by **Minnesota**, June 28, 2000.

WARD, Aaron (WOHRD, AIR-ohn) DET.

Defense. Shoots right. 6'2", 200 lbs. Born, Windsor, Ont., January 17, 1973. Winnipeg's 1st choice, 5th overall, in 1991 Entry Draft.

1988-89	Nepean Raiders	OJHL	54	1	14	15	40	....	....	....	....	....	....	....	....	....	....	....	....	....	....	....	....	....	....	....
1989-90	Nepean Raiders	OJHL	52	6	33	39	85	....	....	....	....	....	....	....	....	....	....	....	....	....	....	....	....	....	....	....
1990-91	U. of Michigan	CCHA	46	8	11	19	126	....	....	....	....	....	....	....	....	....	....	....	....	....	....	....	....	....	....	....
1991-92	U. of Michigan	CCHA	42	7	12	19	64	....	....	....	....	....	....	....	....	....	....	....	....	....	....	....	....	....	....	....
1992-93	U. of Michigan	CCHA	30	5	8	13	73	....	....	....	....	....	....	....	....	....	....	....	....	....	....	....	....	....	....	....
	Canada	Nat-Team	4	0	0	0	8	....	....	....	....	....	....	....	....	....	....	....	....	....	....	....	....	....	....	....
1993-94	**Detroit**	**NHL**	**5**	**1**	**0**	**1**	**4**	**0**	**0**	**0**	**3**	**33.3**	**2**	....	....	....	....	....	....	....	....	....	....	....	....	....
	Adirondack	AHL	58	4	12	16	87	....	....	....	....	....	....	....	....	....	....	....	9	2	6	8	6	....	....	....
1994-95	Adirondack	AHL	76	11	24	35	87	....	....	....	....	....	....	....	....	....	....	....	4	0	1	1	0	....	....	....
	Detroit	**NHL**	**1**	**0**	**1**	**1**	**2**	**0**	**0**	**0**	**0**	**0.0**	**1**	....	....	....	....	....	....	....	....	....	....	....	....	....
1995-96	Adirondack	AHL	74	5	10	15	133	....	....	....	....	....	....	....	....	....	....	....	3	0	0	0	6	....	....	....
1996-97♦	**Detroit**	**NHL**	**49**	**2**	**5**	**7**	**52**	**0**	**0**	**0**	**40**	**5.0**	**–9**	....	....	....	....	....	**19**	**0**	**0**	**0**	**17**	**0**	**0**	**0**
1997-98♦	**Detroit**	**NHL**	**52**	**5**	**5**	**10**	**47**	**0**	**0**	**1**	**47**	**10.6**	**–1**	....	....	....	....	....	....	....	....	....	....	....	....	....
1998-99	**Detroit**	**NHL**	**60**	**3**	**8**	**11**	**52**	**0**	**0**	**0**	**46**	**6.5**	**–5**	**0**	**0.0**	**133**	**37**	**13:55**	**8**	**0**	**1**	**1**	**8**	**0**	**0**	**0**
99-2000	**Detroit**	**NHL**	**36**	**1**	**3**	**4**	**24**	**0**	**0**	**0**	**25**	**4.0**	**–4**	**0**	**0.0**	**87**	**19**	**12:36**	**3**	**0**	**0**	**0**	**0**	**0**	**0**	**0**
	NHL Totals		**203**	**12**	**22**	**34**	**181**	**0**	**0**	**1**	**161**	**7.5**		**0**	**0.0**	**220**	**56**	**13:25**	**30**	**0**	**1**	**1**	**25**	**0**	**0**	**0**

Traded to **Detroit** by **Winnipeg** with Toronto's 4th round choice (previously acquired by Winnipeg - later traded to Detroit - Detroit selected John Jakopin) in 1993 Entry Draft for Paul Ysebaert and future considerations (Alan Kerr, June 18, 1993), June 11, 1993. • Missed majority of 1999-2000 season recovering from shoulder injury suffered in game vs. Vancouver, January 19, 2000.

WARD, Dixon (WOHRD, DIHX-ohn) BUF.

Right wing. Shoots right. 6', 200 lbs. Born, Leduc, Alta., September 23, 1968. Vancouver's 6th choice, 128th overall, in 1988 Entry Draft.

1986-87	Red Deer Rebels	AJHL	59	46	40	86	153	....	....	....	....	....	....	....	....	....	....	....	....	....	....	....	....	....	....	....
1987-88	Red Deer Rebels	AJHL	51	60	71	131	167	....	....	....	....	....	....	....	....	....	....	....	....	....	....	....	....	....	....	....
1988-89	North Dakota	WCHA	37	8	9	17	26	....	....	....	....	....	....	....	....	....	....	....	....	....	....	....	....	....	....	....
1989-90	North Dakota	WCHA	45	35	34	69	44	....	....	....	....	....	....	....	....	....	....	....	....	....	....	....	....	....	....	....
1990-91	North Dakota	WCHA	43	34	35	69	84	....	....	....	....	....	....	....	....	....	....	....	....	....	....	....	....	....	....	....
1991-92	North Dakota	WCHA	38	33	31	64	90	....	....	....	....	....	....	....	....	....	....	....	....	....	....	....	....	....	....	....
1992-93	**Vancouver**	**NHL**	**70**	**22**	**30**	**52**	**82**	**4**	**1**	**0**	**111**	**19.8**	**34**	....	....	....	....	....	**9**	**2**	**3**	**5**	**0**	**2**	**0**	**0**
1993-94	**Vancouver**	**NHL**	**33**	**6**	**1**	**7**	**37**	**2**	**0**	**1**	**46**	**13.0**	**–14**	....	....	....	....	....	....	....	....	....	....	....	....	....
	Los Angeles	**NHL**	**34**	**6**	**2**	**8**	**45**	**2**	**0**	**0**	**44**	**13.6**	**–8**	....	....	....	....	....	....	....	....	....	....	....	....	....
1994-95	**Toronto**	**NHL**	**22**	**0**	**3**	**3**	**31**	**0**	**0**	**0**	**15**	**0.0**	**–4**	....	....	....	....	....	....	....	....	....	....	....	....	....
	St. John's Leafs	AHL	6	3	3	6	19	....	....	....	....	....	....	....	....	....	....	....	....	....	....	....	....	....	....	....
	Detroit Vipers	IHL	7	3	6	9	7	....	....	....	....	....	....	....	....	....	....	....	5	3	0	3	7	....	....	....
1995-96	**Buffalo**	**NHL**	**8**	**2**	**2**	**4**	**6**	**0**	**0**	**1**	**12**	**16.7**	**1**	....	....	....	....	....	....	....	....	....	....	....	....	....
	Rochester	AHL	71	38	56	94	74	....	....	....	....	....	....	....	....	....	....	....	19	11	*24	*35	8	....	....	....
1996-97	**Buffalo**	**NHL**	**79**	**13**	**32**	**45**	**36**	**1**	**2**	**4**	**93**	**14.0**	**17**	....	....	....	....	....	**12**	**2**	**3**	**5**	**6**	**0**	**0**	**1**
1997-98	**Buffalo**	**NHL**	**71**	**10**	**13**	**23**	**42**	**0**	**2**	**3**	**99**	**10.1**	**9**	....	....	....	....	....	**15**	**3**	**8**	**11**	**6**	**0**	**0**	**0**
1998-99	**Buffalo**	**NHL**	**78**	**20**	**24**	**44**	**44**	**2**	**1**	**4**	**101**	**19.8**	**10**	**11**	**54.5**	**45**	**49**	**15:47**	**21**	**7**	**5**	**12**	**32**	**0**	**2**	**3**
99-2000	**Buffalo**	**NHL**	**71**	**11**	**9**	**20**	**41**	**1**	**2**	**2**	**101**	**10.9**	**1**	**8**	**50.0**	**48**	**44**	**13:58**	**5**	**0**	**1**	**1**	**2**	**0**	**0**	**0**
	NHL Totals		**466**	**90**	**116**	**206**	**364**	**12**	**8**	**15**	**622**	**14.5**		**19**	**52.6**	**93**	**93**	**14:55**	**62**	**14**	**20**	**34**	**46**	**2**	**2**	**4**

WCHA Second All-Star Team (1991, 1992) • Won Jack A. Butterfield Trophy (Playoff MVP - AHL) (1996)

Traded to **LA Kings** by **Vancouver** for Jimmy Carson, January 8, 1994. Traded to **Toronto** by **LA Kings** with Guy Leveque, Kelly Fairchild and Shayne Toporowski for Eric Lacroix, Chris Snell and Toronto's 4th round choice (Eric Belanger) in 1996 Entry Draft, October 3, 1994. Signed as a free agent by **Buffalo**, September 20, 1995.

WARD, Ed (WOHRD, EHD) N.J.

Right wing. Shoots right. 6'3", 220 lbs. Born, Edmonton, Alta., November 10, 1969. Quebec's 7th choice, 108th overall, in 1988 Entry Draft.

1986-87	Sherwood Park	AJHL	60	18	28	46	272	....	....	....	....	....	....	....	....	....	....	....	....	....	....	....	....	....	....	....
1987-88	North-Michigan	WCHA	25	0	2	2	40	....	....	....	....	....	....	....	....	....	....	....	....	....	....	....	....	....	....	....
1988-89	North-Michigan	WCHA	42	5	15	20	36	....	....	....	....	....	....	....	....	....	....	....	....	....	....	....	....	....	....	....
1989-90	North-Michigan	WCHA	39	5	11	16	77	....	....	....	....	....	....	....	....	....	....	....	....	....	....	....	....	....	....	....
1990-91	North-Michigan	WCHA	46	13	18	31	109	....	....	....	....	....	....	....	....	....	....	....	....	....	....	....	....	....	....	....
1991-92	Greensboro	ECHL	12	4	8	12	21	....	....	....	....	....	....	....	....	....	....	....	....	....	....	....	....	....	....	....
	Halifax Citadels	AHL	51	7	11	18	65	....	....	....	....	....	....	....	....	....	....	....	....	....	....	....	....	....	....	....
1992-93	Halifax Citadels	AHL	70	13	19	32	56	....	....	....	....	....	....	....	....	....	....	....	....	....	....	....	....	....	....	....
1993-94	**Quebec**	**NHL**	**7**	**1**	**0**	**1**	**5**	**0**	**0**	**0**	**3**	**33.3**	**0**	....	....	....	....	....	....	....	....	....	....	....	....	....
	Cornwall Aces	AHL	60	12	30	42	65	....	....	....	....	....	....	....	....	....	....	....	12	1	3	4	14	....	....	....
1994-95	Cornwall Aces	AHL	56	10	14	24	118	....	....	....	....	....	....	....	....	....	....	....	....	....	....	....	....	....	....	....
	Calgary	**NHL**	**2**	**1**	**1**	**2**	**2**	**0**	**0**	**0**	**1**	**100.0**	**–2**	....	....	....	....	....	....	....	....	....	....	....	....	....
	Saint John Flames	AHL	11	4	5	9	20	....	....	....	....	....	....	....	....	....	....	....	5	1	0	1	10	....	....	....
1995-96	**Calgary**	**NHL**	**41**	**3**	**5**	**8**	**44**	**0**	**0**	**0**	**33**	**9.1**	**–2**	....	....	....	....	....	....	....	....	....	....	....	....	....
	Saint John Flames	AHL	12	1	2	3	45	....	....	....	....	....	....	....	....	....	....	....	16	4	4	8	27	....	....	....
1996-97	**Calgary**	**NHL**	**40**	**5**	**8**	**13**	**49**	**0**	**0**	**1**	**33**	**15.2**	**–3**	....	....	....	....	....	....	....	....	....	....	....	....	....
	Saint John Flames	AHL	1	0	0	0	0	....	....	....	....	....	....	....	....	....	....	....	....	....	....	....	....	....	....	....
	Detroit Vipers	IHL	31	7	6	13	45	....	....	....	....	....	....	....	....	....	....	....	....	....	....	....	....	....	....	....
1997-98	**Calgary**	**NHL**	**64**	**4**	**5**	**9**	**122**	**0**	**0**	**0**	**52**	**7.7**	**–1**	....	....	....	....	....	....	....	....	....	....	....	....	....
1998-99	**Calgary**	**NHL**	**68**	**3**	**5**	**8**	**67**	**0**	**0**	**0**	**56**	**5.4**	**–4**	**6**	**33.3**	**122**	**14**	**8:02**	....	....	....	....	....	....	....	....
99-2000	**Atlanta**	**NHL**	**44**	**5**	**1**	**6**	**44**	**0**	**2**	**0**	**51**	**9.8**	**–5**	**7**	**28.6**	**130**	**15**	**11:26**	....	....	....	....	....	....	....	....
	Anaheim	**NHL**	**8**	**1**	**0**	**1**	**15**	**0**	**0**	**0**	**5**	**20.0**	**–2**	**0**	**0.0**	**13**	**0**	**6:56**	....	....	....	....	....	....	....	....
	NHL Totals		**274**	**23**	**25**	**48**	**348**	**0**	**2**	**1**	**234**	**9.8**		**13**	**30.8**	**265**	**29**	**9:12**	....	....	....	....	....	....	....	....

Traded to **Calgary** by **Quebec** for Francois Groleau, March 23, 1995. Claimed by **Atlanta** from **Calgary** in Expansion Draft, June 25, 1999. Traded to **Anaheim** by **Atlanta** for a conditional choice in 2001 Entry Draft, March 14, 2000. Traded to **New Jersey** by **Anaheim** for New Jersey's 7th round choice in 2001 Entry Draft, June 12, 2000.

WARD, Jason (WOHRD, JAY-suhn) MTL.

Right wing. Shoots right. 6'3", 193 lbs. Born, Chapleau, Ont., January 16, 1979. Montreal's 1st choice, 11th overall, in 1997 Entry Draft.

1994-95	Oshawa Legion	OJHL	47	30	31	61	75	....	....	....	....	....	....	....	....	....	....	....	....	....	....	....	....	....	....	....
1995-96	Niagara Falls	OHL	64	15	35	50	139	....	....	....	....	....	....	....	....	....	....	....	10	6	4	10	23	....	....	....
1996-97	Erie Otters	OHL	58	25	39	64	137	....	....	....	....	....	....	....	....	....	....	....	5	1	2	3	2	....	....	....
1997-98	Erie Otters	OHL	21	7	9	16	42	....	....	....	....	....	....	....	....	....	....	....	....	....	....	....	....	....	....	....
	Windsor Spitfires	OHL	26	19	27	46	34	....	....	....	....	....	....	....	....	....	....	....	....	....	....	....	....	....	....	....
	Fredericton	AHL	7	1	0	1	2	....	....	....	....	....	....	....	....	....	....	....	1	0	0	0	2	....	....	....
1998-99	Windsor Spitfires	OHL	12	8	11	19	25	....	....	....	....	....	....	....	....	....	....	....	....	....	....	....	....	....	....	....
	Plymouth Whalers	OHL	23	14	13	27	28	....	....	....	....	....	....	....	....	....	....	....	11	6	8	14	12	....	....	....
	Fredericton	AHL	....	....	....	....	....	....	....	....	....	....	....	....	....	....	....	....	10	4	2	6	22	....	....	....
99-2000	**Montreal**	**NHL**	**32**	**2**	**1**	**3**	**10**	**1**	**0**	**0**	**24**	**8.3**	**–1**	**86**	**44.2**	**37**	**5**	**9:10**	....	....	....	....	....	....	....	....
	Quebec Citadelles	AHL	40	14	12	26	30	....	....	....	....	....	....	....	....	....	....	....	3	2	1	3	4	....	....	....
	NHL Totals		**32**	**2**	**1**	**3**	**10**	**1**	**0**	**0**	**24**	**8.3**		**86**	**44.2**	**37**	**5**	**9:10**	....	....	....	....	....	....	....	....

WARE, Jeff

(WAIR, JEHF)

Defense. Shoots left. 6'4", 220 lbs. Born, Toronto, Ont., May 19, 1977. Toronto's 1st choice, 15th overall, in 1995 Entry Draft.

			Regular Season																Playoffs							
Season	Club	League	GP	G	A	Pts	PIM	PP	SH	GW	S	%	+/–	TF	F%	H	SB	Min	GP	G	A	Pts	PIM	PP	SH	GW
1993-94	Wexford Raiders	OJHL	45	1	9	10	75	....	....	....	....	....	....	....	....	....	....	....	....	....	....	....	....	....	....	....
1994-95	Oshawa Generals	OHL	55	2	11	13	86	....	....	....	....	....	....	....	....	....	....	....	7	1	1	2	6	....	....	....
1995-96	Oshawa Generals	OHL	62	4	19	23	128	....	....	....	....	....	....	....	....	....	....	....	5	0	1	1	8	....	....	....
	St. John's Leafs	AHL	4	0	0	0	4	....	....	....	....	....	....	....	....	....	....	....	4	0	0	0	2	....	....	....
1996-97	Oshawa Generals	OHL	24	1	10	11	38	....	....	....	....	....	....	....	....	....	....	....	13	0	3	3	34	....	....	....
	Toronto	**NHL**	**13**	**0**	**0**	**0**	**6**	**0**	**0**	**0**	**4**	**0.0**	**2**	....	....	....	....	....	....	....	....	....	....	....	....	....
1997-98	**Toronto**	**NHL**	**2**	**0**	**0**	**0**	**0**	**0**	**0**	**0**	**0**	**0.0**	**1**	....	....	....	....	....	....	....	....	....	....	....	....	....
	St. John's Leafs	AHL	67	0	3	3	182	....	....	....	....	....	....	....	....	....	....	....	4	0	0	0	4	....	....	....
1998-99	St. John's Leafs	AHL	55	1	4	5	130	....	....	....	....	....	....	....	....	....	....	....	....	....	....	....	....	....	....	....
	Florida	**NHL**	**6**	**0**	**1**	**1**	**6**	**0**	**0**	**0**	**1**	**0.0**	**–6**	**0**	**0.0**	**13**	**8**	**15:57**	....	....	....	....	....	....	....	....
	New Haven	AHL	20	0	1	1	26	....	....	....	....	....	....	....	....	....	....	....	....	....	....	....	....	....	....	....
99-2000	Louisville	AHL	51	0	10	10	128	....	....	....	....	....	....	....	....	....	....	....	4	0	0	0	4	....	....	....
	NHL Totals		**21**	**0**	**1**	**1**	**12**	**0**	**0**	**0**	**5**	**0.0**		**0**	**0.0**	**13**	**8**	**15:57**	....	....	....	....	....	....	....	....

Traded to **Florida** by **Toronto** for David Nemirovsky, February 17, 1999.

WARRENER, Rhett

(WAHR-ihn-uhr, REHT) **BUF.**

Defense. Shoots right. 6'1", 206 lbs. Born, Shaunavon, Sask., January 27, 1976. Florida's 2nd choice, 27th overall, in 1994 Entry Draft.

			Regular Season																Playoffs							
Season	Club	League	GP	G	A	Pts	PIM	PP	SH	GW	S	%	+/–	TF	F%	H	SB	Min	GP	G	A	Pts	PIM	PP	SH	GW
1991-92	Saskatoon Blaze	AAHA	33	6	5	11	71	....	....	....	....	....	....	....	....	....	....	....	....	....	....	....	....	....	....	....
	Saskatoon Blades	WHL	2	0	0	0	0	....	....	....	....	....	....	....	....	....	....	....	....	....	....	....	....	....	....	....
1992-93	Saskatoon Blades	WHL	68	2	17	19	100	....	....	....	....	....	....	....	....	....	....	....	9	0	0	0	14	....	....	....
1993-94	Saskatoon Blades	WHL	61	7	19	26	131	....	....	....	....	....	....	....	....	....	....	....	16	0	5	5	33	....	....	....
1994-95	Saskatoon Blades	WHL	66	13	26	39	137	....	....	....	....	....	....	....	....	....	....	....	10	0	3	3	6	....	....	....
1995-96	**Florida**	**NHL**	**28**	**0**	**3**	**3**	**46**	**0**	**0**	**0**	**19**	**0.0**	**4**	....	....	....	....	....	**21**	**0**	**1**	**1**	**0**	**0**	**0**	**0**
	Carolina	AHL	9	0	0	0	4	....	....	....	....	....	....	....	....	....	....	....	....	....	....	....	....	....	....	....
1996-97	**Florida**	**NHL**	**62**	**4**	**9**	**13**	**88**	**1**	**0**	**1**	**58**	**6.9**	**20**	....	....	....	....	....	**5**	**0**	**0**	**0**	**0**	**0**	**0**	**0**
1997-98	**Florida**	**NHL**	**79**	**0**	**4**	**4**	**99**	**0**	**0**	**0**	**66**	**0.0**	**–16**	....	....	....	....	....	....	....	....	....	....	....	....	....
1998-99	**Florida**	**NHL**	**48**	**0**	**7**	**7**	**64**	**0**	**0**	**0**	**33**	**0.0**	**–1**	**0**	**0.0**	**75**	**38**	**19:01**	....	....	....	....	....	....	....	....
	Buffalo	**NHL**	**13**	**1**	**0**	**1**	**20**	**0**	**0**	**0**	**11**	**9.1**	**3**	**0**	**0.0**	**28**	**12**	**18:13**	**20**	**1**	**3**	**4**	**32**	**0**	**0**	**0**
99-2000	**Buffalo**	**NHL**	**61**	**0**	**3**	**3**	**89**	**0**	**0**	**0**	**68**	**0.0**	**18**	**0**	**0.0**	**131**	**79**	**19:51**	**5**	**0**	**0**	**0**	**2**	**0**	**0**	**0**
	NHL Totals		**291**	**5**	**26**	**31**	**406**	**1**	**0**	**1**	**255**	**2.0**		**0**	**0.0**	**234**	**129**	**19:21**	**51**	**1**	**4**	**5**	**34**	**0**	**0**	**0**

Traded to **Buffalo** by **Florida** with Florida's 5th round choice (Ryan Miller) in 1999 Entry Draft for Mike Wilson, March 23, 1999.

WARRINER, Todd

(WAHR-ihn-uhr, TAWD) **T.B.**

Left wing. Shoots left. 6'1", 200 lbs. Born, Blenheim, Ont., January 3, 1974. Quebec's 1st choice, 4th overall, in 1992 Entry Draft.

			Regular Season																Playoffs							
Season	Club	League	GP	G	A	Pts	PIM	PP	SH	GW	S	%	+/–	TF	F%	H	SB	Min	GP	G	A	Pts	PIM	PP	SH	GW
1988-89	Blenheim Blades	OJHL-C	10	1	4	5	0	....	....	....	....	....	....	....	....	....	....	....	....	....	....	....	....	....	....	....
1989-90	Chatham	OJHL-B	40	24	21	45	12	....	....	....	....	....	....	....	....	....	....	....	....	....	....	....	....	....	....	....
1990-91	Windsor Spitfires	OHL	57	36	28	64	26	....	....	....	....	....	....	....	....	....	....	....	11	5	6	11	12	....	....	....
1991-92	Windsor Spitfires	OHL	50	41	41	82	64	....	....	....	....	....	....	....	....	....	....	....	7	5	4	9	6	....	....	....
1992-93	Windsor Spitfires	OHL	23	13	21	34	29	....	....	....	....	....	....	....	....	....	....	....	....	....	....	....	....	....	....	....
	Kitchener	OHL	32	19	24	43	35	....	....	....	....	....	....	....	....	....	....	....	7	5	14	19	14	....	....	....
1993-94	Canada	Nat-Team	50	11	20	31	33	....	....	....	....	....	....	....	....	....	....	....	....	....	....	....	....	....	....	....
	Canada	Olympics	4	1	1	2	0	....	....	....	....	....	....	....	....	....	....	....	....	....	....	....	....	....	....	....
	Kitchener	OHL	....	....	....	....	....	....	....	....	....	....	....	....	....	....	....	....	1	0	1	1	0	....	....	....
	Cornwall Aces	AHL	....	....	....	....	....	....	....	....	....	....	....	....	....	....	....	....	10	1	4	5	4	....	....	....
1994-95	St. John's Leafs	AHL	46	8	10	18	22	....	....	....	....	....	....	....	....	....	....	....	4	1	0	1	2	....	....	....
	Toronto	**NHL**	**5**	**0**	**0**	**0**	**0**	**0**	**0**	**0**	**1**	**0.0**	**–3**	....	....	....	....	....	....	....	....	....	....	....	....	....
1995-96	**Toronto**	**NHL**	**57**	**7**	**8**	**15**	**26**	**1**	**0**	**0**	**79**	**8.9**	**–11**	....	....	....	....	....	**6**	**1**	**1**	**2**	**2**	**0**	**0**	**0**
	St. John's Leafs	AHL	11	5	6	11	16	....	....	....	....	....	....	....	....	....	....	....	....	....	....	....	....	....	....	....
1996-97	**Toronto**	**NHL**	**75**	**12**	**21**	**33**	**41**	**2**	**2**	**0**	**146**	**8.2**	**–3**	....	....	....	....	....	....	....	....	....	....	....	....	....
1997-98	**Toronto**	**NHL**	**45**	**5**	**8**	**13**	**20**	**0**	**0**	**1**	**73**	**6.8**	**5**	....	....	....	....	....	....	....	....	....	....	....	....	....
1998-99	**Toronto**	**NHL**	**53**	**9**	**10**	**19**	**28**	**1**	**0**	**1**	**96**	**9.4**	**–6**	**579**	**47.8**	**52**	**10**	**14:06**	**9**	**0**	**0**	**0**	**2**	**0**	**0**	**0**
99-2000	**Toronto**	**NHL**	**18**	**3**	**1**	**4**	**2**	**0**	**0**	**0**	**33**	**9.1**	**6**	**33**	**45.5**	**18**	**5**	**12:33**	....	....	....	....	....	....	....	....
	Tampa Bay	**NHL**	**55**	**11**	**13**	**24**	**34**	**3**	**1**	**0**	**100**	**11.0**	**–14**	**175**	**52.0**	**72**	**20**	**16:28**	....	....	....	....	....	....	....	....
	NHL Totals		**308**	**47**	**61**	**108**	**151**	**7**	**3**	**2**	**528**	**8.9**		**787**	**48.7**	**142**	**35**	**14:55**	**15**	**1**	**1**	**2**	**4**	**0**	**0**	**0**

OHL First All-Star Team (1992)

Traded to **Toronto** by **Quebec** with Mats Sundin, Garth Butcher and Philadelphia's 1st round choice (previously acquired by Quebec - later traded to Washington - Washington selected Nolan Baumgartner) in 1994 Entry Draft for Wendel Clark, Sylvain Lefebvre, Landon Wilson and Toronto's 1st round choice (Jeffrey Kealty) in 1994 Entry Draft, June 28, 1994. Traded to **Tampa Bay** by **Toronto** for Tampa Bay's 3rd round choice (Mikael Tellqvist) in 2000 Entry Draft, November 29, 1999.

WASHBURN, Steve

(WAWSH-buhrn, STEEV)

Center. Shoots left. 6'2", 198 lbs. Born, Ottawa, Ont., April 10, 1975. Florida's 5th choice, 78th overall, in 1993 Entry Draft.

			Regular Season																Playoffs							
Season	Club	League	GP	G	A	Pts	PIM	PP	SH	GW	S	%	+/–	TF	F%	H	SB	Min	GP	G	A	Pts	PIM	PP	SH	GW
1990-91	Gloucester	OJHL	56	21	30	51	47	....	....	....	....	....	....	....	....	....	....	....	....	....	....	....	....	....	....	....
1991-92	Ottawa 67's	OHL	59	5	17	22	10	....	....	....	....	....	....	....	....	....	....	....	11	2	3	5	4	....	....	....
1992-93	Ottawa 67's	OHL	66	20	38	58	54	....	....	....	....	....	....	....	....	....	....	....	....	....	....	....	....	....	....	....
1993-94	Ottawa 67's	OHL	65	30	50	80	88	....	....	....	....	....	....	....	....	....	....	....	17	7	16	23	10	....	....	....
1994-95	Ottawa 67's	OHL	63	43	63	106	72	....	....	....	....	....	....	....	....	....	....	....	....	....	....	....	....	....	....	....
	Cincinnati	IHL	6	3	1	4	0	....	....	....	....	....	....	....	....	....	....	....	9	1	3	4	4	....	....	....
1995-96	**Florida**	**NHL**	**1**	**0**	**1**	**1**	**0**	**0**	**0**	**0**	**1**	**0.0**	**1**	....	....	....	....	....	**1**	**0**	**1**	**1**	**0**	**0**	**0**	**0**
	Carolina	AHL	78	29	54	83	45	....	....	....	....	....	....	....	....	....	....	....	....	....	....	....	....	....	....	....
1996-97	**Florida**	**NHL**	**18**	**3**	**6**	**9**	**4**	**1**	**0**	**0**	**21**	**14.3**	**2**	....	....	....	....	....	....	....	....	....	....	....	....	....
	Carolina	AHL	60	23	40	63	66	....	....	....	....	....	....	....	....	....	....	....	....	....	....	....	....	....	....	....
1997-98	**Florida**	**NHL**	**58**	**11**	**8**	**19**	**32**	**4**	**0**	**2**	**61**	**18.0**	**–6**	....	....	....	....	....	....	....	....	....	....	....	....	....
	New Haven	AHL	6	3	5	8	4	....	....	....	....	....	....	....	....	....	....	....	3	2	0	2	15	....	....	....
1998-99	**Florida**	**NHL**	**4**	**0**	**0**	**0**	**4**	**0**	**0**	**0**	**0**	**0.0**	**–1**	**21**	**38.1**	**1**	**0**	**6:17**	....	....	....	....	....	....	....	....
	New Haven	AHL	10	4	3	7	6	....	....	....	....	....	....	....	....	....	....	....	....	....	....	....	....	....	....	....
	Vancouver	**NHL**	**8**	**0**	**0**	**0**	**2**	**0**	**0**	**0**	**6**	**0.0**	**0**	**30**	**40.0**	**9**	**1**	**8:05**	....	....	....	....	....	....	....	....
	Syracuse Crunch	AHL	13	1	6	7	6	....	....	....	....	....	....	....	....	....	....	....	....	....	....	....	....	....	....	....
99-2000	Milwaukee	IHL	12	0	4	4	16	....	....	....	....	....	....	....	....	....	....	....	....	....	....	....	....	....	....	....
	Philadelphia	**NHL**	**1**	**0**	**0**	**0**	**0**	**0**	**0**	**0**	**1**	**0.0**	**0**	**8**	**12.5**	**7**	**0**	**14:26**	....	....	....	....	....	....	....	....
	Philadelphia	AHL	61	19	52	71	93	....	....	....	....	....	....	....	....	....	....	....	5	0	2	2	8	....	....	....
	NHL Totals		**90**	**14**	**15**	**29**	**42**	**5**	**0**	**2**	**90**	**15.6**		**59**	**35.6**	**17**	**1**	**8:01**	**1**	**0**	**1**	**1**	**0**	**0**	**0**	**0**

Claimed on waivers by **Vancouver** from **Florida**, February 18, 1999. Signed as a free agent by **Nashville**, August 11, 1999. Traded to **Philadelphia** by **Nashville** for a conditional choice in 2001 Entry Draft, November 16, 1999.

WATT, Mike

(WAHT, MIGHK) **NSH.**

Left wing. Shoots left. 6'2", 212 lbs. Born, Seaforth, Ont., March 31, 1976. Edmonton's 3rd choice, 32nd overall, in 1994 Entry Draft.

			Regular Season																Playoffs							
Season	Club	League	GP	G	A	Pts	PIM	PP	SH	GW	S	%	+/–	TF	F%	H	SB	Min	GP	G	A	Pts	PIM	PP	SH	GW
1990-91	Seaforth	OJHL-D	39	15	23	38	43	....	....	....	....	....	....	....	....	....	....	....	....	....	....	....	....	....	....	....
1991-92	Stratford Cullitons	OJHL-B	40	5	21	26	103	....	....	....	....	....	....	....	....	....	....	....	....	....	....	....	....	....	....	....
1992-93	Stratford Cullitons	OJHL-B	45	20	35	55	100	....	....	....	....	....	....	....	....	....	....	....	....	....	....	....	....	....	....	....
1993-94	Stratford Cullitons	OJHL-B	48	34	34	68	165	....	....	....	....	....	....	....	....	....	....	....	....	....	....	....	....	....	....	....
1994-95	Michigan State	CCHA	39	12	6	18	64	....	....	....	....	....	....	....	....	....	....	....	....	....	....	....	....	....	....	....
1995-96	Michigan State	CCHA	37	17	22	39	60	....	....	....	....	....	....	....	....	....	....	....	....	....	....	....	....	....	....	....
1996-97	Michigan State	CCHA	39	24	17	41	109	....	....	....	....	....	....	....	....	....	....	....	....	....	....	....	....	....	....	....
1997-98	**Edmonton**	**NHL**	**14**	**1**	**2**	**3**	**4**	**0**	**0**	**1**	**14**	**7.1**	**–4**	....	....	....	....	....	....	....	....	....	....	....	....	....
	Hamilton Bulldogs	AHL	63	24	25	49	65	....	....	....	....	....	....	....	....	....	....	....	9	2	2	4	8	....	....	....
1998-99	**NY Islanders**	**NHL**	**75**	**8**	**17**	**25**	**12**	**0**	**0**	**4**	**75**	**10.7**	**–2**	**180**	**50.6**	**73**	**29**	**11:15**	....	....	....	....	....	....	....	....

			Regular Season																Playoffs							
Season	Club	League	GP	G	A	Pts	PIM	PP	SH	GW	S	%	+/-	TF	F%	H	SB	Min	GP	G	A	Pts	PIM	PP	SH	GW
99-2000	NY Islanders	NHL	45	5	6	11	17	0	1	0	49	10.2	-8	81	48.1	45	17	12:02								
	Lowell	AHL	16	6	11	17	6												7	1	1	2	4			
	NHL Totals		134	14	25	39	33	0	1	5	138	10.1		261	49.8	118	46	11:33								

Traded to **NY Islanders** by **Edmonton** for Eric Fichaud, June 18, 1998. Claimed on waivers by **Nashville** from **NY Islanders**, May 23, 2000.

WEBB, Steve

(WEHB, STEEV) **NYI**

Right wing. Shoots right. 6', 195 lbs. Born, Peterborough, Ont., April 30, 1975. Buffalo's 8th choice, 176th overall, in 1994 Entry Draft.

Season	Club	League	GP	G	A	Pts	PIM	PP	SH	GW	S	%	+/-	TF	F%	H	SB	Min	GP	G	A	Pts	PIM	PP	SH	GW
1991-92	Peterborough B's	OJHL-B	37	9	9	18	195																			
1992-93	Windsor Spitfires	OHL	63	14	25	39	184																			
1993-94	Windsor Spitfires	OHL	2	0	1	1	9																			
	Peterborough	OHL	33	6	15	21	117												6	1	1	2	20			
1994-95	Peterborough	OHL	42	8	16	24	109												11	3	3	6	22			
1995-96	Muskegon Fury	ColHL	58	18	24	42	263												5	1	2	3	22			
	Detroit Vipers	IHL	4	0	0	0	24																			
1996-97	NY Islanders	NHL	41	1	4	5	144	1	0	0	21	4.8	-10													
	Kentucky	AHL	25	6	6	12	103												2	0	0	0	19			
1997-98	NY Islanders	NHL	20	0	0	0	35	0	0	0	6	0.0	-2													
	Kentucky	AHL	37	5	13	18	139												3	0	1	1	10			
1998-99	NY Islanders	NHL	45	0	0	0	32	0	0	0	18	0.0	-10	0	0.0	64	1	4:13								
	Lowell	AHL	23	2	4	6	80																			
99-2000	NY Islanders	NHL	65	1	3	4	103	0	0	0	27	3.7	-4	1	0.0	194	12	7:00								
	NHL Totals		171	2	7	9	314	1	0	0	72	2.8		1	0.0	258	13	5:52								

Signed as a free agent by **NY Islanders**, October 10, 1996.

WEIGHT, Doug

(WAYT, DUHG) **EDM.**

Center. Shoots left. 5'11", 200 lbs. Born, Warren, MI, January 21, 1971. NY Rangers' 2nd choice, 34th overall, in 1990 Entry Draft.

Season	Club	League	GP	G	A	Pts	PIM	PP	SH	GW	S	%	+/-	TF	F%	H	SB	Min	GP	G	A	Pts	PIM	PP	SH	GW
1988-89	Bloomfield	NAJHL	34	26	53	79	105																			
1989-90	Lake Superior	CCHA	46	21	48	69	44																			
1990-91	Lake Superior	CCHA	42	29	46	75	86																			
	NY Rangers	NHL																	1	0	0	0	0	0	0	0
1991-92	NY Rangers	NHL	53	8	22	30	23	0	0	2	72	11.1	-3						7	2	2	4	0	1	0	0
	Binghamton	AHL	9	3	14	17	2												4	1	4	5	6			
1992-93	NY Rangers	NHL	65	15	25	40	55	3	0	1	90	16.7	4													
	Edmonton	NHL	13	2	6	8	10	0	0	0	35	5.7	-2													
1993-94	Edmonton	NHL	84	24	50	74	47	4	1	1	188	12.8	-22													
1994-95	SB Rosenheim	DEL	8	2	3	5	18																			
	Edmonton	NHL	48	7	33	40	69	1	0	1	104	6.7	-17													
1995-96	Edmonton	NHL	82	25	79	104	95	9	0	2	204	12.3	-19													
1996-97	Edmonton	NHL	80	21	61	82	80	4	0	2	235	8.9	1						12	3	8	11	8	0	0	0
1997-98	Edmonton	NHL	79	26	44	70	69	9	0	4	205	12.7	1						12	2	7	9	14	2	0	1
	United States	Olympics	4	0	2	2	2																			
1998-99	Edmonton	NHL	43	6	31	37	12	1	0	0	79	7.6	-8	853	49.5	43	16	19:51	4	1	1	2	15	0	0	0
99-2000	Edmonton	NHL	77	21	51	72	54	3	1	4	167	12.6	6	1588	50.4	76	44	20:35	5	3	2	5	4	2	0	1
	NHL Totals		624	155	402	557	514	34	2	17	1379	11.2		2441	50.1	119	60	20:19	41	11	20	31	41	5	0	2

CCHA First All-Star Team (1991) • NCAA West Second All-American Team (1991) • Played in NHL All-Star Game (1996, 1998)

Traded to **Edmonton** by **NY Rangers** for Esa Tikkanen, March 17, 1993.

WEINRICH, Eric

(WIGHN-rihc, AIR-ihk) **MTL.**

Defense. Shoots left. 6'1", 213 lbs. Born, Roanoke, VA, December 19, 1966. New Jersey's 3rd choice, 32nd overall, in 1985 Entry Draft.

Season	Club	League	GP	G	A	Pts	PIM	PP	SH	GW	S	%	+/-	TF	F%	H	SB	Min	GP	G	A	Pts	PIM	PP	SH	GW
1983-84	North Yarmouth	Hi-School	17	23	33	56																				
1984-85	North Yarmouth	Hi-School	20	6	21	27																				
1985-86	U. of Maine	H-East	34	0	14	14	26																			
1986-87	U. of Maine	H-East	41	12	32	44	59																			
1987-88	U. of Maine	H-East	8	4	7	11	22																			
	United States	Nat-Team	38	3	9	12	24																			
	United States	Olympics	3	0	0	0	0																			
1988-89	New Jersey	NHL	2	0	0	0	0	0	0	0	3	0.0	-1													
	Utica Devils	AHL	80	17	27	44	70												5	0	1	1	4			
1989-90	New Jersey	NHL	19	2	7	9	11	1	0	1	16	12.5	1						6	1	3	4	17	0	0	0
	Utica Devils	AHL	57	12	48	60	38																			
1990-91	New Jersey	NHL	76	4	34	38	48	1	0	0	96	4.2	10						7	1	2	3	6	1	0	0
1991-92	New Jersey	NHL	76	7	25	32	55	5	0	0	97	7.2	10						7	0	2	2	4	0	0	0
1992-93	Hartford	NHL	79	7	29	36	76	0	2	2	104	6.7	-11													
1993-94	Hartford	NHL	8	1	1	2	2	1	0	0	10	10.0	-5													
	Chicago	NHL	54	3	23	26	31	1	0	2	105	2.9	6						6	0	2	2	6	0	0	0
1994-95	Chicago	NHL	48	3	10	13	33	1	0	2	50	6.0	1						16	1	5	6	4	0	0	0
1995-96	Chicago	NHL	77	5	10	15	65	0	0	0	76	6.6	14						10	1	4	5	10	1	0	0
1996-97	Chicago	NHL	81	7	25	32	62	1	0	0	115	6.1	19						6	0	1	1	4	0	0	0
1997-98	Chicago	NHL	82	2	21	23	106	0	0	0	85	2.4	10													
1998-99	Chicago	NHL	14	1	3	4	12	0	0	0	24	4.2	-13	0	0.0	27	13	20:12								
	Montreal	NHL	66	6	12	18	77	4	0	1	95	6.3	-12	0	0.0	100	117	24:44								
99-2000	Montreal	NHL	77	4	25	29	39	2	0	0	120	3.3	4	0	0.0	124	152	25:21								
	NHL Totals		759	52	225	277	617	17	2	8	996	5.2		0	0.0	251	282	24:38	58	4	19	23	51	2	0	0

Hockey East First All-Star Team (1987) • NCAA East Second All-American Team (1987) • AHL First All-Star Team (1990) • Won Eddie Shore Award (Outstanding Defenseman - AHL) (1990) • NHL All-Rookie Team (1991)

Traded to **Hartford** by **New Jersey** with Sean Burke for Bobby Holik and Hartford's 2nd round choice (Jay Pandolfo) in 1993 Entry Draft, August 28, 1992. Traded to **Chicago** by **Hartford** with Patrick Poulin for Steve Larmer and Bryan Marchment, November 2, 1993. Traded to **Montreal** by **Chicago** with Jeff Hackett, Alain Nasreddine and Tampa Bay's 4th round choice (previously acquired, Montreal selected Chris Dyment) in 1999 Entry Draft for Jocelyn Thibault, Dave Manson and Brad Brown, November 16, 1998.

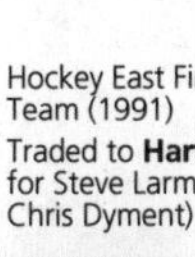

WELLS, Chris

(WEHLS, KRIHS) **DAL.**

Center. Shoots left. 6'6", 223 lbs. Born, Calgary, Alta., November 12, 1975. Pittsburgh's 1st choice, 24th overall, in 1994 Entry Draft.

Season	Club	League	GP	G	A	Pts	PIM	PP	SH	GW	S	%	+/-	TF	F%	H	SB	Min	GP	G	A	Pts	PIM	PP	SH	GW
1990-91	Calgary Royals	AAHA	35	13	14	27	33																			
1991-92	Seattle T-Birds	WHL	64	13	8	21	80												11	0	0	0	15			
1992-93	Seattle T-Birds	WHL	63	18	37	55	111												5	2	3	5	4			
1993-94	Seattle T-Birds	WHL	69	30	44	74	150												9	6	5	11	23			
1994-95	Seattle T-Birds	WHL	69	45	63	108	148												3	0	1	1	4			
	Cleveland	IHL	3	0	1	1	2																			
1995-96	Pittsburgh	NHL	54	2	2	4	59	0	1	0	25	8.0	-6													
1996-97	Cleveland	IHL	15	4	6	10	9																			
	Florida	NHL	47	2	6	8	42	0	0	0	29	6.9	5						3	0	0	0	0	0	0	0
1997-98	Florida	NHL	61	5	10	15	47	0	1	0	57	8.8	4													
1998-99	Florida	NHL	20	0	2	2	31	0	0	0	28	0.0	-4	231	40.7	21	12	11:52								
	New Haven	AHL	9	3	1	4	28																			
99-2000	Florida	NHL	13	0	0	0	14	0	0	0	5	0.0	-5	124	45.2	5	2	8:23								
	Louisville	AHL	31	8	10	18	20																			
	Hartford	AHL	14	2	2	4	6												20	3	4	7	38			
	NHL Totals		195	9	20	29	193	0	2	0	144	6.3		355	42.3	26	14	10:30	3	0	0	0	0	0	0	0

WHL West First All-Star Team (1995)

Traded to **Florida** by **Pittsburgh** for Stu Barnes and Jason Woolley, November 19, 1996. Traded to **NY Rangers** by **Florida** for conditional choice in 2001 Entry Draft, March 13, 2000. Signed as a free agent by **Dallas**, July 28, 2000.

			Regular Season																Playoffs							
Season	Club	League	GP	G	A	Pts	PIM	PP	SH	GW	S	%	+/-	TF	F%	H	SB	Min	GP	G	A	Pts	PIM	PP	SH	GW

WERENKA, Brad — (wuh-REHN-kuh, BRAD) — CGY.

Defense. Shoots left. 6'1", 218 lbs.   Born, Two Hills, Alta., February 12, 1969. Edmonton's 2nd choice, 42nd overall, in 1987 Entry Draft.

Season	Club	League	GP	G	A	Pts	PIM	PP	SH	GW	S	%	+/-	TF	F%	H	SB	Min	GP	G	A	Pts	PIM	PP	SH	GW
1985-86	Ft-Saskatchewan	SJHL	29	12	23	35	24	....	....	....	....	....	....						....	....	....	....	....			
1986-87	North-Michigan	WCHA	30	4	4	8	35	....	....	....	....	....	....						....	....	....	....	....			
1987-88	North-Michigan	WCHA	34	7	23	30	26	....	....	....	....	....	....						....	....	....	....	....			
1988-89	North-Michigan	WCHA	28	7	13	20	16	....	....	....	....	....	....						....	....	....	....	....			
1989-90	North-Michigan	WCHA	8	2	5	7	8	....	....	....	....	....	....						....	....	....	....	....			
1990-91	North-Michigan	WCHA	47	20	43	63	36	....	....	....	....	....	....						....	....	....	....	....			
1991-92	Cape Breton	AHL	66	6	21	27	95	....	....	....	....	....	....						5	0	3	3	6			
1992-93	Canada	Nat-Team	18	3	7	10	10	....	....	....	....	....	....						....	....	....	....	....			
	Edmonton	NHL	27	5	4	9	24	0	1	1	38	13.2	1						....	....	....	....	....			
	Cape Breton	AHL	4	1	1	2	4	....	....	....	....	....	....						16	4	17	21	12			
1993-94	Edmonton	NHL	15	0	4	4	14	0	0	0	11	0.0	-1						....	....	....	....	....			
	Cape Breton	AHL	25	6	17	23	19	....	....	....	....	....	....						....	....	....	....	....			
	Canada	Olympics	8	2	2	4	8	....	....	....	....	....	....						....	....	....	....	....			
	Quebec	NHL	11	0	7	7	8	0	0	0	17	0.0	4						....	....	....	....	....			
	Cornwall Aces	AHL	....	....	....	....	....	....	....	....	....	....	....						12	2	10	12	22			
1994-95	Milwaukee	IHL	80	8	45	53	161	....	....	....	....	....	....						15	3	10	13	36			
1995-96	Chicago	NHL	9	0	0	0	8	0	0	0	2	0.0	-2						....	....	....	....	....			
	Indianapolis Ice	IHL	73	15	42	57	85	....	....	....	....	....	....						5	1	3	4	8			
1996-97	Indianapolis Ice	IHL	82	20	56	76	83	....	....	....	....	....	....						4	1	4	5	6			
1997-98	Pittsburgh	NHL	71	3	15	18	46	2	0	0	50	6.0	15						6	1	0	1	8	0	1	0
1998-99	Pittsburgh	NHL	81	6	18	24	93	1	0	4	77	7.8	17	0	0.0	115	120	21:12	13	1	1	2	6	0	0	0
99-2000	Pittsburgh	NHL	61	3	8	11	69	0	0	1	42	7.1	15	0	0.0	74	78	18:02	....	....	....	....	....			
	Calgary	NHL	12	1	1	2	21	0	0	0	20	5.0	-2	0	0.0	17	17	24:37	....	....	....	....	....			
	NHL Totals		287	18	57	75	283	3	1	6	257	7.0		0	0.0	206	215	20:13	19	2	1	3	14	0	1	0

WCHA First All-Star Team (1991) • NCAA West First All-American Team (1991) • NCAA Championship All-Tournament Team (1991) • IHL First All-Star Team (1997) • Won Governors' Trophy (Top Defenseman - IHL) (1997)
Traded to **Quebec** by **Edmonton** for Steve Passmore, March 21, 1994. Signed as a free agent by **Chicago**, July 20, 1995. Signed as a free agent by **Pittsburgh**, July 31, 1997. Traded to **Calgary** by **Pittsburgh** for Tyler Moss and Rene Corbet, March 14, 2000.

WESENBERG, Brian — (WEE-sehn-buhrg, BRIGH-an) — ATL.

Right wing. Shoots right. 6'3", 187 lbs.   Born, Peterborough, Ont., May 9, 1977. Anaheim's 2nd choice, 29th overall, in 1995 Entry Draft.

Season	Club	League	GP	G	A	Pts	PIM	PP	SH	GW	S	%	+/-	TF	F%	H	SB	Min	GP	G	A	Pts	PIM	PP	SH	GW
1993-94	Cobourg Cougars	OJHL	40	14	18	32	81	....	....	....	....	....	....						....	....	....	....	....			
1994-95	Guelph Storm	OHL	66	17	27	44	81	....	....	....	....	....	....						14	2	3	5	18			
1995-96	Guelph Storm	OHL	66	25	33	58	161	....	....	....	....	....	....						16	4	11	15	34			
1996-97	Guelph Storm	OHL	64	37	43	80	186	....	....	....	....	....	....						18	4	9	13	59			
	Philadelphia	AHL	....	....	....	....	....	....	....	....	....	....	....						3	0	0	0	7			
1997-98	Philadelphia	AHL	74	17	22	39	93	....	....	....	....	....	....						19	1	4	5	34			
1998-99	Philadelphia	NHL	1	0	0	0	5	0	0	0	0	0.0	1	0	0.0	0	0	1:08	....	....	....	....	....			
	Philadelphia	AHL	71	23	20	43	169	....	....	....	....	....	....						16	5	3	8	28			
99-2000	Philadelphia	AHL	22	3	5	8	44	....	....	....	....	....	....						....	....	....	....	....			
	Orlando	IHL	31	9	3	12	50	....	....	....	....	....	....						4	0	0	0	9			
	NHL Totals		1	0	0	0	5	0	0	0	0	0.0		0	0.0	0	0	1:08	....	....	....	....	....			

Traded to **Philadelphia** by **Anaheim** for Anatoli Semenov and Mike Crowley, March 19, 1996. Traded to **Atlanta** by **Philadelphia** for Eric Bertrand, December 9, 1999.

WESLEY, Glen — (WEH-slee, GLEHN) — CAR.

Defense. Shoots left. 6'1", 205 lbs.   Born, Red Deer, Alta., October 2, 1968. Boston's 1st choice, 3rd overall, in 1987 Entry Draft.

Season	Club	League	GP	G	A	Pts	PIM	PP	SH	GW	S	%	+/-	TF	F%	H	SB	Min	GP	G	A	Pts	PIM	PP	SH	GW
1983-84	Red Deer Rustlers	AJHL	57	9	20	29	40	....	....	....	....	....	....						....	....	....	....	....			
	Portland	WHL	3	1	2	3	0	....	....	....	....	....	....						....	....	....	....	....			
1984-85	Portland	WHL	67	16	52	68	76	....	....	....	....	....	....						6	1	6	7	8			
1985-86	Portland	WHL	69	16	75	91	96	....	....	....	....	....	....						15	3	11	14	29			
1986-87	Portland	WHL	63	16	46	62	72	....	....	....	....	....	....						20	8	18	26	27			
1987-88	Boston	NHL	79	7	30	37	69	1	2	0	158	4.4	21						23	6	8	14	22	4	1	0
1988-89	Boston	NHL	77	19	35	54	61	8	1	1	181	10.5	23						10	0	2	2	4	0	0	0
1989-90	Boston	NHL	78	9	27	36	48	5	0	4	166	5.4	6						21	2	6	8	36	0	0	1
1990-91	Boston	NHL	80	11	32	43	78	5	1	1	199	5.5	0						19	2	9	11	19	2	0	0
1991-92	Boston	NHL	78	9	37	46	54	4	0	1	211	4.3	-9						15	2	4	6	16	0	0	0
1992-93	Boston	NHL	64	8	25	33	47	4	1	0	183	4.4	-2						4	0	0	0	4	0	0	0
1993-94	Boston	NHL	81	14	44	58	64	6	1	1	265	5.3	1						13	3	3	6	12	1	0	0
1994-95	Hartford	NHL	48	2	14	16	50	1	0	1	125	1.6	-6						....	....	....	....	....			
1995-96	Hartford	NHL	68	8	16	24	88	6	0	1	129	6.2	-9						....	....	....	....	....			
1996-97	Hartford	NHL	68	6	26	32	40	3	1	0	126	4.8	0						....	....	....	....	....			
1997-98	Carolina	NHL	82	6	19	25	36	1	0	1	121	5.0	7						....	....	....	....	....			
1998-99	Carolina	NHL	74	7	17	24	44	0	0	2	112	6.3	14	1	0.0	121	94	22:31	6	0	0	0	2	0	0	0
99-2000	Carolina	NHL	78	7	15	22	38	1	0	0	99	7.1	-4	0	0.0	116	111	21:32	....	....	....	....	....			
	NHL Totals		955	113	337	450	717	45	7	13	2075	5.4		1	0.0	237	205	22:01	111	15	32	47	111	7	1	1

WHL West First All-Star Team (1986, 1987) • NHL All-Rookie Team (1988) • Played in NHL All-Star Game (1989)
Traded to **Hartford** by **Boston** for Hartford/Carolina's 1st round choices in 1995 (Kyle McLaren), 1996 (Jonathan Aitken) and 1997 (Sergei Samsonov) Entry Drafts, August 26, 1994. Transferred to **Carolina** after **Hartford** franchise relocated, June 25, 1997.

WESTLUND, Tommy — (WEHST-luhnd, TOHM-mee) — CAR.

Right wing. Shoots right. 6', 210 lbs.   Born, Fors, Sweden, December 29, 1974. Carolina's 5th choice, 93rd overall, in 1998 Entry Draft.

Season	Club	League	GP	G	A	Pts	PIM	PP	SH	GW	S	%	+/-	TF	F%	H	SB	Min	GP	G	A	Pts	PIM	PP	SH	GW
1991-92	Avesta BK	Sweden-3	27	11	9	20	8	....	....	....	....	....	....						....	....	....	....	....			
1992-93	Avesta BK	Sweden-2	32	9	5	14	32	....	....	....	....	....	....						....	....	....	....	....			
1993-94	Avesta BK	Sweden-2	31	20	11	31	34	....	....	....	....	....	....						....	....	....	....	....			
1994-95	Avesta BK	Sweden-2	32	17	13	30	22	....	....	....	....	....	....						....	....	....	....	....			
1995-96	Brynas IF	Sweden	18	2	1	3	2	....	....	....	....	....	....						8	1	0	1	4			
	Brynas IF	Sweden-2	18	10	10	20	4	....	....	....	....	....	....						....	....	....	....	....			
1996-97	Brynas IF	Sweden	50	21	13	34	16	....	....	....	....	....	....						3	0	1	1	0			
1997-98	Brynas IF	Sweden	46	29	9	38	45	....	....	....	....	....	....						....	....	....	....	....			
1998-99	New Haven	AHL	50	8	18	26	31	....	....	....	....	....	....						....	....	....	....	....			
99-2000	Carolina	NHL	81	4	8	12	19	0	1	0	67	6.0	-10	336	52.7	86	25	10:23	....	....	....	....	....			
	NHL Totals		81	4	8	12	19	0	1	0	67	6.0		336	52.7	86	25	10:23	....	....	....	....	....			

WHITE, Brian — (WHIGHT, BRIGH-an) — COL.

Defense. Shoots right. 6'1", 195 lbs.   Born, Winchester, MA, February 7, 1976. Tampa Bay's 11th choice, 268th overall, in 1994 Entry Draft.

Season	Club	League	GP	G	A	Pts	PIM	PP	SH	GW	S	%	+/-	TF	F%	H	SB	Min	GP	G	A	Pts	PIM	PP	SH	GW
1993-94	Arlington High	Hi-School	40	14	18	32	81	....	....	....	....	....	....						....	....	....	....	....			
1994-95	U. of Maine	H-East	28	1	1	2	16	....	....	....	....	....	....						....	....	....	....	....			
1995-96	U. of Maine	H-East	39	0	4	4	18	....	....	....	....	....	....						....	....	....	....	....			
1996-97	U. of Maine	H-East	35	4	12	16	36	....	....	....	....	....	....						....	....	....	....	....			
1997-98	U. of Maine	H-East	33	0	12	12	45	....	....	....	....	....	....						....	....	....	....	....			
	Long Beach	IHL	1	0	0	0	0	....	....	....	....	....	....						....	....	....	....	....			
1998-99	Colorado	NHL	2	0	0	0	0	0	0	0	0	0.0	0	0	0.0	1	0	0:40	....	....	....	....	....			
	Hershey Bears	AHL	71	4	8	12	41	....	....	....	....	....	....						4	0	1	1	2			
99-2000	Hershey Bears	AHL	79	3	19	22	78	....	....	....	....	....	....						14	0	3	3	21			
	NHL Totals		2	0	0	0	0	0	0	0	0	0.0		0	0.0	1	0	0:40	....	....	....	....	....			

Signed as a free agent by **Colorado**, July 7, 1998.

WHITE, Colin (WHIGHT, CAWI-ihn) N.J.

Defense. Shoots left. 6'4", 210 lbs. Born, New Glasgow, N.S., December 12, 1977. New Jersey's 5th choice, 49th overall, in 1996 Entry Draft.

			Regular Season																Playoffs							
Season	Club	League	GP	G	A	Pts	PIM	PP	SH	GW	S	%	+/-	TF	F%	H	SB	Min	GP	G	A	Pts	PIM	PP	SH	GW
1994-95	Laval Titan	QMJHL	7	0	1	1	32	....	....	....	....	....	....	....	....	....	....	....	....	....	....	....	....	....	....	....
	Hull Olympiques	QMJHL	5	0	1	1	4	....	....	....	....	....	....	....	....	....	....	....	12	0	0	0	23	....	....	....
1995-96	Hull Olympiques	QMJHL	62	2	8	10	303	....	....	....	....	....	....	....	....	....	....	....	18	0	4	4	42	....	....	....
1996-97	Hull Olympiques	QMJHL	63	3	12	15	297	....	....	....	....	....	....	....	....	....	....	....	14	3	12	15	65	....	....	....
1997-98	Albany River Rats	AHL	76	3	13	16	235	....	....	....	....	....	....	....	....	....	....	....	13	0	0	0	55	....	....	....
1998-99	Albany River Rats	AHL	77	2	12	14	265	....	....	....	....	....	....	....	....	....	....	....	5	0	1	1	8	....	....	....
99-2000♦	**New Jersey**	**NHL**	**21**	**2**	**1**	**3**	**40**	**0**	**0**	**1**	**29**	**6.9**	**3**	**0**	**0.0**	**35**	**26**	**14:45**	**23**	**1**	**5**	**6**	**18**	**0**	**0**	**1**
	Albany River Rats	AHL	52	5	21	26	176	....	....	....	....	....	....	....	....	....	....	....	....	....	....	....	....	....	....	....
	NHL Totals		**21**	**2**	**1**	**3**	**40**	**0**	**0**	**1**	**29**	**6.9**		**0**	**0.0**	**35**	**26**	**14:45**	**23**	**1**	**5**	**6**	**18**	**0**	**0**	**1**

WHITE, Peter (WHIGHT, PEE-tuhr) PHI.

Center. Shoots left. 5'11", 200 lbs. Born, Montreal, Que., March 15, 1969. Edmonton's 4th choice, 92nd overall, in 1989 Entry Draft.

			Regular Season																Playoffs							
Season	Club	League	GP	G	A	Pts	PIM	PP	SH	GW	S	%	+/-	TF	F%	H	SB	Min	GP	G	A	Pts	PIM	PP	SH	GW
1984-85	Lac-St-Louis	QAAA	42	16	32	48	....	....	....	....	....	....	....	....	....	....	....	....	....	....	....	....	....	....	....	....
1985-86	Lac-St-Louis	QAAA	42	38	62	100	....	....	....	....	....	....	....	....	....	....	....	....	....	....	....	....	....	....	....	....
1986-87	Pembroke	OJHL	55	20	34	54	20	....	....	....	....	....	....	....	....	....	....	....	....	....	....	....	....	....	....	....
1987-88	Pembroke	OJHL	56	*90	*136	*226	32	....	....	....	....	....	....	....	....	....	....	....	....	....	....	....	....	....	....	....
1988-89	Michigan State	CCHA	46	20	33	53	17	....	....	....	....	....	....	....	....	....	....	....	....	....	....	....	....	....	....	....
1989-90	Michigan State	CCHA	45	22	40	62	6	....	....	....	....	....	....	....	....	....	....	....	....	....	....	....	....	....	....	....
1990-91	Michigan State	CCHA	37	7	31	38	28	....	....	....	....	....	....	....	....	....	....	....	....	....	....	....	....	....	....	....
1991-92	Michigan State	CCHA	41	26	49	75	32	....	....	....	....	....	....	....	....	....	....	....	....	....	....	....	....	....	....	....
1992-93	Cape Breton	AHL	64	12	28	40	10	....	....	....	....	....	....	....	....	....	....	....	16	3	3	6	12	....	....	....
1993-94	**Edmonton**	**NHL**	**26**	**3**	**5**	**8**	**2**	**0**	**0**	**0**	**17**	**17.6**	**1**	....	....	....	....	....	....	....	....	....	....	....	....	....
	Cape Breton	AHL	45	21	49	70	12	....	....	....	....	....	....	....	....	....	....	....	5	2	3	5	2	....	....	....
1994-95	Cape Breton	AHL	65	36	*69	*105	30	....	....	....	....	....	....	....	....	....	....	....	....	....	....	....	....	....	....	....
	Edmonton	**NHL**	**9**	**2**	**4**	**6**	**0**	**2**	**0**	**0**	**13**	**15.4**	**1**	....	....	....	....	....	....	....	....	....	....	....	....	....
1995-96	**Edmonton**	**NHL**	**26**	**5**	**3**	**8**	**0**	**1**	**0**	**0**	**34**	**14.7**	**–14**	....	....	....	....	....	....	....	....	....	....	....	....	....
	Toronto	**NHL**	**1**	**0**	**0**	**0**	**0**	**1**	**0**	**0**	**0**	**0.0**	**0**	....	....	....	....	....	....	....	....	....	....	....	....	....
	St. John's Leafs	AHL	17	6	7	13	6	....	....	....	....	....	....	....	....	....	....	....	....	....	....	....	....	....	....	....
	Atlanta Knights	IHL	36	21	20	41	4	....	....	....	....	....	....	....	....	....	....	....	3	0	3	3	2	....	....	....
1996-97	Philadelphia	AHL	80	*44	61	*105	28	....	....	....	....	....	....	....	....	....	....	....	10	6	8	14	6	....	....	....
1997-98	Philadelphia	AHL	80	27	*78	*105	28	....	....	....	....	....	....	....	....	....	....	....	20	9	9	18	6	....	....	....
1998-99	**Philadelphia**	**NHL**	**3**	**0**	**0**	**0**	**0**	**0**	**0**	**0**	**0**	**0.0**	**0**	**8**	**37.5**	**0**	**0**	**2:02**	....	....	....	....	....	....	....	....
	Philadelphia	AHL	77	31	59	90	20	....	....	....	....	....	....	....	....	....	....	....	16	4	13	17	12	....	....	....
99-2000	**Philadelphia**	**NHL**	**21**	**1**	**5**	**6**	**6**	**0**	**0**	**0**	**24**	**4.2**	**1**	**277**	**54.5**	**9**	**15**	**13:04**	**16**	**0**	**2**	**2**	**0**	**0**	**0**	**0**
	Philadelphia	AHL	62	20	41	61	38	....	....	....	....	....	....	....	....	....	....	....	....	....	....	....	....	....	....	....
	NHL Totals		**86**	**11**	**17**	**28**	**8**	**4**	**0**	**0**	**88**	**12.5**		**285**	**54.0**	**9**	**15**	**11:41**	**16**	**0**	**2**	**2**	**0**	**0**	**0**	**0**

AHL Second All-Star Team (1995, 1997) • Won John B. Sollenberger Trophy (Top Scorer - AHL) (1995, 1997, 1998)

Traded to **Toronto** by **Edmonton** with Edmonton's 4th round choice (Jason Sessa) in 1996 Entry Draft for Kent Manderville, December 4, 1995. Signed as a free agent by **Philadelphia**, August 19, 1996.

WHITE, Todd (WHIGHT, TAWD) OTT.

Center. Shoots left. 5'10", 180 lbs. Born, Kanata, Ont., May 21, 1975.

			Regular Season																Playoffs							
Season	Club	League	GP	G	A	Pts	PIM	PP	SH	GW	S	%	+/-	TF	F%	H	SB	Min	GP	G	A	Pts	PIM	PP	SH	GW
1990-91	Powassan	OJHL	38	34	38	72	118	....	....	....	....	....	....	....	....	....	....	....	....	....	....	....	....	....	....	....
1991-92	Kanata Valley	OJHL	55	39	49	88	30	....	....	....	....	....	....	....	....	....	....	....	....	....	....	....	....	....	....	....
1992-93	Kanata Valley	OJHL	49	51	87	138	46	....	....	....	....	....	....	....	....	....	....	....	....	....	....	....	....	....	....	....
1993-94	Clarkson	ECAC	33	10	12	22	28	....	....	....	....	....	....	....	....	....	....	....	....	....	....	....	....	....	....	....
1994-95	Clarkson	ECAC	34	13	16	29	44	....	....	....	....	....	....	....	....	....	....	....	....	....	....	....	....	....	....	....
1995-96	Clarkson	ECAC	38	29	43	72	36	....	....	....	....	....	....	....	....	....	....	....	....	....	....	....	....	....	....	....
1996-97	Clarkson	ECAC	37	*38	*36	*74	22	....	....	....	....	....	....	....	....	....	....	....	....	....	....	....	....	....	....	....
1997-98	**Chicago**	**NHL**	**7**	**1**	**0**	**1**	**2**	**0**	**0**	**0**	**3**	**33.3**	**0**	....	....	....	....	....	....	....	....	....	....	....	....	....
	Indianapolis	IHL	65	46	36	82	28	....	....	....	....	....	....	....	....	....	....	....	5	2	3	5	4	....	....	....
1998-99	**Chicago**	**NHL**	**35**	**5**	**8**	**13**	**20**	**2**	**0**	**0**	**43**	**11.6**	**–1**	**452**	**46.0**	**27**	**11**	**13:39**	....	....	....	....	....	....	....	....
	Chicago Wolves	IHL	25	11	13	24	8	....	....	....	....	....	....	....	....	....	....	....	10	1	4	5	8	....	....	....
99-2000	**Chicago**	**NHL**	**1**	**0**	**0**	**0**	**0**	**0**	**0**	**0**	**0**	**0.0**	**0**	**9**	**55.6**	**2**	**0**	**13:02**	....	....	....	....	....	....	....	....
	Cleveland	IHL	42	21	30	51	32	....	....	....	....	....	....	....	....	....	....	....	....	....	....	....	....	....	....	....
	Philadelphia	**NHL**	**3**	**1**	**0**	**1**	**0**	**0**	**0**	**0**	**4**	**25.0**	**–1**	**25**	**40.0**	**1**	**1**	**10:29**	....	....	....	....	....	....	....	....
	Philadelphia	AHL	32	19	24	43	12	....	....	....	....	....	....	....	....	....	....	....	5	2	1	*3	8	....	....	....
	NHL Totals		**46**	**7**	**8**	**15**	**22**	**2**	**0**	**0**	**50**	**14.0**		**486**	**45.9**	**30**	**12**	**13:23**	....	....	....	....	....	....	....	....

ECAC Second All-Star Team (1996) • NCAA East Second All-American Team (1996) • ECAC First All-Star Team (1997) • NCAA East First All-American Team (1997) • Won Garry F. Longman Memorial Trophy (Top Rookie - IHL) (1998)

Signed as a free agent by **Chicago**, August 27, 1997. Traded to **Philadelphia** by **Chicago** for a conditional choice in 2001 Entry Draft, January 26, 2000. Signed as a free agent by **Ottawa**, July 12, 2000.

WHITFIELD, Trent (WHIHT-feeld, TREHNT) WSH.

Center. Shoots left. 5'11", 200 lbs. Born, Estevan, Sask., June 17, 1977. Boston's 5th choice, 100th overall, in 1996 Entry Draft.

			Regular Season																Playoffs							
Season	Club	League	GP	G	A	Pts	PIM	PP	SH	GW	S	%	+/-	TF	F%	H	SB	Min	GP	G	A	Pts	PIM	PP	SH	GW
1993-94	Saskatoon Blaze	SAHA	36	26	22	48	42	....	....	....	....	....	....	....	....	....	....	....	....	....	....	....	....	....	....	....
	Spokane Chiefs	WHL	5	1	1	2	0	....	....	....	....	....	....	....	....	....	....	....	....	....	....	....	....	....	....	....
1994-95	Spokane Chiefs	WHL	48	8	17	25	26	....	....	....	....	....	....	....	....	....	....	....	11	7	6	13	5	....	....	....
1995-96	Spokane Chiefs	WHL	72	33	51	84	75	....	....	....	....	....	....	....	....	....	....	....	18	8	10	18	10	....	....	....
1996-97	Spokane Chiefs	WHL	58	34	42	76	74	....	....	....	....	....	....	....	....	....	....	....	9	5	7	12	10	....	....	....
1997-98	Spokane Chiefs	WHL	65	38	44	82	97	....	....	....	....	....	....	....	....	....	....	....	18	9	10	19	15	....	....	....
1998-99	Portland Pirates	AHL	50	10	8	18	20	....	....	....	....	....	....	....	....	....	....	....	....	....	....	....	....	....	....	....
	Hampton Roads	ECHL	19	13	12	25	12	....	....	....	....	....	....	....	....	....	....	....	4	2	0	2	14	....	....	....
99-2000	Portland Pirates	AHL	79	18	35	53	52	....	....	....	....	....	....	....	....	....	....	....	3	1	1	2	2	....	....	....
	Washington	**NHL**	....	....	....	....	....	....	....	....	....	....	....	....	....	....	....	....	**3**	**0**	**0**	**0**	**0**	**0**	**0**	**0**
	NHL Totals		....	....	....	....	....	....	....	....	....	....	....	....	....	....	....	....	**3**	**0**	**0**	**0**	**0**	**0**	**0**	**0**

WHL West First All-Star Team (1997) • WHL West Second All-Star Team (1998)

Signed as a free agent by **Washington**, September 1, 1998.

WHITNEY, Ray (WHIHT-nee, RAY) FLA.

Left wing. Shoots right. 5'10", 175 lbs. Born, Fort Saskatchewan, Alta., May 8, 1972. San Jose's 2nd choice, 23rd overall, in 1991 Entry Draft.

			Regular Season																Playoffs							
Season	Club	League	GP	G	A	Pts	PIM	PP	SH	GW	S	%	+/-	TF	F%	H	SB	Min	GP	G	A	Pts	PIM	PP	SH	GW
1987-88	Ft-Saskatchewan	AAHA	71	80	155	235	119	....	....	....	....	....	....	....	....	....	....	....	....	....	....	....	....	....	....	....
1988-89	Spokane Chiefs	WHL	71	17	33	50	16	....	....	....	....	....	....	....	....	....	....	....	....	....	....	....	....	....	....	....
1989-90	Spokane Chiefs	WHL	71	57	56	113	50	....	....	....	....	....	....	....	....	....	....	....	6	3	4	7	6	....	....	....
1990-91	Spokane Chiefs	WHL	72	67	118	*185	36	....	....	....	....	....	....	....	....	....	....	....	15	13	18	*31	12	....	....	....
1991-92	Kolner EC	DEL	10	3	6	9	4	....	....	....	....	....	....	....	....	....	....	....	....	....	....	....	....	....	....	....
	Canada	Nat-Team	5	1	0	1	6	....	....	....	....	....	....	....	....	....	....	....	....	....	....	....	....	....	....	....
	San Jose	**NHL**	**2**	**0**	**3**	**3**	**0**	**0**	**0**	**0**	**4**	**0.0**	**–1**	....	....	....	....	....	....	....	....	....	....	....	....	....
	San Diego Gulls	IHL	63	36	54	90	12	....	....	....	....	....	....	....	....	....	....	....	4	0	0	0	0	....	....	....
1992-93	**San Jose**	**NHL**	**26**	**4**	**6**	**10**	**4**	**1**	**0**	**0**	**24**	**16.7**	**–14**	....	....	....	....	....	....	....	....	....	....	....	....	....
	Kansas City	IHL	46	20	33	53	14	....	....	....	....	....	....	....	....	....	....	....	12	5	7	12	2	....	....	....
1993-94	**San Jose**	**NHL**	**61**	**14**	**26**	**40**	**14**	**1**	**0**	**0**	**82**	**17.1**	**2**	....	....	....	....	....	**14**	**0**	**4**	**4**	**8**	**0**	**0**	**0**
1994-95	**San Jose**	**NHL**	**39**	**13**	**12**	**25**	**14**	**4**	**0**	**1**	**67**	**19.4**	**–7**	....	....	....	....	....	**11**	**4**	**4**	**8**	**2**	**0**	**0**	**1**
1995-96	**San Jose**	**NHL**	**60**	**17**	**24**	**41**	**16**	**4**	**2**	**2**	**106**	**16.0**	**–23**	....	....	....	....	....	....	....	....	....	....	....	....	....
1996-97	**San Jose**	**NHL**	**12**	**0**	**2**	**2**	**4**	**0**	**0**	**0**	**24**	**0.0**	**–6**	....	....	....	....	....	....	....	....	....	....	....	....	....
	Kentucky	AHL	9	1	7	8	2	....	....	....	....	....	....	....	....	....	....	....	....	....	....	....	....	....	....	....
	Utah Grizzlies	IHL	43	13	35	48	34	....	....	....	....	....	....	....	....	....	....	....	7	3	1	4	6	....	....	....
1997-98	**Edmonton**	**NHL**	**9**	**1**	**3**	**4**	**0**	**0**	**0**	**0**	**19**	**5.3**	**–1**	....	....	....	....	....	....	....	....	....	....	....	....	....
	Florida	**NHL**	**68**	**32**	**29**	**61**	**28**	**12**	**0**	**2**	**156**	**20.5**	**10**	....	....	....	....	....	....	....	....	....	....	....	....	....

Season	Club	League	GP	G	A	Pts	PIM	PP	SH	GW	S	%	+/–	TF	F%	H	SB	Min	GP	G	A	Pts	PIM	PP	SH	GW
			Regular Season																Playoffs							
1998-99	**Florida**	**NHL**	**81**	**26**	**38**	**64**	**18**	**7**	**0**	**6**	**193**	**13.5**	**–3**	**144**	**43.8**	**14**	**7**	**18:20**	....	....	....	....	....	....	....	....
99-2000	**Florida**	**NHL**	**81**	**29**	**42**	**71**	**35**	**5**	**0**	**3**	**198**	**14.6**	**16**	**198**	**49.0**	**17**	**16**	**18:41**	**4**	**1**	**0**	**1**	**4**	**0**	**0**	**0**
	NHL Totals		**439**	**136**	**185**	**321**	**133**	**34**	**2**	**14**	**873**	**15.6**		**342**	**46.8**	**31**	**23**	**18:31**	**29**	**5**	**8**	**13**	**14**	**0**	**0**	**1**

WHL West First All-Star Team (1991) • Memorial Cup All-Star Team (1991) • Won George Parsons Trophy (Memorial Cup Tournament Most Sportsmanlike Player) (1991) • Played in NHL All-Star Game (2000)

Signed as a free agent by **Edmonton**, October 1, 1997. Claimed on waivers by **Florida** from **Edmonton**, November 6, 1997.

WIEMER, Jason

(WEE-muhr, JAY-suhn) **CGY.**

Center. Shoots left. 6'1", 220 lbs. Born, Kimberley, B.C., April 14, 1976. Tampa Bay's 1st choice, 8th overall, in 1994 Entry Draft.

Season	Club	League	GP	G	A	Pts	PIM	PP	SH	GW	S	%	+/–	TF	F%	H	SB	Min	GP	G	A	Pts	PIM	PP	SH	GW
1991-92	Kimberley	RMJHL	45	33	33	66	211	....	....	....	....	....	....	....	....	....	....	....	....	....	....	....	....	....	....	....
	Portland	WHL	2	0	1	1	0	....	....	....	....	....	....	....	....	....	....	....	....	....	....	....	....	....	....	....
1992-93	Portland	WHL	68	18	34	52	159	....	....	....	....	....	....	....	....	....	....	....	16	7	3	10	27	....	....	....
1993-94	Portland	WHL	72	45	51	96	236	....	....	....	....	....	....	....	....	....	....	....	10	4	4	8	32	....	....	....
1994-95	Portland	WHL	16	10	14	24	63	....	....	....	....	....	....	....	....	....	....	....	....	....	....	....	....	....	....	....
	Tampa Bay	**NHL**	**36**	**1**	**4**	**5**	**44**	**0**	**0**	**0**	**10**	**10.0**	**–2**	....	....	....	....	....	....	....	....	....	....	....	....	....
1995-96	**Tampa Bay**	**NHL**	**66**	**9**	**9**	**18**	**81**	**4**	**0**	**1**	**89**	**10.1**	**–9**	....	....	....	....	....	**6**	**1**	**0**	**1**	**28**	**1**	**0**	**0**
1996-97	**Tampa Bay**	**NHL**	**63**	**9**	**5**	**14**	**134**	**2**	**0**	**0**	**103**	**8.7**	**–13**	....	....	....	....	....	....	....	....	....	....	....	....	....
	Adirondack	AHL	4	1	0	1	7	....	....	....	....	....	....	....	....	....	....	....	....	....	....	....	....	....	....	....
1997-98	**Tampa Bay**	**NHL**	**67**	**8**	**9**	**17**	**132**	**2**	**0**	**0**	**106**	**7.5**	**–9**	....	....	....	....	....	....	....	....	....	....	....	....	....
	Calgary	**NHL**	**12**	**4**	**1**	**5**	**28**	**1**	**0**	**2**	**16**	**25.0**	**–1**	....	....	....	....	....	....	....	....	....	....	....	....	....
1998-99	**Calgary**	**NHL**	**78**	**8**	**13**	**21**	**177**	**1**	**0**	**1**	**128**	**6.3**	**–12**	**867**	**40.9**	**171**	**20**	**13:17**	....	....	....	....	....	....	....	....
99-2000	**Calgary**	**NHL**	**64**	**11**	**11**	**22**	**120**	**2**	**0**	**3**	**104**	**10.6**	**–10**	**955**	**47.6**	**149**	**22**	**14:41**	....	....	....	....	....	....	....	....
	NHL Totals		**386**	**50**	**52**	**102**	**716**	**12**	**0**	**7**	**556**	**9.0**		**1822**	**44.5**	**320**	**42**	**13:55**	**6**	**1**	**0**	**1**	**28**	**1**	**0**	**0**

Traded to **Calgary** by **Tampa Bay** for Sandy McCarthy and Calgary's 3rd (Brad Richards) and 5th (Curtis Rich) round choices in 1998 Entry Draft, March 24, 1998.

WILKIE, David

(WIHL-kee, DAY-vihd) **NYR**

Defense. Shoots right. 6'3", 215 lbs. Born, Ellensburgh, WA, May 30, 1974. Montreal's 1st choice, 20th overall, in 1992 Entry Draft.

Season	Club	League	GP	G	A	Pts	PIM	PP	SH	GW	S	%	+/–	TF	F%	H	SB	Min	GP	G	A	Pts	PIM	PP	SH	GW
1989-90	Seattle North	PIJHL	41	21	27	48	59	....	....	....	....	....	....	....	....	....	....	....	....	....	....	....	....	....	....	....
1990-91	Omaha Lancers	USHL	19	2	2	4	18	....	....	....	....	....	....	....	....	....	....	....	....	....	....	....	....	....	....	....
	Seattle T-Birds	WHL	25	1	1	2	22	....	....	....	....	....	....	....	....	....	....	....	....	....	....	....	....	....	....	....
1991-92	Kamloops Blazers	WHL	71	12	28	40	153	....	....	....	....	....	....	....	....	....	....	....	16	6	5	11	19	....	....	....
1992-93	Kamloops Blazers	WHL	53	11	26	37	109	....	....	....	....	....	....	....	....	....	....	....	6	4	2	6	2	....	....	....
1993-94	Kamloops Blazers	WHL	27	11	18	29	18	....	....	....	....	....	....	....	....	....	....	....	....	....	....	....	....	....	....	....
	Regina Pats	WHL	29	27	21	48	16	....	....	....	....	....	....	....	....	....	....	....	4	1	4	5	4	....	....	....
1994-95	Fredericton	AHL	70	10	43	53	34	....	....	....	....	....	....	....	....	....	....	....	1	0	0	0	0	....	....	....
	Montreal	**NHL**	**1**	**0**	**0**	**0**	**0**	**0**	**0**	**0**	**0**	**0.0**	**0**	....	....	....	....	....	....	....	....	....	....	....	....	....
1995-96	**Montreal**	**NHL**	**24**	**1**	**5**	**6**	**10**	**1**	**0**	**0**	**39**	**2.6**	**–10**	....	....	....	....	....	**6**	**1**	**2**	**3**	**12**	**0**	**0**	**0**
	Fredericton	AHL	23	5	12	17	20	....	....	....	....	....	....	....	....	....	....	....	....	....	....	....	....	....	....	....
1996-97	**Montreal**	**NHL**	**61**	**6**	**9**	**15**	**63**	**3**	**0**	**0**	**65**	**9.2**	**–9**	....	....	....	....	....	**2**	**0**	**0**	**0**	**2**	**0**	**0**	**0**
1997-98	**Montreal**	**NHL**	**5**	**1**	**0**	**1**	**4**	**0**	**0**	**1**	**2**	**50.0**	**–1**	....	....	....	....	....	....	....	....	....	....	....	....	....
	Tampa Bay	**NHL**	**29**	**1**	**5**	**6**	**17**	**0**	**0**	**0**	**46**	**2.2**	**–21**	....	....	....	....	....	....	....	....	....	....	....	....	....
1998-99	**Tampa Bay**	**NHL**	**46**	**1**	**7**	**8**	**69**	**0**	**0**	**0**	**35**	**2.9**	**–19**	**0**	**0.0**	**49**	**48**	**12:18**	....	....	....	....	....	....	....	....
	Cleveland	IHL	2	0	2	2	0	....	....	....	....	....	....	....	....	....	....	....	....	....	....	....	....	....	....	....
99-2000	Houston Aeros	IHL	57	4	24	28	71	....	....	....	....	....	....	....	....	....	....	....	11	1	8	9	10	....	....	....
	Hartford	AHL	1	0	2	2	0	....	....	....	....	....	....	....	....	....	....	....	....	....	....	....	....	....	....	....
	Chicago Wolves	IHL	1	0	0	0	0	....	....	....	....	....	....	....	....	....	....	....	....	....	....	....	....	....	....	....
	NHL Totals		**166**	**10**	**26**	**36**	**163**	**4**	**0**	**1**	**187**	**5.3**		**0**	**0.0**	**49**	**48**	**12:18**	**8**	**1**	**2**	**3**	**14**	**0**	**0**	**0**

Traded to **Tampa Bay** by **Montreal** with Stephane Richer and Darcy Tucker for Patrick Poulin, Mick Vukota and Igor Ulanov, January 15, 1998. Signed as a free agent by **NY Rangers**, September 29, 1999.

WILLIS, Shane

(WIH-lihs, SHAYN) **CAR.**

Right wing. Shoots right. 6', 185 lbs. Born, Edmonton, Alta., June 13, 1977. Carolina's 4th choice, 88th overall, in 1997 Entry Draft.

Season	Club	League	GP	G	A	Pts	PIM	PP	SH	GW	S	%	+/–	TF	F%	H	SB	Min	GP	G	A	Pts	PIM	PP	SH	GW
1992-93	Red Deer Raiders	AAHA	36	32	18	50	88	....	....	....	....	....	....	....	....	....	....	....	....	....	....	....	....	....	....	....
1993-94	Red Deer Chiefs	AAHA	34	40	26	66	103	....	....	....	....	....	....	....	....	....	....	....	....	....	....	....	....	....	....	....
1994-95	Prince Albert	WHL	65	24	19	43	38	....	....	....	....	....	....	....	....	....	....	....	13	3	4	7	6	....	....	....
1995-96	Prince Albert	WHL	69	41	40	81	47	....	....	....	....	....	....	....	....	....	....	....	18	11	10	21	18	....	....	....
1996-97	Prince Albert	WHL	41	34	22	56	63	....	....	....	....	....	....	....	....	....	....	....	....	....	....	....	....	....	....	....
	Lethbridge	WHL	26	22	17	39	24	....	....	....	....	....	....	....	....	....	....	....	19	13	11	24	20	....	....	....
1997-98	Lethbridge	WHL	64	58	54	112	73	....	....	....	....	....	....	....	....	....	....	....	4	2	3	5	6	....	....	....
	New Haven	AHL	1	0	1	1	2	....	....	....	....	....	....	....	....	....	....	....	....	....	....	....	....	....	....	....
1998-99	**Carolina**	**NHL**	**7**	**0**	**0**	**0**	**0**	**0**	**0**	**0**	**1**	**0.0**	**–2**	**0**	**0.0**	**4**	**2**	**2:14**	....	....	....	....	....	....	....	....
	New Haven	AHL	73	31	50	81	49	....	....	....	....	....	....	....	....	....	....	....	....	....	....	....	....	....	....	....
99-2000	**Carolina**	**NHL**	**2**	**0**	**0**	**0**	**0**	**0**	**0**	**0**	**1**	**0.0**	**–1**	**0**	**0.0**	**6**	**0**	**5:50**	....	....	....	....	....	....	....	....
	Cincinnati	IHL	80	35	25	60	64	....	....	....	....	....	....	....	....	....	....	....	11	5	3	8	8	....	....	....
	NHL Totals		**9**	**0**	**0**	**0**	**0**	**0**	**0**	**0**	**2**	**0.0**		**0**	**0.0**	**10**	**2**	**3:02**	....	....	....	....	....	....	....	....

• Re-entered NHL draft. Originally Tampa Bay's 3rd choice, 56th overall, in 1995 Entry Draft.

WHL East First All-Star Team (1997, 1998) • AHL First All-Star Team (1999) • Won Dudley "Red" Garrett Memorial Trophy (Top Rookie - AHL) (1999)

WILLSIE, Brian

(WIHL-see, BRIGH-an) **COL.**

Right wing. Shoots right. 6'1", 195 lbs. Born, London, Ont., March 16, 1978. Colorado's 7th choice, 146th overall, in 1996 Entry Draft.

Season	Club	League	GP	G	A	Pts	PIM	PP	SH	GW	S	%	+/–	TF	F%	H	SB	Min	GP	G	A	Pts	PIM	PP	SH	GW
1993-94	Belmont Bombers	OJHL-D	13	9	5	14	14	....	....	....	....	....	....	....	....	....	....	....	....	....	....	....	....	....	....	....
1994-95	St. Thomas Stars	OJHL-B	45	35	47	82	47	....	....	....	....	....	....	....	....	....	....	....	....	....	....	....	....	....	....	....
1995-96	Guelph Storm	OHL	65	13	21	34	18	....	....	....	....	....	....	....	....	....	....	....	16	4	2	6	6	....	....	....
1996-97	Guelph Storm	OHL	64	37	31	68	37	....	....	....	....	....	....	....	....	....	....	....	18	15	4	19	10	....	....	....
1997-98	Guelph Storm	OHL	57	45	31	76	41	....	....	....	....	....	....	....	....	....	....	....	12	9	5	14	18	....	....	....
1998-99	Hershey Bears	AHL	72	19	10	29	28	....	....	....	....	....	....	....	....	....	....	....	3	1	0	1	0	....	....	....
99-2000	**Colorado**	**NHL**	**1**	**0**	**0**	**0**	**0**	**0**	**0**	**0**	**1**	**0.0**	**0**	**0**	**0.0**	**0**	**0**	**8:16**	....	....	....	....	....	....	....	....
	Hershey Bears	AHL	78	20	39	59	44	....	....	....	....	....	....	....	....	....	....	....	12	2	6	8	8	....	....	....
	NHL Totals		**1**	**0**	**0**	**0**	**0**	**0**	**0**	**0**	**1**	**0.0**		**0**	**0.0**	**0**	**0**	**8:16**	....	....	....	....	....	....	....	....

OHL First All-Star Team (1998)

WILM, Clarke

(WIHLM, KLAHRK) **CGY.**

Center. Shoots left. 6', 202 lbs. Born, Central Butte, Sask., October 24, 1976. Calgary's 5th choice, 150th overall, in 1995 Entry Draft.

Season	Club	League	GP	G	A	Pts	PIM	PP	SH	GW	S	%	+/–	TF	F%	H	SB	Min	GP	G	A	Pts	PIM	PP	SH	GW
1991-92	Saskatoon Blaze	SAHA	36	18	28	46	16	....	....	....	....	....	....	....	....	....	....	....	....	....	....	....	....	....	....	....
	Saskatoon Blades	WHL	....	....	....	....	....	....	....	....	....	....	....	....	....	....	....	....	1	0	0	0	0	....	....	....
1992-93	Saskatoon Blades	WHL	69	14	19	33	71	....	....	....	....	....	....	....	....	....	....	....	9	4	2	6	13	....	....	....
1993-94	Saskatoon Blades	WHL	70	18	32	50	181	....	....	....	....	....	....	....	....	....	....	....	16	0	9	9	19	....	....	....
1994-95	Saskatoon Blades	WHL	71	20	39	59	179	....	....	....	....	....	....	....	....	....	....	....	10	6	1	7	21	....	....	....
1995-96	Saskatoon Blades	WHL	72	49	61	110	83	....	....	....	....	....	....	....	....	....	....	....	4	1	1	2	4	....	....	....
1996-97	Saint John Flames	AHL	62	9	19	28	107	....	....	....	....	....	....	....	....	....	....	....	5	2	0	2	15	....	....	....
1997-98	Saint John Flames	AHL	68	13	26	39	112	....	....	....	....	....	....	....	....	....	....	....	21	5	9	14	8	....	....	....
1998-99	**Calgary**	**NHL**	**78**	**10**	**8**	**18**	**53**	**2**	**2**	**0**	**94**	**10.6**	**11**	**609**	**40.9**	**94**	**21**	**11:32**	....	....	....	....	....	....	....	....
99-2000	**Calgary**	**NHL**	**78**	**10**	**12**	**22**	**67**	**1**	**3**	**0**	**81**	**12.3**	**–6**	**872**	**44.4**	**113**	**34**	**12:38**	....	....	....	....	....	....	....	....
	NHL Totals		**156**	**20**	**20**	**40**	**120**	**3**	**5**	**0**	**175**	**11.4**		**1481**	**42.9**	**207**	**55**	**12:05**	....	....	....	....	....	....	....	....

WILSON, Landon
(WIHL-sohn, LAN-dohn) **PHX.**

Right wing. Shoots right. 6'2", 216 lbs. Born, St. Louis, MO, March 13, 1975. Toronto's 2nd choice, 19th overall, in 1993 Entry Draft.

			Regular Season																Playoffs							
Season	Club	League	GP	G	A	Pts	PIM	PP	SH	GW	S	%	+/-	TF	F%	H	SB	Min	GP	G	A	Pts	PIM	PP	SH	GW
1991-92	California Kings	WSJHL	38	50	42	92	135	....	....	....	....	....	....	....	....	....	....	....	....	....	....	....	....	....	....	....
1992-93	Dubuque Saints	USHL	43	29	36	65	284	....	....	....	....	....	....	....	....	....	....	....	....	....	....	....	....	....	....	....
1993-94	North Dakota	WCHA	35	18	15	33	*147	....	....	....	....	....	....	....	....	....	....	....	....	....	....	....	....	....	....	....
1994-95	North Dakota	WCHA	31	7	16	23	141	....	....	....	....	....	....	....	....	....	....	....	....	....	....	....	....	....	....	....
	Cornwall Aces	AHL	8	4	4	8	25	....	....	....	....	....	....	....	....	....	....	....	13	3	4	7	68	....	....	....
1995-96	**Colorado**	**NHL**	**7**	**1**	**0**	**1**	**6**	0	0	0	6	16.7	3	....	....	....	....	....	....	....	....	....	....	....	....	....
	Cornwall Aces	AHL	53	21	13	34	154	....	....	....	....	....	....	....	....	....	....	....	8	1	3	4	22	....	....	....
1996-97	**Colorado**	**NHL**	**9**	**1**	**2**	**3**	**23**	0	0	0	7	14.3	1	....	....	....	....	....	....	....	....	....	....	....	....	....
	Boston	**NHL**	**40**	**7**	**10**	**17**	**49**	0	0	0	76	9.2	-6	....	....	....	....	....	....	....	....	....	....	....	....	....
	Providence Bruins	AHL	2	2	1	3	2	....	....	....	....	....	....	....	....	....	....	....	10	3	4	7	16	....	....	....
1997-98	**Boston**	**NHL**	**28**	**1**	**5**	**6**	**7**	0	0	0	26	3.8	3	....	....	....	....	....	1	0	0	0	0	0	0	0
	Providence Bruins	AHL	42	18	10	28	146	....	....	....	....	....	....	....	....	....	....	....	....	....	....	....	....	....	....	....
1998-99	**Boston**	**NHL**	**22**	**3**	**3**	**6**	**17**	0	0	0	32	9.4	0	3	0.0	59	2	10:04	8	1	1	2	8	1	0	1
	Providence Bruins	AHL	48	31	22	53	89	....	....	....	....	....	....	....	....	....	....	....	11	7	1	8	19	....	....	....
99-2000	**Boston**	**NHL**	**40**	**1**	**3**	**4**	**18**	0	0	0	67	1.5	-6	14	42.9	84	5	10:09	....	....	....	....	....	....	....	....
	Providence Bruins	AHL	17	5	5	10	45	....	....	....	....	....	....	....	....	....	....	....	9	2	3	5	38	....	....	....
	NHL Totals		**146**	**14**	**23**	**37**	**120**	0	0	0	214	6.5		17	35.3	143	7	10:07	9	1	1	2	8	1	0	1

AHL First All-Star Team (1999)

Traded to **Quebec** by **Toronto** with Wendel Clark, Sylvain Lefebvre and Toronto's 1st round choice (Jeffrey Kealty) in 1994 Entry Draft for Mats Sundin, Garth Butcher, Todd Warriner and Philadelphia's 1st round choice (previously acquired by Quebec - later traded to Washington - Washington selected Nolan Baumgartner) in 1994 Entry Draft, June 28, 1994. Transferred to **Colorado** after **Quebec** franchise relocated, June 21, 1995. Traded to **Boston** by **Colorado** with Anders Myrvold for Boston's 1st round choice (Robyn Regehr) in 1998 Entry Draft, November 22, 1996. Signed as a free agent by **Phoenix**, July 7, 2000.

WILSON, Mike
(WIHL-sohn, MIGHK) **FLA.**

Defense. Shoots left. 6'6", 212 lbs. Born, Brampton, Ont., February 26, 1975. Vancouver's 1st choice, 20th overall, in 1993 Entry Draft.

Season	Club	League	GP	G	A	Pts	PIM	PP	SH	GW	S	%	+/-	TF	F%	H	SB	Min	GP	G	A	Pts	PIM	PP	SH	GW
1991-92	Georgetown	OJHL-B	41	9	13	22	65	....	....	....	....	....	....	....	....	....	....	....	....	....	....	....	....	....	....	....
1992-93	Sudbury Wolves	OHL	53	6	7	13	58	....	....	....	....	....	....	....	....	....	....	....	14	1	1	2	2	....	....	....
1993-94	Sudbury Wolves	OHL	60	4	22	26	62	....	....	....	....	....	....	....	....	....	....	....	9	1	3	4	8	....	....	....
1994-95	Sudbury Wolves	OHL	64	13	34	47	46	....	....	....	....	....	....	....	....	....	....	....	18	1	8	9	10	....	....	....
1995-96	**Buffalo**	**NHL**	**58**	**4**	**8**	**12**	**41**	1	0	1	52	7.7	13	....	....	....	....	....	....	....	....	....	....	....	....	....
	Rochester	AHL	15	0	5	5	38	....	....	....	....	....	....	....	....	....	....	....	....	....	....	....	....	....	....	....
1996-97	**Buffalo**	**NHL**	**77**	**2**	**9**	**11**	**51**	0	0	1	57	3.5	13	....	....	....	....	....	10	0	1	1	2	0	0	0
1997-98	**Buffalo**	**NHL**	**66**	**4**	**4**	**8**	**48**	0	0	1	52	7.7	13	....	....	....	....	....	15	0	1	1	13	0	0	0
1998-99	**Buffalo**	**NHL**	**30**	**1**	**2**	**3**	**47**	0	0	1	40	2.5	10	0	0.0	54	19	16:40	....	....	....	....	....	....	....	....
	Florida	**NHL**	**4**	**0**	**0**	**0**	**0**	0	0	0	8	0.0	2	0	0.0	4	6	19:23	....	....	....	....	....	....	....	....
	Las Vegas	IHL	6	3	1	4	6	....	....	....	....	....	....	....	....	....	....	....	....	....	....	....	....	....	....	....
99-2000	**Florida**	**NHL**	**60**	**4**	**16**	**20**	**35**	0	0	2	65	6.2	10	0	0.0	130	62	18:07	4	0	0	0	0	0	0	0
	NHL Totals		**295**	**15**	**39**	**54**	**222**	1	0	6	274	5.5		0	0.0	188	87	17:42	29	0	2	2	15	0	0	0

Traded to **Buffalo** by **Vancouver** with Mike Peca and Vancouver's 1st round choice (Jay McKee) in 1995 Entry Draft for Alexander Mogilny and Buffalo's 5th round choice (Todd Norman) in 1995 Entry Draft, July 8, 1995. Traded to **Florida** by **Buffalo** for Rhett Warrener and Florida's 5th round choice (Ryan Miller) in 1999 Entry Draft, March 23, 1999.

WISEMAN, Brian
(WIGHS-man, BRIGH-an) **TOR.**

Center. Shoots left. 5'8", 175 lbs. Born, Chatham, Ont., July 13, 1971. NY Rangers' 11th choice, 257th overall, in 1991 Entry Draft.

Season	Club	League	GP	G	A	Pts	PIM	PP	SH	GW	S	%	+/-	TF	F%	H	SB	Min	GP	G	A	Pts	PIM	PP	SH	GW
1986-87	Dresden Kings	OJHL-C	33	12	29	41	53	....	....	....	....	....	....	....	....	....	....	....	....	....	....	....	....	....	....	....
1987-88	Chatham	OJHL-B	41	26	33	59	35	....	....	....	....	....	....	....	....	....	....	....	....	....	....	....	....	....	....	....
1988-89	Chatham	OJHL-B	42	36	*71	*107	34	....	....	....	....	....	....	....	....	....	....	....	....	....	....	....	....	....	....	....
1989-90	Chatham	OJHL-B	40	*70	*77	*147	32	....	....	....	....	....	....	....	....	....	....	....	....	....	....	....	....	....	....	....
1990-91	U. of Michigan	CCHA	47	25	33	58	58	....	....	....	....	....	....	....	....	....	....	....	....	....	....	....	....	....	....	....
1991-92	U. of Michigan	CCHA	44	27	44	71	38	....	....	....	....	....	....	....	....	....	....	....	....	....	....	....	....	....	....	....
1992-93	U. of Michigan	CCHA	35	13	37	50	40	....	....	....	....	....	....	....	....	....	....	....	....	....	....	....	....	....	....	....
1993-94	U. of Michigan	CCHA	40	19	50	69	44	....	....	....	....	....	....	....	....	....	....	....	....	....	....	....	....	....	....	....
1994-95	Chicago Wolves	IHL	75	17	55	72	52	....	....	....	....	....	....	....	....	....	....	....	3	1	1	2	4	....	....	....
1995-96	Chicago Wolves	IHL	73	33	55	88	117	....	....	....	....	....	....	....	....	....	....	....	....	....	....	....	....	....	....	....
1996-97	**Toronto**	**NHL**	**3**	**0**	**0**	**0**	**0**	0	0	0	1	0.0	0	....	....	....	....	....	....	....	....	....	....	....	....	....
	St. John's Leafs	AHL	71	33	62	95	83	....	....	....	....	....	....	....	....	....	....	....	7	5	4	9	8	....	....	....
1997-98	Houston Aeros	IHL	78	26	72	98	86	....	....	....	....	....	....	....	....	....	....	....	4	0	3	3	8	....	....	....
1998-99	Houston Aeros	IHL	77	21	*88	*109	106	....	....	....	....	....	....	....	....	....	....	....	19	3	13	16	26	....	....	....
99-2000	Houston Aeros	IHL	72	15	38	53	52	....	....	....	....	....	....	....	....	....	....	....	3	0	1	1	6	....	....	....
	NHL Totals		**3**	**0**	**0**	**0**	**0**	0	0	0	1	0.0		....	....	....	....	....	....	....	....	....	....	....	....	....

CCHA First All-Star Team (1994) • NCAA West First All-American Team (1994) • IHL First All-Star Team (1998, 1999) • Won Leo P. Lamoureux Memorial Trophy (Top Scorer - IHL) (1999) • Won James Gatschene Memorial Trophy (MVP - IHL) (1999)

Signed as a free agent by **Toronto**, August 14, 1996. Signed as a free agent by **Houston** (IHL), August 4, 1997. Signed as a free agent by **Toronto**, July 13, 1999.

WITEHALL, Johan
(WITH-hall, YOH-han) **NYR**

Left wing. Shoots left. 6'1", 198 lbs. Born, Goteborg, Sweden, January 7, 1972. NY Rangers' 8th choice, 207th overall, in 1998 Entry Draft.

Season	Club	League	GP	G	A	Pts	PIM	PP	SH	GW	S	%	+/-	TF	F%	H	SB	Min	GP	G	A	Pts	PIM	PP	SH	GW
1991-92	Hanhals IF	Sweden-2	32	23	14	37	52	....	....	....	....	....	....	....	....	....	....	....	....	....	....	....	....	....	....	....
1992-93	Hanhals IF	Sweden-2	29	12	7	19	34	....	....	....	....	....	....	....	....	....	....	....	....	....	....	....	....	....	....	....
1993-94	Hanhals IF	Sweden-2	30	13	12	25	66	....	....	....	....	....	....	....	....	....	....	....	....	....	....	....	....	....	....	....
1994-95	Hanhals IF	Sweden-3	32	*38	13	*51	44	....	....	....	....	....	....	....	....	....	....	....	....	....	....	....	....	....	....	....
1995-96	Hanhals IF	Sweden-3	36	*43	17	60	48	....	....	....	....	....	....	....	....	....	....	....	....	....	....	....	....	....	....	....
1996-97	IK Oskarshamn	Sweden-2	32	19	16	35	38	....	....	....	....	....	....	....	....	....	....	....	....	....	....	....	....	....	....	....
1997-98	Leksands IF	Sweden	42	12	4	16	34	....	....	....	....	....	....	....	....	....	....	....	2	0	0	0	2	....	....	....
	Leksands IF	EuroHL	5	3	0	3	2	....	....	....	....	....	....	....	....	....	....	....	....	....	....	....	....	....	....	....
1998-99	**NY Rangers**	**NHL**	**4**	**0**	**0**	**0**	**0**	0	0	0	1	0.0	0	1	100.0	5	0	4:06	....	....	....	....	....	....	....	....
	Hartford	AHL	62	14	15	29	56	....	....	....	....	....	....	....	....	....	....	....	7	1	2	3	6	....	....	....
99-2000	**NY Rangers**	**NHL**	**9**	**1**	**1**	**2**	**2**	0	0	0	6	16.7	0	1	0.0	13	0	8:26	....	....	....	....	....	....	....	....
	Hartford	AHL	73	17	24	41	65	....	....	....	....	....	....	....	....	....	....	....	17	6	7	13	10	....	....	....
	NHL Totals		**13**	**1**	**1**	**2**	**2**	0	0	0	7	14.3		2	50.0	18	0	7:06	....	....	....	....	....	....	....	....

WITT, Brendan
(WITH, BREHN-dohn) **WSH.**

Defense. Shoots left. 6'2", 226 lbs. Born, Humbolt, Sask., February 20, 1975. Washington's 1st choice, 11th overall, in 1993 Entry Draft.

Season	Club	League	GP	G	A	Pts	PIM	PP	SH	GW	S	%	+/-	TF	F%	H	SB	Min	GP	G	A	Pts	PIM	PP	SH	GW
1990-91	Saskatoon Blaze	SAHA	31	5	13	18	42	....	....	....	....	....	....	....	....	....	....	....	....	....	....	....	....	....	....	....
	Seattle T-Birds	WHL	....	....	....	....	....	....	....	....	....	....	....	....	....	....	....	....	1	0	0	0	0	....	....	....
1991-92	Seattle T-Birds	WHL	67	3	9	12	212	....	....	....	....	....	....	....	....	....	....	....	15	1	1	2	84	....	....	....
1992-93	Seattle T-Birds	WHL	70	2	26	28	239	....	....	....	....	....	....	....	....	....	....	....	5	1	2	3	30	....	....	....
1993-94	Seattle T-Birds	WHL	56	8	31	39	235	....	....	....	....	....	....	....	....	....	....	....	9	3	8	11	23	....	....	....
1994-95		DID NOT PLAY																								
1995-96	**Washington**	**NHL**	**48**	**2**	**3**	**5**	**85**	0	0	1	44	4.5	-4	....	....	....	....	....	....	....	....	....	....	....	....	....
1996-97	**Washington**	**NHL**	**44**	**3**	**2**	**5**	**88**	0	0	0	41	7.3	-20	....	....	....	....	....	....	....	....	....	....	....	....	....
	Portland Pirates	AHL	30	2	4	6	56	....	....	....	....	....	....	....	....	....	....	....	5	1	0	1	30	....	....	....
1997-98	**Washington**	**NHL**	**64**	**1**	**7**	**8**	**112**	0	0	0	68	1.5	-11	....	....	....	....	....	16	1	0	1	14	0	0	0
1998-99	**Washington**	**NHL**	**54**	**2**	**5**	**7**	**87**	0	0	0	51	3.9	-6	0	0.0	148	52	15:50	....	....	....	....	....	....	....	....
99-2000	**Washington**	**NHL**	**77**	**1**	**7**	**8**	**114**	0	0	0	64	1.6	5	2	50.0	322	105	20:56	3	0	0	0	0	0	0	0
	NHL Totals		**287**	**9**	**24**	**33**	**486**	0	0	1	268	3.4		2	50.0	470	157	18:50	19	1	0	1	14	0	0	0

WHL West First All-Star Team (1993, 1994) • Canadian Major Junior First All-Star Team (1994)

• Sat out entire 1994-95 season after failing to come to contract terms with Washington.

WOOD, Dody (WUHD, DOH-dee) VAN.

Center. Shoots left. 6', 200 lbs. Born, Chetwynd, B.C., March 18, 1972. San Jose's 4th choice, 45th overall, in 1991 Entry Draft.

			Regular Season																Playoffs							
Season	Club	League	GP	G	A	Pts	PIM	PP	SH	GW	S	%	+/–	TF	F%	H	SB	Min	GP	G	A	Pts	PIM	PP	SH	GW
1989-90	Fort St. John	PCJHL	44	51	73	124	270	....	....	....	....	....	....	....	....	....	....	....	....	....	....	....	....	....	....	....
	Seattle T-Birds	WHL	....	....	....	....	....	....	....	....	....	....	....	....	....	....	....	....	5	0	0	0	2	....	....	....
1990-91	Seattle T-Birds	WHL	69	28	37	65	272	....	....	....	....	....	....	....	....	....	....	....	6	0	1	1	2	....	....	....
1991-92	Seattle T-Birds	WHL	37	13	19	32	232	....	....	....	....	....	....	....	....	....	....	....	....	....	....	....	....	....	....	....
	Swift Current	WHL	3	0	2	2	14	....	....	....	....	....	....	....	....	....	....	....	7	2	1	3	37	....	....	....
1992-93	**San Jose**	**NHL**	**13**	**1**	**1**	**2**	**71**	**0**	**0**	**0**	**10**	**10.0**	**–5**	....	....	....	....	....	....	....	....	....	....	....	....	....
	Kansas City	IHL	36	3	2	5	216	....	....	....	....	....	....	....	....	....	....	....	6	0	1	1	15	....	....	....
1993-94	Kansas City	IHL	48	5	15	20	320	....	....	....	....	....	....	....	....	....	....	....	....	....	....	....	....	....	....	....
1994-95	Kansas City	IHL	44	5	13	18	255	....	....	....	....	....	....	....	....	....	....	....	21	7	10	17	87	....	....	....
	San Jose	**NHL**	**9**	**1**	**1**	**2**	**29**	**0**	**0**	**0**	**5**	**20.0**	**0**	....	....	....	....	....	....	....	....	....	....	....	....	....
1995-96	**San Jose**	**NHL**	**32**	**3**	**6**	**9**	**138**	**0**	**1**	**0**	**33**	**9.1**	**0**	....	....	....	....	....	....	....	....	....	....	....	....	....
1996-97	**San Jose**	**NHL**	**44**	**3**	**2**	**5**	**193**	**0**	**0**	**0**	**43**	**7.0**	**–3**	....	....	....	....	....	....	....	....	....	....	....	....	....
	Kansas City	IHL	6	3	6	9	35	....	....	....	....	....	....	....	....	....	....	....	....	....	....	....	....	....	....	....
1997-98	**San Jose**	**NHL**	**8**	**0**	**0**	**0**	**40**	**0**	**0**	**0**	**4**	**0.0**	**–3**	....	....	....	....	....	....	....	....	....	....	....	....	....
	Kansas City	IHL	2	0	1	1	31	....	....	....	....	....	....	....	....	....	....	....	....	....	....	....	....	....	....	....
	Albany River Rats	AHL	34	4	13	17	185	....	....	....	....	....	....	....	....	....	....	....	13	2	0	2	55	....	....	....
1998-99	Kansas City	IHL	60	11	16	27	286	....	....	....	....	....	....	....	....	....	....	....	3	0	1	1	25	....	....	....
99-2000	Kansas City	IHL	77	13	28	41	*341	....	....	....	....	....	....	....	....	....	....	....	....	....	....	....	....	....	....	....
	NHL Totals		**106**	**8**	**10**	**18**	**471**	**0**	**1**	**0**	**95**	**8.4**		....	....	....	....	....	....	....	....	....	....	....	....	....

Traded to **New Jersey** by **San Jose** with Doug Bodger for John MacLean and Ken Sutton, December 7, 1997. Signed as a free agent by **Vancouver**, September 5, 2000.

WOOLLEY, Jason (WOO-lee, JAY-suhn) BUF.

Defense. Shoots left. 6', 200 lbs. Born, Toronto, Ont., July 27, 1969. Washington's 4th choice, 61st overall, in 1989 Entry Draft.

1986-87	St. Michael's	OJHL-B	35	13	22	35	40	....	....	....	....	....	....	....	....	....	....	....	....	....	....	....	....	....	....	....
1987-88	St. Michael's	OJHL-B	31	19	37	56	22	....	....	....	....	....	....	....	....	....	....	....	....	....	....	....	....	....	....	....
1988-89	Michigan State	CCHA	47	12	25	37	26	....	....	....	....	....	....	....	....	....	....	....	....	....	....	....	....	....	....	....
1989-90	Michigan State	CCHA	45	10	38	48	26	....	....	....	....	....	....	....	....	....	....	....	....	....	....	....	....	....	....	....
1990-91	Michigan State	CCHA	40	15	44	59	24	....	....	....	....	....	....	....	....	....	....	....	....	....	....	....	....	....	....	....
1991-92	Canada	Nat-Team	60	14	30	44	36	....	....	....	....	....	....	....	....	....	....	....	....	....	....	....	....	....	....	....
	Canada	Olympics	8	0	5	5	4	....	....	....	....	....	....	....	....	....	....	....	....	....	....	....	....	....	....	....
	Washington	**NHL**	**1**	**0**	**0**	**0**	**0**	**0**	**0**	**0**	**2**	**0.0**	**1**	....	....	....	....	....	....	....	....	....	....	....	....	....
	Baltimore	AHL	15	1	10	11	6	....	....	....	....	....	....	....	....	....	....	....	....	....	....	....	....	....	....	....
1992-93	**Washington**	**NHL**	**26**	**0**	**2**	**2**	**10**	**0**	**0**	**0**	**11**	**0.0**	**3**	....	....	....	....	....	....	....	....	....	....	....	....	....
	Baltimore	AHL	29	14	27	41	22	....	....	....	....	....	....	....	....	....	....	....	1	0	2	2	0	....	....	....
1993-94	**Washington**	**NHL**	**10**	**1**	**2**	**3**	**4**	**0**	**0**	**0**	**15**	**6.7**	**2**	....	....	....	....	....	**4**	**1**	**0**	**1**	**4**	**0**	**0**	**1**
	Portland Pirates	AHL	41	12	29	41	14	....	....	....	....	....	....	....	....	....	....	....	9	2	2	4	4	....	....	....
1994-95	Detroit Vipers	IHL	48	8	28	36	38	....	....	....	....	....	....	....	....	....	....	....	....	....	....	....	....	....	....	....
	Florida	**NHL**	**34**	**4**	**9**	**13**	**18**	**1**	**0**	**0**	**76**	**5.3**	**–1**	....	....	....	....	....	....	....	....	....	....	....	....	....
1995-96	**Florida**	**NHL**	**52**	**6**	**28**	**34**	**32**	**3**	**0**	**0**	**98**	**6.1**	**–9**	....	....	....	....	....	**13**	**2**	**6**	**8**	**14**	**1**	**0**	**1**
1996-97	**Florida**	**NHL**	**3**	**0**	**0**	**0**	**2**	**0**	**0**	**0**	**7**	**0.0**	**1**	....	....	....	....	....	....	....	....	....	....	....	....	....
	Pittsburgh	**NHL**	**57**	**6**	**30**	**36**	**28**	**2**	**0**	**1**	**79**	**7.6**	**3**	....	....	....	....	....	**5**	**0**	**3**	**3**	**0**	**0**	**0**	**0**
1997-98	**Buffalo**	**NHL**	**71**	**9**	**26**	**35**	**35**	**3**	**0**	**2**	**129**	**7.0**	**8**	....	....	....	....	....	**15**	**2**	**9**	**11**	**12**	**1**	**0**	**1**
1998-99	**Buffalo**	**NHL**	**80**	**10**	**33**	**43**	**62**	**4**	**0**	**2**	**154**	**6.5**	**16**	**0**	**0.0**	**68**	**67**	**18:43**	**21**	**4**	**11**	**15**	**10**	**2**	**0**	**1**
99-2000	**Buffalo**	**NHL**	**74**	**8**	**25**	**33**	**52**	**2**	**0**	**2**	**113**	**7.1**	**14**	**0**	**0.0**	**43**	**57**	**17:51**	**5**	**0**	**2**	**2**	**2**	**0**	**0**	**0**
	NHL Totals		**408**	**44**	**155**	**199**	**243**	**15**	**0**	**7**	**684**	**6.4**		**0**	**0.0**	**111**	**124**	**18:18**	**63**	**9**	**31**	**40**	**42**	**4**	**0**	**4**

CCHA First All-Star Team (1991) • NCAA West First All-American Team (1991)

Signed as a free agent by **Florida**, February 15, 1995. Traded to **Pittsburgh** by **Florida** with Stu Barnes for Chris Wells, November 19, 1996. Traded to **Buffalo** by **Pittsburgh** for Buffalo's 5th round choice (Robert Scuderi) in 1998 Entry Draft, September 24, 1997.

WORRELL, Peter (woh-REHL, PEE-tuhr) FLA.

Left wing. Shoots left. 6'6", 235 lbs. Born, Pierrefonds, Que., August 18, 1977. Florida's 7th choice, 166th overall, in 1995 Entry Draft.

1994-95	Hull Olympiques	QMJHL	56	1	8	9	243	....	....	....	....	....	....	....	....	....	....	....	21	0	1	1	91	....	....	....
1995-96	Hull Olympiques	QMJHL	63	23	36	59	464	....	....	....	....	....	....	....	....	....	....	....	18	11	8	19	81	....	....	....
1996-97	Hull Olympiques	QMJHL	62	17	46	63	437	....	....	....	....	....	....	....	....	....	....	....	14	3	13	16	83	....	....	....
1997-98	**Florida**	**NHL**	**19**	**0**	**0**	**0**	**153**	**0**	**0**	**0**	**15**	**0.0**	**–4**	....	....	....	....	....	....	....	....	....	....	....	....	....
	New Haven	AHL	50	15	12	27	309	....	....	....	....	....	....	....	....	....	....	....	1	0	1	1	6	....	....	....
1998-99	**Florida**	**NHL**	**62**	**4**	**5**	**9**	**258**	**0**	**0**	**2**	**50**	**8.0**	**0**	**0**	**0.0**	**100**	**5**	**6:15**	....	....	....	....	....	....	....	....
	New Haven	AHL	10	3	1	4	65	....	....	....	....	....	....	....	....	....	....	....	....	....	....	....	....	....	....	....
99-2000	**Florida**	**NHL**	**48**	**3**	**6**	**9**	**169**	**2**	**0**	**1**	**45**	**6.7**	**–7**	**1**	**100.0**	**141**	**12**	**8:25**	**4**	**1**	**0**	**1**	**8**	**0**	**0**	**0**
	NHL Totals		**129**	**7**	**11**	**18**	**580**	**2**	**0**	**3**	**110**	**6.4**		**1**	**100.0**	**241**	**17**	**7:12**	**4**	**1**	**0**	**1**	**8**	**0**	**0**	**0**

WOTTON, Mark (WAH-tuhn, MAHRK) DAL.

Defense. Shoots left. 6'1", 195 lbs. Born, Foxwarren, Man., November 16, 1973. Vancouver's 11th choice, 237th overall, in 1992 Entry Draft.

1988-89	Foxwarren Blades	MAHA	60	10	30	40	70	....	....	....	....	....	....	....	....	....	....	....	....	....	....	....	....	....	....	....
1989-90	Saskatoon Blades	WHL	51	2	3	5	31	....	....	....	....	....	....	....	....	....	....	....	7	1	1	2	15	....	....	....
1990-91	Saskatoon Blades	WHL	45	4	11	15	37	....	....	....	....	....	....	....	....	....	....	....	....	....	....	....	....	....	....	....
1991-92	Saskatoon Blades	WHL	64	11	25	36	62	....	....	....	....	....	....	....	....	....	....	....	21	2	6	8	22	....	....	....
1992-93	Saskatoon Blades	WHL	71	15	51	66	90	....	....	....	....	....	....	....	....	....	....	....	9	6	5	11	18	....	....	....
1993-94	Saskatoon Blades	WHL	65	12	34	46	108	....	....	....	....	....	....	....	....	....	....	....	16	3	12	15	32	....	....	....
1994-95	Syracuse Crunch	AHL	75	12	29	41	50	....	....	....	....	....	....	....	....	....	....	....	....	....	....	....	....	....	....	....
	Vancouver	**NHL**	**1**	**0**	**0**	**0**	**0**	**0**	**0**	**0**	**2**	**0.0**	**1**	....	....	....	....	....	**5**	**0**	**0**	**0**	**4**	**0**	**0**	**0**
1995-96	Syracuse Crunch	AHL	80	10	35	45	96	....	....	....	....	....	....	....	....	....	....	....	15	1	12	13	20	....	....	....
1996-97	**Vancouver**	**NHL**	**36**	**3**	**6**	**9**	**19**	**0**	**1**	**0**	**41**	**7.3**	**8**	....	....	....	....	....	....	....	....	....	....	....	....	....
	Syracuse Crunch	AHL	27	2	8	10	25	....	....	....	....	....	....	....	....	....	....	....	2	0	0	0	4	....	....	....
1997-98	**Vancouver**	**NHL**	**5**	**0**	**0**	**0**	**6**	**0**	**0**	**0**	**3**	**0.0**	**–2**	....	....	....	....	....	....	....	....	....	....	....	....	....
	Syracuse Crunch	AHL	56	12	21	33	80	....	....	....	....	....	....	....	....	....	....	....	5	0	0	0	12	....	....	....
1998-99	Syracuse Crunch	AHL	72	4	31	35	74	....	....	....	....	....	....	....	....	....	....	....	....	....	....	....	....	....	....	....
99-2000	Michigan K-Wings	IHL	70	3	7	10	72	....	....	....	....	....	....	....	....	....	....	....	....	....	....	....	....	....	....	....
	NHL Totals		**42**	**3**	**6**	**9**	**25**	**0**	**1**	**0**	**46**	**6.5**		....	....	....	....	....	**5**	**0**	**0**	**0**	**4**	**0**	**0**	**0**

WHL East Second All-Star Team (1994)

Signed as a free agent by **Dallas**, July 19, 1999.

WREN, Bob (REHN, BAWB) ANA.

Center. Shoots left. 5'10", 185 lbs. Born, Preston, Ont., September 16, 1974. Los Angeles' 3rd choice, 94th overall, in 1993 Entry Draft.

1989-90	Guelph Jr. B's	OJHL-B	48	24	36	60	82	....	....	....	....	....	....	....	....	....	....	....	....	....	....	....	....	....	....	....
1990-91	Guelph Jr. B's	OJHL-B	18	17	13	30	51	....	....	....	....	....	....	....	....	....	....	....	....	....	....	....	....	....	....	....
	Kingston	OJHL	14	10	15	25	34	....	....	....	....	....	....	....	....	....	....	....	....	....	....	....	....	....	....	....
1991-92	Detroit	OHL	62	13	36	49	58	....	....	....	....	....	....	....	....	....	....	....	7	3	4	7	19	....	....	....
1992-93	Detroit Jr. Wings	OHL	63	57	88	145	91	....	....	....	....	....	....	....	....	....	....	....	15	4	11	15	20	....	....	....
1993-94	Detroit Jr. Wings	OHL	57	45	64	109	81	....	....	....	....	....	....	....	....	....	....	....	17	12	18	30	20	....	....	....
1994-95	Springfield	AHL	61	16	15	31	118	....	....	....	....	....	....	....	....	....	....	....	....	....	....	....	....	....	....	....
	Richmond	ECHL	2	0	1	1	0	....	....	....	....	....	....	....	....	....	....	....	....	....	....	....	....	....	....	....
1995-96	Detroit Vipers	IHL	1	0	0	0	0	....	....	....	....	....	....	....	....	....	....	....	....	....	....	....	....	....	....	....
	Knoxville	ECHL	50	21	35	56	257	....	....	....	....	....	....	....	....	....	....	....	8	4	11	15	32	....	....	....
1996-97	Baltimore Bandits	AHL	72	23	36	59	97	....	....	....	....	....	....	....	....	....	....	....	3	1	1	2	0	....	....	....
1997-98	**Anaheim**	**NHL**	**3**	**0**	**0**	**0**	**0**	**0**	**0**	**0**	**4**	**0.0**	**0**	....	....	....	....	....	....	....	....	....	....	....	....	....
	Cincinnati Ducks	AHL	77	*42	58	100	151	....	....	....	....	....	....	....	....	....	....	....	....	....	....	....	....	....	....	....

Season	Club	League	GP	G	A	Pts	PIM	PP	SH	GW	S	%	+/-	TF	F%	H	SB	Min	GP	G	A	Pts	PIM	PP	SH	GW
			Regular Season																Playoffs							
1998-99	Cincinnati Ducks	AHL	73	27	43	70	102												3	1	2	3	8			
99-2000	Cincinnati Ducks	AHL	57	24	38	62	61																			
	NHL Totals		**3**	**0**	**0**	**0**	**0**	0	0	0	4	0.0														

OHL Second All-Star Team (1993, 1994)

Signed as a free agent by **Hartford**, September 6, 1994. Signed as a free agent by **Anaheim**, August 1, 1997.

WRIGHT, Jamie

(RIGHT, JAY-mee) **DAL.**

Left wing. Shoots left. 6', 195 lbs. Born, Kitchener, Ont., May 13, 1976. Dallas' 3rd choice, 98th overall, in 1994 Entry Draft.

Season	Club	League	GP	G	A	Pts	PIM	PP	SH	GW	S	%	+/-	TF	F%	H	SB	Min	GP	G	A	Pts	PIM	PP	SH	GW
1991-92	Elmira Kings	OJHL-B	44	17	11	28	46																			
1992-93	Elmira Kings	OJHL-B	47	22	32	54	52																			
1993-94	Guelph Storm	OHL	65	17	15	32	34												8	2	1	3	10			
1994-95	Guelph Storm	OHL	65	43	39	82	36												14	6	8	14	6			
1995-96	Guelph Storm	OHL	55	30	36	66	45												16	10	12	22	35			
1996-97	Michigan K-Wings	IHL	60	6	8	14	34												1	0	0	0	0			
1997-98	**Dallas**	**NHL**	**21**	**4**	**2**	**6**	**2**	0	0	2	15	26.7	8						**5**	**0**	**0**	**0**	**0**	0	0	0
	Michigan K-Wings	IHL	53	15	11	26	31																			
1998-99	**Dallas**	**NHL**	**11**	**0**	**0**	**0**	**0**	0	0	0	10	0.0	-3	0	0.0	18	4	7:37								
	Michigan K-Wings	IHL	64	16	15	31	92												2	0	0	0	2			
99-2000	**Dallas**	**NHL**	**23**	**1**	**4**	**5**	**16**	0	0	0	15	6.7	4	2	50.0	53	5	9:50								
	Michigan K-Wings	IHL	49	12	4	16	64																			
	NHL Totals		**55**	**5**	**6**	**11**	**18**	0	0	2	40	12.5		2	50.0	71	9	9:07	**5**	**0**	**0**	**0**	**0**	0	0	0

WRIGHT, Tyler

(RIGHT, TIGH-luhr) **CBJ**

Center. Shoots right. 6', 185 lbs. Born, Canora, Sask., April 6, 1973. Edmonton's 1st choice, 12th overall, in 1991 Entry Draft.

Season	Club	League	GP	G	A	Pts	PIM	PP	SH	GW	S	%	+/-	TF	F%	H	SB	Min	GP	G	A	Pts	PIM	PP	SH	GW
1988-89	Swift Current	SAHA	36	20	13	33	102																			
1989-90	Swift Current	WHL	67	14	18	32	119												4	0	0	0	12			
1990-91	Swift Current	WHL	66	41	51	92	157												3	0	0	0	6			
1991-92	Swift Current	WHL	63	36	46	82	185												8	2	5	7	16			
1992-93	Swift Current	WHL	37	24	41	65	76												17	9	17	26	*49			
	Edmonton	**NHL**	**7**	**1**	**1**	**2**	**19**	0	0	0	7	14.3	-4													
1993-94	**Edmonton**	**NHL**	**5**	**0**	**0**	**0**	**4**	0	0	0	2	0.0	-3													
	Cape Breton	AHL	65	14	27	41	160												5	2	0	2	11			
1994-95	Cape Breton	AHL	70	16	15	31	184																			
	Edmonton	**NHL**	**6**	**1**	**0**	**1**	**14**	0	0	0	6	16.7	1													
1995-96	**Edmonton**	**NHL**	**23**	**1**	**0**	**1**	**33**	0	0	0	18	5.6	-7													
	Cape Breton	AHL	31	6	12	18	158																			
1996-97	**Pittsburgh**	**NHL**	**45**	**2**	**2**	**4**	**70**	0	0	2	30	6.7	-7													
	Cleveland	IHL	10	4	3	7	34												14	4	2	6	44			
1997-98	**Pittsburgh**	**NHL**	**82**	**3**	**4**	**7**	**112**	1	0	0	46	6.5	-3						**6**	**0**	**1**	**1**	**4**	0	0	0
1998-99	**Pittsburgh**	**NHL**	**61**	**0**	**0**	**0**	**90**	0	0	0	16	0.0	-2	122	46.7	57	3	3:46	**13**	**0**	**0**	**0**	**19**	0	0	0
99-2000	**Pittsburgh**	**NHL**	**50**	**12**	**10**	**22**	**45**	0	0	1	68	17.6	4	698	47.1	89	13	13:24	**11**	**3**	**1**	**4**	**17**	0	0	0
	Wilkes-Barre	AHL	25	5	15	20	86																			
	NHL Totals		**279**	**20**	**17**	**37**	**387**	1	0	3	193	10.4		820	47.1	146	16	8:06	**30**	**3**	**2**	**5**	**40**	0	0	0

Traded to **Pittsburgh** by **Edmonton** for Pittsburgh's 7th round choice (Brandon Lafrance) in 1996 Entry Draft, June 22, 1996. Selected by **Columbus** from **Pittsburgh** in Expansion Draft, June 23, 2000.

YACHMENEV, Vitali

(YATCH-muh-nehv, VIH-tal-ee) **NSH.**

Right wing. Shoots left. 5'11", 195 lbs. Born, Chelyabinsk, USSR, January 8, 1975. Los Angeles' 3rd choice, 59th overall, in 1994 Entry Draft.

Season	Club	League	GP	G	A	Pts	PIM	PP	SH	GW	S	%	+/-	TF	F%	H	SB	Min	GP	G	A	Pts	PIM	PP	SH	GW
1990-91	HC Chelyabinsk	CIS-Jr.	80	88	60	148	72																			
1991-92	HC Chelyabinsk	CIS-Jr.	80	82	70	152	20																			
1992-93	HC Chelyabinsk	CIS-2	51	23	20	43	12																			
1993-94	North Bay	OHL	66	*61	52	113	18												18	13	19	32	12			
1994-95	North Bay	OHL	59	53	52	105	8												6	1	8	9	2			
	Phoenix	IHL																	4	1	0	1	0			
1995-96	**Los Angeles**	**NHL**	**80**	**19**	**34**	**53**	**16**	6	1	2	133	14.3	-3													
1996-97	**Los Angeles**	**NHL**	**65**	**10**	**22**	**32**	**10**	2	0	2	97	10.3	-9													
1997-98	**Los Angeles**	**NHL**	**4**	**0**	**1**	**1**	**4**	0	0	0	4	0.0	1													
	Long Beach	IHL	59	23	28	51	14												17	8	9	17	4			
1998-99	**Nashville**	**NHL**	**55**	**7**	**10**	**17**	**10**	0	1	2	83	8.4	-10	0	0.0	28	21	15:06								
	Milwaukee	IHL	16	7	6	13	0																			
99-2000	**Nashville**	**NHL**	**68**	**16**	**16**	**32**	**12**	1	1	3	120	13.3	5	8	25.0	26	19	15:26								
	NHL Totals		**272**	**52**	**83**	**135**	**52**	9	3	9	437	11.9		8	25.0	54	40	15:17								

Canadian Major Junior Rookie of the Year (1994)

Traded to **Nashville** by **LA Kings** for future considerations, July 7, 1998.

YAKE, Terry

(YAYK, TAIR-ee) **WSH.**

Center. Shoots right. 5'11", 190 lbs. Born, New Westminster, B.C., October 22, 1968. Hartford's 3rd choice, 81st overall, in 1987 Entry Draft.

Season	Club	League	GP	G	A	Pts	PIM	PP	SH	GW	S	%	+/-	TF	F%	H	SB	Min	GP	G	A	Pts	PIM	PP	SH	GW
1984-85	Brandon	WHL	11	1	1	2	0																			
1985-86	Brandon	WHL	72	26	26	52	49																			
1986-87	Brandon	WHL	71	44	58	102	64																			
1987-88	Brandon	WHL	72	55	85	140	59												4	5	6	11	12			
1988-89	**Hartford**	**NHL**	**2**	**0**	**0**	**0**	**0**	0	0	0	0	0.0	1													
	Binghamton	AHL	75	39	56	95	57																			
1989-90	**Hartford**	**NHL**	**2**	**0**	**1**	**1**	**0**	0	0	0	2	0.0	-1													
	Binghamton	AHL	77	13	42	55	37																			
1990-91	**Hartford**	**NHL**	**19**	**1**	**4**	**5**	**10**	0	0	1	19	5.3	-3						**6**	**1**	**1**	**2**	**16**	0	1	0
	Springfield	AHL	60	35	42	77	56												15	9	9	18	10			
1991-92	**Hartford**	**NHL**	**15**	**1**	**1**	**2**	**4**	0	0	0	12	8.3	-2													
	Springfield	AHL	53	21	34	55	63												8	3	4	7	2			
1992-93	**Hartford**	**NHL**	**66**	**22**	**31**	**53**	**46**	4	1	2	98	22.4	3													
	Springfield	AHL	16	8	14	22	27																			
1993-94	**Anaheim**	**NHL**	**82**	**21**	**31**	**52**	**44**	5	0	2	188	11.2	2													
1994-95	**Toronto**	**NHL**	**19**	**3**	**2**	**5**	**2**	1	0	2	26	11.5	1													
	Denver Grizzlies	IHL	2	0	3	3	2												17	4	11	15	16			
1995-96	Milwaukee	IHL	70	32	56	88	70												5	3	6	9	4			
1996-97	Rochester	AHL	78	34	*67	101	77												10	8	8	16	2			
1997-98	**St. Louis**	**NHL**	**65**	**10**	**15**	**25**	**38**	3	1	4	60	16.7	1						**10**	**2**	**1**	**3**	**6**	2	0	1
1998-99	**St. Louis**	**NHL**	**60**	**9**	**18**	**27**	**34**	3	0	4	59	15.3	-9	453	48.1	39	17	14:50	**13**	**1**	**2**	**3**	**14**	1	0	0
	Worcester	AHL	24	8	11	19	26																			
99-2000	**St. Louis**	**NHL**	**26**	**4**	**9**	**13**	**22**	2	0	2	26	15.4	2	129	55.8	18	8	13:51								
	Washington	**NHL**	**35**	**6**	**5**	**11**	**12**	1	0	1	29	20.7	2	219	51.1	9	8	12:36	**3**	**0**	**0**	**0**	**0**	0	0	0
	NHL Totals		**391**	**77**	**117**	**194**	**212**	19	2	18	519	14.8		801	50.2	66	33	13:59	**32**	**4**	**4**	**8**	**36**	3	1	1

Claimed by **Anaheim** from **Hartford** in Expansion Draft, June 24, 1993. Traded to **Toronto** by **Anaheim** for David Sacco, September 28, 1994. Signed as a free agent by **Buffalo**, September 17, 1996. Signed as a free agent by **St. Louis**, July 24, 1997. Claimed by **Atlanta** from **St. Louis** in Expansion Draft, June 25, 1999. Claimed on waivers by **Washington** from **St. Louis**, January 18, 2000.

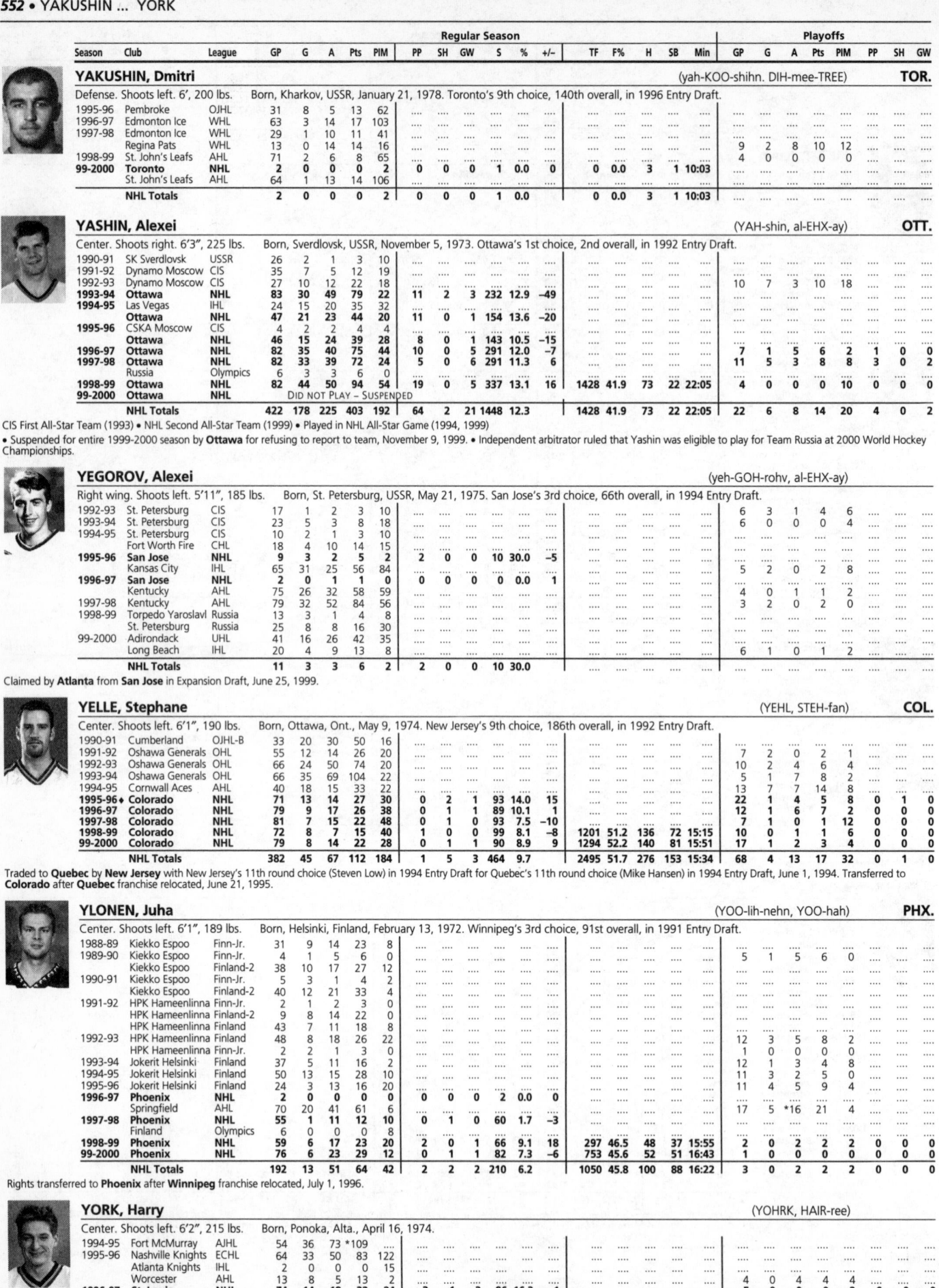

						Regular Season														Playoffs						
Season	Club	League	GP	G	A	Pts	PIM	PP	SH	GW	S	%	+/-	TF	F%	H	SB	Min	GP	G	A	Pts	PIM	PP	SH	GW

YAKUSHIN, Dmitri (yah-KOO-shihn. DIH-mee-TREE) **TOR.**

Defense. Shoots left. 6', 200 lbs. Born, Kharkov, USSR, January 21, 1978. Toronto's 9th choice, 140th overall, in 1996 Entry Draft.

Season	Club	League	GP	G	A	Pts	PIM	PP	SH	GW	S	%	+/-	TF	F%	H	SB	Min	GP	G	A	Pts	PIM	PP	SH	GW
1995-96	Pembroke	OJHL	31	8	5	13	62	....	....	....	....	....	....	....	....	....	....	....	....	....	....	....	....	....	....	....
1996-97	Edmonton Ice	WHL	63	3	14	17	103	....	....	....	....	....	....	....	....	....	....	....	....	....	....	....	....	....	....	....
1997-98	Edmonton Ice	WHL	29	1	10	11	41	....	....	....	....	....	....	....	....	....	....	....	....	....	....	....	....	....	....	....
	Regina Pats	WHL	13	0	14	14	16	....	....	....	....	....	....	....	....	....	....	....	9	2	8	10	12	....	....	....
1998-99	St. John's Leafs	AHL	71	2	6	8	65	....	....	....	....	....	....	....	....	....	....	....	4	0	0	0	0	....	....	....
99-2000	**Toronto**	**NHL**	2	0	0	0	2	0	0	0	1	0.0	0	0	0.0	3	1	10:03	....	....	....	....	....	....	....	....
	St. John's Leafs	AHL	64	1	13	14	106	....	....	....	....	....	....	....	....	....	....	....	....	....	....	....	....	....	....	....
	NHL Totals		2	0	0	0	2	0	0	0	1	0.0		0	0.0	3	1	10:03								

YASHIN, Alexei (YAH-shin, al-EHX-ay) **OTT.**

Center. Shoots right. 6'3", 225 lbs. Born, Sverdlovsk, USSR, November 5, 1973. Ottawa's 1st choice, 2nd overall, in 1992 Entry Draft.

Season	Club	League	GP	G	A	Pts	PIM	PP	SH	GW	S	%	+/-	TF	F%	H	SB	Min	GP	G	A	Pts	PIM	PP	SH	GW
1990-91	SK Sverdlovsk	USSR	26	2	1	3	10	....	....	....	....	....	....	....	....	....	....	....	....	....	....	....	....	....	....	....
1991-92	Dynamo Moscow	CIS	35	7	5	12	19	....	....	....	....	....	....	....	....	....	....	....	....	....	....	....	....	....	....	....
1992-93	Dynamo Moscow	CIS	27	10	12	22	18	....	....	....	....	....	....	....	....	....	....	....	10	7	3	10	18	....	....	....
1993-94	**Ottawa**	**NHL**	83	30	49	79	22	11	2	3	232	12.9	–49	....	....	....	....	....	....	....	....	....	....	....	....	....
1994-95	Las Vegas	IHL	24	15	20	35	32	....	....	....	....	....	....	....	....	....	....	....	....	....	....	....	....	....	....	....
	Ottawa	**NHL**	47	21	23	44	20	11	0	1	154	13.6	–20	....	....	....	....	....	....	....	....	....	....	....	....	....
1995-96	CSKA Moscow	CIS	4	2	2	4	4	....	....	....	....	....	....	....	....	....	....	....	....	....	....	....	....	....	....	....
	Ottawa	**NHL**	46	15	24	39	28	8	0	1	143	10.5	–15	....	....	....	....	....	....	....	....	....	....	....	....	....
1996-97	**Ottawa**	**NHL**	82	35	40	75	44	10	0	5	291	12.0	–7	....	....	....	....	....	7	1	5	6	2	1	0	0
1997-98	**Ottawa**	**NHL**	82	33	39	72	24	5	0	6	291	11.3	6	....	....	....	....	....	11	5	3	8	8	3	0	2
	Russia	Olympics	6	3	3	6	0	....	....	....	....	....	....	....	....	....	....	....	....	....	....	....	....	....	....	....
1998-99	**Ottawa**	**NHL**	82	44	50	94	54	19	0	5	337	13.1	16	1428	41.9	73	22	22:05	4	0	0	0	10	0	0	0
99-2000	**Ottawa**	**NHL**				DID NOT PLAY – SUSPENDED																				
	NHL Totals		422	178	225	403	192	64	2	21	1448	12.3		1428	41.9	73	22	22:05	22	6	8	14	20	4	0	2

CIS First All-Star Team (1993) • NHL Second All-Star Team (1999) • Played in NHL All-Star Game (1994, 1999)
• Suspended for entire 1999-2000 season by **Ottawa** for refusing to report to team, November 9, 1999. • Independent arbitrator ruled that Yashin was eligible to play for Team Russia at 2000 World Hockey Championships.

YEGOROV, Alexei (yeh-GOH-rohv, al-EHX-ay)

Right wing. Shoots left. 5'11", 185 lbs. Born, St. Petersburg, USSR, May 21, 1975. San Jose's 3rd choice, 66th overall, in 1994 Entry Draft.

Season	Club	League	GP	G	A	Pts	PIM	PP	SH	GW	S	%	+/-	TF	F%	H	SB	Min	GP	G	A	Pts	PIM	PP	SH	GW
1992-93	St. Petersburg	CIS	17	1	2	3	10	....	....	....	....	....	....	....	....	....	....	....	6	3	1	4	6	....	....	....
1993-94	St. Petersburg	CIS	23	5	3	8	18	....	....	....	....	....	....	....	....	....	....	....	6	0	0	0	4	....	....	....
1994-95	St. Petersburg	CIS	10	2	1	3	10	....	....	....	....	....	....	....	....	....	....	....	....	....	....	....	....	....	....	....
	Fort Worth Fire	CHL	18	4	10	14	15	....	....	....	....	....	....	....	....	....	....	....	....	....	....	....	....	....	....	....
1995-96	**San Jose**	**NHL**	9	3	2	5	2	2	0	0	10	30.0	–5	....	....	....	....	....	....	....	....	....	....	....	....	....
	Kansas City	IHL	65	31	25	56	84	....	....	....	....	....	....	....	....	....	....	....	5	2	0	2	8	....	....	....
1996-97	**San Jose**	**NHL**	2	0	1	1	0	0	0	0	0	0.0	1	....	....	....	....	....	....	....	....	....	....	....	....	....
	Kentucky	AHL	75	26	32	58	59	....	....	....	....	....	....	....	....	....	....	....	4	0	1	1	2	....	....	....
1997-98	Kentucky	AHL	79	32	52	84	56	....	....	....	....	....	....	....	....	....	....	....	3	2	0	2	0	....	....	....
1998-99	Torpedo Yaroslavl	Russia	13	3	1	4	8	....	....	....	....	....	....	....	....	....	....	....	....	....	....	....	....	....	....	....
	St. Petersburg	Russia	25	8	8	16	30	....	....	....	....	....	....	....	....	....	....	....	....	....	....	....	....	....	....	....
99-2000	Adirondack	UHL	41	16	26	42	35	....	....	....	....	....	....	....	....	....	....	....	....	....	....	....	....	....	....	....
	Long Beach	IHL	20	4	9	13	8	....	....	....	....	....	....	....	....	....	....	....	6	1	0	1	2	....	....	....
	NHL Totals		11	3	3	6	2	2	0	0	10	30.0														

Claimed by **Atlanta** from **San Jose** in Expansion Draft, June 25, 1999.

YELLE, Stephane (YEHL, STEH-fan) **COL.**

Center. Shoots left. 6'1", 190 lbs. Born, Ottawa, Ont., May 9, 1974. New Jersey's 9th choice, 186th overall, in 1992 Entry Draft.

Season	Club	League	GP	G	A	Pts	PIM	PP	SH	GW	S	%	+/-	TF	F%	H	SB	Min	GP	G	A	Pts	PIM	PP	SH	GW
1990-91	Cumberland	OJHL-B	33	20	30	50	16	....	....	....	....	....	....	....	....	....	....	....	....	....	....	....	....	....	....	....
1991-92	Oshawa Generals	OHL	55	12	14	26	20	....	....	....	....	....	....	....	....	....	....	....	7	2	0	2	1	....	....	....
1992-93	Oshawa Generals	OHL	66	24	50	74	20	....	....	....	....	....	....	....	....	....	....	....	10	2	4	6	4	....	....	....
1993-94	Oshawa Generals	OHL	66	35	69	104	22	....	....	....	....	....	....	....	....	....	....	....	5	1	7	8	2	....	....	....
1994-95	Cornwall Aces	AHL	40	18	15	33	22	....	....	....	....	....	....	....	....	....	....	....	13	7	7	14	8	....	....	....
1995-96 ♦	**Colorado**	**NHL**	71	13	14	27	30	0	2	1	93	14.0	15	....	....	....	....	....	22	1	4	5	8	0	1	0
1996-97	**Colorado**	**NHL**	79	9	17	26	38	0	1	1	89	10.1	1	....	....	....	....	....	12	1	6	7	2	0	0	0
1997-98	**Colorado**	**NHL**	81	7	15	22	48	0	1	0	93	7.5	–10	....	....	....	....	....	7	1	0	1	12	0	0	0
1998-99	**Colorado**	**NHL**	72	8	7	15	40	1	0	0	99	8.1	–8	1201	51.2	136	72	15:15	10	0	1	1	6	0	0	0
99-2000	**Colorado**	**NHL**	79	8	14	22	28	0	1	1	90	8.9	9	1294	52.2	140	81	15:51	17	1	2	3	4	0	0	0
	NHL Totals		382	45	67	112	184	1	5	3	464	9.7		2495	51.7	276	153	15:34	68	4	13	17	32	0	1	0

Traded to **Quebec** by **New Jersey** with New Jersey's 11th round choice (Steven Low) in 1994 Entry Draft for Quebec's 11th round choice (Mike Hansen) in 1994 Entry Draft, June 1, 1994. Transferred to **Colorado** after **Quebec** franchise relocated, June 21, 1995.

YLONEN, Juha (YOO-lih-nehn, YOO-hah) **PHX.**

Center. Shoots left. 6'1", 189 lbs. Born, Helsinki, Finland, February 13, 1972. Winnipeg's 3rd choice, 91st overall, in 1991 Entry Draft.

Season	Club	League	GP	G	A	Pts	PIM	PP	SH	GW	S	%	+/-	TF	F%	H	SB	Min	GP	G	A	Pts	PIM	PP	SH	GW
1988-89	Kiekko Espoo	Finn-Jr.	31	9	14	23	8	....	....	....	....	....	....	....	....	....	....	....	....	....	....	....	....	....	....	....
1989-90	Kiekko Espoo	Finn-Jr.	4	1	5	6	0	....	....	....	....	....	....	....	....	....	....	....	5	1	5	6	0	....	....	....
	Kiekko Espoo	Finland-2	38	10	17	27	12	....	....	....	....	....	....	....	....	....	....	....	....	....	....	....	....	....	....	....
1990-91	Kiekko Espoo	Finn-Jr.	5	3	1	4	2	....	....	....	....	....	....	....	....	....	....	....	....	....	....	....	....	....	....	....
	Kiekko Espoo	Finland-2	40	12	21	33	4	....	....	....	....	....	....	....	....	....	....	....	....	....	....	....	....	....	....	....
1991-92	HPK Hameenlinna	Finn-Jr.	2	1	2	3	0	....	....	....	....	....	....	....	....	....	....	....	....	....	....	....	....	....	....	....
	HPK Hameenlinna	Finland-2	9	8	14	22	0	....	....	....	....	....	....	....	....	....	....	....	....	....	....	....	....	....	....	....
	HPK Hameenlinna	Finland	43	7	11	18	8	....	....	....	....	....	....	....	....	....	....	....	....	....	....	....	....	....	....	....
1992-93	HPK Hameenlinna	Finland	48	8	18	26	22	....	....	....	....	....	....	....	....	....	....	....	12	3	5	8	2	....	....	....
	HPK Hameenlinna	Finn-Jr.	2	2	1	3	0	....	....	....	....	....	....	....	....	....	....	....	1	0	0	0	0	....	....	....
1993-94	Jokerit Helsinki	Finland	37	5	11	16	2	....	....	....	....	....	....	....	....	....	....	....	12	1	3	4	8	....	....	....
1994-95	Jokerit Helsinki	Finland	50	13	15	28	10	....	....	....	....	....	....	....	....	....	....	....	11	3	2	5	0	....	....	....
1995-96	Jokerit Helsinki	Finland	50	3	13	16	20	....	....	....	....	....	....	....	....	....	....	....	11	4	5	9	4	....	....	....
1996-97	**Phoenix**	**NHL**	2	0	0	0	0	0	0	0	2	0.0	0	....	....	....	....	....	....	....	....	....	....	....	....	....
	Springfield	AHL	70	20	41	61	6	....	....	....	....	....	....	....	....	....	....	....	17	5	*16	21	4	....	....	....
1997-98	**Phoenix**	**NHL**	55	1	11	12	10	0	1	0	60	1.7	–3	....	....	....	....	....	....	....	....	....	....	....	....	....
	Finland	Olympics	6	0	0	0	8	....	....	....	....	....	....	....	....	....	....	....	....	....	....	....	....	....	....	....
1998-99	**Phoenix**	**NHL**	59	6	17	23	20	2	0	1	66	9.1	18	297	46.5	48	37	15:55	2	0	2	2	2	0	0	0
99-2000	**Phoenix**	**NHL**	76	6	23	29	12	0	1	1	82	7.3	–6	753	45.6	52	51	16:43	1	0	0	0	0	0	0	0
	NHL Totals		192	13	51	64	42	2	2	2	210	6.2		1050	45.8	100	88	16:22	3	0	2	2	2	0	0	0

Rights transferred to **Phoenix** after **Winnipeg** franchise relocated, July 1, 1996.

YORK, Harry (YOHRK, HAIR-ree)

Center. Shoots left. 6'2", 215 lbs. Born, Ponoka, Alta., April 16, 1974.

Season	Club	League	GP	G	A	Pts	PIM	PP	SH	GW	S	%	+/-	TF	F%	H	SB	Min	GP	G	A	Pts	PIM	PP	SH	GW
1994-95	Fort McMurray	AJHL	54	36	73	*109	....	....	....	....	....	....	....	....	....	....	....	....	....	....	....	....	....	....	....	....
1995-96	Nashville Knights	ECHL	64	33	50	83	122	....	....	....	....	....	....	....	....	....	....	....	....	....	....	....	....	....	....	....
	Atlanta Knights	IHL	2	0	0	0	15	....	....	....	....	....	....	....	....	....	....	....	....	....	....	....	....	....	....	....
	Worcester	AHL	13	8	5	13	2	....	....	....	....	....	....	....	....	....	....	....	4	0	4	4	4	....	....	....
1996-97	**St. Louis**	**NHL**	74	14	18	32	24	3	1	3	86	16.3	1	....	....	....	....	....	5	0	0	0	2	0	0	0
1997-98	**St. Louis**	**NHL**	58	4	6	10	31	0	0	0	42	9.5	0	....	....	....	....	....	....	....	....	....	....	....	....	....
	NY Rangers	**NHL**	2	0	0	0	0	0	0	0	2	0.0	–1	....	....	....	....	....	....	....	....	....	....	....	....	....

			Regular Season																Playoffs							
Season	Club	League	GP	G	A	Pts	PIM	PP	SH	GW	S	%	+/-	TF	F%	H	SB	Min	GP	G	A	Pts	PIM	PP	SH	GW
1998-99	**NY Rangers**	**NHL**	**5**	**0**	**0**	**0**	**4**	**0**	**0**	**0**	**5**	**0.0**	**–1**	**33**	**60.6**	**20**	**2**	**10:00**	....	....	....	....	....	....	....	....
	Pittsburgh	**NHL**	**2**	**0**	**0**	**0**	**0**	**0**	**0**	**0**	**0**	**0.0**	**0**	**0**	**0.0**	**1**	**0**	**3:00**	....	....	....	....	....	....	....	....
	Vancouver	**NHL**	**49**	**7**	**9**	**16**	**20**	**1**	**0**	**0**	**55**	**12.7**	**–2**	**496**	**42.9**	**110**	**13**	**14:32**	....	....	....	....	....	....	....	....
99-2000	**Vancouver**	**NHL**	**54**	**4**	**13**	**17**	**20**	**1**	**1**	**0**	**50**	**8.0**	**–4**	**398**	**37.7**	**124**	**16**	**12:35**	....	....	....	....	....	....	....	....
	Syracuse Crunch	AHL	1	0	0	0	15	....	....	....	....	....	....	....	....	....	....	....	....	....	....	....	....	....	....	....
	NHL Totals		**244**	**29**	**46**	**75**	**99**	**5**	**2**	**3**	**240**	**12.1**		**927**	**41.3**	**255**	**31**	**13:09**	**5**	**0**	**0**	**0**	**2**	**0**	**0**	**0**

Named AJHL MVP (1995) • Won AJHL Scoring Title (1995).

Signed as a free agent by **St. Louis**, May 1, 1996. Traded to **NY Rangers** by **St. Louis** for Mike Eastwood, March 24, 1998. Traded to **Pittsburgh** by **NY Rangers** with Alexei Kovalev for Petr Nedved, Chris Tamer and Sean Pronger, November 25, 1998. Claimed on waivers by **Vancouver** from **Pittsburgh**, December 7, 1998. • Played w/ RHI's Chicago Cheetahs in 1995 (24-24-47-71-25).

YORK, Jason

(YOHRK, JAY-suhn) **OTT.**

Defense. Shoots right. 6'1", 200 lbs. Born, Nepean, Ont., May 20, 1970. Detroit's 6th choice, 129th overall, in 1990 Entry Draft.

Season	Club	League	GP	G	A	Pts	PIM	PP	SH	GW	S	%	+/-	TF	F%	H	SB	Min	GP	G	A	Pts	PIM	PP	SH	GW
1986-87	Smiths Falls Bears	OJHL	46	6	13	19	86	....	....	....	....	....	....	....	....	....	....	....	....	....	....	....	....	....	....	....
1987-88	Hamilton Hawks	OHL	58	4	9	13	110	....	....	....	....	....	....	....	....	....	....	....	....	....	....	....	....	....	....	....
1988-89	Windsor Spitfires	OHL	65	19	44	63	105	....	....	....	....	....	....	....	....	....	....	....	....	....	....	....	....	....	....	....
1989-90	Windsor Spitfires	OHL	39	9	30	39	38	....	....	....	....	....	....	....	....	....	....	....	....	....	....	....	....	....	....	....
	Kitchener	OHL	25	11	25	36	17	....	....	....	....	....	....	....	....	....	....	....	17	3	19	22	10	....	....	....
1990-91	Windsor Spitfires	OHL	66	13	80	93	40	....	....	....	....	....	....	....	....	....	....	....	11	3	10	13	12	....	....	....
1991-92	Adirondack	AHL	49	4	20	24	32	....	....	....	....	....	....	....	....	....	....	....	5	0	1	1	0	....	....	....
1992-93	**Detroit**	**NHL**	**2**	**0**	**0**	**0**	**0**	**0**	**0**	**0**	**1**	**0.0**	**0**	....	....	....	....	....	....	....	....	....	....	....	....	....
	Adirondack	AHL	77	15	40	55	86	....	....	....	....	....	....	....	....	....	....	....	11	0	3	3	18	....	....	....
1993-94	**Detroit**	**NHL**	**7**	**1**	**2**	**3**	**2**	**0**	**0**	**0**	**9**	**11.1**	**0**	....	....	....	....	....	....	....	....	....	....	....	....	....
	Adirondack	AHL	74	10	56	66	98	....	....	....	....	....	....	....	....	....	....	....	12	3	11	14	22	....	....	....
1994-95	**Detroit**	**NHL**	**10**	**1**	**2**	**3**	**2**	**0**	**0**	**0**	**6**	**16.7**	**0**	....	....	....	....	....	....	....	....	....	....	....	....	....
	Adirondack	AHL	5	1	3	4	4	....	....	....	....	....	....	....	....	....	....	....	....	....	....	....	....	....	....	....
	Anaheim	**NHL**	**15**	**0**	**8**	**8**	**12**	**0**	**0**	**0**	**22**	**0.0**	**4**	....	....	....	....	....	....	....	....	....	....	....	....	....
1995-96	**Anaheim**	**NHL**	**79**	**3**	**21**	**24**	**88**	**0**	**0**	**0**	**106**	**2.8**	**–7**	....	....	....	....	....	....	....	....	....	....	....	....	....
1996-97	**Ottawa**	**NHL**	**75**	**4**	**17**	**21**	**67**	**1**	**0**	**0**	**121**	**3.3**	**–8**	....	....	....	....	....	**7**	**0**	**0**	**0**	**4**	**0**	**0**	**0**
1997-98	**Ottawa**	**NHL**	**73**	**3**	**13**	**16**	**62**	**0**	**0**	**0**	**109**	**2.8**	**8**	....	....	....	....	....	**7**	**1**	**1**	**2**	**7**	**1**	**0**	**0**
1998-99	**Ottawa**	**NHL**	**79**	**4**	**31**	**35**	**48**	**2**	**0**	**0**	**177**	**2.3**	**17**	**2**	**0.0**	**166**	**127**	**23:49**	**4**	**1**	**1**	**2**	**4**	**0**	**0**	**0**
99-2000	**Ottawa**	**NHL**	**79**	**8**	**22**	**30**	**60**	**1**	**0**	**1**	**159**	**5.0**	**–3**	**0**	**0.0**	**158**	**111**	**23:20**	**6**	**0**	**2**	**2**	**2**	**0**	**0**	**0**
	NHL Totals		**419**	**24**	**116**	**140**	**341**	**4**	**0**	**1**	**710**	**3.4**		**2**	**0.0**	**324**	**238**	**23:35**	**24**	**2**	**4**	**6**	**17**	**1**	**0**	**0**

AHL First All-Star Team (1994)

Traded to **Anaheim** by **Detroit** with Mike Sillinger for Stu Grimson, Mark Ferner and Anaheim's 6th round choice (Magnus Nilsson) in 1996 Entry Draft, April 4, 1995. Traded to **Ottawa** by **Anaheim** with Shaun Van Allen for Ted Drury and the rights to Marc Moro, October 1, 1996.

YORK, Mike

(YOHRK, MIGHK) **NYR**

Center. Shoots right. 5'10", 185 lbs. Born, Waterford, MI, January 3, 1978. NY Rangers' 7th choice, 136th overall, in 1997 Entry Draft.

Season	Club	League	GP	G	A	Pts	PIM	PP	SH	GW	S	%	+/-	TF	F%	H	SB	Min	GP	G	A	Pts	PIM	PP	SH	GW
1992-93	Michigan Nats	MNHL	50	45	50	95	....	....	....	....	....	....	....	....	....	....	....	....	....	....	....	....	....	....	....	....
1993-94	Detroit	MNHL	85	136	140	276	....	....	....	....	....	....	....	....	....	....	....	....	....	....	....	....	....	....	....	....
1994-95	Thornhill Islanders	OJHL	49	39	54	93	44	....	....	....	....	....	....	....	....	....	....	....	11	7	6	13	0	....	....	....
1995-96	Michigan State	CCHA	39	12	27	39	20	....	....	....	....	....	....	....	....	....	....	....	....	....	....	....	....	....	....	....
1996-97	Michigan State	CCHA	37	18	29	47	42	....	....	....	....	....	....	....	....	....	....	....	....	....	....	....	....	....	....	....
1997-98	Michigan State	CCHA	40	27	34	61	38	....	....	....	....	....	....	....	....	....	....	....	....	....	....	....	....	....	....	....
1998-99	Michigan State	CCHA	42	22	32	*54	41	....	....	....	....	....	....	....	....	....	....	....	....	....	....	....	....	....	....	....
	Hartford	AHL	3	2	2	4	0	....	....	....	....	....	....	....	....	....	....	....	6	3	1	4	0	....	....	....
99-2000	**NY Rangers**	**NHL**	**82**	**26**	**24**	**50**	**18**	**8**	**0**	**4**	**177**	**14.7**	....	**0**	**0.0**	**0**	**0**	**0:00**	....	....	....	....	....	....	....	....
	NHL Totals		**82**	**26**	**24**	**50**	**18**	**8**	**0**	**4**	**177**	**14.7**	....	**0**	**0.0**	**0**	**0**	....	....	....	....	....	....	....	....	....

OJHL Bauer Divison Rookie-of-the-Year (1995) • OJHL Bauer Divison All-Star Team (1995) • CCHA Second All-Star Team (1998) • NCAA West First All-American Team (1998, 1999) • CCHA First All-Star Team (1999) • NHL All-Rookie Team (2000)

YOUNG, B.J.

(YUHNG, BEE-JAY) **DET.**

Right wing. Shoots right. 5'10", 178 lbs. Born, Anchorage, AK, July 23, 1977. Detroit's 5th choice, 157th overall, in 1997 Entry Draft.

Season	Club	League	GP	G	A	Pts	PIM	PP	SH	GW	S	%	+/-	TF	F%	H	SB	Min	GP	G	A	Pts	PIM	PP	SH	GW
1992-93	Anchorage Stars	AAHL	50	48	60	108	94	....	....	....	....	....	....	....	....	....	....	....	....	....	....	....	....	....	....	....
1993-94	Tri-City Americans	WHL	54	19	24	43	66	....	....	....	....	....	....	....	....	....	....	....	2	1	1	2	2	....	....	....
1994-95	Tri-City Americans	WHL	30	6	3	9	39	....	....	....	....	....	....	....	....	....	....	....	....	....	....	....	....	....	....	....
	Red Deer Rebels	WHL	21	5	9	14	33	....	....	....	....	....	....	....	....	....	....	....	....	....	....	....	....	....	....	....
1995-96	Red Deer Rebels	WHL	67	49	45	94	144	....	....	....	....	....	....	....	....	....	....	....	8	4	9	13	12	....	....	....
1996-97	Red Deer Rebels	WHL	63	*58	56	114	97	....	....	....	....	....	....	....	....	....	....	....	16	8	14	22	26	....	....	....
1997-98	Adirondack	AHL	65	15	22	37	191	....	....	....	....	....	....	....	....	....	....	....	3	0	2	2	6	....	....	....
1998-99	Adirondack	AHL	58	13	17	30	150	....	....	....	....	....	....	....	....	....	....	....	3	1	0	1	6	....	....	....
99-2000	**Detroit**	**NHL**	**1**	**0**	**0**	**0**	**0**	**0**	**0**	**0**	**1**	**0.0**	**0**	**1**	**100.0**	**0**	**0**	**1:04**	....	....	....	....	....	....	....	....
	Cincinnati Ducks	AHL	71	25	26	51	147	....	....	....	....	....	....	....	....	....	....	....	....	....	....	....	....	....	....	....
	NHL Totals		**1**	**0**	**0**	**0**	**0**	**0**	**0**	**0**	**1**	**0.0**		**1**	**100.0**	**0**	**0**	**1:04**	....	....	....	....	....	....	....	....

WHL East First All-Star Team (1997)

YOUNG, Scott

(YUHNG, SKAWT) **ST.L.**

Right wing. Shoots right. 6'1", 200 lbs. Born, Clinton, MA, October 1, 1967. Hartford's 1st choice, 11th overall, in 1986 Entry Draft.

Season	Club	League	GP	G	A	Pts	PIM	PP	SH	GW	S	%	+/-	TF	F%	H	SB	Min	GP	G	A	Pts	PIM	PP	SH	GW
1984-85	St. Marks	Hi-School	23	28	41	69	....	....	....	....	....	....	....	....	....	....	....	....	....	....	....	....	....	....	....	....
1985-86	Boston University	H-East	38	16	13	29	31	....	....	....	....	....	....	....	....	....	....	....	....	....	....	....	....	....	....	....
1986-87	Boston University	H-East	33	15	21	36	24	....	....	....	....	....	....	....	....	....	....	....	....	....	....	....	....	....	....	....
1987-88	United States	Nat-Team	56	11	47	58	31	....	....	....	....	....	....	....	....	....	....	....	....	....	....	....	....	....	....	....
	United States	Olympics	6	2	6	8	4	....	....	....	....	....	....	....	....	....	....	....	....	....	....	....	....	....	....	....
	Hartford	**NHL**	**7**	**0**	**0**	**0**	**2**	**0**	**0**	**0**	**6**	**0.0**	**–6**	....	....	....	....	....	**4**	**1**	**0**	**1**	**0**	**0**	**0**	**0**
1988-89	**Hartford**	**NHL**	**76**	**19**	**40**	**59**	**27**	**6**	**0**	**2**	**203**	**9.4**	**–21**	....	....	....	....	....	**4**	**2**	**0**	**2**	**4**	**0**	**0**	**0**
1989-90	**Hartford**	**NHL**	**80**	**24**	**40**	**64**	**47**	**10**	**2**	**5**	**239**	**10.0**	**–24**	....	....	....	....	....	**7**	**2**	**0**	**2**	**2**	**0**	**0**	**0**
1990-91	**Hartford**	**NHL**	**34**	**6**	**9**	**15**	**8**	**3**	**1**	**2**	**94**	**6.4**	**–9**	....	....	....	....	....	....	....	....	....	....	....	....	....
	♦ **Pittsburgh**	**NHL**	**43**	**11**	**16**	**27**	**33**	**3**	**1**	**3**	**116**	**9.5**	**3**	....	....	....	....	....	**17**	**1**	**6**	**7**	**2**	**1**	**0**	**0**
1991-92	HC Bolzano	Alpenliga	15	19	11	30	14	....	....	....	....	....	....	....	....	....	....	....	....	....	....	....	....	....	....	....
	HC Bolzano	Italy	18	22	17	39	6	....	....	....	....	....	....	....	....	....	....	....	5	4	3	7	7	....	....	....
	United States	Nat-Team	10	2	4	6	21	....	....	....	....	....	....	....	....	....	....	....	....	....	....	....	....	....	....	....
	United States	Olympics	8	2	1	3	2	....	....	....	....	....	....	....	....	....	....	....	....	....	....	....	....	....	....	....
1992-93	**Quebec**	**NHL**	**82**	**30**	**30**	**60**	**20**	**9**	**6**	**5**	**225**	**13.3**	**5**	....	....	....	....	....	**6**	**4**	**1**	**5**	**0**	**0**	**0**	**2**
1993-94	**Quebec**	**NHL**	**76**	**26**	**25**	**51**	**14**	**6**	**1**	**1**	**236**	**11.0**	**–4**	....	....	....	....	....	....	....	....	....	....	....	....	....
1994-95	EV Landshut	DEL	4	6	1	7	6	....	....	....	....	....	....	....	....	....	....	....	....	....	....	....	....	....	....	....
	Frankfurt Lions	DEL	1	1	0	1	0	....	....	....	....	....	....	....	....	....	....	....	....	....	....	....	....	....	....	....
	Quebec	**NHL**	**48**	**18**	**21**	**39**	**14**	**3**	**3**	**0**	**167**	**10.8**	**9**	....	....	....	....	....	**6**	**3**	**3**	**6**	**2**	**0**	**1**	**0**
1995-96♦	**Colorado**	**NHL**	**81**	**21**	**39**	**60**	**50**	**7**	**0**	**5**	**229**	**9.2**	**2**	....	....	....	....	....	**22**	**3**	**12**	**15**	**10**	**0**	**0**	**0**
1996-97	**Colorado**	**NHL**	**72**	**18**	**19**	**37**	**14**	**7**	**0**	**0**	**164**	**11.0**	**–5**	....	....	....	....	....	**17**	**4**	**2**	**6**	**14**	**2**	**0**	**0**
1997-98	**Anaheim**	**NHL**	**73**	**13**	**20**	**33**	**22**	**4**	**2**	**1**	**187**	**7.0**	**–13**	....	....	....	....	....	....	....	....	....	....	....	....	....
1998-99	**St. Louis**	**NHL**	**75**	**24**	**28**	**52**	**27**	**8**	**0**	**4**	**205**	**11.7**	**8**	**4**	**25.0**	**51**	**18**	**15:14**	**13**	**4**	**7**	**11**	**10**	**1**	**0**	**1**
99-2000	**St. Louis**	**NHL**	**75**	**24**	**15**	**39**	**18**	**6**	**1**	**7**	**244**	**9.8**	**12**	**2**	**50.0**	**63**	**15**	**16:06**	**6**	**6**	**2**	**8**	**8**	**3**	**0**	**0**
	NHL Totals		**822**	**234**	**302**	**536**	**296**	**72**	**17**	**35**	**2315**	**10.1**		**6**	**33.3**	**114**	**33**	**15:40**	**102**	**30**	**33**	**63**	**52**	**7**	**1**	**3**

Traded to **Pittsburgh** by **Hartford** for Rob Brown, December 21, 1990. Traded to **Quebec** by **Pittsburgh** for Bryan Fogarty, March 10, 1992. Transferred to **Colorado** after **Quebec** franchise relocated, June 21, 1995. Traded to **Anaheim** by **Colorado** for Anaheim's 3rd round choice (later traded to Florida - Florida selected Lance Ward) in 1998 Entry Draft, September 17, 1997. Signed as a free agent by **St. Louis**, July 28, 1998.

YUSHKEVICH, Dimitry
(yoosh-KAY-vihch, dih-MEE-tree) **TOR.**

Defense. Shoots right. 5'11", 208 lbs. Born, Yaroslavl, USSR, November 19, 1971. Philadelphia's 6th choice, 122nd overall, in 1991 Entry Draft.

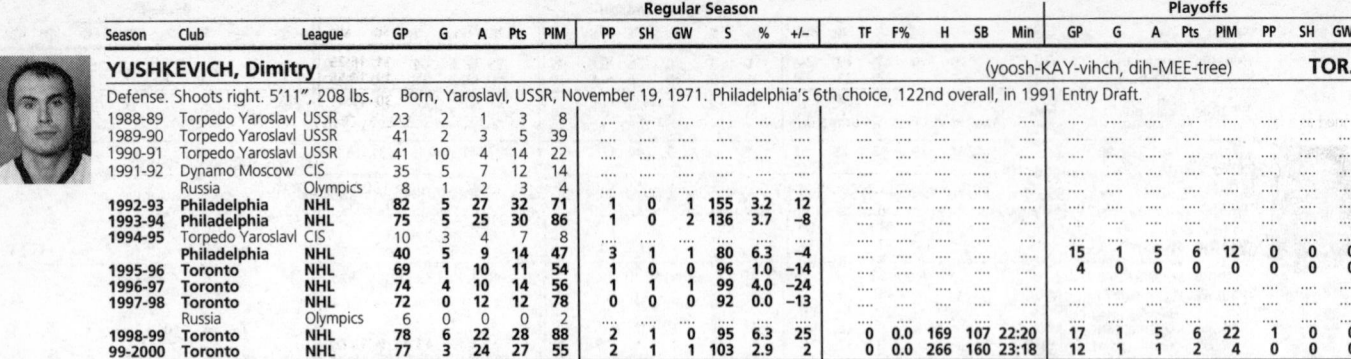

			Regular Season																Playoffs							
Season	Club	League	GP	G	A	Pts	PIM	PP	SH	GW	S	%	+/–	TF	F%	H	SB	Min	GP	G	A	Pts	PIM	PP	SH	GW
1988-89	Torpedo Yaroslavl	USSR	23	2	1	3	8	....	....	....	....	....	....	....	....	....	....	....	....	....	....	....	....	....	....	....
1989-90	Torpedo Yaroslavl	USSR	41	2	3	5	39	....	....	....	....	....	....	....	....	....	....	....	....	....	....	....	....	....	....	....
1990-91	Torpedo Yaroslavl	USSR	41	10	4	14	22	....	....	....	....	....	....	....	....	....	....	....	....	....	....	....	....	....	....	....
1991-92	Dynamo Moscow	CIS	35	5	7	12	14	....	....	....	....	....	....	....	....	....	....	....	....	....	....	....	....	....	....	....
	Russia	Olympics	8	1	2	3	4	....	....	....	....	....	....	....	....	....	....	....	....	....	....	....	....	....	....	....
1992-93	**Philadelphia**	**NHL**	82	5	27	32	71	1	0	1	155	3.2	12	....	....	....	....	....	....	....	....	....	....	....	....	....
1993-94	**Philadelphia**	**NHL**	75	5	25	30	86	1	0	2	136	3.7	–8	....	....	....	....	....	....	....	....	....	....	....	....	....
1994-95	Torpedo Yaroslavl	CIS	10	3	4	7	8	....	....	....	....	....	....	....	....	....	....	....	....	....	....	....	....	....	....	....
	Philadelphia	**NHL**	40	5	9	14	47	3	1	1	80	6.3	–4	....	....	....	....	....	15	1	5	6	12	0	0	0
1995-96	**Toronto**	**NHL**	69	1	10	11	54	1	0	0	96	1.0	–14	....	....	....	....	....	4	0	0	0	0	0	0	0
1996-97	**Toronto**	**NHL**	74	4	10	14	56	1	1	1	99	4.0	–24	....	....	....	....	....	....	....	....	....	....	....	....	....
1997-98	**Toronto**	**NHL**	72	0	12	12	78	0	0	0	92	0.0	–13	....	....	....	....	....	....	....	....	....	....	....	....	....
	Russia	Olympics	6	0	0	0	2	....	....	....	....	....	....	....	....	....	....	....	....	....	....	....	....	....	....	....
1998-99	**Toronto**	**NHL**	78	6	22	28	88	2	1	0	95	6.3	25	0	0.0	169	107	22:20	17	1	5	6	22	1	0	0
99-2000	**Toronto**	**NHL**	77	3	24	27	55	2	1	1	103	2.9	2	0	0.0	266	160	23:18	12	1	1	2	4	0	0	0
	NHL Totals		**567**	**29**	**139**	**168**	**535**	**11**	**4**	**6**	**856**	**3.4**		**0**	**0.0**	**435**	**267**	**22:49**	**48**	**3**	**11**	**14**	**38**	**1**	**0**	**0**

Played in NHL All-Star Game (2000)

Traded to **Toronto** by **Philadelphia** with Philadelphia's 2nd round choice (Francis Larivee) in 1996 Entry Draft for Toronto's 1st round choice (Dainius Zubrus) in 1996 Entry Draft, 2nd round choice (Jean-Marc Pelletier) in 1997 Entry Draft and LA Kings' 4th round choice (previously acquired by Toronto - later traded to LA Kings - LA Kings selected Mikael Simons) in 1996 Entry Draft, August 30, 1995.

YZERMAN, Steve
(IGH-zuhr-muhn, STEEV) **DET.**

Center. Shoots right. 5'11", 185 lbs. Born, Cranbrook, B.C., May 9, 1965. Detroit's 1st choice, 4th overall, in 1983 Entry Draft.

Season	Club	League	GP	G	A	Pts	PIM	PP	SH	GW	S	%	+/–	TF	F%	H	SB	Min	GP	G	A	Pts	PIM	PP	SH	GW
1980-81	Nepean Raiders	OJHL	50	38	*54	92	44	....	....	....	....	....	....	....	....	....	....	....	....	....	....	....	....	....	....	....
1981-82	Peterborough	OHL	58	21	43	64	65	....	....	....	....	....	....	....	....	....	....	....	6	0	1	1	16	....	....	....
1982-83	Peterborough	OHL	56	42	49	91	33	....	....	....	....	....	....	....	....	....	....	....	4	1	4	5	0	....	....	....
1983-84	**Detroit**	**NHL**	80	39	48	87	33	13	0	2	177	22.0	–17	....	....	....	....	....	4	3	3	6	0	1	0	1
1984-85	**Detroit**	**NHL**	80	30	59	89	58	9	0	3	231	13.0	–17	....	....	....	....	....	3	2	1	3	2	0	0	0
1985-86	**Detroit**	**NHL**	51	14	28	42	16	3	0	3	132	10.6	–24	....	....	....	....	....	....	....	....	....	....	....	....	....
1986-87	**Detroit**	**NHL**	80	31	59	90	43	9	1	2	217	14.3	–1	....	....	....	....	....	16	5	13	18	8	1	0	0
1987-88	**Detroit**	**NHL**	64	50	52	102	44	10	6	6	242	20.7	30	....	....	....	....	....	3	1	3	4	6	0	0	0
1988-89	**Detroit**	**NHL**	80	65	90	155	61	17	3	7	388	16.8	17	....	....	....	....	....	6	5	5	10	2	2	0	0
1989-90	**Detroit**	**NHL**	79	62	65	127	79	16	7	8	332	18.7	–6	....	....	....	....	....	....	....	....	....	....	....	....	....
1990-91	**Detroit**	**NHL**	80	51	57	108	34	12	6	4	326	15.6	–2	....	....	....	....	....	7	3	3	6	4	1	0	0
1991-92	**Detroit**	**NHL**	79	45	58	103	64	9	8	9	295	15.3	26	....	....	....	....	....	11	3	5	8	12	0	1	1
1992-93	**Detroit**	**NHL**	84	58	79	137	44	13	7	6	307	18.9	33	....	....	....	....	....	7	4	3	7	4	1	1	1
1993-94	**Detroit**	**NHL**	58	24	58	82	36	7	3	3	217	11.1	11	....	....	....	....	....	3	1	3	4	0	0	0	0
1994-95	**Detroit**	**NHL**	47	12	26	38	40	4	0	1	134	9.0	6	....	....	....	....	....	15	4	8	12	0	2	0	1
1995-96	**Detroit**	**NHL**	80	36	59	95	64	16	2	8	220	16.4	29	....	....	....	....	....	18	8	12	20	4	4	0	1
1996-97 ♦	**Detroit**	**NHL**	81	22	63	85	78	8	0	3	232	9.5	22	....	....	....	....	....	20	7	6	13	4	3	0	2
1997-98 ♦	**Detroit**	**NHL**	75	24	45	69	46	6	2	0	188	12.8	3	....	....	....	....	....	22	6	*18	*24	22	3	1	0
	Canada	Olympics	6	1	1	2	10	....	....	....	....	....	....	....	....	....	....	....	....	....	....	....	....	....	....	....
1998-99	**Detroit**	**NHL**	80	29	45	74	42	13	2	4	231	12.6	8	1600	56.9	46	58	21:35	10	9	4	13	0	4	0	2
99-2000	**Detroit**	**NHL**	78	35	44	79	34	15	2	6	234	15.0	28	1868	56.8	67	56	21:07	8	0	4	4	0	0	0	0
	NHL Totals		**1256**	**627**	**935**	**1562**	**816**	**180**	**49**	**75**	**4103**	**15.3**		**3468**	**56.8**	**113**	**114**	**21:21**	**153**	**61**	**91**	**152**	**68**	**22**	**3**	**9**

NHL All-Rookie Team (1984) • Won Lester B. Pearson Award (1989) • Won Conn Smythe Trophy (1998) • NHL First All-Star Team (2000) • Won Frank J. Selke Trophy (2000) • Played in NHL All-Star Game (1984, 1988, 1989, 1990, 1991, 1992, 1993, 1997, 2000)

ZALAPSKI, Zarley
(zah-LAP-skee, ZAHR-lee)

Defense. Shoots left. 6'1", 215 lbs. Born, Edmonton, Alta., April 22, 1968. Pittsburgh's 1st choice, 4th overall, in 1986 Entry Draft.

Season	Club	League	GP	G	A	Pts	PIM	PP	SH	GW	S	%	+/–	TF	F%	H	SB	Min	GP	G	A	Pts	PIM	PP	SH	GW
1984-85	Ft-Saskatchewan	AJHL	23	17	30	47	14	....	....	....	....	....	....	....	....	....	....	....	....	....	....	....	....	....	....	....
1985-86	Ft-Saskatchewan	AJHL	27	20	33	53	46	....	....	....	....	....	....	....	....	....	....	....	....	....	....	....	....	....	....	....
	Canada	Nat-Team	32	2	4	6	10	....	....	....	....	....	....	....	....	....	....	....	....	....	....	....	....	....	....	....
1986-87	Canada	Nat-Team	74	11	29	40	28	....	....	....	....	....	....	....	....	....	....	....	....	....	....	....	....	....	....	....
1987-88	Canada	Nat-Team	47	3	13	16	32	....	....	....	....	....	....	....	....	....	....	....	....	....	....	....	....	....	....	....
	Canada	Olympics	8	1	3	4	2	....	....	....	....	....	....	....	....	....	....	....	....	....	....	....	....	....	....	....
	Pittsburgh	**NHL**	15	3	8	11	7	0	0	0	31	9.7	10	....	....	....	....	....	....	....	....	....	....	....	....	....
1988-89	**Pittsburgh**	**NHL**	58	12	33	45	57	5	1	2	95	12.6	9	....	....	....	....	....	11	1	8	9	13	1	0	0
1989-90	**Pittsburgh**	**NHL**	51	6	25	31	37	5	0	2	85	7.1	–14	....	....	....	....	....	....	....	....	....	....	....	....	....
1990-91	**Pittsburgh**	**NHL**	66	12	36	48	59	5	1	1	135	8.9	15	....	....	....	....	....	....	....	....	....	....	....	....	....
	Hartford	**NHL**	11	3	3	6	6	3	0	0	21	14.3	–7	....	....	....	....	....	6	1	3	4	8	0	0	1
1991-92	**Hartford**	**NHL**	79	20	37	57	120	4	0	3	230	8.7	–7	....	....	....	....	....	7	2	3	5	6	0	0	0
1992-93	**Hartford**	**NHL**	83	14	51	65	94	8	1	0	192	7.3	–34	....	....	....	....	....	....	....	....	....	....	....	....	....
1993-94	**Hartford**	**NHL**	56	7	30	37	56	0	0	0	121	5.8	–6	....	....	....	....	....	....	....	....	....	....	....	....	....
	Calgary	**NHL**	13	3	7	10	18	1	0	1	35	8.6	0	....	....	....	....	....	7	0	3	3	2	0	0	0
1994-95	**Calgary**	**NHL**	48	4	24	28	46	1	0	1	76	5.3	9	....	....	....	....	....	7	0	4	4	4	0	0	0
1995-96	**Calgary**	**NHL**	80	12	17	29	115	5	0	1	145	8.3	11	....	....	....	....	....	4	0	1	1	10	0	0	0
1996-97	**Calgary**	**NHL**	2	0	0	0	0	0	0	0	7	0.0	–1	....	....	....	....	....	....	....	....	....	....	....	....	....
1997-98	**Calgary**	**NHL**	35	2	7	9	41	2	0	1	46	4.3	–12	....	....	....	....	....	....	....	....	....	....	....	....	....
	Montreal	**NHL**	28	1	5	6	22	0	1	0	27	3.7	–1	....	....	....	....	....	6	0	1	1	4	0	0	0
1998-99	ZSC Zurich	Switz.	11	1	5	6	37	....	....	....	....	....	....	....	....	....	....	....	3	1	0	1	4	....	....	....
99-2000	Long Beach	IHL	7	0	5	5	6	....	....	....	....	....	....	....	....	....	....	....	....	....	....	....	....	....	....	....
	Utah Grizzlies	IHL	56	4	24	28	69	....	....	....	....	....	....	....	....	....	....	....	5	1	1	2	4	....	....	....
	Philadelphia	**NHL**	12	0	2	2	6	0	0	0	6	0.0	0	0	0.0	10	7	14:12	....	....	....	....	....	....	....	....
	NHL Totals		**637**	**99**	**285**	**384**	**684**	**39**	**4**	**12**	**1252**	**7.9**		**0**	**0.0**	**10**	**7**	**14:12**	**48**	**4**	**23**	**27**	**47**	**1**	**0**	**1**

NHL All-Rookie Team (1989) • Played in NHL All-Star Game (1993)

Traded to **Hartford** by **Pittsburgh** with John Cullen and Jeff Parker for Ron Francis, Grant Jennings and Ulf Samuelsson, March 4, 1991. Traded to **Calgary** by **Hartford** with James Patrick and Michael Nylander for Gary Suter, Paul Ranheim and Ted Drury, March 10, 1994. Traded to **Montreal** by **Calgary** with Jonas Hoglund for Valeri Bure and Montreal's 4th round choice (Shaun Sutter) in 1998 Entry Draft, February 1, 1998. Signed as a free agent by **NY Rangers**, August 31, 1998. Signed as a free agent to try-out contract by **Long Beach** (IHL), September 14, 1999. Signed as a free agent by **Utah** (IHL), November 5, 1999. Signed as a free agent by **Philadelphia**, February 15, 2000.

ZAMUNER, Rob
(ZAM-nuhr, RAWB) **OTT.**

Left wing. Shoots left. 6'3", 203 lbs. Born, Oakville, Ont., September 17, 1969. NY Rangers' 3rd choice, 45th overall, in 1989 Entry Draft.

Season	Club	League	GP	G	A	Pts	PIM	PP	SH	GW	S	%	+/–	TF	F%	H	SB	Min	GP	G	A	Pts	PIM	PP	SH	GW
1985-86	Oakville Oaks	OMHA	48	43	50	93	66	....	....	....	....	....	....	....	....	....	....	....	....	....	....	....	....	....	....	....
1986-87	Guelph Jr. B's	OJHL-B	3	6	7	13	15	....	....	....	....	....	....	....	....	....	....	....	....	....	....	....	....	....	....	....
	Guelph Platers	OHL	62	6	15	21	8	....	....	....	....	....	....	....	....	....	....	....	....	....	....	....	....	....	....	....
1987-88	Guelph Platers	OHL	58	20	41	61	18	....	....	....	....	....	....	....	....	....	....	....	....	....	....	....	....	....	....	....
1988-89	Guelph Platers	OHL	66	46	65	111	38	....	....	....	....	....	....	....	....	....	....	....	7	5	5	10	9	....	....	....
1989-90	Flint Spirits	IHL	77	44	35	79	32	....	....	....	....	....	....	....	....	....	....	....	4	1	0	1	6	....	....	....
1990-91	Binghamton	AHL	80	25	58	83	50	....	....	....	....	....	....	....	....	....	....	....	9	7	6	13	35	....	....	....
1991-92	**NY Rangers**	**NHL**	9	1	2	3	2	0	0	0	11	9.1	0	....	....	....	....	....	....	....	....	....	....	....	....	....
	Binghamton	AHL	61	19	53	72	42	....	....	....	....	....	....	....	....	....	....	....	11	8	9	17	8	....	....	....
1992-93	**Tampa Bay**	**NHL**	84	15	28	43	74	1	0	0	183	8.2	–25	....	....	....	....	....	....	....	....	....	....	....	....	....
1993-94	**Tampa Bay**	**NHL**	59	6	6	12	42	0	0	1	109	5.5	–9	....	....	....	....	....	....	....	....	....	....	....	....	....
1994-95	**Tampa Bay**	**NHL**	43	9	6	15	24	0	3	1	74	12.2	–3	....	....	....	....	....	....	....	....	....	....	....	....	....
1995-96	**Tampa Bay**	**NHL**	72	15	20	35	62	0	3	4	152	9.9	11	....	....	....	....	....	6	2	3	5	10	0	1	0
1996-97	**Tampa Bay**	**NHL**	82	17	33	50	56	0	4	3	216	7.9	3	....	....	....	....	....	....	....	....	....	....	....	....	....
1997-98	**Tampa Bay**	**NHL**	77	14	12	26	41	0	3	4	126	11.1	–31	....	....	....	....	....	....	....	....	....	....	....	....	....
	Canada	Olympics	6	1	0	1	8	....	....	....	....	....	....	....	....	....	....	....	....	....	....	....	....	....	....	....

			Regular Season																Playoffs							
Season	Club	League	GP	G	A	Pts	PIM	PP	SH	GW	S	%	+/-	TF	F%	H	SB	Min	GP	G	A	Pts	PIM	PP	SH	GW
1998-99	**Tampa Bay**	**NHL**	**58**	**8**	**11**	**19**	**24**	**1**	**1**	**2**	**89**	**9.0**	**–15**	**34**	**47.1**	**52**	**11**	**16:26**	....	....	....	....	....	....	....	....
99-2000	**Ottawa**	**NHL**	**57**	**9**	**12**	**21**	**32**	**0**	**1**	**0**	**103**	**8.7**	**–6**	**29**	**37.9**	**65**	**19**	**14:56**	**6**	**2**	**0**	**2**	**2**	**0**	**0**	**1**
	NHL Totals		**541**	**94**	**130**	**224**	**357**	**2**	**15**	**15**	**1063**	**8.8**		**63**	**42.9**	**117**	**30**	**15:41**	**12**	**4**	**3**	**7**	**12**	**0**	**1**	**1**

Signed as a free agent by **Tampa Bay**, July 13, 1992. Traded to **Ottawa** by **Tampa Bay** with a conditional 2nd round choice in 2000, 2001 or 2002 Entry Draft for Andreas Johansson, June 29, 1999.

ZEDNIK, Richard

(ZEHD-nihk, REE-khahrd) **WSH.**

Left wing. Shoots left. 6', 199 lbs. Born, Bystrica, Czech., January 6, 1976. Washington's 10th choice, 249th overall, in 1994 Entry Draft.

Season	Club	League	GP	G	A	Pts	PIM	PP	SH	GW	S	%	+/-	TF	F%	H	SB	Min	GP	G	A	Pts	PIM	PP	SH	GW
1993-94	SK Banska	Slovak-2	25	3	6	9	....	....	....	....	....	....	....	....	....	....	....	....	....	....	....	....	....	....	....	....
1994-95	Portland	WHL	65	35	51	86	89	....	....	....	....	....	....	....	....	....	....	....	9	5	5	10	20	....	....	....
1995-96	Portland	WHL	61	44	37	81	154	....	....	....	....	....	....	....	....	....	....	....	7	8	4	12	23	....	....	....
	Washington	**NHL**	**1**	**0**	**0**	**0**	**0**	**0**	**0**	**0**	**0**	**0.0**	**0**	....	....	....	....	....	....	....	....	....	....	....	....	....
	Portland	AHL	1	1	1	2	0	....	....	....	....	....	....	....	....	....	....	....	21	4	5	9	26	....	....	....
1996-97	**Washington**	**NHL**	**11**	**2**	**1**	**3**	**4**	**1**	**0**	**0**	**21**	**9.5**	**–5**	....	....	....	....	....	....	....	....	....	....	....	....	....
	Portland	AHL	56	15	20	35	70	....	....	....	....	....	....	....	....	....	....	....	5	1	0	1	6	....	....	....
1997-98	**Washington**	**NHL**	**65**	**17**	**9**	**26**	**28**	**2**	**0**	**2**	**148**	**11.5**	**–2**	....	....	....	....	....	**17**	**7**	**3**	**10**	**16**	**2**	**0**	**0**
1998-99	**Washington**	**NHL**	**49**	**9**	**8**	**17**	**50**	**1**	**0**	**2**	**115**	**7.8**	**–6**	**2**	**0.0**	**81**	**9**	**15:08**	....	....	....	....	....	....	....	....
99-2000	**Washington**	**NHL**	**69**	**19**	**16**	**35**	**54**	**1**	**0**	**2**	**179**	**10.6**	**6**	**1**	**100.0**	**155**	**27**	**15:34**	**5**	**0**	**0**	**0**	**5**	**0**	**0**	**0**
	NHL Totals		**195**	**47**	**34**	**81**	**136**	**5**	**0**	**6**	**463**	**10.2**		**3**	**33.3**	**236**	**36**	**15:23**	**22**	**7**	**3**	**10**	**21**	**2**	**0**	**0**

WHL West Second All-Star Team (1996)

ZEHR, Jeff

(ZAIR, JEHF) **BOS.**

Left wing. Shoots left. 6'3", 195 lbs. Born, Woodstock, Ont., December 10, 1978. NY Islanders' 3rd choice, 31st overall, in 1997 Entry Draft.

Season	Club	League	GP	G	A	Pts	PIM	PP	SH	GW	S	%	+/-	TF	F%	H	SB	Min	GP	G	A	Pts	PIM	PP	SH	GW
1993-94	Tavistock Braves	OJHL-D	6	2	1	3	6	....	....	....	....	....	....	....	....	....	....	....	....	....	....	....	....	....	....	....
1994-95	Stratford Cullitons	OJHL-B	44	26	32	58	143	....	....	....	....	....	....	....	....	....	....	....	....	....	....	....	....	....	....	....
1995-96	Windsor Spitfires	OHL	56	4	21	25	103	....	....	....	....	....	....	....	....	....	....	....	7	0	1	1	2	....	....	....
1996-97	Windsor Spitfires	OHL	57	27	32	59	196	....	....	....	....	....	....	....	....	....	....	....	5	2	1	3	4	....	....	....
1997-98	Windsor Spitfires	OHL	20	12	18	30	67	....	....	....	....	....	....	....	....	....	....	....	....	....	....	....	....	....	....	....
	Erie Otters	OHL	32	15	24	39	91	....	....	....	....	....	....	....	....	....	....	....	5	0	3	3	24	....	....	....
1998-99	Erie Otters	OHL	28	20	23	43	78	....	....	....	....	....	....	....	....	....	....	....	....	....	....	....	....	....	....	....
	Sarnia Sting	OHL	14	4	10	14	43	....	....	....	....	....	....	....	....	....	....	....	6	3	4	7	27	....	....	....
99-2000	**Boston**	**NHL**	**4**	**0**	**0**	**0**	**2**	**0**	**0**	**0**	**3**	**0.0**	**–1**	**0**	**0.0**	**9**	**0**	**7:25**	....	....	....	....	....	....	....	....
	Providence Bruins	AHL	12	3	3	6	37	....	....	....	....	....	....	....	....	....	....	....	....	....	....	....	....	....	....	....
	NHL Totals		**4**	**0**	**0**	**0**	**2**	**0**	**0**	**0**	**3**	**0.0**		**0**	**0.0**	**9**	**0**	**7:25**	....	....	....	....	....	....	....	....

Signed as a free agent by **Boston**, June 21, 1999. • Missed majority of 1999-2000 season recovering from knee injury suffered in practice, December 22, 1999.

ZELEPUKIN, Valeri

(zeh-leh-POO-kin, VAL-uhr-ee) **CHI.**

Left wing. Shoots left. 6'1", 200 lbs. Born, Voskresensk, USSR, September 17, 1968. New Jersey's 13th choice, 221st overall, in 1990 Entry Draft.

Season	Club	League	GP	G	A	Pts	PIM	PP	SH	GW	S	%	+/-	TF	F%	H	SB	Min	GP	G	A	Pts	PIM	PP	SH	GW
1984-85	HK Khimik	USSR	5	0	0	0	2	....	....	....	....	....	....	....	....	....	....	....	....	....	....	....	....	....	....	....
1985-86	HK Khimik	USSR	33	2	2	4	10	....	....	....	....	....	....	....	....	....	....	....	....	....	....	....	....	....	....	....
1986-87	HK Khimik	USSR	19	1	0	1	4	....	....	....	....	....	....	....	....	....	....	....	....	....	....	....	....	....	....	....
1987-88	CSKA Moscow	USSR	19	3	1	4	8	....	....	....	....	....	....	....	....	....	....	....	....	....	....	....	....	....	....	....
1988-89	CSKA Moscow	USSR	17	2	3	5	2	....	....	....	....	....	....	....	....	....	....	....	....	....	....	....	....	....	....	....
1989-90	HK Khimik	USSR	46	17	14	31	26	....	....	....	....	....	....	....	....	....	....	....	....	....	....	....	....	....	....	....
1990-91	HK Khimik	USSR	34	11	6	17	38	....	....	....	....	....	....	....	....	....	....	....	....	....	....	....	....	....	....	....
1991-92	**New Jersey**	**NHL**	**44**	**13**	**18**	**31**	**28**	**3**	**0**	**3**	**94**	**13.8**	**11**	....	....	....	....	....	**4**	**1**	**1**	**2**	**2**	**0**	**0**	**0**
	Utica Devils	AHL	22	20	9	29	8	....	....	....	....	....	....	....	....	....	....	....	....	....	....	....	....	....	....	....
1992-93	**New Jersey**	**NHL**	**78**	**23**	**41**	**64**	**70**	**5**	**1**	**2**	**174**	**13.2**	**19**	....	....	....	....	....	**5**	**0**	**2**	**2**	**0**	**0**	**0**	**0**
1993-94	**New Jersey**	**NHL**	**82**	**26**	**31**	**57**	**70**	**8**	**0**	**0**	**155**	**16.8**	**36**	....	....	....	....	....	**20**	**5**	**2**	**7**	**14**	**1**	**0**	**0**
1994-95•	**New Jersey**	**NHL**	**4**	**1**	**2**	**3**	**6**	**0**	**0**	**0**	**6**	**16.7**	**3**	....	....	....	....	....	**18**	**1**	**2**	**3**	**12**	**0**	**0**	**1**
1995-96	**New Jersey**	**NHL**	**61**	**6**	**9**	**15**	**107**	**3**	**0**	**1**	**86**	**7.0**	**–10**	....	....	....	....	....	....	....	....	....	....	....	....	....
1996-97	**New Jersey**	**NHL**	**71**	**14**	**24**	**38**	**36**	**3**	**0**	**2**	**111**	**12.6**	**–10**	....	....	....	....	....	**8**	**3**	**2**	**5**	**2**	**1**	**0**	**1**
1997-98	**New Jersey**	**NHL**	**35**	**2**	**8**	**10**	**32**	**0**	**0**	**0**	**54**	**3.7**	**0**	....	....	....	....	....	....	....	....	....	....	....	....	....
	Edmonton	**NHL**	**33**	**2**	**10**	**12**	**57**	**0**	**0**	**0**	**47**	**4.3**	**–2**	....	....	....	....	....	**8**	**1**	**2**	**3**	**2**	**0**	**0**	**0**
	Russia	Olympics	6	1	2	3	0	....	....	....	....	....	....	....	....	....	....	....	....	....	....	....	....	....	....	....
1998-99	**Philadelphia**	**NHL**	**74**	**16**	**9**	**25**	**48**	**0**	**0**	**5**	**129**	**12.4**	**0**	**0**	**0.0**	**85**	**22**	**14:33**	**4**	**1**	**0**	**1**	**4**	**0**	**0**	**1**
99-2000	**Philadelphia**	**NHL**	**77**	**11**	**21**	**32**	**55**	**2**	**0**	**3**	**125**	**8.8**	**–3**	**0**	**0.0**	**104**	**33**	**14:37**	**18**	**1**	**2**	**3**	**12**	**1**	**0**	**0**
	NHL Totals		**559**	**114**	**173**	**287**	**509**	**24**	**1**	**16**	**981**	**11.6**		**0**	**0.0**	**189**	**55**	**14:35**	**85**	**13**	**13**	**26**	**48**	**3**	**0**	**3**

• Missed majority of 1994-95 season recovering from eye injury suffered in practice, January 24, 1995. Traded to **Edmonton** by **New Jersey** with Bill Guerin for Jason Arnott and Bryan Muir, January 4, 1998. Traded to **Philadelphia** by **Edmonton** for Daniel Lacroix, October 5, 1998. Signed as a free agent by **Chicago**, July 18, 2000.

ZENT, Jason

(ZEHNT, JAY-suhn)

Left wing. Shoots left. 5'11", 204 lbs. Born, Buffalo, NY, April 15, 1971. NY Islanders' 3rd choice, 44th overall, in 1989 Entry Draft.

Season	Club	League	GP	G	A	Pts	PIM	PP	SH	GW	S	%	+/-	TF	F%	H	SB	Min	GP	G	A	Pts	PIM	PP	SH	GW
1984-85	Depew Saints	NYAHL	48	40	30	70	26	....	....	....	....	....	....	....	....	....	....	....	....	....	....	....	....	....	....	....
1985-86	Depew Saints	NYAHL	55	50	23	73	24	....	....	....	....	....	....	....	....	....	....	....	....	....	....	....	....	....	....	....
1986-87	Depew Saints	NYAHL	40	44	38	82	56	....	....	....	....	....	....	....	....	....	....	....	....	....	....	....	....	....	....	....
1987-88	Nichols School	Hi-School	21	20	16	36	28	....	....	....	....	....	....	....	....	....	....	....	....	....	....	....	....	....	....	....
1988-89	Nichols School	Hi-School	29	49	32	81	26	....	....	....	....	....	....	....	....	....	....	....	....	....	....	....	....	....	....	....
1989-90	Nichols School	Hi-School	27	36	38	74	....	....	....	....	....	....	....	....	....	....	....	....	....	....	....	....	....	....	....	....
1990-91	U. of Wisconsin	WCHA	39	19	18	37	51	....	....	....	....	....	....	....	....	....	....	....	....	....	....	....	....	....	....	....
1991-92	U. of Wisconsin	WCHA	39	22	17	39	128	....	....	....	....	....	....	....	....	....	....	....	....	....	....	....	....	....	....	....
1992-93	U. of Wisconsin	WCHA	40	26	12	38	92	....	....	....	....	....	....	....	....	....	....	....	....	....	....	....	....	....	....	....
1993-94	U. of Wisconsin	WCHA	42	20	21	41	120	....	....	....	....	....	....	....	....	....	....	....	....	....	....	....	....	....	....	....
1994-95	P.E.I. Senators	AHL	55	15	11	26	46	....	....	....	....	....	....	....	....	....	....	....	9	6	1	7	6	....	....	....
1995-96	P.E.I. Senators	AHL	68	14	5	19	61	....	....	....	....	....	....	....	....	....	....	....	5	2	1	3	4	....	....	....
1996-97	**Ottawa**	**NHL**	**22**	**3**	**3**	**6**	**9**	**0**	**0**	**0**	**20**	**15.0**	**5**	....	....	....	....	....	....	....	....	....	....	....	....	....
	Worcester	AHL	45	14	10	24	45	....	....	....	....	....	....	....	....	....	....	....	5	3	3	6	4	....	....	....
1997-98	**Ottawa**	**NHL**	**3**	**0**	**0**	**0**	**4**	**0**	**0**	**0**	**1**	**0.0**	**0**	....	....	....	....	....	....	....	....	....	....	....	....	....
	Detroit Vipers	IHL	4	1	0	1	0	....	....	....	....	....	....	....	....	....	....	....	....	....	....	....	....	....	....	....
	Worcester	AHL	66	25	17	42	67	....	....	....	....	....	....	....	....	....	....	....	11	2	0	2	6	....	....	....
1998-99	**Philadelphia**	**NHL**	**2**	**0**	**0**	**0**	**0**	**0**	**0**	**0**	**1**	**0.0**	**0**	**0**	**0.0**	**2**	**0**	**2:58**	....	....	....	....	....	....	....	....
	Philadelphia	AHL	64	13	13	26	82	....	....	....	....	....	....	....	....	....	....	....	16	2	4	6	22	....	....	....
99-2000	Philadelphia	AHL	11	0	0	0	22	....	....	....	....	....	....	....	....	....	....	....	....	....	....	....	....	....	....	....
	NHL Totals		**27**	**3**	**3**	**6**	**13**	**0**	**0**	**0**	**22**	**13.6**		**0**	**0.0**	**2**	**0**	**2:58**	....	....	....	....	....	....	....	....

NCAA Championship All-Tournament Team (1992)

Traded to **Ottawa** by **NY Islanders** for Ottawa's 5th round choice (Andy Berenzweig) in 1996 Entry Draft, October 15, 1994. Signed as a free agent by **Philadelphia**, July 28, 1998. • Officially released by **Philadelphia**, December 12, 1999.

ZETTLER, Rob

(ZEHT-luhr, RAWB) **WSH.**

Defense. Shoots left. 6'3", 200 lbs. Born, Sept Iles, Que., March 8, 1968. Minnesota's 5th choice, 55th overall, in 1986 Entry Draft.

Season	Club	League	GP	G	A	Pts	PIM	PP	SH	GW	S	%	+/-	TF	F%	H	SB	Min	GP	G	A	Pts	PIM	PP	SH	GW
1983-84	S.S. Marie Legion	NOHA	40	9	24	33	28	....	....	....	....	....	....	....	....	....	....	....	....	....	....	....	....	....	....	....
1984-85	Sault Ste. Marie	OHL	60	2	14	16	37	....	....	....	....	....	....	....	....	....	....	....	....	....	....	....	....	....	....	....
1985-86	Sault Ste. Marie	OHL	57	5	23	28	92	....	....	....	....	....	....	....	....	....	....	....	....	....	....	....	....	....	....	....
1986-87	Sault Ste. Marie	OHL	64	13	22	35	89	....	....	....	....	....	....	....	....	....	....	....	4	0	0	0	0	....	....	....
1987-88	Sault Ste. Marie	OHL	64	7	41	48	77	....	....	....	....	....	....	....	....	....	....	....	6	2	2	4	9	....	....	....
	Kalamazoo Wings	IHL	2	0	1	1	0	....	....	....	....	....	....	....	....	....	....	....	7	0	2	2	2	....	....	....
1988-89	**Minnesota**	**NHL**	**2**	**0**	**0**	**0**	**0**	**0**	**0**	**0**	**0**	**0.0**	**–1**	....	....	....	....	....	....	....	....	....	....	....	....	....
	Kalamazoo Wings	IHL	80	5	21	26	79	....	....	....	....	....	....	....	....	....	....	....	6	0	1	1	26	....	....	....
1989-90	**Minnesota**	**NHL**	**31**	**0**	**8**	**8**	**45**	**0**	**0**	**0**	**21**	**0.0**	**–7**	....	....	....	....	....	....	....	....	....	....	....	....	....
	Kalamazoo Wings	IHL	41	6	10	16	64	....	....	....	....	....	....	....	....	....	....	....	7	0	0	0	6	....	....	....

			Regular Season																Playoffs							
Season	Club	League	GP	G	A	Pts	PIM	PP	SH	GW	S	%	+/-	TF	F%	H	SB	Min	GP	G	A	Pts	PIM	PP	SH	GW
1990-91	Minnesota	NHL	47	1	4	5	119	0	0	0	30	3.3	-10	....	....	....	....	....	....	....	....	....	....	....	....	....
	Kalamazoo Wings	IHL	1	0	0	0	2	....	....	....	....	....	....	....	....	....	....	....	....	....	....	....	....	....	....	....
1991-92	San Jose	NHL	74	1	8	9	99	0	0	0	72	1.4	-23	....	....	....	....	....	....	....	....	....	....	....	....	....
1992-93	San Jose	NHL	80	0	7	7	150	0	0	0	60	0.0	-50	....	....	....	....	....	....	....	....	....	....	....	....	....
1993-94	San Jose	NHL	42	0	3	3	65	0	0	0	28	0.0	-7	....	....	....	....	....	....	....	....	....	....	....	....	....
	Philadelphia	NHL	33	0	4	4	69	0	0	0	27	0.0	-19	....	....	....	....	....	....	....	....	....	....	....	....	....
1994-95	Philadelphia	NHL	32	0	1	1	34	0	0	0	17	0.0	-3	....	....	....	....	....	1	0	0	0	2	0	0	0
1995-96	Toronto	NHL	29	0	1	1	48	0	0	0	11	0.0	-1	....	....	....	....	....	2	0	0	0	0	0	0	0
1996-97	Toronto	NHL	48	2	12	14	51	0	0	0	31	6.5	8	....	....	....	....	....	....	....	....	....	....	....	....	....
	Utah Grizzlies	IHL	30	0	10	10	60	....	....	....	....	....	....	....	....	....	....	....	....	....	....	....	....	....	....	....
1997-98	Toronto	NHL	59	0	7	7	108	0	0	0	28	0.0	-8	....	....	....	....	....	....	....	....	....	....	....	....	....
1998-99	Nashville	NHL	2	0	0	0	2	0	0	0	0	0.0	-2	0	0.0	5	1	16:16	....	....	....	....	....	....	....	....
	Utah Grizzlies	IHL	77	2	16	18	136	....	....	....	....	....	....	....	....	....	....	....	....	....	....	....	....	....	....	....
99-2000	Washington	NHL	12	0	2	2	19	0	0	0	15	0.0	-1	0	0.0	15	18	15:22	5	0	0	0	2	0	0	0
	Portland Pirates	AHL	23	2	2	4	27	....	....	....	....	....	....	....	....	....	....	....	....	....	....	....	....	....	....	....
	NHL Totals		491	4	57	61	809	0	0	0	340	1.2		0	0.0	20	19	15:30	8	0	0	0	4	0	0	0

Claimed by **San Jose** from **Minnesota** in Dispersal Draft, May 30, 1991. Traded to **Philadelphia** by **San Jose** for Viacheslav Butsayev, February 1, 1994. Traded to **Toronto** by **Philadelphia** for Toronto's 5th round choice (Per-Ragna Bergqvist) in 1996 Entry Draft, July 8, 1995. Claimed by **Nashville** from **Toronto** in Expansion Draft, June 26, 1998. Signed as a free agent by **Washington**, September 7, 1999.
• Missed majority of 1999-2000 season recovering from head injury suffered in game vs. Albany (AHL), October 21, 1999.

ZHAMNOV, Alexei

(ZHAHM-nahf, al-EHX-ay) **CHI.**

Center. Shoots left. 6'1", 200 lbs. Born, Moscow, USSR, October 1, 1970. Winnipeg's 5th choice, 77th overall, in 1990 Entry Draft.

Season	Club	League	GP	G	A	Pts	PIM	PP	SH	GW	S	%	+/-	TF	F%	H	SB	Min	GP	G	A	Pts	PIM	PP	SH	GW
1988-89	Dynamo Moscow	USSR	4	0	0	0	0	....	....	....	....	....	....	....	....	....	....	....	....	....	....	....	....	....	....	....
1989-90	Dynamo Moscow	USSR	43	11	6	17	21	....	....	....	....	....	....	....	....	....	....	....	....	....	....	....	....	....	....	....
1990-91	Dynamo Moscow	USSR	46	16	12	28	24	....	....	....	....	....	....	....	....	....	....	....	....	....	....	....	....	....	....	....
1991-92	Dynamo Moscow	CIS	39	15	21	36	28	....	....	....	....	....	....	....	....	....	....	....	....	....	....	....	....	....	....	....
	Russia	Olympics	8	0	3	3	8	....	....	....	....	....	....	....	....	....	....	....	....	....	....	....	....	....	....	....
1992-93	Winnipeg	NHL	68	25	47	72	58	6	1	4	163	15.3	7	....	....	....	....	....	6	0	2	2	2	0	0	0
1993-94	Winnipeg	NHL	61	26	45	71	62	7	0	1	196	13.3	-20	....	....	....	....	....	....	....	....	....	....	....	....	....
1994-95	Winnipeg	NHL	48	30	35	65	20	9	0	4	155	19.4	5	....	....	....	....	....	....	....	....	....	....	....	....	....
1995-96	Winnipeg	NHL	58	22	37	59	65	5	0	2	199	11.1	-4	....	....	....	....	....	6	2	1	3	8	0	0	0
1996-97	Chicago	NHL	74	20	42	62	56	6	1	2	208	9.6	18	....	....	....	....	....	....	....	....	....	....	....	....	....
1997-98	Chicago	NHL	70	21	28	49	61	6	2	3	193	10.9	16	....	....	....	....	....	....	....	....	....	....	....	....	....
	Russia	Olympics	6	2	1	3	2	....	....	....	....	....	....	....	....	....	....	....	....	....	....	....	....	....	....	....
1998-99	Chicago	NHL	76	20	41	61	50	8	1	2	200	10.0	-10	1299	48.9	40	38	21:30	....	....	....	....	....	....	....	....
99-2000	Chicago	NHL	71	23	37	60	61	5	0	7	175	13.1	7	1171	45.8	28	43	22:08	....	....	....	....	....	....	....	....
	NHL Totals		526	187	312	499	433	52	5	25	1489	12.6		2470	47.4	68	81	21:48	12	2	3	5	10	0	0	0

NHL Second All-Star Team (1995)
Traded to **Chicago** by **Phoenix** with Craig Mills and Phoenix's 1st round choice (Ty Jones) in 1997 Entry Draft for Jeremy Roenick, August 16, 1996.

ZHITNIK, Alexei

(ZHIHT-nihk, al-EHX-ay) **BUF.**

Defense. Shoots left. 5'11", 215 lbs. Born, Kiev, USSR, October 10, 1972. Los Angeles' 3rd choice, 81st overall, in 1991 Entry Draft.

Season	Club	League	GP	G	A	Pts	PIM	PP	SH	GW	S	%	+/-	TF	F%	H	SB	Min	GP	G	A	Pts	PIM	PP	SH	GW
1989-90	Sokol Kiev	USSR	31	3	4	7	16	....	....	....	....	....	....	....	....	....	....	....	....	....	....	....	....	....	....	....
1990-91	Sokol Kiev	USSR	46	1	4	5	46	....	....	....	....	....	....	....	....	....	....	....	....	....	....	....	....	....	....	....
1991-92	CSKA Moscow	CIS	44	2	7	9	52	....	....	....	....	....	....	....	....	....	....	....	....	....	....	....	....	....	....	....
	Russia	Olympics	8	1	0	1	0	....	....	....	....	....	....	....	....	....	....	....	....	....	....	....	....	....	....	....
1992-93	Los Angeles	NHL	78	12	36	48	80	5	0	2	136	8.8	-3	....	....	....	....	....	24	3	9	12	26	2	0	1
1993-94	Los Angeles	NHL	81	12	40	52	101	11	0	1	227	5.3	-11	....	....	....	....	....	....	....	....	....	....	....	....	....
1994-95	Los Angeles	NHL	11	2	5	7	27	2	0	0	33	6.1	-3	....	....	....	....	....	....	....	....	....	....	....	....	....
	Buffalo	NHL	21	2	5	7	34	1	0	0	33	6.1	-3	....	....	....	....	....	5	0	1	1	14	0	0	0
1995-96	Buffalo	NHL	80	6	30	36	58	5	0	0	193	3.1	-25	....	....	....	....	....	....	....	....	....	....	....	....	....
1996-97	Buffalo	NHL	80	7	28	35	95	3	1	0	170	4.1	10	....	....	....	....	....	12	1	0	1	16	0	0	0
1997-98	Buffalo	NHL	78	15	30	45	102	2	3	3	191	7.9	19	....	....	....	....	....	15	0	3	3	36	0	0	0
	Russia	Olympics	6	0	2	2	2	....	....	....	....	....	....	....	....	....	....	....	....	....	....	....	....	....	....	....
1998-99	Buffalo	NHL	81	7	26	33	96	3	1	2	185	3.8	-6	0	0.0	122	109	25:39	21	4	11	15	*52	4	0	2
99-2000	Buffalo	NHL	74	2	11	13	95	1	0	0	139	1.4	-6	0	0.0	117	88	24:48	4	0	0	0	8	0	0	0
	NHL Totals		584	65	211	276	688	33	5	8	1307	5.0		0	0.0	239	197	25:15	81	8	24	32	152	6	0	3

Played in NHL All-Star Game (1999)
Traded to **Buffalo** by **LA Kings** with Robb Stauber, Charlie Huddy and LA Kings' 5th round choice (Marian Menhart) in 1995 Entry Draft for Philippe Boucher, Denis Tsygurov and Grant Fuhr, February 14, 1995.

ZHOLTOK, Sergei

(ZHOL-tok, SAIR-gay) **MTL.**

Center. Shoots right. 6'2", 191 lbs. Born, Riga, Latvia, February 12, 1972. Boston's 2nd choice, 55th overall, in 1992 Entry Draft.

Season	Club	League	GP	G	A	Pts	PIM	PP	SH	GW	S	%	+/-	TF	F%	H	SB	Min	GP	G	A	Pts	PIM	PP	SH	GW
1990-91	Dynamo Riga	USSR	39	4	0	4	16	....	....	....	....	....	....	....	....	....	....	....	....	....	....	....	....	....	....	....
1991-92	Dynamo Riga	CIS	27	6	3	9	6	....	....	....	....	....	....	....	....	....	....	....	....	....	....	....	....	....	....	....
1992-93	Boston	NHL	1	0	1	1	0	0	0	0	2	0.0	1	....	....	....	....	....	....	....	....	....	....	....	....	....
	Providence Bruins	AHL	64	31	35	66	57	....	....	....	....	....	....	....	....	....	....	....	6	3	5	8	4	....	....	....
1993-94	Boston	NHL	24	2	1	3	2	1	0	0	25	8.0	-7	....	....	....	....	....	....	....	....	....	....	....	....	....
	Providence Bruins	AHL	54	29	33	62	16	....	....	....	....	....	....	....	....	....	....	....	....	....	....	....	....	....	....	....
1994-95	Providence Bruins	AHL	78	23	35	58	42	....	....	....	....	....	....	....	....	....	....	....	13	8	5	13	6	....	....	....
1995-96	Las Vegas	IHL	82	51	50	101	30	....	....	....	....	....	....	....	....	....	....	....	15	7	13	20	6	....	....	....
1996-97	Ottawa	NHL	57	12	16	28	19	5	0	0	96	12.5	2	....	....	....	....	....	7	1	1	2	0	1	0	0
	Las Vegas	IHL	19	13	14	27	20	....	....	....	....	....	....	....	....	....	....	....	....	....	....	....	....	....	....	....
1997-98	Ottawa	NHL	78	10	13	23	16	7	0	1	127	7.9	-7	....	....	....	....	....	11	0	2	2	0	0	0	0
1998-99	Montreal	NHL	70	7	15	22	6	2	0	3	102	6.9	-12	522	49.0	23	12	11:11	....	....	....	....	....	....	....	....
	Fredericton	AHL	7	3	4	7	0	....	....	....	....	....	....	....	....	....	....	....	....	....	....	....	....	....	....	....
99-2000	Montreal	NHL	68	26	12	38	28	9	0	7	163	16.0	2	914	48.9	12	18	17:17	....	....	....	....	....	....	....	....
	Quebec Citadelles	AHL	1	0	1	1	2	....	....	....	....	....	....	....	....	....	....	....	....	....	....	....	....	....	....	....
	NHL Totals		298	57	58	115	71	24	0	11	515	11.1		1436	49.0	35	30	14:11	18	1	3	4	0	1	0	0

Signed as a free agent by **Ottawa**, July 10, 1996. Signed as a free agent by **Montreal**, September 9, 1998.

ZMOLEK, Doug

(zuh-MOH-lehk, DUHG) **CHI.**

Defense. Shoots left. 6'2", 222 lbs. Born, Rochester, MN, November 3, 1970. Minnesota's 1st choice, 7th overall, in 1989 Entry Draft.

Season	Club	League	GP	G	A	Pts	PIM	PP	SH	GW	S	%	+/-	TF	F%	H	SB	Min	GP	G	A	Pts	PIM	PP	SH	GW
1987-88	John Marshall	Hi-School	27	4	32	36	....	....	....	....	....	....	....	....	....	....	....	....	....	....	....	....	....	....	....	....
1988-89	John Marshall	Hi-School	29	17	41	58	....	....	....	....	....	....	....	....	....	....	....	....	....	....	....	....	....	....	....	....
1989-90	U. of Minnesota	WCHA	40	1	10	11	52	....	....	....	....	....	....	....	....	....	....	....	....	....	....	....	....	....	....	....
1990-91	U. of Minnesota	WCHA	34	11	6	17	38	....	....	....	....	....	....	....	....	....	....	....	....	....	....	....	....	....	....	....
1991-92	U. of Minnesota	WCHA	41	6	20	26	84	....	....	....	....	....	....	....	....	....	....	....	....	....	....	....	....	....	....	....
1992-93	San Jose	NHL	84	5	10	15	229	2	0	0	94	5.3	-50	....	....	....	....	....	....	....	....	....	....	....	....	....
1993-94	San Jose	NHL	68	0	4	4	122	0	0	0	29	0.0	-9	....	....	....	....	....	....	....	....	....	....	....	....	....
	Dallas	NHL	7	1	0	1	11	0	0	0	3	33.3	1	....	....	....	....	....	7	0	1	1	4	0	0	0
1994-95	Dallas	NHL	42	0	5	5	67	0	0	0	28	0.0	-6	....	....	....	....	....	5	0	0	0	10	0	0	0
1995-96	Dallas	NHL	42	1	5	6	65	0	0	0	26	3.8	1	....	....	....	....	....	....	....	....	....	....	....	....	....
	Los Angeles	NHL	16	1	0	1	22	0	0	0	10	10.0	-6	....	....	....	....	....	....	....	....	....	....	....	....	....
1996-97	Los Angeles	NHL	57	1	0	1	116	0	0	0	28	3.6	-22	....	....	....	....	....	....	....	....	....	....	....	....	....
1997-98	Los Angeles	NHL	46	0	8	8	111	0	0	0	23	0.0	0	....	....	....	....	....	2	0	0	0	2	0	0	0

Season	Club	League	GP	G	A	Pts	PIM	PP	SH	GW	S	%	+/-	TF	F%	H	SB	Min	GP	G	A	Pts	PIM	PP	SH	GW
1998-99	Chicago	NHL	62	0	14	14	102	0	0	0	33	0.0	1	0	0.0	63	54	17:08	....	....	....	....	....	....	....	....
99-2000	Chicago	NHL	43	2	7	9	60	0	0	0	24	8.3	6	0	0.0	49	29	15:15	....	....	....	....	....	....	....	....
	NHL Totals		467	11	53	64	905	2	0	0	298	3.7		0	0.0	112	83	16:22	14	0	1	1	16	0	0	0

WCHA Second All-Star Team (1992) • NCAA West Second All-American Team (1992)

Claimed by **San Jose** from **Minnesota** in Dispersal Draft, May 30, 1991. Traded to **Dallas** by **San Jose** with Mike Lalor for Ulf Dahlen and Dallas' 7th round choice (Brad Mehalko) in 1995 Entry Draft, March 19, 1994. Traded to **LA Kings** by **Dallas** with Shane Churla for Darryl Sydor and LA Kings' 5th round choice (Ryan Christie) in 1996 Entry Draft, February 17, 1996. Traded to **Chicago** by **LA Kings** for Chicago's 3rd round choice (Frantisek Kaberle) in 1999 Entry Draft, September 3, 1998.

ZUBOV, Sergei

(ZOO-bahf, SAIR-gay) **DAL.**

Defense. Shoots right. 6'1", 200 lbs. Born, Moscow, USSR, July 22, 1970. NY Rangers' 6th choice, 85th overall, in 1990 Entry Draft.

Season	Club	League	GP	G	A	Pts	PIM	PP	SH	GW	S	%	+/-	TF	F%	H	SB	Min	GP	G	A	Pts	PIM	PP	SH	GW
1988-89	CSKA Moscow	USSR	29	1	4	5	10	....						....						....							
1989-90	CSKA Moscow	USSR	48	6	2	8	16	....						....						....							
1990-91	CSKA Moscow	USSR	41	6	5	11	12	....						....						....							
1991-92	CSKA Moscow	CIS	44	4	7	11	8	....						....						....							
	Russia	Olympics	8	0	1	1	0	....						....						....							
1992-93	CSKA Moscow	CIS	1	0	1	1	0	....						....						....							
	NY Rangers	NHL	49	8	23	31	4	3	0	0	93	8.6	−1						....							
	Binghamton	AHL	30	7	29	36	14	....						....						11	5	5	10	2	....		
1993-94♦	NY Rangers	NHL	78	12	77	89	39	9	0	1	222	5.4	20						22	5	14	19	0	2	0	0
	Binghamton	AHL	2	1	2	3	0	....						....						....							
1994-95	NY Rangers	NHL	38	10	26	36	18	6	0	0	116	8.6	−2						10	3	8	11	2	1	0	0
1995-96	Pittsburgh	NHL	64	11	55	66	22	3	2	1	141	7.8	28						18	1	14	15	26	1	0	0
1996-97	Dallas	NHL	78	13	30	43	24	1	0	3	133	9.8	19						7	0	3	3	2	0	0	0
1997-98	Dallas	NHL	73	10	47	57	16	5	1	2	148	6.8	16						17	4	5	9	2	3	0	1
1998-99♦	Dallas	NHL	81	10	41	51	20	5	0	3	155	6.5	9	0	0.0	35	41	24:14	23	1	12	13	4	0	0	0
99-2000	Dallas	NHL	77	9	33	42	18	3	1	3	179	5.0	−2	0	0.0	52	58	28:50	18	2	7	9	6	1	1	0
	NHL Totals		538	83	332	415	161	35	4	13	1187	7.0		0	0.0	87	99	26:29	115	16	63	79	42	8	1	1

Played in NHL All-Star Game (1998, 1999, 2000)

Traded to **Pittsburgh** by **NY Rangers** with Petr Nedved for Luc Robitaille and Ulf Samuelsson, August 31, 1995. Traded to **Dallas** by **Pittsburgh** for Kevin Hatcher, June 22, 1996.

ZUBRUS, Dainius

(ZOO-bruhs, DAYN-ihs) **MTL.**

Right wing. Shoots left. 6'4", 227 lbs. Born, Elektrenai, USSR, June 16, 1978. Philadelphia's 1st choice, 15th overall, in 1996 Entry Draft.

Season	Club	League	GP	G	A	Pts	PIM	PP	SH	GW	S	%	+/-	TF	F%	H	SB	Min	GP	G	A	Pts	PIM	PP	SH	GW
1995-96	Pembroke Kings	OJHL	28	19	13	32	73	....						....						....							
	Caledon Canucks	OJHL	7	3	7	10	2	....						....						17	11	12	23	4	....		
1996-97	Philadelphia	NHL	68	8	13	21	22	1	0	2	71	11.3	3						19	5	4	9	12	1	0	1
1997-98	Philadelphia	NHL	69	8	25	33	42	1	0	5	101	7.9	29						5	0	1	1	2	0	0	0
1998-99	Philadelphia	NHL	63	3	5	8	25	0	1	0	49	6.1	−5	29	51.7	54	30	11:00	....							
	Montreal	NHL	17	3	5	8	4	0	0	1	31	9.7	−3	2	50.0	15	6	16:53	....							
99-2000	Montreal	NHL	73	14	28	42	54	3	0	1	139	10.1	−1	212	35.9	99	27	17:37	....							
	NHL Totals		290	36	76	112	147	5	1	9	391	9.2		243	40.7	168	63	14:49	24	5	5	10	14	1	0	1

Traded to **Montreal** by **Philadelphia** with Philadelphia's 2nd round choice (Matt Carkner) in 1999 Entry Draft and NY Islanders' 6th round choice (previously acquired, Montreal selected Scott Selig) in 2000 Entry Draft for Mark Recchi, March 10, 1999.

ZYUZIN, Andrei

(ZYOO-zin, AWN-dray) **T.B.**

Defense. Shoots right. 6'1", 210 lbs. Born, Ufa, USSR, January 21, 1978. San Jose's 1st choice, 2nd overall, in 1996 Entry Draft.

Season	Club	League	GP	G	A	Pts	PIM	PP	SH	GW	S	%	+/-	TF	F%	H	SB	Min	GP	G	A	Pts	PIM	PP	SH	GW
1994-95	Ufa Salavat	CIS	30	3	0	3	16	....						....						....							
1995-96	Ufa Salavat	CIS	41	6	3	9	24	....						....						....							
1996-97	Ufa Salavat	Russia	32	7	10	17	28	....						....						7	1	1	2	4	....		
1997-98	San Jose	NHL	56	6	7	13	66	2	0	2	72	8.3	8						6	1	0	1	14	0	0	1
	Kentucky	AHL	17	4	5	9	28	....						....						....							
1998-99	San Jose	NHL	25	3	1	4	38	2	0	0	44	6.8	5	0	0.0	25	11	15:56	....							
	Kentucky	AHL	23	2	12	14	42	....						....						....							
99-2000	Tampa Bay	NHL	34	2	9	11	33	0	0	0	47	4.3	−11	0	0.0	33	27	20:28	....							
	NHL Totals		115	11	17	28	137	4	0	2	163	6.7		0	0.0	58	38	18:33	6	1	0	1	14	0	0	1

• Suspended for remainder of 1998-99 season by **San Jose** for being leaving team without permission, April 1, 1999. Traded to **Tampa Bay** by **San Jose** with Bill Houlder, Shawn Burr and Steve Guolla for Niklas Sundstrom and NY Rangers' 3rd round choice (previously acquired, later traded to Chicago - Chicago selected Igor Radulov) in 2000 Entry Draft, August 4, 1999. • Missed remainder of 1999-2000 season recovering from shoulder injury suffered in game vs. NY Islanders, January 13, 2000.

Goaltenders

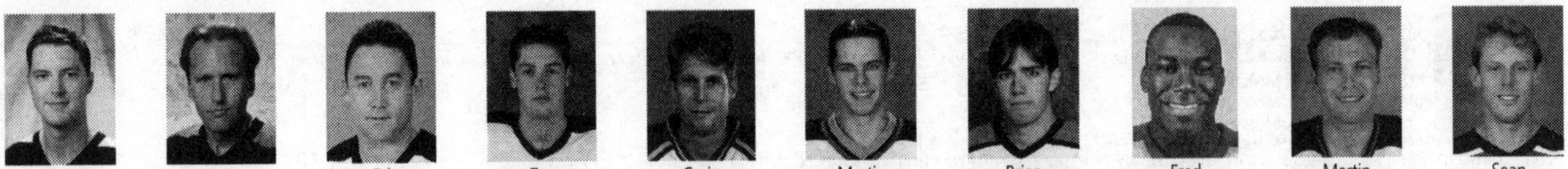

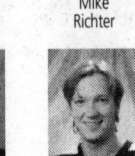

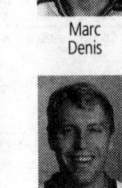

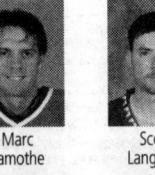

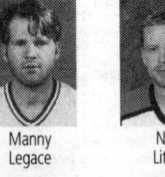

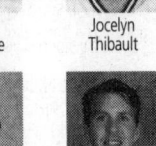

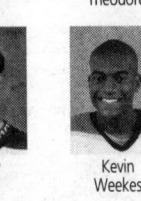

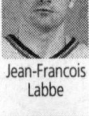

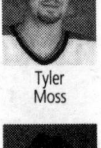

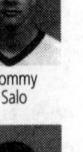

Jean-Sebastien Aubin · Tom Barrasso · Ed Belfour · Zac Bierk · Craig Billington · Martin Biron · Brian Boucher · Fred Braithwaite · Martin Brodeur · Sean Burke

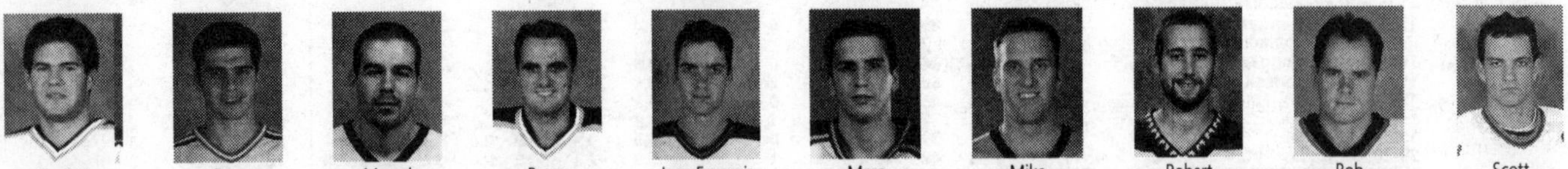

Frederic Chabot · Dan Cloutier · Marcel Cousineau · Byron Dafoe · Jean-Francois Damphousse · Marc Denis · Mike Dunham · Robert Esche · Bob Essensa · Scott Fankhouser

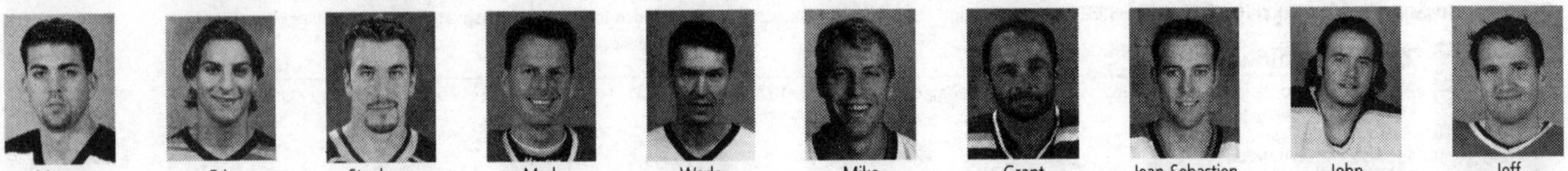

Manny Fernandez · Eric Fichaud · Stephane Fiset · Mark Fitzpatrick · Wade Flaherty · Mike Fountain · Grant Fuhr · Jean-Sebastien Giguere · John Grahame · Jeff Hackett

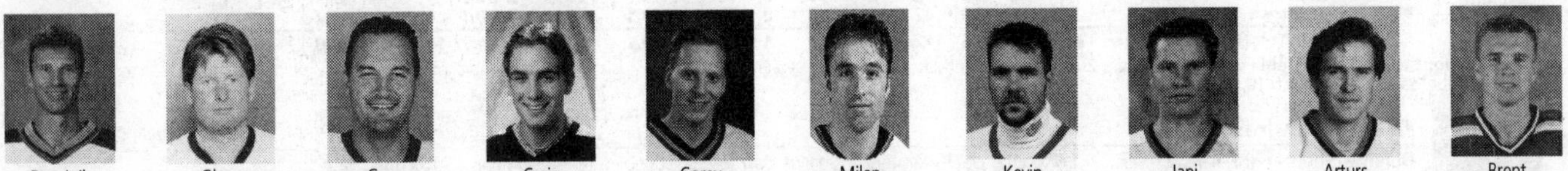

Dominik Hasek · Glenn Healy · Guy Hebert · Craig Hillier · Corey Hirsch · Milan Hnilicka · Kevin Hodson · Jani Hurme · Arturs Irbe · Brent Johnson

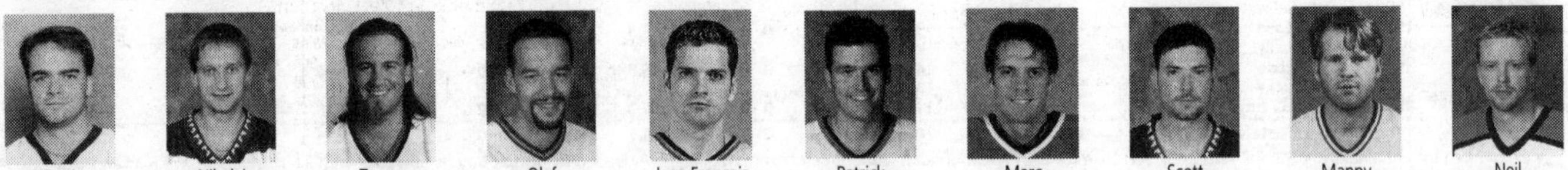

Curtis Joseph · Nikolai Khabibulin · Trevor Kidd · Olaf Kolzig · Jean-Francois Labbe · Patrick Lalime · Marc Lamothe · Scott Langkow · Manny Legace · Neil Little

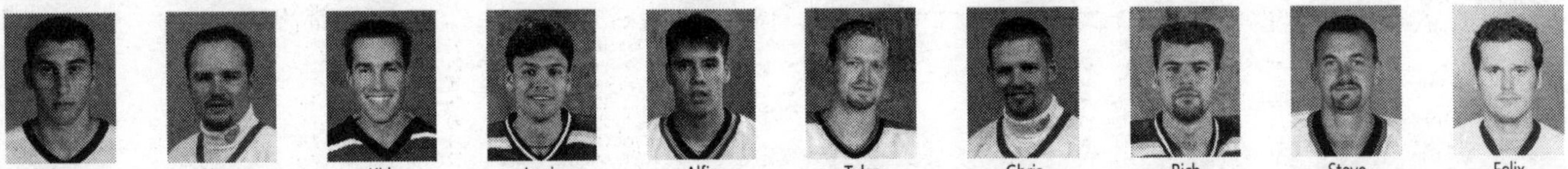

Roberto Luongo · Norm Maracle · Kirk McLean · Jamie McLennan · Alfie Michaud · Tyler Moss · Chris Osgood · Rich Parent · Steve Passmore · Felix Potvin

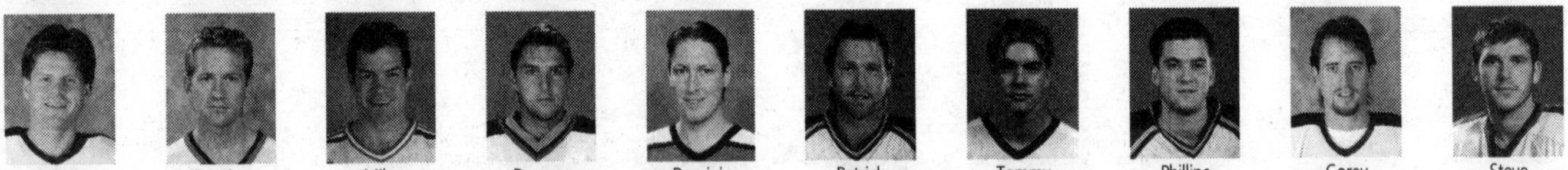

Daren Puppa · Damian Rhodes · Mike Richter · Dwayne Roloson · Dominic Roussel · Patrick Roy · Tommy Salo · Phillipe Sauve · Corey Schwab · Steve Shields

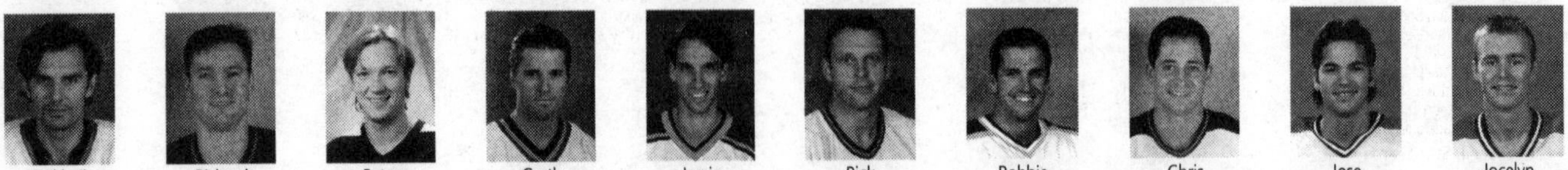

Mikhail Shtalenkov · Richard Shulmistra · Peter Skudra · Garth Snow · Jamie Storr · Rick Tabaracci · Robbie Tallas · Chris Terreri · Jose Theodore · Jocelyn Thibault

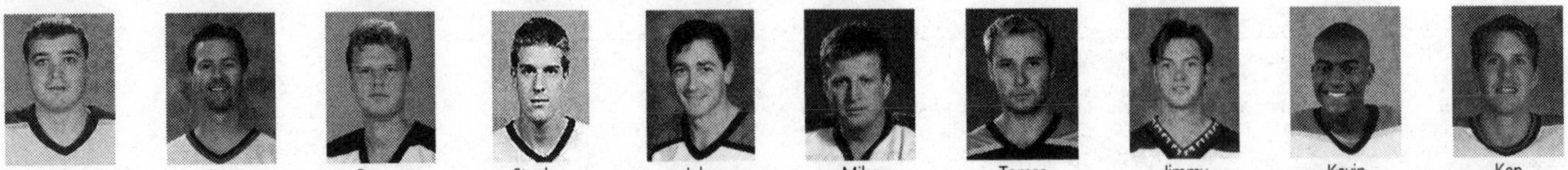

Andrei Trefilov · Ron Tugnutt · Roman Turek · Stephen Valiquette · John Vanbiesbrouck · Mike Vernon · Tomas Vokoun · Jimmy Waite · Kevin Weekes · Ken Wregget

2000-01 Goaltender Register

Note: The 2000-01 Goaltender Register lists every goaltender who appeared in an NHL game in the 1999-2000 season, every goaltender drafted in the first six rounds of the 1999 Entry Draft, goaltenders on NHL Reserve Lists and other goaltenders.

Trades and roster changes are current as of September 5, 2000.

To calculate a goaltender's goals-against-per-game average **(Avg)**, divide goals against **(GA)** by minutes played **(Mins)** and multiply this result by **60**.

Abbreviations: Avg – goals against per game average; **GA** – goals against; **GP** – games played; **L** – losses; **Lea** – league; **SO** – shutouts; **T** – ties; **W** – wins; ♦ – member of Stanley Cup-winning team.

NHL Player Register begins on page 323.

Prospect Register begins on page 265.

League Abbreviations are listed on page 264.

AEBISCHER, David (A-bih-shuhr, DAY-vihd) COL.

Goaltender. Catches left. 6'1", 190 lbs.   Born, Fribourg, Switz., February 7, 1978.
(Colorado's 7th choice, 161st overall, in 1997 Entry Draft).

						Regular Season							Playoffs			
Season	Club	Lea	GP	W	L	T	Mins	GA	SO	Avg	GP	W	L	Mins	GA	SO	Avg
1996-97	HC Fribourg	Switz.	10				577	34	....	3.53	3	....	....	184	13	....	4.24
1997-98	Chesapeake	ECHL	17	5	7	2	930	52	0	3.35							
	Wheeling Nailers	ECHL	10	5	3	1	564	30	1	3.19							
	Hershey Bears	AHL	2	0	0	1	79	5	0	3.76							
	HC Fribourg	Switz.	1	1	0		60	1	0	1.00	4	....	....	240	17	....	4.25
1998-99	Hershey Bears	AHL	38	17	10	5	1932	79	2	2.45	3	1	2	152	6	0	2.37
99-2000	Hershey Bears	AHL	58	29	23	2	3259	180	1	3.31	14	7	6	788	40	2	3.05

AHONEN, Ari (ah-HOH-nuhn, AH-ree) N.J.

Goaltender. Catches left. 6'2", 170 lbs.   Born, Jyvaskyla, Finland, February 6, 1981.
(New Jersey's 1st choice, 27th overall, in 1999 Entry Draft).

						Regular Season							Playoffs			
Season	Club	Lea	GP	W	L	T	Mins	GA	SO	Avg	GP	W	L	Mins	GA	SO	Avg
1997-98	JyP Jyvaskyla	Finn-Jr.	31	....	....	....	1853	64		2.09							
1998-99	JyP Jyvaskyla	Finn-Jr.	24	....	....	....	1447	70		2.90							
99-2000	HIFK Helsinki	Finland	24	11	7	1	1347	70	1	3.12	2	0	2	119	7	0	3.53
	HIFK Helsinki	EuroHL	5	4	1	0	285	15	1	3.16							

ALBAN, Chad DAL.

Goaltender. Catches left. 5'9", 165 lbs.   Born, Kalamazoo, MI, April 27, 1976.

						Regular Season							Playoffs			
Season	Club	Lea	GP	W	L	T	Mins	GA	SO	Avg	GP	W	L	Mins	GA	SO	Avg
1994-95	Michigan State	CCHA	13	8	2	0	636	29	0	2.73							
1995-96	Michigan State	CCHA	40	26	13	1	2286	117	0	3.07							
1996-97	Michigan State	CCHA	39	23	11	4	2272	103	3	2.72							
1997-98	Michigan State	CCHA	40	31	4	5	2438	64	*6	*1.57							
1998-99	Mobile Mysticks	ECHL	34	16	14	3	1960	111	1	3.40	2	0	2	119	9	0	4.54
	Houston Aeros	IHL	5	1	3	0	284	14	0	2.96							
99-2000	Mobile Mysticks	ECHL	39				2334	114	0	2.93	5	2	3	299	20	0	4.01
	Utah Grizzlies	IHL	1	0	1	0	35	3	0	5.16							

CCHA First All-Star Team (1998) • NCAA West First All-American Team (1998)
Signed as a free agent by **Dallas**, August 30, 2000.

AMIDOVSKI, Bujar (D166am-ih-DAWV-skee, BOO-jahr) CAR.

Goaltender. Catches left. 5'11", 180 lbs.   Born, Toronto, Ont., February 19, 1977.

						Regular Season							Playoffs			
Season	Club	Lea	GP	W	L	T	Mins	GA	SO	Avg	GP	W	L	Mins	GA	SO	Avg
1994-95	North York	OJHL	35	....	....	....	2089	137	0	3.93							
1995-96	Kingston	OHL	38	16	16	2	1970	136	1	4.14	4	1	2	194	11	0	3.40
1996-97	Kingston	OHL	36	11	14	1	1797	116	0	3.87	5	1	3	280	24	0	5.14
	Dayton Bombers	ECHL	3	1	1	0	90	5	0	3.31	2	0	2	118	9	0	4.56
1997-98	St. Michael's	OHL	48	12	25	7	2697	153	0	3.40							
1998-99	Louisiana	ECHL	27	17	5	3	1525	59	3	2.32							
	Saint John Flames	AHL	6	2	2	0	243	19	0	4.69							
99-2000	Trenton Titans	ECHL	34	19	11	3	1979	82	2	2.49	5	2	3	254	13	1	3.07
	Philadelphia	AHL	6	3	1	0	250	8	0	1.92							

OHL First All-Star Team (1998)
Signed as a free agent by **Philadelphia**, August 15, 1999. Signed as a free agent by **Carolina**, August 21, 2000.

ANDERSSON, Andreas (AN-duhr-suhn, AN-dree-as) ANA.

Goaltender. Catches left. 6', 180 lbs.   Born, Stora Kopparberg, Sweden, April 4, 1979.
(Anaheim's 8th choice, 245th overall, in 1998 Entry Draft).

						Regular Season							Playoffs			
Season	Club	Lea	GP	W	L	T	Mins	GA	SO	Avg	GP	W	L	Mins	GA	SO	Avg
1997-98	HV Jonkoping	Swede-Jr.	10	....	....	....	600	31	....	3.10							
	HV Jonkoping	Sweden	7	....	....	....	420	20	....	2.86							
1998-99	Mora IK	Swede-Jr.	12	....	....	....	720	28	0	1.92							
	HV Jonkoping	Sweden	12	....	....	....	633	35	0	3.32							
99-2000	Tranas AIF	Swede-2	5	....	....	....	297	17	0	3.44							
	HV Jonkoping	Sweden	1	....	....	....	51	5	0	5.88							

ANDERSSON, Craig (AN-duhr-suhn, KRAYG) CGY.

Goaltender. Catches left. 6'2", 170 lbs.   Born, Park Ridge, IL, May 21, 1981.
(Calgary's 3rd choice, 77th overall, in 1999 Entry Draft).

						Regular Season							Playoffs			
Season	Club	Lea	GP	W	L	T	Mins	GA	SO	Avg	GP	W	L	Mins	GA	SO	Avg
1997-98	Chicago Jets	MEHL	50	....	....	....	2991	143	2	2.86							
1998-99	Chicago Freeze	NAJHL	14	11	3	0	840	40	0	2.56							
	Guelph Storm	OHL	21	12	5	1	1006	52	1	3.10	3	0	2	114	9	0	4.74
99-2000	Guelph Storm	OHL	38	12	17	2	1955	117	0	3.59	3	0	1	110	5	0	2.73

ANTILA, Kristian (AN-tih-luh, KRIHS-tan) EDM.

Goaltender. Catches left. 6'3", 207 lbs.   Born, Vammala, Finland, January 10, 1980.
(Edmonton's 4th choice, 113th overall, in 1998 Entry Draft).

						Regular Season							Playoffs			
Season	Club	Lea	GP	W	L	T	Mins	GA	SO	Avg	GP	W	L	Mins	GA	SO	Avg
1997-98	Ilves Tampere	Finn-Jr.	11	....	....	....	564	28	0	2.97							
1998-99	Ilves Tampere	Finn-Jr.	14	....	....	....	798	35	0	2.63							
	Ilves Tampere	Finland	5	1	2	0	207	12	0	3.48							
99-2000	Ilves Tampere	Finland	25	4	11	4	1239	74	1	3.58	1	0	1	20	4	0	12.00

ASKEY, Tom (AS-kee, TAWM)

Goaltender. Catches left. 6'2", 185 lbs.   Born, Kenmore, NY, October 4, 1974.
(Anaheim's 8th choice, 186th overall, in 1993 Entry Draft).

						Regular Season							Playoffs			
Season	Club	Lea	GP	W	L	T	Mins	GA	SO	Avg	GP	W	L	Mins	GA	SO	Avg
1992-93	Ohio State	CCHA	25	2	19	0	1235	125	0	6.07							
1993-94	Ohio State	CCHA	27	3	19	4	1488	103	0	4.15							
1994-95	Ohio State	CCHA	26	4	19	2	1387	121	0	5.23							
1995-96	Ohio State	CCHA	26	8	11	4	1340	68	0	3.05							
1996-97	Baltimore Bandits	AHL	40	17	18	2	2238	140	1	3.75	0	0	3	137	11	0	4.79
1997-98	**Anaheim**	**NHL**	**7**	**0**	**1**	**2**	**273**	**12**	**0**	**2.64**							
	Cincinnati Ducks	AHL	32	10	16	4	1753	104	3	3.56							
1998-99	Cincinnati Ducks	AHL	53	21	22	3	2893	131	3	2.72	3	0	3	178	13	0	4.38
	Anaheim	**NHL**									**1**	**0**	**1**	**30**	**2**	**0**	**4.00**
99-2000	Kansas City	IHL	13	3	5	3	658	43	0	3.92							
	Houston Aeros	IHL	13	4	7	1	727	33	0	2.72							
	NHL Totals		**7**	**0**	**1**	**2**	**273**	**12**	**0**	**2.64**	**1**	**0**	**1**	**30**	**2**	**0**	**4.00**

CCHA Second All-Star Team (1996)

ASPLUND, Johan (AS-pluhnd, YOH-hahn) NYR

Goaltender. Catches left. 6'1", 180 lbs.   Born, Slutskar, Sweden, December 15, 1980.
(NY Rangers' 4th choice, 79th overall, in 1999 Entry Draft).

						Regular Season							Playoffs			
Season	Club	Lea	GP	W	L	T	Mins	GA	SO	Avg	GP	W	L	Mins	GA	SO	Avg
1998-99	Brynas IF	Sweden	12	....	....	....	646	32	0	2.97							
99-2000	Mora IK	Swede-2	3	3	0	0	180	6	0	2.00							
	Brynas IF	Sweden	10	....	....	....	622	30	0	2.89							

AUBIN, Jean-Sebastien (OH-behn, ZHAWN-suh-BAS-tee-yeh) PIT.

Goaltender. Catches right. 5'11", 176 lbs. Born, Montreal, Que., July 17, 1977.
(Pittsburgh's 2nd choice, 76th overall, in 1995 Entry Draft).

			Regular Season								Playoffs						
Season	Club	Lea	GP	W	L	T	Mins	GA	SO	Avg	GP	W	L	Mins	GA	SO	Avg
1993-94	Montreal-Bourassa	QAAA	27	14	13	0	1524	96	1	3.74	....	....	....	....	....	....	....
1994-95	Sherbrooke	QMJHL	27	13	10	1	1287	73	1	3.40	3	1	2	185	11	0	3.57
1995-96	Sherbrooke	QMJHL	40	18	14	2	2140	127	0	3.57	4	1	3	238	23	0	5.55
1996-97	Laval Titan	QMJHL	11	2	6	1	532	41	0	4.62	....	....	....	....	....	....	....
	Moncton Wildcats	QMJHL	22	9	12	0	1252	67	1	3.21	....	....	....	....	....	....	....
	Sherbrooke	QMJHL	4	3	1	0	249	8	0	1.93	1	0	1	60	4	0	4.00
1997-98	Syracuse Crunch	AHL	8	2	4	1	380	26	0	4.10	....	....	....	....	....	....	....
	Dayton Bombers	ECHL	21	15	2	2	1177	59	1	3.01	3	1	1	142	4	0	1.69
1998-99	**Pittsburgh**	**NHL**	**17**	**4**	**3**	**6**	**756**	**28**	**2**	**2.22**	....	....	....	....	....	....	....
	Kansas City	IHL	13	5	7	1	751	41	0	3.28	....	....	....	....	....	....	....
99-2000	**Pittsburgh**	**NHL**	**51**	**23**	**21**	**3**	**2789**	**120**	**2**	**2.58**	....	....	....	....	....	....	....
	Wilkes-Barre	AHL	11	2	8	0	538	39	0	4.35	....	....	....	....	....	....	....
	NHL Totals		**68**	**27**	**24**	**9**	**3545**	**148**	**4**	**2.50**	....	....	....	....	....	....	....

AULD, Alexander (AWLD, al-ehx-AN-duhr) FLA.

Goaltender. Catches left. 6'4", 197 lbs. Born, Cold Lake, Alta., January 7, 1981.
(Florida's 2nd choice, 40th overall, in 1999 Entry Draft).

			Regular Season								Playoffs						
Season	Club	Lea	GP	W	L	T	Mins	GA	SO	Avg	GP	W	L	Mins	GA	SO	Avg
1996-97	Thunder Bay	TBAHA	35	....	....	....	2100	46	10	1.35	....	....	....	....	....	....	....
1997-98	Sturgeon Falls	NOJHA	11	4	6	0	611	46	0	4.52	....	....	....	....	....	....	....
	North Bay	OHL	6	0	4	0	206	17	0	4.95	....	....	....	....	....	....	....
1998-99	North Bay	OHL	37	9	20	1	1894	106	1	3.36	3	0	3	170	10	0	3.53
99-2000	North Bay	OHL	55	21	26	6	3047	167	2	3.29	6	2	4	374	12	0	*1.93

AYERS, Michael (AY-uhrs) CHI.

Goaltender. Catches left. 5'11", 186 lbs. Born, Weymouth, MA, January 16, 1980.
(Chicago's 8th choice, 177th overall, in 2000 Entry Draft).

			Regular Season								Playoffs						
Season	Club	Lea	GP	W	L	T	Mins	GA	SO	Avg	GP	W	L	Mins	GA	SO	Avg
99-2000	Dubuque Saints	USHL	55	16	35	3	3188	196	0	3.69	....	....	....	....	....	....	....

• Signed Letter of Intent to attend University of New Hampshire, June, 2000.

BACH, Ryan (BAWK, RIGH-yan) FLA.

Goaltender. Catches left. 6'1", 185 lbs. Born, Sherwood Park, Alta., October 21, 1973.
(Detroit's 11th choice, 262nd overall, in 1992 Entry Draft).

			Regular Season								Playoffs						
Season	Club	Lea	GP	W	L	T	Mins	GA	SO	Avg	GP	W	L	Mins	GA	SO	Avg
1991-92	Notre Dame	SJHL	33	16	11	6	1062	124	0	4.00	....	....	....	....	....	....	....
1992-93	Colorado College	WCHA	4	1	3	0	239	11	0	2.76	....	....	....	....	....	....	....
1993-94	Colorado College	WCHA	30	17	7	5	1733	105	0	3.64	....	....	....	....	....	....	....
1994-95	Colorado College	WCHA	27	18	5	1	1522	83	0	3.27	....	....	....	....	....	....	....
1995-96	Colorado College	WCHA	23	*17	4	2	1390	62	2	2.68	....	....	....	....	....	....	....
1996-97	Utica Blizzard	ColHL	2	0	1	1	119	8	0	4.03	....	....	....	....	....	....	....
	Toledo Storm	ECHL	20	5	11	3	1168	74	0	3.80	....	....	....	....	....	....	....
	Adirondack	AHL	13	2	3	1	451	29	0	3.86	1	0	0	46	3	0	3.92
1997-98	Houston Aeros	IHL	43	26	9	6	2452	95	5	2.32	....	....	....	....	....	....	....
1998-99	Utah Grizzlies	IHL	4	2	1	0	197	9	0	2.74	....	....	....	....	....	....	....
	Los Angeles	**NHL**	**3**	**0**	**3**	**0**	**108**	**8**	**0**	**4.44**	....	....	....	....	....	....	....
	Long Beach	IHL	27	10	9	5	1491	74	1	2.98	3	0	2	152	7	0	2.76
99-2000	Louisville	AHL	11	4	4	1	603	33	0	3.28	....	....	....	....	....	....	....
	Wilkes-Barre	AHL	28	8	18	2	1590	100	0	3.77	....	....	....	....	....	....	....
	Kansas City	IHL	6	3	3	0	358	19	0	3.18	....	....	....	....	....	....	....
	NHL Totals		**3**	**0**	**3**	**0**	**108**	**8**	**0**	**4.44**	....	....	....	....	....	....	....

WCHA First All-Star Team (1995, 1996) • NCAA West Second All-American Team (1995) • NCAA West First All-American Team (1996)

Traded to **Los Angeles** by **Detroit** for Los Angeles' 6th round choice (Per Backer) in 2000 Entry Draft, October 22, 1998. Signed as a free agent by **Florida**, July 27, 1999.

BAILEY, Scott (BAY-lee, SKAWT)

Goaltender. Catches left. 6', 195 lbs. Born, Calgary, Alta., May 2, 1972.
(Boston's 3rd choice, 112th overall, in 1992 Entry Draft).

			Regular Season								Playoffs						
Season	Club	Lea	GP	W	L	T	Mins	GA	SO	Avg	GP	W	L	Mins	GA	SO	Avg
1988-89	Moose Jaw	WHL	2	0	1	0	34	7	0	12.35	....	....	....	....	....	....	....
1989-90	Calgary	AAHA	17	....	....	....	991	55	1	3.33	....	....	....	....	....	....	....
1990-91	Spokane Chiefs	WHL	46	33	11	0	2537	157	*4	3.71	....	....	....	....	....	....	....
1991-92	Spokane Chiefs	WHL	65	34	23	5	3798	206	1	3.30	10	5	5	605	43	0	4.26
1992-93	Johnstown Chiefs	ECHL	36	13	15	3	1750	112	1	3.84	....	....	....	....	....	....	....
1993-94	Providence Bruins	AHL	7	2	2	2	377	24	0	3.82	....	....	....	....	....	....	....
	Charlotte	ECHL	36	22	11	3	2180	130	1	3.58	3	1	2	187	12	0	3.83
1994-95	Providence Bruins	AHL	52	25	16	9	2936	147	2	3.00	9	4	4	504	31	*2	3.69
1995-96	**Boston**	**NHL**	**11**	**5**	**1**	**2**	**571**	**31**	**0**	**3.26**	....	....	....	....	....	....	....
	Providence Bruins	AHL	37	15	19	3	2210	120	1	3.26	2	1	1	119	6	0	3.03
1996-97	**Boston**	**NHL**	**8**	**1**	**5**	**0**	**394**	**24**	**0**	**3.65**	....	....	....	....	....	....	....
	Providence Bruins	AHL	31	11	17	2	1735	112	0	3.87	7	3	4	453	23	0	3.05
1997-98	San Antonio	IHL	37	11	17	3	1898	118	1	3.73	....	....	....	....	....	....	....
1998-99	Orlando	IHL	17	5	7	0	749	36	0	2.88	....	....	....	....	....	....	....
	Birmingham Bulls	ECHL	27	16	8	2	1557	90	1	3.47	5	2	3	299	21	0	4.21
99-2000	Tappara Tampere	Finland	6	0	4	2	347	29	0	5.01	....	....	....	....	....	....	....
	Charlotte	ECHL	31	10	16	4	1735	93	2	3.22	....	....	....	....	....	....	....
	Saint John Flames	AHL	4	0	1	0	135	11	0	4.90	....	....	....	....	....	....	....
	NHL Totals		**19**	**6**	**6**	**2**	**965**	**55**	**0**	**3.42**	....	....	....	....	....	....	....

WHL West Second All-Star Team (1991, 1992)

Signed as a free agent by **Charlotte** (ECHL), December 10, 1999. Loaned to **Saint John** (AHL) by **Charlotte** (ECHL), February 6, 2000.

BALES, Mike (BAYLZ, MIGHK) DAL.

Goaltender. Catches left. 6'1", 200 lbs. Born, Prince Albert, Sask., August 6, 1971.
(Boston's 4th choice, 105th overall, in 1990 Entry Draft).

			Regular Season								Playoffs						
Season	Club	Lea	GP	W	L	T	Mins	GA	SO	Avg	GP	W	L	Mins	GA	SO	Avg
1988-89	Estevan Bruins	SJHL	44	....	....	....	2412	197	1	4.90	....	....	....	....	....	....	....
1989-90	Ohio State	CCHA	21	6	13	2	1117	95	0	5.11	....	....	....	....	....	....	....
1990-91	Ohio State	CCHA	*39	11	24	3	*2180	184	0	5.06	....	....	....	....	....	....	....
1991-92	Ohio State	CCHA	36	11	20	5	2060	180	0	5.24	....	....	....	....	....	....	....
1992-93	**Boston**	**NHL**	**1**	**0**	**0**	**0**	**25**	**1**	**0**	**2.40**	....	....	....	....	....	....	....
	Providence Bruins	AHL	44	22	17	0	2363	166	1	4.21	2	0	2	118	8	0	4.07
1993-94	Providence Bruins	AHL	33	9	15	4	1757	130	0	4.44	....	....	....	....	....	....	....
1994-95	P.E.I. Senators	AHL	45	25	16	3	2649	160	2	3.62	9	6	3	530	24	*2	2.72
	Ottawa	**NHL**	**1**	**0**	**0**	**0**	**3**	**0**	**0**	**0.00**	....	....	....	....	....	....	....
1995-96	**Ottawa**	**NHL**	**20**	**2**	**14**	**1**	**1040**	**72**	**0**	**4.15**	....	....	....	....	....	....	....
	P.E.I. Senators	AHL	2	0	2	0	118	11	0	5.58	....	....	....	....	....	....	....
1996-97	**Ottawa**	**NHL**	**1**	**0**	**1**	**0**	**52**	**4**	**0**	**4.62**	....	....	....	....	....	....	....
	Baltimore Bandits	AHL	46	13	21	8	2544	130	3	3.07	....	....	....	....	....	....	....
1997-98	Rochester	AHL	39	13	19	5	2229	127	0	3.42	....	....	....	....	....	....	....
1998-99	Michigan K-Wings	IHL	32	11	17	3	1773	96	1	3.25	....	....	....	....	....	....	....
99-2000	Michigan K-Wings	IHL	25	9	9	5	1341	56	0	2.50	....	....	....	....	....	....	....
	NHL Totals		**23**	**2**	**15**	**1**	**1120**	**77**	**0**	**4.13**	....	....	....	....	....	....	....

Signed as a free agent by **Ottawa**, July 4, 1994. Signed as a free agent by **Buffalo**, September 9, 1997. Signed as a free agent by **Dallas**, July 8, 1998.

BARRASSO, Tom (buh-RAH-soh, TAWM)

Goaltender. Catches right. 6'3", 211 lbs. Born, Boston, MA, March 31, 1965.
(Buffalo's 1st choice, 5th overall, in 1983 Entry Draft).

			Regular Season								Playoffs						
Season	Club	Lea	GP	W	L	T	Mins	GA	SO	Avg	GP	W	L	Mins	GA	SO	Avg
1981-82	Acton-Boxboro	H.S.	23	....	....	....	1035	32	7	1.86	....	....	....	....	....	....	....
1982-83	Acton-Boxboro	H.S.	23	22	0	1	1035	17	10	0.99	....	....	....	....	....	....	....
1983-84	**Buffalo**	**NHL**	**42**	**26**	**12**	**3**	**2475**	**117**	**2**	**2.84**	**3**	**0**	**2**	**139**	**8**	**0**	**3.45**
1984-85	**Buffalo**	**NHL**	**54**	**25**	**18**	**10**	**3248**	**144**	***5**	***2.66**	**5**	**2**	**3**	**300**	**22**	**0**	**4.40**
	Rochester	AHL	5	3	1	1	267	6	1	1.35	....	....	....	....	....	....	....
1985-86	**Buffalo**	**NHL**	**60**	**29**	**24**	**5**	**3561**	**214**	**2**	**3.61**	....	....	....	....	....	....	....
1986-87	**Buffalo**	**NHL**	**46**	**17**	**23**	**2**	**2501**	**152**	**2**	**3.65**	....	....	....	....	....	....	....
1987-88	**Buffalo**	**NHL**	**54**	**25**	**18**	**8**	**3133**	**173**	**2**	**3.31**	**4**	**1**	**3**	**224**	**16**	**0**	**4.29**
1988-89	**Buffalo**	**NHL**	**10**	**2**	**7**	**0**	**545**	**45**	**0**	**4.95**	....	....	....	....	....	....	....
	Pittsburgh	**NHL**	**44**	**18**	**15**	**7**	**2406**	**162**	**0**	**4.04**	**11**	**7**	**4**	**631**	**40**	**0**	**3.80**
1989-90	**Pittsburgh**	**NHL**	**24**	**7**	**12**	**3**	**1294**	**101**	**0**	**4.68**	....	....	....	....	....	....	....
1990-91♦	**Pittsburgh**	**NHL**	**48**	**27**	**16**	**3**	**2754**	**165**	**1**	**3.59**	**20**	**12**	**7**	**1175**	**51**	***1**	***2.60**
1991-92♦	**Pittsburgh**	**NHL**	**57**	**25**	**22**	**9**	**3329**	**196**	**1**	**3.53**	***21**	***16**	**5**	***1233**	**58**	**1**	**2.82**
1992-93	**Pittsburgh**	**NHL**	**63**	***43**	**14**	**5**	**3702**	**186**	**4**	**3.01**	**12**	**7**	**5**	**722**	**35**	***2**	**2.91**
1993-94	**Pittsburgh**	**NHL**	**44**	**22**	**15**	**5**	**2482**	**139**	**2**	**3.36**	**6**	**2**	**4**	**356**	**17**	**0**	**2.87**
1994-95	**Pittsburgh**	**NHL**	**2**	**0**	**1**	**1**	**125**	**8**	**0**	**3.84**	**2**	**0**	**1**	**80**	**8**	**0**	**6.00**
1995-96	**Pittsburgh**	**NHL**	**49**	**29**	**16**	**2**	**2799**	**160**	**2**	**3.43**	**10**	**4**	**5**	**558**	**26**	**1**	**2.80**
1996-97	**Pittsburgh**	**NHL**	**5**	**0**	**5**	**0**	**270**	**26**	**0**	**5.78**	....	....	....	....	....	....	....
1997-98	**Pittsburgh**	**NHL**	**63**	**31**	**14**	**13**	**3542**	**122**	**7**	**2.07**	**6**	**2**	**4**	**376**	**17**	**0**	**2.71**
1998-99	**Pittsburgh**	**NHL**	**43**	**19**	**16**	**3**	**2306**	**98**	**4**	**2.55**	**13**	**6**	**7**	**787**	**35**	**1**	**2.67**
99-2000	**Pittsburgh**	**NHL**	**18**	**5**	**7**	**2**	**870**	**46**	**1**	**3.17**	....	....	....	....	....	....	....
	Ottawa	**NHL**	**7**	**3**	**4**	**0**	**418**	**22**	**0**	**3.16**	**6**	**2**	**4**	**372**	**16**	**0**	**2.58**
	NHL Totals		**733**	**353**	**259**	**81**	**41760**	**2276**	**35**	**3.27**	**119**	**61**	**54**	**6953**	**349**	**6**	**3.01**

NHL All-Rookie Team (1984) • NHL First All-Star Team (1984) • Won Calder Memorial Trophy (1984) • Won Vezina Trophy (1984) • NHL Second All-Star Team (1985, 1993) • Shared William Jennings Trophy with Bob Sauve (1985) • Played in NHL All-Star Game (1985)

Traded to **Pittsburgh** by **Buffalo** with Buffalo's 3rd round choice (Joe Dziedzic) in 1990 Entry Draft for Doug Bodger and Darrin Shannon, November 12, 1988. • Missed majority of 1994-95 season recovering from wrist surgery, January 20, 1995. • Missed majority of 1996-97 season recovering from shoulder injury originally suffered in game vs. Montreal, February 5, 1996. Traded to **Ottawa** by **Pittsburgh** for Ron Tugnutt and Janne Laukkanen, March 14, 2000.

BEAUREGARD, Stephane (BOH-reh-gahrd, STEH-fan) WSH.

Goaltender. Catches right. 5'11", 190 lbs. Born, Cowansville, Que., January 10, 1968.
(Winnipeg's 3rd choice, 52nd overall, in 1988 Entry Draft).

			Regular Season								Playoffs						
Season	Club	Lea	GP	W	L	T	Mins	GA	SO	Avg	GP	W	L	Mins	GA	SO	Avg
1986-87	St-Jean Castors	QMJHL	13	6	7	0	785	58	0	4.43	5	1	3	260	26	0	6.00
1987-88	St-Jean Castors	QMJHL	66	38	20	3	3766	229	2	3.65	7	3	4	423	34	0	4.82
1988-89	Moncton Hawks	AHL	15	4	8	2	824	62	0	4.51	....	....	....	....	....	....	....
	Fort Wayne	IHL	16	9	5	0	830	43	0	3.10	9	4	4	484	21	*1	*2.60
1989-90	**Winnipeg**	**NHL**	**19**	**7**	**8**	**3**	**1079**	**59**	**0**	**3.28**	**4**	**1**	**3**	**238**	**12**	**0**	**3.03**
	Fort Wayne	IHL	33	20	8	3	1949	115	0	3.54	....	....	....	....	....	....	....
1990-91	**Winnipeg**	**NHL**	**16**	**3**	**10**	**1**	**836**	**55**	**0**	**3.95**	....	....	....	....	....	....	....
	Moncton Hawks	AHL	9	3	4	1	504	20	1	2.38	1	1	0	60	1	0	1.00
	Fort Wayne	IHL	32	14	13	2	1761	109	0	3.71	*19	*10	9	*1158	57	0	2.95
1991-92	**Winnipeg**	**NHL**	**26**	**6**	**8**	**6**	**1267**	**61**	**2**	**2.89**	....	....	....	....	....	....	....
1992-93	**Philadelphia**	**NHL**	**16**	**3**	**9**	**0**	**802**	**59**	**0**	**4.41**	....	....	....	....	....	....	....
	Hershey Bears	AHL	13	5	5	3	794	48	0	3.63	....	....	....	....	....	....	....
1993-94	**Winnipeg**	**NHL**	**13**	**0**	**4**	**1**	**418**	**34**	**0**	**4.88**	....	....	....	....	....	....	....
	Moncton Hawks	AHL	37	18	11	6	2082	121	1	3.49	*21	*12	9	*1305	57	*2	2.62
1994-95	Springfield	AHL	24	10	11	3	1381	73	2	3.17	....	....	....	....	....	....	....
1995-96	San Francisco	IHL	*69	*36	24	8	*4022	207	1	3.09	4	1	3	241	10	0	2.49
1996-97	Quebec Rafales	IHL	67	35	20	11	3945	174	4	2.65	9	5	3	498	19	0	2.29
1997-98	Chicago Wolves	IHL	18	10	6	0	917	49	1	3.20	14	10	4	820	36	1	2.63
1998-99	HC Davos	Switz.	*45	....	....	....	2638	151	....	3.44	6	2	4	370	23	0	3.73
99-2000	Schwenningen	DEL	58	....	....	....	*3301	178	4	3.24	....	....	....	....	....	....	....
	NHL Totals		**90**	**19**	**39**	**11**	**4402**	**268**	**2**	**3.65**	**4**	**1**	**3**	**238**	**12**	**0**	**3.03**

QMJHL First All-Star Team (1988) • Canadian Major Junior Goaltender of the year (1988) • IHL First All-Star Team (1996) • Won James Gatschene Memorial Trophy (MVP- IHL) (1996)

Traded to **Buffalo** by **Winnipeg** for Christian Ruuttu and future considerations, June 15, 1992. Traded to **Chicago** by **Buffalo** with Buffalo's 4th round choice (Eric Daze) in 1993 Entry Draft for Dominik Hasek, August 7, 1992. Traded to **Winnipeg** by **Chicago** for Christian Ruuttu, August 10, 1992. Traded to **Philadelphia** by **Winnipeg** for future considerations, October 1, 1992. Traded to **Winnipeg** by **Philadelphia** for future considerations, June 11, 1993. Signed as a free agent by **Washington**, August 20, 1997.

BELFOUR, Ed (BEHL-fohr, EHD) DAL.

Goaltender. Catches left. 5'11", 192 lbs. Born, Carman, Man., April 21, 1965.

			Regular Season								Playoffs						
Season	Club	Lea	GP	W	L	T	Mins	GA	SO	Avg	GP	W	L	Mins	GA	SO	Avg
1983-84	Winkler Flyers	MJHL	14	....	....	....	818	68	0	5.06	....	....	....	....	....	....	....
1984-85	Winkler Flyers	MJHL	34	....	....	....	1973	145	1	4.41	7	....	....	528	41	0	4.66
1985-86	Winkler Flyers	MJHL	33	....	....	....	1943	124	1	3.83	....	....	....	....	....	....	....
1986-87	North Dakota	WCHA	34	29	4	0	2049	81	3	2.43	....	....	....	....	....	....	....
1987-88	Saginaw Hawks	IHL	61	32	25	0	*3446	183	3	3.19	9	4	5	561	33	0	3.53
1988-89	**Chicago**	**NHL**	**23**	**4**	**12**	**3**	**1148**	**74**	**0**	**3.87**	....	....	....	....	....	....	....
	Saginaw Hawks	IHL	29	12	10	0	1760	92	0	3.10	5	2	3	298	14	0	2.82
1989-90	Canada	Nt-Team	33	13	12	6	1808	93	0	3.08	....	....	....	....	....	....	....
	Chicago	**NHL**	....	....	....	....	....	....	....	....	**9**	**4**	**2**	**409**	**17**	**0**	**2.49**
1990-91	**Chicago**	**NHL**	***74**	***43**	**19**	**7**	***4127**	**170**	**4**	***2.47**	**6**	**2**	**4**	**295**	**20**	**0**	**4.07**
1991-92	**Chicago**	**NHL**	**52**	**21**	**18**	**10**	**2928**	**132**	***5**	**2.70**	**18**	**12**	**4**	**949**	**39**	**1**	***2.47**
1992-93	**Chicago**	**NHL**	***71**	**41**	**18**	**11**	***4106**	**177**	***7**	**2.59**	**4**	**0**	**4**	**249**	**13**	**0**	**3.13**
1993-94	**Chicago**	**NHL**	**70**	**37**	**24**	**6**	**3998**	**178**	***7**	**2.67**	**6**	**2**	**4**	**360**	**15**	**0**	**2.50**
1994-95	**Chicago**	**NHL**	**42**	**22**	**15**	**3**	**2450**	**93**	***5**	**2.28**	**16**	**9**	**7**	**1014**	**37**	**1**	**2.19**
1995-96	**Chicago**	**NHL**	**50**	**22**	**17**	**10**	**2956**	**135**	**1**	**2.74**	**9**	**6**	**3**	**666**	**23**	**1**	**2.07**
1996-97	**Chicago**	**NHL**	**33**	**11**	**15**	**6**	**1966**	**88**	**1**	**2.69**	....	....	....	....	....	....	....
	San Jose	**NHL**	**13**	**3**	**9**	**0**	**757**	**43**	**1**	**3.41**	....	....	....	....	....	....	....
1997-98	**Dallas**	**NHL**	**61**	**37**	**12**	**10**	**3581**	**112**	**9**	***1.88**	**17**	**10**	**7**	**1039**	**31**	**1**	***1.79**
1998-99 ♦	**Dallas**	**NHL**	**61**	**35**	**15**	**9**	**3536**	**117**	**5**	**1.99**	***23**	***16**	**7**	***1544**	**43**	***3**	***1.67**
99-2000	**Dallas**	**NHL**	**62**	**32**	**21**	**7**	**3620**	**127**	**4**	**2.10**	***23**	**14**	**9**	**1443**	**45**	***4**	**1.87**
	NHL Totals		**612**	**308**	**195**	**82**	**35173**	**1446**	**49**	**2.47**	**131**	**75**	**51**	**7968**	**283**	**11**	**2.13**

WCHA First All-Star Team (1987) • NCAA Championship All-Tournament Team (1987) • IHL First All-Star Team (1988) • Shared Garry F. Longman Memorial Trophy (Top Rookie - IHL) with John Cullen (1988) • NHL All-Rookie Team (1991) • NHL First All-Star Team (1991, 1993) • Won Trico Goaltender Award (1991) • Won Calder Memorial Trophy (1991) • Won William M. Jennings Trophy (1991, 1993, 1995) • Won Vezina Trophy (1991, 1993) • NHL Second All-Star Team (1995) • Shared William M. Jennings Trophy with Roman Turek (1999) • Played in NHL All-Star Game (1992, 1993, 1996, 1998, 1999)

Signed as a free agent by **Chicago**, September 25, 1987. Traded to **San Jose** by **Chicago** for Chris Terreri, Ulf Dahlen and Michal Sykora, January 25, 1997. Signed as a free agent by **Dallas**, July 2, 1997.

BENDERA, Shane (behn-DEHR-ah) CBJ

Goaltender. Catches left. 6', 170 lbs. Born, St. Albert, Alta., July 13, 1982.
(Columbus' 6th choice, 169th overall, in 2000 Entry Draft).

			Regular Season								Playoffs						
Season	Club	Lea	GP	W	L	T	Mins	GA	SO	Avg	GP	W	L	Mins	GA	SO	Avg
1998-99	Red Deer Rebels	WHL	2	0	1	0	72	7	0	5.83	....	....	....	....	....	....	....
99-2000	Red Deer Rebels	WHL	*69	31	27	9	*4003	202	0	3.03	3	0	2	76	15	0	11.84

BERGQVIST, Per-Ragnar (BUHRG-kvihst, PAIR-RAG-nahr) PHI.

Goaltender. Catches left. 5'11", 183 lbs. Born, Leksand, Sweden, April 11, 1976.
(Philadelphia's 3rd choice, 124th overall, in 1996 Entry Draft).

			Regular Season								Playoffs						
Season	Club	Lea	GP	W	L	T	Mins	GA	SO	Avg	GP	W	L	Mins	GA	SO	Avg
1995-96	Leksands IF	Swede-Jr.	3	....	....	....	180	17	0	5.67	....	....	....	....	....	....	....
	Leksands IF	Sweden	6	....	....	....	327	17	0	3.12	1	....	....	60	1	0	1.00
1996-97	Leksands IF	Sweden	11	....	....	....	660	32	1	2.91	1	....	....	86	5	0	3.49
1997-98	Leksands IF	Sweden	16	....	....	....	909	53	....	3.50	1	0	1	59	5	0	5.08
1998-99	Valerengens IF	Norway	29	....	....	....	1585	52	2	1.96	....	....	....	....	....	....	....
99-2000	Farjestads BK	Sweden	7	....	....	....	379	22	0	3.48	....	....	....	....	....	....	....

BIERK, Zac (BUHRK, ZAK) MIN.

Goaltender. Catches left. 6'4", 205 lbs. Born, Peterborough, Ont., September 17, 1976.
(Tampa Bay's 8th choice, 212th overall, in 1995 Entry Draft).

			Regular Season								Playoffs						
Season	Club	Lea	GP	W	L	T	Mins	GA	SO	Avg	GP	W	L	Mins	GA	SO	Avg
1993-94	Peterborough B's	OJHL	4	....	....	....	205	17	0	4.98	....	....	....	....	....	....	....
	Peterborough	OHL	9	0	4	2	423	37	0	5.22	1	0	0	33	7	0	12.70
1994-95	Peterborough	OHL	35	11	15	5	1779	117	0	3.95	6	2	3	301	24	0	4.78
1995-96	Peterborough	OHL	58	31	16	6	3292	174	2	3.17	*22	*14	7	*1383	83	0	3.60
1996-97	Peterborough	OHL	49	*28	16	0	2744	151	2	3.30	11	6	5	666	35	0	3.15
1997-98	**Tampa Bay**	**NHL**	**13**	**1**	**4**	**1**	**433**	**30**	**0**	**4.16**	....	....	....	....	....	....	....
	Adirondack	AHL	12	1	6	1	557	36	0	3.87	....	....	....	....	....	....	....
1998-99	**Tampa Bay**	**NHL**	**1**	**0**	**1**	**0**	**59**	**2**	**0**	**2.03**	....	....	....	....	....	....	....
	Cleveland	IHL	27	11	12	4	1556	79	0	3.05	....	....	....	....	....	....	....
99-2000	**Tampa Bay**	**NHL**	**12**	**4**	**4**	**1**	**509**	**31**	**0**	**3.65**	....	....	....	....	....	....	....
	Detroit Vipers	IHL	15	4	8	2	846	46	1	3.26	....	....	....	....	....	....	....
	NHL Totals		**26**	**5**	**9**	**2**	**1001**	**63**	**0**	**3.78**	....	....	....	....	....	....	....

OHL First All-Star Team (1997)

• Missed remainder of 1998-99 season recovering from Meniere's Disease which was diagnosed on March 25, 1999. Selected by **Minnesota** from **Tampa Bay** in Expansion Draft, June 23, 2000.

BILLINGTON, Craig (BIHL-lihng-TOHN, KRAYG) WSH.

Goaltender. Catches left. 5'10", 170 lbs. Born, London, Ont., September 11, 1966.
(New Jersey's 2nd choice, 23rd overall, in 1984 Entry Draft).

			Regular Season								Playoffs						
Season	Club	Lea	GP	W	L	T	Mins	GA	SO	Avg	GP	W	L	Mins	GA	SO	Avg
1982-83	London Diamonds	OJHL-B	23	....	....	....	1338	76	0	3.41	....	....	....	....	....	....	....
1983-84	Belleville Bulls	OHL	44	20	19	0	2335	162	1	4.16	1	0	0	30	3	0	6.00
1984-85	Belleville Bulls	OHL	47	26	19	0	2544	180	1	4.25	14	7	5	761	47	1	3.71
1985-86	Belleville Bulls	OHL	3	2	1	0	180	11	0	3.67	20	9	6	1133	68	0	3.60
	New Jersey	**NHL**	**18**	**4**	**9**	**1**	**901**	**77**	**0**	**5.13**	....	....	....	....	....	....	....
1986-87	**New Jersey**	**NHL**	**22**	**4**	**13**	**2**	**1114**	**89**	**0**	**4.79**	....	....	....	....	....	....	....
	Maine Mariners	AHL	20	9	8	2	1151	70	0	3.65	....	....	....	....	....	....	....
1987-88	Utica Devils	AHL	*59	22	27	8	*3404	208	1	3.67	....	....	....	....	....	....	....
1988-89	**New Jersey**	**NHL**	**3**	**1**	**1**	**0**	**140**	**11**	**0**	**4.71**	....	....	....	....	....	....	....
	Utica Devils	AHL	41	17	18	6	2432	150	2	3.70	4	1	3	220	18	0	4.91
1989-90	Utica Devils	AHL	38	20	13	1	2087	138	0	3.97	....	....	....	....	....	....	....
1990-91	Canada	Nt-Team	34	17	14	2	1879	110	2	3.51	....	....	....	....	....	....	....
1991-92	**New Jersey**	**NHL**	**26**	**13**	**7**	**1**	**1363**	**69**	**2**	**3.04**	....	....	....	....	....	....	....
1992-93	**New Jersey**	**NHL**	**42**	**21**	**16**	**4**	**2389**	**146**	**2**	**3.67**	**2**	**0**	**1**	**78**	**5**	**0**	**3.85**
1993-94	**Ottawa**	**NHL**	**63**	**11**	**41**	**4**	**3319**	**254**	**0**	**4.59**	....	....	....	....	....	....	....
1994-95	**Ottawa**	**NHL**	**9**	**0**	**6**	**2**	**472**	**32**	**0**	**4.07**	....	....	....	....	....	....	....
	Boston	**NHL**	**8**	**5**	**1**	**0**	**373**	**19**	**0**	**3.06**	**1**	**0**	**0**	**25**	**1**	**0**	**2.40**
1995-96	**Boston**	**NHL**	**27**	**10**	**13**	**3**	**1380**	**79**	**1**	**3.43**	**1**	**0**	**1**	**60**	**6**	**0**	**6.00**
1996-97	**Colorado**	**NHL**	**23**	**11**	**8**	**2**	**1200**	**53**	**1**	**2.65**	**1**	**0**	**0**	**20**	**1**	**0**	**3.00**
1997-98	**Colorado**	**NHL**	**23**	**8**	**7**	**4**	**1162**	**45**	**1**	**2.32**	**1**	**0**	**0**	**1**	**0**	**0**	**0.00**
1998-99	**Colorado**	**NHL**	**21**	**11**	**8**	**1**	**1086**	**52**	**0**	**2.87**	**1**	**0**	**0**	**9**	**1**	**0**	**6.67**
99-2000	**Washington**	**NHL**	**13**	**3**	**6**	**1**	**611**	**28**	**2**	**2.75**	**1**	**0**	**0**	**20**	**1**	**0**	**3.00**
	NHL Totals		**298**	**102**	**136**	**25**	**15510**	**954**	**9**	**3.69**	**8**	**0**	**2**	**213**	**15**	**0**	**4.23**

OHL First All-Star Team (1985) • Played in NHL All-Star Game (1993)

Traded to **Ottawa** by **New Jersey** with Troy Mallette and New Jersey's 4th round choice (Cosmo Dupaul) in 1993 Entry Draft for Peter Sidorkiewicz and future considerations (Mike Peluso, June 26, 1993), June 20, 1993. Traded to **Boston** by **Ottawa** for NY Islanders' 8th round choice (previously acquired, Ottawa selected Ray Schultz) in 1995 Entry Draft, April 7, 1995. Signed as a free agent by **Florida**, September 5, 1996. Claimed by **Colorado** from **Florida** in NHL Waiver Draft, September 30, 1996. Traded to **Washington** by **Colorado** for future considerations, July 16, 1999.

BIRON, Martin (BIH-rohn, MAHR-tihn) BUF.

Goaltender. Catches left. 6'2", 163 lbs. Born, Lac St. Charles, Que., August 15, 1977.
(Buffalo's 2nd choice, 16th overall, in 1995 Entry Draft).

			Regular Season								Playoffs						
Season	Club	Lea	GP	W	L	T	Mins	GA	SO	Avg	GP	W	L	Mins	GA	SO	Avg
1993-94	Trois-Rivieres	QAAA	23	14	8	1	1412	80	1	3.40	....	....	....	....	....	....	....
1994-95	Beauport Harfangs	QMJHL	56	29	16	9	3193	132	3	*2.48	16	8	7	900	37	*4	2.47
1995-96	Beauport Harfangs	QMJHL	55	29	17	7	3201	152	1	2.85	*19	*12	7	1134	64	0	3.39
	Buffalo	**NHL**	**3**	**0**	**2**	**0**	**119**	**10**	**0**	**5.04**	....	....	....	....	....	....	....
1996-97	Beauport Harfangs	QMJHL	18	6	9	1	928	61	1	3.94	....	....	....	....	....	....	....
	Hull Olympiques	QMJHL	16	11	4	1	974	43	2	2.65	6	3	1	325	19	0	3.51
1997-98	South Carolina	ECHL	2	0	1	1	86	3	0	2.09	....	....	....	....	....	....	....
	Rochester	AHL	41	14	18	6	2312	113	*5	2.93	4	1	3	239	16	0	4.01
1998-99	**Buffalo**	**NHL**	**6**	**1**	**2**	**1**	**281**	**10**	**0**	**2.14**	....	....	....	....	....	....	....
	Rochester	AHL	52	36	13	3	3129	108	*6	*2.07	*20	12	8	1167	42	1	*2.16
99-2000	**Buffalo**	**NHL**	**41**	**19**	**18**	**2**	**2229**	**90**	**5**	**2.42**	....	....	....	....	....	....	....
	Rochester	AHL	6	6	0	0	344	12	1	2.09	....	....	....	....	....	....	....
	NHL Totals		**50**	**20**	**22**	**3**	**2629**	**110**	**5**	**2.51**	....	....	....	....	....	....	....

Canadian Major Junior First All-Star Team (1995) • Canadian Major Junior Goaltender of the Year (1995) • AHL First All-Star Team (1999) • Shared Harry "Hap" Holmes Memorial Trophy (fewest goals against - AHL) with Tom Draper (1999) • Won Baz Bastien Memorial Trophy (Top Goaltender - AHL) (1999)

BLACKBURN, Josh (BLAK-buhrn, JAWSH) PHX.

Goaltender. Catches left. 6', 185 lbs. Born, Delrio, TX, November 13, 1978.
(Phoenix's 6th choice, 116th overall, in 1998 Entry Draft).

			Regular Season								Playoffs						
Season	Club	Lea	GP	W	L	T	Mins	GA	SO	Avg	GP	W	L	Mins	GA	SO	Avg
1996-97	Dubuque Saints	USHL	52	15	32	3	2979	185	1	3.72	....	....	....	....	....	....	....
1997-98	Dubuque Saints	USHL	17	11	15	1	1605	94	0	3.51	....	....	....	....	....	....	....
	Lincoln Stars	USHL	17	13	4	0	1004	41	1	2.45	9	4	5	522	29	0	....
1998-99	U. of Michigan	CCHA	*42	*25	10	6	*2398	91	3	2.28	....	....	....	....	....	....	....
99-2000	U. of Michigan	CCHA	22	14	4	4	1337	53	1	2.38	....	....	....	....	....	....	....

CCHA Second All-Star Team (1999) • NCAA West First All-American Team (1999)

BOUCHER, Brian (BOO-shay, BRIGH-an) PHI.

Goaltender. Catches left. 6'1", 190 lbs. Born, Woonsocket, RI, January 2, 1977.
(Philadelphia's 1st choice, 22nd overall, in 1995 Entry Draft).

			Regular Season								Playoffs						
Season	Club	Lea	GP	W	L	T	Mins	GA	SO	Avg	GP	W	L	Mins	GA	SO	Avg
1993-94	Mount St. Charles	H.S.	15	*14	0	1	*504	*8	*9	*0.57	4	*4	0	*180	*6	*1	*1.20
1994-95	Wexford Raiders	OJHL	8	....	....	....	425	23	0	3.25	....	....	....	....	....	....	....
	Tri-City Americans	WHL	35	17	11	2	1969	108	1	3.29	13	6	5	795	50	0	3.77
1995-96	Tri-City Americans	WHL	55	33	19	2	3183	181	1	3.41	11	6	5	653	37	*2	3.40
1996-97	Tri-City Americans	WHL	41	10	24	6	2458	149	1	3.64	....	....	....	....	....	....	....
1997-98	Philadelphia	AHL	34	16	12	3	1901	101	0	3.19	2	0	0	30	1	0	1.95
1998-99	Philadelphia	AHL	36	20	8	5	2061	89	2	2.59	16	9	7	947	45	0	2.85
99-2000	**Philadelphia**	**NHL**	**35**	**20**	**10**	**3**	**2038**	**65**	**4**	***1.91**	**18**	**11**	**7**	**1183**	**40**	**1**	**2.03**
	Philadelphia	AHL	1	0	0	1	65	3	0	2.77	....	....	....	....	....	....	....
	NHL Totals		**35**	**20**	**10**	**3**	**2038**	**65**	**4**	**1.91**	**18**	**11**	**7**	**1183**	**40**	**1**	**2.03**

WHL West Second All-Star Team (1996) • WHL West First All-Star Team (1997) • NHL All-Rookie Team (2000)

BRATHWAITE, Fred (BRAYTH-wayt, FREHD) CGY.

Goaltender. Catches left. 5'7", 175 lbs. Born, Ottawa, Ont., November 24, 1972.

			Regular Season								Playoffs						
Season	Club	Lea	GP	W	L	T	Mins	GA	SO	Avg	GP	W	L	Mins	GA	SO	Avg
1988-89	Smiths Falls Bears	OJHL	38	16	18	1	2130	187	0	5.27	....	....	....	....	....	....	....
1989-90	OrilliaTerriers	OJHL-B	15	....	....	....	782	47	0	3.61	....	....	....	....	....	....	....
	Oshawa Generals	OHL	20	11	2	1	886	43	1	2.91	10	4	2	451	22	0	*2.93
1990-91	Oshawa Generals	OHL	39	25	6	3	1986	112	1	3.38	13	*9	2	677	43	0	3.81
1991-92	Oshawa Generals	OHL	24	12	7	2	1248	81	0	3.89	....	....	....	....	....	....	....
	London Knights	OHL	23	15	6	2	1325	61	*4	2.76	10	5	5	615	36	0	3.51
1992-93	Detroit Jr. Wings	OHL	37	23	10	4	2192	134	0	3.67	15	9	6	858	48	1	3.36
1993-94	**Edmonton**	**NHL**	**19**	**3**	**10**	**3**	**982**	**58**	**0**	**3.54**	....	....	....	....	....	....	....
	Cape Breton Oilers	AHL	2	1	1	0	119	6	0	3.04	....	....	....	....	....	....	....
1994-95	**Edmonton**	**NHL**	**14**	**2**	**5**	**1**	**601**	**40**	**0**	**3.99**	....	....	....	....	....	....	....
1995-96	**Edmonton**	**NHL**	**7**	**0**	**2**	**0**	**293**	**12**	**0**	**2.46**	....	....	....	....	....	....	....
	Cape Breton Oilers	AHL	31	12	16	0	1699	110	1	3.88	....	....	....	....	....	....	....
1996-97	Manitoba Moose	IHL	58	22	22	5	2945	167	1	3.40	....	....	....	....	....	....	....
1997-98	Manitoba Moose	IHL	51	23	18	4	2736	138	1	3.03	2	0	1	72	4	0	3.30
1998-99	Canada	Nt-Team	24	6	8	3	989	47	2	2.85	....	....	....	....	....	....	....
	Calgary	**NHL**	**28**	**11**	**9**	**7**	**1663**	**68**	**1**	**2.45**	....	....	....	....	....	....	....
99-2000	**Calgary**	**NHL**	**61**	**25**	**25**	**7**	**3448**	**158**	**5**	**2.75**	....	....	....	....	....	....	....
	Saint John Flames	AHL	2	2	0	0	120	4	0	2.00	....	....	....	....	....	....	....
	NHL Totals		**129**	**41**	**51**	**18**	**6987**	**336**	**6**	**2.89**	....	....	....	....	....	....	....

• Scored a goal while with Detroit (OHL), April 20, 1993. • Scored a goal while with Manitoba (IHL), November 9, 1996.

Signed as a free agent by **Edmonton**, October 6, 1993. Signed as a free agent by **Calgary**, January 6, 1999.

BROCHU, Martin (broh-SHOO, MAHR-tihn) CGY.

Goaltender. Catches left. 6', 199 lbs. Born, Anjou, Que., March 10, 1973.

			Regular Season								Playoffs						
Season	Club	Lea	GP	W	L	T	Mins	GA	SO	Avg	GP	W	L	Mins	GA	SO	Avg
1989-90	Montreal-Bourassa	QAAA	27	11	14	1	1471	103	3	4.20	3	1	2	193	10	1	3.10
1990-91	Granby Bisons	QMJHL	16	6	5	0	622	39	....	3.76	....	....	....	....	....	....	....
1991-92	Granby Bisons	QMJHL	52	15	29	2	2772	278	0	4.72	....	....	....	....	....	....	....
1992-93	Hull Olympiques	QMJHL	29	9	15	1	1453	137	0	5.66	2	0	1	69	7	0	6.07
1993-94	Fredericton	AHL	32	10	11	3	1505	76	2	3.03	....	....	....	....	....	....	....
1994-95	Fredericton	AHL	44	18	18	4	2475	145	0	3.51	....	....	....	....	....	....	....
1995-96	Fredericton	AHL	17	6	8	2	986	70	0	4.26	....	....	....	....	....	....	....
	Wheeling	ECHL	19	10	6	2	1060	51	1	2.89	....	....	....	....	....	....	....
	Portland Pirates	AHL	5	2	2	1	287	15	0	3.14	12	7	4	700	28	*2	*2.40
1996-97	Portland Pirates	AHL	55	23	17	7	2962	150	2	3.04	5	2	3	324	13	0	2.41
1997-98	Portland Pirates	AHL	37	16	14	1	1926	96	2	2.99	6	3	2	296	16	0	3.24
1998-99	**Washington**	**NHL**	**2**	**0**	**2**	**0**	**120**	**6**	**0**	**3.00**	....	....	....	....	....	....	....
	Portland Pirates	AHL	20	6	10	3	1164	57	2	2.94	....	....	....	....	....	....	....
	Utah Grizzlies	IHL	5	1	3	1	298	13	0	2.62	....	....	....	....	....	....	....
99-2000	Portland Pirates	AHL	54	32	15	6	3192	116	4	2.18	2	0	2	80	7	0	5.27
	NHL Totals		**2**	**0**	**2**	**0**	**120**	**6**	**0**	**3.00**	....	....	....	....	....	....	....

AHL First All-Star Team (2000) • Won Baz Bastien Memorial Trophy (Top Goaltender - AHL) (2000) • Won Les Cunningham Award (MVP - AHL) (2000)

Signed as a free agent by **Montreal**, September 22, 1992. Traded to **Washington** by **Montreal** for future considerations, March 15, 1996. Signed as a free agent by **Calgary**, August 25, 2000.

BRODEUR, Martin (broh-DOOR, MAHR-tihn) N.J.

Goaltender. Catches left. 6'2", 205 lbs. Born, Montreal, Que., May 6, 1972.
(New Jersey's 1st choice, 20th overall, in 1990 Entry Draft).

			Regular Season								Playoffs						
Season	Club	Lea	GP	W	L	T	Mins	GA	SO	Avg	GP	W	L	Mins	GA	SO	Avg
1988-89	Montreal-Bourassa	QAAA	27	13	12	1	1580	98	0	3.72	....	....	....	....	....	....	....
1989-90	St-Hyacinthe	QMJHL	42	23	13	2	2333	156	0	4.01	12	5	7	678	46	0	4.07
1990-91	St-Hyacinthe	QMJHL	52	22	24	4	2946	162	2	3.30	4	0	4	232	16	0	4.14
1991-92	St-Hyacinthe	QMJHL	48	27	16	4	2846	161	2	3.39	5	2	3	317	14	0	2.65
	New Jersey	**NHL**	**4**	**2**	**1**	**0**	**179**	**10**	**0**	**3.35**	**1**	**0**	**1**	**32**	**3**	**0**	**5.63**
1992-93	Utica Devils	AHL	32	14	13	5	1952	131	0	4.03	4	1	3	258	18	0	4.19
1993-94	**New Jersey**	**NHL**	**47**	**27**	**11**	**8**	**2625**	**105**	**3**	**2.40**	**17**	**8**	**9**	**1171**	**38**	**1**	**1.95**
1994-95♦	**New Jersey**	**NHL**	**40**	**19**	**11**	**6**	**2184**	**89**	**3**	**2.45**	***20**	***16**	**4**	***1222**	**34**	***3**	***1.67**
1995-96	**New Jersey**	**NHL**	**77**	**34**	**30**	**12**	***4433**	**173**	**6**	**2.34**	....	....	....	....	....	....	....
1996-97	**New Jersey**	**NHL**	**67**	**37**	**14**	**13**	**3838**	**120**	***10**	***1.88**	**10**	**5**	**5**	**659**	**19**	**2**	***1.73**
1997-98	**New Jersey**	**NHL**	**70**	***43**	**17**	**8**	**4128**	**130**	**10**	**1.89**	**6**	**2**	**4**	**366**	**12**	**0**	**1.97**
1998-99	**New Jersey**	**NHL**	***70**	***39**	**21**	**10**	***4239**	**162**	**4**	**2.29**	**7**	**3**	**4**	**425**	**20**	**0**	**2.82**
99-2000♦	**New Jersey**	**NHL**	**72**	***43**	**20**	**8**	**4312**	**161**	**6**	**2.24**	***23**	***16**	**7**	***1450**	**39**	**2**	***1.61**
	NHL Totals		**447**	**244**	**125**	**65**	**25938**	**950**	**42**	**2.20**	**84**	**50**	**34**	**5325**	**165**	**8**	**1.86**

QMJHL Second All-Star Team (1992) • NHL All-Rookie Team (1994) • Won Calder Memorial Trophy (1994) • NHL Second All-Star Team (1997, 1998) • Shared William M. Jennings Trophy with Mike Dunham (1997) • Won William M. Jennings Trophy (1998) • Played in NHL All-Star Game (1996, 1997, 1998, 1999, 2000)

• Scored a goal in playoffs vs. Montreal, April 17, 1997.

BRUMBY, David MIN.

Goaltender. Catches Left. 6'1", 190 lbs. Born, Victoria, B.C., May 21, 1975.
(Toronto's 6th choice, 201st overall, in 1993 Entry Draft).

			Regular Season								Playoffs						
Season	Club	Lea	GP	W	L	T	Mins	GA	SO	Avg	GP	W	L	Mins	GA	SO	Avg
1992-93	Tri-City Americans	WHL	30	13	12	0	1529	123	0	4.83	4	0	4	240	20	0	5.00
1993-94	Tri-City Americans	WHL	28	7	16	2	1518	132	0	5.22	2	1	1	120	9	0	4.50
1994-95	Tri-City Americans	WHL	15	5	6	1	851	60	0	4.23	....	....	....	....	....	....	....
	Regina Pats	WHL	4	0	3	0	230	15	0	3.91	....	....	....	....	....	....	....
	Lethbridge	WHL	19	6	11	0	1036	78	0	4.52	....	....	....	....	....	....	....
1995-96	Lethbridge	WHL	50	19	20	2	2502	133	1	3.19	4	0	3	262	14	0	3.21
1996-97	Columbus Chill	ECHL	18	9	5	2	997	68	0	4.09	1	0	0	9	0	0	0.00
	Baltimore Bandits	AHL	2	0	1	0	60	7	0	7.00	....	....	....	....	....	....	....
1997-98	Columbus Chill	ECHL	18	8	8	1	1015	46	*2	2.72	....	....	....	....	....	....	....
	Wheeling Nailers	ECHL	23	15	4	4	1348	64	*2	2.85	15	8	7	983	36	*2	2.24
	Cleveland	IHL	2	0	1	0	99	4	0	2.42	....	....	....	....	....	....	....
1998-99	Wheeling Nailers	ECHL	31	11	14	4	1741	89	0	3.07	....	....	....	....	....	....	....
	Providence Bruins	AHL	2	1	1	0	119	6	0	3.02	....	....	....	....	....	....	....
	Charlotte	ECHL	6	3	1	0	300	18	0	3.60	....	....	....	....	....	....	....
99-2000	Jackson Bandits	ECHL	*59	28	25	4	3368	167	*7	2.97	....	....	....	....	....	....	....
	Providence Bruins	AHL	1	1	0	0	61	1	0	0.98	....	....	....	....	....	....	....

Signed as a free agent by **Minnesota**, June 7, 2000.

BRYZGALOV, Ilja (breez-GAH-lahf, ihl-YUH) ANA.

Goaltender. Catches left. 6'3", 196 lbs. Born, Togliatti, USSR, June 22, 1980.
(Anaheim's 2nd choice, 44th overall, in 2000 Entry Draft).

			Regular Season								Playoffs						
Season	Club	Lea	GP	W	L	T	Mins	GA	SO	Avg	GP	W	L	Mins	GA	SO	Avg
1997-98	Lada Togliatti-2	Russia-3	8	....	....	....	480	28	....	3.50	....	....	....	....	....	....	....
1998-99	Lada Togliatti-2	Russia-4	20	....	....	....	1200	43	....	2.15	....	....	....	....	....	....	....
99-2000	Spartak Moscow	Russia-2	9	....	....	....	500	21	....	2.52	....	....	....	....	....	....	....
	Lada Togliatti	Russia	14	....	....	....	796	18	3	1.36	7	....	....	407	10	1	1.47

BURKE, Sean (BUHRK, SHAWN)

Goaltender. Catches left. 6'4", 210 lbs. Born, Windsor, Ont., January 29, 1967.
(New Jersey's 2nd choice, 24th overall, in 1985 Entry Draft).

			Regular Season								Playoffs						
Season	Club	Lea	GP	W	L	T	Mins	GA	SO	Avg	GP	W	L	Mins	GA	SO	Avg
1983-84	St. Michael's	OJHL-B	25	....	....	....	1482	120	0	4.86	....	....	....	....	....	....	....
1984-85	Toronto Marlies	OHL	49	25	21	3	2987	211	0	4.24	5	1	3	266	25	0	5.64
1985-86	Toronto Marlies	OHL	47	16	27	3	2840	233	0	4.92	4	0	4	238	24	0	6.05
1986-87	Canada	Nt-Team	42	27	13	2	2550	130	0	3.05	....	....	....	....	....	....	....
1987-88	Canada	Nt-Team	37	19	9	2	1962	92	1	2.81	....	....	....	....	....	....	....
	Canada	Olympics	4	1	2	1	238	12	....	3.02	....	....	....	....	....	....	....
	New Jersey	**NHL**	**13**	**10**	**1**	**0**	**689**	**35**	**1**	**3.05**	**17**	**9**	**8**	**1001**	**57**	***1**	**3.42**
1988-89	**New Jersey**	**NHL**	**62**	**22**	**31**	**9**	**3590**	**230**	**3**	**3.84**	....	....	....	....	....	....	....
1989-90	**New Jersey**	**NHL**	**52**	**22**	**22**	**6**	**2914**	**175**	**0**	**3.60**	**2**	**0**	**2**	**125**	**8**	**0**	**3.84**
1990-91	**New Jersey**	**NHL**	**35**	**8**	**12**	**8**	**1870**	**112**	**0**	**3.59**	....	....	....	....	....	....	....
1991-92	Canada	Nt-Team	31	18	6	4	1721	75	1	2.61	....	....	....	....	....	....	....
	Canada	Olympics	7	5	2	0	429	17	0	2.37	....	....	....	....	....	....	....
	San Diego Gulls	IHL	7	4	2	1	424	17	0	2.41	3	0	3	160	13	0	4.88
1992-93	**Hartford**	**NHL**	**50**	**16**	**27**	**3**	**2656**	**184**	**0**	**4.16**	....	....	....	....	....	....	....
1993-94	**Hartford**	**NHL**	**47**	**17**	**24**	**5**	**2750**	**137**	**2**	**2.99**	....	....	....	....	....	....	....
1994-95	**Hartford**	**NHL**	**42**	**17**	**19**	**4**	**2418**	**108**	**0**	**2.68**	....	....	....	....	....	....	....
1995-96	**Hartford**	**NHL**	**66**	**28**	**28**	**6**	**3669**	**190**	**4**	**3.11**	....	....	....	....	....	....	....
1996-97	**Hartford**	**NHL**	**51**	**22**	**22**	**6**	**2985**	**134**	**4**	**2.69**	....	....	....	....	....	....	....
1997-98	**Carolina**	**NHL**	**25**	**7**	**11**	**5**	**1415**	**66**	**1**	**2.80**	....	....	....	....	....	....	....
	Vancouver	**NHL**	**16**	**2**	**9**	**4**	**838**	**49**	**0**	**3.51**	....	....	....	....	....	....	....
	Philadelphia	**NHL**	**11**	**7**	**3**	**0**	**632**	**27**	**1**	**2.56**	**5**	**1**	**4**	**283**	**17**	**0**	**3.60**
1998-99	**Florida**	**NHL**	**59**	**21**	**24**	**14**	**3402**	**151**	**3**	**2.66**	....	....	....	....	....	....	....
99-2000	**Florida**	**NHL**	**7**	**2**	**5**	**0**	**418**	**18**	**0**	**2.58**	....	....	....	....	....	....	....
	Phoenix	**NHL**	**35**	**17**	**14**	**3**	**2074**	**88**	**3**	**2.55**	**5**	**1**	**4**	**296**	**16**	**0**	**3.24**
	NHL Totals		**571**	**218**	**252**	**73**	**32320**	**1704**	**22**	**3.16**	**29**	**11**	**18**	**1705**	**98**	**1**	**3.45**

Played in NHL All-Star Game (1989)

Traded to **Hartford** by **New Jersey** with Eric Weinrich for Bobby Holik and Hartford's 2nd round choice (Jay Pandolfo) in 1993 Entry Draft, August 28, 1992. Transferred to **Carolina** after **Hartford** franchise relocated, June 25, 1997. Traded to **Vancouver** by **Carolina** with Geoff Sanderson and Enrico Ciccone for Kirk McLean and Martin Gelinas, January 3, 1998. Traded to **Philadelphia** by **Vancouver** for Garth Snow, March 4, 1998. Signed as a free agent by **Florida**, September 12, 1998. Traded to **Phoenix** by **Florida** with Florida's 5th round choice (Nate Kiser) in 2000 Entry Draft for Mikhail Shtalenkov and Phoenix's 4th round choice (Chris Eade) in 2000 Entry Draft, November 18, 1999.

BUZAK, Mike (BOO-zehk, MIGHK)

Goaltender. Catches left. 6'3", 220 lbs. Born, Edson, Alta., February 10, 1973.
(St. Louis' 5th choice, 167th overall, in 1993 Entry Draft).

			Regular Season								Playoffs						
Season	Club	Lea	GP	W	L	T	Mins	GA	SO	Avg	GP	W	L	Mins	GA	SO	Avg
1991-92	Michigan State	CCHA	7	4	0	0	311	22	0	4.25	....	....	....	....	....	....	....
1992-93	Michigan State	CCHA	38	22	10	2	*2090	102	0	2.93	....	....	....	....	....	....	....
1993-94	Michigan State	CCHA	*39	21	12	5	*2297	104	2	2.72	....	....	....	....	....	....	....
1994-95	Michigan State	CCHA	31	17	10	3	1796	94	0	3.14	....	....	....	....	....	....	....
1995-96	Worcester	AHL	30	9	10	5	1672	85	0	3.05	....	....	....	....	....	....	....
1996-97	Baton Rouge	ECHL	3	0	2	0	108	7	0	3.87	....	....	....	....	....	....	....
	Worcester	AHL	19	9	4	3	972	41	1	2.53	1	0	1	58	3	0	3.06
1997-98	Long Beach	IHL	31	18	6	5	1763	58	*6	*1.97	5	0	3	215	11	0	3.06
	Tucson	WCHL	2	0	2	0	106	6	0	3.37	....	....	....	....	....	....	....
	Phoenix	WCHL	6	3	3	0	357	27	0	4.53	....	....	....	....	....	....	....
1998-99	Albany River Rats	AHL	48	22	13	3	2382	102	0	2.57	5	2	1	272	12	0	2.65
99-2000	Albany River Rats	AHL	14	3	9	2	776	41	1	3.17	....	....	....	....	....	....	....
	Augusta Lynx	ECHL	3	2	0	0	150	11	0	4.40	....	....	....	....	....	....	....
	Milwaukee	IHL	8	2	5	0	426	24	0	3.38	....	....	....	....	....	....	....
	Utah Grizzlies	IHL	4	0	1	1	168	7	0	2.50	....	....	....	....	....	....	....

CCHA Second All-Star Team (1994, 1995) • Shared James Norris Memorial Trophy (fewest goals against - IHL) with Kay Whitmore (1998)

Signed as a free agent by **New Jersey**, August 14, 1998.

CAMPBELL, Cory (KAM-behl, KOHRY) L.A.

Goaltender. Catches left. 5'11", 195 lbs. Born, Stratford, Ont., July 27, 1981.
(Los Angeles' 4th choice, 92nd overall, in 1999 Entry Draft).

			Regular Season								Playoffs						
Season	Club	Lea	GP	W	L	T	Mins	GA	SO	Avg	GP	W	L	Mins	GA	SO	Avg
1997-98	Waterloo Siskins	OMHA	19	....	....	....	795	31	4	1.75	....	....	....	....	....	....	....
1998-99	Belleville Bulls	OHL	46	28	13	4	2679	156	1	3.49	21	*16	5	1296	65	0	3.01
99-2000	Belleville Bulls	OHL	43	24	14	2	2458	138	0	3.37	13	7	5	685	36	0	3.15

Memorial Cup All-Star Team (1999) • Won Hap Emms Memorial Trophy (Memorial Cup Tournament Top Goaltender) (1999)

CARON, Sebastian (KAIR-aw, suh-BAS-tee-yeh) PIT.

Goaltender. Catches left. 6'1", 160 lbs. Born, Amqui, Que., June 25, 1980.
(Pittsburgh's 4th choice, 86th overall, in 1999 Entry Draft).

			Regular Season								Playoffs						
Season	Club	Lea	GP	W	L	T	Mins	GA	SO	Avg	GP	W	L	Mins	GA	SO	Avg
1997-98	TGV Pentagone	QAAA	17	....	....	....	762	48	1	2.84	....	....	....	....	....	....	....
1998-99	Rimouski Oceanic	QMJHL	30	13	10	3	1570	85	0	3.25	2	1	0	68	0	0	0.00
99-2000	Rimouski Oceanic	QMJHL	54	*38	11	3	3040	179	1	3.53	14	*12	2	828	50	0	3.62

• Memorial Cup All-Star Team (2000) • Won Hap Emms Memorial Trophy (Memorial Cup Tournament Top Goaltender) (2000)

CASSIVI, Frederic (KASS-ih-vee, FREHD-uhr-IHK) COL.

Goaltender. Catches left. 6'4", 205 lbs. Born, Sorel, Que., June 12, 1975.
(Ottawa's 7th choice, 210th overall, in 1994 Entry Draft).

			Regular Season								Playoffs						
Season	Club	Lea	GP	W	L	T	Mins	GA	SO	Avg	GP	W	L	Mins	GA	SO	Avg
1993-94	St-Hyacinthe	QMJHL	35	15	13	3	1751	127	1	4.35	....	....	....	....	....	....	....
1994-95	Halifax	QMJHL	24	9	12	1	1362	105	0	4.63	....	....	....	....	....	....	....
	St-Jean Lynx	QMJHL	19	12	6	0	1021	55	1	3.23	5	2	3	258	18	0	4.19
1995-96	Thunder Bay	ColHL	12	6	4	2	715	51	0	4.28	....	....	....	....	....	....	....
	P.E.I. Senators	AHL	41	20	14	3	2347	128	1	3.27	5	2	3	317	24	0	4.54
1996-97	Syracuse Crunch	AHL	55	23	22	8	3069	164	2	3.21	1	0	1	60	3	0	3.01
1997-98	Worcester	AHL	45	20	22	2	2593	140	1	3.24	6	3	3	326	18	0	3.31
1998-99	Cincinnati	IHL	44	21	17	2	2418	123	1	3.05	3	1	2	139	6	0	2.59
99-2000	Hershey Bears	AHL	31	14	9	3	1554	78	1	3.01	2	0	1	63	5	0	4.75

Signed as a free agent by **Colorado**, August 17, 1999.

CECHMANEK, Roman (chehkh-MAN-ehk) PHI.

Goaltender. Catches left. 6'3", 176 lbs. Born, Gottwaldov, Czech., March 2, 1971.
(Philadelphia's 3rd choice, 171st overall, in 2000 Entry Draft).

			Regular Season								Playoffs						
Season	Club	Lea	GP	W	L	T	Mins	GA	SO	Avg	GP	W	L	Mins	GA	SO	Avg
1994-95	HC Vsetin	Cze-Rep	41	....	....	....	2413	98	5	2.44	11	....	....	619	23	1	2.23
1995-96	HC Vsetin	Cze-Rep	36	....	....	....	2142	77	4	2.16	13	....	....	783	17	2	1.30
1996-97	HC Vsetin	Cze-Rep	48	....	....	....	2762	98	3	2.13	10	....	....	602	11	2	1.10
1997-98	HC Vsetin	Cze-Rep	41	....	....	....	2306	76	....	1.98	10	....	....	600	16	1	1.60
1998-99	HC Vsetin	Cze-Rep	45	....	....	....	2696	77	....	1.71	12	....	....	747	23	1	1.85
99-2000	HC Vsetin	Cze-Rep	37	....	....	....	2141	88	....	2.47	9	....	....	545	15	....	1.65

CENTOMO, Sebastien TOR.

Goaltender. Catches right. 6'1", 193 lbs. Born, Montreal, Que., March 26, 1981.

			Regular Season								Playoffs						
Season	Club	Lea	GP	W	L	T	Mins	GA	SO	Avg	GP	W	L	Mins	GA	SO	Avg
1997-98	Laval-Laurentides	QAAA	30	....	....	....	1696	87	0	2.86	....	....	....	....	....	....	....
1998-99	Rouyn-Noranda	QMJHL	32	14	9	4	1658	104	1	3.76	2	0	1	28	5	0	10.71
99-2000	Rouyn-Noranda	QMJHL	50	24	17	3	2758	160	1	3.48	11	6	5	695	41	0	3.54

Signed as a free agent by **Toronto**, September 10, 1999.

CHABOT, Frederic (shah-BOH, FREHD-uhr-IHK) CBJ

Goaltender. Catches left. 5'11", 187 lbs. Born, Hebertville-Station, Que., February 12, 1968.
(New Jersey's 10th choice, 192nd overall, in 1986 Entry Draft).

			Regular Season								Playoffs						
Season	Club	Lea	GP	W	L	T	Mins	GA	SO	Avg	GP	W	L	Mins	GA	SO	Avg
1985-86	Trois-Rivieres	QAAA	34	25	9	0	2038	139	0	3.90	....	....	....	....	....	....	....
1986-87	Drummondville	QMJHL	62	31	29	0	3508	293	1	5.01	8	2	6	481	40	0	4.99
1987-88	Drummondville	QMJHL	58	27	24	4	3276	237	1	4.34	16	10	6	1019	56	*1	*3.30
1988-89	Moose Jaw	WHL	26	....	....	....	1385	114	....	4.94	....	....	....	....	....	....	....
	Prince Albert	WHL	28	....	....	....	1572	88	....	3.36	4	1	1	199	16	0	4.82
1989-90	Sherbrooke	AHL	2	1	1	0	119	8	0	4.03	....	....	....	....	....	....	....
	Fort Wayne	IHL	23	6	13	3	1208	87	1	4.32	....	....	....	....	....	....	....
1990-91	**Montreal**	**NHL**	**3**	**0**	**0**	**1**	**108**	**6**	**0**	**3.33**	....	....	....	....	....	....	....
	Fredericton	AHL	35	9	15	5	1800	122	0	4.07	....	....	....	....	....	....	....
1991-92	Fredericton	AHL	30	17	9	4	1761	79	2	*2.69	7	3	4	457	20	0	2.63
	Winston-Salem	ECHL	24	15	7	2	1449	71	0	*2.94	....	....	....	....	....	....	....
1992-93	**Montreal**	**NHL**	**1**	**0**	**0**	**0**	**40**	**1**	**0**	**1.50**	....	....	....	....	....	....	....
	Fredericton	AHL	45	22	17	4	2544	141	0	3.33	4	1	3	261	16	0	3.68
1993-94	**Montreal**	**NHL**	**1**	**0**	**1**	**0**	**60**	**5**	**0**	**5.00**	....	....	....	....	....	....	....
	Fredericton	AHL	3	0	1	1	143	12	0	5.03	....	....	....	....	....	....	....
	Las Vegas	IHL	2	1	1	0	110	5	0	2.72	....	....	....	....	....	....	....
	Philadelphia	**NHL**	**4**	**0**	**1**	**1**	**70**	**5**	**0**	**4.29**	....	....	....	....	....	....	....
	Hershey Bears	AHL	28	13	5	6	1464	63	2	*2.58	11	7	4	665	32	0	2.89
1994-95	Cincinnati	IHL	48	25	12	7	2622	128	1	2.93	5	3	2	326	16	0	2.94
1995-96	Cincinnati	IHL	38	23	9	4	2147	88	3	*2.46	14	9	5	854	37	1	2.60
1996-97	Houston Aeros	IHL	*72	*39	26	7	*4265	180	*7	2.53	13	8	5	777	34	*2	2.63
1997-98	**Los Angeles**	**NHL**	**12**	**3**	**3**	**2**	**554**	**29**	**0**	**3.14**	....	....	....	....	....	....	....
	Houston Aeros	IHL	22	12	7	2	1237	46	1	2.23	4	1	3	238	11	0	2.77
1998-99	**Montreal**	**NHL**	**11**	**1**	**3**	**0**	**430**	**16**	**0**	**2.23**	....	....	....	....	....	....	....
	Houston Aeros	IHL	21	16	4	1	1259	49	3	2.34	....	....	....	....	....	....	....
99-2000	Houston Aeros	IHL	*62	*36	19	7	*3695	131	4	2.13	11	6	5	658	20	*3	1.82
	NHL Totals		**32**	**4**	**8**	**4**	**1262**	**62**	**0**	**2.95**	....	....	....	....	....	....	....

WHL East All-Star Team (1989) • Won Baz Bastien Award (Top Goaltender - AHL) (1994) • IHL Second All-Star Team (1996) • IHL First All-Star Team (1997, 2000) • Won James Gatschene Memorial Trophy (MVP - IHL) (1997) • Won James Norris Memorial Trophy (fewest goals against - IHL) (2000) • Won James Gatschene Memorial Trophy (MVP - IHL) (tied with Nikolai Khabibulin) (2000)

Signed as a free agent by **Montreal**, January 16, 1990. Claimed by **Tampa Bay** from **Montreal** in Expansion Draft, June 18, 1992. Traded to **Montreal** by **Tampa Bay** for Jean-Claude Bergeron, June 19, 1992. Traded to **Philadelphia** by **Montreal** for cash, February 21, 1994. Signed as a free agent by **Florida**, August 11, 1994. Signed as a free agent by **LA Kings**, September 3, 1997. Claimed by **Nashville** from **LA Kings** in Expansion Draft, June 26, 1998. Claimed on waivers by **LA Kings** from **Nashville**, July 18, 1998. Claimed by **Montreal** from **LA Kings** in NHL Waiver Draft, October 5, 1998. Selected by **Columbus** from **Montreal** in Expansion Draft, June 23, 2000.

CHARPENTIER, Sebastien (shahr-PUHNT-yay, suh-BAS-tee-yeh) WSH.

Goaltender. Catches left. 5'9", 177 lbs. Born, Drummondville, Que., April 18, 1977.
(Washington's 4th choice, 93rd overall, in 1995 Entry Draft).

			Regular Season								Playoffs						
Season	Club	Lea	GP	W	L	T	Mins	GA	SO	Avg	GP	W	L	Mins	GA	SO	Avg
1991-92	Drummondville	QAAA	14	....	....	....	840	34	2	2.42	....	....	....	....	....	....	....
1992-93	Drummondville	QAAA	20	....	....	....	1215	37	*7	*1.80	....	....	....	....	....	....	....
1993-94	Magog Selectes	QAAA	24	14	5	1	1443	75	1	3.16	....	....	....	....	....	....	....
1994-95	Laval Titan	QMJHL	41	25	12	1	2152	99	2	2.76	16	9	4	886	45	0	3.05
1995-96	Laval Titan	QMJHL	18	4	10	0	938	97	0	6.20	....	....	....	....	....	....	....
	Val-d'Or Foreurs	QMJHL	33	21	9	1	1906	87	1	2.74	13	7	5	740	45	0	3.64
1996-97	Shawinigan	QMJHL	*62	*37	17	4	*3480	177	1	3.05	4	2	1	196	13	0	3.98
1997-98	Portland Pirates	AHL	4	1	3	0	229	10	0	2.61	....	....	....	....	....	....	....
	Hampton Roads	ECHL	43	20	16	6	2388	114	0	2.86	18	*14	4	*1183	38	1	*1.93
1998-99	Quad City Mallards	UHL	6	0	0	0	4	0	0	0.00	....	....	....	....	....	....	....
	Portland Pirates	AHL	3	0	3	0	180	10	0	3.34	....	....	....	....	....	....	....
99-2000	Portland Pirates	AHL	18	10	4	3	1041	48	0	2.77	3	1	1	183	9	0	2.96

QMJHL Second All-Rookie Team (1995) • Named ECHL Playoff MVP (1998)

CHARRON, Jonathon (shuh-RAWN) FLA.

Goaltender. Catches left. 6'2", 180 lbs. Born, Laval, Que., December 9, 1980.
(Florida's 9th choice, 227th overall, in 1999 Entry Draft).

			Regular Season								Playoffs						
Season	Club	Lea	GP	W	L	T	Mins	GA	SO	Avg	GP	W	L	Mins	GA	SO	Avg
1997-98	Laval Titan	QMJHL	23	11	6	1	1145	57	0	2.99	2	0	1	70	5	0	4.25
1998-99	Acadie-Bathurst	QMJHL	19	10	9	0	1065	64	0	3.61	....	....	....	....	....	....	....
	Val-d'Or Foreurs	QMJHL	26	12	8	2	1364	97	0	4.27	1	0	1	21	3	0	8.57
99-2000	Val-d'Or Foreurs	QMJHL	8	2	4	0	391	34	0	5.22	....	....	....	....	....	....	....
	Quebec Remparts	QMJHL	10	3	6	0	513	32	0	3.75	....	....	....	....	....	....	....

CHOUINARD, Mathieu (SHWEE-nuhr, ma-TEW) OTT.

Goaltender. Catches left. 6'1", 211 lbs. Born, Laval, Que., April 11, 1980.
(Ottawa's 2nd choice, 45th overall, in 2000 Entry Draft).

			Regular Season								Playoffs						
Season	Club	Lea	GP	W	L	T	Mins	GA	SO	Avg	GP	W	L	Mins	GA	SO	Avg
1995-96	Amos Forrestiers	QAAA	31	....	....	....	1613	114	1	4.24	....	....	....	....	....	....	....
1996-97	Shawinigan	QMJHL	17	4	7	1	795	51	0	3.85	4	1	3	264	15	0	3.41
1997-98	Shawinigan	QMJHL	55	*32	18	3	3055	142	2	2.79	6	2	4	348	24	0	4.14
1998-99	Shawinigan	QMJHL	56	36	16	4	3288	150	*5	2.74	6	2	4	392	27	0	4.13
99-2000	Shawinigan	QMJHL	*59	32	20	5	*3339	186	4	3.34	13	7	6	769	41	0	3.20

• Re-entered NHL draft. Originally Ottawa's 1st choice, 15th overall, in 1998 Entry Draft.

QMJHL First All-Star Team (1999)

CHOUKALOS, Donald (koo-KAH-luhs, DAWN-ohld) BOS.

Goaltender. Catches left. 6'2", 186 lbs. Born, Calgary, Alta., April 11, 1981.
(Boston's 6th choice, 179th overall, in 1999 Entry Draft).

			Regular Season								Playoffs						
Season	Club	Lea	GP	W	L	T	Mins	GA	SO	Avg	GP	W	L	Mins	GA	SO	Avg
1997-98	Calgary Stars	AMHL	11	2	8	1	644	59	0	5.50	....	....	....	....	....	....	....
	Calgary Hitmen	WHL	9	4	1	1	404	21	0	3.12	....	....	....	....	....	....	....
1998-99	Calgary Hitmen	WHL	10	8	1	0	571	20	1	2.10	....	....	....	....	....	....	....
	Regina Pats	WHL	24	6	12	4	1337	98	0	4.40	....	....	....	....	....	....	....
99-2000	Regina Pats	WHL	58	26	24	4	3259	194	2	3.57	7	3	4	385	24	0	3.74

CLEMMENSEN, Scott (KLEH-mehn-SEHN, SKAWT) N.J.

Goaltender. Catches left. 6'2", 185 lbs. Born, Des Moines, IA, July 23, 1977.
(New Jersey's 7th choice, 215th overall, in 1997 Entry Draft).

			Regular Season								Playoffs						
Season	Club	Lea	GP	W	L	T	Mins	GA	SO	Avg	GP	W	L	Mins	GA	SO	Avg
1995-96	Des Moines	USHL	20	10	7	1	1082	62	0	3.44	....	....	....	....	....	....	....
1996-97	Des Moines	USHL	36	22	9	2	2042	111	1	3.26	4	1	2	200	9	1	2.70
1997-98	Boston College	H-East	37	24	9	4	2205	102	*4	2.78	....	....	....	....	....	....	....
1998-99	Boston College	H-East	*42	26	12	4	*2507	120	1	2.87	....	....	....	....	....	....	....
99-2000	Boston College	H-East	29	19	7	0	1610	59	*5	2.20	....	....	....	....	....	....	....

CLOUTIER, Dan (KLOO-tyay, DAN) T.B.

Goaltender. Catches left. 6'1", 182 lbs. Born, Mont-Laurier, Que., April 22, 1976.
(NY Rangers' 1st choice, 26th overall, in 1994 Entry Draft).

			Regular Season								Playoffs						
Season	Club	Lea	GP	W	L	T	Mins	GA	SO	Avg	GP	W	L	Mins	GA	SO	Avg
1991-92	St. Thomas Stars	OJHL-B	14	....	....	....	823	80	0	5.83	....	....	....	....	....	....	....
1992-93	Timmons Bears	NOJHA	5	4	0	0	255	10	0	2.35	....	....	....	....	....	....	....
	Sault Ste. Marie	OHL	12	4	6	0	572	44	0	4.62	4	1	2	231	12	0	3.12
1993-94	Sault Ste. Marie	OHL	55	28	14	6	2934	174	*2	3.56	14	*10	4	833	52	0	3.75
1994-95	Sault Ste. Marie	OHL	45	15	26	2	2518	185	1	4.41	....	....	....	....	....	....	....
1995-96	Sault Ste. Marie	OHL	13	9	3	0	641	43	0	4.02	....	....	....	....	....	....	....
	Guelph Storm	OHL	17	12	2	2	1004	35	2	2.09	16	11	5	993	52	*2	3.14
1996-97	Binghamton	AHL	60	23	28	8	3367	199	3	3.55	4	1	3	236	13	0	3.31
1997-98	**NY Rangers**	**NHL**	**12**	**4**	**5**	**1**	**551**	**23**	**0**	**2.50**	....	....	....	....	....	....	....
	Hartford	AHL	24	12	8	3	1417	62	0	2.63	8	5	3	478	24	0	3.01
1998-99	**NY Rangers**	**NHL**	**22**	**6**	**8**	**3**	**1097**	**49**	**0**	**2.68**	....	....	....	....	....	....	....
99-2000	**Tampa Bay**	**NHL**	**52**	**9**	**30**	**3**	**2492**	**145**	**0**	**3.49**	....	....	....	....	....	....	....
	NHL Totals		**86**	**19**	**43**	**7**	**4140**	**217**	**0**	**3.14**	....	....	....	....	....	....	....

OHL Second All-Star Team (1996)

Traded to **Tampa Bay** by **NY Rangers** with Niklas Sundstrom and NY Rangers' 1st (Nikita Alexeev) and 3rd (later traded to San Jose - later traded to Chicago - Chicago selected Igor Radulov) round choices in 2000 Entry Draft for Chicago's 1st round choice (previously acquired, NY Rangers selected Pavel Brendl) in 1999 Entry Draft, June 26, 1999.

COUSINEAU, Marcel (koo-ZEE-noh, MAHR-sehl) L.A.

Goaltender. Catches left. 5'9", 183 lbs. Born, Delson, Que., April 30, 1973.
(Boston's 3rd choice, 62nd overall, in 1991 Entry Draft).

			Regular Season								Playoffs						
Season	Club	Lea	GP	W	L	T	Mins	GA	SO	Avg	GP	W	L	Mins	GA	SO	Avg
1989-90	Richelieu Riverains	QAAA	27	22	5	0	1618	104	0	3.83	....	....	....	....	....	....	....
1990-91	Beauport	QMJHL	49	13	29	3	2739	196	1	4.29	....	....	....	....	....	....	....
1991-92	Beauport	QMJHL	*67	26	32	5	*3673	241	0	3.94	....	....	....	....	....	....	....
1992-93	Drummondville	QMJHL	60	20	32	2	3298	225	0	4.09	9	3	6	498	37	*1	4.45
1993-94	St. John's Leafs	AHL	37	13	11	9	2015	118	0	3.51	....	....	....	....	....	....	....
1994-95	St. John's Leafs	AHL	58	22	27	6	3342	171	4	3.07	3	0	3	179	9	0	3.01
1995-96	St. John's Leafs	AHL	62	21	26	13	3629	192	1	3.17	4	1	3	258	11	0	2.56
1996-97	**Toronto**	**NHL**	**13**	**3**	**5**	**1**	**566**	**31**	**1**	**3.29**	....	....	....	....	....	....	....
	St. John's Leafs	AHL	19	7	8	3	1053	58	0	3.30	11	6	5	658	28	0	2.55
1997-98	**Toronto**	**NHL**	**2**	**0**	**0**	**0**	**17**	**0**	**0**	**0.00**	....	....	....	....	....	....	....
	St. John's Leafs	AHL	57	17	25	13	3306	167	1	3.03	4	1	3	254	10	0	2.36
1998-99	**NY Islanders**	**NHL**	**6**	**0**	**4**	**0**	**293**	**14**	**0**	**2.87**	....	....	....	....	....	....	....
	Lowell	AHL	53	26	17	7	3034	139	3	2.75	3	0	3	186	13	0	4.20
99-2000	**Los Angeles**	**NHL**	**5**	**1**	**1**	**0**	**171**	**6**	**0**	**2.11**	....	....	....	....	....	....	....
	Long Beach	IHL	23	15	6	1	1328	62	0	2.80	....	....	....	....	....	....	....
	NHL Totals		**26**	**4**	**10**	**1**	**1047**	**51**	**1**	**2.92**	....	....	....	....	....	....	....

Signed as a free agent by **Toronto**, November 13, 1993. Signed as a free agent by **NY Islanders**, July 29, 1998. Traded to **LA Kings** by **NY Islanders** with Zigmund Palffy, Brian Smolinski and New Jersey's 4th round choice (previously acquired, LA Kings selected Daniel Johanssen) in 1999 Entry Draft for Olli Jokinen, Josh Green, Mathieu Biron and LA Kings' 1st round choice (Taylor Pyatt) in 1999 Entry Draft, June 20, 1999.

CRUICKSHANK, Curtis (KRUHK-shank, KUHR-tihs) WSH.

Goaltender. Catches left. 6'3", 220 lbs. Born, Ottawa, Ont., March 21, 1979.
(Washington's 3rd choice, 89th overall, in 1997 Entry Draft).

			Regular Season								Playoffs						
Season	Club	Lea	GP	W	L	T	Mins	GA	SO	Avg	GP	W	L	Mins	GA	SO	Avg
1995-96	Ottawa	OJHL	24	12	4	0	....	....	0	4.27	....	....	....	....	....	....	....
1996-97	Kingston	OHL	35	13	16	1	1792	118	2	3.95	1	0	1	26	4	0	9.23
1997-98	Kingston	OHL	57	30	20	4	3166	207	2	3.92	12	5	6	702	45	0	3.85
1998-99	Kingston	OHL	16	5	9	0	835	63	1	4.53	....	....	....	....	....	....	....
	Sarnia Sting	OHL	28	18	5	1	1557	66	2	2.54	4	1	0	71	6	0	5.07
99-2000	Portland Pirates	AHL	10	4	5	1	605	30	0	2.98	....	....	....	....	....	....	....
	Hampton Roads	ECHL	7	4	3	0	375	22	0	3.52	1	0	0	12	2	0	10.23

CRUZ, Jomar (KREWZ, YO-mahr) WSH.

Goaltender. Catches left. 6'1", 190 lbs. Born, The Pas, Man., April 5, 1980.
(Washington's 1st choice, 49th overall, in 1998 Entry Draft).

			Regular Season								Playoffs						
Season	Club	Lea	GP	W	L	T	Mins	GA	SO	Avg	GP	W	L	Mins	GA	SO	Avg
1996-97	Notre Dame	SJHL	20	13	6	0	1107	71	2	3.84	....	....	....	....	....	....	....
1997-98	Brandon	WHL	30	16	19	1	1596	81	3	3.05	14	7	6	749	41	0	3.28
1998-99	Brandon	WHL	38	16	17	1	2057	139	1	4.05	1	0	0	23	2	0	5.22
99-2000	Brandon	WHL	21	7	13	1	1151	73	1	3.81	....	....	....	....	....	....	....
	Tri-City Americans	WHL	35	8	22	4	1968	126	0	3.84	3	0	1	51	7	0	8.24

DAFOE, Byron (day-FOH, BRIGH-rohn) BOS.

Goaltender. Catches left. 5'11", 200 lbs. Born, Sussex, England, February 25, 1971.
(Washington's 2nd choice, 35th overall, in 1989 Entry Draft).

			Regular Season								Playoffs						
Season	Club	Lea	GP	W	L	T	Mins	GA	SO	Avg	GP	W	L	Mins	GA	SO	Avg
1987-88	Juan de Fuca	BCJHL	32	....	....	....	1716	129	0	4.51	....	....	....	....	....	....	....
1988-89	Portland	WHL	59	29	24	3	3279	291	1	5.32	*18	10	8	*1091	81	*1	4.45
1989-90	Portland	WHL	40	14	21	3	2265	193	0	5.11	....	....	....	....	....	....	....
1990-91	Portland	WHL	8	1	5	1	414	41	0	5.94	....	....	....	....	....	....	....
	Prince Albert	WHL	32	13	12	4	1839	124	0	4.05	....	....	....	....	....	....	....
1991-92	Baltimore	AHL	33	12	16	4	1847	119	0	3.87	....	....	....	....	....	....	....
	New Haven	AHL	7	3	2	1	364	22	0	3.63	....	....	....	....	....	....	....
	Hampton Roads	ECHL	10	6	4	0	562	26	0	2.78	....	....	....	....	....	....	....
1992-93	**Washington**	**NHL**	**1**	**0**	**0**	**0**	**1**	**0**	**0**	**0.00**	....	....	....	....	....	....	....
	Baltimore	AHL	48	16	20	7	2617	191	1	4.38	5	2	3	241	22	0	5.48
1993-94	**Washington**	**NHL**	**5**	**2**	**2**	**0**	**230**	**13**	**0**	**3.39**	**2**	**0**	**2**	**118**	**5**	**0**	**2.54**
	Portland	AHL	47	24	16	4	2661	148	1	3.34	1	0	0	9	1	0	6.79
1994-95	**Washington**	**NHL**	**4**	**1**	**1**	**1**	**187**	**11**	**0**	**3.53**	**1**	**0**	**0**	**20**	**1**	**0**	**3.00**
	Phoenix	IHL	49	25	16	6	2743	169	2	3.70	....	....	....	....	....	....	....
	Portland	AHL	6	5	0	0	330	16	0	2.91	7	3	4	416	29	0	4.18
1995-96	**Los Angeles**	**NHL**	**47**	**14**	**24**	**8**	**2666**	**172**	**1**	**3.87**	....	....	....	....	....	....	....
1996-97	**Los Angeles**	**NHL**	**40**	**13**	**17**	**5**	**2162**	**112**	**0**	**3.11**	....	....	....	....	....	....	....
1997-98	**Boston**	**NHL**	**65**	**30**	**25**	**9**	**3693**	**138**	**6**	**2.24**	**6**	**2**	**4**	**422**	**14**	**1**	**1.99**
1998-99	**Boston**	**NHL**	**68**	**32**	**23**	**11**	**4001**	**133**	***10**	**1.99**	**12**	**6**	**6**	**768**	**26**	**2**	**2.03**
99-2000	**Boston**	**NHL**	**41**	**13**	**16**	**10**	**2307**	**114**	**3**	**2.96**	....	....	....	....	....	....	....
	NHL Totals		**271**	**105**	**108**	**44**	**15247**	**693**	**20**	**2.73**	**21**	**8**	**12**	**1328**	**46**	**3**	**2.08**

AHL First All-Star Team (1994) • Shared Harry "Hap" Holmes Trophy (fewest goals-against - AHL) with Olaf Kolzig (1994) • NHL Second All-Star Team (1999)

Traded to **Los Angeles** by **Washington** with Dimitri Khristich for Los Angeles' 1st round choice (Alexander Volchkov) and Dallas' 4th round choice (previously acquired, Washington selected Justin Davis) in 1996 Entry Draft, July 8, 1995. Traded to **Boston** by **Los Angeles** with Dimitri Khristich for Jozef Stumpel, Sandy Moger and Boston's 4th round choice (later traded to New Jersey - New Jersey selected Pierre Dagenais) in 1998 Entry Draft, August 29, 1997.

DAMPHOUSSE, Jean-Francois (DAHM-fooz, ZHAWN-fran-SWUH) N.J.

Goaltender. Catches left. 6', 175 lbs. Born, St-Alexis-des-Monts, Que., July 21, 1979.
(New Jersey's 1st choice, 24th overall, in 1997 Entry Draft).

			Regular Season								Playoffs						
Season	Club	Lea	GP	W	L	T	Mins	GA	SO	Avg	GP	W	L	Mins	GA	SO	Avg
1993-94	Ste-Foy Governors	QAAA	18	....	....	....	1078	53	0	2.95	....	....	....	....	....	....	....
1994-95	Ste-Foy Governors	QAAA	16	....	....	....	958	48	0	3.01	....	....	....	....	....	....	....
1995-96	Ste-Foy Governors	QAAA	28	....	....	....	1679	85	2	3.06	....	....	....	....	....	....	....
1996-97	Moncton Wildcats	QMJHL	39	6	25	2	2063	190	0	5.53	....	....	....	....	....	....	....
1997-98	Moncton Wildcats	QMJHL	59	24	26	6	3400	174	1	3.07	10	5	5	595	28	0	2.82
1998-99	Moncton Wildcats	QMJHL	40	19	17	2	2163	121	1	3.36	4	0	4	200	12	0	3.60
	Albany River Rats	AHL	1	0	1	0	59	3	0	3.06	....	....	....	....	....	....	....
99-2000	Augusta Lynx	ECHL	14	4	7	0	676	49	0	4.35	....	....	....	....	....	....	....
	Albany River Rats	AHL	26	9	11	2	1326	62	0	2.81	2	0	1	62	4	0	3.86

DAUBENSPECK, Kirk (DAW-behn-spehk, KUHRK)

Goaltender. Catches left. 6', 190 lbs. Born, Madison, WI, July 16, 1974.
(Philadelphia's 6th choice, 151st overall, in 1992 Entry Draft).

			Regular Season								Playoffs						
Season	Club	Lea	GP	W	L	T	Mins	GA	SO	Avg	GP	W	L	Mins	GA	SO	Avg
1991-92	Culver Academy	H.S.	20	....	....	....	1190	57	0	2.88	....	....	....	....	....	....	....
1992-93	Wisconsin Capitals	USHL	28	5	20	1	1542	123	0	4.79	....	....	....	....	....	....	....
	Sioux City	USHL	9	0	7	1	470	49	0	6.26	....	....	....	....	....	....	....
1993-94	U. of Wisconsin	WCHA	7	2	2	0	280	19	0	4.07	....	....	....	....	....	....	....
1994-95	U. of Wisconsin	WCHA	42	*23	15	4	*2503	146	0	3.51	....	....	....	....	....	....	....
1995-96	U. of Wisconsin	WCHA	*39	*17	20	2	*2357	151	0	3.84	....	....	....	....	....	....	....
1996-97	U. of Wisconsin	WCHA	33	13	18	2	1925	124	1	3.86	....	....	....	....	....	....	....
1997-98	Jacksonville	ECHL	32	20	9	2	1865	92	1	2.96	....	....	....	....	....	....	....
	Indianapolis Ice	IHL	18	6	9	0	953	58	0	3.65	....	....	....	....	....	....	....
1998-99	Indianapolis Ice	IHL	12	2	8	1	650	43	0	3.97	....	....	....	....	....	....	....
	Jacksonville	ECHL	8	5	3	0	424	18	0	2.55	....	....	....	....	....	....	....
	Chesapeake	ECHL	13	7	2	4	774	31	2	2.40	7	3	4	424	12	1	*1.70
99-2000	South Carolina	ECHL	6	4	2	0	360	17	0	2.83	....	....	....	....	....	....	....
	Rochester	AHL	22	7	10	4	1235	53	1	2.57	1	0	0	4	1	0	14.06

WCHA Second All-Star Team (1997) • NCAA West Second All-American Team (1997)

Traded to **Ottawa** by **Philadelphia** with Claude Boivin for Mark Lamb, March 5, 1994. Traded to **Chicago** by **Ottawa** for Ottawa's 6th round choice (previously acquired, Ottawa selected Christopher Neil) in 1998 Entry Draft and future considerations, September 23, 1997.

DENIS, Marc (deh-NEE, MAHRK) CBJ

Goaltender. Catches left. 6', 190 lbs. Born, Montreal, Que., August 1, 1977.
(Colorado's 1st choice, 25th overall, in 1995 Entry Draft).

			Regular Season								Playoffs						
Season	Club	Lea	GP	W	L	T	Mins	GA	SO	Avg	GP	W	L	Mins	GA	SO	Avg
1992-93	Montreal-Bourassa	QAAA	26	....	....	....	1559	74	5	2.87	....	....	....	....	....	....	....
1993-94	Trois-Rivieres	QAAA	36	....	....	....	2093	158	3	4.53	....	....	....	....	....	....	....
1994-95	Chicoutimi	QMJHL	32	17	9	1	1688	98	0	3.48	6	4	2	372	19	1	3.06
1995-96	Chicoutimi	QMJHL	51	23	21	4	2951	157	2	3.19	16	8	8	957	69	0	4.33
1996-97	Chicoutimi	QMJHL	41	22	15	2	2323	104	4	*2.69	*21	*11	10	*1229	70	*1	3.42
	Colorado	**NHL**	**1**	**0**	**1**	**0**	**60**	**3**	**0**	**3.00**	....	....	....	....	....	....	....
	Hershey Bears	AHL	....	....	....	....	....	....	....	....	4	1	0	56	1	0	1.08
1997-98	Hershey Bears	AHL	47	17	23	4	2588	125	1	2.90	6	3	3	346	15	0	2.59
1998-99	**Colorado**	**NHL**	**4**	**1**	**1**	**1**	**217**	**9**	**0**	**2.49**	....	....	....	....	....	....	....
	Hershey Bears	AHL	52	20	23	5	2908	137	4	2.83	3	1	1	143	7	0	2.93
99-2000	**Colorado**	**NHL**	**23**	**9**	**8**	**3**	**1203**	**51**	**3**	**2.54**	....	....	....	....	....	....	....
	NHL Totals		**28**	**10**	**10**	**4**	**1480**	**63**	**3**	**2.55**	....	....	....	....	....	....	....

QMJHL First All-Star Team (1997) • Canadian Major Junior First All-Star Team (1997) • Canadian Major Junior Goaltender of the Year (1997)

Traded to **Columbus** by **Colorado** for Columbus' 2nd round choice (later traded to Carolina - Carolina selected Tomas Kurka) in 2000 Entry Draft, June 7, 2000.

DESROCHERS, Patrick (duh-RAWSH-ai, PAT-rihk) PHX.

Goaltender. Catches left. 6'4", 207 lbs. Born, Penetanguishene, Ont., October 27, 1979.
(Phoenix's 1st choice, 14th overall, in 1998 Entry Draft).

			Regular Season								Playoffs						
Season	Club	Lea	GP	W	L	T	Mins	GA	SO	Avg	GP	W	L	Mins	GA	SO	Avg
1994-95	Barrie Colts	OJHL	26	....	....	....	3205	179	3	3.08	....	....	....	....	....	....	....
1995-96	Sarnia Sting	OHL	29	12	6	2	1265	96	0	4.55	3	0	1	71	5	0	4.23
1996-97	Sarnia Sting	OHL	50	22	17	4	2667	154	*4	3.46	11	6	5	576	42	0	4.38
1997-98	Sarnia Sting	OHL	56	26	17	11	3205	179	1	3.35	4	1	2	160	12	0	4.50
1998-99	Sarnia Sting	OHL	8	3	5	0	425	26	0	3.67	....	....	....	....	....	....	....
	Kingston	OHL	44	14	22	3	2389	177	1	4.45	5	1	4	323	21	0	3.90
	Canada	Nt-Team	1	1	0	0	60	4	0	4.00	....	....	....	....	....	....	....
99-2000	Springfield	AHL	52	21	17	7	2710	137	1	3.03	2	1	1	120	7	1	3.50

DiPIETRO, Rick (dee-pee-EHT-roh) NYI

Goaltender. Catches right. 5'11", 185 lbs. Born, Winthrop, MA, September 19, 1981.
(NY Islanders' 1st choice, 1st overall, in 2000 Entry Draft).

			Regular Season								Playoffs						
Season	Club	Lea	GP	W	L	T	Mins	GA	SO	Avg	GP	W	L	Mins	GA	SO	Avg
1997-98	Team USA	Under-18	46	21	19	0	2526	131	2	3.11	....	....	....	....	....	....	....
1998-99	Team USA	Under-18	46	31	11	2	2760	113	2	2.46	....	....	....	....	....	....	....
99-2000	Boston University	H-East	29	18	5	5	1790	73	2	2.45	....	....	....	....	....	....	....

Hockey East Second All-Star Team (2000)

DUNHAM, Mike (DUHN-uhm, MIGHK) NSH.

Goaltender. Catches left. 6'3", 200 lbs. Born, Johnson City, NY, June 1, 1972.
(New Jersey's 4th choice, 53rd overall, in 1990 Entry Draft).

			Regular Season								Playoffs						
Season	Club	Lea	GP	W	L	T	Mins	GA	SO	Avg	GP	W	L	Mins	GA	SO	Avg
1987-88	Canterbury School	H.S.	29	....	....	....	1740	69	4	2.37	....	....	....	....	....	....	....
1988-89	Canterbury School	H.S.	25	....	....	....	1500	63	2	2.52	....	....	....	....	....	....	....
1989-90	Canterbury School	H.S.	32	....	....	....	1558	68	3	1.96	....	....	....	....	....	....	....
1990-91	U. of Maine	H-East	23	14	5	2	1275	63	0	*2.96	....	....	....	....	....	....	....
1991-92	U. of Maine	H-East	7	6	0	0	382	14	1	2.20	....	....	....	....	....	....	....
	United States	Nt-Team	3	0	1	1	157	10	0	3.82	....	....	....	....	....	....	....
1992-93	U. of Maine	H-East	25	*21	1	1	1429	63	0	2.65	....	....	....	....	....	....	....
1993-94	United States	Nt-Team	33	22	9	2	1983	125	2	3.78	....	....	....	....	....	....	....
	United States	Olympics	3	0	1	2	180	15	0	5.00	....	....	....	....	....	....	....
	Albany River Rats	AHL	5	2	2	1	304	26	0	5.12	....	....	....	....	....	....	....
1994-95	Albany River Rats	AHL	35	20	7	8	2120	99	1	2.80	7	6	1	419	20	1	2.86
1995-96	Albany River Rats	AHL	44	30	10	2	2592	109	1	2.52	3	1	2	182	5	1	1.65
1996-97	**New Jersey**	**NHL**	**26**	**8**	**7**	**1**	**1013**	**43**	**2**	**2.55**	....	....	....	....	....	....	....
	Albany River Rats	AHL	3	1	1	1	184	12	0	3.91	....	....	....	....	....	....	....
1997-98	**New Jersey**	**NHL**	**15**	**5**	**5**	**3**	**773**	**29**	**1**	**2.25**	....	....	....	....	....	....	....
1998-99	**Nashville**	**NHL**	**44**	**16**	**23**	**3**	**2472**	**127**	**1**	**3.08**	....	....	....	....	....	....	....
99-2000	**Nashville**	**NHL**	**52**	**19**	**27**	**6**	**3077**	**146**	**0**	**2.85**	....	....	....	....	....	....	....
	Milwaukee	IHL	1	1	0	0	60	1	0	1.00	....	....	....	....	....	....	....
	NHL Totals		**137**	**48**	**62**	**13**	**7335**	**345**	**4**	**2.82**	....	....	....	....	....	....	....

Hockey East First All-Star Team (1993) • NCAA East First All-American Team (1993) • Shared Harry "Hap" Holmes Memorial Trophy (fewest goals against - AHL) with Corey Schwab (1995) • Shared Jack A. Butterfield Trophy (Playoff MVP - AHL) with Corey Schwab (1995) • AHL Second All-Star Team (1996) • Shared William M. Jennings Trophy with Martin Brodeur (1997)

Claimed by **Nashville** from **New Jersey** in Expansion Draft, June 26, 1998.

ELLIOT, Jason (EHL-lee-awt, JAY-suhn) DET.

Goaltender. Catches left. 6'2", 183 lbs. Born, Inuvik, N.W.T., November 10, 1975.
(Detroit's 7th choice, 205th overall, in 1994 Entry Draft).

			Regular Season								Playoffs						
Season	Club	Lea	GP	W	L	T	Mins	GA	SO	Avg	GP	W	L	Mins	GA	SO	Avg
1994-95	Cornell Big Red	ECAC	16	3	11	1	877	62	0	4.24	....	....	....	....	....	....	....
1995-96	Cornell Big Red	ECAC	19	12	2	1	971	38	2	2.35	....	....	....	....	....	....	....
1996-97	Cornell Big Red	ECAC	27	16	7	2	1475	67	0	2.73	....	....	....	....	....	....	....
1997-98	Cornell Big Red	ECAC	29	14	12	2	1683	74	2	2.64	....	....	....	....	....	....	....
1998-99	Adirondack	AHL	51	14	27	5	2710	146	2	3.23	1	0	1	59	2	0	2.04
99-2000	Manitoba Moose	IHL	43	19	12	9	1187	108	1	2.76	....	....	....	....	....	....	....

ECAC Second All-Star Team (1998)

ELLIS, Dan (EHL-ihs) DAL.

Goaltender. Catches left. 6', 185 lbs. Born, Saskatoon, Sask., June 19, 1980.
(Dallas' 2nd choice, 60th overall, in 2000 Entry Draft).

			Regular Season								Playoffs						
Season	Club	Lea	GP	W	L	T	Mins	GA	SO	Avg	GP	W	L	Mins	GA	SO	Avg
1998-99	Newmarket	OJHL	28	24	3	1	1670	63	3	2.25	....	....	....	....	....	....	....
99-2000	Omaha Lancers	USHL	55	*34	16	4	*3274	123	*11	*2.25	4	1	3	238	10	0	2.52

USHL Player-of-the-Year (2000) • USHL Goaltender-of-the-Year (2000) • USHL First All-Star Team (2000) • Signed Letter of Intent to attend University of Nebraska-Omaha (WCHA).

ESCHE, Robert (EHSH, RAW-buhrt) PHX.

Goaltender. Catches left. 6'1", 200 lbs. Born, Utica, NY, January 22, 1978.
(Phoenix's 5th choice, 139th overall, in 1996 Entry Draft).

			Regular Season								Playoffs						
Season	Club	Lea	GP	W	L	T	Mins	GA	SO	Avg	GP	W	L	Mins	GA	SO	Avg
1994-95	Gloucester	OJHL	20	10	6	0	1034	70	0	4.06	....	....	....	....	....	....	....
1995-96	Detroit Jr. Whalers	OHL	23	13	6	0	1219	76	1	3.74	3	0	2	105	4	0	2.29
1996-97	Detroit Jr. Whalers	OHL	58	24	28	2	3241	206	2	3.81	5	1	4	317	19	0	3.60
1997-98	Plymouth Whalers	OHL	48	29	13	4	2810	135	3	2.88	15	8	7	869	45	0	3.11
1998-99	**Phoenix**	**NHL**	**3**	**0**	**1**	**0**	**130**	**7**	**0**	**3.23**	....	....	....	....	....	....	....
	Springfield	AHL	55	24	20	6	2957	138	1	2.80	1	0	1	60	4	0	4.02
99-2000	**Phoenix**	**NHL**	**8**	**2**	**5**	**0**	**408**	**23**	**0**	**3.38**	....	....	....	....	....	....	....
	Houston Aeros	IHL	7	4	2	1	419	16	2	2.29	....	....	....	....	....	....	....
	Springfield	AHL	21	9	9	2	1207	61	2	3.03	3	1	2	180	12	0	4.01
	NHL Totals		**11**	**2**	**6**	**0**	**538**	**30**	**0**	**3.35**	....	....	....	....	....	....	....

OHL Second All-Star Team (1998)

ESSENSA, Bob (EH-sehn-suh, BAWB) VAN.

Goaltender. Catches left. 6', 188 lbs. Born, Toronto, Ont., January 14, 1965.
(Winnipeg's 5th choice, 71st overall, in 1983 Entry Draft).

			Regular Season								Playoffs						
Season	Club	Lea	GP	W	L	T	Mins	GA	SO	Avg	GP	W	L	Mins	GA	SO	Avg
1981-82	Henry Carr	OJHL	17	....	....	....	948	79	0	4.99	....	....	....	....	....	....	....
1982-83	Henry Carr	OJHL	31	....	....	....	1840	98	2	3.20	....	....	....	....	....	....	....
	Markham Waxers	OJHL	1	1	0	0	60	1	0	1.00	....	....	....	....	....	....	....
1983-84	Michigan State	CCHA	17	11	4	0	946	44	2	2.79	....	....	....	....	....	....	....
1984-85	Michigan State	CCHA	18	15	2	0	1059	29	2	1.64	....	....	....	....	....	....	....
1985-86	Michigan State	CCHA	23	17	4	1	1333	74	1	3.33	....	....	....	....	....	....	....
1986-87	Michigan State	CCHA	25	19	3	1	1383	64	2	2.78	....	....	....	....	....	....	....
1987-88	Moncton Hawks	AHL	27	7	11	1	1287	100	1	4.66	....	....	....	....	....	....	....
1988-89	**Winnipeg**	**NHL**	**20**	**6**	**8**	**3**	**1102**	**68**	**1**	**3.70**	....	....	....	....	....	....	....
	Fort Wayne	IHL	22	14	7	0	1287	70	0	3.26	....	....	....	....	....	....	....
1989-90	**Winnipeg**	**NHL**	**36**	**18**	**9**	**5**	**2035**	**107**	**1**	**3.15**	**4**	**2**	**1**	**206**	**12**	**0**	**3.50**
	Moncton Hawks	AHL	6	3	3	0	358	15	0	2.51	....	....	....	....	....	....	....
1990-91	**Winnipeg**	**NHL**	**55**	**19**	**24**	**6**	**2916**	**153**	**4**	**3.15**	....	....	....	....	....	....	....
	Moncton Hawks	AHL	2	1	0	1	125	6	0	2.88	....	....	....	....	....	....	....
1991-92	**Winnipeg**	**NHL**	**47**	**21**	**17**	**6**	**2627**	**126**	***5**	**2.88**	**1**	**0**	**0**	**33**	**3**	**0**	**5.45**
1992-93	**Winnipeg**	**NHL**	**67**	**33**	**26**	**6**	**3855**	**227**	**2**	**3.53**	**6**	**2**	**4**	**367**	**20**	**0**	**3.27**
1993-94	**Winnipeg**	**NHL**	**56**	**19**	**30**	**6**	**3136**	**201**	**1**	**3.85**	....	....	....	....	....	....	....
	Detroit	**NHL**	**13**	**4**	**7**	**2**	**778**	**34**	**1**	**2.62**	**2**	**0**	**2**	**109**	**9**	**0**	**4.95**
1994-95	San Diego Gulls	IHL	16	6	8	1	919	52	0	3.39	1	0	1	59	3	0	3.05
1995-96	Adirondack	AHL	3	1	2	0	179	11	0	3.69	....	....	....	....	....	....	....
	Fort Wayne	IHL	45	24	14	5	2529	122	1	2.89	5	2	3	299	12	0	2.41
1996-97	**Edmonton**	**NHL**	**19**	**4**	**8**	**0**	**868**	**41**	**1**	**2.83**	....	....	....	....	....	....	....
1997-98	**Edmonton**	**NHL**	**16**	**6**	**6**	**1**	**825**	**35**	**0**	**2.55**	**1**	**0**	**0**	**27**	**1**	**0**	**2.22**
1998-99	**Edmonton**	**NHL**	**39**	**12**	**14**	**6**	**2091**	**96**	**0**	**2.75**	....	....	....	....	....	....	....
99-2000	**Phoenix**	**NHL**	**30**	**13**	**10**	**3**	**1573**	**73**	**1**	**2.78**	....	....	....	....	....	....	....
	NHL Totals		**398**	**155**	**159**	**44**	**21806**	**1161**	**17**	**3.19**	**14**	**4**	**7**	**742**	**45**	**0**	**3.64**

CCHA First All-Star Team (1985) • CCHA Second All-Star Team (1986) • NHL All-Rookie Team (1990)

Traded to **Detroit** by **Winnipeg** with Sergei Bautin for Tim Cheveldae and Dallas Drake, March 8, 1994. Traded to **Edmonton** by **Detroit** for future considerations, June 14, 1996. Signed as a free agent by **Phoenix**, September 5, 1999. Signed as a free agent by **Vancouver**, July 26, 2000.

FANKHOUSER, Scott (FANK-how-suhr, SKAWT) ATL.

Goaltender. Catches left. 6'2", 195 lbs. Born, Bismark, ND, July 1, 1975.
(St. Louis' 8th choice, 276th overall, in 1994 Entry Draft).

			Regular Season								Playoffs						
Season	Club	Lea	GP	W	L	T	Mins	GA	SO	Avg	GP	W	L	Mins	GA	SO	Avg
1994-95	U. Mass-Lowell	H.E.	11	4	4	1	499	37	0	4.44	....	....	....	....	....	....	....
1995-96	Melfort Mustangs	SJHL	45	31	9	4	2544	109	3	2.57	....	....	....	....	....	....	....
1996-97	U. Mass-Lowell	H.E.	11	2	4	1	517	38	0	4.41	....	....	....	....	....	....	....
1997-98	U. Mass-Lowell	H.E.	16	4	7	2	798	48	0	3.61	....	....	....	....	....	....	....
1998-99	U. Mass-Lowell	H.E.	32	16	14	0	1729	80	1	2.78	....	....	....	....	....	....	....
99-2000	**Atlanta**	**NHL**	**16**	**2**	**11**	**2**	**920**	**49**	**0**	**3.20**	....	....	....	....	....	....	....
	Greenville Growl	ECHL	7	6	1	0	419	18	0	2.58	....	....	....	....	....	....	....
	Orlando	IHL	6	2	2	1	320	14	0	2.63	....	....	....	....	....	....	....
	Louisville	AHL	1	0	1	0	59	3	0	3.05	....	....	....	....	....	....	....
	NHL Totals		**16**	**2**	**11**	**2**	**920**	**49**	**0**	**3.20**	....	....	....	....	....	....	....

Signed as a free agent by **Atlanta**, August 24, 1999.

FERNANDEZ, Manny (fuhr-NAN-dehz, MAN-ee) MIN.

Goaltender. Catches left. 6', 180 lbs. Born, Etobicoke, Ont., August 27, 1974.
(Quebec's 4th choice, 52nd overall, in 1992 Entry Draft).

			Regular Season								Playoffs						
Season	Club	Lea	GP	W	L	T	Mins	GA	SO	Avg	GP	W	L	Mins	GA	SO	Avg
1990-91	Lac St-Louis	QAAA	20	13	5	0	1176	69	3	3.52	....	....	....	....	....	....	....
1991-92	Laval Titan	QMJHL	31	14	13	2	1593	99	1	3.73	9	3	5	468	39	0	5.00
1992-93	Laval Titan	QMJHL	43	26	14	2	2347	141	1	3.60	13	*12	1	818	42	0	3.08
1993-94	Laval Titan	QMJHL	51	29	14	1	2776	143	*5	3.09	19	14	5	1116	49	*1	*2.63
1994-95	Kalamazoo Wings	IHL	46	21	10	9	2470	115	2	2.79	14	10	2	753	34	1	2.71
	Dallas	**NHL**	**1**	**0**	**1**	**0**	**59**	**3**	**0**	**3.05**	....	....	....	....	....	....	....
1995-96	**Dallas**	**NHL**	**5**	**0**	**1**	**1**	**249**	**19**	**0**	**4.58**	....	....	....	....	....	....	....
	Michigan K-Wings	IHL	47	22	15	9	2664	133	*4	3.00	6	5	1	372	14	0	*2.26
1996-97	Michigan K-Wings	IHL	48	20	24	2	2720	142	2	3.13	4	1	3	277	15	0	3.25
1997-98	**Dallas**	**NHL**	**2**	**1**	**0**	**0**	**69**	**2**	**0**	**1.74**	**1**	**0**	**0**	**2**	**0**	**0**	**0.00**
	Michigan K-Wings	IHL	55	27	17	5	3022	139	5	2.76	2	0	2	88	7	0	4.73
1998-99	**Dallas**	**NHL**	**1**	**0**	**1**	**0**	**60**	**2**	**0**	**2.00**	....	....	....	....	....	....	....
	Houston Aeros	IHL	50	34	6	9	2949	116	2	2.36	*19	*11	8	*1126	49	1	2.61
99-2000	**Dallas**	**NHL**	**24**	**11**	**8**	**3**	**1353**	**48**	**1**	**2.13**	**1**	**0**	**0**	**17**	**1**	**0**	**3.53**
	NHL Totals		**33**	**12**	**11**	**4**	**1790**	**74**	**1**	**2.48**	**2**	**0**	**0**	**19**	**1**	**0**	**3.16**

QMJHL First All-Star Team (1994) • IHL Second All-Star Team (1995)

Rights traded to **Dallas** by **Quebec** for Tommy Sjodin and Dallas' 3rd round choice (Chris Drury) in 1994 Entry Draft, February 13, 1994. Traded to **Minnesota** by **Dallas** with Brad Lukowich for Minnesota's 3rd round choice (Joel Lundqvist) in 2000 Entry Draft and 4th round choice in 2002 Entry Draft, June 12, 2000.

FICHAUD, Eric (FEE-shoh, AIR-ihk) MTL.

Goaltender. Catches left. 5'11", 171 lbs. Born, Anjou, Que., November 4, 1975.
(Toronto's 1st choice, 16th overall, in 1994 Entry Draft).

			Regular Season								Playoffs						
Season	Club	Lea	GP	W	L	T	Mins	GA	SO	Avg	GP	W	L	Mins	GA	SO	Avg
1991-92	Montreal-Bourassa	QAAA	28	12	15	1	1678	110	0	3.95	....	....	....	....	....	....	....
1992-93	Chicoutimi	QMJHL	43	18	13	1	2039	149	0	4.38	....	....	....	....	....	....	....
1993-94	Chicoutimi	QMJHL	*63	*37	21	3	*3493	192	4	3.30	*26	*16	10	*1560	86	*1	3.31
1994-95	Chicoutimi	QMJHL	46	21	19	4	2637	151	4	3.44	7	2	5	428	20	0	2.80
1995-96	**NY Islanders**	**NHL**	**24**	**7**	**12**	**2**	**1234**	**68**	**1**	**3.31**	....	....	....	....	....	....	....
	Worcester	AHL	34	13	15	6	1989	97	1	2.93	2	1	1	127	7	0	3.30
1996-97	**NY Islanders**	**NHL**	**34**	**9**	**14**	**4**	**1759**	**91**	**0**	**3.10**	....	....	....	....	....	....	....
1997-98	**NY Islanders**	**NHL**	**17**	**3**	**8**	**3**	**807**	**40**	**0**	**2.97**	....	....	....	....	....	....	....
	Utah Grizzlies	IHL	1	0	0	0	40	3	0	4.45	....	....	....	....	....	....	....
1998-99	**Nashville**	**NHL**	**9**	**0**	**6**	**0**	**447**	**24**	**0**	**3.22**	....	....	....	....	....	....	....
	Milwaukee	IHL	8	5	2	1	480	25	0	3.13	....	....	....	....	....	....	....
99-2000	**Carolina**	**NHL**	**9**	**3**	**5**	**1**	**490**	**24**	**1**	**2.94**	....	....	....	....	....	....	....
	Quebec Citadelles	AHL	6	4	1	1	368	17	0	2.77	3	0	3	177	10	0	3.39
	NHL Totals		**93**	**22**	**45**	**10**	**4737**	**247**	**2**	**3.13**	....	....	....	....	....	....	....

Canadian Major Junior Second All-Star Team (1994) • Memorial Cup All-Star Team (1994) • Won Hap Emms Memorial Trophy (Memorial Cup Tournament Top Goaltender) (1994) • QMJHL First All-Star Team (1995)

Traded to **NY Islanders** by **Toronto** for Benoit Hogue, NY Islanders' 3rd round choice (Ryan Pepperall) in 1995 Entry Draft and 5th round choice (Brandon Sugden) in 1996 Entry Draft, April 6, 1995. Traded to **Edmonton** by **NY Islanders** for Mike Watt, June 18, 1998. Traded to **Nashville** by **Edmonton** with Drake Berehowsky and Greg de Vries for Mikhail Shtalenkov and Jim Dowd, October 1, 1998. Traded to **Carolina** by **Nashville** for Toronto's 4th round choice (previously acquired, Nashville selected Yevgeny Pavlov) in 1999 Entry Draft and future considerations, June 26, 1999. Claimed on waivers by **Montreal** from **Carolina**, February 11, 2000.

FINLEY, Brian (FIHN-lee, BRIGH-an) NSH.

Goaltender. Catches right. 6'4", 183 lbs. Born, Sault Ste. Marie, Ont., July 3, 1981.
(Nashville's 1st choice, 6th overall, in 1999 Entry Draft).

			Regular Season								Playoffs						
Season	Club	Lea	GP	W	L	T	Mins	GA	SO	Avg	GP	W	L	Mins	GA	SO	Avg
1996-97	Sault Ste.Marie	NOHA	45	....	....	....	1943	109	3	2.38	....	....	....	....	....	....	....
1997-98	Barrie Colts	OHL	41	23	14	1	2154	105	3	2.92	5	1	3	260	13	0	3.00
1998-99	Barrie Colts	OHL	52	*36	10	4	3063	136	3	2.66	5	4	1	323	15	0	2.79
99-2000	Barrie Colts	OHL	47	24	12	6	2540	130	2	3.07	*23	14	8	1353	58	1	2.57

OHL First All-Star Team (1999)

FISCHER, Kai (FIH-shuhr, KIGH) COL.

Goaltender. Catches left. 5'11", 175 lbs. Born, Forst, West Germany, March 25, 1977.
(Colorado's 8th choice, 160th overall, in 1996 Entry Draft).

			Regular Season								Playoffs						
Season	Club	Lea	GP	W	L	T	Mins	GA	SO	Avg	GP	W	L	Mins	GA	SO	Avg
1995-96	Dusseldorfer EG	DEL-Jr.	1	0	0	1	60	5	0	5.00	....	....	....	....	....	....	....
1996-97	Dusseldorfer EG	DEL	2	1	0	0	125	7	0	3.36	....	....	....	....	....	....	....
1997-98	REV Bremerhaven	DEB-2	45	....	....	....	2674	172	0	3.86	....	....	....	....	....	....	....
1998-99	Moskitos Essen	DEB-2	16	....	....	....	896	56	0	3.75	....	....	....	....	....	....	....
99-2000	Revier Lowen	DEL	17	....	....	....	818	55	0	4.03	....	....	....	....	....	....	....

FISET, Stephane (fih-SEHT, STEH-fan) L.A.

Goaltender. Catches left. 6'1", 215 lbs. Born, Montreal, Que., June 17, 1970.
(Quebec's 3rd choice, 24th overall, in 1988 Entry Draft).

			Regular Season								Playoffs						
Season	Club	Lea	GP	W	L	T	Mins	GA	SO	Avg	GP	W	L	Mins	GA	SO	Avg
1986-87	Montreal-Bourassa	QAAA	29	7	20	1	1445	142	0	5.89	....	....	....	....	....	....	....
1987-88	Victoriaville Tigres	QMJHL	40	15	17	4	2221	146	1	3.94	2	0	2	163	10	0	3.68
1988-89	Victoriaville Tigres	QMJHL	43	25	14	0	2401	138	1	*3.45	12	*9	2	711	33	0	*2.78
1989-90	**Quebec**	**NHL**	**6**	**0**	**5**	**1**	**342**	**34**	**0**	**5.96**	....	....	....	....	....	....	....
	Victoriaville Tigres	QMJHL	24	14	6	3	1383	63	1	*2.73	*14	7	6	*790	49	0	3.72
1990-91	**Quebec**	**NHL**	**3**	**0**	**2**	**1**	**186**	**12**	**0**	**3.87**	....	....	....	....	....	....	....
	Halifax Citadels	AHL	36	10	15	8	1902	131	0	4.13	....	....	....	....	....	....	....
1991-92	**Quebec**	**NHL**	**23**	**7**	**10**	**2**	**1133**	**71**	**1**	**3.76**	....	....	....	....	....	....	....
	Halifax Citadels	AHL	29	8	14	6	1675	110	*3	3.94	....	....	....	....	....	....	....
1992-93	**Quebec**	**NHL**	**37**	**18**	**9**	**4**	**1939**	**110**	**0**	**3.40**	**1**	**0**	**0**	**21**	**1**	**0**	**2.86**
	Halifax Citadels	AHL	3	2	1	0	180	11	0	3.67	....	....	....	....	....	....	....
1993-94	**Quebec**	**NHL**	**50**	**20**	**25**	**4**	**2798**	**158**	**2**	**3.39**	....	....	....	....	....	....	....
	Cornwall Aces	AHL	1	0	1	0	60	4	0	4.00	....	....	....	....	....	....	....
1994-95	**Quebec**	**NHL**	**32**	**17**	**10**	**3**	**1879**	**87**	**2**	**2.78**	**4**	**1**	**2**	**209**	**16**	**0**	**4.59**
1995-96♦	**Colorado**	**NHL**	**37**	**22**	**6**	**7**	**2107**	**103**	**1**	**2.93**	**1**	**0**	**0**	**1**	**0**	**0**	**0.00**
1996-97	**Los Angeles**	**NHL**	**44**	**13**	**24**	**5**	**2482**	**132**	**4**	**3.19**	....	....	....	....	....	....	....
1997-98	**Los Angeles**	**NHL**	**60**	**26**	**25**	**8**	**3497**	**158**	**2**	**2.71**	**2**	**0**	**2**	**93**	**7**	**0**	**4.52**
1998-99	**Los Angeles**	**NHL**	**42**	**18**	**21**	**1**	**2403**	**104**	**3**	**2.60**	....	....	....	....	....	....	....
99-2000	**Los Angeles**	**NHL**	**47**	**20**	**15**	**7**	**2592**	**119**	**1**	**2.75**	**4**	**0**	**3**	**200**	**10**	**0**	**3.00**
	NHL Totals		**381**	**161**	**152**	**43**	**21358**	**1088**	**16**	**3.06**	**12**	**1**	**7**	**524**	**34**	**0**	**3.89**

QMJHL First All-Star Team (1989) • Canadian Major Junior Goaltender of the Year (1989)

Transferred to **Colorado** after **Quebec** franchise relocated, June 21, 1995. Traded to **LA Kings** by **Colorado** with Colorado's 1st round choice (Mathieu Biron) in 1998 Entry Draft for Eric Lacroix and Los Angeles' 1st round choice (Martin Skoula) in 1998 Entry Draft, June 20, 1996.

FITZPATRICK, Mark (FIHTZ-pa-TRIHK, MAHRK)

Goaltender. Catches left. 6'2", 195 lbs. Born, Toronto, Ont., November 13, 1968.
(Los Angeles' 2nd choice, 27th overall, in 1987 Entry Draft).

			Regular Season								Playoffs						
Season	Club	Lea	GP	W	L	T	Mins	GA	SO	Avg	GP	W	L	Mins	GA	SO	Avg
1983-84	Revelstoke	BCJHL	21	....	....	....	1019	90	0	5.30	....	....	....	....	....	....	....
1984-85	Medicine Hat	WHL	3	1	2	0	180	9	0	3.00	1	0	0	20	2	0	6.00
	Calgary Canucks	AJHL	29	....	....	....	1631	102	2	3.75	....	....	....	....	....	....	....
1985-86	Medicine Hat	WHL	41	26	6	1	2074	99	1	*2.86	*19	*11	5	*986	58	0	3.53
1986-87	Medicine Hat	WHL	50	31	11	4	2844	159	4	3.35	20	12	8	1224	71	1	3.48
1987-88	Medicine Hat	WHL	63	36	15	6	3600	194	2	3.23	16	12	4	959	52	*1	*3.25
1988-89	**Los Angeles**	**NHL**	**17**	**6**	**7**	**3**	**957**	**64**	**0**	**4.01**	....	....	....	....	....	....	....
	New Haven	AHL	18	10	5	1	980	54	1	3.31	....	....	....	....	....	....	....
	NY Islanders	**NHL**	**11**	**3**	**5**	**2**	**627**	**41**	**0**	**3.92**	....	....	....	....	....	....	....
1989-90	**NY Islanders**	**NHL**	**47**	**19**	**19**	**5**	**2653**	**150**	**3**	**3.39**	**4**	**0**	**2**	**152**	**13**	**0**	**5.13**
1990-91	**NY Islanders**	**NHL**	**2**	**1**	**1**	**0**	**120**	**6**	**0**	**3.00**	....	....	....	....	....	....	....
	Capital District	AHL	12	3	7	2	734	47	0	3.84	....	....	....	....	....	....	....
1991-92	**NY Islanders**	**NHL**	**30**	**11**	**13**	**5**	**1743**	**93**	**0**	**3.20**	....	....	....	....	....	....	....
	Capital District	AHL	14	6	5	1	782	39	0	2.99	....	....	....	....	....	....	....
1992-93	**NY Islanders**	**NHL**	**39**	**17**	**15**	**5**	**2253**	**130**	**0**	**3.46**	**3**	**0**	**1**	**77**	**4**	**0**	**3.12**
	Capital District	AHL	5	1	3	1	284	18	0	3.80	....	....	....	....	....	....	....
1993-94	**Florida**	**NHL**	**28**	**12**	**8**	**6**	**1603**	**73**	**1**	**2.73**	....	....	....	....	....	....	....
1994-95	**Florida**	**NHL**	**15**	**6**	**7**	**2**	**819**	**36**	**2**	**2.64**	....	....	....	....	....	....	....
1995-96	**Florida**	**NHL**	**34**	**15**	**11**	**3**	**1786**	**88**	**0**	**2.96**	**2**	**0**	**0**	**60**	**6**	**0**	**6.00**
1996-97	**Florida**	**NHL**	**30**	**8**	**9**	**9**	**1680**	**66**	**0**	**2.36**	....	....	....	....	....	....	....
1997-98	**Florida**	**NHL**	**12**	**2**	**7**	**2**	**640**	**32**	**1**	**3.00**	....	....	....	....	....	....	....
	Fort Wayne	IHL	2	1	1	0	119	8	0	4.03	....	....	....	....	....	....	....
	Tampa Bay	**NHL**	**34**	**7**	**24**	**1**	**1938**	**102**	**1**	**3.16**	....	....	....	....	....	....	....
1998-99	**Chicago**	**NHL**	**27**	**6**	**8**	**6**	**1403**	**64**	**0**	**2.74**	....	....	....	....	....	....	....
99-2000	**Carolina**	**NHL**	**3**	**0**	**2**	**0**	**107**	**8**	**0**	**4.49**	....	....	....	....	....	....	....
	Cincinnati	IHL	24	11	11	1	1379	59	4	2.57	....	....	....	....	....	....	....
	NHL Totals		**329**	**113**	**136**	**49**	**18329**	**953**	**8**	**3.12**	**9**	**0**	**3**	**289**	**23**	**0**	**4.78**

WHL East Second All-Star Team (1986, 1988) • Won Hap Emms Memorial Trophy (Memorial Cup Tournament Top Goaltender) (1987, 1988) • Won Bill Masterton Memorial Trophy (1992)

Traded to **NY Islanders** by **Los Angeles** with Wayne McBean and future considerations (Doug Crossman, May 23, 1989) for Kelly Hrudey, February 22, 1989. Traded to **Quebec** by **NY Islanders** with NY Islanders' 1st round choice (Adam Deadmarsh) in 1993 Entry Draft for Ron Hextall and Quebec's 1st round choice (Todd Bertuzzi) in 1993 Entry Draft, June 20, 1993. Claimed by **Florida** from **Quebec** in Expansion Draft, June 24, 1993. Traded to **Tampa Bay** by **Florida** with Jody Hull for Dino Ciccarelli and Jeff Norton, January 15, 1998. Traded to **Chicago** by **Tampa Bay** with Tampa Bay's 4th round choice (later traded to Montreal - Montreal selected Chris Dyment) in 1999 Entry Draft for Michal Sykora, July 17, 1998. Signed as a free agent by **Carolina**, August 19, 1999

FLAHERTY, Wade (FLAY-uhr-tee, WAYD) NYI

Goaltender. Catches left. 6', 170 lbs. Born, Terrace, B.C., January 11, 1968.
(Buffalo's 10th choice, 181st overall, in 1988 Entry Draft).

			Regular Season							Playoffs						
Season	Club	Lea	GP	W	L	T	Mins	GA	SO	Avg	GP	W	L	Mins	GA	SO	Avg
1984-85	Kelowna Wings	WHL	1	0	0	0	55	5	0	5.45	....	....	....	....	....	....	....
1985-86	Seattle T-Birds	WHL	9	1	3	0	271	36	0	7.97	....	....	....	....	....	....	....
	Spokane Chiefs	WHL	5	0	3	0	161	21	0	7.83	....	....	....	....	....	....	....
1986-87	Nanaimo Clippers	BCJHL	15	....	....	....	830	53	0	3.83	....	....	....	....	....	....	....
	Victoria Cougars	WHL	3	0	2	0	127	16	0	7.56	....	....	....	....	....	....	....
1987-88	Victoria Cougars	WHL	36	20	15	0	2052	135	0	3.95	5	2	3	300	18	0	3.60
1988-89	Victoria Cougars	WHL	42	21	19	0	2408	180	4	4.49	....	....	....	....	....	....	....
1989-90	Greensboro	ECHL	27	12	10	0	1308	96	0	4.40	....	....	....	....	....	....	....
1990-91	Kansas City	IHL	*56	16	31	4	2990	224	0	4.49	....	....	....	....	....	....	....
1991-92	**San Jose**	**NHL**	**3**	**0**	**3**	**0**	**178**	**13**	**0**	**4.38**	....	....	....	....	....	....	....
	Kansas City	IHL	43	26	14	3	2603	140	1	3.23	1	0	0	1	0	0	0.00
1992-93	**San Jose**	**NHL**	**1**	**0**	**1**	**0**	**60**	**5**	**0**	**5.00**	....	....	....	....	....	....	....
	Kansas City	IHL	*61	*34	19	7	*3642	195	2	3.21	*12	6	6	733	34	*1	2.78
1993-94	Kansas City	IHL	*60	32	19	9	*3564	202	0	3.40	....	....	....	....	....	....	....
1994-95	**San Jose**	**NHL**	**18**	**5**	**6**	**1**	**852**	**44**	**1**	**3.10**	**7**	**2**	**3**	**377**	**31**	**0**	**4.93**
1995-96	**San Jose**	**NHL**	**24**	**3**	**12**	**1**	**1137**	**92**	**0**	**4.85**	....	....	....	....	....	....	....
1996-97	**San Jose**	**NHL**	**7**	**2**	**4**	**0**	**359**	**31**	**0**	**5.18**	....	....	....	....	....	....	....
	Kentucky	AHL	19	8	6	2	1032	54	1	3.14	3	1	2	200	11	0	3.30
1997-98	**NY Islanders**	**NHL**	**16**	**4**	**4**	**3**	**694**	**23**	**3**	**1.99**	....	....	....	....	....	....	....
	Utah Grizzlies	IHL	24	16	5	3	1341	40	3	1.79	....	....	....	....	....	....	....
1998-99	**NY Islanders**	**NHL**	**20**	**5**	**11**	**2**	**1048**	**53**	**0**	**3.03**	....	....	....	....	....	....	....
	Lowell	AHL	5	1	3	1	305	16	0	3.15	....	....	....	....	....	....	....
99-2000	**NY Islanders**	**NHL**	**4**	**0**	**1**	**1**	**182**	**7**	**0**	**2.31**	....	....	....	....	....	....	....
	NHL Totals		**93**	**19**	**42**	**8**	**4510**	**268**	**4**	**3.57**	**7**	**2**	**3**	**377**	**31**	**0**	**4.93**

WHL West Second All-Star Team (1988) • Playoff MVP - ECHL (1990) • Shared James Norris Memorial Trophy (fewest goals against - IHL) with Arturs Irbe (1992) • IHL Second All-Star Team (1993, 1994)

Signed as a free agent by **San Jose**, September 3, 1991. Signed as a free agent by **NY Islanders**, July 22, 1997.

FORSBERG, Jonas (FOHRZ-buhrg, YOH-nuhs) S.J.

Goaltender. Catches left. 5'10", 150 lbs. Born, Stockholm, Sweden, June 15, 1975.
(San Jose's 12th choice, 210th overall, in 1993 Entry Draft).

			Regular Season							Playoffs						
Season	Club	Lea	GP	W	L	T	Mins	GA	SO	Avg	GP	W	L	Mins	GA	SO	Avg
1992-93	Djurgardens IF	Swede-Jr.	41	....	....	....	2460	114	0	2.78	....	....	....	....	....	....	....
1993-94	Djurgardens IF	Sweden	1	1	0	0	60	4	0	4.00	....	....	....	....	....	....	....
1994-95	Djurgardens IF	Sweden	1	0	1	0	60	6	0	6.00	....	....	....	....	....	....	....
1995-96	Djurgardens IF	Sweden	DID NOT PLAY – INJURED														
1996-97	IF Mangerland	Norway	16	....	....	....	947	76	0	4.81	....	....	....	....	....	....	....
1997-98	Sodertalje SK	Sweden	23	....	....	....	1252	60	0	2.88	....	....	....	....	....	....	....
1998-99	AIK Solna	Sweden	29	....	....	....	1668	81	2	2.91	....	....	....	....	....	....	....
99-2000	AIK Solna	Sweden	30	....	....	....	1696	91	2	3.22	....	....	....	....	....	....	....

FOUNTAIN, Mike (FOWN-tehn, MIGHK) OTT.

Goaltender. Catches left. 6'1", 180 lbs. Born, North York, Ont., January 26, 1972.
(Vancouver's 3rd choice, 45th overall, in 1992 Entry Draft).

			Regular Season							Playoffs						
Season	Club	Lea	GP	W	L	T	Mins	GA	SO	Avg	GP	W	L	Mins	GA	SO	Avg
1988-89	Huntsville	OJHL-C	22	*18	3	2	1306	82	0	3.77	....	....	....	....	....	....	....
1989-90	Chatham Maroons	OJHL-B	21	....	....	....	1249	76	0	3.65	....	....	....	....	....	....	....
1990-91	Sault Ste. Marie	OHL	7	5	2	0	380	19	0	3.00	....	....	....	....	....	....	....
	Oshawa Generals	OHL	30	17	5	1	1483	84	0	3.40	8	1	4	292	26	0	5.34
1991-92	Oshawa Generals	OHL	40	18	13	6	2260	149	1	3.96	7	3	4	429	26	0	3.64
1992-93	Canada	Nt-Team	13	7	5	1	745	37	1	2.98	....	....	....	....	....	....	....
	Hamilton Canucks	AHL	12	2	8	0	618	46	0	4.47	....	....	....	....	....	....	....
1993-94	Hamilton Canucks	AHL	*70	*34	28	6	*4005	241	*4	3.61	3	0	2	146	12	0	4.92
1994-95	Syracuse Crunch	AHL	61	25	29	7	3618	225	2	3.73	....	....	....	....	....	....	....
1995-96	Syracuse Crunch	AHL	54	21	27	3	3060	184	1	3.61	15	8	7	915	57	*2	3.74
1996-97	**Vancouver**	**NHL**	**6**	**2**	**2**	**0**	**245**	**14**	**1**	**3.43**	....	....	....	....	....	....	....
	Syracuse Crunch	AHL	25	8	14	2	1462	78	1	3.20	2	0	2	120	12	0	6.02
1997-98	**Carolina**	**NHL**	**3**	**0**	**3**	**0**	**163**	**10**	**0**	**3.68**	....	....	....	....	....	....	....
	New Haven	AHL	50	25	19	5	2922	139	3	2.85	....	....	....	....	....	....	....
1998-99	New Haven	AHL	51	23	24	3	2989	150	2	3.01	....	....	....	....	....	....	....
99-2000	**Ottawa**	**NHL**	**1**	**0**	**0**	**0**	**16**	**1**	**0**	**3.75**	....	....	....	....	....	....	....
	Grand Rapids	IHL	36	21	7	4	1851	77	3	2.50	1	0	0	20	4	0	12.00
	NHL Totals		**10**	**2**	**5**	**0**	**424**	**25**	**1**	**3.54**	....	....	....	....	....	....	....

OHL First All-Star Team (1992) • AHL Second All-Star Team (1994)

• Recorded shutout (3-0) in NHL debut vs. **New Jersey**, November 14, 1996. Signed as a free agent by **Carolina**, August 19, 1997. Signed as a free agent by **Ottawa**, July 30, 1999.

FRANEK, Petr (FRAH-nehk, PEE-tuhr) COL.

Goaltender. Catches left. 5'11", 187 lbs. Born, Most, Czech., April 6, 1975.
(Quebec's 10th choice, 205th overall, in 1993 Entry Draft).

			Regular Season							Playoffs						
Season	Club	Lea	GP	W	L	T	Mins	GA	SO	Avg	GP	W	L	Mins	GA	SO	Avg
1992-93	CHZ Litvinov	Czech.	5	....	....	....	273	15	0	3.29	....	....	....	....	....	....	....
1993-94	CHZ Litvinov	Cze-Rep	11	....	....	....	535	34	0	3.81	2	....	....	61	10	....	9.83
1994-95	CHZ Litvinov	Cze-Rep	12	....	....	....	657	47	0	4.29	1	0	0	16	0	0	0.00
1995-96	CHZ Litvinov	Cze-Rep	36	....	....	....	2096	85	3	2.43	16	....	....	948	47	1	2.97
1996-97	Hershey Bears	AHL	15	4	1	0	457	23	3	3.02	....	....	....	....	....	....	....
	Brantford Smoke	ColHL	6	4	1	0	321	14	0	2.61	....	....	....	....	....	....	....
	Quebec Rafales	IHL	6	3	3	0	357	18	0	3.02	1	0	1	40	4	0	6.00
1997-98	Hershey Bears	AHL	43	19	14	2	2169	98	2	2.71	1	0	1	60	4	0	4.00
1998-99	Utah Grizzlies	IHL	8	1	6	1	446	26	0	3.50	....	....	....	....	....	....	....
	Las Vegas	IHL	37	17	13	2	1879	107	0	3.42	....	....	....	....	....	....	....
99-2000	EHC Nurnberg	DEL	30	....	....	....	1603	73	2	2.73	....	....	....	....	....	....	....

Rights transferred to **Colorado** after **Quebec** franchise relocated, June 21, 1995.

FRIESEN, Terry (FREE-zehn, TAIR-ree) S.J.

Goaltender. Catches left. 5'11", 195 lbs. Born, Winkler, Man., October 29, 1977.
(San Jose's 3rd choice, 55th overall, in 1996 Entry Draft).

			Regular Season							Playoffs						
Season	Club	Lea	GP	W	L	T	Mins	GA	SO	Avg	GP	W	L	Mins	GA	SO	Avg
1994-95	Winkler Flyers	MJHL	50	....	....	....	1164	72	1	3.71	....	....	....	....	....	....	....
1995-96	Swift Current	WHL	42	19	17	3	2504	155	2	3.71	6	2	4	338	21	0	3.73
1996-97	Swift Current	WHL	53	28	19	3	3090	170	1	3.30	10	6	4	592	27	0	2.74
1997-98	Swift Current	WHL	44	26	10	7	2639	124	1	2.82	12	7	5	754	28	1	*2.23
1998-99	Richmond	ECHL	24	9	13	0	1278	76	1	3.57	1	1	0	20	0	0	0.00
	Kentucky	AHL	1	0	0	0	26	2	0	4.66	....	....	....	....	....	....	....
99-2000	New Orleans Brass	ECHL	26	11	10	2	1356	76	2	3.36	1	0	0	16	1	0	3.86

WHL East Second All-Star Team (1996) • WHL East First All-Star Team (1998)

FUHR, Grant (FYOOR, GRANT) CGY.

Goaltender. Catches right. 5'10", 201 lbs. Born, Spruce Grove, Alta., September 28, 1962.
(Edmonton's 1st choice, 8th overall, in 1981 Entry Draft).

			Regular Season							Playoffs						
Season	Club	Lea	GP	W	L	T	Mins	GA	SO	Avg	GP	W	L	Mins	GA	SO	Avg
1979-80	Victoria Cougars	WHL	43	30	12	0	2488	130	2	3.14	8	5	3	465	22	0	2.84
1980-81	Victoria Cougars	WHL	59	48	9	1	3448	160	*4	*2.78	15	12	3	899	45	*1	*3.00
1981-82	**Edmonton**	**NHL**	**48**	**28**	**5**	**14**	**2847**	**157**	**0**	**3.31**	**5**	**2**	**3**	**309**	**26**	**0**	**5.05**
1982-83	**Edmonton**	**NHL**	**32**	**13**	**12**	**5**	**1803**	**129**	**0**	**4.29**	**1**	**0**	**0**	**11**	**0**	**0**	**0.00**
	Moncton Alpines	AHL	10	4	5	1	604	40	0	3.98	....	....	....	....	....	....	....
1983-84♦	**Edmonton**	**NHL**	**45**	**30**	**10**	**4**	**2625**	**171**	**1**	**3.91**	**16**	**11**	**4**	**883**	**44**	**1**	**2.99**
1984-85♦	**Edmonton**	**NHL**	**46**	**26**	**8**	**7**	**2559**	**165**	**1**	**3.87**	***18**	***15**	**3**	**1064**	**55**	**0**	**3.10**
1985-86	**Edmonton**	**NHL**	**40**	**29**	**8**	**0**	**2184**	**143**	**0**	**3.93**	**9**	**5**	**4**	**541**	**28**	**0**	**3.11**
1986-87♦	**Edmonton**	**NHL**	**44**	**22**	**13**	**3**	**2388**	**137**	**0**	**3.44**	**19**	**14**	**5**	**1148**	**47**	**0**	**2.46**
1987-88♦	**Edmonton**	**NHL**	***75**	***40**	**24**	**9**	***4304**	**246**	***4**	**3.43**	***19**	***16**	**2**	***1136**	**55**	**0**	**2.90**
1988-89	**Edmonton**	**NHL**	**59**	**23**	**26**	**6**	**3341**	**213**	**1**	**3.83**	**7**	**3**	**4**	**417**	**24**	**1**	**3.45**
1989-90♦	**Edmonton**	**NHL**	**21**	**9**	**7**	**3**	**1081**	**70**	**1**	**3.89**	....	....	....	....	....	....	....
	Cape Breton	AHL	2	2	0	0	120	6	0	3.01	....	....	....	....	....	....	....
1990-91	**Edmonton**	**NHL**	**13**	**6**	**4**	**3**	**778**	**39**	**1**	**3.01**	**17**	**8**	**7**	**1019**	**51**	**0**	**3.00**
	Cape Breton	AHL	4	2	2	0	240	17	0	4.25	....	....	....	....	....	....	....
1991-92	**Toronto**	**NHL**	**66**	**25**	**33**	**5**	**3774**	**230**	**2**	**3.66**	....	....	....	....	....	....	....
1992-93	**Toronto**	**NHL**	**29**	**13**	**9**	**4**	**1665**	**87**	**1**	**3.14**	....	....	....	....	....	....	....
	Buffalo	**NHL**	**29**	**11**	**15**	**2**	**1694**	**98**	**0**	**3.47**	**8**	**3**	**4**	**474**	**27**	**1**	**3.42**
1993-94	**Buffalo**	**NHL**	**32**	**13**	**12**	**3**	**1726**	**106**	**2**	**3.68**	....	....	....	....	....	....	....
	Rochester	AHL	5	3	0	2	310	10	0	1.94	....	....	....	....	....	....	....
1994-95	**Buffalo**	**NHL**	**3**	**1**	**2**	**0**	**180**	**12**	**0**	**4.00**	....	....	....	....	....	....	....
	Los Angeles	**NHL**	**14**	**1**	**7**	**3**	**698**	**47**	**0**	**4.04**	....	....	....	....	....	....	....
1995-96	**St. Louis**	**NHL**	***79**	**30**	**28**	**16**	**4365**	**209**	**3**	**2.87**	**2**	**1**	**0**	**69**	**1**	**0**	**0.87**
1996-97	**St. Louis**	**NHL**	**73**	**33**	**27**	**11**	**4261**	**193**	**3**	**2.72**	**6**	**2**	**4**	**357**	**13**	**2**	**2.18**
1997-98	**St. Louis**	**NHL**	**58**	**29**	**21**	**6**	**3274**	**138**	**3**	**2.53**	**10**	**6**	**4**	**616**	**28**	**0**	**2.73**
1998-99	**St. Louis**	**NHL**	**39**	**16**	**11**	**8**	**2193**	**89**	**2**	**2.44**	**13**	**6**	**6**	**790**	**31**	**1**	**2.35**
99-2000	**Calgary**	**NHL**	**23**	**5**	**13**	**2**	**1205**	**77**	**0**	**3.83**	....	....	....	....	....	....	....
	Saint John Flames	AHL	2	0	2	0	99	10	0	6.05	....	....	....	....	....	....	....
	NHL Totals		**868**	**403**	**295**	**114**	**48945**	**2756**	**25**	**3.38**	**150**	**92**	**50**	**8834**	**430**	**6**	**2.92**

WHL First All-Star Team (1980, 1981) • NHL Second All-Star Team (1982) • NHL First All-Star Team (1988) • Won Vezina Trophy (1988) • Shared William M. Jennings Trophy with Dominik Hasek (1994) • Played in NHL All-Star Game (1982, 1984, 1985, 1986, 1988, 1989)

Traded to **Toronto** by **Edmonton** with Glenn Anderson and Craig Berube for Vincent Damphousse, Peter Ing, Scott Thornton, Luke Richardson, future considerations and cash, September 19, 1991. Traded to **Buffalo** by **Toronto** with Toronto's 5th round choice (Kevin Popp) in 1995 Entry Draft for Dave Andreychuk, Daren Puppa and Buffalo's 1st round choice (Kenny Jonsson) in 1993 Entry Draft, February 2, 1993. Traded to **Los Angeles** by **Buffalo** with Philippe Boucher and Denis Tsygurov for Alexei Zhitnik, Robb Stauber, Charlie Huddy and Los Angeles' 5th round choice (Marian Menhart) in 1995 Entry Draft, February 14, 1995. Signed as a free agent by **St. Louis**, July 14, 1995. Traded to **Calgary** by **St. Louis** for Calgary's 3rd round choice (Justin Papineau) in 2000 Entry Draft, September 4, 1999. • Statistics for suspended game vs. Boston on May 24, 1988 are included in playoff record.

GAGE, Joaquin (GAYJ, YOH-ah-keen) EDM.

Goaltender. Catches left. 6', 200 lbs. Born, Vancouver, B.C., October 19, 1973.
(Edmonton's 6th choice, 109th overall, in 1992 Entry Draft).

			Regular Season							Playoffs						
Season	Club	Lea	GP	W	L	T	Mins	GA	SO	Avg	GP	W	L	Mins	GA	SO	Avg
1990-91	Bellingham	BCJHL	16	....	....	....	751	64	0	5.11	....	....	....	....	....	....	....
	Chilliwack Chiefs	BCJHL	2	1	0	0	85	11	0	7.76	....	....	....	....	....	....	....
	Portland	WHL	3	0	3	0	180	17	0	5.70	....	....	....	....	....	....	....
1991-92	Portland	WHL	63	27	30	4	3635	269	2	4.44	6	2	4	366	28	0	4.59
1992-93	Portland	WHL	38	21	16	1	2302	153	2	3.99	8	5	2	427	30	0	4.22
1993-94	Prince Albert	WHL	53	24	25	3	3041	212	1	4.18	....	....	....	....	....	....	....
1994-95	Cape Breton Oilers	AHL	54	17	28	5	3010	207	0	4.13	....	....	....	....	....	....	....
	Edmonton	**NHL**	**2**	**0**	**2**	**0**	**99**	**7**	**0**	**4.24**	....	....	....	....	....	....	....
1995-96	**Edmonton**	**NHL**	**16**	**2**	**8**	**1**	**717**	**45**	**0**	**3.77**	....	....	....	....	....	....	....
	Cape Breton Oilers	AHL	21	8	11	0	1162	80	0	4.13	....	....	....	....	....	....	....
1996-97	Hamilton Bulldogs	AHL	29	7	14	4	1558	91	0	3.50	....	....	....	....	....	....	....
	Wheeling Nailers	ECHL	3	1	0	0	120	8	0	4.00	....	....	....	....	....	....	....
1997-98	Raleigh IceCaps	ECHL	39	19	14	3	2173	116	1	3.20	....	....	....	....	....	....	....
	Syracuse Crunch	AHL	2	1	1	0	120	7	0	3.50	....	....	....	....	....	....	....
1998-99	Augusta Lynx	ECHL	5	5	0	0	300	16	0	3.20	....	....	....	....	....	....	....
	Portland Pirates	AHL	26	8	11	3	1429	69	2	2.90	....	....	....	....	....	....	....
	Providence Bruins	AHL	3	0	2	0	130	9	0	4.16	....	....	....	....	....	....	....
	Syracuse Crunch	AHL	12	2	8	2	706	46	0	3.91	....	....	....	....	....	....	....
99-2000	Canada	Nt-Team	29	13	10	2	1530	83	0	3.25	....	....	....	....	....	....	....
	Hamilton Bulldogs	AHL	2	0	1	1	124	5	0	2.42	10	5	5	580	28	0	2.89
	NHL Totals		**18**	**2**	**10**	**1**	**816**	**52**	**0**	**3.82**	....	....	....	....	....	....	....

Signed as a free agent by **Hamilton** (AHL), April 7, 2000. Signed as a free agent by **Edmonton**, July 25, 2000.

GARDNER, Greg CBJ

Goaltender. Catches left. 6', 190 lbs. Born, Mississauga, Ont., November 21, 1975.

			Regular Season							Playoffs						
Season	Club	Lea	GP	W	L	T	Mins	GA	SO	Avg	GP	W	L	Mins	GA	SO	Avg
1992-93	Caledon	OJHL-B	28	....	....	....	1390	73	1	3.15	....	....	....	....	....	....	....
1993-94	Thornhill Rattlers	OJHL	31	18	11	1	1813	103	1	3.41	....	....	....	....	....	....	....
1994-95	Thornhill Rattlers	OJHL	42	....	....	....	2430	117	4	2.89	11	....	....	677	36	1	3.19
1995-96	Thornhill Rattlers	OJHL	34	....	....	....	2012	99	2	2.95	....	....	....	....	....	....	....
1996-97	Niagara University	ECAC-2	17	8	5	2	939	54	0	3.45	....	....	....	....	....	....	....
	Thornhill Rattlers	OJHL	....	....	....	....	....	....	....	....	18	....	....	1095	59	0	3.23
1997-98	Niagara University	ECAC-2	25	12	10	3	1454	74	0	3.05	....	....	....	....	....	....	....
1998-99	Niagara University	CHA	30	15	10	3	1742	78	4	2.69	....	....	....	....	....	....	....
99-2000	Niagara University	CHA	*41	*29	8	4	*2503	64	*12	*1.53	....	....	....	....	....	....	....

CHA First All-Star Team (2000) • CHA Goaltender-of-the-Year (2000) • CHA Player-of-the-Year (2000)

Signed as a free agent by **Columbus**, May 16, 2000.

GARNER, Tyrone (GAHR-nuhr, TIGH-rohn) CGY.

Goaltender. Catches left. 6'1", 200 lbs. Born, Stoney Creek, Ont., July 27, 1978.
(NY Islanders' 4th choice, 83rd overall, in 1996 Entry Draft).

			Regular Season								Playoffs						
Season	**Club**	**Lea**	**GP**	**W**	**L**	**T**	**Mins**	**GA**	**SO**	**Avg**	**GP**	**W**	**L**	**Mins**	**GA**	**SO**	**Avg**
1994-95	Stoney Creek	OJHL-B	10	....	....	....	589	62	0	6.32	....	....	....	....	....	....	....
1995-96	Hamilton Kilty B's	OJHL	8	....	....	....	419	28	0	4.01	....	....	....	....	....	....	....
	Oshawa Generals	OHL	32	11	15	4	1697	112	0	3.96	....	....	....	....	....	....	....
1996-97	Oshawa Generals	OHL	9	6	1	0	434	20	0	2.76	3	1	0	88	6	0	4.09
1997-98	Oshawa Generals	OHL	54	23	17	8	2946	162	1	3.30	7	3	4	450	25	0	3.33
1998-99	Oshawa Generals	OHL	44	24	15	3	2496	124	4	2.98	15	9	6	901	57	0	3.80
	Calgary	**NHL**	**3**	**0**	**2**	**0**	**139**	**12**	**0**	**5.18**	....	....	....	....	....	....	....
99-2000	Saint John Flames	AHL	19	4	8	4	940	70	0	4.47	....	....	....	....	....	....	....
	Dayton Bombers	ECHL	3	0	2	0	113	11	0	5.86	....	....	....	....	....	....	....
	Johnstown Chiefs	ECHL	17	8	6	3	971	48	0	2.97	1	0	1	59	2	0	2.03
	NHL Totals		**3**	**0**	**2**	**0**	**139**	**12**	**0**	**5.18**	....	....	....	....	....	....	....

OHL Second All-Star Team (1999)

Traded to **Calgary** by **NY Islanders** with Marty McInnis and Calgary's sixth round choice (previously acquired, Calgary selected Ilja Demidov) in 1997 Entry Draft for Robert Reichel, March 18, 1997.

GARON, Mathieu (gah-ROHN, MAT-yoo) MTL.

Goaltender. Catches right. 6'3", 182 lbs. Born, Chandler, Que., January 9, 1978.
(Montreal's 2nd choice, 44th overall, in 1996 Entry Draft).

			Regular Season								Playoffs						
Season	**Club**	**Lea**	**GP**	**W**	**L**	**T**	**Mins**	**GA**	**SO**	**Avg**	**GP**	**W**	**L**	**Mins**	**GA**	**SO**	**Avg**
1995-96	Victoriaville Tigres	QMJHL	51	18	27	0	2709	189	1	4.19	12	7	4	676	38	1	3.39
1996-97	Victoriaville Tigres	QMJHL	53	29	18	3	3032	150	*6	2.97	6	2	4	330	23	0	4.18
1997-98	Victoriaville Tigres	QMJHL	47	27	18	2	2802	125	5	2.68	6	2	4	345	22	0	3.82
1998-99	Fredericton	AHL	40	14	22	2	2222	114	3	3.08	6	1	1	208	12	0	3.47
99-2000	Quebec Citadelles	AHL	53	17	28	3	2884	149	2	3.10	1	0	0	20	3	0	8.82

QMJHL First All-Star Team (1998) • Canadian Major Junior First All-Star Team (1998) • Canadian Major Junior Goaltender of the Year (1998)

GAUTHIER, Sean (GOH-tyay, SHAWN) FLA.

Goaltender. Catches left. 5'11", 200 lbs. Born, Sudbury, Ont., March 28, 1971.
(Winnipeg's 7th choice, 181st overall, in 1991 Entry Draft).

			Regular Season								Playoffs						
Season	**Club**	**Lea**	**GP**	**W**	**L**	**T**	**Mins**	**GA**	**SO**	**Avg**	**GP**	**W**	**L**	**Mins**	**GA**	**SO**	**Avg**
1987-88	Oakville Blades	OJHL-B	28	....	....	....	1491	110	2	4.43	....	....	....	....	....	....	....
1988-89	Kingston Raiders	OHL	37	7	18	1	1528	141	0	5.54	....	....	....	....	....	....	....
1989-90	Kingston	OHL	32	17	9	0	1602	101	0	3.78	2	0	1	76	6	0	4.74
1990-91	Kingston	OHL	59	16	36	3	3200	282	0	5.29	....	....	....	....	....	....	....
1991-92	Moncton Hawks	AHL	25	8	10	5	1415	88	1	3.73	2	0	0	26	2	0	4.62
	Fort Wayne	IHL	18	10	4	2	978	59	1	3.62	2	0	0	48	7	0	8.74
1992-93	Moncton Hawks	AHL	38	10	16	9	2196	145	0	3.96	2	0	1	75	6	0	4.80
1993-94	Moncton Hawks	AHL	13	3	5	1	616	41	0	3.99	....	....	....	....	....	....	....
	Fort Wayne	IHL	22	9	9	3	1139	66	0	3.48	....	....	....	....	....	....	....
1994-95	Fort Wayne	IHL	5	0	2	1	217	15	0	4.13	....	....	....	....	....	....	....
	Canada	Nt-Team	24	....	....	....	1326	53	0	2.40	....	....	....	....	....	....	....
1995-96	South Carolina	ECHL	49	31	11	7	2891	149	0	3.09	8	5	3	478	24	0	3.01
	St. John's Leafs	AHL	5	1	1	0	173	9	0	3.12	....	....	....	....	....	....	....
1996-97	Pensacola	ECHL	46	23	21	1	2692	168	1	3.74	12	8	4	749	44	*1	3.52
1997-98	Pensacola	ECHL	54	29	17	7	3213	194	0	3.62	*19	12	7	1180	58	1	2.95
1998-99	**San Jose**	**NHL**	**1**	**0**	**0**	**0**	**3**	**0**	**0**	**0.00**	....	....	....	....	....	....	....
	Kentucky	AHL	40	18	15	6	2376	99	1	2.50	4	0	1	130	8	0	3.68
99-2000	Louisiana	ECHL	22	12	6	3	1230	62	0	3.02	....	....	....	....	....	....	....
	Louisville Panthers	AHL	39	24	12	2	2259	102	3	2.71	4	1	3	239	14	0	3.52
	NHL Totals		**1**	**0**	**0**	**0**	**3**	**0**	**0**	**0.00**	....	....	....	....	....	....	....

ECHL Second All-Star Team (1996, 1998)

Signed as a free agent by **San Jose**, July 23, 1998. Signed as a free agent by **Florida**, January 13, 2000. • Played w/ RHI's LA Blades in 1995 (22-8-9-5-(3)-1023-133-0-6.24) and 1996 (19-6-8-1-(1)-733-92-0-6.02) and w/ Sacramento River Rats in 1997 (5-2-2-0-(0)-233-35-0-7.22)

GIGUERE, Jean-Sebastien (ZHEE-gair, ZHAWN-suh-BAS-tee-yeh) ANA.

Goaltender. Catches left. 6'1", 175 lbs. Born, Montreal, Que., May 16, 1977.
(Hartford's 1st choice, 13th overall, in 1995 Entry Draft).

			Regular Season								Playoffs						
Season	**Club**	**Lea**	**GP**	**W**	**L**	**T**	**Mins**	**GA**	**SO**	**Avg**	**GP**	**W**	**L**	**Mins**	**GA**	**SO**	**Avg**
1992-93	Laval Regents	QAAA	25	12	11	2	1498	76	0	3.02	....	....	....	....	....	....	....
1993-94	Verdun College	QMJHL	25	13	5	2	1234	66	1	3.21	....	....	....	....	....	....	....
1994-95	Halifax	QMJHL	47	14	27	5	2755	181	2	3.94	7	3	4	417	17	1	*2.45
1995-96	Halifax	QMJHL	55	26	23	2	3230	185	1	3.44	6	1	5	354	24	0	4.07
1996-97	**Hartford**	**NHL**	**8**	**1**	**4**	**0**	**394**	**24**	**0**	**3.65**	....	....	....	....	....	....	....
	Halifax	QMJHL	50	28	19	3	3014	170	2	3.38	16	9	7	954	58	0	3.65
1997-98	Saint John Flames	AHL	31	16	10	3	1758	72	2	2.46	10	5	3	536	27	0	3.02
1998-99	**Calgary**	**NHL**	**15**	**6**	**7**	**1**	**860**	**46**	**0**	**3.21**	....	....	....	....	....	....	....
	Saint John Flames	AHL	39	18	16	3	2145	123	3	3.44	7	3	2	304	21	0	4.14
99-2000	**Calgary**	**NHL**	**7**	**1**	**3**	**1**	**330**	**15**	**0**	**2.73**	....	....	....	....	....	....	....
	Saint John Flames	AHL	41	17	17	3	2243	114	0	3.05	3	0	3	178	9	0	3.03
	NHL Totals		**30**	**8**	**14**	**2**	**1584**	**85**	**0**	**3.22**	....	....	....	....	....	....	....

QMJHL Second All-Star Team (1997) • Shared Harry "Hap" Holmes Memorial Trophy (fewest goals against - AHL) with Tyler Moss (1998)

Transferred to **Carolina** after **Hartford** franchise relocated, June 25, 1997. Traded to **Calgary** by **Carolina** with Andrew Cassels for Gary Roberts and Trevor Kidd, August 25, 1997. Traded to **Anaheim** by **Calgary** for Anaheim's 2nd round choice (later traded to Washington - Washington selected Matt Pettinger) in 2000 Entry Draft, June 10, 2000.

GORDON, Ian (GOHR-dohn, EE-an)

Goaltender. Catches left. 5'10", 160 lbs. Born, Yorkton, Sask., May 15, 1975.

			Regular Season								Playoffs						
Season	**Club**	**Lea**	**GP**	**W**	**L**	**T**	**Mins**	**GA**	**SO**	**Avg**	**GP**	**W**	**L**	**Mins**	**GA**	**SO**	**Avg**
1991-92	Swift Current	SAHA	28	....	....	....	1465	156	0	6.39	....	....	....	....	....	....	....
1992-93	Swift Current	WHL	10	1	6	0	365	31	0	5.10	2	0	0	53	3	0	3.40
1993-94	Swift Current	WHL	65	29	27	4	3657	204	6	3.35	7	3	4	420	21	1	3.00
1994-95	Swift Current	WHL	17	6	9	1	994	62	1	3.74	....	....	....	....	....	....	....
	Saskatoon Blades	WHL	41	24	9	7	2476	129	1	3.13	10	4	6	633	29	1	2.75
1995-96	Saint John Flames	AHL	19	2	12	0	768	56	0	4.37	....	....	....	....	....	....	....
1996-97	Saint John Flames	AHL	21	5	9	1	988	50	0	3.03	....	....	....	....	....	....	....
	Grand Rapids	IHL	5	2	2	0	257	15	0	3.50	1	0	0	0	0	0	0.00
1997-98	Grand Rapids	IHL	49	23	16	4	2573	115	1	2.68	2	0	2	118	7	0	3.54
1998-99	Grand Rapids	IHL	41	16	19	3	2149	123	2	3.43	....	....	....	....	....	....	....
99-2000	Utah Grizzlies	IHL	29	15	7	4	1568	70	2	2.68	....	....	....	....	....	....	....
	Cleveland	IHL	9	2	3	3	480	22	2	2.75	5	2	3	301	11	1	2.20

Signed as a free agent by **Calgary**, October 6, 1995. Traded to **Cleveland** (IHL) by **Utah** (IHL) with Joe Frederick and Sean Berans for Ted Crowley, March 16, 2000.

GRAHAME, John (GRAY-ham, JAWN) BOS.

Goaltender. Catches left. 6'2", 214 lbs. Born, Denver, CO, August 31, 1975.
(Boston's 7th choice, 229th overall, in 1994 Entry Draft).

			Regular Season								Playoffs						
Season	**Club**	**Lea**	**GP**	**W**	**L**	**T**	**Mins**	**GA**	**SO**	**Avg**	**GP**	**W**	**L**	**Mins**	**GA**	**SO**	**Avg**
1993-94	Sioux City	USHL	20	....	....	....	1200	73	0	3.70	....	....	....	....	....	....	....
1994-95	Lake Superior	CCHA	28	16	7	3	1616	75	2	2.79	....	....	....	....	....	....	....
1995-96	Lake Superior	CCHA	29	21	4	2	1558	66	2	2.54	....	....	....	....	....	....	....
1996-97	Lake Superior	CCHA	37	19	13	4	2197	134	3	3.66	....	....	....	....	....	....	....
1997-98	Providence Bruins	AHL	55	15	31	4	3053	164	3	3.22	....	....	....	....	....	....	....
1998-99	Providence Bruins	AHL	48	*37	9	1	2771	134	3	2.90	19	*15	4	*1209	48	1	2.38
99-2000	**Boston**	**NHL**	**24**	**7**	**10**	**5**	**1344**	**55**	**2**	**2.46**	....	....	....	....	....	....	....
	Providence Bruins	AHL	27	11	13	2	1528	86	1	3.38	13	10	3	839	35	0	2.50
	NHL Totals		**24**	**7**	**10**	**5**	**1344**	**55**	**2**	**2.46**	....	....	....	....	....	....	....

GUSTAFSON, Derek MIN.

Goaltender. Catches left. 5'11", 210 lbs. Born, Gresham, OR, June 21, 1979.

			Regular Season								Playoffs						
Season	**Club**	**Lea**	**GP**	**W**	**L**	**T**	**Mins**	**GA**	**SO**	**Avg**	**GP**	**W**	**L**	**Mins**	**GA**	**SO**	**Avg**
1995-96	Seattle Ironmen	BCAHA	16	....	....	....	913	46	0	3.02	....	....	....	....	....	....	....
1996-97	Vernon Vipers	BCJHL	23	....	....	....	1241	70	....	3.38	....	....	....	....	....	....	....
1997-98	Vernon Vipers	BCJHL	42	27	13	2	2270	144	1	3.81	6	2	1	257	13	0	3.04
1998-99	Vernon Vipers	BCJHL	42	39	3	0	2505	94	3	2.25	....	....	....	....	....	....	....
99-2000	St. Lawrence	ECAC	18	12	3	2	992	36	2	2.18	6	5	1	483	15	0	1.86

BCJHL Interior Top Goaltender (1999) • BCJHL First All-Star Team • ECAC Rookie-of-the-Year (2000)

Signed as a free agent by **Minnesota**, June 9, 2000.

HACKETT, Jeff (HA-keht, JEHF) MTL.

Goaltender. Catches left. 6'1", 198 lbs. Born, London, Ont., June 1, 1968.
(NY Islanders' 2nd choice, 34th overall, in 1987 Entry Draft).

			Regular Season								Playoffs						
Season	**Club**	**Lea**	**GP**	**W**	**L**	**T**	**Mins**	**GA**	**SO**	**Avg**	**GP**	**W**	**L**	**Mins**	**GA**	**SO**	**Avg**
1984-85	London Diamonds	OJHL-B	18	....	....	....	1078	73	1	4.06	....	....	....	....	....	....	....
1985-86	London Diamonds	OJHL-B	19	....	....	....	1150	66	0	3.43	....	....	....	....	....	....	....
1986-87	Oshawa Generals	OHL	31	18	9	2	1672	85	2	3.05	15	8	7	895	40	0	2.68
1987-88	Oshawa Generals	OHL	53	30	21	2	3165	205	0	3.89	7	3	4	438	31	0	4.25
1988-89	**NY Islanders**	**NHL**	**13**	**4**	**7**	**0**	**662**	**39**	**0**	**3.53**	....	....	....	....	....	....	....
	Springfield Indians	AHL	29	12	14	2	1677	116	0	4.15	....	....	....	....	....	....	....
1989-90	Springfield Indians	AHL	54	24	25	3	3045	187	1	3.68	*17	*10	5	934	60	0	3.85
1990-91	**NY Islanders**	**NHL**	**30**	**5**	**18**	**1**	**1508**	**91**	**0**	**3.62**	....	....	....	....	....	....	....
1991-92	**San Jose**	**NHL**	**42**	**11**	**27**	**1**	**2314**	**148**	**0**	**3.84**	....	....	....	....	....	....	....
1992-93	**San Jose**	**NHL**	**36**	**2**	**30**	**1**	**2000**	**176**	**0**	**5.28**	....	....	....	....	....	....	....
1993-94	**Chicago**	**NHL**	**22**	**2**	**12**	**3**	**1084**	**62**	**0**	**3.43**	....	....	....	....	....	....	....
1994-95	**Chicago**	**NHL**	**7**	**1**	**3**	**2**	**328**	**13**	**0**	**2.38**	**2**	**0**	**0**	**26**	**1**	**0**	**2.31**
1995-96	**Chicago**	**NHL**	**35**	**18**	**11**	**4**	**2000**	**80**	**4**	**2.40**	**1**	**0**	**1**	**60**	**5**	**0**	**5.00**
1996-97	**Chicago**	**NHL**	**41**	**19**	**18**	**4**	**2473**	**89**	**2**	**2.16**	**6**	**2**	**4**	**345**	**25**	**0**	**4.35**
1997-98	**Chicago**	**NHL**	**58**	**21**	**25**	**11**	**3441**	**126**	**8**	**2.20**	....	....	....	....	....	....	....
1998-99	**Chicago**	**NHL**	**10**	**2**	**6**	**1**	**524**	**33**	**0**	**3.78**	....	....	....	....	....	....	....
	Montreal	**NHL**	**53**	**24**	**20**	**9**	**3091**	**117**	**5**	**2.27**	....	....	....	....	....	....	....
99-2000	**Montreal**	**NHL**	**56**	**23**	**25**	**7**	**3301**	**132**	**3**	**2.40**	....	....	....	....	....	....	....
	NHL Totals		**403**	**132**	**202**	**44**	**22726**	**1106**	**22**	**2.92**	**9**	**2**	**5**	**431**	**31**	**0**	**4.32**

Won Jack A. Butterfield Trophy (Playoff MVP - AHL) (1990)

Claimed by **San Jose** from **NY Islanders** in Expansion Draft, May 30, 1991. Traded to **Chicago** by **San Jose** for Chicago's 3rd round choice (Alexei Yegorov) in 1994 Entry Draft, July 13, 1993. Traded to **Montreal** by **Chicago** with Eric Weinrich, Alain Nasreddine and Tampa Bay's 4th round choice (previously acquired, Montreal selected Chris Dyment) in 1999 Entry Draft for Jocelyn Thibault, Dave Manson and Brad Brown, November 16, 1998.

HAMERLIK, Peter (HAHM-reh-lik) PIT.

Goaltender. Catches left. 6'1", 183 lbs. Born, Myjava, Czech., January 2, 1982.
(Pittsburgh's 3rd choice, 84th overall, in 2000 Entry Draft).

			Regular Season								Playoffs						
Season	**Club**	**Lea**	**GP**	**W**	**L**	**T**	**Mins**	**GA**	**SO**	**Avg**	**GP**	**W**	**L**	**Mins**	**GA**	**SO**	**Avg**
1997-98	HK Skalica-Jr.	Slovakia	49	....	....	....	2969	168	....	3.40	....	....	....	....	....	....	....
1998-99	HK Skalica	Slovakia	1	....	....	....	24	3	0	7.50	....	....	....	....	....	....	....
99-2000	HK Skalica-Jr.	Slovakia	37	....	....	....	1850	121	....	3.92	....	....	....	....	....	....	....
	HK Skalica	Slovakia	7	....	....	....	286	16	....	3.36	....	....	....	....	....	....	....

HASEK, Dominik (HAH-shihk, DOHM-ih-NIHK) BUF.

Goaltender. Catches left. 5'11", 180 lbs. Born, Pardubice, Czech., January 29, 1965.
(Chicago's 11th choice, 207th overall, in 1983 Entry Draft).

			Regular Season								Playoffs						
Season	**Club**	**Lea**	**GP**	**W**	**L**	**T**	**Mins**	**GA**	**SO**	**Avg**	**GP**	**W**	**L**	**Mins**	**GA**	**SO**	**Avg**
1981-82	HC Pardubice	Czech.	12	....	....	....	661	34	....	3.09	....	....	....	....	....	....	....
1982-83	HC Pardubice	Czech.	42	....	....	....	2358	105	....	2.67	....	....	....	....	....	....	....
1983-84	HC Pardubice	Czech.	40	....	....	....	2304	108	....	2.81	....	....	....	....	....	....	....
1984-85	HC Pardubice	Czech.	42	....	....	....	2419	131	....	3.25	....	....	....	....	....	....	....
1985-86	HC Pardubice	Czech.	45	....	....	....	2689	138	....	3.08	....	....	....	....	....	....	....
1986-87	HC Pardubice	Czech.	43	....	....	....	2515	103	....	2.46	....	....	....	....	....	....	....
1987-88	HC Pardubice	Czech.	31	....	....	....	1862	93	....	3.00	....	....	....	....	....	....	....
	Czechoslovakia	Olympics	5	3	2	0	217	18	1	4.98	....	....	....	....	....	....	....
1988-89	HC Pardubice	Czech.	42	....	....	....	2507	114	....	2.73	....	....	....	....	....	....	....
1989-90	Dukla Jihlava	Czech.	40	....	....	....	2251	80	....	2.13	....	....	....	....	....	....	....
1990-91	**Chicago**	**NHL**	**5**	**3**	**0**	**1**	**195**	**8**	**0**	**2.46**	**3**	**0**	**0**	**69**	**3**	**0**	**2.61**
	Indianapolis Ice	IHL	33	20	11	1	1903	80	*5	*2.52	1	1	0	60	3	0	3.00
1991-92	**Chicago**	**NHL**	**20**	**10**	**4**	**1**	**1014**	**44**	**1**	**2.60**	**3**	**0**	**2**	**158**	**8**	**0**	**3.04**
	Indianapolis	IHL	20	7	10	3	1162	69	1	3.56	....	....	....	....	....	....	....
1992-93	**Buffalo**	**NHL**	**28**	**11**	**10**	**4**	**1429**	**75**	**0**	**3.15**	**1**	**1**	**0**	**45**	**1**	**0**	**1.33**
1993-94	**Buffalo**	**NHL**	**58**	**30**	**20**	**6**	**3358**	**109**	***7**	***1.95**	**7**	**3**	**4**	**484**	**13**	**2**	***1.61**
1994-95	HC Pardubice	Cze-Rep	2	1	0	1	124	6	0	2.90	....	....	....	....	....	....	....
	Buffalo	**NHL**	**41**	**19**	**14**	**7**	**2416**	**85**	***5**	***2.11**	**5**	**1**	**4**	**309**	**18**	**0**	**3.50**
1995-96	**Buffalo**	**NHL**	**59**	**22**	**30**	**6**	**3417**	**161**	**2**	**2.83**	....	....	....	....	....	....	....
1996-97	**Buffalo**	**NHL**	**67**	**37**	**20**	**10**	**4037**	**153**	**5**	**2.27**	**3**	**1**	**1**	**153**	**5**	**0**	**1.96**
1997-98	**Buffalo**	**NHL**	***72**	**33**	**23**	**13**	***4220**	**147**	***13**	**2.09**	**15**	**10**	**5**	**948**	**32**	**1**	**2.03**
	Czech-Republic	Olympics	6	*5	1	0	*369	6	*2	*0.97	....	....	....	....	....	....	....
1998-99	**Buffalo**	**NHL**	**64**	**30**	**18**	**14**	**3817**	**119**	**9**	**1.87**	**19**	**13**	**6**	**1217**	**36**	**2**	**1.77**
99-2000	**Buffalo**	**NHL**	**35**	**15**	**11**	**6**	**2066**	**76**	**3**	**2.21**	**5**	**1**	**4**	**301**	**12**	**0**	**2.39**
	NHL Totals		**449**	**210**	**150**	**68**	**25969**	**977**	**45**	**2.26**	**61**	**30**	**26**	**3684**	**128**	**5**	**2.08**

• Czechoslovakian Goaltender-of-the-Year (1986, 1987, 1988, 1989, 1990) • Czechoslovakian Player-of-the-Year (1987, 1989, 1990) • Czechoslovakian First All-Star Team (1988, 1989, 1990) • IHL First All-Star Team (1991) • NHL All-Rookie Team (1992) • NHL First All-Star Team (1994, 1995, 1997, 1998, 1999) • Shared William M. Jennings Trophy with Grant Fuhr (1994) • Won Vezina Trophy (1994, 1995, 1997, 1998, 1999) • Won Lester B. Pearson Award (1997, 1998) • Won Hart Trophy (1997, 1998) • Played in NHL All-Star Game (1996, 1997, 1998, 1999)

Traded to **Buffalo** by **Chicago** for Stephane Beauregard and Buffalo's 4th round choice (Eric Daze) in 1993 Entry Draft, August 7, 1992.

HAUSER, Adam (HOW-uhr, A-dam) EDM.

Goaltender. Catches left. 6'2", 192 lbs. Born, Bovey, MN, May 27, 1980.
(Edmonton's 4th choice, 81st overall, in 1999 Entry Draft).

			Regular Season								Playoffs						
Season	Club	Lea	GP	W	L	T	Mins	GA	SO	Avg	GP	W	L	Mins	GA	SO	Avg
1996-97	Greenway High	H.S.	25	....	....	....	1496	63	0	2.54	....	....	....	....	....	....	....
1997-98	Team USA	Under-18	38	19	10	7	2110	94	4	2.67	....	....	....	....	....	....	....
1998-99	U. of Minnesota	WCHA	*40	14	18	8	*2350	136	3	3.47	....	....	....	....	....	....	....
99-2000	U. of Minnesota	WCHA	36	20	14	2	2114	104	1	2.95	....	....	....	....	....	....	....

HEALY, Glenn (HEE-lee, GLEHN) TOR.

Goaltender. Catches left. 5'9", 190 lbs. Born, Pickering, Ont., August 23, 1962.

			Regular Season								Playoffs						
Season	Club	Lea	GP	W	L	T	Mins	GA	SO	Avg	GP	W	L	Mins	GA	SO	Avg
1979-80	Pickering Panthers	OHA-B	31	....	....	....	1850	123	0	3.99	....	....	....	....	....	....	....
1980-81	Pickering Panthers	OHA-B	35	....	....	....	2080	120	1	3.46	....	....	....	....	....	....	....
1981-82	Western Michigan	CCHA	27	7	19	1	1569	116	0	4.44	....	....	....	....	....	....	....
1982-83	Western Michigan	CCHA	30	8	19	2	1732	116	0	4.01	....	....	....	....	....	....	....
1983-84	Western Michigan	CCHA	38	19	16	3	2241	146	0	3.90	....	....	....	....	....	....	....
1984-85	Western Michigan	CCHA	37	21	14	2	2171	118	0	3.26	....	....	....	....	....	....	....
1985-86	**Los Angeles**	**NHL**	**1**	**0**	**0**	**0**	**51**	**6**	**0**	**7.06**	....	....	....	....	....	....	....
	Toledo	IHL	7	....	....	....	402	28	0	4.18	....	....	....	....	....	....	....
	New Haven	AHL	43	21	15	4	2410	160	0	3.98	2	0	2	49	11	0	5.55
1986-87	New Haven	AHL	47	21	15	0	2828	173	1	3.67	7	3	4	427	19	0	2.67
1987-88	**Los Angeles**	**NHL**	**34**	**12**	**18**	**1**	**1869**	**135**	**1**	**4.33**	**4**	**1**	**3**	**240**	**20**	**0**	**5.00**
1988-89	**Los Angeles**	**NHL**	**48**	**25**	**19**	**2**	**2699**	**192**	**0**	**4.27**	**3**	**0**	**1**	**97**	**6**	**0**	**3.71**
1989-90	**NY Islanders**	**NHL**	**39**	**12**	**19**	**6**	**2197**	**128**	**2**	**3.50**	**4**	**1**	**2**	**166**	**9**	**0**	**3.25**
1990-91	**NY Islanders**	**NHL**	**53**	**18**	**24**	**9**	**2999**	**166**	**0**	**3.32**	....	....	....	....	....	....	....
1991-92	**NY Islanders**	**NHL**	**37**	**14**	**16**	**4**	**1960**	**124**	**1**	**3.80**	....	....	....	....	....	....	....
1992-93	**NY Islanders**	**NHL**	**47**	**22**	**20**	**2**	**2655**	**146**	**1**	**3.30**	**18**	**9**	**8**	**1109**	**59**	**0**	**3.19**
1993-94♦	**NY Rangers**	**NHL**	**29**	**10**	**12**	**2**	**1368**	**69**	**2**	**3.03**	**2**	**0**	**0**	**68**	**1**	**0**	**0.88**
1994-95	**NY Rangers**	**NHL**	**17**	**8**	**6**	**1**	**888**	**35**	**1**	**2.36**	**5**	**2**	**1**	**230**	**13**	**0**	**3.39**
1995-96	**NY Rangers**	**NHL**	**44**	**17**	**14**	**11**	**2564**	**124**	**2**	**2.90**	....	....	....	....	....	....	....
1996-97	**NY Rangers**	**NHL**	**23**	**5**	**12**	**4**	**1357**	**59**	**1**	**2.61**	....	....	....	....	....	....	....
1997-98	**Toronto**	**NHL**	**21**	**4**	**10**	**2**	**1068**	**53**	**0**	**2.98**	....	....	....	....	....	....	....
1998-99	Chicago Wolves	IHL	10	6	3	1	597	33	0	3.32	....	....	....	....	....	....	....
	Toronto	**NHL**	**9**	**6**	**3**	**0**	**546**	**27**	**0**	**2.97**	**1**	**0**	**0**	**20**	**0**	**0**	**0.00**
99-2000	**Toronto**	**NHL**	**20**	**9**	**10**	**0**	**1164**	**59**	**2**	**3.04**	....	....	....	....	....	....	....
	NHL Totals		**422**	**162**	**183**	**44**	**23385**	**1323**	**13**	**3.39**	**37**	**13**	**15**	**1930**	**108**	**0**	**3.36**

CCHA Second All-Star Team (1985) • NCAA West Second All-American Team (1985)

Signed as a free agent by **Los Angeles**, June 13, 1985. Signed as a free agent by **NY Islanders**, August 16, 1989. Claimed by **Anaheim** from **NY Islanders** in Expansion Draft, June 24, 1993. Claimed by **Tampa Bay** from **Anaheim** in Phase II of Expansion Draft, June 25, 1993. Traded to **NY Rangers** by **Tampa Bay** for Tampa Bay's 3rd round choice (previously acquired, Tampa Bay selected Allan Egeland) in 1993 Entry Draft, June 25, 1993. Signed as a free agent by **Toronto**, August 8, 1997.

HEBERT, Guy (ay-BAIR, GEE) ANA.

Goaltender. Catches left. 5'11", 186 lbs. Born, Troy, NY, January 7, 1967.
(St. Louis' 8th choice, 159th overall, in 1987 Entry Draft).

			Regular Season								Playoffs						
Season	Club	Lea	GP	W	L	T	Mins	GA	SO	Avg	GP	W	L	Mins	GA	SO	Avg
1985-86	Hamilton College	NCAA-2	18	4	12	2	1011	69	2	4.09	....	....	....	....	....	....	....
1986-87	Hamilton College	NCAA-2	18	12	5	0	1070	40	3	2.19	2	1	1	134	6	0	2.69
1987-88	Hamilton College	NCAA-2	9	5	3	0	510	22	1	2.58	1	0	1	60	3	0	3.00
1988-89	Hamilton College	NCAA-2	25	18	7	0	1454	62	2	2.56	2	1	1	126	4	0	1.90
1989-90	Peoria Rivermen	IHL	30	7	13	7	1706	124	1	4.36	2	0	1	76	5	0	3.95
1990-91	Peoria Rivermen	IHL	36	24	10	1	2093	100	2	2.87	8	3	4	458	32	0	4.19
1991-92	**St. Louis**	**NHL**	**13**	**5**	**5**	**1**	**738**	**36**	**0**	**2.93**	....	....	....	....	....	....	....
	Peoria Rivermen	IHL	29	20	9	0	1731	98	0	3.40	4	3	1	239	9	0	2.26
1992-93	**St. Louis**	**NHL**	**24**	**8**	**8**	**2**	**1210**	**74**	**1**	**3.67**	**1**	**0**	**0**	**2**	**0**	**0**	**0.00**
1993-94	**Anaheim**	**NHL**	**52**	**20**	**27**	**3**	**2991**	**141**	**2**	**2.83**	....	....	....	....	....	....	....
1994-95	**Anaheim**	**NHL**	**39**	**12**	**20**	**4**	**2092**	**109**	**2**	**3.13**	....	....	....	....	....	....	....
1995-96	**Anaheim**	**NHL**	**59**	**28**	**23**	**5**	**3326**	**157**	**4**	**2.83**	....	....	....	....	....	....	....
1996-97	**Anaheim**	**NHL**	**67**	**29**	**25**	**12**	**3863**	**172**	**4**	**2.67**	**9**	**4**	**4**	**534**	**18**	**1**	**2.02**
1997-98	**Anaheim**	**NHL**	**46**	**13**	**24**	**6**	**2660**	**130**	**3**	**2.93**	....	....	....	....	....	....	....
1998-99	**Anaheim**	**NHL**	**69**	**31**	**29**	**9**	**4083**	**165**	**6**	**2.42**	**4**	**0**	**3**	**208**	**15**	**0**	**4.33**
99-2000	**Anaheim**	**NHL**	**68**	**28**	**31**	**9**	**3976**	**166**	**4**	**2.51**	....	....	....	....	....	....	....
	NHL Totals		**437**	**174**	**192**	**51**	**24939**	**1150**	**26**	**2.77**	**14**	**4**	**7**	**744**	**33**	**1**	**2.66**

IHL Second All-Star Team (1991) • Shared James Norris Memorial Trophy (fewest goals against - IHL) with Pat Jablonski (1991) • Played in NHL All-Star Game (1997)

Claimed by **Anaheim** from **St. Louis** in Expansion Draft, June 24, 1993.

HEDBERG, Johan (HEHD-buhrg, YO-han) S.J.

Goaltender. Catches left. 5'11", 185 lbs. Born, Leksand, Sweden, May 5, 1973.
(Philadelphia's 8th choice, 218th overall, in 1994 Entry Draft).

			Regular Season								Playoffs						
Season	Club	Lea	GP	W	L	T	Mins	GA	SO	Avg	GP	W	L	Mins	GA	SO	Avg
1992-93	Leksands IF	Sweden	10	....	....	....	600	24	....	2.40	....	....	....	....	....	....	....
1993-94	Leksands IF	Sweden	17	....	....	....	1020	48	....	2.81	....	....	....	....	....	....	....
1994-95	Leksands IF	Sweden	17	....	....	....	986	58	....	3.53	....	....	....	....	....	....	....
1995-96	Leksands IF	Sweden	34	....	....	....	2013	95	....	2.83	4	....	....	240	13	....	3.25
1996-97	Leksands IF	Sweden	38	....	....	....	2260	95	3	2.52	8	....	....	581	18	1	1.86
1997-98	Baton Rouge	ECHL	2	1	1	0	100	7	0	4.20	....	....	....	....	....	....	....
	Detroit Vipers	IHL	16	7	2	2	726	32	1	2.64	....	....	....	....	....	....	....
	Manitoba Moose	IHL	14	8	4	1	745	32	1	2.58	2	0	2	105	6	0	3.40
1998-99	Leksands IF	Sweden	*48	....	....	....	*2940	140	0	2.86	4	....	....	255	15	0	3.53
99-2000	Kentucky	AHL	33	18	9	5	1973	88	3	2.68	5	3	2	311	10	1	1.93

Rights traded to **San Jose** by **Philadelphia** for San Jose's 7th round choice (Pavel Kasparik) in 1999 Entry Draft, August 6, 1998.

HEFFLER, Eric (HEH-fluhr, AIR-ihk) EDM.

Goaltender. Catches left. 6'3", 190 lbs. Born, Williamsville, NY, February 29, 1976.

			Regular Season								Playoffs						
Season	Club	Lea	GP	W	L	T	Mins	GA	SO	Avg	GP	W	L	Mins	GA	SO	Avg
1994-95	Oshawa Legion	OJHL	29	....	....	....	1540	111	1	4.32	....	....	....	....	....	....	....
1995-96	St. Lawrence	ECAC	4	0	0	0	55	3	0	3.25	....	....	....	....	....	....	....
1996-97	St. Lawrence	ECAC	12	2	3	1	458	31	0	4.06	....	....	....	....	....	....	....
1997-98	St. Lawrence	ECAC	26	8	14	0	1529	73	2	2.90	....	....	....	....	....	....	....
1998-99	St. Lawrence	ECAC	*37	22	12	3	*2206	88	3	2.39	....	....	....	....	....	....	....
	Hamilton Bulldogs	AHL	2	1	1	0	119	5	0	2.52	....	....	....	....	....	....	....
99-2000	Hamilton Bulldogs	AHL	47	11	25	7	2643	138	5	3.13	....	....	....	....	....	....	....

ECAC Player-of-the-Year (1999) • ECAC First All-Star Team (1999) • NCAA East First All-American Team (1999)

Signed as a free agent by **Edmonton**, April 30, 1999.

HENRY, Frederic (HEHN-ree, FREHD-uhr-IHK) N.J.

Goaltender. Catches left. 5'11", 180 lbs. Born, Cap-Rouge, Que., August 9, 1977.
(New Jersey's 10th choice, 200th overall, in 1995 Entry Draft).

			Regular Season								Playoffs						
Season	Club	Lea	GP	W	L	T	Mins	GA	SO	Avg	GP	W	L	Mins	GA	SO	Avg
1993-94	Ste-Foy Governors	QAAA	30	19	7	1	1571	76	1	2.98	6	2	4	333	15	1	....
1994-95	Granby Predateurs	QMJHL	15	8	5	0	866	47	0	3.26	6	1	2	232	21	0	5.43
1995-96	Granby Predateurs	QMJHL	28	19	5	2	1530	69	*3	2.71	12	9	2	610	21	2	*2.08
1996-97	Granby Predateurs	QMJHL	57	33	16	6	3330	162	4	2.92	5	1	4	251	17	0	4.06
	Albany River Rats	AHL	1	1	0	0	60	3	0	3.00	....	....	....	....	....	....	....
1997-98	Raleigh IceCaps	ECHL	34	13	17	2	1889	119	2	3.78	....	....	....	....	....	....	....
	Albany River Rats	AHL	4	2	0	1	199	8	0	2.41	....	....	....	....	....	....	....
1998-99	Albany River Rats	AHL	35	17	10	3	1690	84	1	2.98	....	....	....	....	....	....	....
99-2000	Albany River Rats	AHL	53	18	23	3	2732	138	1	3.03	4	2	2	236	6	1	1.52

HILLIER, Craig (HIHL-yuhr, KRAYG) PIT.

Goaltender. Catches left. 6'1", 183 lbs. Born, Cole Harbour, N.S., February 28, 1978.
(Pittsburgh's 1st choice, 23rd overall, in 1996 Entry Draft).

			Regular Season								Playoffs						
Season	Club	Lea	GP	W	L	T	Mins	GA	SO	Avg	GP	W	L	Mins	GA	SO	Avg
1993-94	Dartmouth Colts	NSAHA	15	....	....	....	918	42	2	2.75	....	....	....	....	....	....	....
1994-95	Ottawa 67's	OHL	24	6	7	2	1078	69	1	3.84	....	....	....	....	....	....	....
1995-96	Ottawa 67's	OHL	44	24	14	3	2439	117	2	2.88	3	0	2	130	12	0	5.54
1996-97	Ottawa 67's	OHL	36	23	6	4	2007	89	2	2.66	10	4	5	540	33	0	3.67
1997-98	Ottawa 67's	OHL	46	27	12	4	2587	108	*6	*2.50	9	6	2	447	20	1	2.68
1998-99	Syracuse Crunch	AHL	36	9	18	6	1919	126	1	3.94	....	....	....	....	....	....	....
99-2000	Wilkes-Barre	AHL	11	1	6	2	520	36	0	4.15	....	....	....	....	....	....	....
	Johnstown Chiefs	ECHL	5	1	2	0	212	15	0	4.24	....	....	....	....	....	....	....
	Toledo Storm	ECHL	9	1	6	0	375	41	0	6.56	....	....	....	....	....	....	....
	Charlotte	ECHL	3	0	2	0	121	10	0	4.95	....	....	....	....	....	....	....

OHL First All-Star Team (1996)

HIRSCH, Corey (HUHRSH, KOHR-ee)

Goaltender. Catches left. 5'10", 175 lbs. Born, Medicine Hat, Alta., August 10, 1972.
(NY Rangers' 7th choice, 169th overall, in 1991 Entry Draft).

			Regular Season								Playoffs						
Season	Club	Lea	GP	W	L	T	Mins	GA	SO	Avg	GP	W	L	Mins	GA	SO	Avg
1987-88	Calgary Canucks	AJHL	32	....	....	....	1538	91	1	3.55	....	....	....	....	....	....	....
1988-89	Kamloops Blazers	WHL	32	11	12	2	1516	106	2	4.20	5	3	2	245	19	0	4.65
1989-90	Kamloops Blazers	WHL	*63	*48	13	0	3608	230	*3	3.82	*17	*14	3	*1043	60	0	*3.45
1990-91	Kamloops Blazers	WHL	38	26	7	1	1970	100	3	*3.05	11	5	6	623	42	0	4.04
1991-92	Kamloops Blazers	WHL	48	35	10	2	2732	124	*5	*2.72	*16	*11	5	954	35	*2	*2.20
1992-93	**NY Rangers**	**NHL**	**4**	**1**	**2**	**1**	**224**	**14**	**0**	**3.75**	....	....	....	....	....	....	....
	Binghamton	AHL	46	*35	4	5	2692	125	1	*2.79	14	7	7	831	46	0	3.32
1993-94	Canada	Nt-Team	45	24	17	3	2653	124	0	2.80	....	....	....	....	....	....	....
	Canada	Olympics	8	5	2	1	495	18	0	2.18	....	....	....	....	....	....	....
	Binghamton	AHL	10	5	4	1	610	38	0	3.73	....	....	....	....	....	....	....
1994-95	Binghamton	AHL	57	31	20	5	3371	175	0	3.11	....	....	....	....	....	....	....
1995-96	**Vancouver**	**NHL**	**41**	**17**	**14**	**6**	**2338**	**114**	**1**	**2.93**	**6**	**2**	**3**	**338**	**21**	**0**	**3.73**
1996-97	**Vancouver**	**NHL**	**39**	**12**	**20**	**4**	**2127**	**116**	**2**	**3.27**	....	....	....	....	....	....	....
1997-98	**Vancouver**	**NHL**	**1**	**0**	**0**	**0**	**50**	**5**	**0**	**6.00**	....	....	....	....	....	....	....
	Syracuse Crunch	AHL	60	30	22	6	3512	187	1	3.19	5	2	3	297	10	1	*2.02
1998-99	**Vancouver**	**NHL**	**20**	**3**	**8**	**3**	**919**	**48**	**1**	**3.13**	....	....	....	....	....	....	....
	Syracuse Crunch	AHL	5	2	3	0	300	14	0	2.80	....	....	....	....	....	....	....
99-2000	Milwaukee	IHL	19	9	8	1	1098	49	0	2.68	....	....	....	....	....	....	....
	Utah Grizzlies	IHL	17	9	5	1	937	42	3	2.69	2	0	2	121	4	0	1.99
	NHL Totals		**105**	**33**	**44**	**14**	**5658**	**297**	**4**	**3.15**	**6**	**2**	**3**	**338**	**21**	**0**	**3.73**

WHL West Second All-Star Team (1990) • WHL West First All-Star Team (1991, 1992) • Canadian Major Junior Goaltender of the Year (1992) • Memorial Cup All-Star Team (1992) • Won Hap Emms Memorial Trophy (Memorial Cup Tournament Top Goaltender) (1992) • AHL First All-Star Team (1993) • Won Dudley ''Red'' Garrett Memorial Trophy (AHL Rookie of the Year) (1993) • Shared Harry ''Hap'' Holmes Memorial Trophy (fewest goals-against - AHL) with Boris Rousson (1993) • NHL All-Rookie Team (1996)

Traded to **Vancouver** by **NY Rangers** for Nathan Lafayette, April 7, 1995. Signed as a free agent by **Nashville**, August 10, 1999. Traded to **Anaheim** by **Nashville** for future considerations, March 14, 2000.

HNILICKA, Milan (huh-LIHN-ich-kuh, MEE-lan) ATL.

Goaltender. Catches left. 6', 180 lbs. Born, Litomerice, Czech., June 25, 1973.
(NY Islanders' 4th choice, 70th overall, in 1991 Entry Draft).

			Regular Season								Playoffs						
Season	Club	Lea	GP	W	L	T	Mins	GA	SO	Avg	GP	W	L	Mins	GA	SO	Avg
1989-90	Poldi Kladno	Czech.	24	....	....	....	1113	70	....	3.77	....	....	....	....	....	....	....
1990-91	Poldi Kladno	Czech.	40	....	....	....	2122	98	0	2.80	....	....	....	....	....	....	....
1991-92	Poldi Kladno	Czech.	38	....	....	....	2066	128	0	3.73	....	....	....	....	....	....	....
1992-93	Swift Current	WHL	*65	*46	12	2	3679	206	2	3.36	*17	*12	5	*1017	54	*2	3.19
1993-94	Richmond	ECHL	43	18	16	5	2299	155	4	4.05	....	....	....	....	....	....	....
	Salt Lake City	IHL	8	5	1	0	378	25	0	3.97	....	....	....	....	....	....	....
1994-95	Denver Grizzlies	IHL	15	9	4	1	798	47	1	3.53	....	....	....	....	....	....	....
1995-96	Poldi Kladno	Cze-Rep	33	....	....	....	1959	93	1	2.84	8	....	....	493	24	....	2.92
1996-97	Poldi Kladno	Cze-Rep	48	....	....	....	2736	120	4	2.63	3	....	....	151	14	0	5.56
1997-98	Sparta Praha	Cze-Rep	49	....	....	....	2847	99	....	2.09	11	....	....	632	31	....	3.00
1998-99	Sparta Praha	Cze-Rep	*50	....	....	....	*2877	109	....	2.27	8	....	....	507	13	....	*1.54
99-2000	**NY Rangers**	**NHL**	**2**	**0**	**1**	**0**	**86**	**5**	**0**	**3.49**	....	....	....	....	....	....	....
	Hartford	AHL	36	22	11	0	1979	71	5	2.15	3	0	1	99	6	0	3.64
	NHL Totals		**2**	**0**	**1**	**0**	**86**	**5**	**0**	**3.49**	....	....	....	....	....	....	....

• Shared Harry "Hap" Holmes Memorial Trophy (fewest goals against - AHL) with Jean-Francois Labbe (2000)

Signed as a free agent by **NY Rangers**, July 15, 1999. Signed as a free agent by **Atlanta**, July 28, 2000.

HODSON, Jamie (HAWD-suhn, JAY-mee) TOR.

Goaltender. Catches left. 6'2", 206 lbs. Born, Brandon, Man., April 8, 1980.
(Toronto's 3rd choice, 69th overall, in 1998 Entry Draft).

			Regular Season								Playoffs						
Season	Club	Lea	GP	W	L	T	Mins	GA	SO	Avg	GP	W	L	Mins	GA	SO	Avg
1996-97	Yellowhead Chiefs	MAHA	12	....	....	....	720	58	1	4.83	....	....	....	....	....	....	....
1997-98	Brandon	WHL	20	12	2	2	964	52	2	3.24	6	5	0	337	16	0	2.85
1998-99	Brandon	WHL	43	23	12	3	2295	123	4	3.22	5	1	4	275	26	0	5.67
99-2000	Brandon	WHL	39	13	22	3	2321	130	2	3.36	....	....	....	....	....	....	....

HODSON, Kevin (HAWD-suhn, KEH-vihn)

Goaltender. Catches left. 6', 182 lbs. Born, Winnipeg, Man., March 27, 1972.

			Regular Season								Playoffs						
Season	Club	Lea	GP	W	L	T	Mins	GA	SO	Avg	GP	W	L	Mins	GA	SO	Avg
1989-90	Winnipeg Blues	MJHL	35	....	....	....	1900	115	2	3.40	....	....	....	....	....	....	....
1990-91	Sault Ste. Marie	OHL	30	18	11	0	1638	88	*2	*3.22	10	*9	1	581	28	0	*2.89
1991-92	Sault Ste. Marie	OHL	50	28	12	4	2722	151	0	3.33	18	12	6	1116	54	1	2.90
1992-93	Sault Ste. Marie	OHL	26	18	5	2	1470	76	1	*3.10	14	11	2	755	34	0	2.70
	Indianapolis Ice	IHL	14	5	9	0	777	53	0	4.09	....	....	....	....	....	....	....
1993-94	Adirondack	AHL	37	20	10	5	2082	102	2	2.94	3	0	2	89	10	0	6.77
1994-95	Adirondack	AHL	51	19	22	8	2731	161	1	3.54	4	0	4	237	14	0	3.53
1995-96	Detroit	NHL	4	2	0	0	163	3	1	1.10	....	....	....	....	....	....	....
	Adirondack	AHL	32	13	13	2	1654	87	0	3.16	3	0	2	150	8	0	3.21
1996-97	Detroit	NHL	6	2	2	1	294	8	1	1.63	....	....	....	....	....	....	....
	Quebec Rafales	IHL	2	1	1	0	118	7	0	3.54	....	....	....	....	....	....	....
1997-98♦	Detroit	NHL	21	9	3	3	988	44	2	2.67	1	0	0	1	0	0	0.00
1998-99	Detroit	NHL	4	0	2	0	175	9	0	3.09	....	....	....	....	....	....	....
	Adirondack	AHL	6	1	3	2	349	19	0	3.27	....	....	....	....	....	....	....
	Tampa Bay	NHL	5	2	1	1	238	11	0	2.77	....	....	....	....	....	....	....
99-2000	Tampa Bay	NHL	24	2	7	4	769	47	0	3.67	....	....	....	....	....	....	....
	Detroit Vipers	IHL	9	2	6	0	505	22	0	2.61	....	....	....	....	....	....	....
	NHL Totals		64	17	15	9	2627	122	4	2.79	1	0	0	1	0	0	0.00

Memorial Cup All-Star Team (1993) • Won Hap Emms Memorial Trophy (Memorial Cup Tournament Top Goaltender) (1993)

Signed as a free agent by **Chicago**, August 17, 1992. Signed as a free agent by **Detroit**, June 16, 1993. • Played 16 seconds in playoff game vs. Chicago, May 17, 1998. Traded to **Tampa Bay** by **Detroit** with San Jose's 2nd round choice (previously acquired, Tampa Bay selected Sheldon Keefe) in 1999 Entry Draft for Wendel Clark and Detroit's 6th round choice (previously acquired, Detroit selected Kent McDonnell) in 1999 Entry Draft, March 23, 1999. Traded to **Montreal** by **Tampa Bay** for Montreal's 7th round choice (later traded to Philadelphia - Philadelphia selected John Eichelberger) in 2000 Entry Draft, June 2, 2000.

HOLMQVIST, Johan (HOHLM-kvihst, YOH-han) NYR

Goaltender. Catches left. 6'3", 190 lbs. Born, Tolfta, Sweden, May 24, 1978.
(NY Rangers' 9th choice, 175th overall, in 1997 Entry Draft).

			Regular Season								Playoffs						
Season	Club	Lea	GP	W	L	T	Mins	GA	SO	Avg	GP	W	L	Mins	GA	SO	Avg
1996-97	Brynas IF	Sweden	2	0	0	0	80	4	0	3.00	....	....	....	....	....	....	....
1997-98	Brynas IF	Sweden	33	....	....	....	1897	82	....	2.59	3	0	3	180	14	....	4.67
1998-99	Brynas IF	Sweden	41	....	....	....	2383	111	4	2.79	*14	9	5	*855	34	0	2.39
99-2000	Brynas IF	Sweden	41	....	....	....	2402	104	4	2.60	11	....	....	671	30	1	2.68

HURME, Jani (HOOR-meh, YAN-ee) OTT.

Goaltender. Catches left. 6', 187 lbs. Born, Turku, Finland, January 7, 1975.
(Ottawa's 2nd choice, 58th overall, in 1997 Entry Draft).

			Regular Season								Playoffs						
Season	Club	Lea	GP	W	L	T	Mins	GA	SO	Avg	GP	W	L	Mins	GA	SO	Avg
1992-93	TPS Turku	Finn-Jr.	12	....	....	....	669	47	0	4.22	1	....	....	60	0	1	0.00
1993-94	Kiekko-67 Turku	Finn-Jr.	18	....	....	....	1082	57	0	3.16	....	....	....	....	....	....	....
	Kiekko-67 Turku	Finland-2	3	....	....	....	190	7	0	2.21	....	....	....	....	....	....	....
	TPS Turku	Finland	1	....	....	....	2	0	0	0.00	....	....	....	....	....	....	....
1994-95	TPS Turku	Finn-Jr.	2	....	....	....	125	5	0	2.40	....	....	....	....	....	....	....
	Kiekko-67 Turku	Finn-Jr.	9	....	....	....	540	47	....	5.22	....	....	....	....	....	....	....
	Kiekko-67 Turku	Finland-2	19	....	....	....	1049	53	....	3.03	3	....	....	180	6	....	2.00
1995-96	TPS Turku	Finn-Jr.	13	....	....	....	777	34	1	2.63	....	....	....	....	....	....	....
	Kiekko-67 Turku	Finland-2	16	....	....	....	968	39	1	2.42	....	....	....	....	....	....	....
	TPS Turku	Finland	16	....	....	....	946	34	2	2.16	10	....	....	545	22	2	2.42
1996-97	TPS Turku	Finland	48	31	11	6	2917	101	6	2.08	12	6	6	722	39	0	3.24
1997-98	Detroit Vipers	IHL	6	2	2	2	290	20	0	4.13	....	....	....	....	....	....	....
	Indianapolis Ice	IHL	29	11	11	3	1506	83	1	3.30	3	1	0	129	10	0	4.62
1998-99	Detroit Vipers	IHL	12	7	3	1	643	26	1	2.43	....	....	....	....	....	....	....
	Cincinnati	IHL	26	14	9	2	1428	81	0	3.40	....	....	....	....	....	....	....
99-2000	Ottawa	NHL	1	1	0	0	60	2	0	2.00	....	....	....	....	....	....	....
	Grand Rapids	IHL	52	29	15	4	2948	107	4	2.18	*17	*10	7	*1028	37	1	2.16
	NHL Totals		1	1	0	0	60	2	0	2.00	....	....	....	....	....	....	....

Finnish Elite League Rookie-of-the-Year (1997) • IHL Second All-Star Team (2000)

IRBE, Arturs (UHR-bay, AHR-tuhrs) CAR.

Goaltender. Catches left. 5'8", 190 lbs. Born, Riga, Latvia, February 2, 1967.
(Minnesota's 11th choice, 196th overall, in 1989 Entry Draft).

			Regular Season								Playoffs						
Season	Club	Lea	GP	W	L	T	Mins	GA	SO	Avg	GP	W	L	Mins	GA	SO	Avg
1986-87	Dynamo Riga	USSR	2	....	....	....	27	1	0	2.22	....	....	....	....	....	....	....
1987-88	Dynamo Riga	USSR	34	....	....	....	1870	86	4	2.69	....	....	....	....	....	....	....
1988-89	Dynamo Riga	USSR	40	....	....	....	2460	116	4	2.85	....	....	....	....	....	....	....
1989-90	Dynamo Riga	USSR	48	....	....	....	2880	115	2	2.42	....	....	....	....	....	....	....
1990-91	Dynamo Riga	USSR	46	....	....	....	2713	133	5	2.94	....	....	....	....	....	....	....
1991-92	San Jose	NHL	13	2	6	3	645	48	0	4.47	....	....	....	....	....	....	....
	Kansas City	IHL	32	24	7	1	1955	80	0	*2.46	*15	*12	3	914	44	0	*2.89
1992-93	San Jose	NHL	36	7	26	0	2074	142	1	4.11	....	....	....	....	....	....	....
	Kansas City	IHL	6	3	3	0	364	20	0	3.30	....	....	....	....	....	....	....
1993-94	San Jose	NHL	*74	30	28	16	*4412	209	3	2.84	14	7	7	806	50	0	3.72
1994-95	San Jose	NHL	38	14	19	3	2043	111	4	3.26	6	2	4	316	27	0	5.13
1995-96	San Jose	NHL	22	4	12	4	1112	85	0	4.59	....	....	....	....	....	....	....
	Kansas City	IHL	4	1	2	1	226	16	0	4.24	....	....	....	....	....	....	....
1996-97	Dallas	NHL	35	17	12	3	1965	88	3	2.69	1	0	0	13	0	0	0.00
1997-98	Vancouver	NHL	41	14	11	6	1999	91	2	2.73	....	....	....	....	....	....	....
1998-99	Carolina	NHL	62	27	20	12	3643	135	6	2.22	6	2	4	408	15	0	2.21
99-2000	Carolina	NHL	*75	34	28	9	4345	175	5	2.42	....	....	....	....	....	....	....
	NHL Totals		396	149	162	56	22238	1084	24	2.92	27	11	15	1543	92	0	3.58

USSR Rookie-of-the-Year (1988) • IHL First All-Star Team (1992) • Shared James Norris Memorial Trophy (fewest goals against - IHL) with Wade Flaherty (1992) • Played in NHL All-Star Game (1994, 1999)

Claimed by **San Jose** from **Minnesota** in Dispersal Draft, May 30, 1991. Signed as a free agent by **Dallas**, August 19, 1996. Signed as a free agent by **Vancouver**, August 25, 1997. Signed as a free agent by **Carolina**, September 14, 1998.

JABLONSKI, Pat (ja-BLAWN-skee, PAT)

Goaltender. Catches right. 6', 180 lbs. Born, Toledo, OH, June 20, 1967.
(St. Louis' 6th choice, 138th overall, in 1985 Entry Draft).

			Regular Season								Playoffs						
Season	Club	Lea	GP	W	L	T	Mins	GA	SO	Avg	GP	W	L	Mins	GA	SO	Avg
1984-85	Detroit	NAJHL	29	....	....	....	1483	95	0	3.84	....	....	....	....	....	....	....
1985-86	Windsor Spitfires	OHL	29	6	16	4	1600	119	1	4.46	6	0	3	263	20	0	4.56
1986-87	Windsor Spitfires	OHL	41	22	14	2	2328	128	*3	3.30	12	8	4	710	38	0	3.21
1987-88	Peoria Rivermen	IHL	5	2	2	1	285	17	0	3.58	....	....	....	....	....	....	....
	Windsor Spitfires	OHL	18	14	3	0	994	48	2	2.90	9	*8	0	537	28	0	3.13
1988-89	Peoria Rivermen	IHL	35	11	20	0	2051	163	1	4.77	3	0	2	130	13	0	6.00
1989-90	St. Louis	NHL	4	0	3	0	208	17	0	4.90	....	....	....	....	....	....	....
	Peoria Rivermen	IHL	36	14	17	4	2023	165	0	4.89	4	1	3	223	19	0	5.11
1990-91	St. Louis	NHL	8	2	3	3	492	25	0	3.05	3	0	0	90	5	0	3.33
	Peoria Rivermen	IHL	29	23	3	2	1738	87	0	3.00	10	7	2	532	23	0	2.59
1991-92	St. Louis	NHL	10	3	6	0	468	38	0	4.87	....	....	....	....	....	....	....
	Peoria Rivermen	IHL	8	6	1	1	493	29	1	3.53	....	....	....	....	....	....	....
1992-93	Tampa Bay	NHL	43	8	24	4	2268	150	1	3.97	....	....	....	....	....	....	....
1993-94	Tampa Bay	NHL	15	5	6	3	834	54	0	3.88	....	....	....	....	....	....	....
	St. John's Leafs	AHL	16	12	3	1	962	49	1	3.05	11	6	5	676	36	0	3.19
1994-95	Chicago Wolves	IHL	4	0	4	0	216	17	0	4.71	....	....	....	....	....	....	....
	Houston Aeros	IHL	3	1	1	1	179	9	0	3.01	....	....	....	....	....	....	....
1995-96	St. Louis	NHL	1	0	0	0	8	1	0	7.50	....	....	....	....	....	....	....
	Montreal	NHL	23	5	9	6	1264	62	0	2.94	1	0	0	49	1	0	1.22
1996-97	Montreal	NHL	17	4	6	2	754	50	0	3.98	....	....	....	....	....	....	....
	Phoenix	NHL	2	0	1	0	59	2	0	2.03	....	....	....	....	....	....	....
1997-98	Carolina	NHL	5	1	4	0	279	14	0	3.01	....	....	....	....	....	....	....
	Cleveland	IHL	34	13	13	6	1950	98	0	3.01	....	....	....	....	....	....	....
	Quebec Rafales	IHL	7	3	3	0	368	21	0	3.42	....	....	....	....	....	....	....
1998-99	Chicago Wolves	IHL	36	22	7	7	2119	106	1	3.00	3	2	1	185	11	0	3.57
99-2000	Vastra Frolunda	Sweden	27	....	....	....	1624	65	4	2.40	5	....	....	298	18	0	3.62
	NHL Totals		128	28	62	18	6634	413	1	3.74	4	0	0	139	6	0	2.59

Shared James Norris Memorial Trophy (fewest goals against - IHL) with Guy Hebert (1991)

Traded to **Tampa Bay** by **St. Louis** with Steve Tuttle, Darin Kimble and Rob Robinson for future considerations, June 19, 1992. Traded to **Toronto** by **Tampa Bay** for cash, February 21, 1994. Claimed by **St. Louis** from **Toronto** in NHL Waiver Draft, October 2, 1995. Traded to **Montreal** by **St. Louis** for J.J. Daigneault, November 7, 1995. Traded to **Phoenix** by **Montreal** for Steve Cheredaryk, March 18, 1997. Signed as a free agent by **Carolina**, August 12, 1997.

JOHNSON, Brent (JAWN-sohn, BREHNT) ST.L.

Goaltender. Catches left. 6'2", 200 lbs. Born, Farmington, MI, March 12, 1977.
(Colorado's 5th choice, 129th overall, in 1995 Entry Draft).

			Regular Season								Playoffs						
Season	Club	Lea	GP	W	L	T	Mins	GA	SO	Avg	GP	W	L	Mins	GA	SO	Avg
1993-94	Detroit	OJHL	18	....	....	....	1024	49	1	3.52	....	....	....	....	....	....	....
1994-95	Owen Sound	OHL	18	3	9	1	904	75	0	4.98	....	....	....	....	....	....	....
1995-96	Owen Sound	OHL	58	24	28	1	3211	243	1	4.54	6	2	4	371	29	0	4.69
1996-97	Owen Sound	OHL	50	20	28	1	2798	201	1	4.31	4	0	4	253	24	0	5.69
1997-98	Worcester	AHL	42	14	15	7	2240	119	0	3.19	6	3	2	332	19	0	3.43
1998-99	St. Louis	NHL	6	3	2	0	286	10	0	2.10	....	....	....	....	....	....	....
	Worcester	AHL	49	22	22	4	2925	146	2	2.99	4	1	3	238	12	0	3.02
99-2000	Worcester	AHL	58	24	27	5	3319	161	3	2.91	9	4	5	561	23	1	2.46
	NHL Totals		6	3	2	0	286	10	0	2.10	....	....	....	....	....	....	....

Traded to **St. Louis** by **Colorado** for San Jose's third round choice (previously acquired, Colorado selected Rick Berry) in 1997 Entry Draft, May 30, 1997.

JOKELA, Antti (YOH-keh-luh, AHN-tee) CAR.

Goaltender. Catches . 5'11", 165 lbs. Born, Rauma, Finland, May 7, 1981.
(Carolina's 8th choice, 237th overall, in 1999 Entry Draft).

			Regular Season								Playoffs						
Season	Club	Lea	GP	W	L	T	Mins	GA	SO	Avg	GP	W	L	Mins	GA	SO	Avg
1998-99	Lukko Rauma-B	Finn-Jr.	8	....	....	....	480	26	0	3.25	....	....	....	....	....	....	....
	Lukko Rauma	Finn-Jr.	18	....	....	....	1038	66	1	3.81	....	....	....	....	....	....	....
99-2000	Lukko Rauma	Finn-Jr.	21	....	....	....	1196	71	0	3.56	....	....	....	....	....	....	....

JOSEPH, Curtis (JOH-sehf, KUR-this) TOR.

Goaltender. Catches left. 5'11", 190 lbs. Born, Keswick, Ont., April 29, 1967.

			Regular Season								Playoffs						
Season	Club	Lea	GP	W	L	T	Mins	GA	SO	Avg	GP	W	L	Mins	GA	SO	Avg
1984-85	King City Dukes	OJHL-B	18	....	....	....	947	76	0	4.82	....	....	....	....	....	....	....
	Newmarket Flyers	OJHL	2	1	1	0	120	16	0	8.00	....	....	....	....	....	....	....
1985-86	Richmond Hill	OJHL	33	12	18	0	1716	156	1	5.45	....	....	....	....	....	....	....
1986-87	Richmond Hill	OJHL	30	14	7	6	1764	128	1	4.35	....	....	....	....	....	....	....
1987-88	Notre Dame	SJHL	36	25	4	7	2174	94	1	2.59	....	....	....	....	....	....	....
1988-89	U. of Wisconsin	WCHA	38	21	11	5	2267	94	1	2.49	....	....	....	....	....	....	....
1989-90	Peoria Rivermen	IHL	23	10	8	2	1241	80	0	3.87	....	....	....	....	....	....	....
	St. Louis	NHL	15	9	5	1	852	48	0	3.38	6	4	1	327	18	0	3.30
1990-91	St. Louis	NHL	30	16	10	2	1710	89	0	3.12	....	....	....	....	....	....	....
1991-92	St. Louis	NHL	60	27	20	10	3494	175	2	3.01	6	2	4	379	23	0	3.64
1992-93	St. Louis	NHL	68	29	28	9	3890	196	1	3.02	11	7	4	715	27	*2	2.27
1993-94	St. Louis	NHL	71	36	23	11	4127	213	1	3.10	4	0	4	246	15	0	3.66
1994-95	St. Louis	NHL	36	20	10	1	1914	89	1	2.79	7	3	3	392	24	0	3.67
1995-96	Las Vegas	IHL	15	12	2	1	874	29	1	1.99	....	....	....	....	....	....	....
	Edmonton	NHL	34	15	16	2	1936	111	0	3.44	....	....	....	....	....	....	....
1996-97	Edmonton	NHL	72	32	29	9	4100	200	6	2.93	12	5	7	767	36	2	2.82
1997-98	Edmonton	NHL	71	29	31	9	4132	181	8	2.63	12	5	7	716	23	3	1.93
1998-99	Toronto	NHL	67	35	24	7	4001	171	3	2.56	17	9	8	1011	41	1	2.43
99-2000	Toronto	NHL	63	36	20	7	3801	158	4	2.49	12	6	6	729	25	1	2.06
	NHL Totals		587	284	216	68	33957	1631	26	2.88	87	41	44	5282	232	9	2.64

WCHA First All-Star Team (1989) • NCAA West Second All-American Team (1989) • Played in NHL All-Star Game (1994, 2000)

Signed as a free agent by **St. Louis**, June 16, 1989. Traded to **Edmonton** by **St. Louis** with the rights to Michael Grier for St. Louis' 1st round choices (previously acquired) in 1996 (Marty Reasoner) and 1997 (later traded to LA Kings - LA Kings selected Matt Zultek) Entry Drafts, August 4, 1995. Signed as a free agent by **Toronto**, July 15, 1998.

KETTLES, Kyle (KEH-tuhls) NSH.

Goaltender. Catches . 6'3", 180 lbs. Born, Lac du Bonnet, Man., February 19, 1981.
(Nashville's 13th choice, 205th overall, in 1999 Entry Draft).

			Regular Season								Playoffs						
Season	Club	Lea	GP	W	L	T	Mins	GA	SO	Avg	GP	W	L	Mins	GA	SO	Avg
1997-98	Selkirk Steelers	MJHL	32	9	19	1	1613	119	0	4.43	....	....	....	....	....	....	....
	Brandon	WHL	....	....	....	....	....	....	....	....	1	0	0	10	2	0	12.00
1998-99	Selkirk Steelers	MJHL	17	7	8	0	939	65	0	4.15	....	....	....	....	....	....	....
	Neepawa Natives	MJHL	6	2	4	0	361	27	0	4.49	....	....	....	....	....	....	....
99-2000	Medicine Hat	WHL	57	16	33	5	3260	215	1	3.96	....	....	....	....	....	....	....

KHABIBULIN, Nikolai (khah-bee-BOO-lihn, NIH-koh-ligh) PHX.

Goaltender. Catches left. 6'1", 195 lbs. Born, Sverdlovsk, USSR, January 13, 1973.
(Winnipeg's 8th choice, 204th overall, in 1992 Entry Draft).

			Regular Season								Playoffs						
Season	Club	Lea	GP	W	L	T	Mins	GA	SO	Avg	GP	W	L	Mins	GA	SO	Avg
1991-92	CSKA Moscow	CIS	2	0	0	0	34	2	0	3.52	....	....	....	....	....	....	....
1992-93	CSKA Moscow	CIS	13	....	....	....	491	27	....	3.29	....	....	....	....	....	....	....
1993-94	CSKA Moscow	CIS	46	....	....	....	2625	116	....	2.65	3	....	....	193	11	....	3.42
	Russian Pens	IHL	12	2	7	2	639	47	0	4.41	....	....	....	....	....	....	....
1994-95	Springfield	AHL	23	9	9	3	1240	80	0	3.87	....	....	....	....	....	....	....
	Winnipeg	**NHL**	**26**	**8**	**9**	**4**	**1339**	**76**	**0**	**3.41**	....	....	....	....	....	....	....
1995-96	**Winnipeg**	**NHL**	**53**	**26**	**20**	**3**	**2914**	**152**	**2**	**3.13**	**6**	**2**	**4**	**359**	**19**	**0**	**3.18**
1996-97	**Phoenix**	**NHL**	**72**	**30**	**33**	**6**	**4091**	**193**	**7**	**2.83**	**7**	**3**	**4**	**426**	**15**	**1**	**2.11**
1997-98	**Phoenix**	**NHL**	**70**	**30**	**28**	**10**	**4026**	**184**	**4**	**2.74**	**4**	**2**	**1**	**185**	**13**	**0**	**4.22**
1998-99	**Phoenix**	**NHL**	**63**	**32**	**23**	**7**	**3657**	**130**	**8**	**2.13**	**7**	**3**	**4**	**449**	**18**	**0**	**2.41**
99-2000	Long Beach	IHL	33	21	11	1	1936	59	5	*1.83	5	2	3	321	15	0	2.81
	NHL Totals		**284**	**126**	**113**	**30**	**16027**	**735**	**21**	**2.75**	**24**	**10**	**13**	**1419**	**65**	**1**	**2.75**

• Won James Gatschene Memorial Trophy (MVP - IHL) (tied with Frederic Chabot) (2000) • Played in NHL All-Star Game (1998, 1999)

Transferred to **Phoenix** after **Winnipeg** franchise relocated, July 1, 1996. • Sat out entire 1999-2000 NHL season after failing to come to contract terms with **Phoenix**. Signed as a free agent by **Long Beach** (IHL) with **Phoenix** retaining NHL rights, January 14, 2000.

KHLOPTONOV, Denis (khloh-POHT-nahv, DEH-nihs) FLA.

Goaltender. Catches left. 6'4", 198 lbs. Born, Moscow, USSR, January 27, 1978.
(Florida's 8th choice, 209th overall, in 1996 Entry Draft).

			Regular Season								Playoffs						
Season	Club	Lea	GP	W	L	T	Mins	GA	SO	Avg	GP	W	L	Mins	GA	SO	Avg
1996-97	CSKA Moscow	Russia	21	....	....	....	1260	42	0	2.00	....	....	....	....	....	....	....
1997-98	CSKA Moscow	Russia	20	....	....	....	987	58	....	3.53	....	....	....	....	....	....	....
1998-99	Muskegon	UHL	37	21	8	2	1950	98	1	3.02	4	1	1	166	9	0	3.25
99-2000	CSKA Moscow	Russia	10	....	....	....	540	22	1	2.44	2	....	....	119	7	0	3.53

KIDD, Trevor (KIHD, TREH-vohr) FLA.

Goaltender. Catches left. 6'2", 190 lbs. Born, Dugald, Man., March 29, 1972.
(Calgary's 1st choice, 11th overall, in 1990 Entry Draft).

			Regular Season								Playoffs						
Season	Club	Lea	GP	W	L	T	Mins	GA	SO	Avg	GP	W	L	Mins	GA	SO	Avg
1987-88	Eastman Selects	MAHA	14	....	....	....	840	66	0	4.72	....	....	....	....	....	....	....
1988-89	Brandon	WHL	32	11	13	1	1509	102	0	4.06	....	....	....	....	....	....	....
1989-90	Brandon	WHL	*63	24	32	2	*3676	254	2	4.15	....	....	....	....	....	....	....
1990-91	Brandon	WHL	30	10	19	1	1730	117	0	4.06	....	....	....	....	....	....	....
	Spokane Chiefs	WHL	14	8	3	0	749	44	0	3.52	15	*14	1	926	32	2	*2.07
1991-92	Canada	Nat-Team	28	18	4	4	1349	79	2	3.51	....	....	....	....	....	....	....
	Canada	Olympics	1	1	0	0	60	0	1	0.00	....	....	....	....	....	....	....
	Calgary	**NHL**	**2**	**1**	**1**	**0**	**120**	**8**	**0**	**4.00**	....	....	....	....	....	....	....
1992-93	Salt Lake City	IHL	29	10	16	1	1696	111	1	3.93	....	....	....	....	....	....	....
1993-94	**Calgary**	**NHL**	**31**	**13**	**7**	**6**	**1614**	**85**	**0**	**3.16**	....	....	....	....	....	....	....
1994-95	**Calgary**	**NHL**	***43**	**22**	**14**	**6**	***2463**	**107**	**3**	**2.61**	**7**	**3**	**4**	**434**	**26**	**1**	**3.59**
1995-96	**Calgary**	**NHL**	**47**	**15**	**21**	**8**	**2570**	**119**	**3**	**2.78**	**2**	**0**	**1**	**83**	**9**	**0**	**6.51**
1996-97	**Calgary**	**NHL**	**55**	**21**	**23**	**6**	**2979**	**141**	**4**	**2.84**	....	....	....	....	....	....	....
1997-98	**Carolina**	**NHL**	**47**	**21**	**21**	**3**	**2685**	**97**	**3**	**2.17**	....	....	....	....	....	....	....
1998-99	**Carolina**	**NHL**	**25**	**7**	**10**	**6**	**1358**	**61**	**2**	**2.70**	....	....	....	....	....	....	....
99-2000	**Florida**	**NHL**	**28**	**14**	**11**	**2**	**1574**	**69**	**1**	**2.63**	....	....	....	....	....	....	....
	Louisville	AHL	1	0	1	0	60	5	0	5.04	....	....	....	....	....	....	....
	NHL Totals		**278**	**114**	**108**	**37**	**15363**	**687**	**16**	**2.68**	**9**	**3**	**5**	**517**	**35**	**1**	**4.06**

WHL East First All-Star Team (1990) • Canadian Major Junior Goaltender of the Year (1990)

Traded to **Carolina** by **Calgary** with Gary Roberts for Andrew Cassels and Jean-Sebastien Giguere, August 25, 1997. Claimed by **Atlanta** from **Carolina** in Expansion Draft, June 25, 1999. Traded to **Florida** by **Atlanta** for Gord Murphy, Herbert Vasiljevs, Daniel Tjarnqvist and Ottawa's 6th round choice (previously acquired and traded to Dallas - Dallas selected Justin Cox) in 1999 Entry Draft, June 25, 1999.

KIPRUSOFF, Miikka (KIHP-ruh-sohf, MEE-kah) S.J.

Goaltender. Catches left. 6'2", 190 lbs. Born, Turku, Finland, October 26, 1976.
(San Jose's 5th choice, 116th overall, in 1995 Entry Draft).

			Regular Season								Playoffs						
Season	Club	Lea	GP	W	L	T	Mins	GA	SO	Avg	GP	W	L	Mins	GA	SO	Avg
1994-95	TPS Turku	Finn-Jr.	31	....	....	....	1896	92	....	2.91	....	....	....	....	....	....	....
	TPS Turku	Finland	4	....	....	....	240	12	0	3.00	2	....	....	120	7	....	3.50
1995-96	TPS Turku	Finn-Jr.	3	....	....	....	180	9	....	3.00	....	....	....	....	....	....	....
	Kiekko-67 Turku	Finland-2	5	....	....	....	300	7	....	1.40	....	....	....	....	....	....	....
	TPS Turku	Finland	12	....	....	....	550	38	0	4.14	3	....	....	114	4	....	2.11
1996-97	AIK Solna	Sweden	42	....	....	....	2466	104	3	2.53	7	....	....	420	23	0	3.28
1997-98	AIK Solna	Sweden	42	....	....	....	2457	110	....	2.69	....	....	....	....	....	....	....
1998-99	TPS Turku	Finland	39	*26	6	6	2259	70	4	1.86	10	*9	1	580	15	*3	*1.55
99-2000	Kentucky	AHL	47	23	19	4	2759	114	3	2.48	5	1	3	239	13	0	3.27

KOCHAN, Dieter T.B.

Goaltender. Catches left. 6'1", 180 lbs. Born, Saskatoon, SK, May 11, 1974.
(Vancouver's 3rd choice, 98th overall, in 1993 Entry Draft).

			Regular Season								Playoffs						
Season	Club	Lea	GP	W	L	T	Mins	GA	SO	Avg	GP	W	L	Mins	GA	SO	Avg
1991-92	Sioux City	USHL	23	7	10	0	1131	100	0	5.31	....	....	....	....	....	....	....
1992-93	Kelowna Spartans	BCJHL	44	34	8	0	2582	137	1	3.18	15	12	3	927	48	1	3.10
1993-94	North-Michigan	WCHA	20	9	7	0	985	57	2	3.47	....	....	....	....	....	....	....
1994-95	North-Michigan	WCHA	29	8	17	3	1512	107	0	4.25	....	....	....	....	....	....	....
1995-96	North-Michigan	WCHA	31	7	21	2	1627	123	0	4.54	....	....	....	....	....	....	....
1996-97	North-Michigan	WCHA	26	8	15	2	1528	99	0	3.89	....	....	....	....	....	....	....
1997-98	Louisville	ECHL	18	7	9	2	980	61	1	3.73	....	....	....	....	....	....	....
1998-99	Binghamton	UHL	40	18	16	5	2322	115	2	2.97	4	1	2	208	9	0	2.60
99-2000	Binghamton	UHL	43	29	11	3	2544	110	4	2.59	....	....	....	....	....	....	....
	Orlando	IHL	4	4	0	0	240	4	1	1.00	....	....	....	....	....	....	....
	Springfield	AHL	2	1	1	0	120	5	1	2.50	....	....	....	....	....	....	....
	Tampa Bay	**NHL**	**5**	**1**	**4**	**0**	**238**	**17**	**0**	**4.29**	....	....	....	....	....	....	....
	Grand Rapids	IHL	2	1	0	1	93	1	0	0.64	....	....	....	....	....	....	....
	NHL Totals		**5**	**1**	**4**	**0**	**238**	**17**	**0**	**4.29**	....	....	....	....	....	....	....

UHL Second All-Star Team (2000) • Scored goal vs. Winston-Salem (ECHL), January 5, 1999.

Signed as a free agent by **Tampa Bay**, March 27, 2000.

KOLZIG, Olaf (KOHL-zihg, OH-lahf) WSH.

Goaltender. Catches left. 6'3", 225 lbs. Born, Johannesburg, South Africa, April 9, 1970.
(Washington's 1st choice, 19th overall, in 1989 Entry Draft).

			Regular Season								Playoffs						
Season	Club	Lea	GP	W	L	T	Mins	GA	SO	Avg	GP	W	L	Mins	GA	SO	Avg
1986-87	Abbottsford Pilots	BCAHA	17	5	9	0	857	81	0	3.65	....	....	....	....	....	....	....
1987-88	New Westminster	WHL	15	6	5	0	650	48	1	4.43	3	0	3	149	11	0	4.43
1988-89	Tri-City Americans	WHL	30	16	10	2	1671	97	1	*3.48	....	....	....	....	....	....	....
1989-90	**Washington**	**NHL**	**2**	**0**	**2**	**0**	**120**	**12**	**0**	**6.00**	....	....	....	....	....	....	....
	Tri-City Americans	WHL	48	27	27	3	2504	250	1	4.38	6	4	0	318	27	0	5.09
1990-91	Baltimore	AHL	26	10	12	1	1367	72	0	3.16	....	....	....	....	....	....	....
	Hampton Roads	ECHL	21	11	9	1	1248	71	2	3.41	3	1	2	180	14	0	4.66
1991-92	Baltimore	AHL	28	5	17	2	1503	105	1	4.19	....	....	....	....	....	....	....
	Hampton Roads	ECHL	14	11	3	0	847	41	0	2.90	....	....	....	....	....	....	....
1992-93	**Washington**	**NHL**	**1**	**0**	**0**	**0**	**20**	**2**	**0**	**6.00**	....	....	....	....	....	....	....
	Rochester	AHL	49	25	16	4	2737	168	0	3.68	*17	9	8	*1040	61	0	3.52
1993-94	**Washington**	**NHL**	**7**	**0**	**3**	**0**	**224**	**20**	**0**	**5.36**	....	....	....	....	....	....	....
	Portland Pirates	AHL	29	16	8	5	1725	88	3	3.06	17	*12	5	1035	44	0	*2.55
1994-95	**Washington**	**NHL**	**14**	**2**	**8**	**2**	**724**	**30**	**0**	**2.49**	**2**	**1**	**0**	**44**	**1**	**0**	**1.36**
	Portland Pirates	AHL	2	1	0	1	125	3	0	1.44	....	....	....	....	....	....	....
1995-96	**Washington**	**NHL**	**18**	**4**	**8**	**2**	**897**	**46**	**0**	**3.08**	**5**	**2**	**3**	**341**	**11**	**0**	***1.94**
	Portland Pirates	AHL	5	5	0	0	300	7	1	1.40	....	....	....	....	....	....	....
1996-97	**Washington**	**NHL**	**29**	**8**	**15**	**4**	**1645**	**71**	**2**	**2.59**	....	....	....	....	....	....	....
1997-98	**Washington**	**NHL**	**64**	**33**	**18**	**10**	**3788**	**139**	**5**	**2.20**	**21**	**12**	**9**	**1351**	**44**	***4**	**1.95**
	Germany	Olympics	2	2	0	0	120	2	1	1.00	....	....	....	....	....	....	....
1998-99	**Washington**	**NHL**	**64**	**26**	**31**	**3**	**3586**	**154**	**4**	**2.58**	....	....	....	....	....	....	....
99-2000	**Washington**	**NHL**	**73**	**41**	**20**	**11**	***4371**	**163**	**5**	**2.24**	**5**	**1**	**4**	**284**	**16**	**0**	**3.38**
	NHL Totals		**272**	**114**	**105**	**32**	**15375**	**637**	**16**	**2.49**	**33**	**16**	**16**	**2020**	**72**	**4**	**2.14**

WHL West Second All-Star Team (1989) • Shared Harry ''Hap'' Holmes Trophy (fewest goals against - AHL) with Byron Dafoe (1994) • Won Jack Butterfield Trophy (Playoff MVP - AHL) (1994) • NHL First All-Star Team (2000) • Won Vezina Trophy (2000) • Played in NHL All-Star Game (1998, 2000)

• Scored a goal while with Tri-City (WHL), November 29, 1989.

KONSTANTINOV, Evgeny (kohn-stahn-TEE-nahf, EHV-jeh-nee) T.B.

Goaltender. Catches left. 6', 176 lbs. Born, Kazan, USSR, March 29, 1981.
(Tampa Bay's 2nd choice, 67th overall, in 1999 Entry Draft).

			Regular Season								Playoffs						
Season	Club	Lea	GP	W	L	T	Mins	GA	SO	Avg	GP	W	L	Mins	GA	SO	Avg
1997-98	Ak Bars Kazan-2	Russia-3	34	....	....	....	2040	129	....	3.79	....	....	....	....	....	....	....
1998-99	Ak Bars Kazan-2	Russia-4	17	....	....	....	1020	38	....	2.24	....	....	....	....	....	....	....
99-2000	Ak Bars Kazan	Russia	2	....	....	....	59	5	0	5.08	....	....	....	....	....	....	....

KOSTUR, Matus (KAW-stuhr, ma-TOOSH) N.J.

Goaltender. Catches left. 6'2", 185 lbs. Born, Banska Bystrica, Czech., March 28, 1980.
(New Jersey's 10th choice, 164th overall, in 2000 Entry Draft).

			Regular Season								Playoffs						
Season	Club	Lea	GP	W	L	T	Mins	GA	SO	Avg	GP	W	L	Mins	GA	SO	Avg
1997-98	Banska Bystrica	Slovak-Jr.	36	....	....	....	2152	120	0	3.35	....	....	....	....	....	....	....
1998-99	Banska Bystrica	Slovakia	3	....	....	....	133	9	0	4.06	....	....	....	....	....	....	....
99-2000	HKm Zvolen	Slovak-2	10	....	....	....	538	32	0	3.57	....	....	....	....	....	....	....
	HKm Zvolen	Slovakia	20	....	....	....	768	36	0	2.81	2	0	0	41	3	0	4.39

KOTYK, Seamus (koh-TIHK, SHAY-muhs) BOS.

Goaltender. Catches left. 5'11", 187 lbs. Born, London, Ont., October 7, 1980.
(Boston's 5th choice, 147th overall, in 1999 Entry Draft).

			Regular Season								Playoffs						
Season	Club	Lea	GP	W	L	T	Mins	GA	SO	Avg	GP	W	L	Mins	GA	SO	Avg
1996-97	Stratford Cullitons	OJHL-B	28	....	....	....	1615	105	0	3.82	....	....	....	....	....	....	....
1997-98	Ottawa 67's	OHL	31	13	5	5	1422	63	4	2.66	7	3	2	332	11	0	1.99
1998-99	Ottawa 67's	OHL	41	26	7	4	2314	92	5	2.39	5	3	2	338	13	0	*2.31
99-2000	Ottawa 67's	OHL	26	12	6	2	1241	65	1	3.14	....	....	....	....	....	....	....

KRAHN, Brent (KRAWN) CGY.

Goaltender. Catches left. 6'4", 200 lbs. Born, Winnipeg, Man., April 2, 1982.
(Calgary's 1st choice, 9th overall, in 2000 Entry Draft).

			Regular Season								Playoffs						
Season	Club	Lea	GP	W	L	T	Mins	GA	SO	Avg	GP	W	L	Mins	GA	SO	Avg
1997-98	Pembina Valley	MAHA	22	20	0	1	1265	40	3	1.90	2	2	0	120	2	1	1.00
1998-99	Pembina Valley	MAHA	13	10	3	0	770	30	2	2.34	....	....	....	....	....	....	....
99-2000	Calgary Hitman	WHL	39	33	6	0	2315	92	4	2.38	5	2	2	266	13	0	2.93

KULIKOV, Vladimir (kuhl-ee-KAHF) TOR.

Goaltender. Catches left. 5'11", 170 lbs. Born, Moscow, USSR, May 28, 1981.
(Toronto's 7th choice, 211th overall, in 1999 Entry Draft).

			Regular Season								Playoffs						
Season	Club	Lea	GP	W	L	T	Mins	GA	SO	Avg	GP	W	L	Mins	GA	SO	Avg
1998-99	CSKA Moscow	Russia-2	14	....	....	....	848	39	....	2.76	....	....	....	....	....	....	....
99-2000	STATISTICS NOT AVAILABLE																

LABARBERA, Jason (lah-BAR-buhr-uh, JAY-suhn) NYR

Goaltender. Catches left. 6'2", 205 lbs. Born, Prince George, B.C., January 18, 1980.
(NY Rangers' 3rd choice, 66th overall, in 1998 Entry Draft).

			Regular Season								Playoffs						
Season	Club	Lea	GP	W	L	T	Mins	GA	SO	Avg	GP	W	L	Mins	GA	SO	Avg
1995-96	Prince George	BCAHA	31	....	....	....	1860	83	0	2.68	....	....	....	....	....	....	....
1996-97	Tri-City Americans	WHL	2	1	0	0	63	4	0	3.81	....	....	....	....	....	....	....
	Portland	WHL	9	5	1	1	443	18	0	2.44	....	....	....	....	....	....	....
1997-98	Portland	WHL	23	18	4	0	1305	72	1	3.31	....	....	....	....	....	....	....
1998-99	Portland	WHL	51	18	23	9	2991	170	4	3.41	4	0	4	252	19	0	4.52
99-2000	Portland	WHL	34	8	24	2	2005	123	1	3.68	....	....	....	....	....	....	....
	Spokane Chiefs	WHL	21	12	6	2	1146	50	0	2.62	9	6	1	435	18	1	2.48

LABBE, Jean-Francois (lah-BAY, ZHAWN-fran-SWUH) NYR

Goaltender. Catches left. 5'10", 172 lbs. Born, Sherbrooke, Que., June 15, 1972.

			Regular Season								Playoffs						
Season	Club	Lea	GP	W	L	T	Mins	GA	SO	Avg	GP	W	L	Mins	GA	SO	Avg
1988-89	Montreal L'est	QAAA	42	27	14	1	2522	151	0	3.59	....	....	....	....	....	....	....
1989-90	Trois-Rivieres	QMJHL	28	13	10	0	1499	106	1	4.24	3	1	1	132	8	0	3.64
1990-91	Trois-Rivieres	QMJHL	54	*35	14	0	2870	158	5	3.30	5	1	4	230	19	0	4.96
1991-92	Trois-Rivieres	QMJHL	48	*31	13	3	2749	142	1	3.10	*15	*10	3	791	33	*1	*2.50
1992-93	Hull Olympiques	QMJHL	46	26	18	2	2701	156	2	3.46	10	6	3	518	24	*1	*2.78
1993-94	Thunder Bay	ColHL	52	*35	11	4	*2900	150	*2	*3.10	8	7	1	493	18	*2	*2.19
	P.E.I. Senators	AHL	7	4	3	0	389	22	0	3.39	....	....	....	....	....	....	....
1994-95	P.E.I. Senators	AHL	32	13	14	3	1817	94	2	3.10	....	....	....	....	....	....	....
1995-96	Cornwall Aces	AHL	55	25	21	5	2972	144	3	2.91	8	3	5	471	21	1	2.68
1996-97	Hershey Bears	AHL	66	*34	22	9	3811	160	*6	*2.52	*23	*14	8	*1364	59	1	2.60
1997-98	Hamilton Bulldogs	AHL	52	24	17	11	3138	149	2	2.85	7	3	4	413	20	0	2.90
1998-99	Hartford	AHL	*59	28	26	3	*3392	182	2	3.22	7	3	4	447	22	0	2.95
99-2000	**NY Rangers**	**NHL**	**1**	**0**	**1**	**0**	**60**	**3**	**0**	**3.00**	....	....	....	....	....	....	....
	Hartford	AHL	49	27	13	7	2853	120	1	2.52	*22	*15	7	*1320	48	3	2.18
	NHL Totals		**1**	**0**	**1**	**0**	**60**	**3**	**0**	**3.00**	....	....	....	....	....	....	....

QMJHL First All-Star Team (1992) • ColHL First All-Star Team (1994) • Named ColHL's Rookie of the Year (1994) • Named ColHL's Outstanding Goaltender (1994) • Named ColHL's Playoff MVP (1994) • AHL First All-Star Team (1997) • Won Harry "Hap" Holmes Memorial Trophy (fewest goals against - AHL) (1997) • Won Baz Bastien Memorial Trophy (Top Goaltender - AHL) (1997) • Won Les Cunningham Award (MVP - AHL) (1997) • Shared Harry "Hap" Holmes Memorial Trophy (fewest goals against - AHL) with Milan Hnilicka (2000)

Signed as a free agent by **Ottawa**, May 12, 1994. Traded to **Colorado** by **Ottawa** for future considerations, September 20, 1995. Signed as a free agent by **Edmonton**, September 2, 1997. Signed as a free agent by **NY Rangers**, July 30, 1998. • Scored goal with Hartford (AHL) vs. Quebec (AHL), February 5, 2000.

LAJEUNESSE, Simon (lah-ZHUH-nehs, SIGH-mohn) OTT.

Goaltender. Catches left. 6', 175 lbs. Born, Quebec City, Que., January 22, 1981.
(Ottawa's 2nd choice, 48th overall, in 1999 Entry Draft).

			Regular Season								Playoffs						
Season	Club	Lea	GP	W	L	T	Mins	GA	SO	Avg	GP	W	L	Mins	GA	SO	Avg
1996-97	Cap-de-Madelaine	QAAA	23	....	....	....	1300	89	0	4.11	....	....	....	....	....	....	....
1997-98	Moncton Alpines	QMJHL	19	5	6	3	925	51	1	3.31	2	0	0	1	0	0	0.00
1998-99	Moncton Wildcats	QMJHL	36	18	9	3	1993	98	1	2.95	1	0	0	43	2	0	2.79
99-2000	Moncton Wildcats	QMJHL	55	31	15	1	2922	127	6	2.61	16	9	6	910	56	1	3.69

QMJHL First All-Star Team (2000)

LALIME, Patrick (lah-LEEM, PAT-rihk) OTT.

Goaltender. Catches left. 6'3", 185 lbs. Born, St. Bonaventure, Que., July 7, 1974.
(Pittsburgh's 6th choice, 156th overall, in 1993 Entry Draft).

			Regular Season								Playoffs						
Season	Club	Lea	GP	W	L	T	Mins	GA	SO	Avg	GP	W	L	Mins	GA	SO	Avg
1990-91	D'abitibi Forestiers	QAAA	26	9	17	0	1595	151	0	5.81	....	....	....	....	....	....	....
1991-92	Shawinigan	QMJHL	6	....	....	....	272	25	0	5.50	....	....	....	....	....	....	....
1992-93	Shawinigan	QMJHL	44	10	24	4	2467	192	0	4.67	....	....	....	....	....	....	....
1993-94	Shawinigan	QMJHL	48	22	20	0	2733	192	1	4.22	5	1	3	223	25	0	6.73
1994-95	Hampton Roads	ECHL	26	15	7	3	1470	82	2	3.35	....	....	....	....	....	....	....
	Cleveland	IHL	23	7	10	4	1230	91	0	4.44	....	....	....	....	....	....	....
1995-96	Cleveland	IHL	41	20	12	7	2314	149	0	3.86	....	....	....	....	....	....	....
1996-97	**Pittsburgh**	**NHL**	**39**	**21**	**12**	**2**	**2058**	**101**	**3**	**2.94**	....	....	....	....	....	....	....
	Cleveland	IHL	14	6	6	2	834	45	1	3.24	....	....	....	....	....	....	....
1997-98	Grand Rapids	IHL	31	10	10	9	1749	76	2	2.61	1	0	1	77	4	0	3.11
1998-99	Kansas City	IHL	*66	*39	20	4	*3789	190	2	3.01	3	1	2	179	6	1	2.01
99-2000	**Ottawa**	**NHL**	**38**	**19**	**14**	**3**	**2038**	**79**	**3**	**2.33**	....	....	....	....	....	....	....
	NHL Totals		**77**	**40**	**26**	**5**	**4096**	**180**	**6**	**2.64**	....	....	....	....	....	....	....

NHL All-Rookie Team (1997) • IHL First All-Star Team (1999)

Rights traded to **Anaheim** by **Pittsburgh** for Sean Pronger, March 24, 1998. Traded to **Ottawa** by **Anaheim** for Ted Donato and the rights to Antti-Jussi Niemi, June 18, 1999.

LAMOTHE, Marc (luh-MAWTH, MAHRK)

Goaltender. Catches left. 6'2", 210 lbs. Born, New Liskeard, Ont., February 27, 1974.
(Montreal's 6th choice, 92nd overall, in 1992 Entry Draft).

			Regular Season								Playoffs						
Season	Club	Lea	GP	W	L	T	Mins	GA	SO	Avg	GP	W	L	Mins	GA	SO	Avg
1990-91	Ottawa	OJHL	25	13	7	0	1220	82	1	4.03	....	....	....	....	....	....	....
1991-92	Kingston	OHL	42	10	25	2	2378	189	1	4.77	....	....	....	....	....	....	....
1992-93	Kingston	OHL	45	23	12	6	2489	162	1	3.91	15	8	5	753	48	1	3.82
1993-94	Kingston	OHL	48	23	20	5	2828	177	*2	3.76	6	2	2	224	12	0	3.21
1994-95	Fredericton	AHL	9	2	5	0	428	32	0	4.48	....	....	....	....	....	....	....
	Wheeling	ECHL	13	9	2	1	737	38	0	3.10	....	....	....	....	....	....	....
1995-96	Fredericton	AHL	23	5	9	3	1166	73	1	3.76	3	1	2	161	9	0	3.36
1996-97	Indianapolis Ice	IHL	38	20	14	4	2271	100	1	2.64	1	0	0	20	1	0	3.00
1997-98	Indianapolis Ice	IHL	31	18	10	2	1772	72	3	2.44	4	1	3	177	10	0	3.38
1998-99	Indianapolis Ice	IHL	32	9	16	6	1823	115	1	3.78	6	3	3	338	10	*2	1.78
99-2000	**Chicago**	**NHL**	**2**	**1**	**1**	**0**	**116**	**10**	**0**	**5.17**	....	....	....	....	....	....	....
	Cleveland	IHL	44	19	18	4	2455	112	2	2.74	4	2	2	325	12	0	2.21
	NHL Totals		**2**	**1**	**1**	**0**	**116**	**10**	**0**	**5.17**	....	....	....	....	....	....	....

Signed as a free agent by **Chicago**, September 26, 1996.

LANGKOW, Scott (LAING-kow, SKAWT) ATL.

Goaltender. Catches left. 5'11", 190 lbs. Born, Sherwood Park, Alta., April 21, 1975.
(Winnipeg's 2nd choice, 31st overall, in 1993 Entry Draft).

			Regular Season								Playoffs						
Season	Club	Lea	GP	W	L	T	Mins	GA	SO	Avg	GP	W	L	Mins	GA	SO	Avg
1990-91	Sherwood Park	AAHA	32	....	....	....	1920	128	0	4.00	....	....	....	....	....	....	....
1991-92	Abbotsford Pilots	PIJHL	STATISTICS NOT AVAILABLE														
	Portland	WHL	1	0	0	0	33	2	0	3.46	....	....	....	....	....	....	....
1992-93	Portland	WHL	34	24	8	2	2064	119	2	3.46	9	6	3	535	31	0	3.48
1993-94	Portland	WHL	39	27	9	1	2302	121	2	3.15	10	6	4	600	34	0	3.40
1994-95	Portland	WHL	63	20	36	5	*3638	240	1	3.96	8	3	5	510	30	0	3.53
1995-96	**Winnipeg**	**NHL**	**1**	**0**	**0**	**0**	**6**	**0**	**0**	**0.00**	....	....	....	....	....	....	....
	Springfield	AHL	39	18	15	6	2329	116	3	2.99	7	4	2	393	23	0	3.51
1996-97	Springfield	AHL	33	15	9	7	1929	85	0	2.64	....	....	....	....	....	....	....
1997-98	**Phoenix**	**NHL**	**3**	**0**	**1**	**1**	**137**	**10**	**0**	**4.38**	....	....	....	....	....	....	....
	Springfield	AHL	51	30	13	5	2874	128	3	2.67	4	1	3	216	14	0	3.88
1998-99	**Phoenix**	**NHL**	**1**	**0**	**0**	**0**	**35**	**3**	**0**	**5.14**	....	....	....	....	....	....	....
	Las Vegas	IHL	27	7	14	2	1402	97	1	4.15	....	....	....	....	....	....	....
	Utah Grizzlies	IHL	21	10	9	2	1227	59	1	2.89	....	....	....	....	....	....	....
99-2000	**Atlanta**	**NHL**	**15**	**3**	**11**	**0**	**765**	**55**	**0**	**4.31**	....	....	....	....	....	....	....
	Orlando	IHL	27	14	8	2	1487	57	4	2.30	6	2	3	381	16	0	2.52
	NHL Totals		**20**	**3**	**12**	**1**	**943**	**68**	**0**	**4.33**	....	....	....	....	....	....	....

WHL West Second All-Star Team (1994, 1995) • Shared Harry "Hap" Holmes Memorial Trophy (fewest goals against - AHL) with Manny Legace (1996) • AHL First All-Star Team (1998) • Won Baz Bastien Memorial Trophy (Top Goaltender - AHL) (1998)

Transferred to **Phoenix** after **Winnipeg** franchise relocated, July 1, 1996. Traded to **Atlanta** by **Phoenix** for future considerations, June 25, 1999.

LANICEK, Michal (LAN-ih-CHEHK, MIHK-al) T.B.

Goaltender. Catches left. 6'1", 172 lbs. Born, Benesov, Czech., July 6, 1981.
(Tampa Bay's 6th choice, 148th overall, in 1999 Entry Draft).

			Regular Season								Playoffs						
Season	Club	Lea	GP	W	L	T	Mins	GA	SO	Avg	GP	W	L	Mins	GA	SO	Avg
1996-97	Slavia Praha-Jr.	Cze-Rep	22	....	....	....	1260	42	....	2.00	....	....	....	....	....	....	....
1997-98	Slavia Praha-Jr.	Cze-Rep	39	....	....	....	2162	75	....	2.08	....	....	....	....	....	....	....
1998-99	Slavia Praha-Jr.	Cze-Rep	43	....	....	....	2412	87	....	2.16	....	....	....	....	....	....	....
99-2000	Slavia Praha-Jr.	Cze-Rep	18	....	....	....	1020	35	1	2.06	6	....	....	328	7	0	1.28
	HC Bili Liberec-2	Cze-Rep	4	....	....	....	109	11	0	6.06	....	....	....	....	....	....	....
	Berouni Medvedi-2	Cze-Rep	7	....	....	....	365	12	0	1.97	1	0	1	70	4	0	3.43

LANIEL, Jean-Francois (LAN-yehl, ZHAWN-fran-SWUH) FLA.

Goaltender. Catches right. 6'2", 187 lbs. Born, Montreal, Que., June 16, 1981.
(Florida's 4th choice, 80th overall, in 1999 Entry Draft).

			Regular Season								Playoffs						
Season	Club	Lea	GP	W	L	T	Mins	GA	SO	Avg	GP	W	L	Mins	GA	SO	Avg
1997-98	Colonel-Lemoyne	QAAA	36	....	....	....	1972	99	0	3.01	....	....	....	....	....	....	....
1998-99	Shawinigan	QMJHL	18	6	6	0	876	56	0	3.84	....	....	....	....	....	....	....
99-2000	Shawinigan	QMJHL	14	2	7	0	630	40	0	3.81	....	....	....	....	....	....	....
	Val-d'Or Foreurs	QMJHL	11	1	6	0	479	46	0	5.76	....	....	....	....	....	....	....

LAROCQUE, Michel (lah-RAWK, mih-SHEHL) CHI.

Goaltender. Catches left. 5'11", 200 lbs. Born, Lahr, West Germany, October 3, 1976.
(San Jose's 5th choice, 137th overall, in 1996 Entry Draft).

			Regular Season								Playoffs						
Season	Club	Lea	GP	W	L	T	Mins	GA	SO	Avg	GP	W	L	Mins	GA	SO	Avg
1995-96	Boston University	H-East	14	10	1	1	735	42	0	3.43	....	....	....	....	....	....	....
1996-97	Boston University	H-East	24	16	4	4	1466	58	0	*2.37	....	....	....	....	....	....	....
1997-98	Boston University	H-East	24	17	4	1	1370	50	1	2.19	....	....	....	....	....	....	....
1998-99	Boston University	H-East	35	14	18	3	2072	117	0	3.39	....	....	....	....	....	....	....
99-2000	Cleveland	IHL	1	0	0	1	60	2	0	2.00	....	....	....	....	....	....	....
	Wilkes-Barre	AHL	13	5	6	1	727	34	0	2.81	....	....	....	....	....	....	....
	Saint John Flames	AHL	4	2	1	1	243	8	0	1.98	....	....	....	....	....	....	....
	Greensboro	ECHL	4	1	3	0	229	20	0	5.24	....	....	....	....	....	....	....

Hockey East Second All-Star Team (1998) • Hockey East First All-Star Team (1999) • NCAA East Second All-American Team (1999)

Traded to **Chicago** by **San Jose** for Chicago's 5th round choice (Michael Pinc) in 2000 Entry Draft, August 23, 1999.

LASAK, Jan (LA-shak, YAN) NSH.

Goaltender. Catches left. 6'1", 205 lbs. Born, Zvolen, Czech., April 10, 1979.
(Nashville's 6th choice, 65th overall, in 1999 Entry Draft).

			Regular Season								Playoffs						
Season	Club	Lea	GP	W	L	T	Mins	GA	SO	Avg	GP	W	L	Mins	GA	SO	Avg
1996-97	HKm Zvolen-Jr.	Slovakia	49	....	....	....	2940	111	....	2.27	....	....	....	....	....	....	....
1997-98	HKm Zvolen-Jr.	Slovakia	48	....	....	....	2881	119	....	2.48	....	....	....	....	....	....	....
	HK Zilina-2	Slovakia	4	....	....	....	208	12	....	3.46	....	....	....	....	....	....	....
1998-99	HKm Zvolen-Jr.	Slovakia	43	....	....	....	2580	91	....	2.12	....	....	....	....	....	....	....
	HKm Zvolen	Slovakia	8	....	....	....	387	29	....	4.50	....	....	....	....	....	....	....
99-2000	Hampton Roads	ECHL	*59	*36	17	4	*3409	145	0	2.55	10	5	5	610	28	1	2.75

• ECHL First All-Star Team (2000) • Rookie of the Year - ECHL (2000) • Top Goaltender - ECHL (2000)

LEGACE, Manny (LEH-gah-see, MAN-nee) DET.

Goaltender. Catches left. 5'9", 162 lbs. Born, Toronto, Ont., February 4, 1973.
(Hartford's 5th choice, 188th overall, in 1993 Entry Draft).

			Regular Season								Playoffs						
Season	Club	Lea	GP	W	L	T	Mins	GA	SO	Avg	GP	W	L	Mins	GA	SO	Avg
1987-88	Alliston Hornets	OJHL-C	16	7	9	0	960	83	0	5.17	....	....	....	....	....	....	....
1988-89	Vaughan Raiders	OJHL-B	23	....	....	....	1303	92	1	4.24	....	....	....	....	....	....	....
1989-90	Vaughan Raiders	OJHL-B	21	8	11	1	1180	89	1	4.53	....	....	....	....	....	....	....
	Thornhill T-Birds	OJHL-B	8	3	3	2	480	30	0	3.75	....	....	....	....	....	....	....
1990-91	Niagara Falls	OHL	30	13	11	2	1515	107	0	4.24	4	1	1	119	10	0	5.04
1991-92	Niagara Falls	OHL	43	21	16	3	2384	143	0	3.60	14	8	5	791	56	0	4.25
1992-93	Niagara Falls	OHL	48	22	19	3	2630	171	0	3.90	4	0	4	240	18	0	4.50
1993-94	Canada	Nt-Team	16	8	6	0	859	36	2	2.51	....	....	....	....	....	....	....
1994-95	Springfield	AHL	39	12	17	6	2169	128	2	3.54	....	....	....	....	....	....	....
1995-96	Springfield	AHL	37	20	12	4	2196	83	*5	*2.27	4	1	3	220	18	0	4.91
1996-97	Springfield	AHL	36	17	14	5	2119	107	1	3.03	12	9	3	745	25	*2	2.01
	Richmond	ECHL	3	2	1	0	157	8	0	3.05	....	....	....	....	....	....	....
1997-98	Springfield	AHL	6	4	2	0	345	16	0	2.78	....	....	....	....	....	....	....
	Las Vegas	IHL	41	18	16	4	2106	111	1	3.16	4	1	3	237	16	0	4.05
1998-99	**Los Angeles**	**NHL**	**17**	**2**	**9**	**2**	**899**	**39**	**0**	**2.60**	....	....	....	....	....	....	....
	Long Beach	IHL	33	22	8	1	1796	67	2	2.24	6	4	2	338	9	0	*1.60
99-2000	**Detroit**	**NHL**	**4**	**4**	**0**	**0**	**240**	**11**	**0**	**2.75**	....	....	....	....	....	....	....
	Manitoba Moose	IHL	42	17	18	5	2409	104	2	2.59	2	0	2	141	7	0	2.97
	NHL Totals		**21**	**6**	**9**	**2**	**1139**	**50**	**0**	**2.63**							

OHL First All-Star Team (1993) • AHL First All-Star Team (1996) • Shared Harry "Hap" Holmes Memorial Trophy (fewest goals against - AHL) with Scott Langkow (1996) • Won Baz Bastien Memorial Trophy (Top Goaltender - AHL) (1996)

Rights transferred to **Carolina** after **Hartford** franchise relocated, June 25, 1997. Traded to **LA Kings** by **Carolina** for future considerations, July 31, 1998. Signed as a free agent by **Detroit**, August 9, 1999. • Played w/ RHI's Toronto Planets in 1993 (13-10-3-(0)-611-67-0-5.26)

LEHTO, Mika (leh-TOH, MEE-kuh) PIT.

Goaltender. Catches left. 5'11", 172 lbs. Born, Vammala, Finland, April 12, 1979.
(Pittsburgh's 8th choice, 224th overall, in 1998 Entry Draft).

			Regular Season								Playoffs						
Season	Club	Lea	GP	W	L	T	Mins	GA	SO	Avg	GP	W	L	Mins	GA	SO	Avg
1997-98	Assat-Pori	Finn-Jr.	36	....	....	....	2160	103	2	2.86	....	....	....	....	....	....	....
	Assat-Pori	Finland	1	0	0	0	35	1	0	1.71	1	0	0	17	0	0	0.00
1998-99	Assat-Pori	Finn-Jr.	20	....	....	....	1202	68	....	3.39	....	....	....	....	....	....	....
	Assat-Pori	Finland	15	4	6	1	773	38	1	2.95	....	....	....	....	....	....	....
99-2000	Assat-Pori	Finland	23	4	11	3	1099	87	0	4.75	....	....	....	....	....	....	....

LEIGHTON, Michael (LAY-tohn, MIGH-kuhl) CHI.

Goaltender. Catches left. 6'2", 175 lbs. Born, Petrolia, Ont., May 19, 1981.
(Chicago's 5th choice, 165th overall, in 1999 Entry Draft).

			Regular Season								Playoffs						
Season	Club	Lea	GP	W	L	T	Mins	GA	SO	Avg	GP	W	L	Mins	GA	SO	Avg
1997-98	Petrolia Jets	OJHL-B	30	....	....	....	1583	87	2	3.30	....	....	....	....	....	....	....
1998-99	Windsor Spitfires	OHL	28	4	17	2	1389	112	0	4.84	3	0	1	80	10	0	7.50
99-2000	Windsor Spitfires	OHL	42	17	17	2	2272	118	1	3.12	12	5	6	616	32	0	3.12

LINDSAY, Evan (LIHND-say, EE-vawn) MTL.

Goaltender. Catches left. 6', 199 lbs. Born, Calgary, Alta., May 15, 1979.
(Montreal's 4th choice, 107th overall, in 1999 Entry Draft).

			Regular Season								Playoffs						
Season	Club	Lea	GP	W	L	T	Mins	GA	SO	Avg	GP	W	L	Mins	GA	SO	Avg
1995-96	Olds Grizzlys	AJHL	11	4	5	0	....	....	0	3.64	....	....	....	....	....	....	....
1996-97	Prince Albert	WHL	44	20	17	6	2651	153	1	3.46	4	0	4	240	16	0	4.00
1997-98	Prince Albert	WHL	52	14	30	4	3005	193	1	3.85	....	....	....	....	....	....	....
1998-99	Prince Albert	WHL	56	34	16	5	3334	158	1	2.84	14	9	5	780	43	1	3.31
99-2000	Prince Albert	WHL	54	17	30	5	3061	175	1	3.43	6	2	4	359	24	0	4.01

• Re-entered NHL draft. Originally Calgary's 2nd choice, 32nd overall, in 1997 Entry Draft.

WHL East Second All-Star Team (1998, 1999)

LITTLE, Neil (LIHTL, NEEL) PHI.

Goaltender. Catches left. 6'1", 193 lbs. Born, Medicine Hat, Alta., December 18, 1971.
(Philadelphia's 10th choice, 226th overall, in 1991 Entry Draft).

			Regular Season								Playoffs						
Season	Club	Lea	GP	W	L	T	Mins	GA	SO	Avg	GP	W	L	Mins	GA	SO	Avg
1989-90	Estevan Bruins	SJHL	46	21	19	4	2707	150	1	3.32	....	....	....	....	....	....	....
1990-91	RPI Engineers	ECAC	18	9	8	0	1032	71	0	4.13	....	....	....	....	....	....	....
1991-92	RPI Engineers	ECAC	28	11	11	3	1532	96	0	3.76	....	....	....	....	....	....	....
1992-93	RPI Engineers	ECAC	*31	*19	9	3	*1801	88	0	2.93	....	....	....	....	....	....	....
1993-94	RPI Engineers	ECAC	27	16	7	4	1570	88	0	3.36	....	....	....	....	....	....	....
	Hershey Bears	AHL	1	0	0	0	18	1	0	3.33	....	....	....	....	....	....	....
1994-95	Hershey Bears	AHL	19	5	7	3	919	60	0	3.91	....	....	....	....	....	....	....
	Johnstown Chiefs	ECHL	16	7	6	1	897	55	0	3.68	3	0	2	145	11	0	4.55
1995-96	Hershey Bears	AHL	48	21	18	6	2680	149	0	3.34	1	0	1	60	4	0	4.02
1996-97	Philadelphia	AHL	54	31	12	7	3007	145	0	2.89	10	6	4	620	20	1	*1.94
1997-98	Philadelphia	AHL	51	*31	11	7	2960	145	0	2.94	*20	*15	5	*1193	48	*3	2.41
1998-99	Grand Rapids	IHL	50	18	21	5	2740	144	3	3.15	....	....	....	....	....	....	....
99-2000	Philadelphia	AHL	51	26	18	2	2830	144	1	3.03	5	2	3	298	15	0	3.02

ECAC First All-Star Team (1993) • NCAA East Second All-American Team (1993)

LIV, Stefan (LIHV) DET.

Goaltender. Catches left. 6', 172 lbs. Born, Jonkoping, Sweden, December 21, 1980.
(Detroit's 3rd choice, 102nd overall, in 2000 Entry Draft).

			Regular Season								Playoffs						
Season	Club	Lea	GP	W	L	T	Mins	GA	SO	Avg	GP	W	L	Mins	GA	SO	Avg
1997-98	HV-Jonkoping	Swede-Jr.	17	....	....	....	1020	47	....	2.76	....	....	....	....	....	....	....
1998-99	HV-Jonkoping	Sweden	DID NOT PLAY – SPARE GOALTENDER														
99-2000	HV-Jonkoping	Swede-Jr.	10	....	....	....	600	17	2	1.70	....	....	....	....	....	....	....
	Tranas AIF	Swede-2	9	....	....	....	541	20	0	2.17	....	....	....	....	....	....	....
	HV-Jonkoping	Sweden	12	....	....	....	716	24	1	2.01	3	....	....	178	12	0	4.04

LUONGO, Roberto (loo-WAHN-goh, ROH-buhr-TOH) FLA.

Goaltender. Catches left. 6'3", 175 lbs. Born, Montreal, Que., April 4, 1979.
(NY Islanders' 1st choice, 4th overall, in 1997 Entry Draft).

			Regular Season								Playoffs						
Season	Club	Lea	GP	W	L	T	Mins	GA	SO	Avg	GP	W	L	Mins	GA	SO	Avg
1994-95	Montreal-Bourassa	QAAA	25	10	14	0	94	1465	0	3.85	....	....	....	....	....	....	....
1995-96	Val-d'Or Foreurs	QMJHL	23	6	11	4	1201	74	0	3.70	3	0	1	68	5	0	4.41
1996-97	Val-d'Or Foreurs	QMJHL	60	32	22	2	3305	171	2	3.10	13	8	5	777	44	0	3.40
1997-98	Val-d'Or Foreurs	QMJHL	54	27	20	5	3046	157	*7	3.09	*17	*14	3	*1019	37	*2	*2.18
1998-99	Val-d'Or Foreurs	QMJHL	21	6	10	2	1176	77	1	3.93	....	....	....	....	....	....	....
	Acadie-Bathurst	QMJHL	22	14	7	1	1340	74	0	3.31	*23	*16	6	*1400	64	0	2.74
99-2000	**NY Islanders**	**NHL**	**24**	**7**	**14**	**1**	**1292**	**70**	**1**	**3.25**	....	....	....	....	....	....	....
	Lowell	AHL	26	10	12	4	1517	74	1	2.93	6	3	3	359	18	0	3.01
	NHL Totals		**24**	**7**	**14**	**1**	**1292**	**70**	**1**	**3.25**	....	....	....	....	....	....	....

Traded to **Florida** by **NY Islanders** with Olli Jokinen for Mark Parrish and Oleg Kvasha, June 24, 2000.

MAGLIARDITI, Marc CAR.

Goaltender. Catches Left. 6', 180 lbs. Born, Niagara Falls, NY, July 9, 1976.
(Chicago's 6th choice, 146th overall, in 1995 Entry Draft).

			Regular Season								Playoffs						
Season	Club	Lea	GP	W	L	T	Mins	GA	SO	Avg	GP	W	L	Mins	GA	SO	Avg
1994-95	Des Moines	USHL	29	21	2	4	1727	82	0	2.85	8	7	1	490	24	0	2.94
1995-96	Western Michigan	CCHA	36	23	11	2	2110	91	5	2.59	....	....	....	....	....	....	....
1996-97	Spokane Chiefs	WHL	29	12	13	1	1456	74	0	3.05	....	....	....	....	....	....	....
1997-98	Indianapolis Ice	IHL	3	1	2	0	179	10	0	3.35	....	....	....	....	....	....	....
	Columbus Chill	ECHL	28	13	11	3	1644	86	2	3.14	....	....	....	....	....	....	....
	Detroit Vipers	IHL	10	5	4	0	512	30	0	3.51	....	....	....	....	....	....	....
	Fort Wayne	IHL	2	0	1	1	119	6	0	3.01	....	....	....	....	....	....	....
1998-99	Florida Everblades	ECHL	47	*32	10	3	2746	104	5	2.27	5	3	2	332	14	1	2.53
99-2000	Cincinnati	IHL	14	5	6	2	752	35	1	2.79	....	....	....	....	....	....	....
	Florida Everblades	ECHL	33	22	9	0	1794	69	3	2.31	4	1	2	209	12	0	3.44

USHL First All-Star Team (1995) • CCHA Rookie-of-the-Year (1995) • CCHA All-Rookie Team (1995) • CCHA First All-Star Team (1995)

Signed as a free agent by **Carolina**, September 14, 1999.

MARACLE, Norm (MAHR-ah-cuhl, NOHRM) ATL.

Goaltender. Catches left. 5'8", 195 lbs. Born, Belleville, Ont., October 2, 1974.
(Detroit's 6th choice, 126th overall, in 1993 Entry Draft).

			Regular Season								Playoffs						
Season	Club	Lea	GP	W	L	T	Mins	GA	SO	Avg	GP	W	L	Mins	GA	SO	Avg
1990-91	Calgary Stars	AMHL	29	....	....	....	1740	99	0	3.43	....	....	....	....	....	....	....
1991-92	Saskatoon Blades	WHL	29	13	6	3	1529	87	1	3.41	15	9	5	860	37	0	3.38
1992-93	Saskatoon Blades	WHL	53	27	18	3	1939	160	1	3.27	9	4	5	569	33	0	3.48
1993-94	Saskatoon Blades	WHL	56	*41	13	1	3219	148	2	2.76	16	*11	5	940	48	*1	3.06
1994-95	Adirondack	AHL	39	12	15	2	1997	119	0	3.57	....	....	....	....	....	....	....
1995-96	Adirondack	AHL	54	24	18	6	2949	135	2	2.75	1	0	1	30	4	0	8.11
1996-97	Adirondack	AHL	*68	*34	22	9	*3843	173	5	2.70	4	1	3	192	10	1	3.13
1997-98	**Detroit**	**NHL**	**4**	**2**	**0**	**1**	**178**	**6**	**0**	**2.02**	....	....	....	....	....	....	....
	Adirondack	AHL	*66	27	29	8	*3709	190	1	3.07	3	0	3	180	10	0	3.33
1998-99	**Detroit**	**NHL**	**16**	**6**	**5**	**2**	**821**	**31**	**0**	**2.27**	**2**	**0**	**0**	**58**	**3**	**0**	**3.10**
	Adirondack	AHL	6	3	3	0	359	18	0	3.01	....	....	....	....	....	....	....
99-2000	**Atlanta**	**NHL**	**32**	**4**	**19**	**2**	**1618**	**94**	**1**	**3.49**	....	....	....	....	....	....	....
	NHL Totals		**52**	**12**	**24**	**5**	**2617**	**131**	**1**	**3.00**	**2**	**0**	**0**	**58**	**3**	**0**	**3.10**

Won Warwick Trophy (AMHL MVP) (1991) • WHL East Second All-Star Team (1993) • WHL East First All-Star Team (1994) • Canadian Major Junior First All-Star Team (1994) • Canadian Major Junior Goaltender of the Year (1994) • AHL Second All-Star Team (1997, 1998)

Claimed by **Atlanta** from **Detroit** in Expansion Draft, June 25, 1999.

MARSTERS, Nathan (MAHR-stuhrs) L.A.

Goaltender. Catches left. 6'4", 190 lbs. Born, Burlington, Ont., January 20, 1980.
(Los Angeles' 5th choice, 165th overall, in 2000 Entry Draft).

			Regular Season								Playoffs						
Season	Club	Lea	GP	W	L	T	Mins	GA	SO	Avg	GP	W	L	Mins	GA	SO	Avg
1997-98	Bramalea Blues	OJHL	12	....	....	....	539	25	2	2.78	....	....	....	....	....	....	....
1998-99	Chilliwack Chiefs	BCJHL	9	6	2	0	478	29	0	3.65	....	....	....	....	....	....	....
99-2000	Bramalea Blues	OJHL	27	....	....	....	1668	98	2	3.53	....	....	....	....	....	....	....
	Chilliwack Chiefs	BCJHL	15	9	6	0	825	63	0	4.58	20	15	5	1187	62	0	3.13

MASON, Chris (MAY-sohn, KRIHS) NSH.

Goaltender. Catches left. 6', 198 lbs. Born, Red Deer, Alta., April 20, 1976.
(New Jersey's 7th choice, 122nd overall, in 1995 Entry Draft).

			Regular Season								Playoffs						
Season	Club	Lea	GP	W	L	T	Mins	GA	SO	Avg	GP	W	L	Mins	GA	SO	Avg
1992-93	Red Deer Chiefs	AAHA	20	....	....	....	1280	76	0	3.35	....	....	....	....	....	....	....
1993-94	Victoria Cougars	WHL	5	1	4	0	237	27	0	6.84	....	....	....	....	....	....	....
1994-95	Prince George	WHL	44	8	30	1	2288	192	1	5.03	....	....	....	....	....	....	....
1995-96	Prince George	WHL	59	16	37	1	3289	236	1	4.31	....	....	....	....	....	....	....
1996-97	Prince George	WHL	50	19	24	4	2851	172	2	3.62	15	9	6	938	44	*1	2.81
1997-98	Cincinnati Ducks	AHL	47	13	19	7	2368	136	0	3.45	....	....	....	....	....	....	....
1998-99	**Nashville**	**NHL**	**3**	**0**	**0**	**0**	**69**	**6**	**0**	**5.22**	....	....	....	....	....	....	....
	Milwaukee	IHL	34	15	12	6	1901	92	1	2.90	....	....	....	....	....	....	....
99-2000	Milwaukee	IHL	53	20	21	8	2952	137	2	2.78	3	1	2	252	11	0	2.62
	NHL Totals		**3**	**0**	**0**	**0**	**69**	**6**	**0**	**5.22**	....	....	....	....	....	....	....

Signed as a free agent by **Anaheim**, June 27, 1997. Traded to **Nashville** by **Anaheim** with Marc Moro for Dominic Roussel, October 5, 1998.

MAUND, Jeff (MAHND, JEHF) CHI.

Goaltender. Catches left. 6'2", 195 lbs. Born, Mississauga, Ont., April 8, 1976.

			Regular Season								Playoffs						
Season	Club	Lea	GP	W	L	T	Mins	GA	SO	Avg	GP	W	L	Mins	GA	SO	Avg
1996-97	Aurora Tigers	OJHL	30	....	....	....	1731	72	5	2.50	....	....	....	....	....	....	....
1997-98	Ohio State	CCHA	32	22	8	0	1858	73	4	2.36	....	....	....	....	....	....	....
1998-99	Ohio State	CCHA	38	20	14	4	2283	89	3	2.34	....	....	....	....	....	....	....
99-2000	Florida Everblades	ECHL	37	26	6	1	2055	89	3	2.60	2	1	1	89	4	0	2.69

CCHA First All-Star Team (1999) • NCAA West Second All-American Team (1999)

Signed as a free agent by **Chicago**, April 14, 1999.

McLEAN, Jason (muh-KLAYN, JAY-suhn)

Goaltender. Catches left. 6', 200 lbs. Born, Regina, Sask., September 3, 1979.
(NY Rangers' 5th choice, 126th overall, in 1997 Entry Draft).

			Regular Season								Playoffs						
Season	Club	Lea	GP	W	L	T	Mins	GA	SO	Avg	GP	W	L	Mins	GA	SO	Avg
1995-96	Moose Jaw	WHL	11	1	7	1	544	38	0	4.19	....	....	....	....	....	....	....
1996-97	Moose Jaw	WHL	19	7	7	2	1014	60	0	3.55	....	....	....	....	....	....	....
1997-98	Moose Jaw	WHL	5	1	3	0	243	21	0	5.19	....	....	....	....	....	....	....
	Lethbridge	WHL	46	19	18	6	2610	131	2	3.01	4	0	3	190	17	0	5.37
1998-99	Lethbridge	WHL	19	11	4	2	1077	49	1	2.73	2	0	1	75	12	0	9.60
99-2000	Tri-City Americans	WHL	DID NOT PLAY														

McLEAN, Kirk (muh-KLAYN, KUHRK) NYR

Goaltender. Catches left. 6', 180 lbs. Born, Willowdale, Ont., June 26, 1966.
(New Jersey's 6th choice, 107th overall, in 1984 Entry Draft).

			Regular Season								Playoffs						
Season	Club	Lea	GP	W	L	T	Mins	GA	SO	Avg	GP	W	L	Mins	GA	SO	Avg
1982-83	Don Mills Flyers	MTHL	26	....	....	....	1575	52	0	2.01	....	....	....	....	....	....	....
1983-84	Oshawa Generals	OHL	17	5	9	0	940	67	0	4.28	....	....	....	....	....	....	....
1984-85	Oshawa Generals	OHL	47	23	17	2	2581	143	1	*3.32	5	1	3	271	21	0	4.65
1985-86	Oshawa Generals	OHL	51	24	21	2	2830	169	1	3.58	4	1	2	201	18	0	5.37
	New Jersey	**NHL**	**2**	**1**	**1**	**0**	**111**	**11**	**0**	**5.95**	....	....	....	....	....	....	....
1986-87	**New Jersey**	**NHL**	**4**	**1**	**1**	**0**	**160**	**10**	**0**	**3.75**	....	....	....	....	....	....	....
	Maine Mariners	AHL	45	15	23	4	2606	140	1	3.22	....	....	....	....	....	....	....
1987-88	**Vancouver**	**NHL**	**41**	**11**	**27**	**3**	**2380**	**147**	**1**	**3.71**	....	....	....	....	....	....	....
1988-89	**Vancouver**	**NHL**	**42**	**20**	**17**	**3**	**2477**	**127**	**4**	**3.08**	**5**	**2**	**3**	**302**	**18**	**0**	**3.58**
1989-90	**Vancouver**	**NHL**	***63**	**21**	**30**	**10**	***3739**	**216**	**0**	**3.47**	....	....	....	....	....	....	....
1990-91	**Vancouver**	**NHL**	**41**	**10**	**22**	**3**	**1969**	**131**	**0**	**3.99**	**2**	**1**	**1**	**123**	**7**	**0**	**3.41**
1991-92	**Vancouver**	**NHL**	**65**	***38**	**17**	**9**	**3852**	**176**	***5**	**2.74**	**13**	**6**	**7**	**785**	**33**	***2**	**2.52**
1992-93	**Vancouver**	**NHL**	**54**	**28**	**21**	**5**	**3261**	**184**	**3**	**3.39**	**12**	**6**	**6**	**754**	**42**	**0**	**3.34**
1993-94	**Vancouver**	**NHL**	**52**	**23**	**26**	**3**	**3128**	**156**	**3**	**2.99**	***24**	**15**	**9**	***1544**	**59**	***4**	**2.29**
1994-95	**Vancouver**	**NHL**	**40**	**18**	**12**	**10**	**2374**	**109**	**1**	**2.75**	**11**	**4**	**7**	**660**	**36**	**0**	**3.27**
1995-96	**Vancouver**	**NHL**	**45**	**15**	**21**	**9**	**2645**	**156**	**2**	**3.54**	**1**	**0**	**1**	**21**	**3**	**0**	**8.57**
1996-97	**Vancouver**	**NHL**	**44**	**21**	**18**	**3**	**2581**	**138**	**0**	**3.21**	....	....	....	....	....	....	....
1997-98	**Vancouver**	**NHL**	**29**	**6**	**17**	**4**	**1583**	**97**	**1**	**3.68**	....	....	....	....	....	....	....
	Carolina	**NHL**	**8**	**4**	**2**	**0**	**401**	**22**	**0**	**3.29**	....	....	....	....	....	....	....
	Florida	**NHL**	**7**	**4**	**2**	**1**	**406**	**22**	**0**	**3.25**	....	....	....	....	....	....	....
1998-99	**Florida**	**NHL**	**30**	**9**	**10**	**4**	**1597**	**73**	**2**	**2.74**	....	....	....	....	....	....	....
99-2000	**NY Rangers**	**NHL**	**22**	**7**	**8**	**4**	**1206**	**58**	**0**	**2.89**	....	....	....	....	....	....	....
	NHL Totals		**589**	**237**	**252**	**71**	**33870**	**1833**	**22**	**3.25**	**68**	**34**	**34**	**4189**	**198**	**6**	**2.84**

NHL Second All-Star Team (1992) • Played in NHL All-Star Game (1990, 1992)

Traded to **Vancouver** by **New Jersey** with Greg Adams and New Jersey's 2nd round choice (Leif Rohlin) in 1988 Entry Draft for Patrik Sundstrom and Vancouver's 2nd (Jeff Christian) and 4th (Matt Ruchty) round choices in 1988 Entry Draft, September 15, 1987. Traded to **Carolina** by **Vancouver** with Martin Gelinas for Sean Burke, Geoff Sanderson and Enrico Ciccone, January 3, 1998. Traded to **Florida** by **Carolina** for Ray Sheppard, March 24, 1998. Signed as a free agent by **NY Rangers**, July 20, 1999.

McLENNAN, Jamie (muh-KLEH-nuhn, JAY-mee) MIN.

Goaltender. Catches left. 6', 190 lbs. Born, Edmonton, Alta., June 30, 1971.
(NY Islanders' 3rd choice, 48th overall, in 1991 Entry Draft).

			Regular Season								Playoffs						
Season	Club	Lea	GP	W	L	T	Mins	GA	SO	Avg	GP	W	L	Mins	GA	SO	Avg
1987-88	St. Albert Royals	AAHA	21	....	....	....	1224	80	0	3.92	....	....	....	....	....	....	....
1988-89	Spokane Chiefs	WHL	11	....	....	....	578	63	0	6.54	....	....	....	....	....	....	....
	Lethbridge	WHL	7	....	....	....	368	22	0	3.59	....	....	....	....	....	....	....
1989-90	Lethbridge	WHL	34	20	4	2	1690	110	1	3.91	13	6	5	677	44	0	3.90
1990-91	Lethbridge	WHL	56	32	18	4	3230	205	0	3.81	*16	8	8	*970	56	0	3.46
1991-92	Capital District	AHL	18	4	10	2	952	60	1	3.78	....	....	....	....	....	....	....
	Richmond	ECHL	32	16	12	2	1837	114	0	3.72	....	....	....	....	....	....	....
1992-93	Capital District	AHL	38	17	14	6	2171	117	1	3.23	1	0	1	20	5	0	15.00
1993-94	**NY Islanders**	**NHL**	**22**	**8**	**7**	**6**	**1287**	**61**	**0**	**2.84**	**2**	**0**	**1**	**82**	**6**	**0**	**4.39**
	Salt Lake City	IHL	24	8	12	2	1320	80	0	3.64	....	....	....	....	....	....	....
1994-95	**NY Islanders**	**NHL**	**21**	**6**	**11**	**2**	**1185**	**67**	**0**	**3.39**	....	....	....	....	....	....	....
	Denver Grizzlies	IHL	4	3	0	1	239	12	0	3.00	11	8	2	640	23	1	*2.15
1995-96	**NY Islanders**	**NHL**	**13**	**3**	**9**	**1**	**636**	**39**	**0**	**3.68**	....	....	....	....	....	....	....
	Utah Grizzlies	IHL	14	9	2	2	728	29	0	2.39	....	....	....	....	....	....	....
	Worcester	AHL	22	14	7	1	1216	57	0	2.81	2	0	2	119	8	0	4.04
1996-97	Worcester	AHL	39	18	13	4	2152	100	2	2.79	4	2	2	262	16	0	3.67
1997-98	**St. Louis**	**NHL**	**30**	**16**	**8**	**2**	**1658**	**60**	**2**	**2.17**	**1**	**0**	**0**	**14**	**1**	**0**	**4.29**
1998-99	**St. Louis**	**NHL**	**33**	**13**	**14**	**4**	**1763**	**70**	**3**	**2.38**	**1**	**0**	**1**	**37**	**0**	**0**	**0.00**
99-2000	**St. Louis**	**NHL**	**19**	**9**	**5**	**2**	**1009**	**33**	**2**	**1.96**	....	....	....	....	....	....	....
	NHL Totals		**138**	**55**	**54**	**17**	**7538**	**330**	**7**	**2.63**	**4**	**0**	**2**	**133**	**7**	**0**	**3.16**

WHL East First All-Star Team (1991) • Won Bill Masterton Memorial Trophy (1998)

Signed as a free agent by **St. Louis**, July 15, 1996. Selected by **Minnesota** from **St. Louis** in Expansion Draft, June 23, 2000.

MICHAUD, Alfie (mee-SHOH, AL-fee) VAN.

Goaltender. Catches Left. 5'10", 177 lbs. Born, Selkirk, Man., November 6, 1976.

			Regular Season								Playoffs						
Season	Club	Lea	GP	W	L	T	Mins	GA	SO	Avg	GP	W	L	Mins	GA	SO	Avg
1995-96	Lebret Eagles	SJHL	44	....	....	....	2547	121	2	2.85	....	....	....	....	....	....	....
1996-97	U. of Maine	H-East	29	*17	8	1	1515	78	1	3.09	....	....	....	....	....	....	....
1997-98	U. of Maine	H-East	32	15	12	4	1794	94	2	3.14	....	....	....	....	....	....	....
1998-99	U. of Maine	H-East	37	*28	6	3	2147	83	3	2.32	....	....	....	....	....	....	....
99-2000	**Vancouver**	**NHL**	**2**	**0**	**1**	**0**	**69**	**5**	**0**	**4.35**	....	....	....	....	....	....	....
	Syracuse Crunch	AHL	38	10	17	5	2052	132	0	3.86	....	....	....	....	....	....	....
	NHL Totals		**2**	**0**	**1**	**0**	**69**	**5**	**0**	**4.35**	....	....	....	....	....	....	....

NCAA Championship All-Tournament Team (1999) • NCAA Championship Tournament MVP (1999)

Signed as a free agent by **Vancouver**, July 12, 1999.

MILLER, Aren (MIHL-luhr, AIR-ehn) DET.

Goaltender. Catches left. 6'2", 208 lbs. Born, Oxbow, Sask., January 13, 1978.
(Detroit's 2nd choice, 52nd overall, in 1996 Entry Draft).

			Regular Season								Playoffs						
Season	Club	Lea	GP	W	L	T	Mins	GA	SO	Avg	GP	W	L	Mins	GA	SO	Avg
1994-95	Saskatoon Blazers	SAHA	18	....	....	....	977	70	0	4.30	....	....	....	....	....	....	....
1995-96	Spokane Chiefs	WHL	23	8	7	2	965	50	1	3.11	3	0	3	81	8	0	5.93
1996-97	Spokane Chiefs	WHL	52	22	20	3	2834	151	3	3.20	9	4	5	555	28	*1	3.03
1997-98	Spokane Chiefs	WHL	*64	*38	22	3	*3466	187	3	3.24	7	2	3	318	24	0	4.53
1998-99	Toledo Storm	ECHL	7	1	4	1	374	33	0	5.29	....	....	....	....	....	....	....
	Adirondack	AHL	25	3	14	1	1155	68	1	3.53	2	0	2	123	8	0	3.92
99-2000	Cincinnati Ducks	AHL	18	4	10	1	1010	56	1	3.33	....	....	....	....	....	....	....

MILLER, Ryan (MIHL-luhr, RIGH-yan) BUF.

Goaltender. Catches left. 6'1", 150 lbs. Born, East Lansing, MI, July 17, 1980.
(Buffalo's 7th choice, 138th overall, in 1999 Entry Draft).

			Regular Season								Playoffs						
Season	Club	Lea	GP	W	L	T	Mins	GA	SO	Avg	GP	W	L	Mins	GA	SO	Avg
1997-98	Soo Indians	NAJHL	31	17	13	0	1804	72	1	2.39	6	2	4	311	10	0	1.93
1998-99	Soo Indians	NAJHL	47	31	14	1	2711	104	8	2.30	....	....	....	....	....	....	....
99-2000	Michigan State	CCHA	26	16	5	3	1525	39	*8	*1.53	....	....	....	....	....	....	....

CCHA Second All-Star Team (2000)

MINARD, Mike (mih-NAHRD, MIGHK)

Goaltender. Catches left. 6'3", 205 lbs. Born, Owen Sound, Ont., November 1, 1976.
(Edmonton's 4th choice, 83rd overall, in 1995 Entry Draft).

			Regular Season								Playoffs						
Season	Club	Lea	GP	W	L	T	Mins	GA	SO	Avg	GP	W	L	Mins	GA	SO	Avg
1992-93	St. Mary's Lincolns	OJHL-B	23	....	....	....	1374	162	0	3.10	....	....	....	....	....	....	....
1993-94	St. Mary's Lincolns	OJHL-B	31	*25	5	0	1710	78	1	*2.74	....	....	....	....	....	....	....
1994-95	Chilliwack Chiefs	BCJHL	40	....	....	....	2330	136	0	3.50	....	....	....	....	....	....	....
1995-96	Barrie Colts	OHL	1	0	1	0	52	8	0	9.23	....	....	....	....	....	....	....
	Detroit Whalers	OHL	42	25	10	4	2314	128	2	3.32	17	9	6	922	55	1	3.58
1996-97	Hamilton Bulldogs	AHL	3	1	1	0	100	7	0	4.20	....	....	....	....	....	....	....
	Wheeling Nailers	ECHL	23	3	7	1	899	69	0	4.60	3	0	2	148	16	0	6.47
1997-98	Hamilton Bulldogs	AHL	2	1	0	0	80	2	0	1.50	....	....	....	....	....	....	....
	Brantford Smoke	UHL	2	1	1	0	74	7	0	5.63	....	....	....	....	....	....	....
	New Orleans	ECHL	11	6	2	0	429	30	0	4.19	....	....	....	....	....	....	....
	Milwaukee	IHL	8	2	2	0	362	19	0	3.15	....	....	....	....	....	....	....
1998-99	Dayton Bombers	ECHL	15	8	5	2	788	42	1	3.20	....	....	....	....	....	....	....
	Milwaukee	IHL	10	3	5	0	531	27	0	3.05	....	....	....	....	....	....	....
	Hamilton Bulldogs	AHL	11	8	3	0	645	30	1	2.79	1	0	0	20	0	0	0.00
99-2000	**Edmonton**	**NHL**	**1**	**1**	**0**	**0**	**60**	**3**	**0**	**3.00**	....	....	....	....	....	....	....
	Hamilton Bulldogs	AHL	38	16	12	5	1987	102	0	3.08	1	0	0	23	0	0	0.00
	NHL Totals		**1**	**1**	**0**	**0**	**60**	**3**	**0**	**3.00**	....	....	....	....	....	....	....

MORRISON, Michael (MOHR-rihs-ohn, MIGH-kuhl) EDM.

Goaltender. Catches right. 6'3", 194 lbs. Born, Medford, MA, July 11, 1979.
(Edmonton's 8th choice, 186th overall, in 1998 Entry Draft).

			Regular Season								Playoffs						
Season	Club	Lea	GP	W	L	T	Mins	GA	SO	Avg	GP	W	L	Mins	GA	SO	Avg
1997-98	Phillips Exeter	H.S.	27	15	11	2	1632	64	1	2.35	....	....	....	....	....	....	....
1998-99	U. of Maine	H-East	11	3	0	1	347	10	1	1.73	....	....	....	....	....	....	....
99-2000	U. of Maine	H-East	12	7	2	1	608	27	1	2.67	....	....	....	....	....	....	....

MOSS, Tyler (MAWS, TIGH-luhr) CAR.

Goaltender. Catches right. 6', 185 lbs. Born, Ottawa, Ont., June 29, 1975.
(Tampa Bay's 2nd choice, 29th overall, in 1993 Entry Draft).

			Regular Season								Playoffs						
Season	Club	Lea	GP	W	L	T	Mins	GA	SO	Avg	GP	W	L	Mins	GA	SO	Avg
1991-92	Nepean Raiders	OJHL	26	7	12	1	1335	109	0	4.90	....	....	....	....	....	....	....
1992-93	Kingston	OHL	31	13	7	5	1537	97	0	3.79	6	1	2	228	19	0	5.00
1993-94	Kingston	OHL	13	6	4	3	795	42	1	3.17	3	0	2	136	8	0	3.53
1994-95	Kingston	OHL	*57	33	17	5	*3249	164	1	3.03	6	2	4	333	27	0	4.86
1995-96	Atlanta Knights	IHL	40	11	19	4	2030	138	1	4.08	3	0	3	213	11	0	3.10
1996-97	Adirondack	AHL	11	1	5	2	507	42	1	4.97	....	....	....	....	....	....	....
	Grand Rapids	IHL	15	5	6	1	715	35	0	2.94	....	....	....	....	....	....	....
	Muskegon Fury	ColHL	2	1	1	0	119	5	0	2.51	....	....	....	....	....	....	....
	Saint John Flames	AHL	9	6	1	1	534	17	0	1.91	5	2	3	242	15	0	3.72
1997-98	**Calgary**	**NHL**	**6**	**2**	**3**	**1**	**367**	**20**	**0**	**3.27**	....	....	....	....	....	....	....
	Saint John Flames	AHL	39	19	10	7	2194	91	0	2.49	15	8	5	761	37	0	2.91
1998-99	**Calgary**	**NHL**	**11**	**3**	**7**	**0**	**550**	**23**	**0**	**2.51**	....	....	....	....	....	....	....
	Saint John Flames	AHL	9	2	5	1	475	25	0	3.16	....	....	....	....	....	....	....
	Orlando	IHL	9	6	2	1	515	21	1	2.45	17	10	7	1017	53	0	3.13
99-2000	Wilkes-Barre	AHL	4	1	1	1	188	11	0	3.52	....	....	....	....	....	....	....
	Kansas City	IHL	36	18	12	5	2116	105	3	2.98	....	....	....	....	....	....	....
	NHL Totals		**17**	**5**	**10**	**1**	**917**	**43**	**0**	**2.81**	....	....	....	....	....	....	....

OHL First All-Star Team (1995) • Shared Harry "Hap" Holmes Memorial Trophy (fewest goals against - AHL) with Jean-Sebastien Giguere (1998)

Traded to **Calgary** by **Tampa Bay** for Jamie Huscroft, March 18, 1997. Traded to **Pittsburgh** by **Calgary** with Rene Corbet for Brad Werenka, March 14, 2000. Signed as a free agent by **Carolina**, August 9, 2000. • Played w/ RHI's Florida Hammerheads in 1993 (1-0-0-0-8-4-0-24.00)

MUZZATTI, Jason (moo-ZAH-tee, JAY-suhn)

Goaltender. Catches left. 6'2", 210 lbs. Born, Toronto, Ont., February 3, 1970.
(Calgary's 1st choice, 21st overall, in 1988 Entry Draft).

			Regular Season								Playoffs						
Season	Club	Lea	GP	W	L	T	Mins	GA	SO	Avg	GP	W	L	Mins	GA	SO	Avg
1985-86	St. Michael's	OJHL-B	11	6	3	0	517	48	0	5.57	....	....	....	....	....	....	....
1986-87	St. Michael's	OJHL-B	20	10	5	2	1054	69	1	3.93	....	....	....	....	....	....	....
1987-88	Michigan State	CCHA	33	19	9	3	1915	109	0	3.41	....	....	....	....	....	....	....
1988-89	Michigan State	CCHA	42	32	9	1	2515	127	3	*3.03	....	....	....	....	....	....	....
1989-90	Michigan State	CCHA	33	*24	6	0	1976	99	0	3.01	....	....	....	....	....	....	....
1990-91	Michigan State	CCHA	22	8	10	2	1204	75	1	3.74	....	....	....	....	....	....	....
1991-92	Salt Lake City	IHL	52	24	22	5	3033	167	2	3.30	4	1	3	247	18	0	4.37
1992-93	Canada	Nt-Team	16	6	9	0	880	53	0	3.84	....	....	....	....	....	....	....
	Indianapolis Ice	IHL	12	5	6	1	707	48	0	4.07	....	....	....	....	....	....	....
	Salt Lake City	IHL	13	5	6	1	747	52	0	4.18	....	....	....	....	....	....	....
1993-94	**Calgary**	**NHL**	**1**	**0**	**1**	**0**	**60**	**8**	**0**	**8.00**	....	....	....	....	....	....	....
	Saint John Flames	AHL	51	26	21	3	2939	183	2	3.74	7	3	4	415	19	0	2.75
1994-95	**Calgary**	**NHL**	**1**	**0**	**0**	**0**	**10**	**0**	**0**	**0.00**	....	....	....	....	....	....	....
	Saint John Flames	AHL	31	10	14	4	1741	101	2	3.48	....	....	....	....	....	....	....
1995-96	**Hartford**	**NHL**	**22**	**4**	**8**	**3**	**1013**	**49**	**1**	**2.90**	....	....	....	....	....	....	....
	Springfield	AHL	5	4	0	1	300	12	1	2.40	....	....	....	....	....	....	....
1996-97	**Hartford**	**NHL**	**31**	**9**	**13**	**5**	**1591**	**91**	**0**	**3.43**	....	....	....	....	....	....	....
1997-98	**NY Rangers**	**NHL**	**6**	**0**	**3**	**2**	**313**	**17**	**0**	**3.26**	....	....	....	....	....	....	....
	Hartford	AHL	17	11	5	1	999	57	0	3.42	....	....	....	....	....	....	....
	San Jose	**NHL**	**1**	**0**	**0**	**0**	**27**	**2**	**0**	**4.44**	....	....	....	....	....	....	....
	Kentucky	AHL	7	2	3	2	430	25	0	3.49	3	0	3	153	13	0	5.07
1998-99	Eisbaren Berlin	DEL	4	....	....	....	240	12	0	3.00	3	0	3	166	14	0	5.06
99-2000	Tappara Tampere	Finland	41	26	9	5	2479	94	5	2.28	4	1	3	252	14	0	3.33
	NHL Totals		**62**	**13**	**25**	**10**	**3014**	**167**	**1**	**3.32**	....	....	....	....	....	....	....

CCHA Second All-Star Team (1988) • CCHA First All-Star Team (1990) • NCAA West Second All-American Team (1990)

Claimed on waivers by **Hartford** from **Calgary**, October 6, 1995. Transferred to **Carolina** after **Hartford** franchise relocated, June 25, 1997. Traded to **NY Rangers** by **Carolina** for NY Rangers' 4th round choice (Tommy Westlund) in 1998 Entry Draft, August 8, 1997. Traded to **San Jose** by **NY Rangers** for Rich Brennan, March 24, 1998. • Missed majority of 1998-99 season recovering from minor heart surgery, September 1998.

MYERS, Scott (MIGH-yuhrs, SKAWT) PIT.

Goaltender. Catches right. 5'10", 175 lbs. Born, Winnipeg, Man., June 11, 1979.
(Pittsburgh's 4th choice, 110th overall, in 1998 Entry Draft).

			Regular Season								Playoffs						
Season	Club	Lea	GP	W	L	T	Mins	GA	SO	Avg	GP	W	L	Mins	GA	SO	Avg
1995-96	Interlake Lions	AAHA	25	....	....	....	1500	63	0	2.53	....	....	....	....	....	....	....
1996-97	Prince George	WHL	25	6	14	1	1284	94	0	4.39	....	....	....	....	....	....	....
1997-98	Prince George	WHL	48	29	13	4	2822	139	2	2.96	11	5	6	665	25	*2	2.26
1998-99	Prince George	WHL	*66	30	28	6	*3771	214	0	3.40	7	3	4	418	23	0	3.30
99-2000	Prince George	WHL	49	30	15	3	2693	128	1	2.85	13	8	5	796	28	*3	2.11

NABOKOV, Evgeni (nuh-BAW-kahv, ehv-GEH-nee) S.J.

Goaltender. Catches left. 6', 200 lbs. Born, Ust-Kamenogorsk, USSR, July 25, 1975.
(San Jose's 9th choice, 219th overall, in 1994 Entry Draft).

			Regular Season								Playoffs						
Season	Club	Lea	GP	W	L	T	Mins	GA	SO	Avg	GP	W	L	Mins	GA	SO	Avg
1992-93	Ust-Kamenogorsk	CIS	4	....	....	....	109	5	0	2.75	....	....	....	....	....	....	....
1993-94	Ust-Kamenogorsk	CIS	11	....	....	....	539	29	0	3.22	....	....	....	....	....	....	....
1994-95	Dynamo Moscow	CIS	24	....	....	....	1265	40	....	1.89	....	....	....	....	....	....	....
1995-96	Dynamo Moscow	CIS	39	....	....	....	2008	67	5	2.00	6	....	....	298	7	....	1.41
1996-97	Dynamo Moscow	Russia	27	....	....	....	1588	56	2	2.11	4	....	....	255	12	0	2.82
1997-98	Kentucky	AHL	33	10	21	2	1866	122	0	3.92	1	0	0	23	1	0	2.59
1998-99	Kentucky	AHL	43	26	14	1	2429	106	5	2.62	11	6	5	599	30	*2	3.00
99-2000	**San Jose**	**NHL**	**11**	**2**	**2**	**1**	**414**	**15**	**1**	**2.17**	**1**	**0**	**0**	**20**	**0**	**0**	**0.00**
	Cleveland	IHL	20	12	4	3	1164	52	0	2.68	....	....	....	....	....	....	....
	Kentucky	AHL	2	1	1	0	120	3	1	1.50	....	....	....	....	....	....	....
	NHL Totals		**11**	**2**	**2**	**1**	**414**	**15**	**1**	**2.17**	**1**	**0**	**0**	**20**	**0**	**0**	**0.00**

NAUMENKO, Gregg (naw-MEHN-koh, GREHG) ANA.

Goaltender. Catches left. 6'1", 201 lbs. Born, Chicago, IL, March 30, 1977.

			Regular Season								Playoffs						
Season	Club	Lea	GP	W	L	T	Mins	GA	SO	Avg	GP	W	L	Mins	GA	SO	Avg
1995-96	North Iowa	USHL	27	15	12	0	1649	103	1	3.75	4	1	3	239	15	0	3.77
1996-97	North Iowa	USHL	25	11	11	1	1342	85	1	3.80	6	3	2	284	19	0	4.01
1997-98	North Iowa	USHL	38	23	11	3	2171	80	3	2.21	5	4	1	299	11	0	2.21
1998-99	Alaska-Anchorage	WCHA	29	11	13	5	1691	65	1	*2.31	....	....	....	....	....	....	....
99-2000	Cincinnati Ducks	AHL	50	17	25	7	2877	143	2	2.98	....	....	....	....	....	....	....

WCHA First All-Star Team (1999)

Signed as a free agent by **Anaheim**, March 31, 1999.

NIITTYMAKI, Antero (NEE-too-mah-kee, AN-tehr-oh) PHI.

Goaltender. Catches left. 6', 176 lbs. Born, Turku, Finland, June 18, 1980.
(Philadelphia's 7th choice, 168th overall, in 1998 Entry Draft).

			Regular Season								Playoffs						
Season	Club	Lea	GP	W	L	T	Mins	GA	SO	Avg	GP	W	L	Mins	GA	SO	Avg
1998-99	TPS Turku	Finn-Jr.	35	....	....	....	2095	60	0	1.72	....	....	....	....	....	....	....
99-2000	TPS Turku	Finn-Jr.	1	1	0	0	60	1	0	1.00	....	....	....	....	....	....	....
	TPS Turku	Finland	32	23	6	2	1899	68	3	2.15	8	6	1	453	13	0	1.72

NOGUES, Jean-Francois (NOHG, ZHAWN-fran-SWUH) L.A.

Goaltender. Catches left. 6'1", 154 lbs. Born, Acton Vale, Que., May 10, 1981.
(Los Angeles' 7th choice, 133rd overall, in 1999 Entry Draft).

			Regular Season								Playoffs						
Season	Club	Lea	GP	W	L	T	Mins	GA	SO	Avg	GP	W	L	Mins	GA	SO	Avg
1998-99	Victoriaville Tigres	QMJHL	32	11	10	4	1555	108	0	4.17	....	....	....	....	....	....	....
99-2000	Victoriaville Tigres	QMJHL	39	14	17	0	1898	134	0	4.24	5	2	3	259	19	0	4.41

NORONEN, Mika (NOH-rah-nehn, MEE-kah) BUF.

Goaltender. Catches left. 6'1", 206 lbs. Born, Tampere, Finland, June 17, 1979.
(Buffalo's 1st choice, 21st overall, in 1997 Entry Draft).

			Regular Season								Playoffs						
Season	Club	Lea	GP	W	L	T	Mins	GA	SO	Avg	GP	W	L	Mins	GA	SO	Avg
1995-96	Tappara Tampere	Finn-Jr.	16	....	....	....	962	37	2	2.31	....	....	....	....	....	....	....
1996-97	Tappara Tampere	Finland	5	1	3	0	215	17	0	4.73	....	....	....	....	....	....	....
1997-98	Tappara Tampere	Finland	37	14	12	3	1704	83	1	2.92	4	1	2	196	12	0	3.67
1998-99	Tappara Tampere	Finland	43	18	20	5	2494	135	2	3.25	....	....	....	....	....	....	....
99-2000	Rochester	AHL	54	*33	13	4	3089	112	*6	*2.18	21	13	8	1235	37	*6	*1.80

• AHL Second All-Star Team (2000) • Won Dudley "Red" Garrett Memorial Trophy (Top Rookie - AHL) (2000)

ONDRIK, Cam (AWN-drihk, KAM) PHI.

Goaltender. Catches left. 6'1", 170 lbs. Born, Nanaimo, B.C., March 28, 1980.
(Philadelphia's 8th choice, 175th overall, in 1998 Entry Draft).

			Regular Season								Playoffs						
Season	Club	Lea	GP	W	L	T	Mins	GA	SO	Avg	GP	W	L	Mins	GA	SO	Avg
1996-97	Red Deer Rebels	WHL	4	0	0	0	77	10	0	7.79	....	....	....	....	....	....	....
1997-98	Red Deer Rebels	WHL	11	5	3	0	461	31	1	4.03	....	....	....	....	....	....	....
	Medicine Hat	WHL	16	2	7	1	689	53	0	4.62	....	....	....	....	....	....	....
1998-99	Medicine Hat	WHL	39	4	28	0	1922	149	0	4.65	....	....	....	....	....	....	....
99-2000	Medicine Hat	WHL	3	1	2	0	180	8	1	2.67	....	....	....	....	....	....	....
	Saskatoon Blades	WHL	55	29	22	4	3198	151	4	2.83	10	4	6	500	34	2	4.08

O'NEILL, Mike (OH-NEEL, MIGHK)

Goaltender. Catches left. 5'7", 155 lbs. Born, LaSalle, Que., November 3, 1967.
(Winnipeg's 1st choice, 15th overall, in 1988 Supplemental Draft).

			Regular Season								Playoffs						
Season	Club	Lea	GP	W	L	T	Mins	GA	SO	Avg	GP	W	L	Mins	GA	SO	Avg
1981-82	Lac St-Louis	QAAA	22	13	7	2	1318	81	0	3.67	....	....	....	....	....	....	....
1982-83	Lac St-Louis	QAAA	20	7	8	5	1198	107	0	5.34	....	....	....	....	....	....	....
1983-84	Lower Canada	CEGEP	STATISTICS NOT AVAILABLE														
1984-85	Lower Canada	CEGEP	STATISTICS NOT AVAILABLE														
1985-86	Yale University	ECAC	6	3	1	0	389	17	0	3.53	....	....	....	....	....	....	....
1986-87	Yale University	ECAC	16	9	6	1	964	55	2	3.42	....	....	....	....	....	....	....
1987-88	Yale University	ECAC	24	6	17	0	1385	101	0	4.37	....	....	....	....	....	....	....
1988-89	Yale University	ECAC	25	10	14	1	1490	93	0	3.74	....	....	....	....	....	....	....
1989-90	Tappara Tampere	Finland	41	23	13	5	2369	127	2	3.22	7	....	....	420	31	0	4.43
1990-91	Fort Wayne	IHL	8	5	2	1	490	31	0	3.80	....	....	....	....	....	....	....
	Moncton Hawks	AHL	30	13	7	6	1613	84	0	3.12	8	3	4	435	29	0	4.00
1991-92	**Winnipeg**	**NHL**	**1**	**0**	**0**	**0**	**13**	**1**	**0**	**4.62**	....	....	....	....	....	....	....
	Moncton Hawks	AHL	32	14	16	2	1902	108	1	3.41	11	4	7	670	43	*1	3.85
	Fort Wayne	IHL	33	22	6	3	1858	97	*4	3.13	....	....	....	....	....	....	....
1992-93	**Winnipeg**	**NHL**	**2**	**0**	**0**	**1**	**73**	**6**	**0**	**4.93**	....	....	....	....	....	....	....
	Moncton Hawks	AHL	30	13	10	4	1649	88	1	3.20	....	....	....	....	....	....	....
1993-94	**Winnipeg**	**NHL**	**17**	**0**	**9**	**1**	**738**	**51**	**0**	**4.15**	....	....	....	....	....	....	....
	Moncton Hawks	AHL	12	8	4	0	716	33	1	2.76	....	....	....	....	....	....	....
	Fort Wayne	IHL	11	4	4	3	642	38	0	3.55	....	....	....	....	....	....	....
1994-95	Fort Wayne	IHL	28	11	12	4	1603	109	0	4.08	....	....	....	....	....	....	....
	Phoenix	IHL	21	13	4	4	1256	64	1	3.06	9	4	5	535	33	0	3.70
1995-96	Baltimore Bandits	AHL	*74	31	31	7	*4250	250	2	3.53	12	6	6	689	43	0	3.75
1996-97	**Anaheim**	**NHL**	**1**	**0**	**0**	**0**	**31**	**3**	**0**	**5.81**	....	....	....	....	....	....	....
	Long Beach	IHL	45	26	12	6	2644	145	1	3.29	1	0	0	7	0	0	0.00
1997-98	Portland Pirates	AHL	47	16	18	10	2640	135	1	3.07	6	2	3	305	16	0	3.15
1998-99	VSV Villach	Austria	42	35	5	1	2540	104	0	2.49	....	....	....	....	....	....	....
99-2000	Long Beach	IHL	25	7	12	5	1423	71	0	2.99	1	0	1	59	3	0	3.01
	Michigan K-Wings	IHL	4	1	1	0	155	6	1	2.33	....	....	....	....	....	....	....
	NHL Totals		**21**	**0**	**9**	**2**	**855**	**61**	**0**	**4.28**	....	....	....	....	....	....	....

ECAC First All-Star Team (1987, 1989) • NCAA East First All-American Team (1989)

Signed as a free agent by **Anaheim**, July 14, 1995. Signed as a free agent by **Washington**, August 20, 1997. Signed as a free agent by **LA Kings**, July 21, 1999.

OSAER, Phil (OH-shar) ST.L.

Goaltender. Catches . 6'1", 190 lbs. Born, Dearborn, MI, February 10, 1980.
(St. Louis' 6th choice, 203rd overall, in 1999 Entry Draft).

			Regular Season								Playoffs						
Season	Club	Lea	GP	W	L	T	Mins	GA	SO	Avg	GP	W	L	Mins	GA	SO	Avg
1997-98	Waterloo Hawks	USHL	36	12	20	2	2094	107	2	3.07	5	1	4	295	17	0	3.46
1998-99	Ferris State	CCHA	9	2	2	1	399	10	0	1.51	....	....	....	....	....	....	....
99-2000	Ferris State	CCHA	25	13	8	2	1350	49	3	2.18	....	....	....	....	....	....	....

OSGOOD, Chris (AWS-gud, KRIHS) DET.

Goaltender. Catches left. 5'10", 175 lbs. Born, Peace River, Alta., November 26, 1972.
(Detroit's 3rd choice, 54th overall, in 1991 Entry Draft).

			Regular Season								Playoffs						
Season	Club	Lea	GP	W	L	T	Mins	GA	SO	Avg	GP	W	L	Mins	GA	SO	Avg
1988-89	Medicine Hat	AAHA	26	....	....	....	1441	88	0	3.66	....	....	....	....	....	....	....
1989-90	Medicine Hat	WHL	57	24	28	2	3094	228	0	4.42	3	0	3	173	17	0	5.91
1990-91	Medicine Hat	WHL	46	23	18	3	2630	173	2	3.95	12	7	5	712	42	0	3.54
1991-92	Medicine Hat	WHL	15	10	3	0	819	44	0	3.22	....	....	....	....	....	....	....
	Brandon	WHL	16	3	10	1	890	60	1	4.04	....	....	....	....	....	....	....
	Seattle T-Birds	WHL	21	12	7	1	1217	65	1	3.20	15	9	6	904	51	0	3.38
1992-93	Adirondack	AHL	45	19	19	4	2438	159	0	3.91	1	0	1	59	2	0	2.03
1993-94	**Detroit**	**NHL**	**41**	**23**	**8**	**5**	**2206**	**105**	**2**	**2.86**	**6**	**3**	**2**	**307**	**12**	**1**	**2.35**
	Adirondack	AHL	4	3	1	0	239	13	0	3.26	....	....	....	....	....	....	....
1994-95	**Detroit**	**NHL**	**19**	**14**	**5**	**0**	**1087**	**41**	**1**	**2.26**	**2**	**0**	**0**	**68**	**2**	**0**	**1.76**
	Adirondack	AHL	2	1	1	0	120	6	0	3.00	....	....	....	....	....	....	....
1995-96	**Detroit**	**NHL**	**50**	***39**	**6**	**5**	**2933**	**106**	**5**	**2.17**	**15**	**8**	**7**	**936**	**33**	**2**	**2.12**
1996-97♦	**Detroit**	**NHL**	**47**	**23**	**13**	**9**	**2769**	**106**	**6**	**2.30**	**2**	**0**	**0**	**47**	**2**	**0**	**2.55**
1997-98♦	**Detroit**	**NHL**	**64**	**33**	**20**	**11**	**3807**	**140**	**6**	**2.21**	***22**	***16**	**6**	***1361**	**48**	**2**	**2.12**
1998-99	**Detroit**	**NHL**	**63**	**34**	**25**	**4**	**3691**	**149**	**3**	**2.42**	**6**	**4**	**2**	**358**	**14**	**1**	**2.35**
99-2000	**Detroit**	**NHL**	**53**	**30**	**14**	**8**	**3148**	**126**	**6**	**2.40**	**9**	**5**	**4**	**547**	**18**	**2**	**1.97**
	NHL Totals		**337**	**196**	**91**	**42**	**19641**	**773**	**29**	**2.36**	**62**	**36**	**21**	**3624**	**129**	**8**	**2.14**

WHL East Second All-Star Team (1991) • NHL Second All-Star Team (1996) • Shared William M. Jennings Trophy with Mike Vernon (1996) • Played in NHL All-Star Game (1996, 1997, 1998)

• Scored a goal while with Medicine Hat (WHL), January 3, 1991. • Scored a goal vs. Hartford, March 6, 1996.

OUELLET, Maxime (OO-leht, MAX-eem) PHI.

Goaltender. Catches left. 6', 180 lbs. Born, Beauport, Que., June 17, 1981.
(Philadelphia's 1st choice, 22nd overall, in 1999 Entry Draft).

			Regular Season								Playoffs						
Season	Club	Lea	GP	W	L	T	Mins	GA	SO	Avg	GP	W	L	Mins	GA	SO	Avg
1997-98	Quebec Remparts	QMJHL	24	12	7	1	1188	66	0	3.33	7	3	1	305	16	0	3.15
1998-99	Quebec Remparts	QMJHL	*59	*40	12	6	*3447	155	3	*2.70	13	6	7	803	41	*1	3.06
99-2000	Quebec Remparts	QMJHL	53	31	16	4	2984	133	2	2.67	11	7	4	638	28	*2	*2.63

QMJHL Second All-Star Team (1999, 2000)

PARENT, Rich (PEH-ruhn, RIHCH)

Goaltender. Catches left. 6'3", 195 lbs. Born, Montreal, Que., January 12, 1973.

						Regular Season							Playoffs				
Season	Club	Lea	GP	W	L	T	Mins	GA	SO	Avg	GP	W	L	Mins	GA	SO	Avg
1991-92	Fort McMurray	AJHL	23	....	....	....	1363	90	0	3.96	....	....	....	....	....	....	....
	Vernon Lakers	BCJHL	2	0	1	0	52	5	0	5.77	....	....	....	....	....	....	....
1992-93	Spokane Chiefs	WHL	36	12	14	2	1767	129	2	4.38	1	0	0	5	0	0	0.00
1993-94	Fort McMurray	AJHL	29	....	....	....	1712	91	1	3.19	....	....	....	....	....	....	....
1994-95	Muskegon Fury	ColHL	35	17	11	3	1867	112	1	3.60	13	7	3	725	47	1	3.89
1995-96	Muskegon Fury	ColHL	36	23	7	4	2087	85	2	2.44	....	....	....	....	....	....	....
	Rochester	AHL	2	0	1	0	90	6	0	4.02	....	....	....	....	....	....	....
	Detroit Vipers	IHL	19	16	0	1	1040	48	2	2.77	7	3	3	363	22	0	3.64
1996-97	Detroit Vipers	IHL	53	31	13	4	2815	104	4	2.22	15	8	3	786	21	1	*1.60
1997-98	St. Louis	NHL	1	0	0	0	12	0	0	0.00	....	....	....	....	....	....	....
	Manitoba Moose	IHL	26	8	12	2	1334	69	3	3.10	....	....	....	....	....	....	....
	Detroit Vipers	IHL	7	4	0	3	417	15	0	2.15	5	1	0	157	6	0	2.29
1998-99	St. Louis	NHL	10	4	3	1	519	22	1	2.54	....	....	....	....	....	....	....
	Worcester	AHL	20	8	8	2	1100	56	1	3.05	....	....	....	....	....	....	....
99-2000	Utah Grizzlies	IHL	27	17	7	3	1571	58	1	2.21	....	....	....	....	....	....	....
	Tampa Bay	NHL	14	2	7	1	698	43	0	3.70	....	....	....	....	....	....	....
	Detroit Vipers	IHL	10	3	5	1	539	23	1	2.56	....	....	....	....	....	....	....
	NHL Totals		25	6	10	2	1229	65	1	3.17	....	....	....	....	....	....	....

ColHL First All-Star Team (1996) • Named ColHL's Outstanding Goaltender (1996) • Shared James Norris Memorial Trophy (fewest goals against - IHL) with Jeff Reese (1997)

Signed as a free agent by **St. Louis**, July 31, 1997. Traded to **Tampa Bay** by **St. Louis** with Chris McAlpine for Stephane Richer, January 13, 2000. Traded to **Ottawa** by **Tampa Bay** for Ottawa's 7th round choice (later traded to NY Islanders - later traded to Buffalo - Buffalo selected Paul Gaustad) in 2000 Entry Draft, June 4, 2000.

PARLEY, Davis (PAHR-lee) **FLA.**

Goaltender. Catches left. 6'2", 178 lbs. Born, Grenfell, Sask., September 4, 1982.
(Florida's 5th choice, 120th overall, in 2000 Entry Draft).

						Regular Season							Playoffs				
Season	Club	Lea	GP	W	L	T	Mins	GA	SO	Avg	GP	W	L	Mins	GA	SO	Avg
1998-99	Campbell River	VIJHL	23	....	....	....	1380	43	4	1.87	....	....	....	....	....	....	....
99-2000	Kamloops Blazers	WHL	26	8	15	2	1497	80	2	3.21	1	0	0	37	3	0	4.86

PASSMORE, Steve (PAS-mohr, STEEV) **L.A.**

Goaltender. Catches left. 5'9", 165 lbs. Born, Thunder Bay, Ont., January 29, 1973.
(Quebec's 10th choice, 196th overall, in 1992 Entry Draft).

						Regular Season							Playoffs				
Season	Club	Lea	GP	W	L	T	Mins	GA	SO	Avg	GP	W	L	Mins	GA	SO	Avg
1988-89	Tri-City Americans	WHL	1	0	1	0	60	6	0	6.00	....	....	....	....	....	....	....
1989-90	West Island Deltas	BCAHA								STATISTICS NOT AVAILABLE							
	Tri-City Americans	WHL	4	....	....	....	215	17	0	4.74	....	....	....	....	....	....	....
1990-91	Victoria Cougars	WHL	35	3	25	1	1838	190	0	6.20	....	....	....	....	....	....	....
1991-92	Victoria Cougars	WHL	*71	15	50	5	*4228	347	0	4.92	....	....	....	....	....	....	....
1992-93	Victoria Cougars	WHL	43	14	24	2	2402	150	1	3.75	....	....	....	....	....	....	....
	Kamloops Blazers	WHL	25	19	6	0	1479	69	1	2.80	7	4	2	401	22	1	3.29
1993-94	Kamloops Blazers	WHL	36	22	9	2	1927	88	1	*2.74	*18	*11	7	*1099	60	0	3.28
1994-95	Cape Breton Oilers	AHL	25	8	13	3	1455	93	0	3.83	....	....	....	....	....	....	....
1995-96	Cape Breton Oilers	AHL	2	1	0	0	90	2	0	1.33	....	....	....	....	....	....	....
1996-97	Hamilton Bulldogs	AHL	27	12	12	3	1568	70	1	2.68	22	12	10	1325	61	*2	2.76
	Raleigh IceCaps	ECHL	2	1	1	0	118	13	0	6.56	....	....	....	....	....	....	....
1997-98	San Antonio	IHL	14	3	8	2	736	56	0	4.56	....	....	....	....	....	....	....
	Hamilton Bulldogs	AHL	27	11	10	6	1655	87	2	3.15	3	0	2	132	14	0	6.33
1998-99	Edmonton	NHL	6	1	4	1	362	17	0	2.82	....	....	....	....	....	....	....
	Hamilton Bulldogs	AHL	54	24	21	7	3148	117	4	2.23	11	5	6	680	31	0	2.74
99-2000	Chicago	NHL	24	7	12	3	1388	63	1	2.72	....	....	....	....	....	....	....
	Cleveland	IHL	2	1	0	1	120	3	1	1.50	....	....	....	....	....	....	....
	NHL Totals		30	8	16	4	1750	80	1	2.74	....	....	....	....	....	....	....

WHL West First All-Star Team (1993, 1994) • Won Fred Hunt Memorial Trophy (Sportsmanship - AHL) (1997) • AHL Second All-Star Team (1999)

Traded to **Edmonton** by **Quebec** for Brad Werenka, March 21, 1994. • Missed the majority of the 1995-96 season while being treated for a rare blood disorder, October, 1995. Signed as a free agent by **Chicago**, July 8, 1999. Traded to **LA Kings** by **Chicago** for LA Kings' 4th round choice (Olli Malmivaara) in 2000 Entry Draft, May 1, 2000.

PELLETIER, Jean-Marc (PEHL-tyay, ZHAWN-MAHRK) **CAR.**

Goaltender. Catches left. 6'3", 200 lbs. Born, Atlanta, GA, March 4, 1978.
(Philadelphia's 1st choice, 30th overall, in 1997 Entry Draft).

						Regular Season							Playoffs				
Season	Club	Lea	GP	W	L	T	Mins	GA	SO	Avg	GP	W	L	Mins	GA	SO	Avg
1993-94	Richelieu Regents	QAAA	24	14	8	2	1440	91	0	3.79	....	....	....	....	....	....	....
1994-95	Richelieu Regents	QAAA	21	15	6	0	1260	71	0	3.36	....	....	....	....	....	....	....
1995-96	Cornell Big Red	ECAC	5	1	2	0	179	15	0	5.03	....	....	....	....	....	....	....
1996-97	Cornell Big Red	ECAC	11	5	2	3	679	28	1	2.47	....	....	....	....	....	....	....
1997-98	Rimouski Oceanic	QMJHL	34	17	11	3	1913	118	0	3.70	16	11	3	895	51	1	3.42
1998-99	Philadelphia	NHL	1	0	1	0	60	5	0	5.00	....	....	....	....	....	....	....
	Philadelphia	AHL	47	25	16	4	2636	122	2	2.78	1	0	0	27	0	0	0.00
99-2000	Philadelphia	AHL	24	14	10	0	1405	58	3	2.48	....	....	....	....	....	....	....
	Cincinnati	IHL	22	14	4	2	1278	52	2	2.44	3	1	1	160	8	1	3.00
	NHL Totals		1	0	1	0	60	5	0	5.00							

Traded to **Carolina** by **Philadelphia** with Rod Brind'Amour and Philadelphia's 2nd round choice (later traded to Colorado - Colorado selected Argis Saviels) in 2000 Entry Draft for Keith Primeau and Carolina's 5th round choice (later traded to NY Islanders - NY Islanders selected Kristofer Ottoson) in 2000 Entry Draft, January 23, 2000.

PERSSON, Joakim (PEHR-suhn, YOH-kihm) **BOS.**

Goaltender. Catches left. 5'11", 176 lbs. Born, Ostervala, Sweden, May 4, 1970.
(Boston's 10th choice, 259th overall, in 1993 Entry Draft).

						Regular Season							Playoffs				
Season	Club	Lea	GP	W	L	T	Mins	GA	SO	Avg	GP	W	L	Mins	GA	SO	Avg
1992-93	Hammarby IF	Swede-2	40	....	....	....	2395	108	....	2.71	....	....	....	....	....	....	....
1993-94	Hammarby IF	Swede-2	23	....	....	....	1380	59	....	2.57	....	....	....	....	....	....	....
	Providence Bruins	AHL	1	0	0	0	24	0	0	0.00	....	....	....	....	....	....	....
1994-95	AIK Solna	Sweden	30	....	....	....	1800	103	1	3.43	....	....	....	....	....	....	....
1995-96	AIK Solna	Sweden	24	....	....	....	1344	64	....	2.86	....	....	....	....	....	....	....
1996-97	Ratinger Lowen	DEL	35	....	....	....	2111	154	0	4.37	6	....	....	360	29	0	4.83
1997-98	Vasteras IK	Sweden	7	....	....	....	291	24	....	4.95	....	....	....	....	....	....	....
1998-99	Hammarby IF	Swede-2	2	....	....	....	120	10	0	5.00	3	....	....	180	6	0	2.00
99-2000	Hammarby IF	Swede-2	21	....	....	....	1235	48	2	2.33	1	0	1	65	3	0	2.78

PETRUK, Randy (PEHT-ruhk, RAN-dee) **CAR.**

Goaltender. Catches right. 5'9", 180 lbs. Born, Cranbrook, B.C., April 23, 1978.
(Colorado's 5th choice, 107th overall, in 1996 Entry Draft).

						Regular Season							Playoffs				
Season	Club	Lea	GP	W	L	T	Mins	GA	SO	Avg	GP	W	L	Mins	GA	SO	Avg
1993-94	Cranbrook Colts	RMJHL	21	....	....	....	1158	89	0	4.61	....	....	....	....	....	....	....
1994-95	Kamloops Blazers	WHL	27	16	3	4	1462	71	1	2.91	7	5	2	423	19	0	2.70
1995-96	Kamloops Blazers	WHL	52	34	15	1	3071	181	1	3.54	16	9	6	990	58	0	3.52
1996-97	Kamloops Blazers	WHL	*60	25	28	5	*3475	210	0	3.63	....	....	....	....	....	....	....
1997-98	Kamloops Blazers	WHL	57	31	21	1	3097	157	3	3.04	7	3	4	425	21	0	2.96
1998-99	Florida Everblades	ECHL	25	13	10	2	1441	66	1	2.75	1	0	1	60	5	0	5.00
	New Haven	AHL	1	0	0	1	65	3	0	2.77	....	....	....	....	....	....	....
99-2000	Florida Everblades	ECHL	6	5	0	1	339	19	0	3.36	....	....	....	....	....	....	....
	Cincinnati	IHL	26	13	9	3	1436	84	2	3.51	9	4	5	551	27	1	2.94

WHL West Second All-Star Team (1998)

Traded to **Carolina** by **Colorado** for Carolina's 5th round choice (William Magnuson) in 1999 Entry Draft, June 1, 1998.

POTVIN, Felix (PAHT-vihn, FEEL-ihx) **VAN.**

Goaltender. Catches left. 6'1", 190 lbs. Born, Anjou, Que., June 23, 1971.
(Toronto's 2nd choice, 31st overall, in 1990 Entry Draft).

						Regular Season							Playoffs				
Season	Club	Lea	GP	W	L	T	Mins	GA	SO	Avg	GP	W	L	Mins	GA	SO	Avg
1987-88	Montreal-Bourassa	QAAA	27	15	7	3	1585	103	3	3.90	6	2	4	341	20	0	3.51
1988-89	Chicoutimi	QMJHL	*65	25	31	1	*3489	271	*2	4.66	....	....	....	....	....	....	....
1989-90	Chicoutimi	QMJHL	*62	*31	26	2	*3478	231	*2	3.99	....	....	....	....	....	....	....
1990-91	Chicoutimi	QMJHL	54	33	15	4	3216	145	*6	*2.70	*16	*11	5	*992	46	0	*2.78
1991-92	Toronto	NHL	4	0	2	1	210	8	0	2.29	....	....	....	....	....	....	....
	St. John's Leafs	AHL	35	18	10	6	2070	101	2	2.93	11	7	4	642	41	0	3.83
1992-93	Toronto	NHL	48	25	15	7	2781	116	2	*2.50	*21	11	10	*1308	62	1	2.84
	St. John's Leafs	AHL	5	3	0	2	309	18	0	3.50	....	....	....	....	....	....	....
1993-94	Toronto	NHL	66	34	22	9	3883	187	3	2.89	18	9	9	1124	46	3	2.46
1994-95	Toronto	NHL	36	15	13	7	2144	104	0	2.91	7	3	4	424	20	1	2.83
1995-96	Toronto	NHL	69	30	26	11	4009	192	2	2.87	6	2	4	350	19	0	3.26
1996-97	Toronto	NHL	*74	27	36	7	*4271	224	0	3.15	....	....	....	....	....	....	....
1997-98	Toronto	NHL	67	26	33	7	3864	176	5	2.73	....	....	....	....	....	....	....
1998-99	Toronto	NHL	5	3	2	0	299	19	0	3.81	....	....	....	....	....	....	....
	NY Islanders	NHL	11	2	7	1	606	37	0	3.66	....	....	....	....	....	....	....
99-2000	NY Islanders	NHL	22	5	14	3	1273	68	1	3.21	....	....	....	....	....	....	....
	Vancouver	NHL	34	12	13	7	1966	85	0	2.59	....	....	....	....	....	....	....
	NHL Totals		436	179	183	60	25306	1216	13	2.88	52	25	27	3206	147	5	2.75

QMJHL Second All-Star Team (1990) • QMJHL First All-Star Team (1991) • Canadian Major Junior Goaltender of the Year (1991) • Memorial Cup All-Star Team (1991) • Won Hap Emms Memorial Trophy (Memorial Cup Tournament Top Goaltender) (1991) • AHL First All-Star Team (1992) • Won Dudley "Red" Garrett Memorial Trophy (Top Rookie - AHL) (1992) • Won Baz Bastien Memorial Trophy (Top Goaltender - AHL) (1992) • NHL All-Rookie Team (1993) • Played in NHL All-Star Game (1994, 1996)

Traded to **NY Islanders** by **Toronto** with Toronto's 6th round choice (later traded to Tampa Bay - Tampa Bay selected Fedor Fedorov) in 1999 Entry Draft for Bryan Berard and NY Islanders' 6th round choice (Jan Sochor) in 1999 Entry Draft, January 9, 1999. Traded to **Vancouver** by **NY Islanders** with NY Islanders' compensatory 2nd (later traded to New Jersey - New Jersey selected Teemu Laine) and 3rd (Thatcher Bell) round choices in 2000 Entry Draft for Kevin Weekes, Dave Scatchard and Bill Muckalt, December 19, 1999.

PRESTIFILIPPO, J.R. (PREHS-tee-fihl-ih-poh, JAY-AHR) **NYI**

Goaltender. Catches left. 5'10", 170 lbs. Born, Newark, NJ, March 23, 1977.
(NY Islanders' 8th choice, 165th overall, in 1996 Entry Draft).

						Regular Season							Playoffs				
Season	Club	Lea	GP	W	L	T	Mins	GA	SO	Avg	GP	W	L	Mins	GA	SO	Avg
1995-96	Hotchkiss High	H.S.	24	....	....	....	1440	56	3	2.33	....	....	....	....	....	....	....
1996-97	Harvard University	ECAC	31	10	18	3	1866	99	1	3.18	....	....	....	....	....	....	....
1997-98	Harvard University	ECAC	23	9	12	2	1394	80	0	3.44	....	....	....	....	....	....	....
1998-99	Harvard University	ECAC	24	10	13	1	1316	78	0	3.56	....	....	....	....	....	....	....
99-2000	Harvard University	ECAC	25	8	15	2	1468	71	1	2.90	....	....	....	....	....	....	....

PRUSEK, Martin (PREW-sehk, MAHR-tihn) **OTT.**

Goaltender. Catches left. 6', 176 lbs. Born, Ostrava, Czech., December 11, 1975.
(Ottawa's 6th choice, 164th overall, in 1999 Entry Draft).

						Regular Season							Playoffs				
Season	Club	Lea	GP	W	L	T	Mins	GA	SO	Avg	GP	W	L	Mins	GA	SO	Avg
1994-95	HC Vitkovice	Cze-Rep	5	....	....	....	232	18	....	4.65	....	....	....	....	....	....	....
1995-96	HC Vitkovice	Cze-Rep	40	....	....	....	2336	113	1	2.90	4	....	....	250	10	1	2.40
1996-97	HC Vitkovice	Cze-Rep	49	....	....	....	2841	109	8	2.30	9	....	....	546	19	1	2.08
1997-98	HC Vitkovice	Cze-Rep	50	....	....	....	2901	129	....	2.67	9	....	....	529	26	....	3.00
1998-99	HC Vitkovice	Cze-Rep	37	....	....	....	1905	85	....	2.68	4	....	....	250	12	....	2.88
99-2000	HC Vitkovice	Cze-Rep	50	....	....	....	2647	132	....	2.99	....	....	....	....	....	....	....

PUPPA, Daren (POO-puh, DAIR-rehn)

Goaltender. Catches right. 6'4", 205 lbs. Born, Kirkland Lake, Ont., March 23, 1965.
(Buffalo's 6th choice, 76th overall, in 1983 Entry Draft).

			Regular Season								Playoffs						
Season	Club	Lea	GP	W	L	T	Mins	GA	SO	Avg	GP	W	L	Mins	GA	SO	Avg
1983-84	RPI Engineers	ECAC	32	24	6	0	1816	89	0	2.94	....	....	....	....	....	....	....
1984-85	RPI Engineers	ECAC	32	31	1	0	1830	78	0	2.56	....	....	....	....	....	....	....
1985-86	**Buffalo**	**NHL**	**7**	**3**	**4**	**0**	**401**	**21**	**1**	**3.14**	....	....	....	....	....	....	....
	Rochester	AHL	20	8	11	0	1092	79	0	4.34	....	....	....	....	....	....	....
1986-87	**Buffalo**	**NHL**	**3**	**0**	**2**	**1**	**185**	**13**	**0**	**4.22**	....	....	....	....	....	....	....
	Rochester	AHL	57	*33	14	0	3129	146	1	2.80	*16	*10	6	*944	48	*1	3.05
1987-88	**Buffalo**	**NHL**	**17**	**8**	**6**	**1**	**874**	**61**	**0**	**4.19**	**3**	**1**	**1**	**142**	**11**	**0**	**4.65**
	Rochester	AHL	26	14	8	2	1415	65	2	2.76	2	0	1	108	5	0	2.78
1988-89	**Buffalo**	**NHL**	**37**	**17**	**10**	**6**	**1908**	**107**	**1**	**3.36**	....	....	....	....	....	....	....
1989-90	**Buffalo**	**NHL**	**56**	***31**	**16**	**6**	**3241**	**156**	**1**	**2.89**	**6**	**2**	**4**	**370**	**15**	**0**	**2.43**
1990-91	**Buffalo**	**NHL**	**38**	**15**	**11**	**6**	**2092**	**118**	**2**	**3.38**	**2**	**0**	**1**	**81**	**10**	**0**	**7.41**
1991-92	**Buffalo**	**NHL**	**33**	**11**	**14**	**4**	**1757**	**114**	**0**	**3.89**	....	....	....	....	....	....	....
	Rochester	AHL	2	0	2	0	119	9	0	4.54	....	....	....	....	....	....	....
1992-93	**Buffalo**	**NHL**	**24**	**11**	**5**	**4**	**1306**	**78**	**0**	**3.58**	....	....	....	....	....	....	....
	Toronto	**NHL**	**8**	**6**	**2**	**0**	**479**	**18**	**2**	**2.25**	**1**	**0**	**0**	**20**	**1**	**0**	**3.00**
1993-94	**Tampa Bay**	**NHL**	**63**	**22**	**33**	**6**	**3653**	**165**	**4**	**2.71**	....	....	....	....	....	....	....
1994-95	**Tampa Bay**	**NHL**	**36**	**14**	**19**	**2**	**2013**	**90**	**1**	**2.68**	....	....	....	....	....	....	....
1995-96	**Tampa Bay**	**NHL**	**57**	**29**	**16**	**9**	**3189**	**131**	**5**	**2.46**	**4**	**1**	**3**	**173**	**14**	**0**	**4.86**
1996-97	**Tampa Bay**	**NHL**	**6**	**1**	**1**	**2**	**325**	**14**	**0**	**2.58**	....	....	....	....	....	....	....
	Adirondack	AHL	1	1	0	0	62	3	0	2.90	....	....	....	....	....	....	....
1997-98	**Tampa Bay**	**NHL**	**26**	**5**	**14**	**6**	**1456**	**66**	**0**	**2.72**	....	....	....	....	....	....	....
1998-99	**Tampa Bay**	**NHL**	**13**	**5**	**6**	**1**	**691**	**33**	**2**	**2.87**	....	....	....	....	....	....	....
99-2000	**Tampa Bay**	**NHL**	**5**	**1**	**2**	**0**	**249**	**19**	**0**	**4.58**	....	....	....	....	....	....	....
	NHL Totals		**429**	**179**	**161**	**54**	**23819**	**1204**	**19**	**3.03**	**16**	**4**	**9**	**786**	**51**	**0**	**3.89**

AHL First All-Star Team (1987) • NHL Second All-Star Team (1990) • Played in NHL All-Star Game (1990) • Recorded shutout (2-0) in NHL debut vs. **Edmonton**, November 1, 1985.

Traded to **Toronto** by **Buffalo** with Dave Andreychuk and Buffalo's 1st round choice (Kenny Jonsson) in 1993 Entry Draft for Grant Fuhr and Toronto's 5th round choice (Kevin Popp) in 1995 Entry Draft, February 2, 1993. Claimed by **Florida** from **Toronto** in Expansion Draft, June 24, 1993. Claimed by **Tampa Bay** from **Florida** in Phase II of Expansion Draft, June 25, 1993. • Missed majority of 1996-97 season recovering from groin injury suffered in training camp, September, 1997. • Missed majority of 1997-98 and 1998-99 seasons recovering from back injury suffered in game vs. Boston on December 27, 1997.

RACINE, Bruce (ray-SEEN, BREWS)

Goaltender. Catches left. 6', 170 lbs. Born, Cornwall, Ont., August 9, 1966.
(Pittsburgh's 3rd choice, 58th overall, in 1985 Entry Draft).

			Regular Season								Playoffs						
Season	Club	Lea	GP	W	L	T	Mins	GA	SO	Avg	GP	W	L	Mins	GA	SO	Avg
1983-84	Hawkesbury	OJHL	30	....	....	....	1543	121	0	4.70	....	....	....	....	....	....	....
1984-85	Northeastern	H-East	26	11	14	1	1615	103	1	3.83	....	....	....	....	....	....	....
1985-86	Northeastern	H-East	32	17	14	1	1920	147	0	4.56	....	....	....	....	....	....	....
1986-87	Northeastern	H-East	33	12	18	3	1966	133	0	4.06	....	....	....	....	....	....	....
1987-88	Northeastern	H-East	30	15	11	4	1808	108	1	3.58	....	....	....	....	....	....	....
1988-89	Muskegon	IHL	51	*37	11	0	*3039	184	*3	3.63	5	4	1	300	15	0	3.00
1989-90	Muskegon	IHL	49	29	15	4	2911	182	1	3.75	9	5	4	566	32	1	3.34
1990-91	Albany Choppers	IHL	29	7	18	1	1567	104	0	3.98	....	....	....	....	....	....	....
	Muskegon	IHL	9	4	4	1	516	40	0	4.65	....	....	....	....	....	....	....
1991-92	Muskegon	IHL	27	13	10	3	1559	91	1	3.50	1	0	1	60	6	0	6.00
1992-93	Cleveland	IHL	35	13	16	6	1949	140	1	4.31	2	0	0	37	2	0	3.24
1993-94	St. John's Leafs	AHL	37	20	9	2	1875	116	0	3.71	1	0	0	20	1	0	0.00
1994-95	St. John's Leafs	AHL	27	11	10	4	1492	85	1	3.42	2	1	1	119	3	0	1.51
1995-96	**St. Louis**	**NHL**	**11**	**0**	**3**	**0**	**230**	**12**	**0**	**3.13**	**1**	**0**	**0**	**1**	**0**	**0**	**0.00**
	Peoria Rivermen	IHL	22	11	10	1	1228	69	1	3.37	1	0	1	59	3	0	3.05
1996-97	San Antonio	IHL	44	25	14	2	2426	122	6	3.02	6	3	2	325	17	0	3.13
1997-98	San Antonio	IHL	*15	*4	9	1	*836	51	0	3.66	....	....	....	....	....	....	....
	Fort Wayne	IHL	*45	*30	10	4	*2605	109	1	2.51	3	1	2	152	10	0	3.95
1998-99	Fort Wayne	IHL	53	21	18	11	3024	154	1	3.06	1	0	1	60	5	0	5.00
99-2000	Kansas City	IHL	33	12	17	1	1765	84	1	2.86	....	....	....	....	....	....	....
	NHL Totals		**11**	**0**	**3**	**0**	**230**	**12**	**0**	**3.13**	**1**	**0**	**0**	**1**	**0**	**0**	**0.00**

Hockey East Second All-Star Team (1985) • Hockey East First All-Star Team (1987) • NCAA East First All-American Team (1987, 1988) • IHL First All-Star Team (1998)

Signed as a free agent by **Toronto**, August 11, 1993. Signed as a free agent by **St. Louis**, August 10, 1995. Signed as a free agent by **San Jose**, September 8, 1998. Signed as a free agent by **Kansas City** (IHL), July 13, 1999.

RACINE, Jean-Francois (RAY-seen) TOR.

Goaltender. Catches left. 6'3", 183 lbs. Born, St-Hyacinthe, Que., April 27, 1982.
(Toronto's 4th choice, 90th overall, in 2000 Entry Draft).

			Regular Season								Playoffs						
Season	Club	Lea	GP	W	L	T	Mins	GA	SO	Avg	GP	W	L	Mins	GA	SO	Avg
1998-99	Magog Selectes	QAAA	36	....	....	....	2160	107	3	2.98	....	....	....	....	....	....	....
99-2000	Moncton Wildcats	QMJHL	10	3	3	1	410	28	0	4.10	....	....	....	....	....	....	....
	Drummondville	QMJHL	20	14	6	0	1152	63	1	3.28	3	0	0	65	5	0	4.60

RAM, Jamie (RAM, JAY-mee)

Goaltender. Catches left. 5'11", 175 lbs. Born, Scarborough, Ont., January 18, 1971.
(NY Rangers' 9th choice, 213th overall, in 1991 Entry Draft).

			Regular Season								Playoffs						
Season	Club	Lea	GP	W	L	T	Mins	GA	SO	Avg	GP	W	L	Mins	GA	SO	Avg
1988-89	Henry Carr	OJHL-B	24	11	8	2	1200	82	*1	4.10	....	....	....	....	....	....	....
1989-90	Henry Carr	OJHL-B	23	14	5	2	1302	63	1	2.90	....	....	....	....	....	....	....
1990-91	Michigan Tech	WCHA	14	5	9	0	826	57	0	4.14	....	....	....	....	....	....	....
1991-92	Michigan Tech	WCHA	23	9	9	1	1144	83	0	4.35	....	....	....	....	....	....	....
1992-93	Michigan Tech	WCHA	*36	16	14	5	*2078	115	0	3.32	....	....	....	....	....	....	....
1993-94	Michigan Tech	WCHA	39	12	20	5	2192	117	*1	3.20	....	....	....	....	....	....	....
1994-95	Binghamton	AHL	26	12	10	2	1472	81	1	3.30	11	6	5	663	29	1	2.62
1995-96	**NY Rangers**	**NHL**	**1**	**0**	**0**	**0**	**27**	**0**	**0**	**0.00**	....	....	....	....	....	....	....
	Binghamton	AHL	40	18	16	3	2262	151	1	4.01	1	0	0	34	1	0	1.75
1996-97	Kentucky	AHL	50	25	19	5	2937	161	4	3.29	1	0	1	60	3	0	3.00
1997-98	Kentucky	AHL	44	17	18	5	2553	124	3	2.91	....	....	....	....	....	....	....
	Utah Grizzlies	IHL	7	3	4	0	398	24	0	3.61	1	0	1	59	3	0	3.04
1998-99	Cincinnati Ducks	AHL	35	14	19	1	1916	109	2	3.41	....	....	....	....	....	....	....
99-2000	Canada	Nt-Team	32	14	12	4	1759	80	0	2.73	....	....	....	....	....	....	....
	NHL Totals		**1**	**0**	**0**	**0**	**27**	**0**	**0**	**0.00**	....	....	....	....	....	....	....

WCHA First All-Star Team (1993, 1994) • NCAA West First All-American Team (1993, 1994)

Signed as a free agent by **San Jose**, August 19, 1997. Signed as a free agent by **Anaheim**, July 30, 1998.

RANFORD, Bill (RAN-fohrd, BIHL) EDM.

Goaltender. Catches left. 5'11", 185 lbs. Born, Brandon, Man., December 14, 1966.
(Boston's 2nd choice, 52nd overall, in 1985 Entry Draft).

			Regular Season								Playoffs						
Season	Club	Lea	GP	W	L	T	Mins	GA	SO	Avg	GP	W	L	Mins	GA	SO	Avg
1983-84	New Westminster	WHL	27	10	14	0	1450	130	0	5.38	1	0	0	27	2	0	4.44
1984-85	New Westminster	WHL	38	19	17	0	2034	142	0	4.19	7	2	3	309	26	0	5.05
1985-86	New Westminster	WHL	53	17	29	1	2791	225	1	4.84	....	....	....	....	....	....	....
	Boston	**NHL**	**4**	**3**	**1**	**0**	**240**	**10**	**0**	**2.50**	**2**	**0**	**2**	**120**	**7**	**0**	**3.50**
1986-87	**Boston**	**NHL**	**41**	**16**	**20**	**2**	**2234**	**124**	**3**	**3.33**	**2**	**0**	**2**	**123**	**8**	**0**	**3.90**
	Moncton Flames	AHL	3	3	0	0	180	6	0	2.00	....	....	....	....	....	....	....
1987-88	Maine Mariners	AHL	51	27	16	6	2856	165	1	3.47	....	....	....	....	....	....	....
♦	**Edmonton**	**NHL**	**6**	**3**	**0**	**2**	**325**	**16**	**0**	**2.95**	....	....	....	....	....	....	....
1988-89	**Edmonton**	**NHL**	**29**	**15**	**8**	**2**	**1509**	**88**	**1**	**3.50**	....	....	....	....	....	....	....
1989-90♦	**Edmonton**	**NHL**	**56**	**24**	**16**	**9**	**3107**	**165**	**1**	**3.19**	***22**	***16**	**6**	***1401**	**59**	**1**	**2.53**
1990-91	**Edmonton**	**NHL**	**60**	**27**	**27**	**3**	**3415**	**182**	**0**	**3.20**	**3**	**1**	**2**	**135**	**8**	**0**	**3.56**
1991-92	**Edmonton**	**NHL**	**67**	**27**	**26**	**10**	**3822**	**228**	**1**	**3.58**	**16**	**8**	**8**	**909**	**51**	***2**	**3.37**
1992-93	**Edmonton**	**NHL**	**67**	**17**	**38**	**6**	**3753**	**240**	**1**	**3.84**	....	....	....	....	....	....	....
1993-94	**Edmonton**	**NHL**	**71**	**22**	**34**	**11**	**4070**	**236**	**1**	**3.48**	....	....	....	....	....	....	....
1994-95	**Edmonton**	**NHL**	**40**	**15**	**20**	**3**	**2203**	**133**	**2**	**3.62**	....	....	....	....	....	....	....
1995-96	**Edmonton**	**NHL**	**37**	**13**	**18**	**5**	**2015**	**128**	**1**	**3.81**	....	....	....	....	....	....	....
	Boston	**NHL**	**40**	**21**	**12**	**4**	**2307**	**109**	**1**	**2.83**	**4**	**1**	**3**	**239**	**16**	**0**	**4.02**
1996-97	**Boston**	**NHL**	**37**	**12**	**16**	**8**	**2147**	**125**	**2**	**3.49**	....	....	....	....	....	....	....
	Washington	**NHL**	**18**	**8**	**7**	**2**	**1009**	**46**	**0**	**2.74**	....	....	....	....	....	....	....
1997-98	**Washington**	**NHL**	**22**	**7**	**12**	**2**	**1183**	**55**	**0**	**2.79**	....	....	....	....	....	....	....
1998-99	**Tampa Bay**	**NHL**	**32**	**3**	**18**	**3**	**1568**	**102**	**1**	**3.90**	....	....	....	....	....	....	....
	Detroit	**NHL**	**4**	**3**	**0**	**1**	**244**	**8**	**0**	**1.97**	**4**	**2**	**2**	**183**	**10**	**1**	**3.28**
99-2000	**Edmonton**	**NHL**	**16**	**4**	**6**	**3**	**785**	**47**	**0**	**3.59**	....	....	....	....	....	....	....
	NHL Totals		**647**	**240**	**279**	**76**	**35936**	**2042**	**15**	**3.41**	**53**	**28**	**25**	**3110**	**159**	**4**	**3.07**

WHL West Second All-Star Team (1986) • Won Conn Smythe Trophy (1990) • Played in NHL All-Star Game (1991)

Traded to **Edmonton** by **Boston** with Geoff Courtnall and Boston's 2nd round choice (Petro Koivunen) in 1988 Entry Draft for Andy Moog, March 8, 1988. Traded to **Boston** by **Edmonton** for Mariusz Czerkawski, Sean Brown and Boston's 1st round choice (Matthieu Descoteaux) in 1996 Entry Draft, January 11, 1996. Traded to **Washington** by **Boston** with Adam Oates and Rick Tocchet for Jim Carey, Anson Carter, Jason Allison and Washington's 3rd round choice (Lee Goren) in 1997 Entry Draft, March 1, 1997. Traded to **Tampa Bay** by **Washington** for Tampa Bay's 3rd round choice (Todd Hornung) in 1998 Entry Draft and 2nd round choice (Michal Sivek) in 1999 Entry Draft, June 18, 1998. Traded to **Detroit** by **Tampa Bay** for future considerations, March 23, 1999. Signed as a free agent by **Edmonton**, August 4, 1999. • Officially announced retirement, April 24, 2000.

RAYCROFT, Andrew (RAY-kawft, AN-drew) BOS.

Goaltender. Catches left. 6', 150 lbs. Born, Belleville, Ont., May 4, 1980.
(Boston's 4th choice, 135th overall, in 1998 Entry Draft).

			Regular Season								Playoffs						
Season	Club	Lea	GP	W	L	T	Mins	GA	SO	Avg	GP	W	L	Mins	GA	SO	Avg
1996-97	Wellington Dukes	OJHL	27	....	....	....	1402	92	0	3.94	....	....	....	....	....	....	....
1997-98	Sudbury Wolves	OHL	33	8	16	5	1802	125	0	4.16	2	0	1	89	8	0	5.39
1998-99	Sudbury Wolves	OHL	45	17	22	5	2528	173	1	4.11	3	0	2	96	13	0	8.13
99-2000	Kingston	OHL	*61	33	20	5	3340	191	0	3.43	5	1	4	300	21	0	4.20

OHL First All-Star Team (2000) • Canadian Major Junior First All-Star Team (2000) • Canadian Major Junior Goaltender of the Year (2000)

RHODES, Damian (ROHDZ, DAY-mee-an) ATL.

Goaltender. Catches left. 6', 190 lbs. Born, St. Paul, MN, May 28, 1969.
(Toronto's 6th choice, 112th overall, in 1987 Entry Draft).

			Regular Season								Playoffs						
Season	Club	Lea	GP	W	L	T	Mins	GA	SO	Avg	GP	W	L	Mins	GA	SO	Avg
1985-86	Richfield High	H.S.	16	....	....	....	720	56	0	3.50	....	....	....	....	....	....	....
1986-87	Richfield High	H.S.	19	....	....	....	673	51	1	4.55	....	....	....	....	....	....	....
1987-88	Michigan Tech	WCHA	29	16	10	1	1625	114	0	4.20	....	....	....	....	....	....	....
1988-89	Michigan Tech	WCHA	37	15	22	0	2216	163	0	4.41	....	....	....	....	....	....	....
1989-90	Michigan Tech	WCHA	25	6	17	0	1358	119	0	6.26	....	....	....	....	....	....	....
1990-91	**Toronto**	**NHL**	**1**	**1**	**0**	**0**	**60**	**1**	**0**	**1.00**	....	....	....	....	....	....	....
	Newmarket Saints	AHL	38	8	24	3	2154	144	1	4.01	....	....	....	....	....	....	....
1991-92	St. John's Leafs	AHL	43	20	16	5	2454	148	0	3.62	6	4	1	331	16	0	2.90
1992-93	St. John's Leafs	AHL	*52	27	16	8	*3074	184	1	3.59	9	4	5	538	37	0	4.13
1993-94	**Toronto**	**NHL**	**22**	**9**	**7**	**3**	**1213**	**53**	**0**	**2.62**	**1**	**0**	**0**	**1**	**0**	**0**	**0.00**
1994-95	**Toronto**	**NHL**	**13**	**6**	**6**	**1**	**760**	**34**	**0**	**2.68**	....	....	....	....	....	....	....
1995-96	**Toronto**	**NHL**	**11**	**4**	**5**	**1**	**624**	**29**	**0**	**2.79**	....	....	....	....	....	....	....
	Ottawa	**NHL**	**36**	**10**	**22**	**4**	**2123**	**98**	**2**	**2.77**	....	....	....	....	....	....	....
1996-97	**Ottawa**	**NHL**	**50**	**14**	**20**	**14**	**2934**	**133**	**1**	**2.72**	....	....	....	....	....	....	....
1997-98	**Ottawa**	**NHL**	**50**	**19**	**19**	**7**	**2743**	**107**	**5**	**2.34**	**10**	**5**	**5**	**590**	**21**	**0**	**2.14**
1998-99	**Ottawa**	**NHL**	**45**	**22**	**13**	**7**	**2480**	**101**	**3**	**2.44**	**2**	**0**	**2**	**150**	**6**	**0**	**2.40**
99-2000	**Atlanta**	**NHL**	**28**	**5**	**19**	**3**	**1561**	**101**	**1**	**3.88**	....	....	....	....	....	....	....
	NHL Totals		**256**	**90**	**111**	**40**	**14498**	**657**	**12**	**2.72**	**13**	**5**	**7**	**741**	**27**	**0**	**2.19**

• Credited with scoring a goal while with Michigan Tech (WCHA), January 21, 1989. • Credited with scoring a goal vs. New Jersey, January 2, 1999.

• Played 10 seconds of playoff game vs. San Jose, May 6, 1994. Traded to **NY Islanders** by **Toronto** with Ken Belanger for future considerations (Kirk Muller and Don Beaupre, January 23, 1996), January 23, 1996. Traded to **Ottawa** by **NY Islanders** with Wade Redden for Don Beaupre, Martin Straka and Bryan Berard, January 23, 1996. Traded to **Atlanta** by **Ottawa** for future considerations, June 18, 1999.

RICHTER, Mike (RIHK-tuhr, MIGHK) NYR

Goaltender. Catches left. 5'11", 185 lbs. Born, Abington, PA, September 22, 1966.
(NY Rangers' 2nd choice, 28th overall, in 1985 Entry Draft).

			Regular Season								Playoffs						
Season	Club	Lea	GP	W	L	T	Mins	GA	SO	Avg	GP	W	L	Mins	GA	SO	Avg
1983-84	Philadelphia	NEJHL	36	23	10	3	2160	94	0	2.61	....	....	....	....	....	....	....
1984-85	Northwood Prep	H.S.	24	....	....	....	1374	52	2	2.27	....	....	....	....	....	....	....
1985-86	U. of Wisconsin	WCHA	24	14	9	0	1394	92	1	3.96	....	....	....	....	....	....	....
1986-87	U. of Wisconsin	WCHA	36	19	16	1	2136	126	0	3.54	....	....	....	....	....	....	....
1987-88	United States	Nt-Team	29	17	7	2	1559	86	0	3.31	....	....	....	....	....	....	....
	United States	Olympics	4	....	....	....	230	15	0	3.91	....	....	....	....	....	....	....
	Colorado Rangers	IHL	22	16	5	0	1298	68	1	3.14	10	5	3	536	35	0	3.92
1988-89	Denver Rangers	IHL	*57	23	26	0	3031	217	1	4.30	4	0	4	210	21	0	6.00
	NY Rangers	NHL	....	....	....	....	....	....	....	....	1	0	1	58	4	0	4.14
1989-90	NY Rangers	NHL	23	12	5	5	1320	66	0	3.00	6	3	2	330	19	0	3.45
	Flint Spirits	IHL	13	7	4	2	782	49	0	3.76	....	....	....	....	....	....	....
1990-91	NY Rangers	NHL	45	21	13	7	2596	135	0	3.12	6	2	4	313	14	*1	2.68
1991-92	NY Rangers	NHL	41	23	12	2	2298	119	3	3.11	7	4	2	412	24	1	3.50
1992-93	NY Rangers	NHL	38	13	19	3	2105	134	1	3.82	....	....	....	....	....	....	....
	Binghamton	AHL	5	4	0	1	305	6	0	1.18	....	....	....	....	....	....	....
1993-94♦	NY Rangers	NHL	68	*42	12	6	3710	159	5	2.57	23	*16	7	1417	49	*4	2.07
1994-95	NY Rangers	NHL	35	14	17	2	1993	97	2	2.92	7	2	5	384	23	0	3.59
1995-96	NY Rangers	NHL	41	24	13	3	2396	107	3	2.68	11	5	6	661	36	0	3.27
1996-97	NY Rangers	NHL	61	33	22	6	3598	161	4	2.68	15	9	6	939	33	*3	2.11
1997-98	NY Rangers	NHL	*72	21	31	15	4143	184	0	2.66	....	....	....	....	....	....	....
	United States	Olympics	4	1	3	0	237	14	0	3.55	....	....	....	....	....	....	....
1998-99	NY Rangers	NHL	68	27	30	8	3878	170	4	2.63	....	....	....	....	....	....	....
99-2000	NY Rangers	NHL	61	22	31	8	3622	173	0	2.87	....	....	....	....	....	....	....
	NHL Totals		553	252	205	65	31659	1505	22	2.85	76	41	33	4514	202	9	2.68

WCHA Second All-Star Team (1987) • Played in NHL All-Star Game (1992, 1994, 2000)

Claimed by **Nashville** from **NY Rangers** in Expansion Draft, June 26, 1998. Signed as a free agent by **NY Rangers**, July 15, 1998.

ROBITAILLE, Marc (ROH-buh-tigh)

Goaltender. Catches left. 5'10", 185 lbs. Born, Gloucester, Ont., June 7, 1976.

			Regular Season								Playoffs						
Season	Club	Lea	GP	W	L	T	Mins	GA	SO	Avg	GP	W	L	Mins	GA	SO	Avg
1992-93	Hawkesbury	OJHL	15	4	5	0	710	67	0	5.66	....	....	....	....	....	....	....
1993-94	Hawkesbury	OJHL	14	3	7	1	708	50	0	4.24	....	....	....	....	....	....	....
	Smiths Falls Bears	OJHL	8	5	2	1	444	22	1	2.97	....	....	....	....	....	....	....
1994-95	Smiths Falls Bears	OJHL	20	11	5	3	1170	71	0	3.64	....	....	....	....	....	....	....
1995-96	Gloucester	OJHL	35	23	11	0	2000	96	5	2.94	....	....	....	....	....	....	....
1996-97	Northeastern	H-East	*34	7	24	3	*1928	135	3	4.20	....	....	....	....	....	....	....
1997-98	Northeastern	H-East	*39	21	15	3	*2313	123	1	3.19	....	....	....	....	....	....	....
1998-99	St. John's Leafs	AHL	42	13	22	1	2269	124	1	3.28	3	1	2	158	8	0	3.04
99-2000	St. John's Leafs	AHL	27	3	12	4	1369	93	0	4.08	....	....	....	....	....	....	....

Hockey East First All-Star Team (1998) • NCAA East First All-American Team (1998)

Signed as a free agent by **Toronto**, June 4, 1998.

ROLOSON, Dwayne (ROH-loh-suhn, DWAYN) ST.L.

Goaltender. Catches left. 6'1", 190 lbs. Born, Simcoe, Ont., October 12, 1969.

			Regular Season								Playoffs						
Season	Club	Lea	GP	W	L	T	Mins	GA	SO	Avg	GP	W	L	Mins	GA	SO	Avg
1984-85	Simcoe Penguins	OJHL-C	3	....	....	....	100	21	0	12.60	....	....	....	....	....	....	....
1985-86	Simcoe Rams	OJHL-C	1	....	....	....	60	6	0	6.00	....	....	....	....	....	....	....
1986-87	Norwich Merchants	OJHL-C	19	....	....	....	1091	55	0	*3.03	....	....	....	....	....	....	....
1987-88	Belleville Bobcats	OJHL-B	21	9	6	1	1070	60	*2	3.36	....	....	....	....	....	....	....
1988-89	Thorold Hawks	OJHL-B	27	15	6	4	1490	82	0	3.30	....	....	....	....	....	....	....
1989-90	Thorold Hawks	OJHL-B	30	18	8	1	1683	108	0	3.85	....	....	....	....	....	....	....
1990-91	U. Mass-Lowell	H-East	15	5	9	0	823	63	0	4.59	....	....	....	....	....	....	....
1991-92	U. Mass-Lowell	H-East	12	3	8	0	660	52	0	4.73	....	....	....	....	....	....	....
1992-93	U. Mass-Lowell	H-East	*39	20	17	2	*2342	150	0	3.84	....	....	....	....	....	....	....
1993-94	U. Mass-Lowell	H-East	*40	*23	10	7	*2305	106	0	2.76	....	....	....	....	....	....	....
1994-95	Saint John Flames	AHL	46	16	21	8	2734	156	1	3.42	5	1	4	298	13	0	2.61
1995-96	Saint John Flames	AHL	67	*33	22	11	4026	190	1	2.83	16	10	6	1027	49	1	2.86
1996-97	Calgary	NHL	31	9	14	3	1618	78	1	2.89	....	....	....	....	....	....	....
	Saint John Flames	AHL	8	6	2	0	481	22	1	2.75	....	....	....	....	....	....	....
1997-98	Calgary	NHL	39	11	16	8	2205	110	0	2.99	....	....	....	....	....	....	....
	Saint John Flames	AHL	4	3	0	1	245	8	0	1.96	....	....	....	....	....	....	....
1998-99	Buffalo	NHL	18	6	8	2	911	42	1	2.77	4	1	1	139	10	0	4.32
	Rochester	AHL	2	2	0	0	120	4	0	2.00	....	....	....	....	....	....	....
99-2000	Buffalo	NHL	14	1	7	3	677	32	0	2.84	....	....	....	....	....	....	....
	NHL Totals		102	27	45	16	5411	262	2	2.91	4	1	1	139	10	0	4.32

Hockey East First All-Star Team (1994) • NCAA East First All-Ameircan Team (1994)

Signed as a free agent by **Calgary**, July 4, 1994. Signed as a free agent by **Buffalo**, July 15, 1998. Selected by **Columbus** from **Buffalo** in Expansion Draft, June 23, 2000. Signed as a free agent by **St. Louis**, July 14, 2000.

ROSATI, Mike (roh-ZA-tee, MIGHK)

Goaltender. Catches left. 5'10", 170 lbs. Born, Toronto, Ont., January 7, 1968.
(NY Rangers' 6th choice, 131st overall, in 1988 Entry Draft).

			Regular Season								Playoffs						
Season	Club	Lea	GP	W	L	T	Mins	GA	SO	Avg	GP	W	L	Mins	GA	SO	Avg
1984-85	St. Michael's	OJHL-B	19	....	....	....	1027	93	0	5.13	....	....	....	....	....	....	....
1985-86	St. Michael's	OJHL-B	20	8	11	1	1100	95	0	5.18	34	....	....	1648	119	0	4.33
	Hamilton Hawks	OHL	1	0	0	1	70	5	0	4.29	....	....	....	....	....	....	....
1986-87	Hamilton Hawks	OHL	26	....	....	....	1334	85	1	3.82	....	....	....	....	....	....	....
1987-88	Hamilton Hawks	OHL	62	29	25	3	3468	233	1	4.03	14	8	6	833	66	0	4.75
1988-89	Niagara Falls	OHL	52	*28	15	2	2339	174	1	4.46	16	10	4	861	62	0	4.32
1989-90	Erie Panthers	ECHL	18	12	5	0	1056	73	0	4.14	....	....	....	....	....	....	....
1990-91	HC Bolzano	Italy	46	....	....	....	2700	212	0	4.71	....	....	....	....	....	....	....
1991-92	HC Bolzano	Italy	18	11	6	1	1022	58	2	3.22	7	5	2	409	30	0	4.28
1992-93	HC Bolzano	Italy	26	....	....	....	1525	78	1	3.07	....	....	....	....	....	....	....
1993-94	HC Bolzano	Italy	29	....	....	....	1683	104	0	3.71	....	....	....	....	....	....	....
1994-95	HC Bolzano	Italy	47	....	....	....	2705	149	1	3.30	....	....	....	....	....	....	....
1995-96	HC Bolzano	Italy	45	36	5	3	2465	137	3	3.33	....	....	....	....	....	....	....
1996-97	Adler Mannheim	DEL	44	....	....	....	2625	104	6	2.38	9	....	....	514	24	0	2.80
1997-98	Adler Mannheim	EuroHL	2	2	0	0	118	5	1	0.87	....	....	....	....	....	....	....
	Adler Mannheim	DEL	43	....	....	....	2567	116	2	2.71	*10	*9	1	569	17	*1	*2.00
1998-99	Washington	NHL	1	1	0	0	28	0	0	0.00	....	....	....	....	....	....	....
	Portland Pirates	AHL	32	9	23	0	1783	111	1	3.74	....	....	....	....	....	....	....
	Manitoba Moose	IHL	8	5	1	2	479	16	1	2.00	5	2	3	314	18	0	3.44
99-2000	Adler Mannheim	DEL	55	....	....	....	3245	170	3	3.14	5	....	....	280	15	2	3.21
	Adler Mannheim	EuroHL	1	0	0	0	20	1	0	3.00	....	....	....	....	....	....	....
	NHL Totals		1	1	0	0	28	0	0	0.00	....	....	....	....	....	....	....

Signed as a free agent by **Washington**, July 15, 1998.

ROUSSEAU, Ghyslain (roo-SOH, zhihz-LEH) BUF.

Goaltender. Catches left. 6'1", 160 lbs. Born, Black Lake, Que., February 6, 1982.
(Buffalo's 3rd choice, 111th overall, in 2000 Entry Draft).

			Regular Season								Playoffs						
Season	Club	Lea	GP	W	L	T	Mins	GA	SO	Avg	GP	W	L	Mins	GA	SO	Avg
1998-99	Levis Commanders	QAAA	24	2	17	1	1176	112	0	5.71	....	....	....	....	....	....	....
99-2000	Baie-Comeau	QMJHL	46	19	15	1	2301	147	0	3.83	1	0	0	1	0	0	0.00

ROUSSEL, Dominic (roo-SEHL, DOHM-ih-NIHK) ANA.

Goaltender. Catches left. 6'2", 200 lbs. Born, Hull, Que., February 22, 1970.
(Philadelphia's 4th choice, 63rd overall, in 1988 Entry Draft).

			Regular Season								Playoffs						
Season	Club	Lea	GP	W	L	T	Mins	GA	SO	Avg	GP	W	L	Mins	GA	SO	Avg
1986-87	Lac St-Louis	QAAA	24	8	12	0	1334	85	1	3.69	....	....	....	....	....	....	....
1987-88	Trois-Rivieres	QMJHL	51	18	25	4	2905	251	0	5.18	....	....	....	....	....	....	....
1988-89	Shawinigan	QMJHL	46	24	15	2	2555	171	0	4.02	10	6	4	638	36	0	3.39
1989-90	Shawinigan	QMJHL	37	20	14	1	1985	133	0	4.02	2	1	1	120	12	0	6.00
1990-91	Hershey Bears	AHL	45	20	14	7	2507	151	1	3.61	7	3	4	366	21	0	3.44
1991-92	Philadelphia	NHL	17	7	8	2	922	40	1	2.60	....	....	....	....	....	....	....
	Hershey Bears	AHL	35	15	11	6	2040	121	1	3.56	....	....	....	....	....	....	....
1992-93	Philadelphia	NHL	34	13	11	5	1769	111	1	3.76	....	....	....	....	....	....	....
	Hershey Bears	AHL	6	0	3	3	372	23	0	3.71	....	....	....	....	....	....	....
1993-94	Philadelphia	NHL	60	29	20	5	3285	183	1	3.34	....	....	....	....	....	....	....
1994-95	Philadelphia	NHL	19	11	7	0	1075	42	1	2.34	1	0	0	23	0	0	0.00
	Hershey Bears	AHL	1	0	1	0	59	5	0	5.07	....	....	....	....	....	....	....
1995-96	Philadelphia	NHL	9	2	3	2	456	22	1	2.89	....	....	....	....	....	....	....
	Hershey Bears	AHL	12	4	4	3	690	32	0	2.78	....	....	....	....	....	....	....
	Winnipeg	NHL	7	2	2	0	285	16	0	3.37	....	....	....	....	....	....	....
1996-97	Philadelphia	AHL	36	18	9	3	1852	82	2	2.66	1	0	0	26	3	0	6.93
1997-98	Canada	Nt-Team	41	25	12	1	2307	86	5	2.24	....	....	....	....	....	....	....
	SB Rosenheim	DEL	2	0	2	0	120	12	0	6.00	....	....	....	....	....	....	....
1998-99	Anaheim	NHL	18	4	5	4	884	37	1	2.51	....	....	....	....	....	....	....
99-2000	Anaheim	NHL	20	6	5	3	988	52	1	3.16	....	....	....	....	....	....	....
	NHL Totals		184	74	61	21	9664	503	7	3.12	1	0	0	23	0	0	0.00

Traded to **Winnipeg** by **Philadelphia** for Tim Cheveldae and Winnipeg's 3rd round choice (Chester Gallant) in 1996 Entry Draft, February 27, 1996. Signed as a free agent by **Philadelphia**, July 3, 1996. Traded to **Nashville** by **Philadelphia** with Jeff Staples for Nashville's 7th round choice (Cam Ondrik) in 1998 Entry Draft, June 26, 1998. Traded to **Anaheim** by **Nashville** for Chris Mason and Marc Moro, October 5, 1998.

ROY, Patrick (WAH, PAT-rihk) COL.

Goaltender. Catches left. 6'2", 192 lbs. Born, Quebec City, Que., October 5, 1965.
(Montreal's 4th choice, 51st overall, in 1984 Entry Draft).

			Regular Season								Playoffs						
Season	Club	Lea	GP	W	L	T	Mins	GA	SO	Avg	GP	W	L	Mins	GA	SO	Avg
1981-82	Ste-Foy Governors	QAAA	40	27	3	10	2400	156	0	2.63	....	....	....	....	....	....	....
1982-83	Granby Bisons	QMJHL	54	13	35	1	2808	293	0	6.26	....	....	....	....	....	....	....
1983-84	Granby Bisons	QMJHL	61	29	29	1	3585	265	0	4.44	4	0	4	244	22	0	5.41
1984-85	Granby Bisons	QMJHL	44	16	25	1	2463	228	0	5.55	....	....	....	....	....	....	....
	Montreal	NHL	1	1	0	0	20	0	0	0.00	....	....	....	....	....	....	....
	Sherbrooke	AHL	1	1	0	0	60	4	0	4.00	13	10	3	*769	37	0	*2.89
1985-86♦	Montreal	NHL	47	23	18	3	2651	148	1	3.35	20	*15	5	1218	39	*1	1.92
1986-87	Montreal	NHL	46	22	16	6	2686	131	1	2.93	6	4	2	330	22	0	4.00
1987-88	Montreal	NHL	45	23	12	9	2586	125	3	2.90	8	3	4	430	24	0	3.35
1988-89	Montreal	NHL	48	33	5	6	2744	113	4	*2.47	19	13	6	1206	42	2	*2.09
1989-90	Montreal	NHL	54	*31	16	5	3173	134	3	2.53	11	5	6	641	26	1	2.43
1990-91	Montreal	NHL	48	25	15	6	2835	128	1	2.71	13	7	5	785	40	0	3.06
1991-92	Montreal	NHL	67	36	22	8	3935	155	*5	*2.36	11	4	7	686	30	1	2.62
1992-93♦	Montreal	NHL	62	31	25	5	3595	192	2	3.20	20	*16	4	1293	46	0	*2.13
1993-94	Montreal	NHL	68	35	17	11	3867	161	*7	2.50	6	3	3	375	16	0	2.56
1994-95	Montreal	NHL	43	17	20	6	2566	127	1	2.97	....	....	....	....	....	....	....
1995-96	Montreal	NHL	22	12	9	1	1260	62	1	2.95	....	....	....	....	....	....	....
♦	Colorado	NHL	39	22	15	1	2305	103	1	2.68	*22	*16	6	*1454	51	*3	2.10
1996-97	Colorado	NHL	62	*38	15	7	3698	143	7	2.32	17	10	7	1034	38	*3	2.21
1997-98	Colorado	NHL	65	31	19	13	3835	153	4	2.39	7	3	4	430	18	0	2.51
	Canada	Olympics	6	4	2	0	*369	9	1	1.46	....	....	....	....	....	....	....
1998-99	Colorado	NHL	61	32	19	8	3648	139	5	2.29	19	11	8	1173	52	1	2.66
99-2000	Colorado	NHL	63	32	21	8	3704	141	2	2.28	17	11	6	1039	31	3	1.79
	NHL Totals		841	444	264	103	49108	2155	48	2.63	196	121	73	12094	475	15	2.36

NHL All-Rookie Team (1986) • Won Conn Smythe Trophy (1986, 1993) • Shared William Jennings Trophy with Brian Hayward (1987, 1988, 1989) • NHL Second All-Star Team (1988, 1991) • NHL First All-Star Team (1989, 1990, 1992) • Won Trico Goaltending Award (1989, 1990) • Won Vezina Trophy (1989, 1990, 1992) • Won William M. Jennings Trophy (1992) • Played in NHL All-Star Game (1988, 1990, 1991, 1992, 1993, 1994, 1997, 1998)

Traded to **Colorado** by **Montreal** with Mike Keane for Andrei Kovalenko, Martin Rucinsky and Jocelyn Thibault, December 6, 1995.

RUDKOWSKY, Cody (RUHD-kow-SKEE, KOH-dee) ST.L.

Goaltender. Catches left. 6'1", 200 lbs. Born, Willingdon, Alta., July 21, 1978.

			Regular Season								Playoffs						
Season	Club	Lea	GP	W	L	T	Mins	GA	SO	Avg	GP	W	L	Mins	GA	SO	Avg
1995-96	Langley Thunder	BCJHL	23	....	....	....	1172	73	1	3.73	....	....	....	....	....	....	....
	Seattle T-Birds	WHL	2	0	0	0	21	3	0	8.57	....	....	....	....	....	....	....
1996-97	Seattle T-Birds	WHL	40	19	16	1	2162	124	0	3.44	1	1	0	30	0	0	0.00
1997-98	Seattle T-Birds	WHL	53	20	22	3	2805	176	1	3.74	5	1	4	278	18	0	3.88
1998-99	Seattle T-Birds	WHL	64	34	17	10	3665	177	*7	2.90	11	5	6	637	31	1	2.92
99-2000	Worcester	AHL	28	9	7	6	1405	75	0	3.20	....	....	....	....	....	....	....
	Peoria Rivermen	ECHL	10	6	4	0	599	32	0	3.20	2	1	1	119	6	0	3.02

WHL West First All-Star Team (1999) • Canadian Major Junior First All-Star Team (1999) • Canadian Major Junior Goaltender of the Year (1999)

Signed as a free agent by **St. Louis**, March 25, 1999.

RUSSELL, Blaine (RUH-sehL, BLAYN)

Goaltender. Catches left. 5'11", 180 lbs. Born, Wetaskawin, Sask., January 11, 1977.
(Anaheim's 4th choice, 149th overall, in 1996 Entry Draft).

			Regular Season								Playoffs						
Season	Club	Lea	GP	W	L	T	Mins	GA	SO	Avg	GP	W	L	Mins	GA	SO	Avg
1995-96	Spokane Chiefs	WHL	1	0	1	0	37	5	0	8.11	....	....	....	....	....	....	....
	Prince Albert	WHL	34	25	5	2	1920	98	2	3.06	7	4	2	380	20	0	3.16
1996-97	Prince Albert	WHL	29	9	15	3	1690	99	2	3.51	....	....	....	....	....	....	....
	Lethbridge	WHL	6	4	1	1	370	17	0	2.76	14	*13	1	817	29	0	*2.13
1997-98	Columbus Chill	ECHL	4	1	2	0	199	19	0	5.71	....	....	....	....	....	....	....
	Cincinnati Ducks	AHL	20	0	9	2	748	58	0	4.65	....	....	....	....	....	....	....
	Huntington	ECHL	1	0	1	0	60	6	0	6.00	....	....	....	....	....	....	....
	New Orleans	ECHL	4	0	0	2	183	11	0	3.59	....	....	....	....	....	....	....
1998-99	Huntington	ECHL	12	6	1	0	516	25	1	2.91	....	....	....	....	....	....	....
99-2000	Cincinnati Ducks	AHL	2	0	1	0	53	3	0	3.40	....	....	....	....	....	....	....
	Huntington	ECHL	41	20	10	7	2200	119	1	3.24	3	1	1	131	5	1	2.30

• Missed majority of 1998-99 season recovering from knee injury suffered in game vs. Toledo (ECHL), December 4, 1998.

SABOURIN, Dany (SA-boo-rihn, DAN-ee) CGY.

Goaltender. Catches left. 6'2", 182 lbs. Born, Val d'Or, Que., September 2, 1980.
(Calgary's 5th choice, 108th overall, in 1998 Entry Draft).

			Regular Season								Playoffs						
Season	Club	Lea	GP	W	L	T	Mins	GA	SO	Avg	GP	W	L	Mins	GA	SO	Avg
1996-97	Amos Forestiers	QAAA	24	....	....	....	1440	107	0	4.48	....	....	....	....	....	....	....
1997-98	Sherbrooke	QMJHL	37	15	15	2	1906	128	1	4.03	....	....	....	....	....	....	....
1998-99	Sherbrooke	QMJHL	30	8	13	2	1477	102	1	4.14	1	0	1	49	2	0	2.45
	Saint John Flames	AHL	....	....	....	....	....	....	....	....	1	0	1	57	4	0	4.19
99-2000	Sherbrooke	QMJHL	55	25	22	5	3067	181	1	3.54	5	1	4	324	18	0	3.33

SALO, Tommy (SAH-loh, TAWM-mee) EDM.

Goaltender. Catches left. 5'11", 173 lbs. Born, Surahammar, Sweden, February 1, 1971.
(NY Islanders' 5th choice, 118th overall, in 1993 Entry Draft).

			Regular Season								Playoffs						
Season	Club	Lea	GP	W	L	T	Mins	GA	SO	Avg	GP	W	L	Mins	GA	SO	Avg
1990-91	Vasteras IK	Sweden	2	....	....	....	100	11	0	6.60	....	....	....	....	....	....	....
1991-92	Vasteras IK	Swede-Jr.	STATISTICS NOT AVAILABLE														
1992-93	Vasteras IK	Sweden	24	....	....	....	1431	59	2	2.47	2	....	....	120	6	0	3.00
1993-94	Vasteras IK	Sweden	32	....	....	....	1896	106	0	3.35	....	....	....	....	....	....	....
	Sweden	Olympics	6	5	1	0	370	13	1	2.11	....	....	....	....	....	....	....
1994-95	Denver Grizzlies	IHL	*65	*45	14	4	*3810	165	*3	*2.60	8	7	0	390	20	0	3.07
	NY Islanders	**NHL**	**6**	**1**	**5**	**0**	**358**	**18**	**0**	**3.02**	....	....	....	....	....	....	....
1995-96	**NY Islanders**	**NHL**	**10**	**1**	**7**	**1**	**523**	**35**	**0**	**4.02**	....	....	....	....	....	....	....
	Utah Grizzlies	IHL	45	28	15	2	2695	119	*4	2.65	22	*15	7	1342	51	*3	2.28
1996-97	**NY Islanders**	**NHL**	**58**	**20**	**27**	**8**	**3208**	**151**	**5**	**2.82**	....	....	....	....	....	....	....
1997-98	**NY Islanders**	**NHL**	**62**	**23**	**29**	**5**	**3461**	**152**	**4**	**2.64**	....	....	....	....	....	....	....
	Sweden	Olympics	4	2	2	0	238	9	0	2.27	....	....	....	....	....	....	....
1998-99	**NY Islanders**	**NHL**	**51**	**17**	**26**	**7**	**3018**	**132**	**5**	**2.62**	....	....	....	....	....	....	....
	Edmonton	**NHL**	**13**	**8**	**2**	**2**	**700**	**27**	**0**	**2.31**	**4**	**0**	**4**	**296**	**11**	**0**	**2.23**
99-2000	**Edmonton**	**NHL**	**70**	**27**	**28**	**13**	**4164**	**162**	**2**	**2.33**	**5**	**1**	**4**	**297**	**14**	**0**	**2.83**
	NHL Totals		**270**	**97**	**124**	**36**	**15432**	**677**	**16**	**2.63**	**9**	**1**	**8**	**593**	**25**	**0**	**2.53**

IHL First All-Star Team (1995) • Won Garry F. Longman Memorial Trophy (Top Rookie - IHL) (1995) • Won James Norris Memorial Trophy (Fewest goals against - IHL) (1995) • Won James Gatschene Memorial Trophy (MVP - IHL) (1995) • Shared James Norris Memorial Trophy (fewest goals against — IHL) with Mark McArthur (1996) • Won "Bud" Poile Trophy (Playoff MVP - IHL) (1996) • Played in NHL All-Star Game (2000)

Traded to **Edmonton** by **NY Islanders** for Mats Lindgren and Edmonton's 8th round choice (Radek Martinek) in 1999 Entry Draft, March 20, 1999.

SALTARELLI, Erasmo CHI.

Goaltender. Catches left. 5'11", 190 lbs. Born, Montreal, Que., February 20, 1974.

			Regular Season								Playoffs						
Season	Club	Lea	GP	W	L	T	Mins	GA	SO	Avg	GP	W	L	Mins	GA	SO	Avg
1992-93	St-Hubert College	QJHL	22	13	6	2	1322	72	0	3.25	....	....	....	....	....	....	....
1993-94	St-Hubert College	QJHL	29	15	8	4	1735	91	0	3.15	....	....	....	....	....	....	....
1994-95	Princeton	ECAC	8	2	1	0	202	9	0	2.66	....	....	....	....	....	....	....
1995-96	Princeton	ECAC	10	1	4	1	416	24	0	3.46	....	....	....	....	....	....	....
1996-97	Princeton	ECAC	24	9	10	3	1305	63	2	2.90	....	....	....	....	....	....	....
1997-98	Princeton	ECAC	*34	*17	10	7	*2052	99	2	2.89	....	....	....	....	....	....	....
1998-99	Chesapeake	ECHL	27	8	11	5	1421	74	1	3.12	....	....	....	....	....	....	....
	Tallahassee	ECHL	6	1	1	1	216	13	1	3.61	....	....	....	....	....	....	....
99-2000	B.C. Icemen	UHL	29	16	9	4	1700	90	1	3.18	6	2	4	380	19	0	3.00
	Springfield Falcons	AHL	2	0	1	0	88	3	0	2.06	....	....	....	....	....	....	....

Signed as a free agent by **Chicago**, June 7, 2000.

SAUVE, Phillipe (SOH-vay, FIHL-ihp) COL.

Goaltender. Catches left. 6', 180 lbs. Born, Buffalo, NY, February 27, 1980.
(Colorado's 6th choice, 38th overall, in 1998 Entry Draft).

			Regular Season								Playoffs						
Season	Club	Lea	GP	W	L	T	Mins	GA	SO	Avg	GP	W	L	Mins	GA	SO	Avg
1995-96	Laval-Laurentides	QAAA	25	....	....	....	1184	87	1	4.11	....	....	....	....	....	....	....
1996-97	Rimouski Oceanic	QMJHL	26	11	9	2	1334	84	0	3.78	1	0	0	14	3	0	12.90
1997-98	Rimouski Oceanic	QMJHL	40	23	16	0	2326	131	1	3.38	7	0	5	262	33	0	7.55
1998-99	Rimouski Oceanic	QMJHL	44	16	19	4	2401	155	0	3.87	11	6	4	595	30	*1	3.03
99-2000	Drummondville	QMJHL	28	12	12	2	1526	106	0	4.17	....	....	....	....	....	....	....
	Hull Olympiques	QMJHL	17	9	7	1	992	57	0	3.45	12	6	6	735	47	0	3.84

Canadian Major Junior Humanitarian Player of the Year (1999)

SCHAEFER, Nolan (SHAY-fuhr) S.J.

Goaltender. Catches left. 6'1", 175 lbs. Born, Yellow Grass, Sask., January 15, 1980.
(San Jose's 4th choice, 166th overall, in 2000 Entry Draft).

			Regular Season								Playoffs						
Season	Club	Lea	GP	W	L	T	Mins	GA	SO	Avg	GP	W	L	Mins	GA	SO	Avg
1997-98	Nipawin Hawks	SJHL	21	12	4	3	1080	42	*3	*2.33	....	....	....	....	....	....	....
1998-99	Nipawin Hawks	SJHL	STATISTICS NOT AVAILABLE														
99-2000	Providence	H-East	14	6	5	1	778	42	0	3.24	....	....	....	....	....	....	....

SJHL All-Rookie Team (1998)

SCHWAB, Corey (SHWAHB, KOHR-ree) VAN.

Goaltender. Catches left. 6', 180 lbs. Born, North Battleford, Sask., November 4, 1970.
(New Jersey's 12th choice, 200th overall, in 1990 Entry Draft).

			Regular Season								Playoffs						
Season	Club	Lea	GP	W	L	T	Mins	GA	SO	Avg	GP	W	L	Mins	GA	SO	Avg
1988-89	Seattle T-Birds	WHL	10	2	2	0	386	31	0	4.82	....	....	....	....	....	....	....
1989-90	Seattle T-Birds	WHL	27	15	2	1	1150	69	1	3.60	3	0	0	49	2	0	2.45
1990-91	Seattle T-Birds	WHL	*58	32	18	3	*3289	224	0	4.09	6	1	5	382	25	0	3.93
1991-92	Utica Devils	AHL	24	9	12	1	1322	95	0	4.31	....	....	....	....	....	....	....
	Cincinnati	ECHL	8	6	0	1	450	31	0	4.13	9	6	3	540	29	0	3.22
1992-93	Utica Devils	AHL	40	18	16	5	2387	169	*2	4.25	1	0	1	59	6	0	6.10
	Cincinnati	IHL	3	1	2	0	185	17	0	5.51	....	....	....	....	....	....	....
1993-94	Albany River Rats	AHL	51	27	21	3	3058	184	0	3.61	5	1	4	298	20	0	4.02
1994-95	Albany River Rats	AHL	45	25	10	9	2711	117	3	*2.59	7	6	1	425	19	0	2.68
1995-96	**New Jersey**	**NHL**	**10**	**0**	**3**	**0**	**331**	**12**	**0**	**2.18**	....	....	....	....	....	....	....
	Albany River Rats	AHL	5	3	2	0	299	13	0	2.61	....	....	....	....	....	....	....
1996-97	**Tampa Bay**	**NHL**	**31**	**11**	**12**	**1**	**1462**	**74**	**2**	**3.04**	....	....	....	....	....	....	....
1997-98	**Tampa Bay**	**NHL**	**16**	**2**	**9**	**1**	**821**	**40**	**1**	**2.92**	....	....	....	....	....	....	....
1998-99	**Tampa Bay**	**NHL**	**40**	**8**	**25**	**3**	**2146**	**126**	**0**	**3.52**	....	....	....	....	....	....	....
	Cleveland	IHL	8	1	6	1	477	31	0	3.90	....	....	....	....	....	....	....
99-2000	Orlando	IHL	16	9	4	2	868	31	1	2.14	....	....	....	....	....	....	....
	Vancouver	**NHL**	**6**	**2**	**1**	**1**	**269**	**16**	**0**	**3.57**	....	....	....	....	....	....	....
	Syracuse Crunch	AHL	12	7	5	0	720	42	0	3.50	4	1	3	246	11	1	2.69
	NHL Totals		**103**	**23**	**50**	**6**	**5029**	**268**	**3**	**3.20**	....	....	....	....	....	....	....

AHL Second All-Star Team (1995) • Shared Harry "Hap" Holmes Memorial Trophy (fewest goals against - AHL) with Mike Dunham (1995) • Shared Jack A. Butterfield Trophy (Playoff MVP - AHL) with Mike Dunham (1995)

Traded to **Tampa Bay** by **New Jersey** for Jeff Reese, Chicago's 2nd round choice (previously acquired, New Jersey selected Pierre Dagenais) in 1996 Entry Draft and Tampa Bay's 8th round choice (Jason Bertsch) in 1996 Entry Draft, June 22, 1996. Claimed by **Atlanta** from **Tampa Bay** in Expansion Draft, June 25, 1999. Traded to **Vancouver** by **Atlanta** for Vancouver's 4th round choice (Carl Mallette) in 2000 Entry Draft, October 29, 1999.

SCOTT, Travis (SKAWT, TRA-vihs) L.A.

Goaltender. Catches left. 6'2", 185 lbs. Born, Kanata, Ont., September 14, 1975.

			Regular Season								Playoffs						
Season	Club	Lea	GP	W	L	T	Mins	GA	SO	Avg	GP	W	L	Mins	GA	SO	Avg
1992-93	Nepean Raiders	OJHL	36	19	10	2	1968	133	0	4.05	....	....	....	....	....	....	....
1993-94	Windsor Spitfires	OHL	45	20	18	0	2312	158	1	4.10	4	0	4	240	16	0	4.00
1994-95	Windsor Spitfires	OHL	48	26	14	3	2644	147	3	3.34	3	0	1	94	6	1	3.83
1995-96	Oshawa Generals	OHL	31	15	9	4	1763	78	3	2.65	5	1	4	315	23	0	4.38
1996-97	Baton Rouge	ECHL	10	5	2	1	501	22	0	2.63	....	....	....	....	....	....	....
	Worcester	AHL	29	14	10	1	1482	75	1	3.04	....	....	....	....	....	....	....
1997-98	Baton Rouge	ECHL	36	14	11	6	1949	96	1	2.96	....	....	....	....	....	....	....
1998-99	Mississippi	ECHL	44	22	12	5	2337	112	1	2.88	*18	*14	4	*1252	42	3	2.01
99-2000	Lowell	AHL	46	15	23	3	2595	126	3	2.91	1	0	1	60	2	0	2.01

Named ECHL Playoff MVP (1999)

Signed as a free agent by **St. Louis**, December 30, 1996. Signed as a free agent by **LA Kings**, February 18, 2000.

SHIELDS, Steve (SHEELDS, STEEV) S.J.

Goaltender. Catches left. 6'3", 215 lbs. Born, Toronto, Ont., July 19, 1972.
(Buffalo's 5th choice, 101st overall, in 1991 Entry Draft).

			Regular Season								Playoffs						
Season	Club	Lea	GP	W	L	T	Mins	GA	SO	Avg	GP	W	L	Mins	GA	SO	Avg
1989-90	St. Mary's	OJHL-B	26	....	....	....	1512	121	0	4.80	....	....	....	....	....	....	....
1990-91	U. of Michigan	CCHA	37	26	6	3	1963	106	0	3.24	....	....	....	....	....	....	....
1991-92	U. of Michigan	CCHA	*37	*27	7	2	*2090	99	1	2.84	....	....	....	....	....	....	....
1992-93	U. of Michigan	CCHA	*39	*30	6	2	2027	75	2	*2.22	....	....	....	....	....	....	....
1993-94	U. of Michigan	CCHA	36	*28	6	1	1961	87	0	2.66	....	....	....	....	....	....	....
1994-95	Rochester	AHL	13	3	8	0	673	53	0	4.72	1	0	0	20	3	0	9.00
	South Carolina	ECHL	21	11	5	2	1158	52	2	2.69	3	0	2	144	11	0	4.58
1995-96	**Buffalo**	**NHL**	**2**	**1**	**0**	**0**	**75**	**4**	**0**	**3.20**	....	....	....	....	....	....	....
	Rochester	AHL	43	20	17	2	2357	140	1	3.56	*19	*15	3	*1127	47	1	2.50
1996-97	**Buffalo**	**NHL**	**13**	**3**	**8**	**2**	**789**	**39**	**0**	**2.97**	**10**	**4**	**6**	**570**	**26**	**1**	**2.74**
	Rochester	AHL	23	14	6	2	1331	60	1	2.70	....	....	....	....	....	....	....
1997-98	**Buffalo**	**NHL**	**16**	**3**	**6**	**4**	**785**	**37**	**0**	**2.83**	....	....	....	....	....	....	....
	Rochester	AHL	1	0	1	0	59	3	0	3.04	....	....	....	....	....	....	....
1998-99	**San Jose**	**NHL**	**37**	**15**	**11**	**8**	**2162**	**80**	**4**	**2.22**	**1**	**0**	**1**	**60**	**6**	**0**	**6.00**
99-2000	**San Jose**	**NHL**	**67**	**27**	**30**	**8**	**3797**	**162**	**4**	**2.56**	**12**	**5**	**7**	**696**	**36**	**0**	**3.10**
	NHL Totals		**135**	**49**	**55**	**22**	**7608**	**322**	**8**	**2.54**	**23**	**9**	**14**	**1326**	**68**	**1**	**3.08**

CCHA First All-Star Team (1993, 1994) • NCAA West Second All-American Team (1993, 1994)

Traded to **San Jose** by **Buffalo** with Buffalo's 4th round choice (Miroskav Zalesak) in 1998 Entry Draft for Kay Whitmore, Colorado's 2nd round choice (previously acquired, Buffalo selected Jaroslav Kristek) in 1998 Entry Draft and San Jose's 5th round choice (later traded to Columbus - Columbus selected Tyler Kolarik) in 2000 Entry Draft, June 18, 1998.

SHTALENKOV, Mikhail (shtuh-LEHN-kahf, mihk-HAIL)

Goaltender. Catches left. 6'2", 185 lbs. Born, Moscow, USSR, October 20, 1965.
(Anaheim's 5th choice, 108th overall, in 1993 Entry Draft).

			Regular Season								Playoffs						
Season	Club	Lea	GP	W	L	T	Mins	GA	SO	Avg	GP	W	L	Mins	GA	SO	Avg
1986-87	Dynamo Moscow	USSR	17	....	....	....	893	36	1	2.41	....	....	....	....	....	....	....
1987-88	Dynamo Moscow	USSR	25	....	....	....	1302	72	1	3.31	....	....	....	....	....	....	....
1988-89	Dynamo Moscow	USSR	4	....	....	....	80	3	0	2.25	....	....	....	....	....	....	....
1989-90	Dynamo Moscow	USSR	6	....	....	....	20	1	0	3.00	....	....	....	....	....	....	....
1990-91	Dynamo Moscow	USSR	31	....	....	....	1568	56	2	2.14	....	....	....	....	....	....	....
1991-92	Dynamo Moscow	CIS	27	....	....	....	1268	45	1	2.12	....	....	....	....	....	....	....
	Russia	Olympics	8	*7	1	0	440	12	1	1.64	....	....	....	....	....	....	....
1992-93	Milwaukee	IHL	47	26	14	5	2669	135	2	3.03	3	1	2	209	11	0	3.16
1993-94	**Anaheim**	**NHL**	**10**	**3**	**4**	**1**	**543**	**24**	**0**	**2.65**	....	....	....	....	....	....	....
	San Diego Gulls	IHL	28	15	11	2	1616	93	0	3.45	....	....	....	....	....	....	....
1994-95	**Anaheim**	**NHL**	**18**	**4**	**7**	**1**	**810**	**49**	**0**	**3.63**	....	....	....	....	....	....	....
1995-96	**Anaheim**	**NHL**	**30**	**7**	**16**	**3**	**1637**	**85**	**0**	**3.12**	....	....	....	....	....	....	....
1996-97	**Anaheim**	**NHL**	**24**	**7**	**8**	**1**	**1079**	**52**	**2**	**2.89**	**4**	**0**	**3**	**211**	**10**	**0**	**2.84**
1997-98	**Anaheim**	**NHL**	**40**	**13**	**18**	**5**	**2049**	**110**	**1**	**3.22**	....	....	....	....	....	....	....
	Russia	Olympics	5	4	1	0	290	8	0	1.65	....	....	....	....	....	....	....
1998-99	**Edmonton**	**NHL**	**34**	**12**	**17**	**3**	**1819**	**81**	**3**	**2.67**	....	....	....	....	....	....	....
	Phoenix	**NHL**	**4**	**1**	**2**	**1**	**243**	**9**	**0**	**2.22**	....	....	....	....	....	....	....
99-2000	**Phoenix**	**NHL**	**15**	**7**	**6**	**2**	**904**	**36**	**2**	**2.39**	....	....	....	....	....	....	....
	Florida	**NHL**	**15**	**8**	**4**	**2**	**882**	**34**	**0**	**2.31**	....	....	....	....	....	....	....
	NHL Totals		**190**	**62**	**82**	**19**	**9966**	**480**	**8**	**2.89**	**4**	**0**	**3**	**211**	**10**	**0**	**2.84**

USSR Rookie of the Year (1987) • Won Garry F. Longman Memorial Trophy (Top Rookie - IHL) (1993)

Claimed by **Nashville** from **Anaheim** in Expansion Draft, June 26, 1998. Traded to **Edmonton** by **Nashville** with Jim Dowd for Eric Fichaud, Drake Berehowsky and Greg de Vries, October 1, 1998. Traded to **Phoenix** by **Edmonton** for Phoenix's 5th round choice (later traded to Nashville - Nashville selected Matt Koalska) in 2000 Entry Draft, March 11, 1999. Traded to **Florida** by **Phoenix** with Phoenix's 4th round choice (Chris Eade) in 2000 Entry Draft for Sean Burke and Florida's 5th round choice (Nate Kiser) in 2000 Entry Draft, November 18, 1999.

SHULMISTRA, Richard (shuhl-MIHS-trah, RIH-chahrd) FLA.

Goaltender. Catches right. 6'2", 185 lbs. Born, Sudbury, Ont., April 1, 1971.
(Quebec's 1st choice, 4th overall, in 1992 Supplemental Draft).

			Regular Season								Playoffs						
Season	**Club**	**Lea**	**GP**	**W**	**L**	**T**	**Mins**	**GA**	**SO**	**Avg**	**GP**	**W**	**L**	**Mins**	**GA**	**SO**	**Avg**
1988-89	St. Michael's	OJHL-B	12	10	2	0	715	29	*1	2.43	....	....	....	....	....	....	....
1989-90	Thunder Bay	TBJHL	37	....	....	....	2090	131	0	3.76	....	....	....	....	....	....	....
1990-91	U. of Miami-Ohio	CCHA	20	2	12	2	920	80	0	5.21	....	....	....	....	....	....	....
1991-92	U. of Miami-Ohio	CCHA	19	3	5	2	850	67	0	4.72	....	....	....	....	....	....	....
1992-93	U. of Miami-Ohio	CCHA	33	22	6	4	1949	88	1	2.71	....	....	....	....	....	....	....
1993-94	U. of Miami-Ohio	CCHA	27	13	12	1	1521	74	0	2.92	....	....	....	....	....	....	....
1994-95	Cornwall Aces	AHL	20	4	9	2	937	58	0	3.71	8	4	3	446	22	0	2.95
1995-96	Cornwall Aces	AHL	36	9	18	2	1844	100	0	3.25	1	0	0	9	1	0	6.76
1996-97	Albany River Rats	AHL	23	5	9	2	1062	43	2	2.43	2	1	0	77	2	0	1.56
1997-98	Fort Wayne	IHL	11	3	8	0	656	34	1	3.11	....	....	....	....	....	....	....
	New Jersey	**NHL**	**1**	**0**	**1**	**0**	**62**	**2**	**0**	**1.94**	....	....	....	....	....	....	....
	Albany River Rats	AHL	35	20	8	4	2022	78	2	*2.31	13	8	3	696	32	1	2.76
1998-99	Manitoba Moose	IHL	44	25	11	7	2469	117	2	2.84	....	....	....	....	....	....	....
	Albany River Rats	AHL	12	6	4	0	596	34	0	3.42	2	0	2	64	3	0	2.82
99-2000	**Florida**	**NHL**	**1**	**1**	**0**	**0**	**60**	**1**	**0**	**1.00**	....	....	....	....	....	....	....
	Louisville	AHL	27	12	11	2	1447	80	2	3.32	....	....	....	....	....	....	....
	Orlando	IHL	9	5	1	3	520	16	1	1.85	1	0	1	30	3	0	5.90
	NHL Totals		**2**	**1**	**1**	**0**	**122**	**3**	**0**	**1.48**	....	....	....	....	....	....	....

CCHA Second All-Star Team (1993) • AHL Second All-Star Team (1998)

Transferred to **Colorado** after **Quebec** franchise relocated, June 21, 1995. Signed as a free agent by **New Jersey**, December 31, 1997. Signed as a free agent by **Florida**, July 27, 1999.

SKUDRA, Peter (SKOO-druh, PEE-tuhr) PIT.

Goaltender. Catches left. 6'1", 189 lbs. Born, Riga, USSR, April 24, 1973.

			Regular Season								Playoffs						
Season	**Club**	**Lea**	**GP**	**W**	**L**	**T**	**Mins**	**GA**	**SO**	**Avg**	**GP**	**W**	**L**	**Mins**	**GA**	**SO**	**Avg**
1992-93	Pardaugava Riga	CIS	27	....	....	....	1498	74	....	2.96	1	....	....	60	5	0	5.00
1993-94	Pardaugava Riga	CIS	14	....	....	....	783	42	....	3.22	1	....	....	55	4	0	4.36
1994-95	Greensboro	ECHL	33	13	9	5	1612	113	0	4.20	6	2	2	341	28	0	4.92
	Memphis	CHL	2	0	1	0	60	8	0	6.01	....	....	....	....	....	....	....
1995-96	Erie Panthers	ECHL	12	3	8	1	681	47	0	4.14	....	....	....	....	....	....	....
	Johnstown Chiefs	ECHL	30	12	11	4	1657	98	0	3.55	....	....	....	....	....	....	....
1996-97	Hamilton Bulldogs	AHL	32	8	16	2	1615	101	0	3.75	....	....	....	....	....	....	....
	Johnstown Chiefs	ECHL	4	2	1	1	200	11	0	3.30	....	....	....	....	....	....	....
1997-98	**Pittsburgh**	**NHL**	**17**	**6**	**4**	**3**	**851**	**26**	**0**	**1.83**	....	....	....	....	....	....	....
	Houston Aeros	IHL	9	5	3	1	499	23	0	2.77	....	....	....	....	....	....	....
	Kansas City	IHL	13	10	3	0	775	37	0	2.86	8	4	4	512	20	1	*2.34
1998-99	**Pittsburgh**	**NHL**	**37**	**15**	**11**	**5**	**1914**	**89**	**3**	**2.79**	....	....	....	....	....	....	....
99-2000	**Pittsburgh**	**NHL**	**20**	**5**	**7**	**3**	**922**	**48**	**1**	**3.12**	**1**	**0**	**0**	**20**	**1**	**0**	**3.00**
	NHL Totals		**74**	**26**	**22**	**11**	**3687**	**163**	**4**	**2.65**	**1**	**0**	**0**	**20**	**1**	**0**	**3.00**

Signed as a free agent by **Pittsburgh**, September 25, 1997. • Played w/ RHI's Oklahoma Coyotes in 1996 (18-10-4-1-(1)-721-90-0-5.99).

SMANGS, Henrik (SMOHNGS, HEHN-rihk) PHX.

Goaltender. Catches left. 5'11", 174 lbs. Born, Leksand, Sweden, January 19, 1976.
(Winnipeg's 9th choice, 212th overall, in 1994 Entry Draft).

			Regular Season								Playoffs						
Season	**Club**	**Lea**	**GP**	**W**	**L**	**T**	**Mins**	**GA**	**SO**	**Avg**	**GP**	**W**	**L**	**Mins**	**GA**	**SO**	**Avg**
1996-97	Mora IK	Swede-2	5	....	....	....	260	12	....	2.70	....	....	....	....	....	....	....
1997-98	Mora IK	Swede-2	5	....	....	....	300	10	1	2.00	....	....	....	....	....	....	....
1998-99	Tupelo T-Rex	WPHL	31	7	15	1	1497	108	0	4.33	....	....	....	....	....	....	....
99-2000	Tupelo T-Rex	WPHL	3	0	1	1	135	9	0	3.97	....	....	....	....	....	....	....
	Arkansas	ECHL	2	0	1	0	70	8	0	6.83	....	....	....	....	....	....	....

Transferred to **Phoenix** after **Winnipeg** franchise relocated, July 1, 1996.

SMID, Zdenek (SHMIHD, zuh-DEHN-ehk) ATL.

Goaltender. Catches left. 5'10", 172 lbs. Born, Plzen, Czech., February 3, 1980.
(Atlanta's 7th choice, 168th overall, in 2000 Entry Draft).

			Regular Season								Playoffs						
Season	**Club**	**Lea**	**GP**	**W**	**L**	**T**	**Mins**	**GA**	**SO**	**Avg**	**GP**	**W**	**L**	**Mins**	**GA**	**SO**	**Avg**
1996-97	HC Plzen-Jr.	Cze-Rep	23	....	....	....	1304	48	....	2.21	....	....	....	....	....	....	....
1997-98	HC Plzen-Jr.	Cze-Rep	30	....	....	....	1601	91	....	3.41	....	....	....	....	....	....	....
1998-99	Karlovy Vary	Cze-Rep	3	....	....	....	160	11	....	4.13	....	....	....	....	....	....	....
99-2000	Karlovy Vary-Jr.	Cze-Rep	24	....	....	....	1409	54	....	2.30	2	....	....	86	9	....	6.28
	Karlovy Vary	Cze-Rep	14	....	....	....	650	41	0	3.78	3	....	....	150	8	....	3.20

SNEE, Brandon (SNEE) NYR

Goaltender. Catches left. 6'1", 195 lbs. Born, Philadelphia, PA, June 10, 1980.
(NY Rangers' 5th choice, 143rd overall, in 2000 Entry Draft).

			Regular Season								Playoffs						
Season	**Club**	**Lea**	**GP**	**W**	**L**	**T**	**Mins**	**GA**	**SO**	**Avg**	**GP**	**W**	**L**	**Mins**	**GA**	**SO**	**Avg**
1998-99	Union College	ECAC	19	1	12	3	1011	59	1	3.50	....	....	....	....	....	....	....
99-2000	Union College	ECAC	*31	8	22	1	1765	114	0	3.87	....	....	....	....	....	....	....

SNOW, Garth (SNOH, GAHRTH)

Goaltender. Catches left. 6'3", 200 lbs. Born, Wrentham, MA, July 28, 1969.
(Quebec's 6th choice, 114th overall, in 1987 Entry Draft).

			Regular Season								Playoffs						
Season	**Club**	**Lea**	**GP**	**W**	**L**	**T**	**Mins**	**GA**	**SO**	**Avg**	**GP**	**W**	**L**	**Mins**	**GA**	**SO**	**Avg**
1986-87	Mount St. Charles	H.S.	30	....	....	....	1795	53	10	1.77	....	....	....	....	....	....	....
1987-88	Stratford Cullitons	OJHL-B	30	20	6	0	1642	93	2	3.40	....	....	....	....	....	....	....
1988-89	U. of Maine	H-East	5	2	2	0	241	14	1	3.49	....	....	....	....	....	....	....
1989-90	U. of Maine	H-East	DID NOT PLAY – ACADEMICALLY INELIGIBLE														
1990-91	U. of Maine	H-East	25	*18	4	0	1290	64	2	2.98	....	....	....	....	....	....	....
1991-92	U. of Maine	H-East	31	*25	4	2	1792	73	*2	*2.44	....	....	....	....	....	....	....
1992-93	U. of Maine	H-East	23	*21	0	1	1210	42	1	*2.08	....	....	....	....	....	....	....
1993-94	United States	Nt-Team	23	13	5	3	1324	71	1	3.22	....	....	....	....	....	....	....
	United States	Olympics	5	1	3	1	299	17	0	3.41	....	....	....	....	....	....	....
	Quebec	**NHL**	**5**	**3**	**2**	**0**	**279**	**16**	**0**	**3.44**	....	....	....	....	....	....	....
	Cornwall Aces	AHL	16	6	5	3	927	51	0	3.30	13	8	5	790	42	0	3.19
1994-95	Cornwall Aces	AHL	*62	*32	20	7	*3558	162	3	2.73	8	4	3	402	14	*2	*2.09
	Quebec	**NHL**	**2**	**1**	**1**	**0**	**119**	**11**	**0**	**5.55**	**1**	**0**	**0**	**9**	**1**	**0**	**6.67**
1995-96	**Philadelphia**	**NHL**	**26**	**12**	**8**	**4**	**1437**	**69**	**0**	**2.88**	**1**	**0**	**0**	**1**	**0**	**0**	**0.00**
1996-97	**Philadelphia**	**NHL**	**35**	**14**	**8**	**8**	**1884**	**79**	**2**	**2.52**	**12**	**8**	**4**	**699**	**33**	**0**	**2.83**
1997-98	**Philadelphia**	**NHL**	**29**	**14**	**9**	**4**	**1651**	**67**	**1**	**2.43**	....	....	....	....	....	....	....
	Vancouver	**NHL**	**12**	**3**	**6**	**0**	**504**	**26**	**0**	**3.10**	....	....	....	....	....	....	....
1998-99	**Vancouver**	**NHL**	**65**	**20**	**31**	**8**	**3501**	**171**	**6**	**2.93**	....	....	....	....	....	....	....
99-2000	**Vancouver**	**NHL**	**32**	**10**	**15**	**3**	**1712**	**76**	**0**	**2.66**	....	....	....	....	....	....	....
	NHL Totals		**206**	**77**	**80**	**27**	**11087**	**515**	**9**	**2.79**	**14**	**8**	**4**	**709**	**34**	**0**	**2.88**

Hockey East Second All-Star Team (1992, 1993) • NCAA Championship All-Tournament Team (1993)

Transferred to **Colorado** after **Quebec** franchise relocated, June 21, 1995. Traded to **Philadelphia** by **Colorado** for Philadelphia's 3rd (later traded to Washington - Washington selected Shawn McNeil) and 6th (Kai Fischer) round choices in 1996 Entry Draft, July 12, 1995. Traded to **Vancouver** by **Philadelphia** for Sean Burke, March 4, 1998.

STANA, Ratislav (STAN-ah, RAH-tih-slahv) WSH.

Goaltender. Catches left. 6'2", 161 lbs. Born, Kosice, Czech., January 10, 1980.
(Washington's 8th choice, 193rd overall, in 1998 Entry Draft).

			Regular Season								Playoffs						
Season	**Club**	**Lea**	**GP**	**W**	**L**	**T**	**Mins**	**GA**	**SO**	**Avg**	**GP**	**W**	**L**	**Mins**	**GA**	**SO**	**Avg**
1997-98	HC Kosice	Slovak-Jr.	32	....	....	....	1920	56	2	1.75	....	....	....	....	....	....	....
1998-99	Moose Jaw	WHL	36	21	14	1	2131	123	2	3.46	9	4	5	544	30	0	3.31
99-2000	Moose Jaw	WHL	14	4	9	0	730	48	0	3.95	....	....	....	....	....	....	....
	Calgary Hitman	WHL	16	13	2	1	971	37	1	2.29	9	7	2	526	21	1	2.40

STORR, Jamie (STOHR, JAY-mee) L.A.

Goaltender. Catches left. 6'2", 195 lbs. Born, Brampton, Ont., December 28, 1975.
(Los Angeles' 1st choice, 7th overall, in 1994 Entry Draft).

			Regular Season								Playoffs						
Season	**Club**	**Lea**	**GP**	**W**	**L**	**T**	**Mins**	**GA**	**SO**	**Avg**	**GP**	**W**	**L**	**Mins**	**GA**	**SO**	**Avg**
1990-91	Brampton Caps	OJHL-B	24	....	....	....	1145	91	0	4.77	15	....	....	885	60	0	4.07
1991-92	Owen Sound	OHL	34	11	16	1	1732	128	0	4.43	5	1	4	299	28	0	5.62
1992-93	Owen Sound	OHL	41	20	17	3	2362	180	0	4.57	8	4	4	454	35	0	4.63
1993-94	Owen Sound	OHL	35	21	11	1	2004	120	1	3.59	9	4	5	547	44	0	4.83
1994-95	Owen Sound	OHL	17	5	9	2	977	64	0	3.93	....	....	....	....	....	....	....
	Los Angeles	**NHL**	**5**	**1**	**3**	**1**	**263**	**17**	**0**	**3.88**	....	....	....	....	....	....	....
	Windsor Spitfires	OHL	4	3	1	0	241	8	1	1.99	10	6	3	520	34	1	3.92
1995-96	**Los Angeles**	**NHL**	**5**	**3**	**1**	**0**	**262**	**12**	**0**	**2.75**	....	....	....	....	....	....	....
	Phoenix	IHL	48	22	20	4	2711	139	2	3.08	2	1	1	118	4	1	2.03
1996-97	**Los Angeles**	**NHL**	**5**	**2**	**1**	**1**	**265**	**11**	**0**	**2.49**	....	....	....	....	....	....	....
	Phoenix	IHL	44	16	22	4	2441	147	0	3.61	....	....	....	....	....	....	....
1997-98	**Los Angeles**	**NHL**	**17**	**9**	**5**	**1**	**920**	**34**	**2**	**2.22**	**3**	**0**	**2**	**145**	**9**	**0**	**3.72**
	Long Beach	IHL	11	7	2	1	629	31	0	2.96	....	....	....	....	....	....	....
1998-99	**Los Angeles**	**NHL**	**28**	**12**	**12**	**2**	**1525**	**61**	**4**	**2.40**	....	....	....	....	....	....	....
99-2000	**Los Angeles**	**NHL**	**42**	**18**	**15**	**5**	**2206**	**93**	**1**	**2.53**	**1**	**0**	**1**	**36**	**2**	**0**	**3.33**
	NHL Totals		**102**	**45**	**37**	**10**	**5441**	**228**	**7**	**2.51**	**4**	**0**	**3**	**181**	**11**	**0**	**3.65**

OHL First All-Star Team (1994) • NHL All-Rookie Team (1998, 1999)

SWANSON, Kevin (SWAHN-suhn) VAN.

Goaltender. Catches . 5'10", 170 lbs. Born, Calgary, Alta., April 18, 1980.
(Vancouver's 6th choice, 189th overall, in 1999 Entry Draft).

			Regular Season								Playoffs						
Season	**Club**	**Lea**	**GP**	**W**	**L**	**T**	**Mins**	**GA**	**SO**	**Avg**	**GP**	**W**	**L**	**Mins**	**GA**	**SO**	**Avg**
1996-97	Red Deer Chiefs	AMHL	20	....	....	....	1284	94	0	4.39	....	....	....	....	....	....	....
1997-98	Prince George	WHL	28	14	11	1	1532	93	0	3.64	....	....	....	....	....	....	....
1998-99	Kelowna Rockets	WHL	50	18	23	3	2507	144	2	3.45	6	2	4	355	14	0	2.37
99-2000	Kelowna Rockets	WHL	68	25	40	3	3943	194	*7	2.95	5	1	4	297	16	0	3.23

• WHL West First All-Star Team (2000)

SZUPER, Levente (SHOO-puhr, leh-VEHN-Teh) CGY.

Goaltender. Catches left. 5'10", 178 lbs. Born, Budapest, Hungary, June 11, 1980.
(Calgary's 4th choice, 116th overall, in 2000 Entry Draft).

			Regular Season								Playoffs						
Season	**Club**	**Lea**	**GP**	**W**	**L**	**T**	**Mins**	**GA**	**SO**	**Avg**	**GP**	**W**	**L**	**Mins**	**GA**	**SO**	**Avg**
1996-97	TC Budapest-Jr.	Hungary	10	....	....	....	600	9	....	0.90	....	....	....	....	....	....	....
	TC Budapest	Hungary	30	....	....	....	1660	74	3	2.67	....	....	....	....	....	....	....
1997-98	Krefelder EV	DEL-Jr.	40	....	....	....	2300	103	3	2.69	....	....	....	....	....	....	....
1998-99	Ottawa 67's	OHL	32	22	6	3	1800	70	4	2.33	4	2	2	241	11	*1	2.74
99-2000	Ottawa 67's	OHL	53	31	15	2	2862	122	*5	2.56	11	6	5	680	35	1	3.09

TABARACCI, Rick (tab-uh-RA-chee, RIHK) DAL.

Goaltender. Catches left. 6'1", 190 lbs. Born, Toronto, Ont., January 2, 1969.
(Pittsburgh's 2nd choice, 26th overall, in 1987 Entry Draft).

			Regular Season								Playoffs						
Season	**Club**	**Lea**	**GP**	**W**	**L**	**T**	**Mins**	**GA**	**SO**	**Avg**	**GP**	**W**	**L**	**Mins**	**GA**	**SO**	**Avg**
1985-86	Markham Waxers	OJHL	40	19	11	6	2176	188	1	5.18	....	....	....	....	....	....	....
1986-87	Cornwall Royals	OHL	*59	23	32	3	*3347	290	1	5.20	5	1	4	303	26	0	3.17
1987-88	Cornwall Royals	OHL	58	*33	18	6	3448	200	*3	3.48	11	5	6	642	37	0	3.46
	Muskegon	IHL	....	....	....	....	....	....	....	....	1	0	0	13	1	0	4.62
1988-89	**Pittsburgh**	**NHL**	**1**	**0**	**0**	**0**	**33**	**4**	**0**	**7.27**	....	....	....	....	....	....	....
	Cornwall Royals	OHL	50	24	20	5	2974	210	1	4.24	18	10	8	1080	65	*1	3.61
1989-90	Moncton Hawks	AHL	27	10	15	2	1580	107	2	4.06	....	....	....	....	....	....	....
	Fort Wayne	IHL	22	8	9	1	1064	73	0	4.12	3	1	2	159	19	0	7.17
1990-91	**Winnipeg**	**NHL**	**24**	**4**	**9**	**4**	**1093**	**71**	**1**	**3.90**	....	....	....	....	....	....	....
	Moncton Hawks	AHL	11	4	5	2	645	41	0	3.81	....	....	....	....	....	....	....
1991-92	**Winnipeg**	**NHL**	**18**	**6**	**7**	**3**	**966**	**52**	**0**	**3.23**	**7**	**3**	**4**	**387**	**26**	**0**	**4.03**
	Moncton Hawks	AHL	23	10	11	1	1313	80	0	3.66	....	....	....	....	....	....	....
1992-93	**Winnipeg**	**NHL**	**19**	**5**	**10**	**0**	**959**	**70**	**0**	**4.38**	....	....	....	....	....	....	....
	Moncton Hawks	AHL	5	2	1	2	290	18	0	3.72	....	....	....	....	....	....	....
	Washington	**NHL**	**6**	**3**	**2**	**0**	**343**	**10**	**2**	**1.75**	**4**	**1**	**3**	**304**	**14**	**0**	**2.76**
1993-94	**Washington**	**NHL**	**32**	**13**	**14**	**2**	**1770**	**91**	**2**	**3.08**	**2**	**0**	**2**	**111**	**6**	**0**	**3.24**
	Portland Pirates	AHL	3	3	0	0	176	8	0	2.72	....	....	....	....	....	....	....
1994-95	**Washington**	**NHL**	**8**	**1**	**3**	**2**	**394**	**16**	**0**	**2.44**	....	....	....	....	....	....	....
	Chicago Wolves	IHL	2	1	1	0	119	9	0	4.51	....	....	....	....	....	....	....
	Calgary	**NHL**	**5**	**2**	**0**	**1**	**202**	**5**	**0**	**1.49**	**1**	**0**	**0**	**19**	**0**	**0**	**0.00**
1995-96	**Calgary**	**NHL**	**43**	**19**	**16**	**3**	**2391**	**117**	**3**	**2.94**	**3**	**0**	**3**	**204**	**7**	**0**	**2.06**
1996-97	**Calgary**	**NHL**	**7**	**2**	**4**	**0**	**361**	**14**	**1**	**2.33**	....	....	....	....	....	....	....
	Tampa Bay	**NHL**	**55**	**20**	**25**	**6**	**3012**	**138**	**4**	**2.75**	....	....	....	....	....	....	....
1997-98	**Calgary**	**NHL**	**42**	**13**	**22**	**6**	**2419**	**116**	**0**	**2.88**	....	....	....	....	....	....	....
1998-99	**Washington**	**NHL**	**23**	**4**	**12**	**3**	**1193**	**50**	**2**	**2.51**	....	....	....	....	....	....	....
99-2000	Canada	Nt-Team	1	0	1	0	60	4	0	4.00	....	....	....	....	....	....	....
	Atlanta	**NHL**	**1**	**0**	**1**	**0**	**59**	**4**	**0**	**4.07**	....	....	....	....	....	....	....
	Cleveland	IHL	10	5	5	0	568	28	0	2.96	....	....	....	....	....	....	....
	Orlando	IHL	21	11	6	4	1231	53	1	2.58	....	....	....	....	....	....	....
	Colorado	**NHL**	**2**	**1**	**0**	**0**	**60**	**2**	**0**	**2.00**	....	....	....	....	....	....	....
	Utah Grizzlies	IHL	11	4	4	3	626	24	1	2.30	3	1	2	179	7	0	2.34
	NHL Totals		**286**	**93**	**125**	**30**	**15255**	**760**	**15**	**2.99**	**17**	**4**	**12**	**1025**	**53**	**0**	**3.10**

OHL First All-Star Team (1988) • OHL Second All-Star Team (1989)

Traded to **Winnipeg** by **Pittsburgh** with Randy Cunneyworth and Dave McLlwain for Jim Kyte, Andrew McBain and Randy Gilhen, June 17, 1989. Traded to **Washington** by **Winnipeg** for Jim Hrivnak and Washington's 2nd round choice (Alexei Budayev) in 1993 Entry Draft, March 22, 1993. Traded to **Calgary** by **Washington** for Calgary's 5th round choice (Joel Cort) in 1995 Entry Draft, April 7, 1995. Traded to **Tampa Bay** by **Calgary** for Aaron Gavey, November 19, 1996. Traded to **Calgary** by **Tampa Bay** for Calgary's 4th round choice (Eric Beaudoin) in 1998 Entry Draft, June 21, 1997. Traded to **Washington** by **Calgary** for future considerations, August 7, 1998. Signed as a free agent by **Atlanta**, September, 1999. Traded to **Colorado** by **Atlanta** for Shean Donovan, December 8, 1999. Selected by **Columbus** from **Colorado** in Expansion Draft, June 23, 2000. Signed as a free agent by **Dallas**, July 12, 2000.

TALLAS, Robbie (TAL-as, RAW-bee) CHI.

Goaltender. Catches left. 6', 170 lbs. Born, Edmonton, Alta., March 20, 1973.

			Regular Season								Playoffs						
Season	Club	Lea	GP	W	L	T	Mins	GA	SO	Avg	GP	W	L	Mins	GA	SO	Avg
1990-91	Penticton	BCJHL	37				2055	196	0	5.72							
1991-92	Seattle T-Birds	WHL	14	4	7	0	708	52	0	4.41							
	South Surrey	BCJHL	19	6	12	0	1043	112	1	6.44							
1992-93	Seattle T-Birds	WHL	58	24	23	3	3151	194	2	3.69	5	1	4	333	18	0	3.24
1993-94	Seattle T-Birds	WHL	51	23	21	3	2849	188	0	3.96	9	5	4	567	40	0	4.23
1994-95	Charlotte	ECHL	36	21	9	3	2011	114	0	3.40							
	Providence Bruins	AHL	2	1	0	0	82	4	1	2.90							
1995-96	Boston	NHL	1	1	0	0	60	3	0	3.00							
	Providence Bruins	AHL	37	12	16	7	2136	117	1	3.29	2	0	2	135	9	0	4.01
1996-97	Boston	NHL	28	8	12	1	1244	69	1	3.33							
	Providence Bruins	AHL	24	9	14	1	1424	83	0	3.50							
1997-98	Boston	NHL	14	6	3	3	788	24	1	1.83							
	Providence Bruins	AHL	10	1	8	1	575	39	0	4.07							
1998-99	Boston	NHL	17	7	7	2	987	43	1	2.61							
99-2000	Boston	NHL	27	4	13	4	1363	72	0	3.17							
	NHL Totals		87	26	35	10	4442	211	3	2.85							

Signed as a free agent by **Boston**, September 13, 1995. Signed as a free agent by **Chicago**, July 31, 2000.

TARASOV, Vadim (ta-RA-sahf, va-DEEM) MTL.

Goaltender. Catches left. 5'11", 158 lbs. Born, Ust-Kamenogorsk, USSR, December 31, 1976.
(Montreal's 9th choice, 196th overall, in 1999 Entry Draft).

			Regular Season								Playoffs						
Season	Club	Lea	GP	W	L	T	Mins	GA	SO	Avg	GP	W	L	Mins	GA	SO	Avg
1995-96	MK Novokuznetsk	CIS	26				1355	60	1	2.66							
1996-97	MK Novokuznetsk	Russia	34				1971	87	0	2.65							
1997-98	MK Novokuznetsk	Russia	23				1364	61	2	2.68							
	MK Novokuznetsk	Russia-2	STATISTICS NOT AVAILABLE														
1998-99	MK Novokuznetsk	Russia	*41				*2346	56	*8	1.43	6			349	16	0	2.75
99-2000	MK Novokuznetsk	Russia	28				1583	66	1	2.50	14			791	26	1	1.97

TELLQVIST, Mikael (TEHL-kvihst, mih-KIGH-ehl) TOR.

Goaltender. Catches left. 5'11", 174 lbs. Born, Sundbyberg, Sweden, September 19, 1979.
(Toronto's 3rd choice, 70th overall, in 2000 Entry Draft).

			Regular Season								Playoffs						
Season	Club	Lea	GP	W	L	T	Mins	GA	SO	Avg	GP	W	L	Mins	GA	SO	Avg
1997-98	Djurgardens IF	Swede-Jr.	23				1380	55		2.39	2			120	8		4.00
1998-99	Djurgardens IF	Sweden	3				124	8	0	3.87	4			240	11	0	2.75
99-2000	Djurgardens IF	Sweden	30				1909	66	2	2.07	13			814	21	3	1.55

TERRERI, Chris (tuh-RAIR-ee, KRIHS) N.J.

Goaltender. Catches left. 5'9", 170 lbs. Born, Providence, RI, November 15, 1964.
(New Jersey's 3rd choice, 87th overall, in 1983 Entry Draft).

			Regular Season								Playoffs						
Season	Club	Lea	GP	W	L	T	Mins	GA	SO	Avg	GP	W	L	Mins	GA	SO	Avg
1982-83	Providence	ECAC	11	7	1	0	528	17	2	1.93							
1983-84	Providence	ECAC	10	4	2	0	391	20	0	3.07							
1984-85	Providence	H-East	33	15	13	5	1956	116	1	3.35							
1985-86	Providence	H-East	22	6	16	0	1320	84	0	3.74							
1986-87	New Jersey	NHL	7	0	3	1	286	21	0	4.41							
	Maine Mariners	AHL	14	4	9	1	765	57	0	4.47							
1987-88	Utica Devils	AHL	7	5	1	0	399	18	0	2.71							
	United States	Nt-Team	26	17	7	2	1430	81	0	3.40							
	United States	Olympics	3				127	14		6.58							
1988-89	New Jersey	NHL	8	0	4	2	402	18	0	2.69							
	Utica Devils	AHL	39	20	15	3	2314	132	0	3.42	2	0	1	80	6	0	4.50
1989-90	New Jersey	NHL	35	15	12	3	1931	110	0	3.42	4	2	2	238	13	0	3.28
1990-91	New Jersey	NHL	53	24	21	7	2970	144	1	2.91	7	3	4	428	21	0	2.94
1991-92	New Jersey	NHL	54	22	22	10	3186	169	1	3.18	7	3	3	386	23	0	3.58
1992-93	New Jersey	NHL	48	19	21	3	2672	151	2	3.39	4	1	3	219	17	0	4.66
1993-94	New Jersey	NHL	44	20	11	4	2340	106	2	2.72	4	3	0	200	9	0	2.70
1994-95♦	New Jersey	NHL	15	3	7	2	734	31	0	2.53	1	0	0	8	0	0	0.00
1995-96	New Jersey	NHL	4	3	0	0	210	9	0	2.57							
	San Jose	NHL	46	13	29	1	2516	155	0	3.70							
1996-97	San Jose	NHL	22	6	10	3	1200	55	0	2.75							
	Chicago	NHL	7	4	1	2	429	19	0	2.66	2	0	0	44	3	0	4.09
1997-98	Chicago	NHL	21	8	10	2	1222	49	2	2.41							
	Indianapolis Ice	IHL	3	2	0	1	180	3	1	1.00							
1998-99	New Jersey	NHL	12	8	3	1	726	30	1	2.48							
99-2000♦	New Jersey	NHL	12	2	9	0	649	37	0	3.42							
	NHL Totals		388	147	163	41	21473	1104	9	3.08	29	12	12	1523	86	0	3.39

Hockey East First All-Star Team (1985) • NCAA East First All-American Team (1985) • NCAA Championship All-Tournament Team (1985) • NCAA Championship Tournament MVP (1985)

Traded to **San Jose** by **New Jersey** for San Jose's 2nd round choice (later traded to Pittsburgh - Pittsburgh selected Pavel Skrbek) in 1996 Entry Draft, November 15, 1995. Traded to **Chicago** by **San Jose** with Ulf Dahlen and Michal Sykora for Ed Belfour, January 25, 1997. Traded to **New Jersey** by **Chicago** for New Jersey's 2nd round choice (Stepan Mokhov) in 1999 Entry Draft, August 25, 1998. Selected by **Minnesota** from **New Jersey** in Expansion Draft, June 23, 2000. Traded to **New Jersey** by **Minnesota** with Minnesota's 9th round choice (later traded to Tampa Bay - Tampa Bay selected Thomas Ziegler) in 2000 Entry Draft for Brad Bombardir, June 23, 2000.

THEODORE, Jose (THEE-uh-dohr, joh-SAY) MTL.

Goaltender. Catches right. 5'11", 189 lbs. Born, Laval, Que., September 13, 1976.
(Montreal's 2nd choice, 44th overall, in 1994 Entry Draft).

			Regular Season								Playoffs						
Season	Club	Lea	GP	W	L	T	Mins	GA	SO	Avg	GP	W	L	Mins	GA	SO	Avg
1990-91	Richelieu Regents	QAAA	42				2520	80	0	1.90							
1991-92	Richelieu Regents	QAAA	24	9	13	2	1440	96	0	3.99							
1992-93	St-Jean Lynx	QMJHL	34	12	16	2	1776	112	0	3.78	3	0	2	175	11	0	3.77
1993-94	St-Jean Lynx	QMJHL	57	20	29	6	3225	194	0	3.61	5	1	4	296	18	0	3.65
1994-95	Hull Olympiques	QMJHL	*58	*32	22	2	*3348	193	5	3.46	*21	*15	6	*1263	59	*1	2.80
	Fredericton	AHL									1	0	1	60	3	0	3.00
1995-96	Montreal	NHL	1	0	0	0	9	1	0	6.67							
	Hull Olympiques	QMJHL	48	33	11	2	2807	158	0	3.38	5	2	3	299	20	0	4.01
1996-97	Montreal	NHL	16	5	6	2	821	53	0	3.87	2	1	1	168	7	0	2.50
	Fredericton	AHL	26	12	12	0	1469	87	0	3.55							
1997-98	Fredericton	AHL	53	20	23	8	3053	145	2	2.85	4	1	3	237	13	0	3.28
	Montreal	NHL									3	0	1	120	1	0	0.50
1998-99	Montreal	NHL	18	4	12	0	913	50	1	3.29							
	Fredericton	AHL	27	12	13	2	1609	77	2	2.87	13	8	5	694	35	1	3.03
99-2000	Montreal	NHL	30	12	13	2	1655	58	5	2.10							
	NHL Totals		65	21	31	4	3398	162	6	2.86	5	1	2	288	8	0	1.67

QMJHL Second All-Star Team (1995, 1996)

THIBAULT, Jocelyn (tee-BOW, JAW-seh-lihn) CHI.

Goaltender. Catches left. 5'11", 170 lbs. Born, Montreal, Que., January 12, 1975.
(Quebec's 1st choice, 10th overall, in 1993 Entry Draft).

			Regular Season								Playoffs						
Season	Club	Lea	GP	W	L	T	Mins	GA	SO	Avg	GP	W	L	Mins	GA	SO	Avg
1990-91	Laval Regents	QAAA	20	14	5	0	1178	78	1	3.94	5	1	4	300	20	0	4.00
1991-92	Trois-Rivieres	QMJHL	30	14	7	1	1496	77	0	3.09	3	1	1	110	4	0	2.19
1992-93	Sherbrooke	QMJHL	56	34	14	5	3190	159	3	2.99	15	9	6	882	57	0	3.87
1993-94	Quebec	NHL	29	8	13	3	1504	83	0	3.31							
	Cornwall Aces	AHL	4	4	0	0	240	9	1	2.25							
1994-95	Sherbrooke	QMJHL	13	6	6	1	776	38	1	2.94							
	Quebec	NHL	18	12	2	2	898	35	1	2.34	3	1	2	148	8	0	3.24
1995-96	Colorado	NHL	10	3	4	2	558	28	0	3.01							
	Montreal	NHL	40	23	13	3	2334	110	3	2.83	6	2	4	311	18	0	3.47
1996-97	Montreal	NHL	61	22	24	11	3397	164	1	2.90	3	0	3	179	13	0	4.36
1997-98	Montreal	NHL	47	19	15	8	2652	109	2	2.47	2	0	0	43	4	0	5.58
1998-99	Montreal	NHL	10	3	4	2	529	23	1	2.61							
	Chicago	NHL	52	21	26	5	3014	136	4	2.71							
99-2000	Chicago	NHL	60	25	26	7	3438	158	3	2.76							
	NHL Totals		327	136	127	43	18324	846	15	2.77	14	3	9	681	43	0	3.79

QMJHL First All-Star Team (1993) • Canadian Major Junior First All-Star Team (1993) • Canadian Major Junior Goaltender of the Year (1993)

Transferred to **Colorado** after **Quebec** franchise relocated, June 21, 1995. Traded to **Montreal** by **Colorado** with Andrei Kovalenko and Martin Rucinsky for Patrick Roy and Mike Keane, December 6, 1995. Traded to **Chicago** by **Montreal** with Dave Manson and Brad Brown for Jeff Hackett, Eric Weinrich, Alain Nasreddine and Tampa Bay's 4th round choice (previously acquired, Montreal selected Chris Dyment) in 1999 Entry Draft, November 16, 1998.

THOMAS, Tim (TAW-mas, TIHM)

Goaltender. Catches left. 5'11", 180 lbs. Born, Flint, MI, April 15, 1974.
(Quebec's 11th choice, 217th overall, in 1994 Entry Draft).

			Regular Season								Playoffs						
Season	Club	Lea	GP	W	L	T	Mins	GA	SO	Avg	GP	W	L	Mins	GA	SO	Avg
1992-93	Davison Academy	H.S.	27				1580	87		3.30							
1993-94	U. of Vermont	ECAC	*33	15	12	6	1864	94	0	3.03							
1994-95	U. of Vermont	ECAC	34	18	13	2	2010	90	*4	*2.69							
1995-96	U. of Vermont	ECAC	37	*26	7	4	*2254	88	*3	*2.34							
1996-97	U. of Vermont	ECAC	36	22	11	3	2158	101	2	2.81							
1997-98	HIFK Helsinki	Finland	18	13	4	1	1035	28	2	*1.62	*9	*9	0	*551	14	*3	*1.52
	Birmingham Bulls	ECHL	6	4	1	1	360	13	1	2.17							
	Houston Aeros	IHL	1	0	1	0	59	4	0	4.01							
1998-99	HIFK Helsinki	Finland	14	8	3	3	833	31	2	2.23	*11	7	4	*658	25	0	2.28
	Hamilton Bulldogs	AHL	15	6	8	0	837	45	0	3.23							
99-2000	Detroit Vipers	IHL	36	10	21	3	2020	120	1	3.56							

ECAC First All-Star Team (1995, 1996) • NCAA East Second All-American Team (1995) • NCAA East First All-American Team (1996)

Signed as a free agent by **Edmonton**, June 4, 1998.

TOSKALA, Vesa (TAWS-kah-lah, VEH-sa) S.J.

Goaltender. Catches left. 5'9", 175 lbs. Born, Tampere, Finland, May 20, 1977.
(San Jose's 4th choice, 90th overall, in 1995 Entry Draft).

			Regular Season								Playoffs						
Season	Club	Lea	GP	W	L	T	Mins	GA	SO	Avg	GP	W	L	Mins	GA	SO	Avg
1994-95	Ilves Tampere	Finn-Jr.	17				956	36		2.26							
1995-96	Ilves Tampere	Finn-Jr.	3				180	3		1.00							
	KooVee Tampere	Finland-2	2				119	5		2.51							
	Ilves Tampere	Finland	37				2073	109	1	3.16	2			78	11		8.49
1996-97	Ilves Tampere	Finland	40	22	12	5	2270	108	0	2.85	8	3	5	479	29	0	3.63
1997-98	Ilves Tampere	Finland	43	*26	13	3	2555	118	1	2.77	*9	6	3	519	18	1	2.08
1998-99	Ilves Tampere	Finland	33	21	12	0	1966	70	*5	2.14	4	1	3	248	14	0	3.39
99-2000	Farjestads BK	Sweden	44				2652	118	3	2.67	7			439	19	0	2.60

TREFILOV, Andrei (TREH-fee-lahf, AWN-dray) CGY.

Goaltender. Catches left. 6', 190 lbs. Born, Kirovo-Chepetsk, USSR, August 31, 1969.
(Calgary's 14th choice, 261st overall, in 1991 Entry Draft).

			Regular Season								Playoffs						
Season	Club	Lea	GP	W	L	T	Mins	GA	SO	Avg	GP	W	L	Mins	GA	SO	Avg
1990-91	Dynamo Moscow	USSR	20				1070	36	0	2.01							
1991-92	Dynamo Moscow	CIS	28				1326	35	0	1.58							
	Russia	Olympics	4	0	0	0	39	2	0	3.08							
1992-93	Calgary	NHL	1	0	0	1	65	5	0	4.62							
	Salt Lake City	IHL	44	23	17	3	2536	135	0	3.19							
1993-94	Calgary	NHL	11	3	4	2	623	26	2	2.50							
	Saint John Flames	AHL	28	10	10	7	1629	93	0	3.42							
1994-95	Calgary	NHL	6	0	3	0	236	16	0	4.07							
	Saint John Flames	AHL	7	1	5	1	383	20	0	3.13							
1995-96	Buffalo	NHL	22	8	8	1	1094	64	0	3.51							
	Rochester	AHL	5	4	1	0	299	13	0	2.61							
1996-97	Buffalo	NHL	3	0	2	0	159	10	0	3.77	1	0	0	5	0	0	0.00
1997-98	Rochester	AHL	3	1	0	1	138	6	0	2.60							
	Chicago	NHL	6	1	4	0	299	17	0	3.41							
	Indianapolis Ice	IHL	1	0	1	0	59	3	0	3.03							
	Russia	Olympics	2	1	0	0	69	4	0	3.45							
1998-99	AK Bars Kazan	Russia	3				160	7	1	2.63							
	Chicago	NHL	1	0	1	0	25	4	0	9.60							
	Indianapolis Ice	IHL	18	9	6	2	986	39	0	2.37							
	Calgary	NHL	4	0	3	0	162	11	0	4.07							
	Detroit Vipers	IHL	27	17	8	2	1613	53	3	1.97	10	6	4	647	22	0	2.04
99-2000	Chicago Wolves	IHL	37	21	9	3	2060	81	3	2.36	9	7	1	489	11	1	*1.35
	NHL Totals		54	12	25	4	2663	153	2	3.45	1	0	0	5	0	0	0.00

IHL Second All-Star Team (1999) • Shared James Norris Memorial Trophy (fewest goals against - IHL) with Kevin Weekes (1999) • Won "Bud" Poile Trophy (Playoff MVP - IHL) (2000)

Signed as a free agent by **Buffalo**, July 11, 1995. Traded to **Chicago** by **Buffalo** for future considerations, November 12, 1997. Traded to **Calgary** by **Chicago** for future considerations, December 29, 1998.

TUGNUTT, Ron (TUHG-nuht, RAWN) CBJ

Goaltender. Catches left. 5'11", 160 lbs. Born, Scarborough, Ont., October 22, 1967.
(Quebec's 4th choice, 81st overall, in 1986 Entry Draft).

			Regular Season								Playoffs						
Season	Club	Lea	GP	W	L	T	Mins	GA	SO	Avg	GP	W	L	Mins	GA	SO	Avg
1983-84	Toronto Nationals	MTHL	34	....	....	....	1690	91	3	2.67	....	....	....	....	....	....	....
	Weston Dukes	OJHL-B	1	0	0	0	20	2	0	6.00	....	....	....	....	....	....	....
1984-85	Peterborough	OHL	18	7	4	2	938	59	0	3.77	....	....	....	....	....	....	....
1985-86	Peterborough	OHL	26	18	7	0	1543	74	1	2.88	3	2	0	133	6	0	2.71
1986-87	Peterborough	OHL	31	21	7	2	1891	88	2	*2.79	6	3	3	374	21	1	3.37
1987-88	**Quebec**	**NHL**	**6**	**2**	**3**	**0**	**284**	**16**	**0**	**3.38**	....	....	....	....	....	....	....
	Fredericton	AHL	34	20	9	4	1964	118	1	3.60	4	1	2	204	11	0	3.24
1988-89	**Quebec**	**NHL**	**26**	**10**	**10**	**3**	**1367**	**82**	**0**	**3.60**	....	....	....	....	....	....	....
	Halifax Citadels	AHL	24	14	7	2	1368	79	1	3.46	....	....	....	....	....	....	....
1989-90	**Quebec**	**NHL**	**35**	**5**	**24**	**3**	**1978**	**152**	**0**	**4.61**	....	....	....	....	....	....	....
	Halifax Citadels	AHL	6	1	5	0	366	23	0	3.77	....	....	....	....	....	....	....
1990-91	**Quebec**	**NHL**	**56**	**12**	**29**	**10**	**3144**	**212**	**0**	**4.05**	....	....	....	....	....	....	....
	Halifax Citadels	AHL	2	0	1	0	100	8	0	4.80	....	....	....	....	....	....	....
1991-92	**Quebec**	**NHL**	**30**	**6**	**17**	**3**	**1583**	**106**	**1**	**4.02**	....	....	....	....	....	....	....
	Halifax Citadels	AHL	8	3	3	1	447	30	0	4.03	....	....	....	....	....	....	....
	Edmonton	**NHL**	**3**	**1**	**1**	**0**	**124**	**10**	**0**	**4.84**	**2**	**0**	**0**	**60**	**3**	**0**	**3.00**
1992-93	**Edmonton**	**NHL**	**26**	**9**	**12**	**2**	**1338**	**93**	**0**	**4.17**	....	....	....	....	....	....	....
1993-94	**Anaheim**	**NHL**	**28**	**10**	**15**	**1**	**1520**	**76**	**1**	**3.00**	....	....	....	....	....	....	....
	Montreal	**NHL**	**8**	**2**	**3**	**1**	**378**	**24**	**0**	**3.81**	**1**	**0**	**1**	**59**	**5**	**0**	**5.08**
1994-95	**Montreal**	**NHL**	**7**	**1**	**3**	**1**	**346**	**18**	**0**	**3.12**	....	....	....	....	....	....	....
1995-96	Portland Pirates	AHL	58	21	23	6	3068	171	2	3.34	13	7	6	782	36	1	2.76
1996-97	**Ottawa**	**NHL**	**37**	**17**	**15**	**1**	**1991**	**93**	**3**	**2.80**	**7**	**3**	**4**	**425**	**14**	**1**	**1.98**
1997-98	**Ottawa**	**NHL**	**42**	**15**	**14**	**8**	**2236**	**84**	**3**	**2.25**	**2**	**0**	**1**	**74**	**6**	**0**	**4.86**
1998-99	**Ottawa**	**NHL**	**43**	**22**	**10**	**8**	**2508**	**75**	**3**	***1.79**	**2**	**0**	**2**	**118**	**6**	**0**	**3.05**
99-2000	**Ottawa**	**NHL**	**44**	**18**	**12**	**8**	**2435**	**103**	**4**	**2.54**	....	....	....	....	....	....	....
	Pittsburgh	**NHL**	**7**	**4**	**2**	**0**	**374**	**15**	**0**	**2.41**	**11**	**6**	**5**	**746**	**22**	**2**	**1.77**
	NHL Totals		**398**	**134**	**170**	**49**	**21606**	**1159**	**15**	**3.22**	**25**	**9**	**13**	**1482**	**56**	**3**	**2.27**

OHL First All-Star Team (1987) • Played in NHL All-Star Game (1999)

Traded to **Edmonton** by **Quebec** with Brad Zavisha for Martin Rucinsky, March 10, 1992. Claimed by **Anaheim** from **Edmonton** in Expansion Draft, June 24, 1993. Traded to **Montreal** by **Anaheim** for Stephan Lebeau, February 20, 1994. Signed as a free agent by **Washington**, September 25, 1995. Signed as a free agent by **Ottawa**, August 14, 1996. Traded to **Pittsburgh** by **Ottawa** with Janne Laukkanen for Tom Barrasso, March 14, 2000. Signed as a free agent by **Columbus**, July 4, 2000.

TURCO, Marty (TUHR-koh, MAHR-tee) DAL.

Goaltender. Catches left. 5'11", 183 lbs. Born, Sault Ste. Marie, Ont., August 13, 1975.
(Dallas' 4th choice, 124th overall, in 1994 Entry Draft).

			Regular Season								Playoffs						
Season	Club	Lea	GP	W	L	T	Mins	GA	SO	Avg	GP	W	L	Mins	GA	SO	Avg
1993-94	Cambridge Hawks	OJHL	34	19	10	3	1973	114	0	3.47	....	....	....	....	....	....	....
1994-95	U. of Michigan	CCHA	37	*27	7	1	2063	95	1	2.76	....	....	....	....	....	....	....
1995-96	U. of Michigan	CCHA	*42	*34	7	1	*2335	84	*5	*2.16	....	....	....	....	....	....	....
1996-97	U. of Michigan	CCHA	*41	*33	4	4	*2296	87	*4	*2.27	....	....	....	....	....	....	....
1997-98	U. of Michigan	CCHA	*45	*33	10	1	*2640	95	4	2.16	....	....	....	....	....	....	....
1998-99	Michigan K-Wings	IHL	54	24	17	10	3127	136	1	2.61	5	2	3	300	14	0	2.80
99-2000	Michigan K-Wings	IHL	60	23	27	*7	3399	139	7	2.45	....	....	....	....	....	....	....

NCAA Championship All-Tournament Team (1996, 1998) • CCHA First All-Star Team (1997) • NCAA West First All-American Team (1997) • CCHA Second All-Star Team (1998) • NCAA Championship Tournament MVP (1998) • Won Garry F. Longman Memorial Trophy (Top Rookie - IHL) (1999)

TUREK, Roman (TOOR-ehk, ROH-man) ST.L.

Goaltender. Catches right. 6'3", 190 lbs. Born, Pisek, Czech., May 21, 1970.
(Minnesota's 6th choice, 113th overall, in 1990 Entry Draft).

			Regular Season								Playoffs						
Season	Club	Lea	GP	W	L	T	Mins	GA	SO	Avg	GP	W	L	Mins	GA	SO	Avg
1990-91	MC Budejovice	Czech.	26	....	....	....	1244	98	0	4.70	....	....	....	....	....	....	....
1991-92	MC Budejovice	Czech-2							STATISTICS NOT AVAILABLE								
1992-93	MC Budejovice	Czech.	43	....	....	....	2555	121	....	2.84	....	....	....	....	....	....	....
1993-94	MC Budejovice	Cze-Rep	44	....	....	....	2584	111	....	2.51	3	....	....	180	12	0	4.00
	Czech-Republic	Olympics	2	2	0	0	120	3	....	1.50	....	....	....	....	....	....	....
1994-95	MC Budejovice	Cze-Rep	44	....	....	....	2587	119	....	2.76	9	....	....	498	25	....	3.01
1995-96	EHC Nurnberg	DEL	48	....	....	....	2787	154	....	3.31	5	....	....	338	14	....	2.48
1996-97	**Dallas**	**NHL**	**6**	**3**	**1**	**0**	**263**	**9**	**0**	**2.05**	....	....	....	....	....	....	....
	Michigan K-Wings	IHL	29	8	13	4	1555	77	0	2.97	....	....	....	....	....	....	....
1997-98	**Dallas**	**NHL**	**23**	**11**	**10**	**1**	**1324**	**49**	**1**	**2.22**	....	....	....	....	....	....	....
	Michigan K-Wings	IHL	2	1	1	0	119	5	0	2.51	....	....	....	....	....	....	....
1998-99 ♦	**Dallas**	**NHL**	**26**	**16**	**3**	**3**	**1382**	**48**	**1**	**2.08**	....	....	....	....	....	....	....
99-2000	**St. Louis**	**NHL**	**67**	**42**	**15**	**9**	**3960**	**129**	***7**	**1.95**	**7**	**3**	**4**	**415**	**19**	**0**	**2.75**
	NHL Totals		**122**	**72**	**29**	**13**	**6929**	**235**	**9**	**2.03**	**7**	**3**	**4**	**415**	**19**	**0**	**2.75**

Czech Republic Player of the Year (1994) • Shared William M. Jennings Trophy with Ed Belfour (1999) • NHL Second All-Star Team (2000) • Won William M. Jennings Trophy (2000) • Played in NHL All-Star Game (2000)

Transferred to **Dallas** after **Minnesota** franchise relocated, June 9, 1993. Traded to **St. Louis** by **Dallas** for St. Louis' compensatory 2nd round choice (Dan Jancevski) in 1999 Entry Draft, June 20, 1999.

UNDERHILL, Matt (UHN-duhr-HIHL, MAT) CGY.

Goaltender. Catches left. 6'2", 195 lbs. Born, Merritt, B.C., September 16, 1979.
(Calgary's 8th choice, 170th overall, in 1999 Entry Draft).

			Regular Season								Playoffs						
Season	Club	Lea	GP	W	L	T	Mins	GA	SO	Avg	GP	W	L	Mins	GA	SO	Avg
1997-98	Notre Dame	SJHL	43	18	22	3	2573	132	2	3.07	....	....	....	....	....	....	....
1998-99	Cornell Big Red	ECAC	25	7	10	4	1320	65	1	2.95	....	....	....	....	....	....	....
99-2000	Cornell Big Red	ECAC	18	8	7	1	912	44	1	2.89	....	....	....	....	....	....	....

VALIQUETTE, Stephen (val-ih-KEHT) NYI

Goaltender. Catches left. 6'5", 190 lbs. Born, Etobicoke, Ont., August 20, 1977.
(Los Angeles' 8th choice, 190th overall, in 1996 Entry Draft).

			Regular Season								Playoffs						
Season	Club	Lea	GP	W	L	T	Mins	GA	SO	Avg	GP	W	L	Mins	GA	SO	Avg
1993-94	Burlington	OJHL	30	....	....	....	1663	112	1	4.04	....	....	....	....	....	....	....
1994-95	Smiths Falls Bears	OJHL	21	10	8	3	1275	75	0	3.53	....	....	....	....	....	....	....
	Sudbury Wolves	OHL	4	2	0	0	138	6	0	2.61	....	....	....	....	....	....	....
1995-96	Sudbury Wolves	OHL	39	13	16	2	1887	123	0	3.91	....	....	....	....	....	....	....
1996-97	Sudbury Wolves	OHL	*61	21	29	7	3311	232	1	4.20	....	....	....	....	....	....	....
	Dayton Bombers	ECHL	3	1	0	0	89	6	0	4.03	2	1	1	118	5	0	2.54
1997-98	Sudbury Wolves	OHL	14	5	7	1	807	50	0	3.72	....	....	....	....	....	....	....
	Erie Otters	OHL	28	16	7	3	1525	65	3	2.56	7	3	4	467	15	1	1.93
1998-99	Hampton Roads	ECHL	31	18	7	3	1713	84	1	2.94	2	0	1	60	7	0	7.00
	Lowell	AHL	1	0	1	0	59	3	0	3.05	....	....	....	....	....	....	....
99-2000	**NY Islanders**	**NHL**	**6**	**2**	**0**	**0**	**193**	**6**	**0**	**1.87**	....	....	....	....	....	....	....
	Lowell	AHL	14	8	5	0	727	36	0	2.97	....	....	....	....	....	....	....
	Providence Bruins	AHL	1	1	0	0	60	3	0	3.00	....	....	....	....	....	....	....
	Trenton	ECHL	12	5	6	1	692	36	1	3.12	....	....	....	....	....	....	....
	NHL Totals		**6**	**2**	**0**	**0**	**193**	**6**	**0**	**1.87**	....	....	....	....	....	....	....

Signed as a free agent by **NY Islanders**, August 18, 1998.

VANBIESBROUCK, John (van-BEES-bruhk, JAWN) NYI

Goaltender. Catches left. 5'8", 176 lbs. Born, Detroit, MI, September 4, 1963.
(NY Rangers' 5th choice, 72nd overall, in 1981 Entry Draft).

			Regular Season								Playoffs						
Season	Club	Lea	GP	W	L	T	Mins	GA	SO	Avg	GP	W	L	Mins	GA	SO	Avg
1980-81	Sault Ste. Marie	OMJHL	56	31	16	1	2941	203	0	4.14	11	3	3	457	24	1	3.15
1981-82	Sault Ste. Marie	OHL	31	12	12	2	1686	102	0	3.62	7	1	4	276	20	0	4.35
	NY Rangers	**NHL**	**1**	**1**	**0**	**0**	**60**	**1**	**0**	**1.00**	....	....	....	....	....	....	....
1982-83	Sault Ste. Marie	OHL	*62	39	21	1	3471	209	0	3.61	16	7	6	944	56	*1	3.56
1983-84	**NY Rangers**	**NHL**	**3**	**2**	**1**	**0**	**180**	**10**	**0**	**3.33**	**1**	**0**	**0**	**1**	**0**	**0**	**0.00**
	Tulsa Oilers	CHL	37	20	13	2	2153	124	*3	3.46	4	4	0	240	10	0	*2.50
1984-85	**NY Rangers**	**NHL**	**42**	**12**	**24**	**3**	**2358**	**166**	**1**	**4.22**	**1**	**0**	**0**	**20**	**0**	**0**	**0.00**
1985-86	**NY Rangers**	**NHL**	**61**	***31**	**21**	**5**	**3326**	**184**	**3**	**3.32**	**16**	**8**	**8**	**899**	**49**	***1**	**3.27**
1986-87	**NY Rangers**	**NHL**	**50**	**18**	**20**	**5**	**2656**	**161**	**0**	**3.64**	**4**	**1**	**3**	**195**	**11**	**1**	**3.38**
1987-88	**NY Rangers**	**NHL**	**56**	**27**	**22**	**7**	**3319**	**187**	**2**	**3.38**	....	....	....	....	....	....	....
1988-89	**NY Rangers**	**NHL**	**56**	**28**	**21**	**4**	**3207**	**197**	**0**	**3.69**	**2**	**0**	**1**	**107**	**6**	**0**	**3.36**
1989-90	**NY Rangers**	**NHL**	**47**	**19**	**19**	**7**	**2734**	**154**	**1**	**3.38**	**6**	**2**	**3**	**298**	**15**	**0**	**3.02**
1990-91	**NY Rangers**	**NHL**	**40**	**15**	**18**	**6**	**2257**	**126**	**3**	**3.35**	**1**	**0**	**0**	**52**	**1**	**0**	**1.15**
1991-92	**NY Rangers**	**NHL**	**45**	**27**	**13**	**3**	**2526**	**120**	**2**	**2.85**	**7**	**2**	**5**	**368**	**23**	**0**	**3.75**
1992-93	**NY Rangers**	**NHL**	**48**	**20**	**18**	**7**	**2757**	**152**	**4**	**3.31**	....	....	....	....	....	....	....
1993-94	**Florida**	**NHL**	**57**	**21**	**25**	**11**	**3440**	**145**	**1**	**2.53**	....	....	....	....	....	....	....
1994-95	**Florida**	**NHL**	**37**	**14**	**15**	**4**	**2087**	**86**	**4**	**2.47**	....	....	....	....	....	....	....
1995-96	**Florida**	**NHL**	**57**	**26**	**20**	**7**	**3178**	**142**	**2**	**2.68**	***22**	**12**	**10**	**1332**	**50**	**1**	**2.25**
1996-97	**Florida**	**NHL**	**57**	**27**	**19**	**10**	**3347**	**128**	**2**	**2.29**	**5**	**1**	**4**	**328**	**13**	**1**	**2.38**
1997-98	**Florida**	**NHL**	**60**	**18**	**29**	**11**	**3451**	**165**	**4**	**2.87**	....	....	....	....	....	....	....
	United States	Olympics	1	0	0	0	1	0	0	0.00	....	....	....	....	....	....	....
1998-99	**Philadelphia**	**NHL**	**62**	**27**	**18**	**15**	**3712**	**135**	**6**	**2.18**	**6**	**2**	**4**	**369**	**9**	**1**	**1.46**
99-2000	**Philadelphia**	**NHL**	**50**	**25**	**15**	**9**	**2950**	**108**	**3**	**2.20**	....	....	....	....	....	....	....
	NHL Totals		**829**	**358**	**318**	**114**	**47545**	**2367**	**38**	**2.99**	**71**	**28**	**38**	**3969**	**177**	**5**	**2.68**

OHL Second All-Star Team (1983) • CHL First All-Star Team (1984) • Shared Terry Sawchuk Trophy (fewest goals against - CHL) with Ron Scott (1984) • Shared Tommy Ivan Trophy (MVP - CHL) with Bruce Affleck (1984) • NHL First All-Star Team (1986) • Won Vezina Trophy (1986) • NHL Second All-Star Team (1994) • Played in NHL All-Star Game (1994, 1996, 1997)

Traded to **Vancouver** by **NY Rangers** for future considerations (Doug Lidster, June 25, 1993), June 20, 1993. Claimed by **Florida** from **Vancouver** in Expansion Draft, June 24, 1993. Signed as a free agent by **Philadelphia**, July 16, 1998. Traded to **NY Islanders** by **Philadelphia** for NY Islanders' 4th round choice in 2001 Entry Draft, June 25, 2000.

VERNON, Mike (VUHR-nohn, MIGHK) CGY.

Goaltender. Catches left. 5'9", 180 lbs. Born, Calgary, Alta., February 24, 1963.
(Calgary's 2nd choice, 56th overall, in 1981 Entry Draft).

			Regular Season								Playoffs						
Season	Club	Lea	GP	W	L	T	Mins	GA	SO	Avg	GP	W	L	Mins	GA	SO	Avg
1979-80	Calgary Canucks	AJHL	31	21	7	0	1796	88	0	2.95	....	....	....	....	....	....	....
1980-81	Calgary Wranglers	WHL	59	33	17	1	3154	198	1	3.77	22	14	8	1271	82	1	3.87
1981-82	Calgary Wranglers	WHL	42	22	14	2	2329	143	3	3.68	9	5	4	527	30	0	3.42
	Oklahoma City	CHL	....	....	....	....	....	....	....	....	1	0	1	70	4	0	3.43
1982-83	Calgary Wranglers	WHL	50	29	18	2	2856	155	*3	*3.26	16	9	7	925	60	0	3.89
	Calgary	**NHL**	**2**	**0**	**2**	**0**	**100**	**11**	**0**	**6.59**	....	....	....	....	....	....	....
1983-84	**Calgary**	**NHL**	**1**	**0**	**1**	**0**	**11**	**4**	**0**	**22.22**	....	....	....	....	....	....	....
	Colorado Flames	CHL	46	30	13	2	2648	148	1	*3.35	6	2	4	347	21	0	3.63
1984-85	Moncton Flames	AHL	41	10	20	4	2050	134	0	3.92	....	....	....	....	....	....	....
1985-86	**Calgary**	**NHL**	**18**	**9**	**3**	**3**	**921**	**52**	**1**	**3.39**	***21**	**12**	***9**	***1229**	**60**	**0**	**2.93**
	Moncton Flames	AHL	6	3	1	2	374	21	0	3.37	....	....	....	....	....	....	....
	Salt Lake City	IHL	10	6	4	0	600	34	1	3.40	....	....	....	....	....	....	....
1986-87	**Calgary**	**NHL**	**54**	**30**	**21**	**1**	**2957**	**178**	**1**	**3.61**	**5**	**2**	**3**	**263**	**16**	**0**	**3.65**
1987-88	**Calgary**	**NHL**	**64**	**39**	**16**	**7**	**3565**	**210**	**1**	**3.53**	**9**	**4**	**4**	**515**	**34**	**0**	**3.96**
1988-89 ♦	**Calgary**	**NHL**	**52**	***37**	**6**	**5**	**2938**	**130**	**0**	**2.65**	***22**	***16**	**5**	***1381**	**52**	***3**	**2.26**
1989-90	**Calgary**	**NHL**	**47**	**23**	**14**	**9**	**2795**	**146**	**0**	**3.13**	**6**	**2**	**3**	**342**	**19**	**0**	**3.33**
1990-91	**Calgary**	**NHL**	**54**	**31**	**19**	**3**	**3121**	**172**	**1**	**3.31**	**7**	**3**	**4**	**427**	**21**	**0**	**2.95**
1991-92	**Calgary**	**NHL**	**63**	**24**	**30**	**9**	**3640**	**217**	**0**	**3.58**	....	....	....	....	....	....	....
1992-93	**Calgary**	**NHL**	**64**	**29**	**26**	**9**	**3732**	**203**	**2**	**3.26**	**4**	**1**	**1**	**150**	**15**	**0**	**6.00**
1993-94	**Calgary**	**NHL**	**48**	**26**	**17**	**5**	**2798**	**131**	**3**	**2.81**	**7**	**3**	**4**	**466**	**23**	**0**	**2.96**
1994-95	**Detroit**	**NHL**	**30**	**19**	**6**	**4**	**1807**	**76**	**1**	**2.52**	**18**	**12**	**6**	**1063**	**41**	**1**	**2.31**
1995-96	**Detroit**	**NHL**	**32**	**21**	**7**	**2**	**1855**	**70**	**3**	**2.26**	**4**	**2**	**2**	**243**	**11**	**0**	**2.72**
1996-97 ♦	**Detroit**	**NHL**	**33**	**13**	**11**	**8**	**1952**	**79**	**0**	**2.43**	***20**	***16**	**4**	***1229**	**36**	**1**	**1.76**
1997-98	**San Jose**	**NHL**	**62**	**30**	**22**	**8**	**3564**	**146**	**5**	**2.46**	**6**	**2**	**4**	**348**	**14**	**1**	**2.41**
1998-99	**San Jose**	**NHL**	**49**	**16**	**22**	**10**	**2831**	**107**	**4**	**2.27**	**5**	**2**	**3**	**321**	**13**	**0**	**2.43**
99-2000	**San Jose**	**NHL**	**15**	**6**	**5**	**1**	**772**	**32**	**0**	**2.49**	....	....	....	....	....	....	....
	Florida	**NHL**	**34**	**18**	**13**	**2**	**2019**	**83**	**1**	**2.47**	**4**	**0**	**4**	**237**	**12**	**0**	**3.04**
	NHL Totals		**722**	**371**	**241**	**86**	**41378**	**2047**	**23**	**2.97**	**138**	**77**	**56**	**8214**	**367**	**6**	**2.68**

WHL First All-Star Team (1982, 1983) • Won Hap Emms Memorial Trophy (Memorial Cup Tournament Top Goaltender) (1983) • CHL Second All-Star Team (1984) • NHL Second All-Star Team (1989) • Shared William M. Jennings Trophy with Chris Osgood (1996) • Won Conn Smythe Trophy (1997) • Played in NHL All-Star Game (1988, 1989, 1990, 1991, 1993)

Traded to **Detroit** by **Calgary** for Steve Chiasson, June 29, 1994. Traded to **San Jose** by **Detroit** with Detroit's 5th round choice (Andrei Maximenko) in 1999 Entry Draft for San Jose's 2nd round choice (later traded to St. Louis - St. Louis selected Maxim Linnik) in 1998 Entry Draft and San Jose's 2nd round choice (later traded to Tampa Bay - Tampa Bay selected Sheldon Keefe) in 1999 Entry Draft, August 18, 1997. Traded to **Florida** by **San Jose** with San Jose's 3rd round choice (Sean O'Connor) in 2000 Entry Draft and future considerations for Radek Dvorak, December 30, 1999. Selected by **Minnesota** from **Florida** in Expansion Draft, June 23, 2000. Traded to **Calgary** by **Minnesota** for the rights to Dan Cavanaugh and Calgary's 8th round choice in 2001 Entry Draft, June 23, 2000.

VOKOUN, Tomas
(voh-KOHN, TAW-mas) **NSH.**

Goaltender. Catches right. 6', 197 lbs. Born, Karlovy Vary, Czech., July 2, 1976.
(Montreal's 11th choice, 226th overall, in 1994 Entry Draft).

			Regular Season								Playoffs						
Season	Club	Lea	GP	W	L	T	Mins	GA	SO	Avg	GP	W	L	Mins	GA	SO	Avg
1993-94	Poldi Kladno	Cze-Rep	1	0	0	0	20	2	0	6.01	....	....	....	....	....	....	....
1994-95	Poldi Kladno	Cze-Rep	26	....	....	....	1368	70	....	3.07	5	....	....	240	19	....	4.75
1995-96	Wheeling	ECHL	35	20	10	2	1912	117	0	3.67	7	4	3	436	19	0	2.61
	Fredericton	AHL	....	....	....	....	....	....	....	....	1	0	1	59	4	0	4.09
1996-97	Montreal	NHL	1	0	0	0	20	4	0	12.00	....	....	....	....	....	....	....
	Fredericton	AHL	47	12	26	7	2645	154	2	3.49	....	....	....	....	....	....	....
1997-98	Fredericton	AHL	31	13	13	2	1735	90	0	3.11	....	....	....	....	....	....	....
1998-99	Nashville	NHL	37	12	18	4	1954	96	1	2.95	....	....	....	....	....	....	....
	Milwaukee	IHL	9	3	2	4	539	22	1	2.45	2	0	2	149	8	0	3.22
99-2000	Nashville	NHL	33	9	20	1	1879	87	1	2.78	....	....	....	....	....	....	....
	Milwaukee	IHL	7	5	2	0	364	17	0	2.80	....	....	....	....	....	....	....
	NHL Totals		71	21	38	5	3853	187	2	2.91	....	....	....	....	....	....	....

Claimed by **Nashville** from **Montreal** in Expansion Draft, June 26, 1998.

VOLKOV, Alexei
(VOHL-kawf, al-EHX-ay) **L.A.**

Goaltender. Catches left. 6'1", 195 lbs. Born, Yekaterinburg, USSR, March 15, 1980.
(Los Angeles' 3rd choice, 76th overall, in 1998 Entry Draft).

			Regular Season								Playoffs						
Season	Club	Lea	GP	W	L	T	Mins	GA	SO	Avg	GP	W	L	Mins	GA	SO	Avg
1995-96	SKA Yekaterinburg	Russia-2	42	....	....	....	2520	78	....	1.87	....	....	....	....	....	....	....
1996-97	SKA Yekaterinburg	Russia-3	34	....	....	....	2040	66	....	1.94	....	....	....	....	....	....	....
	Krylja Sovetov	Russia-Jr.	8	....	....	....	48	9	....	1.25	....	....	....	....	....	....	....
1997-98	Krylja Sovetov	Russia-3	27	....	....	....	1620	72	....	2.67	....	....	....	....	....	....	....
1998-99	Halifax	QMJHL	39	25	9	3	2332	105	2	2.70	5	1	4	282	21	0	4.47
99-2000	Halifax	QMJHL	40	23	13	2	2222	124	1	3.35	8	3	4	417	29	0	4.18

WAGNER, Stephen
(WAG-nuhr, STEEV-vuhn) **ST.L.**

Goaltender. Catches left. 6'2", 200 lbs. Born, Red Deer, Alta., January 17, 1977.
(St. Louis' 5th choice, 159th overall, in 1996 Entry Draft).

			Regular Season								Playoffs						
Season	Club	Lea	GP	W	L	T	Mins	GA	SO	Avg	GP	W	L	Mins	GA	SO	Avg
1995-96	Olds Grizzlys	AJHL	47	....	....	....	2787	139	2	2.99	....	....	....	....	....	....	....
1996-97	U. of Denver	WCHA	22	13	6	0	1202	57	1	2.85	....	....	....	....	....	....	....
1997-98	U. of Denver	WCHA	29	9	17	1	1615	113	0	4.20	....	....	....	....	....	....	....
1998-99	U. of Denver	WCHA	*40	*24	13	1	2318	114	*4	2.95	....	....	....	....	....	....	....
99-2000	U. of Denver	WCHA	33	13	18	1	1870	102	2	3.27	....	....	....	....	....	....	....

WAITE, Jimmy
(WAYT, JIHM-ee) **TOR.**

Goaltender. Catches left. 6'1", 180 lbs. Born, Sherbrooke, Que., April 15, 1969.
(Chicago's 1st choice, 8th overall, in 1987 Entry Draft).

			Regular Season								Playoffs						
Season	Club	Lea	GP	W	L	T	Mins	GA	SO	Avg	GP	W	L	Mins	GA	SO	Avg
1984-85	L'estrie-Maurice	QAAA	10	6	4	0	598	52	0	5.22	....	....	....	....	....	....	....
1985-86	L'estrie-Maurice	QAAA	29	11	15	1	1643	143	0	5.22	....	....	....	....	....	....	....
1986-87	Chicoutimi	QMJHL	50	23	17	3	2569	209	2	4.48	11	4	6	576	54	1	5.63
1987-88	Chicoutimi	QMJHL	36	17	16	1	2000	150	0	4.50	4	1	2	222	17	0	4.59
1988-89	Chicago	NHL	11	0	7	1	494	43	0	5.22	....	....	....	....	....	....	....
	Saginaw Hawks	IHL	5	3	1	0	304	10	0	1.97	....	....	....	....	....	....	....
1989-90	Chicago	NHL	4	2	0	0	183	14	0	4.59	....	....	....	....	....	....	....
	Indianapolis Ice	IHL	54	*34	14	5	*3207	135	*5	*2.53	*10	*9	1	*602	19	*1	*1.89
1990-91	Chicago	NHL	1	1	0	0	60	2	0	2.00	....	....	....	....	....	....	....
	Indianapolis Ice	IHL	49	*26	18	4	2888	167	3	3.47	6	2	4	369	20	0	3.25
1991-92	Chicago	NHL	17	4	7	4	877	54	0	3.69	....	....	....	....	....	....	....
	Indianapolis Ice	IHL	13	4	7	1	702	53	0	4.53	....	....	....	....	....	....	....
	Hershey Bears	AHL	11	6	4	1	631	44	0	4.18	6	2	4	360	19	0	3.17
1992-93	Chicago	NHL	20	6	7	1	996	49	2	2.95	....	....	....	....	....	....	....
1993-94	San Jose	NHL	15	3	7	0	697	50	0	4.30	2	0	0	40	3	0	4.50
1994-95	Chicago	NHL	2	1	1	0	119	5	0	2.52	....	....	....	....	....	....	....
	Indianapolis Ice	IHL	4	2	1	1	239	13	0	3.25	....	....	....	....	....	....	....
1995-96	Chicago	NHL	1	0	0	0	31	0	0	0.00	....	....	....	....	....	....	....
	Indianapolis Ice	IHL	56	28	18	6	3157	179	0	3.40	5	2	3	298	15	1	3.02
1996-97	Chicago	NHL	2	0	1	1	105	7	0	4.00	....	....	....	....	....	....	....
	Indianapolis Ice	IHL	41	22	15	4	2450	112	4	2.74	4	1	3	222	13	0	3.51
1997-98	Phoenix	NHL	17	5	6	1	793	28	1	2.12	4	0	3	171	11	0	3.86
1998-99	Phoenix	NHL	16	6	5	4	898	41	1	2.74	....	....	....	....	....	....	....
	Springfield Falcons	AHL	8	3	4	1	483	19	0	2.36	2	0	2	118	6	0	3.05
	Utah Grizzlies	IHL	11	6	3	2	622	30	0	2.89	....	....	....	....	....	....	....
99-2000	St. John's Leafs	AHL	*62	20	37	4	*3461	176	6	3.05	....	....	....	....	....	....	....
	NHL Totals		106	28	41	12	5253	293	4	3.35	6	0	3	211	14	0	3.98

QMJHL Second All-Star Team (1987) • IHL First All-Star Team (1990) • Won James Norris Memorial Trophy (fewest goals against - IHL) (1990)

Traded to **San Jose** by **Chicago** for future considerations (Neil Wilkinson, July 9, 1993), June 18, 1993. Traded to **Chicago** by **San Jose** for Chicago's 4th round choice (later traded to NY Rangers - NY Rangers selected Tomi Kallarsson) in 1997 Entry Draft, February 5, 1995. Claimed by **Phoenix** from **Chicago** in NHL Waiver Draft, September 28, 1997. Signed as a free agent by **Toronto**, August 19, 1999.

WANDLER, Bryce
NYR

Goaltender. Catches left. 6', 180 lbs. Born, Lacombe, Alta., February 25, 1979.

			Regular Season								Playoffs						
Season	Club	Lea	GP	W	L	T	Mins	GA	SO	Avg	GP	W	L	Mins	GA	SO	Avg
1996-97	Kamloops Blazers	WHL	1	0	0	0	34	3	0	5.29	....	....	....	....	....	....	....
	Edmonton Ice	WHL	19	2	11	1	936	84	0	5.38	....	....	....	....	....	....	....
1997-98	Edmonton Ice	WHL	47	12	27	4	2576	180	1	4.19	....	....	....	....	....	....	....
1998-99	Swift Current	WHL	51	23	20	4	2882	123	3	2.56	6	2	4	364	17	1	2.80
99-2000	Swift Current	WHL	56	*37	15	2	3255	112	6	*2.06	10	5	5	597	29	0	2.91

Signed as a free agent by **NY Rangers**, March 15, 2000.

WEEKES, Kevin
(WEEKS, KEH-vihn) **T.B.**

Goaltender. Catches left. 6', 195 lbs. Born, Toronto, Ont., April 4, 1975.
(Florida's 2nd choice, 41st overall, in 1993 Entry Draft).

			Regular Season								Playoffs						
Season	Club	Lea	GP	W	L	T	Mins	GA	SO	Avg	GP	W	L	Mins	GA	SO	Avg
1990-91	St. Michael's	OJHL-B	1	0	0	0	41	1	0	1.46	....	....	....	....	....	....	....
1991-92	Toronto Wings	OJHL	35	....	....	....	1575	68	4	1.94	....	....	....	....	....	....	....
	St. Michael's	MTHL	2	0	1	1	127	11	0	5.20	4	1	2	214	15	1	4.21
1992-93	Owen Sound	OHL	29	9	12	5	1645	143	0	5.22	1	0	0	26	5	0	11.50
1993-94	Owen Sound	OHL	34	13	19	1	1974	158	0	4.80	....	....	....	....	....	....	....
1994-95	Ottawa 67's	OHL	41	13	23	4	2266	153	1	4.05	....	....	....	....	....	....	....
1995-96	Carolina	AHL	60	24	25	8	3404	229	2	4.04	....	....	....	....	....	....	....
1996-97	Carolina	AHL	51	17	28	4	2899	172	1	3.56	....	....	....	....	....	....	....
1997-98	Florida	NHL	11	0	5	1	485	32	0	3.96	....	....	....	....	....	....	....
	Fort Wayne	IHL	12	9	2	1	719	34	1	2.84	....	....	....	....	....	....	....
1998-99	Vancouver	NHL	11	0	8	1	532	34	0	3.83	....	....	....	....	....	....	....
	Detroit Vipers	IHL	33	19	5	7	1857	64	*4	*2.07	....	....	....	....	....	....	....
99-2000	Vancouver	NHL	20	6	7	4	987	47	1	2.86	....	....	....	....	....	....	....
	NY Islanders	NHL	36	10	20	4	2026	115	1	3.41	....	....	....	....	....	....	....
	NHL Totals		78	16	40	10	4030	228	2	3.39	....	....	....	....	....	....	....

Shared James Norris Memorial Trophy (fewest goals against - IHL) with Andrei Trefilov (1999)

Traded to **Vancouver** by **Florida** with Ed Jovanovski, Dave Gagner, Mike Brown and Florida's 1st round choice (Nathan Smith) in 2000 Entry Draft for Pavel Bure, Bret Hedican, Brad Ference and Vancouver's 3rd round choice (Robert Fried) in 2000 Entry Draft, January 17, 1999. Traded to **NY Islanders** by **Vancouver** with Dave Scatchard and Bill Muckalt for Felix Potvin and NY Islanders' compensatory 2nd (later traded to New Jersey - New Jersey selected Teemu Laine) and 3rd (Thatcher Bell) round choices in 2000 Entry Draft, December 19, 1999. Traded to **Tampa Bay** by **NY Islanders** with the rights to Kristian Kudroc and NY Islanders' 2nd round choice in 2001 Entry Draft for Tampa Bay's 1st round choice (Raffi Torres) in 2000 Entry Draft, Calgary's 4th round choice (previously acquired, NY Islanders selected Vladimir Gorbunov) in 2000 Entry Draft and NY Islanders' 7th round choice (previously acquired, NY Islanders selected Ryan Caldwell) in 2000 Entry Draft, June 24, 2000.

WENINGER, Dave
(WHEN-ihn-juhr, DAYV) **WSH.**

Goaltender. Catches left. 6'1", 180 lbs. Born, Calgary, Alta., February 8, 1976.
(Washington's 5th choice, 74th overall, in 1996 Entry Draft).

			Regular Season								Playoffs						
Season	Club	Lea	GP	W	L	T	Mins	GA	SO	Avg	GP	W	L	Mins	GA	SO	Avg
1995-96	Michigan Tech	WCHA	25	11	7	2	1300	70	0	3.23	....	....	....	....	....	....	....
1996-97	Michigan Tech	WCHA	18	1	13	0	855	59	1	4.14	....	....	....	....	....	....	....
1997-98	Michigan Tech	WCHA	34	14	16	2	1911	119	1	3.74	....	....	....	....	....	....	....
1998-99	Michigan Tech	WCHA	32	9	21	1	1802	100	0	3.33	....	....	....	....	....	....	....
99-2000	Wheeling Nailers	ECHL	1	0	1	0	60	4	0	4.00	....	....	....	....	....	....	....
	Wilkes-Barre	AHL	25	6	9	3	1277	76	0	3.57	....	....	....	....	....	....	....
	Dayton Bombers	ECHL	5	0	1	0	104	8	0	4.62	1	0	0	10	0	0	0.00

WHITMORE, Kay
(WHIHT-mohr, KAY) **BOS.**

Goaltender. Catches left. 5'11", 175 lbs. Born, Sudbury, Ont., April 10, 1967.
(Hartford's 2nd choice, 26th overall, in 1985 Entry Draft).

			Regular Season								Playoffs						
Season	Club	Lea	GP	W	L	T	Mins	GA	SO	Avg	GP	W	L	Mins	GA	SO	Avg
1982-83	Sudbury Legion	NOJHA	43	....	....	....	2580	108	4	2.51	....	....	....	....	....	....	....
1983-84	Peterborough	OHL	29	17	8	0	1471	110	0	4.49	....	....	....	....	....	....	....
1984-85	Peterborough	OHL	*53	*35	16	2	*3077	172	*2	3.35	17	10	4	1020	58	0	3.41
1985-86	Peterborough	OHL	41	27	12	2	2467	114	*3	*2.77	14	8	5	837	40	0	2.87
1986-87	Peterborough	OHL	36	14	17	5	2159	118	1	3.28	7	3	3	366	17	1	2.79
1987-88	Binghamton	AHL	38	17	15	4	2137	121	*3	3.40	2	0	2	118	10	0	5.08
1988-89	Hartford	NHL	3	2	1	0	180	10	0	3.33	2	0	2	135	10	0	4.44
	Binghamton	AHL	*56	21	29	4	*3200	241	1	4.52	....	....	....	....	....	....	....
1989-90	Hartford	NHL	9	4	2	1	442	26	0	3.53	....	....	....	....	....	....	....
	Binghamton	AHL	24	3	19	2	1386	109	0	4.72	....	....	....	....	....	....	....
1990-91	Hartford	NHL	18	3	9	3	850	52	0	3.67	....	....	....	....	....	....	....
	Springfield	AHL	33	22	9	1	1916	98	1	3.07	*15	*11	4	*926	37	0	*2.40
1991-92	Hartford	NHL	45	14	21	6	2567	155	3	3.62	1	0	0	19	1	0	3.16
1992-93	Vancouver	NHL	31	18	8	4	1817	94	1	3.10	....	....	....	....	....	....	....
1993-94	Vancouver	NHL	32	18	14	0	1921	113	0	3.53	....	....	....	....	....	....	....
1994-95	Vancouver	NHL	11	0	6	2	558	37	0	3.98	1	0	0	20	2	0	6.00
1995-96	Detroit Vipers	IHL	10	3	5	0	501	33	0	3.95	....	....	....	....	....	....	....
	Los Angeles	IHL	30	10	9	7	1563	99	1	3.80	....	....	....	....	....	....	....
	Syracuse Crunch	AHL	11	6	4	1	663	37	0	3.35	....	....	....	....	....	....	....
	Binghamton	AHL	....	....	....	....	....	....	....	....	2	0	2	127	9	0	4.27
1996-97	Sodertalje SK	Sweden	25	....	....	....	1320	85	0	3.86	....	....	....	....	....	....	....
1997-98	Long Beach	IHL	46	28	12	3	2516	109	3	2.60	14	9	5	838	43	0	3.08
1998-99	Hartford	AHL	18	8	8	2	1080	47	0	2.61	....	....	....	....	....	....	....
	Milwaukee	IHL	23	10	6	4	1304	64	0	2.94	....	....	....	....	....	....	....
99-2000	Providence Bruins	AHL	43	17	19	3	2393	127	1	3.18	1	0	1	59	2	0	2.04
	NHL Totals		149	59	61	16	8335	487	4	3.51	4	0	2	174	13	0	4.48

OHL First All-Star Team (1986) • Won Jack A. Butterfield Trophy (Playoff MVP - AHL) (1991) • Shared James Norris Memorial Trophy (fewest goals against - IHL) with Mike Buzak (1998)

Traded to **Vancouver** by **Hartford** for Corrie D'Alessio and cash, October 1, 1992. Traded to **NY Rangers** by **Vancouver** for Joe Kocur, March 20, 1996. Signed as a free agent by **San Jose**, September 10, 1997. Traded to **Buffalo** by **San Jose** with Colorado's 2nd round choice (previously acquired, Buffalo selected Jaroslav Kristek) in 1998 Entry Draft and San Jose's 5th round choice (later traded to Columbus - Columbus selected Tyler Kolarik) in 2000 Entry Draft for Steve Shields and Buffalo's 4th round choice (Miroslav Zalesak) in 1998 Entry Draft, June 18, 1998. Signed as a free agent by **NY Rangers**, August 17, 1998. Signed as a free agent by **Boston**, August 25, 1999. Traded to **Edmonton** by **Boston** for Mike Matteucci, December 28, 1999. Traded to **Boston** by **Edmonton** for future considerations, July 20, 2000.

WILKINSON, Derek (WIHL-kihn-sohn, DAIR-ehk)

Goaltender. Catches left. 6', 170 lbs. Born, Lasalle, Ont., July 29, 1974.
(Tampa Bay's 7th choice, 145th overall, in 1992 Entry Draft).

			Regular Season								Playoffs						
Season	Club	Lea	GP	W	L	T	Mins	GA	SO	Avg	GP	W	L	Mins	GA	SO	Avg
1989-90	Windsor Bulldogs	OJHL-B	3	1	1	0	164	18	0	6.59	....	....	....	....	....	....	....
	Belle River	OJHL-C	2	....	....	....	115	2	1	1.04	....	....	....	....	....	....	....
1990-91	Chatham Macs	OJHL-B	24	....	....	....	1429	86	0	3.61	....	....	....	....	....	....	....
1991-92	Detroit	OHL	38	16	17	1	1943	138	1	4.26	7	3	2	313	28	0	5.37
1992-93	Detroit Jr. Wings	OHL	*4	1	2	1	*245	18	0	4.41	....	....	....	....	....	....	....
	Belleville Bulls	OHL	*59	21	24	11	*3370	237	0	4.22	7	3	4	434	29	0	4.01
1993-94	Belleville Bulls	OHL	*56	24	16	4	2860	179	*2	3.76	12	6	6	700	39	*1	3.34
1994-95	Atlanta Knights	IHL	46	22	17	2	2414	121	1	3.01	4	2	1	197	8	0	2.43
1995-96	**Tampa Bay**	**NHL**	**4**	**0**	**3**	**0**	**200**	**15**	**0**	**4.50**	....	....	....	....	....	....	....
	Atlanta Knights	IHL	28	11	11	2	1433	98	1	4.10	....	....	....	....	....	....	....
1996-97	**Tampa Bay**	**NHL**	**5**	**0**	**2**	**1**	**169**	**12**	**0**	**4.26**	....	....	....	....	....	....	....
	Cleveland	IHL	46	20	17	6	2595	138	1	3.19	14	8	6	893	44	0	2.95
1997-98	**Tampa Bay**	**NHL**	**8**	**2**	**4**	**1**	**311**	**17**	**0**	**3.28**	....	....	....	....	....	....	....
	Cleveland	IHL	25	9	12	2	1295	63	1	2.92	1	0	0	27	1	0	2.19
1998-99	**Tampa Bay**	**NHL**	**5**	**1**	**3**	**1**	**253**	**13**	**0**	**3.08**	....	....	....	....	....	....	....
	Cleveland	IHL	34	10	15	2	1760	108	1	3.68	....	....	....	....	....	....	....
99-2000	Charlotte	ECHL	31	11	13	2	1435	83	0	3.47	....	....	....	....	....	....	....
	Chicago Wolves	IHL	1	0	0	1	60	5	0	5.00	....	....	....	....	....	....	....
	NHL Totals		**22**	**3**	**12**	**3**	**933**	**57**	**0**	**3.67**	....	....	....	....	....	....	....

WREGGET, Ken (REHG-eht, KEHN) DET.

Goaltender. Catches left. 6'1", 201 lbs. Born, Brandon, Man., March 25, 1964.
(Toronto's 4th choice, 45th overall, in 1982 Entry Draft).

			Regular Season								Playoffs						
Season	Club	Lea	GP	W	L	T	Mins	GA	SO	Avg	GP	W	L	Mins	GA	SO	Avg
1981-82	Lethbridge	WHL	36	19	12	0	1713	118	0	4.13	3	2	0	84	3	0	2.14
1982-83	Lethbridge	WHL	48	26	17	1	2696	157	1	3.49	*20	14	5	*1154	58	*1	*3.02
1983-84	**Toronto**	**NHL**	**3**	**1**	**1**	**1**	**165**	**14**	**0**	**5.09**	....	....	....	....	....	....	....
	Lethbridge	WHL	53	32	20	0	3053	161	0	*3.16	4	1	3	210	18	0	5.14
1984-85	**Toronto**	**NHL**	**23**	**2**	**15**	**3**	**1278**	**103**	**0**	**4.84**	....	....	....	....	....	....	....
	St. Catharines	AHL	12	2	8	1	688	48	0	4.19	....	....	....	....	....	....	....
1985-86	**Toronto**	**NHL**	**30**	**9**	**13**	**4**	**1566**	**113**	**0**	**4.33**	**10**	**6**	**4**	**607**	**32**	***1**	**3.16**
	St. Catharines	AHL	18	8	9	0	1058	78	1	4.42	....	....	....	....	....	....	....
1986-87	**Toronto**	**NHL**	**56**	**22**	**28**	**3**	**3026**	**200**	**0**	**3.97**	**13**	**7**	**6**	**761**	**29**	**1**	**2.29**
1987-88	**Toronto**	**NHL**	**56**	**12**	**35**	**4**	**3000**	**222**	**2**	**4.44**	**2**	**0**	**1**	**108**	**11**	**0**	**6.11**
1988-89	**Toronto**	**NHL**	**32**	**9**	**20**	**2**	**1888**	**139**	**0**	**4.42**	....	....	....	....	....	....	....
	Philadelphia	**NHL**	**3**	**1**	**1**	**0**	**130**	**13**	**0**	**6.00**	**5**	**2**	**2**	**268**	**10**	**0**	**2.24**
1989-90	**Philadelphia**	**NHL**	**51**	**22**	**24**	**3**	**2961**	**169**	**0**	**3.42**	....	....	....	....	....	....	....
1990-91	**Philadelphia**	**NHL**	**30**	**10**	**14**	**3**	**1484**	**88**	**0**	**3.56**	....	....	....	....	....	....	....
1991-92	**Philadelphia**	**NHL**	**23**	**9**	**8**	**3**	**1259**	**75**	**0**	**3.57**	....	....	....	....	....	....	....
♦	**Pittsburgh**	**NHL**	**9**	**5**	**3**	**0**	**448**	**31**	**0**	**4.15**	**1**	**0**	**0**	**40**	**4**	**0**	**6.00**
1992-93	**Pittsburgh**	**NHL**	**25**	**13**	**7**	**2**	**1368**	**78**	**0**	**3.42**	....	....	....	....	....	....	....
1993-94	**Pittsburgh**	**NHL**	**42**	**21**	**12**	**7**	**2456**	**138**	**1**	**3.37**	....	....	....	....	....	....	....
1994-95	**Pittsburgh**	**NHL**	**38**	***25**	**9**	**2**	**2208**	**118**	**0**	**3.21**	**11**	**5**	**6**	**661**	**33**	**1**	**3.00**
1995-96	**Pittsburgh**	**NHL**	**37**	**20**	**13**	**2**	**2132**	**115**	**3**	**3.24**	**9**	**7**	**2**	**599**	**23**	**0**	**2.30**
1996-97	**Pittsburgh**	**NHL**	**46**	**17**	**17**	**6**	**2514**	**136**	**2**	**3.25**	**5**	**1**	**4**	**297**	**18**	**0**	**3.64**
1997-98	**Pittsburgh**	**NHL**	**15**	**3**	**6**	**2**	**611**	**28**	**0**	**2.75**	....	....	....	....	....	....	....
1998-99	**Calgary**	**NHL**	**27**	**10**	**12**	**4**	**1590**	**67**	**1**	**2.53**	....	....	....	....	....	....	....
99-2000	**Detroit**	**NHL**	**29**	**14**	**10**	**2**	**1579**	**70**	**0**	**2.66**	....	....	....	....	....	....	....
	NHL Totals		**575**	**225**	**248**	**53**	**31663**	**1917**	**9**	**3.63**	**56**	**28**	**25**	**3341**	**160**	**3**	**2.87**

WHL East First All-Star Team (1984)

Traded to **Philadelphia** by **Toronto** for Philadelphia's 1st round choice (Rob Pearson) and Calgary's 1st round choice (previously acquired, Toronto selected Steve Bancroft) in 1989 Entry Draft, March 6, 1989. Traded to **Pittsburgh** by **Philadelphia** with Rick Tocchet, Kjell Samuelsson and Philadelphia's 3rd round choice (Dave Roche) in 1993 Entry Draft for Mark Recchi, Brian Benning and Los Angeles' 1st round choice (previously acquired, Philadelphia selected Jason Bowen) in 1992 Entry Draft, February 19, 1992. Traded to **Calgary** by **Pittsburgh** with Dave Roche for German Titov and Todd Hlushko, June 17, 1998. Signed as a free agent by **Detroit**, July 23, 1999.

YEATS, Matthew (YAYTS, MAT-thew) L.A.

Goaltender. Catches left. 5'11", 165 lbs. Born, Montreal, Que., April 6, 1979.
(Los Angeles' 9th choice, 248th overall, in 1998 Entry Draft).

			Regular Season								Playoffs						
Season	Club	Lea	GP	W	L	T	Mins	GA	SO	Avg	GP	W	L	Mins	GA	SO	Avg
1996-97	Olds Grizzlys	AJHL	32	....	....	....	1678	95	1	3.41	....	....	....	....	....	....	....
1997-98	Olds Grizzlys	AJHL	26	12	12	1	1498	96	0	3.85	....	....	....	....	....	....	....
1998-99	U. of Maine	H-East	DID NOT PLAY – ACADEMICALLY INELIGIBLE														
99-2000	U. of Maine	H-East	32	20	6	4	1821	79	0	2.60	....	....	....	....	....	....	....

YEREMEYEV, Vitali (yehr-eh-MAY-ehv, VIH-tal-ee) NYR

Goaltender. Catches left. 5'10", 167 lbs. Born, Ust-Kamenogorsk, USSR, September 23, 1975.
(NY Rangers' 11th choice, 209th overall, in 1994 Entry Draft).

			Regular Season								Playoffs						
Season	Club	Lea	GP	W	L	T	Mins	GA	SO	Avg	GP	W	L	Mins	GA	SO	Avg
1993-94	Ust-Kamenogorsk	CIS	19	....	....	....	1015	38	....	2.24	....	....	....	....	....	....	....
1994-95	CSKA Moscow	CIS	49	....	....	....	2733	97	....	2.13	2	....	....	120	8	....	4.00
1995-96	CSKA Moscow	CIS	25	....	....	....	1339	37	5	1.66	3	....	....	179	7	....	2.34
1996-97	CSKA Moscow	Russia	14	....	....	....	635	35	0	3.31	1	....	....	59	3	0	3.05
1997-98	Torpedo Yaroslavl	Russia	17	....	....	....	979	19	3	*1.16	....	....	....	....	....	....	....
	Kazakhstan	Olympics	*7	....	....	....	292	28	....	5.76	....	....	....	....	....	....	....
1998-99	CSKA Moscow	Russia-2	19	....	....	....	1100	33	....	1.80	....	....	....	....	....	....	....
99-2000	Dynamo Moscow	Russia	26	....	....	....	1564	32	*7	*1.23	*17	....	....	*1039	22	*4	*1.27

YOUNG, Wendell (YUHNG, WEHN-dawl)

Goaltender. Catches left. 5'9", 181 lbs. Born, Halifax, N.S., August 1, 1963.
(Vancouver's 3rd choice, 73rd overall, in 1981 Entry Draft).

			Regular Season								Playoffs						
Season	Club	Lea	GP	W	L	T	Mins	GA	SO	Avg	GP	W	L	Mins	GA	SO	Avg
1979-80	Cole Harbour Colts	MJrHL	25	....	....	....	1446	94	0	3.90	....	....	....	....	....	....	....
1980-81	Kitchener Rangers	OMJHL	42	19	15	0	2215	164	1	4.44	14	9	1	800	42	*1	3.15
1981-82	Kitchener Rangers	OHL	*60	*38	17	2	*3470	195	1	3.37	15	12	1	900	35	*1	*2.33
1982-83	Kitchener Rangers	OHL	61	*41	19	0	*3611	231	1	3.84	12	6	5	720	43	0	3.58
1983-84	Fredericton	AHL	11	7	3	0	569	39	1	4.11	....	....	....	....	....	....	....
	Milwaukee	IHL	6	4	1	1	339	17	0	3.01	....	....	....	....	....	....	....
	Salt Lake City	CHL	20	11	6	0	1094	80	0	4.39	4	0	2	122	11	0	5.42
1984-85	Fredericton	AHL	22	7	11	3	1242	83	0	4.01	....	....	....	....	....	....	....
1985-86	**Vancouver**	**NHL**	**22**	**4**	**9**	**3**	**1023**	**61**	**0**	**3.58**	**1**	**0**	**1**	**60**	**5**	**0**	**5.00**
	Fredericton	AHL	24	12	8	4	1457	78	0	3.21	....	....	....	....	....	....	....
1986-87	**Vancouver**	**NHL**	**8**	**1**	**6**	**1**	**420**	**35**	**0**	**5.00**	....	....	....	....	....	....	....
	Fredericton	AHL	30	11	16	0	1676	118	0	4.22	....	....	....	....	....	....	....
1987-88	**Philadelphia**	**NHL**	**6**	**3**	**2**	**0**	**320**	**20**	**0**	**3.75**	....	....	....	....	....	....	....
	Hershey Bears	AHL	51	*33	15	1	2922	135	1	2.77	12	*12	0	*767	28	*1	*2.19
1988-89	**Pittsburgh**	**NHL**	**22**	**12**	**9**	**0**	**1150**	**92**	**0**	**4.80**	**1**	**0**	**0**	**39**	**1**	**0**	**1.54**
	Muskegon	IHL	2	1	0	1	125	7	0	3.36	....	....	....	....	....	....	....
1989-90	**Pittsburgh**	**NHL**	**43**	**16**	**20**	**3**	**2318**	**161**	**1**	**4.17**	....	....	....	....	....	....	....
1990-91♦	**Pittsburgh**	**NHL**	**18**	**4**	**6**	**2**	**773**	**52**	**0**	**4.04**	....	....	....	....	....	....	....
1991-92♦	**Pittsburgh**	**NHL**	**18**	**7**	**6**	**0**	**838**	**53**	**0**	**3.79**	....	....	....	....	....	....	....
1992-93	**Tampa Bay**	**NHL**	**31**	**7**	**19**	**2**	**1591**	**97**	**0**	**3.66**	....	....	....	....	....	....	....
	Atlanta Knights	IHL	3	3	0	0	183	8	0	2.62	....	....	....	....	....	....	....
1993-94	**Tampa Bay**	**NHL**	**9**	**2**	**3**	**1**	**480**	**20**	**1**	**2.50**	....	....	....	....	....	....	....
	Atlanta Knights	IHL	2	2	0	0	120	6	0	3.00	....	....	....	....	....	....	....
1994-95	Chicago Wolves	IHL	37	14	11	7	1882	112	0	3.57	....	....	....	....	....	....	....
	Pittsburgh	**NHL**	**10**	**3**	**6**	**0**	**497**	**27**	**0**	**3.26**	....	....	....	....	....	....	....
1995-96	Chicago Wolves	IHL	61	30	20	6	3285	199	1	3.63	9	4	5	540	30	0	3.33
1996-97	Chicago Wolves	IHL	52	25	21	4	2931	170	1	3.48	4	1	3	256	13	0	3.04
1997-98	Chicago Wolves	IHL	51	31	14	3	2912	149	2	3.07	9	5	3	515	24	1	2.79
1998-99	Chicago Wolves	IHL	35	20	10	4	2047	84	3	2.46	7	4	3	421	19	1	2.71
99-2000	Chicago Wolves	IHL	48	32	12	4	2781	128	6	2.76	9	5	3	488	27	0	3.32
	NHL Totals		**187**	**59**	**86**	**12**	**9410**	**618**	**2**	**3.94**	**2**	**0**	**1**	**99**	**6**	**0**	**3.64**

AHL First All-Star Team (1988) • Won Baz Bastien Memorial Trophy (Top Goaltender - AHL) (1988) • Won Jack Butterfield Trophy (Playoff MVP - AHL) (1988)

Traded to **Philadelphia** by **Vancouver** with Vancouver's 3rd round choice (Kimbi Daniels) in 1990 Entry Draft for Darren Jensen and Daryl Stanley, August 31, 1987. Traded to **Pittsburgh** by **Philadelphia** with Philadelphia's 7th round choice (Mika Valila) in 1990 Entry Draft for Pittsburgh's 3rd round choice (Chris Therien) in 1990 Entry Draft, Steptember 1, 1988. Claimed by **Tampa Bay** from **Pittsburgh** in Expansion Draft, June 18, 1992. Traded to **Pittsburgh** by **Tampa Bay** for future considerations, February 16, 1995. • Only goaltender to win Memorial Cup (1982); Calder Cup (1988); Stanley Cup (1991, 1992) and Turner Cup (1998, 2000).

ZEPP, Rob (ZEHP, RAWB) ATL.

Goaltender. Catches left. 6'1", 160 lbs. Born, Scarborough, Ont., September 7, 1981.
(Atlanta's 5th choice, 99th overall, in 1999 Entry Draft).

			Regular Season								Playoffs						
Season	Club	Lea	GP	W	L	T	Mins	GA	SO	Avg	GP	W	L	Mins	GA	SO	Avg
1997-98	Newmarket 87's	OJHL	3	....	....	....	181	13	0	4.31	....	....	....	....	....	....	....
1998-99	Plymouth Whalers	OHL	31	19	3	4	1662	76	3	2.74	3	1	0	100	10	0	6.00
99-2000	Plymouth Whalers	OHL	53	*36	11	3	3005	119	3	*2.38	*23	*15	8	1374	52	2	2.27

OHL Second All-Star Team (2000)

Notes:

Retired Players and Goaltenders
Research Project

Throughout the Retired Players and Retired Goaltenders sections of this book, you will notice many players with a bullet (•) by their names. These players, according to our records, are deceased. The editors recognize that our information on the death dates of NHLers is incomplete. If you have documented information on the passing of any player not marked with a bullet (•) in this edition, we would like to hear from you. Please send this information to:

Retired Player Research Project
c/o NHL Publishing
194 Dovercourt Road
Toronto, Ontario
M6J 3C8   Canada
Fax: 416/531-3939

Many thanks to the following contributors in 1999-2000:

Patricia Barry, Paul R. Carroll, Jr., Bob Duff, Peter Fillman, Ernie Fitzsimmons, Mel Foster, Glen Goodhand, Bob Gregoire, Michelle G. Keller, Christopher MacDonald, John Paton, Gary J. Pearce, Ed Sweeney, Marie Woodruff.

Retired NHL Player Index

Abbreviations: Teams/Cities: — **Ana.** – Anaheim; **Atl.** – Atlanta; **Bos.** – Boston, **Bro.** – Brooklyn; **Buf.** – Buffalo; **Cal.** – California; **Cgy.** – Calgary; **Cle.** – Cleveland; **Col.** – Colorado; **Dal.** – Dallas; **Det.** – Detroit; **Edm.** – Edmonton; **Fla.** – Florida; **Ham.** – Hamilton; **Hfd.** – Hartford; **K.C.** – Kansas City; **L.A.** – Los Angeles; **Min.** — Minnesota; **Mtl.** – Montreal; **Mtl. M.** – Montreal Maroons; **Mtl. W.** – Montreal Wanderers; **N.J.** – New Jersey; **NYA** – NY Americans; **NYI** – New York Islanders; **NYR** – New York Rangers; **Oak.** – Oakland; **Ott.** – Ottawa; **Phi.** – Philadelphia; **Phx.** – Phoenix; **Pit.** – Pittsburgh; **Que.** – Quebec; **St. L.** – St. Louis; **S.J.** – San Jose; **T.B.** – Tampa Bay; **Tor.** – Toronto; **Van.** – Vancouver; **Wpg.** – Winnipeg; **Wsh.** – Washington.

Total seasons are rounded off to the nearest full season. **A** – assists; **G** – goals; **GP** – games played; **PIM** – penalties in minutes; **TP** – total points. ● – deceased. Assists not recorded during 1917-18 season ‡ – Remains active in other leagues.

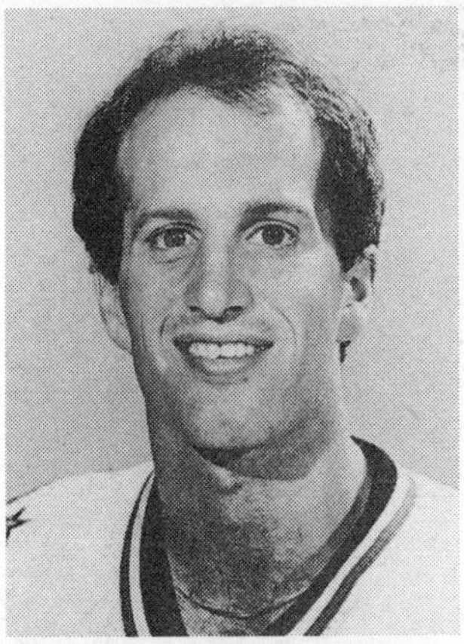

Keith Acton

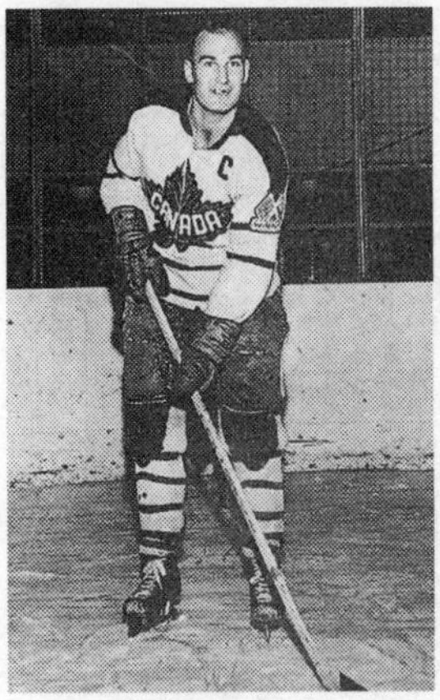

Gary Aldcorn

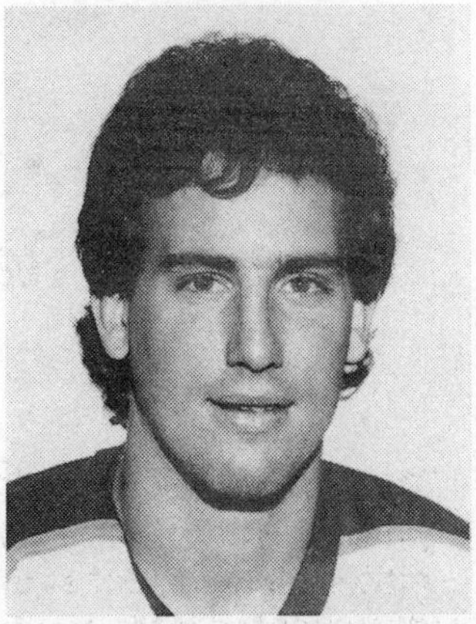

Scott Arniel

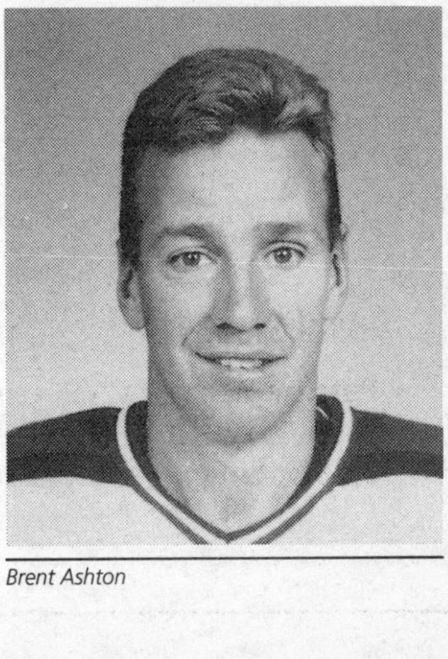

Brent Ashton

			Regular Schedule					Playoffs					NHL	First	Last
Name	NHL Teams	NHL Seasons	GP	G	A	TP	PIM	GP	G	A	TP	PIM	Cup Wins	NHL Season	NHL Season
A															
Abbott, Reg	Mtl.	1	3	0	0	0	0	....	....	....	....	....	....	1952-53	1952-53
● Abel, Clarence	NYR, Chi.	8	333	19	18	37	359	38	1	1	2	58	2	1926-27	1933-34
Abel, Gerry	Det.	1	1	0	0	0	0	....	....	....	....	....	....	1966-67	1966-67
● Abel, Sid	Det., Chi.	14	612	189	283	472	376	97	28	30	58	79	3	1938-39	1953-54
Abgrall, Dennis	L.A.	1	13	0	2	2	4	....	....	....	....	....	....	1975-76	1975-76
Abrahamsson, Thommy	Hfd.	1	32	6	11	17	16	....	....	....	....	....	....	1980-81	1980-81
Achtymichuk, Gene	Mtl., Det.	4	32	3	5	8	2	....	....	....	....	....	....	1951-52	1958-59
Acomb, Doug	Tor.	1	2	0	1	1	0	....	....	....	....	....	....	1969-70	1969-70
Acton, Keith	Mtl., Min., Edm., Phi., Wsh., NYI	17	1023	226	358	584	1172	66	12	21	33	88	1	1979-80	1993-94
Adam, Douglas	NYR	1	4	0	1	1	0	....	....	....	....	....	....	1949-50	1949-50
Adam, Russ	Tor.	1	8	1	2	3	11	....	....	....	....	....	....	1982-83	1982-83
Adams, Greg	Phi., Hfd., Wsh., Edm., Van., Que., Det.	10	545	84	143	227	1173	43	2	11	13	153	....	1980-81	1989-90
● Adams, Jack	Tor., Ott.	7	173	83	32	115	366	10	1	0	1	13	2	1917-18	1926-27
Adams, John	Mtl.	1	42	6	12	18	11	3	0	0	0	0	....	1940-41	1940-41
● Adams, Stew	Chi., Tor.	4	95	9	26	35	60	11	3	3	6	14	....	1929-30	1932-33
Adduono, Rick	Bos., Atl.	2	4	0	0	0	2	....	....	....	....	....	....	1975-76	1979-80
Affleck, Bruce	St.L., Van., NYI	7	280	14	66	80	86	8	0	0	0	0	....	1974-75	1983-84
Agnew, Jim	Van., Hfd.	7	81	0	1	1	257	4	0	0	0	6	....	1986-87	1993-94
Ahern, Fred	Cal., Cle., Col.	4	146	31	30	61	130	2	0	1	1	2	....	1974-75	1977-78
Ahlin, Tony	Chi.	1	1	0	0	0	0	....	....	....	....	....	....	1937-38	1937-38
‡ Ahola, Peter	L.A., Pit., S.J., Cgy.	3	123	10	17	27	137	6	0	0	0	2	....	1991-92	1993-94
Ahrens, Chris	Min.	6	52	0	3	3	84	1	0	0	0	0	....	1972-73	1977-78
Ailsby, Lloyd	NYR	1	3	0	0	0	2	....	....	....	....	....	....	1951-52	1951-52
Aitken, Brad	Pit., Edm.	2	14	1	3	4	25	....	....	....	....	....	....	1987-88	1990-91
● Albright, Clint	NYR	1	59	14	5	19	19	....	....	....	....	....	....	1948-49	1948-49
Aldcorn, Gary	Tor., Det., Bos.	5	226	41	56	97	78	6	1	2	3	4	....	1956-57	1960-61
Alexander, Claire	Tor., Van.	4	155	18	47	65	36	16	2	4	6	4	....	1974-75	1977-78
● Alexandre, Art	Mtl.C.	2	11	0	2	2	8	4	0	0	0	0	....	1931-32	1932-33
Allan, Jeff	Cle.	1	4	0	0	0	2	....	....	....	....	....	....	1977-78	1977-78
Allen, George	NYR, Chi., Mtl.	8	339	82	115	197	179	41	9	10	19	32	....	1938-39	1946-47
Allen, Keith	Det.	2	28	0	4	4	8	5	0	0	0	0	1	1953-54	1954-55
● Allen, Vivian	NYA	1	6	0	1	1	0	....	....	....	....	....	....	1940-41	1940-41
Alley, Steve	Hfd.	2	15	3	3	6	11	3	0	1	1	0	....	1979-80	1980-81
Allison, Dave	Mtl.	2	3	0	0	0	12	....	....	....	....	....	....	1983-84	1983-84
Allison, Mike	NYR, Tor., L.A.	10	499	102	166	268	630	82	9	17	26	135	....	1980-81	1989-90
Allison, Ray	Hfd., Phi.	7	238	64	93	157	223	12	2	3	5	20	....	1979-80	1986-87
● Allum, Bill	NYR	1	1	0	1	1	0	....	....	....	....	....	....	1940-41	1940-41
● Amadio, Dave	Det., L.A.	3	125	5	11	16	163	16	1	2	3	18	....	1957-58	1968-69
‡ Ambroziak, Peter	Buf.	1	12	0	1	1	0	....	....	....	....	....	....	1994-95	1994-95
Amodeo, Mike	Wpg.	1	19	0	0	0	2	....	....	....	....	....	....	1979-80	1979-80
● Anderson, Bill	Bos.	1	....	....	....	....	....	1	0	0	0	0	....	1942-43	1942-43
Anderson, Dale	Det.	1	13	0	0	0	6	2	0	0	0	0	....	1956-57	1956-57
Anderson, Doug	Mtl.	1	....	....	....	....	....	2	0	0	0	0	1	1952-53	1952-53
Anderson, Earl	Det., Bos.	3	109	19	19	38	22	5	0	1	1	0	....	1974-75	1976-77
Anderson, Glenn	Edm., Tor., NYR, St.L.	16	1129	498	601	1099	1120	225	93	121	214	442	6	1980-81	1995-96
Anderson, Jim	L.A.	1	7	1	2	3	2	....	....	....	....	....	....	1967-68	1967-68
Anderson, John	Tor., Que., Hfd.	12	814	282	349	631	263	37	9	18	27	2	....	1977-78	1988-89
Anderson, Murray	Wsh.	1	40	0	1	1	68	....	....	....	....	....	....	1974-75	1974-75
Anderson, Perry	St.L., N.J., S.J.	10	400	50	59	109	1051	36	2	1	3	161	....	1981-82	1991-92
Anderson, Ron	Det., L.A., St.L., Buf.	5	251	28	30	58	146	5	0	0	0	4	....	1967-68	1971-72
Anderson, Ron	Wsh.	1	28	9	7	16	8	....	....	....	....	....	....	1974-75	1974-75
Anderson, Russ	Pit., Hfd., L.A.	9	519	22	99	121	1086	10	0	3	3	28	....	1976-77	1984-85
‡ Anderson, Shawn	Buf., Que., Wsh., Phi.	8	255	11	51	62	117	19	1	1	2	16	....	1986-87	1994-95
● Anderson, Tom	Det., NYA, Bro.	8	319	62	127	189	180	16	2	7	9	8	....	1934-35	1941-42
Andersson, Kent-Erik	Min., NYR	7	456	72	103	175	78	50	4	11	15	4	....	1977-78	1983-84
Andersson, Peter	Wsh., Que.	3	172	10	41	51	81	7	0	2	2	2	....	1983-84	1985-86
‡ Andersson, Peter	NYR, Fla.	2	47	6	13	19	20	....	....	....	....	....	....	1992-93	1993-94
Andrascik, Steve	NYR	1	....	....	....	....	....	1	0	0	0	0	....	1971-72	1971-72
Andrea, Paul	NYR, Pit., Cal., Buf.	4	150	31	49	80	10	....	....	....	....	....	....	1965-66	1970-71
● Andrews, Lloyd	Tor.	4	53	8	5	13	10	2	0	0	0	0	....	1921-22	1924-25
‡ Andrievski, Alexander	Chi.	1	1	0	0	0	0	....	....	....	....	....	....	1992-93	1992-93
Andruff, Ron	Mtl., Col.	5	153	19	36	55	54	2	0	0	0	0	....	1974-75	1978-79
Angotti, Lou	NYR, Chi., Phi., Pit., St.L.	10	653	103	186	289	228	65	8	8	16	17	....	1964-65	1973-74
Anholt, Darrel	Chi.	1	1	0	0	0	0	....	....	....	....	....	....	1983-84	1983-84
Anslow, Hub	NYR	1	2	0	0	0	0	....	....	....	....	....	....	1947-48	1947-48
Antonovich, Mike	Min., Hfd., N.J.	6	87	10	15	25	37	....	....	....	....	....	....	1975-76	1983-84
Antoski, Shawn	Van., Phi., Pit., Ana.	8	183	3	5	8	599	36	1	3	4	74	....	1990-91	1997-98
● Apps, Syl	Tor.	10	423	201	231	432	56	69	25	29	54	8	3	1936-37	1947-48
Apps, Syl Jr.	NYR, Pit., L.A.	10	727	183	423	606	311	23	5	5	10	23	....	1970-71	1979-80
Arbour, Al	Det., Chi., Tor., St.L.	16	626	12	58	70	617	86	1	8	9	92	4	1953-54	1970-71
● Arbour, Amos	Mtl.C., Ham., Tor.	6	113	52	20	72	77	....	....	....	....	....	....	1918-19	1923-24
● Arbour, Jack	Det., Tor.	2	47	5	1	6	56	....	....	....	....	....	....	1926-27	1928-29
Arbour, John	Bos., Pit., Van., St.L.	5	106	1	9	10	149	5	0	0	0	0	....	1965-66	1971-72
● Arbour, Ty	Pit., Chi.	5	207	28	28	56	112	11	2	0	2	6	....	1926-27	1930-31
Archambault, Michel	Chi.	1	3	0	0	0	0	....	....	....	....	....	....	1976-77	1976-77
Archibald, Jim	Min.	3	16	1	2	3	45	....	....	....	....	....	....	1984-85	1986-87
Areshenkoff, Ron	Edm.	1	4	0	0	0	0	....	....	....	....	....	....	1979-80	1979-80
Armstrong, Bill	Phi.	1	1	0	1	1	0	....	....	....	....	....	....	1990-91	1990-91
● Armstrong, Bob	Bos.	12	542	13	86	99	671	42	1	7	8	28	....	1950-51	1961-62
Armstrong, George	Tor.	21	1187	296	417	713	721	110	26	34	60	52	4	1949-50	1970-71
Armstrong, Murray	Tor., NYA, Bro., Det.	8	270	67	121	188	72	30	4	6	10	2	....	1937-38	1945-46
● Armstrong, Norm	Tor.	1	7	1	1	2	2	....	....	....	....	....	....	1962-63	1962-63
Armstrong, Tim	Tor.	1	11	1	0	1	6	....	....	....	....	....	....	1988-89	1988-89
Arnason, Chuck	Mtl., Atl., Pit., K.C., Col., Cle., Min., Wsh.	8	401	109	90	199	122	9	2	4	6	4	....	1971-72	1978-79
Arniel, Scott	Wpg., Buf., Bos.	11	730	149	189	338	599	34	3	3	6	39	....	1981-82	1991-92
Arthur, Fred	Hfd., Phi.	3	80	1	8	9	49	4	0	0	0	2	....	1980-81	1982-83
Arundel, John	Tor.	1	3	0	0	0	9	....	....	....	....	....	....	1949-50	1949-50
● Ashbee, Barry	Bos., Phi.	6	284	15	70	85	291	17	0	4	4	22	1	1965-66	1973-74
● Ashby, Don	Tor., Col., Edm.	6	188	40	56	96	40	12	1	0	1	4	....	1975-76	1980-81
Ashton, Brent	Van., Col., N.J., Min., Que., Det., Wpg., Bos., Cgy.	14	998	284	345	629	635	85	24	25	49	70	....	1979-80	1992-93
Ashworth, Frank	Chi.	1	18	5	4	9	2	....	....	....	....	....	....	1946-47	1946-47
Asmundson, Oscar	NYR, Det., St.L., NYA, Mtl.C.	5	111	11	23	34	30	9	0	2	2	4	1	1932-33	1937-38
‡ Astley, Mark	Buf.	3	75	4	19	23	92	2	0	0	0	0	....	1993-94	1995-96
● Atanas, Walt	NYR	1	49	13	8	21	40	....	....	....	....	....	....	1944-45	1944-45
Atkinson, Steve	Bos., Buf., Wsh.	6	302	60	51	111	104	1	0	0	0	0	....	1968-69	1974-75
Attwell, Bob	Col.	2	22	1	5	6	0	....	....	....	....	....	....	1979-80	1980-81
Attwell, Ron	St.L., NYR	1	22	1	7	8	8	....	....	....	....	....	....	1967-68	1967-68

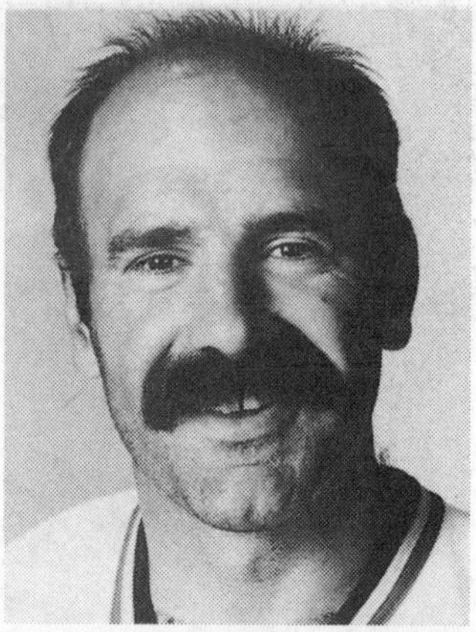

Dave Babych

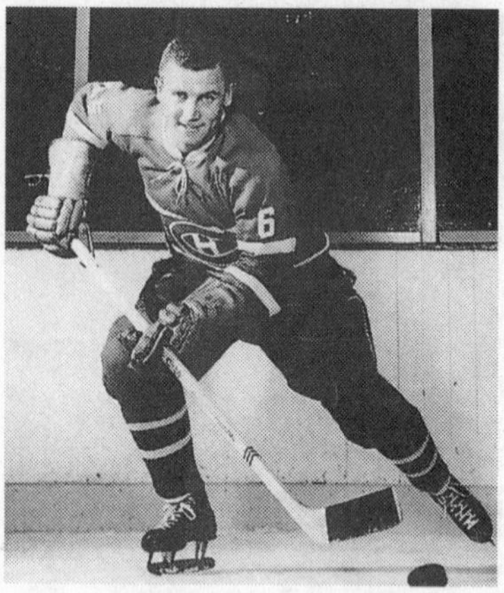

Ralph Backstrom

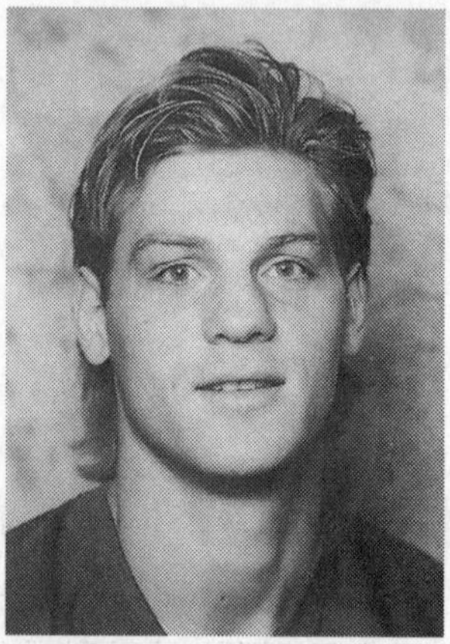

Ken Baumgartner

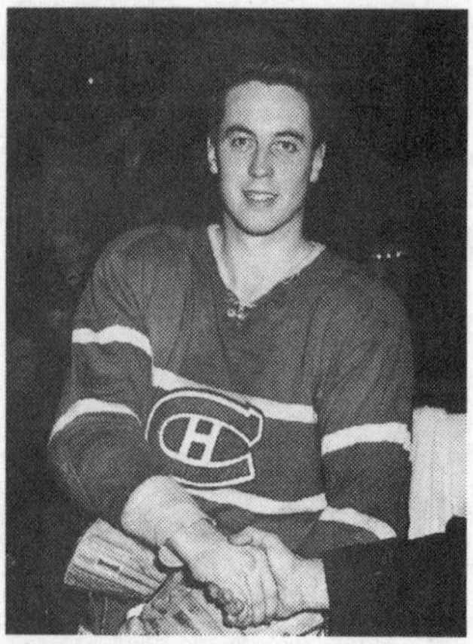

Jean Beliveau

			Regular Schedule					Playoffs					NHL	First	Last
Name	NHL Teams	NHL Seasons	GP	G	A	TP	PIM	GP	G	A	TP	PIM	Cup Wins	NHL Season	NHL Season
Aubin, Norm	Tor.	2	69	18	13	31	30	1	0	0	0	0	....	1981-82	1982-83
Aubry, Pierre	Que., Det.	5	202	24	26	50	133	20	1	1	2	32	....	1980-81	1984-85
Aubuchon, Ossie	Bos., NYR	2	50	20	12	32	4	6	1	0	1	0	....	1942-43	1943-44
Auge, Les	Col.	1	6	0	3	3	4	....	....	....	....	....	....	1980-81	1980-81
• Aurie, Larry	Det.	12	489	147	129	276	279	24	6	9	15	10	2	1927-28	1938-39
Awrey, Don	Bos., St.L., Mtl., Pit., NYR, Col.	16	979	31	158	189	1065	71	0	18	18	150	3	1963-64	1978-79
• Ayres, Vern	NYA, Mtl., St.L., NYR	6	211	6	11	17	350	....	....	....	....	....	....	1930-31	1935-36
B															
Babando, Pete	Bos., Det., Chi., NYR	6	351	86	73	159	194	17	3	3	6	6	1	1947-48	1952-53
Babcock, Bobby	Wsh.	2	2	0	0	0	2	....	....	....	....	....	....	1990-91	1992-93
Babe, Warren	Min.	4	21	2	5	7	23	2	0	0	0	0	....	1987-88	1990-91
Babin, Mitch	St.L.	1	8	0	0	0	0	....	....	....	....	....	....	1975-76	1975-76
Baby, John	Cle., Min.	2	26	2	8	10	26	....	....	....	....	....	....	1977-78	1978-79
‡ Babych, Dave	Wpg., Hfd., Van., Phi., L.A.	19	1195	142	581	723	970	114	21	41	62	113	....	1980-81	1998-99
Babych, Wayne	St.L., Pit., Que., Hfd.	9	519	192	246	438	498	41	7	9	16	24	....	1978-79	1986-87
‡ Baca, Jergus	Hfd.	2	10	0	2	2	14	....	....	....	....	....	....	1990-91	1991-92
Backman, Mike	NYR	3	18	1	6	7	18	10	2	2	4	2	....	1981-82	1983-84
• Backor, Pete	Tor.	1	36	4	5	9	6	....	....	....	....	....	1	1944-45	1944-45
Backstrom, Ralph	Mtl., L.A., Chi.	17	1032	278	361	639	386	116	27	32	59	68	6	1956-57	1972-73
• Bailey, Ace	Tor.	8	313	111	82	193	472	21	3	4	7	12	1	1926-27	1933-34
Bailey, Bob	Tor., Det., Chi.	5	150	15	21	36	207	15	0	4	4	22	....	1953-54	1957-58
Bailey, Garnet	Bos., Det., St.L., Wsh.	10	568	107	171	278	633	15	2	4	6	28	2	1968-69	1977-78
Bailey, Reid	Phi., Tor., Hfd.	4	40	1	3	4	105	16	0	2	2	25	....	1980-81	1983-84
Baillargeon, Joel	Wpg., Que.	3	20	0	2	2	31	....	....	....	....	....	....	1986-87	1988-89
Baird, Ken	Cal.	1	10	0	2	2	15	....	....	....	....	....	....	1971-72	1971-72
Baker, Bill	Mtl., Col., St.L., NYR	3	143	7	25	32	175	6	0	0	0	0	....	1980-81	1982-83
Baker, Jamie	Que., Ott., S.J., Tor.	10	404	71	79	150	271	25	5	4	9	42	....	1989-90	1998-99
Bakovic, Peter	Van.	1	10	2	0	2	48	....	....	....	....	....	....	1987-88	1987-88
Balderis, Helmut	Min.	1	26	3	6	9	2	....	....	....	....	....	....	1989-90	1989-90
Baldwin, Doug	Tor., Det., Chi.	3	24	0	1	1	8	....	....	....	....	....	....	1945-46	1947-48
Balfour, Earl	Tor., Chi.	7	288	30	22	52	78	26	0	3	3	4	1	1951-52	1960-61
• Balfour, Murray	Mtl., Chi., Bos.	8	306	67	90	157	393	40	9	10	19	45	1	1956-57	1964-65
Ball, Terry	Phi., Buf.	4	74	7	19	26	26	....	....	....	....	....	....	1967-68	1971-72
Balon, Dave	NYR, Mtl., Min., Van.	14	776	192	222	414	607	78	14	21	35	109	2	1959-60	1972-73
Baltimore, Bryon	Edm.	1	2	0	0	0	4	....	....	....	....	....	....	1979-80	1979-80
Baluik, Stan	Bos.	1	7	0	0	0	2	....	....	....	....	....	....	1959-60	1959-60
Bandura, Jeff	NYR	1	2	0	1	1	0	....	....	....	....	....	....	1980-81	1980-81
Banks, Darren	Bos.	2	20	2	2	4	73	....	....	....	....	....	....	1992-93	1993-94
‡ Barahona, Ralph	Bos.	2	6	2	2	4	0	....	....	....	....	....	....	1990-91	1991-92
Barbe, Andy	Tor.	1	1	0	0	0	2	....	....	....	....	....	....	1950-51	1950-51
Barber, Bill	Phi.	14	903	420	463	883	623	129	53	55	108	109	2	1972-73	1983-84
Barber, Don	Min., Wpg., Que., S.J.	4	115	25	32	57	64	11	4	4	8	10	....	1988-89	1991-92
• Barilko, Bill	Tor.	5	252	26	36	62	456	47	5	7	12	104	4	1946-47	1950-51
Barkley, Doug	Chi., Det.	8	253	24	80	104	382	30	0	9	9	63	....	1957-58	1967-68
Barlow, Bob	Min.	2	77	16	17	33	10	6	2	2	4	6	....	1969-70	1970-71
Barnes, Blair	L.A.	1	1	0	0	0	0	....	....	....	....	....	....	1982-83	1982-83
Barnes, Norm	Phi., Hfd.	5	156	6	38	44	178	12	0	0	0	8	....	1976-77	1981-82
Baron, Normand	Mtl., St.L.	2	27	2	0	2	51	3	0	0	0	22	....	1983-84	1985-86
Barr, Dave	Bos., NYR, St.L., Hfd., Det., N.J., Dal.	13	614	128	204	332	520	71	12	10	22	70	....	1981-82	1993-94
Barrault, Doug	Min., Fla.	2	4	0	0	0	2	....	....	....	....	....	....	1992-93	1993-94
Barrett, Fred	Min., L.A.	13	745	25	123	148	671	44	0	2	2	60	....	1970-71	1983-84
Barrett, John	Det., Wsh., Min.	8	488	20	77	97	604	16	2	2	4	50	....	1980-81	1987-88
Barrie, Doug	Pit., Buf., L.A.	3	158	10	42	52	268	....	....	....	....	....	....	1968-69	1971-72
Barry, Ed	Bos.	1	19	1	3	4	2	....	....	....	....	....	....	1946-47	1946-47
• Barry, Marty	NYA, Bos., Det., Mtl.	12	509	195	192	387	231	43	15	18	33	34	2	1927-28	1939-40
Barry, Ray	Bos.	1	18	1	2	3	6	....	....	....	....	....	....	1951-52	1951-52
Bartel, Robin	Cgy., Van.	2	41	0	1	1	14	6	0	0	0	16	....	1985-86	1986-87
Bartlett, Jim	Mtl., NYR, Bos.	5	191	34	23	57	273	2	0	0	0	0	....	1954-55	1960-61
• Barton, Cliff	Pit., Phi., NYR	3	85	10	9	19	22	....	....	....	....	....	....	1929-30	1939-40
Bathe, Frank	Det., Phi.	9	224	3	28	31	542	27	1	3	4	42	....	1974-75	1983-84
Bathgate, Andy	NYR, Tor., Det., Pit.	17	1069	349	624	973	624	54	21	14	35	76	1	1952-53	1970-71
Bathgate, Frank	NYR	1	2	0	0	0	2	....	....	....	....	....	....	1952-53	1952-53
• Batters, Jeff	St.L.	2	16	0	0	0	28	....	....	....	....	....	....	1993-94	1994-95
‡ Batyrshin, Ruslan	L.A.	1	2	0	0	0	6	....	....	....	....	....	....	1995-96	1995-96
• Bauer, Bobby	Bos.	9	327	123	137	260	36	48	11	8	19	6	2	1936-37	1951-52
Baumgartner, Ken	L.A., NYI, Tor., Ana., Bos.	13	696	13	41	54	2244	51	1	2	3	106	....	1987-88	1998-99
Baumgartner, Mike	K.C.	1	17	0	0	0	0	....	....	....	....	....	....	1974-75	1974-75
Baun, Bob	Tor., Oak., Det.	17	964	37	187	224	1493	96	3	12	15	171	4	1956-57	1972-73
‡ Bautin, Sergei	Wpg., Det., S.J.	3	132	5	25	30	176	6	0	0	0	2	....	1992-93	1995-96
‡ Bawa, Robin	Wsh., Van., S.J., Ana.	4	61	6	1	7	60	1	0	0	0	0	....	1989-90	1993-94
Baxter, Paul	Que., Pit., Cgy.	11	472	48	121	169	1564	40	0	5	5	162	....	1979-80	1986-87
Beadle, Sandy	Wpg.	1	6	1	0	1	2	....	....	....	....	....	....	1980-81	1980-81
Beaton, Frank	NYR	2	25	1	1	2	43	....	....	....	....	....	....	1978-79	1979-80
• Beattie, Red	Bos., Det., NYA	9	334	62	85	147	137	24	4	2	6	8	....	1930-31	1938-39
Beaudin, Norm	St.L., Min.	2	25	1	2	3	4	....	....	....	....	....	....	1967-68	1970-71
Beaudoin, Serge	Atl.	1	3	0	0	0	0	....	....	....	....	....	....	1979-80	1979-80
‡ Beaudoin, Yves	Wsh.	3	11	0	0	0	5	....	....	....	....	....	....	1985-86	1987-88
Beck, Barry	Col., NYR, L.A.	10	615	104	251	355	1016	51	10	23	33	77	....	1977-78	1989-90
Beckett, Bob	Bos.	4	68	7	6	13	18	....	....	....	....	....	....	1956-57	1963-64
Bedard, James	Chi.	2	22	1	1	2	8	....	....	....	....	....	....	1949-50	1950-51
Bednarski, John	NYR, Edm.	4	100	2	18	20	114	1	0	0	0	17	....	1974-75	1979-80
‡ Beers, Bob	Bos., T.B., Edm., NYI	8	258	28	79	107	225	21	1	1	2	22	....	1989-90	1996-97
Beers, Eddy	Cgy., St.L.	6	250	94	116	210	256	41	7	10	17	47	....	1981-82	1986-87
• Behling, Dick	Det.	2	5	1	0	1	2	....	....	....	....	....	....	1940-41	1942-43
Beisler, Frank	NYA	2	2	0	0	0	0	....	....	....	....	....	....	1936-37	1939-40
Belanger, Alain	Tor.	1	9	0	1	1	6	....	....	....	....	....	....	1977-78	1977-78
Belanger, Roger	Pit.	1	44	3	5	8	32	....	....	....	....	....	....	1984-85	1984-85
Belisle, Danny	NYR	1	4	2	0	2	0	....	....	....	....	....	....	1960-61	1960-61
Beliveau, Jean	Mtl.	20	1125	507	712	1219	1029	162	79	97	176	211	10	1950-51	1970-71
• Bell, Billy	Mtl., Mtl.C., Ott.	6	72	4	2	6	14	5	0	0	0	0	....	1917-18	1923-24
Bell, Bruce	Que., St.L., NYR, Edm.	5	209	12	64	76	113	34	3	5	8	41	....	1984-85	1989-90
Bell, Harry	NYR	1	1	0	1	1	0	....	....	....	....	....	....	1946-47	1946-47
Bell, Joe	NYR	2	62	8	9	17	18	....	....	....	....	....	....	1942-43	1946-47
Belland, Neil	Van., Pit.	6	109	13	32	45	54	21	2	9	11	23	....	1981-82	1986-87
• Bellefeuille, Pete	Tor., Det.	4	92	26	4	30	58	....	....	....	....	....	....	1925-26	1929-30
• Bellemer, Andy	Mtl.M.	1	15	0	0	0	0	....	....	....	....	....	....	1932-33	1932-33
Bellows, Brian	Min., Mtl., T.B., Ana., Wsh.	17	1188	485	537	1022	718	143	51	71	122	143	1	1982-83	1998-99
• Bend, Lin	NYR	1	8	3	1	4	2	....	....	....	....	....	....	1942-43	1942-43
Bennett, Adam	Chi., Edm.	3	69	3	8	11	69	....	....	....	....	....	....	1991-92	1993-94
Bennett, Bill	Bos., Hfd.	2	31	4	7	11	65	....	....	....	....	....	....	1978-79	1979-80
Bennett, Curt	St.L., NYR, Atl.	10	580	152	182	334	347	21	1	1	2	57	....	1970-71	1979-80
Bennett, Frank	Det.	1	7	0	1	1	2	....	....	....	....	....	....	1943-44	1943-44
Bennett, Harvey	Pit., Wsh., Phi., Min., St.L.	5	268	44	46	90	347	4	0	0	0	2	....	1974-75	1978-79
• Bennett, Max	Mtl.C.	1	1	0	0	0	0	....	....	....	....	....	....	1935-36	1935-36
Bennett, Rick	NYR	3	15	1	1	2	13	....	....	....	....	....	....	1989-90	1991-92
Benning, Brian	St.L., L.A., Phi., Edm., Fla.	11	568	63	233	296	963	48	3	20	23	74	....	1984-85	1994-95
Benning, Jim	Tor., Van.	9	605	52	191	243	461	7	1	1	2	2	....	1981-82	1989-90
• Benoit, Joe	Mtl.	5	185	75	69	144	94	11	6	3	9	11	1	1940-41	1946-47
Benson, Bill	NYA, Bro.	2	67	11	25	36	35	....	....	....	....	....	....	1940-41	1941-42
• Benson, Bobby	Bos.	1	8	0	1	1	4	....	....	....	....	....	....	1924-25	1924-25
• Bentley, Doug	Chi., NYR	13	566	219	324	543	217	23	9	8	17	12	....	1939-40	1953-54
• Bentley, Max	Chi., Tor., NYR	12	646	245	299	544	179	51	18	27	45	14	3	1940-41	1953-54
Bentley, Reggie	Chi.	1	11	1	2	3	2	....	....	....	....	....	....	1942-43	1942-43
Beraldo, Paul	Bos.	2	10	0	0	0	4	....	....	....	....	....	....	1987-88	1988-89
Berenson, Red	Mtl., NYR, St.L., Det.	21	987	261	397	658	305	85	23	14	37	49	1	1961-62	1977-78
Berezan, Perry	Cgy., Min., S.J.	9	378	61	75	136	279	31	4	7	11	34	....	1984-85	1992-93
Berg, Bill	NYI, Tor., NYR, Ott.	10	546	55	67	122	488	61	3	4	7	34	....	1988-89	1998-99
• Bergdinon, Fred	Bos.	1	2	0	0	0	0	....	....	....	....	....	....	1925-26	1925-26
Bergen, Todd	Phi.	2	14	11	5	16	4	17	4	9	13	8	....	1984-85	1985-86
‡ Berger, Mike	Min.	2	30	3	1	4	67	....	....	....	....	....	....	1987-88	1988-89

Name	NHL Teams	NHL Seasons	Regular Schedule					Playoffs					NHL Cup Wins	First NHL Season	Last NHL Season
			GP	G	A	TP	PIM	GP	G	A	TP	PIM			
Bergeron, Michel	Det., NYI, Wsh.	5	229	80	58	138	165	....	....	....	....	....	....	1974-75	1978-79
Bergeron, Yves	Pit.	2	3	0	0	0	0	....	....	....	....	....	....	1974-75	1976-77
‡ Bergkvist, Stefan	Pit.	2	7	0	0	0	9	4	0	0	0	2	....	1995-96	1996-97
Bergland, Tim	Wsh., T.B.	5	182	17	26	43	75	26	2	2	4	22	....	1989-90	1993-94
Bergloff, Bob	Min.	1	2	0	0	0	5	....	....	....	....	....	....	1982-83	1982-83
Berglund, Bo	Que., Min., Phi.	3	130	28	39	67	40	9	2	0	2	6	....	1983-84	1985-86
Bergman, Gary	Det., Min., K.C.	12	838	68	299	367	1249	21	0	5	5	20	....	1964-65	1975-76
Bergman, Thommie	Det.	6	246	21	44	65	243	7	0	2	2	2	....	1972-73	1979-80
Bergqvist, Jonas	Cgy.	1	22	2	5	7	10	....	....	....	....	....	....	1989-90	1989-90
● Berlinquette, Louis	Mtl.C., Mtl.M., Pit.	8	193	45	33	78	129	11	0	4	4	9	....	1917-18	1925-26
Bernier, Serge	Phi., L.A., Que.	7	302	78	119	197	234	5	1	1	2	0	....	1968-69	1980-81
Berry, Bob	Mtl., L.A.	16	541	159	191	350	344	26	2	6	8	6	....	1968-69	1976-77
Berry, Brad	Wpg., Min., Dal.	9	241	4	28	32	323	13	0	1	1	16	....	1985-86	1993-94
Berry, Doug	Col.	2	121	10	33	43	25	....	....	....	....	....	....	1979-80	1980-81
Berry, Fred	Det.	1	3	0	0	0	0	....	....	....	....	....	....	1976-77	1976-77
Berry, Ken	Edm., Van.	4	55	8	10	18	30	....	....	....	....	....	....	1981-82	1988-89
● Besler, Phil	Bos., Chi., Det.	2	30	1	4	5	18	....	....	....	....	....	....	1935-36	1938-39
● Bessone, Pete	Det.	1	6	0	1	1	6	....	....	....	....	....	....	1937-38	1937-38
Bethel, John	Wpg.	1	17	0	2	2	4	....	....	....	....	....	....	1979-80	1979-80
‡ Bets, Maxim	Ana.	1	3	0	0	0	0	....	....	....	....	....	....	1993-94	1993-94
Bettio, Sam	Bos.	1	44	9	12	21	32	....	....	....	....	....	....	1949-50	1949-50
Beukeboom, Jeff	Edm., NYR	14	804	30	129	159	1890	99	3	16	19	197	4	1985-86	1998-99
Beverley, Nick	Bos., Pit., NYR, Min., L.A., Col.	17	502	18	94	112	156	7	0	1	1	0	....	1966-67	1979-80
Bialowas, Dwight	Atl., Min.	4	164	11	46	57	46	....	....	....	....	....	....	1973-74	1976-77
Bianchin, Wayne	Pit., Edm.	7	276	68	41	109	137	3	0	1	1	6	....	1973-74	1979-80
Bidner, Todd	Wsh.	1	12	2	1	3	7	....	....	....	....	....	....	1981-82	1981-82
Biggs, Don	Min., Phi.	2	12	2	0	2	8	....	....	....	....	....	....	1984-85	1989-90
Bignell, Larry	Pit.	2	20	0	3	3	2	3	0	0	0	2	....	1973-74	1974-75
Bilodeau, Gilles	Que.	1	9	0	1	1	25	....	....	....	....	....	....	1979-80	1979-80
Bionda, Jack	Tor., Bos.	4	93	3	9	12	113	11	0	1	1	14	....	1955-56	1958-59
‡ Bissett, Tom	Det.	1	5	0	0	0	0	....	....	....	....	....	....	1990-91	1990-91
Bjugstad, Scott	Min., Pit., L.A.	9	317	76	68	144	144	9	0	1	1	2	....	1983-84	1991-92
Black, Stephen	Det., Chi.	2	113	11	20	31	77	13	0	0	0	13	1	1949-50	1950-51
Blackburn, Bob	NYR, Pit.	3	135	8	12	20	105	6	0	0	0	4	....	1968-69	1970-71
Blackburn, Don	Bos., Phi., NYR, NYI, Min.	6	185	23	44	67	87	12	3	0	3	10	....	1962-63	1972-73
Blade, Hank	Chi.	2	24	2	3	5	2	....	....	....	....	....	....	1946-47	1947-48
Bladon, Tom	Phi., Pit., Edm., Wpg., Det.	9	610	73	197	270	392	86	8	29	37	70	2	1972-73	1980-81
● Blaine, Garry	Mtl.	1	1	0	0	0	0	....	....	....	....	....	....	1954-55	1954-55
● Blair, Andy	Tor., Chi.	9	402	74	86	160	323	38	6	6	12	32	1	1928-29	1936-37
Blair, Chuck	Tor.	1	1	0	0	0	0	....	....	....	....	....	....	1948-49	1948-49
Blair, Dusty	Tor.	1	2	0	0	0	0	....	....	....	....	....	....	1950-51	1950-51
Blaisdell, Mike	Det., NYR, Pit., Tor.	9	343	70	84	154	166	6	1	2	3	10	....	1980-81	1988-89
Blake, Bob	Bos.	1	12	0	0	0	0	....	....	....	....	....	....	1935-36	1935-36
● Blake, Mickey	Mtl.M., St.L., Tor.	3	10	1	1	2	4	....	....	....	....	....	....	1932-33	1935-36
● Blake, Toe	Mtl.M., Mtl.C., Mtl.	14	577	235	292	527	272	58	25	37	62	23	3	1934-35	1947-48
Blight, Rick	Van., L.A.	7	326	96	125	221	170	5	0	5	5	2	....	1975-76	1982-83
● Blinco, Russ	Mtl.M., Chi.	6	268	59	66	125	24	19	3	3	6	4	1	1933-34	1938-39
Block, Ken	Van.	1	1	0	0	0	0	....	....	....	....	....	....	1970-71	1970-71
Bloemberg, Jeff	NYR	4	43	3	6	9	25	7	0	3	3	5	....	1988-89	1991-92
Blomqvist, Timo	Wsh., N.J.	5	243	4	53	57	293	13	0	0	0	24	....	1981-82	1986-87
‡ Blomsten, Arto	Wpg., L.A.	3	25	0	4	4	8	....	....	....	....	....	....	1993-94	1995-96
Bloom, Mike	Wsh., Det.	3	201	30	47	77	215	....	....	....	....	....	....	1974-75	1976-77
Blum, John	Edm., Bos., Wsh., Det.	8	250	7	34	41	610	20	0	2	2	27	....	1982-83	1989-90
Bodak, Bob	Cgy., Hfd.	2	4	0	0	0	29	....	....	....	....	....	....	1987-88	1989-90
Boddy, Gregg	Van.	5	273	23	44	67	263	3	0	0	0	0	....	1971-72	1975-76
Bodnar, Gus	Tor., Chi., Bos.	12	667	142	254	396	207	32	4	3	7	10	2	1943-44	1954-55
Boehm, Ron	Oak.	1	16	2	1	3	10	....	....	....	....	....	....	1967-68	1967-68
● Boesch, Garth	Tor.	4	197	9	28	37	205	34	2	5	7	18	3	1946-47	1949-50
Boh, Rick	Min.	1	8	2	1	3	4	....	....	....	....	....	....	1987-88	1987-88
Boileau, Marc	Det.	2	54	5	6	11	8	....	....	....	....	....	....	1961-62	1961-62
Boileau, Rene	NYA	1	7	0	0	0	0	....	....	....	....	....	....	1925-26	1925-26
Boimistruck, Fred	Tor.	2	83	4	14	18	45	....	....	....	....	....	....	1981-82	1982-83
Boisvert, Serge	Tor., Mtl.	5	46	5	7	12	8	23	3	7	10	4	1	1982-83	1987-88
‡ Boivin, Claude	Phi., Ott.	4	132	12	19	31	364	....	....	....	....	....	....	1991-92	1994-95
Boivin, Leo	Tor., Bos., Det., Pit., Min.	19	1150	72	250	322	1192	54	3	10	13	59	....	1951-52	1969-70
Boland, Mike	Phi.	1	2	0	0	0	0	....	....	....	....	....	....	1974-75	1974-75
Boland, Mike J.	K.C., Buf.	2	23	1	2	3	29	3	1	0	1	2	....	1974-75	1978-79
Boldirev, Ivan	Bos., Cal., Chi., Atl., Van., Det.	15	1052	361	505	866	507	48	13	20	33	14	....	1970-71	1984-85
Bolduc, Danny	Det., Cgy.	3	102	22	19	41	33	1	0	0	0	0	....	1978-79	1983-84
Bolduc, Michel	Que.	2	10	0	0	0	6	....	....	....	....	....	....	1981-82	1982-83
● Boll, Buzz	Tor., NYA, Bro., Bos.	12	437	133	130	263	148	31	7	3	10	13	....	1932-33	1943-44
Bolonchuk, Larry	Van., Wsh.	4	74	3	9	12	97	....	....	....	....	....	....	1972-73	1977-78
● Bolton, Hugh	Tor.	8	235	10	51	61	221	17	0	5	5	14	....	1949-50	1956-57
Bonar, Dan	L.A.	3	170	25	39	64	208	14	3	4	7	22	....	1980-81	1982-83
Bonin, Marcel	Det., Bos., Mtl.	9	454	97	175	272	336	50	11	14	25	51	4	1952-53	1961-62
Boo, Jim	Min.	1	6	0	0	0	22	....	....	....	....	....	....	1977-78	1977-78
Boone, Buddy	Bos.	2	34	5	3	8	28	22	2	1	3	25	....	1956-57	1957-58
Boothman, George	Tor.	2	58	17	19	36	18	5	2	1	3	2	....	1942-43	1943-44
Bordeleau, Christian	Mtl., St.L., Chi.	4	205	38	65	103	82	19	4	7	11	17	1	1968-69	1971-72
Bordeleau, J.P.	Chi.	10	519	97	126	223	143	48	3	6	9	12	....	1969-70	1979-80
Bordeleau, Paulin	Van.	4	183	33	56	89	47	5	2	1	3	0	....	1973-74	1975-76
Borotsik, Jack	St.L.	1	1	0	0	0	0	....	....	....	....	....	....	1974-75	1974-75
‡ Borsato, Luciano	Wpg.	5	203	35	55	90	113	7	1	0	1	4	....	1990-91	1994-95
Borschevsky, Nikolai	Tor., Cgy., Dal.	4	162	49	73	122	44	31	4	9	13	4	....	1992-93	1995-96
Boschman, Laurie	Tor., Edm., Wpg., N.J., Ott.	14	1009	229	348	577	2265	57	8	13	21	140	....	1979-80	1992-93
Bossy, Mike	NYI	10	752	573	553	1126	210	129	85	75	160	38	4	1977-78	1986-87
Bostrom, Helge	Chi.	4	96	3	3	6	58	13	0	0	0	16	....	1929-30	1932-33
Botell, Mark	Phi.	1	32	4	10	14	31	....	....	....	....	....	....	1981-82	1981-82
Bothwell, Tim	NYR, St.L., Hfd.	11	502	28	93	121	382	49	0	3	3	56	....	1978-79	1988-89
Botting, Cam	Atl.	1	2	0	1	1	0	....	....	....	....	....	....	1975-76	1975-76
Boucha, Henry	Det., Min., K.C., Col.	6	247	53	49	102	157	....	....	....	....	....	....	1971-72	1976-77
Bouchard, Butch	Mtl.	15	785	49	144	193	863	113	11	21	32	121	4	1941-42	1955-56
Bouchard, Dick	NYR	1	1	0	0	0	0	....	....	....	....	....	....	1954-55	1954-55
● Bouchard, Edmond	Mtl.C., Ham., NYA, Pit.	8	211	19	21	40	117	....	....	....	....	....	....	1921-22	1928-29
Bouchard, Pierre	Mtl., Wsh.	12	595	24	82	106	433	76	3	10	13	56	5	1970-71	1981-82
● Boucher, Billy	Mtl.C., Bos., NYA	7	213	93	38	131	409	14	3	0	3	17	....	1921-22	1927-28
● Boucher, Bobby	Mtl.C.	1	11	1	0	1	0	2	0	0	0	0	....	1923-24	1923-24
● Boucher, Clarence	NYA	2	47	2	2	4	133	....	....	....	....	....	....	1926-27	1927-28
● Boucher, Frank	Ott., NYR	18	557	160	263	423	119	55	16	20	36	12	2	1921-22	1943-44
● Boucher, Georges	Ott., Mtl.M., Chi.	16	449	117	87	204	838	28	5	3	8	88	1	1917-18	1931-32
Boudreau, Bruce	Tor., Chi.	8	141	28	42	70	46	9	2	0	2	0	....	1976-77	1985-86
Boudrias, Andre	Mtl., Min., Chi., St.L., Van.	12	662	151	340	491	216	34	6	10	16	12	....	1963-64	1975-76
Boughner, Barry	Oak., Cal.	2	20	0	0	0	11	....	....	....	....	....	....	1969-70	1970-71
Bourbonnais, Dan	Hfd.	2	59	3	25	28	11	....	....	....	....	....	....	1981-82	1983-84
Bourbonnais, Rick	St.L.	3	71	9	15	24	29	4	0	1	1	0	....	1975-76	1977-78
● Bourcier, Conrad	Mtl.C.	1	6	0	0	0	0	....	....	....	....	....	....	1935-36	1935-36
Bourcier, Jean	Mtl.C.	1	9	0	1	1	0	....	....	....	....	....	....	1935-36	1935-36
● Bourgeault, Leo	Tor., NYR, Ott., Mtl.C.	8	307	24	20	44	269	24	1	1	2	18	1	1926-27	1934-35
Bourgeois, Charlie	Cgy., St.L., Hfd.	7	290	16	54	70	788	40	2	3	5	194	....	1981-82	1987-88
Bourne, Bob	NYI, L.A.	14	964	258	324	582	605	139	40	56	96	108	4	1974-75	1987-88
‡ Bourque, Phil	Pit., NYR, Ott.	12	477	88	111	199	516	56	13	12	25	107	2	1983-84	1995-96
Boutette, Pat	Tor., Hfd., Pit.	10	756	171	282	453	1354	46	10	14	24	109	....	1975-76	1984-85
Boutilier, Paul	NYI, Bos., Min., NYR, Wpg.	8	288	27	83	110	358	41	1	9	10	45	1	1981-82	1988-89
Bowman, Kirk	Chi.	3	88	11	17	28	19	7	1	0	1	0	....	1976-77	1978-79
● Bowman, Ralph	Ott., St.L., Det.	7	274	8	17	25	260	22	2	2	4	6	2	1933-34	1939-40
Bownass, Jack	Mtl., NYR	4	80	3	8	11	58	....	....	....	....	....	....	1957-58	1961-62
Bowness, Rick	Atl., Det., St.L., Wpg.	15	173	18	37	55	191	5	0	0	0	2	....	1975-76	1981-82
● Boyd, Bill	NYR, NYA	4	138	15	7	22	72	10	0	0	0	4	1	1926-27	1929-30
Boyd, Irvin	Bos., Det.	4	96	10	10	20	30	5	0	1	1	4	....	1931-32	1943-44
Boyd, Randy	Pit., Chi., NYI, Van.	8	257	20	67	87	328	13	0	2	2	26	....	1981-82	1988-89
Boyer, Wally	Tor., Chi., Oak., Pit.	7	365	54	105	159	163	15	1	3	4	0	....	1965-66	1971-72
Boyer, Zac	Dal.	2	3	0	0	0	0	2	0	0	0	0	....	1994-95	1995-96

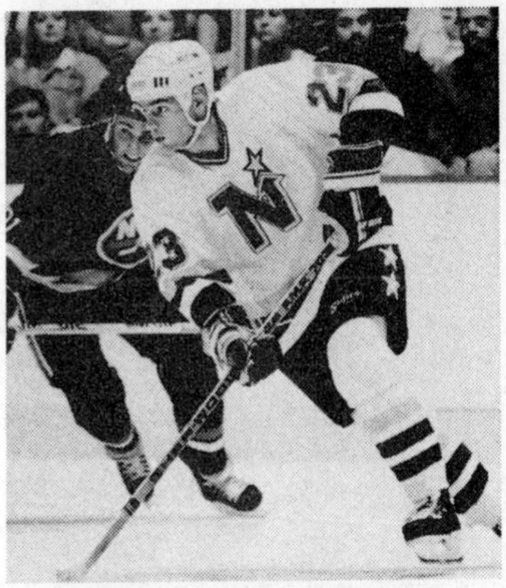

Brian Bellows

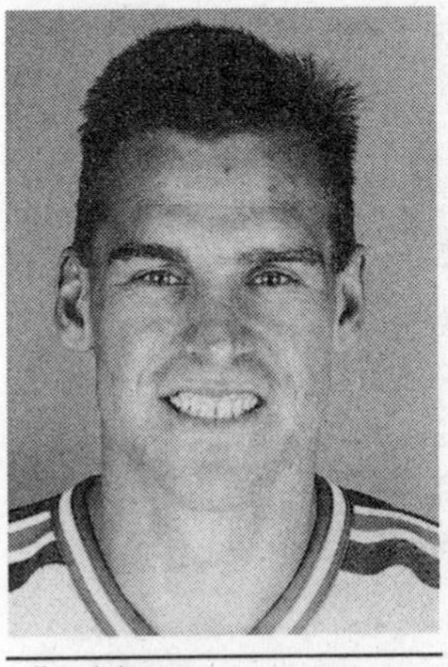

Jeff Beukeboom

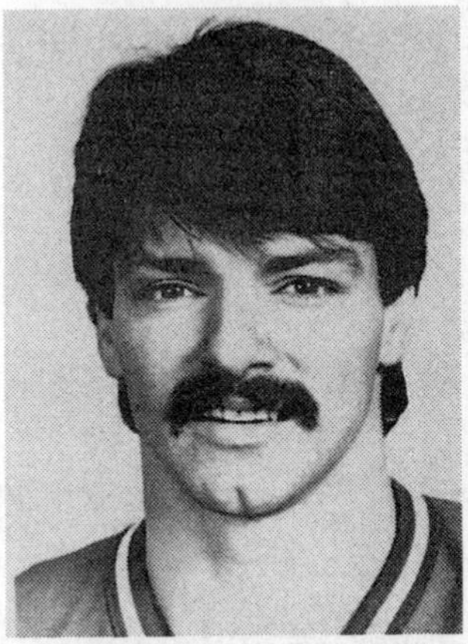

Serge Boisvert

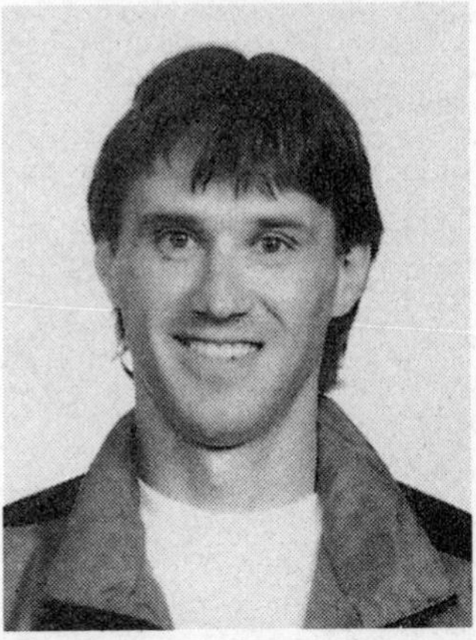

Laurie Boschman

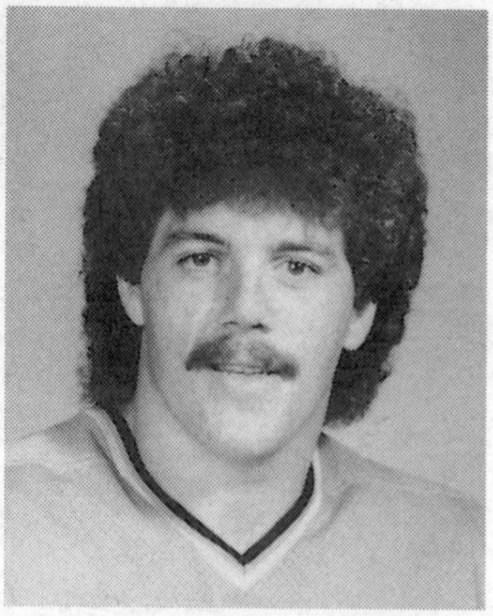

Mike Bullard

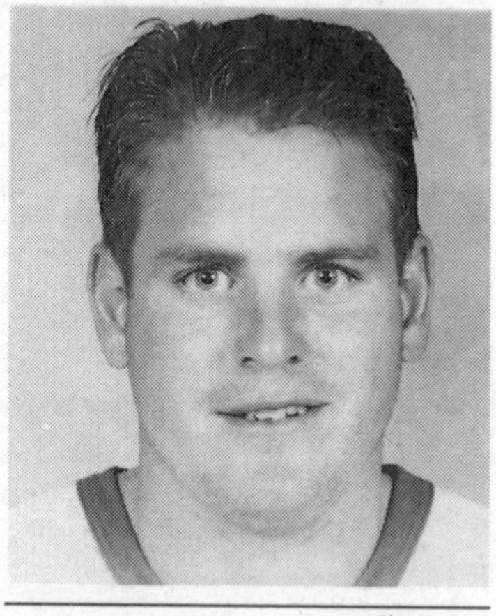

Shawn Burr

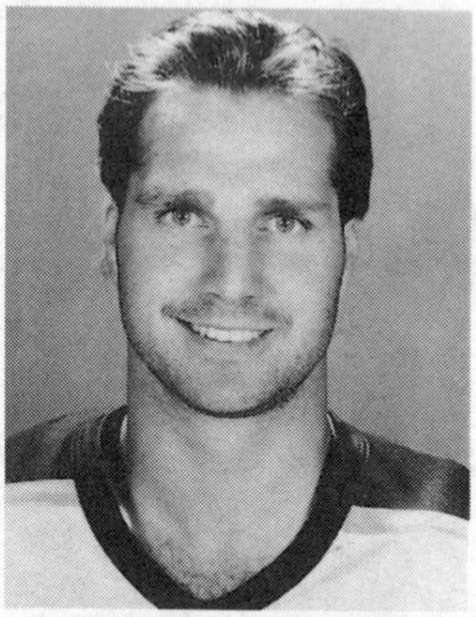

Randy Burridge

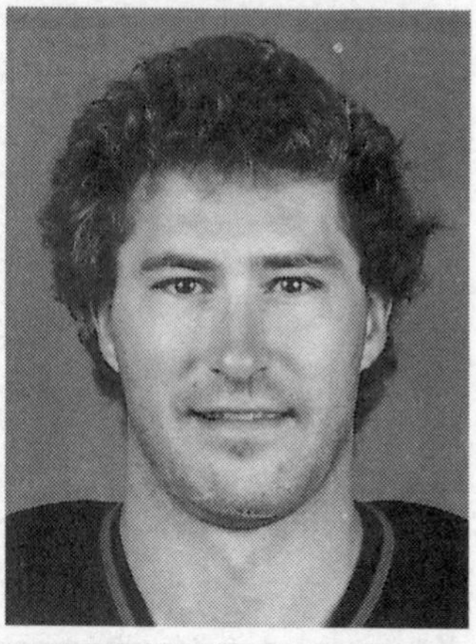

Bobby Carpenter

			Regular Schedule					Playoffs					NHL	First	Last
Name	NHL Teams	NHL Seasons	GP	G	A	TP	PIM	GP	G	A	TP	PIM	Cup Wins	NHL Season	NHL Season
Boyko, Darren	Wpg.	1	1	0	0	0	0	....	....	....	....	....	....	1988-89	1988-89
Bozek, Steve	L.A., Cgy., St.L., Van., S.J.	11	641	164	167	331	309	58	12	11	23	69	....	1981-82	1991-92
‡ Bozon, Philippe	St.L.	4	144	16	25	41	101	19	2	0	2	31	....	1991-92	1994-95
● Brackenborough, John	Bos.	1	7	0	0	0	0	....	....	....	....	....	....	1925-26	1925-26
Brackenbury, Curt	Que., Edm., St.L.	4	141	9	17	26	226	2	0	0	0	0	....	1979-80	1982-83
Bradley, Bart	Bos.	1	1	0	0	0	0	....	....	....	....	....	....	1949-50	1949-50
Bradley, Brian	Cgy., Van., Tor., T.B.	14	651	182	321	503	528	13	3	7	10	16	....	1985-86	1998-99
Bradley, Lyle	Cal., Cle.	2	6	1	0	1	2	....	....	....	....	....	....	1973-74	1976-77
‡ Brady, Neil	N.J., Ott., Dal.	5	89	9	22	31	95	....	....	....	....	....	....	1989-90	1993-94
Bragnalo, Rick	Wsh.	4	145	15	35	50	46	....	....	....	....	....	....	1975-76	1978-79
● Branigan, Andy	NYA, Bro.	2	27	1	2	3	31	....	....	....	....	....	....	1940-41	1941-42
Brasar, Per-Olov	Min., Van.	5	348	64	142	206	33	13	1	2	3	0	....	1977-78	1981-82
● Brayshaw, Russ	Chi.	1	43	5	9	14	24	....	....	....	....	....	....	1944-45	1944-45
Breault, Francois	L.A.	3	27	2	4	6	42	....	....	....	....	....	....	1990-91	1992-93
Breitenbach, Ken	Buf.	4	68	1	13	14	49	8	0	1	1	4	....	1975-76	1978-79
Brennan, Dan	L.A.	2	8	0	1	1	9	....	....	....	....	....	....	1983-84	1985-86
Brennan, Doug	NYR	3	123	9	7	16	152	16	1	0	1	21	1	1931-32	1933-34
Brennan, Tom	Bos.	3	12	2	2	4	2	....	....	....	....	....	....	1943-44	1945-46
Brenneman, John	Chi., NYR, Tor., Det., Oak.	5	152	21	19	40	46	....	....	....	....	....	1	1964-65	1968-69
Bretto, Joe	Chi.	1	3	0	0	0	4	....	....	....	....	....	....	1944-45	1944-45
Brewer, Carl	Tor., Det., St.L.	12	604	25	198	223	1037	72	3	17	20	146	3	1957-58	1979-80
Brickley, Andy	Phi., Pit., N.J., Bos., Wpg.	11	385	82	140	222	81	17	1	4	5	4	....	1982-83	1993-94
● Briden, Archie	Bos., Det., Pit.	2	71	9	5	14	56	....	....	....	....	....	....	1926-27	1929-30
Bridgman, Mel	Phi., Cgy., N.J., Det., Van.	14	977	252	449	701	1625	125	28	39	67	298	....	1975-76	1988-89
● Briere, Michel	Pit.	1	76	12	32	44	20	10	5	3	8	17	....	1969-70	1969-70
Brindley, Doug	Tor.	1	3	0	0	0	0	....	....	....	....	....	....	1970-71	1970-71
● Brink, Milt	Chi.	1	5	0	0	0	0	....	....	....	....	....	....	1936-37	1936-37
Brisson, Gerry	Mtl.	1	4	0	2	2	4	....	....	....	....	....	....	1962-63	1962-63
Britz, Greg	Tor., Hfd.	3	8	0	0	0	4	....	....	....	....	....	....	1983-84	1986-87
● Broadbent, Punch	Ott., Mtl.M., NYA	11	303	121	51	172	564	23	4	5	9	50	....	1918-19	1928-29
‡ Brochu, Stephane	NYR	1	1	0	0	0	0	....	....	....	....	....	....	1988-89	1988-89
Broden, Connie	Mtl.	3	6	2	1	3	2	7	0	1	1	0	2	1955-56	1957-58
Brooke, Bob	NYR, Min., N.J.	7	447	69	97	166	520	34	9	9	18	59	....	1983-84	1989-90
Brooks, Gord	St.L., Wsh.	3	70	7	18	25	37	....	....	....	....	....	....	1971-72	1974-75
● Brophy, Bernie	Mtl.M., Det.	3	62	4	4	8	25	2	0	0	0	2	....	1925-26	1929-30
Brossart, Willie	Phi., Tor., Wsh.	6	129	1	14	15	88	1	0	0	0	0	....	1970-71	1975-76
Broten, Aaron	Col., N.J., Min., Que., Tor., Wpg.	12	748	186	329	515	441	34	7	18	25	40	....	1980-81	1991-92
Broten, Neal	Min., Dal., N.J., L.A.	17	1099	289	634	923	569	135	35	63	98	77	1	1980-81	1996-97
Broten, Paul	NYR, Dal., St.L.	7	322	46	55	101	264	38	4	6	10	18	....	1989-90	1995-96
● Brown, Adam	Det., Chi., Bos.	10	391	104	113	217	378	26	2	4	6	14	1	1941-42	1951-52
Brown, Arnie	Tor., NYR, Det., NYI, Atl.	12	681	44	141	185	738	22	0	6	6	23	....	1961-62	1973-74
‡ Brown, Cam	Van.	1	1	0	0	0	7	....	....	....	....	....	....	1990-91	1990-91
● Brown, Connie	Det.	5	73	15	24	39	12	14	2	3	5	0	1	1938-39	1942-43
Brown, David	Phi., Edm., S.J.	14	729	45	52	97	1789	80	2	3	5	209	1	1982-83	1995-96
● Brown, Fred	Mtl.M.	1	19	1	0	1	0	9	0	0	0	0	....	1927-28	1927-28
Brown, George	Mtl.C.	3	79	6	22	28	34	7	0	0	0	2	....	1936-37	1938-39
● Brown, Gerry	Det.	2	23	4	5	9	2	12	2	1	3	4	....	1941-42	1945-46
‡ Brown, Greg	Buf., Pit., Wpg.	4	94	4	14	18	86	6	0	1	1	4	....	1990-91	1994-95
Brown, Harold	NYR	1	13	2	1	3	2	....	....	....	....	....	....	1945-46	1945-46
Brown, Jeff	Que., St.L., Van., Hfd., Car., Tor., Wsh.	13	747	154	430	584	498	87	20	45	65	59	....	1985-86	1997-98
Brown, Jim	L.A.	1	3	0	1	1	5	....	....	....	....	....	....	1982-83	1982-83
Brown, Keith	Chi., Fla.	16	876	68	274	342	916	103	4	32	36	184	....	1979-80	1994-95
Brown, Larry	NYR, Det., Phi., L.A.	9	455	7	53	60	180	35	0	4	4	10	....	1969-70	1977-78
● Brown, Stan	NYR, Det.	2	48	8	2	10	18	2	0	0	0	0	....	1926-27	1927-28
Brown, Wayne	Bos.	1	....	....	....	....	....	4	0	0	0	2	....	1953-54	1953-54
● Browne, Cecil	Chi.	1	13	2	0	2	4	....	....	....	....	....	....	1927-28	1927-28
Brownschidle, Jack	St.L., Hfd.	9	494	39	162	201	151	26	0	5	5	18	....	1977-78	1985-86
Brownschidle, Jeff	Hfd.	2	7	0	1	1	2	....	....	....	....	....	....	1981-82	1982-83
Brubaker, Jeff	Hfd., Mtl., Cgy., Tor., Edm., NYR, Det.	8	178	16	9	25	512	2	0	0	0	27	....	1979-80	1988-89
Bruce, David	Van., St.L., S.J.	8	234	48	39	87	338	3	0	0	0	2	....	1985-86	1993-94
● Bruce, Gordie	Bos.	3	28	4	9	13	13	7	2	3	5	4	1	1940-41	1945-46
● Bruce, Morley	Ott.	4	71	8	3	11	27	3	0	0	0	2	1	1917-18	1921-22
Brumwell, Murray	Min., N.J.	7	128	12	31	43	70	2	0	0	0	2	....	1980-81	1987-88
Bruneteau, Eddie	Det.	7	180	40	42	82	35	31	7	6	13	0	....	1940-41	1948-49
● Bruneteau, Mud	Det.	11	411	139	138	277	80	77	23	14	37	22	3	1935-36	1945-46
● Brydge, Bill	Tor., Det., NYA	9	368	26	52	78	506	2	0	0	0	4	....	1926-27	1935-36
Brydges, Paul	Buf.	1	15	2	2	4	6	....	....	....	....	....	....	1986-87	1986-87
● Brydson, Glenn	Mtl.M., St.L., NYR, Chi.	8	299	56	79	135	203	11	0	0	0	8	....	1930-31	1937-38
Brydson, Gord	Tor.	1	8	2	0	2	8	....	....	....	....	....	....	1929-30	1929-30
Bubla, Jiri	Van.	5	256	17	101	118	202	6	0	0	0	7	....	1981-82	1985-86
● Buchanan, Al	Tor.	2	4	0	1	1	2	....	....	....	....	....	....	1948-49	1949-50
Buchanan, Bucky	NYR	1	2	0	0	0	0	....	....	....	....	....	....	1948-49	1948-49
Buchanan, Jeff	Col.	1	6	0	0	0	6	....	....	....	....	....	....	1998-99	1998-99
Buchanan, Mike	Chi.	1	1	0	0	0	0	....	....	....	....	....	....	1951-52	1951-52
Buchanan, Ron	Bos., St.L.	2	5	0	0	0	0	....	....	....	....	....	....	1966-67	1969-70
Bucyk, John	Det., Bos.	23	1540	556	813	1369	497	124	41	62	103	42	2	1955-56	1977-78
Bucyk, Randy	Mtl., Cgy.	2	19	4	2	6	8	2	0	0	0	0	1	1985-86	1987-88
Buhr, Doug	K.C.	1	6	0	2	2	4	....	....	....	....	....	....	1974-75	1974-75
Bukovich, Tony	Det.	2	17	7	3	10	6	6	0	1	1	0	....	1943-44	1944-45
‡ Bullard, Mike	Pit., Cgy., St.L., Phi., Tor.	11	727	329	345	674	703	40	11	18	29	44	....	1980-81	1991-92
● Buller, Hy	Det., NYR	5	188	22	58	80	215	....	....	....	....	....	....	1943-44	1953-54
Bulley, Ted	Chi., Wsh., Pit.	8	414	101	113	214	704	29	5	5	10	24	....	1976-77	1983-84
‡ Burakovsky, Robert	Ott.	1	23	2	3	5	6	....	....	....	....	....	....	1993-94	1993-94
● Burch, Billy	Ham., NYA, Bos., Chi.	11	390	137	61	198	255	2	0	0	0	0	....	1922-23	1932-33
● Burchell, Fred	Mtl.	2	4	0	0	0	2	....	....	....	....	....	....	1950-51	1953-54
Burdon, Glen	K.C.	1	11	0	2	2	0	....	....	....	....	....	....	1974-75	1974-75
Burega, Bill	Tor.	1	4	0	1	1	4	....	....	....	....	....	....	1955-56	1955-56
● Burke, Eddie	Bos., NYA	4	106	29	20	49	55	....	....	....	....	....	....	1931-32	1934-35
● Burke, Marty	Mtl.C., Pit., Ott., Chi.	11	494	19	47	66	560	31	2	4	6	44	2	1927-28	1937-38
● Burmeister, Roy	NYA	3	67	4	3	7	2	....	....	....	....	....	....	1929-30	1931-32
Burnett, Kelly	NYR	1	3	1	0	1	0	....	....	....	....	....	....	1952-53	1952-53
Burns, Bobby	Chi.	3	20	1	0	1	8	....	....	....	....	....	....	1927-28	1929-30
Burns, Charlie	Det., Bos., Oak., Pit., Min.	11	749	106	198	304	252	31	5	4	9	6	....	1958-59	1972-73
Burns, Gary	NYR	2	11	2	2	4	18	5	0	0	0	2	....	1980-81	1981-82
● Burns, Norm	NYR	1	11	0	4	4	2	....	....	....	....	....	....	1941-42	1941-42
Burns, Robin	Pit., K.C.	5	190	31	38	69	139	....	....	....	....	....	....	1970-71	1975-76
‡ Burr, Shawn	Det., T.B., S.J.	16	878	181	259	440	1069	91	16	19	35	95	....	1984-85	1999-00
Burridge, Randy	Bos., Wsh., L.A., Buf.	13	706	199	251	450	458	107	18	34	52	103	....	1985-86	1997-98
Burrows, Dave	Pit., Tor.	10	724	29	135	164	373	29	1	5	6	25	....	1971-72	1980-81
● Burry, Bert	Ott.	1	4	0	0	0	0	....	....	....	....	....	....	1932-33	1932-33
Burton, Cummy	Det.	3	43	0	2	2	21	3	0	0	0	0	....	1955-56	1958-59
Burton, Nelson	Wsh.	2	8	1	0	1	21	....	....	....	....	....	....	1977-78	1978-79
● Bush, Eddie	Det.	2	26	4	6	10	40	11	1	6	7	23	....	1938-39	1941-42
Buskas, Rod	Pit., Van., L.A., Chi.	11	556	19	63	82	1294	18	0	3	3	45	....	1982-83	1992-93
Busniuk, Mike	Phi.	2	143	3	23	26	297	25	2	5	7	34	....	1979-80	1980-81
Busniuk, Ron	Buf.	2	6	0	3	3	13	....	....	....	....	....	....	1972-73	1973-74
● Buswell, Walt	Det., Mtl.C., Mtl.	8	368	10	40	50	164	24	2	1	3	10	....	1932-33	1939-40
Butcher, Garth	Van., St.L., Que., Tor.	14	897	48	158	206	2302	50	6	5	11	122	....	1981-82	1994-95
Butler, Dick	Chi.	1	7	2	0	2	0	....	....	....	....	....	....	1947-48	1947-48
Butler, Jerry	NYR, St.L., Tor., Van., Wpg.	11	641	99	120	219	515	48	3	3	6	79	....	1972-73	1982-83
Butters, Bill	Min.	2	72	1	4	5	77	....	....	....	....	....	....	1977-78	1978-79
Buttrey, Gord	Chi.	1	10	0	0	0	0	....	....	....	....	....	....	1943-44	1943-44
Buynak, Gord	St.L.	1	4	0	0	0	2	....	....	....	....	....	....	1974-75	1974-75
‡ Byakin, Ilja	Edm., S.J.	2	57	8	25	33	44	....	....	....	....	....	....	1993-94	1994-95
Byce, John	Bos.	3	21	2	3	5	6	8	2	0	2	2	....	1989-90	1991-92
Byers, Gord	Bos.	1	1	0	1	1	0	....	....	....	....	....	....	1949-50	1949-50
Byers, Jerry	Min., Atl., NYR	4	43	3	4	7	15	....	....	....	....	....	....	1972-73	1977-78
Byers, Lyndon	Bos., S.J.	10	279	28	43	71	1081	37	2	2	4	96	....	1983-84	1992-93
Byers, Mike	Tor., Phi., L.A., Buf.	4	166	42	34	76	39	4	0	1	1	0	....	1967-68	1971-72
Byram, Shawn	NYI, Chi.	2	5	0	0	0	14	....	....	....	....	....	....	1990-91	1991-92

Name	NHL Teams	NHL Seasons	Regular Schedule					Playoffs					NHL Cup Wins	First NHL Season	Last NHL Season
			GP	G	A	TP	PIM	GP	G	A	TP	PIM			
C															
• Caffery, Jack	Tor., Bos.	3	57	3	2	5	22	10	1	0	1	4	....	1954-55	1957-58
Caffery, Terry	Chi., Min.	2	14	0	0	0	0	1	0	0	0	0	....	1969-70	1970-71
• Cahan, Larry	Tor., NYR, Oak., L.A.	13	666	38	92	130	700	29	1	1	2	38	....	1954-55	1970-71
• Cahill, Charles	Bos.	2	32	0	1	1	4	....	....	....	....	....	....	1925-26	1926-27
• Cain, Francis	Mtl.M., Tor.	2	61	4	0	4	35	....	....	....	....	....	....	1924-25	1925-26
• Cain, Herb	Mtl.M., Mtl.C., Bos.	13	570	206	194	400	178	67	16	13	29	13	2	1933-34	1945-46
Cairns, Don	K.C., Col.	2	9	0	1	1	2	....	....	....	....	....	....	1975-76	1976-77
Calder, Eric	Wsh.	2	2	0	0	0	0	....	....	....	....	....	....	1981-82	1982-83
• Calladine, Norm	Bos.	3	63	19	29	48	8	....	....	....	....	....	....	1942-43	1944-45
Callander, Drew	Phi., Van.	4	39	6	2	8	7	....	....	....	....	....	....	1976-77	1979-80
Callighen, Brett	Edm.	3	160	56	89	145	132	14	4	6	10	8	....	1979-80	1981-82
Callighen, Patsy	NYR	1	36	0	0	0	32	9	0	0	0	0	1	1927-28	1927-28
‡ Camazzola, James	Chi.	2	3	0	0	0	0	....	....	....	....	....	....	1983-84	1986-87
Camazzola, Tony	Wsh.	1	3	0	0	0	4	....	....	....	....	....	....	1981-82	1981-82
Cameron, Al	Det., Wpg.	6	282	11	44	55	356	7	0	1	1	2	....	1975-76	1980-81
• Cameron, Billy	Mtl.C., NYA	2	39	0	0	0	2	2	0	0	0	0	....	1923-24	1925-26
Cameron, Craig	Det., St.L., Min., NYI	9	552	87	65	152	196	27	3	1	4	17	....	1966-67	1975-76
Cameron, Dave	Col., N.J.	3	168	25	28	53	238	....	....	....	....	....	....	1981-82	1983-84
• Cameron, Harry	Tor., Ott., Mtl.C.	6	128	88	51	139	189	11	5	4	9	16	....	1917-18	1922-23
• Cameron, Scotty	NYR	1	35	8	11	19	0	....	....	....	....	....	....	1942-43	1942-43
Campbell, Bryan	L.A., Chi.	5	260	35	71	106	74	22	3	4	7	2	....	1967-68	1971-72
Campbell, Colin	Pit., Col., Edm., Van., Det.	11	636	25	103	128	1292	45	4	10	14	181	....	1974-75	1984-85
• Campbell, Dave	Mtl.C.	1	2	0	0	0	0	....	....	....	....	....	....	1920-21	1920-21
Campbell, Don	Chi.	1	17	1	3	4	8	....	....	....	....	....	....	1943-44	1943-44
• Campbell, Earl	Ott., NYA	3	76	6	3	9	14	1	0	0	0	6	....	1923-24	1925-26
Campbell, Scott	Wpg., St.L.	3	80	4	21	25	243	....	....	....	....	....	....	1979-80	1981-82
Campbell, Wade	Wpg., Bos.	6	213	9	27	36	305	10	0	0	0	20	....	1982-83	1987-88
Campeau, Tod	Mtl.	3	42	5	9	14	16	1	0	0	0	0	....	1943-44	1948-49
Campedelli, Dom	Mtl.	1	2	0	0	0	0	....	....	....	....	....	....	1985-86	1985-86
Capuano, Dave	Pit., Van., T.B., S.J.	4	104	17	38	55	56	6	1	1	2	5	....	1989-90	1993-94
Capuano, Jack	Tor., Van., Bos.	3	6	0	0	0	0	....	....	....	....	....	....	1989-90	1991-92
Carbol, Leo	Chi.	1	6	0	1	1	4	....	....	....	....	....	....	1942-43	1942-43
Cardin, Claude	St.L.	1	1	0	0	0	0	....	....	....	....	....	....	1967-68	1967-68
Cardwell, Steve	Pit.	3	53	9	11	20	35	4	0	0	0	2	....	1970-71	1972-73
• Carey, George	Mtl., Que., Ham., Tor.	6	72	21	12	33	20	....	....	....	....	....	....	1917-18	1923-24
Carkner, Terry	NYR, Que., Phi., Det., Fla.	13	858	42	188	230	1588	54	1	9	10	48	....	1986-87	1998-99
Carleton, Wayne	Tor., Bos., Cal.	7	278	55	73	128	172	18	2	4	6	14	1	1965-66	1971-72
Carlin, Brian	L.A.	1	5	1	0	1	0	....	....	....	....	....	....	1971-72	1971-72
Carlson, Jack	Min., St.L.	7	236	30	15	45	417	25	1	2	3	72	....	1978-79	1986-87
Carlson, Kent	Mtl., St.L., Wsh.	6	113	7	11	18	148	8	0	0	0	13	....	1983-84	1988-89
Carlson, Steve	L.A.	1	52	9	12	21	23	4	1	1	2	7	....	1979-80	1979-80
‡ Carlsson, Anders	N.J.	3	104	7	26	33	34	3	1	0	1	2	....	1986-87	1988-89
Carlyle, Randy	Tor., Pit., Wpg.	19	1055	148	499	647	1400	69	9	24	33	120	....	1976-77	1992-93
‡ Carnback, Patrik	Mtl., Ana.	4	154	24	38	62	122	....	....	....	....	....	....	1992-93	1995-96
• Caron, Alain	Oak., Mtl.	2	60	9	13	22	18	....	....	....	....	....	....	1967-68	1968-69
Carpenter, Bob	Wsh., NYR, L.A., Bos., N.J.	19	1178	320	408	728	919	140	21	38	59	136	1	1981-82	1998-99
• Carpenter, Ed	Que., Ham.	2	45	10	5	15	41	....	....	....	....	....	....	1919-20	1920-21
Carr, Gene	St.L., NYR, L.A., Pit., Atl.	8	465	79	136	215	365	35	5	8	13	66	....	1971-72	1978-79
Carr, Lorne	NYR, NYA, Tor.	13	580	204	222	426	132	53	10	9	19	13	2	1933-34	1945-46
Carr, Red	Tor.	1	5	0	1	1	2	....	....	....	....	....	....	1943-44	1943-44
Carriere, Larry	Buf., Atl., Van., L.A., Tor.	7	367	16	74	90	462	27	0	3	3	42	....	1972-73	1979-80
• Carrigan, Gene	NYR, Det., St.L.	3	37	2	1	3	13	4	0	0	0	0	....	1930-31	1934-35
Carroll, Billy	NYI, Edm., Det.	7	322	30	54	84	113	71	6	12	18	18	4	1980-81	1986-87
• Carroll, George	Mtl.M., Bos.	1	16	0	0	0	11	....	....	....	....	....	....	1924-25	1924-25
Carroll, Greg	Wsh., Det., Hfd.	2	131	20	34	54	44	....	....	....	....	....	....	1978-79	1979-80
Carruthers, Dwight	Det., Phi.	2	2	0	0	0	0	....	....	....	....	....	....	1965-66	1967-68
Carse, Bill	NYR, Chi.	4	124	28	43	71	38	13	3	2	5	0	....	1938-39	1941-42
Carse, Bob	Chi., Mtl.	5	167	32	55	87	52	10	0	2	2	2	....	1939-40	1947-48
• Carson, Bill	Tor., Bos.	4	159	54	24	78	156	11	3	0	3	14	1	1926-27	1929-30
• Carson, Frank	Mtl.M., NYA, Det.	7	248	42	48	90	166	27	0	2	2	9	....	1925-26	1933-34
• Carson, Gerry	Mtl.C., NYR, Mtl.M.	7	261	12	11	23	205	22	0	0	0	12	1	1928-29	1936-37
Carson, Jimmy	L.A., Edm., Det., Van., Hfd.	10	626	275	286	561	254	55	17	15	32	22	....	1986-87	1995-96
Carson, Lindsay	Phi., Hfd.	7	373	66	80	146	524	49	4	10	14	56	....	1981-82	1987-88
Carter, Billy	Mtl., Bos.	3	16	0	0	0	6	....	....	....	....	....	....	1957-58	1961-62
Carter, John	Bos., S.J.	8	244	40	50	90	201	31	7	5	12	51	....	1985-86	1992-93
Carter, Ron	Edm.	1	2	0	0	0	0	....	....	....	....	....	....	1979-80	1979-80
• Carveth, Joe	Det., Bos., Mtl.	11	504	150	189	339	81	69	21	16	37	28	2	1940-41	1950-51
Cashman, Wayne	Bos.	23	1027	277	516	793	1041	145	31	57	88	250	2	1964-65	1982-83
‡ Casselman, Mike	Fla.	1	3	0	0	0	0	....	....	....	....	....	....	1995-96	1995-96
Cassidy, Bruce	Chi.	6	36	4	13	17	10	1	0	0	0	0	....	1983-84	1989-90
Cassidy, Tom	Pit.	1	26	3	4	7	15	....	....	....	....	....	....	1977-78	1977-78
Cassolato, Tony	Wsh.	3	23	1	6	7	4	....	....	....	....	....	....	1979-80	1981-82
Caufield, Jay	NYR, Min., Pit.	7	208	5	8	13	759	17	0	0	0	42	1	1986-87	1992-93
‡ Cavallini, Gino	Cgy., St.L., Que.	9	593	114	159	273	507	74	14	19	33	66	....	1984-85	1992-93
Cavallini, Paul	Wsh., St.L., Dal.	10	564	56	177	233	750	69	8	27	35	114	....	1986-87	1995-96
Ceresino, Ray	Tor.	1	12	1	1	2	2	....	....	....	....	....	....	1948-49	1948-49
Cernik, Frantisek	Det.	1	49	5	4	9	13	....	....	....	....	....	....	1984-85	1984-85
‡ Chabot, John	Mtl., Pit., Det.	8	508	84	228	312	85	33	6	20	26	2	....	1983-84	1990-91
• Chad, John	Chi.	3	80	15	22	37	29	10	0	1	1	2	....	1939-40	1945-46
• Chalmers, Chick	NYR	1	1	0	0	0	0	....	....	....	....	....	....	1953-54	1953-54
Chalupa, Milan	Det.	1	14	0	5	5	6	....	....	....	....	....	....	1984-85	1984-85
• Chamberlain, Murph	Tor., Mtl., Bro., Bos.	12	510	100	175	275	769	66	14	17	31	96	2	1937-38	1948-49
Champagne, Andre	Tor.	1	2	0	0	0	0	....	....	....	....	....	....	1962-63	1962-63
‡ Chapdelaine, Rene	L.A.	3	32	0	2	2	32	....	....	....	....	....	....	1990-91	1992-93
• Chapman, Art	Bos., NYA	12	438	62	176	238	140	26	1	5	6	9	....	1930-31	1939-40
Chapman, Blair	Pit., St.L.	7	402	106	125	231	158	25	4	6	10	15	....	1976-77	1982-83
‡ Chapman, Brian	Hfd.	1	3	0	0	0	29	....	....	....	....	....	....	1990-91	1990-91
‡ Charbonneau, Jose	Mtl., Van.	4	71	9	13	22	67	11	1	0	1	8	....	1987-88	1994-95
Charbonneau, Stephane	Que.	1	2	0	0	0	0	....	....	....	....	....	....	1991-92	1991-92
Charlebois, Bob	Min.	1	7	1	0	1	0	....	....	....	....	....	....	1967-68	1967-68
Charlesworth, Todd	Pit., NYR	6	93	3	9	12	47	....	....	....	....	....	....	1983-84	1989-90
Charron, Guy	Mtl., Det., K.C., Wsh.	14	734	221	309	530	146	....	....	....	....	....	....	1969-70	1980-81
Chartier, Dave	Wpg.	1	1	0	0	0	0	....	....	....	....	....	....	1980-81	1980-81
Chartraw, Rick	Mtl., L.A., NYR, Edm.	10	420	28	64	92	399	75	7	9	16	80	5	1974-75	1983-84
Chasse, Denis	St.L., Wsh., Wpg., Ott.	4	132	11	14	25	292	7	1	7	8	23	....	1993-94	1996-97
Check, Lude	Det., Chi.	2	27	6	2	8	4	....	....	....	....	....	....	1943-44	1944-45
Chernoff, Mike	Min.	1	1	0	0	0	0	....	....	....	....	....	....	1968-69	1968-69
Chernomaz, Rich	Col., N.J., Cgy.	7	51	9	7	16	18	....	....	....	....	....	....	1981-82	1991-92
Cherry, Dick	Bos., Phi.	3	145	12	10	22	45	4	1	0	1	4	....	1956-57	1969-70
Cherry, Don	Bos.	3	....	....	....	....	....	1	0	0	0	0	....	1954-55	1954-55
‡ Chervyakov, Denis	Bos.	1	2	0	0	0	2	....	....	....	....	....	....	1992-93	1992-93
• Chevrefils, Real	Bos., Det.	8	387	104	97	201	185	30	5	4	9	20	....	1951-52	1958-59
• Chiasson, Steve	Det., Cgy., Hfd., Car.	13	751	93	305	398	1107	63	16	19	35	119	....	1986-87	1998-99
‡ Chibirev, Igor	Hfd.	2	45	7	12	19	2	....	....	....	....	....	....	1993-94	1994-95
Chicoine, Dan	Cle., Min.	3	31	1	2	3	12	1	0	0	0	0	....	1977-78	1979-80
Chinnick, Rick	Min.	2	4	0	2	2	0	....	....	....	....	....	....	1973-74	1974-75
Chipperfield, Ron	Edm., Que.	2	83	22	24	46	34	....	....	....	....	....	....	1979-80	1980-81
Chisholm, Art	Bos.	1	3	0	0	0	0	....	....	....	....	....	....	1960-61	1960-61
Chisholm, Colin	Min.	1	1	0	0	0	0	....	....	....	....	....	....	1986-87	1986-87
• Chisholm, Lex	Tor.	2	54	10	8	18	19	3	1	0	1	0	....	1939-40	1940-41
Chorney, Marc	Pit., L.A.	4	210	8	27	35	209	7	0	1	1	2	....	1980-81	1983-84
• Chouinard, Gene	Ott.	1	8	0	0	0	0	....	....	....	....	....	....	1927-28	1927-28
Chouinard, Guy	Atl., Cgy., St.L.	10	578	205	370	575	120	46	9	28	37	12	....	1974-75	1983-84
Christian, Dave	Wpg., Wsh., Bos., St.L., Chi.	15	1009	340	433	773	284	102	32	25	57	27	....	1979-80	1993-94
Christie, Mike	Cal., Cle., Col., Van.	7	412	15	101	116	550	2	0	0	0	0	....	1974-75	1980-81
Christoff, Steve	Min., Cgy., L.A.	5	248	77	64	141	108	35	16	12	28	25	....	1979-80	1983-84
Chrystal, Bob	NYR	2	132	11	14	25	112	....	....	....	....	....	....	1953-54	1954-55
• Church, Jack	Tor., Bro., Bos.	5	130	4	19	23	154	25	1	1	2	18	....	1938-39	1945-46

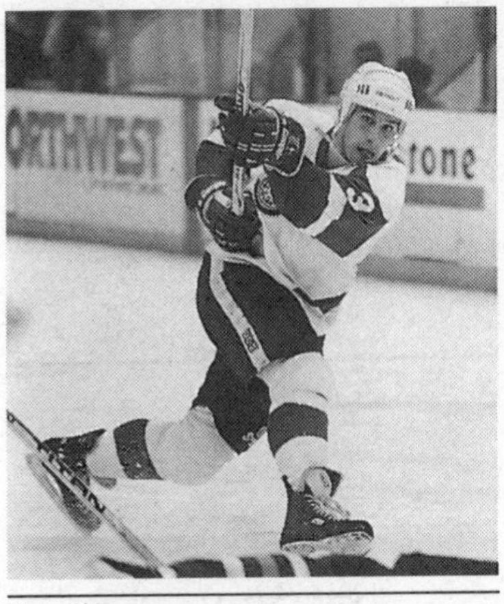

Steve Chiasson

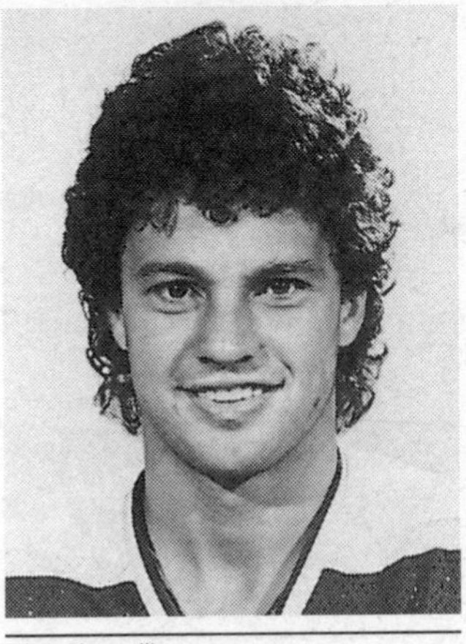

Dino Ciccarelli

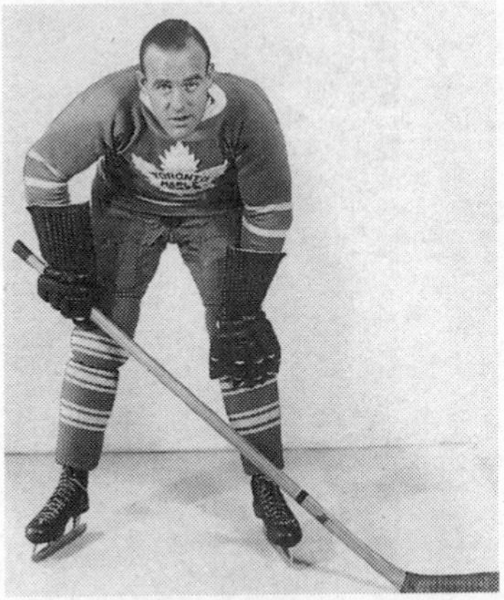

King Clancy

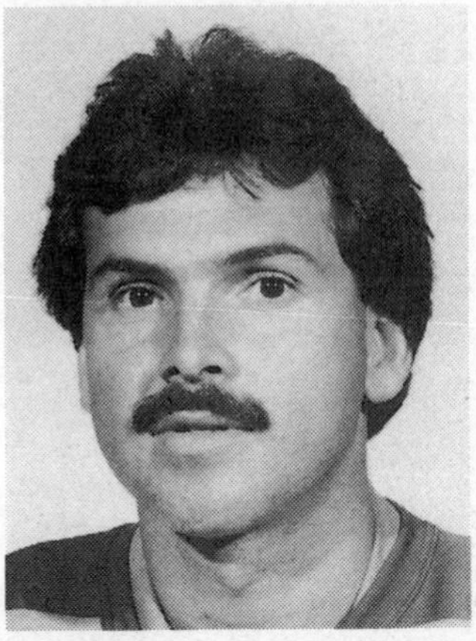

Real Cloutier

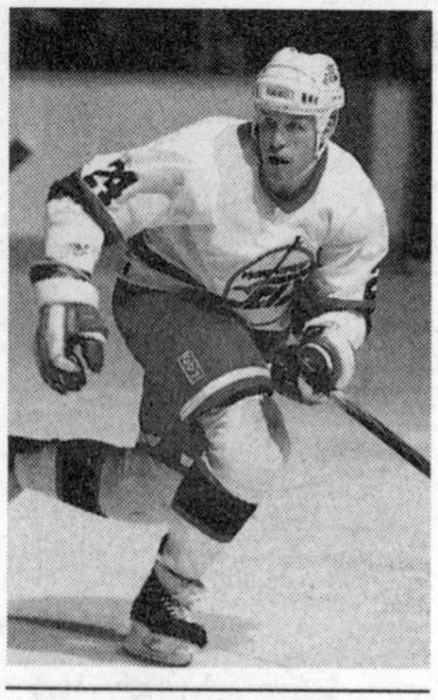
Danton Cole

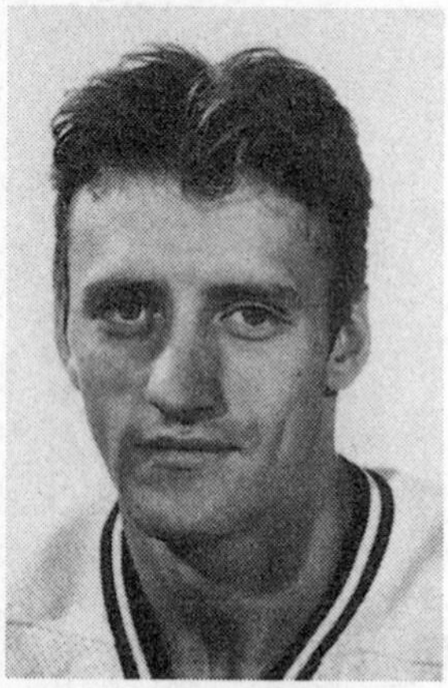
Tim Coulis

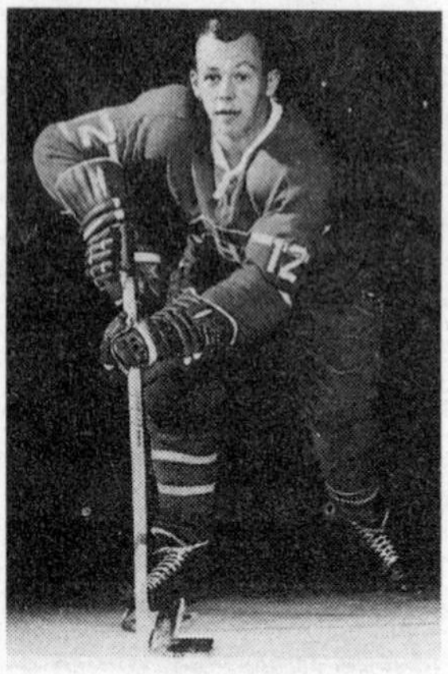
Yvan Cournoyer

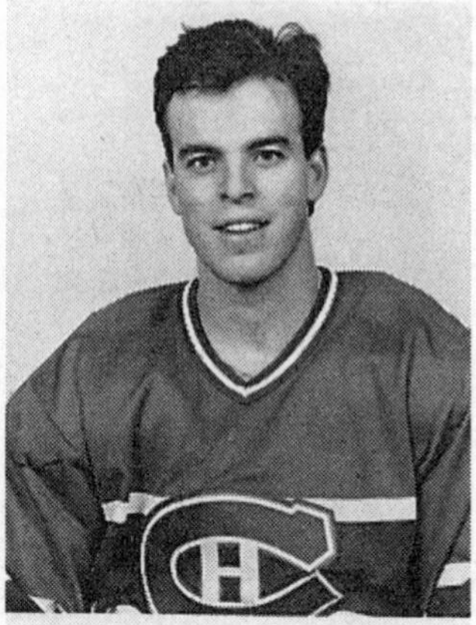
Russ Courtnall

Name	NHL Teams	NHL Seasons	Regular Schedule GP	G	A	TP	PIM	Playoffs GP	G	A	TP	PIM	NHL Cup Wins	First NHL Season	Last NHL Season
Churla, Shane	Hfd., Cgy., Min., Dal., L.A., NYR	12	488	26	45	71	2301	78	5	7	12	282	....	1986-87	1997-98
Chychrun, Jeff	Phi., L.A., Pit., Edm.	8	262	3	22	25	744	19	0	2	2	65	....	1986-87	1993-94
Chynoweth, Dean	NYI, Bos.	9	241	4	18	22	667	6	0	0	0	26	....	1988-89	1997-98
‡ Ciavaglia, Peter	Buf.	2	5	0	0	0	0	....	....	....	....	....	....	1991-92	1992-93
Ciccarelli, Dino	Min., Wsh., Det., T.B., Fla.	19	1232	608	592	1200	1425	141	73	45	118	211	....	1980-81	1998-99
Cichocki, Chris	Det., N.J.	4	68	11	12	23	27	....	....	....	....	....	....	1985-86	1988-89
● Ciesla, Hank	Chi., NYR	4	269	26	51	77	87	6	0	2	2	0	....	1955-56	1958-59
‡ Cimellaro, Tony	Ott.	1	2	0	0	0	0	....	....	....	....	....	....	1992-93	1992-93
‡ Cimetta, Robert	Bos., Tor.	4	103	16	16	32	66	1	0	0	0	15	....	1988-89	1991-92
Cirella, Joe	Col., N.J., Que., NYR, Fla., Ott.	16	828	64	211	275	1446	38	0	13	13	98	....	1981-82	1995-96
‡ Cirone, Jason	Wpg.	1	3	0	0	0	2	....	....	....	....	....	....	1991-92	1991-92
Clackson, Kim	Pit., Que.	2	106	0	8	8	370	8	0	0	0	70	....	1979-80	1980-81
● Clancy, King	Ott., Tor.	17	592	136	147	283	914	55	8	8	16	92	2	1921-22	1936-37
Clancy, Terry	Oak., Tor.	4	93	6	6	12	39	....	....	....	....	....	....	1967-68	1972-73
● Clapper, Dit	Bos.	21	833	228	246	474	462	82	13	17	30	50	3	1927-28	1946-47
Clark, Dan	NYR	1	4	0	1	1	6	....	....	....	....	....	....	1978-79	1978-79
Clark, Dean	Edm.	1	1	0	0	0	0	....	....	....	....	....	....	1983-84	1983-84
Clark, Gordie	Bos.	2	8	0	1	1	0	1	0	0	0	0	....	1974-75	1975-76
● Clark, Nobby	Bos.	1	5	0	0	0	0	....	....	....	....	....	....	1927-28	1927-28
Clarke, Bobby	Phi.	20	1144	358	852	1210	1453	136	42	77	119	152	2	1969-70	1983-84
● Cleghorn, Odie	Mtl.C., Pit.	10	181	95	34	129	142	12	7	1	8	2	....	1918-19	1927-28
● Cleghorn, Sprague	Ott., Tor., Mtl.C., Bos.	10	259	83	55	138	538	21	4	2	6	28	....	1918-19	1927-28
Clement, Bill	Phi., Wsh., Atl., Cgy.	11	719	148	208	356	383	50	5	3	8	26	2	1971-72	1981-82
Cline, Bruce	NYR	1	30	2	3	5	10	....	....	....	....	....	....	1956-57	1956-57
Clippingdale, Steve	L.A., Wsh.	2	19	1	2	3	9	1	0	0	0	0	....	1976-77	1979-80
Cloutier, Real	Que., Buf.	6	317	146	198	344	119	25	7	5	12	20	....	1979-80	1984-85
Cloutier, Rejean	Det.	2	5	0	2	2	2	....	....	....	....	....	....	1979-80	1981-82
Cloutier, Roland	Det., Que.	3	34	8	9	17	2	....	....	....	....	....	....	1977-78	1979-80
● Clune, Wally	Mtl.	1	5	0	0	0	6	....	....	....	....	....	....	1955-56	1955-56
Coalter, Gary	Cal., K.C.	2	34	2	4	6	2	....	....	....	....	....	....	1973-74	1974-75
Coates, Steve	Det.	1	5	1	0	1	24	....	....	....	....	....	....	1976-77	1976-77
Cochrane, Glen	Phi., Van., Chi., Edm.	10	411	17	72	89	1556	18	1	1	2	31	....	1978-79	1988-89
Coflin, Hugh	Chi.	1	31	0	3	3	33	....	....	....	....	....	....	1950-51	1950-51
‡ Cole, Danton	Wpg., T.B., N.J., NYI, Chi.	7	318	58	60	118	125	1	0	0	0	0	1	1989-90	1995-96
Colley, Tom	Min.	1	1	0	0	0	2	....	....	....	....	....	....	1974-75	1974-75
Collings, Norm	Mtl.C.	1	1	0	1	1	0	....	....	....	....	....	....	1934-35	1934-35
Collins, Bill	Min., Mtl., Det., St.L., NYR, Phi., Wsh.	11	768	157	154	311	415	18	3	5	8	12	....	1967-68	1977-78
Collins, Gary	Tor.	1	....	....	....	....	....	2	0	0	0	0	....	1958-59	1958-59
Collyard, Bob	St.L.	1	10	1	3	4	4	....	....	....	....	....	....	1973-74	1973-74
● Colman, Michael	S.J.	1	15	0	1	1	32	....	....	....	....	....	....	1991-92	1991-92
Colville, Mac	NYR	9	353	71	104	175	130	40	9	10	19	14	1	1935-36	1946-47
● Colville, Neil	NYR	12	464	99	166	265	213	46	7	19	26	32	1	1935-36	1948-49
Colwill, Les	NYR	1	69	7	6	13	16	....	....	....	....	....	....	1958-59	1958-59
Comeau, Rey	Mtl., Atl., Col.	9	564	98	141	239	175	9	2	1	3	8	....	1971-72	1979-80
Conacher, Brian	Tor., Det.	5	155	28	28	56	84	12	3	2	5	21	1	1961-62	1971-72
● Conacher, Charlie	Tor., Det., NYA	12	459	225	173	398	523	49	17	18	35	49	1	1929-30	1940-41
Conacher, Jim	Det., Chi., NYR	8	328	85	117	202	91	19	5	2	7	4	....	1945-46	1952-53
● Conacher, Lionel	Pit., NYA, Mtl.M., Chi.	12	498	80	105	185	882	35	2	2	4	34	2	1925-26	1936-37
Conacher, Pat	NYR, Edm., N.J., L.A., Cgy., NYI	14	521	63	76	139	235	66	11	10	21	40	1	1979-80	1995-96
Conacher, Pete	Chi., NYR, Tor.	6	229	47	39	86	57	7	0	0	0	0	....	1951-52	1957-58
● Conacher, Roy	Bos., Det., Chi.	11	490	226	200	426	90	42	15	15	30	14	2	1938-39	1951-52
● Conn, Red	NYA	2	96	9	28	37	22	....	....	....	....	....	....	1933-34	1934-35
Conn, Rob	Chi., Buf.	2	30	2	5	7	20	....	....	....	....	....	....	1991-92	1995-96
● Connelly, Bert	NYR, Chi.	3	87	13	15	28	37	14	1	0	1	0	1	1934-35	1937-38
Connelly, Wayne	Mtl., Bos., Min., Det., St.L., Van.	10	543	133	174	307	156	24	11	7	18	4	....	1960-61	1971-72
Connor, Cam	Mtl., Edm., NYR	5	89	9	22	31	256	20	5	0	5	6	1	1978-79	1982-83
● Connor, Harry	Bos., NYA, Ott.	4	134	16	5	21	149	10	0	0	0	2	....	1927-28	1930-31
● Connors, Bob	NYA, Det.	3	78	17	10	27	110	2	0	0	0	10	....	1926-27	1929-30
‡ Conroy, Al	Phi.	3	114	9	14	23	156	....	....	....	....	....	....	1991-92	1993-94
Contini, Joe	Col., Min.	3	68	17	21	38	34	2	0	0	0	0	....	1977-78	1980-81
Convery, Brandon	Tor., Van., L.A.	4	72	9	19	28	36	5	0	0	0	2	....	1995-96	1998-99
● Convey, Eddie	NYA	3	36	1	1	2	33	....	....	....	....	....	....	1930-31	1932-33
● Cook, Bill	NYR	11	474	229	138	367	386	46	13	11	24	68	2	1926-27	1936-37
● Cook, Bob	Van., Det., NYI, Min.	4	72	13	9	22	22	....	....	....	....	....	....	1970-71	1974-75
● Cook, Bud	Bos., Ott., St.L.	3	50	5	4	9	22	....	....	....	....	....	....	1931-32	1934-35
● Cook, Bun	NYR, Bos.	11	473	158	144	302	444	46	15	3	18	50	2	1926-27	1936-37
● Cook, Lloyd	Bos.	1	4	1	0	1	0	....	....	....	....	....	....	1924-25	1924-25
● Cook, Tom	Chi., Mtl.M.	9	349	77	98	175	184	24	2	4	6	19	1	1929-30	1937-38
● Cooper, Carson	Bos., Mtl.C., Det.	8	294	110	57	167	111	7	0	0	0	2	....	1924-25	1931-32
Cooper, Ed	Col.	2	49	8	7	15	46	....	....	....	....	....	....	1980-81	1981-82
● Cooper, Hal	NYR	1	8	0	0	0	2	....	....	....	....	....	....	1944-45	1944-45
● Cooper, Joe	NYR, Chi.	11	420	30	66	96	442	35	3	5	8	58	....	1935-36	1946-47
Copp, Bob	Tor.	2	40	3	9	12	26	....	....	....	....	....	....	1942-43	1950-51
● Corbeau, Bert	Mtl.C., Ham., Tor.	10	258	63	49	112	629	9	2	2	4	38	....	1917-18	1926-27
Corbett, Mike	L.A.	1	....	....	....	....	....	2	0	1	1	2	....	1967-68	1967-68
Corcoran, Norm	Bos., Det., Chi.	4	29	1	3	4	21	4	0	0	0	6	....	1949-50	1955-56
● Cormier, Roger	Mtl.C.	1	1	0	0	0	0	....	....	....	....	....	....	1925-26	1925-26
‡ Cornforth, Mark	Bos.	1	6	0	0	0	4	....	....	....	....	....	....	1995-96	1995-96
Corrigan, Chuck	Tor., NYA	2	19	2	2	4	2	....	....	....	....	....	....	1937-38	1940-41
Corrigan, Mike	L.A., Van., Pit.	10	594	152	195	347	698	17	2	3	5	20	....	1967-68	1977-78
● Corriveau, Andre	Mtl.	1	3	0	1	1	0	....	....	....	....	....	....	1953-54	1953-54
‡ Corriveau, Yvon	Wsh., Hfd., S.J.	9	280	48	40	88	310	29	5	7	12	50	....	1985-86	1993-94
Cory, Ross	Wpg.	2	51	2	10	12	41	....	....	....	....	....	....	1979-80	1980-81
Cossette, Jacques	Pit.	3	64	8	6	14	29	3	0	1	1	4	....	1975-76	1978-79
Costello, Les	Tor.	3	15	2	3	5	11	6	2	2	4	2	1	1947-48	1949-50
Costello, Murray	Chi., Bos., Det.	4	162	13	19	32	54	5	0	0	0	2	....	1953-54	1956-57
Costello, Rich	Tor.	2	12	2	2	4	2	....	....	....	....	....	....	1983-84	1985-86
● Cotch, Charlie	Ham., Tor.	1	12	1	0	1	0	....	....	....	....	....	....	1924-25	1924-25
Cote, Alain	Que.	10	696	103	190	293	383	67	9	15	24	44	....	1979-80	1988-89
‡ Cote, Alain	Bos., Wsh., Mtl., T.B., Que.	9	119	2	18	20	124	11	0	2	2	26	....	1985-86	1993-94
Cote, Ray	Edm.	3	15	0	0	0	4	14	3	2	5	0	....	1982-83	1984-85
● Cotton, Baldy	Pit., Tor., NYA	12	503	101	103	204	419	43	4	9	13	46	1	1925-26	1936-37
● Coughlin, Jack	Tor., Que., Mtl.C., Ham.	3	19	2	0	2	3	....	....	....	....	....	1	1917-18	1920-21
Coulis, Tim	Wsh., Min.	5	47	4	5	9	138	3	1	0	1	2	....	1978-79	1985-86
Coulson, D'arcy	Phi.	1	28	0	0	0	103	....	....	....	....	....	....	1930-31	1930-31
Coulter, Art	Chi., NYR	11	465	30	82	112	543	49	4	5	9	61	2	1931-32	1941-42
Coulter, Neal	NYI	3	26	5	5	10	11	....	....	....	....	....	....	1985-86	1987-88
Cournoyer, Yvan	Mtl.	16	968	428	435	863	255	147	64	63	127	47	10	1963-64	1978-79
Courteau, Yves	Cgy., Hfd.	3	22	2	5	7	4	1	0	0	0	0	....	1984-85	1986-87
Courtenay, Ed	S.J.	2	44	7	13	20	10	....	....	....	....	....	....	1991-92	1992-93
Courtnall, Russ	Tor., Mtl., Min., Dal., Van., NYR, L.A.	16	1029	297	447	744	557	129	39	44	83	83	....	1983-84	1998-99
● Coutu, Billy	Mtl.C., Ham., Bos.	10	244	33	21	54	478	19	1	1	2	35	....	1917-18	1926-27
● Couture, Gerry	Det., Mtl., Chi.	10	385	86	70	156	89	45	9	7	16	4	1	1944-45	1953-54
● Couture, Rosie	Chi., Mtl.C.	8	309	48	56	104	184	23	1	5	6	15	1	1928-29	1935-36
‡ Couturier, Sylvain	L.A.	3	33	4	5	9	4	....	....	....	....	....	....	1988-89	1991-92
Cowick, Bruce	Phi., Wsh., St.L.	3	70	5	6	11	43	8	0	0	0	9	1	1973-74	1975-76
‡ Cowie, Rob	L.A.	2	78	7	12	19	52	....	....	....	....	....	....	1994-95	1995-96
● Cowley, Bill	St.L., Bos.	13	549	195	353	548	143	64	12	34	46	22	2	1934-35	1946-47
● Cox, Danny	Tor., Ott., Det., NYR	8	319	47	49	96	128	10	0	1	1	6	....	1926-27	1933-34
‡ Coxe, Craig	Van., Cgy., St.L., S.J.	8	235	14	31	45	713	5	1	0	1	18	....	1984-85	1991-92
‡ Craighead, John	Tor.	1	5	0	0	0	10	....	....	....	....	....	....	1996-97	1996-97
Crashley, Bart	Det., K.C., L.A.	6	140	7	36	43	50	....	....	....	....	....	....	1965-66	1975-76
Crawford, Bob	St.L., Hfd., NYR, Wsh.	7	246	71	71	142	72	11	0	1	1	8	....	1979-80	1986-87
Crawford, Bobby	Col., Det.	2	16	1	3	4	6	....	....	....	....	....	....	1980-81	1982-83
● Crawford, Jack	Bos.	13	548	38	140	178	202	66	3	13	16	36	2	1937-38	1949-50
Crawford, Lou	Bos.	2	26	2	1	3	29	1	0	0	0	0	....	1989-90	1991-92
Crawford, Marc	Van.	9	176	19	31	50	229	20	1	2	3	44	....	1981-82	1986-87
● Crawford, Rusty	Ott., Tor.	2	38	10	8	18	117	2	2	1	3	9	1	1917-18	1918-19
Creighton, Adam	Buf., Chi., NYI, T.B., St.L.	14	708	187	216	403	1077	61	11	14	25	137	....	1983-84	1996-97
Creighton, Dave	Bos., Tor., Chi., NYR	12	616	140	174	314	223	51	11	13	24	20	....	1948-49	1959-60

			Regular Schedule					Playoffs					NHL	First	Last
Name	NHL Teams	NHL Seasons	GP	G	A	TP	PIM	GP	G	A	TP	PIM	Cup Wins	NHL Season	NHL Season
• Creighton, Jimmy	Det.	1	11	1	0	1	2	....	....	....	....	....	....	1930-31	1930-31
Cressman, Dave	Min.	2	85	6	8	14	37	....	....	....	....	....	....	1974-75	1975-76
Cressman, Glen	Mtl.	1	4	0	0	0	2	....	....	....	....	....	....	1956-57	1956-57
Crisp, Terry	Bos., St.L., NYI, Phi.	11	536	67	134	201	135	110	15	28	43	40	2	1965-66	1976-77
Cristofoli, Ed	Mtl.	1	9	0	1	1	4	....	....	....	....	....	....	1989-90	1989-90
• Croghan, Maurice	Mtl.M.	1	16	0	0	0	4	....	....	....	....	....	....	1937-38	1937-38
Crombeen, Mike	Cle., St.L., Hfd.	8	475	55	68	123	218	27	6	2	8	32	....	1977-78	1984-85
Cronin, Shawn	Wsh., Wpg., Phi., S.J.	7	292	3	18	21	877	32	1	0	1	38	....	1988-89	1994-95
• Crossett, Stan	Phi.	1	21	0	0	0	10	....	....	....	....	....	....	1930-31	1930-31
Crossman, Doug	Chi., Phi., L.A., NYI, Hfd., Det., T.B., St.L.	14	914	105	359	464	534	97	12	39	51	105	....	1980-81	1993-94
Croteau, Gary	L.A., Det., Cal., K.C., Col.	12	684	144	175	319	143	11	3	2	5	8	....	1968-69	1979-80
Crowder, Bruce	Bos., Pit.	4	243	47	51	98	156	31	8	4	12	41	....	1981-82	1984-85
Crowder, Keith	Bos., L.A.	10	662	223	271	494	1354	85	14	22	36	218	....	1980-81	1989-90
Crowder, Troy	N.J., Det., L.A., Van.	8	150	9	7	16	433	4	0	0	0	22	....	1987-88	1996-97
Crozier, Joe	Tor.	1	5	0	3	3	2	....	....	....	....	....	....	1959-60	1959-60
• Crutchfield, Nels	Mtl.C.	1	41	5	5	10	20	2	0	1	1	22	....	1934-35	1934-35
Culhane, Jim	Hfd.	1	6	0	1	1	4	....	....	....	....	....	....	1989-90	1989-90
Cullen, Barry	Tor., Det.	5	219	32	52	84	111	6	0	0	0	2	....	1955-56	1959-60
Cullen, Brian	Tor., NYR	7	326	56	100	156	92	19	3	0	3	2	....	1954-55	1960-61
Cullen, John	Pit., Hfd., Tor., T.B.	12	621	187	363	550	898	53	12	22	34	58	....	1988-89	1998-99
Cullen, Ray	NYR, Det., Min., Van.	6	313	92	123	215	120	20	3	10	13	2	....	1965-66	1970-71
Cummins, Barry	Cal.	1	36	1	2	3	39	....	....	....	....	....	....	1973-74	1973-74
Cunningham, Bob	NYR	2	4	0	1	1	0	....	....	....	....	....	....	1960-61	1961-62
Cunningham, Jim	Phi.	1	1	0	0	0	4	....	....	....	....	....	....	1977-78	1977-78
Cunningham, Les	NYA, Chi.	2	60	7	19	26	21	1	0	0	0	0	....	1936-37	1939-40
Cupolo, Bill	Bos.	1	47	11	13	24	10	7	1	2	3	0	....	1944-45	1944-45
Curran, Brian	Bos., NYI, Tor., Buf., Wsh.	10	381	7	33	40	1461	24	0	1	1	122	....	1983-84	1993-94
‡ Currie, Dan	Edm., L.A.	4	22	2	1	3	4	....	....	....	....	....	....	1990-91	1993-94
Currie, Glen	Wsh., L.A.	8	326	39	79	118	100	12	1	3	4	4	....	1979-80	1987-88
Currie, Hugh	Mtl.	1	1	0	0	0	0	....	....	....	....	....	....	1950-51	1950-51
Currie, Tony	St.L., Van., Hfd.	8	290	92	119	211	83	16	4	12	16	14	....	1977-78	1984-85
Curry, Floyd	Mtl.	11	601	105	99	204	147	91	23	17	40	38	4	1947-48	1957-58
Curtale, Tony	Cgy.	1	2	0	0	0	0	....	....	....	....	....	....	1980-81	1980-81
Curtis, Paul	Mtl., L.A., St.L.	4	185	3	34	37	161	5	0	0	0	2	....	1969-70	1972-73
Cushenan, Ian	Chi., Mtl., NYR, Det.	5	129	3	11	14	134	....	....	....	....	....	1	1956-57	1963-64
Cusson, Jean	Oak.	1	2	0	0	0	0	....	....	....	....	....	....	1967-68	1967-68
Cyr, Denis	Cgy., Chi., St.L.	6	193	41	43	84	36	4	0	0	0	0	....	1980-81	1985-86
Cyr, Paul	Buf., NYR, Hfd.	10	470	101	140	241	623	24	4	6	10	31	....	1982-83	1991-92
D															
Dahlin, Kjell	Mtl.	3	166	57	59	116	10	35	6	11	17	6	1	1985-86	1987-88
Dahlquist, Chris	Pit., Min., Cgy., Ott.	11	532	19	71	90	488	39	4	7	11	30	....	1985-86	1995-96
Dahlstrom, Cully	Chi.	8	342	88	118	206	58	29	6	8	14	4	1	1937-38	1944-45
Daigle, Alain	Chi.	6	389	56	50	106	122	17	0	1	1	0	....	1974-75	1979-80
Dailey, Bob	Van., Phi.	9	561	94	231	325	814	63	12	34	46	105	....	1973-74	1981-82
• Daley, Frank	Det.	1	5	0	0	0	0	2	0	0	0	0	....	1928-29	1928-29
Daley, Pat	Wpg.	2	12	1	0	1	13	....	....	....	....	....	....	1979-80	1980-81
Dalgarno, Brad	NYI	11	321	49	71	120	332	27	2	4	6	37	....	1985-86	1995-96
Dallman, Marty	Tor.	2	6	0	1	1	0	....	....	....	....	....	....	1987-88	1988-89
Dallman, Rod	NYI, Phi.	4	6	1	0	1	26	1	0	1	1	0	....	1987-88	1991-92
Dame, Bunny	Mtl.	1	34	2	5	7	4	....	....	....	....	....	....	1941-42	1941-42
Damore, Hank	NYR	1	4	1	0	1	2	....	....	....	....	....	....	1943-44	1943-44
‡ Daniels, Kimbi	Phi.	2	27	1	2	3	4	....	....	....	....	....	....	1990-91	1991-92
Daniels, Scott	Hfd., Phi., N.J.	6	149	8	12	20	667	1	0	0	0	0	....	1992-93	1998-99
Daoust, Dan	Mtl., Tor.	8	522	87	167	254	544	32	7	5	12	83	....	1982-83	1989-90
Dark, Michael	St.L.	2	43	5	6	11	14	....	....	....	....	....	....	1986-87	1987-88
• Darragh, Harold	Pit., Phi., Bos., Tor.	8	308	68	49	117	50	16	1	3	4	4	1	1925-26	1932-33
• Darragh, Jack	Ott.	6	121	66	46	112	113	11	3	0	3	9	1	1917-18	1923-24
David, Richard	Que.	3	31	4	4	8	10	1	0	0	0	0	....	1979-80	1982-83
• Davidson, Bob	Tor.	12	491	94	160	254	398	79	5	17	22	76	2	1934-35	1945-46
• Davidson, Gord	NYR	2	51	3	6	9	8	....	....	....	....	....	....	1942-43	1943-44
• Davie, Bob	Bos.	3	41	0	1	1	25	....	....	....	....	....	....	1933-34	1935-36
Davies, Buck	NYR	1	....	....	....	....	....	1	0	0	0	0	....	1947-48	1947-48
• Davis, Bob	Det.	1	3	0	0	0	0	....	....	....	....	....	....	1932-33	1932-33
Davis, Kim	Pit., Tor.	4	36	5	7	12	51	4	0	0	0	0	....	1977-78	1980-81
Davis, Lorne	Mtl., Chi., Det., Bos.	6	95	8	12	20	20	18	3	1	4	10	1	1951-52	1959-60
Davis, Mal	Det., Buf.	6	100	31	22	53	34	7	1	0	1	0	....	1978-79	1985-86
• Davison, Murray	Bos.	1	1	0	0	0	0	....	....	....	....	....	....	1965-66	1965-66
‡ Davydov, Evgeny	Wpg., Fla., Ott.	4	155	40	39	79	120	11	2	2	4	2	....	1991-92	1994-95
Dawes, Bobby	Tor., Mtl.	4	32	2	7	9	6	10	0	0	0	2	1	1946-47	1950-51
• Day, Hap	Tor., NYA	14	581	86	116	202	601	53	4	7	11	56	1	1924-25	1937-38
Day, Joe	Hfd., NYI	3	72	1	10	11	87	....	....	....	....	....	....	1991-92	1993-94
Dea, Billy	NYR, Det., Chi., Pit.	8	397	67	54	121	44	11	2	1	3	6	....	1953-54	1970-71
• Deacon, Don	Det.	3	30	6	4	10	6	2	2	1	3	0	....	1936-37	1939-40
Deadmarsh, Butch	Buf., Atl., K.C.	5	137	12	5	17	155	4	0	0	0	17	....	1970-71	1974-75
Dean, Barry	Col., Phi.	3	165	25	56	81	146	....	....	....	....	....	....	1976-77	1978-79
Debenedet, Nelson	Det., Pit.	2	46	10	4	14	13	....	....	....	....	....	....	1973-74	1974-75
DeBlois, Lucien	NYR, Col., Wpg., Mtl., Que., Tor.	15	993	249	276	525	814	52	7	6	13	38	1	1977-78	1991-92
Debol, Dave	Hfd.	2	92	26	26	52	4	3	0	0	0	0	....	1979-80	1980-81
Defazio, Dean	Pit.	1	22	0	2	2	28	....	....	....	....	....	....	1983-84	1983-84
DeGray, Dale	Cgy., Tor., L.A., Buf.	5	153	18	47	65	195	13	1	3	4	28	....	1985-86	1989-90
• Delmonte, Armand	Bos.	1	1	0	0	0	0	....	....	....	....	....	....	1945-46	1945-46
Delorme, Gilbert	Mtl., St.L., Que., Det., Pit.	10	541	31	92	123	520	56	1	9	10	56	....	1981-82	1990-91
Delorme, Ron	Col., Van.	9	524	83	83	166	667	25	1	2	3	59	....	1976-77	1984-85
Delory, Val	NYR	1	1	0	0	0	0	....	....	....	....	....	....	1948-49	1948-49
Delparte, Guy	Col.	1	48	1	8	9	18	....	....	....	....	....	....	1976-77	1976-77
Delvecchio, Alex	Det.	25	1549	456	825	1281	383	121	35	69	104	29	3	1950-51	1973-74
DeMarco, Ab Jr.	NYR, St.L., Pit., Van., L.A., Bos.	9	344	44	80	124	75	25	1	2	3	17	....	1969-70	1978-79
• DeMarco, Ab Sr.	Chi., Tor., Bos., NYR	7	209	72	93	165	53	11	3	0	3	2	....	1938-39	1946-47
• Demers, Tony	Mtl.C., Mtl., NYR	6	83	20	22	42	23	2	0	0	0	0	....	1937-38	1943-44
Denis, Jean-Paul	NYR	2	10	0	2	2	2	....	....	....	....	....	....	1946-47	1949-50
Denis, Lulu	Mtl.	2	3	0	1	1	0	....	....	....	....	....	....	1949-50	1950-51
• Denneny, Corb	Tor., Ham., Chi.	9	176	103	42	145	148	6	1	0	1	4	....	1917-18	1927-28
• Denneny, Cy	Ott., Bos.	12	328	248	85	333	301	25	16	2	18	17	2	1917-18	1928-29
Dennis, Norm	St.L.	4	12	3	0	3	11	5	0	0	0	2	....	1968-69	1971-72
• Denoird, Gerry	Tor.	1	17	0	1	1	0	....	....	....	....	....	....	1922-23	1922-23
DePalma, Larry	Min., S.J., Pit.	7	148	21	20	41	408	3	0	0	0	6	....	1985-86	1993-94
Derlago, Bill	Van., Tor., Bos., Wpg., Que.	9	555	189	227	416	247	13	5	0	5	8	....	1978-79	1986-87
• Desaulniers, Gerard	Mtl.	3	8	0	2	2	4	....	....	....	....	....	....	1950-51	1953-54
• Desilets, Joffre	Mtl.C., Chi.	5	192	37	45	82	57	7	1	0	1	7	....	1935-36	1939-40
Desjardins, Martin	Mtl.	1	8	0	2	2	2	....	....	....	....	....	....	1989-90	1989-90
• Desjardins, Vic	Chi., NYR	2	87	6	15	21	27	16	0	0	0	0	....	1930-31	1931-32
Deslauriers, Jacques	Mtl.	1	2	0	0	0	0	....	....	....	....	....	....	1955-56	1955-56
Devine, Kevin	NYI	1	2	0	1	1	8	....	....	....	....	....	....	1982-83	1982-83
• Dewar, Tom	NYR	1	9	0	2	2	4	....	....	....	....	....	....	1943-44	1943-44
Dewsbury, Al	Det., Chi.	9	347	30	78	108	365	14	1	5	6	16	1	1946-47	1955-56
Deziel, Michel	Buf.	1	....	....	....	....	....	1	0	0	0	0	....	1974-75	1974-75
Dheere, Marcel	Mtl.	1	11	1	2	3	2	5	0	0	0	6	....	1942-43	1942-43
‡ Di Pietro, Paul	Mtl., Tor., L.A.	6	192	31	49	80	96	31	11	10	21	10	1	1991-92	1996-97
Diachuk, Edward	Det.	1	12	0	0	0	19	....	....	....	....	....	....	1960-61	1960-61
Dick, Harry	Chi.	1	12	0	1	1	12	....	....	....	....	....	....	1946-47	1946-47
Dickens, Ernie	Tor., Chi.	6	278	12	44	56	98	13	0	0	0	4	1	1941-42	1950-51
Dickenson, Herb	NYR	2	48	18	17	35	10	....	....	....	....	....	....	1951-52	1952-53
Dietrich, Don	Chi., N.J.	2	28	0	7	7	10	....	....	....	....	....	....	1983-84	1985-86
• Dill, Bob	NYR	2	76	15	15	30	135	....	....	....	....	....	....	1943-44	1944-45
• Dillabough, Bob	Det., Bos., Pit., Oak.	9	283	32	54	86	76	17	3	0	3	0	....	1961-62	1969-70
• Dillon, Cecil	NYR, Det.	10	453	167	131	298	105	43	14	9	23	14	1	1930-31	1939-40
Dillon, Gary	Col.	1	13	1	1	2	29	....	....	....	....	....	....	1980-81	1980-81
Dillon, Wayne	NYR, Wpg.	4	229	43	66	109	60	3	0	1	1	0	....	1975-76	1979-80
Dineen, Bill	Det., Chi.	5	323	51	44	95	122	37	1	1	2	18	2	1953-54	1957-58

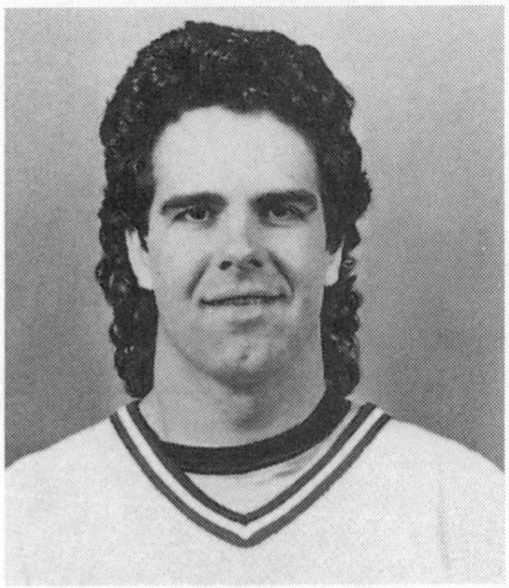
John Cullen

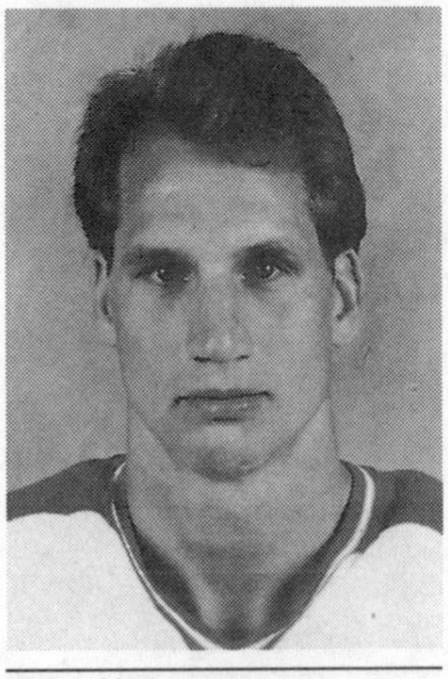
Chris Dahlquist

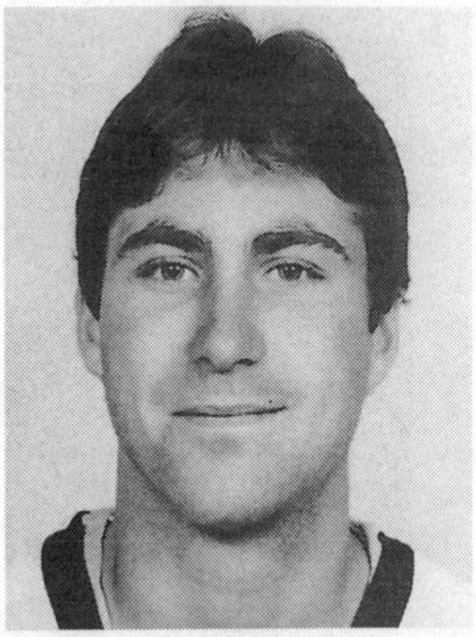
Dave Donnelly

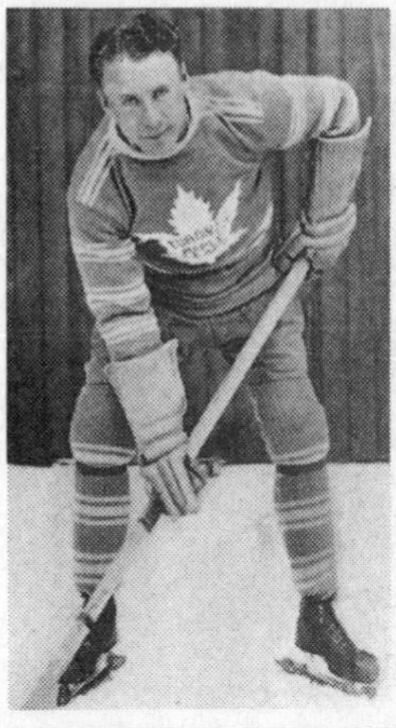
Ken Doraty

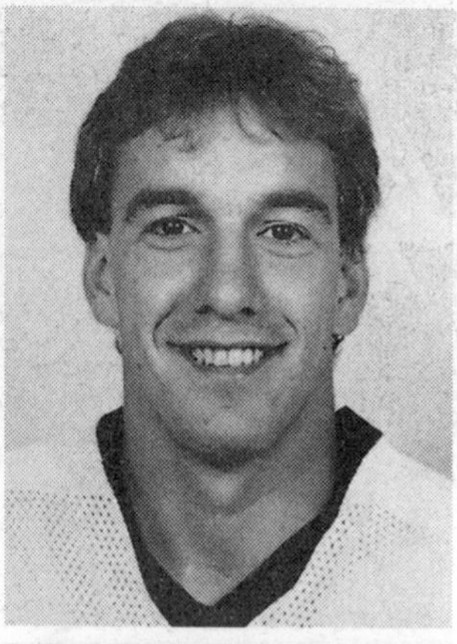

Luc Dufour

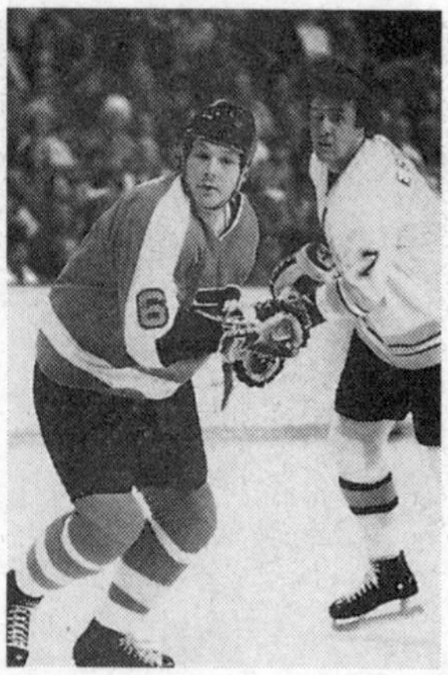

Andre Dupont

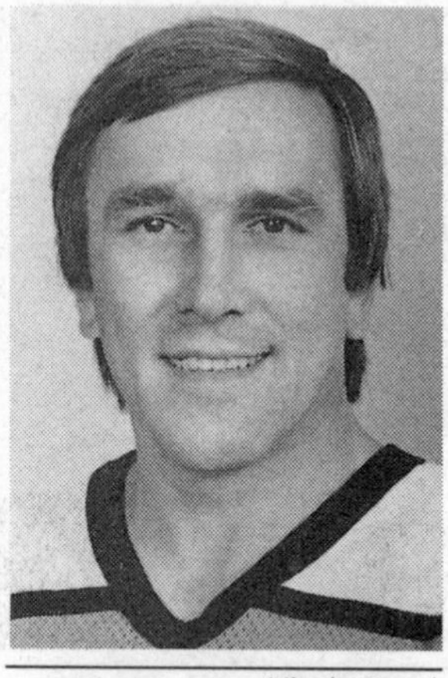

Miroslav Dvorak

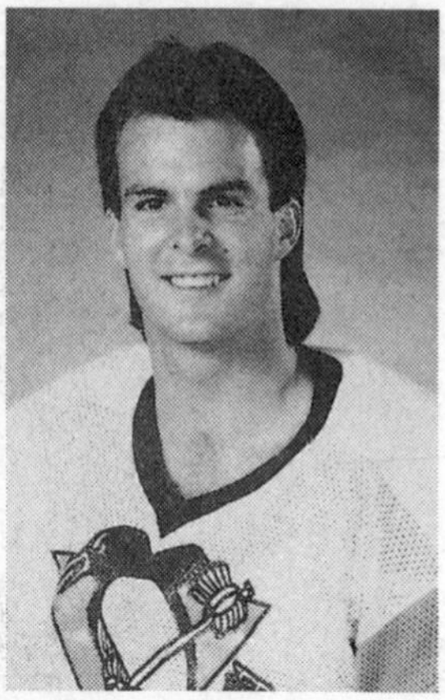

Bob Errey

			Regular Schedule					Playoffs					NHL	First	Last
Name	NHL Teams	NHL Seasons	GP	G	A	TP	PIM	GP	G	A	TP	PIM	Cup Wins	NHL Season	NHL Season
Dineen, Gary	Min.	1	4	0	1	1	0	....	....	....	....	....	....	1968-69	1968-69
‡ Dineen, Gord	NYI, Min., Pit., Ott.	13	528	16	90	106	695	40	1	7	8	68	....	1982-83	1994-95
Dineen, Peter	L.A., Det.	2	13	0	2	2	13	....	....	....	....	....	....	1986-87	1989-90
• Dinsmore, Dinny	Mtl.M.	4	100	6	2	8	50	8	1	0	1	2	....	1924-25	1929-30
Dionne, Marcel	Det., L.A., NYR	18	1348	731	1040	1771	600	49	21	24	45	17	....	1971-72	1988-89
Dirk, Robert	St.L., Van., Chi., Ana., Mtl.	9	402	13	29	42	786	39	0	1	1	56	....	1987-88	1995-96
‡ Djoos, Per	Det., NYR	3	82	2	31	33	58	....	....	....	....	....	....	1990-91	1992-93
Doak, Gary	Det., Bos., Van., NYR	16	789	23	107	130	908	78	2	4	6	121	1	1965-66	1980-81
Dobbin, Brian	Phi., Bos.	5	63	7	8	15	61	2	0	0	0	17	....	1986-87	1991-92
Dobson, Jim	Min., Col., Que.	4	12	0	0	0	6	....	....	....	....	....	....	1979-80	1983-84
• Doherty, Fred	Mtl.C.	1	1	0	0	0	0	....	....	....	....	....	....	1918-19	1918-19
Donaldson, Gary	Chi.	1	1	0	0	0	0	....	....	....	....	....	....	1973-74	1973-74
Donatelli, Clark	Min., Bos.	2	35	3	4	7	39	2	0	0	0	0	....	1989-90	1991-92
• Donnelly, Babe	Mtl.M.	1	34	0	1	1	14	2	0	0	0	0	....	1926-27	1926-27
Donnelly, Dave	Bos., Chi., Edm.	5	137	15	24	39	150	5	0	0	0	0	....	1983-84	1987-88
‡ Donnelly, Gord	Que., Wpg., Buf., Dal.	12	554	28	41	69	2069	26	0	2	2	61	....	1983-84	1994-95
Donnelly, Mike	NYR, Buf., L.A., Dal., NYI	11	465	114	121	235	255	47	12	12	24	30	....	1986-87	1996-97
• Doran, John	NYA, Det., Mtl.	5	98	5	10	15	110	3	0	0	0	0	....	1933-34	1939-40
Doran, Lloyd	Det.	1	24	3	2	5	10	....	....	....	....	....	....	1946-47	1946-47
• Doraty, Ken	Chi., Tor., Det.	5	103	15	26	41	24	15	7	2	9	2	....	1926-27	1937-38
Dore, Andre	NYR, St.L., Que.	7	257	14	81	95	261	23	1	2	3	32	....	1978-79	1984-85
Dore, Daniel	Que.	2	17	2	3	5	59	....	....	....	....	....	....	1989-90	1990-91
Dorey, Jim	Tor., NYR	4	232	25	74	99	553	11	0	2	2	40	....	1968-69	1971-72
Dorion, Dan	N.J.	2	4	1	1	2	2	....	....	....	....	....	....	1985-86	1987-88
Dornhoefer, Gary	Bos., Phi.	14	787	214	328	542	1291	80	17	19	36	203	2	1963-64	1977-78
Dorohoy, Eddie	Mtl.	1	16	0	0	0	6	....	....	....	....	....	....	1948-49	1948-49
Douglas, Jordy	Hfd., Min., Wpg.	6	268	76	62	138	160	6	0	0	0	4	....	1979-80	1984-85
Douglas, Kent	Tor., Oak., Det.	7	428	33	115	148	631	19	1	3	4	33	3	1962-63	1968-69
Douglas, Les	Det.	4	52	6	12	18	8	10	3	2	5	2	1	1940-41	1946-47
• Downie, Dave	Tor.	1	11	0	1	1	2	....	....	....	....	....	....	1932-33	1932-33
‡ Doyon, Mario	Chi., Que.	3	28	3	4	7	16	....	....	....	....	....	....	1988-89	1990-91
• Draper, Bruce	Tor.	1	1	0	0	0	0	....	....	....	....	....	....	1962-63	1962-63
• Drillon, Gordie	Tor., Mtl.	7	311	155	139	294	56	50	26	15	41	10	1	1936-37	1942-43
Driscoll, Peter	Edm.	2	60	3	8	11	97	3	0	0	0	0	....	1979-80	1980-81
Driver, Bruce	N.J., NYR	15	922	96	390	486	670	108	10	40	50	64	1	1983-84	1997-98
Drolet, Rene	Phi., Det.	2	2	0	0	0	0	....	....	....	....	....	....	1971-72	1974-75
‡ Droppa, Ivan	Chi.	2	19	0	1	1	14	....	....	....	....	....	....	1993-94	1995-96
• Drouillard, Clarence	Det.	1	10	0	1	1	0	....	....	....	....	....	....	1937-38	1937-38
Drouin, Jude	Mtl., Min., NYI, Wpg.	12	666	151	305	456	346	72	27	41	68	33	....	1968-69	1980-81
• Drouin, Polly	Mtl.C., Mtl.	7	160	23	50	73	80	5	0	1	1	5	....	1934-35	1940-41
‡ Druce, John	Wsh., Wpg., L.A., Phi.	10	531	113	126	239	347	53	17	6	23	38	....	1988-89	1997-98
• Drummond, Jim	NYR	1	2	0	0	0	0	....	....	....	....	....	....	1944-45	1944-45
• Drury, Herb	Pit., Phi.	6	213	24	13	37	203	4	1	1	2	0	....	1925-26	1930-31
Dube, Gilles	Mtl., Det.	2	12	1	2	3	2	2	0	0	0	0	1	1949-50	1953-54
Dube, Norm	K.C.	2	57	8	10	18	54	....	....	....	....	....	....	1974-75	1975-76
Duberman, Justin	Pit.	1	4	0	0	0	0	....	....	....	....	....	....	1993-94	1993-94
Duchesne, Gaetan	Wsh., Que., Min., S.J., Fla.	14	1028	179	254	433	617	84	14	13	27	97	....	1981-82	1994-95
Dudley, Rick	Buf., Wpg.	6	309	75	99	174	292	25	7	2	9	69	....	1972-73	1980-81
Duff, Dick	Tor., NYR, Mtl., L.A., Buf.	18	1030	283	289	572	743	114	30	49	79	78	6	1954-55	1971-72
Dufour, Luc	Bos., Que., St.L.	3	167	23	21	44	199	18	1	0	1	32	....	1982-83	1984-85
Dufour, Marc	NYR, L.A.	3	14	1	0	1	2	....	....	....	....	....	....	1963-64	1968-69
Dufresne, Donald	Mtl., T.B., L.A., St.L., Edm.	9	268	6	36	42	258	34	1	3	4	47	1	1988-89	1996-97
• Duggan, John	Ott.	1	27	0	0	0	0	2	0	0	0	0	....	1925-26	1925-26
Duggan, Ken	Min.	1	1	0	0	0	0	....	....	....	....	....	....	1987-88	1987-88
Duguay, Ron	NYR, Det., Pit., L.A.	12	864	274	346	620	582	89	31	22	53	118	....	1977-78	1988-89
• Duguid, Lorne	Mtl.M., Det., Bos.	6	135	9	15	24	57	4	1	0	1	6	....	1931-32	1936-37
• Dukowski, Duke	Chi., NYA, NYR	5	200	16	30	46	172	6	0	0	0	6	....	1926-27	1933-34
Dumart, Woody	Bos.	16	772	211	218	429	99	88	12	15	27	23	2	1935-36	1953-54
Dunbar, Dale	Van., Bos.	2	2	0	0	0	2	....	....	....	....	....	....	1985-86	1988-89
• Duncan, Art	Det., Tor.	6	156	18	16	34	225	5	0	0	0	4	....	1926-27	1930-31
Duncan, Iain	Wpg.	4	127	34	55	89	149	11	0	3	3	6	....	1986-87	1990-91
Duncanson, Craig	L.A., Wpg., NYR	7	38	5	4	9	61	....	....	....	....	....	....	1985-86	1992-93
Dundas, Rocky	Tor.	1	5	0	0	0	14	....	....	....	....	....	....	1989-90	1989-90
• Dunlap, Frank	Tor.	1	15	0	1	1	2	....	....	....	....	....	....	1943-44	1943-44
Dunlop, Blake	Min., Phi., St.L., Det.	11	550	130	274	404	172	40	4	10	14	18	....	1973-74	1983-84
Dunn, Dave	Van., Tor.	3	184	14	41	55	313	10	1	1	2	41	....	1973-74	1975-76
Dunn, Richie	Buf., Cgy., Hfd.	12	483	36	140	176	314	36	3	15	18	24	....	1977-78	1988-89
Dupere, Denis	Tor., Wsh., St.L., K.C., Col.	8	421	80	99	179	66	16	1	0	1	0	....	1970-71	1977-78
Dupont, Andre	NYR, St.L., Phi., Que.	13	800	59	185	244	1986	140	14	18	32	352	2	1970-71	1982-83
Dupont, Jerome	Chi., Tor.	6	214	7	29	36	468	20	0	2	2	56	....	1981-82	1986-87
Dupont, Norm	Mtl., Wpg., Hfd.	5	256	55	85	140	52	13	4	2	6	0	....	1979-80	1983-84
• Dupre, Yanick	Phi.	3	35	2	0	2	16	....	....	....	....	....	....	1991-92	1995-96
Durbano, Steve	St.L., Pit., K.C., Col.	6	220	13	60	73	1127	5	0	2	2	8	....	1972-73	1978-79
Duris, Vitezslav	Tor.	2	89	3	20	23	62	3	0	1	1	2	....	1980-81	1982-83
Dussault, Norm	Mtl.	4	206	31	62	93	47	7	3	1	4	0	....	1947-48	1950-51
• Dutton, Red	Mtl.M., NYA	10	449	29	67	96	871	18	1	0	1	33	....	1926-27	1935-36
Dvorak, Miroslav	Phi.	3	193	11	74	85	51	18	0	2	2	6	....	1982-83	1984-85
Dwyer, Mike	Col., Cgy.	4	31	2	6	8	25	1	1	0	1	0	....	1978-79	1981-82
• Dyck, Henry	NYR	1	1	0	0	0	0	....	....	....	....	....	....	1943-44	1943-44
• Dye, Babe	Tor., Ham., Chi., NYA	11	271	201	47	248	221	10	2	0	2	11	....	1919-20	1930-31
Dykstra, Steve	Buf., Edm., Pit., Hfd.	5	217	8	32	40	545	1	0	0	0	2	....	1985-86	1989-90
Dyte, Jack	Chi.	1	27	1	0	1	31	....	....	....	....	....	....	1943-44	1943-44
Dziedzic, Joe	Pit., Phx.	3	130	14	14	28	131	21	1	3	4	23	....	1995-96	1998-99
E															
Eakin, Bruce	Cgy., Det.	4	13	2	2	4	4	....	....	....	....	....	....	1981-82	1985-86
Eatough, Jeff	Buf.	1	1	0	0	0	0	....	....	....	....	....	....	1981-82	1981-82
Eaves, Mike	Min., Cgy.	11	324	83	143	226	80	43	7	10	17	14	....	1978-79	1985-86
Eaves, Murray	Wpg., Det.	8	57	4	13	17	9	4	0	1	1	2	....	1980-81	1989-90
Ecclestone, Tim	St.L., Det., Tor., Atl.	11	692	126	233	359	344	48	6	11	17	76	....	1967-68	1977-78
Edberg, Rolf	Wsh.	3	184	45	58	103	24	....	....	....	....	....	....	1978-79	1980-81
• Eddolls, Frank	Mtl., NYR, Chi.	9	317	23	43	66	114	31	0	2	2	10	1	1944-45	1954-55
Edestrand, Darryl	St.L., Phi., Pit., Bos., L.A.	10	455	34	90	124	404	42	3	9	12	57	....	1967-68	1978-79
Edmundson, Garry	Mtl., Tor.	3	43	4	6	10	49	11	0	1	1	8	....	1951-52	1960-61
Edur, Tom	Col., Pit.	2	158	17	70	87	67	....	....	....	....	....	....	1976-77	1977-78
Egan, Pat	NYA, Bro., Det., Bos., NYR	11	554	77	153	230	776	46	9	4	13	48	....	1939-40	1950-51
Egers, Jack	NYR, St.L., Wsh.	7	284	64	69	133	154	32	5	6	11	32	....	1969-70	1975-76
Ehman, Gerry	Bos., Det., Tor., Oak., Cal.	9	429	96	118	214	100	41	10	10	20	12	1	1957-58	1970-71
‡ Eisenhut, Neil	Van., Cgy.	2	16	1	3	4	21	....	....	....	....	....	....	1993-94	1994-95
Eklund, Per-Erik	Phi., Dal.	9	594	120	335	455	109	66	10	36	46	8	....	1985-86	1993-94
Eldebrink, Anders	Van., Que.	2	55	3	11	14	29	14	0	0	0	10	....	1981-82	1982-83
Elik, Bo	Det.	1	3	0	0	0	0	....	....	....	....	....	....	1962-63	1962-63
‡ Elik, Todd	L.A., Min., Edm., S.J., St.L., Bos.	8	448	110	219	329	453	52	15	27	42	48	....	1989-90	1996-97
• Elliot, Fred	Ott.	1	43	2	0	2	6	....	....	....	....	....	....	1928-29	1928-29
Ellis, Ron	Tor.	16	1034	332	308	640	207	70	18	8	26	20	1	1963-64	1980-81
Eloranta, Kari	Cgy., St.L.	5	267	13	103	116	155	26	1	7	8	19	....	1981-82	1986-87
Elynuik, Pat	Wpg., Wsh., T.B., Ott.	9	506	154	188	342	459	20	6	9	15	25	....	1987-88	1995-96
Emberg, Eddie	Mtl.	1	....	....	....	....	....	2	1	0	1	0	....	1944-45	1944-45
Emmons, Gary	S.J.	1	3	1	0	1	0	....	....	....	....	....	....	1993-94	1993-94
• Emms, Hap	Mtl.M., NYA, Det., Bos.	10	320	36	53	89	311	14	0	0	0	12	....	1926-27	1937-38
Endean, Craig	Wpg.	1	2	0	1	1	0	....	....	....	....	....	....	1986-87	1986-87
Engblom, Brian	Mtl., Wsh., L.A., Buf., Cgy.	11	659	29	177	206	599	48	3	9	12	43	3	1976-77	1986-87
Engele, Jerry	Min.	3	100	2	13	15	162	2	0	1	1	0	....	1975-76	1977-78
English, John	L.A.	1	3	1	3	4	4	1	0	0	0	0	....	1987-88	1987-88
Ennis, Jim	Edm.	1	5	1	0	1	10	....	....	....	....	....	....	1987-88	1987-88
Erickson, Aut	Bos., Chi., Tor., Oak.	7	226	7	24	31	182	7	0	0	0	2	1	1959-60	1969-70
Erickson, Bryan	Wsh., L.A., Pit., Wpg.	9	351	80	125	205	141	14	3	4	7	7	....	1983-84	1993-94
Erickson, Grant	Bos., Min.	2	6	1	0	1	0	....	....	....	....	....	....	1968-69	1969-70
Eriksson, Peter	Edm.	1	20	3	3	6	24	....	....	....	....	....	....	1989-90	1989-90
Eriksson, Roland	Min., Van.	3	193	48	95	143	26	2	1	0	1	0	....	1976-77	1978-79

Name	NHL Teams	NHL Seasons	Regular Schedule GP	G	A	TP	PIM	Playoffs GP	G	A	TP	PIM	NHL Cup Wins	First NHL Season	Last NHL Season
Eriksson, Thomas	Phi.	5	208	22	76	98	107	19	0	3	3	12	....	1980-81	1985-86
Erixon, Jan	NYR	10	556	57	159	216	167	58	7	7	14	16	....	1983-84	1992-93
Errey, Bob	Pit., Buf., S.J., Det., Dal., NYR	15	895	170	212	382	1005	99	13	16	29	109	2	1983-84	1997-98
‡ Esau, Len	Tor., Que., Cgy., Edm.	4	27	0	10	10	24	....	....	....	....	....	....	1991-92	1994-95
Esposito, Phil	Chi., Bos., NYR	18	1282	717	873	1590	910	130	61	76	137	138	2	1963-64	1980-81
Evans, Chris	Tor., Buf., St.L., Det., K.C.	5	241	19	42	61	143	12	1	1	2	8	....	1969-70	1974-75
Evans, Daryl	L.A., Wsh., Tor.	6	113	22	30	52	25	11	5	8	13	12	....	1981-82	1986-87
Evans, Doug	St.L., Wpg., Phi.	8	355	48	87	135	502	22	3	4	7	38	....	1985-86	1992-93
• Evans, Jack	NYR, Chi.	14	752	19	80	99	989	56	2	2	4	97	1	1948-49	1962-63
Evans, John Paul	Phi.	3	103	14	25	39	34	1	0	0	0	0	....	1978-79	1982-83
‡ Evans, Kevin	Min., S.J.	2	9	0	1	1	44	....	....	....	....	....	....	1990-91	1991-92
Evans, Paul	Tor.	2	11	1	1	2	21	2	0	0	0	0	....	1976-77	1977-78
Evans, Shawn	St.L., NYI	2	9	1	0	1	2	....	....	....	....	....	....	1985-86	1989-90
• Evans, Stewart	Det., Mtl.M., Mtl.C.	8	367	28	49	77	425	26	0	0	0	20	1	1930-31	1938-39
Evason, Dean	Wsh., Hfd., S.J., Dal., Cgy.	13	803	139	233	372	1002	55	9	20	29	132	....	1983-84	1995-96
Ewen, Todd	St.L., Mtl., Ana., S.J.	12	518	36	40	76	1911	26	0	0	0	87	1	1986-87	1997-98
Ezinicki, Bill	Tor., Bos., NYR	9	368	79	105	184	713	40	5	8	13	87	3	1944-45	1954-55

F

Name	NHL Teams	NHL Seasons	Regular Schedule GP	G	A	TP	PIM	Playoffs GP	G	A	TP	PIM	NHL Cup Wins	First NHL Season	Last NHL Season
Fahey, Trevor	NYR	1	1	0	0	0	0	....	....	....	....	....	....	1964-65	1964-65
Fairbairn, Bill	NYR, Min., St.L.	11	658	162	261	423	173	54	13	22	35	42	....	1968-69	1978-79
Falkenberg, Bob	Det.	5	54	1	5	6	26	....	....	....	....	....	....	1966-67	1971-72
Farrant, Walt	Chi.	1	1	0	0	0	0	....	....	....	....	....	....	1943-44	1943-44
Farrish, Dave	NYR, Que., Tor.	8	430	17	110	127	440	14	0	2	2	24	....	1976-77	1983-84
Fashoway, Gordie	Chi.	1	13	3	2	5	14	....	....	....	....	....	....	1950-51	1950-51
Faubert, Mario	Pit.	7	231	21	90	111	292	10	2	2	4	6	....	1974-75	1981-82
Faulkner, Alex	Tor., Det.	3	101	15	17	32	15	12	5	0	5	2	....	1961-62	1963-64
Fauss, Ted	Tor.	2	28	0	2	2	15	....	....	....	....	....	....	1986-87	1987-88
‡ Faust, Andre	Phi.	2	47	10	7	17	14	....	....	....	....	....	....	1992-93	1993-94
Feamster, Dave	Chi.	4	169	13	24	37	154	33	3	5	8	61	....	1981-82	1984-85
Featherstone, Tony	Oak., Cal., Min.	3	130	17	21	38	65	2	0	0	0	0	....	1969-70	1973-74
Federko, Bernie	St.L., Det.	14	1000	369	761	1130	487	91	35	66	101	83	....	1976-77	1989-90
‡ Fedotov, Anatoli	Wpg., Ana.	2	4	0	2	2	0	....	....	....	....	....	....	1992-93	1993-94
‡ Felix, Chris	Wsh.	4	35	1	12	13	10	2	0	1	1	0	....	1987-88	1990-91
‡ Felsner, Denny	St.L.	4	18	1	4	5	6	10	2	3	5	2	....	1991-92	1994-95
Feltrin, Tony	Pit., NYR	6	48	3	3	6	65	....	....	....	....	....	....	1980-81	1985-86
Fenton, Paul	Hfd., NYR, L.A., Wpg., Tor., Cgy., S.J.	8	411	100	83	183	198	17	4	1	5	27	....	1984-85	1991-92
Fenyves, David	Buf., Phi.	9	206	3	32	35	119	11	0	0	0	9	....	1982-83	1990-91
Fergus, Tom	Bos., Tor., Van.	12	726	235	346	581	499	65	21	17	38	48	....	1981-82	1992-93
Ferguson, George	Tor., Pit., Min.	12	797	160	238	398	431	86	14	23	37	44	....	1972-73	1983-84
Ferguson, John	Mtl.	8	500	145	158	303	1214	85	20	18	38	260	5	1963-64	1970-71
Ferguson, Lorne	Bos., Det., Chi.	8	422	82	80	162	193	31	6	3	9	24	....	1949-50	1958-59
Ferguson, Norm	Oak., Cal.	4	279	73	66	139	72	10	1	4	5	7	....	1968-69	1971-72
‡ Ferner, Mark	Buf., Wsh., Ana., Det.	6	91	3	10	13	51	....	....	....	....	....	....	1986-87	1994-95
Fetisov, Viacheslav	N.J., Det.	10	546	36	192	228	656	116	2	26	28	147	2	1989-90	1997-98
Fidler, Mike	Cle., Min., Hfd., Chi.	7	271	84	97	181	124	....	....	....	....	....	....	1976-77	1982-83
• Field, Wilf	NYA, Bro., Mtl., Chi.	6	219	17	25	42	151	2	0	0	0	2	....	1936-37	1944-45
Fielder, Guyle	Chi., Det., Bos.	4	9	0	0	0	2	6	0	0	0	2	....	1950-51	1957-58
‡ Filimonov, Dmitri	Ott.	1	30	1	4	5	18	....	....	....	....	....	....	1993-94	1993-94
Fillion, Bob	Mtl.	7	327	42	61	103	84	33	7	4	11	10	2	1943-44	1949-50
• Fillion, Marcel	Bos.	1	1	0	0	0	0	....	....	....	....	....	....	1944-45	1944-45
• Filmore, Tommy	Det., NYA, Bos.	4	117	15	12	27	33	....	....	....	....	....	....	1930-31	1933-34
• Finkbeiner, Lloyd	NYA	1	2	0	0	0	0	....	....	....	....	....	....	1940-41	1940-41
Finn, Steven	Que., T.B., L.A.	12	725	34	78	112	1724	23	0	4	4	39	....	1985-86	1996-97
Finney, Sid	Chi.	3	59	10	7	17	4	7	0	2	2	0	....	1951-52	1953-54
• Finnigan, Ed	St.L., Bos.	2	15	1	1	2	2	....	....	....	....	....	....	1934-35	1935-36
• Finnigan, Frank	Ott., Tor., St.L.	14	553	115	88	203	407	38	6	9	15	22	2	1923-24	1936-37
Fiorentino, Peter	NYR	1	1	0	0	0	0	....	....	....	....	....	....	1991-92	1991-92
Fischer, Ron	Buf.	2	18	0	7	7	6	....	....	....	....	....	....	1981-82	1982-83
• Fisher, Alvin	Tor.	1	9	1	0	1	4	....	....	....	....	....	....	1924-25	1924-25
Fisher, Dunc	NYR, Bos., Det.	7	275	45	70	115	104	21	4	4	8	14	....	1947-48	1958-59
Fisher, Joe	Det.	4	65	8	12	20	13	12	2	1	3	6	1	1939-40	1942-43
Fitchner, Bob	Que.	2	78	12	20	32	59	3	0	0	0	10	....	1979-80	1980-81
‡ Fitzgerald, Rusty	Pit.	2	25	2	2	4	12	5	0	0	0	4	....	1994-95	1995-96
Fitzpatrick, Ross	Phi.	4	20	5	2	7	0	....	....	....	....	....	....	1982-83	1985-86
Fitzpatrick, Sandy	NYR, Min.	2	22	3	6	9	8	12	0	0	0	0	....	1964-65	1967-68
Flaman, Fern	Bos., Tor.	17	910	34	174	208	1370	63	4	8	12	93	1	1944-45	1960-61
Flatley, Pat	NYI, NYR	14	780	170	340	510	686	70	18	15	33	75	....	1983-84	1996-97
Fleming, Gerry	Mtl.	2	11	0	0	0	42	....	....	....	....	....	....	1993-94	1994-95
Fleming, Reggie	Mtl., Chi., Bos., NYR, Phi., Buf.	12	749	108	132	240	1468	50	3	6	9	106	1	1959-60	1970-71
Flesch, John	Min., Pit., Col.	4	124	18	23	41	117	....	....	....	....	....	....	1974-75	1979-80
Fletcher, Steven	Mtl., Wpg.	2	3	0	0	0	5	1	0	0	0	5	....	1987-88	1988-89
• Flett, Bill	L.A., Phi., Tor., Atl., Edm.	11	689	202	215	417	501	52	7	16	23	42	1	1967-68	1979-80
Flichel, Todd	Wpg.	3	6	0	1	1	4	....	....	....	....	....	....	1987-88	1989-90
Flockhart, Rob	Van., Min.	5	55	2	5	7	14	1	1	0	1	2	....	1976-77	1980-81
Flockhart, Ron	Phi., Pit., Mtl., St.L., Bos.	9	453	145	183	328	208	19	4	6	10	14	....	1980-81	1988-89
Floyd, Larry	N.J.	2	12	2	3	5	9	....	....	....	....	....	....	1982-83	1983-84
‡ Fogarty, Bryan	Que., Pit., Mtl.	6	156	22	52	74	119	....	....	....	....	....	....	1989-90	1994-95
Fogolin, Lee Jr.	Buf., Edm.	13	924	44	195	239	1318	108	5	19	24	173	2	1974-75	1986-87
Fogolin, Lee Sr.	Det., Chi.	9	427	10	48	58	575	28	0	2	2	30	1	1947-48	1955-56
Folco, Peter	Van.	1	2	0	0	0	0	....	....	....	....	....	....	1973-74	1973-74
Foley, Gerry	Tor., NYR, L.A.	4	142	9	14	23	99	9	0	1	1	2	....	1954-55	1968-69
Foley, Rick	Chi., Phi., Det.	3	67	11	26	37	180	4	0	1	1	4	....	1970-71	1973-74
Foligno, Mike	Det., Buf., Tor., Fla.	16	1018	355	372	727	2049	57	15	17	32	185	....	1979-80	1993-94
Folk, Bill	Det.	2	12	0	0	0	4	....	....	....	....	....	....	1951-52	1952-53
Fontaine, Len	Det.	2	46	8	11	19	10	....	....	....	....	....	....	1972-73	1973-74
Fontas, Jon	Min.	2	2	0	0	0	0	....	....	....	....	....	....	1979-80	1980-81
Fonteyne, Val	Det., NYR, Pit.	13	820	75	154	229	26	59	3	10	13	8	....	1959-60	1971-72
Fontinato, Lou	NYR, Mtl.	9	535	26	78	104	1247	21	0	2	2	42	....	1954-55	1962-63
Forbes, Dave	Bos., Wsh.	6	363	64	64	128	341	45	1	4	5	13	....	1973-74	1978-79
Forbes, Mike	Bos., Edm.	3	50	1	11	12	41	....	....	....	....	....	....	1977-78	1981-82
Forey, Connie	St.L.	1	4	0	0	0	2	....	....	....	....	....	....	1973-74	1973-74
• Forsey, Jack	Tor.	1	19	7	9	16	10	3	0	1	1	0	....	1942-43	1942-43
• Forslund, Gus	Ott.	1	48	4	9	13	2	....	....	....	....	....	....	1932-33	1932-33
‡ Forslund, Tomas	Cgy.	2	44	5	11	16	12	....	....	....	....	....	....	1991-92	1992-93
Forsyth, Alex	Wsh.	1	1	0	0	0	0	....	....	....	....	....	....	1976-77	1976-77
Fortier, Dave	Tor., NYI, Van.	4	205	8	21	29	335	20	0	2	2	33	....	1972-73	1976-77
‡ Fortier, Marc	Que., Ott., L.A.	6	212	42	60	102	135	....	....	....	....	....	....	1987-88	1992-93
Fortin, Ray	St.L.	3	92	2	6	8	33	6	0	0	0	8	....	1967-68	1969-70
‡ Foster, Corey	N.J., Phi., Pit., NYI	4	45	5	6	11	24	3	0	0	0	4	....	1988-89	1996-97
Foster, Dwight	Bos., Col., N.J., Det.	10	541	111	163	274	420	35	5	12	17	4	....	1977-78	1986-87
Foster, Herb	NYR	2	6	1	0	1	5	....	....	....	....	....	....	1940-41	1947-48
• Foster, Yip	NYR, Bos., Det.	4	83	3	2	5	32	....	....	....	....	....	....	1929-30	1934-35
Fotiu, Nick	NYR, Hfd., Cgy., Phi., Edm.	14	646	60	77	137	1362	38	0	4	4	67	....	1976-77	1988-89
• Fowler, Jimmy	Tor.	3	135	18	29	47	39	18	0	3	3	2	....	1936-37	1938-39
Fowler, Tom	Chi.	1	24	0	1	1	18	....	....	....	....	....	....	1946-47	1946-47
Fox, Greg	Atl., Chi., Pit.	8	494	14	92	106	637	44	1	9	10	67	....	1977-78	1984-85
Fox, Jim	L.A.	10	578	186	293	479	143	22	4	8	12	0	....	1980-81	1989-90
• Foyston, Frank	Det.	2	64	17	7	24	32	....	....	....	....	....	....	1926-27	1927-28
Frampton, Bob	Mtl.	1	2	0	0	0	0	3	0	0	0	0	....	1949-50	1949-50
Franceschetti, Lou	Wsh., Tor., Buf.	10	459	59	81	140	747	44	3	2	5	111	....	1981-82	1991-92
Francis, Bobby	Det.	3	14	2	0	2	0	....	....	....	....	....	....	1982-83	1982-83
• Fraser, Archie	NYR	1	3	0	1	1	0	....	....	....	....	....	....	1943-44	1943-44
• Fraser, Charles	Ham.	1	1	0	0	0	0	....	....	....	....	....	....	1923-24	1923-24
Fraser, Curt	Van., Chi., Min.	13	704	193	240	433	1306	65	15	18	33	198	....	1978-79	1989-90
• Fraser, Gord	Chi., Det., Mtl.C., Pit., Phi.	5	144	24	12	36	224	2	1	0	1	6	....	1926-27	1930-31
Fraser, Harvey	Chi.	1	21	5	4	9	0	....	....	....	....	....	....	1944-45	1944-45
‡ Fraser, Iain	NYI, Que., Dal., Edm., Wpg., S.J.	5	94	23	23	46	31	4	0	0	0	0	....	1992-93	1996-97
Fraser, Scott	Mtl., Edm., NYR	3	72	16	15	31	24	11	1	1	2	0	....	1995-96	1998-99
Frawley, Dan	Chi., Pit.	6	273	37	40	77	674	1	0	0	0	0	....	1983-84	1988-89

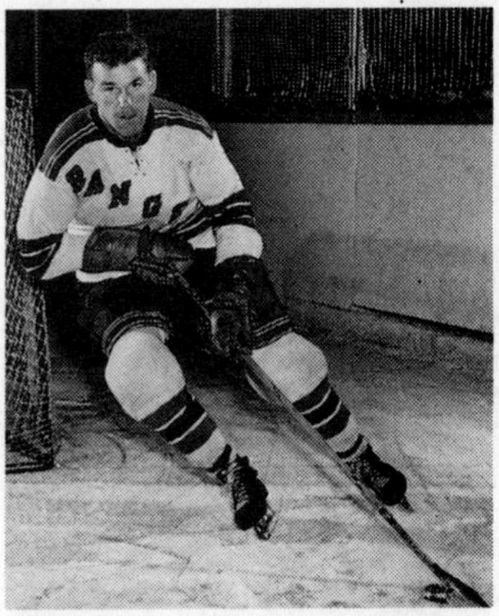

Jack Evans

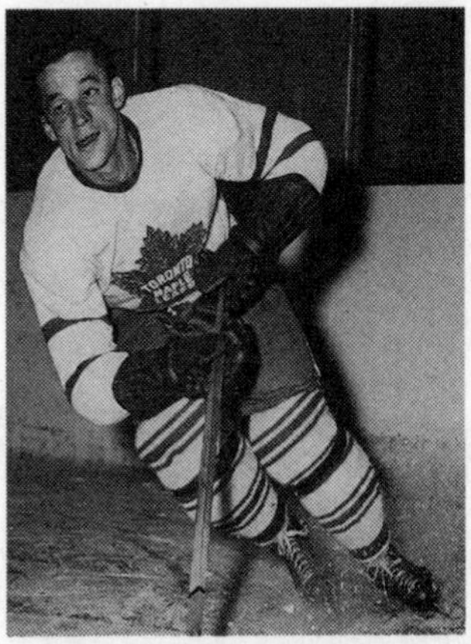

Bill Ezinicki

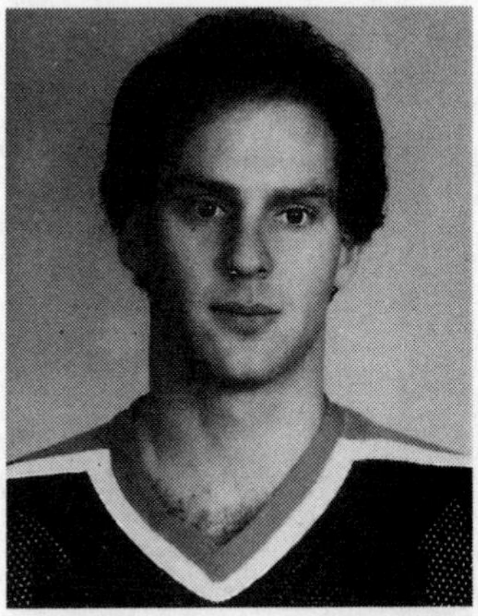

Lee Fogolin

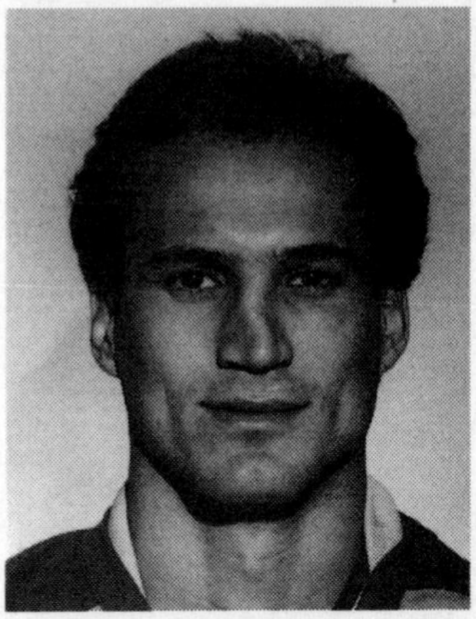

Mike Foligno

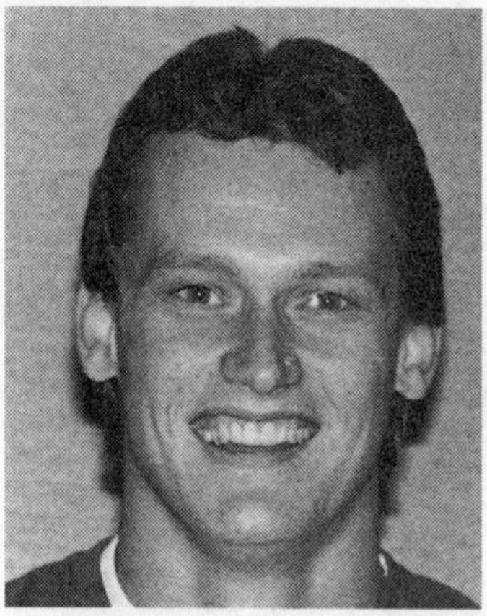

Miroslav Frycer

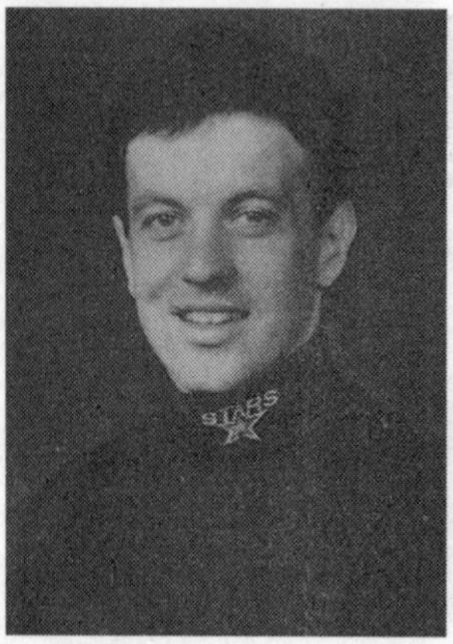

Dave Gagner

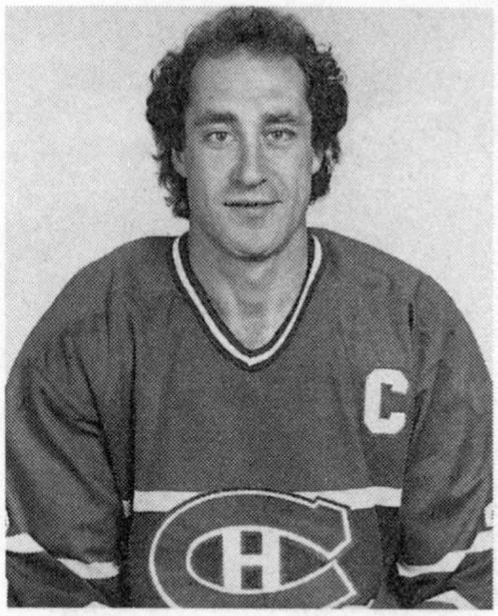

Bob Gainey

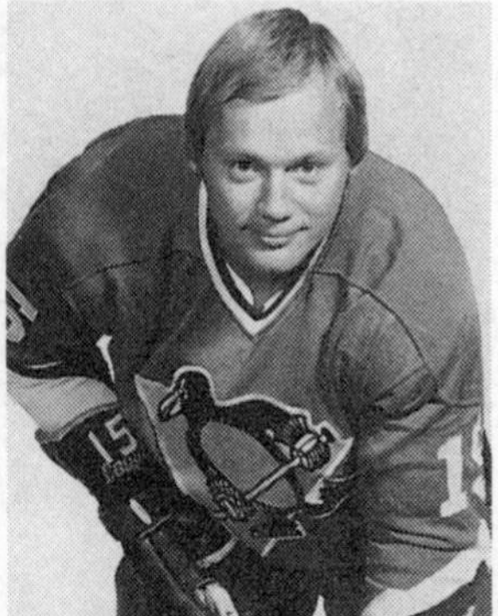

Stan Gilbertson

Name	NHL Teams	NHL Seasons	Regular Schedule GP	G	A	TP	PIM	Playoffs GP	G	A	TP	PIM	NHL Cup Wins	First NHL Season	Last NHL Season
• Fredrickson, Frank	Det., Bos., Pit.	5	161	39	34	73	206	10	2	3	5	24	....	1926-27	1930-31
• Frew, Irv	Mtl.M., St.L., Mtl.C.	3	96	2	5	7	146	4	0	0	0	6	....	1933-34	1935-36
Friday, Tim	Det.	1	23	0	3	3	6	....	....	....	....	....	....	1985-86	1985-86
Fridgen, Dan	Hfd.	2	13	2	3	5	2	....	....	....	....	....	....	1981-82	1982-83
Friest, Ron	Min.	3	64	7	7	14	191	6	1	0	1	7	....	1980-81	1982-83
Frig, Len	Chi., Cal., Cle., St.L.	7	311	13	51	64	479	14	2	1	3	0	....	1972-73	1979-80
Frost, Harry	Bos.	1	4	0	0	0	0	1	0	0	0	0	1	1938-39	1938-39
Frycer, Miroslav	Que., Tor., Det., Edm.	8	415	147	183	330	486	17	3	8	11	16	....	1981-82	1988-89
Fryday, Bob	Mtl.	2	5	1	0	1	0	....	....	....	....	....	....	1949-50	1951-52
Ftorek, Robbie	Det., Que., NYR	13	334	77	150	227	262	19	9	6	15	28	....	1972-73	1984-85
Fullan, Larry	Wsh.	1	4	1	0	1	0	....	....	....	....	....	....	1974-75	1974-75
Fusco, Mark	Hfd.	2	80	3	12	15	42	....	....	....	....	....	....	1983-84	1984-85

G

Name	NHL Teams	NHL Seasons	Regular Schedule GP	G	A	TP	PIM	Playoffs GP	G	A	TP	PIM	NHL Cup Wins	First NHL Season	Last NHL Season
Gadsby, Bill	Chi., NYR, Det.	20	1248	130	438	568	1539	67	4	23	27	92	....	1946-47	1965-66
‡ Gaetz, Link	Min., S.J.	3	65	6	8	14	412	....	....	....	....	....	....	1988-89	1991-92
Gage, Jody	Det., Buf.	6	68	14	15	29	26	....	....	....	....	....	....	1980-81	1991-92
• Gagne, Art	Mtl.C., Bos., Ott., Det.	6	228	67	33	100	257	11	2	1	3	20	....	1926-27	1931-32
Gagne, Paul	Col., N.J., Tor., NYI	10	390	110	101	211	127	....	....	....	....	....	....	1980-81	1989-90
Gagne, Pierre	Bos.	1	2	0	0	0	0	....	....	....	....	....	....	1959-60	1959-60
Gagner, Dave	NYR, Min., Dal., Tor., Cgy., Fla., Van.	15	946	318	401	719	1018	57	22	26	48	64	....	1984-85	1998-99
Gagnon, Germaine	Mtl., NYI, Chi., K.C.	5	259	40	101	141	72	19	2	3	5	2	....	1971-72	1975-76
• Gagnon, Johnny	Mtl.C., Bos., Mtl., NYA	10	454	120	141	261	295	32	12	12	24	37	1	1930-31	1939-40
Gainey, Bob	Mtl.	19	1160	239	262	501	585	182	25	48	73	151	5	1973-74	1988-89
• Gainor, Norm	Bos., NYR, Ott., Mtl.M.	7	246	51	56	107	129	22	2	1	3	14	2	1927-28	1934-35
‡ Galarneau, Michel	Hfd.	3	78	7	10	17	34	....	....	....	....	....	....	1980-81	1982-83
• Galbraith, Percy	Bos., Ott.	8	347	29	31	60	224	31	4	7	11	24	1	1926-27	1933-34
• Gallagher, John	Mtl.M., Det., NYA	7	205	14	19	33	153	24	2	3	5	27	1	1930-31	1938-39
Gallant, Gerard	Det., T.B.	11	615	211	269	480	1674	58	18	21	39	178	....	1984-85	1994-95
Gallimore, Jamie	Min.	1	2	0	0	0	0	....	....	....	....	....	....	1977-78	1977-78
• Gallinger, Don	Bos.	5	222	65	88	153	89	23	5	5	10	19	....	1942-43	1947-48
Gamble, Dick	Mtl., Chi., Tor.	8	195	41	41	82	66	14	1	2	3	4	1	1950-51	1966-67
Gambucci, Gary	Min.	2	51	2	7	9	9	....	....	....	....	....	....	1971-72	1973-74
Ganchar, Perry	St.L., Mtl., Pit.	4	42	3	7	10	36	7	3	1	4	0	....	1983-84	1988-89
Gans, Dave	L.A.	2	6	0	0	0	2	....	....	....	....	....	....	1982-83	1985-86
• Gardiner, Herb	Mtl.C., Chi.	3	108	10	9	19	52	9	0	1	1	16	....	1926-27	1928-29
Gardner, Bill	Chi., Hfd.	9	380	73	115	188	68	45	3	8	11	17	....	1980-81	1988-89
Gardner, Cal	NYR, Tor., Chi., Bos.	12	696	154	238	392	517	61	7	10	17	20	2	1945-46	1956-57
Gardner, Dave	Mtl., St.L., Cal., Cle., Phi.	7	350	75	115	190	41	....	....	....	....	....	....	1972-73	1979-80
Gardner, Paul	Col., Tor., Pit., Wsh., Buf.	13	447	201	201	402	207	16	2	6	8	14	....	1976-77	1985-86
Gare, Danny	Buf., Det., Edm.	13	827	354	331	685	1285	64	25	21	46	195	....	1974-75	1986-87
Gariepy, Ray	Bos., Tor.	2	36	1	6	7	43	....	....	....	....	....	....	1953-54	1955-56
• Garland, Scott	Tor., L.A.	3	91	13	24	37	115	7	1	2	3	35	....	1975-76	1978-79
Garner, Rob	Pit.	1	1	0	0	0	0	....	....	....	....	....	....	1982-83	1982-83
• Garrett, Red	NYR	1	23	1	1	2	18	....	....	....	....	....	....	1942-43	1942-43
Gartner, Mike	Wsh., Min., NYR, Tor., Phx.	19	1432	708	627	1335	1159	122	43	50	93	125	....	1979-80	1997-98
• Gassoff, Bob	St.L.	4	245	11	47	58	866	9	0	1	1	16	....	1973-74	1976-77
Gassoff, Brad	Van.	4	122	19	17	36	163	3	0	0	0	0	....	1975-76	1978-79
Gatzos, Steve	Pit.	4	89	15	20	35	83	1	0	0	0	0	....	1981-82	1984-85
Gaudreau, Rob	S.J., Ott.	4	231	51	54	105	69	14	2	0	2	0	....	1992-93	1995-96
Gaudreault, Armand	Bos.	1	44	15	9	24	27	7	0	2	2	8	....	1944-45	1944-45
• Gaudreault, Leo	Mtl.C.	3	67	8	4	12	30	....	....	....	....	....	....	1927-28	1932-33
Gaulin, Jean-Marc	Que.	4	26	4	3	7	8	1	0	0	0	0	....	1982-83	1985-86
Gaume, Dallas	Hfd.	1	4	1	1	2	0	....	....	....	....	....	....	1988-89	1988-89
• Gauthier, Art	Mtl.C.	1	13	0	0	0	0	1	0	0	0	0	....	1926-27	1926-27
‡ Gauthier, Daniel	Chi.	1	5	0	0	0	0	....	....	....	....	....	....	1994-95	1994-95
• Gauthier, Fern	NYR, Mtl., Det.	6	229	46	50	96	35	22	5	1	6	7	....	1943-44	1948-49
Gauthier, Jean	Mtl., Phi., Bos.	10	166	6	29	35	150	14	1	3	4	22	1	1960-61	1969-70
Gauthier, Luc	Mtl.	2	3	0	0	0	2	....	....	....	....	....	....	1990-91	1990-91
Gauvreau, Jocelyn	Mtl.	1	2	0	0	0	0	....	....	....	....	....	....	1983-84	1983-84
Gavin, Stew	Tor., Hfd., Min.	14	768	130	155	285	584	66	14	20	34	75	....	1980-81	1992-93
Geale, Bob	Pit.	1	1	0	0	0	2	....	....	....	....	....	....	1984-85	1984-85
• Gee, George	Chi., Det.	9	551	135	183	318	345	41	6	13	19	32	1	1945-46	1953-54
Geldart, Gary	Min.	1	4	0	0	0	5	....	....	....	....	....	....	1970-71	1970-71
Gendron, Jean-Guy	NYR, Bos., Mtl., Phi.	14	863	182	201	383	701	42	7	4	11	47	....	1955-56	1971-72
Geoffrion, Bernie	Mtl., NYR	16	883	393	429	822	689	132	58	60	118	88	6	1950-51	1967-68
Geoffrion, Danny	Mtl., Wpg.	3	111	20	32	52	99	2	0	0	0	7	....	1979-80	1981-82
• Geran, Gerry	Mtl., Bos.	2	37	5	1	6	6	....	....	....	....	....	....	1917-18	1925-26
• Gerard, Eddie	Ott.	6	128	50	48	98	108	16	4	0	4	61	....	1917-18	1922-23
Germain, Eric	L.A.	1	4	0	1	1	13	1	0	0	0	4	....	1987-88	1987-88
Getliffe, Ray	Bos., Mtl.	10	393	136	137	273	250	45	9	10	19	30	2	1935-36	1944-45
Giallonardo, Mario	Col.	2	23	0	3	3	6	....	....	....	....	....	....	1979-80	1980-81
Gibbs, Barry	Bos., Min., Atl., St.L., L.A.	13	797	58	224	282	945	36	4	2	6	67	....	1967-68	1979-80
Gibson, Don	Van.	1	14	0	3	3	20	....	....	....	....	....	....	1990-91	1990-91
Gibson, Doug	Bos., Wsh.	3	63	9	19	28	0	1	0	0	0	0	....	1973-74	1977-78
Gibson, John	L.A., Tor., Wpg.	3	48	0	2	2	120	....	....	....	....	....	....	1980-81	1983-84
Giesebrecht, Gus	Det.	4	135	27	51	78	13	17	2	3	5	0	....	1938-39	1941-42
Giffin, Lee	Pit.	2	27	1	3	4	9	....	....	....	....	....	....	1986-87	1987-88
Gilbert, Ed	K.C., Pit.	3	166	21	31	52	22	....	....	....	....	....	....	1974-75	1976-77
Gilbert, Greg	NYI, Chi., NYR, St.L.	15	837	150	228	378	576	133	17	33	50	162	3	1981-82	1995-96
Gilbert, Jeannot	Bos.	2	9	0	1	1	4	....	....	....	....	....	....	1962-63	1964-65
Gilbert, Rod	NYR	18	1065	406	615	1021	508	79	34	33	67	43	....	1960-61	1977-78
Gilbertson, Stan	Cal., St.L., Wsh., Pit.	6	428	85	89	174	148	3	1	1	2	2	....	1971-72	1976-77
Giles, Curt	Min., NYR, St.L.	14	895	43	199	242	733	103	6	16	22	118	....	1979-80	1992-93
Gilhen, Randy	Hfd., Wpg., Pit., L.A., NYR, T.B., Fla.	11	457	55	60	115	314	33	3	2	5	26	1	1982-83	1995-96
Gillen, Don	Phi., Hfd.	2	35	2	4	6	22	....	....	....	....	....	....	1979-80	1981-82
• Gillie, Farrand	Det.	1	1	0	0	0	0	....	....	....	....	....	....	1928-29	1928-29
Gillies, Clark	NYI, Buf.	14	958	319	378	697	1023	164	47	47	94	287	4	1974-75	1987-88
Gillis, Jere	Van., NYR, Que., Buf., Phi.	9	386	78	95	173	230	19	4	7	11	9	....	1977-78	1986-87
Gillis, Mike	Col., Bos.	6	246	33	43	76	186	27	2	5	7	10	....	1978-79	1983-84
Gillis, Paul	Que., Chi., Hfd.	12	624	88	154	242	1498	42	3	14	17	156	....	1982-83	1992-93
Gingras, Gaston	Mtl., Tor., St.L.	10	476	61	174	235	161	52	6	18	24	20	1	1979-80	1988-89
Girard, Bob	Cal., Cle., Wsh.	5	305	45	69	114	140	....	....	....	....	....	....	1975-76	1979-80
Girard, Kenny	Tor.	3	7	0	1	1	2	....	....	....	....	....	....	1956-57	1959-60
• Giroux, Art	Mtl.C., Bos., Det.	3	54	6	4	10	14	2	0	0	0	0	....	1932-33	1935-36
Giroux, Larry	St.L., K.C., Det., Hfd.	7	274	15	74	89	333	5	0	0	0	4	....	1973-74	1979-80
Giroux, Pierre	L.A.	1	6	1	0	1	17	....	....	....	....	....	....	1982-83	1982-83
Gladney, Bob	L.A., Pit.	2	14	1	5	6	4	....	....	....	....	....	....	1982-83	1983-84
Gladu, Jean-Paul	Bos.	1	40	6	14	20	2	7	2	2	4	0	....	1944-45	1944-45
Glennie, Brian	Tor., L.A.	10	572	14	100	114	621	32	0	1	1	66	....	1969-70	1978-79
Glennon, Matt	Bos.	1	3	0	0	0	2	....	....	....	....	....	....	1991-92	1991-92
Gloeckner, Lorry	Det.	1	13	0	2	2	6	....	....	....	....	....	....	1978-79	1978-79
Gloor, Dan	Van.	1	2	0	0	0	0	....	....	....	....	....	....	1973-74	1973-74
Glover, Fred	Det., Chi.	5	92	13	11	24	62	8	0	0	0	0	1	1948-49	1952-53
Glover, Howie	Chi., Det., NYR, Mtl.	5	144	29	17	46	101	11	1	2	3	2	....	1958-59	1968-69
Glynn, Brian	Cgy., Min., Edm., Ott., Van., Hfd.	10	431	25	79	104	410	57	6	10	16	40	....	1987-88	1996-97
Godden, Ernie	Tor.	1	5	1	1	2	6	....	....	....	....	....	....	1981-82	1981-82
• Godfrey, Warren	Bos., Det.	16	786	32	125	157	752	52	1	4	5	42	....	1952-53	1967-68
Godin, Eddy	Wsh.	2	27	3	6	9	12	....	....	....	....	....	....	1977-78	1978-79
• Godin, Sam	Ott., Mtl.C.	3	83	4	3	7	36	....	....	....	....	....	....	1927-28	1933-34
‡ Godynyuk, Alexander	Tor., Cgy., Fla., Hfd.	7	223	10	39	49	224	....	....	....	....	....	....	1990-91	1996-97
Goegan, Pete	Det., NYR, Min.	11	383	19	67	86	365	33	1	3	4	61	....	1957-58	1967-68
Goertz, Dave	Pit.	1	2	0	0	0	2	....	....	....	....	....	....	1987-88	1987-88
• Goldham, Bob	Tor., Chi., Det.	12	650	28	143	171	400	66	3	14	17	53	4	1941-42	1955-56
• Goldsworthy, Bill	Bos., Min., NYR	14	771	283	258	541	793	40	18	19	37	30	....	1964-65	1977-78
• Goldsworthy, Leroy	NYR, Det., Chi., Mtl.C., Bos., NYA	10	336	66	57	123	79	24	1	0	1	4	1	1928-29	1938-39
Goldup, Glenn	Mtl., L.A.	9	291	52	67	119	303	16	4	3	7	22	....	1973-74	1981-82
Goldup, Hank	Tor., NYR	6	202	63	80	143	97	26	5	1	6	6	1	1939-40	1945-46
• Gooden, Bill	NYR	2	53	9	11	20	15	....	....	....	....	....	....	1942-43	1943-44
Goodenough, Larry	Phi., Van.	6	242	22	77	99	179	22	3	15	18	10	1	1974-75	1979-80
• Goodfellow, Ebbie	Det.	14	557	134	190	324	511	45	8	8	16	65	3	1929-30	1942-43

Name	NHL Teams	NHL Seasons	Regular Schedule GP	G	A	TP	PIM	Playoffs GP	G	A	TP	PIM	NHL Cup Wins	First NHL Season	Last NHL Season
‡ Gordiouk, Viktor	Buf.	2	26	3	8	11	0	....	....	....	....	....	....	1992-93	1994-95
Gordon, Fred	Det., Bos.	2	81	8	7	15	68	2	0	0	0	0	....	1926-27	1927-28
Gordon, Jackie	NYR	3	36	3	10	13	0	9	1	1	2	7	....	1948-49	1950-51
Gorence, Tom	Phi., Edm.	6	303	58	53	111	89	37	9	6	15	47	....	1978-79	1983-84
Goring, Butch	L.A., NYI, Bos.	19	1107	375	513	888	102	134	38	50	88	32	4	1969-70	1984-85
Gorman, Dave	Atl.	1	3	0	0	0	0	....	....	....	....	....	....	1979-80	1979-80
● Gorman, Ed	Ott., Tor.	4	111	14	6	20	108	8	0	0	0	2	1	1924-25	1927-28
Gosselin, Benoit	NYR	1	7	0	0	0	33	....	....	....	....	....	....	1977-78	1977-78
Gosselin, Guy	Wpg.	1	5	0	0	0	6	....	....	....	....	....	....	1987-88	1987-88
Gotaas, Steve	Pit., Min.	3	49	6	9	15	53	3	0	1	1	5	....	1987-88	1990-91
● Gottselig, Johnny	Chi.	17	589	176	195	371	203	43	13	13	26	18	2	1928-29	1944-45
Gould, Bobby	Atl., Cgy., Wsh., Bos.	11	697	145	159	304	572	78	15	13	28	58	....	1979-80	1989-90
Gould, John	Buf., Van., Atl.	9	504	131	138	269	113	14	3	2	5	4	....	1971-72	1979-80
Gould, Larry	Van.	1	2	0	0	0	0	....	....	....	....	....	....	1973-74	1973-74
Goulet, Michel	Que., Chi.	15	1089	548	604	1152	825	92	39	39	78	110	....	1979-80	1993-94
Goupille, Red	Mtl.C., Mtl.	8	222	12	28	40	256	8	2	0	2	6	....	1935-36	1942-43
‡ Govedaris, Chris	Hfd., Tor.	4	45	4	6	10	24	4	0	0	0	2	....	1989-90	1993-94
Goyer, Gerry	Chi.	1	40	1	2	3	4	3	0	0	0	2	....	1967-68	1967-68
Goyette, Phil	Mtl., NYR, St.L., Buf.	16	941	207	467	674	131	94	17	29	46	26	4	1956-57	1971-72
Graboski, Tony	Mtl.	3	66	6	10	16	24	3	0	0	0	6	....	1940-41	1942-43
● Gracie, Bob	Tor., Bos., NYA, Mtl.M., Mtl.C., Chi.	9	379	82	109	191	205	33	4	7	11	4	2	1930-31	1938-39
Gradin, Thomas	Van., Bos.	9	677	209	384	593	298	42	17	25	42	20	....	1978-79	1986-87
Graham, Dirk	Min., Chi.	12	772	219	270	489	917	90	17	27	44	92	....	1983-84	1994-95
● Graham, Leth	Ott., Ham.	6	27	3	0	3	0	1	0	0	0	0	1	1920-21	1925-26
Graham, Pat	Pit., Tor.	3	103	11	17	28	136	4	0	0	0	2	....	1981-82	1983-84
Graham, Rod	Bos.	1	14	2	1	3	7	....	....	....	....	....	....	1974-75	1974-75
● Graham, Teddy	Chi., Mtl.M., Det., St.L., Bos., NYA	9	346	14	25	39	300	24	3	1	4	30	....	1927-28	1936-37
Grant, Danny	Mtl., Min., Det., L.A.	13	736	263	273	536	239	43	10	14	24	19	1	1965-66	1978-79
Gratton, Dan	L.A.	1	7	1	0	1	5	....	....	....	....	....	....	1987-88	1987-88
Gratton, Norm	NYR, Atl., Buf., Min.	5	201	39	44	83	64	6	0	1	1	2	....	1971-72	1975-76
Gravelle, Leo	Mtl., Det.	5	223	44	34	78	42	17	4	1	5	2	....	1946-47	1950-51
Graves, Hilliard	Cal., Atl., Van., Wpg.	9	556	118	163	281	209	2	0	0	0	0	....	1970-71	1979-80
Graves, Steve	Edm.	3	35	5	4	9	10	....	....	....	....	....	....	1983-84	1987-88
● Gray, Alex	NYR, Tor.	2	50	7	0	7	32	13	1	0	1	0	1	1927-28	1928-29
Gray, Terry	Bos., Mtl., L.A., St.L.	6	147	26	28	54	64	35	5	5	10	22	....	1961-62	1970-71
● Green, Red	Ham., NYA, Bos., Det.	6	195	59	26	85	290	1	0	0	0	0	1	1923-24	1928-29
Green, Rick	Wsh., Mtl., Det., NYI	15	845	43	220	263	588	100	3	16	19	73	1	1976-77	1991-92
● Green, Shorty	Ham., NYA	5	103	33	20	53	151	....	....	....	....	....	....	1923-24	1926-27
Green, Ted	Bos.	17	620	48	206	254	1029	31	4	8	12	54	1	1960-61	1971-72
‡ Greenlaw, Jeff	Wsh., Fla.	6	57	3	6	9	108	2	0	0	0	21	....	1986-87	1993-94
Gregg, Randy	Edm., Van.	10	474	41	152	193	333	137	13	38	51	127	5	1981-82	1991-92
Greig, Bruce	Cal.	2	9	0	1	1	46	....	....	....	....	....	....	1973-74	1974-75
Grenier, Lucien	Mtl., L.A., Atl.	5	151	14	14	28	18	2	0	0	0	0	1	1968-69	1972-73
Grenier, Richard	NYI	1	10	1	1	2	2	....	....	....	....	....	....	1972-73	1972-73
Greschner, Ron	NYR	16	982	179	431	610	1226	84	17	32	49	106	....	1974-75	1989-90
‡ Gretzky, Brent	T.B.	2	13	1	3	4	2	....	....	....	....	....	....	1993-94	1994-95
Gretzky, Wayne	Edm., L.A., St.L., NYR	20	1487	894	1963	2857	577	208	122	260	382	66	4	1979-80	1998-99
Grieve, Brent	NYI, Edm., Chi., L.A.	4	97	20	16	36	87	....	....	....	....	....	....	1993-94	1996-97
Grigor, George	Chi.	1	2	1	0	1	0	1	0	0	0	0	....	1943-44	1943-44
Grisdale, John	Tor., Van.	6	250	4	39	43	346	10	0	1	1	15	....	1972-73	1978-79
Gronsdahl, Lloyd	Bos.	1	10	1	2	3	0	....	....	....	....	....	....	1941-42	1941-42
Gronstrand, Jari	Min., NYR, Que., NYI	5	185	8	26	34	135	3	0	0	0	4	....	1986-87	1990-91
Gross, Lloyd	Tor., NYA, Bos., Det.	3	62	11	5	16	20	1	0	0	0	0	....	1926-27	1934-35
● Grosso, Don	Det., Chi., Bos.	9	336	87	117	204	90	48	15	14	29	63	1	1938-39	1946-47
Grosvenor, Len	Ott., NYA, Mtl.C.	6	149	9	11	20	78	4	0	0	0	2	....	1927-28	1932-33
Groulx, Wayne	Que.	1	1	0	0	0	0	....	....	....	....	....	....	1984-85	1984-85
Gruen, Danny	Det., Col.	3	49	9	13	22	19	....	....	....	....	....	....	1972-73	1976-77
Gruhl, Scott	L.A., Pit.	3	20	3	3	6	6	....	....	....	....	....	....	1981-82	1987-88
Gryp, Bob	Bos., Wsh.	3	74	11	13	24	33	....	....	....	....	....	....	1973-74	1975-76
‡ Guay, Francois	Buf.	1	1	0	0	0	0	....	....	....	....	....	....	1989-90	1989-90
Guay, Paul	Phi., L.A., Bos., NYI	7	117	11	23	34	92	9	0	1	1	12	....	1983-84	1990-91
‡ Guerard, Daniel	Ott.	1	2	0	0	0	0	....	....	....	....	....	....	1994-95	1994-95
Guerard, Stephane	Que.	4	34	0	0	0	40	....	....	....	....	....	....	1987-88	1991-92
Guevremont, Jocelyn	Van., Buf., NYR	9	571	84	223	307	319	40	4	17	21	18	....	1971-72	1979-80
Guidolin, Aldo	NYR	4	182	9	15	24	117	....	....	....	....	....	....	1952-53	1955-56
Guidolin, Bep	Bos., Det., Chi.	9	519	107	171	278	606	24	5	7	12	35	....	1942-43	1951-52
Guindon, Bobby	Wpg.	1	6	0	1	1	0	....	....	....	....	....	....	1979-80	1979-80
‡ Gusmanov, Ravil	Wpg.	1	4	0	0	0	0	....	....	....	....	....	....	1995-96	1995-96
Gustafsson, Bengt-Ake	Wsh.	9	629	196	359	555	196	32	9	19	28	16	....	1979-80	1988-89
Gustavsson, Peter	Col.	1	2	0	0	0	0	....	....	....	....	....	....	1981-82	1981-82
Guy, Kevan	Cgy., Van.	6	156	5	20	25	138	5	0	1	1	23	....	1986-87	1991-92

H

Name	NHL Teams	NHL Seasons	Regular Schedule GP	G	A	TP	PIM	Playoffs GP	G	A	TP	PIM	NHL Cup Wins	First NHL Season	Last NHL Season
Haanpaa, Ari	NYI	3	60	6	11	17	37	6	0	0	0	10	....	1985-86	1987-88
‡ Haas, David	Edm., Cgy.	2	7	2	1	3	7	....	....	....	....	....	....	1990-91	1993-94
Habscheid, Marc	Edm., Min., Det., Cgy.	11	345	72	91	163	171	12	1	3	4	13	....	1981-82	1991-92
‡ Hachborn, Len	Phi., L.A.	3	102	20	39	59	29	7	0	3	3	7	....	1983-84	1985-86
Haddon, Lloyd	Det.	1	8	0	0	0	2	1	0	0	0	0	....	1959-60	1959-60
Hadfield, Vic	NYR, Pit.	16	1002	323	389	712	1154	73	27	21	48	117	....	1961-62	1976-77
● Haggarty, Jim	Mtl.	1	5	1	1	2	0	3	2	1	3	0	....	1941-42	1941-42
● Hagglund, Roger	Que.	1	3	0	0	0	0	....	....	....	....	....	....	1984-85	1984-85
Hagman, Matti	Bos., Edm.	4	237	56	89	145	36	20	5	2	7	6	....	1976-77	1981-82
Haidy, Gord	Det.	1	....	....	....	....	....	1	0	0	0	0	1	1949-50	1949-50
Hajdu, Richard	Buf.	2	5	0	0	0	4	....	....	....	....	....	....	1985-86	1986-87
Hajt, Bill	Buf.	14	854	42	202	244	433	80	2	16	18	70	....	1973-74	1986-87
Hakansson, Anders	Min., Pit., L.A.	5	330	52	46	98	141	6	0	0	0	2	....	1981-82	1985-86
● Halderson, Harold	Det., Tor.	1	44	3	2	5	65	....	....	....	....	....	....	1926-27	1926-27
Hale, Larry	Phi.	4	196	5	37	42	90	8	0	0	0	12	....	1968-69	1971-72
Haley, Len	Det.	2	30	2	2	4	14	6	1	3	4	6	....	1959-60	1960-61
Halkidis, Bob	Buf., L.A., Tor., Det., T.B., NYI	11	256	8	32	40	825	20	0	1	1	51	....	1984-85	1995-96
● Hall, Bob	NYA	1	8	0	0	0	0	....	....	....	....	....	....	1925-26	1925-26
Hall, Del	Cal.	3	9	2	0	2	2	....	....	....	....	....	....	1971-72	1973-74
● Hall, Joe	Mtl.C.	2	38	15	8	23	189	7	0	1	1	29	....	1917-18	1918-19
Hall, Murray	Chi., Det., Min., Van.	9	164	35	48	83	46	6	0	0	0	0	....	1961-62	1971-72
Hall, Taylor	Van., Bos.	5	41	7	9	16	29	....	....	....	....	....	....	1983-84	1987-88
Hall, Wayne	NYR	1	4	0	0	0	0	....	....	....	....	....	....	1960-61	1960-61
● Halliday, Milt	Ott.	3	67	1	0	1	4	6	0	0	0	0	1	1926-27	1928-29
Hallin, Mats	NYI, Min.	5	152	17	14	31	193	15	1	0	1	13	1	1982-83	1986-87
Halward, Doug	Bos., L.A., Van., Det., Edm.	14	653	69	224	293	774	47	7	10	17	113	....	1975-76	1988-89
Hamel, Gilles	Buf., Wpg., L.A.	9	519	127	147	274	276	27	4	5	9	10	....	1980-81	1988-89
● Hamel, Herb	Tor.	1	2	0	0	0	4	....	....	....	....	....	....	1930-31	1930-31
Hamel, Jean	St.L., Det., Que., Mtl.	12	699	26	95	121	766	33	0	2	2	44	....	1972-73	1983-84
● Hamill, Red	Bos., Chi.	12	419	128	94	222	160	24	1	2	3	20	1	1937-38	1950-51
Hamilton, Al	NYR, Buf., Edm.	7	257	10	78	88	258	7	0	0	0	2	....	1965-66	1979-80
Hamilton, Chuck	Mtl., St.L.	2	4	0	2	2	2	....	....	....	....	....	....	1961-62	1972-73
● Hamilton, Jack	Tor.	3	102	28	32	60	20	11	2	1	3	0	....	1942-43	1945-46
Hamilton, Jim	Pit.	8	95	14	18	32	28	6	3	0	3	0	....	1977-78	1984-85
● Hamilton, Reg	Tor., Chi.	12	424	21	87	108	412	64	3	8	11	46	1	1935-36	1946-47
Hammarstrom, Inge	Tor., St.L.	6	427	116	123	239	86	13	2	3	5	4	....	1973-74	1978-79
Hammond, Ken	L.A., Edm., NYR, Tor., Bos., S.J., Van., Ott.	8	193	18	29	47	290	15	0	0	0	24	....	1984-85	1992-93
Hampson, Gord	Cgy.	1	4	0	0	0	5	....	....	....	....	....	....	1982-83	1982-83
Hampson, Ted	Tor., NYR, Det., Oak., Cal., Min.	12	676	108	245	353	94	35	7	10	17	2	....	1959-60	1971-72
Hampton, Rick	Cal., Cle., L.A.	6	337	59	113	172	147	2	0	0	0	0	....	1974-75	1979-80
‡ Hamr, Radek	Ott.	2	11	0	0	0	0	....	....	....	....	....	....	1992-93	1993-94
Hamway, Mark	NYI	3	53	5	13	18	9	1	0	0	0	0	....	1984-85	1986-87
‡ Handy, Ron	NYI, St.L.	2	14	0	3	3	0	....	....	....	....	....	....	1984-85	1987-88
Hangsleben, Al	Hfd., Wsh., L.A.	3	185	21	48	69	396	....	....	....	....	....	....	1979-80	1981-82
Hankinson, Ben	N.J., T.B.	3	43	3	3	6	45	2	1	0	1	4	....	1992-93	1994-95
Hanna, John	NYR, Mtl., Phi.	5	198	6	26	32	206	....	....	....	....	....	....	1958-59	1967-68
Hannan, Dave	Pit., Edm., Tor., Buf., Col., Ott.	16	841	114	191	305	942	63	6	7	13	46	2	1981-82	1996-97

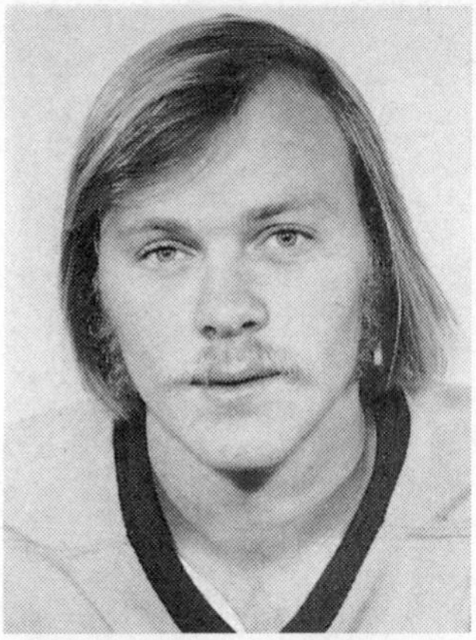

Butch Goring

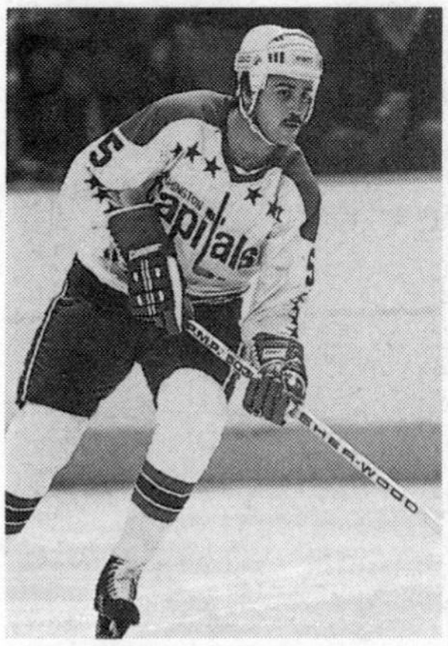

Rick Green

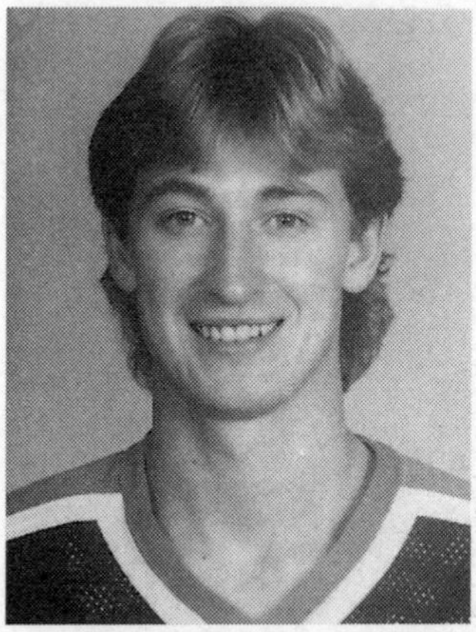

Wayne Gretzky

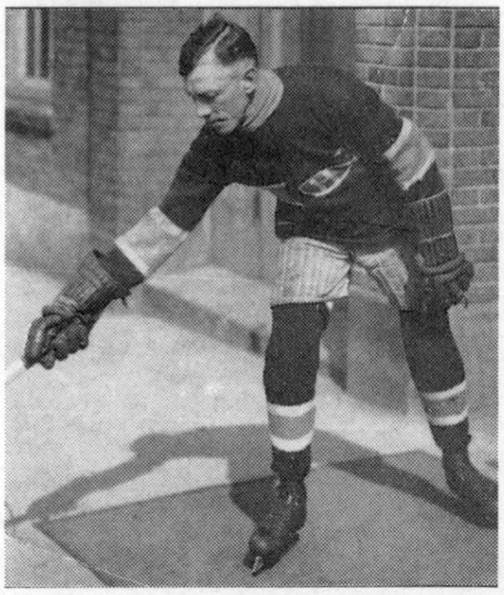

Joe Hall

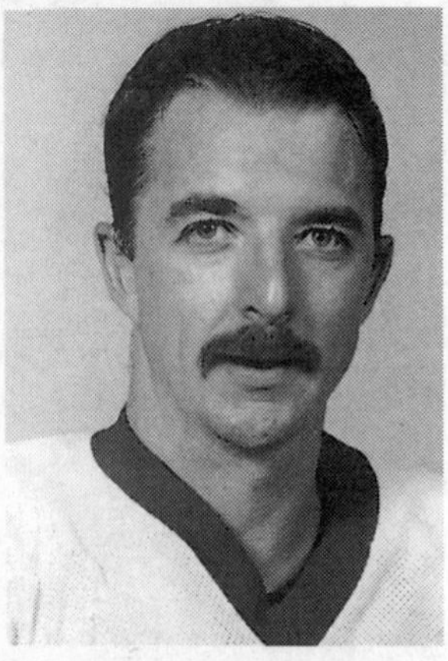

Doug Halward

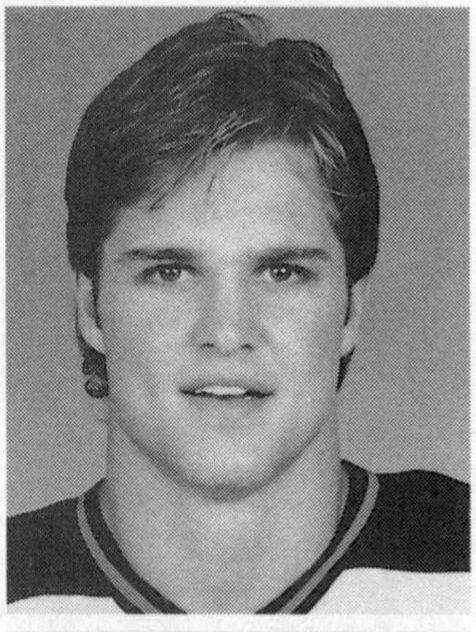

Ben Hankinson

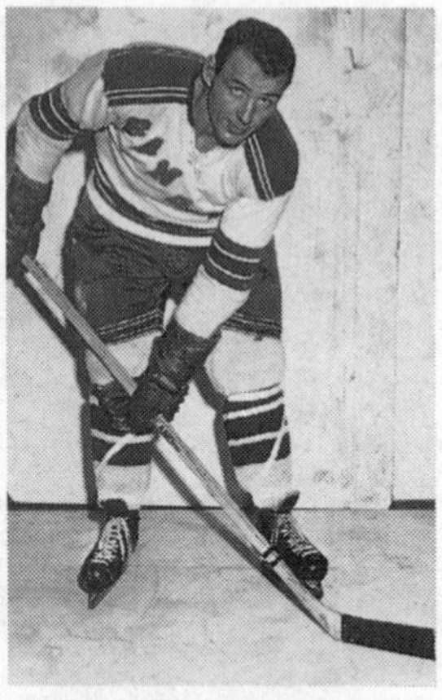

Andy Hebenton

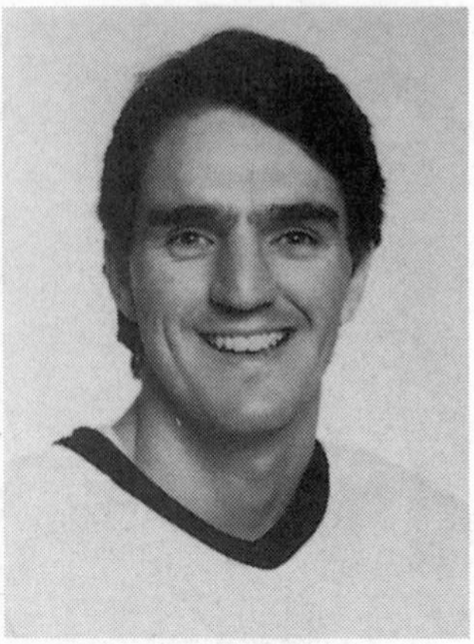

Randy Hillier

			Regular Schedule					Playoffs					NHL	First	Last
Name	NHL Teams	NHL Seasons	GP	G	A	TP	PIM	GP	G	A	TP	PIM	Cup Wins	NHL Season	NHL Season
• Hannigan, Gord	Tor.	4	161	29	31	60	117	9	2	0	2	8	....	1952-53	1955-56
Hannigan, Pat	Tor., NYR, Phi.	5	182	30	39	69	116	11	1	2	3	11	....	1959-60	1968-69
Hannigan, Ray	Tor.	1	3	0	0	0	2	....	....	....	....	....	....	1948-49	1948-49
Hansen, Richie	NYI, St.L.	4	20	2	8	10	4	....	....	....	....	....	....	1976-77	1981-82
Hanson, Dave	Det., Min.	2	33	1	1	2	65	....	....	....	....	....	....	1978-79	1979-80
• Hanson, Emil	Det.	1	7	0	0	0	6	....	....	....	....	....	....	1932-33	1932-33
Hanson, Keith	Cgy.	1	25	0	2	2	77	....	....	....	....	....	....	1983-84	1983-84
Hanson, Oscar	Chi.	1	8	0	0	0	0	....	....	....	....	....	....	1937-38	1937-38
Harbaruk, Nick	Pit., St.L.	5	364	45	75	120	273	14	3	1	4	20	....	1969-70	1973-74
Harding, Jeff	Phi.	2	15	0	0	0	47	....	....	....	....	....	....	1988-89	1989-90
Hardy, Joe	Oak., Cal.	2	63	9	14	23	51	4	0	0	0	0	....	1969-70	1970-71
Hardy, Mark	L.A., NYR, Min.	16	915	62	306	368	1293	67	5	16	21	158	....	1979-80	1993-94
Hargreaves, Jim	Van.	2	66	1	7	8	105	....	....	....	....	....	....	1970-71	1972-73
‡ Harkins, Todd	Cgy., Hfd.	3	48	3	3	6	78	....	....	....	....	....	....	1991-92	1993-94
Harlow, Scott	St.L.	1	1	0	1	1	0	....	....	....	....	....	....	1987-88	1987-88
Harmon, Glen	Mtl.	9	452	50	96	146	334	53	5	10	15	37	2	1942-43	1950-51
Harms, John	Chi.	2	44	5	5	10	21	4	3	0	3	2	....	1943-44	1944-45
• Harnott, Walter	Bos.	1	6	0	0	0	2	....	....	....	....	....	....	1933-34	1933-34
Harper, Terry	Mtl., L.A., Det., St.L., Col.	19	1066	35	221	256	1362	112	4	13	17	140	5	1962-63	1980-81
Harrer, Tim	Cgy.	1	3	0	0	0	2	....	....	....	....	....	....	1982-83	1982-83
• Harrington, Hago	Bos., Mtl.C.	3	72	9	3	12	15	4	1	0	1	2	....	1925-26	1932-33
Harris, Billy	Tor., Det., Oak., Pit.	13	769	126	219	345	205	62	8	10	18	30	3	1955-56	1968-69
Harris, Billy	NYI, L.A., Tor.	12	897	231	327	558	394	71	19	19	38	48	....	1972-73	1983-84
Harris, Duke	Min., Tor.	1	26	1	4	5	4	....	....	....	....	....	....	1967-68	1967-68
• Harris, Henry	Bos.	1	32	2	4	6	20	....	....	....	....	....	....	1930-31	1930-31
Harris, Hugh	Buf.	1	60	12	26	38	17	3	0	0	0	0	....	1972-73	1972-73
Harris, Ron	Det., Oak., Atl., NYR	11	476	20	91	111	474	28	4	3	7	33	....	1962-63	1975-76
• Harris, Smokey	Bos.	1	6	3	1	4	8	....	....	....	....	....	....	1924-25	1924-25
Harris, Ted	Mtl., Min., Det., St.L., Phi.	12	788	30	168	198	1000	100	1	22	23	230	5	1963-64	1974-75
Harrison, Ed	Bos., NYR	4	194	27	24	51	53	9	1	0	1	2	....	1947-48	1950-51
Harrison, Jim	Bos., Tor., Chi., Edm.	8	324	67	86	153	435	13	1	1	2	43	....	1968-69	1979-80
Hart, Gerry	Det., NYI, Que., St.L.	15	730	29	150	179	1240	78	3	12	15	175	....	1968-69	1982-83
• Hart, Gizzy	Det., Mtl.C.	3	104	6	8	14	12	8	0	1	1	0	....	1926-27	1932-33
Hartman, Mike	Buf., Wpg., T.B., NYR	9	397	43	35	78	1388	21	0	0	0	106	....	1986-87	1994-95
Hartsburg, Craig	Min.	14	570	98	315	413	818	61	15	27	42	70	....	1979-80	1988-89
Harvey, Buster	Min., Atl., K.C., Det.	7	407	90	118	208	131	14	0	2	2	8	....	1970-71	1976-77
• Harvey, Doug	Mtl., NYR, Det., St.L.	20	1113	88	452	540	1216	137	8	64	72	152	6	1947-48	1968-69
Harvey, Hugh	K.C.	2	18	1	1	2	4	....	....	....	....	....	....	1974-75	1975-76
Hassard, Bob	Tor., Chi.	5	126	9	28	37	22	....	....	....	....	....	....	1949-50	1954-55
Hatoum, Ed	Det., Van.	3	47	3	6	9	25	....	....	....	....	....	....	1968-69	1970-71
Hawerchuk, Dale	Wpg., Buf., St.L., Phi.	16	1188	518	891	1409	730	97	30	69	99	67	....	1981-82	1996-97
‡ Hawkins, Todd	Van., Tor.	3	10	0	0	0	15	....	....	....	....	....	....	1988-89	1991-92
Haworth, Alan	Buf., Wsh., Que.	8	524	189	211	400	425	42	12	16	28	28	....	1980-81	1987-88
Haworth, Gord	NYR	1	2	0	1	1	0	....	....	....	....	....	....	1952-53	1952-53
Hawryliw, Neil	NYI	1	1	0	0	0	0	....	....	....	....	....	....	1981-82	1981-82
Hay, Bill	Chi.	8	506	113	273	386	244	67	15	21	36	62	1	1959-60	1966-67
• Hay, George	Chi., Det.	7	239	74	60	134	84	8	2	3	5	2	....	1926-27	1933-34
Hay, Jim	Det.	3	75	1	5	6	22	9	1	0	1	2	1	1952-53	1954-55
Hayek, Peter	Min.	1	1	0	0	0	0	....	....	....	....	....	....	1981-82	1981-82
Hayes, Chris	Bos.	1	....	....	....	....	....	1	0	0	0	0	1	1971-72	1971-72
• Haynes, Paul	Mtl.M., Bos., Mtl.C., Mtl.	11	391	61	134	195	164	24	2	8	10	13	....	1930-31	1940-41
‡ Hayward, Rick	L.A.	1	4	0	0	0	5	....	....	....	....	....	....	1990-91	1990-91
Hazlett, Steve	Van.	1	1	0	0	0	0	....	....	....	....	....	....	1979-80	1979-80
Head, Galen	Det.	1	1	0	0	0	0	....	....	....	....	....	....	1967-68	1967-68
• Headley, Fern	Bos., Mtl.C.	1	30	1	3	4	10	1	0	0	0	0	....	1924-25	1924-25
Healey, Rich	Det.	1	1	0	0	0	2	....	....	....	....	....	....	1960-61	1960-61
‡ Heaphy, Shawn	Cgy.	1	1	0	0	0	0	....	....	....	....	....	....	1992-93	1992-93
Heaslip, Mark	NYR, L.A.	3	117	10	19	29	110	5	0	0	0	2	....	1976-77	1978-79
Heath, Randy	NYR	2	13	2	4	6	15	....	....	....	....	....	....	1984-85	1985-86
Hebenton, Andy	NYR, Bos.	9	630	189	202	391	83	22	6	5	11	8	....	1955-56	1963-64
Hedberg, Anders	NYR	7	465	172	225	397	144	58	22	24	46	31	....	1978-79	1984-85
• Heffernan, Frank	Tor.	1	19	0	1	1	10	....	....	....	....	....	....	1919-20	1919-20
Heffernan, Gerry	Mtl.	3	83	33	35	68	27	11	3	3	6	8	1	1941-42	1943-44
Heidt, Michael	L.A.	1	6	0	1	1	7	....	....	....	....	....	....	1983-84	1983-84
• Heindl, Bill	Min., NYR	3	18	2	1	3	0	....	....	....	....	....	....	1970-71	1972-73
Heinrich, Lionel	Bos.	1	35	1	1	2	33	....	....	....	....	....	....	1955-56	1955-56
Heiskala, Earl	Phi.	3	127	13	11	24	294	....	....	....	....	....	....	1968-69	1970-71
Helander, Peter	L.A.	1	7	0	1	1	0	....	....	....	....	....	....	1982-83	1982-83
• Heller, Ott	NYR	15	647	55	176	231	465	61	6	8	14	61	2	1931-32	1945-46
Helman, Harry	Ott.	3	44	1	0	1	7	2	0	0	0	0	....	1922-23	1924-25
‡ Helminen, Raimo	NYR, Min., NYI	3	117	13	46	59	16	2	0	0	0	0	....	1985-86	1988-89
• Hemmerling, Tony	NYA	2	22	3	3	6	4	....	....	....	....	....	....	1935-36	1936-37
Henderson, Archie	Wsh., Min., Hfd.	3	23	3	1	4	92	....	....	....	....	....	....	1980-81	1982-83
Henderson, Murray	Bos.	8	405	24	62	86	305	41	2	3	5	23	....	1944-45	1951-52
Henderson, Paul	Det., Tor., Atl.	13	707	236	241	477	304	56	11	14	25	28	....	1962-63	1979-80
Hendrickson, John	Det.	3	5	0	0	0	4	....	....	....	....	....	....	1957-58	1961-62
Henning, Lorne	NYI	15	544	73	111	184	102	81	7	7	14	8	2	1972-73	1980-81
• Henry, Camille	NYR, Chi., St.L.	14	727	279	249	528	88	47	6	12	18	7	....	1953-54	1969-70
Hepple, Alan	N.J.	3	3	0	0	0	7	....	....	....	....	....	....	1983-84	1985-86
• Herbert, Jimmy	Bos., Tor., Det.	6	206	83	31	114	253	9	3	0	3	10	....	1924-25	1929-30
Herchenratter, Art	Det.	1	10	1	2	3	2	....	....	....	....	....	....	1940-41	1940-41
Hergerts, Fred	NYA	2	20	2	4	6	2	....	....	....	....	....	....	1934-35	1935-36
Hergesheimer, Philip	Chi., Bos.	4	125	21	41	62	19	6	0	0	0	2	....	1939-40	1942-43
Hergesheimer, Wally	NYR, Chi.	7	351	114	85	199	106	5	1	0	1	0	....	1951-52	1958-59
Heron, Red	Tor., Bro., Mtl.	4	106	21	19	40	38	21	2	2	4	6	....	1938-39	1941-42
Heroux, Yves	Que.	1	1	0	0	0	0	....	....	....	....	....	....	1986-87	1986-87
‡ Herter, Jason	NYI	1	1	0	1	1	0	....	....	....	....	....	....	1995-96	1995-96
Hervey, Matt	Wpg., Bos., T.B.	3	35	0	5	5	97	5	0	0	0	6	....	1988-89	1992-93
Hess, Bob	St.L., Buf., Hfd.	8	329	27	95	122	178	4	1	1	2	2	....	1974-75	1983-84
Heximer, Obs	NYR, Bos., NYA	3	84	13	7	20	16	5	0	0	0	2	....	1929-30	1934-35
Hextall, Bryan Jr.	NYR, Pit., Atl., Det., Min.	8	549	99	161	260	738	18	0	4	4	59	....	1962-63	1975-76
• Hextall, Bryan Sr.	NYR	11	449	187	175	362	227	37	8	9	17	19	1	1936-37	1947-48
Hextall, Dennis	NYR, L.A., Cal., Min., Det., Wsh.	13	681	153	350	503	1398	22	3	3	6	45	....	1967-68	1979-80
Heyliger, Vic	Chi.	2	33	2	3	5	2	....	....	....	....	....	....	1937-38	1943-44
Hicke, Bill	Mtl., NYR, Oak., Cal., Pit.	14	729	168	234	402	395	42	3	10	13	41	2	1958-59	1971-72
Hicke, Ernie	Cal., Atl., NYI, Min., L.A.	8	520	132	140	272	407	2	1	0	1	0	....	1970-71	1977-78
Hickey, Greg	NYR	1	1	0	0	0	0	....	....	....	....	....	....	1977-78	1977-78
Hickey, Pat	NYR, Col., Tor., Que., St.L.	10	646	192	212	404	351	55	5	11	16	37	....	1975-76	1984-85
Hicks, Doug	Min., Chi., Edm., Wsh.	9	561	37	131	168	442	18	2	1	3	15	....	1974-75	1982-83
Hicks, Glenn	Det.	2	108	6	12	18	127	....	....	....	....	....	....	1979-80	1980-81
• Hicks, Henry	Mtl.M., Det.	3	96	7	2	9	72	....	....	....	....	....	....	1928-29	1930-31
Hicks, Wayne	Chi., Bos., Mtl., Phi., Pit.	5	115	13	23	36	22	2	0	1	1	2	1	1959-60	1967-68
Hidi, Andre	Wsh.	2	7	2	1	3	9	2	0	0	0	0	....	1983-84	1984-85
Hiemer, Uli	N.J.	3	143	19	54	73	176	....	....	....	....	....	....	1984-85	1986-87
Higgins, Paul	Tor.	2	25	0	0	0	152	1	0	0	0	0	....	1981-82	1982-83
Higgins, Tim	Chi., N.J., Det.	11	706	154	198	352	719	65	5	8	13	77	....	1978-79	1988-89
Hildebrand, Ike	NYR, Chi.	2	41	7	11	18	16	....	....	....	....	....	....	1953-54	1954-55
Hill, Al	Phi.	8	221	40	55	95	227	51	8	11	19	43	....	1976-77	1987-88
Hill, Brian	Hfd.	1	19	1	1	2	4	....	....	....	....	....	....	1979-80	1979-80
• Hill, Mel	Bos., Bro., Tor.	9	324	89	109	198	128	43	12	7	19	18	3	1937-38	1945-46
Hiller, Dutch	NYR, Det., Bos., Mtl.	9	383	91	113	204	163	48	9	8	17	21	2	1937-38	1945-46
‡ Hiller, Jim	L.A., Det., NYR	2	63	8	12	20	116	2	0	0	0	4	....	1992-93	1993-94
Hillier, Randy	Bos., Pit., NYI, Buf.	11	543	16	110	126	906	28	0	2	2	93	1	1981-82	1991-92
Hillman, Floyd	Bos.	1	6	0	0	0	10	....	....	....	....	....	....	1956-57	1956-57
Hillman, Larry	Det., Bos., Tor., Min., Mtl., Phi., L.A., Buf.	19	790	36	196	232	579	74	2	9	11	30	4	1954-55	1972-73
• Hillman, Wayne	Chi., NYR, Min., Phi.	13	691	18	86	104	534	28	0	3	3	19	1	1960-61	1972-73
Hilworth, John	Det.	3	57	1	1	2	89	....	....	....	....	....	....	1977-78	1979-80
• Himes, Normie	NYA	9	402	106	113	219	127	2	0	0	0	0	....	1926-27	1934-35
Hindmarch, Dave	Cgy.	4	99	21	17	38	25	10	0	0	0	6	....	1980-81	1983-84
Hinse, Andre	Tor.	1	4	0	0	0	0	....	....	....	....	....	....	1967-68	1967-68
Hinton, Dan	Chi.	1	14	0	0	0	16	....	....	....	....	....	....	1976-77	1976-77

Name	NHL Teams	NHL Seasons	Regular Schedule					Playoffs					NHL Cup Wins	First NHL Season	Last NHL Season
			GP	G	A	TP	PIM	GP	G	A	TP	PIM			
Hirsch, Tom	Min.	5	31	1	7	8	30	12	0	0	0	6	....	1983-84	1987-88
• Hirschfeld, Bert	Mtl.	2	33	1	4	5	2	5	1	0	1	0	....	1949-50	1950-51
Hislop, Jamie	Que., Cgy.	8	345	75	103	178	86	28	3	2	5	11	....	1979-80	1983-84
• Hitchman, Lionel	Ott., Bos.	12	417	28	34	62	523	35	3	1	4	73	1	1922-23	1933-34
Hlinka, Ivan	Van.	3	137	42	81	123	28	16	3	10	13	8	....	1981-82	1982-83
Hodge, Ken	Chi., Bos., NYR	14	881	328	472	800	779	97	34	47	81	120	2	1964-65	1977-78
Hodge, Ken	Min., Bos., T.B.	4	142	39	48	87	32	15	4	6	10	6	....	1988-89	1992-93
‡ Hodgson, Dan	Tor., Van.	4	114	29	45	74	64	....	....	....	....	....	....	1985-86	1988-89
Hodgson, Rick	Hfd.	1	6	0	0	0	6	1	0	0	0	0	....	1979-80	1979-80
Hodgson, Ted	Bos.	1	4	0	0	0	0	....	....	....	....	....	....	1966-67	1966-67
Hoekstra, Cec	Mtl.	1	4	0	0	0	0	....	....	....	....	....	....	1959-60	1959-60
Hoekstra, Ed	Phi.	1	70	15	21	36	6	7	0	1	1	0	....	1967-68	1967-68
Hoene, Phil	L.A.	3	37	2	4	6	22	....	....	....	....	....	....	1972-73	1974-75
Hoffinger, Val	Chi.	2	28	0	1	1	30	....	....	....	....	....	....	1927-28	1928-29
Hoffman, Mike	Hfd.	3	9	1	3	4	2	....	....	....	....	....	....	1982-83	1985-86
Hoffmeyer, Bob	Chi., Phi., N.J.	6	198	14	52	66	325	3	0	1	1	25	....	1977-78	1984-85
Hofford, Jim	Buf., L.A.	3	18	0	0	0	47	....	....	....	....	....	....	1985-86	1988-89
Hogaboam, Bill	Atl., Det., Min.	8	332	80	109	189	100	2	0	0	0	0	....	1972-73	1979-80
Hoganson, Dale	L.A., Mtl., Que.	7	343	13	77	90	186	11	0	3	3	12	....	1969-70	1981-82
‡ Holan, Milos	Phi., Ana.	3	49	5	11	16	42	....	....	....	....	....	....	1993-94	1995-96
Holbrook, Terry	Min.	2	43	3	6	9	4	6	0	0	0	0	....	1972-73	1973-74
Holland, Jerry	NYR	2	37	8	4	12	6	....	....	....	....	....	....	1974-75	1975-76
• Hollett, Flash	Tor., Ott., Bos., Det.	13	562	132	181	313	358	79	8	26	34	38	2	1933-34	1945-46
• Hollingworth, Gord	Chi., Det.	4	163	4	14	18	201	3	0	0	0	2	....	1954-55	1957-58
Holloway, Bruce	Van.	1	2	0	0	0	0	....	....	....	....	....	....	1984-85	1984-85
• Holmes, Bill	Mtl.C., NYA	3	52	6	4	10	35	....	....	....	....	....	....	1925-26	1929-30
Holmes, Chuck	Det.	2	23	1	3	4	10	....	....	....	....	....	....	1958-59	1961-62
Holmes, Lou	Chi.	2	59	1	4	5	6	2	0	0	0	2	....	1931-32	1932-33
Holmes, Warren	L.A.	3	45	8	18	26	7	....	....	....	....	....	....	1981-82	1983-84
Holmgren, Paul	Phi., Min.	10	527	144	179	323	1684	82	19	32	51	195	....	1975-76	1984-85
• Holota, John	Det.	2	15	2	0	2	0	....	....	....	....	....	....	1942-43	1945-46
Holst, Greg	NYR	3	11	0	0	0	0	....	....	....	....	....	....	1975-76	1977-78
Holt, Gary	Cal., Cle., St.L.	5	101	13	11	24	133	....	....	....	....	....	....	1973-74	1977-78
Holt, Randy	Chi., Cle., Van., L.A., Cgy., Wsh., Phi.	10	395	4	37	41	1438	21	2	3	5	83	....	1974-75	1983-84
• Holway, Albert	Tor., Mtl.M., Pit.	5	112	7	2	9	48	6	0	0	0	0	....	1923-24	1928-29
Homenuke, Ron	Van.	1	1	0	0	0	0	....	....	....	....	....	....	1972-73	1972-73
Hoover, Ron	Bos., St.L.	3	18	4	0	4	31	8	0	0	0	18	....	1989-90	1991-92
Hopkins, Dean	L.A., Edm., Que.	6	223	23	51	74	306	18	1	5	6	29	....	1979-80	1988-89
Hopkins, Larry	Tor., Wpg.	4	60	13	16	29	26	6	0	0	0	2	....	1977-78	1982-83
Horacek, Tony	Phi., Chi.	5	154	10	19	29	316	2	1	0	1	2	....	1989-90	1994-95
‡ Horava, Miloslav	NYR	3	80	5	17	22	38	2	0	1	1	0	....	1988-89	1990-91
Horbul, Doug	K.C.	1	4	1	0	1	2	....	....	....	....	....	....	1974-75	1974-75
Hordy, Mike	NYI	2	11	0	0	0	7	....	....	....	....	....	....	1978-79	1979-80
Horeck, Pete	Chi., Det., Bos.	8	426	106	118	224	340	34	6	8	14	43	....	1944-45	1951-52
• Horne, George	Mtl.M., Tor.	3	54	9	3	12	34	4	0	0	0	4	1	1925-26	1928-29
Horner, Red	Tor.	12	490	42	110	152	1254	71	7	10	17	170	1	1928-29	1939-40
Hornung, Larry	St.L.	2	48	2	9	11	10	11	0	2	2	2	....	1970-71	1971-72
• Horton, Tim	Tor., NYR, Pit., Buf.	24	1446	115	403	518	1611	126	11	39	50	183	4	1949-50	1973-74
Horvath, Bronco	NYR, Mtl., Bos., Chi., Tor., Min.	9	434	141	185	326	319	36	12	9	21	18	....	1955-56	1967-68
Hospodar, Ed	NYR, Hfd., Phi., Min., Buf.	9	450	17	51	68	1314	44	4	1	5	208	....	1979-80	1987-88
‡ Hostak, Martin	Phi.	2	55	3	11	14	24	....	....	....	....	....	....	1990-91	1991-92
Hotham, Greg	Tor., Pit.	6	230	15	74	89	139	5	0	3	3	6	....	1979-80	1984-85
Houck, Paul	Min.	3	16	1	2	3	2	....	....	....	....	....	....	1985-86	1987-88
Houde, Claude	K.C.	2	59	3	6	9	40	....	....	....	....	....	....	1974-75	1975-76
Hough, Mike	Que., Fla., NYI	13	707	100	156	256	675	42	5	5	10	38	....	1986-87	1998-99
Houle, Rejean	Mtl.	12	635	161	247	408	395	90	14	34	48	66	5	1969-70	1982-83
Houston, Ken	Atl., Cgy., Wsh., L.A.	9	570	161	167	328	624	35	10	9	19	66	....	1975-76	1983-84
Howard, Jack	Tor.	1	2	0	0	0	0	....	....	....	....	....	....	1936-37	1936-37
Howatt, Garry	NYI, Hfd., N.J.	12	720	112	156	268	1836	87	12	14	26	289	2	1972-73	1983-84
Howe, Gordie	Det., Hfd.	26	1767	801	1049	1850	1685	157	68	92	160	220	4	1946-47	1979-80
Howe, Mark	Hfd., Phi., Det.	16	929	197	545	742	455	101	10	51	61	34	....	1979-80	1994-95
Howe, Marty	Hfd., Bos.	6	197	2	29	31	99	15	1	2	3	9	....	1979-80	1984-85
• Howe, Syd	Ott., Phi., Tor., St.L., Det.	17	698	237	291	528	212	70	17	27	44	10	3	1929-30	1945-46
Howe, Vic	NYR	3	33	3	4	7	10	....	....	....	....	....	....	1950-51	1954-55
Howell, Harry	NYR, Oak., Cal., L.A.	21	1411	94	324	418	1298	38	3	3	6	32	....	1952-53	1972-73
• Howell, Ron	NYR	2	4	0	0	0	0	....	....	....	....	....	....	1954-55	1955-56
Howse, Don	L.A.	1	33	2	5	7	6	2	0	0	0	0	....	1979-80	1979-80
Howson, Scott	NYI	2	18	5	3	8	4	....	....	....	....	....	....	1984-85	1985-86
Hoyda, Dave	Phi., Wpg.	4	132	6	17	23	299	12	0	0	0	17	....	1977-78	1980-81
Hrdina, Jiri	Cgy., Pit.	5	250	45	85	130	92	46	2	5	7	24	3	1987-88	1991-92
Hrechkosy, Dave	Cal., St.L.	4	140	42	24	66	41	3	1	0	1	2	....	1973-74	1976-77
Hrycuik, Jim	Wsh.	1	21	5	5	10	12	....	....	....	....	....	....	1974-75	1974-75
Hrymnak, Steve	Chi., Det.	2	18	2	1	3	4	2	0	0	0	0	....	1951-52	1952-53
Hrynewich, Tim	Pit.	2	55	6	8	14	82	....	....	....	....	....	....	1982-83	1983-84
Huard, Rolly	Tor.	1	1	1	0	1	0	....	....	....	....	....	....	1930-31	1930-31
Huber, Willie	Det., NYR, Van., Phi.	10	655	104	217	321	950	33	5	5	10	35	....	1978-79	1987-88
Hubick, Greg	Tor., Van.	2	77	6	9	15	10	....	....	....	....	....	....	1975-76	1979-80
Huck, Fran	Mtl., St.L.	3	94	24	30	54	38	11	3	4	7	2	....	1969-70	1972-73
Hucul, Fred	Chi., St.L.	5	164	11	30	41	113	6	1	0	1	10	....	1950-51	1967-68
Huddy, Charlie	Edm., L.A., Buf., St.L.	19	1017	99	354	453	785	183	19	66	85	135	5	1980-81	1996-97
Hudson, Dave	NYI, K.C., Col.	6	409	59	124	183	89	2	1	1	2	0	....	1972-73	1977-78
Hudson, Lex	Pit.	1	2	0	0	0	0	2	0	0	0	0	....	1978-79	1978-79
Hudson, Mike	Chi., Edm., NYR, Pit., Tor., St.L., Phx.	9	416	49	87	136	414	49	4	10	14	64	1	1988-89	1996-97
Hudson, Ron	Det.	2	33	5	2	7	2	....	....	....	....	....	....	1937-38	1939-40
Huffman, Kerry	Phi., Que., Ott.	10	401	37	108	145	361	11	0	0	0	2	....	1986-87	1995-96
Huggins, Al	Mtl.M.	1	20	1	1	2	2	....	....	....	....	....	....	1930-31	1930-31
Hughes, Albert	NYA	2	60	6	8	14	22	....	....	....	....	....	....	1930-31	1931-32
Hughes, Brent	L.A., Phi., St.L., Det., K.C.	8	435	15	117	132	440	22	1	3	4	53	....	1967-68	1974-75
Hughes, Brent	Wpg., Bos., Buf., NYI	8	357	41	39	80	831	29	4	1	5	53	....	1988-89	1996-97
Hughes, Frank	Cal.	1	5	0	0	0	0	....	....	....	....	....	....	1971-72	1971-72
Hughes, Howie	L.A.	3	168	25	32	57	30	14	2	0	2	2	....	1967-68	1969-70
Hughes, Jack	Col.	2	46	2	5	7	104	....	....	....	....	....	....	1980-81	1981-82
Hughes, James	Det.	1	40	0	1	1	48	....	....	....	....	....	....	1929-30	1929-30
Hughes, John	Van., Edm., NYR	2	70	2	14	16	211	7	0	1	1	16	....	1979-80	1980-81
Hughes, Pat	Mtl., Pit., Edm., Buf., St.L., Hfd.	10	573	130	128	258	646	71	8	25	33	77	3	1977-78	1986-87
Hughes, Ryan	Bos.	1	3	0	0	0	0	....	....	....	....	....	....	1995-96	1995-96
Hull, Bobby	Chi., Wpg., Hfd.	16	1063	610	560	1170	640	119	62	67	129	102	1	1957-58	1979-80
Hull, Dennis	Chi., Det.	14	959	303	351	654	261	104	33	34	67	30	....	1964-65	1977-78
• Hunt, Fred	NYA, NYR	2	59	15	14	29	6	....	....	....	....	....	....	1940-41	1944-45
Hunter, Dale	Que., Wsh., Col.	20	1407	323	697	1020	3565	186	42	76	118	729	....	1980-81	1998-99
Hunter, Dave	Edm., Pit., Wpg.	10	746	133	190	323	918	105	16	24	40	211	3	1979-80	1988-89
Hunter, Mark	Mtl., St.L., Cgy., Hfd., Wsh.	12	628	213	171	384	1426	79	18	20	38	230	1	1981-82	1992-93
Hunter, Tim	Cgy., Que., Van., S.J.	17	815	62	76	138	3146	132	5	7	12	426	1	1981-82	1996-97
Huras, Larry	NYR	1	2	0	0	0	0	....	....	....	....	....	....	1976-77	1976-77
Hurlburt, Bob	Van.	1	1	0	0	0	2	....	....	....	....	....	....	1974-75	1974-75
Hurley, Paul	Bos.	1	1	0	1	1	0	....	....	....	....	....	....	1968-69	1968-69
Hurst, Ron	Tor.	2	64	9	7	16	70	3	0	2	2	4	....	1955-56	1956-57
Huston, Ron	Cal.	2	79	15	31	46	8	....	....	....	....	....	....	1973-74	1974-75
Hutchinson, Ron	NYR	1	9	0	0	0	0	....	....	....	....	....	....	1960-61	1960-61
Hutchison, Dave	L.A., Tor., Chi., N.J.	10	584	19	97	116	1550	48	2	12	14	149	....	1974-75	1983-84
• Hutton, Bill	Bos., Ott., Phi.	2	64	3	2	5	8	2	0	0	0	0	....	1929-30	1930-31
• Hyland, Harry	Mtl., Ott.	1	17	14	2	16	65	....	....	....	....	....	....	1917-18	1917-18
Hynes, Dave	Bos.	2	22	4	0	4	2	....	....	....	....	....	....	1973-74	1974-75
‡ Hynes, Gord	Bos., Phi.	2	52	3	9	12	22	12	1	2	3	6	....	1991-92	1992-93

I

Iafrate, Al	Tor., Wsh., Bos., S.J., Car.	15	799	152	311	463	1301	71	19	16	35	77	....	1984-85	1998-99
‡ Ihnacak, Miroslav	Tor., Det.	3	56	8	9	17	39	1	0	0	0	0	....	1985-86	1988-89
Ihnacak, Peter	Tor.	8	417	102	165	267	175	28	4	10	14	25	....	1982-83	1989-90
Imlach, Brent	Tor.	2	3	0	0	0	0	....	....	....	....	....	....	1965-66	1966-67
Ingarfield, Earl	NYR, Pit., Oak., Cal.	13	746	179	226	405	239	21	9	8	17	10	....	1958-59	1970-71
Ingarfield, Earl Jr.	Atl., Cgy., Det.	2	39	4	4	8	22	2	0	1	1	0	....	1979-80	1980-81

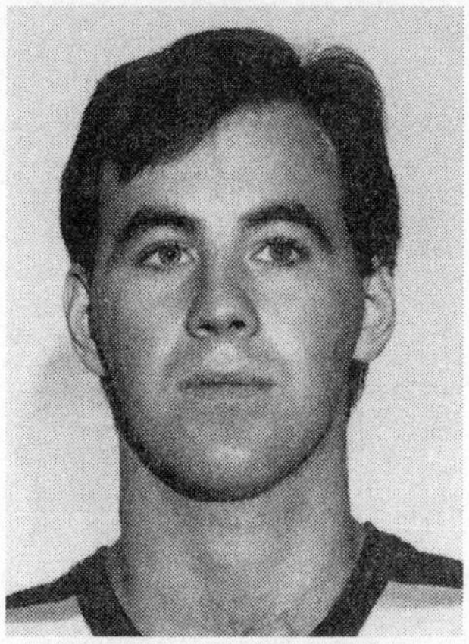
Jim Hofford

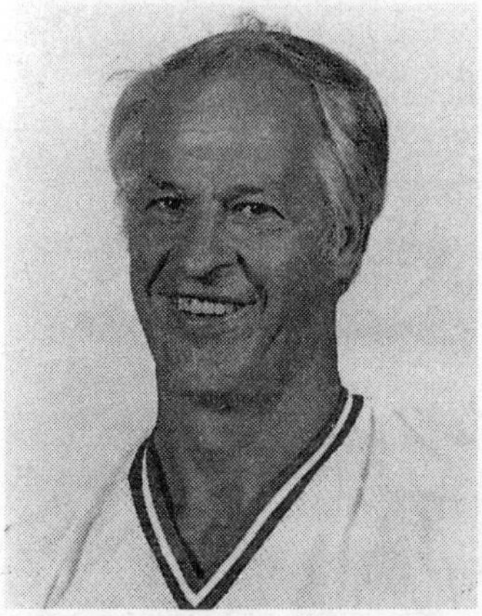
Gordie Howe

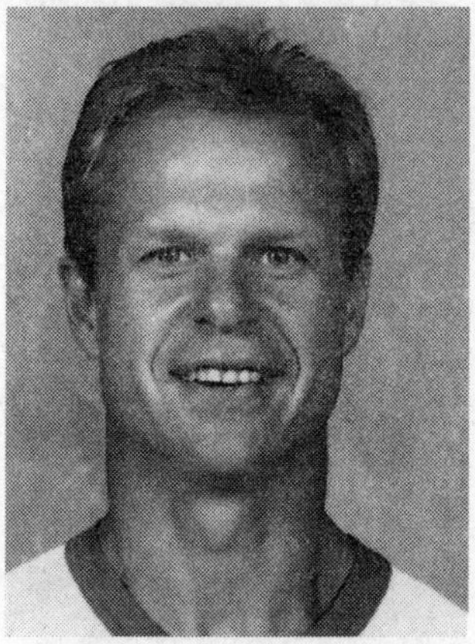
Mark Howe

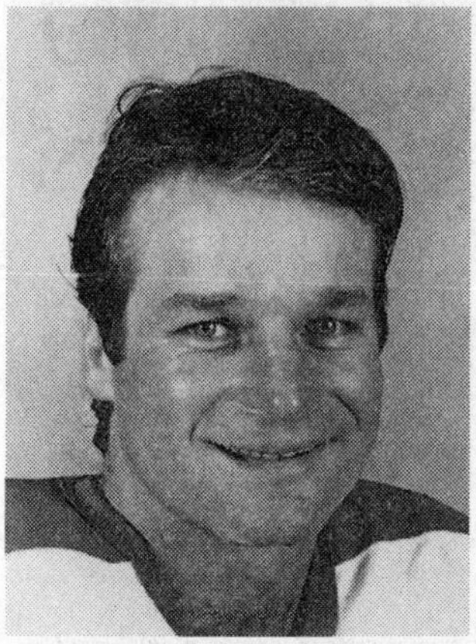
Dale Hunter

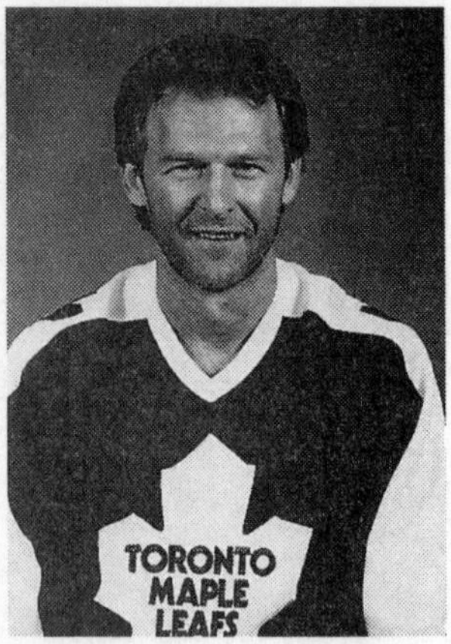

Peter Ihnacak

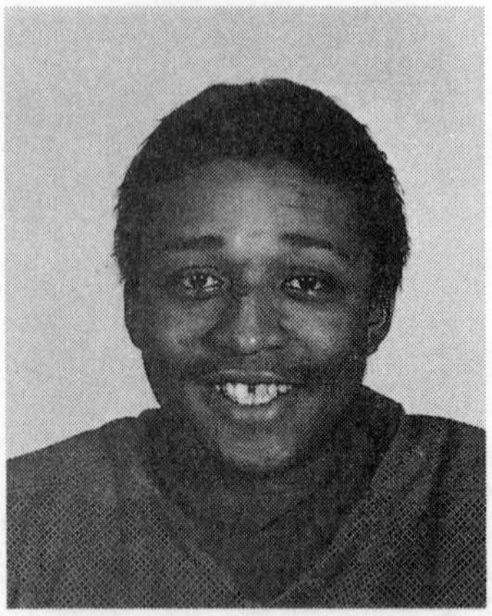

Brian Johnson

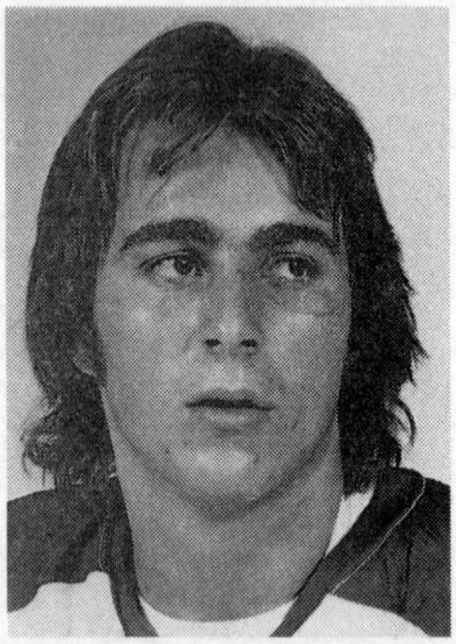

Greg Joly

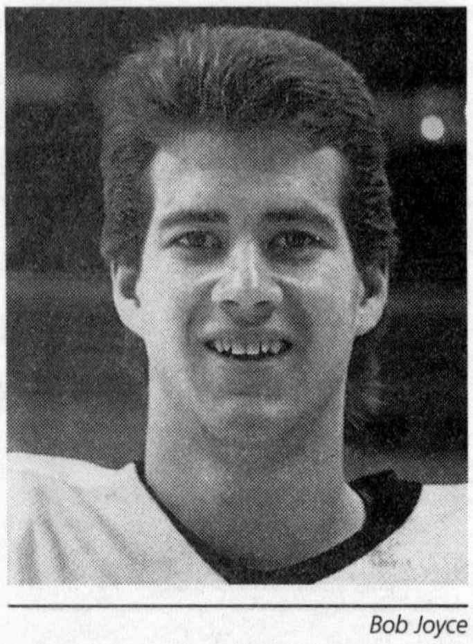

Bob Joyce

Name	NHL Teams	NHL Seasons	Regular Schedule GP	G	A	TP	PIM	Playoffs GP	G	A	TP	PIM	NHL Cup Wins	First NHL Season	Last NHL Season
Inglis, Billy	L.A., Buf.	3	36	1	3	4	4	11	1	2	3	4	....	1967-68	1970-71
● Ingoldsby, Johnny	Tor.	2	29	5	1	6	15	....	....	....	....	....	....	1942-43	1943-44
Ingram, Frank	Chi.	3	101	24	16	40	69	11	0	1	1	2	....	1929-30	1931-32
● Ingram, John J.	Bos.	1	1	0	0	0	0	....	....	....	....	....	....	1924-25	1924-25
Ingram, Ron	Chi., Det., NYR	4	114	5	15	20	81	2	0	0	0	0	....	1956-57	1964-65
● Irvin, Dick	Chi.	3	94	29	23	52	78	2	2	0	2	4	....	1926-27	1928-29
Irvine, Ted	Bos., L.A., NYR, St.L.	11	724	154	177	331	657	83	16	24	40	115	....	1963-64	1976-77
Irwin, Ivan	Mtl., NYR	5	155	2	27	29	214	5	0	0	0	8	....	1952-53	1957-58
Isaksson, Ulf	L.A.	1	50	7	15	22	10	....	....	....	....	....	....	1982-83	1982-83
Issel, Kim	Edm.	1	4	0	0	0	0	....	....	....	....	....	....	1988-89	1988-89

J

Name	NHL Teams	NHL Seasons	Regular Schedule GP	G	A	TP	PIM	Playoffs GP	G	A	TP	PIM	NHL Cup Wins	First NHL Season	Last NHL Season
● Jackson, Art	Tor., Bos., NYA	11	468	123	178	301	144	52	8	12	20	29	2	1934-35	1944-45
● Jackson, Busher	Tor., NYA, Bos.	15	633	241	234	475	437	71	18	12	30	53	1	1929-30	1943-44
Jackson, Don	Min., Edm., NYR	12	311	16	52	68	640	53	4	5	9	147	2	1977-78	1986-87
● Jackson, Harold	Chi., Det.	8	219	17	34	51	208	31	1	2	3	33	2	1936-37	1946-47
Jackson, Jack	Chi.	1	48	2	5	7	38	....	....	....	....	....	....	1946-47	1946-47
Jackson, Jeff	Tor., NYR, Que., Chi.	8	263	38	48	86	313	6	1	1	2	16	....	1984-85	1991-92
Jackson, Jim	Cgy., Buf.	4	112	17	30	47	20	14	3	2	5	6	....	1982-83	1987-88
● Jackson, Lloyd	NYA	1	14	1	1	2	0	....	....	....	....	....	....	1936-37	1936-37
● Jackson, Stan	Tor., Bos., Ott.	5	86	9	6	15	75	....	....	....	....	....	....	1921-22	1926-27
Jackson, Walter	NYA, Bos.	4	84	16	11	27	18	....	....	....	....	....	....	1932-33	1935-36
● Jacobs, Paul	Tor.	1	1	0	0	0	0	....	....	....	....	....	....	1918-19	1918-19
Jacobs, Tim	Cal.	1	46	0	10	10	35	....	....	....	....	....	....	1975-76	1975-76
Jalo, Risto	Edm.	1	3	0	3	3	0	....	....	....	....	....	....	1985-86	1985-86
Jalonen, Kari	Cgy., Edm.	2	37	9	6	15	4	5	1	0	1	0	....	1982-83	1983-84
James, Gerry	Tor.	6	149	14	26	40	257	15	1	0	1	8	....	1954-55	1959-60
James, Val	Buf., Tor.	2	11	0	0	0	30	....	....	....	....	....	....	1981-82	1986-87
Jamieson, Jim	NYR	1	1	0	1	1	0	....	....	....	....	....	....	1943-44	1943-44
Jankowski, Lou	Det., Chi.	4	127	19	18	37	15	1	0	0	0	0	....	1950-51	1954-55
Janney, Craig	Bos., St.L., S.J., Wpg., Phx., T.B., NYI	12	760	188	563	751	170	120	24	86	110	53	....	1987-88	1998-99
‡ Jantunen, Marko	Cgy.	1	3	0	0	0	0	....	....	....	....	....	....	1996-97	1996-97
Jarrett, Doug	Chi., NYR	13	775	38	182	220	631	99	7	16	23	82	....	1964-65	1976-77
Jarrett, Gary	Tor., Det., Oak., Cal.	7	341	72	92	164	131	11	3	1	4	9	....	1960-61	1971-72
Jarry, Pierre	NYR, Tor., Det., Min.	7	344	88	117	205	142	5	0	1	1	0	....	1971-72	1977-78
Jarvenpaa, Hannu	Wpg.	3	114	11	26	37	83	....	....	....	....	....	....	1986-87	1988-89
Jarvi, Iiro	Que.	2	116	18	43	61	58	....	....	....	....	....	....	1988-89	1989-90
Jarvis, Doug	Mtl., Wsh., Hfd.	15	964	139	264	403	263	105	14	27	41	42	4	1975-76	1987-88
Jarvis, Jim	Pit., Phi., Tor.	3	112	17	15	32	62	....	....	....	....	....	....	1929-30	1936-37
Jarvis, Wes	Wsh., Min., L.A., Tor.	9	237	31	55	86	98	2	0	0	0	2	....	1979-80	1987-88
Javanainen, Arto	Pit.	1	14	4	1	5	2	....	....	....	....	....	....	1984-85	1984-85
Jay, Bob	L.A.	1	3	0	1	1	0	....	....	....	....	....	....	1993-94	1993-94
Jeffrey, Larry	Det., Tor., NYR	9	368	39	62	101	293	38	4	10	14	42	1	1961-62	1969-70
Jelinek, Tomas	Ott.	2	49	7	6	13	52	....	....	....	....	....	....	1992-93	1992-93
Jenkins, Dean	L.A.	1	5	0	0	0	2	....	....	....	....	....	....	1983-84	1983-84
Jenkins, Roger	Chi., Tor., Mtl.C., Bos., Mtl.M., NYA	8	325	15	39	54	253	25	1	7	8	12	2	1930-31	1938-39
Jennings, Bill	Det., Bos.	5	108	32	33	65	45	20	4	4	8	6	....	1940-41	1944-45
Jennings, Grant	Wsh., Hfd., Pit., Tor., Buf.	9	389	14	43	57	804	54	2	1	3	68	2	1987-88	1995-96
Jensen, Chris	NYR, Phi.	6	74	9	12	21	27	....	....	....	....	....	....	1985-86	1991-92
Jensen, David	Min.	3	18	0	2	2	11	....	....	....	....	....	....	1983-84	1985-86
Jensen, David	Hfd., Wsh.	4	69	9	13	22	22	11	0	0	0	2	....	1984-85	1987-88
Jensen, Steve	Min., L.A.	7	438	113	107	220	318	12	0	3	3	9	....	1975-76	1981-82
● Jeremiah, Ed	NYA, Bos.	1	15	0	1	1	0	....	....	....	....	....	....	1931-32	1931-32
Jerrard, Paul	Min.	1	5	0	0	0	4	....	....	....	....	....	....	1988-89	1988-89
● Jerwa, Frank	Bos., St.L.	4	81	11	16	27	53	....	....	....	....	....	....	1931-32	1934-35
● Jerwa, Joe	NYR, Bos., NYA	7	234	29	58	87	309	17	2	3	5	16	....	1930-31	1938-39
Jirik, Jaroslav	St.L.	1	3	0	0	0	0	....	....	....	....	....	....	1969-70	1969-70
● Joanette, Rosario	Mtl.	1	2	0	1	1	4	....	....	....	....	....	....	1944-45	1944-45
Jodzio, Rick	Col., Cle.	1	70	2	8	10	71	....	....	....	....	....	....	1977-78	1977-78
Johannesen, Glenn	NYI	1	2	0	0	0	0	....	....	....	....	....	....	1985-86	1985-86
Johannson, John	N.J.	1	5	0	0	0	0	....	....	....	....	....	....	1983-84	1983-84
Johansen, Bill	Tor.	1	1	0	0	0	0	....	....	....	....	....	....	1949-50	1949-50
Johansen, Trevor	Tor., Col., L.A.	5	286	11	46	57	282	13	0	3	3	21	....	1977-78	1981-82
Johansson, Bjorn	Cle.	2	15	1	1	2	10	....	....	....	....	....	....	1976-77	1977-78
‡ Johansson, Roger	Cgy., Chi.	4	161	9	34	43	163	5	0	1	1	2	....	1989-90	1994-95
Johns, Don	NYR, Mtl., Min.	6	153	2	21	23	76	....	....	....	....	....	....	1960-61	1967-68
Johnson, Al	Mtl., Det.	4	105	21	28	49	30	11	2	2	4	6	....	1956-57	1962-63
Johnson, Brian	Det.	1	3	0	0	0	5	....	....	....	....	....	....	1983-84	1983-84
● Johnson, Ching	NYR, NYA	12	436	38	48	86	808	61	5	2	7	161	2	1926-27	1937-38
● Johnson, Danny	Tor., Van., Det.	3	121	18	19	37	24	....	....	....	....	....	....	1969-70	1971-72
Johnson, Earl	Det.	1	1	0	0	0	0	....	....	....	....	....	....	1953-54	1953-54
Johnson, Jim	NYR, Phi., L.A.	8	302	75	111	186	73	7	0	2	2	2	....	1964-65	1971-72
Johnson, Jim	Pit., Min., Dal., Wsh., Phx.	13	829	29	166	195	1197	51	1	11	12	132	....	1985-86	1997-98
Johnson, Mark	Pit., Min., Hfd., St.L., N.J.	11	669	203	305	508	260	37	16	12	28	10	....	1979-80	1989-90
Johnson, Norm	Bos., Chi.	3	61	5	20	25	41	14	4	0	4	6	....	1957-58	1959-60
Johnson, Terry	Que., St.L., Cgy., Tor.	9	285	3	24	27	580	38	0	4	4	118	....	1979-80	1987-88
Johnson, Tom	Mtl., Bos.	17	978	51	213	264	960	111	8	15	23	109	6	1947-48	1964-65
● Johnson, Virgil	Chi.	3	75	1	11	12	27	19	0	3	3	4	1	1937-38	1944-45
Johnston, Bernie	Hfd.	2	57	12	24	36	16	3	0	1	1	0	....	1979-80	1980-81
Johnston, George	Chi.	4	58	20	12	32	2	....	....	....	....	....	....	1941-42	1946-47
‡ Johnston, Greg	Bos., Tor.	9	187	26	29	55	124	22	2	1	3	12	....	1983-84	1991-92
Johnston, Jay	Wsh.	2	8	0	0	0	13	....	....	....	....	....	....	1980-81	1981-82
Johnston, Joey	Min., Cal., Chi.	6	331	85	106	191	320	....	....	....	....	....	....	1968-69	1975-76
Johnston, Larry	L.A., Det., K.C., Col.	7	320	9	64	73	580	....	....	....	....	....	....	1967-68	1976-77
Johnston, Marshall	Min., Cal.	14	251	14	52	66	58	6	0	0	0	2	....	1967-68	1973-74
Johnston, Randy	NYI	1	4	0	0	0	4	....	....	....	....	....	....	1979-80	1979-80
Johnstone, Eddie	NYR, Det.	10	426	122	136	258	375	55	13	10	23	83	....	1975-76	1986-87
Johnstone, Ross	Tor.	2	42	5	4	9	14	3	0	0	0	0	1	1943-44	1944-45
● Joliat, Aurel	Mtl.C.	16	655	270	190	460	771	46	9	13	22	66	2	1922-23	1937-38
● Joliat, Rene	Mtl.C.	1	1	0	0	0	0	....	....	....	....	....	....	1924-25	1924-25
Joly, Greg	Wsh., Det.	9	365	21	76	97	250	5	0	0	0	8	....	1974-75	1982-83
Joly, Yvan	Mtl.	3	2	0	0	0	0	1	0	0	0	0	....	1979-80	1982-83
Jonathan, Stan	Bos., Pit.	8	411	91	110	201	751	63	8	4	12	137	....	1975-76	1982-83
Jones, Bob	NYR	1	2	0	0	0	0	....	....	....	....	....	....	1968-69	1968-69
Jones, Brad	Wpg., L.A., Phi.	6	148	25	31	56	122	9	1	1	2	2	....	1986-87	1991-92
Jones, Buck	Det., Tor.	4	50	2	2	4	36	12	0	1	1	18	....	1938-39	1942-43
Jones, Jim	Cal.	1	2	0	0	0	0	....	....	....	....	....	....	1971-72	1971-72
Jones, Jimmy	Tor.	3	148	13	18	31	68	19	1	5	6	11	....	1977-78	1979-80
Jones, Ron	Bos., Pit., Wsh.	5	54	1	4	5	31	....	....	....	....	....	....	1971-72	1975-76
Jonsson, Tomas	NYI, Edm.	8	552	85	259	344	482	80	11	26	37	97	2	1981-82	1988-89
Joseph, Tony	Wpg.	1	2	1	0	1	0	....	....	....	....	....	....	1988-89	1988-89
Joyal, Eddie	Det., Tor., L.A., Phi.	9	466	128	134	262	103	50	11	8	19	18	....	1962-63	1971-72
‡ Joyce, Bob	Bos., Wsh., Wpg.	6	158	34	49	83	90	46	15	9	24	29	....	1987-88	1992-93
Joyce, Duane	Dal.	1	3	0	0	0	0	....	....	....	....	....	....	1993-94	1993-94
Juckes, Bing	NYR	2	16	2	1	3	6	....	....	....	....	....	....	1947-48	1949-50
‡ Juhlin, Patrik	Phi.	2	56	7	6	13	23	13	1	0	1	2	....	1994-95	1995-96
Julien, Claude	Que.	2	14	0	1	1	25	....	....	....	....	....	....	1984-85	1985-86
‡ Junker, Steve	NYI	2	5	0	0	0	0	3	0	1	1	0	....	1992-93	1993-94
Jutila, Timo	Buf.	1	10	1	5	6	13	....	....	....	....	....	....	1984-85	1984-85
Juzda, Bill	NYR, Tor.	9	398	14	54	68	398	42	0	3	3	46	2	1940-41	1951-52

K

Name	NHL Teams	NHL Seasons	Regular Schedule GP	G	A	TP	PIM	Playoffs GP	G	A	TP	PIM	NHL Cup Wins	First NHL Season	Last NHL Season
Kabel, Bob	NYR	2	48	5	13	18	34	....	....	....	....	....	....	1959-60	1960-61
Kachowski, Mark	Pit.	3	64	6	5	11	209	....	....	....	....	....	....	1987-88	1989-90
Kachur, Ed	Chi.	2	96	10	14	24	35	....	....	....	....	....	....	1956-57	1957-58
Kaese, Trent	Buf.	1	1	0	0	0	0	....	....	....	....	....	....	1988-89	1988-89
Kaiser, Vern	Mtl.	1	50	7	5	12	33	2	0	0	0	0	....	1950-51	1950-51
● Kalbfleish, Walter	Ott., St.L., NYA, Bos.	4	36	0	4	4	32	5	0	0	0	2	....	1933-34	1936-37
● Kaleta, Alex	Chi., NYR	7	387	92	121	213	190	17	1	6	7	2	....	1941-42	1950-51
Kallur, Anders	NYI	6	383	101	110	211	149	78	12	23	35	32	4	1979-80	1984-85

Name	NHL Teams	NHL Seasons	Regular Schedule GP	G	A	TP	PIM	Playoffs GP	G	A	TP	PIM	NHL Cup Wins	First NHL Season	Last NHL Season
‡ Kamensky, Valeri	Que., Col., NYR	9	518	179	267	446	327	64	25	35	60	72	1	1991-92	1999-00
• Kaminsky, Max	Ott., Bos., St.L., Mtl.M.	4	130	22	34	56	38	4	0	0	0	0	....	1933-34	1936-37
Kaminsky, Yan	Wpg., NYI	2	26	3	2	5	4	2	0	0	0	4	....	1993-94	1994-95
• Kampman, Rudolph	Tor.	5	189	14	30	44	287	47	1	4	5	38	1	1937-38	1941-42
Kane, Francis	Det.	1	2	0	0	0	0	....	....	....	....	....	....	1943-44	1943-44
Kannegiesser, Gord	St.L.	2	23	0	1	1	15	....	....	....	....	....	....	1967-68	1971-72
Kannegiesser, Sheldon	Pit., NYR, L.A., Van.	8	366	14	67	81	292	18	0	2	2	10	....	1970-71	1977-78
‡ Karabin, Ladislav	Pit.	1	9	0	0	0	2	....	....	....	....	....	....	1993-94	1993-94
‡ Karamnov, Vitali	St.L.	3	92	12	20	32	65	2	0	0	0	2	....	1992-93	1994-95
‡ Karjalainen, Kyosti	L.A.	1	28	1	8	9	12	3	0	1	1	2	....	1991-92	1991-92
Karlander, Al	Det.	4	212	36	56	92	70	4	0	1	1	0	....	1969-70	1972-73
‡ Karpov, Valeri	Ana.	3	76	14	15	29	32	....	....	....	....	....	....	1994-95	1996-97
Kasatonov, Alexei	N.J., Ana., St.L., Bos.	7	383	38	122	160	326	33	4	7	11	40	....	1989-90	1995-96
Kasper, Steve	Bos., L.A., Phi., T.B.	13	821	177	291	468	554	94	20	28	48	82	....	1980-81	1992-93
Kastelic, Ed	Wsh., Hfd.	7	220	11	10	21	719	8	1	0	1	32	....	1985-86	1991-92
Kaszycki, Mike	NYI, Wsh., Tor.	5	226	42	80	122	108	19	2	6	8	10	....	1977-78	1982-83
• Kea, Ed	Atl., St.L.	10	583	30	145	175	508	32	2	4	6	39	....	1973-74	1982-83
Kearns, Dennis	Van.	10	677	31	290	321	386	11	1	2	3	8	....	1971-72	1980-81
• Keating, Jack	Det.	2	11	3	0	3	4	....	....	....	....	....	....	1938-39	1939-40
• Keating, John	NYA	2	35	5	5	10	17	....	....	....	....	....	....	1931-32	1932-33
Keating, Mike	NYR	1	1	0	0	0	0	....	....	....	....	....	....	1977-78	1977-78
Keats, Duke	Bos., Det., Chi.	3	82	30	19	49	113	....	....	....	....	....	....	1926-27	1928-29
• Keeling, Butch	Tor., NYR	12	525	157	63	220	331	47	11	11	22	34	1	1926-27	1937-38
Keenan, Larry	Tor., St.L., Buf., Phi.	6	233	38	64	102	28	46	15	16	31	12	....	1961-62	1971-72
Kehoe, Rick	Tor., Pit.	18	906	371	396	767	120	39	4	17	21	4	....	1971-72	1984-85
Kekalainen, Jarmo	Bos., Ott.	3	55	5	8	13	28	....	....	....	....	....	....	1989-90	1993-94
Keller, Ralph	NYR	1	3	1	0	1	6	....	....	....	....	....	....	1962-63	1962-63
Kellgren, Christer	Col.	1	5	0	0	0	0	....	....	....	....	....	....	1981-82	1981-82
Kelly, Bob	Phi., Wsh.	12	837	154	208	362	1454	101	9	14	23	172	2	1970-71	1981-82
Kelly, Bob	St.L., Pit., Chi.	6	425	87	109	196	687	23	6	3	9	40	....	1973-74	1978-79
Kelly, Dave	Det.	1	16	2	0	2	4	....	....	....	....	....	....	1976-77	1976-77
Kelly, John Paul	L.A.	7	400	54	70	124	366	18	1	1	2	41	....	1979-80	1985-86
Kelly, Pete	St.L., Det., NYA, Bro.	7	177	21	38	59	68	19	3	1	4	2	2	1934-35	1941-42
Kelly, Red	Det., Tor.	21	1316	281	542	823	327	164	33	59	92	51	8	1947-48	1966-67
• Kelly, Regis	Tor., Chi., Bro.	8	288	74	53	127	105	38	7	6	13	10	....	1934-35	1941-42
• Kemp, Kevin	Hfd.	1	3	0	0	0	4	....	....	....	....	....	....	1980-81	1980-81
Kemp, Stan	Tor.	1	1	0	0	0	2	....	....	....	....	....	....	1948-49	1948-49
• Kendall, Bill	Chi., Tor.	5	131	16	10	26	28	6	0	0	0	0	1	1933-34	1937-38
Kennedy, Dean	L.A., NYR, Buf., Wpg., Edm.	12	717	26	108	134	1118	36	1	7	8	59	....	1982-83	1994-95
Kennedy, Forbes	Chi., Det., Bos., Phi., Tor.	11	603	70	108	178	988	12	2	4	6	64	....	1956-57	1968-69
Kennedy, Sheldon	Det., Cgy., Bos.	8	310	49	58	107	233	24	6	4	10	20	....	1989-90	1996-97
Kennedy, Ted	Tor.	14	696	231	329	560	432	78	29	31	60	32	5	1942-43	1956-57
• Kenny, Ernest	NYR, Chi.	2	10	0	0	0	18	....	....	....	....	....	....	1930-31	1934-35
Keon, Dave	Tor., Hfd.	18	1296	396	590	986	117	92	32	36	68	6	4	1960-61	1981-82
‡ Kerch, Alexander	Edm.	1	5	0	0	0	2	....	....	....	....	....	....	1993-94	1993-94
Kerr, Alan	NYI, Det., Wpg.	9	391	72	94	166	826	38	5	4	9	70	....	1984-85	1992-93
Kerr, Reg	Cle., Chi., Edm.	6	263	66	94	160	169	7	1	0	1	7	....	1977-78	1983-84
Kerr, Tim	Phi., NYR, Hfd.	13	655	370	304	674	596	81	40	31	71	58	....	1980-81	1992-93
Kessell, Rick	Pit., Cal.	5	135	4	24	28	6	....	....	....	....	....	....	1969-70	1973-74
Ketola, Veli-Pekka	Col.	1	44	9	5	14	4	....	....	....	....	....	....	1981-82	1981-82
Ketter, Kerry	Atl.	1	41	0	2	2	58	....	....	....	....	....	....	1972-73	1972-73
‡ Kharin, Sergei	Wpg.	1	7	2	3	5	2	....	....	....	....	....	....	1990-91	1990-91
Khmylev, Yuri	Buf., St.L.	5	263	64	88	152	133	26	8	6	14	24	....	1992-93	1996-97
Kidd, Ian	Van.	2	20	4	7	11	25	....	....	....	....	....	....	1987-88	1988-89
Kiessling, Udo	Min.	1	1	0	0	0	2	....	....	....	....	....	....	1981-82	1981-82
Kilrea, Brian	Det., L.A.	2	26	3	5	8	12	....	....	....	....	....	....	1957-58	1967-68
• Kilrea, Hec	Ott., Det., Tor.	15	633	167	129	296	438	48	8	7	15	18	3	1925-26	1939-40
• Kilrea, Ken	Det.	5	91	16	23	39	8	15	2	2	4	4	....	1938-39	1943-44
Kilrea, Wally	Ott., Phi., NYA, Mtl.M., Det.	9	329	35	58	93	87	25	2	4	6	6	2	1929-30	1937-38
‡ Kimble, Darin	Que., St.L., Bos., Chi.	7	311	23	20	43	1082	23	0	0	0	52	....	1988-89	1994-95
Kindrachuk, Orest	Phi., Pit., Wsh.	10	508	118	261	379	648	76	20	20	40	53	2	1972-73	1981-82
King, Frank	Mtl.	1	10	1	0	1	2	....	....	....	....	....	....	1950-51	1950-51
King, Wayne	Cal.	3	73	5	18	23	34	....	....	....	....	....	....	1973-74	1975-76
Kinsella, Brian	Wsh.	2	10	0	1	1	0	....	....	....	....	....	....	1975-76	1976-77
• Kinsella, Ray	Ott.	1	14	0	0	0	0	....	....	....	....	....	....	1930-31	1930-31
‡ Kiprusoff, Marko	Mtl.	1	24	0	4	4	8	....	....	....	....	....	....	1995-96	1995-96
• Kirk, Bobby	NYR	1	39	4	8	12	14	....	....	....	....	....	....	1937-38	1937-38
Kirkpatrick, Bob	NYR	1	49	12	12	24	6	....	....	....	....	....	....	1942-43	1942-43
Kirton, Mark	Tor., Det., Van.	6	266	57	56	113	121	4	1	2	3	7	....	1979-80	1984-85
Kisio, Kelly	Det., NYR, S.J., Cgy.	14	761	229	429	658	768	39	6	15	21	52	....	1982-83	1994-95
Kitchen, Bill	Mtl., Tor.	4	41	1	4	5	40	3	0	1	1	0	....	1981-82	1984-85
• Kitchen, Hobie	Mtl.M., Det.	2	47	5	4	9	58	....	....	....	....	....	1	1925-26	1926-27
Kitchen, Mike	Col., N.J.	10	474	12	62	74	370	2	0	0	0	2	....	1976-77	1983-84
Klassen, Ralph	Cal., Cle., Col., St.L.	9	497	52	93	145	120	26	4	2	6	12	....	1975-76	1983-84
• Klein, Lloyd	Bos., NYA	8	164	30	24	54	68	5	0	0	0	2	1	1928-29	1937-38
Kleinendorst, Scot	NYR, Hfd., Wsh.	8	281	12	46	58	452	26	2	7	9	40	....	1982-83	1989-90
Klima, Petr	Det., Edm., T.B., L.A., Pit.	13	786	313	260	573	671	95	28	24	52	83	1	1985-86	1998-99
‡ Klimovich, Sergei	Chi.	1	1	0	0	0	2	....	....	....	....	....	....	1996-97	1996-97
Klingbeil, Ike	Chi.	1	5	1	2	3	2	....	....	....	....	....	....	1936-37	1936-37
Klukay, Joe	Tor., Bos.	11	566	109	127	236	189	71	13	10	23	23	4	1942-43	1955-56
Kluzak, Gord	Bos.	9	299	25	98	123	543	46	6	13	19	129	....	1982-83	1990-91
Knibbs, Bill	Bos.	1	53	7	10	17	4	....	....	....	....	....	....	1964-65	1964-65
• Knott, Nick	Bro.	1	14	3	1	4	9	....	....	....	....	....	....	1941-42	1941-42
Knox, Paul	Tor.	1	1	0	0	0	0	....	....	....	....	....	....	1954-55	1954-55
‡ Kolesar, Mark	Tor.	2	28	2	2	4	14	3	1	0	1	2	....	1995-96	1996-97
Kolstad, Dean	Min., S.J.	3	40	1	7	8	69	....	....	....	....	....	....	1988-89	1992-93
Komadoski, Neil	L.A., St.L.	8	502	16	76	92	632	23	0	2	2	47	....	1972-73	1979-80
Konik, George	Pit.	1	52	7	8	15	26	....	....	....	....	....	....	1967-68	1967-68
Konroyd, Steve	Cgy., NYI, Chi., Hfd., Det., Ott.	15	895	41	195	236	863	97	10	15	25	99	....	1980-81	1994-95
Konstantinov, Vladimir	Det.	7	446	47	128	175	838	82	5	14	19	107	1	1991-92	1997-98
Kontos, Chris	NYR, Pit., L.A., T.B.	8	230	54	69	123	103	20	11	0	11	12	....	1982-83	1992-93
• Kopak, Russ	Bos.	1	24	7	9	16	0	....	....	....	....	....	....	1943-44	1943-44
Korab, Jerry	Chi., Van., Buf., L.A.	15	975	114	341	455	1629	93	8	18	26	201	....	1970-71	1984-85
Kordic, Dan	Phi.	6	197	4	8	12	584	12	1	0	1	22	....	1991-92	1998-99
• Kordic, John	Mtl., Tor., Wsh., Que.	7	244	17	18	35	997	41	4	3	7	131	1	1985-86	1991-92
Korn, Jim	Det., Tor., Buf., N.J., Cgy.	11	597	66	122	188	1801	16	1	2	3	109	....	1979-80	1989-90
Korney, Mike	Det., NYR	4	77	9	10	19	59	....	....	....	....	....	....	1973-74	1978-79
Koroll, Cliff	Chi.	11	814	208	254	462	376	85	19	29	48	67	....	1969-70	1979-80
Kortko, Roger	NYI	2	79	7	17	24	28	10	0	3	3	17	....	1984-85	1985-86
Kostynski, Doug	Bos.	2	15	3	1	4	4	....	....	....	....	....	....	1983-84	1984-85
Kotanen, Dick	NYR	1	1	0	0	0	0	....	....	....	....	....	....	1950-51	1950-51
Kotsopoulos, Chris	NYR, Hfd., Tor., Det.	10	479	44	109	153	827	31	1	3	4	91	....	1980-81	1989-90
Kowal, Joe	Buf.	2	22	0	5	5	13	2	0	0	0	0	....	1976-77	1977-78
Kozak, Don	L.A., Van.	7	437	96	86	182	480	29	7	2	9	69	....	1972-73	1978-79
Kozak, Les	Tor.	1	12	1	0	1	2	....	....	....	....	....	....	1961-62	1961-62
• Kraftcheck, Stephen	Bos., NYR, Tor.	4	157	11	18	29	83	6	0	0	0	7	....	1950-51	1958-59
Krake, Skip	Bos., L.A., Buf.	7	249	23	40	63	182	10	1	0	1	17	....	1963-64	1970-71
‡ Kravets, Mikhail	S.J.	2	2	0	0	0	0	....	....	....	....	....	....	1991-92	1992-93
Krentz, Dale	Det.	3	30	5	3	8	9	2	0	0	0	0	....	1986-87	1988-89
• Krol, Joe	NYR, Bro.	3	26	10	4	14	8	....	....	....	....	....	....	1936-37	1941-42
Kromm, Rich	Cgy., NYI	9	372	70	103	173	138	36	2	6	8	22	....	1983-84	1992-93
Krook, Kevin	Col.	1	3	0	0	0	2	....	....	....	....	....	....	1978-79	1978-79
Krulicki, Jim	NYR, Det.	1	41	0	3	3	6	....	....	....	....	....	....	1970-71	1970-71
Kruppke, Gord	Det.	3	23	0	0	0	32	....	....	....	....	....	....	1990-91	1993-94
Krushelnyski, Mike	Bos., Edm., L.A., Tor., Det.	14	897	241	328	569	699	139	29	43	72	106	3	1981-82	1994-95
Krutov, Vladimir	Van.	1	61	11	23	34	20	....	....	....	....	....	....	1989-90	1989-90
Kryskow, Dave	Chi., Wsh., Det., Atl.	4	231	33	56	89	174	12	2	0	2	4	....	1972-73	1975-76
Kryzanowski, Ed	Bos., Chi.	5	237	15	22	37	65	18	0	1	1	4	....	1948-49	1952-53
‡ Kudashov, Alexei	Tor.	1	25	1	0	1	4	....	....	....	....	....	....	1993-94	1993-94
Kudelski, Bob	L.A., Ott., Fla.	9	442	139	102	241	218	22	4	4	8	4	....	1987-88	1995-96
• Kuhn, Gord	NYA	1	12	1	1	2	4	....	....	....	....	....	....	1932-33	1932-33

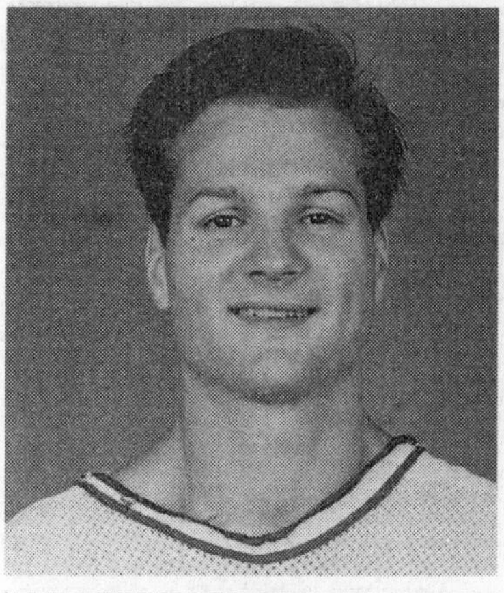
Ed Kastelic

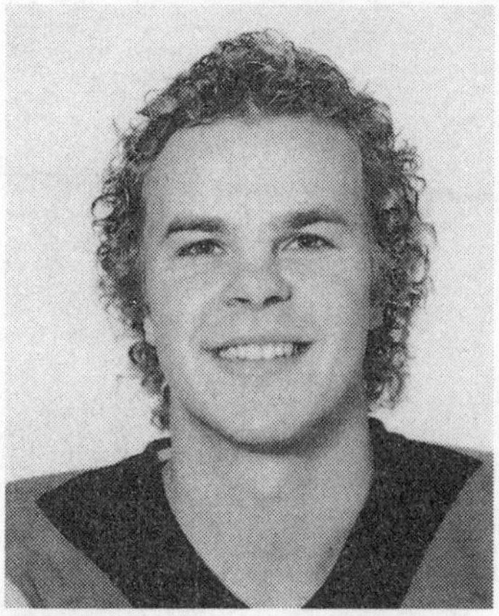
Mark Kirton

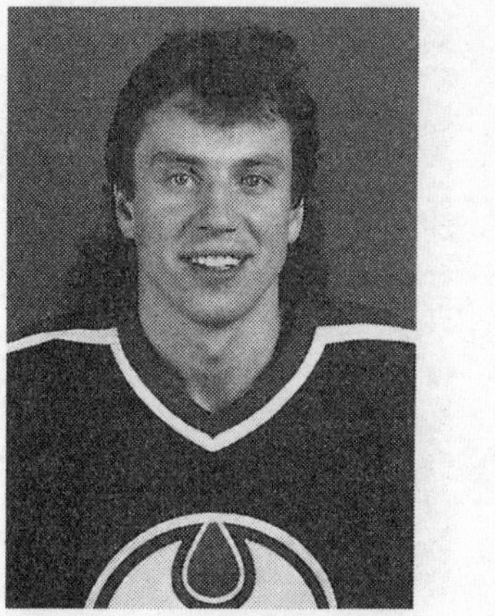
Petr Klima

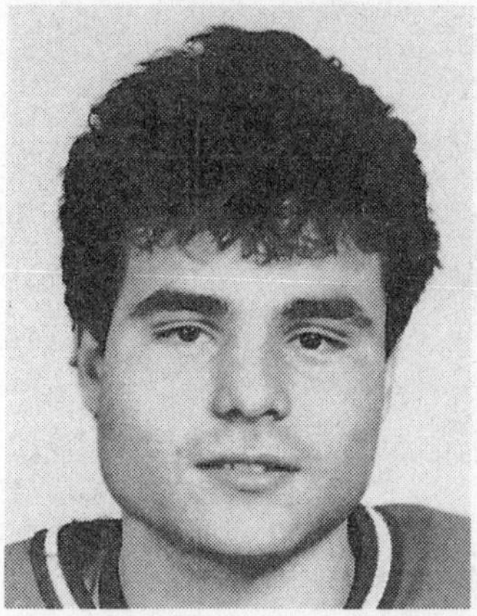
John Kordic

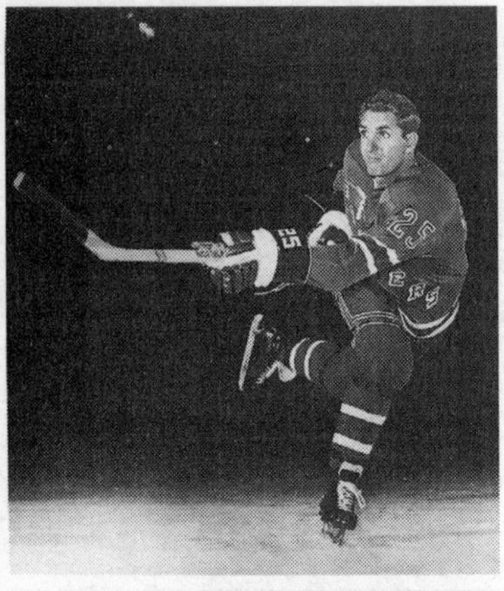

Orland Kurtenbach

Name	NHL Teams	NHL Seasons	Regular Schedule GP	G	A	TP	PIM	Playoffs GP	G	A	TP	PIM	NHL Cup Wins	First NHL Season	Last NHL Season
Kukulowicz, Aggie	NYR	2	4	1	0	1	0	....	....	....	....	....	....	1952-53	1953-54
‡ Kulak, Stu	Van., Edm., NYR, Que., Wpg.	4	90	8	4	12	130	3	0	0	0	2	....	1982-83	1988-89
Kullman, Arnie	Bos.	2	13	0	1	1	11	....	....	....	....	....	....	1947-48	1949-50
● Kullman, Eddie	NYR	6	343	56	70	126	298	6	1	0	1	2	....	1947-48	1953-54
Kumpel, Mark	Que., Det., Wpg.	6	288	38	46	84	113	39	6	4	10	14	....	1984-85	1990-91
● Kuntz, Alan	NYR	2	45	10	12	22	12	6	1	0	1	2	....	1941-42	1945-46
Kuntz, Murray	St.L.	1	7	1	2	3	0	....	....	....	....	....	....	1974-75	1974-75
Kurri, Jari	Edm., L.A., NYR, Ana., Col.	17	1251	601	797	1398	545	200	106	127	233	123	5	1980-81	1997-98
Kurtenbach, Orland	NYR, Bos., Tor., Van.	13	639	119	213	332	628	19	2	4	6	70	....	1960-61	1973-74
Kurvers, Tom	Mtl., Buf., N.J., Tor., Van., NYI, Ana.	11	659	93	328	421	350	57	8	22	30	68	1	1984-85	1994-95
Kuryluk, Merv	Chi.	1	....	....	....	....	....	2	0	0	0	0	....	1961-62	1961-62
Kushner, Dale	NYI, Phi.	3	84	10	13	23	215	....	....	....	....	....	....	1989-90	1991-92
Kuzyk, Ken	Cle.	2	41	5	9	14	8	....	....	....	....	....	....	1976-77	1977-78
‡ Kvartalnov, Dmitri	Bos.	2	112	42	49	91	26	4	0	0	0	0	....	1992-93	1993-94
Kwong, Larry	NYR	1	1	0	0	0	0	....	....	....	....	....	....	1947-48	1947-48
● Kyle, Bill	NYR	2	3	0	3	3	0	....	....	....	....	....	....	1949-50	1950-51
● Kyle, Gus	NYR, Bos.	3	203	6	20	26	362	14	1	2	3	34	....	1949-50	1951-52
‡ Kyllonen, Markku	Wpg.	1	9	0	2	2	2	....	....	....	....	....	....	1988-89	1988-89
Kypreos, Nick	Wsh., Hfd., NYR, Tor.	9	442	46	44	90	1210	34	1	3	4	65	1	1989-90	1997-98
Kyte, Jim	Wpg., Pit., Cgy., Ott., S.J.	13	598	17	49	66	1342	42	0	6	6	94	....	1982-83	1995-96

L

Name	NHL Teams	NHL Seasons	Regular Schedule GP	G	A	TP	PIM	Playoffs GP	G	A	TP	PIM	NHL Cup Wins	First NHL Season	Last NHL Season
L'Abbe, Moe	Chi.	1	5	0	1	1	0	....	....	....	....	....	....	1972-73	1972-73
Labadie, Mike	NYR	1	3	0	0	0	0	....	....	....	....	....	....	1952-53	1952-53
Labatte, Neil	St.L.	2	26	0	2	2	19	....	....	....	....	....	....	1978-79	1981-82
‡ Labelle, Marc	Dal.	1	9	0	0	0	46	....	....	....	....	....	....	1996-97	1996-97
Labine, Leo	Bos., Det.	11	643	128	193	321	730	60	12	11	23	82	....	1951-52	1961-62
Labossiere, Gord	NYR, L.A., Min.	6	215	44	62	106	75	10	2	3	5	28	....	1963-64	1971-72
Labovitch, Max	NYR	1	5	0	0	0	4	....	....	....	....	....	....	1943-44	1943-44
Labraaten, Dan	Det., Cgy.	4	268	71	73	144	47	8	1	0	1	4	....	1978-79	1981-82
Labre, Yvon	Pit., Wsh.	9	371	14	87	101	788	....	....	....	....	....	....	1970-71	1980-81
Labrie, Guy	Bos., NYR	2	42	4	9	13	16	....	....	....	....	....	....	1943-44	1944-45
Lach, Elmer	Mtl.	14	664	215	408	623	478	76	19	45	64	36	3	1940-41	1953-54
Lachance, Michel	Col.	1	21	0	4	4	22	....	....	....	....	....	....	1978-79	1978-79
Lacombe, Francois	Oak., Buf., Que.	4	78	2	17	19	54	3	1	0	1	0	....	1968-69	1979-80
Lacombe, Normand	Buf., Edm., Phi.	7	319	53	62	115	196	26	5	1	6	49	1	1984-85	1990-91
Lacroix, Andre	Phi., Chi., Hfd.	6	325	79	119	198	44	16	2	5	7	0	....	1967-68	1979-80
Lacroix, Pierre	Que., Hfd.	4	274	24	108	132	197	8	0	2	2	10	....	1979-80	1982-83
Ladouceur, Randy	Det., Hfd., Ana.	14	930	30	126	156	1322	40	5	8	13	59	....	1982-83	1995-96
Lafleur, Guy	Mtl., NYR, Que.	17	1126	560	793	1353	399	128	58	76	134	67	5	1971-72	1990-91
● Lafleur, Roland	Mtl.C.	1	1	0	0	0	0	....	....	....	....	....	....	1924-25	1924-25
LaFontaine, Pat	NYI, Buf., NYR	15	865	468	545	1013	552	69	26	36	62	36	....	1983-84	1997-98
Laforce, Ernie	Mtl.	1	1	0	0	0	0	....	....	....	....	....	....	1942-43	1942-43
LaForest, Bob	L.A.	1	5	1	0	1	2	....	....	....	....	....	....	1983-84	1983-84
Laforge, Claude	Mtl., Det., Phi.	8	193	24	33	57	82	5	1	2	3	15	....	1957-58	1968-69
‡ Laforge, Marc	Hfd., Edm.	2	14	0	0	0	64	....	....	....	....	....	....	1989-90	1993-94
Laframboise, Pete	Cal., Wsh., Pit.	4	227	33	55	88	70	9	1	0	1	0	....	1971-72	1974-75
Lafrance, Adie	Mtl.C.	1	3	0	0	0	2	2	0	0	0	0	....	1933-34	1933-34
● Lafrance, Leo	Mtl.C., Chi.	2	33	2	0	2	6	....	....	....	....	....	....	1926-27	1927-28
‡ Lafreniere, Jason	Que., NYR, T.B.	5	146	34	53	87	22	15	1	5	6	19	....	1986-87	1993-94
Lafreniere, Roger	Det., St.L.	2	13	0	0	0	4	....	....	....	....	....	....	1962-63	1972-73
Lagace, Jean-Guy	Pit., Buf., K.C.	6	197	9	39	48	251	....	....	....	....	....	....	1968-69	1975-76
Laidlaw, Tom	NYR, L.A.	10	705	25	139	164	717	69	4	17	21	78	....	1980-81	1989-90
Laird, Robbie	Min.	1	1	0	0	0	0	....	....	....	....	....	....	1979-80	1979-80
Lajeunesse, Serge	Det., Phi.	5	103	1	4	5	103	....	....	....	....	....	....	1970-71	1974-75
Lalande, Hec	Chi., Det.	4	151	21	39	60	120	....	....	....	....	....	....	1953-54	1957-58
Lalonde, Bobby	Van., Atl., Bos., Cgy.	11	641	124	210	334	298	16	4	2	6	6	....	1971-72	1981-82
● Lalonde, Newsy	Mtl.C., NYA	6	99	124	41	165	183	7	15	24	19	23	....	1917-18	1926-27
Lalonde, Ron	Pit., Wsh.	7	397	45	78	123	106	....	....	....	....	....	....	1972-73	1978-79
Lalor, Mike	Mtl., St.L., Wsh., Wpg., S.J., Dal.	12	687	17	88	105	677	92	5	10	15	167	1	1985-86	1996-97
● Lamb, Joe	Mtl.M., Ott., NYA, Bos., Mtl.C., St.L., Det.	11	443	108	101	209	601	18	1	1	2	51	....	1927-28	1937-38
‡ Lamb, Mark	Cgy., Det., Edm., Ott., Phi., Mtl.	11	403	46	100	146	291	70	7	19	26	51	1	1985-86	1995-96
‡ Lambert, Dan	Que.	2	29	6	9	15	22	....	....	....	....	....	....	1990-91	1991-92
‡ Lambert, Lane	Det., NYR, Que.	6	283	58	66	124	521	17	2	4	6	40	....	1983-84	1988-89
Lambert, Yvon	Mtl., Buf.	10	683	206	273	479	340	90	27	22	49	67	4	1972-73	1981-82
Lamby, Dick	St.L.	3	22	0	5	5	22	....	....	....	....	....	....	1978-79	1980-81
● Lamirande, Jean-Paul	NYR, Mtl.	4	49	5	5	10	26	8	0	0	0	4	....	1946-47	1954-55
Lammens, Hank	Ott.	1	27	1	2	3	22	....	....	....	....	....	....	1993-94	1993-94
● Lamoureux, Leo	Mtl.	6	235	19	79	98	175	28	1	6	7	16	2	1941-42	1946-47
Lamoureux, Mitch	Pit., Phi.	3	73	11	9	20	59	....	....	....	....	....	....	1983-84	1987-88
Lampman, Mike	St.L., Van., Wsh.	4	96	17	20	37	34	....	....	....	....	....	....	1972-73	1976-77
Lancien, Jack	NYR	4	63	1	5	6	35	6	0	1	1	2	....	1946-47	1950-51
Landon, Larry	Mtl., Tor.	2	9	0	0	0	2	....	....	....	....	....	....	1983-84	1984-85
Lane, Gord	Wsh., NYI	10	539	19	94	113	1228	75	3	14	17	214	4	1975-76	1984-85
● Lane, Myles	NYR, Bos.	3	71	4	1	5	41	11	0	0	0	0	1	1928-29	1933-34
Langdon, Steve	Bos.	3	7	0	1	1	2	4	0	0	0	0	....	1974-75	1977-78
Langelle, Pete	Tor.	4	136	22	51	73	11	41	5	9	14	4	1	1938-39	1941-42
Langevin, Chris	Buf.	2	22	3	1	4	22	....	....	....	....	....	....	1983-84	1985-86
Langevin, Dave	NYI, Min., L.A.	8	513	12	107	119	530	87	2	17	19	106	4	1979-80	1986-87
Langlais, Alain	Min.	2	25	4	4	8	10	....	....	....	....	....	....	1973-74	1974-75
Langlois, Albert	Mtl., NYR, Det., Bos.	9	497	21	91	112	488	53	1	5	6	50	3	1957-58	1965-66
● Langlois, Charlie	Ham., NYA, Pit., Mtl.C.	4	151	22	5	27	189	2	0	0	0	0	....	1924-25	1927-28
Langway, Rod	Mtl., Wsh.	15	994	51	278	329	849	104	5	22	27	97	1	1978-79	1992-93
Lanthier, Jean-Marc	Van.	4	105	16	16	32	29	....	....	....	....	....	....	1983-84	1987-88
Lanyon, Ted	Pit.	1	5	0	0	0	4	....	....	....	....	....	....	1967-68	1967-68
Lanz, Rick	Van., Tor., Chi.	10	569	65	221	286	448	28	3	8	11	35	....	1980-81	1991-92
‡ Laperriere, Daniel	St.L., Ott.	4	48	2	5	7	27	....	....	....	....	....	....	1992-93	1995-96
Laperriere, Jacques	Mtl.	15	691	40	242	282	674	88	9	22	31	101	6	1962-63	1973-74
Lapointe, Guy	Mtl., St.L., Bos.	17	884	171	451	622	893	123	26	44	70	138	6	1968-69	1983-84
● Lapointe, Rick	Det., Phi., St.L., Que., L.A.	11	664	44	176	220	831	46	2	7	9	64	....	1975-76	1985-86
Lappin, Peter	Min., S.J.	2	7	0	0	0	2	....	....	....	....	....	....	1989-90	1991-92
Laprade, Edgar	NYR	10	500	108	172	280	42	18	4	9	13	4	....	1945-46	1954-55
LaPrairie, Benjamin	Chi.	1	7	0	0	0	0	....	....	....	....	....	....	1936-37	1936-37
Lariviere, Garry	Que., Edm.	4	219	6	57	63	167	14	0	5	5	8	....	1979-80	1982-83
Larmer, Jeff	Col., N.J., Chi.	5	158	37	51	88	57	5	1	0	1	2	....	1981-82	1985-86
Larmer, Steve	Chi., NYR	15	1006	441	571	1012	532	140	56	75	131	89	1	1980-81	1994-95
● Larochelle, Wildor	Mtl.C., Chi.	12	474	92	74	166	211	34	6	4	10	24	2	1925-26	1936-37
Larocque, Denis	L.A.	1	8	0	1	1	18	....	....	....	....	....	....	1987-88	1987-88
● Larose, Bonner	Bos.	1	6	0	0	0	0	....	....	....	....	....	....	1925-26	1925-26
Larose, Claude	Mtl., Min., St.L.	16	943	226	257	483	887	97	14	18	32	143	5	1962-63	1977-78
Larose, Claude	NYR	2	25	4	7	11	2	2	0	0	0	0	....	1979-80	1981-82
‡ Larose, Guy	Wpg., Tor., Cgy., Bos.	6	70	10	9	19	63	4	0	0	0	0	....	1988-89	1994-95
Larouche, Pierre	Pit., Mtl., Hfd., NYR	14	812	395	427	822	237	64	20	34	54	16	2	1974-75	1987-88
Larson, Norm	NYA, Bro., NYR	3	89	25	18	43	12	....	....	....	....	....	....	1940-41	1946-47
Larson, Reed	Det., Bos., Edm., NYI, Min., Buf.	14	904	222	463	685	1391	32	4	7	11	63	....	1976-77	1989-90
Larter, Tyler	Wsh.	1	1	0	0	0	0	....	....	....	....	....	....	1989-90	1989-90
Latal, Jiri	Phi.	3	92	12	36	48	24	....	....	....	....	....	....	1989-90	1991-92
Latos, James	NYR	1	1	0	0	0	0	....	....	....	....	....	....	1988-89	1988-89
Latreille, Phil	NYR	1	4	0	0	0	2	....	....	....	....	....	....	1960-61	1960-61
Latta, David	Que.	4	36	4	8	12	4	....	....	....	....	....	....	1985-86	1990-91
Lauder, Martin	Bos.	1	3	0	0	0	2	....	....	....	....	....	....	1927-28	1927-28
Lauen, Mike	Wpg.	1	4	0	1	1	0	....	....	....	....	....	....	1983-84	1983-84
Laughlin, Craig	Mtl., Wsh., L.A., Tor.	8	549	136	205	341	364	33	6	6	12	20	....	1981-82	1988-89
Laughton, Mike	Oak., Cal.	4	189	39	48	87	101	11	2	4	6	0	....	1967-68	1970-71
Laurence, Don	Atl., St.L.	2	79	15	22	37	14	....	....	....	....	....	....	1978-79	1979-80
LaVallee, Kevin	Cgy., L.A., St.L., Pit.	7	366	110	125	235	85	32	5	8	13	21	....	1980-81	1986-87
LaVarre, Mark	Chi.	3	78	9	16	25	58	1	0	0	0	2	....	1985-86	1987-88
Lavender, Brian	St.L., NYI, Det., Cal.	4	184	16	26	42	174	3	0	0	0	2	....	1971-72	1974-75
‡ Lavigne, Eric	L.A.	1	1	0	0	0	0	....	....	....	....	....	....	1994-95	1994-95
● Laviolette, Jack	Mtl.C.	1	18	2	1	3	6	2	0	0	0	0	....	1917-18	1917-18
Laviolette, Peter	NYR	1	12	0	0	0	6	....	....	....	....	....	....	1988-89	1988-89

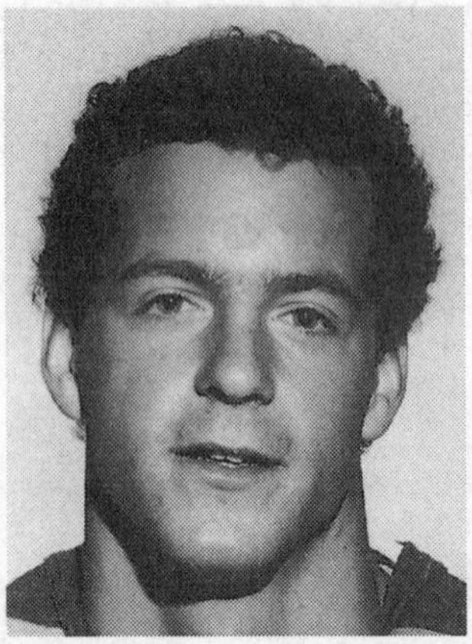

Normand LaCombe

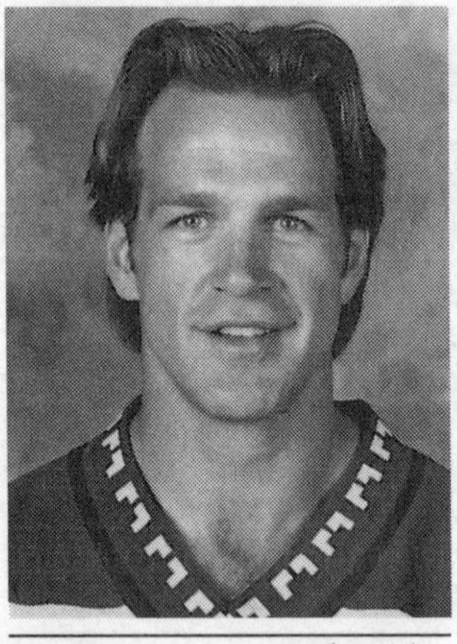

Jocelyn Lemieux

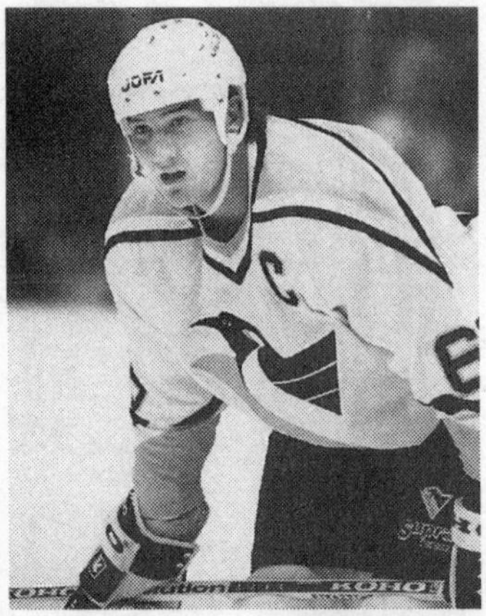

Mario Lemieux

Name	NHL Teams	NHL Seasons	Regular Schedule GP	G	A	TP	PIM	Playoffs GP	G	A	TP	PIM	NHL Cup Wins	First NHL Season	Last NHL Season
‡ Lavoie, Dominic	St.L., Ott., Bos., L.A.	6	38	5	8	13	32	....	....	....	....	....	....	1988-89	1993-94
Lawless, Paul	Hfd., Phi., Van., Tor.	7	239	49	77	126	54	3	0	2	2	2	....	1982-83	1989-90
Lawson, Danny	Det., Min., Buf.	5	219	28	29	57	61	16	0	1	1	2	....	1967-68	1971-72
Lawton, Brian	Min., NYR, Hfd., Que., Bos., S.J.	9	483	112	154	266	401	11	1	1	2	12	....	1983-84	1992-93
Laxdal, Derek	Tor., NYI	6	67	12	7	19	88	1	0	2	2	2	....	1984-85	1990-91
● Laycoe, Hal	NYR, Mtl., Bos.	11	531	25	77	102	292	40	2	5	7	39	....	1945-46	1955-56
‡ Lazaro, Jeff	Bos., Ott.	3	102	14	23	37	114	28	3	3	6	32	....	1990-91	1992-93
Leach, Jamie	Pit., Hfd., Fla.	5	81	11	9	20	12	....	....	....	....	....	....	1989-90	1993-94
Leach, Larry	Bos.	3	126	13	29	42	91	7	1	1	2	8	....	1958-59	1961-62
Leach, Reggie	Bos., Cal., Phi., Det.	13	934	381	285	666	387	94	47	22	69	22	1	1970-71	1982-83
Leavins, Jim	Det., NYR	2	41	2	12	14	30	....	....	....	....	....	....	1985-86	1986-87
‡ Lebeau, Stephan	Mtl., Ana.	7	373	118	159	277	105	30	9	7	16	12	1	1988-89	1994-95
LeBlanc, Fern	Det.	3	34	5	6	11	0	....	....	....	....	....	....	1976-77	1978-79
LeBlanc, J.P.	Chi., Det.	5	153	14	30	44	87	2	0	0	0	0	....	1968-69	1978-79
LeBlanc, John	Van., Edm., Wpg.	8	83	26	13	39	28	1	0	0	0	0	....	1986-87	1994-95
LeBrun, Al	NYR	2	6	0	2	2	4	....	....	....	....	....	....	1960-61	1965-66
Lecaine, Bill	Pit.	1	4	0	0	0	0	....	....	....	....	....	....	1968-69	1968-69
Leclair, Jackie	Mtl.	3	160	20	40	60	56	20	6	1	7	6	2	1954-55	1956-57
Leclerc, Rene	Det.	2	87	10	11	21	105	....	....	....	....	....	....	1968-69	1970-71
Lecuyer, Doug	Chi., Wpg., Pit.	4	126	11	31	42	178	7	4	0	4	15	....	1978-79	1982-83
Ledingham, Walt	Chi., NYI	3	15	0	2	2	4	....	....	....	....	....	....	1972-73	1976-77
● LeDuc, Albert	Mtl.C., Ott., NYR	10	383	57	35	92	614	28	5	6	11	32	2	1925-26	1934-35
LeDuc, Rich	Bos., Que.	4	130	28	38	66	69	5	0	0	0	9	....	1972-73	1980-81
● Lee, Bobby	Mtl.	1	1	0	0	0	0	....	....	....	....	....	....	1942-43	1942-43
Lee, Edward	Que.	1	2	0	0	0	5	....	....	....	....	....	....	1984-85	1984-85
Lee, Peter	Pit.	6	431	114	131	245	257	19	0	8	8	4	....	1977-78	1982-83
Leeman, Gary	Tor., Cgy., Mtl., Van., St.L.	14	667	199	267	466	531	36	8	16	24	36	1	1982-83	1996-97
● Lefley, Bryan	NYI, K.C., Col.	5	228	7	29	36	101	2	0	0	0	0	....	1972-73	1977-78
Lefley, Chuck	Mtl., St.L.	9	407	128	164	292	137	29	5	8	13	10	2	1970-71	1980-81
● Leger, Roger	NYR, Mtl.	5	187	18	53	71	71	20	0	7	7	14	....	1943-44	1949-50
Legge, Barry	Que., Wpg.	3	107	1	11	12	144	....	....	....	....	....	....	1979-80	1981-82
Legge, Randy	NYR	1	12	0	2	2	2	....	....	....	....	....	....	1972-73	1972-73
Lehman, Tommy	Bos., Edm.	3	36	5	5	10	16	....	....	....	....	....	....	1987-88	1989-90
Lehto, Petteri	Pit.	1	6	0	0	0	4	....	....	....	....	....	....	1984-85	1984-85
Lehtonen, Antero	Wsh.	1	65	9	12	21	14	....	....	....	....	....	....	1979-80	1979-80
Lehvonen, Henri	K.C.	1	4	0	0	0	0	....	....	....	....	....	....	1974-75	1974-75
Leier, Edward	Chi.	2	16	2	1	3	2	....	....	....	....	....	....	1949-50	1950-51
Leinonen, Mikko	NYR, Wsh.	4	162	31	78	109	71	20	2	11	13	28	....	1981-82	1984-85
Leiter, Bobby	Bos., Pit., Atl.	10	447	98	126	224	144	8	3	0	3	2	....	1962-63	1975-76
Leiter, Ken	NYI, Min.	5	143	14	36	50	62	15	0	6	6	8	....	1984-85	1989-90
Lemaire, Jacques	Mtl.	16	853	366	469	835	217	145	61	78	139	63	8	1967-68	1978-79
‡ Lemay, Moe	Van., Edm., Bos., Wpg.	8	317	72	94	166	442	28	6	3	9	55	1	1981-82	1988-89
Lemelin, Roger	K.C., Col.	4	36	1	2	3	27	....	....	....	....	....	....	1974-75	1977-78
Lemieux, Alain	St.L., Que., Pit.	6	119	28	44	72	38	19	4	6	10	0	....	1981-82	1986-87
Lemieux, Bob	Oak.	1	19	0	1	1	12	....	....	....	....	....	....	1967-68	1967-68
Lemieux, Jacques	L.A.	3	19	0	4	4	8	1	0	0	0	0	....	1967-68	1969-70
Lemieux, Jean	Atl., Wsh.	5	204	23	63	86	39	3	1	1	2	0	....	1973-74	1977-78
Lemieux, Jocelyn	St.L., Mtl., Chi., Hfd., N.J., Cgy., Phx.	12	598	80	84	164	740	60	5	10	15	88	....	1986-87	1997-98
Lemieux, Mario	Pit.	13	745	613	881	1494	737	89	70	85	155	83	2	1984-85	1996-97
● Lemieux, Real	Det., L.A., NYR, Buf.	8	456	51	104	155	262	18	2	4	6	10	....	1966-67	1973-74
Lemieux, Richard	Van., K.C., Atl.	5	274	39	82	121	132	2	0	0	0	0	....	1971-72	1975-76
Lenardon, Tim	N.J., Van.	2	15	2	1	3	4	....	....	....	....	....	....	1986-87	1989-90
● Lepine, Hec	Mtl.C.	1	33	5	2	7	2	....	....	....	....	....	....	1925-26	1925-26
● Lepine, Pit	Mtl.C.	14	526	143	98	241	392	41	7	5	12	26	2	1925-26	1937-38
Leroux, Gaston	Mtl.C.	1	2	0	0	0	0	....	....	....	....	....	....	1935-36	1935-36
Lesieur, Art	Mtl.C., Chi.	4	100	4	2	6	50	14	0	0	0	4	1	1928-29	1935-36
Lessard, Rick	Cgy., S.J.	3	15	0	4	4	18	....	....	....	....	....	....	1988-89	1991-92
Lesuk, Bill	Bos., Phi., L.A., Wsh., Wpg.	8	388	44	63	107	368	9	1	0	1	12	1	1968-69	1979-80
● Leswick, Jack	Chi.	1	37	1	7	8	16	....	....	....	....	....	....	1933-34	1933-34
Leswick, Pete	NYA, Bos.	2	3	1	0	1	0	....	....	....	....	....	....	1936-37	1944-45
Leswick, Tony	NYR, Det., Chi.	12	740	165	159	324	900	59	13	10	23	91	3	1945-46	1957-58
Levandoski, Joe	NYR	1	8	1	1	2	0	....	....	....	....	....	....	1946-47	1946-47
Leveille, Normand	Bos.	2	75	17	25	42	49	....	....	....	....	....	....	1981-82	1982-83
Leveque, Guy	L.A.	2	17	2	2	4	21	....	....	....	....	....	....	1992-93	1993-94
Lever, Don	Van., Atl., Cgy., Col., N.J., Buf.	17	1020	313	367	680	593	30	7	10	17	26	....	1972-73	1986-87
Levie, Craig	Wpg., Min., St.L., Van.	6	183	22	53	75	177	16	2	3	5	32	....	1981-82	1986-87
● Levinsky, Alex	Tor., NYR, Chi.	9	367	19	49	68	307	37	2	1	3	26	2	1930-31	1938-39
Levo, Tapio	Col., N.J.	2	107	16	53	69	36	....	....	....	....	....	....	1981-82	1982-83
Lewicki, Danny	Tor., NYR, Chi.	9	461	105	135	240	177	28	0	4	4	8	1	1950-51	1958-59
Lewis, Dale	NYR	1	8	0	0	0	0	....	....	....	....	....	....	1975-76	1975-76
Lewis, Dave	NYI, L.A., N.J., Det.	16	1008	36	187	223	953	91	1	20	21	143	....	1973-74	1987-88
Lewis, Doug	Mtl.	1	3	0	0	0	0	....	....	....	....	....	....	1946-47	1946-47
● Lewis, Herbie	Det.	11	483	148	161	309	248	38	13	10	23	6	2	1928-29	1938-39
Ley, Rick	Tor., Hfd.	12	310	12	72	84	528	14	0	2	2	20	....	1968-69	1980-81
‡ Liba, Igor	NYR, L.A.	1	37	7	18	25	36	2	0	0	0	2	....	1988-89	1988-89
Libby, Jeff	NYI	1	1	0	0	0	0	....	....	....	....	....	....	1997-98	1997-98
Libett, Nick	Det., Pit.	14	982	237	268	505	472	16	6	2	8	2	....	1967-68	1980-81
Licari, Tony	Det.	1	9	0	1	1	0	....	....	....	....	....	....	1946-47	1946-47
Liddington, Bob	Tor.	1	11	0	1	1	2	....	....	....	....	....	....	1970-71	1970-71
Lidster, Doug	Van., NYR, St.L., Dal.	16	897	75	268	343	679	80	6	15	21	64	2	1983-84	1998-99
‡ Lilley, John	Ana.	3	23	3	8	11	13	....	....	....	....	....	....	1993-94	1995-96
‡ Lindberg, Chris	Cgy., Que.	3	116	17	25	42	47	2	0	1	1	2	....	1991-92	1993-94
‡ Lindbom, Johan	NYR	1	38	1	3	4	28	....	....	....	....	....	....	1997-98	1997-98
Linden, Jamie	Fla.	1	4	0	0	0	17	....	....	....	....	....	....	1994-95	1994-95
Lindgren, Lars	Van., Min.	6	394	25	113	138	325	40	5	6	11	20	....	1978-79	1983-84
‡ Lindholm, Mikael	L.A.	1	18	2	2	4	2	....	....	....	....	....	....	1989-90	1989-90
Lindros, Brett	NYI	2	51	2	5	7	147	....	....	....	....	....	....	1994-95	1995-96
Lindsay, Ted	Det., Chi.	17	1068	379	472	851	1808	133	47	49	96	194	4	1944-45	1964-65
Lindstrom, Willy	Wpg., Edm., Pit.	8	582	161	162	323	200	57	14	18	32	24	2	1979-80	1986-87
Linseman, Ken	Phi., Edm., Bos., Tor.	14	860	256	551	807	1727	113	43	77	120	325	1	1978-79	1991-92
Liscombe, Carl	Det.	9	373	137	140	277	117	59	22	19	41	20	1	1937-38	1945-46
Litzenberger, Ed	Mtl., Chi., Det., Tor.	12	618	178	238	416	283	40	5	13	18	34	4	1952-53	1963-64
‡ Loach, Lonnie	Ott., L.A., Ana.	2	56	10	13	23	29	1	0	0	0	0	....	1992-93	1993-94
● Locas, Jacques	Mtl.	2	59	7	8	15	66	....	....	....	....	....	....	1947-48	1948-49
Lochead, Bill	Det., Col., NYR	6	330	69	62	131	180	7	3	0	3	6	....	1974-75	1979-80
● Locking, Norm	Chi.	2	48	2	6	8	26	....	....	....	....	....	....	1934-35	1935-36
‡ Loewen, Darcy	Buf., Ott.	5	135	4	8	12	211	....	....	....	....	....	....	1989-90	1993-94
Lofthouse, Mark	Wsh., Det.	6	181	42	38	80	73	....	....	....	....	....	....	1977-78	1982-83
Logan, Dave	Chi., Van.	6	218	5	29	34	470	12	0	0	0	10	....	1975-76	1980-81
Logan, Robert	Buf., L.A.	3	42	10	5	15	0	....	....	....	....	....	....	1986-87	1988-89
Loiselle, Claude	Det., N.J., Que., Tor., NYI	13	616	92	117	209	1149	41	4	11	15	60	....	1981-82	1993-94
Lomakin, Andrei	Phi., Fla.	4	215	42	62	104	92	....	....	....	....	....	....	1991-92	1994-95
‡ Loney, Brian	Van.	1	12	2	3	5	6	....	....	....	....	....	....	1995-96	1995-96
Loney, Troy	Pit., Ana., NYI, NYR	12	624	87	110	197	1091	67	8	14	22	97	2	1983-84	1994-95
Long, Barry	L.A., Det., Wpg.	5	280	11	68	79	250	5	0	1	1	18	....	1972-73	1981-82
● Long, Stanley	Mtl.	1	....	....	....	....	....	3	0	0	0	0	....	1951-52	1951-52
Lonsberry, Ross	Bos., L.A., Phi., Pit.	15	968	256	310	566	806	100	21	25	46	87	2	1966-67	1980-81
Loob, Hakan	Cgy.	6	450	193	236	429	189	73	26	28	54	16	1	1983-84	1988-89
Loob, Peter	Que.	1	8	1	2	3	0	....	....	....	....	....	....	1984-85	1984-85
Lorentz, Jim	Bos., St.L., NYR, Buf.	10	659	161	238	399	208	54	12	10	22	30	1	1968-69	1977-78
Lorimer, Bob	NYI, Col., N.J.	10	529	22	90	112	431	49	3	10	13	83	2	1976-77	1985-86
● Lorrain, Rod	Mtl.C., Mtl.	6	179	28	39	67	30	11	0	3	3	0	....	1935-36	1941-42
● Loughlin, Clem	Det., Chi.	3	101	8	6	14	77	....	....	....	....	....	....	1926-27	1928-29
● Loughlin, Wilf	Tor.	1	14	0	0	0	2	....	....	....	....	....	....	1923-24	1923-24
Lovsin, Ken	Wsh.	1	1	0	0	0	0	....	....	....	....	....	....	1990-91	1990-91
Lowdermilk, Dwayne	Wsh.	1	2	0	1	1	2	....	....	....	....	....	....	1980-81	1980-81
Lowe, Darren	Pit.	1	8	1	2	3	0	....	....	....	....	....	....	1983-84	1983-84
Lowe, Kevin	Edm., NYR	21	1254	84	347	431	1498	214	10	48	58	192	6	1979-80	1997-98
Lowe, Odie	NYR	1	4	1	1	2	0	....	....	....	....	....	....	1949-50	1949-50
● Lowe, Ross	Bos., Mtl.	3	77	6	8	14	82	2	0	0	0	0	....	1949-50	1951-52
● Lowrey, Ed	Ott., Ham.	3	27	2	2	4	6	....	....	....	....	....	....	1917-18	1920-21
● Lowrey, Fred	Mtl.M., Pit.	2	53	1	1	2	10	2	0	0	0	....	....	1924-25	1925-26

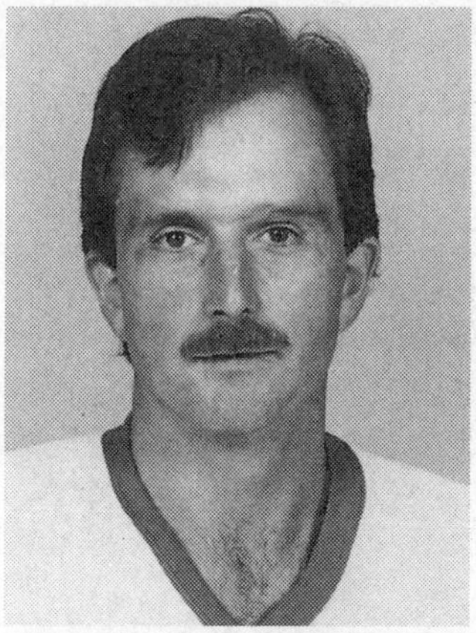

Dave Lewis

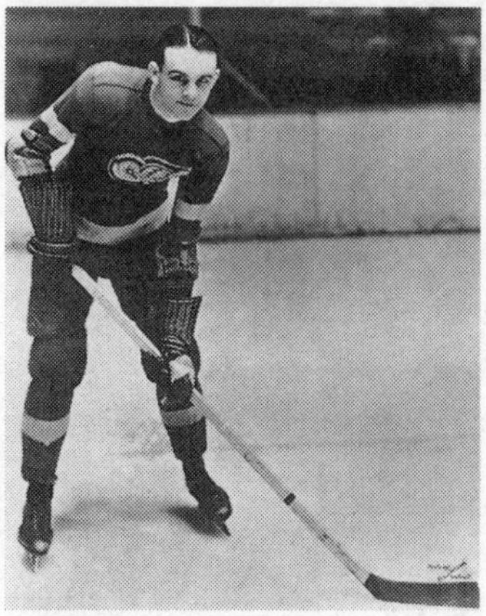

Herbie Lewis

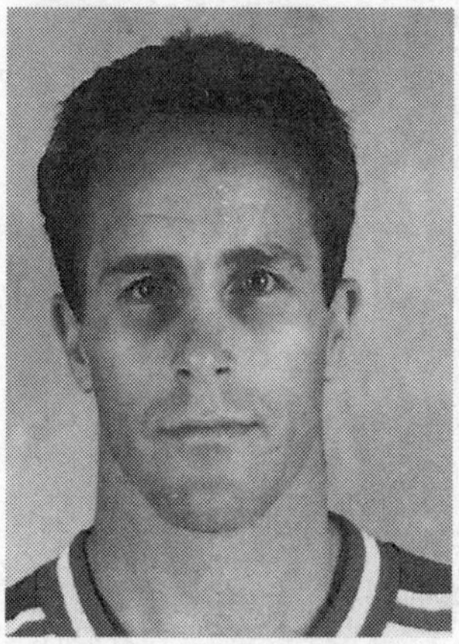

Doug Lidster

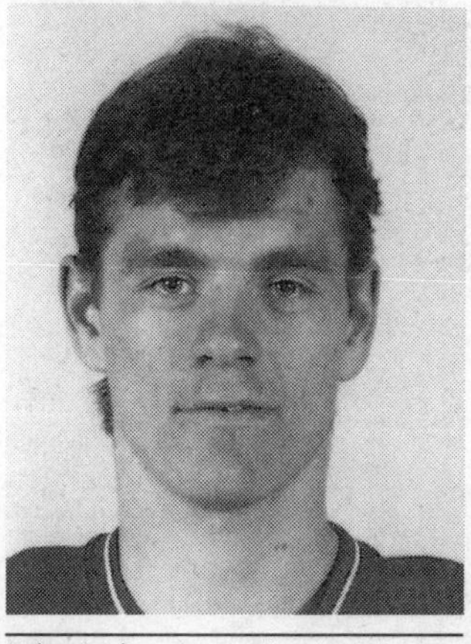

Hakan Loob

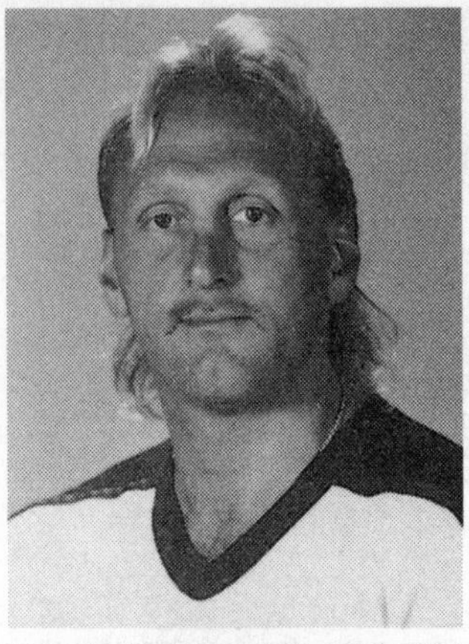

Craig Ludwig

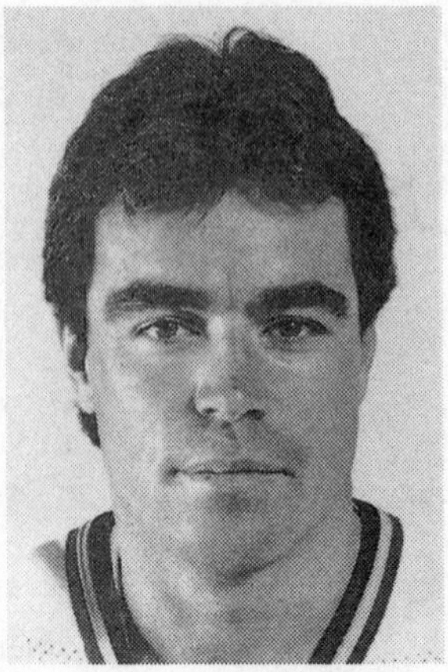

Brian MacLellan

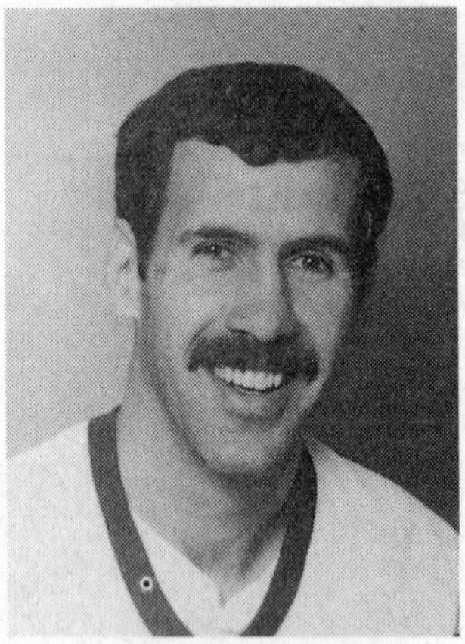

Jamie Macoun

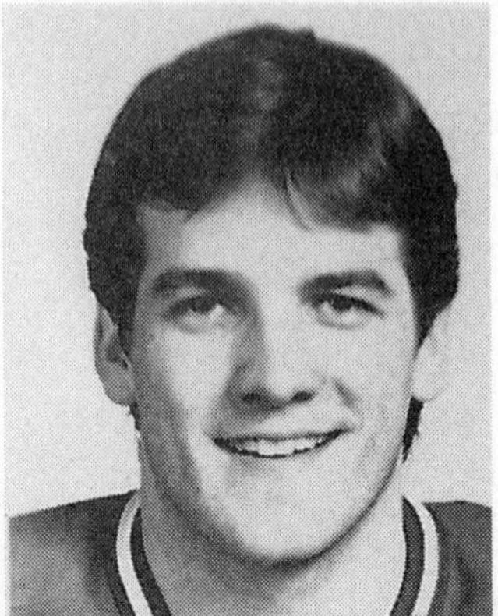

David Maley

Name	NHL Teams	NHL Seasons	Regular Schedule GP	G	A	TP	PIM	Playoffs GP	G	A	TP	PIM	NHL Cup Wins	First NHL Season	Last NHL Season
● Lowrey, Gerry	Tor., Pit., Phi., Chi., Ott.	6	211	48	48	96	148	2	1	0	1	2	....	1927-28	1932-33
Lucas, Danny	Phi.	1	6	1	0	1	0	....	....	....	....	....	....	1978-79	1978-79
Lucas, Dave	Det.	1	1	0	0	0	0	....	....	....	....	....	....	1962-63	1962-63
Luce, Don	NYR, Det., Buf., L.A., Tor.	13	894	225	329	554	364	71	17	22	39	52	....	1969-70	1981-82
Ludvig, Jan	N.J., Buf.	7	314	54	87	141	418	....	....	....	....	....	....	1982-83	1988-89
Ludwig, Craig	Mtl., NYI, Min., Dal.	18	1256	38	184	222	1437	177	4	25	29	244	2	1982-83	1998-99
Ludzik, Steve	Chi., Buf.	10	424	46	93	139	333	44	4	8	12	70	....	1981-82	1989-90
Lukowich, Bernie	Pit., St.L.	2	79	13	15	28	34	2	0	0	0	0	....	1973-74	1974-75
Lukowich, Morris	Wpg., Bos., L.A.	8	582	199	219	418	584	11	0	2	2	24	....	1979-80	1986-87
Luksa, Charlie	Hfd.	1	8	0	1	1	4	....	....	....	....	....	....	1979-80	1979-80
Lumley, Dave	Mtl., Edm., Hfd.	9	437	98	160	258	680	61	6	8	14	131	2	1978-79	1986-87
Lund, Pentti	Bos., NYR	7	259	44	55	99	40	19	7	5	12	0	....	1946-47	1952-53
Lundberg, Brian	Pit.	1	1	0	0	0	2	....	....	....	....	....	....	1982-83	1982-83
Lunde, Len	Det., Chi., Min., Van.	8	321	39	83	122	75	20	3	2	5	2	....	1958-59	1970-71
Lundholm, Bengt	Wpg.	5	275	48	95	143	72	14	3	4	7	14	....	1981-82	1985-86
Lundrigan, Joe	Tor., Wsh.	2	52	2	8	10	22	....	....	....	....	....	....	1972-73	1974-75
Lundstrom, Tord	Det.	1	11	1	1	2	0	....	....	....	....	....	....	1973-74	1973-74
Lundy, Pat	Det., Chi.	5	150	37	32	69	31	16	2	2	4	2	....	1945-46	1950-51
‡ Luongo, Chris	Det., Ott., NYI	5	218	8	23	31	176	....	....	....	....	....	....	1990-91	1995-96
Lupien, Gilles	Mtl., Pit., Hfd.	5	226	5	25	30	416	25	0	0	0	21	2	1977-78	1981-82
Lupul, Gary	Van.	7	293	70	75	145	243	25	4	7	11	11	....	1979-80	1985-86
Lyle, George	Det., Hfd.	4	99	24	38	62	51	....	....	....	....	....	....	1979-80	1982-83
Lynch, Jack	Pit., Det., Wsh.	7	382	24	106	130	336	....	....	....	....	....	....	1972-73	1978-79
Lynn, Vic	NYR, Det., Mtl., Tor., Bos., Chi.	11	327	49	76	125	274	47	7	10	17	46	3	1942-43	1953-54
Lyon, Steve	Pit.	1	3	0	0	0	2	....	....	....	....	....	....	1976-77	1976-77
Lyons, Ron	Bos., Phi.	1	36	2	4	6	27	5	0	0	0	0	....	1930-31	1930-31
Lysiak, Tom	Atl., Chi.	13	919	292	551	843	567	76	25	38	63	49	....	1973-74	1985-86

M

Name	NHL Teams	NHL Seasons	Regular Schedule GP	G	A	TP	PIM	Playoffs GP	G	A	TP	PIM	NHL Cup Wins	First NHL Season	Last NHL Season
MacAdam, Al	Phi., Cal., Cle., Min., Van.	12	864	240	351	591	509	64	20	24	44	21	1	1973-74	1984-85
MacDermid, Paul	Hfd., Wpg., Wsh., Que.	14	690	116	142	258	1303	43	5	11	16	116	....	1981-82	1994-95
MacDonald, Blair	Edm., Van.	4	219	91	100	191	65	11	0	6	6	2	....	1979-80	1982-83
MacDonald, Brett	Van.	1	1	0	0	0	0	....	....	....	....	....	....	1987-88	1987-88
‡ MacDonald, Doug	Buf.	3	11	1	0	1	2	....	....	....	....	....	....	1992-93	1994-95
MacDonald, Kevin	Ott.	1	1	0	0	0	2	....	....	....	....	....	....	1993-94	1993-94
● MacDonald, Kilby	NYR	4	151	36	34	70	47	15	1	2	3	4	1	1939-40	1944-45
MacDonald, Lowell	Det., L.A., Pit.	14	506	180	210	390	92	30	11	11	22	12	....	1961-62	1977-78
MacDonald, Parker	Tor., NYR, Det., Bos., Min.	14	676	144	179	323	253	75	14	14	28	20	....	1952-53	1968-69
MacDougall, Kim	Min.	1	1	0	0	0	0	....	....	....	....	....	....	1974-75	1974-75
MacEachern, Shane	St.L.	1	1	0	0	0	0	....	....	....	....	....	....	1987-88	1987-88
Macey, Hub	NYR, Mtl.	3	30	6	9	15	0	8	0	0	0	0	....	1941-42	1946-47
MacGregor, Bruce	Det., NYR	14	893	213	257	470	217	107	19	28	47	44	....	1960-61	1973-74
MacGregor, Randy	Hfd.	1	2	1	1	2	2	....	....	....	....	....	....	1981-82	1981-82
MacGuigan, Garth	NYI	2	5	0	1	1	2	....	....	....	....	....	....	1979-80	1983-84
MacIntosh, Ian	NYR	1	4	0	0	0	4	....	....	....	....	....	....	1952-53	1952-53
MacIver, Don	Wpg.	1	6	0	0	0	2	....	....	....	....	....	....	1979-80	1979-80
Maciver, Norm	NYR, Hfd., Edm., Ott., Pit., Wpg., Phx.	12	500	55	230	285	350	56	3	11	14	32	....	1986-87	1997-98
MacKasey, Blair	Tor.	1	1	0	0	0	2	....	....	....	....	....	....	1976-77	1976-77
MacKay, Calum	Det., Mtl.	8	237	50	55	105	214	38	5	13	18	20	1	1946-47	1954-55
MacKay, Dave	Chi.	1	29	3	0	3	26	5	0	1	1	2	....	1940-41	1940-41
● MacKay, Mickey	Chi., Pit., Bos.	4	147	44	19	63	79	11	0	0	0	6	1	1926-27	1929-30
● MacKay, Murdo	Mtl.	4	19	0	3	3	0	15	1	2	3	0	....	1945-46	1948-49
MacKell, Fleming	Tor., Bos.	13	665	149	220	369	562	80	22	41	63	75	2	1947-48	1959-60
● MacKell, Jack	Ott.	2	45	4	2	6	59	2	0	0	0	0	1	1919-20	1920-21
MacKenzie, Barry	Min.	1	6	0	1	1	6	....	....	....	....	....	....	1968-69	1968-69
● MacKenzie, Bill	Chi., Mtl.M., NYR, Mtl.C.	7	264	15	14	29	145	21	1	1	2	11	1	1932-33	1939-40
‡ Mackey, David	Chi., Min., St.L.	6	126	8	12	20	305	3	0	0	0	2	....	1987-88	1993-94
● Mackey, Reg	NYR	1	34	0	0	0	16	1	0	0	0	0	....	1926-27	1926-27
● Mackie, Howie	Det.	2	20	1	0	1	4	8	0	0	0	0	1	1936-37	1937-38
MacKinnon, Paul	Wsh.	5	147	5	23	28	91	....	....	....	....	....	....	1979-80	1983-84
MacLean, Paul	St.L., Wpg., Det.	12	719	324	349	673	968	53	21	14	35	110	....	1980-81	1990-91
MacLeish, Rick	Phi., Hfd., Pit., Det.	14	846	349	410	759	434	114	54	53	107	38	2	1970-71	1983-84
MacLellan, Brian	L.A., NYR, Min., Cgy., Det.	10	606	172	241	413	551	47	5	9	14	42	1	1982-83	1991-92
‡ MacLeod, Pat	Min., S.J., Dal.	4	53	5	13	18	14	....	....	....	....	....	....	1990-91	1995-96
MacMillan, Billy	Tor., Atl., NYI	7	446	74	77	151	184	53	6	6	12	40	....	1970-71	1976-77
MacMillan, Bob	NYR, St.L., Atl., Cgy., Col., N.J., Chi.	11	753	228	349	577	260	31	8	11	19	16	....	1974-75	1984-85
MacMillan, John	Tor., Det.	5	104	5	10	15	32	12	0	1	1	2	2	1960-61	1964-65
MacNeil, Al	Tor., Mtl., Chi., NYR, Pit.	12	524	17	75	92	617	37	0	4	4	67	....	1955-56	1967-68
MacNeil, Bernie	St.L.	1	4	0	0	0	0	....	....	....	....	....	....	1973-74	1973-74
Macoun, Jamie	Cgy., Tor., Det.	17	1128	76	282	358	1208	159	10	32	42	169	2	1982-83	1998-99
● MacPherson, Bud	Mtl.	7	259	5	33	38	233	29	0	3	3	21	1	1948-49	1956-57
● MacSweyn, Ralph	Phi.	5	47	0	5	5	10	8	0	0	0	6	....	1967-68	1971-72
MacTavish, Craig	Bos., Edm., NYR, Phi., St.L.	20	1093	213	267	480	891	193	20	38	58	218	4	1979-80	1996-97
MacWilliam, Mike	NYI	1	6	0	0	0	14	....	....	....	....	....	....	1995-96	1995-96
Madigan, Connie	St.L.	1	20	0	3	3	25	5	0	0	0	4	....	1972-73	1972-73
Madill, Jeff	N.J.	1	14	4	0	4	46	7	0	2	2	8	....	1990-91	1990-91
Magee, Dean	Min.	1	7	0	0	0	4	....	....	....	....	....	....	1977-78	1977-78
Maggs, Daryl	Chi., Cal., Tor.	3	135	14	19	33	54	4	0	0	0	0	....	1971-72	1979-80
Magnan, Marc	Tor.	1	4	0	1	1	5	....	....	....	....	....	....	1982-83	1982-83
Magnuson, Keith	Chi.	12	589	14	125	139	1442	68	3	9	12	164	....	1969-70	1979-80
Maguire, Kevin	Tor., Buf., Phi.	6	260	29	30	59	782	11	0	0	0	86	....	1986-87	1991-92
Mahaffy, John	Mtl., NYR	3	37	11	25	36	4	1	0	1	1	0	....	1942-43	1944-45
Mahovlich, Frank	Tor., Det., Mtl.	18	1181	533	570	1103	1056	137	51	67	118	163	6	1956-57	1973-74
Mahovlich, Pete	Det., Mtl., Pit.	16	884	288	485	773	916	88	30	42	72	134	4	1965-66	1980-81
‡ Mailhot, Jacques	Que.	1	5	0	0	0	33	....	....	....	....	....	....	1988-89	1988-89
Mailley, Frank	Mtl.	1	1	0	0	0	0	....	....	....	....	....	....	1942-43	1942-43
Mair, Jim	Phi., NYI, Van.	5	76	4	15	19	49	3	1	2	3	4	....	1970-71	1974-75
● Majeau, Fern	Mtl.	2	56	22	24	46	43	1	0	0	0	0	1	1943-44	1944-45
Major, Bruce	Que.	1	4	0	0	0	0	....	....	....	....	....	....	1990-91	1990-91
Makarov, Sergei	Cgy., S.J., Dal.	7	424	134	250	384	317	34	12	11	23	8	....	1989-90	1996-97
Makela, Mikko	NYI, L.A., Buf., Bos.	7	423	118	147	265	139	18	3	8	11	14	....	1985-86	1994-95
Maki, Chico	Chi.	15	841	143	292	435	345	113	17	36	53	43	1	1960-61	1975-76
● Maki, Wayne	Chi., St.L., Van.	6	246	57	79	136	184	2	1	0	1	2	....	1967-68	1972-73
Makkonen, Kari	Edm.	1	9	2	2	4	0	....	....	....	....	....	....	1979-80	1979-80
‡ Maley, David	Mtl., N.J., Edm., S.J., NYI	9	466	43	81	124	1043	46	5	5	10	111	1	1985-86	1993-94
Malinowski, Merlin	Col., N.J., Hfd.	5	282	54	111	165	121	....	....	....	....	....	....	1978-79	1982-83
Mallette, Troy	NYR, Edm., N.J., Ott., Bos., T.B.	9	456	51	68	119	1226	15	2	2	4	99	....	1989-90	1997-98
Malone, Cliff	Mtl.	1	3	0	0	0	0	....	....	....	....	....	....	1951-52	1951-52
Malone, Greg	Pit., Hfd., Que.	11	704	191	310	501	661	20	3	5	8	32	....	1976-77	1986-87
● Malone, Joe	Mtl.C., Que., Ham.	7	126	143	32	175	57	9	6	0	6	3	1	1917-18	1923-24
Maloney, Dan	Chi., L.A., Det., Tor.	11	737	192	259	451	1489	40	4	7	11	35	....	1970-71	1981-82
Maloney, Dave	NYR, Buf.	11	657	71	246	317	1154	49	7	17	24	91	....	1974-75	1984-85
Maloney, Don	NYR, Hfd., NYI	17	765	214	350	564	815	94	22	35	57	101	....	1978-79	1990-91
Maloney, Phil	Bos., Tor., Chi.	5	158	28	43	71	16	6	0	0	0	0	....	1949-50	1959-60
Maluta, Ray	Bos.	2	25	2	3	5	6	2	0	0	0	0	....	1975-76	1976-77
Manastersky, Tom	Mtl.	1	6	0	0	0	11	....	....	....	....	....	....	1950-51	1950-51
Mancuso, Gus	Mtl.C., Mtl., NYR	4	42	7	9	16	17	....	....	....	....	....	....	1937-38	1942-43
Mandich, Dan	Min.	4	111	5	11	16	303	7	0	0	0	2	....	1982-83	1985-86
Manery, Kris	Cle., Min., Van., Wpg.	4	250	63	64	127	91	....	....	....	....	....	....	1977-78	1980-81
Manery, Randy	Det., Atl., L.A.	10	582	50	206	256	415	13	0	2	2	12	....	1970-71	1979-80
Mann, Jack	NYR	2	9	3	4	7	0	....	....	....	....	....	....	1943-44	1944-45
Mann, Jimmy	Wpg., Que., Pit.	9	293	10	20	30	895	22	0	0	0	89	....	1979-80	1987-88
Mann, Ken	Det.	1	1	0	0	0	0	....	....	....	....	....	....	1975-76	1975-76
Mann, Norm	Tor.	3	31	0	3	3	4	2	0	0	0	0	....	1935-36	1940-41
● Manners, Rennison	Pit., Phi.	2	37	3	2	5	14	....	....	....	....	....	....	1929-30	1930-31
Manno, Bob	Van., Tor., Det.	8	371	41	131	172	274	17	2	4	6	12	....	1976-77	1984-85
Manson, Ray	Bos., NYR	2	2	0	1	1	0	....	....	....	....	....	....	1947-48	1948-49
● Mantha, Georges	Mtl.C., Mtl.	13	488	89	102	191	148	36	6	2	8	24	2	1928-29	1940-41
Mantha, Moe	Wpg., Pit., Edm., Min., Phi.	12	656	81	289	370	501	17	5	10	15	18	....	1980-81	1991-92
● Mantha, Sylvio	Mtl.C., Bos.	14	542	63	78	141	671	39	5	5	10	64	2	1923-24	1936-37
● Maracle, Bud	NYR	1	11	1	3	4	4	4	0	0	0	0	....	1930-31	1930-31

Name	NHL Teams	NHL Seasons	Regular Schedule GP	G	A	TP	PIM	Playoffs GP	G	A	TP	PIM	NHL Cup Wins	First NHL Season	Last NHL Season
Marcetta, Milan	Tor., Min.	3	54	7	15	22	10	17	7	7	14	4	1	1966-67	1968-69
March, Mush	Chi.	17	759	153	230	383	540	45	12	15	27	41	2	1928-29	1944-45
Marchinko, Brian	Tor., NYI	4	47	2	6	8	0	....	....	....	....	....	....	1970-71	1973-74
Marcinyshyn, Dave	N.J., Que., NYR	3	16	0	1	1	49	....	....	....	....	....	....	1990-91	1992-93
Marcon, Lou	Det.	3	60	0	4	4	42	....	....	....	....	....	....	1958-59	1962-63
Marcotte, Don	Bos.	15	868	230	254	484	317	132	34	27	61	81	2	1965-66	1981-82
Marini, Hector	NYI, N.J.	5	154	27	46	73	246	10	3	6	9	14	1	1978-79	1983-84
• Mario, Frank	Bos.	2	53	9	19	28	24	....	....	....	....	....	....	1941-42	1944-45
• Mariucci, John	Chi.	5	223	11	34	45	308	12	0	3	3	26	....	1940-41	1947-48
Mark, Gordon	N.J., Edm.	4	85	3	10	13	187	....	....	....	....	....	....	1986-87	1994-95
Markell, John	Wpg., St.L., Min.	4	55	11	10	21	36	....	....	....	....	....	....	1979-80	1984-85
• Marker, Gus	Det., Mtl.M., Tor., Bro.	10	322	64	69	133	133	46	5	7	12	36	1	1932-33	1941-42
Markham, Ray	NYR	1	14	1	1	2	21	7	1	0	1	24	....	1979-80	1979-80
• Markle, Jack	Tor.	1	8	0	1	1	0	....	....	....	....	....	....	1935-36	1935-36
• Marks, Jack	Mtl., Tor., Que.	2	7	0	0	0	4	....	....	....	....	....	1	1917-18	1919-20
Marks, John	Chi.	10	657	112	163	275	330	57	5	9	14	60	....	1972-73	1981-82
Markwart, Nevin	Bos., Cgy.	8	309	41	68	109	794	19	1	0	1	33	....	1983-84	1991-92
‡ Marois, Daniel	Tor., NYI, Bos., Dal.	9	350	117	93	210	419	19	3	3	6	28	....	1987-88	1995-96
Marois, Mario	NYR, Van., Que., Wpg., St.L.	15	955	76	357	433	1746	100	4	34	38	182	....	1977-78	1991-92
Marotte, Gilles	Bos., Chi., L.A., NYR, St.L.	12	808	56	265	321	919	29	3	3	6	26	....	1965-66	1976-77
Marquess, Mark	Bos.	1	27	5	4	9	6	4	0	0	0	0	....	1946-47	1946-47
Marsh, Brad	Atl., Cgy., Phi., Tor., Det., Ott.	15	1086	23	175	198	1241	97	6	18	24	124	....	1978-79	1992-93
Marsh, Gary	Det., Tor.	2	7	1	3	4	4	....	....	....	....	....	....	1967-68	1968-69
Marsh, Peter	Wpg., Chi.	5	278	48	71	119	224	26	1	5	6	33	....	1979-80	1983-84
Marshall, Bert	Det., Oak., Cal., NYR, NYI	14	868	17	181	198	926	72	4	22	26	99	....	1965-66	1978-79
Marshall, Don	Mtl., NYR, Buf., Tor.	19	1176	265	324	589	127	94	8	15	23	14	5	1951-52	1971-72
Marshall, Paul	Pit., Tor., Hfd.	4	95	15	18	33	17	1	0	0	0	0	....	1979-80	1982-83
Marshall, Willie	Tor.	4	33	1	5	6	2	....	....	....	....	....	....	1952-53	1958-59
Marson, Mike	Wsh., L.A.	6	196	24	24	48	233	....	....	....	....	....	....	1974-75	1979-80
• Martin, Clare	Bos., Det., Chi., NYR	6	237	12	28	40	78	27	0	2	2	6	1	1941-42	1951-52
‡ Martin, Craig	Wpg., Fla.	2	21	0	1	1	24	....	....	....	....	....	....	1994-95	1996-97
Martin, Frank	Bos., Chi.	6	282	11	46	57	122	10	0	2	2	2	....	1952-53	1957-58
Martin, Grant	Van., Wsh.	4	44	0	4	4	55	1	1	0	1	2	....	1983-84	1986-87
Martin, Jack	Tor.	1	1	0	0	0	0	....	....	....	....	....	....	1960-61	1960-61
Martin, Pit	Det., Bos., Chi., Van.	17	1101	324	485	809	609	100	27	31	58	56	....	1961-62	1978-79
Martin, Rick	Buf., L.A.	11	685	384	317	701	477	63	24	29	53	74	....	1971-72	1981-82
• Martin, Ron	NYA	2	94	13	16	29	36	....	....	....	....	....	....	1932-33	1933-34
Martin, Terry	Buf., Que., Tor., Edm., Min.	10	479	104	101	205	202	21	4	2	6	26	....	1975-76	1984-85
Martin, Tom	Tor.	1	3	1	0	1	0	....	....	....	....	....	....	1967-68	1967-68
Martin, Tom	Wpg., Hfd., Min.	6	92	12	11	23	249	4	0	0	0	6	....	1984-85	1989-90
Martineau, Don	Atl., Min., Det.	4	90	6	10	16	63	....	....	....	....	....	....	1973-74	1976-77
‡ Martini, Darcy	Edm.	1	2	0	0	0	0	....	....	....	....	....	....	1993-94	1993-94
Martinson, Steve	Det., Mtl., Min.	4	49	2	1	3	244	1	0	0	0	10	....	1987-88	1991-92
Maruk, Dennis	Cal., Cle., Min., Wsh.	14	888	356	522	878	761	34	14	22	36	26	....	1975-76	1988-89
Masnick, Paul	Mtl., Chi., Tor.	6	232	18	41	59	139	33	4	5	9	27	1	1950-51	1957-58
• Mason, Charley	NYR, NYA, Det., Chi.	4	95	7	18	25	44	4	0	1	1	0	....	1934-35	1938-39
• Massecar, George	NYA	3	100	12	11	23	46	....	....	....	....	....	....	1929-30	1931-32
Masters, Jamie	St.L.	3	33	1	13	14	2	2	0	0	0	0	....	1975-76	1978-79
• Masterton, Bill	Min.	1	38	4	8	12	4	....	....	....	....	....	....	1967-68	1967-68
Mathers, Frank	Tor.	3	23	1	3	4	4	....	....	....	....	....	....	1948-49	1951-52
Mathiasen, Dwight	Pit.	3	33	1	7	8	18	....	....	....	....	....	....	1985-86	1987-88
Mathieson, Jim	Wsh.	1	2	0	0	0	4	....	....	....	....	....	....	1989-90	1989-90
• Matte, Joe	Tor., Ham., Bos., Mtl.C.	4	68	17	15	32	54	....	....	....	....	....	....	1919-20	1925-26
• Matte, Joe	Det., Chi.	2	24	0	3	3	8	....	....	....	....	....	....	1929-30	1942-43
Mattiussi, Dick	Pit., Oak., Cal.	4	200	8	31	39	124	8	0	1	1	6	....	1967-68	1970-71
• Matz, Johnny	Mtl.C.	1	30	2	3	5	0	1	0	0	0	0	....	1924-25	1924-25
Maxner, Wayne	Bos.	2	62	8	9	17	48	....	....	....	....	....	....	1964-65	1965-66
Maxwell, Brad	Min., Que., Tor., Van., NYR	10	612	98	270	368	1292	79	12	49	61	178	....	1977-78	1986-87
Maxwell, Bryan	Min., St.L., Wpg., Pit.	9	331	18	77	95	745	15	1	1	2	86	....	1977-78	1984-85
Maxwell, Kevin	Min., Col., N.J.	3	66	6	15	21	61	16	3	4	7	24	....	1980-81	1983-84
Maxwell, Wally	Tor.	1	2	0	0	0	0	....	....	....	....	....	....	1952-53	1952-53
May, Alan	Bos., Edm., Wsh., Dal., Cgy.	8	393	31	45	76	1348	40	1	2	3	80	....	1987-88	1994-95
‡ Mayer, Derek	Ott.	1	17	2	2	4	8	....	....	....	....	....	....	1993-94	1993-94
Mayer, Jim	NYR	1	4	0	0	0	0	....	....	....	....	....	....	1979-80	1979-80
Mayer, Pat	Pit.	1	1	0	0	0	4	....	....	....	....	....	....	1987-88	1987-88
Mayer, Shep	Tor.	1	12	1	2	3	4	....	....	....	....	....	....	1942-43	1942-43
• Mazur, Eddie	Mtl., Chi.	6	107	8	20	28	120	25	4	5	9	22	1	1950-51	1956-57
‡ Mazur, Jay	Van.	4	47	11	7	18	20	6	0	1	1	8	....	1988-89	1991-92
McAdam, Gary	Buf., Pit., Det., Cgy., Wsh., N.J., Tor.	11	534	96	132	228	243	30	6	5	11	16	....	1975-76	1985-86
• McAdam, Sam	NYR	1	5	0	0	0	0	....	....	....	....	....	....	1930-31	1930-31
• McAndrew, Hazen	Bro.	1	7	0	1	1	6	....	....	....	....	....	....	1941-42	1941-42
McAneeley, Ted	Cal.	3	158	8	35	43	141	....	....	....	....	....	....	1972-73	1974-75
McAtee, Jud	Det.	3	46	15	13	28	6	14	2	1	3	0	....	1942-43	1944-45
McAtee, Norm	Bos.	1	13	0	1	1	0	....	....	....	....	....	....	1946-47	1946-47
• McAvoy, George	Mtl.	1	....	....	....	....	....	4	0	0	0	0	....	1954-55	1954-55
McBain, Andrew	Wpg., Pit., Van., Ott.	11	608	129	172	301	633	24	5	7	12	39	....	1983-84	1993-94
McBean, Wayne	L.A., NYI, Wpg., Pit.	7	211	10	39	49	168	2	1	1	2	0	....	1987-88	1994-95
McBride, Cliff	Mtl.M., Tor.	2	2	0	0	0	0	....	....	....	....	....	....	1928-29	1929-30
McBurney, Jim	Chi.	1	1	0	1	1	0	....	....	....	....	....	....	1952-53	1952-53
• McCabe, Stan	Det., Mtl.M.	4	78	9	4	13	49	....	....	....	....	....	....	1929-30	1933-34
• McCaffrey, Bert	Tor., Pit., Mtl.C.	7	260	43	30	73	202	8	2	1	3	10	1	1924-25	1930-31
McCahill, John	Col.	1	1	0	0	0	0	....	....	....	....	....	....	1977-78	1977-78
McCaig, Doug	Det., Chi.	7	263	8	21	29	255	7	0	1	1	10	....	1941-42	1950-51
• McCallum, Dunc	NYR, Pit.	5	187	14	35	49	230	10	1	2	3	12	....	1965-66	1970-71
• McCalmon, Eddie	Chi., Phi.	2	39	5	0	5	14	....	....	....	....	....	....	1927-28	1930-31
McCann, Rick	Det.	6	43	1	4	5	6	....	....	....	....	....	....	1967-68	1974-75
McCarthy, Dan	NYR	1	5	4	0	4	4	....	....	....	....	....	....	1980-81	1980-81
McCarthy, Kevin	Phi., Van., Pit.	10	537	67	191	258	527	21	2	3	5	20	....	1977-78	1986-87
• McCarthy, Thomas	Que., Ham.	2	35	22	7	29	10	....	....	....	....	....	....	1919-20	1920-21
McCarthy, Tom	Det., Bos.	4	60	8	9	17	8	....	....	....	....	....	....	1956-57	1960-61
McCarthy, Tom	Min., Bos.	9	460	178	221	399	330	68	12	26	38	67	....	1979-80	1987-88
• McCartney, Walt	Mtl.C.	1	2	0	0	0	0	....	....	....	....	....	....	1932-33	1932-33
McCaskill, Ted	Min.	1	4	0	2	2	0	....	....	....	....	....	....	1967-68	1967-68
McClanahan, Rob	Buf., Hfd., NYR	5	224	38	63	101	126	34	4	12	16	31	....	1979-80	1983-84
McClelland, Kevin	Pit., Edm., Det., Tor., Wpg.	12	588	68	112	180	1672	98	11	18	29	281	4	1981-82	1993-94
McCord, Bob	Bos., Det., Min., St.L.	7	316	10	58	68	262	14	2	5	7	10	....	1963-64	1972-73
McCord, Dennis	Van.	1	3	0	0	0	6	....	....	....	....	....	....	1973-74	1973-74
McCormack, John	Tor., Mtl., Chi.	8	311	25	49	74	35	22	1	1	2	0	2	1947-48	1954-55
‡ McCosh, Shawn	L.A., NYR	2	9	1	0	1	6	....	....	....	....	....	....	1991-92	1994-95
McCourt, Dale	Det., Buf., Tor.	7	532	194	284	478	124	21	9	7	16	6	....	1977-78	1983-84
McCreary, Bill Jr.	Tor.	1	12	1	0	1	4	....	....	....	....	....	....	1980-81	1980-81
McCreary, Bill Sr.	NYR, Det., Mtl., St.L.	8	309	53	62	115	108	48	6	16	22	14	....	1953-54	1970-71
McCreary, Keith	Mtl., Pit., Atl.	10	532	131	112	243	294	16	0	4	4	6	....	1961-62	1974-75
• McCreedy, Johnny	Tor.	2	64	17	12	29	25	21	4	3	7	16	2	1941-42	1944-45
McCrimmon, Brad	Bos., Phi., Cgy., Det., Hfd., Phx.	19	1222	81	322	403	1416	116	11	18	29	176	1	1979-80	1996-97
McCrimmon, Jim	St.L.	1	2	0	0	0	0	....	....	....	....	....	....	1974-75	1974-75
McCulley, Bob	Mtl.C.	1	1	0	0	0	0	....	....	....	....	....	....	1934-35	1934-35
• McCurry, Duke	Pit.	4	148	21	11	32	119	4	0	2	2	4	....	1925-26	1928-29
McCutcheon, Brian	Det.	3	37	3	1	4	7	....	....	....	....	....	....	1974-75	1976-77
McCutcheon, Darwin	Tor.	1	1	0	0	0	2	....	....	....	....	....	....	1981-82	1981-82
McDill, Jeff	Chi.	1	1	0	0	0	0	....	....	....	....	....	....	1976-77	1976-77
McDonagh, Bill	NYR	1	4	0	0	0	2	....	....	....	....	....	....	1949-50	1949-50
McDonald, Ab	Mtl., Chi., Bos., Det., Pit., St.L.	15	762	182	248	430	200	84	21	29	50	42	4	1957-58	1971-72
McDonald, Brian	Chi., Buf.	2	12	0	0	0	29	8	0	0	0	2	....	1967-68	1970-71
• McDonald, Bucko	Det., Tor., NYR	11	446	35	88	123	206	50	6	1	7	24	3	1934-35	1944-45
McDonald, Butch	Det., Chi.	2	66	8	20	28	2	5	0	2	2	10	....	1939-40	1944-45
McDonald, Gerry	Hfd.	2	8	0	0	0	4	....	....	....	....	....	....	1981-82	1983-84
• McDonald, Jack	Mtl., Mtl.C., Que., Tor.	5	69	26	14	40	30	7	1	1	2	3	....	1917-18	1921-22
McDonald, Jack	NYR	1	43	10	9	19	6	....	....	....	....	....	....	1943-44	1943-44
McDonald, Lanny	Tor., Col., Cgy.	16	1111	500	506	1006	899	117	44	40	84	120	1	1973-74	1988-89
McDonald, Robert	NYR	1	1	0	0	0	0	....	....	....	....	....	....	1943-44	1943-44
McDonald, Terry	K.C.	1	8	0	1	1	6	....	....	....	....	....	....	1975-76	1975-76

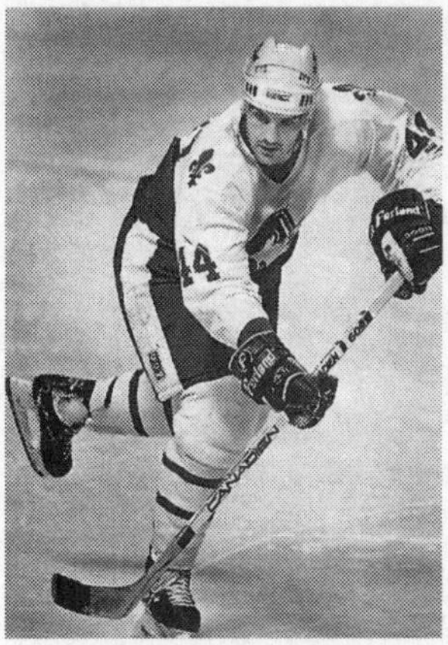
Mario Marois

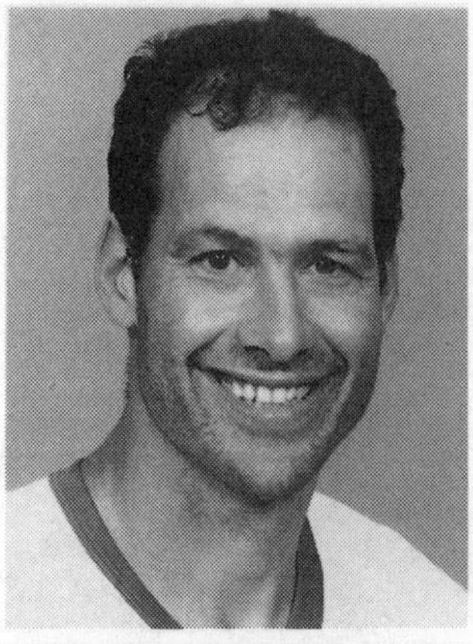
Brad Marsh

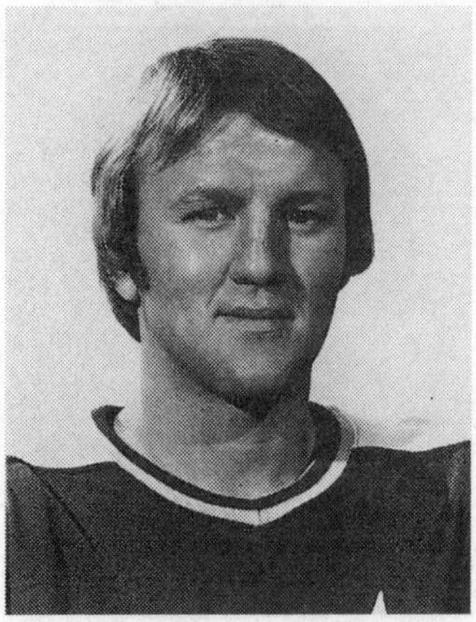
Don Martineau

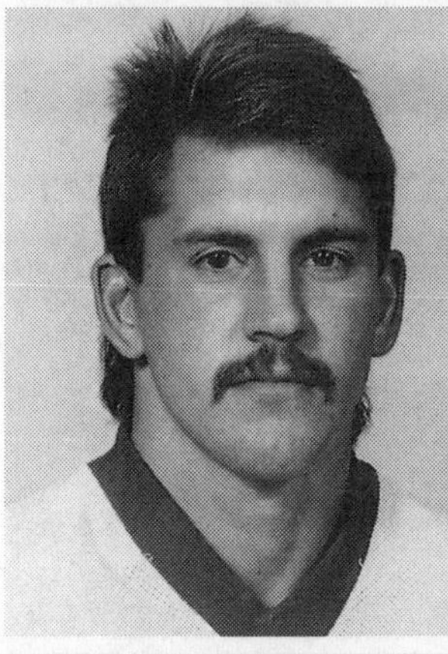
Steve Martinson

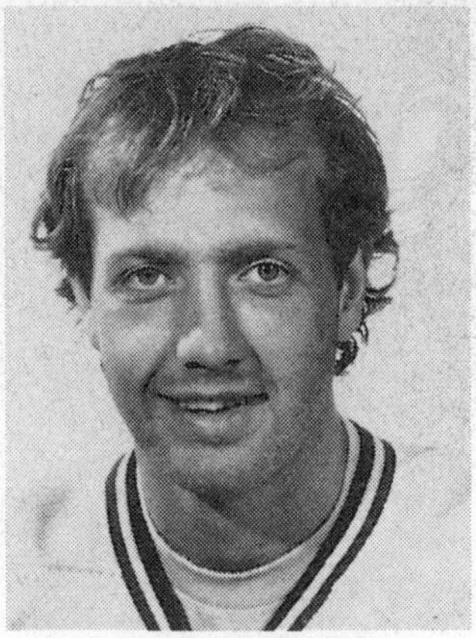

Brad Maxwell

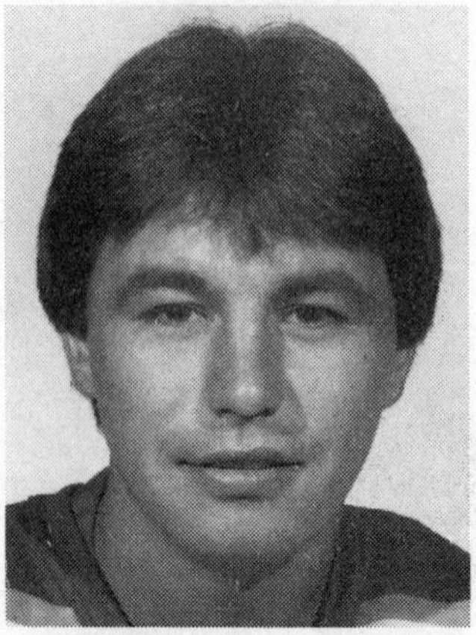

Dale McCourt

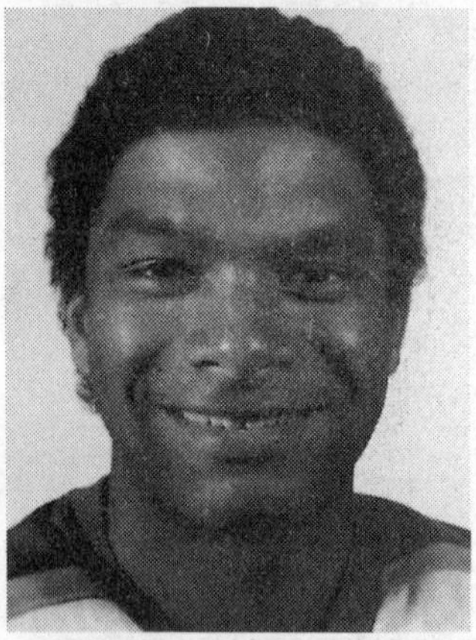

Tony McKegney

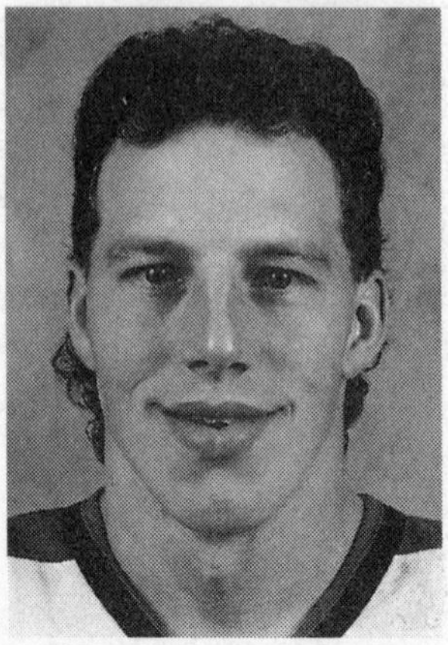

Corey Millen

			Regular Schedule					Playoffs					NHL	First	Last
Name	NHL Teams	NHL Seasons	GP	G	A	TP	PIM	GP	G	A	TP	PIM	Cup Wins	NHL Season	NHL Season
McDonnell, Joe	Van., Pit.	3	50	2	10	12	34	....	....	....	....	....	....	1981-82	1985-86
● McDonnell, Moylan	Ham.	1	22	1	2	3	2	....	....	....	....	....	....	1920-21	1920-21
McDonough, Al	L.A., Pit., Atl., Det.	5	237	73	88	161	73	8	0	1	1	2	....	1970-71	1977-78
McDonough, Hubie	L.A., NYI, S.J.	5	195	40	26	66	67	5	1	0	1	4	....	1988-89	1992-93
McDougal, Mike	NYR, Hfd.	4	61	8	10	18	43	....	....	....	....	....	....	1978-79	1982-83
‡ McDougall, Bill	Det., Edm., T.B.	3	28	5	5	10	12	1	0	0	0	0	....	1990-91	1993-94
McElmury, Jim	Min., K.C., Col.	5	180	14	47	61	49	....	....	....	....	....	....	1972-73	1977-78
McEwen, Mike	NYR, Col., NYI, L.A., Wsh., Det., Hfd.	12	716	108	296	404	460	78	12	36	48	48	3	1976-77	1987-88
McFadden, Jim	Det., Chi.	8	412	100	126	226	89	49	10	9	19	30	1	1946-47	1953-54
McFadyen, Don	Chi.	4	179	12	33	45	77	11	2	2	4	5	1	1932-33	1935-36
McFall, Dan	Wpg.	2	9	0	1	1	0	....	....	....	....	....	....	1984-85	1985-86
● McFarlane, Gord	Chi.	1	2	0	0	0	0	....	....	....	....	....	....	1926-27	1926-27
‡ McGeough, Jim	Wsh., Pit.	4	57	7	10	17	32	....	....	....	....	....	....	1981-82	1986-87
● McGibbon, Irv	Mtl.	1	1	0	0	0	2	....	....	....	....	....	....	1942-43	1942-43
McGill, Bob	Tor., Chi., S.J., Det., NYI, Hfd.	13	705	17	55	72	1766	49	0	0	0	88	....	1981-82	1993-94
● McGill, Jack	Mtl.C.	3	134	27	10	37	71	3	2	0	2	0	....	1934-35	1936-37
McGill, Jack	Bos.	4	97	23	36	59	42	27	7	4	11	17	....	1941-42	1946-47
McGill, Ryan	Chi., Phi., Edm.	4	151	4	15	19	391	....	....	....	....	....	....	1991-92	1994-95
McGregor, Sandy	NYR	1	2	0	0	0	2	....	....	....	....	....	....	1963-64	1963-64
● McGuire, Mickey	Pit.	2	36	3	0	3	6	....	....	....	....	....	....	1926-27	1927-28
McHugh, Mike	Min., S.J.	4	20	1	0	1	16	....	....	....	....	....	....	1988-89	1991-92
McIlhargey, Jack	Phi., Van., Hfd.	11	393	11	36	47	1102	27	0	3	3	68	....	1974-75	1981-82
● McInenly, Bert	Det., NYA, Ott., Bos.	6	166	19	15	34	144	4	0	0	0	2	....	1930-31	1935-36
McIntosh, Bruce	Min.	1	2	0	0	0	0	....	....	....	....	....	....	1972-73	1972-73
McIntosh, Paul	Buf.	2	48	0	2	2	66	2	0	0	0	7	....	1974-75	1975-76
● McIntyre, Jack	Bos., Chi., Det.	11	499	109	102	211	173	29	7	6	13	4	....	1949-50	1959-60
McIntyre, John	Tor., L.A., NYR, Van.	6	351	24	54	78	516	44	0	6	6	54	....	1989-90	1994-95
McIntyre, Larry	Tor.	2	41	0	3	3	26	....	....	....	....	....	....	1969-70	1972-73
McKay, Doug	Det.	1	....	....	....	....	....	1	0	0	0	0	1	1949-50	1949-50
McKay, Ray	Chi., Buf., Cal.	6	140	2	16	18	102	....	....	....	....	....	....	1968-69	1973-74
McKay, Scott	Ana.	1	1	0	0	0	0	....	....	....	....	....	....	1993-94	1993-94
McKechnie, Walt	Min., Cal., Bos., Det., Wsh., Cle., Tor., Col.	16	955	214	392	606	469	15	7	5	12	7	....	1967-68	1982-83
McKee, Mike	Que.	1	48	3	12	15	41	....	....	....	....	....	....	1993-94	1993-94
McKegney, Ian	Chi.	1	3	0	0	0	2	....	....	....	....	....	....	1976-77	1976-77
McKegney, Tony	Buf., Que., Min., NYR, St.L., Det., Chi.	13	912	320	319	639	517	79	24	23	47	56	....	1978-79	1990-91
McKendry, Alex	NYI, Cgy.	4	46	3	6	9	21	6	2	2	4	0	1	1977-78	1980-81
McKenna, Sean	Buf., L.A., Tor.	9	414	82	80	162	181	15	1	2	3	2	....	1981-82	1989-90
McKenney, Don	Bos., NYR, Tor., Det., St.L.	13	798	237	345	582	211	58	18	29	47	10	1	1954-55	1967-68
McKenny, Jim	Tor., Min.	14	604	82	247	329	294	37	7	9	16	10	....	1965-66	1978-79
McKenzie, Brian	Pit.	1	6	1	1	2	4	....	....	....	....	....	....	1971-72	1971-72
McKenzie, John	Chi., Det., NYR, Bos.	12	691	206	268	474	917	69	15	32	47	133	2	1958-59	1971-72
‡ McKim, Andrew	Bos., Det.	3	38	1	4	5	6	....	....	....	....	....	....	1992-93	1994-95
● McKinnon, Alex	Ham., NYA, Chi.	5	193	19	11	30	237	....	....	....	....	....	....	1924-25	1928-29
● McKinnon, John	Mtl.C., Pit., Phi.	6	208	28	11	39	224	2	0	0	0	4	....	1925-26	1930-31
McLean, Don	Wsh.	1	9	0	0	0	6	....	....	....	....	....	....	1975-76	1975-76
● McLean, Fred	Que., Ham.	2	8	0	0	0	2	....	....	....	....	....	....	1919-20	1920-21
McLean, Jack	Tor.	3	67	14	24	38	76	13	2	2	4	8	1	1942-43	1944-45
‡ McLean, Jeff	S.J.	1	6	1	0	1	0	....	....	....	....	....	....	1993-94	1993-94
● McLellan, John	Tor.	1	2	0	0	0	0	....	....	....	....	....	....	1951-52	1951-52
McLellan, Scott	Bos.	1	2	0	0	0	0	....	....	....	....	....	....	1982-83	1982-83
McLellan, Todd	NYI	1	5	1	1	2	0	....	....	....	....	....	....	1987-88	1987-88
● McLenahan, Rollie	Det.	1	9	2	1	3	10	2	0	0	0	0	....	1945-46	1945-46
McLeod, Al	Det.	1	26	2	2	4	24	....	....	....	....	....	....	1973-74	1973-74
McLeod, Jackie	NYR	5	106	14	23	37	12	7	0	0	0	0	....	1949-50	1954-55
‡ McLlwain, Dave	Pit., Wpg., Buf., NYI, Tor., Ott.	10	501	100	107	207	292	20	0	2	2	2	....	1987-88	1996-97
● McMahon, Mike	Mtl., Bos.	3	57	7	18	25	102	13	1	2	3	30	1	1942-43	1945-46
McMahon, Mike	NYR, Min., Chi., Det., Pit., Buf.	8	224	15	68	83	171	14	3	7	10	4	....	1963-64	1971-72
McManama, Bob	Pit.	3	99	11	25	36	28	8	0	1	1	6	....	1973-74	1975-76
● McManus, Sammy	Mtl.M., Bos.	2	26	0	1	1	8	1	0	0	0	0	1	1934-35	1936-37
McMurchy, Tom	Chi., Edm.	4	55	8	4	12	65	....	....	....	....	....	....	1983-84	1987-88
McNab, Max	Det.	4	128	16	19	35	24	25	1	0	1	4	1	1947-48	1950-51
McNab, Peter	Buf., Bos., Van., N.J.	14	954	363	450	813	179	107	40	42	82	20	....	1973-74	1986-87
● McNabney, Sid	Mtl.	1	....	....	....	....	....	5	0	1	1	2	....	1950-51	1950-51
● McNamara, Howard	Mtl.C.	1	10	1	0	1	4	....	....	....	....	....	....	1919-20	1919-20
● McNaughton, George	Que.	1	1	0	0	0	0	....	....	....	....	....	....	1919-20	1919-20
McNeill, Billy	Det.	6	257	21	46	67	142	4	1	1	2	4	....	1956-57	1963-64
‡ McNeill, Mike	Chi., Que.	2	63	5	11	16	18	....	....	....	....	....	....	1990-91	1991-92
McNeill, Stu	Det.	3	10	1	1	2	2	....	....	....	....	....	....	1957-58	1959-60
McPhee, George	NYR, N.J.	9	115	24	25	49	257	29	5	3	8	69	....	1982-83	1988-89
McPhee, Mike	Mtl., Min., Dal.	11	744	200	199	399	661	134	28	27	55	193	1	1983-84	1993-94
McRae, Basil	Que., Tor., Det., Min., T.B., St.L., Chi.	16	576	53	83	136	2457	78	8	4	12	349	....	1981-82	1996-97
McRae, Chris	Tor., Det.	3	21	1	0	1	122	....	....	....	....	....	....	1987-88	1989-90
McRae, Ken	Que., Tor.	7	137	14	21	35	364	6	0	0	0	4	....	1987-88	1993-94
McReavy, Pat	Bos., Det.	4	55	5	10	15	4	22	3	3	6	9	1	1938-39	1941-42
McReynolds, Brian	Wpg., NYR, L.A.	3	30	1	5	6	8	....	....	....	....	....	....	1989-90	1993-94
McSheffrey, Bryan	Van., Buf.	3	90	13	7	20	44	....	....	....	....	....	....	1972-73	1974-75
‡ McSween, Don	Buf., Ana.	5	47	3	10	13	55	....	....	....	....	....	....	1987-88	1995-96
McTaggart, Jim	Wsh.	2	71	3	10	13	205	....	....	....	....	....	....	1980-81	1981-82
McTavish, Gord	St.L., Wpg.	2	11	1	3	4	2	....	....	....	....	....	....	1978-79	1979-80
● McVeigh, Charley	Chi., NYA	9	397	84	88	172	138	4	0	0	0	2	....	1926-27	1934-35
● McVicar, Jack	Mtl.M.	2	88	2	4	6	63	6	0	0	0	2	....	1930-31	1931-32
Meagher, Rick	Mtl., Hfd., N.J., St.L.	12	691	144	165	309	383	62	8	7	15	41	....	1979-80	1990-91
Meehan, Gerry	Tor., Phi., Buf., Van., Atl., Wsh.	10	670	180	243	423	111	10	0	1	1	0	....	1968-69	1978-79
Meeke, Brent	Cal., Cle.	5	75	9	22	31	8	....	....	....	....	....	....	1972-73	1976-77
Meeker, Howie	Tor.	9	346	83	102	185	329	42	6	9	15	50	4	1946-47	1953-54
Meeker, Mike	Pit.	1	4	0	0	0	5	....	....	....	....	....	....	1978-79	1978-79
● Meeking, Harry	Tor., Det., Bos.	3	64	18	12	30	66	9	3	0	3	6	....	1917-18	1926-27
Meger, Paul	Mtl.	6	212	39	52	91	118	35	3	8	11	16	1	1949-50	1954-55
Meighan, Ron	Min., Pit.	2	48	3	7	10	18	....	....	....	....	....	....	1981-82	1982-83
Meissner, Barrie	Min.	2	6	0	1	1	4	....	....	....	....	....	....	1967-68	1968-69
Meissner, Dick	Bos., NYR	5	171	11	15	26	37	....	....	....	....	....	....	1959-60	1964-65
Melametsa, Anssi	Wpg.	1	27	0	3	3	2	....	....	....	....	....	....	1985-86	1985-86
Melin, Roger	Min.	2	3	0	0	0	0	....	....	....	....	....	....	1980-81	1981-82
Mellor, Tom	Det.	2	26	2	4	6	25	....	....	....	....	....	....	1973-74	1974-75
Melnyk, Gerry	Det., Chi., St.L.	6	269	39	77	116	34	53	6	6	12	6	....	1955-56	1967-68
Melnyk, Larry	Bos., Edm., NYR, Van.	10	432	11	63	74	686	66	2	9	11	127	2	1980-81	1989-90
Melrose, Barry	Wpg., Tor., Det.	6	300	10	23	33	728	7	0	2	2	38	....	1979-80	1985-86
Menard, Hillary	Chi.	1	1	0	0	0	0	....	....	....	....	....	....	1953-54	1953-54
Menard, Howie	Det., L.A., Chi., Oak.	4	151	23	42	65	87	19	3	7	10	36	....	1963-64	1969-70
Mercredi, Vic	Atl.	1	2	0	0	0	0	....	....	....	....	....	....	1974-75	1974-75
Meredith, Greg	Cgy.	2	38	6	4	10	8	5	3	1	4	4	....	1980-81	1982-83
Merkosky, Glenn	Hfd., N.J., Det.	5	66	5	12	17	22	....	....	....	....	....	....	1981-82	1989-90
● Meronek, Bill	Mtl.	2	19	5	8	13	0	1	0	0	0	0	....	1939-40	1942-43
Merrick, Wayne	St.L., Cal., Cle., NYI	12	774	191	265	456	303	102	19	30	49	30	4	1972-73	1983-84
● Merrill, Horace	Ott.	2	8	0	0	0	3	....	....	....	....	....	1	1917-18	1919-20
Messier, Joby	NYR, NYI	4	25	0	4	4	24	....	....	....	....	....	....	1992-93	1995-96
Messier, Mitch	Min.	4	20	0	2	2	11	....	....	....	....	....	....	1987-88	1990-91
Messier, Paul	Col.	1	9	0	0	0	4	....	....	....	....	....	....	1978-79	1978-79
‡ Metcalfe, Scott	Edm., Buf.	3	19	1	2	3	18	....	....	....	....	....	....	1987-88	1989-90
Metz, Don	Tor.	9	172	20	35	55	42	42	7	8	15	12	5	1938-39	1948-49
● Metz, Nick	Tor.	12	518	131	119	250	149	76	19	20	39	31	4	1934-35	1947-48
Michaluk, Art	Chi.	1	5	0	0	0	0	....	....	....	....	....	....	1947-48	1947-48
Michaluk, John	Chi.	1	1	0	0	0	0	....	....	....	....	....	....	1950-51	1950-51
Michayluk, Dave	Phi., Pit.	3	14	2	6	8	8	7	1	1	2	0	1	1981-82	1991-92
Micheletti, Joe	St.L., Col.	3	158	11	60	71	114	11	1	11	12	10	....	1979-80	1981-82
Micheletti, Pat	Min.	1	12	2	0	2	8	....	....	....	....	....	....	1987-88	1987-88
● Mickey, Larry	Chi., NYR, Tor., Mtl., L.A., Phi., Buf.	11	292	39	53	92	160	9	1	0	1	10	....	1964-65	1974-75
Mickoski, Nick	NYR, Chi., Det., Bos.	13	703	158	185	343	319	18	1	6	7	6	....	1947-48	1959-60
Middendorf, Max	Que., Edm.	4	13	2	4	6	6	....	....	....	....	....	....	1986-87	1990-91
Middleton, Rick	NYR, Bos.	14	1005	448	540	988	157	114	45	55	100	19	....	1974-75	1987-88
‡ Miehm, Kevin	St.L.	2	22	1	4	5	8	2	0	1	1	0	....	1992-93	1993-94

			Regular Schedule					Playoffs					NHL	First	Last
Name	NHL Teams	NHL Seasons	GP	G	A	TP	PIM	GP	G	A	TP	PIM	Cup Wins	NHL Season	NHL Season
Migay, Rudy	Tor.	10	418	59	92	151	293	15	1	0	1	20	....	1949-50	1959-60
Mikita, Stan	Chi.	22	1394	541	926	1467	1270	155	59	91	150	169	1	1958-59	1979-80
Mikkelson, Bill	L.A., NYI, Wsh.	4	147	4	18	22	105	....	....	....	....	....	....	1971-72	1976-77
Mikol, Jim	Tor., NYR	2	34	1	4	5	8	....	....	....	....	....	....	1962-63	1964-65
‡ Mikulchik, Oleg	Wpg., Ana.	3	37	0	3	3	33	....	....	....	....	....	....	1993-94	1995-96
Milbury, Mike	Bos.	15	754	49	189	238	1552	86	4	24	28	219	....	1975-76	1986-87
• Milks, Hib	Pit., Phi., NYR, Ott.	8	317	87	41	128	179	11	0	0	0	2	....	1925-26	1932-33
Millar, Hugh	Det.	1	4	0	0	0	0	1	0	0	0	0	....	1946-47	1946-47
‡ Millar, Mike	Hfd., Wsh., Bos., Tor.	5	78	18	18	36	12	....	....	....	....	....	....	1986-87	1990-91
‡ Millen, Corey	NYR, L.A., N.J., Dal., Cgy.	8	335	90	119	209	236	47	5	7	12	22	....	1989-90	1996-97
• Miller, Bill	Mtl.M., Mtl.C.	3	95	7	3	10	16	12	0	0	0	0	1	1934-35	1936-37
Miller, Bob	Bos., Col., L.A.	6	404	75	119	194	220	36	4	7	11	27	....	1977-78	1984-85
‡ Miller, Brad	Buf., Ott., Cgy.	6	82	1	5	6	321	....	....	....	....	....	....	1988-89	1993-94
• Miller, Earl	Chi., Tor.	5	109	19	14	33	124	10	1	0	1	6	1	1927-28	1931-32
Miller, Jack	Chi.	2	17	0	0	0	4	....	....	....	....	....	....	1949-50	1950-51
‡ Miller, Jason	N.J.	3	6	0	0	0	0	....	....	....	....	....	....	1990-91	1992-93
Miller, Jay	Bos., L.A.	7	446	40	44	84	1723	48	2	3	5	243	....	1985-86	1991-92
Miller, Kelly	NYR, Wsh.	15	1057	181	282	463	512	119	20	34	54	65	....	1984-85	1998-99
Miller, Paul	Col.	1	3	0	3	3	0	....	....	....	....	....	....	1981-82	1981-82
Miller, Perry	Det.	4	217	10	51	61	387	....	....	....	....	....	....	1977-78	1980-81
Miller, Tom	Det., NYI	4	118	16	25	41	34	....	....	....	....	....	....	1970-71	1974-75
Miller, Warren	NYR, Hfd.	4	262	40	50	90	137	6	1	0	1	0	....	1979-80	1982-83
‡ Miner, John	Edm.	1	14	2	3	5	16	....	....	....	....	....	....	1987-88	1987-88
Minor, Gerry	Van.	5	140	11	21	32	173	12	1	3	4	25	....	1979-80	1983-84
Miszuk, John	Det., Chi., Phi., Min.	6	237	7	39	46	232	19	0	3	3	19	....	1963-64	1969-70
Mitchell, Bill	Det.	1	1	0	0	0	0	....	....	....	....	....	....	1963-64	1963-64
• Mitchell, Herb	Bos.	2	44	6	0	6	36	....	....	....	....	....	....	1924-25	1925-26
Mitchell, Red	Chi.	3	83	4	5	9	67	....	....	....	....	....	....	1941-42	1944-45
‡ Mitchell, Roy	Min.	1	3	0	0	0	0	....	....	....	....	....	....	1992-93	1992-93
• Moe, Bill	NYR	5	261	11	42	53	163	1	0	0	0	0	....	1944-45	1948-49
Moffat, Lyle	Tor., Wpg.	3	97	12	16	28	51	....	....	....	....	....	....	1972-73	1979-80
• Moffat, Ron	Det.	3	37	1	1	2	8	7	0	0	0	0	....	1932-33	1934-35
Moher, Mike	N.J.	1	9	0	1	1	28	....	....	....	....	....	....	1982-83	1982-83
Mohns, Doug	Bos., Chi., Min., Atl., Wsh.	22	1390	248	462	710	1250	94	14	36	50	122	....	1953-54	1974-75
Mohns, Lloyd	NYR	1	1	0	0	0	0	....	....	....	....	....	....	1943-44	1943-44
Mokosak, Carl	Cgy., L.A., Phi., Pit., Bos.	6	83	11	15	26	170	1	0	0	0	0	....	1981-82	1988-89
Mokosak, John	Det.	2	41	0	2	2	96	....	....	....	....	....	....	1988-89	1989-90
Molin, Lars	Van.	3	172	33	65	98	37	19	2	9	11	7	....	1981-82	1983-84
Moller, Mike	Buf., Edm.	7	134	15	28	43	41	3	0	1	1	0	....	1980-81	1986-87
Moller, Randy	Que., NYR, Buf., Fla.	14	815	45	180	225	1692	78	6	16	22	197	....	1981-82	1994-95
Molloy, Mitch	Buf.	1	2	0	0	0	10	....	....	....	....	....	....	1989-90	1989-90
Molyneaux, Larry	NYR	2	45	0	1	1	20	10	0	0	0	8	....	1937-38	1938-39
‡ Momesso, Sergio	Mtl., St.L., Van., Tor., NYR	13	710	152	193	345	1557	119	18	26	44	311	....	1983-84	1996-97
Monahan, Garry	Mtl., Det., L.A., Tor., Van.	12	748	116	169	285	484	22	3	1	4	13	....	1967-68	1978-79
Monahan, Hartland	Cal., NYR, Wsh., Pit., L.A., St.L.	7	334	61	80	141	163	6	0	0	0	4	....	1973-74	1980-81
• Mondou, Armand	Mtl.C., Mtl.	12	386	47	71	118	99	32	3	5	8	12	2	1928-29	1939-40
Mondou, Pierre	Mtl.	9	548	194	262	456	179	69	17	28	45	26	3	1976-77	1984-85
‡ Mongeau, Michel	St.L., T.B.	4	54	6	19	25	10	2	0	1	1	0	....	1989-90	1992-93
Mongrain, Bob	Buf., L.A.	6	81	13	14	27	14	11	1	2	3	2	....	1979-80	1985-86
Monteith, Hank	Det.	3	77	5	12	17	6	4	0	0	0	0	....	1968-69	1970-71
Moore, Dickie	Mtl., Tor., St.L.	14	719	261	347	608	652	135	46	64	110	122	6	1951-52	1967-68
• Moran, Amby	Mtl.C., Chi.	2	35	1	1	2	24	....	....	....	....	....	....	1926-27	1927-28
• Morenz, Howie	Mtl.C., Chi., NYR	14	550	271	201	472	546	39	13	9	22	58	2	1923-24	1936-37
Moretto, Angelo	Cle.	1	5	1	2	3	2	....	....	....	....	....	....	1976-77	1976-77
• Morin, Pete	Mtl.	1	31	10	12	22	7	1	0	0	0	0	....	1941-42	1941-42
• Morin, Stephane	Que., Van.	5	90	16	39	55	52	....	....	....	....	....	....	1989-90	1993-94
• Morris, Bernie	Bos.	1	6	1	0	1	0	....	....	....	....	....	....	1924-25	1924-25
Morris, Jon	N.J., S.J., Bos.	6	103	16	33	49	47	11	1	7	8	25	....	1988-89	1993-94
• Morris, Moe	Tor., NYR	4	135	13	29	42	58	18	4	2	6	16	1	1943-44	1948-49
Morrison, Dave	L.A., Van.	5	39	3	3	6	4	....	....	....	....	....	....	1980-81	1984-85
Morrison, Don	Det., Chi.	3	112	18	28	46	12	3	0	1	1	0	....	1947-48	1950-51
Morrison, Doug	Bos.	4	23	7	3	10	15	....	....	....	....	....	....	1979-80	1984-85
Morrison, Gary	Phi.	3	43	1	15	16	70	5	0	1	1	2	....	1979-80	1981-82
Morrison, George	St.L.	2	115	17	21	38	13	3	0	0	0	0	....	1970-71	1971-72
Morrison, Jim	Bos., Tor., Det., NYR, Pit.	12	704	40	160	200	542	36	0	12	12	38	....	1951-52	1970-71
• Morrison, John	NYA	1	18	0	0	0	0	....	....	....	....	....	....	1925-26	1925-26
Morrison, Kevin	Col.	1	41	4	11	15	23	....	....	....	....	....	....	1979-80	1979-80
Morrison, Lew	Phi., Atl., Wsh., Pit.	9	564	39	52	91	107	17	0	0	0	2	....	1969-70	1977-78
Morrison, Mark	NYR	2	10	1	1	2	0	....	....	....	....	....	....	1981-82	1983-84
• Morrison, Rod	Det.	1	34	8	7	15	4	3	0	0	0	0	....	1947-48	1947-48
Morrow, Ken	NYI	10	550	17	88	105	309	127	11	22	33	97	4	1979-80	1988-89
‡ Morrow, Scott	Cgy.	1	4	0	0	0	0	....	....	....	....	....	....	1994-95	1994-95
Morton, Dean	Det.	1	1	1	0	1	2	....	....	....	....	....	....	1989-90	1989-90
Mortson, Gus	Tor., Chi., Det.	13	797	46	152	198	1380	54	5	8	13	68	4	1946-47	1958-59
Mosdell, Kenny	Bro., Mtl., Chi.	16	693	141	168	309	475	80	16	13	29	48	4	1941-42	1958-59
• Mosienko, Bill	Chi.	14	711	258	282	540	121	22	10	4	14	15	....	1941-42	1954-55
Mott, Morris	Cal.	3	199	18	32	50	49	....	....	....	....	....	....	1972-73	1974-75
• Motter, Alex	Bos., Det.	8	255	39	64	103	135	41	3	9	12	41	1	1934-35	1942-43
Moxey, Jim	Cal., Cle., L.A.	3	127	22	27	49	59	....	....	....	....	....	....	1974-75	1976-77
Mulhern, Richard	Atl., L.A., Tor., Wpg.	6	303	27	93	120	217	7	0	3	3	5	....	1975-76	1980-81
Mullen, Brian	Wpg., NYR, S.J., NYI	11	832	260	362	622	414	62	12	18	30	30	....	1982-83	1992-93
Mullen, Joe	St.L., Cgy., Pit., Bos.	17	1062	502	561	1063	241	143	60	46	106	42	3	1979-80	1996-97
Muloin, Wayne	Det., Oak., Cal., Min.	3	147	3	21	24	93	11	0	0	0	2	....	1963-64	1970-71
Mulvenna, Glenn	Pit., Phi.	2	2	0	0	0	4	....	....	....	....	....	....	1991-92	1992-93
Mulvey, Grant	Chi., N.J.	10	586	149	135	284	816	42	10	5	15	70	....	1974-75	1983-84
Mulvey, Paul	Wsh., Pit., L.A.	4	225	30	51	81	613	....	....	....	....	....	....	1978-79	1981-82
• Mummery, Harry	Tor., Que., Mtl.C., Ham.	6	106	33	19	52	226	2	1	1	2	17	....	1917-18	1922-23
Muni, Craig	Tor., Edm., Chi., Buf., Wpg., Pit., Dal.	16	819	28	119	147	775	113	0	17	17	108	3	1981-82	1997-98
• Munro, Dunc	Mtl.M., Mtl.C.	8	239	28	18	46	172	21	2	2	4	18	....	1924-25	1931-32
• Munro, Gerry	Mtl.M., Tor.	2	34	1	0	1	37	....	....	....	....	....	....	1924-25	1925-26
Murdoch, Bob	Mtl., L.A., Atl., Cgy.	16	757	60	218	278	764	69	4	18	22	92	2	1970-71	1981-82
Murdoch, Bob	Cal., Cle., St.L.	4	260	72	85	157	127	....	....	....	....	....	....	1975-76	1978-79
Murdoch, Don	NYR, Edm., Det.	8	320	121	117	238	155	24	10	8	18	16	....	1976-77	1981-82
Murdoch, Murray	NYR	11	508	84	108	192	197	55	9	12	21	28	2	1926-27	1936-37
Murphy, Brian	Det.	1	1	0	0	0	0	....	....	....	....	....	....	1974-75	1974-75
Murphy, Mike	St.L., NYR, L.A.	12	831	238	318	556	514	66	13	23	36	54	....	1971-72	1982-83
‡ Murphy, Rob	Van., Ott., L.A.	7	125	9	12	21	152	4	0	0	0	2	....	1987-88	1993-94
Murphy, Ron	NYR, Chi., Det., Bos.	18	889	205	274	479	460	53	7	8	15	26	1	1952-53	1969-70
Murray, Allan	NYA	7	271	5	9	14	163	14	0	0	0	10	....	1933-34	1939-40
Murray, Bob	Atl., Van.	4	194	6	16	22	98	10	1	1	2	15	....	1973-74	1976-77
Murray, Bob	Chi.	15	1008	132	382	514	873	112	19	37	56	106	....	1975-76	1989-90
Murray, Jim	L.A.	1	30	0	2	2	14	....	....	....	....	....	....	1967-68	1967-68
Murray, Ken	Tor., NYI, Det., K.C.	5	106	1	10	11	135	....	....	....	....	....	....	1969-70	1975-76
• Murray, Leo	Mtl.C.	1	6	0	0	0	2	....	....	....	....	....	....	1932-33	1932-33
‡ Murray, Mike	Phi.	1	1	0	0	0	0	....	....	....	....	....	....	1987-88	1987-88
Murray, Pat	Phi.	2	25	3	1	4	15	....	....	....	....	....	....	1990-91	1991-92
Murray, Randy	Tor.	1	3	0	0	0	2	....	....	....	....	....	....	1969-70	1969-70
Murray, Terry	Cal., Phi., Det., Wsh.	15	302	4	76	80	199	18	2	2	4	10	....	1972-73	1981-82
Murray, Troy	Chi., Wpg., Ott., Pit., Col.	15	915	230	354	584	875	113	17	26	43	145	1	1981-82	1995-96
Murzyn, Dana	Hfd., Cgy., Van.	14	838	52	152	204	1571	82	9	10	19	166	1	1985-86	1998-99
Myers, Hap	Buf.	1	13	0	0	0	6	....	....	....	....	....	....	1970-71	1970-71
Myles, Vic	NYR	1	45	6	9	15	57	....	....	....	....	....	....	1942-43	1942-43

N

Nachbaur, Don	Hfd., Edm., Phi.	8	223	23	46	69	465	11	1	1	2	24	....	1980-81	1989-90
Nahrgang, Jim	Det.	3	57	5	12	17	34	....	....	....	....	....	....	1974-75	1976-77
Nanne, Lou	Min.	11	635	68	157	225	356	32	4	10	14	8	....	1967-68	1977-78
Nantais, Rich	Min.	3	63	5	4	9	79	....	....	....	....	....	....	1974-75	1976-77
Napier, Mark	Mtl., Min., Edm., Buf.	11	767	235	306	541	157	82	18	24	42	11	2	1978-79	1988-89
Naslund, Mats	Mtl., Bos.	9	651	251	383	634	111	102	35	57	92	33	1	1982-83	1994-95

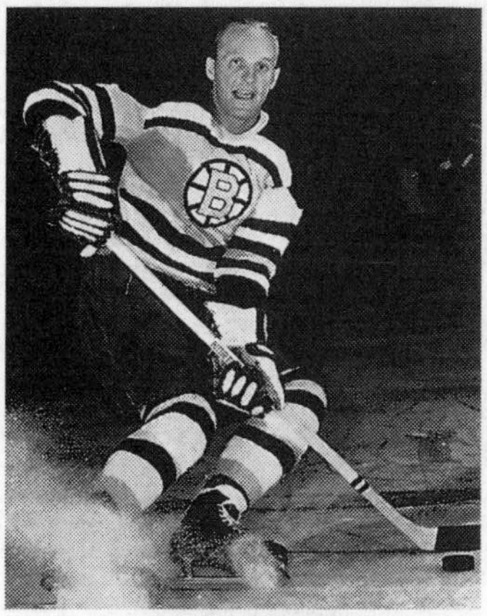
Doug Mohns

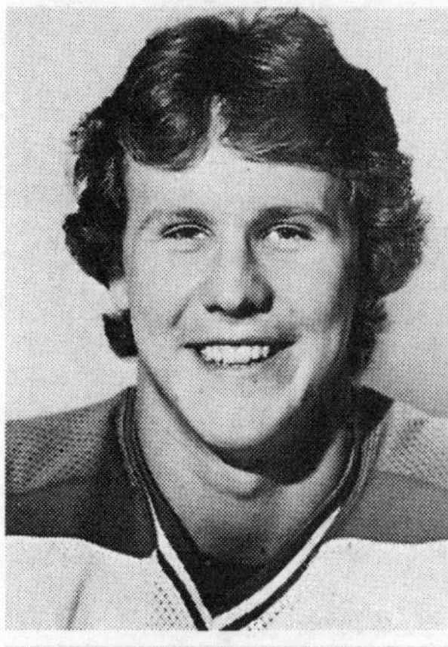
Brian Mullen

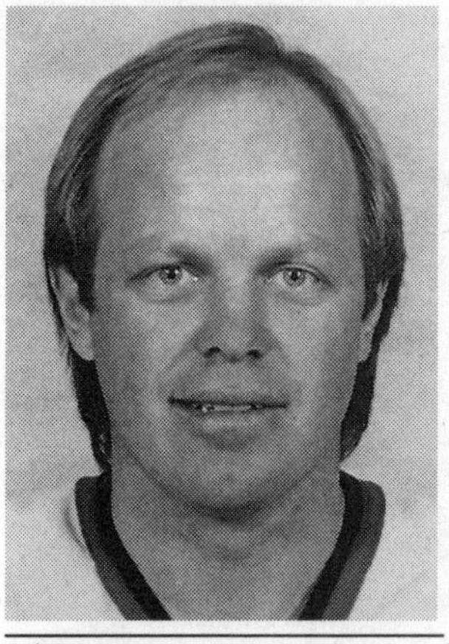
Bob Murray

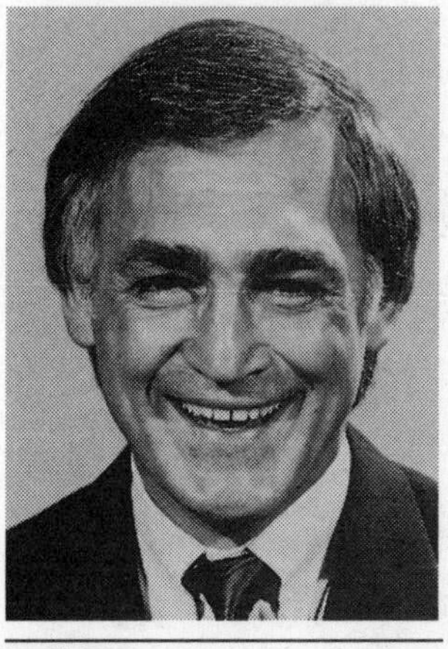
Lou Nanne

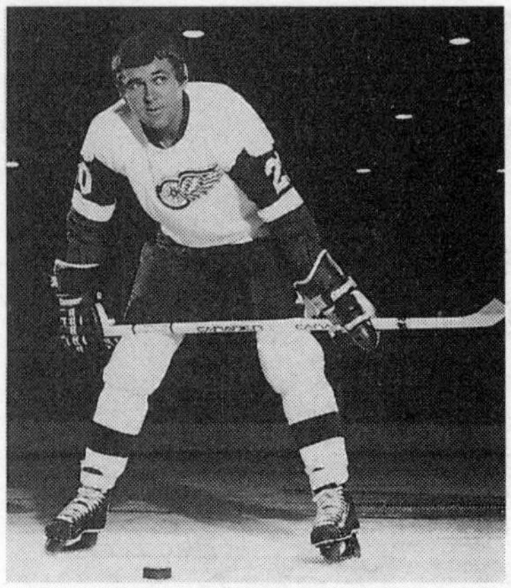

Vaclav Nedomansky

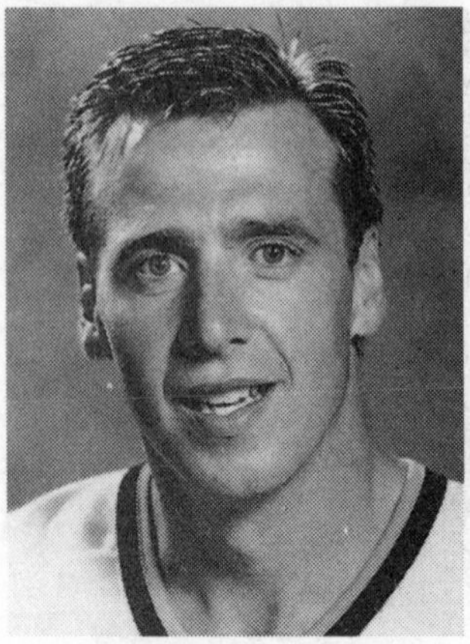

Bernie Nicholls

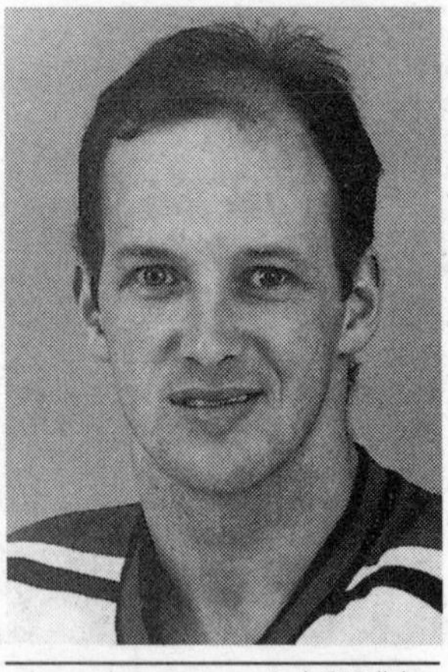

Jack O'Callahan

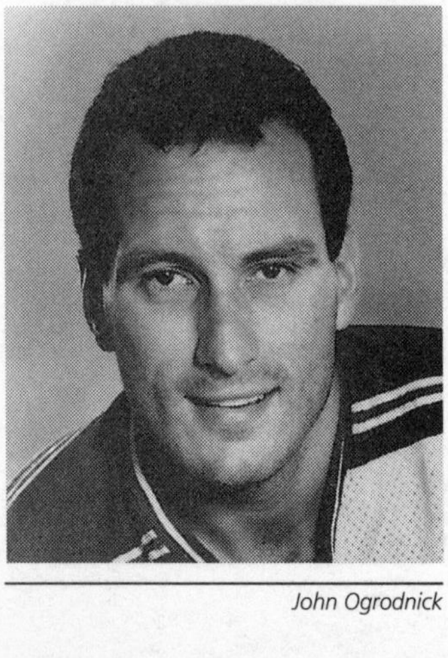

John Ogrodnick

			Regular Schedule					Playoffs							
Name	NHL Teams	NHL Seasons	GP	G	A	TP	PIM	GP	G	A	TP	PIM	NHL Cup Wins	First NHL Season	Last NHL Season
Nattrass, Ralph	Chi.	4	223	18	38	56	308	....	....	....	....	....	....	1946-47	1949-50
Nattress, Ric	Mtl., St.L., Cgy., Tor., Phi.	11	536	29	135	164	377	67	5	10	15	60	1	1982-83	1992-93
Natyshak, Mike	Que.	1	4	0	0	0	0	....	....	....	....	....	....	1987-88	1987-88
‡ Neaton, Pat	Pit.	1	9	1	1	2	12	....	....	....	....	....	....	1993-94	1993-94
Nechayev, Viktor	L.A.	1	3	1	0	1	0	....	....	....	....	....	....	1982-83	1982-83
Nedomansky, Vaclav	Det., NYR, St.L.	6	421	122	156	278	88	7	3	5	8	0	....	1977-78	1982-83
Needham, Mike	Pit., Dal.	3	86	9	5	14	16	14	2	0	2	4	1	1991-92	1993-94
Neely, Bob	Tor., Col.	5	283	39	59	98	266	26	5	7	12	15	....	1973-74	1977-78
Neely, Cam	Van., Bos.	13	726	395	299	694	1241	93	57	32	89	168	....	1983-84	1995-96
Neilson, Jim	NYR, Cal., Cle.	16	1023	69	299	368	904	65	1	17	18	61	....	1962-63	1977-78
Nelson, Gordie	Tor.	1	3	0	0	0	11	....	....	....	....	....	....	1969-70	1969-70
‡ Nelson, Todd	Pit., Wsh.	2	3	1	0	1	2	4	0	0	0	0	....	1991-92	1993-94
Nemeth, Steve	NYR	1	12	2	0	2	2	....	....	....	....	....	....	1987-88	1987-88
Nesterenko, Eric	Tor., Chi.	21	1219	250	324	574	1273	124	13	24	37	127	1	1951-52	1971-72
Nethery, Lance	NYR, Edm.	2	41	11	14	25	14	14	5	3	8	9	....	1980-81	1981-82
Neufeld, Ray	Hfd., Wpg., Bos.	11	595	157	200	357	816	28	8	6	14	55	....	1979-80	1989-90
• Neville, Mike	Tor., NYA	3	65	5	5	10	14	2	0	0	0	0	....	1924-25	1930-31
Nevin, Bob	Tor., NYR, Min., L.A.	18	1128	307	419	726	211	84	16	18	34	24	2	1957-58	1975-76
Newberry, John	Mtl., Hfd.	4	22	0	4	4	6	2	0	0	0	0	....	1982-83	1985-86
Newell, Rick	Det.	2	6	0	0	0	0	....	....	....	....	....	....	1972-73	1973-74
Newman, Dan	NYR, Mtl., Edm.	4	126	17	24	41	63	3	0	0	0	4	....	1976-77	1979-80
• Newman, John	Det.	1	8	1	1	2	0	....	....	....	....	....	....	1930-31	1930-31
Nicholls, Bernie	L.A., NYR, Edm., N.J., Chi., S.J.	18	1127	475	734	1209	1292	118	42	72	114	164	....	1981-82	1998-99
Nicholson, Al	Bos.	2	19	0	1	1	4	....	....	....	....	....	....	1955-56	1956-57
• Nicholson, Ed	Det.	1	1	0	0	0	0	....	....	....	....	....	....	1947-48	1947-48
• Nicholson, Hickey	Chi.	1	2	1	0	1	0	....	....	....	....	....	....	1937-38	1937-38
Nicholson, Neil	Oak., NYI	4	39	3	1	4	23	2	0	0	0	0	....	1969-70	1977-78
Nicholson, Paul	Wsh.	3	62	4	8	12	18	....	....	....	....	....	....	1974-75	1976-77
Nicolson, Graeme	Bos., Col., NYR	3	52	2	7	9	60	....	....	....	....	....	....	1978-79	1982-83
‡ Nieckar, Barry	Hfd., Cgy., Ana.	4	8	0	0	0	21	....	....	....	....	....	....	1992-93	1997-98
Niekamp, Jim	Det.	2	29	0	2	2	37	....	....	....	....	....	....	1970-71	1971-72
Nielsen, Kirk	Bos.	1	6	0	0	0	0	....	....	....	....	....	....	1997-98	1997-98
‡ Nienhuis, Kraig	Bos.	3	87	20	16	36	39	2	0	0	0	14	....	1985-86	1987-88
• Nighbor, Frank	Ott., Tor.	13	349	139	98	237	249	20	4	9	13	13	1	1917-18	1929-30
Nigro, Frank	Tor.	2	68	8	18	26	39	3	0	0	0	2	....	1982-83	1983-84
‡ Nikulin, Igor	Ana.	1	....	....	....	....	....	1	0	0	0	0	....	1996-97	1996-97
Nilan, Chris	Mtl., NYR, Bos.	13	688	110	115	225	3043	111	8	9	17	541	1	1979-80	1991-92
Nill, Jim	St.L., Van., Bos., Wpg., Det.	11	524	58	87	145	854	59	10	5	15	203	....	1981-82	1989-90
Nilsson, Kent	Atl., Cgy., Min., Edm.	9	553	264	422	686	116	59	11	41	52	14	1	1979-80	1994-95
Nilsson, Ulf	NYR	4	170	57	112	169	85	25	8	14	22	27	....	1978-79	1982-83
Nistico, Lou	Col.	1	3	0	0	0	0	....	....	....	....	....	....	1977-78	1977-78
• Noble, Reg	Tor., Mtl.M., Det.	16	510	168	106	274	916	18	2	2	4	33	....	1917-18	1932-33
Noel, Claude	Wsh.	1	7	0	0	0	0	....	....	....	....	....	....	1979-80	1979-80
• Nolan, Paddy	Tor.	1	2	0	0	0	0	....	....	....	....	....	....	1921-22	1921-22
Nolan, Ted	Det., Pit.	3	78	6	16	22	105	....	....	....	....	....	....	1981-82	1985-86
Nolet, Simon	Phi., K.C., Pit., Col.	10	562	150	182	332	187	34	6	3	9	8	1	1967-68	1976-77
‡ Nordmark, Robert	St.L., Van.	4	236	13	70	83	254	7	3	2	5	8	....	1987-88	1990-91
Noris, Joe	Pit., St.L., Buf.	3	55	2	5	7	22	....	....	....	....	....	....	1971-72	1973-74
‡ Norris, Dwayne	Que., Ana.	3	20	2	4	6	8	....	....	....	....	....	....	1993-94	1995-96
Norrish, Rod	Min.	2	21	3	3	6	2	....	....	....	....	....	....	1973-74	1974-75
• Northcott, Baldy	Mtl.M., Chi.	11	446	133	112	245	273	31	8	5	13	14	1	1928-29	1938-39
Norwich, Craig	Wpg., St.L., Col.	2	104	17	58	75	60	....	....	....	....	....	....	1979-80	1980-81
Norwood, Lee	Que., Wsh., St.L., Det., N.J., Hfd., Cgy.	12	503	58	153	211	1099	65	6	22	28	171	....	1980-81	1993-94
Novy, Milan	Wsh.	1	73	18	30	48	16	2	0	0	0	0	....	1982-83	1982-83
Nowak, Hank	Pit., Det., Bos.	4	180	26	29	55	161	13	1	0	1	8	....	1973-74	1976-77
Nykoluk, Mike	Tor.	1	32	3	1	4	20	....	....	....	....	....	....	1956-57	1956-57
Nylund, Gary	Tor., Chi., NYI	11	608	32	139	171	1235	24	0	6	6	63	....	1982-83	1992-93
• Nyrop, Bill	Mtl., Min.	4	207	12	51	63	101	35	1	7	8	22	3	1975-76	1981-82
Nystrom, Bob	NYI	14	900	235	278	513	1248	157	39	44	83	236	4	1972-73	1985-86

O

O'Brien, Dennis	Min., Col., Cle., Bos.	10	592	31	91	122	1017	34	1	2	3	101	....	1970-71	1979-80
O'Brien, Ellard	Bos.	1	2	0	0	0	0	....	....	....	....	....	....	1955-56	1955-56
O'Callahan, Jack	Chi., N.J.	7	389	27	104	131	541	32	4	11	15	41	....	1982-83	1988-89
O'Connell, Mike	Chi., Bos., Det.	13	860	105	334	439	605	82	8	24	32	64	....	1977-78	1989-90
• O'Connor, Buddy	Mtl., NYR	10	509	140	257	397	34	53	15	21	36	6	2	1941-42	1950-51
O'Connor, Myles	N.J., Ana.	4	43	3	4	7	69	....	....	....	....	....	....	1990-91	1993-94
O'Donnell, Fred	Bos.	2	115	15	11	26	98	5	0	1	1	5	....	1972-73	1973-74
O'Donoghue, Don	Oak., Cal.	3	125	18	17	35	35	3	0	0	0	0	....	1969-70	1971-72
O'Dwyer, Bill	L.A., Bos.	5	120	9	13	22	108	10	0	0	0	2	....	1983-84	1989-90
O'Flaherty, Gerry	Tor., Van., Atl.	8	438	99	95	194	168	7	2	2	4	6	....	1971-72	1978-79
O'Flaherty, Peanuts	NYA, Bro.	2	21	5	1	6	0	....	....	....	....	....	....	1940-41	1941-42
• O'Grady, George	Mtl.	1	4	0	0	0	0	....	....	....	....	....	....	1917-18	1917-18
• O'Neil, Jim	Bos., Mtl.	6	156	6	30	36	109	9	1	1	2	13	....	1933-34	1941-42
O'Neil, Paul	Van., Bos.	2	6	0	0	0	0	....	....	....	....	....	....	1973-74	1975-76
• O'Neill, Tom	Tor.	2	66	10	12	22	53	4	0	0	0	6	1	1943-44	1944-45
O'Ree, Willie	Bos.	2	45	4	10	14	26	....	....	....	....	....	....	1957-58	1960-61
O'Regan, Tom	Pit.	3	61	5	12	17	10	....	....	....	....	....	....	1983-84	1985-86
O'Reilly, Terry	Bos.	14	891	204	402	606	2095	108	25	42	67	335	....	1971-72	1984-85
O'Shea, Danny	Min., Chi., St.L.	5	369	64	115	179	265	39	3	7	10	61	....	1968-69	1972-73
O'Shea, Kevin	Buf., St.L.	3	134	13	18	31	85	12	2	1	3	10	....	1970-71	1972-73
• Oatman, Russell	Det., Mtl.M., NYR	3	120	20	9	29	100	15	1	0	1	18	....	1926-27	1928-29
Oddleifson, Chris	Bos., Van.	9	524	95	191	286	464	14	1	6	7	8	....	1972-73	1980-81
Odelein, Selmar	Edm.	3	18	0	2	2	35	....	....	....	....	....	....	1985-86	1988-89
Odrowski, Gerry	Det., Oak., St.L.	6	309	12	19	31	111	30	0	1	1	16	....	1960-61	1971-72
Ogilvie, Brian	Chi., St.L.	6	90	15	21	36	29	....	....	....	....	....	....	1972-73	1978-79
Ogrodnick, John	Det., Que., NYR	14	928	402	425	827	260	41	18	8	26	6	....	1979-80	1992-93
‡ Ojanen, Janne	N.J.	4	98	21	23	44	28	3	0	2	2	0	....	1988-89	1992-93
Okerlund, Todd	NYI	1	4	0	0	0	2	....	....	....	....	....	....	1987-88	1987-88
Oksiuta, Roman	Edm., Van., Ana., Pit.	4	153	46	41	87	100	10	2	3	5	0	....	1993-94	1996-97
• Oliver, Harry	Bos., NYA	11	463	127	85	212	147	35	10	6	16	24	1	1926-27	1936-37
Oliver, Murray	Det., Bos., Tor., Min.	17	1127	274	454	728	320	35	9	16	25	10	....	1957-58	1974-75
Olmstead, Bert	Chi., Mtl., Tor.	14	848	181	421	602	884	115	16	43	59	101	5	1948-49	1961-62
‡ Olsen, Darryl	Cgy.	1	1	0	0	0	0	....	....	....	....	....	....	1991-92	1991-92
Olson, Dennis	Det.	1	4	0	0	0	0	....	....	....	....	....	....	1957-58	1957-58
‡ Olsson, Christer	St.L., Ott.	2	56	4	12	16	24	3	0	0	0	0	....	1995-96	1996-97
Orban, Bill	Chi., Min.	3	114	8	15	23	67	3	0	0	0	0	....	1967-68	1969-70
Orlando, Gates	Buf.	3	98	18	26	44	51	5	0	4	4	14	....	1984-85	1986-87
Orlando, Jimmy	Det.	6	199	6	25	31	375	36	0	9	9	105	1	1936-37	1942-43
Orleski, Dave	Mtl.	2	2	0	0	0	0	....	....	....	....	....	....	1980-81	1981-82
Orr, Bobby	Bos., Chi.	12	657	270	645	915	953	74	26	66	92	107	2	1966-67	1978-79
‡ Osborne, Keith	St.L., T.B.	2	16	1	3	4	16	....	....	....	....	....	....	1989-90	1992-93
Osborne, Mark	Det., NYR, Tor., Wpg.	14	919	212	319	531	1152	87	12	16	28	141	....	1981-82	1994-95
Osburn, Randy	Tor., Phi.	2	27	0	2	2	0	....	....	....	....	....	....	1972-73	1974-75
Osiecki, Mark	Cgy., Ott., Wpg., Min.	2	93	3	11	14	43	....	....	....	....	....	....	1991-92	1992-93
Otevrel, Jaroslav	S.J.	2	16	3	4	7	2	....	....	....	....	....	....	1992-93	1993-94
Otto, Joel	Cgy., Phi.	14	943	195	313	508	1934	122	27	47	74	207	1	1984-85	1997-98
Ouellette, Eddie	Chi.	1	43	3	2	5	11	1	0	0	0	0	....	1935-36	1935-36
Ouellette, Gerry	Bos.	1	34	5	4	9	0	....	....	....	....	....	....	1960-61	1960-61
Owchar, Dennis	Pit., Col.	6	288	30	85	115	200	10	1	1	2	8	....	1974-75	1979-80
• Owen, George	Bos.	5	183	44	33	77	151	21	2	5	7	25	1	1928-29	1932-33

P

Pachal, Clayton	Bos., Col.	3	35	2	3	5	95	....	....	....	....	....	....	1976-77	1978-79
Paddock, John	Wsh., Phi., Que.	9	87	8	14	22	86	5	2	0	2	0	....	1975-76	1982-83
‡ Paek, Jim	Pit., L.A., Ott.	5	217	5	29	34	155	27	1	4	5	8	2	1990-91	1994-95
Paiement, Rosaire	Phi., Van.	5	190	48	52	100	343	3	3	0	3	0	....	1967-68	1971-72
Paiement, Wilf	K.C., Col., Tor., Que., NYR, Buf., Pit.	14	946	356	458	814	1757	69	18	17	35	185	....	1974-75	1987-88
Palangio, Pete	Mtl.C., Det., Chi.	5	71	13	10	23	28	7	0	0	0	0	1	1926-27	1937-38

Name	NHL Teams	NHL Seasons	Regular Schedule GP	G	A	TP	PIM	Playoffs GP	G	A	TP	PIM	NHL Cup Wins	First NHL Season	Last NHL Season
Palazzari, Aldo	Bos., NYR	2	35	8	3	11	4	....	....	....	....	....	....	1943-44	1944-45
Palazzari, Doug	St.L.	4	108	18	20	38	23	2	0	0	0	0	....	1974-75	1978-79
Palmer, Brad	Min., Bos.	3	168	32	38	70	58	29	9	5	14	16	....	1980-81	1982-83
Palmer, Rob	Chi.	3	16	0	3	3	2	....	....	....	....	....	....	1973-74	1975-76
Palmer, Robert	L.A., N.J.	7	320	9	101	110	115	8	1	2	3	6	....	1977-78	1983-84
● Panagabko, Ed	Bos.	2	29	0	3	3	38	....	....	....	....	....	....	1955-56	1956-57
‡ Panteleev, Grigori	Bos., NYI	4	54	8	6	14	12	....	....	....	....	....	....	1992-93	1995-96
● Papike, Joe	Chi.	3	20	3	3	6	4	5	0	2	2	0	....	1940-41	1944-45
Pappin, Jim	Tor., Chi., Cal., Cle.	14	767	278	295	573	667	92	33	34	67	101	2	1963-64	1976-77
Paradise, Bob	Min., Atl., Pit., Wsh.	8	368	8	54	62	393	12	0	1	1	19	....	1971-72	1978-79
Pargeter, George	Mtl.	1	4	0	0	0	0	....	....	....	....	....	....	1946-47	1946-47
Parise, Jean-Paul	Bos., Tor., Min., NYI, Cle.	14	890	238	356	594	706	86	27	31	58	87	....	1965-66	1978-79
Parizeau, Michel	St.L., Phi.	1	58	3	14	17	18	....	....	....	....	....	....	1971-72	1971-72
Park, Brad	NYR, Bos., Det.	17	1113	213	683	896	1429	161	35	90	125	217	....	1968-69	1984-85
Parker, Jeff	Buf., Hfd.	5	141	16	19	35	163	5	0	0	0	26	....	1986-87	1990-91
● Parkes, Ernie	Mtl.M.	1	17	0	0	0	2	....	....	....	....	....	....	1924-25	1924-25
‡ Parks, Greg	NYI	3	23	1	2	3	6	2	0	0	0	0	....	1990-91	1992-93
● Parsons, George	Tor.	3	78	12	13	25	20	7	3	2	5	11	....	1936-37	1938-39
● Pasek, Dusan	Min.	1	48	4	10	14	30	2	1	0	1	0	....	1988-89	1988-89
Pasin, Dave	Bos., L.A.	2	76	18	19	37	50	3	0	1	1	0	....	1985-86	1988-89
Paslawski, Greg	Mtl., St.L., Wpg., Buf., Que., Phi., Cgy.	11	650	187	185	372	169	60	19	13	32	25	....	1983-84	1993-94
Paterson, Joe	Det., Phi., L.A., NYR	9	291	19	37	56	829	22	3	4	7	77	....	1980-81	1988-89
Paterson, Mark	Hfd.	4	29	3	3	6	33	....	....	....	....	....	....	1982-83	1985-86
Paterson, Rick	Chi.	9	430	50	43	93	136	61	7	10	17	51	....	1978-79	1986-87
Patey, Doug	Wsh.	3	45	4	2	6	8	....	....	....	....	....	....	1976-77	1978-79
Patey, Larry	Cal., St.L., NYR	12	717	153	163	316	631	40	8	10	18	57	....	1973-74	1984-85
Patrick, Craig	Cal., St.L., K.C., Wsh.	11	401	72	91	163	61	2	0	1	1	0	....	1971-72	1978-79
Patrick, Glenn	St.L., Cal., Cle.	4	38	2	3	5	72	....	....	....	....	....	....	1973-74	1976-77
● Patrick, Lester	NYR	3	1	0	0	0	2	....	....	....	....	....	....	1926-27	1926-27
● Patrick, Lynn	NYR	10	455	145	190	335	240	44	10	6	16	22	1	1934-35	1945-46
● Patrick, Muzz	NYR	5	166	5	26	31	133	25	4	0	4	34	1	1937-38	1945-46
Patrick, Steve	Buf., NYR, Que.	6	250	40	68	108	242	12	0	1	1	12	....	1980-81	1985-86
Patterson, Colin	Cgy., Buf.	10	504	96	109	205	239	85	12	17	29	57	1	1983-84	1992-93
Patterson, Dennis	K.C., Phi.	3	138	6	22	28	67	....	....	....	....	....	....	1974-75	1979-80
● Patterson, George	Tor., Mtl.C., NYA, Bos., Det., St.L.	9	284	51	27	78	218	3	0	0	0	2	....	1926-27	1934-35
● Paul, Butch	Det.	1	3	0	0	0	0	....	....	....	....	....	....	1964-65	1964-65
● Paulhus, Rollie	Mtl.C.	1	33	0	0	0	0	....	....	....	....	....	....	1925-26	1925-26
Pavelich, Mark	NYR, Min., S.J.	7	355	137	192	329	340	23	7	17	24	14	....	1981-82	1991-92
Pavelich, Marty	Det.	10	634	93	159	252	454	91	13	15	28	74	4	1947-48	1956-57
Pavese, Jim	St.L., NYR, Det., Hfd.	8	328	13	44	57	689	34	0	6	6	81	....	1981-82	1988-89
● Payer, Evariste	Mtl.C.	1	1	0	0	0	0	....	....	....	....	....	....	1917-18	1917-18
‡ Payne, Davis	Bos.	2	22	0	1	1	14	....	....	....	....	....	....	1995-96	1996-97
Payne, Steve	Min.	10	613	228	238	466	435	71	35	35	70	60	....	1978-79	1987-88
Paynter, Kent	Chi., Wsh., Wpg., Ott.	7	37	1	3	4	69	4	0	0	0	10	....	1987-88	1993-94
Peake, Pat	Wsh.	5	134	28	41	69	105	13	2	2	4	20	....	1993-94	1997-98
● Pearson, Mel	NYR, Pit.	5	38	2	6	8	25	....	....	....	....	....	....	1959-60	1967-68
Pedersen, Allen	Bos., Min., Hfd.	8	428	5	36	41	487	64	0	0	0	91	....	1986-87	1993-94
Pederson, Barry	Bos., Van., Pit., Hfd.	12	701	238	416	654	472	34	22	30	52	25	1	1980-81	1991-92
‡ Pederson, Mark	Mtl., Phi., S.J., Det.	5	169	35	50	85	77	2	0	0	0	0	....	1989-90	1993-94
‡ Pederson, Tom	S.J., Tor.	5	240	20	49	69	142	24	1	11	12	10	....	1992-93	1996-97
Peer, Bert	Det.	1	1	0	0	0	0	....	....	....	....	....	....	1939-40	1939-40
Peirson, Johnny	Bos.	11	545	153	173	326	315	49	10	16	26	26	....	1946-47	1957-58
Pelensky, Perry	Chi.	1	4	0	0	0	5	....	....	....	....	....	....	1983-84	1983-84
Pelletier, Roger	Phi.	1	1	0	0	0	0	....	....	....	....	....	....	1967-68	1967-68
Peloffy, Andre	Wsh.	1	9	0	0	0	0	....	....	....	....	....	....	1974-75	1974-75
Peluso, Mike	Chi., Ott., N.J., St.L., Cgy.	9	458	38	52	90	1951	62	3	4	7	107	1	1989-90	1997-98
Pelyk, Mike	Tor.	9	441	26	88	114	566	40	0	3	3	41	....	1967-68	1977-78
Penney, Chad	Ott.	1	3	0	0	0	2	....	....	....	....	....	....	1993-94	1993-94
Pennington, Cliff	Mtl., Bos.	3	101	17	42	59	6	....	....	....	....	....	....	1960-61	1962-63
Peplinski, Jim	Cgy.	11	711	161	263	424	1467	99	15	31	46	382	1	1980-81	1994-95
Perlini, Fred	Tor.	2	8	2	3	5	0	....	....	....	....	....	....	1981-82	1983-84
Perreault, Fern	NYR	2	3	0	0	0	0	....	....	....	....	....	....	1947-48	1949-50
Perreault, Gilbert	Buf.	17	1191	512	814	1326	500	90	33	70	103	44	....	1970-71	1986-87
Perry, Brian	Oak., Buf.	3	96	16	29	45	24	8	1	1	2	4	....	1968-69	1970-71
Persson, Stefan	NYI	9	622	52	317	369	574	102	7	50	57	69	4	1977-78	1985-86
Pesut, George	Cal.	2	92	3	22	25	130	....	....	....	....	....	....	1974-75	1975-76
● Peters, Frank	NYR	1	43	0	0	0	59	4	0	0	0	2	....	1930-31	1930-31
Peters, Garry	Mtl., NYR, Phi., Bos.	8	311	34	34	68	261	9	2	2	4	31	1	1964-65	1971-72
Peters, Jimmy Jr.	Det., L.A.	9	309	37	36	73	48	11	0	2	2	2	....	1964-65	1974-75
Peters, Jimmy Sr.	Mtl., Bos., Det., Chi.	9	574	125	150	275	186	60	5	9	14	22	3	1945-46	1953-54
Peters, Steve	Col.	1	2	0	1	1	0	....	....	....	....	....	....	1979-80	1979-80
Peterson, Brent	Det., Buf., Van., Hfd.	13	620	72	141	213	484	31	4	4	8	65	....	1978-79	1988-89
‡ Petit, Michel	Van., NYR, Que., Tor., Cgy., L.A., T.B., Edm., Phi., Phx.	16	827	90	238	328	1839	19	0	2	2	61	....	1982-83	1997-98
‡ Petrenko, Sergei	Buf.	1	14	0	4	4	0	....	....	....	....	....	....	1993-94	1993-94
Pettersson, Jorgen	St.L., Hfd., Wsh.	6	435	174	192	366	117	44	15	12	27	4	....	1980-81	1985-86
● Pettinger, Eric	Bos., Tor., Ott.	3	98	7	12	19	83	4	1	0	1	8	....	1928-29	1930-31
● Pettinger, Gord	NYR, Det., Bos.	8	292	42	74	116	77	47	4	5	9	11	4	1932-33	1939-40
Phair, Lyle	L.A.	3	48	6	7	13	12	1	0	0	0	0	....	1985-86	1987-88
Phillipoff, Harold	Atl., Chi.	3	141	26	57	83	267	6	0	2	2	9	....	1977-78	1979-80
● Phillips, Batt	Mtl.M.	1	27	1	1	2	6	4	0	0	0	2	....	1929-30	1929-30
Phillips, Charlie	Mtl.	1	17	0	0	0	6	....	....	....	....	....	....	1942-43	1942-43
● Phillips, Merlyn	Mtl.M., NYA	8	302	52	31	83	232	24	5	1	6	19	....	1925-26	1932-33
Picard, Noel	Mtl., St.L., Atl.	7	335	12	63	75	616	50	2	11	13	167	1	1964-65	1972-73
Picard, Robert	Wsh., Tor., Mtl., Wpg., Que., Det.	13	899	104	319	423	1025	36	5	15	20	39	....	1977-78	1989-90
Picard, Roger	St.L.	1	15	2	2	4	21	....	....	....	....	....	....	1967-68	1967-68
Pichette, Dave	Que., St.L., N.J., NYR	7	322	41	140	181	348	28	3	7	10	54	....	1980-81	1987-88
Picketts, Hal	NYA	1	48	3	1	4	32	....	....	....	....	....	....	1933-34	1933-34
Pidhirny, Harry	Bos.	1	2	0	0	0	0	....	....	....	....	....	....	1957-58	1957-58
Pierce, Randy	Col., N.J., Hfd.	8	277	62	76	138	223	2	0	0	0	0	....	1977-78	1984-85
Pike, Alf	NYR	6	234	42	77	119	145	21	4	2	6	12	1	1939-40	1946-47
Pilote, Pierre	Chi., Tor.	14	890	80	418	498	1251	86	8	53	61	102	1	1955-56	1968-69
Pinder, Gerry	Chi., Cal.	3	223	55	69	124	135	17	0	4	4	6	....	1969-70	1971-72
Pirus, Alex	Min., Det.	4	159	30	28	58	94	2	0	1	1	2	....	1976-77	1979-80
● Pitre, Didier	Mtl.C.	6	127	64	34	98	84	9	2	4	6	16	....	1917-18	1922-23
● Plager, Barclay	St.L.	10	614	44	187	231	1115	68	3	20	23	182	....	1967-68	1976-77
Plager, Bill	Min., St.L., Atl.	9	263	4	34	38	294	31	0	2	2	26	....	1967-68	1975-76
Plager, Bob	NYR, St.L.	14	644	20	126	146	802	74	2	17	19	195	....	1964-65	1977-78
Plamondon, Gerry	Mtl.	5	74	7	13	20	10	11	5	2	7	2	1	1945-46	1950-51
Plante, Cam	Tor.	1	2	0	0	0	0	....	....	....	....	....	....	1984-85	1984-85
Plante, Pierre	Phi., St.L., Chi., NYR, Que.	9	599	125	172	297	599	33	2	6	8	51	....	1971-72	1979-80
Plantery, Mark	Wpg.	1	25	1	5	6	14	....	....	....	....	....	....	1980-81	1980-81
‡ Plavsic, Adrien	St.L., Van., T.B., Ana.	8	214	16	56	72	161	13	1	7	8	4	....	1989-90	1996-97
● Plaxton, Hugh	Mtl.M.	1	15	1	2	3	4	....	....	....	....	....	....	1932-33	1932-33
Playfair, Jim	Edm., Chi.	3	21	2	4	6	51	....	....	....	....	....	....	1983-84	1988-89
Playfair, Larry	Buf., L.A.	12	688	26	94	120	1812	43	0	6	6	111	....	1978-79	1989-90
Pleau, Larry	Mtl.	3	94	9	15	24	27	4	0	0	0	0	....	1969-70	1971-72
Pletsch, Charles	Ham.	1	1	0	0	0	0	....	....	....	....	....	....	1920-21	1920-21
Plett, Willi	Atl., Cgy., Min., Bos.	13	834	222	215	437	2572	83	24	22	46	466	....	1975-76	1987-88
Plumb, Rob	Det.	2	14	3	2	5	2	....	....	....	....	....	....	1977-78	1978-79
Plumb, Ron	Hfd.	1	26	3	4	7	14	....	....	....	....	....	....	1979-80	1979-80
Pocza, Harvie	Wsh.	2	3	0	0	0	2	....	....	....	....	....	....	1979-80	1981-82
Poddubny, Walt	Edm., Tor., NYR, Que., N.J.	11	468	184	238	422	454	19	7	2	9	12	....	1981-82	1991-92
‡ Podloski, Ray	Bos.	1	8	0	1	1	17	....	....	....	....	....	....	1988-89	1988-89
Podolsky, Nels	Det.	1	1	0	0	0	0	7	0	0	0	4	....	1948-49	1948-49
Poeta, Tony	Chi.	1	1	0	0	0	0	....	....	....	....	....	....	1951-52	1951-52
Poile, Bud	Tor., Chi., Det., NYR, Bos.	7	311	107	122	229	91	23	4	5	9	8	1	1942-43	1949-50
Poile, Don	Det.	2	66	7	9	16	12	4	0	0	0	0	....	1954-55	1957-58
Poirier, Gordie	Mtl.	1	10	0	0	0	0	....	....	....	....	....	....	1939-40	1939-40
Polanic, Tom	Min.	2	19	0	2	2	53	5	1	1	2	4	....	1969-70	1970-71
Polich, John	NYR	2	3	0	1	1	0	....	....	....	....	....	....	1939-40	1940-41
Polich, Mike	Mtl., Min.	5	226	24	29	53	57	23	2	1	3	2	1	1976-77	1980-81

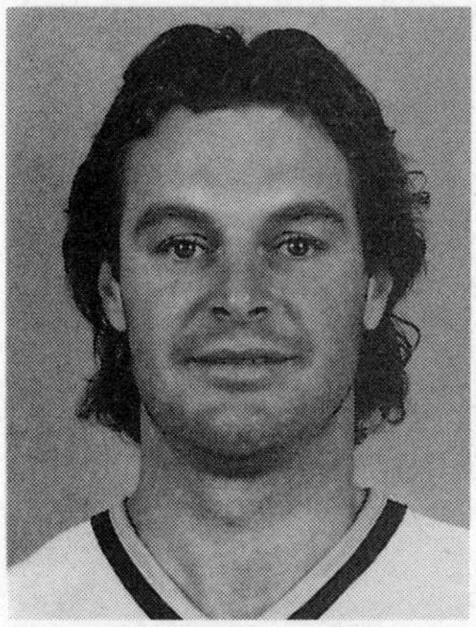
Michel Petit

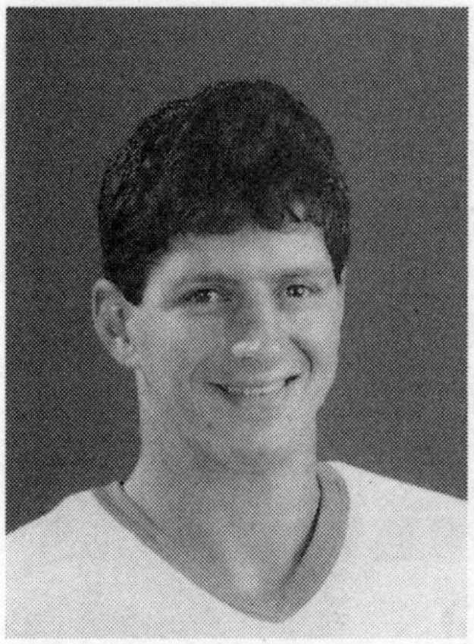
Robert Picard

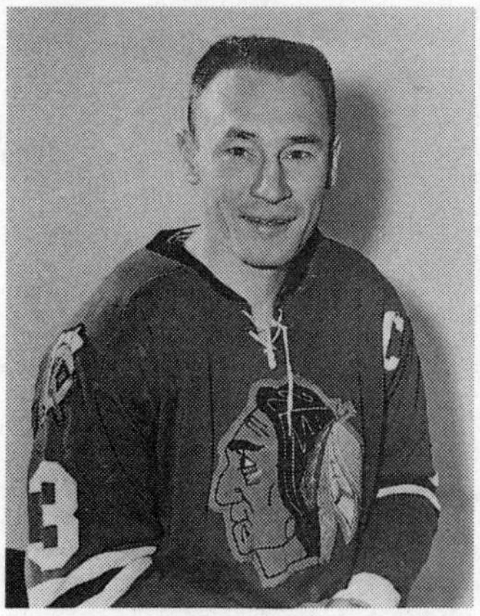
Pierre Pilote

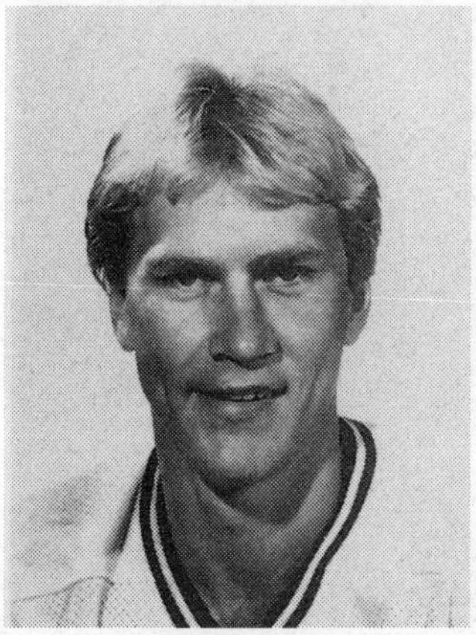
Willi Plett

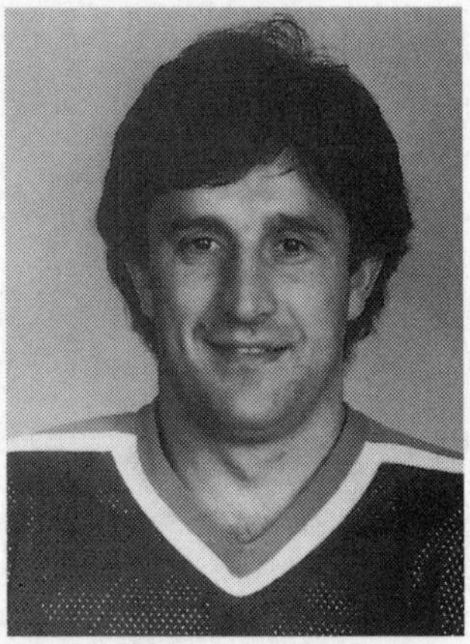

Jaroslav Pouzar

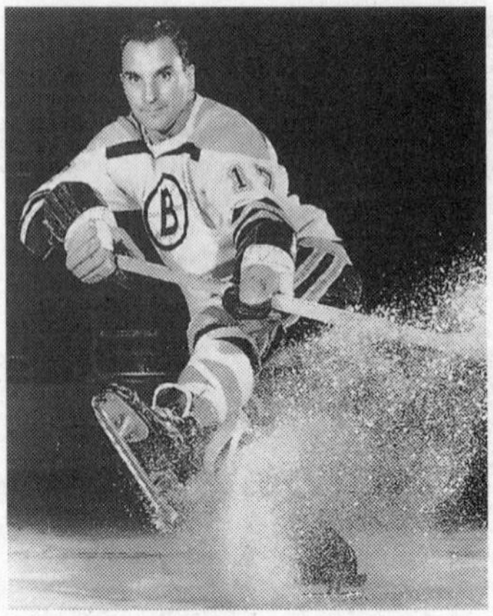

Dean Prentice

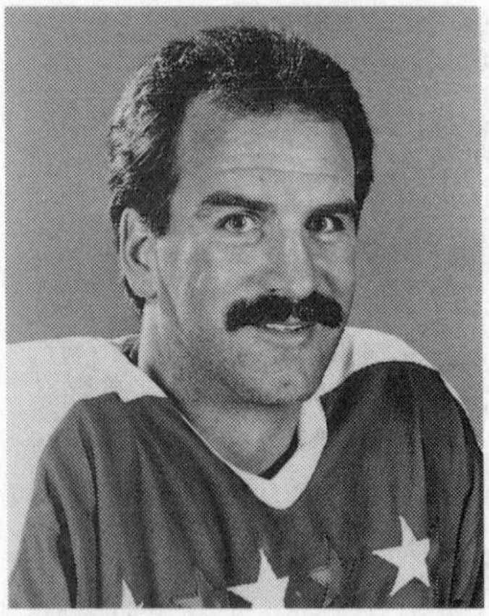

Joel Quenneville

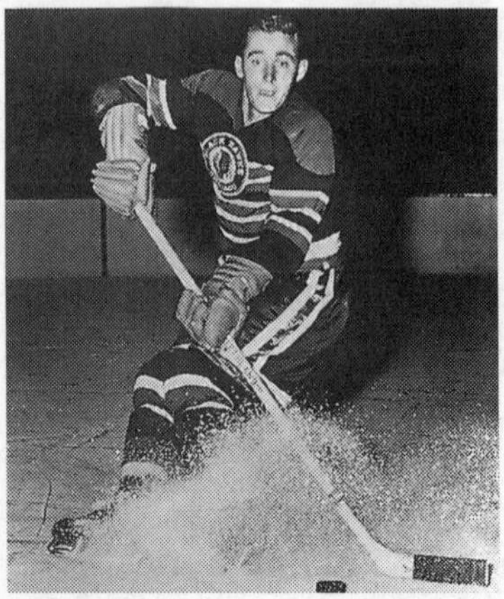

Clare Raglan

Name	NHL Teams	NHL Seasons	Regular Schedule GP	G	A	TP	PIM	Playoffs GP	G	A	TP	PIM	NHL Cup Wins	First NHL Season	Last NHL Season
Polis, Greg	Pit., St.L., NYR, Wsh.	10	615	174	169	343	391	7	0	2	2	6	....	1970-71	1979-80
Poliziani, Dan	Bos.	1	1	0	0	0	0	3	0	0	0	0	....	1958-59	1958-59
Polonich, Dennis	Det.	8	390	59	82	141	1242	7	1	0	1	19	....	1974-75	1982-83
Pooley, Paul	Wpg.	2	15	0	3	3	0	....	....	....	....	....	....	1984-85	1985-86
Popein, Larry	NYR, Oak.	8	449	80	141	221	162	16	1	4	5	6	....	1954-55	1967-68
Popiel, Poul	Bos., L.A., Det., Van., Edm.	7	224	13	41	54	210	4	1	0	1	4	....	1965-66	1979-80
• Portland, Jack	Mtl.C., Bos., Chi., Mtl.	10	381	15	56	71	323	33	1	3	4	25	1	1933-34	1942-43
Porvari, Jukka	Col., N.J.	2	39	3	9	12	4	....	....	....	....	....	....	1981-82	1982-83
Posa, Victor	Chi.	1	2	0	0	0	2	....	....	....	....	....	....	1985-86	1985-86
Posavad, Mike	St.L.	2	8	0	0	0	0	....	....	....	....	....	....	1985-86	1986-87
Potvin, Denis	NYI	15	1060	310	742	1052	1356	185	56	108	164	253	4	1973-74	1987-88
Potvin, Jean	L.A., Phi., NYI, Cle., Min.	11	613	63	224	287	478	39	2	9	11	17	....	1970-71	1980-81
Potvin, Marc	Det., L.A., Hfd., Bos.	6	121	3	5	8	456	13	0	1	1	50	....	1990-91	1995-96
‡ Poudrier, Daniel	Que.	3	25	1	5	6	10	....	....	....	....	....	....	1985-86	1987-88
Poulin, Daniel	Min.	1	3	1	1	2	2	....	....	....	....	....	....	1981-82	1981-82
Poulin, Dave	Phi., Bos., Wsh.	13	724	205	325	530	482	129	31	42	73	132	....	1982-83	1994-95
Pouzar, Jaroslav	Edm.	4	186	34	48	82	135	29	6	4	10	16	3	1982-83	1986-87
Powell, Ray	Chi.	1	31	7	15	22	2	....	....	....	....	....	....	1950-51	1950-51
Powis, Geoff	Chi.	1	2	0	0	0	0	....	....	....	....	....	....	1967-68	1967-68
Powis, Lynn	Chi., K.C.	2	130	19	33	52	25	1	0	0	0	0	....	1973-74	1974-75
Prajsler, Petr	L.A., Bos.	4	46	3	10	13	51	4	0	0	0	0	....	1987-88	1991-92
• Pratt, Babe	NYR, Tor., Bos.	12	517	83	209	292	463	63	12	17	29	90	2	1935-36	1946-47
Pratt, Jack	Bos.	2	37	2	0	2	42	4	0	0	0	0	....	1930-31	1931-32
Pratt, Kelly	Pit.	1	22	0	6	6	15	....	....	....	....	....	....	1974-75	1974-75
Pratt, Tracy	Oak., Pit., Buf., Van., Col., Tor.	10	580	17	97	114	1026	25	0	1	1	62	....	1967-68	1976-77
Prentice, Dean	NYR, Bos., Det., Pit., Min.	22	1378	391	469	860	484	54	13	17	30	38	....	1952-53	1973-74
Prentice, Eric	Tor.	1	5	0	0	0	4	....	....	....	....	....	....	1943-44	1943-44
Presley, Wayne	Chi., S.J., Buf., NYR, Tor.	12	684	155	147	302	953	83	26	17	43	142	....	1984-85	1995-96
Preston, Rich	Chi., N.J.	10	580	127	164	291	348	47	4	18	22	56	....	1979-80	1986-87
Preston, Yves	Phi.	2	28	7	3	10	4	....	....	....	....	....	....	1978-79	1980-81
Priakin, Sergei	Cgy.	3	46	3	8	11	2	1	0	0	0	0	1	1988-89	1990-91
Price, Jack	Chi.	3	57	4	6	10	24	4	0	0	0	0	....	1951-52	1953-54
Price, Noel	Tor., NYR, Det., Mtl., Pit., L.A., Atl.	14	499	14	114	128	333	12	0	1	1	8	1	1957-58	1975-76
Price, Pat	NYI, Edm., Pit., Que., NYR, Min.	13	726	43	218	261	1456	74	2	10	12	195	....	1975-76	1987-88
Price, Tom	Cal., Cle., Pit.	5	29	0	2	2	12	....	....	....	....	....	....	1974-75	1978-79
‡ Priestlay, Ken	Buf., Pit.	6	168	27	34	61	63	14	0	0	0	21	1	1986-87	1991-92
• Primeau, Joe	Tor.	9	310	66	177	243	105	38	5	18	23	12	1	1927-28	1935-36
Primeau, Kevin	Van.	1	2	0	0	0	4	....	....	....	....	....	....	1980-81	1980-81
• Pringle, Ellie	NYA	1	6	0	0	0	0	....	....	....	....	....	....	1930-31	1930-31
• Prodgers, Goldie	Tor., Ham.	6	111	63	29	92	39	....	....	....	....	....	....	1919-20	1924-25
‡ Prokhorov, Vitali	St.L.	3	83	19	11	30	35	4	0	0	0	0	....	1992-93	1994-95
Pronovost, Andre	Mtl., Bos., Det., Min.	10	556	94	104	198	408	70	11	11	22	58	4	1956-57	1967-68
Pronovost, Jean	Pit., Atl., Wsh.	14	998	391	383	774	413	35	11	9	20	14	....	1968-69	1981-82
Pronovost, Marcel	Det., Tor.	21	1206	88	257	345	851	134	8	23	31	104	5	1949-50	1969-70
Propp, Brian	Phi., Bos., Min., Hfd.	15	1016	425	579	1004	830	160	64	84	148	151	....	1979-80	1993-94
‡ Proulx, Christian	Mtl.	1	7	1	2	3	20	....	....	....	....	....	....	1993-94	1993-94
• Provost, Claude	Mtl.	15	1005	254	335	589	469	126	25	38	63	86	9	1955-56	1969-70
Pryor, Chris	Min., NYI	6	82	1	4	5	122	....	....	....	....	....	....	1984-85	1989-90
Prystai, Metro	Chi., Det.	11	674	151	179	330	231	43	12	14	26	8	2	1947-48	1957-58
• Pudas, Al	Tor.	1	4	0	0	0	0	....	....	....	....	....	....	1926-27	1926-27
Pulford, Bob	Tor., L.A.	17	1079	281	362	643	792	89	25	26	51	126	4	1956-57	1971-72
Pulkkinen, Dave	NYI	1	2	0	0	0	0	....	....	....	....	....	....	1972-73	1972-73
Purpur, Fido	St.L., Chi., Det.	5	144	25	35	60	46	16	1	2	3	4	....	1934-35	1944-45
‡ Purves, John	Wsh.	1	7	1	0	1	0	....	....	....	....	....	....	1990-91	1990-91
• Pusie, Jean	Mtl.C., NYR, Bos.	5	61	1	4	5	28	7	0	0	0	0	1	1930-31	1935-36
Pyatt, Nelson	Det., Wsh., Col.	7	296	71	63	134	69	....	....	....	....	....	....	1973-74	1979-80

Q

Name	NHL Teams	NHL Seasons	Regular Schedule GP	G	A	TP	PIM	Playoffs GP	G	A	TP	PIM	NHL Cup Wins	First NHL Season	Last NHL Season
• Quackenbush, Bill	Det., Bos.	14	774	62	222	284	95	80	2	19	21	8	....	1942-43	1955-56
Quackenbush, Max	Bos., Chi.	2	61	4	7	11	30	6	0	0	0	4	....	1950-51	1951-52
Quenneville, Joel	Tor., Col., N.J., Hfd., Wsh.	15	803	54	136	190	705	32	0	8	8	22	....	1978-79	1990-91
• Quenneville, Leo	NYR	1	25	0	3	3	10	3	0	0	0	0	....	1929-30	1929-30
• Quilty, John	Mtl., Bos.	4	125	36	34	70	81	13	3	5	8	9	....	1940-41	1947-48
Quinn, Dan	Cgy., Pit., Van., St.L., Phi., Min., Ott., L.A.	14	805	266	419	685	533	65	22	26	48	62	....	1983-84	1996-97
Quinn, Pat	Tor., Van., Atl.	9	606	18	113	131	950	11	0	1	1	21	....	1968-69	1976-77
‡ Quinney, Ken	Que.	3	59	7	13	20	23	....	....	....	....	....	....	1986-87	1990-91
‡ Quintin, Jean-Francois	S.J.	2	22	5	5	10	4	....	....	....	....	....	....	1991-92	1992-93

R

Name	NHL Teams	NHL Seasons	Regular Schedule GP	G	A	TP	PIM	Playoffs GP	G	A	TP	PIM	NHL Cup Wins	First NHL Season	Last NHL Season
‡ Racine, Yves	Det., Phi., Mtl., S.J., Cgy., T.B.	9	508	37	194	231	439	25	5	4	9	37	....	1989-90	1997-98
• Radley, Yip	NYA, Mtl.M.	2	18	0	1	1	13	....	....	....	....	....	....	1930-31	1936-37
Raglan, Herb	St.L., Que., T.B., Ott.	9	343	33	56	89	775	32	3	6	9	50	....	1985-86	1993-94
Raglan, Rags	Det., Chi.	3	100	4	9	13	52	3	0	0	0	0	....	1950-51	1952-53
Raleigh, Don	NYR	10	535	101	219	320	96	18	6	5	11	6	....	1943-44	1955-56
Ramage, Rob	Col., St.L., Cgy., Tor., Min., T.B., Mtl., Phi.	15	1044	139	425	564	2226	84	8	42	50	218	2	1979-80	1993-94
• Ramsay, Beattie	Tor.	1	43	0	2	2	10	....	....	....	....	....	....	1927-28	1927-28
Ramsay, Craig	Buf.	21	1070	252	420	672	201	89	17	31	48	27	....	1971-72	1984-85
Ramsay, Les	Chi.	1	11	2	2	4	2	....	....	....	....	....	....	1944-45	1944-45
Ramsey, Mike	Buf., Pit., Det.	20	1070	79	266	345	1012	115	8	29	37	176	....	1979-80	1996-97
Ramsey, Wayne	Buf.	1	2	0	0	0	0	....	....	....	....	....	....	1977-78	1977-78
• Randall, Ken	Tor., Ham., NYA	10	218	68	50	118	533	6	2	1	3	27	....	1917-18	1926-27
Ranieri, George	Bos.	1	2	0	0	0	0	....	....	....	....	....	....	1956-57	1956-57
Ratelle, Jean	NYR, Bos.	21	1281	491	776	1267	276	123	32	66	98	24	....	1960-61	1980-81
Rathwell, Jake	Bos.	1	1	0	0	0	0	....	....	....	....	....	....	1974-75	1974-75
‡ Ratushny, Dan	Van.	1	1	0	1	1	2	....	....	....	....	....	....	1992-93	1992-93
Rausse, Errol	Wsh.	3	31	7	3	10	0	....	....	....	....	....	....	1979-80	1981-82
Rautakallio, Pekka	Atl., Cgy.	3	235	33	121	154	122	23	2	5	7	8	....	1979-80	1981-82
Ravlich, Matt	Bos., Chi., Det., L.A.	10	410	12	78	90	364	24	1	5	6	16	....	1962-63	1972-73
• Raymond, Armand	Mtl.C., Mtl.	2	22	0	2	2	10	....	....	....	....	....	....	1937-38	1939-40
• Raymond, Paul	Mtl.C.	4	76	2	3	5	6	5	0	0	0	2	....	1932-33	1938-39
Read, Mel	NYR	1	1	0	0	0	0	....	....	....	....	....	....	1946-47	1946-47
Reardon, Ken	Mtl.	7	341	26	96	122	604	31	2	5	7	62	1	1940-41	1949-50
• Reardon, Terry	Bos., Mtl.	7	193	47	53	100	73	30	8	10	18	12	1	1938-39	1946-47
Reaume, Marc	Tor., Det., Mtl., Van.	9	344	8	43	51	273	21	0	2	2	8	....	1954-55	1970-71
Reay, Billy	Det., Mtl.	10	479	105	162	267	202	63	13	16	29	43	2	1943-44	1952-53
Redahl, Gord	Bos.	1	18	0	1	1	2	....	....	....	....	....	....	1958-59	1958-59
• Redding, George	Bos.	2	55	3	2	5	23	....	....	....	....	....	....	1924-25	1925-26
Redmond, Craig	L.A., Edm.	5	191	16	68	84	134	3	1	0	1	2	....	1984-85	1988-89
Redmond, Dick	Min., Cal., Chi., St.L., Atl., Bos.	13	771	133	312	445	504	66	9	22	31	27	....	1969-70	1981-82
Redmond, Keith	L.A.	1	12	1	0	1	20	....	....	....	....	....	....	1993-94	1993-94
Redmond, Mickey	Mtl., Det.	9	538	233	195	428	219	16	2	3	5	2	2	1967-68	1975-76
Reeds, Mark	St.L., Hfd.	8	365	45	114	159	135	53	8	9	17	23	....	1981-82	1988-89
• Regan, Bill	NYR, NYA	3	67	3	2	5	67	8	0	0	0	2	....	1929-30	1932-33
Regan, Larry	Bos., Tor.	5	280	41	95	136	71	42	7	14	21	18	....	1956-57	1960-61
Regier, Darcy	Cle., NYI	3	26	0	2	2	35	....	....	....	....	....	....	1977-78	1983-84
Reibel, Earl	Det., Chi., Bos.	6	409	84	161	245	75	39	6	14	20	4	2	1953-54	1958-59
• Reid, Dave	Tor.	3	7	0	0	0	0	....	....	....	....	....	....	1952-53	1955-56
Reid, Gerry	Det.	1	....	....	....	....	....	2	0	0	0	2	....	1948-49	1948-49
Reid, Gord	NYA	1	1	0	0	0	2	....	....	....	....	....	....	1936-37	1936-37
• Reid, Reg	Tor.	2	39	1	0	1	4	2	0	0	0	0	....	1924-25	1925-26
Reid, Tom	Chi., Min.	11	701	17	113	130	654	42	1	13	14	49	....	1967-68	1977-78
Reierson, Dave	Cgy.	1	2	0	0	0	2	....	....	....	....	....	....	1988-89	1988-89
Reigle, Ed	Bos.	1	17	0	2	2	25	....	....	....	....	....	....	1950-51	1950-51
Reinhart, Paul	Atl., Cgy., Van.	11	648	133	426	559	277	83	23	54	77	42	....	1979-80	1989-90
• Reinikka, Ollie	NYR	1	16	0	0	0	0	....	....	....	....	....	....	1926-27	1926-27
Reise Jr., Leo	Chi., Det., NYR	9	494	28	81	109	399	52	8	5	13	68	2	1945-46	1953-54
• Reise Sr., Leo	Ham., NYA, NYR	8	241	43	43	86	187	6	0	0	0	16	....	1920-21	1929-30

			Regular Schedule					Playoffs					NHL	First	Last
Name	NHL Teams	NHL Seasons	GP	G	A	TP	PIM	GP	G	A	TP	PIM	Cup Wins	NHL Season	NHL Season
Renaud, Mark	Hfd., Buf.	5	152	6	50	56	86	....	....	....	....	....	....	1979-80	1983-84
‡ Reynolds, Bobby	Tor.	1	7	1	1	2	0	....	....	....	....	....	....	1989-90	1989-90
Ribble, Pat	Atl., Chi., Tor., Wsh., Cgy.	8	349	19	60	79	365	8	0	1	1	12	....	1975-76	1982-83
Rice, Steven	NYR, Edm., Hfd., Car.	8	329	64	61	125	275	2	2	1	3	6	....	1990-91	1997-98
Richard, Henri	Mtl.	20	1256	358	688	1046	928	180	49	80	129	181	11	1955-56	1974-75
Richard, Jacques	Atl., Buf., Que.	10	556	160	187	347	307	35	5	5	10	34	....	1972-73	1982-83
‡ Richard, Jean-Marc	Que.	2	5	2	1	3	2	....	....	....	....	....	....	1987-88	1989-90
● Richard, Maurice	Mtl.	18	978	544	421	965	1285	133	82	44	126	188	8	1942-43	1959-60
‡ Richard, Mike	Wsh.	2	7	0	2	2	0	....	....	....	....	....	....	1987-88	1989-90
‡ Richards, Todd	Hfd.	2	8	0	4	4	4	11	0	3	3	6	....	1990-91	1991-92
‡ Richards, Travis	Dal.	2	3	0	0	0	2	....	....	....	....	....	....	1994-95	1995-96
Richardson, Dave	NYR, Chi., Det.	4	45	3	2	5	27	....	....	....	....	....	....	1963-64	1967-68
Richardson, Glen	Van.	1	24	3	6	9	19	....	....	....	....	....	....	1975-76	1975-76
Richardson, Ken	St.L.	3	49	8	13	21	16	....	....	....	....	....	....	1974-75	1978-79
Richer, Bob	Buf.	1	3	0	0	0	0	....	....	....	....	....	....	1972-73	1972-73
‡ Richer, Stephane	T.B., Bos., Fla.	3	27	1	5	6	20	3	0	0	0	0	....	1992-93	1994-95
Richmond, Steve	NYR, Det., N.J., L.A.	5	159	4	23	27	514	4	0	0	0	12	....	1983-84	1988-89
Richter, Dave	Min., Phi., Van., St.L.	9	365	9	40	49	1030	22	1	0	1	80	....	1981-82	1989-90
Ridley, Mike	NYR, Wsh., Tor., Van.	12	866	292	466	758	424	104	28	50	78	70	....	1985-86	1996-97
Riley, Bill	Wsh., Wpg.	5	139	31	30	61	320	....	....	....	....	....	....	1974-75	1979-80
Riley, Jack	Det., Mtl.C., Bos.	4	104	10	22	32	8	4	0	3	3	0	....	1932-33	1935-36
● Riley, Jim	Chi., Det.	1	9	0	2	2	14	....	....	....	....	....	....	1926-27	1926-27
Riopelle, Rip	Mtl.	3	169	27	16	43	73	8	1	1	2	2	....	1947-48	1949-50
Rioux, Gerry	Wpg.	1	8	0	0	0	6	....	....	....	....	....	....	1979-80	1979-80
‡ Rioux, Pierre	Cgy.	1	14	1	2	3	4	....	....	....	....	....	....	1982-83	1982-83
● Ripley, Vic	Chi., Bos., NYR, St.L.	7	278	51	49	100	173	20	4	1	5	10	....	1928-29	1934-35
Risebrough, Doug	Mtl., Cgy.	13	740	185	286	471	1542	124	21	37	58	238	4	1974-75	1986-87
Rissling, Gary	Wsh., Pit.	7	221	23	30	53	1008	5	0	1	1	4	....	1978-79	1984-85
Ritchie, Bob	Phi., Det.	2	29	8	4	12	10	....	....	....	....	....	....	1976-77	1977-78
● Ritchie, Dave	Mtl., Ott., Tor., Que., Mtl.C.	6	58	15	6	21	50	1	0	0	0	0	....	1917-18	1925-26
Ritson, Alex	NYR	1	1	0	0	0	0	....	....	....	....	....	....	1944-45	1944-45
Rittinger, Alan	Bos.	1	19	3	7	10	0	....	....	....	....	....	....	1943-44	1943-44
Rivard, Bob	Pit.	1	27	5	12	17	4	....	....	....	....	....	....	1967-68	1967-68
● Rivers, Gus	Mtl.C.	3	88	4	5	9	12	16	2	0	2	2	2	1929-30	1931-32
Rivers, Shawn	T.B.	1	4	0	2	2	2	....	....	....	....	....	....	1992-93	1992-93
Rivers, Wayne	Det., Bos., St.L., NYR	7	108	15	30	45	94	....	....	....	....	....	....	1961-62	1968-69
Rizzuto, Garth	Van.	1	37	3	4	7	16	....	....	....	....	....	....	1970-71	1970-71
● Roach, Mickey	Tor., Ham., NYA	8	211	77	34	111	54	....	....	....	....	....	....	1919-20	1926-27
‡ Roberge, Mario	Mtl.	5	112	7	7	14	314	15	0	0	0	24	1	1990-91	1994-95
‡ Roberge, Serge	Que.	1	9	0	0	0	24	....	....	....	....	....	....	1990-91	1990-91
Robert, Claude	Mtl.	1	23	1	0	1	9	....	....	....	....	....	....	1950-51	1950-51
Robert, Rene	Tor., Pit., Buf., Col.	12	744	284	418	702	597	50	22	19	41	73	....	1970-71	1981-82
Roberto, Phil	Mtl., St.L., Det., K.C., Col., Cle.	8	385	75	106	181	464	31	9	8	17	69	1	1969-70	1976-77
‡ Roberts, David	St.L., Edm., Van.	5	125	20	33	53	85	9	0	0	0	16	....	1993-94	1997-98
Roberts, Doug	Det., Oak., Cal., Bos.	10	419	43	104	147	342	16	2	3	5	46	....	1965-66	1974-75
Roberts, Gordie	Hfd., Min., Phi., St.L., Pit., Bos.	15	1097	61	359	420	1582	153	10	47	57	273	2	1979-80	1993-94
Roberts, Jim	Min.	3	106	17	23	40	33	2	0	0	0	0	....	1976-77	1978-79
Roberts, Jimmy	Mtl., St.L.	19	1006	126	194	320	621	153	20	16	36	160	5	1963-64	1977-78
● Robertson, Fred	Tor., Det.	2	34	1	0	1	35	7	0	0	0	0	1	1931-32	1933-34
Robertson, Geordie	Buf.	1	5	1	2	3	7	....	....	....	....	....	....	1982-83	1982-83
Robertson, George	Mtl.	2	31	2	5	7	6	....	....	....	....	....	....	1947-48	1948-49
Robertson, Torrie	Wsh., Hfd., Det.	10	442	49	99	148	1751	22	2	1	3	90	....	1980-81	1989-90
Robidoux, Florent	Chi.	4	52	7	4	11	75	....	....	....	....	....	....	1980-81	1983-84
Robinson, Doug	Chi., NYR, L.A.	7	239	44	67	111	34	11	4	3	7	0	....	1963-64	1970-71
● Robinson, Earl	Mtl.M., Chi., Mtl.	11	417	83	98	181	133	25	5	4	9	0	1	1928-29	1939-40
Robinson, Larry	Mtl., L.A.	23	1384	208	750	958	793	227	28	116	144	211	6	1972-73	1991-92
Robinson, Moe	Mtl.	1	1	0	0	0	0	....	....	....	....	....	....	1979-80	1979-80
Robinson, Rob	St.L.	1	22	0	1	1	8	....	....	....	....	....	....	1991-92	1991-92
Robinson, Scott	Min.	1	1	0	0	0	2	....	....	....	....	....	....	1989-90	1989-90
Robitaille, Mike	NYR, Det., Buf., Van.	8	382	23	105	128	280	13	0	1	1	4	....	1969-70	1976-77
● Roche, Des	Mtl.M., Ott., St.L., Mtl.C., Det.	4	113	20	18	38	44	....	....	....	....	....	....	1930-31	1934-35
● Roche, Earl	Mtl.M., Bos., Ott., St.L., Det.	4	147	25	27	52	48	2	0	0	0	0	....	1930-31	1934-35
Roche, Ernie	Mtl.	1	4	0	0	0	2	....	....	....	....	....	....	1950-51	1950-51
Rochefort, Dave	Det.	1	1	0	0	0	0	....	....	....	....	....	....	1966-67	1966-67
Rochefort, Leon	NYR, Mtl., Phi., L.A., Det., Atl., Van.	15	617	121	147	268	93	39	4	4	8	16	2	1960-61	1975-76
Rochefort, Normand	Que., NYR, T.B.	13	598	39	119	158	570	69	7	5	12	82	....	1980-81	1993-94
● Rockburn, Harvey	Det., Ott.	3	94	4	2	6	254	....	....	....	....	....	....	1929-30	1932-33
● Rodden, Eddie	Chi., Tor., Bos., NYR	4	97	6	14	20	60	2	0	1	1	0	....	1926-27	1930-31
Rogers, John	Min.	2	14	2	4	6	0	....	....	....	....	....	....	1973-74	1974-75
Rogers, Mike	Hfd., NYR, Edm.	7	484	202	317	519	184	17	1	13	14	6	....	1979-80	1985-86
Rohlicek, Jeff	Van.	2	9	0	0	0	8	....	....	....	....	....	....	1987-88	1988-89
‡ Rohlin, Leif	Van.	2	96	8	24	32	40	5	0	0	0	0	....	1995-96	1996-97
Rolfe, Dale	Bos., L.A., Det., NYR	9	509	25	125	150	556	71	5	24	29	89	....	1959-60	1974-75
Romanchych, Larry	Chi., Atl.	6	298	68	97	165	102	7	2	2	4	4	....	1970-71	1976-77
‡ Romaniuk, Russell	Wpg., Phi.	5	102	13	14	27	63	2	0	0	0	0	....	1991-92	1995-96
Rombough, Doug	Buf., NYI, Min.	4	150	24	27	51	80	....	....	....	....	....	....	1972-73	1975-76
● Romnes, Doc	Chi., Tor., NYA	10	360	68	136	204	42	45	7	18	25	4	2	1930-31	1939-40
Ronan, Ed	Mtl., Wpg., Buf.	6	182	13	23	36	101	27	4	3	7	16	1	1991-92	1996-97
● Ronan, Skene	Ott.	1	11	0	0	0	6	....	....	....	....	....	....	1918-19	1918-19
Ronson, Len	NYR, Oak.	2	18	2	1	3	10	....	....	....	....	....	....	1960-61	1968-69
Ronty, Paul	Bos., NYR, Mtl.	8	488	101	211	312	103	21	1	7	8	6	....	1947-48	1954-55
Rooney, Steve	Mtl., Wpg., N.J.	5	154	15	13	28	496	25	3	2	5	86	1	1984-85	1988-89
Root, Bill	Mtl., Tor., St.L., Phi.	6	247	11	23	34	180	22	1	2	3	25	....	1982-83	1987-88
● Ross, Art	Mtl.	1	3	1	0	1	12	....	....	....	....	....	....	1917-18	1917-18
Ross, Jim	NYR	2	62	2	11	13	29	....	....	....	....	....	....	1951-52	1952-53
Rossignol, Roly	Det., Mtl.	3	14	3	5	8	6	1	0	0	0	2	....	1943-44	1945-46
Rota, Darcy	Chi., Atl., Van.	11	794	256	239	495	973	60	14	7	21	147	....	1973-74	1983-84
Rota, Randy	Mtl., L.A., K.C., Col.	5	212	38	39	77	60	5	0	1	1	0	....	1972-73	1976-77
● Rothschild, Sam	Mtl.M., Pit., NYA	4	100	8	6	14	25	6	0	0	0	0	....	1924-25	1927-28
● Roulston, Rolly	Det.	3	24	0	6	6	10	....	....	....	....	....	....	1935-36	1937-38
Roulston, Tom	Edm., Pit.	5	195	47	49	96	74	21	2	2	4	2	....	1980-81	1985-86
Roupe, Magnus	Phi.	2	40	3	5	8	42	....	....	....	....	....	....	1987-88	1988-89
Rousseau, Bobby	Mtl., Min., NYR	15	942	245	458	703	359	128	27	57	84	69	4	1960-61	1974-75
‡ Rousseau, Guy	Mtl.	2	4	0	1	1	0	....	....	....	....	....	....	1954-55	1956-57
Rousseau, Roland	Mtl.	1	2	0	0	0	0	....	....	....	....	....	....	1952-53	1952-53
‡ Routhier, Jean-Marc	Que.	1	8	0	0	0	9	....	....	....	....	....	....	1989-90	1989-90
● Rowe, Bobby	Bos.	1	4	1	0	1	0	....	....	....	....	....	....	1924-25	1924-25
Rowe, Mike	Pit.	3	11	0	0	0	11	....	....	....	....	....	....	1984-85	1986-87
Rowe, Ron	NYR	1	5	1	0	1	0	....	....	....	....	....	....	1947-48	1947-48
Rowe, Tom	Wsh., Hfd., Det.	7	357	85	100	185	615	3	2	0	2	0	....	1976-77	1982-83
‡ Roy, Jean-Yves	NYR, Ott., Bos.	4	61	12	16	28	26	....	....	....	....	....	....	1994-95	1997-98
‡ Roy, Stephane	Min.	1	12	1	0	1	0	....	....	....	....	....	....	1987-88	1987-88
Rozzini, Gino	Bos.	1	31	5	10	15	20	6	1	2	3	6	....	1944-45	1944-45
Rucinski, Mike	Chi.	2	1	0	0	0	0	2	0	0	0	0	....	1987-88	1988-89
Ruelle, Bernie	Det.	1	2	1	0	1	0	....	....	....	....	....	....	1943-44	1943-44
‡ Ruff, Jason	St.L., T.B.	2	14	3	3	6	10	....	....	....	....	....	....	1992-93	1993-94
Ruff, Lindy	Buf., NYR	14	691	105	195	300	1264	52	11	13	24	193	....	1979-80	1990-91
Ruhnke, Kent	Bos.	1	2	0	1	1	0	....	....	....	....	....	....	1975-76	1975-76
Rundqvist, Thomas	Mtl.	1	2	0	1	1	0	....	....	....	....	....	....	1984-85	1984-85
● Runge, Paul	Bos., Mtl.M., Mtl.C.	7	140	18	22	40	57	7	0	0	0	6	....	1930-31	1937-38
Ruotsalainen, Reijo	NYR, Edm., N.J.	7	446	107	237	344	180	86	15	32	47	44	2	1981-82	1989-90
Rupp, Duane	NYR, Tor., Min., Pit.	10	374	24	93	117	220	10	2	2	4	8	....	1962-63	1972-73
Ruskowski, Terry	Chi., L.A., Pit., Min.	10	630	113	313	426	1354	21	1	6	7	86	....	1979-80	1988-89
● Russell, Church	NYR	3	90	20	16	36	12	....	....	....	....	....	....	1945-46	1947-48
Russell, Phil	Chi., Atl., Cgy., N.J., Buf.	15	1016	99	325	424	2038	73	4	22	26	202	....	1972-73	1986-87
Ruuttu, Christian	Buf., Chi., Van.	9	621	134	298	432	714	42	4	9	13	49	....	1986-87	1994-95
‡ Ruzicka, Vladimir	Edm., Bos., Ott.	5	233	82	85	167	129	30	4	14	18	2	....	1989-90	1993-94
Rychel, Warren	Chi., L.A., Tor., Col., Ana.	9	406	38	39	77	1422	70	8	13	21	121	1	1988-89	1998-99
‡ Rymsha, Andy	Que.	1	6	0	0	0	23	....	....	....	....	....	....	1991-92	1991-92

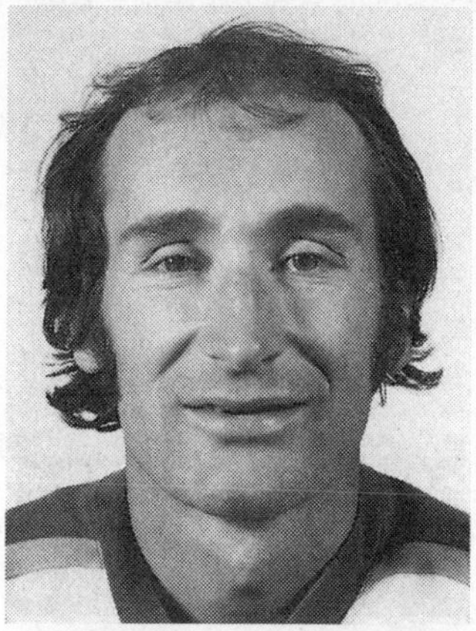

Craig Ramsay

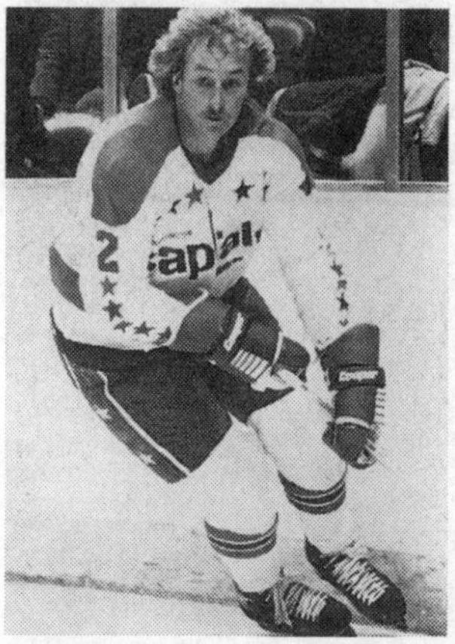

Pat Ribble

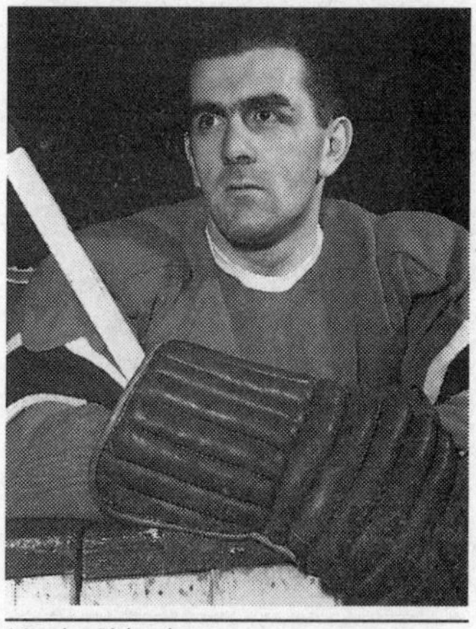

Maurice Richard

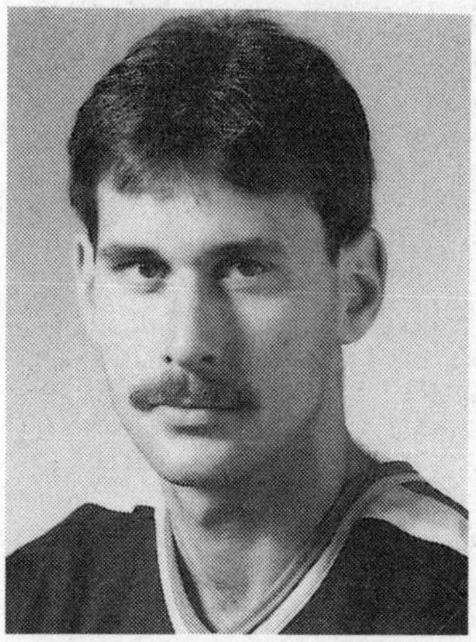

Dave Richter

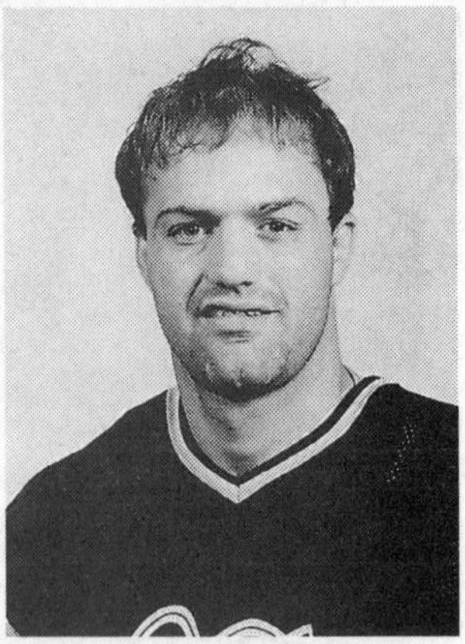

Gary Rissling

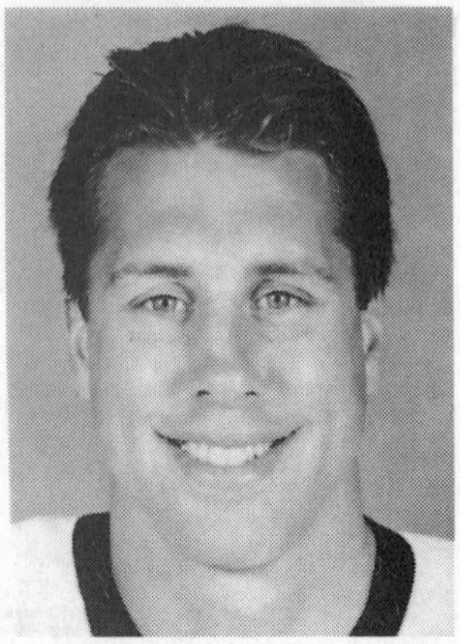

Warren Rychel

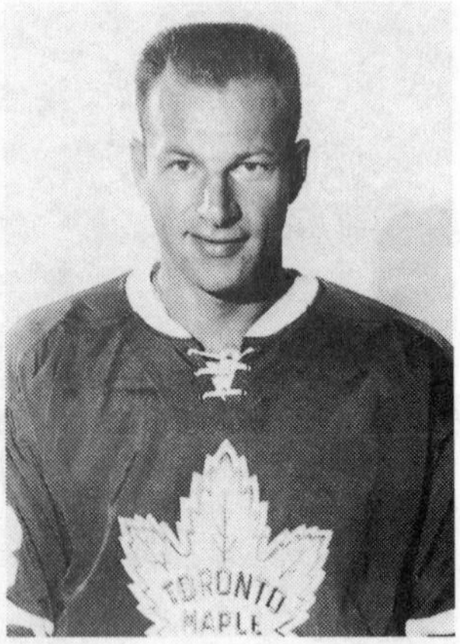

Eddie Shack

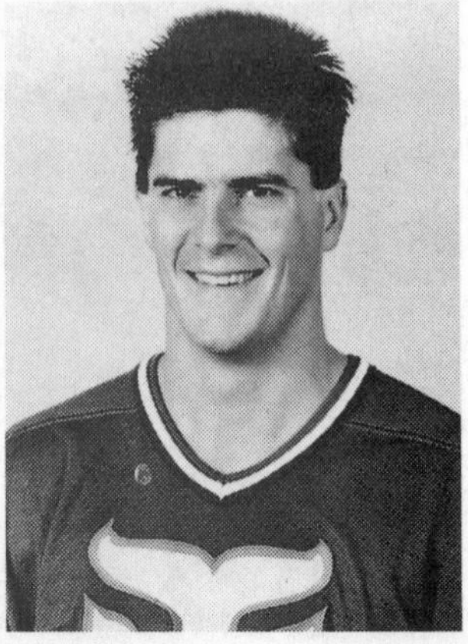

Brad Shaw

			Regular Schedule					Playoffs					NHL	First	Last
Name	NHL Teams	NHL Seasons	GP	G	A	TP	PIM	GP	G	A	TP	PIM	Cup Wins	NHL Season	NHL Season
S															
Saarinen, Simo	NYR	1	8	0	0	0	0	....	....	....	....	....	....	1984-85	1984-85
Sabol, Shaun	Phi.	1	2	0	0	0	0	....	....	....	....	....	....	1989-90	1989-90
Sabourin, Bob	Tor.	1	1	0	0	0	2	....	....	....	....	....	....	1951-52	1951-52
Sabourin, Gary	St.L., Tor., Cal., Cle.	10	627	169	188	357	397	62	19	11	30	58	....	1967-68	1976-77
Sabourin, Ken	Cgy., Wsh.	4	74	2	8	10	201	12	0	0	0	34	1	1988-89	1991-92
Sacco, David	Tor., Ana.	3	35	5	13	18	22	....	....	....	....	....	....	1993-94	1995-96
Sacharuk, Larry	NYR, St.L.	5	151	29	33	62	42	2	1	1	2	2	....	1972-73	1976-77
Saganiuk, Rocky	Tor., Pit.	6	259	57	65	122	201	6	1	0	1	15	....	1978-79	1983-84
Saleski, Don	Phi., Col.	9	543	128	125	253	629	82	13	17	30	131	2	1971-72	1979-80
Salming, Borje	Tor., Det.	17	1148	150	637	787	1344	81	12	37	49	91	....	1973-74	1989-90
Salovaara, Barry	Det.	2	90	2	13	15	70	....	....	....	....	....	....	1974-75	1975-76
Salvian, Dave	NYI	1	....	....	....	....	....	1	0	1	1	2	....	1976-77	1976-77
Samis, Phil	Tor.	2	2	0	0	0	0	5	0	1	1	2	1	1947-48	1949-50
Sampson, Gary	Wsh.	4	105	13	22	35	25	12	1	0	1	0	....	1983-84	1986-87
Samuelsson, Kjell	NYR, Phi., Pit., T.B.	14	813	48	138	186	1225	123	4	20	24	178	1	1985-86	1998-99
Sandelin, Scott	Mtl., Phi., Min.	4	25	0	4	4	2	....	....	....	....	....	....	1986-87	1991-92
Sanderson, Derek	Bos., NYR, St.L., Van., Pit.	13	598	202	250	452	911	56	18	12	30	187	2	1965-66	1977-78
Sandford, Ed	Bos., Det., Chi.	9	502	106	145	251	355	42	13	11	24	27	....	1947-48	1955-56
Sandlak, Jim	Van., Hfd.	11	549	110	119	229	821	33	7	10	17	30	....	1985-86	1995-96
• Sands, Charlie	Tor., Bos., Mtl., NYR	12	427	99	109	208	58	34	6	6	12	4	1	1932-33	1943-44
Sanipass, Everett	Chi., Que.	5	164	25	34	59	358	5	2	0	2	4	....	1986-87	1990-91
Sargent, Gary	L.A., Min.	8	402	61	161	222	273	20	5	7	12	8	....	1975-76	1982-83
Sarner, Craig	Bos.	1	7	0	0	0	0	....	....	....	....	....	....	1974-75	1974-75
Sarrazin, Dick	Phi.	3	100	20	35	55	22	4	0	0	0	0	....	1968-69	1971-72
Saskamoose, Fred	Chi.	1	11	0	0	0	6	....	....	....	....	....	....	1953-54	1953-54
Sasser, Grant	Pit.	1	3	0	0	0	0	....	....	....	....	....	....	1983-84	1983-84
Sather, Glen	Bos., Pit., NYR, St.L., Mtl., Min.	14	658	80	113	193	724	72	1	5	6	86	....	1966-67	1975-76
Saunders, Bernie	Que.	2	10	0	1	1	8	....	....	....	....	....	....	1979-80	1980-81
Saunders, David	Van.	1	56	7	13	20	10	....	....	....	....	....	....	1987-88	1987-88
Saunders, Ted	Ott.	1	18	1	3	4	4	....	....	....	....	....	....	1933-34	1933-34
Sauve, Jean-Francois	Buf., Que.	7	290	65	138	203	114	36	9	12	21	10	....	1980-81	1986-87
‡ Savage, Joel	Buf.	1	3	0	1	1	0	....	....	....	....	....	....	1990-91	1990-91
• Savage, Tony	Bos., Mtl.C.	1	49	1	5	6	6	2	0	0	0	0	....	1934-35	1934-35
Savard, Andre	Bos., Buf., Que.	17	790	211	271	482	411	85	13	18	31	77	....	1973-74	1984-85
Savard, Denis	Chi., Mtl., T.B.	18	1196	473	865	1338	1336	169	66	109	175	256	1	1980-81	1996-97
Savard, Jean	Chi., Hfd.	3	43	7	12	19	29	....	....	....	....	....	....	1977-78	1979-80
Savard, Serge	Mtl., Wpg.	17	1040	106	333	439	592	130	19	49	68	88	8	1966-67	1982-83
Scamurra, Peter	Wsh.	4	132	8	25	33	59	....	....	....	....	....	....	1975-76	1979-80
Sceviour, Darin	Chi.	1	1	0	0	0	0	....	....	....	....	....	....	1986-87	1986-87
Schaeffer, Butch	Chi.	1	5	0	0	0	6	....	....	....	....	....	....	1936-37	1936-37
Schamehorn, Kevin	Det., L.A.	3	10	0	0	0	17	....	....	....	....	....	....	1976-77	1980-81
Schella, John	Van.	2	115	2	18	20	224	....	....	....	....	....	....	1970-71	1971-72
Scherza, Chuck	Bos., NYR	2	36	6	6	12	35	....	....	....	....	....	....	1943-44	1944-45
Schinkel, Ken	NYR, Pit.	12	636	127	198	325	163	19	7	2	9	4	....	1959-60	1972-73
‡ Schlegel, Brad	Wsh., Cgy.	3	48	1	8	9	10	7	0	1	1	2	....	1991-92	1993-94
Schliebener, Andy	Van.	3	84	2	11	13	74	6	0	0	0	0	....	1981-82	1984-85
Schmautz, Bobby	Chi., Van., Bos., Edm., Col.	13	764	271	286	557	988	84	28	33	61	92	....	1967-68	1980-81
Schmautz, Cliff	Buf., Phi.	1	56	13	19	32	33	....	....	....	....	....	....	1970-71	1970-71
• Schmidt, Clarence	Bos.	1	7	1	0	1	2	....	....	....	....	....	....	1943-44	1943-44
Schmidt, Jackie	Bos.	1	45	6	7	13	6	5	0	0	0	0	....	1942-43	1942-43
Schmidt, Milt	Bos.	17	776	229	346	575	466	86	24	25	49	60	2	1936-37	1954-55
Schmidt, Norm	Pit.	4	125	23	33	56	73	....	....	....	....	....	....	1983-84	1987-88
Schmidt, Otto	Bos.	1	2	0	0	0	0	....	....	....	....	....	....	1943-44	1943-44
• Schnarr, Werner	Bos.	2	26	0	0	0	0	....	....	....	....	....	....	1924-25	1925-26
‡ Schneider, Andy	Ott.	1	10	0	0	0	15	....	....	....	....	....	....	1993-94	1993-94
Schock, Danny	Bos., Phi.	2	20	1	2	3	0	1	0	0	0	0	1	1969-70	1970-71
Schock, Ron	Bos., St.L., Pit., Buf.	15	909	166	351	517	260	55	4	16	20	29	....	1963-64	1977-78
Schoenfeld, Jim	Buf., Det., Bos.	13	719	51	204	255	1132	75	3	13	16	151	....	1972-73	1984-85
Schofield, Dwight	Det., Mtl., St.L., Wsh., Pit., Wpg.	7	211	8	22	30	631	9	0	0	0	55	....	1976-77	1987-88
‡ Schreiber, Wally	Min.	2	41	8	10	18	12	....	....	....	....	....	....	1987-88	1988-89
• Schriner, Sweeney	NYA, Tor.	11	484	201	204	405	148	59	18	11	29	54	2	1934-35	1945-46
Schulte, Paxton	Que., Cgy.	2	2	0	0	0	4	....	....	....	....	....	....	1993-94	1996-97
Schultz, Dave	Phi., L.A., Pit., Buf.	9	535	79	121	200	2294	73	8	12	20	412	2	1971-72	1979-80
Schurman, Maynard	Hfd.	1	7	0	0	0	0	....	....	....	....	....	....	1979-80	1979-80
Schutt, Rod	Mtl., Pit., Tor.	8	286	77	92	169	177	22	8	6	14	26	....	1977-78	1985-86
Scissons, Scott	NYI	3	2	0	0	0	0	1	0	0	0	0	....	1990-91	1993-94
Sclisizzi, Enio	Det., Chi.	6	81	12	11	23	26	13	0	0	0	6	....	1946-47	1952-53
• Scott, Ganton	Tor., Ham., Mtl.M.	3	57	1	1	2	0	....	....	....	....	....	....	1922-23	1924-25
• Scott, Laurie	NYA, NYR	2	62	6	3	9	28	....	....	....	....	....	1	1926-27	1927-28
Scremin, Claudio	S.J.	2	17	0	1	1	29	....	....	....	....	....	....	1991-92	1992-93
Scruton, Howard	L.A.	1	4	0	4	4	9	....	....	....	....	....	....	1982-83	1982-83
Seabrooke, Glen	Phi.	3	19	1	6	7	4	....	....	....	....	....	....	1986-87	1988-89
Secord, Al	Bos., Chi., Tor., Phi.	12	766	273	222	495	2093	102	21	34	55	382	....	1978-79	1989-90
Sedlbauer, Ron	Van., Chi., Tor.	7	430	143	86	229	210	19	1	3	4	27	....	1974-75	1980-81
Seftel, Steve	Wsh.	1	4	0	0	0	2	....	....	....	....	....	....	1990-91	1990-91
Seguin, Dan	Min., Van.	2	37	2	6	8	50	....	....	....	....	....	....	1970-71	1973-74
Seguin, Steve	L.A.	1	5	0	0	0	9	....	....	....	....	....	....	1984-85	1984-85
• Seibert, Earl	NYR, Chi., Det.	15	645	89	187	276	746	66	11	8	19	76	2	1931-32	1945-46
Seiling, Ric	Buf., Det.	10	738	179	208	387	573	62	14	14	28	36	....	1977-78	1986-87
Seiling, Rod	Tor., NYR, Wsh., St.L., Atl.	17	979	62	269	331	601	77	4	8	12	55	....	1962-63	1978-79
‡ Sejba, Jiri	Buf.	1	11	0	2	2	8	....	....	....	....	....	....	1990-91	1990-91
Selby, Brit	Tor., Phi., St.L.	8	350	55	62	117	163	16	1	1	2	8	....	1964-65	1971-72
Self, Steve	Wsh.	1	3	0	0	0	0	....	....	....	....	....	....	1976-77	1976-77
Selwood, Brad	Tor., L.A.	3	163	7	40	47	153	6	0	0	0	4	....	1970-71	1979-80
‡ Semak, Alexander	N.J., T.B., NYI, Van.	6	289	83	91	174	187	8	1	1	2	0	....	1991-92	1996-97
Semchuk, Brandy	L.A.	1	1	0	0	0	2	....	....	....	....	....	....	1992-93	1992-93
Semenko, Dave	Edm., Hfd., Tor.	9	575	65	88	153	1175	73	6	6	12	208	2	1979-80	1987-88
Semenov, Anatoli	Edm., T.B., Van., Ana., Phi., Buf.	8	362	68	126	194	122	49	9	13	22	12	1	1989-90	1996-97
Senick, George	NYR	1	13	2	3	5	8	....	....	....	....	....	....	1952-53	1952-53
Seppa, Jyrki	Wpg.	1	13	0	2	2	6	....	....	....	....	....	....	1983-84	1983-84
Serafini, Ron	Cal.	1	2	0	0	0	2	....	....	....	....	....	....	1973-74	1973-74
Serowik, Jeff	Tor., Bos., Pit.	4	28	0	6	6	16	....	....	....	....	....	....	1990-91	1998-99
Servinis, George	Min.	1	5	0	0	0	0	....	....	....	....	....	....	1987-88	1987-88
‡ Sevcik, Jaroslav	Que.	1	13	0	2	2	2	....	....	....	....	....	....	1989-90	1989-90
Shack, Eddie	NYR, Tor., Bos., L.A., Buf., Pit.	17	1047	239	226	465	1437	74	6	7	13	151	4	1958-59	1974-75
• Shack, Joe	NYR	2	70	9	27	36	20	....	....	....	....	....	....	1942-43	1944-45
‡ Shafranov, Konstantin	St.L.	1	5	2	1	3	0	....	....	....	....	....	....	1996-97	1996-97
Shakes, Paul	Cal.	1	21	0	4	4	12	....	....	....	....	....	....	1973-74	1973-74
Shanahan, Sean	Mtl., Col., Bos.	3	40	1	3	4	47	....	....	....	....	....	....	1975-76	1977-78
Shand, Dave	Atl., Tor., Wsh.	8	421	19	84	103	544	26	1	2	3	83	....	1976-77	1984-85
‡ Shank, Daniel	Det., Hfd.	3	77	13	14	27	175	5	0	0	0	22	....	1989-90	1991-92
Shannon, Chuck	NYA	1	4	0	0	0	2	....	....	....	....	....	....	1939-40	1939-40
• Shannon, Gerry	Ott., St.L., Bos., Mtl.M.	5	180	23	29	52	80	9	0	1	1	2	....	1933-34	1937-38
‡ Sharples, Jeff	Det.	3	105	14	35	49	70	7	0	3	3	6	....	1986-87	1988-89
Sharpley, Glen	Min., Chi.	8	389	117	161	278	199	27	7	11	18	24	....	1976-77	1984-85
Shaunessy, Scott	Que.	2	7	0	0	0	23	....	....	....	....	....	....	1986-87	1988-89
Shaw, Brad	Hfd., Ott., Wsh., St.L.	12	377	22	137	159	208	23	4	8	12	6	....	1985-86	1998-99
Shaw, David	Que., NYR, Edm., Min., Bos., T.B.	16	769	41	153	194	906	45	3	9	12	81	....	1982-83	1997-98
• Shay, Norm	Bos., Tor.	2	53	5	3	8	34	....	....	....	....	....	....	1924-25	1925-26
• Shea, Pat	Chi.	1	10	1	0	1	0	....	....	....	....	....	....	1931-32	1931-32
Shedden, Doug	Pit., Det., Que., Tor.	8	416	139	186	325	176	....	....	....	....	....	....	1981-82	1990-91
Sheehan, Bobby	Mtl., Cal., Chi., Det., NYR, Col., L.A.	9	310	48	63	111	40	25	4	3	7	8	1	1969-70	1981-82
Sheehy, Neil	Cgy., Hfd., Wsh.	9	379	18	47	65	1311	54	0	3	3	241	....	1983-84	1991-92
Sheehy, Tim	Det., Hfd.	2	27	2	1	3	0	....	....	....	....	....	....	1977-78	1979-80
Shelton, Doug	Chi.	1	5	0	1	1	2	....	....	....	....	....	....	1967-68	1967-68
• Sheppard, Frank	Det.	1	8	1	1	2	0	....	....	....	....	....	....	1927-28	1927-28
Sheppard, Gregg	Bos., Pit.	10	657	205	293	498	243	82	32	40	72	31	....	1972-73	1981-82
• Sheppard, Johnny	Det., NYA, Bos., Chi.	8	308	68	58	126	224	10	0	0	0	0	1	1926-27	1933-34
• Sherf, John	Det.	5	19	0	0	0	8	8	0	1	1	2	1	1935-36	1943-44

			Regular Schedule					Playoffs							
Name	NHL Teams	NHL Seasons	GP	G	A	TP	PIM	GP	G	A	TP	PIM	NHL Cup Wins	First NHL Season	Last NHL Season
• Shero, Fred	NYR	3	145	6	14	20	137	13	0	2	2	8	....	1947-48	1949-50
Sherritt, Gordon	Det.	1	8	0	0	0	12	....	....	....	....	....	....	1943-44	1943-44
‡ Sherven, Gord	Edm., Min., Hfd.	5	97	13	22	35	33	3	0	0	0	0	....	1983-84	1987-88
• Shewchuck, Jack	Bos.	6	187	9	19	28	160	20	0	1	1	19	....	1938-39	1944-45
Shibicky, Alex	NYR	8	324	110	91	201	161	39	12	12	24	12	1	1935-36	1945-46
• Shields, Al	Ott., Phi., NYA, Mtl.M., Bos.	11	459	42	46	88	637	17	0	1	1	14	1	1927-28	1937-38
Shill, Bill	Bos.	3	79	21	13	34	18	7	1	2	3	2	....	1942-43	1946-47
• Shill, Jack	Tor., Bos., NYA, Chi.	6	160	15	20	35	70	25	1	6	7	23	1	1933-34	1938-39
Shinske, Rick	Cle., St.L.	3	63	5	16	21	10	....	....	....	....	....	....	1976-77	1978-79
Shires, Jim	Det., St.L., Pit.	3	56	3	6	9	32	....	....	....	....	....	....	1970-71	1972-73
Shmyr, Paul	Chi., Cal., Min., Hfd.	7	343	13	72	85	528	34	3	3	6	44	....	1968-69	1981-82
Shoebottom, Bruce	Bos.	4	35	1	4	5	53	14	1	2	3	77	....	1987-88	1990-91
• Shore, Eddie	Bos., NYA	14	550	105	179	284	1047	55	6	13	19	181	2	1926-27	1939-40
• Shore, Hamby	Ott.	1	18	3	8	11	51	....	....	....	....	....	....	1917-18	1917-18
Short, Steve	L.A., Det.	2	6	0	0	0	2	....	....	....	....	....	....	1977-78	1978-79
‡ Shuchuk, Gary	Det., L.A.	5	142	13	26	39	70	20	2	2	4	12	....	1990-91	1995-96
‡ Shudra, Ron	Edm.	1	10	0	5	5	6	....	....	....	....	....	....	1987-88	1987-88
Shutt, Steve	Mtl., L.A.	13	930	424	393	817	410	99	50	48	98	65	5	1972-73	1984-85
• Siebert, Babe	Mtl.M., NYR, Bos., Mtl.C.	14	592	140	156	296	982	49	7	5	12	62	1	1925-26	1938-39
Silk, Dave	NYR, Bos., Det., Wpg.	7	249	54	59	113	271	13	2	4	6	13	....	1979-80	1985-86
Siltala, Mike	Wsh., NYR	3	7	1	0	1	2	....	....	....	....	....	....	1981-82	1987-88
Siltanen, Risto	Edm., Hfd., Que.	8	562	90	265	355	266	32	6	12	18	30	....	1979-80	1986-87
Sim, Trevor	Edm.	1	3	0	1	1	2	....	....	....	....	....	....	1989-90	1989-90
Simard, Martin	Cgy., T.B.	3	44	1	5	6	183	....	....	....	....	....	....	1990-91	1992-93
Simmer, Charlie	Cal., Cle., L.A., Bos., Pit.	14	712	342	369	711	544	24	9	9	18	32	....	1974-75	1987-88
Simmons, Al	Cal., Bos.	3	11	0	1	1	21	1	0	0	0	0	....	1971-72	1975-76
• Simon, Cully	Det., Chi.	3	130	4	11	15	121	14	1	0	1	6	1	1942-43	1944-45
Simon, Thain	Det.	1	3	0	0	0	0	....	....	....	....	....	....	1946-47	1946-47
‡ Simon, Todd	Buf.	1	15	0	1	1	0	5	1	0	1	0	....	1993-94	1993-94
Simonetti, Frank	Bos.	4	115	5	8	13	76	12	0	1	1	8	....	1984-85	1987-88
Simpson, Bobby	Atl., St.L., Pit.	5	175	35	29	64	98	6	0	1	1	2	....	1976-77	1982-83
• Simpson, Cliff	Det.	2	6	0	1	1	0	2	0	0	0	2	....	1946-47	1947-48
Simpson, Craig	Pit., Edm., Buf.	10	634	247	250	497	659	67	36	32	68	56	2	1985-86	1994-95
• Simpson, Joe	NYA	6	228	21	19	40	156	2	0	0	0	0	....	1925-26	1930-31
Sims, Al	Bos., Hfd., L.A.	12	475	49	116	165	286	41	0	2	2	14	....	1973-74	1982-83
Sinclair, Reg	NYR, Det.	3	208	49	43	92	139	3	1	0	1	0	....	1950-51	1952-53
• Singbush, Alex	Mtl.	1	32	0	5	5	15	3	0	0	0	4	....	1940-41	1940-41
Sinisalo, Ilkka	Phi., Min., L.A.	11	582	204	222	426	208	68	21	11	32	6	....	1981-82	1991-92
Siren, Ville	Pit., Min.	5	290	14	68	82	276	7	0	0	0	6	....	1985-86	1989-90
Sirois, Bob	Phi., Wsh.	6	286	92	120	212	42	....	....	....	....	....	....	1974-75	1979-80
Sittler, Darryl	Tor., Phi., Det.	15	1096	484	637	1121	948	76	29	45	74	137	....	1970-71	1984-85
• Sjoberg, Lars-Erik	Wpg.	1	79	7	27	34	48	....	....	....	....	....	....	1979-80	1979-80
‡ Sjodin, Tommy	Min., Dal., Que.	2	106	8	40	48	52	....	....	....	....	....	....	1992-93	1993-94
• Skaare, Bjorn	Det.	1	1	0	0	0	0	....	....	....	....	....	....	1978-79	1978-79
Skarda, Randy	St.L.	2	26	0	5	5	11	....	....	....	....	....	....	1989-90	1991-92
• Skilton, Raymie	Mtl.	1	1	0	0	0	0	....	....	....	....	....	....	1917-18	1917-18
• Skinner, Alf	Tor., Bos., Mtl.M., Pit.	4	71	26	10	36	87	2	0	1	1	9	....	1917-18	1925-26
Skinner, Larry	Col.	4	47	10	12	22	8	2	0	0	0	0	....	1976-77	1979-80
Skov, Glen	Det., Chi., Mtl.	12	650	106	136	242	413	53	7	7	14	48	3	1949-50	1960-61
Skriko, Petri	Van., Bos., Wpg., S.J.	9	541	183	222	405	246	28	5	9	14	4	....	1984-85	1992-93
Sleaver, John	Chi.	2	13	1	0	1	6	....	....	....	....	....	....	1953-54	1956-57
Sleigher, Louis	Que., Bos.	7	194	46	53	99	146	17	1	1	2	64	....	1979-80	1986-87
Sloan, Tod	Tor., Chi.	13	745	220	262	482	831	47	9	12	21	47	2	1947-48	1960-61
• Slobodian, Peter	NYA	1	41	3	2	5	54	....	....	....	....	....	....	1940-41	1940-41
• Slowinski, Eddie	NYR	6	291	58	74	132	63	16	2	6	8	6	....	1947-48	1952-53
Sly, Darryl	Tor., Min., Van.	4	79	1	2	3	20	....	....	....	....	....	....	1965-66	1970-71
Smail, Doug	Wpg., Min., Que., Ott.	13	845	210	249	459	602	42	9	2	11	49	....	1980-81	1992-93
Smart, Alex	Mtl.	1	8	5	2	7	0	....	....	....	....	....	....	1942-43	1942-43
Smedsmo, Dale	Tor.	1	4	0	0	0	0	....	....	....	....	....	....	1972-73	1972-73
Smillie, Don	Bos.	1	12	2	2	4	4	....	....	....	....	....	....	1933-34	1933-34
• Smith, Alex	Ott., Det., Bos., NYA	11	443	41	50	91	645	19	0	2	2	28	1	1924-25	1934-35
• Smith, Art	Tor., Ott.	4	144	15	10	25	249	4	1	1	2	8	....	1927-28	1930-31
Smith, Barry	Bos., Col.	3	114	7	7	14	10	....	....	....	....	....	....	1975-76	1980-81
Smith, Bobby	Min., Mtl.	15	1077	357	679	1036	917	184	64	96	160	245	1	1978-79	1992-93
Smith, Brad	Van., Atl., Cgy., Det., Tor.	9	222	28	34	62	591	20	3	3	6	49	....	1978-79	1986-87
Smith, Brian	Det.	3	61	2	8	10	12	5	0	0	0	0	....	1957-58	1960-61
• Smith, Brian	L.A., Min.	2	67	10	10	20	33	7	0	0	0	0	....	1967-68	1968-69
• Smith, Carl	Det.	1	7	1	1	2	2	....	....	....	....	....	....	1943-44	1943-44
Smith, Clint	NYR, Chi.	11	483	161	236	397	24	42	10	14	24	2	1	1936-37	1946-47
Smith, Dallas	Bos., NYR	16	890	55	252	307	959	86	3	29	32	128	2	1959-60	1977-78
Smith, Dennis	Wsh., L.A.	2	8	0	0	0	4	....	....	....	....	....	....	1989-90	1990-91
Smith, Derek	Buf., Det.	8	335	78	116	194	60	30	9	14	23	13	....	1975-76	1982-83
‡ Smith, Derrick	Phi., Min., Dal.	10	537	82	92	174	373	82	14	11	25	79	....	1984-85	1993-94
• Smith, Des	Mtl.M., Mtl.C., Chi., Bos.	5	196	22	25	47	236	25	1	4	5	18	1	1937-38	1941-42
• Smith, Don	Mtl.C.	1	12	1	0	1	6	....	....	....	....	....	....	1919-20	1919-20
Smith, Don	NYR	1	11	1	1	2	0	1	0	0	0	0	....	1949-50	1949-50
Smith, Doug	L.A., Buf., Edm., Van., Pit.	9	535	115	138	253	624	18	4	2	6	21	....	1981-82	1989-90
Smith, Floyd	Bos., NYR, Det., Tor., Buf.	13	616	129	178	307	207	48	12	11	23	16	....	1954-55	1971-72
Smith, Geoff	Edm., Fla., NYR	10	462	18	73	91	282	13	0	1	1	8	1	1989-90	1998-99
Smith, Glen	Chi.	1	2	0	0	0	0	....	....	....	....	....	....	1950-51	1950-51
• Smith, Glenn	Tor.	1	9	0	0	0	0	....	....	....	....	....	....	1921-22	1921-22
Smith, Gord	Wsh., Wpg.	6	299	9	30	39	284	....	....	....	....	....	....	1974-75	1979-80
Smith, Greg	Cal., Cle., Min., Det., Wsh.	13	829	56	232	288	1110	63	4	7	11	106	....	1975-76	1987-88
• Smith, Hooley	Ott., Mtl.M., Bos., NYA	17	715	200	225	425	1013	54	11	8	19	109	2	1924-25	1940-41
Smith, Ken	Bos.	7	331	78	93	171	49	30	8	13	21	6	....	1944-45	1950-51
Smith, Nakina	Det.	1	10	1	2	3	0	....	....	....	....	....	....	1943-44	1943-44
Smith, Randy	Min.	2	3	0	0	0	0	....	....	....	....	....	....	1985-86	1986-87
Smith, Rick	Bos., Cal., St.L., Det., Wsh.	11	687	52	167	219	560	78	3	23	26	73	1	1968-69	1980-81
• Smith, Rodger	Pit., Phi.	6	210	20	4	24	172	4	3	0	3	0	....	1925-26	1930-31
Smith, Ron	NYI	1	11	1	1	2	14	....	....	....	....	....	....	1972-73	1972-73
Smith, Sid	Tor.	12	601	186	183	369	94	44	17	10	27	2	3	1946-47	1957-58
Smith, Stan	NYR	2	9	2	1	3	0	1	0	0	0	0	1	1939-40	1940-41
Smith, Steve	Phi., Phialdelphia, Buf.	6	18	0	1	1	15	....	....	....	....	....	....	1981-82	1988-89
Smith, Stu	Mtl.	2	4	2	2	4	2	1	0	0	0	0	....	1940-41	1941-42
Smith, Stu	Hfd.	4	77	2	10	12	95	....	....	....	....	....	....	1979-80	1982-83
• Smith, Tommy	Que.	1	10	0	1	1	11	....	....	....	....	....	....	1919-20	1919-20
Smith, Vern	NYI	1	1	0	0	0	0	....	....	....	....	....	....	1984-85	1984-85
Smith, Wayne	Chi.	1	2	1	1	2	2	1	0	0	0	0	....	1966-67	1966-67
Smrke, John	St.L., Que.	3	103	11	17	28	33	....	....	....	....	....	....	1977-78	1979-80
• Smrke, Stan	Mtl.	2	9	0	3	3	0	....	....	....	....	....	....	1956-57	1957-58
Smyl, Stan	Van.	14	896	262	411	673	1556	41	16	17	33	64	....	1978-79	1990-91
• Smylie, Rod	Tor., Ott.	6	74	4	2	6	12	4	0	0	0	2	....	1920-21	1925-26
Smyth, Greg	Phi., Que., Cgy., Fla., Tor., Chi.	10	229	4	16	20	783	12	0	0	0	40	....	1986-87	1996-97
Smyth, Kevin	Hfd.	3	58	6	8	14	31	....	....	....	....	....	....	1993-94	1995-96
‡ Snell, Chris	Tor., L.A.	2	34	2	7	9	24	....	....	....	....	....	....	1993-94	1994-95
Snell, Ron	Pit.	2	7	3	2	5	6	....	....	....	....	....	....	1968-69	1969-70
Snell, Ted	Pit., K.C., Det.	2	104	7	18	25	22	....	....	....	....	....	....	1973-74	1974-75
Snepsts, Harold	Van., Min., Det., St.L.	18	1033	38	195	233	2009	93	1	14	15	231	....	1974-75	1990-91
Snow, Sandy	Det.	1	3	0	0	0	2	....	....	....	....	....	....	1968-69	1968-69
Snuggerud, Dave	Buf., S.J., Phi.	4	265	30	54	84	127	12	1	3	4	6	....	1989-90	1992-93
Sobchuk, Dennis	Det., Que.	2	35	5	6	11	2	....	....	....	....	....	....	1979-80	1982-83
• Sobchuk, Gene	Van.	1	1	0	0	0	0	....	....	....	....	....	....	1973-74	1973-74
Solheim, Ken	Chi., Min., Det., Edm.	5	135	19	20	39	34	3	1	1	2	2	....	1980-81	1985-86
Solinger, Bob	Tor., Det.	5	99	10	11	21	19	....	....	....	....	....	....	1951-52	1959-60
• Somers, Art	Chi., NYR	6	222	33	56	89	189	30	1	5	6	20	1	1929-30	1934-35
Sommer, Roy	Edm.	2	3	1	0	1	7	....	....	....	....	....	....	1980-81	1980-81
Songin, Tom	Bos.	3	43	5	5	10	22	....	....	....	....	....	....	1978-79	1980-81
Sonmor, Glen	NYR	2	28	2	0	2	21	....	....	....	....	....	....	1953-54	1954-55
• Sorrell, John	Det., NYA	11	490	127	119	246	100	42	12	15	27	10	2	1930-31	1940-41
• Sparrow, Emory	Bos.	1	8	0	0	0	4	....	....	....	....	....	....	1924-25	1924-25
Speck, Fred	Det., Van.	3	28	1	2	3	2	....	....	....	....	....	....	1968-69	1971-72

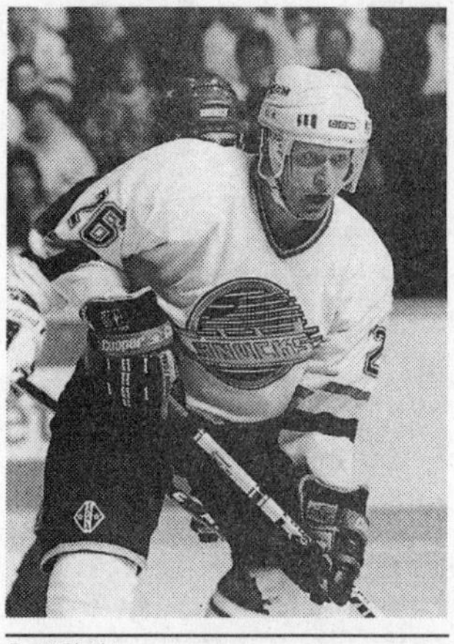

Petri Skriko

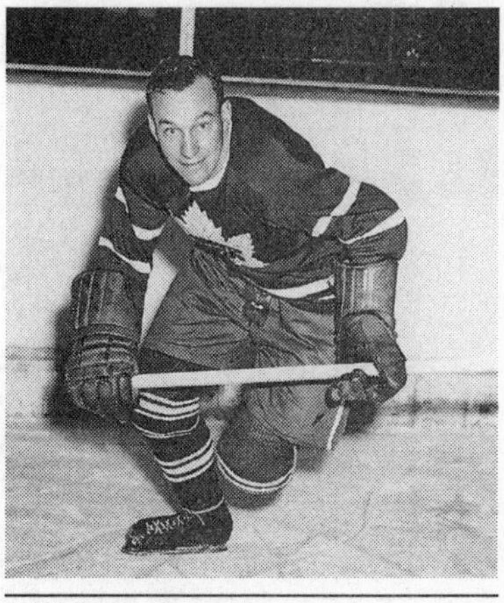

Bob Solinger

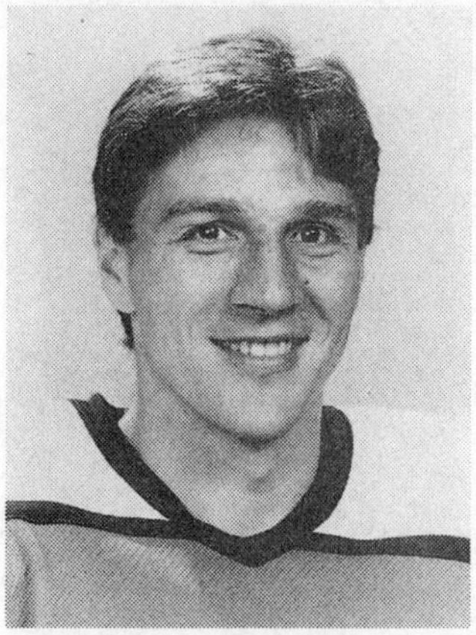

Doug Sulliman

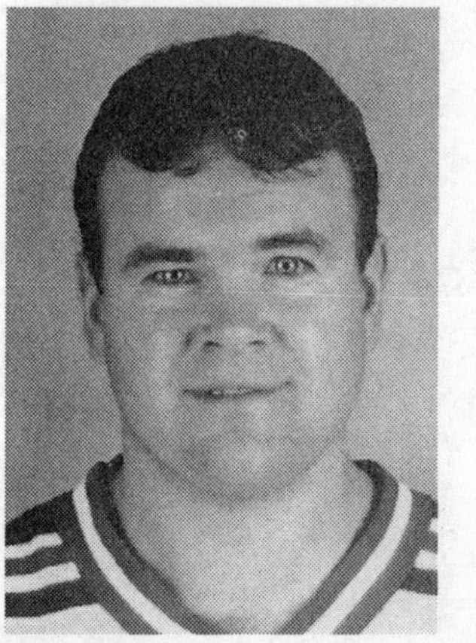

Tim Sweeney

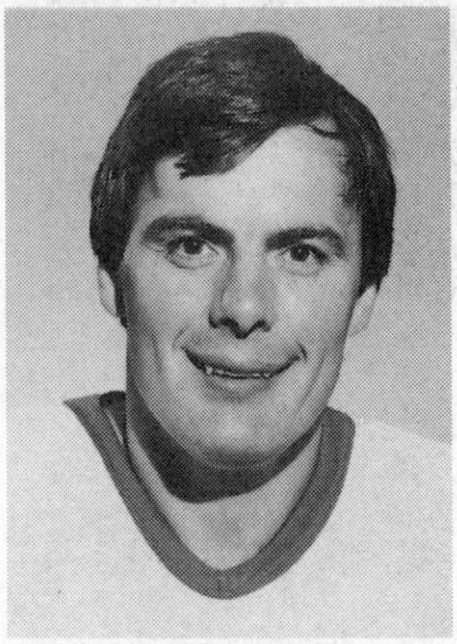

Marc Tardif

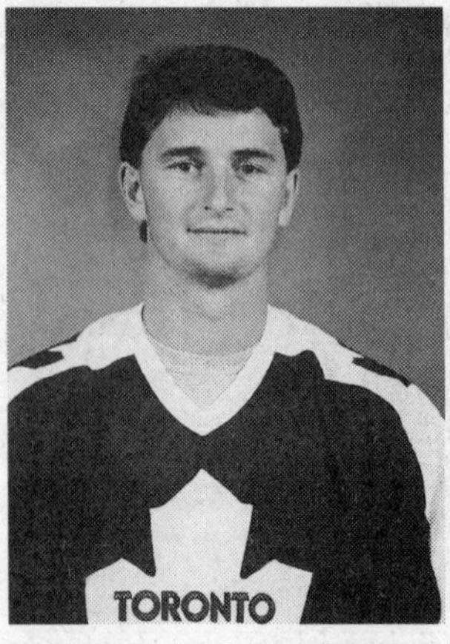

Greg Terrion

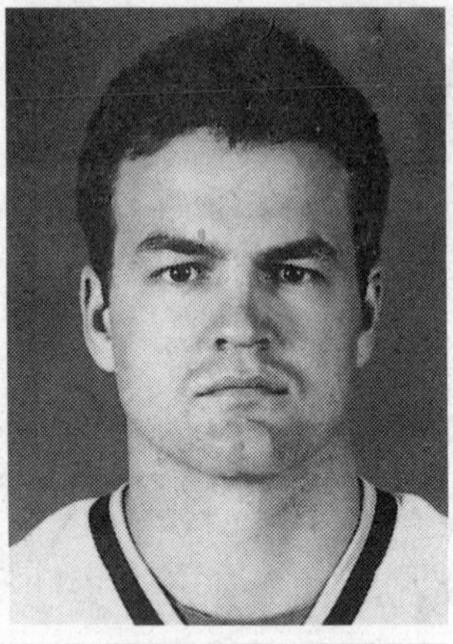

Dave Thomlinson

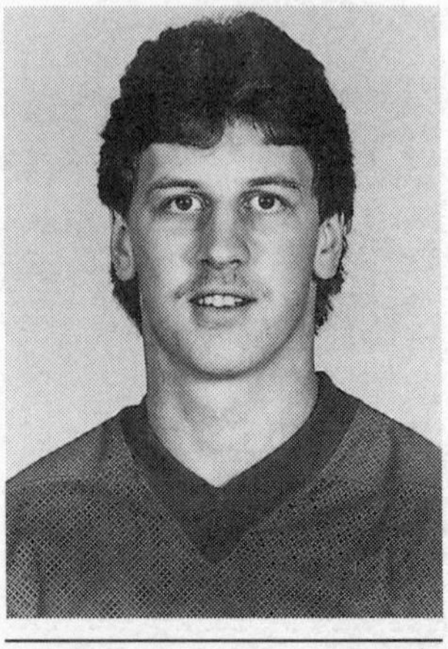

Larry Trader

			Regular Schedule					Playoffs					NHL	First	Last
Name	**NHL Teams**	**NHL Seasons**	**GP**	**G**	**A**	**TP**	**PIM**	**GP**	**G**	**A**	**TP**	**PIM**	**Cup Wins**	**NHL Season**	**NHL Season**
● Speer, Bill	Pit., Bos.	4	130	5	20	25	79	8	1	0	1	4	1	1967-68	1970-71
Speers, Ted	Det.	1	4	1	1	2	0	....	....	....	....	....	....	1985-86	1985-86
● Spence, Gordon	Tor.	1	3	0	0	0	0	....	....	....	....	....	....	1925-26	1925-26
● Spencer, Brian	Tor., NYI, Buf., Pit.	10	553	80	143	223	634	37	1	5	6	29	....	1969-70	1978-79
Spencer, Irv	NYR, Bos., Det.	8	230	12	38	50	127	16	0	0	0	8	....	1959-60	1967-68
● Speyer, Chris	Tor., NYA	3	14	0	0	0	0	....	....	....	....	....	....	1923-24	1933-34
Spring, Don	Wpg.	4	259	1	54	55	80	6	0	0	0	10	....	1980-81	1983-84
Spring, Frank	Bos., St.L., Cal., Cle.	5	61	14	20	34	12	....	....	....	....	....	....	1969-70	1976-77
● Spring, Jesse	Ham., Pit., Tor., NYA	6	133	11	4	15	74	2	0	2	2	2	....	1923-24	1929-30
Spruce, Andy	Van., Col.	3	172	31	42	73	111	2	0	2	2	0	....	1976-77	1978-79
‡ Srsen, Tomas	Edm.	1	2	0	0	0	0	....	....	....	....	....	....	1990-91	1990-91
‡ St. Amour, Martin	Ott.	1	1	0	0	0	2	....	....	....	....	....	....	1992-93	1992-93
St. Laurent, Andre	NYI, Det., L.A., Pit.	11	644	129	187	316	749	59	8	12	20	48	....	1973-74	1983-84
St. Laurent, Dollard	Mtl., Chi.	12	652	29	133	162	496	92	2	22	24	87	5	1950-51	1961-62
St. Marseille, Frank	St.L., L.A.	10	707	140	285	425	242	88	20	25	45	18	....	1967-68	1976-77
St. Sauveur, Claude	Atl.	1	79	24	24	48	23	2	0	0	0	0	....	1975-76	1975-76
Stackhouse, Ron	Cal., Det., Pit.	12	889	87	372	459	824	32	5	8	13	38	....	1970-71	1981-82
● Stackhouse, Ted	Tor.	1	13	0	0	0	2	1	0	0	0	0	....	1921-22	1921-22
● Stahan, Butch	Mtl.	1	....	....	....	....	....	3	0	1	1	2	....	1944-45	1944-45
‡ Stajduhar, Nick	Edm.	1	2	0	0	0	4	....	....	....	....	....	....	1995-96	1995-96
Staley, Al	NYR	1	1	0	1	1	0	....	....	....	....	....	....	1948-49	1948-49
Stamler, Lorne	L.A., Tor., Wpg.	4	116	14	11	25	16	....	....	....	....	....	....	1976-77	1979-80
Standing, George	Min.	1	2	0	0	0	0	....	....	....	....	....	....	1967-68	1967-68
Stanfield, Fred	Chi., Bos., Min., Buf.	14	914	211	405	616	134	106	21	35	56	10	2	1964-65	1977-78
Stanfield, Jack	Chi.	1	....	....	....	....	....	1	0	0	0	0	....	1965-66	1965-66
Stanfield, Jim	L.A.	3	7	0	1	1	0	....	....	....	....	....	....	1969-70	1971-72
Stankiewicz, Ed	Det.	2	6	0	0	0	2	....	....	....	....	....	....	1953-54	1955-56
Stankiewicz, Myron	St.L., Phi.	1	35	0	7	7	36	1	0	0	0	0	....	1968-69	1968-69
Stanley, Allan	NYR, Chi., Bos., Tor., Phi.	21	1244	100	333	433	792	109	7	36	43	80	4	1948-49	1968-69
● Stanley, Barney	Chi.	1	1	0	0	0	0	....	....	....	....	....	....	1927-28	1927-28
Stanley, Daryl	Phi., Van.	6	189	8	17	25	408	17	0	0	0	30	....	1983-84	1989-90
Stanowski, Wally	Tor., NYR	10	428	23	88	111	160	60	3	14	17	13	4	1939-40	1950-51
‡ Stanton, Paul	Pit., Bos., NYI	5	295	14	49	63	262	44	2	10	12	66	2	1990-91	1994-95
Stapleton, Brian	Wsh.	1	1	0	0	0	0	....	....	....	....	....	....	1975-76	1975-76
Stapleton, Pat	Bos., Chi.	10	635	43	294	337	353	65	10	39	49	38	....	1961-62	1972-73
Starikov, Sergei	N.J.	1	16	0	1	1	8	....	....	....	....	....	....	1989-90	1989-90
● Starr, Harold	Ott., Mtl.M., Mtl.C., NYR	7	205	6	5	11	186	15	1	0	1	4	....	1929-30	1935-36
Starr, Wilf	NYA, Det.	4	87	8	6	14	25	7	0	2	2	2	....	1932-33	1935-36
Stasiuk, Vic	Chi., Det., Bos.	14	745	183	254	437	669	69	16	18	34	40	3	1949-50	1962-63
Stastny, Anton	Que.	9	650	252	384	636	150	66	20	32	52	31	....	1980-81	1988-89
Stastny, Marian	Que., Tor.	5	322	121	173	294	110	32	5	17	22	7	....	1981-82	1985-86
Stastny, Peter	Que., N.J., St.L.	15	977	450	789	1239	824	93	33	72	105	123	....	1980-81	1994-95
Staszak, Ray	Det.	1	4	0	1	1	7	....	....	....	....	....	....	1985-86	1985-86
● Steele, Frank	Det.	1	1	0	0	0	0	....	....	....	....	....	....	1930-31	1930-31
Steen, Anders	Wpg.	1	42	5	11	16	22	....	....	....	....	....	....	1980-81	1980-81
Steen, Thomas	Wpg.	14	950	264	553	817	753	56	12	32	44	62	....	1981-82	1994-95
Stefaniw, Morris	Atl.	1	13	1	1	2	2	....	....	....	....	....	....	1972-73	1972-73
Stefanski, Bud	NYR	1	1	0	0	0	0	....	....	....	....	....	....	1977-78	1977-78
Stemkowski, Pete	Tor., Det., NYR, L.A.	15	967	206	349	555	866	83	25	29	54	136	1	1963-64	1977-78
Stenlund, Vern	Cle.	1	4	0	0	0	0	....	....	....	....	....	....	1976-77	1976-77
Stephenson, Bob	Hfd., Tor.	1	18	2	3	5	4	....	....	....	....	....	....	1979-80	1979-80
Sterner, Ulf	NYR	1	4	0	0	0	0	....	....	....	....	....	....	1964-65	1964-65
Stevens, John	Phi., Hfd.	5	53	0	10	10	48	....	....	....	....	....	....	1986-87	1993-94
‡ Stevens, Mike	Van., Bos., NYI, Tor.	4	23	1	4	5	29	....	....	....	....	....	....	1984-85	1989-90
● Stevens, Phil	Mtl., Mtl.C., Bos.	3	25	1	0	1	3	....	....	....	....	....	....	1917-18	1925-26
‡ Stevenson, Shayne	Bos., T.B.	3	27	0	2	2	35	....	....	....	....	....	....	1990-91	1992-93
Stewart, Allan	N.J., Bos.	6	64	6	4	10	243	....	....	....	....	....	....	1985-86	1991-92
Stewart, Bill	Buf., St.L., Tor., Min.	9	261	7	64	71	424	13	1	3	4	11	....	1977-78	1985-86
Stewart, Blair	Det., Wsh., Que.	7	229	34	44	78	326	....	....	....	....	....	....	1973-74	1979-80
Stewart, Bob	Bos., Cal., Cle., St.L., Pit.	9	575	27	101	128	809	5	1	1	2	2	....	1971-72	1979-80
Stewart, Gaye	Tor., Chi., Det., NYR, Mtl.	11	502	185	159	344	274	25	2	9	11	16	2	1941-42	1953-54
● Stewart, Jack	Det., Chi.	12	565	31	84	115	765	80	5	14	19	143	2	1938-39	1951-52
Stewart, John	Pit., Atl., Cal.	5	258	58	60	118	158	4	0	0	0	10	....	1970-71	1974-75
Stewart, John	Que.	1	2	0	0	0	0	....	....	....	....	....	....	1979-80	1979-80
● Stewart, Ken	Chi.	1	6	1	1	2	2	....	....	....	....	....	....	1941-42	1941-42
● Stewart, Nels	Mtl.M., Bos., NYA	15	650	324	191	515	953	50	9	12	21	47	....	1925-26	1939-40
Stewart, Paul	Que.	1	21	2	0	2	74	....	....	....	....	....	....	1979-80	1979-80
Stewart, Ralph	Van., NYI	7	252	57	73	130	28	19	4	4	8	2	....	1970-71	1977-78
Stewart, Ron	Tor., Bos., St.L., NYR, Van., NYI	21	1353	276	253	529	560	119	14	21	35	60	3	1952-53	1972-73
Stewart, Ryan	Wpg.	1	3	1	0	1	0	....	....	....	....	....	....	1985-86	1985-86
Stienburg, Trevor	Que.	4	71	8	4	12	161	1	0	0	0	0	....	1985-86	1988-89
Stiles, Tony	Cgy.	1	30	2	7	9	20	....	....	....	....	....	....	1983-84	1983-84
Stoddard, Jack	NYR	2	80	16	15	31	31	....	....	....	....	....	....	1951-52	1952-53
Stoltz, Roland	Wsh.	1	14	2	2	4	14	....	....	....	....	....	....	1981-82	1981-82
Stone, Steve	Van.	1	2	0	0	0	0	....	....	....	....	....	....	1973-74	1973-74
Storm, Jim	Hfd., Dal.	3	84	7	15	22	44	....	....	....	....	....	....	1993-94	1995-96
Stothers, Mike	Phi., Tor.	4	30	0	2	2	65	5	0	0	0	11	....	1984-85	1987-88
Stoughton, Blaine	Pit., Tor., Hfd., NYR	8	526	258	191	449	204	8	4	2	6	2	....	1973-74	1983-84
Stoyanovich, Steve	Hfd.	1	23	3	5	8	11	....	....	....	....	....	....	1983-84	1983-84
● Strain, Neil	NYR	1	52	11	13	24	12	....	....	....	....	....	....	1952-53	1952-53
Strate, Gord	Det.	3	61	0	0	0	34	....	....	....	....	....	....	1956-57	1958-59
Stratton, Art	NYR, Det., Chi., Pit., Phi.	4	95	18	33	51	24	5	0	0	0	0	....	1959-60	1967-68
Strobel, Art	NYR	1	7	0	0	0	0	....	....	....	....	....	....	1943-44	1943-44
Strong, Ken	Tor.	3	15	2	2	4	6	....	....	....	....	....	....	1982-83	1984-85
Struch, David	Cgy.	1	4	0	0	0	4	....	....	....	....	....	....	1993-94	1993-94
‡ Strueby, Todd	Edm.	3	5	0	1	1	2	....	....	....	....	....	....	1981-82	1983-84
● Stuart, Billy	Tor., Bos.	7	195	30	20	50	151	12	1	1	2	6	....	1920-21	1926-27
Stumpf, Bob	St.L., Pit.	1	10	1	1	2	20	....	....	....	....	....	....	1974-75	1974-75
Sturgeon, Peter	Col.	2	6	0	1	1	2	....	....	....	....	....	....	1979-80	1980-81
Suikkanen, Kai	Buf.	2	2	0	0	0	0	....	....	....	....	....	....	1981-82	1982-83
Sulliman, Doug	NYR, Hfd., N.J., Phi.	11	631	160	168	328	175	16	1	3	4	2	....	1979-80	1989-90
Sullivan, Barry	Det.	1	1	0	0	0	0	....	....	....	....	....	....	1947-48	1947-48
Sullivan, Bob	Hfd.	1	62	18	19	37	18	....	....	....	....	....	....	1982-83	1982-83
Sullivan, Brian	N.J.	1	2	0	1	1	0	....	....	....	....	....	....	1992-93	1992-93
Sullivan, Frank	Tor., Chi.	4	8	0	0	0	2	....	....	....	....	....	....	1949-50	1955-56
Sullivan, Peter	Wpg.	2	126	28	54	82	40	....	....	....	....	....	....	1979-80	1980-81
Sullivan, Red	Bos., Chi., NYR	12	557	107	239	346	441	18	1	2	3	6	....	1949-50	1960-61
Summanen, Raimo	Edm., Van.	5	151	36	40	76	35	10	2	5	7	0	1	1983-84	1987-88
● Summerhill, Bill	Mtl.C., Mtl., Bro.	4	72	14	17	31	70	3	0	0	0	2	....	1937-38	1941-42
‡ Sundblad, Niklas	Cgy.	1	2	0	0	0	0	....	....	....	....	....	....	1995-96	1995-96
‡ Sundin, Ronnie	NYR	1	1	0	0	0	0	....	....	....	....	....	....	1997-98	1997-98
Sundstrom, Patrik	Van., N.J.	10	679	219	369	588	349	37	9	17	26	25	....	1982-83	1991-92
Sundstrom, Peter	NYR, Wsh., N.J.	6	338	61	83	144	120	23	3	3	6	8	....	1983-84	1989-90
● Suomi, Al	Chi.	1	5	0	0	0	0	....	....	....	....	....	....	1936-37	1936-37
Sutherland, Bill	Mtl., Phi., Tor., St.L., Det.	6	250	70	58	128	99	14	2	4	6	0	....	1962-63	1971-72
● Sutherland, Max	Bos.	1	2	0	0	0	0	....	....	....	....	....	....	1931-32	1931-32
Sutter, Brent	NYI, Chi.	18	1111	363	466	829	1054	144	30	44	74	164	2	1980-81	1997-98
Sutter, Brian	St.L.	15	779	303	333	636	1786	65	21	21	42	249	....	1976-77	1987-88
Sutter, Darryl	Chi.	13	406	161	118	279	288	51	24	19	43	26	....	1979-80	1986-87
Sutter, Duane	NYI, Chi.	11	731	139	203	342	1333	161	26	32	58	405	4	1979-80	1989-90
Sutter, Rich	Pit., Phi., Van., St.L., Chi., T.B., Tor.	13	874	149	166	315	1411	78	13	5	18	133	....	1982-83	1994-95
Suzor, Mark	Phi., Col.	2	64	4	16	20	60	....	....	....	....	....	....	1976-77	1977-78
Svensson, Leif	Wsh.	2	121	6	40	46	49	....	....	....	....	....	....	1978-79	1979-80
‡ Svensson, Magnus	Fla.	2	46	4	14	18	31	....	....	....	....	....	....	1994-95	1995-96
Swain, Garry	Pit.	1	9	1	1	2	0	....	....	....	....	....	....	1968-69	1968-69
Swarbrick, George	Oak., Pit., Phi.	4	132	17	25	42	173	....	....	....	....	....	....	1967-68	1970-71
● Sweeney, Bill	NYR	1	4	1	0	1	0	....	....	....	....	....	....	1959-60	1959-60
‡ Sweeney, Bob	Bos., Buf., NYI, Cgy.	10	639	125	163	288	799	103	15	18	33	197	....	1986-87	1995-96
Sweeney, Tim	Cgy., Bos., Ana., NYR	8	291	55	83	138	123	4	0	0	0	2	....	1990-91	1997-98
Sykes, Bob	Tor.	1	2	0	0	0	0	....	....	....	....	....	....	1974-75	1974-75
Sykes, Phil	L.A., Wpg.	10	456	79	85	164	519	26	0	3	3	29	....	1982-83	1991-92
Szura, Joe	Oak.	2	90	10	15	25	30	7	2	3	5	2	....	1967-68	1968-69

			Regular Schedule					Playoffs					NHL	First	Last
Name	NHL Teams	NHL Seasons	GP	G	A	TP	PIM	GP	G	A	TP	PIM	Cup Wins	NHL Season	NHL Season
T															
Taft, John	Det.	1	15	0	2	2	4	....	....	....	....	....	....	1978-79	1978-79
Taglianetti, Peter	Wpg., Min., Pit., T.B.	11	451	18	74	92	1106	53	2	8	10	103	2	1984-85	1994-95
Talafous, Dean	Atl., Min., NYR	8	497	104	154	258	163	21	4	7	11	11	....	1974-75	1981-82
Talakoski, Ron	NYR	2	9	0	1	1	33	....	....	....	....	....	....	1986-87	1987-88
Talbot, Jean-Guy	Mtl., Min., Det., St.L., Buf.	17	1056	43	242	285	1006	150	4	26	30	142	7	1954-55	1970-71
Tallon, Dale	Van., Chi., Pit.	10	642	98	238	336	568	33	2	10	12	45	....	1970-71	1979-80
Tambellini, Steve	NYI, Col., N.J., Cgy., Van.	10	553	160	150	310	105	2	0	1	1	0	1	1978-79	1987-88
Tanguay, Christian	Que.	1	2	0	0	0	0	....	....	....	....	....	....	1981-82	1981-82
Tannahill, Don	Van.	2	111	30	33	63	25	....	....	....	....	....	....	1972-73	1973-74
Tanti, Tony	Chi., Van., Pit., Buf.	11	697	287	273	560	661	30	3	12	15	27	....	1981-82	1991-92
Tardif, Marc	Mtl., Que.	8	517	194	207	401	443	62	13	15	28	75	2	1969-70	1982-83
Tatarinov, Mikhail	Wsh., Que., Bos.	4	161	21	48	69	184	....	....	....	....	....	....	1990-91	1993-94
Tatchell, Spence	NYR	1	1	0	0	0	0	....	....	....	....	....	....	1942-43	1942-43
• Taylor, Billy	Tor., Det., Bos., NYR	7	323	87	180	267	120	33	6	18	24	13	1	1939-40	1947-48
• Taylor, Bob	Bos.	1	8	0	0	0	6	....	....	....	....	....	....	1929-30	1929-30
Taylor, Dave	L.A.	17	1111	431	638	1069	1589	92	26	33	59	145	....	1977-78	1993-94
Taylor, Harry	Tor., Chi.	3	66	5	10	15	30	1	0	0	0	0	1	1946-47	1951-52
Taylor, Mark	Phi., Pit., Wsh.	5	209	42	68	110	73	6	0	0	0	0	....	1981-82	1985-86
• Taylor, Ralph	Chi., NYR	3	99	4	1	5	169	4	0	0	0	10	....	1927-28	1929-30
Taylor, Ted	NYR, Det., Min., Van.	6	166	23	35	58	181	....	....	....	....	....	....	1964-65	1971-72
Taylor Jr., Billy	NYR	1	2	0	0	0	0	....	....	....	....	....	....	1964-65	1964-65
Teal, Jeff	Mtl.	1	6	0	1	1	0	....	....	....	....	....	....	1984-85	1984-85
Teal, Skip	Bos.	1	1	0	0	0	0	....	....	....	....	....	....	1954-55	1954-55
Teal, Vic	NYI	1	1	0	0	0	0	....	....	....	....	....	....	1973-74	1973-74
Tebbutt, Greg	Que., Pit.	2	26	0	3	3	35	....	....	....	....	....	....	1979-80	1983-84
Tepper, Stephen	Chi.	1	1	0	0	0	0	....	....	....	....	....	....	1992-93	1992-93
Terbenche, Paul	Chi., Buf.	5	189	5	26	31	28	12	0	0	0	0	....	1967-68	1973-74
Terrion, Greg	L.A., Tor.	8	561	93	150	243	339	35	2	9	11	41	....	1980-81	1987-88
Terry, Bill	Min.	1	5	0	0	0	0	....	....	....	....	....	....	1987-88	1987-88
• Tertyshny, Dimitri	Phi.	1	62	2	8	10	30	1	0	0	0	0	....	1998-99	1998-99
Tessier, Orval	Mtl., Bos.	3	59	5	7	12	6	....	....	....	....	....	....	1954-55	1960-61
Theberge, Greg	Wsh.	5	153	15	63	78	73	4	0	1	1	0	....	1979-80	1983-84
Thelin, Mats	Bos.	3	163	8	19	27	107	5	0	0	0	6	....	1984-85	1986-87
Thelven, Michael	Bos.	5	207	20	80	100	217	34	4	10	14	34	....	1985-86	1989-90
Therrien, Gaston	Que.	3	22	0	8	8	12	9	0	1	1	4	....	1980-81	1982-83
‡ Thibaudeau, Gilles	Mtl., NYI, Tor.	5	119	25	37	62	40	8	3	3	6	2	....	1986-87	1990-91
Thibeault, Lorrain	Det., Mtl.	2	5	0	2	2	2	....	....	....	....	....	....	1944-45	1945-46
Thiffault, Leo	Min.	1	....	....	....	....	....	5	0	0	0	0	....	1967-68	1967-68
Thomas, Cy	Chi., Tor.	1	14	2	2	4	12	....	....	....	....	....	....	1947-48	1947-48
Thomas, Reg	Que.	1	39	9	7	16	6	....	....	....	....	....	....	1979-80	1979-80
Thomlinson, Dave	St.L., Bos., L.A.	5	42	1	3	4	50	9	3	1	4	4	....	1989-90	1994-95
Thompson, Cliff	Bos.	2	13	0	1	1	2	....	....	....	....	....	....	1941-42	1948-49
Thompson, Errol	Tor., Det., Pit.	10	599	208	185	393	184	34	7	5	12	11	....	1970-71	1980-81
• Thompson, Ken	Mtl.	1	1	0	0	0	0	....	....	....	....	....	....	1917-18	1917-18
• Thompson, Paul	NYR, Chi.	14	582	153	179	332	336	48	11	11	22	54	3	1926-27	1938-39
• Thoms, Bill	Tor., Chi., Bos.	13	548	135	206	341	154	44	6	10	16	6	....	1932-33	1944-45
• Thomson, Bill	Det.	2	9	2	2	4	0	2	0	0	0	0	....	1938-39	1943-44
Thomson, Floyd	St.L.	8	411	56	97	153	341	10	0	2	2	6	....	1971-72	1979-80
Thomson, Jim	Wsh., Hfd., N.J., L.A., Ott., Ana.	7	115	4	3	7	416	1	0	0	0	0	....	1986-87	1993-94
• Thomson, Jimmy	Tor., Chi.	13	787	19	215	234	920	63	2	13	15	135	4	1945-46	1957-58
• Thomson, Rhys	Mtl., Tor.	2	25	0	2	2	38	....	....	....	....	....	....	1939-40	1942-43
Thornbury, Tom	Pit.	1	14	1	8	9	16	....	....	....	....	....	....	1983-84	1983-84
• Thorsteinson, Joe	NYA	1	4	0	0	0	0	....	....	....	....	....	....	1932-33	1932-33
• Thurier, Fred	NYA, Bro., NYR	3	80	25	27	52	18	....	....	....	....	....	....	1940-41	1944-45
Thurlby, Tom	Oak.	1	20	1	1	2	4	....	....	....	....	....	....	1967-68	1967-68
Thyer, Mario	Min.	1	5	0	0	0	0	1	0	0	0	2	....	1989-90	1989-90
Tichy, Milan	Chi., NYI	3	23	0	5	5	40	....	....	....	....	....	....	1992-93	1995-96
Tidey, Alex	Buf., Edm.	3	9	0	0	0	8	2	0	0	0	0	....	1976-77	1979-80
‡ Tilley, Tom	St.L.	4	174	4	38	42	89	14	1	3	4	19	....	1988-89	1993-94
• Timgren, Ray	Tor., Chi.	6	251	14	44	58	70	30	3	9	12	6	2	1948-49	1954-55
Tippett, Dave	Hfd., Wsh., Pit., Phi.	12	721	93	169	262	317	62	6	16	22	34	....	1983-84	1993-94
Titanic, Morris	Buf., Buffalo Sabres	3	19	0	0	0	0	....	....	....	....	....	....	1974-75	1976-77
Tkaczuk, Walt	NYR	14	945	227	451	678	556	93	19	32	51	119	....	1967-68	1980-81
Toal, Mike	Edm.	1	3	0	0	0	0	....	....	....	....	....	....	1979-80	1979-80
Todd, Kevin	N.J., Edm., Chi., L.A., Ana.	9	383	70	133	203	225	12	3	2	5	16	....	1988-89	1997-98
Tomalty, Glenn	Wpg.	1	1	0	0	0	0	....	....	....	....	....	....	1979-80	1979-80
Tomlak, Mike	Hfd.	4	141	15	22	37	103	10	0	1	1	4	....	1989-90	1993-94
‡ Tomlinson, Dave	Tor., Wpg., Fla.	4	42	1	3	4	28	....	....	....	....	....	....	1991-92	1994-95
Tomlinson, Kirk	Min.	1	1	0	0	0	0	....	....	....	....	....	....	1987-88	1987-88
Tomson, Jack	NYA	3	15	1	1	2	0	2	0	0	0	0	....	1938-39	1940-41
Tonelli, John	NYI, Cgy., L.A., Chi., Que.	14	1028	325	511	836	911	172	40	75	115	200	4	1978-79	1991-92
Tookey, Tim	Wsh., Que., Pit., Phi., L.A.	7	106	22	36	58	71	10	1	3	4	2	....	1980-81	1988-89
Toomey, Sean	Min.	1	1	0	0	0	0	....	....	....	....	....	....	1986-87	1986-87
Toppazzini, Jerry	Bos., Chi., Det.	12	783	163	244	407	436	40	13	9	22	13	....	1952-53	1963-64
Toppazzini, Zellio	Bos., NYR, Chi.	5	123	21	22	43	49	2	0	0	0	0	....	1948-49	1956-57
‡ Torgaev, Pavel	Cgy., T.B.	2	55	6	14	20	20	1	0	0	0	0	....	1995-96	1999-00
‡ Torkki, Jari	Chi.	1	4	1	0	1	0	....	....	....	....	....	....	1988-89	1988-89
‡ Tormanen, Antti	Ott.	1	50	7	8	15	28	....	....	....	....	....	....	1995-96	1995-96
• Touhey, Bill	Mtl.M., Ott., Bos.	7	280	65	40	105	107	2	1	0	1	0	....	1927-28	1933-34
• Toupin, Jacques	Chi.	1	8	1	2	3	0	4	0	0	0	0	....	1943-44	1943-44
• Townsend, Art	Chi.	1	5	0	0	0	0	....	....	....	....	....	....	1926-27	1926-27
Townshend, Graeme	Bos., NYI, Ott.	5	45	3	7	10	28	....	....	....	....	....	....	1989-90	1993-94
Trader, Larry	Det., St.L., Mtl.	4	91	5	13	18	74	3	0	0	0	0	....	1982-83	1987-88
• Trainor, Wes	NYR	1	17	1	2	3	6	....	....	....	....	....	....	1948-49	1948-49
• Trapp, Bob	Chi.	2	82	4	4	8	129	2	0	0	0	4	....	1926-27	1927-28
Trapp, Doug	Buf.	1	2	0	0	0	0	....	....	....	....	....	....	1986-87	1986-87
• Traub, Percy	Chi., Det.	3	130	3	3	6	217	4	0	0	0	6	....	1926-27	1928-29
Tredway, Brock	L.A.	1	....	....	....	....	....	1	0	0	0	0	....	1981-82	1981-82
Tremblay, Brent	Wsh.	2	10	1	0	1	6	....	....	....	....	....	....	1978-79	1979-80
Tremblay, Gilles	Mtl.	9	509	168	162	330	161	48	9	14	23	4	3	1960-61	1968-69
• Tremblay, J.C.	Mtl.	13	794	57	306	363	204	108	14	51	65	58	5	1959-60	1971-72
Tremblay, Marcel	Mtl.C.	1	10	0	2	2	0	....	....	....	....	....	....	1938-39	1938-39
Tremblay, Mario	Mtl.	12	852	258	326	584	1043	101	20	29	49	187	5	1974-75	1985-86
• Tremblay, Nil	Mtl.	2	3	0	1	1	0	2	0	0	0	0	....	1944-45	1945-46
Trimper, Tim	Chi., Wpg., Min.	6	190	30	36	66	153	2	0	0	0	2	....	1979-80	1984-85
Trottier, Bryan	NYI, Pit.	21	1279	524	901	1425	912	221	71	113	184	277	6	1975-76	1993-94
• Trottier, Dave	Mtl.M., Det.	11	446	121	113	234	517	31	4	3	7	39	1	1928-29	1938-39
Trottier, Guy	NYR, Tor.	3	115	28	17	45	37	9	1	0	1	16	....	1968-69	1971-72
Trottier, Rocky	N.J.	2	38	6	4	10	2	....	....	....	....	....	....	1983-84	1984-85
• Trudel, Lou	Chi., Mtl.C., Mtl.	8	306	49	69	118	122	24	1	3	4	4	2	1933-34	1940-41
Trudell, Rene	NYR	3	129	24	28	52	72	5	0	0	0	2	....	1945-46	1947-48
‡ Tsulygin, Nikolai	Ana.	1	22	0	1	1	8	....	....	....	....	....	....	1996-97	1996-97
‡ Tsygurov, Denis	Buf., L.A.	3	51	1	5	6	45	....	....	....	....	....	....	1993-94	1995-96
‡ Tucker, John	Buf., Wsh., NYI, T.B.	12	656	177	259	436	285	31	10	18	28	24	....	1983-84	1995-96
• Tudin, Connie	Mtl.	1	4	0	1	1	4	....	....	....	....	....	....	1941-42	1941-42
Tudor, Rob	Van., St.L.	3	28	4	4	8	19	3	0	0	0	0	....	1978-79	1982-83
Tuer, Allan	L.A., Min., Hfd.	4	57	1	1	2	208	....	....	....	....	....	....	1985-86	1989-90
Turcotte, Alfie	Mtl., Wpg., Wsh.	7	112	17	29	46	49	5	0	0	0	0	....	1983-84	1990-91
‡ Turgeon, Sylvain	Hfd., N.J., Mtl., Ott.	12	669	269	226	495	691	36	4	7	11	22	....	1983-84	1994-95
Turlick, Gord	Bos.	1	2	0	0	0	2	....	....	....	....	....	....	1959-60	1959-60
Turnbull, Ian	Tor., L.A., Pit.	10	628	123	317	440	736	55	13	32	45	94	....	1973-74	1982-83
Turnbull, Perry	St.L., Mtl., Wpg.	9	608	188	163	351	1245	34	6	7	13	86	....	1979-80	1987-88
Turnbull, Randy	Cgy.	1	1	0	0	0	2	....	....	....	....	....	....	1981-82	1981-82
Turner, Bob	Mtl., Chi.	8	478	19	51	70	307	68	1	4	5	44	5	1955-56	1962-63
Turner, Brad	NYI	1	3	0	0	0	0	....	....	....	....	....	....	1991-92	1991-92
Turner, Dean	NYR, Col., L.A.	4	35	1	0	1	59	....	....	....	....	....	....	1978-79	1982-83
• Tustin, Norm	NYR	1	18	2	4	6	0	....	....	....	....	....	....	1941-42	1941-42
Tuten, Aut	Chi.	2	39	4	8	12	48	....	....	....	....	....	....	1941-42	1942-43

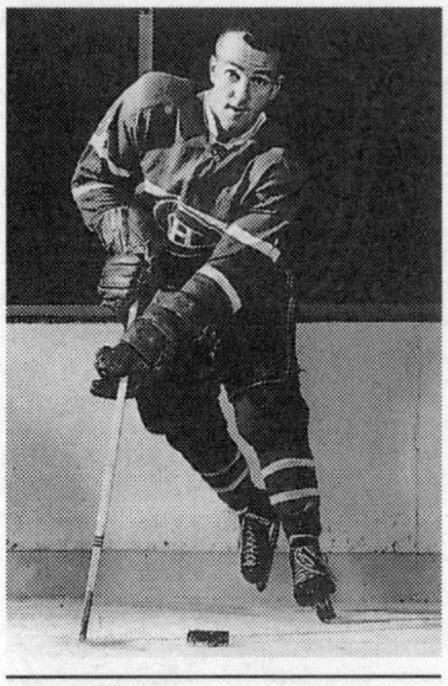

J.C. Tremblay

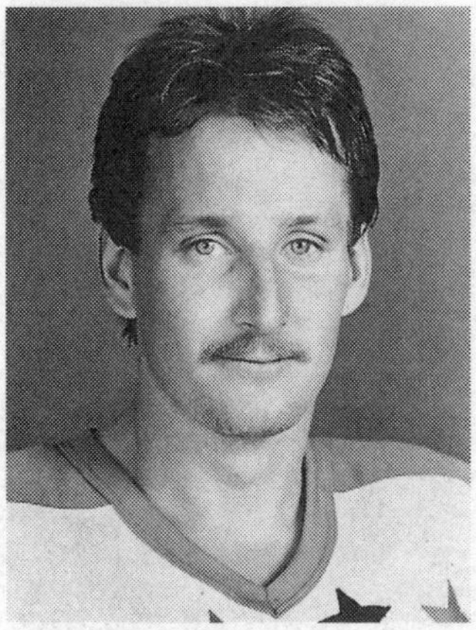

Darren Veitch

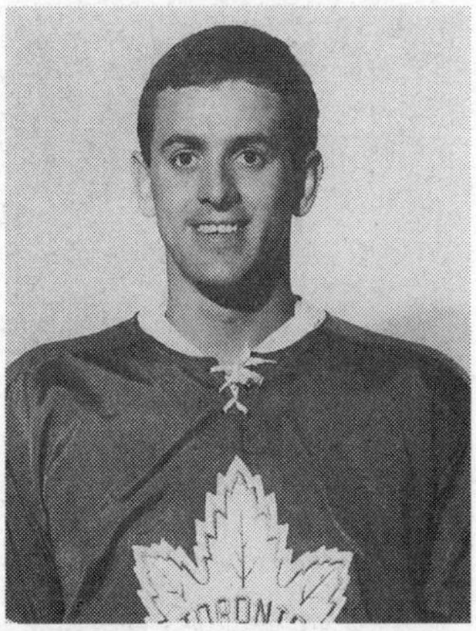

Mike Walton

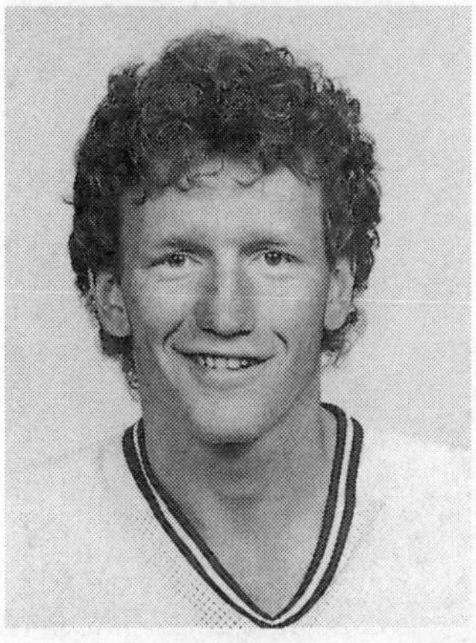

Blake Wesley

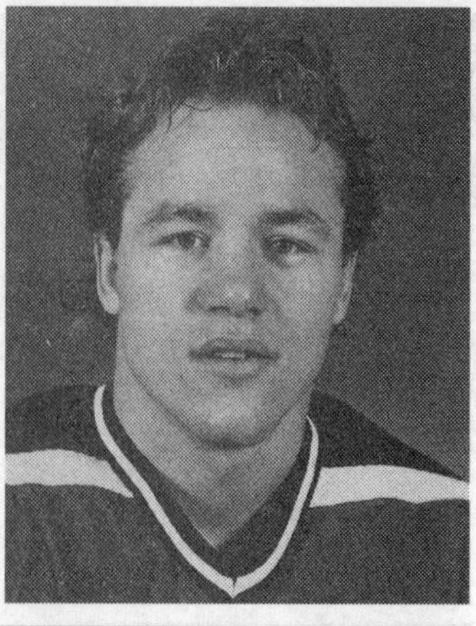

Mitch Wilson

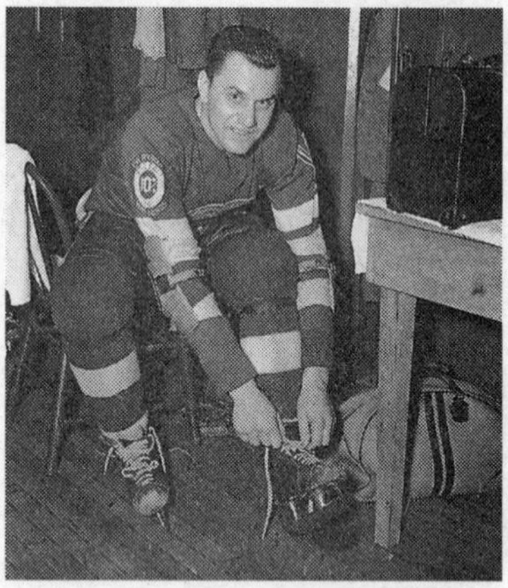

Steve Wojciechowski

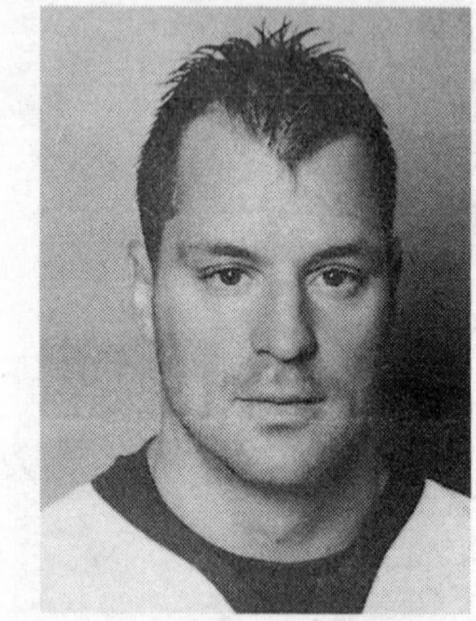

Craig Wolanin

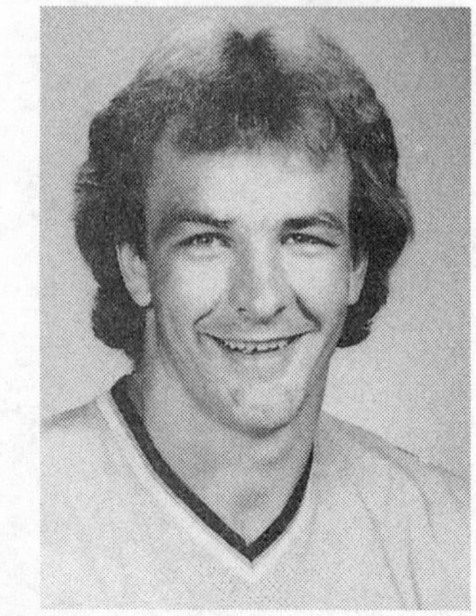

Bennett Wolf

Name	NHL Teams	NHL Seasons	Regular Schedule GP	G	A	TP	PIM	Playoffs GP	G	A	TP	PIM	NHL Cup Wins	First NHL Season	Last NHL Season
‡ Tutt, Brian	Wsh.	1	7	1	0	1	2	....	....	....	....	....	....	1989-90	1989-90
Tuttle, Steve	St.L.	3	144	28	28	56	12	17	1	6	7	2	....	1988-89	1990-91

U V

Name	NHL Teams	NHL Seasons	GP	G	A	TP	PIM	GP	G	A	TP	PIM	NHL Cup Wins	First NHL Season	Last NHL Season
Ubriaco, Gene	Pit., Oak., Chi.	3	177	39	35	74	50	11	2	0	2	4	....	1967-68	1969-70
Ullman, Norm	Det., Tor.	20	1410	490	739	1229	712	106	30	53	83	67	....	1955-56	1974-75
Unger, Garry	Tor., Det., St.L., Atl., L.A., Edm.	16	1105	413	391	804	1075	52	12	18	30	105	....	1967-68	1982-83
Vachon, Nick	NYI	1	1	0	0	0	0	....	....	....	....	....	....	1996-97	1996-97
Vadnais, Carol	Mtl., Oak., Cal., Bos., NYR, N.J.	17	1087	169	418	587	1813	106	10	40	50	185	2	1966-67	1982-83
Vail, Eric	Atl., Cgy., Det.	9	591	216	260	476	281	20	5	6	11	6	....	1973-74	1981-82
• Vail, Sparky	NYR	2	50	4	1	5	18	10	0	0	0	2	....	1928-29	1929-30
Vaive, Rick	Van., Tor., Chi., Buf.	13	876	441	347	788	1445	54	27	16	43	111	....	1979-80	1991-92
Valentine, Chris	Wsh.	3	105	43	52	95	127	2	0	0	0	4	....	1981-82	1983-84
Valiquette, Jack	Tor., Col.	7	350	84	134	218	79	23	3	6	9	4	....	1974-75	1980-81
‡ Vallis, Lindsay	Mtl.	1	1	0	0	0	0	....	....	....	....	....	....	1993-94	1993-94
Van Boxmeer, John	Mtl., Col., Buf., Que.	11	588	84	274	358	465	38	5	15	20	37	1	1973-74	1983-84
Van Dorp, Wayne	Edm., Pit., Chi., Que.	6	125	12	12	24	565	27	0	1	1	42	1	1986-87	1991-92
Van Impe, Ed	Chi., Phi., Pit.	11	700	27	126	153	1025	66	1	12	13	131	2	1966-67	1976-77
‡ Varvio, Jarkko	Dal.	2	13	3	4	7	4	....	....	....	....	....	....	1993-94	1994-95
Vaske, Dennis	NYI, Bos.	9	235	5	41	46	253	22	0	7	7	16	....	1990-91	1998-99
• Vasko, Moose	Chi., Min.	13	786	34	166	200	719	78	2	7	9	73	1	1956-57	1969-70
Vasko, Rick	Det.	3	31	3	7	10	29	....	....	....	....	....	....	1977-78	1980-81
Vautour, Yvon	NYI, Col., N.J., Que.	6	204	26	33	59	401	....	....	....	....	....	....	1979-80	1984-85
Vaydik, Greg	Chi.	1	5	0	0	0	0	....	....	....	....	....	....	1976-77	1976-77
Veitch, Darren	Wsh., Det., Tor.	10	511	48	209	257	296	33	4	11	15	33	....	1980-81	1990-91
Velischek, Randy	Min., N.J., Que.	10	509	21	76	97	401	44	2	5	7	32	....	1982-83	1991-92
Vellucci, Mike	Hfd.	1	2	0	0	0	11	....	....	....	....	....	....	1987-88	1987-88
Venasky, Vic	L.A.	7	430	61	101	162	66	21	1	5	6	12	....	1972-73	1978-79
Veneruzzo, Gary	St.L.	2	7	1	1	2	0	9	0	2	2	2	....	1967-68	1971-72
Vermette, Mark	Que.	4	67	5	13	18	33	....	....	....	....	....	....	1988-89	1991-92
‡ Verret, Claude	Buf.	2	14	2	5	7	2	....	....	....	....	....	....	1983-84	1984-85
Verstraete, Leigh	Tor.	3	8	0	1	1	14	....	....	....	....	....	....	1982-83	1987-88
Ververgaert, Dennis	Van., Phi., Wsh.	8	583	176	216	392	247	8	1	2	3	6	....	1973-74	1980-81
Vesey, Jim	St.L., Bos.	3	15	1	2	3	7	....	....	....	....	....	....	1988-89	1991-92
Veysey, Sid	Van.	1	1	0	0	0	0	....	....	....	....	....	....	1977-78	1977-78
Vickers, Steve	NYR	10	698	246	340	586	330	68	24	25	49	58	....	1972-73	1981-82
Vigneault, Alain	St.L.	4	42	2	5	7	82	4	0	1	1	26	....	1981-82	1982-83
‡ Viitakoski, Vesa	Cgy.	3	23	2	4	6	8	....	....	....	....	....	....	1993-94	1995-96
‡ Vilgrain, Claude	Van., N.J., Phi.	5	89	21	32	53	78	11	1	1	2	17	....	1987-88	1993-94
Vincelette, Dan	Chi., Que.	6	193	20	22	42	351	12	0	0	0	4	....	1986-87	1991-92
Vipond, Pete	Cal.	1	3	0	0	0	0	....	....	....	....	....	....	1972-73	1972-73
Virta, Hannu	Buf.	5	245	25	101	126	66	17	1	3	4	6	....	1981-82	1985-86
‡ Visheau, Mark	Wpg., L.A.	2	29	1	3	4	107	....	....	....	....	....	....	1993-94	1998-99
‡ Vitolinsh, Harijs	Wpg.	1	8	0	0	0	4	....	....	....	....	....	....	1993-94	1993-94
‡ Viveiros, Emanuel	Min.	3	29	1	11	12	6	....	....	....	....	....	....	1985-86	1987-88
• Vokes, Ed	Chi.	1	5	0	0	0	0	....	....	....	....	....	....	1930-31	1930-31
Volcan, Mickey	Hfd., Cgy.	4	162	8	33	41	146	....	....	....	....	....	....	1980-81	1983-84
Volek, David	NYI	7	396	95	154	249	201	15	5	5	10	2	....	1988-89	1994-95
Volmar, Doug	Det., L.A.	4	62	13	8	21	26	2	1	0	1	0	....	1969-70	1972-73
• Voss, Carl	Tor., NYR, Det., Ott., St.L., NYA, Mtl.M., Chi.	9	261	34	70	104	50	24	5	3	8	0	1	1926-27	1938-39
Vyazmikin, Igor	Edm.	1	4	1	0	1	0	....	....	....	....	....	....	1990-91	1990-91

W

Name	NHL Teams	NHL Seasons	GP	G	A	TP	PIM	GP	G	A	TP	PIM	NHL Cup Wins	First NHL Season	Last NHL Season
Waddell, Don	L.A.	3	1	0	0	0	0	....	....	....	....	....	....	1980-81	1980-81
• Waite, Frank	NYR	1	17	1	3	4	4	....	....	....	....	....	....	1930-31	1930-31
Walker, Gord	NYR, L.A.	4	31	3	4	7	23	....	....	....	....	....	....	1986-87	1989-90
Walker, Howard	Wsh., Cgy.	3	83	2	13	15	133	....	....	....	....	....	....	1980-81	1982-83
• Walker, Jack	Det.	2	80	5	8	13	18	....	....	....	....	....	....	1926-27	1927-28
Walker, Kurt	Tor.	3	71	4	5	9	142	16	0	0	0	34	....	1975-76	1977-78
Walker, Russ	L.A.	2	17	1	0	1	41	....	....	....	....	....	....	1976-77	1977-78
Wall, Bob	Det., L.A., St.L.	8	322	30	55	85	155	22	0	3	3	2	....	1964-65	1971-72
Wallin, Peter	NYR	2	52	3	14	17	14	14	2	6	8	6	....	1980-81	1981-82
Walsh, Jim	Buf.	1	4	0	1	1	4	....	....	....	....	....	....	1981-82	1981-82
Walsh, Mike	NYI	2	14	2	0	2	4	....	....	....	....	....	....	1987-88	1988-89
Walter, Ryan	Wsh., Mtl., Van.	15	1003	264	382	646	946	113	16	35	51	62	1	1978-79	1992-93
• Walton, Bobby	Mtl.	1	4	0	0	0	0	....	....	....	....	....	....	1943-44	1943-44
Walton, Mike	Tor., Bos., Van., St.L., Chi.	12	588	201	247	448	357	47	14	10	24	45	2	1965-66	1978-79
Wappel, Gord	Atl., Cgy.	3	20	1	1	2	10	2	0	0	0	4	....	1979-80	1981-82
Ward, Don	Chi., Bos.	2	34	0	1	1	16	....	....	....	....	....	....	1957-58	1959-60
• Ward, Jimmy	Mtl.M., Mtl.C.	12	527	147	127	274	455	36	4	4	8	26	1	1927-28	1938-39
Ward, Joe	Col.	1	4	0	0	0	2	....	....	....	....	....	....	1980-81	1980-81
Ward, Ron	Tor., Van.	2	89	2	5	7	6	....	....	....	....	....	....	1969-70	1971-72
Ware, Michael	Edm.	2	5	0	1	1	15	....	....	....	....	....	....	1988-89	1989-90
Wares, Eddie	NYR, Det., Chi.	9	321	60	102	162	161	45	5	7	12	34	1	1936-37	1946-47
Warner, Bob	Tor.	2	10	1	1	2	4	4	0	0	0	0	....	1975-76	1976-77
Warner, Jim	Hfd.	1	32	0	3	3	10	....	....	....	....	....	....	1979-80	1979-80
Warwick, Bill	NYR	2	14	3	3	6	16	....	....	....	....	....	....	1942-43	1943-44
Warwick, Grant	NYR, Bos., Mtl.	9	395	147	142	289	220	16	2	4	6	6	....	1941-42	1949-50
• Wasnie, Nick	Chi., Mtl.C., NYA, Ott., St.L.	7	248	57	34	91	176	20	6	3	9	20	2	1927-28	1934-35
Watson, Bill	Chi.	4	115	23	36	59	12	6	0	2	2	0	....	1985-86	1988-89
Watson, Bryan	Mtl., Det., Oak., Pit., St.L., Wsh.	16	878	17	135	152	2212	32	2	0	2	70	....	1963-64	1978-79
Watson, Dave	Col.	3	18	0	1	1	10	....	....	....	....	....	....	1978-79	1980-81
Watson, Harry	Bro., Det., Tor., Chi.	14	809	236	207	443	150	62	16	9	25	27	5	1941-42	1956-57
Watson, Jim	Det., Buf.	8	221	4	19	23	345	....	....	....	....	....	....	1963-64	1971-72
Watson, Jimmy	Phi.	10	613	38	148	186	492	101	5	34	39	89	2	1972-73	1981-82
Watson, Joe	Bos., Phi., Col.	14	835	38	178	216	447	84	3	12	15	82	2	1964-65	1978-79
• Watson, Phil	NYR, Mtl.	13	590	144	265	409	532	54	10	25	35	67	2	1935-36	1947-48
Watters, Tim	Wpg., L.A.	14	741	26	151	177	1289	82	1	5	6	115	....	1981-82	1994-95
Watts, Brian	Det.	1	4	0	0	0	0	....	....	....	....	....	....	1975-76	1975-76
• Webster, Aubrey	Phi., Mtl.M.	2	5	0	0	0	0	....	....	....	....	....	....	1930-31	1934-35
• Webster, Don	Tor.	1	27	7	6	13	28	5	0	0	0	12	....	1943-44	1943-44
Webster, John	NYR	1	14	0	0	0	4	....	....	....	....	....	....	1949-50	1949-50
Webster, Tom	Bos., Det., Cal.	5	102	33	42	75	61	1	0	0	0	0	....	1968-69	1979-80
• Weiland, Cooney	Bos., Ott., Det.	12	509	173	160	333	147	45	12	10	22	12	2	1928-29	1938-39
Weir, Stan	Cal., Tor., Edm., Col., Det.	10	642	139	207	346	183	37	6	5	11	4	....	1972-73	1982-83
Weir, Wally	Que., Hfd., Pit.	6	320	21	45	66	625	23	0	1	1	96	....	1979-80	1984-85
• Wellington, Alex	Que.	1	1	0	0	0	0	....	....	....	....	....	....	1919-20	1919-20
Wells, Jay	L.A., Phi., Buf., NYR, St.L., T.B.	18	1098	47	216	263	2359	114	3	14	17	213	1	1979-80	1996-97
Wensink, John	St.L., Bos., Que., Col., N.J.	8	403	70	68	138	840	43	2	6	8	86	....	1973-74	1982-83
• Wentworth, Cy	Chi., Mtl.M., Mtl.C., Mtl.	13	575	39	68	107	355	35	5	6	11	20	1	1927-28	1939-40
Wesley, Blake	Phi., Hfd., Que., Tor.	7	298	18	46	64	486	19	2	2	4	30	....	1979-80	1985-86
Westfall, Ed	Bos., NYI	18	1220	231	394	625	544	95	22	37	59	41	2	1961-62	1978-79
Wharram, Kenny	Chi.	14	766	252	281	533	222	80	16	27	43	38	1	1951-52	1968-69
Wharton, Len	NYR	1	1	0	0	0	0	....	....	....	....	....	....	1944-45	1944-45
‡ Wheeldon, Simon	NYR, Wpg.	3	15	0	2	2	10	....	....	....	....	....	....	1987-88	1990-91
• Wheldon, Donald	St.L.	1	2	0	0	0	0	....	....	....	....	....	....	1974-75	1974-75
Whelton, Bill	Wpg.	1	2	0	0	0	0	....	....	....	....	....	....	1980-81	1980-81
Whistle, Rob	NYR, St.L.	2	51	7	5	12	16	4	0	0	0	2	....	1985-86	1987-88
White, Bill	L.A., Chi.	10	604	50	215	265	495	91	7	32	39	76	....	1967-68	1976-77
White, Moe	Mtl.	1	4	0	1	1	2	....	....	....	....	....	....	1945-46	1945-46
• White, Sherman	NYR	2	4	0	2	2	0	....	....	....	....	....	....	1946-47	1949-50
• White, Tex	Pit., NYA, Phi.	6	203	33	12	45	141	4	0	0	0	4	....	1925-26	1930-31
White, Tony	Wsh., Min.	5	164	37	28	65	104	....	....	....	....	....	....	1974-75	1979-80
Whitelaw, Bob	Det.	2	32	0	2	2	2	8	0	0	0	0	....	1940-41	1941-42
Whitlock, Bob	Min.	1	1	0	0	0	0	....	....	....	....	....	....	1969-70	1969-70
‡ Whyte, Sean	L.A.	2	21	0	2	2	12	....	....	....	....	....	....	1991-92	1992-93
• Wickenheiser, Doug	Mtl., St.L., Van., NYR, Wsh.	10	556	111	165	276	286	41	4	7	11	18	....	1980-81	1989-90
• Widing, Juha	NYR, L.A., Cle.	8	575	144	226	370	208	8	1	2	3	2	....	1969-70	1976-77

Name	NHL Teams	NHL Seasons	Regular Schedule GP	G	A	TP	PIM	Playoffs GP	G	A	TP	PIM	NHL Cup Wins	First NHL Season	Last NHL Season
‡ Widmer, Jason	NYI, S.J.	3	7	0	1	1	7	....	....	....	....	....	....	1994-95	1996-97
• Wiebe, Art	Chi.	11	414	14	27	41	201	31	1	3	4	10	1	1932-33	1943-44
Wiemer, Jim	Buf., NYR, Edm., L.A., Bos.	11	325	29	72	101	378	62	5	8	13	63	1	1982-83	1993-94
• Wilcox, Archie	Mtl.M., Bos., St.L.	6	208	8	14	22	158	12	1	0	1	8	....	1929-30	1934-35
Wilcox, Barry	Van.	2	33	3	2	5	15	....	....	....	....	....	....	1972-73	1974-75
Wilder, Arch	Det.	1	18	0	2	2	2	....	....	....	....	....	....	1940-41	1940-41
Wiley, Jim	Pit., Van.	5	63	4	10	14	8	....	....	....	....	....	....	1972-73	1976-77
Wilkie, Bob	Det., Phi.	2	18	2	5	7	10	....	....	....	....	....	....	1990-91	1993-94
Wilkins, Barry	Bos., Van., Pit.	9	418	27	125	152	663	6	0	1	1	4	....	1966-67	1975-76
• Wilkinson, John	Bos.	1	9	0	0	0	6	....	....	....	....	....	....	1943-44	1943-44
Wilkinson, Neil	Min., S.J., Chi., Wpg., Pit.	10	460	16	67	83	813	53	3	6	9	41	....	1989-90	1998-99
Wilks, Brian	L.A.	4	48	4	8	12	27	....	....	....	....	....	....	1984-85	1988-89
Willard, Rod	Tor.	1	1	0	0	0	0	....	....	....	....	....	....	1982-83	1982-83
• Williams, Burr	Det., St.L., Bos.	3	19	0	1	1	28	7	0	0	0	8	....	1933-34	1936-37
Williams, Butch	St.L., Cal.	3	108	14	35	49	131	....	....	....	....	....	....	1973-74	1975-76
Williams, Darryl	L.A.	1	2	0	0	0	10	....	....	....	....	....	....	1992-93	1992-93
Williams, David	S.J., Ana.	4	173	11	53	64	157	....	....	....	....	....	....	1991-92	1994-95
Williams, Fred	Det.	1	44	2	5	7	10	....	....	....	....	....	....	1976-77	1976-77
Williams, Gord	Phi.	2	2	0	0	0	2	....	....	....	....	....	....	1981-82	1982-83
Williams, Sean	Chi.	1	2	0	0	0	4	....	....	....	....	....	....	1991-92	1991-92
Williams, Tiger	Tor., Van., Det., L.A., Hfd.	14	962	241	272	513	3966	83	12	23	35	455	....	1974-75	1987-88
Williams, Tom	NYR, L.A.	8	397	115	138	253	73	29	8	7	15	4	....	1971-72	1978-79
• Williams, Tommy	Bos., Min., Cal., Wsh.	13	663	161	269	430	177	10	2	5	7	2	....	1961-62	1975-76
Willson, Don	Mtl.C.	2	22	2	7	9	0	3	0	0	0	0	....	1937-38	1938-39
Wilson, Behn	Phi., Chi., Van.	11	601	98	260	358	1480	67	12	29	41	190	....	1978-79	1988-89
• Wilson, Bert	NYR, St.L., L.A., Cgy.	8	478	37	44	81	646	21	0	2	2	42	....	1973-74	1980-81
Wilson, Bob	Chi.	1	1	0	0	0	0	....	....	....	....	....	....	1953-54	1953-54
Wilson, Carey	Cgy., Hfd., NYR	10	552	169	258	427	314	52	11	13	24	14	....	1983-84	1992-93
• Wilson, Cully	Tor., Mtl.C., Ham., Chi.	5	127	59	28	87	243	2	1	0	1	6	....	1919-20	1926-27
Wilson, Doug	Chi., S.J.	16	1024	237	590	827	830	95	19	61	80	88	....	1977-78	1992-93
Wilson, Gord	Bos.	1	....	....	....	....	....	2	0	0	0	0	....	1954-55	1954-55
Wilson, Hub	NYA	1	2	0	0	0	0	....	....	....	....	....	....	1931-32	1931-32
Wilson, Jerry	Mtl.	1	3	0	0	0	2	....	....	....	....	....	....	1956-57	1956-57
Wilson, Johnny	Det., Chi., Tor., NYR	13	688	161	171	332	190	66	14	13	27	11	4	1949-50	1961-62
• Wilson, Larry	Det., Chi.	6	152	21	48	69	75	4	0	0	0	0	1	1949-50	1955-56
Wilson, Mitch	N.J., Pit.	2	26	2	3	5	104	....	....	....	....	....	....	1984-85	1986-87
Wilson, Murray	Mtl., L.A.	7	386	94	95	189	162	53	5	14	19	32	3	1972-73	1978-79
Wilson, Rick	Mtl., St.L., Det.	8	239	6	26	32	165	3	0	0	0	0	....	1973-74	1976-77
Wilson, Rik	St.L., Cgy., Chi.	6	251	25	65	90	220	22	0	4	4	23	....	1981-82	1987-88
Wilson, Roger	Chi.	1	7	0	2	2	6	....	....	....	....	....	....	1974-75	1974-75
Wilson, Ron	Tor., Min.	10	177	26	67	93	68	20	4	13	17	8	....	1977-78	1987-88
Wilson, Ron	Wpg., St.L., Mtl.	14	832	110	216	326	415	63	10	12	22	64	....	1979-80	1993-94
Wilson, Wally	Bos.	1	53	11	8	19	18	1	0	0	0	0	....	1947-48	1947-48
Wing, Murray	Det.	1	1	0	1	1	0	....	....	....	....	....	....	1973-74	1973-74
‡ Winnes, Chris	Bos., Phi.	4	33	1	6	7	6	1	0	0	0	0	....	1990-91	1993-94
• Wiseman, Eddie	Det., NYA, Bos.	10	456	115	165	280	136	43	10	10	20	16	1	1932-33	1941-42
Wiste, Jim	Chi., Van.	3	52	1	10	11	8	....	....	....	....	....	....	1968-69	1970-71
Witherspoon, Jim	L.A.	1	2	0	0	0	2	....	....	....	....	....	....	1975-76	1975-76
Witiuk, Steve	Chi.	1	33	3	8	11	14	....	....	....	....	....	....	1951-52	1951-52
Woit, Benny	Det., Chi.	7	334	7	26	33	170	41	2	6	8	18	3	1950-51	1956-57
Wojciechowski, Steve	Det.	2	54	19	20	39	17	6	0	1	1	0	....	1944-45	1946-47
Wolanin, Craig	N.J., Que., Col., T.B., Tor.	13	695	40	133	173	894	35	4	6	10	67	1	1985-86	1997-98
Wolf, Bennett	Pit.	3	30	0	1	1	133	....	....	....	....	....	....	1980-81	1982-83
Wong, Mike	Det.	1	22	1	1	2	12	....	....	....	....	....	....	1975-76	1975-76
Wood, Randy	NYI, Buf., Tor., Dal.	11	741	175	159	334	603	51	8	9	17	40	....	1986-87	1996-97
Wood, Robert	NYR	1	1	0	0	0	0	....	....	....	....	....	....	1950-51	1950-51
Woodley, Dan	Van.	1	5	2	0	2	17	....	....	....	....	....	....	1987-88	1987-88
Woods, Paul	Det.	7	501	72	124	196	276	7	0	5	5	4	....	1977-78	1983-84
‡ Wortman, Kevin	Cgy.	1	5	0	0	0	2	....	....	....	....	....	....	1993-94	1993-94
• Woytowich, Bob	Bos., Min., Pit., L.A.	8	503	32	126	158	352	24	1	3	4	20	....	1964-65	1971-72
Wright, John	Van., St.L., K.C.	3	127	16	36	52	67	....	....	....	....	....	....	1972-73	1974-75
Wright, Keith	Phi.	1	1	0	0	0	0	....	....	....	....	....	....	1967-68	1967-68
Wright, Larry	Phi., Cal., Det.	5	106	4	8	12	19	....	....	....	....	....	....	1971-72	1977-78
Wycherley, Ralph	NYA, Bro.	2	28	4	7	11	6	....	....	....	....	....	....	1940-41	1941-42
• Wylie, Bill	NYR	1	1	0	0	0	0	....	....	....	....	....	....	1950-51	1950-51
Wylie, Duane	Chi.	2	14	3	3	6	2	....	....	....	....	....	....	1974-75	1976-77
Wyrozub, Randy	Buf.	4	100	8	10	18	10	....	....	....	....	....	....	1970-71	1973-74

Y Z

Name	NHL Teams	NHL Seasons	Regular Schedule GP	G	A	TP	PIM	Playoffs GP	G	A	TP	PIM	NHL Cup Wins	First NHL Season	Last NHL Season
• Yackel, Ken	Bos.	1	6	0	0	0	2	2	0	0	0	2	....	1958-59	1958-59
Yaremchuk, Gary	Tor.	4	34	1	4	5	28	....	....	....	....	....	....	1981-82	1984-85
Yaremchuk, Ken	Chi., Tor.	6	235	36	56	92	106	31	6	8	14	49	....	1983-84	1988-89
Yates, Ross	Hfd.	1	7	1	1	2	4	....	....	....	....	....	....	1983-84	1983-84
Yawney, Trent	Chi., Cgy., St.L.	13	593	27	102	129	783	60	9	17	26	81	....	1987-88	1998-99
Young, Brian	Chi.	1	8	0	2	2	6	....	....	....	....	....	....	1980-81	1980-81
Young, C.J.	Cgy., Bos.	1	43	7	7	14	32	....	....	....	....	....	....	1992-93	1992-93
• Young, Doug	Det., Mtl.	10	388	35	45	80	303	28	1	5	6	16	1	1931-32	1940-41
• Young, Howie	Det., Chi., Van.	8	336	12	62	74	851	19	2	4	6	46	....	1960-61	1970-71
Young, Tim	Min., Wpg., Phi.	10	628	195	341	536	438	36	7	24	31	27	....	1975-76	1984-85
Young, Warren	Min., Pit., Det.	7	236	72	77	149	472	....	....	....	....	....	....	1981-82	1987-88
Younghans, Tom	Min., NYR	6	429	44	41	85	373	24	2	1	3	21	....	1976-77	1981-82
‡ Ysebaert, Paul	N.J., Det., Wpg., Chi., T.B.	11	532	149	187	336	217	30	4	3	7	20	....	1988-89	1998-99
‡ Zabransky, Libor	St.L.	2	40	1	6	7	50	....	....	....	....	....	....	1996-97	1997-98
Zaharko, Miles	Atl., Chi.	4	129	5	32	37	84	3	0	0	0	0	....	1977-78	1981-82
Zaine, Rod	Pit., Buf.	2	61	10	6	16	25	....	....	....	....	....	....	1970-71	1971-72
Zanussi, Joe	NYR, Bos., St.L.	3	87	1	13	14	46	4	0	1	1	2	....	1974-75	1976-77
Zanussi, Ron	Min., Tor.	5	299	52	83	135	373	17	0	4	4	17	....	1977-78	1981-82
Zavisha, Brad	Edm.	2	2	0	0	0	0	....	....	....	....	....	....	1992-93	1993-94
Zeidel, Larry	Det., Chi., Phi.	5	158	3	16	19	198	12	0	1	1	12	1	1951-52	1968-69
Zemlak, Richard	Que., Min., Pit., Cgy.	5	132	2	12	14	587	1	0	0	0	10	....	1986-87	1991-92
Zeniuk, Ed	Det.	1	2	0	0	0	0	....	....	....	....	....	....	1954-55	1954-55
Zetterstrom, Lars	Van.	1	14	0	1	1	2	....	....	....	....	....	....	1978-79	1978-79
Zezel, Peter	Phi., St.L., Wsh., Tor., Dal., N.J., Van.	15	873	219	389	608	435	131	25	39	64	83	....	1984-85	1998-99
Zoborosky, Marty	Chi.	1	1	0	0	0	2	....	....	....	....	....	....	1944-45	1944-45
Zombo, Rick	Det., St.L., Bos.	12	652	24	130	154	728	60	1	11	12	127	....	1984-85	1995-96
Zuke, Mike	St.L., Hfd.	8	455	86	196	282	220	26	6	6	12	12	....	1978-79	1985-86
Zunich, Rudy	Det.	1	2	0	0	0	2	....	....	....	....	....	....	1943-44	1943-44

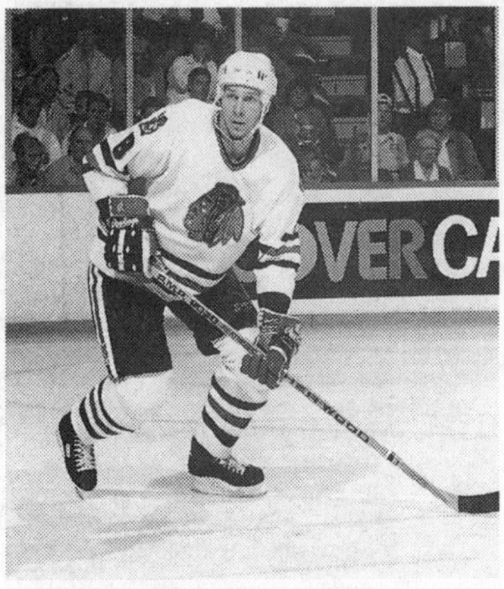

Trent Yawney

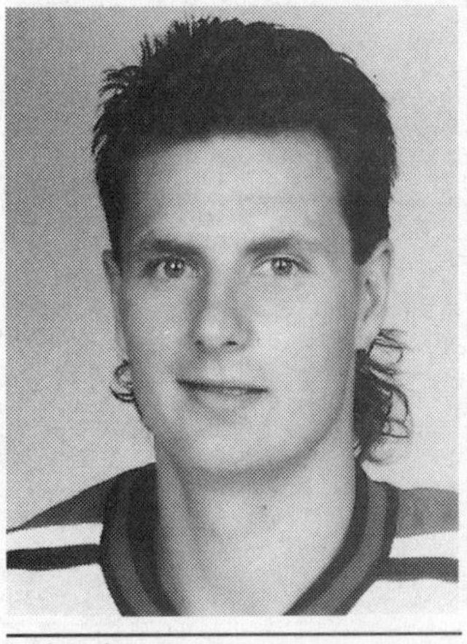

Paul Yserbart

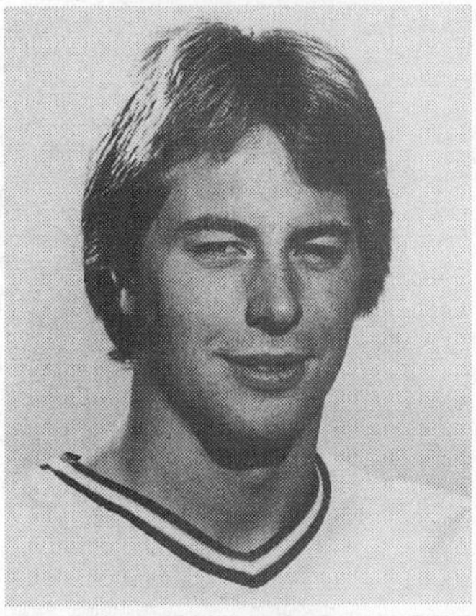

Ron Zanussi

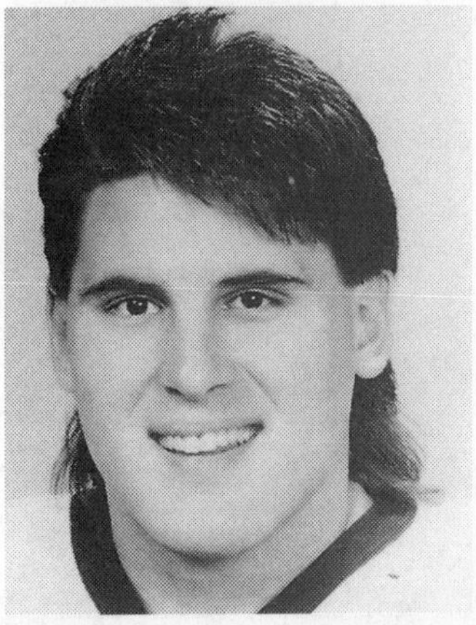

Peter Zezel

Clint Benedict

Bob Froese

Pokey Reddick

Johnny Bower

Ron Hextall

Jeff Reese

Jim Carey

Bob Janecyk

Kari Takko

Jacques Caron

Frank Pietrangelo

Tiny Thompson

Retired NHL Goaltender Index

Abbreviations: Teams/Cities: — **Ana.** – Anaheim; **Atl.** – Atlanta; **Bos.** – Boston, **Bro.** – Brooklyn; **Buf.** – Buffalo; **Cal.** – California; **Cgy.** – Calgary; **Cle.** – Cleveland; **Col.** – Colorado; **Dal.** – Dallas; **Det.** – Detroit; **Edm.** – Edmonton; **Fla.** – Florida; **Ham.** – Hamilton; **Hfd.** – Hartford; **K.C.** – Kansas City; **L.A.** – Los Angeles; **Min.** — Minnesota; **Mtl.** – Montreal; **Mtl. M.** – Montreal Maroons; **Mtl. W.** – Montreal Wanderers; **N.J.** – New Jersey; **NYA** – NY Americans; **NYI** – New York Islanders; **NYR** – New York Rangers; **Oak.** – Oakland; **Ott.** – Ottawa; **Phi.** – Philadelphia; **Pit.** – Pittsburgh; **Que.** – Quebec; **St. L.** – St. Louis; **S.J.** – San Jose; **T.B.** – Tampa Bay; **Tor.** – Toronto; **Van.** – Vancouver; **Wpg.** – Winnipeg; **Wsh.** – Washington.

Avg. – goals against per 60 minutes played; **GA** – goals against; **GP** – games played; **Mins** – minutes played; **SO** – shutouts.

● – deceased. § – Forward, defenseman or coach who appeared in goal. For complete career, see Retired Player Index. ‡ – Remains active in other leagues.

			Regular Schedule								Playoffs										
Name	NHL Teams	NHL Seasons	GP	W	L	T	Mins	GA	SO	Avg	GP	W	L	T	Mins	GA	SO	Avg	NHL Cup Wins	First NHL Season	Last NHL Season
Abbott, George	Bos.	1	1	0	1	0	60	7	0	7.00	....	....	....	....	....	....	....	....		1943-44	1943-44
Adams, John	Bos., Wsh.	2	22	9	10	1	1180	85	1	4.32	....	....	....	....	....	....	....	....		1972-73	1974-75
Aiken, Don	Mtl.	1	1	0	1	0	34	6	0	10.59	....	....	....	....	....	....	....	....		1957-58	1957-58
● Aitkenhead, Andy	NYR	3	106	47	43	16	6570	257	11	2.35	10	6	2	2	608	15	3	1.48	1	1932-33	1934-35
Almas, Red	Det., Chi.	3	3	0	2	1	180	13	0	4.33	5	1	3	....	263	13	0	2.97		1946-47	1952-53
● Anderson, Lorne	NYR	1	3	1	2	0	180	18	0	6.00	....	....	....	....	....	....	....	....		1951-52	1951-52
Astrom, Hardy	NYR, Col.	3	83	17	44	12	4456	278	0	3.74	....	....	....	....	....	....	....	....		1977-78	1980-81
Baker, Steve	NYR	4	57	20	20	11	3081	190	3	3.70	14	7	7	....	826	55	0	4.00		1979-80	1982-83
Bannerman, Murray	Van., Chi.	8	289	116	125	33	16470	1051	8	3.83	40	20	18	....	2322	165	0	4.26		1977-78	1986-87
Baron, Marco	Bos., L.A., Edm.	6	86	34	38	9	4822	292	1	3.63	1	0	1	....	20	3	0	9.00		1979-80	1984-85
Bassen, Hank	Chi., Det., Pit.	9	156	46	66	31	8759	434	5	2.97	5	1	3	....	274	11	0	2.41		1954-55	1967-68
● Bastien, Baz	Tor.	1	5	0	4	1	300	20	0	4.00	....	....	....	....	....	....	....	....		1945-46	1945-46
Bauman, Gary	Mtl., Min.	3	35	6	18	6	1718	102	0	3.56	....	....	....	....	....	....	....	....		1966-67	1968-69
Beaupre, Don	Min., Wsh., Ott., Tor.	17	667	268	277	75	37396	2151	17	3.45	72	33	31	....	3943	220	3	3.35		1980-81	1996-97
Bedard, Jim	Wsh.	2	73	17	40	13	4232	278	1	3.94	....	....	....	....	....	....	....	....		1977-78	1978-79
Behrend, Marc	Wpg.	3	39	12	19	3	1991	160	1	4.82	7	1	3	0	312	19	0	3.65		1983-84	1985-86
Belanger, Yves	St.L., Atl., Bos.	6	78	29	33	6	4134	259	2	3.76	....	....	....	....	....	....	....	....		1974-75	1979-80
Belhumeur, Michel	Phi., Wsh.	3	65	9	36	7	3306	254	0	4.61	1	0	0	....	10	1	0	6.00		1972-73	1975-76
● Bell, Gordie	Tor., NYR	2	8	3	5	0	480	31	0	3.88	2	1	1	....	120	9	0	4.50		1945-46	1955-56
● Benedict, Clint	Ott., Mtl.M.	13	362	190	143	28	22367	863	58	2.32	28	12	11	3	1707	53	9	1.86		1917-18	1929-30
Bennett, Harvey	Bos.	1	25	10	12	2	1470	103	0	4.20	....	....	....	....	....	....	....	....		1944-45	1944-45
‡ Bergeron, Jean-Claude	Mtl., T.B., L.A.	6	72	21	33	7	3772	232	1	3.69	....	....	....	....	....	....	....	....		1990-91	1996-97
Bernhardt, Tim	Cgy., Tor.	4	67	17	36	7	3748	267	0	4.27	....	....	....	....	....	....	....	....		1982-83	1986-87
‡ Berthiaume, Daniel	Wpg., Min., L.A., Bos., Ott.	9	215	81	90	21	11662	714	5	3.67	14	5	9	....	807	50	0	3.72		1985-86	1993-94
Bester, Allan	Tor., Det., Dal.	10	219	73	99	17	11773	786	7	4.01	11	2	6	....	508	37	0	4.37		1983-84	1995-96
● Beveridge, Bill	Det., Ott., St.L., Mtl.M., NYR	9	297	87	166	42	18375	879	18	2.87	5	2	3	....	300	11	0	2.20		1929-30	1942-43
● Bibeault, Paul	Mtl., Tor., Bos., Chi.	7	214	81	107	25	12890	785	10	3.65	20	6	14	....	1237	71	2	3.44		1940-41	1946-47
Binette, Andre	Mtl.	1	1	1	0	0	60	4	0	4.00	....	....	....	....	....	....	....	....		1954-55	1954-55
Binkley, Les	Pit.	5	196	58	94	34	11046	575	11	3.12	7	5	2	....	428	15	0	2.10		1967-68	1971-72
Bittner, Richard	Bos.	1	1	0	0	1	60	3	0	3.00	....	....	....	....	....	....	....	....		1949-50	1949-50
Blake, Mike	L.A.	3	40	13	15	5	2117	150	0	4.25	....	....	....	....	....	....	....	....		1981-82	1983-84
Blue, John	Bos., Buf.	3	46	16	18	7	2521	126	1	3.00	2	0	1	....	96	5	0	3.13		1992-93	1995-96
Boisvert, Gilles	Det.	1	3	0	3	0	180	9	0	3.00	....	....	....	....	....	....	....	....		1959-60	1959-60
Bouchard, Dan	Atl., Cgy., Que., Wpg.	14	655	286	232	113	37919	2061	27	3.26	43	13	30	....	2549	147	1	3.46		1972-73	1985-86
● Bourque, Claude	Mtl., Det.	2	62	16	38	8	3830	193	4	3.02	3	1	2	....	188	8	1	2.55		1938-39	1939-40
Boutin, Rollie	Wsh.	3	22	7	10	1	1137	75	0	3.96	....	....	....	....	....	....	....	....		1978-79	1980-81
Bouvrette, Lionel	NYR	1	1	0	1	0	60	6	0	6.00	....	....	....	....	....	....	....	....		1942-43	1942-43
Bower, Johnny	NYR, Tor.	15	552	250	195	90	32016	1340	37	2.51	74	35	34	....	4378	180	5	2.47	4	1953-54	1969-70
§ ● Branigan, Andy	NYA	1	1	0	0	0	7	0	0	0.00	....	....	....	....	....	....	....	....		1940-41	1940-41
● Brimsek, Frank	Bos., Chi.	10	514	252	182	80	31210	1404	40	2.70	68	32	36	....	4395	186	2	2.54	2	1938-39	1949-50
● Broda, Turk	Tor.	14	629	302	224	101	38167	1609	62	2.53	101	60	39	....	6389	211	13	1.98	5	1936-37	1951-52
Broderick, Ken	Min., Bos.	3	27	11	12	1	1464	74	1	3.03	....	....	....	....	....	....	....	....		1969-70	1974-75
Broderick, Len	Mtl.	1	1	1	0	0	60	2	0	2.00	....	....	....	....	....	....	....	....		1957-58	1957-58
Brodeur, Richard	NYI, Van., Hfd.	9	385	131	175	62	21968	1410	6	3.85	33	13	20	....	2009	111	1	3.32		1979-80	1987-88
Bromley, Gary	Buf., Van.	6	136	54	44	28	7427	425	7	3.43	7	2	5	....	360	25	0	4.17		1973-74	1980-81
● Brooks, Art	Tor.	1	4	2	2	0	220	23	0	6.27	....	....	....	....	....	....	....	....		1917-18	1917-18
Brooks, Ross	Bos.	3	54	37	7	6	3047	134	4	2.64	1	0	0	....	20	3	0	9.00		1972-73	1974-75
● Brophy, Frank	Que.	1	21	3	18	0	1249	148	0	7.11	....	....	....	....	....	....	....	....		1919-20	1919-20
Brown, Andy	Det., Pit.	3	62	22	26	9	3373	213	1	3.79	....	....	....	....	....	....	....	....		1971-72	1973-74
Brown, Ken	Chi.	1	1	0	0	0	18	1	0	3.33	....	....	....	....	....	....	....	....		1970-71	1970-71
‡ Brunetta, Mario	Que.	3	40	12	17	1	1967	128	0	3.90	....	....	....	....	....	....	....	....		1987-88	1989-90
Bullock, Bruce	Van.	3	16	3	9	3	927	74	0	4.79	....	....	....	....	....	....	....	....		1972-73	1976-77
Buzinski, Steve	NYR	1	9	2	6	1	560	55	0	5.89	....	....	....	....	....	....	....	....		1942-43	1942-43
Caley, Don	St.L.	1	1	0	0	0	30	3	0	6.00	....	....	....	....	....	....	....	....		1967-68	1967-68
Caprice, Frank	Van.	6	102	31	46	11	5589	391	1	4.20	....	....	....	....	....	....	....	....		1982-83	1987-88
Carey, Jim	Wsh., Bos., St.L.	5	172	79	65	16	9668	416	16	2.58	10	2	5	....	455	35	0	4.62		1994-95	1998-99
Caron, Jacques	L.A., St.L., Van.	5	72	24	29	11	3846	211	2	3.29	12	4	7	....	639	34	0	3.19		1967-68	1973-74
Carter, Lyle	Cal.	1	15	4	7	0	721	50	0	4.16	....	....	....	....	....	....	....	....		1971-72	1971-72
Casey, Jon	Min., Bos., St.L.	12	425	170	157	55	23255	1246	16	3.21	66	32	31	....	3743	192	3	3.08		1983-84	1996-97
● Chabot, Lorne	NYR, Tor., Mtl.C., Chi., Mtl.M., NYA	11	411	201	148	62	25307	860	73	2.04	37	13	17	6	2498	64	5	1.54	2	1926-27	1936-37
Chadwick, Ed	Tor., Bos.	6	184	57	92	35	11040	541	14	2.94	....	....	....	....	....	....	....	....		1955-56	1961-62
Champoux, Bob	Det., Cal.	2	17	2	11	3	923	80	0	5.20	1	1	0	....	55	4	0	4.36		1963-64	1973-74
Cheevers, Gerry	Tor., Bos.	14	418	230	102	74	24394	1174	26	2.89	88	53	34	....	5396	242	8	2.69	2	1961-62	1979-80
Cheveldae, Tim	Det., Wpg., Bos.	9	340	149	136	37	19172	1116	10	3.49	25	9	15	....	1418	71	2	3.00		1988-89	1996-97
Chevrier, Alain	N.J., Wpg., Chi., Pit., Det.	6	234	91	100	14	12202	845	2	4.16	16	9	7	....	1013	44	0	2.61		1985-86	1990-91
§ ● Clancy, King	Ott., Tor.	2	2	0	0	0	3	1	0	20.00	....	....	....	....	....	....	....	....		1924-25	1931-32
§ ● Cleghorn, Odie	Pit.	1	1	1	0	0	60	2	0	2.00	....	....	....	....	....	....	....	....		1925-26	1925-26
§ ● Cleghorn, Sprague	Ott., Mtl.C.	2	2	0	0	0	5	0	0	0.00	....	....	....	....	....	....	....	....		1918-19	1921-22
Clifford, Chris	Chi.	2	2	0	0	0	24	0	0	0.00	....	....	....	....	....	....	....	....		1984-85	1988-89
Cloutier, Jacques	Buf., Chi., Que.	14	255	82	102	24	12826	778	3	3.64	8	1	5	....	413	18	1	2.62		1981-82	1993-94
Colvin, Les	Bos.	1	1	0	1	0	60	4	0	4.00	....	....	....	....	....	....	....	....		1948-49	1948-49
§ ● Conacher, Charlie	Tor., Det.	3	4	0	0	0	10	0	0	0.00	....	....	....	....	....	....	....	....		1932-33	1938-39
● Connell, Alex	Ott., Det., NYA, Mtl.M.	12	417	193	156	67	26050	830	81	1.91	21	8	5	8	1309	26	4	1.19	2	1924-25	1936-37
Corsi, Jim	Edm.	1	26	8	14	3	1366	83	0	3.65	....	....	....	....	....	....	....	....		1979-80	1979-80
Courteau, Maurice	Bos.	1	6	2	4	0	360	33	0	5.50	....	....	....	....	....	....	....	....		1943-44	1943-44
‡ Cowley, Wayne	Edm.	1	1	0	1	0	57	3	0	3.16	....	....	....	....	....	....	....	....		1993-94	1993-94
Cox, Abbie	Mtl.M., NYA, Det., Mtl.C.	3	5	1	1	2	263	11	0	2.51	....	....	....	....	....	....	....	....		1929-30	1935-36
Craig, Jim	Atl., Bos., Min.	3	30	11	10	7	1588	100	0	3.78	....	....	....	....	....	....	....	....		1979-80	1983-84
Crha, Jiri	Tor.	2	69	28	27	11	3942	261	0	3.97	5	0	4	....	186	21	0	6.77		1979-80	1980-81
● Crozier, Roger	Det., Buf., Wsh.	14	518	206	197	70	28567	1446	30	3.04	32	14	16	....	1789	82	1	2.75		1963-64	1976-77
● Cude, Wilf	Phi., Bos., Chi., Mtl.C., Det., Mtl.	10	282	100	132	49	17586	798	24	2.72	19	7	11	1	1257	51	1	2.43		1930-31	1940-41
Cutts, Don	Edm.	1	6	1	2	1	269	16	0	3.57	....	....	....	....	....	....	....	....		1979-80	1979-80
● Cyr, Claude	Mtl.	1	1	0	0	0	20	1	0	3.00	....	....	....	....	....	....	....	....		1958-59	1958-59
Dadswell, Doug	Cgy.	2	27	8	8	3	1346	99	0	4.41	....	....	....	....	....	....	....	....		1986-87	1987-88
D'Alessio, Corrie	Hfd.	1	1	0	0	0	11	0	0	0.00	....	....	....	....	....	....	....	....		1992-93	1992-93
Daley, Joe	Pit., Buf., Det.	4	105	34	44	19	5836	326	3	3.35	....	....	....	....	....	....	....	....		1968-69	1971-72
Damore, Nick	Bos.	1	1	1	0	0	60	3	0	3.00	....	....	....	....	....	....	....	....		1941-42	1941-42
D'Amour, Marc	Cgy., Phi.	2	16	2	4	2	579	32	0	3.32	....	....	....	....	....	....	....	....		1985-86	1988-89
Daskalakis, Cleon	Bos.	3	12	3	4	1	506	41	0	4.86	....	....	....	....	....	....	....	....		1984-85	1986-87
Davidson, John	St.L., NYR	10	301	123	124	39	17109	1004	7	3.52	31	16	14	....	1862	77	1	2.48		1973-74	1982-83
Decourcy, Bob	NYR	1	1	0	1	0	29	6	0	12.41	....	....	....	....	....	....	....	....		1947-48	1947-48
Defelice, Norm	Bos.	1	10	3	5	2	600	30	0	3.00	....	....	....	....	....	....	....	....		1956-57	1956-57
DeJordy, Denis	Chi., L.A., Mtl., Det.	11	316	124	128	51	17798	929	15	3.13	18	6	9	....	946	55	0	3.49		1962-63	1973-74
DelGuidice, Matt	Bos.	2	11	2	5	1	434	28	0	3.87	....	....	....	....	....	....	....	....		1990-91	1991-92
‡ DeRouville, Philippe	Pit.	2	3	1	2	0	171	9	0	3.16	....	....	....	....	....	....	....	....		1994-95	1996-97
Desjardins, Gerry	L.A., Chi., NYI, Buf.	10	331	122	153	44	19014	1042	12	3.29	35	15	15	....	1874	108	0	3.46		1968-69	1977-78
● Dickie, Bill	Chi.	1	1	1	0	0	60	3	0	3.00	....	....	....	....	....	....	....	....		1941-42	1941-42

			Regular Schedule								Playoffs										
Name	NHL Teams	NHL Seasons	GP	W	L	T	Mins	GA	SO	Avg	GP	W	L	T	Mins	GA	SO	Avg	NHL Cup Wins	First NHL Season	Last NHL Season
Dion, Connie	Det.	2	38	23	11	4	2280	119	1	3.13	5	1	4	....	300	17	0	3.40		1943-44	1944-45
Dion, Michel	Que., Wpg., Pit.	6	227	60	118	32	12695	898	2	4.24	5	2	3	....	304	22	0	4.34		1979-80	1984-85
Dolson, Dolly	Det.	3	93	35	41	17	5820	192	16	1.98	2	0	2	0	120	7	0	3.50		1928-29	1930-31
‡ Dopson, Rob	Pit.	1	2	0	0	0	45	3	0	4.00	....	....	....	....	....	....	....	....		1993-94	1993-94
Dowie, Bruce	Tor.	1	2	0	1	0	72	4	0	3.33	....	....	....	....	....	....	....	....		1983-84	1983-84
‡ Draper, Tom	Wpg., Buf., NYI	6	53	19	23	5	2807	173	1	3.70	7	3	4	....	433	19	1	2.63		1988-89	1995-96
Dryden, Dave	NYR, Chi., Buf., Edm.	9	203	66	76	31	10424	555	9	3.19	3	0	2	....	133	9	0	4.06		1961-62	1979-80
Dryden, Ken	Mtl.	8	397	258	57	74	23352	870	46	2.24	112	80	32	....	6846	274	10	2.40	6	1970-71	1978-79
‡ Duffus, Parris	Phx.	1	1	0	0	0	29	1	0	2.07	....	....	....	....	....	....	....	....		1996-97	1996-97
Dumas, Michel	Chi.	3	8	2	1	2	362	24	0	3.98	1	0	0	....	19	1	0	3.16		1974-75	1976-77
Dupuis, Bob	Edm.	1	1	0	1	0	60	4	0	4.00	....	....	....	....	....	....	....	....		1979-80	1979-80
• Durnan, Bill	Mtl.	7	383	208	112	62	22945	901	34	2.36	45	27	18	....	2871	99	2	2.07	2	1943-44	1949-50
Dyck, Ed	Van.	3	49	8	28	5	2453	178	1	4.35	....	....	....	....	....	....	....	....		1971-72	1973-74
Edwards, Don	Buf., Cgy., Tor.	10	459	208	155	74	26181	1449	16	3.32	42	16	21	....	2302	132	1	3.44		1976-77	1985-86
Edwards, Gary	St.L., L.A., Cle., Min., Edm., Pit.	13	286	88	125	51	16002	973	11	3.65	11	5	4	....	537	34	0	3.80		1968-69	1981-82
Edwards, Marv	Pit., Tor., Cal.	4	61	15	34	7	3467	218	2	3.77	....	....	....	....	....	....	....	....		1968-69	1973-74
• Edwards, Roy	Det., Pit.	7	236	97	88	38	13109	637	12	2.92	4	0	3	....	206	11	0	3.20		1967-68	1973-74
Eliot, Darren	L.A., Det., Buf.	5	89	25	41	12	4931	377	1	4.59	1	0	0	....	40	7	0	10.50		1984-85	1988-89
Ellacott, Ken	Van.	1	12	2	3	4	555	41	0	4.43	....	....	....	....	....	....	....	....		1982-83	1982-83
‡ Erickson, Chad	N.J.	1	2	1	1	0	120	9	0	4.50	....	....	....	....	....	....	....	....		1991-92	1991-92
Esposito, Tony	Mtl., Chi.	16	886	423	306	151	52585	2563	76	2.92	99	45	53	....	6017	308	6	3.07	1	1968-69	1983-84
• Evans, Claude	Mtl., Bos.	2	5	1	2	1	260	16	0	3.69	....	....	....	....	....	....	....	....		1954-55	1957-58
Exelby, Randy	Mtl., Edm.	2	2	0	1	0	63	5	0	4.76	....	....	....	....	....	....	....	....		1988-89	1989-90
Farr, Rocky	Buf.	3	19	2	6	3	722	42	0	3.49	....	....	....	....	....	....	....	....		1972-73	1974-75
Favell, Doug	Phi., Tor., Col.	12	373	123	153	69	20771	1096	18	3.17	21	6	15	....	1270	66	1	3.12		1967-68	1978-79
• Forbes, Jake	Tor., Ham., NYA, Phi.	14	210	85	114	11	12922	594	19	2.76	2	0	2	0	120	7	0	3.50		1919-20	1932-33
Ford, Brian	Que., Pit.	2	11	3	7	0	580	61	0	6.31	....	....	....	....	....	....	....	....		1983-84	1984-85
Foster, Norm	Bos., Edm.	2	13	7	4	0	623	34	0	3.27	....	....	....	....	....	....	....	....		1990-91	1991-92
Fowler, Hec	Bos.	1	7	1	6	0	409	42	0	6.16	....	....	....	....	....	....	....	....		1924-25	1924-25
Francis, Emile	Chi., NYR	6	95	31	52	11	5660	355	1	3.76	....	....	....	....	....	....	....	....		1946-47	1951-52
• Franks, Jim	Det., NYR, Bos.	4	42	12	23	7	2520	181	1	4.31	1	0	1	....	30	2	0	4.00	1	1936-37	1943-44
Frederick, Ray	Chi.	1	5	0	4	1	300	22	0	4.40	....	....	....	....	....	....	....	....		1954-55	1954-55
Friesen, Karl	N.J.	1	4	0	2	1	130	16	0	7.38	....	....	....	....	....	....	....	....		1986-87	1986-87
Froese, Bob	Phi., NYR	8	242	128	72	20	13451	694	13	3.10	18	3	9	....	830	55	0	3.98		1982-83	1989-90
‡ Gagnon, David	Det.	1	2	0	1	0	35	6	0	10.29	....	....	....	....	....	....	....	....		1990-91	1990-91
• Gamble, Bruce	NYR, Bos., Tor., Phi.	10	327	110	150	46	18442	988	22	3.21	5	0	4	....	206	25	0	7.28	1	1958-59	1971-72
Gamble, Troy	Van.	4	72	22	29	9	3804	229	1	3.61	4	1	3	....	249	16	0	3.86		1986-87	1991-92
Gardiner, Bert	NYR, Mtl., Chi., Bos.	6	144	49	68	27	8760	554	4	3.79	9	4	5	....	647	20	0	1.85		1935-36	1943-44
• Gardiner, Charlie	Chi.	7	316	112	152	52	19687	664	42	2.02	21	12	6	3	1472	35	5	1.43	1	1927-28	1933-34
Gardner, George	Det., Van.	5	66	16	30	6	3313	207	0	3.75	....	....	....	....	....	....	....	....		1965-66	1971-72
Garrett, John	Hfd., Que., Van.	6	207	68	91	37	11763	837	1	4.27	9	4	3	....	461	33	0	4.30		1979-80	1984-85
Gatherum, Dave	Det.	1	3	2	0	1	180	3	1	1.00	....	....	....	....	....	....	....	....		1953-54	1953-54
Gauthier, Paul	Mtl.C.	1	1	0	0	1	70	2	0	1.71	....	....	....	....	....	....	....	....		1937-38	1937-38
• Gelineau, Jack	Bos., Chi.	4	143	46	64	33	8580	447	7	3.13	4	1	2	....	260	7	1	1.62		1948-49	1953-54
Giacomin, Ed	NYR, Det.	13	610	289	208	97	35693	1675	54	2.82	65	29	35	....	3838	180	1	2.81		1965-66	1977-78
Gilbert, Gilles	Min., Bos., Det.	14	416	192	143	60	23677	1290	18	3.27	32	17	15	....	1919	97	3	3.03		1969-70	1982-83
Gill, Andre	Bos.	1	5	3	2	0	270	13	1	2.89	....	....	....	....	....	....	....	....		1967-68	1967-68
• Goodman, Paul	Chi.	3	52	23	20	9	3240	117	6	2.17	3	0	3	....	187	10	0	3.21	1	1937-38	1940-41
Gordon, Scott	Que.	2	23	2	16	0	1082	101	0	5.60	....	....	....	....	....	....	....	....		1989-90	1990-91
Gosselin, Mario	Que., L.A., Hfd.	9	241	91	107	14	12857	801	6	3.74	32	16	15	....	1816	99	0	3.27		1983-84	1993-94
‡ Goverde, David	L.A.	3	5	1	4	0	278	29	0	6.26	....	....	....	....	....	....	....	....		1991-92	1993-94
Grahame, Ron	Bos., L.A., Que.	4	114	50	43	15	6472	409	5	3.79	4	2	1	....	202	7	0	2.08		1977-78	1980-81
• Grant, Benny	Tor., NYA, Bos.	6	50	17	26	4	2990	187	4	3.75	....	....	....	....	....	....	....	....		1928-29	1943-44
Grant, Doug	Det., St.L.	7	77	27	34	8	4199	280	2	4.00	....	....	....	....	....	....	....	....		1973-74	1979-80
Gratton, Gilles	St.L., NYR	2	47	13	18	9	2299	154	0	4.02	....	....	....	....	....	....	....	....		1975-76	1976-77
Gray, Gerry	Det., NYI	2	8	1	5	1	440	35	0	4.77	....	....	....	....	....	....	....	....		1970-71	1972-73
Gray, Harrison	Det.	1	1	0	1	0	40	5	0	7.50	....	....	....	....	....	....	....	....		1963-64	1963-64
Greenlay, Mike	Edm.	1	2	0	0	0	20	4	0	12.00	....	....	....	....	....	....	....	....		1989-90	1989-90
Guenette, Steve	Pit., Cgy.	5	35	19	16	0	1958	122	1	3.74	....	....	....	....	....	....	....	....		1986-87	1990-91
• Hainsworth, George	Mtl.C., Tor.	11	465	246	145	74	29087	937	94	1.93	52	22	25	5	3486	112	8	1.93	2	1926-27	1936-37
Hall, Glenn	Det., Chi., St.L.	18	906	407	326	163	53484	2222	84	2.49	115	49	65	....	6899	320	6	2.78	1	1952-53	1970-71
Hamel, Pierre	Tor., Wpg.	4	69	13	41	7	3766	276	0	4.40	....	....	....	....	....	....	....	....		1974-75	1980-81
Hanlon, Glen	Van., St.L., NYR, Det.	15	477	167	202	61	26037	1561	13	3.60	35	11	15	....	1756	92	4	3.14		1977-78	1990-91
Harrison, Paul	Min., Tor., Pit., Buf.	7	109	28	59	9	5806	408	2	4.22	4	0	1	....	157	9	0	3.44		1975-76	1981-82
Hayward, Brian	Wpg., Mtl., Min., S.J.	11	357	143	156	37	20025	1242	8	3.72	37	11	18	....	1803	104	0	3.46		1982-83	1992-93
Head, Don	Bos.	1	38	9	26	3	2280	158	2	4.16	....	....	....	....	....	....	....	....		1961-62	1961-62
• Hebert, Sammy	Tor., Ott.	2	4	2	1	0	200	19	0	5.70	....	....	....	....	....	....	....	....	1	1917-18	1923-24
Heinz, Rick	St.L., Van.	5	49	14	19	5	2356	159	2	4.05	1	0	0	....	8	1	0	7.50		1980-81	1984-85
Henderson, John	Bos.	2	46	15	15	15	2688	113	5	2.52	2	0	2	....	120	8	0	4.00		1954-55	1955-56
• Henry, Gord	Bos.	4	3	1	2	0	180	5	1	1.67	5	0	4	....	283	21	0	4.45		1948-49	1952-53
Henry, Jim	NYR, Chi., Bos.	9	406	161	173	70	24355	1166	27	2.87	29	11	18	....	1741	81	2	2.79		1941-42	1954-55
Herron, Denis	Pit., K.C., Mtl.	14	462	146	203	76	25608	1579	10	3.70	15	5	10	....	901	50	0	3.33		1972-73	1985-86
Hextall, Ron	Phi., Que., NYI	13	608	296	214	69	34750	1723	23	2.97	93	47	43	....	5456	276	2	3.04		1986-87	1998-99
Highton, Hec	Chi.	1	24	10	14	0	1440	108	0	4.50	....	....	....	....	....	....	....	....		1943-44	1943-44
§ • Himes, Normie	NYA	2	2	0	1	0	79	3	0	2.28	....	....	....	....	....	....	....	....		1927-28	1928-29
Hodge, Charlie	Mtl., Oak., Van.	13	358	151	124	61	20593	925	24	2.70	16	7	8	....	804	32	2	2.39	4	1954-55	1970-71
Hoffort, Bruce	Phi.	2	9	4	0	3	368	22	0	3.59	....	....	....	....	....	....	....	....		1989-90	1990-91
Hoganson, Paul	Pit.	1	2	0	1	0	57	7	0	7.37	....	....	....	....	....	....	....	....		1970-71	1970-71
Hogosta, Goran	NYI, Que.	2	22	5	12	3	1208	83	1	4.12	....	....	....	....	....	....	....	....		1977-78	1979-80
Holden, Mark	Mtl., Wpg.	4	8	2	2	1	372	25	0	4.03	....	....	....	....	....	....	....	....		1981-82	1984-85
Holland, Ken	Hfd., Det.	5	4	0	2	1	206	17	0	4.95	....	....	....	....	....	....	....	....		1980-81	1983-84
Holland, Robbie	Pit.	2	44	11	22	9	2513	171	1	4.08	....	....	....	....	....	....	....	....		1979-80	1980-81
• Holmes, Hap	Tor., Det.	4	103	39	54	10	6510	264	17	2.43	2	1	1	0	120	7	0	3.50		1917-18	1927-28
§ Horner, Red	Tor.	1	1	0	0	0	1	1	0	60.00	....	....	....	....	....	....	....	....		1931-32	1931-32
‡ Hrivnak, Jim	Wsh., Wpg., St.L.	5	85	34	30	3	4217	262	0	3.73	....	....	....	....	....	....	....	....		1989-90	1993-94
Hrudey, Kelly	NYI, L.A., S.J.	15	677	271	265	88	38084	2174	17	3.43	85	36	46	....	5163	283	0	3.29		1983-84	1997-98
Ing, Peter	Tor., Edm., Det.	4	74	20	37	9	3941	266	1	4.05	....	....	....	....	....	....	....	....		1989-90	1993-94
Inness, Gary	Pit., Phi., Wsh.	7	162	58	61	27	8710	494	2	3.40	9	5	4	....	540	24	0	2.67		1973-74	1980-81
Ireland, Randy	Buf.	1	2	0	0	0	30	3	0	6.00	....	....	....	....	....	....	....	....		1978-79	1978-79
Irons, Robbie	St.L.	1	1	0	0	0	3	0	0	0.00	....	....	....	....	....	....	....	....		1968-69	1968-69
• Ironstone, Joe	Ott., NYA, Tor.	3	2	0	0	1	110	3	1	1.64	....	....	....	....	....	....	....	....		1924-25	1927-28
Jackson, Doug	Chi.	1	6	2	3	1	360	42	0	7.00	....	....	....	....	....	....	....	....		1947-48	1947-48
Jackson, Percy	Bos., NYA, NYR	4	7	1	3	1	392	26	0	3.98	....	....	....	....	....	....	....	....		1931-32	1935-36
‡ Jaks, Pauli	L.A.	1	1	0	0	0	40	2	0	3.00	....	....	....	....	....	....	....	....		1994-95	1994-95
Janaszak, Steve	Min., Col.	2	3	0	1	1	160	15	0	5.63	....	....	....	....	....	....	....	....		1979-80	1981-82
Janecyk, Bob	Chi., L.A.	6	110	43	47	13	6250	432	2	4.15	3	0	3	....	184	10	0	3.26		1983-84	1988-89
§ Jenkins, Roger	NYA	1	1	0	1	0	30	7	0	14.00	....	....	....	....	....	....	....	....		1938-39	1938-39
Jensen, Al	Det., Wsh., L.A.	7	179	95	53	18	9974	557	8	3.35	12	5	5	....	598	32	0	3.21		1980-81	1986-87
Jensen, Darren	Phi.	2	30	15	10	1	1496	95	2	3.81	....	....	....	....	....	....	....	....		1984-85	1985-86
Johnson, Bob	St.L., Pit.	2	24	9	9	1	1059	66	0	3.74	....	....	....	....	....	....	....	....		1972-73	1974-75
Johnston, Eddie	Bos., Tor., St.L., Chi.	24	592	234	257	80	34216	1852	32	3.25	18	7	10	....	1023	57	1	3.34	2	1962-63	1977-78
Junkin, Joe	Bos.	1	1	0	0	0	8	0	0	0.00	....	....	....	....	....	....	....	....		1968-69	1968-69
Kaarela, Jari	Col.	1	5	2	2	0	220	22	0	6.00	....	....	....	....	....	....	....	....		1980-81	1980-81
Kamppuri, Hannu	N.J.	1	13	1	10	1	645	54	0	5.02	....	....	....	....	....	....	....	....		1984-85	1984-85
• Karakas, Mike	Chi., Mtl.	8	336	114	169	53	20616	1002	28	2.92	23	11	12	0	1434	72	3	3.01	1	1935-36	1945-46
Keans, Doug	L.A., Bos.	9	210	96	64	26	11388	666	4	3.51	9	2	6	....	432	34	0	4.72		1979-80	1987-88
Keenan, Don	Bos.	1	1	0	1	0	60	4	0	4.00	....	....	....	....	....	....	....	....		1958-59	1958-59

Name	NHL Teams	NHL Seasons	Regular Schedule								Playoffs								NHL Cup Wins	First NHL Season	Last NHL Season
			GP	W	L	T	Mins	GA	SO	Avg	GP	W	L	T	Mins	GA	SO	Avg			
• Kerr, Davey	Mtl.M., NYA, NYR	11	427	203	148	75	26639	954	51	2.15	40	18	19	3	2616	76	8	1.74	1	1930-31	1940-41
King, Scott	Det.	2	2	0	0	0	61	3	0	2.95	....	....	....	....	....	....	....	....		1990-91	1991-92
Kleisinger, Terry	NYR	1	4	0	2	0	191	14	0	4.40	....	....	....	....	....	....	....	....		1985-86	1985-86
Klymkiw, Julian	NYR	1	1	0	0	0	19	2	0	6.32	....	....	....	....	....	....	....	....		1958-59	1958-59
Knickle, Rick	L.A.	2	14	7	6	0	706	44	0	3.74	....	....	....	....	....	....	....	....		1992-93	1993-94
Kuntar, Les	Mtl.	1	6	2	2	0	302	16	0	3.18	....	....	....	....	....	....	....	....		1993-94	1993-94
Kurt, Gary	Cal.	1	16	1	7	5	838	60	0	4.30	....	....	....	....	....	....	....	....		1971-72	1971-72
‡ Labrecque, Patrick	Mtl.	1	2	0	1	0	98	7	0	4.29	....	....	....	....	....	....	....	....		1995-96	1995-96
Lacher, Blaine	Bos.	2	47	22	16	4	2636	123	4	2.80	5	1	4	....	283	12	0	2.54		1994-95	1995-96
• Lacroix, Frenchy	Mtl.C.	2	5	1	4	0	280	16	0	3.43	....	....	....	....	....	....	....	....		1925-26	1926-27
LaFerriere, Rick	Col.	1	1	0	0	0	20	1	0	3.00	....	....	....	....	....	....	....	....		1981-82	1981-82
LaForest, Mark	Det., Phi., Tor., Ott.	6	103	25	54	4	5032	354	2	4.22	2	1	0	....	48	1	0	1.25		1985-86	1993-94
• Larocque, Michel	Mtl., Tor., Phi., St.L.	11	312	160	89	45	17615	978	17	3.33	14	6	6	....	759	37	1	2.92	4	1973-74	1983-84
Laskowski, Gary	L.A.	2	59	19	27	5	2942	228	0	4.65	....	....	....	....	....	....	....	....		1982-83	1983-84
Laxton, Gord	Pit.	4	17	4	9	0	800	74	0	5.55	....	....	....	....	....	....	....	....		1975-76	1978-79
‡ LeBlanc, Ray	Chi.	1	1	1	0	0	60	1	0	1.00	....	....	....	....	....	....	....	....		1991-92	1991-92
§ • LeDuc, Albert	Mtl.C.	1	1	0	0	0	2	1	0	30.00	....	....	....	....	....	....	....	....		1931-32	1931-32
Legris, Claude	Det.	2	4	0	1	1	91	4	0	2.64	....	....	....	....	....	....	....	....		1980-81	1981-82
• Lehman, Hugh	Chi.	2	48	20	24	4	3047	136	6	2.68	2	0	1	1	120	10	0	5.00		1926-27	1927-28
Lemelin, Reggie	Atl., Cgy., Bos.	15	507	236	162	63	28006	1613	12	3.46	59	23	25	....	3119	186	2	3.58		1978-79	1992-93
‡ Lenarduzzi, Mike	Hfd.	2	4	1	1	1	189	10	0	3.17	....	....	....	....	....	....	....	....		1992-93	1993-94
Lessard, Mario	L.A.	6	240	92	97	39	13529	843	9	3.74	20	6	12	....	1136	83	0	4.38		1978-79	1983-84
Levasseur, Jean-Louis	Min.	1	1	0	1	0	60	7	0	7.00	....	....	....	....	....	....	....	....		1979-80	1979-80
§ • Levinsky, Alex	Tor.	1	1	0	0	0	1	1	0	60.00	....	....	....	....	....	....	....	....		1931-32	1931-32
• Lindbergh, Pelle	Phi.	5	157	87	49	15	9150	503	7	3.30	23	12	10	....	1214	63	3	3.11		1981-82	1985-86
• Lindsay, Bert	Mtl., Tor.	2	20	6	14	0	1238	118	0	5.72	....	....	....	....	....	....	....	....		1917-18	1918-19
‡ Littman, David	Buf., T.B.	3	3	0	2	0	141	14	0	5.96	....	....	....	....	....	....	....	....		1990-91	1992-93
Liut, Mike	St.L., Hfd., Wsh.	13	663	293	271	74	38155	2219	25	3.49	67	29	32	....	3814	215	2	3.38		1979-80	1991-92
Lockett, Ken	Van.	2	55	13	15	8	2348	131	2	3.35	1	0	1	....	60	6	0	6.00		1974-75	1975-76
• Lockhart, Howard	Tor., Que., Ham., Bos.	5	59	16	41	0	3413	287	1	5.05	....	....	....	....	....	....	....	....		1919-20	1924-25
LoPresti, Pete	Min., Edm.	6	175	43	102	20	9858	668	5	4.07	2	0	2	....	77	6	0	4.68		1974-75	1980-81
• LoPresti, Sam	Chi.	2	74	30	38	6	4530	236	4	3.13	8	3	5	....	530	17	1	1.92		1940-41	1941-42
‡ Lorenz, Danny	NYI	3	8	1	5	0	357	25	0	4.20	....	....	....	....	....	....	....	....		1990-91	1992-93
Loustel, Ron	Wpg.	1	1	0	1	0	60	10	0	10.00	....	....	....	....	....	....	....	....		1980-81	1980-81
Low, Ron	Tor., Wsh., Det., Que., Edm., N.J.	13	382	102	203	38	20502	1463	4	4.28	7	1	6	....	452	29	0	3.85		1972-73	1984-85
Lozinski, Larry	Det.	1	30	6	11	7	1459	105	0	4.32	....	....	....	....	....	....	....	....		1980-81	1980-81
• Lumley, Harry	Det., NYR, Chi., Tor., Bos.	16	803	330	329	142	48044	2206	71	2.75	76	29	47	....	4778	198	7	2.49	1	1943-44	1959-60
MacKenzie, Shawn	N.J.	1	4	0	1	0	130	15	0	6.92	....	....	....	....	....	....	....	....		1982-83	1982-83
Madeley, Darrin	Ott.	3	39	4	23	5	1928	140	0	4.36	....	....	....	....	....	....	....	....		1992-93	1994-95
Malarchuk, Clint	Que., Wsh., Buf.	10	338	141	130	45	19030	1100	12	3.47	15	2	9	0	781	56	0	4.30		1981-82	1991-92
Maneluk, George	NYI	1	4	1	1	0	140	15	0	6.43	....	....	....	....	....	....	....	....		1990-91	1990-91
Maniago, Cesare	Tor., Mtl., NYR, Min., Van.	15	568	189	259	96	32570	1773	30	3.27	36	15	21	....	2245	100	3	2.67		1960-61	1977-78
Marois, Jean	Tor., Chi.	2	3	1	2	0	180	15	0	5.00	....	....	....	....	....	....	....	....		1943-44	1953-54
Martin, Seth	St.L.	1	30	8	10	7	1552	67	1	2.59	2	0	0	....	73	5	0	4.11		1967-68	1967-68
Mason, Bob	Wsh., Chi., Que., Van.	8	145	55	65	16	7988	500	1	3.76	5	2	3	....	369	12	1	1.95		1983-84	1990-91
Mattsson, Markus	Wpg., Min., L.A.	4	92	21	46	14	5007	343	6	4.11	....	....	....	....	....	....	....	....		1979-80	1983-84
May, Darrell	St.L.	2	6	1	5	0	364	31	0	5.11	....	....	....	....	....	....	....	....		1985-86	1987-88
Mayer, Gilles	Tor.	4	9	2	6	1	540	24	0	2.67	....	....	....	....	....	....	....	....		1949-50	1955-56
McAuley, Ken	NYR	2	96	17	64	15	5740	537	1	5.61	....	....	....	....	....	....	....	....		1943-44	1944-45
McCartan, Jack	NYR	2	12	2	7	3	680	42	1	3.71	....	....	....	....	....	....	....	....		1959-60	1960-61
• McCool, Frank	Tor.	2	72	34	31	7	4320	242	4	3.36	13	8	5	....	807	30	4	2.23	1	1944-45	1945-46
McDuffe, Peter	St.L., NYR, K.C., Det.	5	57	11	36	6	3207	218	0	4.08	1	0	1	....	60	7	0	7.00		1971-72	1975-76
McGrattan, Tom	Det.	1	1	0	0	0	8	1	0	7.50	....	....	....	....	....	....	....	....		1947-48	1947-48
McKay, Ross	Hfd.	1	1	0	0	0	35	3	0	5.14	....	....	....	....	....	....	....	....		1990-91	1990-91
McKenzie, Bill	Det., K.C., Col.	6	91	18	49	13	4776	326	2	4.10	....	....	....	....	....	....	....	....		1973-74	1979-80
McKichan, Steve	Van.	1	1	0	0	0	20	2	0	6.00	....	....	....	....	....	....	....	....		1990-91	1990-91
McLachlan, Murray	Tor.	1	2	0	1	0	25	4	0	9.60	....	....	....	....	....	....	....	....		1970-71	1970-71
McLelland, Dave	Van.	1	2	1	1	0	120	10	0	5.00	....	....	....	....	....	....	....	....		1972-73	1972-73
McLeod, Don	Det., Phi.	2	18	3	10	1	879	74	0	5.05	....	....	....	....	....	....	....	....		1970-71	1971-72
McLeod, Jim	St.L.	1	16	6	6	4	880	44	0	3.00	....	....	....	....	....	....	....	....		1971-72	1971-72
McNamara, Gerry	Tor.	2	7	2	2	1	323	14	0	2.60	....	....	....	....	....	....	....	....		1960-61	1969-70
McNeil, Gerry	Mtl.	7	276	119	105	52	16535	649	28	2.36	35	17	18	....	2284	72	5	1.89	2	1947-48	1956-57
McRae, Gord	Tor.	5	71	30	22	10	3799	221	1	3.49	8	2	5	....	454	22	0	2.91		1972-73	1977-78
Melanson, Rollie	NYI, Min., L.A., N.J., Mtl.	12	291	129	106	33	16452	995	6	3.63	23	4	9	....	801	59	0	4.42	3	1980-81	1991-92
Meloche, Gilles	Chi., Cal., Cle., Min., Pit.	18	788	270	351	131	45401	2756	20	3.64	45	21	19	....	2464	143	2	3.48		1970-71	1987-88
‡ Micalef, Corrado	Det.	5	113	26	59	15	5794	409	2	4.24	3	0	0	....	49	8	0	9.80		1981-82	1985-86
Middlebrook, Lindsay	Wpg., Min., N.J., Edm.	4	37	3	23	6	1845	152	0	4.94	....	....	....	....	....	....	....	....		1979-80	1982-83
• Millar, Al	Bos.	1	6	1	4	1	360	25	0	4.17	....	....	....	....	....	....	....	....		1957-58	1957-58
Millen, Greg	Pit., Hfd., St.L., Que., Chi., Det.	14	604	215	284	89	35377	2281	17	3.87	59	27	29	....	3383	193	0	3.42		1978-79	1991-92
• Miller, Joe	NYA, NYR, Pit., Phi.	4	127	24	87	16	7871	383	16	2.92	3	2	1	0	180	3	1	1.00	1	1927-28	1930-31
Mio, Eddie	Edm., NYR, Det.	7	192	64	73	30	10428	705	4	4.06	17	9	7	....	986	63	0	3.83		1979-80	1985-86
• Mitchell, Ivan	Tor.	3	22	10	9	0	1190	88	0	4.44	....	....	....	....	....	....	....	....		1919-20	1921-22
Moffat, Mike	Bos.	3	19	7	7	2	979	70	0	4.29	11	6	5	....	663	38	0	3.44		1981-82	1983-84
Moog, Andy	Edm., Bos., Dal., Mtl.	18	713	372	209	88	40151	2097	28	3.13	132	68	57	....	7452	377	4	3.04	3	1980-81	1997-98
Moore, Alfie	NYA, Chi., Det.	4	21	7	14	0	1290	81	1	3.77	3	1	2	....	180	7	0	2.33	1	1936-37	1939-40
Moore, Robbie	Phi., Wsh.	2	6	3	1	1	257	8	2	1.87	5	3	2	....	268	18	0	4.03		1978-79	1982-83
Morissette, Jean-Guy	Mtl.	1	1	0	1	0	36	4	0	6.67	....	....	....	....	....	....	....	....		1963-64	1963-64
• Mowers, Johnny	Det.	4	152	65	61	26	9350	399	15	2.56	32	19	13	....	2000	85	2	2.55	1	1940-41	1946-47
Mrazek, Jerome	Phi.	1	1	0	0	0	6	1	0	10.00	....	....	....	....	....	....	....	....		1975-76	1975-76
§ • Mummery, Harry	Que., Ham.	2	4	2	1	0	192	20	0	6.25	....	....	....	....	....	....	....	....		1919-20	1921-22
§ • Munro, Dunc	Mtl.M.	1	1	0	0	0	2	0	0	0.00	....	....	....	....	....	....	....	....		1924-25	1924-25
• Murphy, Hal	Mtl.	1	1	1	0	0	60	4	0	4.00	....	....	....	....	....	....	....	....		1952-53	1952-53
• Murray, Mickey	Mtl.C.	1	1	0	1	0	60	4	0	4.00	....	....	....	....	....	....	....	....		1929-30	1929-30
‡ Myllys, Jarmo	Min., S.J.	4	39	4	27	1	1846	161	0	5.23	....	....	....	....	....	....	....	....		1988-89	1991-92
Mylnikov, Sergei	Que.	1	10	1	7	2	568	47	0	4.96	....	....	....	....	....	....	....	....		1989-90	1989-90
Myre, Phil	Mtl., Atl., St.L., Phi., Col., Buf.	14	439	149	198	76	25220	1482	14	3.53	12	6	5	....	747	41	1	3.29	1	1969-70	1982-83
Newton, Cam	Pit.	2	16	4	7	1	814	51	0	3.76	....	....	....	....	....	....	....	....		1970-71	1972-73
Norris, Jack	Bos., Chi., L.A.	4	58	20	25	4	3119	202	2	3.89	....	....	....	....	....	....	....	....		1964-65	1970-71
Oleschuk, Bill	K.C., Col.	4	55	7	28	10	2835	188	1	3.98	....	....	....	....	....	....	....	....		1975-76	1979-80
• Olesevich, Dan	NYR	1	1	0	0	1	29	2	0	4.14	....	....	....	....	....	....	....	....		1961-62	1961-62
Ouimet, Ted	St.L.	1	1	0	1	0	60	2	0	2.00	....	....	....	....	....	....	....	....		1968-69	1968-69
Pageau, Paul	L.A.	1	1	0	1	0	60	8	0	8.00	....	....	....	....	....	....	....	....		1980-81	1980-81
Paille, Marcel	NYR	7	107	32	52	22	6342	362	2	3.42	....	....	....	....	....	....	....	....		1957-58	1964-65
Palmateer, Mike	Tor., Wsh.	8	356	149	138	52	20131	1183	17	3.53	29	12	17	....	1765	89	2	3.03		1976-77	1983-84
Pang, Darren	Chi.	3	81	27	35	7	4252	287	0	4.05	6	1	3	....	250	18	0	4.32		1984-85	1988-89
Parent, Bernie	Bos., Phi., Tor.	13	608	271	198	121	35136	1493	54	2.55	71	38	33	....	4302	174	6	2.43	2	1965-66	1978-79
Parent, Bob	Tor.	2	3	0	2	0	160	15	0	5.63	....	....	....	....	....	....	....	....		1981-82	1982-83
Parro, Dave	Wsh.	4	77	21	36	10	4015	274	2	4.09	....	....	....	....	....	....	....	....		1980-81	1983-84
§ • Patrick, Lester	NYR	1	....	....	....	....	....	....	....	....	1	1	0	0	46	1	0	1.30	1	1927-28	1927-28
Peeters, Pete	Phi., Bos., Wsh.	13	489	246	155	51	27699	1424	21	3.08	71	35	35	....	4200	232	2	3.31		1978-79	1990-91
Pelletier, Marcel	Chi., NYR	2	8	1	6	0	395	32	0	4.86	....	....	....	....	....	....	....	....		1950-51	1962-63
Penney, Steve	Mtl., Wpg.	5	91	35	38	12	5194	313	1	3.62	27	15	12	....	1604	72	4	2.69		1983-84	1987-88
• Perreault, Bob	Mtl., Det., Bos.	3	31	8	16	7	1827	103	3	3.38	....	....	....	....	....	....	....	....		1955-56	1962-63
Pettie, Jim	Bos.	3	21	9	7	2	1157	71	1	3.68	....	....	....	....	....	....	....	....		1976-77	1978-79
‡ Pietrangelo, Frank	Pit., Hfd.	7	141	46	59	6	7141	490	1	4.12	12	7	5	....	713	34	1	2.86	1	1987-88	1993-94
• Plante, Jacques	Mtl., NYR, St.L., Tor., Bos.	18	837	435	247	145	49493	1964	82	2.38	112	71	36	....	6651	237	14	2.14	6	1952-53	1972-73
Plasse, Michel	St.L., Mtl., K.C., Pit., Col., Que.	11	299	92	136	54	16760	1058	2	3.79	4	1	2	....	195	9	1	2.77	1	1970-71	1981-82
§ • Plaxton, Hugh	Mtl.M.	1	1	0	1	0	57	5	0	5.26	....	....	....	....	....	....	....	....		1932-33	1932-33
Pronovost, Claude	Bos., Mtl.	2	3	1	1	0	120	7	1	3.50	....	....	....	....	....	....	....	....		1955-56	1958-59

	Name	NHL Teams	NHL Seasons	Regular Schedule								Playoffs								NHL Cup Wins	First NHL Season	Last NHL Season
				GP	W	L	T	Mins	GA	SO	Avg	GP	W	L	T	Mins	GA	SO	Avg			
	Pusey, Chris	Det.	1	1	0	0	0	40	3	0	4.50	....	....	....	....	....	....	....	....		1985-86	1985-86
‡	Racicot, Andre	Mtl.	5	68	26	23	8	3357	196	2	3.50	4	0	1	....	31	4	0	7.74	1	1989-90	1993-94
	Raymond, Alain	Wsh.	1	1	0	1	0	40	2	0	3.00	....	....	....	....	....	....	....	....		1987-88	1987-88
	Rayner, Chuck	NYA, Bro., NYR	10	424	138	208	77	25491	1294	25	3.05	18	9	9	....	1135	46	1	2.43		1940-41	1952-53
	Reaugh, Daryl	Edm., Hfd.	3	27	8	9	1	1246	72	1	3.47	....	....	....	....	....	....	....	....		1984-85	1990-91
‡	Reddick, Pokey	Wpg., Edm., Fla.	6	132	46	58	16	7162	443	0	3.71	4	0	2	....	168	10	0	3.57	1	1986-87	1993-94
•	Redding, George	Bos.	1	1	0	0	0	11	1	0	5.45	....	....	....	....	....	....	....	....		1924-25	1924-25
	Redquest, Greg	Pit.	1	1	0	0	0	13	3	0	13.85	....	....	....	....	....	....	....	....		1977-78	1977-78
	Reece, Dave	Bos.	1	14	7	5	2	777	43	2	3.32	....	....	....	....	....	....	....	....		1975-76	1975-76
‡	Reese, Jeff	Tor., Cgy., Hfd., T.B., N.J.	12	174	53	65	17	8667	529	5	3.66	11	3	5	....	515	35	0	4.08		1987-88	1999-00
	Resch, Chico	NYI, Col., N.J., Phi.	14	571	231	224	82	32279	1761	26	3.27	41	17	17	....	2044	85	2	2.50	1	1973-74	1986-87
•	Rheaume, Herb	Mtl.C.	1	31	10	20	1	1889	92	0	2.92	....	....	....	....	....	....	....	....		1925-26	1925-26
	Ricci, Nick	Pit.	4	19	7	12	0	1087	79	0	4.36	....	....	....	....	....	....	....	....		1979-80	1982-83
	Richardson, Terry	Det., St.L.	5	20	3	11	0	906	85	0	5.63	....	....	....	....	....	....	....	....		1973-74	1978-79
	Ridley, Curt	NYR, Van., Tor.	6	104	27	47	16	5498	355	1	3.87	2	0	2	....	120	8	0	4.00		1974-75	1980-81
‡	Riendeau, Vincent	Mtl., St.L., Det., Bos.	8	184	85	65	20	10423	573	5	3.30	25	11	12	....	1277	71	1	3.34		1987-88	1994-95
	Riggin, Dennis	Det.	2	18	6	10	2	999	52	1	3.12	....	....	....	....	....	....	....	....		1959-60	1962-63
	Riggin, Pat	Atl., Cgy., Wsh., Bos., Pit.	9	350	153	120	52	19872	1135	11	3.43	25	8	13	....	1336	72	0	3.23		1979-80	1987-88
	Ring, Bob	Bos.	1	1	0	0	0	33	4	0	7.27	....	....	....	....	....	....	....	....		1965-66	1965-66
	Rivard, Fern	Min.	4	55	9	26	11	2865	190	2	3.98	....	....	....	....	....	....	....	....		1968-69	1974-75
•	Roach, John Ross	Tor., NYR, Det.	14	492	219	204	68	30444	1246	58	2.46	29	12	14	3	1901	60	7	1.89		1921-22	1934-35
•	Roberts, Moe	Bos., NYA, Chi.	4	10	3	5	0	501	31	0	3.71	....	....	....	....	....	....	....	....		1925-26	1951-52
•	Robertson, Earl	Det., NYA, Bro.	6	190	60	95	34	11820	575	16	2.92	15	7	7	....	995	29	2	1.75	1	1936-37	1941-42
•	Rollins, Al	Tor., Chi., NYR	9	430	141	205	83	25723	1192	28	2.78	13	6	7	....	755	30	0	2.38	1	1949-50	1959-60
	Romano, Roberto	Pit., Bos.	6	126	46	63	8	7111	471	4	3.97	....	....	....	....	....	....	....	....		1982-83	1993-94
	Rupp, Pat	Det.	1	1	0	1	0	60	4	0	4.00	....	....	....	....	....	....	....	....		1963-64	1963-64
	Rutherford, Jim	Det., Pit., Tor., L.A.	13	457	151	227	59	25895	1576	14	3.65	8	2	5	....	440	28	0	3.82		1970-71	1982-83
	Rutledge, Wayne	L.A.	3	82	28	37	9	4325	241	2	3.34	8	2	4	....	378	20	0	3.17		1967-68	1969-70
	St. Croix, Rick	Phi., Tor.	8	130	49	54	18	7295	451	2	3.71	11	4	6	....	562	29	1	3.10		1977-78	1984-85
	St. Laurent, Sam	N.J., Det.	5	34	7	12	4	1572	92	1	3.51	1	0	0	....	10	1	0	6.00		1985-86	1989-90
§ •	Sands, Charlie	Mtl.	1	1	0	0	0	25	5	0	12.00	....	....	....	....	....	....	....	....		1939-40	1939-40
	Sands, Mike	Min.	2	6	0	5	0	302	26	0	5.17	....	....	....	....	....	....	....	....		1984-85	1986-87
	Sarjeant, Geoff	St.L., S.J.	2	8	1	2	1	291	20	0	4.12	....	....	....	....	....	....	....	....		1994-95	1995-96
	Sauve, Bob	Buf., Det., Chi., N.J.	13	420	182	154	54	23711	1377	8	3.48	34	15	16	....	1850	95	4	3.08		1976-77	1988-89
•	Sawchuk, Terry	Det., Bos., Tor., L.A., NYR	21	971	447	330	172	57194	2389	103	2.51	106	54	48	....	6290	266	12	2.54	4	1949-50	1969-70
	Schaefer, Joe	NYR	2	2	0	2	0	86	8	0	5.58	....	....	....	....	....	....	....	....		1959-60	1960-61
‡	Schafer, Paxton	Bos.	1	3	0	0	0	77	6	0	4.68	....	....	....	....	....	....	....	....		1996-97	1996-97
	Scott, Ron	NYR, L.A.	5	28	8	13	4	1450	91	0	3.77	1	0	0	....	32	4	0	7.50		1983-84	1989-90
	Sevigny, Richard	Mtl., Que.	8	176	80	54	20	9485	507	5	3.21	4	0	3	....	208	13	0	3.75		1979-80	1986-87
	Sharples, Scott	Cgy.	1	1	0	0	1	65	4	0	3.69	....	....	....	....	....	....	....	....		1991-92	1991-92
§ •	Shields, Al	NYA	1	2	0	0	0	41	9	0	13.17	....	....	....	....	....	....	....	....		1931-32	1931-32
	Sidorkiewicz, Peter	Hfd., Ott., N.J.	8	246	79	128	27	13884	832	8	3.60	15	5	10	....	912	55	0	3.62		1987-88	1997-98
	Simmons, Don	Bos., Tor., NYR	11	248	101	100	41	14495	698	20	2.89	24	13	11	....	1436	62	3	2.59	3	1956-57	1968-69
	Simmons, Gary	Cal., Cle., L.A.	4	107	30	57	15	6162	366	5	3.56	1	0	0	....	20	1	0	3.00		1974-75	1977-78
	Skidmore, Paul	St.L.	1	2	1	1	0	120	6	0	3.00	....	....	....	....	....	....	....	....		1981-82	1981-82
	Skorodenski, Warren	Chi., Edm.	5	35	12	11	4	1732	100	2	3.46	2	0	0	....	33	6	0	10.91		1981-82	1987-88
	Smith, Al	Tor., Pit., Det., Buf., Hfd., Col.	10	233	74	99	36	12752	735	10	3.46	6	1	4	....	317	21	0	3.97		1965-66	1980-81
	Smith, Billy	L.A., NYI	20	680	305	233	105	38431	2031	22	3.17	132	88	36	....	7645	348	5	2.73	4	1971-72	1988-89
	Smith, Gary	Tor., Oak., Cal., Chi., Van., Min., Wsh., Wpg.	14	532	173	261	74	29619	1675	26	3.39	20	5	13	....	1153	62	1	3.23		1965-66	1979-80
•	Smith, Normie	Mtl.M., Det.	8	199	81	83	35	12357	479	17	2.33	12	9	2	0	820	18	3	1.32	2	1931-32	1944-45
	Sneddon, Bob	Cal.	1	5	0	2	0	225	21	0	5.60	....	....	....	....	....	....	....	....		1970-71	1970-71
‡	Soderstrom, Tommy	Phi., NYI	5	156	45	69	19	8189	496	10	3.63	....	....	....	....	....	....	....	....		1992-93	1996-97
	Soetaert, Doug	NYR, Wpg., Mtl.	12	284	110	104	42	15583	1030	6	3.97	5	1	2	....	180	14	0	4.67	1	1975-76	1986-87
‡	Soucy, Christian	Chi.	1	1	0	0	0	3	0	0	0.00	....	....	....	....	....	....	....	....		1993-94	1993-94
•	Spooner, Red	Pit.	1	1	0	1	0	60	6	0	6.00	....	....	....	....	....	....	....	....		1929-30	1929-30
§ •	Spring, Jesse	Ham.	1	1	0	0	0	2	0	0	0.00	....	....	....	....	....	....	....	....		1924-25	1924-25
	Staniowski, Ed	St.L., Wpg., Hfd.	10	219	67	104	21	12075	818	2	4.06	8	1	6	....	428	28	0	3.93		1975-76	1984-85
§ •	Starr, Harold	Mtl.M.	1	1	0	0	0	3	0	0	0.00	....	....	....	....	....	....	....	....		1931-32	1931-32
	Stauber, Robb	L.A., Buf.	4	62	21	23	9	3295	209	1	3.81	4	3	1	....	240	16	0	4.00		1989-90	1994-95
	Stefan, Greg	Det.	9	299	115	127	30	16333	1068	5	3.92	30	12	17	....	1681	99	1	3.53		1981-82	1989-90
	Stein, Phil	Tor.	1	1	0	0	1	70	2	0	1.71	....	....	....	....	....	....	....	....		1939-40	1939-40
	Stephenson, Wayne	St.L., Phi., Wsh.	10	328	146	103	49	18343	937	14	3.06	26	11	12	....	1522	79	2	3.11	1	1971-72	1980-81
	Stevenson, Doug	Chi., NYR	3	8	2	6	0	480	39	0	4.88	....	....	....	....	....	....	....	....		1942-43	1945-46
	Stewart, Charles	Bos.	3	77	30	41	5	4742	194	10	2.45	....	....	....	....	....	....	....	....		1924-25	1926-27
	Stewart, Jim	Bos.	1	1	0	1	0	20	5	0	15.00	....	....	....	....	....	....	....	....		1979-80	1979-80
•	Stuart, Herb	Det.	1	3	1	2	0	180	5	0	1.67	....	....	....	....	....	....	....	....		1926-27	1926-27
	Sylvestri, Don	Bos.	1	3	0	0	2	102	6	0	3.53	....	....	....	....	....	....	....	....		1984-85	1984-85
‡	Takko, Kari	Min., Edm.	6	142	37	71	14	7317	475	1	3.90	4	0	1	....	109	7	0	3.85		1985-86	1990-91
	Tanner, John	Que.	3	21	2	11	5	1084	65	1	3.60	....	....	....	....	....	....	....	....		1989-90	1991-92
	Tataryn, Dave	NYR	1	2	1	1	0	80	10	0	7.50	....	....	....	....	....	....	....	....		1976-77	1976-77
	Taylor, Bobby	Phi., Pit.	5	46	15	17	6	2268	155	0	4.10	....	....	....	....	....	....	....	....	1	1971-72	1975-76
•	Teno, Harvey	Det.	1	5	2	3	0	300	15	0	3.00	....	....	....	....	....	....	....	....		1938-39	1938-39
	Thomas, Wayne	Mtl., Tor., NYR	9	243	103	93	34	13768	766	10	3.34	15	6	8	....	849	50	1	3.53		1972-73	1980-81
•	Thompson, Tiny	Bos., Det.	12	553	284	194	75	34175	1183	81	2.08	44	20	24	0	2974	93	7	1.88	1	1928-29	1939-40
§	Toppazzini, Jerry	Bos.	1	1	0	0	0	1	0	0	0.00	....	....	....	....	....	....	....	....		1960-61	1960-61
‡	Torchia, Mike	Dal.	1	6	3	2	1	327	18	0	3.30	....	....	....	....	....	....	....	....		1994-95	1994-95
	Tremblay, Vincent	Tor., Pit.	5	58	12	26	8	2785	223	1	4.80	....	....	....	....	....	....	....	....		1979-80	1983-84
	Tucker, Ted	Cal.	1	5	1	1	1	177	10	0	3.39	....	....	....	....	....	....	....	....		1973-74	1973-74
•	Turner, Joe	Det.	1	1	0	0	1	70	3	0	2.57	....	....	....	....	....	....	....	....		1941-42	1941-42
	Vachon, Rogie	Mtl., L.A., Det., Bos.	16	795	355	291	127	46298	2310	51	2.99	48	23	23	....	2876	133	2	2.77	3	1966-67	1981-82
	Veisor, Mike	Chi., Hfd., Wpg.	10	139	41	62	26	7806	532	5	4.09	4	0	2	....	180	15	0	5.00		1973-74	1983-84
•	Vezina, Georges	Mtl.C.	9	190	103	81	5	11592	633	13	3.28	13	9	4	1	780	36	2	2.77		1917-18	1925-26
	Villemure, Gilles	NYR, Chi.	10	205	100	64	29	11581	542	13	2.81	14	5	5	....	656	32	0	2.93		1963-64	1976-77
	Wakaluk, Darcy	Buf., Min., Dal., Phx.	8	191	67	75	21	9756	524	9	3.22	8	4	2	....	364	18	0	2.97		1988-89	1996-97
	Wakely, Ernie	Mtl., St.L.	5	113	41	42	17	6244	290	8	2.79	10	2	6	....	509	37	1	4.36		1962-63	1971-72
•	Walsh, Flat	Mtl.M., NYA	7	108	48	43	16	6641	256	12	2.31	8	2	4	2	570	16	2	1.68		1926-27	1932-33
	Wamsley, Rick	Mtl., St.L., Cgy., Tor.	13	407	204	131	46	23123	1287	12	3.34	27	7	18	....	1397	81	0	3.48	1	1980-81	1992-93
	Watt, Jim	St.L.	1	1	0	0	0	20	2	0	6.00	....	....	....	....	....	....	....	....		1973-74	1973-74
	Weeks, Steve	NYR, Hfd., Van., NYI, L.A., Ott.	13	290	111	119	33	15879	989	5	3.74	12	3	5	....	486	27	0	3.33		1980-81	1992-93
	Wetzel, Carl	Det., Min.	2	7	1	3	1	301	22	0	4.39	....	....	....	....	....	....	....	....		1964-65	1967-68
	Willis, Jordan	Dal.	1	1	0	1	0	19	1	0	3.16	....	....	....	....	....	....	....	....		1995-96	1995-96
	Wilson, Dunc	Phi., Van., Tor., NYR, Pit.	10	287	80	150	33	15851	988	8	3.74	....	....	....	....	....	....	....	....		1969-70	1978-79
	Wilson, Lefty	Det., Tor., Bos.	3	3	0	0	1	81	1	0	0.74	....	....	....	....	....	....	....	....		1953-54	1957-58
•	Winkler, Hal	NYR, Bos.	2	75	35	26	14	4739	126	21	1.60	10	2	3	5	640	18	2	1.69		1926-27	1927-28
	Wolfe, Bernie	Wsh.	4	120	20	61	21	6104	424	1	4.17	....	....	....	....	....	....	....	....		1975-76	1978-79
	Wood, Alex	NYA	1	1	0	1	0	70	3	0	2.57	....	....	....	....	....	....	....	....		1936-37	1936-37
	Worsley, Gump	NYR, Mtl., Min.	21	861	335	352	150	50183	2407	43	2.88	70	40	26	....	4084	189	5	2.78	4	1952-53	1973-74
•	Worters, Roy	Pit., NYA, Mtl.C.	12	484	171	229	83	30175	1143	67	2.27	11	3	6	2	690	24	3	2.09		1925-26	1936-37
	Worthy, Chris	Oak., Cal.	3	26	5	10	4	1326	98	0	4.43	....	....	....	....	....	....	....	....		1968-69	1970-71
§ •	Young, Doug	Det.	1	1	0	0	0	21	1	0	2.86	....	....	....	....	....	....	....	....		1933-34	1933-34
‡	Zanier, Mike	Edm.	1	3	1	1	1	185	12	0	3.89	....	....	....	....	....	....	....	....		1984-85	1984-85

1999-2000 Transactions

September, 1999

30 – **NHL Waiver Draft**

Pos.	Player	Claimed By	Claimed From
RW	**Ladislav Kohn**	Atlanta	Toronto
C	**Viachselev Butsayev**	Tampa Bay	Ottawa
D	**Chris Joseph**	Vancouver	Ottawa
D	**Jamie Rivers**	NY Islanders	St. Louis
D	**Ken Sutton**	Washington	New Jersey
D	**Rich Brennan**	Los Angeles	Nashville
C	**Jeff Williams**	Atlanta	New Jersey
D	**John Namestnikov**	Vancouver	Rangers
C	**Terry Yake**	St. Louis	Atlanta
D	**Ladislav Benysek**	Anaheim	Edmonton

October, 1999

1 – Tampa Bay trades **Cory Cross** and a 7th round pick in 2001 to Toronto for **Fredrik Modin**.

3 – Tampa Bay trades **Alexandre Daigle** to NY Rangers for future considerations.

5 – Washington trades **Ken Sutton** to New Jersey for future considerations.

7 – Tampa Bay trades **Steve Kelly** to New Jersey for New Jersey's 7th round pick in 2000 (**Brian Eklund**).

8 – Toronto trades **Sylvain Cote** to Chicago for a 2nd round pick in 2001 and future considerations.

15 – Atlanta trades **Jody Hull** to Philadelphia for future considerations.

20 – Philadelphia trades **Karl Dykhuis** to Montreal for future considerations.

20 – Toronto trades **Derek King** and a conditional pick in 2000 to St. Louis for **Tyler Harlton** and a conditional pick in 2000 (Toronto has the option to switch 8th round picks).

20 – Boston trades **Dmitri Khristich** to Toronto for a 2nd round pick in 2000 (**Ivan Huml**).

29 – Tampa Bay trades **Mikko Kuparinen** to Atlanta for future considerations.

29 – Atlanta trades **Corey Schwab** to Vancouver for a 2nd round pick in 2000 (**Libor Ustrnul**).

29 – Anaheim trades **Ted Drury** to NY Islanders for **Tony Hrkac** and **Dean Malkoc**.

November, 1999

1 – Atlanta trades **Sylvain Cloutier, Jeff Williams** and a 7th round pick in 2000 (**Ken Magowan**) to **New Jersey** for **Wesley Mason** and **Eric Bertrand**.

3 – New Jersey trades **Brian Rolston** to Colorado for **Claude Lemieux**, Colorado's second-round pick in 2000 (**Matt DeMarchi**) and the option to switch first round picks in 2000.

11 – Tampa Bay trades **Colin Forbes** to Ottawa for **Bruce Gardiner**.

12 – Tampa Bay trades **Michael Nylander** to Chicago for **Bryan Muir** and **Reid Simpson**.

16 – Nashville trades **Steve Washburn** to Philadelphia for a conditional pick in 2001.

18 – Phoenix trades **Mikhail Shtalenkov** and a 4th round pick in 2000 (**Chris Eade**) to Florida for **Sean Burke** and a 5th round pick in 2000 (**Nate Kiser**).

20 – Calgary trades **Nils Ekman** and a 4th round pick in 2000 (later traded to NY Isladers. NY Islanders selected **Vladimir Gorbunov**) to Tampa Bay for **Andreas Johansson**.

26 – Tampa Bay trades **Mike McBain** to Montreal for **Gordie Dwyer**.

29 – Tampa Bay trades a 3rd round pick in 2000 (**Mikael Tellqvist**) to Toronto for **Todd Warriner**.

30 – Phoenix trades **Rob Murray** to Edmonton for **Eric Houde**.

December, 1999

8 – Atlanta trades **Rick Tabaracci** to Colorado for **Shean Donovan**.

9 – Atlanta trades **Eric Bertrand** to Philadelphia for **Brian Wesenberg**.

15 – Atlanta trades **Kevin Dean** to Dallas for a 9th round pick in 2000 (**Mark McRae**).

19 – Vancouver trades **Kevin Weekes, Dave Scatchard** and **Bill Muckalt** to NY Islanders for **Felix Potvin**, a 2nd round pick in 2000 (Later traded to New Jersey. New Jersey selected **Teemu Laine**) and a 3rd round pick in 2000 (**Thatcher Bell**).

28 – Boston trades **Kay Whitmore** to Edmonton for **Mike Matteucci**.

30 – San Jose trades **Mike Vernon**, a 3rd round pick in 2000 (**Sean O'Connor**) and future considerations to Florida for **Radek Dvorak**.

30 – San Jose trades **Radek Dvorak** to NY Rangers for **Todd Harvey** and a 4th round pick in 2001.

January, 2000

13 – Tampa Bay trades **Stephane Richer** to St. Louis for **Rich Parent** and **Chris McAlpine**.

14 – New Jersey trades **Vadim Sharifijanov** and a draft pick to Vancouver for draft picks.

17 – Tampa Bay trades draft picks to Washington for **Jaroslav Svejkovsky**.

22 – Dallas trades **Juha Lind** to Montreal for **Scott Thornton**.

23 – Philadelphia trades **Rod Brind'Amour, Jean-Marc Pelletier** and a 2nd round pick in 2000 (later traded to Colorado. Colorado selected **Agris Saviels**) to Carolina for **Keith Primeau** and a 5th round pick in 2000 (later traded to NY Islanders. NY Islanders selected **Kristofer Ottoson**).

24 – Los Angeles trades **Vladimir Tsyplakov** to Buffalo for an 8th round pick in 2000 (**Dan Welch**).

25 – Los Angeles trades **Bill Huard** to Atlanta for future considerations.

26 – Chicago trades **Todd White** to Philadelphia for a conditional pick in 2001.

29 – Pittsburgh trades **Kip Miller** to Anaheim for a conditional pick in 2000 (**Roman Simicek**).

February, 2000

2 – Washington trades **Stewart Malgunas** to Nashville for conditional pick in 2001.

3 – NY Rangers trade **John Namestnikov** to Nashville for **Jason Dawe**.

7 – Washington trades **Alexander Volchkov** to Edmonton for a conditional pick in 2001.

8 – Chicago trades **Dave Manson** and **Sylvain Cote** to Dallas for **Kevin Dean, Derek Plante** and a 2nd round pick in 2001.

9 – Tampa Bay trades **Darcy Tucker** and draft picks to Toronto for **Mike Johnson, Marek Posmyk** and draft picks.

9 – St. Louis trades **Rory Fitzpatrick** to Nashville for **Dan Keczmer**.

11 – Atlanta trades **Darryl Shannon** and **Jason Botterill** to Calgary for **Hnat Domenichelli** and **Dmitri Vlasenkov**.

14 – Philadelphia trades **Eric Bertrand** to Nashville for future considerations.

15 – NY Islanders trade **Gino Odjick** to Philadelphia for **Mikael Andersson** and Carolina's 5th round pick in 2000 (Previously acquired. NY Islanders selected **Kristofer Ottoson**.).

18 – Calgary trades **Allan Egeland** to Los Angeles for future considerations.

18 – Calgary trades **Joel Irving** to Atlanta for future considerations.

23 – Toronto trades **Craig Charron** to Los Angeles for **Donald MacLean**.

March, 2000

1 – Montreal trades **Vladimir Malakhov** to New Jersey for **Sheldon Souray, Josh DeWolf** and New Jersey's 2nd round pick in 2001.

3 – NY Islanders trade **Dallas Eakins** to Chicago for future considerations.

6 – Calgary trades **Travis Brigley** and a 6th round pick in 2001 to Philadelphia for **Marc Bureau**.

6 – Colorado trades **Brian Rolston, Samuel Pahlsson, Martin Grenier** and a 1st round pick in 2000 (**Martin Samuelsson**) to Boston for **Ray Bourque** and **Dave Andreychuk**.

7 – New Jersey trades **Lyle Odelein** to Phoenix for **Deron Quint** and a draft pick in 2001.

8 – Tampa Bay trades **Jeff Shevalier** to Ottawa for future considerations.

8 – Philadelphia trades **Mikael Renberg** to Phoenix for **Rick Tocchet**.

9 – Tampa Bay trades **Ian Herbers** to NY Islanders for a 7th round pick in 2000 (Later traded back to NY Islanders. NY Islanders selected Ryan Caldwell.).

9 – Edmonton trades **Christian Laflamme** and **Matthieu Descoteaux** to Montreal for **Igor Ulanov** and **Alain Nasreddine**.

9 – Buffalo trades **Cory Sarich, Wayne Primeau, Brian Holzinger** and a 3rd round pick in 2000 (**Alexander Kharitonov**) to Tampa Bay for **Chris Gratton** and a 2nd round pick in 2001.

10 – Buffalo trades **Michal Grosek** to Chicago for **Doug Gilmour, J.P. Dumont** and a conditional pick in 2001 or 2002.

10 – Boston trades **Rob DiMaio** to NY Rangers for **Mike Knuble**.

11 – Anaheim trades **Johan Davidsson** and a conditional pick in 2001 to NY Islanders for **Jorgen Jonsson**.

11 – Tampa Bay trades **Chris McAlpine** to Atlanta for **Mikko Kuparinen**.

13 – Nashville trades **Bob Boughner** to Pittsburgh for **Pavel Skrbek**.

13 – Phoenix trades **Todd Gill** to Detroit for **Philippe Audet**.

13 – Los Angeles trades **Donald Audette** and **Frantisek Kaberle** to Atlanta for **Kelly Buchberger** and **Nelson Emerson**.

13 – Florida trades **Chris Wells** to NY Rangers for a conditional pick in 2001.

14 – Anaheim trades **Dan Trebil** to Pittsburgh for a 5th-round pick in 2000 (**Bill Cass**).

14 – Atlanta trades **Ed Ward** to Anaheim for a conditional pick in 2001.

14 – Atlanta trades **Kirby Law** to Philadelphia for Vancouver's 6th-round pick in 2000 (Previously acquired by Philadelphia. Atlanta selected **Jeff Dwyer**) and a conditional pick in 2001.

14 – Calgary trades **Cale Hulse** and a 3rd-round pick in 2001 to Nashville for **Sergei Krivokrasov**.

14 – Calgary trades **Tyler Moss** and **Rene Corbet** to Pittsburgh for **Brad Werenka**.

14 – Carolina trades **Kent Manderville** to Philadelphia for **Sandy McCarthy**.

14 – Edmonton trades **Josef Beranek** to Pittsburgh for **German Titov**.

14 – Florida trades **Ryan Johnson** and **Dwayne Hay** to Tampa Bay for **Mike Sillinger**.

14 – Nashville trades **Corey Hirsch** to Anaheim for future considerations.

14 – New Jersey trades **Brendan Morrison** and **Denis Pederson** to Vancouver for **Alexander Mogilny**.

14 – Ottawa trades **Ron Tugnutt** and **Janne Laukkanen** to Pittsburgh for **Tom Barrasso**.

14 – NY Islanders trade **Petr Sachl** to Nashville for a 9th-round pick in 2000 (**Tomi Pettinen**).

16 – Calgary trades **Rocky Thompson** to Florida for **Filip Kuba**.

May, 2000

1 – Chicago trades **Steve Passmore** to Los Angeles for a conditional pick in 2000 (**Olli Malmivaara**).

11 – NY Islanders trade **Chris Nielsen** to Columbus for a 4th round pick in 2000 (Later traded to Anaheim. Anaheim selected **Jonas Ronnqvist**.) and a 9th round pick in 2000 (**Sean Kotray**).

23 – Anaheim trades **Trent Hunter** to NY Islanders for Columbus' 4th round pick in 2000 (Previously acquired by NY Islanders. Anaheim selected selected **Jonas Ronnqvist**.).

25 – Anaheim trades **Espen Knutsen** to Columbus for Columbus' 4th round pick in 2001.

31 – Carolina trades **Paul Ranheim** to Philadelphia for an 8th round pick in 2002.

June, 2000

1 – Anaheim trades **Stephen Peat** to Washington for a 4th round pick in 2000 (Later traded to Montreal. Later traded to Pittsburgh. Pittsburgh selected **Michel Ouellet**).

1 – Tampa Bay trades **Eric Beaudon** to Florida for a 7th round pick in 2000 (**Marek Priechodsky**).

2 – Tampa Bay trades **Kevin Hodson** to Montreal for a 7th round pick in 2000 (Later traded to Philadelphia. Philadelphia selected **John Eichelberger**.).

2 – Montreal trades a 6th round pick in 2000 (**Darcy Hordichuk**) to Atlanta for future considerations.

7 – Tampa Bay trades **Rich Parent** to Ottawa for a 7th round pick in 2000 (Later traded to Buffalo. Buffalo selected **Paul Gaustad**).

7 – Colorado trades **Marc Denis** to Columbus for a 2nd round pick in 2000 (Later traded to Carolina. Carolina selected **Tomas Kurka**).

9 – Calgary trades **J.S. Giguere** to Anaheim for a 2nd round pick in the 2000 Entry Draft (Later traded to Washington. Washington selected **Matt Pettinger**.)

11 – San Jose trades **Jan Caloun**, a 9th round pick in the 2000 Entry Draft (**Martin Paroulek**) and a conditional pick in the 2001 Entry Draft to Columbus for future considerations.

11 – San Jose trades **Andy Sutton**, a 7th round pick in the 2000 Entry Draft (**Peter Bartos**) and 3rd round pick in the 2001 Entry Draft to Minnesota for an 8th round pick in the 2001 Entry Draft.

11 – Ottawa trades **Patrick Traverse** to Anaheim for **Joel Kwiatkowski**.

12 – Atlanta trades **Steve Staios** to New Jersey for a 9th round pick (**Simon Gamache**) in the 2000 Entry Draft.

12 – Philadelphia trades a 9th round pick in the 2000 Entry Draft (**Arne Ramholt**) to Chicago for **Mark Janssens**.

12 – Dallas trades **Manny Fernandez** and **Brad Lukowich** to Minnesota for a 3rd round pick in the 2000 Entry Draft (**Joel Lundqvist**) and 4th round pick in the 2002 Entry Draft.

12 – Nashville trades **Patrick Cote** to Edmonton for Phoenix's 5th round pick (**Matt Koalska**) in the 2000 Entry Draft (previously acquired by Edmonton).

12 – Anaheim trades **Ed Ward** to New Jersey for a 7th round pick in the 2001 Entry Draft.

12 – New Jersey trades **Krzysztof Oliwa** and future considerations (**Deron Quint**, June 23, 2000) to Columbus for a 3rd round pick in the 2001 Entry Draft and future considerations (**Turner Stevenson**, June 23, 2000).

12 – Minnesota transfers a 6th round pick in the 2001 Entry Draft to Montreal as compensation for Minnesota signing **Jacques Lemaire** as head coach.

23 – Calgary trades the rights to **Dan Cavanaugh** and an 8th round pick in the 2001 Entry Draft to Minnesota for **Mike Vernon**.

23 – Minnesota trades **Joe Juneau** to Phoenix for **Rickard Wallin**.

23 – Montreal trades San Jose's 2nd round pick in the 2001 Entry Draft (previously acquired) to Columbus for future considerations.

23 – Boston trades a 5th round pick (**Scott Heffernan**) in the 2000 Entry Draft to Columbus for future considerations.

23 – Buffalo trades **Jean-Luc Grand-Pierre, Matt Davidson**, San Jose's 5th round pick (**Tyler Kolarik**) in the 2000 Entry Draft (**previously acquired**) and a 5th round pick in the 2001 Entry Draft to Columbus for future considerations.

23 – Minnesota trades **Chris Terreri** and a 9th round pick (Later traded to Tampa Bay. Tampa Bay selected **Thomas Ziegler**.) in the 2000 Entry Draft to New Jersey for **Brad Bombardir**.

24 – NY Islanders trade **Kevin Weekes, Kristian Kudroc** and a 2nd round pick in the 2001 Entry Draft to Tampa Bay for Tampa Bay's 1st round pick in the 2000 Entry Draft (**Raffi Torres**), Calgary's 4th round pick in 2000 (previously acquired, **Vladimir Gorbunov**) and NY Islanders' 7th round pick in 2000 (previously acquired, **Ryan Caldwell**).

24 – Vancouver trades **Brad May** to Phoenix for a conditional pick in the 2001 Entry Draft.

24 – NY Islanders trade **Roberto Luongo** and **Olli Jokinen** to Florida for **Mark Parrish** and **Oleg Kvasha**.

24 – Colorado trades **Sandis Ozolinsh** and Columbus' 2nd round pick in the 2000 Entry Draft (previously acquired, **Tomas Kurka**) to Carolina for **Nolan Pratt**, Carolina's 1st round pick in the 2000 Entry Draft (**Vaclav Nedorost**), 2nd round pick in 2000 (**Jared Aulin**) and Philadelphia's 2nd round pick in 2000 (previously acquired, **Agris Saviels**).

24 – New York Islanders trade **Eric Brewer, Josh Green** and the NY Islanders' 2nd round pick in the 2000 Entry Draft (**Brad Winchester**) to Edmonton for **Roman Hamrlik**.

24 – Washington trades **Miika Elomo** and Buffalo's 4th round compensatory pick in the 2000 Entry Draft (previously acquired, **Levente Szuper**) to Calgary for Anaheim's 2nd round pick in the 2000 Entry Draft (previously acquired, **Matt Pettinger**).

24 – Vancouver trades a 2nd round pick in the 2000 Entry Draft (**Libor Ustrnul**) to Atlanta for a conditional pick in the 2001 Entry Draft.

24 – Chicago trades a 2nd round pick in the 2000 Entry Draft (**Tero Maatta**) to San Jose for San Jose's 2nd round pick in 2000 (**Jonas Nordqvist**) and NY Rangers' 3rd round pick in 2000 (previously acquired, **Igor Radulov**).

24 – NY Rangers trade a 2nd round pick in the 2000 Entry Draft (**Tomas Kopecky**) to Detroit for Detroit's 2nd round pick in 2000 (**Filip Novak**) and 3rd round pick in 2000 (**Dominic Moore**).

24 – Montreal trades a 2nd round pick in the 2000 Entry Draft (**Igor Bryzgalov**) to Anaheim for Anaheim's 3rd round pick in 2000 (**Jozef Balej**), Washington's 4th round pick in 2000 (previously acquired, **Michel Ouellet**) and Anaheim's 5th round pick in 2000 (**Glenn Ryan**).

25 – Dallas trades **Aaron Gavey, Pavel Patera**, an 8th round pick in the

2000 Entry Draft (**Eric Johannon**) and Minnesota's 4th round pick in 2002 (previously acquired) to Minnesota for **Brad Lukowich** and Minnesota's 3rd and 9th round picks in 2001.

25 – Philadelphia trades **John Vanbiesbrouck** to NY Islanders for NY Islanders' 4th round pick in the 2001 Entry Draft.

25 – Washington trades Tampa Bay's 7th round pick in the 2000 Entry Draft (previously acquired, **Yevgeny Federov**) and Calgary's 7th round pick in 2000 (previously acquired, **Tim Eriksson**) to Los Angeles for Los Angeles' 5th round compensatory pick in 2000 (Later traded to Chicago. Chicago selected **Alexander Barkunov**).

25 – Detroit trades a 3rd round pick in the 2001 Entry Draft to Nashville for Nashville's 4th round pick in 2000 (**Stefan Liv**).

25 – Carolina trades Anaheim's 4th round pick (previously acquired, **Blake Robson**), Carolina's 5th round compensatory pick (Matt McRae) and 8th round pick (**Eric Bowen**) in the 2000 Entry Draft to Atlanta for Atlanta's 4th round pick in 2000 (**Niclas Wallin**).

25 – NY Rangers trade a 4th round pick in the 2000 Entry Draft (**Jon Disalvatore**) to San Jose for San Jose's 4th round pick (**Premsyl Duben**) and 5th round compensatory pick (**Brandon Snee**) in 2000.

25 – Philadelphia trades a 4th round pick in the 2000 Entry Draft (**Johan Hagglund**) to Tampa Bay for Tampa Bay's 6th round pick (**Roman Cechmanek**), Montreal's 7th round pick (previously acquired, **John Eichelberger**) and Toronto's 9th round pick (previously acquired, **Milan Kopecky**) in 2000.

25 – Pittsburgh trades a 4th round pick in the 2000 Entry Draft (**Christian Larrivee**) to Montreal in exchange for Washington's 4th round pick (previously acquired and later traded to Pittsburgh. Pittsburgh selected

Michel Ouellet) and Montreal's 5th round pick (**David Koci**) in 2000.

25 – Chicago trades Toronto's 4th round pick in the 2000 Entry Draft (previously acquired, **Ryan Vanbuskirk**) to Washington for Los Angeles' 5th round compensatory pick (previously acquired, **Alexander Barkunov**) and Washington's 6th round pick (**Joey Martin**) in 2000.

25 – Los Angeles trades a 5th round pick (**Greg Zanon**) and 5th round compensatory pick (**Grant Potulny**) in the 2000 Entry Draft to Ottawa for Ottawa's 4th round pick (**Lubomir Vishnovsky**) in 2000.

25 – Chicago trades the rights to **Ben Simon** to Atlanta for Atlanta's 9th round pick (**Peter Flache**) in the 2000 Entry Draft.

25 – Detroit trades **Shayne Hnidy** to Ottawa for Ottawa's 8th round pick (**Todd Jackson**) in the 2000 Entry Draft.

25 – Toronto trades the rights to **Jonathan Hedstrom** to Anaheim for Anaheim's 6th round pick (**Vadim Sozinov**) and 7th round pick (**Markus Seikola**) in the 2000 Entry Draft.

25 – Buffalo trades a 6th round pick in the 2000 Entry Draft (**Petr Chvojka**) to Montreal for Montreal's 5th round pick in 2001.

25 – Detroit trades a 9th round pick in the 2000 Entry Draft (**Louie Mandeville**) to Columbus for Columbus' 9th round pick in 2002.

25 – Tampa Bay trades Ottawa's 7th round pick in the 2000 Entry Draft (previously acquired, **Paul Gaustad**) to Buffalo for Buffalo's 7th and 9th round picks in 2001.

25 – Washington trades an 8th round pick in the 2000 Entry Draft (**Pasi Saarinen**) to San Jose for San Jose's 8th round pick in the 2001 Entry Draft.

25 – Edmonton trades a 9th round pick in the 2000 Entry Draft (**Andreas Lindstrom**) to Boston for Boston's 9th round pick in 2001.

25 – Calgary trades an 8th round compensatory pick in the 2000 Entry Draft (**Sean McMorrow**) to Buffalo for Buffalo's 8th round pick in 2001.

25 – New Jersey trades Minnesota's 9th round pick in the 2000 Entry Draft (previously acquired, **Thomas Ziegler**) to Tampa Bay for Tampa Bay's 8th round pick in 2001.

25 – Florida trades a 9th round pick in the 2000 Entry Draft (**Andrej Nedorost**) to Columbus for Columbus' 9th round pick in 2001.

July, 2000

10 – New Jersey trades **Steve Staios** to Atlanta for future considerations.

20 – Edmonton trades **Kay Whitmore** to Boston for future considerations.

20 – Washington trades **Nolan Baumgartner** to Chicago for **Remi Royer**.

August, 2000

4 – NY Rangers trade **Darren Langdon** and **Rob DiMaio** to Carolina for **Sandy McCarthy** and a conditional pick in the 2001 Entry Draft.

11 – Chicago trades the rights to **David Ling** to Dallas for a conditional pick in the 2001 Entry Draft.

14 – Columbus trades a conditional pick in the 2003 Entry Draft to Detroit for **Kent McDonell**.

Trades and free agent signings that occurred after September 1, 2000 are listed on page 264.

Hockey Fights Cancer is a joint initiative created by the National Hockey League and the National Hockey League Players' Association that honors those in the hockey community who have struggled, or continue to struggle, with the disease.

The goal of Hockey Fights Cancer is to raise money and visibility for local cancer care or research, as well as to support the American Cancer Society and Canadian Cancer Society national organizations. Founded by the NHL and the NHLPA, Hockey Fights Cancer is supported by NHL member clubs, NHL Alumni, the NHL Officials Association, Professional Hockey Trainers and Equipment Managers, corporate marketing partners, broadcast partners and fans throughout North America.

Join the Fight! If you would like to make a contribution to Hockey Fights Cancer, please forward a check made payable to Hockey Fights Cancer to one of the following addresses:

For Canadian Residents:
Hockey Fights Cancer
P.O. Box 1282, Station B
Montreal, Quebec H3B 3K9

For U.S. Residents:
Hockey Fights Cancer
P.O. Box 5037
New York, NY 10185-5037

Please include your name and current address so that your donation can be acknowledged. All donations are tax-deductible.

For more information, log on to www.hockeyfightscancer.com or call 1-800-540-6500.

THREE STAR SELECTION...

NHL PUBLICATIONS
ORDER FORM

Please send

☐ copies of **next** year's
NHL Guide & Record Book/2001-2002 (available Sept. 2001)

☐ copies of **this** year's
NHL Guide & Record Book/2001 (available now)

☐ copies of **next** year's
NHL Yearbook 2002 magazine (available Sept. 2001)

☐ copies of **this** year's
NHL Yearbook 2001 magazine (available now)

☐ copies of **next** year's
NHL Rule Book/2001-2002 (available Sept. 2001)

☐ copies of **this** year's
NHL Rule Book/2000-2001 (available now)

PRICES:	CANADA	USA	OVERSEAS
GUIDE & RECORD BOOK	$25.95	$23.95	$23.95 U.S.$
Handling (per copy)	$ 5.36	$ 9.00	$13.00 U.S.$
7% GST	$ 2.19	—	—
Total (per copy)	**$33.50**	**$32.95**	**$36.95** U.S.$
Add Extra for airmail	$ 9.00	$ 9.00	$17.00 U.S.$
YEARBOOK	$ 7.95	$ 7.95	$ 7.95 U.S.$
Handling (per copy)	$ 4.55	$ 5.50	$ 7.00 U.S.$
7% GST	$ .87	—	—
Total (per copy)	**$13.37**	**$13.45**	**$14.95** U.S.$
RULE BOOK	$ 9.95	$ 7.95	$ 7.95 U.S.$
Handling (per copy)	$ 3.05	$ 3.00	$ 3.55 U.S.$
7% GST	$ .91	—	—
Total (per copy)	**$13.91**	**$10.95**	**$11.50** U.S.$

Charge my   ☐ Visa   ☐ MasterCard/EuroCard   ☐ Am Ex

_____   _____
Credit Card Account Number   Expiry Date (important)

_____
Signature

☐ Enclosed is my cheque or money order.

_____
Name

_____
Address

_____   _____
Province/State   Postal/Zip Code

IN CANADA
Mail completed form to:
NHL Official Guide
194 Dovercourt Rd.
Toronto, Ontario
M6J 3C8

IN USA
Mail completed form to:
NHL Official Guide
194 Dovercourt Rd.
Toronto, Ontario
CANADA M6J 3C8
Remit in U.S. funds

OVERSEAS
Mail completed form to:
NHL Official Guide
194 Dovercourt Rd.
Toronto, Ontario
CANADA M6J 3C8
**Money order or
credit card only.
No cheques please.**

DELIVERY: Canada & USA – up to three weeks. Overseas – up to five weeks.

NHL PUBLISHING
*IS PLEASED TO OFFER
THREE OF THE GAME'S
LEADING ANNUAL
PUBLICATIONS*

1. **THE NHL OFFICIAL
GUIDE & RECORD BOOK**
*The NHL's authoritative
information source.
69th year in print.
624 pages.
The "Bible of Hockey".
Read worldwide.*

2. **THE NHL YEARBOOK**
*264-page, full-color magazine
with features on each club.
Award winners, All-Stars
and special statistics.*

3. **THE NHL RULE BOOK**
*Complete playing rules,
rink dimensions and
officials' signals.*

Free Book List with each order.

**Credit card holders
can order by FAX or E-MAIL**
FAX **416/531-3939** or
(OVERSEAS CUSTOMERS: USE INTERNATIONAL DIALING CODE FOR CANADA)
E-MAIL **dda.nhl@sympatico.ca**
24 HOURS
*PLEASE INCLUDE YOUR CARD'S EXPIRY DATE
As for a free book list by return e-mail.*

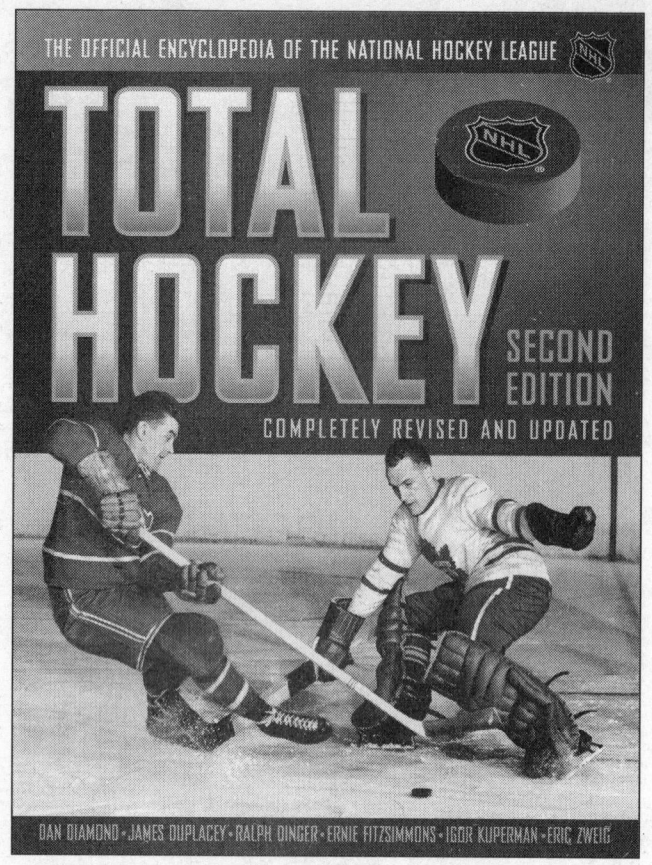